Income Tax Regulations

Including Proposed Regulations

As of July 14, 2003

Volume 3
§1.441-0–§1.865-2

CCH Editorial Staff Publication

CCH INCORPORATED
Chicago
A WoltersKluwer Company

This publication is designed to provide accurate and authoritative information in regard to the subject matter covered. It is sold with the understanding that the publisher is not engaged in rendering legal, accounting, or other professional service. If legal advice or other expert assistance is required, the services of a competent professional person should be sought.

ISBN 0-8080-1008-5

©2003, **CCH** INCORPORATED

4025 W. Peterson Ave.
Chicago, IL 60646-6085
1 800 248 3248
http://tax.cchgroup.com

No claim is made to original government works; however, within this Product or Publication, the following are subject to CCH's copyright: (1) the gathering, compilation, and arrangement of such government materials; (2) the magnetic translation and digital conversion of data, if applicable; (3) the historical, statutory and other notes and references; and (4) the commentary and other materials.

All Rights Reserved
Printed in the United States of America

ACCOUNTING PERIODS AND METHODS

Accounting Periods

[Reg. § 1.441-0]

§ 1.441-0. Table of contents.—This section lists the captions contained in §§ 1.441-1 through 1.441-4 as follows:

§ 1.441-1. Period for computation of taxable income.

(a) Computation of taxable income.

(1) In general.

(2) Length of taxable year.

(b) General rules and definitions.

(1) Taxable year.

(2) Required taxable year.

(i) In general.

(ii) Exceptions.

(A) 52-53-week taxable years.

(B) Partnerships, S corporations, and PSCs.

(C) Specified foreign corporations.

(3) Annual accounting period.

(4) Calendar year.

(5) Fiscal year.

(i) Definition.

(ii) Recognition.

(6) Grandfathered fiscal year.

(7) Books.

(8) Taxpayer.

(c) Adoption of taxable year.

(1) In general.

(2) Approval required.

(i) Taxpayers with required taxable years.

(ii) Taxpayers without books.

(d) Retention of taxable year.

(e) Change of taxable year.

(f) Obtaining approval of the Commissioner or making a section 444 election.

§ 1.441-2. Election of taxable year consisting of 52-53 weeks.

(a) In general.

(1) Election.

(2) Effect.

(3) Eligible taxpayer.

(4) Example.

(b) Procedures to elect a 52-53-week taxable year.

(1) Adoption of a 52-53-week taxable year.

(i) In general.

(ii) Filing requirement.

(2) Change to (or from) a 52-53-week taxable year.

(i) In general.

(ii) Special rules for short period required to effect the change.

(3) Examples.

(c) Application of effective dates.

(1) In general.

(2) Examples.

(3) Changes in tax rates.

(4) Examples.

(d) Computation of taxable income.

(e) Treatment of taxable years ending with reference to the same calendar month.

(1) Pass-through entities.

(2) Personal service corporations and employee-owners.

(3) Definitions.

(i) Pass-through entity.

(ii) Owner of a pass-through entity.

(4) Examples.

(5) Transition rule.

§ 1.441-3. Taxable year of a personal service corporation.

(a) Taxable year.

(1) Required taxable year.

(2) Exceptions.

(b) Adoption, change, or retention of taxable year.

(1) Adoption of taxable year.

(2) Change in taxable year.

(3) Retention of taxable year.

(4) Procedures for obtaining approval or making a section 444 election.

(5) Examples.

(c) Personal service corporation defined.

(1) In general.

(2) Testing period.

(i) In general.

(ii) New corporations.

(3) Examples.

(d) Performance of personal services.

(1) Activities described in section 448(d)(2)(A).

(2) Activities not described in section 448(d)(2)(A).

Reg. § 1.441-0

(e) *Principal activity.*

(1) General rule.

(2) Compensation cost.

(i) Amounts included.

(ii) Amounts excluded.

(3) Attribution of compensation cost to personal service activity.

(i) Employees involved only in the performance of personal services.

(ii) Employees involved only in activities that are not treated as the performance of personal services.

(iii) Other employees.

(A) Compensation cost attributable to personal service activity.

(B) Compensation cost not attributable to personal service activity.

(f) Services substantially performed by employee-owners.

(1) General rule.

(2) Compensation cost attributable to personal services.

(3) Examples.

(g) Employee-owner defined.

(1) General rule.

(2) Special rule for independent contractors who are owners.

(h) Special rules for affiliated groups filing consolidated returns.

(1) In general.

(2) Examples.

§ 1.441-4. Effective date.

[Reg. § 1.441-0.]

☐ [*T.D.* 8996, 5-16-2002.]

[Reg. § 1.441-1]

§ 1.441-1. Period for computation of taxable income.—(a) *Computation of taxable income*—(1) *In general.* Taxable income must be computed and a return must be made for a period known as the taxable year. For rules relating to methods of accounting, the taxable year for which items of gross income are included and deductions are taken, inventories, and adjustments, see parts II and III (section 446 and following), subchapter E, chapter 1 of the Internal Revenue Code, and the regulations thereunder.

(2) *Length of taxable year.* Except as otherwise provided in the Internal Revenue Code and the regulations thereunder (e.g., § 1.441-2 regarding 52-53-week taxable years), a taxable year may not cover a period of more than 12 calendar months.

Reg. § 1.441-1(a)(1)

(b) *General rules and definitions.* The general rules and definitions in this paragraph (b) apply for purposes of sections 441 and 442 and the regulations thereunder.

(1) *Taxable year. Taxable year* means—

(i) The period for which a return is made, if a return is made for a period of less than 12 months (short period). See section 443 and the regulations thereunder;

(ii) Except as provided in paragraph (b)(1)(i) of this section, the taxpayer's required taxable year (as defined in paragraph (b)(2) of this section), if applicable;

(iii) Except as provided in paragraphs (b)(1)(i) and (ii) of this section, the taxpayer's annual accounting period (as defined in paragraph (b)(3) of this section), if it is a calendar year or a fiscal year; or

(iv) Except as provided in paragraphs (b)(1)(i) and (ii) of this section, the calendar year, if the taxpayer keeps no books, does not have an annual accounting period, or has an annual accounting period that does not qualify as a fiscal year.

(2) *Required taxable year*—(i) *In general.* Certain taxpayers must use the particular taxable year that is required under the Internal Revenue Code and the regulations thereunder (the required taxable year). For example, the required taxable year is—

(A) In the case of a foreign sales corporation or domestic international sales corporation, the taxable year determined under section 441(h) and § 1.921-1T(a)(11), (b)(4), and (b)(6);

(B) In the case of a personal service corporation (PSC), the taxable year determined under section 441(i) and § 1.441-3;

(C) In the case of a nuclear decommissioning fund, the taxable year determined under § 1.468A-4(c)(1);

(D) In the case of a designated settlement fund or a qualified settlement fund, the taxable year determined under § 1.468B-2(j);

(E) In the case of a common trust fund, the taxable year determined under section 584(i);

(F) In the case of certain trusts, the taxable year determined under section 644;

(G) In the case of a partnership, the taxable year determined under section 706 and § 1.706-1;

(H) In the case of an insurance company, the taxable year determined under section 843 and § 1.1502-76(a)(2);

(I) In the case of a real estate investment trust, the taxable year determined under section 859;

(J) In the case of a real estate mortgage investment conduit, the taxable year determined under section 860D(a)(5) and § 1.860D-1(b)(6);

(K) In the case of a specified foreign corporation, the taxable year determined under section 898(c)(1)(A);

(L) In the case of an S corporation, the taxable year determined under section 1378 and § 1.1378-1; or

(M) In the case of a member of an affiliated group that makes a consolidated return, the taxable year determined under § 1.1502-76.

(ii) *Exceptions.* Notwithstanding paragraph (b)(2)(i) of this section, the following taxpayers may have a taxable year other than their required taxable year:

(A) *52-53-week taxable years.* Certain taxpayers may elect to use a 52-53-week taxable year that ends with reference to their required taxable year. See, for example, §§ 1.441-3 (PSCs), 1.706-1 (partnerships), 1.1378-1 (S corporations), and 1.1502-76(a)(1) (members of a consolidated group).

(B) *Partnerships, S corporations, and PSCs.* A partnership, S corporation, or PSC may use a taxable year other than its required taxable year if the taxpayer elects to use a taxable year other than its required taxable year under section 444, elects a 52-53-week taxable year that ends with reference to its required taxable year as provided in paragraph (b)(2)(ii)(A) of this section or to a taxable year elected under section 444, or establishes a business purpose to the satisfaction of the Commissioner under section 442 (such as a grandfathered fiscal year).

(C) *Specified foreign corporations.* A specified foreign corporation (as defined in section 898(b)) may use a taxable year other than its required taxable year if it elects a 52-53-week taxable year that ends with reference to its required taxable year as provided in paragraph (b)(2)(ii)(A) of this section or makes a one-month deferral election under section 898(c)(1)(B).

(3) *Annual accounting period.* Annual accounting period means the annual period (calendar year or fiscal year) on the basis of which the taxpayer regularly computes its income in keeping its books.

(4) *Calendar year.* Calendar year means a period of 12 consecutive months ending on December 31. A taxpayer who has not established a fiscal year must make its return on the basis of a calendar year.

(5) *Fiscal year*—(i) *Definition.* Fiscal year means—

(A) A period of 12 consecutive months ending on the last day of any month other than December; or

(B) A 52-53-week taxable year, if such period has been elected by the taxpayer. See § 1.441-2.

(ii) *Recognition.* A fiscal year will be recognized only if the books of the taxpayer are kept in accordance with such fiscal year.

(6) *Grandfathered fiscal year.* Grandfathered fiscal year means a fiscal year (other than a year that resulted in a three month or less deferral of income) that a partnership or an S corporation received permission to use on or after July 1, 1974, by a letter ruling (i.e., not by automatic approval).

(7) *Books.* Books include the taxpayer's regular books of account and such other records and data as may be necessary to support the entries on the taxpayer's books and on the taxpayer's return, as for example, a reconciliation of any difference between such books and the taxpayer's return. Records that are sufficient to reflect income adequately and clearly on the basis of an annual accounting period will be regarded as the keeping of books. See section 6001 and the regulations thereunder for rules relating to the keeping of books and records.

(8) *Taxpayer.* Taxpayer has the same meaning as the term *person* as defined in section 7701(a)(1) (e.g., an individual, trust, estate, partnership, association, or corporation) rather than the meaning of the term taxpayer as defined in section 7701(a)(14) (any person subject to tax).

(c) *Adoption of taxable year*—(1) *In general.* Except as provided in paragraph (c)(2) of this section, a new taxpayer may adopt any taxable year that satisfies the requirements of section 441 and the regulations thereunder without the approval of the Commissioner. A taxable year of a new taxpayer is adopted by filing its first Federal income tax return using that taxable year. The filing of an application for automatic extension of time to file a Federal income tax return (e.g., Form 7004, "Application for Automatic Extension of Time To File Corporation Income Tax Return"), the filing of an application for an employer identification number (i.e., Form SS-4, "Application for Employer Identification Number"), or the payment of estimated taxes, for a particular taxable year do not constitute an adoption of that taxable year.

(2) *Approval required*—(i) *Taxpayers with required taxable years.* A newly-formed partner-

Reg. § 1.441-1(c)(2)

ship, S corporation, or PSC that wants to adopt a taxable year other than its required taxable year, a taxable year elected under section 444, or a 52-53-week taxable year that ends with reference to its required taxable year or a taxable year elected under section 444 must establish a business purpose and obtain the approval of the Commissioner under section 442.

(ii) *Taxpayers without books.* A taxpayer that must use a calendar year under section 441(g) and paragraph (f) of this section may not adopt a fiscal year without obtaining the approval of the Commissioner.

(d) *Retention of taxable year.* In certain cases, a partnership, S corporation, electing S corporation, or PSC will be required to change its taxable year unless it obtains the approval of the Commissioner under section 442, or makes an election under section 444, to retain its current taxable year. For example, a corporation using a June 30 fiscal year that either becomes a PSC or elects to be an S corporation and, as a result, is required to use the calendar year under section 441(i) or 1378, respectively, must obtain the approval of the Commissioner to retain its current fiscal year. Similarly, a partnership using a taxable year that corresponds to its required taxable year must obtain the approval of the Commissioner to retain such taxable year if its required taxable year changes as a result of a change in ownership. However, a partnership that previously established a business purpose to the satisfaction of the Commissioner to use a taxable year is not required to obtain the approval of the Commissioner if its required taxable year changes as a result of a change in ownership.

(e) *Change of taxable year.* Once a taxpayer has adopted a taxable year, such taxable year must be used in computing taxable income and making returns for all subsequent years unless the taxpayer obtains approval from the Commissioner to make a change or the taxpayer is otherwise authorized to change without the approval of the Commissioner under the Internal Revenue Code (e.g., section 444 or 859) or the regulations thereunder.

(f) *Obtaining approval of the Commissioner or making a section 444 election.* See § 1.442-1(b) for procedures for obtaining approval of the Commissioner (automatically or otherwise) to adopt, change, or retain an annual accounting period. See §§ 1.444-1T and 1.444-2T for qualifications, and 1.444-3T for procedures, for making an election under section 444. [Reg. § 1.441-1.]

☐ [T.D. 8996, 5-16-2002.]

[Reg. § 1.441-2]

§ 1.441-2. **Election of taxable year consisting of 52-53 weeks.**—(a) *In general*—(1) *Election.* An eligible taxpayer may elect to compute its taxable income on the basis of a fiscal year that—

(i) Varies from 52 to 53 weeks;

(ii) Ends always on the same day of the week; and

(iii) Ends always on—

(A) Whatever date this same day of the week last occurs in a calendar month; or

(B) Whatever date this same day of the week falls that is the nearest to the last day of the calendar month.

(2) *Effect.* In the case of a taxable year described in paragraph (a)(1)(iii)(A) of this section, the year will always end within the month and may end on the last day of the month, or as many as six days before the end of the month. In the case of a taxable year described in paragraph (a)(1)(iii)(B) of this section, the year may end on the last day of the month, or as many as three days before or three days after the last day of the month.

(3) *Eligible taxpayer.* A taxpayer is eligible to elect a 52-53-week taxable year if such fiscal year would otherwise satisfy the requirements of section 441 and the regulations thereunder. For example, a taxpayer that is required to use a calendar year under § 1.441-1(b)(2)(i)(D) is not an eligible taxpayer.

(4) *Example.* The provisions of this paragraph (a) are illustrated by the following example:

Example. If the taxpayer elects a taxable year ending always on the last Saturday in November, then for the year 2001, the taxable year would end on November 24, 2001. On the other hand, if the taxpayer had elected a taxable year ending always on the Saturday nearest to the end of November, then for the year 2001, the taxable year would end on December 1, 2001.

(b) *Procedures to elect a 52-53-week taxable year*—(1) *Adoption of a 52-53-week taxable year*—(i) *In general.* A new eligible taxpayer elects a 52-53-week taxable year by adopting such year in accordance with § 1.441-1(c). A newly-formed partnership, S corporation or personal service corporation (PSC) may adopt a 52-53-week taxable year without the approval of the Commissioner if such year ends with reference to either the taxpayer's required taxable year (as defined in § 1.441-1(b)(2)) or the taxable year elected under section 444. See §§ 1.441-3, 1.706-1, and 1.1378-1. Similarly, a newly-formed specified foreign corporation (as defined in section 898(b))

Reg. § 1.441-2(a)(1)

may adopt a 52-53-week taxable year if such year ends with reference to the taxpayer's required taxable year, or, if the one-month deferral election under section 898(c)(1)(B) is made, with reference to the month immediately preceding the required taxable year. See § 1.1502-76(a)(1) for special rules regarding subsidiaries adopting 52-53-week taxable years.

(ii) *Filing requirement.* A taxpayer adopting a 52-53-week taxable year must file with its Federal income tax return for its first taxable year a statement containing the following information—

(A) The calendar month with reference to which the 52-53-week taxable year ends;

(B) The day of the week on which the 52-53-week taxable year always will end; and

(C) Whether the 52-53-week taxable year will always end on the date on which that day of the week last occurs in the calendar month, or on the date on which that day of the week falls that is nearest to the last day of that calendar month.

(2) *Change to (or from) a 52-53-week taxable year*—(i) *In general.* An election of a 52-53-week taxable year by an existing eligible taxpayer with an established taxable year is treated as a change in annual accounting period that requires the approval of the Commissioner in accordance with § 1.442-1. Thus, a taxpayer must obtain approval to change from its current taxable year to a 52-53-week taxable year, even if such 52-53-week taxable year ends with reference to the same calendar month. Similarly, a taxpayer must obtain approval to change from a 52-53-week taxable year, or to change from one 52-53-week taxable year to another 52-53-week taxable year. However, a taxpayer may obtain approval for 52-53-week taxable year changes automatically to the extent provided in administrative procedures published by the Commissioner. See § 1.442-1(b) for procedures for obtaining such approval.

(ii) *Special rules for the short period required to effect the change.* If a change to or from a 52-53-week taxable year results in a short period (within the meaning of § 1.443-1(a)) of 359 days or more, or six days or less, the tax computation under § 1.443-1(b) does not apply. If the short period is 359 days or more, it is treated as a full taxable year. If the short period is six days or less, such short period is not a separate taxable year but instead is added to and deemed a part of the following taxable year. (In the case of a change to or from a 52-53-week taxable year not involving a change of the month with reference to which the taxable year ends, the tax computation under § 1.443-1(b) does not apply because the short period will always be 359 days or more, or six days or less.) In the case of a short period which is more than six days and less than 359 days, taxable income for the short period is placed on an annual basis for purposes of § 1.443-1(b) by multiplying such income by 365 and dividing the result by the number of days in the short period. In such case, the tax for the short period is the same part of the tax computed on such income placed on an annual basis as the number of days in the short period is of 365 days (unless § 1.443-1(b)(2), relating to the alternative tax computation, applies). For an adjustment in deduction for personal exemption, see § 1.443-1(b)(1)(v).

(3) *Examples.* The following examples illustrate paragraph (b)(2)(ii) of this section:

Example 1. A taxpayer having a fiscal year ending April 30, obtains approval to change to a 52-53-week taxable year ending the last Saturday in April for taxable years beginning after April 30, 2001. This change involves a short period of 362 days, from May 1, 2001, to April 27, 2002, inclusive. Because the change results in a short period of 359 days or more, it is not placed on an annual basis and is treated as a full taxable year.

Example 2. Assume the same conditions as *Example 1*, except that the taxpayer changes for taxable years beginning after April 30, 2002, to a taxable year ending on the Thursday nearest to April 30. This change results in a short period of two days, May 1 to May 2, 2002. Because the short period is less than seven days, tax is not separately computed. This short period is added to and deemed part of the following 52-53-week taxable year, which would otherwise begin on May 3, 2002, and end on May 1, 2003.

(c) *Application of effective dates*—(1) *In general.* Except as provided in paragraph (c)(3) of this section, for purposes of determining the effective date (e.g., of legislative, regulatory, or administrative changes) or the applicability of any provision of the internal revenue laws that is expressed in terms of taxable years beginning, including, or ending with reference to the first or last day of a specified calendar month, a 52-53-week taxable year is deemed to begin on the first day of the calendar month nearest to the first day of the 52-53-week taxable year, and is deemed to end or close on the last day of the calendar month nearest to the last day of the 52-53-week taxable year, as the case may be. Examples of provisions of this title, the applicability of which is expressed in terms referred to in the preceding sentence, include the provisions relating to the time for filing returns and other documents, paying tax, or performing other acts, and the provisions of part II, subchapter B, chapter 6 (section

Reg. § 1.441-2(c)(1)

1561 and following) relating to surtax exemptions of certain controlled corporations.

(2) *Examples.* The provisions of paragraph (c)(1) of this section may be illustrated by the following examples:

Example 1. Assume that an income tax provision is applicable to taxable years beginning on or after January 1, 2001. For that purpose, a 52-53-week taxable year beginning on any day within the period December 26, 2000, to January 4, 2001, inclusive, is treated as beginning on January 1, 2001.

Example 2. Assume that an income tax provision requires that a return must be filed on or before the 15th day of the third month following the close of the taxable year. For that purpose, a 52-53-week taxable year ending on any day during the period May 25 to June 3, inclusive, is treated as ending on May 31, the last day of the month ending nearest to the last day of the taxable year, and the return, therefore, must be made on or before August 15.

Example 3. Assume that a revenue procedure requires the performance of an act by the taxpayer within "the first 90 days of the taxable year," by "the 75th day of the taxable year," or, alternately, by "the last day of the taxable year." The taxpayer employs a 52-53-week taxable year that ends always on the Saturday closest to the last day of December. These requirements are not expressed in terms of taxable years beginning, including, or ending with reference to the first or last day of a specified calendar month, and are accordingly outside the scope of the rule stated in § 1.441-2(c)(1). Accordingly, the taxpayer must perform the required act by the 90th, 75th, or last day, respectively, of its taxable year.

Example 4. X, a corporation created on January 1, 2001,elects a 52-53-week taxable year ending on the Friday nearest the end of December. Thus, X's first taxable year begins on Monday, January 1, 2001, and ends on Friday, December 28, 2001; its next taxable year begins on Saturday, December 29, 2001, and ends on Friday, January 3, 2003; and its next taxable year begins on Saturday, January 4, 2003, and ends on Friday, January 2, 2004. For purposes of applying the provisions of Part II, subchapter B, chapter 6 of the Internal Revenue Code, X's first taxable year is deemed to end on December 31, 2001; its next taxable year is deemed to begin on January 1, 2002, and end on December 31, 2002, and its next taxable year is deemed to begin on January 1, 2003, and end on December 31, 2003. Accordingly, each such taxable year is treated as including one and only one December 31st.

(3) *Changes in tax rates.* If a change in the rate of tax is effective during a 52-53-week taxable year (other than on the first day of such year as determined under paragraph (c)(1) of this section), the tax for the 52-53-week taxable year must be computed in accordance with section 15, relating to effect of changes, and the regulations thereunder. For the purpose of the computation under section 15, the determination of the number of days in the period before the change, and in the period on and after the change, is to be made without regard to the provisions of paragraph (b)(1) of this paragraph.

(4) *Examples.* The provisions of paragraph (c)(3) of this section may be illustrated by the following examples:

Example 1. Assume a change in the rate of tax is effective for taxable years beginning after June 30, 2002. For a 52-53-week taxable year beginning on Friday, November 2, 2001, the tax must be computed on the basis of the old rates for the actual number of days from November 2, 2001, to June 30, 2002, inclusive, and on the basis of the new rates for the actual number of days from July 1, 2002, to Thursday, October 31, 2002, inclusive.

Example 2. Assume a change in the rate of tax is effective for taxable years beginning after June 30, 2001. For this purpose, a 52-53-week taxable year beginning on any of the days from June 25 to July 4, inclusive, is treated as beginning on July 1. Therefore, no computation under section 15 will be required for such year because of the change in rate.

(d) *Computation of taxable income.* The principles of section 451, relating to the taxable year for inclusion of items of gross income, and section 461, relating to the taxable year for taking deductions, generally are applicable to 52-53-week taxable years. Thus, except as otherwise provided, all items of income and deduction must be determined on the basis of a 52-53-week taxable year. However, a taxpayer may determine particular items as though the 52-53-week taxable year were a taxable year consisting of 12 calendar months, provided that practice is consistently followed by the taxpayer and clearly reflects income. For example, an allowance for depreciation or amortization may be determined on the basis of a 52-53-week taxable year, or as though the 52-53-week taxable year is a taxable year consisting of 12 calendar months, provided the taxpayer consistently follows that practice with respect to all depreciable or amortizable items.

(e) *Treatment of taxable years ending with reference to the same calendar month*—(1) *Pass-through entities.* If a pass-through entity (as de-

Reg. § 1.441-2(c)(2)

fined in paragraph (e)(3)(i) of this section) or an owner of a pass-through entity (as defined in paragraph (e)(3)(ii) of this section), or both, use a 52-53-week taxable year and the taxable year of the pass-through entity and the owner end with reference to the same calendar month, then, for purposes of determining the taxable year in which items of income, gain, loss, deductions, or credits from the pass-through entity are taken into account by the owner of the pass-through, the owner's taxable year will be deemed to end on the last day of the pass-through's taxable year. Thus, if the taxable year of a partnership and a partner end with reference to the same calendar month, then for purposes of determining the taxable year in which that partner takes into account items described in section 702 and items that are deductible by the partnership (including items described in section 707(c)) and includible in the income of that partner, that partner's taxable year will be deemed to end on the last day of the partnership's taxable year. Similarly, if the taxable year of an S corporation and a shareholder end with reference to the same calendar month, then for purposes of determining the taxable year in which that shareholder takes into account items described in section 1366(a) and items that are deductible by the S corporation and includible in the income of that shareholder, that shareholder's taxable year will be deemed to end on the last day of the S corporation's taxable year.

(2) *Personal service corporations and employee-owners.* If the taxable year of a PSC (within the meaning of § 1.441-3(c)) and an employee-owner (within the meaning of § 1.441-3(g)) end with reference to the same calendar month, then for purposes of determining the taxable year in which an employee-owner takes into account items that are deductible by the PSC and includible in the income of the employee-owner, the employee-owner's taxable year will be deemed to end on the last day of the PSC's taxable year.

(3) *Definitions*—(i) *Pass-through entity.* For purposes of this section, a pass-through entity means a partnership, S corporation, trust, estate, closely-held real estate investment trust (within the meaning of section 6655(e)(5)(B)), common trust fund (within the meaning of section 584(i)), controlled foreign corporation (within the meaning of section 957), foreign personal holding company (within the meaning of section 552), or passive foreign investment company that is a qualified electing fund (within the meaning of section 1295).

(ii) *Owner of a pass-through entity.* For purposes of this section, an owner of a pass-through entity generally means a taxpayer that owns an interest in, or stock of, a pass-through entity. For example, an owner of a pass-through entity includes a partner in a partnership, a shareholder of an S corporation, a beneficiary of a trust or an estate, an owner of a closely-held real estate investment trust (within the meaning of section 6655(e)(5)(A)), a participant in a common trust fund, a U.S. shareholder (as defined in section 951(b)) of a controlled foreign corporation, a U.S. shareholder (as defined in section 551(a)) of a foreign personal holding company, or a U.S. person that holds stock in a passive foreign investment company that is a qualified electing fund with respect to that shareholder.

(4) *Examples.* The provisions of paragraph (e)(2) of this section may be illustrated by the following examples:

Example 1. ABC Partnership uses a 52-53-week taxable year that ends on the Wednesday nearest to December 31, and its partners, A, B, and C, are individual calendar year taxpayers. Assume that, for ABC's taxable year ending January 3, 2001, each partner's distributive share of ABC's taxable income is $10,000. Under section 706(a) and paragraph (e)(1) of this section, for the taxable year ending December 31, 2000, A, B, and C each must include $10,000 in income with respect to the ABC year ending January 3, 2001. Similarly, if ABC makes a guaranteed payment to A on January 2, 2001, A must include the payment in income for A's taxable year ending December 31, 2000.

Example 2. X, a PSC, uses a 52-53-week taxable year that ends on the Wednesday nearest to December 31, and all of the employee-owners of X are individual calendar year taxpayers. Assume that, for its taxable year ending January 3, 2001, X pays a bonus of $10,000 to each employee-owner on January 2, 2001. Under paragraph (e)(2) of this section, each employee-owner must include its bonus in income for the taxable year ending December 31, 2000.

(5) *Transition rule.* In the case of an owner of a pass-through entity (other than the owner of a partnership or S corporation) that is required by this paragraph (e) to include in income for its first taxable year ending on or after May 17, 2002, amounts attributable to two taxable years of a pass-through entity, the amount that otherwise would be required to be included in income for such first taxable year by reason of this paragraph (e) should be included in income ratably over the four-taxable-year period beginning with such first taxable year under principles similar to § 1.702-3T, unless the owner of the pass-through entity elects to include all such income in its first

Reg. § 1.441-2(e)(5)

taxable year ending on or after May 17, 2002. [Reg. § 1.441-2.]

☐ [*T.D.* 8996, 5-16-2002.]

[Reg. § 1.441-3]

§ 1.441-3. **Taxable year of a personal service corporation.**—(a) *Taxable year*—(1) *Required taxable year.* Except as provided in paragraph (a)(2) of this section, the taxable year of a personal service corporation (PSC) (as defined in paragraph (c) of this section) must be the calendar year.

(2) *Exceptions.* A PSC may have a taxable year other than its required taxable year (i.e., a fiscal year) if it makes an election under section 444, elects to use a 52-53-week taxable year that ends with reference to the calendar year or a taxable year elected under section 444, or establishes a business purpose for such fiscal year and obtains the approval of the Commissioner under section 442.

(b) *Adoption, change, or retention of taxable year*—(1) *Adoption of taxable year.* A PSC may adopt, in accordance with § 1.441-1(c), the calendar year, a taxable year elected under section 444, or a 52-53-week taxable year ending with reference to the calendar year or a taxable year elected under section 444 without the approval of the Commissioner. See § 1.441-1. A PSC that wants to adopt any other taxable year must establish a business purpose and obtain the approval of the Commissioner under section 442.

(2) *Change in taxable year.* A PSC that wants to change its taxable year must obtain the approval of the Commissioner under section 442 or make an election under section 444. However, a PSC may obtain automatic approval for certain changes, including a change to the calendar year or to a 52-53-week taxable year ending with reference to the calendar year, pursuant to administrative procedures published by the Commissioner.

(3) *Retention of taxable year.* In certain cases, a PSC will be required to change its taxable year unless it obtains the approval of the Commissioner under section 442, or makes an election under section 444, to retain its current taxable year. For example, a corporation using a June 30 fiscal year that becomes a PSC and, as a result, is required to use the calendar year must obtain the approval of the Commissioner to retain its current fiscal year.

(4) *Procedures for obtaining approval or making a section 444 election.* See § 1.442-1(b) for procedures to obtain the approval of the Commissioner (automatically or otherwise) to adopt, change, or retain a taxable year. See §§ 1.444-1T and 1.444-2T for qualifications, and 1.444-3T for procedures, for making an election under section 444.

(5) *Examples.* The provisions of paragraph (b)(4) of this section may be illustrated by the following examples:

Example 1. X, whose taxable year ends on January 31, 2001, becomes a PSC for its taxable year beginning February 1, 2001, and does not obtain the approval of the Commissioner for using a fiscal year. Thus, for taxable years ending before February 1, 2001, this section does not apply with respect to X. For its taxable year beginning on February 1, 2001, however, X will be required to comply with paragraph (a) of this section. Thus, unless X obtains approval of the Commissioner to use a January 31 taxable year, or makes a section 444 election, X will be required to change its taxable year to the calendar year under paragraph (b) of this section by using a short taxable year that begins on February 1, 2001, and ends on December 31, 2001. Under paragraph (b)(1) of this section, X may obtain automatic approval to change its taxable year to a calendar year. See § 1.442-1(b).

Example 2. Assume the same facts as in *Example 1*, except that X desires to change to a 52-53-week taxable year ending with reference to the month of December. Under paragraph (b)(1) of this section X may obtain automatic approval to make the change. See § 1.442-1(b).

(c) *Personal service corporation defined*—(1) *In general.* For purposes of this section and section 442, a taxpayer is a PSC for a taxable year only if—

(i) The taxpayer is a C corporation (as defined in section 1361(a)(2)) for the taxable year;

(ii) The principal activity of the taxpayer during the testing period is the performance of personal services;

(iii) During the testing period, those services are substantially performed by employee-owners (as defined in paragraph (g) of this section); and

(iv) Employee-owners own (as determined under the attribution rules of section 318, except that the language "any" applies instead of "50 percent" in section 318(a)(2)(C)) more than 10 percent of the fair market value of the outstanding stock in the taxpayer on the last day of the testing period.

(2) *Testing period*—(i) *In general.* Except as otherwise provided in paragraph (c)(2)(ii) of this section, the testing period for any taxable year is the immediately preceding taxable year.

(ii) *New corporations.* The testing period for a taxpayer's first taxable year is the period

Reg. § 1.441-3(a)(1)

beginning on the first day of that taxable year and ending on the earlier of—

(A) The last day of that taxable year; or

(B) The last day of the calendar year in which that taxable year begins.

(3) *Examples.* The provisions of paragraph (c)(2)(ii) of this section may be illustrated by the following examples:

Example 1. Corporation A's first taxable year begins on June 1, 2001, and A desires to use a September 30 taxable year. However, if A is a personal service corporation, it must obtain the Commissioner's approval to use a September 30 taxable year. Pursuant to paragraph (c)(2)(ii) of this section, A's testing period for its first taxable year beginning June 1, 2001, is the period June 1, 2001 through September 30, 2001. Thus, if, based upon such testing period, A is a personal service corporation, A must obtain the Commissioner's permission to use a September 30 taxable year.

Example 2. The facts are the same as in Example 1, except that A desires to use a March 31 taxable year. Pursuant to paragraph (c)(2)(ii) of this section, A's testing period for its first taxable year beginning June 1, 2001, is the period June 1, 2001, through December 31, 2001. Thus, if, based upon such testing period, A is a personal service corporation, A must obtain the Commissioner's permission to use a March 31 taxable year.

(d) *Performance of personal services*—(1) *Activities described in section 448(d)(2)(A).* For purposes of this section, any activity of the taxpayer described in section 448(d)(2)(A) or the regulations thereunder will be treated as the performance of personal services. Therefore, any activity of the taxpayer that involves the performance of services in the fields of health, law, engineering, architecture, accounting, actuarial science, performing arts, or consulting (as such fields are defined in § 1.448-1T) will be treated as the performance of personal services for purposes of this section.

(2) *Activities not described in section 448(d)(2)(A).* For purposes of this section, any activity of the taxpayer not described in section 448(d)(2)(A) or the regulations thereunder will not be treated as the performance of personal services.

(e) *Principal activity*—(1) *General rule.* For purposes of this section, the principal activity of a corporation for any testing period will be the performance of personal services if the cost of the corporation's compensation (the compensation cost) for such testing period that is attributable to its activities that are treated as the performance of personal services within the meaning of paragraph (d) of this section (i.e., the total compensation for personal service activities) exceeds 50 percent of the corporation's total compensation cost for such testing period.

(2) *Compensation cost*—(i) *Amounts included.* For purposes of this section, the compensation cost of a corporation for a taxable year is equal to the sum of the following amounts allowable as a deduction, allocated to a long-term contract, or otherwise chargeable to a capital account by the corporation during such taxable year—

(A) Wages and salaries; and

(B) Any other amounts, attributable to services performed for or on behalf of the corporation by a person who is an employee of the corporation (including an owner of the corporation who is treated as an employee under paragraph (g)(2) of this section) during the testing period. Such amounts include, but are not limited to, amounts attributable to deferred compensation, commissions, bonuses, compensation includible in income under section 83, compensation for services based on a percentage of profits, and the cost of providing fringe benefits that are includible in income.

(ii) *Amounts excluded.* Notwithstanding paragraph (e)(2)(i) of this section, compensation cost does not include amounts attributable to a plan qualified under section 401(a) or 403(a), or to a simplified employee pension plan defined in section 408(k).

(3) *Attribution of compensation cost to personal service activity*—(i) *Employees involved only in the performance of personal services.* The compensation cost for employees involved only in the performance of activities that are treated as personal services under paragraph (d) of this section, or employees involved only in supporting the work of such employees, are considered to be attributable to the corporation's personal service activity.

(ii) *Employees involved only in activities that are not treated as the performance of personal services.* The compensation cost for employees involved only in the performance of activities that are not treated as personal services under paragraph (d) of this section, or for employees involved only in supporting the work of such employees, are not considered to be attributable to the corporation's personal service activity.

(iii) *Other employees.* The compensation cost for any employee who is not described in either paragraph (e)(3)(i) or (ii) of this section (a mixed-activity employee) is allocated as follows—

(A) *Compensation cost attributable to personal service activity.* That portion of the com-

Reg. § 1.441-3(e)(3)

pensation cost for a mixed activity employee that is attributable to the corporation's personal service activity equals the compensation cost for that employee multiplied by the percentage of the total time worked for the corporation by that employee during the year that is attributable to activities of the corporation that are treated as the performance of personal services under paragraph (d) of this section. That percentage is to be determined by the taxpayer in any reasonable and consistent manner. Time logs are not required unless maintained for other purposes;

(B) *Compensation cost not attributable to personal service activity.* That portion of the compensation cost for a mixed activity employee that is not considered to be attributable to the corporation's personal service activity is the compensation cost for that employee less the amount determined in paragraph (e)(3)(iii)(A) of this section.

(f) *Services substantially performed by employee-owners*—(1) *General rule.* Personal services are substantially performed during the testing period by employee-owners of the corporation if more than 20 percent of the corporation's compensation cost for that period attributable to its activities that are treated as the performance of personal services within the meaning of paragraph (d) of this section (i.e., the total compensation for personal service activities) is attributable to personal services performed by employee-owners.

(2) *Compensation cost attributable to personal services.* For purposes of paragraph (f)(1) of this section—

(i) The corporation's compensation cost attributable to its activities that are treated as the performance of personal services is determined under paragraph (e)(3) of this section; and

(ii) The portion of the amount determined under paragraph (f)(2)(i) of this section that is attributable to personal services performed by employee-owners is to be determined by the taxpayer in any reasonable and consistent manner.

(3) *Examples.* The provisions of this paragraph (f) may be illustrated by the following examples:

Example 1. For its taxable year beginning February 1, 2001, Corp A's testing period is the taxable year ending January 31, 2000. During that testing period, A's only activity was the performance of personal services. The total compensation cost of A (including compensation cost attributable to employee-owners) for the testing period was $1,000,000. The total compensation cost attributable to employee-owners of A for the testing period was $210,000. Pursuant to paragraph (f)(1) of this section, the employee-owners of A substantially performed the personal services of A during the testing period because the compensation cost of A's employee-owners was more than 20 percent of the total compensation cost for all of A's employees (including employee-owners).

Example 2. Corp B has the same facts as corporation A in *Example 1,* except that during the taxable year ending January 31, 2001, B also participated in an activity that would not be characterized as the performance of personal services under this section. The total compensation cost of B (including compensation cost attributable to employee-owners) for the testing period was $1,500,000 ($1,000,000 attributable to B's personal service activity and $500,000 attributable to B's other activity). The total compensation cost attributable to employee-owners of B for the testing period was $250,000 ($210,000 attributable to B's personal service activity and $40,000 attributable to B's other activity). Pursuant to paragraph (f)(1) of this section, the employee-owners of B substantially performed the personal services of B during the testing period because more than 20 percent of B's compensation cost during the testing period attributable to its personal service activities was attributable to personal services performed by employee-owners ($210,000).

(g) *Employee-owner defined*—(1) *General rule.* For purposes of this section, a person is an employee-owner of a corporation for a testing period if—

(i) The person is an employee of the corporation on any day of the testing period; and

(ii) The person owns any outstanding stock of the corporation on any day of the testing period.

(2) *Special rule for independent contractors who are owners.* Any person who is an owner of the corporation within the meaning of paragraph (g)(1)(ii) of this section and who performs personal services for, or on behalf of, the corporation is treated as an employee for purposes of this section, even if the legal form of that person's relationship to the corporation is such that the person would be considered an independent contractor for other purposes.

(h) *Special rules for affiliated groups filing consolidated returns*—(1) *In general.* For purposes of applying this section to the members of an affiliated group of corporations filing a consolidated return for the taxable year—

(i) The members of the affiliated group are treated as a single corporation;

Reg. § 1.441-3(f)(1)

(ii) The employees of the members of the affiliated group are treated as employees of such single corporation; and

(iii) All of the stock of the members of the affiliated group that is not owned by any other member of the affiliated group is treated as the outstanding stock of that corporation.

(2) *Examples.* The provisions of this paragraph (h) may be illustrated by the following examples:

Example 1. The affiliated group AB, consisting of corporation A and its wholly owned subsidiary B, filed a consolidated Federal income tax return for the taxable year ending January 31, 2001, and AB is attempting to determine whether it is affected by this section for its taxable year beginning February 1, 2001. During the testing period (i.e., the taxable year ending January 31, 2001), A did not perform personal services. However, B's only activity was the performance of personal services. On the last day of the testing period, employees of A did not own any stock in A. However, some of B's employees own stock in A. In the aggregate, B's employees own 9 percent of A's stock on the last day of the testing period. Pursuant to paragraph (h)(1) of this section, this section is effectively applied on a consolidated basis to members of an affiliated group filing a consolidated Federal income tax return. Because the only employee-owners of AB are the employees of B, and because B's employees do not own more than 10 percent of AB on the last day of the testing period, AB is not a PSC subject to the provisions of this section. Thus, AB is not required to determine on a consolidated basis whether, during the testing period, its principal activity is the providing of personal services, or the personal services are substantially performed by employee-owners.

Example 2. The facts are the same as in *Example 1,* except that on the last day of the testing period A owns only 80 percent of B. The remaining 20 percent of B is owned by employees of B. The fair market value of A, including its 80 percent interest in B, as of the last day of the testing period, is $1,000,000. In addition, the fair market value of the 20 percent interest in B owned by B's employees is $50,000 as of the last day of the testing period. Pursuant to paragraphs (c)(1)(iv) and (h)(1) of this section, AB must determine whether the employee-owners of A and B (i.e., B's employees) own more than 10 percent of the fair market value of A and B as of the last day of the testing period. Because the $140,000 [($1,000,000×.09)+$50,000] fair market value of the stock held by B's employees is greater than 10 percent of the aggregate fair market value of A

and B as of the last day of the testing period, or $105,000 [$1,000,000+$50,000×.10], AB may be subject to this section if, on a consolidated basis during the testing period, the principal activity of AB is the performance of personal services and the personal services are substantially performed by employee-owners. [Reg. § 1.441-3.]

☐ [*T.D.* 8996, 5-16-2002.]

[Reg. § 1.441-4]

§ 1.441-4. Effective date.—Sections 1.441-0 through 1.441-3 are applicable for taxable years ending on or after May 17, 2002. [Reg. § 1.441-4.]

☐ [*T.D.* 8996, 5-16-2002.]

[Reg. § 1.442-1]

§ 1.442-1. Change of annual accounting period.—(a) *Approval of the Commissioner.* A taxpayer that has adopted an annual accounting period (as defined in § 1.441-1(b)(3)) as its taxable year generally must continue to use that annual accounting period in computing its taxable income and for making its Federal income tax returns. If the taxpayer wants to change its annual accounting period and use a new taxable year, it must obtain the approval of the Commissioner, unless it is otherwise authorized to change without the approval of the Commissioner under either the Internal Revenue Code (e.g., section 444 and section 859) or the regulations thereunder (e.g., paragraph (c) of this section). In addition, as described in § 1.441-1(c) and (d), a partnership, S corporation, electing S corporation, or personal service corporation (PSC) generally is required to secure the approval of the Commissioner to adopt or retain an annual accounting period other than its required taxable year. The manner of obtaining approval from the Commissioner to adopt, change, or retain an annual accounting period is provided in paragraph (b) of this section. However, special rules for obtaining approval may be provided in other sections.

(b) *Obtaining approval*—(1) *Time and manner for requesting approval.* In order to secure the approval of the Commissioner to adopt, change, or retain an annual accounting period, a taxpayer must file an application, generally on Form 1128, "Application To Adopt, Change, or Retain a Tax Year," with the Commissioner within such time and in such manner as is provided in administrative procedures published by the Commissioner.

(2) *General requirements for approval.* An adoption, change, or retention in annual accounting period will be approved where the taxpayer establishes a business purpose for the requested annual accounting period and agrees to the Commissioner's prescribed terms, conditions, and ad-

justments for effecting the adoption, change, or retention. In determining whether a taxpayer has established a business purpose and which terms, conditions, and adjustments will be required, consideration will be given to all the facts and circumstances relating to the adoption, change, or retention, including the tax consequences resulting therefrom. Generally, the requirement of a business purpose will be satisfied, and adjustments to neutralize any tax consequences will not be required, if the requested annual accounting period coincides with the taxpayer's required taxable year (as defined in § 1.441-1(b)(2)), ownership taxable year, or natural business year. In the case of a partnership, S corporation, electing S corporation, or PSC, deferral of income to partners, shareholders, or employee-owners will not be treated as a business purpose.

(3) *Administrative procedures.* The Commissioner will prescribe administrative procedures under which a taxpayer may be permitted to adopt, change, or retain an annual accounting period. These administrative procedures will describe the business purpose requirements (including an ownership taxable year and a natural business year) and the terms, conditions, and adjustments necessary to obtain approval. Such terms, conditions, and adjustments may include adjustments necessary to neutralize the tax effects of a substantial distortion of income that would otherwise result from the requested annual accounting period including: a deferral of a substantial portion of the taxpayer's income, or shifting of a substantial portion of deductions, from one taxable year to another; a similar deferral or shifting in the case of any other person, such as a beneficiary in an estate; the creation of a short period in which there is a substantial net operating loss, capital loss, or credit (including a general business credit); or the creation of a short period in which there is a substantial amount of income to offset an expiring net operating loss, capital loss, or credit. See, for example, Rev. Proc. 2002-39, 2002-22 I.R.B., procedures for obtaining the Commissioner's prior approval of an adoption, change, or retention in annual accounting period through application to the national office; Rev. Proc. 2002-37, 2002-22 I.R.B., automatic approval procedures for certain corporations; Rev. Proc. 2002-38, 2002-22 I.R.B., automatic approval procedures for partnerships, S corporations, electing S corporations, and PSCs; and Rev. Proc. 66-50, 1966-2 C.B. 1260, automatic approval procedures for individuals. For availability of Revenue Procedures and Notices, see § 601.601(d)(2) of this chapter.

(4) *Taxpayers to whom section 441(g) applies.* If section 441(g) and § 1.441-1(b)(1)(iv) apply to a taxpayer, the adoption of a fiscal year is treated as a change in the taxpayer's annual accounting period under section 442. Therefore, that fiscal year can become the taxpayer's taxable year only with the approval of the Commissioner. In addition to any other terms and conditions that may apply to such a change, the taxpayer must establish and maintain books that adequately and clearly reflect income for the short period involved in the change and for the fiscal year proposed.

(c) *Special rule for change of annual accounting period by subsidiary corporation.* A subsidiary corporation that is required to change its annual accounting period under § 1.1502-76, relating to the taxable year of members of an affiliated group that file a consolidated return, does not need to obtain the approval of the Commissioner or file an application on Form 1128 with respect to that change.

(d) *Special rule for newly married couples.* (1) A newly married husband or wife may obtain automatic approval under this paragraph (d) to change his or her annual accounting period in order to use the annual accounting period of the other spouse so that a joint return may be filed for the first or second taxable year of that spouse ending after the date of marriage. Such automatic approval will be granted only if the newly married husband or wife adopting the annual accounting period of the other spouse files a Federal income tax return for the short period required by that change on or before the 15th day of the 4th month following the close of the short period. See section 443 and the regulations thereunder. If the due date for any such short-period return occurs before the date of marriage, the first taxable year of the other spouse ending after the date of marriage cannot be adopted under this paragraph (d). The short-period return must contain a statement at the top of page one of the return that it is filed under the authority of this paragraph (d). The newly married husband or wife need not file Form 1128 with respect to a change described in this paragraph (d). For a change of annual accounting period by a husband or wife that does not qualify under this paragraph (d), see paragraph (b) of this section.

(2) The provisions of this paragraph (d) may be illustrated by the following example:

Example. H & W marry on September 25, 2001. H is on a fiscal year ending June 30, and W is on a calendar year. H wishes to change to a calendar year in order to file joint returns with W. W's first taxable year after marriage ends on December 31, 2001. H may not change to a calendar year for 2001 since, under this paragraph (d),

Reg. § 1.442-1(b)(3)

he would have had to file a return for the short period from July 1 to December 31, 2000, by April 16, 2001. Since the date of marriage occurred subsequent to this due date, the return could not be filed under this paragraph (d). Therefore, H cannot change to a calendar year for 2001. However, H may change to a calendar year for 2002 by filing a return under this paragraph (d) by April 15, 2002, for the short period from July 1 to December 31, 2001. If H files such a return, H and W may file a joint return for calendar year 2002 (which is W's second taxable year ending after the date of marriage).

(e) *Effective date.* The rules of this section are applicable for taxable years ending on or after May 17, 2002. [Reg. § 1.442-1.]

☐ [T.D. 6226, 2-27-57. Amended by T.D. 6432, 12-18-59, T.D. 6614, 10-12-62, T.D. 7235, 12-27-72, T.D. 7286, 9-26-73, T.D. 7323, 9-24-74, T.D. 7470, 2-28-77, T.D. 7767, 2-3-81, T.D. 7936, 1-17-84; T.D. 8123, 2-5-87 and T.D. 8996, 5-16-2002.]

[Reg. § 1.443-1]

§ 1.443-1. **Returns for periods of less than 12 months.**—(a) *Returns for short period.* A return for a short period, that is, for a taxable year consisting of a period of less than 12 months, shall be made under any of the following circumstances:

(1) *Change of annual accounting period.* In the case of a change in the annual accounting period of a taxpayer, a separate return must be filed for the short period of less than 12 months beginning with the day following the close of the old taxable year and ending with the day preceding the first day of the new taxable year. However, such a return is not required for a short period of six days or less, or 359 days or more, resulting from a change from or to a 52-53-week taxable year. See section 441(f) and § 1.441-2. The computation of the tax for a short period required to effect a change of annual accounting period is described in paragraph (b) of this section. In general, a return for a short period resulting from a change of annual accounting period shall be filed and the tax paid within the time prescribed for filing a return for a taxable year of 12 months ending on the last day of the short period. For rules applicable to a subsidiary corporation which becomes a member of an affiliated group which files a consolidated return, see § 1.1502-76.

(2) *Taxpayer not in existence for entire taxable year.* If a taxpayer is not in existence for the entire taxable year, a return is required for the short period during which the taxpayer was in existence. For example, a corporation organized on August 1 and adopting the calendar year as its annual accounting period is required to file a return for the short period from August 1 to December 31, and returns for each calendar year thereafter. Similarly, a dissolving corporation which files its returns for the calendar year is required to file a return for the short period from January 1 to the date it goes out of existence. Income for the short period is not required to be annualized if the taxpayer is not in existence for the entire taxable year, and, in the case of a taxpayer other than a corporation, the deduction under section 151 for personal exemptions (or deductions in lieu thereof) need not be reduced under section 443(c). In general, the requirements with respect to the filing of returns and the payment of tax for a short period where the taxpayer has not been in existence for the entire taxable year are the same as for the filing of a return and the payment of tax for a taxable year of 12 months ending on the last day of the short period. Although the return of a decedent is a return for the short period beginning with the first day of his last taxable year and ending with the date of his death, the filing of a return and the payment of tax for a decedent may be made as though the decedent had lived throughout his last taxable year.

(b) *Computation of tax for short period on change of annual accounting period*—(1) *General rule.* (i) If a return is made for a short period resulting from a change of annual accounting period, the taxable income for the short period shall be placed on an annual basis by multiplying such income by 12 and dividing the result by the number of months in the short period. Unless section 443(b)(2) and subparagraph (2) of this paragraph apply, the tax for the short period shall be the same part of the tax computed on the annual basis as the number of months in the short period is of 12 months.

(ii) If a return is made for a short period of more than 6 days, but less than 359 days, resulting from a change from or to a 52-53-week taxable year, the taxable income for the short period shall be annualized and the tax computed on a daily basis, as provided in section 441(f)(2)(B)(iii) and § 1.441-2(b)(2)(ii).

(iii) For method of computation of income for a short period in the case of a subsidiary corporation required to change its annual accounting period to conform to that of its parent, see § 1.1502-76(b).

(iv) An individual taxpayer making a return for a short period resulting from a change of annual accounting period is not allowed to take the standard deduction provided in section 141 in computing his taxable income for the short period. See section 142(b)(3).

(v) In computing the taxable income of a taxpayer other than a corporation for a short period (which income is to be annualized in order to determine the tax under section 443(b)(1)) the personal exemptions allowed individuals under section 151 (and any deductions allowed other taxpayers in lieu thereof, such as the deduction under section 642(b)) shall be reduced to an amount which bears the same ratio to the full amount of the exemptions as the number of months in the short period bears to 12. In the case of the taxable income for a short period resulting from a change from or to a 52-53-week taxable year to which section 441(f)(2)(B)(iii) applies, the computation required by the preceding sentence shall be made on a daily basis, that is, the deduction for personal exemptions (or any deduction in lieu thereof) shall be reduced to an amount which bears the same ratio to the full deduction as the number of days in the short period bears to 365.

(vi) If the amount of a credit against the tax (for example, the credits allowable under section 34 (for dividends received on or before December 31, 1964), and 35 (for partially tax-exempt interest)) is dependent upon the amount of any item of income or deduction, such credit shall be computed upon the amount of the item annualized separately in accordance with the foregoing rules. The credit so computed shall be treated as a credit against the tax computed on the basis of the annualized taxable income. In any case in which a limitation on the amount of a credit is based upon taxable income, taxable income shall mean the taxable income computed on the annualized basis.

(vii) The provisions of this subparagraph may be illustrated by the following examples:

Example (1). A taxpayer with one dependent who has been granted permission under section 442 to change his annual accounting period files a return for the short period of 10 months ending October 31, 1956. He has income and deductions as follows:

```
Income
    Interest income ...................................................... $10,000.00
    Partially tax-exempt interest with respect to which a credit is allowable under
        section 35 ........................................................     500.00
    Dividends to which sections 34 and 116 are applicable ..................     750.00
                                                                             $11,250.00
Deductions
    Real estate taxes ....................................................  $   200.00
    2 personal exemptions at $600 on an annual basis......................    1,200.00
The tax for the 10-month period is computed as follows:
Total income as above ....................................................              11,250.00
Less: Exclusion for dividends received ........................  $   50.00
      2 personal exemptions ($1,200 × 10/12) ..................   1,000.00
      Real estate taxes ....................................       200.00              $ 1,250.00

Taxable income for 10-month period before annualizing....................              $10,000.00
Taxable income annualized ($10,000 × 12/10) ..............................              12,000.00
Tax on $12,000 before credits ............................................               3,400.00
Deduct credits:
    Dividends received for 10-month period .........    $750.00
    Less: Excluded portion .........................      50.00

    Included in gross income .......................    $700.00
    Dividend income annualized ($700 × 12/10) ......     840.00
    Credit (4 percent of $840)......................                   $   33.60
    Partially tax-exempt interest included in gross income
        for 10-month period ........................    $500.00
    Partially tax-exempt interest (annualized) ($500 ×
        12/10) .....................................     600.00
    Credit (3 percent of $600) .....................                      18.00        $    51.60

Tax on $12,000 (after credits).............................................            $ 3,348.40

Tax for 10-month period ($3,348.40 × 10/12) ..............................             $ 2,790.33
```

Example (2). The X Corporation makes a return for the one-month period ending September 30, 1956, because of a change in annual account-

Reg. § 1.443-1(b)(1)

ing period permitted under section 442. Income and expenses for the short period are as follows:

Gross operating income		$126,000
Business expenses		130,000
Net loss from operations		$ (4,000)
Dividends received from taxable domestic corporations		30,000
Gross income for short period before annualizing		$ 26,000
Dividends received deduction (85 percent of $30,000, but not in excess of 85 percent of $26,000)		22,100
Taxable income for short period before annualizing		$ 3,900
Taxable income annualized ($3,900 × 12)		46,800
Tax on annual basis: $46,800 at 52 percent	$24,336	
Less surtax exemption	5,500	$ 18,836
Tax for one-month period ($18,836 × 1/12)		$ 1,570

Example (3). The Y Corporation makes a return for the six-month period ending June 30, 1957, because of a change in annual accounting period permitted under section 442. Income for the short period is as follows:

Taxable income exclusive of net long-term capital gain		$ 40,000
Net long-term capital gain		10,000
Taxable income for short period before annualizing		$ 50,000
Taxable income annualized ($50,000 × 12/6)		100,000
Regular tax computation		
Taxable income annualized		$100,000
Tax on annual basis:		
$100,000 at 52 percent	$52,000	
Less surtax exemption	5,500	46,500
Tax for 6-month period ($46,500 × 6/12)		23,250
Alternative tax computation		
Taxable income annualized		$100,000
Less annualized capital gain ($10,000 × 12/6)		20,000
Annualized taxable income subject to partial tax		$ 80,000
Partial tax on annual basis		
$80,000 at 52 percent	$41,600	
Less surtax exemption	5,500	$ 36,100
25 percent of annualized capital gain ($20,000)		5,000
Alternative tax on annual basis		$ 41,100
Alternative tax for 6-month period ($41,100 × 6/12)		20,550

Since the alternative tax of $20,550 is less than the tax computed in the regular manner ($23,250), the corporation's tax for the 6-month short period is $20,550.

(2) *Exception: computation based on 12-month period.* (i) A taxpayer whose tax would otherwise be computed under section 443(b)(1) (or section 441(f)(2)(B)(iii) in the case of certain changes from or to a 52-53-week taxable year) for the short period resulting from a change of annual accounting period may apply to the district director to have his tax computed under the provisions of section 443(b)(2) and this subparagraph. If such application is made, as provided in subdivision (v) of this subparagraph, and if the taxpayer establishes the amount of his taxable income for the 12-month period described in subdivision (ii) of this subparagraph, then the tax for the short period shall be the greater of the following—

(*a*) An amount which bears the same ratio to the tax computed on the taxable income which the taxpayer has established for the 12-month period as the taxable income computed on the basis of the short period bears to the taxable income for such 12-month period; or

(*b*) The tax computed on the taxable income for the short period without placing the taxable income on an annual basis.

However, if the tax computed under section 443(b)(2) and this subparagraph is not less than the tax for the short period computed under section 443(b)(1) (or section 441(f)(2)(B)(iii) in the

Reg. § 1.443-1(b)(2)

case of certain changes from or to a 52-53-week taxable year), then section 443(b)(2) and this subparagraph do not apply.

(ii) The term "12-month period" referred to in subdivision (i) of this subparagraph means the 12-month period beginning on the first day of the short period. However, if the taxpayer is not in existence at the end of such 12-month period, or if the taxpayer is a corporation which has disposed of substantially all of its assets before the end of such 12-month period, the term "12-month period" means the 12-month period ending at the close of the last day of the short period. For the purposes of the preceding sentence, a corporation which has ceased business and distributed so much of the assets used in its business that it cannot resume its customary operations with the remaining assets, will be considered to have disposed of substantially all of its assets. In the case of a change from a 52-53-week taxable year, the term "12-month period" means the period of 52 or 53 weeks (depending on the taxpayer's 52-53-week taxable year) beginning on the first day of the short period.

(iii) (a) The taxable income for the 12-month period is computed under the same provisions of law as are applicable to the short period and is computed as if the 12-month period were an actual annual accounting period of the taxpayer. All items which fall in such 12-month period must be included even if they are extraordinary in amount or of an unusual nature. If the taxpayer is a member of a partnership, his taxable income for the 12-month period shall include his distributive share of partnership income for any taxable year of the partnership ending within or with such 12-month period, but no amount shall be included with respect to a taxable year of the partnership ending before or after such 12-month period. If any other item partially applicable to such 12-month period can be determined only at the end of a taxable year which includes only part of the 12-month period, the taxpayer subject to review by the Commissioner, shall apportion such item to the 12-month period in such manner as will most clearly reflect income for the 12-month period.

(b) In the case of a taxpayer permitted or required to use inventories, the cost of goods sold during a part of the 12-month period included in a taxable year shall be considered, unless a more exact determination is available, as such part of the cost of goods sold during the entire taxable year as the gross receipts from sales for such part of the 12-month period is of the gross receipts from sales for the entire taxable year. For example, the 12-month period of a corporation engaged in the sale of merchandise, which has a short period from January 1, 1956, to September 30, 1956, is the calendar year 1956. The three-month period, October 1, 1956, to December 31, 1956, is part of the taxpayer's taxable year ending September 30, 1957. The cost of goods sold during the three-month period, October 1, 1956, to December 31, 1956, is such part of the cost of goods sold during the entire fiscal year ending September 30, 1957, as the gross receipts from sales for such three-month period are of the gross receipts from sales for the entire fiscal year.

(c) The Commissioner may, in granting permission to a taxpayer to change his annual accounting period, require, as a condition to permitting the change, that the taxpayer must take a closing inventory upon the last day of the 12-month period if he wishes to obtain the benefits of section 443(b)(2). Such closing inventory will be used only for the purposes of section 443(b)(2), and the taxpayer will not be required to use such inventory in computing the taxable income for the taxable year in which such inventory is taken.

(iv) The provisions of this subparagraph may be illustrated by the following examples:

Example (1). The taxpayer in example (1) under paragraph (b)(1)(vii) of this section establishes his taxable income for the 12-month period from January 1, 1956, to December 31, 1956. The taxpayer has a short period of 10 months, from January 1, 1956, to October 31, 1956. The taxpayer files an application in accordance with subdivision (v) of this subparagraph to compute his tax under section 443(b)(2). The taxpayer's income and deductions for the 12-month period, as so established, follow:

Income
- Interest income $11,000
- Partially tax-exempt interest with respect to which a credit is allowable under section 35 600
- Dividends to which sections 34 and 116 are applicable 850

$12,450

Deductions
- Real estate taxes .... $ 200
- 2 personal exemptions at $600 1,200

Tax computation for short period under section 443(b)(2)(A)(i)
- Total income as above $12,450

Reg. § 1.443-1(b)(2)

Accounting Periods

See p. 20,601 for regulations not amended to reflect law changes

Less: Exclusion for dividends received	$ 50	
Personal exemptions	1,200	
Deduction for taxes	200	1,450
Taxable income for 12-month period		$11,000
Tax before credits		$ 3,020
Credit for partially tax-exempt interest (3 percent of $600)	$ 18	
Credit for dividends received (4 percent of ($850 − 50))	32	50
Tax under section 443(b)(2)(A)(i) for 12-month period		$ 2,970
Taxable income for 10-month short period from example (1) of paragraph (b)(1)(vii) of this section before annualizing		10,000
Tax for short period under section 443(b)(2)(A)(i) ($2,970 × $10,000 (taxable income for short period)/$11,000 (taxable income for 12-month period))		2,700

Tax computation for short period under section 443(b)(2)(A)(ii)

Total income for 10-month short period		$11,250
Less: Exclusion for dividends received	$ 50	
2 personal exemptions	1,200	
Real estate taxes	200	1,450
Taxable income for short period without annualizing and without proration of personal exemptions		$ 9,800
Tax before credits		$ 2,572
Less credits: Partially tax-exempt interest (3 per cent of $500)	$ 15	
Dividends received (4 percent of ($750 − 50))	28	$ 43
Tax for short period under section 443(b)(2)(A)(ii)		$ 2,529

The tax of $2,700 computed under section 443(b)(2)(A)(i) is greater than the tax of $2,529, computed under section 443(b)(2)(A)(ii), and is, therefore, the tax under section 443(b)(2). Since the tax of $2,700 (computed under section 443(b)(2)) is less than the tax of $2,790.33 (computed under section 443(b)(1)) on the annualized income of the short period (see example (1) of paragraph (b)(1)(vii) of this section), the taxpayer's tax for the 10-month short period is $2,700.

Example (2). Assume the same facts as in example (1) of this subdivision, except that, during the month of November 1956, the taxpayer suffered a casualty loss of $5,000. The tax computation for the short period under section 443(b)(2) would be as follows:

Tax computation for short period under section 443(b)(2)(A)(i)

Taxable income for 12-month period from example (1)		$11,000
Less: Casualty loss		5,000
Taxable income for 12-month period		$ 6,000
Tax before credits	$1,360	
Credits from example (1)	50	
Tax under section 443(b)(2)(A)(i) for 12-month period		$ 1,310
Tax for short period ($1,310 × $10,000/$6,000) under section 443(b)(2)(A)(i)		$ 2,183

Tax computation for short period under section 443(b)(2)(A)(ii)

Total income for the short period		$11,250
Less: Exclusion for dividends received	$ 50	
2 personal exemptions	1,200	
Real estate taxes	200	1,450
Taxable income for short period without annualizing and without proration of personal exemptions		$ 9,800
Tax before credits		2,572
Less credits: Partially tax-exempt interest (3 percent of $500)	$ 15	
Dividends received (4 percent of ($750 − 50))	28	43
Tax for short period under section 433(b)(2)(A)(ii)		$ 2,529

The tax of $2,529, computed under section 443(b)(2)(A)(ii) is greater than the tax of $2,183 computed under section 443(b)(2)(A)(i) and is, therefore, the tax under section 443(b)(2). Since this tax is less than the tax of $2,790.33, computed under section 443(b)(1) (see example (1) of paragraph (b)(1)(vii) of this section), the tax-

Reg. § 1.443-1(b)(2)

payer's tax for the 10-month short period is $2,529.

(v) (*a*) A taxpayer who wishes to compute his tax for a short period resulting from a change of annual accounting period under section 443(b)(2) must make an application therefor. Except as provided in (*b*) of this subdivision, the taxpayer shall first file his return for the short period and compute his tax under section 443(b)(1). The application for the benefits of section 443(b)(2) shall subsequently be made in the form of a claim for credit or refund. The claim shall set forth the computation of the taxable income and the tax thereon for the 12-month period and must be filed not later than the time (including extensions) prescribed for filing the return for the taxpayer's first taxable year which ends on or after the day which is 12 months after the beginning of the short period. For example, assume that a taxpayer changes his annual accounting period from the calendar year to a fiscal year ending September 30, and files a return for the short period from January 1, 1956, to September 30, 1956. His application for the benefits of section 443(b)(2) must be filed not later than the time prescribed for filing his return for his first taxable year which ends on or after the last day of December 1956, the twelfth month after the beginning of the short period. Thus, the taxpayer must file his application not later than the time prescribed for filing the return for his fiscal year ending September 30, 1957. If he obtains an extension of time for filing the return for such fiscal year, he may file his application during the period of such extension. If the district director determines that the taxpayer has established the amount of his taxable income for the 12-month period, any excess of the tax paid for the short period over the tax computed under section 443(b)(2) will be credited or refunded to the taxpayer in the same manner as in the case of an overpayment.

(*b*) If at the time the return for the short period is filed, the taxpayer is able to determine that the 12-month period ending with the close of the short period (see section 443(b)(2)(B)(ii) and subparagraph (2)(ii) of this paragraph) will be used in the computations under section 443(b)(2), then the tax on the return for the short period may be determined under the provisions of section 443(b)(2). In such case, a return covering the 12-month period shall be attached to the return for the short period as a part thereof, and the return and attachment will then be considered as an application for the benefits of section 443(b)(2).

(c) *Adjustment in deduction for personal exemption.* For adjustment in the deduction for personal exemptions in computing the tax for a short period resulting from a change of annual accounting period under section 443(b)(1) (or under section 441(f)(2)(B)(iii) in the case of certain changes from or to a 52-53-week taxable year), see paragraph (b)(1)(v) of this section.

(d) *Adjustment in exclusion for computing minimum tax for tax preferences.* (1) If a return is made for a short period on account of any of the reasons specified in subsection (a) of section 443, the $30,000 amount specified in section 56 (relating to minimum tax for tax preferences), modified as provided by section 58 and the regulations thereunder, shall be reduced to the amount which bears the same ratio to such specified amount as the number of days in the short period bears to 365.

(2) *Example.* The provisions of this paragraph may be illustrated by the following example:

Example. A taxpayer who is an unmarried individual has been granted permission under section 442 to change his annual accounting period files a return for the short period of 4 months ending April 30, 1970. The $30,000 amount specified in section 56 is reduced as follows:

$$\frac{120}{365} \times \$30{,}000 = \$9{,}863.01.$$

(e) *Cross references.* For inapplicability of section 443(b) and paragraph (b) of this section in computing—

(1) Accumulated earnings tax, see section 536 and the regulations thereunder;

(2) Personal holding company tax, see section 546 and the regulations thereunder;

(3) Undistributed foreign personal holding company income, see section 557 and the regulations thereunder;

(4) The taxable income of a regulated investment company, see section 852(b)(2)(E) and the regulations thereunder; and

(5) The taxable income of a real estate investment trust, see section 857(b)(2)(C) and the regulations thereunder. [Reg. § 1.443-1.]

☐ [*T.D. 6226, 2-27-57. Amended by T.D. 6598, 4-25-62; T.D. 6777, 12-15-64; T.D. 7244, 12-29-72; T.D. 7564, 9-11-78; T.D. 7575, 12-15-78; T.D. 7767, 2-3-81 and T.D. 8996, 5-16-2002.*]

Reg. § 1.443-1(c)

Accounting Periods

[Reg. § 1.444-0T]

§ 1.444-0T. Table of contents (temporary).—This section lists the captions that appear in the temporary regulations under section 444.

§ 1.444-1T. Election to use a taxable year other than the required taxable year (temporary).

(a) General rules.

(1) Year other than required year.

(2) Effect of section 444 election.

(i) In general.

(ii) Duration of section 444 election.

(3) Section 444 election not required for certain years.

(4) Required taxable year.

(5) Termination of section 444 election.

(i) In general.

(ii) Effective date of termination.

(iii) Example.

(iv) Special rule for entity that liquidates or is sold prior to making a section 444 election, required return, or required payment.

(6) Re-activating certain S elections.

(i) Certain corporations electing S status that did not make a back-up calendar year request.

(ii) Certain corporations that revoked their S status.

(iii) Procedures for re-activating an S election.

(iv) Examples.

(b) Limitation on taxable years that may be elected.

(1) General rule.

(2) Changes in taxable year.

(i) In general.

(ii) Special rule for certain existing corporations electing S status.

(iii) Deferral period of the taxable year that is being changed.

(iv) Examples.

(3) Special rule for entities retaining 1986 taxable year.

(4) Deferral period.

(i) Retentions of taxable year.

(ii) Adoptions of and changes in taxable year.

(A) In general.

(B) Special rule.

(C) Examples.

(5) Miscellaneous rules.

(i) Special rule for determining the taxable year of a corporation electing S status.

(ii) Special procedure for cases where an income tax return is superseded.

(A) In general.

(B) Procedure for superseding return.

(iii) Anti-abuse rule.

(iv) Special rules for partial months and 52-53-week taxable years.

(c) Effective date.

(d) Examples.

(1) Changes in taxable year.

(2) Special rule for entities retaining their 1986 taxable year.

§ 1.444-2T. Tiered structure (temporary).

(a) General rule.

(b) Definition of a member of a tiered structure.

(1) In general.

(2) Deferral entity.

(i) In general.

(ii) Grantor trusts.

(3) Anti-abuse rule.

(c) De minimis rules.

(1) In general.

(2) Downstream de minimis rule.

(i) General rule.

(ii) Definition of testing period.

(iii) Definition of adjusted taxable income.

(A) Partnership.

(B) S corporation.

(C) Personal service corporation.

(iv) Special rules.

(A) Pro-forma rule.

(B) Reasonable estimates allowed.

(C) Newly formed entities.

(*1*) Newly formed deferral entities.

(*2*) Newly formed partnership, S corporation, or personal service corporation desiring to make a section 444 election.

(3) Upstream de minimis rule.

(d) Date for determining the existence of a tiered structure.

(1) General rule.

(2) Special rule for taxable years beginning in 1987.

(e) Same taxable year exception.

(1) In general.

(2) Definition of tiered structure.

(i) General rule.

Reg. § 1.444-0T

(ii) Special flow-through rule for downstream controlled partnerships.

(3) Determining the taxable year of a partnership or S corporation.

(4) Special rule for 52-53-week taxable years.

(5) Interaction with de minimis rules.

(i) Downstream de minimis rule.

(A) In general.

(B) Special rule for members of a tiered structure directly owned by a downstream controlled partnership.

(ii) Upstream de minimis rule.

(f) Examples.

(g) Effective date.

§ 1.444-3T. *Manner and time of making section 444 election (temporary).*

(a) In general.

(b) Manner and time of making election.

(1) General rule.

(2) Special extension of time for making an election.

(3) Corporation electing to be an S corporation.

(i) In general.

(ii) Examples.

(4) Back-up section 444 election.

(i) General rule.

(ii) Procedures for making a back-up section 444 election.

(iii) Procedures for activating a back-up section 444 election.

(A) Partnerships and S corporations.

(*1*) In general.

(*2*) Special rule if Form 720 used to satisfy return requirement.

(B) Personal service corporations.

(iv) Examples.

(c) Administrative relief.

(1) Extension of time to file income tax returns.

(i) Automatic extension.

(ii) Additional extensions.

(iii) Examples.

(2) No penalty for certain late payments.

(i) In general.

(ii) Example.

(d) Effective date.

[Temporary Reg. § 1.444-0T.]

☐ [*T.D.* 8205, 5-24-88.]

[Reg. § 1.444-1T]

§ 1.444-1T. **Election to use a taxable year other than the required taxable year (temporary).**—(a) *General rules*—(1) *Year other than required year.* Except as otherwise provided in this section and § 1.444-2T, a partnership, S corporation, or personal service corporation (as defined in § 1.441-3(c)) may make or continue an election (a "section 444 election") to have a taxable year other than its required taxable year. See paragraph (b) of this section for limitations on the taxable year that may be elected. See § 1.444-2T for rules that generally prohibit a partnership, S corporation, or personal service corporation that is a member of a tiered structure from making or continuing a section 444 election. See § 1.444-3T for rules explaining how and when to make a section 444 election.

(2) *Effect of section 444 election*—(i) *In general.* A partnership or S corporation that makes or continues a section 444 election shall file returns and make payments as required by §§ 1.7519-1T and 1.7519-2T. A personal service corporation that makes or continues a section 444 election is subject to the deduction limitation of § 1.280H-1T.

(ii) *Duration of section 444 election.* A section 444 election shall remain in effect until the election is terminated pursuant to paragraph (a)(5) of this section.

(3) *Section 444 election not required for certain years.* A partnership, S corporation, or personal service corporation is not required to make a section 444 election to use—

(i) A taxable year for which such entity establishes a business purpose to the satisfaction of the Commissioner (*i.e.,* approved under section 4 or 6 of Rev. Proc. 87-32, 1987-28 I.R.B. 14, or any successor revenue ruling or revenue procedure), or

(ii) A taxable year that is a "grandfathered fiscal year," within the meaning of section 5.01(2) of Rev. Proc. 87-32 or any successor revenue ruling or revenue procedure.

Although a partnership, S corporation or personal service corporation qualifies to use a taxable year described in paragraph (a)(3)(i) or (ii) of this section, such entity may, if otherwise qualified, make a section 444 election to use a different taxable year. Thus, for example, assume that a personal service corporation that historically used a January 31 taxable year established to the satisfaction of the Commissioner, under section 6 of Rev. Proc. 87-32, a business purpose to use a September 30 taxable year for its taxable year beginning February 1, 1987. Pursuant to this paragraph (a)(3), such personal service corporation

Reg. § 1.444-1T(a)(1)

may use a September 30 taxable year without making a section 444 election. However, the corporation may, if otherwise qualified, make a section 444 election to use a year ending other than September 30 for its taxable year beginning February 1, 1987.

(4) *Required taxable year.* For purposes of this section, the term "required taxable year" means the taxable year determined under section 706(b), 1378, or 441(i) without taking into account any taxable year which is allowable either—

(i) By reason of business purpose (*i.e.*, approved under section 4 or 6 of Rev. Proc. 87-32 or any successor revenue ruling or procedure), or

(ii) As a "grandfathered fiscal year" within the meaning of section 5.01(2) of Rev. Proc. 87-32, or any successor revenue ruling or procedure.

(5) *Termination of section 444 election*—(i) *In general.* A section 444 election is terminated when—

(A) A partnership, S corporation, or personal service corporation changes to its required taxable year; or

(B) A partnership, S corporation, or personal service corporation liquidates (including a deemed liquidation of a partnership under § 1.708-1(b)(1)(iv)); or

(C) A partnership, S corporation, or personal service corporation willfully fails to comply with the requirements of section 7519 or 280H, whichever is applicable; or

(D) A partnership, S corporation, or personal service corporation becomes a member of a tiered structure (within the meaning of § 1.444-2T), unless it is a partnership or S corporation that meets the same taxable year exception under § 1.444-2T(e); or

(E) An S corporation's S election is terminated; or

(F) A personal service corporation ceases to be a personal service corporation.

However, if a personal service corporation, that has a section 444 election in effect, elects to be an S corporation, the S corporation may continue the section 444 election of the personal service corporation. Similarly, if an S corporation that has a section 444 election in effect terminates its S election and immediately becomes a personal service corporation, the personal service corporation may continue the section 444 election of the S corporation. If a section 444 election is terminated under this paragraph (a)(5), the partnership, S corporation, or personal service corporation may not make another section 444 election for any taxable year.

(ii) *Effective date of termination.* A termination of a section 444 election shall be effective—

(A) In the case of a change to the required year, on the first day of the short year caused by the change;

(B) In the case of a liquidating entity, on the date the liquidation is completed for tax purposes;

(C) In the case of willful failure to comply, on the first day of the taxable year (determined as if a section 444 election had never been made) determined in the discretion of the District Director;

(D) In the case of membership in a tiered structure, on the first day of the taxable year in which the entity is considered to be a member of a tiered structure, or such other taxable year determined in the discretion of the District Director;

(E) In the case of termination of S status, on the first day of the taxable year for which S status no longer exists;

(F) In the case of a personal service corporation that changes status, on the first day of the taxable year, for which the entity is no longer a personal service corporation.

In the case of a termination under this paragraph (a)(5) that results in a short taxable year, an income tax return is required for the short period. In order to allow the Service to process the affected income tax return in an efficient manner, a partnership, S corporation, or personal service corporation that files such a short period return should type or legibly print at the top of the first page of the income tax return for the short taxable year—"SECTION 444 ELECTION TERMINATED." In addition, a personal service corporation that changes its taxable year to the required taxable year is required to annualize its income for the short period.

(iii) *Example.* The provisions of paragraph (a)(5)(ii) of this section may be illustrated by the following example.

Example. Assume a partnership that is 100 percent owned, at all times, by calendar year individuals has historically used a June 30 taxable year. Also assume the partnership makes a valid section 444 election to retain a year ending June 30 for its taxable year beginning July 1, 1987. However, for its taxable year beginning July 1, 1988, the partnership changes to a calendar year, its required year. Based on these facts, the partnership's section 444 election is terminated on

Reg. § 1.444-1T(a)(5)

July 1, 1988, and the partnership must file a short period return for the period July 1, 1988—December 31, 1988. Furthermore, pursuant to § 1.702-3T(a)(1), the partners in such partnership are not entitled to a 4-year spread with respect to partnership items of income and expense for the taxable year beginning July 1, 1988 and ending December 31, 1988.

(iv) *Special rule for entity that liquidates or is sold prior to making a section 444 election, required return, or required payment.* A partnership, S corporation, or personal service corporation that is liquidated or sold for tax purposes before a section 444 election, required return, or required payment is made for a particular year may, nevertheless, make or continue a section 444 election, if otherwise qualified. (See §§ 1.7519-2T(a)(2) and 1.7519-1T(a)(3), respectively, for a description of the required return and a definition of the term "required payment.") However, the partnership, S corporation, or personal service corporation (or a trustee or agent thereof) must comply with the requirements for making or continuing a section 444 election. Thus, if applicable, required payments must be made and a subsequent claim for refund must be made in accordance with § 1.7519-2T(a)(6). The following examples illustrate the application of this paragraph (a)(5)(iv).

Example (1). Assume an existing S corporation historically used a June 30 taxable year and desires to make a section 444 election for its taxable year beginning July 1, 1987. Assume further that the S corporation is liquidated for tax purposes on February 15, 1988. If otherwise qualified, the S corporation (or a trustee or agent thereof) may make a section 444 election to have a taxable year beginning July 1, 1987, and ending February 15, 1988. However, if the S corporation makes a section 444 election, it must comply with the requirements for making a section 444 election, including making required payments.

Example (2). The facts are the same as in example (1), except that instead of liquidating on February 15, 1988, the shareholders of the S corporation sell their stock to a corporation on February 15, 1988. Thus, the corporation's S election is terminated on February 15, 1988. If otherwise qualified, the corporation may make a section 444 election to have a taxable year beginning July 1, 1987, and ending February 14, 1988.

Example (3). The facts are the same as in example (2), except that the new shareholders are individuals. Furthermore, the corporation's S election is not terminated. Based on these facts, the S corporation, if otherwise qualified, may make a section 444 election to retain a year ending June 30 for its taxable year beginning July 1, 1987. Furthermore, the S corporation may, if otherwise qualified, continue its section 444 election for subsequent taxable years.

(6) *Re-activating certain S elections*—(i) *Certain corporations electing S status that did not make a back-up calendar year request.* If a corporation that timely filed Form 2553, Election by a Small Business Corporation, effective for its first taxable year beginning in 1987—

(A) Requested a fiscal year based on business purpose,

(B) Did not agree to use a calendar year in the event its business purpose request was denied, and

(C) Such business purpose request is denied or withdrawn,

such corporation may retroactively re-activate its S election by making a valid section 444 election for its first taxable year beginning in 1987 and complying with the procedures in paragraph (a)(6)(iii) of this section.

(ii) *Certain corporations that revoked their S status.* If a corporation that used a fiscal year revoked its S election (pursuant to section 1362(d)(1)) for its first taxable year beginning in 1987, such corporation may retroactively re-activate its S election (*i.e.,* rescind its revocation) by making a valid section 444 election for its first taxable year beginning in 1987 and complying with the procedures in paragraph (a)(6)(iii) of this section.

(iii) *Procedures for re-activating an S election.* A corporation re-activating its S election pursuant to paragraph (a)(6)(i) or (ii) of this section must—

(A) Obtain the consents of all shareholders who have owned stock in the corporation since the first day of the first taxable year of the corporation beginning after December 31, 1986,

(B) Include the following statement at the top of the first page of the corporation's Form 1120S for its first taxable year beginning in 1987—"SECTION 444 ELECTION—RE-ACTIVATES S STATUS," and

(C) Include the following statement with Form 1120S—"RE-ACTIVATION CONSENTED TO BY ALL SHAREHOLDERS WHO HAVE OWNED STOCK AT ANY TIME SINCE THE FIRST DAY OF THE FIRST TAXABLE YEAR OF THIS CORPORATION BEGINNING AFTER DECEMBER 31, 1986."

(iv) *Examples.* The provisions of this paragraph (a)(6) may be illustrated by the following examples.

Reg. § 1.444-1T(a)(6)

Example (1). Assume a corporation historically used a June 30 taxable year and such corporation timely filed Form 2553, Election by a Small Business Corporation, to be effective for its taxable year beginning July 1, 1987. On its Form 2553, the corporation requested permission to retain its June 30 taxable year based on business purpose. However, the corporation did not agree to use a calendar year in the event its business purpose request was denied. On April 1, 1988, the Internal Revenue Service notified the corporation that its business purpose request was denied and therefore the corporation's S election was not effective. Pursuant to paragraph (a)(6)(i) of this section, the corporation may re-activate its S election by making a valid section 444 election and complying with the procedures in paragraph (a)(6)(iii) of this section.

Example (2). The facts are the same as in example (1), except that as of July 26, 1988 the Internal Revenue Service has not yet determined whether the corporation has a valid business purpose to retain a June 30 taxable year. Based on these facts, the corporation may, if otherwise qualified, make a back-up section 444 election as provided in § 1.444-3T(b)(4). If the corporation's business purpose request is subsequently denied, the corporation should follow the procedures in § 1.444-3T(b)(4)(iii) for activating a back-up section 444 election rather than the procedures provided in this paragraph (a)(6) for re-activating an S election.

Example (3). Assume a corporation has historically been an S corporation with a March 31 taxable year. However, for its taxable year beginning April 1, 1987, the corporation revoked its S election pursuant to section 1362(d)(1). Pursuant to paragraph (a)(6)(ii) of this section, such corporation may retroactively rescind its S election revocation by making a valid section 444 election for its taxable year beginning April 1, 1987, and complying with the procedures provided in paragraph (a)(6)(iii) of this section. If the corporation retroactively rescinds its S revocation, the corporation shall file a Form 1120S for its taxable year beginning April 1, 1987.

(b) *Limitation on taxable years that may be elected*—(1) *General rule.* Except as provided in paragraphs (b)(2) and (3) of this section, a section 444 election may be made only if the deferral period (as defined in paragraph (b)(4) of this section) of the taxable year to be elected is not longer than three months.

(2) *Changes in taxable year*—(i) *In general.* In the case of a partnership, S corporation, or personal service corporation changing its taxable year, such entity may make a section 444 election only if the deferral period of the taxable year to be elected is not longer than the shorter of—

(A) Three months, or

(B) The deferral period of the taxable year that is being changed, as defined in paragraph (b)(2)(iii) of this section.

(ii) *Special rule for certain existing corporations electing S status.* If a corporation with a taxable year other than the calendar year—

(A) Elected after September 18, 1986, and before January 1, 1988, under section 1362 of the Code to be an S corporation, and

(B) Elected to have the calendar year as the taxable year of the S corporation,

then, for taxable years beginning before 1989, paragraph (b)(2)(i) of this section shall be applied by taking into account the deferral period of the last taxable year of the corporation prior to electing to be an S corporation, rather than the deferral period of the taxable year that is being changed. Thus, the provisions of the preceding sentence do not apply to a corporation that elected to be an S corporation for its first taxable year.

(iii) *Deferral period of the taxable year that is being changed.* For purposes of paragraph (b)(2)(i)(B) of this section, the phrase "deferral period of the taxable year that is being changed" means the deferral period of the taxable year immediately preceding the taxable year for which the taxpayer desires to make a section 444 election. Furthermore, the deferral period of such year will be determined by using the required taxable year of the taxable year for which the taxpayer desires to make a section 444 election. For example, assume P, a partnership that has historically used a March 31 taxable year, desires to change to a September 30 taxable year by making a section 444 election for its taxable year beginning April 1, 1987. Furthermore, assume that pursuant to paragraph (a)(4) of this section, P's required taxable year for the taxable year beginning April 1, 1987 is a year ending December 31. Based on these facts, the deferral period of the taxable year being changed is nine months (the period from March 31 to December 31).

(iv) *Examples.* See paragraph (d)(1) of this section for examples that illustrate the provisions of this paragraph (b)(2).

(3) *Special rule for entities retaining 1986 taxable year.* Notwithstanding paragraph (b)(2) of this section, a partnership, S corporation, or personal service corporation may, for its first taxable year beginning after December 31, 1986, if otherwise qualified, make a section 444 election to have a taxable year that is the same as the en-

Reg. § 1.444-1T(b)(3)

tity's last taxable year beginning in 1986. See paragraph (d)(2) of this section for examples that illustrate the provisions of this paragraph (b)(3).

(4) *Deferral period*—(i) *Retentions of taxable year.* For a partnership, S corporation, or personal service corporation that desires to retain its taxable year by making a section 444 election, the term "deferral period" means the months between the beginning of such year and the close of the first required taxable year (as defined in paragraph (a)(4) of this section). The following example illustrates the application of this paragraph (b)(4)(i).

Example. AB partnership has historically used a taxable year ending July 31. AB desires to retain its July 31 taxable year by making a section 444 election for its taxable year beginning August 1, 1987. Calendar year individuals, A and B, each own 50 percent of the profits and capital of AB; thus, under paragraph (a)(4) of this section AB's required taxable year is the year ending December 31. Pursuant to this paragraph (b)(4)(i), if AB desires to retain its year ending July 31, the deferral period is five months (the months between July 31 and December 31).

(ii) *Adoptions of and changes in taxable year*—(A) *In general.* For a partnership, S corporation, or personal service corporation that desires to adopt or change its taxable year by making a section 444 election, the term "deferral period" means the months that occur after the end of the taxable year desired under section 444 and before the close of the required taxable year.

(B) *Special rule.* If a partnership, S corporation or personal service corporation is using the required taxable year as its taxable year, the deferral period is deemed to be zero.

(C) *Examples.* The provisions of this paragraph (b)(4)(ii) may be illustrated by the following examples.

Example (1). Assume that CD partnership has historically used the calendar year and that CD's required taxable year is the calendar year. Under the special rule provided in paragraph (b)(4)(ii)(B) of this section, CD's deferral period is zero. See paragraph (b)(2)(i) of this section for rules that preclude CD from making a section 444 election to change its taxable year.

Example (2). E, a newly formed partnership, began operations on December 1, 1987, and is owned by calendar year individuals. E desires to make a section 444 election to adopt a September 30 taxable year. E's required taxable year is December 31. Pursuant to paragraph (b)(4)(ii)(A) of this section, E's deferral period for the taxable year beginning December 1, 1987, is three months (the number of months between September 30 and December 31).

Example (3). Assume that F, a personal service corporation, has historically used a June 30 taxable year. F desires to make a section 444 election to change to an August 31 taxable year, effective for its taxable year beginning July 1, 1987. For purposes of determining the availability of a section 444 election for changing to the taxable year ending August 31, the deferral period of an August 31 taxable year is four months (the number of months between August 31 and December 31). The deferral period for F's existing June 30 taxable year is six months (the number of months between June 30 and December 31). Pursuant to § 1.444-1T(b)(2)(i), F may not make a section 444 election to change to an August 31 taxable year.

(5) *Miscellaneous rules*—(i) *Special rule for determining the taxable year of a corporation electing S status.* For purposes of this section, and only for purposes of this section, a corporation that elected to be an S corporation for a taxable year beginning in 1987 or 1988 and which elected to be an S corporation prior to September 26, 1988, will not be considered to have adopted or changed its taxable year by virtue of information included on Form 2553, Election by a Small Business Corporation. See example (8) in paragraph (d) of this section.

(ii) *Special procedure for cases where an income tax return is superseded*—(A) *In general.* In the case of a partnership, S corporation, or personal service corporation that filed an income tax return for its first taxable year beginning after December 31, 1986, but subsequently makes a section 444 election that would result in a different year end for such taxable year, the income tax return filed pursuant to the section 444 election will supersede the original return. However, any payments of income tax made with respect to such superseded return will be credited to the taxpayer's superseding return and the taxpayer may file a claim for refund for such payments. See examples (5) and (7) in paragraph (d)(2) of this section.

(B) *Procedure for superseding return.* In order to allow the Service to process the affected income tax returns in an efficient manner, a partnership, S corporation, or personal service corporation that desires to supersede an income tax return in accordance with paragraph (b)(5)(ii)(A) of this section should type or legibly print at the top of the first page of the income tax return for the taxable year elected—"SECTION 444 ELECTION—SUPERSEDES PRIOR RETURN."

Reg. § 1.444-1T(b)(4)

(iii) *Anti-abuse rule*—If an existing partnership, S corporation or personal service corporation ("predecessor entities"), or the owners thereof, transfer assets to a related party and the principal purpose of such transfer is to—

(A) Create a deferral period greater than the deferral period of the predecessor entity's taxable year, or

(B) Make a section 444 election following the termination of the predecessor entity's section 444 election,

then such transfer will be disregarded for purposes of section 444 and this section, even if the deferral created by such change is effectively eliminated by a required payment (within the meaning of section 7519) or deferral of a deduction (to a personal service corporation under section 280H). The following example illustrates the application of this paragraph (b)(5)(iii).

Example. Assume that P1 is a partnership that historically used the calendar year and is owned by calendar year partners. Assume that P1 desires to make a section 444 election to change to a September year for the taxable year beginning January 1, 1988. P1 may not make a section 444 election to change taxable years under section 444(b)(2) because its current deferral period is zero. Assume further that P1 transfers a substantial portion of its assets to a newly-formed partnership (P2), which is owned by the partners of P1. Absent paragraph (b)(5)(iii) of this section, P2 could, if otherwise qualified, make a section 444 election under paragraph (b)(1) of this section to use a taxable year with a three month or less deferral period (*i.e.*, a September 30, October 31, or November 30 taxable year). However, if the principal purpose of the asset transfer was to create a one-, two-, or three-month deferral period by P2 making a section 444 election, the section 444 election shall not be given effect, even if the deferral would be effectively eliminated by P2 making a required payment under section 7519.

(iv) *Special rules for partial months and 52-53-week taxable years.* Except as otherwise provided in § 1.280H-1T(c)(2)(i)(A), for purposes of this section and §§ 1.7519-1T, 1.7519-2T and 1.280H-1T—

(A) A month of less than 16 days is disregarded, and a month of more than 15 days is treated as a full month; and

(B) A 52-53-week taxable year with reference to the end of a particular month will be considered to be the same as a taxable year ending with reference to the last day of such month.

(c) *Effective date.* This section is effective for taxable years beginning after December 31, 1986.

(d) *Examples*—(1) *Changes in taxable year.* The following examples illustrate the provisions of paragraph (b)(2) of this section.

Example (1). A is a personal service corporation that historically used a June 30 taxable year. A desires to make a section 444 election to change to an August 31 taxable year, effective with its taxable year beginning July 1, 1987. Under paragraph (b)(4)(ii) of this section, the deferral period of the taxable year to be elected is four months (the number of months between August 31 and December 31). Furthermore, the deferral period of the taxable year that is being changed is six months (the number of months between June 30 and December 31). Pursuant to paragraph (b)(2)(i) of this section, a taxpayer may, if otherwise qualified, make a section 444 election to change to a taxable year only if the deferral period of the taxable year to be elected is not longer than the shorter of three months or the deferral period of the taxable year being changed. Since the deferral period of the taxable year to be elected (August 31) is greater than three months, A may not make a section 444 election to change to the taxable year ending August 31. However, since the deferral period of the taxable year that is being changed is three months or more, A may, if otherwise qualified, make a section 444 election to change to a year ending September 30, 1987 (three-month deferral period), a year ending October 31, 1987 (two-month deferral period), or a year ending November 30, 1987 (one-month deferral period). In addition, instead of making a section 444 election to change its taxable year, A could, if otherwise qualified, make a section 444 election to retain its June year end, pursuant to paragraph (b)(3) of this section.

Example (2). B, a corporation that historically used an August 31 taxable year, elected on November 1, 1986 to be an S corporation for its taxable year beginning September 1, 1986. As a condition to having the S election accepted, B agreed on Form 2553 to use a calendar year. Pursuant to the general effective date provided in paragraph (c) of this section, B may not make a section 444 election for its taxable year beginning in 1986. Thus, B must file a short period income tax return for the period September 1 to December 31, 1986.

Example (3). The facts are the same as in example (2), except that B desires to make a section 444 election for its taxable year beginning January 1, 1987. Absent paragraph (b)(2)(ii) of this section, B would not be allowed to change its taxable year because the deferral period of the taxable year being changed (*i.e.*, the calendar year) is zero. However, pursuant to the special

Reg. § 1.444-1T(d)(1)

rule provided in paragraph (b)(2)(ii) of this section, B shall apply paragraph (b)(2)(i) of this section by taking into account the deferral period of the last taxable year of B prior to B's election to be an S corporation (four months), rather than the deferral period of B's taxable year that is being changed (zero months). Thus, if otherwise qualified, B may make a section 444 election to change to a taxable year ending September 30, October 31, or November 30, for its taxable year beginning January 1, 1987.

Example (4). The facts are the same as in example (3), except that B files a calendar year income tax return for 1987 rather than making a section 444 election. However, for its taxable year beginning January 1, 1988, B desires to change its taxable year by making a section 444 election. Given that the special rule provided in paragraph (b)(2)(ii) of this section applies to section 444 elections made in taxable years beginning before 1989, B may, if otherwise qualified, make a section 444 election to change to a taxable year ending September 30, October 31, or November 30 for its taxable year beginning January 1, 1988.

Example (5). C, a corporation that historically used a June 30 taxable year, elected on December 15, 1986 to be an S corporation for its taxable year beginning July 1, 1987. As a condition to having the S election accepted, C agreed on Form 2553 to use a calendar year. Although, pursuant to paragraph (b)(3) of this section, C would, if otherwise qualified, be allowed to retain its June 30 taxable year, C desires to change to a September 30 taxable year by making a section 444 election. Pursuant to paragraph (b)(2) of this section, a taxpayer may, if otherwise qualified, make a section 444 election to change to a taxable year only if the deferral period of the taxable year to be elected is not longer than the shorter of three months or the deferral period of the taxable year being changed. Given these facts, the deferral period of the taxable year to be elected is 3 months (September 30 to December 31) while the deferral period of the taxable year being changed is 6 months (June 30 to December 31). Thus, C may, if otherwise qualified, change to a September 30 taxable year for its taxable year beginning July 1, 1987, by making a section 444 election. The fact that C agreed on Form 2553 to use a calendar year is not relevant.

Example (6). D, a corporation that historically used a March 31 taxable year, elects on June 1, 1988 to be an S corporation for its taxable year beginning April 1, 1988. D desires to change to a June 30 taxable year by making a section 444 election for its taxable year beginning April 1, 1988. Pursuant to paragraph (b)(2)(i) of this section, D may not change to a June 30 taxable year because such year would have a deferral period greater than 3 months. However, if otherwise qualified, D may make a section 444 election to change to a taxable year ending September 30, October 31, or November 30 for its taxable year beginning April 1, 1988.

Example (7). E, a corporation that began operations on November 1, 1986, elected to be an S corporation on December 15, 1986, for its taxable year beginning November 1, 1986. E filed a short period income tax return for the period November 1 to December 31, 1986. E desires to change to a September 30 taxable year by making a section 444 election for its taxable year beginning January 1, 1987. Although E elected to be an S corporation after September 18, 1986, and before January 1, 1988, paragraph (b)(2)(ii) of this section does not apply to E since E was not a C corporation prior to electing S status. Thus, E may not change its taxable year for the taxable year beginning January 1, 1987, by making a section 444 election.

Example (8). The facts are the same as in example (7), except that E began operations on April 15, 1987, and elected to be an S corporation on June 1, 1987, for its taxable year beginning April 15, 1987. As a condition to being an S corporation, E agreed on Form 2553 to use a calendar year. E desires to make a section 444 election to use a year ending September 30 for its taxable year beginning April 15, 1987. Pursuant to paragraph (b)(5)(i) of this section, E's agreement to use a calendar year on Form 2553 does not mean that E has adopted a calendar year. Thus, E's desire to make a section 444 election to use a September 30 taxable year will not be considered a change in taxable year and thus paragraph (b)(2) of this section will not apply. Instead, E will be subject to paragraph (b)(1) of this section. Since a September 30 taxable year would result in only a three-month deferral period (September 30 to December 31), E may, if otherwise qualified, make a section 444 election to use a year ending September 30 for its taxable year beginning April 15, 1987.

(2) *Special rule for entities retaining their 1986 taxable year.* The following examples illustrate the provisions of paragraph (b)(3) of this section.

Example (1). F, an S corporation that elected to be an S corporation several years ago, has historically used a June 30 taxable year. F desires to retain its June 30 taxable year by making a section 444 election for its taxable year beginning July 1, 1987. Pursuant to paragraph (b)(4)(i) of this section, the deferral period of the taxable year

Reg. § 1.444-1T(d)(2)

being retained is 6 months (June 30 to December 31, F's required taxable year). Absent the special rule provided in paragraph (b)(3) of this section, F would be subject to the general rule provided in paragraph (b)(1) of this section which limits the deferral period of the taxable year elected to three months or less. However, pursuant to paragraph (b)(3) of this section, F may, if otherwise qualified, make a section 444 election to retain its year ending June 30 for its taxable year beginning July 1, 1987.

Example (2). The facts are the same as in example (1), except that F received permission from the Commissioner to change its taxable year to the calendar year, and filed a short period income tax return for the period July 1 to December 31, 1986. F desires to make a section 444 election to use a year ending June 30 for its taxable year beginning January 1, 1987. Given that F had a December 31 taxable year for its last taxable year beginning in 1986, the special rule provided in paragraph (b)(3) of this section does not allow F to use a June 30 taxable year for its taxable year beginning January 1, 1987. Furthermore, pursuant to paragraph (b)(2)(i) of this section, F is not allowed to change its taxable year from December 31 to June 30 because the deferral period of the taxable year being changed is zero months.

Example (3). G, a corporation that historically used an August 31 taxable year, elected to be an S corporation on November 15, 1986, for its taxable year beginning September 1, 1986. As a condition to obtaining S status, G agreed to use a calendar year. Thus, G filed its first S corporation return for the period September 1 to December 31, 1986. G desires to make a section 444 election to use a year ending August 31 for its taxable year beginning January 1, 1987. Since G's last taxable year beginning in 1986 was a calendar year, G cannot use paragraph (b)(3) of this section, relating to retentions of taxable years, to elect an August 31 taxable year. Thus, G is subject to paragraph (b)(2)(i) of this section, relating to changes in taxable year. Although G, if otherwise qualified, may use the special rule provided in paragraph (b)(2)(ii) of this section, G may only change from its current taxable year (*i.e.*, the calendar year) to a taxable year that has no more than a three-month deferral period (*i.e.*, September 30, October 31, or November 30).

Example (4). The facts are the same as in example (3), except that G elected to be an S corporation for its taxable year beginning September 1, 1987, rather than its taxable year beginning September 1, 1986. As a condition to making its S election, G agreed, on Form 2553, to use the calendar year. However, G has not yet filed a short period income tax return for the period September 1 to December 31, 1987. Given these facts, paragraph (b)(3) of this section would allow G, if otherwise qualified, to make a section 444 election to retain an August 31 taxable year for its taxable year beginning September 1, 1987.

Example (5). The facts are the same as in example (4), except that G has already filed a short period income tax return for the period September 1 to December 31, 1987. Pursuant to paragraph (b)(5)(ii)(A) of this section, G may supersede the return it filed for the period September 1 to December 31, 1987. Thus, pursuant to paragraph (b)(3) of this section, G may, if otherwise qualified, make a section 444 election to retain an August 31 taxable year for the taxable year beginning September 1, 1987. In addition, G should follow the special procedures set forth in paragraph (b)(5)(ii)(B) of this section.

Example (6). H, a corporation that historically used a May 31 taxable year, elects to be an S corporation on June 15, 1988 for its taxable year beginning June 1, 1988. H desires to make a section 444 election to use a taxable year other than the calendar year. Since the taxable year in issue is not H's first taxable year beginning after December 31, 1986, H may not use the special rule provided in paragraph (b)(3)(i) and thus may not retain its May 31 year. However, H may, if otherwise qualified, make a section 444 election under paragraph (b)(2)(i) of this section, to change to a taxable year that has no more than a three-month deferral period (*i.e.*, September 30, October 31, or November 30) for its taxable year beginning June 1, 1988.

Example (7). I is a partnership that has historically used a calendar year. Sixty percent of the profits and capital of I are owned by Q, a corporation (that is neither an S corporation nor a personal service corporation) that has a June 30 taxable year, and 40 percent of the profits and capital are owned by R, a calendar year individual. Since the partner that has more than a fifty percent interest in I has a June 30 taxable year, I's required taxable year is June 30. Accordingly, I filed an income tax return for the period January 1 to June 30, 1987. Based on these facts, I may, pursuant to paragraph (b)(5)(ii)(A) of this section, disregard the income tax return filed for the period January 1 to June 30, 1987. Thus, if otherwise qualified, I may make a section 444 election under paragraph (b)(2)(i) of this section to use a calendar year for its taxable year beginning January 1, 1987. If I makes such a section 444 election, I should follow the special proce-

Reg. § 1.444-1T(d)(2)

dures set forth in paragraph (b)(5)(ii)(B) of this section. [Temporary Reg. § 1.444-1T.]

☐ [*T.D.* 8205, 5-24-88. *Amended by T.D.* 8996, 5-16-2002.]

[Reg. § 1.444-2T]

§ 1.444-2T. Tiered structure (temporary).— (a) *General rule.* Except as provided in paragraph (e) of this section, no section 444 election shall be made or continued with respect to a partnership, S corporation, or personal service corporation that is a member of a tiered structure on the date specified in paragraph (d) of this section. For purposes of this section, the term "personal service corporation" means a personal service corporation as defined in § 1.441-3(c).

(b) *Definition of a member of a tiered structure*—(1) *In general.* A partnership, S corporation, or personal service corporation is considered a member of a tiered structure if—

(i) The partnership, S corporation, or personal service corporation directly owns any portion of a deferral entity, or

(ii) A deferral entity directly owns any portion of the partnership, S corporation, or personal service corporation.

However, see paragraph (c) of this section for certain de minimis rules, and see paragraph (b)(3) of this section for an anti-abuse rule. In addition, for purposes of this section, a beneficiary of a trust shall be considered to own an interest in the trust.

(2) *Deferral entity*—(i) *In general.* For purposes of this section, the term "deferral entity" means an entity that is a partnership, S corporation, personal service corporation, or trust. In the case of an affiliated group of corporations filing a consolidated income tax return that is treated as a personal service corporation pursuant to § 1.441-4T(i), such affiliated group is considered to be a single deferral entity.

(ii) *Grantor trusts.* The term "deferral entity" does not include a trust (or a portion of a trust) which is treated as owned by the grantor or beneficiary under Subpart E, part I, subchapter J, chapter 1, of the Code (relating to grantor trusts), including a trust that is treated as a grantor trust pursuant to section 1361(d)(1)(A) of the Code (relating to qualified subchapter S trusts). Thus, any taxpayer treated under subpart E as owning a portion of a trust shall be treated as owning the assets of the trust attributable to that ownership. The following examples illustrate the provisions of this paragraph (b)(2)(ii).

Example (1). A, an individual, is the sole beneficiary of T. T is a trust that owns 50 percent of the profits and capital of X, a partnership that desires to make a section 444 election. Furthermore, pursuant to Subpart E, Part I, subchapter J, chapter 1 of the Code, A is treated as an owner of X. Based upon these facts, T is not a deferral entity and 50 percent of X is considered to be directly owned by A.

Example (2). The facts are the same as in example (1), except that A is a personal service corporation rather than an individual. Given these facts, 50 percent of X is considered to be directly owned by A, a deferral entity. Thus, X is considered to be a member of a tiered structure.

(3) *Anti-abuse rule.* Notwithstanding paragraph (b)(1) of this section, a partnership, S corporation, or personal service corporation is considered a member of a tiered structure if the partnership, S corporation, personal service corporation, or related taxpayers have organized or reorganized their ownership structure or operations for the principal purpose of obtaining a significant unintended tax benefit from making or continuing a section 444 election. For purposes of the preceding sentence, a significant unintended tax benefit results when a partnership, S corporation, or personal service corporation makes a section 444 election and, as a result, a taxpayer (not limited to the entity making the election) obtains a significant deferral of income substantially all of which is not eliminated by a required payment under section 7519. See examples (15) through (19) in paragraph (f) of this section.

(c) *De minimis rules*—(1) *In general.* For rules relating to a de minimis exception to paragraph (b)(1)(i) of this section (the "downstream de minimis rule"), see paragraph (c)(2) of this section. For rules relating to a de minimis exception to paragraph (b)(1)(ii) of this section (the "upstream de minimis rule"), see paragraph (c)(3) of this section. For rules relating to the interaction of the de minimis rules provided in this paragraph (c) and the "same taxable year exception" provided in paragraph (e) of this section, see paragraph (e)(5) of this section.

(2) *Downstream de minimis rule*—(i) *General rule.* If a partnership, S corporation, or personal service corporation directly owns any portion of one or more deferral entities as of the date specified in paragraph (d) of this section, such ownership is disregarded for purposes of paragraph (b)(1)(i) of this section if, in the aggregate, all such deferral entities accounted for—

(A) Not more than 5 percent of the partnership's, S corporation's, or personal service corporation's adjusted taxable income for the testing period ("5 percent adjusted taxable income test"), or

Reg. § 1.444-2T(a)

(B) Not more than 2 percent of the partnership's, S corporation's, or personal service corporation's gross income for the testing period ("2 percent gross income test"). See section 702(c) for rules relating to the determination of gross income of a partner in a partnership.

See examples (3) through (5) in paragraph (f) of this section.

(ii) *Definition of testing period.* For purposes of this paragraph (c)(2), the term "testing period" means the taxable year that ends immediately prior to the taxable year for which the partnership, S corporation, or personal service corporation desires to make or continue a section 444 election. However, see the special rules provided in paragraph (c)(2)(iv) of this section for certain special cases (*e.g.,* the partnership, S corporation, personal service corporation or deferral entity was not in existence during the entire testing period). The following example illustrates the application of this paragraph (c)(2)(ii).

Example. A partnership desires to make a section 444 election for its taxable year beginning November 1, 1987. The testing period for purposes of determining whether deferral entities owned by such partnership are de minimis under paragraph (c)(2) of this section is the taxable year ending October 31, 1987. If either the partnership or the deferral entities were not in existence for the entire taxable year ending October 1, 1987, see the special rules provided in paragraph (c)(2)(iv) of this section.

(iii) *Definition of adjusted taxable income*—(A) *Partnership.* In the case of a partnership, adjusted taxable income for purposes of paragraph (c)(2) of this section is an amount equal to the sum of the—

(*1*) Aggregate amount of the partnership items described in section 702(a) (other than credits and tax-exempt income),

(*2*) Applicable payments defined in section 7519(d)(3) that are deducted in determining the amount described in paragraph (c)(2)(iii)(A)(*1*) of this section, and

(*3*) Guaranteed payments defined in section 707(c) that are deducted in determining the amount described in paragraph (c)(2)(iii)(A)(*1*) of this section and are not otherwise included in paragraph (c)(2)(iii)(A)(*2*) of this section. For purposes of determining the aggregate amount of partnership items under paragraph (c)(2)(iii)(A)(*1*) of this section, deductions and losses are treated as negative income. Thus, for example, if under section 702(a) a partnership has $1,000 of ordinary taxable income, $500 of specially allocated deductions, and $300 of capital loss, the partnership's aggregate amount of partnership items under paragraph (c)(2)(iii)(A)(*1*) of this section is $200 ($1,000 − $500 − $300).

(B) *S corporation.* In the case of an S corporation, adjusted taxable income for purposes of paragraph (c)(2) of this section is an amount equal to the sum of the—

(*1*) Aggregate amount of the S corporation items described in section 1366(a) (other than credits and tax-exempt income), and

(*2*) Applicable payments defined in section 7519(d)(3) that are deducted in determining the amount described in paragraph (c)(2)(iii)(B)(*1*) of this section.

For purposes of determining the aggregate amount of S corporation items under paragraph (c)(2)(iii)(B)(*1*) of this section, deductions and losses are treated as negative income. Thus, for example, if under section 1366(a) an S corporation has $2,000 of ordinary taxable income, $1,000 of deductions described in section 1366(a)(1)(A) of the Code, and $500 of capital loss, the S corporation's aggregate amount of S corporation items under paragraph (c)(2)(iii)(B)(*1*) of this section is $500 ($2,000 − $1,000 − $500).

(C) *Personal service corporation.* In the case of a personal service corporation, adjusted taxable income for purposes of paragraph (c)(2) of this section is an amount equal to the sum of the—

(*1*) Taxable income of the personal service corporation, and

(*2*) Applicable amounts defined in section 280H(f)(1) that are deducted in determining the amount described in paragraph (c)(2)(iii)(C)(*1*) of this section.

(iv) *Special rules*—(A) *Pro-forma rule.* Except as provided in paragraph (c)(2)(iv)(C)(*2*) of this section, if a partnership, S corporation, or personal service corporation directly owns any interest in a deferral entity as of the date specified in paragraph (d) of this section and such ownership interest is different in amount from the partnership's, S corporation's, or personal service corporation's interest on any day during the testing period, the 5 percent adjusted taxable income test and the 2 percent gross income test must be applied on a pro-forma basis (*i.e.,* adjusted taxable income and gross income must be calculated for the testing period assuming that the partnership, S corporation, or personal service corporation owned the same interest in the deferral entity that it owned as of the date specified in paragraph (d) of this section). The following example illustrates the application of this paragraph (c)(2)(iv)(A).

Reg. § 1.444-2T(c)(2)

Example. A personal service corporation desiring to make a section 444 election for its taxable year beginning October 1, 1987, acquires a 25 percent ownership interest in a partnership on or after October 1, 1987. Furthermore, the partnership has been in existence for several years. The personal service corporation must modify its calculations of the 5 percent adjusted taxable income test and the 2 percent gross income test for the testing period ended September 30, 1987, by assuming that the personal service corporation owned 25 percent of the partnership during such testing period and the personal service corporation's adjusted taxable income and gross income were correspondingly adjusted.

(B) *Reasonable estimates allowed.* If the information necessary to complete the pro-forma calculation described in paragraph (c)(2)(iv)(A) of this section is not readily available, the partnership, S corporation, or personal service corporation may make a reasonable estimate of such information.

(C) *Newly formed entities*—(1) *Newly formed deferral entities.* If a partnership, S corporation, or personal service corporation owns any portion of a deferral entity on the date specified in paragraph (d) of this section and such deferral entity was not in existence during the entire testing period (hereinafter referred to as a "newly formed deferral entity"), both the 5 percent adjusted taxable income test and the 2 percent gross income test are modified as follows. First, the partnership, S corporation, or personal service corporation shall calculate the percentage of its adjusted taxable income or gross income that is attributable to deferral entities, excluding newly formed deferral entities. Second, the partnership, S corporation, or personal service corporation shall calculate (on the date specified in paragraph (d) of this section) the percentage of the tax basis of its assets that are attributable to its tax basis with respect to its ownership interests in all newly formed deferral entities. If the sum of the two percentages is 5 percent or less, the deferral entities are considered de minimis and are disregarded for purposes of paragraph (b)(1)(i) of this section. If the sum of the two percentages is greater than 5 percent, the deferral entities do not qualify for the de minimis rule provided in paragraph (c)(2) of this section and thus the partnership, S corporation, or personal service corporation is considered to be a member of a tiered structure for purposes of this section.

(2) *Newly formed partnership, S corporation, or personal service corporation desiring to make a section 444 election.* If a partnership, S corporation, or personal service corporation desires to make a section 444 election for the first taxable year of its existence, the 5 percent adjusted taxable income test and the 2 percent gross income test are replaced by a 5 percent of assets test. Thus, if on the date specified in paragraph (d) of this section, 5 percent or less of the assets (measured by reference to the tax basis of the assets) of the newly formed partnership, S corporation, or personal service corporation are attributable to the tax basis with respect to its ownership interests in the deferral entities, the deferral entities will be considered de minimis and will be disregarded for purposes of paragraph (b)(1)(i) of this section.

(3) *Upstream de minimis rule.* If a partnership, S corporation or personal service corporation is directly owned by one or more deferral entities as of the date specified in paragraph (d) of this section, such ownership is disregarded for purposes of paragraph (b)(1)(ii) of this section if on the date specified in paragraph (d) of this section the deferral entities directly own, in the aggregate, 5 percent or less of—

(i) An interest in the current profits of the partnership, or

(ii) The stock (measured by value) of the S corporation or personal service corporation.

See examples (6) and (7) in paragraph (f) of this section.

(d) *Date for determining the existence of a tiered structure*—(1) *General rule.* For purposes of paragraph (a) of this section, a partnership, S corporation, or personal service corporation will be considered a member of a tiered structure for a particular taxable year if the partnership, S corporation, or personal service corporation is a member of a tiered structure on the last day of the required taxable year (as defined in section 444(e) of the Code) ending within such year. If a particular taxable year does not include the last day of the required taxable year for such year, the partnership, S corporation, or personal service corporation will not be considered a member of a tiered structure for such year. The following examples illustrate the application of this paragraph (d)(1).

Example (1). Assume that a newly formed partnership whose first taxable year begins November 1, 1988, desires to adopt a September 30 taxable year by making a section 444 election. Furthermore, assume that for its taxable year beginning November 1, 1988, the partnership's required taxable year is December 31. If the partnership is a member of a tiered structure on December 31, 1988, it will not be eligible to make a section 444 election for a taxable year beginning

Reg. § 1.444-2T(d)(1)

November 1, 1988, and ending September 30, 1989.

Example (2). Assume an S corporation that historically used a June 30 taxable year desires to make a section 444 election to change to a year ending September 30 for its taxable year beginning July 1, 1987. If the S corporation can make the section 444 election, it will have a short taxable year beginning July 1, 1987, and ending September 30, 1987. Given these facts, the short taxable year beginning July 1, 1987, does not include the last day of the S corporation's required taxable year for such year (*i.e.*, December 31, 1987). Thus, pursuant to paragraph (d)(1) of this section, the S corporation will not be considered a member of a tiered structure for its taxable year beginning July 1, 1987, and ending September 30, 1987.

(2) *Special rule for taxable years beginning in 1987.* For purposes of paragraph (a) of this section, a partnership, S corporation, or personal service corporation will not be considered a member of a tiered structure for a taxable year beginning in 1987 if the partnership, S corporation, or personal service corporation is not a member of a tiered structure on the day the partnership, S corporation, or personal service corporation timely files its section 444 election for such year. The following examples illustrate the application of this paragraph (d)(2).

Example (1). Assume that a partnership desires to retain a June 30 taxable year by making a section 444 election for its taxable year beginning July 1, 1987. Furthermore, assume that the partnership's required taxable year for such year is December 31 and that the partnership was a member of a tiered structure on such date. Also assume that the partnership was not a member of a tiered structure as of the date it timely filed its section 444 election for its taxable year beginning July 1, 1987. Based upon the special rule provided in this paragraph (d)(2), the partnership will not be considered a member of a tiered structure for its taxable year beginning July 1, 1987.

Example (2). Assume the same facts as in example (1), except that the partnership was a member of a tiered structure on the date it filed its section 444 election for its taxable year beginning July 1, 1987, but was not a member of a tiered structure on December 31, 1987. Paragraph (d)(1) of this section would still apply and thus the partnership would not be considered part of a tiered structure for its taxable year beginning July 1, 1987. However, the partnership would be considered a member of a tiered structure for its taxable year beginning July 1, 1988, if the partnership was a member of a tiered structure on December 31, 1988.

(e) *Same taxable year exception*—(1) *In general.* Although a partnership or S corporation is a member of a tiered structure as of the date specified in paragraph (d) of this section, the partnership or S corporation may make or continue a section 444 election if the tiered structure (as defined in paragraph (e)(2) of this section) consists entirely of partnerships or S corporations (or both), all of which have the same taxable year as determined under paragraph (e)(3) of this section. However, see paragraph (e)(5) of this section for the interaction of the de minimis rules provided in paragraph (c) of this section with the same taxable year exception. For purposes of this paragraph (e), two or more entities are considered to have the same taxable year if their taxable years end on the same day, even though they begin on different days. See examples (8) through (14) in paragraph (f) of this section.

(2) *Definition of tiered structure*—(i) *General rule.* For purposes of the same taxable year exception, the members of a tiered structure are defined to include the following entities—

(A) The partnership or S corporation that desires to qualify for the same taxable year exception,

(B) A deferral entity (or entities) directly owned (in whole or in part) by the partnership or S corporation that desires to qualify for the same taxable year exception,

(C) A deferral entity (or entities) directly owning any portion of the partnership or S corporation that desires to qualify for the same taxable year exception, and

(D) A deferral entity (or entities) directly owned (in whole or in part) by a "downstream controlled partnership," as defined in paragraph (e)(2)(ii) of this section.

(ii) *Special flow-through rule for downstream controlled partnerships.* If more than 50 percent of a partnership's profits and capital are owned by a partnership or S corporation that desires to qualify for the same taxable year exception, such owned partnership is considered a downstream controlled partnership for purposes of paragraph (e)(2)(i) of this section. Furthermore, if more than 50 percent of a partnership's profits and capital are owned by a downstream controlled partnership, such owned partnership is considered a downstream controlled partnership for purposes of paragraph (e)(2)(i) of this section.

(3) *Determining the taxable year of a partnership or S corporation.* The taxable year of a partnership or S corporation to be taken into

Reg. § 1.444-2T(e)(3)

account for purposes of paragraph (e)(1) of this section is the taxable year ending with or prior to the date specified in paragraph (d) of this section. Furthermore, the determination of such taxable year will take into consideration any section 444 elections made by the partnership or S corporation. See examples (10) and (11) in paragraph (f) of this section.

(4) *Special rule for 52-53-week taxable years.* For purposes of this paragraph (e), a 52-53-week taxable year with reference to the end of a particular month will be considered to be the same as a taxable year ending with reference to the last day of such month.

(5) *Interaction with de minimis rules*— (i) Downstream de minimis rule—(A) *In general.* If a partnership or S corporation that desires to make or continue a section 444 election is a member of a tiered structure (as defined in paragraph (e)(2) of this section) and directly owns any member (or members) of the tiered structure with a taxable year different from the taxable year of the partnership or S corporation, such ownership is disregarded for purposes of the same taxable year exception of paragraph (e)(1) of this section provided that, in the aggregate, the de minimis rule of paragraph (c)(2) of this section is satisfied with respect to such owned member (or members). The following example illustrates the application of this paragraph (e)(5)(i)(A).

Example. P, a partnership with a June 30 taxable year, owns 60 percent of P1, another partnership with a June 30 taxable year. P also owns 1 percent of P2 and P3, calendar year partnerships. If, in the aggregate, P's ownership interests in P2 and P3 are considered de minimis under paragraph (c)(2) of this section, P meets the same taxable year exception and may make a section 444 election to retain its June 30 taxable year.

(B) *Special rule for members of a tiered structure directly owned by a downstream controlled partnership.* For purposes of paragraph (e)(5)(i)(A) of this section, a partnership or S corporation desiring to make or continue a section 444 election is considered to directly own any member of the tiered structure (as defined in paragraph (e)(2) of this section) directly owned by a downstream controlled partnership (as defined in paragraph (e)(2)(ii) of this section). The adjusted taxable income or gross income of the partnership or S corporation that is attributable to a member of a tiered structure directly owned by a downstream controlled partnership equals the adjusted taxable income or gross income of such member multiplied by the partnership's or S corporation's indirect ownership percentage of such member. The following example illustrates the application of this paragraph (e)(5)(i)(B).

Example. P, a partnership, desires to retain its June 30 taxable year by making a section 444 election. However, as of the date specified in paragraph (d) of this section, P owns 75 percent of P1, a June 30 partnership, and P1 owns 40 percent of P2, a calendar year partnership. P also owns 25 percent of P3, a calendar year partnership. Pursuant to paragraphs (e)(5)(i)(A) and (B) of this section, P may only qualify to use the same taxable year exception if, in the aggregate, P2 and P3 are de minimis with respect to P. Pursuant to paragraph (e)(5)(i)(B) of this section, P's adjusted taxable income or gross income attributable to P2 equals 30 percent (75 percent times 40 percent) of P2's adjusted taxable income or gross income.

(ii) *Upstream de minimis rule.* If a partnership or S corporation that desires to make or continue a section 444 election is a member of a tiered structure (as defined in paragraph (e)(2) of this section) and is owned directly by a member (or members) of the tiered structure with taxable years different from the taxable year of the partnership or S corporation, such ownership is disregarded for purposes of the same taxable year exception of paragraph (e)(1) of this section provided that, in the aggregate, the de minimis rule of paragraph (c)(3) of this section is satisfied with respect to such owning member (or members). See example (12) of paragraph (f) of this section.

(f) *Examples.* The provisions of this section may be illustrated by the following examples.

Example (1). A, a partnership, desires to make or continue a section 444 election. However, on the date specified in paragraph (d) of this section, A is owned by a combination of individuals and S corporations. The S corporations are deferral entities, as defined in paragraph (b)(2) of this section. Thus, pursuant to paragraph (b)(1)(ii) of this section, A will be a member of a tiered structure unless under paragraph (c)(3) of this section, the S corporations, in the aggregate, own a de minimis portion of A. If the S corporations' ownership in A is not considered de minimis under paragraph (c)(3) of this section, A is a member of a tiered structure and will be allowed to make or continue a section 444 election only if it meets the same taxable year exception provided in paragraph (e) of this section.

Example (2). B, a partnership, desires to make or continue a section 444 election. However, on the date specified in paragraph (d) of this section, B is a partner in two partnerships, B1 and B2. B1 and B2 are deferral entities, as defined in paragraph (b)(2) of this section. Thus, under paragraph (b)(1)(i) of this section, B will be a member of a tiered structure unless B's aggregate ownership interests in B1 and B2 are considered de minimis under paragraph (c)(2) of this section. If B is a member of a tiered structure on the date specified in paragraph (d) of this section, B will be allowed to make or continue a section 444 election only if it meets the same taxable year exception provided in paragraph (e) of this section.

Example (3). C, a partnership with a September 30 taxable year, is 100 percent owned by calendar year individuals. C desires to make a section 444 election for its taxable year beginning October 1, 1987. However, on the date specified in paragraph (d) of this section, C owns a 1 percent interest in C1, a partnership. C does not own any other interest in a deferral entity. For the taxable year ended September 30, 1987, 10 percent of C's adjusted taxable income (as defined in paragraph (c)(2)(iii) of this section) was attributable to C's partnership interest in C1. Furthermore, 4 percent of C's gross income for the taxable year ended September 30, 1987, was attributable to C's partnership interest in C1. Under paragraph (c)(2) of this section, C's partnership interest in C1 is not de minimis because during the testing period more than 5 percent of C's adjusted taxable income is attributable to C1 and more than 2 percent of C's gross income is attributable to C1. Thus, C is a member of a tiered structure for its taxable year beginning October 1, 1987.

Example (4). The facts are the same as example (3), except that for the taxable year ended September 30, 1987, only 2 percent of C's adjusted taxable income was attributable to C1. Under paragraph (c)(2) of this section, C's partnership interest in C1 is considered de minimis for purposes of determining whether C is a member of a tiered structure because not more than 5 percent of C's adjusted taxable income during the testing period is attributable to C1. Thus, C is not a member of a tiered structure for its taxable year beginning October 1, 1987.

Example (5). The facts are the same as example (4), except that in addition to owning C1, C also owns 15 percent of C2, another partnership. For the taxable year ended September 30, 1987, 2 percent of C's adjusted taxable income is attributable to C1 and an additional 4 percent is attributable to C2. Furthermore, for the taxable year ended September 30, 1987, 4 percent of C's gross income is attributable to C1 while 3 percent is attributable to C2. Under paragraph (c)(2) of this section, C1 and C2 must be aggregated for purposes of determining whether C meets either the 5 percent adjusted taxable income test or the 2 percent gross income test. Since C's adjusted taxable income attributable to C1 and C2 is 6 percent (2 percent + 4 percent) and C's gross income attributable to C1 and C2 is 7 percent (4 percent + 3 percent), C does not meet the downstream de minimis rule provided in paragraph (c)(2) of this section. Thus, C is a member of a tiered structure for its taxable year beginning October 1, 1987.

Example (6). The facts are the same as example (3), except that instead of determining whether C is part of a tiered structure, the issue is whether C1 is part of a tiered structure. In addition, assume that on the date specified in paragraph (d) of this section, the remaining 99 percent of C1 is owned by calendar year individuals and C1 does not own an interest in any deferral entity. Although C in Example (3) was considered to be a part of a tiered structure by virtue of its ownership interest in C1, C1 must be tested separately to determine whether it is part of a tiered structure. Since C's interest in C1 is 5 percent or less, C's interest in C1 is de minimis with respect to C1. See paragraph (c)(3) of this section. Thus, based upon these facts, C1 is not part of a tiered structure.

Example (7). The facts are the same as example (6), except that the remaining 99 percent of C1 is owned 94 percent by calendar year individuals and 5 percent by C3, another partnership. Thus, deferral entities own 6 percent of C1 (1 percent owned by C and 5 percent owned by C3). Under paragraph (c)(3) of this section, deferral entities own more than a de minimis interest (*i.e.*, 5 percent) of C1, and thus C1 is part of a tiered structure.

Example (8). D, a partnership with a September 30 taxable year, desires to make a section 444 election for its taxable year beginning October 1, 1987. On December 31, 1987, the date D plans to file its section 444 election, D is 10 percent owned by D1, a personal service corporation with a September 30 taxable year, and 90 percent owned by calendar year individuals. Furthermore, D1 will retain its September 30 taxable year because it previously established a business purpose for such year. Since D is owned in part by D1, a personal service corporation, and the ownership interest is not *de minimis* under paragraph (c)(3) of this section, D is considered a member of a tiered structure for its taxable year beginning October 1, 1987. Furthermore, although D and D1 have the same taxable year, D does not qualify for the same taxable year exception provided in paragraph (e) of this section because D1 is a personal service corporation rather than a partnership or S corporation. Thus, pursuant to paragraph (a) of this section, D may not make a section 444 elec-

Reg. § 1.444-2T(f)

tion for its taxable year beginning October 1, 1987.

Example (9). The facts are the same as example (8), except that D1 is a partnership rather than a personal service corporation. Based upon these facts, D qualifies for the same taxable year exception provided in paragraph (e) of this section. Thus, D may make a section 444 election for its taxable year beginning October 1, 1987.

Example (10). The facts are the same as example (9), except that D1 has not established a business purpose for a September 30 taxable year. In addition, D1 does not desire to make a section 444 election and, under section 706(b), D1 will be required to change to a calendar year for its taxable year beginning October 1, 1987. Pursuant to paragraph (e)(3) of this section, D and D1 do not have the same taxable year for purposes of the same taxable year exception provided in paragraph (e) of this section. Thus, D may not make a section 444 election for its taxable year beginning October 1, 1987.

Example (11). The facts are the same as example (8), except that D1 is a partnership with a March 31 taxable year. Furthermore, for its taxable year beginning April 1, 1987, D1 will change to a September 30 taxable year by making a section 444 election. Pursuant to paragraph (e)(3) of this section, D1 is considered to have a September 30 taxable year for purposes of determining whether D qualifies for the same taxable year exception provided in paragraph (e) of this section. Since both D and D1 will have the same taxable year as of the date specified in paragraph (d) of this section, D may make a section 444 election for its taxable year beginning October 1, 1987.

Example (12). The facts are the same as example (11), except that instead of the remaining 90 percent of D being owned by calendar year individuals, it is owned 86 percent by individuals and 4 percent by D2, a calendar year partnership. Thus, D, a September 30 partnership, is 10 percent owned by D1, a September 30 partnership, 86 percent owned by calendar year individuals, and 4 percent owned by D2, a calendar year partnership. Under paragraph (e)(5)(ii) of this section, D2's ownership interest in D is considered *de minimis* for purposes of the same taxable year exception. Since D2's ownership interest in D is considered *de minimis*, it is disregarded for purposes of determining whether D qualifies for the same taxable year exception provided in paragraph (e) of this section. Thus, since both D and D1 will have the same taxable year as of the date specified in paragraph (d) of this section, D may make a section 444 election for its taxable year beginning October 1, 1987.

Example (13). E, a partnership with a June 30 taxable year, desires to make a section 444 election for its taxable year beginning July 1, 1987. On the date specified in paragraph (d) of this section, E is 100 percent owned by calendar year individuals; E owns 99 percent of the profits and capital of E1, a partnership with a June 30 taxable year; and E1 owns 30 percent of the profits and capital of E2, a partnership with a September 30 taxable year. E owns no other deferral entities. Pursuant to paragraph (b)(1)(i) of this section, E is considered to be a member of a tiered structure. Furthermore, pursuant to paragraph (e) of this section, E does not qualify for the same taxable year exception because E2 does not have the same taxable year as E and E1.

Example (14). The facts are the same as example (13), except that E owns only 49 percent (rather than 99 percent) of the profits and capital of E1. Pursuant to paragraph (e) of this section, E qualifies for the same taxable year exception because E and E1 have the same taxable year. Pursuant to paragraph (e) of this section, E1's ownership interest in E2 is disregarded since E does not own more than 50 percent of E1's profits and capital.

Example (15). Prior to consideration of the anti-abuse rule provided in paragraph (b)(3) of this section, H, a partnership that commenced operations on October 1, 1987, is eligible to make a section 444 election for its taxable year beginning October 1, 1987. Although H may obtain a significant deferral of income substantially all of which is not eliminated by a required payment under section 7519 (since there will be no required payment for H's first taxable year), the anti-abuse rule of paragraph (b)(3) will not apply unless the principal purpose of organizing H was the attainment of a significant deferral of income that would result from making a section 444 election.

Example (16). F, a partnership with a January 31 taxable year, desires to make a section 444 election to retain its January 31 taxable year for the taxable year beginning February 1, 1987. F is 100 percent owned by calendar year individuals. Prior to the date specified in paragraph (d) of this section, F contributes substantially all of its assets to F1, a partnership, in exchange for a 51 percent interest in F1. The remaining 49 percent of F1 is owned by the calendar year individuals owning 100 percent of F. If F is allowed to make a section 444 election to retain its January 31 taxable year, F1's required taxable year will be January 31 since a majority of F1's partners use a January 31

Reg. § 1.444-2T(f)

taxable year (see § 1.706-3T). F's principal purpose for creating F1 and contributing its assets to F1 is to obtain an 11-month deferral on 49 percent of the income previously earned by F and now earned by F1. Pursuant to paragraph (b)(3) of this section, F is not allowed to make a section 444 election for its taxable year beginning February 1, 1987.

Example (17). The facts are the same as in example (16), except that F does not create F1 and contribute its assets to F1 until immediately after F makes its section 444 election for the taxable year beginning February 1, 1987. Thus, F is allowed to make a section 444 election for its taxable year beginning February 1, 1987. However, pursuant to paragraph (b)(3) of this section, F will have its section 444 election terminated for subsequent years unless the tax deferral inherent in the structure is eliminated (*e.g.*, F1 is liquidated or the individual owners of F contribute their interests in F1 to F) prior to the date specified in paragraph (d) of this section for subsequent taxable years beginning on or after February 1, 1988.

Example (18). The facts are the same as in example (16), except that F1 is 99 percent owned by F and none of the individual owners of F own any portion of F1. Furthermore, F obtained no tax benefit from creating and contributing assets to F1. Given these facts paragraph (b)(3) of this section does not apply and thus, F may make a section 444 election for its taxable year beginning February 1, 1987.

Example (19). G, a partnership with an October 31 taxable year, desires to retain its October 31 taxable year for its taxable year beginning November 1, 1987. However, as of December 31, 1987, G owns a 30 percent interest in G1, a calendar year partnership. G owns no other deferral entity, and G is 100 percent owned by calendar year individuals. Furthermore, G's interest in G1 does not meet the *de minimis* rule provided in paragraph (c)(3) of this section. Thus, in order to avoid being a tiered structure, G sells its interest in G1 to an unrelated third party prior to the date G timely makes its section 444 election for its taxable year beginning November 1, 1987. Although the sale of G1 allows G to qualify to make a section 444 election, and therefore to obtain a significant tax benefit, such benefit is not unintended. Thus, paragraph (b)(3) of this section does not apply, and G may make a section 444 election for its taxable year beginning November 1, 1987.

(g) *Effective date.* This section is effective for taxable years beginning after December 31, 1986. [Temporary Reg. § 1.444-2T.]

☐ [*T.D. 8205, 5-24-88. Amended by T.D. 8996, 5-16-2002.*]

[Reg. § 1.444-3T]

§ 1.444-3T. **Manner and time of making section 444 election (temporary).**—(a) *In general.* A section 444 election shall be made in the manner and at the time provided in this section.

(b) *Manner and time of making election*—(1) *General rule.* A section 444 election shall be made by filing a properly prepared Form 8716, "Election to Have a Tax Year Other Than a Required Tax Year," with the Service Center indicated by the instructions to Form 8716. Except as provided in paragraphs (b)(2) and (4) of this section, Form 8716 must be filed by the earlier of—

(i) The 15th day of the fifth month following the month that includes the first day of the taxable year for which the election will first be effective, or

(ii) The due date (without regard to extensions) of the income tax return resulting from the section 444 election.

In addition, a copy of Form 8716 must be attached to Form 1065 or Form 1120 series form, whichever is applicable, for the first taxable year for which the section 444 election is made. Form 8716 shall be signed by any person who is authorized to sign Form 1065 or Form 1120 series form, whichever is applicable. (See sections 6062 and 6063, relating to the signing of returns). The provisions of this paragraph (b)(1) may be illustrated by the following examples.

Example (1). A, a partnership that began operations on September 10, 1988, is qualified to make a section 444 election to use a September 30 taxable year for its taxable year beginning September 10, 1988. Pursuant to paragraph (b)(1) of this section, A must file Form 8716 by the earlier of the 15th day of the fifth month following the month that includes the first day of the taxable year for which the election will first be effective (*i.e.*, February 15, 1989) or the due date (without regard to extensions) of the partnership's tax return for the period September 10, 1988 to September 30, 1988 (*i.e.*, January 15, 1989). Thus, A must file Form 8716 by January 15, 1989.

Example (2). The facts are the same as in example (1), except that A began operations on October 20, 1988. Based upon these facts, A must file Form 8716 by March 15, 1989, the 15th day of the fifth month following the month that includes the first day of the taxable year for which the election will first be effective.

Example (3). B is a corporation that first becomes a personal service corporation for its taxable year beginning September 1, 1988. B qualifies to make a section 444 election to use a September 30 taxable year for its taxable year beginning September 1, 1988. Pursuant to this paragraph (b)(1), B must file Form 8716 by December 15, 1988, the due date of the income tax return for the short period September 1 to September 30, 1988.

(2) *Special extension of time for making an election.* If, pursuant to paragraph (b)(1) of this section, the due date for filing Form 8716 is prior to July 26, 1988, such date is extended to July 26, 1988. The provisions of this paragraph (b)(2) may be illustrated by the following examples.

Example (1). B, a partnership that historically used a June 30 taxable year, is qualified to make a section 444 election to retain a June 30 taxable year for its taxable year beginning July 1, 1987. Absent paragraph (b)(2) of this section, B would be required to file Form 8716 by December 15, 1987. However, pursuant to paragraph (b)(2) of this section, B's due date for filing Form 8716 is extended to July 26, 1988.

Example (2). C, a partnership that began operations on January 20, 1988, is qualified to make a section 444 election to use a year ending September 30 for its taxable year beginning January 20, 1988. Absent paragraph (b)(2) of this section, C is required to file Form 8716 by June 15, 1988 (the 15th day of the fifth month following the month that includes the first day of the taxable year for which the election will first be effective). However, pursuant to paragraph (b)(2) of this section, the due date for filing Form 8716 is July 26, 1988.

(3) *Corporation electing to be an S corporation*—(i) *In general.* A corporation electing to be an S corporation is subject to the same time and manner rules for filing Form 8716 as any other taxpayer making a section 444 election. Thus, a corporation electing to be an S corporation that desires to make a section 444 election is not required to file Form 8716 with its Form 2553, "Election by a Small Business Corporation." However, a corporation electing to be an S corporation after September 26, 1988, is required to state on Form 2553 its intention to—

(A) Make a section 444 election, if qualified, or

(B) Make a "back-up section 444 election" as described in paragraph (b)(4) of this section.

If a corporation electing to be an S corporation fails to state either of the above intentions, the District Director may, at his discretion, disregard any section 444 election for such taxpayer.

(ii) *Examples.* The provisions of this paragraph (b)(3) may be illustrated by the following examples.

Example (1). D is a corporation that commences operations on October 1, 1988, and elects to be an S corporation for its taxable year beginning October 1, 1988. All of D's shareholders use the calendar year as their taxable year. D desires to adopt a September 30 taxable year. D does not believe it has a business purpose for a September 30 taxable year and thus it must make a section 444 election to use such year. Based on these facts, D must, pursuant to the instructions to Form 2553, state on Form 2553 that, if qualified, it will make a section 444 election to adopt a year ending September 30 for its taxable year beginning October 1, 1988. If D is qualified (*i.e.*, D is not a member of a tiered structure on December 31, 1988) to make a section 444 election for its taxable year beginning October 1, 1988, D must file Form 8716 by March 15, 1989. If D ultimately is not qualified to make a section 444 election for its taxable year beginning October 1, 1988, D's election to be an S corporation will not be effective unless, pursuant to the instructions to Form 2553, D made a back-up calendar year election (*i.e.*, an election to adopt the calendar year in the event D ultimately is not qualified to make a section 444 election for such year).

Example (2). The facts are the same as in example (1), except that D believes it can establish, to the satisfaction of the Commissioner, a business purpose for adopting a September 30 taxable year. However, D desires to make a "back-up section 444 election" (see paragraph (b)(4) of this section) in the event that the Commissioner does not grant permission to adopt a September 30 taxable year based upon business purpose. Based on these facts, D must, pursuant to the instructions to Form 2553, state on Form 2553 its intention, if qualified, to make a back-up section 444 election to adopt a September 30 taxable year. If, by March 15, 1989, D has not received permission to adopt a September 30 taxable year and D is qualified to make a section 444 election, D must make a back-up election in accordance with paragraph (b)(4) of this section.

(4) *Back-up section 444 election*—(i) *General rule.* A taxpayer that has requested (or is planning to request) permission to use a particular taxable year based upon business purpose, may, if otherwise qualified, file a section 444 election (referred to as a "back-up section 444 election"). If the Commissioner subsequently denies the business purpose request, the taxpayer will, if otherwise qualified, be required to activate the back-up

Reg. § 1.444-3T(b)(2)

section 444 election. See examples (1) and (2) in paragraph (b)(4)(iv) of this section.

(ii) *Procedures for making a back-up section 444 election.* In addition to following the general rules provided in this section, a taxpayer making a back-up section 444 election should, in order to allow the Service to process the affected returns in an efficient manner, type or legibly print the words "BACK-UP ELECTION" at the top of Form 8716, "Election to Have a Tax Year Other Than a Required Tax Year." However, if such Form 8716 is filed on or after the date a Form 1128, Application for Change in Accounting Period, is filed with respect to a period that begins on the same date, the words "FORM 1128 BACK-UP ELECTION" should be typed or legibly printed at the top of Form 8716.

(iii) *Procedures for activating a back-up section 444 election*—(A) *Partnerships and S corporations*—(*1*) *In general.* A back-up section 444 election made by a partnership or S corporation is activated by filing the return required in § 1.7519-2T(a)(2)(i) and making the payment required in § 1.7519-1T. The due date for filing such return and payment will be the later of—

(*i*) The due dates provided in § 1.7519-2T, or

(*ii*) 60 days from the date the Commissioner denies the business purpose request.

However, interest will be assessed (at the rate provided in section 6621(a)(2)) on any required payment made after the due date (without regard to any extension for a back-up election) provided in § 1.7519-2T(a)(4)(i) or (a)(4)(ii), whichever is applicable, for such payment. Interest will be calculated from such due date to the date such amount is actually paid. Interest assessed under this paragraph will be separate from any required payments. Thus, interest will not be subject to refund under § 1.7519-2T.

(*2*) *Special rule if Form 720 used to satisfy return requirement.* If, pursuant to § 1.7519-2T(a)(3), a partnership or S corporation must use Form 720, "Quarterly Federal Excise Tax Return," to satisfy the return requirement of § 1.7519-2T(a)(2), then in addition to following the general rules provided in § 1.7519-2T, the partnership or S corporation must type or legibly print the words "ACTIVATING BACK-UP ELECTION" on the top of Form 720. A partnership or S corporation that would otherwise file a Form 720 on or before the date specified in paragraph (b)(4)(iii)(A)(*1*) of this section may satisfy the return requirement by including the necessary information on such Form 720. Alternatively, such partnership or S corporation may file an additional Form 720 (*i.e.*, a Form 720 separate from the Form 720 it would otherwise file). Thus, for example, if the due date for activating an S corporation's back-up election is November 15, 1988, and the S corporation must file a Form 720 by October 31, 1988, to report manufacturers excise tax for the third quarter of 1988, the S corporation may use that Form 720 to activate its back-up election. Alternatively, the S corporation may file its regular Form 720 that is due October 31, 1988, and file an additional Form 720 by November 15, 1988, activating its back-up election.

(B) *Personal service corporations.* A back-up section 444 election made by a personal service corporation is activated by filing Form 8716 with the personal service corporation's original or amended income tax return for the taxable year in which the election is first effective, and typing or legibly printing the words—"ACTIVATING BACK-UP ELECTION" on the top of such income tax return.

(iv) *Examples.* The provisions of this paragraph (b)(4) may be illustrated by the following examples. Also see example (2) in paragraph (b)(3) of this section.

Example (1). E, a partnership that historically used a June 30 taxable year, requested (pursuant to section 6 of Rev. Proc. 87-32, 1987-28 I.R.B. 14) permission from the Commissioner to retain a June 30 taxable year for its taxable year beginning July 1, 1987. Furthermore, E is qualified to make a section 444 election to retain a June 30 taxable year for its taxable year beginning July 1, 1987. However, as of the date specified in paragraph (b)(2) of this section, the Commissioner has not determined whether E has a valid business purpose for retaining its June 30 taxable year. Based on these facts, E may, by the date specified in paragraph (b)(2) of this section, make a back-up section 444 election to retain its June 30 taxable year.

Example (2). The facts are the same as in example (1). In addition, on August 12, 1988, the Internal Revenue Service notifies E that its business purpose request is denied. E asks for reconsideration of the Service's decision, and the Service sustains the original denial on September 30, 1988. Based on these facts, E must activate its back-up section 444 election within 60 days after September 30, 1988.

Example (3). The facts are the same as in example (1), except that E desires to make a section 444 election to use a year ending September 30 for its taxable year beginning July 1, 1987. Although E qualifies to make a section 444 election to retain its June 30 taxable year, E may

Reg. § 1.444-3T(b)(4)

make a back-up section 444 election for a September 30 taxable year.

(c) *Administrative relief*—(1) *Extension of time to file income tax returns*—(i) *Automatic extension.* If a partnership, S corporation, or personal service corporation makes a section 444 election (or does not make a section 444 election, either because it is ineligible or because it decides not to make the election, and therefore changes to its required taxable year) for its first taxable year beginning after December 31, 1986, the due date for filing its income tax return for such year shall be the later of—

(A) The due date established under—

(*1*) Section 6072, in the case of Form 1065,

(*2*) § 1.6037-1(b), in the case of Form 1120S,

(*3*) Section 6072(b), in the case of other Form 1120 series form; or

(B) August 15, 1988.

The words "SECTION 444 RETURN" should, in order to allow the Service to process the affected returns in an efficient manner, be typed or legibly printed at the top of the Form 1065 or Form 1120 series form, whichever is applicable, filed under this paragraph (c)(1)(i).

(ii) *Additional extensions.* If the due date of the income tax return for the first taxable year beginning after December 31, 1986, extended as provided in paragraph (c)(1)(i)(B) of this section, occurs before the date that is 6 months after the date specified in paragraph (c)(1)(i)(A) of this section, the partnership, S corporation, or personal service corporation may request an additional extension or extensions of time (up to 6 months after the date specified in paragraph (c)(1)(i)(A) of this section) to file its income tax return for such first taxable year. The request must be made by the later of the date specified in paragraph (c)(1)(i)(A) or (c)(1)(i)(B) of this section and must be made on Form 7004, "Application for Automatic Extension of Time To File Corporation Income Tax Return", or Form 2758, "Application for Extension of Time to File U.S. Partnership, Fiduciary, and Certain Other Returns," whichever is applicable, in accordance with the form and its instructions. In addition, the following words should be typed or legibly printed at the top of the form—"SECTION 444 REQUEST FOR ADDITIONAL EXTENSION."

(iii) *Examples.* The provisions of paragraph (c)(1) of this section may be illustrated by the following examples.

Example (1). G, a partnership that historically used a January 31 taxable year, makes a section 444 election to retain such year for its taxable year beginning February 1, 1987. Absent paragraph (c)(1)(i) of this section, G's Form 1065 for the taxable year ending January 31, 1988, is due on or before May 15, 1988. However, if G types or legibly prints "SECTION 444 RETURN" at the top of Form 1065 for such year, paragraph (c)(1)(i) of this section automatically extends the due date of such return to August 15, 1988.

Example (2). The facts are the same as in example (1), except that G desires to extend the due date of its income tax return for the year ending January 31, 1988, to a date beyond August 15, 1988. Pursuant to paragraph (c)(1)(ii) of this section, G may extend such return to November 15, 1988 (*i.e.*, the date that is up to 6 months after May 15, 1988, the normal due date of the return). However, in order to obtain this additional extension, G must file Form 2758 pursuant to paragraph (c)(1)(ii) of this section on or before August 15, 1988.

Example (3). H, a partnership that historically used a May 31 taxable year, makes a section 444 election to use a year ending September 30 for its taxable year beginning on June 1, 1987. Absent paragraph (c)(1)(i) of this section, H's Form 1065 for the taxable year beginning June 1, 1987, and ending September 30, 1987, is due on or before January 15, 1988. However, if H types or legibly prints "SECTION 444 RETURN" at the top of Form 1065 for such year, paragraph (c)(1)(i) of this section automatically extends the due date of such return to August 15, 1988.

Example (4). The facts are the same as in example (3), except H desires to further extend (*i.e.*, extend beyond August 15, 1988) the due date of its income tax return for its taxable year beginning June 1, 1987, and ending September 30, 1987. Since August 15, 1988, is 6 months or more after the due date (without extensions) of such return, paragraph (c)(1)(ii) of this section prevents H from further extending the time for filing such return.

Example (5). I, a partnership that historically used a June 30 taxable year, considered making a section 444 election to retain such taxable year, but eventually decided to change to a December 31 taxable year (I's required taxable year). Absent paragraph (c)(1)(i) of this section, I's Form 1065 for the taxable year beginning July 1, 1987, and ending December 31, 1987, is due on or before April 15, 1988. Pursuant to paragraph (c)(1)(i) of this section, if I types or legibly prints "SECTION 444 RETURN" at the top of Form 1065 for such year, paragraph (c)(1)(i) of this section automatically extends the due date of such return to August 15, 1988. In addition, I may further extend such return pursuant to paragraph (c)(1)(ii) of this section.

(2) *No penalty for certain late payments*—(i) *In general.* In the case of a personal service corporation or S corporation described in paragraph (c)(1)(i) of this section, no penalty under section 6651(a)(2) will be imposed for failure to pay income tax (if any) for the first taxable year beginning after December 31, 1986, but only for the period beginning with the last date for payment and ending with the later of the date specified in paragraph (c)(1)(i) or paragraph (c)(1)(ii) of this section.

(ii) *Example.* The provisions of paragraph (c)(2)(i) of this section may be illustrated by the following example.

Example. J, a personal service corporation that historically used a January 31 taxable year, makes a section 444 election to retain such year for its taxable year beginning February 1, 1987. The last date (without extension) for payment of J's income tax (if any) for its taxable year beginning February 1, 1987, is April 15, 1988. However, under paragraph (c)(2)(i) of this section, no penalty under section 6651(a)(2) will be imposed on any underpayment of income tax for the period beginning April 15, 1988 and ending August 15, 1988.

(d) *Effective date.* This section is effective for taxable years beginning after December 31, 1986. [Temporary Reg. § 1.444-3T.]

☐ [T.D. 8205, 5-24-88.]

[Reg. § 1.444-4]

§ 1.444-4. **Tiered structure.**—(a) *Electing small business trusts.* For purposes of § 1.444-2T, solely with respect to an S corporation shareholder, the term *deferral entity* does not include a trust that is treated as an electing small business trust under section 1361(e). An S corporation with an electing small business trust as a shareholder may make an election under section 444. This paragraph is applicable to taxable years beginning on and after December 29, 2000; however, taxpayers may voluntarily apply it to taxable years of S corporations beginning after December 31, 1996.

(b) *Certain tax-exempt trusts.* For purposes of § 1.444-2T, solely with respect to an S corporation shareholder, the term *deferral entity* does not include a trust that is described in section 401(a) or 501(c)(3), and is exempt from taxation under section 501(a). An S corporation with a trust as a shareholder that is described in section 401(a) or section 501(c)(3), and is exempt from taxation under section 501(a) may make an election under section 444. This paragraph is applicable to taxable years beginning on and after December 29, 2000; however taxpayers may voluntarily apply it to taxable years of S corporations beginning after December 31, 1997.

(c) *Certain terminations disregarded*—(1) *In general.* An S corporation that is described in this paragraph (c)(1) may request that a termination of its election under section 444 be disregarded, and that the S corporation be permitted to resume use of the year it previously elected under section 444, by following the procedures of paragraph (c)(2) of this section. An S corporation is described in this paragraph if the S corporation is otherwise qualified to make a section 444 election, and its previous election was terminated under § 1.444-2T(a) solely because—

(i) In the case of a taxable year beginning after December 31, 1996, a trust that is treated as an electing small business trust became a shareholder of such S corporation; or

(ii) In the case of a taxable year beginning after December 31, 1997, a trust that is described in section 401(a) or 501(c)(3), and is exempt from taxation under section 501(a) became a shareholder of such S corporation.

(2) *Procedure*—(i) *In general.* An S corporation described in paragraph (c)(1) of this section that wishes to make the request described in paragraph (c)(1) of this section must do so by filing Form 8716, "Election To Have a Tax Year Other Than a Required Tax Year," and typing or printing legibly at the top of such form—"CONTINUATION OF SECTION 444 ELECTION UNDER § 1.444-4." In order to assist the Internal Revenue Service in updating the S corporation's account, on Line 5 the Box "Changing to" should be checked. Additionally, the election month indicated must be the last month of the S corporation's previously elected section 444 election year, and the effective year indicated must end in 2002.

(ii) *Time and place for filing Form 8716.* Such form must be filed on or before October 15, 2002, with the service center where the S corporation's returns of tax (Forms 1120S) are filed. In addition, a copy of the Form 8716 should be attached to the S corporation's short period Federal income tax return for the first election year beginning on or after January 1, 2002.

(3) *Effect of request*—(i) *Taxable years beginning on or after January 1, 2002.* An S corporation described in paragraph (c)(1) of this section that requests, in accordance with this paragraph, that a termination of its election under section 444 be disregarded will be permitted to resume use of the year it previously elected under section 444, commencing with its first taxable year begin-

Reg. § 1.444-4(c)(3)

ning on or after January 1, 2002. Such S corporation will be required to file a return under § 1.7519-2T for each taxable year beginning on or after January 1, 2002. No payment under section 7519 will be due with respect to the first taxable year beginning on or after January 1, 2002. However, a required payment will be due on or before May 15, 2003, with respect to such S corporation's second continued section 444 election year that begins in calendar year 2002.

(ii) *Taxable years beginning prior to January 1, 2002.* An S corporation described in paragraph (c)(1) of this section that requests, in accordance with this paragraph, that a termination of its election under section 444 be disregarded will not be required to amend any prior Federal income tax returns, make any required payments under section 7519, or file any returns under § 1.7519-2T, with respect to taxable years beginning on or after the date the termination of its section 444 election was effective and prior to January 1, 2002.

(iii) *Section 7519: required payments and returns.* The Internal Revenue Service waives any requirement for an S corporation described in paragraph (c)(1) of this section to file the federal tax returns and make any required payments under section 7519 for years prior to the taxable year of continuation as described in paragraph (c)(3)(i) of this section, if for such years the S corporation filed its federal income tax returns on the basis of its required taxable year. [Reg. § 1.444-4.]

☐ [*T.D.* 8994, 5-13-2002.]

Methods of Accounting

[Reg. § 1.446-1]

§ 1.446-1. General rule for methods of accounting.—(a) *General rule.*—(1) Section 446(a) provides that taxable income shall be computed under the method of accounting on the basis of which a taxpayer regularly computes his income in keeping his books. The term "method of accounting" includes not only the over-all method of accounting of the taxpayer but also the accounting treatment of any item. Examples of such over-all methods are the cash receipts and disbursements method, an accrual method, combinations of such methods, and combinations of the foregoing with various methods provided for the accounting treatment of special items. These methods of accounting for special items include the accounting treatment prescribed for research and experimental expenditures, soil and water conservation expenditures, depreciation, net operating losses, etc. Except for deviations permitted or required by such special accounting treatment, taxable income shall be computed under the method of accounting on the basis of which the taxpayer regularly computes his income in keeping his books. For requirement respecting the adoption or change of accounting method, see section 446(e) and paragraph (e) of this section.

(2) It is recognized that no uniform method of accounting can be prescribed for all taxpayers. Each taxpayer shall adopt such forms and systems as are, in his judgment, best suited to his needs. However, no method of accounting is acceptable unless, in the opinion of the Commissioner, it clearly reflects income. A method of accounting which reflects the consistent application of generally accepted accounting principles in a particular trade or business in accordance with accepted conditions or practices in that trade or business will ordinarily be regarded as clearly reflecting income, provided all items of gross income and expense are treated consistently from year to year.

(3) Items of gross income and expenditures which are elements in the computation of taxable income need not be in the form of cash. It is sufficient that such items can be valued in terms of money. For general rules relating to the taxable year for inclusion of income and for taking deductions, see sections 451 and 461, and the regulations thereunder.

(4) Each taxpayer is required to make a return of his taxable income for each taxable year and must maintain such accounting records as will enable him to file a correct return. See section 6001 and the regulations thereunder. Accounting records include the taxpayer's regular books of account and such other records and data as may be necessary to support the entries on his books of account and on his return, as for example, a reconciliation of any differences between such books and his return. The following are among the essential features that must be considered in maintaining such records:

(i) In all cases in which the production, purchase, or sale of merchandise of any kind in an income-producing factor, merchandise on hand (including finished goods, work in process, raw materials, and supplies) at the beginning and end of the year shall be taken into account in computing the taxable income of the year. (For rules relating to computation of inventories, see sections 263A, 471 and 472, and the regulations thereunder.)

(ii) Expenditures made during the year shall be properly classified as between capital and expense. For example, expenditures for such items as plant and equipment, which have a useful life extending substantially beyond the taxable year, shall be charged to a capital account and not to an expense account.

(iii) In any case in which there is allowable with respect to an asset a deduction for depreciation, amortization, or depletion, any expenditures (other than ordinary repairs) made to restore the asset or prolong its useful life shall be added to the asset account or charged against the appropriate reserve.

(b) *Exceptions*—(1) If the taxpayer does not regularly employ a method of accounting which clearly reflects his income, the computation of taxable income shall be made in a manner which, in the opinion of the Commissioner, does clearly reflect income.

(2) A taxpayer whose sole source of income is wages need not keep formal books in order to have an accounting method. Tax returns, copies thereof, or other records may be sufficient to establish the use of the method of accounting used in the preparation of the taxpayer's income tax returns.

(c) *Permissible methods*—(1) *In general.* Subject to the provisions of paragraphs (a) and (b) of this section, a taxpayer may compute his taxable income under any of the following methods of accounting:

(i) *Cash receipts and disbursements method.* Generally, under the cash receipts and disbursements method in the computation of taxable income, all items which constitute gross income (whether in the form of cash, property, or services) are to be included for the taxable year in which actually or constructively received. Expenditures are to be deducted for the taxable year in which actually made. For rules relating to constructive receipt, see § 1.451-2. For treatment of an expenditure attributable to more than one taxable year, see section 461(a) and paragraph (a)(1) of § 1.461-1.

(ii) *Accrual method*—(A) Generally, under an accrual method, income is to be included for the taxable year when all the events have occurred that fix the right to receive the income and the amount of the income can be determined with reasonable accuracy. Under such a method, a liability is incurred, and generally is taken into account for Federal income tax purposes, in the taxable year in which all the events have occurred that establish the fact of the liability, the amount of the liability can be determined with reasonable accuracy, and economic performance has occurred with respect to the liability. (See paragraph (a)(2)(iii)(A) of § 1.461-1 for examples of liabilities that may not be taken into account until after the taxable year incurred, and see §§ 1.461-4 through 1.461-6 for rules relating to economic performance.) Applicable provisions of the Code, the Income Tax Regulations, and other guidance published by the Secretary prescribe the manner in which a liability that has been incurred is taken into account. For example, section 162 provides that a deductible liability generally is taken into account in the taxable year incurred through a deduction from gross income. As a further example, under section 263 or 263A, a liability that relates to the creation of an asset having a useful life extending substantially beyond the close of the taxable year is taken into account in the taxable year incurred through capitalization (within the meaning of § 1.263A-1(c)(3)), and may later affect the computation of taxable income through depreciation or otherwise over a period including subsequent taxable years, in accordance with applicable Internal Revenue Code sections and related guidance.

(B) The term "liability" includes any item allowable as a deduction, cost, or expense for Federal income tax purposes. In addition to allowable deductions, the term includes any amount otherwise allowable as a capitalized cost, as a cost taken into account in computing cost of goods sold, as a cost allocable to a long-term contract, or as any other cost or expense. Thus, for example, an amount that a taxpayer expends or will expend for capital improvements to property must be incurred before the taxpayer may take the amount into account in computing its basis in the property. The term "liability" is not limited to items for which a legal obligation to pay exists at the time of payment. Thus, for example, amounts prepaid for goods or services and amounts paid without a legal obligation to do so may not be taken into account by an accrual basis taxpayer any earlier than the taxable year in which those amounts are incurred.

(C) No method of accounting is acceptable unless, in the opinion of the Commissioner, it clearly reflects income. The method used by the taxpayer in determining when income is to be accounted for will generally be acceptable if it accords with generally accepted accounting principles, is consistently used by the taxpayer from year to year, and is consistent with the Income Tax Regulations. For example, a taxpayer engaged in a manufacturing business may account for sales of the taxpayer's product when the goods are shipped, when the product is delivered or accepted, or when title to the goods passes to the customers, whether or not billed, depending on the method regularly employed in keeping the taxpayer's books.

Reg. § 1.446-1(c)(1)

(iii) *Other permissible methods.* Special methods of accounting are described elsewhere in chapter 1 of the Code and the regulations thereunder. For example, see the following sections and the regulations thereunder: Sections 61 and 162, relating to the crop method of accounting; section 453, relating to the installment method; section 460, relating to the long-term contract methods. In addition, special methods of accounting for particular items of income and expense are provided under other sections of chapter 1. For example, see section 174, relating to research and experimental expenditures, and section 175, relating to soil and water conservation expenditures.

(iv) *Combinations of the foregoing methods.* (*a*) In accordance with the following rules, any combination of the foregoing methods of accounting will be permitted in connection with a trade or business if such combination clearly reflects income and is consistently used. Where a combination of methods of accounting includes any special methods, such as those referred to in subdivision (iii) of this subparagraph, the taxpayer must comply with the requirements relating to such special methods. A taxpayer using an accrual method of accounting with respect to purchases and sales may use the cash method in computing all other items of income and expense. However, a taxpayer who uses the cash method of accounting in computing gross income from his trade or business shall use the cash method in computing expenses of such trade or business. Similarly, a taxpayer who uses an accrual method of accounting in computing business expenses shall use an accrual method in computing items affecting gross income from his trade or business.

(*b*) A taxpayer using one method of accounting in computing items of income and deductions of his trade or business may compute other items of income and deductions not connected with his trade or business under a different method of accounting.

(2) *Special rules*—(i) In any case in which it is necessary to use an inventory the accrual method of accounting must be used with regard to purchases and sales unless otherwise authorized under subdivision (ii) of this subparagraph.

(ii) No method of accounting will be regarded as clearly reflecting income unless all items of gross profit and deductions are treated with consistency from year to year. The Commissioner may authorize a taxpayer to adopt or change to a method of accounting permitted by this chapter although the method is not specifically described in this part if, in the opinion of the Commissioner, income is clearly reflected by the use of such method. Further, the Commissioner may authorize a taxpayer to continue the use of a method of accounting consistently used by the taxpayer, even though not specifically authorized by the regulations in this part, if, in the opinion of the Commissioner, income is clearly reflected by the use of such method. See section 446(a) and paragraph (a) of this section, which require that taxable income shall be computed under the method of accounting on the basis of which the taxpayer regularly computes his income in keeping his books, and section 446(e) and paragraph (e) of this section, which require the prior approval of the Commissioner in the case of changes in accounting method.

(iii) The timing rules of § 1.1502-13 are a method of accounting for intercompany transactions (as defined in § 1.1502-13(b)(1)(i)), to be applied by each member of a consolidated group in addition to the member's other methods of accounting. See § 1.1502-13(a)(3)(i). This paragraph (c)(2)(iii) is applicable to consolidated return years beginning on or after November 7, 2001.

(d) *Taxpayer engaged in more than one business*—(1) Where a taxpayer has two or more separate and distinct trades or businesses, a different method of accounting may be used for each trade or business, provided the method used for each trade or business clearly reflects the income of that particular trade or business. For example, a taxpayer may account for the operations of a personal service business on the cash receipts and disbursements method and of a manufacturing business on an accrual method, provided such businesses are separate and distinct and the methods used for each clearly reflect income. The method first used in accounting for business income and deductions in connection with each trade or business, as evidenced in the taxpayer's income tax return in which such income or deductions are first reported, must be consistently followed thereafter.

(2) No trade or business will be considered separate and distinct for purposes of this paragraph unless a complete and separable set of books and records is kept for such trade or business.

(3) If, by reason of maintaining different methods of accounting, there is a creation or shifting of profits or losses between the trades or businesses of the taxpayer (for example, through inventory adjustments, sales, purchases, or expenses) so that income of the taxpayer is not clearly reflected, the trades or businesses of the taxpayer will not be considered to be separate and distinct.

Reg. § 1.446-1(c)(2)

(e) *Requirement respecting the adoption or change of accounting method*—(1) A taxpayer filing his first return may adopt any permissible method of accounting in computing taxable income for the taxable year covered by such return. See section 446(c) and paragraph (c) of this section for permissible methods. Moreover, a taxpayer may adopt any permissible method of accounting in connection with each separate and distinct trade or business, the income from which is reported for the first time. See section 446(d) and paragraph (d) of this section. See also section 446(a) and paragraph (a) of this section.

(2)(i) Except as otherwise expressly provided in chapter 1 of the Code and the regulations thereunder, a taxpayer who changes the method of accounting employed in keeping his books shall, before computing his income upon such new method for purposes of taxation, secure the consent of the Commissioner. Consent must be secured whether or not such method is proper or is permitted under the Internal Revenue Code or the regulations thereunder.

(ii)(*a*) A change in the method of accounting includes a change in the overall plan of accounting for gross income or deductions or a change in the treatment of any material item used in such overall plan. Although a method of accounting may exist under this definition without the necessity of a pattern of consistent treatment of an item, in most instances a method of accounting is not established for an item without such consistent treatment. A material item is any item which involves the proper time for the inclusion of the item in income or the taking of a deduction. Changes in method of accounting include a change from the cash receipts and disbursements method to an accrual method, or vice versa, a change involving the method or basis used in the valuation of inventories (see sections 471 and 472 and the regulations thereunder), a change from the cash or accrual method to a long-term contract method, or vice versa (see § 1.460-4), a change involving the adoption, use or discontinuance of any other specialized method of computing taxable income, such as the crop method, and a change where the Internal Revenue Code and regulations thereunder specifically require that the consent of the Commissioner must be obtained before adopting such a change.

(*b*) A change in method of accounting does not include correction of mathematical or posting errors, or errors in the computation of tax liability (such as errors in computation of the foreign tax credit, net operating loss, percentage depletion or investment credit). Also, a change in method of accounting does not include adjustment of any item of income or deduction which does not involve the proper time for the inclusion of the item of income or the taking of a deduction. For example, corrections of items that are deducted as interest or salary, but which are in fact payments of dividends, and of items that are deducted as business expenses, but which are in fact personal expenses, are not changes in method of accounting. In addition, a change in the method of accounting does not include an adjustment with respect to the addition to a reserve for bad debts or an adjustment in the useful life of a depreciable asset. Although such adjustments may involve the question of the proper time for the taking of a deduction, such items are traditionally corrected by adjustments in the current and future years. For the treatment of the adjustment of the addition to a bad debt reserve, see the regulations under section 166 of the Code; for the treatment of a change in the useful life of a depreciable asset, see the regulations under section 167(b) of the Code. A change in the method of accounting also does not include a change in treatment resulting from a change in underlying facts. On the other hand, for example, a correction to require depreciation in lieu of a deduction for the cost of a class of depreciable assets which had been consistently treated as an expense in the year of purchase involves the question of the proper timing of an item, and is to be treated as a change in method of accounting.

(*c*) A change in an overall plan or system of identifying or valuing items in inventory is a change in method of accounting. Also a change in the treatment of any material item used in the overall plan for identifying or valuing items in inventory is a change in method of accounting.

(iii) A change in the method of accounting may be illustrated by the following examples:

Example (1). Although the sale of merchandise is an income producing factor, and therefore inventories are required, a taxpayer in the retail jewelry business reports his income on the cash receipts and disbursements method of accounting. A change from the cash receipts and disbursements method of accounting to the accrual method of accounting is a change in the overall plan of accounting and thus is a change in method of accounting.

Example (2). A taxpayer in the wholesale dry goods business computes its income and expenses on the accrual method of accounting and files its Federal income tax returns on such basis except for real estate taxes which have been reported on the cash receipts and disbursements method of accounting. A change in the treatment of real estate taxes from the cash receipts and disbursements method to the accrual method is a change in method of accounting because such change is a change in the treatment of a material item within his overall accounting practice.

Example (3). A taxpayer in the wholesale dry goods business computes its income and expenses on the accrual method of accounting and files its Federal income tax returns on such basis. Vacation pay has been deducted in the year in which paid because the taxpayer did not have a completely vested vacation pay plan, and, therefore, the liability for payment did not accrue until that year. Subsequently, the taxpayer adopts a completely vested vacation pay plan that changes its year for accruing the deduction from the year in which payment is made to the year in which the liability to make the payment now arises. The change for the year of deduction of the vacation pay plan is not a change in method of accounting but results, instead, because the underlying facts (that is, the type of vacation pay plan) have changed.

Example (4). From 1968 through 1970, a taxpayer has fairly allocated indirect overhead costs to the value of inventories on a fixed percentage of direct costs. If the ratio of indirect overhead costs to direct costs increases in 1971, a change in the underlying facts has occurred. Accordingly, an increase in the percentage in 1971 to fairly reflect the increase in the relative level of indirect overhead costs is not a change in method of accounting but is a change in treatment resulting from a change in the underlying facts.

Example (5). A taxpayer values inventories at cost. A change in the basis for valuation of inventories from cost to the lower of cost or market is a change in an overall practice of valuing items in inventory. The change, therefore, is a change of method of accounting for inventories.

Example (6). A taxpayer in the manufacturing business has for many taxable years valued its inventories at cost. However, cost has been improperly computed since no overhead costs have been included in valuing the inventories at cost. The failure to allocate an appropriate portion of overhead to the value of inventories is contrary to the requirement of the Internal Revenue Code and the regulations thereunder. A change requiring appropriate allocation of overhead is a change in method of accounting because it involves a change in the treatment of a material item used in the overall practice of identifying or valuing items in inventory.

Example (7). A taxpayer has for many taxable years valued certain inventories by a method which provides for deducting 20 percent of the cost of the inventory items in determining the final inventory valuation. The 20 percent adjustment is taken as a "reserve for price changes." Although this method is not a proper method of valuing inventories under the Internal Revenue Code or the regulations thereunder, it involves the treatment of a material item used in the overall practice of valuing inventory. A change in such practice or procedure is a change of method of accounting for inventories.

Example (8). A taxpayer has always used a base stock system of accounting for inventories. Under this system a constant price is applied to an assumed constant normal quantity of goods in stock. The base stock system is an overall plan of accounting for inventories which is not recognized as a proper method of accounting for inventories under the regulations. A change in this practice is, nevertheless, a change of method of accounting for inventories.

(3)(i) Except as otherwise provided under the authority of paragraph (e)(3)(ii) of this section, to secure the Commissioner's consent to a taxpayer's change in method of accounting the taxpayer must file an application on Form 3115 with the Commissioner during the taxable year in which the taxpayer desires to make the change in method of accounting. To the extent applicable, the taxpayer must furnish all information requested on the Form 3115. This information includes all classes of items that will be treated differently under the new method of accounting, any amounts that will be duplicated or omitted as a result of the proposed change, and the taxpayer's computation of any adjustments necessary to prevent such duplications or omissions. The Commissioner may require such other information as may be necessary to determine whether the proposed change will be permitted. Permission to change a taxpayer's method of accounting will not be granted unless the taxpayer agrees to the Commissioner's prescribed terms and conditions for effecting the change, including the taxable year or years in which any adjustment necessary to prevent amounts from being duplicated or omitted is to be taken into account. See section 481 and the regulations thereunder, relating to certain adjustments resulting from accounting method changes, and section 472 and the regulations thereunder, relating to adjustments for changes to and from the last-in, first-out inventory method. For any Form 3115 filed on or after May 15, 1997, see § 1.446-1T(e)(3)(i)(B).

(ii) Notwithstanding the provisions of paragraph (e)(3)(i) of this section, the Commissioner may prescribe administrative procedures under which taxpayers will be permitted to change their method of accounting. The administrative proce-

Reg. § 1.446-1(e)(3)

dures shall prescribe those terms and conditions necessary to obtain the Commissioner's consent to effect the change and to prevent amounts from being duplicated or omitted. The terms and conditions that may be prescribed by the Commissioner may include terms and conditions that require the change in method of accounting to be effected on a cut-off basis or by an adjustment under section 481(a) to be taken into account in the taxable year or years prescribed by the Commissioner.

(iii) This paragraph (e)(3) applies to Forms 3115 filed on or after December 31, 1997. For other Forms 3115, see § 1.446-1(e)(3) in effect prior to December 31, 1997 (§ 1.446-1(e)(3) as contained in the 26 CFR part 1 edition revised as of April 1, 1997). [Reg. § 1.446-1.]

☐ [T.D. 6282, 12-24-57. Amended by T.D. 6584, 12-20-61; T.D. 7073, 11-17-70; T.D. 7285, 9-14-73; T.D. 8067, 12-30-85; T.D. 8131, 3-24-87; T.D. 8408, 4-9-92; T.D. 8482, 8-6-93; T.D. 8608, 8-4-95; T.D. 8719, 5-14-97; T.D. 8742, 12-30-97; T.D. 8929, 1-10-2001 and T.D. 9025, 12-13-2002.]

[Reg. § 1.446-2]

§ 1.446-2. Method of accounting for interest.—(a) *Applicability*—(1) *In general.* This section provides rules for determining the amount of interest that accrues during an accrual period (other than interest described in paragraph (a)(2) of this section) and for determining the portion of a payment that consists of accrued interest. For purposes of this section, interest includes original issue discount and amounts treated as interest (whether stated or unstated) any lending or deferred payment transaction. Accrued interest determined under this section is taken into account by a taxpayer under the taxpayer's regular method of accounting (e.g., an accrual method or the cash receipts and disbursements method). Application of an exception described in paragraph (a)(2) of this section to one party to a transaction does not affect the application of this section to any other party to the transaction.

(2) *Exceptions*—(i) *Interest included or deducted under certain other provisions.* This section does not apply to interest that is taken into account under—

(A) Sections 1272(a), 1275, and 163(e) (income and deductions relating to original issue discount);

(B) Section 467(a)(2) (certain payments for the use of property or services);

(C) Sections 1276 through 1278 (market discount);

(D) Sections 1281 through 1283 (discount on certain short-term obligations);

(E) Section 7872(a) (certain loans with below-market interest rates); or

(F) Section 1.1272-3 (an election by a holder to treat all interest on a debt instrument as original issue discount).

(ii) *De minimis original issue discount.* This section does not apply to de minimis original issue discount (other than de minimis original issue discount treated as qualified stated interest) as determined under § 1.1273-1(d). See § 1.163-7 for the treatment of de minimis original issue discount by the issuer and § § 1.1273-1(d) and 1.1272-3 for the treatment of de minimis original issue discount by the holder.

(b) *Accrual of qualified stated interest.* Qualified stated interest (as defined in § 1.1273-1(c)) accrues ratably over the accrual period (or periods) to which it is attributable and accrues at the stated rate for the period (or periods).

(c) *Accrual of interest other than qualified stated interest.* Subject to the modifications in paragraph (d) of this section, the amount of interest (other than qualified stated interest) that accrues for any accrual period is determined under rules similar to those in the regulations under sections 1272 and 1275 for the accrual of original issue discount. The preceding sentence applies regardless of any contrary formula agreed to by the parties.

(d) *Modifications*—(1) *Issue price.* The issue price of the loan or contract is equal to—

(i) In the case of a contract for the sale or exchange of property to which section 483 applies, the amount described in § 1.483-2(a)(1)(i) or (ii), whichever is applicable;

(ii) In the case of a contract for the sale or exchange of property to which section 483 does not apply, the stated principal amount; or

(iii) In any other case, the amount loaned.

(2) *Principal payments that are not deferred payments.* In the case of a contract to which section 483 applies, principal payments that are not deferred payments are ignored for purposes of determining yield and adjusted issue price.

(e) *Allocation of interest to payments*—(1) *In general.* Except as provided in paragraphs (e)(2), (e)(3), and (e)(4) of this section, each payment under a loan (other than payments of additional interest or similar charges provided with respect to amounts that are not paid when due) is treated as a payment of interest to the extent of the accrued and unpaid interest determined under paragraphs (b) and (c) of this section as of the date the payment becomes due.

(2) *Special rule for points deductible under section 461(g)(2).* If a payment of points is de-

Reg. § 1.446-2(e)(2)

ductible by the borrower under section 461(g)(2), the payment is treated by the borrower as a payment of interest.

(3) *Allocation respected in certain small transactions.* [Reserved]

(4) *Pro rata prepayments.* Accrued but unpaid interest is allocated to a pro rata prepayment under rules similar to those for allocating accrued but unpaid original issue discount to a pro rata prepayment under § 1.1275-2(f). For purposes of the preceding sentence, a pro rata prepayment is a payment that is made prior to maturity that—

(i) Is not made pursuant to the contract's payment schedule; and

(ii) Results in a substantially pro rata reduction of each payment remaining to be paid on the contract.

(f) *Aggregation rule.* For purposes of this section, all contracts calling for deferred payments arising from the same transaction (or a series of related transactions) are treated as a single contract. This rule, however, generally only applies to contracts involving a single borrower and a single lender.

(g) *Debt instruments denominated in a currency other than the U.S. dollar.* This section applies to a debt instrument that provides for all payments denominated in, or determined by reference to, the functional currency of the taxpayer or qualified business unit of the taxpayer (even if that currency is other than the U.S. dollar). See § 1.988-2(b) to determine interest income or expense for debt instruments that provide for payments denominated in, or determined by reference to, a nonfunctional currency.

(h) *Example.* The following example illustrates the rules of this section.

Example. Allocation of unstated interest to deferred payments—(i) *Facts.* On July 1, 1996, A sells his personal residence to B for a stated purchase price of $1,297,143.66. The property is not personal use property (within the meaning of section 1275(b)(3)) in the hands of B. Under the loan agreement, B is required to make two installment payments of $648,571.83 each, the first due on June 30, 1998, and the second due on June 30, 2000. Both A and B use the cash receipts and disbursements method of accounting and use a calendar year for their taxable year.

(ii) *Amount of unstated interest.* Under section 483, the agreement does not provide for adequate stated interest. Thus, the loan's yield is the test rate of interest determined under § 1.483-3. Assume that both A and B use annual accrual periods and that the test rate of interest is 9.2 percent, compounded annually. Under § 1.483-2, the present value of the deferred payments is $1,000,000. Thus, the agreement has unstated interest of $297,143.66.

(iii) *First two accrual periods.* Under paragraph (d)(1) of this section, the issue price at the beginning of the first accrual period is $1,000,000 (the amount described in § 1.483-2(a)(1)(i)). Under paragraph (c) of this section, the amount of interest that accrues for the first accrual period is $92,000 ($1,000,000 × .092) and the amount of interest that accrues for the second accrual period is $100,464 ($1,092,000 × .092). Thus, $192,464 of interest has accrued as of the end of the second accrual period. Under paragraph (e)(1) of this section, the $648,571.83 payment made on June 30, 1998, is treated first as a payment of interest to the extent of $192,464. The remainder of the payment ($456,107.83) is treated as a payment of principal. Both A and B take the payment of interest ($192,464) into account in 1998.

(iv) *Second two accrual periods.* The adjusted issue price at the beginning of the third accrual period is $543,892.17 ($1,092,000 + $100,464 − $648,571.83). The amount of interest that accrues for the third accrual period is $50,038.08 ($543,892.17 × .092) and the amount of interest that accrues for the final accrual period is $54,641.58, the excess of the amount payable at maturity ($648,571.83), over the adjusted issue price at the beginning of the accrual period ($593,930.25). As of the date the second payment becomes due, $104,679.66 of interest has accrued. Thus, of the $648,571.83 payment made on June 30, 2000, $104,679.66 is treated as interest and $543,892.17 is treated as principal. Both A and B take the payment of interest ($104,679.66) into account in 2000.

(i) [Reserved]

(j) *Effective date.* This section applies to debt instruments issued on or after April 4, 1994, and to lending transactions, sales, and exchanges that occur on or after April 4, 1994. Taxpayers, however, may rely on this section for debt instruments issued after December 21, 1992, and before April 4, 1994, and for lending transactions, sales, and exchanges that occur after December 21, 1992, and before April 4, 1994. [Reg. § 1.446-2.]

☐ [*T.D.* 8517, 1-27-94.]

[Reg. § 1.446-3]

§ 1.446-3. **Notional principal contracts.**—(a) *Table of contents.* This paragraph (a) lists captioned paragraphs contained in § 1.446-3.

§ 1.446-3. Notional principal contracts.

(a) Table of contents.

Methods of Accounting

See p. 20,601 for regulations not amended to reflect law changes

(b) Purpose.
(c) Definitions and scope.
   (1) Notional principal contract.
      (i) In general.
      (ii) Excluded contracts.
      (iii) Transactions within section 475.
      (iv) Transactions within section 988.
   (2) Specified index.
   (3) Notional principal amount.
   (4) Special definitions.
      (i) Related person and party to the contract.
      (ii) Objective financial information.
      (iii) Dealer in notional principal contracts.
(d) Taxable year of inclusion and deduction.
(e) Periodic payments.
   (1) Definition.
   (2) Recognition rules.
      (i) In general.
      (ii) Rate set in arrears.
      (iii) Notional principal amount set in arrears.
   (3) Examples.
(f) Nonperiodic payments.
   (1) Definition.
   (2) Recognition rules.
      (i) In general.
      (ii) General rule for swaps.
      (iii) Alternative methods for swaps.
         (A) Prepaid swaps.
         (B) Other nonperiodic swap payments.
      (iv) General rule for caps and floors.
      (v) Alternative methods for caps and floors that hedge debt instruments.
         (A) Prepaid caps and floors.
         (B) Other caps and floors.
         (C) Special method for collars.
      (vi) Additional methods.
   (3) Term of extendible or terminable contracts.
   (4) Examples.
(g) Special rules.
   (1) Disguised notional principal contracts.
   (2) Hedged notional principal contracts.
   (3) Options and forwards to enter into notional principal contracts.
   (4) Swaps with significant nonperiodic payments.
   (5) Caps and floors that are significantly in-the-money. [Reserved]
   (6) Examples.
(h) Termination payments.
   (1) Definition.
   (2) Taxable year of inclusion and deduction by original parties.
   (3) Taxable year of inclusion and deduction by assignees.
   (4) Special rules.
      (i) Assignment of one leg of a contract.
      (ii) Substance over form.
   (5) Examples.
(i) Anti-abuse rule.
(j) Effective date.

(b) *Purpose.* The purpose of this section is to enable the clear reflection of the income and deductions from notional principal contracts by prescribing accounting methods that reflect the economic substance of such contracts.

(c) *Definitions and scope*—(1) *Notional principal contract*—(i) *In general.* A notional principal contract is a financial instrument that provides for the payment of amounts by one party to another at specified intervals calculated by reference to a specified index upon a notional principal amount in exchange for specified consideration or a promise to pay similar amounts. An agreement between a taxpayer and a qualified business unit (as defined in section 989(a)) of the taxpayer, or among qualified business units of the same taxpayer, is not a notional principal contract because a taxpayer cannot enter into a contract with itself. Notional principal contracts governed by this section include interest rate swaps, currency swaps, basis swaps, interest rate caps, interest rate floors, commodity swaps, equity swaps, equity index swaps, and similar agreements. A collar is not itself a notional principal contract, but certain caps and floors that comprise a collar may be treated as a single notional principal contract under paragraph (f)(2)(v)(C) of this section. A contract may be a notional principal contract governed by this section even though the term of the contract is subject to termination or extension. Each confirmation under a master agreement to enter into agreements governed by this section is treated as a separate notional principal contract.

      (ii) *Excluded contracts.* A contract described in section 1256(b), a futures contract, a forward contract, and an option are not notional principal contracts. An instrument or contract that constitutes indebtedness under general principles of Federal income tax law is not a notional

Reg. § 1.446-3(c)(1)

principal contract. An option or forward contract that entitles or obligates a person to enter into a notional principal contract is not a notional principal contract but payments made under such an option or forward contract may be governed by paragraph (g)(3) of this section.

(iii) *Transactions within section 475.* To the extent that the rules provided in paragraphs (e) and (f) of this section are inconsistent with the rules that apply to any notional principal contract that is governed by section 475 and regulations thereunder, the rules of section 475 and the regulations thereunder govern.

(iv) *Transactions within section 988.* To the extent that the rules provided in this section are inconsistent with the rules that apply to any notional principal contract that is also a section 988 transaction or that is integrated with other property or debt pursuant to section 988(d), the rules of section 988 and the regulations thereunder govern.

(2) *Specified index.* A specified index is—

(i) A fixed rate, price, or amount;

(ii) A fixed rate, price, or amount applicable in one or more specified periods followed by one or more different fixed rates, prices, or amounts applicable in other periods;

(iii) An index that is based on objective financial information (as defined in paragraph (c)(4)(ii) of this section); and

(iv) An interest rate index that is regularly used in normal lending transactions between a party to the contract and unrelated persons.

(3) *Notional principal amount.* For purposes of this section, a notional principal amount is any specified amount of money or property that, when multiplied by a specified index, measures a party's rights and obligations under the contract, but is not borrowed or loaned between the parties as part of the contract. The notional principal amount may vary over the term of the contract, provided that it is set in advance or varies based on objective financial information (as defined in paragraph (c)(4)(ii) of this section).

(4) *Special definitions*—(i) *Related person and party to the contract.* A related person is a person related (within the meaning of section 267(b) or 707(b)(1)) to one of the parties to the notional principal contract or a member of the same consolidated group (as defined in § 1.1502-1(h)) as one of the parties to the contract. For purposes of this paragraph (c), a related person is considered to be a party to the contract.

(ii) *Objective financial information.* For purposes of this paragraph (c), objective financial information is any current, objectively determinable financial or economic information that is not within the control of any of the parties to the contract and is not unique to one of the parties' circumstances (such as one party's dividends, profits, or the value of its stock). Thus, for example, a notional principal amount may be based on a broadly-based equity index or the outstanding balance of a pool of mortgages, but not on the value of a party's stock.

(iii) *Dealer in notional principal contracts.* A dealer in notional principal contracts is a person who regularly offers to enter into, assume, offset, assign, or otherwise terminate positions in notional principal contracts with customers in the ordinary course of a trade or business.

(d) *Taxable year of inclusion and deduction.* For all purposes of the Code, the net income or net deduction from a notional principal contract for a taxable year is included in or deducted from gross income for that taxable year. The net income or net deduction from a notional principal contract for a taxable year equals the total of all of the periodic payments that are recognized from that contract for the taxable year under paragraph (e) of this section and all of the nonperiodic payments that are recognized from that contract for the taxable year under paragraph (f) of this section.

(e) *Periodic payments*—(1) *Definition.* Periodic payments are payments made or received pursuant to a notional principal contract that are payable at intervals of one year or less during the entire term of the contract (including any extension periods provided for in the contract), that are based on a specified index described in paragraph (c)(2)(i), (iii), or (iv) of this section (appropriately adjusted for the length of the interval), and that are based on either a single notional principal amount or a notional principal amount that varies over the term of the contract in the same proportion as the notional principal amount that measures the other party's payments. Payments to purchase or sell a cap or a floor, however, are not periodic payments.

(2) *Recognition rules*—(i) *In general.* All taxpayers, regardless of their method of accounting, must recognize the ratable daily portion of a periodic payment for the taxable year to which that portion relates.

(ii) *Rate set in arrears.* If the amount of a periodic payment is not determinable at the end of a taxable year because the value of the specified index is not fixed until a date that occurs after the end of the taxable year, the ratable daily portion of a periodic payment that relates to that taxable year is generally based on the specified index that would have applied if the specified index were fixed as of the last day of the taxable

Reg. § 1.446-3(c)(2)

year. If a taxpayer determines that the value of the specified index as of the last day of the taxable year does not provide a reasonable estimate of the specified index that will apply when the payment is fixed, the taxpayer may use a reasonable estimate of the specified index each year, provided that the taxpayer (and any related person that is a party to the contract) uses the same method to make the estimate consistently from year to year and uses the same estimate for purposes of all financial reports to equity holders and creditors. The taxpayer's treatment of notional principal contracts with substantially similar specified indices will be considered in determining whether the taxpayer's estimate of the specified index is reasonable. Any difference between the amount that is recognized under this paragraph (e)(2)(ii) and the corresponding portion of the actual payment that becomes fixed under the contract is taken into account as an adjustment to the net income or net deduction from the notional principal contract for the taxable year during which the payment becomes fixed.

(iii) *Notional principal amount set in arrears.* Rules similar to the rules of paragraph (e)(2)(ii) of this section apply if the amount of a periodic payment is not determinable at the end of a taxable year because the notional principal amount is not fixed until a date that occurs after the end of the taxable year.

(3) *Examples.* The following examples illustrate the application of paragraph (e) of this section.

Example 1. Accrual of periodic swap payments. (a) On April 1, 1995, A enters into a contract with unrelated counterparty B under which, for a term of five years, A is obligated to make a payment to B each April 1, beginning April 1, 1996, in an amount equal to the London Interbank Offered Rate (LIBOR), as determined on the immediately preceding April 1, multiplied by a notional principal amount of $100 million. Under the contract, B is obligated to make a payment to A each April 1, beginning April 1, 1996, in an amount equal to 8% multiplied by the same notional principal amount. A and B are calendar year taxpayers that use the accrual method of accounting. On April 1, 1995, LIBOR is 7.80%.

(b) This contract is a notional principal contract as defined by paragraph (c)(1) of this section, and both LIBOR and a fixed interest rate of 8% are specified indices under paragraph (c)(2) of this section. All of the payments to be made by A and B are periodic payments under paragraph (e)(1) of this section because each party's payments are based on a specified index described in paragraphs (c)(2)(iii) and (c)(2)(i) of this section, respectively, are payable at periodic intervals of one year or less throughout the term of the contract, and are based on a single notional principal amount.

(c) Under the terms of the swap agreement, on April 1, 1996, B is obligated to make a payment to A of $8,000,000 (8% × $100,000,000) and A is obligated to make a payment to B of $7,800,000 (7.80% × $100,000,000). Under paragraph (e)(2)(i) of this section, the ratable daily portions for 1995 are the amounts of these periodic payments that are attributable to A's and B's taxable year ending December 31, 1995. The ratable daily portion of the 8% fixed leg is $6,010,929 (275 days/366 days × $8,000,000), and the ratable daily portion of the floating leg is $5,860,656 (275 days/366 days × $7,800,000). The net amount for the taxable year is the difference between the ratable daily portions of the two periodic payments, or $150,273 ($6,010,929 −$5,860,656). Accordingly, A has net income of $150,273 from this swap for 1995, and B has a corresponding net deduction of $150,273.

(d) The $49,727 unrecognized balance of the $200,000 net periodic payment that is made on April 1, 1996, is included in A's and B's net income or net deduction from the contract for 1996.

(e) If the parties had entered into the contract on February 1, 1995, the result would not change because no portion of either party's obligation to make a payment under the swap relates to the period prior to April 1, 1995. Consequently, under paragraph (e)(2) of this section, neither party would accrue any income or deduction from the swap for the period from February 1, 1995, through March 31, 1995.

Example 2. Accrual of periodic swap payments by cash method taxpayer. (a) On April 1, 1995, C enters into a contract with unrelated counterparty D under which, for a period of five years, C is obligated to make a fixed payment to D each April 1, beginning April 1, 1996, in an amount equal to 8% multiplied by a notional principal amount of $100 million. D is obligated to make semi-annual payments to C each April 1 and October 1, beginning October 1, 1995, in an amount equal to one-half of the LIBOR amount as of the first day of the preceding 6-month period multiplied by the notional principal amount. The payments are to be calculated using a 30/360 day convention. C is a calendar year taxpayer that uses the accrual method of accounting. D is a calendar year taxpayer that uses the cash receipts and disbursements method of accounting. LIBOR

Reg. § 1.446-3(e)(3)

is 7.80% on April 1, 1995, and 7.46% on October 1, 1995.

(b) This contract is a notional principal contract as defined by paragraph (c)(1) of this section, and LIBOR and the fixed interest rate of 8% are each specified indices under paragraph (c)(2) of this section. All of the payments to be made by C and D are periodic payments under paragraph (e)(1) of this section because they are each based on appropriate specified indices, are payable at periodic intervals of one year or less throughout the term of the contract, and are based on a single notional principal amount.

(c) Under the terms of the swap agreement, D pays C $3,900,000 (0.5 × 7.8% × $100,000,000) on October 1, 1995. In addition, D is obligated to pay C $3,730,000 (0.5 × 7.46% × $100,000,000) on April 1, 1996. C is obligated to pay D $8,000,000 on April 1, 1996. Under paragraph (e)(2)(i) of this section, C's and D's ratable daily portions for 1995 are the amounts of the periodic payments that are attributable to their taxable year ending December 31, 1995. The ratable daily portion of the 8% fixed leg is $6,000,000 (270 days/360 days × $8,000,000), and the ratable daily portion of the floating leg is $5,765,000 ($3,900,000 + (90 days/180 days × $3,730,000)). Thus, C's net deduction from the contract for 1995 is $235,000 ($6,000,000 − $5,765,000) and D reports $235,000 of net income from the contract for 1995.

(d) The net unrecognized balance of $135,000 ($2,000,000 balance of the fixed leg − $1,865,000 balance of the floating leg) is included in C's and D's net income or net deduction from the contract for 1996.

Example 3. Accrual of swap payments on index set in arrears. (a) The facts are the same as in *Example 1*, except that A's obligation to make payments based upon LIBOR is determined by reference to LIBOR on the day each payment is due. LIBOR is 8.25% on December 31, 1995, and 8.16% on April 1, 1996.

(b) On December 31, 1995, the amount that A is obligated to pay B is not known because it will not become fixed until April 1, 1996. Under paragraph (e)(2)(ii) of this section, the ratable daily portion of the periodic payment from A to B for 1995 is based on the value of LIBOR on December 31, 1995 (unless A or B determines that the value of LIBOR on that day does not reasonably estimate the value of the specified index). Thus, the ratable daily portion of the floating leg is $6,198,770 (275 days/366 days × 8.25% × $100,000,000), while the ratable daily portion of the fixed leg is $6,010,929 (275 days/366 days × $8,000,000). The net amount for 1995 on this swap is $187,841 ($6,198,770 − $6,010,929). Accordingly, B has $187,841 of net income from the swap in 1995, and A has a net deduction of $187,841.

(c) On April 1, 1996, A makes a net payment to B of $160,000 ($8,160,000 payment on the floating leg − $8,000,000 payment on the fixed leg). For purposes of determining their net income or net deduction from this contract for the year ended December 31, 1996, B and A must adjust the net income and net deduction they recognized in 1995 by $67,623 (275 days/366 days × ($8,250,000 presumed payment on the floating leg − $8,160,000 actual payment on the floating leg)).

(f) *Nonperiodic payments*—(1) *Definition.* A nonperiodic payment is any payment made or received with respect to a notional principal contract that is not a periodic payment (as defined in paragraph (e)(1) of this section) or a termination payment (as defined in paragraph (h) of this section). Examples of nonperiodic payments are the premium for a cap or floor agreement (even if it is paid in installments), the payment for an off-market swap agreement, the prepayment of part or all of one leg of a swap, and the premium for an option to enter into a swap if and when the option is exercised.

(2) *Recognition rules*—(i) *In general.* All taxpayers, regardless of their method of accounting, must recognize the ratable daily portion of a nonperiodic payment for the taxable year to which that portion relates. Generally, a nonperiodic payment must be recognized over the term of a notional principal contract in a manner that reflects the economic substance of the contract.

(ii) *General rule for swaps.* A nonperiodic payment that relates to a swap must be recognized over the term of the contract by allocating it in accordance with the forward rates (or, in the case of a commodity, the forward prices) of a series of cash-settled forward contracts that reflect the specified index and the notional principal amount. For purposes of this allocation, the forward rates or prices used to determine the amount of the nonperiodic payment will be respected, if reasonable. See paragraph (f)(4) *Example 7* of this section.

(iii) *Alternative methods for swaps.* Solely for purposes of determining the timing of income and deductions, a nonperiodic payment made or received with respect to a swap may be allocated to each period of the swap contract using one of the methods described in this paragraph (f)(2)(iii). The alternative methods may not be used by a dealer in notional principal contracts (as defined in paragraph (c)(4)(iii) of this section)

Reg. § 1.446-3(f)(1)

for swaps entered into or acquired in its capacity as a dealer.

(A) *Prepaid swaps.* An upfront payment on a swap may be amortized by assuming that the nonperiodic payment represents the present value of a series of equal payments made throughout the term of the swap contract (the level payment method), adjusted as appropriate to take account of increases or decreases in the notional principal amount. The discount rate used in this calculation must be the rate (or rates) used by the parties to determine the amount of the nonperiodic payment. If that rate is not readily ascertainable, the discount rate used must be a rate that is reasonable under the circumstances. Under this method, an upfront payment is allocated by dividing each equal payment into its principal recovery and time value components. The principal recovery components of the equal payments are treated as periodic payments that are deemed to be made on each of the dates that the swap contract provides for periodic payments by the payor of the nonperiodic payment or, if none, on each of the dates that the swap contract provides for periodic payments by the recipient of the nonperiodic payment. The time value component is needed to compute the amortization of the nonperiodic payment, but is otherwise disregarded. See paragraph (f)(4) *Example 5* of this section.

(B) *Other nonperiodic swap payments.* Nonperiodic payments on a swap other than an upfront payment may be amortized by treating the contract as if it provided for a single upfront payment (equal to the present value of the nonperiodic payments) and a loan between the parties. The discount rate (or rates) used in determining the deemed upfront payment and the time value component of the deemed loan is the same as the rate (or rates) used in the level payment method. The single upfront payment is then amortized under the level payment method described in paragraph (f)(2)(iii)(A) of this section. The time value component of the loan is not treated as interest, but, together with the amortized amount of the deemed upfront payment, is recognized as a periodic payment. See paragraph (f)(4) *Example 6* of this section. If both parties make nonperiodic payments, this calculation is done separately for the nonperiodic payments made by each party.

(iv) *General rule for caps and floors.* A payment to purchase or sell a cap or floor must be recognized over the term of the agreement by allocating it in accordance with the prices of a series of cash-settled option contracts that reflect the specified index and the notional principal amount. For purposes of this allocation, the option pricing used by the parties to determine the total amount paid for the cap or floor will be respected, if reasonable. Only the portion of the purchase price that is allocable to the option contract or contracts that expire during a particular period is recognized for that period. Thus, under this paragraph (f)(2)(iv), straight-line or accelerated amortization of a cap premium is generally not permitted. See paragraph (f)(4) *Examples 1* and *2* of this section.

(v) *Alternative methods for caps and floors that hedge debt instruments.* Solely for purposes of determining the timing of income and deductions, if a cap or floor is entered into primarily to reduce risk with respect to a specific debt instrument or group of debt instruments held or issued by the taxpayer, the taxpayer may amortize a payment to purchase or sell the cap or floor using the methods described in this paragraph (f)(2)(v), adjusted as appropriate to take account of increases or decreases in the notional principal amount. The alternative methods may not be used by a dealer in notional principal contracts (as defined in paragraph (c)(4)(iii) of this section) for caps or floors entered into or acquired in its capacity as a dealer.

(A) *Prepaid caps and floors.* A premium paid upfront for a cap or a floor may be amortized using the "level payment method" described in paragraph (f)(2)(iii)(A) of this section. See paragraph (f)(4) *Example 3* of this section.

(B) *Other caps and floors.* Nonperiodic payments on a cap or floor other than an upfront payment are amortized by treating the contract as if it provided for a single upfront payment (equal to the present value of the nonperiodic payments) and a loan between the parties as described in paragraph (f)(2)(iii)(B) of this section. Under the level payment method, a cap or floor premium paid in level annual installments over the term of the contract is effectively included or deducted from income ratably, in accordance with the level payments. See paragraph (f)(4) *Example 4* of this section.

(C) *Special method for collars.* A taxpayer may also treat a cap and a floor that comprise a collar as a single notional principal contract and may amortize the net nonperiodic payment to enter into the cap and floor over the term of the collar in accordance with the methods prescribed in this paragraph (f)(2)(v).

(vi) *Additional methods.* The Commissioner may, by a revenue ruling or a revenue procedure published in the Internal Revenue Bulletin, provide alternative methods for allocating nonperiodic payments that relate to a notional principal contract to each year of the contract. See § 601.601(d)(2)(ii)(*b*) of this chapter.

Reg. § 1.446-3(f)(2)

(3) *Term of extendible or terminable contracts.* For purposes of this paragraph (f), the term of a notional principal contract that is subject to extension or termination is the reasonably expected term of the contract.

(4) *Examples.* The following examples illustrate the application of paragraph (f) of this section.

Example 1. Cap premium amortized using general rule. (a) On January 1, 1995, when LIBOR is 8%, F pays unrelated party E $600,000 for a contract that obligates E to make a payment to F each quarter equal to one-quarter of the excess, if any, of three-month LIBOR over 9% with respect to a notional principal amount of $25 million. Both E and F are calendar year taxpayers. E provides F with a schedule of allocable premium amounts indicating that the cap was priced according to a reasonable variation of the Black-Scholes option pricing formula and that the total premium is allocable to the following periods:

	Pricing allocation
1995	$ 55,000
1996	225,000
1997	320,000
	$600,000

(b) This contract is a notional principal contract as defined by paragraph (c)(1) of this section, and LIBOR is a specified index under paragraph (c)(2)(iii) of this section. Any payments made by E to F are periodic payments under paragraph (e)(1) of this section because they are payable at periodic intervals of one year or less throughout the term of the contract, are based on an appropriate specified index, and are based on a single notional principal amount. The $600,000 cap premium paid by F to E is a nonperiodic payment as defined in paragraph (f)(1) of this section.

(c) The Black-Scholes model is recognized in the financial industry as a standard technique for pricing interest rate cap agreements. Therefore, because E has used a reasonable option pricing model, the schedule generated by E is consistent with the economic substance of the cap, and may be used by both E and F for calculating their ratable daily portions of the cap premium. Under paragraph (f)(2)(iv) of this section, E recognizes the ratable daily portion of the cap premium as income, and F recognizes the ratable daily portion of the cap premium as a deduction based on the pricing schedule. Thus, E and F account for the contract as follows:

	Ratable daily portion
1995	$ 55,000
1996	225,000
1997	320,000
	$600,000

(d) Any periodic payments under the cap agreement (that is, payments that E makes to F because LIBOR exceeds 9%) are included in the parties' net income or net deduction from the contract in accordance with paragraph (e)(2) of this section.

Example 2. Cap premium allocated to proper period. (a) The facts are the same as in *Example 1*, except that the cap is purchased by F on November 1, 1994. The first determination date under the cap agreement is January 31, 1995 (the last day of the first quarter to which the contract relates). LIBOR is 9.1% on December 31, 1994, and is 9.15% on January 31, 1995.

(b) E and F recognize $9,192 (61 days/365 days × $55,000) as the ratable daily portion of the nonperiodic payment for 1994, and include that amount in their net income or net deduction from the contract for 1994. If E's pricing model allocated the cap premium to each quarter covered by the contract, the ratable daily portion would be 61 days/92 days times the premium allocated to the first quarter.

(c) Under paragraph (e)(2)(ii) of this section, E and F calculate the payments using LIBOR as of December 31, 1994. F recognizes as income the ratable daily portion of the presumed payment, or $4,144 (61 days/92 days × .25 × .001 × $25,000,000). Thus, E reports $5,048 of net income from the contract for 1994 ($9,192 − $4,144), and F reports a net deduction from the contract of $5,048.

(d) On January 31, 1995, E pays F $9,375 (.25 × .0015 × $25,000,000) under the terms of the cap agreement. For purposes of determining their net income or net deduction from this con-

Reg. § 1.446-3(f)(3)

tract for the year ended December 31, 1995, E and F must adjust their respective net income and net deduction from the cap by $2,072 (61 days/92 days × ($9,375 actual payment under the cap on January 31, 1995 − $6,250 presumed payment under the cap on December 31, 1994)).

Example 3. Cap premium amortized using alternative method. (a) The facts are the same as in *Example 1*, except that the cap provides for annual payments by E and is entered into by F primarily to reduce risk with respect to a debt instrument issued by F. F elects to amortize the cap premium using the alternative level payment method provided under paragraph (f)(2)(v)(A) of this section. Under that method, F amortizes the cap premium by assuming that the $600,000 is repaid in 3 equal annual payments of $241,269, assuming a discount rate of 10%. Each payment is divided into a time value component and a principal component, which are set out below.

	Level Payment	Time Value Component	Principal Component
1995	$241,269	$ 60,000	$181,269
1996	241,269	41,873	199,396
1997	241,269	21,934	219,335
	$723,807	$123,807	$600,000

(b) The net of the ratable daily portions of the principal component and the payments, if any, received from E comprise F's annual net income or net deduction from the cap. The time value components are needed only to compute the ratable daily portions of the cap premium, and are otherwise disregarded.

Example 4. Cap premium paid in level installments and amortized using alternative method. (a) The facts are the same as in *Example 3*, except that F agrees to pay for the cap in three level installments of $241,269 (a total of $723,807) on December 31, 1995, 1996, and 1997. The present value of three payments of $241,269, discounted at 10%, is $600,000. For purposes of amortizing the cap premium under the alternative method provided in paragraph (f)(2)(v)(B) of this section, F is treated as paying $600,000 for the cap on January 1, 1995, and borrowing $600,000 from E that will be repaid in three annual installments of $241,269. The time value component of the loan is computed as follows:

	Loan Balance	Time Value Component	Principal Component
1995	$600,000	$ 60,000	$181,269
1996	418,731	41,873	199,396
1997	219,335	21,934	219,335
		$123,807	$600,000

(b) F is treated as making periodic payments eqaul to the amortized principal components from a $600,000 cap paid in advance (as described in *Example 3*), increased by the time value components of the $600,000 loan, which totals $241,269 each year. The time value components of the $600,000 loan are included in the periodic payments made by F, but are not characterized as interest income or expense. The effect of the alternative method in this situation is to allow F to amortize the cap premium in level installments, the same way it is paid. The net of the ratable daily portions of F's deemed periodic payments and the payments, if any, received from E comprise F's annual net income or net deduction from the cap.

Example 5. Upfront interest rate swap payment amortized using alternative method. (a) On January 1, 1995, G enters into an interest rate swap agreement with unrelated counterparty H under which, for a term of five years, G is obligated to make annual payments at 11% and H is obligated to make annual payments at LIBOR on a notional principal amount of $100 million. At the time G and H enter into this swap agreement, the rate for similar on-market swaps is LIBOR to 10%. To compensate for this difference, on January 1, 1995, H pays G a yield adjustment fee of $3,790,786. G provides H with information that indicates that the amount of the yield adjustment fee was determined as the present value, at 10% compounded annually, of five annual payments of $1,000,000 (1% × $100,000,000). G and H are calendar year taxpayers.

(b) This contract is a notional principal contract as defined by paragraph (c)(1) of this section. The yield adjustment fee is a nonperiodic payment as defined in paragraph (f)(1) of this section.

(c) Under the alternative method described in paragraph (f)(2)(iii)(A) of this section, the yield adjustment fee is recognized over the life of the agreement by assuming that the $3,790,786 is repaid in five level payments. Assuming a constant yield to maturity and annual compounding

Reg. § 1.446-3(f)(4)

Methods of Accounting

See p. 20,601 for regulations not amended to reflect law changes

at 10%, the ratable daily portions are computed as follows:

	Level Payment	Time Value Component	Principal Component
1995	$1,000,000	$ 379,079	$ 620,921
1996	1,000,000	316,987	683,013
1997	1,000,000	248,685	751,315
1998	1,000,000	173,554	826,446
1999	1,000,000	90,909	909,091
	$5,000,000	$1,209,214	$3,790,786

(d) G also makes swap payments to H at 11%, while H makes swap payments to G based on LIBOR. The net of the ratable daily portions of the 11% payments by G, the LIBOR payments by H, and the principal component of the yield adjustment fee paid by H determines the annual net income or net deduction from the contract for both G and H. The time value components are needed only to compute the ratable daily portions of the yield adjustment fee paid by H, and are otherwise disregarded.

Example 6. Backloaded interest rate swap payment amortized using alternative method. (a) The facts are the same as in *Example 5*, but H agrees to pay G a yield adjustment fee of $6,105,100 on December 31, 1999. Under the alternative method in paragraph (f)(2)(iii)(B) of this section, H is treated as paying a yield adjustment fee of $3,790,786 (the present value of $6,105,100, discounted at a 10% rate with annual compounding) on January 1, 1995. Solely for timing purposes, H is treated as borrowing $3,790,786 from G. Assuming annual compounding at 10%, the time value component is computed as follows:

	Loan Balance	Time Value Component	Principal Component
1995	$3,790,786	$379,079	$ –0–
1996	4,169,865	416,987	–0–
1997	4,586,852	458,685	–0–
1998	5,045,537	504,554	–0–
1999	5,550,091	555,009	6,105,100

(b) The amortization of H's yield adjustment fee is equal to the amortization of a yield adjustment fee of $3,790,786 paid in advance (as described in *Example 5*), increased by the time value component of the $3,790,786 deemed loan from G to H. Thus, the amount of H's yield adjustment fee that is allocated to 1995 is $1,000,000 ($620,921 + $379,079). The time value components of the $3,790,786 loan are included in the periodic payments paid by H, but are not characterized as interest income or expense. The net of the ratable daily portions of the 11% swap payments by G, and the LIBOR payments by H, added to the principal components from *Example 5* and the time value components from this *Example 6*, determines the annual net income or net deduction from the contract for both G and H.

Example 7. Nonperiodic payment on a commodity swap amortized under general rule. (a) On January 1, 1995, I enters into a commodity swap agreement with unrelated counterparty J under which, for a term of three years, I is obligated to make annual payments based on a fixed price of $2.35 per bushel times a notional amount of 100,000 bushels of corn and J is obligated to make annual payments equal to the spot price times the same notional amount. Assume that on January 1, 1995, the price of a one year forward for corn is $2.40 per bushel, of a two year forward $2.55 per bushel, and of a 3 year forward $2.75 per bushel. To compensate for the below-market fixed price provided in the swap agreement, I pays J $53,530 for entering into the swap. I and J are calendar year taxpayers.

(b) This contract is a notional principal contract as defined by paragraph (c)(1) of this section, and $2.35 and the spot price of corn are specified indices under paragraphs (c)(2)(i) and (iii) of this section, respectively. The $53,530 payment is a nonperiodic payment as defined by paragraph (f)(1) of this section.

(c) Assuming that I does not use the alternative methods provided under paragraph (f)(2)(iii) of this section, paragraph (f)(2)(ii) of this section requires that I recognize the nonperiodic payment over the term of the agreement by allocating the payment to each forward contract in accordance with the forward price of corn. Solely for timing purposes, I treats the $53,530 nonperiodic payment as a loan that J will repay in three installments of $5,000, $20,000, and $40,000, the expected payouts on the in-the-money forward

Reg. § 1.446-3(f)(4)

contracts. With annual compounding at 8%, the ratable daily portions are computed as follows:

	Expected Forward Payment	Time Value Component	Principal Component
1995	$ 5,000	$ 4,282	$ 718
1996	20,000	4,225	15,775
1997	40,000	2,963	37,037
	$65,000	$11,470	$53,530

(d) The ratable daily portion of the principal component is added to I's periodic payments in computing its net income or net deduction from the notional principal contract for each taxable year. The time value components are needed only to compute the principal components, and are otherwise disregarded.

(g) *Special rules*—(1) *Disguised notional principal contracts.* The Commissioner may recharacterize all or part of a transaction (or series of transactions) if the effect of the transaction (or series of transactions) is to avoid the application of this section.

(2) *Hedged notional principal contracts.* If a taxpayer, either directly or through a related person (as defined in paragraph (c)(4)(i) of this section), reduces risk with respect to a notional principal contract by purchasing, selling, or otherwise entering into other notional principal contracts, futures, forwards, options, or other financial contracts (other than debt instruments), the taxpayer may not use the alternative methods provided in paragraphs (f)(2)(iii) and (v) of this section. Moreover, where such positions are entered into to avoid the appropriate timing or character of income from the contracts taken together, the Commissioner may require that amounts paid to or received by the taxpayer under the notional principal contract be treated in a manner that is consistent with the economic substance of the transaction as a whole.

(3) *Options and forwards to enter into notional principal contracts.* An option or forward contract that entitles or obligates a person to enter into a notional principal contract is subject to the general rules of taxation for options or forward contracts. Any payment with respect to the option or forward contract is treated as a nonperiodic payment for the underlying notional principal contract under the rules of paragraphs (f) and (g)(4) or (g)(5) of this section if and when the underlying notional principal contract is entered into.

(4) *Swaps with significant nonperiodic payments.* A swap with significant nonperiodic payments is treated as two separate transactions consisting of an on-market, level payment swap and a loan. The loan must be accounted for by the parties to the contract independently of the swap. The time value component associated with the loan is not included in the net income or net deduction from the swap under paragraph (d) of this section, but is recognized as interest for all purposes of the Internal Revenue Code. See paragraph (g)(6) *Example 3* of this section. For purposes of section 956, the Commissioner may treat any nonperiodic swap payment, whether or not it is significant, as one or more loans.

(5) *Caps and floors that are significantly in-the-money.* [Reserved]

(6) *Examples.* The following examples illustrate the application of paragraph (g) of this section.

Example 1. Cap hedged with options. (a) On January 1, 1995, K sells to unrelated counterparty L three cash settlement European-style put options on Eurodollar time deposits with a strike rate of 9%. The options have exercise dates of January 1, 1996, January 1, 1997, and January 1, 1998, respectively. If LIBOR exceeds 9% on any of the exercise dates, L will be entitled, by exercising the relevant option, to receive from K an amount that corresponds to the excess of LIBOR over 9% times $25 million. L pays K $650,000 for the three options. Furthermore, K is related to F, the cap purchaser in paragraph (f)(4) *Example 1* of this section.

(b) K's option agreements with L reduce risk with respect to F's cap agreement with E. Accordingly, under paragraph (g)(2) of this section, F cannot use the alternative methods provided in paragraph (f)(2)(v) of this section to amortize the premium paid under the cap agreement. F must amortize the cap premium it paid in accordance with paragraph (f)(2)(iv) of this section.

(c) The method that E may use to account for its agreement with F is not affected by the application of paragraph (g)(2) of this section to F.

Example 2. Nonperiodic payment that is not significant. (a) On January 1, 1995, G enters into an interest rate swap agreement with unrelated counterparty H under which, for a term of five years, G is obligated to make annual payments at 11% and H is obligated to make annual payments

Reg. § 1.446-3(g)(6)

at LIBOR on a notional principal amount of $100 million. At the time G and H enter into this swap agreement, the rate for similar on-market swaps is LIBOR to 10%. To compensate for this difference, on January 1, 1995, H pays G a yield adjustment fee of $3,790,786. G provides H with information that indicates that the amount of the yield adjustment fee was determined as the present value, at 10% compounded annually, of five annual payments of $1,000,000 (1% × $100,000,000). G and H are calendar year taxpayers. (These facts are the same as in paragraph (f)(4) *Example 5* of this section.)

(b) In this situation, the yield adjustment fee of $3,790,786 is not a significant nonperiodic payment within the meaning of paragraph (g)(4) of this section, in light of the amount of the fee in proportion to the present value of the total amount of fixed payments due under the contract. Accordingly, no portion of the swap is recharacterized as a loan for purposes of this section.

Example 3. Significant nonperiodic payment. (a) On January 1, 1995, unrelated parties M and N enter into an interest rate swap contract. Under the terms of the contract, N agrees to make five annual payments to M equal to LIBOR times a notional principal amount of $100 million. In return, M agrees to pay N 6% of $100 million annually, plus $15,163,147 on January 1, 1995. At the time M and N enter into this swap agreement the rate for similar on-market swaps is LIBOR to 10%, and N provides M with information that the amount of the initial payment was determined as the present value, at 10% compounded annually, of five annual payments from M to N of $4,000,000 (4% of $100,000,000).

(b) Although the parties have characterized this transaction as an interest rate swap, the $15,163,147 payment from M to N is significant when compared to the present value of the total fixed payments due under the contract. Accordingly, under paragraph (g)(4) of this section, the transaction is recharacterized as consisting of both a $15,163,147 loan from M to N that N repays in installments over the term of the agreement, and an interest rate swap between M and N in which M immediately pays the installment payments on the loan back to N as part of its fixed payments on the swap in exchange for the LIBOR payments by N.

(c) The yield adjustment fee is recognized over the life of the agreement by treating the $15,163,147 as a loan that will be repaid with level payments over five years. Assuming a constant yield to maturity and annual compounding at 10%, M and N account for the principal and interest on the loan as follows:

	Level Payment	Interest Component	Principal Component
1995	$ 4,000,000	$1,516,315	$ 2,483,685
1996	4,000,000	1,267,946	2,732,054
1997	4,000,000	994,741	3,005,259
1998	4,000,000	694,215	3,305,785
1999	4,000,000	363,636	3,636,364
	$20,000,000	$4,836,853	$15,163,147

(d) M recognizes interest income, and N claims an interest deduction, each taxable year equal to the interest component of the deemed installment payments on the loan. These interest amounts are not included in the parties' net income or net deduction from the swap contract under paragraph (d) of this section. The principal components are needed only to compute the interest component of the level payment for the following period, and do not otherwise affect the parties' net income or net deduction from this contract.

(e) N also makes swap payments to M based on LIBOR, and receives swap payments from M at a fixed rate that is equal to the sum of the stated fixed rate and the rate calculated by dividing the deemed level annual payments on the loan by the notional principal amount. Thus, the fixed rate on this swap is 10%, which is the sum of the stated rate of 6% and the rate calculated by dividing the annual loan payment of $4,000,000 by the notional principal amount of $100,000,000, or 4%. Using the methods provided in paragraph (e)(2) of this section, the swap payments from M to N of $10,000,000 (10% of $100,000,000) and the LIBOR swap payments from N to M are included in the parties' net income or net deduction from the contract for each taxable year.

Example 4. Swaps recharacterized as a loan. (a) The facts are the same as in *Example 3*, except that on January 1, 1995, N also enters into an interest rate swap agreement with unrelated counterparty O under which, for a term of five years, N is obligated to make annual payments at 12% and O is obligated to make annual payments at LIBOR on a notional principal amount of $100 million. At the time N and O enter into this swap agreement, the rate for similar on-market swaps is LIBOR to 10%. To compensate for this difference,

Reg. § 1.446-3(g)(6)

Methods of Accounting 36,757
See p. 20,601 for regulations not amended to reflect law changes

O pays N an upfront yield adjustment fee of $7,581,574. This yield adjustment fee equals the present value, at 10% compounded annually, of five annual payments of $2,000,000 (2% of $100,000,000).

(b) In substance, these two interest rate swaps are the equivalent of a fixed rate borrowing by N of $22,744,721 ($15,163,147 from M plus $7,581,574 from O). Under paragraph (g)(2) of this section, if these positions were entered into to avoid interest character on a net loan position, the Commissioner may recharacterize the swaps as a loan which N will repay with interest in five annual installments of $6,000,000 each (the difference between the 12% N pays under the swap with O and the 6% N receives under the swap with M, multiplied by the $100,000,000 notional principal amount).

(c) N recognizes no net income or net deduction from these contracts under paragraph (d) of this section because, as to N, there is no notional principal contract income or expense. However, the recharacterization of N's separate transactions as a loan has no effect on the way M and O must each account for their notional principal contracts under paragraphs (d) through (g) of this section.

(h) *Termination payments*—(1) *Definition.* A payment made or received to extinguish or assign all or a proportionate part of the remaining rights and obligations of any party under a notional principal contract is a termination payment to the party making the termination payment and the party receiving the payment. A termination payment includes a payment made between the original parties to the contract (an extinguishment), a payment made between one party to the contract and a third party (an assignment), and any gain or loss realized on the exchange of one notional principal contract for another. Where one party assigns its remaining rights and obligations to a third party, the original nonassigning counterparty realizes gain or loss if the assignment results in a deemed exchange of contracts and a realization event under section 1001.

(2) *Taxable year of inclusion and deduction by original parties.* Except as otherwise provided (for example, in section 453, section 1092, or § 1.446-4), a party to a notional principal contract recognizes a termination payment in the year the contract is extinguished, assigned, or exchanged. When the termination payment is recognized, the party also recognizes any other payments that have been made or received pursuant to the notional principal contract, but that have not been recognized under paragraph (d) of this section. If only a proportionate part of a party's rights and obligations is extinguished, assigned, or exchanged, then only that proportion of the unrecognized payments is recognized under the previous sentence.

(3) *Taxable year of inclusion and deduction by assignees.* A termination payment made or received by an assignee pursuant to an assignment of a notional principal contract is recognized by the assignee under the rules of paragraphs (f) and (g)(4) or (g)(5) of this section as a nonperiodic payment for the notional principal contract that is in effect after the assignment.

(4) *Special rules*—(i) *Assignment of one leg of a contract.* A payment is not a termination payment if it is made or received by a party in exchange for assigning all or a portion of one leg of a notional principal contract at a time when a substantially proportionate amount of the other leg remains unperformed and unassigned. The payment is either an amount loaned, an amount borrowed, or a nonperiodic payment, depending on the economic substance of the transaction to each party. This paragraph (h)(4)(i) applies whether or not the original notional principal contract is terminated as a result of the assignment.

(ii) *Substance over form.* Any economic benefit that is given or received by a taxpayer in lieu of a termination payment is a termination payment.

(5) *Examples.* The following examples illustrate the application of this paragraph (h). The contracts in the examples are not hedging transactions as defined in § 1.1221-2(b), and all of the examples assume that no loss deferral rules apply.

Example 1. Termination by extinguishment. (a) On January 1, 1995, P enters into an interest rate swap agreement with unrelated counterparty Q under which, for a term of seven years, P is obligated to make annual payments based on 10% and Q is obligated to make semi-annual payments based on LIBOR and a notional principal amount of $100 million. P and Q are both calendar year taxpayers. On January 1, 1997, when the fixed rate on a comparable LIBOR swap has fallen to 9.5%, P pays Q $1,895,393 to terminate the swap.

(b) The payment from P to Q extinguishes the swap contract and is a termination payment, as defined in paragraph (h)(1) of this section, for both parties. Accordingly, under paragraph (h)(2) of this section, P recognizes a loss of $1,895,393 in 1997 and Q recognizes $1,895,393 of gain in 1997.

Example 2. Termination by assignment. (a) The facts are the same as in *Example 1*, except that on January 1, 1997, P pays unrelated party R $1,895,393 to assume all of P's rights and obligations under the swap with Q. In return for this payment, R agrees to pay 10% of $100 mil-

Reg. § 1.446-3(h)(5)

lion annually to Q and to receive LIBOR payments from Q for the remaining five years of the swap.

(b) The payment from P to R terminates P's interest in the swap contract with Q and is a termination payment, as defined in paragraph (h)(1) of this section, for P. Under paragraph (h)(2) of this section, P recognizes a loss of $1,895,393 in 1997. Whether Q also has a termination payment with respect to the payment from P to R is determined under section 1001.

(c) Under paragraph (h)(3) of this section, the assignment payment that R receives from P is a nonperiodic payment for an interest rate swap. Because the assignment payment is not a significant nonperiodic payment within the meaning of paragraph (g)(1) of this section, R amortizes the $1,895,393 over the five year term of the swap agreement under paragraph (f)(2) of this section.

Example 3. Assignment of swap with yield adjustment fee. (a) The facts are the same as in *Example 2*, except that on January 1, 1995, Q paid P a yield adjustment fee to enter into the seven year interest rate swap. In accordance with paragraph (f)(2) of this section, P and Q included the ratable daily portions of that nonperiodic payment in their net income or net deduction from the contract for 1995 and 1996. On January 1, 1997, $300,000 of the nonperiodic payment has not yet been recognized by P and Q.

(b) Under paragraph (h)(2) of this section, P recognizes a loss of $1,595,393 ($1,895,393 − $300,000) in 1997. R accounts for the termination payment in the same way it did in *Example 2*; the existence of an unamortized payment with respect [to] the original swap has no effect on R.

Example 4. Assignment of one leg of a swap. (a) On January 1, 1995, S enters into an interest rate swap agreement with unrelated counterparty T under which, for a term of five years, S will make annual payments at 10% and T will make annual payments at LIBOR on a notional principal amount of $50 million. On January 1, 1996, unrelated party U pays T $15,849,327 for the right to receive the four remaining $5,000,000 payments from S. Under the terms of the agreement between S and T, S is notified of this assignment, and S is contractually bound thereafter to make its payments to U on the appropriate payment dates. S's obligation to pay U is conditioned on T making its LIBOR payment to S on the appropriate payment dates.

(b) Because T has assigned to U its rights to the fixed rate payments, but not its floating rate obligations under the notional principal contract, U's payment to T is not a termination payment as defined in paragraph (h)(1) of this section, but is covered by paragraph (h)(4)(i) of this section. The economic substance of the transaction between T and U is a loan that does not affect the way that S and T account for the notional principal contract under this section.

(i) *Anti-abuse rule.* If a taxpayer enters into a transaction with a principal purpose of applying the rules of this section to produce a material distortion of income, the Commissioner may depart from the rules of this section as necessary to reflect the appropriate timing of income and deductions from the transaction.

(j) *Effective date.* These regulations are effective for notional principal contracts entered into on or after December 13, 1993. [Reg. § 1.446-3.]

☐ [T.D. 8491, 10-8-93. Amended by T.D. 8554, 7-13-94.]

[Reg. § 1.446-4]

§ 1.446-4. Hedging transactions.—(a) *In general.* Except as provided in this paragraph (a), a hedging transaction as defined in § 1.1221-2(b) (whether or not the character of gain or loss from the transaction is determined under § 1.1221-2) must be accounted for under the rules of this section. To the extent that provisions of any other regulations governing the timing of income, deductions, gain, or loss are inconsistent with the rules of this section, the rules of this section control.

(1) *Trades or businesses excepted.* A taxpayer is not required to account for hedging transactions under the rules of this section for any trade or business in which the cash receipts and disbursements method of accounting is used or in which § 1.471-6 is used for inventory valuations if, for all prior taxable years ending on or after September 30, 1993, the taxpayer met the $5,000,000 gross receipts test of section 448(c) (or would have met that test if the taxpayer were a corporation or partnership). A taxpayer not required to use the rules of this section may nonetheless use a method of accounting that is consistent with these rules.

(2) *Coordination with other sections.* This section does not apply to—

(i) Any position to which section 475(a) applies;

(ii) An integrated transaction subject to § 1.1275-6;

(iii) Any section 988 hedging transaction if the transaction is integrated under § 1.988-5 or if other regulations issued under section 988(d) (or an advance ruling described in § 1.988-5(e)) govern when gain or loss from the transaction is taken into account; or

(iv) The determination of the issuer's yield on an issue of tax-exempt bonds for purposes of the arbitrage restrictions to which § 1.148-4(h) applies.

(b) *Clear reflection of income.* The method of accounting used by a taxpayer for a hedging transaction must clearly reflect income. To clearly reflect income, the method used must reasonably match the timing of income, deduction, gain, or loss from the hedging transaction with the timing of income, deduction, gain, or loss from the item or items being hedged. Taking gains and losses into account in the period in which they are realized may clearly reflect income in the case of certain hedging transactions. For example, where a hedge and the item being hedged are disposed of in the same taxable year, taking realized gain or loss into account on both items in that taxable year may clearly reflect income. In the case of many hedging transactions, however, taking gains and losses into account as they are realized does not result in the matching required by this section.

(c) *Choice of method and consistency.* For any given type of hedging transaction, there may be more than one method of accounting that satisfies the clear reflection requirement of paragraph (b) of this section. A taxpayer is generally permitted to adopt a method of accounting for a particular type of hedging transaction that clearly reflects the taxpayer's income from that type of transaction. See paragraph (e) of this section for requirements and limitations on the taxpayer's choice of method. Different methods of accounting may be used for different types of hedging transactions and for transactions that hedge different types of items. Once a taxpayer adopts a method of accounting, however, that method must be applied consistently and can only be changed with the consent of the Commissioner, as provided by section 446(e) and the regulations and procedures thereunder.

(d) *Recordkeeping requirements*—(1) *In general.* The books and records maintained by a taxpayer must contain a description of the accounting method used for each type of hedging transaction. The description of the method or methods used must be sufficient to show how the clear reflection requirement of paragraph (b) of this section is satisfied.

(2) *Additional identification.* In addition to the identification required by § 1.1221-2(f), the books and records maintained by a taxpayer must contain whatever more specific identification with respect to a transaction is necessary to verify the application of the method of accounting used by the taxpayer for the transaction. This additional identification may relate to the hedging transaction or to the item, items, or aggregate risk being hedged. The additional identification must be made at the time specified in § 1.1221-2(f)(2) and must be made on, and retained as part of, the taxpayer's books and records.

(3) *Transactions in which character of gain or loss is not determined under § 1.1221-2.* A section 988 transaction, as defined in section 988(c)(1), or a qualified fund, as defined in section 988(c)(1)(E)(iii), is subject to the identification and recordkeeping requirements of § 1.1221-2(f). See § 1.1221-2(a)(4).

(e) *Requirements and limitations with respect to hedges of certain assets and liabilities.* In the case of certain hedging transactions, this paragraph (e) provides guidance in determining whether a taxpayer's method of accounting satisfies the clear reflection requirement of paragraph (b) of this section. Even if these rules are satisfied, however, the taxpayer's method, as actually applied to the taxpayer's hedging transactions, must clearly reflect income by meeting the matching requirement of paragraph (b) of this section.

(1) *Hedges of aggregate risk*—(i) *In general.* The method of accounting used for hedges of aggregate risk must comply with the matching requirements of paragraph (b) of this section. Even though a taxpayer may not be able to associate the hedging transaction with any particular item being hedged, the timing of income, deduction, gain, or loss from the hedging transaction must be matched with the timing of the aggregate income, deduction, gain, or loss from the items being hedged. For example, if a notional principal contract hedges a taxpayer's aggregate risk, taking into account income, deduction, gain, or loss under the provisions of § 1.446-3 may clearly reflect income. See paragraph (e)(5) of this section.

(ii) *Mark-and-spread method.* The following method may be appropriate for taking into account income, deduction, gain, or loss from hedges of aggregate risk:

(A) The hedging transactions are marked to market at regular intervals for which the taxpayer has the necessary data, but no less frequently than quarterly; and

(B) The income, deduction, gain, or loss attributable to the realization or periodic marking to market of hedging transactions is taken into account over the period for which the hedging transactions are intended to reduce risk. Although the period over which the hedging transactions are intended to reduce risk may change, the period must be reasonable and consistent with the taxpayer's hedging policies and strategies.

Reg. § 1.446-4(e)(1)

(2) *Hedges of items marked to market.* In the case of a transaction that hedges an item that is marked to market under the taxpayer's method of accounting, marking the hedge to market clearly reflects income.

(3) *Hedges of inventory*—(i) *In general.* If a hedging transaction hedges purchases of inventory, gain or loss on the hedging transaction may be taken into account in the same period that it would be taken into account if the gain or loss were treated as an element of the cost of inventory. Similarly, if a hedging transaction hedges sales of inventory, gain or loss on the hedging transaction may be taken into account in the same period that it would be taken into account if the gain or loss were treated as an element of sales proceeds. If a hedge is associated with a particular purchase or sales transaction, the gain or loss on the hedge may be taken into account when it would be taken into account if it were an element of cost incurred in, or sales proceeds from, that transaction. As with hedges of aggregate risk, however, a taxpayer may not be able to associate hedges of inventory purchases or sales with particular purchase or sales transactions. In order to match the timing of income, deduction, gain, or loss from the hedge with the timing of aggregate income, deduction, gain, or loss from the hedged purchases or sales, it may be appropriate for a taxpayer to account for its hedging transactions in the manner described in paragraph (e)(1)(ii) of this section, except that the gain or loss that is spread to each period is taken into account when it would be if it were an element of cost incurred (purchase hedges), or an element of proceeds from sales made (sales hedges), during that period.

(ii) *Alternative methods for certain inventory hedges.* In lieu of the method described in paragraph (e)(3)(i) of this section, other simpler, less precise methods may be used in appropriate cases where the clear reflection requirement of paragraph (b) of this section is satisfied. For example:

(A) Taking into account realized gains and losses on both hedges of inventory purchases and hedges of inventory sales when they would be taken into account if the gains and losses were elements of inventory cost in the period realized may clearly reflect income in some situations, but does not clearly reflect income for a taxpayer that uses the last-in, first-out method of accounting for the inventory; and

(B) Marking hedging transactions to market with resulting gain or loss taken into account immediately may clearly reflect income even though the inventory that is being hedged is not marked to market, but only if the inventory is not accounted for under either the last-in, first-out method or the lower-of-cost-or-market method and only if items are held in inventory for short periods of time.

(4) *Hedges of debt instruments.* Gain or loss from a transaction that hedges a debt instrument issued or to be issued by a taxpayer, or a debt instrument held or to be held by a taxpayer, must be accounted for by reference to the terms of the debt instrument and the period or periods to which the hedge relates. A hedge of an instrument that provides for interest to be paid at a fixed rate or a qualified floating rate, for example, generally is accounted for using constant yield principles. Thus, assuming that a fixed rate or qualified floating rate instrument remains outstanding, hedging gain or loss is taken into account in the same periods in which it would be taken into account if it adjusted the yield of the instrument over the term to which the hedge relates. For example, gain or loss realized on a transaction that hedged an anticipated fixed rate borrowing for its entire term is accounted for, solely for purposes of this section, as if it decreased or increased the issue price of the debt instrument. Similarly, gain or loss realized on a transaction that hedges a contingent payment on a debt instrument subject to § 1.1275-4(c) (a contingent payment debt instrument issued for nonpublicly traded property) is taken into account when the contingent payment is taken into account under § 1.1275-4(c).

(5) *Notional principal contracts.* The rules of § 1.446-3 govern the timing of income and deductions with respect to a notional principal contract unless, because the notional principal contract is part of a hedging transaction, the application of those rules would not result in the matching that is needed to satisfy the clear reflection requirement of paragraph (b) and, as applicable, (e)(4) of this section. For example, if a notional principal contract hedges a debt instrument, the method of accounting for periodic payments described in § 1.446-3(e) and the methods of accounting for nonperiodic payments described in § 1.446-3(f)(2)(iii) and (v) generally clearly reflect the taxpayer's income. The methods described in § 1.446-3(f)(2)(ii) and (iv), however, generally do not clearly reflect the taxpayer's income in that situation.

(6) *Disposition of hedged asset or liability.* If a taxpayer hedges an item and disposes of, or terminates its interest in, the item but does not dispose of or terminate the hedging transaction, the taxpayer must appropriately match the built-in gain or loss on the hedging transaction to the gain or loss on the disposed item. To meet this

Reg. § 1.446-4(e)(2)

requirement, the taxpayer may mark the hedge to market on the date it disposes of the hedged item. If the taxpayer intends to dispose of the hedging transaction within a reasonable period, however, it may be appropriate to match the realized gain or loss on the hedging transaction with the gain or loss on the disposed item. If the taxpayer intends to dispose of the hedging transaction within a reasonable period and the hedging transaction is not actually disposed of within that period, the taxpayer must match the gain or loss on the hedge at the end of the reasonable period with the gain or loss on the disposed item. For purposes of this paragraph (e)(6), a reasonable period is generally 7 days.

(7) *Recycled hedges.* If a taxpayer enters into a hedging transaction by recycling a hedge of a particular hedged item to serve as a hedge of a different item, as described in § 1.1221-2(d)(4), the taxpayer must match the built-in gain or loss at the time of the recycling to the gain or loss on the original hedged item, items, or aggregate risk. Income, deduction, gain, or loss attributable to the period after the recycling must be matched to the new hedged item, items, or aggregate risk under the principles of paragraph (b) of this section.

(8) *Unfulfilled anticipatory transactions*—(i) *In general.* If a taxpayer enters into a hedging transaction to reduce risk with respect to an anticipated asset acquisition, debt issuance, or obligation, and the anticipated transaction is not consummated, any income, deduction, gain, or loss from the hedging transaction is taken into account when realized.

(ii) *Consummation of anticipated transaction.* A taxpayer consummates a transaction for purposes of paragraph (e)(8)(i) of this section upon the occurrence (within a reasonable interval around the expected time of the anticipated transaction) of either the anticipated transaction or a different but similar transaction for which the hedge serves to reasonably reduce risk.

(9) *Hedging by members of a consolidated group*—(i) *General rule: single-entity approach.* In general, a member of a consolidated group must account for its hedging transactions as if all of the members were separate divisions of a single corporation. Thus, the timing of the income, deduction, gain, or loss on a hedging transaction must match the timing of income, deduction, gain, or loss from the item or items being hedged. Because all of the members are treated as if they were divisions of a single corporation, intercompany transactions are neither hedging transactions nor hedged items for these purposes.

(ii) *Separate-entity election.* If a consolidated group makes an election under § 1.1221-2(e)(2), then paragraph (e)(9)(i) of this section does not apply. Thus, in that case, each member of the consolidated group must account for its hedging transactions in a manner that meets the requirements of paragraph (b) of this section. For example, the income, deduction, gain, or loss from intercompany hedging transactions (as defined in § 1.1221-2(e)(2)(ii)) is taken into account under the timing rules of § 1.446-4 rather than under the timing rules of § 1.1502-13.

(iii) *Definitions.* For definitions of consolidated group, divisions of a single corporation, intercompany transaction, and member, see section 1502 and the regulations thereunder.

(iv) *Effective date.* This paragraph (e)(9) applies to transactions entered into on or after March 8, 1996.

(f) *Type or character of income and deduction.* The rules of this section govern the timing of income, deduction, gain, or loss on hedging transactions but do not affect the type or character of income, deduction, gain, or loss produced by the transaction. Thus, for example, the rules of paragraph (e)(3) of this section do not affect the computation of cost of goods sold or sales proceeds for a taxpayer that hedges inventory purchases or sales. Similarly, the rules of paragraph (e)(4) of this section do not increase or decrease the interest income or expense of a taxpayer that hedges a debt instrument or a liability.

(g) *Effective date.* This section applies to hedging transactions entered into on or after October 1, 1994.

(h) *Consent to change methods of accounting.* The Commissioner grants consent for a taxpayer to change its methods of accounting for transactions that are entered into on or after October 1, 1994, and that are described in paragraph (a) of this section. This consent is granted only for changes for the taxable year containing October 1, 1994. The taxpayer must describe its new methods of accounting in a statement that is included in its Federal income tax return for that taxable year. [Reg. § 1.446-4.]

☐ [T.D. 8554, 7-13-94. Amended by T.D. 8653, 1-5-96; T.D. 8674, 6-11-96 and T.D. 8985, 3-15-2002.]

[Reg. § 1.448-1]

§ 1.448-1. **Limitation on the use of the cash receipts and disbursements method of accounting.**—(a) through (f). [Reserved]

(g) *Treatment of accounting method change and timing rules for section 481(a) adjustment*—(1) *Treatment of change in accounting method.*

Notwithstanding any other procedure published prior to January 7, 1991, concerning changes from the cash method, any taxpayer to whom section 448 applies must change its method of accounting in accordance with the provisions of this paragraph (g) and paragraph (h) of this section. In the case of any taxpayer required by this section to change its method of accounting for any taxable year, the change shall be treated as a change initiated by the taxpayer. The adjustments required under section 481(a) with respect to the change in method of accounting of such a taxpayer shall not be reduced by amounts attributable to taxable years preceding the Internal Revenue Code of 1954. Paragraph (h)(2) of this section provides procedures under which a taxpayer may change to an overall accrual method of accounting for the first taxable year the taxpayer is subject to this section ("first section 448 year"). If the taxpayer complies with the provisions of paragraph (h)(2) of this section for its first section 448 year, the change shall be treated as made with the consent of the Commissioner. Paragraph (h)(3) of this section provides procedures under which a taxpayer may change to other than an overall accrual method of accounting for its first section 448 year. Unless the taxpayer complies with the provisions of paragraph (h)(2) or (h)(3) of this section for its first section 448 year, the taxpayer must comply with the provisions of paragraph (h)(4) of this section. See paragraph (h) of this section for rules to effect a change in method of accounting.

(2) *Timing rules for section 481(a) adjustment*—(i) *In general.* Except as otherwise provided in paragraphs (g)(2)(ii) and (g)(3) of this section, a taxpayer required by this section to change from the cash method must take the section 481(a) adjustment into account ratably (beginning with the year of change) over the shorter of—

(A) The number of taxable years the taxpayer used the cash method, or

(B) 4 taxable years, provided the taxpayer complies with the provisions of paragraph (h)(2) or (h)(3) of this section for its first section 448 year.

(ii) *Hospital timing rules*—(A) *In general.* In the case of a hospital that is required by this section to change from the cash method, the section 481(a) adjustment shall be taken into account ratably (beginning with the year of change) over 10 years, provided the taxpayer complies with the provisions of paragraph (h)(2) or (h)(3) of this section for its first section 448 year.

(B) *Definition of hospital.* For purposes of paragraph (g) of this section, a hospital is an institution—

(1) Accredited by the Joint Commission on Accreditation of Healthcare Organizations or its predecessor (the JCAHO) (or accredited or approved by a program of the qualified governmental unit in which such institution is located if the Secretary of Health and Human Services has found that the accreditation or comparable approval standards of such qualified governmental unit are essentially equivalent to those of the JCAHO);

(2) Used primarily to provide, by or under the supervision of physicians, to inpatients diagnostic services and therapeutic services for medical diagnosis, treatment, and care of injured, disabled, or sick persons;

(3) Requiring every patient to be under the care and supervision of a physician; and

(4) Providing 24-hour nursing services rendered or supervised by a registered professional nurse and having a licensed practical nurse or registered nurse on duty at all times.

For purposes of this section, an entity need not be owned by or on behalf of a governmental unit or by a section 501(c)(3) organization, or operated by a section 501(c)(3) organization, in order to be considered a hospital. In addition, for purposes of this section, a hospital does not include a rest or nursing home, continuing care facility, daycare center, medical school facility, research laboratory, or ambulatory care facility.

(C) *Dual function facilities.* With respect to any taxpayer whose operations consist both of a hospital, and other facilities not qualifying as a hospital, the portion of the adjustment required by section 481(a) that is attributable to the hospital shall be taken into account in accordance with the rules of paragraph (g)(2) of this section relating to hospitals. The portion of the adjustment required by section 481(a) that is not attributable to the hospital shall be taken into account in accordance with the rules of paragraph (g)(2) of this section not relating to hospitals.

(iii) *Untimely change in method of accounting to comply with this section.* Unless a taxpayer (including a hospital and a cooperative) required by this section to change from the cash method complies with the provisions of paragraph (h)(2) or (h)(3) of this section for its first section 448 year within the time prescribed by those paragraphs, the taxpayer must take the section 481(a) adjustment into account under the provisions of any applicable administrative procedure that is prescribed by the Commissioner after January 7, 1991, specifically for purposes of comply-

Reg. § 1.448-1(g)(2)

ing with this section. Absent such an administrative procedure, a taxpayer must request a change under § 1.446-1(e)(3) and shall be subject to any terms and conditions (including the year of change) as may be imposed by the Commissioner.

(3) *Special timing rules for section 481(a) adjustment*—(i) *One-third rule.* If, during the period the section 481(a) adjustment is to be taken into account, the balance of the taxpayer's accounts receivable as of the last day of each of two consecutive taxable years is less than 66⅔ percent of the taxpayer's accounts receivable balance at the beginning of the first year of the section 481(a) adjustment, the balance of the section 481(a) adjustment (relating to accounts receivable) not previously taken into account shall be included in income in the second taxable year. This paragraph (g)(3)(i) shall not apply to any hospital (within the meaning of paragraph (g)(2)(ii) of this section).

(ii) *Cooperatives.* Notwithstanding paragraph (g)(2)(i) of this section, in the case of a cooperative (within the meaning of section 1381(a)) that is required by this section to change from the cash method, the entire section 481(a) adjustment may, at the cooperative's option, be taken into account in the year of change, provided the cooperative complies with the provisions of paragraph (h)(2) or (h)(3) of this section for its first section 448 year.

(iii) *Cessation of trade or business.* If the taxpayer ceases to engage in the trade or business to which the section 481(a) adjustment relates, or if the taxpayer operating the trade or business terminates existence, and such cessation or termination occurs prior to the expiration of the adjustment period described in paragraph (g)(2)(i) or (ii) of this section, the taxpayer must take into account, in the taxable year of such cessation or termination, the balance of the adjustment not previously taken into account in computing taxable income. For purposes of this paragraph (g)(3)(iii), the determination as to whether a taxpayer has ceased to engage in the trade or business to which the section 481(a) adjustment relates, or has terminated its existence, is to be made under the principles of § 1.446-1(e)(3)(ii) and its underlying administrative procedures.

(iv) *De minimis rule for a taxpayer other than a cooperative.* Notwithstanding paragraph (g)(2)(i) and (ii) of this section, a taxpayer other than a cooperative (within the meaning of section 1381(a)) that is required to change from the cash method by this section may elect to use, in lieu of the adjustment period described in paragraph (g)(2)(i) and (ii) of this section, the adjustment period for de minimis section 481(a) adjustments provided in the applicable administrative procedure issued under § 1.446-1(e)(3)(ii) for obtaining the Commissioner's consent to a change in accounting method. A taxpayer may make an election under this paragraph (g)(3)(iv) only if—

(A) The taxpayer's entire net section 481(a) adjustment (whether positive or negative) is a de minimis amount as determined under the applicable administrative procedure issued under § 1.446-1(e)(3)(ii) for obtaining the Commissioner's consent to a change in accounting method,

(B) The taxpayer complies with the provisions of paragraph (h)(2) or (3) of this section for its first section 448 year,

(C) The return for such year is due (determined with regard to extensions) after December 27, 1993, and

(D) The taxpayer complies with any applicable instructions to Form 3115 that specify the manner of electing the adjustment period for de minimis section 481(a) adjustments.

(4) *Additional rules relating to section 481(a) adjustment.* In addition to the rules set forth in paragraph (g)(2) and (3) of this section, the following rules shall apply in taking the section 481(a) adjustment into account—

(i) Any net operating loss and tax credit carryforwards will be allowed to offset any positive section 481(a) adjustment,

(ii) Any net operating loss arising in the year of change or in any subsequent year that is attributable to a negative section 481(a) adjustment may be carried back to earlier taxable years in accordance with section 172, and

(iii) For purposes of determining estimated income tax payments under sections 6654 and 6655, the section 481(a) adjustment will be recognized in taxable income ratably throughout a taxable year.

(5) *Outstanding section 481(a) adjustment from previous change in method of accounting.* If a taxpayer changed its method of accounting to the cash method for a taxable year prior to the year the taxpayer was required by this section to change from the cash method (the section 448 year), any section 481(a) adjustment from such prior change in method of accounting that is outstanding as of the section 448 year shall be taken into account in accordance with the provisions of this paragraph (g)(5). A taxpayer shall account for any remaining portion of the prior section 481(a) adjustment outstanding as of the section 448 year by continuing to take such remaining portion into account under the provisions and

conditions of the prior change in method of accounting, or, at the taxpayer's option, combining or netting the remaining portion of the prior section 481(a) adjustment with the section 481(a) adjustment required under this section, and taking into account under the provisions of this section the resulting net amount of the adjustment. Any taxpayer choosing to combine or net the section 481(a) adjustments as described in the preceding sentence shall indicate such choice on the Form 3115 required to be filed by such taxpayer under the provisions of paragraph (h) of this section.

(6) *Examples.* The following examples illustrate the provisions of paragraph (g) of this section:

Example (1). Y is required by this section to change from the cash method of accounting for its taxable year beginning January 1, 1987. Y changes to an overall accrual method. The adjustment required by section 481(a) to effect the change is $10,000. Y has been using the cash method for the 10-year period preceding the year of change. Y is required by paragraph (g)(2)(i) to include the section 481(a) adjustment in taxable income ratably over four consecutive taxable years, beginning with 1987, i.e., $2,500 of the section 481(a) adjustment should be included in income for each of the four years.

Example (2). The facts are the same as in example (1), except that Y is required to change from the cash method and changes to an overall accrual method of accounting for its taxable year beginning January 1, 1989. The result is the same as in example (1), except that the four-year period for ratably taking the section 481(a) adjustment into account begins with the 1989 taxable year.

Example (3). Assume that X is required by this section to change from the cash method and that it changes to an overall accrual method for its taxable year beginning January 1, 1987. The adjustment required by section 481(a) to effect the change is $10,000. X was formed on January 1, 1986, and began business operations during that year. Since X only used the cash method for one year, X is required by paragraph (g)(2)(i) of this section to include all ($10,000) of the section 481(a) adjustment in taxable income for the 1987 taxable year.

Example (4). The facts are the same as in example (1). In addition, Y previously changed from an accrual method of accounting to the cash method for its taxable year beginning January 1, 1983. As a result of that prior change, Y was required to take into account a $5,000 negative section 481(a) adjustment ratably over a ten-year period, beginning with the 1983 taxable year. As of the beginning of the 1987 taxable year $3,000 of that adjustment had not been taken into account. Y may continue to take the remaining negative $3,000 section 481(a) adjustment into account ratably over the remaining adjustment period for the prior change in method of accounting (i.e., six remaining years). Alternatively, Y may combine or net the negative $3,000 adjustment with the positive $10,000 section 481(a) adjustment required by this section, and include the resulting $7,000 amount in taxable income ratably over four consecutive taxable years, beginning with 1987. Y is not allowed to take the entire unamortized amount of the prior section 481(a) adjustment into account for its 1987 taxable year.

(h) *Procedures for change in method of accounting*—(1) *Applicability.* Paragraph (h) of this section applies to taxpayers who change from the cash method as required by this section. Paragraph (h) of this section does not apply to a change in accounting method required by any Code section (or regulations thereunder) other than this section.

(2) *Automatic rule for changes to an overall accrual method*—(i) *Timely changes in method of accounting.* Notwithstanding any other available procedures to change to the accrual method of accounting, a taxpayer to whom paragraph (h) of this section applies who desires to make a change to an overall accrual method for its first section 448 year must make that change under the provisions of this paragraph (h)(2). A taxpayer changing to an overall accrual method under this paragraph (h)(2) must file a current Form 3115 by the time prescribed in paragraph (h)(2)(ii). In addition, the taxpayer must set forth on a statement accompanying the Form 3115 the period over which the section 481(a) adjustment will be taken into account and the basis for such conclusion. Moreover, the taxpayer must type or legibly print the following statement at the top of page 1 of the Form 3115: "Automatic Change to Accrual Method—Section 448." The consent of the Commissioner to the change in method of accounting is granted to taxpayers who change to an overall accrual method under this paragraph (h)(2). See paragraph (g)(2)(i), (g)(2)(ii), or (g)(3) of this section, whichever is applicable, for rules to account for the section 481(a) adjustment.

(ii) *Time and manner for filing Form 3115*—(A) *In general.* Except as provided in paragraph (h)(2)(ii)(B) of this section, the Form 3115 required by paragraph (h)(2)(i) must be filed no later than the due date (determined with regard to extensions) of the taxpayer's federal income tax return for the first section 448 year and must be attached to that return.

Reg. § 1.448-1(g)(6)

(B) *Extension of filing deadline.* Notwithstanding paragraph (h)(2)(ii)(A) of this section, the filing of the Form 3115 required by paragraph (h)(2)(i) shall not be considered late if such Form 3115 is attached to a timely filed amended income tax return for the first section 448 year, provided that—

(*1*) The taxpayer's first section 448 year is a taxable year that begins (or, pursuant to § 1.441-2(c), is deemed to begin) in 1987, 1988, 1989, or 1990,

(*2*) The taxpayer has not been contacted for examination, is not before appeals, and is not before a federal court with respect to an income tax issue (each as defined in applicable administrative pronouncements), unless the taxpayer also complies with any requirements for approval in those applicable administrative pronouncements, and

(*3*) Any amended return required by this paragraph (h)(2)(ii)(B) is filed on or before July 8, 1991.

Filing an amended return under this paragraph (h)(2)(ii)(B) does not extend the time for making any other election. Thus, for example, taxpayers that comply with this section by filing an amended return pursuant to this paragraph (h)(2)(ii)(B) may not elect out of section 448 pursuant to paragraph (i)(2) of this section.

(3) *Changes to a method other than overall accrual method*—(i) *In general.* A taxpayer to whom paragraph (h) of this section applies who desires to change to a special method of accounting must make that change under the provisions of this paragraph (h)(3), except to the extent other special procedures have been promulgated regarding the special method of accounting. Such a taxpayer includes taxpayers who change to both an accrual method of accounting and a special method of accounting such as a long-term contract method. In order to change an accounting method under this paragraph (h)(3), a taxpayer must submit an application for change in accounting method under the applicable administrative procedures in effect at the time of change, including the applicable procedures regarding the time and place of filing the application for change in method. Moreover, a taxpayer who changes an accounting method under this paragraph (h)(3) must type or legibly print the following statement on the top of page 1 of Form 3115: "Change to a Special Method of Accounting—Section 448." The filing of a Form 3115 by any taxpayer requesting a change of method of accounting under this paragraph (h)(3) for its taxable year beginning in 1987 will not be considered late if the form is filed with the appropriate office of the Internal Revenue Service on or before the later of: the date that is the 180th day of the taxable year of change; or September 14, 1987. If the Commissioner approves the taxpayer's application for change in method of accounting, the timing of the adjustment required under section 481(a), if applicable, will be determined under the provisions of paragraph (g)(2)(i), (g)(2)(ii), or (g)(3) of this section, whichever is applicable. If the Commissioner denies the taxpayer's application for change in accounting method, or if the taxpayer's application is untimely, the taxpayer must change to an overall accrual method of accounting under the provisions of either paragraph (h)(2) or (h)(4) of this section, whichever is applicable.

(ii) *Extension of filing deadline.* Notwithstanding paragraph (h)(3)(i) of this section, if the events or circumstances which under section 448 disqualify a taxpayer from using the cash method occur after the time prescribed under applicable procedures for filing the Form 3115, the filing of such form shall not be considered late if such form is filed on or before 30 days after the close of the taxable year.

(4) *Untimely change in method of accounting to comply with this section.* Unless a taxpayer to whom paragraph (h) of this section applies complies with the provisions of paragraph (h)(2) or (h)(3) of this section for its first section 448 year, the taxpayer must comply with the requirements of § 1.446-1(e)(3) (including any applicable administrative procedure that is prescribed thereunder after January 7, 1991, specifically for purposes of complying with this section) in order to secure the consent of the Commissioner to change to a method of accounting that is in compliance with the provisions of this section. The taxpayer shall be subject to any terms and conditions (including the year of change) as may be imposed by the Commissioner.

(i) *Effective date*—(1) *In general.* Except as provided in paragraph (i)(2), (3), and (4) of this section, this section applies to any taxable year beginning after December 31, 1986.

(2) *Election out of section 448*—(i) *In general.* A taxpayer may elect not to have this section apply to any (A) transaction with a related party (within the meaning of section 267(b) of the Internal Revenue Code of 1954, as in effect on October 21, 1986), (B) loan, or (C) lease, if such transaction, loan, or lease was entered into on or before September 25, 1985. Any such election described in the preceding sentence may be made separately with respect to each transaction, loan or lease. For rules relating to the making of such election, see § 301.9100-7T (temporary regulations relating to elections under the Tax Reform Act of 1986).

Reg. § 1.448-1(i)(2)

Notwithstanding the provisions of this paragraph (i)(2), the gross receipts attributable to a transaction, loan, or lease described in this paragraph (i)(2) shall be taken into account for purposes of the $5,000,000 gross receipts test described in paragraph (f) of this section.

(ii) *Special rules for loans.* If the taxpayer makes an election under paragraph (i)(2)(i) of this section with respect to a loan entered into on or before September 25, 1985, the election shall apply only with respect to amounts that are attributable to the loan balance outstanding on September 25, 1985. The election shall not apply to any amounts advanced or lent after September 25, 1985, regardless of whether the loan agreement was entered into on or before such date. Moreover, any payments made on outstanding loan balances after September 25, 1985, shall be deemed to first extinguish loan balances outstanding on September 25, 1985, regardless of any contrary treatment of such loan payments by the borrower and lender.

(3) *Certain contracts entered into before September 25, 1985.* This section does not apply to a contract for the acquisition or transfer of real property or a contract for services related to the acquisition or development of real property if—

(i) The contract was entered into before September 25, 1985; and

(ii) The sole element of the contract which was not performed as of September 25, 1985, was payment for such property or services.

(4) *Transitional rule for paragraphs (g) and (h) of this section.* To the extent the provisions of paragraphs (g) and (h) of this section were not reflected in paragraphs (g) and (h) of § 1.448-1T (as set forth in 26 CFR Part 1 as revised on April 1, 1993), paragraphs (g) and (h) of this section will not be adversely applied to a taxpayer with respect to transactions entered into before December 27, 1993. [Reg. § 1.448-1.]

☐ [*T.D.* 8514, 12-23-93. *Amended by T.D.* 8996, 5-16-2002.]

[Reg. § 1.448-1T]

§ 1.448-1T. Limitation on the use of the cash receipts and disbursements method of accounting (temporary).—(a) *Limitation on accounting method*—(1) *In general.* This section prescribes regulations under section 448 relating to the limitation on the use of the cash receipts and disbursements method of accounting (the cash method) by certain taxpayers.

(2) *Limitation rule.* Except as otherwise provided in this section, the computation of taxable income using the cash method is prohibited in the case of a—

(i) C corporation,

(ii) Partnership with a C corporation as a partner, or

(iii) Tax shelter.

A partnership is described in paragraph (a)(2)(ii) of this section, if the partnership has a C corporation as a partner at any time during the partnership's taxable year beginning after December 31, 1986.

(3) *Meaning of C corporation.* For purposes of this section, the term "C corporation" includes any corporation that is not an S corporation. For example, a regulated investment company (as defined in section 851) or a real estate investment trust (as defined in section 856) is a C corporation for purposes of this section. In addition, a trust subject to tax under section 511(b) shall be treated, for purposes of this section, as a C corporation, but only with respect to the portion of its activities that constitute an unrelated trade or business. Similarly, for purposes of this section, a corporation that is exempt from federal income taxes under section 501(a) shall be treated as a C corporation only with respect to the portion of its activities that constitute an unrelated trade or business. Moreover, for purposes of determining whether a partnership has a C corporation as a partner, any partnership described in paragraph (a)(2)(ii) of this section is treated as C corporation. Thus, if partnership ABC has a partner that is a partnership with a C corporation, then, for purposes of this section, partnership ABC is treated as a partnership with a C corporation partner.

(4) *Treatment of a combination of methods.* For purposes of this section, the use of a method of accounting that records some, but not all, items on the cash method shall be considered the use of the cash method. Thus, a C corporation that uses a combination of accounting methods including the use of the cash method is subject to this section.

(b) *Tax shelter defined*—(1) *In general.* For purposes of this section, the term "tax shelter" means any—

(i) Enterprise (other than a C corporation) if at any time (including taxable years beginning before January 1, 1987) interests in such enterprise have been offered for sale in any offering required to be registered with any federal or state agency having the authority to regulate the offering of securities for sale,

(ii) Syndicate (within the meaning of paragraph (b)(2) of this section), or

(iii) Tax shelter within the meaning of section 6661(b)(2)(C)(ii) (relating to (A) a part-

Reg. § 1.448-1T(a)(1)

nership or other entity, (B) any investment plan or arrangement, or (C) any other plan or arrangement, whose principal purpose is the avoidance or evasion of Federal income tax).

(2) *Requirement of registration.* For purposes of paragraph (b)(1)(i) of this section, an offering is required to be registered with a federal or state agency if, under the applicable federal or state law, failure to register the offering would result in a violation of the applicable federal or state law (regardless of whether the offering is in fact registered). In addition, an offering is required to be registered with a federal or state agency if, under the applicable federal or state law, failure to file a notice of exemption from registration would result in a violation of the applicable federal or state law (regardless of whether the notice is in fact filed).

(3) *Meaning of syndicate.* For purposes of paragraph (b)(1)(ii) of this section, the term "syndicate" means a partnership or other entity (other than a C corporation) if more than 35 percent of the losses of such entity during the taxable year (for taxable years beginning after December 31, 1986) are allocated to limited partners or limited entrepreneurs. For purposes of this paragraph (b)(3), the term "limited entrepreneur" has the same meaning given such term in section 464(e)(2). In addition, in determining whether an interest in a partnership is held by a limited partner, or an interest in an entity or enterprise is held by a limited entrepreneur, section 464(c)(2) shall apply in the case of the trade or business of farming (as defined in paragraph (d)(2) of this section), and section 1256(e)(3)(C) shall apply in any other case. Moreover, for purposes of this paragraph (b)(3), the losses of a partnership, entity, or enterprise (the enterprise) means the excess of the deductions allowable to the enterprise over the amount of income recognized by such enterprise under the enterprise's method of accounting used for federal income tax purposes (determined without regard to this section). For this purpose, gains or losses from the sale of capital assets or section 1221(2) assets are not taken into account.

(4) *Presumed tax avoidance.* For purposes of paragraph (b)(1)(iii) of this section, marketed arrangements in which persons carry on farming activities using the services of a common managerial or administrative service will be presumed to have the principal purpose of tax avoidance if such persons use borrowed funds to prepay a substantial portion of their farming expenses (*e.g.,* payment for farm supplies that will not be used or consumed until a taxable year subsequent to the taxable year of payment).

(5) *Taxable year tax shelter must change accounting method.* A partnership, entity, or enterprise that is a tax shelter must change from the cash method for the later of (i) the first taxable year beginning after December 31, 1986, or (ii) the taxable year that such partnership, entity, or enterprise becomes a tax shelter.

(c) *Effect of section 448 on other provisions.* Nothing in section 448 shall have any effect on the application of any other provision of law that would otherwise limit the use of the cash method, and no inference shall be drawn from section 448 with respect to the application of any such provision. For example, nothing in section 448 affects the requirement of section 447 that certain corporations must use an accrual method of accounting in computing taxable income from farming, or the requirement of § 1.446-1(c)(2) that an accrual method be used with regard to purchases and sales of inventory. Similarly, nothing in section 448 affects the authority of the Commissioner under section 446(b) to require the use of an accounting method that clearly reflects income, or the requirement under section 446(e) that a taxpayer secure the consent of the Commissioner before changing its method of accounting. For example, a taxpayer using the cash method may be required to change to an accrual method of accounting under section 446(b) because such method clearly reflects that taxpayer's income, even though the taxpayer is not prohibited by section 448 from using the cash method. Similarly, a taxpayer using an accrual method of accounting that is not prohibited by section 448 from using the cash method may not change to the cash method unless the taxpayer secures the consent of the Commissioner under section 446(e), and, in the opinion of the Commissioner, the use of the cash method clearly reflects that taxpayer's income under section 446(b).

(d) *Exception for farming business*—(1) *In general.* Except in the case of a tax shelter, this section shall not apply to any farming business. A taxpayer engaged in a farming business and a separate nonfarming business is not prohibited by this section from using the cash method with respect to the farming business, even though the taxpayer may be prohibited by this section from using the cash method with respect to the nonfarming business.

(2) *Meaning of farming business.* For purposes of paragraph (d) of this section, the term "farming business" means—

(i) The trade or business of farming as defined in section 263A(e)(4) (including the operation of a nursery or sod farm, or the raising or harvesting of trees bearing fruit, nuts, or other crops, or ornamental trees), or

(ii) The raising, harvesting, or growing of trees described in section 263A(c)(5) (relating to trees raised, harvested, or grown by the taxpayer other than trees described in paragraph (d)(2)(i) of this section).

Thus, for purposes of this section, the term "farming business" includes the raising of timber. For purposes of this section, the term "farming business" does not include the processing of commodities or products beyond those activities normally incident to the growing, raising or harvesting of such products. For example, assume that a C corporation taxpayer is in the business of growing and harvesting wheat and other grains. The taxpayer processes the harvested grains to produce breads, cereals, and similar food products which it sells to customers in the course of its business. Although the taxpayer is in the farming business with respect to the growing and harvesting of grain, the taxpayer is not in the farming business with respect to the processing of such grains to produce food products which the taxpayer sells to customers. Similarly, assume that a taxpayer is in the business of raising poultry or other livestock. The taxpayer uses the livestock in a meat processing operation in which the livestock are slaughtered, processed, and packaged or canned for sale to customers. Although the taxpayer is in the farming business with respect to the raising of livestock, the taxpayer is not in the farming business with respect to the meat processing operation. However, under this section the term "farming business" does include processing activities which are normally incident to the growing, raising or harvesting of agricultural products. For example, assume a taxpayer is in the business of growing fruits and vegetables. When the fruits and vegetables are ready to be harvested, the taxpayer picks, washes, inspects, and packages the fruits and vegetables for sale. Such activities are normally incident to the raising of these crops by farmers. The taxpayer will be considered to be in the business of farming with respect to the growing of fruits and vegetables, and the processing activities incident to the harvest.

(e) *Exception for qualified personal service corporation*—(1) *In general.* Except in the case of a tax shelter, this section does not apply to a qualified personal service corporation.

(2) *Certain treatment for qualified personal service corporation.* For purposes of paragraph (a)(2)(ii) of this section (relating to whether a partnership has a C corporation as a partner), a qualified personal service corporation shall be treated as an individual.

(3) *Meaning of qualified personal service corporation.* For purposes of this section, the term "qualified personal service corporation" means any corporation that meets—

(i) The function test of paragraph (e)(4) of this section, and

(ii) The ownership test of paragraph (e)(5) of this section.

(4) *Function test*—(i) *In general.* A corporation meets the function test if substantially all the corporation's activities for a taxable year involve the performance of services in one or more of the following fields—

(A) Health,

(B) Law,

(C) Engineering (including surveying and mapping),

(D) Architecture,

(E) Accounting,

(F) Actuarial science,

(G) Performing arts, or

(H) Consulting.

Substantially all of the activities of a corporation are involved in the performance of services in any field described in the preceding sentence (a qualifying field), only if 95 percent or more of the time spent by employees of the corporation, serving in their capacity as such, is devoted to the performance of services in a qualifying field. For purposes of determining whether this 95 percent test is satisfied, the performance of any activity incident to the actual performance of services in a qualifying field is considered the performance of services in that field. Activities incident to the performance of services in a qualifying field include the supervision of employees engaged in directly providing services to clients, and the performance of administrative and support services incident to such activities.

(ii) *Meaning of services performed in the field of health.* For purposes of paragraph (e)(4)(i)(A) of this section, the performance of services in the field of health means the provision of medical services by physicians, nurses, dentists, and other similar health-care professionals. The performance of services in the field of health does not include the provisions of services not directly related to a medical field, even though the services may purportedly relate to the health of the service recipient. For example, the performance of services in the field of health does not include the operation of health clubs or health spas that provide physical exercise or conditioning to their customers.

Reg. § 1.448-1T(e)(1)

(iii) *Meaning of services performed in the field of performing arts.* For purposes of paragraph (e)(4)(i)(G) of this section, the performance of services in the field of the performing arts means the provision of services by actors, actresses, singers, musicians, entertainers, and similar artists in their capacity as such. The performance of services in the field of the performing arts does not include the provision of services by persons who themselves are not performing artists (*e.g.*, persons who may manage or promote such artists, and other persons in a trade or business that relates to the performing arts). Similarly, the performance of services in the field of the performing arts does not include the provision of services by persons who broadcast or otherwise disseminate the performances of such artists to members of the public (*e.g.*, employees of a radio station that broadcasts the performances of musicians and singers). Finally, the performance of services in the field of the performing arts does not include the provision of services by athletes.

(iv) *Meaning of services performed in the field of consulting*—(A) *In general.* For purposes of paragraph (e)(4)(i)(H) of this section, the performance of services in the field of consulting means the provision of advice and counsel. The performance of services in the field of consulting does not include the performance of services other than advice and counsel, such as sales or brokerage services, or economically similar services. For purposes of the preceding sentence, the determination of whether a person's services are sales or brokerage services, or economically similar services, shall be based on all the facts and circumstances of that person's business. Such facts and circumstances include, for example, the manner in which the taxpayer is compensated for the services provided (*e.g.*, whether the compensation for the services is contingent upon the consummation of the transaction that the services were intended to effect).

(B) *Examples.* The following examples illustrate the provisions of paragraph (e)(4)(iv)(A) of this section. The examples do not address all types of services that may or may not qualify as consulting. The determination of whether activities not specifically addressed in the examples qualify as consulting shall be made by comparing the service activities in question to the types of service activities discussed in the examples. With respect to a corporation which performs services which qualify as consulting under this section, and other services which do not qualify as consulting, see paragraph (e)(4)(i) of this section which requires that substantially all of the corporation's activities involve the performance of services in a qualifying field.

Example (1). A taxpayer is in the business of providing economic analyses and forecasts of business prospects for its clients. Based on these analyses and forecasts, the taxpayer advises its clients on their business activities. For example, the taxpayer may analyze the economic conditions and outlook for a particular industry which a client is considering entering. The taxpayer will then make recommendations and advise the client on the prospects of entering the industry, as well as on other matters regarding the client's activities in such industry. The taxpayer provides similar services to other clients, involving, for example, economic analyses and evaluations of business prospects in different areas of the United States or in other countries, or economic analyses of overall economic trends and the provision of advice based on these analyses and evaluations. The taxpayer is considered to be engaged in the performance of services in the field of consulting.

Example (2). A taxpayer is in the business of providing services that consist of determining a client's electronic data processing needs. The taxpayer will study and examine the client's business, focusing on the types of data and information relevant to the client and the needs of the client's employees for access to this information. The taxpayer will then make recommendations regarding the design and implementation of data processing systems intended to meet the needs of the client. The taxpayer does not, however, provide the client with additional computer programming services distinct from the recommendations made by the taxpayer with respect to the design and implementation of the client's data processing systems. The taxpayer is considered to be engaged in the performance of services in the field of consulting.

Example (3). A taxpayer is in the business of providing services that consist of determining a client's management and business structure needs. The taxpayer will study the client's organization, including, for example, the departments assigned to perform specific functions, lines of authority in the managerial hierarchy, personnel hiring, job responsibility, and personnel evaluations and compensation. Based on the study, the taxpayer will then advise the client on changes in the client's management and business structure, including, for example, the restructuring of the client's departmental systems or its lines of managerial authority. The taxpayer is considered to be engaged in the performance of services in the field of consulting.

Example (4). A taxpayer is in the business of providing financial planning services. The taxpayer will study a particular client's financial

Reg. § 1.448-1T(e)(4)

situation, including, for example, the client's present income, savings and investments, and anticipated future economic and financial needs. Based on this study, the taxpayer will then assist the client in making decisions and plans regarding the client's financial activities. Such financial planning includes the design of a personal budget to assist the client in monitoring the client's financial situation, the adoption of investment strategies tailored to the client's needs, and other similar services. The taxpayer is considered to be engaged in the performance of services in the field of consulting.

Example (5). A taxpayer is in the business of executing transactions for customers involving various types of securities or commodities generally traded through organized exchanges or other similar networks. The taxpayer provides its clients with economic analyses and forecasts of conditions in various industries and businesses. Based on these analyses, the taxpayer makes recommendations regarding transactions in securities and commodities. Clients place orders with the taxpayer to trade securities or commodities based on the taxpayer's recommendations. The taxpayer's compensation for its services is typically based on the trade orders. The taxpayer is not considered to be engaged in the performance of services in the field of consulting. The taxpayer is engaged in brokerage services. Relevant to this determination is the fact that the compensation of the taxpayer for its services is contingent upon the consummation of the transaction the services were intended to effect (i.e., the execution of trade orders for its clients).

Example (6). A taxpayer is in the business of studying a client's needs regarding its data processing facilities and making recommendations to the client regarding the design and implementation of data processing systems. The client will then order computers and other data processing equipment through the taxpayer based on the taxpayer's recommendations. The taxpayer's compensation for its services is typically based on the equipment orders made by the clients. The taxpayer is not considered to be engaged in the performance of services in the field of consulting. The taxpayer is engaged in the performance of sales services. Relevant to this determination is the fact that the compensation of the taxpayer for its services is contingent upon the consummation of the transaction the services were intended to effect (i.e., the execution of equipment orders for its clients).

Example (7). A taxpayer is in the business of assisting businesses in meeting their personnel requirements by referring job applicants to employers with hiring needs in a particular area. The taxpayer may be informed by potential employers of their need for job applicants, or, alternatively, the taxpayer may become aware of the client's personnel requirements after the taxpayer studies and examines the client's management and business structure. The taxpayer's compensation for its services is typically based on the job applicants, referred by the taxpayer to the clients, who accept employment positions with the clients. The taxpayer is not considered to be engaged in the performance of services in the field of consulting. The taxpayer is involved in the performance of services economically similar to brokerage services. Relevant to this determination is the fact that the compensation of the taxpayer for its services is contingent upon the consummation of the transaction the services were intended to effect (i.e., the hiring of a job applicant by the client).

Example (8). The facts are the same as in example (7), except that the taxpayer's clients are individuals who use the services of the taxpayer to obtain employment positions. The taxpayer is typically compensated by its clients who obtain employment as a result of the taxpayer's services. For the reasons set forth in example (7), the taxpayer is not considered to be engaged in the performance of services in the field of consulting.

Example (9). A taxpayer is in the business of assisting clients in placing advertisements for their goods and services. The taxpayer analyzes the conditions and trends in the client's particular industry, and then makes recommendations to the client regarding the types of advertisements which should be placed by the client and the various types of advertising media (e.g., radio, television, magazines, etc.) which should be used by the client. The client will then purchase, through the taxpayer, advertisements in various media based on the taxpayer's recommendations. The taxpayer's compensation for its services is typically based on the particular orders for advertisements which the client makes. The taxpayer is not considered to be engaged in the performance of services in the field of consulting. The taxpayer is engaged in the performance of services economically similar to brokerage services. Relevant to this determination is the fact that the compensation of the taxpayer for its services is contingent upon the consummation of the transaction the services were intended to effect (i.e., the placing of advertisements by clients).

Example (10). A taxpayer is in the business of selling insurance (including life and casualty insurance), annuities, and other similar

Reg. § 1.448-1T(e)(4)

insurance products to various individual and business clients. The taxpayer will study the particular client's financial situation, including, for example, the client's present income, savings and investments, business and personal insurance risks, and anticipated future economic and financial needs. Based on this study, the taxpayer will then make recommendations to the client regarding the desirability of various insurance products. The client will then purchase these various insurance products through the taxpayer. The taxpayer's compensation for its services is typically based on the purchases made by the clients. The taxpayer is not considered to be engaged in the performance of services in the field of consulting. The taxpayer is engaged in the performance of brokerage or sales services. Relevant to this determination is the fact that the compensation of the taxpayer for its services is contingent upon the consummation of the transaction the services were intended to effect (i.e., the purchase of insurance products by its clients).

(5) *Ownership test*—(i) *In general.* A corporation meets the ownership test, if at all times during the taxable year, substantially all the corporation's stock, by value, is held, directly or indirectly, by—

(A) Employees performing services for such corporation in connection with activities involving a field referred to in paragraph (e)(4) of this section,

(B) Retired employees who had performed such services for such corporation,

(C) The estate of any individual described in paragraph (e)(5)(i)(A) or (B), or

(D) Any other person who acquired such stock by reason of the death of an individual described in paragraph (e)(5)(i)(A) or (B), but only for the 2-year period beginning on the date of the death of such individual.

For purposes of this paragraph (e)(5), the term "substantially all" means an amount equal to or greater than 95 percent.

(ii) *Definition of employee.* For purposes of the ownership test of this paragraph (e)(5), a person shall not be considered an employee of a corporation unless the services performed by that person for such corporation, based on the facts and circumstances, are more than de minimis. In addition, a person who is an employee of a corporation shall not be treated as an employee of another corporation merely by reason of the employer corporation and the other corporation being members of the same affiliated group or otherwise related.

(iii) *Attribution rules.* For purposes of this paragraph (e)(5), a corporation's stock is considered held indirectly by a person if, and to the extent, such person owns a proportionate interest in a partnership, S corporation, or qualified personal service corporation that owns such stock. No other arrangement or type of ownership shall constitute indirect ownership of a corporation's stock for purposes of this paragraph (e)(5). Moreover, stock of a corporation held by a trust is considered held by a person if, and to the extent, such person is treated under subpart E, part I, subchapter J, chapter 1 of the Code as the owner of the portion of the trust that consists of such stock.

(iv) *Disregard of community property laws.* For purposes of this paragraph (e)(5), community property laws shall be disregarded. Thus, in determining the stock ownership of a corporation, stock owned by a spouse solely by reason of community property laws shall be treated as owned by the other spouse.

(v) *Treatment of certain stock plans.* For purposes of this paragraph (e)(5), stock held by a plan described in section 401(a) that is exempt from tax under section 501(a) shall be treated as held by an employee described in paragraph (e)(5)(i)(A) of this section.

(vi) *Special election for certain affiliated groups.* For purposes of determining whether the stock ownership test of this paragraph (e)(5) has been met, at the election of the common parent of an affiliated group (within the meaning of section 1504(a)), all members of such group shall be treated as one taxpayer if substantially all (within the meaning of paragraph (e)(4)(i) of this section) the activities of all such members (in the aggregate) are in the same field described in paragraph (e)(4)(i)(A)-(H) of this section. For rules relating to the making of the election, see 26 CFR 5h.5 (temporary regulations relating to elections under the Tax Reform Act of 1986).

(vii) *Examples.* The following examples illustrate the provisions of paragraph (e) of this section:

Example (1). (i) X, a C corporation, is engaged in the business of providing accounting services to its clients. These services consist of the preparation of audit and financial statements and the preparation of tax returns. For purposes of section 448, such services consist of the performance of services in the field of accounting. In addition, for purposes of section 448, the supervision of employees directly preparing the statements and returns, and the performance of all administrative and support services incident to such activities (including secretarial, janitorial, purchasing, personnel, security, and payroll ser-

Reg. § 1.448-1T(e)(5)

vices) are the performance of services in the field of accounting.

(ii) In addition, X owns and leases a portion of an office building. For purposes of this section, the following types of activities undertaken by the employees of X shall be considered as the performance of services in a field other than the field of accounting: (A) services directly relating to the leasing activities, e.g., time spent in leasing and maintaining the leased portion of the building; (B) supervision of employees engaged in directly providing services in the leasing activity; and (C) all administrative and support services incurred incident to services described in (A) and (B). The leasing activities of X are considered the performance of services in a field other than the field of accounting, regardless of whether such leasing activities constitute a trade or business under the Code. If the employees of X spend 95% or more of their time in the performance of services in the field of accounting, X satisfies the function test of paragraph (e)(4) of this section.

Example (2). Assume that Y, a C corporation, meets the function test of paragraph (e)(4) of this section. Assume further that all the employees of Y are performing services for Y in a qualifying field as defined in paragraph (e)(4) of this section. P, a partnership, owns 40%, by value, of the stock of Y. The remaining 60% of the stock of Y is owned directly by employees of Y. Employees of Y have an aggregate interest of 90% in the capital and profits of P. Thus, 96% of the stock of Y is held directly, or indirectly, by employees of Y performing services in a qualifying field. Accordingly, Y meets the ownership test of paragraph (e)(5) of this section and is a qualified personal service corporation.

Example (3). The facts are the same as in example (2), except that 40% of the stock of Y is owned by Z, a C corporation. The remaining 60% of the stock is owned directly by the employees of Y. Employees of Y own 90% of the stock, by value, of Z. Assume that Z independently qualifies as a personal service corporation. The result is the same as in example (2), i.e., 96% of the stock of Y is held, directly or indirectly, by employees of Y performing services in a qualifying field. Thus, Y is a qualified personal service corporation.

Example (4). The facts are the same as in example (3), except that Z does not independently qualify as a personal service corporation. Because Z is not a qualified personal service corporation, the Y stock owned by Z is not treated as being held indirectly by the Z shareholders. Consequently, only 60% of the stock of Y is held, directly or indirectly, by employees of Y. Thus, Y does not meet the ownership test of paragraph (e)(5) of this section, and is not a qualified personal service corporation.

Example (5). Assume that W, a C corporation, meets the function test of paragraph (e)(4) of this section. In addition, assume that all the employees of W are performing services for W in a qualifying field. Nominal legal title to 100% of the stock of W is held by employees of W. However, due solely to the operation of community property laws, 20% of the stock of W is held by spouses of such employees who themselves are not employees of W. In determining the ownership of the stock, community property laws are disregarded. Thus, Y meets the ownership test of paragraph (e)(5) of this section, and is a qualified personal service corporation.

Example (6). Assume that 90% of the stock of T, a C corporation, is directly owned by the employees of T. Spouses of T's employees directly own 5% of the stock of T. The spouses are not employees of T, and their ownership does not occur solely by operation of community property laws. In addition, 5% of the stock of T is held by trusts (other than a trust described in section 401(a) that is exempt from tax under section 501(a)), the sole beneficiaries of which are employees of T. The employees are not treated as owners of the trusts under subpart E, part I, subchapter J, chapter 1 of the Code. Since a person is not treated as owning the stock of a corporation owned by that person's spouse, or by any portion of a trust that is not treated as owned by such person under subpart E, only 90% of the stock of T is treated as held, directly or indirectly, by employees of T. Thus, T does not meet the ownership test of paragraph (e)(5) of this section, and is not a qualified personal service corporation.

Example (7). Assume that Y, a C corporation, directly owns all the stock of three subsidiaries, F, G, and H. Y is a common parent of an affiliated group within the meaning of section 1504(a) consisting of Y, F, G, and H. Y is not engaged in the performance of services in a qualifying field. Instead, Y is a holding company whose activities consist of its ownership and investment in its operating subsidiaries. Substantially all the activities of F involve the performance of services in the field of engineering. In addition, a majority of (but not substantially all) the activities of G involve the performance of services in the field of engineering; the remainder of G's services involve the performance of services in a nonqualifying field. Moreover, a majority of (but not substantially all) the activities of H involve the performance of services in the field of engineering; the remainder of H's activities involve the performance of services in the field of architecture. Never-

Reg. § 1.448-1T(e)(5)

theless, substantially all the activities of the group consisting of Y, F, G, and H, in the aggregate, involve the performance of services in the field of engineering. Accordingly, Y elects under paragraph (e)(5)(vi) of this section to be treated as one taxpayer for determining the ownership test of paragraph (e)(5) of this section. Assume that substantially all the stock of Y (by value) is held by employees of F, G, or H who perform services in connection with a qualifying field (engineering or architecture). Thus, for purposes of determining whether any member corporation is a qualified personal service corporation, the ownership test of paragraph (e)(5) of this section has been satisfied. Since F and H satisfy the function test of paragraph (e)(4) of this section, F and H are qualified personal service corporations. However, since Y and G each fail the function test of paragraph (e)(4) of this section, neither corporation is a qualified personal service corporation.

Example (8). The facts are the same as in example (7), except that less than substantially all the activities of the group consisting of Y, F, G, and H, in the aggregate, are performed in the field of engineering. Substantially all the activities of the group consisting of Y, F, G, and H, are, in the aggregate, performed in two fields, the fields of engineering and architecture. Y may not elect to have the affiliated group treated as one taxpayer for purposes of determining whether group members meet the ownership test of paragraph (e)(5) of this section. The election is available only if substantially all the activities of the group, in the aggregate, involve the performance of services in only one qualifying field. Moreover, none of the group members are qualified personal service corporations. Y fails the function test of paragraph (e)(4) of this section because less than substantially all the activities of Y are performed in a qualifying field. In addition, F, G, and H, fail the ownership test of paragraph (e)(5) of this section because substantially all their stock is owned by Y and not by their employees. The owners of Y are not deemed to indirectly own the stock owned by Y because Y is not a qualified personal service corporation.

Example (9). (i) The facts are the same as in example (8), except that Y itself satisfies the function test of paragraph (e)(4) of this section because substantially all the activities of Y involve the performance of services in the field of engineering. In addition, assume that all employees of Y are involved in the performance of services in the field of engineering, and that all such employees own 100% of Y's stock. Moreover, assume that one-third of all the employees of Y are separately employed by F. Similarly, another one-third of the employees of Y are separately employed by G and H, respectively. None of the employees of Y are employed by more than one of Y's subsidiaries. Also, no other persons except the employees of Y are employed by any of the subsidiaries.

(ii) Y is a personal service corporation under section 448 because Y satisfies both the function and the ownership test of paragraphs (e)(4) and (5) of this section. As in example (8), Y is unable to make the election to have the affiliated group treated as one taxpayer for purposes of determining whether group members meet the ownership test of paragraph (e)(5) of this section because less than substantially all the activities, in the aggregate, of the group members are performed in one of the qualifying fields. However, because Y is a personal service corporation, the stock owned by Y is treated as indirectly owned, proportionately, by the owners of Y. Thus, the employees of F are collectively treated as owning one-third of the stock of F, G, and H. The employees of G and H are similarly treated as owning one-third of each subsidiary's stock.

(iii) F, G, and H each fail the ownership test of paragraph (e)(5) of this section because less than substantially all of each corporation's stock is owned by the employees of the respective corporation. Only one-third of each corporation's stock is owned by employees of that corporation. Thus, F, G, and H are not qualified personal service corporations.

Example (10). (i) Assume that Y, a C corporation, directly owns all the stock of three subsidiaries, F, G, and Z. Y is a common parent of an affiliated group within the meaning of section 1504(a) consisting of Y, F, and G. Z is a foreign corporation and is excluded from the affiliated group under section 1504. Assume that Y is a holding company whose activities consist of its ownership and investment in its operating subsidiaries. Substantially all the activities of F, G, and Z involve the performance of services in the field of engineering. Assume that employees of Z own one-third of the stock of Y and that none of these employees are also employees of Y, F, or G. In addition, assume that Y elects to be treated as one taxpayer for determining whether group members meet the ownership test of paragraph (e)(5) of this section. Thus, Y, F, and G are treated as one taxpayer for purposes of the ownership test.

(ii) None of the members of the group are qualified personal service corporations. Y, F, and G fail the ownership test of paragraph (e)(5) of this section because less than substantially all the stock of Y is owned by employees of either Y, F, or G. Moreover, Z fails the ownership test of paragraph (e)(5) of this section because substantially

Reg. § 1.448-1T(e)(5)

all its stock is owned by Y and not by its employees.

(6) *Application of function and ownership tests.* A corporation that fails the function test of paragraph (e)(4) of this section for any taxable year, or that fails the ownership test of paragraph (e)(5) of this section at any time during any taxable year, shall change from the cash method effective for the year in which the corporation fails to meet the function test or the ownership test. For example, if a personal service corporation fails the function test for taxable year 1987, such corporation must change from the cash method effective for taxable year 1987. A corporation that fails the function or ownership test for a taxable year shall not be treated as a qualified personal service corporation for any part of that taxable year.

(f) *Exception for entities with gross receipts of not more than $5 million*—(1) *In general.* Except in the case of a tax shelter, this section shall not apply to any C corporation or partnership with a C corporation as a partner for any taxable year if, for all prior taxable years beginning after December 31, 1985, such corporation or partnership (or any predecessor thereof) meets the $5,000,000 gross receipts test of paragraph (f)(2) of this section.

(2) *The $5,000,000 gross receipts test*—(i) *In general.* A corporation meets the $5,000,000 gross receipts test of this paragraph (f)(2) for any prior taxable year if the average annual gross receipts of such corporation for the 3 taxable years (or, if shorter, the taxable years during which such corporation was in existence) ending with such prior taxable year does not exceed $5,000,000. In the case of a C corporation exempt from federal income taxes under section 501(a), or a trust subject to tax under section 511(b) that is treated as a C corporation under paragraph (a)(3) of this section, only gross receipts from the activities of such corporation or trust that constitute unrelated trades or businesses are taken into account in determining whether the $5,000,000 gross receipts test is satisfied. A partnership with a C corporation as a partner meets the $5,000,000 gross receipts test of this paragraph (f)(2) for any prior taxable year if the average annual gross receipts of such partnership for the 3 taxable years (or, if shorter, the taxable years during which such partnership was in existence) ending with such prior year does not exceed $5,000,000. The gross receipts of the corporate partner are not taken into account in determining whether the partnership meets the $5,000,000 gross receipts test.

(ii) *Aggregation of gross receipts.* For purposes of determining whether the $5,000,000 gross receipts test has been satisfied, all persons treated as a single employer under section 52(a) or (b), or section 414(m) or (o) (or who would be treated as a single employer under such sections if they had employees) shall be treated as one person. Gross receipts attributable to transactions between persons who are treated as a common employer under this paragraph shall not be taken into account in determining whether the $5,000,000 gross receipts test is satisfied.

(iii) *Treatment of short taxable year.* In the case of any taxable year of less than 12 months (a short taxable year), the gross receipts shall be annualized by (A) multiplying the gross receipts for the short period by 12 and (B) dividing the result by the number of months in the short period.

(iv) *Determination of gross receipts*—(A) *In general.* The term "gross receipts" means gross receipts of the taxable year in which such receipts are properly recognized under the taxpayer's accounting method used in that taxable year (determined without regard to this section) for federal income tax purposes. For this purpose, gross receipts include total sales (net of returns and allowances) and all amounts received for services. In addition, gross receipts include any income from investments, and from incidental or outside sources. For example, gross receipts include interest (including original issue discount and tax-exempt interest within the meaning of section 103), dividends, rents, royalties, and annuities, regardless of whether such amounts are derived in the ordinary course of the taxpayer's trade or business. Gross receipts are not reduced by cost of goods sold or by the cost of property sold if such property is described in section 1221(1), (3), (4) or (5). With respect to sales of capital assets as defined in section 1221, or sales of property described in 1221(2) (relating to property used in a trade or business), gross receipts shall be reduced by the taxpayer's adjusted basis in such property. Gross receipts do not include the repayment of a loan or similar instrument (*e.g.*, a repayment of the principal amount of a loan held by a commercial lender). Finally, gross receipts do not include amounts received by the taxpayer with respect to sales tax or other similar state and local taxes if, under the applicable state or local law, the tax is legally imposed on the purchaser of the good or service, and the taxpayer merely collects and remits the tax to the taxing authority. If, in contrast, the tax is imposed on the taxpayer under the applicable law, then gross receipts shall include the amounts received that are allocable to the payment of such tax.

Reg. § 1.448-1T(e)(6)

(3) *Examples.* The following examples illustrate the provisions of paragraph (f) of this section:

Example (1). X, a calendar year C corporation, was formed on January 1, 1986. Assume that in 1986 X has gross receipts of $15 million. For taxable year 1987, this section applies to X because in 1986, the period during which X was in existence, X has average annual gross receipts of more than $5 million.

Example (2). Y, a calendar year C corporation that is not a qualified personal service corporation, has gross receipts of $10 million, $9 million, and $4 million for taxable years 1984, 1985, and 1986, respectively. In taxable year 1986, X has average annual gross receipts for the 3-taxable-year period ending with 1986 of $7.67 million (10 million + 9 million + 4 million/3). Thus, for taxable year 1987, this section applies and Y must change from the cash method for such year.

Example (3). Z, a C corporation which is not a qualified personal service corporation, has a 5% partnership interest in ZAB partnership, a calendar year cash method taxpayer. All other partners of ZAB partnership are individuals. Z corporation has average annual gross receipts of $100,000 for the 3-taxable-year period ending with 1986, (*i.e.,* 1984, 1985 and 1986). The ZAB partnership has average annual gross receipts of $6 million for the same 3-taxable-year period. Since ZAB fails to meet the $5,000,000 gross receipts test for 1986, this section applies to ZAB for its taxable year beginning January 1, 1987. Accordingly, ZAB must change from the cash method for its 1987 taxable year. The gross receipts of Z corporation are not relevant in determining whether ZAB is subject to this section.

Example (4). The facts are the same as in example (3), except that during the 1987 taxable year of ZAB, the Z corporation transfers its partnership interest in ZAB to an individual. Under paragraph (a)(1) of this section, ZAB is treated as a partnership with a C corporation as a partner. Thus, this section requires ZAB to change from the cash method effective for its taxable year 1987. If ZAB later desires to change its method of accounting to the cash method for its taxable year beginning January 1, 1988 (or later), ZAB must comply with all requirements of law, including sections 446(b), 446(e), and 481, to effect the change.

Example (5). X, a C corporation that is not a qualified personal service corporation, was formed on January 1, 1986, in a transaction described in section 351. In the transaction, A, an individual, contributed all of the assets and liabilities of B, a trade or business, to X, in return for the receipt of all of the outstanding stock of X. Assume that in 1986 X had gross receipts of $4 million. In 1984 and 1985, the gross receipts of B, the trade or business, were $10 million and $7 million, respectively. The gross receipts test is applied for the period during which X and its predecessor trade or business were in existence. X has average annual gross receipts for the 3-taxable-year period ending with 1986 of $7 million ($10 million + $7 million + $4 million/3). Thus, for taxable year 1987, this section applies and X must change from the cash method for such year. [Temporary Reg. § 1.448-1T.]

☐ *T.D. 8143, 6-12-87. Amended by T.D. 8329, 1-4-91 and T.D. 8514, 12-23-93.*]

[Reg. § 1.448-2T]

§ 1.448-2T. Nonaccrual of certain amounts by service providers (temporary).—(a) *In general.* Except as otherwise provided, this section applies to any person using an accrual method of accounting with respect to amounts to be received from the performance of services by such person. This section applies to such persons regardless of whether such persons changed their method of accounting from the cash method under section 448. For example, this section applies to a taxpayer who used an overall accrual method of accounting in taxable years prior to 1987.

(b) *Nonaccrual-experience method; treatment as method of accounting.* Any person to whom this section applies is not required to accrue any portion of amounts to be received from the performance of services which, on the basis of experience, will not be collected. This nonaccrual of amounts to be received for the performance of services shall be treated as a method of accounting under the Code (the nonaccrual-experience method).

(c) *Method not available if interest charged on amounts due*—(1) *In general.* The nonaccrual-experience method of accounting may not be used with respect to amounts due for which interest is required to be paid, or for which there is any penalty for failure to timely pay any amounts due. For this purpose, interest or penalties for late payment will be deemed to be charged by a taxpayer if such treatment is in accordance with the economic substance of a transaction, regardless of the characterization of the transaction by the parties, or the treatment of the transaction under state or local law. However, the offering of a discount for early payment of an amount due will not be regarded as the charging of interest or penalties for late payment under this section, if (i) the full amount due is otherwise accrued as gross income by the taxpayer at the time the services are provided, and (ii) the discount for early payment is treated as an adjustment to gross income in the year of payment, if payment is received within the time required for allowance of such discount.

(2) *Example.* The provisions of this paragraph (c) may be illustrated by the following example:

Example. X uses an accrual method of accounting for amounts to be received from the provision of services. For such amounts, X has two billing methods. Under one method, for amounts that are more than 90 days past due, X charges interest at a market rate until such amounts (together with interest) are paid. Under the other billing method, X charges no interest for amounts past due. X cannot use the nonaccrual-experience method of accounting with respect to any of the amounts billed under the method that charges interest on amounts that are more than 90 days past due. X may, however, use the nonaccrual-experience method with respect to the amounts billed under the method that does not charge interest for amounts past due.

(d) *Method not available for certain receivables.* The nonaccrual-experience method of accounting may be used only with respect to amounts earned by the taxpayer and otherwise recognized in income (an account receivable) through the performance of services by such taxpayer. For example, the nonaccrual-experience method may not be used with respect to amounts owed to the taxpayer by reason of the taxpayer's activities with respect to (1) lending money; (2) selling goods; or (3) acquiring receivables or other rights to receive payment from other persons (including persons related to the taxpayer) regardless of whether those other persons earned such amounts through the provision of services.

(e) *Use of experience to estimate uncollectible amounts*—(1) *In general.* In determining the portion of any amount due which, on the basis of experience, will not be collected, the formula prescribed by paragraph (e)(2) of this section shall be used by the taxpayer with respect to each separate trade or business of the taxpayer. No other method or formula may be used by a taxpayer in determining the uncollectible amounts under this section.

(2) *Six-year moving average*—(i) *General rule.* For any taxable year the uncollectible amount of a receivable is the amount of that receivable which bears the same ratio to the account receivable outstanding at the close of the taxable year as (A) the total bad debts (with respect to accounts receivable) sustained throughout the period consisting of the taxable year and the five preceding taxable years (or, with the approval of the Commissioner, a shorter period), adjusted for recoveries of bad debts during such period, bears to (B) the sum of the accounts receivable earned throughout the entire six (or fewer) taxable year period (i.e., the total amount of sales resulting in accounts receivable) throughout the period. Accounts receivable described in paragraphs (c) and (d) of this section are not taken into account in computing the ratio.

(ii) *Period of less than six years.* A period shorter than six years generally will be appropriate only if there is a change in the type of a substantial portion of the outstanding accounts receivable such that the risk of loss is substantially increased. A decline in the general economic conditions in the area, which substantially increases the risk of loss, is a relevant factor in determining whether a shorter period is appropriate. However, approval to use a shorter period will not be granted unless the taxpayer supplies specific evidence that the loans outstanding at the close of the taxable years for the shorter period requested are not comparable in nature and risk to loans outstanding at the close of the six taxable years. A substantial increase in a taxpayer's bad debt experience, is not, by itself, sufficient to justify the use of a shorter period. If approval is granted to use a shorter period, the experience for the excluded taxable years shall not be used for any subsequent year. A request for approval to exclude the experience of a prior taxable year shall be made in accordance with the applicable procedures for requesting a letter ruling and shall include a statement of the reasons such experience should be excluded. A request will not be considered unless it is sent to the Commissioner at least 30 days before the close of the first taxable year for which such approval is requested.

(iii) *Special rule for new taxpayers.* In the case of any current taxable year which is preceded by less than 5 taxable years, paragraph (e)(2)(i) of this section shall be applied by using the experience of the current year and the actual number of preceding taxable years. However, for this purpose, experience from preceding taxable years of a predecessor trade or business may be used in applying paragraph (e)(2)(i) of this section.

(3) *Mechanics of nonaccrual-experience method.* The nonaccrual-experience method shall be applied with respect to each account receivable of the taxpayer which is eligible for such method. With respect to a particular account receivable, the taxpayer will determine, in the manner prescribed in paragraph (e) of this section, the amount of such account receivable that is not expected to be collected. Such determination shall

be made only once with respect to each account receivable, regardless of the term of such receivable. The estimated uncollectible amount shall not be recognized as gross income. Thus, the amount recognized as gross income shall be the amount that would otherwise be recognized as gross income with respect to the account receivable, less the amount which is not expected to be collected. Upon the collection of the account receivable, additional gross income shall be recognized with respect to the collection of any amount not initially expected to be collected. Similarly, no bad debt deduction under section 166 for a wholly or partially worthless account receivable shall be allowed for any amount not previously taken into income under the nonaccrual-experience method.

(4) *Examples.* The following examples illustrate the provisions of paragraph (e) of this section:

Example (1). X is a calendar year service provider that uses an accrual method of accounting with respect to the amounts (accounts receivable) to be received from the provision of services. X does not require the payment of interest or penalties with respect to past due accounts receivable. Assume that under this section, X adopts for taxable year 1987 the nonaccrual-experience method of accounting with respect to its accounts receivable. Further, assume that X's total accounts receivable and bad debt experience for the current and five preceding taxable years is as follows:

Years	Total accounts receivable	Bad debts adjusted for recoveries
1982	$ 30,000	$ 5,700
1983	40,000	7,200
1984	50,000	11,000
1985	60,000	10,200
1986	70,000	14,000
1987	80,000	16,800
	$330,000	$64,900

Thus, the ratio of the bad debts (adjusted for recoveries) for the current and five preceding taxable years to the total accounts receivable over the same period is 19.67% ($64,900/$330,000). Assume that $49,300 of the total $80,000 of accounts receivable earned throughout the taxable year 1987 are outstanding as of the close of such year. Assume further that the $49,300 of the accounts receivable outstanding as of the close of the tax year 1987 consist of 10 separate accounts receivable. The uncollectible amount of each receivable is 19.67%. The amount of these accounts receivable and the uncollectible amount of each is as follows:

	Accounts receivable	Applicable ratio	Uncollectible amount
1.	$ 5,200	.1967	$1,022.84
2.	7,300	.1967	1,435.91
3.	3,200	.1967	629.44
4.	4,300	.1967	845.81
5.	1,700	.1967	334.39
6.	4,000	.1967	786.80
7.	6,300	.1967	1,239.21
8.	8,000	.1967	1,573.60
9.	3,200	.1967	629.44
10.	6,100	.1967	1,199.87
	$49,300		$9,697.31

For taxable year 1987, X will not accrue as income $9,697.31 of its accounts receivable of $49,300 outstanding as of the close of the year.

Example (2). The facts are the same as in example (1). In 1988 the entire amount of account receivable number 8 becomes wholly worthless. Since in 1987 X did not accrue as income under the nonaccrual-experience method $1,573.60 of that account receivable, no deduction under section 166 is allowable with respect to that amount of the account receivable; a deduction of $6,426.40 under section 166 is allowable for 1988.

Example (3). The facts are the same as in example (1). In 1988 X collects, in full, account receivable number 5. Accordingly, in 1988 X must recognize additional gross income of $334.39, the amount of the account receivable that was initially considered uncollectible.

(5) *Special rule for estimated tax.* For purposes of section 6654 or 6655 only (relating to the addition to tax for underpayment of estimated tax), a taxpayer's income does not include eligible income attributable to the period before May 16, 1988, taxpayer's eligible income is the excess (if any) of—

(i) Income (including the amount of any adjustment required under section 481(a)) computed with a bad debt experience ratio using accounts receivable earned throughout the period ending at the close of the six-year period (or other shorter period) described in paragraph (e)(2)(i) of this section, over

(ii) Income (including the amount of any adjustment required under section 481(a)) computed with a bad debt experience ratio using the year-end balances of accounts receivable over such six-year (or other shorter) period.

(f) [Reserved].

(g) *Coordination of change in accounting method with section 481*—(1) *Taxpayers required to change their method of accounting under section 448.* The provisions of this paragraph (g)(1) apply to taxpayers who under § 1.448-1T(h) change from the cash method as required by section 448 and who also change under paragraph (h)

Reg. § 1.448-2T(g)(1)

of this section to a method of accounting that includes the nonaccrual-experience method. With respect to such taxpayers, the section 481(a) adjustment resulting from the change in method of accounting to the nonaccrual-experience method shall be combined or netted with the section 481(a) adjustment applicable to the change in method of accounting required under section 448. The resulting amount shall then be taken into account in accordance with the provisions of § 1.448-1T (g) applicable to the change in method of accounting required by section 448.

(2) *Taxpayers not required to change their method of accounting under section 448.* The provisions of this paragraph (g)(2) apply to taxpayers who are not required by section 448 to change their method of accounting (*e.g.,* taxpayers who were using an accrual method of accounting for taxable years preceding 1987) and who change to the nonaccrual-experience method under paragraph (h)(3) of this section. With respect to such taxpayers, the section 481(a) adjustment resulting from the change in method of accounting to the nonaccrual-experience method shall be taken into account ratably over four taxable years. The provisions of this paragraph (g)(2) shall apply to any taxpayer regardless of whether such taxpayer was required to change its method of accounting for bad debts under section 805 of the Tax Reform Act of 1986.

(h) *Changes in method of accounting to nonaccrual-experience method*—(1) *Automatic changes to overall accrual method.* The provisions of this paragraph (h)(1) apply to taxpayers who change from the cash method as required by section 448, and change to an overall accrual method of accounting under the automatic change provisions of § 1.448-1T (h)(2). Taxpayers to whom this paragraph (h)(1) applies may automatically change their method of accounting to the nonaccrual-experience method under this paragraph (h)(1), if they otherwise qualify under this section for the use of such method. Taxpayers changing to the nonaccrual-experience method under this paragraph (h)(1) shall comply with the provisions of § 1.448-1T (h)(2). Moreover, such taxpayers shall type or legibly print the following statement at the top of page 1 of Form 3115: Automatic Change to Nonaccrual Experience Method—Section 448." The consent of the Commissioner to the change in method of accounting is granted to taxpayers changing to the nonaccrual-experience method under this paragraph (h)(1).

(2) *Changes to a method other than overall accrual method.* The provisions of this paragraph (h)(2) apply to taxpayers who change from the cash method as required by section 448 and who also change to a permissible special method of accounting under § 1.448-1T (h)(3). Taxpayers to whom this paragraph (h)(2) applies may change their method of accounting to the nonaccrual-experience method under this paragraph (h)(2). Taxpayers changing to the nonaccrual-experience method under this paragraph (h)(2) shall comply with the provisions of § 1.448-1T (h)(3). Moreover, such taxpayers shall type or legibly print the following statement on the top of page 1 of Form 3115: "Change to Nonaccrual-Experience Method and Special Method of Accounting-Section 448." The consent of the Commissioner to the change in method of accounting is granted to taxpayers changing to the nonaccrual-experience method under this paragraph (h)(2).

(3) *Taxpayers not required to change their method of accounting under section 448.* The provisions of this paragraph (h)(3) apply to taxpayers who are not required by section 448 to change their method of accounting for the taxable year in which such taxpayers desire to adopt the nonaccrual-experience method (*e.g.,* taxpayers who were using an accrual method of accounting for taxable years preceding 1987). Such taxpayers may automatically change their method of accounting to the nonaccrual-experience method under the provisions of this paragraph (h)(3), for their taxable year beginning in 1987, if they otherwise qualify under the provisions of this section for the use of such method. Taxpayers changing to the nonaccrual-experience method for their taxable year beginning in 1987 shall complete and file a current Form 3115. The Form 3115 shall be filed no later than the due date (including extension) of the taxpayer's federal income tax return for the year of change and shall be attached to that return. Moreover, the taxpayer shall type or legibly print the following statement at the top of page 1 of Form 3115: "Automatic Change to Nonaccrual Experience Method—Taxpayer Not Required to Change Method of Accounting Under Section 448." The consent of the Commissioner to the change in method of accounting is granted to taxpayers changing to the nonaccrual-experience method for their taxable year beginning in 1987 under this paragraph (h)(3). With respect to taxpayers described in this paragraph (h)(3) who desire to change to the nonaccrual-experience method for a taxable year beginning after December 31, 1987, such taxpayers shall submit an application for change in accounting method under the administrative procedures applicable to taxpayers at the time of change, including the applicable procedures regarding the time and place of filing the application for change in method. Taxpayers described in the preceding sentence include taxpayers who were required to

Reg. § 1.448-2T(g)(2)

change their method of accounting under section 448 for an earlier taxable year, but who did not change to the nonaccrual-experience method at that time.

(i) *Effective date.* This section applies to any taxable year beginning after December 31, 1986. [Temporary Reg. § 1.448-2T.]

☐ [T.D. 8143, 6-12-87. Amended by T.D. 8194, 4-14-88.]

[Reg. § 1.451-1]

§ 1.451-1. General rule for taxable year of inclusion.—(a) *General rule.* Gains, profits, and income are to be included in gross income for the taxable year in which they are actually or constructively received by the taxpayer unless includible for a different year in accordance with the taxpayer's method of accounting. Under an accrual method of accounting, income is includible in gross income when all the events have occurred which fix the right to receive such income and the amount thereof can be determined with reasonable accuracy. Therefore, under such a method of accounting if, in the case of compensation for services, no determination can be made as to the right to such compensation or the amount thereof until the services are completed, the amount of compensation is ordinarily income from the taxable year in which the determination can be made. Under the cash receipts and disbursements method of accounting, such an amount is includible in gross income when actually or constructively received. Where an amount of income is properly accrued on the basis of a reasonable estimate and the exact amount is subsequently determined, the difference, if any, shall be taken into account for the taxable year in which such determination is made. To the extent that income is attributable to the recovery of bad debts for accounts charged off in prior years, it is includible in the year of recovery in accordance with the taxpayer's method of accounting, regardless of the date when the amounts were charged off. For treatment of bad debts and bad debt recoveries, see sections 166 and 111 and the regulations thereunder. For rules relating to the treatment of amounts received in crop shares, see section 61 and the regulations thereunder. For the year in which a partner must include his distributive share of partnership income, see section 706(a) and paragraph (a) of § 1.706-1. If a taxpayer ascertains that an item should have been included in gross income in a prior taxable year, he should, if within the period of limitation, file an amended return and pay any additional tax due. Similarly, if a taxpayer ascertains that an item was improperly included in gross income in a prior taxable year, he should, if within the period of limitation, file claim for credit or refund of any overpayment of tax arising therefrom.

(b) *Special rule in case of death.* (1) A taxpayer's taxable year ends on the date of his death. See section 443(a)(2) and paragraph (a)(2) of § 1.443-1. In computing taxable income for such year, there shall be included only amounts properly includible under the method of accounting used by the taxpayer. However, if the taxpayer used an accrual method of accounting, amounts accrued only by reason of his death shall not be included in computing taxable income for such year. If the taxpayer uses no regular accounting method, only amounts actually or constructively received during such year shall be included. (For rules relating to the inclusion of partnership income in the return of a decedent partner, see subchapter K of chapter 1 of the Code and the regulations thereunder.)

(2) If the decedent owned an installment obligation the income from which was taxable to him under section 453, no income is required to be reported in the return of the decedent by reason of the transmission at death of such obligation. See section 453(d)(3). For the treatment of installment obligations acquired by the decedent's estate or by any person by bequest, devise, or inheritance from the decedent, see section 691(a)(4) and the regulations thereunder.

(c) *Special rule for employee tips.* Tips reported by an employee to his employer in a written statement furnished to the employer pursuant to section 6053(a) shall be included in gross income of the employee for the taxable year in which the written statement is furnished the employer. For provisions relating to the reporting of tips by an employee to his employer, see section 6053 and § 31.6053-1 of this chapter (Employment Tax Regulations).

(d) *Special rule for ratable inclusion of original issue discount.* For ratable inclusion of original issue discount in respect of certain corporate obligations issued after May 27, 1969, see section 1232(a)(3).

(e) *Special rule for inclusion of qualified tax refund effected by allocation.* For rules relating to the inclusion in income of an amount paid by a taxpayer in respect of his liability for a qualified State individual income tax and allocated or reallocated in such a manner as to apply it toward the taxpayer's liability for the Federal income tax, see paragraph (f)(1) of § 301.6361-1 of this chapter (Regulations on Procedure and Administration).

(f) *Timing of income from notional principal contracts.* For the timing of income with respect to notional principal contracts, see § 1.446-3.

(g) *Timing of income from section 467 rental agreements.* For the timing of income with respect to section 467 rental agreements, see section 467 and the regulations thereunder. [Reg. § 1.451-1.]

☐ [T.D. 6282, 12-24-57. *Amended by* T.D. 7001, 1-17-69; T.D. 7154, 12-27-71; T.D. 7577, 12-19-78; T.D. 8491, 10-8-93 *and* T.D. 8820, 5-17-99.]

[Reg. § 1.451-2]

§ 1.451-2. Constructive receipts of income.— (a) *General rule.* Income although not actually reduced to a taxpayer's possession is constructively received by him in the taxable year during which it is credited to his account, set apart for him, or otherwise made available so that he may draw upon it at any time, or so that he could have drawn upon it during the taxable year if notice of intention to withdraw had been given. However, income is not constructively received if the taxpayer's control of its receipt is subject to substantial limitations or restrictions. Thus, if a corporation credits its employees with bonus stock, but the stock is not available to such employees until some future date, the mere crediting on the books of the corporation does not constitute receipt. In the case of interest, dividends, or other earnings (whether or not credited) payable in respect of any deposit or account in a bank, building and loan association, savings and loan association, or similar institution, the following are not substantial limitations or restrictions on the taxpayer's control over the receipt of such earnings:

(1) A requirement that the deposit or account, and the earnings thereon, must be withdrawn in multiples of even amounts;

(2) The fact that the taxpayer would, by withdrawing the earnings during the taxable year, receive earnings that are not substantially less in comparison with the earnings for the corresponding period to which the taxpayer would be entitled had he left the account on deposit until a later date (for example, if an amount equal to three months' interest must be forfeited upon withdrawal or redemption before maturity of a one year or less certificate of deposit, time deposit, bonus plan, or other deposit arrangement then the earnings payable on premature withdrawal or redemption would be substantially less when compared with the earnings available at maturity);

(3) A requirement that the earnings may be withdrawn only upon a withdrawal of all or part of the deposit or account. However, the mere fact that such institutions may pay earnings on withdrawals, total or partial, made during the last three business days of any calendar month ending a regular quarterly or semiannual earnings period at the applicable rate calculated to the end of such calendar month shall not constitute constructive receipt of income by any depositor or account holder in any such institution who has not made a withdrawal during such period;

(4) A requirement that a notice of intention to withdraw must be given in advance of the withdrawal. In any case when the rate of earnings payable in respect of such a deposit or account depends on the amount of notice of intention to withdraw that is given, earnings at the maximum rate are constructively received during the taxable year regardless of how long the deposit or account was held during the year or whether, in fact, any notice of intention to withdraw is given during the year. However, if in the taxable year of withdrawal the depositor or account holder receives a lower rate of earnings because he failed to give the required notice of intention to withdraw, he shall be allowed an ordinary loss in such taxable year in an amount equal to the difference between the amount of earnings previously included in gross income and the amount of earnings actually received. See section 165 and the regulations thereunder.

(b) *Examples of constructive receipt.* Amounts payable with respect to interest coupons which have matured and are payable but which have not been cashed are constructively received in the taxable year during which the coupons mature, unless it can be shown that there are no funds available for payment of the interest during such year. Dividends on corporate stock are constructively received when unqualifiedly made subject to the demand of the shareholder. However, if a dividend is declared payable on December 31 and the corporation followed its usual practice of paying the dividends by checks mailed so that the shareholders would not receive them until January of the following year, such dividends are not considered to have been constructively received in December. Generally, the amount of dividends or interest credited on savings bank deposits or to shareholders of organizations such as building and loan associations or cooperative banks is income to the depositors or shareholders for the taxable year when credited. However, if any portion of such dividends or interest is not subject to withdrawal at the time credited, such portion is not constructively received and does not constitute income to the depositor or shareholder until the taxable year in which the portion first may be withdrawn. Accordingly, if, under a bonus or forfeiture plan, a portion of the dividends or interest is accumulated and may not be withdrawn until the maturity of the plan, the crediting of such portion to the account of the shareholder or depositor does not constitute constructive receipt. In this case, such

Methods of Accounting

credited portion is income to the depositor or shareholder in the year in which the plan matures. However, in the case of certain deposits made after December 31, 1970, in banks, domestic building and loan associations, and similar financial institutions, the ratable inclusion rules of section 1232(a)(3) apply. See § 1.1232-3A. Accrued interest on unwithdrawn insurance policy dividends is gross income to the taxpayer for the first taxable year during which such interest may be withdrawn by him. [Reg. § 1.451-2.]

☐ [T.D. 6282, 12-24-57. Amended by T.D. 6723, 4-20-64; T.D. 7154, 12-27-71 and T.D. 7663, 12-21-79.]

[Reg. § 1.451-4]

§ 1.451-4. **Accounting for redemption of trading stamps and coupons.**—(a) *In general*—(1) *Subtraction from receipts.* If an accrual method taxpayer issues trading stamps or premium coupons with sales, or an accrual method taxpayer is engaged in the business of selling trading stamps or premium coupons, and such stamps or coupons are redeemable by such taxpayer in merchandise, cash, or other property, the taxpayer should, in computing the income from such sales, subtract from gross receipts with respect to sales of such stamps or coupons (or from gross receipts with respect to sales with which trading stamps or coupons are issued) an amount equal to—

(i) The cost to the taxpayer of merchandise, cash, and other property used for redemptions in the taxable year,

(ii) Plus the net addition to the provision for future redemptions during the taxable year (or less the net subtraction from the provision for future redemptions during the taxable year).

(2) *Trading stamp companies.* For purposes of this section, a taxpayer will be considered as being in the business of selling trading stamps or premium coupons if—

(i) The trading stamps or premium coupons sold by him are issued by purchasers to promote the sale of their merchandise or services,

(ii) The principal activity of the trade or business is the sale of such stamps or coupons,

(iii) Such stamps or coupons are redeemable by the taxpayer for a period of at least 1 year from the date of sale, and

(iv) Based on his overall experience, it is estimated that not more than two-thirds of the stamps or coupons sold which it is estimated, pursuant to paragraph (c) of this section, will be ultimately redeemed, will be redeemed within 6 months of the date of sale.

(b) *Computation of the net addition to or subtraction from the provision for future redemptions*—(1) *Determination of the provision for future redemptions.* (i) The provision for future redemptions as of the end of a taxable year is computed by multiplying "estimated future redemptions" (as defined in subdivision (ii) of this subparagraph) by the estimated average cost of redeeming each trading stamp or coupon (computed in accordance with subdivision (iii) of this subparagraph).

(ii) For purposes of this section, the term "estimated future redemptions" as of the end of a taxable year means the number of trading stamps or coupons outstanding as of the end of such year that it is reasonably estimated will ultimately be presented for redemption. Such estimate shall be determined in accordance with the rules contained in paragraph (c) of this section.

(iii) For purposes of this section, the estimated average cost of redeeming each trading stamp or coupon shall be computed by including only the costs to the taxpayer of acquiring the merchandise, cash, or other property needed to redeem such stamps or coupons. The term "the costs to the taxpayer of acquiring the merchandise, cash, or other property needed to redeem such stamps or coupons" includes only the price charged by the seller (less trade or other discounts, except strictly cash discounts approximating a fair interest rate, which may be deducted or not at the option of the taxpayer provided a consistent course is followed) plus transportation or other necessary charges in acquiring possession of the goods. Items such as the costs of advertising, catalogs, operating redemption centers, transporting merchandise or other property from a central warehouse to a branch warehouse (or from a warehouse to a redemption center), and storing the merchandise or other property used to redeem stamps or coupons should not be included in costs of redeeming stamps or premium coupons, but rather should be accounted for in accordance with the provisions of sections 162 and 263.

(2) *Changes in provision for future redemptions.* For purposes of this section, a "net addition to" or "net subtraction from" the provision for future redemptions for a taxable year is computed as follows:

(i) Carry over the provision for future redemptions (if any) as of the end of the preceding taxable year,

(ii) Compute the provision for future redemptions as of the end of the taxable year in accordance with subparagraph (1) of this paragraph, and

Reg. § 1.451-4(b)(2)

(iii) If the amount referred to in subdivision (ii) of this subparagraph exceeds the amount referred to in subdivision (i) of this paragraph, such excess is the net addition to the provision for future redemptions for the taxable year. On the other hand, if the amount referred to in such subdivision (i) exceeds the amount referred to in such subdivision (ii), such excess is the net subtraction from the provision for future redemptions for the taxable year.

(3) *Example.* The provisions of this paragraph and paragraph (a)(1) of this section may be illustrated by the following example:

Example. (a) X Company, a calendar year accrual method taxpayer, is engaged in the business of selling trading stamps to merchants. In 1971, its first year of operation, X sells 10 million stamps at $5 per 1,000; it redeems 3 million stamps for merchandise and cash of an average value of $3 per 1,000 stamps. At the end of 1971 it is estimated (pursuant to paragraph (c) of this section) that a total of 9 million stamps of the 10 million stamps issued in 1971 will eventually be presented for redemption. At this time it is estimated that the average cost of redeeming stamps (as described in subparagraph (1)(iii) of this paragraph) would continue to be $3 per 1,000 stamps. Under these circumstances, X computes its gross income from sales of trading stamps as follows:

Gross receipts from sales (10 million stamps at $5 per 1,000)		$50,000
Less:		
Cost of actual redemptions (3 million stamps at $3 per 1,000)	$ 9,000	
Provision for future redemptions on December 31, 1971 (9 million stamps—3 million stamps × $3 per 1,000)	$18,000	$27,000
1971 Gross income from sales of stamps		$23,000

(b) In 1972, X also sells 10 million stamps at $5 per 1,000 stamps. During 1972 X redeems 7 million stamps at an average cost of $3.01 per 1,000 stamps. At the end of 1972 it is determined that the estimated future redemptions (within the meaning of subparagraph (1)(ii) of this paragraph) is 8 million. It is further determined that the estimated average cost of redeeming stamps would continue to be $3.01 per 1,000 stamps. X thus computes its gross income from sales of trading stamps for 1972 as follows:

Gross receipts from sales (10 million stamps at $5 per 1,000)		$50,000
Less:		
Cost of actual redemptions: (7 million stamps at $3.01 per 1,000)	$21,070	
Plus:		
Provision for future redemptions on Dec. 31, 1972 (8 million stamps at $3.01 per 1,000)	$24,080	
Minus provision for future redemptions on Dec. 31, 1971	18,000	
Addition to provision for future redemptions	$ 6,080	
Total cost of redemptions		$27,150
1972 Gross income from sales of stamps		$22,850

(c) *Estimated future redemptions*—(1) *In general.* A taxpayer may use any method of determining the estimated future redemptions as of the end of a year so long as—

(i) Such method results in a reasonably accurate estimate of the stamps or coupons outstanding at the end of such year that will ultimately be presented for redemption,

(ii) Such method is used consistently, and

(iii) Such taxpayer complies with the requirements of this paragraph and paragraphs (d) and (e) of this section.

(2) *Utilization of prior redemption experience.* Normally, the estimated future redemptions of a taxpayer shall be determined on the basis of such taxpayer's prior redemption experience. However, if the taxpayer does not have sufficient redemption experience to make a reasonable determination of his "estimated future redemptions", or if because of a change in his mode of operation or other relevant factors the determination cannot reasonably be made completely on the basis of the taxpayer's own experience, the experiences of similarly situated taxpayers may be used to establish an experience factor.

(3) *One method of determining estimated future redemptions.* One permissible method of determining the estimated future redemptions as of the end of the current taxable year is as follows:

(i) Estimate for each preceding taxable year and the current taxable year the number of trading stamps or coupons issued for each such year which will ultimately be presented for redemption.

(ii) Determine the sum of the estimates under subdivision (i) of this subparagraph for

Reg. § 1.451-4(b)(3)

each taxable year prior to and including the current taxable year.

(iii) The difference between the sum determined under subdivision (ii) of this subparagraph and the total number of trading stamps or coupons which have already been presented for redemption is the estimated future redemptions as of the end of the current taxable year.

(4) *Determination of an "estimated redemption percentage."* For purposes of applying subparagraph (3)(i) of this paragraph, one permissible method of estimating the number of trading stamps or coupons issued for a taxable year that will ultimately be presented for redemption is to multiply such number of stamps issued for such year by an "estimated redemption percentage". For purposes of this section the term "estimated redemption percentage" for a taxable year means a fraction, the numerator of which is the number of trading stamps or coupons issued during a taxable year that it is reasonably estimated will ultimately be redeemed, and the denominator of which is the number of trading stamps or coupons issued during such year. Consequently, the product of such percentage and the number of stamps issued for such year equals the number of trading stamps or coupons issued for such year that it is estimated will ultimately be redeemed.

(5) *Five-year rule.* (i) One permissible method of determining the "estimated redemption percentage" for a taxable year is to—

(*a*) Determine the percentage which the total number of stamps or coupons redeemed in the taxable year and the 4 preceding taxable years is of the total number of stamps or coupons issued or sold in such 5 years; and

(*b*) Multiply such percentage by an appropriate growth factor as determined pursuant to guidelines published by the Commissioner.

(ii) If a taxpayer uses the method described in subdivision (i) of this subparagraph for a taxable year, it will normally be presumed that such taxpayer's "estimated redemption percentage" is reasonably accurate.

(6) *Other methods of determining estimated future redemptions.* (i) If a taxpayer uses a method of determining his "estimated future redemptions" (other than a method which applies the 5-year rule as described in subparagraph (5)(i) of this paragraph) such as a probability sampling technique, the appropriateness of the method (including the appropriateness of the sampling technique, if any) and the accuracy and reliability of the results obtained must, if requested, be demonstrated to the satisfaction of the district director.

(ii) No inference shall be drawn from subdivision (i) of this subparagraph that the use of any method to which such subdivision applies is less acceptable than the method described in subparagraph (5)(i) of this paragraph. Therefore, certain probability sampling techniques used in determining estimated future redemptions may result in reasonably accurate and reliable estimates. Such a sampling technique will be considered appropriate if the sampling is—

(*a*) Taken in accordance with sound statistical sampling principles,

(*b*) In accordance with such principles, sufficiently broad to produce a reasonably accurate result, and

(*c*) Taken with sufficient frequency as to produce a reasonably accurate result.

In addition, if the sampling technique is appropriate, the results obtained therefrom in determining estimated future redemptions will be considered accurate and reliable if the evaluation of such results is consistent with sound statistical principles. Ordinarily, samplings and recomputations of the estimated future redemptions will be required annually. However, the facts and circumstances in a particular case may justify such a recomputation being taken less frequently than annually. In addition, the Commissioner may prescribe procedures indicating that samples made to update the results of a sample of stamps redeemed in a prior year need not be the same size as the sample of such prior year.

(d) *Consistency with financial reporting*—(1) *Estimated future redemptions.* For taxable years beginning after August 22, 1972, the estimated future redemptions must be no greater than the estimate that the taxpayer uses for purposes of all reports (including consolidated financial statements) to shareholders, partners, beneficiaries, other proprietors, and for credit purposes.

(2) *Average cost of redeeming stamps.* For taxable years beginning after August 22, 1972, the estimated average cost of redeeming each stamp or coupon must be no greater than the average cost of redeeming each stamp or coupon (computed in accordance with paragraph (b)(1)(iii) of this section) that the taxpayer uses for purposes of all reports (including consolidated financial statements) to shareholders, partners, beneficiaries, other proprietors, and for credit purposes.

(e) *Information to be furnished with return*—(1) *In general.* For taxable years beginning after August 22, 1972, a taxpayer described in paragraph (a) of this section who uses a method of determining the "estimated future redemptions" other than that described in paragraph (c)(5)(i) of this section shall file a statement with his return showing such information as is necessary to establish the correctness of the amount subtracted from gross receipts in the taxable year.

(2) *Taxpayers using the 5-year rule.* If a taxpayer uses the method of determining estimated future redemptions described in paragraph (c)(5)(i) of this section, he shall file a statement with his return showing, with respect to the taxable year and the 4 preceding taxable years—

(i) The total number of stamps or coupons issued or sold during each year, and

(ii) The total number of stamps or coupons redeemed in each such year.

(3) *Trading stamp companies.* In addition to the information required by subparagraph (1) or (2) of this paragraph, a taxpayer engaged in the trade or business of selling trading stamps or premium coupons shall include with the statement described in subparagraph (1) or (2) of this paragraph such information as may be necessary to satisfy the requirements of paragraph (a)(2)(iv) of this section. [Reg. § 1.451-4.]

☐ [T.D. 6282, 12-24-57. Amended by T.D. 7201, 8-22-72.]

[Reg. § 1.451-5]

§ 1.451-5. **Advance payments for goods and long-term contracts.**—(a) *Advance payment defined*—(1) For purposes of this section, the term "advance payment" means any amount which is received in a taxable year by a taxpayer using an accrual method of accounting for purchases and sales or a long-term contract method of accounting (described in § 1.451-3), pursuant to, and to be applied against, an agreement:

(i) For the sale or other disposition in a future taxable year of goods held by the taxpayer primarily for sale to customers in the ordinary course of his trade or business, or

(ii) For the building, installing, constructing or manufacturing by the taxpayer of items where the agreement is not completed within such taxable year.

(2) For purposes of subparagraph (1) of this paragraph:

(i) The term "agreement" includes (*a*) a gift certificate that can be redeemed for goods, and (*b*) an agreement which obligates a taxpayer to perform activities described in subparagraph (1)(i) or (ii) of this paragraph and which also contains an obligation to perform services that are to be performed as an integral part of such activities; and

(ii) Amounts due and payable are considered "received".

(3) If a taxpayer (described in subparagraph (1) of this paragraph) receives an amount pursuant to, and to be applied against, an agreement that not only obligates the taxpayer to perform the activities described in subparagraph (1)(i) and (ii) of this paragraph, but also obligates the taxpayer to perform services that are not to be performed as an integral part of such activities, such amount will be treated as an "advance payment" (as defined in subparagraph (1) of this paragraph) only to the extent such amount is properly allocable to the obligation to perform the activities described in subparagraph (1)(i) and (ii) of this paragraph. The portion of the amount not so allocable will not be considered an "advance payment" to which this section applies. If, however, the amount not so allocable is less than five percent of the total contract price, such amount will be treated as so allocable except that such treatment can not result in delaying the time at which the taxpayer would otherwise accrue the amounts attributable to the activities described in subparagraph (1)(i) and (ii) of this paragraph.

(b) *Taxable year of inclusion*—(1) *In general.* Advance payments must be included in income either—

(i) In the taxable year of receipt; or

(ii) Except as provided in paragraph (c) of this section.

(*a*) In the taxable year in which properly accruable under the taxpayer's method of accounting for tax purposes if such method results in including advance payments in gross receipts no later than the time such advance payments are included in gross receipts for purposes of all of his reports (including consolidated financial statements) to shareholders, partners, beneficiaries, other proprietors, and for credit purposes, or

(*b*) If the taxpayer's method of accounting for purposes of such reports results in advance payments (or any portion of such payments) being included in gross receipts earlier than for tax purposes, in the taxable year in which includible in gross receipts pursuant to his method of accounting for purposes of such reports.

(2) *Examples.* This paragraph may be illustrated by the following examples:

Example (1). S, a retailer who uses for tax purposes and for purposes of the reports referred to in subparagraph (1)(ii)(a) of this paragraph, an accrual method of accounting under which it accounts for its sales of goods when the goods are shipped, receives advance payments for such goods. Such advance payments must be included in gross receipts for tax purposes either in the taxable year the payments are received or in the taxable year such goods are shipped (except as provided in paragraph (c) of this section).

Example (2). T, a manufacturer of household furniture, is a calendar year taxpayer who uses an accrual method of accounting pursuant to which income is accrued when furniture is shipped for purposes of its financial reports (referred to in subparagraph (1)(ii)(*a*) of this paragraph) and an accrual method of accounting pursuant to which the income is accrued when furniture is delivered and accepted for tax purposes. See § 1.446-1(c)(1)(ii). In 1974, T receives an advance payment of $8,000 from X with respect to an order of furniture to be manufactured for X for a total price of $20,000. The furniture is shipped to X in December 1974, but it is not delivered to and accepted by X until January 1975. As a result of this contract, T must include the entire advance payment in its gross income for tax purposes in 1974 pursuant to subparagraph (1)(ii)(*b*) of this paragraph. T must include the remaining $12,000 of the gross contract price in its gross income in 1975 for tax purposes.

(3) *Long-term contracts*. In the case of a taxpayer accounting for advance payments for tax purposes pursuant to a long-term contract method of accounting under § 1.460-4, or of a taxpayer accounting for advance payments with respect to a long-term contract pursuant to an accrual method of accounting referred to in the succeeding sentence, advance payments shall be included in income in the taxable year in which properly included in gross receipts pursuant to such method of accounting (without regard to the financial reporting requirement contained in subparagraph (1)(ii)(*a*) or (*b*) of this paragraph). An accrual method of accounting to which the preceding sentence applies shall consist of any method of accounting under which the income is accrued when, and costs are accumulated until, the subject matter of the contract (or, if the subject matter of the contract consists of more than one item, an item) is shipped, delivered, or accepted.

(4) *Installment method*. The financial reporting requirement of subparagraph (1)(ii)(*a*) or (*b*) of this paragraph shall not be construed to prevent the use of the installment method under section 453. See § 1.446-1(c)(1)(ii).

(c) *Exception for inventoriable goods*. (1)(i) If a taxpayer receives an advance payment in a taxable year with respect to an agreement for the sale of goods properly includible in his inventory, or with respect to an agreement (such as a gift certificate) which can be satisfied with goods or a type of goods that cannot be identified in such taxable year, and on the last day of such taxable year the taxpayer—

(*a*) Is accounting for advance payments pursuant to a method described in paragraph (b)(1)(ii) of this section for tax purposes,

(*b*) Has received "substantial advance payments" (as defined in subparagraph (3) of this paragraph) with respect to such agreement, and

(*c*) Has on hand (or available to him in such year through his normal source of supply) goods of substantially similar kind and in sufficient quantity to satisfy the agreement in such year.

then all advance payments received with respect to such agreement by the last day of the second taxable year following the year in which such substantial advance payments are received, and not previously included in income in accordance with the taxpayer's accrual method of accounting, must be included in income in such second taxable year.

(ii) If advance payments are required to be included in income in a taxable year solely by reason of subdivision (i) of this subparagraph, the taxpayer must take into account in such taxable year the costs and expenditures included in inventory at the end of such year with respect to such goods (or substantially similar goods) on hand or, if no such goods are on hand by the last day of such second taxable year, the estimated cost of goods necessary to satisfy the agreement.

(iii) Subdivision (ii) of this subparagraph does not apply if the goods or type of goods with respect to which the advance payment is received are not identifiable in the year the advance payments are required to be included in income by reason of subdivision (i) of this subparagraph (for example, where an amount is received for a gift certificate).

(2) If subparagraph (1)(i) of this paragraph is applicable to advance payments received with respect to an agreement, any advance payments received with respect to such agreement subsequent to such second taxable year must be included in gross income in the taxable year of receipt. To the extent estimated costs of goods are taken into account in a taxable year pursuant to subparagraph (1)(ii) of this paragraph, such costs may not again be taken into account in another year. In addition, any variances between the costs or estimated costs taken into account pursuant to subparagraph (1)(ii) of this paragraph and the costs actually incurred in fulfilling the taxpayer's obligations under the agreement must be taken into account as an adjustment to the cost of goods sold in the year the taxpayer completes his obligations under such agreement.

(3) For purposes of subparagraph (1) of this paragraph, a taxpayer will be considered to have

Reg. § 1.451-5(c)(3)

received "substantial advance payments" with respect to an agreement by the last day of a taxable year if the advance payments received with respect to such agreement during such taxable year plus the advance payments received prior to such taxable year pursuant to such agreement, equal or exceed the total costs and expenditures reasonably estimated as includible in inventory with respect to such agreement. Advance payments received in a taxable year with respect to an agreement (such as a gift certificate) under which the goods or type of goods to be sold are not identifiable in such year shall be treated as "substantial advance payments" when received.

(4) The application of this paragraph is illustrated by the following example:

Example. In 1971, X, a calendar year accrual method taxpayer, enters into a contract for the sale of goods (properly includible in X's inventory) with a total contract price of $100. X estimates that his total inventoriable costs and expenditures for the goods will be $50. X receives the following advance payments with respect to the contract:

1971	$35
1972	20
1973	15
1974	10
1975	10
1976	10

The goods are delivered pursuant to the customer's request in 1977. X's closing inventory for 1972 of the type of goods involved in the contract is sufficient to satisfy the contract. Since advance payments received by the end of 1972 exceed the inventoriable costs X estimates that he will incur, such payments constitute "substantial advance payments". Accordingly, all payments received by the end of 1974, the end of the second taxable year following the taxable year during which "substantial advance payments" are received, are includible in gross income for 1974. Therefore, for taxable year 1974 X must include $80 in his gross income. X must include in his cost of goods sold for 1974 the cost of such goods (or similar goods) on hand or, if no such goods are on hand, the estimated inventoriable costs necessary to satisfy the contract. Since no further deferral is allowable for such contract, X must include in his gross income for the remaining years of the contract, the advance payment received each year. Any variance between estimated costs and the costs actually incurred in fulfilling the contract is to be taken into account in 1977, when the goods are delivered. See paragraph (c)(2) of this section.

(d) *Information schedule.* If a taxpayer accounts for advance payments pursuant to paragraph (b)(1)(ii) of this section, he must attach to his income tax return for each taxable year to which such provision applies an annual information schedule reflecting the total amount of advance payments received in the taxable year, the total amount of advance payments received in prior taxable years which has not been included in gross income before the current taxable year, and the total amount of such payments received in prior taxable years which has been included in gross income for the current taxable year.

(e) *Adoption of method.* (1) For taxable years ending on or after December 31, 1969, and before January 1, 1971, a taxpayer (even if he has already filed an income tax return for a taxable year ending within such period) may secure the consent of the Commissioner to change his method of accounting for such year to a method prescribed in paragraph (b)(1)(ii) of this section in the manner prescribed in section 446 and the regulations thereunder, if an application to secure such consent is filed on Form 3115 within 180 days after March 23, 1971.

(2) A taxpayer who is already reporting his income in accordance with a method prescribed in paragraph (b)(1)(ii)(*a*) of this section need not secure the consent of the Commissioner to continue to utilize this method. However, such a taxpayer, for all taxable years ending after March 23, 1971, must comply with the requirements of paragraphs (b)(1)(ii)(*a*) (including the financial reporting requirement) and (d) (relating to an annual information schedule) of this section.

(f) *Cessation of taxpayer's liability.* If a taxpayer has adopted a method prescribed in paragraph (b)(1)(ii) of this section, and if in a taxable year the taxpayer dies, ceases to exist in a transaction other than one to which section 381(a) applies, or his liability under the agreement otherwise ends, then so much of the advance payment as was not includible in his gross income in preceding taxable years shall be included in his gross income for such taxable year.

(g) *Special rule for certain transactions concerning natural resources.* A transaction which is treated as creating a mortgage loan pursuant to section 636 and the regulations thereunder rather than as a sale shall not be considered a "sale or other disposition" within the meaning of paragraph (a)(1) of this section. Consequently, any payment received pursuant to such a transaction, which payment would otherwise qualify as an "advance payment", will not be treated as an "advance payment" for purposes of this section. [Reg. § 1.451-5.]

☐ [*T.D.* 7103, 3-23-71. *Amended by T.D.* 7397, 1-14-76; *T.D.* 8067, 12-30-85 *and T.D.* 8929, 1-10-2001.]

Reg. § 1.451-5(c)(4)

Methods of Accounting

See p. 20,601 for regulations not amended to reflect law changes

[Reg. § 1.451-6]

§ 1.451-6. **Election to include crop insurance proceeds in gross income in the taxable year following the taxable year of destruction or damage.**—(a) *In general*—(1) For taxable years ending after December 30, 1969, a taxpayer reporting gross income on the cash receipts and disbursements method of accounting may elect to include insurance proceeds received as a result of the destruction of, or damage to, crops in gross income for the taxable year following the taxable year of the destruction or damage, if the taxpayer establishes that, under the taxpayer's normal business practice, the income from those crops would have been included in gross income for any taxable year following the taxable year of the destruction or damage. However, if the taxpayer receives the insurance proceeds in the taxable year following the taxable year of the destruction or damage, the taxpayer shall include the proceeds in gross income for the taxable year of receipt without having to make an election under section 451(d) and this section. For the purposes of this section only, federal payments received as a result of destruction or damage to crops caused by drought, flood, or any other natural disaster or, the inability to plant crops because of such a natural disaster, shall be treated as insurance proceeds received as a result of destruction or damage to crops. The preceding sentence shall apply to payments that are received by the taxpayer after December 31, 1973.

(2) In the case of a taxpayer who receives insurance proceeds as a result of the destruction of, or damage to, two or more specific crops, if such proceeds may, under section 451(d) or this section, be included in gross income for the taxable year following the taxable year of such destruction or damage, and if such taxpayer makes an election under section 451(d) and this section with respect to any portion of such proceeds, then such election will be deemed to cover all of such proceeds which are attributable to crops representing a single trade or business under section 446(d). A separate election must be made with respect to insurance proceeds attributable to each crop which represents a separate trade or business under section 446(d).

(b)(1) *Time and manner of making election.* The election to include in gross income insurance proceeds received as a result of destruction of, or damage to, the taxpayer's crops in the taxable year following the taxable year of such destruction or damage shall be made by means of a statement attached to the taxpayer's return (or an amended return) for the taxable year of destruction or damage. The statement shall include the name and address of the taxpayer (or his duly authorized representative), and shall set forth the following information:

(i) A declaration that the taxpayer is making an election under section 451(d) and this section;

(ii) Identification of the specific crop or crops destroyed or damaged;

(iii) A declaration that under the taxpayer's normal business practice the income derived from the crops which were destroyed or damaged would have been included in his gross income for a taxable year following the taxable year of such destruction or damage;

(iv) The cause of destruction or damage of crops and the date or dates on which such destruction or damage occurred;

(v) The total amount of payments received from insurance carriers, itemized with respect to each specific crop and with respect to the date each payment was received;

(vi) The name(s) of the insurance carrier or carriers from whom payments were received.

(2) *Scope of election.* Once made, an election under section 451(d) is binding for the taxable year for which made unless the district director consents to a revocation of such election. Requests for consent to revoke an election under section 451(d) shall be made by means of a letter to the district director for the district in which the taxpayer is required to file his return, setting forth the taxpayer's name, address, and identification number, the year for which it is desired to revoke the election, and the reasons therefor. [Reg. § 1.451-6.]

☐ [T.D. 7097, 3-18-71. Amended by T.D. 7526, 12-23-77 and T.D. 8429, 8-25-92.]

[Reg. § 1.451-7]

§ 1.451-7. **Election relating to livestock sold on account of drought.**—(a) *In general.* Section 451(e) provides that for taxable years beginning after December 31, 1975, a taxpayer whose principal trade or business is farming (within the meaning of § 6420(c)(3)) and who reports taxable income on the cash receipts and disbursements method of accounting may elect to defer for one year a certain portion of income. The income which may be deferred is the amount of gain realized during the taxable year from the sale or exchange of that number of livestock sold or exchanged solely on account of a drought which caused an area to be designated as eligible for assistance by the Federal Government (regardless of whether the designation is made by the President or by an agency or department of the Federal Government). That number is equal to the

Reg. § 1.451-7(a)

excess of the number of livestock sold or exchanged over the number which would have been sold or exchanged had the taxpayer followed its usual business practices in the absence of such drought. For example, if in the past it has been a taxpayer's practice to sell or exchange annually 400 head of beef cattle but due to qualifying drought conditions 550 head were sold in a given taxable year, only income from the sale of 150 head may qualify for deferral under this section. The election is not available with respect to livestock described in section 1231(b)(3) (relating to cattle, horses (and other livestock) held by the taxpayer for 24 months (12 months) and used for draft, breeding, dairy, or sporting purposes).

(b) *Usual business practice.* The determination of the number of animals which a taxpayer would have sold if it had followed its usual business practice in the absence of drought will be made in light of all the facts and circumstances. In the case of taxpayers who have not established a usual business practice, reliance will be placed upon the usual business practice of similarly situated taxpayers in the same general region as the taxpayer.

(c) *Special rules.* (1) *Connection with drought area.* To qualify under section 451(e) and this section, the livestock need not be raised, and the sale or exchange need not take place, in a drought area. However, the sale or exchange of the livestock must occur solely on account of drought conditions, the existence of which affected the water, grazing, or other requirements of the livestock so as to necessitate their sale or exchange.

(2) *Sale prior to designation of area as eligible for Federal assistance.* The provisions of this section will apply regardless of whether all or a portion of the excess number of animals were sold or exchanged before an area becomes eligible for Federal assistance, so long as the drought which caused such dispositions also caused the area to be designated as eligible for Federal assistance.

(d) *Classifications of livestock with respect to which the election may be made.* The election to have the provisions of section 451(e) apply must be made separately for each broad generic classification of animals (*e.g.,* hogs, sheep, cattle) for which the taxpayer wishes the provisions to apply. Separate elections shall not be made solely by reason of the animals' age, sex, or breed.

(e) *Computation*—(1) *Determination of amount deferred.* The amount of income which may be deferred for a classification of livestock pursuant to this section shall be determined in the following manner. The total amount of income realized from the sale or exchange of all livestock in the classification during the taxable year shall be divided by the total number of all such livestock sold. The resulting quotient shall then be multiplied by the excess number of such livestock sold on account of drought.

(2) *Example.* The provisions of this paragraph may be illustrated by the following example:

Example. A, a calendar year taxpayer, normally sells 100 head of beef cattle a year. As the result of drought conditions existing during 1976, A sells 135 head during that year. A realizes $35,100 of income from the sale of the 135 head. On August 9, 1976, as a result of the drought, the affected area was declared a disaster area thereby eligible for Federal assistance. The amount of income which A may defer until 1977, presuming the other provisions of this section are met, is determined as follows:

$$\frac{\$35{,}100 \text{ (Total income from sales of beef cattle)}}{135 \text{ (total number of beef cattle sold)}} \times 35 \text{ (excess number of beef cattle sold, i.e. } 135 - 100)$$

$$= \$9{,}100 \text{ (amount which A may defer until 1977)}$$

(f) *Successive elections.* If a taxpayer makes an election under section 451(e) for successive years, the amount deferred from one year to the next year shall not be deemed to have been received from the sale or exchange of livestock during the later year. In addition, in determining the taxpayer's normal business practice for the later year, earlier years for which an election under section 451(e) was made shall not be considered.

(g) *Time and manner of making election.* The election provided for in this section must be made by the later of (1) the due date for filing the income tax return (determined with regard to any extensions of time granted the taxpayer for filing such return) for the taxable year in which the early sale of livestock occurs, or (2) March 27, 1978. The election must be made separately for each taxable year to which it is to apply. It must be made by attaching a statement to the return or an amended return for such taxable year. The statement shall include the name and address of the taxpayer and shall set forth the following information for each classification of livestock for which the election is made:

(1) A declaration that the taxpayer is making an election under section 451(e);

Reg. § 1.451-7(b)

(2) Evidence of the existence of the drought conditions which forced the early sale or exchange of the livestock and the date, if known, on which an area was designated as eligible for assistance by the Federal Government as a result of the drought conditions;

(3) A statement explaining the relationship of the drought area to the taxpayer's early sale or exchange of the livestock;

(4) The total number of animals sold in each of the three preceding years;

(5) The number of animals which would have been sold in the taxable year had the taxpayer followed its normal business practice in the absence of drought;

(6) The total number of animals sold, and the number sold on account of drought, during the taxable year; and

(7) A computation, pursuant to paragraph (e) of this section, of the amount of income to be deferred for each such classification.

(h) *Revocation of election.* Once an election under this section is made for a taxable year, it may be revoked only with the approval of the Commissioner.

(i) *Cross reference.* For provisions relating to the involuntary conversion of livestock sold on account of drought see section 1033(e) and the regulations thereunder. [Reg. § 1.451-7.]

☐ [T.D. 7526, 12-23-77.]

[Reg. § 15A.453-0]

§ 15A.453-0. **Taxable years affected (Temporary).**—(a) *In general.* Except as otherwise provided, the provisions of § 15A.453-1(a) through (e) generally apply to installment method reporting for sales of real property and casual sales of personal property occurring after October 19, 1980. See 26 CFR § 1.453-1 (rev. as of April 1, 1980) for the provisions relating to installment method reporting for sales of real property and casual sales before October 20, 1980 (except as provided in paragraph (b) of this section) and for provisions relating to installment sales by dealers in personal property occurring before October 20, 1980.

(b) *Certain limitations.* The provisions of prior law (section 453(b) of the Internal Revenue Code of 1954, in effect as of October 18, 1980) which required that the buyer receive no more than 30 percent of the selling price in the taxable year of the installment sale and that at least two payments be received shall not apply to reporting for casual installment sales of personal property and installment sales of real property occurring in a taxable year ending after October 19, 1980. [Temporary Reg. § 15A.453-0.]

☐ [T.D. 7768, 1-30-81.]

[Reg. § 15A.453-1]

§ 15A.453-1. **Installment method reporting for sales of real property and casual sales of personal property (Temporary).**—(a) *In general.* Unless the taxpayer otherwise elects in the manner prescribed in paragraph (d)(3) of this section, income from a sale of real property or a casual sale of personal property, where any payment is to be received in a taxable year after the year of sale, is to be reported on the installment method.

(b) *Installment sale defined*—(1) *In general.* The term "installment sale" means a disposition of property (except as provided in paragraph (b)(4) of this section) where at least one payment is to be received after the close of the taxable year in which the disposition occurs. The term "installment sale" includes dispositions from which payment is to be received in a lump sum in a taxable year subsequent to the year of sale. For purposes of this paragraph, the taxable year in which payments are to be received is to be determined without regard to section 453(e) (relating to related party sales), section (f)(3) (relating to the definition of a "payment") and section (g) (relating to sales of depreciable property to a spouse or 80-percent-owned entity).

(2) *Installment method defined*—(i) *In general.* Under the installment method, the amount of any payment which is income to the taxpayer is that portion of the installment payment received in that year which the gross profit realized or to be realized bears to the total contract price (the "gross profit ratio"). See paragraph (c) of this section for rules describing installment method reporting of contingent payment sales.

(ii) *Selling price defined.* The term "selling price" means the gross selling price without reduction to reflect any existing mortgage or other encumbrance on the property (whether assumed or taken subject to by the buyer) and, for installment sales in taxable years ending after October 19, 1980, without reduction to reflect any selling expenses. Neither interest, whether stated or unstated, nor original issue discount is considered to be a part of the selling price. See paragraph (c) of this section for rules describing installment method reporting of contingent payment sales.

(iii) *Contract price defined.* The term "contract price" means the total contract price equal to selling price reduced by that portion of any qualifying indebtedness (as defined in paragraph (b)(2)(iv) of this section), assumed or taken subject to by the buyer, which does not exceed the seller's basis in the property (adjusted, for installment sales in taxable years ending after October 19, 1980, to reflect commissions and other selling expenses as provided in paragraph (b)(2)(v) of this section). See paragraph (c) of this section for rules describing installment method reporting of contingent payment sales.

(iv) *Qualifying indebtedness.* The term "qualifying indebtedness" means a mortgage or other indebtedness encumbering the property and indebtedness, not secured by the property but incurred or assumed by the purchaser incident to the purchaser's acquisition, holding, or operation in the ordinary course of business or investment, of the property. The term "qualifying indebtedness" does not include an obligation of the taxpayer incurred incident to the disposition of the property (*e.g.,* legal fees relating to the taxpayer's sale of the property) or an obligation functionally unrelated to the acquisition, holding, or operating of the property (*e.g.,* the taxpayer's medical bill). Any obligation created subsequent to the taxpayer's acquisition of the property and incurred or assumed by the taxpayer or placed as an encumbrance on the property in contemplation of disposition of the property is not qualifying indebtedness if the arrangement results in accelerating recovery of the taxpayer's basis in the installment sale.

(v) *Gross profit defined.* The term "gross profit" means the selling price less the adjusted basis as defined in section 1011 and the regulations thereunder. For sales in taxable years ending after October 19, 1980, in the case of sales of real property by a person other than a dealer and casual sales of personal property, commissions and other selling expenses shall be added to basis for purposes of determining the proportion of payments which is gross profit attributable to the disposition. Such additions to basis will not be deemed to affect the taxpayer's holding period in the transferred property.

(3) *Payment*—(i) *In general.* Except as provided in paragraph (e) of this section (relating to purchaser evidences of indebtedness payable on demand or readily tradable), the term "payment" does not include the receipt of evidences of indebtedness of the person acquiring the property ("installment obligation"), whether or not payment of such indebtedness is guaranteed by a third party (including a government agency). For special rules regarding the receipt of an evidence of indebtedness of a transferee of a qualified intermediary, see §§ 1.1031(b)-2(b) and 1.1031(k)-1(j)(2)(iii) of this chapter. A standby letter of credit (as defined in paragraph (b)(3)(iii) of this section) shall be treated as a third party guarantee. Payments include amounts actually or constructively received in the taxable year under an installment obligation. For a special rule regarding a transfer of property to a qualified intermediary followed by the sale of such property by the qualified intermediary, see § 1.1031(k)-1(j)(2)(ii) of this chapter. Receipt of an evidence of indebtedness which is secured directly or indirectly by cash or a cash equivalent, such as a bank certificate of deposit or a treasury note, will be treated as the receipt of payment. For a special rule regarding a transfer of property in exchange for an obligation that is secured by cash or a cash equivalent held in a qualified escrow account or a qualified trust, see § 1.1031(k)-1(j)(2)(i) of this chapter. Payment may be received in cash or other property, including foreign currency, marketable securities, and evidences of indebtedness which are payable on demand or readily tradable. However, for special rules relating to the receipt of certain property with respect to which gain is not recognized, see paragraph (f) of this section (relating to transactions described in sections 351, 356(a) and 1031). Except as provided in § 15A.453-2 of these regulations (relating to distributions of installment obligations in corporate liquidations described in section 337), payment includes receipt of an evidence of indebtedness of a person other than the person acquiring the property from the taxpayer. For purposes of determining the amount of payment received in the taxable year, the amount of qualifying indebtedness (as defined in paragraph (b)(2)(iv) of this section) assumed or taken subject to by the person acquiring the property shall be included only to the extent that it exceeds the basis of the property (determined after adjustment to reflect selling expenses). For purposes of the preceding sentence, an arrangement under which the taxpayer's liability on qualifying indebtedness is eliminated incident to the disposition (*e.g.,* a novation) shall be treated as an assumption of the qualifying indebtedness. If the taxpayer sells property to a creditor of the taxpayer and indebtedness of the taxpayer is cancelled in consideration of the sale, such cancellation shall be treated as payment. To the extent that cancellation is not in consideration of the sale, see §§ 1.61-12(b)(1) and 1.1001-2(a)(2) relating to discharges of indebtedness. If the taxpayer sells property which is encumbered by a mortgage or other indebtedness on which the taxpayer is not personally liable, and the person acquiring the property is the obligee, the taxpayer shall be treated as having received payment in the amount of such indebtedness.

(ii) *Wrap-around mortgage.* This paragraph (b)(3)(ii) shall apply generally to any installment sale after March 4, 1981 unless the

Reg. § 15A.453-1(b)(3)

installment sale was completed before June 1, 1981 pursuant to a written obligation binding on the seller that was executed on or before March 4, 1981. A "wrap-around mortgage" means an agreement in which the buyer initially does not assume and purportedly does not take subject to part or all of the mortgage or other indebtedness encumbering the property ("wrapped indebtedness") and, instead, the buyer issues to the seller an installment obligation the principal amount of which reflects such wrapped indebtedness. Ordinarily, the seller will use payments received on the installment obligation to service the wrapped indebtedness. The wrapped indebtedness shall be deemed to have been taken subject to even though title to the property has not passed in the year of sale and even though the seller remains liable for payments on the wrapped indebtedness. In the hands of the seller, the wrap-around installment obligation shall have a basis equal to the seller's basis in the property which was the subject of the installment sale, increased by the amount of gain recognized in the year of sale, and decreased by the amount of cash and the fair market value of other nonqualifying property received in the year of sale. For purposes of this paragraph (b)(3)(ii), the amount of any indebtedness assumed or taken subject to by the buyer (other than wrapped indebtedness) is to be treated as cash received by the seller in the year of sale. Therefore, except as otherwise required by section 483 or 1232, the gross profit ratio with respect to the wrap-around installment obligation is a fraction, the numerator of which is the face value of the obligation less the taxpayer's basis in the obligation and the denominator of which is the face value of the obligation.

(iii) *Standby letter of credit.* The term "standby letter of credit" means a non-negotiable, nontransferable (except together with the evidence of indebtedness which it secures) letter of credit, issued by a bank or other financial institution, which serves as a guarantee of the evidence of indebtedness which is secured by the letter of credit. Whether or not the letter of credit explicitly states it is non-negotiable and nontransferable, it will be treated as non-negotiable and nontransferable if applicable local law so provides. The mere right of the secured party (under applicable local law) to transfer the proceeds of a letter of credit shall be disregarded in determining whether the instrument qualifies as a standby letter of credit. A letter of credit is not a standby letter of credit if it may be drawn upon in the absence of default in payment of the underlying evidence of indebtedness.

(4) *Exceptions.* The term "installment sale" does not include, and the provisions of section 453 do not apply to, dispositions of personal property on the installment plan by a person who regularly sells or otherwise disposes of personal property on the installment plan, or to dispositions of personal property of a kind which is required to be included in the inventory of the taxpayer if on hand at the close of the taxable year. See section 453A and the regulations thereunder for rules relating to installment sales by dealers in personal property. A dealer in real property or a farmer who is not required under his method of accounting to maintain inventories may report the gain on the installment method under section 453.

(5) *Examples.* The following examples illustrate installment method reporting under this section:

Example (1). In 1980, A, a calendar year taxpayer, sells Blackacre, an unencumbered capital asset in A's hands, to B for $100,000: $10,000 down and the remainder payable in equal annual installments over the next 9 years, together with adequate stated interest. A's basis in Blackacre, exclusive of selling expenses, is $38,000. Selling expenses paid by A are $2,000. Therefore, the gross profit is $60,000 ($100,000 selling price — $40,000 basis inclusive of selling expenses). The gross profit ratio is 3/5 (gross profit of $60,000 divided by $100,000 contract price). Accordingly, $6,000 (3/5 of $10,000) of each $10,000 payment received is gain attributable to the sale and $4,000 ($10,000 — $6,000) is recovery of basis. The interest received in addition to principal is ordinary income to A.

Example (2). C sells Whiteacre to D for a selling price of $160,000. Whiteacre is encumbered by a longstanding mortgage in the principal amount of $60,000. D will assume or take subject to the $60,000 mortgage and pay the remaining $100,000 in 10 equal annual installments together with adequate stated interest. C's basis in Whiteacre is $90,000. There are no selling expenses. The contract price is $100,000, the $160,000 selling price reduced by the mortgage of $60,000 assumed or taken subject to. Gross profit is $70,000 ($160,000 selling price less C's basis of $90,000). C's gross profit ratio is 7/10 (gross profit of $70,000 divided by $100,000 contract price). Thus, $7,000 (7/10 of $10,000) of each $10,000 annual payment is gain attributable to the sale, and $3,000 ($10,000 — $7,000) is recovery of basis.

Example (3). The facts are the same as in example (2), except that C's basis in the land is $40,000. In the year of the sale C is deemed to have received payment of $20,000 ($60,000 — $40,000, the amount by which the mortgage D assumed or took subject to exceeds C's basis). Since basis is fully recovered in the year of sale, the gross profit ratio is 1 ($120,000/$120,000) and C will report 100% of the $20,000 deemed payment in the year of sale and each $10,000 annual payment as gain attributable to the sale.

Example (4). E sells Blackacre, an unencumbered capital gain property in E's hands, to F on January 2, 1981. F makes a cash down payment of $500,000 and issues a note to E obliging F to pay an additional $500,000 on the fifth anniversary date. The note does not require a payment of interest. In determining selling price, section 483 will apply to recharacterize as interest a portion of the $500,000 future payment. Assume that under section 483 and the applicable regulations $193,045 is treated as total unstated interest, and the selling price is $806,955 ($1 million less unstated interest). Assuming E's basis (including selling expenses) in Blackacre is $200,000, gross profit is $606,955 ($806,955 − $200,000) and the gross profit ratio is 75.21547%. Accordingly, of the $500,000 cash down payment received by E in 1981, $376,077 (75.21547% of $500,000) is gain attributable to the sale and $123,923 is recovery of basis ($500,000 − $376,077).

Example (5). In 1982, G sells to H Blackacre, which is encumbered by a first mortgage with a principal amount of $500,000 and a second mortgage with a principal amount of $400,000, for a selling price of $2 million. G's basis in Blackacre is $700,000. Under the agreement between G and H, passage of title is deferred and H does not assume and purportedly does not take subject to either mortgage in the year of sale. H pays G $200,000 in cash and issues a wrap-around mortgage note with a principal amount of $1,800,000 bearing adequate stated interest. H is deemed to have acquired Blackacre subject to the first and second mortgages (wrapped indebtedness) totalling $900,000. The contract price is $1,300,000 (selling price of $2 million less $700,000 mortgages within the seller's basis assumed or taken subject to). Gross profit is also $1,300,000 (selling price of $2 million less $700,000 basis). Accordingly in the year of sale, the gross profit ratio is 1 ($1,300,000/$1,300,000). Payment in the year of sale is $400,000 ($200,000 cash received plus $200,000 mortgage in excess of basis ($900,000 − $700,000)). Therefore, G recognizes $400,000 gain in the year of sale ($400,000 × 1). In the hands of G the wrap-around installment obligation has a basis of $900,000, equal to G's basis in Blackacre ($700,000) increased by the gain recognized by G in the year of sale ($400,000) reduced by the cash received by G in the year of sale ($200,000). G's gross profit with respect to the note is $900,000 ($1,800,000 face amount less $900,000 basis in the note) and G's contract price with respect to the note is its face amount of $1,800,000. Therefore, the gross profit ratio with respect to the note is 1/2 ($900,000/$1,800,000).

Example (6). The facts are the same as example (5) except that under the terms of the agreement H assumes the $500,000 first mortgage on Blackacre. H does not assume and purportedly does not take subject to the $400,000 second mortgage on Blackacre. The wrap-around installment obligation issued by H to G has a face amount of $1,300,000. The tax results in the year of sale to G are the same as example (5) ($400,000 payment received and gain recognized). In the hands of G, basis in the wrap-around installment obligation is $400,000 ($700,000 basis in Blackacre plus $400,000 gain recognized in the year of sale minus $700,000 ($200,000 cash received and $500,000 treated as cash received as a result of H's assumption of the first mortgage)). G's gross profit with respect to the note is $900,000 ($1,300,000 face amount of the wrap-around installment obligation less $400,000 basis in that note) and G's contract price with respect to the note is its face value of $1,300,000. Therefore, the gross profit ratio with respect to the note is 9/13

$$\frac{\$\ 900{,}000)}{(\$1{,}300{,}000)}.$$

Example (7). A sells the stock of X corporation to B for a $1 million installment obligation payable in equal annual installments over the next 10 years with adequate stated interest. The installment obligation is secured by a standby letter of credit (within the meaning of paragraph (b)(3)(iii) of this section) issued by M bank. Under the agreement between B and M bank, B is required to maintain a compensating balance in an account B maintains with M bank and is required by the M bank to post additional collateral, which may include cash or a cash equivalent, with M bank. Under neither the standby letter of credit nor any other agreement or arrangement is A granted a direct lien upon or other security interest in such cash or cash equivalent collateral. Receipt of B's installment obligation secured by the standby letter of credit will not be treated as the receipt of payment by A.

Example (8). The facts are the same as in example (7) except that the standby letter of credit is in the drawable sum of $600,000. To secure fully its $1 million note issued to A, B deposits in escrow $400,000 in cash and Treasury bills. Under the escrow agreement, upon default in payment of the note A may look directly to the escrowed collateral. Receipt of B's installment obligation will be treated as the receipt payment by A in the sum of $400,000.

(c) *Contingent payment sales*—(1) *In general.* Unless the taxpayer otherwise elects in the manner prescribed in paragraph (d)(3) of this section, contingent payment sales are to be reported on the installment method. As used in this section, the term "contingent payment sale" means a sale or other disposition of property in which the aggregate selling price cannot be determined by the close of the taxable year in which such sale or other disposition occurs.

The term "contingent payment sale" does not include transactions with respect to which the installment obligation represents, under applicable principles of tax law, a retained interest in the property which is the subject of the transaction, an interest in a joint venture or a partnership, an equity interest in a corporation or similar transactions, regardless of the existence of a stated maximum selling price or a fixed payment term. See paragraph (c)(8) of this section, describing the extent to which the regulations under section 385 apply to the determination of whether an installment obligation represents an equity interest in a corporation.

This paragraph prescribes the rules to be applied in allocating the taxpayer's basis (including selling expenses except for selling expenses of dealers in real estate) to payments received and to be received in a contingent payment sale. The rules are designed appropriately to distinguish contingent payment sales for which a maximum selling price is determinable, sales for which a maximum selling price is not determinable but the time over which payments will be received is determinable, and sales for which neither a maximum selling price nor a definite payment term is determinable. In addition, rules are prescribed under which, in appropriate circumstances, the taxpayer will be permitted to recover basis under an income forecast computation.

(2) *Stated maximum selling price*—(i) *In general.* (A) A contingent payment sale will be treated as having a stated maximum selling price if, under the terms of the agreement, the maximum amount of sale proceeds that may be received by the taxpayer can be determined as of the end of the taxable year in which the sale or other disposition occurs. The stated maximum selling price shall be determined by assuming that all of the contingencies contemplated by the agreement are met or otherwise resolved in a manner that will maximize the selling price and accelerate payments to the earliest date or dates permitted under the agreement. Except as provided in paragraph (c)(2)(ii) and (7) of this section (relating to certain payment recomputations), the taxpayer's basis shall be allocated to payments received and to be received under a stated maximum selling price agreement by treating the stated maximum selling price as the selling price for purposes of paragraph (b) of this section. The stated maximum selling price, as initially determined, shall thereafter be treated as the selling price unless and until that maximum amount is reduced, whether pursuant to the terms of the original agreement, by subsequent amendment, by application of the payment recharacterization rule (described in paragraph (c)(2)(ii) of this section), or by a subsequent supervening event such as bankruptcy of the obligor. When the maximum amount is subsequently reduced, the gross profit ratio will be recomputed with respect to payments received in or after the taxable year in which an event requiring reduction occurs. If, however, application of the foregoing rules in a particular case would substantially and inappropriately accelerate or defer recovery of the taxpayer's basis, a special rule will apply. See paragraph (c)(7) of this section.

(B) The following examples illustrate the provisions of paragraph (c)(2)(i) of this section. In each example, it is assumed that application of the rules illustrated will not substantially and inappropriately defer or accelerate recovery of the taxpayer's basis.

Example (1). A sells all of the stock of X corporation to B for $100,000 payable at closing plus an amount equal to 5% of the net profits of X for each of the next nine years, the contingent payments to be made annually together with adequate stated interest. The agreement provides that the maximum amount A may receive, inclusive of the $100,000 down payment but exclusive of interest, shall be $2,000,000. A's basis in the stock of X inclusive of selling expenses, is $200,000. Selling price and contract price are considered to be $2,000,000. Gross profit is $1,800,000, and the gross profit ratio is 9/10 ($1,800,000/$2,000,000). Accordingly, of the $100,000 received by A in the year of sale, $90,000 is reportable as gain attributable to the sale and $10,000 is recovery of basis.

Example (2). C owns Blackacre which is encumbered by a long-standing mortgage of $100,000. On January 15, 1981, C sells Blackacre to D under the following payment arrangement: $100,000 in cash on closing; nine equal annual installment payments of $100,000 commencing January 15, 1982; and nine annual payments (the first to be made on March 30, 1982) equal to 5% of the gross annual rental receipts from Blackacre generated during the preceding calendar year. The agreement provides that each deferred payment shall be accompanied by a payment of interest calculated at the rate of 12% per annum and that the maximum amount payable to C under

Reg. § 15A.453-1(c)(2)

the agreement (exclusive of interest) shall be $2,100,000. The agreement also specifies that D will assume the long-standing mortgage. C's basis (inclusive of selling expenses) in Blackacre is $300,000. Accordingly, selling price is $2,100,000 and contract price is $2,000,000 (selling price of $2,100,000 less the $100,000 mortgage). The gross profit ratio is 9/10 (gross profit of $1,800,000 divided by $2,000,000 contract price). Of the $100,000 cash payment received by C in 1981, $90,000 is gain attributable to the sale of Blackacre and $10,000 is recovery of basis.

(ii) *Certain interest recomputations.* When interest is stated in the contingent price sale agreement at a rate equal to or greater than the applicable prescribed test rate referred to in § 1.483-1(d)(1)(ii) and such stated interest is payable in addition to the amounts otherwise payable under the agreement, such stated interest is not considered a part of the selling price. In other circumstances (i.e., section 483 is applicable because no interest is stated or interest is stated below the applicable test rate, or interest is stated under a payment recharacterization provision of the sale agreement), the special rule set forth in this (ii) shall be applied in the initial computation and subsequent recomputations of selling price, contract price, and gross profit ratio. The special rule is referred to in this section as the "price-interest recomputation rule." As used in this section, the term "payment recharacterization" refers to a contractual arrangement under which a computed amount otherwise payable as part of the selling price is denominated an interest payment. The amount of unstated interest determined under section 483 or (if section 483 is inapplicable in the particular case) the amount of interest determined under a payment recharacterization arrangement is collectively referred to in this section as "internal interest" amounts. The price-interest recomputation rule is applicable to any stated maximum selling price agreement which contemplates receipt of internal interest by the taxpayer. Under the rule, stated maximum selling price will be determined as of the end of the taxpayer's taxable year in which the sale or other disposition occurs, taking into account all events which have occurred and are subject to prompt subsequent calculation and verification and assuming that all amounts that may become payable under the agreement will be paid on the earliest date or dates permitted under the agreement. With respect to the year of sale, the amount (if any) of internal interest then shall be determined taking account of the respective components of that calculation. The maximum amount initially calculated, minus the internal interest so determined, is the initial stated maximum selling price under the price-interest recomputation rule. For each subsequent taxable year, stated maximum selling price (and thus selling price, contract price, and gross profit ratio) shall be recomputed, taking into account all events which have occurred and are subject to prompt subsequent calculation and verification and assuming that all amounts that may become payable under the agreement will be paid on the earliest date or dates permitted under the agreement. The redetermined gross profit ratio, adjusted to reflect payments received and gain recognized in prior taxable years, shall be applied to payments received in that taxable year.

(iii) *Examples.* The following examples illustrate installment method reporting of a contingent payment sale under which there is a stated maximum selling price. In each example, it is assumed that application of the rules described will not substantially and inappropriately defer or accelerate recovery of the taxpayer's basis.

Example (1). A owns all of the stock of X corporation with a basis to A of $20 million. On July 1, 1981, A sells the stock of X to B under an agreement calling for fifteen annual payments respectively equal to 5% of the net profits of X earned in the immediately preceding fiscal year beginning with the fiscal year ending March 31, 1982. Each payment is to be made on the following June 15th, commencing June 15, 1982, together with adequate stated interest. The agreement specifies that the maximum amount (exclusive of interest) payable to A shall not exceed $60 million. Since stated interest is payable as an addition to the selling price and the specified rate is not below the section 483 test rate, there is no internal interest under the agreement. The stated maximum selling price is $60 million. The gross profit ratio is 2/3 (gross profit of $40 million divided by $60 million contract price). Thus, if on June 15, 1982, A receives a payment of $3 million (exclusive of interest) under the agreement, in that year A will report $2 million ($3 million × 2/3) as gain attributable to the sale, and $1 million as recovery of basis.

Example (2). (i) The facts are the same as in example (1) except that the agreement does not call for the payment of any stated interest but does provide for an initial cash payment of $3 million on July 1, 1981. The maximum amount payable, including the $3 million initial payment, remains $60 million. Since section 483 will apply to each payment received by A more than one year following the date of sale (section 483 is inapplicable to the contingent payment that will be received on June 15, 1982 since that date is within one year following the July 1, 1981 sale

Reg. § 15A.453-1(c)(2)

date), the agreement contemplates internal interest and the price-interest recomputation rule is applicable. Under the rule, an initial determination must be made for A's taxable year 1981. On December 31, 1981, the last day of the taxable year, no events with regard to the first fiscal year have occurred which are subject to prompt subsequent calculation and verification because that fiscal year will end March 31, 1982. Under the price-interest recomputation rule, on December 31, 1981 A is required to assume that the maximum amount subsequently payable under the agreement ($57 million, equal to $60 million less the $3 million initial cash payment received by A in 1981) will be paid on the earliest date permissible under the agreement, *i.e.*, on June 15, 1982. Since no part of a payment received on that date would be treated as interest under section 483, the initial stated maximum selling price, applicable to A's 1981 tax calculation, is deemed to be $60 million. Thus, the 1981 gross profit ratio is 2/3 and for the taxable year 1981 A will report $2 million as gain attributable to the sale.

(ii) The net profits of X for its fiscal year ending March 31, 1982 are $100 million. On June 15, 1982 A receives a payment from B equal to 5% of that amount, or $6 million. On December 31, 1982, A knows that the maximum amount he may subsequently receive under the agreement is $51 million, and A is required to assume that this amount will be paid to him on the earliest permissible date, June 15, 1983. Section 483 does not treat as interest any part of the $6 million received by A on June 15, 1982, but section 483 will treat as unstated interest a computed part of the $51 million it is assumed A will receive on June 15, 1983. Assuming that under the tables in the regulations under section 483, it is determined that the principal component of a payment received more than 21 months but less than 27 months after the date of sale is considered to be .82270, $41,957,700 of the presumed $51 million payment will be treated as principal. The balance of $9,042,300 is interest. Accordingly, in A's 1982 tax calculations stated maximum selling price will be $50,957,700, which amount is equal to the stated maximum selling price that was determined in the 1981 tax calculations ($60 million) reduced by the section 483 interest component of the $6 million payment received by A in 1982 ($0) and further reduced by the section 483 interest component of the $51 million presumed payment to be received by A on June 15, 1983 ($9,042,300). Similarly, in determining gross profit for 1982 tax calculations, the gross profit of $40 million determined in the 1981 tax calculations must be reduced by the same section 483 interest amounts, yielding a recomputed gross profit of $30,957,700 ($40,000,000 − $9,042,300). Further, since prior to 1982 A received payment under the agreement (1981 payment of $3 million of which $2 million was profit), the appropriate amounts must be subtracted in the 1982 tax calculation. The total previously received selling price payment of $3 million is subtracted from the recomputed maximum selling price of $50,957,700, yielding an adjusted selling price of $47,957,700. The total previously recognized gain of $2 million is subtracted from the recomputed maximum gross profit of $30,957,700, yielding an adjusted gross profit of $28,957,700. The gross profit percentage applicable to 1982 tax calculations thus is determined to be 60.38175%, equal to the quotient of dividing the adjusted gross profit of $28,957,700 by the adjusted selling price of $47,957,700. Accordingly, of the $6 million received by A in 1982, no part of which is unstated interest under section 483, A will report $3,622,905 (60.38175% of $6 million) as gain attributable to the sale and $2,377,095 ($6,000,000 − $3,622,905) as recovery of basis.

(iii) The net profits of X for its fiscal year ending March 31, 1983 are $200 million. On June 15, 1983 A receives a payment from B equal to $10 million. On December 31, 1983, A knows that the maximum amount he may subsequently receive under the agreement is $41 million, and A is required to assume that this amount will be paid to him on the earliest permissible date, June 15, 1984. Assuming that under the tables in the regulations under section 483 it is determined that the principal component of a payment received more than 33 months but less than 39 months after the date of sale is .74622, $30,595,020 of the presumed $41 million ($51 million − $10 million) payment will be treated as principal and $10,404,980 is interest. Based upon the assumed factor for 21 months but less than 27 months (.82270) $8,227,000 of the $10 million payment is principal and $1,733,000 is interest. Accordingly, in A's 1983 tax calculations stated maximum selling price will be $47,822,020, which amount is equal to the stated maximum selling price determined in the 1981 calculation ($60 million) reduced by the section 483 interest component of the $6 million 1982 payment ($0), the section 483 interest component of the 1983 payment ($1,773,000) and by the section 483 interest component of the presumed $41 million payment to be received in 1984 ($10,404,980). The recomputed gross profit is $27,822,020 ($40 million − $10,404,980 − $1,773,000). The previously reported payments must be deducted for the 1983 calculation. Selling price is reduced to $38,822,020 by subtracting the $3 million 1981 payment and the $6 million 1982 payment

Reg. § 15A.453-1(c)(2)

($47,822,020 − $9 million) and gross profit is reduced to $22,199,115 by subtracting the 1981 profit of $2 million and the 1982 profit of $3,622,905 ($27,822,020 − $5,622,905), yielding a gross profit percentage of 57.18176% ($22,199,115/$38,822,020). Accordingly, of the $10 million received in 1983, A will report $1,773,000 as interest under section 483, and of the remaining principal component of $8,227,000, $4,704,343 as gain attributable to the sale ($8,227,000 × 57.18176%) and $3,522,657 ($8,227,000 − $4,704,343) as recovery of basis.

Example (3). The facts are the same as in example (2) except that X is a collapsible corporation as defined in section 341(b)(1) and no limitation or exception under section 341(d), (e), or (f) is applicable. Under section 341(a), all of A's gain on the sale will be ordinary income. Accordingly, section 483 will not apply to treat as interest any part of the payments to be received by A under his agreement with B. See section 483(f)(3). Therefore, the price-interest recomputation rule is inapplicable and the tax results to A in each year in which payment is received will be determined in a manner consistent with example (1).

Example (4). The facts are the same as in example (2) (maximum amount payable under the agreement $60 million) except that the agreement between A and B contains the following "payment recharacterization" provision:

"Any payment made more than one year after the (July 1, 1981) date of sale shall be composed of an interest element and a principal element, the interest element being computed on the principal element at an interest rate of 9% per annum computed from the date of sale to the date of payment."

The results reached in example (2), with respect to the $3 million initial cash payment received by A in 1981 remain the same because, under the payment recharacterization formula, no amount received or assumed to be received prior to July 1, 1982 is treated as interest. The 1982 tax computation method described in example (2) is equally applicable to the $6 million payment received in 1982. However, the adjusted gross profit ratio determined in this example (4) will differ from the ratio determined in example (2). The difference is attributable to the difference between a 9% stated interest rate calculation (in this example (4)) and the compound rate of unstated interest required under section 483 and used in calculating the results in example (2).

Example (5). The facts are the same as in example (1). In 1992 X is adjudged a bankrupt and it is determined that, in and after 1992, B will not be required to make any further payments under the agreement, *i.e.*, B's contingent payment obligation held by A now has become worthless. Assume that A previously received aggregate payments (exclusive of interest) of $45 million and out of those payments recovered $15 million of A's total $20 million basis. For 1992 A will report a loss of $5 million attributable to the sale, taken at the time determined to be appropriate under the rules generally applicable to worthless debts.

Example (6). (i) C owns all of the stock of Z corporation, a calendar year taxpayer. On July 1, 1981, C sells the stock of Z to D under an agreement calling for payment, each year for the next ten years, of an amount equal to 10% of the net profits of Z earned in the immediately preceding calendar year beginning with the year ending December 31, 1981. Each payment is to be made on the following April 1st, commencing April 1, 1982. In addition, C is to receive a payment of $5 million on closing. The agreement specifies that the maximum amount payable to C, including the $5 million cash payment at closing, is $24 million. The agreement does not call for the payment of any stated interest. Since section 483 will apply to each payment received by C more than one year following the date of sale (section 483 is inapplicable to the payment that will be received on April 1, 1982, since that date is within one year following the July 1, 1981 sale date), the agreement contemplates internal interest and the price interest recomputation rule is applicable. Under that rule, C must make an initial determination for his taxable year 1981.

(ii) On December 31, 1981, the exact amount of Z's 1981 net profit is not known, since it normally takes a number of weeks to compile the relevant information. However, the events which will determine the amount of the payment C will receive on April 1, 1982 have already occurred, and the information (Z's 1981 financial statement) will be promptly calculated and verified and will be available prior to the time C's 1981 tax return is timely filed. On March 15, 1982, Z reports net income of $14 million, and on April 1, 1982 D pays C $1.4 million.

(iii) Under the price-interest recomputation rule, C is required to determine the gross profit ratio for the 1981 $5 million payment on the basis of the events which occurred by the close of that taxable year and which are verifiable before the due date of the 1981 return. Because at the end of C's 1981 taxable year all events which will determine the amount of the April 1, 1982 payment have occurred and because the actual facts are known prior to the due date of C's return, C will take those facts into account when

Methods of Accounting 36,797
See p. 20,601 for regulations not amended to reflect law changes

calculating the gross profit ratio. Thus, because C knows that the 1982 payment is $1.4 million, C knows that the remaining amount to be recovered under the contract is $17.6 million ($24 million − ($5 million + $1.4 million)). For purposes of this paragraph C must assume that the entire $17.6 million will be paid on the earliest possible date, April 1, 1983. Because section 483 will apply to that payment, and assuming that under the tables in the regulations under section 483 the principal component of a payment received 21 months after the date of sale is considered to be .86384, $15,203,584 of the $17.6 million would be principal and $2,396,416 ($17,600,000 − $15,203,584) would be interest. Therefore C must assume, for purposes of reporting the $5 million payment received in 1981, that the selling price is $21,603,584 calculated as follows:

$24,000,000	Total selling price
− 2,396,416	Interest component of the $17,600,000 payment which C must assume will be made April 1, 1983.
$21,603,584	Adjusted selling price to be used when reporting the 1981 payment.

(iv) Assume that on March 15, 1982, Z reports net income of $15 million for 1982 and that on April 1, 1983 D pays C $1.5 million. Because section 483 will apply to that payment, and assuming that under the tables in the regulations under section 483 the principal component of a payment received 21 months after the date of sale is considered to be .86384, $1,295,760 of the $1,500,000 payment will be principal and $204,240 ($1,500,000 − $1,295,760) will be interest. Because C knows the amount of the 1983 payment when filing the 1982 tax return, C must assume that the remaining amount to be received under the contract, $16.1 million ($24 million − ($5 million + $1.4 million + $1.5 million)), will be received as a lump sum on April 1, 1984. Because section 483 will again apply, and assuming that the principal component of a payment made 34 months after the date of the sale is .74622, $12,014,142 of the $16.1 million would be principal, and $4,085,858 ($16,100,000 − $12,014,142) would be interest. Therefore, C must assume, for purpose of reporting the $1.4 million payment made April 1, 1982, that the adjusted selling price (within the meaning of example (2)) is $14,709,902, calculated as follows:

$24,000,000	Total selling price
− 204,240	Interest component of the $1,500,000 payment made April 1, 1983.
− $ 4,085,858	Interest component of the $16,100,000 payment which C must assume will be made April 1, 1984.
− 5,000,000	Payment made in 1981.
$14,709,902	Adjusted selling price for calculations for reporting the 1982 payment.

(3) *Fixed period*—(i) *In general.* When a stated maximum selling price cannot be determined as of the close of the taxable year in which the sale or other disposition occurs, but the maximum period over which payments may be received under the contingent sale price agreement is fixed, the taxpayer's basis (inclusive of selling expenses) shall be allocated to the taxable years in which payment may be received under the agreement in equal annual increments. In making the allocation it is not relevant whether the buyer is required to pay adequate stated interest. However, if the terms of the agreement incorporate an arithmetic component that is not identical for all taxable years, basis shall be allocated among the taxable years to accord with that component unless, taking into account all of the payment terms of the agreement, it is inappropriate to presume that payments under the contract are likely to accord with the variable component. If in any taxable year no payment is received or the amount of payment received (exclusive of interest) is less than the basis allocated to that taxable year, no loss shall be allowed unless the taxable year is the final payment year under the agreement or unless it is otherwise determined in accordance with the rules generally applicable to worthless debts that the future payment obligation under the agreement has become worthless. When no loss is allowed, the unrecovered portion of the basis allocated to the taxable year shall be carried forward to the next succeeding taxable year. If application of the foregoing rules to a particular case would substantially and inappropriately defer or accelerate recovery of the taxpayer's basis, a special rule will apply. See paragraph (c)(7) of this section.

(ii) *Examples.* The following examples illustrate the rules for recovery of basis in a contingent payment sale in which stated maximum selling price cannot be determined but the period over which payments are to be received under the

Reg. § 15A.453-1(c)(3)

agreement is fixed. In each case, it is assumed that application of the described rules will not substantially and inappropriately defer or accelerate recovery of the taxpayer's basis.

Example (1). A sells Blackacre to B for 10 percent of Blackacre's gross yield for each of the next 5 years. A's basis in Blackacre is $5 million. Since the sales price is indefinite and the maximum selling price is not ascertainable from the terms of the contract, basis is recovered ratably over the period during which payment may be received under the contract. Thus, assuming A receives the payments (exclusive of interest) listed in the following table, A will report the following:

Year	Payment	Basis Recovered	Gain Attributable to the Sale
1	$1,300,000	$1,000,000	$ 300,000
2	$1,500,000	$1,000,000	$ 500,000
3	$1,400,000	$1,000,000	$ 400,000
4	$1,800,000	$1,000,000	$ 800,000
5	$2,100,000	$1,000,000	$1,100,000

Example (2). The facts are the same as in example (1), except that the payment in year 1 is only $900,000. Since the installment payment is less than the amount of basis allocated to that year, the unrecovered basis, $100,000, is carried forward to year 2.

Year	Payment	Basis Recovered	Gain Attributable to the Sale
1	$900,000	$900,000	—0—
2	$1,500,000	$1,100,000	$ 400,000
3	$1,400,000	$1,000,000	$ 400,000
4	$1,800,000	$1,000,000	$ 800,000
5	$2,100,000	$1,000,000	$1,100,000

Example (3). C owns all of the stock of X corporation with a basis of $100,000 (inclusive of selling expenses). D purchases the X stock from C and agrees to make four payments computed in accordance with the following formula: 40% of the net profits of X in year 1, 30% in year 2, 20% in year 3, and 10% in year 4. Accordingly, C's basis is allocated as follows: $40,000 to year 1, $30,000 to year 2, $20,000 to year 3, and $10,000 to year 4.

Example (4). The facts are the same as in example (3), but the agreement also requires that D make fixed installment payments in accordance with the following schedule: no payment in year 1, $100,000 in year 2, $200,000 in year 3, $300,000 in year 4, and $400,000 in year 5. Thus, while it is reasonable to project that the contingent component of the payments will decrease each year, the fixed component of the payments will increase each year. Accordingly, C is required to allocate $20,000 of basis to each of the taxable years 1 through 5.

(4) *Neither stated maximum selling price nor fixed period.* If the agreement neither specifies a maximum selling price nor limits payments to a fixed period, a question arises whether a sale realistically has occurred or whether, in economic effect, payments received under the agreement are in the nature of rent or royalty income. Arrangements of this sort will be closely scrutinized. If, taking into account all of the pertinent facts, including the nature of the property, the arrangement is determined to qualify as a sale, the taxpayer's basis (including selling expenses) shall be recovered in equal annual increments over a period of 15 years commencing with the date of sale. However, if in any taxable year no payment is received or the amount of payment received (exclusive of interest) is less than basis allocated to the year, no loss shall be allowed unless it is otherwise determined in accordance with the timing rules generally applicable to worthless debts that the future payment obligation under the agreement has become worthless; instead the excess basis shall be reallocated in level amounts over the balance of the 15-year term. Any basis not recovered at the end of the 15th year shall be carried forward to the next succeeding year, and to the extent unrecovered thereafter shall be carried forward from year to year until all basis has been recovered or the future payment obligation is determined to be worthless. The general rule requiring initial level allocation of basis over 15 years shall not apply if the taxpayer can establish to the satisfaction of the Internal Revenue Service that application of the general rule would substantially and inappropriately defer recovery of the taxpayer's basis. See paragraph (c)(7) of this section. If the Service determines that initially allocating basis in level amounts over the first 15 years will substantially and inappropriately accelerate recovery of the taxpayer's basis in early years of that 15-year term, the Service may require that basis be reallocated within the 15-year term but the Service will not require that basis initially be allocated over more than 15 years. See paragraph (c)(7) of this section.

(5) *Foreign currency and other fungible payment units*—(i) *In general.* An installment sale may call for payment in foreign currency. For federal income tax purposes, foreign currency is property. Because the value of foreign currency will vary over time in relation to the United States dollar, an installment sale requiring payment in foreign currency is a contingent payment sale. However, when the consideration payable under an installment sale agreement is specified in foreign currency, the taxpayer's basis (including selling expenses) shall be recovered in the same manner as basis would have been recovered

Reg. § 15A.453-1(c)(4)

had the agreement called for payment in United States dollars. This rule is equally applicable to any installment sale in which the agreement specifies that payment shall be made in identified, fungible units of property the value of which will or may vary over time in relation to the dollar (*e.g.*, bushels of wheat or ounces of gold).

(ii) *Example.* The following example illustrates the provisions of this subparagraph:

Example. A sells Blackacre to B for 4 million Swiss francs payable 1 million in year 2 and 3 million in year 3, together with adequate stated interest. A's basis (including selling expenses) in Blackacre is $100,000. Twenty-five thousand dollars of A's basis (¼ of total basis) is allocable to the year 2 payment of 1 million Swiss francs and $75,000 of A's basis is allocable to the year 3 payment of 3 million Swiss francs.

(6) *Income forecast method for basis recovery*—(i) *In general.* The rules for ratable recovery of basis set forth in paragraph (c)(2) through (4) of this section focus on the payment terms of the contingent selling price agreement. Except to the extent contemplated by paragraph (c)(7) of this section (relating to a special rule to prevent substantial distortion of basis recovery), the nature and productivity of the property sold is not independently relevant to the basis to be recovered in any payment year. The special rule for an income forecast method of basis recovery set forth in paragraph (c)(6) of this section recognizes that there are cases in which failure to take account of the nature or productivity of the property sold may be expected to result in distortion of the taxpayer's income over time. Specifically, when the property sold is depreciable property of a type normally eligible for depreciation on the income forecast method, or is depletable property of a type normally eligible for cost depletion in which total future production must be estimated, and payments under the contingent selling price agreement are based upon receipts or units produced by or from the property, the taxpayer's basis may appropriately be recovered by using an income forecast method.

(ii) *Availability of methods.* In lieu of applying the rules set forth in paragraph (c)(2) through (4) of this section, in an appropriate case the taxpayer may elect (on its tax return timely filed for the first year under the contingent payment agreement in which a payment is received) to recover basis using the income forecast method of basis recovery. No special form of election is prescribed. An appropriate case is one meeting the criteria set forth in paragraph (c)(6)(i) of this section in which the property sold is a mineral property, a motion picture film, a television film, or a taped television show. The Internal Revenue Service may from time to time specify other properties of a similar character which, in appropriate circumstances, will be eligible for recovery of basis on the income forecast method. In addition, a taxpayer may seek a ruling from the Service as to whether a specific property qualifies as property of a similar character eligible, in appropriate circumstances, for income forecast recovery of basis.

(iii) *Required calculations.* The income forecast method requires application of a fraction, the numerator of which is the payment (exclusive of interest) received in the taxable year under a contingent payment agreement, and the denominator of which is the forecast or estimated total payments (exclusive of interest) to be received under the agreement. This fraction is multiplied by the taxpayer's basis in the property sold to determine the basis recovered with respect to the payment received in the taxable year. If in a subsequent year it is found that the income forecast was substantially overestimated or underestimated by reason of circumstances occurring in such subsequent year, an adjustment of the income forecast for such subsequent year shall be made. In such case, the formula for computing recovery of basis would be as follows: payment received in the taxable year (exclusive of interest) divided by the revised estimated total payments (exclusive of interest) then and thereafter to be made under the agreement (the current year's payment and total estimated future payments), multiplied by the taxpayer's unrecovered basis remaining as of the beginning of the taxable year. If the agreement contemplates internal interest (as defined in paragraph (c)(2)(ii) of this section), in making the initial income forecast computation and in making any required subsequent recomputation the amount of internal interest (which shall not be treated as payment under the agreement) shall be calculated by assuming that each future contingent selling price payment will be made in the amount and at the time forecast. The total forecast of estimated payments to be received under the agreement shall be based on the conditions known to exist at the end of the taxable year for which the return is filed. If a subsequent upward or downward revision of this estimate is required, the revision shall be made at the end of the subsequent taxable year based on additional information which became available after the last prior estimate. No loss shall be allowed unless the taxable year is the final payment year under the agreement or unless it is otherwise determined in accordance with the rules generally applicable to the time a debt becomes worthless that the future

Reg. § 15A.453-1(c)(6)

payment obligation under the agreement has become worthless.

(iv) *Examples.* The following examples illustrate the income forecast method of basis recovery:

Example (1). A sells a television film to B for 5% of annual gross receipts from the exploitation of the film. The film is an ordinary income asset in the hands of A. A reasonably forecasts that total payments to be received under the contingent selling price agreement will be $1,200,000, and that A will be paid $600,000 in year 1, $150,000 in year 2, $300,000 in year 3, $100,000 in year 4, and $50,000 in year 5. A reasonably anticipates no or only insignificant receipts thereafter. A's basis in the film is $100,000. Under the income forecast method, A's basis initially is allocated to the five taxable years of forecasted payment as follows:

Year	Percentage	Basis
1	50.00%	$50,000
2	12.50%	$12,500
3	25.00%	$25,000
4	8.33%	$ 8,333
5	4.17%	$ 4,167

Payments are received and A reports the sale under the installment method as follows:

Year	Payment Received	Basis Recovered	Gain on Sale
1	$600,000	$50,000	$550,000
2	$150,000	$12,500	$137,500
3	$300,000	$25,000	$275,000
4	$100,000	$ 8,333	$ 91,667
5	$ 50,000	$ 4,167	$ 45,833

Example (2). The facts are the same as in example (1), except that in year 2 A receives no payment. In year 3 A receives a payment of $300,000 and reasonably estimates that in subsequent years he will receive total additional payments of only $100,000. In year 2 A will be allowed no loss. At the beginning of year 3 A's unrecovered basis is $50,000. In year 3 A must recompute the applicable basis recovery fraction based upon facts known and forecast as at the end of year 3: year 3 payment of $300,000 divided by estimated current and future payments of $400,000, equaling 75%. Thus, in year 3 A recovers $37,500 (75% of $50,000) of A's previously unrecovered basis.

(7) *Special rule to avoid substantial distortion*—(i) *In general.* The normal basis recovery rules set forth in paragraph (c)(2) through (4) of this section may, with respect to a particular contingent payment sale, substantially and inappropriately defer or accelerate recovery of the taxpayer's basis.

(ii) *Substantial and inappropriate deferral.* The taxpayer may use an alternative method of basis recovery if the taxpayer is able to demonstrate prior to the due date of the return including extensions for the taxable year in which the first payment is received, that application of the normal basis recovery rule will substantially and inappropriately defer recovery of basis. To demonstrate that application of the normal basis recovery rule will substantially and inappropriately defer recovery of basis, the taxpayer must show (A) that the alternative method is a reasonable method of ratably recovering basis and, (B) that, under that method, it is reasonable to conclude that over time the taxpayer likely will recover basis at a rate twice as fast as the rate at which basis would have been recovered under the otherwise applicable normal basis recovery rule. The taxpayer must receive a ruling from the Internal Revenue Service before using an alternative method of basis recovery described in paragraph (c)(7)(ii) of this section.

The request for a ruling shall be made in accordance with all applicable procedural rules set forth in the Statement of Procedural Rules (26 CFR Part 601) and any applicable revenue procedures relating to submission of ruling requests. The request shall be submitted to the Commissioner of Internal Revenue, Attention: Assistant Commissioner (Technical), Washington, DC 20224. The taxpayer must file a request for a ruling prior to the due date for the return including extensions. In demonstrating that application of the normal basis recovery rule would substantially and inappropriately defer recovery of the taxpayer's basis, the taxpayer in appropriate circumstances may rely upon contemporaneous or immediate past relevant sales, profit, or other factual data that are subject to verification. The taxpayer ordinarily is not permitted to rely upon projections of future productivity, receipts, profits, or the like. However, in special circumstances a reasonable projection may be acceptable if the projection is based upon a specific event that already has occurred (*e.g.,* corporate stock has been sold for future payments contingent on profits and an inadequately insured major plant facility of the corporation has been destroyed).

(iii) *Substantial and inappropriate acceleration.* Notwithstanding the other provisions of this paragraph, the Internal Revenue Service may find that the normal basis recovery rule will substantially and inappropriately accelerate recovery of basis. In such a case, the Service may require an alternate method of basis recovery, unless the taxpayer is able to demonstrate either (A) that the method of basis recovery required by the Service is not a reasonable method of ratable recovery, or (B) that it is not reasonable to conclude that the taxpayer over time is likely to

Reg. § 15A.453-1(c)(7)

recover basis at a rate twice as fast under the normally applicable basis recovery rule as the rate at which basis would be recovered under the method proposed by the Service. In making such demonstrations the taxpayer may rely in appropriate circumstances upon contemporaneous or immediate past relevant sales, profit, or other factual data subject to verification. In special circumstances a reasonable projection may be acceptable, but only with the consent of the Service, if the projection is based upon a specific event that has already occurred.

(iv) *Subsequent recomputation.* A contingent payment sale may initially and properly have been reported under the normally applicable basis recovery rule and, during the term of the agreement, circumstances may show that continued reporting on the original method will substantially and inappropriately defer or accelerate recovery of the unrecovered balance of the taxpayer's basis. In this event, the special rule provided in this paragraph is applicable.

(v) *Examples.* The following examples illustrate the application of the special rule of this paragraph. In examples (1) and (2) it is assumed that rulings consistent with paragraph (c)(7)(ii) of this section have been requested.

Example (1). A owns all of the stock of X corporation with a basis of $100,000. A sells the stock of X to B for a cash down payment of $1,800,000 and B's agreement to pay A an amount equal to 1% of the net profits of X in each of the next 10 years (together with adequate stated interest). The agreement further specifies that the maximum amount that may be paid to A (exclusive of interest) shall not exceed $10 million. A is able to demonstrate that current and recent profits of X have approximated $2 million annually, and that there is no reason to anticipate a major increase in the annual profits of X during the next 10 years. One percent of $2 million annual profits is $20,000, a total of $200,000 over 10 years. Under the basis recovery rule normally applicable to a maximum contingent selling price agreement, in the year of sale A would recover $18,000 of A's total $100,000 basis, and would not recover more than a minor part of the balance until the final year under the agreement. On a $2 million selling price ($200,000 plus $1,800,000 down payment), A would recover $90,000 of A's total $100,000 basis in the year of sale and 5% of each payment ($100,000/$2,000,000) received up to a maximum of $10,000 over the next ten years. Since the rate of basis recovery under the demonstrated method is more than twice the rate under the normal rule, A will be permitted to recover $90,000 basis in the year of sale.

Example (2). The facts are the same as in example (1) except that no maximum contingent selling price is stated in the agreement. Under the basis recovery rule normally applicable when no maximum amount is stated but the payment term is fixed, in the year of sale and in each subsequent year A would recover approximately $9,100 (1/11 of $100,000) of A's total basis. A will be permitted to recover $90,000 of A's total basis in the year of sale.

Example (3). The facts are the same as in example (1) except that A sells the X stock to B on the following terms: 1% of the annual net profits of X in each of the next 10 years and a cash payment of $1,800,000 in the eleventh year, all payments to be made together with adequate stated interest. No maximum contingent selling price is stated. Under the normally applicable basis recovery rule, A would recover 1/11 of A's total $100,000 basis in each of the 11 payment years under the agreement. On the facts (see example (1)), A cannot demonstrate that application of the normal rule would not substantially and inappropriately accelerate recovery of A's basis. Accordingly, A will be allowed to recover only $1,000 of A's total basis in each of the 10 contingent payment years under the agreement, and will recover the $90,000 balance of A's basis in the final year in which the large fixed cash payment will be made.

(8) *Coordination with regulations under section 385.*

(i) *In general.* The regulations under section 385 do not apply to an instrument (as defined in § 1.385-3(c)) providing for a contingent payment of principal (with or without stated interest) issued in connection with a sale or other disposition of property to a corporation if § 1.385-6 (relating to proportionality) does not apply to such instrument (or to a class of instruments which includes such instrument). Thus, such instrument will be treated as stock or indebtedness under applicable principles of law without reference to the regulations under section 385.

(ii) *Examples.* The following examples illustrate the application of this paragraph:

Example (1). On January 1, 1982, corporation X buys a factory from Y, an independent creditor (within the meaning of § 1.385-6(b)). In exchange for the factory, Y receives $200,000 in cash on January 1, 1982. In addition, on January 1, 1984, Y will receive a payment in the range of $100,000 to $300,000, plus adequate stated interest, depending on the factory's output. Based on these facts, § 1.385-6 does not apply to X's obligation to Y (see § 1.385-6(a)(3)(ii)) and the regulations under section 385 do not apply to X's obligation to Y.

Example (2). The facts are the same as in example (1), except that the contingent payment due on January 1, 1984 will be in the range of $50,000 to $250,000. In addition, on January 1, 1982, Y receives a $50,000 noninterest-bearing note due absolutely and unconditionally on January 1, 1984. Based on these facts, the $50,000 note is treated as stock or indebtedness under the regulations under section 385.

(d) *Election not to report an installment sale on the installment method*—(1) *In general.* An installment sale is to be reported on the installment method unless the taxpayer elects otherwise in accordance with the rules set forth in paragraph (d)(3) of this section.

(2) *Treatment of an installment sale when a taxpayer elects not to report on the installment method*—(i) *In general.* A taxpayer who elects not to report an installment sale on the installment method must recognize gain on the sale in accordance with the taxpayer's method of accounting. The fair market value of an installment obligation shall be determined in accordance with paragraph (d)(2)(ii) and (iii) of this section. In making such determination, any provision of contract or local law restricting the transferability of the installment obligation shall be disregarded. Receipt of an installment obligation shall be treated as a receipt of property, in an amount equal to the fair market value of the installment obligation, whether or not such obligation is the equivalent of cash. An installment obligation is considered to be property and is subject to valuation, as provided in paragraph (d)(2)(ii) and (iii) of this section, without regard to whether the obligation is embodied in a note, an executory contract, or any other instrument, or is an oral promise enforceable under local law.

(ii) *Fixed amount obligations.* (A) A fixed amount obligation means an installment obligation the amount payable under which is fixed. Solely for the purpose of determining whether the amount payable under an installment obligation is fixed, the provisions of section 483 and any "payment recharacterization" arrangement (as defined in paragraph (c)(2)(ii) of this section) shall be disregarded. If the fixed amount payable is stated in identified, fungible units of property the value of which will or may vary over time in relation to the United States dollar (*e.g.*, foreign currency, ounces of gold, or bushels of wheat), such units shall be converted to United States dollars at the rate of exchange or dollar value on the date the installment sale is made. A taxpayer using the cash receipts and disbursements methods of accounting shall treat as an amount realized in the year of sale the fair market value of the installment obligation. In no event will the fair market value of the installment obligation be considered to be less than the fair market value of the property sold (minus any another consideration received by the taxpayer on the sale). A taxpayer using the accrual method of accounting shall treat as an amount realized in the year of sale the total amount payable under the installment obligation. For this purpose, neither interest (whether stated or unstated) nor original issue discount is considered to be part of the amount payable. If the amount payable is otherwise fixed, but because the time over which payments may be made is contingent, a portion of the fixed amount will or may be treated as internal interest (as defined in paragraph (c)(2)(ii) of this section), the amount payable shall be determined by applying the price interest recomputation rule (described in paragraph (c)(2)(ii) of this section). Under no circumstances will an installment sale for a fixed amount obligation be considered an "open" transaction. For purposes of this (ii) remote or incidental contingencies are not to be taken into account.

(B) The following examples illustrate the provisions of paragraph (d)(2) of this section.

Example (1). A, an accrual method taxpayer, owns all of the stock of X corporation with a basis of $20 million. On July 1, 1981, A sells the stock of X corporation to B for $60 million payable on June 15, 1992. The agreement also provides that, against this fixed amount, B shall make annual prepayments (on June 15) equal to 5% of the net profits of X earned in the immediately preceding fiscal year beginning with the fiscal year ending March 31, 1982. Thus, the first prepayment will be made on June 15, 1982. No stated interest is payable under the agreement and thus the unstated interest provisions of section 483 are applicable. Under section 483, no part of any payment made on June 15, 1982 (which is within one year following the July 1, 1981 sale date), will be treated as unstated interest. Under the price interest recomputation rule, it is presumed that the entire $60 million fixed amount will be paid on June 15, 1982. Accordingly, if A elects not to report the transaction on the installment method, in 1981 A must report $60 million as the amount realized on the sale and must report $40 million as gain on the sale in that year.

Example (2). The facts are the same as in example (1) except that A uses the cash receipts and disbursements method of accounting. In 1981 A must report as an amount realized on the sale the fair market value of the installment obligation and must report as gain on the sale in 1981 the excess of that amount realized over A's basis of $20 million. In no event will the fair market value of the installment obligation be considered to be less than the fair market value of the stock of X. In determining the fair market value of the installment obligation, any contractual or legal restrictions on the transferability of the installment obligation, and any remote or incidental contingencies otherwise affecting the amount payable or time of payments under the installment obligation, shall be disregarded.

(iii) *Contingent payment obligations.* Any installment obligation which is not a fixed amount obligation (as defined in paragraph (d)(2)(ii) of this section) is a contingent payment obligation. If an installment obligation contains both a fixed amount component and a contingent payment component, the fixed amount component shall be treated under the rules of paragraph (d)(2)(ii) of this section and the contingent amount component shall be treated under the rules of this (iii). The fair market value of a contingent payment obligation shall be determined by disregarding any restrictions on transfer imposed by agreement or under local law. The fair market value of a contingent payment obligation may be ascertained from, and in no event shall be considered to be less than, the fair market value of the property sold (less the amount of any other consideration received in the sale). Only in those rare and extraordinary cases involving sales for a contingent payment obligation in which the fair market value of the obligation (determinable under the preceding sentences) cannot reasonably be ascertained will the taxpayer be entitled to assert that the transaction is "open." Any such transaction will be carefully scrutinized to determine whether a sale in fact has taken place. A taxpayer using the cash receipts and disbursements method of accounting must report as an amount realized in the year of sale the fair market value of the contingent payment obligation. A taxpayer using the accrual method of accounting must report an amount realized in the year of sale determined in accordance with that method of accounting, but in no event less than the fair market value of the contingent payment obligation.

(3) *Time and manner for making election—* (i) *In general.* An election under paragraph (d)(1) of this section must be made on or before the due date prescribed by law (including extensions) for filing the taxpayer's return for the taxable year in which the installment sale occurs. The election must be made in the manner prescribed by the appropriate forms for the taxpayer's return for the taxable year of the sale. A taxpayer who reports an amount realized equal to the selling price including the full face amount of any installment obligation on the tax return filed for the taxable year in which the installment sale occurs will be considered to have made an effective election under paragraph (d)(1) of this section. A cash method taxpayer receiving an obligation the fair market value of which is less than the face value must make the election in the manner prescribed by appropriate instructions for the return filed for the taxable year of the sale.

(ii) *Election made after the due date.* Elections after the time specified in paragraph (d)(3)(i) of this section will be permitted only in those rare circumstances when the Internal Revenue Service concludes that the taxpayer had good cause for failing to make a timely election. A recharacterization of a transaction as a sale in a taxable year subsequent to the taxable year in which the transaction occurred (*e.g.*, a transaction initially reported as a lease later is determined to have been an installment sale) will not justify a late election. No conditional elections will be permitted. For a special transitional rule relating to certain taxable years for which a return is filed prior to February 19, 1981, see paragraph (d)(5) of this section.

(4) *Revoking an election.* Generally, an election made under paragraph (d)(1) is irrevocable. An election may be revoked only with the consent of the Internal Revenue Service. A revocation is retroactive. A revocation will not be permitted when one of its purposes is the avoidance of federal income taxes, or when the taxable year in which any payment was received has closed. For a special transitional rule relating to certain taxable years for which a return is filed prior to February 19, 1981, see paragraph (d)(5) of this section.

(5) *Transitional rules.* The following transitional rules shall apply with respect to any contingent payment sale made after October 19, 1980 in a taxable year, ending after that date, for which the taxpayer has filed a federal income tax return prior to February 19, 1981. If in such tax return the taxpayer has treated the contingent payment sale under the installment method, consent of the Internal Revenue Service to a late election by the taxpayer not to report the transaction on the installment method will generally be granted if the request for election out of installment method treatment is filed by May 5, 1981. If in such tax return the taxpayer has elected not to report the contingent payment sale under the installment method, consent of the Service to revocation of the election by the taxpayer will generally be granted if the request for revocation is filed by May 5, 1981.

Reg. § 15A.453-1(d)(5)

(e) *Purchaser evidences of indebtedness payable on demand or readily tradable*—(1) *Treatment as payment.* (i) *In general.* A bond or other evidence of indebtedness (hereinafter in this section referred to as an obligation) issued by any person and payable on demand shall be treated as a payment in the year received, not as installment obligations payable in future years. In addition, an obligation issued by a corporation or a government or political subdivision thereof—

(A) With interest coupons attached (whether or not the obligation is readily tradable in an established securities market),

(B) In registered form (other than an obligation issued in registered form which the taxpayer establishes will not be readily tradable in an established securities market), or

(C) In any other form designed to render such obligation readily tradable in an established securities market,

shall be treated as a payment in the year received, not as an installment obligation payable in future years. For purposes of this paragraph, an obligation is to be considered in registered form if it is registered as to principal, interest, or both and if its transfer must be effected by the surrender of the old instrument and either the reissuance by the corporation of the old instrument to the new holder or the issuance by the corporation of a new instrument to the new holder.

(ii) *Examples.* The rules stated in this paragraph may be illustrated by the following examples:

Example (1). On July 1, 1981, A, an individual on the cash method of accounting reporting on a calendar year basis, transferred all of his stock in corporation X (traded on an established securities market and having a fair market value of $1,000,000) to corporation Y in exchange for 250 of Y's registered bonds (which are traded in an over-the-counter market) each with a principal amount and fair market value of $1,000 (with interest payable at the rate of 12 percent per year), and Y's unsecured promissory note with a principal amount of $750,000. At the time of such exchange A's basis in the X stock is $900,000. The promissory note is payable at the rate of $75,000 annually, due on July 1 of each year following 1981 until the principal balance is paid. The note provides for the payment of interest at the rate of 12 percent per year also payable on July 1 of each year. Under the rule stated in paragraph (e)(1)(i) of this section, the 250 registered bonds of Y are treated as a payment in 1981 in the amount of the value of the bonds, $250,000.

Example (2). Assume the same facts as in example (1). Assume further that on July 1, 1982, Y makes its first installment payment to A under the terms of the unsecured promissory note with 75 more of its $1,000 registered bonds. A must include $7,500 (*i.e.*, 10 percent gross profit percentage times $75,000), A's gross income for calendar year 1982. In addition, A includes the interest payment made by Y on July 1 in A's gross income for 1982.

(2) *Amounts treated as payment.* If under paragraph (e)(1) of this section an obligation is treated as a payment in the year received, the amount realized by reason of such payment shall be determined in accordance with the taxpayer's method of accounting. If the taxpayer uses the cash receipts and disbursements method of accounting, the amount realized on such payment is the fair market value of the obligation. If the taxpayer uses the accrual method of accounting, the amount realized on receipt of an obligation payable on demand is the face amount of the obligation, and the amount realized on receipt of an obligation with coupons attached or a readily tradable obligation is the stated redemption price at maturity less any original issue discount (as defined in section 1232(b)(1)) or, if there is no original issue discount, the amount realized is the stated redemption price at maturity appropriately discounted to reflect total unstated interest (as defined in section 483(b)), if any.

(3) *Payable on demand.* An obligation shall be treated as payable on demand only if the obligation is treated as payable on demand under applicable state or local law.

(4) *Designed to be readily tradable in an established securities market* —(i) *In general.* Obligations issued by a corporation or government or political subdivision thereof will be deemed to be in a form designed to render such obligations readily tradable in an established securities market if—

(A) Steps necessary to create a market for them are taken at the time of issuance (or later, if taken pursuant to an expressed or implied agreement or understanding which existed at the time of issuance),

(B) If they are treated as readily tradable in an established securities market under paragraph (e)(4)(ii) of this section, or

(C) If they are convertible obligations to which paragraph (e)(5) of this section applies.

(ii) *Readily tradable in an established securities market.* An obligation will be treated as readily tradable in an established securities market if—

Reg. § 15A.453-1(e)(1)

(A) The obligation is part of an issue or series of issues which are readily tradable in an established securities market, or

(B) The corporation issuing the obligation has other obligations of a comparable character which are described in paragraph (e)(4)(ii)(A) of this section.

For purposes of paragraph (e)(4)(ii)(B) of this section, the determination as to whether there exist obligations of a comparable character depends upon the particular facts and circumstances. Factors to be considered in making such determination include, but are not limited to, substantial similarity with respect to the presence and nature of security for the obligation, the number of obligations issued (or to be issued), the number of holders of such obligation, the principal amount of the obligation, and other relevant factors.

(iii) *Readily tradable.* For purposes of paragraph (e)(4)(ii)(A) of this section, an obligation shall be treated as readily tradable if it is regularly quoted by brokers or dealers making a market in such obligation or is part of an issue a portion of which is in fact traded in an established securities market.

(iv) *Established securities market.* For purposes of this paragraph, the term "established securities market" includes (A) a national securities exchange which is registered under section 6 of the Securities Exchange Act of 1934 (15 U.S.C. 78f), (B) an exchange which is exempted from registration under section 5 of the Securities Exchange Act of 1934 (15 U.S.C. 78e) because of its limited volume of transactions, and (C) any over-the-counter market. For purposes of this (iv), an over-the-counter market is reflected by the existence of an interdealer quotation system. An interdealer quotation system is any system of general circulation to brokers and dealers which regularly disseminates quotations of obligations by identified brokers or dealers, other than a quotation sheet prepared and distributed by a broker or dealer in the regular course of business and containing only quotations of such broker or dealer.

(v) *Examples.* The rules stated in this paragraph may be illustrated by the following examples:

Example (1). On June 1, 1982, 25 individuals owning equal interests in a tract of land with a fair market value of $1 million sell the land to corporation Y. The $1 million sales price is represented by 25 bonds issued by Y, each having a face value of $40,000. The bonds are not in registered form and do not have interest coupons attached, and, in addition, are payable in 120 equal installments, each due on the first business day of each month. In addition, the bonds are negotiable and may be assigned by the holder to any other person. However, the bonds are not quoted by any brokers or dealers who deal in corporate bonds, and, furthermore, there are no comparable obligations of Y (determined with reference to the characteristics set forth in paragraph (e)(2) of this section) which are so quoted. Therefore, the bonds are not treated as readily tradable in an established securities market. In addition, under the particular facts and circumstances stated, the bonds will not be considered to be in a form designed to render them readily tradable in an established securities market. The receipt of such bonds by the holder is not treated as a payment for purposes of section 453(f)(4), notwithstanding that they are freely assignable.

Example (2). On April 1, 1981, corporation M purchases in a casual sale of personal property a fleet of trucks from corporation N in exchange for M's negotiable notes, not in registered form and without coupons attached. The M notes are comparable to earlier notes issued by M, which notes are quoted in the Eastern Bond section of the National Daily Quotation Sheet, which is an interdealer quotation system. Both issues of notes are unsecured, held by more than 100 holders, have a maturity date of more than 5 years, and were issued for a comparable principle [sic] amount. On the basis of these similar characteristics it appears that the latest notes will also be readily tradable. Since an interdealer system reflects an over-the-counter market, the earlier notes are treated as readily tradable in an established securities market. Since the later notes are obligations comparable to the earlier ones, which are treated as readily tradable in an established securities market, the later notes are also treated as readily tradable in an established securities market (whether or not such notes are actually traded).

(5) *Special rule for convertible securities.* (i) *General rule.* If an obligation contains a right whereby the holder of such obligation may convert it directly or indirectly into another obligation which would be treated as a payment under paragraph (e)(1) of this section or may convert it directly or indirectly into stock which would be treated as readily tradable or designed to be readily tradable in an established securities market under paragraph (e)(4) of this section, the convertible obligation shall be considered to be in a form designed to render such obligation readily tradable in an established securities market unless such obligation is convertible only at a substantial discount. In determining whether the stock or obligation into which an obligation is convertible

Reg. § 15A.453-1(e)(5)

is readily tradable or designed to be readily tradable in an established securities market, the rules stated in paragraph (e)(4) of this section shall apply, and for purposes of such paragraph (e)(4) if such obligation is convertible into stock then the term "stock" shall be substituted for the term "obligation" wherever it appears in such paragraph (e)(4).

(ii) *Substantial discount rule.* Whether an obligation is convertible at a substantial discount depends upon the particular facts and circumstances. A substantial discount shall be considered to exist if at the time the convertible obligation is issued, the fair market value of the stock or obligation into which the obligation is convertible is less than 80 percent of the fair market value of the obligation (determined by taking into account all relevant factors, including proper discount to reflect the fact that the convertible obligation is not readily tradable in an established securities market and any additional consideration required to be paid by the taxpayer). Also, if a privilege to convert an obligation into stock or an obligation which is readily tradable in an established securities market may not be exercised within a period of one year from the date the obligation is issued, a substantial discount shall be considered to exist.

(6) *Effective date.* The provisions of this paragraph (e) shall apply to sales or other dispositions occurring after May 27, 1969, which are not made pursuant to a binding written contract entered into on or before such date. No inference shall be drawn from this section as to any questions of law concerning the application of section 453 to sales or other dispositions occurring on or before May 27, 1969. [Temporary Reg. § 15A.453-1.]

☐ [T.D. 7768, 1-30-81, Amended by T.D. 7788, 9-30-81 and T.D. 8535, 4-19-94.]

[Reg. § 1.453-4]

§ 1.453-4. Sale of real property involving deferred periodic payments—(a) *In general.* Sales of real property involving deferred payments include (1) agreements of purchase and sale which contemplate that a conveyance is not to be made at the outset, but only after all or a substantial portion of the selling price has been paid, and (2) sales in which there is an immediate transfer of title, the vendor being protected by a mortgage or other lien as to deferred payments.

(b) *Classes of sales.* Such sales, under either paragraph (a)(1) or (2) of this section, fall into two classes when considered with respect to the terms of sale, as follows:

(1) Sales of real property which may be accounted for on the installment method, that is, sales of real property in which (i) there are no payments during the taxable year of the sale or (ii) the payments in such taxable year (exclusive of evidences of indebtedness of the purchaser) do not exceed 30 percent of the selling price, or

(2) Deferred-payment sales of real property in which the payments received in cash or property other than evidences of indebtedness of the purchaser during the taxable year in which the sale is made exceed 30 percent of the selling price.

(c) *Determination of "selling price".* In the sale of mortgaged property the amount of the mortgage, whether the property is merely taken subject to the mortgage or whether the mortgage is assumed by the purchaser, shall, for the purpose of determining whether a sale is on the installment plan, be included as a part of the "selling price"; and for the purpose of determining the payments and the total contract price as those terms are used in section 453, and §§ 1.453-1 through 1.453-7, the amount of such mortgage shall be included only to the extent that it exceeds the basis of the property. The term "payments" does not include amounts received by the vendor in the year of sale from the disposition to a third person of notes given by the vendee as part of the purchase price which are due and payable in subsequent years. Commissions and other selling expenses paid or incurred by the vendor shall not reduce the amount of the payments, the total contract price, or the selling price. [Reg. § 1.453-4.]

☐ [T.D. 6314, 9-17-58. Amended by T.D. 6500, 11-26-60.]

[Reg. § 1.453-5]

§ 1.453-5. Sale of real property treated on installment method—(a) *In general.* In any transaction described in paragraph (b)(1) of § 1.453-4, that is, sales of real property in which there are no payments during the year of sale or the payments in that year do not exceed 30 percent of the selling price, the vendor may return as income from each such transaction in any taxable year that proportion of the installment payments actually received in that year which the gross profit (as described in paragraph (b) of § 1.453-1) realized or to be realized when the property is paid for bears to the total contract price. In any case, the sale of each lot or parcel of a subdivided tract must be treated as a separate transaction and gain or loss computed accordingly. (See paragraph (a) of § 1.61-6.)

(b) *Defaults and repossessions*—(1) *Effective date.* This paragraph shall apply only with respect to taxable years beginning before September 3, 1964, in respect of which an election has not been properly made to have the provisions of section 1038 apply. For rules applicable to taxable years beginning after September 2, 1964, and for taxable years beginning after December 31, 1957, to which such an election applies, see §§ 1.1038 through 1.1038-3.

(2) *Gain or loss on reacquisition of property.* If the purchaser of real property on the installment plan defaults in any of his payments, and the vendor returning income on the installment method reacquires the property sold, whether title thereto had been retained by the vendor or transferred to the purchaser, gain or loss for the year in which the reacquisition occurs is to be computed upon any installment obligations of the purchaser which are satisfied or discharged upon the reacquisition or are applied by the vendor to the purchase or bid price of the property. Such gain or loss is to be measured by the difference between the fair market value at the date of reacquisition of the property reacquired (including the fair market value of any fixed improvements placed on the property by the purchaser) and the basis in the hands of the vendor of the obligations of the purchaser which are so satisfied, discharged, or applied, with proper adjustment for any other amounts realized or costs incurred in connection with the reacquisition.

(3) *Fair market value of reacquired property.* If the property reacquired is bid in by the vendor at a foreclosure sale, the fair market value of the property shall be presumed to be the purchase or bid price thereof in the absence of clear and convincing proof to the contrary.

(4) *Basis of obligations.* The basis in the hands of the vendor of the obligations of the purchaser satisfied, discharged, or applied upon the reacquisition of the property will be the excess of the face value of such obligations over an amount equal to the income which would be returnable were the obligations paid in full. For definition of the basis of an installment obligation, see section 453(d)(2) and paragraph (b)(2) of § 1.453-9.

(5) *Bad debt deduction.* No deduction for a bad debt shall in any case be taken on account of any portion of the obligations of the purchaser which are treated by the vendor as not having been satisfied, discharged, or applied upon the reacquisition of the property, unless it is clearly shown that after the property was reacquired the purchaser remained liable for such portion; and in no event shall the amount of the deduction exceed the basis in the hands of the vendor of the portion of the obligations with respect to which the purchaser remained liable after the reacquisition. See section 166 and the regulations thereunder.

(6) *Basis of reacquired property.* If the property reacquired is subsequently sold, the basis for determining gain or loss is the fair market value of the property at the date of reacquisition, including the fair market value of any fixed improvements placed on the property by the purchaser. [Reg. § 1.453-5.]

☐ [*T.D.* 6314, 9-17-58. *Amended by T.D.* 6500, 11-26-60 *and T.D.* 6916, 4-12-67.]

[Reg. § 1.453-6]

§ 1.453-6. **Deferred payment sale of real property not on installment method.**—(a) *Value of obligations.* (1) In transactions included in paragraph (b)(2) of § 1.453-4, that is, sales of real property involving deferred payments in which the payments received during the year of sale exceed 30 percent of the selling price, the obligations of the purchaser received by the vendor are to be considered as an amount realized to the extent of their fair market value in ascertaining the profit or loss from the transaction. Such obligations, however, are not considered in determining whether the payments during the year of sale exceed 30 percent of the selling price.

(2) If the obligations received by the vendor have no fair market value, the payments in cash or other property having a fair market value shall be applied against and reduce the basis of the property sold and, if in excess of such basis, shall be taxable to the extent of the excess. Gain or loss is realized when the obligations are disposed of or satisfied, the amount thereof being the difference between the reduced basis as provided in the preceding sentence and the amount realized therefor. Only in rare and extraordinary cases does property have no fair market value.

(b) *Repossession of property where title is retained by vendor*—(1) *Gain or loss on repossession.* If the vendor in sales referred to in paragraph (a) of this section has retained title to the property and the purchaser defaults in any of his payments, and the vendor repossesses the property, the difference between—

(i) The entire amount of the payments actually received on the contract and retained by the vendor plus the fair market value at the time of repossession of fixed improvements placed on the property by the purchaser, and

(ii) The sum of the profits previously returned as income in connection therewith and an amount representing what would have been a proper adjustment for exhaustion, wear and tear, obsolescence, amortization, and depletion of the property during the period the property was in the hands of the purchaser had the sale not been made, will constitute gain or loss, as the case may

Reg. § 1.453-6(b)(1)

be, to the vendor for the year in which the property is repossessed.

(2) *Basis of repossessed property.* The basis of the property described in subparagraph (2) of this paragraph in the hands of the vendor will be the original basis at the time of the sale plus the fair market value at the time of repossession of fixed improvements placed on the property by the purchaser, except that, with respect to repossessions occurring after September 18, 1958, the basis of the property shall be reduced by what would have been a proper adjustment for exhaustion, wear and tear, obsolescence, amortization, and depletion of the property during the period the property was in the hands of the purchaser if the sale had not been made.

(c) *Reacquisition of property where title is transferred to purchaser*—(1) *Gain or loss on reacquisition.* If the vendor in sales described in paragraph (a) of this section has previously transferred title to the purchaser, and the purchaser defaults in any of his payments, and the vendor accepts a voluntary reconveyance of the property, in partial or full satisfaction of the unpaid portion of the purchase price, the receipt of the property so reacquired, to the extent of its fair market value at that time, including the fair market value of fixed improvements placed on the property by the purchaser, shall be considered as the receipt of payment on the obligations satisfied. If the fair market value of the property is greater than the basis of the obligations of the purchaser so satisfied (generally, such basis being the fair market value of such obligations previously recognized in computing income), the excess constitutes ordinary income. If the value of such property is less than the basis of such obligations, the difference may be deducted as a bad debt if uncollectible, except that, if the obligations satisfied are securities (as defined in section 165(g)(2)(C)), any gain or loss resulting from the transaction is a capital gain or loss subject to the provisions of sections 1201 through 1241.

(2) *Basis of reacquired property.* If the reacquired property described in subparagraph (1) of this paragraph is subsequently sold, the basis for determining gain or loss is the fair market value of the property at the date of reacquisition, including the fair market value of the fixed improvements placed on the property by the purchaser. See section 166 and the regulations thereunder with respect to property reacquired by the vendor in a foreclosure proceeding.

(d) *Effective date.* Paragraphs (b) and (c) of this section shall apply only with respect to taxable years beginning before September 3, 1964, in respect of which an election has not been properly made to have the provisions of section 1038 apply. For rules applicable to taxable years beginning after September 2, 1964, and for taxable years beginning after December 31, 1957, to which such an election applies, see §§ 1.1038 through 1.1038-3. [Reg. § 1.453-6.]

☐ [T.D. 6314, 9-17-58. Amended by T.D. 6916, 4-12-67.]

[Reg. § 1.453-9]

§ 1.453-9. **Gain or loss on disposition of installment obligations.**—(a) *In general.* Subject to the exceptions contained in section 453(d)(4) and paragraph (c) of this section, the entire amount of gain or loss resulting from any disposition or satisfaction of installment obligations, computed in accordance with section 453(d), is recognized in the taxable year of such disposition or satisfaction and shall be considered as resulting from the sale or exchange of the property in respect of which the installment obligation was received by the taxpayer.

(b) *Computation of gain or loss.* (1) The amount of gain or loss resulting under paragraph (a) of this section is the difference between the basis of the obligation and (i) the amount realized, in the case of satisfaction at other than face value or in the case of a sale or exchange, or (ii) the fair market value of the obligation at the time of disposition, if such disposition is other than by sale or exchange.

(2) The basis of an installment obligation shall be the excess of the face value of the obligation over an amount equal to the income which would be returnable were the obligation satisfied in full.

(3) The application of subparagraphs (1) and (2) of this paragraph may be illustrated by the following examples:

Example (1). In 1960 the M Corporation sold a piece of unimproved real estate to B for $20,000. The company acquired the property in 1948 at a cost of $10,000. During 1960 the company received $5,000 cash and vendee's notes for the remainder of the selling price, or $15,000, payable in subsequent years. In 1962, before the vendee made any further payments, the company sold the notes for $13,000 in cash. The corporation makes its returns on the calendar year basis. The income to be reported for 1962 is $5,500, computed as follows:

Methods of Accounting 36,809
See p. 20,601 for regulations not amended to reflect law changes

Proceeds of sale of notes		$13,000
Selling price of property	$20,000	
Cost of property	10,000	
Total profit	10,000	
Total contract price	20,000	

Percent of profit, or proportion of each payment returnable as income, $10,000 divided by $20,000, 50 percent.

Face value of notes	$15,000
Amount of income returnable were the notes satisfied in full, 50 percent of $15,000	7,500
Basis of obligation—excess of face value or notes over amount of income returnable were the notes satisfied in full	$ 7,500
Taxable income to be reported for 1962	5,500

Example (2). Suppose in example (1) the M Corporation, instead of selling the notes, distributed them in 1962 to its shareholders as a dividend, and at the time of such distribution, the fair market value of the notes was $14,000.

The income to be reported for 1962 is $6,500, computed as follows:

Fair market value of notes	$14,000
Basis of obligation—excess of face value of notes over amount of income returnable were the notes satisfied in full (computed as in example (1))	7,500
Taxable income to be reported for 1962	6,500

(c) *Disposition from which no gain or loss is recognized.* (1)(i) Under section 453(d)(4)(A), no gain or loss shall be recognized to a distributing corporation with respect to the distribution made after November 13, 1966, of installment obligations if (*a*) the distribution is made pursuant to a plan for the complete liquidation of a subsidiary under section 332, and (*b*) the basis of such obligations in the hands of the distributee is determined under section 334(b)(1).

(ii) Under section 453(d)(4)(B), no gain or loss shall be recognized to a distributing corporation with respect to the distribution of installment obligations if the distribution is made, pursuant to a plan for the complete liquidation of a corporation which meets the requirements of section 337, under conditions whereby no gain or loss would have been recognized to the corporation had such installment obligations been sold or exchanged on the day of the distribution. The preceding sentence shall not apply to the extent that under section 453(d)(1) gain to the distributing corporation would be considered as gain to which section 341(f)(2), 617(d)(1), 1245(a)(1), 1250(a)(1), 1251(c)(1), 1252(a)(1), or 1254(a)(1) applies, computed under the principles of the regulations under such provisions. See paragraph (d) of § 1.1245-6, paragraph (c)(6) of § 1.1250-1, paragraph (e)(6) of § 1.1251-1, paragraph (d)(3) of § 1.1252-1, and paragraph (d) of § 1.1254-1.

(2) Where the Code provides for exceptions to the recognition of gain or loss in the case of certain dispositions, no gain or loss shall result under section 453(d) in the case of a disposition of an installment obligation. Such exceptions include: Certain transfers to corporations under sections 351 and 361; contributions of property to a partnership by a partner under section 721; and distributions by a partnership to a partner under section 731 (except as provided by section 736 and section 751).

(3) Any amount received by a person in payment or settlement of an installment obligation acquired in a transaction described in subparagraphs (1) or (2) of this paragraph (other than an amount received by a stockholder with respect to an installment obligation distributed to him pursuant to section 337) shall be considered to have the character it would have had in the hands of the person from whom such installment obligation was acquired.

(d) *Carryover of installment method.* For the treatment of income derived from installment obligations received in transactions to which section 381(a) is applicable, see section 381(c)(8) and the regulations thereunder.

(e) *Installment obligations transmitted at death.* Where installment obligations are transmitted at death, see section 691(a)(4) and the regulations thereunder for the treatment of amounts considered income in respect of a decedent.

(f) *Losses.* See subchapter P (sections 1201 and following), Chapter 1 of the Code, as to the limitation on capital losses sustained by corporations and the limitation as to both capital gains and capital losses of individuals.

(g) *Disposition of installment obligations to life insurance companies.* (1) Notwithstanding the provisions of section 453(d)(4) and paragraph (c)

Reg. § 1.453-9(g)

of this section or any provision of subtitle A relating to the nonrecognition of gain, the entire amount of any gain realized on the disposition of an installment obligation by any person, other than a life insurance company (as defined in section 801(a) and paragraph (b) of § 1.801-3), to a life insurance company or to a partnership of which a life insurance company is a partner shall be recognized and treated in accordance with section 453(d)(1) and paragraphs (a) and (b) of this section. If a corporation which is a life insurance company for the taxable year was a corporation which was not a life insurance company for the preceding taxable year, such corporation shall be treated, for purposes of section 453 (d)(1) and this paragraph, as having transferred to a life insurance company, on the last day of the preceding taxable year, all installment obligations which it held on such last day. The gain, if any, realized by reason of the installment obligations being so transferred shall be recognized and treated in accordance with section 453(d)(1) and paragraphs (a) and (b) of this section. Similarly, a partnership of which a life insurance company becomes a partner shall be treated, for purposes of section 453(d)(1) and this paragraph, as having transferred to a life insurance company, on the last day of the preceding taxable year of such partnership, all installment obligations which it holds at the time such life insurance company becomes a partner. The gain, if any, realized by reason of the installment obligations being so transferred shall be recognized and treated in accordance with section 453(d)(1) and paragraphs (a) and (b) of this section.

(2) The provisions of section 453(d)(5) and subparagraph (1) of this paragraph shall not apply to losses sustained in connection with the disposition of installment obligations to a life insurance company.

(3) For the effective date of the provisions of section 453(d)(5) and this paragraph, see paragraph (f) of § 1.453-10.

(4) Application of the provisions of this paragraph may be illustrated by the following examples:

Example (1). A, an individual, in a transaction to which section 351 applies, transfers in 1961 certain assets, including installment obligations, to a new corporation, X, which qualifies as a life insurance company (as defined in section 801(a)) for the year 1961. A makes his return on the calendar year basis. Section 453(d)(5) provides that the nonrecognition provisions of section 351 will not apply to the installment obligations transferred by A to X Corporation. Therefore, the entire amount of any gain realized by A on the transfer of the installment obligations shall be recognized in 1961, with the amount of any such gain computed in accordance with the provisions of section 453(d)(1) and paragraph (b) of this section.

Example (2). The M Corporation did not qualify as a life insurance company (as defined in section 801(a)) for the taxable year 1958. On December 31, 1958, it held $60,000 of installment obligations. The M Corporation qualified as a life insurance company for the taxable year 1959. Accordingly, the M Corporation is treated as having transferred to a life insurance company, on December 31, 1958, the $60,000 of installment obligations it held on such date. The gain, if any, realized by M by reason of such installment obligations being so transferred shall be recognized in the taxable year 1958, with the amount of any such gain computed in accordance with the provisions of section 453(d)(1) and paragraph (b) of this section.

Example (3). During its taxable year 1958, none of the partners of the N partnership qualified as a life insurance company (as defined in section 801(a)). The N partnership held $30,000 of installment obligations on December 31, 1958. On July 30, 1959, the O Corporation, a life insurance company (as defined in section 801(a)), became a partner in the partnership. The N partnership held $50,000 of installment obligations on July 30, 1959. Pursuant to section 453(d)(5), the N partnership is treated as having transferred to a life insurance company, on December 31, 1958, the $50,000 of installment obligations it held on July 30, 1959. The gain, if any, realized by the N partnership by reason of such installment obligations being so transferred shall be recognized in the taxable year 1958, with the amount of any such gain computed in accordance with the provisions of section 453(d)(1) and paragraph (b) of this section.

Example (4). In 1960, the P Corporation, in a reorganization qualifying under section 368(a), transferred certain assets (including installment obligations) to the R Corporation, a life insurance company as defined in section 801(a). P realized a loss upon the transfer of the installment obligations, which was not recognized under section 361. Pursuant to subparagraph (2) of paragraph (c) of this section, no loss with respect to the transfer of these obligations will be recognized to P under section 453(d)(1). [Reg. § 1.453-9.]

☐ [T.D. 6314, 9-17-58. Amended by T.D. 6590, 2-12-62; T.D. 6832, 7-6-65; T.D. 7084, 1-7-71; T.D. 7418, 5-6-76 and T.D. 8586, 1-9-95.]

[Reg. § 1.453-10]

§ 1.453-10. Effective date.—(a) Except as provided in this section, the provisions of section 453 and §§ 1.453-1 through 1.453-9 shall apply to

Methods of Accounting

taxable years beginning after December 31, 1953, and ending after August 16, 1954.

(b) The provisions of paragraphs (a)(2) and (3), (b), and (c) of § 1.453-8 shall apply to taxable years ending after December 17, 1958.

(c) Under the provisions of sections 453(b) and 7851(a)(1)(C), section 453(b)(1) and the regulations with respect thereto shall also apply—

(1) To a sale or other disposition during a taxable year beginning before January 1, 1954, only if the income was returnable (by reason of section 44(b) of the Internal Revenue Code of 1939) on the basis and in the manner prescribed in section 44(a) of such code.

(2) To a sale or other disposition during a taxable year beginning after December 31, 1953, and ending before August 17, 1954, though such taxable year is subject to the provisions of the Internal Revenue Code of 1939.

(d) Under the provisions of sections 453(c)(1)(B) and 7851(a)(1)(C), section 453(c) and the regulations with respect thereto shall also apply to taxable years beginning after December 31, 1953, and ending before August 17, 1954, though such taxable years are subject to the provisions of the Internal Revenue Code of 1939.

(e) The provisions of paragraph (b)(3) of § 1.453-6 shall apply to repossessions occurring after December 18, 1958.

(f) The provisions of section 453(d)(5) and paragraph (g) of § 1.453-9 shall apply to taxable years ending after December 31, 1957, but only as to transfers or other dispositions of installment obligations occurring after such date. [Reg. § 1.453-10.]

☐ [T.D. 6314, 9-17-58. Amended by T.D. 6590, 2-12-62 and T.D. 6682, 10-15-63.]

[Reg. § 1.453-11]

§ 1.453-11. **Installment obligations received from a liquidating corporation.**—(a) *In general*—(1) *Overview.* Except as provided in section 453(h)(1)(C) (relating to installment sales of depreciable property to certain closely related persons), a qualifying shareholder (as defined in paragraph (b) of this section) who receives a qualifying installment obligation (as defined in paragraph (c) of this section) in a liquidation that satisfies section 453(h)(1)(A) treats the receipt of payments in respect of the obligation, rather than the receipt of the obligation itself, as a receipt of payment for the shareholder's stock. The shareholder reports the payments received on the installment method unless the shareholder elects otherwise in accordance with § 15a.453-1(d) of this chapter.

(2) *Coordination with other provisions*—(i) *Deemed sale of stock for installment obligation.* Except as specifically provided in section 453(h)(1)(C), a qualifying shareholder treats a qualifying installment obligation, for all purposes of the Internal Revenue Code, as if the obligation is received by the shareholder from the person issuing the obligation in exchange for the shareholder's stock in the liquidating corporation. For example, if the stock of a corporation that is liquidating is traded on an established securities market, an installment obligation distributed to a shareholder of the corporation in exchange for the shareholder's stock does not qualify for installment reporting pursuant to section 453(k)(2).

(ii) *Special rules to account for the qualifying installment obligation*—(A) *Issue price.* A qualifying installment obligation is treated by a qualifying shareholder as newly issued on the date of the distribution. The issue price of the qualifying installment obligation on that date is equal to the sum of the adjusted issue price of the obligation on the date of the distribution (as determined under § 1.1275-1(b)) and the amount of any qualified stated interest (as defined in § 1.1273-1(c)) that has accrued prior to the distribution but that is not payable until after the distribution. For purposes of the preceding sentence, if the qualifying installment obligation is subject to § 1.446-2 (e.g., a debt instrument that has unstated interest under section 483), the adjusted issue price of the obligation is determined under § 1.446-2(c) and (d).

(B) *Variable rate debt instrument.* If the qualifying installment obligation is a variable rate debt instrument (as defined in § 1.1275-5), the shareholder uses the equivalent fixed rate debt instrument (within the meaning of § 1.1275-5(e)(3)(ii)) constructed for the qualifying installment obligation as of the date the obligation was issued to the liquidating corporation to determine the accruals of original issue discount, if any, and interest on the obligation.

(3) *Liquidating distributions treated as selling price.* All amounts distributed or treated as distributed to a qualifying shareholder incident to the liquidation, including cash, the issue price of qualifying installment obligations as determined under paragraph (a)(2)(ii)(A) of this section, and the fair market value of other property (including obligations that are not qualifying installment obligations) are considered as having been received by the shareholder as the selling price (as defined in § 15a.453-1(b)(2)(ii) of this chapter) for the shareholder's stock in the liquidating corporation. For the proper method of reporting liquidating distributions received in more than one

Reg. § 1.453-11(a)(3)

taxable year of a shareholder, see paragraph (d) of this section. An election not to report on the installment method an installment obligation received in the liquidation applies to all distributions received in the liquidation.

(4) *Assumption of corporate liability by shareholders.* For purposes of this section, if in the course of a liquidation a shareholder assumes secured or unsecured liabilities of the liquidating corporation, or receives property from the corporation subject to such liabilities (including any tax liabilities incurred by the corporation on the distribution), the amount of the liabilities is added to the shareholder's basis in the stock of the liquidating corporation. These additions to basis do not affect the shareholder's holding period for the stock. These liabilities do not reduce the amounts received in computing the selling price.

(5) *Examples.* The provisions of this paragraph (a) are illustrated by the following examples. Except as otherwise provided, assume in each example that A, an individual who is a calendar-year taxpayer, owns all of the stock of T corporation. A's adjusted tax basis in that stock is $100,000. On February 1, 1998, T, an accrual method taxpayer, adopts a plan of complete liquidation that satisfies section 453(h)(1)(A) and immediately sells all of its assets to unrelated B corporation in a single transaction. The examples are as follows:

Example 1. (i) The stated purchase price for T's assets is $3,500,000. In consideration for the sale, B makes a down payment of $500,000 and issues a 10-year installment obligation with a stated principal amount of $3,000,000. The obligation provides for interest payments of $150,000 on January 31 of each year, with the total principal amount due at maturity.

(ii) Assume that for purposes of section 1274, the test rate on February 1, 1998, is 8 percent, compounded semi-annually. Also assume that a semi-annual accrual period is used. Under § 1.1274-2, the issue price of the obligation on February 1, 1998, is $2,368,450. Accordingly, the obligation has $631,550 of original issue discount ($3,000,000 − $2,368,450). Between February 1 and July 31, $19,738 of original issue discount and $75,000 of qualified stated interest accrue with respect to the obligation and are taken into account by T.

(iii) On July 31, 1998, T distributes the installment obligation to A in exchange for A's stock. No other property is ever distributed to A. On January 31, 1999, A receives the first annual payment of $150,000 from B.

(iv) When the obligation is distributed to A on July 31, 1998, it is treated as if the obligation is received by A in an installment sale of shares directly to B on that date. Under § 1.1275-1(b), the adjusted issue price of the obligation on that date is $2,388,188 (original issue price of $2,368,450 plus accrued original issue discount of $19,738). Accordingly, the issue price of the obligation under paragraph (a)(2)(ii)(A) of this section is $2,463,188, the sum of the adjusted issue price of the obligation on that date ($2,388,188) and the amount of accrued but unpaid qualified stated interest ($75,000).

(v) The selling price and contract price of A's stock in T is $2,463,188, and the gross profit is $2,363,188 ($2,463,188 selling price less A's adjusted tax basis of $100,000). A's gross profit ratio is thus 96 percent (gross profit of $2,363,188 divided by total contract price of $2,463,188).

(vi) Under §§ 1.446-2(e)(1) and 1.1275-2(a), $98,527 of the $150,000 payment is treated as a payment of the interest and original issue discount that accrued on the obligation from July 31, 1998, to January 31, 1999 ($75,000 of qualified stated interest and $23,527 of original issue discount). The balance of the payment ($51,473) is treated as a payment of principal. A's gain recognized in 1999 is $49,414 (96 percent of $51,473).

Example 2. (i) T owns Blackacre, unimproved real property, with an adjusted tax basis of $700,000. Blackacre is subject to a mortgage (underlying mortgage) of $1,100,000. A is not personally liable on the underlying mortgage and the T shares held by A are not encumbered by the underlying mortgage. The other assets of T consist of $400,000 of cash and $600,000 of accounts receivable attributable to sales of inventory in the ordinary course of business. The unsecured liabilities of T total $900,000.

(ii) On February 1, 1998, T adopts a plan of complete liquidation complying with section 453(h)(1)(A), and promptly sells Blackacre to B for a 4-year mortgage note (bearing adequate stated interest and otherwise meeting all of the requirements of section 453) in the face amount of $4 million. Under the agreement between T and B, T (or its successor) is to continue to make principal and interest payments on the underlying mortgage. Immediately thereafter, T completes its liquidation by distributing to A its remaining cash of $400,000 (after payment of T's tax liabilities), accounts receivable of $600,000, and the $4 million B note. A assumes T's $900,000 of unsecured liabilities and receives the distributed property subject to the obligation to make payments on the $1,100,000 underlying mortgage. A receives no payments from B on the B note during 1998.

Reg. § 1.453-11(a)(4)

Methods of Accounting

(iii) Unless A elects otherwise, the transaction is reported by A on the installment method. The selling price is $5 million (cash of $400,000, accounts receivable of $600,000, and the B note of $4 million). The total contract price also is $5 million. A's adjusted tax basis in the T shares, initially $100,000, is increased by the $900,000 of unsecured T liabilities assumed by A and by the obligation (subject to which A takes the distributed property) to make payments on the $1,100,000 underlying mortgage on Blackacre, for an aggregate adjusted tax basis of $2,100,000. Accordingly, the gross profit is $2,900,000 (selling price of $5 million less aggregate adjusted tax basis of $2,100,000). The gross profit ratio is 58 percent (gross profit of $2,900,000 divided by the total contract price of $5 million). The 1998 payments to A are $1 million ($400,000 cash plus $600,000 receivables) and A recognizes gain in 1998 of $580,000 (58 percent of $1 million).

(iv) In 1999, A receives payment from B on the B note of $1 million (exclusive of interest). A's gain recognized in 1999 is $580,000 (58 percent of $1 million).

(b) *Qualifying shareholder.* For purposes of this section, *qualifying shareholder* means a shareholder to which, with respect to the liquidating distribution, section 331 applies. For example, a creditor that receives a distribution from a liquidating corporation, in exchange for the creditor's claim, is not a qualifying shareholder as a result of that distribution regardless of whether the liquidation satisfies section 453(h)(1)(A).

(c) *Qualifying installment obligation*—(1) *In general.* For purposes of this section, *qualifying installment obligation* means an installment obligation (other than an evidence of indebtedness described in § 15a.453-1(e) of this chapter, relating to obligations that are payable on demand or are readily tradable) acquired in a sale or exchange of corporate assets by a liquidating corporation during the 12-month period beginning on the date the plan of liquidation is adopted. See paragraph (c)(4) of this section for an exception for installment obligations acquired in respect of certain sales of inventory. Also see paragraph (c)(5) of this section for an exception for installment obligations attributable to sales of certain property that do not generally qualify for installment method treatment.

(2) *Corporate assets.* Except as provided in section 453(h)(1)(C), in paragraph (c)(4) of this section (relating to certain sales of inventory), and in paragraph (c)(5) of this section (relating to certain tax avoidance transactions), the nature of the assets sold by, and the tax consequences to, the selling corporation do not affect whether an installment obligation is a qualifying installment obligation. Thus, for example, the fact that the fair market value of an asset is less than the adjusted basis of that asset in the hands of the corporation; or that the sale of an asset will subject the corporation to depreciation recapture (e.g., under section 1245 or section 1250); or that the assets of a trade or business sold by the corporation for an installment obligation include depreciable property, certain marketable securities, accounts receivable, installment obligations, or cash; or that the distribution of assets to the shareholder is or is not taxable to the corporation under sections 336 and 453B, does not affect whether installment obligations received in exchange for those assets are treated as qualifying installment obligations by the shareholder. However, an obligation received by the corporation in exchange for cash, in a transaction unrelated to a sale or exchange of noncash assets by the corporation, is not treated as a qualifying installment obligation.

(3) *Installment obligations distributed in liquidations described in section 453(h)(1)(E)*—(i) *In general.* In the case of a liquidation to which section 453(h)(1)(E) (relating to certain liquidating subsidiary corporations) applies, a qualifying installment obligation acquired in respect of a sale or exchange by the liquidating subsidiary corporation will be treated as a qualifying installment obligation if distributed by a controlling corporate shareholder (within the meaning of section 368(c)) to a qualifying shareholder. The preceding sentence is applied successively to each controlling corporate shareholder, if any, above the first controlling corporate shareholder.

(i) *Examples.* The provisions of this paragraph (c)(3) are illustrated by the following examples:

Example 1. (i) A, an individual, owns all of the stock of T corporation, a C corporation. T has an operating division and three wholly-owned subsidiaries, X, Y, and Z. On February 1, 1998, T, Y, and Z all adopt plans of complete liquidation.

(ii) On March 1, 1998, the following sales are made to unrelated purchasers: T sells the assets of its operating division to B for cash and an installment obligation. T sells the stock of X to C for an installment obligation. Y sells all of its assets to D for an installment obligation. Z sells all of its assets to E for cash. The B, C, and D installment obligations bear adequate stated interest and meet the requirements of section 453.

(iii) In June 1998, Y and Z completely liquidate, distributing their respective assets (the D installment obligation and cash) to T. In July 1998, T completely liquidates, distributing to A

Reg. § 1.453-11(c)(3)

cash and the installment obligations respectively issued by B, C, and D. The liquidation of T is a liquidation to which section 453(h) applies and the liquidations of Y and Z into T are liquidations to which section 332 applies.

(iv) Because T is in control of Y (within the meaning of section 368(c)), the D obligation acquired by Y is treated as acquired by T pursuant to section 453(h)(1)(E). A is a qualifying shareholder and the installment obligations issued by B, C, and D are qualifying installment obligations. Unless A elects otherwise, A reports the transaction on the installment method as if the cash and installment obligations had been received in an installment sale of the stock of T corporation. Under section 453B(d), no gain or loss is recognized by Y on the distribution of the D installment obligation to T. Under sections 453B(a) and 336, T recognizes gain or loss on the distribution of the B, C, and D installment obligations to A in exchange for A's stock.

Example 2. (i) A, a cash-method individual taxpayer, owns all of the stock of P corporation, a C corporation. P owns 30 percent of the stock of Q corporation. The balance of the Q stock is owned by unrelated individuals. On February 1, 1998, P adopts a plan of complete liquidation and sells all of its property, other than its Q stock, to B, an unrelated purchaser for cash and an installment obligation bearing adequate stated interest. On March 1, 1998, Q adopts a plan of complete liquidation and sells all of its property to an unrelated purchaser, C, for cash and installment obligations. Q immediately distributes the cash and installment obligations to its shareholders in completion of its liquidation. Promptly thereafter, P liquidates, distributing to A cash, the B installment obligation, and a C installment obligation that P received in the liquidation of Q.

(ii) In the hands of A, the B installment obligation is a qualifying installment obligation. In the hands of P, the C installment obligation was a qualifying installment obligation. However, in the hands of A, the C installment obligation is not treated as a qualifying installment obligation because P owned only 30 percent of the stock of Q. Because P did not own the requisite 80 percent stock interest in Q, P was not a controlling corporate shareholder of Q (within the meaning of section 368(c)) immediately before the liquidation. Therefore, section 453(h)(1)(E) does not apply. Thus, in the hands of A, the C obligation is considered to be a third-party note (not a purchaser's evidence of indebtedness) and is treated as a payment to A in the year of distribution. Accordingly, for 1998, A reports as payment the cash and the fair market value of the C obligation distributed to A in the liquidation of P.

(iii) Because P held 30 percent of the stock of Q, section 453B(d) is inapplicable to P. Under sections 453B(a) and 336, Q recognizes gain or loss on the distribution of the C obligation. P also recognizes gain or loss on the distribution of the B and C installment obligations to A in exchange for A's stock. See sections 453B and 336.

(4) *Installment obligations attributable to certain sales of inventory*—(i) *In general.* An installment obligation acquired by a corporation in a liquidation that satisfies section 453(h)(1)(A) in respect of a broken lot of inventory is not a qualifying installment obligation. If an installment obligation is acquired in respect of a broken lot of inventory and other assets, only the portion of the installment obligation acquired in respect of the broken lot of inventory is not a qualifying installment obligation. The portion of the installment obligation attributable to other assets is a qualifying installment obligation. For purposes of this section, the term *broken lot of inventory* means inventory property that is sold or exchanged other than in bulk to one person in one transaction involving substantially all of the inventory property attributable to a trade or business of the corporation. See paragraph (c)(4)(ii) of this section for rules for determining what portion of an installment obligation is not a qualifying installment obligation and paragraph (c)(4)(iii) of this section for rules determining the application of payments on an installment obligation only a portion of which is a qualifying installment obligation.

(ii) *Rules for determining nonqualifying portion of an installment obligation.* If a broken lot of inventory is sold to a purchaser together with other corporate assets for consideration consisting of an installment obligation and either cash, other property, the assumption of (or taking property subject to) corporate liabilities by the purchaser, or some combination thereof, the installment obligation is treated as having been acquired in respect of a broken lot of inventory only to the extent that the fair market value of the broken lot of inventory exceeds the sum of unsecured liabilities assumed by the purchaser, secured liabilities which encumber the broken lot of inventory and are assumed by the purchaser or to which the broken lot of inventory is subject, and the sum of the cash and fair market value of other property received. This rule applies solely for the purpose of determining the portion of the installment obligation (if any) that is attributable to the broken lot of inventory.

Reg. § 1.453-11(c)(4)

Methods of Accounting

(iii) *Application of payments.* If, by reason of the application of paragraph (c)(4)(ii) of this section, a portion of an installment obligation is not a qualifying installment obligation, then for purposes of determining the amount of gain to be reported by the shareholder under section 453, payments on the obligation (other than payments of qualified stated interest) shall be applied first to the portion of the obligation that is not a qualifying installment obligation.

(iv) *Example.* The following example illustrates the provisions of this paragraph (c)(4). In this example, assume that all obligations bear adequate stated interest within the meaning of section 1274(c)(2) and that the fair market value of each nonqualifying installment obligation equals its face amount. The example is as follows:

Example. (i) P corporation has three operating divisions, X, Y, and Z, each engaged in a separate trade or business, and a minor amount of investment assets. On July 1, 1998, P adopts a plan of complete liquidation that meets the criteria of section 453(h)(1)(A). The following sales are promptly made to purchasers unrelated to P: P sells all of the assets of the X division (including all of the inventory property) to B for $30,000 cash and installment obligations totalling $200,000. P sells substantially all of the inventory property of the Y division to C for a $100,000 installment obligation, and sells all of the other assets of the Y division (excluding cash but including installment receivables previously acquired in the ordinary course of the business of the Y division) to D for a $170,000 installment obligation. P sells 1/3 of the inventory property of the Z division to E for $100,000 cash, 1/3 of the inventory property of the Z division to F for a $100,000 installment obligation, and all of the other assets of the Z division (including the remaining 1/3 of the inventory property worth $100,000) to G for $60,000 cash, a $240,000 installment obligation, and the assumption by G of the liabilities of the Z division. The liabilities assumed by G, which are unsecured liabilities and liabilities encumbering the inventory property acquired by G, aggregate $30,000. Thus, the total purchase price G pays is $330,000.

(ii) P immediately completes its liquidation, distributing the cash and installment obligations, which otherwise meet the requirements of section 453, to A, an individual cash-method taxpayer who is its sole shareholder. In 1999, G makes a payment to A of $100,000 (exclusive of interest) on the $240,000 installment obligation.

(iii) In the hands of A, the installment obligations issued by B, C, and D are qualifying installment obligations because they were timely acquired by P in a sale or exchange of its assets. In addition, the installment obligation issued by C is a qualifying installment obligation because it arose from a sale to one person in one transaction of substantially all of the inventory property of the trade or business engaged in by the Y division.

(iv) The installment obligation issued by F is not a qualifying installment obligation because it is in respect of a broken lot of inventory. A portion of the installment obligation issued by G is a qualifying installment obligation and a portion is not a qualifying installment obligation, determined as follows: G purchased part of the inventory property (with a fair market value of $100,000) and all of the other assets of the Z division by paying cash ($60,000), issuing an installment obligation ($240,000), and assuming liabilities of the Z division ($30,000). The assumed liabilities ($30,000) and cash ($60,000) are attributed first to the inventory property. Therefore, only $10,000 of the $240,000 installment obligation is attributed to inventory property. Accordingly, in the hands of A, the G installment obligation is a qualifying installment obligation to the extent of $230,000, but is not a qualifying installment obligation to the extent of the $10,000 attributable to the inventory property.

(v) In the 1998 liquidation of P, A receives a liquidating distribution as follows:

Item	Qualifying Installment Obligations	Cash and Other Property
cash		$190,000
B note	$200,000	
C note	$100,000	
D note	$170,000	
F note		$100,000
G note [1]	$230,000	$ 10,000
Total	$700,000	$300,000

[1] Face amount $240,000.

Reg. § 1.453-11(c)(4)

(vi) Assume that A's adjusted tax basis in the stock of P is $100,000. Under the installment method, A's selling price and the contract price are both $1 million, the gross profit is $900,000 (selling price of $1 million less adjusted tax basis of $100,000), and the gross profit ratio is 90 percent (gross profit of $900,000 divided by the contract price of $1 million). Accordingly, in 1998, A reports gain of $270,000 (90 percent of $300,000 payment in cash and other property). A's adjusted tax basis in each of the qualifying installment obligations is an amount equal to 10 percent of the obligation's respective face amount. A's adjusted tax basis in the F note, a nonqualifying installment obligation, is $100,000, i.e., the fair market value of the note when received by A. A's adjusted tax basis in the G note, a mixed obligation, is $33,000 (10 percent of the $230,000 qualifying installment obligation portion of the note, plus the $10,000 nonqualifying portion of the note).

(vii) With respect to the $100,000 payment received from G in 1999, $10,000 is treated as the recovery of the adjusted tax basis of the nonqualifying portion of the G installment obligation and $9,000 (10 percent of $90,000) is treated as the recovery of the adjusted tax basis of the portion of the note that is a qualifying installment obligation. The remaining $81,000 (90 percent of $90,000) is reported as gain from the sale of A's stock. See paragraph (c)(4)(iii) of this section.

(5) *Installment obligations attributable to sales of certain property*—(i) *In general.* An installment obligation acquired by a liquidating corporation, to the extent attributable to the sale of property described in paragraph (c)(5)(ii) of this section, is not a qualifying obligation if the corporation is formed or availed of for a principal purpose of avoiding section 453(b)(2) (relating to dealer dispositions and certain other dispositions of personal property), section 453(i) (relating to sales of property subject to recapture), or section 453(k) (relating to dispositions under a revolving credit plan and sales of stock or securities traded on an established securities market) through the use of a party bearing a relationship, either directly or indirectly, described in section 267(b) to any shareholder of the corporation.

(ii) *Covered property.* Property is described in this paragraph (c)(5)(ii) if, within 12 months before or after the adoption of the plan of liquidation, the property was owned by any shareholder and—

(A) The shareholder regularly sold or otherwise disposed of personal property of the same type on the installment plan or the property is real property that the shareholder held for sale to customers in the ordinary course of a trade or business (provided the property is not described in section 453(l)(2) (relating to certain exceptions to the definition of dealer dispositions));

(B) The sale of the property by the shareholder would result in recapture income (within the meaning of section 453(i)(2)), but only if the amount of the recapture income is equal to or greater than 50 percent of the property's fair market value on the date of the sale by the corporation;

(C) The property is stock or securities that are traded on an established securities market; or

(D) The sale of the property by the shareholder would have been under a revolving credit plan.

(iii) *Safe harbor.* Paragraph (c)(5)(i) of this section will not apply to the liquidation of a corporation if, on the date the plan of complete liquidation is adopted and thereafter, less than 15 percent of the fair market value of the corporation's assets is attributable to property described in paragraph (c)(5)(ii) of this section.

(iv) *Example.* The provisions of this paragraph (c)(5) are illustrated by the following example:

Example. Ten percent of the fair market value of the assets of T is attributable to stock and securities traded on an established securities market. T owns no other assets described in paragraph (c)(5)(ii) of this section. T, after adopting a plan of complete liquidation, sells all of its stock and securities holdings to C corporation in exchange for an installment obligation bearing adequate stated interest, sells all of its other assets to B corporation for cash, and distributes the cash and installment obligation to its sole shareholder, A, in a complete liquidation that satisfies section 453(h)(1)(A). Because the C installment obligation arose from a sale of publicly traded stock and securities, T cannot report the gain on the sale under the installment method pursuant to section 453(k)(2). In the hands of A, however, the C installment obligation is treated as having arisen out of a sale of the stock of T corporation. In addition, the general rule of paragraph (c)(5)(i) of this section does not apply, even if a principal purpose of the liquidation was the avoidance of section 453(k)(2), because the fair market value of the publicly traded stock and securities is less than 15 percent of the total fair market value of T's assets. Accordingly, section 453(k)(2) does not apply to A, and A may use the installment method to report the gain recognized on the payments it receives in respect of the obligation.

(d) *Liquidating distributions received in more than one taxable year.* If a qualifying shareholder receives liquidating distributions to which this section applies in more than one taxable year, the shareholder must reasonably estimate the gain attributable to distributions received in each taxable year. In allocating basis to calculate the gain for a taxable year, the shareholder must reasonably estimate the anticipated aggregate distributions. For this purpose, the shareholder must take into account distributions and other relevant events or information that the shareholder knows or reasonably could know up to the date on which the federal income tax return for that year is filed. If the gain for a taxable year is properly taken into account on the basis of a reasonable estimate and the exact amount is subsequently determined the difference, if any, must be taken into account for the taxable year in which the subsequent determination is made. However, the shareholder may file an amended return for the earlier year in lieu of taking the difference into account for the subsequent taxable year.

(e) *Effective date.* This section is applicable to distributions of qualifying installment obligations made on or after January 28, 1998. [Reg. § 1.453-11.]

☐ [*T.D.* 8762, 1-27-98.]

[Reg. § 1.453-12]

§ 1.453-12. **Allocation of unrecaptured section 1250 gain reported on the installment method.**—(a) *General rule.* Unrecaptured section 1250 gain, as defined in section 1(h)(7), is reported on the installment method if that method otherwise applies under section 453 or 453A and the corresponding regulations. If gain from an installment sale includes unrecaptured section 1250 gain and adjusted net capital gain (as defined in section 1(h)(4)), the unrecaptured section 1250 gain is taken into account before the adjusted net capital gain.

(b) *Installment payments from sales before May 7, 1997.* The amount of unrecaptured section 1250 gain in an installment payment that is properly taken into account after May 6, 1997, from a sale before May 7, 1997, is determined as if, for all payments properly taken into account after the date of sale but before May 7, 1997, unrecaptured section 1250 gain had been taken into account before adjusted net capital gain.

(c) *Installment payments received after May 6, 1997, and on or before August 23, 1999.* If the amount of unrecaptured section 1250 gain in an installment payment that is properly taken into account after May 6, 1997, and on or before August 23, 1999, is less than the amount that would have been taken into account under this section, the lesser amount is used to determine the amount of unrecaptured section 1250 gain that remains to be taken into account.

(d) *Examples.* In each example, the taxpayer, an individual whose taxable year is the calendar year, does not elect out of the installment method. The installment obligation bears adequate stated interest, and the property sold is real property held in a trade or business that qualifies as both section 1231 property and section 1250 property. In all taxable years, the taxpayer's marginal tax rate on ordinary income is 28 percent. The following examples illustrate the rules of this section:

Example 1. General rule. This example illustrates the rule of paragraph (a) of this section as follows:

(i) In 1999, A sells property for $10,000, to be paid in ten equal annual installments beginning on December 1, 1999. A originally purchased the property for $5000, held the property for several years, and took straight-line depreciation deductions in the amount of $3000. In each of the years 1999-2008, A has no other capital or section 1231 gains or losses.

(ii) A's adjusted basis at the time of the sale is $2000. Of A's $8000 of section 1231 gain on the sale of the property, $3000 is attributable to prior straight-line depreciation deductions and is unrecaptured section 1250 gain. The gain on each installment payment is $800.

(iii) As illustrated in the table in this paragraph (iii) of this *Example 1.*, A takes into account the unrecaptured section 1250 gain first. Therefore, the gain on A's first three payments, received in 1999, 2000, and 2001, is taxed at 25 percent. Of the $800 of gain on the fourth payment, received in 2002, $600 is taxed at 25 percent and the remaining $200 is taxed at 20 percent. The gain on A's remaining six installment payments is taxed at 20 percent. The table is as follows:

	1999	2000	2001	2002	2003	2004-2008	Total gain
Installment gain	800	800	800	800	800	4000	8000
Taxed at 25%	800	800	800	600	...	...	3000
Taxed at 20%	...	...	...	200	800	4000	5000
Remaining to be taxed at 25%	2200	1400	600	...	...	...	...

Example 2. Installment payments from sales prior to May 7, 1997. This example illustrates the rule of paragraph (b) of this section as follows:

(i) The facts are the same as in *Example 1* except that A sold the property in 1994, received the first of the ten annual installment payments on December 1, 1994, and had no other capital or section 1231 gains or losses in the years 1994-2003.

(ii) As in *Example 1*, of A's $8000 of gain on the sale of the property, $3000 was attributable to prior straight-line depreciation deductions and is unrecaptured section 1250 gain.

(iii) As illustrated in the following table, A's first three payments, in 1994, 1995, and 1996, were received before May 7, 1997, and taxed at 28 percent. Under the rule described in paragraph (b) of this section, A determines the allocation of unrecaptured section 1250 gain for each installment payment after May 6, 1997, by taking unrecaptured section 1250 gain into account first, treating the general rule of paragraph (a) of this section as having applied since the time the property was sold, in 1994. Consequently, of the $800 of gain on the fourth payment, received in 1997, $600 is taxed at 25 percent and the remaining $200 is taxed at 20 percent. The gain on A's remaining six installment payments is taxed at 20 percent. The table is as follows:

	1994	1995	1996	1997	1998	1999-2003	Total gain
Installment gain	800	800	800	800	800	4000	8000
Taxed at 28%	800	800	800	....	....	....	2400
Taxed at 25%	....	....	....	600	....	....	600
Taxed at 20%	....	....	....	200	800	4000	5000
Remaining to be taxed at 25%	2200	1400	600	....	....	....	....

Example 3. Effect of section 1231(c) recapture. This example illustrates the rule of paragraph (a) of this section when there are non-recaptured net section 1231 losses, as defined in section 1231(c)(2), from prior years as follows:

(i) The facts are the same as in *Example 1*, except that in 1999 A has non-recaptured net section 1231 losses from the previous four years of $1000.

(ii) As illustrated in the table in paragraph (iv) of this *Example 3*, in 1999, all of A's $800 installment gain is recaptured as ordinary income under section 1231(c). Under the rule described in paragraph (a) of this section, for purposes of determining the amount of unrecaptured section 1250 gain remaining to be taken into account, the $800 recaptured as ordinary income under section 1231(c) is treated as reducing unrecaptured section 1250 gain, rather than adjusted net capital gain. Therefore, A has $2200 of unrecaptured section 1250 gain remaining to be taken into account.

(iii) In the year 2000, A's installment gain is taxed at two rates. First, $200 is recaptured as ordinary income under section 1231(c). Second, the remaining $600 of gain on A's year 2000 installment payment is taxed at 25 percent. Because the full $800 of gain reduces unrecaptured section 1250 gain, A has $1400 of unrecaptured section 1250 gain remaining to be taken into account.

(iv) The gain on A's installment payment received in 2001 is taxed at 25 percent. Of the $800 of gain on the fourth payment, received in 2002, $600 is taxed at 25 percent and the remaining $200 is taxed at 20 percent. The gain on A's remaining six installment payments is taxed at 20 percent. The table is as follows:

	1999	2000	2001	2002	2003	2004-2008	Total gain
Installment gain	800	800	800	800	800	4000	8000
Taxed at ordinary rates under section 1231(c)	800	200	....	....	....	....	1000
Taxed at 25%	....	600	800	600	....	....	2000
Taxed at 20%	....	....	....	200	800	4000	5000
Remaining non-recaptured net section 1231 losses	200	....	....	....	....	....	....
Remaining to be taxed at 25%	2200	1400	600	....	....	....	....

Example 4. Effect of a net section 1231 loss. This example illustrates the application of paragraph (a) of this section when there is a net section 1231 loss as follows:

(i) The facts are the same as in *Example 1* except that A has section 1231 losses of $1000 in 1999.

(ii) In 1999, A's section 1231 installment gain of $800 does not exceed A's section 1231 losses of $1000. Therefore, A has a net section 1231 loss of

Reg. § 1.453-12(d)

$200. As a result, under section 1231(a) all of A's section 1231 gains and losses are treated as ordinary gains and losses. As illustrated in the following table, A's entire $800 of installment gain is ordinary gain. Under the rule described in paragraph (a) of this section, for purposes of determining the amount of unrecaptured section 1250 gain remaining to be taken into account, A's $800 of ordinary section 1231 installment gain in 1999 is treated as reducing unrecaptured section 1250 gain. Therefore, A has $2200 of unrecaptured section 1250 gain remaining to be taken into account.

(iii) In the year 2000, A has $800 of section 1231 installment gain, resulting in a net section 1231 gain of $800. A also has $200 of non-recaptured net section 1231 losses. The $800 gain is taxed at two rates. First, $200 is taxed at ordinary rates under section 1231(c), recapturing the $200 net section 1231 loss sustained in 1999. Second, the remaining $600 of gain on A's year 2000 installment payment is taxed at 25 percent. As in *Example 3*, the $200 of section 1231(c) gain is treated as reducing unrecaptured section 1250 gain, rather than adjusted net capital gain. Therefore, A has $1400 of unrecaptured section 1250 gain remaining to be taken into account.

(iv) The gain on A's installment payment received in 2001 is taxed at 25 percent, reducing the remaining unrecaptured section 1250 gain to $600. Of the $800 of gain on the fourth payment, received in 2002, $600 is taxed at 25 percent and the remaining $200 is taxed at 20 percent. The gain on A's remaining six installment payments is taxed at 20 percent. The table is as follows:

	1999	2000	2001	2002	2003	2004-2008	Total gain
Installment gain	800	800	800	800	800	4000	8000
Ordinary gain under section 1231(a)	800	....	....	....	....	....	800
Taxed at ordinary rates under section 1231(c)	....	200	....	....	....	....	200
Taxed at 25%	....	600	800	600	....	....	2000
Taxed at 20%	....	....	....	200	800	4000	5000
Net section 1231 loss	200	....	....	....	....	....	....
Remaining to be taxed at 25%	2200	1400	600	....	....	....	....

(e) *Effective date.* This section applies to installment payments properly taken into account after August 23, 1999. [Reg. § 1.453-12.]

☐ [T.D. 8836, 8-20-99.]

[Reg. § 1.453A-0]

§ 1.453A-0. Table of contents.

This section lists the paragraphs and subparagraphs contained in §§ 1.453A-1 through 1.453A-3.

§ 1.453A-1. *Installment method of reporting income by dealers in personal property.*

(a) In general.

(b) Effect of security.

(c) Definition of dealer, sale, and sale on the installment plan.

(d) Installment plans.

(1) Traditional installment plans.

(2) Revolving credit plans.

(e) Installment income of dealers in personal property.

(1) In general.

(2) Gross profit and total contract price.

(3) Carrying charges not included in total contract price.

(f) Other accounting methods.

(g) Records.

(h) Effective date.

§ 1.453A-2. *Treatment of revolving credit plans; taxable years beginning on or before December 31, 1986.*

(a) In general.

(b) Coordination with traditional installment plan.

(c) Revolving credit plans.

(d) Effective date.

§ 1.453A-3. *Requirements for adoption of or change to installment method by dealers in personal property.*

(a) In general.

(b) Time and manner of electing installment method reporting.

(1) Time for election.

(2) Adoption of installment method.

(3) Change to installment method.

(4) Deemed elections.

(c) Consent.

(d) Cut-off method for amounts previously accrued.

(e) Effective date. [Reg. § 1.453A-0.]

☐ [T.D. 8270, 11-2-89.]

Reg. § 1.453A-0

[Reg. § 1.453A-1]

§ 1.453A-1. **Installment method of reporting income by dealers in personal property.**

(a) *In general.* A dealer (as defined in paragraph (c)(1) of this section) may elect to return the income from the sale of personal property on the installment method if such sale is a sale on the installment plan (as defined in paragraphs (c)(3) and (d) of this section). Under the installment method of accounting, a taxpayer may return as income from installment sales in any taxable year that proportion of the installment payments actually received in that year which the gross profit realized or to be realized when the property is paid for bears to the total contract price. For this purpose, gross profit means sales less cost of goods sold. See paragraph (d) of this section for additional rules relating to the computation of income under the installment method of accounting. In addition, see § 1.453A-2 for rules treating revolving credit plans as installment plans for taxable years beginning on or before December 31, 1986.

(b) *Effect of security.* A dealer may adopt (but is not required to do so) one of the following four ways of protecting against loss in case of default by the purchaser:

(1) An agreement that title is to remain in the vendor until performance of the purchaser's part of the transaction is completed;

(2) A form of contract in which title is conveyed to the purchaser immediately, but subject to a lien for the unpaid portion of the selling price;

(3) A present transfer of title to the purchaser, who at the same time executes a reconveyance in the form of a chattel mortgage to the vendor; or

(4) A conveyance to a trustee pending performance of the contract and subject to its provisions.

(c) *Definitions of dealer, sale, and sale on the installment plan.* For purposes of the regulations under section 453A—

(1) The term "dealer" means a person who regularly sells or otherwise disposes of personal property on the installment plan;

(2) The term "sale" includes sales and other dispositions; and

(3) Except as provided in paragraph (d)(2) of this section, the term "sale on the installment plan" means—

(i) A sale of personal property by the taxpayer under any plan for the sale of personal property, which plan, by its terms and conditions, contemplates that each sale under the plan will be paid for in two or more payments; or

(ii) A sale of personal property by the taxpayer under any plan for the sale of personal property—

(A) Which plan, by its terms and conditions, contemplates that such sale will be paid for in two or more payments; and

(B) Which sale is in fact paid for in two or more payments.

(d) *Installment plans*—(1) *Traditional installment plans.* A traditional installment plan usually has the following characteristics:

(i) The execution of a separate installment contract for each sale or disposition of personal property; and

(ii) The retention by the dealer of some type of security interest in such property.

Normally, a sale under a traditional installment plan meets the requirements of paragraph (c)(3)(i) of this section.

(2) *Revolving credit plans.* Sales under a revolving credit plan (within the meaning of § 1.453A-2(c)(1))—

(i) Are treated, for taxable years beginning on or before December 31, 1986, as sales on the installment plan to the extent provided in § 1.453A-2, which provides for the application of the requirements of paragraph (c)(3)(ii) of this section to sales under revolving credit plans; and

(ii) Are not treated as sales on the installment plan for taxable years beginning after December 31, 1986.

(e) *Installment income of dealers in personal property*—(1) *In general.* The income from sales on the installment plan of a dealer may be ascertained by treating as income that proportion of the total payments received in the taxable year from sales on the installment plan (such payments being allocated to the year against the sales of which they apply) which the gross profit realized or to be realized on the total sales on the installment plan made during each year bears to the total contract price of all such sales made during that respective year. However, if the dealer demonstrates to the satisfaction of the district director that income from sales on the installment plan is clearly reflected, the income from such sales may be ascertained by treating as income that proportion of the total payments received in the taxable year from sales on the installment plan (such payments being allocated to the year against the sales of which they apply) which either:

(i) The gross profit realized or to be realized on the total credit sales made during each year bears to the total contract price of all credit sales during that respective year, or

(ii) The gross profit realized or to be realized on all sales made during each year bears to the total contract price of all sales made during that respective year. A dealer who desires to compute income by the installment method shall maintain accounting records in such a manner as to enable an accurate computation to be made by such method in accordance with the provisions of this section, section 446 and § 1.446-1.

(2) *Gross profit and total contract price.* For purposes of paragraph (e)(1) of this section, in computing the gross profit realized or to be realized on the total sales on the installment plan, there shall be included in the total selling price and, thus, in the total contract price of all such sales,

(i) The amount of carrying charges or interest which is determined at the time of each sale and is added to the established cash selling price of such property and is treated as part of the selling price for customer billing purposes, and

(ii) In the case of sales made in taxable years beginning on or after January 1, 1960, the amount of carrying charges or interest determined with respect to such sales which are added contemporaneously with the sale on the books of account of the seller but are treated as periodic service charges for customer billing purposes.

Any change in the amount of the carrying charges or interest in a year subsequent to the sale will not affect the computation of the gross profit for the year of sale but will be taken into account at the time the carrying charges or interest are adjusted. The application of this paragraph (e)(2) to carrying charges or interest described in paragraph (e)(2)(ii) of this section may be illustrated by the following example:

Example. X Corporation makes sales on the traditional installment plan. The customer's order specifies that the total price consists of a cash price plus a "time price differential" of 1½ percent per month on the outstanding balance in the customer's account, and the customer is billed in this manner. On its books and for purposes of reporting to stockholders, X Corporation consistently makes the following entries each month when it records its sales. A debit entry is made to accounts receivable (for the total price) and balancing credit entries are made to sales (for the established selling price) and to a reserve account for collection expense (for the amount of the time price differential). In computing the gross profit realized or to be realized on the total sales on the installment plan, the total selling price and, thus, the total contract price for purposes of this paragraph (e) would, with respect to sales made in taxable years beginning on or after January 1, 1960, include the time price differential.

(3) *Carrying charges not included in total contract price.* In the case of sales by dealers in personal property made during taxable years beginning after December 31, 1963, the income from which is returned on the installment method, if the carrying charges or interest with respect to such sales in not included in the total contract price, payments received with respect to such sales shall be treated as applying first against such carrying charges or interest.

(f) *Other accounting methods.* If the vendor chooses as a matter of consistent practice to return the income from installment sales on an accrual method (,) such a course is permissible.

(g) *Records.* In adopting the installment method of accounting the seller must maintain such records as are necessary to clearly reflect income in accordance with this section, section 446 and § 1.446-1.

(h) *Effective date.* This section applies for taxable years beginning after December 31, 1953, and ending after August 16, 1954, but generally does not apply to sales made after December 31, 1987, in taxable years ending after such date. For sales made after December 31, 1987, sales made by a dealer in personal or real property shall not be treated as sales on the installment plan. (However, see section 453(l)(2) for exceptions to this rule.) [Reg. § 1.453A-1.]

☐ [*T.D. 8270, 11-2-89.*]

[Reg. § 1.453A-2]

§ 1.453A-2. Treatment of revolving credit plans; taxable years beginning on or before December 31, 1986.

(a) *In general.* If a dealer sells or otherwise disposes of personal property under a revolving credit plan—

(1) Such sales will be treated as sales on the installment plan to the extent provided in paragraph (c) of this section;

(2) Income from sales treated as sales on the installment plan under paragraph (c) of this section may be returned on the installment method; and

(3) Income returned on the installment method is computed in accordance with § 1.453A-1, except that—

(i) The gross profit on such sales is computed without regard to § 1.453A-1(e)(2);

(ii) Under the circumstances described in paragraph (c)(6)(vi) of this section, the taxpayer may, in computing income for a taxable year, treat all such sales as sales made in such taxable year for purposes of applying the gross profit percentage; and

(iii) The rule contained in § 1.453A-1(e)(3) is applied in accordance with paragraph (c)(6)(v) of this section.

(b) *Coordination with traditional installment plan.* A dealer who makes sales of personal property under both a revolving credit plan and a traditional installment plan (1) may elect to report only sales under the traditional installment plan on the installment method, (2) may elect to report only sales under the revolving credit plan on the installment method, or (3) may elect to report both sales under the revolving credit plan and the traditional installment plan on the installment method.

(c) *Revolving credit plans.* (1) To the extent provided in this paragraph (c) sales under a revolving credit plan will be treated as sales on the installment plan. The term "revolving credit plan" includes cycle budget accounts, flexible budget accounts, continuous budget accounts, and other similar plans or arrangements for the sale of personal property under which the customer agrees to pay each billing-month (as defined in paragraph (c)(6)(iii) of this section) a part of the outstanding balance of the customer's account. Sales under a revolving credit plan do not constitute sales on the installment plan merely by reason of the fact that the total debt at the end of a billing-month is paid in installments. The terms and conditions of a revolving credit plan do not contemplate that each sale under the plan will be paid for in two or more payments and thus do not meet the requirements of § 1.453A-1(c)(3)(i). In addition, since under a revolving credit plan payments are not generally applied to liquidate any particular sale, and since the terms and conditions of such plan contemplate that account balances may be paid in full or in installments, it is generally impossible to determine that a particular sale under a revolving credit plan is to be or is in fact paid for in installments so as to meet the requirements of § 1.453A-1(c)(3)(ii). However, paragraphs (c)(2) and (3) of this section provides rules under which a certain percentage of charges under a revolving credit plan will be treated as sales on the installment plan. For purposes of arriving at this percentage, these rules, in general, treat as sales on the plan those sales under a revolving installment credit plan:

(i) Which are of the type which the terms and conditions of the plan contemplate will be paid for in two or more installments, and

(ii) Which are charged to accounts on which subsequent payments indicate that such sales are being paid for in two or more installments.

(2)(i) The percentage of charges under a revolving credit plan which will be treated as sales on the installment plan shall be computed by making an actual segregation of charges in a probability sample of the revolving credit accounts and by applying the rules contained in paragraph (c)(3) of this section to determine what percentage of charges in the sample is to be treated as sales on the installment plan. (See paragraph (c)(5) of this section for rules to be used if some of the sales under a revolving credit plan are nonpersonal property sales (as defined in paragraph (c)(6)(iv) of this section).) Such segregation shall be made of charges which make up the balances in the sample accounts as of the end of each customer's last billing-month ending within the taxable year. (See paragraph (c)(6)(v) of this section for rules to be used in determining which charges make up the balance of an account.) However, in making such segregation, any account to which a sale is charged during the taxable year on which no payment is credited after the billing-month within which the sale is made (hereinafter called the "billing-month of sale") and on or before the end of the first billing-month ending in the taxpayer's next taxable year shall be disregarded and not taken into account in the determination of what percentage of charges in the sample is to be treated as sales on the installment plan. In order to obtain a probability sample, the accounts shall be selected in accordance with generally accepted probability sampling techniques. The appropriateness of the sampling technique and the accuracy and reliability of the results obtained must, if requested, be demonstrated to the satisfaction of the district director. If the district director is not satisfied that the taxpayer's sample is appropriate or that the results obtained are accurate and reliable, the taxpayer shall recompute the sample percentage or make appropriate adjustments to the original computations in a manner satisfactory to the district director. The taxpayer shall maintain records in sufficient detail to show the method of computing and applying the sample.

(ii) For taxable years ending before January 31, 1964, a taxpayer who has reported for income tax purposes all or a portion of sales under a revolving credit plan as sales on the installment method may apply the percentage obtained for the first taxable year ending on or after such date in determining the percentage of charges under a revolving credit plan for such prior taxable year (or years) which will be treated as sales on the installment plan. However, in computing the percentage to be applied in determining the percent-

Reg. § 1.453A-2(b)

age of charges under a revolving credit plan which will be treated as sales on the installment plan for such prior taxable year (or years), the rule stated in § 1.453A-1(e)(3) shall not apply. See paragraph (c)(6)(v) of this section for rules relating to the application of payments to finance charges for such prior taxable years.

(3) For the purpose of determining the percentage described in paragraph (c)(2) of this section, a charge under a revolving credit plan will be treated as a sale on the installment plan only if such charge is a sale (as defined in paragraph (c)(6) of this section) and meets the following requirements:

(i) The sale must be of the type which the terms and conditions of the plan contemplate will be paid for in two or more installments. If the aggregate of sales charged during a billing-month to an account under a revolving credit plan exceeds the required monthly payment, then all sales during such billing-month shall be considered to be of the type which the terms and conditions of such plan contemplate will be paid for in two or more installments. The required monthly payment shall be the amount of the payment which the terms and conditions of the revolving credit contract require the customer to make with respect to a billing-month. If the amount of such payment is not fixed at the date the contract is entered into, but is dependent upon the balance of the account, then such amount shall be the amount that the customer is required to pay (but not including any past-due payments) as shown on the statement either:

(A) For the last billing-month ending within the taxpayer's taxable year or

(B) For the billing-month of sale, whichever method the taxpayer adopts for all accounts. A taxpayer shall not change such method of determining the required monthly payment based upon the balance of the account without obtaining the consent of the district director. In any case where the required monthly payment is not set in accordance with a consistent method used during the entire taxable year, the district director may determine the required monthly payment in accordance with the method used during the major portion of such taxable year if the use of such method is necessary in order to reflect properly the income from sales under a revolving credit plan. The requirements stated in this paragraph (c)(3)(i) may be illustrated by the following examples:

Example (1). Under the terms of a revolving credit plan the required monthly payment to be made by customer A is $20. During the billing-month ending in December, sales aggregating $80 are charged to customer A's account, and during the next billing-month, ending in January, sales aggregating $19.95 and finance charges of $.60 are charged to A's account. Since the aggregate of sales charged to customer A's account during the billing-month ending in December ($80) exceeds the required monthly payment ($20), the terms and conditions of the plan contemplate that the sales charged during such billing-month are of the type which will be paid for in two or more installments. Since the aggregate of sales charged to customer A's account during the billing-month ending in January ($19.95) does not exceed the required monthly payment, the sales making up the aggregate of sales in such billing-month are not of the type which the terms and conditions of the plan contemplate will be paid for in two or more installments.

Example (2). The terms of a revolving credit plan require a payment of 20 percent of the balance of the customer's account as of the end of the billing-month for which the statement is rendered. A customer makes purchases aggregating $25 in the customer's next to the last billing-month ending within the taxpayer's taxable year, and the balance at the end of that month is $150. At the end of the customer's last billing-month ending within the taxpayer's taxable year, the balance of the account has decreased to $110. If the taxpayer determines the required monthly payment by reference to the payment required on the statement for the last billing-month ending within the taxable year and applies such method consistently to all accounts, then the sales making up the $25 aggregate of sales are of the type which the terms and conditions of the plan contemplate will be paid for in two or more installments. Although such aggregate was less than the $30 payment (20% × $150) required on the statement rendered for the billing-month of sales. It was more than the $22 (20% × $110) that the customer was required to pay on the statement rendered for his last billing-month ending within the taxable year, and thus meets the requirements of this paragraph (c)(3)(i). If, however, the taxpayer determines the required monthly payment by reference to the payment required on the statement for the billing-month of sale, then the sales making up the aggregate of sales during such billing-month do not meet the requirements of this paragraph (c)(3)(i) because such aggregate was less than the $30 payment required on the statement rendered for such month.

(ii) The sale must be charged to an account on which the first payment after the billing-month of sale indicates that the sale is being paid in installments. The first payment after the billing-month of sale indicates that the sale is being

Reg. § 1.453A-2(c)(3)

paid in installments if, and only if, such payment is an amount which is less than the balance of the account as of the close of the billing-month of sale. For purposes of this paragraph (c)(3)(ii), such balance shall be reduced by any return or allowance credited to the account after the close of the billing-month of sale and before the close of the billing-month within which the first payment after the billing-month of sale is credited to the account, unless the taxpayer demonstrates that the return or allowance was attributable to a charge made in a month subsequent to the billing-month of sale. The requirements stated in this paragraph (c)(3)(ii) may be illustrated by the following examples, in which it is assumed that the taxpayer's annual accounting period ends on January 31.

Example (1). Customer A's revolving credit account shows the following sales and payments:

Month ending	Aggregate sales in month	Payments	Balance
December 20	$150	0	$150
January 20	75	$30	195
February 20	0	195	0

All sales made in the billing-month ending December 20 meet the requirements of this paragraph (c)(3)(ii) because the first payment on the account after such billing-month ($30) was less than the balance of the account as of the close of such billing-month ($150); and none of the sales made in the billing-month ending January 20 meets the requirements of this paragraph (c)(3)(ii) because the balance of the account as of the end of such billing-month was liquidated in one payment. By application of the rules of paragraph (c)(6)(v) of this section, the balance in the account as of the last billing-month ending in the taxable year ($195) consists of $120 of the $150 of sales made in the billing-month ending December 20 and all of the $75 of sales made in the billing-month ending January 20. Therefore, $120 of the account balance meets the requirements of this paragraph (c)(3)(ii) and $75 does not.

Example (2). Customer B's revolving credit account shows the following sales and payments:

Month ending	Aggregate sales in month	Payments	Balance
December 20	$50	0	$50
January 20	100	0	150
February 20	0	$50	100

None of the sales made in the billing-month ending December 20 meets the requirements of this paragraph (c)(3)(ii) because the first payment credited to the account after such billing-month ($50) is not less than the balance of the account as of the close of such month ($50). All of the sales made in the billing-month ending January 20 meet the requirements of this paragraph (c)(3)(ii) because the first payment after such billing-month ($50) is less than the balance of the account as of the close of such month ($150).

Example (3). Customer C's revolving credit account shows the following purchases and credits:

Month ending	Item	Charges	Credits	Balance
January 20	Coat	$55		
	Dress	40		
	Shirt	5		$100
February 20	Return		$5	
	Payments		95	0

None of the sales made in the billing-month ending January 20 meets the requirements of this paragraph (c)(3)(ii) because the first payment credited to the account after such billing-month ($95) was equal to the balance of the account as of the end of such billing-month, $95. For this purpose, the balance of $100 is reduced by the $5 return which was credited to the account after the close of the billing-month of sale and before the close of the billing-month within which the first payment after the billing-month of sale is credited.

Reg. § 1.453A-2(c)(3)

Methods of Accounting

(4) The provisions of paragraphs (c)(2) and (3) of this section may be illustrated by the following examples in which it is assumed that the taxpayer is a dealer whose annual accounting period ends on January 31.

Example (1). Customer A's revolving credit ledger account shows the following:

Month ending	Aggregate sales in month [1]	Returns and allowances	Payments	Finance charges	Balance
January 20	$15.00	0	0	0	$15.00
February 20	0	0	0	$0.15	15.15

[1] Including sales of personal property and nonpersonal property sales.

For purposes of the segregation provided for in paragraph (c)(2)(i) of this section, customer A's account will be disregarded and not taken into account in the determination of what percentage of charges in the sample is to be treated as sales on the installment plan because no payment was credited to that account after the billing-month of sale and on or before February 20.

Example (2). This example is applicable with respect to sales made during taxable years beginning before January 1, 1964. Under the terms of corporation X's revolving credit plan, payments are required in accordance with the following schedule:

Unpaid balance:	Required monthly payment
0 to $99.99	$20
$100 to $199.99	40
$200 to $299.99	60

Customer B's revolving credit ledger account for the period beginning on September 21, 1963, and ending February 20, 1964, shows the following:

Month ending	Aggregate sales in month [1]	Returns and allowances	Payments	Finance charges	Balances
October 20	$55.00	0	0	0	$55.00
November 20	45.00	0	$20.00	$0.35	80.35
December 20	20.00	0	20.00	.60	80.95
January 20	26.00	$ 5.00	20.00	.61	82.56
February 20	0	10.00	72.56	0	0

[1] Including sales of personal property and nonpersonal property sales.

The three $20 payments and the $5 return or allowance made in the billing-months ending in the taxable year are applied under the rules in paragraph (c)(6)(v) of this section to liquidate the earliest outstanding charges, first to the $55 aggregate of sales in the billing-month ending October 20 and next to $10 of the aggregate of sales made in the billing-month ending November 20. Thus, the balance of the account as of the close of the billing-month ending January 20, $82.56, is made up as follows:

Remainder of sales in billing-month ending Nov. 20 ($45–$10)	$35.00
Finance charges for billing-month ending Nov. 20	0.35
Sales for billing-month ending Dec. 20	20.00
Finance charge for billing-month ending Dec. 20	0.60
Sales for billing-month ending Jan. 20	26.00
Finance charge for billing-month ending Jan. 20	0.61
Total	82.56

The sales of $35 remaining from the aggregate of sales for the billing-month ending November 20 meet the requirements of paragraph (c)(3)(i) of this section because the aggregate of sales charged during such billing-month ($45) exceeds the required monthly payment ($20), and such sales meet the requirements of paragraph (c)(3)(ii) of this section because the first payment after the billing-month of sale ($20) is an amount less than the balance of the account as of the close of such month ($80.35). Therefore, $35 of sales will be treated as sales on the installment plan. The $20 aggregate of sales charged during the billing-month ending December 20 does not meet the requirements of paragraph (c)(3)(i) of this section because it is in an amount which does not exceed the required monthly payment ($20). (The finance charge of $0.60 added in the billing-month does not enter into the determination of the aggregate of sales for the month because the term "sales" (as defined in paragraph (c)(6)(i) of this section) does not include finance charges.) The

Reg. § 1.453A-2(c)(4)

$26 aggregate of sales for the billing-month ending January 20 does not meet the requirements of paragraph (c)(3)(ii) of this section because the first payment after such billing-month ($72.56) was equal to the balance of the account as of the close of such billing-month ($72.56). For this purpose, the balance of $82.56 is reduced by the $10 return or allowance which was credited after the billing-month of sale and before February 20. Thus, of the $82.56 balance of B's account as of the close of the last billing-month ending within corporation X's taxable year, $35 will be treated as sales on the installment plan for purposes of determining the percentage provided for paragraph (c)(2) of this section.

Example (3). This example is applicable with respect to sales made during taxable years beginning after December 31, 1963. Assume the facts in example (2), except that Customer B's revolving credit ledger account is for the period beginning on September 21, 1964 and ending February 20, 1965. Since payments received are first used to liquidate any outstanding finance charges under the rule in paragraph (c)(6)(v) of this section, the $20 payment in December liquidated the $0.35 finance charge accrued at the end of the November billing-month and the $20 payment in January liquidated the $0.60 finance charge accrued at the end of the December billing-month. The balance of the three $20 payments ($59.05) and the $5 return or allowance are applied (under the rules in paragraph (c)(6)(v) of this section) to liquidate the earliest outstanding sales, first to the $55 aggregate of sales in the billing-month ending October 20 and next to $9.05 of the aggregate of sales made in the billing-month ending November 20. Thus, the balance of the account as of the close of the billing-month ending January 20, $82.56, is made up as follows:

Remainder of sales in billing-month ending Nov. 20 ($45-$9.05)	$35.95
Sales for billing-month ending Dec. 20	20.00
Sales for billing-month ending Jan. 20	26.00
Finance charge for billing-month ending Jan. 20	0.61
Total	82.56

The sales of $35.95 remaining from the aggregate of sales for the billing-month ending November 20 meet the requirements of paragraph (c)(3)(i) of this section because the aggregate of sales charged during such billing-month ($45) exceeds the required monthly payment ($20), and such sales meet the requirements of paragraph (c)(3)(ii) of this section because the first payment after the billing-month of sale ($20) is an amount less than the balance of the account as of the close of such month ($80.35). Therefore, $35.95 of sales will be treated as sales on the installment plan. The $20 aggregate of sales charged during the billing-month ending December 20 does not meet the requirements of paragraph (c)(3)(i) of this section because it is in an amount which does not exceed the required monthly payment ($20). The $26 aggregate of sales for the billing-month ending January 20 does not meet the requirements of paragraph (c)(3)(ii) of this section because the first payment after such billing-month ($72.56) was equal to the balance of the account as of the close of such billing-month ($72.56). For this purpose, the balance of $82.56 is reduced by the $10 return or allowance which was credited after the billing-month of sale and before February 20. Thus, of the $82.56 balance of B's account as of the close of the last billing-month ending within corporation X's taxable year $35.95 will be treated as sales on the installment plan for purposes of determining the percentage provided for in paragraph (c)(2) of this section.

(5) Sales under a revolving credit plan which are nonpersonal property sales (as defined in paragraph (c)(6)(iv) of this section) do not constitute sales on the installment plan. Therefore, the charges under a revolving credit plan must be reduced by the nonpersonal property sales, if any, under such plan, before application of the sample percentage as provided for in paragraph (c)(2)(i) of this section. The taxpayer may treat as the nonpersonal property sales under the plan for the taxable year an amount which bears the same ratio to the total sales under the revolving credit plan made in the taxable year as the total nonpersonal property sales made in such year bears to the total sales made in such year.

(6) For purposes of this paragraph (c)—

(i) The term "sales" includes sales of services, such as a charge for watch repair, as well as sales of property, but does not include finance or service charges.

(ii) The term "charges" includes sales of services and property as well as finance or service charges.

(iii) A billing-month is that period of time for which a periodic statement of charges and credits is rendered to a customer.

(iv) The term "nonpersonal property sales" means all sales which are not sales of personal property made by the taxpayer. Thus, sales of a department leased by the taxpayer to another are nonpersonal property sales. Likewise, charges for services rendered by the taxpayer are nonpersonal property sales unless such services are incidental to and rendered contemporaneously with the sale of personal property, in which case such charges shall be considered as constituting part of the selling price of such property.

(v) Except as otherwise provided in this paragraph (c)(6)(v), each payment received from

Reg. § 1.453A-2(c)(5)

a customer under a revolving credit plan before the close of the last billing-month ending in the taxable year shall be applied to liquidate the earliest outstanding charges under such plan, notwithstanding any rule of law or contract provision to the contrary. For purposes of determining which charges remain in the balance of an account at the end of the last billing-month ending in the taxable year, the taxpayer may apply returns and allowances which are credited before the close of the last billing-month ending in the taxable year either (A) to liquidate or reduce the charge for the specific item so returned or for which an allowance is permitted, or (B) to liquidate or reduce the earliest outstanding charges. The method so selected for applying returns and allowances shall be followed on a consistent basis from year to year unless the district director consents to a change. Additionally, finance or service charges which are computed on the basis of the balance of the account at the end of the previous billing-month (usually reduced by payments during the current billing-month) are accrued at the end of the current billing-month and are therefore considered, for purposes of determining the earliest outstanding charges, as charged to the account after any sales made during the current billing month. However, for purposes of determining which charges remain in the balance of an account at the end of the last billing-month ending in a taxable year which began after December 31, 1963, payments received during such year shall be applied first against any finance or service charges which were outstanding at the time such payment was received. The preceding sentence shall not apply with respect to a computation made for purposes of applying the rule described in paragraph (c)(2)(ii) of this section.

(vi) The taxpayer shall allocate those sales under a revolving credit plan which are treated as sales on the installment plan to the proper year of sale in order to apply the appropriate gross profit percentage as provided for in § 1.453A-1(e). This allocation shall be made on the basis of the percentages of charges treated as sales on the installment plan which are attributable to each taxable year as determined in the sample of accounts described in paragraph (c)(2) of this section. However, if the taxpayer demonstrates to the satisfaction of the district director that income from sales on the installment plan is clearly reflected, all sales may be considered as being made in the taxable year for purposes of applying the gross profit percentage.

(7) The provisions of this paragraph (c) may be illustrated by the following example:

Example. Corporation X is a dealer and has elected to report on the installment method those sales under its revolving credit plan which may be treated as sales on the installment plan. Corporation X's taxable year ends on January 31, and the total balance of all its revolving credit accounts as of January 31, 1964, is $2,000,000. The total sales made in the taxable year are $10,000,000 of which $500,000 are nonpersonal property sales. The gross profit percentage realized or to be realized on all sales made in the taxable year is 40 percent. The amount of the gross profit contained in the year-end balance of $2,000,000 which may be deferred to succeeding years is computed as follows:

(i) In order to reduce the charges appearing in the year-end balance of revolving credit accounts receivable by the nonpersonal property sales contained therein, corporation X determines the amount of such nonpersonal property sales under the method permitted in paragraph (c)(5) of this section. Corporation X first determines the ratio which total nonpersonal property sales made during the year ($500,000) bears to total sales made during the year ($10,000,000), and then applies the percentage (5 percent) thus obtained to the year-end balance of revolving credit accounts receivable ($2,000,000). The nonpersonal property sales thus determined ($100,000) is subtracted from such year-end balance to obtain the charges under the revolving credit plan appearing in the year-end balance ($1,900,000) to which the sample percentage is to be applied.

(ii) In accordance with generally accepted sampling techniques, the taxpayer selects a probability sample of all revolving credit accounts having balances for billing-months ending in January 1964. The technique employed results in a random selection of accounts with total balances of $100,000.

(iii) Analysis of these sample accounts discloses that of the $100,000 of balances, $10,000 of balances are in accounts on which no payment was credited after a billing-month of sale and on or before the end of the first billing-month ending in the taxable year beginning February 1, 1964. These balances are, therefore, disregarded and not taken into account in the determination of what percentage of sales in the sample is to be treated as sales on the installment plan. Of the remaining $90,000 of balances, the taxpayer determines, by analyzing the ledger cards in the sample, that $63,000 of balances are composed of sales which meet the requirements of paragraphs (c)(3)(i) and (ii) of this section and are thus treated as sales on the installment plan. The remaining $27,000 of balances either did not meet the requirements of paragraphs (c)(3)(i) and (ii) of this section or were not sales (as defined in paragraph (c)(6)(i) of this section). The percentage of charges in the sample treated as sales on the installment plan is, therefore, 70 percent ($63,000 ÷ $90,000).

Reg. § 1.453A-2(c)(7)

(iv) The charges in the year-end balance which are to be treated as sales on the installment plan, $1,330,000, are computed by multiplying the charges to which the sample percentage is applied ($1,900,000) by the sample percentage (70 percent).

(v) The deferred gross profit attributable to sales under the revolving credit plan for the taxable year, $532,000, is determined by multiplying the amount treated as sales on the installment plan ($1,330,000), by the gross profit percentage (40 percent). (Corporation X will be able to demonstrate to the satisfaction of the district director that (A) since the gross profit percentage for all sales does not vary materially from the gross profit percentage for all sales made under the revolving credit plan, (B) since only an insubstantial amount of sales included in year-end account balances was made prior to the taxable year, and (C) since the prior year's gross profit percentage does not vary materially from the gross profit percentage for the taxable year, income from sales on the installment plan will be clearly reflected by applying the current year's gross profit percentage for all sales under the revolving credit plan treated as sales on the installment plan.)

(d) *Effective date.* This section applies for taxable years beginning after December 31, 1953, and ending after August 16, 1954, but does not apply for any taxable year beginning after December 31, 1986. For taxable years beginning after December 31, 1986, sales under a revolving credit plan shall not be treated as sales on the installment plan. [Reg. § 1.453A-2.]

□ [T.D. 8270, 11-2-89.]

[Reg. § 1.453A-3]

§ 1.453A-3. **Requirements for adoption of or change to installment method by dealers in personal property.**—(a) *In general.* A dealer (within the meaning of § 1.453A-1(c)(1)) may adopt or change to the installment method for a type or types of sales on the installment plan (within the meaning of § 1.453A-1(c)(3) and (d)) in the manner prescribed in this section. This section applies only to dealers and only with respect to their sales on the installment plan.

(b) *Time and manner of electing installment method reporting*—(1) *Time for election.* An election to adopt or change to the installment method for a type or types of sales must be made on an income tax return for the taxable year of the election, filed on or before the time specified (including extensions thereof) for filing such return.

(2) *Adoption of installment method.* A taxpayer who adopts the installment method for the first taxable year in which sales are made on an installment plan of any kind must indicate in the income tax return for that taxable year that the installment method of accounting is being adopted and specify the type or types of sales included within the election. If a taxpayer in the year of the initial election made only one type of sale on the installment plan, but during a subsequent taxable year makes another type of sale on the installment plan and adopts the installment method for that other type of sale, the taxpayer must indicate in the income tax return for the subsequent year that an election is being made to adopt the installment method of accounting for the additional type of sale.

(3) *Change to installment method.* A taxpayer who changes to the installment method for a particular type or types of sales on the installment plan in accordance with this section must, for each type of sale on the installment plan for which the installment method is to be used, attach a separate statement to the income tax return for the taxable year with respect to which the change is made. Each statement must show the method of accounting used in computing taxable income before the change and the type of sale on the installment plan for which the installment method is being elected.

(4) *Deemed elections.* A dealer (including a person who is a dealer as a result of the recharacterization of transactions as sales) is deemed to have elected the installment method if the dealer treats a sale on the installment plan as a transaction other than a sale and fails to report the full amount of gain in the year of the sale. For example, if a transaction treated by a dealer as a lease is recharacterized by the Internal Revenue Service as a sale on the installment plan, the dealer will be deemed to have elected the installment method assuming the dealer failed to report the full amount of gain in the year of the transaction.

(c) *Consent.* A dealer may adopt or change to the installment method for sales on the installment plan without the consent of the Commissioner. However, a dealer may not change from the installment method to the accrual method of accounting or to any other method of accounting without the consent of the Commissioner.

(d) *Cut-off method for amounts previously accrued.* An election to change to the installment method for a type of sale applies only with respect to sales made on or after the first day of the taxable year of change. Thus, payments received in the taxable year of the change, or in subsequent years, in respect of an installment obligation which arose in a taxable year prior to the taxable year of change are not taken into account on the installment method, but rather must be accounted for under the taxpayer's method of accounting in use in the prior year.

(e) *Effective date.* This section applies to sales by dealers in taxable years ending after October 19, 1980, but generally does not apply to sales made after December 31, 1987. For sales made after December 31, 1987, sales by a dealer in personal or real property shall not be treated as sales on the installment plan. (However, see section 453(l)(2) for certain exceptions to this rule.) For rules relating to sales by dealers in taxable years ending before October 20, 1980, see 26 CFR 1.453-7 and 1.453-8 (rev. as of April 1, 1987). [Reg. § 1.453A-3.]

☐ [T.D. 8269, 11-2-89.]

[Reg. § 1.454-1]

§ 1.454-1. Obligations issued at discount.—(a) *Certain non-interest-bearing obligations issued at discount* —(1) *Election to include increase in income currently.* If a taxpayer owns—

(i) A non-interest-bearing obligation issued at a discount and redeemable for fixed amounts increasing at stated intervals (other than an obligation issued by a corporation after May 27, 1969, as to which ratable inclusion of original issue discount is required under section 1232(a)(3)), or

(ii) An obligation of the United States, other than a current income obligation, in which he retains his investment in a matured series E United States savings bond, or

(iii) A nontransferable obligation (whether or not a current income obligation) of the United States for which a series E United States savings bond was exchanged (whether or not at final maturity) in an exchange upon which gain is not recognized because of section 1037(a) (or so much of section 1031(b) as relates to section 1037),

and if the increase, if any, in redemption price of such obligation described in subdivision (i), (ii), or (iii) of this subparagraph during the taxable year (as described in subparagraph (2) of this paragraph) does not constitute income for such year under the method of accounting used in computing his taxable income, then the taxpayer may, at his election, treat the increase as constituting income for the year in which such increase occurs. If the election is not made and section 1037 (or so much of section 1031 as relates to section 1037) does not apply, the taxpayer shall treat the increase as constituting income for the year in which the obligation is redeemed or disposed of, or finally matures, whichever is earlier. Any such election must be made in the taxpayer's return and may be made for any taxable year. If an election is made with respect to any such obligation described in subdivision (i), (ii), or (iii) of this subparagraph, it shall apply also to all other obligations of the type described in such subdivisions owned by the taxpayer at the beginning of the first taxable year to which the election applies, and to those thereafter acquired by him, and shall be binding for the taxable year for which the return is filed and for all subsequent taxable years, unless the Commissioner permits the taxpayer to change to a different method of reporting income from such obligations. See section 446(e) and paragraph (e) of § 1.446-1, relating to requirement respecting a change of accounting method. Although the election once made is binding upon the taxpayer, it does not apply to a transferee of the taxpayer.

(2) *Amount of increase in case of non-interest-bearing obligations.* In any case in which an election is made under section 454, the amount which accrues in any taxable year to which the election applies is measured by the actual increase in the redemption price occurring in that year. This amount does not accrue ratably between the dates on which the redemption price changes. For example, if two dates on which the redemption price increases (February 1 and August 1) fall within a taxable year and if the redemption price increases in the amount of 50 cents on each such date, the amount accruing in that year would be $1.00 ($0.50 on February 1 and $0.50 on August 1). If the taxpayer owns a non-interest-bearing obligation of the character described in subdivision (i), (ii), or (iii) of subparagraph (1) of this paragraph acquired prior to the first taxable year to which his election applies, he must also include in gross income for such first taxable year (i) the increase in the redemption price of such obligation occurring between the date of acquisition of the obligation and the first day of such first taxable year and (ii), in a case where a series E bond was exchanged for such obligation, the increase in the redemption price of such series E bond occurring between the date of acquisition of such series E bond and the date of exchange.

(3) *Amount of increase in case of current income obligations.* If an election is made under section 454 and the taxpayer owns, at the beginning of the first taxable year to which the election applies, a current income obligation of the character described in subparagraph (1)(iii) of this paragraph acquired prior to such taxable year, he must also include in gross income for such first taxable year the increase in the redemption price of the series E bond which was surrendered to the United States in exchange for such current income obligation; the amount of the increase is that occurring between the date of acquisition of the series E bond and the date of the exchange.

(4) *Illustrations.* The application of this paragraph may be illustrated by the following examples:

Example (1). Throughout the calendar year 1954, a taxpayer who uses the cash receipts and disbursements method of accounting holds series

Reg. § 1.454-1(a)(4)

E United States savings bonds having a maturity value of $5,000 and a redemption value at the beginning of the year 1954 of $4,050 and at the end of the year 1954 of $4,150. He purchased the bonds on January 1, 1949, for $3,750, and holds no other obligation of the type described in this section. If the taxpayer exercises the election in his return for the calendar year 1954, he is required to include $400 in taxable income with respect to such bonds. Of this amount, $300 represents the increase in the redemption price before 1954 and $100 represents the increase in the redemption price in 1954. The increases in redemption value occurring in subsequent taxable years are includible in gross income for such taxable years.

Example (2). In 1958 B, a taxpayer who uses the cash receipts and disbursements method of accounting and the calendar year as his taxable year, purchased for $7,500 a series E United States savings bond with a face value of $10,000. In 1965, when the stated redemption value of the series E bond is $9,760, B surrenders it to the United States in exchange solely for a $10,000 series H United States current income savings bond in an exchange qualifying under section 1037(a), after paying $240 additional consideration. On the exchange of the series E bond for the series H bond in 1965, B realizes a gain of $2,260 ($9,760 less $7,500), none of which is recognized for that year by reason of section 1037(a). B retains the series H bond and redeems it at maturity in 1975 for $10,000, but in 1966 he exercises the election under section 454(a) in his return for that year with respect to five series E bonds he purchased in 1960. B is required to include in gross income for 1966 the increase in redemption price occurring before 1966 and in 1966 with respect to the series E bonds purchased in 1960; he is also required to include in gross income for 1966 the $2,260 increase in redemption price of the series E bond which was exchanged in 1965 for the series H bond.

(b) *Short-term obligations issued on a discount basis.* In the case of obligations of the United States or any of its possessions, or of a State, or Territory, or any political subdivision thereof, or of the District of Columbia, issued on a discount basis and payable without interest at a fixed maturity date not exceeding one year from the date of issue, the amount of discount at which such obligation originally sold does not accrue until the date on which such obligation is redeemed, sold, or otherwise disposed of. This rule applies regardless of the method of accounting used by the taxpayer. For examples illustrating rules for computation of income from sale or other disposition of certain obligations of the type described in this paragraph, see section 1221 and the regulations thereunder.

(c) *Matured United States savings bonds*—(1) *Inclusion of increase in income upon redemption or final maturity.* If a taxpayer (other than a corporation) holds—

(i) A matured series E United States savings bond,

(ii) An obligation of the United States, other than a current income obligation, in which he retains his investment in a matured series E United States savings bond, or

(iii) A nontransferable obligation (whether or not a current income obligation) of the United States for which a series E United States savings bond was exchanged (whether or not at final maturity) in an exchange upon which gain is not recognized because of section 1037(a) (or so much of section 1031(b) as relates to section 1037(a)),

the increase in redemption price of the series E bond in excess of the amount paid for such series E bond shall be included in the gross income of such taxpayer for one taxable year in which the obligation described in subdivision (i), (ii), or (iii) of this subparagraph is redeemed or disposed of, or finally matures, whichever is earlier, but only to the extent such increase has not previously been includible in the gross income of such taxpayer or any other taxpayer. If such obligation is partially redeemed before final maturity, or partially disposed of by being partially reissued to another owner, such increase in redemption price shall be included in the gross income of such taxpayer for such taxable year on a basis proportional to the total denomination of obligations redeemed or disposed of. The provisions of section 454(c) and of this subparagraph shall not apply in the case of any taxable year for which the taxpayer's taxable income is computed under an accrual method of accounting or for a taxable year for which an election made by the taxpayer under section 454(a) and paragraph (a) of this section applies. For rules respecting the character of the gain realized upon the disposition or redemption of an obligation described in subdivision (iii) of this subparagraph, see paragraph (b) of § 1.1037-1.

(2) *Illustrations.* The application of this paragraph may be illustrated by the following examples, in which it is assumed that the taxpayer uses the cash receipts and disbursements method of accounting and the calendar year as his taxable year:

Example (1). On June 1, 1941, A purchased for $375 a series E United States savings bond which was redeemable at maturity (10 years from issue date) for $500. At maturity of the bond, A

Reg. § 1.454-1(b)

exercised the option of retaining the matured series E bond for the 10-year extended maturity period. On June 2, 1961, A redeemed the series E bond, at which time the stated redemption value was $674.60. A never elected under section 454(a) to include the annual increase in redemption price in gross income currently. Under section 454(c), A is required to include $299.60 ($674.60 less $375) in gross income for 1961 by reason of his redemption of the bond.

Example (2). The facts are the same as in example (2) in paragraph (a)(4) of this section. On redemption of the series H bond received in exchange qualifying under section 1037(a), B realizes a gain of $2,260, determined as provided in example (5) in paragraph (b)(4) of § 1.1037-1. None of this amount is includible in B's gross income for 1975, such amount having already been includible in his gross income for 1966 because of his election under section 454(a).

Example (3). C, who had elected under section 454(a) to include the annual increase in the redemption price of his non-interest-bearing obligations in gross income currently, owned a $1,000 series E United States savings bond, which was purchased on October 1, 1949, for $750. C died on February 1, 1955, when the redemption value of the bond was $820. The bond was immediately reissued to D, his only heir, who has not made an election under section 454(a). On January 15, 1960, when the redemption value of the bond is $1,000, D surrenders it to the United States in exchange solely for a $1,000 series H United States savings bond in an exchange qualifying under the provisions of section 1037(a). For 1960 D properly does not return any income from the exchange of bonds, although he returns the interest payments on the series H bond for the taxable years in which they are received. On September 1, 1964, prior to maturity of the series H bond, D redeems it for $1,000. For 1964, D must include $180 in gross income under section 454(c) from the redemption of the series H bond, that is, the amount of the increase in the redemption price of the series E bond ($1,000 less $820) occurring between February 1, 1955, and January 15, 1960, the period during which he owned the series E bond. [Reg. § 1.454-1.]

☐ [*T.D. 6282, 12-24-57. Amended by T.D. 6935, 11-16-67 and by T.D. 7154, 12-27-71.*]

[Reg. § 1.455-1]

§ 1.455-1. Treatment of prepaid subscription income.—Effective with respect to taxable years beginning after December 31, 1957, section 455 permits certain taxpayers to elect with respect to a trade or business in connection with which prepaid subscription income is received, to include such income in gross income for the taxable years during which a liability exists to furnish or deliver a newspaper, magazine, or other periodical. If a taxpayer does not elect to treat prepaid subscription income under the provisions of section 455, such income is includible in gross income for the taxable year in which received by the taxpayer, unless under the method or practice of accounting used in computing taxable income such amount is to be properly accounted for as of a different period. [Reg. § 1.455-1.]

☐ [*T.D. 6591, 2-26-62.*]

[Reg. § 1.455-2]

§ 1.455-2. Scope of election under section 455.—(a) If a taxpayer makes an election under section 455 and § 1.455-6 with respect to a trade or business, all prepaid subscription income from such trade or business shall be included in gross income for the taxable years during which the liability exists to furnish or deliver a newspaper, magazine, or other periodical. Such election shall be applicable to all prepaid subscription income received in connection with the trade or business for which the election is made; except that the taxpayer may further elect to include in gross income for the taxable year of receipt (as described in section 455(d)(3) and paragraph (c) of § 1.455-5) the entire amount of any prepaid subscription income if the liability from which it arose is to end within 12 months after the date of receipt, hereinafter sometimes referred to as "within 12 months" election.

(b) If the taxpayer is engaged in more than one trade or business in which a liability is incurred to furnish or deliver a newspaper, magazine, or other periodical, a separate election may be made under section 455 with respect to each such trade or business. In addition, a taxpayer may make a separate "within 12 months" election for each separate trade or business for which it has made an election under section 455.

(c) An election made under section 455 shall be binding for the first taxable year for which the election is made and for all subsequent taxable years, unless the taxpayer secures the consent of the Commissioner to the revocation of such election. Thus, in any case where the taxpayer has elected a method prescribed by section 455 for the inclusion of prepaid subscription income in gross income, such method of reporting income may not be changed without the prior approval of the Commissioner. In order to secure the Commissioner's consent to the revocation of such election, an application must be filed with the Commissioner in accordance with section 446(e) and the regulations thereunder. For purposes of subtitle A of the Code, the computation of taxable income

Reg. § 1.455-2(c)

under an election made under section 455 shall be treated as a method of accounting. For adjustments required by changes in method of accounting, see section 481 and the regulations thereunder.

(d) An election made under section 455 shall not apply to any prepaid subscription income received before the first taxable year to which the election applies. For example, Corporation M, which computes its taxable income under an accrual method of accounting and files its income tax returns on the calendar year basis, publishes a monthly magazine and customarily sells subscriptions on a 3-year basis. In 1958 it received $135,000 of 3-year prepaid subscription income for subscriptions beginning during 1958, and in 1959 it received $142,000 of prepaid subscription income for subscriptions beginning after December 31, 1958. In February, 1959 it elected, with the consent of the Commissioner, to report its prepaid subscription income under the provisions of section 455 for the year 1959 and subsequent taxable years. The $135,000 received in 1958 from prepaid subscriptions must be included in gross income in full in that year, and no part of such 1958 income shall be allocated to the years 1959, 1960, and 1961 during which M was under a liability to deliver its magazine. The $142,000 received in 1959 from prepaid subscriptions shall be allocated to the years 1959, 1960, 1961, and 1962.

(e) No election may be made under section 455 with respect to a trade or business if, in computing taxable income, the cash receipts and disbursements method of accounting is used with respect to such trade or business. However, if the taxpayer is on a "combination" method of accounting under section 446(c)(4) and the regulations thereunder, it may elect the benefits of section 455 if it uses an accrual method of accounting for subscription income. [Reg. § 1.455-2.]

☐ [T.D. 6591, 2-26-62.]

[Reg. § 1.455-3]

§ 1.455-3. Method of allocation.—(a) Prepaid subscription income to which section 455 applies shall be included in gross income for the taxable years during which the liability to which the income relates is discharged or is deemed to be discharged on the basis of the taxpayer's experience.

(b) For purposes of determining the period or periods over which the liability of the taxpayer extends, and for purposes of allocating prepaid subscription income to such periods, the taxpayer may aggregate similar transactions during the taxable year in any reasonable manner, provided the method of aggregation and allocation is consistently followed. [Reg. § 1.455-3.]

☐ [T.D. 6591, 2-26-62.]

[Reg. § 1.455-4]

§ 1.455-4. Cessation of taxpayer's liability.—(a) If a taxpayer has elected to apply the provisions of section 455 to a trade or business in connection with which prepaid subscription income is received, and if its liability to furnish or deliver a newspaper, magazine, or other periodical ends for any reason, then so much of the prepaid subscription income attributable to such liability as was not includible in its gross income under section 455 for preceding taxable years shall be included in its gross income for the taxable year in which such liability ends. A taxpayer's liability may end, for example, because of the cancellation of a subscription. See section 381(c)(4) and the regulations thereunder for the treatment of prepaid subscription income in a transaction to which section 381(a) applies.

(b) If a taxpayer who has elected to apply the provisions of section 455 to a trade or business dies or ceases to exist, then so much of the prepaid subscription income attributable to such trade or business which was not includible in its gross income under section 455 for preceding taxable years shall be included in its gross income for the taxable year in which such death or cessation of existence occurs. See section 381(c)(4) and the regulations thereunder for the treatment of prepaid subscription income in a transaction to which section 381(a) applies. [Reg. § 1.455-4.]

☐ [T.D. 6591, 2-26-62.]

[Reg. § 1.455-5]

§ 1.455-5. Definitions and other rules.—(a) *Prepaid subscription income.* (1) The term "prepaid subscription income" means any amount includible in gross income which is received in connection with, and is directly attributable to, a liability of the taxpayer which extends beyond the close of the taxable year in which such amount is received and which is income from a newspaper, magazine, or other periodical. For example where Corporation X, a publisher of newspapers, magazines, and other periodicals makes sales on a subscription basis and the purchaser pays the subscription price in advance, prepaid subscription income would include the amounts actually received by X in connection with its liability to furnish or deliver the newspaper, magazine, or other periodical.

(2) For purposes of section 455, prepaid subscription income does not include amounts re-

Reg. § 1.455-3(a)

ceived by a taxpayer in connection with sales of subscriptions on a prepaid basis where such taxpayer does not have the liability to furnish or deliver a newspaper, magazine, or other periodical. The provisions of this subparagraph may be illustrated by the following example. Corporation D has a contract with each of several large publishers which grants it the right to sell subscriptions to their periodicals. Corporation D collects the subscription price from the subscribers, retains a portion thereof as its commission and remits the balance to the publishers. The amount retained by Corporation D represents commissions on the sale of subscriptions, and is not prepaid subscription income for purposes of section 455 since the commissions represent compensation for services rendered and are not directly attributable to a liability of Corporation D to furnish or deliver a newspaper, magazine, or other periodical.

(b) *Liability.* The term "liability" means a liability of the taxpayer to furnish or deliver a newspaper, magazine, or other periodical.

(c) *Receipt of prepaid subscription income.* For purposes of section 455, prepaid subscription income shall be treated as received during the taxable year for which it is includible in gross income under section 451, relating to general rule for taxable year of inclusion, without regard to section 455.

(d) *Treatment of prepaid subscription income under an established accounting method.* Notwithstanding the provisions of section 455 and § 1.455–1, any taxpayer who, for taxable years beginning before January 1, 1958, has reported prepaid subscription income for income tax purposes under an established and consistent method or practice of deferring such income may continue to report such income in accordance with such method or practice for all subsequent taxable years to which section 455 applies without making an election under section 455. [Reg. § 1.455-5.]

☐ [T.D. 6591, 2-26-62.]

[Reg. § 1.455-6]

§ 1.455-6. **Time and manner of making election.**—(a) *Election without consent.* (1) A taxpayer may, without consent, elect to treat prepaid subscription income of a trade or business under section 455 for the first taxable year—

(i) Which begins after December 31, 1957 and

(ii) In which there is received prepaid subscription income from the trade or business for which the election is made.

Such an election shall be made not later than the time prescribed by law for filing the income tax return for such year (including extensions thereof), and shall be made by means of a statement attached to such return.

(2) The statement shall indicate that the taxpayer is electing to apply the provisions of section 455 to his trade or business, and shall contain the following information:

(i) The name and a description of the taxpayer's trade or business to which the election is to apply;

(ii) The method of accounting used in such trade or business;

(iii) The total amount of prepaid subscription income from such trade or business for the taxable year;

(iv) The period or periods over which the liability of the taxpayer to furnish or deliver a newspaper, magazine, or other periodical extends;

(v) The amount of prepaid subscription income applicable to each such period; and

(vi) A description of the method used in allocating the prepaid subscription income to each such period.

In any case in which prepaid subscription income is received from more than one trade or business, the statement shall set forth the required information with respect to each trade or business subject to the election.

(3) See paragraph (c) of this section for additional information required to be submitted with the statement if the taxpayer also elects to include in gross income for the taxable year of receipt the entire amount of prepaid subscription income attributable to a liability which is to end within 12 months after the date of receipt.

(b) *Election with consent.* A taxpayer may, with the consent of the Commissioner, elect at any time to apply the provisions of section 455 to any trade or business in which it receives prepaid subscription income. The request for such consent shall be in writing, signed by the taxpayer or its authorized representative, and shall be addressed to the Commissioner of Internal Revenue, Attention: T:R:C, Washington 25, D.C. The request must be filed on or before the later of the following dates: (1) 90 days after the beginning of the first taxable year to which the election is to apply, or (2) May 28, 1962, and must contain the information described in paragraph (a)(2) of this section. See paragraph (c) of this section for additional information required to be submitted with the request if the taxpayer who elects to include in gross income for the taxable year of receipt the entire amount of prepaid subscription income attributable to a liability which is to end within 12 months after the date of receipt.

(c) *"Within 12 months" election.* (1) A taxpayer who elects to apply the provisions of section 455 to any trade or business may also elect to include in gross income for the taxable year of receipt (as described in section 455(d)(3) and paragraph (c) of § 1.455-5) the entire amount of any prepaid subscription income from such trade or business if the liability from which it arose is to end within 12 months after the date of receipt. Any such election is binding for the first taxable year for which it is effective and for all subsequent taxable years, unless the taxpayer secures permission from the Commissioner to treat such income differently. Application to revoke or change a "within 12 months" election shall be made in accordance with the provisions of section 446(e) and the regulations thereunder.

(2) The "within 12 months" election shall be made by including in the statement required by paragraph (a) of this section or the request described in paragraph (b) of this section, whichever is applicable, a declaration that the taxpayer elects to include such income in gross income in the taxable year of receipt, and the amount of such income. If the taxpayer is engaged in more than one trade or business for which the election under section 455 is made, it must include, in such statement or request, a declaration for each trade or business for which it makes the "within 12 months" election. See also paragraph (e) of § 1.455-2.

(3) If the taxpayer does not make the "within 12 months" election for its trade or business at the time prescribed for making the election to include prepaid subscription income in gross income for the taxable years during which its liability to furnish or deliver a newspaper, magazine, or other periodical exists for such trade or business, but later wishes to make such election it must apply for permission from the Commissioner. Such application shall be made in accordance with the provisions of section 446(e) and the regulations thereunder. [Reg. § 1.455-6.]

☐ [T.D. 6591, 2-26-62.]

[Reg. § 1.456-1]

§ 1.456-1. **Treatment of prepaid dues income.**—Effective for taxable years beginning after December 31, 1960, a taxpayer which is a membership organization (as described in par. (c) of § 1.456-5) and which receives prepaid dues income as described in par. (a) of § 1.456-5 in connection with its trade or business of rendering services or making available membership privileges may elect under section 456 to include such income in gross income ratably over the taxable years during which its liability (as described in par. (b) of § 1.456-5) to render such services or extend such privileges exists, if such liability does not extend over a period of time in excess of 36 months. If the taxpayer does not elect to treat prepaid dues income under section 456, or if such income may not be reported under section 456, as for example, where the income relates to a liability to render services or make available membership privileges which extends beyond 36 months, then such income is includible in gross income for the taxable year in which it is received (as described in par. (d) of § 1.456-5). [Reg. § 1.456-1.]

☐ [T.D. 6937, 11-29-67.]

[Reg. § 1.456-2]

§ 1.456-2. **Scope of election under section 456.**—(a) An election made under section 456 and § 1.456-6, shall be applicable to all prepaid dues income received in connection with the trade or business for which the election is made. However, the taxpayer may further elect to include in gross income for the taxable year of receipt the entire amount of any prepaid dues income attributable to a liability extending beyond the close of the taxable year but ending within 12 months after the date of receipt, hereinafter referred to as the "within 12 months" election.

(b) If the taxpayer is engaged in more than one trade or business in connection with which prepaid dues income is received, a separate election may be made under section 456 with respect to each such trade or business. In addition, a taxpayer may make a separate "within 12 months" election for each separate trade or business for which it has made an election under section 456.

(c) A section 456 election and a "within 12 months" election shall be binding for the first taxable year for which the election is made and for all subsequent taxable years, unless the taxpayer secures the consent of the Commissioner to the revocation of either election. In order to secure the Commissioner's consent to the revocation of the section 456 election or the "within 12 months" election, an application must be filed with the Commissioner in accordance with section 446(e) and the regulations thereunder. However, an application for consent to revoke the section 456 election or the "within 12 months" election in the case of all taxable years which end before November 30, 1967, must be filed on or before February 28, 1968. For purposes of subtitle A of the Code, the computation of taxable income under an election made under section 456 or under the "within 12 months" election shall be treated as a method of accounting. For adjustments required

Reg. § 1.456-1

by changes in method of accounting, see section 481 and the regulations thereunder.

(d) Except as provided in section 456(d) and § 1.456-7, an election made under section 456 shall not apply to any prepaid dues income received before the first taxable year to which the election applies. For example, Corporation X, a membership organization which files its income tax returns on a calendar year basis, customarily sells 3-year memberships, payable in advance. In 1961 it received $160,000 of prepaid dues income for 3-year memberships beginning during 1961, and in 1962 it received $185,000 of prepaid dues income for 3-year memberships beginning on January 1, 1962. In March 1962 it elected, with the consent of the Commissioner, to report its prepaid dues income under the provisions of section 456 for the year 1962 and subsequent taxable years. The $160,000 received in 1961 from prepaid dues must be included in gross income in full in that year, and except as provided in section 456(d) and § 1.456-7, no part of such income shall be allocated to the taxable years 1962, 1963, and 1964 during which X was under a liability to make available its membership privileges. The $185,000 received in 1962 from prepaid dues income shall be allocated to the years 1962, 1963, and 1964.

(e) No election may be made under section 456 with respect to a trade or business if, in computing taxable income, the cash receipts and disbursements method (or a hybrid thereof) of accounting is used with respect to such trade or business, [unless] the combination of the section 456 election and the taxpayer's hybrid method of accounting does not result in a material distortion of income. [Reg. § 1.456-2.]

☐ [T.D. 6937, 11-29-67.]

[Reg. § 1.456-3]

§ 1.456-3. Method of allocation.—(a) Prepaid dues income for which an election has been made under section 456 shall be included in gross income over the period of time during which the liability to render services or make available membership privileges exists. The liability to render the services or make available the membership privileges shall be deemed to exist ratably over the period of time such services are required to be rendered, or such membership privileges are required to be made available. Thus, the prepaid dues income shall be included in gross income ratably over the period of the membership contract. For example, Corporation X, a membership organization, which files its income tax returns on a calendar year basis, elects, for its taxable year beginning January 1, 1961, to report its prepaid dues income in accordance with the provisions of section 456. On March 31, 1961, it sells a 2-year membership for $48 payable in advance, the membership to extend from May 1, 1961 to April 30, 1963. X shall include in its gross income for the taxable year 1961 8/24 of the $48, or $16, and for the taxable year 1962 12/24 of the $48, or $24, and for the taxable year 1963 4/24 of the $48, or $8.

(b) For purposes of determining the period or periods over which the liability of the taxpayer exists, and for purposes of allocating prepaid dues income to such periods, the taxpayer may aggregate similar transactions during the taxable year in any reasonable manner, provided the method of aggregation and allocation is consistently followed. [Reg. § 1.456-3.]

☐ [T.D. 6937, 11-29-67.]

[Reg. § 1.456-4]

§ 1.456-4. Cessation of liability or existence.—(a) If a taxpayer has elected to apply the provisions of section 456 to a trade or business in connection with which prepaid dues income is received, and if the taxpayer's liability to render services or make available membership privileges ends for any reason, as for example, because of the cancellation of a membership, then so much of the prepaid dues income attributable to such liability as was not includible in the taxpayer's gross income under section 456 for preceding taxable years shall be included in gross income for the taxable year in which such liability ends. This paragraph shall not apply to amounts includible in gross income under § 1.456-7.

(b) If a taxpayer which has elected to apply the provisions of section 456 ceases to exist, then the prepaid dues income which was not includible in gross income under section 456 for preceding taxable years shall be included in the taxpayer's gross income for the taxable year in which such cessation of existence occurs. This paragraph shall not apply to amounts includible in gross income under § 1.456-7.

(c) If a taxpayer is a party to a transaction to which section 381(a) applies and the taxpayer's method of accounting with respect to prepaid dues income is used by the acquiring corporation under the provisions of section 381(c)(4), then neither the liability nor the existence of the taxpayer shall be deemed to have ended or ceased. In such cases see section 381(c)(4) and the regulations thereunder for the treatment of the portion of prepaid dues income which was not included in gross income under section 456 for preceding taxable years. [Reg. § 1.456-4.]

☐ [T.D. 6937, 11-29-67.]

36,836

Methods of Accounting

See p. 20,601 for regulations not amended to reflect law changes

[Reg. § 1.456-5]

§ 1.456-5. Definitions and other rules.—(a) *Prepaid dues income.* (1) The term "prepaid dues income" means any amount for membership dues includible in gross income which is received by a membership organization in connection with, and is directly attributable to, a liability of the taxpayer to render services or make available membership privileges over a period of time which extends beyond the close of the taxable year in which such amount is received.

(2) For purposes of section 456, prepaid dues income does not include amounts received by a taxpayer in connection with sales of memberships on a prepaid basis where the taxpayer does not have the liability to furnish the services or make available the membership privileges. For example, where a taxpayer has a contract with several membership organizations to sell memberships in such organizations and retains a portion of the amounts received from the sale of such memberships and remits the balance to the membership organizations, the amounts retained by such taxpayer represent commissions and do not constitute prepaid dues income for purposes of section 456.

(b) *Liability.* The term "liability" means a liability of the taxpayer to render services or make available membership privileges over a period of time which does not exceed 36 months. Thus, if during the taxable year a taxpayer sells memberships for more than 36 months and also memberships for 36 months or less, section 456 does not apply to the income from the sale of memberships for more than 36 months. For the purpose of determining the duration of a liability, a bona fide renewal of a membership shall not be considered to be a part of the existing membership.

(c) *Membership organization.* (1)The term "membership organization" means a corporation, association, federation, or other similar organization meeting the following requirements:

(i) It is organized without capital stock of any kind,

(ii) Its charter, bylaws, or other written agreement or contract expressly prohibits the distribution of any part of the net earnings directly or indirectly, in money, property, or services, to any member, and

(iii) No part of the net earnings of which is in fact distributed to any member either directly or indirectly, in money, property, or services.

(2) For purposes of this paragraph an increase in services or reduction in dues to all members shall generally not be considered distributions of net earnings.

(3) If a corporation, association, federation, or other similar organization subsequent to the time it elects to report its prepaid dues income in accordance with the provisions of section 456, (i) issues any kind of capital stock either to any member or nonmember, (ii) amends its charter, bylaws, or other written agreement or contract to permit distributions of its net earnings to any member or, (iii) in fact, distributes any part of its net earnings either in money, property, or services to any member, then immediately after such event the organization shall not be considered a membership organization within the meaning of section 456(e)(3).

(d) *Receipt of prepaid dues income.* For purposes of section 456, prepaid dues income shall be treated as received during the taxable year for which it is includible in gross income under section 451, relating to the general rule for taxable year of inclusion, without regard to section 456. [Reg. § 1.456-5.]

☐ [*T.D.* 6937, 11-29-67.]

[Reg. § 1.456-6]

§ 1.456-6. Time and manner of making election.—(a) *Election without consent.* A taxpayer may make an election under section 456 without the consent of the Commissioner for the first taxable year beginning after December 31, 1960, in which it receives prepaid dues income in the trade or business for which such election is made. The election must be made not later than the time prescribed by law for filing the income tax return for such year (including extensions thereof). The election must be made by means of a statement attached to such return. In addition, there should be attached a copy of a typical membership contract used by the organization and a copy of its charter, bylaws, or other written agreement or contract of organization or association. The statement shall indicate that the taxpayer is electing to apply the provisions of section 456 to the trade or business, and shall contain the following information:

(1) The taxpayer's name and a description of the trade or business to which the election is to apply.

(2) The method of accounting used for prepaid dues income in the trade or business during the first taxable year for which the election is to be effective and during each of 3 preceding taxable years, and if there was a change in the method of accounting for prepaid dues income during such 3-year period, a detailed explanation of such change including the adjustments necessary to prevent duplications or omissions of income.

Reg. § 1.456-5(a)(2)

(3) Whether any type of deferral method for prepaid dues income has been used during any of the 3 taxable years preceding the first taxable year for which the election is effective. Where any type of such deferral method has been used during this period, an explanation of the method and a schedule showing the amounts received in each such year and the amounts deferred to each succeeding year.

(4) A schedule with appropriate explanations showing:

(i) The total amount of prepaid dues income received in the trade or business in the first taxable year for which the election is effective and the amount of such income to be included in each taxable year in accordance with the election,

(ii) The total amount, if any, of prepayments of dues received in the first taxable year for which the election is effective which are directly attributable to a liability of the taxpayer to render services or make available membership privileges over a period of time in excess of 36 months, and

(iii) The total amount, if any, of prepaid dues income received in the trade or business in—

(*a*) The taxable year preceding the first taxable year for which the election is effective if all memberships sold by the taxpayer are for periods of 1 year or less,

(*b*) Each of the 2 taxable years preceding the first taxable year for which the election is effective if any memberships are sold for periods in excess of 1 year but none are sold for periods in excess of 2 years, or

(*c*) Each of the 3 taxable years preceding the first taxable year for which the election is effective if any memberships are sold for periods in excess of 2 years.

In each case there shall be set forth the amount of such income which would have been includible in each taxable year had the election been effective for the years for which the information is required.

In any case in which prepaid dues income is received from more than one trade or business, the statement shall set forth separately the required information with respect to each trade or business for which the election is made. See paragraph (c) of this section for additional information required to be submitted with the statement if the taxpayer also elects to include in gross income for the taxable year of receipt the entire amount of prepaid dues income attributable to a liability which is to end within 12 months after the date of receipt.

(b) *Election with consent.* A taxpayer may elect with the consent of the Commissioner, to apply the provisions of section 456 to any trade or business in which it receives prepaid dues income. The request for such consent shall be in writing, signed by the taxpayer or its authorized representative, and shall be addressed to the Commissioner of Internal Revenue, Washington, D.C. 20224. The request must be filed on or before the later of the following dates: (1) 90 days after the beginning of the first taxable year to which the election is to apply, or (2) February 28, 1968, and should contain the information described in paragraph (a) of this section. See paragraph (c) of this section for additional information required to be submitted with the request if the taxpayer also elects to include in gross income for the taxable year of receipt the entire amount of prepaid dues income attributable to a liability which is to end within 12 months after the date of receipt.

(c) *"Within 12 months" election.* (1) The "within 12 months" election shall be made by including in the statement required by paragraph (a) of this section or the request described in paragraph (b) of this section, whichever is applicable, a declaration that the taxpayer elects to include such income in gross income in the taxable year of receipt, and the amount of such income for each taxable year to which the election is to apply which has ended prior to the time such statement or request is filed. If the taxpayer is engaged in more than one trade or business for which the election under section 456 is made, it must include, in such statement or request, a declaration for each trade or business for which it wishes to make the "within 12 months" election.

(2) If the taxpayer does not make the "within 12 months" election for a trade or business at the time it makes the election under paragraph (a) or (b) of this section, but later wishes to make such election, it must apply for permission from the Commissioner. Such application shall be made in accordance with the provisions of section 446(e) and § 1.446(e)(3). [Reg. § 1.456-6.]

☐ [*T.D.* 6937, 11-29-67.]

[Reg. § 1.456-7]

§ 1.456-7. *Transitional rule.*—(a) Under section 456(d)(1), a taxpayer making an election under section 456 shall include in its gross income for the first taxable year to which the election applies and for each of the 2 succeeding taxable years not only that portion of prepaid dues income which is includible in gross income for each such taxable year under section 456(a), but also an additional amount equal to that portion of the total prepaid dues income received in each of the 3 taxable years preceding the first taxable year to which the election applies which would have been includible in gross income for such first taxable year and such two succeeding taxable years had

Reg. § 1.456-7(a)

the election under section 456 been effective during such 3 preceding taxable years. In computing such additional amounts—

(1) In the case of taxpayers who did not include in gross income for the taxable year preceding the first taxable year for which the election is effective, that portion of the prepaid dues income received in such year attributable to a liability which is to end within 12 months after the date of receipt, no effect shall be given to a "within 12 months" election made under paragraph (c) of § 1.456-6, and

(2) There shall be taken into account only prepaid dues income arising from a trade or business with respect to which an election is made under section 456 and § 1.456-6.

Section 481 and the regulations thereunder shall have no application to the additional amounts includible in gross income under section 456(d) and this section, but section 481 and the regulations thereunder shall apply to prevent other amounts from being duplicated or omitted.

(b) A taxpayer who makes an election with respect to prepaid dues income, and who includes in gross income for any taxable year to which the election applies an additional amount computed under section 456(d)(1) and paragraph (a) of this section, shall be permitted under section 456(d)(2) to deduct for such taxable year and for each of the 4 succeeding taxable years an amount equal to one-fifth of such additional amount, but only to the extent that such additional amount was also included in the taxpayer's gross income for any of the 3 taxable years preceding the first taxable year to which such election applies. The taxpayer shall maintain books and records in sufficient detail to enable the district director to determine upon audit that the additional amounts were included in the taxpayer's gross income for any of the 3 taxable years preceding such first taxable year. If, however, the taxpayer ceases to exist, as described in paragraph (b) of § 1.456-4, and there is included in gross income, under such paragraph, of the year of cessation the entire portion of prepaid dues income not previously includible in gross income under section 456 for preceding taxable years (other than for amounts received prior to the first year for which an election was made), all the amounts not previously deducted under this paragraph shall be permitted as a deduction in the year of cessation of existence.

(c) The provisions of this section may be illustrated by the following example:

Example. (1) Assume that X Corporation, a membership organization qualified to make the election under section 456, elects to report its prepaid dues income in accordance with the provisions of section 456 for its taxable year ending December 31, 1961. Assume further that X Corporation receives in the middle of each taxable year $3,000 of prepaid dues income in connection with a liability to render services over a 3-year period beginning with the date of receipt. Under section 456(a), X Corporation will report income received in 1961 and subsequent years as follows:

Year of Receipt	Total Receipts	1961	1962	1963	1964	1965	1966	1967	1968
1961	$3,000	$500	$1,000	$1,000	$500	....	....	....	....
1962	3,000	....	500	1,000	1,000	500	....	....	....
1963	3,000	....	....	500	1,000	1,000	$500	....	....
1964	3,000	....	....	....	500	1,000	1,000	$500	....
1965	3,000	....	....	....	....	500	1,000	1,000	$500
1966	3,000	....	....	....	....	....	500	1,000	1,000
1967	3,000	....	....	....	....	....	....	500	1,000
1968	3,000	....	....	....	....	....	....	....	500
Total reportable under section 456(a)		$500	$1,500	$2,500	$3,000	$3,000	$3,000	$3,000	$3,000

(2) Under section 456(d)(1), X Corporation must include in its gross income for the first taxable year to which the election applies and for each of the two succeeding taxable years, the amounts which would have been included in those years had the election been effective 3 years earlier. If the election had been effective in 1958, the following amounts received in 1958, 1959, and 1960 would have been reported in 1961 and subsequent years:

		Years of Including Additional Amounts		
Year of Receipt	Amount Received	1961	1962	1963
1958	$3,000	$500	...	...
1959	3,000	1,000	$500	...
1960	3,000	1,000	1,000	$500
Total additional amounts to be included under section 456(d)(1)		$2,500	$1,500	$500

Reg. § 1.456-7(a)(1)

(3) Having included the additional amounts as required by section 456(d)(1), and assuming such amounts were actually included in gross income in the 3 taxable years preceding the first taxable year for which the election is effective, X Corporation is entitled to deduct under section 456(d)(2) in the year of inclusion and in each of the succeeding 4 years an amount equal to one-fifth of the amounts included, as follows:

Year of Inclusion	Amount	1961	1962	1963	1964	1965	1966	1967
1961	$2,500	$500	$500	$500	$500	$500	...	...
1962	1,500	...	300	300	300	300	$300	...
1963	500	...	...	100	100	100	100	$100
Total amount deductible under section 456(d)(2)		$500	$800	$900	$900	$900	$400	$100

(4) The net result of the inclusions under section 456(d)(1) and the deductions under section 456(d)(2) may be summarized as follows:

	1961	1962	1963	1964	1965	1966	1967	1968
Amount includible under section 456(a)	$500	$1,500	$2,500	$3,000	$3,000	$3,000	$3,000	$3,000
Amount includible under section 456(d)(1)	2,500	1,500	500	...	...	...	...	...
Total	$3,000	$3,000	$3,000	$3,000	$3,000	$3,000	$3,000	$3,000
Amount deductible under section 456(d)(2)	500	800	900	900	900	400	100	...
Net amount reportable under section 456	$2,500	$2,200	$2,100	$2,100	$2,100	$2,600	$2,900	$3,000

[Reg. § 1.456-7.]

☐ [T.D. 6937, 11-29-67.]

[Reg. § 1.457-1]

§ 1.457-1. General overviews of section 457.—Section 457 provides rules for nonqualified deferred compensation plans established by eligible employers as defined under § 1.457-2(d). Eligible employers can establish either deferred compensation plans that are eligible plans and that meet the requirements of section 457(b) and §§ 1.457-3 through 1.457-10, or deferred compensation plans or arrangements that do not meet the requirements of section 457(b) and §§ 1.457-3 through 1.457-10 and that are subject to tax treatment under section 457(f) and § 1.457-11. [Reg. § 1.457-1.]

☐ [T.D. 7836, 9-23-82. Amended by T.D. 9075, 7-10-2003.]

[Reg. § 1.457-2]

§ 1.457-2. Definitions.—This section sets forth the definitions that are used under §§ 1.457-1 through 1.457-11.

(a) *Amount(s) deferred.* Amount(s) deferred means the total annual deferrals under an eligible plan in the current and prior years, adjusted for gain or loss. Except as provided at §§ 1.457-4(c)(1)(iii) and 1.457-6(a), amount(s) deferred includes any rollover amount held by an eligible plan as provided under § 1.457-10(e).

(b) *Annual deferral(s)*—(1) Annual deferral(s) means, with respect to a taxable year, the amount of compensation deferred under an eligible plan, whether by salary reduction or by nonelective employer contribution. The amount of compensation deferred under an eligible plan is taken into account as an annual deferral in the taxable year of the participant in which deferred, or, if later, the year in which the amount of compensation deferred is no longer subject to a substantial risk of forfeiture.

(2) If the amount of compensation deferred under the plan during a taxable year is not subject to a substantial risk of forfeiture, the amount taken into account as an annual deferral is not adjusted to reflect gain or loss allocable to the compensation deferred. If, however, the amount of compensation deferred under the plan during the taxable year is subject to a substantial risk of forfeiture, the amount of compensation deferred that is taken into account as an annual deferral in the taxable year in which the substantial risk of forfeiture lapses must be adjusted to reflect gain or loss allocable to the compensation deferred until the substantial risk of forfeiture lapses.

(3) If the eligible plan is a defined benefit plan within the meaning of section 414(j), the

Reg. § 1.457-2(b)(3)

annual deferral for a taxable year is the present value of the increase during the taxable year of the participant's accrued benefit that is not subject to a substantial risk of forfeiture (disregarding any such increase attributable to prior annual deferrals). For this purpose, present value must be determined using actuarial assumptions and methods that are reasonable (both individually and in the aggregate), as determined by the Commissioner.

(4) For purposes solely of applying § 1.457-4 to determine the maximum amount of the annual deferral for a participant for a taxable year under an eligible plan, the maximum amount is reduced by the amount of any deferral for the participant under a plan described at paragraph (k)(4)(i) of this section (relating to certain plans in existence before January 1, 1987) as if that deferral were an annual deferral under another eligible plan of the employer.

(c) *Beneficiary.* Beneficiary means a person who is entitled to benefits in respect of a participant following the participant's death or an alternate payee as described in § 1.457-10(c).

(d) *Catch-up.* Catch-up amount or *catch-up* limitation for a participant for a taxable year means the annual deferral permitted under section 414(v) (as described in § 1.457-4(c)(2)) or section 457(b)(3) (as described in § 1.457-4(c)(3)) to the extent the amount of the annual deferral for the participant for the taxable year is permitted to exceed the plan ceiling applicable under section 457(b)(2) (as described in § 1.457-4(c)(1)).

(e) *Eligible employer.* Eligible employer means an entity that is a State that establishes a plan or a tax-exempt entity that establishes a plan. The performance of services as an independent contractor for a State or local government or a tax-exempt entity is treated as the performance of services for an eligible employer. The term *eligible employer* does not include a church as defined in section 3121(w)(3)(A), a qualified church-controlled organization as defined in section 3121(w)(3)(B), or the Federal government or any agency or instrumentality thereof. Thus, for example, a nursing home which is associated with a church, but which is not itself a church (as defined in section 3121(w)(3)(A)) or a qualified church-controlled organization as defined in section 3121(w)(3)(B)), would be an eligible employer if it is a tax-exempt entity as defined in paragraph (m) of this section.

(f) *Eligible plan.* An *eligible plan* is a plan that meets the requirements of §§ 1.457-3 through 1.457-10 that is established and maintained by an eligible employer. An *eligible governmental plan* is an eligible plan that is established and maintained by an eligible employer as defined in paragraph (l) of this section. An arrangement does not fail to constitute a single eligible governmental plan merely because the arrangement is funded through more than one trustee, custodian, or insurance carrier. An *eligible plan of a tax-exempt entity* is an eligible plan that is established and maintained by an eligible employer as defined in paragraph (m) of this section.

(g) *Includible compensation.* Includible *compensation* of a participant means, with respect to a taxable year, the participant's compensation, as defined in section 415(c)(3), for services performed for the eligible employer. The amount of includible compensation is determined without regard to any community property laws.

(h) *Ineligible plan.* Ineligible *plan* means a plan established and maintained by an eligible employer that is not maintained in accordance with §§ 1.457-3 through 1.457-10. A plan that is not established by an eligible employer as defined in paragraph (e) of this section is neither an eligible nor an ineligible plan.

(i) *Nonelective employer contribution.* A *nonelective employer contribution* is a contribution made by an eligible employer for the participant with respect to which the participant does not have the choice to receive the contribution in cash or property. Solely for purposes of section 457 and §§ 1.457-2 through 1.457-11, the term *nonelective employer contribution* includes employer contributions that would be described in section 401(m) if they were contributions to a qualified plan.

(j) *Participant.* Participant in an eligible plan means an individual who is currently deferring compensation, or who has previously deferred compensation under the plan by salary reduction or by nonelective employer contribution and who has not received a distribution of his or her entire benefit under the eligible plan. Or.ly individuals who perform services for the eligible employer, either as an employee or as an independent contractor, may defer compensation under the eligible plan.

(k) *Plan.* Plan includes any agreement or arrangement between an eligible employer and a participant or participants (including an individual employment agreement) under which the payment of compensation is deferred (whether by salary reduction or by nonelective employer contribution). The following types of plans are not treated as agreements or arrangement under which compensation is deferred: a bona fide vacation leave, sick leave, compensatory time, severance pay, disability pay, or death benefit plan described in section 457(e)(11)(A)(i) and any plan paying length of service awards to bona fide volunteers (and their beneficiaries) on account of qualified services performed by such volunteers as described in section 457(e)(11)(A)(ii). Further, the term *plan* does not include any of the following (and section 457 and §§ 1.457-2 through 1.457-11 do not apply to any of the following)—

(1) Any nonelective deferred compensation under which all individuals (other than those who have not satisfied any applicable initial service requirement) with the same relationship with the eligible employer are covered under the same plan with no individual variations or options under the plan as described in section 457(e)(12), but only to the extent the compensation is attributable to services performed as an independent contractor;

(2) An agreement or arrangement described in § 1.457-11(b);

(3) Any plan satisfying the conditions in section 1107(c)(4) of the Tax Reform Act of 1986 (100 Stat. 2494) (TRA '86) (relating to certain plans for State judges); and

(4) Any of the following plans or arrangements (to which specific transitional statutory exclusions apply)—

(i) A plan or arrangement of a tax-exempt entity in existence prior to January 1, 1987, if the conditions of section 1107(c)(3)(B) of the TRA '86, as amended by section 1011(e)(6) of Technical and Miscellaneous Revenue Act of 1988 (102 Stat. 3700) (TAMRA), are satisfied (see § 1.457-2(b)(4) for a special rule regarding such plan);

(ii) A collectively bargained nonelective deferred a compensation plan in effect on December 31, 1987, if the conditions of section 6064(d)(2) of TAMRA are satisfied;

(iii) Amounts described in section 6064(d)(3) of TAMRA (relating to certain nonelective deferred compensation arrangements in effect before 1989); and

(iv) Any plan satisfying the conditions in section 1107(c)(4) or (5) of TRA '86 (relating to certain plans for certain individuals with respect to which the Service issued guidance before 1977).

(l) *State.* State means a State (treating the District of Columbia as a State as provided under section 7701(a)(10)), a political subdivision of a State, and any agency or instrumentality of a State.

(m) *Tax-exempt entity.* Tax-exempt entity includes any organization exempt from tax under subtitle A of the Internal Revenue Code, except that a governmental unit (including an international governmental organization) is not a tax-exempt entity.

(n) *Trust.* Trust means a trust described under section 457(g) and § 1.457-8. Custodial accounts and contracts described in section 401(f) are treated as trusts under the rules described in § 1.457-8(a)(2). [Reg. § 1.457-2.]

☐ [T.D. 7836, 9-23-82. Amended by T.D. 9075, 7-10-2003.]

[Reg. § 1.457-3]

§ 1.457-3. General introduction to eligible plans.—(a) *Compliance in form and operation.* An eligible plan is a written plan established and maintained by an eligible employer that is maintained, in both form and operation, in accordance with the requirements of §§ 1.457-4 through 1.457-10. An eligible plan must contain all the material terms and conditions for benefits under the plan. An eligible plan may contain certain optional features not required for plan eligibility under section 457(b), such as distributions for unforeseeable emergencies, loans, plan-to-plan transfers, additional deferral elections, acceptance of rollovers to the plan, and distributions of smaller accounts to eligible participants. However, except as otherwise specifically provided in §§ 1.457-4 through 1.457-10, if an eligible plan contains any optional provisions, the optional provisions must meet, in both form and operation, the relevant requirements under section 457 and §§ 1.457-2 through 1.457-10.

(b) *Treatment as single plan.* In any case in which multiple plans are used to avoid or evade the requirements of §§ 1.457-4 through 1.457-10, the Commissioner may apply the rules under §§ 1.457-4 through 1.457-10 as if the plans were a single plan. See also § 1.457-4(c)(3)(v) (requiring an eligible employer to have no more than one normal retirement age for each participant under all of the eligible plans it sponsors), the second sentence of § 1.457-4(e)(2) (treating deferrals under all eligible plans under which an individual participates by virtue of his or her relationship with a single employer as a single plan for purposes of determining excess deferrals), and § 1.457-5 (combining annual deferrals under all eligible plans). [Reg. § 1.457-3.]

☐ [T.D. 7836, 9-23-82. Amended by T.D. 9075, 7-10-2003.]

[Reg. § 1.457-4]

§ 1.457-4. Annual deferrals, deferral limitations, and deferral agreements under eligible plans.—(a) *Taxation of annual deferrals.* Annual deferrals that satisfy the requirements of paragraphs (b) and (c) of this section are excluded from the gross income of a participant in the year deferred or contributed and are not includible in gross income until paid to the participant in the case of an eligible governmental plan, or until paid or otherwise made available to the participant in the case of an eligible plan of a tax-exempt entity. See § 1.457-7.

(b) *Agreement for deferral.* In order to be an eligible plan, the plan must provide that compensation may be deferred for any calendar month by salary reduction only if an agreement providing for the deferral has been entered into before the first day of the month in which the compensation is paid or made available. A new employee may defer compensation payable in the calendar month during which the participant first becomes an employee if an agreement providing for the deferral is entered into on or before the first day on which the participant performs services for the eligible employer. An eligible plan may provide that if a participant enters into an agreement providing for deferral by salary reduction under the plan, the agreement will remain in effect until the participant revokes or alters the terms of the agreement. Nonelective employer contributions are treated as being made under an agreement entered into before the first day of the calendar month.

(c) *Maximum deferral limitations*—(1) *Basic annual limitation*—(i) Except as described in paragraphs (c)(2) and (3) of this section, in order to be an eligible plan, the plan must provide that the annual deferral amount for a taxable year (the plan ceiling) may not exceed the lesser of—

(A) The applicable annual dollar amount specified in section 457(e)(15): $11,000 for 2002; $12,000 for 2003; $13,000 for 2004; $14,000 for 2005; and $15,000 for 2006 and thereafter. After 2006, the $15,000 amount is adjusted for cost-of-living in the manner described in paragraph (c)(4) of this section; or

(B) 100 percent of the participant's includible compensation for the taxable year.

(ii) The amount of annual deferrals permitted by the 100 percent of includible compensation limitation under paragraph (c)(1)(i)(B) of this section is determined under section 457(e)(5) and § 1.457-2(g).

(iii) For purposes of determining the plan ceiling under this paragraph (c), the annual deferral amount does not include any rollover amounts received by the eligible plan under § 1.457-10(e).

(iv) The provisions of this paragraph (c)(1) are illustrated by the following examples:

Example 1 (i) *Facts.* Participant A, who earns $14,000 a year, enters into a salary reduction agreement in 2006 with A's eligible employer and elects to defer $13,000 of A's compensation for that year. Participant A is not eligible for the catch-up described in paragraph (c)(2) or (3) of this section, participates in no other retirement plan, and has no other income exclusions taken into account in computing includible compensation.

(ii) *Conclusion.* The annual deferral limit for A in 2006 is the lesser of $15,000 or 100 percent of includible compensation, $14,000. A's annual deferral of $13,000 is permitted under the plan because it is not in excess of $14,000 and thus does not exceed 100 percent of A's includible compensation.

Example 2. (i) *Facts.* Assume the same facts as in *Example 1*, except that A's eligible employer provides an immediately vested, matching employer contribution under the plan for participants who make salary reduction deferrals under A's eligible plan. The matching contribution is equal to 100 percent of elective contributions, but not in excess of 10 percent of compensation (in A's case, $1,400).

(ii) *Conclusion.* Participant A's annual deferral exceeds the limitations of this paragraph (c)(1). A's maximum deferral limitation in 2006 is $14,000. A's salary reduction deferral of $13,000 combined with A's eligible employer's nonelective employer contribution of $1,400 exceeds the basic annual limitation of this paragraph (c)(1) because A's annual deferrals total $14,400. A has an excess deferral for the taxable year of $400, the amount exceeding A's permitted annual deferral limitation. The $400 excess deferral is treated as described in paragraph (e) of this section.

Example 3. (i) *Facts.* Beginning in year 2002, Eligible Employer X contributes $3,000 per year for five years to Participant B's eligible plan account. B's interest in the account vests in 2006. B has annual compensation of $50,000 in each of the five years 2002 through 2006. Participant B is 41 years old. B is not eligible for the catch-up described in paragraph (c)(2) or (3) of this section, participates in no other retirement plan, and has no other income exclusions taken into account in computing includible compensation. Adjusted for gain or loss, the value of B's benefit when B's interest in the account vests in 2006 is $17,000.

(ii) *Conclusion.* Under this vesting schedule, $17,000 is taken into account as an annual deferral in 2006. B's annual deferrals under the plan are limited to a maximum of $15,000 in 2006. Thus, the aggregate of the amounts deferred, $17,000, is in excess of the B's maximum deferral limitation by $2,000. The $2,000 is treated as an excess deferral described in paragraph (e) of this section.

(2) *Age 50 catch-up*—(i) *In general.* In accordance with section 414(v) and the regulations

Reg. § 1.457-4(b)

thereunder, an eligible governmental plan may provide for catch-up contributions for a participant who is age 50 by the end of the year, provided that such age 50 catch-up contributions do not exceed the catch-up limit under section 414(v)(2) for the taxable year. The maximum amount of age 50 catch-up contributions for a taxable year under section 414(v) is as follows: $1,000 for 2002; $2,000 for 2003; $3,000 for 2004; $4,000 for 2005; and $5,000 for 2006 and thereafter. After 2006, the $5,000 amount is adjusted for cost-of-living. For additional guidance, see regulations under section 414(v).

(ii) *Coordination with special section 457 catch-up*. In accordance with sections 414(v)(6)(C) and 457(e)(18), the age 50 catch-up described in this paragraph (c)(2) does not apply for any taxable year for which a higher limitation applies under the special section 457 catch-up under paragraph (c)(3) of this section. Thus, for purposes of this paragraph (c)(2)(ii) and paragraph (c)(3) of this section, the special section 457 catch-up under paragraph (c)(3) of this section applies for any taxable year if and only if the plan ceiling taking into account paragraph (c)(1) of this section and the special section 457 catch-up described in paragraph (c)(3) of this section (and disregarding the age 50 catch-up described in this paragraph (c)(2)) is larger than the plan ceiling taking into account paragraph (c)(1) of this section and the age 50 catch-up described in this paragraph (c)(2) (and disregarding the special section 457 catch-up described in paragraph (c)(3) of this section). Thus, if a plan so provides, a participant who is eligible for the age 50 catch-up for a year and for whom the year is also one of the participant's last three taxable years ending before the participant attains normal retirement age is eligible for the larger of—

(A) The plan ceiling under paragraph (c)(1) of this section and the age 50 catch-up described in this paragraph (c)(2) (and disregarding the special section 457 catch-up described in paragraph (c)(3) of this section) or

(B) The plan ceiling under paragraph (c)(1) of this section and the special section 457 catch-up described in paragraph (c)(3) of this section (and disregarding the age 50 catch-up described in this paragraph (c)(2)).

(iii) *Examples*. The provisions of this paragraph (c)(2) are illustrated by the following examples:

Example 1. (i) *Facts.* Participant C, who is 55, is eligible to participate in an eligible governmental plan in 2006. The plan provides a normal retirement age of 65. The plan provides limitations on annual deferrals up to the maximum permitted under paragraphs (c)(1) and (3) of this section and the age 50 catch-up described in this paragraph (c)(2). For 2006, C will receive compensation of $40,000 from the eligible employer. C desires to defer the maximum amount possible in 2006. The applicable basic dollar limit of paragraph (c)(1)(i)(A) of this section is $15,000 for 2006 and the additional dollar amount permitted under the age 50 catch-up is $5,000 for 2006.

(ii) *Conclusion.* C is eligible for the age 50 catch-up in 2006 because C is 55 in 2006. However, C is not eligible for the special section 457 catch-up under paragraph (c)(3) of this section in 2006 because 2006 is not one of the last three taxable years ending before C attains normal retirement age. Accordingly, the maximum that C may defer for 2006 is $20,000.

Example 2. (i) *Facts.* The facts are the same as in *Example 1*, except that, in 2006, C will attain age 62. The maximum amount that C can elect under the special section 457 catch-up under paragraph (c)(3) of this section is $2,000 for 2006.

(ii) *Conclusion.* The maximum that C may defer for 2006 is $20,000. This is the sum of the basic plan ceiling under paragraph (c)(1) of this section equal to $15,000 and the age 50 catch-up equal to $5,000. The special section 457 catch-up under paragraph (c)(3) of this section is not applicable since it provides a smaller plan ceiling.

Example 3. (i) *Facts.* The facts are the same as in *Example 2*, except that the maximum additional amount that C can elect under the special section 457 catch-up under paragraph (c)(3) of this section is $7,000 for 2006.

(ii) *Conclusion.* The maximum that C may defer for 2006 is $22,000. This is the sum of the basic plan ceiling under paragraph (c)(1) of this section equal to $15,000, plus the additional special section 457 catch-up under paragraph (c)(3) of this section equal to $7,000. The additional dollar amount permitted under the age 50 catch-up is not applicable to C for 2006 because it provides a smaller plan ceiling.

(3) *Special section 457 catch-up*—(i) *In general.* Except as provided in paragraph (c)(2)(ii) of this section, an eligible plan may provide that, for one or more of the participant's last three taxable years ending before the participant attains normal retirement age, the plan ceiling is an amount not in excess of the lesser of—

(A) Twice the dollar amount in effect under paragraph (c)(1)(i)(A) of this section; or

(B) The underutilized limitation determined under paragraph (c)(3)(ii) of this section.

Reg. § 1.457-4(c)(3)

(ii) *Underutilized limitation.* The underutilized amount determined under this paragraph (c)(3)(ii) is the sum of—

(A) The plan ceiling established under paragraph (c)(1) of this section for the taxable year; plus

(B) The plan ceiling established under paragraph (c)(1) of this section (or under section 457(b)(2) for any year before the applicability date of this section) for any prior taxable year or years, less the amount of annual deferrals under the plan for such prior taxable year or years (disregarding any annual deferrals under the plan permitted under the age 50 catch-up under paragraph (c)(2) of this section).

(iii) *Determining underutilized limitation under paragraph (c)(3)(ii)(B) of this section.* A prior taxable year is taken into account under paragraph (c)(3)(ii)(B) of this section only if it is a year beginning after December 31, 1978, in which the participant was eligible to participate in the plan, and in which compensation deferred (if any) under the plan during the year was subject to a plan ceiling established under paragraph (c)(1) of this section. This paragraph (c)(3)(iii) is subject to the special rules in paragraph (c)(3)(iv) of this section.

(iv) *Special rules concerning application of the coordination limit for years prior to 2002 for purposes of determining the underutilized limitation*—(A) *General rule.* For purposes of determining the underutilized limitation for years prior to 2002, participants remain subject to the rules in effect prior to the repeal of the coordination limitation under section 457(c)(2). Thus, the applicable basic annual limitation under paragraph (c)(1) of this section and the special section 457 catch-up under this paragraph (c)(3) for years in effect prior to 2002 are reduced, for purposes of determining a participant's underutilized amount under a plan, by amounts excluded from the participant's income for any prior taxable year by reason of a nonelective employer contribution, salary reduction or elective contribution under any other eligible section 457(b) plan, or a salary reduction or elective contribution under any 401(k) qualified cash or deferred arrangement, section 402(h)(1)(B) simplified employee pension (SARSEP), section 403(b) annuity contract, and section 408(p) simple retirement account, or under any plan for which a deduction is allowed because of a contribution to an organization described in section 501(c)(18) (pre-2002 coordination plans). Similarly, in applying the section 457(b)(2)(B) limitation for includible compensation for years prior to 2002, the limitation is 33 1/3 percent of the participant's compensation includible in gross income.

(B) *Coordination limitation applied to participant.* For purposes of determining the underutilized limitation for years prior to 2002, the coordination limitation applies to pre-2002 coordination plans of all employers for whom a participant has performed services, whether or not those are plans of the participant's current eligible employer. Thus, for purposes of determining the amount excluded from a participant's gross income in any prior taxable year under paragraph (c)(3)(ii)(B) of this section, the participant's annual deferrals under an eligible plan, and salary reduction or elective deferrals under all other pre-2002 coordination plans, must be determined on an aggregate basis. To the extent that the combined deferrals for years prior to 2002 exceeded the maximum deferral limitations, the amount is treated as an excess deferral under paragraph (e) of this section for those prior years.

(C) *Special rule where no annual deferrals under the eligible plan.* A participant who, although eligible, did not defer any compensation under the eligible plan in any year before 2002 is not subject to the coordinated deferral limit, even though the participant may have deferred compensation under one of the other pre-2002 coordination plans. An individual is treated as not having deferred compensation under an eligible plan for a prior taxable year if all annual deferrals under the plan are distributed in accordance with paragraph (e) of this section. Thus, to the extent that a participant participated solely in one or more of the other pre-2002 coordination plans during a prior taxable year (and not the eligible plan), the participant is not subject to the coordinated limitation for that prior taxable year. However, the participant is treated as having deferred an amount in a prior taxable year, for purposes of determining the underutilized limitation for that prior taxable year under this paragraph (c)(3)(iv)(C), to the extent of the participant's aggregate salary reduction contributions and elective deferrals under all pre-2002 coordination plans up to the maximum deferral limitations in effect under section 457(b) for that prior taxable year. To the extent an employer did not offer an eligible plan to an individual in a prior given year, no underutilized limitation is available to the individual for that prior year, even if the employee subsequently becomes eligible to participate in an eligible plan of the employer.

(D) *Examples.* The provisions of this paragraph (c)(3)(iv) are illustrated by the following examples:

Reg. § 1.457-4(c)(3)

Example 1. (i) *Facts.* In 2001 and in years prior to 2001, Participant D earned $50,000 a year and was eligible to participate in both an eligible plan and a section 401(k) plan. However, D had always participated only in the section 401(k) plan and had always deferred the maximum amount possible. For each year before 2002, the maximum amount permitted under section 401(k) exceeded the limitation of paragraph (c)(3)(i) of this section. In 2002, D is in the 3-year period prior to D's attainment of the eligible plan's normal retirement age of 65, and D now wants to participate in the eligible plan and make annual deferrals of up to $30,000 under the plan's special section 457 catch-up provisions.

(ii) *Conclusion.* Participant D is treated as having no underutilized amount under paragraph (c)(3)(ii)(B) of this section for 2002 for purposes of the catch-up limitation under section 457(b)(3) and paragraph (c)(3) of this section because, in each of the years before 2002, D has deferred an amount equal to or in excess of the limitation of paragraph (c)(3)(i) of this section under all of D's coordinated plans.

Example 2. (i) *Facts.* Assume the same facts as in *Example 1*, except that D only deferred $2,500 per year under the section 401(k) plan for one year before 2002.

(ii) *Conclusion.* D is treated as having an underutilized amount under paragraph (c)(3)(ii)(B) of this section for 2002 for purposes of the special section 457 catch-up limitation. This is because D has deferred an amount for prior years that is less than the limitation of paragraph (c)(1)(i) of this section under all of D's coordinated plans.

Example 3. (i) *Facts.* Participant E, who earned $15,000 for 2000, entered into a salary reduction agreement in 2000 with E's eligible employer and elected to defer $3,000 for that year under E's eligible plan. For 2000, E's eligible employer provided an immediately vested, matching employer contribution under the plan for participants who make salary reduction deferrals under E's eligible plan. The matching contribution was equal to 67 percent of elective contributions, but not in excess of 10 percent of compensation before salary reduction deferrals (in E's case, $1,000). For 2000, E was not eligible for any catch-up contribution, participated in no other retirement plan, and had no other income exclusions taken into account in computing taxable compensation.

(ii) *Conclusion.* Participant E's annual deferral equaled the maximum limitation of section 457(b) for 2000. E's maximum deferral limitation in 2000 was $4,000 because E's includible compensation was $12,000 ($15,000 minus the deferral of $3,000) and the applicable limitation for 2000 was one third of the individual's includible compensation (one-third of $12,000 equals $4,000). E's salary reduction deferral of $3,000 combined with E's eligible employer's matching contribution of $1,000 equals the limitation of section 457(b) for 2000 because E's annual deferrals totaled $4,000. E's underutilized amount for 2000 is zero.

(v) *Normal retirement age*—(A) *General rule.* For purposes of the special section 457 catch-up in this paragraph (c)(3), a plan must specify the normal retirement age under the plan. A plan may define normal retirement age as any age that is on or after the earlier of age 65 or the age at which participants have the right to retire and receive, under the basic defined benefit pension plan of the State or tax-exempt entity (or a money purchase pension plan in which the participant also participates if the participant is not eligible to participate in a defined benefit plan), immediate retirement benefits without actuarial or similar reduction because of retirement before some later specified age, and that is not later than age 70½. Alternatively, a plan may provide that a participant is allowed to designate a normal retirement age within these ages. For purposes of the special section 457 catch-up in this paragraph (c)(3), an entity sponsoring more than one eligible plan may not permit a participant to have more than one normal retirement age under the eligible plans it sponsors.

(B) *Special rule for eligible plans of qualified police or firefighters.* An eligible plan with participants that include qualified police or firefighters as defined under section 415(b)(2)(H)(ii)(I) may designate a normal retirement age for such qualified police or firefighters that is earlier than the earliest normal retirement age designated under the general rule of paragraph (c)(3)(i)(A) of this section, but in no event may the normal retirement age be earlier than age 40. Alternatively, a plan may allow a qualified police or firefighter participant to designate a normal retirement age that is between age 40 and age 70½.

(vi) *Examples.* The provisions of this paragraph (c)(3) are illustrated by the following examples:

Example 1. (i) *Facts.* Participant F, who will turn 61 on April 1, 2006, becomes eligible to participate in an eligible plan on January 1, 2006. The plan provides a normal retirement age of 65. The plan provides limitations on annual deferrals up to the maximum permitted under paragraphs (c)(1) through (3) of this section. For 2006, F will receive compensation of $40,000 from the eligible employer. F desires to defer the maximum amount possible in 2006. The applicable basic dollar limit of paragraph (c)(1)(i)(A) of this section is $15,000 for 2006 and the additional dollar amount permitted under the age 50 catch-up in paragraph (c)(2) of this section for an individual who is at least age 50 is $5,000 for 2006.

(ii) *Conclusion.* F is not eligible for the special section 457 catch-up under paragraph (c)(3) of this section in 2006 because 2006 is not one of the last three taxable years ending before F attains normal retirement age. Accordingly, the maximum that F may defer for 2006 is $20,000. See also paragraph (c)(2)(iii) *Example 1* of this section.

Example 2. (i) *Facts.* The facts are the same as in *Example 1* except that, in 2006, F elects to defer only $2,000 under the plan (rather than the maximum permitted amount of $20,000). In addition, assume that the applicable basic dollar limit of paragraph (c)(1)(i)(A) of this section continues to be $15,000 for 2007 and the additional dollar amount permitted under the age 50 catch-up in paragraph (c)(2) of this section for an individual who is at least age 50 continues to be $5,000 for 2007. In F's taxable year 2007, which is one of the last three taxable years ending before F attains the plan's normal retirement age of 65, F again receives a salary of $40,000 and elects to defer the maximum amount permissible under the plan's catch-up provisions prescribed under paragraph (c) of this section.

(ii) *Conclusion.* For 2007, which is one of the last three taxable years ending before F attains the plan's normal retirement age of 65, the applicable limit on deferrals for F is the larger of the amount under the special section 457 catch-up or $20,000, which is the basic annual limitation ($15,000) and the age 50 catch-up limit of section 414(v) ($5,000). For 2007, F's special section 457 catch-up amount is the lesser of two times the basic annual limitation ($30,000) or the sum of the basic annual limitation ($15,000) plus the $13,000 underutilized limitation under paragraph (c)(3)(ii) of this section (the $15,000 plan ceiling in 2006, minus the $2,000 contributed for F in 2006), or $28,000. Thus, the maximum amount that F may defer in 2007 is $28,000.

Example 3. (i) *Facts.* The facts are the same as in *Examples 1* and *2*, except that F does not make any contributions to the plan before 2010. In addition, assume that the applicable basic dollar limitation of paragraph (c)(1)(i)(A) of this section continues to be $15,000 for 2010 and the additional dollar amount permitted under the age 50 catch-up in paragraph (c)(2) of this section for an individual who is at least age 50 continues to be $5,000 for 2010. In F's taxable year 2010, the year in which F attains age 65 (which is the normal retirement age under the plan), F desires to defer the maximum amount possible under the plan. F's compensation for 2010 is again $40,000.

(ii) *Conclusion.* For 2010, the maximum amount that F may defer is $20,000. The special section 457 catch-up provisions under paragraph (c)(3) of this section are not applicable because 2010 is not a taxable year ending before the year in which F attains normal retirement age.

(4) *Cost-of-living adjustment.* For years beginning after December 31, 2006, the $15,000 dollar limitation in paragraph (c)(1)(i)(A) of this section will be adjusted to take into account increases in the cost-of-living. The adjustment in the dollar limitation is made at the same time and in the same manner as under section 415(d) (relating to qualified plans under section 401(a)), except that the base period is the calendar quarter beginning July 1, 2005 and any increase which is not a multiple of $500 will be rounded to the next lowest multiple of $500.

(d) *Deferral of sick, vacation, and back pay under an eligible plan*—(1) *In general.* An eligible plan may provide that a participant may elect to defer accumulated sick pay, accumulated vacation pay, and back pay under an eligible plan if the requirements of section 457(b) are satisfied. For example, the plan must provide, in accordance with paragraph (b) of this section, that these amounts may be deferred for any calendar month only if an agreement providing for the deferral is entered into before the beginning of the month in which the amounts would otherwise be paid or made available and the participant is an employee in that month. In the case of accumulated sick pay, vacation pay, or back pay that is payable before the participant has a severance from employment, the requirements of the preceding sentence are deemed to be satisfied if the agreement providing for the deferral is entered into before the amount is currently available (as defined in regulations under section 401(k)).

(2) *Examples.* The provisions of this paragraph (d) are illustrated by the following examples:

Example 1. (i) *Facts.* Participant G, who is age 62 in 2003, is an employee who participates in an eligible plan providing a normal retirement age of 65. Under the terms of G's employer's eligible plan and G's sick leave plan, G may, during November of 2003 (which is one of the three years prior to normal retirement age), make a one-time election to contribute amounts representing accumulated sick pay to the eligible plan

Reg. § 1.457-4(c)(4)

in December of 2003 (within the maximum deferral limitations). Alternatively, such amounts may remain in the "bank" under the sick leave plan. No cash out of the sick pay is available until the month in which a participant ceases to be employed by the employer. The total value of G's accumulated sick pay (determined, in accordance with the terms of the sick leave plan, by reference to G's current salary) is $4,000 in December of 2003.

(ii) *Conclusion.* Under the terms of the eligible plan and sick leave plan, G may elect before December of 2003 to defer the $4,000 value of accumulated sick pay under the eligible plan, provided that G's other annual deferrals to the eligible plan for 2003, when added to the $4,000, do not exceed G's maximum deferral limitation for the year.

Example 2. (i) *Facts.* Same facts as in *Example 1*, except that G will separate from service on January 17, 2004, and elects, on January 4, 2004, to defer G's accumulated sick and vacation pay (which totals $12,000) that is payable on January 15, 2004.

(ii) *Conclusion.* G may elect before January 15, 2004 to defer the accumulated sick and vacation pay under the eligible plan, even if the election is made after the beginning of January, because the agreement providing for the deferral is entered into before the amount is currently available and G does not cease to be an employee before the amount is currently available. G will have $12,000 of includible compensation in 2004 because the deferral is taken into account in the definition of includible compensation.

Example 3. (i) *Facts.* Employer X maintains an eligible plan and a vacation leave plan. Under the terms of the vacation leave plan, employees generally accrue three weeks of vacation per year. Up to one week's unused vacation may be carried over from one year to the next, so that in any single year an employee may have a maximum of four weeks vacation time. At the beginning of each calendar year, under the terms of the eligible plan (which constitutes an agreement providing for the deferral), the value of any unused vacation time from the prior year in excess of one week is automatically contributed to the eligible plan, to the extent of the employee's maximum deferral limitations. Amounts in excess of the maximum deferral limitations are forfeited.

(ii) *Conclusion.* The value of the unused vacation pay contributed to X's eligible plan pursuant to the terms of the plan and the terms of the vacation leave plan is treated as an annual deferral to the eligible plan in the calendar year the contribution is made. No amounts contributed to the eligible plan will be considered made available to a participant in X's eligible plan.

(e) *Excess deferrals under an eligible plan*—(1) *In general.* Any amount deferred under an eligible plan for the taxable year of a participant that exceeds the maximum deferral limitations set forth in paragraphs (c)(1) through (3) of this section, and any amount that exceeds the individual limitation under § 1.457-5, constitutes an excess deferral that is taxable in accordance with § 1.457-11 for that taxable year. Thus, an excess deferral is includible in gross income in the taxable year deferred or, if later, the first taxable year in which there is no substantial risk of forfeiture.

(2) *Excess deferrals under an eligible governmental plan other than as a result of the individual limitation.* In order to be an eligible governmental plan, the plan must provide that any excess deferral resulting from a failure of a plan to apply the limitations of paragraphs (c)(1) through (3) of this section to amounts deferred under the eligible plan (computed without regard to the individual limitation under § 1.457-5) will be distributed to the participant, with allocable net income, as soon as administratively practicable after the plan determines that the amount is an excess deferral. For purposes of determining whether there is an excess deferral resulting from a failure of a plan to apply the limitations of paragraphs (c)(1) through (3) of this section, all plans under which an individual participates by virtue of his or her relationship with a single employer are treated as a single plan (without regard to any differences in funding). An eligible governmental plan does not fail to satisfy the requirements of paragraphs (a) through (d) of this section or §§ 1.457-6 through 1.457-10 (including the distribution rules under § 1.457-6 and the funding rules under § 1.457-8) solely by reason of a distribution made under this paragraph (e)(2). If such excess deferrals are not corrected by distribution under this paragraph (e)(2), the plan will be an ineligible plan under which benefits are taxable in accordance with § 1.457-11.

(3) *Excess deferrals under an eligible plan of a tax-exempt employer other than as a result of the individual limitation.* If a plan of a tax-exempt employer fails to comply with the limitations of paragraphs (c)(1) through (3) of this section, the plan will be an ineligible plan under which benefits are taxable in accordance with § 1.457-11. However, a plan may distribute to a participant any excess deferrals (and any income allocable to such amount) not later than the first April 15 following the close of the taxable year of the excess deferrals. In such a case, the plan will continue to be treated as an eligible plan. How-

ever, any excess deferral is included in the gross income of a participant for the taxable year of the excess deferral. If the excess deferrals are not corrected by distribution under this paragraph (e)(3), the plan is an ineligible plan under which benefits are taxable in accordance with § 1.457-11. For purposes of determining whether there is an excess deferral resulting from a failure of a plan to apply the limitations of paragraphs (c)(1) through (3) of this section, all eligible plans under which an individual participates by virtue of his or her relationship with a single employer are treated as a single plan.

(4) *Excess deferrals arising from application of the individual limitation.* An eligible plan may provide that an excess deferral that is a result solely of a failure to comply with the individual limitation under § 1.457-5 for a taxable year may be distributed to the participant, with allocable net income, as soon as administratively practicable after the plan determines that the amount is an excess deferral. An eligible plan does not fail to satisfy the requirements of paragraphs (a) through (d) of this section or §§ 1.457-6 through 1.457-10 (including the distribution rules under § 1.457-6 and the funding rules under § 1.457-8) solely by reason of a distribution made under this paragraph (e)(4). Although a plan will still maintain eligible status if excess deferrals are not distributed under this paragraph (e)(4), a participant must include the excess amounts in income as provided in paragraph (e)(1) of this section.

(5) *Examples.* The provisions of this paragraph (e) are illustrated by the following examples:

Example 1. (i) *Facts.* In 2006, the eligible plan of State Employer X in which Participant H participates permits a maximum deferral of the lesser of $15,000 or 100 percent of includible compensation. In 2006, H, who has compensation of $28,000, nevertheless defers $16,000 under the eligible plan. Participant H is age 45 and normal retirement age under the plan is age 65. For 2006, the applicable dollar limit under paragraph (c)(1)(i)(A) of this section is $15,000. Employer X discovers the error in January of 2007 when it completes H's 2006 Form W-2 and promptly distributes $1,022 to H (which is the sum of the $1,000 excess and $22 of allocable net income).

(ii) *Conclusion.* Participant H has deferred $1,000 in excess of the $15,000 limitation provided for under the plan for 2006. The $1,000 excess must be included by H in H's income for 2006. In order to correct the failure and still be an eligible plan, the plan must distribute the excess deferral, with allocable net income, as soon as administratively practicable after determining that the amount exceeds the plan deferral limitations. In this case, $22 of the distribution of $1,022 is included in H's gross income for 2007 (and is not an eligible rollover distribution). If the excess deferral were not distributed, the plan would be an ineligible plan with respect to which benefits are taxable in accordance with § 1.457-11.

Example 2. (i) *Facts.* The facts are the same as in *Example 1*, except that X uses a number of separate arrangements with different trustees and annuity insurers to permit employees to defer and H elects deferrals under several of the funding arrangements none of which exceeds $15,000 for any individual funding arrangement, but which total $16,000.

(ii) *Conclusion.* The conclusion is the same as in *Example 1.*

Example 3. (i) *Facts.* The facts are the same as in *Example 1*, except that H's deferral under the eligible plan is limited to $11,000 and H also makes a salary reduction contribution of $5,000 to an annuity contract under section 403(b) with the same Employer X.

(ii) *Conclusion.* H's deferrals are within the plan deferral limitations of Employer X. Because of the repeal of the application of the coordination limitation under former paragraph (2) of section 457(c), H's salary reduction deferrals under the annuity contract are no longer considered in determining H's applicable deferral limits under paragraphs (c)(1) through (3) of this section.

Example 4. (i) *Facts.* The facts are the same as in *Example 1*, except that H's deferral under the eligible governmental plan is limited to $14,000 and H also makes a deferral of $4,000 to an eligible governmental plan of a different employer. Participant H is age 45 and normal retirement age under both eligible plans is age 65.

(ii) *Conclusion.* Because of the application of the individual limitation under § 1.457-5, H has an excess deferral of $3,000 (the sum of $14,000 plus $4,000 equals $18,000, which is $3,000 in excess of the dollar limitation of $15,000). The $3,000 excess deferral, with allocable net income, may be distributed from either plan as soon as administratively practicable after determining that the combined amount exceeds the deferral limitations. If the $3,000 excess deferral is not distributed to H, each plan will continue to be an eligible plan, but the $3,000 must be included by H in H's income for 2006.

Example 5. (i) *Facts.* Assume the same facts as in *Example 3*, except that H's deferral under the eligible governmental plan is limited to $14,000 and H also makes a deferral of $4,000 to

Reg. § 1.457-4(e)(4)

an eligible plan of Employer Y, a tax-exempt entity.

(ii) *Conclusion.* The results are the same as in *Example 3*, namely, because of the application of the individual limitation under § 1.457-5, H has an excess deferral of $3,000. If the $3,000 excess deferral is not distributed to H, each plan will continue to be an eligible plan, but the $3,000 must be included by H in H's income for 2006.

Example 6. (i) Facts. Assume the same facts as in *Example 5*, except that X is a tax-exempt entity and thus its plan is an eligible plan of a tax-exempt entity.

(ii) *Conclusion.* The results are the same as in Example 5, namely, because of the application of the individual limitation under § 1.457-5, H has an excess deferral of $3,000. If the $3,000 excess deferral is not distributed to H, each plan will continue to be an eligible plan, but the $3,000 must be included by H into H's income for 2006.

[Reg. § 1.457-4.]

☐ [*T.D.* 7836, 9-23-82. *Amended by T.D.* 9075, 7-10-2003.]

[Reg. § 1.457-5]

§ 1.457-5. Individual limitation for combined annual deferrals under multiple eligible plans.—(a) *General rule.* The individual limitation under section 457(c) and this section equals the basic annual deferral limitation under § 1.457-4(c)(1)(i)(A), plus either the age 50 catch-up amount under § 1.457-4(c)(2), or the special section 457 catch-up amount under § 1.457-4(c)(3), applied by taking into account the combined annual deferral for the participant for any taxable year under all eligible plans. While an eligible plan may include provisions under which it will limit deferrals to meet the individual limitation under section 457(c) and this section, annual deferrals by a participant that exceed the individual limit under section 457(c) and this section (but do not exceed the limits under § 1.457-4(c)) will not cause a plan to lose its eligible status. However, to the extent the combined annual deferrals for a participant for any taxable year exceed the individual limitation under section 457(c) and this section for that year, the amounts are treated as excess deferrals as described in § 1.457-4(e).

(b) *Limitation applied to participant.* The individual limitation in this section applies to eligible plans of all employers for whom a participant has performed services, including both eligible governmental plans and eligible plans of a tax-exempt entity and both eligible plans of the employer and eligible plans of other employers. Thus, for purposes of determining the amount excluded from a participant's gross income in any taxable year (including the underutilized limitation under § 1.457-4 (c)(3)(ii)(B)), the participant's annual deferral under an eligible plan, and the participant's annual deferrals under all other eligible plans, must be determined on an aggregate basis. To the extent that the combined annual deferral amount exceeds the maximum deferral limitation applicable under § 1.457-4 (c)(1)(i)(A), (c)(2), or (c)(3), the amount is treated as an excess deferral under § 1.457-4(e).

(c) *Special rules for catch-up amounts under multiple eligible plans.* For purposes of applying section 457(c) and this section, the special section 457 catch-up under § 1.457-4 (c)(3) is taken into account only to the extent that an annual deferral is made for a participant under an eligible plan as a result of plan provisions permitted under § 1.457-4 (c)(3). In addition, if a participant has annual deferrals under more than one eligible plan and the applicable catch-up amount under § 1.457-4 (c)(2) or (3) is not the same for each such eligible plan for the taxable year, section 457(c) and this section are applied using the catch-up amount under whichever plan has the largest catch-up amount applicable to the participant.

(d) *Examples.* The provisions of this section are illustrated by the following examples:

Example 1. (i) *Facts.* Participant F is age 62 in 2006 and participates in two eligible plans during 2006, Plans J and K, which are each eligible plans of two different governmental entities. Each plan includes provisions allowing the maximum annual deferral permitted under § 1.457-4(c)(1) through (3). For 2006, the underutilized amount under § 1.457-4 (c)(3)(ii)(B) is $20,000 under Plan J and is $40,000 under Plan K. Normal retirement age is age 65 under both plans. Participant F defers $15,000 under each plan. Participant F's includible compensation is in each case in excess of the deferral. Neither plan designates the $15,000 contribution as a catch-up permitted under each plan's special section 457 catch-up provisions.

(ii) *Conclusion.* For purposes of applying this section to Participant F for 2006, the maximum exclusion is $20,000. This is equal to the sum of $15,000 plus $5,000, which is the age 50 catch-up amount. Thus, F has an excess amount of $10,000 which is treated as an excess deferral for Participant F for 2006 under § 1.457-4(e).

Example 2. (i) *Facts.* Participant E, who will turn 63 on April 1, 2006, participates in four eligible plans during 2006: Plan W which is an eligible governmental plan; and Plans X, Y, and Z which are each eligible plans of three different tax-exempt entities. For 2006, the limitation that applies to Participant E under all four plans under § 1.457-4 (c)(1)(i)(A) is $15,000. For 2006, the additional age 50 catch-up limitation that applies to Participant E under all four plans under § 1.457-4 (c)(2) is $5,000. Further, for 2006, different limitations under § 1.457-4(c)(3) and (c)(3)(ii)(B) apply to Participant E under each of these plans, as follows: under Plan W, the underutilized limitation under § 1.457-4 (c)(3)(ii)(B) is $7,000; under Plan X, the underutilized limitation under § 1.457-4 (c)(3)(ii)(B) is $2,000; under Plan Y, the underutilized limitation under § 1.457-4 (c)(3)(ii)(B) is $8,000; and under Plan Z, § 1.457-4 (c)(3) is not applicable since normal retirement age is age 62 under Plan Z. Participant E's includible compensation is in each case in excess of any applicable deferral.

(ii) *Conclusion.* For purposes of applying this section to Participant E for 2006, Participant E could elect to defer $23,000 under Plan Y, which is the maximum deferral limitation under § 1.457-4 (c)(1) through (3), and to defer no amount under Plans W, X, and Z. The $23,000 maximum amount is equal to the sum of $15,000 plus $8,000, which is the catch-up amount applicable to Participant E under Plan Y and which is the largest catch-up amount applicable to Participant E under any of the four plans for 2006. Alternatively, Participant E could instead elect to defer the following combination of amounts: an aggregate total of $20,000 to any of the four plans; or $22,000 to Plan W and none to any of the other three plans.

(iii) If the underutilized amount under Plans W, X, and Y for 2006 were in each case zero (because E had always contributed the maximum amount or E was a new participant) or an amount not in excess of $5,000, the maximum exclusion under this section would be $20,000 for Participant E for 2006 ($15,000 plus the $5,000 age 50 catch-up amount), which Participant E could contribute to any of the plans.

[Reg. § 1.457-5.]

☐ [T.D. 9075, 7-10-2003.]

[Reg. § 1.457-6]

§ 1.457-6. Timing of distributions under eligible plans.—(a) *In general.* Except as provided in paragraph (c) of this section (relating to distributions on account of an unforeseeable emergency), paragraph (e) of this section (relating to distributions of small accounts), § 1.457-10(a) (relating to plan terminations), or § 1.457-10(c) (relating to domestic relations orders), amounts deferred under an eligible governmental plan may not be paid to a participant or beneficiary before the participant has a severance from employment with the eligible employer or when the participant attains age 70½, if earlier. For rules relating to loans, see paragraph (f) of this section. This section does not apply to distributions of excess amounts under § 1.457-4(e). However, except to the extent set forth by the Commissioner in revenue rulings, notices, and other guidance published in the Internal Revenue Bulletin, this section applies to amounts held in a separate account for eligible rollover distributions maintained by an eligible governmental plan as described in § 1.457-10(e)(2).

(b) *Severance from employment*—(1) *Employees.* An employee has a severance from employment with the eligible employer if the employee dies, retires, or otherwise has a severance from employment with the eligible employer. See regulations under section 401(k) for additional guidance concerning severance from employment.

(2) *Independent contractors*—(i) *In general.* An independent contractor is considered to have a severance from employment with the eligible employer upon the expiration of the contract (or in the case of more than one contract, all contracts) under which services are performed for the eligible employer if the expiration constitutes a good-faith and complete termination of the contractual relationship. An expiration does not constitute a good faith and complete termination of the contractual relationship if the eligible employer anticipates a renewal of a contractual relationship or the independent contractor becoming an employee. For this purpose, an eligible employer is considered to anticipate the renewal of the contractual relationship with an independent contractor if it intends to contract again for the services provided under the expired contract, and neither the eligible employer nor the independent contractor has eliminated the independent contractor as a possible provider of services under any such new contract. Further, an eligible employer is considered to intend to contract again for the services provided under an expired contract if the eligible employer's doing so is conditioned only upon incurring a need for the services, the availability of funds, or both.

(ii) *Special rule.* Notwithstanding paragraph (b)(2)(i) of this section, the plan is considered to satisfy the requirement described in paragraph (a) of this section that no amounts deferred under the plan be paid or made available to the participant before the participant has a severance from employment with the eligible employer if, with respect to amounts payable to a participant who is an independent contractor, an eligible plan provides that—

(A) No amount will be paid to the participant before a date at least 12 months after the day on which the contract expires under which services are performed for the eligible employer (or, in the case of more than one contract, all such contracts expire); and

(B) No amount payable to the participant on that date will be paid to the participant if, after the expiration of the contract (or contracts) and before that date, the participant performs services for the eligible employer as an independent contractor or an employee.

(c) *Rules applicable to distributions for unforeseeable emergencies*—(1) *In general.* An eligible plan may permit a distribution to a participant or beneficiary faced with an unforeseeable emergency. The distribution must satisfy the requirements of paragraph (c)(2) of this section.

(2) *Requirements*—(i) *Unforeseeable emergency defined.* An unforeseeable emergency must be defined in the plan as a severe financial hardship of the participant or beneficiary resulting from an illness or accident of the participant or beneficiary, the participant's or beneficiary's spouse, or the participant's or beneficiary's dependent (as defined in section 152(a)); loss of the participant's or beneficiary's property due to casualty (including the need to rebuild a home following damage to a home not otherwise covered by homeowner's insurance, e.g., as a result of a natural disaster); or other similar extraordinary and unforeseeable circumstances arising as a result of events beyond the control of the participant or the beneficiary. For example, the imminent foreclosure of or eviction from the participant's or beneficiary's primary residence may constitute an unforeseeable emergency. In addition, the need to pay for medical expenses, including non-refundable deductibles, as well as for the cost of prescription drug medication, may constitute an unforeseeable emergency. Finally, the need to pay for the funeral expenses of a spouse or a dependent (as defined in section 152(a)) may also constitute an unforeseeable emergency. Except as otherwise specifically provided in this paragraph (c)(2)(i), the purchase of a home and the payment of college tuition are not unforeseeable emergencies under this paragraph (c)(2)(i).

(ii) *Unforeseeable emergency distribution standard.* Whether a participant or beneficiary is faced with an unforeseeable emergency permitting a distribution under this paragraph (c) is to be determined based on the relevant facts and circumstances of each case, but, in any case, a distribution on account of unforeseeable emergency may not be made to the extent that such emergency is or may be relieved through reimbursement or compensation from insurance or otherwise, by liquidation of the participant's assets, to the extent the liquidation of such assets would not itself cause severe financial hardship, or by cessation of deferrals under the plan.

(iii) *Distribution necessary to satisfy emergency need.* Distributions because of an unforeseeable emergency must be limited to the amount reasonably necessary to satisfy the emergency need (which may include any amounts necessary to pay any federal, state, or local income taxes or penalties reasonably anticipated to result from the distribution).

(d) *Minimum required distributions for eligible plans.* In order to be an eligible plan, a plan must meet the distribution requirements of section 457(d)(1) and (2). Under section 457(d)(2), a plan must meet the minimum distribution requirements of section 401(a)(9). See section 401(a)(9) and the regulations thereunder for these requirements. Section 401(a)(9) requires that a plan begin lifetime distributions to a participant no later than April 1 of the calendar year following the later of the calendar year in which the participant attains age 70½ or the calendar year in which the participant retires.

(e) *Distributions of smaller accounts*—(1) *In general.* An eligible plan may provide for a distribution of all or a portion of a participant's benefit if this paragraph (e)(1) is satisfied. This paragraph (e)(1) is satisfied if the participant's total amount deferred (the participant's total account balance) which is not attributable to rollover contributions (as defined in section 411(a)(11)(D)) is not in excess of the dollar limit under section 411(a)(11)(A), no amount has been deferred under the plan by or for the participant during the two-year period ending on the date of the distribution, and there has been no prior distribution under the plan to the participant under this paragraph (e). An eligible plan is not required to permit distributions under this paragraph (e).

(2) *Alternative provisions possible.* Consistent with the provisions of paragraph (e)(1) of this section, a plan may provide that the total amount deferred for a participant or beneficiary will be distributed automatically to the participant or beneficiary if the requirements of paragraph (e)(1) of this section are met. Alternatively, if the requirements of paragraph (e)(1) of this section are met, the plan may provide for the total amount deferred for a participant or beneficiary to be distributed to the participant or beneficiary only if the participant or beneficiary so elects. The plan is permitted to substitute a specified dollar amount that is less than the total amount deferred. In addition, these two alternatives can

Reg. § 1.457-6(e)(2)

be combined; for example, a plan could provide for automatic distributions for up to $500, but allow participants or beneficiary to elect a distribution if the total account balance is above $500.

(f) *Loans from eligible plans*—(1) *Eligible plans of tax-exempt entities.* If a participant or beneficiary receives (directly or indirectly) any amount deferred as a loan from an eligible plan of a tax-exempt entity, that amount will be treated as having been paid or made available to the individual as a distribution under the plan, in violation of the distribution requirements of section 457(d).

(2) *Eligible governmental plans.* The determination of whether the availability of a loan, the making of a loan, or a failure to repay a loan made from a trustee (or a person treated as a trustee under section 457(g)) of an eligible governmental plan to a participant or beneficiary is treated as a distribution (directly or indirectly) for purposes of this section, and the determination of whether the availability of the loan, the making of the loan, or a failure to repay the loan is in any other respect a violation of the requirements of section 457(b) and the regulations, depends on the facts and circumstances. Among the facts and circumstances are whether the loan has a fixed repayment schedule and bears a reasonable rate of interest, and whether there are repayment safeguards to which a prudent lender would adhere. Thus, for example, a loan must bear a reasonable rate of interest in order to satisfy the exclusive benefit requirement of section 457(g)(1) and § 1.457-8(a)(1). See also § 1.457-7(b)(3) relating to the application of section 72(p) with respect to the taxation of a loan made under an eligible governmental plan, and § 1.72(p)-1 relating to section 72(p)(2).

(3) *Example.* The provisions of paragraph (f)(2) of this section are illustrated by the following example:

Example. (i) *Facts.* Eligible Plan X of State Y is funded through Trust Z. Plan X permits an employee's account balance under Plan X to be paid in a single sum at severance from employment with State Y. Plan X includes a loan program under which any active employee with a vested account balance may receive a loan from Trust Z. Loans are made pursuant to plan provisions regarding loans that are set forth in the plan under which loans bear a reasonable rate of interest and are secured by the employee's account balance. In order to avoid taxation under § 1.457-7(b)(3) and section 72(p)(1), the plan provisions limit the amount of loans and require loans to be repaid in level installments as required under section 72(p)(2). Participant J's vested account balance under Plan X is $50,000. J receives a loan from Trust Z in the amount of $5,000 on December 1, 2003, to be repaid in level installments made quarterly over the 5-year period ending on November 30, 2008. Participant J makes the required repayments until J has a severance from employment from State Y in 2005 and subsequently fails to repay the outstanding loan balance of $2,250. The $2,250 loan balance is offset against J's $80,000 account balance benefit under Plan X, and J elects to be paid the remaining $77,750 in 2005.

(ii) *Conclusion.* The making of the loan to J will not be treated as a violation of the requirements of section 457(b) or the regulations. The cancellation of the loan at severance from employment does not cause Plan X to fail to satisfy the requirements for plan eligibility under section 457. In addition, because the loan satisfies the maximum amount and repayment requirements of section 72(p)(2), J is not required to include any amount in income as a result of the loan until 2005, when J has income of $2,250 as a result of the offset (which is a permissible distribution under this section) and income of $77,750 as a result of the distribution made in 2005.

[Reg. § 1.457-6.]

☐ [T.D. 9075, 7-10-2003.]

[Reg. § 1.457-7]

§ 1.457-7. Taxation of distributions under eligible plans.—(a) *General rules for when amounts are included in gross income.* The rules for determining when an amount deferred under an eligible plan is includible in the gross income of a participant or beneficiary depend on whether the plan is an eligible governmental plan or an eligible plan of a tax-exempt entity. Paragraph (b) of this section sets forth the rules for an eligible governmental plan. Paragraph (c) of this section sets forth the rules for an eligible plan of a tax-exempt entity.

(b) *Amounts included in gross income under an eligible governmental plan*—(1) *Amounts included in gross income in year paid under an eligible governmental plan.* Except as provided in paragraphs (b)(2) and (3) of this section (or in § 1.457-10(c) relating to payments to a spouse or former spouse pursuant to a qualified domestic relations order), amounts deferred under an eligible governmental plan are includible in the gross income of a participant or beneficiary for the taxable year in which paid to the participant or beneficiary under the plan.

(2) *Rollovers to individual retirement arrangements and other eligible retirement plans.* A trustee-to-trustee transfer in accordance with section 401(a)(31) (generally referred to as a direct

Reg. § 1.457-7(a)

rollover) from an eligible government plan is not includible in gross income of a participant or beneficiary in the year transferred. In addition, any payment made from an eligible government plan in the form of an eligible rollover distribution (as defined in section 402(c)(4)) is not includible in gross income in the year paid to the extent the payment is transferred to an eligible retirement plan (as defined in section 402(c)(8)(B)) within 60 days, including the transfer to the eligible retirement plan of any property distributed from the eligible governmental plan. For this purpose, the rules of section 402(c)(2) through (7) and (9) apply. Any trustee-to-trustee transfer under this paragraph (b)(2) from an eligible government plan is a distribution that is subject to the distribution requirements of § 1.457-6.

(3) *Amounts taxable under section 72(p)(1).* In accordance with section 72(p), the amount of any loan from an eligible governmental plan to a participant or beneficiary (including any pledge or assignment treated as a loan under section 72(p)(1)(B)) is treated as having been received as a distribution from the plan under section 72(p)(1), except to the extent set forth in section 72(p)(2) (relating to loans that do not exceed a maximum amount and that are repayable in accordance with certain terms) and § 1.72(p)-1. Thus, except to the extent a loan satisfies section 72(p)(2), any amount loaned from an eligible governmental plan to a participant or beneficiary (including any pledge or assignment treated as a loan under section 72(p)(1)(B)) is includible in the gross income of the participant or beneficiary for the taxable year in which the loan is made. See generally § 1.72(p)-1.

(4) *Examples.* The provisions of this paragraph (b) are illustrated by the following examples:

Example 1. (i) *Facts.* Eligible Plan G of a governmental entity permits distribution of benefits in a single sum or in installments of up to 20 years, with such benefits to commence at any date that is after severance from employment (up to the later of severance from employment or the plan's normal retirement age of 65). Effective for participants who have a severance from employment after December 31, 2001, Plan X allows an election—as to both the date on which payments are to begin and the form in which payments are to be made—to be made by the participant at any time that is before the commencement date selected. However, Plan X chooses to require elections to be filed at least 30 days before the commencement date selected in order for Plan X to have enough time to be able to effectuate the election.

(ii) *Conclusion.* No amounts are included in gross income before actual payments begin. If installment payments begin (and the installment payments are payable over at least 10 years so as not to be eligible rollover distributions), the amount included in gross income for any year is equal to the amount of the installment payment paid during the year.

Example 2. (i) *Facts.* Same facts as in *Example 1*, except that the same rules are extended to participants who had a severance from employment before January 1, 2002.

(ii) *Conclusion.* For all participants (that is, both those who have a severance from employment after December 31, 2001, and those who have a severance from employment before January 1, 2002, including those whose benefit payments have commenced before January 1, 2002), no amounts are included in gross income before actual payments begin. If installment payments begin (and the installment payments are payable over at least 10 years so as not to be eligible rollover distributions), the amount included in gross income for any year is equal to the amount of the installment payment paid during the year.

(c) *Amounts included in gross income under an eligible plan of a tax-exempt entity*—(1) *Amounts included in gross income in year paid or made available under an eligible plan of a tax-exempt entity.* Amounts deferred under an eligible plan of a tax-exempt entity are includible in the gross income of a participant or beneficiary for the taxable year in which paid or otherwise made available to the participant or beneficiary under the plan. Thus, amounts deferred under an eligible plan of a tax-exempt entity are includible in the gross income of the participant or beneficiary in the year the amounts are first made available under the terms of the plan, even if the plan has not distributed the amounts deferred. Amounts deferred under an eligible plan of a tax-exempt entity are not considered made available to the participant or beneficiary solely because the participant or beneficiary is permitted to choose among various investments under the plan.

(2) *When amounts deferred are considered to be made available under an eligible plan of a tax-exempt entity*—(i) *General rule.* Except as provided in paragraphs (c)(2)(ii) through (iv) of this section, amounts deferred under an eligible plan of a tax-exempt entity are considered made available (and, thus, are includible in the gross income of the participant or beneficiary under this paragraph (c)) at the earliest date, on or after severance from employment, on which the plan allows distributions to commence, but in no event later than the date on which distributions must com-

mence pursuant to section 401(a)(9). For example, in the case of a plan that permits distribution to commence on the date that is 60 days after the close of the plan year in which the participant has a severance from employment with the eligible employer, amounts deferred are considered to be made available on that date. However, distributions deferred in accordance with paragraphs (c)(2)(ii) through (iv) of this section are not considered made available prior to the applicable date under paragraphs (c)(2)(ii) through (iv) of this section. In addition, no portion of a participant or beneficiary's account is treated as made available (and thus currently includible in income) under an eligible plan of a tax-exempt entity merely because the participant or beneficiary under the plan may elect to receive a distribution in any of the following circumstances:

(A) A distribution in the event of an unforeseeable emergency to the extent the distribution is permitted under § 1.457-6(c).

(B) A distribution from an account for which the total amount deferred is not in excess of the dollar limit under section 411(a)(11)(A) to the extent the distribution is permitted under § 1.457-6(e).

(ii) *Initial election to defer commencement of distributions*—(A) *In general.* An eligible plan of a tax-exempt entity may provide a period for making an initial election during which the participant or beneficiary may elect, in accordance with the terms of the plan, to defer the payment of some or all of the amounts deferred to a fixed or determinable future time. The period for making this initial election must expire prior to the first time that any such amounts would be considered made available under the plan under paragraph (c)(2)(i) of this section.

(B) *Failure to make initial election to defer commencement of distributions.* Generally, if no initial election is made by a participant or beneficiary under this paragraph (c)(2)(ii), then the amounts deferred under an eligible plan of a tax-exempt entity are considered made available and taxable to the participant or beneficiary in accordance with paragraph (c)(2)(i) of this section at the earliest time, on or after severance from employment (but in no event later than the date on which distributions must commence pursuant to section 401(a)(9)), that distribution is permitted to commence under the terms of the plan. However, the plan may provide for a default payment schedule that applies if no election is made. If the plan provides for a default payment schedule, the amounts deferred are includible in the gross income of the participant or beneficiary in the year the amounts deferred are first made available under the terms of the default payment schedule.

(iii) *Additional election to defer commencement of distribution.* An eligible plan of a tax-exempt entity is permitted to provide that a participant or beneficiary who has made an initial election under paragraph (c)(2)(ii)(A) of this section may make one additional election to defer (but not accelerate) commencement of distributions under the plan before distributions have commenced in accordance with the initial deferral election under paragraph (c)(2)(ii)(A) of this section. Amounts payable to a participant or beneficiary under an eligible plan of a tax-exempt entity are not treated as made available merely because the plan allows the participant to make an additional election under this paragraph (c)(2)(iii). A participant or beneficiary is not precluded from making an additional election to defer commencement of distributions merely because the participant or beneficiary has previously received a distribution under § 1.457-6(c) because of an unforeseeable emergency, has received a distribution of smaller amounts under § 1.457-6(e), has made (and revoked) other deferral or method of payment elections within the initial election period, or is subject to a default payment schedule under which the commencement of benefits is deferred (for example, until a participant is age 65).

(iv) *Election as to method of payment.* An eligible plan of a tax-exempt entity may provide that an election as to the method of payment under the plan may be made at any time prior to the time the amounts are distributed in accordance with the participant or beneficiary's initial or additional election to defer commencement of distributions under paragraph (c)(2)(ii) or (iii) of this section. Where no method of payment is elected, the entire amount deferred will be includible in the gross income of the participant or beneficiary when the amounts first become made available in accordance with a participant's initial or additional elections to defer under paragraphs (c)(2)(ii) and (iii) of this section, unless the eligible plan provides for a default method of payment (in which case amounts are considered made available and taxable when paid under the terms of the default payment schedule). A method of payment means a distribution or a series of periodic distributions commencing on a date determined in accordance with paragraph (c)(2)(ii) or (iii) of this section.

(3) *Examples.* The provisions of this paragraph (c) are illustrated by the following examples:

Example 1. (i) *Facts.* Eligible Plan X of a tax-exempt entity provides that a participant's total account balance, representing all amounts deferred under the plan, is payable to a participant in a single sum 60 days after severance from employment throughout these examples, unless, during a 30-day period immediately following the severance, the participant elects to receive the single sum payment at a later date (that is not later than the plan's normal retirement age of 65) or elects to receive distribution in 10 annual installments to begin 60 days after severance from employment (or at a later date, if so elected, that is not later than the plan's normal retirement age of 65). On November 13, 2004, participant K, a calendar year taxpayer, has a severance from employment with the eligible employer. K does not, within the 30-day window period, elect to postpone distributions to a later date or to receive payment in 10 fixed annual installments.

(ii) *Conclusion.* The single sum payment is payable to K 60 days after the date K has a severance from employment (January 12, 2005), and is includible in the gross income of K in 2005 under section 457(a).

Example 2. (i) *Facts.* The terms of eligible Plan X are the same as described in *Example 1.* Participant L participates in eligible Plan X. On November 11, 2003, L has a severance from the employment of the eligible employer. On November 24, 2003, L makes an initial deferral election not to receive the single-sum payment payable 60 days after the severance, and instead elects to receive the amounts in 10 annual installments to begin 60 days after severance from employment.

(ii) *Conclusion.* No portion of L's account is considered made available in 2003 or 2004 before a payment is made and no amount is includible in the gross income of L until distributions commence. The annual installment payable in 2004 will be includible in L's gross income in 2004.

Example 3. (i) *Facts.* The facts are the same as in *Example 1,* except that eligible Plan X also provides that those participants who are receiving distributions in 10 annual installments may, at any time and without restriction, elect to receive a cash out of all remaining installments. Participant M elects to receive a distribution in 10 annual installments commencing in 2004.

(ii) *Conclusion.* M's total account balance, representing the total of the amounts deferred under the plan, is considered made available and is includible in M's gross income in 2004.

Example 4. (i) *Facts.* The facts are the same as in *Example 3,* except that, instead of providing for an unrestricted cashout of remaining payments, the plan provides that participants or beneficiaries who are receiving distributions in 10 annual installments may accelerate the payment of the amount remaining payable to the participant upon the occurrence of an unforeseeable emergency as described in § 1.457-6(c)(1) in an amount not exceeding that described in § 1.457-6(c)(2).

(ii) *Conclusion.* No amount is considered made available to participant M on account of M's right to accelerate payments upon the occurrence of an unforeseeable emergency.

Example 5. (i) *Facts.* Eligible Plan Y of a tax-exempt entity provides that distributions will commence 60 days after a participant's severance from employment unless the participant elects, within a 30-day window period following severance from employment, to defer distributions to a later date (but no later than the year following the calendar year the participant attains age 70½). The plan provides that a participant who has elected to defer distributions to a later date may make an election as to form of distribution at any time prior to the 30th day before distributions are to commence.

(ii) *Conclusion.* No amount is considered made available prior to the date distributions are to commence by reason of a participant's right to defer or make an election as to the form of distribution.

Example 6. (i) *Facts.* The facts are the same as in *Example 1,* except that the plan also permits participants who have made an initial election to defer distribution to make one additional deferral election at any time prior to the date distributions are scheduled to commence. Participant N has a severance from employment at age 50. The next day, during the 30-day period provided in the plan, N elects to receive distribution in the form of 10 annual installment payments beginning at age 55. Two weeks later, within the 30-day window period, N makes a new election permitted under the plan to receive 10 annual installment payments beginning at age 60 (instead of age 55). When N is age 59, N elects under the additional deferral election provisions, to defer distributions until age 65.

(ii) *Conclusion.* In this example, N's election to defer distributions until age 65 is a valid election. The two elections N makes during the 30-day window period are not additional deferral elections described in paragraph (c)(2)(iii) of this section because they are made before the first permissible payout date under the plan. Therefore, the plan is not precluded from allowing N to make the additional deferral election. However, N can make no further election to defer distributions beyond age 65 (or accelerate distribution before

Reg. § 1.457-7(c)(3)

age 65) because this additional deferral election can only be made once.

[Reg. § 1.457-7.]

☐ [T.D. 9075, 7-10-2003.]

[Reg. § 1.457-8]

§ 1.457-8. Funding rules for eligible plans.—
(a) *Eligible governmental plans*—(1) *In general.* In order to be an eligible governmental plan, all amounts deferred under the plan, all property and rights purchased with such amounts, and all income attributable to such amounts, property, or rights, must be held in trust for the exclusive benefit of participants and their beneficiaries. A trust described in this paragraph (a) that also meets the requirements of §§ 1.457-3 through 1.457-10 is treated as an organization exempt from tax under section 501(a), and a participant's or beneficiary's interest in amounts in the trust is includible in the gross income of the participants and beneficiaries only to the extent, and at the time, provided for in section 457(a) and §§ 1.457-4 through 1.457-10.

(2) *Trust requirement*—(i) A trust described in this paragraph (a) must be established pursuant to a written agreement that constitutes a valid trust under State law. The terms of the trust must make it impossible, prior to the satisfaction of all liabilities with respect to participants and their beneficiaries, for any part of the assets and income of the trust to be used for, or diverted to, purposes other than for the exclusive benefit of participants and their beneficiaries.

(ii) Amounts deferred under an eligible governmental plan must be transferred to a trust within a period that is not longer than is reasonable for the proper administration of the participant accounts (if any). For purposes of this requirement, the plan may provide for amounts deferred for a participant under the plan to be transferred to the trust within a specified period after the date the amounts would otherwise have been paid to the participant. For example, the plan could provide for amounts deferred under the plan at the election of the participant to be contributed to the trust within 15 business days following the month in which these amounts would otherwise have been paid to the participant.

(3) *Custodial accounts and annuity contracts treated as trusts*—(i) *In general.* For purposes of the trust requirement of this paragraph (a), custodial accounts and annuity contracts described in section 401(f) that satisfy the requirements of this paragraph (a)(3) are treated as trusts under rules similar to the rules of section 401(f). Therefore, the provisions of § 1.401(f)-1(b) will generally apply to determine whether a custodial account or an annuity contract is treated as a trust. The use of a custodial account or annuity contract as part of an eligible governmental plan does not preclude the use of a trust or another custodial account or annuity contract as part of the same plan, provided that all such vehicles satisfy the requirements of section 457(g)(1) and (3) and paragraphs (a)(1) and (2) of this section and that all assets and income of the plan are held in such vehicles.

(ii) *Custodial accounts*—(A) *In general.* A custodial account is treated as a trust, for purposes of section 457(g)(1) and paragraphs (a)(1) and (2) of this section, if the custodian is a bank, as described in section 408(n), or a person who meets the nonbank trustee requirements of paragraph (a)(3)(ii)(B) of this section, and the account meets the requirements of paragraphs (a)(1) and (2) of this section, other than the requirement that it be a trust.

(B) *Nonbank trustee status.* The custodian of a custodial account may be a person other than a bank only if the person demonstrates to the satisfaction of the Commissioner that the manner in which the person will administer the custodial account will be consistent with the requirements of section 457(g)(1) and (3). To do so, the person must demonstrate that the requirements of § 1.408-2(e)(2) through (6) (relating to nonbank trustees) are met. The written application must be sent to the address prescribed by the Commissioner in the same manner as prescribed under § 1.408-2(e). To the extent that a person has already demonstrated to the satisfaction of the Commissioner that the person satisfies the requirements of § 1.408-2(e) in connection with a qualified trust (or custodial account or annuity contract) under section 401(a), that person is deemed to satisfy the requirements of this paragraph (a)(3)(ii)(B).

(iii) *Annuity contracts.* An annuity contract is treated as a trust for purposes of section 457(g)(1) and paragraph (a)(1) of this section if the contract is an annuity contract, as defined in section 401(g), that has been issued by an insurance company qualified to do business in the State, and the contract meets the requirements of paragraphs (a)(1) and (2) of this section, other than the requirement that it be a trust. An annuity contract does not include a life, health or accident, property, casualty, or liability insurance contract.

(4) *Combining assets.* [Reserved]

(b) *Eligible plans maintained by tax-exempt entity*—(1) *General rule.* In order to be an eligible plan of a tax-exempt entity, the plan must be unfunded and plan assets must not be set aside for participants or their beneficiaries. Under section

457(b)(6) and this paragraph (b), an eligible plan of a tax-exempt entity must provide that all amounts deferred under the plan, all property and rights to property (including rights as a beneficiary of a contract providing life insurance protection) purchased with such amounts, and all income attributable to such amounts, property, or rights, must remain (until paid or made available to the participant or beneficiary) solely the property and rights of the eligible employer (without being restricted to the provision of benefits under the plan), subject only to the claims of the eligible employer's general creditors.

(2) *Additional requirements.* For purposes of a paragraph (b)(1) of this section, the plan must be unfunded regardless of whether or not the amounts were deferred pursuant to a salary reduction agreement between the eligible employer and the participant. Any funding arrangement under an eligible plan of a tax-exempt entity that sets aside assets for the exclusive benefit of participants violates this requirement, and amounts deferred are generally immediately includible in the gross income of plan participants and beneficiaries. Nothing in this paragraph (b) prohibits an eligible plan from permitting participants and their beneficiaries to make an election among different investment options available under the plan, such as an election affecting the investment of the amounts described in paragraph (b)(1) of this section. [Reg. § 1.457-8.]

☐ [T.D. 9075, 7-10-2003.]

[Reg. § 1.457-9]

§ 1.457-9. **Effect on eligible plans when not administered in accordance with eligibility requirements.**—(a) *Eligible governmental plans.* A plan of a State ceases to be an eligible governmental plan on the first day of the first plan year beginning more than 180 days after the date on which the Commissioner notifies the State in writing that the plan is being administered in a manner that is inconsistent with one or more of the requirements of §§ 1.457-3 through 1.457-8, or 1.457-10. However, the plan may correct the plan inconsistencies specified in the written notification before the first day of that plan year and continue to maintain plan eligibility. If a plan ceases to be an eligible governmental plan, amounts subsequently deferred by participants will be includible in income when deferred, or, if later, when the amounts deferred cease to be subject to a substantial risk of forfeiture, as provided at § 1.457-11. Amounts deferred before the date on which the plan ceases to be an eligible governmental plan, and any earnings thereon, will be treated as if the plan continues to be an eligible governmental plan and will not be includible in participant's or beneficiary's gross income until paid to the participant or beneficiary.

(b) *Eligible plans of tax-exempt entities.* A plan of a tax-exempt entity ceases to be an eligible plan on the first day that the plan fails to satisfy one or more of the requirements of §§ 1.457-3 through 1.457-8, or § 1.457-10. See § 1.457-11 for rules regarding the treatment of an ineligible plan. [Reg. § 1.457-9.]

☐ [T.D. 9075, 7-10-2003.]

[Reg. § 1.457-10]

§ 1.457-10. **Miscellaneous provisions.**—(a) *Plan terminations and frozen plans*—(1) *In general.* An eligible employer may amend its plan to eliminate future deferrals for existing participants or to limit participation to existing participants and employees. An eligible plan may also contain provisions that permit plan termination and permit amounts deferred to be distributed on termination. In order for a plan to be considered terminated, amounts deferred under an eligible plan must be distributed to all plan participants and beneficiaries as soon as administratively practicable after termination of the eligible plan. The mere provision for, and making of, distributions to participants or beneficiaries upon a plan termination will not cause an eligible plan to cease to satisfy the requirements of section 457(b) or the regulations.

(2) *Employers that cease to be eligible employers*—(i) *Plan not terminated.* An eligible employer that ceases to be an eligible employer may no longer maintain an eligible plan. If the employer was a tax-exempt entity and the plan is not terminated as permitted under a paragraph (a)(2)(ii) of this section, the tax consequences to participants and beneficiaries in the previously eligible (unfunded) plan of an ineligible employer are determined in accordance with either section 451 if the employer becomes an entity other than a State or § 1.457-11 if the employer becomes a State. If the employer was a State and the plan is neither terminated as permitted under paragraph (a)(2)(ii) of this section nor transferred to another eligible plan of that State as permitted under paragraph (b) of this section, the tax consequences to participants in the previously eligible governmental plan of an ineligible employer, the assets of which are held in trust pursuant to § 1.457-8(a), are determined in accordance with section 402(b) (section 403(c) in the case of an annuity contract) and the trust is no longer to be treated as a trust that is exempt from tax under section 501(a).

(ii) *Plan termination.* As an alternative to determining the tax consequences to the plan and participants under paragraph (a)(2)(i) of this section, the employer may terminate the plan and distribute the amounts deferred (and all plan assets) to all plan participants as soon as administratively practicable in accordance with paragraph (a)(1) of this section. Such distribution may include eligible rollover distributions in the case of a plan that was an eligible governmental plan. In addition, if the employer is a State, another alternative to determining the tax consequences under paragraph (a)(2)(i) of this section is to transfer the assets of the eligible governmental plan to an eligible governmental plan of another eligible employer within the same State under the plan-to-plan transfer rules of paragraph (b) of this section.

(3) *Examples.* The provisions of this paragraph (a) are illustrated by the following examples:

Example 1. (i) *Facts.* Employer Y, a corporation that owns a State hospital, sponsors an eligible governmental plan funded through a trust. Employer Y is acquired by a for-profit hospital and Employer Y ceases to be an eligible employer under section 457(e)(1) or § 1.457-2(e). Employer Y terminates the plan and, during the next 6 months, distributes to participants and beneficiaries all amounts deferred that were under the plan.

(ii) *Conclusion.* The termination and distribution does not cause the plan to fail to be an eligible governmental plan. Amounts that are distributed as eligible rollover distributions may be rolled over to an eligible retirement plan described in section 402(c)(8)(B).

Example 2. (i) *Facts.* The facts are the same as in *Example 1,* except that Employer Y decides to continue to maintain the plan.

(ii) *Conclusion.* If Employer Y continues to maintains the plan, the tax consequences to participants and beneficiaries will be determined in accordance with either section 402(b) if the compensation deferred is funded through a trust, section 403(c) if the compensation deferred is funded through annuity contracts, or § 1.457-11 if the compensation deferred is not funded through a trust or annuity contract. In addition, if Employer Y continues to maintain the plan, the trust will no longer be treated as exempt from tax under section 501(a).

Example 3. (i) *Facts.* Employer Z, a corporation that owns a tax-exempt hospital, sponsors an unfunded eligible plan. Employer Z is acquired by a for-profit hospital and is no longer an eligible employer under section 457(e)(1) or § 1.457-2(e). Employer Z terminates the plan and distributes all amounts deferred under the eligible plan to participants and beneficiaries within a one-year period.

(ii) *Conclusion.* Distributions under the plan are treated as made under an eligible plan of a tax-exempt entity and the distributions of the amounts deferred are includible in the gross income of the participant or beneficiary in the year distributed.

Example 4. (i) *Facts.* The facts are the same as in *Example 3,* except that Employer Z decides to maintain instead of terminate the plan.

(ii) *Conclusion.* If Employer Z maintains the plan, the tax consequences to participants and beneficiaries in the plan will thereafter be determined in accordance with section 451.

(b) *Plan-to-plan transfers*—(1) *General rule.* An eligible governmental plan may provide for the transfer of amounts deferred by a participant or beneficiary to another eligible governmental plan if the conditions in paragraph (b)(2), (3), or (4) of this section are met. An eligible plan of a tax-exempt entity may provide for transfers of amounts deferred by a participant to another eligible plan of a tax-exempt entity if the conditions in paragraph (b)(5) of this section are met. In addition, an eligible governmental plan may accept transfers from another eligible governmental plan as described in the first sentence of this paragraph (b)(1), and an eligible plan of a tax-exempt entity may accept transfers from another eligible plan of a tax-exempt entity as described in the preceding sentence. However, a State may not transfer the assets of its eligible governmental plan to a tax-exempt entity's eligible plan and the plan of a tax-exempt entity may not accept such a transfer. Similarly, a tax-exempt entity may not transfer the assets of its eligible plan to an eligible governmental plan and an eligible governmental plan may not accept such a transfer. In addition, if the conditions in paragraph (b)(4) of this section (relating to permissive past service credit and repayments under section 415) are met, an eligible governmental plan of a State may provide for the transfer of amounts deferred by a participant or beneficiary to a qualified plan (under section 401(a)) maintained by a State. However, a qualified plan may not transfer assets to an eligible governmental plan or to an eligible plan of a tax-exempt entity, and an eligible governmental plan or the plan of a tax-exempt entity may not accept such a transfer.

(2) *Requirements for post-severance plan-to-plan transfers among eligible governmental plans.* A transfer under paragraph (b)(1) of this section from an eligible governmental plan to another eligible governmental plan is permitted if the following conditions are met—

Reg. § 1.457-10(a)(3)

(i) The transferor plan provides for transfers;

(ii) The receiving plan provides for the receipt of transfers;

(iii) The participant or beneficiary whose amounts deferred are being transferred will have an amount deferred immediately after the transfer at least equal to the amount deferred with respect to that participant or beneficiary immediately before the transfer; and

(iv) In the case of a transfer for a participant, the participant has had a severance from employment with the transferring employer and is performing services for the entity maintaining the receiving plan.

(3) *Requirements for plan-to-plan transfers of all plan assets of eligible governmental plan.* A transfer under paragraph (b)(1) of this section from an eligible governmental plan to another eligible governmental plan is permitted if the following conditions are met—

(i) The transfer is from an eligible governmental plan to another eligible governmental plan within the same State;

(ii) All of the assets held by the transferor plan are transferred;

(iii) The transferor plan provides for transfers;

(iv) The receiving plan provides for the receipt of transfers;

(v) The participant or beneficiary whose amounts deferred are being transferred will have an amount deferred immediately after the transfer at least equal to the amount deferred with respect to that participant or beneficiary immediately before the transfer; and

(vi) The participants or beneficiaries whose deferred amounts are being transferred are not eligible for additional annual deferrals in the receiving plan unless they are performing services for the entity maintaining the receiving plan.

(4) *Requirements for plan-to-plan transfers among eligible governmental plans of the same employer.* A transfer under paragraph (b)(1) of this section from an eligible governmental plan to another eligible governmental plan is permitted if the following conditions are met—

(i) The transfer is from an eligible governmental plan to another eligible governmental plan of the same employer (and, for this purpose, the employer is not treated as the same employer if the participant's compensation is paid by a different entity);

(ii) The transferor plan provides for transfers;

(iii) The receiving plan provides for the receipt of transfers;

(iv) The participant or beneficiary whose amounts deferred are being transferred will have an amount deferred immediately after the transfer at least equal to the amount deferred with respect to that participant or beneficiary immediately before the transfer; and

(v) The participant or beneficiary whose deferred amounts are being transferred is not eligible for additional annual deferrals in the receiving plan unless the participant or beneficiary is performing services for the entity maintaining the receiving plan.

(5) *Requirements for post-severance plan-to-plan transfers among eligible plans of tax-exempt entities.* A transfer under paragraph (b)(1) of this section from an eligible plan of a tax-exempt employer to another eligible plan of a tax-exempt employer is permitted if the following conditions are met—

(i) The transferor plan provides for transfers;

(ii) The receiving plan provides for the receipt of transfers;

(iii) The participant or beneficiary whose amounts deferred are being transferred will have an amount deferred immediately after the transfer at least equal to the amount deferred with respect to that participant or beneficiary immediately before the transfer; and

(iv) In the case of a transfer for a participant, the participant has had a severance from employment with the transferring employer and is performing services for the entity maintaining the receiving plan.

(6) *Treatment of amount transferred following a plan-to-plan transfer between eligible plans.* Following a transfer of any amount between eligible plans under paragraphs (b)(1) through (b)(5) of this section—

(i) the transferred amount is subject to the restrictions of § 1.457-6 (relating to when distributions are permitted to be made to a participant under an eligible plan) in the receiving plan in the same manner as if the transferred amount had been originally been deferred under the receiving plan if the participant is performing services for the entity maintaining the receiving plan, and

(ii) in the case of a transfer between eligible plans of tax-exempt entities, except as otherwise determined by the Commissioner, the transferred amount is subject to § 1.457-7(c)(2) (relating to when amounts are considered to be made available under an eligible plan of a tax-exempt entity) in the same manner as if the elections made by the participant or beneficiary under the transferor plan had been made under the receiving plan.

(7) *Examples.* The provisions of paragraphs (b)(1) through (6) of this section are illustrated by the following examples:

Example 1. (i) *Facts.* Participant A, the president of City X's hospital, has accepted a position with another hospital which is a tax-exempt entity. A participates in the eligible governmental plan of City X. A would like to transfer the amounts deferred under City X's eligible governmental plan to the eligible plan of the tax-exempt hospital.

(ii) *Conclusion.* City X's plan may not transfer A's amounts deferred to the tax-exempt employer's eligible plan. In addition, because the amounts deferred would no longer be held in trust for the exclusive benefit of participants and their beneficiaries, the transfer would violate the exclusive benefit rule of section 457(g) and § 1.457-8(a).

Example 2. (i) *Facts.* County M, located in State S, operates several health clinics and maintains an eligible governmental plan for employees of those clinics. One of the clinics operated by County M is being acquired by a hospital operated by State S, and employees of that clinic will become employees of State S. County M permits those employees to transfer their balances under County M's eligible governmental plan to the eligible governmental plan of State S.

(ii) *Conclusion.* If the eligible governmental plans of County M and State S provide for the transfer and acceptance of the transfer (and the other requirements of paragraph (b)(1) of this section are satisfied), then the requirements of paragraph (b)(2) of this section are satisfied and, thus, the transfer will not cause either plan to violate the requirements of section 457 or these regulations.

Example 3. (i) *Facts.* City Employer Z, a hospital, sponsors an eligible governmental plan. City Employer Z is located in State B. All of the assets of City Employer Z are being acquired by a tax-exempt hospital. City Employer Z, in accordance with the plan-to-plan transfer rules of paragraph (b) of this section, would like to transfer the total amount of assets deferred under City Employer Z's eligible governmental plan to the acquiring tax-exempt entity's eligible plan.

(ii) *Conclusion.* City Employer Z may not permit participants to transfer the amounts to the eligible plan of the tax-exempt entity. In addition, because the amounts deferred would no longer be held in trust for the exclusive benefit of participants and their beneficiaries, the transfer would violate the exclusive benefit rule of section 457(g) and § 1.457-8(a).

Example 4. (i) *Facts.* The facts are the same as in *Example 3*, except that City Employer Z, instead of transferring all of its assets to the eligible plan of the tax-exempt entity, decides to transfer all of the amounts deferred under City Z's eligible governmental plan to the eligible governmental plan of County B in which City Z is located. County B's eligible plan does not cover employees of City Z, but is willing to allow the assets of City Z's plan to be transferred to County B's plan, a related state government entity, also located in State B.

(ii) *Conclusion.* If City Employer Z's (transferor) eligible governmental plan provides for such transfer and the eligible governmental plan of County B permits the acceptance of such a transfer (and the other requirements of paragraph (b)(1) of this section are satisfied), then the requirements of paragraph (b)(3) of this section are satisfied and, thus, City Employer Z may transfer the total amounts deferred under its eligible governmental plan, prior to termination of that plan, to the eligible governmental plan maintained by County B. However, the participants of City Employer Z whose deferred amounts are being transferred are not eligible to participate in the eligible governmental plan of County B, the receiving plan, unless they are performing services for County B.

Example 5. (i) *Facts.* State C has an eligible governmental plan. Employees of City U in State C are among the eligible employees for State C's plan and City U decides to adopt another eligible governmental plan only for its employees. State C decides to allow employees to elect to transfer all of the amounts deferred for an employee under State C's eligible governmental plan to City U's eligible governmental plan.

(ii) *Conclusion.* If State C's (transferor) eligible governmental plan provides for such transfer and the eligible governmental plan of City U permits the acceptance of such a transfer (and the other requirements of paragraph (b)(1) of this section are satisfied), then the requirements of paragraph (b)(4) of this section are satisfied and, thus, State C may transfer the total amounts deferred under its eligible governmental plan to the eligible governmental plan maintained by City U.

(8) *Purchase of permissive past service credit by plan-to-plan transfers from an eligible governmental plan to a qualified plan*—(i) *General rule.* An eligible governmental plan of a State may provide for the transfer of amounts deferred by a participant or beneficiary to a defined benefit

Reg. § 1.457-10(b)(7)

governmental plan (as defined in section 414(d)), and no amount shall be includible in gross income by reason of the transfer, if the conditions in paragraph (b)(8)(ii) of this section are met. A transfer under this paragraph (b)(8) is not treated as a distribution for purposes of § 1.457-6. Therefore, such a transfer may be made before severance from employment.

(ii) *Conditions for plan-to-plan transfers from an eligible governmental plan to a qualified plan.* A transfer may be made under this paragraph (b)(8) only if the transfer is either—

(A) For the purchase of permissive past service credit (as defined in section 415(n)(3)(A)) under the receiving defined benefit governmental plan; or

(B) A repayment to which section 415 does not apply by reason of section 415(k)(3).

(iii) *Example.* The provisions of this paragraph (b)(8) are illustrated by the following example:

Example. (i) *Facts.* Plan X is an eligible governmental plan maintained by County Y for its employees. Plan X provides for distributions only in the event of death, an unforeseeable emergency, or severance from employment with County Y (including retirement from County Y). Plan S is a qualified defined benefit plan maintained by State T for its employees. County Y is within State T. Employee A is an employee of County Y and is a participant in Plan X. Employee A previously was an employee of State T and is still entitled to benefits under Plan S. Plan S includes provisions allowing participants in certain plans, including Plan X, to transfer assets to Plan S for the purchase of past service credit under Plan S and does not permit the amount transferred to exceed the amount necessary to fund the benefit resulting from the past service credit. Although not required to do so, Plan X allows Employee A to transfer assets to Plan S to provide a past service benefit under Plan S.

(ii) *Conclusion.* The transfer is permitted under this paragraph (b)(8).

(c) *Qualified domestic relations orders under eligible plans*—(1) *General rule.* An eligible plan does not become an ineligible plan described in section 457(f) solely because its administrator or sponsor complies with a qualified domestic relations order as defined in section 414(p), including an order requiring the distribution of the benefits of a participant to an alternate payee in advance of the general rules for eligible plan distributions under § 1.457-6. If a distribution or payment is made from an eligible plan to an alternate payee pursuant to a qualified domestic relations order, rules similar to the rules of section 402(e)(1)(A) shall apply to the distribution or payment.

(2) *Examples.* The provisions of this paragraph (c) are illustrated by the following examples:

Example 1. (i) *Facts.* Participant C and C's spouse D are divorcing. C is employed by State S and is a participant in an eligible plan maintained by State S. C has an account valued at $100,000 under the plan. Pursuant to the divorce, a court issues a qualified domestic relations order on September 1, 2003 that allocates 50 percent of C's $100,000 plan account to D and specifically provides for an immediate distribution to D of D's share within 6 months of the order. Payment is made to D in January of 2004.

(ii) *Conclusion.* State S's eligible plan does not become an ineligible plan described in section 457(f) and § 1.457-11 solely because its administrator or sponsor complies with the qualified domestic relations order requiring the immediate distribution to D in advance of the general rules for eligible plan distributions under § 1.457-6. In accordance with section 402(e)(1)(A), D (not C) must include the distribution in gross income. The distribution is includible in D's gross income in 2004. If the qualified domestic relations order were to provide for distribution to D at a future date, amounts deferred attributable to D's share will be includible in D's gross income when paid to D.

Example 2. (i) *Facts.* The facts are the same as in *Example 1,* except that S is a tax-exempt entity, instead of a State.

(ii) *Conclusion.* State S's eligible plan does not become an ineligible plan described in section 457(f) and § 1.457-11 solely because its administrator or sponsor complies with the qualified domestic relations order requiring the immediate distribution to D in advance of the general rules for eligible plan distributions under § 1.457-6. In accordance with section 402(e)(1)(A), D (not C) must include the distribution in gross income. The distribution is includible in D's gross income in 2004, assuming that the plan did not make the distribution available to D in 2003. If the qualified domestic relations order were to provide for distribution to D at a future date, amounts deferred attributable to D's share would be includible in D's gross income when paid or made available to D.

(d) *Death benefits and life insurance proceeds.* A death benefit plan under section 457(e)(11) is not an eligible plan. In addition, no amount paid or made available under an eligible plan as death benefits or life insurance proceeds is excludable from gross income under section 101.

Reg. § 1.457-10(d)

(e) *Rollovers to eligible governmental plans*—(1) *General rule.* An eligible governmental plan may accept contributions that are eligible rollover distributions (as defined in section 402(c)(4)) made from another eligible retirement plan (as defined in section 402(c)(8)(B)) if the conditions in paragraph (e)(2) of this section are met. Amounts contributed to an eligible governmental plan as eligible rollover distributions are not taken into account for purposes of the annual limit on annual deferrals by a participant in § 1.457-4(c) or § 1.457-5, but are otherwise treated in the same manner as amounts deferred under section 457 for purposes of §§ 1.457-3 through 1.457-9 and this section.

(2) *Conditions for rollovers to an eligible governmental plan.* An eligible governmental plan that permits eligible rollover distributions made from another eligible retirement plan to be paid into the eligible governmental plan is required under this paragraph (e)(2) to provide that it will separately account for any eligible rollover distributions it receives. A plan does not fail to satisfy this requirement if it separately accounts for particular types of eligible rollover distributions (for example, if it maintains a separate account for eligible rollover distributions attributable to annual deferrals that were made under other eligible governmental plans and a separate account for amounts attributable to other eligible rollover distributions), but this requirement is not satisfied if any such separate account includes any amount that is not attributable to an eligible rollover distribution.

(3) *Example.* The provisions of this paragraph (e) are illustrated by the following example:

Example. (i) *Facts.* Plan T is an eligible governmental plan that provides that employees who are eligible to participate in Plan T may make rollover contributions to Plan T from amounts distributed to an employee from an eligible retirement plan. An eligible retirement plan is defined in Plan T as another eligible governmental plan, a qualified section 401(a) or 403(a) plan, or a section 403(b) contract, or an individual retirement arrangement (IRA) that holds such amounts. Plan T requires rollover contributions to be paid by the eligible retirement plan directly to Plan T (a direct rollover) or to be paid by the participant within 60 days after the date on which the participant received the amount from the other eligible retirement plan. Plan T does not take rollover contributions into account for purposes of the plan's limits on amounts deferred that conform to § 1.457-4(c). Rollover contributions paid to Plan T are invested in the trust in the same manner as amounts deferred under Plan T and rollover contributions (and earnings thereon) are available for distribution to the participant at the same time and in the same manner as amounts deferred under Plan T. In addition, Plan T provides that, for each participant who makes a rollover contribution to Plan T, the Plan T record-keeper is to establish a separate account for the participant's rollover contributions. The record-keeper calculates earnings and losses for investments held in the rollover account separately from earnings and losses on other amounts held under the plan and calculates disbursements from and payments made to the rollover account separately from disbursements from and payments made to other amounts held under the plan.

(ii) *Conclusion.* Plan T does not lose its status as an eligible governmental plan as a result of the receipt of rollover contributions. The conclusion would not be different if the Plan T record-keeper were to establish two separate accounts, one of which is for the participant's rollover contributions attributable to annual deferrals that were made under an eligible governmental plan and the other of which is for other rollover contributions.

(f) *Deemed IRAs under eligible governmental plans.* See regulations under section 408(q) for guidance regarding the treatment of separate accounts or annuities as individual retirement plans (IRAs). [Reg. § 1.457-10.]

☐ [*T.D.* 9075, 7-10-2003.]

[Reg. § 1.457-11]

§ 1.457-11. Tax treatment of participants if plan is not an eligible plan.—(a) *In general.* Under section 457(f), if an eligible employer provides for a deferral of compensation under any agreement or arrangement that is an ineligible plan—

(1) Compensation deferred under the agreement or arrangement is includible in the gross income of the participant or beneficiary for the first taxable year in which there is no substantial risk of forfeiture (within the meaning of section 457(f)(3)(B)) of the rights to such compensation;

(2) If the compensation deferred is subject to a substantial risk of forfeiture, the amount includible in gross income for the first taxable year in which there is no substantial risk of forfeiture includes earnings thereon to the date on which there is no substantial risk of forfeiture;

(3) Earnings credited on the compensation deferred under the agreement or arrangement that are not includible in gross income under paragraph (a)(2) of this section are includible in the gross income of the participant or beneficiary only when paid or made available to the partici-

pant or beneficiary, provided that the interest of the participant or beneficiary in any assets (including amounts deferred under the plan) of the entity sponsoring the agreement or arrangement is not senior to the entity's general creditors; and

(4) Amounts paid or made available to a participant or beneficiary under the agreement or arrangement are includible in the gross income of the participant or beneficiary under section 72, relating to annuities.

(b) *Exceptions.* Paragraph (a) of this section does not apply with respect to—

(1) A plan described in section 401(a) which includes a trust exempt from tax under section 501(a);

(2) An annuity plan or contract described in section 403;

(3) That portion of any plan which consists of a transfer of property described in section 83;

(4) That portion of any plan which consists of a trust to which section 402(b) applies; or

(5) A qualified governmental excess benefit arrangement described in section 415(m).

(c) *Amount included in income.* The amount included in gross income on the applicable date under paragraphs (a)(1) and (a)(2) of this section is equal to the present value of the compensation (including earnings to the extent provided in paragraph (a)(2) of this section) on that date. For purposes of applying section 72 on the applicable date under paragraphs (a)(3) and (4) of this section, the participant is treated as having paid investment in the contract (or basis) to the extent that the deferred compensation has been taken into account by the participant in accordance with paragraphs (a)(1) and (a)(2) of this section.

(d) *Coordination of section 457(f) with section 83*—(1) *General rules.* Under paragraph (b)(3) of this section, section 457(f) and paragraph (a) of this section do not apply to that portion of any plan which consists of a transfer of property described in section 83. For this purpose, a transfer of property described in section 83 means a transfer of property to which section 83 applies. Section 457(f) and paragraph (a) of this section do not apply if the date on which there is no substantial risk of forfeiture with respect to compensation deferred under an agreement or arrangement that is not an eligible plan is on or after the date on which there is a transfer of property to which section 83 applies. However, section 457(f) and paragraph (a) of this section apply if the date on which there is no substantial risk of forfeiture with respect to compensation deferred under an agreement or arrangement that is not an eligible plan precedes the date on which there is a transfer of property to which section 83 applies. If deferred compensation payable in property is includible in gross income under section 457(f), then, as provided in section 72, the amount includible in gross income when that property is later transferred or made available to the service provider is the excess of the value of the property at that time over the amount previously included in gross income under section 457(f).

(2) *Examples.* The provisions of this paragraph (d) are illustrated in the following examples:

Example 1. (i) *Facts.* As part of an arrangement for the deferral of compensation, an eligible employer agrees on December 1, 2002 to pay an individual rendering services for the eligible employer a specified dollar amount on January 15, 2005. The arrangement provides for the payment to be made in the form of property having a fair market value equal to the specified dollar amount. The individual's rights to the payment are not subject to a substantial risk of forfeiture (within the meaning of section 457(f)(3)(B)).

(ii) *Conclusion.* In this *Example 1*, because there is no substantial risk of forfeiture with respect to the agreement to transfer property in 2005, the present value (as of December 1, 2002) of the payment is includible in the individual's gross income for 2002. Under paragraph (a)(4) of this section, when the payment is made on January 15, 2005, the amount includible in the individual's gross income is equal to the excess of the fair market value of the property when paid, over the amount that was includible in gross income for 2002 (which is the basis allocable to that payment).

Example 2. (i) *Facts.* As part of an arrangement for the deferral of compensation, individuals A and B rendering services for a tax-exempt entity each receive in 2010 property that is subject to a substantial risk of forfeiture (within the meaning of section 457(f)(3)(B) and within the meaning of section 83(c)(1)). Individual A makes an election to include the fair market value of the property in gross income under section 83(b) and individual B does not make this election. The substantial risk of forfeiture for the property transferred to individual A lapses in 2012 and the substantial risk of forfeiture for the property transferred to individual B also lapses in 2012. Thus, the property transferred to individual A is included in A's gross income for 2010 when A makes an section 83(b) election and the property transferred to individual B is included in B's gross income for 2012 when the substantial risk of forfeiture for the property lapses.

Reg. § 1.457-11(d)(2)

(ii) *Conclusion.* In this *Example 2,* in each case, the compensation deferred is not subject to section 457(f) or this section because section 83 applies to the transfer of property on or before the date on which there is no substantial risk of forfeiture with respect to compensation deferred under the arrangement.

Example 3. (i) *Facts.* In 2004, Z, a tax-exempt entity, grants an option to acquire property to employee C. The option lacks a readily ascertainable fair market value, within the meaning of section 83(e)(3), has a value on the date of grant equal to $100,000, and is not subject to a substantial risk of forfeiture (within the meaning of section 457(f)(3)(B) and within the meaning of section 83(c)(1)). Z exercises the option in 2012 by paying an exercise price of $75,000 and receives property that has a fair market value (for purposes of section 83) equal to $300,000.

(ii) *Conclusion.* In this *Example 3,* under section 83(e)(3), section 83 does not apply to the grant of the option. Accordingly, C has income of $100,000 in 2004 under section 457(f). In 2012, C has income of $125,000, which is the value of the property transferred in 2012, minus the allocable portion of the basis that results from the $100,000 of income in 2004 and the $75,000 exercise price.

Example 4. (i) *Facts.* In 2010, X, a tax-exempt entity, agrees to pay deferred compensation to employee D. The amount payable is $100,000 to be paid 10 years later in 2020. The commitment to make the $100,000 payment is not subject to a substantial risk of forfeiture. In 2010, the present value of the $100,000 is $50,000. In 2018, X transfers to D property having a fair market value (for purposes of section 83) equal to $70,000. The transfer is in partial settlement of the commitment made in 2010 and, at the time of the transfer in 2018, the present value of the commitment is $80,000. In 2020, X pays D the $12,500 that remains due.

(ii) *Conclusion.* In this *Example 4,* D has income of $50,000 in 2010. In 2018, D has income of $30,000, which is the amount transferred in 2018, minus the allocable portion of the basis that results from the $50,000 of income in 2010. (Under section 72(e)(2)(B), income is allocated first. The income is equal to $30,000 ($80,000 minus the $50,000 basis), with the result that the allocable portion of the basis is equal to $40,000 ($70,000 minus the $30,000 of income).) In 2020, D has income of $2,500 ($12,500 minus $10,000, which is the excess of the original $50,000 basis over the $40,000 basis allocated to the transfer made in 2018).

[Reg. § 1.457-11.]

☐ [T.D. 9075, 7-10-2003.]

Reg. § 1.457-12(a)

[Reg. § 1.457-12]

§ 1.457-12. Effective dates.—(a) *General effective date.* Except as otherwise provided in this section, §§ 1.457-1 through 1.457-11 apply for taxable years beginning after December 31, 2001.

(b) *Transition period for eligible plans to comply with EGTRRA.* For taxable years beginning after December 31, 2001, and before January 1, 2004, a plan does not fail to be an eligible plan as a result of requirements imposed by the Economic Growth and Tax Relief Reconciliation Act of 2001 (115 Stat. 385) (EGTRRA) (Public Law 107-16) June 7, 2001, if it is operated in accordance with a reasonable, good faith interpretation of EGTRRA.

(c) *Special rule for distributions from rollover accounts.* The last sentence of § 1.457-6(a) (relating to distributions of amounts held in a separate account for eligible rollover distributions) applies for taxable years beginning after December 31, 2003.

(d) *Special rule for options.* Section 1.457-11(d) does not apply with respect to an option without a readily ascertainable fair market value (within the meaning of section 83(e)(3)) that was granted on or before May 8, 2002.

(e) *Special rule for qualified domestic relations orders.* Section 1.457-10(c) (relating to qualified domestic relations orders) applies for transfers, distributions, and payments made after December 31, 2001. [Reg. § 1.457-12.]

☐ [T.D. 9075, 7-10-2003.]

[Reg. § 1.458-1]

§ 1.458-1. Exclusion for certain returned magazines, paperbacks, or records.—(a) *In general*—(1) *Introduction.* For taxable years beginning after September 30, 1979, section 458 allows accrual basis taxpayers to elect to use a method of accounting that excludes from gross income some or all of the income attributable to qualified sales during the taxable year of magazines, paperbacks, or records that are returned before the close of the applicable merchandise return period for that taxable year. Any amount so excluded cannot be excluded or deducted from gross income for the taxable year in which the merchandise is returned to the taxpayer. For the taxable year in which the taxpayer first uses this method of accounting, the taxpayer is not allowed to exclude from gross income amounts attributable to merchandise returns received during the taxable year that would have been excluded from gross income for the prior taxable year had the taxpayer used this method of accounting for that prior year. (See paragraph (e) of this section for rules describing how this amount should be taken into account.) The election to use this method of accounting shall be made in accordance with the rules contained in section 458(c) and in § 1.458-2 and this section. A taxpayer that does not elect to use this method of accounting can reduce income for returned merchandise only for the taxable year in which the merchandise is actually returned unsold by the purchaser.

(2) *Effective date.* While this section is generally effective only for taxable years beginning after August 31, 1984, taxpayers may rely on the provisions of paragraphs (a) through (f) of this section in taxable years beginning after September 30, 1979.

(b) *Definitions*—(1) *Magazine.* "Magazine" means a publication, usually paper-backed and sometimes illustrated, that is issued at regular intervals and contains stories, poems, articles, features, etc. This term includes periodicals, but does not include newspapers or volumes of a single publication issued at various intervals. However, volumes of a single publication that are issued at least annually, are related by title or subject matter to a magazine, and would otherwise qualify as a magazine, will be treated as a magazine.

(2) *Paperback.* "Paperback" means a paperback book other than a magazine. Unlike a hardback book, which usually has stiff front and back covers that enclose pages bound to a separate spine, a paperback book is characterized by a flexible outer cover to which the pages of the book are directly affixed.

(3) *Record.* "Record" means a disc, tape, or similar item on which music, spoken or other sounds are recorded. However, the term does not include blank records, tapes, etc., on which it is expected the ultimate purchaser will record. The following items, provided they carry pre-recorded sound, are examples of "records": audio and video cassettes, eight-track tapes, reel-to-reel tapes, cylinders, and flat, compact, and laser discs.

(4) *Qualified sale.* In order for a sale to be considered a qualified sale, both of the following conditions must be met:

(i) The taxpayer must be under a legal obligation (as determined by applicable State law), at the time of sale, to adjust the sales price of the magazine, paperback, or record on account of the purchaser's failure to resell it; and

(ii) The taxpayer must actually adjust the sales price of the magazine, paperback, or record to reflect the purchaser's failure to resell the merchandise. The following are examples of adjustments to the sales price of unsold merchandise: cash refunds, credits to the account of the purchaser, and repurchases of the merchandise. The adjustment need not be equal to the full amount of the sales price of the item. However, a markdown of the sales price under an agreement whereby the purchaser continues to hold the merchandise for sale or other disposition (other than solely for scrap) does not constitute an adjustment resulting from a failure to resell.

(5) *Merchandise return period*—(i) *In general.* Unless the taxpayer elects a shorter period, the "merchandise return period" is the period that ends 2 months and 15 days after the close of the taxable year for sales of magazines and 4 months and 15 days after the close of the taxable year for sales of paperbacks and records.

(ii) *Election to use shorter period.* The taxpayer may select a shorter merchandise return period than the applicable period set forth in paragraph (b)(5)(i) of this section.

(iii) *Change in merchandise return period.* Any change in the merchandise return period after its initial establishment will be treated as a change in method of accounting.

(c) *Amount of the exclusion*—(1) *In general.* Except as otherwise provided in paragraph (g) of this section, the amount of the gross income exclusion with respect to any qualified sale is equal to the lesser of—

(i) The amount covered by the legal obligation referred to in paragraph (b)(4)(i) of this section; or

(ii) The amount of the adjustment agreed to by the taxpayer before the close of the merchandise return period.

(2) *Price adjustment in excess of legal obligation.* The excess, if any, of the amount described in paragraph (c)(1)(ii) of this section over the amount described in paragraph (c)(1)(i) of this section should be excluded in the taxable year in which it is properly accruable under section 461.

(d) *Return of the merchandise*—(1) *In general.* (i) The exclusion from gross income allowed by section 458 applies with respect to a qualified sale of merchandise only if the seller receives, before the close of the merchandise return period, either—

(A) The physical return of the merchandise; or

(B) Satisfactory evidence that the merchandise has not been and will not be resold (as defined in paragraph (d)(2) of this section).

(ii) For purposes of this paragraph (d), evidence of a return received by an agent of the seller (other than the purchaser who purchased the merchandise from the seller) will be considered to be received by the seller at the time the agent receives the merchandise or evidence.

(2) *Satisfactory evidence.* Evidence that merchandise has not been and will not be resold is satisfactory only if the seller receives—

(i) Physical return of some portion of the merchandise (e.g., covers) provided under either the agreement between the seller and the purchaser or industry practice (such return evidencing the fact that the purchaser has not and will not resell the merchandise); or

(ii) A written statement from the purchaser specifying the quantities of each title not resold, provided either—

(A) The statement contains a representation that the items specified will not be resold by the purchaser; or

(B) The past dealings, if any, between the parties and industry practice indicate that such statement constitutes a promise by the purchaser not to resell the items.

(3) *Retention of evidence.* In the case of a return of merchandise (described in paragraph (d)(1)(i)(A) of this section) or portion thereof (described in paragraph (d)(2)(i) of this section), the seller has no obligation to retain physical evidence of the returned merchandise or portion thereof, provided the seller maintains documentary evidence that describes the quantity of physical items returned to the seller and indicates that the items were returned before the close of the merchandise return period.

(e) *Transitional adjustment*—(1) *In general.* An election to change from some other method of accounting for the return of magazines, paperbacks, or records to the method of accounting described in section 458 is a change in method of accounting that requires a transitional adjustment. Section 458 provides special rules for transitional adjustments that must be taken into account as a result of this change. See paragraph (e)(2) of this section for special rules applicable to magazines and paragraphs (e)(3) and (4) of this section for special rules applicable to paperbacks and records.

(2) *Magazines: 5-year spread of decrease in taxable income.* For taxpayers who have elected to use the method of accounting described in section 458 to account for returned magazines for a taxable year, section 458(d) and this paragraph (e)(2) provide a special rule for taking into account any decrease in taxable income resulting from the adjustment required by section 481(a)(2). Under these provisions, one-fifth of the transitional adjustment must be taken into account in the taxable year of the change and in each of the 4 succeeding taxable years. For example, if the application of section 481(a)(2) would produce a decrease in taxable income of $50 for 1980, the year of change, then $10 (one-fifth of $50) must be taken into account as a decrease in taxable income for 1980, 1981, 1982, 1983, and 1984.

(3) *Suspense account for paperbacks and records*—(i) *In general.* For taxpayers who have elected to use the method of accounting described in section 458 to account for returned paperbacks and records for a taxable year, section 458(e) provides that, in lieu of applying section 481, an electing taxpayer must establish a separate suspense account for its paperback business and its record business. The initial opening balance of the suspense account is described in paragraph (e)(3)(ii)(A) of this section. An initial adjustment to gross income for the year of election is described in paragraph (e)(3)(ii)(B) of this section. Annual adjustments to the suspense account are described in paragraph (e)(3)(iii)(A) of this section. Gross income adjustments are described in paragraph (e)(3)(iii)(B) of this section. Examples are provided in paragraph (e)(4) of this section. The effect of the suspense account is to defer all, or some part, of the deduction of the transitional adjustment until the taxpayer is no longer engaged in the trade or business of selling paperbacks or records, whichever is applicable.

(ii) *Establishing a suspense account*—(A) *Initial opening balance.* To compute the initial opening balance of the suspense account for the first taxable year for which an election is effective, the taxpayer must determine the section 458 amount (as defined in paragraph (e)(3)(ii)(C) of this section) for each of the three preceding taxable years. The initial opening balance of the account is the largest of the section 458 amounts.

(B) *Initial year adjustment.* If the initial opening balance in the suspense account exceeds the section 458 amount (as defined in paragraph (e)(3)(ii)(C) of this section) for the taxable year immediately preceding the year of election, the excess is included in the taxpayer's gross income for the first taxable year for which the election was made.

(C) *Section 458 amount.* For purposes of paragraph (e)(3)(ii) of this section, the section 458 amount for a taxable year is the dollar amount of merchandise returns that would have been excluded from gross income under section 458(a) for that taxable year if the section 458 election had been in effect for that taxable year.

(iii) *Annual adjustments*—(A) *Adjustment to the suspense account.* Adjustments are made to the suspense account each year to account for fluctuations in merchandise returns. To compute the annual adjustment, the taxpayer must determine the amount to be excluded under the election from gross income under section 458(a) for the taxable year. If the amount is less than the opening balance in the suspense account for the taxable year, the balance in the suspense account is reduced by the difference. Conversely, if the amount is greater than the opening balance in the

Reg. § 1.458-1(d)(3)

suspense account for the taxable year, the account is increased by the difference, but not to an amount in excess of the initial opening balance described in paragraph (e)(3)(ii)(A) of this section. Therefore, the balance in the suspense account will never be greater than the initial opening balance in the suspense account determined in paragraph (e)(3)(ii)(A) of this section. However, the balance in the suspense account after adjustments may be less than this initial opening balance in the suspense account.

(B) *Gross income adjustments.* Adjustments to the suspense account for years subsequent to the year of election also produce adjustments in the taxpayer's gross income. Adjustments which reduce the balance in the suspense account reduce gross income for the year in which the adjustment to the suspense account is made. Adjustments which increase the balance in the suspense account increase gross income for the year in which the adjustment to the suspense account is made.

(4) *Example.* The provisions of paragraph (e)(3) of this section may be illustrated by the following example:

Example. (i) X corporation, a paperback distributor, makes a timely section 458 election for its taxable year ending December 31, 1980. If the election had been in effect for the taxable years ending on December 31, 1977, 1978, and 1979, the dollar amounts of the qualifying returns would have been $5, $8, and $6, respectively. The initial opening balance of X's suspense account on January 1, 1980, is $8, the largest of these amounts. Since the initial opening balance ($8), is larger than the qualifying returns for 1979 ($6), the initial adjustment to gross income for 1980 is $2 ($8 − $6).

(ii) X has $5 in qualifying returns for its taxable year ending December 31, 1980. X must reduce its suspense account by $3, which is the excess of the opening balance ($8) over the amount of qualifying returns for the 1980 taxable year ($5). X also reduces its gross income for 1980 by $3. Thus, the net amount excludable from gross income for the 1980 taxable year after taking into account the qualifying returns, the gross income adjustment, and the initial year adjustment is $6 ($3 + $5 − $2).

(iii) X has qualifying returns of $7 for its taxable year ending December 31, 1981. X must increase its suspense account balance by $2, which is the excess of the amount of qualifying returns for 1981 ($7) over X's opening balance in the suspense account ($5). X must also increase its gross income by $2. Thus, the net amount excludable from gross income for the 1981 taxable year after taking into account the qualifying returns and the gross income adjustment is $5 ($7 − $2).

(iv) X has qualifying returns of $10 for its taxable year ending December 31, 1982. The opening balance in X's suspense account of $7 will not be increased in excess of the initial opening balance ($8). X must also increase gross income by $1. Thus, the net amount excludable from gross income for the 1982 taxable year is $9 ($10 − $1).

(v) This example is summarized by the following table:

Years Ending Dec. 31

Facts:	1977	1978	1979	1980 [1]	1981	1982
Qualifying returns during merchandise return period for the taxable year	$5	$8	$6	$ 5	$ 7	$ 10
Adjustment to suspense account:						
Opening balance				$ 8	$ 5	$ 7
Addition to account [2]					2	1
Reduction to account [3]				(3)		
Opening balance for next year				$ 5	$ 7	$ 8
Amount excludable from income:						
Initial year adjustment				$ (2)		
Amount excludable as qualifying returns in merchandise return period				$ 5	$ 7	$ 10
Adjustment for increase in suspense account					(2)	(1)
Adjustment for decrease in suspense account				3		
Net amount excludable for the year				$ 6	$ 5	$ 9

[1] Year of Change.
[2] Applies when qualifying returns during the merchandise return period exceed the opening balance; the addition is not to cause the suspense account to exceed the initial opening balance.
[3] Applies when qualifying returns during the merchandise return period are less than the opening balance.

Reg. § 1.458-1(e)(4)

(f) *Subchapter C transactions*—(1) *General rule.* If a transfer of substantially all the assets of a trade or business in which paperbacks or records are sold is made to an acquiring corporation, and if the acquiring corporation determines its basis in these assets, in whole or part, with reference to the basis of these assets in the hands of the transferor, then for the purposes of section 458(e) the principles of section 381 and § 1.381(c)(4)-1 will apply. The application of this rule is not limited to the transactions described in section 381(a). Thus, the rule also applies, for example, to transactions described in section 351.

(2) *Special rules.* If, in the case of a transaction described in paragraph (f)(1) of this section, an acquiring corporation acquires assets that were used in a trade or business that was not subject to a section 458 election from a transferor that is owned or controlled directly (or indirectly through a chain of corporations) by the same interests, and if the acquiring corporation uses the acquired assets in a trade or business for which the acquiring corporation later makes an election to use section 458, then the acquiring corporation must establish a suspense account by taking into account not only its own experience but also the transferor's experience when the transferor held the assets in its trade or business. Furthermore, the transferor is not allowed a deduction or exclusion for merchandise returned after the date of the transfer attributable to sales made by the transferor before the date of the transfer. Such returns shall be considered to be received by the acquiring corporation.

(3) *Example.* The provisions of paragraph (f)(2) of this section may be illustrated by the following example.

Example. Corporation S, a calendar year taxpayer, is a wholly owned subsidiary of Corporation P, a calendar year taxpayer. On December 31, 1982, S acquires from P substantially all of the assets used in a trade or business in which records are sold. P had not made an election under section 458 with respect to the qualified sale of records made in connection with that trade or business. S makes an election to use section 458 for its taxable year ending December 31, 1983, for the trade or business in which the acquired assets are used. P's qualified record returns within the 4 month and 15 day merchandise return period *following* the 1980 and 1981 taxable years were $150 and $170, respectively. S's qualified record returns during the merchandise return period following 1982 were $160. S must establish a suspense account by taking into account both P's and S's experience for the 3 immediately preceding taxable years. Thus, the initial opening balance of S's suspense account is $170. S must also make an initial year adjustment of $10 ($170 − $160), which S must include in income for S's taxable year ending December 31, 1983. P is not entitled to a deduction or exclusion for merchandise received after the date of the transfer (December 31, 1982) attributable to sales made by the transferor before the date of transfer. Thus, P is not entitled to a deduction or exclusion for the $160 of merchandise received by S during the first 4 months and 15 days of 1983.

(g) *Adjustment to inventory and cost of goods sold.* (1) If a taxpayer makes adjustments to gross receipts for a taxable year under the method of accounting described in section 458, the taxpayer, in determining excludable gross income, is also required to make appropriate correlative adjustments to purchases or closing inventory and to cost of goods sold for the same taxable year. Adjustments are appropriate, for example, where the taxpayer holds the merchandise returned for resale or where the taxpayer is entitled to receive a price adjustment from the person or entity that sold the merchandise to the taxpayer. Cost of goods sold must be properly adjusted in accordance with the provisions of § 1.61-3 which provides, in pertinent part, that gross income derived from a manufacturing or merchandising business equals total sales less cost of goods sold.

(2) The provisions of this paragraph (g) may be illustrated by the following examples. These examples do not, however, reflect any required adjustments under paragraph (e)(3) of this section.

Example 1. (i) In 1986, P, a publisher, properly elects under section 458 of the Code not to include in its gross income in the year of sale, income attributable to qualified sales of paperback books returned within the specified statutory merchandise return period of 4 months and 15 days. P and D, a distributor, agree that P shall provide D with a full refund for paperback books that D purchases from P and is unable to resell, provided the merchandise is returned to P within four months following the original sale. The agreement constitutes a legal obligation. The agreement provides that D's return of the covers of paperback books within the first four months following their sale constitutes satisfactory evidence that D has not resold and will not resell the paperback books. During P's 1989 taxable year,

Reg. § 1.458-1(f)(1)

pursuant to the agreement, P sells D 500 paperback books for $1 each. In 1990, during the merchandise return period, D returns covers from 100 unsold paperback books representing $100 of P's 1989 sales of paperback books. P's cost attributable to the returned books is $25. No adjustment to cost of goods sold is required under paragraph (g)(1) of this section because P is not holding returned merchandise for resale. P's proper amount excluded from its 1989 gross income under section 458 is $100.

(ii) If D returns the paperback books, rather than the cover, to P and these same books are then held by P for resale to other customers, paragraph (g)(1) of this section applies. Under paragraph (g)(1), P is required to decrease its cost of goods sold by $25, the amount of P's cost attributable to the returned merchandise. The proper amount excluded from P's 1989 gross income under section 458 is $75, resulting from adjustments to sales and cost of sales [(100 × $1) − $25].

Example 2. (i) In 1986, D, a distributor, properly elects under section 458 of the Code not to include in its gross income in the year of sale, income attributable to qualified sales of paperback books returned within the specified statutory merchandise return period of four months and 15 days. D and R, a retailer, agree that D shall provide a full refund for paperback books that R purchases from it and is unable to resell. D and R also have agreed that the merchandise must be returned to D within four months following the original sale. The agreement constitutes a legal obligation. D is similarly entitled to a full refund from P, the publisher, for the same paperback books. In 1990, during the merchandise return period, R returns paperback books to D representing $100 of 1989 sales. D's cost relating to these sale is $50. Under paragraph (g)(1) of this section, D must decrease its cost of goods sold by $50. D's proper amount excluded from its 1989 gross income under section 458 is $50 resulting from adjustments to sales and cost of sales ($100 − $50).

(ii) If D is instead only entitled to a 50 percent refund from P, D is required under paragraph (g)(1) of this section to decrease its cost of goods sold by $25, the amount of refund from P. D's proper amount excluded from its 1989 gross income under section 458 is $75, resulting from adjustments to sales and cost of sales ($100 − $25). [Reg. § 1.458-1.]

☐ [T.D. 8426, 8-25-92.]

[Reg. § 1.458-2]

§ 1.458-2. Manner of and time for making election.—(a) *Scope.* For taxable years beginning after September 30, 1979, section 458 provides a special method of accounting for taxpayers who account for sales of magazines, paperbacks, or records using an accrual method of accounting. In order to use the special method of accounting under section 458, a taxpayer must make an election in the manner prescribed in this section. The election does not require the prior consent of the Internal Revenue Service. The election is effective for the taxable year for which it is made and for all subsequent taxable years, unless the taxpayer secures the prior consent of the Internal Revenue Service to revoke such election.

(b) *Separate election for each trade or business.* An election is made with respect to each trade or business of a taxpayer in connection with which qualified sales (as defined in section 458(b)(5)) of a category of merchandise were made. Magazines, paperbacks, and records are each treated as a separate category of merchandise. If qualified sales of two or more categories of merchandise are made in connection with the same trade or business, then solely for purposes of section 458, each category is treated as a separate trade or business. For example, if a taxpayer makes qualified sales of both magazines and paperbacks in the same trade or business, then solely for purposes of section 458, the qualified sales relating to magazines are considered one trade or business and the qualified sales relating to paperbacks are considered a separate trade or business. Thus, if the taxpayer wishes to account under section 458 for the qualified sales of both magazines and paperbacks, such taxpayer must make a separate election for each category.

(c) *Manner of, and time for, making election.* An election is made under section 458 and this section by filing a statement of election containing the information described in paragraph (d) of this section with the taxpayer's income tax return for first taxable year for which the election is made. The election must be made no later than the time prescribed by law (including extensions) for filing the income tax return for the first taxable year for which the election is made. Thus, the election may not be filed with an amended income tax return after the prescribed date (including extensions) for filing the original return for such year.

(d) *Required information.* The statement of election required by paragraph (c) of this section must indicate that an election is being made under section 458(c) and must set forth the following information:

(1) The taxpayer's name, address, and identification number;

(2) A description of each trade or business for which an election is made;

(3) The first taxable year for which an election is made for each trade or business;

(4) The merchandise return period (as defined in section 458(b)(7)) for each trade or business for which an election is made;

(5) With respect to an election that applies to magazines, the amount of the adjustment computed under section 481(a) resulting from the change to the method of accounting described in section 458; and

(6) With respect to an election that applies to paperbacks or records, the initial opening balance (computed in accordance with section 458(e)) in the suspense account for each trade or business for which an election is made.

The statement of election should be made on a Form 3115 which need contain no information other than that required by this paragraph. [Reg. § 1.458-2.]

☐ [T.D. 7628, 6-8-79. Redesignated by T.D. 8426, 8-25-92.]

[Reg. § 1.460-0]

§ 1.460-0. Outline of regulations under section 460.—This section lists the paragraphs contained in § 1.460-1 through § 1.460-6.

§ 1.460-1. Long-term contracts.

(a) Overview.

(1) In general.

(2) Exceptions to required use of PCM.

(i) Exempt construction contract.

(ii) Qualified ship or residential construction contract.

(b) Terms.

(1) Long-term contract.

(2) Contract for the manufacture, building, installation, or construction of property.

(i) In general.

(ii) De minimis construction activities.

(3) Allocable contract costs.

(4) Related party.

(5) Contracting year.

(6) Completion year.

(7) Contract commencement date.

(8) Incurred.

(9) Independent research and development expenses.

(10) Long-term contract methods of accounting.

(c) Entering into and completing long-term contracts.

(1) In general.

(2) Date contract entered into.

(i) In general.

(ii) Options and change orders.

(3) Date contract completed.

(i) In general.

(ii) Secondary items.

(iii) Subcontracts.

(iv) Final completion and acceptance.

(A) In general.

(B) Contingent compensation.

(C) Assembly or installation.

(D) Disputes.

(d) Allocation among activities.

(1) In general.

(2) Non-long-term contract activity.

(e) Severing and aggregating contracts.

(1) In general.

(2) Facts and circumstances.

(i) Pricing.

(ii) Separate delivery or acceptance.

(iii) Reasonable businessperson.

(3) Exceptions.

(i) Severance for PCM.

(ii) Options and change orders.

(4) Statement with return.

(f) Classifying contracts.

(1) In general.

(2) Hybrid contracts.

(i) In general.

(ii) Elections.

(3) Method of accounting.

(4) Use of estimates.

(i) Estimating length of contract.

(ii) Estimating allocable contract costs.

(g) Special rules for activities benefitting long-term contracts of a related party.

(1) Related party use of PCM.

(i) In general.

(ii) Exception for components and subassemblies.

(2) Total contract price.

(3) Completion factor.

(h) Effective date.

(1) In general.

(2) Change in method of accounting.

(i) [Reserved]

Reg. § 1.460-0

Methods of Accounting

(j) Examples.
§ 1.460-2. Long-term manufacturing contracts.
  (a) In general.
  (b) Unique.
    (1) In general.
    (2) Safe harbors.
      (i) Short production period.
      (ii) Customized item.
      (iii) Inventoried item.
  (c) Normal time to complete.
    (1) In general.
    (2) Production by related parties.
  (d) Qualified ship contracts.
  (e) Examples.
§ 1.460-3. Long-term construction contracts.
  (a) In general.
  (b) Exempt construction contracts.
    (1) In general.
    (2) Home construction contract.
      (i) In general.
      (ii) Townhouses and rowhouses.
      (iii) Common improvements.
      (iv) Mixed use costs.
    (3) $10,000,000 gross receipts test.
      (i) In general.
      (ii) Single employer.
      (iii) Attribution of gross receipts.
  (c) Residential construction contracts.
§ 1.460-4. Methods of accounting for long-term contracts.
  (a) Overview.
  (b) Percentage-of-completion method.
    (1) In general.
    (2) Computations.
    (3) Post-completion-year income.
    (4) Total contract price.
      (i) In general.
        (A) Definition.
        (B) Contingent compensation.
        (C) Non-long-term contract activities.
      (ii) Estimating total contract price.
    (5) Completion factor.
      (i) Allocable contract costs.
      (ii) Cumulative allocable contract costs.
      (iii) Estimating total allocable contract costs.
      (iv) Pre-contracting-year costs.
      (v) Post-completion-year costs.
    (6) 10-percent method.
      (i) In general.
      (ii) Election.
    (7) Terminated contract.
      (i) Reversal of income.
      (ii) Adjusted basis.
      (iii) Look-back method.
  (c) Exempt contract methods.
    (1) In general.
    (2) Exempt-contract percentage-of-completion method.
      (i) In general.
      (ii) Determination of work performed.
  (d) Completed-contract method.
    (1) In general.
    (2) Post-completion-year income and costs.
    (3) Gross contract price.
    (4) Contracts with disputed claims.
      (i) In general.
      (ii) Taxpayer assured of profit or loss.
      (iii) Taxpayer unable to determine profit or loss.
      (iv) Dispute resolved.
  (e) Percentage-of-completion/capitalized-cost method.
  (f) Alternative minimum taxable income.
    (1) In general.
    (2) Election to use regular completion factors.
  (g) Method of accounting.
  (h) Examples.
  (i) [Reserved]
  (j) Consolidated groups and controlled groups.
    (1) Intercompany transactions.
      (i) In general.
      (ii) Definitions and nomenclature.
    (2) Example.
    (3) Effective dates.
      (i) In general.
      (ii) Prior law.
    (4) Consent to change method of accounting.
  (k) Mid-contract change in taxpayer.
    (1) In general.
    (2) Constructive completion transactions.
      (i) Scope.
      (ii) Old taxpayer.
      (iii) New taxpayer.
      (iv) Special rules relating to distributions of certain contracts by a partnership. [Reserved.]

Reg. § 1.460-0

(3) Step-in-the-shoes transactions.
(i) Scope.
(ii) Old taxpayer.
(A) In general.
(B) Gain realized on the transaction.
(iii) New taxpayer.
(A) Method of accounting.
(B) Contract price.
(C) Contract costs.
(iv) Special rules related to certain corporate transactions.
(A) Old taxpayer—basis adjustment.
(*1*) In general.
(*2*) Basis adjustment in excess of stock basis.
(*3*) Subsequent dispositions of certain contracts.
(B) New taxpayer.
(*1*) Contract price adjustment.
(*2*) Basis in contract.
(v) Special rules related to certain partnership transactions. [Reserved.]
(4) Anti-abuse rule.
(5) Examples.
(6) Effective date.
§ 1.460-5. *Cost allocation rules.*
(a) Overview.
(b) Cost allocation method for contracts subject to PCM.
(1) In general.
(2) Special rules.
(i) Direct material costs.
(ii) Components and subassemblies.
(iii) Simplified production methods.
(iv) Costs identified under cost-plus long-term contracts and federal long-term contracts.
(v) Interest.
(A) In general.
(B) Production period.
(C) Application of section 263A(f).
(vi) Research and experimental expenses.
(vii) Service costs.
(A) Simplified service cost method.
(*1*) In general.
(*2*) Example.
(B) Jobsite costs.
(C) Limitation on other reasonable cost allocation methods.

(c) Simplified cost-to-cost method for contracts subject to the PCM.
(1) In general.
(2) Election.
(d) Cost allocation rules for exempt construction contracts reported using CCM.
(1) In general.
(2) Indirect costs.
(i) Indirect costs allocable to exempt construction contracts.
(ii) Indirect costs not allocable to exempt construction contracts.
(3) Large homebuilders.
(e) Cost allocation rules for contracts subject to the PCCM.
(f) Special rules applicable to costs allocated under this section.
(1) Nondeductible costs.
(2) Costs incurred for non-long-term contract activities.
(g) Method of accounting.
§ 1.460-6. *Look-back method.*
(a) In general.
(1) Introduction.
(2) Overview.
(b) Scope of look-back method.
(1) In general.
(2) Exceptions from section 460.
(3) De minimis exception.
(4) Alternative minimum tax.
(5) Effective date.
(c) Operation of the look-back method.
(1) Overview.
(i) In general.
(ii) Post-completion revenue and expenses.
(A) In general.
(B) Completion.
(C) Discounting of contract price and contract cost adjustments subsequent to completion; election not to discount.
(*1*) General rule.
(*2*) Election not to discount.
(*3*) Year-end discounting convention.
(D) Revenue acceleration rule.
(2) Look-back Step One.
(i) Hypothetical reallocation of income among prior tax years.
(ii) Treatment of estimated future costs in year of completion.
(iii) Interim reestimates not considered.

Reg. § 1.460-0

Methods of Accounting

(iv) Tax years in which income is affected.

(v) Costs incurred prior to contract execution; 10-percent method.

    (A) General rule.

    (B) Example.

(vi) Amount treated as contract price.

    (A) General rule.

    (B) Contingencies.

    (C) Change orders.

(3) Look-back Step Two: Computation of hypothetical overpayment or underpayment of tax.

    (i) In general.

    (ii) Redetermination of tax liability.

    (iii) Hypothetical underpayment or overpayment.

    (iv) Cumulative determination of tax liability.

    (v) Years affected by look-back only.

    (vi) Definition of tax liability.

(4) Look-back Step Three: Calculation of interest on underpayment or overpayment.

    (i) In general.

    (ii) Changes in the amount of a loss or credit carryback or carryover.

    (iii) Changes in the amount of tax liability that generated a subsequent refund.

(d) Simplified marginal impact method.

    (1) Introduction.

    (2) Operation.

        (i) In general.

        (ii) Applicable tax rate.

        (iii) Overpayment ceiling.

        (iv) Example.

    (3) Anti-abuse rule.

    (4) Application.

        (i) Required use by certain pass-through entities.

            (A) General rule.

            (B) Closely held.

            (C) Examples.

            (D) Domestic contracts.

                (*1*) General rule.

                (*2*) Portion of contract income sourced.

            (E) Application to foreign contracts.

            (F) Effective date.

        (ii) Elective use.

            (A) General rule.

            (B) Election requirements.

            (C) Consolidated group consistency rule.

(e) Delayed reapplication method.

    (1) In general.

    (2) Time and manner of making election.

    (3) Examples.

(f) Look-back reporting.

    (1) Procedure.

    (2) Treatment of interest on return.

        (i) General rule.

        (ii) Timing of look-back interest.

    (3) Statutes of limitations and compounding of interest on look-back interest.

(g) Mid-contract change in taxpayer.

    (1) In general.

    (2) Constructive completion transactions.

    (3) Step-in-the-shoes transactions.

        (i) General rules.

        (ii) Application of look-back method to pre-transaction period.

            (A) Contract Price

            (B) Method.

            (C) Interest accrual period.

            (D) Information old taxpayer must provide.

        (iii) Application of look-back method to post-transaction years.

        (iv) S corporation elections.

    (4) Effective date.

(h) Examples.

    (1) Overview.

    (2) Step One.

    (3) Step Two.

    (4) Post-completion adjustments.

    (5) Alternative minimum tax.

    (6) Credit carryovers.

    (7) Net operating losses.

    (8) Alternative minimum tax credit.

    (9) Period for interest.

(i) [Reserved.]

(j) Election not to apply look-back method in de minimis cases.

[Reg. § 1.460-0.]

[*T.D.* 8315, 10-12-90. Amended by *T.D.* 8597, 7-12-95; *T.D.* 8756, 1-12-98; *T.D.* 8775, 7-1-98; *T.D.* 8929, 1-10-2001 *and T.D.* 8995, 5-14-2002.]

[Reg. § 1.460-1]

§ 1.460-1. **Long-term contracts.**—(a) *Overview*—(1) *In general.* This section provides rules for determining whether a contract for the manufacture, building, installation, or construction of property is a long-term contract under section 460 and what activities must be accounted for as a single long-term contract. Specific rules for long-term manufacturing and construction contracts are provided in §§ 1.460-2 and 1.460-3, respectively. A taxpayer generally must determine the income from a long-term contract using the percentage-of-completion method described in § 1.460-4(b) (PCM) and the cost allocation rules described in § 1.460-5(b) or (c). In addition, after a contract subject to the PCM is completed, a taxpayer generally must apply the look-back method described in § 1.460-6 to determine the amount of interest owed on any hypothetical underpayment of tax, or earned on any hypothetical overpayment of tax, attributable to accounting for the long-term contract under the PCM.

(2) *Exceptions to required use of PCM*—(i) *Exempt construction contract.* The requirement to use the PCM does not apply to any exempt construction contract described in § 1.460-3(b). Thus, a taxpayer may determine the income from an exempt construction contract using any accounting method permitted by § 1.460-4(c) and, for contracts accounted for using the completed-contract method (CCM), any cost allocation method permitted by § 1.460-5(d). Exempt construction contracts that are not subject to the PCM or CCM are not subject to the cost allocation rules of § 1.460-5 except for the production-period interest rules of § 1.460-5(b)(2)(v). Exempt construction contractors that are large homebuilders described in § 1.460-5(d)(3) must capitalize costs under section 263A. All other exempt construction contractors must account for the cost of construction using the appropriate rules contained in other sections of the Internal Revenue Code or regulations.

(ii) *Qualified ship or residential construction contract.* The requirement to use the PCM applies only to a portion of a *qualified ship contract* described in § 1.460-2(d) or *residential construction contract* described in § 1.460-3(c). A taxpayer generally may determine the income from a qualified ship contract or residential construction contract using the percentage-of-completion/capitalized-cost method (PCCM) described in § 1.460-4(e), but must use a cost allocation method described in § 1.460-5(b) for the entire contract.

(b) *Terms*—(1) *Long-term contract.* A *long-term contract* generally is any contract for the manufacture, building, installation, or construction of property if the contract is not completed within the contracting year, as defined in paragraph (b)(5) of this section. However, a contract for the manufacture of property is a long-term contract only if it also satisfies either the unique item or 12-month requirements described in § 1.460-2. A contract for the manufacture of personal property is a *manufacturing contract*. In contrast, a contract for the building, installation, or construction of real property is a *construction contract*.

(2) *Contract for the manufacture, building, installation, or construction of property*—(i) *In general.* A contract is a *contract for the manufacture, building, installation, or construction of property* if the manufacture, building, installation, or construction of property is necessary for the taxpayer's contractual obligations to be fulfilled and if the manufacture, building, installation, or construction of that property has not been completed when the parties enter into the contract. If a taxpayer has to manufacture or construct an item to fulfill its obligations under the contract, the fact that the taxpayer is not required to deliver that item to the customer is not relevant. Whether the customer has title to, control over, or bears the risk of loss from, the property manufactured or constructed by the taxpayer also is not relevant. Furthermore, how the parties characterize their agreement (e.g., as a contract for the sale of property) is not relevant.

(ii) *De minimis construction activities.* Notwithstanding paragraph (b)(2)(i) of this section, a contract is not a construction contract under section 460 if the contract includes the provision of land by the taxpayer and the estimated total allocable contract costs, as defined in paragraph (b)(3) of this section, attributable to the taxpayer's construction activities are less than 10 percent of the contract's total contract price, as defined in § 1.460-4(b)(4)(i). For the purposes of this paragraph (b)(2)(ii), the allocable contract costs attributable to the taxpayer's construction activities do not include the cost of the land provided to the customer. In addition, a contract's estimated total allocable contract costs include a proportionate share of the estimated cost of any common improvement that benefits the subject matter of the contract if the taxpayer is contractually obligated, or required by law, to construct the common improvement.

(3) *Allocable contract costs. Allocable contract costs* are costs that are allocable to a long-term contract under § 1.460-5.

(4) *Related party.* A *related party* is a person whose relationship to a taxpayer is described in section 707(b) or 267(b), determined without regard to section 267(f)(1)(A) and determined by replacing "at least 80 percent" with "more than 50 percent" for the purposes of determining the ownership of the stock of a corporation in sections 267(b)(2), (8), (10)(A), and (12).

Reg. § 1.460-1(a)(2)

(5) *Contracting year.* The *contracting year* is the taxable year in which a taxpayer enters into a contract as described in paragraph (c)(2) of this section.

(6) *Completion year.* The *completion year* is the taxable year in which a taxpayer completes a contract as described in paragraph (c)(3) of this section.

(7) *Contract commencement date.* The *contract commencement date* is the date that a taxpayer or related party first incurs any allocable contract costs, such as design and engineering costs, other than expenses attributable to bidding and negotiating activities. Generally, the contract commencement date is relevant in applying § 1.460-6(b)(3) (concerning the de minimis exception to the look-back method under section 460(b)(3)(B)); § 1.460-5(b)(2)(v)(B)(*1*)(*i*) (concerning the production period subject to interest allocation); § 1.460-2(d) (concerning qualified ship contracts); and § 1.460-3(b)(1)(ii) (concerning the construction period for exempt construction contracts).

(8) *Incurred.* Incurred has the meaning given in § 1.461-1(a)(2) (concerning the taxable year a liability is incurred under the accrual method of accounting), regardless of a taxpayer's overall method of accounting. See § 1.461-4(d)(2)(ii) for economic performance rules concerning the PCM.

(9) *Independent research and development expenses. Independent research and development expenses* are any expenses incurred in the performance of research or development, except that this term does not include any expenses that are directly attributable to a particular long-term contract in existence when the expenses are incurred and this term does not include any expenses under an agreement to perform research or development.

(10) *Long-term contract methods of accounting. Long-term contract methods of accounting,* which include the PCM, the CCM, the PCCM, and the exempt-contract percentage-of-completion method (EPCM), are methods of accounting that may be used only for long-term contracts.

(c) *Entering into and completing long-term contracts*—(1) *In general.* To determine when a contract is entered into under paragraph (c)(2) of this section and completed under paragraph (c)(3) of this section, a taxpayer must consider all relevant allocable contract costs incurred and activities performed by itself, by related parties on its behalf, and by the customer, that are incident to or necessary for the long-term contract. In addition, to determine whether a contract is completed in the contracting year, the taxpayer may not consider when it expects to complete the contract.

(2) *Date contract entered into*—(i) *In general.* A taxpayer enters into a contract on the date that the contract binds both the taxpayer and the customer under applicable law, even if the contract is subject to unsatisfied conditions not within the taxpayer's control (such as obtaining financing). If a taxpayer delays entering into a contract for a principal purpose of avoiding section 460, however, the taxpayer will be treated as having entered into a contract not later than the contract commencement date.

(ii) *Options and change orders.* A taxpayer enters into a new contract on the date that the customer exercises an option or similar provision in a contract if that option or similar provision must be severed from the contract under paragraph (e) of this section. Similarly, a taxpayer enters into a new contract on the date that it accepts a change order or other similar agreement if the change order or other similar agreement must be severed from the contract under paragraph (e) of this section.

(3) *Date contract completed*—(i) *In general.* A taxpayer's contract is completed upon the earlier of—

(A) Use of the subject matter of the contract by the customer for its intended purpose (other than for testing) and at least 95 percent of the total allocable contract costs attributable to the subject matter have been incurred by the taxpayer; or

(B) Final completion and acceptance of the subject matter of the contract.

(ii) *Secondary items.* The date a contract accounted for using the CCM is completed is determined without regard to whether one or more secondary items have been used or finally completed and accepted. If any secondary items are incomplete at the end of the taxable year in which the primary subject matter of a contract is completed, the taxpayer must separate the portion of the gross contract price and the allocable contract costs attributable to the incomplete secondary item(s) from the completed contract and account for them using a permissible method of accounting. A permissible method of accounting includes a long-term contract method of accounting only if a separate contract for the secondary item(s) would be a long-term contract, as defined in paragraph (b)(1) of this section.

(iii) *Subcontracts.* In the case of a subcontract, a subcontractor's customer is the general contractor. Thus, the subject matter of the subcontract is the relevant subject matter under paragraph (c)(3)(i) of this section.

(iv) *Final completion and acceptance*—(A) *In general.* Except as otherwise provided in this

Reg. § 1.460-1(c)(3)

paragraph (c)(3)(iv), to determine whether final completion and acceptance of the subject matter of a contract have occurred, a taxpayer must consider all relevant facts and circumstances. Nevertheless, a taxpayer may not delay the completion of a contract for the principal purpose of deferring federal income tax.

(B) *Contingent compensation.* Final completion and acceptance is determined without regard to any contractual term that provides for additional compensation that is contingent on the successful performance of the subject matter of the contract. A taxpayer must account for all contingent compensation that is not includible in total contract price under § 1.460-4(b)(4)(i), or in gross contract price under § 1.460-4(d)(3), using a permissible method of accounting. For application of the look-back method for contracts accounted for using the PCM, see § 1.460-6(c)(1)(ii) and (2)(vi).

(C) *Assembly or installation.* Final completion and acceptance is determined without regard to whether the taxpayer has an obligation to assist or supervise assembly or installation of the subject matter of the contract where the assembly or installation is not performed by the taxpayer or a related party. A taxpayer must account for the gross receipts and costs attributable to such an obligation using a permissible method of accounting, other than a long-term contract method.

(D) *Disputes.* Final completion and acceptance is determined without regard to whether a dispute exists at the time the taxpayer tenders the subject matter of the contract to the customer. For contracts accounted for using the CCM, see § 1.460-4(d)(4). For application of the look-back method for contracts accounted for using the PCM, see § 1.460-6(c)(1)(ii) and (2)(vi).

(d) *Allocation among activities*—(1) *In general.* Long-term contract methods of accounting apply only to the gross receipts and costs attributable to long-term contract activities. Gross receipts and costs attributable to long-term contract activities means amounts included in total contract price or gross contract price, whichever is applicable, as determined under § 1.460-4, and costs allocable to the contract, as determined under § 1.460-5. Gross receipts and costs attributable to non-long-term contract activities (as defined in paragraph (d)(2) of this section) generally must be taken into account using a permissible method of accounting other than a long-term contract method. See section 446(c) and § 1.446-1(c). However, if the performance of a *non-long-term contract activity* is incident to or necessary for the manufacture, building, installation, or construction of the subject matter of one or more of the taxpayer's long-term contracts, the gross receipts and costs attributable to that activity must be allocated to the long-term contract(s) benefitted as provided in §§ 1.460-4(b)(4)(i) and 1.460-5(f)(2), respectively. Similarly, if a single long-term contract requires a taxpayer to perform a non-long-term contract activity that is not incident to or necessary for the manufacture, building, installation, or construction of the subject matter of the long-term contract, the gross receipts and costs attributable to that non-long-term contract activity must be separated from the contract and accounted for using a permissible method of accounting other than a long-term contract method. But see paragraph (g) of this section for related party rules.

(2) *Non-long-term contract activity.* Non-*long-term contract activity* means the performance of an activity other than manufacturing, building, installation, or construction, such as the provision of architectural, design, engineering, and construction management services, and the development or implementation of computer software. In addition, performance under a guaranty, warranty, or maintenance agreement is a non-long-term contract activity that is never incident to or necessary for the manufacture or construction of property under a long-term contract.

(e) *Severing and aggregating contracts*—(1) *In general.* After application of the allocation rules of paragraph (d) of this section, the severing and aggregating rules of this paragraph (e) may be applied by the Commissioner or the taxpayer as necessary to clearly reflect income (e.g., to prevent the unreasonable deferral (or acceleration) of income or the premature recognition (or deferral) of loss). Under the severing and aggregating rules, one agreement may be treated as two or more contracts, and two or more agreements may be treated as one contract. Except as provided in paragraph (e)(3)(ii) of this section, a taxpayer must determine whether to sever an agreement or to aggregate two or more agreements based on the facts and circumstances known at the end of the contracting year.

(2) *Facts and circumstances.* Whether an agreement should be severed, or two or more agreements should be aggregated, depends on the following factors:

(i) *Pricing.* Independent pricing of items in an agreement is necessary for the agreement to be severed into two or more contracts. In the case of an agreement for similar items, if the price to be paid for the items is determined under different terms or formulas (e.g., if some items are priced under a cost-plus incentive fee arrangement and later items are to be priced under a fixed-price

Reg. § 1.460-1(d)(1)

arrangement), then the difference in the pricing terms or formulas indicates that the items are independently priced. Similarly, interdependent pricing of items in separate agreements is necessary for two or more agreements to be aggregated into one contract. A single price negotiation for similar items ordered under one or more agreements indicates that the items are interdependently priced.

(ii) *Separate delivery or acceptance.* An agreement may not be severed into two or more contracts unless it provides for separate delivery or separate acceptance of items that are the subject matter of the agreement. However, the separate delivery or separate acceptance of items by itself does not necessarily require an agreement to be severed.

(iii) *Reasonable businessperson.* Two or more agreements to perform manufacturing or construction activities may not be aggregated into one contract unless a reasonable businessperson would not have entered into one of the agreements for the terms agreed upon without also entering into the other agreement(s). Similarly, an agreement to perform manufacturing or construction activities may not be severed into two or more contracts if a reasonable businessperson would not have entered into separate agreements containing terms allocable to each severed contract. Analyzing the reasonable businessperson standard requires an analysis of all the facts and circumstances of the business arrangement between the taxpayer and the customer. For purposes of this paragraph (e)(2)(iii), a taxpayer's expectation that the parties would enter into another agreement, when agreeing to the terms contained in the first agreement, is not relevant.

(3) *Exceptions*—(i) *Severance for PCM.* A taxpayer may not sever under this paragraph (e) a long-term contract that would be subject to the PCM without obtaining the Commissioner's prior written consent.

(ii) *Options and change orders.* Except as provided in paragraph (e)(3)(i) of this section, a taxpayer must sever an agreement that increases the number of units to be supplied to the customer, such as through the exercise of an option or the acceptance of a change order, if the agreement provides for separate delivery or separate acceptance of the additional units.

(4) *Statement with return.* If a taxpayer severs an agreement or aggregates two or more agreements under this paragraph (e) during the taxable year, the taxpayer must attach a statement to its original federal income tax return for that year. This statement must contain the following information—

(i) The legend NOTIFICATION OF SEVERANCE OR AGGREGATION UNDER SEC. 1.460-1(e);

(ii) The taxpayer's name; and

(iii) The taxpayer's employer identification number or social security number.

(f) *Classifying contracts*—(1) *In general.* After applying the severing and aggregating rules of paragraph (e) of this section, a taxpayer must determine the classification of a contract (e.g., as a long-term manufacturing contract, long-term construction contract, non-long-term contract) based on all the facts and circumstances known no later than the end of the contracting year. Classification is determined on a contract-by-contract basis. Consequently, a requirement to manufacture a single unique item under a long-term contract will subject all other items in that contract to section 460.

(2) *Hybrid contracts*—(i) *In general.* A long-term contract that requires a taxpayer to perform both manufacturing and construction activities (hybrid contract) generally must be classified as two contracts, a manufacturing contract and a construction contract. A taxpayer may elect, on a contract-by-contract basis, to classify a hybrid contract as a long-term construction contract if at least 95 percent of the estimated total allocable contract costs are reasonably allocable to construction activities. In addition, a taxpayer may elect, on a contract-by-contract basis, to classify a hybrid contract as a long-term manufacturing contract subject to the PCM.

(ii) *Elections.* A taxpayer makes an election under this paragraph (f)(2) by using its method of accounting for similar construction contracts or for manufacturing contracts, whichever is applicable, to account for a hybrid contract entered into during the taxable year of the election on its original federal income tax return for the election year. If an electing taxpayer's method is the PCM, the taxpayer also must use the PCM to apply the look-back method under § 1.460-6 and to determine alternative minimum taxable income under § 1.460-4(f).

(3) *Method of accounting.* Except as provided in paragraph (f)(2)(ii) of this section, a taxpayer's method of classifying contracts is a method of accounting under section 446 and, thus, may not be changed without the Commissioner's consent. If a taxpayer's method of classifying contracts is unreasonable, that classification method is an impermissible accounting method.

(4) *Use of estimates*—(i) *Estimating length of contract.* A taxpayer must use a reasonable estimate of the time required to complete a contract when necessary to classify the contract (e.g.,

Reg. § 1.460-1(f)(4)

to determine whether the five-year completion rule for qualified ship contracts under § 1.460-2(d), or the two-year completion rule for exempt construction contracts under § 1.460-3(b), is satisfied, but not to determine whether a contract is completed within the contracting year under paragraph (b)(1) of this section). To be considered reasonable, an estimate of the time required to complete the contract must include anticipated time for delay, rework, change orders, technology or design problems, or other problems that reasonably can be anticipated considering the nature of the contract and prior experience. A contract term that specifies an expected completion or delivery date may be considered evidence that the taxpayer reasonably expects to complete or deliver the subject matter of the contract on or about the date specified, especially if the contract provides bona fide penalties for failing to meet the specified date. If a taxpayer classifies a contract based on a reasonable estimate of completion time, the contract will not be reclassified based on the actual (or another reasonable estimate of) completion time. A taxpayer's estimate of completion time will not be considered unreasonable if a contract is not completed within the estimated time primarily because of unforeseeable factors not within the taxpayer's control, such as third-party litigation, extreme weather conditions, strikes, or delays in securing permits or licenses.

(ii) *Estimating allocable contract costs.* A taxpayer must use a reasonable estimate of total allocable contract costs when necessary to classify the contract (e.g., to determine whether a contract is a home construction contract under § 1.460-(3)(b)(2)). If a taxpayer classifies a contract based on a reasonable estimate of total allocable contract costs, the contract will not be reclassified based on the actual (or another reasonable estimate of) total allocable contract costs.

(g) *Special rules for activities benefitting long-term contracts of a related party*—(1) *Related party use of PCM*—(i) *In general.* Except as provided in paragraph(g)(1)(ii) of this section, if a related party and its customer enter into a long-term contract subject to the PCM, and a taxpayer performs any activity that is incident to or necessary for the related party's long-term contract, the taxpayer must account for the gross receipts and costs attributable to this activity using the PCM, even if this activity is not otherwise subject to section 460(a). This type of activity may include, for example, the performance of engineering and design services, and the production of components and subassemblies that are reasonably expected to be used in the production of the subject matter of the related party's contract.

(ii) *Exception for components and subassemblies.* A taxpayer is not required to use the PCM under this paragraph (g) to account for a component or subassembly that benefits a related party's long-term contract if more than 50 percent of the average annual gross receipts attributable to the sale of this item for the 3-taxable-year-period ending with the contracting year comes from unrelated parties.

(2) *Total contract price.* If a taxpayer is required to use the PCM under paragraph (g)(1)(i) of this section, the total contract price (as defined in § 1.460-4(b)(4)(i)) is the fair market value of the taxpayer's activity that is incident to or necessary for the performance of the related party's long-term contract. The related party also must use the fair market value of the taxpayer's activity as the cost it incurs for the activity. The fair market value of the taxpayer's activity may or may not be the same as the amount the related party pays the taxpayer for that activity.

(3) *Completion factor.* To compute a contract's completion factor (as described in § 1.460-4(b)(5)), the related party must take into account the fair market value of the taxpayer's activity that is incident to or necessary for the performance of the related party's long-term contract when the related party incurs the liability to the taxpayer for the activity, rather than when the taxpayer incurs the costs to perform the activity.

(h) *Effective date*—(1) *In general.* Except as otherwise provided, this section and §§ 1.460-2 through 1.460-5 are applicable for contracts entered into on or after January 11, 2001.

(2) *Change in method of accounting.* Any change in a taxpayer's method of accounting necessary to comply with this section and §§ 1.460-2 through 1.460-5 is a change in method of accounting to which the provisions of section 446 and the regulations thereunder apply. For the first taxable year that includes January 11, 2001, a taxpayer is granted the consent of the Commissioner to change its method of accounting to comply with the provisions of this section and §§ 1.460-2 through 1.460-5 for long-term contracts entered into on or after January 11, 2001. A taxpayer that wants to change its method of accounting under this paragraph (h)(2) must follow the automatic consent procedures in Rev. Proc. 99-49 (1999-52 I.R.B. 725) (see § 601.601(d)(2) of this chapter), except that the scope limitations in section 4.02 of Rev. Proc. 99-49 do not apply. Because a change under this paragraph (h)(2) is made on a cut-off basis, a section 481(a) adjustment is not permitted or required. Moreover, the taxpayer does not receive audit protection under section 7 of Rev.

Reg. § 1.460-1(g)(1)

Proc. 99-49 for a change in method of accounting under this paragraph (h)(2). A taxpayer that wants to change its exempt-contract method of accounting is not granted the consent of the Commissioner under this paragraph (h)(2) and must file a Form 3115, "Application for Change in Accounting Method," to obtain consent. See Rev. Proc. 97-27 (1997-1 C.B. 680) (see § 601.601(d)(2) of this chapter).

(i) [Reserved]

(j) *Examples.* The following examples illustrate the rules of this section:

Example 1. Contract for manufacture of property. B notifies C, an aircraft manufacturer, that it wants to purchase an aircraft of a particular type. At the time C receives the order, C has on hand several partially completed aircraft of this type; however, C does not have any completed aircraft of this type on hand. C and B agree that B will purchase one of these aircraft after it has been completed. C retains title to and risk of loss with respect to the aircraft until the sale takes place. The agreement between C and B is a contract for the manufacture of property under paragraph (b)(2)(i) of this section, even if labeled as a contract for the sale of property, because the manufacture of the aircraft is necessary for C's obligations under the agreement to be fulfilled and the manufacturing was not complete when B and C entered into the agreement.

Example 2. De minimis construction activity. C, a master developer whose taxable year ends December 31, owns 5,000 acres of undeveloped land with a cost basis of $5,000,000 and a fair market value of $50,000,000. To obtain permission from the local county government to improve this land, a service road must be constructed on this land to benefit all 5,000 acres. In 2001, C enters into a contract to sell a 1,000-acre parcel of undeveloped land to B, a residential developer, for its fair market value, $10,000,000. In this contract, C agrees to construct a service road running through the land that C is selling to B and through the 4,000 adjacent acres of undeveloped land that C has sold or will sell to other residential developers for its fair market value, $40,000,000. C reasonably estimates that it will incur allocable contract costs of $50,000 (excluding the cost of the land) to construct this service road, which will be owned and maintained by the county. C must reasonably allocate the cost of the service road among the benefitted parcels. The portion of the estimated total allocable contract costs that C allocates to the 1,000-acre parcel being sold to B (based upon its fair market value) is $10,000 ($50,000 × ($10,000,000 ÷ $50,000,000)). Construction of the service road is finished in 2002. Because the estimated total allocable contract costs attributable to C's construction activities, $10,000, are less than 10 percent of the contract's total contract price, $10,000,000, C's contract with B is not a construction contract under paragraph (b)(2)(ii) of this section. Thus, C's contract with B is not a long-term contract under paragraph (b)(2)(i) of this section, notwithstanding that construction of the service road is not completed in 2001.

Example 3. Completion—customer use. In 2002, C, whose taxable year ends December 31, enters into a contract to construct a building for B. In November of 2003, the building is completed in every respect necessary for its intended use, and B occupies the building. In early December of 2003, B notifies C of some minor deficiencies that need to be corrected, and C agrees to correct them in January 2004. C reasonably estimates that the cost of correcting these deficiencies will be less than five percent of the total allocable contract costs. C's contract is complete under paragraph (c)(3)(i)(A) of this section in 2003 because in that year, B used the building and C had incurred at least 95 percent of the total allocable contract costs attributable to the building. C must use a permissible method of accounting for any deficiency-related costs incurred after 2003.

Example 4. Completion—customer use. In 2001, C, whose taxable year ends December 31, agrees to construct a shopping center, which includes an adjoining parking lot, for B. By October 2002, C has finished constructing the retail portion of the shopping center. By December 2002, C has graded the entire parking lot, but has paved only one-fourth of it because inclement weather conditions prevented C from laying asphalt on the remaining three-fourths. In December 2002, B opens the retail portion of the shopping center and the paved portion of the parking lot to the general public. C reasonably estimates that the cost of paving the remaining three-fourths of the parking lot when weather permits will exceed five percent of C's total allocable contract costs. Even though B is using the subject matter of the contract, C's contract is not completed in December 2002 under paragraph (c)(3)(i)(A) of this section because C has not incurred at least 95 percent of the total allocable contract costs attributable to the subject matter.

Example 5. Completion—customer use. In 2001, C, whose taxable year ends December 31, agrees to manufacture 100 machines for B. By December 31, 2002, C has delivered 99 of the machines to B. C reasonably estimates that the cost of finishing the related work on the contract will be less than five percent of the total allocable

Reg. § 1.460-1(j)

contract costs. C's contract is not complete under paragraph (c)(3)(i)(A) of this section in 2002 because in that year, B is not using the subject matter of the contract (all 100 machines) for its intended purpose.

Example 6. Non-long-term contract activity. On January 1, 2001, C, whose taxable year ends December 31, enters into a single long-term contract to design and manufacture a satellite and to develop computer software enabling B to operate the satellite. At the end of 2001, C has not finished manufacturing the satellite. Designing the satellite and developing the computer software are non-long-term contract activities that are incident to and necessary for the taxpayer's manufacturing of the subject matter of a long-term contract because the satellite could not be manufactured without the design and would not operate without the software. Thus, under paragraph (d)(1) of this section, C must allocate these non-long-term contract activities to the long-term contract and account for the gross receipts and costs attributable to designing the satellite and developing computer software using the PCM.

Example 7. Non-long-term contract activity. C agrees to manufacture equipment for B under a long-term contract. In a separate contract, C agrees to design the equipment being manufactured for B under the long-term contract. Under paragraph (d)(1) of this section, C must allocate the gross receipts and costs related to the design to the long-term contract because designing the equipment is a non-long-term contract activity that is incident to and necessary for the manufacture of the subject matter of the long-term contract.

Example 8. Severance. On January 1, 2001, C, a construction contractor, and B, a real estate investor, enter into an agreement requiring C to build two office buildings in different areas of a large city. The agreement provides that the two office buildings will be completed by C and accepted by B in 2002 and 2003, respectively, and that C will be paid $1,000,000 and $1,500,000 for the two office buildings, respectively. The agreement will provide C with a reasonable profit from the construction of each building. Unless C is required to use the PCM to account for the contract, C is required to sever this contract under paragraph (e)(2) of this section because the buildings are independently priced, the agreement provides for separate delivery and acceptance of the buildings, and, as each building will generate a reasonable profit, a reasonable businessperson would have entered into separate agreements for the terms agreed upon for each building.

Example 9. Severance. C, a large construction contractor whose taxable year ends December 31, accounts for its construction contracts using the PCM and has elected to use the 10-percent method described in § 1.460-4(b)(6). In September 2001, C enters into an agreement to construct four buildings in four different cities. The buildings are independently priced and the contract provides a reasonable profit for each of the buildings. In addition, the agreement requires C to complete one building per year in 2002, 2003, 2004, and 2005. As of December 31, 2001, C has incurred 25 percent of the estimated total allocable contract costs attributable to one of the buildings, but only five percent of the estimated total allocable contract costs attributable to all four buildings included in the agreement. C does not request the Commissioner's consent to sever this contract. Using the 10-percent method, C does not take into account any portion of the total contract price or any incurred allocable contract costs attributable to this agreement in 2001. Upon examination of C's 2001 tax return, the Commissioner determines that C entered into one agreement for four buildings rather than four separate agreements each for one building solely to take advantage of the deferral obtained under the 10-percent method. Consequently, to clearly reflect the taxpayer's income, the Commissioner may require C to sever the agreement into four separate contracts under paragraph (e)(2) of this section because the buildings are independently priced, the agreement provides for separate delivery and acceptance of the buildings, and a reasonable businessperson would have entered into separate agreements for these buildings.

Example 10. Aggregation. In 2001, C, a shipbuilder, enters into two agreements with the Department of the Navy as the result of a single negotiation. Each agreement obligates C to manufacture a submarine. Because the submarines are of the same class, their specifications are similar. Because C has never manufactured submarines of this class, however, C anticipates that it will incur substantially higher costs to manufacture the first submarine, to be delivered in 2007, than to manufacture the second submarine, to be delivered in 2010. If the agreements are treated as separate contracts, the first contract probably will produce a substantial loss, while the second contract probably will produce substantial profit. Based upon these facts, aggregation is required under paragraph (e)(2) of this section because the submarines are interdependently priced and a reasonable businessperson would not have entered the first agreement without also entering into the second.

Reg. § 1.460-1(j)

Example 11. Aggregation. In 2001, C, a manufacturer of aircraft and related equipment, agrees to manufacture 10 military aircraft for foreign government B and to deliver the aircraft by the end of 2003. When entering into the agreement, C anticipates that it might receive production orders from B over the next 20 years for as many as 300 more of these aircraft. The negotiated contract price reflects C's and B's consideration of the expected total cost of manufacturing the 10 aircraft, the risks and opportunities associated with the agreement, and the additional factors the parties considered relevant. The negotiated price provides a profit on the sale of the 10 aircraft even if C does not receive any additional production orders from B. It is unlikely, however, that C actually would have wanted to manufacture the 10 aircraft but for the expectation that it would receive additional production orders from B. In 2003, B accepts delivery of the 10 aircraft. At that time, B orders an additional 20 aircraft of the same type for delivery in 2007. When negotiating the price for the additional 20 aircraft, C and B consider the fact that the expected unit cost for this production run of 20 aircraft will be lower than the unit cost of the 10 aircraft completed and accepted in 2003, but substantially higher than the expected unit cost of future production runs. Based upon these facts, aggregation is not permitted under paragraph (e)(2) of this section. Because the parties negotiated the prices of both agreements considering only the expected production costs and risks for each agreement standing alone, the terms and conditions agreed upon for the first agreement are independent of the terms and conditions agreed upon for the second agreement. The fact that the agreement to manufacture 10 aircraft provides a profit for C indicates that a reasonable businessperson would have entered into that agreement without entering into the agreement to manufacture the additional 20 aircraft.

Example 12. Classification and completion. In 2001, C, whose taxable year ends December 31, agrees to manufacture and install an industrial machine for B. C elects under paragraph (f) of this section to classify the agreement as a long-term manufacturing contract and to account for it using the PCM. The agreement requires C to deliver the machine in August 2003 and to install and test the machine in B's factory. In addition, the agreement requires B to accept the machine when the tests prove that the machine's performance will satisfy the environmental standards set by the Environmental Protection Agency (EPA), even if B has not obtained the required operating permit. Because of technical difficulties, C cannot deliver the machine until December 2003, when B conditionally accepts delivery. C installs the machine in December 2003 and then tests it through February 2004. B accepts the machine in February 2004, but does not obtain the operating permit from the EPA until January 2005. Under paragraph (c)(3)(i)(B) of this section, C's contract is finally completed and accepted in February 2004, even though B does not obtain the operating permit until January 2005, because C completed all its obligations under the contract and B accepted the machine in February 2004.

[Reg. § 1.460-1.]

☐ [*T.D.* 8315, 10-12-90. *Amended by T.D.* 8929, 1-10-2001.]

[Reg. § 1.460-2]

§ 1.460-2. Long-term manufacturing contracts.—(a) *In general.* Section 460 generally requires a taxpayer to determine the income from a long-term manufacturing contract using the percentage-of-completion method described in § 1.460-4(b) (PCM). A contract not completed in the contracting year is a long-term manufacturing contract if it involves the manufacture of personal property that is—

(1) A unique item of a type that is not normally carried in the finished goods inventory of the taxpayer; or

(2) An item that normally requires more than 12 calendar months to complete (regardless of the duration of the contract or the time to complete a deliverable quantity of the item).

(b) *Unique*—(1) *In general. Unique* means designed for the needs of a specific customer. To determine whether an item is designed for the needs of a specific customer, a taxpayer must consider the extent to which research, development, design, engineering, retooling, and similar activities (customizing activities) are required to manufacture the item and whether the item could be sold to other customers with little or no modification. A contract may require the taxpayer to manufacture more than one unit of a unique item. If a contract requires a taxpayer to manufacture more than one unit of the same item, the taxpayer must determine whether that item is unique by considering the customizing activities that would be needed to produce only the first unit. For the purposes of this paragraph (b), a taxpayer must consider the activities performed on its behalf by a subcontractor.

(2) *Safe harbors.* Notwithstanding paragraph (b)(1) of this section, an item is not unique if it satisfies one or more of the safe harbors in this paragraph (b)(2). If an item does not satisfy one or more safe harbors, the determination of unique-

ness will depend on the facts and circumstances. The safe harbors are:

(i) *Short production period.* An item is not unique if it normally requires 90 days or less to complete. In the case of a contract for multiple units of an item, the item is not unique only if it normally requires 90 days or less to complete each unit of the item in the contract.

(ii) *Customized item.* An item is not unique if the total allocable contract costs attributable to customizing activities that are incident to or necessary for the manufacture of the item do not exceed 10 percent of the estimated total allocable contract costs allocable to the item. In the case of a contract for multiple units of an item, this comparison must be performed on the first unit of the item and the total allocable contract costs attributable to customizing activities that are incident to or necessary for the manufacture of the first unit of the item must be allocated to that first unit.

(iii) *Inventoried item.* A unique item ceases to be unique no later than when the taxpayer normally includes similar items in its finished goods inventory.

(c) *Normal time to complete*—(1) *In general.* The amount of time normally required to complete an item is the item's reasonably expected *production period,* as described in § 1.263A-12, determined at the end of the contracting year. Thus, in general, the expected production period for an item begins when a taxpayer incurs at least five percent of the costs that would be allocable to the item under § 1.460-5 and ends when the item is ready to be held for sale and all reasonably expected production activities are complete. In the case of components that are assembled or reassembled into an item or unit at the customer's facility by the taxpayer's employees or agents, the production period ends when the components are assembled or reassembled into an operable item or unit. To the extent that several distinct activities related to the production of the item are expected to occur simultaneously, the period during which these distinct activities occur is not counted more than once. Furthermore, when determining the normal time to complete an item, a taxpayer is not required to consider activities performed or costs incurred that would not be allocable contract costs under section 460 (e.g., independent research and development expenses (as defined in § 1.460-1(b)(9)) and marketing expenses). Moreover, the time normally required to design and manufacture the first unit of an item for which the taxpayer intends to produce multiple units generally does not indicate the normal time to complete the item.

(2) *Production by related parties.* To determine the time normally required to complete an item, a taxpayer must consider all relevant production activities performed and costs incurred by itself and by related parties, as defined in § 1.460-1(b)(4). For example, if a taxpayer's item requires a component or subassembly manufactured by a related party, the taxpayer must consider the time the related party takes to complete the component or subassembly and, for purposes of determining the beginning of an item's production period, the costs incurred by the related party that are allocable to the component or subassembly. However, if both requirements of the exception for components and subassemblies under § 1.460-1(g)(1)(ii) are satisfied, a taxpayer does not consider the activities performed or the costs incurred by a related party when determining the normal time to complete an item.

(d) *Qualified ship contracts.* A taxpayer may determine the income from a long-term manufacturing contract that is a qualified ship contract using either the PCM or the percentage-of-completion/capitalized-cost method (PCCM) of accounting described in § 1.460-4(e). A *qualified ship contract* is any contract entered into after February 28, 1986, to manufacture in the United States not more than 5 seagoing vessels if the vessels will not be manufactured directly or indirectly for the United States Government and if the taxpayer reasonably expects to complete the contract within 5 years of the contract commencement date. Under § 1.460-1(e)(3)(i), a contract to produce more than 5 vessels for which the PCM would be required cannot be severed in order to be classified as a qualified ship contract.

(e) *Examples.* The following examples illustrate the rules of this section:

Example 1. Unique item and classification. In December 2001, C enters into a contract with B to design and manufacture a new type of industrial equipment. C reasonably expects the normal production period for this type of equipment to be eight months. Because the new type of industrial equipment requires a substantial amount of research, design, and engineering to produce, C determines that the equipment is a unique item and its contract with B is a long-term contract. After delivering the equipment to B in September 2002, C contracts with B to produce five additional units of that industrial equipment with certain different specifications. These additional units, which also are expected to take eight months to produce, will be delivered to B in 2003. C determines that the research, design, engineering, retooling, and similar customizing costs necessary to produce the five additional units of equipment

Reg. § 1.460-2(c)(1)

does not exceed 10 percent of the first unit's share of estimated total allocable contract costs. Consequently, the additional units of equipment satisfy the safe harbor in paragraph (b)(2)(ii) of this section and are not unique items. Although C's contract with B to produce the five additional units is not completed within the contracting year, the contract is not a long-term contract since the additional units of equipment are not unique items and do not normally require more than 12 months to produce. C must classify its second contract with B as a non-long term contract, notwithstanding that it classified the previous contract with B for a similar item as a long-term contract, because the determination of whether a contract is a long-term contract is made on a contract-by-contract basis. A change in classification is not a change in method of accounting because the change in classification results from a change in underlying facts.

Example 2. 12-month rule—related party. C manufactures cranes. C purchases one of the crane's components from R, a related party under § 1.460-1(b)(4). Less than 50 percent of R's gross receipts attributable to the sale of this component comes from sales to unrelated parties; thus, the exception for components and subassemblies under § 1.460-1(g)(1)(ii) is not satisfied. Consequently, C must consider the activities of R as R incurs costs and performs the activities rather than as C incurs a liability to R. The normal time period between the time that both C and R incur five percent of the costs allocable to the crane and the time that R completes the component is five months. C normally requires an additional eight months to complete production of the crane after receiving the integral component from R. C's crane is an item of a type that normally requires more than 12 months to complete under paragraph (c) of this section because the production period from the time that both C and R incur five percent of the costs allocable to the crane until the time that production of the crane is complete is normally 13 months.

Example 3. 12-month rule—duration of contract. The facts are the same as in *Example 2*, except that C enters into a sales contract with B on December 31, 2001 (the last day of C's taxable year), and delivers a completed crane to B on February 1, 2002. C's contract with B is a long-term contract under paragraph (a)(2) of this section because the contract is not completed in the contracting year, 2001, and the crane is an item that normally requires more than 12 calendar months to complete (regardless of the duration of the contract).

Example 4. 12-month rule—normal time to complete. The facts are the same as in *Example 2*, except that C (and R) actually complete B's crane in only 10 calendar months. The contract is a long-term contract because the normal time to complete a crane, not the actual time to complete a crane, is the relevant criterion for determining whether an item is subject to paragraph (a)(2) of this section.

Example 5. Normal time to complete. C enters into a multi-unit contract to produce four units of an item. C does not anticipate producing any additional units of the item. C expects to perform the research, design, and development that are directly allocable to the particular item and to produce the first unit in the first 24 months. C reasonably expects the production period for each of the three remaining units will be 3 months. This contract is not a contract that involves the manufacture of an item that normally requires more than 12 months to complete because the normal time to complete the item is 3 months. However, the contract does not satisfy the 90-day safe harbor for unique items because the normal time to complete the first unit of this item exceeds 90 days. Thus, the contract might involve the manufacture of a unique item depending on the facts and circumstances.

[Reg. § 1.460-2.]

☐ [*T.D.* 8315, 10-12-90. *Amended by T.D.* 8929, 1-10-2001 (*corrected* 4-5-2001).]

[Reg. § 1.460-3]

§ 1.460-3. Long-term construction contracts.—(a) *In general.* Section 460 generally requires a taxpayer to determine the income from a long-term construction contract using the percentage-of-completion method described in § 1.460-4(b) (PCM). A contract not completed in the contracting year is a long-term construction contract if it involves the building, construction, reconstruction, or rehabilitation of real property; the installation of an integral component to real property; or the improvement of real property (collectively referred to as construction). *Real property* means land, buildings, and *inherently permanent structures*, as defined in § 1.263A-8(c)(3), such as roadways, dams, and bridges. Real property does not include vessels, offshore drilling platforms, or unsevered natural products of land. An *integral component to real property* includes property not produced at the site of the real property but intended to be permanently affixed to the real property, such as elevators and central heating and cooling systems. Thus, for example, a contract to install an elevator in a building is a construction contract because a building is real property, but a contract to

Reg. § 1.460-3(a)

install an elevator in a ship is not a construction contract because a ship is not real property.

(b) *Exempt construction contracts*—(1) *In general.* The general requirement to use the PCM and the cost allocation rules described in § 1.460-5(b) or (c) does not apply to any long-term construction contract described in this paragraph (b) (exempt construction contract). *Exempt construction contract* means any—

(i) Home construction contract; and

(ii) Other construction contract that a taxpayer estimates (when entering into the contract) will be completed within 2 years of the contract commencement date, provided the taxpayer satisfies the $10,000,000 gross receipts test described in paragraph (b)(3) of this section.

(2) *Home construction contract*—(i) *In general.* A long-term construction contract is a *home construction contract* if a taxpayer (including a subcontractor working for a general contractor) reasonably expects to attribute 80 percent or more of the estimated total allocable contract costs (including the cost of land, materials, and services), determined as of the close of the contracting year, to the construction of—

(A) Dwelling units, as defined in section 168(e)(2)(A)(ii)(I), contained in buildings containing 4 or fewer dwelling units (including buildings with 4 or fewer dwelling units that also have commercial units); and

(B) Improvements to real property directly related to, and located at the site of, the dwelling units.

(ii) *Townhouses and rowhouses.* Each townhouse or rowhouse is a separate building.

(iii) *Common improvements.* A taxpayer includes in the cost of the dwelling units their allocable share of the cost that the taxpayer reasonably expects to incur for any common improvements (e.g., sewers, roads, clubhouses) that benefit the dwelling units and that the taxpayer is contractually obligated, or required by law, to construct within the tract or tracts of land that contain the dwelling units.

(iv) *Mixed use costs.* If a contract involves the construction of both commercial units and dwelling units within the same building, a taxpayer must allocate the costs among the commercial units and dwelling units using a reasonable method or combination of reasonable methods, such as specific identification, square footage, or fair market value.

(3) *$10,000,000 gross receipts test*—(i) *In general.* Except as otherwise provided in paragraphs (b)(3)(ii) and (iii) of this section, the $10,000,000 gross receipts test is satisfied if a taxpayer's (or predecessor's) average annual gross receipts for the 3 taxable years preceding the contracting year do not exceed $10,000,000, as determined using the principles of the gross receipts test for small resellers under § 1.263A-3(b).

(ii) *Single employer.* To apply the gross receipts test, a taxpayer is not required to aggregate the gross receipts of persons treated as a single employer solely under section 414(m) and any regulations prescribed under section 414.

(iii) *Attribution of gross receipts.* A taxpayer must aggregate a proportionate share of the construction-related gross receipts of any person that has a five percent or greater interest in the taxpayer. In addition, a taxpayer must aggregate a proportionate share of the construction-related gross receipts of any person in which the taxpayer has a five percent or greater interest. For this purpose, a taxpayer must determine ownership interests as of the first day of the taxpayer's contracting year and must include indirect interests in any corporation, partnership, estate, trust, or sole proprietorship according to principles similar to the constructive ownership rules under sections 1563(e), (f)(2), and (f)(3)(A). However, a taxpayer is not required to aggregate under this paragraph (b)(3)(iii) any construction-related gross receipts required to be aggregated under paragraph (b)(3)(i) of this section.

(c) *Residential construction contracts.* A taxpayer may determine the income from a long-term construction contract that is a residential construction contract using either the PCM or the percentage-of-completion/capitalized-cost method (PCCM) of accounting described in § 1.460-4(e). A *residential construction contract* is a home construction contract, as defined in paragraph (b)(2) of this section, except that the building or buildings being constructed contain more than 4 dwelling units. [Reg. § 1.460-3.]

☐ [*T.D.* 8315, 10-12-90. Amended by T.D. 8929, 1-10-2001.]

[Reg. § 1.460-4]

§ 1.460-4. Methods of accounting for long-term contracts.—(a) *Overview.* This section prescribes permissible methods of accounting for long-term contracts. Paragraph (b) of this section describes the percentage-of-completion method under section 460(b) (PCM) that a taxpayer generally must use to determine the income from a long-term contract. Paragraph (c) of this section lists permissible methods of accounting for exempt construction contracts described in § 1.460-3(b)(1) and describes the exempt-contract percentage-of-completion method (EPCM). Paragraph (d) of this section describes the completed-

Methods of Accounting

contract method (CCM), which is one of the permissible methods of accounting for exempt construction contracts. Paragraph (e) of this section describes the percentage-of-completion/capitalized-cost method (PCCM), which is a permissible method of accounting for qualified ship contracts described in § 1.460-2(d) and residential construction contracts described in § 1.460-3(c). Paragraph (f) of this section provides rules for determining the alternative minimum taxable income (AMTI) from long-term contracts that are not exempted under section 56. Paragraph (g) of this section provides rules concerning consistency in methods of accounting for long-term contracts. Paragraph (h) of this section provides examples illustrating the principles of this section. Paragraph (j) of this section provides rules for taxpayers that file consolidated tax returns. Finally, paragraph (k) of this section provides rules relating to a mid-contract change in taxpayer of a contract accounted for using a long-term contract method of accounting.

(b) *Percentage-of-completion method*—(1) *In general*. Under the PCM, a taxpayer generally must include in income the portion of the *total contract price*, as defined in paragraph (b)(4)(i) of this section, that corresponds to the percentage of the entire contract that the taxpayer has completed during the taxable year. The percentage of completion must be determined by comparing allocable contract costs incurred with estimated total allocable contract costs. Thus, the taxpayer includes a portion of the total contract price in gross income as the taxpayer incurs allocable contract costs.

(2) *Computations*. To determine the income from a long-term contract, a taxpayer—

(i) Computes the *completion factor* for the contract, which is the ratio of the cumulative allocable contract costs that the taxpayer has incurred through the end of the taxable year to the estimated total allocable contract costs that the taxpayer reasonably expects to incur under the contract;

(ii) Computes the amount of *cumulative gross receipts* from the contract by multiplying the completion factor by the total contract price;

(iii) Computes the amount of *current-year gross receipts*, which is the difference between the amount of cumulative gross receipts for the current taxable year and the amount of cumulative gross receipts for the immediately preceding taxable year (the difference can be a positive or negative number); and

(iv) Takes both the current-year gross receipts and the allocable contract costs incurred during the current year into account in computing taxable income.

(3) *Post-completion-year income*. If a taxpayer has not included the total contract price in gross income by the completion year, as defined in § 1.460-1(b)(6), the taxpayer must include the remaining portion of the total contract price in gross income for the taxable year following the completion year. For the treatment of post-completion-year costs, see paragraph (b)(5)(v) of this section. See § 1.460-6(c)(1)(ii) for application of the look-back method as a result of adjustments to total contract price.

(4) *Total contract price*—(i) *In general*—(A) *Definition*. *Total contract price* means the amount that a taxpayer reasonably expects to receive under a long-term contract, including holdbacks, retainages, and cost reimbursements. See § 1.460-6(c)(1)(ii) and (2)(vi) for application of the look-back method as a result of changes in total contract price.

(B) *Contingent compensation*. Any amount related to a contingent right under a contract, such as a bonus, award, incentive payment, and amount in dispute, is included in total contract price as soon as the taxpayer can reasonably predict that the amount will be earned, even if the all events test has not yet been met. For example, if a bonus is payable to a taxpayer for meeting an early completion date, the bonus is includible in total contract price at the time and to the extent that the taxpayer can reasonably predict the achievement of the corresponding objective. Similarly, a portion of the contract price that is in dispute is includible in total contract price at the time and to the extent that the taxpayer can reasonably predict that the dispute will be resolved in the taxpayer's favor (regardless of when the taxpayer actually receives payment or when the dispute is finally resolved). Total contract price does not include compensation that might be earned under any other agreement that the taxpayer expects to obtain from the same customer (e.g., exercised option or follow-on contract) if that other agreement is not aggregated under § 1.460-1(e). For the purposes of this paragraph (b)(4)(i)(B), a taxpayer can reasonably predict that an amount of contingent income will be earned not later than when the taxpayer includes that amount in income for financial reporting purposes under generally accepted accounting principles. If a taxpayer has not included an amount of contingent compensation in total contract price under this paragraph (b)(4)(i) by the taxable year following the completion year, the taxpayer must account for that amount of contingent compensation using a permissible method of

Reg. § 1.460-4(b)(4)

accounting. If it is determined after the taxable year following the completion year that an amount included in total contract price will not be earned, the taxpayer should deduct that amount in the year of the determination.

(C) *Non-long-term contract activities.* Total contract price includes an allocable share of the gross receipts attributable to a non-long-term contract activity, as defined in § 1.460-1(d)(2), if the activity is incident to or necessary for the manufacture, building, installation, or construction of the subject matter of the long-term contract. Total contract price also includes amounts reimbursed for independent research and development expenses (as defined in § 1.460-1(b)(9)), or for bidding and proposal costs, under a federal or cost-plus long-term contract (as defined in section 460(d)), regardless of whether the research and development, or bidding or proposal, activities are incident to or necessary for the performance of that long-term contract.

(ii) *Estimating total contract price.* A taxpayer must estimate the total contract price based upon all the facts and circumstances known as of the last day of the taxable year. For this purpose, an event that occurs after the end of the taxable year must be taken into account if its occurrence was reasonably predictable and its income was subject to reasonable estimation as of the last day of that taxable year.

(5) *Completion factor*—(i) *Allocable contract costs.* A taxpayer must use a cost allocation method permitted under either § 1.460-5(b) or (c) to determine the amount of cumulative allocable contract costs and estimated total allocable contract costs that are used to determine a contract's completion factor. Allocable contract costs include a reimbursable cost that is allocable to the contract.

(ii) *Cumulative allocable contract costs.* To determine a contract's completion factor for a taxable year, a taxpayer must take into account the cumulative allocable contract costs that have been incurred, as defined in § 1.460-1(b)(8), through the end of the taxable year.

(iii) *Estimating total allocable contract costs.* A taxpayer must estimate total allocable contract costs for each long-term contract based upon all the facts and circumstances known as of the last day of the taxable year. For this purpose, an event that occurs after the end of the taxable year must be taken into account if its occurrence was reasonably predictable and its cost was subject to reasonable estimation as of the last day of that taxable year. To be considered reasonable, an estimate of total allocable contract costs must include costs attributable to delay, rework, change orders, technology or design problems, or other problems that reasonably can be predicted considering the nature of the contract and prior experience. However, estimated total allocable contract costs do not include any contingency allowance for costs that, as of the end of the taxable year, are not reasonably predicted to be incurred in the performance of the contract. For example, estimated total allocable contract costs do not include any costs attributable to factors not reasonably predictable at the end of the taxable year, such as third-party litigation, extreme weather conditions, strikes, and delays in securing required permits and licenses. In addition, the estimated costs of performing other agreements that are not aggregated with the contract under § 1.460-1(e) that the taxpayer expects to incur with the same customer (e.g., follow-on contracts) are not included in estimated total allocable contract costs for the initial contract.

(iv) *Pre-contracting-year costs.* If a taxpayer reasonably expects to enter into a long-term contract in a future taxable year, the taxpayer must capitalize all costs incurred prior to entering into the contract that will be allocable to that contract (e.g., bidding and proposal costs). A taxpayer is not required to compute a completion factor, or to include in gross income any amount, related to allocable contract costs for any taxable year ending before the contracting year or, if applicable, the 10-percent year defined in paragraph (b)(6)(i) of this section. In that year, the taxpayer is required to compute a completion factor that includes all allocable contract costs that have been incurred as of the end of that taxable year (whether previously capitalized or deducted) and to take into account in computing taxable income the related gross receipts and the previously capitalized allocable contract costs. If, however, a taxpayer determines in a subsequent year that it will not enter into the long-term contract, the taxpayer must account for these pre-contracting-year costs in that year (e.g., as a deduction or an inventoriable cost) using the appropriate rules contained in other sections of the Code or regulations.

(v) *Post-completion-year costs.* If a taxpayer incurs an allocable contract cost after the completion year, the taxpayer must account for that cost using a permissible method of accounting. See § 1.460-6(c)(1)(ii) for application of the look-back method as a result of adjustments to allocable contract costs.

(6) *10-percent method*—(i) *In general.* Instead of determining the income from a long-term contract beginning with the contracting year, a taxpayer may elect to use the 10-percent method

Reg. § 1.460-4(b)(5)

under section 460(b)(5). Under the 10-percent method, a taxpayer does not include in gross income any amount related to allocable contract costs until the taxable year in which the taxpayer has incurred at least 10 percent of the estimated total allocable contract costs (10-percent year). A taxpayer must treat costs incurred before the 10-percent year as pre-contracting-year costs described in paragraph (b)(5)(iv) of this section.

(ii) *Election.* A taxpayer makes an election under this paragraph (b)(6) by using the 10-percent method for all long-term contracts entered into during the taxable year of the election on its original federal income tax return for the election year. This election is a method of accounting and, thus, applies to all long-term contracts entered into during and after the taxable year of the election. An electing taxpayer must use the 10-percent method to apply the look-back method under § 1.460-6 and to determine alternative minimum taxable income under paragraph (f) of this section. This election is not available if a taxpayer uses the simplified cost-to-cost method described in § 1.460-5(c) to compute the completion factor of a long-term contract.

(7) *Terminated contract*—(i) *Reversal of income.* If a long-term contract is terminated before completion and, as a result, the taxpayer retains ownership of the property that is the subject matter of that contract, the taxpayer must reverse the transaction in the taxable year of termination. To reverse the transaction, the taxpayer reports a loss (or gain) equal to the cumulative allocable contract costs reported under the contract in all prior taxable years less the cumulative gross receipts reported under the contract in all prior taxable years.

(ii) *Adjusted basis.* As a result of reversing the transaction under paragraph (b)(7)(i) of this section, a taxpayer will have an adjusted basis in the retained property equal to the cumulative allocable contract costs reported under the contract in all prior taxable years. However, if the taxpayer received and retains any consideration or compensation from the customer, the taxpayer must reduce the adjusted basis in the retained property (but not below zero) by the fair market value of that consideration or compensation. To the extent that the amount of the consideration or compensation described in the preceding sentence exceeds the adjusted basis in the retained property, the taxpayer must include the excess in gross income for the taxable year of termination.

(iii) *Look-back method.* The look-back method does not apply to a terminated contract that is subject to this paragraph (b)(7).

(c) *Exempt contract methods*—(1) *In general.* An *exempt contract method* means the method of accounting that a taxpayer must use to account for all its long-term contracts (and any portion of a long-term contract) that are exempt from the requirements of section 460(a). Thus, an exempt contract method applies to exempt construction contracts, as defined in § 1.460-3(b); the non-PCM portion of a qualified ship contract, as defined in § 1.460-2(d); and the non-PCM portion of a residential construction contract, as defined in § 1.460-3(c). Permissible exempt contract methods include the PCM, the EPCM described in paragraph (c)(2) of this section, the CCM described in paragraph (d) of this section, or any other permissible method. See section 446.

(2) *Exempt-contract percentage-of-completion method*—(i) *In general.* Similar to the PCM described in paragraph (b) of this section, a taxpayer using the EPCM generally must include in income the portion of the total contract price, as described in paragraph (b)(4) of this section, that corresponds to the percentage of the entire contract that the taxpayer has completed during the taxable year. However, under the EPCM, the percentage of completion may be determined as of the end of the taxable year by using any method of cost comparison (such as comparing direct labor costs incurred to date to estimated total direct labor costs) or by comparing the work performed on the contract with the estimated total work to be performed, rather than by using the cost-to-cost comparison required by paragraphs (b)(2)(i) and (5) of this section, provided such method is used consistently and clearly reflects income. In addition, paragraph (b)(3) of this section (regarding post-completion-year income), paragraph (b)(6) of this section (regarding the 10-percent method) and § 1.460-6 (regarding the look-back method) do not apply to the EPCM.

(ii) *Determination of work performed.* For purposes of the EPCM, the criteria used to compare the work performed on a contract as of the end of the taxable year with the estimated total work to be performed must clearly reflect the earning of income with respect to the contract. For example, in the case of a roadbuilder, a standard of completion solely based on miles of roadway completed in a case where the terrain is substantially different may not clearly reflect the earning of income with respect to the contract.

(d) *Completed-contract method*—(1) *In general.* Except as otherwise provided in paragraph (d)(4) of this section, a taxpayer using the CCM to account for a long-term contract must take into account in the contract's completion year, as defined in § 1.460-1(b)(6), the gross contract price

Reg. § 1.460-4(d)(1)

and all allocable contract costs incurred by the completion year. A taxpayer may not treat the cost of any materials and supplies that are allocated to a contract, but actually remain on hand when the contract is completed, as an allocable contract cost.

(2) *Post-completion-year income and costs.* If a taxpayer has not included an item of contingent compensation (i.e., amounts for which the all events test has not been satisfied) in gross contract price under paragraph (d)(3) of this section by the completion year, the taxpayer must account for this item of contingent compensation using a permissible method of accounting. If a taxpayer incurs an allocable contract cost after the completion year, the taxpayer must account for that cost using a permissible method of accounting.

(3) *Gross contract price.* Gross contract price includes all amounts (including holdbacks, retainages, and reimbursements) that a taxpayer is entitled by law or contract to receive, whether or not the amounts are due or have been paid. In addition, gross contract price includes all bonuses, awards, and incentive payments, such as a bonus for meeting an early completion date, to the extent the all events test is satisfied. If a taxpayer performs a non-long-term contract activity, as defined in § 1.460-1(d)(2), that is incident to or necessary for the manufacture, building, installation, or construction of the subject matter of one or more of the taxpayer's long-term contracts, the taxpayer must include an allocable share of the gross receipts attributable to that activity in the gross contract price of the contract(s) benefitted by that activity. Gross contract price also includes amounts reimbursed for independent research and development expenses (as defined in § 1.460-1(b)(9)), or bidding and proposal costs, under a federal or cost-plus long-term contract (as defined in section 460(d)), regardless of whether the research and development, or bidding and proposal, activities are incident to or necessary for the performance of that long-term contract.

(4) *Contracts with disputed claims*—(i) *In general.* The special rules in this paragraph (d)(4) apply to a long-term contract accounted for using the CCM with a dispute caused by a customer's requesting a reduction of the gross contract price or the perfomance of additional work under the contract or by a taxpayer's requesting an increase in gross contract price, or both, on or after the date a taxpayer has tendered the subject matter of the contract to the customer.

(ii) *Taxpayer assured of profit or loss.* If the disputed amount relates to a customer's claim for either a reduction in price or additional work and the taxpayer is assured of either a profit or a loss on a long-term contract regardless of the outcome of the dispute, the gross contract price, reduced (but not below zero) by the amount reasonably in dispute, must be taken into account in the completion year. If the disputed amount relates to a taxpayer's claim for an increase in price and the taxpayer is assured of either a profit or a loss on a long-term contract regardless of the outcome of the dispute, the gross contract price must be taken into account in the completion year. If the taxpayer is assured a profit on the contract, all allocable contract costs incurred by the end of the completion year are taken into account in that year. If the taxpayer is assured a loss on the contract, all allocable contract costs incurred by the end of the completion year, reduced by the amount reasonably in dispute, are taken into account in the completion year.

(iii) *Taxpayer unable to determine profit or loss.* If the amount reasonably in dispute affects so much of the gross contract price or allocable contract costs that a taxpayer cannot determine whether a profit or loss ultimately will be realized from a long-term contract, the taxpayer may not take any of the gross contract price or allocable contract costs into account in the completion year.

(iv) *Dispute resolved.* Any part of the gross contract price and any allocable contract costs that have not been taken into account because of the principles described in paragraph (d)(4)(i), (ii), or (iii) of this section must be taken into account in the taxable year in which the dispute is resolved. If a taxpayer performs additional work under the contract because of the dispute, the term *taxable year in which the dispute is resolved* means the taxable year the additional work is completed, rather than the taxable year in which the outcome of the dispute is determined by agreement, decision, or otherwise.

(e) *Percentage-of-completion/capitalized-cost method.* Under the PCCM, a taxpayer must determine the income from a long-term contract using the PCM for the applicable percentage of the contract and its exempt contract method, as defined in paragraph (c) of this section, for the remaining percentage of the contract. For residential construction contracts described in § 1.460-3(c), the applicable percentage is 70 percent, and the remaining percentage is 30 percent. For qualified ship contracts described in § 1.460-2(d), the applicable percentage is 40 percent, and the remaining percentage is 60 percent.

(f) *Alternative minimum taxable income*—(1) *In general.* Under section 56(a)(3), a taxpayer (not exempt from the AMT under section 55(e))

Reg. § 1.460-4(d)(2)

must use the PCM to determine its AMTI from any long-term contract entered into on or after March 1, 1986, that is not a home construction contract, as defined in § 1.460-3(b)(2). For AMTI purposes, the PCM must include any election under paragraph (b)(6) of this section (concerning the 10-percent method) or under § 1.460-5(c) (concerning the simplified cost-to-cost method) that the taxpayer has made for regular tax purposes. For exempt construction contracts described in § 1.460-3(b)(1)(ii), a taxpayer must use the simplified cost-to-cost method to determine the completion factor for AMTI purposes. Except as provided in paragraph (f)(2) of this section, a taxpayer must use AMTI costs and AMTI methods, such as the depreciation method described in section 56(a)(1), to determine the completion factor of a long-term contract (except a home construction contract) for AMTI purposes.

(2) *Election to use regular completion factors.* Under this paragraph (f)(2), a taxpayer may elect for AMTI purposes to determine the completion factors of all of its long-term contracts using the methods of accounting and allocable contract costs used for regular federal income tax purposes. A taxpayer makes this election by using regular methods and regular costs to compute the completion factors of all long-term contracts entered into during the taxable year of the election for AMTI purposes on its original federal income tax return for the election year. This election is a method of accounting and, thus, applies to all long-term contracts entered into during and after the taxable year of the election. Although a taxpayer may elect to compute the completion factor of its long-term contracts using regular methods and regular costs, an election under this paragraph (f)(2) does not eliminate a taxpayer's obligation to comply with the requirements of section 55 when computing AMTI. For example, although a taxpayer may elect to use the depreciation methods used for regular tax purposes to compute the completion factor of its long-term contracts for AMTI purposes, the taxpayer must use the depreciation methods permitted by section 56 to compute AMTI.

(g) *Method of accounting.* A taxpayer that uses the PCM, EPCM, CCM, or PCCM, or elects the 10-percent method or special AMTI method (or changes to another method of accounting with the Commissioner's consent) must apply the method(s) consistently for all similarly classified long-term contracts, until the taxpayer obtains the Commissioner's consent under section 446(e) to change to another method of accounting. A taxpayer-initiated change in method of accounting will be permitted only on a cut-off basis (i.e., for contracts entered into on or after the year of change), and thus, a section 481(a) adjustment will not be permitted or required.

(h) *Examples.* The following examples illustrate the rules of this section:

Example 1. PCM—estimating total contract price. C, whose taxable year ends December 31, determines the income from long-term contracts using the PCM. On January 1, 2001, C enters into a contract to design and manufacture a satellite (a unique item). The contract provides that C will be paid $10,000,000 for delivering the completed satellite by December 1, 2002. The contract also provides that C will receive a $3,000,000 bonus for delivering the satellite by July 1, 2002, and an additional $4,000,000 bonus if the satellite successfully performs its mission for five years. C is unable to reasonably predict if the satellite will successfully perform its mission for five years. If on December 31, 2001, C should reasonably expect to deliver the satellite by July 1, 2002, the estimated total contract price is $13,000,000 ($10,000,000 unit price + $3,000,000 production-related bonus). Otherwise, the estimated total contract price is $10,000,000. In either event, the $4,000,000 bonus is not includible in the estimated total contract price as of December 31, 2001, because C is unable to reasonably predict that the satellite will successfully perform its mission for five years.

Example 2. PCM—computing income. (i) C, whose taxable year ends December 31, determines the income from long-term contracts using the PCM. During 2001, C agrees to manufacture for the customer, B, a unique item for a total contract price of $1,000,000. Under C's contract, B is entitled to retain 10 percent of the total contract price until it accepts the item. By the end of 2001, C has incurred $200,000 of allocable contract costs and estimates that the total allocable contract costs will be $800,000. By the end of 2002, C has incurred $600,000 of allocable contract costs and estimates that the total allocable contract costs will be $900,000. In 2003, after completing the contract, C determines that the actual cost to manufacture the item was $750,000.

(ii) For each of the taxable years, C's income from the contract is computed as follows:

Reg. § 1.460-4(h)

Methods of Accounting

See p. 20,601 for regulations not amended to reflect law changes

		Taxable Year		
		2001	2002	2003
(A)	Cumulative incurred costs	$ 200,000	$ 600,000	$ 750,000
(B)	Estimated total costs	800,000	900,000	750,000
(C)	Completion factor: (A) ÷ (B)	25.00%	66.67%	100.00%
(D)	Total contract price	1,000,000	1,000,000	1,000,000
(E)	Cumulative gross receipts: (C) × (D)	250,000	666,667	1,000,000
(F)	Cumulative gross receipts (prior year):	(0)	(250,000)	(666,667)
(G)	Current-year gross receipts	250,000	416,667	333,333
(H)	Cumulative incurred costs	200,000	600,000	750,000
(I)	Cumulative incurred costs (prior year):	(0)	(200,000)	(600,000)
(J)	Current-year costs	200,000	400,000	150,000
(K)	Gross income: (G) − (J)	$ 50,000	$ 16,667	$ 183,333

Example 3. *PCM—computing income with cost sharing.* (i) C, whose taxable year ends December 31, determines the income from long-term contracts using the PCM. During 2001, C enters into a contract to manufacture a unique item. The contract specifies a target price of $1,000,000, a target cost of $600,000, and a target profit of $400,000. C and B will share the savings of any cost underrun (actual total incurred cost is less than target cost) and the additional cost of any cost overrun (actual total incurred cost is greater than target cost) as follows: 30 percent to C and 70 percent to B. By the end of 2001, C has incurred $200,000 of allocable contract costs and estimates that the total allocable contract costs will be $600,000. By the end of 2002, C has incurred $300,000 of allocable contract costs and estimates that the total allocable contract costs will be $400,000. In 2003, after completing the contract, C determines that the actual cost to manufacture the item was $700,000.

(ii) For each of the taxable years, C's income from the contract is computed as follows (note that the sharing of any cost underrun or cost overrun is reflected as an adjustment to C's target price under paragraph (b)(4)(i) of this section):

		Taxable Year		
		2001	2002	2003
(A)	Cumulative incurred costs	$ 200,000	$ 300,000	$ 700,000
(B)	Estimated total costs	600,000	400,000	700,000
(C)	Completion factor: (A) ÷ (B)	33.33%	75.00%	100.00%
(D)	Target price	$1,000,000	$1,000,000	$1,000,000
(E)	Estimated total costs	600,000	400,000	700,000
(F)	Target costs	600,000	600,000	600,000
(G)	Cost (underrun)/overrun: (E) − (F)	0	(200,000)	100,000
(H)	Adjustment rate	70%	70%	70%
(I)	Target price adjustment	0	(140,000)	70,000
(J)	Total contract price: (D) + (I)	$1,000,000	$ 860,000	$1,070,000
(K)	Cumulative gross receipts: (C) × (J)	$ 333,333	$ 645,000	$1,070,000
(L)	Cumulative gross receipts (prior year):	(0)	(333,333)	(645,000)
(M)	Current-year gross receipts	333,333	311,667	425,000
(N)	Cumulative incurred costs	200,000	300,000	700,000
(O)	Cumulative incurred costs (prior year):	(0)	(200,000)	(300,000)
(P)	Current-year costs	200,000	100,000	400,000
(Q)	Gross income: (M) − (P)	$ 133,333	$ 211,667	$ 25,000

Example 4. *PCM—10 percent method.* (i) C, whose taxable year ends December 31, determines the income from long-term contracts using the PCM. In November 2001, C agrees to manufacture a unique item for $1,000,000. C reasonably estimates that the total allocable contract costs will be $600,000. By December 31, 2001, C has received $50,000 in progress payments and in-

Reg. § 1.460-4(h)

curred $40,000 of costs. C elects to use the 10 percent method effective for 2001 and all subsequent taxable years. During 2002, C receives $500,000 in progress payments and incurs $260,000 of costs. In 2003, C incurs an additional $300,000 of costs, C finishes manufacturing the item, and receives the final $450,000 payment.

(ii) For each of the taxable years, C's income from the contract is computed as follows:

		Taxable Year		
		2001	2002	2003
(A)	Cumulative incurred costs	$ 40,000	$ 300,000	$ 600,000
(B)	Estimated total costs	600,000	600,000	600,000
(C)	Completion factor (A) ÷ (B)	6.67%	50.00%	100.00%
(D)	Total contract price	1,000,000	1,000,000	1,000,000
(E)	Cumulative gross receipts: (C) × (D)*	0	500,000	1,000,000
(F)	Cumulative gross receipts (prior year):	(0)	(0)	(500,000)
(G)	Current-year gross receipts	0	500,000	500,000
(H)	Cumulative incurred costs	0	300,000	600,000
(I)	Cumulative incurred costs (prior year):	(0)	(0)	(300,000)
(J)	Current-year costs	0	300,000	300,000
(K)	Gross income: (G) − (J)	$ 0	$ 200,000	$ 200,000

* Unless (C) < 10 percent.

Example 5. PCM-contract terminated. C, whose taxable year ends December 31, determines the income from long-term contracts using the PCM. During 2001, C buys land and begins constructing a building that will contain 50 condominium units on that land. C enters into a contract to sell one unit in this condominium to B for $240,000. B gives C a $5,000 deposit toward the purchase price. By the end of 2001, C has incurred $50,000 of allocable contract costs on B's unit and estimates that the total allocable contract costs on B's unit will be $150,000. Thus, for 2001, C reports gross receipts of $80,000 ($50,000 ÷ $150,000 × $240,000), current-year costs of $50,000, and gross income of $30,000 ($80,000 − $50,000). In 2002, after C has incurred an additional $25,000 of allocable contract costs on B's unit, B files for bankruptcy protection and defaults on the contract with C, who is permitted to keep B's $5,000 deposit as liquidated damages. In 2002, C reverses the transaction with B under paragraph(b)(7) of this section and reports a loss of $30,000 ($50,000 − $80,000). In addition, C obtains an adjusted basis in the unit sold to B of $70,000 ($50,000 (current-year costs deducted in 2001) − $5,000 (B's forfeited deposit) + $25,000 (current-year costs incurred in 2002). C may not apply the look-back method to this contract in 2002.

Example 6. CCM-contracts with disputes from customer claims. In 2001, C, whose taxable year ends December 31, uses the CCM to account for exempt construction contracts. C enters into a contract to construct a bridge for B. The terms of the contract provide for a $1,000,000 gross contract price. C finishes the bridge in 2002 at a cost of $950,000. When B examines the bridge, B insists that C either repaint several girders or reduce the contract price. The amount reasonably in dispute is $10,000. In 2003, C and B resolve their dispute, C repaints the girders at a cost of $6,000, and C and B agree that the contract price is not to be reduced. Because C is assured a profit of $40,000 ($1,000,000 − $10,000 − $950,000) in 2002 even if the dispute is resolved in B's favor, C must take this $40,000 into account in 2002. In 2003, C will earn an additional $4,000 profit ($1,000,000 − $956,000 − $40,000) from the contract with B. Thus, C must take into account an additional $10,000 of gross contract price and $6,000 of additional contract costs in 2003.

Example 7. CCM-contracts with disputes from taxpayer claims. In 2003, C, whose taxable year ends December 31, uses the CCM to account for exempt construction contracts. C enters into a contract to construct a building for B. The terms of the contract provide for a $1,000,000 gross contract price. C finishes the building in 2004 at a cost of $1,005,000. B examines the building in 2004 and agrees that it meets the contract's specifications; however, at the end of 2004, C and B are unable to agree on the merits of C's claim for an additional $10,000 for items that C alleges are changes in contract specifications and B alleges are within the scope of the contract's original specifications. In 2005, B agrees to pay C an additional $2,000 to satisfy C's claims under the contract. Because the amount in dispute affects so much of the gross contract price that C cannot determine in 2004 whether a profit or loss will

Reg. § 1.460-4(h)

ultimately be realized, C may not taken any of the gross contract price or allocable contract costs into account in 2004. C must take into account $1,002,000 of gross contract price and $1,005,000 of allocable contract costs in 2005.

Example 8. CCM-contracts with disputes from taxpayer and customer claims. C, whose taxable year ends December 31, uses the CCM to account for exempt construction contracts. C constructs a factory for B pursuant to a long-term contract. Under the terms of the contract, B agrees to pay C a total of $1,000,000 for construction of the factory. C finishes construction of the factory in 2002 at a cost of $1,020,000. When B takes possession of the factory and begins operations in December 2002, B is dissatisfied with the location and workmanship of certain heating ducts. As of the end of 2002, C contends that the heating ducts are constructed in accordance with contract specifications. The amount of the gross contract price reasonably in dispute with respect to the heating ducts is $6,000. As of this time, C is claiming $14,000 in addition to the original contract price for certain changes in contract specifications which C alleges have increased his costs. B denies that these changes have increased C's costs. In 2003, the disputes between C and B are resolved by performance of additional work by C at a cost of $1,000 and by an agreement that the contract price would be revised downward to $996,000. Under these circumstances, C must include in his gross income for 2002, $994,000 (the gross contract price less the amount reasonably in dispute because of B's claim, or $1,000,000 − $6,000). In 2002, C must also take into account $1,000,000 of allocable contract costs (costs incurred less the amounts in dispute attributable to both B's and C's claims, or $1,020,000 − $6,000 − $14,000). In 2003, C must take into account an additional $2,000 of gross contract price ($996,000 − $994,000) and $21,000 of allocable contract costs ($1,021,000 − $1,000,000).

(i) [Reserved]

(j) *Consolidated groups and controlled groups*—(1) *Intercompany transactions*—(i) *In general.* Section 1.1502-13 does not apply to the income, gain, deduction, or loss from an intercompany transaction between members of a consolidated group, and section 267(f) does not apply to these items from an intercompany sale between members of a controlled group, to the extent—

(A) The transaction or sale directly or indirectly benefits, or is intended to benefit, another member's long-term contract with a nonmember;

(B) The selling member is required under section 460 to determine any part of its gross income from the transaction or sale under the percentage-of-completion method (PCM); and

(C) The member with the long-term contract is required under section 460 to determine any part of its gross income from the long-term contract under the PCM.

(ii) *Definitions and nomenclature.* The definitions and nomenclature under § 1.1502-13 and § 1.267(f)-1 apply for purposes of this paragraph (j).

(2) *Example.* The following example illustrates the principles of paragraph (j)(1) of this section.

Example. Corporations P, S, and B file consolidated returns on a calendar-year basis. In 1996, B enters into a long-term contract with X, a nonmember, to manufacture 5 airplanes for $500 million, with delivery scheduled for 1999. Section 460 requires B to determine the gross income from its contract with X under the PCM. S enters into a contract with B to manufacture for $50 million the engines that B will install on X's airplanes. Section 460 requires S to determine the gross income from its contract with B under the PCM. S estimates that it will incur $40 million of total contract costs during 1997 and 1998 to manufacture the engines. S incurs $10 million of contract costs in 1997 and $30 million in 1998. Under paragraph (j) of this section, S determines its gross income from the long-term contract under the PCM rather than taking its income or loss into account under section 267(f) or § 1.1502-13. Thus, S includes $12.5 million of gross receipts and $10 million of contract costs in gross income in 1997 and includes $37.5 million of gross receipts and $30 million of contract costs in gross income in 1998.

(3) *Effective dates*—(i) *In general.* This paragraph (j) applies with respect to transactions and sales occurring pursuant to contracts entered into in years beginning on or after July 12, 1995.

(ii) *Prior law.* For transactions and sales occurring pursuant to contracts entered into in years beginning before July 12, 1995, see the applicable regulations issued under sections 267(f) and 1502, including §§ 1.267(f)-1T, 1.267(f)-2T, and 1.1502-13(n) (as contained in the 26 CFR part 1 edition revised as of April 1, 1995).

(4) *Consent to change method of accounting.* For transactions and sales to which this paragraph (j) applies, the Commissioner's consent under section 446(e) is hereby granted to the extent any changes in method of accounting are necessary solely to comply with this section, provided the changes are made in the first taxable year of the taxpayer to which the rules of this paragraph (j) apply. Changes in method of ac-

counting for these transactions are to be effected on a cut-off basis.

(k) *Mid-contract change in taxpayer*—(1) *In general.* The rules in this paragraph (k) apply if prior to the completion of a long-term contract accounted for using a long-term contract method by a taxpayer (old taxpayer), there is a transaction that makes another taxpayer (new taxpayer) responsible for accounting for income from the same contract. For purposes of this paragraph (k) and § 1.460-6(g), an old taxpayer also includes any old taxpayer(s) (e.g., predecessors) of the old taxpayer. In addition, a change in status from taxable to tax exempt or from domestic to foreign, or vice versa, will be considered a change in taxpayer. Finally, a contract will be treated as the same contract if the terms of the contract are not substantially changed in connection with the transaction, whether or not the customer agrees to release the old taxpayer from any or all of its obligations under the contract. The rules governing constructive completion transactions are provided in paragraph (k)(2) of this section, while the rules governing step-in-the-shoes transactions are provided in paragraph (k)(3) of this section. Special rules related to the treatment of certain partnership transactions are reserved under paragraphs (k)(2)(iv) and (k)(3)(v) of this section. For application of the look-back method to mid-contract changes in taxpayers for contracts accounted for using the PCM, see § 1.460-6(g).

(2) *Constructive completion transactions*—(i) *Scope.* The constructive completion rules in this paragraph (k)(2) apply to transactions (constructive completion transactions) that result in a change in the taxpayer responsible for reporting income from a contract and that are not described in paragraph (k)(3)(i) of this section. Constructive completion transactions generally include, for example, taxable sales under section 1001 and deemed asset sales under section 338.

(ii) *Old taxpayer.* The old taxpayer is treated as completing the contract on the date of the transaction. The total contract price (or, gross contract price in the case of a long-term contract accounted for under the CCM) for the old taxpayer is the sum of any amounts realized from the transaction that are allocable to the contract and any amounts the old taxpayer has received or reasonably expects to receive under the contract. Total contract price (or gross contract price) is reduced by any amount paid by the old taxpayer to the new taxpayer, and by any transaction costs, that are allocable to the contract. Thus, the old taxpayer's allocable contract costs determined under paragraph (b)(5) of this section do not include any consideration paid, or costs incurred, as a result of the transaction that are allocable to the contract. In the case of a transaction subject to section 338 or 1060, the amount realized from the transaction allocable to the contract is determined by using the residual method under §§ 1.338-6 and 1.338-7.

(iii) *New taxpayer.* The new taxpayer is treated as entering into a new contract on the date of the transaction. The new taxpayer must evaluate whether the new contract should be classified as a long-term contract within the meaning of § 1.460-1(b) and account for the contract under a permissible method of accounting. For a new taxpayer who accounts for a contract using the PCM, the total contract price is any amount the new taxpayer reasonably expects to receive under the contract consistent with paragraph (b)(4) of this section. Total contract price is reduced by the amount of any consideration paid by the new taxpayer as a result of the transaction, and by any transaction costs, that are allocable to the contract and is increased by the amount of any consideration received by the new taxpayer as a result of the transaction that is allocable to the contract. Similarly, the gross contract price for a contract accounted for using the CCM is all amounts the new taxpayer is entitled by law or contract to receive consistent with paragraph (d)(3) of this section, adjusted for any consideration paid (or received) by the new taxpayer as a result of the transaction, and for any transaction costs, that are allocable to the contract. Thus, the new taxpayer's allocable contract costs determined under paragraph (b)(5) of this section do not include any consideration paid, or costs incurred, as a result of the transaction that are allocable to the contract. In the case of a transaction subject to sections 338 or 1060, the amount of consideration paid that is allocable to the contract is determined by using the residual method under §§ 1.338-6 and 1.338-7.

(iv) *Special rules relating to distributions of certain contracts by a partnership.* [Reserved]

(3) *Step-in-the-shoes transactions*—(i) *Scope.* The step-in-the-shoes rules in this paragraph (k)(3) apply to the following transactions that result in a change in the taxpayer responsible for reporting income from a contract accounted for using a long-term contract method of accounting (step-in-the-shoes transactions)—

(A) Transfers to which section 361 applies if the transfer is in connection with a reorganization described in section 368(a)(1)(A), (C) or (F);

(B) Transfers to which section 361 applies if the transfer is in connection with a reorganization described in section 368(a)(1)(D) or (G), provided the requirements of section 354(b)(1)(A) and (B) are met;

Reg. § 1.460-4(k)(3)

(C) Distributions to which section 332 applies, provided the contract is transferred to an 80-percent distributee;

(D) Transfers described in section 351;

(E) Transfers to which section 361 applies if the transfer is in connection with a reorganization described in section 368(a)(1)(D) with respect to which the requirements of section 355 (or so much of section 356 as relates to section 355) are met;

(F) Transfers (e.g., sales) of S corporation stock;

(G) Conversion to or from an S corporation;

(H) Members joining or leaving a consolidated group;

(I) Contributions to which section 721(a) applies;

(J) Transfers of partnership interests;

(K) Distributions to which section 731 applies (other than the distribution of the contract); and

(L) Any other transaction designated in the Internal Revenue Bulletin by the Internal Revenue Service. See § 601.601(d)(2)(ii) of this chapter.

(ii) *Old taxpayer*—(A) *In general.* The new taxpayer will "step into the shoes" of the old taxpayer with respect to the contract. Thus, the old taxpayer's obligation to account for the contract terminates on the date of the transaction and is assumed by the new taxpayer, as set forth in paragraph (k)(3)(iii) of this section. As a result, an old taxpayer using the PCM is required to recognize income from the contract based on the cumulative allocable contract costs incurred as of the date of the transaction. Similarly, an old taxpayer using the CCM is not required to recognize any revenue and may not deduct allocable contract costs incurred with respect to the contract.

(B) *Gain realized on the transaction.* The amount of gain the old taxpayer realizes on the transfer of a contract in a step-in-the-shoes transaction must be determined after application of paragraph (k)(3)(ii)(A) of this section using the rules of paragraph (k)(2) of this section that apply to constructive completion transactions. (The amount of gain realized on a transfer of a contract is relevant, for example, in determining the amount of gain recognized with respect to the contract in a section 351 transaction in which the old taxpayer receives from the new taxpayer money or property other than stock of the transferee.)

(iii) *New taxpayer*—(A) *Method of accounting.* Beginning on the date of the transaction, the new taxpayer must account for the long-term contract by using the same method of accounting used by the old taxpayer prior to the transaction. The same method of accounting must be used for such contract regardless of whether the old taxpayer's method is the new taxpayer's principal method of accounting under § 1.381(c)(4)-1(b)(3) or whether the new taxpayer is otherwise eligible to use the old taxpayer's method. Thus, if the old taxpayer uses the PCM to account for the contract, the new taxpayer steps into the shoes of the old taxpayer with respect to its completion factor and percentage of completion methods (such as the 10-percent method), even if the new taxpayer has not elected such methods for similarly classified contracts. Similarly, if the old taxpayer uses the CCM, the new taxpayer steps into the shoes of the old taxpayer with respect to the CCM, even if the new taxpayer is not otherwise eligible to use the CCM. However, the new taxpayer is not necessarily bound by the old taxpayer's method for similarly classified contracts entered into by the new taxpayer subsequent to the transaction and must apply general tax principles, including section 381, to determine the appropriate method to account for these subsequent contracts. To the extent that general tax principles allow the taxpayer to account for similarly classified contracts using a method other than the old taxpayer's method, the taxpayer is not required to obtain the consent of the Commissioner to begin using such other method.

(B) *Contract price.* In the case of a long-term contract that has been accounted for under PCM, the total contract price for the new taxpayer is the sum of any amounts the old taxpayer or the new taxpayer has received or reasonably expects to receive under the contract consistent with paragraph (b)(4) of this section. Similarly, the gross contract price in the case of a long-term contract accounted for under the CCM includes all amounts the old taxpayer or the new taxpayer is entitled by law or by contract to receive consistent with paragraph (d)(3) of this section.

(C) *Contract costs.* Total allocable contract costs for the new taxpayer are the allocable contract costs as defined under paragraph (b)(5) of this section incurred by either the old taxpayer prior to, or the new taxpayer after, the transaction. Thus, any payments between the old taxpayer and the new taxpayer with respect to the contract in connection with the transaction are not treated as allocable contract costs.

(iv) *Special rules related to certain corporate transactions*—(A) *Old taxpayer—basis adjustment*—(*1*) *In general.* Except as provided in paragraph (k)(3)(iv)(A)(2) of this section, in the case of a transaction described in paragraph (k)(3)(i)(D) or (E) of this section, the old taxpayer must adjust its basis in the stock of the new taxpayer by—

(i) Increasing such basis by the amount of gross receipts the old taxpayer has recognized under the contract; and

(ii) Reducing such basis by the amount of gross receipts the old taxpayer has received or reasonably expects to receive under the contract.

(2) *Basis adjustment in excess of stock basis.* If the old and new taxpayer do not join in the filing of a consolidated Federal income tax return, the old taxpayer may not adjust its basis in the stock of the new taxpayer under paragraph (k)(3)(iv)(A)(1) of this section below zero and the old taxpayer must recognize ordinary income to the extent the basis in the stock of the new taxpayer otherwise would be adjusted below zero. If the old and new taxpayer join in the filing of a consolidated Federal income tax return, the old taxpayer must create an (or increase an existing) excess loss account to the extent the basis in the stock of the new taxpayer otherwise would be adjusted below zero under paragraph (k)(3)(iv)(A)(1) of this section. See §§ 1.1502-19 and 1.1502-32(a)(3)(ii).

(3) *Subsequent dispositions of certain contracts.* If the old taxpayer disposes of a contract in a transaction described in paragraph (k)(3)(i)(D) or (E) of this section that the old taxpayer acquired in a transaction described in paragraph (k)(3)(i)(D) or (E) of this section, the basis adjustment rule of this paragraph (k)(3)(iv)(A) is applied by treating the old taxpayer as having recognized the amount of gross receipts recognized by the previous old taxpayer under the contract and any amount recognized by the previous old taxpayer with respect to the contract in connection with the transaction in which the old taxpayer acquired the contract. In addition, the old taxpayer is treated as having received or as reasonably expecting to receive under the contract any amount the previous old taxpayer received or reasonably expects to receive under the contract. Similar principles will apply in the case of multiple successive transfers described in paragraph (k)(3)(i)(D) or (E) of this section involving the contract.

(B) *New taxpayer*—(1) *Contract price adjustment.* Generally, payments between the old taxpayer and the new taxpayer with respect to the contract in connection with the transaction do not affect the contract price. Notwithstanding the preceding sentence and paragraph (k)(3)(iii)(B) of this section, however, in the case of transactions described in paragraph (k)(3)(i)(B), (D) or (E) of this section, the total contract price (or gross contract price) must be reduced to the extent of any amount recognized by the old taxpayer with respect to the contract in connection with the transaction (e.g., any amount recognized under section 351(b) or 357 that is attributable to the contract and any income recognized by the old taxpayer pursuant to the basis adjustment rule of paragraph (k)(3)(iv)(A)).

(2) *Basis in contract.* The new taxpayer's basis in a contract (including the uncompleted property, if applicable) acquired in a transaction described in paragraphs (k)(3)(i)(A) through (E) of this section will be computed under section 362 or section 334, as applicable. Upon a new taxpayer's completion (actual or constructive) of a CCM or a PCM contract acquired in a transaction described in paragraphs (k)(3)(i)(A) through (E) of this section, the new taxpayer's basis in the contract (including the uncompleted property, if applicable) is reduced to zero. The new taxpayer is not entitled to a deduction or loss in connection with any basis reduction pursuant to this paragraph (k)(3)(iv)(B)(2).

(v) *Special rules related to certain partnership transactions.* [Reserved]

(4) *Anti-abuse rule.* Notwithstanding this paragraph (k), in the case of a transaction entered into with a principal purpose of shifting the tax consequences associated with a long-term contract in a manner that substantially reduces the aggregate U.S. Federal income tax liability of the parties with respect to that contract, the Commissioner may allocate to the old (or new) taxpayer the income from that contract properly allocable to the old (or new) taxpayer. For example, the Commissioner may reallocate income from a long-term contract in a transaction in which a contract accounted for using the CCM, or using the PCM where the old taxpayer has received advance payments in excess of its contribution to the contract, is transferred to a tax indifferent party (e.g., a foreign person not subject to U.S. Federal income tax).

(5) *Examples.* The following examples illustrate the rules of this paragraph (k). For purposes of these examples, it is assumed that the contract is a long-term construction contract accounted for using the PCM prior to the transaction unless stated otherwise and the contract is not transferred with a principal purpose of shifting the tax consequences associated with a long-term contract in a manner that substantially reduces the aggregate U.S. Federal income tax liability of the par-

Reg. § 1.460-4(k)(5)

ties with respect to that contract. The examples are as follows:

Example 1. Constructive completion—PCM—(i) *Facts.* In Year 1, X enters into a contract. The total contract price is $1,000,000 and the estimated total allocable contract costs are $800,000. In Year 1, X incurs costs of $200,000. In Year 2, X incurs additional costs of $400,000 before selling the contract as part of a taxable sale of its business in Year 2 to Y, an unrelated party. At the time of sale, X has received $650,000 in progress payments under the contract. The consideration allocable to the contract under section 1060 is $150,000. Pursuant to the sale, the new taxpayer Y immediately assumes X's contract obligations and rights. Y is required to account for the contract using the PCM. In Year 2, Y incurs additional allocable contract costs of $50,000. Y correctly estimates at the end of Year 2 that it will have to incur an additional $75,000 of allocable contract costs in Year 3 to complete the contract.

(ii) *Old taxpayer.* For Year 1, X reports receipts of $250,000 (the completion factor multiplied by total contract price ($200,000/$800,000 × $1,000,000) and costs of $200,000, for a profit of $50,000. X is treated as completing the contract in Year 2 because it sold the contract. For purposes of applying the PCM in Year 2, the total contract price is $800,000 (the sum of the amounts received under the contract and the amount realized in the sale ($650,000 + $150,000)) and the total allocable contract costs are $600,000 (the sum of the costs incurred in Year 1 and Year 2 ($200,000 + $400,000)). Thus, in Year 2, X reports receipts of $550,000 (total contract price minus receipts already reported ($800,000 − $250,000) and costs incurred in year 2 of $400,000, for a profit of $150,000.

(iii) *New taxpayer.* Y is treated as entering into a new contract in Year 2. The total contract price is $200,000 (the amount remaining to be paid under the terms of the contract less the consideration paid allocable to the contract ($1,000,000 − $650,000 − $150,000)). The estimated total allocable contract costs at the end of Year 2 are $125,000 (the allocable contract costs that Y reasonably expects to incur to complete the contract ($50,000 + $75,000)). In Year 2, Y reports receipts of $80,000 (the completion factor multiplied by the total contract price [($50,000/$125,000) × $200,000] and costs of $50,000 (the costs incurred after the purchase), for a profit of $30,000. For Year 3, Y reports receipts of $120,000 (total contract price minus receipts already reported ($200,000 − $80,000)) and costs of $75,000, for a profit of $45,000.

Example 2. Constructive completion—CCM—(i) *Facts.* The facts are the same as in Example 1, except that X and Y properly account for the contract under the CCM.

(ii) *Old taxpayer.* X does not report any income or costs from the contract in Year 1. In Year 2, the contract is deemed complete for X, and X reports its gross contract price of $800,000 (the sum of the amounts received under the contract and the amount realized in the sale ($650,000 + $150,000)) and its total allocable contract costs of $600,000 (the sum of the costs incurred in Year 1 and Year 2 ($200,000 + $400,000)) in that year, for a profit of $200,000.

(iii) *New taxpayer.* Y is treated as entering into a new contract in Year 2. Under the CCM, Y reports no gross receipts or costs in Year 2. Y reports its gross contract price of $200,000 (the amount remaining to be paid under the terms of the contract less the consideration paid allocable to the contract ($1,000,000 − $650,000 − $150,000)) and its total allocable contract costs of $125,000 (the allocable contract costs that Y incurred to complete the contract ($50,000 + $75,000)) in Year 3, the completion year, for a profit of $75,000.

Example 3. Step-in-the-shoes—PCM—(i) Facts. The facts are the same as in Example 1, except that X transfers the contract (including the uncompleted property) to Y in exchange for stock of Y in a transaction that qualifies as a statutory merger described in section 368(a)(1)(A) and does not result in gain or loss to X under section 361(a).

(ii) *Old taxpayer.* For Year 1, X reports receipts of $250,000 (the completion factor multiplied by total contract price ($200,000/$800,000 × $1,000,000)) and costs of $200,000, for a profit of $50,000. Because the mid-contract change in taxpayer results from a transaction described in paragraph (k)(3)(i) of this section, X is not treated as completing the contract in Year 2. In Year 2, X reports receipts of $500,000 (the completion factor multiplied by the total contract price and minus the Year 1 gross receipts [($600,000/$800,000 × $1,000,000) − $250,000]) and costs of $400,000, for a profit of $100,000.

(iii) *New taxpayer.* Because the mid-contract change in taxpayer results from a step-in-the-shoes transaction, Y must account for the contract using the same methods of accounting used by X prior to the transaction. Total contract price is the sum of any amounts that X and Y have received or reasonably expect to receive under the contract, and total allocable contract costs are the allocable contract costs of X and Y. Thus, the

Reg. § 1.460-4(k)(5)

estimated total allocable contract costs at the end of Year 2 are $725,000 (the cumulative allocable contract costs of X and the estimated total allocable contract costs of Y ($200,000 + $400,000 + $50,000 + $75,000)). In Year 2, Y reports receipts of $146,552 (the completion factor multiplied by the total contract price minus receipts reported by the old taxpayer ([($650,000/$725,000) × $1,000,000] − $750,000) and costs of $50,000, for a profit of $96,552. For Year 3, Y reports receipts of $103,448 (the total contract price minus prior year receipts ($1,000,000 − $896,552)) and costs of $75,000, for a profit of $28,448.

Example 4. Step-in-the-shoes—CCM—(i) *Facts.* The facts are the same as in *Example 3,* except that X properly accounts for the contract under the CCM.

(ii) *Old taxpayer.* X reports no income or costs from the contract in Years 1, 2 or 3.

(iii) *New taxpayer.* Because the mid-contract change in taxpayer results from a step-in-the-shoes transaction, Y must account for the contract using the same method of accounting used by X prior to the transaction. Thus, in Year 3, the completion year, Y reports receipts of $1,000,000 and total contract costs of $725,000, for a profit of $275,000.

Example 5. Step in the shoes—PCM—basis adjustment. The facts are the same as in *Example 3,* except that X transfers the contract (including the uncompleted property) with a basis of $0 and $125,000 of cash to a new corporation, Z, in exchange for all of the stock of Z in a section 351 transaction. Thus, under section 358(a), X's basis in the Z stock is $125,000. Pursuant to paragraph (k)(3)(iv)(A)(*1*) of this section, X must increase its basis in the Z stock by the amount of gross receipts X recognized under the contract, $750,000 ($250,000 receipts in Year 1 + $500,000 receipts in Year 2), and reduce its basis by the amount of gross receipts X received under the contract, the $650,000 in progress payments. Accordingly, X's basis in the Z stock is $225,000. All other results are the same.

Example 6. Step in the shoes—CCM—basis adjustment—(i) *Facts.* The facts are the same as in *Example 4,* except that X receives progress payments of $800,000 (rather than $650,000) and transfers the contract (including the uncompleted property) with a basis of $600,000 and $125,000 of cash to a new corporation, Z, in exchange for all of the stock of Z in a section 351 transaction. X and Z do not join in filing a consolidated Federal income tax return.

(ii) *Old taxpayer.* X reports no income or costs under the contract in Years 1, 2, or 3. Under section 358(a), X's basis in Z is $725,000. Pursuant to paragraph (k)(3)(iv)(A)(*1*), X must reduce its basis in the stock of Z by $800,000, the progress payments received by X. However, X may not reduce its basis in the Z stock below zero pursuant paragraph (k)(3)(iv)(A)(*2*) of this section. Accordingly, X's basis in the Z stock is reduced by $725,000 to zero and X must recognize ordinary income of $75,000.

(iii) *New taxpayer.* Upon completion of the contract in Year 3, Z reports gross receipts of $925,000 ($1,000,000 original contract price − $75,000 income recognized by the old taxpayer pursuant to the basis adjustment rule of paragraph (k)(3)(iv)(A)) and total contract costs of $725,000, for a profit of $200,000.

Example 7. Step in the shoes—PCM—gain recognized in transaction—(i) *Facts.* The facts are the same as in *Example 3,* except that X transfers the contract (including the uncompleted property) with a basis of $0 and an unrelated capital asset with a value of $100,000 and a basis of $0 to a new corporation, Z, in exchange for stock of Z with a value of $200,000 and $50,000 of cash in a section 351 transaction.

(ii) *Old taxpayer.* For year 1, X reports receipts of $250,000 ($200,000/$800,000 × $1,000,000) and costs of $200,000, for a profit of $50,000. X is not treated as completing the contract in Year 2. In Year 2, X reports receipts of $500,000 (($600,000/$800,000 × $1,000,000 = $750,000 cumulative gross receipts) × $250,000 prior year cumulative gross receipts) and costs of $400,000, for a profit of $100,000. Under paragraph (k)(3)(ii)(B) of this section, X determines that the gain realized on the transfer of the contract to Z under the constructive completion rules of paragraph (k)(2)(ii) of this section is $50,000 (total contract price of $800,000 ($150,000 value allocable to the contract + $650,000 progress payments) − $750,000 previously recognized cumulative gross receipts − $0 costs incurred but not recognized). The gain realized on the transfer of the unrelated capital asset to Z is $100,000. The amount of gain X must recognize due to the receipt of $50,000 cash in the exchange is $50,000, of which $30,000 is allocated to the contract ($150,000 value of contract/$250,000 total value of property transferred to Z × $50,000) and is treated as ordinary income, and $20,000 is allocated to the unrelated capital asset ($100,000 value of capital asset/$250,000 total value of property transferred to Z × $50,000). Under section 358(a), X's basis in the Z stock is $0. However, pursuant to paragraph (k)(3)(iv)(A)(*1*) of this section, X must increase its basis in the Z stock by $750,000, the amount of gross receipts

Reg. § 1.460-4(k)(5)

recognized under the contract, and must reduce its basis in the Z stock by $650,000, the amount of gross receipts X received under the contract. Therefore, X's basis in the Z stock is $100,000.

(iii) *New taxpayer.* Z must account for the contract using the same PCM method used by X prior to the transaction. Pursuant to paragraph (k)(3)(iv)(B)(*1*) of this section, the total contract price is $970,000 ($1,000,000 amount X and Z have received or reasonably expect to receive under the contract − $30,000 income recognized by X with respect to the contract as a result of the receipt of $50,000 cash in the transaction). In Year 2, Z reports gross receipts of $119,655 ($650,000/$725,000 × $970,000 = $869,655 current year cumulative gross receipts − $750,000 cumulative gross receipts reported by the old taxpayer) and costs of $50,000, for a profit of $69,655. In Year 3, Z reports gross receipts of $100,345 ($970,000 − $869,655) and costs of $75,000, for a profit of $25,345.

Example 8. Step in the shoes—CCM—gain recognized in transaction—(i) *Facts.* The facts are the same as in *Example 4*, except that X transfers the contract (including the uncompleted property) with a basis of $600,000 and an unrelated capital asset with a value of $125,000 and a basis of $0 to a new corporation, Z, in exchange for all the stock of Z with a value of $175,000 and $100,000 of cash in a section 351 transaction. X and Z do not join in filing a consolidated Federal income tax return.

(ii) *Old taxpayer.* X reports no income or costs under the contract in Years 1, 2, or 3. Under paragraph (k)(3)(ii)(B), X determines that the gain realized on the transfer of the contract to Z under the constructive completion rules of paragraph (k)(2)(ii) of this section is $200,000 ($800,000 total contract price ($150,000 value allocable to the contract + $650,000 progress payments) − $600,000 costs incurred but not recognized). The gain realized on the transfer of the unrelated capital asset to Z is $125,000. The amount of gain X must recognize due to the reciept of $100,000 of cash in the exchange is $100,000, of which $54,545 is allocated to the contract ($150,000 value of the contract/$275,000 total value of property transferred to Z × $100,000) and is treated as ordinary income, and $45,455 is allocated to the unrelated capital asset ($125,000 value of capital asset/$275,000 total value of property transferred to Z × $100,000). Under section 358(a), X's basis in the Z stock is $600,000 ($600,000 basis in the contract and unrelated capital asset transferred − $100,000 cash received + $100,000 gain recognized). Pursuant to paragraph (k)(3)(iv)(A)(*1*) of this section, X must reduce its basis in the stock of Z by $650,000, the progress payments received under the contract. However, X may not reduce its basis in the Z stock below zero pursuant to paragraph (k)(3)(iv)(A)(*2*) of this section. Accordingly, X's basis in the Z stock is reduced by $600,000 to zero and X must recognize income of $50,000.

(iii) *New taxpayer.* Z must account for the contract using the same CCM used by X prior to the transaction. Pursuant to paragraph (k)(3)(iv)(B)(1) of this section, the total contract price is $895,455 ($1,000,000 original contract price − $54,545 income recognized by old taxpayer with respect to the contract as a result of the receipt of cash in the transaction − $50,000 income recognized by the old taxpayer pursuant to the basis adjustment rule of paragraph (k)(3)(iv)(A)). Accordingly, upon completion of the contract in Year 3, Z reports gross receipts of $895,455 and total contract costs of $725,000, for a profit of $170,455.

(6) *Effective date.* This paragraph (k) is applicable for transactions on or after May 15, 2002. Application of the rules of this paragraph (k) to a transaction that occurs on or after May 15, 2002 is not a change in method of accounting. [Reg. § 1.460-4.]

[*T.D.* 8315, 10-12-90. Amended by *T.D.* 8597, 7-12-95; *T.D.* 8929, 1-10-2001 (*corrected 4-5-2001*) *and T.D.* 8995, 5-14-2002.]

[Reg. § 1.460-5]

§ 1.460-5. Cost allocation rules.—(a) *Overview.* This section prescribes methods of allocating costs to long-term contracts accounted for using the percentage-of-completion method described in § 1.460-4(b) (PCM), the completed-contract method described in § 1.460-4(d) (CCM), or the percentage-of-completion/capitalized-cost method described in § 1.460-4(e) (PCCM). Exempt construction contracts described in § 1.460-3(b) accounted for using a method other than the PCM or CCM are not subject to the cost allocation rules of this section (other than the requirement to allocate production-period interest under paragraph (b)(2)(v) of this section). Paragraph (b) of this section describes the regular cost allocation methods for contracts subject to the PCM. Paragraph (c) of this section describes an elective simplified cost allocation method for contracts subject to the PCM. Paragraph (d) of this section describes the cost allocation methods for exempt construction contracts reported using the CCM. Paragraph (e) of this section describes the cost allocation rules for contracts subject to the PCCM. Paragraph (f) of this section describes additional rules applicable to the cost allocation

Reg. § 1.460-5(a)

methods described in this section. Paragraph (g) of this section provides rules concerning consistency in method of allocating costs to long-term contracts.

(b) *Cost allocation method for contracts subject to PCM*—(1) *In general.* Except as otherwise provided in paragraph (b)(2) of this section, a taxpayer must allocate costs to each long-term contract subject to the PCM in the same manner that direct and indirect costs are capitalized to property produced by a taxpayer under § 1.263A-1(e) through (h). Thus, a taxpayer must allocate to each long-term contract subject to the PCM all direct costs and certain indirect costs properly allocable to the long-term contract (i.e., all costs that directly benefit or are incurred by reason of the performance of the long-term contract). However, see paragraph (c) of this section concerning an election to allocate contract costs using the simplified cost-to-cost method. As in section 263A, the use of the practical capacity concept is not permitted. See § 1.263A-2(a)(4).

(2) *Special rules*—(i) *Direct material costs.* The costs of direct materials must be allocated to a long-term contract when dedicated to the contract under principles similar to those in § 1.263A-11(b)(2). Thus, a taxpayer dedicates direct materials by associating them with a specific contract, including by purchase order, entry on books and records, or shipping instructions. A taxpayer maintaining inventories under § 1.471-1 must determine allocable contract costs attributable to direct materials using its method of accounting for those inventories (e.g., FIFO, LIFO, specific identification).

(ii) *Components and subassemblies.* The costs of a component or subassembly (component) produced by the taxpayer must be allocated to a long-term contract as the taxpayer incurs costs to produce the component if the taxpayer reasonably expects to incorporate the component into the subject matter of the contract. Similarly, the cost of a purchased component (including a component purchased from a related party) must be allocated to a long-term contract as the taxpayer incurs the cost to purchase the component if the taxpayer reasonably expects to incorporate the component into the subject matter of the contract. In all other cases, the cost of a component must be allocated to a long-term contract when the component is dedicated, under principles similar to those in § 1.263A-11(b)(2). A taxpayer maintaining inventories under § 1.471-1 must determine allocable contract costs attributable to components using its method of accounting for those inventories (e.g., FIFO, LIFO, specific identification).

(iii) *Simplified production methods.* A taxpayer may not determine allocable contract costs using the simplified production methods described in § 1.263A-2(b) and (c).

(iv) *Costs identified under cost-plus long-term contracts and federal long-term contracts.* To the extent not otherwise allocated to the contract under this paragraph (b), a taxpayer must allocate any identified costs to a cost-plus long-term contract or federal long-term contract (as defined in section 460(d)). *Identified cost* means any cost, including a charge representing the time-value of money, identified by the taxpayer or related person as being attributable to the taxpayer's cost-plus long-term contract or federal long-term contract under the terms of the contract itself or under federal, state, or local law or regulation.

(v) *Interest*—(A) *In general.* If property produced under a long-term contract is *designated property*, as defined in § 1.263A-8(b) (without regard to the exclusion for long-term contracts under § 1.263A-8(d)(2)(v)), a taxpayer must allocate interest incurred during the production period to the long-term contract in the same manner as interest is allocated to property produced by a taxpayer under section 263A(f). See §§ 1.263A-8 to 1.263A-12 generally.

(B) *Production period.* Notwithstanding § 1.263A-12(c) and (d), for purposes of this paragraph (b)(2)(v), the production period of a long-term contract—

(*1*) Begins on the later of—

(*i*) The contract commencement date, as defined in § 1.460-1(b)(7); or

(*ii*) For a taxpayer using the accrual method of accounting for long-term contracts, the date by which 5 percent or more of the total estimated costs, including design and planning costs, under the contract have been incurred; and

(*2*) Ends on the date that the contract is completed, as defined in § 1.460-1(c)(3).

(C) *Application of section 263A(f).* For purposes of this paragraph (b)(2)(v), section 263A(f)(1)(B)(iii) (regarding an estimated production period exceeding 1 year and a cost exceeding $1,000,000) must be applied on a contract-by-contract basis; except that, in the case of a taxpayer using an accrual method of accounting, that section must be applied on a property-by-property basis.

(vi) *Research and experimental expenses.* Notwithstanding § 1.263A-1(e)(3)(ii)(P) and (iii)(B), a taxpayer must allocate research and experimental expenses, other than independent

Reg. § 1.460-5(b)(2)

research and development expenses (as defined in § 1.460-1(b)(9)), to its long-term contracts.

(vii) *Service costs*—(A) *Simplified service cost method*—(*1*) *In general.* To use the simplified service cost method under § 1.263A-1(h), a taxpayer must allocate the otherwise capitalizable mixed service costs among its long-term contracts using a reasonable method. For example, otherwise capitalizable mixed service costs may be allocated to each long-term contract based on labor hours or contract costs allocable to the contract. To be considered reasonable, an allocation method must be applied consistently and must not disproportionately allocate service costs to contracts expected to be completed in the near future.

(*2*) *Example.* The following example illustrates the rule of this paragraph (b)(2)(vii)(A):

Example. Simplified service cost method. During 2001, C, whose taxable year ends December 31, produces electronic equipment for inventory and enters into long-term contracts to manufacture specialized electronic equipment. C's method of allocating mixed service costs to the property it produces is the labor-based, simplified service cost method described in § 1.263A-1(h)(4). For 2001, C's total mixed service costs are $100,000, C's section 263A labor costs are $500,000, C's section 460 labor costs (i.e., labor costs allocable to C's long-term contracts) are $250,000, and C's total labor costs are $1,000,000. To determine the amount of mixed service costs capitalizable under section 263A for 2001, C multiplies its total mixed service costs by its section 263A allocation ratio (section 263A labor costs ÷ total labor costs). Thus, C's capitalizable mixed service costs for 2001 are $50,000 ($100,000 × $500,000 ÷ $1,000,000). Thereafter, C allocates its capitalizable mixed service costs to produced property remaining in ending inventory using its 263A allocation method (e.g., burden rate, simplified production). Similarly, to determine the amount of mixed service costs that are allocable to C's long-term contracts for 2001, C multiplies its total mixed service costs by its section 460 allocation ratio (section 460 labor ÷ total labor costs). Thus, C's allocable mixed service contract costs for 2001 are $25,000 ($100,000 × $250,000 ÷ $1,000,000). Thereafter, C allocates its allocable mixed service costs to its long-term contracts proportionately based on its section 460 labor costs allocable to each long-term contract.

(B) *Jobsite costs.* If an administrative, service, or support function is performed solely at the jobsite for a specific long-term contract, the taxpayer may allocate all the direct and indirect costs of that administrative, service, or support function to that long-term contract. Similarly, if an administrative, service, or support function is performed at the jobsite solely for the taxpayer's long-term contract activities, the taxpayer may allocate all the direct and indirect costs of that administrative, service, or support function among all the long-term contracts performed at that jobsite. For this purpose, *jobsite* means a production plant or a construction site.

(C) *Limitation on other reasonable cost allocation methods.* A taxpayer may use any other reasonable method of allocating service costs, as provided in § 1.263A-1(f)(4), if, for the taxpayer's long-term contracts considered as a whole, the—

(*1*) Total amount of service costs allocated to the contracts does not differ significantly from the total amount of service costs that would have been allocated to the contracts under § 1.263A-1(f)(2) or (3);

(*2*) Service costs are not allocated disproportionately to contracts expected to be completed in the near future because of the taxpayer's cost allocation method; and

(*3*) Taxpayer's cost allocation method is applied consistently.

(c) *Simplified cost-to-cost method for contracts subject to the PCM*—(1) *In general.* Instead of using the cost allocation method prescribed in paragraph (b) of this section, a taxpayer may elect to use the simplified cost-to-cost method, which is authorized under section 460(b)(3)(A), to allocate costs to a long-term contract subject to the PCM. Under the simplified cost-to-cost method, a taxpayer determines a contract's completion factor based upon only direct material costs; direct labor costs; and depreciation, amortization, and cost recovery allowances on equipment and facilities directly used to manufacture or construct the subject matter of the contract. For this purpose, the costs associated with any manufacturing or construction activities performed by a subcontractor are considered either direct material or direct labor costs, as appropriate, and therefore must be allocated to the contract under the simplified cost-to-cost method. An electing taxpayer must use the simplified cost-to-cost method to apply the look-back method under § 1.460-6 and to determine alternative minimum taxable income under § 1.460-4(f).

(2) *Election.* A taxpayer makes an election under this paragraph (c) by using the simplified cost-to-cost method for all long-term contracts entered into during the taxable year of the election on its original federal income tax return for the election year. This election is a method of accounting and, thus, applies to all long-term con-

Reg. § 1.460-5(c)(1)

tracts entered into during and after the taxable year of the election. This election is not available if a taxpayer does not use the PCM to account for all long-term contracts or if a taxpayer elects to use the 10-percent method described in § 1.460-4(b)(6).

(d) *Cost allocation rules for exempt construction contracts reported using the CCM*—(1) *In general.* For exempt construction contracts reported using the CCM, other than contracts described in paragraph (d)(3) of this section (concerning contracts of homebuilders that do not satisfy the $10,000,000 gross receipts test described in § 1.460-3(b)(3) or will not be completed within two years of the contract commencement date), a taxpayer must annually allocate the cost of any activity that is incident to or necessary for the taxpayer's performance under a long-term contract. A taxpayer must allocate to each exempt construction contract all direct costs as defined in § 1.263A-1(e)(2)(i) and all indirect costs either as provided in § 1.263A-1(e)(3) or as provided in paragraph (d)(2) of this section.

(2) *Indirect costs*—(i) *Indirect costs allocable to exempt construction contracts.* A taxpayer allocating costs under this paragraph (d)(2) must allocate the following costs to an exempt construction contract, other than a contract described in paragraph (d)(3) of this section, to the extent incurred in the performance of that contract—

(A) Repair of equipment or facilities;

(B) Maintenance of equipment or facilities;

(C) Utilities, such as heat, light, and power, allocable to equipment or facilities;

(D) Rent of equipment or facilities;

(E) Indirect labor and contract supervisory wages, including basic compensation, overtime pay, vacation and holiday pay, sick leave pay (other than payments pursuant to a wage continuation plan under section 105(d) as it existed prior to its repeal in 1983), shift differential, payroll taxes, and contributions to a supplemental unemployment benefits plan;

(F) Indirect materials and supplies;

(G) Noncapitalized tools and equipment;

(H) Quality control and inspection;

(I) Taxes otherwise allowable as a deduction under section 164, other than state, local, and foreign income taxes, to the extent attributable to labor, materials, supplies, equipment, or facilities;

(J) Depreciation, amortization, and cost-recovery allowances reported for the taxable year for financial purposes on equipment and facilities to the extent allowable as deductions under chapter 1 of the Internal Revenue Code;

(K) Cost depletion;

(L) Administrative costs other than the cost of selling or any return on capital;

(M) Compensation paid to officers other than for incidental or occasional services;

(N) Insurance, such as liability insurance on machinery and equipment; and

(O) Interest, as required under paragraph (b)(2)(v) of this section.

(ii) *Indirect costs not allocable to exempt construction contracts.* A taxpayer allocating costs under this paragraph (d)(2) is not required to allocate the following costs to an exempt construction contract reported using the CCM—

(A) Marketing and selling expenses, including bidding expenses;

(B) Advertising expenses;

(C) Other distribution expenses;

(D) General and administrative expenses attributable to the performance of services that benefit the taxpayer's activities as a whole (e.g., payroll expenses, legal and accounting expenses);

(E) Research and experimental expenses (described in section 174 and the regulations thereunder);

(F) Losses under section 165 and the regulations thereunder;

(G) Percentage of depletion in excess of cost depletion;

(H) Depreciation, amortization, and cost recovery allowances on equipment and facilities that have been placed in service but are temporarily idle (for this purpose, an asset is not considered to be temporarily idle on non-working days, and an asset used in construction is considered to be idle when it is neither en route to nor located at a job-site), and depreciation, amortization and cost recovery allowances under chapter 1 of the Internal Revenue Code in excess of depreciation, amortization, and cost recovery allowances reported by the taxpayer in the taxpayer's financial reports;

(I) Income taxes attributable to income received from long-term contracts;

(J) Contributions paid to or under a stock bonus, pension, profit-sharing, or annuity plan or other plan deferring the receipt of compensation whether or not the plan qualifies under section 401(a), and other employee benefit expenses paid or accrued on behalf of labor, to the extent the contributions or expenses are otherwise allowable as deductions under chapter 1 of the

Reg. § 1.460-5(d)(2)

Internal Revenue Code. Other employee benefit expenses include (but are not limited to): worker's compensation; amounts deductible or for whose payment reduction in earnings and profits is allowed under section 404A and the regulations thereunder; payments pursuant to a wage continuation plan under section 105(d) as it existed prior to its repeal in 1983; amounts includible in the gross income of employees under a method or arrangement of employer contributions or compensation which has the effect of a stock bonus, pension, profit-sharing, or annuity plan, or other plan deferring the receipt of compensation or providing deferred benefits; premiums on life and health insurance; and miscellaneous benefits provided for employees such as safety, medical treatment, recreational and eating facilities, membership dues, etc.;

(K) Cost attributable to strikes, rework labor, scrap and spoilage; and

(L) Compensation paid to officers attributable to the performance of services that benefit the taxpayer's activities as a whole.

(3) *Large homebuilders.* A taxpayer must capitalize the costs of home construction contracts under section 263A and the regulations thereunder, unless the contract will be completed within two years of the contract commencement date and the taxpayer satisfies the $10,000,000 gross receipts test described in § 1.460-3(b)(3).

(e) *Cost allocation rules for contracts subject to the PCCM.* A taxpayer must use the cost allocation rules described in paragraph (b) of this section to determine the costs allocable to the entire qualified ship contract or residential construction contract accounted for using the PCCM and may not use the simplified cost-to-cost method described in paragraph (c) of this section.

(f) *Special rules applicable to costs allocated under this section*—(1) *Nondeductible costs.* A taxpayer may not allocate any otherwise allocable contract cost to a long-term contract if any section of the Internal Revenue Code disallows a deduction for that type of payment or expenditure (e.g., an illegal bribe described in section 162(c)).

(2) *Costs incurred for non-long-term contract activities.* If a taxpayer performs a non-long-term contract activity, as defined in § 1.460-1(d)(2), that is incident to or necessary for the manufacture, building, installation, or construction of the subject matter of one or more of the taxpayer's long-term contracts, the taxpayer must allocate the costs attributable to that activity to such contract(s).

(g) *Method of accounting.* A taxpayer that adopts or elects a cost allocation method of accounting (or changes to another cost allocation method of accounting with the Commissioner's consent) must apply that method consistently for all similarly classified contracts, until the taxpayer obtains the Commissioner's consent under section 446(e) to change to another cost allocation method. A taxpayer-initiated change in cost allocation method will be permitted only on a cut-off basis (i.e., for contracts entered into on or after the year of change, and thus, a section 481(a) adjustment will not be permitted or required. [Reg. § 1.460-5.]

☐ [*T.D.* 8315, 10-12-90. Amended by T.D. 8929, 1-10-2001.]

[Reg. § 1.460-6]

§ 1.460-6. **Look-back method.**—(a) *In general*—(1) *Introduction.* With respect to income from any long-term contract reported under the percentage of completion method, a taxpayer is required to pay or is entitled to receive interest under section 460(b) on the amount of tax liability that is deferred or accelerated as a result of overestimating or underestimating total contract price or contract costs. Under this look-back method, taxpayers are required to pay interest for any deferral of tax liability resulting from the underestimation of the total contract price or the overestimation of total contract costs. Conversely, if the total contract price is overestimated or the total contract costs are underestimated, taxpayers are entitled to receive interest for any resulting acceleration of tax liability. The computation of the amount of deferred or accelerated tax liability under the look-back method is hypothetical; application of the look-back method does not result in an adjustment to the taxpayer's tax liability as originally reported, as reported on an amended return, or as adjusted on examination. Thus, the look-back method does not correct for differences in tax liability that result from over- or underestimation of contract price and costs and that are permanent because, for example, tax rates change during the term of the contract.

(2) *Overview.* Paragraph (b) explains which situations require application of the look-back method to income from a long-term contract. Paragraph (c) explains the operation of the three computational steps for applying the look-back method. Paragraph (d) provides guidance concerning the simplified marginal impact method. Paragraph (e) provides an elective method to minimize the number of times the look-back method must be reapplied to a single long-term contract. Paragraph (f) describes the reporting requirements for the look-back method and the tax treatment of look-back interest. Paragraph (g) provides rules for applying the look-back method

when there is a transaction that changes the taxpayer that reports income from a long-term contract prior to the completion of a contract. Paragraph (h) provides examples illustrating the three computational steps for applying the look-back method. Paragraph (j) of this section provides guidance concerning the election not to apply the look-back method in de minimis cases.

(b) *Scope of look-back method*—(1) *In general.* The look-back method applies to any income from a long-term contract within the meaning of section 460(f) that is required to be reported under the percentage of completion method (as modified by section 460) for regular income tax purposes or for alternative minimum tax purposes. If a taxpayer uses the percentage of completion-capitalized cost method for long-term contracts, the look-back method applies for regular tax purposes only to the portion (40, 70, or 90 percent, whichever applies) of the income from the contract that is reported under the percentage of completion method. To the extent that the percentage of completion method is required to be used under § 1.460-1(g) with respect to income and expenses that are attributable to activities that benefit a related party's long-term contract, the look-back method also applies to these amounts, even if those activities are not performed under a contract entered into directly by the taxpayer.

(2) *Exceptions from section 460.* The look-back method generally does not apply to the regular taxable income from any long-term construction contract within the meaning of section 460(e)(4) that

(i) is a home construction contract within the meaning of section 460(e)(1)(A), or

(ii) is not a home construction contract but is estimated to be completed within a 2-year period by a taxpayer whose average annual gross receipts for the 3 tax years preceding the tax year the contract is entered into do not exceed $10,000,000 (as provided in section 460(e)(1)(B)). These contracts are not subject to the look-back method for regular tax purposes, even if the taxpayer uses a version of the percentage of completion method permitted under § 1.451-3, unless the taxpayer has properly changed its method of accounting for these contracts to the percentage of completion method as modified by section 460(b). The look-back method, however, applies to the alternative minimum taxable income from a contract of this type, unless it is exempt from the required use of the percentage of completion method under section 56(a)(3).

(3) *De minimis exception.* Notwithstanding that the percentage of completion method is otherwise required to be used, the look-back method does not apply to any long-term contract that (i) is completed within 2 years of the contract commencement date, and (ii) has a gross contract price (as of the completion of the contract) that does not exceed the lesser of $1,000,000 or 1 percent of the average annual gross receipts of the taxpayer for the 3 tax years preceding the tax year in which the contract is completed. This de minimis exception is mandatory and, therefore, precludes application of the look-back method to any contract that meets the requirements of the exception. The de minimis exception applies for purposes of computing both regular taxable income and alternative minimum taxable income. Solely for this purpose, the determination of whether a long-term contract meets the gross receipts test for both alternative minimum tax and regular tax purposes is made based only on the taxpayer's regular taxable income.

(4) *Alternative minimum tax.* For purposes of computing alternative minimum taxable income, section 56(a)(3) generally requires long-term contracts within the meaning of section 460(f) (generally without regard to the exceptions in section 460(e)) to be accounted for using only the percentage of completion method as defined in section 460(b), including the look-back method of section 460(b), with respect to tax years beginning after December 31, 1986. However, section 56(a)(3) (and thus the look-back method) does not apply to any long-term contract entered into after June 20, 1988, and before the beginning of the first tax year that begins after September 30, 1990, that meets the conditions of both section 460(e)(1)(A) and clauses (i) and (ii) of section 460(e)(1)(B), and does not apply to any long-term contract entered into in a tax year that begins after September 30, 1990, that meets the conditions of section 460(e)(1)(A). A taxpayer that applies the percentage of completion method (and thus the look-back method) to income from a long-term contract only for purposes of determining alternative minimum taxable income, and not regular taxable income, must apply the look-back method to the alternative minimum taxable income in the year of contract completion and other filing years whether or not the taxpayer was liable for the alternative minimum tax for the filing year or for any prior year. Interest is computed under the look-back method to the extent that the taxpayer's total tax liability (including the alternative minimum tax liability) would have differed if the percentage of completion method had been applied using actual, rather than estimated, contract price and contract costs.

(5) *Effective date.* The look-back method, including the de minimis exception, applies to long-term contracts entered into after February

Reg. § 1.460-6(b)(5)

28, 1986. With respect to activities that are subject to section 460 solely because they benefit a long term contract of a related party, the look-back method generally applies only if the related party's long-term contract was entered into after June 20, 1988, unless a principal purpose of the related-party arrangement is to avoid the requirements of section 460.

(c) *Operation of the look-back method*—(1) *Overview*—(i) *In general.* The amount of interest charged or credited to a taxpayer under the look-back method is computed in three steps. This paragraph (c) describes the three steps for applying the look-back method. These steps are illustrated by the examples in paragraph (h). The first step is to hypothetically reapply the percentage of completion method to all long-term contracts that are completed or adjusted in the current year (the "filing year"), using the actual, rather than estimated, total contract price and contract costs. Based on this reapplication, the taxpayer determines the amount of taxable income (and alternative minimum taxable income) that would have been reported for each year prior to the filing year that is affected by contracts completed or adjusted in the filing year if the actual, rather than estimated, total contract price and costs had been used in applying the percentage of completion method to these contracts, and to any other contracts completed or adjusted in a year preceding the filing year. If the percentage of completion method only applies to alternative minimum taxable income for contracts completed or adjusted in the filing year, only alternative minimum taxable income is recomputed in the first step. The second step is to compare what the tax liability would have been under the percentage of completion method (as reapplied in the first step) for each tax year for which the tax liability is affected by income from contracts completed or adjusted in the filing year (a "redetermination year") with the most recent determination of tax liability for that year to produce a hypothetical underpayment or overpayment of tax. The third step is to apply the rate of interest on overpayments designated under section 6621 of the Code, compounded daily, to the hypothetical underpayment or overpayment of tax for each redetermination year to compute interest that runs, generally, from the due date (determined without regard to extensions) of the return for the redetermination year to the due date (determined without regard to extensions) of the return for the filing year. The net amount of interest computed under the third step is paid by or credited to the taxpayer for the filing year. Paragraph (d) provides a simplified marginal impact method that simplifies the second step—the computation of hypothetical underpayments or overpayments of tax liability for redetermination years—and, in some cases, the third step—the determination of the time period for computing interest.

(ii) *Post-completion revenue and expenses*—(A) *In general.* Except as otherwise provided in section 460(b)(6) (see § 1.460-6(j) for method of electing) or § 1.460-6(e), a taxpayer must apply the look-back method to a long-term contract in the completion year and in any post-completion year for which the taxpayer must adjust total contract price or total allocable contract costs, or both, under the PCM. Any year in which the look-back method must be reapplied is treated as a filing year. See Example (3) of paragraph (h)(4) for an illustration of how the look-back method is applied to post-completion adjustments.

(B) *Completion.* A contract is considered to be completed for purposes of the look-back method in the year in which final completion and acceptance within the meaning of § 1.460-1(c)(3) have occurred.

(C) *Discounting of contract price and contract cost adjustments subsequent to completion; election not to discount*—(1) *General rule.* The amount of any post-completion adjustment to the total contract price or contract costs is discounted, solely for purposes of applying the look-back method, from its value at the time the amount is taken into account in computing taxable income to its value at the completion of the contract. The discount rate for this purpose is the Federal mid-term rate under section 1274(d) in effect at the time the amount is properly taken into account. For purposes of applying the look-back method for the completion year, no amounts are discounted, even if they are received after the completion year.

(2) *Election not to discount.* Notwithstanding the general requirement to discount post-completion adjustments, a taxpayer may elect not to discount contract price and contract cost adjustments with respect to any contract. The election not to discount is to be made on a contract-by-contract basis and is binding with respect to all post-completion adjustments that arise with respect to a contract for which an election has been made. An election not to discount with respect to any contract is made by stating that an election is being made on the taxpayer's timely filed federal income tax return (determined with regard to extensions) for the first tax year after completion in which the taxpayer takes into account (*i.e.*, includes in income or deducts) any adjustment to the contract price or contract costs. See § 301.9100-8 of this chapter.

Reg. § 1.460-6(c)(1)

(*3*) *Year-end discounting convention.* In the absence of an election not to discount, any revisions to the contract price and contract costs must be discounted to their value as of the completion of the contract in reapplying the look-back method. For this purpose, the period of discounting is the period between the completion date of the contract and the date that any adjustment is taken into account in computing taxable income. Although taxpayers may use the period between the months in which these two events actually occur, in many cases, these dates may not be readily identifiable. Therefore, for administrative convenience, taxpayers are permitted to use the period between the end of the tax years in which these events occur as the period of discounting provided that the convention is used consistently with respect to all post-completion adjustments for all contracts of the taxpayer the adjustments to which are discounted. In that case, the taxpayer must use as the discount rate the Federal mid-term rate under section 1274(d) as of the end of the tax year in which any revision is taken into account in computing taxable income.

(D) *Revenue acceleration rule.* Section 460(b)(1) imposes a special rule that requires a taxpayer to include in gross income, for the tax year immediately following the year of completion, any previously unreported portion of the total contract price (including amounts that the taxpayer expects to receive in the future) determined as of that year, even if the percentage of completion ratio is less than 100 percent because the taxpayer expects to incur additional allocable contract costs in a later year. At the time any remaining portion of the contract price is includible in income under this rule, no offset against this income is permitted for estimated future contract costs. To achieve the requirement to report all remaining contract revenue without regard to additional estimated costs, a taxpayer must include only costs actually incurred through the end of the tax year in the denominator of the percentage of completion ratio in applying the percentage of completion method for any tax years after the year of completion. The look-back method also must be reapplied for the year immediately following the year of completion if any portion of the contract price is includible in income in that year by reason of section 460(b)(1). For purposes of reapplying the look-back method as a result of this inclusion in income, the taxpayer must only include in the denominator of the percentage of completion ratio the actual contract costs incurred as of the end of the year, even if the taxpayer reasonably expects to incur additional allocable contract costs. To the extent that costs are incurred in a subsequent tax year, the look-back method is reapplied in that year (or a later year if the delayed reapplication method is used), and the taxpayer is entitled to receive interest for the post-completion adjustment to contract costs. Because this reapplication occurs subsequent to the completion year, only the cumulative costs incurred as of the end of the reapplication year are includible in the denominator of the percentage of completion ratio.

(2) *Look-back Step One*—(i) *Hypothetical reallocation of income among prior tax years.* For each filing year, a taxpayer must allocate total contract income among prior tax years, by hypothetically applying the percentage of completion method to all contracts that are completed or adjusted in the filing year using the rules of this paragraph (c)(2). The taxpayer must reallocate income from those contracts among all years preceding the filing year that are affected by those contracts using the total contract price and contract costs, as determined as of the end of the filing year ("actual contract price and costs"), rather than the estimated contract price and contract costs. The taxpayer then must determine the amount of taxable income and the amount of alternative minimum taxable income that would have been reported for each affected tax year preceding the filing year if the percentage of completion method had been applied on the basis of actual contract price and contract costs in reporting income from all contracts completed or adjusted in the filing year and in any preceding year. If the percentage of completion method only applies to alternative minimum taxable income from the contract, only alternative minimum taxable income is recomputed in the first step. For purposes of reallocating income (and costs if the 10-percent year changes for a taxpayer using the 10-percent method of section 460(b)(5)) under the look-back method, the method of computing the percentage of completion ratio is the same method used to report income from the contract on the taxpayer's return. (Thus, an election to use the 10-percent method or the simplified cost-to-cost method is taken into account). See Example (1) of paragraph (h)(2) for an illustration of Step One.

(ii) *Treatment of estimated future costs in year of completion.* If a taxpayer reasonably expects to incur additional allocable contract costs in a tax year subsequent to the year in which the contract is completed, the taxpayer includes the actual costs incurred as of the end of the completion year plus the additional allocable contract costs that are reasonably expected to be incurred (to the extent includible under the taxpayer's percentage of completion method) in the denominator of the percentage of completion ratio. The completion year is the only filing year for which

Reg. § 1.460-6(c)(2)

the taxpayer may include additional estimated costs in the denominator of the percentage of completion ratio in applying the look-back method. If the look-back method is reapplied in any year after the completion year, only the cumulative costs incurred as of the end of the year of reapplication are includible in the denominator of the percentage of completion ratio in reapplying the look-back method.

(iii) *Interim reestimates not considered.* The look-back method cannot be applied to a contract before it is completed. Accordingly, for purposes of applying Step One, the actual total contract price and contract costs are substituted for the previous estimates of total contract price and contract costs only with respect to contracts that have been completed in the filing year and in a tax year preceding the filing year. No adjustments are made under Step One for contracts that have not been completed prior to the end of the current filing year, even if, as of the end of this year, the estimated total contract price or contract costs for these uncompleted contracts is different from the estimated amount that was used during any tax year for which taxable income is recomputed with respect to completed contracts under the look-back method for the current filing year.

(iv) *Tax years in which income is affected.* In general, because income under the percentage of completion method is generally reported as costs are incurred, the taxable income and alternative minimum taxable income are recomputed only for each year in which allocable contract costs were incurred. However, there will be exceptions to this general rule. For example, a taxpayer may be required to cumulatively adjust the income from a contract in a year in which no allocable contract costs are incurred if the estimated total contract price or contract costs was revised in that year. However, in applying the look-back method, no contract income is allocated to that year. Thus, there may be a difference between the amount of contract income originally reported for that year and the amount of contract income as reallocated. Similarly, because of the revenue acceleration rule of section 460(b)(1), income may be reported in the year immediately following the completion year even though no costs were incurred during that year and, in applying the look-back method in that year or another year, if additional costs are incurred or the contract price is adjusted in a later year, no income is allocated to the year immediately following the completion year.

(v) *Costs incurred prior to contract execution; 10-percent method*—(A) *General rule.* The look-back method does not require allocation of contract income to tax years before the contract was entered into. Costs incurred prior to the year a contract is entered into are first taken into account in the numerator of the percentage of completion ratio in the year the contract is entered into. A taxpayer using the 10-percent method must also use the 10-percent method in applying the look-back method, using actual total contract costs to determine the 10-percent year. Thus, contract income is never reallocated to a year before the 10-percent year as determined on the basis of actual contract costs. If the 10-percent year is earlier as a result of applying Step One of the look-back method, contract costs incurred up to and including the new 10-percent year (as determined based on actual contract costs), are reallocated from the original 10 percent year to the new 10-percent, and costs incurred in later years but before the old 10-percent year are reallocated to those years. If the 10-percent year is later as a result of applying Step One of the look-back method, contract costs incurred up to and including the new 10-percent year are reallocated from all prior years to the new 10-percent year. This is the only case in which costs are reallocated under the look-back method.

(B) *Example.* The application of the look-back method by a taxpayer using the 10-percent method is illustrated by the following example:

Example. Z elected to use the 10-percent method of section 460(b)(5) for reporting income under the percentage of completion method. Z entered into a contract in 1990 for a fixed price of $1,000x. During 1990, Z incurred allocable contract costs of $80x and estimated that it would incur a total of $900x for the entire contract. Since $80x is less than 10 percent of total estimated contract costs, Z reported no revenue from the contract in 1990 and deferred the $80x of costs incurred. In 1991, Z incurred an additional $620x of contract costs, and completed the contract. Accordingly, in its 1991 return, Z reported the entire contract price of $1,000x, and deducted the $620x of costs incurred in 1991 and the $80x of costs incurred in 1990.

Under section 460(b)(5), the 10-percent method applies both for reporting contract income and the look-back method. Under the look-back method, since the costs incurred in 1990 ($80x) exceed 10 percent of the actual total contract costs ($700x), Z is required to allocate $114x of contract revenue ($80x/$700x × $1,000x) and the $80x of costs incurred to 1990. Thus, application of the look-back method results in a net increase

Reg. § 1.460-6(c)(2)

in taxable income for 1990 of $34x, solely for purposes of the look-back method.

(vi) *Amount treated as contract price*—(A) *General rule.* The amount that is treated as total contract price for purposes of applying the percentage of completion method and reapplying the percentage of completion method under the look-back method under Step One includes all amounts that the taxpayer expects to receive from the customer. Thus, amounts are treated as part of the contract price as soon as it is reasonably estimated that they will be received, even if the all-events test has not yet been met.

(B) *Contingencies.* Any amounts related to contingent rights or obligations, such as incentive fees or amounts in dispute, are not separated from the contract and accounted for under a non-long-term contract method of accounting, notwithstanding any provision in § 1.460-4(b)(4)(i), to the contrary. Instead, those amounts are treated as part of the total contract price in applying the look-back method. For example, if an incentive fee under a contract to manufacture a satellite is payable to the taxpayer after a specified period of successful performance, the incentive fee is includible in the total contract price at the time and to the extent that it can reasonably be predicted that the performance objectives will be met. A portion of the contract price that is in dispute is included in the total contract price at the time and to the extent that the taxpayer can reasonably expect the dispute will be resolved in the taxpayer's favor (without regard to when the taxpayer receives payment for the amount in dispute or when the dispute is finally resolved).

(C) *Change orders.* In applying the look-back method, a change order with respect to a contract is not treated as a separate contract unless the change order would be treated as a separate contract under the rules for severing and aggregating contracts provided in § 1.460-1(e). Thus, if a change order is not treated as a separate contract, the contract price and contract costs attributable to the change order must be taken into account in allocating contract income to all tax years affected by the underlying contract.

(3) *Look-back Step Two: Computation of hypothetical overpayment or underpayment of tax*—(i) *In general.* Step Two involves the computation of a hypothetical overpayment or underpayment of tax for each year in which the tax liability is affected by income from contracts that are completed or adjusted in the filing year (a "redetermination year"). The application of Step Two depends on whether the taxpayer uses the simplified marginal impact method contained in paragraph (d) or the actual method described in this paragraph (c)(3). The remainder of this paragraph (c)(3) does not apply if a taxpayer uses the simplified marginal impact method.

(ii) *Redetermination of tax liability.* Under the method described in this paragraph (c)(3) (the "actual method"), a taxpayer, first, must determine what its regular and alternative minimum tax liability would have been for each redetermination year if the amounts of contract income allocated in Step One for all contracts completed or adjusted in the filing year and in any prior year were substituted for the amounts of contract income reported under the percentage of completion method on the taxpayer's original return (or as subsequently adjusted on examination, or by amended return). See Example (2) of paragraph (h)(3) for an illustration of Step Two.

(iii) *Hypothetical underpayment or overpayment.* After redetermining the income tax liability for each tax year affected by the reallocation of contract income, the taxpayer then determines the amount, if any, of the hypothetical underpayment or overpayment of tax for each of these redetermination years. The hypothetical underpayment or overpayment for each affected year is the difference between the tax liability as redetermined under the look-back method for that year and the amount of tax liability determined as of the latest of the following:

(A) the original return date;

(B) the date of a subsequently amended or adjusted return (if, however, the amended return is due to a carryback described in section 6611(f), see paragraph (c)(4)(iii)); or,

(C) the last previous application of the look-back method (in which case, the previous hypothetical tax liability is used).

(iv) *Cumulative determination of tax liability.* The redetermination of tax liability resulting from previous applications of the look-back method is cumulative. Thus, for example, in computing the amount of a hypothetical overpayment or underpayment of tax for a redetermination year, the current hypothetical tax liability is compared to the hypothetical tax liability for that year determined as of the last previous application of the look-back method.

(v) *Years affected by look-back only.* A redetermination of income tax liability under Step Two is required for every tax year for which the tax liability would have been affected by a change in the amount of income or loss for any other year for which a redetermination is required. For example, if the allocation of contract income under Step One changed the amount of a net operating loss that was carried back to a year preceding the

Reg. § 1.460-6(c)(3)

year the taxpayer entered into the contract, the tax liability for the earlier year must be redetermined.

(vi) *Definition of tax liability.* For purposes of Step Two, the income tax liability must be redetermined by taking into account all applicable additions to tax, credits, and net operating loss carrybacks and carryovers. Thus, the tax, if any, imposed under section 55 (relating to alternative minimum tax) must be taken into account. For example, if the taxpayer did not pay alternative minimum tax, but would have paid alternative minimum tax for that year if actual rather than estimated contract price and costs had been used in determining contract income for the year, the amount of any hypothetical overpayment or underpayment of tax must be determined by comparing the hypothetical total tax liability (including hypothetical alternative minimum tax liability) with the actual tax liability for that year. The effect of taking these items into account in applying the look-back method is illustrated in Examples (4) through (7) of paragraphs (h)(5) through (h)(8) below.

(4) *Look-back Step Three: Calculation of interest on underpayment or overpayment*—(i) *In general.* After determining a hypothetical underpayment or overpayment of tax for each redetermination year, the taxpayer must determine the interest charged or credited on each of these amounts. Interest on the amount determined under Step Two is determined by applying the overpayment rate designated under section 6621, compounded daily. In general, the time period over which interest is charged on hypothetical underpayments or credited on hypothetical overpayments begins at the due date (not including extensions) of the return for the redetermination year for which the hypothetical underpayment or overpayment determined in Step Two is computed. This time period generally ends on the earlier of

(A) the due date (not including extensions) of the return for the filing year, and

(B) the date both

(*1*) the income tax return for the filing year is filed, and

(*2*) the tax for that year has been paid in full.

If a taxpayer uses the simplified marginal impact method contained in paragraph (d), the remainder of this paragraph (c)(4) does not apply.

(ii) *Changes in the amount of a loss or credit carryback or carryover.* The time period for determining interest may be different in cases involving loss or credit carrybacks or carryovers in order to properly reflect the time period during which the taxpayer (in the case of an underpayment) or the Government (in the case of an overpayment) had the use of the amount determined to be a hypothetical underpayment or overpayment. Thus, if a reallocation of contract income under Step One results in an increase or decrease to a net operating loss carryback (but not a carryforward), the interest due or to be refunded must be computed on the increase or decrease in tax attributable to the change to the carryback only from the due date (not including extensions) of the return for the redetermination year that generated the carryback and not from the due date of the return for the redetermination year in which the carryback was absorbed. In the case of a change in the amount of a carryover as a result of applying the look-back method, interest is computed from the due date of the return for the year in which the carryover was absorbed. See Examples (8) and (9) of paragraph (h)(9) for an illustration of these rules.

(iii) *Changes in the amount of tax liability that generated a subsequent refund.* If the amount of tax liability for a redetermination year (as reported on the taxpayer's original return, as subsequently adjusted on examination, as adjusted by amended return, or as redetermined by the last previous application of the look-back method) is decreased by the application of the look-back method, and any portion of the redetermination year tax liability was absorbed by a loss or credit carryback arising in a year subsequent to the redetermination year, the look-back method applies as follows to properly reflect the time period of the use of the tax overpayment. To the extent the amount of tax absorbed because of the carryback exceeds the total hypothetical tax liability for the year (as redetermined under the look-back method) the taxpayer is entitled to receive interest only until the due date (not including extensions) of the return for the year in which the carryback arose.

Example. Upon the completion of a long-term contract in 1990, the taxpayer redetermines its tax liability for 1988 under the look-back method. This redetermination results in a hypothetical reduction of tax liability from $1,500x (actual liability originally reported) to $1,200x (hypothetical liability). In addition, the taxpayer had already received a refund of some or all of the actual 1988 tax by carrying back a net operating loss (NOL) that arose in 1989. The time period over which interest would be computed on the hypothetical overpayment of $300x for 1988 would depend on the amount of the refund generated by the carryback, as illustrated by the following three alternative situations:

Reg. § 1.460-6(c)(4)

(A) If the amount refunded because of the NOL is $1,500x$: interest is credited to the taxpayer on the entire hypothetical overpayment of $300x$ from the due date of the 1988 return, when the hypothetical overpayment occurred, until the due date of the 1989 return, when the taxpayer received a refund for the entire amount of the 1988 tax, including the hypothetical overpayment.

(B) If the amount refunded because of the NOL is $1,000x$: interest is credited to the taxpayer on the entire amount of the hypothetical overpayment of $300x$ from the due date of the 1988 return, when the hypothetical overpayment occurred, until the due date of the 1990 return. In this situation interest is credited until the due date of the return for the completion year of the contract, rather than the due date of the return for the year in which the carryback arose, because the amount refunded was less than the redetermined tax liability. Therefore, no portion of the hypothetical overpayment is treated as having been refunded to the taxpayer before the filing year.

(C) If the amount refunded because of the NOL is $1,300x$: interest is credited to the taxpayer on $100x$ ($1,300x - 1,200x$) from the due date of the 1988 return until the due date of the 1989 return because only this portion of the total hypothetical overpayment is treated as having been refunded to the taxpayer before the filing year. However, the taxpayer did not receive a refund for the remaining $200x$ of the overpayment at that time and, therefore, is credited with interest on $200x$ through the due date of the tax return for 1990, the filing year. See Examples (10) and (11) of paragraph (h)(9) for a further illustration of this rule.

(d) *Simplified marginal impact method*—(1) *Introduction.* This paragraph (d) provides a simplified method for calculating look-back interest. Any taxpayer may elect this simplified marginal impact method, except that pass-through entities described in paragraph (d)(4) of this section are required to apply the simplified marginal impact method at the entity level with respect to domestic contracts and the owners of those entities do not apply the look-back method to those contracts. Under the simplified marginal impact method, a taxpayer calculates the hypothetical underpayments or overpayments of tax for a prior year based on an assumed marginal tax rate. A taxpayer electing to use the simplified marginal impact method must use the method for each long-term contract for which it reports income (except with respect to domestic contracts if the taxpayer is an owner in a widely held pass-through entity that is required to use the simplified marginal impact method at the entity level for those contracts).

(2) *Operation*—(i) *In general.* Under the simplified marginal impact method, income from those contracts that are completed or adjusted in the filing year is first reallocated in accordance with the procedures of Step One contained in paragraph (c)(2) of this section. Step Two is modified in the following manner. The hypothetical underpayment or overpayment of tax for each year of the contract (a "redetermination year") is determined by multiplying the applicable regular tax rate (as defined in paragraph (d)(2)(iii)) by the increase or decrease in regular taxable income (or, if it produces a greater amount, by multiplying the applicable alternative minimum tax rate by the increase or decrease in alternative minimum taxable income, whether or not the taxpayer would have been subject to the alternative minimum tax) that results from reallocating income to the tax year under Step One. Generally, the product of the alternative minimum tax rate and the increase or decrease in alternative minimum taxable income will be the greater of the two amounts described in the preceding sentence only with respect to contracts for which a taxpayer uses the full percentage of completion method only for alternative minimum tax purposes and uses the completed contract method, or the percentage of completion-capitalized cost method, for regular tax purposes. Step Three is then applied. Interest is credited to the taxpayer on the net overpayment and is charged to the taxpayer on the net underpayment for each redetermination year from the due date (determined without regard to extensions) of the return for the redetermination year until the earlier of

(A) the due date (determined without regard to extensions) of the return for the filing year, and

(B) the first date by which both the return is filed and the tax is fully paid.

(ii) *Applicable tax rate.* For purposes of determining hypothetical underpayments or overpayments of tax under the simplified marginal impact method, the applicable regular tax rate is the highest rate of tax in effect for the redetermination year under section 1 in the case of an individual and under section 11 in the case of a corporation. The applicable alternative minimum tax rate is the rate of tax in effect for the taxpayer under section 55(b)(1). The highest rate is determined without regard to the taxpayer's actual rate bracket and without regard to any additional surtax imposed for the purpose of phasing out multiple tax brackets or exemptions.

Reg. § 1.460-6(d)(2)

(iii) *Overpayment ceiling.* The net hypothetical overpayment of tax for any redetermination year is limited to the taxpayer's total federal income tax liability for the redetermination year reduced by the cumulative amount of net hypothetical overpayments of tax for that redetermination year resulting from earlier applications of the look-back method. If the reallocation of contract income results in a net overpayment of tax and this amount exceeds the actual tax liability (as of the filing year) for the redetermination year, as adjusted for past applications of the look-back method and taking into account net operating loss, capital loss, or credit carryovers and carrybacks to that year, the actual tax so adjusted is treated as the overpayment for the redetermination year. This overpayment ceiling does not apply when the simplified marginal impact method is applied at the entity level by a widely held pass-through entity in accordance with paragraph (d)(4) of this section.

(iv) *Example.* The application of the simplified marginal impact method is illustrated by the following example:

Example. Corporation X, a calendar-year taxpayer, reports income from long-term contracts and elected the simplified marginal impact method when it filed its income tax return for 1989. X uses only the percentage of completion method for both regular taxable income and alternative minimum taxable income. X completed contracts A, B, and C in 1989 and, therefore, was required to apply the look-back method in 1989. Income was actually reported for these contracts in 1987, 1988, and 1989. X's applicable tax rate, as determined under section 11, for the redetermination years 1987 and 1988 was 40 percent and 34 percent, respectively. The amount of contract income originally reported and reallocated for contracts A, B, and C, and the net overpayments and underpayments for the redetermination years are as follows:

	1987	1988
Contract A:		
Originally reported	$5,000x	$4,000x
Reallocated	3,000x	5,000x
Increase/(Decrease)	(2,000x)	1,000x
Contract B:		
Originally reported	6,000x	2,000x
Reallocated	7,000x	1,500x
Increase/(Decrease)	1,000x	(500x)
Contract C:		
Originally reported	8,000x	5,000x
Reallocated	4,000x	7,000x
Increase/(Decrease)	(4,000x)	2,000x
Net Increase/(Decrease)	(5,000x)	2,500x
Tentative (Underpayment)/Overpayment		
.40	2,000x	
.34		(850x)
Ceiling:		
Actual Tax Liability (After Carryovers and Carrybacks)	1,500x	500x
Final (Underpayment)/Overpayment	1,500x	(850x)

Under the simplified marginal impact method, X determined a tentative hypothetical net overpayment for 1987 and a net underpayment for 1988. X determined these amounts by first aggregating the difference for contracts A, B, and C between the amount of contract price originally reported and the amount of contract price as reallocated and, then, applying the highest regular tax rate to the aggregate decrease in income for 1987 and the aggregate increase in income for 1988.

However, X's overpayment for 1987 is subject to a ceiling based on X's total tax liability. Because the tentative net overpayment of tax for 1987 exceeds the actual tax liability for that year after taking into account carryovers and carrybacks to that year, the final overpayment under the simplified marginal impact method is the amount of tax liability paid instead of the tentative net overpayment. Since application of the look-back method for 1988 results in a tentative underpayment of tax, it is not subject to a ceiling. If the look-back method is applied in 1991, the ceiling amount for 1987 will be zero and the ceiling amount for 1988 will be $1,350.

X is entitled to receive interest on the hypothetical overpayment from March 15, 1988, to March 15, 1990. X is required to pay interest on the underpayment from March 15, 1989, to March 15, 1990.

(3) *Anti-abuse rule.* If the simplified marginal impact method is used with respect to any

Reg. § 1.460-6(d)(3)

long-term contract (including a contract of a widely held pass-through entity), the district director may recompute interest for the contract (including domestic contracts of widely held pass-through entities) under the look-back method using the actual method (and without regard to the simplified marginal impact method). The district director may make such a recomputation only if the amount of income originally reported with respect to the contract for any redetermination year exceeds the amount of income reallocated under the look-back method with respect to that contract for that year (using actual contract price and contract costs) by the lesser of $1,000,000 or 20 percent of the amount of income as reallocated (i.e., based on actual contract price and contract costs) under the look-back method with respect to that contract for that year. In determining whether to exercise this authority upon examination of the Form 8697, the district director may take into account whether the taxpayer overreported income for a purpose of receiving interest under the look-back method on a hypothetical overpayment determined at the applicable tax rate. The district director also may take into account whether the taxpayer underreported income for the year in question with respect to other contracts. Notwithstanding the look-back method, the district director may require an adjustment to the tax liability for any open tax year if the taxpayer did not apply the percentage of completion method properly on its original return.

(4) *Application*—(i) *Required use by certain pass-through entities*—(A) *General rule.* The simplified marginal impact method is required to be used with respect to income reported from domestic contracts by a pass-through entity that is either a partnership, an S corporation, or a trust, and that is not closely held. With respect to contracts described in the preceding sentence, the simplified marginal impact method is applied by the pass-through entity at the entity level. For determining the amount of any hypothetical underpayment or overpayment, the applicable regular and alternative minimum tax rates, respectively, are generally the highest rates of tax in effect for corporations under section 11 and section 55(b)(1). However, the applicable regular and alternative minimum tax rates are the highest rates of tax imposed on individuals under section 1 and section 55(b)(1) if, at all times during the redetermination year involved (i.e., the year in which the hypothetical increase or decrease in income arises), more than 50 percent of the interests in the entity were held by individuals directly or through 1 or more pass through entities.

(B) *Closely held.* A pass-through entity is closely held if, at any time during any redetermination year, 50 percent or more (by value) of the beneficial interests in that entity are held (directly or indirectly) by or for 5 or fewer persons. For this purpose, the term "person" has the same meaning as in section 7701(a)(1), except that a pass-through entity is not treated as a person. In addition, the constructive ownership rules of section 1563(e) apply by substituting the term "beneficial interest" for the term "stock" and by substituting the term "pass-through entity" for the term "corporation" used in that section, as appropriate, for purposes of determining whether a beneficial interest in a pass-through entity is indirectly owned by any person.

(C) *Examples.* The following examples illustrate the application of the rules of paragraph (d)(4)(i):

Example (1). P, a partnership, began a long-term contract on March 1, 1986, and completed this contract in its tax year ending December 31, 1989. P used the percentage of completion method for all contract income. Substantially all of the income from the contract arose from U.S. sources. At all times during all of the years for which income was required to be reported under the contract, exactly 25 percent of the value of P's interests was owned by Corporation M. The remaining 75 percent of the value of P's interests was owned in equal shares by 15 unrelated individuals, who are also unrelated to Corporation M. M's ownership of P represents less than 50 percent of the value of the beneficial interests in P, and, therefore, viewed alone, is insufficient to make P a closely held partnership. In addition, because no 4 of the individual owners together own 25 percent or more of the remaining value of P's beneficial interests, there is no group of 5 owners that together own, directly or indirectly, 50 percent or more by value of the beneficial interests in P. Therefore, P is not a closely held pass-through entity.

Because P is not a closely held pass-through entity, and because P completed the contract after the effective date of section 460(b)(4), P is required to use the simplified marginal impact method. Any interest computed under the look-back method will be paid to, or collected from, P, rather than its partners, and must be reported to each of the partners on Form 1065 as interest income or expense. Further, assume that, for the redetermination years, Corporation M is subject to alternative minimum tax at the rate of 20 percent and 3 of the individuals who own interests in P are subject to the highest marginal tax rate of 33 percent in 1988. Regardless of the

Reg. § 1.460-6(d)(4)

actual marginal tax rates of its partners, P is required to determine the underpayment or overpayment of tax for each redetermination year at the entity level by applying a single rate to the increase or decrease in income resulting from the reallocation of contract income under the lookback method. Because more than 50 percent of the interests in P are held by individuals, P must use the highest rate specified in section 1 for each redetermination year. Thus, the rate applied by P is 50 percent for 1986, 38.5 percent for 1987, and 28 percent for 1988.

Example (2). Assume the same facts as in Example (1), except that one of the individuals, Individual I, who directly owns 5 percent of the value of the interests of P, also owns 100 percent of the stock of Corporation M. Section 1563(e)(4) of the Code provides that stock owned directly or indirectly by or for a corporation is considered to be owned by any person who owns 5 percent or more in value of its stock in that proportion which the value of the stock which that person so owns bears to the value of all the stock in that corporation. Because section 460(b)(4)(C)(iii) and this paragraph (d)(4) provide that rules similar to the constructive ownership rules of section 1563(e) apply in determining whether a pass-through entity is closely held, all of M's interest in P is attributed to I because I owns 100 percent of the value of the stock in M. Accordingly, because I's direct 5 percent and constructive 25 percent ownership of P, plus the interests owned by any 4 other individual partners, equals 50 percent or more of the value of the beneficial interests of P, P is a closely held pass-through entity within the meaning of section 460(b)(4)(C)(iii). Therefore, P cannot use the simplified marginal impact method at the entity level. Accordingly, each of the partners of P must separately apply the lookback method to their respective interests in the income and expenses attributable to the contract, but each partner may elect to use the simplified marginal impact method with respect to the partner's share of income from the contract.

(D) *Domestic contracts*—(*1*) *General rule.* A domestic contract is any contract substantially all of the income of which is from sources in the United States. For this purpose, "substantially all" of the income from a long-term contract is considered to be from United States sources if 95 percent or more of the gross income from the contract is from sources within the United States as determined under the rules in sections 861 through 865.

(*2*) *Portion of contract income sourced.* In determining whether substantially all of the gross income from a long-term contract is from United States sources, taxpayers must apply the allocation and apportionment principles of sections 861 through 865 only to the portion of the contract accounted for under the percentage of completion method. Under the percentage of completion method, gross income from a long-term contract includes all payments to be received under the contract (*i.e.*, any amounts treated as contract price). Similarly, all costs taken into account in the computation of taxable income under the percentage of completion method are deducted from gross income rather than added to a cost of goods sold account that reduces gross income. Therefore, allocable contract costs are not considered in determining whether a long-term contract is a domestic contract or a foreign contract, even if, under the taxpayer's facts, the allocation of contract costs to any portion of a contract not accounted for under the percentage of completion method would affect the relative percentages of United States and foreign source gross income from the entire contract if this portion of the contract were taken into account in applying the 95-percent test.

(E) *Application to foreign contracts.* If a widely held pass-through entity has some foreign contracts and some domestic contracts, the owners of the pass-through entity each apply the lookback method (using, if they elect, the simplified marginal impact method) to their respective share of the income and expense from foreign contracts. Moreover, in applying the look-back method to foreign contracts at the owner level, the owners do not take into account their share of increases or decreases in contract income resulting from the application of the simplified marginal impact method with respect to domestic contracts at the entity level.

(F) *Effective date.* The simplified marginal impact method must be applied to pass-through entities described in paragraph (d)(4)(i) of this section with respect to domestic contracts completed or adjusted in tax years for which the due date of the return (determined with regard to extensions) of the pass-through entity is after November 9, 1988.

(ii) *Elective use*—(A) *General rule.* As provided in paragraph (d)(4)(i) of this section, the simplified marginal impact method must be used by certain pass-through entities with respect to domestic contracts. C corporations, individuals, and owners of closely held pass-through entities may elect the simplified marginal impact method. Owners of other pass-through entities may also elect the simplified marginal impact method with respect to all contracts other than those for which the simplified marginal impact method is required to be applied at the entity level. This rule applies to foreign contracts of widely held pass-through entities. In the case of an electing owner in a pass-through entity, the simplified marginal impact method is applied at the owner level, instead of at the entity level, with respect to the owner's share of the long-term contract income and expense reported by the pass-through entity.

(B) *Election requirements.* A taxpayer elects the simplified marginal impact method by stating that the election is being made on a timely filed income tax return (determined with regard to extensions) for the first tax year the election is to apply. An election to use the simplified marginal impact method applies to all applications of the look-back method to all eligible long-term contracts for the tax year for which the election is made and for any subsequent tax year. The election may not be revoked without the consent of the Commissioner.

(C) *Consolidated group consistency rule.* In the case of a consolidated group of corporations, as defined in § 1.1502-1(h), an election to use the simplified marginal impact method is made by the common parent of the group. The election is binding on all other affected members of the group (including members that join the group after the election is made with respect to all applications of the look-back method after joining). If a member subsequently leaves the group, the election remains binding as to that member unless the Commissioner consents to a revocation of the election. If a corporation using the simplified marginal impact method joins a group that does not use the method, the election is automatically revoked with respect to all applications of the look-back method after it joins the group.

(e) *Delayed reapplication method*—(1) *In general.* For purposes of reapplying the look-back method after the year of contract completion, a taxpayer may elect the delayed reapplication method to minimize the number of required reapplications of the look-back method. Under this method, the look-back method is reapplied after the year of completion of a contract (or after a subsequent application of the look-back method) only when the first one of the following conditions is met with respect to the contract:

(i) the net undiscounted value of increases or decreases in the contract price occurring since the time of the last application of the look-back method exceeds the lesser of $1,000,000 or 10 percent of the total contract price as of that time,

(ii) the net undiscounted value of increases or decreases in contract costs occurring since the time of the last application of the look-back method exceeds the lesser of $1,000,000 or 10 percent of the total actual contract costs as of that time,

(iii) the taxpayer goes out of existence,

(iv) the taxpayer reasonably believes the contract is finally settled and closed, or

(v) neither condition (i), (ii), (iii) nor (iv) above is met by the end of the fifth tax year that begins after the last previous application of the look-back method.

(2) *Time and manner of making election.* An election to use the delayed reapplication method may be made for any filing year for which the due date of the return (determined with regard to extensions) is after June 12, 1990. The election is made by a statement to that effect on the taxpayer's timely filed federal income tax return (determined with regard to extensions) for the first tax year the election is to be effective. An election to use the delayed reapplication method is binding with respect to all long-term contracts for which the look-back method would be reapplied without regard to the election in the year of election and any subsequent year unless the Commissioner consents to a revocation of the election. In the case of a consolidated group of corporations, as defined in § 1.1502-1(h), an election to use the delayed reapplication method is made by the common parent of the group. The election is binding on all other affected members of the group (including members that join the group after the election is made with respect to contracts adjusted after joining). If a member subsequently leaves the group, the election remains binding as to that member unless the Commissioner consents to a revocation of the election. If a corporation that has made the election joins a consolidated group that has not made the election, the election is treated as revoked with respect to contracts adjusted after joining.

(3) *Examples.* The operation of this delayed reapplication method is illustrated by the following examples:

Example (1). X completes a contract in 1987, and applies the look-back method when its return for 1987 is filed. X properly uses $600,000 as the actual contract price in applying the look-back method. In 1990, as a result of the settlement of a dispute with its customer, X redetermines total contract price to be $640,000, and includes $40,000 in gross income. On its return for 1990, X states that it is electing the delayed reapplication method. X is not required to reapply the look-back method at that time, because $40,000 does not exceed the lesser of $1,000,000 or 10 percent of the unadjusted contract price of $600,000, and 5 years have not passed since the last application of the look-back method.

Reg. § 1.460-6(e)(3)

Example (2). Assume the same facts as in Example (1), except that at the end of 1992, the fifth year after completion of the contract, no other adjustments to contract price or contract costs have occurred. X is required to reapply the look-back method in 1992 and, accordingly, redetermine its tax liability for each redetermination year. After redetermining the underpayment of tax for those years, X must compute the amount of interest charged on the underpayments. Although 1992 is the filing year, interest is due on the amount of each underpayment resulting from the adjustment only from the due date of the return for each redetermination year to the due date of the return for 1990 because the tax liability for the adjustment was fully paid in 1990. However, from the due date of the 1990 return until the due date of the 1992 return, when the look-back method is reapplied for the adjustment, interest is due on the amount of interest attributable to the underpayments.

(f) *Look-back reporting*—(1) *Procedure.* The amount of any interest due from, or payable to, a taxpayer as a result of applying the look-back method is computed on Form 8697 for any filing year. In general, the look-back method is applied by the taxpayer that reports income from a long-term contract. See paragraph (g) of this section to determine who is responsible for applying the look-back method when, prior to the completion of a long-term contract, there is a transaction that changes the taxpayer that reports income from the contract.

(2) *Treatment of interest on return*—(i) *General rule.* The amount of interest required to be paid by a taxpayer is treated as an income tax under subtitle A, but only for purposes of subtitle F of the Code (other than sections 6654 and 6655), which addresses tax procedures and administration. Thus, a taxpayer that fails to pay the amount of interest due is subject to any applicable penalties under subtitle F, including, for example, an underpayment penalty under section 6651, and the taxpayer also is liable for underpayment interest under section 6601. However, interest required to be paid under the look-back method is treated as interest expense for purposes of computing taxable income under subtitle A, even though it is treated as income tax liability for subtitle F purposes. Interest received under the look-back method is treated as taxable interest income for all purposes, and is not treated as a reduction in tax liability or a tax refund. The determination of whether or not interest computed under the look-back method is treated as tax is determined on a "net" basis for each filing year. Thus, if a taxpayer computes for the current filing year both hypothetical overpayments and hypothetical underpayments for prior years, the taxpayer has an increase in tax only if the interest computed on the underpayments for all those prior years exceeds the interest computed on the overpayments for all those prior years, for all contracts completed or adjusted for the year.

(ii) *Timing of look-back interest.* For purposes of determining taxable income under subtitle A of the Code, any amount of interest payable to the taxpayer under the look-back method is includible in gross income as interest income in the tax year it is properly taken into account under the taxpayer's method of accounting for interest income. Any amount of interest required to be paid is taken into account as interest expense arising from an underpayment of income tax in the tax year it is properly taken into account under the taxpayer's method of accounting for interest expense. Thus, look-back interest required to be paid by an individual, or by a pass-through entity on behalf of an individual owner (or beneficiary) under the simplified marginal impact method, is personal interest and, therefore, is disallowed in accordance with § 1.163-9T(b)(2). Interest determined at the entity level under the simplified marginal impact method is allocated among the owners (or beneficiaries) for reporting purposes in the same manner that interest income and interest expense are allocated to owners (or beneficiaries) and subject to the requirements of section 704 and any other applicable rules.

(3) *Statute of limitations and compounding of interest on look-back interest.* For guidance on the statute of limitations applicable to the assessment and collection of look-back interest owed by a taxpayer, see sections 6501 and 6502. A taxpayer's claim for credit or refund of look-back interest previously paid by or collected from a taxpayer is a claim for credit or refund of an overpayment of tax and is subject to the statute of limitations provided in section 6511. A taxpayer's claim for look-back interest (or interest payable on look-back interest) that is not attributable to an amount previously paid by or collected from a taxpayer is a general, non-tax claim against the federal government. For guidance on the statute of limitations that applies to general, non-tax claims against the federal government, see 28 U.S.C. sections 2401 and 2501. For guidance applicable to the compounding of interest when the look-back interest is not paid, see sections 6601 to 6622.

(g) *Mid-contract change in taxpayer*—(1) *In general.* The rules in this paragraph (g) apply if, as described in § 1.460-4(k), prior to the completion of a long-term contract accounted for using the PCM or the PCCM by a taxpayer (old taxpayer), there is a transaction that makes another taxpayer (new taxpayer) responsible for accounting for income from the same contract. The rules governing constructive completion transactions are provided in paragraph (g)(2) of this section, while the rules governing step-in-the-shoes transactions are provided in paragraph (g)(3) of this section. For purposes of this paragraph, pre-transaction years are all taxable years of the old taxpayer in which the old taxpayer accounted for (or should have accounted for) gross receipts from the contract, and post-transaction years are all taxable years of the new taxpayer in which the new taxpayer accounted for (or should have accounted for) gross receipts from the contract.

(2) *Constructive completion transactions.* In the case of a transaction described in § 1.460-4(k)(2)(i) (constructive completion transaction), the look-back method is applied by the old taxpayer with respect to pre-transaction years upon the date of the transaction and, if the new taxpayer uses the PCM or the PCCM to account for the contract, by the new taxpayer with respect to post-transaction years upon completion of the contract. The contract price and allocable contract costs to be taken into account by the old taxpayer or the new taxpayer in applying the look-back method are described in § 1.460-4(k)(2).

(3) *Step-in-the-shoes transactions*—(i) *General rules.* In the case of a transaction described in § 1.460-4(k)(3)(i) (step-in-the-shoes transaction), the look-back method is not applied at the time of the transaction, but is instead applied for the first time when the contract is completed by the new taxpayer. Upon completion of the contract, the look-back method is applied by the new taxpayer with respect to both pre-transaction years and post-transaction years, taking into account all amounts reasonably expected to be received by either the old or new taxpayer and all allocable contract costs incurred during both periods as described in § 1.460-4(k)(3). The new taxpayer is liable for filing the Form 8697 and for interest computed on hypothetical underpayments of tax, and is entitled to receive interest with respect to hypothetical overpayments of tax, for both pre- and post-transaction years. The old taxpayer will be secondarily liable for any interest required to be paid with respect to pre-transaction years reduced by any interest on pre-transaction overpayments.

(ii) *Application of look-back method to pre-transaction period*—(A) *Contract price.* The actual contract price for pre-transaction taxable years must be determined by the new taxpayer without regard to any contract price adjustment described in paragraph (k)(3)(iv)(B)(1) of this section.

(B) *Method.* The new taxpayer may apply the look-back method to each pre-transaction taxable year that is a redetermination year using the simplified marginal impact method described in paragraph (d) of this section (regardless of whether or not the old taxpayer would have actually used that method and without regard to the tax liability ceiling). But see paragraph (d)(4) of this section, which requires use of the simplified marginal impact method by certain pass-through entities.

(C) *Interest accrual period.* With respect to any hypothetical underpayment or overpayment of tax for a pre-transaction taxable year, interest accrues from the due date of the old taxpayer's tax return (not including extensions) for the taxable year of the underpayment or overpayment until the due date of the new taxpayer's return (not including extensions) for the completion year or the year of a post-completion adjustment, whichever is applicable.

(D) *Information old taxpayer must provide.* In order to help the new taxpayer to apply the look-back method with respect to pre-transaction taxable years, any old taxpayer that accounted for income from a long-term contract under the PCM or PCCM for either regular or alternative minimum tax purposes is required to provide the information described in this paragraph to the new taxpayer by the due date (not including extensions) of the old taxpayer's income tax return for the first taxable year ending on or after a step-in-the-shoes transaction described in § 1.460-4(k)(3)(i). The required information is as follows—

(*1*) The portion of the contract reported by the old taxpayer under PCM for regular and alternative minimum tax purposes (i.e., whether the old taxpayer used PCM, the 40/60 PCCM method, or the 70/30 PCCM method);

(*2*) Any submethods used in the application of PCM (e.g., the simplified cost-to-cost method or the 10-percent method);

(*3*) The amount of total contract price reported by year;

(*4*) The numerator and the denominator of the completion factor by year;

(*5*) The due date (not including extensions) of the old taxpayer's income tax returns for each taxable year in which income was required to be reported;

(*6*) Whether the old taxpayer was a corporate or a noncorporate taxpayer by year; and

Reg. § 1.460-6(g)(3)

(7) Any other information required by the Commissioner by administrative pronouncement.

(iii) *Application of look-back method to post-transaction years.* With respect to post-transaction taxable years, the new taxpayer must use the same look-back method it uses for other contracts (i.e., the simplified marginal impact method or the actual method) to determine the amount of any hypothetical overpayment or underpayment of tax and the time period for computing interest on these amounts.

(iv) *S corporation elections.* Following the conversion of a C corporation into an S corporation, the look-back method is applied at the entity level with respect to contracts entered into prior to the conversion, notwithstanding section 460(b)(4)(B)(i).

(4) *Effective date.* This paragraph (g) is applicable for transactions on or after May 15, 2002.

(h) *Examples*—(1) *Overview.* This paragraph provides computational examples of the rules of this section. Except as otherwise noted, the examples involve calendar-year taxpayers and involve long-term contracts subject to section 460 that are accounted for using the percentage of completion method, rather than the percentage of completion-capitalized cost method. If the percentage of completion-capitalized cost method were used by a taxpayer described in the examples, the amounts of contract income and expenses shown in the examples would be reduced, for purposes of determining regular taxable income, to the appropriate fraction (40, 70, or 90 percent) of contract items accounted for under the percentage of completion method. Tens of thousands of dollars ($00,000's) are omitted from the figures in the examples. The contracts described in the examples are assumed to be the taxpayers' only contracts that are subject to the look-back method of section 460. Except as otherwise stated, the examples assume that the taxpayer has no adjustments and preferences for purposes of section 55, so that alternative minimum taxable income is the same as taxable income, and no alternative minimum tax is imposed for the years involved. The examples assume that the taxpayer does not elect the 10-percent method, the simplified marginal impact method, or the delayed reapplication method.

(2) *Step One.* The following example illustrates the application of paragraph (c)(2):

Example (1). In 1989, W completes three long-term contracts, A, B, and C, entered into on January 1 of 1986, 1987, and 1988, respectively. For Contract A, W used the completed contract method of accounting. For Contract B, W used the percentage of completion-capitalized cost method of accounting, taking into account 60 percent of contract income under W's normal method of accounting, which was the completed contract method. For Contract C, W used the percentage of completion method of accounting. The total price for each contract was $1,000. In computing alternative minimum taxable income, W is required to use the percentage of completion method for Contracts B and C. W used regular tax costs for purposes of determining the degree of contract completion under the alternative minimum tax.

Contract A is not taken into account for purposes of applying the look-back method, because it is subject to neither section 460 nor section 56(a)(3). Thus, even if W had used the percentage of completion method as permitted under § 1.451-3, instead of the completed contract method, the look-back method would not be applicable because the Contract A was entered into before the effective date of section 460.

The actual costs allocated to Contracts B and C under section 460(c) and incurred in each year of the contract were as follows:

Contract	1987	1988	1989	Total
B	$200	$400	$200	$800
C		100	300	400	800

In applying the look-back method, the first step is to allocate the contract price among tax years preceding and including the completion year. That allocation would produce the following amounts of gross income for purposes of the regular tax. Note that no income from Contract C is allocated to 1987, the year before the contract was entered into, even though contract costs were incurred in 1987:

Contract	1987	1988	1989
B	$100	$200	$700
	(40% × $200/$800 × $1000)	((40% × $600/$800 × $1000) − $100)	
C	0		500	500
		($400/$800 × $1000)	

Because the percentage of completion-capitalized cost method may not be used for alternative minimum tax purposes, the allocation of contract income would produce the following amounts of

Reg. § 1.460-6(g)(4)

Methods of Accounting

See p. 20,601 for regulations not amended to reflect law changes

gross income for purposes of computing alternative minimum taxable income:

Contract	1987	1988	1989
B	$250 ($200/$800 × $1000)	$500 (($600/$800 × $1000) − $250)	$250
C	0	500	500

(3) *Step Two.* The following example illustrates the application of paragraph (c)(3):

e = estimate
a = amount originally reported (actual)
h = hypothetical

Example (2). (i) X enters into two long-term contracts (D and E) in 1988. X determines its tax liability for 1988 as follows:

1988

	D	E	Total
1988 contract costs	$ 3,000a	$ 2,000a	
Total contract costs	8,000e	8,000e	
Total contract price	10,000e	10,000e	
1988 completion %	37.5%e	25%e	
1988 gross income	3,750a	2,500a	
less, 1988 costs	(3,000a)	(2,000a)	
1988 net contract income	750a	500a	$ 1,250a
Other 1988 net income (loss)			(2,000a)
Taxable income (NOL)			(750a)
Tax			-0-a
Refund from NOL carryback fully absorbed in 1985, at 46%			345a

(ii) X completes Contract D during 1989. X determines its taxable income for 1989 as follows:

1989

	D	E	Total
1989 contract costs	$ 3,000a	$ -0-a	
Total contract costs	6,000a	9,000e	
Total contract price	10,000a	10,000e	
1989 completion %	100%a	22.2%e	
1989 gross income/(loss)	6,250a	(278a)	
less, 1989 costs	(3,000a)	-0-a	
1989 net contract income	3,250a	(278a)	$ 2,972a
Other 1989 net income (loss)			-0-a
Taxable income (NOL)			2,972a
Tax at 34%			1,011a

(iii) For purposes of the look-back method, X must reallocate the actual total contract D price between 1988 and 1989 based on the actual total contract D costs. This results in the following hypothetical underpayment of tax for 1988 for purposes of the look-back method. Note that X does not reallocate the contract E price in applying the look-back method in 1989 because contract E has not been completed, even though X's estimate of contract E costs has changed. The following computation is only for purposes of applying the look-back method, and does not result in the assessment of a tax deficiency.

1988

	D	E	Total
1988 contract costs	$ 3,000a	$ 2,000a	
Total contract costs	6,000a	8,000e	
Total contract price	10,000a	10,000e	
1988 completion %	50%a	25%e	
1988 gross income	5,000h	2,500a	
less, 1988 costs	(3,000a)	(2,000a)	
1988 net contract income	2,000h	500a	$ 2,500h
Other 1988 net income (loss)			(2,000a)

Reg. § 1.460-6(h)(3)

Methods of Accounting

See p. 20,601 for regulations not amended to reflect law changes

Taxable income (NOL)	500h
Tax at 34%	170h
less, previously computed tax	-0-a
Underpayment of 1988 tax	170h
Underpayment of 1985 tax from NOL carryback refund in 1988	345h
Total underpayment of tax	515h

For purposes of any subsequent application of the look-back method for which 1989 is a redetermination year, because the reallocation of contract income and redetermination of tax liability are cumulative, X will use for 1989 the amount of contract D income and the amount of tax liability that would have been reported in 1989 if X had used actual contract costs instead of the amounts that were originally reported using the estimate of $8,000. Assuming no subsequent revisions (due to, for example, adjustments to contract D price and costs determined after the end of 1989), this amount would be determined as follows:

1989

	D	E	Total
1989 contract costs	$ 3,000a	$ -0-a	
Total contract costs	6,000a	9,000e	
Total contract price	10,000a	10,000e	
1989 completion %	100%a	22.2%e	
1989 gross income	5,000h	(278a)	
less, 1989 costs	(3,000a)	-0-a	
1989 net contract income	2,000h	(278a)	$ 1,722h
Other 1989 net income (loss)			-0-a
Taxable income (NOL)			1,722h
Tax at 34%			585h

(iv) X completes contract E during 1990. X determines its taxable income for 1990 as follows:

1990

	D	E	Total
1990 contract costs		$ 7,000a	
Total contract costs		9,000a	
Total contract price		10,000a	
1990 completion %		100%a	
1990 gross income		7,778a	
less, 1990 costs		(7,000a)	
1990 net contract income		778a	$ 778a
Other 1990 net income (loss)			-0-a
Taxable income (NOL)			778a
Tax at 34%			265a

(v) For purposes of the look-back method, X must reallocate the actual total contract E price between 1988, 1989, and 1990, based on the actual total contract E costs. This results in the following hypothetical overpayment of tax for 1988. Note that X uses the amount of income for contract D determined in the last previous application of the look-back method, and not the amount of income actually reported:

1988

	D	E	Total
1988 contract costs	$ 3,000a	$ 2,000a	
Total contract costs	6,000a	9,000a	
Total contract price	10,000a	10,000a	
1988 completion %	50%a	22.2%a	
1988 gross income	5,000h	2,222h	
less, 1988 costs	(3,000a)	(2,000a)	
1988 net contract income	2,000h	222h	$ 2,222h
Other 1988 net income (loss)			(2,000a)
Taxable income (NOL)			222h
Tax at 34%			75h

Reg. § 1.460-6(h)(3)

Methods of Accounting

See p. 20,601 for regulations not amended to reflect law changes

less, previously computed tax (based on most recent application of the look-back method) 170h
Overpayment of 1988 tax .... (95h)

In applying the look-back method to 1989, X again uses the amounts substituted as of the last previous application of the look-back method with respect to contract D. Thus, X computes its hypothetical underpayment for 1989 as follows:

1989

	D	E	Total
1989 contract costs	$ 3,000a	$ -0-a	
Total contract costs	6,000a	9,000a	
Total contract price	10,000a	10,000a	
1989 completion %	100%a	22.2%a	
1989 gross income	5,000h	-0-h	
less, 1989 costs	(3,000a)	(-0-a)	
1989 net contract income	2,000h	-0-a	$ 2,000h
Other 1989 net income (loss)			(-0-a)
Taxable income (NOL)			2,000h
Tax at 34%			680h
less, previously computed tax			585h
Underpayment of 1989 tax			95h

For purposes of any subsequent application of the look-back method for which 1990 is a redetermination year, X will use for 1990 the amount of Contract E income, and the amount of tax liability, that was originally reported in 1990 because X's estimate of the total contract costs from $8,000 to $9,000 did not change after 1989. Without regard to any subsequent revisions, these amounts are the same as in the table in paragraph (h)(3)(iv) above.

(4) *Post-completion adjustments.* The following example illustrates the application of paragraph (c)(1)(ii):

Example (3). The facts are the same as in Example (2). In 1991, X settles a lawsuit against its customer in Contract E. The customer pays X an additional $3,000, without interest, in 1991. Applying the Federal mid-term rate then in effect, this $3,000 has a discounted value at the time of contract completion in 1990 of $2,700. X is required to apply the look-back method for 1991 even though no contract was completed in 1991. X must include the full $3,000 adjustment (which was not previously includible in total contract price) in gross income for 1991. X does not elect not to discount adjustments to the contract price or costs. Thus, X adjusts the contract price by the discounted amount of the adjustment and, therefore, uses $12,700 (not $13,000) for total Contract E price, rather than $10,000, which was used when the look-back method was first applied with respect to Contract E.

For purposes of the look-back method, X must allocate the revised total Contract E price of $12,700 between 1988, 1989 and 1990 based on the actual total Contract E costs, and compare the resulting revised tax liability with the tax liability determined for the last previous application of the look-back method involving those years. This results in the following hypothetical underpayments of tax for purposes of the look-back method:

r = revised

1988

	D	E	Total
1988 contract costs	$ 3,000a	$ 2,000a	
Total contract costs	6,000a	9,000a	
Total contract price	10,000a	12,700r	
1988 completion %	50%a	22.2%a	
1988 gross income	5,000h	2,822rh	
less, 1988 costs	(3,000a)	(2,000a)	
1988 net contract income	2,000h	822rh	$ 2,822rh
Other 1988 net income/(loss)			(2,000a)
Taxable income			822rh
Tax at 34%			279rh
less, previously computed tax			75h
Underpayment of 1988 tax			204rh

Reg. § 1.460-6(h)(4)

36,920   Methods of Accounting

See p. 20,601 for regulations not amended to reflect law changes

No Contract E costs were incurred in 1989, and there is no hypothetical underpayment for 1989.

1990

	D	E	Total
1990 contract costs		$ 7,000a	
Total contract costs		9,000a	
Total contract price		12,700r	
1990 completion %		100%a	
1990 gross income		9,878rh	
less, 1990 costs		(7,000a)	
1990 net contract income		2,878rh	$ 2,878rh
Other 1990 net income (loss)			-0-a
Taxable income (NOL)			2,878rh
Tax at 34%			978rh
less, previously computed tax			265h
Underpayment of 1990 tax			713rh

In 1992, X incurs an additional cost of $1,000 allocable to the contract, which was not previously includible in total contract costs. Applying the Federal mid-term rate then in effect, the $1,000 has a discounted value at the time of contract completion of $800. X deducts this additional $1,000 in expenses in 1992. Based on this increase to contract costs, X reapplies the look-back method, and determines the following hypothetical overpayments for 1988, 1989 and 1990 for purposes of the look-back method:

1988

	D	E	Total
1988 contract costs	$ 3,000a	$ 2,000a	
Total contract costs	6,000a	9,800r	
Total contract price	10,000a	12,700r	
1988 completion %	50%a	20.4%r	
1988 gross income	5,000h	2,592rh	
less, 1988 costs	(3,000a)	(2,000a)	
1988 net contract income	2,000h	592rh	$ 2,592rh
Other 1988 net income (loss)			(2,000a)
Taxable income (NOL)			592rh
Tax at 34%			201rh
less, previously computed tax			279rh
Overpayment of 1988 tax			(78rh)

No Contract E costs were incurred in 1989, and there is no hypothetical underpayment for 1989.

1990

	D	E	Total
1990 contract costs		$ 7,000a	
Total contract costs		9,800r	
Total contract price		12,700r	
1990 completion %		92%a	
1990 gross income		9,071rh	
less, 1990 costs		(7,000a)	
1990 net contract income		2,071rh	$ 2,071rh
Other 1990 net income (loss)			-0-a
Taxable income (NOL)			2,071rh
Tax at 34%			704rh
less, previously computed tax			978rh
Overpayment of 1990 tax			(274rh)

(5) *Alternative minimum tax.* The operation of the look-back method in the case of a taxpayer liable for the alternative minimum tax as provided in paragraph (c)(3)(vi) is illustrated by the following example:

Example (4). Y enters into a long-term contract in 1988 that is completed in 1989. Y used regular tax costs for purposes of determining the degree of contract completion under the alternative minimum tax.

Reg. § 1.460-6(h)(5)

Methods of Accounting

See p. 20,601 for regulations not amended to reflect law changes

(i) Y determines its tax liability for 1988 as follows:

1988 contract costs	$ 4,000a
Total contract costs	8,000e
Total contract price	20,000e
1988 completion %	50%e
1988 gross income	10,000a
less, 1988 contract costs	(4,000a)
1988 net contract income	6,000a
Other 1988 net income/(loss)	(3,400a)
Taxable income	2,600a
Regular tax at 34%	884a
Adjustments and preferences to produce alternative minimum taxable income	600a
Alternative minimum taxable income	3,200a
Tentative minimum tax at 20%	640a
Tax liability	884a

In 1989, Y determines the following amounts:

1989 contract costs	$ 6,000a
Total contract costs	10,000a
Total contract price	20,000a

(ii) For purposes of applying the look-back method, Y redetermines its tax liability for 1988, which results in a hypothetical overpayment of tax. This hypothetical overpayment is determined by comparing Y's original regular tax liability for 1988 with the hypothetical total tax liability (including alternative minimum tax liability) for that year because Y would have paid the alternative minimum tax if Y had used its actual contract costs to report income:

1988 contract costs	$ 4,000a
Total contract costs	10,000a
Total contract price	20,000a
1988 completion %	40%a
1988 gross income	8,000h
less, 1988 contract costs	(4,000a)
1988 net contract income	4,000h
Other 1988 net income/(loss)	(3,400a)
Taxable income	600h
Regular tax at 34%	204h
Adjustments and preferences to produce alternative minimum taxable income	600a
Alternative minimum taxable income	1,200h
Tentative minimum tax at 20%	240h
Alternative minimum tax	36h
Total tax liability	240h
less, previously computed tax	884a
Underpayment/(overpayment)	(644h)

(6) *Credit carryovers.* The operation of the look-back method in the case of credit carryovers as provided in paragraph (c)(3)(v) is illustrated by the following example:

Example (5). Z enters into a contract in 1986 that is completed in 1987. Z determines its tax liability for 1986 as follows:

1986 contract costs	$ 400a
Total contract costs	1,000e
Total contract price	2,000e
1986 completion %	40%e
1986 gross income	800a
less, 1986 costs	(400a)
1986 net contract income	400a
Other 1986 net income	-0-a
Taxable income	400a
Tax at 46%	184a
Unused tax credits carried forward from 1985 allowable in 1986	350a
Net tax due	-0-a

Z determines the following amounts for 1987:

1987 contract costs	$ 400a
Total contract price	2,000a
Total contract costs	800a

Reg. § 1.460-6(h)(6)

If Z had used actual rather than estimated contract costs in determining gross income for 1986, Z would have reported tax liability of $276 (46% × $600) rather than $184. However, Z would have paid no additional tax for 1986 because its unused tax credits carried forward from 1985 would have been sufficient to offset this increased tax liability. Therefore, there is no hypothetical underpayment for 1986 for purposes of the look-back method. However, this hypothetical earlier use of the credit may increase the hypothetical tax liability for 1987 (or another subsequent year) for purposes of subsequent applications of the look-back method.

(7) *Net operating losses.* The operation of the look-back method in the case of net operating loss ("NOL") carryovers as provided in paragraph (c)(3)(v) is illustrated by the following example:

Example (6). A entered into a long-term contract in 1986, which was completed in 1987. A determined its tax liability for 1986 as follows:

1986 contract costs	$ 400a
Total contract costs	1,000e
Total contract price	2,000e
1986 completion %	40%e
1986 gross income	800a
less, 1986 costs	(400a)
1986 net contract income	400a
Other 1986 net income/(loss)	(1,000a)
Taxable income/(NOL)	(600a)
Tax	-0-a

A elected to carry this loss forward to 1987 pursuant to section 172(b)(3)(C).

For 1987, A determined the following amounts:

1987 contract costs	$ 400a
Total contract costs	800a
Total contract price	2,000a

If actual rather than estimated contract costs had been used in determining gross income for 1986, A would have reported $1,000 of gross income from the contract rather than $800, and thus would have reported a loss of $400 rather than $600. However, since A would have paid no tax for 1986 regardless of whether actual or estimated contract costs had been used, A does not have an underpayment for 1986 for purposes of the look-back method. If A had, instead, carried back the 1986 NOL, and this NOL had been absorbed in the tax years 1983 through 1985, it would have resulted in refunds of tax for those years in 1986. When A applies the look-back method, a hypothetical underpayment of tax would have resulted for those years due to a hypothetical reduction in the amount that would have been refunded if income had been reported on the basis of actual contract costs. See Example (2)(iii).

(8) *Alternative minimum tax credit.* The following example illustrates the application of the look-back method if affected by the alternative minimum tax credit as provided in paragraph (c)(3)(vi):

Example (4), above, illustrates that the reallocation of contract income under the look-back method can result in a hypothetical underpayment or overpayment determined using the alternative minimum tax rate, even though the taxpayer actually paid only the regular tax for that year. However, application of the look-back method had no effect on the difference between the amount of alternative minimum taxable income and the amount of regular taxable income taken into account in that year because the taxpayer was required to use the percentage of completion method for both regular and alternative minimum tax purposes and used the same version of the percentage of completion method for both regular and alternative minimum tax purposes (*i.e.,* the taxpayer had made an election to use regular tax costs in determining the percentage of completion for purposes of computing alternative minimum taxable income).

The following example illustrates the application of the look-back method in the case of a taxpayer that does not use the percentage of completion method of accounting for long-term contracts in computing taxable income for regular tax purposes and thus must make an adjustment to taxable income to determine alternative minimum taxable income. The example also shows how interest is computed under the look-back method when the taxpayer is entitled to a credit under section 53 for minimum tax paid because of this adjustment.

Example (7). X is a taxpayer engaged in the construction of real property under contracts that are completed within a 24-month period and whose average annual gross receipts do not exceed $10,000,000. As permitted by section 460(e)(1)(B), X uses the completed contract method ("CCM") for regular tax purposes. However, X is engaged in the construction of commer-

Reg. § 1.460-6(h)(7)

Methods of Accounting

cial real property and, therefore, is required to use the percentage of completion method ("PCM") for alternative minimum tax ("AMT") purposes.

Assume that for 1988, 1989, and 1990, X has only one long-term contract, which is entered into in 1988 and completed in 1990. Assume further that X estimates gross income from the contract to be $2,000, total contract costs to be $1,000, and that the contract is 25 percent complete in 1988 and 75 percent complete in 1989. In 1990, the year of completion, the percentage of completion does not change but, upon completion, gross income from the contract is actually $3,000, instead of $2,000, and costs are actually $1,000.

For 1988, 1989, and 1990, X's income and tax liability using estimated contract price and costs are as follows:

Estimates	1988	1989	1990
Regular tax			
Long-term Contract-CCM	$-0-	$ -0-	$2,000
Other Income	-0-	5,000	-0-
Total Income	-0-	5,000	2,000
Tax 34%	-0-	1,700	680
AMT			
Gross Income	500	1,000	1,500
Deductions	(250)	(500)	(250)
Total long-term Contract-PCM	250	500	1,250
Other Income	-0-	5,000	-0-
Total Income	250	5,500	1,250
Tax 20%	50	1,100	250
Tentative Minimum Tax	50	1,100	250
Regular Tax	-0-	1,700	680
Minimum Tax Credit	-0-	(50)	-0-
Net Tax Liability	50	1,650	680

When X files its tax return for 1990, X applies the look-back method to the contract. For 1988, 1989, and 1990, X's income and tax liability using actual contract price and costs are as follows:

Actual	1988	1989	1990
Regular tax			
Long-term Contract-CCM	$-0-	$ -0-	$2,000
Other Income	-0-	5,000	-0-
Total Income	-0-	5,000	2,000
Tax 34%	-0-	1,700	680
AMT			
Gross Income	750	1,500	750
Deductions	(250)	(500)	(250)
Total long-term Contract-PCM	500	1,000	500
Other Income	-0-	5,000	-0-
Total Income	500	6,000	500
Tax 20%	100	1,200	100
Tentative Minimum Tax	100	1,200	100
Regular Tax	-0-	1,700	680
Minimum Tax Credit	-0-	(100)	-0-
Net Tax Liability	100	1,600	680
Underpayment	50		
Overpayment		50	

As shown above, application of the look-back method results in a hypothetical underpayment of $50 for 1988 because X was subject to the alternative minimum tax for that year. Interest is charged to X on this $50 underpayment from the due date of X's 1988 return until the due date of X's 1990 return.

In 1989, although X was required to compute alternative minimum taxable income using the percentage of completion method, X was not re-

Reg. § 1.460-6(h)(8)

36,924 Methods of Accounting

See p. 20,601 for regulations not amended to reflect law changes

quired to pay alternative minimum tax. Nevertheless, the look-back method must be applied to 1989 because use of actual rather than estimated contract price in computing alternative minimum taxable income for 1988 would have changed the amount of the alternative minimum tax credit carried to 1989. Interest is paid to X on the resulting $50 overpayment from the due date of X's 1989 return until the due date of X's 1990 return.

(9) *Period for interest.* The following Examples (8) through (11) illustrate how to determine the period for computing interest as provided in paragraph (c)(4):

Example (8). The facts are the same as in Example (6), except that the contract is completed in 1988, and A determined the following amounts for 1987 and 1988:

for 1987:

1987 contract costs	$ –0–
Total contract costs	1,000e
Total contract price	2,000e
1987 completion %	40%e
1987 gross income	–0–a
less, 1987 costs	–0–a
Other 1987 net income	600a
Net operating loss carryforward from 1986	(600a)
taxable income	–0–a
tax	–0–a

for 1988:

1988 contract costs	400a
Total contract costs	800a
Total contract price	2,000a

If actual rather than estimated contract costs had been used in determining gross income for 1986, A would have reported $1,000 of gross income from the contract for 1986 rather than $800, and would have reported a net operating loss carryforward to 1987 of $400 rather than $600. Therefore, A would have reported taxable income of $200, and would have paid tax of $80 (*i.e.*, $200 × 40%) for 1987. The due date for filing A's Federal income tax return for its 1988 taxable year is March 15. A obtains an extension and files its 1988 return on September 15, 1989. Under the look-back method, A is required to pay interest on the amount of this hypothetical underpayment ($80) computed from the due date (determined without regard to extensions) for A's return for 1987 (not 1986, even though 1986 was the year in which the net operating loss arose) until March 15 (not September 15), the due date (without regard to extensions) of A's return for 1988. A is required to pay additional interest from March 15 until September 15 on the amount of interest outstanding as of March 15 with respect to the hypothetical underpayment of $80.

Example (9). The facts are the same as in Example (6), except that A carries the net operating loss of $600 back to 1983 rather than forward to 1987, and receives a refund of $276 ($600 reduction in 1983 taxable income × 46% rate in effect in 1983). As in Example (6), if actual contract costs had been used, A would have reported a loss for 1986 of $400 rather than $600. Thus, A would have received a refund of 1983 tax of $184 ($400 × 46%) rather than $276. Under the look-back method A is required to pay interest on the difference in these two amounts ($92) computed from the due date (determined without regard to extensions) of A's return for 1986 (the year in which the carryback arose rather than 1983, the year in which it was used) until the due date of A's return for 1988.

Example (10). B enters into a long-term contract in 1986 that is completed in 1988. B determines its 1986 tax liability as follows:

1986 contract costs	$ 400a
Total contract costs	1,000e
Total contract price	2,000e
1986 completion %	40%e
1986 gross income	800a
less, 1986 costs	(400a)
1986 net contract income	400a
Other 1986 net income	2,000a
Taxable income	2,400a
Tax at 46%	1,104a

B determines its tax liability for 1987 as follows:

1987 contract costs	$ 400a
Total contract costs	1,600e
Total contract price	2,000e
1987 completion %	50%e
1987 gross income (= (50% × $2,000) − $800 previously reported)	200a
less, 1987 costs	(400a)
1987 net contract income	(200a)
Other 1987 net income/(loss)	(2,200a)
Taxable income (NOL)	(2,400a)
Tax	–0–a

Assume that B had no taxable income in either 1984 or 1985, so that the entire amount of the $2,400 net operating loss is carried back to 1986, and B receives a refund, with interest from the due date of B's 1987 return, of the entire $1,104 in tax that it paid for 1986.

In 1988, B determines the following amounts:

1988 contract costs	$ 800a
Total contract costs	1,600a
Total contract price	2,000a

If B had used actual contract costs rather than estimated costs in determining its gross income for 1986, B would have had gross income from the contract of $500 rather than $800, and thus would have had taxable income of $2,100 rather than $2,400, and would have paid tax of $966 rather than $1,104. B is entitled to receive

Reg. § 1.460-6(h)(9)

interest on the difference between these two amounts, the hypothetical overpayment of tax of $138. Interest is computed from the due date (without regard to extensions) of B's return for 1986 until the due date for B's return for 1987. Interest stops running at this date, because B's hypothetical overpayment of tax ended when B filed its original 1987 return and received a refund for the carryback to 1986, and interest on this refund began to run only from the due date of B's 1987 return. See section 6611(f).

Example (11). C enters into a long-term contract in 1986, its first year in business, which is completed in 1988. C determines its tax liability for 1986 as follows:

1986 contract costs	$ 400a
Total contract costs	1,000e
Total contract price	2,000e
1986 completion %	40%e
1986 gross income	800a
less, 1986 costs	(400a)
1986 net contract income	400a
Other 1986 net income	2,000a
Taxable income (NOL)	2,400a
Tax at 46%	1,104a

C determines its tax liability for 1987 as follows:

1987 contract costs	$ 400a
Total contract costs	1,066e
Total contract price	2,000e
1987 completion %	75%e
1987 gross income	700a
less, 1987 costs	(400a)
1987 net contract income	300a
Other 1987 net income	(2,450a)
Taxable income (NOL)	(2,150a)
Tax	–0–a

C carries back the net operating loss to 1986, and files an amended return for 1986, showing taxable income of $250, and receives a refund of $989 (46% × $2,150). Interest on this refund begins to run only as of the due date of C's 1987 return. See section 6611(f).

In 1988, when the contract is completed, C determines the following amounts:

1988 contract costs	$ 800a
Total contract costs	1,600a
Total contract price	2,000a

If C had used actual contract price and contract costs in determining gross income for 1986, it would have reported gross income from the contract of $500 rather than $800, taxable income of $2,100 rather than $2,400, and tax liability of $966 rather than $1,104.

If C had used actual contract price and contract costs in determining gross income for 1987, it would have reported gross income from the contract of $500 rather than $700, and would have reported a net operating loss of $2,350, rather than $2,150, which would have been carried back to 1986.

Under the look-back method, C receives interest with respect to a total 1986 hypothetical overpayment of $138 ($1,104 minus $966). C is credited with interest on $23 of this amount only from the due date of C's 1986 return until the due date of C's 1987 tax return, because this portion of C's total hypothetical overpayment for 1986 was refunded to C with interest computed from the due date of C's 1987 return and, therefore, was no longer held by the government. However, because the remainder of the total hypothetical overpayment of $115 was not refunded to C, C is credited with interest on this amount from the due date of C's 1986 return until the due date of C's 1988 tax return.

Under the look-back method, C receives no interest with respect to 1987, because C had no tax liability for 1987 using either estimated or actual contract price and costs.

(i) [Reserved].

(j) *Election not to apply look-back method in de minimis cases.* Section 460(b)(6) provides taxpayers with an election not to apply the look-back method to long-term contracts in de minimis cases, effective for contracts completed in taxable years ending after August 5, 1997. To make an election, a taxpayer must attach a statement to its timely filed original federal income tax return (including extensions) for the taxable year the election is to become effective or to an amended return for that year, provided the amended return is filed on or before March 31, 1998. This statement must have the legend "NOTIFICATION OF ELECTION UNDER SECTION 460(b)(6)"; provide the taxpayer's name and identifying number and the effective date of the election; and identify the trades or businesses that involve long-term contracts. An election applies to all long-term contracts completed during and after the taxable year for which the election is effective. An election may not be revoked without the Commissioner's consent. For taxpayers who elected to use the delayed reapplication method under paragraph (e) of this section, an election under this paragraph (j) automatically revokes the election to use the delayed reapplication method for contracts subject to section 460(b)(6). A consolidated group of corporations, as defined in § 1.1502-1(h), is subject to consistency rules analogous to those in paragraph (e)(2) of this section and in paragraph (d)(4)(ii)(C) of this section (concerning election to use simplified marginal impact method). [Reg. § 1.460-6.]

Reg. § 1.460-6(j)

Methods of Accounting

See p. 20,601 for regulations not amended to reflect law changes

☐ [T.D. 8315, 10-12-90. Amended by T.D. 8775, 7-1-98; T.D. 8929, 1-10-2001 and T.D. 8995, 5-14-2002.]

[Reg. § 1.461-0]

§ 1.461-0. Table of contents.—This section lists the captions that appear in the regulations under section 461 of the Internal Revenue Code.

§ 1.461-1. General rule for taxable year of deduction.

(a) General rule.

(1) Taxpayer using cash receipts and disbursements method.

(2) Taxpayer using an accrual method.

(3) Effect in current taxable year of improperly accounting for a liability in a prior taxable year.

(4) Deductions attributable to certain foreign income.

(b) Special rule in case of death.

(c) Accrual of real property taxes.

(1) In general.

(2) Special rules.

(3) When election may be made.

(4) Binding effect of election.

(5) Apportionment of taxes on real property between seller and purchaser.

(6) Examples.

(d) Limitation on acceleration of accrual of taxes.

(e) Dividends or interest paid by certain savings institutions on certain deposits or withdrawable accounts.

(1) Deduction not allowable.

(2) Computation of amounts not allowed as a deduction.

(3) When amounts allowable.

§ 1.461-2. Contested liabilities.

(a) General rule.

(1) Taxable year of deduction.

(2) Exception.

(3) Refunds includible in gross income.

(4) Examples.

(5) Liabilities described in paragraph (g) of § 1.461-4. [Reserved]

(b) Contest of asserted liability.

(1) Asserted liability.

(2) Definition of the term "contest."

(3) Example.

(c) Transfer to provide for the satisfaction of an asserted liability.

(1) In general.

(2) Examples.

(d) Contest exists after transfer.

(e) Deduction otherwise allowed.

(1) In general.

(2) Example.

(f) Treatment of money or property transferred to an escrowee, trustee, or court and treatment of any income attributable thereto. [Reserved]

(g) Effective dates.

§ 1.461-3. Prepaid interest. [Reserved]

§ 1.461-4. Economic performance.

(a) Introduction.

(1) In general.

(2) Overview.

(b) Exceptions to the economic performance requirement.

(c) Definitions.

(1) Liability.

(2) Payment.

(d) Liabilities arising out of the provision of services, property, or the use of property.

(1) In general.

(2) Services or property provided to the taxpayer.

(3) Use of property provided to the taxpayer.

(4) Services or property provided by the taxpayer.

(5) Liabilities that are assumed in connection with the sale of a trade or business.

(6) Rules relating to the provision of services or property to a taxpayer.

(7) Examples.

(e) Interest.

(f) Timing of deductions from notional principal contracts. [Reserved]

(g) Certain liabilities for which payment is economic performance.

(1) In general.

(2) Liabilities arising under a workers compensation act or out of any tort, breach of contract, or violation of law.

(3) Rebates and refunds.

(4) Awards, prizes, and jackpots.

(5) Insurance, warranty, and service contracts.

(6) Taxes.

(7) Other liabilities.

(8) Examples.

Reg. § 1.461-0

(h) Liabilities arising under the Nuclear Waste Policy Act of 1982.

(i) [Reserved]

(j) Contingent liabilities. [Reserved]

(k) Special effective dates.

(1) In general.

(2) Long-term contracts.

(3) Payment liabilities.

(l) [Reserved]

(m) Change in method of accounting required by this section.

(1) In general.

(2) Change in method of accounting for long-term contracts and payment liabilities.

§ 1.461-5. Recurring item exception.

(a) In general.

(b) Requirements for use of the exception.

(1) General rule.

(2) Amended returns.

(3) Liabilities that are recurring in nature.

(4) Materiality requirement.

(5) Matching requirement.

(c) Types of liabilities not eligible for treatment under the recurring item exception.

(d) Time and manner of adopting the recurring item exception.

(1) In general.

(2) Change to the recurring item exception method for the first taxable year beginning after December 31, 1991.

(3) Retroactive change to the recurring item exception method.

(e) Examples.

§ 1.461-6. Economic performance when certain liabilities are assigned or are extinguished by the establishment of a fund.

(a) Qualified assignments of certain personal injury liabilities under section 130.

(b) Section 468B.

(c) Payments to other funds or persons that constitute economic performance. [Reserved]

(d) Effective dates.

[Reg. § 1.461-0.]

☐ [T.D. 8408, 4-9-92. Amended by T.D. 8593, 4-7-95.]

[Reg. § 1.461-1]

§ 1.461-1. General rule for taxable year of deduction.—(a) *General rule*—(1) *Taxpayer using cash receipts and disbursements method.* Under the cash receipts and disbursements method of accounting, amounts representing allowable deductions shall, as a general rule, be taken into account for the taxable year in which paid. Further, a taxpayer using this method may also be entitled to certain deductions in the computation of taxable income which do not involve cash disbursements during the taxable year, such as the deductions for depreciation, depletion, and losses under sections 167, 611, and 165, respectively. If an expenditure results in the creation of an asset having a useful life which extends substantially beyond the close of the taxable year, such an expenditure may not be deductible, or may be deductible only in part, for the taxable year in which made. An example is an expenditure for the construction of improvements by the lessee on leased property where the estimated life of the improvements is in excess of the remaining period of the lease. In such a case, in lieu of the allowance for depreciation provided by section 167, the basis shall be amortized ratably over the remaining period of the lease. See section 178 and the regulations thereunder for rules governing the effect to be given renewal options in determining whether the useful life of the improvements exceeds the remaining term of the lease where a lessee begins improvements on leased property after July 28, 1958, other than improvements which on such date and at all times thereafter, the lessee was under a binding legal obligation to make. See section 263 and the regulations thereunder for rules relating to capital expenditures. See section 467 and the regulations thereunder for rules under which a liability arising out of the use of property pursuant to a section 467 rental agreement is taken into account.

(2) *Taxpayer using an accrual method*—(i) *In general.* Under an accrual method of accounting, a liability (as defined in § 1.446-1(c)(1)(ii)(B)) is incurred, and generally is taken into account for Federal income tax purposes, in the taxable year in which all the events have occurred that establish the fact of the liability, the amount of the liability can be determined with reasonable accuracy, and economic performance has occurred with respect to the liability. (See paragraph (a)(2)(iii)(A) of this section for examples of liabilities that may not be taken into account until a taxable year subsequent to the taxable year incurred, and see § § 1.461-4 through 1.461-6 for rules relating to economic performance.) Applicable provisions of the Code, the Income Tax Regulations, and other guidance published by the Secretary prescribe the manner in which a liability that has been incurred is taken into account. For example, section 162 provides that a deductible liability generally is taken into account in the taxable year incurred through a deduction from gross income. As a further exam-

ple, under section 263 or 263A, a liability that relates to the creation of an asset having a useful life extending substantially beyond the close of the taxable year is taken into account in the taxable year incurred through capitalization (within the meaning of § 1.263A-1(c)(3)), and may later affect the computation of taxable income through depreciation or otherwise over a period including subsequent taxable years, in accordance with applicable Internal Revenue Code sections and guidance published by the Secretary. The principles of this paragraph (a)(2) also apply in the calculation of earnings and profits and accumulated earnings and profits.

(ii) *Uncertainty as to the amount of a liability.* While no liability shall be taken into account before economic performance and all of the events that fix the liability have occurred, the fact that the exact amount of the liability cannot be determined does not prevent a taxpayer from taking into account that portion of the amount of the liability which can be computed with reasonable accuracy within the taxable year. For example, A renders services to B during the taxable year for which A charges $10,000. B admits a liability to A for $6,000 but contests the remainder. B may take into account only $6,000 as an expense for the taxable year in which the services were rendered.

(iii) *Alternative timing rules.* (A) If any provision of the Code requires a liability to be taken into account in a taxable year later than the taxable year provided in paragraph (a)(2)(i) of this section, the liability is taken into account as prescribed in that Code provision. See, for example, section 267 (transactions between related parties) and section 464 (farming syndicates).

(B) If the liability of a taxpayer is subject to section 170 (charitable contributions), section 192 (black lung benefit trusts), section 194A (employer liability trusts), section 468 (mining and solid waste disposal reclamation and closing costs), or section 468A(a) (certain nuclear decommissioning costs), the liability is taken into account as determined under that section and not under section 461 or the regulations thereunder. For special rules relating to certain loss deductions, see sections 165(e), 165(i), and 165(l), relating to theft losses, disaster losses, and losses from certain deposits in qualified financial institutions.

(C) Section 461 and the regulations thereunder do not apply to any amount allowable under a provision of the Code as a deduction for a reserve for estimated expenses.

(D) Except as otherwise provided in any Internal Revenue regulation, revenue procedure, or revenue ruling, the economic performance requirement of section 461(h) and the regulations thereunder is satisfied to the extent that any amount is otherwise deductible under section 404 (employer contributions to a plan of deferred compensation), section 404A (certain foreign deferred compensation plans), or section 419 (welfare benefit funds). See § 1.461-4(d)(2)(iii).

(E) Except as otherwise provided by regulations or other published guidance issued by the Commissioner (See § 601.601(b)(2) of this chapter), in the case of a liability arising out of the use of property pursuant to a section 467 rental agreement, the all events test (including economic performance) is considered met in the taxable year in which the liability is to be taken into account under section 467 and the regulations thereunder.

(3) *Effect in current taxable year of improperly accounting for a liability in a prior taxable year.* Each year's return should be complete in itself, and taxpayers shall ascertain the facts necessary to make a correct return. The expenses, liabilities, or loss of one year generally cannot be used to reduce the income of a subsequent year. A taxpayer may not take into account in a return for a subsequent taxable year liabilities that, under the taxpayer's method of accounting, should have been taken into account in a prior taxable year. If a taxpayer ascertains that a liability should have been taken into account in a prior taxable year, the taxpayer should, if within the period of limitation, file a claim for credit or refund of any overpayment of tax arising therefrom. Similarly, if a taxpayer ascertains that a liability was improperly taken into account in a prior taxable year, the taxpayer should, if within the period of limitation, file an amended return and pay any additional tax due. However, except as provided in section 905(c) and the regulations thereunder, if a liability is properly taken into account in an amount based on a computation made with reasonable accuracy and the exact amount of the liability is subsequently determined in a later taxable year, the difference, if any, between such amounts shall be taken into account for the later taxable year.

(4) *Deductions attributable to certain foreign income.* In any case in which, owing to monetary, exchange, or other restrictions imposed by a foreign country, an amount otherwise constituting gross income for the taxable year from sources without the United States is not includible in gross income of the taxpayer for that year, the deductions and credits properly chargeable against the amount so restricted shall not be deductible in such year but shall be deductible proportionately in any subsequent taxable year in which such amount or portion thereof is includible

Reg. § 1.461-1(a)(3)

Methods of Accounting

in gross income. See paragraph (b) of § 1.905-1 for rules relating to credit for foreign income taxes when foreign income is subject to exchange controls.

(b) *Special rule in case of death.* A taxpayer's taxable year ends on the date of his death. See section 443(a)(2) and paragraph (a)(2) of § 1.443-1. In computing taxable income for such year, there shall be deducted only amounts properly deductible under the method of accounting used by the taxpayer. However, if the taxpayer used an accrual method of accounting, no deduction shall be allowed for amounts accrued only by reason of his death. For rules relating to the inclusion of items of partnership deduction, loss, or credit in the return of a decedent partner, see subchapter K, chapter 1 of the Code, and the regulations thereunder.

(c) *Accrual of real property taxes*—(1) *In general.* If the accrual of real property taxes is proper in connection with one of the methods of accounting described in section 446(c), any taxpayer using such a method of accounting may elect to accrue any real property tax, which is related to a definite period of time, ratably over that period in the manner described in this paragraph. For example, assume that such an election is made by a calendar-year taxpayer whose real property taxes, applicable to the period from July 1, 1955, to June 30, 1956, amount to $1,200. Under section 461(c), $600 of such taxes accrue in the calendar year 1955, and the balance accrues in 1956. For special rule in the case of certain contested real property taxes in respect of which the taxpayer transfers money or other property to provide for the satisfaction of the contested tax, see § 1.461-2. For general rules relating to deductions for taxes, see section 164 and the regulations thereunder.

(2) *Special rules*—(i) *Effective date.* Section 461(c) and this paragraph do not apply to any real property tax allowable as a deduction under the Internal Revenue Code of 1939 for any taxable year beginning before January 1, 1954.

(ii) If real property taxes which relate to a period prior to the taxpayer's first taxable year beginning on or after January 1, 1954, would, but for section 461(c), be deductible in such first taxable year, the portion of such taxes which applies to the prior period is deductible in such first taxable year (in addition to the amount allowable under section 461(c)(1)).

(3) *When election may be made*—(i) *Without consent.* A taxpayer may elect to accrue real property taxes ratably in accordance with section 461(c) and this paragraph without the consent of the Commissioner for his first taxable year beginning after December 31, 1953, and ending after August 16, 1954, in which the taxpayer incurs real property taxes. Such election must be made not later than the time prescribed by law for filing the return for such year (including extensions thereof). An election may be made by the taxpayer for each separate trade or business (and for nonbusiness activities, if accounted for separately). Such an election shall apply to all real property taxes of the trade, business, or nonbusiness activity for which the election is made. The election shall be made in a statement submitted with the taxpayer's return for the first taxable year to which the election is applicable. The statement should set forth:

(*a*) The trades or businesses, or nonbusiness activity, to which the election is to apply, and the method of accounting used therein;

(*b*) The period of time to which the taxes are related; and

(*c*) The computation of the deduction for real property taxes for the first year of the election (or a summary of such computation).

(ii) *With consent.* A taxpayer may elect with the consent of the Commissioner to accrue real property taxes ratably in accordance with section 461(c) and this paragraph. A written request for permission to make such an election shall be submitted to the Commissioner of Internal Revenue, Washington 25, D.C., within 90 days after the beginning of the taxable year to which the election is first applicable, or before March 26, 1958, publication in the FEDERAL REGISTER of the regulations under section 461, whichever date is later. The request for permission shall state:

(*a*) The name and address of the taxpayer;

(*b*) The trades or businesses, or nonbusiness activity, to which the election is to apply, and the method of accounting used therein;

(*c*) The taxable year to which the election first applies;

(*d*) The period to which the real property taxes relate;

(*e*) The computation of the deduction for real property taxes for the first year of election (or a summary of such computation); and

(*f*) An adequate description of the manner in which all real property taxes were deducted in the year prior to the year of election.

(4) *Binding effect of election.* An election to accrue real property taxes ratably under section 461(c) is binding upon the taxpayer unless the consent of the Commissioner is obtained under section 446(e) and paragraph (e) of § 1.446-1 to change such method of deducting real property

Reg. § 1.461-1(c)(4)

Methods of Accounting

taxes. If the last day prescribed by law for filing a return for any taxable year (including extensions thereof) to which section 461(c) is applicable falls before March 25, 1958, consent is hereby given for the taxpayer to revoke an election previously made to accrue real property taxes in the manner prescribed by section 461(c). If the taxpayer revokes his election under the preceding sentence, he must, on or before March 25, 1958, notify the district director for the district in which the return was filed of such revocation. For any taxable year for which such revocation is applicable, an amended return reflecting such revocation shall be filed on or before March 25, 1958.

(5) *Apportionment of taxes on real property between seller and purchaser.* For apportionment of taxes on real property between seller and purchaser, see section 164(d) and the regulations thereunder.

(6) *Examples.* The provisions of this paragraph are illustrated by the following examples:

Example (1). A taxpayer on an accrual method reports his taxable income for the taxable year ending June 30. He elects to accrue real property taxes ratably for the taxable year ending June 30, 1955 (which is his first taxable year beginning on or after January 1, 1954). In the absence of an election under section 461(c), such taxes would accrue on January 1 of the calendar year to which they are related. The real property taxes are $1,200 for 1954; $1,600 for 1955; and $1,800 for 1956. Deductions for such taxes for the fiscal years ending June 30, 1955, and June 30, 1956, are computed as follows:

Fiscal year ending June 30, 1955	
July through December 1954	[1] None
January through June 1955 (6/12 of $1,600)	$ 800
Deduction for fiscal year ending June 30, 1955	800
Fiscal year ending June 30, 1956	
July through December 1955 (6/12 of $1,600)	$ 800
January through June 1956 (6/12 of $1,800)	900
Deduction for fiscal year ending June 30, 1956	1,700

[1] The taxes for 1954 were deductible in the fiscal year ending June 30, 1954, since such taxes accrued on January 1, 1954.

Example (2). A calendar-year taxpayer on an accrual method elects to accrue real property taxes ratably for 1954. In the absence of an election under section 461(c), such taxes would accrue on July 1 and are assessed for the 12-month period beginning on that date. The real property taxes assessed for the year ending June 30, 1954, are $1,200; $1,600 for the year ending June 30, 1955; and $1,800 for the year ending June 30, 1956. Deductions for such taxes for the calendar years 1954 and 1955 are computed as follows:

Year ending December 31, 1954	
January through June 1954	[1] None
July through December 1954 (6/12 of $1,600)	$ 800
Deduction for year ending December 31, 1954	800
Year ending December 31, 1955	
January through June 1955 (6/12 of $1,600)	$ 800
July through December 1955 (6/12 of $1,800)	900
Deduction for year ending December 31, 1955	1,700

[1] The entire tax of $1,200 for the year ended June 30, 1954, was deductible in the return for 1953, since such tax accrued on July 1, 1953.

Example (3). A calendar-year taxpayer on an accrual method elects to accrue real property taxes ratably for 1954. In the absence of an election under section 461(c), such taxes, which relate to the calendar year 1954, are accruable on December 1 of the preceding calendar year. No deduction for real property taxes is allowable for the taxable year 1954 since such taxes accrued in the taxable year 1953 under section 23(c) of the Internal Revenue Code of 1939.

Example (4). A taxpayer on an accrual method reports his taxable income for the taxable year ending March 31. He elects to accrue real property taxes ratably for the taxable year ending March 31, 1955. In the absence of an election under section 461(c), such taxes are accruable on June 1 of the calendar year to which they relate. The real property taxes are $1,200 for 1954; $1,600 for 1955; and $1,800 for 1956. Deductions for such taxes for the taxable years ending March

Reg. § 1.461-1(c)(5)

31, 1955, and March 31, 1956, are computed as follows:

Fiscal year ending March 31, 1955

April through December 1954 (9/12 of $1,200)	$ 900
January through March 1955 (3/12 of $1,600)	400
Taxes accrued ratably in fiscal year ending March 31, 1955	1,300
Tax relating to period January through March 1954, paid in June 1954, and not deductible in prior taxable years (3/12 of $1,200)	300
Deduction for fiscal year ending March 31, 1955	1,600

Fiscal year ending March 31, 1956

April through December 1955 (9/12 of $1,600)	$1,200
January through March 1956 (3/12 of $1,800)	450
Deduction for fiscal year ending March 31, 1956	1,650

Example (5). The facts are the same as in example (4) except that in June 1955, when the taxpayer pays his $1,600 real property taxes for 1955, he pays $400 of such amount under protest. Deductions for taxes for the taxable years ending March 31, 1955, and March 31, 1956, are computed as follows:

Fiscal year ending March 31, 1955

April through December 1954 (9/12 of $1,200)	$ 900
January through March 1955 (3/12 of $1,200, that is, $1,600 minus $400 (the contested portion which is not properly accruable))	300
Taxes accrued ratably in fiscal year ending March 31, 1955	1,200
Tax relating to period January through March 1954, paid in June 1954, and not deductible in prior taxable years (3/12 of $1,200)	300
Deduction for fiscal year ending March 31, 1955	1,500

Fiscal year ending March 31, 1956

April through December 1955 (9/12 of $1,200)	$ 900
January through March 1956 (3/12 of $1,800)	450
Taxes accrued ratably in fiscal year ending March 31, 1956	1,350
Contested portion of tax relating to period January through December 1955, paid in June 1955, and deductible, under section 461(f), for taxpayer's fiscal year ending March 31, 1956	400
Deduction for fiscal year ending March 31, 1956	1,750

(d) *Limitation on acceleration of accrual of taxes.* (1) Section 461(d)(1) provides that, in the case of a taxpayer whose taxable income is computed under an accrual method of accounting, to the extent that the time for accruing taxes is earlier than it would be but for any action of any taxing jurisdiction taken after December 31, 1960, such taxes are to be treated as accruing at the time they would have accrued but for such action. Any such action which, but for the provisions of section 461(d) and this paragraph, would accelerate the time for accruing a tax is to be disregarded in determining the time for accruing such tax for purposes of the deduction allowed for such tax. Such action is to be disregarded not only with respect to a taxpayer (whose taxable income is computed under an accrual method of accounting) upon whom the tax is imposed at the time of the action, but also with respect to such a taxpayer upon whom the tax is imposed at any time subsequent to such action. Thus, in the case of a tax imposed on property, the acceleration of the time for accruing taxes is to be disregarded not only with respect to the taxpayer who owned the property at the time of such acceleration, but also with respect to any subsequent owner of the property whose taxable income is computed under an accrual method of accounting. Similarly, such action is to be disregarded with respect to all property subject to such tax, even if such property is acquired after the action. Whenever the time for accruing taxes is to be disregarded in accordance with the provisions of this paragraph, the taxpayer shall accrue the tax at the time (original accrual date) the tax would have accrued but for such action, and shall, in the absence of any action of the taxing jurisdiction placing the time for accruing such tax at a time subsequent to the original accrual date, continue to accrue the tax as of the original accrual date for all future taxable years.

(2) For purposes of this paragraph—

Reg. § 1.461-1(d)(2)

(i) The term "a taxpayer whose taxable income is computed under an accrual method of accounting" means a taxpayer who, for Federal income tax purposes, accounts for any tax which is the subject of "any action" (as defined in subdivision (iii) of this subparagraph) under an accrual method of accounting. See section 446 and the regulations thereunder. If a taxpayer uses an accrual method as his overall method of accounting, it shall be presumed that he is "a taxpayer whose taxable income is computed under an accrual method of accounting." However, if the taxpayer establishes to the satisfaction of the district director that he has, for Federal income tax purposes, consistently accounted for such tax under the cash method of accounting, he shall be considered not to be "a taxpayer whose taxable income is computed under an accrual method of accounting."

(ii) The time for accruing taxes shall be determined under section 461 and the regulations in this section.

(iii) The term "any action" includes the enactment or reenactment of legislation, the adoption of an ordinance, the exercise of any taxing or administrative authority, or the taking of any other step, the result of which is an acceleration of the accrual event of any tax. The term also applies to the substitution of a substantially similar tax by either the original taxing jurisdiction or a substitute jurisdiction. However, the term does not include either a judicial interpretation, or an administrative determination by the Internal Revenue Service, as to the event which fixes the accrual date for the tax.

(iv) The term "any taxing jurisdiction" includes the District of Columbia, any State, possession of the United States, city, county, municipality, school district, or other political subdivision or authority, other than the United States, which imposes, assesses, or collects a tax.

(3) The provisions of this paragraph may be illustrated by the following examples:

Example (1). State X imposes a tax on intangible and tangible personal property used in a trade or business conducted in the State. The tax is assessed as of July 1, and becomes a lien as of that date. As a result of administrative and judicial decisions, July 1 is recognized as the proper date on which accrual method taxpayers may accrue their personal property tax for Federal income tax purposes. In 1961 State X, by legislative action, changes the assessment and lien dates from July 1, 1962, to December 31, 1961, for the property tax year 1962. The action taken by State X is considered to be "any action" of a taxing jurisdiction which results in the time for accruing taxes being earlier than it would have been but for that action. Therefore, for purposes of the deduction allowed for such tax, the personal property tax imposed by State X, for the property tax year 1962, shall be treated as though it accrued on July 1, 1962.

Example (2). Assume the same facts as in example (1) except that State X repeals the personal property tax and in lieu thereof enacts a franchise tax which is imposed on the privilege of conducting a trade or business within State X, and is based on the value of intangible and tangible personal property used in the trade or business. The franchise tax is to be assessed and will become a lien as of December 31, 1961, for the franchise tax year 1962, and on December 31 for all subsequent franchise tax years. Since the franchise tax is substantially similar to the former personal property tax and since the enactment of the franchise tax has the effect of accelerating the accrual date of the personal property tax from July 1, 1962, to December 31, 1961, the action taken by State X is considered to be "any action" of a taxing jurisdiction which results in the time for accruing taxes being earlier than it would have been but for that action. Therefore, for purposes of the deduction allowed for such tax, the franchise tax imposed by State X shall be treated as though it accrued on July 1, 1962, for the franchise tax year 1962, and on July 1 for all subsequent franchise tax years.

Example (3). Assume the same facts as in example (1) except that State X repealed the personal property tax and empowered the counties within the State to impose a personal property tax. Assuming the counties in State X subsequently imposed a personal property tax and chose December 31 of the preceding year as the assessment and lien date, the action of each of the counties would be considered to be "any action" of a taxing jurisdiction which results in the time for accruing taxes being earlier than it would have been but for that action since it is immaterial whether the original taxing jurisdiction or a substitute jurisdiction took the action.

(4) Section 461(d)(1) shall not be applicable to the extent that it would prevent the taxpayer and all other persons, including successors in interest, from ever taking into account, for Federal income tax purposes, any tax to which that section would otherwise apply. For example, assume that State Y imposes a personal property tax on tangible personal property used in a trade or business conducted in the State during a calendar year. The tax is assessed as of February 1 of the year following the personal property tax year, and becomes a lien as of that date. As a result of administrative and judicial decisions, February 1

Reg. § 1.461-1(d)(3)

of the following year is recognized as the proper date on which accrual method taxpayers may accrue the personal property tax for Federal income tax purposes. In 1962 State Y, by legislative action, changes the assessment and lien dates for the personal property tax year 1962 from February 1, 1963, to December 1, 1962, and to December 1 of the personal property tax year for all subsequent years. Corporation A, an accrual method taxpayer which uses the calendar year as its taxable year, pays the tax for 1962 on December 10, 1962. On December 15, 1962, the property which was taxed is completely destroyed and, on December 20, 1962, corporation A transfers all of its remaining assets to its shareholders, and is dissolved. Since corporation A is not in existence in 1963, and therefore could not take the personal property tax into account in computing its 1963 Federal income tax if February 1, 1963, is considered to be the time for accruing the tax, and no other person could ever take such tax into account in computing his Federal income tax, such tax shall be treated as accruing as of December 1, 1962. To the extent that any person other than the taxpayer may at any time take such tax into account in computing his taxable income, the provisions of section 461(d)(1) shall apply. Thus, upon the dissolution of a corporation or the termination of a partnership between the time which, but for the provisions of section 461(d)(1) and this paragraph, would be the time for accruing any tax which was the subject of "any action" (as defined in subdivision (iii) of subparagraph (2)), and the original accrual date, the corporation or the partnership would be entitled to a deduction for only that portion, if any, of such tax with respect to which it can establish, to the satisfaction of the district director, that no other taxpayer can properly take into account in computing his taxable income. However, to the extent that the corporation or partnership cannot establish, at the time of its dissolution or termination, as the case may be, that no other taxpayer would be entitled to take such tax into account in computing his taxable income, and it is subsequently determined that no other taxpayer is entitled to take such tax into account in computing his taxable income, the corporation or partnership may file a claim for refund for the year of its dissolution or termination (subject to the limitations prescribed in section 6511) and claim as a deduction therein the portion of such tax determined to be not deductible by any other taxpayer.

(5) Section 461(d) and this paragraph shall apply to taxable years ending after December 31, 1960.

(e) *Dividends or interest paid by certain savings institutions on certain deposits or withdrawable accounts*—(1) *Deduction not allowable*—(i) *In general.* Except as otherwise provided in this paragraph, pursuant to section 461(e) amounts paid to, or credited to the accounts of, depositors or holders of accounts as dividends or interest on their deposits or withdrawable accounts (if such amounts paid or credited are withdrawable on demand subject only to customary notice to withdraw) by a mutual savings bank not having capital stock represented by shares, a domestic building and loan association, or a cooperative bank shall not be allowed as a deduction for the taxable year to the extent such amounts are paid or credited for periods representing more than 12 months. The provisions of section 461(e) are applicable with respect to taxable years ending after December 31, 1962. Whether amounts are paid or credited for periods representing more than 12 months depends upon all the facts and circumstances in each case. For example, payments or credits which under all the facts and circumstances are in the nature of bona fide bonus interest or dividends paid or credited because a shareholder or depositor maintained a certain balance for more than 12 months, will not be considered made for more than 12 months, providing the regular payments or credits represent a period of 12 months or less. The nonallowance of a deduction to the taxpayer under section 461(e) and this subparagraph has no effect either on the proper time for reporting dividends or interest by a depositor or holder of a withdrawable account, or on the obligation of the taxpayer to make a return setting forth, among other things, the aggregate amounts paid to a depositor or shareholder under section 6049 (relating to returns regarding payments of interest) and the regulations thereunder. With respect to a short period (a taxable year consisting of a period of less than 12 months), amounts of dividends or interest paid or credited shall not be allowed as a deduction to the extent that such amounts are paid or credited for a period representing more than the number of months in such short period. In such a case, the rules contained in section 461(e) and this paragraph apply to the short period in a manner consistent with the application of such rules to a 12-month taxable year. Subparagraph (2) of this paragraph provides rules for computing amounts not allowed in the taxable year and subparagraph (3) provides rules for determining when such amounts are allowed. See section 7701(a)(19) and (32) and the regulations thereunder for the definitions of domestic building and loan association and cooperative bank.

(ii) *Exceptions.* The rule of nonallowance set forth in subdivision (i) of this subparagraph is not applicable to a taxpayer in the year in which

Reg. § 1.461-1(e)

Methods of Accounting

See p. 20,601 for regulations not amended to reflect law changes

it liquidates (other than following, or as part of, an acquisition of its assets in which the acquiring corporation, pursuant to section 381(a), takes into account certain items of the taxpayer, which for purposes of this paragraph shall be referred to as an acquisition described in section 381(a)). In addition, such rule of nonallowance is not applicable to a taxpayer which pays or credits grace interest or dividends to terminating depositors or shareholders, provided the total amount of the grace interest or dividends paid or credited during the payment or crediting period (for example, a quarterly or semi-annual period) does not exceed 10 percent of the total amount of the interest or dividends paid or credited during such period, computed without regard to the grace interest or dividends. For example, providing the 10 percent limitation is met, the rule of nonallowance does not apply in a case in which a calendar year taxpayer, with regular interest payment dates of January 1, April 1, July 1, and October 1, pays grace interest for the period beginning October 1 to a depositor who terminates his account on December 10.

(2) *Computation of amounts not allowed as a deduction*—(i) *Method of computation.* The amount of the dividends or interest to which subparagraph (1) of this paragraph applies, which is not allowed as a deduction, shall be computed under the rules of this subparagraph. The amount which is not allowed as a deduction is the difference between the total amount of dividends or interest paid or credited to that class of accounts with respect to which a deduction is not allowed under subparagraph (1) of this paragraph during the taxable year (or short period, if applicable) and an amount which bears the same ratio to such total as the number 12 (or number of months in the short period) bears to the number of months with respect to which such amounts of dividends or interest are paid or credited.

(ii) *Examples.* The provisions of subdivision (i) of this subparagraph may be illustrated by the following examples:

Example (1). X Association, a domestic building and loan association filing its return on the basis of a calendar year, regularly credits dividends on its withdrawable accounts quarterly on the first day of the quarter following the quarter with respect to which they are earned. X changes the time of crediting dividends commencing with the credit for the fourth quarter of 1964. Such credit and all subsequent credits are made on the last day of the quarter with respect to which they are earned. As a result of this change X's credits for the year 1964 are as follows:

Period with respect to which earned	Date credited in 1964	Amount
Fourth Quarter, 1963	Jan. 1	$ 250,000
First Quarter, 1964	Apr. 1	300,000
Second Quarter, 1964	July 1	300,000
Third Quarter, 1964	Oct. 1	300,000
Fourth Quarter, 1964	Dec. 31	350,000
Total dividends credited		1,500,000

Since the change in the time of crediting dividends results in the crediting in 1964 of amounts of dividends representing periods totaling 15 months (October 1963 through December 1964), amounts shall not be allowed as a deduction in 1964 which are in excess of $1,200,000, which is the amount which bears the same ratio to the amounts of dividends credited during the year ($1,500,000) as the number 12 bears to the number of months (15) with respect to which such dividends are credited. Thus, $300,000 ($1,500,000 minus $1,200,000) is not allowed as a deduction in 1964.

Example (2). Y Association, a domestic building and loan association filing its return on the basis of a calendar year, regularly credits dividends on its withdrawable accounts on the basis of a semiannual period on March 31 and September 30 of each year. Y changes the period with respect to which credits are made from the semiannual period to the quarterly basis, commencing with the last quarter in 1964. The credit for this last quarter and all subsequent credits are made on the last day of the quarter with respect to which they are earned. As a result of this change, Y's credits for the year 1964 are as follows:

Period with respect to which earned	Date credited in 1964	Amount
Six-month period ending Mar. 31, 1964	Mar. 31	$300,000
Six-month period ending Sept. 30, 1964	Sept. 30	400,000
Fourth Quarter, 1964	Dec. 31	200,000
Total dividends credited		900,000

Since the change in the basis of crediting dividends results in a crediting in 1964 of dividends representing periods totaling 15 months (October 1963 through December 1964), amounts shall not be allowed as a deduction in 1964 which are in excess of $720,000, which is the amount which bears the same ratio to the amounts of dividends credited during the year ($900,000) as the number 12 bears to the number of months (15) with respect to which such dividends are credited. Thus, $180,000 ($900,000 minus $720,000) is not allowed as a deduction in 1964.

Example (3). Z Association, a domestic building and loan association regularly files its return on the basis of a fiscal year ending on the

Reg. § 1.461-1(e)(2)

last day of February and regularly credits dividends on its withdrawable accounts quarterly on the last day of the quarter with respect to which they are earned. Z receives approval from the Commissioner of Internal Revenue to change its accounting period to a calendar year and effects the change by filing a return for a short period ending on December 31, 1964. Dividend credits for the short period beginning on March 1 and ending on December 31, 1964, are as follows:

Period with respect to which earned	Date credited in 1964	Amount
Jan.-Mar., 1964	Mar. 31	$250,000
April-June, 1964	June 30	300,000
July-Sept., 1964	Sept. 30	300,000
Oct.-Dec., 1964	Dec. 31	350,000
Total dividends credited		1,200,000

Since the change of accounting period results in amounts of dividends credited ($1,200,000) representing periods totaling 12 months (January through December 1964), and such periods represent more than the number of months (10) in the short period, an amount shall not be allowed as a deduction in such short period which is in excess of $1,000,000, which is the amount which bears the same ratio to the amount of dividends credited in the short period ($1,200,000) as the number of months (10) in the short period bears to the number of months (12) with respect to which such dividends are credited. Thus, $200,000 ($1,200,000 minus $1,000,000) is not allowed as a deduction in the short period.

(3) *When amounts allowable.* The amount of dividends or interest not allowed as a deduction under subparagraph (1) of this paragraph shall be allowed as follows (subject to the limitation that the total of the amounts so allowed shall not exceed the amount not allowed under subparagraph (1)):

(i) Such amount shall be allowed as a deduction in a later taxable year or years subject to the limitation that, when taken together with the deductions otherwise allowable in the later taxable year or years, it does not bring the deductions for any later taxable year to a total representing a period of more than 12 months (or number of months in the short period, if applicable). However, in any event, an amount otherwise allowable under subdivision (ii) of this subparagraph shall be allowed notwithstanding the fact that it may bring the deductions allowable to a total representing a period of more than 12 months (or number of months in the short period, if applicable).

(ii) In any case in which it is established to the satisfaction of the Commissioner that the taxpayer does not intend to avoid taxes, one-tenth of such amount shall be allowed as a deduction in each of the 10 succeeding taxable years—

(*a*) Commencing with the taxable year for which such amount is not allowed as a deduction under subparagraph (1), or

(*b*) In the case of such amount not allowed for a taxable year ending before July 1, 1964, commencing with either the first or second taxable year after the taxable year for which such amount is not allowed as a deduction under subparagraph (1) if the taxpayer has not taken a deduction on his return, or filed a claim for credit or refund, in respect of such amount under (*a*).

Normally, if the deduction not allowed under subparagraph (1) is a result of a change, not requested by the taxpayer, in the taxpayer's annual accounting period or dividend or interest payment or crediting dates solely as a consequence of a requirement of a Federal or State regulatory authority, or if the deduction is not allowed solely as a result of the taxpayer being a party to an acquisition to which section 381(a) applies, the Commissioner will permit the allowance of the amount not allowed in the manner provided in this subdivision. Nothing set forth in this subdivision shall be construed as permitting the allowance of a credit or refund for any year which is barred by the limitations on credit or refund provided by section 6511.

(iii) If the total of the amounts, if any, allowed under subdivisions (i) and (ii) of this subparagraph before the taxable year in which the taxpayer liquidates or otherwise ceases to engage in trade or business is less than the amount not allowed under subparagraph (1), there shall be allowed a deduction in such taxable year for the difference between the amount not allowed under subparagraph (1) and the amounts allowed, if any, as deductions under subdivisions (i) and (ii) unless the circumstances under which the taxpayer ceased to do business constitute an acquisition described in section 381(a) (relating to carryovers in certain corporate acquisitions). If the circumstances under which the taxpayer ceased to do business constitute an acquisition described in section 381(a), the acquiring corporation shall succeed to and take into account the balance of the amounts not allowed on the same basis as the taxpayer, had it not ceased to engage in business. [Reg. § 1.461-1.]

☐ [*T.D.* 6282, 12-24-57. *Amended by T.D.* 6520, 12-23-60; *T.D.* 6710, 3-17-64; *T.D.* 6735, 5-18-64; *T.D.* 6772, 11-23-64; *T.D.* 6917, 5-1-67; *T.D.* 8408, 4-9-92; *T.D.* 8482, 8-6-93; *T.D.* 8554, 7-13-94 *and T.D.* 8820, 5-17-99.]

Reg. § 1.461-1(e)(3)

[Reg. § 1.461-2]

§ 1.461-2. Contested liabilities.—(a) *General rule*—(1) *Taxable year of deduction.* If—

(i) The taxpayer contests an asserted liability,

(ii) The taxpayer transfers money or other property to provide for the satisfaction of the asserted liability,

(iii) The contest with respect to the asserted liability exists after the time of the transfer, and

(iv) But for the fact that the asserted liability is contested, a deduction would be allowed for the taxable year of the transfer (or, in the case of an accrual method taxpayer, for an earlier taxable year for which such amount would be accruable),

then the deduction with respect to the contested amount shall be allowed for the taxable year of the transfer.

(2) *Exception.* Subparagraph (1) of this paragraph shall not apply in respect of the deduction for income, war profits, and excess profits taxes imposed by the authority of any foreign country or possession of the United States, including a tax paid in lieu of a tax on income, war profits, or excess profits otherwise generally imposed by any foreign country or by any possession of the United States.

(3) *Refunds includible in gross income.* If any portion of the contested amount which is deducted under subparagraph (1) of this paragraph for the taxable year of transfer is refunded when the contest is settled, such portion is includible in gross income except as provided in § 1.111-1, relating to recovery of certain items previously deducted or credited. Such refunded amount is includible in gross income for the taxable year of receipt, or for an earlier taxable year if properly accruable for such earlier year.

(4) *Examples.* The provisions of this paragraph are illustrated by the following examples:

Example (1). X Corporation, which uses an accrual method of accounting, in 1964 contests $20 of a $100 asserted real property tax liability but pays the entire $100 to the taxing authority. In 1968, the contest is settled and X receives a refund of $5. X deducts $100 for the taxable year 1964, and includes $5 in gross income for the taxable year 1968 (assuming § 1.111-1 does not apply to such amount). If in 1964 X pays only $80 to the taxing authority, X deducts only $80 for 1964. The result would be the same if X Corporation used the cash method of accounting.

Example (2). Y Corporation makes its return on the basis of a calendar year and uses an accrual method of accounting. Y's real property taxes are assessed and become a lien on December 1, but are not payable until March 1 of the following year. On December 10, 1964, Y contests $20 of the $100 asserted real property tax which was assessed and became a lien on December 1, 1964. On March 1, 1965, Y pays the entire $100 to the taxing authority. In 1968, the contest is settled and Y receives a refund of $5. Y deducts $80 for the taxable year 1964, deducts $20 for the taxable year 1965, and includes $5 in gross income for the taxable year 1968 (assuming § 1.111-1 does not apply to such amount).

(5) *Liabilities described in paragraph (g) of § 1.461-4.* [Reserved]

(b) *Contest of asserted liability*—(1) *Asserted liability.* For purposes of paragraph (a)(1) of this section, the term "asserted liability" means an item with respect to which, but for the existence of any contest in respect of such item, a deduction would be allowable under an accrual method of accounting. For example, a notice of a local real estate tax assessment and a bill received for services may represent asserted liabilities.

(2) *Definition of the term "contest".* Any contest which would prevent accrual of a liability under section 461(a) shall be considered to be a contest in determining whether the taxpayer satisfies paragraph (a)(1)(i) of this section. A contest arises when there is a bona fide dispute as to the proper evaluation of the law or the facts necessary to determine the existence or correctness of the amount of an asserted liability. It is not necessary to institute suit in a court of law in order to contest an asserted liability. An affirmative act denying the validity or accuracy, or both, of an asserted liability to the person who is asserting such liability, such as including a written protest with payment of the asserted liability, is sufficient to commence a contest. Thus, lodging a protest in accordance with local law is sufficient to contest an asserted liability for taxes. It is not necessary that the affirmative act denying the validity or accuracy, or both, of an asserted liability be in writing if, upon examination of all the facts and circumstances, it can be established to the satisfaction of the Commissioner that a liability has been asserted and contested.

(3) *Example.* The provisions of this paragraph are illustrated by the following example:

Example: O Corporation makes its return on the basis of a calendar year and uses an accrual method of accounting. O receives a large shipment of typewriter ribbons from S Company on January 30, 1964, which O pays for in full on February 10, 1964. Subsequent to their receipt, several of the ribbons prove defective because of inferior materials used by the manufacturer. On August 9, 1964, O orally notifies S and demands refund of the full purchase price of the ribbons. After negotiations prove futile and a written demand is rejected by S, O institutes an action for the full purchase price. For purposes of paragraph (a)(1)(i) of this section, S has asserted a liability against O which O contests on August 9, 1964. O deducts the contested amount for 1964.

(c) *Transfer to provide for the satisfaction of an asserted liability*—(1) *In general.* A taxpayer may provide for the satisfaction of an asserted liability by transferring money or other property beyond his control (i) to the person who is asserting the liability, (ii) to an escrowee or trustee pursuant to a written agreement (among the escrowee or trustee, the taxpayer, and the person who is asserting the liability) that the money or other property be delivered in accordance with the settlement of the contest, or (iii) to an escrowee or trustee pursuant to an order of the United States, any State or political subdivision thereof, or any agency or instrumentality of the foregoing, or a court that the money or other property be delivered in accordance with the settlement of the contest. A taxpayer may also provide for the satisfaction of an asserted liability by transferring money or other property beyond his control to a court with jurisdiction over the contest. Purchasing a bond to guarantee payment of the asserted liability, an entry on the taxpayer's books of account, and a transfer to an account which is within the control of the taxpayer are not transfers to provide for the satisfaction of an asserted liability. In order for money or other property to be beyond the control of a taxpayer, the taxpayer must relinquish all authority over such money or other property.

(2) *Examples.* The provisions of this paragraph are illustrated by the following examples:

Example (1). M Corporation contests a $5,000 liability asserted against it by L Company for services rendered. To provide for the contingency that it might have to pay the liability, M establishes a separate bank account in its own name. M then transfers $5,000 from its general account to such separate account. Such transfer does not qualify as a transfer to provide for the satisfaction of an asserted liability because M has not transferred the money beyond its control.

Example (2). M Corporation contests a $5,000 liability asserted against it by L Company for services rendered. To provide for the contingency that it might have to pay the liability, M transfers $5,000 to an irrevocable trust pursuant to a written agreement among the trustee, M (the taxpayer), and L (the person who is asserting the liability) that the money shall be held until the contest is settled and then disbursed in accordance with the settlement. Such transfer qualifies as a transfer to provide for the satisfaction of an asserted liability.

(d) *Contest exists after transfer.* In order for a contest with respect to an asserted liability to exist after the time of transfer, such contest must be pursued subsequent to such time. Thus, the contest must have been neither settled nor abandoned at the time of the transfer. A contest may be settled by a decision, judgment, decree, or other order of any court of competent jurisdiction which has become final, or by written or oral agreement between the parties. For example, Z Corporation, which uses an accrual method of accounting, in 1964 contests a $100 asserted liability. In 1967 the contested liability is settled as being $80 which Z accrues and deducts for such year. In 1968 Z pays the $80. Section 461(f) does not apply to Z with respect to the transfer because a contest did not exist after the time of such transfer.

(e) *Deduction otherwise allowed*—(1) *In general.* The existence of the contest with respect to an asserted liability must prevent (without regard to section 461(f)) and be the only factor preventing a deduction for the taxable year of the transfer (or, in the case of an accrual method taxpayer, for an earlier taxable year for which such amount would be accruable) to provide for the satisfaction of such liability. Nothing in section 461(f) or this section shall be construed to give rise to a deduction since section 461(f) and this section relate only to the timing of deductions which are otherwise allowable under the Code.

(2) *Example.* The provisions of this paragraph are illustrated by the following example:

Example. A, an individual, makes a gift of certain property to B, an individual. A pays the entire amount of gift tax assessed against him but contests his liability for such tax. Section 275(a)(3) provides that gift taxes are not deductible. A does not satisfy the requirement of paragraph (a)(1)(iv) of this section since a deduction would not be allowed for the taxable year of the transfer even if A did not contest his liability to such tax.

(f) *Treatment of money or property transferred to an escrowee, trustee, or court and treatment of any income attributable thereto.* [Reserved]

(g) *Effective dates.* Paragraphs (a) through (e) of this section apply to transfers of money or property made in taxable years beginning after December 31, 1953, and ending after August 16, 1954. [Reg. § 1.461-2.]

☐ [T.D. 6772, 11-23-64. *Amended by* T.D. 8408, 4-9-92.]

Reg. § 1.461-2(g)

Methods of Accounting

See p. 20,601 for regulations not amended to reflect law changes

[Reg. § 1.461-3]

§ 1.461-3. Prepaid interest. [Reserved]

☐ [T.D. 8408, 4-9-92.]

[Reg. § 1.461-4]

§ 1.461-4. Economic performance.—(a) *Introduction*—(1) *In general.* For purposes of determining whether an accrual basis taxpayer can treat the amount of any liability (as defined in § 1.446-1(c)(1)(ii)(B)) as incurred, the all events test is not treated as met any earlier than the taxable year in which economic performance occurs with respect to the liability.

(2) *Overview.* Paragraph (b) of this section lists exceptions to the economic performance requirement. Paragraph (c) of this section provides cross-references to the definitions of certain terms for purposes of section 461(h) and the regulations thereunder. Paragraphs (d) through (m) of this section and § 1.461-6 provide rules for determining when economic performance occurs. Section 1.461-5 provides rules relating to an exception under which certain recurring items may be incurred for the taxable year before the year during which economic performance occurs.

(b) *Exceptions to the economic performance requirement.* Paragraph (a)(2)(iii)(B) of § 1.461-1 provides examples of liabilities that are taken into account under rules that operate without regard to the all events test (including economic performance).

(c) *Definitions.* The following cross-references identify certain terms defined for purposes of section 461(h) and the regulations thereunder:

(1) *Liability.* See paragraph (c)(1)(ii)(B) of § 1.446-1 for the definition of "liability."

(2) *Payment.* See paragraph (g)(1)(ii) of this section for the definition of "payment."

(d) *Liabilities arising out of the provision of services, property, or the use of property*—(1) *In general.* The principles of this paragraph (d) determine when economic performance occurs with respect to liabilities arising out of the performance of services, the transfer of property, or the use of property. This paragraph (d) does not apply to liabilities described in paragraph (e) (relating to interest expense) or paragraph (g) (relating to breach of contract, workers compensation, tort, etc.) of this section. In addition, except as otherwise provided in Internal Revenue regulations, revenue procedures, or revenue rulings this paragraph (d) does not apply to amounts paid pursuant to a notional principal contract. The Commissioner may provide additional rules in regulations, revenue procedures, or revenue rulings concerning the time at which economic performance occurs for items described in this paragraph (d).

(2) *Services or property provided to the taxpayer*—(i) *In general.* Except as otherwise provided in paragraph (d)(5) of this section, if the liability of a taxpayer arises out of the providing of services or property to the taxpayer by another person, economic performance occurs as the services or property is provided.

(ii) *Long-term contracts.* In the case of any liability of a taxpayer described in paragraph (d)(2)(i) of this section that is an expense attributable to a long-term contract with respect to which the taxpayer uses the percentage of completion method, economic performance occurs—

(A) As the services or property is provided; or, if earlier,

(B) As the taxpayer makes payment (as defined in paragraph (g)(1)(ii) of this section) in satisfaction of the liability to the person providing the services or property. See paragraph (k)(2) of this section for the effective date of this paragraph (d)(2)(ii).

(iii) *Employee benefits*—(A) *In general.* Except as otherwise provided in any Internal Revenue regulation, revenue procedure, or revenue ruling, the economic performance requirement is satisfied to the extent that any amount is otherwise deductible under section 404 (employer contributions to a plan of deferred compensation), section 404A (certain foreign deferred compensation plans), and section 419 (welfare benefit funds). See § 1.461-1(a)(2)(iii)(D).

(B) *Property transferred in connection with performance of services.* [Reserved]

(iv) *Cross-references.* See *Examples 4* through *6* of paragraph (d)(7) of this section. See paragraph (d)(6) of this section for rules relating to when a taxpayer may treat services or property as provided to the taxpayer.

(3) *Use of property provided to the taxpayer*—(i) *In general.* Except as otherwise provided in this paragraph (d)(3) and paragraph (d)(5) of this section, if the liability of a taxpayer arises out of the use of property by the taxpayer, economic performance occurs ratably over the period of time the taxpayer is entitled to the use of the property (taking into account any reasonably expected renewal periods when necessary to carry out the purposes of section 461(h)). See *Examples 6* through *9* of paragraph (d)(7) of this section.

(ii) *Exceptions*—(A) *Volume, frequency of use, or income.* If the liability of a taxpayer arises out of the use of property by the taxpayer and all or a portion of the liability is determined by reference to the frequency or volume of use of the

Reg. § 1.461-3

property or the income from the property, economic performance occurs for the portion of the liability determined by reference to the frequency or volume of use of the property or the income from the property as the taxpayer uses the property or includes income from the property. See Examples 8 and 9 of paragraph (d)(7) of this section. This paragraph (d)(3)(ii) shall not apply if the District Director determines, that based on the substance of the transaction, the liability of the taxpayer for use of the property is more appropriately measured ratably over the period of time the taxpayer is entitled to the use of the property.

(B) *Section 467 rental agreements.* In the case of a liability arising out of the use of property pursuant to a section 467 rental agreement, economic performance occurs as provided in § 1.461-1(a)(2)(iii)(E).

(4) *Services or property provided by the taxpayer*—(i) *In general.* Except as otherwise provided in paragraph (d)(5) of this section, if the liability of a taxpayer requires the taxpayer to provide services or property to another person, economic performance occurs as the taxpayer incurs costs (within the meaning of § 1.446-1(c)(1)(ii)) in connection with the satisfaction of the liability. See *Examples 1* through *3* of paragraph (d)(7) of this section.

(ii) *Barter transactions.* If the liability of a taxpayer requires the taxpayer to provide services, property, or the use of property, and arises out of the use of property by the taxpayer, or out of the provision of services or property to the taxpayer by another person, economic performance occurs to the extent of the lesser of—

(A) The cumulative extent to which the taxpayer incurs costs (within the meaning of § 1.446-1(c)(1)(ii)) in connection with its liability to provide the services or property; or

(B) The cumulative extent to which the services or property is provided to the taxpayer.

(5) *Liabilities that are assumed in connection with the sale of a trade or business*—(i) *In general.* If, in connection with the sale or exchange of a trade or business by a taxpayer, the purchaser expressly assumes a liability arising out of the trade or business that the taxpayer but for the economic performance requirement would have been entitled to incur as of the date of the sale, economic performance with respect to that liability occurs as the amount of the liability is properly included in the amount realized on the transaction by the taxpayer. See § 1.1001-2 for rules relating to the inclusion in amount realized from a discharge of liabilities resulting from a sale or exchange.

(ii) *Trade or business.* For purposes of this paragraph (d)(5), a trade or business is a specific group of activities carried on by the taxpayer for the purpose of earning income or profit if every operation that is necessary to the process of earning income or profit is included in the group. Thus, for example, the group of activities generally must include the collection of income and the payment of expenses.

(iii) *Tax avoidance.* This paragraph (d)(5) does not apply if the District Director determines that tax avoidance is one of the taxpayer's principal purposes for the sale or exchange.

(6) *Rules relating to the provision of services or property to a taxpayer.* The following rules apply for purposes of this paragraph (d):

(i) Services or property provided to a taxpayer include services or property provided to another person at the direction of the taxpayer.

(ii) A taxpayer is permitted to treat services or property as provided to the taxpayer as the taxpayer makes payment to the person providing the services or property (as defined in paragraph (g)(1)(ii) of this section), if the taxpayer can reasonably expect the person to provide the services or property within 3 1/2 months after the date of payment.

(iii) A taxpayer is permitted to treat property as provided to the taxpayer when the property is delivered or accepted, or when title to the property passes. The method used by the taxpayer to determine when property is provided is a method of accounting that must comply with the rules of § 1.446-1(e). Thus, the method of determining when property is provided must be used consistently from year to year, and cannot be changed without the consent of the Commissioner.

(iv) If different services or items of property are required to be provided to a taxpayer under a single contract or agreement, economic performance generally occurs over the time each service is provided and as each item of property is provided. However, if a service or item of property to be provided to the taxpayer is incidental to other services or property to be provided under a contract or agreement, the taxpayer is not required to allocate any portion of the total contract price to the incidental service or property. For purposes of this paragraph (d)(6)(iv), services or property is treated as incidental only if—

(A) The cost of the services or property is treated on the taxpayer's books and records as part of the cost of the other services or property provided under the contract; and

Reg. § 1.461-4(d)(6)

(B) The aggregate cost of the services or property does not exceed 10 percent of the total contract price.

(7) *Examples.* The following examples illustrate the principles of this paragraph (d). For purposes of these examples, it is assumed that the requirements of the all events test other than economic performance have been met, and that the recurring item exception is not used. Assume further that the examples do not involve section 467 rental agreements and, therefore, section 467 is not applicable. The examples are as follows:

Example 1. Services or property provided by the taxpayer. (i) X corporation, a calendar year, accrual method taxpayer, is an oil company. During March 1990, X enters into an oil and gas lease with Y. In November 1990, X installs a platform and commences drilling. The lease obligates X to remove its offshore platform and well fixtures upon abandonment of the well or termination of the lease. During 1998, X removes the platform and well fixtures at a cost of $200,000.

(ii) Under paragraph (d)(4)(i) of this section, economic performance with respect to X's liability to remove the offshore platform and well fixtures occurs as X incurs costs in connection with that liability. X incurs these costs in 1998 as, for example, X's employees provide X with removal services (see paragraph (d)(2) of this section). Consequently, X incurs $200,000 for the 1998 taxable year. Alternatively, assume that during 1990 X pays Z $130,000 to remove the platform and fixtures, and that Z performs these removal services in 1998. Under paragraph (d)(2) of this section, X does not incur this cost until Z performs the services. Thus, economic performance with respect to the $130,000 X pays Z occurs in 1998.

Example 2. Services or property provided by the taxpayer. (i) W corporation, a calendar year, accrual method taxpayer, sells tractors under a three-year warranty that obligates W to make any reasonable repairs to each tractor it sells. During 1990, W sells ten tractors. In 1992 W repairs, at a cost of $5,000, two tractors sold during 1990.

(ii) Under paragraph (d)(4)(i) of this section, economic performance with respect to W's liability to perform services under the warranty occurs as W incurs costs in connection with that liability. W incurs these costs in 1992 as, for example, replacement parts are provided to W (see paragraph (d)(2) of this section). Consequently, $5,000 is incurred by W for the 1992 taxable year.

Example 3. Services or property provided by the taxpayer; Long-term contracts. (i) W corporation, a calendar year, accrual method taxpayer, manufactures machine tool equipment. In November 1992, W contracts to provide X corporation with certain equipment. The contract is not a long-term contract under section 460 or § 1.451-3. In 1992, W pays Z corporation $50,000 to lease from Z, for the one-year period beginning on January 1, 1993, testing equipment to perform quality control tests required by the agreement with X. In 1992, pursuant to the terms of a contract, W pays Y corporation $100,000 for certain parts necessary to manufacture the equipment. The parts are provided to W in 1993. W's employees provide W with services necessary to manufacture the equipment during 1993, for which W pays $150,000 in 1993.

(ii) Under paragraph (d)(4) of this section, economic performance with respect to W's liability to provide the equipment to X occurs as W incurs costs in connection with that liability. W incurs these costs during 1993, as services, property, and the use of property necessary to manufacture the equipment are provided to W (see paragraphs (d)(2) and (d)(3) of this section). Thus, $300,000 is incurred by W for the 1993 taxable year. See section 263A and the regulations thereunder for rules relating to the capitalization and inclusion in inventory of these incurred costs.

(iii) Alternatively, assume that the agreement with X is a long-term contract as defined in section 460(f), and that W takes into account all items with respect to such contracts under the percentage of completion method as described in section 460 (b)(1). Under paragraph (d)(2)(ii) of this section, the $100,000 W pays in 1992 for parts is incurred for the 1992 taxable year, for purposes of determining the percentage of completion under section 460(b)(1)(A). W's other costs under the agreement are incurred for the 1993 taxable year for this purpose.

Example 4. Services or property provided to the taxpayer. (i) LP1, a calendar year, accrual method limited partnership, owns the working interest in a parcel of property containing oil and gas. During December 1990, LP1 enters into a turnkey contract with Z corporation pursuant to which LP1 pays Z $200,000 and Z is required to provide a completed well by the close of 1992. In May 1992, Z commences drilling the well, and, in December 1992, the well is completed.

(ii) Under paragraph (d)(2) of this section, economic performance with respect to LP1's liability for drilling and development services provided to LP1 by Z occurs as the services are provided. Consequently, $200,000 is incurred by LP1 for the 1992 taxable year.

Example 5. Services or property provided to the taxpayer. (i) X corporation, a calendar year,

Reg. § 1.461-4(d)(7)

accrual method taxpayer, is an automobile dealer. On January 15, 1990, X agrees to pay an additional $10 to Y, the manufacturer of the automobiles, for each automobile purchased by X from Y. Y agrees to provide advertising and promotional activities to X.

(ii) During 1990, X purchases from Y 1,000 new automobiles and pays to Y an additional $10,000 as provided in the agreement. Y, in turn, uses this $10,000 to provide advertising and promotional activities during 1992.

(iii) Under paragraph (d)(2) of this section, economic performance with respect to X's liability for advertising and promotional services provided to X by Y occurs as the services are provided. Consequently, $10,000 is incurred by X for the 1992 taxable year.

Example 6. Use of property provided to the taxpayer; services or property provided to the taxpayer. (i) V corporation, a calendar year, accrual method taxpayer, charters aircraft. On December 20, 1990, V leases a jet aircraft from L for the four-year period that begins on January 1, 1991. The lease obligates V to pay L a base rental of $500,000 per year. In addition, the lease requires V to pay $25 to an escrow account for each hour that the aircraft is flown. The escrow account funds are held by V and are to be used by L to make necessary repairs to the aircraft. Any amount remaining in the escrow account upon termination of the lease is payable to V. During 1991, the aircraft is flown 1,000 hours and V pays $25,000 to the escrow account. The aircraft is repaired by L in 1993. In 1994, $20,000 is released from the escrow account to pay L for the repairs.

(ii) Under paragraph (d)(3)(i) of this section, economic performance with respect to V's base rental liability occurs ratably over the period of time V is entitled to use the jet aircraft. Consequently, the $500,000 rent is incurred by V for the 1991 taxable year and for each of the next three taxable years. Under paragraph (d)(2) of this section, economic performance with respect to the liability to place amounts in escrow occurs as the aircraft is repaired. Consequently, V incurs $20,000 for the 1993 taxable year.

Example 7. Use of property provided to the taxpayer. (i) X corporation, a calendar year, accrual method taxpayer, manufactures and sells electronic circuitry. On November 15, 1990, X enters into a contract with Y that entitles X to the exclusive use of a product owned by Y for the five-year period beginning on January 1, 1991. Pursuant to the contract, X pays Y $100,000 on December 30, 1990.

(ii) Under paragraph (d)(3)(i) of this section, economic performance with respect to X's liability for the use of property occurs ratably over the period of time X is entitled to use the product. Consequently, $20,000 is incurred by X for 1991 and for each of the succeeding four taxable years.

Example 8. Use of property provided to the taxpayer. (i) Y corporation, a calendar year, accrual method taxpayer, enters into a five-year lease with Z for the use of a copy machine on July 1, 1991. Y also receives delivery of the copy machine on July 1, 1991. The lease obligates Y to pay Z a base rental payment of $6,000 per year at the beginning of each lease year and an additional charge of 5 cents per copy 30 days after the end of each lease year. The machine is used to make 50,000 copies during the first lease year: 20,000 copies in 1991 and 30,000 copies from January 1, 1992, to July 1, 1992. Y pays the $6,000 base rental payment to Z on July 1, 1991, and the $2,500 variable use payment on July 30, 1992.

(ii) Under paragraph (d)(3)(i) of this section, economic performance with respect to Y's base rental liability occurs ratably over the period of time Y is entitled to use the copy machine. Consequently, $3,000 rent is incurred by Y for the 1991 taxable year. Under paragraph (d)(3)(ii) of this section, economic performance with respect to Y's variable use portion of the liability occurs as Y uses the machine. Thus, the $1,000 of the $2,500 variable-use liability that relates to the 20,000 copies made in 1991 is incurred by Y for the 1991 taxable year.

Example 9. Use of property provided to the taxpayer. (i) X corporation, a calendar year, accrual method taxpayer, enters into a five-year product distribution agreement with Y, on January 1, 1992. The agreement provides for a payment of $100,000 on January 1, 1992, plus 10 percent of the gross profits earned by X from distribution of the product. The variable income portion of X's liability is payable on April 1 of each subsequent year. On January 1, 1992, X pays Y $100,000. On April 1, 1993, X pays Y $3 million representing 10 percent of X's gross profits from January 1 through December 31, 1992.

(ii) Under paragraph (d)(3)(i) of this section, economic performance with respect to X's $100,000 payment occurs ratably over the period of time X is entitled to use the product. Consequently, $20,000 is incurred by X for each year of the agreement beginning with 1992. Under paragraph (d)(3)(ii) of this section, economic performance with respect to X's variable income portion of the liability occurs as the income is earned by X. Thus, the $3 million variable-income liability is incurred by X for the 1992 taxable year.

Reg. § 1.461-4(d)(7)

(e) *Interest.* In the case of interest, economic performance occurs as the interest cost economically accrues, in accordance with the principles of relevant provisions of the Code.

(f) *Timing of deductions from notional principal contracts.* Economic performance on a notional principal contract occurs as provided under § 1.446-3.

(g) *Certain liabilities for which payment is economic performance*—(1) *In general*—(i) *Person to which payment must be made.* In the case of liabilities described in paragraphs (g)(2) through (7) of this section, economic performance occurs when, and to the extent that, payment is made to the person to which the liability is owed. Thus, except as otherwise provided in paragraph (g)(1)(iv) of this section and § 1.461-6, economic performance does not occur as a taxpayer makes payments in connection with such a liability to any other person, including a trust, escrow account, court-administered fund, or any similar arrangement, unless the payments constitute payment to the person to which the liability is owed under paragraph (g)(1)(ii)(B) of this section. Instead, economic performance occurs as payments are made from that other person or fund to the person to which the liability is owed. The amount of economic performance that occurs as payment is made from the other person or fund to the person to which the liability is owed may not exceed the amount the taxpayer transferred to the other person or fund. For special rules relating to the taxation of amounts transferred to "qualified settlement funds," see section 468B and the regulations thereunder. The Commissioner may provide additional rules in regulations, revenue procedures, and revenue rulings concerning the time at which economic performance occurs for items described in this paragraph (g).

(ii) *Payment to person to which liability is owed.* Paragraph (d)(6) of this section provides that for purposes of paragraph (d) of this section (relating to the provision of services or property to the taxpayer) in certain cases a taxpayer may treat services or property as provided to the taxpayer as the taxpayer makes payments to the person providing the services or property. In addition, this paragraph (g) provides that in the case of certain liabilities of a taxpayer, economic performance occurs as the taxpayer makes payment to persons specified therein. For these and all other purposes of section 461(h) and the regulations thereunder:

(A) *Payment.* The term "payment" has the same meaning as is used when determining whether a taxpayer using the cash receipts and disbursements method of accounting has made a payment. Thus, for example, payment includes the furnishing of cash or cash equivalents and the netting of offsetting accounts. Payment does not include the furnishing of a note or other evidence of indebtedness of the taxpayer, whether or not the evidence is guaranteed by any other instrument (including a standby letter of credit) or by any third party (including a government agency). As a further example, payment does not include a promise of the taxpayer to provide services or property in the future (whether or not the promise is evidenced by a contract or other written agreement). In addition, payment does not include an amount transferred as a loan, refundable deposit, or contingent payment.

(B) *Person to which payment is made.* Payment to a particular person is accomplished if paragraph (g)(1)(ii)(A) of this section is satisfied and a cash basis taxpayer in the position of that person would be treated as having actually or constructively received the amount of the payment as gross income under the principles of section 451 (without regard to section 104(a) or any other provision that specifically excludes the amount from gross income). Thus, for example, the purchase of an annuity contract or any other asset generally does not constitute payment to the person to which a liability is owed unless the ownership of the contract or other asset is transferred to that person.

(C) *Liabilities that are assumed in connection with the sale of a trade or business.* Paragraph (d)(5) of this section provides rules that determine when economic performance occurs in the case of liabilities that are assumed in connection with the sale of a trade or business. The provisions of paragraph (d)(5) of this section also apply to any liability described in paragraph (g)(2) through (7) of this section that the purchaser expressly assumes in connection with the sale or exchange of a trade or business by a taxpayer, provided the taxpayer (but for the economic performance requirement) would have been entitled to incur the liability as of the date of the sale.

(iii) *Person.* For purposes of this paragraph (g), "person" has the same meaning as in section 7701(a)(1), except that it also includes any foreign state, the United States, any State or political subdivision thereof, any possession of the United States, and any agency or instrumentality of any of the foregoing.

(iv) *Assignments.* If a person that has a right to receive payment in satisfaction of a liability described in paragraphs (g)(2) through (7) of this section makes a valid assignment of that right to a second person, or if the right is assigned to the second person through operation of law, then payment to the second person in satisfaction of that liability constitutes payment to the person to which the liability is owed.

(2) *Liabilities arising under a workers compensation act or out of any tort, breach of contract, or violation of law.* If the liability of a taxpayer requires a payment or series of payments to another person and arises under any workers compensation act or out of any tort, breach of contract, or violation of law, economic performance occurs as payment is made to the person to which the liability is owed. See *Example 1* of paragraph (g)(8) of this section. For purposes of this paragraph (g)(2)—

(i) A liability to make payments for services, property, or other consideration provided under a contract is not a liability arising out of a breach of that contract unless the payments are in the nature of incidental, consequential, or liquidated damages; and

(ii) A liability arising out of a tort, breach of contract, or violation of law includes a liability arising out of the settlement of a dispute in which a tort, breach of contract, or violation of law, respectively, is alleged.

(3) *Rebates and refunds.* If the liability of a taxpayer is to pay a rebate, refund, or similar payment to another person (whether paid in property, money, or as a reduction in the price of goods or services to be provided in the future by the taxpayer), economic performance occurs as payment is made to the person to which the liability is owed. This paragraph (g)(3) applies to all rebates, refunds, and payments or transfers in the nature of a rebate or refund regardless of whether they are characterized as a deduction from gross income, an adjustment to gross receipts or total sales, or an adjustment or addition to cost of goods sold. In the case of a rebate or refund made as a reduction in the price of goods or services to be provided in the future by the taxpayer, "payment" is deemed to occur as the taxpayer would otherwise be required to recognize income resulting from a disposition at an unreduced price. See *Example 2* of paragraph (g)(8) of this section. For purposes of determining whether the recurring item exception of § 1.461-5 applies, a liability that arises out of a tort, breach of contract, or violation of law is not considered a rebate or refund.

(4) *Awards, prizes, and jackpots.* If the liability of a taxpayer is to provide an award, prize, jackpot, or other similar payment to another person, economic performance occurs as payment is made to the person to which the liability is owed. See *Examples 3* and *4* of paragraph (g)(8) of this section.

(5) *Insurance, warranty, and service contracts.* If the liability of a taxpayer arises out of the provision to the taxpayer of insurance, or a warranty or service contract, economic performance occurs as payment is made to the person to which the liability is owed. See *Examples 5* through *7* of paragraph (g)(8) of this section. For purposes of this paragraph (g)(5)—

(i) A warranty or service contract is a contract that a taxpayer enters into in connection with property bought or leased by the taxpayer, pursuant to which the other party to the contract promises to replace or repair the property under specified circumstances.

(ii) The term "insurance" has the same meaning as is used when determining the deductibility of amounts paid or incurred for insurance under section 162.

(6) *Taxes*—(i) *In general.* Except as otherwise provided in this paragraph (g)(6), if the liability of a taxpayer is to pay a tax, economic performance occurs as the tax is paid to the governmental authority that imposed the tax. For purposes of this paragraph (g)(6), payment includes payments of estimated income tax and payments of tax where the taxpayer subsequently files a claim for credit or refund. In addition, for purposes of this paragraph (g)(6), a tax does not include a charge collected by a governmental authority for specific extraordinary services or property provided to a taxpayer by the governmental authority. Examples of such a charge include the purchase price of a parcel of land sold to a taxpayer by a governmental authority and a charge for labor engaged in by government employees to improve that parcel. In certain cases, a liability to pay a tax is permitted to be taken into account in the taxable year before the taxable year during which economic performance occurs under the recurring item exception of § 1.461-5. See *Example 8* of paragraph (g)(8) of this section.

(ii) *Licensing fees.* If the liability of a taxpayer is to pay a licensing or permit fee required by a governmental authority, economic performance occurs as the fee is paid to the governmental authority, or as payment is made to any other person at the direction of the governmental authority.

(iii) *Exceptions*—(A) *Real property taxes.* If a taxpayer has made a valid election under section 461(c), the taxpayer's accrual for real property taxes is determined under section 461(c). Otherwise, economic performance with respect to a property tax liability occurs as the tax is paid, as specified in paragraph (g)(6)(i) of this section.

Reg. § 1.461-4(g)(6)

(B) *Certain foreign taxes.* If the liability of a taxpayer is to pay an income, war profits, or excess profits tax that is imposed by the authority of any foreign country or possession of the United States and is creditable under section 901 (including a creditable tax described in section 903 that is paid in lieu of such a tax), economic performance occurs when the requirements of the all events test (as described in § 1.446-1(c)(1)(ii)) other than economic performance are met, whether or not the taxpayer elects to credit such taxes under section 901(a).

(7) *Other liabilities.* In the case of a taxpayer's liability for which economic performance rules are not provided elsewhere in this section or in any other Internal Revenue regulation, revenue ruling or revenue procedure, economic performance occurs as the taxpayer makes payments in satisfaction of the liability to the person to which the liability is owed. This paragraph (g)(7) applies only if the liability cannot properly be characterized as a liability covered by rules provided elsewhere in this section. If a liability may properly be characterized as, for example, a liability arising from the provision of services or property to, or by, a taxpayer, the determination as to when economic performance occurs with respect to that liability is made under paragraph (d) of this section and not under this paragraph (g)(7).

(8) *Examples.* The following examples illustrate the principles of this paragraph (g). For purposes of these examples, it is assumed that the requirements of the all events test other than economic performance have been met and, except as otherwise provided, that the recurring item exception is not used.

Example 1. Liabilities arising out of a tort. (i) During the period 1970 through 1975, Z corporation, a calendar year, accrual method taxpayer, manufactured and distributed industrial products that contained carcinogenic substances. In 1992, a number of lawsuits are filed against Z alleging damages due to exposure to these products. In settlement of a lawsuit maintained by A, Z agrees to purchase an annuity contract that will provide annual payments to A of $50,000 for a period of 25 years. On December 15, 1992, Z pays W, an unrelated life insurance company, $491,129 for such an annuity contract. Z retains ownership of the annuity contract.

(ii) Under paragraph (g)(2) of this section, economic performance with respect to Z's liability to A occurs as each payment is made to A. Consequently, $50,000 is incurred by Z for each taxable year that a payment is made to A under the annuity contract. (Z must also include in income a portion of amounts paid under the annuity, pursuant to section 72.) The result is the same if in 1992 Z secures its obligation with a standby letter of credit.

(iii) If Z later transfers ownership of the annuity contract to A, an amount equal to the fair market value of the annuity on the date of transfer is incurred by Z in the taxable year of the transfer (see paragraph (g)(1)(ii)(B) of this section). In addition, the transfer constitutes a transaction to which section 1001 applies.

Example 2. Rebates and refunds. (i) X corporation, a calendar year, accrual method taxpayer, manufactures and sells hardware products. X enters into agreements that entitle each of its distributors to a rebate (or discount on future purchases) from X based on the amount of purchases made by the distributor from X during any calendar year. During the 1992 calendar year, X becomes liable to pay a $2,000 rebate to distributor A. X pays A $1,200 of the rebate on January 15, 1993, and the remaining $800 on October 15, 1993. Assume the rebate is deductible (or allowable as an adjustment to gross receipts or cost of goods sold) when incurred.

(ii) If X does not adopt the recurring item exception described in § 1.461-5 with respect to rebates and refunds, then under paragraph (g)(3) of this section, economic performance with respect to the $2,000 rebate liability occurs in 1993. However, if X has made a proper election under § 1.461-5, and as of December 31, 1992, all events have occurred that determine the fact of the rebate liability, X incurs $1,200 for the 1992 taxable year. Because economic performance (payment) with respect to the remaining $800 does not occur until October 15, 1993 (more than 8½ months after the end of 1992), X cannot use the recurring item exception for this portion of the liability (see § 1.461-5). Thus, the $800 is not incurred by X until the 1993 taxable year. If, instead of making the cash payments to A during 1993, X adjusts the price of hardware purchased by A that is delivered to A during 1993, X's "payment" occurs as X would otherwise be required to recognize income resulting from a disposition at an unreduced price.

Example 3. Awards, prizes, and jackpots. (i) W corporation, a calendar year, accrual method taxpayer, produces and sells breakfast cereal. W conducts a contest pursuant to which the winner is entitled to $10,000 per year for a period of 20 years. On December 1, 1992, A is declared the winner of the contest and is paid $10,000 by W. In addition, on December 1 of each of the next nineteen years, W pays $10,000 to A.

(ii) Under paragraph (g)(4) of this section, economic performance with respect to the

Reg. § 1.461-4(g)(7)

$200,000 contest liability occurs as each of the $10,000 payments is made by W to A. Consequently, $10,000 is incurred by W for the 1992 taxable year and for each of the succeeding nineteen taxable years.

Example 4. Awards, prizes, and jackpots. (i) Y corporation, a calendar year, accrual method taxpayer, owns a casino that contains progressive slot machines. A progressive slot machine provides a guaranteed jackpot amount that increases as money is gambled through the machine until the jackpot is won or until a maximum predetermined amount is reached. On July 1, 1993, the guaranteed jackpot amount on one of Y's slot machines reaches the maximum predetermined amount of $50,000. On October 1, 1994, the $50,000 jackpot is paid to B.

(ii) Under paragraph (g)(4) of this section, economic performance with respect to the $50,000 jackpot liability occurs on the date the jackpot is paid to B. Consequently, $50,000 is incurred by Y for the 1994 taxable year.

Example 5. Insurance, warranty, and service contracts. (i) V corporation, a calendar year, accrual method taxpayer, manufactures toys. V enters into a contract with W, an unrelated insurance company, on December 15, 1992. The contract obligates V to pay W a premium of $500,000 before the end of 1995. The contract obligates W to satisfy any liability of V resulting from claims made during 1993 or 1994 against V by any third party for damages attributable to defects in toys manufactured by V. Pursuant to the contract, V pays W a premium of $500,000 on October 1, 1995.

(ii) Assuming the arrangement constitutes insurance, under paragraph (g)(5) of this section economic performance occurs as the premium is paid. Thus, $500,000 is incurred by V for the 1995 taxable year.

Example 6. Insurance, warranty, and service contracts. (i) Y corporation, a calendar year, accrual method taxpayer, is a common carrier. On December 15, 1992, Y enters into a contract with Z, an unrelated insurance company, under which Z must satisfy any liability of Y that arises during the succeeding 5 years for damages under a workers compensation act or out of any tort, provided the event that causes the damages occurs during 1993 or 1994. Under the contract, Y pays $360,000 to Z on December 31, 1993.

(ii) Assuming the arrangement constitutes insurance, under paragraph (g)(5) of this section economic performance occurs as the premium is paid. Consequently, $360,000 is incurred by Y for the 1993 taxable year. The period for which the $360,000 amount is permitted to be taken into account is determined under the capitalization rules because the insurance contract is an asset having a useful life extending substantially beyond the close of the taxable year.

Example 7. Insurance, warranty, and service contracts. Assume the same facts as in *Example 6*, except that Y is obligated to pay the first $5,000 of any damages covered by the arrangement with Z. Y is, in effect, self-insured to the extent of this $5,000 "deductible." Thus, under paragraph (g)(2) of this section, economic performance with respect to the $5,000 liability does not occur until the amount is paid to the person to which the tort or workers compensation liability is owed.

Example 8. Taxes. (i) The laws of State A provide that every person owning personal property located in State A on the first day of January shall be liable for tax thereon and that a lien for the tax shall attach as of that date. In addition, the laws of State A provide that 60% of the tax is due on the first day of December following the lien date and the remaining 40% is due on the first day of July of the succeeding year. On January 1, 1992, X corporation, a calendar year, accrual method taxpayer, owns personal property located in State A. State A imposes a $10,000 tax on X with respect to that property on January 1, 1992. X pays State A $6,000 of the tax on December 1, 1992, and the remaining $4,000 on July 1, 1993.

(ii) Under paragraph (g)(6) of this section, economic performance with respect to $6,000 of the tax liability occurs on December 1, 1992. Consequently, $6,000 is incurred by X for the 1992 taxable year. Economic performance with respect to the remaining $4,000 of the tax liability occurs on July 1, 1993. If X has adopted the recurring item exception described in § 1.461-5 as a method of accounting for taxes, and as of December 31, 1992, all events have occurred that determine the liability of X for the remaining $4,000, X also incurs $4,000 for the 1992 taxable year. If X does not adopt the recurring item exception method, the $4,000 is not incurred by X until the 1993 taxable year.

(h) *Liabilities arising under the Nuclear Waste Policy Act of 1982.* Notwithstanding the principles of paragraph (d) of this section, economic performance with respect to the liability of an owner or generator of nuclear waste to make payments to the Department of Energy ("DOE") pursuant to a contract required by the Nuclear Waste Policy Act of 1982 (Pub. L. 97-425, 42 U.S.C. 10101-10226 (1982)) occurs as each payment under the contract is made to DOE and not when DOE satisfies its obligations under the con-

Reg. § 1.461-4(h)

tract. This rule applies to the continuing fee required by 42 U.S.C. 10222(a)(2) (1982), as well as the one-time fee required by 42 U.S.C. 10222(a)(3) (1982). For rules relating to when economic performance occurs with respect to interest, see paragraph (e) of this section.

(i) [Reserved]

(j) *Contingent liabilities.* [Reserved]

(k) *Special effective dates*— (1) *In general.* Except as otherwise provided in this paragraph (k), section 461(h) and this section apply to liabilities that would, under the law in effect before the enactment of section 461(h), be allowable as a deduction or otherwise incurred after July 18, 1984. For example, the economic performance requirement applies to all liabilities arising under a workers compensation act or out of any tort that would, under the law in effect before the enactment of section 461(h), be incurred after July 18, 1984. For taxable years ending before April 7, 1995, see Q&A-2 of § 1.461-7T (as it appears in 26 CFR part 1 revised April 1, 1995), which provides an election to make this change in method of accounting applicable to either the portion of the first taxable year that occurs after July 18, 1984 (part-year change method), or the entire first taxable year ending after July 18, 1984 (full-year change method). With respect to the effective date rules for interest, section 461(h) applies to interest accruing under any obligation (whether or not evidenced by a debt instrument) if the obligation is incurred in any transaction occurring after June 8, 1984, and is not incurred under a written contract which was binding on March 1, 1984, and at all times thereafter until the obligation is incurred. Interest accruing under an obligation described in the preceding sentence is subject to section 461(h) even if the interest accrues before July 19, 1984. Similarly, interest accruing under any obligation incurred in a transaction occurring before June 9, 1984, (or under a written contract which was binding on March 1, 1984, and at all times thereafter until the obligation is incurred) is not subject to section 461(h) even to the extent the interest accrues after July 18, 1984.

(2) *Long-term contracts.* Except as otherwise provided in paragraph (m)(2) of this section, in the case of liabilities described in paragraph (d)(2)(ii) of this section (relating to long-term contracts), paragraph (d)(2)(ii) of this section applies to liabilities that would, but for the enactment of section 461(h), be allowable as a deduction or otherwise incurred for taxable years beginning after December 31, 1991.

(3) *Payment liabilities.* Except as otherwise provided in paragraph (m)(2) of this section, in the case of liabilities described in paragraph (g) of this section (other than liabilities arising under a workers compensation act or out of any tort described in paragraph (g)(2) of this section), paragraph (g) of this section applies to liabilities that would, but for the enactment of section 461(h), be allowable as a deduction or otherwise incurred for taxable years beginning after December 31, 1991.

(l) [Reserved]

(m) *Change in method of accounting required by this section*—(1) *In general.* For the first taxable year ending after July 18, 1984, a taxpayer is granted the consent of the Commissioner to change its method of accounting for liabilities to comply with the provisions of this section pursuant to any of the following procedures:

(i) For taxable years ending before April 7, 1995, the part-year change in method election described in Q&A-2 through Q&A-6 and Q&A-8 through Q&A-10 of § 1.461-7T (as it appears in 26 CFR part 1 revised April 1, 1995);

(ii) For taxable years ending before April 7, 1995, the full-year change in method election described in Q&A-2 through Q&A-6 and Q&A-8 through Q&A-10 of § 1.461-7T (as it appears in 26 CFR part 1 revised April 1, 1995); or

(iii) For taxable years ending before April 7, 1995, if no election is made, the cut-off method described in Q&A-1 and Q&A-11 of § 1.461-7T (as it appears in 26 CFR part 1 revised April 1, 1995).

(2) *Change in method of accounting for long-term contracts and payment liabilities*—(i) *First taxable year beginning after December 31, 1991.* For the first taxable year beginning after December 31, 1991, a taxpayer is granted the consent of the Commissioner to change its method of accounting for long-term contract liabilities described in paragraph (d)(2)(ii) of this section and payment liabilities described in paragraph (g) of this section (other than liabilities arising under a workers compensation act or out of any tort described in paragraph (g)(2) of this section) to comply with the provisions of this section. The change must be made in accordance with paragraph (m)(1)(ii) or (m)(1)(iii) of this section, except the effective date is the first day of the first taxable year beginning after December 31, 1991.

(ii) *Retroactive change in method of accounting for long-term contracts and payment liabilities.* For the first taxable year beginning after December 31, 1989, or the first taxable year beginning after December 31, 1990, a taxpayer is granted the consent of the Commissioner to change its method of accounting for long-term contract liabilities described in paragraph (d)(2)(ii) of this section and payment liabilities

Reg. § 1.461-4(i)

described in paragraph (g) of this section (other than liabilities arising under a workers compensation act or out of any tort described in paragraph (g)(2) of this section) to comply with the provisions of this section. The change must be made in accordance with paragraph (m)(1)(ii) or (m)(1)(iii) of this section, except the effective date is the first day of the first taxable year beginning after December 31, 1989, or the first day of the first taxable year beginning after December 31, 1990. For taxable years ending before April 7, 1995, the taxpayer may make the change in method of accounting, including a full-year change in method election under paragraph (m)(1)(ii) of this section and Q&A-5 of § 1.461-7T (as it appears in 26 CFR part 1 revised April 1, 1995), by filing an amended return for such year, provided the amended return is filed on or before October 7, 1992. [Reg. § 1.461-4.]

☐ [T.D. 8408, 4-9-92. Amended by T.D. 8491, 10-8-93; T.D. 8593, 4-7-95 and T.D. 8820, 5-17-99.]

[Reg. § 1.461-5]

§ 1.461-5. Recurring item exception.—(a) *In general.* Except as otherwise provided in paragraph (c) of this section, a taxpayer using an accrual method of accounting may adopt the recurring item exception described in paragraph (b) of this section as a method of accounting for one or more types of recurring items incurred by the taxpayer. In the case of the "other payment liabilities" described in § 1.461-4(g)(7), the Commissioner may provide for the application of the recurring item exception by regulation, revenue procedure or revenue ruling.

(b) *Requirements for use of the exception*—(1) *General rule.* Under the recurring item exception, a liability is treated as incurred for a taxable year if—

(i) As of the end of that taxable year, all events have occurred that establish the fact of the liability and the amount of the liability can be determined with reasonable accuracy;

(ii) Economic performance with respect to the liability occurs on or before the earlier of—

(A) The date the taxpayer files a timely (including extensions) return for that taxable year; or

(B) The 15th day of the 9th calendar month after the close of that taxable year;

(iii) The liability is recurring in nature; and

(iv) Either—

(A) The amount of the liability is not material; or

(B) The accrual of the liability for that taxable year results in a better matching of the liability with the income to which it relates than would result from accruing the liability for the taxable year in which economic performance occurs.

(2) *Amended returns.* A taxpayer may file an amended return treating a liability as incurred under the recurring item exception for a taxable year if economic performance with respect to the liability occurs after the taxpayer files a return for that year, but within 8½ months after the close of that year.

(3) *Liabilities that are recurring in nature.* A liability is recurring if it can generally be expected to be incurred from one taxable year to the next. However, a taxpayer may treat such a liability as recurring in nature even if it is not incurred by the taxpayer in each taxable year. In addition, a liability that has never previously been incurred by a taxpayer may be treated as recurring if it is reasonable to expect that the liability will be incurred on a recurring basis in the future.

(4) *Materiality requirement.* For purposes of this paragraph (b):

(i) In determining whether a liability is material, consideration shall be given to the amount of the liability in absolute terms and in relation to the amount of other items of income and expense attributable to the same activity.

(ii) A liability is material if it is material for financial statement purposes under generally accepted accounting principles.

(iii) A liability that is immaterial for financial statement purposes under generally accepted accounting principles may be material for purposes of this paragraph (b).

(5) *Matching requirement.* (i) In determining whether the matching requirement of paragraph (b)(1)(iv)(B) of this section is satisfied, generally accepted accounting principles are an important factor, but are not dispositive.

(ii) In the case of a liability described in paragraph (g)(3) (rebates and refunds), paragraph (g)(4) (awards, prizes, and jackpots), paragraph (g)(5) (insurance, warranty, and service contracts), paragraph (g)(6) (taxes), or paragraph (h) (continuing fees under the Nuclear Waste Policy Act of 1982) of § 1.461-4, the matching requirement of paragraph (b)(1)(iv)(B) of this section shall be deemed satisfied.

(c) *Types of liabilities not eligible for treatment under the recurring item exception.* The recurring item exception does not apply to any liability of a taxpayer described in paragraph (e) (interest), paragraph (g)(2) (workers compensation, tort, breach of contract, and violation of law), or paragraph (g)(7) (other liabilities) of § 1.461-4. Moreover, the recurring item exception does not apply to any liability incurred by a tax shelter, as defined in section 461(i) and § 1.448-1T(b).

(d) *Time and manner of adopting the recurring item exception*—(1) *In general.* The recurring item exception is a method of accounting that must be consistently applied with respect to a type of item, or for all items, from one taxable year to the next in order to clearly reflect income. A taxpayer is permitted to adopt the recurring item exception as part of its method of accounting for any type of item for the first taxable year in which that type of item is incurred. Except as otherwise provided, the rules of section 446(e) and § 1.446-1(e) apply to changes to or from the recurring item exception as a method of accounting. For taxable years ending before April 7, 1995, see Q&A-7 of § 1.461-7T (as it appears in 26 CFR part 1 revised April 1, 1995) for rules concerning the time and manner of adopting the recurring item exception for taxable years that include July 19, 1984. For purposes of this section, items are to be classified by type in a manner that results in classifications that are no less inclusive than the classifications of production costs provided in the full-absorption regulations of § 1.471-11(b) and (c), whether or not the taxpayer is required to maintain inventories.

(2) *Change to the recurring item exception method for the first taxable year beginning after December 31, 1991*—(i) *In general.* For the first taxable year beginning after December 31, 1991, a taxpayer is granted the consent of the Commissioner to change to the recurring item exception method of accounting. A taxpayer is also granted the consent of the Commissioner to expand or modify its use of the recurring item exception method for the first taxable year beginning after December 31, 1991. For each trade or business for which a taxpayer elects to use the recurring item exception method, the taxpayer must use the same method of change (cut-off or full-year change) it is using for that trade or business under § 1.461-4(m). For taxable years ending before April 7, 1995, see Q&A-11 of § 1.461-7T (as it appears in 26 CFR part 1 revised April 1, 1995) for an explanation of how amounts are taken into account under the cut-off method (except that, for purposes of this paragraph (d)(2), the change applies to all amounts otherwise incurred on or after the first day of the first taxable year beginning after December 31, 1991). For taxable years ending before April 7, 1995, see Q&A-6 of § 1.461-7T (as it appears in 26 CFR part 1 revised April 1, 1995) for an explanation of how amounts are taken into account under the full-year change method (except that the change in method occurs on the first day of the first taxable year beginning after December 31, 1991). For taxable years ending before April 7, 1995, the full-year change in method may result in a section 481(a) adjustment that must be taken into account in the manner described in Q&A-8 and Q&A-9 of § 1.461-7T (as it appears in 26 CFR part 1 revised April 1, 1995) (except that the taxable year of change is the first taxable beginning after December 31, 1991).

(ii) *Manner of changing to the recurring item exception method.* For the first taxable year beginning after December 31, 1991, a taxpayer may change to the recurring item exception method by accounting for the item on its timely filed original return for such taxable year (including extensions). For taxable years ending before April 7, 1995, the automatic consent of the Commissioner is limited to those items accounted for under the recurring item exception method on the timely filed return, unless the taxpayer indicates a wider scope of change by filing the statement provided in Q&A-7(b)(2) of § 1.461-7T (as it appears in 26 CFR part 1 revised April 1, 1995).

(3) *Retroactive change to the recurring item exception method.* For the first taxable year beginning after December 31, 1989, or December 31, 1990, a taxpayer is granted consent of the Commissioner to change to the recurring item exception method of accounting, provided the taxpayer complies with paragraph (d)(2) of this section on either the original return for such year or on an amended return for such year filed on or before October 7, 1992. For this purpose the effective date is the first day of the first taxable year beginning after December 31, 1989, or the first day of the first taxable year beginning after December 31, 1990. A taxpayer is also granted the consent of the Commissioner to expand or modify its use of the recurring item exception method for the first taxable year beginning after December 31, 1989, December 31, 1990, or December 31, 1991.

(e) *Examples.* The following examples illustrate the principles of this section:

Example 1. Requirements for use of the recurring item exception. (i) Y corporation, a calendar year, accrual method taxpayer, manufactures and distributes video cassette recorders. Y timely files its federal income tax return for each taxable year on the extended due date for the return (September 15, of the following taxable year). Y offers to refund the price of a recorder to any purchaser not satisfied with the recorder. During 1992, 100 purchasers request a refund of the $500 purchase price. Y refunds $30,000 on or before September

15, 1993, and the remaining $20,000 after such date but before the end of 1993.

(ii) Under paragraph (g)(3) of § 1.461-4, economic performance with respect to $30,000 of the refund liability occurs on September 15, 1993. Assume the refund is deductible (or allowable as an adjustment to gross receipts or cost of goods sold) when incurred. If Y does not adopt the recurring item exception with respect to rebates and refunds, the $30,000 refund is incurred by Y for the 1993 taxable year. However, if Y has properly adopted the recurring item exception method of accounting under this section, and as of December 31, 1992, all events have occurred that determine the fact of the liability for the $30,000 refund, Y incurs that amount for the 1992 taxable year. Because economic performance (payment) with respect to the remaining $20,000 occurs after September 15, 1993 (more than 8½ months after the end of 1992), that amount is not eligible for recurring item treatment under this section. Thus, the $20,000 amount is not incurred by Y until the 1993 taxable year.

Example 2. Requirements for use of the recurring item exception; amended returns. The facts are the same as in *Example 2,* except that Y files its income tax return for 1992 on March 15, 1993, and Y does not refund the price of any recorder before that date. Under paragraph (b)(1) of this section, the refund liability is not eligible for the recurring item exception because economic performance with respect to the refund does not occur before Y files a return for the taxable year for which the item would have been incurred under the exception. However, since economic performance occurs within 8½ months after 1992, Y may file an amended return claiming the $30,000 as incurred for its 1992 taxable year (see paragraph (b)(2) of this section). [Reg. § 1.461-5.]

☐ [T.D. 8408, 4-9-92. Amended by T.D. 8593, 4-7-95.]

[Reg. § 1.461-6]

§ 1.461-6. Economic performance when certain liabilities are assigned or are extinguished by the establishment of a fund.—(a) *Qualified assignments of certain personal injury liabilities under section 130.* In the case of a qualified assignment (within the meaning of section 130(c)), economic performance occurs as a taxpayer-assignor makes payments that are excludible from the income of the assignee under section 130(a).

(b) *Section 468B.* Economic performance occurs as a taxpayer makes qualified payments to a designated settlement fund under section 468B, relating to special rules for designated settlement funds.

(c) *Payments to other funds or persons that constitute economic performance.* [Reserved]

(d) *Effective dates.* The rules in paragraph (a) of this section apply to payments after July 18, 1984. [Reg. § 1.461-6.]

☐ [T.D. 8408, 4-9-92.]

[Reg. § 1.463-1T]

§ 1.463-1T. Transitional rule for vested accrued vacation pay (Temporary).—(a) *Introduction.* Section 91(i) of the Tax Reform Act of 1984 provides a transitional rule for the election under section 463, relating to accrual of vacation pay. Section 91(i) applies only in the case of taxpayers with respect to which a deduction was allowable (other than under section 463) for vested accrued vacation pay for the last taxable year ending on or before July 18, 1984.

(b) *Election under transitional rule.* A taxpayer described in paragraph (a) of this section that makes an election under section 463 for the first taxable year ending after July 18, 1984, shall compute the opening balance of the account described in section 463(a)(1) ("accrual account") with respect to such vacation pay under the rules provided in paragraph (e)(3) of this section.

(c) *Multiple vacation pay accounts within a single trade or business.* (1) An election under section 463 must be made with respect to all vacation pay accounts maintained by the taxpayer within a single trade or business whether the liability is for vested accrued vacation pay or for vacation pay that is contingent.

(2) If a taxpayer has elected, in a taxable year ending on or before July 18, 1984, to treat contingent vacation pay with respect to a single trade or business under section 463, the taxpayer may elect, under the provisions of section 91(i) of the Tax Reform Act of 1984, to treat vested accrued vacation pay with respect to the same trade or business under section 463. However, no election may be made with respect to vacation pay for which a prior section 463 election was made and that is accounted for under section 463.

(d) *Time for making election.* A taxpayer described in paragraph (a) of this section that makes an election under section 463 for the first taxable year ending after July 18, 1984, must make the election on or before the due date (determined with regard to extensions) for filing the taxpayer's income tax return for such taxable year. However, if the taxpayer's income tax return was filed for the first taxable year ending after July 18, 1984, prior to March 6, 1986, the taxpayer must make the election by the later of the due date (determined with regard to extensions) for filing the taxpayer's income tax return,

Reg. § 1.463-1T(d)

or May 5, 1986. In this case, the election must be made by filing an amended return (showing adjustments, if any) for such year and attaching the statement required by paragraph (e) of this section on or before the later of the due date (determined with regard to extensions) for filing the taxpayer's income tax return, or May 5, 1986.

(e) *Manner of making election.* A taxpayer must make the election described in paragraph (b) of this section by attaching a statement to the taxpayer's income tax return for the first taxable year ending after July 18, 1984. The statement must indicate that the taxpayer is electing to apply the provisions of section 463 with respect to vested accrued vacation pay for the taxpayer's first taxable year ending after July 18, 1984. The statement must contain the following information:

(1) The taxpayer's name and a description of the vacation pay plans to which the election applies.

(2) If a taxpayer has more than one trade or business and is not making the election with respect to all trades or businesses, a description of the trades or businesses to which the election applies.

(3) The opening balance in the taxpayer's accrual account. This balance equals the amount determined as if the taxpayer had maintained an account for the last taxable year ending on or before July 18, 1984, representing the taxpayer's liability for vested accrued vacation pay earned by employees before the close of the last taxable year ending on or before July 18, 1984, and payable during that taxable year or within 12 months following the close of that taxable year. If the taxpayer's liability for vacation pay includes both vested accrued vacation pay and vacation pay the liability for which is contingent, the amount in the opening balance of the accrual account that represents the taxpayer's liability for contingent vacation pay is to be determined under the rules provided in section 463(b)(2).

(4) The opening balance in the taxpayer's suspense account. This balance equals the amount determined under paragraph (e)(3) of this section less the portion allowed as deductions under section 162 for prior taxable years for vacation pay earned but not paid at the close of the last taxable year ending on or before July 18, 1984.

(f) *Vested accrued vacation pay.* For purposes of paragraphs (a) through (e) of this section, "vested accrued vacation pay" means any amount allowable as deductions under section 162(a) for a taxable year with respect to vacation pay of employees of the taxpayer (determined without regard to section 463). For purposes of this section, vacation pay will be considered vested accrued vacation pay even though there is a limit or ceiling on the amount of vacation pay an employee is entitled to as of the close of any plan year. For example, if under a vacation pay plan an employee may accumulate no more than 40 days of vacation leave by the end of any plan year and any unused days in excess of 40 days are forfeited, the taxpayer is considered to have vested accrued vacation pay (even though the plan is not fully vested) and may make an election under the transitional rule. [Temporary Reg. § 1.463-1T.]

☐ [T.D. 8073, 1-29-86.]

[Reg. § 10.2]

§ 10.2. **Election to accrue vacation pay (Temporary).**—[Reg. § 10.2 was redesignated as Reg. § 301.9100-16T by T.D. 8435, 9-18-92.—CCH.]

[Reg. § 1.465-1T]

§ 1.465-1T. **Aggregation of certain activities (Temporary).**—(a) *General rule.* A partner in a partnership or an S corporation shareholder may aggregate and treat as a single activity—

(1) The holding, production, or distribution of more than one motion picture film or video tape by the partnership or S corporation,

(2) The farming (as defined in section 464(e)) of more than one farm by the partnership or S corporation,

(3) The exploration for, or exploitation of, oil and gas resources with respect to more than one oil and gas property by the partnership or S corporation, or

(4) The exploration for, or exploitation of, geothermal deposits (within the meaning of section 613(e)(3)) with respect to more than one geothermal property by the partnership or S corporation.

Thus, for example, if a partnership or S corporation is engaged in the activity of exploring for, or exploiting, oil and gas resources with respect to 10 oil and gas properties, a partner or S corporation shareholder may aggregate those properties and treat the aggregated oil and gas activities as a single activity. If that partnership or S corporation also is engaged in the activity of farming with respect to two farms, the partner or shareholder may aggregate the farms and treat the aggregated farming activities as a single separate activity. Except as provided in section 465(c)(2)(B)(ii), the partner or shareholder cannot aggregate the farming activity with the oil and gas activity.

Reg. § 10.2

Methods of Accounting

(b) *Effective date.* This section shall apply to taxable years beginning during 1984. [Temporary Reg. § 1.465-1T.]

☐ [T.D. 8012, 3-7-85.]

[Reg. § 7.465-1]

§ 7.465-1. Amounts at risk with respect to activities begun prior to effective date; in general (Temporary).—Section 465 provides that a taxpayer (other than a corporation which is not a subchapter S corporation or a personal holding company) engaged in certain activities may not deduct losses from such activity to the extent the losses exceed the amount the taxpayer is at risk with respect to the activity. For the types of activities to which section 465 applies and for determining what constitutes a separate activity, see section 465(c). Section 465 generally applies to losses attributable to amounts paid or incurred in taxable years beginnning after December 31, 1975. For the purposes of applying the at risk limitation to activities begun before the effective date of the provision (and which were not expected from application of the provision), it is necessary to determine the amount at risk as of the first day of the first taxable year beginning after December 31, 1975. The amount at risk in an activity as of the first day of the first taxable year of the taxpayer beginning after December 31, 1975, (for the purposes of § 7.465-1 through 7.465-5 such first day shall be referred to as the effective date) shall be determined according to the rules provided in sections 7.465-2 through 7.465-5. [Temporary Reg. § 7.465-1.]

☐ [T.D. 7504, 8-19-77.]

[Reg. § 7.465-2]

§ 7.465-2. Determination of amount at risk (Temporary).—(a) *Initial amount.* The amount a taxpayer is at risk on the effective date with respect to an activity to which section 465 applies shall be determined in accordance with this section. The initial amount the taxpayer is at risk in the activity shall be the taxpayer's initial basis in the activity as modified by disregarding amounts described in section 465(b)(3) or (4) (relating generally to amounts protected against loss or borrowed from related persons).

(b) *Succeeding adjustments.* For each taxable year ending before the effective date, the initial amount at risk shall be increased and decreased by the items which increased and decreased the taxpayer's basis in the activity in that year as modified by disregarding the amounts described in section 465(b)(3) or (4).

(c) *Application of losses and withdrawals.* (1) Losses described in section 465(d) which are incurred in taxable years beginning prior to January 1, 1976 and deducted in such taxable years, will be treated as reducing first that portion of the taxpayer's basis which is attributable to amounts not at risk. On the other hand, withdrawals made in taxable years beginning before January 1, 1976, will be treated as reducing the amount which the taxpayer is at risk.

(2) Therefore, if in a taxable year beginning prior to January 1, 1976 there is a loss described in section 465(d), it shall reduce the amount at risk only to the extent it exceeds the amount of the taxpayer's basis which is not at risk. For the purposes of this paragraph, the taxpayer's basis which is not at risk is that portion of the taxpayer's basis in the activity (as of the close of the taxable year and prior to reduction for the loss) which is attributable to amounts described in section 465(b)(3) or (4).

(d) *Amount at risk shall not be less than zero.* If, after determining the amount described in paragraphs (a), (b), and (c) of this section, the amount at risk (but for this paragraph) would be less than zero, the amount at risk on the effective date shall be zero. [Temporary Reg. § 7.465-2.]

☐ [T.D. 7504, 8-19-77.]

[Reg. § 7.465-3]

§ 7.465-3. Allocation of loss for different taxable years (Temporary).—If the taxable year of the entity conducting the activity differs from that of the taxpayer, the loss attributable to the activity for the first taxable year of the entity ending after the beginning of the first taxable year of the taxpayer beginning after December 31, 1975, shall be allocated in the following manner. That portion of the loss from the activity for such taxable year of the entity which bears the same ratio as the number of days in such taxable year before January 1, 1976, divided by the total number of days in the taxable year, shall be attributable to taxable years of the taxpayer beginning before January 1, 1976. Consequently, that portion shall be treated in accordance with § 7.465-2. [Temporary Reg. § 7.465-3.]

☐ [T.D. 7504, 8-19-77.]

[Reg. § 7.465-4]

§ 7.465-4. Insufficient records (Temporary).—If sufficient records do not exist to accurately determine under § 7.465-2 the amount which a taxpayer is at risk on the effective date, the amount at risk shall be the taxpayer's basis in the activity reduced (but not below zero) by the taxpayer's share of amounts described in section 465(b)(3) or (4) with respect to the activity on the

Reg. § 7.465-4

Methods of Accounting

day before the effective date. [Temporary Reg. § 7.465-4.]

☐ [T.D. 7504, 8-19-77.]

[Reg. § 7.465-5]

§ 7.465-5. **Examples (Temporary).**—The provisions of § 7.465-1 and § 7.465-2 may be illustrated by the following examples:

Example (1). J and K, as equal partners, form partnership JK on January 1, 1975. Partnership JK is engaged solely in an activity described in section 465(c)(1). On January 1, 1975, each partner contributes $10,000 in cash from personal assets to JK. On July 1, 1975, JK borrows $40,000 (of which J's share is $20,000) from a bank under a nonrecourse financing arrangement secured only by the new equipment (for use in the activity) purchased with the $40,000. On September 1, 1975, JK reduces the amount due on the loan to $36,000 (of which J's share is $18,000). On October 1, 1975, JK distributes $3,000 to each partner. For taxable year 1975, JK has no income or loss. Although J's basis in the activity is $25,000 ($10,000 + $18,000 − $3,000) J's amount at risk on the effective date is $7,000 determined as follows:

Initial amount at risk		$10,000
Plus:		
Items which increased basis other than amounts described in section 465(b)(3) or (4)	$ 0	0
Total		$10,000
Less:		
Distribution	$3,000	$ 3,000
J's amount at risk on effective date		$ 7,000

Example (2). Assume the same facts as in Example (1) except that JK has a loss (as described in section 465(d)) for 1975 of which J's share is $12,000. Although J's basis in the activity is $13,000 ($10,000 + $18,000 − ($3,000 + $12,000)) J's amount at risk on the effective date is $7,000 determined as follows:

Initial amount at risk		$10,000
Plus:		
Items which increased basis other than amounts described in section 465(b)(3) or (4)	0	0
Total		$10,000
Less:		
Distribution	$3,000	3,000
Portion of loss ($12,000) in excess of portion of basis not at risk ($18,000)		0
J's amount at risk on effective date		$ 7,000

Example (3). Assume the same facts as in Example (1) except that JK has a loss (as described in section 465(d)) for 1975, and J's share is $23,000. J's basis in the activity is $2,000 ($10,000 + $18,000 − ($3,000 + $23,000)). The amount at risk on the effective date is determined as follows:

Initial amount at risk		$10,000
Plus:		
Items which increased basis other than amounts described in section 465(b)(3) or (4)	0	0
		$10,000
Less:		
Distribution	$3,000	
Portion of loss ($23,000) in excess of portion of basis not at risk ($18,000)	5,000	8,000
J's amount at risk on the effective date		$ 2,000

[Reg. § 7.465-5.]

☐ [T.D. 7504, 8-19-77.]

[Reg. § 1.465-27]

§ 1.465-27. **Qualified nonrecourse financing.**—(a) *In general.* Notwithstanding any provision of section 465(b) or the regulations under section 465(b), for an activity of holding real property, a taxpayer is considered at risk for the taxpayer's share of any qualified nonrecourse financing which is secured by real property used in such activity.

(b) *Qualified nonrecourse financing secured by real property*—(1) *In general.* For purposes of section 465(b)(6) and this section, the term *qualified nonrecourse financing* means any financing—

Reg. § 7.465-5

(i) Which is borrowed by the taxpayer with respect to the activity of holding real property;

(ii) Which is borrowed by the taxpayer from a qualified person or represents a loan from any federal, state, or local government or instrumentality thereof, or is guaranteed by any federal, state, or local government;

(iii) For which no person is personally liable for repayment, taking into account paragraphs (b)(3), (4), and (5) of this section; and

(iv) Which is not convertible debt.

(2) *Security for qualified nonrecourse financing*—(i) *Types of property.* For a taxpayer to be considered at risk under section 465(b)(6), qualified nonrecourse financing must be secured only by real property used in the activity of holding real property. For this purpose, however, property that is incidental to the activity of holding real property will be disregarded. In addition, for this purpose, property that is neither real property used in the activity of holding real property nor incidental property will be disregarded if the aggregate gross fair market value of such property is less than 10 percent of the aggregate gross fair market value of all the property securing the financing.

(ii) *Look-through rule for partnerships.* For purposes of paragraph (b)(2)(i) of this section, a borrower shall be treated as owning directly its proportional share of the assets in a partnership in which the borrower owns (directly or indirectly through a chain of partnerships) an equity interest.

(3) *Personal liability; partial liability.* If one or more persons are personally liable for repayment of a portion of a financing, the portion of the financing for which no person is personally liable may qualify as qualified nonrecourse financing.

(4) *Partnership liability.* For purposes of section 465(b)(6) and this paragraph (b), the personal liability of any partnership for repayment of a financing is disregarded and, provided the requirements contained in paragraphs (b)(1)(i), (ii), and (iv) of this section are satisfied, the financing will be treated as qualified nonrecourse financing secured by real property if—

(i) The only persons personally liable to repay the financing are partnerships;

(ii) Each partnership with personal liability holds only property described in paragraph (b)(2)(i) of this section (applying the principles of paragraph (b)(2)(ii) of this section in determining the property held by each partnership); and

(iii) In exercising its remedies to collect on the financing in a default or default-like situation, the lender may proceed only against property that is described in paragraph (b)(2)(i) of this section and that is held by the partnership or partnerships (applying the principles of paragraph (b)(2)(ii) of this section in determining the property held by the partnership or partnerships).

(5) *Disregarded entities.* Principles similar to those described in paragraph (b)(4) of this section shall apply in determining whether a financing of an entity that is disregarded for federal tax purposes under § 301.7701-3 of this chapter is treated as qualified nonrecourse financing secured by real property.

(6) *Examples.* The following examples illustrate the rules of this section:

Example 1. Personal liability of a partnership; incidental property. (i) X is a limited liability company that is classified as a partnership for federal tax purposes. X engages only in the activity of holding real property. In addition to real property used in the activity of holding real property, X owns office equipment, a truck, and maintenance equipment that it uses to support the activity of holding real property. X borrows $500 to use in the activity. X is personally liable on the financing, but no member of X and no other person is liable for repayment of the financing under local law. The lender may proceed against all of X's assets if X defaults on the financing.

(ii) Under paragraph (b)(2)(i) of this section, the personal property is disregarded as incidental property used in the activity of holding real property. Under paragraph (b)(4) of this section, the personal liability of X for repayment of the financing is disregarded and, provided the requirements contained in paragraphs (b)(1)(i), (ii), and (iv) of this section are satisfied, the financing will be treated as qualified nonrecourse financing secured by real property.

Example 2. Bifurcation of a financing. The facts are the same as in *Example 1*, except that A, a member of X, is personally liable for repayment of $100 of the financing. If the requirements contained in paragraphs (b)(1)(i), (ii), and (iv) of this section are satisfied, then under paragraph (b)(3) of this section, the portion of the financing for which A is not personally liable for repayment ($400) will be treated as qualified nonrecourse financing secured by real property.

Example 3. Personal liability; tiered partnerships. (i) UTP1 and UTP2, both limited liability companies classified as partnerships, are the only

Reg. § 1.465-27(b)(6)

general partners in Y, a limited partnership. Y borrows $500 with respect to the activity of holding real property. The financing is a general obligation of Y. UTP1 and UTP2, therefore, are personally liable to repay the financing. Under section 752, UTP1's share of the financing is $300, and UTP2's share is $200. No person other than Y, UTP1, and UTP2 is personally liable to repay the financing. Y, UTP1, and UTP2 each hold only real property.

(ii) Under paragraph (b)(4) of this section, the personal liability of Y, UTP1, and UTP2 to repay the financing is disregarded and, provided the requirements of paragraphs (b)(1)(i), (ii), and (iv) of this section are satisfied, UTP1's $300 share of the financing and UTP2's $200 share of the financing will be treated as qualified nonrecourse financing secured by real property.

Example 4. Personal liability; tiered partnerships. The facts are the same as in *Example 3*, except that Y's general partners are UTP1 and B, an individual. Because B, an individual, is also personally liable to repay the $500 financing, the entire financing fails to satisfy the requirement in paragraph (b)(1)(iii) of this section. Accordingly, UTP1's $300 share of the financing will not be treated as qualified nonrecourse financing secured by real property.

Example 5. Personal liability; tiered partnerships. The facts are the same as in *Example 3*, except that Y is a limited liability company and UTP1 and UTP2 are not personally liable for the debt. However, UTP1 and UTP2 each pledge property as security for the loan that is other than real property used in the activity of holding real property and other than property that is incidental to the activity of holding real property. The fair market value of the property pledged by UTP1 and UTP2 is greater than 10 percent of the sum of the aggregate gross fair market value of the property held by Y and the aggregate gross fair market value of the property pledged by UTP1 and UTP2. Accordingly, the financing fails to satisfy the requirement in paragraph (b)(1)(iii) of this section by virtue of its failure to satisfy paragraph (b)(4)(iii) of this section. Therefore, the financing is not qualified nonrecourse financing secured by real property.

Example 6. Personal liability; Disregarded entity. (i) X is a single member limited liability company that is disregarded as an entity separate from its owner for federal tax purposes under § 301.7701-3 of this chapter. X owns certain real property and property that is incidental to the activity of holding the real property. X does not own any other property. For federal tax purposes, A, the sole member of X, is considered to own all of the property held by X and is engaged in the activity of holding real property through X. X borrows $500 and uses the proceeds to purchase additional real property that is used in the activity of holding real property. X is personally liable to repay the financing, but A is not personally liable for repayment of the financing under local law. The lender may proceed against all of X's assets if X defaults on the financing.

(ii) X is disregarded so that the assets and liabilities of X are treated as the assets and liabilities of A. However, A is not personally liable for the $500 liability. Provided that the requirements contained in paragraphs (b)(1)(i), (ii), and (iv) of this section are satisfied, the financing will be treated as qualified nonrecourse financing secured by real property with respect to A.

(c) *Effective date.* This section is effective for any financing incurred on or after August 4, 1998. Taxpayers, however, may apply this section retroactively for financing incurred before August 4, 1998. [Reg. § 1.465-27.]

☐ [*T.D.* 8777, 8-3-98.]

[Reg. § 1.466-1]

§ 1.466-1. **Method of accounting for the redemption cost of qualified discount coupons.**—(a) *Introduction.* Section 466 permits taxpayers who elect to use the method of accounting described in section 466 to deduct the redemption cost (as defined in paragraph (b) of this section) of qualified discount coupons (as defined in paragraph (c) of this section) outstanding at the end of the taxable year and redeemed during the redemption period (within the meaning of paragraph (d)(2) of this section) in addition to the redemption cost of qualified discount coupons redeemed during the taxable year which were not deducted for a prior taxable year. For the taxable year in which the taxpayer first uses this method of accounting, the taxpayer is not allowed to deduct the redemption costs of qualified discount coupons redeemed during the taxable year that would have been deductible for the prior taxable year had the taxpayer used this method of accounting for such prior year. (See paragraph (e) of this section for rules describing how this amount should be taken into account.) A taxpayer must use the accrual method of accounting for any trade or business for which an election is made under section 466. Furthermore, the taxpayer must make an election in accordance with the rules in section 466(d) and § 1.466-3 for that trade or business. The method of accounting in section 466 is applicable only to the taxpayer's redemption of qualified discount coupons. Section 466 does not apply to trading stamps or premium coupons, which are subject to the method of accounting in § 1.451-4, or to discount coupons that are not qualified discount coupons.

(b) *Redemption costs*—(1) *Costs deductible under section 466.* The deduction allowed by section 466 applies only to the redemption cost of qualified discount coupons. The term "redemption cost" means an amount equal to:

(i) The lesser of:

(A) The amount of the discount stated on the coupon, or

(B) The cost incurred by the taxpayer for paying the discount; plus

(ii) The amount payable to the retailer (or other person redeeming the coupon from the person receiving the price discount) for services in redeeming the coupon.

The amount payable to the retailer or other person for services in redeeming the coupon is allowed only if the amount payable is stated on the coupon.

(2) *Costs not deductible under section 466.* The term "redemption cost" includes only the amounts stated in paragraph (b)(1) of this section. Amounts other than those mentioned in paragraph (b)(1) of this section cannot be deducted under the method of accounting described in section 466 even though such amounts are incurred in relation to the redemption of qualified discount coupons. Therefore, those amounts must be taken into account as if section 466 did not apply. Examples of such amounts are fees paid to the redemption center or clearinghouse and amounts payable to the retailer in excess of the amount stated on the coupon.

(c) *Qualified discount coupons*—(1) *General rule.* In order for a discount coupon (as defined in paragraph (c)(2)(i) of this section) to be considered a qualified discount coupon, all of the following requirements must be met:

(i) The coupon must have been issued by and must be redeemable by the taxpayer;

(ii) The coupon must allow a discount on the purchase price of merchandise or other tangible personal property;

(iii) The face amount of the coupon must not exceed five dollars;

(iv) The coupon, by its terms, may not be used with other coupons to bring about a price discount reimbursable by the issuer of more than five dollars with respect to any item; and

(v) There must exist a redemption chain (as defined in paragraph (c)(2)(ii) of this section) with respect to the coupon.

(2) *Definitions*—(i) *Discount coupon.* A discount coupon is a sales promotion device used to encourage the purchase of a specific product by allowing a purchaser of that product to receive a discount on its purchase price. The term "discount coupon" does not include trading stamps or premium coupons, which are subject to the method of accounting in § 1.451-4. A discount coupon may or may not be issued as part of a prior purchase. A discount coupon normally entitles its holders to receive nothing more than a reduction in the sales price of one of the issuer's products. The discount may be stated in terms of a cash amount, a percentage or fraction of the purchase price, a "two for the price of one" deal, or any other similar provision. A discount coupon need not be printed on paper in the form usually associated with coupons; it may be a token or other object so long as it functions as a coupon.

(ii) *Redemption chain.* A redemption chain exists when the issuer redeems the coupon from some person other than the customer who used the coupon to receive the price discount. Thus, in order to be treated as a qualified discount coupon, the coupon must not be issued by the person that initially redeems the coupon from the customer. For purposes of determining whether a redemption chain exists, corporations that are members of the same controlled group of corporations (as defined in section 1563(a)) as the issuer of the coupon shall be treated as the issuer. Thus, if the issuer of the coupon and the retailer that initially redeems the coupon from the customer are members of the same controlled group of corporations, the coupon shall not be treated as a qualified discount coupon.

(d) *Deduction for coupons redeemed during the redemption period*—(1) *General rule.* Two special conditions must be met before the cost of redeeming qualified discount coupons during the redemption period can be deducted from the taxpayer's gross income for the taxable year preceding the redemption period. First, the qualified discount coupons must have been outstanding at the close of such taxable year. Second, the qualified discount coupons must have been received by the taxpayer before the close of the redemption period for that taxable year.

(2) *Redemption period.* The taxpayer can select any redemption period so long as the period

Reg. § 1.466-1(d)(2)

does not extend longer than 6 months after the close of the taxpayer's taxable year. A change in the redemption period so selected shall be treated as a change in method of accounting.

(3) *Coupons received.* The deduction provided for in section 466(a)(1) is limited to the redemption costs associated with coupons that are actually received by the taxpayer within the redemption period. For purposes of this paragraph, if the issuer uses a redemption agent or clearinghouse to group, count, and verify coupons after they have been redeemed by a retailer, the coupons received by the redemption agent or clearinghouse will be considered to have been received by the issuer. Nothing in section 466, however, allows deductions to be made on the basis of estimated redemptions, whether such estimates are made by either the issuer or some other party.

(e) *Transitional adjustment*—(1) *In general.* An election to change from some other method of accounting for the redemption of discount coupons to the method of accounting described in section 466 is a change in method of accounting that requires a transitional adjustment. Unless the taxpayer can qualify for a waiver of the suspense account requirement as provided for in section 373(c) of the Revenue Act of 1978 (92 Stat. 2865), the taxpayer should compute the transitional adjustment described in section 481(a)(2) according to the rules contained in this section. This adjustment should be taken into account according to the special rules in subsections (e) and (f) of section 466.

(2) *Net increase in taxable income.* In the case of a transitional adjustment that would result in a net increase in taxable income under section 481(a)(2) for the year of change, that increase should be taken into income over a ten-year period consisting of the year of change and the immediately succeeding nine taxable years. For example, assume that A, a calendar year taxpayer, makes an election to use the method of accounting described in section 466 for the year 1980 and for subsequent years. Assume further that the amount of the transitional adjustment computed under section 481(a)(2) would result in a net increase of taxable income of $100 for 1980. Under these facts, A should increase taxable income for 1980 and each of the next nine taxable years by $10.

(3) *Suspense account*—(i) *In general.* In the case of a transitional adjustment that would result in a net decrease in taxable income under section 481(a)(2) for the year of change, in lieu of applying section 481, the taxpayer must establish a separate suspense account for each trade or business for which the taxpayer has made an election to use section 466. The computation of the initial opening balance in the suspense account is described in paragraph (e)(3)(ii)(A) of this section. An initial adjustment to gross income for the year of election is described in paragraph (e)(3)(ii)(B) of this section. Annual adjustments to the suspense account are described in paragraph (e)(3)(iii)(A) of this section, and gross income adjustments are described in paragraph (e)(3)(iii)(B) of this section. Examples are provided in paragraph (e)(4) of this section. The effect of the suspense account is to defer some part of, or all of, the deduction of the transitional adjustment until the taxpayer no longer redeems discount coupons in connection with the trade or business to which the suspense account relates.

(ii) *Establishing a suspense account*—(A) *Initial opening balance.* To compute the initial opening balance of the suspense account for the first taxable year for which the election to use section 466 is effective, the taxpayer must determine the dollar amount of the deduction that would have been allowed for qualified discount coupon redemption costs during the redemption period for each of the three immediately preceding taxable years had the election to use section 466 been in effect for those years. The initial opening balance of the suspense account is the largest such dollar amount reduced by the sum of the adjustments attributable to the change in method of accounting that increase income for the year of change.

(B) *Initial year adjustment.* If, in computing the initial opening balance, the largest dollar amount of deduction that would have been allowed in any of the three prior years exceeds the actual cost of redeeming qualified discount coupons received during the redemption period following the close of the year immediately preceding the year of election, the excess is included in income in the year of election. Section 481(b) does not apply to this increase in gross income.

(iii) *Annual adjustments*—(A) *Adjustment to the suspense account.* Adjustments are made to the suspense account each year to account for fluctuations in coupon redemptions. To compute the annual adjustment, the taxpayer must determine the amount to be deducted under section 466(a)(1) for the taxable year. If the amount is less than the opening balance in the suspense account for the taxable year, the balance in the suspense account is reduced by the difference.

Reg. § 1.466-1(d)(3)

Conversely, if such amount is greater than the opening balance in the suspense account for the taxable year, the account is increased by the difference (but not to an amount in excess of the initial opening balance described in paragraph (e)(3)(ii) of this section). Therefore, the balance in the suspense account will never be greater than the initial opening balance in the suspense account determined in paragraph (e)(3)(ii) of this section. However, the balance in the suspense account after adjustments may be less than this initial opening balance in the suspense account.

(B) *Gross income adjustments.* Adjustments to the suspense account for years subsequent to the year of the election also produce adjustments in the taxpayer's gross income. Adjustments which reduce the balance in the suspense account reduce gross income for the year in which the adjustment to the suspense account is made. Adjustments which increase the balance in the suspense account increase gross income for the year in which the adjustment to the suspense account is made.

(4) *Examples.* (i) The provisions of paragraph (e)(3) of this section may be illustrated by the following examples:

Example (1). Assume that the issuer of qualified discount coupons makes a timely election under section 466 for its taxable year ending December 31, 1979, and does not select a coupon redemption period shorter than the statutory period of 6 months. Assume further that the taxpayer's qualified discount coupon redemption costs in the first 6 months of 1977, 1978, and 1979 were $7, $13, and $8 respectively, and that the accounting change adjustments that increase income for 1979 are $10. Since the accounting change adjustment that increases income for 1979, ($10), is greater than the taxpayer's discount coupon redemptions during the first 6 months of 1979, ($8), the net section 481(a)(2) adjustment for the year of change results in a positive adjustment. Because of this, a suspense account is not required. The taxpayer should instead follow the rules in section 466(f) and in paragraph (e)(2) of this section in order to take this positive transitional adjustment into account.

Example (2). Assume the same facts as in example (1), except that the sum of the accounting change adjustments that increase income for 1979 is equal to $2. Under these facts the initial opening balance in the suspense account on January 1, 1979 would be $11 (that is, the largest dollar amount of qualified coupon redemption costs in the pertinent years ($13), reduced by the sum of the accounting change adjustments that increase income in the year of change ($2)). Since the coupon redemption costs taken into account in determining the initial opening balance ($13 in 1978) exceed the actual redemption costs in the first 6 months of the taxable year for which the election is first effective ($8 in 1979), the excess of $5 is added to gross income for the year of election (1979).

Example (3). Assume, in addition to the facts of example (2), that coupon redemption costs during the redemption period for the 1979 taxable year are $7. Since the qualifying redemption costs ($7) during the redemption period for the taxable year are less than the opening balance in the suspense account ($11) the taxpayer must reduce the suspense account balance by the difference ($4). The taxpayer is also allowed to take a deduction equal to the amount of this adjustment to the suspense account. Thus, the net amount deductible for the 1979 taxable year after taking into account the coupon redemptions during the redemption period, the amount deductible because of the decrease in the suspense account, and the initial year adjustment determined in example (2) is $6 ($7 + $4 − $5).

Example (4). Assume, in addition to the facts of example (3), that coupon redemption costs during the redemption period for the 1980 taxable year are $10. Since the qualifying redemption costs during the redemption period for the taxable year ($10) exceed the opening balance of the suspense account at the beginning of the taxable year ($7), the suspense account must be increased by the difference ($3). The taxpayer must also include $3 in gross income for the taxable year. Thus, the net amount deductible for the 1980 taxable year is $7 ($10 − $3).

Example (5). Assume, in addition to the facts of example (4), that coupon redemption costs during the redemption period for the 1981 taxable year are $12. Since the qualifying redemption costs for the 1981 taxable year ($12) exceed the opening balance of the suspense account at the beginning of the taxable year ($10), the suspense account must be increased by the difference ($2) but not above the initial opening balance ($11). Thus, the taxpayer will increase the balance by $1. The taxpayer must also include $1 in gross income for the taxable year. Thus, the net amount deductible for the 1981 taxable year is $11 ($12 − $1).

(ii) The following table summarizes examples (2) through (5):

Reg. § 1.466-1(e)(4)

Methods of Accounting

See p. 20,601 for regulations not amended to reflect law changes

	Years Ending Dec. 31—					
	1977	1978	1979	1980	1981	1982
Facts:						
Actual coupon redemption costs in first six months	$7	$13	$8	$7	$10	$12
Accounting change adjustments that increase income in year of change			2			
Net adjustment decreasing income in year of change under sec. 481(a)(2)			$6			
Adjustment to suspense account:						
Opening balance			$11	$7	$10	$11
Addition to account				3	1	
Reduction to account			(4)			
Opening balance for next year			$7	$10	$11	
Amount deductible:						
Initial year adjustment			$(5)			
Amount deductible as actual coupon redemptions during redemption period			7	$10	$12	
Adjustment for increase in suspense account				(3)	(1)	
Adjustment for decrease in suspense account			4			
Net amount deductible for the year for coupons redeemed during the redemption period			$6	$7	$11	

(f) *Subchapter C transactions*—(1) *General rule.* If a transfer of substantially all the assets of a trade or business in which discount coupons are redeemed is made to an acquiring corporation, and if the acquiring corporation determines its basis in these assets, in whole or part, with reference to the basis of these assets in the hands of the transferor, then for the purposes of section 466(e) the principles of section 381 and § 1.381(c)(4)-1 will apply. The application of this rule is not limited to the transactions described in section 381(a). Thus, the rule also applies, for example, to transactions described in section 351.

(2) *Special rules.* If, in the case of a transaction described in paragraph (f)(1) of this section, an acquiring corporation acquires assets that were used in a trade or business that was not subject to a section 466 election from a transferor that is owned or controlled directly (or indirectly through a chain of corporations) by the same interests, and if the acquiring corporation uses the acquired assets in a trade or business for which the acquiring corporation later makes an election to use section 466, then the acquiring corporation must establish a suspense account by taking into account not only its own experience but also the transferor's experience when the transferor held the assets in its trade or business. Furthermore, the transferor is not allowed a deduction for qualified discount coupons redeemed after the date of the transfer attributable to discount coupons issued by the transferor before the date of the transfer. Such redemptions shall be considered to be made by the acquiring corporation.

(3) *Example.* The provisions of paragraph (f)(2) of this section may be illustrated by the following example:

Example. Corporation S, a calendar year taxpayer, is a wholly owned subsidiary of Corporation P, a calendar year taxpayer. On December 31, 1982, S acquires from P substantially all of the assets used in a trade or business in which qualified discount coupons are redeemed. P had not made an election under section 466 with respect to the redemption costs of the qualified discount coupons issued in connection with that trade or business. S makes an election to use section 466 for its taxable year ending December 31, 1983, for the trade or business in which the acquired assets are used, and selects a redemption period of 6 months. Assume that P's qualified discount coupon redemption costs in the first 6 months of 1981 and 1982 were $120 and $140 respectively. Assume further that S's qualified discount coupon redemption costs in the first 6 months of 1983 were $130, and that there are no accounting change adjustments that increase income with respect to the election. S must establish a suspense account by taking into account the largest dollar amount of deductions that would have been allowed under section 466(a)(1) for the 3 immediately preceding taxable years of P, including both P's and S's experience with respect to costs actually incurred during the redemption periods relating to those years. Thus, the initial opening balance of S's suspense account is $140. S must also make an initial year adjustment of $10 ($140-$130), which S must include in income for S's taxable year ending December 31, 1983. P may not take a deduction for the qualified coupon redemptions made after December 31, 1982, that are attributable to coupons issued by P before December 31, 1982. Thus, none of the $130 qualified discount coupon redemption costs incurred by

Reg. § 1.466-1(f)(1)

S during the first six months of 1983 may be deducted by P. [Reg. § 1.466-1.]

☐ [T.D. 8022, 4-30-85.]

[Reg. § 1.466-2]

§ 1.466-2. **Special protective election for certain taxpayers.**—(a) *General rule.* Section 373(c) of the Revenue Act of 1978 (92 Stat. 2865) allows certain taxpayers, who in prior years have accounted for discount coupons under a method of accounting reasonably similar to the method described in § 1.451-4, to elect to treat that method of accounting as a proper one for those prior years. There are several differences between this protective election and the section 466(d) election. First, the protective election applies only to a single continuous period of taxable years the last year of which ends before January 1, 1979. Second, an otherwise qualifying protective election may apply to coupons which are discount coupons but which would not be treated as qualified discount coupons under Code section 466. Third, certain expenses such as the cost of redemption center service fees, and amounts that are payable to the retailer (or other person redeeming the coupons from the person receiving the price discount) for services in redeeming the coupons but that are not stated on the coupon, can be subtracted from gross receipts for prior years covered by a protective election (if treated as deductible under the accounting method for such years), even though such expenses would not be deductible under Code section 466.

(b) *Requirements.* In order to qualify for this special protective election, the following conditions must be met:

(1) For a continuous period of one or more prior taxable years, (the last year of which ends before January 1, 1979), the taxpayer must have used a method of accounting for discount coupons that is reasonably similar to the method provided in § 1.451-4 or its predecessors under the Internal Revenue Code of 1954;

(2) The taxpayer must make an election under section 466 of the Internal Revenue Code of 1954 according to the rules contained in § 1.466-3 for its first taxable year ending after December 31, 1978; and

(3) The taxpayer must make an election under section 373(c) of the Revenue Act of 1978 according to the rules contained in § 1.466-4 for its first taxable year ending after December 31, 1978.

(c) *Amount to be subtracted from gross receipts.* The amount the taxpayer may subtract under this section for the redemption costs of coupons shall include only:

(1) Costs of the type permitted by § 1.451-4 to be included in the estimated average cost of redeeming coupons, plus

(2) Any amount designated or referred to on the coupon payable by the taxpayer to the person who allowed the discount on a sale by such person to the user of the coupon.

Nothing in this paragraph shall allow an item to be deducted more than once.

(d) *Right to amend prior tax returns.* This paragraph applies only to those taxpayers who have agreed in a prior year to discontinue the use of the method of accounting described in § 1.451-4 for discount coupon redemptions. If the taxpayer used such method of accounting on the original return filed for the prior taxable year, and if any such year is not closed under the statute of limitations or by reason of a closing agreement with the Internal Revenue Service, a taxpayer who has made a protective election may file an amended return and a claim for refund for such years. In this amended return, the taxpayer should account for its discount coupon redemptions according to the method of accounting described in § 1.451-4. This is not to be construed, however, to abrogate in any way the rules regarding the close of taxable years due to the statute of limitations or a binding closing agreement between the Internal Revenue Service and the taxpayer.

(e) *Suspense account not required.* If the following three conditions are satisfied, the taxpayer need not establish the suspense account otherwise required by section 466(e). First, the taxpayer must make a timely election under these rules to protect prior years. Second, the method of accounting used in those years must have been used for all discount coupons issued by the taxpayer in those years in all the taxpayer's separate trades or businesses in which coupons were issued. Third, either before or after an amendment to the taxpayer's tax returns as described in paragraph (d) of this section, a method of accounting reasonably similar to the method of accounting described in § 1.451-4 must have been used for the taxable year ending on or before December 31, 1978. If these conditions are met, the taxpayer will treat the election of the method under section 466 as a change in method of accounting to which the rules in section 481 and the regulations thereunder apply.

(f) *Definition: reasonably similar.* For purposes of paragraphs (b)(1) and (e) of this section, a taxpayer will be considered to have used a method of accounting for discount coupons that is "reasonably similar" to the method of accounting provided in § 1.451-4 if the taxpayer followed the method of accounting described in § 1.451-4 as if that method were a valid method of accounting for discount coupon redemptions. [Reg. § 1.466-2.]

☐ [T.D. 8022, 4-30-85.]

[Reg. § 1.466-3]

§ 1.466-3. **Manner of and time for making election under section 466.**—(a) *In general.* Section 466 provides a special method of accounting for accrual basis taxpayers who issue qualified discount coupons (as defined in section 466(b)). In order to use the special method under section 466, a taxpayer must make an election with respect to the trade or business in connection with which the qualified discount coupons are issued. If a taxpayer issues qualified discount coupons in connection with more than one trade or business, the taxpayer may use the special method of accounting under section 466 only with respect to the qualified discount coupons issued in connection with a trade or business for which an election is made. The election must be made in the manner prescribed in this section. The election does not require the prior consent of the Internal Revenue Service. An election under section 466 is effective for the taxable year for which it is made and for all subsequent taxable years, unless the taxpayer secures the prior consent of the Internal Revenue Service to revoke such election.

(b) *Manner of and time for making election*— (1) *General rule.* Except as provided in paragraph (b)(2) of this section, an election is made under section 466 and this section by filing a statement of election containing the information described in paragraph (c) of this section with the taxpayer's income tax return for the taxpayer's first taxable year for which the election is made. The election must be made not later than the time prescribed by law (including extensions thereof) for filing the income tax return for the first taxable year for which the election is made. Thus, the election may not be made for a taxable year by filing an amended income tax return after the time prescribed (including extensions) for filing the original return for such year.

(2) *Transitional rule.* If the last day of the time prescribed by law (including extensions thereof) for filing a taxpayer's income tax return for the taxpayer's first taxable year ending after December 31, 1978, falls before December 3, 1979, and the taxpayer does not make an election under section 466 with respect to such taxable year in the manner prescribed by paragraph (b)(1) of this section, an election is made under section 466 and this section with respect to such taxable year if—

(i) Within the time prescribed by law (including extensions thereof) for filing the taxpayer's income tax return for such taxable year, the taxpayer has made a reasonable effort to notify the Commissioner of the taxpayer's intent to make an election under section 466 with respect to such taxable year, and

(ii) Before January 2, 1980, the taxpayer files a statement of election containing the information described in paragraph (c) of this section to be associated with the taxpayer's income tax return for such taxable year.

For purposes of paragraph (b)(2)(i) of this section, a reasonable effort to notify the Commissioner of an intent to make an election under section 466 with respect to a taxable year includes the timely filing of an income tax return for such taxable year if the taxable income reported on the return reflects a deduction for the redemption costs of qualified discount coupons as determined under section 466(a).

(c) *Required information.* The statement of election required by paragraph (b) of this section must indicate that the taxpayer (identified by name, address, and taxpayer identification number) is making an election under section 466 and must set forth the following information:

(1) A description of each trade or business for which the election is made;

(2) The first taxable year for which the election is made;

(3) The redemption period (as defined in section 466(c)(2)) for each trade or business for which the election is made;

(4) If the taxpayer is required to establish a suspense account under section 466(e) for a trade or business for which the election is made, the initial opening balance of such account (as defined in section 466(e)(2)) for each such trade or business; and

(5) In the case of an election under section 466 that results in a net increase in taxable income under section 481(a)(2), the amount of such net increase.

The statement of election should be made on a Form 3115, which need contain no information other than that required by this paragraph or paragraph (c) of § 1.466-4. [Reg. § 1.466-3.]

☐ [T.D. 8022, 4-30-85.]

[Reg. § 1.466-4]

§ 1.466-4. **Manner of and time for making election under section 373(c) of the Revenue Act of 1978.**—(a) *In general.* Section 373(c)(2) of the Revenue Act of 1978 (92 Stat. 2865) provides an election for taxpayers who satisfy the requirements of section 373(c)(2)(A)(i) and (ii) of the Act. The election is made with respect to a method of accounting for the redemption costs of discount coupons used by the electing taxpayer in a continuous period of one or more taxable years ending before January 1, 1979. The election must be made in the manner prescribed by this section. The election does not require the prior consent of the Internal Revenue Service.

(b) *Manner of and time for making election*—(1) *General rule.* Except as provided in paragraph (b)(2) of this section, the election under section 373(c) of the Revenue Act of 1978 is made by filing a statement of election containing the information described in paragraph (c) of this section with the taxpayer's income tax return for the taxpayer's first taxable year ending after December 31, 1978. The election must be made not later than the time prescribed by law (including extensions thereof) for filing the income tax return for the taxpayer's first taxable year ending after December 31, 1978. Thus, the election may not be made with an amended income tax return for such year filed after the time prescribed (including extensions) for filing the original return.

(2) *Transitional rule.* If the last day of the time prescribed by law (including extensions thereof) for filing a taxpayer's income tax return for the taxpayer's first taxable year ending after December 31, 1978, falls before December 3, 1979, and the taxpayer does not make an election in the manner prescribed by paragraph (b)(1) of this section, an election is made under section 373(c) of the Act and this section with respect to a continuous period if—

(i) Within the time prescribed by law (including extensions thereof) for filing the taxpayer's income tax return for the taxpayer's first taxable year ending after December 31, 1978, the taxpayer has made a reasonable effort to notify the Commissioner of the taxpayer's intent to make an election under section 373(c) of the Act with respect to the continuous period, and

(ii) Before January 2, 1980, the taxpayer files a statement of election containing the information described in paragraph (c) of this section to be associated with the taxpayer's income tax return for the taxpayer's first taxable year ending after December 31, 1978.

(c) *Required information.* The statement of election required by paragraph (b) of this section must indicate that the taxpayer (identified by name, address, and taxpayer identification number) is making an election under section 373(c) of the Revenue Act of 1978 and must set forth the taxable years in the continuous period for which the election is made. The statement of election should be made on the same Form 3115 on which the taxpayer has made a statement of election under section 466. The Form 3115 need contain no information other than that required by this paragraph or paragraph (c) of § 1.466-3. [Reg. § 1.466-4.]

☐ [T.D. 8022, 4-30-85.]

[Reg. § 1.467-0]

§ 1.467-0. **Table of contents.**—This section lists the captions that appear in §§ 1.467-1 through 1.467-9.

§ *1.467-1 Treatment of lessors and lessees generally.*

(a) Overview.
   (1) In general.
   (2) Cases in which rules are inapplicable.
   (3) Summary of rules.
      (i) Basic rules.
      (ii) Special rules.
   (4) Scope of rules.
   (5) Application of other authorities.
(b) Method of accounting for section 467 rental agreements.
(c) Section 467 rental agreements.
   (1) In general.
   (2) Increasing or decreasing rent.
      (i) Fixed rent.
         (A) In general.
         (B) Certain rent holidays disregarded.
      (ii) Fixed rent allocated to a rental period.
         (A) Specific allocation.
            (*1*) In general.
            (*2*) Rental agreements specifically allocating fixed rent.
         (B) No specific allocation.
      (iii) Contingent rent.
         (A) In general.
         (B) Certain contingent rent disregarded.
   (3) Deferred or prepaid rent.
      (i) Deferred rent.
      (ii) Prepaid rent.
      (iii) Rent allocated to a calendar year.
      (iv) Examples.
   (4) Rental agreements involving total payments of $250,000 or less.
      (i) In general.
      (ii) Special rules in computing amount described in paragraph (c)(4)(i) of this section.
(d) Section 467 rent.
   (1) In general.
   (2) Fixed rent for a rental period.
      (i) Constant rental accrual.
      (ii) Proportional rental accrual.
      (iii) Section 467 rental agreement accrual.
(e) Section 467 interest.
   (1) In general.
   (2) Interest on fixed rent for a rental period.
      (i) In general.

(ii) Section 467 rental agreements with adequate interest.
(3) Treatment of interest.
(f) Substantial modification of a rental agreement.
(1) Treatment as new agreement.
(i) In general.
(ii) Limitation.
(2) Post-modification agreement; in general.
(3) Other effects of a modification.
(4) Special rules.
(i) Carryover of character; leasebacks.
(ii) Carryover of character; long-term agreements.
(iii) Carryover of character; disqualified agreements.
(iv) Allocation of rent.
(v) Difference between aggregate rent and interest and aggregate payments.
(A) In general.
(B) Constant rental accrual prior to the modification.
(C) Agreements described in this paragraph (f)(4)(v)(C).
(vi) Principal purpose of tax avoidance.
(5) Definitions.
(6) Safe harbors.
(7) Special rules for certain transfers.
(i) In general.
(ii) Exception.
(g) Treatment of amounts payable by lessor to lessee.
(1) Interest.
(2) Other amounts. [Reserved]
(h) Meaning of terms.
(i) [Reserved]
(j) Computational rules.
(1) Counting conventions.
(2) Conventions regarding timing of rent and payments.
(i) In general.
(ii) Time amount is payable.
(3) Annualized fixed rent.
(4) Allocation of fixed rent within a period.
(5) Rental period length.

§ 1.467-2 Rent accrual for section 467 rental agreements without adequate interest.
(a) Section 467 rental agreements for which proportional rental accrual is required.
(b) Adequate interest on fixed rent.
(1) In general.

(2) Section 467 rental agreements that provide for a variable rate of interest.
(3) Agreements with both deferred and prepaid rent.
(c) Computation of proportional rental amount.
(1) In general.
(2) Section 467 rental agreements that provide for a variable rate of interest.
(d) Present value.
(e) Applicable Federal rate.
(1) In general.
(2) Source of applicable Federal rates.
(3) 110 percent of applicable Federal rate.
(4) Term of the section 467 rental agreement.
(i) In general.
(ii) Section 467 rental agreements with variable interest.
(f) Examples.

§ 1.467-3 Disqualified leasebacks and long-term agreements.
(a) General rule.
(b) Disqualified leaseback or long-term agreement.
(1) In general.
(2) Leaseback.
(3) Long-term agreement.
(i) In general.
(ii) Statutory recovery period.
(A) In general.
(B) Special rule for rental agreements relating to properties having different statutory recovery periods.
(c) Tax avoidance as principal purpose for increasing or decreasing rent.
(1) In general.
(2) Tax avoidance.
(i) In general.
(ii) Significant difference in tax rates.
(iii) Special circumstances.
(3) Safe harbors.
(4) Uneven rent test.
(i) In general.
(ii) Special rule for real estate.
(iii) Operating rules.
(d) Calculating constant rental amount.
(1) In general.
(2) Initial or final short periods.
(3) Method to determine constant rental amount; no short periods.
(i) Step 1.
(ii) Step 2.

Reg. § 1.467-0

Methods of Accounting

(iii) Step 3.
(e) Examples.
§ 1.467-4 Section 467 loan.
 (a) In general.
  (1) Overview.
  (2) No section 467 loan in the case of certain section 467 rental agreements.
  (3) Rental agreements subject to constant rental accrual.
  (4) Special rule in applying the provisions of § 1.467-7(e), (f), or (g).
 (b) Principal balance.
  (1) In general.
  (2) Section 467 rental agreements that provide for prepaid fixed rent and adequate interest.
  (3) Timing of payments.
 (c) Yield.
  (1) In general.
   (i) Method of determining yield.
   (ii) Method of stating yield.
   (iii) Rounding adjustments.
  (2) Yield of section 467 rental agreements for which constant rental amount or proportional rental amount is computed.
  (3) Yield for purposes of applying paragraph (a)(4) of this section.
  (4) Determination of present values.
 (d) Contingent payments.
 (e) Section 467 rental agreements that call for payments before or after the lease term.
 (f) Examples.
§ 1.467-5 Section 467 rental agreements with variable interest.
 (a) Variable interest on deferred or prepaid rent.
  (1) In general.
  (2) Exceptions.
 (b) Variable rate treated as fixed.
  (1) In general.
  (2) Variable interest adjustment amount.
   (i) In general.
   (ii) Positive or negative adjustment.
  (3) Section 467 loan balance.
 (c) Examples.
§ 1.467-6 Section 467 rental agreements with contingent payments. [Reserved]
§ 1.467-7 Section 467 recapture and other rules relating to dispositions and modifications.
 (a) Section 467 recapture.
 (b) Recapture amount.
  (1) In general.
  (2) Prior understated inclusion.

  (3) Section 467 gain.
   (i) In general.
   (ii) Certain dispositions.
 (c) Special rules.
  (1) Gifts.
  (2) Dispositions at death.
  (3) Certain tax-free exchanges.
   (i) In general.
   (ii) Dispositions covered.
    (A) In general.
    (B) Transfers to certain tax-exempt organizations.
  (4) Dispositions by transferee.
  (5) Like-kind exchanges and involuntary conversions.
  (6) Installment sales.
  (7) Dispositions covered by section 170(e), 341(e)(12), or 751(c).
 (d) Examples.
 (e) Other rules relating to dispositions.
  (1) In general.
  (2) Treatment of section 467 loan.
  (3) [Reserved]
  (4) Examples.
 (f) Treatment of assignments by lessee and lessee-financed renewals.
  (1) Substitute lessee use.
  (2) Treatment of section 467 loan.
  (3) Lessor use.
  (4) Examples.
 (g) Application of section 467 following a rental agreement modification.
  (1) Substantial modifications.
   (i) Treatment of pre-modification items.
   (ii) Computations with respect to post-modification items.
   (iii) Adjustments.
    (A) Adjustment relating to certain prepayments.
    (B) Adjustment relating to retroactive beginning of lease term.
   (iv) Coordination with rules relating to dispositions and assignments.
    (A) Dispositions.
    (B) Assignments.
  (2) Other modifications.
   (i) Computation of section 467 loan for modified agreement.
   (ii) Change in balance of section 467 loan.
   (iii) Section 467 rent and interest after the modification.
   (iv) Applicable Federal rate.

Reg. § 1.467-0

(v) Modification effective within a rental period.

(vi) Other adjustments.

(vii) Coordination with rules relating to dispositions and assignments.

(viii) Exception for agreements entered into prior to effective date of section 467.

(3) Adjustment by Commissioner.

(4) Effective date of modification.

(5) Examples.

(h) Omissions or duplications.

(1) In general.

(2) Example.

§ 1.467-8 Automatic consent to change to constant rental accrual for certain rental agreements.

(a) General rule.

(b) Agreements to which automatic consent applies.

§ 1.467-9 Effective dates and automatic method changes for certain agreements.

(a) In general.

(b) Automatic consent for certain rental agreements.

(c) Application of regulation project IA-292-84 to certain leasebacks and long-term agreements.

(d) Entered into.

(e) Change in method of accounting.

(1) In general.

(2) Application of regulation project IA-292-84.

(3) Automatic change procedures.

[Reg. § 1.467-0.]

☐ [T.D. 8820, 5-17-99. Amended by T.D. 8917, 1-4-2001.]

[Reg. § 1.467-1]

§ 1.467-1. **Treatment of lessors and lessees generally.**—(a) *Overview*—(1) *In general.* When applicable, section 467 requires a lessor and lessee of tangible property to treat rents consistently and to use the accrual method of accounting (and time value of money principles) regardless of their overall method of accounting. In addition, in certain cases involving tax avoidance, the lessor and lessee must take rent and stated or imputed interest into account under a constant rental accrual method, pursuant to which the rent is treated as accruing ratably over the entire lease term.

(2) *Cases in which rules are inapplicable.* Section 467 applies only to leases (or other similar arrangements) that constitute section 467 rental agreements as defined in paragraph (c) of this section. For example, a rental agreement is not a section 467 rental agreement, and, therefore, is not subject to the provisions of this section and §§ 1.467-2 through 1.467-9 (the section 467 regulations), if it specifies equal amounts of rent for each month throughout the lease term and all payments of rent are due in the calendar year to which the rent relates (or in the preceding or succeeding calendar year). In addition, the section 467 regulations do not apply to a rental agreement that requires total rents of $250,000 or less. For purposes of determining whether the agreement has total rents of $250,000 or less, certain specified contingent rent is disregarded.

(3) *Summary of rules*—(i) *Basic rules.* Paragraph (c) of this section provides rules for determining whether a rental agreement is a section 467 rental agreement. Paragraphs (d) and (e) of this section provide rules for determining the amount of rent and interest, respectively, required to be taken into account by a lessor and lessee under a section 467 rental agreement. Paragraphs (f) through (h) and (j) of this section provide various definitions and special rules relating to the application of the section 467 regulations. Paragraph (i) of this section is reserved.

(ii) *Special rules.* Section 1.467-2 provides rules for section 467 rental agreements that have deferred or prepaid rents without providing for adequate interest. Section 1.467-3 provides rules for application of the constant rental accrual method, including criteria for determining whether an agreement is subject to this method. Section 1.467-4 provides rules for establishing and adjusting a section 467 loan (the amount that a lessor is deemed to have loaned to the lessee, or vice versa, pursuant to the application of the section 467 regulations). Section 1.467-5 provides rules for applying the section 467 regulations where a rental agreement requires payments of interest at a variable rate. Section 1.467-6, relating to the treatment of certain section 467 rental agreements with contingent payments, is reserved. Section 1.467-7 provides rules for the treatment of dispositions by a lessor of property subject to a section 467 rental agreement and the treatment of assignments by lessees and certain lessee-financed renewals of a section 467 rental agreement. Section 1.467-7 also provides rules for the treatment of modified rental agreements. Section 1.467-8 provides special transitional rules relating to the method of accounting for certain rental agreements entered into on or before May 18, 1999. Finally, § 1.467-9 provides the effective date rules for the section 467 regulations.

(4) *Scope of rules.* No inference should be drawn from any provision of this section or §§ 1.467-2 through 1.467-9 concerning whether—

(i) For Federal tax purposes, an arrangement constitutes a lease; or

(ii) For Federal tax purposes, any obligation of the lessee under a rental agreement is treated as rent.

Reg. § 1.467-1(a)(1)

Methods of Accounting

See p. 20,601 for regulations not amended to reflect law changes

(5) *Application of other authorities.* Notwithstanding section 467 and the regulations thereunder, other authorities such as section 446(b) clear-reflection-of-income principles, section 482, and the substance-over-form doctrine, may be applied by the Commissioner to determine the income and expense from a rental agreement (including the proper allocation of fixed rent under a rental agreement).

(b) *Method of accounting for section 467 rental agreements.* If a rental agreement is a section 467 rental agreement, as described in paragraph (c) of this section, the lessor and lessee must each take into account for any taxable year the sum of—

(1) The section 467 rent for the taxable year (as defined in paragraph (d) of this section); and

(2) The section 467 interest for the taxable year (as defined in paragraph (e) of this section).

(c) *Section 467 rental agreements*—(1) *In general.* Except as otherwise provided in paragraph (c)(4) of this section, the term *section 467 rental agreement* means a rental agreement, as defined in paragraph (h)(12) of this section, that has increasing or decreasing rents (as described in paragraph (c)(2) of this section), or deferred or prepaid rents (as described in paragraph (c)(3) of this section).

(2) *Increasing or decreasing rent*—(i) *Fixed rent*—(A) *In general.* A rental agreement has increasing or decreasing rent if the annualized fixed rent, as described in paragraph (j)(3) of this section, allocated to any rental period exceeds the annualized fixed rent allocated to any other rental period in the lease term.

(B) *Certain rent holidays disregarded.* Notwithstanding the provisions of paragraph (c)(2)(i)(A) of this section, a rental agreement does not have increasing or decreasing rent if the increasing or decreasing rent is solely attributable to a rent holiday provision allowing reduced rent (or no rent) for a period of three months or less at the beginning of the lease term.

(ii) *Fixed rent allocated to a rental period*—(A) *Specific allocation*—(*1*) *In general.* If a rental agreement provides a specific allocation of fixed rent, as described in paragraph (c)(2)(ii)(A)(*2*) of this section, the amount of fixed rent allocated to each rental period during the lease term is the amount of fixed rent allocated to that period by the rental agreement.

(*2*) *Rental agreements specifically allocating fixed rent.* A rental agreement specifically allocates fixed rent if the rental agreement unambiguously specifies, for periods no longer than a year, a fixed amount of rent for which the lessee becomes liable on account of the use of the property during that period, and the total amount of fixed rent specified is equal to the total amount of fixed rent payable under the lease. For example, a rental agreement providing that rent is $100,000 per calendar year, and providing for total payments of fixed rent equal to the total amount specified, specifically allocates rent. A rental agreement stating only when rent is payable does not specifically allocate rent.

(B) *No specific allocation.* If a rental agreement does not provide a specific allocation of fixed rent (for example, because the total amount of fixed rent specified is not equal to the total amount of fixed rent payable under the lease), the amount of fixed rent allocated to a rental period is the amount of fixed rent payable during that rental period. If an amount of fixed rent is payable before the beginning of the lease term, it is allocated to the first rental period in the lease term. If an amount of fixed rent is payable after the end of the lease term, it is allocated to the last rental period in the lease term.

(iii) *Contingent rent*—(A) *In general.* A rental agreement has increasing or decreasing rent if it requires (or may require) the payment of contingent rent (as defined in paragraph (h)(2) of this section), other than contingent rent described in paragraph (c)(2)(iii)(B) of this section.

(B) *Certain contingent rent disregarded.* For purposes of this paragraph (c)(2)(iii), rent is disregarded to the extent it is contingent as the result of one or more of the following provisions—

(*1*) A qualified percentage rents provision, as defined in paragraph (h)(8) of this section;

(*2*) An adjustment based on a reasonable price index, as defined in paragraph (h)(10) of this section;

(*3*) A provision requiring the lessee to pay third-party costs, as defined in paragraph (h)(15) of this section;

(*4*) A provision requiring the payment of late payment charges, as defined in paragraph (h)(4) of this section;

(*5*) A loss payment provision, as defined in paragraph (h)(7) of this section;

(*6*) A qualified TRAC provision, as defined in paragraph (h)(9) of this section;

(*7*) A residual condition provision, as defined in paragraph (h)(13) of this section;

(*8*) A tax indemnity provision, as defined in paragraph (h)(14) of this section;

(*9*) A variable interest rate provision, as defined in paragraph (h)(16) of this section; or

Reg. § 1.467-1(c)(2)

(*10*) Any other provision provided in regulations or other published guidance issued by the Commissioner, but only if the provision is designated as contingent rent to be disregarded for purposes of this paragraph (c)(2)(iii).

(3) *Deferred or prepaid rent*—(i) *Deferred rent.* A rental agreement has deferred rent under this paragraph (c)(3) if the cumulative amount of rent allocated as of the close of a calendar year (determined under paragraph (c)(3)(iii) of this section) exceeds the cumulative amount of rent payable as of the close of the succeeding calendar year.

(ii) *Prepaid rent.* A rental agreement has prepaid rent under this paragraph (c)(3) if the cumulative amount of rent payable as of the close of a calendar year exceeds the cumulative amount of rent allocated as of the close of the succeeding calendar year (determined under paragraph (c)(3)(iii) of this section).

(iii) *Rent allocated to a calendar year.* For purposes of this paragraph (c)(3), the rent allocated to a calendar year is the sum of—

(A) The fixed rent allocated to any rental period (determined under paragraph (c)(2)(ii) of this section) that begins and ends in the calendar year;

(B) A ratable portion of the fixed rent allocated to any other rental period that begins or ends in the calendar year; and

(C) Any contingent rent that accrues during the calendar year.

(iv) *Examples.* The following examples illustrate the application of this paragraph (c)(3):

Example 1. (i) A and B enter into a rental agreement that provides for the lease of property to begin on January 1, 2000, and end on December 31, 2003. The rental agreement provides that rent of $100,000 accrues during each year of the lease term. Under the rental agreement, no rent is payable during calendar year 2000, a payment of $100,000 is to be made on December 31, 2001, and December 31, 2002, and a payment of $200,000 is to be made on December 31, 2003. A and B both select the calendar year as their rental period. Thus, the amount of rent allocated to each rental period under paragraph (c)(2)(ii) of this section is $100,000. Therefore, the rental agreement does not have increasing or decreasing rent as described in paragraph (c)(2)(i) of this section.

(ii) Under paragraph (c)(3)(i) of this section, a rental agreement has deferred rent if, at the close of a calendar year, the cumulative amount of rent allocated under paragraph (c)(3)(iii) of this section exceeds the cumulative amount of rent payable as of the close of the succeeding year. In this example, there is no deferred rent: the rent allocated to 2000 ($100,000) does not exceed the cumulative rent payable as of December 31, 2001 ($100,000); the rent allocated to 2001 and preceding years ($200,000) does not exceed the cumulative rent payable as of December 31, 2002 ($200,000); the rent allocated to 2002 and preceding years ($300,000) does not exceed the cumulative rent payable as of December 31, 2003 ($400,000); and the rent allocated to 2003 and preceding years ($400,000) does not exceed the cumulative rent payable as of December 31, 2004 ($400,000). Therefore, because the rental agreement does not have increasing or decreasing rent and does not have deferred or prepaid rent, the rental agreement is not a section 467 rental agreement.

Example 2. (i) A and B enter into a rental agreement that provides for a 10-year lease of personal property, beginning on January 1, 2000, and ending on December 31, 2009. The rental agreement provides for accruals of rent of $10,000 during each month of the lease term. Under paragraph (c)(3)(iii) of this section, $120,000 is allocated to each calendar year. The rental agreement provides for a $1,200,000 payment on December 31, 2000.

(ii) The rental agreement does not have increasing or decreasing rent as described in paragraph (c)(2)(i) of this section. The rental agreement, however, provides prepaid rent under paragraph (c)(3)(ii) of this section because the cumulative amount of rent payable as of the close of a calendar year exceeds the cumulative amount of rent allocated as of the close of the succeeding calendar year. For example, the cumulative amount of rent payable as of the close of 2000 ($1,200,000 is payable on December 31, 2000) exceeds the cumulative amount of rent allocated as of the close of 2001, the succeeding calendar year ($240,000). Accordingly, the rental agreement is a section 467 rental agreement.

(4) *Rental agreements involving total payments of $250,000 or less*—(i) *In general.* A rental agreement is not a section 467 rental agreement if, as of the agreement date (as defined in paragraph (h)(1) of this section), it is not reasonably expected that the sum of the aggregate amount of rental payments under the rental agreement and the aggregate value of all other consideration to be received for the use of property (taking into account any payments of contingent rent, and any other contingent consideration) will exceed $250,000.

(ii) *Special rules in computing amount described in paragraph (c)(4)(i) of this section.* The

Reg. § 1.467-1(c)(3)

following rules apply in determining the amount described in paragraph (c)(4)(i) of this section:

(A) Stated interest on deferred rent is not taken into account. However, the Commissioner may recharacterize a portion of stated interest as additional rent if a rental agreement provides for interest on deferred rent at a rate that, in light of all of the facts and circumstances, is clearly greater than the arm's-length rate of interest that would have been charged in a lending transaction between the lessor and lessee.

(B) Consideration that does not involve a cash payment is taken into account at its fair market value. A liability that is either assumed or secured by property acquired subject to the liability is taken into account at the sum of its remaining principal amount and accrued interest (if any) thereon or, in the case of an obligation originally issued at a discount, at the sum of its adjusted issue price and accrued qualified stated interest (if any), within the meaning of § 1.1273-1(c)(1).

(C) All rental agreements that are part of the same transaction or a series of related transactions involving the same lessee (or any related person) and the same lessor (or any related person) are treated as a single rental agreement. Whether two or more rental agreements are part of the same transaction or a series of related transactions depends on all the facts and circumstances.

(D) If an agreement includes a provision increasing or decreasing rent payable solely as a result of an adjustment based on a reasonable price index, the amount described in paragraph (c)(4)(i) of this section must be determined as if the applicable price index did not change during the lease term.

(E) If an agreement includes a variable interest rate provision (as defined in paragraph (h)(16) of this section), the amount described in paragraph (c)(4)(i) of this section must be determined by using fixed rate substitutes (determined in the same manner as under § 1.1275-5(e), treating the agreement date as the issue date) for the variable rates of interest applicable to the lessor's indebtedness.

(F) Contingent rent described in paragraphs (c)(2)(iii)(B)(*3*) through (*8*) of this section is not taken into account.

(d) *Section 467 rent*—(1) *In general.* The section 467 rent for a taxable year is the sum of—

(i) The fixed rent for any rental period (determined under paragraph (d)(2) of this section) that begins and ends in the taxable year;

(ii) A ratable portion of the fixed rent for any other rental period beginning or ending in the taxable year; and

(iii) In the case of a section 467 rental agreement that provides for contingent rent, the contingent rent that accrues during the taxable year.

(2) *Fixed rent for a rental period*—(i) *Constant rental accrual.* In the case of a section 467 rental agreement that is a disqualified leaseback or long-term agreement (as described in § 1.467-3(b)), the fixed rent for a rental period is the constant rental amount (as determined under § 1.467-3(d)).

(ii) *Proportional rental accrual.* In the case of a section 467 rental agreement that is not described in paragraph (d)(2)(i) of this section, and does not provide adequate interest on fixed rent (as determined under § 1.467-2(b)), the fixed rent for a rental period is the proportional rental amount (as determined under § 1.467-2(c)).

(iii) *Section 467 rental agreement accrual.* In the case of a section 467 rental agreement that is not described in either paragraph (d)(2)(i) or (ii) of this section, the fixed rent for a rental period is the amount of fixed rent allocated to the rental period under the rental agreement, as determined under paragraph (c)(2)(ii) of this section.

(e) *Section 467 interest*—(1) *In general.* The section 467 interest for a taxable year is the sum of—

(i) The interest on fixed rent for any rental period that begins and ends in the taxable year;

(ii) A ratable portion of the interest on fixed rent for any other rental period beginning or ending in the taxable year; and

(iii) In the case of a section 467 rental agreement that provides for contingent rent, any interest that accrues on the contingent rent during the taxable year.

(2) *Interest on fixed rent for a rental period*—(i) *In general.* Except as provided in paragraph (e)(2)(ii) of this section and § 1.467-5(b)(1)(ii), the interest on fixed rent for a rental period is equal to the product of—

(A) The principal balance of the section 467 loan (as described in § 1.467-4(b)) at the beginning of the rental period; and

(B) The yield of the section 467 loan (as described in § 1.467-4(c)).

(ii) *Section 467 rental agreements with adequate interest.* Except in the case of a section 467 rental agreement that is a disqualified leaseback or long-term agreement, if a section 467 rental agreement provides adequate interest

Reg. § 1.467-1(e)(2)

under § 1.467-2(b)(1)(i) (agreements with no deferred or prepaid rent) or § 1.467-2(b)(1)(ii) (agreements with adequate interest stated at a single fixed rate), the interest on fixed rent for a rental period is the amount of interest provided in the rental agreement for the period.

(3) *Treatment of interest.* If the section 467 interest for a rental period is a positive amount, the lessor has interest income and the lessee has an interest expense. If the section 467 interest for a rental period is a negative amount, the lessee has interest income and the lessor has an interest expense. Section 467 interest is treated as interest for all purposes of the Internal Revenue Code.

(f) *Substantial modification of a rental agreement*—(1) *Treatment as new agreement*—(i) *In general.* If a substantial modification of a rental agreement occurs after June 3, 1996, the post-modification agreement is treated as a new agreement and the date on which the modification occurs is treated as the agreement date in applying section 467 and the regulations thereunder to the post-modification agreement. Thus, for example, the post-modification agreement is treated as a new agreement entered into on the date the modification occurs for purposes of determining whether it is a section 467 rental agreement under this section, whether it is a disqualified leaseback or long-term agreement under § 1.467-3, and whether it is entered into after the applicable effective date in § 1.467-9.

(ii) *Limitation.* In the case of a substantial modification of a rental agreement occurring on or before May 18, 1999, this paragraph (f) applies only if—

(A) The rental agreement was a disqualified leaseback or long-term agreement before the modification and the agreement date, determined without regard to the modification, is after June 3, 1996; or

(B) The post-modification agreement would, after application of the rules in this paragraph (f) (other than the special rule for disqualified agreements in paragraph (f)(4)(iii) of this section), be a disqualified leaseback or long-term agreement.

(2) *Post-modification agreement; in general.* For purposes of determining whether a post-modification agreement is a section 467 rental agreement or a disqualified leaseback or long-term agreement under paragraph (f)(1) of this section, the terms of the post-modification agreement are, except as provided in paragraph (f)(4) of this section, only those terms that provide for rights and obligations relating to post-modification items (within the meaning of paragraph (f)(5)(iv) of this section).

(3) *Other effects of a modification.* For rules relating to amounts that must be taken into account following certain modifications, see § 1.467-7(g).

(4) *Special rules*—(i) *Carryover of character; leasebacks.* If an agreement is a leaseback prior to its modification and the lessee prior to the modification (or a related person) is the lessee after the modification, the post-modification agreement is a leaseback even if the post-modification lessee did not have an interest in the property at any time during the two-year period ending on the date on which the modification occurs.

(ii) *Carryover of character; long-term agreements.* If an agreement is a long-term agreement prior to its modification and the entire agreement (as modified) would be a long-term agreement, the post-modification agreement is a long-term agreement.

(iii) *Carryover of character; disqualified agreements.* If an agreement (as in effect before its modification) is a disqualified leaseback or long-term agreement as the result of a determination (whether occurring before or after the modification) under § 1.467-3(b)(1)(ii) and the post-modification agreement is a section 467 rental agreement (or the entire agreement (as modified) would be a section 467 rental agreement), the post-modification agreement will, notwithstanding its treatment as a new agreement under paragraph (f)(1)(i) of this section, be subject to constant rental accrual unless the Commissioner determines that, because of the absence of tax avoidance potential, the post-modification agreement should not be treated as a disqualified leaseback or long-term agreement.

(iv) *Allocation of rent.* If the entire agreement (as modified) provides a specific allocation of fixed rent, as described in paragraph (c)(2)(ii)(A)(*2*) of this section, the post-modification agreement is treated as an agreement that provides a specific allocation of fixed rent. If the entire agreement (as modified) does not provide a specific allocation of fixed rent, the fixed rent allocated to rental periods during the lease term of the post-modification agreement is determined by applying the rules of paragraph (c)(2)(ii)(B) of this section to the entire agreement (as modified).

(v) *Difference between aggregate rent and interest and aggregate payments*—(A) *In general.* Except as provided in paragraph (f)(4)(v)(B) of this section, a post-modification agreement described in paragraph (f)(4)(v)(C) of this section is treated as a section 467 rental agreement subject to proportional rental accrual (determined under § 1.467-2(c)).

Reg. § 1.467-1(e)(3)

(B) *Constant rental accrual prior to the modification.* A post-modification agreement described in paragraph (f)(4)(v)(C) of this section is treated as a section 467 rental agreement subject to constant rental accrual if—

(*1*) Constant rental accrual is required under paragraph (f)(4)(iii) of this section; or

(*2*) The post-modification agreement involves total payments of more than $250,000 (as described in paragraph (c)(4) of this section), and the Commissioner determines that the post-modification agreement is a disqualified leaseback or long-term agreement.

(C) *Agreements described in this paragraph (f)(4)(v)(C).* A post-modification agreement is described in this paragraph (f)(4)(v)(C) if the aggregate amount of fixed rent and stated interest treated as post-modification items does not equal the aggregate amount of payments treated as post-modification items.

(vi) *Principal purpose of tax avoidance.* If a principal purpose of a substantial modification is to avoid the purpose or intent of section 467 or the regulations thereunder, the Commissioner may treat the entire agreement (as modified) as a single agreement for purposes of section 467 and the regulations thereunder.

(5) *Definitions.* The following definitions apply for purposes of this paragraph (f) and § 1.467-7(g):

(i) A *modification* of a rental agreement is any alteration, including any deletion or addition, in whole or in part, of a legal right or obligation of the lessor or lessee thereunder, whether the alteration is evidenced by an express agreement (oral or written), conduct of the parties, or otherwise.

(ii) A modification is *substantial* only if, based on all of the facts and circumstances, the legal rights or obligations that are altered and the degree to which they are altered are economically substantial. A modification of a rental agreement will not be treated as substantial solely because it is not described in paragraph (f)(6) of this section.

(iii) A modification *occurs* on the earlier of the first date on which there is a binding contract that substantially sets forth the terms of the modification or the date on which agreement to such terms is otherwise evidenced.

(iv) *Post-modification items* with respect to any modification of a rental agreement are all items (other than pre-modification items) provided under the terms of the entire agreement (as modified).

(v) *Pre-modification items* with respect to any modification of a rental agreement are pre-modification rent, interest thereon, and payments allocable thereto (whether payable before or after the modification.) For this purpose—

(A) Pre-modification rent is rent allocable to periods before the effective date of the modification, but only to the extent such rent is payable under the entire agreement (as modified) at the time such rent was due under the agreement in effect before the modification; and

(B) Pre-modification items are identified by applying payments, in the order payable under the entire agreement (as modified) unless the agreement specifies otherwise, to rent and interest thereon in the order in which amounts accrue.

(vi) The *entire agreement (as modified)* with respect to any modification is the agreement consisting of pre-modification terms providing for rights and obligations that are not affected by the modification and post-modification terms providing for rights and obligations that differ from the rights and obligations under the agreement in effect before the modification. For example, if a 10-year rental agreement that provides for rent of $25,000 per year is modified at the end of the 5th year to provide for rent of $30,000 per year in subsequent years, the entire agreement (as modified) provides for a 10-year lease term and provides for rent of $25,000 per year in years 1 through 5 and rent of $30,000 per year in years 6 through 10. The result would be the same if the modification provided for both the increase in rent and the substitution of a new lessee.

(6) *Safe harbors.* Notwithstanding the provisions of paragraph (f)(5) of this section, a modification of a rental agreement is not a substantial modification if the modification occurs solely as the result of one or more of the following—

(i) The refinancing of any indebtedness incurred by the lessor to acquire the property subject to the rental agreement and secured by such property (or any refinancing thereof) but only if all of the following conditions are met—

(A) Neither the amount, nor the time for payment, of the principal amount of the new indebtedness differs from the amount and time for payment of the remaining principal amount of the refinanced indebtedness, except for de minimis changes;

(B) For each of the remaining rental periods, the rent allocation schedule, the payments of rent and interest, and the amount accrued under section 467 are changed only to the extent necessary to take into account the change in financing costs, and such changes are made pursuant to the terms of the rental agreement in effect before the modification;

(C) The lessor and the lessee are not related persons to each other or to any lender to the lessor with respect to the property (whether under the refinanced indebtedness or the new indebtedness); and

(D) With respect to the indebtedness being refinanced, the lessor was granted a unilateral option (within the meaning of § 1.1001-3(c)(3)) by the creditor to repay the refinanced indebtedness, exercisable with or without the lessee's consent;

(ii) A change in the obligation of the lessee to make any of the contingent payments described in paragraphs (c)(2)(iii)(B)(*3*) through (*8*) of this section; or

(iii) A change in the amount of fixed rent allocated to a rental period that, when combined with all previous changes in the amount of fixed rent allocated to the rental period, does not exceed one percent of the fixed rent allocated to that rental period prior to the modification.

(7) *Special rules for certain transfers*—(i) *In general.* For purposes of this paragraph (f), a substitution of a new lessee or a sale, exchange, or other disposition by a lessor of property subject to a rental agreement will not, by itself, be treated as a substantial modification unless a principal purpose of the transaction giving rise to the modification is the avoidance of Federal income tax. In determining whether a principal purpose of the transaction giving rise to the modification is the avoidance of Federal income tax—

(A) The safe harbors and other principles of § 1.467-3(c) are taken into account; and

(B) The Commissioner may treat the post-modification agreement as a new agreement or treat the entire agreement (as modified) as a single agreement.

(ii) *Exception.* Notwithstanding the provisions of paragraph (f)(7)(i) of this section, the continuing lessor and the new lessee (in the case of a substitution of a new lessee) or the new lessor and the continuing lessee (in the case of a sale, exchange, or other disposition by a lessor of property subject to a rental agreement) may, in appropriate cases, request the Commissioner to treat the transaction as if it were a substantial modification in order to have the provisions of paragraph (f)(4)(iii) of this section and § 1.467-7(g)(1) apply to the transaction.

(g) *Treatment of amounts payable by lessor to lessee*—(1) *Interest.* For purposes of determining present value, any amounts payable by the lessor to the lessee as interest on prepaid rent are treated as negative amounts.

(2) *Other amounts.* [Reserved]

(h) *Meaning of terms.* The following meanings apply for purposes of this section and §§ 1.467-2 through 1.467-9:

(1) *Agreement date* means the earlier of the lease date or the first date on which there is a binding written contract that substantially sets forth the terms under which the property will be leased.

(2) *Contingent rent* means any rent that is not fixed rent, including any amount reflecting an adjustment based on a reasonable price index (as defined in paragraph (h)(10) of this section) or a variable interest rate provision (as defined in paragraph (h)(16) of this section).

(3) *Fixed rent* means any rent to the extent its amount and the time at which it is required to be paid are fixed and determinable under the terms of the rental agreement as of the lease date. The following rules apply for the purpose of determining the extent to which rent is fixed rent:

(i) The possibility of a breach, default, or other early termination of the rental agreement and any adjustments based on a reasonable price index or a variable interest rate provision are disregarded.

(ii) Rent will not fail to be treated as fixed rent merely because of the possibility of impairment by insolvency, bankruptcy, or other similar circumstances.

(iii) If the lease term (as defined in paragraph (h)(6) of this section) includes one or more periods as to which either the lessor or the lessee has an option to renew or extend the term of the agreement, rent will not fail to be treated as fixed rent merely because the option has not been exercised.

(iv) If the lease term includes one or more periods during which a substitute lessee or lessor may have use of the property, rent will not fail to be treated as fixed rent merely because the contingencies relating to the obligation of the lessee (or a related person) to make payments in the nature of rent have not occurred.

(v) If either the lessor or the lessee has an unconditional option or options, exercisable on one or more dates during the lease term, that, if exercised, require payments of rent to be made under an alternative payment schedule or schedules, the amount of fixed rent and the dates on which such rent is required to be paid are determined on the basis of the payment schedule that, as of the agreement date, is most likely to occur. If payments of rent are made under an alternative payment schedule that differs from the payment schedule assumed in applying the preceding sentence, then, for purposes of paragraph (f) of

Reg. § 1.467-1(f)(7)

this section, the rental agreement is treated as having been modified at the time the option to make payments on such alternative schedule is exercised.

(4) *Late payment charge* means any amount required to be paid by the lessee to the lessor as additional compensation for the lessee's failure to make any payment of rent under a rental agreement when due.

(5) *Lease date* means the date on which the lessee first has the right to use of the property that is the subject of the rental agreement.

(6) *Lease term* means the period during which the lessee has use of the property subject to the rental agreement, including any option of the lessor to renew or extend the term of the agreement. An option of the lessee to renew or extend the term of the agreement is included in the lease term only if it is expected, as of the agreement date, that the option will be exercised. For this purpose, a lessee is generally expected to exercise an option if, for example, as of the agreement date, the rent for the option period is less than the expected fair market value rental for such period. The lessor's or lessee's determination that an option period is either included in or excluded from the lease term is not binding on the Commissioner. If the lessee (or a related person) agrees that one or both of them will or could be obligated to make payments in the nature of rent (within the meaning of § 1.168(i)-2(b)(2)) for a period when another lessee (the substitute lessee) or the lessor will have use of the property subject to the rental agreement, the Commissioner may, in appropriate cases, treat the period when the substitute lessee or lessor will have use of the property as part of the lease term. See § 1.467-7(f) for special rules applicable to the lessee, substitute lessee, and lessor. This paragraph (h)(6) applies to section 467 rental agreements entered into after March 6, 2001. However, taxpayers may choose to apply this paragraph (h)(6) to any rental agreement that is described in § 1.467-9(a) and is entered into on or before March 6, 2001.

(7) A *loss payment provision* means a provision that requires the lessee to pay the lessor a sum of money (which may be either a stipulated amount or an amount determined by reference to a formula or other objective measure) if the property subject to the rental agreement is lost, stolen, damaged or destroyed, or otherwise rendered unsuitable for any use (other than for scrap purposes).

(8) A *qualified percentage rents provision* means a provision pursuant to which the rent is equal to a fixed percentage of the lessee's receipts or sales (whether or not receipts or sales are adjusted for returned merchandise or Federal, state, or local sales taxes), but only if the percentage does not vary throughout the lease term. A provision will not fail to be treated as a qualified percentage rents provision solely by reason of one or more of the following additional terms:

(i) Differing percentages of receipts or sales apply to different departments or separate floors of a retail store, but only if the percentage applicable to a particular department or floor does not vary throughout the lease term.

(ii) The percentage is applied to receipts or sales in excess of determinable dollar amounts, but only if the determinable dollar amounts are fixed and do not vary throughout the lease term.

(9) A *qualified TRAC provision* means a terminal rental adjustment clause (as defined in section 7701(h)(3)) contained in a qualified motor vehicle operating agreement (as defined in section 7701(h)(2)), but only if the adjustment to the rental price is based on a reasonable estimate, determined as of any date between the agreement date and the lease date (or, in the event the agreement date is the same as or later than the lease date, determined as of the agreement date), of the fair market value of the motor vehicle (including any trailer) at the end of the lease term.

(10) An adjustment is *based on a reasonable price index* if the adjustment reflects inflation or deflation occurring over a period during the lease term and is determined consistently under a generally recognized index for measuring inflation or deflation (for example, the non-seasonally adjusted U.S. City Average All Items Consumer Price Index for All Urban Consumers (CPI-U), which is published by the Bureau of Labor Statistics of the Department of Labor). An adjustment will not fail to be treated as one that is based on a reasonable price index merely because the adjustment may be limited to a fixed percentage, but only if the parties reasonably expect, as of any date between the agreement date and the lease date (or, in the event the agreement date is the same as the lease date, as of such date), that the fixed percentage will actually limit the amount of the rent payable during less than 50 percent of the lease term.

(11) For purposes of determining whether a section 467 rental agreement is a leaseback within the meaning of § 1.467-3(b)(2), two persons are *related persons* if they are related persons within the meaning of section 465(b)(3)(C). In all other cases, two persons are *related persons* if they either have a relationship to each other that is specified in section 267(b) or section 707(b)(1) or

are related entities within the meaning of sections 168(h)(4)(A), (B), or (C).

(12) *Rental agreement* includes any agreement, whether written or oral, that provides for the use of tangible property and is treated as a lease for Federal income tax purposes.

(13) A *residual condition provision* means a provision in a rental agreement that requires a payment to be made by either the lessor or the lessee to the other party based on the difference between the actual condition of the property subject to the agreement, determined as of the expiration of the lease term, and the expected condition of the property at the expiration of the lease term, as set forth in the rental agreement. The amount of any such payment may be determined by reference to any objective measure relating to the use or condition of the property, such as miles, hours or other duration of use, units of production, or similar measure. A provision will be treated as a residual condition provision only if the payment represents compensation for the use of, or wear and tear on, the property in excess of, or below, a standard set forth in the rental agreement, and the standard is reasonably expected, as of any date between the agreement date and the lease date (or, in the event the agreement date is the same as or later than the lease date, as of the agreement date), to be met at the expiration of the lease term.

(14) A *tax indemnity provision* means a provision in a rental agreement that may require the lessee to make one or more payments to the lessor in the event that the Federal, foreign, state, or local income tax consequences actually realized by a lessor from owning the property subject to the rental agreement and leasing it to the lessee differ from the consequences reasonably expected by the lessor, but only if the differences in such consequences result from a misrepresentation, act, or failure to act on the part of the lessee, or any other factor not within the control of the lessor or any related person.

(15) *Third-party costs* include any real estate taxes, insurance premiums, maintenance costs, and any other costs (excluding a debt service cost) that relate to the leased property and are not within the control of the lessor or lessee or any person related to the lessor or lessee.

(16) A *variable interest rate provision* means a provision in a rental agreement that requires the rent payable by the lessee to the lessor to be adjusted by the dollar amount of changes in the amount of interest payable by the lessor on any indebtedness that was incurred to acquire the property subject to the rental agreement (or any refinancing thereof), but—

(i) Only to the extent the changes are attributable to changes in the interest rate; and

(ii) Only if the indebtedness provides for interest at one or more qualified floating rates (within the meaning of § 1.1275-5(b)), or the changes are attributable to a refinancing at a fixed rate or one or more qualified floating rates.

(i) [Reserved].

(j) *Computational rules.* For purposes of this section and §§ 1.467-2 through 1.467-9, the following rules apply—

(1) *Counting conventions.* Any reasonable counting convention may be used (for example, 30 days per month/360 days per year) to determine the length of a rental period or to perform any computation. Rental periods of the same descriptive length, for example annual, semiannual, quarterly, or monthly, may be treated as being of equal length.

(2) *Conventions regarding timing of rent and payments*—(i) *In general.* For purposes of determining present values and yield only, except as otherwise provided in this section and §§ 1.467-2 through 1.467-8—

(A) The rent allocated to a rental period is taken into account on the last day of the rental period;

(B) Any amount payable during the first half of the first rental period is treated as payable on the first day of that rental period;

(C) Any amount payable during the first half of any other rental period is treated as payable on the last day of the preceding rental period;

(D) Any amount payable during the second half of a rental period is treated as payable on the last day of the rental period; and

(E) Any amount payable at the midpoint of a rental period is treated, in applying this paragraph (j)(2), as an amount payable during the first half of the rental period.

(ii) *Time amount is payable.* For purposes of this section and §§ 1.467-2 through 1.467-9, an amount is payable on the last day for timely payment (that is, the last day such amount may be paid without incurring interest, computed at an arm's-length rate, a substantial penalty, or other substantial detriment (such as giving the lessor the right to terminate the agreement, bring an action to enforce payment, or exercise other similar remedies under the terms of the agreement or applicable law)). This paragraph (j)(2)(ii) applies to section 467 rental agreements entered into after March 6, 2001. However, taxpayers may choose to apply this paragraph (j)(2)(ii) to any rental agreement that is described in

Reg. § 1.467-1(h)(12)

§ 1.467-9(a) and is entered into on or before March 6, 2001.

(3) *Annualized fixed rent.* Annualized fixed rent is determined by multiplying the fixed rent allocated to the rental period under paragraph (c)(2)(ii) of this section by the number of periods of the rental period's length in a calendar year. Thus, if the fixed rent allocated to a rental period is $10,000 and the rental period is one month, the annualized fixed rent for that rental period is $120,000 ($10,000 times 12).

(4) *Allocation of fixed rent within a period.* A rental agreement that allocates fixed rent to any period is treated as allocating fixed rent ratably within that period. Thus, if a rental agreement provides that $120,000 is allocated to each calendar year in the lease term, $10,000 of rent is allocated to each calendar month.

(5) *Rental period length.* Except as provided in § 1.467-3(d)(1) (relating to agreements for which constant rental accrual is required), rental periods may be of any length, may vary in length, and may be different as between the lessor and the lessee as long as—

(i) The rental periods are one year or less, cover the entire lease term, and do not overlap;

(ii) Each scheduled payment under the rental agreement (other than a payment scheduled to occur before or after the lease term) occurs within 30 days of the beginning or end of a rental period; and

(iii) In the case of a rental agreement that does not provide a specific allocation of fixed rent, the rental periods selected do not cause the agreement to be treated as a section 467 rental agreement unless all alternative rental period schedules would result in such treatment. [Reg. § 1.467-1.]

☐ [*T.D. 8820, 5-17-99. Amended by T.D. 8917, 1-4-2001.*]

[Reg. § 1.467-2]

§ 1.467-2. **Rent accrual for section 467 rental agreements without adequate interest.**—(a) *Section 467 rental agreements for which proportional rental accrual is required.* Under § 1.467-1(d)(2)(ii), the fixed rent for each rental period is the proportional rental amount, computed under paragraph (c) of this section, if—

(1) The section 467 rental agreement is not a disqualified leaseback or long-term agreement under § 1.467-3(b); and

(2) The section 467 rental agreement does not provide adequate interest on fixed rent under paragraph (b) of this section.

(b) *Adequate interest on fixed rent*—(1) *In general.* A section 467 rental agreement provides adequate interest on fixed rent if, disregarding any contingent rent—

(i) The rental agreement has no deferred or prepaid rent as described in § 1.467-1(c)(3);

(ii) The rental agreement has deferred or prepaid rent, and—

(A) The rental agreement provides interest (the stated rate of interest) on deferred or prepaid fixed rent at a single fixed rate (as defined in § 1.1273-1(c)(1)(iii));

(B) The stated rate of interest on fixed rent is no lower than 110 percent of the applicable Federal rate (as defined in paragraph (e)(3) of this section);

(C) The amount of deferred or prepaid fixed rent on which interest is charged is adjusted at least annually to reflect the amount of deferred or prepaid fixed rent as of a date no earlier than the date of the preceding adjustment and no later than the date of the succeeding adjustment; and

(D) The rental agreement requires interest to be paid or compounded at least annually;

(iii) The rental agreement provides for deferred rent but no prepaid rent, and the sum of the present values (within the meaning of paragraph (d) of this section) of all amounts payable by the lessee as fixed rent (and interest, if any, thereon) is equal to or greater than the sum of the present values of the fixed rent allocated to each rental period; or

(iv) The rental agreement provides for prepaid rent but no deferred rent, and the sum of the present values of all amounts payable by the lessee as fixed rent, plus the sum of the negative present values of all amounts payable by the lessor as interest, if any, on prepaid fixed rent, is equal to or less than the sum of the present values of the fixed rent allocated to each rental period.

(2) *Section 467 rental agreements that provide for a variable rate of interest.* For purposes of the adequate interest test under paragraph (b)(1) of this section, if a section 467 rental agreement provides for variable interest, the rental agreement is treated as providing for fixed rates of interest on deferred or prepaid fixed rent equal to the fixed rate substitutes (determined in the same manner as under § 1.1275-5(e), treating the agreement date as the issue date) for the variable rates called for by the rental agreement. For purposes of this section, a rental agreement provides for variable interest if all stated interest provided by the agreement is paid or compounded at least annually at a rate or rates that meet the requirements of § 1.1275-5(a)(3)(i)(A) or (B) and (a)(4).

(3) *Agreements with both deferred and prepaid rent.* If an agreement has both deferred and

prepaid rent, the agreement provides adequate interest under paragraph (b)(1) of this section if the conditions set forth in paragraph (b)(1)(ii)(A) through (D) of this section are met for both the prepaid and the deferred rent. For purposes of this paragraph (b)(3), an agreement will be considered to meet the condition set forth in paragraph (b)(1)(ii)(A) of this section if the agreement provides a single fixed rate of interest on the deferred rent and a single fixed rate of interest on the prepaid rent, even if those rates are not the same. This paragraph (b)(3) applies to section 467 rental agreements entered into after March 6, 2001. However, taxpayers may choose to apply this paragraph (b)(3) to any rental agreement that is described in § 1.467-9(a) and is entered into on or before March 6, 2001.

(c) *Computation of proportional rental amount*—(1) *In general.* The proportional rental amount for a rental period is the amount of fixed rent allocated to the rental period under § 1.467-1(c)(2)(ii), multiplied by a fraction. The numerator of the fraction is the sum of the present values of the amounts payable under the terms of the section 467 rental agreement as fixed rent and interest thereon. The denominator of the fraction is the sum of the present values of the fixed rent allocated to each rental period under the rental agreement.

(2) *Section 467 rental agreements that provide for a variable rate of interest.* To calculate the proportional rental amount for a section 467 rental agreement that provides for a variable rate of interest, see § 1.467-5.

(d) *Present value.* For purposes of determining adequate interest under paragraph (b) of this section or the proportional rental amount under paragraph (c) of this section, the present value of any amount is determined using a discount rate equal to 110 percent of the applicable Federal rate. In general, present values are determined as of the first day of the first rental period in the lease term. However, if a section 467 rental agreement calls for payments of fixed rent prior to the lease term, present values are determined as of the first day a fixed rent payment is called for by the agreement. For purposes of the present value determination under paragraph (b)(1)(iv) of this section, the fixed rent allocated to a rental period must be discounted from the first day of the rental period. For other conventions and rules relating to the determination of present value, see § 1.467-1(g) and (j).

(e) *Applicable Federal rate*—(1) *In general.* The applicable Federal rate for a section 467 rental agreement is the applicable Federal rate in effect on the agreement date. The *applicable Federal rate* for a rental agreement means—

(i) The Federal short-term rate if the term of the rental agreement is not over 3 years;

(ii) The Federal mid-term rate if the term of the rental agreement is over 3 years but not over 9 years; and

(iii) The Federal long-term rate if the term of the rental agreement is over 9 years.

(2) *Source of applicable Federal rates.* The Internal Revenue Service publishes the applicable Federal rates, based on annual, semiannual, quarterly, and monthly compounding, each month in the Internal Revenue Bulletin (see § 601.601(d) of this chapter). However, the applicable Federal rates may be based on any compounding assumption. To convert a rate based on one compounding assumption to an equivalent rate based on a different compounding assumption, see § 1.1272-1(j), *Example 1.*

(3) *110 percent of applicable Federal rate.* For purposes of § 1.467-1, this section and §§ 1.467-3 through 1.467-9, 110 percent of the applicable Federal rate means 110 percent of the applicable Federal rate based on semiannual compounding or any rate based on a different compounding assumption that is equivalent to 110 percent of the applicable Federal rate based on semiannual compounding. The Internal Revenue Service publishes 110 percent of the applicable Federal rates, based on annual, semiannual, quarterly, and monthly compounding, each month in the Internal Revenue Bulletin (see § 601.601(d)(2) of this chapter).

(4) *Term of the section 467 rental agreement*—(i) *In general.* For purposes of determining the applicable Federal rate under this paragraph (e), the term of the section 467 rental agreement includes the lease term, any period before the lease term beginning with the first day an amount of fixed rent is payable under the terms of the rental agreement, and any period after the lease term ending with the last day an amount of fixed rent or interest thereon is payable under the rental agreement.

(ii) *Section 467 rental agreements with variable interest.* If a section 467 rental agreement provides variable interest on deferred or prepaid fixed rent, the term of the rental agreement for purposes of calculating the applicable Federal rate is the longest period between interest rate adjustment dates, or, if the rental agreement provides an initial fixed rate of interest on deferred or prepaid fixed rent, the period between the agreement date and the last day the fixed rate applies, if this period is longer. If, as described in § 1.1274-4(c)(2)(ii), the rental agreement provides

Reg. § 1.467-2(c)(1)

for a qualified floating rate (as defined in § 1.1275-5(b)) that in substance resembles a fixed rate, the applicable Federal rate is determined by reference to the lease term.

(f) *Examples.* The following examples illustrate the application of this section. In each of these examples it is assumed that the rental agreement is not a disqualified leaseback or long-term agreement subject to constant rental accrual. The examples are as follows:

Example 1. (i) C agrees to lease property from D for five years beginning on January 1, 2000, and ending on December 31, 2004. The section 467 rental agreement provides that rent of $100,000 accrues in each calendar year in the lease term and that rent of $500,000 plus $120,000 of interest is payable on December 31, 2004. Assume that the parties select the calendar year as the rental period and that 110 percent of the applicable Federal rate is 10 percent, compounded annually.

(ii) The rental agreement has deferred rent under § 1.467-1(c)(3)(i) because the fixed rent allocated to calendar years 2000, 2001, and 2002 is not paid until 2004. In addition, because the rental agreement does not state an interest rate, the rental agreement does not satisfy the requirements of paragraph (b)(1)(ii) of this section.

(iii)(A) Because the rental agreement has deferred fixed rent and no prepaid rent, the agreement has adequate interest only if the present value test provided in paragraph (b)(1)(iii) of this section is met. The present value of all fixed rent and interest payable under the rental agreement is $384,971.22, determined as follows: $620,000/(1.10)$^{-5}$ = $384,971.22. The present value of all fixed rent allocated under the rental agreement (discounting the amount of fixed rent allocated to a rental period from the last day of the rental period) is $379,078.68, determined as follows:

$$\$379{,}078.68 = \$100{,}000 \times \frac{1 - (1.10)^{-5}}{.10}$$

(B) The rental agreement provides adequate interest on fixed rent because the present value of the single amount payable under the section 467 rental agreement exceeds the sum of the present values of fixed rent allocated.

(iv) For an example illustrating the computation of the yield on the rental agreement and the allocation of the interest and rent provided for under the rental agreement, see § 1.467-4(f), *Example 2.*

Example 2. (i) E and F enter into a section 467 rental agreement for the lease of equipment beginning on January 1, 2000, and ending on December 31, 2004. The rental agreement provides that rent of $100,000 accrues for each calendar month during the lease term. All rent is payable on December 31, 2004, together with interest on accrued rent at a qualified floating rate set at a current value (as defined in § 1.1275-5(a)(4)) that is compounded at the end of each calendar month and adjusted at the beginning of each calendar month throughout the lease term. Therefore, the rental agreement provides for variable interest within the meaning of paragraph (b)(2) of this section.

(ii) On the agreement date the qualified floating rate is 7.5 percent, and 110 percent of the applicable Federal rate, as defined in paragraph (e)(3) of this section, based on monthly compounding, is 7 percent. Under paragraph (b)(2) of this section, the fixed rate substitute for the qualified floating rate is 7.5 percent and the agreement is treated as providing for interest at this fixed rate for purposes of determining whether adequate interest is provided under paragraph (b) of this section. Accordingly, the requirements of paragraph (b)(1)(ii) of this section are satisfied, and the rental agreement has adequate interest.

Example 3. (i) X and Y enter into a section 467 rental agreement for the lease of real property beginning on January 1, 2000, and ending on December 31, 2002. The rental agreement provides that rent of $800,000 is allocable to 2000, $1,000,000 is allocable to 2001, and $1,200,000 is allocable to 2002. Under the rental agreement, Y must make a $3,000,000 payment on December 31, 2002. Assume that both X and Y choose the calendar year as the rental period, X and Y are calendar year taxpayers, and 110 percent of the applicable Federal rate is 8.5 percent compounded annually.

(ii) The rental agreement fails to provide adequate interest under paragraph (b)(1) of this section. Therefore, under § 1.467-1(d)(2)(ii), the fixed rent for each rental period is the proportional rental amount.

(iii)(A) The proportional rental amount is computed under paragraph (c) of this section. Because the rental agreement does not call for any fixed rent payments prior to the lease term, under paragraph (d) of this section, the present value is determined as of the first day of the first rental period in the lease term. The present value of the single amount payable by the lessee under the rental agreement is computed as follows:

$$\$2{,}348{,}724.30 = \frac{\$3{,}000{,}000}{(1 + .085)^3}$$

(B) The sum of the present values of the fixed rent allocated to each rental period (discounting the fixed rent allocated to a rental period from the

Reg. § 1.467-2(f)

last day of such rental period) is computed as follows:

$$2,526,272.20 = \frac{\$800,000}{(1 + .085)} + \frac{\$1,000,000}{(1 + .085)^2} + \frac{\$1,200,000}{(1 + .085)^3}$$

(C) Thus, the fraction for determining the proportional rental amount is .9297194 ($2,348,724.30/$2,526,272.20). The section 467 interest for each of the taxable years within the lease term is computed and taken into account as provided in § 1.467-4. The section 467 rent for each of the taxable years within the lease term is as follows:

Taxable year	Section 467 rent	
2000	$ 743,775.52	($ 800,000 × .9297194)
2001	929,719.40	($1,000,000 × .9297194)
2002	1,115,663.28	($1,200,000 × .9297194)

[Reg. § 1.467-2.]

☐ [T.D. 8820, 5-17-99. Amended by T.D. 8917, 1-4-2001.]

[Reg. § 1.467-3]

§ 1.467-3. Disqualified leasebacks and long-term agreements.—(a) *General rule.* Under § 1.467-1(d)(2)(i), constant rental accrual (as described under paragraph (d) of this section) must be used to determine the fixed rent for each rental period in the lease term if the section 467 rental agreement is a disqualified leaseback or long-term agreement within the meaning of paragraph (b) of this section. Constant rental accrual may not be used in the absence of a determination by the Commissioner, pursuant to paragraph (b)(1)(ii) of this section, that the rental agreement is disqualified. Such determination may be made either on a case-by-case basis or in regulations or other guidance published by the Commissioner (see § 601.601(d)(2) of this chapter) providing that a certain type or class of leaseback or long-term agreement will be treated as disqualified and subject to constant rental accrual.

(b) *Disqualified leaseback or long-term agreement*—(1) *In general.* A leaseback (as defined in paragraph (b)(2) of this section) or a long-term agreement (as defined in paragraph (b)(3) of this section) is disqualified only if—

(i) A principal purpose for providing increasing or decreasing rent is the avoidance of Federal income tax (as described in paragraph (c) of this section);

(ii) The Commissioner determines that, because of the tax avoidance purpose, the agreement should be treated as a disqualified leaseback or long-term agreement; and

(iii) For section 467 rental agreements entered into before July 19, 1999, the amount determined with respect to the rental agreement under § 1.467-1(c)(4), (relating to the exception for rental agreements involving total payments of $250,000 or less) exceeds $2,000,000.

(2) *Leaseback.* A section 467 rental agreement is a leaseback if the lessee (or a related person) had any interest (other than a de minimis interest) in the property at any time during the two-year period ending on the agreement date. For this purpose, interests in property include options and agreements to purchase the property (whether or not the lessee or related person was considered the owner of the property for Federal income tax purposes) and, in the case of subleased property, any interest as a sublessor.

(3) *Long-term agreement*—(i) *In general.* A section 467 rental agreement is a long-term agreement if the lease term exceeds 75 percent of the property's statutory recovery period.

(ii) *Statutory recovery period*—(A) *In general.* The term *statutory recovery period* means—

(*1*) In the case of property depreciable under section 168, the applicable period determined under section 467(e)(3)(A);

(*2*) In the case of land, 19 years; and

(*3*) In the case of any other tangible property, the period that would apply under section 467(e)(3)(A) if the property were property to which section 168 applied.

(B) *Special rule for rental agreements relating to properties having different statutory recovery periods.* In the case of a rental agreement relating to two or more related properties that have different statutory recovery periods, the statutory recovery period for purposes of paragraph (b)(3)(ii)(A) of this section is the weighted average, based on the fair market values of the properties on the agreement date, of the statutory recovery periods of each of the properties.

(c) *Tax avoidance as principal purpose for increasing or decreasing rent*—(1) *In general.* In determining whether a principal purpose for providing increasing or decreasing rent is the avoidance of Federal income tax, all relevant facts and circumstances are taken into account. However, an agreement will not be treated as a disqualified leaseback or long-term agreement if either of the

Reg. § 1.467-3(a)

safe harbors set forth in paragraph (c)(3) of this section is met. The mere failure of a leaseback or long-term agreement to meet one of these safe harbors will not, by itself, cause the agreement to be treated as one in which tax avoidance was a principal purpose for providing increasing or decreasing rent.

(2) *Tax avoidance*—(i) *In general.* If, as of the agreement date, a significant difference between the marginal tax rates of the lessor and lessee can reasonably be expected at some time during the lease term, the agreement will be closely scrutinized and clear and convincing evidence will be required to establish that tax avoidance is not a principal purpose for providing increasing or decreasing rent. The term "marginal tax rate" means the percentage determined by dividing one dollar into the amount of the increase or decrease in the Federal income tax liability of the taxpayer that would result from an additional dollar of rental income or deduction.

(ii) *Significant difference in tax rates.* A significant difference between the marginal tax rates of the lessor and lessee is reasonably expected if—

(A) The rental agreement has increasing rents and the lessor's marginal tax rate is reasonably expected to exceed the lessee's marginal tax rate by more than 10 percentage points during any rental period to which the rental agreement allocates annualized fixed rent that is less than the average rent allocated to all calendar years (determined by taking into account the rules set forth in paragraph (c)(4)(iii) of this section); or

(B) The rental agreement has decreasing rents and the lessee's marginal tax rate is reasonably expected to exceed the lessor's marginal tax rate by more than 10 percentage points during any rental period to which the rental agreement allocates annualized fixed rent that is greater than the average rent allocated to all calendar years (determined by taking into account the rules set forth in paragraph (c)(4)(iii) of this section).

(iii) *Special circumstances.* In determining the expected marginal tax rates of the lessor and lessee, net operating loss and credit carryovers and any other attributes or special circumstances reasonably expected to affect the Federal income tax liability of the taxpayer (including the alternative minimum tax) are taken into account. For example, in the case of a partnership or S corporation, the amount of rental income or deduction that would be allocable to the partners or shareholders, respectively, is taken into account.

(3) *Safe harbors.* Tax avoidance will not be considered a principal purpose for providing increasing or decreasing rent if—

(i) The uneven rent test (as defined in paragraph (c)(4) of this section) is met; or

(ii) The increase or decrease in rent is wholly attributable to one or more of the following provisions—

(A) A contingent rent provision set forth in § 1.467-1(c)(2)(iii)(B); or

(B) A single rent holiday provision allowing reduced rent (or no rent) for one consecutive period during the lease term, but only if—

(*1*) The rent holiday is for a period of three months or less at the beginning of the lease term and for no other period; or

(*2*) The duration of the rent holiday is reasonable, determined by reference to commercial practice (as of the agreement date) in the locality where the use of the property occurs, and does not exceed the lesser of 24 months or 10 percent of the lease term.

(4) *Uneven rent test*—(i) *In general.* The uneven rent test is met if the rent allocated to each calendar year does not vary from the average rent allocated to all calendar years (determined in accordance with the rules set forth in paragraph (c)(4)(iii) of this section) by more than 10 percent.

(ii) *Special rule for real estate.* Paragraph (c)(4)(i) of this section is applied by substituting "15 percent" for "10 percent" if the rental agreement is a long-term agreement and at least 90 percent of the property subject to the agreement (determined on the basis of fair market value as of the agreement date) consists of real property (as defined in § 1.856-3(d)).

(iii) *Operating rules.* In determining whether the uneven rent test has been met, the following rules apply:

(A) Any contingent rent attributable to a provision set forth in § 1.467-1(c)(2)(iii)(B)(*3*) through (*9*) is disregarded.

(B) If the lease term includes one or more partial calendar years (a period less than a complete calendar year), the average rent allocated to each calendar year is the total rent allocated under the rental agreement, divided by the actual length (in years) of the lease term. The rent allocated to a partial calendar year is annualized by multiplying the allocated rent by the number of periods of the partial calendar year's length in a full calendar year and the annualized rent is treated as the amount of rent allocated to that year in determining whether the uneven rent test is met.

Reg. § 1.467-3(c)(4)

(C) In the case of a rental agreement not described in paragraph (c)(4)(ii) of this section, an initial rent holiday period and any rent allocated to such period are disregarded for purposes of this paragraph (c)(4) if taking such period and rent into account would cause the agreement to fail to meet the uneven rent test. For purposes of this paragraph (c)(4), an initial rent holiday period is any period of three months or less at the beginning of the lease term during which annualized fixed rent (determined by treating such period as a rental period for purposes of § 1.467-1(j)(3)) is less than the average rent allocated to all calendar years (determined before the application of this paragraph (c)(4)(iii)(C)).

(D) In the case of a rental agreement described in paragraph (c)(4)(ii) of this section, one qualified rent holiday period and any rent allocated to such period are disregarded for purposes of this paragraph (c)(4) if taking such period and rent into account would cause the agreement to fail the uneven rent test. For this purpose, a qualified rent holiday period is a consecutive period that is an initial rent holiday period or that meets the following conditions:

(*1*) The period does not exceed the lesser of 24 months or 10 percent of the lease term (determined before the application of this paragraph (c)(4)(iii)(D)).

(*2*) Annualized fixed rent during the period (determined by treating the period as a rental period for purposes of § 1.467-1(j)(3)) is less than the average rent allocated to all calendar years (determined before the application of this paragraph (c)(4)(iii)(D)).

(*3*) Providing less than average rent for the period is reasonable, determined by reference to commercial practice (as of the agreement date) in the locality where the use of the property occurs.

(E) If the rental agreement contains a variable interest rate provision, the uneven rent test is applied by treating the rent as having been fixed under the terms of the rental agreement for the entire lease term using fixed rate substitutes (determined in the same manner as § 1.1275-5(e), treating the agreement date as the issue date) for the variable rates of interest provided under the terms of the lessor's indebtedness.

(d) *Calculating constant rental amount*—(1) *In general.* Except as provided in paragraph (d)(2) of this section, the constant rental amount is the amount that, if paid at the end of each rental period, would result in a present value equal to the present value of all amounts payable under the disqualified leaseback or long-term agreement as rent and interest. In computing the constant rental amount, the rules for determining present value are the same as those provided in § 1.467-2(d) for computing the proportional rental amount. If constant rental accrual is required, all rental periods (other than an initial or final short period of not more than one month) must be equal in length and satisfy the requirements of § 1.467-1(j)(5).

(2) *Initial or final short periods.* If a disqualified leaseback or long-term agreement has an initial or final short rental period, the constant rental amount for the initial or final short period may be determined under any reasonable method. However, the sum of the present values of all the constant rental amounts must equal the present values of all amounts payable under the disqualified leaseback or long-term agreement as rent and interest. Any adjustment necessary to eliminate the section 467 loan balance because of the method used to determine the constant rental amount for short periods must be taken into account as section 467 rent for the final rental period.

(3) *Method to determine constant rental amount; no short periods*—(i) *Step 1.* Determine the present value of amounts payable under the disqualified leaseback or long-term agreement as rent or interest.

(ii) *Step 2.* Determine the present value of $1 to be received at the end of each rental period during the lease term as of the first day of the first rental period during the lease term (or, if earlier, the first day a rent payment is required under the rental agreement).

(iii) *Step 3.* Divide the amount determined in paragraph (d)(3)(i) of this section (Step 1) by the number of dollars determined in paragraph (d)(3)(ii) of this section (Step 2).

(e) *Examples.* The following examples illustrate the application of this section:

Example 1. (i) K, lessor, and L, lessee, enter into a long-term agreement for a 10-year lease of personal property beginning on January 1, 2000. K and L are C corporations that use the calendar year as their taxable year. K does not have any unused losses or credits from taxable years preceding 2000. In addition, as of the agreement date, K expects that it will be subject to the maximum rate of tax imposed by section 11 in 2000 and that it will not be limited in its ability to use any losses or credits. As of the agreement date, L expects that it will be subject to the alternative minimum tax imposed by section 55 in 2000. The rental agreement provides for rent allocations in each year of the lease term, as follows:

Reg. § 1.467-3(d)(1)

Year	Amount
2000	$427,500
2001	442,500
2002	457,500
2003	472,500
2004	487,500
2005	502,500
2006	517,500
2007	532,500
2008	547,500
2009	562,500

(ii) As described in paragraph (c)(2) of this section, as of the agreement date, a significant difference between the marginal tax rates of the lessor and lessee can reasonably be expected at some time during the lease term. First, the rental agreement has increasing rents. Second, the lessor's marginal tax rate exceeds the lessee's marginal tax rate by more than 10 percentage points during a rental period to which the rental agreement allocates less than a ratable portion of the aggregate amount of rent payable under the agreement. For example, for the year 2000, the lessor's expected marginal tax rate is 35 percent, the percentage determined by dividing the increase in the Federal income tax liability of K that would result from an additional dollar of rental income ($.35) by $1. Because the lessee is subject to the alternative minimum tax, the lessee's expected marginal tax rate for 2000 is 20 percent, the percentage determined by dividing the decrease in the Federal income tax liability (taking into account both the decrease in the lessee's regular tax and the increase in the lessee's alternative minimum tax) that would result from an additional dollar of rental deduction ($.20) by $1. Further, for the year 2000, the rent allocated in accordance with the rental agreement is $427,500, which is less than a ratable portion of the aggregate amount of rental payments, $495,000, determined by dividing the total rents payable under the agreement ($4,950,000) by the number of years in the lease term (10). Thus, because a significant difference between the marginal tax rates of the lessor and lessee can reasonably be expected during the lease term, the agreement will be closely scrutinized and clear and convincing evidence will be required to establish that tax avoidance is not a principal purpose for providing increasing rent.

Example 2. (i) A and B enter into a long-term agreement for a 5-year lease of personal property beginning on July 1, 2000, and ending on June 30, 2005. The rental agreement provides that the rent is allocated to the calendar years in the lease term in accordance with the following schedule and is paid at successive six-month intervals (on December 31 and June 30) during the lease term:

Year	Amount
2000	$ 450,000
2001	900,000
2002	900,000
2003	1,100,000
2004	1,100,000
2005	550,000

(ii) In determining whether the uneven rent test described in paragraph (c)(4)(i) of this section is met, the total amount of rent allocated under the rental agreement is $5,000,000, and the lease term is five years. The average rent for each year is $1,000,000 (see paragraph (c)(4)(iii)(B) of this section), and the uneven rent test is met if the rent for each year is not less than $900,000 and not more than $1,100,000. The test is met for 2000 because the annualized rent for that year is $900,000. The test is met for 2005 because the annualized rent for that year is $1,100,000. The test is met for each of the years 2001 through 2004 because the rent for each of these years is not less than $900,000 and not more than $1,100,000. Accordingly, because the uneven rent test of paragraph (c)(4)(i) of this section is met, the long-term agreement will not be treated as disqualified.

Example 3. (i) C and D enter into a long-term agreement for a lease of personal property beginning on October 1, 1999, and ending on December 31, 2005. The rental agreement provides that the rent is allocated to the calendar years in the lease term in accordance with the following schedule and is paid at successive six-month intervals (on December 31 and June 30) during the lease term:

Year	Amount
1999	$ 0
2000	900,000
2001	900,000
2002	900,000
2003	1,100,000
2004	1,100,000
2005	1,100,000

(ii) The three-month rent holiday period at the beginning of the lease term is an initial rent holiday within the meaning of paragraph (c)(4)(iii)(C) of this section. Moreover, the agreement would fail the uneven rent test if the rent holiday period and the rent allocated to the period were taken into account. Thus, under paragraph (c)(4)(iii)(C) of this section, the period and the rent allocated to the period are disregarded for purposes of applying the uneven rent test. In that case, the lease term is six years, and the uneven rent test is met because the average rent for each

Reg. § 1.467-3(e)

year in the lease term is $1,000,000 and the rent for each calendar year in the lease term is not less than $900,000 nor more than $1,100,000. Accordingly, the long-term agreement will not be treated as disqualified.

Example 4. (i) E and F enter into a long-term agreement for a 6-year lease of personal property beginning on January 1, 2000, and ending on December 31, 2005. The rental agreement provides that the rent allocated to the calendar years in the lease term and paid at successive six-month intervals (on June 30 and December 31) during the lease term is the sum of the interest on the lessor's indebtedness, in the amount of $4,637,577, and an amount determined in accordance with the following schedule:

Year	Amount
2000	$ 539,574
2001	583,603
2002	631,225
2003	886,733
2004	959,090
2005	1,037,352

(ii) Assume further that the lessor's indebtedness bears interest at the rate of 2 percent in excess of the 6-month London Interbank Offered Rate (LIBOR) in effect on the first day of the 6-month period for each rental period and that, on the agreement date, the interest rate under this formula would be 8 percent. If the interest rate remained fixed during the entire lease term, the formula for determining the rent payable by the lessee would result in payments of rent in the amount of $450,000 for each six-month period in 2000, 2001, and 2002, and $550,000 for each six-month period in 2003, 2004, and 2005.

(iii) Under paragraph (c)(4)(iii)(E) of this section, the fixed rate substitute for the variable interest rate provision produces a schedule of fixed rents that meets the uneven rent test of paragraph (c)(4)(i) of this section. Thus, even if the actual rents payable under the rental agreement do not meet the uneven rent test because of fluctuations in the 6-month LIBOR, the uneven rent test will be treated as having been met, and the long-term agreement will not be treated as disqualified.

Example 5. (i) G and H enter into a long-term agreement for a 5-year lease of personal property beginning on January 1, 2000, and ending on December 31, 2004. The rental agreement provides that the rent is payable to G at the rate of $40,000 per month in arrears, subject to an adjustment based on changes in prevailing interest rates during the lease term. Under this adjustment, the lessor is entitled to receive an amount equal to the sum of a specified dollar amount, which increases each month as payments of rent are made, and interest on a notional principal amount (as defined in § 1.446-3(c)(3)) at a qualified floating rate (as defined in § 1.1275-5(b)). The notional principal amount is initially established at 80 percent of the cost of the property. As each payment of rent is made, the notional principal amount is reduced (but not below zero) to an amount that would represent the outstanding principal balance of a loan the payments on which are equal to the monthly payments of rent. As of the agreement date, the value of the qualified floating rate is 9 percent. Although G did not incur indebtedness specifically for the purpose of acquiring the property, the parties agreed to the adjustment provisions in order to compensate G for its general costs of borrowing.

(ii) The adjustment provision produces a schedule of rent payments that is virtually identical to the schedule that would have resulted if G had actually borrowed money in an amount and on terms identical to the terms used in determining interest on the notional principal amount and the adjustment were based on that indebtedness. An adjustment based on actual indebtedness of the lessor would have been a variable interest rate provision eligible for a safe harbor under paragraph (c)(3)(ii)(A) of this section. Accordingly, based on all the facts and circumstances, the adjustment provision did not have as one of its principal purposes the avoidance of Federal income tax, and thus the long-term agreement will not be treated as disqualified.

Example 6. (i) X and Y enter into a leaseback for a 5-year lease of personal property beginning on January 1, 1998, and ending on December 31, 2002. The rental agreement provides that $0 of rent is allocated to years 1998, 1999, and 2000, and that rent of $17,500,000 is allocated to years 2001 and 2002. The rental agreement provides that the rent allocated to each year is payable on December 31 of that year. Assume all rental periods are the calendar year. Assume also that 110 percent of the applicable Federal rate based on annual compounding is 12 percent.

(ii)(A) If the Commissioner determines that the leaseback is disqualified, the constant rental amount is computed as follows:

(B) Step 1 in calculating the constant rental amount is to determine the present value of the two payments due under the rental agreement as follows:

$$\$21{,}051{,}536 = \frac{\$17{,}500{,}000}{(1.12)^4} + \frac{\$17{,}500{,}000}{(1.12)^5}$$

Reg. § 1.467-3(e)

(iii) Because no amounts of rent are payable before the lease term, Step 2 in calculating the constant rental amount is to determine the present value as of the first day of the lease term of $1 to be received at the end of each rental period during the lease term. This results in a present value of $3.6047762. In Step 3 the amount determined in Step 1 is divided by the number of dollars determined in Step 2. Thus, the constant rental amount is $5,839,901 for each calendar year during the lease term computed as follows:

$$\$5{,}839{,}901 = \frac{\$21{,}051{,}536}{3.6047762}$$

[Reg. § 1.467-3.]

☐ [T.D. 8820, 5-17-99. *Amended by T.D.* 8917, 1-4-2001.]

[Reg. § 1.467-4]

§ 1.467-4. Section 467 loan.—(a) *In general*—(1) *Overview.* Except as provided in paragraph (a)(2) of this section, the section 467 loan rules of this section apply to a section 467 rental agreement if, as of the first day of a rental period, there is a difference between the amount of fixed rent payable under the rental agreement on or before the first day and the amount of fixed rent required to be accrued in accordance with § 1.467-1(d)(2) before the first day. Paragraph (b) of this section provides rules for computing the principal balance of a section 467 loan at the beginning of any rental period. The principal balance of a section 467 loan may be positive or negative. For Federal tax purposes, if the principal balance is positive, the amount represents a loan from the lessor to the lessee, and if the principal balance is negative, the amount represents a loan from the lessee to the lessor.

(2) *No section 467 loan in the case of certain section 467 rental agreements.* Except as provided in paragraphs (a)(3) and (4) of this section, this section does not apply to section 467 rental agreements that provide adequate interest under § 1.467-2(b)(1)(i) (agreements with no deferred or prepaid rent) or § 1.467-2(b)(1)(ii) (agreements with deferred or prepaid rent that provide adequate stated interest at a single fixed rate).

(3) *Rental agreements subject to constant rental accrual.* Notwithstanding the provisions of paragraph (a)(2) of this section, this section applies to rental agreements subject to constant rental accrual under § 1.467-3 (relating to disqualified leasebacks or long-term agreements).

(4) *Special rule in applying the provisions of § 1.467-7(e), (f), or (g).* Notwithstanding the provisions of paragraph (a)(2) of this section, section 467 loan balances must be computed for section 467 rental agreements that are not subject to constant rental accrual under § 1.467-3 and that provide adequate interest under § 1.467-2(b)(1)(i) or (ii), but only for purposes of applying the provisions of § 1.467-7(e) (relating to dispositions of property subject to a section 467 rental agreement), § 1.467-7(f) (relating to assignments by lessees and lessee-financed renewals), and § 1.467-7(g) (relating to modifications of rental agreements).

(b) *Principal balance*—(1) *In general.* Except as provided in paragraph (b)(2) of this section or in § 1.467-7(e), (f), or (g), the principal balance of the section 467 loan at the beginning of a rental period equals—

(i) The fixed rent accrued in preceding rental periods;

(ii) Increased by the sum of—

(A) The interest on fixed rent includible in the gross income of the lessor for preceding rental periods; and

(B) Any amount payable by the lessor on or before the first day of the rental period as interest on prepaid fixed rent; and

(iii) Decreased by the sum of—

(A) The interest on prepaid fixed rent includible in the gross income of the lessee for preceding rental periods; and

(B) Any amount payable by the lessee on or before the first day of the rental period as fixed rent or interest thereon.

(2) *Section 467 rental agreements that provide for prepaid fixed rent and adequate interest.* If a section 467 rental agreement calls for prepaid fixed rent and provides adequate interest under § 1.467-2(b)(1)(iv), the principal balance of the section 467 loan at the beginning of a rental period equals the principal balance determined under paragraph (b)(1) of this section, plus the fixed rent accrued for that rental period.

(3) *Timing of payments.* For purposes of this paragraph (b), the day on which an amount is payable is determined under the rules of § 1.467-1(j)(2)(i)(B) through (E) and § 1.467-1(j)(2)(ii).

(c) *Yield*—(1) *In general*—(i) *Method of determining yield.* Except as provided in paragraphs (c)(2) and (3) of this section, the yield of a section 467 loan is the discount rate at which the sum of the present values of all amounts payable by the lessee as fixed rent and interest on fixed rent, plus the sum of the present values of all amounts payable by the lessor as interest on prepaid fixed rent, equals the sum of the present values of the fixed rent that accrues in accordance with § 1.467-1(d)(2). The yield must be constant over the term of the section 467 rental agreement and, when expressed as a percentage, must be calculated to at least two decimal places.

(ii) *Method of stating yield.* In determining the section 467 interest for a rental period, the yield of the section 467 loan must be stated appropriately by taking into account the length of the rental period. Section 1.1272-1(j), Example 1, provides a formula for converting a yield based on a period of one length to an equivalent yield based on a period of a different length.

(iii) *Rounding adjustments.* Any adjustment necessary to eliminate the section 467 loan because of rounding the yield to two or more decimal places must be taken into account as an adjustment to the section 467 interest for the final rental period determined as provided in paragraph (e) of this section.

(2) *Yield of section 467 rental agreements for which constant rental amount or proportional rental amount is computed.* In the case of a section 467 rental agreement to which § 1.467-1(d)(2)(i) or (ii) applies, the yield of the section 467 loan equals 110 percent of the applicable Federal rate (based on a compounding period equal to the length of the rental period).

(3) *Yield for purposes of applying paragraph (a)(4) of this section.* For purposes of applying paragraph (a)(4) of this section, the yield of the section 467 loan balance of any party, or prior party, to a section 467 rental agreement for a period is the same for all parties and is the yield that results in the net accrual of positive or negative interest for that period equal to the amount of such interest that accrues under the terms of the rental agreement for that period. For example, if property subject to a section 467 rental agreement is sold (transferred) and the beginning section 467 loan balance of the transferor (as described in § 1.467-7(e)(2)(i)) is positive and the beginning section 467 loan balance of the transferee (as described in § 1.467-7(e)(2)(ii)) is negative, the yield on each of these loan balances for any period is the same for all parties and is the yield that results in the net accrual of positive or negative interest, taking into account the aggregate positive or negative interest on the section 467 loan balances of both the transferor and transferee, equal to the amount of such interest that accrues under the terms of the rental agreement for that period.

(4) *Determination of present values.* The rules for determining present value in computing the yield of a section 467 loan are the same as those provided in § 1.467-2(d) for computing the proportional rental amount.

(d) *Contingent payments.* Except as otherwise required, contingent payments are not taken into account in calculating either the yield or the principal balance of a section 467 loan.

(e) *Section 467 rental agreements that call for payments before or after the lease term.* If a section 467 rental agreement calls for the payment of fixed rent or interest thereon before the beginning of the lease term, this section is applied by treating the period beginning on the first day an amount is payable and ending on the day before the beginning of the first rental period of the lease term as one or more rental periods. If a rental agreement calls for the payment of fixed rent or interest thereon after the end of the lease term, this section is applied by treating the period beginning on the day after the end of the last rental period of the lease term and ending on the last day an amount of fixed rent or interest thereon is payable as one or more rental periods. Rental period length for the period before the lease term or after the lease term is determined in accordance with the rules of § 1.467-1(j)(5).

(f) *Examples.* The following examples illustrate the application of this section:

Example 1. (i)(A) A leases property to B for a three-year period beginning on January 1, 2000, and ending on December 31, 2002. The section 467 rental agreement has the following rent allocation schedule and payment schedule:

	Rent Allocation	Payment
2000	$ 400,000	
2001	600,000	
2002	800,000	$1,800,000

(B) The rental agreement requires a $1.8 million payment to be made on December 31, 2002, but does not provide for interest on deferred rent. Assume A and B choose the calendar year as the rental period length and that 110 percent of the applicable Federal rate based on annual compounding is 10 percent. Assume also that the agreement is not a leaseback or long-term agreement and, therefore, is not subject to constant rental accrual.

(ii) Because the section 467 rental agreement does not provide adequate interest under § 1.467-2(b) and is not subject to constant rental accrual, the fixed rent that accrues during each rental period is the proportional rental amount as described in § 1.467-2(c). The proportional rental amounts for each rental period are as follows:

2000	$370,370.37
2001	555,555.56
2002	740,740.73

(iii) A section 467 loan arises at the beginning of the second rental period because the rent payable on or before that day (zero) is less than the fixed rent accrued under § 1.467-1(d)(2) in all

Reg. § 1.467-4(c)(2)

preceding rental periods ($370,370.37). Under paragraph (c)(2) of this section, the yield of the loan is equal to 110 percent of the applicable Federal rate (10 percent compounded annually). Because no payments are treated as made on or before the first day of the second rental period, the principal balance of the loan at the beginning of the second rental period is $370,370.37. The interest for the second rental period on fixed rent is $37,037.04 (.10 × $370,370.37) and, under § 1.467-1(e)(3), is treated as interest income of the lessor and as an interest expense of the lessee.

(iv) Because no payments are made on or before the first day of the third rental period, the principal balance of the loan at the beginning of the third rental period is equal to the fixed rent accrued during the first and second rental periods plus the lessor's interest income on fixed rent for the second rental period ($962,962.97 = $370,370.37 + $555,555.56 + $37,037.04). The interest for the third rental period on fixed rent is $96,296.30 (.10 × $962,962.97). Thus, the sum of the fixed rent and interest on fixed rent for the three rental periods is equal to the total amount paid over the lease term (first year fixed rent accrual, $370,370.37, plus second year fixed rent and interest accrual, $555,555.56 + $37,037.04, plus third year fixed rent and interest accrual, $740,740.73 + $96,296.30, equals $1,800,000). B takes the amounts of interest and rent into account as interest and rent expense, respectively, and A takes such amounts into account as interest and rent income, respectively, for the calendar years identified above, regardless of their respective overall methods of accounting.

Example 2. (i) The facts are the same as in *Example 1,* § 1.467-2(f). C agrees to lease property from D for five years beginning on January 1, 2000, and ending on December 31, 2004. The section 467 rental agreement provides that rent of $100,000 accrues in each calendar year in the lease term and that rent of $500,000 plus $120,000 of interest is payable on December 31, 2004. The parties select the calendar year as the rental period, and 110 percent of the applicable Federal rate is 10 percent, compounded annually. The rental agreement has deferred rent but provides adequate interest on fixed rent.

(ii)(A) Pursuant to paragraph (c)(1) of this section, the yield of the section 467 loan is 10.775078%, compounded annually. The following is a schedule of the rent allocable to each rental period during the lease term, the balance of the section 467 loan as of the end of each rental period (determined, in the case of the calendar year 2004, without regard to the single payment of rent and interest in the amount of $620,000 payable on the last day of the lease term), and the interest on the section 467 loan allocable to each rental period:

Calendar Year	Section 467 Interest	Section 467 Rent	Section 467 Loan Balance
2000	$0	$100,000.00	$100,000.00
2001	10,775.08	100,000.00	210,775.08
2002	22,711.18	100,000.00	333,486.26
2003	35,933.41	100,000.00	469,419.67
2004	50,580.33	100,000.00	620,000.00

(B) C takes the amounts of interest and rent into account as expense and D takes such amounts into account as income for the calendar years identified above, regardless of their respective overall methods of accounting.

[Reg. § 1.467-4.]

☐ [T.D. 8820, 5-17-99.]

[Reg. § 1.467-5]

§ 1.467-5. **Section 467 rental agreements with variable interest.**—(a) *Variable interest on deferred or prepaid rent*—(1) *In general.* This section provides rules for computing section 467 rent and interest in the case of section 467 rental agreements providing variable interest. For purposes of this section, a rental agreement provides for variable interest if the rental agreement provides for stated interest that is paid or compounded at least annually at a rate or rates that meet the requirements of § 1.1275-5(a)(3)(i)(A) or (B) and (a)(4). If a section 467 rental agreement provides for interest that is neither variable interest nor fixed interest, the agreement provides for contingent payments.

(2) *Exceptions.* This section is not applicable to section 467 rental agreements that provide adequate interest under § 1.467-2(b)(1)(i) (agreements with no deferred or prepaid rent) or (b)(1)(ii) (rental agreements with stated interest at a single fixed rate). The exceptions in this paragraph (a)(2) do not apply to rental agreements subject to constant rental accrual under § 1.467-3.

(b) *Variable rate treated as fixed*—(1) *In general.* If a section 467 rental agreement provides variable interest—

(i) The fixed rate substitutes (determined in the same manner as under § 1.1275-5(e), treating the agreement date as the issue date) for the variable rates of interest on deferred or prepaid fixed rent provided by the rental agreement must be used in computing the proportional rental amount under § 1.467-2(c), the constant rental amount under § 1.467-3(d), the principal balance of a section 467 loan under § 1.467-4(b), and the yield of a section 467 loan under § 1.467-4(c); and

(ii) The interest on fixed rent for any rental period is equal to the amount that would be determined under § 1.467-1(e)(2) if the section 467 rental agreement did not provide variable interest, using the fixed rate substitutes determined under paragraph (b)(1)(i) of this section in place of the variable rates called for by the rental agreement, plus the variable interest adjustment amount provided in paragraph (b)(2) of this section.

(2) *Variable interest adjustment amount*—(i) *In general.* The variable interest adjustment amount for a rental period equals the difference between—

(A) The amount of interest that, without regard to section 467, would have accrued during the rental period under the terms of the section 467 rental agreement; and

(B) The amount of interest that, without regard to section 467, would have accrued during the rental period under the terms of the section 467 rental agreement using the fixed rate substitutes determined under paragraph (b)(1)(i) of this section in place of the variable interest rates called for by the rental agreement.

(ii) *Positive or negative adjustment.* If the amount determined under paragraph (b)(2)(i)(A) of this section is greater than the amount determined under paragraph (b)(2)(i)(B) of this section, the variable interest adjustment amount is positive. If the amount determined under paragraph (b)(2)(i)(A) of this section is less than the amount determined under paragraph (b)(2)(i)(B) of this section, the variable interest adjustment amount is negative.

(3) *Section 467 loan balance.* The variable interest adjustment amount is not taken into account in determining the principal balance of a section 467 loan under § 1.467-4(b). Instead, the section 467 loan balance is computed as if all amounts payable under the section 467 rental agreement were based on the fixed rate substitutes determined under paragraph (b)(1)(i) of this section.

(c) *Examples.* The following examples illustrate the application of this section:

Example 1. (i) X and Y enter into a section 467 rental agreement for the lease of personal property beginning on January 1, 2000, and ending on December 31, 2002. The rental agreement allocates $100,000 of rent to 2000, $200,000 to 2001, and $100,000 to 2002, and requires the lessee to pay all $400,000 of rent on December 31, 2002. The rental agreement requires the accrual of interest on unpaid accrued rent at two different qualified floating rates (as defined in § 1.1275-5(b)), one for 2001 and the other for 2002, such interest to be paid on December 31 of the year it accrues. The rental agreement provides that the qualified floating rate is set at a current value within the meaning of § 1.1275-5(a)(4). Assume that on the agreement date, 110 percent of the applicable Federal rate is 10 percent, compounded annually. Assume also that the agreement is not a leaseback or long-term agreement and, therefore, is not subject to constant rental accrual.

(ii) To determine if the section 467 rental agreement provides for adequate interest under § 1.467-2(b), § 1.467-2(b)(2) requires the use of fixed rate substitutes (in this example determined in the same manner as under § 1.1275-5(e)(3)(i) treating the agreement date as the issue date) in place of the variable rates called for by the rental agreement. Assume that on the agreement date the qualified floating rates, and therefore the fixed rate substitutes, relating to 2001 and 2002 are 10 and 15 percent compounded annually. Taking into account the fixed rate substitutes, the sum of the present values of all amounts payable by the lessee as fixed rent and interest thereon is greater than the sum of the present values of the fixed rent allocated to each rental period. Accordingly, the rental agreement provides adequate interest under § 1.467-2(b)(1)(iii) and the fixed rent accruing in each calendar year during the rental agreement is the fixed rent allocated under the rental agreement.

(iii) Because the section 467 rental agreement provides for variable interest on unpaid accrued fixed rent at qualified floating rates and the qualified floating rates are set at a current value, the requirements of § 1.1275-5(a)(3)(i)(A) and (4) are met and the rental agreement provides for variable interest within the meaning of paragraph (a)(1) of this section. Therefore, under paragraph (b)(1)(i) of this section, the yield of the section 467 loan is computed based on the fixed rate substitutes. Under § 1.467-4(c), the constant yield (rounded to two decimal places) equals 13.63 percent compounded annually. Based on the fixed rate substitutes, the fixed rent, interest on fixed rent, and the principal balance of the section 467 loan, for each calendar year during the lease term, are as follows:

Reg. § 1.467-5(b)(2)

Methods of Accounting

See p. 20,601 for regulations not amended to reflect law changes

	Accrued Rent	Accrued Interest	Projected Payment	Cumulative Loan
2000	$100,000	$ 0	$ 0	$100,000
2001	200,000	13,630	(10,000)	303,630
2002	100,000	41,370	(445,000)	0

(iv) To compute the actual reported interest on fixed rent for each calendar year, the variable interest adjustment amount, as described in paragraph (b)(2) of this section, must be added to the accrued interest determined in paragraph (iii) of this *Example 1*. Assume that the variable rates for 2001 and 2002 are actually 11 and 14 percent, respectively. Without regard to section 467, the interest that would have accrued during each calendar year under the terms of the section 467 rental agreement, and the interest that would have accrued under the terms of the rental agreement using the fixed rate substitutes determined under paragraph (b)(1)(i) of this section are as follows:

	Accrued Interest Under Rental Agreement	Accrued Interest Using Fixed Rate Substitutes
2000	$ 0	$ 0
2001	11,000	10,000
2002	42,000	45,000

(v) Under paragraph (b)(2) of this section, the variable interest adjustment amount is $1,000 ($11,000 − $10,000) for 2001 and is −$3,000 ($42,000 − $45,000) for 2002. Thus, under paragraph (b)(1)(ii) of this section, the actual interest on fixed rent for 2001 is $14,630 ($13,630 + $1,000) and for 2002 is $38,370 ($41,370 − $3,000).

Example 2. (i) The facts are the same as in *Example 1* except that 110 percent of the applicable Federal rate is 15 percent compounded annually and the section 467 rental agreement does not provide adequate interest under § 1.467-2(b). Consequently, the fixed rent for each calendar year during the lease is the proportional rental amount.

(ii) The sum of the present values of the fixed rent provided for each calendar year during the lease term, discounted at 15 percent compounded annually, equals $303,936.87.

(iii)(A) Paragraph (b)(1)(i) of this section requires the proportional rental amount to be computed based on the assumption that interest will accrue and be paid based on the fixed rate substitutes. Thus, the sum of the present values of the projected payments under the section 467 rental agreement equals $300,156.16, computed as follows:

$$\begin{aligned} \$ \ 10{,}000/(1.15)^2 &= \$ \ \ \ 7{,}561.44 \\ 445{,}000/(1.15)^3 &= \ \ \underline{292{,}594.72} \\ & \ \ \ \$300{,}156.16 \end{aligned}$$

(B) The fraction for computing the proportional rental amount equals .9875609 ($300,156.16/$303,936.87).

(iv) Based on the fixed rate substitutes, the fixed rent, interest on fixed rent, and the balance of the section 467 loan for each calendar year during the lease term are as follows:

	Proportional Rent	Accrued Interest	Projected Payment	Cumulative Loan
2000	$ 98,756.09	$ 0.00	$ 0	$ 98,756.09
2001	197,512.18	14,813.41	(10,000)	301,081.68
2002	98,756.09	45,162.23	(445,000)	0.00

(v) The variable interest adjustment amount in this example is the same as in *Example 1*. Under paragraph (b)(1)(ii) of this section, the actual interest on fixed rent for 2001 is $15,813.41 ($14,813.41 + $1,000) and for 2002 is $42,162.23 ($45,162.23 − $3,000).

[Reg. § 1.467-5.]

☐ [T.D. 8820, 5-17-99.]

[Reg. § 1.467-6]

§ 1.467-6. Section 467 rental agreements with contingent payments. [Reserved].

☐ [T.D. 8820, 5-17-99.]

[Reg. § 1.467-7]

§ 1.467-7. Section 467 recapture and other rules relating to dispositions and modifications.—(a) *Section 467 recapture.* Notwithstanding any other provision of the Internal Revenue Code, except as provided in paragraph (c) of this section, a lessor disposing of property in a transaction to which this paragraph (a) applies must recognize the recapture amount (determined under paragraph (b) of this section) and treat

Reg. § 1.467-7(a)

that amount as ordinary income. This paragraph (a) applies to any disposition of property subject to a section 467 rental agreement that—

(1) Is a leaseback (as defined in § 1.467-3(b)(2)) or a long-term agreement (as defined in § 1.467-3(b)(3));

(2) Is not disqualified under § 1.467-3(b)(1); and

(3) Allocates to any rental period fixed rent that, when annualized, exceeds the annualized fixed rent allocated to any preceding rental period.

(b) *Recapture amount*—(1) *In general.* The recapture amount for a disposition is the lesser of—

(i) The prior understated inclusion (determined under paragraph (b)(2) of this section); or

(ii) The section 467 gain (determined under paragraph (b)(3) of this section).

(2) *Prior understated inclusion.* The prior understated inclusion is the excess (if any) of—

(i) The aggregate amount of section 467 rent and section 467 interest for the period during which the lessor held the property, determined as if the section 467 rental agreement were a disqualified leaseback or long-term agreement subject to constant rental accrual under § 1.467-3; over

(ii) The aggregate amount of section 467 rent and section 467 interest accrued by the lessor during that period.

(3) *Section 467 gain*—(i) *In general.* Except as otherwise provided in paragraph (b)(3)(ii) of this section, the section 467 gain is the excess (if any) of—

(A) The amount realized from the disposition; over

(B) The sum of the adjusted basis of the property and the amount of any gain from the disposition that is treated as ordinary income under any provision of subtitle A of the Internal Revenue Code other than section 467(c) (for example, section 1245 or 1250).

(ii) *Certain dispositions.* In the case of a disposition that is not a sale or exchange, the section 467 gain is the excess (if any) of the fair market value of the property on the date of disposition over the amount determined under paragraph (b)(3)(i)(B) of this section.

(c) *Special rules*—(1) *Gifts.* Paragraph (a) of this section does not apply to a disposition by gift. However, see paragraph (c)(4) of this section for dispositions by transferees. If a disposition is in part a sale or exchange and in part a gift, paragraph (a) of this section applies to the disposition but the prior understated inclusion is determined by taking into account only section 467 rent and section 467 interest properly allocable to the portion of the property not disposed of by gift.

(2) *Dispositions at death.* Paragraph (a) of this section does not apply to a disposition if the basis of the property in the hands of the transferee is determined under section 1014(a). This paragraph (c)(2) does not apply to property which constitutes a right to receive an item of income in respect of a decedent. See sections 691 and 1014(c).

(3) *Certain tax-free exchanges*—(i) *In general.* The recapture amount in the case of a disposition to which this paragraph (c)(3) applies is limited to the amount of gain recognized to the transferor (determined without regard to paragraph (a) of this section), reduced by the amount of any gain from the disposition that is treated as ordinary income under any provision of subtitle A of the Internal Revenue Code other than section 467(c). However, see paragraph (c)(4) of this section for dispositions by transferees.

(ii) *Dispositions covered*—(A) *In general.* Except as provided in paragraph (c)(3)(ii)(B) of this section, this paragraph (c)(3) applies to a disposition of property if the basis of the property in the hands of the transferee is determined by reference to its basis in the hands of the transferor by reason of the application of section 332, 351, 361, 721, or 731.

(B) *Transfers to certain tax-exempt organizations.* This paragraph (c)(3) does not apply to a disposition to an organization (other than a cooperative described in section 521) which is exempt from tax imposed by chapter 1, subtitle A of the Internal Revenue Code (a tax-exempt entity) except to the extent the property is used in an activity the income from which is subject to tax under section 511(a) (a section 511(a) activity). However, if assets used to any extent in a section 511(a) activity are disposed of by the tax-exempt entity, then, notwithstanding any other provision of law (except section 1031 or section 1033) the recapture amount with respect to such disposition, to the extent attributable under paragraph (c)(4) of this section to the period of the transferor's ownership of the property prior to the first disposition, shall be included in the tax-exempt entity's unrelated business taxable income. To the extent that the tax-exempt entity ceases to use the property in a section 511(a) activity, the entity will be treated for purposes of this paragraph (c)(3) and paragraph (c)(4) of this section as having disposed of the property to such extent on the date of the cessation.

(4) *Dispositions by transferee.* If the recapture amount with respect to a disposition of prop-

Reg. § 1.467-7(a)(1)

erty (the first disposition) is limited under paragraph (c)(1) or (3) of this section and the transferee subsequently disposes of the property in a transaction to which paragraph (a) of this section applies, the prior understated inclusion determined under paragraph (b)(2) of this section is computed by taking into account the amounts attributable to the period of the transferor's ownership of the property prior to the first disposition. Thus, for example, the section 467 rent and section 467 interest that would have been taken into account by the transferee if the section 467 rental agreement were a disqualified leaseback or long-term agreement subject to constant rental accrual include the amounts that would have been taken into account by the transferor, and the aggregate amount of section 467 rent and section 467 interest accrued by the transferee includes the aggregate amount of section 467 rent and section 467 interest that was taken into account by the transferor. The prior understated inclusion determined under this paragraph (c)(4) must be reduced by any recapture amount taken into account under paragraph (a) of this section by the transferor.

(5) *Like-kind exchanges and involuntary conversions.* If property is disposed of or converted and, before the application of paragraph (a) of this section, gain is not recognized in whole or in part under section 1031 or 1033, then the amount of section 467 gain taken into account by the lessor is limited to the sum of—

(i) The amount of gain recognized on the disposition or conversion of the property (determined without regard to paragraph (a) of this section); and

(ii) The fair market value of property acquired that is not subject to the same section 467 rental agreement and that is not taken into account under paragraph (c)(5)(i) of this section.

(6) *Installment sales.* In the case of an installment sale of property to which paragraph (a) of this section applies—

(i) The recapture amount is recognized and treated as ordinary income in the year of the disposition; and

(ii) Any gain in excess of the recapture amount is reported under the installment method of accounting if and to the extent that method is otherwise available under section 453.

(7) *Dispositions covered by section 170(e), 341(e)(12), or 751(c).* For purposes of sections 170(e), 341(e)(12), and 751(c), amounts treated as ordinary income under paragraph (a) of this section must be treated in the same manner as amounts treated as ordinary income under section 1245 or 1250.

(d) *Examples.* The following examples illustrate the application of paragraphs (a), (b), and (c) of this section. In each of these examples the transferor of property subject to a section 467 rental agreement is entitled to the rent for the day of the disposition. The examples are as follows:

Example 1. (i)(A) X and Y enter into a section 467 rental agreement for a 5-year lease of personal property beginning on January 1, 2000, and ending on December 31, 2004. The rental agreement provides that the calendar year will be the rental period and that rents accrue and are paid in the following pattern:

	Allocation	Payment
2000	$ 0	$ 0
2001	87,500	0
2002	87,500	175,000
2003	87,500	175,000
2004	87,500	0

(B) Assume that both X and Y are calendar year taxpayers and that 110 percent of the applicable Federal rate is 11 percent, compounded annually. Assume also that the rental agreement is a long-term agreement (as defined in § 1.467-3(b)(3)), but it is not a disqualified leaseback or long-term agreement. Further, because the agreement does not provide prepaid or deferred rent, proportional rental accrual is not applicable. (See § 1.467-2(b)(1)(i)). Therefore, the rent taken into account under § 1.467-1(d)(2) is the fixed rent allocated to the rental periods under § 1.467-1(c)(2)(ii).

(ii) On December 31, 2000, X sells the property subject to the section 467 rental agreement to an unrelated person for $575,000. At the time of the sale, X's adjusted basis in the property is $175,000. Thus, X's gain on the sale of the property is $400,000. Assume that $175,000 of this gain would be treated as ordinary income under provisions of the Internal Revenue Code other than section 467(c). Under paragraph (a) of this section, X is required to take the recapture amount into account as ordinary income. Under paragraph (b) of this section, the recapture amount is the lesser of the prior understated inclusion or the section 467 gain.

(iii)(A) In computing the prior understated inclusion under paragraph (b)(2) of this section, assume that the section 467 rent and section 467

Reg. § 1.467-7(d)

36,988   Methods of Accounting

See p. 20,601 for regulations not amended to reflect law changes

interest (based on constant rental accrual) would be taken into account as follows if the section 467 rental agreement were a disqualified long-term agreement:

	Section 467 Rent	Section 467 Interest
2000	$65,812.55	$ 0
2001	65,812.55	7,239.38
2002	65,812.55	15,275.09
2003	65,812.55	4,944.73
2004	65,812.55	(6,521.95)

(B) The total amount of section 467 rent and section 467 interest for 2000, based on constant rental accrual, is $65,812.55. Since X did not take any section 467 rent or section 467 interest into account in 2000, the prior understated inclusion is also $65,812.55. X's section 467 gain is $225,000, which is the excess of the gain realized ($400,000) over the amount of that gain treated as ordinary income under non-section 467 provisions ($175,000). Accordingly, the recapture amount (the lesser of the prior understated inclusion or the section 467 gain) treated as ordinary income is $65,812.55.

Example 2. (i) The facts are the same as in Example 1, except that the section 467 rental agreement specifies that rents accrue and are paid in the following pattern:

	Allocation	Payment
2000	$60,000	$ 0
2001	65,000	0
2002	70,000	175,000
2003	75,000	175,000
2004	80,000	0

(ii)(A) Assume the section 467 rental agreement does not provide for adequate interest under § 1.467-2(b), and, therefore, the fixed rent for a rental period is the proportional rental amount. See § 1.467-1(d)(2)(ii). Under § 1.467-2(c), the following amounts would be required to be taken into account:

	Section 467 Rent	Section 467 Interest
2000	$57,260.43	$ 0
2001	62,032.13	6,298.65
2002	66,803.83	13,815.03
2003	71,575.53	3,433.11
2004	76,347.23	(7,565.94)

(B) The amount of section 467 rent and section 467 interest taken into account by X for 2000 is $57,260.43. Thus, the prior understated inclusion is $8,552.12 (the excess of the amount of section 467 rent and section 467 interest based on constant rental accrual for 2000, $65,812.55, over the amount of section 467 rent and section 467 interest actually taken into account, $57,260.43). Since the prior understated inclusion is less than the section 467 gain ($225,000, as determined in Example 1(iii)(B)), the recapture amount treated as ordinary income is also $8,552.12.

Example 3. (i) The facts are the same as in Example 1, except that, instead of selling the property, X transfers the property to S on December 31, 2002, in exchange for stock of S in a transaction that meets the requirements of section 351(a). Under paragraph (c)(3) of this section, because of the application of section 351, X is not required to take into account any section 467 recapture.

(ii) On December 31, 2003, S sells the property subject to the section 467 rental agreement to an unrelated person for $450,000. At the time of the sale, S's adjusted basis in the property is $105,000. Thus, S's gain on the sale of the property is $345,000. Assume that $245,000 of this gain would be treated as ordinary income under provisions of the Internal Revenue Code other than section 467(c). Under paragraph (a) of this section, S is required to take the recapture amount into account as ordinary income which, under paragraph (b) of this section, is the lesser of the prior understated inclusion or the section 467 gain.

(iii) S owned the property in 2003 and, under paragraph (c)(4) of this section, for purposes of determining S's prior understated inclusion, S is treated as if it had owned the property during the years 2000 through 2002. In computing S's prior understated inclusion under paragraph (b)(2) of this section, the section 467 rent and section 467 interest based on constant rental accrual are the same as the amounts set forth in the schedule in Example 1(iii)(A). Thus, the constant rental amount for 2000, 2001, 2002, and 2003 is $290,709.40 ((4 × $65,812.55) + $7,239.38 + $15,275.09 + $4,944.73). The section 467 rent

Reg. § 1.467-7(d)

Methods of Accounting

and section 467 interest actually taken into account prior to the disposition is $262,500. Thus, S's prior understated inclusion is $28,209.40 ($290,709.40 minus $262,500 (3 × $87,500)). S's section 467 gain is $100,000, the difference between the gain realized on the disposition ($345,000) and the amount of gain that is treated as ordinary income under non-section 467 Code provisions ($245,000). Accordingly, S's recapture amount, the lesser of the prior understated inclusion or the section 467 gain, is $28,209.40.

(e) *Other rules relating to dispositions*—(1) *In general.* If there is a sale, exchange, or other disposition of property subject to a section 467 rental agreement (the transfer), the section 467 rent and, if applicable, section 467 interest for a period are taken into account by the owner of the property during the period. The following rules apply in determining the section 467 rent and section 467 interest for the portion of the rental period ending immediately prior to the transfer:

(i) The section 467 rent and section 467 interest for the portion of the rental period ending immediately prior to the transfer are a pro rata portion of the section 467 rent and the section 467 interest, respectively, for the rental period. Such amounts are also taken into account in determining the transferor's section 467 loan balance, prior to any adjustment thereof that may be required under paragraph (h) of this section, immediately before the transfer.

(ii) If the transferor of the property is entitled to the rent for the day of transfer, the transfer is treated as occurring at the end of the day of the transfer.

(iii) If the transferee of the property is entitled to the rent for the day of transfer, the transfer is treated as occurring at the beginning of the day of the transfer.

(2) *Treatment of section 467 loan.* If there is a transfer described in paragraph (e)(1) of this section, the following rules apply in determining the transferor's and the transferee's section 467 loans for the period after the transfer, the amount realized by the transferor, and the transferee's basis in the property:

(i) The beginning balance of the transferor's section 467 loan is equal to the net present value at the time of the transfer (but after giving effect to the transfer) of all subsequent amounts payable as fixed rent and interest on fixed rent to the transferor and all subsequent amounts payable as interest on prepaid fixed rent by the transferor. The transferor must continue to take into account interest on the transferor's section 467 loan balance after the date of the transfer.

(ii) The beginning balance of the transferee's section 467 loan is equal to the principal balance of the transferor's section 467 loan immediately before the transfer reduced (below zero, if appropriate) by the beginning balance of the transferor's section 467 loan. Amounts payable to the transferor are not taken into account in adjusting the transferee's section 467 loan balance.

(iii) If the beginning balance of the transferee's section 467 loan is negative, the transferor and transferee must treat the balance as a liability that is either assumed in connection with the transfer of the property or secured by the property acquired subject to the liability. If the beginning balance of the transferee's section 467 loan is positive, the transferor and transferee must treat the balance as an additional asset acquired in connection with the transfer of the property. In the case of a positive beginning balance of the transferee's section 467 loan, the transferee will have an initial cost basis in the section 467 loan equal to the lesser of the beginning balance of the loan or the aggregate consideration for the transfer of the property subject to the section 467 rental agreement and the transfer of the transferor's interest in the section 467 loan.

(3) [Reserved].

(4) *Examples.* The following examples illustrate the application of this paragraph (e). In each of these examples the transferor of property subject to a section 467 rental agreement is entitled to the rent for the day of the transfer. The examples are as follows:

Example 1. (i) Q and R enter into a section 467 rental agreement for a 5-year lease of personal property beginning on January 1, 2000, and ending on December 31, 2004. The rental agreement provides that $0 of rent is allocated to 2000, 2001, and 2002, and $1,750,000 is allocated to each of the years 2003 and 2004. The rental agreement provides that the calendar year will be the rental period and that the rent allocated to each calendar year is payable on the last day of that calendar year. Assume that both Q and R are calendar year taxpayers and that 110 percent of the applicable Federal rate is 11 percent, compounded annually. Assume further that the rental agreement is a disqualified long-term agreement (as defined in § 1.467-3(b)(3)) and that the section 467 rent, the section 467 interest, and the section 467 loan balance would be the following amounts:

Reg. § 1.467-7(e)(4)

Calendar Year	Payment	Section 467 Interest	Section 467 Rent	Section 467 Loan Balance
2000	$ 0	$ 0	$592,905.87	$ 592,905.87
2001	0	65,219.65	592,905.87	1,251,031.39
2002	0	137,613.45	592,905.87	1,981,550.71
2003	1,750,000.00	217,970.58	592,905.87	1,042,427.16
2004	1,750,000.00	114,666.97	592,905.87	0

(ii) On December 31, 2002, Q sells the property subject to the section 467 rental agreement to P, an unrelated person, for $3,000,000. Q does not retain the right to receive any amounts payable by R under the rental agreement after the date of sale, but the agreement is not otherwise modified. At the time of the sale, Q's adjusted basis in the property is $975,000. Assume that, under § 1.467-1(f)(7), the disposition is not a substantial modification. Further, the Commissioner does not determine that the treatment of the agreement as a disqualified long-term agreement should be changed and, under § 1.467-1(f)(4)(iii), the agreement remains subject to constant rental accrual. Thus, under paragraph (g)(2)(iii) of this section, section 467 rent and section 467 interest for periods after the disposition will be taken into account on the basis of constant rental accrual applied to the terms of the entire agreement (as modified).

(iii) Under paragraph (e)(2)(ii) of this section, the beginning balance of P's section 467 loan is $1,981,550.71. P's section 467 loan balance is computed by reducing the balance of the section 467 loan immediately before the transfer ($1,981,550.71) by the beginning balance of the transferor's section 467 loan ($0 because Q does not retain the right to receive any amounts payable under the rental agreement subsequent to the transfer).

(iv) Q will be treated as if it had received $1,981,550.71 from the disposition of the section 467 loan and $1,018,449.29 from the sale of the property subject to the rental agreement. Thus, Q's gain on the sale of the property is $43,449.29 ($1,018,449.29 amount realized less $975,000 adjusted basis). Q's gain is not subject to the recapture provisions of section 467(c) and paragraph (a) of this section because the rental agreement was disqualified under § 1.467-3(b)(1) and, thus, the requirement of paragraph (a)(2) of this section is not met. Q recognizes no gain on the disposition of the section 467 loan because Q's basis in the loan equals the amount considered received for the loan. Further, Q does not take into account any of the section 467 rent or section 467 interest attributable to periods after the transfer of the property.

(v) P is treated as if it had acquired the property and the positive balance in the transferee's section 467 loan. P's cost basis in the property is $1,018,449.29, and its cost basis in the section 467 loan immediately following the transfer is $1,981,550.71. P takes section 467 rent and section 467 interest into account for the calendar years 2002 and 2003 under the constant rental accrual method and, accordingly, treats payments received under the rental agreement as recoveries of the principal balance of the section 467 loan (as adjusted from time to time).

Example 2. (i) The facts are the same as *Example 1*, except that on December 31, 2002, Q transfers the property to P in exchange for stock of P having a fair market value of $3,000,000 and the transaction meets the requirements of section 351(a).

(ii) Q is treated as having transferred two assets to P, the property subject to the rental agreement and the positive balance of the section 467 loan. Under section 351(a), because only stock of P is received by Q, Q does not recognize any of the gain realized on the transaction. Pursuant to section 358(a), the basis of Q in the P stock received in the exchange is the same as the aggregate basis of the property exchanged, or $2,956,550.71 (the sum of the balance of the section 467 loan, $1,981,550.71, and the adjusted basis of the property, $975,000). Q does not take into account any of the section 467 rent or section 467 interest attributable to periods after the transfer of the property.

(iii) P is treated as if it had acquired the property and the positive balance in the transferee's section 467 loan in the transaction. Pursuant to section 362(a), P's basis in each asset is the same as the basis of Q immediately preceding the transfer. Thus, the basis of P in the property subject to the rental agreement is $975,000, and the basis of P in the section 467 loan immediately following the transfer is $1,981,550.71. P takes section 467 rent and section 467 interest into account for the calendar years 2003 and 2004 under the constant rental accrual method and, accordingly, treats payments received under the rental agreement as recoveries of the principal balance of the section 467 loan (as adjusted from time to time).

(f) *Treatment of assignments by lessee and lessee-financed renewals*—(1) *Substitute lessee use.* If a lessee assigns its interest in a section 467 rental agreement to a substitute lessee, or if a period when a substitute lessee has the use of property subject to a section 467 rental agreement

Reg. § 1.467-7(f)(1)

is otherwise included in the lease term under § 1.467-1(h)(6), the section 467 rent for a period is taken into account by the person having the use of the property during the period. The following rules apply in determining the section 467 rent and section 467 interest for the portion of the rental period ending immediately prior to the assignment:

(i) The section 467 rent and section 467 interest for the portion of the rental period ending immediately prior to the assignment are a pro rata portion of the section 467 rent and the section 467 interest, respectively, for the rental period. Such amounts are also taken into account in determining the lessee's section 467 loan balance, prior to any adjustment thereof that may be required under paragraph (h) of this section, immediately before the substitute lessee first has use of the property.

(ii) If the lessee is liable for the rent for the day that the substitute lessee first has use of the property, the substitute lessee's use shall be treated as beginning at the end of that day.

(iii) If the substitute lessee is liable for the rent for the day that the substitute lessee first has use of the property, the substitute lessee's use shall be treated as beginning at the beginning of that day.

(2) *Treatment of section 467 loan.* If, as described in paragraph (f)(1) of this section, a lessee assigns its interest in a section 467 rental agreement to a substitute lessee or a period when a substitute lessee has the use of property subject to a section 467 rental agreement is otherwise included in the lease term under § 1.467-1(h)(6), the following rules apply in determining the amount of the lessee's and the substitute lessee's section 467 loans for the period when the substitute lessee has use of the property and in computing the taxable income of the lessee and substitute lessee:

(i) The beginning balance of the lessee's section 467 loan is equal to the net present value, as of the time the substitute lessee first has use of the property (but after giving effect to the transfer of the right to use the property), of all amounts subsequently payable by the lessee as fixed rent and interest on fixed rent and all amounts subsequently payable as interest on prepaid fixed rent to the lessee. For purposes of this paragraph (f), any amount otherwise payable by the lessee is not treated as an amount subsequently payable by the lessee to the extent that such payment, if made by the lessee, would give rise to a right of contribution or other similar claim against the substitute lessee or any other person. The lessee must continue to take into account interest on the lessee's section 467 loan balance after the substitute lessee first has use of the property.

(ii) The beginning balance of the substitute lessee's section 467 loan is equal to the principal balance of the lessee's section 467 loan immediately before the substitute lessee first has use of the property reduced (below zero, if appropriate) by the beginning balance of the lessee's section 467 loan. Amounts payable by the lessee to any person other than the substitute lessee (or a related person) or payable to the lessee by any person other than the substitute lessee (or a related person) are not taken into account in adjusting the substitute lessee's section 467 loan balance.

(iii) If the beginning balance of the substitute lessee's section 467 loan is positive, the beginning balance is treated as—

(A) Gross receipts of the lessee for the taxable year in which the substitute lessee first has use of the property; and

(B) A liability that is either assumed in connection with the transfer of the leasehold interest to the substitute lessee or secured by property acquired subject to the liability.

(iv) If the beginning balance of the substitute lessee's section 467 loan is negative, the following rules apply:

(A) If the principal balance of the lessee's section 467 loan immediately before the substitute lessee first has use of the property was negative, any consideration paid by the substitute lessee to the lessee in conjunction with the transfer of the use of the property shall be treated as a nontaxable return of capital to the lessee to the extent that—

(*1*) The consideration does not exceed the amount owed to the lessee under the lessee's section 467 loan balance immediately before the substitute lessee first has use of the property; and

(*2*) The lessee has basis in the principal balance of the lessee's section 467 loan immediately before the substitute lessee first has use of the property.

(B) Except as provided in paragraph (f)(2)(iv)(D) of this section, the excess, if any, of the beginning balance of the amount owed to the substitute lessee under the section 467 loan, over any consideration paid by the substitute lessee to the lessee in conjunction with the transfer of the use of the property, is treated as an amount incurred by the lessee for the taxable year in which the substitute lessee first has use of the property.

Reg. § 1.467-7(f)(2)

(C) To the extent the beginning balance of the amount owed to the substitute lessee under the section 467 loan exceeds any consideration paid by the substitute lessee to the lessee in conjunction with the transfer of the use of the property, repayments of the beginning balance are items of gross income of the substitute lessee in the taxable year in which repayment occurs (determined by applying any repayment first to the beginning balance of the substitute lessee's section 467 loan).

(D) Any amount incurred by the lessee under paragraph (f)(2)(iv)(B) of this section with respect to a transfer of the use of property (the current transfer) shall be reduced (but not below zero) to the extent that the lessee, in its capacity, if any, as a substitute lessee with respect to an earlier transfer of the use of the property would have recognized additional gross income under paragraph (f)(2)(iv)(C) of this section if the current transfer had not occurred.

(v) For purposes of paragraph (f)(2)(iv)(C) of this section, repayments occur as the negative balance is amortized through the net accrual of rent and negative interest.

(3) *Lessor use.* If a period when the lessor has the use of property subject to a section 467 rental agreement is included in the lease term under § 1.467-1(h)(6), the section 467 rent for the period is not taken into account and the lessor is treated as a substitute lessee for purposes of this paragraph (f).

(4) *Examples.* The following examples illustrate the application of this paragraph (f). In each of these examples, the substitute lessee is liable for the rent for the day on which the substitute lessee first has use of the property subject to the section 467 rental agreement. Further, assume that in each example the lessee assignment is not a substantial modification under § 1.467-1(f). The examples are as follows:

Example 1. (i) The facts are the same as in *Example 1* of paragraph (e)(4) of this section, except that on December 31, 2001, R, the lessee, contracts to assign its entire remaining interest in the leasehold to S, a calendar year taxpayer. The assignment becomes effective at the beginning of January 1, 2002. Pursuant to the terms of the assignment, R agrees with S that R will make $1,400,000 of the $1,750,000 rental payment required on December 31, 2003.

(ii) Under paragraph (f)(2)(i) of this section, R's section 467 loan balance as of the beginning of January 1, 2002, the time S first has use of the property, is $1,136,271.41 ($1,400,000/$(1.11)^2$). Under paragraph (f)(2)(ii) of this section, S's section 467 loan balance as of the beginning of January 1, 2002, is $114,759.98 (the principal balance of R's section 467 loan immediately before S has use of the property ($1,251,031.39), less R's section 467 loan balance at the beginning of January 1, 2002 ($1,136,271.41)).

(iii) Because S's $114,759.98 section 467 loan balance is positive, under paragraph (f)(2)(iii)(A) of this section, such amount is treated as gross receipts of R for 2002, R's taxable year in which S first has use of the property. R will treat the $114,759.98 as an amount received in exchange for the transfer of the leasehold interest. Under paragraph (f)(2)(iii)(B) of this section, S will treat that amount as a liability assumed in acquiring the leasehold interest. Thus, S's cost basis in the leasehold interest is $114,759.98.

(iv) Under paragraph (f)(1) of this section, S takes the section 467 rent attributable to the property into account for the period beginning on January 1, 2002. For 2002, S takes section 467 interest into account based on S's section 467 loan balance at the beginning of 2002. S's amounts payable, section 467 rent, section 467 interest, and end-of-year section 467 loan balances for calendar years 2002 through 2004 are as follows:

Calendar Year	Payment	Section 467 Interest	Section 467 Rent	Section 467 Loan Balance
Beginning				$ 114,759.98
2002	$ 0	$ 12,623.60	$592,905.87	720,289.45
2003	350,000.00	79,231.83	592,905.87	1,042,427.15
2004	1,750,000.00	114,666.98	592,905.87	0

(v) Under paragraph (f)(2)(i) of this section, R must continue to take into account section 467 interest on R's section 467 loan balance after S first has use of the property. R's section 467 loan balance beginning when S first has use of the property is $1,136,271.41. R's section 467 interest and end-of-year section 467 loan balances for calendar years 2002 through 2003 are as follows:

Calendar Year	Payment	Section 467 Interest	Section 467 Loan Balance
Beginning			$1,136,271.41
2002	$ 0	$124,989.85	1,261,261.26
2003	1,400,000.00	138,738.74	0

Reg. § 1.467-7(f)(3)

Methods of Accounting

Example 2. (i) On January 1, 2000, B leases tangible personal property from C for a period of five years. The rental agreement provides that the rental period is the calendar year and that rent payments are due at the end of the calendar year. The rental agreement does not provide for interest on prepaid rent. Assume that B and C are both calendar year taxpayers and that 110 percent of the applicable Federal rate is 10 percent, compounded annually. The rental agreement allocates rents and provides for payments of rent as follows:

Calendar Year	Rent	Payments
2000	$200,000	$400,000
2001	200,000	300,000
2002	200,000	200,000
2003	200,000	100,000
2004	200,000	0

(ii) The rental agreement has prepaid rent within the meaning of § 1.467-1(c)(3)(ii) because the cumulative amount of rent payable through the end of 2001 ($700,000) exceeds the cumulative amount of rent allocated to calendar years 2000 through 2002 ($600,000). Because the rental agreement does not provide for adequate interest on prepaid fixed rent, the rent for each calendar year during the lease term is the proportional rental amount, as described in § 1.467-2(c). The amounts payable, section 467 rent, section 467 interest, and end-of-year section 467 loan balances for each calendar year are as follows:

Calendar Year	Payment	Section 467 Interest	Section 467 Rent	Section 467 Loan Balance
2000	$400,000	$ 0	$218,987.40	($181,012.60)
2001	300,000	(18,101.26)	218,987.40	(280,126.46)
2002	200,000	(28,012.64)	218,987.40	(289,151.70)
2003	100,000	(28,915.17)	218,987.40	(199,079.47)
2004	0	(19,907.93)	218,987.40	0

(iii) On December 31, 2001, B contracts to assign its entire remaining interest in the leasehold to D, a calendar year taxpayer. The assignment becomes effective at the beginning of January 1, 2002. D pays B $278,000 on January 1, 2002, in conjunction with the assignment of the leasehold interest. Under the terms of the assignment, B is not obligated to make any rental payments due after the assignment.

(iv) Under paragraph (f)(2)(i) of this section, B's section 467 loan balance as of the beginning of January 1, 2002, the time D first has use of the property, is zero because D is obligated to make all rent payments due after the assignment of the leasehold interest. Under paragraph (f)(2)(ii) of this section, D's section 467 loan balance as of the beginning of January 1, 2002, is negative $280,126.46 (the principal balance of B's section 467 loan immediately before D has use of the property (negative $280,126.46), less B's section 467 loan balance when D first has use of the property (zero)). Because D's beginning section 467 loan balance is negative, paragraph (f)(2)(iv) of this section applies.

(v) Because B's $280,126.46 section 467 loan balance at the end of 2001 (that is, immediately before D has use of the property) is negative, paragraph (f)(2)(iv)(A) of this section applies. B's loan balance is the amount owed to B under the section 467 loan and consists of the excess of B's payments to C over the net amount of rent and negative interest B has taken into account through the end of 2001. Thus, B's basis in the negative section 467 loan balance at the end of 2001 is $280,126.46. Because the $278,000 paid by D to B in conjunction with the transfer of the leasehold interest does not exceed the amount owed to B under the section 467 loan at the end of 2001, and does not exceed B's basis in that loan balance, under paragraph (f)(2)(iv)(A) of this section B treats the $278,000 payment from D as a nontaxable return of capital.

(vi) The beginning balance of the amount owed to D under the section 467 loan ($280,126.46) exceeds by $2,126.46 the $278,000 paid by D to B in conjunction with the transfer of the leasehold interest. Paragraph (f)(2)(iv)(B) of this section treats the $2,126.46 as an amount incurred by B in 2002, B's taxable year in which D first has use of the property. Paragraph (f)(2)(iv)(D) of this section does not apply to reduce the amount incurred by B because B is the original lessee under the section 467 rental agreement.

(vii) Under paragraph (f)(1) of this section, D takes the section 467 rent into account for the period beginning when D first has use of the property. D takes section 467 interest into account based on a beginning section 467 loan balance of negative $280,126.46.

(viii) The beginning balance of the amount owed to D under the section 467 loan ($280,126.46) exceeds by $2,126.46 the $278,000

Reg. § 1.467-7(f)(4)

paid by D to B in conjunction with the transfer of the leasehold interest. Under paragraph (f)(2)(iv)(C) of this section, D must include this amount in gross income in 2002, the year in which this amount of D's beginning section 467 loan balance is paid through the net accrual of rent and negative interest. This inclusion in gross income ensures that the reductions in D's taxable income attributable to the section 467 rental agreement will not exceed the actual amount of D's expenditures.

(g) *Application of section 467 following a rental agreement modification*—(1) *Substantial modifications.* The following rules apply to any substantial modification of a rental agreement occurring after May 18, 1999, unless the entire agreement (as modified) is treated as a single agreement under § 1.467-1(f)(4)(vi):

(i) *Treatment of pre-modification items.* The lessor and lessee must take pre-modification items (within the meaning of § 1.467-1(f)(5)(v)) into account under their method of accounting used before the modification to report income and expense attributable to the rental agreement.

(ii) *Computations with respect to post-modification items.* In computing section 467 rent, section 467 interest, and the amount of the section 467 loan with respect to post-modification items—

(A) Post-modification items are treated as provided under a rental agreement (the post-modification agreement) separate from the agreement under which pre-modification items are provided;

(B) The lease term of the post-modification agreement begins at the beginning of the first period for which rent other than pre-modification rent is provided; and

(C) The applicable Federal rate for the post-modification agreement is the applicable Federal rate in effect on the day on which the modification occurs.

(iii) *Adjustments*—(A) *Adjustment relating to certain prepayments.* If any payments before the beginning of the lease term of the post-modification agreement are post-modification items, the lessor and lessee must take into account, in the taxable year in which the modification occurs, any adjustment necessary to prevent duplication with respect to such payments or the omission of interest thereon for periods before the beginning of the lease term.

(B) *Adjustment relating to retroactive beginning of lease term.* If the lease term of a post-modification agreement begins before the date on which the modification occurs, the lessor and lessee must take into account in the taxable year in which the modification occurs any amount necessary to prevent the duplication or omission of rent or interest for the period after the beginning of the lease term of the post-modification agreement and before the beginning of the taxable year in which the modification occurs. For this purpose, the amount necessary to prevent duplication or omission is determined after taking into account any adjustments required by the Commissioner for taxable years ending prior to the beginning of the taxable year in which the modification occurs. In determining any adjustments required by the Commissioner for taxable years ending prior to the beginning of the taxable year in which the modification occurs, the Commissioner will disregard the modification.

(iv) *Coordination with rules relating to dispositions and assignments*—(A) *Dispositions.* If the modification involves a sale, exchange, or other disposition of the property subject to the rental agreement—

(*1*) Adjustments required under this paragraph (g) are taken into account before applying paragraphs (a), (b), (c), and (e) of this section;

(*2*) The prior understated inclusion for purposes of paragraph (b) of this section is the sum of the prior understated inclusion with respect to pre-modification items and the prior understated inclusion with respect to post-modification items; and

(*3*) Paragraph (e) of this section applies separately with respect to pre-modification items and post-modification items.

(B) *Assignments.* If the modification involves an assignment of the lessee's interest in the rental agreement to a substitute lessee or a substitute lessee having use of the property during a period otherwise included in the lease term—

(*1*) Adjustments required under this paragraph (g) are taken into account before applying paragraph (f) of this section; and

(*2*) Paragraph (f) of this section applies separately with respect to pre-modification items and post-modification items.

(2) *Other modifications.* The following rules apply to a modification (other than a substantial modification) of a rental agreement occurring after May 18, 1999:

(i) *Computation of section 467 loan for modified agreement.* The amount of the section 467 loan relating to the agreement is computed as of the effective date of the modification. The section 467 rent and section 467 interest for periods before the effective date of the modification

Reg. § 1.467-7(g)(1)

are determined, solely for purposes of computing the amount of the section 467 loan, under the terms of the entire agreement (as modified).

(ii) *Change in balance of section 467 loan.*—(A) If the balance of the section 467 loan determined under paragraph (g)(2)(i) of this section is greater than the balance of the section 467 loan immediately before the effective date of the modification, the difference is taken into account, in the taxable year in which the modification occurs, as additional rent.

(B) If the balance of the section 467 loan determined under paragraph (g)(2)(i) of this section is less than the balance of the section 467 loan immediately before the effective date of the modification, the difference is taken into account, in the taxable year in which the modification occurs, as a reduction of the rent previously taken into account by the lessor and lessee.

(C) For purposes of this paragraph (g)(2)(ii), a negative balance is less than a positive balance, a zero balance, or any other negative balance that is closer to a zero balance.

(iii) *Section 467 rent and interest after the modification.* The section 467 rent and section 467 interest for periods after the effective date of the modification are determined under the terms of the entire agreement (as modified).

(iv) *Applicable Federal rate.* The applicable Federal rate for the agreement does not change as a result of the modification.

(v) *Modification effective within a rental period.* If the effective date of a modification does not coincide with the beginning or end of a rental period under the agreement in effect before the modification, the section 467 rent and section 467 interest for the portion of the rental period ending immediately prior to the effective date of the modification are a pro rata portion of the section 467 rent and the section 467 interest, respectively, for the rental period. Such amounts are also taken into account in determining the section 467 loan balance, prior to any adjustment thereof that may be required under paragraph (h) of this section, immediately before the effective date of the modification. Similar rules apply with respect to the section 467 rent and section 467 interest determined under the terms of the entire agreement (as modified) for purposes of computing the amount of the section 467 loan under paragraph (g)(2)(i) of this section and the section 467 rent and section 467 interest for a partial rental period beginning on the effective date of the modification.

(vi) *Other adjustments.* The lessor and lessee must take into account, in the taxable year in which a retroactive modification occurs, any amount necessary to prevent the duplication or omission of rent or interest for the period before the beginning of the taxable year in which the modification occurs.

(vii) *Coordination with rules relating to dispositions and assignments.* If the modification involves a sale, exchange, or other disposition of the property subject to the rental agreement, an assignment of the lessee's interest in the rental agreement to a substitute lessee or a substitute lessee having use of the property during a period otherwise included in the lease term, adjustments required under this paragraph (g) are taken into account before applying paragraphs (a), (b), (c), (e), and (f) of this section.

(viii) *Exception for agreements entered into prior to effective date of section 467.* This paragraph (g)(2) does not apply to a modification of a rental agreement that is not subject to section 467 because of the effective date provisions of section 92(c) of the Tax Reform Act of 1984 (Public Law 98-369 (98 Stat. 612)).

(3) *Adjustment by Commissioner.* If the entire agreement (as modified) is treated as a single agreement under § 1.467-1(f)(4)(vi), the Commissioner may require adjustments to taxable income to reflect the effect of the modification, including adjustments that are similar to those required under paragraph (g)(2) of this section.

(4) *Effective date of modification.* The effective date of a modification of a rental agreement occurs at the earliest of—

(i) The date on which the modification occurs;

(ii) The beginning of the first period for which the amount of rent or interest provided under the entire agreement (as modified) differs from the amount of rent or interest provided under the agreement in effect before the modification;

(iii) The due date of the first payment, under either the entire agreement (as modified) or the agreement in effect before the modification, that is not identical, in due date and amount, under both such agreements;

(iv) The date, in the case of a modification involving the substitution of a new lessor, on which the property subject to the rental agreement is transferred; or

(v) The date, in the case of a modification involving the substitution of a new lessee, on which the substitute lessee first has use of the property subject to the rental agreement.

(5) *Examples.* The following examples illustrate the application of this paragraph (g):

Reg. § 1.467-7(g)(5)

36,996   Methods of Accounting

See p. 20,601 for regulations not amended to reflect law changes

Example 1. (i) F, a cash method lessor, and G, an accrual method lessee, agree to a 7-year lease of tangible personal property for the period beginning on January 1, 1998, and ending on December 31, 2004. The rental agreement allocates $100,000 of rent to each calendar year during the lease term, such rent to be paid December 31 following the close of the calendar year to which it is allocated. Because the rental agreement does not provide for increasing rent, or deferred rent within the meaning of section 467(d)(1)(A), section 467 does not apply to the rental agreement.

(ii) Prior to January 1, 2001, G timely makes the $100,000 rental payments required as of December 31, 1999, and December 31, 2000. On January 1, 2001, F and G modify the rental agreement payment schedule to provide for a single final payment of $500,000 on December 31, 2004. Assume that the change is a substantial modification within the meaning of § 1.467-1(f)(5)(ii). Because the modification occurs after May 18, 1999, the post-modification agreement is treated, under § 1.467-1(f)(1), as a new agreement for purposes of determining whether it is a section 467 rental agreement.

(iii) Under § 1.467-1(f)(5)(v), the $200,000 of rent allocated to calendar years 1998 and 1999 (periods prior to the modification) constitutes pre-modification rent, and the $100,000 rent payments made on December 31, 1999, and December 31, 2000, constitute pre-modification payments. Although calendar year 2000 is also prior to the modification, the rent allocated to calendar year 2000 is not pre-modification rent and the related payment is not a pre-modification payment because the modification changed the time at which that rent is payable. See § 1.467-1(f)(5)(v)(A).

(iv) Under paragraph (g)(1)(i) of this section, F and G take pre-modification rent and pre-modification payments into account under the method of accounting they used to report income and deductions attributable to the pre-modification agreement.

(v) Under § 1.467-1(f)(1)(i), the post-modification agreement providing rent for the period beginning on January 1, 2000, and ending on December 31, 2004, is treated as a new rental agreement. This rental agreement allocates $100,000 of rent to each of the calendar years 2000 through 2004 and provides for a single rental payment of $500,000 on December 31, 2004. Because the post-modification agreement provides for deferred rent under § 1.467-1(c)(3)(i), section 467 applies. Further, the post-modification agreement does not provide for adequate interest on fixed rent, and therefore F and G must account for fixed rent and interest on fixed rent using proportional rental accrual. Under paragraph (g)(1)(iii) of this section, for their taxable years which include January 1, 2001, F and G must adjust reported rent for the difference between the rent taken into account for the calendar year 2000 under the unmodified agreement and the proportional rental amount for that year under the postmodification agreement.

Example 2. (i) On January 1, 2000, X, lessee, and Y, lessor, enter into a rental agreement for a 6-year lease of tangible personal property beginning January 1, 2000, and ending December 31, 2005. The agreement provides that the calendar year is the rental period and all rent payments are due on July 15 of all years in which a payment is required. Assume the agreement is not a disqualified leaseback or long-term agreement within the meaning of § 1.467-3(b), and has the following allocation schedule and payment schedule:

Year	Allocation	Payment
2000	$ 800,000	$ 0
2001	900,000	0
2002	1,000,000	1,500,000
2003	1,000,000	1,500,000
2004	1,100,000	1,500,000
2005	1,200,000	1,500,000

(ii) The rental agreement has deferred rent within the meaning of § 1.467-1(c)(3)(i) because the rent allocated to 2000 is not payable until 2002 and some of the rent allocable to 2001 is not payable until 2003. Further, the rental agreement does not provide adequate interest on fixed rent within the meaning of § 1.467-2(b). Therefore, the rent amount to be accrued by X and Y for each rental period is the proportional rental amount, as described in § 1.467-2(c). Assuming 110 percent of the applicable Federal rate is 10 percent compounded annually, the section 467 rent, interest, and loan balances are as follows:

Year	Rent	Interest	Loan Balance
2000	$ 736,949.55	$ 0	$ 736,949.55
2001	829,068.24	73,694.96	1,639,712.75
2002	921,186.94	163,971.28	1,224,870.97

Reg. § 1.467-7(g)(5)

Methods of Accounting

See p. 20,601 for regulations not amended to reflect law changes

Year			
2003	921,186.94	122,487.10	768,545.01
2004	1,013,305.63	76,854.50	358,705.14
2005	1,105,424.33	35,870.53	0

(iii)(A) On January 1, 2004, X and Y agree that the $1,500,000 payment scheduled for July 15, 2005, will be made in three equal installments on June 15, 2005, July 15, 2005, and August 15, 2005. Under § 1.467-1(j)(2)(i)(C) (relating to timing conventions), the payment to be made on June 15, 2005, is treated as if it were payable on December 31, 2004, for purposes of determining present values and yield of the section 467 loan. Assume that this change, which results in the following allocation schedule and payment schedule, is not a substantial modification within the meaning of § 1.467-1(f)(5)(ii):

Year	Allocation	Payment
2000	$ 800,000	$ 0
2001	900,000	0
2002	1,000,000	1,500,000
2003	1,000,000	1,500,000
2004	1,100,000	2,000,000
2005	1,200,000	1,000,000

(B) The agreement remains subject to proportional rental accrual after the modification because it has deferred rent and does not provide adequate interest on fixed rent within the meaning of § 1.467-2(b).

(iv) Because the modification occurs after May 18, 1999, and is not substantial within the meaning of § 1.467-1(f)(5)(ii), paragraph (g)(2) of this section applies. Under paragraph (g)(2)(i) of this section, the amount of the section 467 loan relating to the modified agreement is computed as of the effective date of the modification, and, solely for purposes of recomputing the amount of the section 467 loan, the section 467 rent and section 467 interest for periods before the modification are determined under the terms of the entire agreement (as modified). In addition, the applicable Federal rate does not change as a result of the modification. Thus, the recomputed section 467 rent, interest, and loan balances are as follows:

Year	Rent	Interest	Loan Balance
2000	$ 742,242.59	$ 0	$ 742,242.59
2001	835,022.91	74,224.26	1,651,489.76
2002	927,803.24	165,148.98	1,244,441.98
2003	927,803.24	124,444.20	796,689.42
2004	1,020,583.56	79,668.94	(103,058.08)
2005	1,113,363.88	(10,305.80)	0

(v) Under paragraph (g)(2)(ii) of this section, the difference between the section 467 loan balance immediately before the effective date of the modification and the recomputed section 467 loan balance as of the effective date of the modification is taken into account. In this example, the loan balance immediately before the effective date of the modification is $768,545.01 and the recomputed loan balance as of the effective date of the modification is $796,689.42. Thus, because the recomputed loan balance exceeds the original loan balance, the difference ($28,144.41) is taken into account, in the taxable year in which the modification occurs, as additional rent. Beginning on January 1, 2004, section 467 rent and interest are taken into account by X and Y in accordance with the recomputed rent schedule set forth in paragraph (iv) of this example.

(h) *Omissions or duplications*—(1) *In general.* In applying the rules of this section in conjunction with the rules of §§ 1.467-1 through 1.467-5, adjustments must be made to the extent necessary to prevent the omission or duplication of items of income, deduction, gain, or loss. For example, if a transferee lessor acquires property subject to a section 467 rental agreement at other than the beginning or end of a rental period, and the transferee lessor's beginning section 467 loan balance differs from the transferor lessor's section 467 loan balance immediately prior to the transfer, it will be necessary to treat the rental period that includes the day of transfer as consisting of two rental periods, one beginning at the beginning of the rental period that includes the day of transfer and ending with or immediately prior to the transfer and one beginning with or immediately after the transfer and ending immediately prior to the beginning of the succeeding rental period. Because the substitution of two rental periods for one rental period may change the proportional rental amount or constant rental amount, the change in rental periods should be treated as a modification of the rental agreement that occurs immediately prior to the transfer. The change in rental periods, by itself, is not treated as a substantial modification of the rental agreement al-

Reg. § 1.467-7(h)(1)

though the substitution of a new lessor may constitute a substantial modification of the rental agreement. Likewise, § 1.467-1(j)(2), which provides rules regarding when amounts are treated as payable, is designed to simplify calculations of present values, section 467 loan balances, and proportional and constant rental amounts. These simplifying conventions assume that there will be no change in the lessor or lessee under a section 467 rental agreement and that the terms of the section 467 rental agreement will not be modified. Therefore, as illustrated in the example in paragraph (h)(2) of this section, when actual events do not reflect these assumptions, it may be necessary to alter the application of these rules to properly reflect taxable income.

(2) *Example.* The following example illustrates an application of this paragraph (h):

Example. (i) J leases tangible personal property from K for five years beginning on January 1, 2000, and ending on December 31, 2004. Under the rental agreement, rent is payable on July 15 of the calendar year to which it is allocated. Both J and K treat the calendar year as the rental period. The allocation of rent and payments of rent required under the rental agreement are as follows:

Calendar Year	Rent	Payments
2000	$200,000	$450,000
2001	200,000	250,000
2002	200,000	200,000
2003	200,000	100,000
2004	200,000	0

(ii) The rental agreement does not provide for interest on prepaid rent. The rental agreement has prepaid rent under § 1.467-1(c)(3)(ii) because the rent payable at the end of 2000 exceeds the cumulative amount of rent allocated to 2000 and 2001. Therefore, J and K must take section 467 rent into account under the proportional rental method of § 1.467-2(c). Assume that 110 percent of the applicable Federal rate is 10 percent, compounded annually. The section 467 rent, section 467 interest, amounts payable, and section 467 loan balances for each of the calendar years under the terms of the rental agreement are as follows:

Calendar Year	Section 467 Rent	Section 467 Interest	Payments	Section 467 Loan Balance
2000	$220,077.48	$0	$450,000	$(229,922.52)
2001	220,077.48	(22,992.25)	250,000	(282,837.29)
2002	220,077.48	(28,283.73)	200,000	(291,043.54)
2003	220,077.48	(29,104.35)	100,000	(200,070.41)
2004	220,077.48	(20,007.07)	0	0

(iii) On January 1, 2002, J and K amend the terms of the rental agreement to advance the due date of the $200,000 payment originally due on July 15, 2002, to June 15, 2002. This change in the payment schedule constitutes a modification of the terms of the rental agreement within the meaning of § 1.467-1(f)(5)(i). Assume, however, that the change is not a substantial modification within the meaning of § 1.467-1(f)(5)(ii). Because the modification occurs after May 18, 1999, and is not substantial, paragraph (g)(2) of this section applies. Thus, the section 467 loan balance at the beginning of 2002 must be recomputed as if the June 15, 2002, payment date had been included in the terms of the pre-modification rental agreement. If this had been the case, the section 467 rent, section 467 interest, amounts payable, and section 467 loan balances for each of the calendar years under the terms of the rental agreement would have been as follows:

Calendar Year	Section 467 Rent	Section 467 Interest	Payments	Section 467 Loan Balance
2000	$224,041.38	$0	$450,000	$(225,958.62)
2001	224,041.38	(22,595.86)	450,000	(474,513.10)
2002	224,041.38	(47,451.31)	0	(297,923.03)
2003	224,041.38	(29,792.30)	100,000	(203,673.95)
2004	224,041.38	(20,367.43)	0	0

(iv) Section 1.467-4(b)(3) incorporates the conventions of § 1.467-1(j)(2) in determining when amounts are treated as payable for purposes of determining the section 467 loan balance. Section 1.467-1(j)(2)(i)(C) treats amounts payable during the first half of any rental period except the first rental period as payable on the last day of the preceding rental period. Therefore, because June 15, 2002, occurs in the first half of 2002, in determining the section 467 loan balance at the beginning of 2002 under the amended terms of the rental agreement, the $200,000 payment due on June 15, 2002, is treated as payable on December 31, 2001.

Reg. § 1.467-7(h)(2)

(v) Under paragraph (g)(2)(ii)(B) of this section, if the recomputed section 467 loan balance is less than the section 467 loan balance immediately before the modification, the difference is taken into account as a reduction of the rent previously taken into account by the lessor and the lessee. In this example, the recomputed section 467 loan balance immediately after the modification is negative $474,513.10 and the section 467 loan balance immediately before the modification is negative $282,837.29. However, the section 467 loan balance immediately before the modification does not take into account the $200,000 payment originally payable on July 15, 2002, whereas, under the conventions of § 1.467-1(j)(2)(i)(C), the recomputed section 467 loan balance immediately after the modification takes into account that $200,000 payment because it is now payable in the first half of the rental period (June 15). Under these circumstances, if the recomputed section 467 loan balance immediately after the modification is treated as negative $474,513.10 for purposes of applying paragraph (g)(2)(ii)(B) of this section, K's gross income and J's deductions attributable to the section 467 rental agreement will be understated by $200,000. Therefore, under paragraph (h)(1) of this section, only for purposes of applying paragraph (g)(2)(ii)(B) of this section, the $200,000 payment due on June 15, 2002, should not be taken into account in determining the recomputed section 467 loan balance immediately after the modification.

[Reg. § 1.467-7.]

☐ [T.D. 8820, 5-17-99.]

[Reg. § 1.467-8]

§ 1.467-8. Automatic consent to change to constant rental accrual for certain rental agreements.—(a) *General rule.* For the first taxable year ending after May 18, 1999, a taxpayer may change to the constant rental accrual method, as described in § 1.467-3, for all of its section 467 rental agreements described in paragraph (b) of this section. A change to the constant rental accrual method is a change in method of accounting to which the provisions of sections 446 and 481 and the regulations thereunder apply. A taxpayer changing its method of accounting in accordance with this section must follow the automatic change in accounting method provisions of Rev. Proc. 98-60 (see § 601.601(d)(2) of this chapter) except, for purposes of this paragraph (a), the scope limitations in section 4.02 of Rev. Proc. 98-60 are not applicable. Taxpayers changing their method of accounting in accordance with this section must do so for all of their section 467 rental agreements described in paragraph (b) of this section.

(b) *Agreements to which automatic consent applies.* A section 467 rental agreement is described in this paragraph (b) if—

(1) The property subject to the section 467 rental agreement is financed with an "exempt facility bond" within the meaning of section 142;

(2) The facility subject to the section 467 rental agreement is described in section 142(a)(1), (2), (3), or (12);

(3) The section 467 rental agreement does not include a specific allocation of fixed rent within the meaning of § 1.467-1(c)(2)(ii)(A)(*2*); and

(4) The section 467 rental agreement was entered into on or before May 18, 1999. [Reg. § 1.467-8.]

☐ [T.D. 8820, 5-17-99.]

[Reg. § 1.467-9]

§ 1.467-9. Effective dates and automatic method changes for certain agreements.—(a) *In general.* Sections 1.467-1 through 1.467-7 are applicable for—

(1) Disqualified leasebacks and long-term agreements entered into after June 3, 1996; and

(2) Rental agreements not described in paragraph (a)(1) of this section that are entered into after May 18, 1999.

(b) *Automatic consent for certain rental agreements.* Section 1.467-8 applies only to rental agreements described in § 1.467-8.

(c) *Application of regulation project IA-292-84 to certain leasebacks and long-term agreements.* In the case of any leaseback or long-term agreement (other than a disqualified leaseback or long-term agreement) entered into after June 3, 1996, and on or before May 18, 1999, a taxpayer may choose to apply the provisions of regulation project IA-292-84 (1996-2 C.B. 462) (see § 601.601(d)(2) of this chapter).

(d) *Entered into.* For purposes of this section and § 1.467-8, a rental agreement is entered into on its agreement date (within the meaning of § 1.467-1(h)(1) and, if applicable, § 1.467-1(f)(1)(i)).

(e) *Change in method of accounting*—(1) *In general.* For the first taxable year ending after May 18, 1999, a taxpayer is granted consent of the Commissioner to change its method of accounting for rental agreements described in paragraph (a)(2) of this section to comply with the provisions of §§ 1.467-1 through 1.467-7.

Reg. § 1.467-9(e)(1)

Methods of Accounting

See p. 20,601 for regulations not amended to reflect law changes

(2) *Application of regulation project IA-292-84.* For the first taxable year ending after May 18, 1999, a taxpayer is granted consent of the Commissioner to change its method of accounting for any rental agreement described in paragraph (c) of this section to comply with the provisions of regulation project IA-292-84 (1996-2 C.B. 462) (see § 601.601(d)(2) of this chapter).

(3) *Automatic change procedures.* A taxpayer changing its method of accounting in accordance with this paragraph (e) must follow the automatic change in accounting method provisions of Rev. Proc. 98-60 (see § 601.601(d)(2) of this chapter) except, for purposes of this paragraph (e), the scope limitations in section 4.02 of Rev.Proc. 98-60 are not applicable. A method change in accordance with paragraph (e)(1) of this section is made on a cut-off basis so no adjustment under section 481(a) is required. [Reg. § 1.467-9.]

☐ [T.D. 8820, 5-17-99.]

[Reg. § 1.468A-0]

§ 1.468A-0. **Nuclear decommissioning costs; table of contents.**—This section lists the paragraphs contained in §§ 1.468A-1 through 1.468A-8.

§ 1.468A-1. *Nuclear decommissioning costs; general rules.*

(a) Introduction.

(b) Definitions.

(c) Special rules applicable to certain experimental nuclear facilities.

(d) Special rules for electing taxpayers whose rates are under the jurisdiction of the Rural Electrification Administration.

§ 1.468A-2. *Treatment of electing taxpayer.*

(a) In general.

(b) Limitation on payments to a nuclear decommissioning fund.

　(1) In general.

　(2) Cost of service amount.

(c) Deemed payment rules.

(d) Treatment of distributions.

　(1) In general.

　(2) Exceptions to inclusion in gross income.

　　(i) Payment of administrative costs and incidental expenses.

　　(ii) Withdrawals of excess contributions.

　　(iii) Actual distributions of amounts included in gross income as deemed distributions.

(e) Deduction when economic performance occurs.

(f) Effect of interim rate orders and retroactive adjustments to such orders.

　(1) In general.

　(2) Special rule permitting withdrawal of excess contribution that results from retroactive adjustment to interim rate order.

　(3) Revised schedule of ruling amounts.

　(4) Example.

§ 1.468A-3. *Ruling amount.*

(a) In general.

(b) Level funding limitation.

(c) Funding period.

　(1) General rule.

　(2) Examples.

(d) Decommissioning costs allocable to a fund.

　(1) General rule.

　(2) Total estimated cost of decommissioning.

　(3) Taxpayer's share.

　(4) Qualifying percentage.

(e) Determination of estimated dates.

(f) Special rules in the case of rates established or approved by two or more public utility commissions.

(g) Requirement of determination by public utility commission of decommissioning costs to be included in cost of service.

(h) Manner of requesting schedule of ruling amounts.

　(1) In general.

　(2) Information required.

　(3) Administrative procedures.

(i) Review and revision of schedule of ruling amounts.

　(1) Mandatory review.

　(2) Elective review.

　(3) Determination of revised schedule of ruling amounts.

(j) Special rule permitting payments to a nuclear decommissioning fund before receipt of an initial or revised ruling amount applicable to a taxable year.

§ 1.468A-4. *Treatment of nuclear decommissioning fund.*

(a) In general.

(b) Modified gross income.

(c) Special rules.

　(1) Period for computation of modified gross income.

　(2) Gain or loss upon distribution of property by a fund.

　(3) Denial of credits against tax.

Methods of Accounting

(4) Other corporate taxes inapplicable.

(d) Treatment as corporation for purposes of subtitle F.

§ 1.468A-5. Nuclear decommissioning fund—miscellaneous provisions.

(a) Qualification requirements.

(1) In general.

(2) Limitation on contributions.

(3) Limitation on use of fund.

(i) In general.

(ii) Definition of administrative costs and expenses.

(4) Trust provisions.

(b) Prohibitions against self-dealing.

(1) In general.

(2) Self-dealing defined.

(3) Disqualified person defined.

(c) Disqualification of nuclear decommissioning fund.

(1) In general.

(2) Exception to disqualification.

(i) In general.

(ii) Excess contribution defined.

(iii) Taxation of income attributable to an excess contribution.

(3) Effect of disqualification.

(d) Termination of nuclear decommissioning fund upon substantial completion of decommissioning.

(1) In general.

(2) Substantial completion of decommissioning defined.

§ 1.468A-6. Disposition of an interest in a nuclear power plant.

(a) In general.

(b) Requirements.

(c) Tax consequences.

(1) The transferor and its Fund.

(2) The transferee and its Fund.

(3) Basis.

(d) Determination of proportionate amount.

(e) Calculation of schedule of ruling amounts for dispositions described in this section.

(1) Transferor.

(2) Transferee.

(3) Example.

(f) Calculation of the qualifying percentage after dispositions described in this section.

(1) In general.

(2) Special rule.

(g) Other.

(1) Anti-abuse provision.

(2) Relief provision.

(h) Effective date.

§ 1.468A-7. Manner of and time for making election.

(a) In general.

(b) Required information.

§ 1.468A-8. Effective date and transitional rules.

(a) Effective date.

(1) In general.

(2) Cut-off method applicable to electing taxpayers.

(b) Transitional rules.

(1) Time for filing request for schedule of ruling amounts.

(2) Manner of and time for making contributions to a nuclear decommissioning fund.

(3) Manner of and time for making election.

(4) Determination of cost of service limitation.

(5) Assumptions and determinations to be used in determining ruling amounts.

(6) Exception to level funding limitation.

(7) Determination of qualifying percentage.

(8) Limitation on payments to a nuclear decommissioning fund.

(9) Denial of interest on overpayment.

(10) Determination of addition to tax for failure to pay estimated tax.

(11) Nuclear decommissioning fund qualification requirements.

[Reg. § 1.468A-0.]

☐ [T.D. 8184, 2-29-88. Amended by T.D. 8461, 12-29-92 and T.D. 8580, 12-23-94.]

[Reg. § 1.468A-1]

§ 1.468A-1. Nuclear decommissioning costs; general rules.—(a) *Introduction.* Section 468A provides an elective method for taking into account nuclear decommissioning costs for Federal income tax purposes. In general, an eligible taxpayer that elects the application of section 468A pursuant to the rules contained in § 1.468A-7 is allowed a deduction (as determined under § 1.468A-2) for the taxable year in which the taxpayer makes a cash payment to a nuclear decommissioning fund. Taxpayers using an accrual method of accounting that do not elect the application of section 468A are not allowed a deduction for nuclear decommissioning costs prior to the taxable year in which economic performance occurs with respect to such costs (see section 461(h)).

(b) *Definitions*. The following terms are defined for purposes of section 468A and the regulations thereunder:

(1) The term "eligible taxpayer" means any taxpayer that possesses a qualifying interest in a nuclear power plant (including a nuclear power plant that is under construction).

(2) The term "qualifying interest" means—

(i) A direct ownership interest; and

(ii) A leasehold interest in any portion of a nuclear power plant if—

(A) The holder of the leasehold interest is subject to the jurisdiction of a public utility commission with respect to such portion of the nuclear power plant;

(B) The holder of the leasehold interest is primarily liable under Federal or State law for decommissioning such portion of the nuclear power plant; and

(C) No other person establishes a nuclear decommissioning fund with respect to such portion of the nuclear power plant.

A direct ownership interest includes an interest held as a tenant in common or joint tenant, but does not include stock in a corporation that owns a nuclear power plant or an interest in a partnership that owns a nuclear power plant. Thus, in the case of a partnership that owns a nuclear power plant, the election under section 468A must be made by the partnership and not by the partners. In the case of an unincorporated organization described in § 1.761-2(a)(3) that elects under section 761(a) to be excluded from the application of subchapter K, each taxpayer that is a co-owner of the nuclear power plant is eligible to make a separate election under section 468A.

(3) The terms "nuclear decommissioning fund" and "qualified nuclear decommissioning fund" mean a fund that satisfies the requirements of § 1.468A-5. The term "nonqualified decommissioning fund" means a fund that does not satisfy those requirements.

(4) The term "nuclear power plant" means any nuclear power reactor that is used predominantly in the trade or business of the furnishing or sale of electric energy, if the rates for the furnishing or sale, as the case may be, eithher have been established or approved by a public utility commission or are under the jurisdiction of the Rural Electrification Administration. Each unit (i.e., nuclear reactor) located on a multi-unit site is a separate nuclear power plant. The term "nuclear power plant" also includes the portion of the common facilities of a multi-unit site allocable to a unit on that site.

(5) The term "nuclear decommissioning costs" or "decommissioning costs" means all otherwise deductible expenses to be incurred in connection with the entombment, decontamination, dismantlement, removal and disposal of the structures, systems and components of a nuclear power plant that has permanently ceased the production of electric energy. Such term includes all otherwise deductible expenses to be incurred in connection with the preparation for decommissioning, such as engineering and other planning expenses, and all otherwise deductible expenses to be incurred with respect to the plant after the actual decommissioning occurs, such as physical security and radiation monitoring expenses. Such term does not include otherwise deductible expenses to be incurred in connection with the disposal of spent nuclear fuel under the Nuclear Waste Policy Act of 1982 (Pub. L. 97-425). An expense is otherwise deductible for purposes of this paragraph (b)(5) if it would be deductible under chapter 1 of the Internal Revenue Code without regard to section 280B.

(6) The term "public utility commission" means any State or political subdivision thereof, any agency, instrumentality or judicial body of the United States, or any judicial body, commission or other similar body of the District of Columbia or of any State or any political subdivision thereof that establishes or approves rates for the furnishing or sale of electric energy.

(7) The term "ratemaking proceeding" means any proceeding before a public utility commission in which rates for the furnishing or sale of electric energy are established or approved. Such term includes a generic proceeding that applies to two or more taxpayers that are subject to the jurisdiction of a single public utility commission.

(c) *Special rules applicable to certain experimental nuclear facilities.* (1) The owner of a qualifying interest in an experimental nuclear facility possesses a qualifying interest in a nuclear power plant for purposes of paragraph (b) of this section if—

(i) Such person is engaged in the trade or business of the furnishing or sale of electric energy;

(ii) The rates charged for electric energy furnished or sold by such person are established or approved by a public utility commission; and

(iii) The cost of decommissioning the facility is included in the cost of service of such person.

Reg. § 1.468A-1(b)(1)

(2) An owner of stock in a corporation that owns an experimental nuclear facility possesses a qualifying interest in a nuclear power plant for purposes of paragraph (b)(1) of this section if—

(i) Such stockholder satisfies the conditions of paragraph (c)(1)(i) through (iii) of this section; and

(ii) The corporation that directly owns the facility is not engaged in the trade or business of the furnishing or sale of electric energy.

(3) For purposes of this paragraph (c), an experimental nuclear facility is a nuclear power reactor that is used predominantly for the purpose of conducting experimentation and research.

(d) *Special rules for electing taxpayers whose rates are under the jurisdiction of the Rural Electrification Administration.* Notwithstanding any other provision of the regulations under section 468A, a schedule of ruling amounts may be provided to a taxpayer with respect to a nuclear power plant if the rates for the furnishing or sale of the plant's electricity are under the jurisdiction of the Rural Electrification Administration. This schedule will be determined on the basis of all facts and circumstances in a manner consistent with section 468A. No taxpayer will be provided a schedule of ruling amounts under section 468A for any taxable year unless the portion of the rates attributable to the decommissioning costs of that taxpayer with respect to such taxable year are treated by the taxpayer as though they were subject to section 88. [Reg. § 1.468A-1.]

☐ [*T.D.* 8184, 2-29-88. *Amended by T.D.* 8461, 12-29-92 *and T.D.* 8580, 12-23-94.]

[Reg. § 1.468A-2]

§ 1.468A-2. **Treatment of electing taxpayer.**—(a) *In general.* An eligible taxpayer that elects the application of section 468A pursuant to the rules contained in § 1.468A-7 (an "electing taxpayer") is allowed a deduction for the taxable year in which the taxpayer makes a cash payment (or is deemed to make a cash payment as provided in paragraph (c) of this section) to a nuclear decommissioning fund. The amount of the deduction for any taxable year equals the total amount of cash payments made (or deemed made) by the electing taxpayer to a nuclear decommissioning fund (or nuclear decommissioning funds) during such taxable year. A payment may not be made (or deemed made) to a nuclear decommissioning fund before the first taxable year in which all of the following conditions are satisfied:

(1) The construction of the nuclear power plant to which the nuclear decommissioning fund relates has commenced.

(2) Nuclear decommissioning costs of the nuclear power plant to which the nuclear decommissioning fund relates are included in the taxpayer's cost of service for ratemaking purposes (see paragraph (b) of this section).

(3) A ruling amount is applicable to the nuclear decommissioning fund (see § 1.468A-3).

(b) *Limitation on payments to a nuclear decommissioning fund*—(1) *In general.* For purposes of paragraph (a) of this section, the maximum amount of cash payments made (or deemed made) to a nuclear decommissioning fund during any taxable year shall not exceed the lesser of—

(i) The cost of service amount applicable to the nuclear decommissioning fund for such taxable year (as defined in paragraph (b)(2) of this section); or

(ii) The ruling amount applicable to the nuclear decommissioning fund for such taxable year (as determined under § 1.468A-3).

If the amount of cash payments made (or deemed made) to a nuclear decommissioning fund during any taxable year exceeds the limitation of this paragraph (b)(1), the excess is not deductible by the electing taxpayer. In addition, see paragraph (c) of § 1.468A-5 for rules which provide that the Internal Revenue Service may disqualify a nuclear decommissioning fund if the amount of cash payments made (or deemed made) to a nuclear decommissioning fund during any taxable year exceeds the limitation of this paragraph (b)(1).

(2) *Cost of service amount.* (i) For purposes of section 468A and the regulations thereunder, the "cost of service amount applicable to a nuclear decommissioning fund for a taxable year" is the amount of decommissioning costs included in the electing taxpayer's cost of service for ratemaking purposes for such taxable year. Decommissioning costs are included in cost of service for a taxable year only to the extent such costs are directly or indirectly charged to customers of the taxpayer by reason of electric energy consumed during such taxable year or are otherwise required to be included in the taxpayer's income under section 88 and the regulations thereunder.

(ii) Except as otherwise provided in paragraph (b)(4)(i) of § 1.468A-8 (relating to a special transitional rule), decommissioning costs shall generally not be considered included in cost of service for purposes of this section unless—

(A) The order or opinion of the applicable public utility commission identifies the amount of decommissioning costs that is included in cost of service for ratemaking purposes; or

(B) The written records of the ratemaking proceeding clearly and unambiguously indicate the amount of decommissioning costs that is included in cost of service for ratemaking purposes.

(iii) Except as otherwise provided in paragraph (f)(2) of this section (relating to a special rule that applies to certain retroactive adjustments to interim rate orders), orders or opinions of a public utility commission that are issued after the close of any taxable year shall not be considered in determining the amount of decommissioning costs included in cost of service for such taxable year.

(iv) If a taxpayer possesses a qualifying interest in two or more nuclear power plants that are the subject of a single ratemaking proceeding, the amount of decommissioning costs included in cost of service pursuant to such ratemaking proceeding must be allocated among such nuclear power plants. Such allocation must be reasonable and consistent, and must take into account the assumptions and determinations, if any, used by the public utility commission in establishing or approving the amount of decommissioning costs included in cost of service.

(c) *Deemed payment rules.*—(1) The amount of any cash payment made by an electing taxpayer to a nuclear decommissioning fund on or before the 15th day of the third calendar month after the close of any taxable year (the "deemed payment deadline date") shall be deemed made during such taxable year if the electing taxpayer irrevocably designates the amount as relating to such taxable year on its timely filed Federal income tax return for such taxable year (see paragraph (b)(4)(iv) of § 1.468A-7 for rules relating to such designation).

(2) The amount of any cash payment made by a customer of an electing taxpayer to a nuclear decommissioning fund of such electing taxpayer shall be deemed made by the electing taxpayer if the amount is included in the gross income of the electing taxpayer in the manner prescribed by section 88 and § 1.88-1.

(d) *Treatment of distributions*—(1) *In general.* Except as otherwise provided in paragraph (d)(2) of this section, the amount of any actual or deemed distribution from a nuclear decommissioning fund shall be included in the gross income of the electing taxpayer for the taxable year in which the distribution occurs. The amount of any distribution of property equals the fair market value of the property on the date of the distribution. A distribution from a nuclear decommissioning fund shall include an expenditure from the fund or the use of the fund's assets—

(i) To satisfy, in whole or in part, the liability of the electing taxpayer for decommissioning costs of the nuclear power plant to which the fund relates; and

(ii) To pay administrative costs and other incidental expenses of the fund.

See paragraphs (c) and (d) of § 1.468A-5 for rules relating to the deemed distribution of the assets of a nuclear decommissioning fund in the case of a disqualification or termination of the fund.

(2) *Exceptions to inclusion in gross income*—(i) *Payment of administrative costs and incidental expenses.* The amount of any payment by a nuclear decommissioning fund for administrative costs or other incidental expenses of such fund (as defined in paragraph (a)(3)(ii) of § 1.468A-5) shall not be included in the gross income of the electing taxpayer unless such amount is paid to the electing taxpayer (in which case the amount of the payment is included in the gross income of the electing taxpayer under section 61).

(ii) *Withdrawals of excess contributions.* The amount of a withdrawal of an excess contribution (as defined in paragraph (c)(2)(ii) of § 1.468A-5) by an electing taxpayer pursuant to the rules of paragraph (c) (2) of § 1.468A-5 shall not be included in the gross income of the electing taxpayer. See paragraph (b)(1) of this section, which provides that the payment of such amount to the nuclear decommissioning fund is not deductible by the electing taxpayer.

(iii) *Actual distributions of amounts included in gross income as deemed distributions.* If the amount of a deemed distribution is included in the gross income of the electing taxpayer for the taxable year in which the deemed distribution occurs, no further amount is required to be included in gross income when the amount of the deemed distribution is actually distributed by the nuclear decommissioning fund. The amount of a deemed distribution is actually distributed by a nuclear decommissioning fund as the first actual distributions are made by the nuclear decommissioning fund on or after the date of the deemed distribution.

(e) *Deduction when economic performance occurs.* An electing taxpayer using an accrual method of accounting is allowed a deduction for nuclear decommissioning costs no earlier than the taxable year in which economic performance occurs with respect to such costs (see section 461(h)(2)). The amount of nuclear decommissioning costs that is deductible under this paragraph (e) is determined without regard to section 280B (see paragraph (b)(5) of § 1.468A-1). A deduction is allowed under this paragraph (e) whether or not a deduction was allowed with respect to such costs under section 468A(a) and paragraph (a) of this section for an earlier taxable year (see paragraph (a)(2) of § 1.468A-8, however, for the effective date applicable to this paragraph (e)).

(f) *Effect of interim rate orders and retroactive adjustments to such orders*—(1) *In general.* (i) The amount of decommissioning costs included in cost of service for any taxable year that ends before the date of a retroactive adjustment to an interim rate order or interim determination of a public utility commission shall include amounts authorized pursuant to such interim rate order or interim determination unless a taxpayer elects the application of paragraph (f)(2) of this section for such taxable year. For purposes of this paragraph (f), a retroactive adjustment occurs on the effective date of the revised rate schedule that implements the retroactive adjustment.

(ii) If a retroactive adjustment to an interim rate order or interim determination reduces the amount of decommissioning costs included in cost of service for one or more taxable years ending before the date of the adjustment, the amount of such reduction must be subtracted from the amount of decommissioning costs included in cost of service (as determined under paragraph (b)(2) of this section) for one or more taxable years ending on or after the date of the adjustment. For this purpose, the amount of such reduction must be taken into account in the following manner:

(A) If the retroactive adjustment reduces the amount of decommissioning costs included in cost of service for one taxable year ending before the date of the adjustment, the total amount of the reduction must be taken into account for the taxable year that includes the date of the adjustment.

(B) If the retroactive adjustment reduces the amount of decommissioning costs included in cost of service for two taxable years ending before the date of the adjustment, at least one-half of the total amount of the reduction must be taken into account for the first taxable year ending on or after the date of the adjustment and the total amount of the reduction must be taken into account over the first two taxable years ending on or after the date of the adjustment.

(C) If the retroactive adjustment reduces the amount of decommissioning costs included in cost of service for three or more taxable years ending before the date of the adjustment, at least one-third of the total amount of the reduction must be taken into account for the first taxable year ending on or after the date of the adjustment, at least two-thirds of the total amount of the reduction must be taken into account over the first two taxable years ending on or after the date of the adjustment, and the total amount of the reduction must be taken into account over the first three taxable years ending on or after the date of the adjustment.

(2) *Special rule permitting withdrawal of excess contribution that results from retroactive adjustment to interim rate order.* (i) If a retroactive adjustment that reduces the amount of decommissioning costs included in cost of service for a taxable year occurs on or before the date prescribed by law (including extensions) for filing the return of the nuclear decommissioning fund for such taxable year, a taxpayer may elect the application of this paragraph (f)(2) for such taxable year by—

(A) Including in the amount of decommissioning costs included in cost of service for such taxable year only the amount of decommissioning costs authorized for such taxable year under the retroactive adjustment; and

(B) Withdrawing any excess contribution that results from such treatment in accordance with the rules of paragraph (c)(2) of § 1.468A-5.

(ii) If a taxpayer elects the application of this paragraph (f)(2) for any taxable year, the retroactive adjustment shall not be treated for purposes of paragraph (f)(1)(ii) of this section as a reduction in the amount of decommissioning costs included in cost of service for such taxable year.

(3) *Revised schedule of ruling amounts.* (i) If the rules provided in this paragraph (f) result in a cost of service amount applicable to a nuclear decommissioning fund for any taxable year that is less than the cost of service amount applicable to the nuclear decommissioning fund for the immediately preceding taxable year, the taxpayer must request a revised schedule of ruling amounts on or before the deemed payment deadline date for the taxable year in which the retroactive adjustment occurs. The first taxable year to which the revised schedule of ruling amount applies shall be the taxable year in which the retroactive adjustment occurs.

(ii) The requirement of this paragraph (f)(3) does not apply if the taxpayer determines its schedule of ruling amounts under a formula or method obtained under § 1.468A-3(a)(4) and the cost of service amount is a variable element of that formula or method.

(4) *Example.* The following example illustrates the application of the principles of this paragraph (f):

Example. (i) X corporation is a calendar year, accrual method taxpayer engaged in the sale of electric energy generated by a nuclear power plant owned by X. During 1989, X is authorized pursuant to an interim rate order issued by the

Reg. § 1.468A-2(f)(4)

public utility commission of State A to collect nuclear decommissioning costs of $500,000 per year beginning on January 1, 1990. On May 1, 1992, the public utility commission of State A issues a final rate order that is effective on July 1, 1992. The final rate order authorizes X to collect decommissioning costs of $400,000 per year and requires X to refund to the ratepayers of State A excess decommissioning costs of $250,000 collected between January 1, 1990, and July 1, 1992.

(ii) If X elects the application of paragraph (f)(2) of this section for the 1991 taxable year, the amount of decommissioning costs included in cost of service for such taxable year is $400,000. If X made a contribution of $500,000 to a nuclear decommissioning fund for the 1991 taxable year, X must withdraw $100,000 from the nuclear decommissioning fund on or before the date prescribed by law (including extensions) for filing the return of the nuclear decommissioning fund for the 1991 taxable year (see paragraph (c)(2) of § 1.468A-5).

(iii) In addition, under paragraph (f)(1)(i) of this section, the amount of decommissioning costs included in cost of service for the 1990 taxable year is $500,000, and, under paragraph (f)(1)(ii) of this section, the amount of decommissioning costs included in cost of service for the 1992 taxable year is $300,000. Because the cost of service amount for the 1991 taxable year ($400,000) is less than the cost of service amount for the 1990 taxable year ($500,000), paragraph (f)(3) of this section applies and X must file a request for a revised schedule of ruling amounts for the period beginning with the 1992 taxable year on or before March 15, 1993.

(iv) Alternatively, if X does not elect the application of paragraph (f)(2) of this section for the 1991 taxable year, under paragraph (f)(1)(i) of this section, the amount of decommissioning costs included in cost of service for the 1990 and 1991 taxable years is $500,000, and, under paragraph (f)(1)(ii) of this section, the amount of decommissioning costs included in cost of service for the 1992 taxable year may not exceed $300,000. Because the cost of service amount for the 1992 taxable year is less than the cost of service amount for the 1991 taxable year, paragraph (f)(3) of this section applies and X must file a request for a revised schedule of ruling amounts for the period beginning with the 1992 taxable year on or before March 15, 1993. [Reg. § 1.468A-2.]

☐ [T.D. 8184, 2-29-88. Amended by T.D. 8461, 12-29-92 and T.D. 8758, 1-16-98.]

Reg. § 1.468A-3(a)(1)

[Reg. § 1.468A-3]

§ 1.468A-3. Ruling amount.—(a) *In general.*—(1) Except as otherwise provided in paragraph (j) of this section, an electing taxpayer is allowed a deduction under section 468A(a) for the taxable year in which the taxpayer makes a cash payment (or is deemed to make a cash payment) to a nuclear decommissioning fund only if the taxpayer has received a schedule of ruling amounts for the nuclear decommissioning fund that includes a ruling amount for such taxable year. Except as provided in paragraph (a)(4) or (5) of this section, a schedule of ruling amounts for a nuclear decommissioning fund ("schedule of ruling amounts") is a ruling (within the meaning of paragraph (a)(2) of § 601.201) specifying the annual payments ("ruling amounts") that, over the taxable years remaining in the "funding period" as of the date the schedule first applies, will result in a projected balance of the nuclear decommissioning fund as of the last day of the funding period equal to (and in no event greater than) the "amount of decommissioning costs allocable to the fund." The projected balance of a nuclear decommissioning fund as of the last day of the funding period shall be calculated by taking into account the fair market value of the assets of the fund as of the first day of the first taxable year to which the schedule of ruling amounts applies and the estimated rate of return to be earned by the assets of the fund after payment of the estimated administrative costs and incidental expenses to be incurred by the fund (as defined in paragraph (a)(3)(ii) of § 1.468A-5), including all Federal, State and local income taxes to be incurred by the fund (the "after-tax rate of return"). See paragraph (c) of this section for a definition of funding period and paragraph (d) of this section for guidance with respect to the amount of decommissioning costs allocable to a fund.

(2) To the extent consistent with the principles and provisions of this section, each schedule of ruling amounts shall be based on the reasonable assumptions and determinations used by the applicable public utility commission(s) in establishing or approving the amount of decommissioning costs to be included in cost of service for ratemaking purposes, taking into account amounts that are otherwise required to be included in the taxpayer's income under section 88 and the regulations thereunder. Thus, for example, each schedule of ruling amounts shall be based on the public utility commission's reasonable assumptions concerning—

(i) The after-tax rate of return to be earned by the amounts collected for decommissioning;

(ii) The total estimated cost of decommissioning the nuclear power plant (see paragraph (d)(2) of this section); and

(iii) The frequency of contributions to a nuclear decommissioning fund for a taxable year (*e.g.*, monthly, quarterly, semi-annual or annual contributions).

(3) The Internal Revenue Service shall provide a schedule of ruling amounts that is identical to the schedule of ruling amounts proposed by the taxpayer in connection with the taxpayer's request for a schedule of ruling amounts (see paragraph (h)(2)(viii) of this section), but no schedule of ruling amounts shall be provided unless the taxpayer's proposed schedule of ruling amounts is consistent with the principles and provisions of this section. If a proposed schedule of ruling amounts is not consistent with the principles and provisions of this section, the taxpayer may propose an amended schedule of ruling amounts that is consistent with such principles and provisions.

(4) The Internal Revenue Service will approve, at the request of the taxpayer, a formula or method for determining a schedule of ruling amounts (rather than a schedule specifying a dollar amount for each taxable year) that is consistent with the principles and provisions of this section. See paragraph (i)(1)(ii) of this section for a special rule relating to the mandatory review of ruling amounts that are determined pursuant to a formula or method.

(5) The Internal Revenue Service may, in its discretion, provide a schedule of ruling amounts that is determined on a basis other than the rules of paragraphs (a) through (g) of this section if—

(i) In connection with its request for a schedule of ruling amounts, the taxpayer explains the need for special treatment and sets forth an alternative basis for determining the schedule of ruling amounts; and

(ii) The Internal Revenue Service determines that special treatment is consistent with the purpose of section 468A.

(b) *Level funding limitation.*—(1) Except as otherwise provided in paragraph (b)(4) of this section and paragraph (b)(6) of § 1.468A-8 (relating to a special transitional rule), the ruling amount specified in a schedule of ruling amounts for any taxable year in the level funding limitation period shall not be less than the ruling amount specified in such schedule for any earlier taxable year.

(2) For purposes of this section, the level funding limitation period for a nuclear decommissioning fund is the period that—

(i) Begins on the first day of the first taxable year for which a deductible payment is made (or deemed made) to such nuclear decommissioning fund (see paragraph (a) of § 1.468A-2 for rules relating to the first taxable year for which a payment may be made (or deemed made) to a nuclear decommissioning fund); and

(ii) Ends on the last day of the taxable year that includes the estimated date on which the nuclear power plant to which the nuclear decommissioning fund relates will no longer be included in the taxpayer's rate base for ratemaking purposes (see paragraphs (e)(2) and (4) of this section).

(3) The ruling amount specified in a schedule of ruling amounts for a taxable year after the end of the level funding limitation period may be less than the ruling amount specified in such schedule for an earlier taxable year.

(4) The ruling amount specified in a schedule of ruling amounts for the last taxable year in the level funding limitation period may be less than the ruling amount specified in such schedule for any earlier taxable year if the applicable public utility commission assumes for cost of service purposes that decommissioning costs will be included in cost of service for only a portion of the last taxable year in the level funding limitation period. The ruling amount for the last taxable year in the level funding limitation period, however, may not be less than the amount that bears the same relationship to the ruling amount for the preceding taxable year as the period for which decommissioning costs will be included in cost of service for such last taxable year bears to one year.

(c) *Funding period*—(1) *General rule.* For purposes of this section, the funding period for a nuclear decommissioning fund is the period that—

(i) Begins on the first day of the first taxable year for which a deductible payment is made (or deemed made) to such nuclear decommissioning fund (see paragraph (a)(1) of § 1.468A-2 for rules relating to the first taxable year for which a payment may be made (or deemed made) to a nuclear decommissioning fund); and

(ii) Ends on the later of—

(A) The last day of the taxable year that includes the estimated date on which decommissioning costs of the nuclear power plant to which the nuclear decommissioning fund relates will no longer be included in the taxpayer's cost of service for ratemaking purposes (see paragraph (e)(1) of this section); or

Reg. § 1.468A-3(c)(1)

(B) The last day of the taxable year that includes the estimated date on which the nuclear power plant to which the nuclear decommissioning fund relates will no longer be included in the taxpayer's rate base for ratemaking purposes (see paragraph (e)(2) of this section).

(2) *Examples.* The following examples illustrate the application of the principles of paragraphs (a), (b) and (c) of this section:

Example (1). (i) X corporation is a calendar year, accrual method taxpayer engaged in the sale of electric energy generated by power plants owned by X. On March 15, 1995, X commences the construction of a nuclear power plant in State A. On May 15, 1995, the public utility commission of State A issues a final rate order for the four-year period beginning on January 1, 1995, that authorizes X to collect decommissioning costs from ratepayers residing in State A. For the 1995 taxable year, X is authorized to collect decommissioning costs of $500,000, and, for each taxable year during the remainder of the period to which the rate order applies, X is authorized to collect decommissioning costs in an amount equal to 105 percent of the amount authorized to be collected for the preceding taxable year.

(ii) In determining the amount of decommissioning costs to be collected from ratepayers residing in State A, the public utility commission assumes that (A) decommissioning costs will be included in cost of service for each taxable year in the period that begins with 1995 and ends with 2025 and (B) decommissioning costs collected pursuant to subsequent rate orders will increase in the same manner as amounts collected pursuant to the rate order issued on May 15, 1995. In addition, in determining the rate of return to be earned by X with respect to the nuclear power plant, the public utility commission assumes that the nuclear power plant will be included in rate base for each year in the period that begins with 2000 and ends with 2025.

(iii) X requests a schedule of ruling amounts in accordance with the rules of paragraph (h) of this section for the period beginning with the 1995 taxable year. In determining the level funding limitation period and the funding period, the Internal Revenue Service shall assume that a deductible payment will be made to a nuclear decommissioning fund for the 1995 taxable year. Thus, under paragraph (b) of this section, the level funding limitation period begins on January 1, 1995, and ends on December 31, 2025. Under paragraph (c)(1) of this section, the funding period begins on January 1, 1995, and ends on December 31, 2025.

(iv) In its request for a schedule of ruling amounts, X proposes a ruling amount for each taxable year in the funding period that corresponds to the projected cost of service amount for such taxable year. If (A) the assumptions and determinations used by the public utility commission in establishing the amount of decommissioning costs to be included in cost of service are reasonable and (B) the amounts collected pursuant to the proposed schedule, combined with the after-tax earnings on such amounts, will result in a projected balance of the nuclear decommissioning fund as of December 31, 2025, equal to the amount of decommissioning costs allocable to the fund, then, under paragraph (a)(3) of this section, each ruling amount in the initial schedule of ruling amounts shall equal the ruling amount proposed by X in connection with its request for a schedule of ruling amounts. Thus, the ruling amount for the 1995 taxable year would be $500,000, and the ruling amount for each subsequent taxable year would be 105 percent of the ruling amount for the preceding taxable year.

Example (2). (i) Assume the same facts as in Example (1), except that on May 15, 1995, the public utility commission of State A issues a final rate order for the four-year period beginning on January 1, 1995, that authorizes X to collect decommissioning costs of $600,000 per year from ratepayers residing in State A. In determining the amount of decommissioning costs to be collected from ratepayers residing in State A, the public utility commission assumes that decommissioning costs of $600,000 will be collected for each taxable year in the period that begins with 1995 and ends with 2004 and that decommissioning costs of $200,000 will be collected for each taxable year in the period that begins with 2005 and ends with 2025.

(ii) X requests a schedule of ruling amounts in accordance with the rules of paragraph (h) of this section for the period beginning with the 1995 taxable year. In determining the level funding limitation period and the funding period, the Internal Revenue Service shall assume that a deductible payment will be made to a nuclear decommissioning fund for the 1995 taxable year. Thus, under paragraph (b) of this section, the level funding limitation period begins on January 1, 1995, and ends on December 31, 2025. Under paragraph (c)(1) of this section, the funding period begins on January 1, 1995, and ends on December 31, 2025.

(iii) In its request for a schedule of ruling amounts, X proposes a ruling amount for each taxable year in the funding period that corresponds to the projected cost of service amount for

Reg. § 1.468A-3(c)(2)

such taxable year. A schedule of ruling amounts based on the projected cost of service amount would be inconsistent with the level funding limitation of paragraph (b) of this section because the projected cost of service amount for 2005 is less than the projected cost of service amount for 2004. Consequently, under paragraph (a)(3) of this section, no schedule of ruling amounts shall be provided to X unless X proposes an amended schedule of ruling amounts that is consistent with the level funding limitation and the other principles and provisions of this section.

(iv) Assume that X proposes an amended schedule of ruling amounts that provides for ruling amounts of $400,000 for each taxable year in the funding period. If (A) the schedule of ruling amounts proposed by X is based on the reasonable assumptions and determinations used by the public utility commission in establishing the amount of decommissioning costs to be included in cost of service and (B) the amounts collected pursuant to the proposed schedule, combined with the after-tax earnings on such amounts, will result in a projected balance of the nuclear decommissioning fund as of December 31, 2025, equal to the amount of decommissioning costs allocable to the fund, then, under paragraph (a)(3) of this section, each ruling amount in the initial schedule of ruling amounts shall equal the ruling amount proposed by X in connection with its request for a schedule of ruling amounts. Thus, the ruling amount for the 1995 taxable year and for each subsequent taxable year through 2025 would be $400,000.

(v) Under section 468A(b) and paragraph (b)(1) of § 1.468A-2, the maximum amount of cash payments that X can make to a nuclear decommissioning fund for any taxable year shall not exceed the lesser of (A) the cost of service amount for such taxable year or (B) the ruling amount for such taxable year. If the projected cost of service amount that was assumed in determining rates under the rate order that was issued on May 15, 1995, is the actual cost of service amount for each taxable year in the funding period and the ruling amounts provided in the initial schedule of ruling amounts are not changed by a subsequent schedule of ruling amounts, then X would be allowed to make a deductible contribution of $400,000 to a nuclear decommissioning fund for each taxable year in the period that begins with 1995 and ends with 2004 and to make a deductible contribution of $200,000 to such nuclear decommissioning fund for each taxable year in the period that begins with 2005 and ends with 2025.

Example (3). (i) Y corporation is a calendar year, accrual method taxpayer engaged in the sale of electric energy generated by power plants owned by Y. On June 1, 1990, a nuclear power plant owned by Y began commercial operations in State B. In the first ratemaking proceeding in which the nuclear power plant was included in rate base, the public utility commission of State B assumed that the nuclear power plant would be included in rate base for each year in the period that began with 1990 and ended with 2020. In addition, for each taxable year in the period that began with 1990 and ended with 2017, Y made a deductible contribution of $750,000 to a nuclear decommissioning fund established by Y. The $750,000 contribution equalled the cost of service amount and the ruling amount for each taxable year in the 28-year period.

(ii) On August 30, 2017, the public utility commission of State B issues a final rate order for the six-year period beginning on January 1, 2018, that authorizes Y to collect decommissioning costs of: (A) $500,000 for 2018, 2019 and 2020; (B) $1,500,000 for 2021; (C) $1,000,000 for 2022; and (D) $750,000 for 2023. In determining the amount of decommissioning costs to be collected from ratepayers residing in State B, the public utility commission assumes that decommissioning costs will no longer be included in cost of service after 2023. In addition, in determining the rate of return to be earned by Y with respect to the nuclear power plant, the public utility commission assumes that the nuclear power plant will no longer be included in rate base after 2020.

(iii) Under paragraph (i)(1)(iii) of this section, Y is required to request a revised schedule of ruling amounts on or before March 15, 2019. Assume that Y makes a timely request for a revised schedule of ruling amounts in accordance with the rules of paragraph (h) of this section. In its request, Y proposes a ruling amount for each taxable year in the period that begins with 2018 and ends with 2023 that corresponds to the amount of decommissioning costs to be included in cost of service under the rate order of August 30, 2017.

(iv) Under paragraph (b) of this section, the level funding limitation period begins on January 1, 1990, and ends on December 31, 2020. Under paragraph (c)(1) of this section, the funding period begins on January 1, 1990, and ends on December 31, 2023.

(v) If (A) the assumptions and determinations used by the public utility commission in establishing the amount of decommissioning costs to be included in cost of service are reasonable and (B) the projected balance of the nuclear

Reg. § 1.468A-3(c)(2)

decommissioning fund as of December 31, 2023 (taking into account the fair market value of the assets of the fund as of January 1, 2018, and the estimated after-tax rate of return to be earned by the assets of the fund) will equal the amount of decommissioning costs allocable to the fund, then, under paragraph (a)(3) of this section, each ruling amount in the revised schedule of ruling amounts shall equal the ruling amount proposed by Y in connection with its request for a schedule of ruling amounts. Thus, the ruling amount for 2018, 2019 and 2020 would be $500,000, the ruling amount for 2021 would be $1,500,000, the ruling amount for 2022 would be $1,000,000 and the ruling amount for 2023 would be $750,000.

(vi) Although the ruling amount specified in the revised schedule of ruling amounts for 2018, 2019 and 2020 is less than a ruling amount specified in a prior schedule of ruling amounts for years prior to 2018, the revised schedule of ruling amounts is consistent with the level funding limitation. Under paragraph (i)(3) of this section, a ruling amount specified in a revised schedule of ruling amounts for any taxable year in the level funding limitation period may be less than one or more ruling amounts specified in a prior schedule of ruling amounts for a prior taxable year. In addition, although the ruling amount specified in the revised schedule of ruling amounts for 2022 and 2023 is less than a ruling amount specified in such schedule for a prior taxable year, the revised schedule of ruling amounts is consistent with the level funding limitation because the level funding limitation period ends on December 31, 2020.

(d) *Decommissioning costs allocable to a fund.* The amount of decommissioning costs allocable to a nuclear decommissioning fund is determined for purposes of this section by applying the following rules and definitions:

(1) *General rule.* The amount of decommissioning costs allocable to a nuclear decommissioning fund is the taxpayer's share of the total estimated cost of decommissioning the nuclear power plant to which the fund relates, multiplied by the qualifying percentage.

(2) *Total estimated cost of decommissioning.* (i) Except as otherwise provided in paragraph (d)(2)(ii) of this section, the total estimated cost of decommissioning a nuclear power plant is the reasonably estimated cost of decommissioning used by the applicable public utility commission in establishing or approving the amount of decommissioning costs to be included in cost of service for ratemaking purposes. If, in establishing or approving the amount of decommissioning costs to be included in cost of service, the public utility commission uses an estimated cost of decommissioning that is equal to a generic estimate of the cost of decommissioning as determined by the Nuclear Regulatory Commission (or an estimated cost that is based on the generic estimate adjusted for inflation), the Internal Revenue Service may, at its discretion, accept such amount as a reasonable estimate of the cost of decommissioning. In addition, if the estimated costs used by the applicable public utility commission are expected to be paid in any taxable year other than the taxable year that includes the last day of the funding period or the immediately succeeding taxable year, such costs must be adjusted (increased or decreased, as the case may be) by discounting or compounding such costs at the after-tax rate of return from the date such costs are expected to be paid to the last day of the funding period.

(ii) If, in establishing or approving the amount of decommissioning costs to be included in cost of service, the applicable public utility commission assumes a projected balance of amounts set aside for decommissioning (whether or not such amounts are provided by a nuclear decommissioning fund) that is less than the total estimated cost of decommissioning assumed by the public utility commission, the total estimated cost of decommissioning for purposes of determining the schedule of ruling amounts shall equal the projected balance of amounts set aside for decommissioning that was assumed by the public utility commission.

(3) *Taxpayer's share.* The taxpayer's share of the total estimated cost of decommissioning a nuclear power plant equals the total estimated cost of decommissioning such nuclear power plant multiplied by the percentage of such nuclear power plant that the qualifying interest of the taxpayer represents (see paragraph (b)(2) of § 1.468A-1 for circumstances in which a taxpayer possesses a qualifying interest in a nuclear power plant).

(4) *Qualifying percentage.* (i) Except as otherwise provided in paragraph (b)(7)(iii) of § 1.468A-8 (relating to a special transitional rule), the qualifying percentage for any nuclear decommissioning fund is equal to the fraction, the numerator of which is the number of taxable years in the estimated period for which the nuclear decommissioning fund is to be in effect and the denominator of which is the number of taxable years in the estimated useful life of the applicable nuclear power plant.

(ii) Except as otherwise provided in paragraph (b)(7)(i) or (ii) of § 1.468A-8 (relating to special transitional rules), the estimated period for which a nuclear decommissioning fund is to be in effect—

Reg. § 1.468A-3(d)(1)

(A) Begins on the later of—

(*1*) The first day of the first taxable year for which a deductible payment is made (or deemed made) to such nuclear decommissioning fund; or

(*2*) The first day of the taxable year that includes the date that the nuclear power plant to which such nuclear decommissioning fund relates begins commercial operations; and

(B) Ends on the last day of the taxable year that includes the estimated date on which the nuclear power plant to which such nuclear decommissioning fund relates will no longer be included in the taxpayer's rate base for ratemaking purposes (see paragraph (e)(3) and (4) of this section).

(iii) Except as otherwise provided in paragraph (b)(7)(ii) of § 1.468A-8 (relating to a special transitional rule), the estimated useful life of a nuclear power plant—

(A) Begins on the first day of the taxable year that includes the date that the nuclear power plant begins commercial operations; and

(B) Ends on the last day of the taxable year that includes the estimated date on which the nuclear power plant will no longer be included in the taxpayer's rate base for ratemaking purposes (see paragraph (e)(3) and (4) of this section).

(e) *Determination of estimated dates.*—(1) For purposes of paragraph (c)(1)(ii)(A) of this section (relating to the funding period), the estimated date on which decommissioning costs of the nuclear power plant to which the nuclear decommissioning fund relates will no longer be included in the taxpayer's cost of service for ratemaking purposes is determined under the ratemaking assumptions that were used to determine the last rates (whether interim or final) that were established or approved by the applicable public utility commission prior to the filing of the current request for a schedule of ruling amounts.

(2) For purposes of paragraphs (b)(2)(ii) and (c)(1)(ii)(B) of this section (relating to the level funding limitation period and the funding period), the estimated date on which the nuclear power plant to which the nuclear decommissioning fund relates will no longer be included in the taxpayer's rate base for ratemaking purposes is determined under the ratemaking assumptions that were used to determine the last rates (whether interim or final) that were established or approved by the applicable public utility commission prior to the filing of the current request for a schedule of ruling amounts.

(3) For purposes of paragraph (d)(4)(ii)(B) and (iii)(B) of this section (relating to the qualifying percentage), the estimated date on which the nuclear power plant to which the nuclear decommissioning fund relates will no longer be included in the taxpayer's rate base for ratemaking purposes is determined under the ratemaking assumptions used by the applicable public utility commission in establishing or approving rates during the first ratemaking proceeding in which the nuclear power plant was included in the taxpayer's rate base.

(4) For purposes of this section, in the case of a taxpayer whose interest in the nuclear power plant is described in paragraph (b)(2)(ii) of § 1.468A-1, the date corresponding to "the estimated date on which the nuclear power plant to which the nuclear decommissioning fund relates will no longer be included in the taxpayer's rate base" will be determined upon the basis of all the facts and circumstances in a manner consistent with the provisions of this section and section 468A of the Code.

(5) A formula or method obtained under paragraph (a)(4) of this section may provide for changes in an estimated date described in paragraph (e)(1) or (2) of this section to reflect changes in the ratemaking assumptions used to determine rates (whether interim or final) that are established or approved by the applicable public utility commission after the filing of the request for approval of a formula or method.

(f) *Special rules in the case of rates established or approved by two or more public utility commissions.* If two or more public utility commissions establish or approve rates for electric energy generated by a single nuclear power plant, the following rules shall apply in determining the schedule of ruling amounts for the nuclear decommissioning fund that relates to such nuclear power plant.

(1) A schedule of ruling amounts shall be separately determined pursuant to the rules of paragraphs (a) through (e) of this section for each public utility commission that has determined the amount of decommissioning costs to be included in cost of service for ratemaking purposes with respect to such nuclear power plant (see paragraph (g) of this section).

(2) The separate determination with respect to a public utility commission shall be based on the reasonable assumptions and determinations used by such public utility commission and shall take into account only that portion of the total estimated cost of decommissioning the nuclear power plant that is properly allocable to the ratepayers whose rates are established or approved by such public utility commission.

Reg. § 1.468A-3(f)(2)

(3) The ruling amount applicable to the nuclear decommissioning fund for any taxable year is the sum of the ruling amounts for such taxable year determined under the separate schedules of ruling amounts.

(4) The schedule of ruling amounts for the nuclear decommissioning fund is the schedule of the ruling amounts determined under paragraph (f)(3) of this section.

(g) *Requirement of determination by public utility commission of decommissioning costs to be included in cost of service.* The Internal Revenue Service shall not provide a taxpayer with a schedule of ruling amounts for any nuclear decommissioning fund unless a public utility commission that establishes or approves rates for electric energy generated by the nuclear power plant to which the nuclear decommissioning fund relates has—

(1) Determined the amount of decommissioning costs of such nuclear power plant to be included in the taxpayer's cost of service for ratemaking purposes; and

(2) Disclosed the after-tax return and any other assumptions and determinations used in establishing or approving such amount for any taxable year beginning on or after January 1, 1987.

(h) *Manner of requesting schedule of ruling amounts*—(1) *In general.* (i) In order to receive a ruling amount for any taxable year, a taxpayer must file a request for a schedule of ruling amounts that complies with the requirements of this paragraph (h), the applicable procedural rules set forth in paragraph (e) of § 601.201 (Statement of Procedural Rules) and the requirements of any applicable revenue procedure that is in effect on the date the request is filed.

(ii) A separate request for a schedule of ruling amounts is required for each nuclear decommissioning fund established by a taxpayer (see paragraph (a) of § 1.468A-5 for rules relating to the number of nuclear decommissioning funds that a taxpayer can establish).

(iii) Except as provided by § 1.468A-5(a)(1)(iv) (relating to certain unincorporated organizations that may be taxable as corporations), a request for a schedule of ruling amounts must not contain a request for a ruling on any other issue, whether the issue involves section 468A or another section of the Internal Revenue Code.

(iv) In the case of an affiliated group of corporations that join in the filing of a consolidated return, the common parent of the group may request a schedule of ruling amounts for each member of the group that possesses a qualifying interest in the same nuclear power plant by filing a single submission with the Internal Revenue Service.

(v) Except as otherwise provided in paragraph (b)(1) of § 1.468A-8, the Internal Revenue Service shall not provide or revise a ruling amount applicable to a taxable year in response to a request for a schedule of ruling amounts that is filed after the deemed payment deadline date (as defined in paragraph (c)(1) of § 1.468A-2) for such taxable year. In determining the date when a request is filed, the principles of sections 7502 and 7503 shall apply.

(vi) Except as provided in paragraph (h)(1)(vii) of this section, a request for a schedule of ruling amounts shall be considered filed only if such request complies substantially with the requirements of this paragraph (h).

(vii) (A) If a request does not comply substantially with the requirements of this paragraph (h), the Internal Revenue Service will notify the taxpayer of that fact. If the information or materials necessary to comply substantially with the requirements of this paragraph (h) are provided to the Internal Revenue Service within 30 days after this notification, the request will be considered filed on the date of the original submission. If the information or materials necessary to comply substantially with the requirements of this paragraph (h) are not provided within 30 days after this notification, the request will be considered filed on the date that all information or materials necessary to comply with the requirements of this paragraph (h) are provided.

(B) The Internal Revenue Service may waive the requirements of paragraph (h)(1)(vii)(A) of this section if the Service determines that the electing taxpayer is making a good faith effort to comply with the deadline and if the waiver is consistent with the purposes of section 468A.

(2) *Information required.* A request for a schedule of ruling amounts must contain the following information:

(i) The taxpayer's name, address and taxpayer identification number.

(ii) Whether the request is for an initial schedule of ruling amounts, a mandatory review of the schedule of ruling amounts (see paragraph (i)(1) of this section) or an elective review of the schedule of ruling amounts (see paragraph (i)(2) of this section).

(iii) The name and location of the nuclear power plant with respect to which a schedule of ruling amounts is requested.

(iv) A description of the taxpayer's qualifying interest in the nuclear power plant and the percentage of such nuclear power plant that the qualifying interest of the taxpayer represents.

(v) An identification of each public utility commission that establishes or approves rates for the furnishing or sale by the taxpayer of electric energy generated by the nuclear power plant, and, for each public utility commission identified—

(A) Whether the public utility commission has determined the amount of decommissioning costs to be included in the taxpayer's cost of service for ratemaking purposes; and

(B) Whether a proceeding is pending before the public utility commission that may result in an increase or decrease in the amount of decommissioning costs to be included in cost of service.

(vi) For each public utility commission that has determined the amount of decommissioning costs to be included in the taxpayer's cost of service for ratemaking purposes—

(A) The amount of decommissioning costs that are to be included in the taxpayer's cost of service for each taxable year under the current determination and amounts that otherwise are required to be included in the taxpayer's income under section 88 and the regulations thereunder;

(B) A description of the assumptions, estimates and other factors that were used in determining the amounts described in paragraph (h)(2)(vi)(A) of this section, including each of the following if applicable—

(1) A description of the proposed method of decommissioning the nuclear power plant (for example, prompt removal/dismantlement, safe storage entombment with delayed dismantlement, or safe storage mothballing with delayed dismantlement);

(2) The estimated year in which substantial decommissioning costs will first be incurred;

(3) The estimated year in which the decommissioning of the nuclear power plant will be substantially complete (see paragraph (d)(2) of § 1.468A-5 for a definition of substantial completion of decommissioning);

(4) The total estimated cost of decommissioning expressed in current dollars (i.e., based on price levels in effect at the time of the current determination);

(5) The total estimated cost of decommissioning expressed in future dollars (i.e., based on anticipated price levels when expenses are expected to be paid);

(6) For each taxable year in the period that begins with the year specified in paragraph (h)(2)(vi)(B)(2) of this section ("the estimated year in which substantial decommissioning costs will first be incurred") and ends with the year specified in paragraph (h)(2)(vi)(B)(3) of this section ("the estimated year in which the decommissioning of the nuclear power plant will be substantially complete"), the estimated cost of decommissioning expressed in future dollars;

(7) A description of the methodology used in converting the estimated cost of decommissioning expressed in current dollars to the estimated cost of decommissioning expressed in future dollars;

(8) The assumed after-tax rate of return to be earned by the amounts collected for decommissioning (if two or more after-tax rates of return are assumed by the public utility commission, each assumed after-tax rate of return and the amounts collected for decommissioning to which each assumed after-tax rate of return applies);

(9) The proposed period over which decommissioning costs will be included in the cost of service of the taxpayer and the projected amount that will be included in cost of service for each taxable year in the proposed period;

(10) The estimated date on which the nuclear power plant will no longer be included in the taxpayer's rate base for ratemaking purposes as determined under the ratemaking assumptions that were used to determine the last rates (whether interim or final) that were established or approved by the applicable public utility commission prior to the filing of the current request for a schedule of ruling amounts (or a corresponding date in the case of a taxpayer whose interest in the nuclear power plant is described in paragraph (b)(2)(ii) of § 1.468A-1; see paragraph (e)(4) of this section); and

(11) The estimated date on which the nuclear power plant will no longer be included in the taxpayer's rate base for ratemaking purposes as determined under the ratemaking assumptions that were used by the applicable public utility commission in establishing or approving rates during the first ratemaking proceeding in which the nuclear power plant was included in the taxpayer's rate base (or a corresponding date in the case of a taxpayer whose interest in the nuclear power plant is described in paragraph (b)(2)(ii) of § 1.468A-1; see paragraph (e)(4) of this section);

(C) A copy of such portions of any order or opinion of the public utility commission as pertain to the commission's most recent determi-

Reg. § 1.468A-3(h)(2)

nation of the amount of decommissioning costs to be included in cost of service; and

(D) A copy of each engineering or cost study that was relied on or used by the taxpayer or the public utility commission in determining the amount of decommissioning costs to be included in the taxpayer's cost of service under the current determination.

(vii) For each proceeding pending before a public utility commission that may result in an increase or decrease in the amount of decommissioning costs to be included in the taxpayer's cost of service—

(A) A description of the stage of the proceeding;

(B) The amount of decommissioning costs that are proposed to be included in the taxpayer's cost of service for each taxable year;

(C) A description of the assumptions, estimates and other factors that were used in determining the amount of decommissioning costs that are proposed to be included in the taxpayer's cost of service for each taxable year, including each of the items described in paragraph (h)(2)(vi)(B) of this section if applicable; and

(D) A copy of each engineering or cost study that was relied on or used by the taxpayer or the public utility commission in determining the amount of decommissioning costs that are proposed to be included in the taxpayer's cost of service.

(viii) A proposed schedule of ruling amounts for each taxable year remaining in the funding period as of the date the schedule of ruling amounts will first apply.

(ix) A description of the assumptions, estimates and other factors that were used in determining the proposed schedule of ruling amounts, including each of the following if applicable—

(A) The level funding limitation period (as such term is defined in paragraph (b)(2) of this section);

(B) The funding period (as such term is defined in paragraph (c) of this section);

(C) The assumed after-tax rate of return to be earned by the assets of the nuclear decommissioning fund;

(D) The fair market value of the assets (if any) of the nuclear decommissioning fund as of the first day of the first taxable year to which the schedule of ruling amounts will apply;

(E) The amount expected to be earned by the assets of the nuclear decommissioning fund (based on the after-tax rate of return applicable to the fund) over the period that begins on the first day of the first taxable year to which the schedule of ruling amounts will apply and ends on the last day of the funding period;

(F) The amount of decommissioning costs allocable to the nuclear decommissioning fund (as determined under paragraph (d) of this section);

(G) The total estimated cost of decommissioning (as such term is defined in paragraph (d)(2) of this section);

(H) The taxpayer's share of the total estimated cost of decommissioning (as such term is defined in paragraph (d)(3) of this section);

(I) The qualifying percentage (as such term is defined in paragraph (d)(4)(i) of this section);

(J) The estimated period for which the nuclear decommissioning fund is to be in effect (as such term is defined in paragraph (d)(4)(ii) of this section); and

(K) The estimated useful life of the nuclear power plant (as such term is defined in paragraph (d)(4)(iii) of this section).

(x) If the request is for a revised schedule of ruling amounts, the after-tax rate of return earned by the assets of the nuclear decommissioning fund for each taxable year in the period that begins with the date of the initial contribution to the fund and ends with the first day of the first taxable year to which the revised schedule of ruling amounts applies.

(xi) If applicable, an explanation of the need for a schedule of ruling amounts determined on a basis other than the rules of paragraphs (a) through (g) of this section and a description of an alternative basis for determining a schedule of ruling amounts (see paragraph (a)(5) of this section).

(xii) A chart or table, based upon the assumed after-tax rate of return to be earned by the assets of the nuclear decommissioning fund, setting forth the years the fund will be in existence, the annual contribution to the fund, the estimated annual earnings of the fund and the cumulative total balance in the fund.

(xiii) If the request is for a revised schedule of ruling amounts, a copy of the most recently issued schedule of ruling amounts for the nuclear power plant to which the request relates that has been issued to the taxpayer (or a predecessor in interest) making the request.

(xiv) If the request for a schedule of ruling amounts contains a request, pursuant to § 1.468A-5(a)(1)(iv), that the Service rule whether an unincorporated organization through which the assets of the fund are invested is an association

Reg. § 1.468A-3(h)(2)

taxable as a corporation for federal tax purposes, a copy of the legal documents establishing or otherwise governing the organization.

(xv) Any other information required by the Internal Revenue Service that may be necessary or useful in determining the schedule of ruling amounts.

(3) *Administrative procedures.* The Internal Revenue Service may prescribe administrative procedures that supplement the provisions of paragraph (h)(1) and (2) of this section. In addition, the Internal Revenue Service may, in its discretion, waive the requirements of paragraph (h)(1) and (2) of this section under appropriate circumstances.

(i) *Review and revision of schedule of ruling amounts*—(1) *Mandatory review.* (i) Any taxpayer that has obtained a schedule of ruling amounts pursuant to paragraph (h) of this section must file a request for a revised schedule of ruling amounts on or before the deemed payment deadline date for the 10th taxable year that begins after the taxable year in which the most recent schedule of ruling amounts was received. The first taxable year to which the revised schedule of ruling amounts applies shall be the 10th taxable year that begins after the taxable year in which the most recent schedule of ruling amounts was received.

(ii)(A) Any taxpayer that has obtained a formula or method for determining a schedule of ruling amounts for any taxable year under paragraph (a)(4) of this section must file a request for a revised schedule on or before the earlier of the deemed payment deadline for the fifth taxable year that begins after its taxable year in which the most recent formula or method was approved or the deemed payment deadline for the first taxable year that begins after a taxable year in which there is a substantial variation in the ruling amount determined under the most recent formula or method. There is a substantial variation in the ruling amount determined under the formula or method in effect for a taxable year if the ruling amount for the year and the ruling amount for any earlier year since the most recent formula or method was approved differ by more than 50 percent of the smaller amount.

(B) Any taxpayer that has determined its ruling amount for any taxable year under a formula prescribed by § 1.468A-6 (which prescribes ruling amounts for the taxable year in which there is a disposition of a qualifying interest in a nuclear power plant) must file a request for a revised schedule of ruling amounts on or before the deemed payment deadline for its first taxable year that begins after the disposition.

(iii) A taxpayer is required to request a revised schedule of ruling amounts for a nuclear decommissioning fund if—

(A) Any public utility commission that establishes or approves rates for the furnishing or sale of electric energy generated by a nuclear power plant to which the nuclear decommissioning fund relates—

(*1*) Increases the proposed period over which decommissioning costs of such nuclear power plant will be included in cost of service for ratemaking purposes;

(*2*) Adjusts the estimated date on which such nuclear power plant will no longer be included in the taxpayer's rate base for ratemaking purposes; or

(*3*) Reduces the amount of decommissioning costs to be included in cost of service for any taxable year;

(B) The taxpayer's most recent request for a schedule of ruling amounts did not provide notice to the Internal Revenue Service of such action by the public utility commission; and

(C) In the case of a taxpayer that determines its schedule of ruling amounts under a formula or method obtained under paragraph (a)(4) of this section, the item increased, adjusted, or reduced is a fixed (rather than a variable) element of that formula or method.

(iv) If a taxpayer is required to request a revised schedule of ruling amounts by reason of an action described in paragraph (i)(1)(iii) of this section, the taxpayer must file the request for a revised schedule of ruling amounts on or before the deemed payment deadline date for the first taxable year in which rates that reflect such action become effective. The first taxable year to which the revised schedule of ruling amounts applies shall be the first taxable year in which such rates become effective.

(v) A request for a schedule of ruling amounts required by this paragraph (i)(1) must be made in accordance with the rules of paragraph (h) of this section. If a taxpayer does not properly file a request for a revised schedule of ruling amounts by the date provided in paragraph (i)(1)(i), (ii) or (iv) of this section (whichever is applicable), the taxpayer's ruling amount for the first taxable year to which the revised schedule of ruling amounts would have applied and for all succeeding taxable years until a new schedule is obtained shall be zero, unless, in its discretion, the Internal Revenue Service provides otherwise in such new schedule of ruling amounts.

(vi) See paragraph (f)(3) of § 1.468A-2 for the application of the rules in paragraph

Reg. § 1.468A-3(i)(1)

(i)(1)(iii), (iv), and (v) of this section in the case of certain retroactive adjustments to interim rate orders.

(2) *Elective review.* Any taxpayer that has obtained a schedule of ruling amounts pursuant to paragraph (h) of this section can request a revised schedule of ruling amounts. Such a request must be made in accordance with the rules of paragraph (h) of this section; thus, the Internal Revenue Service shall not provide a revised ruling amount applicable to a taxable year in response to a request for a schedule of ruling amounts that is filed after the deemed payment deadline date for such taxable year (see paragraph (h)(1)(vi) of this section).

(3) *Determination of revised schedule of ruling amounts.* A revised schedule of ruling amounts for a nuclear decommissioning fund shall be determined under this section without regard to any schedule of ruling amounts for such nuclear decommissioning fund that was issued prior to such revised schedule. Thus, a ruling amount specified in a revised schedule of ruling amounts for any taxable year in the level funding limitation period can be less than one or more ruling amounts specified in a prior schedule of ruling amounts for a prior taxable year.

(j) *Special rule permitting payments to a nuclear decommissioning fund before receipt of an initial or revised ruling amount applicable to a taxable year.*—(1) If an electing taxpayer has filed a timely request for an initial or revised ruling amount for a taxable year beginning on or after January 1, 1987, and does not receive the ruling amount on or before the deemed payment deadline date for such taxable year, the taxpayer may make a payment to a nuclear decommissioning fund on the basis of the ruling amount proposed in the taxpayer's request. Thus, under the preceding sentence, an electing taxpayer may make a payment to a nuclear decommissioning fund for such taxable year that does not exceed the lesser of—

(i) The cost of service amount applicable to the nuclear decommissioning fund for such taxable year; or

(ii) The ruling amount proposed by the taxpayer for such taxable year in a timely filed request for a schedule of ruling amounts.

(2) If an electing taxpayer makes a payment to a nuclear decommissioning fund for any taxable year pursuant to paragraph (j)(1) of this section and the ruling amount that is provided by the Internal Revenue Service is greater than the ruling amount proposed by the taxpayer for such taxable year, the taxpayer is not allowed to make an additional payment to the fund for such taxable year after the deemed payment deadline date for such taxable year.

(3) If—

(i) An electing taxpayer makes a payment to a nuclear decommissioning fund for any taxable year pursuant to paragraph (j)(1) of this section,

(ii) The ruling amount that is provided by the Internal Revenue Service is less than the ruling amount proposed by the taxpayer for such taxable year, and

(iii) As a result, there is an excess contribution (as defined in paragraph (c)(2)(ii) of § 1.468A-5) for such taxable year,

then the amount of the excess contribution is not deductible (see paragraph (b)(1) of § 1.468A-2) and must be withdrawn by the taxpayer pursuant to the rules of paragraph (c)(2)(i) of § 1.468A-5. Thus, an electing taxpayer that files a return based on a payment made pursuant to paragraph (j)(1) of this section should file an amended return if an excess contribution results when the ruling amount is issued for such taxable year. [Reg. § 1.468A-3.]

☐ [T.D. 8184, 2-29-88. Amended by T.D. 8461, 12-29-92; T.D. 8580, 12-23-94 and T.D. 8758, 1-16-98.]

[Reg. § 1.468A-4]

§ 1.468A-4. Treatment of nuclear decommissioning fund.—(a) *In general.* A nuclear decommissioning fund is subject to tax on all of its modified gross income (as defined in paragraph (b) of this section). The rate of tax is 22 percent for taxable years beginning in calendar year 1994 or 1995, 20 percent for taxable years beginning after December 31, 1995, and the highest rate of tax specified by section 11(b) for other years. This tax is in lieu of any other tax that may be imposed under subtitle A of the Internal Revenue Code on the income earned by the assets of the nuclear decommissioning fund.

(b) *Modified gross income.* For purposes of this section, the term "modified gross income" means gross income as defined under section 61 computed with the following modifications:

(1) The amount of any payment to the nuclear decommissioning fund with respect to which a deduction is allowed under section 468A(a) is excluded from gross income.

(2) A deduction is allowed for the amount of administrative costs and other incidental expenses of the nuclear decommissioning fund (including taxes, legal expenses, accounting expenses, actuarial expenses and trustee expenses, but not including decommissioning costs) that are otherwise deductible and that are paid by the nuclear

Reg. § 1.468A-4(a)

decommissioning fund to any person other than the electing taxpayer. An expense is otherwise deductible for purposes of this paragraph (b)(2) if it would be deductible under chapter 1 of the Internal Revenue Code in determining the taxable income of a corporation. For example, because Federal income taxes are not deductible under chapter 1 of the Internal Revenue Code in determining the taxable income of a corporation, the tax imposed by section 468A(e)(2) and paragraph (a) of this section is not deductible in determining the modified gross income of a nuclear decommissioning fund. Similarly, because certain expenses allocable to tax-exempt interest income are not deductible under section 265 of the Internal Revenue Code in determining the taxable income of a corporation, such expenses are not deductible in determining the modified gross income of a nuclear decommissioning fund.

(3) A deduction is allowed for the amount of an otherwise deductible loss that is sustained by the nuclear decommissioning fund in connection with the sale, exchange or worthlessness of any investment. A loss is otherwise deductible for purposes of this paragraph (b)(3) if such loss would be deductible by a corporation under section 165(f) or (g) and sections 1211(a) and 1212(a).

(4) A deduction is allowed for the amount of an otherwise deductible net operating loss of the nuclear decommissioning fund. For purposes of this paragraph (b), the net operating loss of a nuclear decommissioning fund for a taxable year is the amount by which the deductions allowable under paragraph (b)(2) and (3) of this section exceed the gross income of the nuclear decommissioning fund computed with the modification described in paragraph (b)(1) of this section. A net operating loss is otherwise deductible for purposes of this paragraph (b)(4) if such a net operating loss would be deductible by a corporation under section 172(a).

(c) *Special rules*—(1) *Period for computation of modified gross income.* The modified gross income of a nuclear decommissioning fund must be computed on the basis of the taxable year of the electing taxpayer. If an electing taxpayer changes its taxable year, each nuclear decommissioning fund of the electing taxpayer must change to the new taxable year. See section 442 and § 1.442-1 for rules relating to the change to a new taxable year.

(2) *Gain or loss upon distribution of property by a fund.* A distribution of property by a nuclear decommissioning fund (whether an actual distribution or a deemed distribution) shall be considered a disposition of property by the nuclear decommissioning fund for purposes of section 1001. In determining the amount of gain or loss from such disposition, the amount realized by the nuclear decommissioning fund shall be the fair market value of the property on the date of disposition.

(3) *Denial of credits against tax.* The tax imposed on the modified gross income of a nuclear decommissioning fund under paragraph (a) of this section is not to be reduced or offset by any credits against tax provided by part IV of subchapter A of chapter 1 of the Internal Revenue Code other than the credit provided by section 31(c) for amounts withheld under section 3406 (back-up withholding).

(4) *Other corporate taxes inapplicable.* Although the modified gross income of a nuclear decommissioning fund is subject to tax at the rate specified by section 468A(e)(2) and paragraph (a) of this section, a nuclear decommissioning fund is not subject to the other taxes imposed on corporations under subtitle A of the Internal Revenue Code. For example, a nuclear decommissioning fund is not subject to the alternative minimum tax imposed by section 55, the accumulated earnings tax imposed by section 531, the personal holding company tax imposed by section 541, and the alternative tax imposed on a corporation under section 1201(a).

(d) *Treatment as corporation for purposes of subtitle F.* For purposes of subtitle F of the Internal Revenue Code and the regulations thereunder, a nuclear decommissioning fund is to be treated as if it were a corporation and the tax imposed by section 468A(e)(2) and paragraph (a) of this section is to be treated as a tax imposed by section 11. Thus, for example, the following rules apply:

(1) A nuclear decommissioning fund must file a return with respect to the tax imposed by section 468A(e)(2) and paragraph (a) of this section for each taxable year (or portion thereof) that the fund is in existence even though no amount is included in the gross income of the fund for such taxable year. The return is to be made on Form 1120-ND in accordance with the instructions relating to such form. For purposes of this paragraph (d)(1), a nuclear decommissioning fund is in existence for the period that—

(i) Begins on the date that the first deductible payment is actually made to such nuclear decommissioning fund; and

(ii) Ends on the date of termination (see paragraph (d) of § 1.468A-5), the date that the entire fund is disqualified (see paragraph (c) of § 1.468A-5), or the date that the electing taxpayer disposes of its entire qualifying interest in the nuclear power plant to which the nuclear decom-

Reg. § 1.468A-4(d)(1)

missioning fund relates (see § 1.468A-6), whichever is applicable.

(2) For each taxable year of the nuclear decommissioning fund, the return described in paragraph (d)(1) of this section must be filed on or before the 15th day of the third month following the close of such taxable year unless the nuclear decommissioning fund is granted an extension of time for filing under section 6081. If such an extension is granted for any taxable year, the return for such taxable year must be filed on or before the extended due date for such taxable year. In no event will the filing of the initial return of a nuclear decommissioning fund be required before January 6, 1987.

(3) A nuclear decommissioning fund must provide its employer identification number on returns, statements and other documents as required by the forms and instructions relating thereto. The employer identification number is obtained by filing a Form SS-4 in accordance with the instructions relating thereto.

(4) A nuclear decommissioning fund must deposit all payments of tax imposed by section 468A(e)(2) and paragraph (a) of this section (including any payments of estimated tax) with an authorized government depositary in accordance with § 1.6302-1.

(5) A nuclear decommissioning fund is subject to the addition to tax imposed by section 6655 in case of a failure to pay estimated income tax. For purposes of section 6655 and this section—

(i) The tax with respect to which the amount of the underpayment is computed in the case of a nuclear decommissioning fund is the tax imposed by section 468A(e)(2) and paragraph (a) of this section; and

(ii) The taxable income with respect to which the nuclear decommissioning fund's status as a "large corporation" is measured is "modified gross income" (as defined by paragraph (b) of this section). [Reg. § 1.468A-4.]

☐ [T.D. 8184, 2-29-88. Amended by T.D. 8461, 12-29-92.]

[Reg. § 1.468A-5]

§ 1.468A-5. Nuclear decommissioning fund qualification requirements; prohibitions against self-dealing; disqualification of nuclear decommissioning fund; termination of fund upon substantial completion of decommissioning.—(a) *Qualification requirements*— (1) *In general.* (i) A nuclear decommissioning fund must be established and maintained at all times in the United States pursuant to an arrangement that qualifies as a trust under State law. Such trust must be established for the exclusive purpose of providing funds for the decommissioning of one or more nuclear power plants, but a single trust agreement may establish multiple funds for such purpose. Thus—

(A) Two or more nuclear decommissioning funds can be established and maintained pursuant to a single trust agreement; and

(B) One or more funds that are to be used for the decommissioning of a nuclear power plant and that do not qualify as nuclear decommissioning funds under this paragraph (a) can be established and maintained pursuant to a trust agreement that governs one or more nuclear decommissioning funds.

(ii) A separate nuclear decommissioning fund is required for each electing taxpayer and for each nuclear power plant with respect to which an electing taxpayer possesses a qualifyng interest. The Internal Revenue Service shall issue a separate schedule of ruling amounts with respect to each nuclear decommissioning fund and each nuclear decommissioning fund must file a separate income tax return even if other nuclear decommissioning funds or nonqualifed decommissioning funds are established and maintained pursuant to the trust agreement governing such fund or the assets of other nuclear decommissioning funds or nonqualified decommissioning funds are pooled with the assets of such fund.

(iii) An electing taxpayer can maintain only one nuclear decommissioning fund for each nuclear power plant with respect to which the taxpayer elects the application of section 468A. If a nuclear power plant is subject to the ratemaking jurisdiction of two or more public utility commissions and any such public utility commission requires a separate fund to be maintained for the benefit of ratepayers whose rates are established or approved by the public utility commission, the separate funds maintained for such plant (whether or not established and maintained pursuant to a single trust agreement) shall be considered a single nuclear decommissioning fund for purposes of section 468A and §§ 1.468A-1 through 1.468A-5, 1.468A-7 and 1.468A-8. Thus, for example, the Internal Revenue Service shall issue one schedule of ruling amounts with respect to such nuclear power plant (see paragraph (f) of § 1.468A-3), the nuclear decommissioning fund must file a single income tax return (see paragraph (d)(1) of § 1.468A-4), and, if the Internal Revenue Service disqualifies the nuclear decommissioning fund, the assets of each separate fund are treated as distributed on the date of disqualification (see paragraph (c)(3) of this section).

(iv) If assets of a nuclear decommissioning fund are (or will be) invested through an unincorporated organization, within the meaning of § 301.7701-2 of this chapter, the Internal Revenue Service will rule, if requested, whether the organization is an association taxable as a corporation for federal tax purposes. A request for such a ruling may be made by the electing taxpayer as part of its request for a schedule of ruling amounts.

(2) *Limitation on contributions.* Except as otherwise provided in paragraph (b)(2)(ii) of § 1.468A-8 (relating to a special transitional rule), a nuclear decommissioning fund is not permitted to accept any contributions in cash or property other than cash payments with respect to which a deduction is allowed under section 468A(a) and paragraph (a) of § 1.468A-2. Thus, for example, unless the exception contained in paragraph (b)(2)(ii) of § 1.468A-8 applies, securities may not be contributed to a nuclear decommissioning fund even if the taxpayer or a fund established by the taxpayer previously held such securities for the purpose of providing funds for the decommissioning of a nuclear power plant.

(3) *Limitation on use of fund*—(i) *In general.* The assets of a nuclear decommissioning fund are to be used exclusively—

(A) To satisfy, in whole or in part, the liability of the electing taxpayer for decommissioning costs of the nuclear power plant to which the nuclear decommissioning fund relates;

(B) To pay administrative costs and other incidental expenses of the nuclear decommissioning fund; and

(C) To the extent that the assets of the nuclear decommissioning fund are not currently required for the purposes described in paragraph (a)(3)(i)(A) or (B) of this section, to make investments.

(ii) *Definition of administrative costs and expenses.* For purposes of paragraph (a)(3)(i) of this section, the term "administrative costs and other incidental expenses of a nuclear decommissioning fund" means all ordinary and necessary expenses incurred in connection with the operation of the nuclear decommissioning fund. Such term includes the tax imposed by section 468A(e)(2) and paragraph (a) of § 1.468A-4, any State or local tax imposed on the income or the assets of the fund, legal expenses, accounting expenses, actuarial expenses and trustee expenses. Such term does not include decommissioning costs. Such term also does not include the excise tax imposed on the trustee or other disqualified person under section 4951 or the reimbursement of any expenses incurred in connection with the assertion of such tax unless such expenses are considered reasonable and necessary under section 4951(d)(2)(C) and it is determined that the trustee or other disqualified person is not liable for the excise tax.

(4) *Trust provisions.* By December 31, 1996, each qualified nuclear decommissioning fund trust agreement must provide that assets in the fund must be used as authorized by section 468A and the regulations thereunder and that the agreement may not be amended so as to violate section 468A or the regulations thereunder.

(b) *Prohibitions against self-dealing*—(1) *In general.* Except as otherwise provided in this paragraph (b), the excise taxes imposed by section 4951 shall apply to each act of self-dealing between a disqualified person and a nuclear decommissioning fund.

(2) *Self-dealing defined.* For purposes of this paragraph (b), the term "self-dealing" means any act described in section 4951(d), except—

(i) A payment by a nuclear decommissioning fund for the purpose of satisfying, in whole or in part, the liability of the electing taxpayer for decommissioning costs of the nuclear power plant to which the nuclear decommissioning fund relates;

(ii) A withdrawal of an excess contribution by the electing taxpayer pursuant to the rules of paragraph (c)(2) of this section;

(iii) A withdrawal by the electing taxpayer of amounts that have been treated as distributed under paragraph (c)(3) of this section;

(iv) A payment of amounts remaining in a nuclear decommissioning fund to the electing taxpayer after the termination of such fund (as determined under paragraph (d) of this section);

(v) Any act described in section 4951(d)(2)(B) or (C);

(vi) Any act described in § 53.4951-1(c) of this chapter only if undertaken to facilitate the temporary investment of assets or the payment of reasonable administrative expenses of the nuclear decommissioning fund; or

(vii) A payment by a nuclear decommissioning fund for the performance of trust functions and certain general banking services by a bank or trust company which is a disqualified person, where the banking services are reasonable and necessary to carry out the purposes of the fund, if the compensation paid to the bank or trust company, taking into account the fair interest rate for the use of the funds by the bank or trust company, for such services is not excessive. The general banking services allowed by this paragraph (b)(2)(vii) are—

Reg. § 1.468A-5(b)(2)

(A) Checking accounts, as long as the bank does not charge interest on any overwithdrawals,

(B) Savings accounts, as long as the fund may withdraw its funds on no more than 30 days' notice without subjecting itself to a loss of interest on its money for the time during which the money was on deposit, and

(C) Safekeeping activities. (See example 3 of § 53.4941(d)-3(c)(2).)

(3) *Disqualified person defined.* For purposes of this paragraph (b), the term "disqualified person" includes each person described in section 4951(e)(4) and paragraph (d) of § 53.4951-1.

(c) *Disqualification of nuclear decommissioning fund*—(1) *In general.* Except as otherwise provided in paragraph (c)(2) of this section, if at any time during a taxable year of a nuclear decommissioning fund—

(i) The nuclear decommissioning fund does not satisfy the requirements of paragraph (a) of this section, or

(ii) The nuclear decommissioning fund and a disqualified person engage in an act of self-dealing (as defined in paragraph (b)(2) of this section),

the Internal Revenue Service may, in its discretion, disqualify all or any portion of the fund as of the date that the fund does not satisfy the requirements of paragraph (a) of this section or the date on which the act of self-dealing occurs, whichever is applicable, or as of any subsequent date ("date of disqualification"). The Internal Revenue Service shall notify the electing taxpayer of the disqualification of a nuclear decommissioning fund and the date of disqualification by registered or certified mail to the last known address of the electing taxpayer (the "notice of disqualification"). For further guidance regarding the definition of last known address, see § 301.6212-2 of this chapter.

(2) *Exception to disqualification*—(i) *In general.* A nuclear decommissioning fund will not be disqualified under paragraph (c)(1) of this section by reason of an excess contribution or the withdrawal of such excess contribution by an electing taxpayer if the amount of the excess contribution is withdrawn by the electing taxpayer on or before the date prescribed by law (including extensions) for filing the return of the nuclear decommissioning fund for the taxable year to which the excess contribution relates. In the case of an excess contribution that is the result of a payment made pursuant to paragraph (j)(1) of § 1.468A-3, a nuclear decommissioning fund will not be disqualified under paragraph (c)(1) of this section if the amount of the excess contribution is withdrawn by the electing taxpayer on or before the later of—

(A) The date prescribed by law (including extensions) for filing the return of the nuclear decommissioning fund for the taxable year to which the excess contribution relates; or

(B) The date that is 30 days after the date that the taxpayer receives the ruling amount for such taxable year.

(ii) *Excess contribution defined.* For purposes of this section, an excess contribution is the amount by which cash payments made (or deemed made) to a nuclear decommissioning fund during any taxable year exceed the payment limitation contained in section 468A(b) and paragraph (b) of § 1.468A-2.

(iii) *Taxation of income attributable to an excess contribution.* The income of a nuclear decommissioning fund attributable to an excess contribution is required to be included in the gross income of the nuclear decommissioning fund under paragraph (b) of § 1.468A-4.

(3) *Effect of disqualification.* If all or any portion of a nuclear decommissioning fund is disqualified under paragraph (c)(1) of this section, the portion of the nuclear decommissioning fund that is disqualified is treated as distributed to the electing taxpayer on the date of disqualification. Such a distribution shall be treated for purposes of section 1001 as a disposition of property held by the nuclear decommissioning fund (see paragraph (c)(2) of § 1.468A-4). In addition, the electing taxpayer must include in gross income for the taxable year that includes the date of disqualification an amount equal to the product of—

(i) The fair market value of the assets of the fund determined as of the date of disqualification, reduced by—

(A) The amount of any excess contribution that was not withdrawn before the date of disqualification if no deduction was allowed with respect to such excess contribution;

(B) The amount of any deemed distribution that was not actually distributed before the date of disqualification (as determined under paragraph (d)(2)(iii) of § 1.468A-2) if the amount of the deemed distribution was included in the gross income of the electing taxpayer for the taxable year in which the deemed distribution occurred; and

(C) The amount of any tax that—

(*1*) Is imposed on the income of the fund;

(*2*) Is attributable to income taken into account before the date of disqualification or as a result of the disqualification; and

Reg. § 1.468A-5(b)(3)

(*3*) Has not been paid as of the date of disqualification; and

(ii) The fraction of the nuclear decommissioning fund that was disqualified under paragraph (c)(1) of this section.

Contributions made to a disqualified fund after the date of disqualification are not deductible under section 468A(a) and paragraph (a) of § 1.468A-2, or, if the fund is disqualified only in part, are deductible only to the extent provided in the notice of disqualification. In addition, if any assets of the fund that are deemed distributed under this paragraph (c)(3) are held by the fund after the date of disqualification (or if additional assets are acquired with nondeductible contributions made to the fund after the date of disqualification), the income earned by such assets after the date of disqualification must be included in the gross income of the electing taxpayer (see section 671) to the extent that such income is otherwise includible under chapter 1 of the Internal Revenue Code. An electing taxpayer can establish a nuclear decommissioning fund to replace a fund that has been disqualified in its entirety only if the Internal Revenue Service specifically consents to the establishment of a replacement fund in connection with the issuance of an initial schedule of ruling amounts for such replacement fund.

(d) *Termination of nuclear decommissioning fund upon substantial completion of decommissioning*—(1) *In general.* Upon substantial completion of the decommissioning of a nuclear power plant to which a nuclear decommissioning fund relates, such nuclear decommissioning fund shall be considered terminated and treated as having distributed all of its assets on the date the termination occurs. Such a distribution shall be treated for purposes of section 1001 as a disposition of property held by the nuclear decommissioning fund (see paragraph (c)(2) of § 1.468A-4). In addition, the electing taxpayer shall include in gross income for the taxable year in which the termination occurs an amount equal to the fair market value of the assets of the fund determined as of the date of termination, reduced by—

(i) The amount of any deemed distribution that was not actually distributed before the date of termination if the amount of the deemed distribution was included in the gross income of the electing taxpayer for the taxable year in which the deemed distribution occurred; and

(ii) The amount of any tax that—

(A) Is imposed on the income of the fund;

(B) Is attributable to income taken into account before the date the termination occurs or as a result of the termination; and

(C) Has not been paid as of the date the termination occurs.

Contributions made to a nuclear decommissioning fund after the termination date are not deductible under section 468A(a) and paragraph (a) of § 1.468A-2. In addition, if any assets are held by the fund after the termination date, the income earned by such assets after the termination date must be included in the gross income of the electing taxpayer (see section 671) to the extent that such income is otherwise includible under chapter 1 of the Internal Revenue Code. Finally, an electing taxpayer using an accrual method of accounting is allowed a deduction for nuclear decommissioning costs that are incurred during any taxable year (see paragraph (e) of § 1.468A-2) even if such costs are incurred after substantial completion of decommissioning (*e.g.,* expenses incurred to monitor or safeguard the plant site).

(2) *Substantial completion of decommissioning defined.* (i) Except as otherwise provided in paragraph (d)(2)(ii) of this section, the substantial completion of the decommissioning of a nuclear power plant occurs on the date that the maximum acceptable radioactivity levels mandated by the Nuclear Regulatory Commission with respect to a decommissioned nuclear power plant are satisfied (the "substantial completion date").

(ii) If a significant portion of the total estimated decommissioning costs with respect to a nuclear power plant are not incurred on or before the substantial completion date, an electing taxpayer may request, and the Internal Revenue Service shall issue, a ruling that designates the date on which substantial completion of decommissioning occurs. The date designated in the ruling shall not be later than the last day of the third taxable year after the taxable year that includes the substantial completion date. The request for a ruling under this paragraph (d)(2)(ii) must be filed during the taxable year that includes the substantial completion date and must comply with the procedural rules in effect at the time of the request. [Reg. § 1.468A-5.]

☐ [*T.D.* 8184, 2-29-88. *Amended by T.D.* 8461, 12-29-92; *T.D.* 8580, 12-23-94 *and T.D.* 8939, 1-11-2001.]

[Reg. § 1.468A-6]

§ 1.468A-6. Disposition of an interest in a nuclear power plant.—(a) *In general.* This section describes the federal income tax consequences of a transfer of the assets of a nuclear decommissioning fund (Fund) within the meaning of § 1.468A-1(b)(3) in connection with a sale, exchange, or other disposition by a taxpayer (transferor) of all or a portion of its qualifying interest in a nuclear power plant to another taxpayer (transferee). This section also explains how a schedule of ruling amounts will be determined for the transferor and transferee.

(b) *Requirements.* This section applies if—

(1) Immediately before the disposition, the transferor maintained a Fund with respect to the interest disposed of; and

(2) Immediately after the disposition—

(i) The transferee maintains a Fund with respect to the interest acquired;

(ii) The interest acquired is a qualifying interest of the transferee in the nuclear power plant;

(iii) Either a proportionate amount (which could include all) of the assets of the transferor's Fund is transferred to a Fund of the transferee, or the transferor's entire Fund is transferred to the transferee, provided in the latter case (or if the transferee receives all of the assets in the transferor's Fund, but not the transferor's Fund) that the transferee acquires the transferor's entire qualifying interest in the plant; and

(iv) The transferee continues to satisfy the requirements of § 1.468A-5(a)(iii), which permits an electing taxpayer to maintain only one Fund for each plant.

(c) *Tax consequences.* A disposition that satisfies the requirements of paragraph (b) of this section will have the following tax consequences at the time it occurs:

(1) *The transferor and its Fund.* Neither the transferor nor the transferor's Fund will recognize gain or loss or otherwise take any income or deduction into account by reason of the transfer of a proportionate amount of the assets of the transferor's Fund to the transferee's Fund (or by reason of the transfer of the transferor's entire Fund to the transferee). For purposes of the regulations under section 468A, this transfer (or the transfer of the transferor's Fund) will not be considered a distribution of assets by the transferor's Fund.

(2) *The transferee and its Fund.* Neither the transferee nor the transferee's Fund will recognize gain or loss or otherwise take any income or deduction into account by reason of the transfer of a proportionate amount of the assets of the transferor's Fund to the transferee's Fund (or by reason of the transfer of the transferor's Fund to the transferee). For purposes of the regulations under section 468A, this transfer (or the transfer of the transferor's Fund) will not constitute a payment or a contribution of assets by the transferee to its Fund.

(3) *Basis.* Transfers of assets of a Fund to which this section applies do not affect basis. Thus, the transferee's Fund will have a basis in the assets received from the transferor's Fund that is the same as the basis of those assets in the transferor's Fund immediately before the disposition.

(d) *Determination of proportionate amount.* For purposes of this section, a transferor of a qualifying interest in a nuclear power plant is considered to transfer a proportionate amount of the assets of its Fund to a Fund of a transferee of the interest if, on the date of the transfer of the interest, the percentage of the fair market value of the Fund's assets that are transferred equals the percentage of the transferor's qualifying interest that is transferred.

(e) *Calculation of schedule of ruling amounts for dispositions described in this section*—(1) *Transferor.* If a transferor disposes of all or a portion of its qualifying interest in a nuclear power plant in accordance with this section, the transferor's schedule of ruling amounts with respect to the interests disposed of and retained (if any) will be determined in accordance with paragraphs (e)(1)(i) and (ii) of this section.

(i) *Taxable year of disposition.* If a transferor does not file a request for a revised schedule of ruling amounts on or before the deemed payment deadline for the taxable year of the transferor in which the disposition of its interest in the nuclear power plant occurs (that is, the date that is two and one-half months after the close of that year), the transferor's ruling amount with respect to that plant for that year will equal the sum of—

(A) The ruling amount contained in the transferor's current schedule of ruling amounts with respect to that plant for that taxable year multiplied by the portion of the qualifying interest that is retained (if any); and

(B) The ruling amount contained in the transferor's current schedule of ruling amounts with respect to that plant for that taxable year multiplied by the product of—

(*1*) The portion of the transferor's qualifying interest that is disposed of; and

(*2*) A fraction, the numerator of which is the number of days in that taxable year that precede the date of disposition, and the denominator of which is the number of days in that taxable year.

(ii) *Taxable years after the year of disposition.* A transferor that retains a qualifying interest in a nuclear power plant must file a request for a revised schedule of ruling amounts with respect to that interest on or before the deemed payment deadline for the first taxable year of the transferor beginning after the disposition. See § 1.468A-3(i)(1)(ii)(B). If the transferor does not timely file such a request, the transferor's ruling amount with respect to that interest for the affected year or years will be zero, unless the Internal Revenue Service waives the application of this paragraph (e)(1)(ii) upon a showing of good cause for the delay.

(2) *Transferee.* If a transferee acquires all or a portion of a transferor's qualifying interest in a nuclear power plant under this section, the transferee's schedule of ruling amounts with respect to the interest acquired will be determined under paragraphs (e)(2)(i) and (ii) of this section.

(i) *Taxable year of disposition.* If a transferee does not file a request for a schedule of ruling amounts on or before the deemed payment deadline for the taxable year of the transferee in which the disposition occurs (that is, the date that is two and one-half months after the close of that year), the transferee's ruling amount with respect to the interest acquired in the nuclear power plant for that year is the amount described in the following sentence. This amount is the amount contained in the transferor's current schedule of ruling amounts for that plant for the taxable year of the transferor in which the disposition occurred, multiplied by the product of—

(A) The portion of the transferor's qualifying interest that is transferred; and

(B) A fraction, the numerator of which is the number of days in the taxable year of the transferor including and following the date of disposition, and the denominator of which is the number of days in that taxable year.

(ii) *Taxable years after the year of disposition.* A transferee of a qualifying interest in a nuclear power plant must file a request for a revised schedule of ruling amounts with respect to that interest on or before the deemed payment deadline for the first taxable year of the transferee beginning after the disposition. See § 1.468A-3(i)(1)(ii)(B). If the transferee does not timely file such a request, the transferee's ruling amount with respect to that interest for the affected year or years will be zero, unless the Internal Revenue Service waives the application of this paragraph (e)(2)(ii) upon a showing of good cause for the delay.

(3) *Example.* The following example illustrates the provisions of this paragraph (e).

Example. (i) X Corporation is a calendar year taxpayer engaged in the sale of electric energy generated by a nuclear power plant. The plant is owned entirely by X. On May 27, 1995, X transfers a 60 percent qualifying interest in the plant to Y Corporation, a calendar year taxpayer. Before the transfer, X had received a schedule of ruling amounts containing an annual ruling amount of $10 million for the taxable years 1993 through 2013. For 1995, neither X nor Y files a request for a revised schedule of ruling amounts.

(ii) Under paragraph (e)(1)(i) of this section, X's ruling amount for 1995 is calculated as follows: ($10,000,000 × 40%) + ($10,000,000 × 60% × 146/365) = $6,400,000. Under paragraph (e)(2)(i) of this section, Y's ruling amount for 1995 is calculated as follows: $10,000,000 × 60% × 219/365 = $3,600,000. Under paragraphs (e)(1)(ii) and (e)(2)(ii) of this section, X and Y must file requests for revised schedules of ruling amounts by March 15, 1997.

(f) *Calculation of the qualifying percentage after dispositions described in this section*—(1) *In general.* If a transferee acquires an interest in a nuclear power plant in a transaction that satisfies the requirements of this section, the transferee's qualifying percentage (within the meaning of § 1.468A-3(d)(4)) for the interest acquired is the transferor's qualifying percentage for that interest immediately before the disposition. If the Internal Revenue Service has not approved a qualifying percentage for the transferor with respect to the interest transferred, the qualifying percentage for that interest is determined under § 1.468A-3(d)(4).

(2) *Special rule.* The Internal Revenue Service may, in its discretion, determine a qualifying percentage for an interest in a nuclear power plant acquired by a transferee on a basis other than the rule set forth in paragraph (f)(1) of this section if—

(i) In connection with its first request for a schedule of ruling amounts after the disposition, the transferee requests special treatment, explains the need for such treatment, and sets forth an alternative basis for determining the qualifying percentage; and

(ii) The Internal Revenue Service determines that the special treatment is consistent with the purposes of section 468A.

(g) *Other*—(1) *Anti-abuse provision.* The Internal Revenue Service may treat a disposition occurring on or after December 27, 1994 as satisfying the requirements of this section if the Internal Revenue Service determines that this treatment is necessary or appropriate to carry out the purposes of section 468A and the regulations thereunder.

(2) *Relief provision.* Upon request of the electing taxpayer, the Internal Revenue Service

Reg. § 1.468A-6(g)(2)

Methods of Accounting

See p. 20,601 for regulations not amended to reflect law changes

may treat a disposition occurring after July 17, 1984, and before December 27, 1994 as satisfying the requirements of this section if the Internal Revenue Service determines that this treatment is necessary or appropriate to carry out the purposes of section 468A and the regulations thereunder.

(h) *Effective date.* Section 1.468A-6 is effective for a disposition of an interest in a nuclear power plant on or after December 27, 1994. [Reg. § 1.468A-6.]

☐ [*T.D.* 8580, 12-23-94.]

[Reg. § 1.468A-7]

§ 1.468A-7. **Manner of and time for making election.**—(a) *In general.* An eligible taxpayer is allowed a deduction for the taxable year in which the taxpayer makes a cash payment (or is deemed to make a cash payment) to a nuclear decommissioning fund only if the taxpayer elects the application of section 468A. A separate election is required for each nuclear decommissioning fund and for each taxable year with respect to which payments are to be deducted under section 468A. In the case of an affiliated group of corporations that join in the filing of a consolidated return for a taxable year, the common parent must make a separate election on behalf of each member whose payments to a nuclear decommissioning fund during such taxable year are to be deducted under section 468A. The election under section 468A for any taxable year is irrevocable and must be made by attaching a statement ("Election Statement") and a copy of the schedule of ruling amounts provided pursuant to the rules of § 1.468A-3 to the taxpayer's Federal income tax return (or, in the case of an affiliated group of corporations that join in the filing of a consolidated return, the consolidated return) for such taxable year. Except as otherwise provided in paragraph (b)(3) of § 1.468A-8, the return to which the Election Statement and a copy of the schedule of ruling amounts is attached must be filed on or before the time prescribed by law (including extensions) for filing the return for the taxable year with respect to which payments are to be deducted under section 468A.

(b) *Required information.* The Election Statement must include the following information:

(1) The legend "Election Under Section 468A" typed or legibly printed at the top of the first page.

(2) The electing taxpayer's name, address and taxpayer identification number (or, in the case of an affiliated group of corporations that join in the filing of a consolidated return, the name, address and taxpayer identification number of each electing taxpayer).

(3) The taxable year for which the election is made.

(4) For each nuclear decommissioning fund for which an election is made—

(i) The name and location of the nuclear power plant to which the fund relates;

(ii) The name and employer identification number of the nuclear decommissioning fund;

(iii) The total amount of actual cash payments made to the nuclear decommissioning fund during the taxable year that were not treated as deemed cash payments under paragraph (c)(1) of § 1.468A-2 for a prior taxable year;

(iv) The total amount of cash payments deemed made to the nuclear decommissioning fund under paragraph (c)(1) of § 1.468A-2 for the taxable year; and

(v) The cost of service amount for the taxable year (see paragraph (b)(2) of § 1.468A-2). [Reg. § 1.468A-7.]

☐ [*T.D.* 8184, 2-29-88.]

[Reg. § 1.468A-8]

§ 1.468A-8. **Effective date and transitional rules.**—(a) *Effective date*—(1) *In general.* Section 468A and §§ 1.468A-1 through 1.468A-8 are effective on July 18, 1984, and apply with respect to taxable years ending on or after such date.

(2) *Cut-off method applicable to electing taxpayers.* Any amount of nuclear decommissioning costs taken into account before July 18, 1984, for a taxable year beginning before such date, is not allowable as a deduction after July 17, 1984, under section 468A(c)(2) and paragraph (e) of § 1.468A-2.

(b) *Transitional rules*—(1) *Time for filing request for schedule of ruling amounts.* The Internal Revenue Service shall provide a ruling amount for any taxable year that ends on or after July 18, 1984, and begins before January 1, 1987, if—

(i) Paragraph (g) of § 1.468A-3 is satisfied for the taxable year; and

(ii) The taxpayer files a request for a schedule of ruling amounts that includes a proposed ruling amount for the taxable year on or before June 3, 1988.

(2) *Manner of and time for making contributions to a nuclear decommissioning fund.* (i) The amount of any contribution (including a contribution of property allowed under paragraph (b)(2)(ii) of this section) to a nuclear decommissioning fund that relates to a taxable year that ends on or after July 18, 1984, and begins before January 1, 1987, shall be deemed made during such taxable year if—

Reg. § 1.468A-7(a)

(A) The taxpayer makes such contribution on or before the 30th day after the date the taxpayer receives a ruling amount applicable to such taxable year; and

(B) The taxpayer irrevocably designates the amount of such contribution as relating to such taxable year on the Election Statement attached to its Federal income tax return (or amended return) for such taxable year.

(ii)(A) An electing taxpayer may contribute property to a nuclear decommissioning fund if the property—

(*1*) Is described in paragraph (a)(3)(i)(C) of § 1.468A-5;

(*2*) Was acquired after July 18, 1984, and before March 3, 1988; and

(*3*) Is contributed for any taxable year ending after July 18, 1984, and beginning before March 3, 1988.

(B) If a taxpayer contributes property to a nuclear decommissioning fund under this paragraph (b)(2)(ii)—

(*1*) The amount of the contribution (and the basis of the property to the nuclear decommissioning fund) shall equal the fair market value of the property on the date the property is contributed to the nuclear decommissioning fund;

(*2*) The contribution of the property to the nuclear decommissioning fund shall be considered a sale or exchange of the property by the taxpayer for purposes of section 1001; and

(*3*) For purposes of section 1001, the amount realized by the taxpayer shall be the fair market value of the property on the date the property was contributed to the nuclear decommissioning fund.

(iii) A fund established by a taxpayer for the purpose of paying the decommissioning costs of a nuclear power plant is not treated as a nuclear decommissioning fund before the earlier of—

(A) The date the taxpayer receives an initial schedule of ruling amounts with respect to the fund, or

(B) The first day of the first taxable year of the taxpayer that begins on or after January 1, 1987,

even if the taxpayer elects the application of section 468A for a taxable year that begins before such date. Any income earned before such date by the assets of a fund that satisfies the requirements of § 1.468A-5 must be included in the gross income of the taxpayer treated under section 671 as the owner of such assets.

(iv) If a fund is first treated as a nuclear decommissioning fund on the date described in paragraph (b)(2)(iii) of this section—

(A) The assets held in the fund on such date shall be treated for purposes of this paragraph (b)(2) as assets contributed to the nuclear decommissioning fund on such date; and

(B) The withdrawal of any such assets on or before the date prescribed by law (including extensions) for filing the return of the nuclear decommissioning fund for the taxable year that includes such date shall be treated in the same manner as the withdrawal of an excess contribution (see paragraph (c)(2) of § 1.468A-5).

(3) *Manner of and time for making election.* A taxpayer may elect the application of section 468A for a taxable year that ends on or after July 18, 1984, and begins before January 1, 1987, by attaching the Election Statement and a copy of the schedule of ruling amounts to—

(i) A return that is filed on or before the time prescribed by law (including extensions) for filing a return for such taxable year; or

(ii) An amended return for such taxable year that is filed on or before the 90th day after the date that the taxpayer receives a ruling amount for such taxable year.

(4) *Determination of cost of service limitation.* (i) For purposes of section 468A(b)(1) and paragraph (b)(2)(ii) of § 1.468A-2, decommissioning costs included in cost of service for any taxable year beginning before January 1, 1987, shall include decommissioning costs that can be accurately determined from information contained in the regulated books of account or other written records of the taxpayer.

(ii) For purposes of section 468A(b)(1) and paragraph (b)(2) of § 1.468A-2, the cost of service amount applicable to a nuclear decommissioning fund for the taxable year that includes July 18, 1984, is the amount determined under paragraph (b)(2) of § 1.468A-2 multiplied by a fraction, the numerator of which is the amount of nuclear decommissioning costs that is directly or indirectly charged to customers in such taxable year and that is included in the taxable income of the taxpayer for such taxable year and the denominator of which is the amount of nuclear decommissioning costs that is directly or indirectly charged to customers in such taxable year and that would have been included in the gross income of the taxpayer if such costs were taken into account by the taxpayer in the same manner as amounts charged for electric energy (see § 1.88-1). Under the preceding sentence, an amount of decommissioning costs is included in the taxable income of a taxpayer for the taxable year that includes July

Reg. § 1.468A-8(b)(4)

18, 1984, if the amount is included in gross income for such taxable year and no deduction (other than a deduction allowed under section 468A(a) and paragraph (a) of § 1.468A-2) is claimed with respect to such amount for such taxable year.

(5) *Assumptions and determinations to be used in determining ruling amounts.* (i) To the extent consistent with the principles and provisions of § 1.468A-3, a ruling amount for any taxable year beginning before January 1, 1987, shall be based on the reasonable assumptions and determinations used by the applicable public utility commission(s) in establishing or approving the amount of decommissioning costs included in cost of service for ratemaking purposes for such taxable year.

(ii) If the applicable public utility commission(s) did not disclose the after-tax rate of return used in establishing or approving the amount of decommissioning costs included in cost of service for any period during a taxable year that ends on or after July 18, 1984, and begins before January 1, 1987, the after-tax rate of return during such period is equal to 54 percent of the overpayment rate in effect under section 6621 during such period.

(iii) If the applicable public utility commission(s) did not disclose the other assumptions and determinations used in establishing or approving the amount of decommissioning costs included in cost of service for any taxable year that ends on or after July 18, 1984, and begins before January 1, 1987, a ruling amount for each such taxable year shall be determined by taking into account—

(A) The amount of decommissioning costs included in cost of service for such taxable year;

(B) The qualifying percentage (as determined under paragraph (d)(4) of § 1.468A-3 and paragraph (b)(7) of this section); and

(C) The amount of decommissioning costs included in cost of service for any earlier taxable year.

(6) *Exception to level funding limitation.* Notwithstanding paragraph (b) of § 1.468A-3, the Internal Revenue Service may, in its discretion, provide a schedule of ruling amounts specifying a ruling amount for a taxable year that ends on or after July 18, 1984, and begins before January 1, 1987, that is greater than the ruling amount specified in such schedule for a later taxable year.

(7) *Determination of qualifying percentage.* (i) (A) The qualifying percentage shall be determined under this paragraph (b)(7)(i) if a nuclear power plant began commercial operations on or before July 10, 1986, and a taxpayer—

(*1*) Files a request for a schedule of ruling amounts for the nuclear decommissioning fund maintained with respect to such nuclear power plant on or before June 3, 1988; and

(*2*) Elects the application of this paragraph (b)(7)(i) in its request for a schedule of ruling amounts.

(B) If the qualifying percentage is determined under this paragraph (b)(7)(i), the estimated period for which the nuclear decommissioning fund is to be in effect for purposes of paragraph (d)(4)(ii) of § 1.468A-3 begins on the later of—

(*1*) The first day of the taxable year that includes the date that the nuclear power plant began commercial operations; or

(*2*) The first day of the taxable year that includes July 18, 1984.

(ii)(A) The qualifying percentage shall be determined under this paragraph (b)(7)(ii) if a nuclear power plant began commercial operations before July 18, 1984, and a taxpayer—

(*1*) Files a request for a schedule of ruling amounts for the nuclear decommissioning fund maintained with respect to such nuclear power plant on or before June 3, 1988; and

(*2*) Elects the application of this paragraph (b)(7)(ii) in its request for a schedule of ruling amounts.

(B) If the qualifying percentage is determined under this paragraph (b)(7)(ii), the estimated period for which the nuclear decommissioning fund is to be in effect for purposes of paragraph (d)(4)(ii) of § 1.468A-3 and the estimated useful life of the nuclear power plant for purposes of paragraph (d)(4)(iii) of § 1.468A-3 shall end on the earlier of—

(*1*) the last day of the taxable year in which it is estimated that decommissioning will begin; or

(*2*) the last day of the taxable year that includes the expiration date of the Nuclear Regulatory Commission operating license as in effect on July 18, 1984, without regard to any extensions or amendments thereto.

(iii) In the case of a nuclear power plant that began commercial operations before July 18, 1984, and whose estimated useful life for ratemaking purposes was adjusted by a public utility commission before July 18, 1984, a taxpayer may elect in its request for a schedule of ruling amounts to compute the qualifying percentage in accordance with the following rules:

Reg. § 1.468A-8(b)(5)

(A) If the taxpayer files a request for a schedule of ruling amounts for the nuclear decommissioning fund maintained with respect to such nuclear power plant on or before June 3, 1988, the qualifying percentage equals the percentage of original depreciation costs (determined without regard to capitalized decommissioning costs) with respect to the nuclear power plant that remains to be recovered for ratemaking purposes as of the first day of the taxable year that includes July 18, 1984.

(B) If a taxpayer does not file a request for a schedule of ruling amounts for the nuclear decommissioning fund maintained with respect to such nuclear power plant on or before June 3, 1988, the qualifying percentage equals the percentage of original depreciation costs (determined without regard to capitalized decommissioning costs) with respect to the nuclear power plant that remains to be recovered for ratemaking purposes as of the first day of the first taxable year for which a deductible payment is made to the nuclear decommissioning fund that relates to such nuclear power plant.

(C) For purposes of this paragraph (b)(7)(iii), original depreciation costs with respect to a nuclear power plant include only those costs that were taken into account in determining the amount of depreciation with respect to such plant in the first ratemaking proceeding in which such depreciation was treated as a cost of service.

(8) *Limitation on payments to a nuclear decommissioning fund*—(i) The limitation on payments to a nuclear decommissioning fund (see section 468A(b) and paragraph (b) of § 1.468A-2) for a taxable year that ends on or after July 18, 1984, and begins before January 1, 1987, shall be determined under paragraph (b)(8)(ii) of this section if—

(A) The electing taxpayer receives a ruling amount applicable to such taxable year after the deemed payment deadline date for such taxable year; and

(B) The requirements of paragraph (b)(8)(iii) of this section are satisfied.

(ii) If the limitation on payments to a nuclear decommissioning fund for a taxable year is determined under this paragraph (b)(8)(ii), the maximum amount of payments made (or deemed made) to the nuclear decommissioning fund during such taxable year shall not exceed the sum of—

(A) The amount determined under section 468A(b) and paragraph (b) of § 1.468A-2 (*i.e.*, the lesser of the cost of service amount or the ruling amount) after application of the transitional rules contained in paragraph (b)(4), (5), (6) and (7) of this section; and

(B) The amount of after-tax earnings that would have accumulated to the date of actual payment to the nuclear decommissioning fund if the amount described in paragraph (b)(8)(ii)(A) of this section had been contributed to the nuclear decommissioning fund on the deemed payment deadline date for such taxable year.

In determining the after-tax earnings that would have accumulated to the date of payment, an electing taxpayer must use the after-tax rate of return of the nuclear decommissioning fund that was used in determining the initial schedule of ruling amounts.

(iii) In order to compute the payment limitation under paragraph (b)(8)(ii) of this section for any taxable year, an electing taxpayer must—

(A) Indicate on the Election Statement for the taxable year that the amount of the deductible payment is greater than the amount determined under section 468A(b) and paragraph (b) of § 1.468A-2 because paragraph (b)(8) of § 1.468A-8 applies;

(B) Not have claimed a deduction for the taxable year under section 468A(a) or paragraph (a) of § 1.468A-2 on any return that is filed before the date that a ruling amount is received for the taxable year;

(C) Not have taken a deduction under section 468A(a) or paragraph (a) of § 1.468A-2 into account in determining the amount properly estimated as tax for the taxable year under section 6081(b) (relating to the automatic extension for filing corporate income tax returns); and

(D) Not take the deduction allowed with respect to such payment into account in determining the amount of any overpayment of tax (within the meaning of section 6611) or underpayment of tax (within the meaning of section 6601) for the period ending on the date of such payment (see paragraph (b)(9) of this section).

(iv) The following example illustrates the application of the principles of paragraph (b)(8) of this section:

Example. X corporation is a calendar year, accrual method taxpayer engaged in the sale of electric energy generated by a nuclear power plant owned by X. On September 15, 1987, X receives a schedule of ruling amounts from the Internal Revenue Service that includes a ruling amount of $1,000,000 for the 1986 taxable year. For purposes of this example, assume that the cost of service amount applicable to the nuclear decommissioning fund for the 1986 taxable year is

Reg. § 1.468A-8(b)(8)

also $1,000,000 and that the after-tax rate of return of the nuclear decommissioning fund that was used in determining the schedule of ruling amounts is 10 percent compounded semi-annually. On September 15, 1987, X makes a contribution of $1,050,000 to a nuclear decommissioning fund established by X. Under paragraph (b)(8)(ii) of this section, this contribution does not exceed the limitation on payments for the 1986 taxable year and the entire amount of the contribution is deductible for such year. The additional $50,000 deductible payment that is allowed under this paragraph (b)(8) reflects the foregone earnings of the fund for the six-month period beginning on the deemed payment deadline date for the 1986 taxable year (March 15, 1987) and ending on the date of the contribution (September 15, 1987).

(9) *Denial of interest on overpayment.* If a deduction is allowed by reason of paragraph (b)(2) of this section for the amount of any payment made after the 15th day of the third calendar month after the close of the taxable year to which such payment relates, such deduction shall not be taken into account in determining the amount of any overpayment of tax (within the meaning of section 6611) or underpayment of tax (within the meaning of section 6601) for the period ending on the date of such payment.

(10) *Determination of addition to tax for failure to pay estimated tax.* In the case of any taxable year that ends on or after July 18, 1984, and begins before January 1, 1987, the tax shown on the return for such taxable year for purposes of section 6655(b) shall equal the tax that would be shown on the return if a deduction were allowed for the lesser of—

(i) The amount of the payment made to the nuclear decommissioning fund for such taxable year; or

(ii) The amount determined under section 468A(b) and paragraph (b) of § 1.468A-2 (*i.e.*, the lesser of the cost of service amount or the ruling amount) after application of the transitional rules contained in paragraph (b)(4), (5), (6) and (7) of this section but without regard to the transitional rule contained in paragraph (b)(8) of this section.

(11) *Nuclear decommissioning fund qualification requirements.* For tax years beginning prior to January 1, 1995, the Service will not assert that an unincorporated organization referred to in § 1.468A-5(a)(1)(iv), established prior to January 1, 1993, through which the assets of a nuclear decommissioning fund are invested, is an association taxable as a corporation for federal tax purposes.

(12) *Use of formula or method.* Section 1.468A-2(f)(3)(ii) and § 1.468A-3(a)(4) (to the extent it permits a formula or method when the applicable public utility commission estimates the cost of decommissioning in future dollars), (e)(5), (i)(1)(ii)(A) (to the extent it requires the taxpayer to file a request for a revised schedule because of a substantial variation in ruling amounts), and (i)(1)(iii)(C) apply only to requests for a formula or method submitted on or after January 20, 1998, and to formulas and methods obtained in response to those requests. [Reg. § 1.468A-8.]

☐ [*T.D.* 8184, 2-29-88. Amended by *T.D.* 8461, 12-29-92 and *T.D.* 8758, 1-16-98.]

[Reg. § 1.468B]

§ 1.468B. **Designated settlement funds.**—A designated settlement fund, as defined in section 468B(d)(2), is taxed in the manner described in § 1.468B-2. The rules for transferors to a qualified settlement fund described in § 1.468B-3 apply to transferors to a designated settlement fund. Similarly, the rules for claimants of a qualified settlement fund described in § 1.468B-4 apply to claimants of a designated settlement fund. A fund, account, or trust that does not qualify as a designated settlement fund is, however, a qualified settlement fund if it meets the requirements of a qualified settlement fund described in § 1.468B-1. [Reg. § 1.468B.]

☐ [*T.D.* 8459, 12-18-92.]

[Reg. § 1.468B-0]

§ 1.468B-0. **Table of contents.**—This section contains a listing of the headings of §§ 1.468B-1 through 1.468B-5.

§ 1.468B-1. Qualified settlement funds.

(a) In general.

(b) Coordination with other entity classifications.

(c) Requirements.

(d) Definitions.

(1) Transferor.

(2) Related person.

(e) Governmental order or approval requirement.

(1) In general.

(2) Arbitration panels.

(f) Resolve or satisfy requirement.

(1) Liabilities to provide property or services.

(2) CERCLA liabilities.

(g) Excluded liabilities.

(h) Segregation requirement.

(1) In general.

Methods of Accounting 37,029
See p. 20,601 for regulations not amended to reflect law changes

(2) Classification of fund established to resolve or satisfy allowable and non-allowable claims.

(i) [Reserved]

(j) Classification of fund prior to satisfaction of requirements in paragraph (c) of this section.

(1) In general.

(2) Relation-back rule.

(i) In general.

(ii) Relation-back election.

(k) Examples.

§ 1.468B-2. Taxation of qualified settlement funds and related administrative requirements.

(a) In general.

(b) Modified gross income.

(c) Partnership interests held by a qualified settlement fund on February 14, 1992.

(1) In general.

(2) Limitation on changes in partnership agreements and capital contributions.

(d) Distributions to transferors and claimants.

(e) Basis of property transferred to a qualified settlement fund.

(f) Distribution of property.

(g) Other taxes.

(h) Denial of credits against tax.

(i) [RESERVED]

(j) Taxable year and accounting method.

(k) Treatment as corporation for purposes of subtitle F.

(l) Information reporting and withholding requirements.

(1) Payments to a qualified settlement fund.

(2) Payments and distributions by a qualified settlement fund.

(i) In general.

(ii) Special rules.

(m) Request for prompt assessment.

(n) Examples.

§ 1.468B-3. Rules applicable to the transferor.

(a) Transfer of property.

(1) In general.

(2) Anti-abuse rule.

(b) Qualified appraisal requirement for transfers of certain property.

(1) In general.

(2) Provision of copies.

(3) Qualified appraisal.

(4) Information included in a qualified appraisal.

(5) Effect of signature of the qualified appraiser.

(c) Economic performance.

(1) In general.

(2) Right to a refund or reversion.

(i) In general.

(ii) Right extinguished.

(3) Obligations of a transferor.

(d) Payment of insurance amounts.

(e) Statement to the qualified settlement fund and the Internal Revenue Service.

(1) In general.

(2) Required statement.

(i) In general.

(ii) Combined statements.

(f) Distributions to transferors.

(1) In general.

(2) Deemed distributions.

(i) Other liabilities.

(ii) Constructive receipt.

(3) Tax benefit rule.

(g) Example.

§ 1.468B-4. Taxability of distributions to claimants.

§ 1.468B-5. Effective dates and transition rules.

(a) In general.

(b) Taxation of certain pre-1996 fund income.

(1) Reasonable method.

(i) In general.

(ii) Qualified settlement funds established after February 14, 1992, but before January 1, 1993.

(iii) Use of cash method of accounting.

(iv) Unreasonable position.

(v) Waiver of penalties.

(2) Election to apply qualified settlement fund rules.

(i) In general.

(ii) Election statement.

(iii) Due date of returns and amended returns.

(iv) Computation of interest and waiver of penalties.

[Reg. § 1.468B-0.]

☐ [T.D. 8459, 12-18-92.]

[§ 1.468B-1]

§ 1.468B-1. Qualified settlement funds.—(a) *In general.* A qualified settlement fund is a fund, account, or trust that satisfies the requirements of paragraph (c) of this section.

Reg. § 1.468B-1(a)

(b) *Coordination with other entity classifications.* If a fund, account, or trust that is a qualified settlement fund could be classified as a trust within the meaning of § 301.7701-4 of this chapter, it is classified as a qualified settlement fund for all purposes of the Internal Revenue Code (Code). If a fund, account, or trust, organized as a trust under applicable state law, is a qualified settlement fund, and could be classified as either an association (within the meaning of § 301.7701-2 of this chapter) or a partnership (within the meaning of § 301.7701-3 of this chapter), it is classified as a qualified settlement fund for all purposes of the Code. If a fund, account, or trust, established for contested liabilities pursuant to § 1.461-2(c)(1) is a qualified settlement fund, it is classified as a qualified settlement fund for all purposes of the Code.

(c) *Requirements.* A fund, account, or trust satisfies the requirements of this paragraph (c) if—

(1) It is established pursuant to an order of, or is approved by, the United States, any state (including the District of Columbia), territory, possession, or political subdivision thereof, or any agency or instrumentality (including a court of law) of any of the foregoing and is subject to the continuing jurisdiction of that governmental authority;

(2) It is established to resolve or satisfy one or more contested or uncontested claims that have resulted or may result from an event (or related series of events) that has occurred and that has given rise to at least one claim asserting liability—

(i) Under the Comprehensive Environmental Response, Compensation and Liability Act of 1980 (hereinafter referred to as CERCLA), as amended, 42 U.S.C. 9601 et seq.; or

(ii) Arising out of a tort, breach of contract, or violation of law; or

(iii) Designated by the Commissioner in a revenue ruling or revenue procedure; and

(3) The fund, account, or trust is a trust under applicable state law, or its assets are otherwise segregated from other assets of the transferor (and related persons).

(d) *Definitions.* For purposes of this section—

(1) *Transferor.* A "transferor" is a person that transfers (or on behalf of whom an insurer or other person transfers) money or property to a qualified settlement fund to resolve or satisfy claims described in paragraph (c)(2) of this section against that person.

(2) *Related person.* A "related person" is any person who is related to the transferor within the meaning of sections 267(b) or 707(b)(1).

(e) *Governmental order or approval requirement*—(1) *In general.* A fund, account, or trust is "ordered by" or "approved by" a governmental authority described in paragraph (c)(1) of this section when the authority issues its initial or preliminary order to establish, or grants its initial or preliminary approval of, the fund, account, or trust, even if that order or approval may be subject to review or revision. Except as otherwise provided in paragraph (j)(2) of this section, the governmental authority's order or approval has no retroactive effect and does not permit a fund, account, or trust to be a qualified settlement fund prior to the date the order is issued or the approval is granted.

(2) *Arbitration panels.* An arbitration award that orders the establishment of, or approves, a fund, account, or trust is an order or approval of a governmental authority described in paragraph (c)(1) of this section if—

(i) The arbitration award is judicially enforceable;

(ii) The arbitration award is issued pursuant to a bona fide arbitration proceeding in accordance with rules that are approved by a governmental authority described in paragraph (c)(1) of this section (such as self-regulatory organization-administered arbitration proceedings in the securities industry); and

(iii) The fund, account, or trust is subject to the continuing jurisdiction of the arbitration panel, the court of law that has jurisdiction to enforce the arbitration award, or the governmental authority that approved the rules of the arbitration proceeding.

(f) *Resolve or satisfy requirement*—(1) *Liabilities to provide services or property.* Except as otherwise provided in paragraph (f)(2) of this section, a liability is not described in paragraph (c)(2) of this section if it is a liability for the provision of services or property, unless the transferor's obligation to provide services or property is extinguished by a transfer or transfers to the fund, account, or trust.

(2) *CERCLA liabilities.* A transferor's liability under CERCLA to provide services or property is described in paragraph (c)(2) of this section if following its transfer to a fund, account, or trust the transferor's only remaining liability to the Environmental Protection Agency (if any) is a remote, future obligation to provide services or property.

Reg. § 1.468B-1(b)

(g) *Excluded liabilities.* A liability is not described in paragraph (c)(2) of this section if it—

(1) Arises under a workers compensation act or a self-insured health plan;

(2) Is an obligation to refund the purchase price of, or to repair or replace, products regularly sold in the ordinary course of the transferor's trade or business;

(3) Is an obligation of the transferor to make payments to its general trade creditors or debtholders that relates to a title 11 or similar case (as defined in section 368(a)(3)(A)), or a workout; or

(4) Is designated by the Commissioner in a revenue ruling or a revenue procedure (see § 601.601(d)(2)(ii)(*b*) of this chapter).

(h) *Segregation requirement*—(1) *In general.* If it is not a trust under applicable state law, a fund, account, or trust satisfies the requirements of paragraph (c)(3) of this section if its assets are physically segregated from other assets of the transferor (and related persons). For example, cash held by a transferor in a separate bank account satisfies the segregation requirement of paragraph (c)(3) of this section.

(2) *Classification of fund established to resolve or satisfy allowable and non-allowable claims.* If a fund, account, or trust is established to resolve or satisfy claims described in paragraph (c)(2) of this section as well as other types of claims (*i.e.,* non-allowable claims) arising from the same event or related series of events, the fund is a qualified settlement fund. However, under § 1.468B-3(c), economic performance does not occur with respect to transfers to the qualified settlement fund for non-allowable claims.

(i) [Reserved]

(j) *Classification of fund prior to satisfaction of requirements in paragraph (c) of this section*—(1) *In general.* If a fund, account, or trust is established to resolve or satisfy claims described in paragraph (c)(2) of this section, the assets of the fund, account, or trust are treated as owned by the transferor of those assets until the fund, account, or trust also meets the requirements of paragraphs (c)(1) and (3) of this section. On the date the fund, account, or trust satisfies all the requirements of paragraph (c) of this section, the transferor is treated as transferring the assets to a qualified settlement fund.

(2) *Relation-back rule*—(i) *In general.* If a fund, account, or trust meets the requirements of paragraphs (c)(2) and (c)(3) of this section prior to the time it meets the requirements of paragraph (c)(1) of this section, the transferor and administrator (as defined in § 1.468B-2(k)(3)) may jointly elect (a relation-back election) to treat the fund, account, or trust as coming into existence as a qualified settlement fund on the later of the date the fund, account, or trust meets the requirements of paragraphs (c)(2) and (c)(3) of this section or January 1 of the calendar year in which all the requirements of paragraph (c) of this section are met. If a relation-back election is made, the assets held by the fund, account, or trust on the date the qualified settlement fund is treated as coming into existence are treated as transferred to the qualified settlement fund on that date.

(ii) *Relation-back election.* A relation-back election is made by attaching a copy of the election statement, signed by each transferor and the administrator, to (and as part of) the timely filed income tax return (including extensions) of the qualified settlement fund for the taxable year in which the fund is treated as coming into existence. A copy of the election statement must also be attached to (and as part of) the timely filed income tax return (including extensions), or an amended return that is consistent with the requirements of §§ 1.468B-1 through 1.468B-4, of each transferor for the taxable year of the transferor that includes the date on which the qualified settlement fund is treated as coming into existence. The election statement must contain—

(A) A legend, "§ 1.468B-1 Relation-Back Election", at the top of the first page;

(B) Each transferor's name, address, and taxpayer identification number;

(C) The qualified settlement fund's name, address, and employer identification number;

(D) The date as of which the qualified settlement fund is treated as coming into existence; and

(E) A schedule describing each asset treated as transferred to the qualified settlement fund on the date the fund is treated as coming into existence. The schedule of assets does not have to identify the amount of cash or the property treated as transferred by a particular transferor. If the schedule does not identify the transferor of each asset, however, each transferor must include with the copy of the election statement that is attached to its income tax return (or amended return) a schedule describing each asset the transferor is treated as transferring to the qualified settlement fund.

(k) *Examples.* The following examples illustrate the rules of this section:

Example 1. In a class action brought in a United States federal district court, the court

Reg. § 1.468B-1(k)

holds that the defendant, Corporation X, violated certain securities laws and must pay damages in the amount of $150 million. Pursuant to an order of the court, Corporation X transfers $50 million in cash and transfers property with a fair market value of $75 million to a state law trust. The trust will liquidate the property and distribute the cash proceeds to the plaintiffs in the class action. The trust is a qualified settlement fund because it was established pursuant to the order of a federal district court to resolve or satisfy claims against Corporation X for securities law violations that have occurred.

Example 2. (i) Assume the same facts as in *Example 1*, except that Corporation X and the class of plaintiffs reach an out-of-court settlement that requires Corporation X to establish and fund a state law trust before the settlement agreement is submitted to the court for approval.

(ii) The trust is not a qualified settlement fund because it neither is established pursuant to an order of, nor has it been approved by, a governmental authority described in paragraph (c)(1) of this section.

Example 3. On June 1, 1994, Corporation Y establishes a fund to resolve or satisfy claims against it arising from the violation of certain securities laws. On that date, Corporation Y transfers $10 million to a segregated account. On December 1, 1994, a federal district court approves the fund. Assuming Corporation Y and the administrator of the qualified settlement fund do not make a relation-back election, Corporation Y is treated as the owner of the $10 million, and is taxable on any income earned on that money, from June 1 through November 30, 1994. The fund is a qualified settlement fund beginning on December 1, 1994.

Example 4. (i) On September 1, 1993, Corporation X, which has a taxable year ending on October 31, enters into a settlement agreement with a plaintiff class for asserted tort liabilities. Under the settlement agreement, Corporation X makes two $50 million payments into a segregated fund, one on September 1, 1993, and one on October 1, 1993, to resolve or satisfy the tort liabilities. A federal district court approves the settlement agreement on November 1, 1993.

(ii) The administrator of the fund and Corporation X elect to treat the fund as a qualified settlement fund prior to governmental approval under the relation-back rule of paragraph (j)(2) of this section. The administrator must attach the relation-back election statement to the fund's income tax return for calendar year 1993, and Corporation X must attach the election to its original or amended income tax return for its taxable year ending October 31, 1993.

(iii) Pursuant to the relation-back election, the fund begins its existence as a qualified settlement fund on September 1, 1993, and Corporation X is treated as transferring $50 million to the qualified settlement fund on September 1, 1993, and $50 million on October 1, 1993.

(iv) With respect to these transfers, Corporation X must provide the statement described in § 1.468B-3(e) to the administrator of the qualified settlement fund by February 15, 1994, and must attach a copy of this statement to its original or amended income tax return for its taxable year ending October 31, 1993.

Example 5. Assume the same facts as in *Example 4*, except that the court approves the settlement on May 1, 1994. The administrator must attach the relation-back election statement to the fund's income tax return for calendar year 1994, and Corporation X must attach the election statement to its original or amended income tax return for its taxable year ending October 31, 1994. Pursuant to this election, the fund begins its existence as a qualified settlement fund on January 1, 1994. In addition, Corporation X is treated as transferring to the qualified settlement fund all amounts held in the fund on January 1, 1994. With respect to the transfer, Corporation X must provide the statement described in § 1.468B-3(e) to the administrator of the qualified settlement fund by February 15, 1995, and must attach a copy of this statement to its income tax return for its taxable year ending October 31, 1994.

Example 6. Corporation Z establishes a fund that meets all the requirements of section 468B(d)(2) for a designated settlement fund, except that Corporation Z does not make the election under section 468B(d)(2)(F). Although the fund does not qualify as a designated settlement fund, it is a qualified settlement fund because the fund meets the requirements of paragraph (c) of this section.

Example 7. Corporation X owns and operates a landfill in State A. State A requires Corporation X to transfer money to a trust annually based on the total tonnage of material placed in the landfill during the year. Under the laws of State A, Corporation X will be required to perform (either itself or through contractors) specified closure activities when the landfill is full, and the trust assets will be used to reimburse Corporation X for those closure costs. The trust is not a qualified settlement fund because it is established to secure the liability of Corporation X to perform the closure activities. [Reg. § 1.468B-1.]

☐ [T.D. 8459, 12-18-92.]

Reg. § 1.468B-1(k)

[§ 1.468B-2]

§ 1.468B-2. **Taxation of qualified settlement funds and related administrative requirements.**—(a) *In general.* A qualified settlement fund is a United States person and is subject to tax on its modified gross income for any taxable year at a rate equal to the maximum rate in effect for that taxable year under section 1(e).

(b) *Modified gross income.* The "modified gross income" of a qualified settlement fund is its gross income, as defined in section 61, computed with the following modifications—

(1) In general, amounts transferred to the qualified settlement fund by, or on behalf of, a transferor to resolve or satisfy a liability for which the fund is established are excluded from gross income. However, dividends on stock of a transferor (or a related person), interest on debt of a transferor (or a related person), and payments in compensation for late or delayed transfers, are not excluded from gross income.

(2) A deduction is allowed for administrative costs and other incidental expenses incurred in connection with the operation of the qualified settlement fund that would be deductible under chapter 1 of the Internal Revenue Code in determining the taxable income of a corporation. Administrative costs and other incidental expenses include state and local taxes, legal, accounting, and actuarial fees relating to the operation of the qualified settlement fund, and expenses arising from the notification of claimants and the processing of their claims. Administrative costs and other incidental expenses do not include legal fees incurred by, or on behalf of, claimants.

(3) A deduction is allowed for losses sustained by the qualified settlement fund in connection with the sale, exchange, or worthlessness of property held by the fund to the extent the losses would be deductible in determining the taxable income of a corporation under section 165(f) or (g), and sections 1211(a) and 1212(a).

(4) A deduction is allowed for the amount of a net operating loss of the qualified settlement fund to the extent the loss would be deductible in determining the taxable income of a corporation under section 172(a). For purposes of this paragraph (b)(4), the net operating loss of a qualified settlement fund for a taxable year is the amount by which the deductions allowed under paragraphs (b)(2) and (b)(3) of this section exceed the gross income of the fund computed with the modification described in paragraph (b)(1) of this section.

(c) *Partnership interests held by a qualified settlement fund on February 14, 1992*—(1) *In general.* For taxable years ending prior to January 1, 2003, a qualified settlement fund that holds a partnership interest it acquired prior to February 15, 1992, is allowed a deduction for its distributive share of that partnership's items of loss, deduction, or credit described in section 702(a) that would be deductible in determining the taxable income (or in the case of a credit, the income tax liability) of a corporation to the extent of the fund's distributive share of that partnership's items of income and gain described in section 702(a) for the same taxable year. For purposes of this paragraph (c)(1), a distributive share of a partnership credit is treated as a deduction in an amount equal to the amount of the credit divided by the rate described in paragraph (a) of this section.

(2) *Limitation on chances in partnership agreements and capital contributions.* For purposes of paragraph (c)(1) of this section, changes in a qualified settlement fund's distributive share of items of income, gain, loss, deduction, or credit are disregarded if—

(i) They result from a change in the terms of the partnership agreement on or after December 18, 1992 or a capital contribution to the partnership on or after December 18, 1992 unless the partnership agreement as in effect prior to December 18, 1992 requires the contribution; and

(ii) A principal purpose of the change in the terms of the partnership agreement or the capital contribution is to circumvent the limitation described in paragraph (c)(1) of this section.

(d) *Distributions to transferors and claimants.* Amounts that are distributed by a qualified settlement fund to, or on behalf of, a transferor or a claimant are not deductible by the fund.

(e) *Basis of property transferred to a qualified settlement fund.* A qualified settlement fund's initial basis in property it receives from a transferor (or from an insurer or other person on behalf of a transferor) is the fair market value of that property on the date of transfer to the fund.

(f) *Distribution of property.* A qualified settlement fund must treat a distribution of property as a sale or exchange of that property for purposes of section 1001(a). In computing gain or loss, the amount realized by the qualified settlement fund is the fair market value of the property on the date of distribution.

(g) *Other taxes.* The tax imposed under paragraph (a) of this section is in lieu of any other taxation of the income of a qualified settlement fund under subtitle A of the Internal Revenue Code. Thus, a qualified settlement fund is not subject to the alternative minimum tax of section 55, the accumulated earnings tax of section 531, the personal holding company tax of section 541,

Reg. § 1.468B-2(g)

or the maximum capital gains rate of section 1(h). A qualified settlement fund is, however, subject to taxes that are not imposed on the income of a taxpayer, such as the tax on transfers of property to foreign entities under section 1491.

(h) *Denial of credits against tax.* The tax imposed on the modified gross income of a qualified settlement fund under paragraph (a) of this section may not be reduced or offset by any credits against tax provided by part IV of subchapter A of chapter 1 of the Internal Revenue Code.

(i) [Reserved]

(j) *Taxable year and accounting method.* The taxable year of a qualified settlement fund is the calendar year. A qualified settlement fund must use an accrual method of accounting within the meaning of section 446(c).

(k) *Treatment as corporation for purposes of subtitle F.* Except as otherwise provided in § 1.468B-5(b), for purposes of subtitle F of the Internal Revenue Code, a qualified settlement fund is treated as a corporation and any tax imposed under paragraph (a) of this section is treated as a tax imposed by section 11. Subtitle F rules that apply to qualified settlement funds include, but are not limited to—

(1) A qualified settlement fund must file an income tax return with respect to the tax imposed under paragraph (a) of this section for each taxable year that the fund is in existence, whether or not the fund has gross income for that taxable year.

(2) A qualified settlement fund is in existence for the period that—

(i) Begins on the first date on which the fund is treated as a qualified settlement fund under § 1.468B-1; and

(ii) Ends on the earlier of the date the fund—

(A) No longer satisfies the requirements of § 1.468B-1; or

(B) No longer has any assets and will not receive any more transfers. (See paragraph (m) of this section for procedures for the prompt assessment of tax).

(3) The income tax return of the qualified settlement fund must be filed on or before March 15 of the year following the close of the taxable year of the qualified settlement fund unless the fund is granted an extension of time for filing under section 6081. The return must be made by the administrator of the qualified settlement fund. The "administrator" (which may include a trustee if the qualified settlement fund is a trust) of a qualified settlement fund is, in order of priority—

(i) The person designated, or approved, by the governmental authority that ordered or approved the fund for purposes of § 1.468B-1(c)(1);

(ii) The person designated in the escrow agreement, settlement agreement, or other similar agreement governing the fund;

(iii) The escrow agent, custodian, or other person in possession or control of the fund's assets; or

(iv) The transferor or, if there are multiple transferors, all the transferors, unless an agreement signed by all the transferors designates a single transferor as the administrator.

(4) The administrator of a qualified settlement fund must obtain an employer identification number for the fund.

(5) A qualified settlement fund must deposit all payments of tax imposed under paragraph (a) of this section (including any payments of estimated tax) with an authorized government depositary in accordance with § 1.6302-1.

(6) A qualified settlement fund is subject to the addition to tax imposed by section 6655 in the case of an underpayment of estimated tax computed with respect to the tax imposed under paragraph (a) of this section. For purposes of section 6655(g)(2), a qualified settlement fund's taxable income is its modified gross income and a transferor is not considered a predecessor of a qualified settlement fund.

(l) *Information reporting and withholding requirements*—(1) *Payments to a qualified settlement fund.* Payments to a qualified settlement fund are treated as payments to a corporation for purposes of the information reporting requirements of part III of subchapter A of chapter 61 of the Internal Revenue Code.

(2) *Payments and distributions by a qualified settlement fund*—(i) *In general.* Payments and distributions by a qualified settlement fund are subject to the information reporting requirements of part III of subchapter A of chapter 61 of the Internal Revenue Code (Code), and the withholding requirements of subchapter A of chapter 3 of subtitle A and subtitle C of the Code.

(ii) *Special rules.* The following rules apply with respect to payments and distributions by a qualified settlement fund—

(A) A qualified settlement fund must make a return for, or must withhold tax on, a distribution to a claimant if one or more transferors would have been required to make a return or withhold tax had that transferor made the distribution directly to the claimant;

(B) For purposes of sections 6041(a) and 6041A, if a qualified settlement fund makes a

Reg. § 1.468B-2(h)

payment or distribution to a transferor, the fund is deemed to make the payment or distribution to the transferor in the course of a trade or business;

(C) For purposes of sections 6041(a) and 6041A, if a qualified settlement fund makes a payment or distribution on behalf of a transferor or a claimant, the fund is deemed to make the payment or distribution to the recipient of that payment or distribution in the course of a trade or business;

(D) With respect to a distribution or payment described in paragraph (l)(2)(ii)(C) of this section and the information reporting requirements of part III of subchapter A of chapter 61 of the Internal Revenue Code, the qualified settlement fund is also deemed to have made the distribution or payment to the transferor or claimant.

(m) *Request for prompt assessment.* A qualified settlement fund is eligible to request the prompt assessment of tax under section 6501(d). For purposes of section 6501(d), a qualified settlement fund is treated as dissolving on the date the fund no longer has any assets (other than a reasonable reserve for potential tax liabilities and related professional fees) and will not receive any more transfers.

(n) *Examples.* The following examples illustrate the rules of this section:

Example 1. On June 30, 1993, a United States federal district court approves the settlement of a lawsuit under which Corporation X must transfer $10,833,000 to a qualified settlement fund on August 1, 1993. The $10,833,000 includes $10 million of damages incurred by plaintiffs on October 1, 1992, and $833,000 of interest calculated at 10 percent annually from October 1, 1992, to August 1, 1993. The $833,000 of interest is not a payment to the qualified settlement fund in compensation for a late or delayed transfer to the fund within the meaning of paragraph (b)(1) of this section because the payment of $10,833,000 to the fund is not due until August 1, 1993.

Example 2. Assume the same facts as in *Example 1* except that the settlement agreement also provides for interest to accrue at a rate of 12 percent annually on any amount not transferred to the qualified settlement fund on August 1, 1993, and the only transfer Corporation X makes to the fund is $11,374,650 on January 1, 1994. The additional payment of $541,650 ($11,374,650 paid on January 1, 1994, less $10,833,000 due on August 1, 1993) is a payment to the qualified settlement fund in compensation for a late or delayed transfer to the fund within the meaning of paragraph (b)(1) of this section. [Reg. § 1.468B-2.]

☐ [*T.D.* 8459, 12-18-92.]

[§ 1.468B-3]

§ 1.468B-3. **Rules applicable to the transferor.**—(a) *Transfer of property*—(1) *In general.* A transferor must treat a transfer of property to a qualified settlement fund as a sale or exchange of that property for purposes of section 1001(a). In computing the gain or loss, the amount realized by the transferor is the fair market value of the property on the date the transfer is made (or is treated as made under § 1.468B-1(g)) to the qualified settlement fund. Because the issuance of a transferor's debt, obligation to provide services or property in the future, or obligation to make a payment described in § 1.461-4(g), is generally not a transfer of property by the transferor, it generally does not result in gain or loss to the transferor under this paragraph (a)(1). If a person other than the transferor transfers property to a qualified settlement fund, there may be other tax consequences as determined under general federal income tax principles.

(2) *Anti-abuse rule.* The Commissioner may disallow a loss resulting from the transfer of property to a qualified settlement fund if the Commissioner determines that a principal purpose for the transfer was to claim the loss and—

(i) The transferor places significant restrictions on the fund's ability to use or dispose of the property; or

(ii) The property (or substantially similar property) is distributed to the transferor (or a related person).

(b) *Qualified appraisal requirement for transfers of certain property*—(1) *In general.* A transferor must obtain a qualified appraisal to support a loss or deduction it claims with respect to a transfer to a qualified settlement fund of the following types of property—

(i) Nonpublicly traded securities (as defined in § 1.170A-13(c)(7)(ix)) issued by the transferor (or a related person); and

(ii) Interests in the transferor (if the transferor is a partnership) and in a partnership in which the transferor (or a related person) is a direct or indirect partner.

(2) *Provision of copies.* The transferor must provide a copy of the qualified appraisal to the administrator of the qualified settlement fund no later than February 15 of the year following the calendar year in which the property is transferred. The transferor also must attach a copy of the qualified appraisal to (and as part of) its timely filed income tax return (including extensions) for the taxable year of the transferor in which the transfer is made.

Reg. § 1.468B-3(b)(2)

(3) *Qualified appraisal.* A "qualified appraisal" is a written appraisal that—

(i) Is made within 60 days before or after the date the property is transferred to the qualified settlement fund;

(ii) Is prepared, signed, and dated by an individual who is a qualified appraiser within the meaning of § 1.170A-13(c)(5);

(iii) Includes the information required by paragraph (b)(4) of this section; and

(iv) Does not involve an appraisal fee of the type prohibited by § 1.170A-13(c)(6).

(4) *Information included in a qualified appraisal.* A qualified appraisal must include the following information—

(i) A description of the appraised property;

(ii) The date (or expected date) of the property's transfer to the qualified settlement fund;

(iii) The appraised fair market value of the property on the date (or expected date) of transfer;

(iv) The method of valuing the property, such as the comparable sales approach;

(v) The specific basis for the valuation, such as specific comparable sales or statistical sampling, including a justification for using comparable sales or statistical sampling and an explanation of the procedure employed;

(vi) The terms of any agreement or understanding entered into (or expected to be entered into) by or on behalf of the transferor (or a related person) or the qualified settlement fund that relates to the use, sale, or other disposition of the transferred property, including, for example, the terms of any agreement or understanding that temporarily or permanently—

(A) Restricts the qualified settlement fund's right to use or dispose of the property; or

(B) Reserves to, or confers upon, any person other than the qualified settlement fund any right (including designating another person as having the right) to income from the property, to possess the property (including the right to purchase or otherwise acquire the property), or to exercise any voting rights with respect to the property;

(vii) The name, address, and taxpayer identification number of the qualified appraiser; and if the qualified appraiser is acting in his or her capacity as a partner in a partnership, an employee of any person, or an independent contractor engaged by a person other than the transferor, the name, address, and taxpayer identification number of the partnership or the person who employs or engages the qualified appraiser;

(viii) The qualifications of the qualified appraiser, including the appraiser's background, experience, education, and membership, if any, in professional appraisal associations; and

(ix) A statement that the appraisal was prepared for income tax purposes.

(5) *Effect of signature of the qualified appraiser.* Any appraiser who falsely or fraudulently overstates the value of the transferred property referred to in a qualified appraisal may be subject to a civil penalty under section 6701 for aiding and abetting an understatement of tax liability and may have appraisals disregarded pursuant to 31 U.S.C. 330(c).

(c) *Economic performance*—(1) *In general.* Except as otherwise provided in this paragraph (c), for purposes of section 461(h), economic performance occurs with respect to a liability described in § 1.468B-1(c)(2)(determined with regard to § 1.468B-1(f) and (g)) to the extent the transferor makes a transfer to a qualified settlement fund to resolve or satisfy the liability.

(2) *Right to a refund or reversion*—(i) *In general.* Economic performance does not occur to the extent—

(A) The transferor (or a related person) has a right to a refund or reversion of a transfer if that right is exercisable currently and without the agreement of an unrelated person that is independent or has an adverse interest (e.g., the court or agency that approved the fund, or the fund claimants); or

(B) Money or property is transferred under conditions that allow its refund or reversion by reason of the occurrence of an event that is certain to occur, such as the passage of time, or if restrictions on its refund or reversion are illusory.

(ii) *Right extinguished.* With respect to a transfer described in paragraph (c)(2)(i) of this section, economic performance is deemed to occur on the date, and to the extent, the transferor's right to a refund or reversion is extinguished.

(3) *Obligations of a transferor.* Economic performance does not occur when a transferor transfers to a qualified settlement fund its debt (or the debt of a related person). Instead, economic performance occurs as the transferor (or related person) makes principal payments on the debt. Similarly, economic performance does not occur when a transferor transfers to a qualified settlement fund its obligation (or the obligation of a related person) to provide services or property in the future, or to make a payment described in § 1.461-4(g). Instead, economic performance with

Reg. § 1.468B-3(b)(3)

respect to such an obligation occurs as services, property or payments are provided or made to the qualified settlement fund or a claimant.

(d) *Payment of insurance amounts.* No deduction is allowed to a transferor for a transfer to a qualified settlement fund to the extent the transferred amounts represent amounts received from the settlement of an insurance claim and are excludable from gross income. If the settlement of an insurance claim occurs after a transferor makes a transfer to a qualified settlement fund for which a deduction has been taken, the transferor must include in income the amounts received from the settlement of the insurance claim to the extent of the deduction.

(e) *Statement to the qualified settlement fund and the Internal Revenue Service*—(1) *In general.* A transferor must provide the statement described in paragraph (e)(2) of this section to the administrator of a qualified settlement fund no later than February 15 of the year following each calendar year in which the transferor (or an insurer or other person on behalf of the transferor) makes a transfer to the fund. The transferor must attach a copy of the statement to (and as part of) its timely filed income tax return (including extensions) for the taxable year of the transferor in which the transfer is made.

(2) *Required statement*—(i) *In general.* The statement required by this paragraph (e) must provide the following information—

(A) A legend, "§ 1.468B-3 Statement", at the top of the first page;

(B) The transferor's name, address, and taxpayer identification number;

(C) The qualified settlement fund's name, address, and employer identification number;

(D) The date of each transfer;

(E) The amount of cash transferred; and

(F) A description of property transferred and its fair market value on the date of transfer.

(ii) *Combined statements.* If a qualified settlement fund has more than one transferor, any two or more of the transferors may provide a combined statement to the administrator that does not identify the amount of cash or the property transferred by a particular transferor. If a combined statement is used, however, each transferor must include with its copy of the statement that is attached to its income tax return a schedule describing each asset that the transferor transferred to the qualified settlement fund.

(f) *Distributions to transferors*—(1) *In general.* A transferor must include in gross income any distribution (including a deemed distribution described in paragraph (f)(2) of this section) it receives from a qualified settlement fund. If property is distributed, the amount includible in gross income and the basis in that property, is the fair market value of the property on the date of the distribution.

(2) *Deemed distributions*—(i) *Other liabilities.* If a qualified settlement fund makes a distribution on behalf of a transferor to a person that is not a claimant, or to a claimant to resolve or satisfy a liability of the transferor (or a related person) other than a liability described in § 1.468B-1(c)(2) for which the fund was established, the distribution is deemed made by the fund to the transferor. The transferor, in turn, is deemed to have made a payment to the actual recipient.

(ii) *Constructive receipt.* To the extent a transferor acquires a right to a refund or reversion described in paragraph (c)(2) of this section of all or a portion of the assets of a qualified settlement fund subsequent to the transfer of those assets to the fund, the fund is deemed to distribute those assets to the transferor on the date the right is acquired.

(3) *Tax benefit rule.* A distribution described in paragraph (f)(1) or (f)(2) of this section is excluded from the gross income of a transferor to the extent provided by section 111(a).

(g) *Example.* The following example illustrates the rules of this section:

Example. On March 1, 1993, Individual A transfers $1 million to a qualified settlement fund to resolve or satisfy claims against him resulting from certain violations of securities laws. Individual A uses the cash receipts and disbursements method of accounting. Since Individual A does not use the accrual method of accounting, the economic performance rules of paragraph (c) of this section are not applicable. Therefore, whether, when, and to what extent Individual A can deduct the transfer is determined under applicable provisions of the Internal Revenue Code, such as sections 162 and 461. [Reg. § 1.468B-3.]

☐ [T.D. 8459, 12-18-92.]

[§ 1.468B-4]

§ 1.468B-4. Taxability of distributions to claimants.—Whether a distribution to a claimant is includible in the claimant's gross income is generally determined by reference to the claim in respect of which the distribution is made and as if the distribution were made directly by the transferor. For example, to the extent a distribution is in satisfaction of damages on account of personal injury or sickness, the distribution may be exclud-

Reg. § 1.468B-4

able from gross income under section 104(a)(2). Similarly, to the extent a distribution is in satisfaction of a claim for foregone taxable interest, the distribution is includible in the claimant's gross income under section 61(a)(4). [Reg. § 1.468B-4.]

☐ [T.D. 8459, 12-18-92.]

[§ 1.468B-5]

§ 1.468B-5. Effective dates and transition rules.—(a) *In general.* Section 468B, including section 468B(g), is effective as provided in the Tax Reform Act of 1986 and the Technical and Miscellaneous Revenue Act of 1988. Except as otherwise provided in this section, § § 1.468B-1 through 1.468B-4 are effective on January 1, 1993. Thus, the regulations apply to income of a qualified settlement fund earned after December 31, 1992, transfers to a fund after December 31, 1992, and distributions from a fund after December 31, 1992. For purposes of § 1.468B-3(c)(relating to economic performance), previously transferred assets held by a qualified settlement fund on the date these regulations first apply to the fund (i.e., January 1, 1993, or the earlier date provided under paragraph (b)(2) of this section) are treated as transferred to the fund on that date, to the extent no taxpayer has previously claimed a deduction for the transfer.

(b) *Taxation of certain pre-1996 fund income*—(1) *Reasonable method*—(i) *In general.* With respect to a fund, account, or trust established after August 16, 1986, but prior to February 15, 1992, that satisfies (or, if it no longer exists, would have satisfied) the requirements of § 1.468B-1(c), the Internal Revenue Service will not challenge a reasonable, consistently applied method of taxation for transfers to the fund, income earned by the fund, and distributions made by the fund after August 16, 1986, but prior to January 1, 1996. A method is generally considered reasonable if, depending on the facts and circumstances, all transferors and the administrator of the fund have consistently treated transfers to the fund, income earned by the fund, and distributions made by the fund after August 16, 1986, as if the fund were—

(A) A grantor trust and the transferors are the grantors;

(B) A complex trust and the transferors are the grantors; or

(C) A designated settlement fund.

(ii) *Qualified settlement funds established after February 14, 1992, but before January 1, 1993.* With respect to a fund, account, or trust established after February 14, 1992, but prior to January 1, 1993, that satisfies the requirements of § 1.468B-1(c), the Internal Revenue Service will not challenge a reasonable, consistently applied method of taxation as described in paragraph (b)(1)(i) of this section for transfers to, income earned by, and distributions made by the fund prior to January 1, 1993. However, pursuant to paragraph (a) of this section, sections 1.468B-1 through 1.468B-4 apply to transfers to, income earned by, and distributions made by the qualified settlement fund after 1992.

(iii) *Use of cash method of accounting.* For purposes of paragraphs (b)(i) and (b)(ii) of this section, for taxable years beginning prior to January 1, 1996, the Internal Revenue Service will not challenge the use of the cash receipts and disbursement method of accounting by a fund, account, or trust.

(iv) *Unreasonable position.* In no event is it a reasonable position to assert, pursuant to Rev. Rul. 71-119 (see § 601.601(d)(2)(ii)(*b*) of this Chapter), that there is no current taxation of the income of a fund established after August 16, 1986.

(v) *Waiver of penalties.* For taxable years beginning prior to January 1, 1993, if a fund, account or trust is subject to section 468B(g) and the Internal Revenue Service does not challenge the method of taxation for transfers to, income earned by, and distributions made by, the fund pursuant to paragraph (b)(1)(i) or (b)(1)(ii) of this section, penalties will not be imposed in connection with the use of such method. For example, the penalties under section 6655 for failure to pay estimated tax, section 6651(a)(1) for failure to file a return, section 6651(a)(2) for failure to pay tax, section 6656 for failure to make deposit of taxes, and section 6662 for accuracy-related underpayments will generally not be imposed.

(2) *Election to apply qualified settlement fund rules*—(i) *In general.* The person that will be the administrator of a qualified settlement fund may elect to apply § § 1.468B-1 through 1.468B-4 to transfers to, income earned by, and distributions made by, the fund in taxable years ending after August 16, 1986. The election is effective beginning on the first day of the earliest open taxable year of the qualified settlement fund. For purposes of this paragraph (b)(2), a taxable year is considered open if the period for assessment and collection of tax has not expired pursuant to the rules of section 6501. The election statement must provide the information described in paragraph (b)(2)(ii) of this section and must be signed by the person that will be the administrator. Such person must also provide each transferor of the qualified settlement fund with a copy of the election statement on or before March 15, 1993.

Methods of Accounting

See p. 20,601 for regulations not amended to reflect law changes

(ii) *Election statement.* The election statement must provide the following information—

(A) A legend, "§ 1.468B-5(b)(2) Election", at the top of the first page;

(B) Each transferor's name, address, and taxpayer identification number;

(C) The qualified settlement fund's name, address, and employer identification number; and

(D) The date the qualified settlement fund was established within the meaning of § 1.468B-1(j).

(iii) *Due date of returns and amended returns.* The election statement described in paragraph (b)(2)(ii) of this section must be filed with, and as part of, the qualified settlement fund's timely filed tax return for the taxable year ended December 31, 1992. In addition, the qualified settlement fund must file an amended return that is consistent with the requirements of §§ 1.468B-1 through 1.468B-4 for any taxable year to which the election applies in which the fund took a position inconsistent with those requirements. Any such amended return must be filed no later than March 15, 1993, and must include a copy of the election statement described in paragraph (b)(2)(ii) of this section.

(iv) *Computation of interest and waiver of penalties.* For purposes of section 6601 and section 6611, the income tax return for each taxable year of the qualified settlement fund to which the election applies is due on March 15 of the year following the taxable year of the fund. For taxable years of a qualified settlement fund ending prior to January 1, 1993, the income earned by the fund is deemed to have been earned on December 31 of each taxable year for purposes of section 6655. Thus, the addition to tax for failure to pay estimated tax under section 6655 will not be imposed. The penalty for failure to file a return under section 6651(a)(1), the penalty for failure to pay tax under section 6651(a)(2), the penalty for failure to make deposit of taxes under section 6656, and the accuracy-related penalty under section 6662 will not be imposed on a qualified settlement fund if the fund files its tax returns for taxable years ending prior to January 1, 1993, and pays any tax due for those taxable years, on or before March 15, 1993. [Reg. § 1.468B-5.]

☐ [*T.D.* 8459, 12-18-92.]

[Reg. § 1.469-0]

§ 1.469-0. **Table of contents.**—This section lists the captions that appear in the regulations under section 469.

§ 1.469-1. General rules.

(a) through (c)(7) [Reserved].

(c)(8) Consolidated groups.

(c)(9) through (d)(1) [Reserved].

(2) Coordination with sections 613A(d) and 1211.

(d)(3) through (e)(1) [Reserved].

(2) Trade or business activity.

(e)(3)(i) through (e)(3)(ii) [Reserved].

(iii) Average period of customer use.

(A) In general.

(B) Average use factor.

(C) Average period of customer use for class of property.

(D) Period of customer use.

(E) Class of property.

(F) Gross rental income and daily rent.

(e)(3)(iv) through (e)(3)(vi)(C) [Reserved].

(D) Lodging rented for convenience of employer.

(E) Unadjusted basis.

(e)(3)(vii) through (e)(4)(iii) [Reserved].

(iv) Definition of "working interest."

(e)(4)(v) through (vi) [Reserved].

(5) Rental of dwelling unit.

(e)(6) through (f)(3)(iii) [Reserved].

(4) Carryover of disallowed deductions and credits.

(i) In general.

(ii) Operations continued through C corporations or similar entities.

(iii) Examples.

(g)(1) through (g)(4)(ii)(B) [Reserved].

(g)(4)(ii)(C) (no paragraph heading).

(g)(5) [Reserved].

(h)(1) In general.

(h)(2) Definitions.

(h)(3) [Reserved].

(4) Status and participation of members.

(i) Determination by reference to status and participation of group.

(ii) Determination of status and participation of consolidated group.

(h)(5) [Reserved].

(h)(6) Intercompany transactions.

(i) In general.

(ii) Example.

(iii) Effective date.

(h)(7) through (k) [Reserved].

§ 1.469-1T. General rules (temporary).

Reg. § 1.469-0

(a) Passive activity loss and credit disallowed.
   (1) In general.
   (2) Exceptions.
(b) Taxpayers to whom these rules apply.
(c) Cross references.
   (1) Definition of passive activity.
   (2) Passive activity loss.
   (3) Passive activity credit.
   (4) Effect of rules for other purposes.
   (5) Special rule for oil and gas working interests.
   (6) Treatment of disallowed losses and credits.
   (7) Corporations subject to section 469.
   (8) [Reserved].
   (9) Joint returns
   (10) Material participation.
   (11) Effective date and transition rules.
   (12) Future regulations.
(d) Effect of section 469 and the regulations thereunder for other purposes.
   (1) Treatment of items of passive activity income and gain.
   (2) Coordination with sections 613A(d) and 1211 [Reserved].
   (3) Treatment of passive activity losses.
(e) Definition of "passive activity".
   (1) In general.
   (2) Trade or business activity [Reserved].
   (3) Rental activity.
     (i) In general.
     (ii) Exceptions.
     (iii) Average period of customer use [Reserved].
       (A) In general [Reserved].
       (B) Average use factor [Reserved].
       (C) Average period of customer use for class of property [Reserved].
       (D) Period of customer use [Reserved].
       (E) Class of property [Reserved].
       (F) Gross rental income and daily rent [Reserved].
     (iv) Significant personal services.
       (A) In general.
       (B) Excluded services.
     (v) Extraordinary personal services.
     (vi) Rental of property incidental to a nonrental activity of the taxpayer.
       (A) In general.
       (B) Property held for investment.
       (C) Property used in a trade or business.
       (D) Lodging rented for convenience of employer [Reserved].
       (E) Unadjusted basis [Reserved].
     (vii) Property made available for use in a nonrental activity conducted by a partnership, S corporation or joint venture in which the taxpayer owns an interest.
     (viii) Examples.
   (4) Special rules for oil and gas working interests.
     (i) In general.
     (ii) Exception for deductions attributable to a period during which liability is limited.
       (A) In general.
       (B) Coordination with rules governing the identification of disallowed passive activity deductions.
       (C) Meaning of certain terms.
         (*1*) Allocable deductions.
         (*2*) Disqualified deductions.
         (*3*) Net loss.
         (*4*) Ratable portion.
     (iii) Examples.
     (iv) Definition of "working interest" [Reserved].
     (v) Entities that limit liability.
       (A) General rule.
       (B) Other limitations disregarded.
       (C) Examples.
     (vi) Cross reference to special rule for income from certain oil or gas properties.
   (5) Rental of dwelling unit [Reserved].
   (6) Activity of trading personal property.
     (i) In general.
     (ii) Personal property.
     (iii) Example.
(f) Treatment of disallowed passive activity losses and credits.
   (1) Scope of this paragraph.
   (2) Identification of disallowed passive activity deductions.
     (i) Allocation of disallowed passive activity deductions.
       (A) General rule.
       (B) Loss from an activity.
       (C) Significant participation passive activities.
       (D) Examples.
     (ii) Allocation with loss activities.

Reg. § 1.469-0

Methods of Accounting 37,041

See p. 20,601 for regulations not amended to reflect law changes

(A) In general.

(B) Excluded deductions.

(iii) Separately identified deductions.

(3) Identification of disallowed credits from passive activities.

(i) General rule.

(ii) Coordination rule.

(iii) Separately identified credits.

(4) Carryover of disallowed deductions and credits [Reserved].

(i) In general.

(ii) Operations continued through C corporations or similar entities.

(iii) Examples.

(g) Application of these rules to C corporations.

(1) In general.

(2) Definitions.

(3) Participation of corporations.

(i) Material participation.

(ii) Significant participation.

(iii) Participation of individual.

(4) Modified computation of passive activity loss in the case of closely held corporations.

(i) In general.

(ii) Net active income.

(iii) Examples.

(5) Allowance of passive activity credit of closely held corporations to extent of net active income tax liability.

(i) In general.

(ii) Net active income tax liability.

(h) Special rules for affiliated group filing consolidated return.

(1) [Reserved].

(2) [Reserved].

(3) Disallowance of consolidated group's passive activity loss or credit.

(4) Status and participation of members [Reserved].

(i) Determination by reference to status and participation of group [Reserved].

(ii) Determination of status and participation of consolidated group [Reserved].

(5) Modification of rules for identifying disallowed passive activity deductions and credits.

(i) Identification of disallowed deductions.

(ii) Ratable portion of disallowed passive activity losses.

(iii) Identification of disallowed credits.

(6) [Reserved].

(7) Disposition of stock of a member of an affiliated group.

(8) Dispositions of property used in multiple activities.

(i) [Reserved].

(j) Spouses filing joint returns.

(1) In general.

(2) Exceptions of treatment as one taxpayer.

(i) Identification of disallowed deductions and credits.

(ii) Treatment of deductions disallowed under sections 704(d), 1366(d) and 465.

(iii) Treatment of losses from working interests.

(3) Joint return no longer filed.

(4) Participation of spouses.

(k) Former passive activities and changes in status of corporations [Reserved].

§ 1.469-2. Passive activity loss.

(a) through (c)(2)(ii) [Reserved].

(iii) Disposition of substantially appreciated property formerly used in a nonpassive activity.

(A) In general.

(B) Date of disposition.

(C) Substantially appreciated property.

(D) Investment property.

(E) Coordination with § 1.469-2T(c)(2)(ii).

(F) Coordination with section 163(d).

(G) Examples.

(iv) Taxable acquisitions.

(v) Property held for sale to customers.

(A) Sale incidental to another activity.

(*1*) Applicability.

(*i*) In general.

(*ii*) Principal purpose.

(*2*) Dealing activity not taken into account.

(B) Use in a nondealing activity incidental to sale.

(C) Examples.

(c)(3) through (c)(5) [Reserved].

(6) Gross income from certain oil or gas properties.

(i) In general.

(ii) Gross and net passive income from the property.

(iii) Property.

(iv) Examples 1 and 2.

Reg. § 1.469-0

(c)(6)(iv) Example 3 through (c)(7)(iii) [Reserved].

(c)(7)(iv) through (vi) (no paragraph headings).

(d)(1) through (d)(2)(viii) [Reserved].

(d)(2)(ix) through (d)(2)(xii) (no paragraph headings).

(d)(2)(x) through (d)(2)(xi) [Reserved].

(d)(2)(xii) (no paragraph heading).

(d)(3) through (d)(5)(ii) [Reserved].

(d)(5)(iii)(A) Applicability of rules in § 1.469-2T(c)(2).

(d)(5)(iii)(B) through (d)(6)(v)(D) [Reserved].

(d)(6)(v)(E) (no paragraph heading).

(d)(6)(v)(F) through (d)(7) [Reserved].

(8) Taxable year in which item arises.

(e)(1) through (e)(2)(i) [Reserved].

(ii) Section 707(c).

(iii) Payments in liquidation of a partner's interest in partnership property.

(A) In general.

(B) Payments in liquidation of a partner's interest in unrealized receivables and goodwill under section 736(a).

(e)(3)(ii) through (iii)(A) [Reserved].

(e)(3)(iii)(B) (no paragraph heading).

(e)(3)(iii)(C) through (f)(4) [Reserved].

(5) Net income from certain property rented incidental to development activity.

(i) In general.

(ii) Commencement of use.

(iii) Services performed for the purpose of enhancing the value of property.

(iv) Examples.

(6) Property rented to a nonpassive activity.

(f)(7) through (f)(9)(ii) [Reserved].

(f)(9)(iii) through (f)(9)(iv) (no paragraph heading).

(10) Coordination with section 163(d).

(f)(11) [Reserved].

§ 1.469-2T. Passive activity loss (temporary).

(a) Scope of this section.

(b) Definition of passive activity loss.

(1) In general.

(2) Cross references.

(c) Passive activity group income.

(1) In general.

(2) Treatment of gain from disposition of an interest in an activity or an interest in property used in an activity.

(i) In general.

(A) Treatment of gain.

(B) Dispositions of partnership interest and S corporation stock.

(C) Interest in property.

(D) Examples.

(ii) Disposition of property used in more than one activity in 12-month period preceding disposition.

(iii) Disposition of substantially appreciated property used in nonpassive activity [Reserved].

(A) In general [Reserved].

(B) Date of disposition [Reserved].

(C) Substantially appreciated property [Reserved].

(D) Investment property [Reserved].

(E) Coordination with paragraph (c)(2)(ii) of this section [Reserved].

(F) Coordination with section 163(d) [Reserved].

(G) Examples [Reserved].

(iv) Taxable acquisitions [Reserved].

(v) Property held for sale to customers [Reserved].

(A) Sale incidental to another activity [Reserved].

(*1*) Applicability [Reserved].

(*i*) In general [Reserved].

(*ii*) Principal purpose [Reserved].

(*2*) Dealing activity not taken into account [Reserved].

(B) Use in a nondealing activity incidental to sale [Reserved].

(C) Examples [Reserved].

(3) Items of portfolio income specifically excluded.

(i) In general.

(ii) Gross income derived in the ordinary course of a trade or business.

(iii) Special rules.

(A) Income from property held for investment by dealer.

(B) Royalties derived in the ordinary course of the trade or business of licensing intangible property.

(*1*) In general.

(*2*) Substantial services or costs.

Reg. § 1.469-0

Methods of Accounting

See p. 20,601 for regulations not amended to reflect law changes

(*i*) In general.
(*ii*) Exception.
(*iii*) Expenditures takes into account.
(*3*) Passthrough entities.
(*4*) Cross reference.
(C) Mineral production payments.
(iv) Examples.
(4) Items of personal service income specifically excluded.
(i) In general.
(ii) Example.
(5) Income from section 481 adjustments.
(i) In general.
(ii) Positive section 481 adjustments.
(iii) Ratable portion.
(6) Gross income from certain oil or gas properties [Reserved].
(i) In general [Reserved].
(ii) Gross and net passive income from the properties [Reserved].
(iii) Property [Reserved].
(iv) Examples.
(7) Other items specifically excluded.
(d) Passive activity deductions.
(1) In general.
(2) Exceptions.
(3) Interest expense.
(4) Clearly and directly allocable expenses.
(5) Treatment of loss from disposition.
(i) In general.
(ii) Disposition of property used in more than one activity in 12-month period preceding disposition.
(iii) Other applicable rules.
(A) Applicability of rules in paragraph (c)(2).
(B) Dispositions of partnership interest and S corporation stock.
(6) Coordination with other limitations on deductions that apply before section 469.
(i) In general.
(ii) Proration of deductions disallowed under basis limitations.
(A) Deductions disallowed under section 704(d).
(B) Deductions disallowed under section 1366(d).
(iii) Proration of deductions disallowed under at-risk limitations.

(iv) Coordination of basis and at-risk limitations.
(v) Separately identified items of deduction and loss.
(7) Deductions from section 481 adjustment.
(i) In general.
(ii) Negative section 481 adjustment.
(iii) Ratable portion.
(8) Taxable year in which item arises.
(e) Special rules for partners and S corporation shareholders.
(1) In general.
(2) Payments under sections 707(a), 707(c), and 736(b).
(i) Section 707(a).
(ii) Section 707(c).
(iii) Payments in liquidation of a partner's interest in partnership property.
(A) In general.
(B) Payments in liquidation of a partner's interest of a partnership property.
(3) Sale or exchange of interest in passthrough entity.
(i) Application of this paragraph (e)(3).
(ii) General rule.
(A) Allocation among activities.
(B) Ratable portion.
(*1*) Disposition on which gain is recognized.
(*2*) Disposition on which loss is recognized.
(C) Default rule.
(D) Special rules.
(*1*) Applicable valuation date.
(*i*) In general.
(*ii*) Exception.
(*2*) Basis adjustment.
(*3*) Tiered passthrough entities.
(E) Meaning of certain terms.
(iii) Treatment of gain allocated to certain passive activities as not from a passive activity.
(iv) Dispositions occurring in taxable years beginning before February 19, 1988.
(A) In general.
(B) Exceptions.
(v) Treatment of portfolio assets.
(vi) Definitions.
(vii) Examples.
(f) Recharacterization of passive income in certain situations.
(1) In general.
(2) Special rule for significant participation.

Reg. § 1.469-0

(i) In general.
(ii) Significant participation passive activity.
(iii) Example.
(3) Rental of nondepreciable property.
(4) Net interest income from passive equity-financed lending activity.
(i) In general.
(ii) Equity-financed lending activity.
(A) In general.
(B) Certain liabilities not taken into account.
(iii) Equity-financed interest income.
(iv) Net interest income.
(v) Interest-bearing assets.
(vi) Liabilities incurred in the activity.
(vii) Average outstanding balance.
(viii) Example.
(5) Net income from certain property rented incidental to development activity.
(i) In general.
(ii) Commencement of use [Reserved].
(iii) Services performed for the purpose of enhancing the value of property [Reserved].
(iv) Examples [Reserved].
(6) Property rented to a nonpassive activity.
(7) Special rules applicable to the acquisition of an interest of a passthrough entity engaged in the trade or business of licensing intangible property.
(i) In general.
(ii) Royalty income from property.
(iii) Exceptions.
(iv) Capital expenditures.
(v) Example.
(8) Limitation on recharacterized income.
(9) Meaning of certain terms.
(10) Coordination with section 163(d).
(11) Effective date.

§ 1.469-3. Passive activity credit.
(a) through (d) [Reserved].
(e) Coordination with section 38(b).
(f) Coordination with section 50.
(g) [Reserved].

§ 1.469-3T. Passive activity credit (temporary).
(a) Computation of passive activity credit.
(b) Credits subject to section 469.
(1) In general.
(2) Treatment of credits attributed to qualified progress expenditures.
(3) Special rule for partners and S corporations shareholders.
(4) Exception for pre-1987 credits.
(c) Taxable year to which credit is attributable.
(d) Regular tax liability allocable to passive activities.
(1) In general.
(2) Regular tax liability.
(e) Coordination with section 38(b) [Reserved].
(f) Coordination with section 47 [Reserved].
(g) Examples.

§ 1.469-4. Definition of activity.
(a) Scope and purpose.
(b) Definitions.
(1) Trade or business activities.
(2) Rental activities.
(c) General rules for grouping activities.
(1) Appropriate economic unit.
(2) Facts and circumstances test.
(3) Examples.
(d) Limitation on grouping certain activities.
(1) Grouping rental activities with other trade or business activities.
(i) Rule.
(ii) Examples.
(2) Grouping real property rentals and personal property rentals prohibited.
(3) Certain activities of limited partners and limited entrepreneurs.
(i) In general.
(ii) Example.
(4) Other activities identified by the Commissioner.
(5) Activities conducted through section 469 entities.
(i) In general.
(ii) Cross reference.
(e) Disclosure and consistency requirements.
(1) Original groupings.
(2) Regroupings.
(f) Grouping by Commissioner to prevent tax avoidance.
(1) Rule.
(2) Example.
(g) Treatment of partial dispositions.
(h) Rules for grouping rental real estate activities for taxpayers qualifying under section 469(c)(7).

§ 1.469-5. Material participation.
(a) through (e) [Reserved].

Reg. § 1.469-0

Methods of Accounting

(f) Participation.

(1) In general.

(f)(2) through (h)(2) [Reserved].

(3) Coordination with rules governing the treatment of passthroughs entities.

(i) [Reserved].

(j) Material participation for preceding taxable years.

(1) In general.

(2) Material participation test for taxable years beginning before January 1, 1987.

(k) Examples (1) through (4) [Reserved].

(k) Example (5).

(k) Examples (6) through (8) [Reserved].

§ 1.469-5T. Material participation (temporary).

(a) In general.

(b) Facts and circumstances.

(1) In general [Reserved].

(2) Certain participation insufficient to constitute material participation under this paragraph (b).

(i) Participation satisfying standards not contained in section 469.

(ii) Certain management activities.

(iii) Participation less than 100 hours.

(c) Significant participation activity.

(1) In general.

(2) Significant participation.

(d) Personal service activity.

(e) Treatment of limited partners.

(1) General rule.

(2) Exceptions.

(3) Limited partnership interest.

(i) In general.

(ii) Limited partner holding general partner interest.

(f) Participation [Reserved].

(1) In general [Reserved].

(2) Exceptions.

(i) Certain work not customarily done by owners.

(ii) Participation as an investor.

(A) In general.

(B) Work done in individual's capacity as an investor.

(3) Participation of spouses.

(4) Methods of proof.

(g) Material participation of trust and estates [Reserved].

(h) Miscellaneous rules.

(1) Participation of corporations.

(2) Treatment of certain retired farmers and surviving spouses of retired or disabled farmers.

(3) Coordination with rules governing the treatment of passthrough entities [Reserved].

(i) [Reserved].

(j) Material participation for preceding taxable years [Reserved].

(1) In general [Reserved].

(2) Material participation for taxable years beginning before January 1, 1987 [Reserved].

(k) Examples.

§ 1.469-6. Treatment of losses upon certain dispositions. [Reserved]

§ 1.469-7 Treatment of self-charged items of interest income and deduction.

(a) In general.

(1) Applicability and effect of rules.

(2) Priority of rules in this section.

(b) Definitions.

(1) Passthrough entity.

(2) Taxpayer's share.

(3) Taxpayer's indirect interest.

(4) Entity taxable year.

(5) Deductions for a taxable year.

(c) Taxpayer loans to passthrough entity.

(1) Applicability.

(2) General rule.

(3) Applicable percentage.

(d) Passthrough entity loans to taxpayer.

(1) Applicability.

(2) General rule.

(3) Applicable percentage.

(e) Identically-owned passthrough entities.

(1) Applicability.

(2) General rule.

(3) Example.

(f) Identification of properly allocable deductions.

(g) Election to avoid application of the rules of this section.

(1) In general.

(2) Form of election.

(3) Period for which election applies.

(4) Revocation.

(h) Examples.

§ 1.469-8. Application of section 469 to trust, estates, and their beneficiaries. [Reserved]

§ 1.469-9. Rules for certain rental real estate activities.

Reg. § 1.469-0

Methods of Accounting

See p. 20,601 for regulations not amended to reflect law changes

(a) Scope and purpose.
(b) Definitions.
   (1) Trade or business.
   (2) Real property trade or business.
   (3) Rental real estate.
   (4) Personal services.
   (5) Material participation.
   (6) Qualifying taxpayer.
(c) Requirements for qualifying taxpayers.
   (1) In general.
   (2) Closely held C corporations.
   (3) Requirement of material participation in the real property trades or businesses.
   (4) Treatment of spouses.
   (5) Employees in real property trades or businesses.
(d) General rule for determining real property trades or businesses.
   (1) Facts and circumstances.
   (2) Consistency requirement.
(e) Treatment of rental real estate activities of a qualifying taxpayer.
   (1) In general.
   (2) Treatment as a former passive activity.
   (3) Grouping rental real estate activities with other activities.
     (i) In general.
     (ii) Special rule for certain management activities.
   (4) Example.
(f) Limited partnership interests in rental real estate activities.
   (1) In general.
   (2) De minimis exception.
(g) Election to treat all interests in rental real estate as a single rental real estate activity.
   (1) In general.
   (2) Certain changes not material.
   (3) Filing a statement to make or revoke the election.
(h) Interests in rental real estate held by certain passthrough entities.
   (1) General rule.
   (2) Special rule if a qualifying taxpayer holds a fifty-percent or greater interest in a passthrough entity.
   (3) Special rule for interests held in tiered passthrough entities.
   (i) [Reserved].

(j) $25,000 offset for rental real estate activities of qualifying taxpayers.
   (1) In general.
   (2) Example.

§ 1.469-10. Application of section 469 to publicly traded partnerships. [Reserved]

§ 1.469-11. Effective date and transition rules.
(a) Generally applicable effective dates.
(b) Additional effective dates.
   (1) Application of 1992 amendments for taxable years beginning before October 4, 1994.
   (2) Additional transition rule for 1992 amendments.
   (3) Fresh starts under consistency rules.
     (i) Regrouping when tax liability is first determined under Project PS-1-89.
     (ii) Regrouping when tax liability is first determined under § 1.469-4.
     (iii) Regrouping when taxpayer is first subject to section 469(c)(7).
   (4) Certain investment credit property.
(c) Special rules.
   (1) Application of certain income recharacterization rules and self-charged rules.
     (i) Certain recharacterization rules inapplicable in 1987.
     (ii) Property rented to a nonpassive activity.
     (iii) Self-charged rules.
   (2) Qualified low-income housing projects.
   (3) Effect of events occurring in years prior to 1987.
(d) Examples.
[Reg. § 1.469-0.]

☐ [*T.D.* 8417, 5-11-92. Amended by *T.D.* 8477, 2-22-93; *T.D.* 8495, 11-3-93; *T.D.* 8565, 10-3-94; *T.D.* 8597, 7-12-95; *T.D.* 8645, 12-21-95 and *T.D.* 9013, 8-20-2002.]

[Reg. § 1.469-1]

§ 1.469-1. General rules.

(a) through (c)(7). [Reserved]

(c)(8) *Consolidated groups.* Rules relating to the application of section 469 to consolidated groups are contained in paragraph (h) of this section.

(c)(9) through (d)(1). [Reserved]

(d)(2) *Coordination with sections 613A(d) and 1211.* A passive activity deduction that is not disallowed for the taxable year under section 469 and the regulations thereunder may nonetheless be disallowed for the taxable year under section

Reg. § 1.469-1

613A(d) or 1211. The following example illustrates the application of this paragraph (d)(2):

Example. In 1993, an individual derives $10,000 of ordinary income from passive activity X, no gains from the sale or exchange of capital assets or assets used in a trade or business, $12,000 of capital loss from passive activity Y, and no income, gain, deductions, or losses from any other passive activity. The capital loss from activity Y is a passive activity deduction (within the meaning of § 1.469-2T(d)). Under section 469 and the regulations thereunder, the taxpayer is allowed $10,000 of the $12,000 passive activity deduction and has a $2,000 passive activity loss for the taxable year. Since the $10,000 passive activity deduction allowed under section 469 is a capital loss, such deduction is allowable for the taxable year only to the extent provided under section 1211. Therefore, the taxpayer is allowed $3,000 of the $10,000 capital loss under section 1211 and has a $7,000 capital loss carryover (within the meaning of section 1212(b)) to the succeeding taxable year.

(d)(3) through (e)(1). [Reserved]

(e)(2) *Trade or business activities. Trade or business activities* are activities that constitute trade or business activities within the meaning of § 1.469-4(b)(1).

(e)(3)(i) through (e)(3)(ii). [Reserved]

(e)(3)(iii) *Average period of customer use*—(A) *In general.* For purposes of this paragraph (e)(3), the average period of customer use for property held in connection with an activity (the *activity's average period of customer use*) is the sum of the average use factors for each class of property held in connection with the activity.

(B) *Average use factor.* The average use factor for a class of property held in connection with an activity is the average period of customer use for that class of property multiplied by the fraction obtained by dividing—

(*1*) The activity's gross rental income attributable to that class of property; by

(*2*) The activity's gross rental income.

(C) *Average period of customer use for class of property.* In determining an activity's average period of customer use for a taxable year, the average period of customer use for a class of property held in connection with an activity is determined by dividing—

(*1*) The aggregate number of days in all periods of customer use for property in the class (taking into account only periods that end during the taxable year or that include the last day of the taxable year); by

(*2*) The number of those periods of customer use.

(D) *Period of customer use.* Each period during which a customer has a continuous or recurring right to use an item of property held in connection with the activity (without regard to whether the customer uses the property for the entire period or whether the right to use the property is pursuant to a single agreement or to renewals thereof) is treated for purposes of this paragraph (e)(3)(iii) as a separate period of customer use. The duration of a period of customer use that includes the last day of a taxable year may be determined on the basis of reasonable estimates.

(E) *Class of property.* Taxpayers may organize property into classes for purposes of this paragraph (e)(3)(iii) using any method under which items of property for which the amount of the daily rent differs significantly are not included in the same class.

(F) *Gross rental income and daily rent.* In determining an activity's average period of customer use for a taxable year—

(*1*) The activity's gross rental income is the gross income from the activity for the taxable year taking into account only income that is attributable to amounts paid for the use of property;

(*2*) The activity's gross rental income attributable to a class of property is the gross income from the activity for the taxable year taking into account only income that is attributable to amounts paid for the use of property in that class; and

(*3*) The daily rent for items of property may be determined on any basis that reasonably reflects differences during the taxable year in the amounts ordinarily paid for one day's use of those items of property.

(e)(3)(iv) through (e)(3)(vi)(C) [Reserved]

(e)(3)(vi)(D) *Lodging rented for convenience of employer.* The provision of lodging to an employee or to an employee's spouse or dependents is treated as incidental to the activity (or activities) of the taxpayer in which the employee performs services if the lodging is furnished for the taxpayer's convenience (within the meaning of section 119).

(E) *Unadjusted basis.* For purposes of this paragraph (e)(3)(vi), the term "unadjusted basis" means adjusted basis determined without regard to any adjustment described in section 1016 that decreases basis.

(e)(3)(vii) through (e)(4)(iii) [Reserved]

Reg. § 1.469-1

(e)(4)(iv) *Definition of "working interest."* For purposes of section 469 and the regulations thereunder, the term "working interest" means a working or operating mineral interest in any tract or parcel of land (within the meaning of § 1.612-4(a)).

(e)(4)(v) through (f)(3) [Reserved]

(f)(4) *Carryover of disallowed deductions and credits*—(i) *In general.* In the case of an activity of a taxpayer with respect to which any deductions or credits are disallowed for a taxable year under § 1.469-1T(f)(2) or (f)(3) (the loss activity)—

(A) The disallowed deductions or credits is allocated among the taxpayer's activities for the succeeding taxable year in a manner that reasonably reflects the extent to which each activity continues the loss activity; and

(B) The disallowed deductions or credits allocated to an activity under paragraph (f)(4)(i)(A) of this section shall be treated as deductions or credits from the activity for the succeeding taxable year.

(ii) *Business continued through C corporations or similar entities.* If a taxpayer continues part or all of a loss activity through a C corporation or similar entity (C corporation entity), the taxpayer's interest in the C corporation entity shall be treated for purposes of this paragraph (f)(4) as an interest in a passive activity that continues that loss activity in whole or part. An entity is similar to a C corporation for this purpose if the owners of interests in the entity derive only portfolio income (within the meaning of § 1.469-2T(c)(3)(i)) from the interests.

(iii) *Examples.* The following examples illustrate the application of this paragraph (f)(4). In each example, the taxpayer is an individual whose taxable year is the calendar year.

Example 1. (i) The taxpayer owns interests in a convenience store and an apartment building. In each taxable year, the taxpayer's interests in the convenience store and the apartment building are treated under § 1.469-4 as interests in two separate passive activities of the taxpayer. A $5,000 loss from the convenience-store activity and a $3,000 loss from the apartment-building activity are disallowed under § 1.469-1T(f)(2) for 1993. Under § 1.469-1T(f)(2), the $5,000 loss from the convenience-store activity is allocated among the passive activity deductions from that activity for 1993, and the $3,000 loss from the apartment-building activity is treated similarly.

(ii) In 1994, the convenience store is continued in a single activity, and the section 469 activities that constituted the apartment building is similarly continued in a separate activity. Thus, the disallowed deductions from the convenience-store activity for 1993 must be allocated under paragraph (f)(4)(i)(A) of this section to the taxpayer's convenience-store activity in 1994. Similarly, the disallowed deductions from the apartment-building activity for 1993 must be allocated to the taxpayer's apartment-building activity in 1994. Under paragraph (f)(4)(i)(B) of this section, the disallowed deductions allocated to the convenience-store activity in 1994 are treated as deductions from that activity for 1994, and the disallowed deductions allocated to the apartment-building activity for 1994 are treated as deductions from the apartment-building activity for 1994.

Example 2. (i) In 1993, the taxpayer acquires a restaurant and a catering business. Assume that in 1993 and 1994 the restaurant and the catering business are treated under § 1.469-4 as an interest in a single passive activity of the taxpayer (the restaurant and catering activity). A $10,000 loss from the activity is disallowed under § 1.469-1T(f)(2) for 1994. Assume that in 1995, the taxpayer's interests in the restaurant and the catering business are treated under § 1.469-4 as interests in two separate passive activities of the taxpayer.

(ii) Under § 1.469-1T(f)(2), the $10,000 loss from the restaurant and catering activity is allocated among the passive activity deductions from that activity for 1994. In 1995, the businesses that constituted the restaurant and catering activity are continued, but are treated as two separate activities under § 1.469-4. Thus, the disallowed deductions from the restaurant and catering activity for 1994 must be allocated under paragraph (f)(4)(i)(A) of this section between the restaurant activity and the catering activity in 1995 in a manner that reasonably reflects the extent to which each of the activities continues the single restaurant and catering activity. Under paragraph (f)(4)(i)(B) of this section, the disallowed deductions allocated to the restaurant activity in 1995 are treated as deductions from the restaurant activity for 1995, and the disallowed deductions allocated to the catering activity in 1995 are treated as deductions from the catering activity for 1995.

Example 3. (i) In 1993, the taxpayer acquires a restaurant and a catering business. Assume that in 1993 and 1994 the restaurant and the catering business are treated under § 1.469-4 as an interest in a single passive activity of the taxpayer (the restaurant and catering activity). A $10,000 loss from the activity is disallowed under

§ 1.469-1T(f)(2) for 1994. Assume that in 1995, the taxpayer's interests in the restaurant and the catering business are treated under § 1.469-4 as interests in two separate passive activities of the taxpayer. In addition, a $20,000 loss from the activity was disallowed under § 1.469-1T(f)(2) for 1993, and the gross income and deductions (including deductions that were disallowed for 1993 under § 1.469-1T(f)(2)) from the restaurant and catering business for 1993 and 1994 are as follows:

	Restaurant	Catering business
1993:		
Gross income	$20,000	$60,000
Deductions	40,000	60,000
Net income (loss)	($20,000)	—
1994:		
Gross income	$40,000	$50,000
Deductions	30,000*	70,000**
Net income (loss)	$10,000	($20,000)

* Includes $8,000 of deductions that were disallowed for 1993 ($20,000 × $40,000/$100,000).

** Includes $12,000 of deductions that were disallowed for 1993 ($20,000 × $60,000/$100,000).

(ii) Under paragraph (f)(4)(i)(A) of this section, the disallowed deductions from the restaurant and catering activity must be allocated among the taxpayer's activities for the succeeding year in a manner that reasonably reflects the extent to which those activities continue the restaurant and catering activity. The remainder of this example describes a number of allocation methods that will ordinarily satisfy the requirement of paragraph (f)(4)(i)(A) of this section. The description of specific allocation methods in this example does not preclude the use of other reasonable allocation methods for purposes of paragraph (f)(4)(i)(A) of this section.

(iii) Ordinarily, an allocation of disallowed deductions from the restaurant to the restaurant activity and disallowed deductions from the catering business to the catering activity would satisfy the requirement of paragraph (f)(4)(i)(A) of this section. Under § 1.469-1T(f)(2)(ii), a ratable portion of each deduction from the restaurant and catering activity is disallowed for 1994. Thus, $3,000 of the 1994 deductions from the restaurant are disallowed ($10,000 × $30,000/$100,000), and $7,000 of the 1994 deductions from the catering business are disallowed ($10,000 × $70,000/$100,000). Thus, the taxpayer can ordinarily treat $3,000 of the disallowed deductions as deductions from the restaurant activity for 1995, and $7,000 of the disallowed deductions as deductions from the catering activity for 1995.

(iv) Ordinarily, an allocation of disallowed deductions between the restaurant activity and catering activity in proportion to the losses from the restaurant and from the catering business for 1994 would also satisfy the requirement of paragraph (f)(4)(i)(A) of this section. If the restaurant and the catering business had been treated as separate activities in 1994, the restaurant activity would have had net income of $10,000 and the catering activity would have had a $20,000 loss. Thus, the taxpayer can ordinarily treat all $10,000 of disallowed deductions as deductions from the catering activity for 1995.

(v) Ordinarily, an allocation of disallowed deductions between the restaurant activity and catering activity in proportion to the losses from the restaurant and from the catering business for 1994 (determined as if the restaurant and the catering business had been separate activities for all taxable years) would also satisfy the requirement of paragraph (f)(4)(i)(A) of this section. If the restaurant and the catering business had been treated as separate activities for all taxable years, the entire $20,000 loss from the restaurant in 1993 would have been allocated to the restaurant activity in 1994, and the gross income and deductions from the separate activities for 1994 would be as follows:

	Restaurant	Catering business
Gross income	$40,000	$50,000
Deductions	42,000	58,000
Net income (loss)	($ 2,000)	($ 8,000)

Thus, the taxpayer can ordinarily treat $2,000 of the disallowed deductions as deductions from the restaurant activity for 1995, and $8,000 of the disallowed deductions as deductions from the catering activity for 1995.

Example 4. (i) The taxpayer is a partner in a law partnership that acquires a building in December 1993 for use in the partnership's law practice. In taxable year 1993, four floors that are not needed in the law practice are leased to tenants; in taxable year 1994, two floors are leased to tenants; in taxable years after 1994, only one floor is leased to tenants and the rental operations are insubstantial. Assume that under § 1.469-4, the law practice and the rental property are treated as a trade or business activity and a separate rental activity for taxable years 1993 and 1994. Assume further that the law practice and the rental operations are a single trade or business activity for taxable years after 1994 under § 1.469-4. The trade or business activity is not a passive activity of the taxpayer. The rental activity, however, is a passive activity. Under § 1.469-[1]T(f)(2), a $12,000 loss from the rental

Reg. § 1.469-1

activity is disallowed for 1993 and a $9,000 loss from the rental activity is disallowed for 1994.

(ii) Under § 1.469-1T(f)(2), the $12,000 loss from the rental activity for 1993 is allocated among the passive activity deductions from that activity for 1993. In 1994, the business of the rental activity is continued in two separate activities. Only two floors of the building remain in the rental activity, and the other two floors (i.e., the floors that were leased to tenants in 1993, but not in 1994) are used in the taxpayer's law-practice activity. Thus, the disallowed deductions from the rental activity for 1993 must be allocated under paragraph (f)(4)(i)(A) of this section between the rental activity and the law-practice activity in a manner that reasonably reflects the extent to which each of the activities continues business on the four floors that were leased to tenants in 1993. In these circumstances, the requirement of paragraph (f)(4)(i)(A) of this section would ordinarily be satisfied by any of the allocation methods illustrated in Example 3 or by an allocation of 50 percent of the disallowed deductions to each activity. Under paragraph (f)(4)(i)(B) of this section, the disallowed deductions allocated to the rental activity in 1994 are treated as deductions from the rental activity for 1994, and the disallowed deductions ($6,000) allocated to the law-practice activity in 1994 are treated as deductions from the law-practice activity for 1994.

(iii) Under § 1.469-1T(f)(2), the $9,000 loss from the rental activity for 1994 is allocated among the passive activity deductions from that activity for 1994. In 1995, the rental activity is continued in the taxpayer's law-practice activity. Thus, the disallowed deductions from the rental activity for 1994 must be allocated under paragraph (f)(4)(ii) of this section to the taxpayer's law-practice activity in 1995. Under paragraph (f)(4)(i)(B) of this section, the disallowed deductions allocated to the law-practice activity are treated as deductions from the law-practice activity for 1995.

(iv) Rules relating to former passive activities will be contained in paragraph (k) of this section. Under those rules, any disallowed deductions from the rental activity that are treated as deductions from the law-practice activity will be treated as unused deductions that are allocable to a former passive activity.

Example 5. (i) The taxpayer owns stock in a corporation that is an S corporation for the taxpayer's 1993 taxable year and a C corporation thereafter. The only activity of the corporation is a rental activity. For 1993, the taxpayer's pro rata share of the corporation's loss from the rental activity is $5,000, and the entire loss is disallowed under § 1.469-1T(f)(2) of this section.

(ii) Under § 1.469-1T(f)(2), the taxpayer's $5,000 loss from the rental activity is allocated among the taxpayer's deductions from that activity for 1993. In 1994, the rental activity is continued through a C corporation, and the taxpayer's interest in the C corporation is treated under paragraph (f)(4)(ii) of this section as a passive activity that continues the rental activity (the C corporation activity) for purposes of allocating the previously disallowed loss. Thus, the disallowed deductions from the rental activity for 1993 must be allocated under paragraph (f)(4)(i)(A) of this section to the taxpayer's C corporation activity in 1994, and are treated under paragraph (f)(4)(i)(B) of this section as deductions from the C corporation activity for 1994.

(iii) Treating the taxpayer's interest in the C corporation as an interest in a passive activity that continues the business of the rental activity does not change the character of the taxpayer's dividend income from the C corporation. Thus, the taxpayer's dividend income is portfolio income (within the meaning of § 1.469-2T(c)(3)(i)) and is not included in passive activity gross income. Accordingly, the taxpayer's loss from the C corporation activity for 1994 is $5,000.

Example 6. (i) The taxpayer owns stock in a corporation that is an S corporation for the taxpayer's 1993 taxable year and a C corporation thereafter. The only activity of the corporation is a rental activity. For 1993, the taxpayer's pro rata share of the corporation's loss from the rental activity is $5,000, and the entire loss is disallowed under § 1.469-1T(f)(2). The taxpayer has $2,000 in income from other passive activities for 1994, and as a result, only 60% of the taxpayer's loss from the C corporation activity ($3,000) is disallowed for 1994 under § 1.469-1T(f)(2).

(ii) Under § 1.469-1T(f)(2), the $3,000 disallowed loss from the C corporation activity is allocated among the passive activity deductions from that activity for 1994. In effect, therefore, 60 percent of each disallowed deduction from the rental activity for 1993 is again disallowed for 1994.

(iii) Under paragraph (f)(4) of this section, the taxpayer's interest in the C corporation is treated as a loss activity and as an interest in a passive activity that continues the business of that loss activity for 1995. Thus, the disallowed deductions from the C corporation activity for 1994 must be allocated under paragraph (f)(4)(i)(A) of this section to the taxpayer's C corporation activity in 1995, and are treated

Reg. § 1.469-1

under paragraph (f)(4)(i)(B) of this section as deductions from that activity for 1995.

(g)(1) through (g)(4)(ii)(B) [Reserved]

(g)(4)(ii)(C) Portfolio income (within the meaning of § 1.469-2T(c)(3)(i)), including any gross income that is treated as portfolio income under any other provision of the regulations (See, e.g., § 1.469-2(c)(2)(iii)(F) (relating to gain from the disposition of substantially appreciated property formerly held for investment) and § 1.469-2(f)(10) (relating to certain recharacterized passive activity gross income)).

(g)(5) [Reserved]

(h)(1) *In general.* This paragraph (h) provides rules for applying section 469 in computing a consolidated group's consolidated taxable income and consolidated tax liability (and the separate taxable income and tax liability of each member).

(2) *Definitions.* The definitions and nomenclature in the regulations under section 1502 apply for purposes of this paragraph (h). See, e.g., §§ 1.1502-1 (definitions of group, consolidated group, member, subsidiary, and consolidated return year), 1.1502-2 (consolidated tax liability), 1.1502-11 (consolidated taxable income), 1.1502-12 (separate taxable income), 1.1502-13 (intercompany transactions), 1.1502-21 (net operating losses), and 1.1502-22 (consolidated net capital gain and loss).

(3) [Reserved]

(h)(4) *Status and participation of members*— (i) *Determination by reference to status and participation of group.* For purposes of section 469 and the regulations thereunder—

(A) Each member of a consolidated group shall be treated as a closely held corporation or personal service corporation, respectively, for the taxable year, if and only if the consolidated group is treated (under the rules of paragraph (h)(4)(ii) of this section) as a closely held corporation or personal service corporation for that year; and

(B) The determination of whether a trade or business activity (within the meaning of paragraph (e)(2) of this section) conducted by one or more members of a consolidated group is a passive activity of the members is made by reference to the consolidated group's participation in the activity.

(ii) *Determination of status and participation of consolidated group.* For purposes of determining under § 1.469-1T(g)(2) whether a consolidated group is treated as a closely held corporation or a personal service corporation, and determining under § 1.469-1T(g)(3) whether the consolidated group materially or significantly participates in any activity conducted by one or more members of the group—

(A) The members of the consolidated group shall be treated as one corporation;

(B) Only the outstanding stock of the common parent shall be treated as outstanding stock of the corporation;

(C) An employee of any member of the group shall be treated as an employee of the corporation; and

(D) An activity is treated as the principal activity of the corporation if and only if it is the principal activity (within the meaning of § 1.441-3(e)) of the consolidated group.

(5) [Reserved]

(6) *Intercompany transactions*—(i) *In general.* Section 1.1502-13 applies to determine the treatment under section 469 of intercompany items and corresponding items from intercompany transactions between members of a consolidated group. For example, the matching rule of § 1.1502-13(c) treats the selling member (S) and the buying member (B) as divisions of a single corporation for purposes of determining whether S's intercompany items and B's corresponding items are from a passive activity. Thus, for purposes of applying § 1.469-2(c)(2)(iii) and § 1.469-2T(d)(5)(ii) to property sold by S to B in an intercompany transaction—

(A) S and B are treated as divisions of a single corporation for determining the uses of the property during the 12-month period preceding its disposition to a nonmember, and generally have an aggregate holding period for the property; and

(B) § 1.469-2(c)(2)(iv) does not apply.

(ii) *Example.* The following example illustrates the application of this paragraph (h)(6).

Example. (i) P, a closely held corporation, is the common parent of the P consolidated group. P owns all of the stock of S and B. X is a person unrelated to any member of the P group. S owns and operates equipment that is not used in a passive activity. On January 1 of Year 1, S sells the equipment to B at a gain. B uses the equipment in a passive activity and does not dispose of the equipment before it has been fully depreciated.

(ii) Under the matching rule of § 1.1502-13(c), S's gain taken into account as a result of B's depreciation is treated as gain from a passive activity even though S used the equipment in a nonpassive activity.

(iii) The facts are the same as in paragraph (a) of this *Example,* except that B sells the equipment to X on December 1 of Year 3 at a

Reg. § 1.469-1

further gain. Assume that if S and B were divisions of a single corporation, gain from the sale to X would be passive income attributable to a passive activity. To the extent of B's depreciation before the sale, the results are the same as in paragraph (ii) of this *Example*. B's gain and S's remaining gain taken into account as a result of B's sale are treated as attributable to a passive activity.

(iv) The facts are the same as in paragraph (iii) of this *Example*, except that B recognizes a loss on the sale to X. B's loss and S's gain taken into account as a result of B's sale are treated as attributable to a passive activity.

(iii) *Effective dates.* This paragraph (h)(6) applies with respect to transactions occurring in years beginning on or after July 12, 1995. For transactions occurring in years beginning before July 12, 1995, see § 1.469-1T(h)(6) (as contained in the 26 CFR part 1 edition revised as of April 1, 1995).

(h)(7) through (k) [Reserved]

[Reg. § 1.469-1.]

☐ [T.D. 8417, 5-11-92. Amended by T.D. 8597, 7-12-95; T.D. 8677, 6-26-96; T.D. 8823, 6-25-99 and T.D. 8996, 5-16-2002.]

[Reg. § 1.469-1T]

§ 1.469-1T. General rules (temporary).—(a) *Passive activity loss and credit disallowed*—(1) *In general.* Except as otherwise provided in paragraph (a)(2) of this section—

(i) The passive activity loss for the taxable year shall not be allowed as a deduction; and

(ii) The passive activity credit for the taxable year shall not be allowed.

(2) *Exceptions.* Paragraph (a)(1) of this section shall not apply to the passive activity loss or the passive activity credit for the taxable year to the extent provided in—

(i) Section 469(i) and the rules to be contained in § 1.469-9T (relating to losses and credits attributable to certain rental real estate activities); and

(ii) Section 1.469-11T (relating to losses and credits attributable to certain pre-enactment interests in activities).

(b) *Taxpayers to whom these rules apply.* The rules of section 469 and the regulations thereunder generally apply to—

(1) Individuals;

(2) Trusts (other than trusts (or portions of trusts) described in section 671);

(3) Estates;

(4) Personal service corporations (within the meaning of paragraph (g)(2)(i) of this section); and

(5) Closely held corporations (within the meaning of paragraph this section).

(c) *Cross references*—(1) *Definition of "passive activity."* Rules relating to the definition of the term "passive activity" are contained in paragraph (e) of this section.

(2) *Passive activity loss.* Rules relating to the computation of the passive activity loss for the taxable year are contained in § 1.469-2T.

(3) *Passive activity credit.* Rules relating to the computation of the passive activity credit for the taxable year are contained in § 1.469-3T.

(4) *Effect of rules for other purposes.* Rules relating to the effect of section 469 and the regulations thereunder for other purposes under the Code are contained in paragraph (d) of this section.

(5) *Special rule for oil and gas working interests.* Rules relating to the treatment of losses and credits from certain interests in oil and gas wells are contained in paragraph (e)(4) of this section.

(6) *Treatment of disallowed losses and credits.* Paragraph (f) of this section contains rules relating to—

(i) The treatment of deductions from passive activities in taxable years in which the passive activity loss is disallowed in whole or in part under paragraph (a)(1)(i) of this section; and

(ii) The treatment of credits from passive activities in taxable years in which the passive activity credit is disallowed in whole or in part under paragraph (a)(1)(ii) of this section.

(7) *Corporations subject to section 469.* Rules relating to the application of section 469 and regulations thereunder to C corporations are contained in paragraph (g) of this section.

(8) [Reserved.]

(9) *Joint returns.* Rules relating to the application of section 469 and the regulations thereunder to spouses filing a joint return for the taxable year are contained in paragraph (j) of this section.

(10) *Material participation.* Rules defining the term "material participation" are contained in § 1.469-5T.

(11) *Effective date and transition rules.* Rules relating to the effective date of section 469 and the regulations thereunder and transition rules applicable to pre-enactment interests in activities are contained in § 1.469-11T.

(12) *Future regulations.* (i) Rules relating to former passive activities and changes in corporate

Reg. § 1.469-1T(a)(1)

Methods of Accounting 37,053

status will be contained in paragraph (k) of this section.

(ii) Rules relating to the definition of "activity" will be contained in § 1.469-4T.

(iii) Rules relating to the treatment of deductions from activities that are disposed of in certain transactions will be contained in § 1.469-6T.

(iv) Rules relating to the treatment of self-charged items of income and expense will be contained in § 1.469-7T.

(v) Rules relating to the application of section 469 and the regulations thereunder to trusts, estates, and their beneficiaries will be contained in § 1.469-8T.

(vi) Rules relating to the treatment of income, deductions, and credits from certain rental real estate activities of individuals and certain estates will be contained in § 1.469-9T.

(vii) Rules relating to the application of section 469 to publicly traded partnerships will be contained in § 1.469-10T.

(d) *Effect of section 469 and the regulations thereunder for other purposes*—(1) *Treatment of items of passive activity income and gain.* Neither the provisions of section 469(a)(1) and paragraph (a)(1) of this section nor the characterization of items of income or deduction as passive activity gross income (within the meaning of § 1.469-2T(c)) or passive activity deductions (within the meaning of § 1.469-2T(d)) affects the treatment of any item of income or gain under any provision of the Internal Revenue Code other than section 469. The following example illustrates the application of this paragraph (d)(1):

Example. (i) In 1991, an individual's only income and loss from passive activities are a $10,000 capital gain from passive activity X and a $12,000 ordinary loss from passive activity Y. The taxpayer also has a $10,000 capital loss that is not derived from a passive activity.

(ii) Under § 1.469-2T(b), the taxpayer has a $2,000 passive activity loss for the taxable year. The only effect of section 469 and the regulations thereunder is to disallow a deduction for the taxpayer's $2,000 passive activity loss for the taxable year. Thus, the taxpayer's capital loss for the taxable year is allowed because the $10,000 capital gain from passive activity X is taken into account under section 1211(b) in computing the taxpayer's allowable capital loss for the year.

(2) *Coordination with sections 613A(d) and 1211.* [Reserved] See § 1.469-1(d)(2) for rules relating to this paragraph.

(3) *Treatment of passive activity losses.* Except as otherwise provided by regulations, a deduction that is disallowed for a taxable year under section 469 and regulations thereunder is not taken into account as a deduction that is allowed for the taxable year in computing the amount subject to any tax imposed by subtitle A of the Internal Revenue Code. The following example illustrates the application of this paragraph (d)(3):

Example. An individual has a $5,000 passive activity loss for a taxable year, all of which is disallowed under paragraph (a)(1) of this section. All of the disallowed loss is allocated under paragraph (f) of this section to activities that are trades or businesses (within the meaning of section 1402(c)). Such loss is not taken into account for the taxable year in computing the taxpayer's taxable income subject to tax under section 1. In addition, under this paragraph (d)(3), such loss is not taken into account for the taxable year in computing the taxpayer's net earnings from self-employment subject to tax under section 1401.

(e) *Definition of "passive activity"*—(1) *In general.* Except as otherwise provided in this paragraph (e), an activity is a passive activity of the taxpayer for a taxable year if and only if the activity—

(i) Is a trade or business activity (within the meaning of paragraph (e)(2) of this section) in which the taxpayer does not materially participate for such taxable year; or

(ii) Is a rental activity (within the meaning of paragraph (e)(3) of this section), without regard to whether or to what extent the taxpayer participates in such activity.

(2) *Trade or business activity.* [Reserved] See § 1.469-1(e)(2) for rules relating to this paragraph.

(3) *Rental activity*—(i) *In general.* Except as otherwise provided in this paragraph (e)(3), an activity is a rental activity for a taxable year if—

(A) During such taxable year, tangible property held in connection with the activity is used by customers or held for use by customers; and

(B) The gross income attributable to the conduct of the activity during such taxable year represents (or, in the case of an activity in which property is held for use by customers, the expected gross income from the conduct of the activity will represent) amounts paid or to be paid principally for the use of such tangible property (without regard to whether the use of the property by customers is pursuant to a lease or pursuant to a service contract or other arrangement that is not denominated a lease).

Reg. § 1.469-1T(e)(3)

(ii) *Exceptions.* For purposes of this paragraph (e)(3), an activity involving the use of tangible property is not a rental activity for a taxable year if for such taxable year—

(A) The average period of customer use for such property is seven days or less;

(B) The average period of customer use for such property is 30 days or less, and significant personal services (within the meaning of paragraph (e)(3)(iv) of this section) are provided by or on behalf of the owner of the property in connection with making the property available for use by customers;

(C) Extraordinary personal services (within the meaning of paragraph (e)(3)(v) of this section) are provided by or on behalf of the owner of the property in connection with making such property available for use by customers (without regard to the average period of customer use);

(D) The rental of such property is treated as incidental to a nonrental activity of the taxpayer under paragraph (e)(3)(vi) of this section;

(E) The taxpayer customarily makes the property available during defined business hours for nonexclusive use by various customers; or

(F) The provision of the property for use in an activity conducted by a partnership, S corporation, or joint venture in which the taxpayer owns an interest is not a rental activity under paragraph (e)(3)(vii) of this section.

(iii) *Average period of customer use.* [Reserved] See § 1.469-1(e)(3)(iii) for rules relating to this paragraph.

(iv) *Significant personal services*—(A) *In general.* For purposes of paragraph (e)(3)(ii)(B) of this section, personal services include only services performed by individuals, and do not include excluded services (within the meaning of paragraph (e)(3)(iv)(B) of this section). In determining whether personal services provided in connection with making property available for use by customers are significant, all of the relevant facts and circumstances shall be taken into account. Relevant facts and circumstances include the frequency with which such services are provided, the type and amount of labor required to perform such services, and the value of such services relative to the amount charged for the use of the property.

(B) *Excluded services.* For purposes of paragraph (e)(3)(iv)(A) this section, the term "excluded services" means, with respect to any property made available for use by customers—

(*1*) Services necessary to permit the lawful use of the property;

(*2*) Services performed in connection with the construction of incidental to the activity (or activities) of the taxpayer in which the employee performs improvements to the property, or in connection with the performance of repairs that extend the property's useful life for a period substantially longer than the average period for which such property is used by customers; and

(*3*) Services, provided in connection with the use of any improved real property, that are similar to those commonly provided in connection with long-term rentals of high-grade commercial or residential real property (e.g., cleaning and maintenance of common areas, routine repairs, trash collection, elevator service, and security at entrances or perimeters).

(v) *Extraordinary personal services.* For purposes of paragraph (e)(3)(ii)(C) of this section, extraordinary personal services are provided in connection with making property available for use by customers only if the services provided in connection with the use of the property are performed by individuals, and the use by customers of the property is incidental to their receipt of such services. For example, the use by patients of a hospital's boarding facilities generally is incidental to their receipt of the personal services provided by the hospital's medical and nursing staff. Similarly, the use by students of a boarding school's dormitories generally is incidental to their receipt of the personal services provided by the school's teaching staff.

(vi) *Rental of property incidental to a nonrental activity of the taxpayer*—(A) *In general.* For purposes of paragraph (e)(3)(ii)(D) of this section, the rental of property shall be treated as incidental to a nonrental activity of the taxpayer only to the extent provided in this paragraph (e)(3)(vi).

(B) *Property held for investment.* The rental of property during a taxable year shall be treated as incidental to an activity of holding such property for investment if and only if—

(*1*) The principal purpose for holding the property during such taxable year is to realize gain from the appreciation of the property (without regard to whether it is expected that such gain will be realized from the sale or exchange of the property in its current state of development); and

(*2*) The gross rental income from the property for such taxable year is less than two percent of the lesser of—

(*i*) The unadjusted basis of such property; and

(*ii*) The fair market value of such property.

Reg. § 1.469-1T(e)(3)

(C) *Property used in a trade or business.* The rental of property during a taxable year shall be treated as incidental to a trade or business activity (within the meaning of paragraph (e)(2) of this section) if and only if—

(*1*) The taxpayer owns an interest in such trade or business activity during the taxable year;

(*2*) The property was predominantly used in such trade or business activity during the taxable year or during at least two of the five taxable years that immediately precede the taxable year; and

(*3*) The gross rental income from such property for the taxable year is less than two percent of the lesser of—

(*i*) The unadjusted basis of such property; and

(*ii*) The fair market value of such property.

(D) *Lodging rented for convenience of employer.* [Reserved] See § 1.469-1(e)(3)(vi)(D) for rules relating to this paragraph.

(E) *Unadjusted basis.* [Reserved] See § 1.469-1(e)(3)(vi)(E) for rules relating to this paragraph.

(vii) *Property made available for use in a nonrental activity conducted by a partnership, S corporation, or joint venture in which the taxpayer owns an interest.* If the taxpayer owns an interest in a partnership, S corporation, or joint venture conducting an activity other than a rental activity, and the taxpayer provides property for use in the activity in the taxpayer's capacity as an owner of an interest in such partnership, S corporation, or joint venture, the provision of such property is not a rental activity. Thus, if a partner contributes the use of property to a partnership, none of the partner's distributive share of partnership income is income from a rental activity unless the partnership is engaged in a rental activity. In addition, a partner's gross income attributable to a payment described in section 707(c) is not income from a rental activity under any circumstances (see § 1.469-2T(e)(2)). The determination of whether property used in an activity is provided by the taxpayer in the taxpayer's capacity as an owner of an interest in a partnership, S corporation, or joint venture shall be made on the basis of all of the facts and circumstances.

(viii) *Examples.* The following examples illustrate the application of this paragraph (e)(3):

Example (1). The taxpayer is engaged in an activity of leasing photocopying equipment. The average period of customer use for the equipment exceeds 30 days. Pursuant to the lease agreements, skilled technicians employed by the taxpayer maintain the equipment and service malfunctioning equipment for no additional charge. Service calls occur frequently (three times per week on average) and require substantial labor. The value of the maintenance and repair services (measured by the cost to the taxpayer of employees performing these services) exceeds 50 percent of the amount charged for the use of the equipment. Under these facts, services performed by individuals are provided in connection with the use of the photocopying equipment, but the customers' use of the photocopying equipment is not incidental to their receipt of the services. Therefore, extraordinary personal services (within the meaning of paragraph (e)(3)(v) of this section) are not provided in connection with making the photocopying equipment available for use by customers, and the activity is a rental activity.

Example (2). The facts are the same as in example (1), except that the average period of customer use for the photocopying equipment exceeds seven days but does not exceed 30 days. Under these facts, significant personal services (within the meaning of paragraph (e)(3)(iv) of this section) are provided in connection with making the photocopying equipment available for use by customers and, under paragraph (e)(3)(ii)(B) of this section, the activity is not a rental activity.

Example (3). The taxpayer is engaged in an activity of transporting goods for customers. In conducting the activity, the taxpayer provides tractor-trailers to transport goods for customers pursuant to arrangements under which the tractor-trailers are selected by the taxpayer, may be replaced at the sole option of the taxpayer, and are operated and maintained by drivers and mechanics employed by the taxpayer. The average period of customer use for the tractor-trailers exceeds 30 days. Under these facts, the use of tractor-trailers by the taxpayer's customers is incidental to their receipt of personal services provided by the taxpayer. Accordingly, the services performed in the activity are extraordinary personal services (within the meaning of paragraph (e)(3)(v) of this section) and, under paragraph (e)(3)(ii)(C) of this section, the activity is not a rental activity.

Example (4). The taxpayer is engaged in an activity of owning operating a residential apartment hotel. For the taxable year, the average period of customer use for apartments exceeds seven days but does not exceed 30 days. In addition to cleaning public entrances, exits, stairways, and lobbies, and collecting and removing trash, the taxpayer provides a daily maid and linen

Reg. § 1.469-1T(e)(3)

service at no additional charge. All of the services other than maid and linen service are excluded services (within the meaning of paragraph (e)(3)(iv)(B) of this section), because such services are similar to those commonly provided in connection with long-term rentals of high-grade residential real property. The value of the maid and linen services (measured by the cost to the taxpayer of employees performing such services) is less than 10 percent of the amount charged to tenants for occupancy of apartments. Under these facts, neither significant personal services (within the meaning of paragraph (e)(3)(iv) of this section) nor extraordinary personal services (within the meaning of paragraph (e)(3)(v) of this section) are provided in connection with making apartments available for use by customers. Accordingly, the activity is a rental activity.

Example (5). The taxpayer owns 1,000 acres of unimproved land with a fair market value of $350,000 and an unadjusted basis of $210,000. The taxpayer holds the land for the principal purpose of realizing gain from appreciation. In order to defray the cost of carrying the land, the taxpayer leases the land to a rancher, who uses the land to graze cattle and pays rent of $4,000 per year. Thus, the gross rental income from the land is less than two percent of the lesser of the fair market value and the unadjusted basis of the land (.02 × $210,000 = $4,200). Accordingly, under paragraph (e)(3)(ii)(D) of this section, the rental of the land is not a rental activity because the rental is treated under paragraph (e)(3)(vi)(B) of this section as incidental to an activity of holding the property for investment.

Example (6). (i) A calendar year taxpayer owns an interest in a farming activity which is a trade or business activity (within the meaning of paragraph (e)(2) of this section) and owns farmland which was used in the farming activity in 1985 and 1986. The fair market value of the farmland is $350,000 and its unadjusted basis is $210,000. In 1987, 1988, and 1989, the taxpayer continues to own an interest in the farming activity but does not use the land in the activity. In 1987, the taxpayer leases the land for $4,000 to a rancher, who uses the land to graze cattle. In 1988, the taxpayer leases the land for $10,000 to a film production company, which uses the land to film scenes for a movie. In 1989, the taxpayer again leases the land for $4,000 to the rancher.

(ii) For 1987 and 1989, the taxpayer owns an interest in a trade or business activity, and the farmland which the taxpayer leases to the rancher was used in such activity for two out of the five immediately preceding taxable years. In addition, the gross rental income from the land ($4,000) is less than two percent of the lesser of the fair market value and the unadjusted basis of the land (.02 × $210,000 = $4,200). Accordingly, the taxpayer's rental of the land is treated under paragraph (e)(3)(vi)(C) of this section as incidental to the taxpayer's farming activity, and is not a rental activity.

(iii) Because the taxpayer's gross rental income from the land for 1988 ($10,000) is not less than two percent of the lesser of the fair market value and the unadjusted basis of the land, the requirement of paragraph (e)(3)(vi)(C)(*3*) of this section is not met. Therefore, the taxpayer's rental of the land in 1988 is not treated as incidental to the taxpayer's farming activity and is a rental activity.

Example (7). (i) In 1988, the taxpayer acquires vacant land for the purpose of constructing a shopping mall. Before commencing construction, the taxpayer leases the land under a one-year lease to an automobile dealer, who uses the land to park cars held in its inventory. The taxpayer commences construction of the shopping mall in 1989.

(ii) The taxpayer acquired the land for the principal purpose of constructing the shopping mall, not for the principal purpose of realizing gain from the appreciation of the property. Therefore, the rental of the property in 1988 is not treated under paragraph (e)(3)(vi)(B) of this section as incidental to an activity of holding the property for investment.

(iii) The land has not been used in any taxable year in any trade or business of the taxpayer. Therefore, the rental of the property in 1988 is not treated under paragraph (e)(3)(vi)(C) of this section as incidental to a trade or business activity.

(iv) Since the rental of the land in 1988 is not treated under paragraph (e)(3)(vi) of this section as incidental to a nonrental activity of the taxpayer, the rental of the land in 1988 is a rental activity. See § 1.469-2T(f)(3) for a special rule relating to the treatment of gross income from the rental of nondepreciable property.

Example (8). The taxpayer makes farmland available to a tenant farmer pursuant to an arrangement designated a "crop-share lease." Under the arrangement, the tenant is required to use the tenant's best efforts to farm the land and produce marketable crops. The taxpayer is obligated to pay 50 percent of the costs incurred in the activity (without regard to whether any crops are successfully produced or marketed), and is entitled to 50 percent of the crops produced (or 50 percent of the proceeds from marketing the crops). For purposes of paragraph (e)(3)(vii) of

Reg. § 1.469-1T(e)(3)

this section, the taxpayer is treated as providing the farmland for use in a farming activity conducted by a joint venture in the taxpayer's capacity as an owner of an interest in the joint venture. Accordingly, under paragraph (e)(3)(ii)(F) of this section, the taxpayer is not engaged in a rental activity, without regard to whether the taxpayer performs any services in the farming activity.

Example (9). The taxpayer owns a taxicab which the taxpayer operates during the day and leases to another driver for use at night under a one-year lease. Under the terms of the lease, the other driver is charged a fixed rental for use of the taxicab. Assume that, under the rules to be contained in § 1.469-4T, the taxpayer is engaged in two separate activities, an activity of operating the taxicab and an activity of making the taxicab available for use by the other driver. Under these facts, the period for which the other driver uses the taxicab exceeds 30 days, and the taxpayer does not provide extraordinary personal services in connection with making the taxicab available to the other driver. Accordingly, the lease of the taxicab is a rental activity.

Example (10). The taxpayer operates a golf course. Some customers of the golf course pay greens fees upon each use of the golf course, while other customers purchase weekly, monthly, or annual passes. The golf course is open to all customers from sunrise to sunset every day of the year except certain holidays and days on which the taxpayer determines that the course is too wet for play. The taxpayer thus makes the golf course available during prescribed hours for nonexclusive use by various customers. Accordingly, under paragraph (e)(3)(ii)(E) of this section, the taxpayer is not engaged in a rental activity, without regard to the average period of customer use for the golf course.

(4) *Special rule for oil and gas working interests*—(i) *In general.* Except as otherwise provided in paragraph (e)(4)(ii) of this section, an interest in an oil or gas well drilled or operated pursuant to a working interest (within the meaning of paragraph (e)(4)(iv) of this section) of a taxpayer is not an interest in a passive activity for the taxpayer's taxable year (without regard to whether the taxpayer materially participates in such activity) if at any time during such taxable year the taxpayer holds such working interest either—

(A) Directly; or

(B) Through an entity that does not limit the liability of the taxpayer with respect to the drilling or operation of such well pursuant to such working interest.

(ii) *Exception for deductions attributable to a period during which liability is limited*—(A) *In general.* If paragraph (e)(4)(i) of this section applies for a taxable year to the taxpayer's interest in an oil or gas well that would, but for the application of paragraph (e)(4)(i) of this section, be an interest in a passive activity for the taxable year, and the taxpayer has a net loss (within the meaning of paragraph (e)(4)(ii)(C)(*3*) of this section) from the well for the taxable year—

(*1*) The taxpayer's disqualified deductions (within the meaning of paragraph (e)(4)(ii)(C)(*2*) of this section) from such oil or gas well for such year shall be treated as passive activity deductions for such year (within the meaning of § 1.469-2T (d)); and

(*2*) A ratable portion (within the meaning of paragraph (e)(4)(ii)(C)(*4*) of this section) of the taxpayer's gross income from such oil or gas well for such year shall be treated as passive activity gross income for such year (within the meaning of § 1.469-2T(c)).

(B) *Coordination with rules governing the identification of disallowed passive activity deductions.* If gross income and deductions from an activity for a taxable year are treated as passive activity gross income and passive activity deductions under paragraph (e)(4)(ii)(A) of this section, such activity shall be treated as a passive activity for such year for purposes of applying paragraph (f)(2) and (4) of this section.

(C) *Meaning of certain terms.* For purposes of this paragraph (e)(4)(ii), the following terms shall have the meanings set forth below:

(*1*) *Allocable deductions.* The deductions allocable to a taxable year are any deductions that arise in such year (within the meaning of § 1.469-2T(d)(8)) and any deductions that are treated as deductions for such year under paragraph (f)(4) of this section.

(*2*) *Disqualified deductions.* The taxpayer's "disqualified deductions" from an oil or gas well for a taxable year are the taxpayer's deductions—

(*i*) That are attributable to such well and allocable to the taxable year; and

(*ii*) With respect to which economic performance (within the meaning of section 461(h), without regard to section 461(h)(3) or (i)(2)) occurs at a time during which the taxpayer's only interest in the working interest is held through an entity that limits the taxpayer's liability with respect to the drilling or operation of such well.

(*3*) *Net loss.* The "net loss" of a taxpayer from an oil or gas well for a taxable year equals the amount by which the taxpayer's deductions that are attributable to such oil or gas well

Reg. § 1.469-1T(e)(4)

and allocable to such year exceeds the gross income of the taxpayer from such well for such year.

(4) *Ratable portion.* The "ratable portion" of the taxpayer's gross income from an oil or gas well for a taxable year equals the total amount of such gross income multiplied by the fraction obtained by dividing—

(*i*) The disqualified deductions from such oil or gas well for the taxable year; by

(*ii*) The total amount of the deductions that are attributable to such oil or gas well and allocable to the taxable year.

(iii) *Examples.* The following examples illustrate the application of paragraphs (e)(4)(i) and (ii) of this section:

Example (1). (i) A, a calendar year individual, acquires on January 1, 1987, a general partnership interest in P, a calendar year partnership that holds a working interest in an oil or gas property. Pursuant to the partnership agreement, A is entitled to convert the general partnership interest into a limited partnership interest at any time. On December 1, 1987, pursuant to a contract with D, an independent drilling contractor, P commences drilling a single well pursuant to the working interest. Under the drilling contract, P pays D for the drilling only as the work is performed. All drilling costs are deducted by P in the year in which they are paid. At the end of 1987, A converts the general partnership interest into a limited partnership interest, effective immediately. The drilling of the well is completed on February 28, 1988. A's interest in the well would but for this paragraph (e)(4) be an interest in a passive activity.

(ii) Throughout 1987, A holds the working interest through an entity that does not limit A's liability with respect to the drilling of the well pursuant to the working interest. In 1988, however, A holds the working interest through an entity that limits A's liability with respect to the drilling and operation of the well throughout such year. Accordingly, under paragraph (e)(4)(i) of this section, A's interest in P's well is not an interest in a passive activity for 1987 but is an interest in a passive activity for 1988. Moreover, since economic performance occurs in 1987 with respect to all items of deduction for drilling costs that are allocable to 1987, A has no disqualified deductions for 1987.

Example (2). The facts are the same as in example (1), except that all costs of drilling under the contract with D (including costs of drilling performed after 1987) are paid before the end of 1987 and A has a net loss for 1987. In addition, A has $15,000 of total deductions that are attributable to the well and allocable to 1987, but economic performance (as that term is used in paragraph (e)(4)(ii)(C)(*2*)(*ii*) of this section) does not occur with respect to $5,000 of those deductions until 1988. Under paragraph (e)(4)(ii) of this section, the $5,000 of deductions with respect to which economic performance occurs in 1988 are disqualified deductions and are treated as passive activity deductions for 1987. In addition, one-third ($5,000/$15,000) of A's gross income from the well for 1987 is treated as passive activity gross income.

(iv) *Definition of "working interest."* [Reserved] See § 1.469-1(e)(4)(iv) for rules relating to this paragraph.

(v) *Entities that limit liability*—(A) *General rule.* For purposes of paragraph (e)(4)(i)(B) of this section, an entity limits the liability of the taxpayer with respect to the drilling or operation of a well pursuant to a working interest held through such entity if the taxpayer's interest in the entity is in the form of—

(*1*) A limited partnership interest in a partnership in which the taxpayer is not a general partner;

(*2*) Stock in a corporation; or

(*3*) An interest in any entity (other than a limited partnership or corporation) that, under applicable State law, limits the potential liability of a holder of such an interest for all obligations of the entity to a determinable fixed amount (for example, the sum of the taxpayer's capital contributions).

(B) *Other limitations disregarded.* For purposes of this paragraph (e)(4), protection against loss through any of the following is not taken into account in determining whether a taxpayer holds a working interest through an entity that limits the taxpayer's liability:

(*1*) An indemnification agreement;

(*2*) A stop loss arrangement;

(*3*) Insurance;

(*4*) Any similar arrangement; or

(*5*) Any combination of the foregoing.

(C) *Examples.* The following examples illustrate the application of this paragraph (e)(4)(v):

Example (1). A owns a 20 percent interest as a general partner in the capital and profits of P, a partnership which owns oil or gas working interests. The other partners of P agree to indemnify A against liability in excess of A's capital contribution for any of P's costs and expenses with respect to P's working interests. As a general partner, however, A is jointly and severally liable for all of P's liabilities and, under paragraph

Reg. § 1.469-1T(e)(4)

(e)(4)(v)(B)(*1*) of this section, the indemnification agreement is not taken into account in determining whether A holds the working interests through an entity that limits A's liability. Accordingly, the partnership does not limit A's liability with respect to the drilling or operation of wells pursuant to the working interests.

Example (2). B owns a 10 percent interest in X, an entity (other than a limited partnership or corporation) created under applicable State law to hold working interests in oil or gas properties. Under applicable State law, B is liable without limitation for 10 percent of X's costs and expenses with respect to X's working interests but is not liable for the remaining 90 percent of such costs and expenses. Since B's liability for the obligations of X is not limited to a determinable fixed amount (within the meaning of paragraph (e)(4)(v)(A)(*3*) of this section), the entity does not limit B's liability with respect to the drilling or operation of wells pursuant to the working interests.

Example (3). C is both a general partner and a limited partner in a partnership that owns a working interest in oil or gas property. Because C owns an interest as a general partner in each well drilled pursuant to the working interest, C's entire interest in each well drilled pursuant to the working interest is treated under paragraph (e)(4)(i) of this section as an interest in an activity that is not a passive activity (without regard to whether C materially participates in such activity).

(vi) *Cross reference to special rule for income from certain oil or gas properties.* A special rule relating to the treatment of income from certain interests in oil or gas properties is contained in § 1.469-2T(c)(6).

(5) *Rental of dwelling unit.* [Reserved] See § 1.469-1(d)(2)(xii) for rules relating to this paragraph.

(6) *Activity of trading personal property*—(i) *In general.* An activity of trading personal property for the account of owners of interests in the activity is not a passive activity (without regard to whether such activity is a trade or business activity (within the meaning of paragraph (e)(2) of this section)).

(ii) *Personal property.* For purposes of this paragraph (e)(6), the term "personal property" means personal property (within the meaning of section 1092(d), without regard to paragraph (3) thereof).

(iii) *Example.* The following example illustrates the application of this paragraph (e)(6):

Example. A partnership is a trader of stocks, bonds, and other securities (within the meaning of section 1236(c)). The capital employed by the partnership in the trading activity consists of amounts contributed by the partners in exchange for their partnership interests, and funds borrowed by the partnership. The partnership derives gross income from the activity in the form of interest, dividends, and capital gains. Under these facts, the partnership is treated as conducting an activity of trading personal property for the account of its partners. Accordingly, under this paragraph (e)(6), the activity is not a passive activity.

(f) *Treatment of disallowed passive activity losses and credits*—(1) *Scope of this paragraph.* The rules in this paragraph (f)—

(i) Identify the passive activity deductions that are disallowed for any taxable year in which all or a portion of the taxpayer's passive activity loss is disallowed under paragraph (a)(1)(i) of this section;

(ii) Identify the credits from passive activities that are disallowed for any taxable year in which all or a portion of the taxpayer's passive activity credit is disallowed under paragraph (a)(1)(ii) of this section; and

(iii) Provide for the carryover of disallowed deductions and credits.

(2) *Identification of disallowed passive activity deductions*—(i) *Allocation of disallowed passive activity loss among activities*—(A) *General rule.* If all or any portion of the taxpayer's passive activity loss is disallowed for the taxable year under paragraph (a)(1)(i) of this section, a ratable portion of the loss (if any) from each passive activity of the taxpayer is disallowed. For purposes of the preceding sentence, the ratable portion of a loss from an activity is computed by multiplying the passive activity loss that is disallowed for the taxable year by the fraction obtained by dividing—

(*1*) The loss from the activity for the taxable year; by

(*2*) The sum of the losses for the taxable year from all activities having losses for such year.

(B) *Loss from an activity.* For purposes of this paragraph (f)(2)(i), the term "loss from an activity" means—

(*1*) The amount by which the passive activity deductions from the activity for the taxable year (within the meaning of § 1.469-2T(d)) exceed the passive activity gross income from the activity for the taxable year (within the meaning of § 1.469-2T(c)); reduced by

Reg. § 1.469-1T(f)(2)

(2) Any part of such amount that is allowed under section 469(i) and the rules to be contained in § 1.469-9T (relating to the $25,000 allowance for certain rental real estate activities).

(C) *Significant participation passive activities.* If the taxpayer's passive activity gross income from significant participation passive activities (within the meaning of § 1.469-2T(f)(2)(ii)) for the taxable year (determined without regard to § 1.469-2T(f)(2) through (4)) exceeds the taxpayer's passive activity deductions from such activities for the taxable year, such activities shall be treated, solely for purposes of applying this paragraph (f)(2)(i) for the taxable year, as a single activity that does not have a loss for such taxable year.

(D) *Examples.* The following examples illustrate the application of this paragraph (f)(2)(i):

Example (1). An individual holds interests in three passive activities, A, B, and C. The gross income and deductions from these activities for the taxable year are as follows:

	A	B	C	Total
Gross income	$7,000	$4,000	$12,000	$23,000
Deductions	(16,000)	(20,000)	(8,000)	(44,000)
Net income (loss)	($9,000)	($16,000)	$4,000	($21,000)
Total				$21,000

The taxpayer's $21,000 passive activity loss for the taxable year is disallowed under paragraph (a)(1)(i) of this section. Therefore, a ratable portion of the losses from activities A and B is disallowed. The disallowed portion of each loss is determined as follows:

A: $21,000 × $ 9,000/$25,000 = $ 7,560
B: $21,000 × $16,000/$25,000 = $13,440

Example (2). An individual holds interests in four passive activities, A, B, C, and D. The results of operations of these activities for the taxable year are as follows:

	A	B	C	D	Total
Gross income	$15,000	$5,000	$10,000	$10,000	40,000
Deductions	(5,000)	(10,000)	(20,000)	(8,000)	(43,000)
Net income (loss)	10,000	(5,000)	(10,000)	2,000	(3,000)

Activities A and B are significant participation passive activities (within the meaning of § 1.469-2T(f)(2)(ii)). The gross income from those activities for the taxable year ($20,000) exceeds the passive activity deductions from those activities for the taxable year ($15,000) by $5,000 and, under § 1.469-2T(f)(2), $5,000 of gross income from those activities is treated as not from a passive activity. Therefore, solely for purposes of applying this paragraph (f)(2)(i) for the taxable year, activities A and B are treated as a single activity that does not have a loss for the taxable year. Under § 1.469-2T(b), the taxpayer's passive activity loss for the taxable year is $8,000 ($43,000 of passive activity deductions minus $35,000 of passive activity gross income). The result of treating activities A and B as a single activity that does not have a loss for the taxable year is that none of the $8,000 passive activity loss is allocated under this paragraph (f)(2)(i) to activity B for the taxable year, even though the taxpayer incurred a loss in that activity for the taxable year.

(ii) *Allocation within loss activities*—(A) *In general.* If all or any portion of a taxpayer's loss from an activity is disallowed under paragraph (f)(2)(i) of this section for the taxable year, a ratable portion of each passive activity deduction (other than an excluded deduction (within the meaning of paragraph (f)(2)(ii)(B) of this section)) of the taxpayer from such activity is disallowed. For purposes of the preceding sentence, the ratable portion of a passive activity deduction of a taxpayer is the amount of the disallowed portion of the taxpayer's loss from the activity (within the meaning of paragraph (f)(2)(i)(B) of this section) for the taxable year multiplied by the fraction obtained by dividing—

(1) The amount of such deduction; by

(2) The sum of all passive activity deductions (other than excluded deductions (within the meaning of paragraph (f)(2)(ii)(B) of this section)) of the taxpayer from such activity for the taxable year.

(B) *Excluded deductions.* The term "excluded deduction" means any passive activity deduction of a taxpayer that is taken into account in computing the taxpayer's net income from an item of property for a taxable year in which an amount of the taxpayer's gross income from such

Reg. § 1.469-1T(f)(2)

item of property is treated as not from a passive activity under § 1.469-2T(c)(6) or § 1.469-2T(f)(5), (6), or (7).

(iii) *Separately identified deductions.* In identifying the deductions from an activity that are disallowed under this paragraph (f)(2), the taxpayer need not account separately for a deduction unless such deduction may, if separately taken into account, result in an income tax liability for any taxable year different from that which would result were such deduction not taken into account separately. For related rules applicable to partnerships and S corporations, see § 1.702-1(a)(8)(ii) and section 1366(a)(1)(A), respectively. Deductions that must be accounted for separately include (but are not limited to) deductions that—

(A) Arise in a rental real estate activity (within the meaning of section 469(i) and the rules to be contained in § 1.469-9T) in taxable years in which the taxpayer actively participates (within the meaning of section 469(i) and the rules to be contained in § 1.469-9T) in such activity;

(B) Arise in a rental real estate activity (within the meaning of section 469(i) and the rules to be contained in § 1.469-9T) in taxable years in which the taxpayer does not actively participate (within the meaning of section 469(i) and the rules to be contained in § 1.469-9T) in such activity; or

(C) Are taken into account under section 1211 (relating to the limitation on capital losses) or section 1231 (relating to property used in a trade or business and involuntary conversions).

(3) *Identification of disallowed credits from passive activities*—(i) *General rule.* If all or any portion of the taxpayer's passive activity credit is disallowed for the taxable year under paragraph (a)(1)(ii) of this section, a ratable portion of each credit from each passive activity of the taxpayer is disallowed. For purposes of the preceding sentence, the ratable portion of a credit of a taxpayer is computed by multiplying the portion of the taxpayer's passive activity credit that is disallowed for the taxable year by the fraction obtained by dividing—

(A) The amount of the credit; by

(B) The sum of all of the taxpayer's credits from passive activities for the taxable year.

(ii) *Coordination rule.* For purposes of paragraph (f)(3)(i) of this section, the credits from a passive activity do not include any credit or portion of a credit that—

(A) Is allowed for the taxable year under section 469(i) and the rules to be contained in § 1.469-9T (relating to the $25,000 allowance for certain rental real estate activities); or

(B) Increases the basis of property during the taxable year under section 469(j)(9) and the rules to be contained in § 1.469-6T (relating to the election to increase the basis of certain property by disallowed credits).

(iii) *Separately identified credits.* In identifying the credits from an activity that are disallowed under this paragraph (f)(3), the taxpayer need not account separately for any credit unless such credit may, if separately taken into account, result in an income tax liability for any taxable year different from that which would result were such credit not taken into account separately. For related rules applicable to partnerships and S corporations, see § 1.702-1(a)(8)(ii) and section 1366(a)(1)(A), respectively. Credits that must be accounted for separately include (but are not limited to)—

(A) Credits (other than the low-income housing and rehabilitation investment credits) from a rental real estate activity (within the meaning of section 469(i) and the rules to be contained in § 1.469-9T) that arise in a taxable year in which the taxpayer actively participates (within the meaning of section 469(i) and the rules to be contained in § 1.469-9T) in such activity;

(B) Credits (other than the low-income housing and rehabilitation investment credits) from a rental real estate activity (within the meaning of section 469(i) and the rules to be contained in § 1.469-9T) that arise in a taxable year in which the taxpayer does not actively participate (within the meaning of section 469(i) and the rules to be contained in § 1.469-9T) in such activity;

(C) Low-income housing and rehabilitation investment credits from a rental real estate activity (within the meaning of section 469(i) and the rules to be contained in § 1.469-9T); and

(D) Any credit that is subject to the limitations of sections 26(a), 28(d)(2), 29(b)(5), or 38(c) in a manner that differs from the manner in which any other credit is subject to such limitations.

(4) *Carryover of disallowed deductions and credits.* [Reserved] See § 1.469-1(f)(4) for rules relating to this paragraph.

(g) *Application of these rules to C corporations*—(1) *In general.* Except as otherwise provided in the rules to be contained in paragraph (k) of this section, section 469 and the regulations

Reg. § 1.469-1T(g)(1)

thereunder do not apply to any corporation that is not a personal service corporation or a closely held corporation for the taxable year. See paragraph (g)(4) and (5) of this section for special rules for computing the passive activity loss and passive activity credit, respectively, of a closely held corporation.

(2) *Definitions.* For purposes of section 469 and the regulations thereunder—

(i) The term "personal service corporation" means a C corporation that is a personal service corporation for the taxable year (within the meaning of § 1.441-3(c)); and

(ii) The term "closely held corporation" means a C corporation that meets the stock ownership requirements of section 542(a)(2) (taking into account the modifications in section 465(a)(3)) for the taxable year and is not a personal service corporation for such year.

(3) *Participation of corporations*—(i) *Material participation.* For purposes of section 469 and the regulations thereunder, a corporation described in paragraph (g)(2) of this section shall be treated as materially participating in an activity for a taxable year if and only if—

(A) One or more individuals, each of whom is treated under paragraph (g)(3)(iii) of this section as materially participating in such activity for the taxable year, directly or indirectly hold (in the aggregate) more than 50 percent (by value) of the outstanding stock of such corporation; or

(B) In the case of a closely held corporation (within the meaning of paragraph (g)(2)(ii) of this section), the requirements of section 465(c)(7)(C) (without regard to clause (iv) thereof and taking into account section 465(c)(7)(D)) are met with respect to such activity.

(ii) *Significant participation.* For purposes of § 1.469-2T(f)(2), an activity of a corporation described in paragraph (g)(2) of this section shall be treated as a significant participation passive activity for a taxable year if and only if—

(A) The corporation is not treated as materially participating in such activity for the taxable year; and

(B) One or more individuals, each of whom is treated under paragraph (g)(3)(iii) of this section as significantly participating in such activity, directly or indirectly hold (in the aggregate) more than 50 percent (by value) of the outstanding stock of such corporation.

(iii) *Participation of individual.* Whether an individual is treated for purposes of this paragraph (g)(3) as materially participating or significantly participating in an activity of a corporation shall be determined under the rules of § 1.469-5T, except that in applying such rules—

(A) All activities of the corporation shall be treated as activities which the individual holds an interest in determining whether the individual participates (within the meaning of § 1.469-5T(f)) in an activity of the corporation; and

(B) The individual's participation in all activities other than activities of the corporation shall be disregarded in determining whether the individual's participation in an activity of the corporation is treated as material participation under § 1.469-5T(a)(4) (relating to material participation in significant participation activities).

(4) *Modified computation of passive activity loss in the case of closely held corporations*—(i) *In general.* A closely held corporation's passive activity loss for the taxable year is the amount, if any, by which the corporation's passive activity deductions for the taxable year (within the meaning of § 1.469-2T(d)) exceed the sum of—

(A) The corporation's passive activity gross income for the taxable year (within the meaning of § 1.469-2T(c)); and

(B) The corporation's net active income for the taxable year.

(ii) *Net active income.* For purposes of this paragraph (g)(4), a corporation's net active income for the taxable year is such corporation's taxable income for the taxable year, determined without regard to the following items for the year:

(A) Passive activity gross income;

(B) Passive activity deductions;

(C) [Reserved] See § 1.469-1(g)(4)(ii)(C) for rules relating to this paragraph.

(D) Gross income that is treated under § 1.469-2T(c)(6) (relating to gross income from certain oil or gas properties) as not from a passive activity;

(E) Gross income and deductions from any trade or business activity (within the meaning of paragraph (e)(2) of this section) that is described in paragraph (e)(6) of this section (relating to certain activities of trading personal property) but only if the corporation did not materially participate in such activity for the taxable year;

(F) Deductions described in § 1.469-2T(d)(2)(i), (ii), and (iv) (relating to certain deductions attributable to portfolio income); and

(G) Interest expense allocated under § 1.163-8T to a portfolio expenditure (within the meaning of § 1.163-8T(b)(6)).

Reg. § 1.469-1T(g)(2)

Methods of Accounting   37,063
See p. 20,601 for regulations not amended to reflect law changes

(iii) *Examples.* The following examples illustrate the application of this paragraph (g)(4):

Example (1). (i) For 1987, X, a closely held corporation, is engaged in two activities, a trade or business activity in which X materially participates for 1987 and a rental activity. X also holds portfolio investments. For 1987, X has the following gross income and deductions:

Gross Income:

Rents	$ 60,000
Gross income from business	100,000
Portfolio income	35,000
Total	$195,000

Deductions:

Rental deductions	($100,000)
Business deductions	(80,000)
Interest expense allocable to portfolio expenditures under § 1.163-8T	(10,000)
Deductions (other than interest expense) clearly and directly allocable to portfolio income	(5,000)
Total	($195,000)

(ii) The corporation's net active income for 1987 is $20,000, computed as follows:

Gross income		$195,000	
Amounts not taken into account in computing net active income:			
Rents (see paragraph (g) (4)(ii)(A) of this section)	$60,000		
Portfolio income (see paragraph (g) (4)(ii)(C) of this section)	$35,000		
	$95,000	($95,000)	
Gross income taken into account in computing net active income		$100,000	$100,000
Deductions		($195,000)	
Amounts not taken into account in computing net active income:			
Rental deductions (see paragraph (g)(4)(ii) (B) of this section)	($100,000)		
Interest expense allocated to portfolio expenditures (see paragraph (g)(4)(ii) (G) of this section)	($10,000)		
Other deductions clearly and directly allocable to portfolio income (see paragraph (g) (4)(ii)(F) of this section)	($5,000)		
	($115,000)	$115,000	
Deductions taken into account in computing net active income		($80,000)	($80,000)
Net active income			$20,000

(iii) Under paragraph (g)(4)(i) of this section, X's passive activity loss for 1987 is $20,000, the amount by which the passive activity deductions for the taxable year ($100,000) exceed the sum of (a) the passive activity gross income for the taxable year ($60,000) and (b) the net active income for the taxable year ($20,000). Under paragraph (f)(4) of this section, the $20,000 of deductions from X's rental activity that are disallowed for 1987 are treated as deductions from the rental activity for 1988. If computed without regard to the net active income for the taxable year, X's passive activity loss would be $40,000 ($100,000 of rental deductions minus $60,000 of rental income). Thus, the effect of the rule in paragraph (g)(4)(i) of this section is to reduce the corporation's passive activity loss for the taxable year by the amount of the corporation's net active income for such year.

(iv) Under these facts, X's taxable income for 1987 is $20,000, computed as follows:

Gross income		$195,000
Deductions		
Total deductions	($195,000)	
Passive activity loss	$20,000	
Allowable deductions	($175,000)	($175,000)
Taxable income		$20,000

Example (2). (i) The facts are the same as in example (1), except that, in 1988, X has a loss from the trade or business activity, and a net operating loss ("NOL") of $15,000 that is carried back under section 172(b) to 1987. Since NOL carrybacks are taken into account in computing

Reg. § 1.469-1T(g)(4)

net active income, X's net active income for 1987 must be recomputed as follows:

Net active income before NOL carryback	$20,000
NOL carryback	($15,000)
Net active income	$5,000

(ii) Under these facts, X's disallowed passive activity loss for 1987 is $35,000, the amount by which the passive activity deductions for the taxable year ($100,000) exceed the sum of (a) the passive activity gross income for the taxable year ($60,000) and (b) the net active income for the taxable year ($5,000).

(iii) Under paragraph (f)(4) of this section, the $35,000 of deductions from X's rental activity that are disallowed for 1987 are treated as deductions from the rental activity for 1988. X's taxable income for 1987 is $20,000, computed as follows:

Gross income		$195,000
Deductions		
Total deductions	($210,000)	
Passive activity loss	$35,000	
Allowable deductions	($175,000)	($175,000)
Taxable income		$20,000

Thus, taking the NOL carryback into account in computing net active income for 1987 does not affect X's taxable income for 1987, but increases the deductions treated under paragraph (f)(4) as deductions from X's rental activity for 1988 and decreases X's NOL carryover to years other than 1987.

(5) *Allowance of passive activity credit of closely held corporations to extent of net active income tax liability*—(i) *In general.* Solely for purposes of determining the amount disallowed under paragraph (a)(1)(ii) of this section, a closely held corporation's passive activity credit for the taxable year shall be reduced by such corporation's net active income tax liability for such year.

(ii) *Net active income tax liability.* For purposes of paragraph (g)(5)(i) of this section, a corporation's net active income tax liability for a taxable year is the amount (if any) by which—

(A) The corporation's regular tax liability (within the meaning of section 26(b)) for the taxable year, determined by reducing the corporation's taxable income for such year by an amount equal to the excess (if any) of the corporation's passive activity gross income for such year over the corporation's passive activity deductions for such year; exceeds

(B) The sum of—

(1) The corporation's regular tax liability for the taxable year, determined by reducing the corporation's taxable income for such year by an amount equal to the excess (if any) of the sum of the corporation's net active income (within the meaning of paragraph (g)(4)(ii) of this section) and passive activity gross income for such year over the corporation's passive activity deductions for such year; and

(2) The corporation's credits (other than credits from passive activities) that are allowable for the taxable year (without regard to the limitations contained in sections 26(a), 28(d)(2), 29(b)(5), 38(c), and 469).

(h) *Special rules for affiliated group filing consolidated return*—(1) [Reserved.]

(2) [Reserved.]

(3) *Disallowance of consolidated group's passive activity loss or credit.* A consolidated group's passive activity loss or passive activity credit for the taxable year shall be disallowed to the extent provided in paragraph (a) of this section. For purposes of the preceding sentence, a consolidated group's passive activity loss and passive activity credit determined by taking into account the following items of each member of such group:

(i) Passive activity gross income;

(ii) Passive activity deductions;

(iii) Net active income (in the case of a consolidated group treated as a closely held corporation under paragraph (h)(4)(ii) of this section); and

(iv) Credits from passive activities.

(4) [Reserved] See § 1.469-1(h)(4) for rules relating to this paragraph.

(5) *Modification of rules for identifying disallowed passive activity deductions and credits*—(i) *Identification of disallowed deductions.* In applying paragraph (f)(2) and (4) of this section to a consolidated group for purposes of identifying the passive activity deductions of such consolidated group and of each member of such consolidated group that are disallowed for the taxable year and treated as deductions from activities for the succeeding taxable year, the following rules shall apply:

(A) A ratable portion (within the meaning of paragraph (h)(5)(ii) of this section) of the passive activity loss of the consolidated group that is disallowed for the taxable year shall be allocated to each member of the group;

(B) Paragraph (f)(2) of this section shall then be applied to each member of the group as if—

(1) Such member were a separate taxpayer; and

Reg. § 1.469-1T(g)(5)

(2) The amount allocated to such member under paragraph (h)(5)(i)(A) of this section were the amount of such member's passive activity loss that is disallowed for the taxable year; and

(C) Paragraph (f)(4) of this section shall be applied to each member of the group as if it were a separate taxpayer.

(ii) *Ratable portion of disallowed passive activity loss.* For purposes of paragraph (h)(5)(i)(A) of this section, a member's ratable portion of the disallowed passive activity loss of the consolidated group is the amount of such disallowed loss multiplied by the fraction obtained by dividing—

(A) The amount of the passive activity loss of such member of the consolidated group that would be disallowed for the taxable year if the items of gross income and deduction of such member were the only items of the group for such year; by

(B) The sum of the amounts described in paragraph (h)(5)(ii)(A) of this section for all members of the group.

(iii) *Identification of disallowed credits.* In applying paragraph (f)(3) of this section to a consolidated group for purposes of identifying the credits from passive activities of members of such consolidated group that are disallowed for the taxable year, the consolidated group shall be treated as one taxpayer. Thus, a ratable portion of each of the group's credits from passive activities is disallowed.

(6) [Reserved.]

(7) *Disposition of stock of a member of an affiliated group.* Any gain recognized by a member on the disposition of stock of a subsidiary (including income resulting from the recognition of an excess loss account under § 1.1502-19) shall be treated as portfolio income (within the meaning of § 1.469-2T(c)(3)(i)).

(8) *Dispositions of property used in multiple activities.* The determination of whether § 1.469-2T(c)(2)(ii) or (iii) or (d)(5)(ii) applies to a disposition (including a deemed disposition described in paragraph (h)(6)(iii)(C)(*1*) of this section) of property by a member of a consolidated group shall be made by treating such member as having held the property for the entire period that the group has owned such property and as having used the property in all of the activities in which the group has used such property.

(i) [Reserved.]

(j) *Spouses filing joint return*—(1) *In general.* Except as otherwise regulations under section 469, spouses filing a joint return for a taxable year shall be treated for such year as one taxpayer for purposes of section 469 and the regulations thereunder. Thus, for example, spouses filing a joint return are treated as one taxpayer for purposes of—

(i) Section 1.469-2T (relating generally to the computation of such taxpayer's passive activity loss); and

(ii) Paragraph (f) of this section (relating to the allocation of such taxpayer's disallowed passive activity loss and passive activity credit among activities and the identification of disallowed passive activity deductions and credits from passive activities).

(2) *Exceptions to treatment as one taxpayer*—(i) *Identification of disallowed deductions and credits.* For purposes of paragraph (f)(2)(iii) and (3)(iii) of this section, spouses filing a joint return for the taxable year must account separately for the deductions and credits attributable to the interests of each spouse in any activity.

(ii) *Treatment of deductions disallowed under sections 704(d), 1366(d), and 465.* Notwithstanding any other provision of this section or § 1.469-2T, this paragraph (j) shall not affect the application of section 704(d), section 1366(d), or section 465 to taxpayers filing a joint return for the taxable year.

(iii) *Treatment of losses from working interests.* Paragraph (e)(4) of this section (relating to losses and credits from certain interests in oil and gas wells) shall be applied by treating a husband and wife (whether or not filing a joint return) as separate taxpayers.

(3) *Joint return no longer filed.* If an individual—

(A) Does not file a joint return for the taxable year; and

(B) Filed a joint return for the immediately preceding taxable year;

then the passive activity deductions and credits allocable to such individual's activities for the taxable year under paragraph (f)(4) of this section shall be determined by taking into account the items of deduction and credit attributable to such individual's interest in passive activities for the immediately preceding taxable year. See paragraph (j)(2)(i) of this section.

(4) *Participation of spouses.* Rules treating an individual's participation in an activity as participation of such individual's spouse in such activity (without regard to whether the spouses file a joint return) are contained in § 1.469-5T(f)(3).

(k) *Former passive activities and changes in status of corporations.* [Reserved.]

Reg. § 1.469-1T(k)

[Temporary Reg. § 1.469-1T.]

☐ [T.D. 8175, 2-19-88. Amended by T.D. 8253, 5-11-89; T.D. 8319, 11-19-90; T.D. 8417, 5-11-92; T.D. 8560, 8-12-94; T.D. 8597, 7-12-95 and T.D. 8996, 5-16-2002.]

[Reg. § 1.469-2]

§ 1.469-2. Passive activity loss.—(a) through (c)(2)(ii) [Reserved]

(c)(2)(iii) *Disposition of substantially appreciated property formerly used in nonpassive activity*—(A) *In general*. If an interest in property used in an activity is substantially appreciated at the time of its disposition, any gain from the disposition shall be treated as not from a passive activity unless the interest in property was used in a passive activity for either—

(*1*) 20 percent of the period during which the taxpayer held the interest in property; or

(*2*) The entire 24-month period ending on the date of the disposition.

(B) *Date of disposition*. For purposes of this paragraph (c)(2)(iii), a disposition of an interest in property is deemed to occur on the date that the interest in property becomes subject to an oral or written agreement that either requires the owner or gives the owner an option to transfer the interest in property for consideration that is fixed or otherwise determinable on that date.

(C) *Substantially appreciated property*. For purposes of this paragraph (c)(2)(iii), an interest in property is substantially appreciated if the fair market value of the interest in property exceeds 120 percent of the adjusted basis of the interest.

(D) *Investment property*. For purposes of this paragraph (c)(2)(iii), an interest in property is treated as an interest in property used in an activity other than a passive activity and as an interest in property held for investment for any period during which the interest is held through a C corporation or similar entity. An entity is similar to a C corporation for this purpose if the owners of interests in the entity derive only portfolio income (within the meaning of § 1.469-2T) from the interests.

(E) *Coordination with § 1.469-2T(c)(2)(ii)*. If § 1.469-2T(c)(2)(ii) applies to the disposition of an interest in property, this paragraph (c)(2)(iii) applies only to that portion of the gain from the disposition of the interest in property that is characterized as gain from a passive activity after the application of § 1.469-2T(c)(2)(ii).

(F) *Coordination with section 163(d)*. Gain that is treated as not from a passive activity under this paragraph (c)(2)(iii) is treated as income described in section 469(e)(1)(A) and § 1.469-2T(c)(3)(i) if and only if the gain is from the disposition of an interest in property that was held for investment for more than 50 percent of the period during which the taxpayer held that interest in property in activities other than passive activities.

(G) *Examples*. The following examples illustrate the application of this paragraph (c)(2)(iii):

Example 1. A acquires a building on January 1, 1993, and uses the building in a trade or business activity in which A materially participates until March 31, 2004. On April 1, 2004, A leases the building to B. On December 31, 2005, A sells the building. At the time of the sale, A's interest in the building is substantially appreciated (within the meaning of paragraph (c)(2)(iii)(C) of this section). Assuming A's lease of the building to B constitutes a rental activity (within the meaning of § 1.469-1T(e)(3)), the building is used in a passive activity for 21 months (April 1, 2004, through December 31, 2005). Thus, the building was not used in a passive activity for the entire 24-month period ending on the date of the sale. In addition, the 21-month period during which the building was used in a passive activity is less than 20 percent of A's holding period for the building (13 years). Therefore, the gain from the sale is treated under this paragraph (c)(2)(iii) as not from a passive activity.

Example 2. (i) A, an individual, is a stockholder of corporation X. X is a C corporation until December 31, 1993, and is an S corporation thereafter. X acquires a building on January 1, 1993, and sells the building on March 1, 1994. At the time of the sale, A's interest in the building held through X is substantially appreciated (within the meaning of paragraph (c)(2)(iii)(C) of this section). The building is leased to various tenants at all times during the period in which it is held by X. Assume that the lease of the building would constitute a rental activity (within the meaning of § 1.469-1T(e)(3)) with respect to a person that holds the building directly or through an S corporation.

(ii) Paragraph (c)(2)(iii)(D) of this section provides that an interest in property is treated for purposes of this paragraph (c)(2)(iii) as used in an activity other than a passive activity and as held for investment for any period during which the interest is held through a C corporation. Thus, for purposes of determining the

Reg. § 1.469-2(a)

character of A's gain from the sale of the building, A's interest in the building is treated as an interest in property held for investment for the period from January 1, 1993, to December 31, 1993, and as an interest in property used in a passive activity for the period from January 1, 1994, to February 28, 1994.

(iii) A's interest in the building was not used in a passive activity for the entire 24-month period ending on the date of the sale. In addition, the 2-month period during which A's interest in the building was used in a passive activity is less than 20 percent of the period during which A held an interest in the building (14 months). Therefore, the gain from the sale is treated under this paragraph (c)(2)(iii) as not from a passive activity.

(iv) Under paragraph (c)(2)(iii)(F) of this section, gain that is treated as nonpassive under this paragraph (c)(2)(iii) is treated as portfolio income (within the meaning of § 1.469-2T(c)(3)(i)) if the gain is from the disposition of an interest in property that was held for investment for more than 50 percent of the period during which the taxpayer held the interest in activities other than passive activities. In this case, A's interest in the building was treated as held for investment for the entire period during which it was used in activities other than passive activities (*i.e.*, the 12-month period from January 1, 1993, to December 31, 1993). Accordingly, A's gain from the sale is treated under this paragraph (c)(2)(iii) as portfolio income.

(iv) *Taxable acquisitions.* If a taxpayer acquires an interest in property in a transaction other than a nonrecognition transaction (within the meaning of section 7701(a)(45)), the ownership and use of the interest in property before the transaction is not taken into account for purposes of applying this paragraph (c)(2) to any subsequent disposition of the interest in property by the taxpayer.

(v) *Property held for sale to customers*—(A) *Sale incidental to another activity*—(*1*) *Applicability*—(*i*) *In general.* This paragraph (c)(2)(v)(A) applies to the disposition of a taxpayer's interest in property if and only if—

(A) At the time of the disposition, the taxpayer holds the interest in property in an activity that, for purposes of section 1221(1), involves holding the property or similar property primarily for sale to customers in the ordinary course of a trade or business (a *dealing activity*);

(B) One or more other activities of the taxpayer do not involve holding similar property for sale to customers in the ordinary course of a trade or business (*nondealing activities*) and the interest in property was used in the nondealing activity or activities for more than 80 percent of the period during which the taxpayer held the interest in property; and

(C) The interest in property was not acquired and held by the taxpayer for the principal purpose of selling the interest to customers in the ordinary course of a trade or business.

(*ii*) *Principal purpose.* For purposes of this paragraph (c)(2)(v)(A), a taxpayer is rebuttably presumed to have acquired and held an interest in property for the principal purpose of selling the interest to customers in the ordinary course of a trade or business if—

(A) The period during which the interest in property was used in nondealing activities of the taxpayer does not exceed the lesser of 24 months or 20 percent of the recovery period (within the meaning of section 168) applicable to the property; or

(B) The interest in property was simultaneously offered for sale to customers and used in a nondealing activity of the taxpayer for more than 25 percent of the period during which the interest in property was used in nondealing activities of the taxpayer.

For purposes of the preceding sentence, an interest in property is not considered to be offered for sale to customers solely because a lessee of the property has been granted an option to purchase the property.

(*2*) *Dealing activity not taken into account.* If paragraph (c)(2)(v)(A) applies to the disposition of a taxpayer's interest in property, holding the interest in the dealing activity is treated, for purposes of § 1.469-2T(c)(2), as the use of the interest in the last nondealing activity of the taxpayer in which the interest in property was used prior to its disposition.

(B) *Use in a nondealing activity incidental to sale.* If paragraph (c)(2)(v)(A) of this section does not apply to the disposition of a taxpayer's interest in property that is held in a dealing activity of the taxpayer at the time of disposition, the use of the interest in property in a nondealing activity of the taxpayer for any period during which the interest in property is also offered for sale to customers is treated, for purposes of § 1.469-2T(c)(2), as the use of the interest in property in the dealing activity of the taxpayer.

(C) *Examples.* The following examples illustrate the application of this paragraph (c)(2)(v):

Example 1. (i) The taxpayer acquires a residential apartment building on January 1, 1993, and uses the building in a rental activity. In January 1996, the taxpayer converts the apart-

Reg. § 1.469-2(c)

ments into condominium units. After the conversion, the taxpayer holds the condominium units for sale to customers in the ordinary course of a trade or business of dealing in condominium units. (Assume that these are dealing operations treated as separate activities under § 1.469-4, and that the taxpayer materially participates in the activity.) In addition, the taxpayer continues to use the units in the rental activity until they are sold. The units are first held for sale on January 1, 1996, and the last unit is sold on December 31, 1996.

(ii) This paragraph (c)(2)(v) provides that holding an interest in property in a dealing activity (the marketing of the property) is treated for purposes of § 1.469-2T(c)(2) as the use of the interest in a nondealing activity if the marketing of the property is incidental to the nondealing use. Under paragraph (c)(2)(v)(A)(*2*) of this section, the interests in property are treated as used in the last nondealing activity in which they were used prior to their disposition. In addition, paragraph (c)(2)(v)(A)(*1*) of this section provides rules for determining whether the marketing of the property is incidental to the use of an interest in property in a nondealing activity. Under these rules, the marketing of the property is treated as incidental to the use in a nondealing activity if the interest in property was used in nondealing activities for more than 80 percent of the taxpayer's holding period in the property (the holding period requirement) and the taxpayer did not acquire and hold the interest in property for the principal purpose of selling it to customers in the ordinary course of a trade or business (a dealing purpose).

(iii) In this case, the apartments were used in a rental activity for the entire period during which they were held by the taxpayer. Thus, the apartments were used in a nondealing activity for more than 80 percent of the taxpayer's holding period in the property, and the marketing of the property satisfies the holding period requirement.

(iv) Paragraph (c)(2)(v)(A)(*1*)(*ii*) of this section provides that a taxpayer is rebuttably presumed to have a dealing purpose unless the interest in property was used in nondealing activities for more than 24 months or 20 percent of the property's recovery period (whichever is less). The same presumption applies if the interest in property was offered for sale to customers during more than 25 percent of the period in which the interest was held in nondealing activities. In this case, the taxpayer used each apartment in a nondealing activity (the rental activity) for a period of 36 to 48 months (*i.e.*, from January 1, 1993, to the date of sale in the period from January through December 1996). Thus, the apartments were used in nondealing activities for more than 24 months, and the first of the rebuttable presumptions described above does not apply. In addition, the apartments were offered for sale to customers for up to 12 months (depending on the month in which the apartment was sold) during the period in which the apartments were used in a nondealing activity. The percentage obtained by dividing the period during which an apartment was held for sale to customers by the period during which the apartment was used in nondealing activities ranges from zero in the case of apartments sold on January 1, 1996, to 25 percent (*i.e.*, 12 months/48 months) in the case of apartments sold on December 31, 1996. Thus, no apartment was offered for sale to customers during more than 25 percent of the period in which it was used in nondealing activities, and the second rebuttable presumption does not apply.

(v) Because neither of the rebuttable presumptions in paragraph (c)(2)(v)(A)(*1*)(*ii*) of this section applies in this case, the taxpayer will not be treated as having a dealing purpose unless other facts and circumstances establish that the taxpayer acquired and held the apartments for the principal purpose of selling the apartments to customers in the ordinary course of a trade or business. Assume that none of the facts and circumstances suggest that the taxpayer had such a purpose. If that is the case, the taxpayer does not have a dealing purpose.

(vi) The marketing of the property satisfies the holding period requirement, and the taxpayer does not have a dealing purpose. Thus, holding the apartments in the taxpayer's dealing activity is treated for purposes of this paragraph (c)(2) as the use of the apartments in a nondealing activity. In this case, the rental activity is the only nondealing activity in which the apartments were used prior to their disposition. Thus, the apartments are treated under paragraph (c)(2)(v)(A)(*2*) of this section as interests in property that were used only in the rental activity for the entire period during which the taxpayer held the interests. Accordingly, the rules in § 1.469-2T(c)(2)(ii) and paragraph (c)(2)(iii) of this section do not apply, and all gain from the sale of the apartments is treated as passive activity gross income.

Example 2. (i) The taxpayer acquires a residential apartment building on January 1, 1993, and uses the building in a rental activity. The taxpayer converts the apartments into condominium units on July 1, 1993. After the conversion, the taxpayer holds the condominium units

Reg. § 1.469-2(c)

for sale to customers in the ordinary course of a trade or business of dealing in condominium units. (Assume that these are dealing operations treated as separate activities under § 1.469-4, and that the taxpayer materially participates in the activities.) In addition, the taxpayer continues to use the units in the rental activity until they are sold. The first unit is sold on January 1, 1994, and the last unit is sold on December 31, 1996.

(ii) In this case, all of the apartments were simultaneously offered for sale to customers and used in a nondealing activity of the taxpayer for more than 25 percent of the period during which the apartments were used in nondealing activities. Thus, the taxpayer is rebuttably presumed to have acquired the apartments (including apartments that are used in the rental activity for at least 24 months) for the principal purpose of selling them to customers in the ordinary course of a trade or business. Assume that the facts and circumstances do not rebut this presumption. If that is the case, the taxpayer has a dealing purpose, and paragraph (c)(2)(v)(A) of this section does not apply to the disposition of the apartments.

(iii) Paragraph (c)(2)(v)(B) of this section provides that if paragraph (c)(2)(v)(A) of this section does not apply to the disposition of a taxpayer's interest in property that is held in a dealing activity of the taxpayer at the time of the disposition, the use of the interest in property in any nondealing activity of the taxpayer for any period during which the interest is also offered for sale to customers is treated as incidental to the use of the interest in the dealing activity. Accordingly, for purposes of applying the rules of § 1.469-2T(c)(2) to the disposition of the apartments, the rental of the apartments after July 1, 1993, is treated as the use of the apartments in the taxpayer's dealing activity.

Example 3. (i) The taxpayer acquires a residential apartment building on January 1, 1993, and uses the building in a rental activity. In January 1996, the taxpayer converts the apartments into condominium units. After the conversion, the taxpayer holds the condominium units for sale to customers in the ordinary course of a trade or business of dealing in condominium units. (Assume that these are dealing operations treated as separate activities under § 1.469-4, and that the taxpayer materially participates in the activities.) In addition, the taxpayer continues to use the units in the rental activity until they are sold. The units are first held for sale on January 1, 1996, and the last unit is sold in 1997.

(ii) The treatment of apartments sold in 1996 is the same as in Example 1. The apartments sold in 1997, however, were simultaneously offered for sale to customers and used in a nondealing activity for more than 25 percent of the period during which the apartments were used in nondealing activities. (For example, an apartment that is sold on January 31, 1997, has been offered for sale for 13 months or 26.1 percent of the 49-month period during which it was used in nondealing activities.) Thus, the taxpayer is rebuttably presumed to have acquired the apartments sold in 1997 for the principal purpose of selling them to customers in the ordinary course of a trade or business. Assume that the facts and circumstances do not rebut this presumption. In that case, the marketing of the apartments sold in 1997 does not satisfy the principal purpose requirement, and paragraph (c)(2)(v)(A) of this section does not apply to the disposition of those apartments. Accordingly, for purposes of applying the rules of § 1.469-2T(c)(2) to the disposition of the apartments sold in 1997, the rental of the apartments after January 1, 1996, is treated, under paragraph (c)(2)(v)(B) of this section, as the use of the apartments in the taxpayer's dealing activity.

(c)(3) through (c)(5) [Reserved]

(c)(6) *Gross income from certain oil or gas properties*—(i) *In general.* Notwithstanding any other provision of the regulations under section 469, passive activity gross income for any taxable year does not include an amount of the taxpayer's gross passive income for the year from a property described in this paragraph (c)(6)(i) equal to the taxpayer's net passive income from the property for the year. Property is described in this paragraph (c)(6)(i) if the property is—

(A) An oil or gas property that includes an oil or gas well if, for any prior taxable year beginning after December 31, 1986, any of the taxpayer's loss from the well was treated, solely by reason of § 1.469-1T(e)(4) (relating to a special rule for losses from oil and gas working interests), and not by reason of the taxpayer's material participation in the activity, as a loss that is not from a passive activity; or

(B) Any property the basis of which is determined in whole or in part by reference to the basis of property described in paragraph (c)(6)(i)(A) of this section.

(ii) *Gross and net passive income from the property.* For purposes of this paragraph (c)(6)—

(A) The taxpayer's gross passive income for any taxable year from any property described in paragraph (c)(6)(i) of this section is any passive activity gross income for the year (determined without regard to this paragraph (c)(6) and § 1.469-2T(f)) from the property;

Reg. § 1.469-2(c)

(B) The taxpayer's net passive income for any taxable year from any property described in paragraph (c)(6)(i) of this section is the excess, if any, of—

(1) The taxpayer's gross passive income for the taxable year from the property; over

(2) Any passive activity deductions for the taxable year (including any deduction treated as a deduction for the year under § 1.469-1T(f)(4)) that are reasonably allocable to the income; and

(C) If any oil or gas well or other item of property (the item) is included in two or more properties described in paragraph (c)(6)(i) of this section (the properties), the taxpayer must allocate the passive activity gross income (determined without regard to this paragraph (c)(6) and § 1.469-2T(f)) from the item and the passive activity deductions reasonably allocable to the item among the properties.

(iii) *Property.* For purposes of paragraph (c)(6)(i)(A) of this section, the term "property" does not have the meaning given the term by section 614(a) or the regulations thereunder, and an oil or gas property that includes an oil or gas well is—

(A) The well; and

(B) Any other item of property (including any oil or gas well) the value of which is directly enhanced by any drilling, logging, seismic testing, or other activities the costs of which were taken into account in determining the amount of the taxpayer's income or loss from the well.

(iv) *Examples.* The following examples illustrate the application of this paragraph (c)(6):

Example 1. A is a general partner in partnership P and a limited partner in partnership R. P and R own oil and gas working interests in two separate tracts of land acquired from two separate landowners. In 1993, P drills a well on its tract, and A's distributive share of P's losses from drilling the well are treated under § 1.469-1T(e)(4) as not from a passive activity. In the course of selecting the drilling site and drilling the well, P develops information indicating that the reservoir in which the well was drilled underlies R's tract as well as P's. Under these facts, P's and R's tracts are treated as one property for purposes of this paragraph (c)(6), even if A's interests in the mineral deposits in the tracts are treated as separate properties under section 614(a). Accordingly, in 1994 and subsequent years, A's distributive share of both P's and R's income and expenses from their respective tracts is taken into account in computing A's net passive income from the property for purposes of this paragraph (c)(6).

Example 2. B is a general partner in partnership S. S owns an oil and gas working interest in a single tract of land. In 1993, S drills a well, and B's distributive share of S's losses from drilling the well is treated under § 1.469-1T(e)(4) as not from a passive activity. In the course of drilling the well, S discovers two oil-bearing formations, one underlying the other. On December 1, 1993, S completes the well in the underlying formation. On January 1, 1994, B converts B's entire general partnership interest in S into a limited partnership interest. In 1994, S completes in, and commences production from, the shallow formation. Under these facts, the two mineral deposits in S's tract are treated as one property for purposes of this paragraph (c)(6), even if they are treated as separate properties under section 614(a). Accordingly, B's distributive share of S's income and expenses from both the underlying formation and from recompletion in and production from the shallow formation is taken into account in computing B's net passive income from the property for purposes of this paragraph (c)(6).

(c)(6)(iv) *Example 3* through (c)(7)(iii) [Reserved]

(c)(7)(iv) Gross income of an individual from a covenant by such individual not to compete;

(v) Gross income that is treated as not from a passive activity under any provision of the regulations under section 469, including but not limited to § 1.469-1T(h)(6) (relating to income from intercompany transactions of members of an affiliated group of corporations filing a consolidated return) and § 1.469-2T(f) and paragraph (f) of this section (relating to recharacterized passive income);

(vi) Gross income attributable to the reimbursement of a loss from fire, storm, shipwreck, or other casualty, or from theft (as such terms are used in section 165(c)(3)) if—

(A) The reimbursement is included in gross income under § 1.165-1(d)(2)(iii) (relating to reimbursements of losses that the taxpayer deducted in a prior taxable year); and

(B) The deduction for the loss was not a passive activity deduction; and [sic]

(c)(7)(vii) Gross income or gain allocable to business or rental use of a dwelling unit for any taxable year in which section 280A(c)(5) applies to such business or rental use.

(d)(1) through (d)(2)(viii) [Reserved]

(d)(2)(ix) An item of loss or deduction that is carried to the taxable year under section 172(a),

Reg. § 1.469-2(d)

Methods of Accounting 37,071

See p. 20,601 for regulations not amended to reflect law changes

section 613A(d), section 1212(a)(1) (in the case of corporations), or section 1212(b) (in the case of taxpayers other than corporations);

(x) An item of loss or deduction that would have been allowed for a taxable year beginning before January 1, 1987, but for section 704(d), 1366, or 465;

(xi) A deduction for a loss from fire, storm, shipwreck, or other casualty, or from theft (as such terms are used in section 165(c)(3)) if losses that are similar in cause and severity do not recur regularly in the conduct of the activity; and

(d)(2)(xii) A deduction or loss allocable to business or rental use of a dwelling unit for any taxable year in which section 280A(c)(5) applies to such business or rental use.

(d)(3) through (d)(5)(ii) [Reserved]

(d)(5)(iii) *Other applicable rules*—(A) *Applicability of rules in § 1.469-2T(c)(2).* For purposes of this paragraph (d)(5), a taxpayer's interests in property used in an activity and the amounts allocated to the interests shall be determined under § 1.469-2T(c)(2)(i)(C). In addition, the rules contained in paragraph (c)(2)(iv) and (v) of this section apply in determining for purposes of this paragraph (d)(5) the activity (or activities) in which an interest in property is used at the time of its disposition and during the 12-month period ending on the date of its disposition.

(d)(5)(iii)(B) through (d)(6)(v)(D) [Reserved]

(d)(6)(v)(E) Are taken into account under section 613A(d) (relating to limitations on certain depletion deductions), section 1211 (relating to the limitation on capital losses), or section 1231 (relating to property used in a trade or business and involuntary conversions); or

(d)(6)(v)(F) through (d)(7) [Reserved]

(d)(8) *Taxable year in which item arises.* For purposes of § 1.469-2T(d), an item of deduction arises in the taxable year in which the item would be allowable as a deduction under the taxpayer's method of accounting if taxable income for all taxable years were determined without regard to sections 469, 613A(d) and 1211.

(e)(1) through (e)(2)(i) [Reserved]

(e)(2)(ii) *Section 707(c).* Except as provided in paragraph (e)(2)(iii)(B) of this section, any payment to a partner for services or the use of capital that is described in section 707(c), including any payment described in section 736(a)(2) (relating to guaranteed payments made in liquidation of the interest of a retiring or deceased partner), is characterized as a payment for services or as the payment of interest, respectively, and not as a distributive share of partnership income.

(iii) *Payments in liquidation of a partner's interest in partnership property*—(A) *In general.* If any gain or loss is taken into account by a retiring partner (or any other person that owns (directly or indirectly) an interest in the partner if the partner is a passthrough entity) or a deceased partner's successor in interest as a result of a payment to which section 736(b) (relating to payments made in exchange for a retired or deceased partner's interest in partnership property) applies, the gain or loss is treated as passive activity gross income or a passive activity deduction only to the extent that the gain or loss would have been passive activity gross income or a passive activity deduction of the retiring or deceased partner (or the other person) if it had been recognized at the time the liquidation of the partner's interest commenced.

(B) *Payments in liquidation of a partner's interest in unrealized receivables and goodwill under section 736(a).* (*1*) If a payment is made in liquidation of a retiring or deceased partner's interest, the payment is described in section 736(a), and any income—

(*i*) Is taken into account by the retiring partner (or any other person that owns (directly or indirectly) an interest in the partner if the partner is a passthrough entity) or the deceased partner's successor in interest as a result of the payment; and

(*ii*) Is attributable to the portion (if any) of the payment that is allocable to the unrealized receivables (within the meaning of section 751(c)) and goodwill of the partnership;

the percentage of the income that is treated as passive activity gross income shall not exceed the percentage of passive activity gross income that would be included in the gross income that the retiring or deceased partner (or the other person) would have recognized if the unrealized receivables and goodwill had been sold at the time that the liquidation of the partner's interest commenced.

(*2*) For purposes of this paragraph (e)(2)(iii)(B), the portion (if any) of a payment under section 736(a) that is allocable to unrealized receivables and goodwill of a partnership shall be determined in accordance with the principles employed under § 1.736-1(b) for determining the portion of a payment made under section 736 that is treated as a distribution under section 736(b).

(e)(3)(i) through (iii)(A) [Reserved]

Reg. § 1.469-2(e)

(e)(3)(iii)(B) An amount of gain that would have been treated as gain that is not from a passive activity under paragraph (c)(2)(iii) of this section (relating to substantially appreciated property formerly used in a nonpassive activity), paragraph (c)(6) of this section (relating to certain oil or gas properties), § 1.469-2T(f)(5) (relating to certain property rented incidental to development), paragraph (f)(6) of this section (relating to property rented to a nonpassive activity), or § 1.469-2T(f)(7) (relating to certain interests in a passthrough entity engaged in the trade or business of licensing intangible property) would have been allocated to the holder (or such other person) with respect to the interest if all of the property used in the passive activity had been sold immediately prior to the disposition for its fair market value on the applicable valuation date (within the meaning of § 1.469-2T(e)(3)(ii)(D)(*1*)); and

(e)(3)(iii)(C) through (f)(4) [Reserved]

(f)(5) *Net income from certain property rented incidental to development activity*—(i) *In general.* An amount of the taxpayer's gross rental activity income for the taxable year from an item of property equal to the net rental activity income for the year from the item of property shall be treated as not from a passive activity if—

(A) Any gain from the sale, exchange, or other disposition of the item of property is included in the taxpayer's income for the taxable year;

(B) The taxpayer's use of the item of property in an activity involving the rental of the property commenced less than 12 months before the date of the disposition (within the meaning of paragraph (c)(2)(iii)(B) of this section) of such property; and

(C) The taxpayer materially participated (within the meaning of § 1.469-5T) or significantly participated (within the meaning of § 1.469-5T(c)(2)) for any taxable year in an activity that involved for such year the performance of services for the purpose of enhancing the value of such item of property (or any other item of property if the basis of the item of property that is sold, exchanged, or otherwise disposed of is determined in whole or in part by reference to the basis of such other item of property).

(ii) *Commencement of use*—(A) *In general.* For purposes of paragraph (f)(5)(i)(B) of this section, a taxpayer's use of an item of property in an activity involving the rental of the property commences on the first date on which—

(1) The taxpayer owns an interest in the property;

(2) Substantially all of the property is rented (or is held out for rent and is in a state of readiness for rental); and

(3) No significant value-enhancing services (within the meaning of paragraph (f)(5)(ii)(B) of this section) remain to be performed.

(B) *Value-enhancing services.* For purposes of this paragraph (f)(5)(ii), the term value-enhancing services means the services described in paragraphs (f)(5)(i)(C) and (iii) of this section, except that the term does not include lease-up. Thus, in cases in which this paragraph (f)(5) applies solely because substantial lease-up remains to be performed (see paragraph (f)(5)(iii)(C) of this section), the twelve month period described in paragraph (f)(5)(i)(B) of this section will begin when the taxpayer acquires an interest in the property if substantially all of the property is held out for rent and is in a state of readiness for rental on that date.

(iii) *Services performed for the purpose of enhancing the value of property.* For purposes of paragraph (f)(5)(i)(C) of this section, services that are treated as performed for the purpose of enhancing the value of an item of property include but are not limited to—

(A) Construction;

(B) Renovation; and

(C) Lease-up (unless more than 50 percent of the property is leased on the date that the taxpayer acquires an interest in the property).

(iv) *Examples.* The following examples illustrate the application of this paragraph (f)(5):

Example 1. (i) A, a calendar year individual, is a partner in P, a calendar year partnership, which develops real estate. In 1993, P acquires an interest in undeveloped land and arranges for the financing and construction of an office building on the land. Construction is completed in February 1995, and substantially all of the building is either rented or held out for rent and in a state of readiness for rental beginning on March 1, 1995. Twenty percent of the building is leased as of March 1, 1995.

(ii) P rents the building (or holds it out for rent) for the remainder of 1995 and all of 1996, and sells the building on February 1, 1997, pursuant to a contract entered into on January 15, 1996. P did not hold the building (or any other buildings) for sale to customers in the ordinary course of P's trade or business (see paragraph (c)(2)(v) of this section). A's distributive share of P's taxable losses from the rental of the building is $50,000 for 1995 and $30,000 for 1996. All of A's losses from the rental of the building are disal-

Reg. § 1.469-2(f)

lowed under § 1.469-1(a)(1)(i) (relating to the disallowance of the passive activity loss for the taxable year). A's distributive share of P's gain from the sale of the building is $150,000. A has no other gross income or deductions from the activity of renting the building.

(iii) The real estate development activity that A holds through P in 1993, 1994, and 1995 involves the performance of services (e.g., construction) for the purpose of enhancing the value of the building. Accordingly, an amount equal to A's net rental activity income from the building may be treated as gross income that is not from a passive activity if A's use of the building in an activity involving the rental of the building commenced less that 12 months before the date of the disposition of the building. In this case, the date of the disposition of the building is January 15, 1996, the date of the binding contract for its sale.

(iv) (A) A taxpayer's use of an item of property in an activity involving the rental of the property commences on the first date on which—

(*1*) The taxpayer owns an interest in the item of property;

(*2*) Substantially all of the property is rented (or is held out for rent and is in a state of readiness for rental); and

(*3*) No significant value-enhancing services (within the meaning of paragraph (f)(5)(ii)(B) of this section) remain to be performed.

(B) In this case, A's use of the building in an activity involving the rental of the building commenced on March 1, 1995, less than 12 months before January 15, 1996, the date of disposition. Accordingly, if A materially (or significantly) participated in the real estate development activity in 1993, 1994, or 1995 (without regard to whether A materially participated in the activity in more than one of those years), an amount of A's gross rental activity income from the building for 1997 equal to A's net rental activity income from the building for 1997 is treated under this paragraph (f)(5) as gross income that is not from a passive activity. Under paragraph (f)(9)(iv) of this section, A's net rental activity income from the building for 1997 is $70,000 ($150,000 distributive share of gain from the disposition of the building minus $80,000 of reasonably allocable passive activity deductions).

Example 2. (i) X, a calendar year taxpayer subject to section 469, acquires a building on February 1, 1994, when the building is 25 percent leased. During 1994, X rents the building (or holds it out for rent) and materially participates in an activity that involves the lease-up of the building. X's activities do not otherwise involve the performance of construction or other services for the purpose of enhancing the value of the building, and X does not hold the building (or any other building) for sale to customers in the ordinary course of X's trade or business. X sells the building on December 1, 1994.

(ii)(A) Under paragraph (f)(5)(iii)(C) of this section, lease-up is considered a service performed for the purpose of enhancing the value of property unless more than 50 percent of the property is leased on the date the taxpayer acquires an interest in the property. Under paragraph (f)(5)(ii)(B) of this section, however, lease-up is not considered a value-enhancing service for purposes of determining when the taxpayer commences using an item of property in an activity involving the rental of the property. Accordingly, X's acquisition of the building constitutes a commencement of X's use of the building in a rental activity, because February 1, 1994, is the first date on which—

(*1*) The taxpayer owns an interest in the item of property;

(*2*) Substantially all of the property is held out for rent; and

(*3*) No significant value-enhancing services (within the meaning of paragraph (f)(5)(ii)(B) of this section) remain to be performed.

(B) In this case, X disposes of the property within 12 months of the date X commenced using the building in a rental activity. Accordingly, an amount of X's gross rental activity income for 1994 equal to X's net rental activity income from the building for 1994 is treated under this paragraph (f)(5) as gain that is not from a passive activity.

Example 3. The facts are the same as in *Example 2,* except that at the time X acquires the building it is 60 percent leased. Under paragraph (f)(5)(iii)(C) of this section, lease-up is not considered a service performed for the purpose of enhancing the value of property if more than 50 percent of the property is leased on the date the taxpayer acquires an interest in the property. Therefore, additional lease-up performed by X is not taken into account under this paragraph (f)(5). Since X's activities do not otherwise involve the performance of services for the purpose of enhancing the value of the building, none of X's gross rental activity income from the building will be treated as income that is not from a passive activity under this paragraph (f)(5).

(f)(6) *Property rented to a nonpassive activity.* An amount of the taxpayer's gross rental activity income for the taxable year from an item of property equal to the net rental activity in-

Reg. § 1.469-2(f)

come for the year from that item of property is treated as not from a passive activity if the property—

(i) Is rented for use in a trade or business activity (within the meaning of paragraph (e)(2) of this section) in which the taxpayer materially participates (within the meaning of § 1.469-5T) for the taxable year; and

(ii) Is not described in § 1.469-2T(f)(5).

(f)(7) through (f)(9)(ii) [Reserved]

(f)(9)(iii) The gross rental activity income for a taxable year from an item of property is any passive activity gross income (determined without regard to § 1.469-2T(f)(2) through (f)(6)) that—

(A) Is income for the year from the rental or disposition of such item of property; and

(B) In the case of income from the disposition of such item of property, is income from an activity that involved the rental of such item of property during the 12-month period ending on the date of the disposition (see § 1.469-2T(c)(2)(ii)); and

(iv) The net rental activity income from an item of property for the taxable year is the excess, if any, of—

(A) The gross rental activity income from the item of property for the taxable year; over

(B) Any passive activity deductions for the taxable year (including any deduction treated as a deduction for the year under § 1.469-1(f)(4)) that are reasonably allocable to the income.

(10) *Coordination with section 163(d).* Gross income that is treated as not from a passive activity under § 1.469-2T(f)(3), (4), or (7) is treated as income described in section 469(e)(1)(A) and § 1.469-2T(c)(3)(i) except in determining whether—

(i) Any property is treated for purposes of section 469(e)(1)(A)(ii)(I) and § 1.469-2T(c)(3)(i)(C) as property that produces income of a type described in § 1.469-2T(c)(3)(i)(A);

(ii) Any property is treated for purposes of section 469(e)(1)(A)(ii)(II) and § 1.469-2T(c)(3)(i)(D) as property held for investment;

(iii) An expense (other than interest expense) is treated for purposes of section 469(e)(1)(A)(i)(II) and § 1.469-2T(d)(4) as clearly and directly allocable to portfolio income (within the meaning of § 1.469-2T(c)(3)(i); and

(iv) Interest expense is allocated under § 1.163-8T to an investment expenditure (within the meaning of § 1.163-8T(b)(3)) or to a passive activity expenditure (within the meaning of § 1.163-8T(b)(4)).

(11) [Reserved] [Reg. § 1.469-2.]

☐ [*T.D. 8417, 5-11-92. Amended by T.D. 8477, 2-22-93 and T.D. 8495, 11-3-93.*]

[Reg. § 1.469-2T]

§ 1.469-2T. **Passive activity loss (temporary).**—(a) *Scope of this section.* This section contains rules for determining the amount of the taxpayer's passive activity loss for the taxable year for purposes of section 469 and the regulations thereunder. The rules contained in this section—

(1) Provide general guidance for identifying items of income and deduction that are taken into account in determining the amount of the passive activity loss for the taxable year;

(2) Specify particular items of income and deduction that are not taken into account in determining the amount of the passive activity loss for the taxable year; and

(3) Specify the manner in which provisions of the Internal Revenue Code and the regulations, other than section 469 and the regulations thereunder, are applied for purposes of determining the extent to which items of deduction are taken into account for a taxable year in computing the amount of the passive activity loss for such year.

(b) *Definition of passive activity loss*—(1) *In general.* In the case of a taxpayer other than a closely held corporation (within the meaning of § 1.469-1T(g)(2)(ii)), the passive activity loss for the taxable year is the amount, if any, by which the passive activity deductions for the taxable year exceed the passive activity gross income for the taxable year.

(2) *Cross references.* See paragraph (c) of this section for the definition of "passive activity gross income," paragraph (d) of this section for the definition of "passive activity deduction," and § 1.469-1T(g)(4) for the computation of the passive activity loss of a closely held corporation.

(c) *Passive activity gross income*—(1) *In general.* Except as otherwise provided in the regulations under section 469, passive activity gross income for a taxable year includes an item of gross income if and only if such income is from a passive activity.

(2) *Treatment of gain from disposition of an interest in an activity or an interest in property used in an activity*—(i) *In general*—(A) *Treatment of gain.* Except as otherwise provided in the regulations under section 469, any gain recognized upon the sale, exchange, or other disposition (a "disposition") of an interest in property used in

Reg. § 1.469-2T(a)(1)

an activity at the time of the disposition or of an interest in an activity held through a partnership or S corporation is treated in the following manner:

(1) The gain is treated as gross income from such activity for the taxable year or years in which it is recognized;

(2) If the activity is a passive activity of the taxpayer for the taxable year of the disposition, the gain is treated as passive activity gross income for the taxable year or years in which it is recognized; and

(3) If the activity is not a passive activity of the taxpayer for the taxable year of the disposition, the gain is treated as not from a passive activity.

(B) *Dispositions of partnership interests and S corporation stock.* A partnership interest or S corporation stock is not property used in an activity for purposes of this paragraph (c)(2). See paragraph (e)(3) of this section for rules treating the gain recognized upon the disposition of a partnership interest or S corporation stock as gain from the disposition of interests in the activities in which the partnership or S corporation has an interest.

(C) *Interest in property.* For purposes of applying this paragraph (c)(2) to a disposition of property—

(1) Any material portion of the property that was used, at any time before the disposition, in any activity at a time when the remainder of the property was not used in such activity shall be treated as a separate interest in property; and

(2) The amount realized from the disposition and the adjusted basis of the property must be allocated among the separate interests in a reasonable manner.

(D) *Examples.* The following examples illustrate the application of this paragraph (c)(2)(i):

Example (1). A owns an interest in a trade or business activity in which A has never materially participated. In 1987, A sells equipment that was used exclusively in the activity and realizes a gain on the sale. Under paragraph (c)(2)(i)(A)(*2*) of this section, the gain is passive activity gross income.

Example (2). B owns an interest in a trade or business activity in which B materially participates for 1987. In 1987, B sells a building used in the activity in an installment sale and realizes a gain on the sale. B does not materially participate in the activity for 1988 or any subsequent year. Under paragraph (c)(2)(i)(A)(*3*) of this section, none of B's gain from the sale (including gain taken into account after 1987) is passive activity gross income.

Example (3). C enters into a contract to acquire property used by the seller in a rental activity. Before acquiring the property pursuant to the contract, C sells all rights under the contract and realizes a gain on the sale. Since C's rights under the contract are not property used in a rental activity, the gain is not income from a rental activity. The result would be the same if C owned an option to acquire the property and sold the option.

Example (4). D sells a ten-floor office building. D owned the building for three years preceding the sale and at all times during that period used seven floors of the building in a trade or business activity and three floors in a rental activity. The fair market value per square foot is substantially the same throughout the building, and D did not maintain a separate adjusted basis for any part of the building. Under paragraph (c)(2)(i)(C)(*1*) of this section, the seven floors used in the trade or business activity and the three floors used in the rental activity are treated as separate interests in property. Under paragraph (c)(2)(i)(C)(*2*) of this section, the amount realized and the adjusted basis of the building must be allocated between the separate interests in a reasonable manner. Under these facts, an allocation based on the square footage of the parts of the building used in each activity would be reasonable.

Example (5). The facts are the same as in example (4), except that two of the seven floors used in the trade or business activity were used in the rental activity until five months before the sale. Under paragraph (c)(2)(i)(C)(*1*) of this section, the five floors used exclusively in the trade or business activity and the two floors used first in the rental activity and then in the trade or business activity are treated as separate interests in property. See paragraph (c)(2)(ii) of this section for rules for allocating amount realized and adjusted basis upon a disposition of an interest in property used in more than one activity during the 12-month period ending on the date of the disposition.

(ii) *Disposition of property used in more than one activity in 12-month period preceding disposition.* In the case of a disposition of an interest in property that is used in more than one activity during the 12-month period ending on the date of the disposition, the amount realized from the disposition and the adjusted basis of such interest must be allocated among such activities on a basis that reasonably reflects the use of such interest in property during such 12-month period.

Reg. § 1.469-2T(c)(2)

For purposes of this paragraph (c)(2)(ii), an allocation of the amount realized and adjusted basis solely to the activity in which an interest in property is predominantly used during the 12-month period ending on the date of the disposition reasonably reflects the use of such interest in property if the fair market value of such interest does not exceed the lesser of—

(A) $10,000; and

(B) 10 percent of the sum of the fair market value of such interest and the fair market value of all other property used in such activity immediately before the disposition.

The following examples illustrate the application of this paragraph (c)(2)(ii):

Example (1). The facts are the same as in example (5) of paragraph (c)(2)(i)(D) of this section. Under paragraph (c)(2)(i)(C)(*2*) of this section, D allocates the amount realized and adjusted basis of the building 30 percent to the three floors used exclusively in the rental activity, 50 percent to the five floors used exclusively in exceed the lesser of—the trade or business activity, and 20 percent to the two floors used first in the rental activity and then in the trade or business activity. Under this paragraph (c)(2)(ii), the amount realized and adjusted basis allocated to the two floors that were used in both activities during the 12-month period ending on the date of the disposition must also be allocated between such activities. Under these facts, an allocation of 7/12 of such amounts to the rental activity and 5/12 of such amounts to the trade or business activity would reasonably reflect the use of the two floors during the 12-month period ending on the date of the disposition.

Example (2). B is a limited partner in a partnership that sells a tractor-trailer. During the 12-month period ending on the date of the sale, the tractor-trailer was used in several activities, and the partnership allocates the amount realized from the disposition and the adjusted basis of the tractor-trailer among the activities based on the number of days during the 12-month period that the partnership used the tractor-trailer in each activity. Under these facts, the partnership's allocation reasonably reflects the use of the tractor-trailer during the 12-month period ending on the date of the sale.

Example (3). C sells a personal computer for $8,000. During the 12-month period ending on the date of the sale, 70 percent of C's use of the computer was in a passive activity. Immediately before the sale, the fair market value of all property used in the passive activity (including the personal computer) was $200,000. Under these facts, the computer was predominantly used in the passive activity during the 12-month period ending on the date of the sale, and the value of the computer, as measured by its sale price ($8,000), does not exceed the lesser of (a) $10,000, and (b) 10 percent of the value of all property used in the activity immediately before the sale ($20,000). C allocates the amount realized and the adjusted basis solely to the passive activity. Under this paragraph (c)(2)(ii), C's allocation reasonably reflects the use of the computer during the 12-month period ending on the date of the sale.

(iii) *Disposition of substantially appreciated property formerly used in nonpassive activity.* [Reserved] See § 1.469-2(c)(2)(iii) for rules relating to this paragraph.

(iv) *Taxable acquisitions.* [Reserved] See § 1.469-2(c)(2)(iv) for rules relating to this paragraph.

(v) *Property held for sale to customers.* [Reserved] See § 1.469-2(c)(2)(v) for rules relating to this paragraph.

(3) *Items of portfolio income specifically excluded*—(i) *In general.* Passive activity gross income does not include portfolio income. For purposes of the preceding sentence, portfolio income includes all gross income, other than income derived in the ordinary course of a trade or business (within the meaning of paragraph (c)(3)(ii) of this section), that is attributable to—

(A) Interest (including amounts treated as interest under paragraph (e)(2)(ii) of this section, relating to certain payments to partners for the use of capital); annuities; royalties (including fees and other payments for the use of intangible property); dividends on C corporation stock; and income (including dividends) from a real estate investment trust (within the meaning of section 856), regulated investment company (within the meaning of section 851), real estate mortgage investment conduit (within the meaning of section 860D), common trust fund (within the meaning of section 584), controlled foreign corporation (within the meaning of section 957), qualified electing fund (within the meaning of section 1295(a)), or cooperative (within the meaning of section 1381(a));

(B) Dividends on S corporation stock (within the meaning of section 1368(c)(2));

(C) The disposition of property that produces income of a type described in paragraph (c)(3)(i)(A) of this section; and

(D) The disposition of property held for investment (within the meaning of section 163(d)).

(ii) *Gross income derived in the ordinary course of a trade or business.* Solely for purposes of

Reg. § 1.469-2T(c)(3)

paragraph (c)(3)(i) of this section, gross income derived in the ordinary course of a trade or business includes only—

(A) Interest income on loans and investments made in the ordinary course of a trade or business of lending money;

(B) Interest on accounts receivable arising from the performance of services or the sale of property in the ordinary course of a trade or business of performing such services or selling such property, but only if credit is customarily offered to customers of the business;

(C) Income from investments made in the ordinary course of a trade or business of furnishing insurance or annuity contracts or reinsuring risks underwritten by insurance companies;

(D) Income or gain derived in the ordinary course of an activity of trading or dealing in any property if such activity constitutes a trade or business (but see paragraph (c)(3)(iii)(A) of this section);

(E) Royalties derived by the taxpayer in the ordinary course of a trade or business of licensing intangible property (within the meaning of paragraph (c)(3)(iii)(B) of this section);

(F) Amounts included in the gross income of a patron of a cooperative (within the meaning of section 1381(a), without regard to paragraph (2)(A) or (C) thereof) by reason of any payment or allocation to the patron based on patronage occurring with respect to a trade or business of the patron; and

(G) Other income identified by the Commissioner as income derived by the taxpayer in the ordinary course of a trade or business.

(iii) *Special rules*—(A) *Income from property held for investment by dealer.* For purposes of paragraph (c)(3)(i) of this section, a dealer's income or gain from an item of property is not derived by the dealer in the ordinary course of a trade or business of dealing in such property if the dealer held the property for investment at any time before such income or gain is recognized.

(B) *Royalties derived in the ordinary course of the trade or business of licensing intangible property*—(*1*) *In general.* Royalties received by any person with respect to a license or other transfer of any rights in intangible property shall be considered to be derived in the ordinary course of the trade or business of licensing such property only if such person—

(*i*) Created such property; or

(*ii*) Performed substantial services or incurred substantial costs with respect to the development or marketing of such property.

(*2*) *Substantial services or costs*—(*i*) *In general.* Except as provided in paragraph (c)(3)(iii)(B)(*2*)(*ii*) of this section, the determination of whether a person has performed substantial services or incurred substantial costs with respect to the development or marketing of an item of intangible property shall be made on the basis of all the facts and circumstances.

(*ii*) *Exception.* A person has performed substantial services or incurred substantial costs for a taxable year with respect to the development or marketing of an item of intangible property if—

(*a*) The expenditures reasonably incurred by such person in such taxable year with respect to the development or marketing of the property exceed 50 percent of the gross royalties from licensing such property that are includible in such person's gross income for the taxable year; or

(*b*) The expenditures reasonably incurred by such person in such taxable year and all prior taxable years with respect to the development or marketing of the property exceed 25 percent of the aggregate capital expenditures (without any adjustment for amortization) made by such person with respect to the property in all such taxable years.

(*iii*) *Expenditures taken into account.* For purposes of paragraph (c)(3)(iii)(B)(*2*)(*ii*) of this section, expenditures in a taxable year include amounts chargeable to capital account for such year without regard to the year or years (if any) in which any deduction for such expenditure is allowed.

(*3*) *Passthrough entities.* For purposes of this paragraph (c)(3)(iii)(B), in the case of any intangible property held by a partnership, S corporation, estate, or trust, the determination of whether royalties from such property are derived in the ordinary course of a trade or business shall be made by applying the rules of this paragraph (c)(3)(iii)(B) to such entity and not to any holder of an interest in such entity.

(*4*) *Cross reference.* For special rules applicable to certain gross income from a trade or business of licensing intangible property, see paragraph (f)(7) of this section.

(C) *Mineral production payments.* For purposes of section 469 and the regulations thereunder—

(*1*) If a mineral production payment is treated as a loan under section 636, the portion of any payment in discharge of the production payment that is the equivalent of interest shall be treated as interest; and

Reg. § 1.469-2T(c)(3)

(2) If a mineral production payment is not treated as a loan under section 636, payments in discharge of the production payment shall be treated as royalties.

(iv) *Examples.* The following examples illustrate the application of this paragraph (c)(3):

Example (1). A, an individual engaged in the trade or business of farming, disposes of farmland in an installment sale. A is not engaged in a trade or business of selling farmland. Therefore, A's interest income from the installment note is not gross income derived in the ordinary course of a trade or business.

Example (2). P, a partnership, operates a rental apartment building for low-income tenants in City Y. Under Y's laws relating to the operation of low-income housing, P is required to maintain a reserve fund to pay for the maintenance and repair of the building. P invests the reserve fund in short-term interest-bearing deposits. Because P's interest income from the investment of the reserve fund is not interest income described in paragraph (c)(3)(ii) of this section, such income is not treated as derived in the ordinary course of a trade or business. Accordingly, P's interest income from the deposits is portfolio income (within the meaning of paragraph (c)(3)(i) of this section).

Example (3). (i) B is a partner in a partnership that is engaged in an activity involving the conduct of a trade or business of dealing in securities. On February 1, the partnership acquires certain securities for investment (within the meaning of section 163(d)). On February 2, before recognizing any income with respect to the securities, the partnership determines that it would be advisable to hold the securities primarily for sale to customers and subsequently sells them to customers in the ordinary course of its business.

(ii) Under paragraph (c)(3)(iii)(A) of this section, income or gain from any security (including any security acquired pursuant to an investment of working capital) held by a dealer for investment at any time before such income or gain is recognized is not treated for purposes of paragraph (c)(3)(i) of this section as derived by the dealer in the ordinary course of its trade or business of dealing in securities. Accordingly, B's distributive share of the partnership's interest, dividends, or gains from the securities acquired by the partnership for investment on February 1 is portfolio income of B, notwithstanding that such securities were held by the partnership, subsequent to February 1, primarily for sale to customers in the ordinary course of the partnership's trade or business of dealing in securities.

Example (4). C is a partner in a partnership that is engaged in an activity of trading or dealing in royalty interests in mineral properties. The partnership derives royalty income from royalty interests held in the activity. If the activity is a trade or business activity, C's distributive share of the partnership's royalty income from such royalty interests is treated under paragraph (c)(3)(ii)(D) of this section as derived in the ordinary course of the partnership's trade or business.

Example (5). (i) D, a calendar year individual, is a partner in a calendar year partnership that is engaged in an activity of developing and marketing a design for a system that reduces air pollution in office buildings. D has a 10 percent distributive share of all items of partnership income, gain, loss, deduction, and credit. In 1987, the partnership acquired the rights to the design for $100,000. In 1987, 1988, and 1989, the partnership incurs expenditures with respect to the development and marketing of the design, and derives gross royalties from licensing the design, in the amounts set forth in the table below. The expenditures incurred in 1987 and 1988 are currently deductible expenses. The expenditures incurred in 1989 are capitalized and may be deducted only in subsequent taxable years.

Year	Gross Royalties	Expenditures	Cumulative Capital Expenditures
1987	$20,000	$8,000	$100,000
1988	20,000	12,000	100,000
1989	60,000	15,000	115,000
1990	120,000	-0-	115,000

(ii) Under paragraph (c)(3)(iii)(B)(*3*) of this section, the determination of whether royalties from intangible property are derived in the ordinary course of a trade or business of a partnership is made by applying the rules of paragraph (c)(3)(iii)(B) of this section to the partnership rather than the partners. The expenditures reasonably incurred by the partnership in 1987 with respect to the development or marketing of the design ($8,000) do not exceed 50 percent of the partnership's gross royalties for such year from licensing the design ($20,000). In addition, the sum of such expenditures incurred in 1987 and all prior taxable years ($8,000) does not exceed 25 percent of the aggregate capital expenditures made by the partnership in all such taxable years with respect to the design ($100,000). Accordingly, for 1987, the partnership is not treated under paragraph (c)(3)(iii)(B)(*2*)(*ii*) of this section as performing substantial services or incurring substantial costs with respect to the development or marketing of the design. Therefore, unless all of the facts and circumstances indicate that the partnership performed substantial services or incurred substantial costs with respect to the development or marketing of the

Reg. § 1.469-2T(c)(3)

design, D's distributive share of the partnership's royalty income for 1987 is portfolio income.

(iii) As of the end of 1988, the sum of the expenditures reasonably incurred by the partnership during such taxable year and all prior taxable years with respect to the development or marketing of the design ($20,000) does not exceed 25 percent of the aggregate capital expenditures made by the partnership in all such years with respect to the design ($100,000). However, the amount of such expenditures incurred by the partnership in 1988 ($12,000) exceeds 50 percent of the partnership's gross royalties for such year from licensing the design ($20,000). Accordingly, for 1988, under paragraph (c)(3)(iii)(B)(*2*)(*ii*)(*a*) of this section, the partnership is treated as performing substantial services or incurring substantial costs with respect to the development or marketing of the design, and D's distributive share of the partnership's royalty income for 1988 is considered for purposes of paragraph (c)(3)(i) of this section to be derived in the ordinary course of a trade or business and therefore is not portfolio income.

(iv) The expenditures reasonably incurred by the partnership in 1989 with respect to the development or marketing of the design ($15,000) do not exceed 50 percent of the partnership's gross royalties for such year from licensing the design ($60,000). However, the sum of such expenditures incurred by the partnership in 1989 and all prior taxable years ($35,000) exceeds 25 percent of the partnership's aggregate capital expenditures made in all such years with respect to the design ($115,000). Accordingly, for 1989, under paragraph (c)(3)(iii)(B)(*2*)(*ii*)(*b*) of this section, the partnership is treated as performing substantial services or incurring substantial costs with respect to the development or marketing of the design, and D's distributive share of the partnership's royalty income in 1989 is considered for purposes of paragraph (c)(3)(i) of this section to be derived in the ordinary course of a trade or business and therefore is not portfolio income.

(v) The result for 1990 is the same as for 1989, notwithstanding that the partnership incurs no expenditures in 1990 with respect to the development or marketing of the design.

Example (6). The facts are the same as in example (5), except that, for 1987, D's distributive share of the partnership's development and marketing costs is 15 percent, while D's distributive share of the partnership's gross royalties is 10 percent. Although D's distributive share of the expenditures reasonably incurred by the partnership during 1987 with respect to the development and marketing of the design ($1,200) is more than 50 percent of D's distributive share of the partnership's gross royalties from licensing the design ($2,000), D is not treated as performing substantial services or incurring substantial costs with respect to the development or marketing of the design for 1987 under paragraph (c)(3)(iii)(B)(*2*)(*ii*)(*a*) of this section. This is because, under paragraph (c)(3)(iii)(B)(*3*) of this section, the determination of whether the royalties are derived in the ordinary course of a trade or business is made by applying paragraph (c)(3)(iii)(B) of this section to the partnership, and not to D.

(4) *Items of personal service income specifically excluded*—(i) *In general.* Passive activity gross income does not include compensation paid to or on behalf of an individual for personal services performed or to be performed by such individual at any time. For purposes of this paragraph (c)(4), compensation for personal services includes only—

(A) Earned income (within the meaning of section 911(d)(2)(A)), including gross income from a payment described in paragraph (e)(2) of this section that represents compensation for the performance of services by a partner;

(B) Amounts includible in gross income under section 83;

(C) Amounts includible in gross income under sections 402 and 403;

(D) Amounts (other than amounts described in paragraph (c)(4)(i)(C) of this section) paid pursuant to retirement, pension, and other arrangements for deferred compensation for services;

(E) Social security benefits (within the meaning of section 86(d)) includible in gross income under section 86; and

(F) Other income identified by the Commissioner as income derived by the taxpayer from personal services;

provided, however, that no portion of a partner's distributive share of partnership income (within the meaning of section 704(b)) or a shareholder's pro rata share of income from an S corporation (within the meaning of section 1377(a)) shall be treated as compensation for personal services.

(ii) *Example.* The following example illustrates the application of this paragraph (c)(4):

Example. C owns 50 percent of the stock of X, an S corporation. X owns rental real estate, which it manages. X pays C a salary for services performed by C on behalf of X in connection with the management of X's rental properties. Under this paragraph (c)(4), although C's pro rata share of X's gross rental income is passive activity gross

Reg. § 1.469-2T(c)(4)

income (even if the salary paid to C is less than the fair market value of C's services), the salary paid to C does not constitute passive activity gross income.

(5) *Income from section 481 adjustment*—(i) *In general.* If a change in accounting method results in a positive section 481 adjustment with respect to an activity, a ratable portion (within the meaning of paragraph (c)(5)(iii) of this section) of the amount taken into account for a taxable year as a net positive section 481 adjustment by reason of such change shall be treated as gross income from the activity for such taxable year, and such gross income shall be treated as passive activity gross income if and only if such activity is a passive activity for the year of the change (within the meaning of section 481(a)).

(ii) *Positive section 481 adjustments.* For purposes of applying this paragraph (c)(5)—

(A) The term "net positive section 481 adjustment" means the increase (if any) in taxable income taken into account under section 481(a) to prevent amounts from being duplicated or omitted by reason of a change in accounting method; and

(B) The term "positive section 481 adjustment with respect to an activity" means the increase (if any) in taxable income that would be taken into account under section 481(a) to prevent only the duplication or omission of amounts from such activity by reason of the change in accounting method.

(iii) *Ratable portion.* The ratable portion of the amount taken into account as a net positive section 481 adjustment for a taxable year by reason of a change in accounting method is determined with respect to an activity by multiplying such amount by the fraction obtained by dividing—

(A) The positive section 481 adjustment with respect to the activity; by

(B) The sum of the positive section 481 adjustments with respect to all of the activities of the taxpayer.

(6) *Gross income from certain oil or gas properties*—(i) *In general.* [Reserved] See § 1.469-2(c)(6)(i) for rules relating to this paragraph.

(ii) *Gross and net passive income from the property.* [Reserved] See § 1.469-2(c)(6)(ii) for rules relating to this paragraph.

(iii) *Property.* [Reserved] See § 1.469-2(c)(6)(iii) for rules relating to this paragraph.

(iv) *Examples.* The following examples illustrate the application of this paragraph (c)(6):

Example (1). [Reserved] See § 1.469-2(c)(6)(iv) Example 1.

Example (2). [Reserved] See § 1.469-2(c)(6)(iv) Example 2.

Example (3). C is a general partner in partnership T and a limited partner in partnership U. T and U both own oil and gas working interests in tracts of land in County X. In 1987, T drills a well, and C's distributive share of T's losses from drilling the well is treated under § 1.469-1T(e)(4) as not from a passive activity. In the course of selecting the drilling site and drilling the well, T develops information indicating a significant probability that substantial oil and gas reserves underlie most portions of County X. As a result, the value of all oil and gas properties in County X is enhanced. The information developed by T does not, however, indicate that the reservoir in which T's well is drilled underlies U's tract. Under these facts, T's and U's tracts are not treated as one property for purposes of this paragraph (c)(6), because the value of U's tract is not directly enhanced by T's activities.

(7) *Other items specifically excluded.* Notwithstanding any other provision of the regulations under section 469, passive activity gross income does not include the following:

(i) Gross income of an individual from intangible property, such as a patent, copyright, or literary, musical, or artistic composition, if the taxpayer's personal efforts significantly contributed to the creation of such property;

(ii) Gross income from a qualified low-income housing project (within the meaning of section 502 of the Tax Reform Act of 1986) for any taxable year in the relief period (within the meaning of section 502(b) of such Act);

(iii) Gross income attributable to a refund of any state, local, or foreign income, war profits, or excess profits tax;

(iv) [Reserved] See § 1.469-2(c)(7)(iv) for rules relating to this paragraph (c)(7)(iv).

(v) [Reserved] See § 1.469-2(c)(7)(v) for rules relating to this paragraph (c)(7)(v).

(vi) [Reserved] See § 1.469-2(c)(7)(vi) for rules relating to this paragraph (c)(7)(vi).

(d) *Passive activity deductions*—(1) *In general.* Except as otherwise provided in section 469 and the regulations thereunder, a deduction is a passive activity deduction for a taxable year if and only if such deduction—

(i) Arises (within the meaning of paragraph (d)(8) of this section) in connection with the conduct of an activity that is a passive activity for the taxable year; or

Reg. § 1.469-2T(c)(5)

(ii) Is treated as a deduction from an activity under § 1.469-1T (f)(4) for the taxable year.

The following example illustrates the application of this paragraph (d)(1):

Example. (i) In 1987, A, a calendar year individual, acquires a partnership interest in R, a calendar year partnership. R's only activity is a trade or business activity in which A materially participates for 1987. R incurs a loss in 1987. A's distributive share of R's 1987 loss is $1,000. However, A's basis in the partnership interest at the end of 1987 (without regard to A's distributive share of partnership loss) is $600; accordingly, section 704(d) disallows any deduction in 1987 for $400 of A's distributive share of R's loss. The remainder of A's distributive share of R's loss would be allowed as a deduction for 1987 if taxable income for all taxable years were determined without regard to sections 469, 613A(d), and 1211. See paragraph (d)(8) of this section.

(ii) A does not materially participate in R's activity for 1988. In 1988, R again incurs a loss, and A's distributive share of the loss is again $1,000. At the end of 1988, A's basis in the partnership interest (without regard to A's distributive share of partnership loss) is $2,000; accordingly, in 1988 section 704(d) does not limit A's deduction for either A's $1,000 distributive share of R's 1988 loss or the $400 loss carried over from 1987 under the second sentence of section 704(d). These losses would be allowed as a deduction for 1988 if taxable income for all taxable years were determined without regard to sections 469, 613A(d), and 1211. See paragraph (d)(8) of this section.

(iii) Under these facts, only $400 of A's distributive share of R's deductions from the activity are disallowed under section 704(d) in 1987. A's remaining deductions from the activity are treated as deductions that arise in connection with the activity for 1987 under paragraph (d)(8) of this section. Because A materially participates in the activity for 1987, the activity is not a passive activity (within the meaning of § 1.469-1T(e)(1)) of A for such year. Accordingly, the deductions that are not disallowed in 1987 are not passive activity deductions.

(iv) A does not materially participate in R's activity for 1988. Accordingly, the activity is a passive activity of A for such year. No portion of A's distributive share of R's deductions from the activity is disallowed under section 704(d) in 1988. Accordingly, A's distributive share of R's deductions for 1988 and the $400 of deductions carried over from 1987 are both treated under paragraph (d)(8) of this section as deductions that arise in 1988. Since the activity is a passive activity for 1988, such deductions are passive activity deductions.

(2) *Exceptions.* Passive activity deductions do not include—

(i) A deduction for an item of expense (other than interest) that is clearly and directly allocable (within the meaning of paragraph (d)(4) of this section) to portfolio income (within the meaning of paragraph (c)(3)(i) of this section);

(ii) A deduction allowed under section 243, 244, or 245 with respect to any dividend that is not included in passive activity gross income;

(iii) Interest expense (other than interest expense described in paragraph (d)(3) of this section);

(iv) a deduction for a loss from the disposition of property of a type that produces portfolio income (within the meaning of paragraph (c)(3)(i) of this section);

(v) A deduction that, under section 469(g) and § 1.469-6T (relating to the allowance of passive activity losses upon certain dispositions of interests in passive activities), is treated as a deduction that is not a passive activity deduction;

(vi) A deduction for any state, local, or foreign income, war profits, or excess profits tax;

(vii) A miscellaneous itemized deduction (within the meaning of section 67(b)) that is subject to disallowance in whole or in part under section 67(a) (without regard to whether any amount of such deduction is disallowed under section 67);

(viii) A deduction allowed under section 170 for a charitable contribution;

(ix) [Reserved] See § 1.469-2(d)(2)(ix) for rules relating to this paragraph;

(x) [Reserved] See § 1.469-2(d)(2)(x) for rules relating to this paragraph (d)(2)(x);

(xi) [Reserved] See § 1.469-2(d)(2)(xi) for rules relating to this paragraph (d)(2)(xi);

(xii) [Reserved] See § 1.469-2(d)(2)(xii) for rules relating to this paragraph (d)(2)(xii).

(3) *Interest expense.* Except as otherwise provided in the regulations under section 469, interest expense is taken into account as a passive activity deduction if and only if such interest expense—

(i) Is allocated under § 1.163-8T to a passive activity expenditure (within the meaning of § 1.163-8T(b)(4)); and

(ii) Is not—

(A) Qualified residence interest (within the meaning of § 1.163-10T); or

Reg. § 1.469-2T(d)(3)

(B) Capitalized pursuant to a capitalization provision (within the meaning of § 1.163-8T(m)(7)(i)).

(4) *Clearly and directly allocable expenses.* For purposes of section 469 and regulations thereunder, an expense (other than interest expense) is clearly and directly allocable to portfolio income (within the meaning of paragraph (c)(3)(i) of this section) if and only if such expense is incurred as a result of, or incident to, an activity in which such gross income is derived or in connection with property from which such gross income is derived. For example, general and administrative expenses and compensation paid to officers attributable to the performance of services that do not directly benefit or are not incurred by reason of a particular activity or particular property are not clearly and directly allocable to portfolio income (within the meaning of paragraph (c)(3)(i) of this section).

(5) *Treatment of loss from disposition*—(i) *In general.* Except as otherwise provided in the regulations under section 469—

(A) Any loss recognized in any year upon the sale, exchange, or other disposition (a "disposition") of an interest in property used in an activity at the time of the disposition or of an interest in an activity held through a partnership or S corporation and any deduction allowed on account of the abandonment or worthlessness of such an interest is treated as a deduction from such activity; and

(B) Any such deduction is a passive activity deduction if and only if the activity is a passive activity of the taxpayer for the taxable year of the disposition (or other event giving rise to the deduction).

(ii) *Disposition of property used in more than one activity in 12-month period preceding disposition.* In the case of a disposition of an interest in property that is used in more than one activity during the 12-month period ending on the date of the disposition, the amount realized from the disposition and the adjusted basis of such interest must be allocated among such activities in the manner described in paragraph (c)(2)(ii) of this section.

(iii) *Other applicable rules*—(A) *Applicability of rules in paragraph (c)(2).* [Reserved] See § 1.469-2(d)(5)(iii)(A) for rules relating to this paragraph.

(B) *Dispositions of partnership interests and S corporation stock.* A partnership interest or S corporation stock is not property used in an activity for purposes of this paragraph (d)(5). See paragraph (e)(3) of this section for rules treating the loss recognized upon the disposition of a partnership interest or S corporation stock as loss from the disposition of interests in the activities in which the partnership or S corporation has an interest.

(6) *Coordination with other limitations on deductions that apply before section 469*—(i) *In general.* A item of deduction from a passive activity that is disallowed for a taxable year under section 704(d), 1366(d), or 465 is not a passive activity deduction for the taxable year. Paragraphs (d)(6)(ii) and (iii) of this section provide rules for determining the extent to which items of deduction from a passive activity are disallowed for a taxable year under sections 704(d), 1366(d), and 465.

(ii) *Proration of deductions disallowed under basis limitations*—(A) *Deductions disallowed under section 704(d).* If any amount of a partner's distributive share of a partnership's loss for the taxable year is disallowed under section 704(d), a ratable portion of the partner's distributive share of each item of deduction or loss of the partnership is disallowed for the taxable year. For purposes of the preceding sentence, the ratable portion of an item of deduction or loss is the amount of such item multiplied by the fraction obtained by dividing—

(*1*) The amount of the partner's distributive share of partnership loss that is disallowed for the taxable year; by

(*2*) The sum of the partner's distributive shares of all items of deduction and loss of the partnership for the taxable year.

(B) *Deductions disallowed under section 1366(d).* If any amount of an S corporation shareholder's pro rata share of an S corporation's loss for the taxable year is disallowed under section 1366(d), a ratable portion of the taxpayer's pro rata share of each item of deduction or loss of the S corporation is disallowed for the taxable year. For purposes of the preceding sentence, the ratable portion of an item of such item multiplied by the fraction obtained by dividing—

(*1*) The amount of the shareholder's pro rata share of S corporation loss that is disallowed for the taxable year; by

(*2*) The sum of the shareholder's pro rata shares of all items of deduction and loss of the corporation for the taxable year.

(iii) *Proration of deductions disallowed under at-risk limitation.* If any amount of the taxpayer's loss from an activity (within the meaning of section 465(c)) is disallowed under section 465 for the taxable year, a ratable portion of each item of deduction or loss from the activity is disallowed for the taxable year. For purposes of the preceding sentence, the ratable portion of an

Reg. § 1.469-2T(d)(4)

item of deduction or loss is the amount of such item multiplied by the fraction obtained by dividing—

(*1*) The amount of the loss from the activity that is disallowed for the taxable year; by

(*2*) The sum of all deductions from the activity for the taxable year.

(iv) *Coordination of basis and at-risk limitations.* The portion of any item of deduction or loss that is disallowed for the taxable year under section 704(d) or 1366(d) is not taken into account for the taxable year in determining the loss from an activity (within the meaning of section 465(c)) for purposes of applying section 465.

(v) *Separately identified items of deduction and loss.* In identifying the items of deduction and loss from an activity that are not disallowed under sections 704(d), 1366(d), and 465 (and that therefore may be treated as passive activity deductions), the taxpayer need not account separately for any item of deduction or loss unless such item may, if separately taken into account, result in an income tax liability different from that which would result were such item of deduction or loss not taken into account separately. For related rules applicable to partnerships and S corporations, see § 1.702-1(a)(8)(ii) and section 1366(a)(1)(A), respectively. Items of deduction or loss that must be accounted for separately include (but are not limited to) items of deduction or loss that—

(A) Are attributable to separate activities (within the meaning of the rules to be contained in § 1.469-4T);

(B) Arise in a rental real estate activity (within the meaning of section 469(i) and the rules to be contained in § 1.469-9T) in taxable years in which the taxpayer actively participates (within the meaning of section 469(i) and the rules to be contained in § 1.469-9T) in such activity;

(C) Arise in a rental real estate activity (within the meaning of section 469(i) and the rules to be contained in § 1.469-9T) in taxable years in which the taxpayer does not actively participate (within the meaning of section 469(i) and the rules to be contained in § 1.469-9T) in such activity;

(D) Arose in a taxable year beginning before 1987 and were not allowed for such taxable year under section 704(d), 1366(d), or 465(a)(2);

(E) [Reserved] See § 1.469-2(d)(6)(v)(E) for rules relating to this paragraph.

(F) Are attributable to pre-enactment interests in activities (within the meaning of § 1.469-11T(c)).

(7) *Deductions from section 481 adjustment*—(i) *In general.* If a change in accounting method results in a negative section 481 adjustment with respect to an activity, a ratable portion (within the meaning of paragraph (d)(7)(iii) of this section) of the amount taken into account for a taxable year as a net negative section 481 adjustment by reason of such change shall be treated as a deduction from the activity for such taxable year, and such deduction shall be treated as a passive activity deduction if and only if such activity is a passive activity for the year of the change (within the meaning of section 481(a)). See the rules to be contained in § 1.469-1T(k) for the treatment of passive activity deductions from an activity in taxable years in which the activity is a former passive activity.

(ii) *Negative section 481 adjustments.* For purposes of applying this paragraph (d)(7)—

(A) The term "net negative section 481 adjustment" means the decrease (if any) in taxable income taken into account under section 481(a) to prevent amounts from being duplicated or omitted by reason of a change in accounting method; and

(B) The term "negative section 481 adjustment with respect to an activity" means the decrease (if any) in taxable income that would be taken into account under section 481(a) to prevent only the duplication or omission of amounts from such activity by reason of the change in accounting method.

(iii) *Ratable portion.* The ratable portion of the amount taken into account as a net negative section 481 adjustment for a taxable year by reason of a change in accounting method is determined with respect to an activity by multiplying such amount by the fraction obtained by dividing—

(A) The negative section 481 adjustment with respect to the activity; by

(B) The sum of the negative section 481 adjustments with respect to all of the activities of the taxpayer.

(8) *Taxable year in which item arises.* [Reserved] See § 1.469-2(d)(8) for rules relating to this paragraph.

(e) *Special rules for partners and S corporation shareholders*—(1) *In general.* For purposes of section 469 and the regulations thereunder, the character (as an item of passive activity gross income or passive activity deduction) of each item of gross income and deduction allocated to a taxpayer from a partnership or S corporation (a "passthrough entity") shall be determined, in any case in which participation is relevant, by refer-

Reg. § 1.469-2T(e)(1)

ence to the participation of the taxpayer in the activity (or activities) that generated such item. Such participation is determined for the taxable year of the passthrough entity (and not the taxable year of the taxpayer). The following example illustrates the application of this paragraph (e)(1):

Example. A, a calendar year individual, is a partner in a partnership that has a taxable year ending January 31. During its taxable year ending on January 31, 1988, the partnership engages in a single trade or business activity. For the period from February 1, 1987, through January 31, 1988, A does not materially participate in this activity. In A's calendar year 1988 return, A's distributive share of the partnership's gross income and deductions from the activity must be treated as passive activity gross income and passive activity deductions, without regard to A's participation in the activity from February 1, 1988, through December 31, 1988. See also § 1.469-11T(a)(4) (relating to the effective date of, and transition rules under, section 469 and the regulations thereunder).

(2) *Payments under sections 707(a), 707(c), and 736(b).* Items of gross income and deduction attributable to a transaction described in section 707(a), 707(c), or 736(b) shall be characterized for purposes of section 469 and the regulations thereunder in accordance with the following rules:

(i) *Section 707(a).* Any item of gross income or deduction attributable to a transaction that is treated under section 707(a) as a transaction between a partnership and a partner acting in a capacity other than as a member of such partnership shall be characterized for purposes of section 469 and the regulations thereunder in a manner that is consistent with the treatment of such transaction under section 707(a).

(ii) *Section 707(c).* [Reserved] See § 1.469-2(e)(2)(ii) for rules relating to this paragraph.

(iii) *Payments in liquidation of a partner's interest in partnership property.* [Reserved] See § 1.469-2(e)(2)(iii) for rules relating to this paragraph.

(3) *Sale or exchange of interest in passthrough entity*—(i) *Application of this paragraph (e)(3).* In the case of the sale, exchange, or other disposition (a "disposition") of an interest in a passthrough entity, the amount of the seller's gain or loss from each activity in which such entity has an interest is determined, for purposes of section 469 and the regulations thereunder, under this paragraph (e)(3). In the case of any such disposition, except as otherwise provided in paragraph (e)(3)(iii) or (iv) of this section, paragraph (e)(3)(ii) of this section shall apply. See paragraphs (c)(2) and (d)(5) of this section for rules for determining the character of gain or loss, respectively, recognized upon a disposition of an interest in an activity held through a passthrough entity.

(ii) *General rule*—(A) *Allocation among activities.* Except as otherwise provided in this paragraph (e)(3)(ii) or in paragraph (e)(3)(iii) or (iv) of this section, if a holder of an interest in a passthrough entity disposes of such interest, a ratable portion (within the meaning of paragraph (e)(3)(ii)(B) of this section) of any gain or loss from such disposition shall be treated as gain or loss from the disposition of an interest in each trade or business, rental, or investment activity in which such passthrough entity owns an interest on the applicable valuation date.

(B) *Ratable portion*—(*1*) *Dispositions on which gain is recognized.* The ratable portion of any gain from the disposition of an interest in a passthrough entity that is allocable to an activity described in paragraph (e)(3)(ii)(A) of this section is determined by multiplying the amount of such gain by the fraction obtained by dividing—

(*i*) The amount of net gain (within the meaning of paragraph (e)(3)(ii)(E)(*3*) of this section) that would have been allocated to the holder of such interest with respect thereto if the passthrough entity had sold its entire interest in such activity for its fair market value on the applicable valuation date; by

(*ii*) The sum of the accounts of net gain that would have been allocated to the holder of such interest with respect thereto if the passthrough entity had sold its entire interest in each appreciated activity (within the meaning of paragraph (e)(3)(ii)(E)(*1*) of this section) described in paragraph (e)(3)(ii)(A) of this section for the fair market value of each such activity on the applicable valuation date.

(*2*) *Dispositions on which loss is recognized.* The ratable portion of any loss from the disposition of an interest in a passthrough entity that is allocable to an activity described in paragraph (e)(3)(ii)(A) of this section is determined by multiplying the amount of such loss by the fraction obtained by dividing—

(*i*) The amount of net loss (within the meaning of paragraph (e)(3)(ii)(E)(*4*) of this section) that would have been allocated to the holder of such interest with respect thereto if the passthrough entity had sold its entire interest in such activity for its fair market value on the applicable valuation date; by

(*ii*) The sum of the amounts of net loss that would have been allocated to the holder

Reg. § 1.469-2T(e)(2)

of such interest with respect thereto if the passthrough entity had sold its entire interest in each depreciated activity (within the meaning of paragraph (e)(3)(ii)(E)(*2*) of this section) described in paragraph (e)(3)(ii)(A) of this section for the fair market value of each such activity on the applicable valuation date.

(C) *Default rule.* If the gain or loss recognized upon the disposition of an interest in a passthrough entity cannot be allocated under paragraph (e)(3)(ii)(A) of this section, such gain or loss shall be allocated among the activities described in paragraph (e)(3)(ii)(A) of this section in proportion to the respective fair market values of the passthrough entity's interest in such activities at the applicable valuation date and the gain or loss allocated to each activity of the passthrough entity shall be treated as gain or loss from the disposition of an interest in such activity.

(D) *Special rules.* For purposes of this paragraph (e)(3)(ii), the following rules shall apply:

(*1*) *Applicable valuation date*—(*i*) *In general.* Except as otherwise provided in paragraph (e)(3)(ii)(D)(*1*)(*ii*) of this section, the applicable valuation date with respect to any disposition of an interest in a passthrough entity is whichever one of the following dates is selected by the passthrough entity:

(*a*) The beginning of the taxable year of the passthrough entity in which such disposition occurs; or

(*b*) The date on which such disposition occurs.

(*ii*) *Exception.* If, after the beginning of a passthrough entity's taxable year in which a holder's disposition of an interest in such passthrough entity occurs and before the time of such disposition—

(*a*) The passthrough entity disposes of more than 10 percent of its interest (by value as of the beginning of such taxable year) in any activity;

(*b*) More than 10 percent of the property (by value as of the beginning of such taxable year) used in any activity of the passthrough entity is disposed of; or

(*c*) The holder of such interest contributes to the passthrough entity substantially appreciated property or substantially depreciated property with a total fair market value or adjusted basis, respectively, which exceeds 10 percent of the total fair market value of the holder's interest in the passthrough entity as of the beginning of such taxable year;

then the applicable valuation date shall be the date immediately preceding the date on which such disposition occurs.

(*2*) *Basis adjustments.* Any adjustment to the basis of partnership property under section 743(b) made with respect to the holder of an interest in a partnership shall be taken into account in computing the net gain or net loss that would have been allocated to the holder with respect to such interest if the partnership had sold its entire interest in an activity.

(*3*) *Tiered passthrough entities.* In the case of a disposition of an interest in a passthrough entity (the "subsidiary passthrough entity") by a holder that is also a passthrough entity, any gain or loss from such disposition that is taken into account by any person that owns (directly or indirectly) an interest in such holder shall be allocated among the activities of the subsidiary passthrough entity by applying the rules of this paragraph (e)(3)(ii) to the person taking such gain or loss into account as if such person had been the holder of an interest in such subsidiary passthrough entity and had recognized such gain or loss as a result of a disposition of such interest.

(E) *Meaning of certain terms.* For purposes of this paragraph (e)(3)(ii)—

(*1*) An activity is an appreciated activity with respect to a holder that has disposed of an interest in a passthrough entity if a net gain would have been allocated to the holder with respect to such interest if the passthrough entity had sold its entire interest in such activity for its fair market value on the applicable valuation date;

(*2*) An activity is a depreciated activity with respect to a holder that has disposed of an interest in a passthrough entity if a net loss would have been allocated to the holder with respect to such interest if the passthrough entity had sold its entire interest in such activity for its fair market value on the applicable valuation date;

(*3*) The term "net gain" means, with respect to the sale of a passthrough entity's entire interest in an activity, the amount by which the gains from the sale of all of the property used by (or representing the interest of) the passthrough entity in such activity exceed the losses (if any) from such sale;

(*4*) The term "net loss" means, with respect to the sale of a passthrough entity's entire interest in an activity, the amount by which the losses from the sale of all of the property used by (or representing the interest of) the passthrough

Reg. § 1.469-2T(e)(3)

entity in such activity exceed the gains (if any) from such sale.

(iii) *Treatment of gain allocated to certain passive activities as not from a passive activity.* If, in the case of a disposition of an interest in a passthrough entity—

(A) An amount of gain recognized on account of such disposition by the holder of such interest (or any other person that owns (directly or indirectly) an interest in such holder if such holder is a passthrough entity) is allocated to a passive activity of such holder (or such other person) under paragraph (e)(3)(ii) of this section;

(B) [Reserved] See § 1.469-2(e)(3)(iii)(B) for rules relating to this paragraph.

(C) The amount of the gain of the holder (or such other person) described in paragraph (e)(3)(iii)(B) of this section exceeds 10 percent of the amount of the gain of the holder (or such other person) described in paragraph (e)(3)(iii)(A) of this section;

then the gain of the holder (or such other person) that is described in paragraph (e)(3)(iii)(A) of this section shall be treated as gain that is not from a passive activity to the extent that such gain does not exceed the amount of the gain of the holder (or such other person) described in paragraph (e)(3)(iii)(B) of this section. For purposes of applying the preceding sentence to the disposition of an interest in a partnership, the amount of gain that would have been allocated to the holder (or such other person) if all of the property used in an activity had been sold shall be determined by taking into account any adjustment to the basis of partnership property made with respect to such holder (or such other person) under section 743(b).

(iv) *Dispositions occurring in taxable years beginning before February 19, 1988*—(A) *In general.* Except as otherwise provided in this paragraph (e)(3)(iv), if the holder of an interest in a passthrough entity sells, exchanges, or otherwise disposes of all or part of such interest during a taxable year of such entity beginning prior to February 19, 1988, any gain or loss recognized from such disposition shall be allocated among the activities of the passthrough entity under any reasonable method selected by the passthrough entity, and the gain or loss allocated to each activity of the passthrough entity shall be treated as gain or loss from the disposition of an interest in such activity. For purposes of the preceding sentence, a reasonable method shall include the method prescribed by paragraph (e)(3)(ii) of this section. In addition, a method that allocates gain or loss among the passthrough entity's activities on the basis of the fair market value, cost, or adjusted basis of the property used in such activities shall generally be considered a reasonable method for purposes of this paragraph (e)(3)(iv).

(B) *Exceptions.* This paragraph (e)(3)(iv) shall not apply to any disposition of an interest in a passthrough entity occurring after February 19, 1988, if after such date, but before the holder's disposition of such interest, the holder (or any other person that owns (directly or indirectly) an interest in such holder if such holder is a passthrough entity) contributes to the passthrough entity substantially appreciated portfolio assets or any other substantially appreciated property that was used in any trade or business activity (within the meaning of § 1.469-1T(e)) of the holder (or such other person) during—

(*1*) The taxable year of such person in which such contribution occurs; or

(*2*) The immediately preceding taxable year of such person;

but only if such person materially participated (within the meaning of § 1.469-5T) in the activity for such year.

(v) *Treatment of portfolio assets.* For purposes of this paragraph (e)(3), all portfolio assets owned by a passthrough entity shall be treated as held in a single investment activity.

(vi) *Definitions.* For purposes of this paragraph (e)(3)—

(A) The term "portfolio asset" means any property of a type that produces portfolio income (within the meaning of paragraph (c)(3)(i) of this section);

(B) The term "substanitally appreciated property" means property with a fair market value that exceeds 120 percent of its adjusted basis; and

(C) The term "substantially depreciated property" means property with an adjusted basis that exceeds 120 percent of its fair market value.

(vii) *Examples.* The following examples illustrate the application of this paragraph (e)(3):

Example (1). (i) A owns a one-half interest in P, a calendar year partnership. In 1993, A sells 50 percent of such interest for $50,000. A's adjusted basis for the interest sold is $30,000. Thus, A recognizes $20,000 of gain from the sale. P is engaged in three trade or business activities, X, Y, and Z, and owns marketable securities that are portfolio assets. For 1993, A materially participates in activity Z, but does not participate in activities X and Y. Paragraph (c)(2)(iii) of this section would not have applied to any of the gain that A would have been allocated if, immediately before A's sale, P had disposed of all of the property used in its trade or business activities. Dur-

Methods of Accounting

See p. 20,601 for regulations not amended to reflect law changes

ing the portion of 1993 preceding A's sale, P did not sell any of the property used in its activities, and A did not contribute any property to P.

(ii) Under paragraph (e)(3)(ii) of this section, a ratable portion of A's $20,000 gain is allocated to each appreciated activity in which P owned an interest on the applicable valuation date (within the meaning of paragraph (e)(3)(ii)(D)(*1*) of this section). For this purpose, paragraph (e)(3)(v) of this section treats the marketable securities owned by P as a single investment activity.

(iii) P selects the beginning of 1993 as the applicable valuation date pursuant to paragraph (e)(3)(ii)(D)(*1*)(*i*) of this section. P is not required to use the date of A's sale as the applicable valuation date under paragraph (e)(3)(ii)(D)(*1*)(*ii*) of this section because during the portion of 1993 preceding A's sale, P did not sell any of its property and A did not contribute any property to P. At the beginning of 1993, the fair market value and adjusted basis of the property used in P's activities are as follows:

	Adjusted Basis	Fair Market Value
X	$ 68,000	$ 48,000
Y	30,000	62,000
Z	20,000	80,000
Marketable securities	2,000	10,000
Total	$120,000	$200,000

(iv) Under paragraph (e)(3)(ii)(B) of this section, the portion of A's $20,000 gain that is allocated to an appreciated activity of P (i.e., activities Y and Z and the marketable securities) is the amount of such gain multiplied by the fraction obtained by dividing (a) the net gain that would have been allocated to A with respect to the interest sold by A if P had sold its entire interest in such activity at the beginning of 1993 by (b) the sum of the amounts of net gain that would have been allocated to A with respect to the interest sold by A if P had sold its entire interest in each appreciated activity at the beginning of 1993.

(v) If P had sold its entire interest in activities Y and Z and the marketable securities at the beginning of 1993, A would have been allocated the following amounts of net gain with respect to the interest in P that A sold in 1993:

Activity	Net Gain
Y	$ 8,000
Z	15,000
Marketable securities	2,000
Total	$25,000

(vi) Accordingly, under paragraph (e)(3)(ii) of this section, $6,400 of A's $20,000 gain ($20,000 × $8,000/$25,000) is allocated to activity Y, $12,000 of A's $20,000 gain ($20,000 × $15,000/$25,000) is allocated to activity Z, and $1,600 of A's $20,000 gain ($20,000 × $2,000/$25,000) is allocated to the marketable securities. The gain allocated to activity Y is passive activity gross income. None of that gain is treated as gain that is not from a passive activity under paragraph (e)(3)(iii) of this section because (c)(2)(iii) of this section would not have applied to any of the gain that A would have been allocated if P had sold all of the property used in activity Y immediately prior to A's sale.

Example (2). (i) B and C, calendar year individuals, are equal partners in calendar year partnership R, which they formed on January 1, 2005, with contributions of property and money. The only item of property (other than money) contributed by B was a building that B had used for 12 years preceding the contribution in an activity that was not a passive activity during such period. At the time of its contribution, the building had an adjusted basis of $40,000 and a fair market value of $66,000. R is engaged in a single activity: the sale of equipment to customers in the ordinary course of the business of dealing in such property. R uses the building contributed by B in the dealership activity. B did not materially participate in the dealership activity during 2005. On July 1, 2005, D purchases one-half of B's interest in R for $37,500 in cash. At the time of the sale, the balance sheet of R, which uses the accrual method of accounting, is as follows:

Reg. § 1.469-2T(e)(3)

Methods of Accounting

See p. 20,601 for regulations not amended to reflect law changes

Assets

	Adjusted basis per books	Fair market value
Cash	$ 30,000	$ 30,000
Accounts receivable—Dealership	20,000	18,000
Inventory—Dealership	52,000	66,000
Building	40,000	66,000
Total	$142,000	$180,000

Liabilities and Capital

	Adjusted basis per books	Fair market value
Liabilities	$ 30,000	$ 30,000
Capital B	47,000	75,000
C	65,000	75,000
Total	$142,000	$180,000

Thus, B's gain from the sale is $14,000 ($45,000 amount realized from the sale (consisting of $37,500 of cash and $7,500 of liabilities assumed by the purchaser) minus B's $31,000 adjusted basis for the interest sold (one-half of B's total adjusted basis of $62,000)).

(ii) Under paragraph (e)(3)(ii) of this section, all $14,000 of B's gain from the sale is allocated to R's dealership activity, which is a passive activity of B for 2005. If, however, R had sold its interest in the building immediately prior to B's sale for its fair market value on the applicable valuation date (the valuation date selected by R is irrelevant since the building had a fair market value of $66,000 at the beginning of 2005 and at the time of the sale), B would have been allocated $13,000 of gain under section 704(c) with respect to the interest in R that B sold to D. This gain would have been treated as gain that is not from a passive activity under paragraph (c)(2)(iii) of this section and would have exceeded 10 percent of the total amount of B's gain that is allocated to the dealership activity under paragraph (e)(3)(ii) of this section. Accordingly, under paragraph (e)(3)(iii) of this section, B's gain from the sale ($14,000) is treated as gain that is not from a passive activity to the extent that such gain does not exceed the amount of gain subject to paragraph (c)(2)(iii) of this section that B would have been allocated with respect to the interest sold to D if R had sold all of the property used in the dealership activity immediately prior to B's sale ($13,000). Thus, $13,000 of B's gain from the sale is treated as gain that is not from a passive gain activity.

(f) *Recharacterization of passive income in certain situations*—(1) *In general.* This paragraph (f) sets forth rules that require income from certain passive activities to be treated as income that is not from a passive activity (regardless of whether such income is treated as passive activity gross income under section 469 or any other provision of the regulations thereunder. For definitions of certain terms used in this paragraph (f), see paragraph (f)(9) of this section.

(2) *Special rule for significant participation*—(i) *In general.* An amount of the taxpayer's gross income from each significant participation passive activity for the taxable year equal to a ratable portion of the taxpayer's net passive income from such activity for the taxable year shall be treated as not from a passive activity if the taxpayer's passive activity gross income from all significant participation passive activities for the taxable year (determined without regard to paragraph (f)(2) through paragraph (4) of this section) exceeds the taxpayer's passive activity deductions from all such activities for such year. For purposes of this paragraph (f)(2), the ratable portion of the net passive income from an activity is determined by multiplying the amount of such income by the fraction obtained by dividing—

(A) The amount of the excess described in the preceding sentence; by

(B) The amount of the excess described in the preceding sentence taking into account only significant participation passive activities from which the taxpayer has net passive income for the taxable year.

(ii) *Significant participation passive activity.* For purposes of this paragraph (f)(2), the term "significant participation passive activity" means any trade or business activity (within the meaning of § 1.469-1T(e)(2)) in which the taxpayer significantly participates (within the meaning of § 1.469-5T(c)(2)) for the taxable year but in which the taxpayer does not materially participate (within the meaning of § 1.469-5T) for such year.

Reg. § 1.469-2T(f)(1)

(iii) *Example.* The following example illustrates the application of this paragraph (f)(2):

Example. (i) A owns interests in three trade or business activities, X, Y, and Z. A does not materially participate in any of these activities for the taxable year, but participates in activity X for 110 hours, in activity Y for 160 hours, and in activity Z for 125 hours. A owns no interest in any other trade or business activity in which A does not materially participate for the taxable year but in which A participates for more than 100 hours during the taxable year. A's net passive income (or loss) for the taxable year from activities X, Y, and Z is as follows:

	X	Y	Z
Passive activity gross income	$600	$ 700	$900
Passive activity deductions	(200)	(1,000)	(300)
Net passive income	$400	($ 300)	$600

(ii) Under paragraph (f)(2)(ii) of this section, activities X, Y, and Z are A's only significant participation passive activities for the taxable year. A's passive activity gross income from significant participation passive activities ($2,200) exceeds A's passive activity deductions from significant participation passive activities ($1,500) by $700 for such year. Therefore, under paragraph (f)(2)(i) of this section, a ratable portion of A's gross income from activities X and Z (A's significant participation passive activities with net passive income for the taxable year) is treated as gross income that is not from a passive activity. The ratable portion is determined by dividing (a) the amount by which A's passive activity gross income from significant participation passive activities exceeds A's passive activity deductions from significant participation passive activities for the taxable year ($700) by (b) such excess taking into account only A's significant participation passive activities having net passive income for the taxable year ($1,000). Accordingly, $280 of gross income from activity X ($400 × 700/1000) and $420 of gross income from activity Z ($600 × 700/1000) is treated as gross income that is not from a passive activity.

(3) *Rental of nondepreciable property.* If less than 30 percent of the unadjusted basis of the property used or held for use by customers in a rental activity (within the meaning of § 1.469-1T(e)(3)) during the taxable year is subject to the allowance for depreciation under section 167, an amount of the taxpayer's gross income from the activity equal to the taxpayer's net passive income from the activity shall be treated as not from a passive activity. For purposes of this paragraph (f)(3), the term "unadjusted basis" means adjusted basis determined without regard to any adjustment described in section 1016 that decreases basis. The following example illustrates the application of this paragraph (f)(3):

Example. C is a limited partner in a partnership. The partnership acquires vacant land for $300,000, constructs improvements on the land at a cost of $100,000, and leases the land and improvements to a tenant. The partnership then sells the land and improvements for $600,000, thereby realizing a gain on the disposition. The unadjusted basis of the improvements ($100,000) equals 25 percent of the unadjusted basis of all property ($400,000) used in the rental activity. Therefore, under this paragraph (f)(3), an amount of C's gross income from the activity equal to the net passive income from the activity (which is computed by taking into account the gain from the disposition, including gain allocable to the improvements) is treated as not from a passive activity.

(4) *Net interest income from passive equity-financed lending activity*—(i) *In general.* An amount of the taxpayer's gross income for the taxable year from any equity-financed lending activity equal to the lesser of—

(A) The taxpayer's equity-financed interest income from the activity for such year; and

(B) The taxpayer's net passive income from the activity for such year

shall be treated as not from a passive activity.

(ii) *Equity-financed lending activity*—(A) *In general.* For purposes of this paragraph (f)(4), an activity is an equity-financed lending activity for a taxable year if—

(*1*) The activity involves a trade or business of lending money; and

(*2*) The average outstanding balance of the liabilities incurred in the activity for the taxable year does not exceed 80 percent of the average outstanding balance of the interest-bearing assets held in the activity for such year.

(B) *Certain liabilities not taken into account.* For purposes of paragraph (f)(4)(ii)(A)(*2*) of this section, liabilities incurred principally for the purpose of increasing the percentage described in paragraph (f)(4)(ii)(A)(*2*) of this section shall not be taken into account in computing such percentage.

Reg. § 1.469-2T(f)(4)

(iii) *Equity-financed interest income.* For purposes of this paragraph (f)(4), the taxpayer's equity-financed interest income from an activity for a taxable year is the amount of the taxpayer's net interest income from the activity for such year multiplied by the fraction obtained by dividing—

(A) The excess of the average outstanding balance for such year of the interest-bearing assets held in the activity over the average outstanding balance such year of the liabilities incurred in the activity; by

(B) The average outstanding balance for such year of the interest-bearing assets held in the activity.

(iv) *Net interest income.* For purposes of this paragraph (f)(4), the net interest income from an activity for a taxable year is—

(A) The gross interest income from the activity for such year; reduced by

(B) Expenses from the activity (other than interest on liabilities described in paragraph (f)(4)(vi) of this section) for such year that are reasonably allocable to such gross interest income.

(v) *Interest-bearing assets.* For purposes of this paragraph (f)(4), the interest-bearing assets held in an activity include all assets that produce interest income, including loans to customers.

(vi) *Liabilities incurred in the activity.* For purposes of this paragraph (f)(4), liabilities incurred in an activity include all fixed and determinable liabilities incurred in the activity that bear interest or are issued with original issue discount other than debts secured by tangible property used in the activity. In the case of an activity conducted by an entity in which the taxpayer owns an interest, liabilities incurrred in an activity include only liabilities with respect to which the entity is the borrower.

(vii) *Average outstanding balance.* For purposes of this paragraph (f)(4), the average outstanding balance of liabilities incurred in an activity or of the interest-bearing assets held in an activity may be computed on a daily, monthly, or quarterly basis at the option of the taxpayer.

(viii) *Example.* The following example illustrates the application of this paragraph (f)(4):

Example. (i) A, a calendar year individual, acquires on January 1, 1988, a limited partnership interest in P, a calendar year partnership. Under the partnership agreement, A has a one percent share of each item of income, gain, loss, deduction, and credit of P. A acquires the partnership interest for $90,000, using $50,000 of unborrowed funds and $40,000 of proceeds of a loan bearing interest at an annual rate of 10 percent. A pays $4,000 of interest on the loan in 1988.

(ii) P's sole activity is a trade or business of lending money. A does not materially participate in the activity for 1988. During 1988, the average outstanding balance of P's interest-bearing assets (including loans to customers, temporary deposits with other lending institutions, and government and corporate securities) is $20 million. P incurs numerous interest-bearing liabilities in connection with its lending activity, including liabilities for deposits taken from customers, unsecured short-term and long-term loans from other lending institutions, and a mortgage loan secured by the building, owed by P, in which P conducts its business. For 1988, the average outstanding balance of all of these liabilities (other than the mortgage loan) is $11 million. None of these liabilities was incurred by P principally for the purpose of increasing the percentage described in paragraph (f)(4)(ii)(A)(*2*) of this section.

(iii) The interest income derived by P for 1988 from its interest-bearing assets is $2.2 million. The interest expense paid by P for 1988, with respect to the liabilities incurred in connection with its lending activity (other than the mortgage loan) is $990,000. P's other expenses for 1988 that are reasonably allocable to P's gross interest income (including expenses for advertising, loan processing and servicing, and insurance and depreciation on P's building) total $250,000. P's interest expense for 1988 on the mortgage loan secured by the building used in P's lending activity is $50,000. All of the interest expense paid or incurred by P for 1988 is allocated under § 1.163-8T to expenditures in connection with P's lending activity.

(iv) Under paragraph (f)(4)(ii) of this section, P's activity is an equity-financed lending activity for 1988, since, for 1988, the activity involves a trade or business of lending money and the average outstanding balance of the liabilities incurred in the activity ($11 million) does not exceed 80 percent of the average outstanding balance of the interest-bearing assets held in the activity ($20 million). Accordingly, under paragraph (f)(4)(i) of this section, an amount of A's gross income from the activity equal to the lesser of (a) A's equity-financed interest income from the activity for 1988, or (b) A's net passive income from the activity for 1988, is treated as income that is not from a passive activity.

(v) Under paragraph (f)(4)(iii) of this section, A's equity-financed interest income from the activity for 1988 is determined by multiplying A's net interest income from the activity for 1988 by the fraction obtained by dividing $9 million (the

Reg. § 1.469-2T(f)(4)

excess of the average interest-bearing assets for 1988 over the average interest-bearing liabilities for 1988) by $20 million (the average interest-bearing assets for 1988). Under paragraph (f)(4)(iv) of this section, A's net interest income from the activity for 1988 is $19,000 (A's distributive share of $2.2 million of gross interest income less A's distributive share of $300,000 of expenses described in paragraph (f)(4)(iv)(B) of this section, including interest expense on the mortgage loan). A's distributive share of P's other interest expense ($990,000) is not taken into account in computing A's net interest income for 1988. Accordingly, A's equity-financed interest income from the activity for 1988 is $8,550 ($19,000 × $9 million/$20 million).

(vi) Under paragraph (f)(9)(i) of this section, A's net passive income from the activity for 1988 is determined by taking into account A's distributive share of P's gross income and deductions from the activity for 1988, as well as any interest expense incurred by A individually that is taken into account under § 1.163-8T in determining A's income or loss from the activity for 1988. Assuming that for 1988 all $4,000 of interest expense on the loan that A used to finance the acquisition of A's interest in P is allocated under § 1.163-8T to expenditures of A in connection with the lending activity for 1988, A's net passive income from the activity for 1988 is $5,100, computed as set forth in the following table:

Gross income:	
Interest income	$22,000
Deductions:	
Distributive share of P's expenses from the activity	(12,900)
Interest expense on A's acquisition debt	(4,000)
Net passive income	$ 5,100

(vii) A's net passive income from the activity for 1988 ($5,100) is less than A's equity-financed income from the activity for 1988 ($8,550). Accordingly, under this paragraph (f)(4), $5,100 of A's gross income from the activity for 1988 is treated as not from a passive activity.

(5) *Net income from certain property rented incidental to development activity*—(i) *In general.* [Reserved] See § 1.469(f)(5)(i) for rules relating to this paragraph.

(ii) *Commencement.* [Reserved] See § 1.469-2(f)(5)(ii) for rules relating to this paragraph (f)(5)(ii).

(iii) *Services performed for the purpose of enhancing the value of property.* [Reserved] See § 1.469-2(f)(5)(iii) for rules relating to this paragraph (f)(5)(iii).

(iv) *Examples.* [Reserved] See § 1.469-2(f)(5)(iv) for examples relating to this paragraph (f)(5)(iv).

(6) *Property rented to a nonpassive activity.* [Reserved] See § 1.469(f)(6) for rules relating to this paragraph.

(7) *Special rules applicable to the acquisition of an interest in a passthrough entity engaged in the trade or business of licensing intangible property*—(i) *In general.* If a taxpayer acquires an interest in an entity described in paragraph (c)(3)(iii)(B)(*3*) of this section (the "development entity") after the development entity has created an item of intangible property or performed substantial services or incurred substantial costs with respect to the development or marketing of an item of intangible property, an amount of the taxpayer's gross royalty income for the taxable year from such item of property equal to the taxpayer's net royalty income for the year from such item of property shall be treated as not from a passive activity.

(ii) *Royalty income from property.* For purposes of this paragraph (f)(7)—

(A) A taxpayer's gross royalty income for a taxable year from an item of property is the taxpayer's share of passive activity gross income for such year (determined without regard to paragraphs (f)(2) through (7) of this section) from the licensing or transfer of any right in such property; and

(B) A taxpayer's net royalty income for a taxable year from an item of property is the excess, if any, of—

(*1*) The taxpayer's gross royalty income for the taxable year from such item of property; over

(*2*) Any passive activity deductions for such taxable year (including any deduction treated as a deduction for such year under § 1.469-1T(f)(4)) that are reasonably allocable to such item of property.

(iii) *Exceptions.* Paragraph (f)(7)(i) of this section shall not apply to a taxpayer's gross royalty income for a taxable year from the licensing of an item of intangible property if—

(A) The expenditures reasonably incurred by the development entity for the taxable

Reg. § 1.469-2T(f)(7)

year of the entity ending with or within the taxpayer's taxable year with respect to the development or marketing of such property satisfy paragraph (c)(3)(iii)(B)(*2*)(*ii*)(*a*) of this section; or

(B) The taxpayer's share of the expenditures reasonably incurred by the development entity with respect to the development or marketing of such property for all taxable years of the entity beginning with the taxable year of the entity in which year the taxpayer acquired the interest in the entity and ending with the taxable year of the entity ending with or within the taxpayer's current taxable year exceeds 25 percent of the fair market value of the taxpayer's interest in such property at the time the taxpayer acquired the interest in the entity.

(iv) *Capital expenditures.* For purposes of paragraph (f)(7)(iii)(B) of this section, a capital expenditure shall be taken into account for the taxable year of the entity in which such expenditure is chargeable to capital account, and the taxpayer's share of such expenditure shall be determined as though such expenditure were allowed as a deduction for such year.

(v) *Example.* The following example illustrates the application of this paragraph (f)(7):

Example. (i) The facts are the same as in example (5) in paragraph (c)(3)(iv) of this section, except that, in 1988, D's 10 percent partnership interest is sold to F for $13,000, all of which is attributable to the design licensed by the partnership.

(ii) For 1988, the expenditures reasonably incurred by the partnership with respect to the development or marketing of the design satisfy paragraph (c)(3)(iii)(B)(*2*)(*ii*)(*a*) of this section. Accordingly, under paragraph (f)(7)(iii)(A) of this section, paragraph (f)(7)(i) of this section does not apply to F's distributive share of the partnership's gross income from licensing the design.

(iii) For 1989, the expenditures reasonably incurred by the partnership with respect to the development or marketing of the design do not satisfy paragraph (c)(3)(iii)(B)(*2*)(*ii*)(*a*) of this section. Moreover, F's distributive share of such expenditures reasonably incurred by the partnership for 1988 and 1989 ($27,000 $\times$ .10 = $2,700) does not exceed 25 percent of the fair market value of F's interest in the design at the time F acquired the partnership interest ($13,000). Accordingly, neither of the exceptions provided in paragraph (f)(7)(iii) of this section applies for 1989 and, under paragraph (f)(7)(i) of this section, an amount of F's gross royalty income from the design equal to F's net royalty income from the design is treated as not from a passive activity.

(8) *Limitation on recharacterized income.* The amount of gross income from an activity that is treated as not from a passive activity for the taxable year under subparagraphs (f)(2) through (4) of this paragraph (f) shall not exceed the greatest amount of gross income treated as not from a passive activity under any one of such subparagraphs.

(9) *Meaning of certain terms.* For purposes of this paragraph (f), the terms set forth below shall have the following meanings:

(i) The net passive income from an activity for a taxable year is the amount by which the taxpayer's passive activity gross income from the activity for the taxable year (determined without regard to paragraphs (f)(2) through (4) of this section) exceeds the taxpayer's passive activity deductions from the activity for such year;

(ii) The net passive loss from an activity for a taxable year is the amount by which the taxpayer's passive activity deductions from the activity for the taxable year exceeds the taxpayer's passive activity gross income from the activity for such year (determined without regard to paragraphs (f)(2) through (4) of this section).

(iii) [Reserved] See § 1.469-2(f)(9)(iii) for rules relating to this paragraph.

(iv) [Reserved] See § 1.469-2(f)(9)(iv) for rules relating to this paragraph.

(10) *Coordination with section 163(d).* [Reserved] See § 1.469-2(f)(10) for rules relating to this paragraph.

(11) *Effective date.* For the effective date of the rules in this paragraph (f), see § 1.469-11T (relating to effective date and transition rules). [Temporary Reg. § 1.469-2T.]

☐ [*T.D.* 8175, 2-19-88. Amended by *T.D.* 8253, 5-11-89; *T.D.* 8290, 2-23-90; *T.D.* 8318, 11-16-90; *T.D.* 8417, 5-11-92; *T.D.* 8477, 2-22-93 and *T.D.* 8495, 11-3-93.]

[Reg. § 1.469-3]

§ 1.469-3. **Passive activity credit.**—(a) through (d) [Reserved]

(e) *Coordination with section 38(b).* Any credit described in section 38(b)(1) through (5) is taken into account in computing the current year business credit for the first taxable year in which the credit is subject to section 469 and is not disallowed by section 469 and the regulations thereunder.

(f) *Coordination with section 50.* In the case of any cessation described in section 50(a)(1) or (2), the credits allocable to the taxpayer's activities

Reg. § 1.469-3(a)

under § 1.469-1(f)(4) shall be adjusted by reason of the cessation.

(g) [Reserved] [Reg. § 1.469-3.]

☐ [T.D. 8417, 5-11-92.]

[Reg. § 1.469-3T]

§ 1.469-3T. Passive activity credit (Temporary).—(a) *Computation of passive activity credit.* The taxpayer's passive activity credit for the taxable year is the amount (if any) by which—

(1) The sum of all of the taxpayer's credits that are subject to section 469 for such year; exceeds

(2) The taxpayer's regular tax liability allocable to all passive activities for such year.

(b) *Credits subject to section 469*—(1) *In general.* Except as otherwise provided in this paragraph (b), a credit is subject to section 469 for a taxable year if and only if—

(i) Such credit—

(A) Is attributable to such taxable year and arises in connection with the conduct of an activity that is a passive activity for such taxable year; and

(B) Is described in—

(*1*) Section 38(b)(1) through (5) (relating to general business credits);

(*2*) Section 27(b) (relating to corporations described in section 936);

(*3*) Section 28 (relating to clinical testing of certain drugs); or

(*4*) Section 29 (relating to fuel from nonconventional sources); or

(ii) Such credit is allocable to an activity for such taxable year under § 1.469-1T(f)(4).

(2) *Treatment of credits attributable to qualified progress expenditures.* Any credit attributable to an increase in qualified investment under section 46(d)(1)(A) (relating to qualified progress expenditures) with respect to progress expenditure property (as defined in section 46(d)(2)) is subject to section 469 for a taxable year if—

(i) Such credit is attributable to such taxable year;

(ii) Such credit is described in paragraph (b)(1)(i)(B) of this section; and

(iii) It is reasonable to believe that such progress expenditure property will be used in a passive activity of the taxpayer when it is placed in service.

(3) *Special rule for partners and S corporation shareholders.* The character of a credit of a taxpayer arising in connection with an activity conducted by a partnership or S corporation (as a credit subject to section 469) shall be determined, in any case in which participation is relevant, by reference to the participation of the taxpayer in such activity. Such participation is determined for the taxable year of the partnership or S corporation (and not the taxable year of the taxpayer). See § 1.469-2T(e)(1).

(4) *Exception for pre-1987 credits.* A credit is not subject to section 469 if it is attributable to a taxable year of the taxpayer beginning prior to January 1, 1987.

(c) *Taxable year to which credit is attributable.* A credit is taxable year in which such credit would be (or would have been) allowed if the credits allowed for all taxable years were determined without regard to the limitations contained in sections 26(a), 28(d)(2), 29(b)(5), 38(c), and 469.

(d) *Regular tax liability allocable to passive activities*—(1) *In general.* For purposes of paragraph (a)(2) of this section, the taxpayer's regular tax liability allocable to all passive activities for the taxable year is the excess (if any) of—

(i) The taxpayer's regular tax liability for such taxable year; over

(ii) The amount of such regular tax liability determined by reducing the taxpayer's taxable income for such year by the excess (if any) of the taxpayer's passive activity gross income for such year over the taxpayer's passive activity deductions for such year.

(2) *Regular tax liability.* For purposes of this section, the term "regular tax liability" has the meaning given such term in section 26(b).

(e) *Coordination with section 38(b).* [Reserved] See § 1.469-3(e) for rules relating to this paragraph.

(f) *Coordination with section 50.* [Reserved] See § 1.469-3(f) for rules relating to this paragraph.

(g) *Examples.* The following examples illustrate the application of this section:

Example (1). (i) A, a calendar year individual, is a general partner in calendar year partnership P. P purchases a building in 1987 and, in 1987, 1988, and 1989, incurs rehabilitation costs with respect to the building. The building is placed in service in the rental activity in 1989. P's rehabilitation costs are qualified rehabilitation expenditures (within the meaning of section 48(g)(2)) and are taken into account in determining the amount of the investment credit for rehabilitation expenditures. P's qualified rehabilitation expenditures are not qualified progress expenditures (within the meaning of section 46(d)).

37,094   Methods of Accounting

See p. 20,601 for regulations not amended to reflect law changes

(ii) Because, under section 46(c)(1), the credit is allowable for the taxable year in which the rehabilitated property is placed in service, the credit allowable for P's qualified rehabilitation expenditures arises in connection with the activity in which the property is placed in service. In addition, the credit is attributable to 1989, the year in which the property is placed in service, because it would be allowed for such year if A's credits allowed for all taxable years were determined without regard to the limitations contained in sections 26(a), 28(d)(2), 29(b)(5), 38(c), and 469. Accordingly, under paragraph (b)(1) of this section, A's distributive share of the credit is subject to section 469 for 1989 because the credit arises in connection with a rental activity for such year.

Example (2). The facts are the same as in example (1), except that the rehabilitation costs are incurred in anticipation of placing the building in service in a rental activity, the qualified rehabilitation expenditures in 1987 and 1988 are qualified progress expenditures ("QPEs") (within the meaning of section 46(d)(3)), the improvements resulting from the expenditures are progress expenditure property (within the meaning of paragraph (d)(2) of this section), and it is reasonable to expect that such property will be transition property (within the meaning of section 49 (e)) when the property is placed in service. Therefore, under section 46(d)(1)(A), the qualified investment for 1987 and 1988 is increased by an amount equal to the aggregate of the applicable percentage of the qualified rehabilitation expenditures incurred in such years. The credits that are based on these expenditures are attributable (under paragraph (c) of this section) to 1987 and 1988, respectively. It is reasonable to believe in 1987 and 1988 that the progress expenditure property will be used in a rental activity when it is placed in service. Accordingly, under paragraph (b)(2) of this section, A's distributive share of the credit for 1987 and 1988 is subject to section 469. Under paragraph (b)(1) of this section (as in example (1)), A's distributive share of the credit for 1989 is also subject to section 469.

Example (3). (i) B, a single individual, acquires an interest in a partnership that, in 1988, rehabilitates a building and places it in service in a trade or business activity in which B does not materially participate. For 1988, B has the following items of gross income, deduction, and credit:

Gross income		
Income other than passive activity gross income	$110,000	
Passive activity gross income	20,000	$130,000
Deductions		
Deductions other than passive activity deductions	$23,950	
Passive activity deductions	18,000	(41,950)
Taxable income		($88,050)
Credits		
Rehabilitation credit from the passive activity		$8,000

(ii) For 1988, the amount by which B's passive activity gross income exceeds B's passive activity deductions (B's net passive income) is $2,000. Under paragraph (d) of this section, B's regular tax liability allocable to passive activities for 1988 is determined as follows:

(A) Taxable income	$88,050.00	
(B) Regular tax liability		$24,578.50
(C) Taxable income minus net passive income	86,050.00	
(D) Regular tax liability for taxable income of $86,050.00		23,918.50
(E) Regular tax liability allocable to passive activities ((B) minus (D))		$660.00

Reg. § 1.469-3T(g)

(iii) Under paragraph (a) of this section, B's passive activity credit for 1988 is the amount by which B's credits that are subject to section 469 for 1988 ($8,000) exceed B's regular tax liability allocable to passive activities for 1988 ($660.00). Accordingly, B's passive activity credit for 1988 is $7,340.

Example (4). (i) The facts are the same as in example (3) except that, in 1988, B also has additional deductions of $100,000 from a trade or business activity in which B materially participates for 1988. Thus, B has a taxable loss for 1988 of $11,950, determined as follows:

Gross income:		
Income other than passive activity gross income		$110,000
Passive activity gross income	20,000	$130,000
Deductions:		
Deductions other than passive activity deductions	$123,950	
Passive activity deductions	18,000	(141,950)
Taxable income		($11,950)

(ii) Under section 26(b) and paragraph (d)(2) of this section, the regular tax liability for a taxable year cannot exceed the tax imposed by chapter 1 of subtitle A of the Internal Revenue Code for the taxable year. Therefore, under paragraph (d)(1) of this section, B's regular tax liability allocable to passive activities for 1988 is zero. Although B's net operating loss for the taxable year is reduced by B's net passive income, and B's regular tax liability for other taxable years may increase as a result of the reduction, such an increase does not change B's regular tax liability allocable to passive activities for 1988. Accordingly, B's passive activity credit for 1988 is $8,000. [Temporary Reg. § 1.469-3T.]

☐ [*T.D.* 8175, 2-19-88. *Amended by T.D.* 8253, 5-11-89 *and T.D.* 8417, 5-11-92.]

[Reg. § 1.469-4]

§ 1.469-4. Definition of activity.—(a) *Scope and purpose.* This section sets forth the rules for grouping a taxpayer's trade or business activities and rental activities for purposes of applying the passive activity loss and credit limitation rules of section 469. A taxpayer's activities include those conducted through C corporations that are subject to section 469, S corporations, and partnerships.

(b) *Definitions.* The following definitions apply for purposes of this section—

(1) *Trade or business activities.* Trade or business activities are activities, other than rental activities or activities that are treated under § 1.469-1T(e)(3)(vi)(B) as incidental to an activity of holding property for investment, that—

(i) Involve the conduct of a trade or business (within the meaning of section 162);

(ii) Are conducted in anticipation of the commencement of a trade or business; or

(iii) Involve research or experimental expenditures that are deductible under section 174 (or would be deductible if the taxpayer adopted the method described in section 174(a)).

(2) *Rental activities. Rental activities* are activities that constitute rental activities within the meaning of § 1.469-1T(e)(3).

(c) *General rules for grouping activities*—(1) *Appropriate economic unit.* One or more trade or business activities or rental activities may be treated as a single activity if the activities constitute an appropriate economic unit for the measurement of gain or loss for purposes of section 469.

(2) *Facts and circumstances test.* Except as otherwise provided in this section, whether activities constitute an appropriate economic unit and, therefore, may be treated as a single activity depends upon all the relevant facts and circumstances. A taxpayer may use any reasonable method of applying the relevant facts and circumstances in grouping activities. The factors listed below, not all of which are necessary for a taxpayer to treat more than one activity as a single activity, are given the greatest weight in determining whether activities constitute an appropriate economic unit for the measurement of gain or loss for purposes of section 469—

(i) Similarities and differences in types of trades or businesses;

(ii) The extent of common control;

(iii) The extent of common ownership;

(iv) Geographical location; and

(v) Interdependencies between or among the activities (for example, the extent to which the activities purchase or sell goods between or among themselves, involve products or services that are normally provided together, have the same customers, have the same employees, or are accounted for with a single set of books and records).

(3) *Examples.* The following examples illustrate the application of this paragraph (c).

Reg. § 1.469-4(c)(3)

Example 1. Taxpayer *C* has a significant ownership interest in a bakery and a movie theater at a shopping mall in Baltimore and in a bakery and a movie theater in Philadelphia. In this case, after taking into account all the relevant facts and circumstances, there may be more than one reasonable method for grouping *C*'s activities. For instance, depending on the relevant facts and circumstances, the following groupings may or may not be permissible: a single activity; a movie theater activity and a bakery activity; a Baltimore activity and a Philadelphia activity; or four separate activities. Moreover, once *C* groups these activities into appropriate economic units, paragraph (e) of this section requires *C* to continue using that grouping in subsequent taxable years unless a material change in the facts and circumstances makes it clearly inappropriate.

Example 2. Taxpayer *B*, an individual, is a partner in a business that sells non-food items to grocery stores (partnership *L*). *B* also is a partner in a partnership that owns and operates a trucking business (partnership *Q*). The two partnerships are under common control. The predominant portion of *Q*'s business is transporting goods for *L*, and *Q* is the only trucking business in which *B* is involved. Under this section, *B* appropriately treats *L*'s wholesale activity and *Q*'s trucking activity as a single activity.

(d) *Limitation on grouping certain activities.* The grouping of activities under this section is subject to the following limitations:

(1) *Grouping rental activities with other trade or business activities*—(i) *Rule.* A rental activity may not be grouped with a trade or business activity unless the activities being grouped together constitute an appropriate economic unit under paragraph (c) of this section and—

(A) The rental activity is insubstantial in relation to the trade or business activity;

(B) The trade or business activity is insubstantial in relation to the rental activity; or

(C) Each owner of the trade or business activity has the same proportionate ownership interest in the rental activity, in which case the portion of the rental activity that involves the rental of items of property for use in the trade or business activity may be grouped with the trade or business activity.

(ii) *Examples.* The following examples illustrate the application of paragraph (d)(1)(i) of this section:

Example 1. (i) *H* and *W* are married and file a joint return. *H* is the sole shareholder of an S corporation that conducts a grocery store trade or business activity. *W* is the sole shareholder of an S corporation that owns and rents out a building. Part of the building is rented to *H*'s grocery store trade or business activity (the grocery store rental). The grocery store rental and the grocery store trade or business are not insubstantial in relation to each other.

(ii) Because they file a joint return, *H* and *W* are treated as one taxpayer for purposes of section 469. See § 1.469-1T(j). Therefore, the sole owner of the trade or business activity (taxpayer *H-W*) is also the sole owner of the rental activity. Consequently, each owner of the trade or business activity has the same proportionate ownership interest in the rental activity. Accordingly, the grocery store rental and the grocery store trade or business activity may be grouped together (under paragraph (d)(1)(i) of this section) into a single trade or business activity, if the grouping is appropriate under paragraph (c) of this section.

Example 2. Attorney *D* is a sole practitioner in town *X*. *D* also wholly owns residential real estate in town *X* that *D* rents to third parties. *D*'s law practice is a trade or business activity within the meaning of paragraph (b)(1) of this section. The residential real estate is a rental activity within the meaning of § 1.469-1T(e)(3) and is insubstantial in relation to *D*'s law practice. Under the facts and circumstances, the law practice and the residential real estate do not constitute an appropriate economic unit under paragraph (c) of this section. Therefore, *D* may not treat the law practice and the residential real estate as a single activity.

(2) *Grouping real property rentals and personal property rentals prohibited.* An activity involving the rental of real property and an activity involving the rental of personal property (other than personal property provided in connection with the real property or real property provided in connection with the personal property) may not be treated as a single activity.

(3) *Certain activities of limited partners and limited entrepreneurs*—(i) *In general.* Except as provided in this paragraph, a taxpayer that owns an interest, as a limited partner or a limited entrepreneur (as defined in section 464(e)(2)), in an activity described in section 465(c)(1), may not group that activity with any other activity. A taxpayer that owns an interest as a limited partner or a limited entrepreneur in an activity described in the preceding sentence may group that activity with another activity in the same type of business if the grouping is appropriate under the provisions of paragraph (c) of this section.

(ii) *Example.* The following example illustrates the application of this paragraph (d)(3):

Example. (i) Taxpayer *A*, an individual, owns and operates a farm. *A* is also a member of *M*, a limited liability company that conducts a

Reg. § 1.469-4(d)(1)

cattle-feeding business. *A* does not actively participate in the management of *M* (within the meaning of section 464(e)(2)(B)). In addition, *A* is a limited partner in *N*, a limited partnership engaged in oil and gas production.

(ii) Because *A* does not actively participate in the management of *M*, *A* is a limited entrepreneur in *M*'s activity. *M*'s cattle-feeding business is described in section 465(c)(1)(B) (relating to farming) and may not be grouped with any other activity that does not involve farming. Moreover, *A*'s farm may not be grouped with the cattle-feeding activity unless the grouping constitutes an appropriate economic unit for the measurement of gain or loss for purposes of section 469.

(iii) Because *A* is a limited partner in *N* and *N*'s activity is described in section 465(c)(1)(D) (relating to exploring for, or exploiting, oil and gas resources), *A* may not group *N*'s oil and gas activity with any other activity that does not involve exploring for, or exploiting, oil and gas resources. Thus, *N*'s activity may not be grouped with *A*'s farm or with *M*'s cattle-feeding business.

(4) *Other activities identified by the Commissioner.* A taxpayer that owns an interest in an activity identified in guidance issued by the Commissioner as an activity covered by this paragraph (d)(4) may not group that activity with any other activity, except as provided in the guidance issued by the Commissioner.

(5) *Activities conducted through section 469 entities*—(i) *In general.* A C corporation subject to section 469, an S corporation, or a partnership (a section 469 entity) must group its activities under the rules of this section. Once the section 469 entity groups its activities, a shareholder or partner may group those activities with each other, with activities conducted directly by the shareholder or partner, and with activities conducted through other section 469 entities, in accordance with the rules of this section. A shareholder or partner may not treat activities grouped together by a section 469 entity as separate activities.

(ii) *Cross reference.* An activity that a taxpayer conducts through a C corporation subject to section 469 may be grouped with another activity of the taxpayer, but only for purposes of determining whether the taxpayer materially or significantly participates in the other activity. See § 1.469-2T(c)(3)(i)(A) and (c)(4)(i) for the rules regarding dividends on C corporation stock and compensation paid for personal services.

(e) *Disclosure and consistency requirements*—

(1) *Original groupings.* Except as provided in paragraph (e)(2) of this section and § 1.469-11, once a taxpayer has grouped activities under this section, the taxpayer may not regroup those activities in subsequent taxable years. Taxpayers must comply with disclosure requirements that the Commissioner may prescribe with respect to both their original groupings and the addition and disposition of specific activities within those chosen groupings in subsequent taxable years.

(2) *Regroupings.* If it is determined that a taxpayer's original grouping was clearly inappropriate or a material change in the facts and circumstances has occurred that makes the original grouping clearly inappropriate, the taxpayer must regroup the activities and must comply with disclosure requirements that the Commissioner may prescribe.

(f) *Grouping by Commissioner to prevent tax avoidance*—(1) *Rule.* The Commissioner may regroup a taxpayer's activities if any of the activities resulting from the taxpayer's grouping is not an appropriate economic unit and a principal purpose of the taxpayer's grouping (or failure to regroup under paragraph (e) of this section) is to circumvent the underlying purposes of section 469.

(2) *Example.* The following example illustrates the application of this paragraph (f):

Example. (i) Taxpayers *D, E, F, G,* and *H* are doctors who operate separate medical practices. *D* invested in a tax shelter several years ago that generates passive losses and the other doctors intend to invest in real estate that will generate passive losses. The taxpayers form a partnership to engage in the trade or business of acquiring and operating X-ray equipment. In exchange for equipment contributed to the partnership, the taxpayers receive limited partnership interests. The partnership is managed by a general partner selected by the taxpayers; the taxpayers do not materially participate in its operations. Substantially all of the partnership's services are provided to the taxpayers or their patients, roughly in proportion to the doctors' interests in the partnership. Fees for the partnership's services are set at a level equal to the amounts that would be charged if the partnership were dealing with the taxpayers at arm's length and are expected to assure the partnership a profit. The taxpayers treat the partnership's services as a separate activity from their medical practices and offset the income generated by the partnership against their passive losses.

(ii) For each of the taxpayers, the taxpayer's own medical practice and the services provided by the partnership constitute an appropriate economic unit, but the services provided by the partnership do not separately constitute an appropriate economic unit. Moreover, a principal purpose of treating the medical practices and the partnership's services as separate activities is to

Reg. § 1.469-4(f)(2)

circumvent the underlying purposes of section 469. Accordingly, the Commissioner may require the taxpayers to treat their medical practices and their interests in the partnership as a single activity, regardless of whether the separate medical practices are conducted through C corporations subject to section 469, S corporations, partnerships, or sole proprietorships. The Commissioner may assert penalties under section 6662 against the taxpayers in appropriate circumstances.

(g) *Treatment of partial dispositions.* A taxpayer may, for the taxable year in which there is a disposition of substantially all of an activity, treat the part disposed of as a separate activity, but only if the taxpayer can establish with reasonable certainty—

(1) The amount of deductions and credits allocable to that part of the activity for the taxable year under § 1.469-1(f)(4) (relating to carryover of disallowed deductions and credits); and

(2) The amount of gross income and of any other deductions and credits allocable to that part of the activity for the taxable year.

(h) *Rules for grouping rental real estate activities for taxpayers qualifying under section 469(c)(7).* See § 1.469-9 for rules for certain rental real estate activities. [Reg. § 1.469-4.]

☐ [T.D. 8565, 10-3-94. Amended by T.D. 8645, 12-21-95.]

[Reg. § 1.469-5]

§ 1.469-5. **Material participation.**—(a) through (e) [Reserved]

(f) *Participation*—(1) *In general.* Except as otherwise provided in this paragraph (f), any work done by an individual (without regard to the capacity in which the individual does the work) in connection with an activity in which the individual owns an interest at the time the work is done shall be treated for purposes of this section as participation of the individual in the activity.

(f)(2) through (h)(2) [Reserved]

(h)(3) *Coordination with rules governing the treatment of passthrough entities.* If a taxpayer takes into account for a taxable year of the taxpayer any item of gross income or deduction from a partnership or S corporation that is characterized as an item of gross income or deduction from an activity in which the taxpayer materially participated under § 1.469-2T(e)(1), the taxpayer is treated as materially participating in the activity for the taxable year for purposes of applying § 1.469-5T(a)(5) and (6) to any succeeding taxable year of the taxpayer.

(i) [Reserved]

(j) *Material participation for preceding taxable years*—(1) *In general.* For purposes of § 1.469-5T(a)(5) and (6), a taxpayer has materially participated in an activity for a preceding taxable year if the activity includes significant section 469 activities that are substantially the same as significant section 469 activities that were included in an activity in which the taxpayer materially participated (determined without regard to § 1.469-5T(a)(5)) for the preceding taxable year.

(2) *Material participation for taxable years beginning before January 1, 1987.* In any case in which it is necessary to determine whether an individual materially participated in any activity for a taxable year beginning before January 1, 1987 (other than a taxable year of a partnership, S corporation, estate, or trust ending after December 31, 1986), the determination shall be made without regard to paragraphs (a)(2) through (7) of this section.

(k) *Examples.*

Example (1) through *Example (4)* [Reserved.]

Example (5). In 1993, D, an individual, acquires stock in an S corporation engaged in a trade or business activity (within the meaning of § 1.469-1(e)(2)). For every taxable year from 1993 through 1997, D is treated as materially participating (without regard to § 1.469-5T(a)(5)) in the activity. D retires from the activity at the beginning of 1998, and would not be treated as materially participating in the activity for 1998 and subsequent taxable years if material participation for those years were determined without regard to § 1.469-5T(a)(5). Under § 1.469-5T(a)(5) of this section, however, D is treated as materially participating in the activity for taxable years 1998 through 2003 because D materially participated in the activity (determined without regard to § 1.469-5T(a)(5)) for five taxable years during the ten taxable years that immediately precede each of those years. D is not treated under § 1.469-5T(a)(5) as materially participating in the activity for taxable years beginning after 2003 because for those years D has not materially participated in the activity (determined without regard to § 1.469-5T(a)(5) for five of the last ten immediately preceding taxable years. [Reg. § 1.469-5.]

☐ [T.D. 8417, 5-11-92.]

[Reg. § 1.469-5T]

§ 1.469-5T. **Material participation (Temporary).**—(a) *In general.* Except as provided in paragraphs (e) and ((h)(2) of this section, an individual shall be treated, for purposes of section 469 and the regulations thereunder, as materially participating in an activity for the taxable year if and only if—

(1) The individual participates in the activity for more than 500 hours during such year;

(2) The individual's participation in the activity for the taxable year constitutes substantially all of the participation in such activity of all individuals (including individuals who are not owners of interests in the activity) for such year;

Reg. § 1.469-5(a)

(3) The individual participates in the activity for more than 100 hours during the taxable year, and such individual's participation in the activity for the taxable year is not less than the participation in the activity of any other individual (including individuals who are not owners of interests in the activity) for such year;

(4) The activity is a significant participation activity (within the meaning of paragraph (c) of this section) for the taxable year, and the individual's aggregate participation in all significant participation activities during such year exceeds 500 hours;

(5) The individual materially participated in the activity (determined without regard to this paragraph (a)(5)) for any five taxable years (whether or not consecutive) during the ten taxable years that immediately precede the taxable year;

(6) The activity is a personal service activity (within the meaning of paragraph (d) of this section), and the individual materially participated in the activity for any three taxable years (whether or not consecutive) preceding the taxable year; or

(7) Based on all of the facts and circumstances (taking into account the rules in paragraph (b) of this section), the individual participates in the activity on a regular, continuous, and substantial basis during such year.

(b) *Facts and circumstances*—(1) *In general.* [Reserved.]

(2) *Certain participation insufficient to constitute material participation under this paragraph (b)*—(i) *Participation satisfying standards not contained in section 469.* Except as provided in section 469(h)(3) and paragraph (h)(2) of this section (relating to certain retired individuals and surviving spouses in the case of farming activities), the fact that an individual satisfies the requirements of any participation standard (whether or not referred to as "material participation") under any provision (including sections 1402 and 2032A and the regulations thereunder) other than section 469 and the regulations thereunder shall not be taken into account in determining whether such individual materially participates in any activity for any taxable year for purposes of section 469 and the regulations thereunder.

(ii) *Certain management activities.* An individual's services performed in the management of an activity shall not be taken into account in determining whether such individual is treated as materially participating in such activity for the taxable year under paragraph (a)(7) of this section unless, for such taxable year—

(A) No person (other than such individual) who performs services in connection with the management of the activity receives compensation described in section 911(d)(2)(A) in consideration for such services; and

(B) No individual performs services in connection with the management of the activity that exceed (by hours) the amount of such services performed by such individual.

(iii) *Participation less than 100 hours.* If an individual participates in an activity for 100 hours or less during the taxable year, such individual shall not be treated as materially participating in such activity for the taxable year under paragraph (a)(7) of this section.

(c) *Significant participation activity*—(1) *In general.* For purposes of paragraph (a)(4) of this section, an activity is a significant participation activity of an individual if and only if such activity—

(i) Is a trade or business activity (within the meaning of § 1.469-1T(e)(2)) in which the individual significantly participates for the taxable year; and

(ii) Would be an activity in which the individual does not materially participate for the taxable year if material participation for such year were determined without regard to paragraph (a)(4) of this section.

(2) *Significant participation.* An individual is treated as significantly participating in an activity for a taxable year if and only if the individual participates in the activity for more than 100 hours during such year.

(d) *Personal service activity.* An activity constitutes a personal service activity for purposes of paragraph (a)(6) of this section if such activity involves the performance of personal services in—

(1) The fields of health, law, engineering, architecture, accounting, actuarial science, performing arts, or consulting; or

(2) Any other trade or business in which capital is not a material income-producing factor.

(e) *Treatment of limited partners*—(1) *General rule.* Except as otherwise provided in this paragraph (e), an individual shall not be treated as materially participating in any activity of a limited partnership for purposes of applying section 469 and the regulations thereunder to—

(i) The individual's share of any income, gain, loss, deduction, or credit from such activity that is attributable to a limited partnership interest in the partnership; and

(ii) Any gain or loss from such activity recognized upon a sale or exchange of such an interest.

Reg. § 1.469-5T(e)(1)

(2) *Exceptions.* Paragraph (e)(1) of this section shall not apply to an individual's share of income, gain, loss, deduction, and credit for a taxable year from any activity in which the individual would be treated as materially participating for the taxable year under paragraph (a)(1), (5) or (6) of this section if the individual were not a limited partner for such taxable year.

(3) *Limited partnership interest*—(i) *In general.* Except as provided in paragraph (e)(3)(ii) of this section, for purposes of section 469(h)(2) and this paragraph (e), a partnership interest shall be treated as a limited partnership interest if—

(A) Such interest is designated a limited partnership interest in the limited partnership agreement or the certificate of limited partnership, without regard to whether the liability of the holder of such interest for obligations of the partnership is limited under the applicable State law; or

(B) The liability of the holder of such interest for obligations of the partnership is limited, under the law of the State in which the partnership is organized, to a determinable fixed amount (for example, the sum of the holder's capital contributions to the partnership and contractual obligations to make additional capital contributions to the partnership).

(ii) *Limited partner holding general partner interest.* A partnership interest of an individual shall not be treated as a limited partnership interest for the individual's taxable year if the individual is a general partner in the partnership at all times during the partnership's taxable year ending with or within the individual's taxable year (or portion of the partnership's taxable year during which the individual (directly or indirectly) owns such limited partnership interest).

(f) *Participation*—(1) [Reserved] See § 1.469-5(f)(1) for rules relating to this paragraph.

(2) *Exceptions*—(i) *Certain work not customarily done by owners.* Work done in connection with an activity shall not be treated as participation in the activity for purposes of this section if—

(A) Such work is not of a type that is customarily done by an owner of such activity; and

(B) One of the principal purposes for the performance of such work is to avoid the disallowance, under section 469 and the regulations thereunder, of any loss or credit from such activity.

(ii) *Participation as an investor*—(A) *In general.* Work done by an individual in the individual's capacity as an investor in an activity shall not be treated as participation in the activity for purposes of this section unless the individual is directly involved in the day-to-day management or operations of the activity.

(B) *Work done in individual's capacity as an investor.* For purposes of this paragraph (f)(2)(ii), work done by an individual in the individual's capacity as an investor in an activity includes—

(1) Studying and reviewing financial statements or reports on operations of the activity;

(2) Preparing or compiling summaries or analyses of the finances or operations of the activity for the individual's own use; and

(3) Monitoring the finances or operations of the activity in a non-managerial capacity.

(3) *Participation of spouse.* In the case of any person who is a married individual (within the meaning of section 7703) for the taxable year, any participation by such person's spouse in the activity during the taxable year (without regard to whether the spouse owns an interest in the activity and without regard to whether the spouses file a joint return for the taxable year) shall be treated, for purposes of applying section 469 and the regulations thereunder to such person, as participation by such person in the activity during the taxable year.

(4) *Methods of proof.* The extent of an individual's participation in an activity may be established by any reasonable means. Contemporaneous daily time reports, logs, or similar documents are not required if the extent of such participation may be established by other reasonable means. Reasonable means for purposes of this paragraph may include but are not limited to the identification of services performed over a period of time and the approximate number of hours spent performing such services during such period, based on appointment books, calendars, or narrative summaries.

(g) *Material participation of trusts and estates.* [Reserved.]

(h) *Miscellaneous rules*—(1) *Participation of corporations.* For rules relating to the participation in an activity of a personal service corporation (within the meaning of § 1.469-1T(g)(2)(i)) or a closely held corporation (within the meaning of § 1.469-1T(g)(2)(ii)), see § 1.469-1T(g)(3).

(2) *Treatment of certain retired farmers and surviving spouses of retired or disabled farmers.* An individual shall be treated as materially participating for a taxable year in any trade or business activity of farming if paragraph (4) or (5) of section 2032A(b) would cause the requirements of section 2032A(b)(1)(C)(ii) to be met with respect

to real property used in such activity had the individual died during such taxable year.

(3) *Coordination with rules governing the treatment of passthrough entities.* [Reserved] See § 1.469-5(h)(3) for rules relating to this paragraph.

(i) [Reserved.]

(j) *Material participation for preceding taxable years.* [Reserved] See § 1.469-5(j) for rules relating to this paragraph.

(k) *Examples.* The following examples illustrate the application of this section:

Example (1). A, a calendar year individual, owns all of the stock of X, a C corporation. X is the general partner, and A is the limited partner, in P, a calendar year partnership. P has a single activity, a restaurant, which is a trade or business activity (within the meaning of § 1.469-1T(e)(2)). During the taxable year, A works for an average of 30 hours per week in connection with P's restaurant activity. Under paragraphs (a)(1) and (e)(2) of this section, A is treated as materially participating in the activity for the taxable year because A participates in the restaurant activity during such year for more than 500 hours. In addition, under § 1.469-1T(g)(3)(i), A's participation will cause X to be treated as materially participating in the restaurant activity.

Example (2). The facts are the same as in example (1), except that the partnership agreement provides that P's restaurant activity is to be managed by X, and A's work in the activity is performed pursuant to an employment contract between A and X. Under paragraph (f)(1) of this section, work done by A in connection with the activity in any capacity is treated as participation in the activity by A. Accordingly, the conclusion is the same as in example (1). The conclusion would be the same if A owned no stock in X at any time, although in that case A's participation would not be taken into account in determining whether X materially participates in the restaurant activity.

Example (3). B, an individual, is employed full-time as a carpenter. B also owns an interest in a partnership which is engaged in a van conversion activity, which is a trade or business activity (within the meaning of § 1.469-1T(e)(2)). B and C, the other partner, are the only participants in the activity for the taxable year. The activity is conducted entirely on Saturdays. Each Saturday throughout the taxable year, B and C work for eight hours in the activity. Although B does not participate in the activity for more than 500 hours during the taxable year, under paragraph (a)(3) of this section, B is treated for such year as materially participating in the activity because B participates in the activity for more than 100 hours during the taxable year, and B's participation in the activity for such year is not less than the participation of any other person in the activity for such year.

Example (4). C, an individual, is employed full-time as an accountant. C also owns interests in a restaurant and a shoe store. The restaurant and shoe store are trade or business activities (within the meaning of § 1.469-1T(e)(2)) that are treated as separate activities under the rules to be contained in § 1.469-4T. Each activity has several full-time employees. During the taxable year, C works in the restaurant activity for 400 hours and in the shoe store activity for 150 hours. Under paragraph (c) of this section, both the restaurant and shoe store activities are significant participation activities of C for the taxable year. Accordingly, since C's aggregate participation in the restaurant and shoe store activities during the taxable year exceeds 500 hours, C is treated under paragraph (a)(4) of this section as materially participating in both activities.

Example (5). [Reserved] See § 1.469-5(k) Example 5 for this example.

Example (6). The facts are the same as in example (5), except that D does not acquire any stock in the S corporation until 1994. Under paragraph (f)(1) of this section, D is not treated as participating in the activity for any taxable year prior to 1994 because D does not own an interest in the activity for any such taxable year. Accordingly, D materially participates in the activity for only one taxable year prior to 1995, and D is not treated under paragraph (a)(5) of this section as materially participating in the activity for 1995 or subsequent taxable years.

Example (7). (i) E, a married individual filing a separate return for the taxable year, is employed full-time as an attorney. E also owns an interest in a professional football team that is a trade or business activity (within the meaning of § 1.469-1T(e)(2)). E does no work in connection with this activity. E anticipates that, for the taxable year, E's deductions from the activity will exceed E's gross income from the activity and that, if E does not materially participate in the activity for the taxable year, part or all of E's passive activity loss for the taxable year will be disallowed under § 1.469-1T(a)(1)(i). Accordingly, E pays E's spouse to work as an office receptionist in connection with the activity for an average of 15 hours per week during the taxable year.

(ii) Under paragraph (f)(3) of this section, any participation in the the activity by E's spouse is treated as participation in the activity by E. However, under paragraph (f)(2)(i) of this section,

Reg. § 1.469-5T(k)

the work done by E's spouse is not treated as participation in the activity because work as an office receptionist is not work of a type customarily done by an owner of a football team, and one of E's principal purposes for paying E's spouse to do this work is to avoid the disallowance under § 1.469-1T(a)(1)(i) of E's passive activity loss. Accordingly, E is not treated as participating in the activity for the taxable year.

Example (8). (i) F, an individual, owns an interest in a partnership that feeds and sells cattle. The general partner of the partnership periodically mails F a letter setting forth certain proposed actions and decisions with respect to the cattle-feeding operation. Such actions and decisions include, for example, what kind of feed to purchase, how much to purchase, and when to purchase it, how often to feed cattle, and when to sell cattle. The letters explain the proposed actions and decisions, emphasize that taking or not taking a particular action or decision is solely within the discretion of F and other partners, and ask F to indicate a decision with respect to each proposed action by answering certain questions. The general partner receives a fee that constitutes earned income (within the meaning of section 911(d)(2)(A)) for managing the cattle-feeding operation. F is not treated as materially participating in the cattle-feeding operation under paragraph (a)(1) through (6) of this section.

(ii) F's only participation in the cattle-feeding operation is to make certain managerial decisions. Under paragraph (b)(2)(ii) of this section, such management services are not taken into account in determining whether the taxpayer is treated as materially participating in the activity for a taxable year under paragraph (a)(7) of this section if any other person performs services in connection with the management of the activity and receives compensation described in section 911(d)(2)(A) for such services. Therefore, F is not treated as materially participating for the taxable year in the cattle-feeding operation. [Reg. § 1.469-5T.]

☐ [T.D. 8175, 2-19-88. Amended by T.D. 8253, 5-11-89 and T.D. 8417, 5-11-92.]

[Reg. § 1.469-6]

§ 1.469-6. Treatment of losses upon certain dispositions. [Reserved]

[Reg. § 1.469-7]

§ 1.469-7. Treatment of self-charged items of interest income and deduction.—(a) *In general*—(1) *Applicability and effect of rules.* This section sets forth rules that apply, for purposes of section 469 and the regulations thereunder, in the case of a lending transaction (including guaranteed payments for the use of capital under section 707(c)) between a taxpayer and a passthrough entity in which the taxpayer owns a direct or indirect interest, or between certain passthrough entities. The rules apply only to items of interest income and interest expense that are recognized in the same taxable year. The rules—

(i) Treat certain interest income resulting from these lending transactions as passive activity gross income;

(ii) Treat certain deductions for interest expense that is properly allocable to the interest income as passive activity deductions; and

(iii) Allocate the passive activity gross income and passive activity deductions resulting from this treatment among the taxpayer's activities.

(2) *Priority of rules in this section.* The character of amounts treated under the rules of this section as passive activity gross income and passive activity deductions and the activities to which these amounts are allocated are determined under the rules of this section and not under the rules of §§ 1.163-8T, 1.469-2(c) and (d), and 1.469-2T(c) and (d).

(b) *Definitions.* The following definitions set forth the meaning of certain terms for purposes of this section:

(1) *Passthrough entity.* The term *passthrough entity* means a partnership or an S corporation.

(2) *Taxpayer's share.* A *taxpayer's share* of an item of income or deduction of a passthrough entity is the amount treated as an item of income or deduction of the taxpayer for the taxable year under section 702 (relating to the treatment of distributive shares of partnership items as items of partners) or section 1366 (relating to the treatment of pro rata shares of S corporation items as items of shareholders).

(3) *Taxpayer's indirect interest.* The taxpayer has an indirect interest in an entity if the interest is held through one or more passthrough entities.

(4) *Entity taxable year.* In applying this section for a taxable year of a taxpayer, the term *entity taxable year* means the taxable year of the passthrough entity for which the entity reports items that are taken into account under section 702 or section 1366 for the taxpayer's taxable year.

(5) *Deductions for a taxable year.* The term *deductions for a taxable year* means deductions that would be allowable for the taxable year if the taxpayer's taxable income for all taxable years were determined without regard to sections 163(d), 170(b), 469, 613A(d), and 1211.

Reg. § 1.469-6

(c) *Taxpayer loans to passthrough entity*—(1) *Applicability*. Except as provided in paragraph (g) of this section, this paragraph (c) applies with respect to a taxpayer's interest in a passthrough entity (borrowing entity) for a taxable year if—

(i) The borrowing entity has deductions for the entity taxable year for interest charged to the borrowing entity by persons that own direct or indirect interests in the borrowing entity at any time during the entity taxable year (the borrowing entity's self-charged interest deductions);

(ii) The taxpayer owns a direct or an indirect interest in the borrowing entity at any time during the entity taxable year and has gross income for the taxable year from interest charged to the borrowing entity by the taxpayer or a passthrough entity through which the taxpayer holds an interest in the borrowing entity (the taxpayer's income from interest charged to the borrowing entity); and

(iii) The taxpayer's share of the borrowing entity's self-charged interest deductions includes passive activity deductions.

(2) *General rule*. If any of the borrowing entity's self-charged interest deductions are allocable to an activity for a taxable year in which this paragraph (c) applies, the passive activity gross income and passive activity deductions from that activity are determined under the following rules—

(i) The applicable percentage of each item of the taxpayer's income for the taxable year from interest charged to the borrowing entity is treated as passive activity gross income from the activity; and

(ii) The applicable percentage of each deduction for the taxable year for interest expense that is properly allocable (within the meaning of paragraph (f) of this section) to the taxpayer's income from the interest charged to the borrowing entity is treated as a passive activity deduction from the activity.

(3) *Applicable percentage*. In applying this paragraph (c) with respect to a taxpayer's interest in a borrowing entity, the applicable percentage is separately determined for each of the taxpayer's activities. The percentage applicable to an activity for a taxable year is obtained by dividing—

(i) The taxpayer's share for the taxable year of the borrowing entity's self-charged interest deductions that are treated as passive activity deductions from the activity by

(ii) The greater of—

(A) The taxpayer's share for the taxable year of the borrowing entity's aggregate self-charged interest deductions for all activities (regardless of whether these deductions are treated as passive activity deductions); or

(B) The taxpayer's aggregate income for the taxable year from interest charged to the borrowing entity for all activities of the borrowing entity.

(d) *Passthrough entity loans to taxpayer*—(1) *Applicability*. Except as provided in paragraph (g) of this section, this paragraph (d) applies with respect to a taxpayer's interest in a passthrough entity (lending entity) for a taxable year if—

(i) The lending entity has gross income for the entity taxable year from interest charged by the lending entity to persons that own direct or indirect interests in the lending entity at any time during the entity taxable year (the lending entity's self-charged interest income);

(ii) The taxpayer owns a direct or an indirect interest in the lending entity at any time during the entity taxable year and has deductions for the taxable year for interest charged by the lending entity to the taxpayer or a passthrough entity through which the taxpayer holds an interest in the lending entity (the taxpayer's deductions for interest charged by the lending entity); and

(iii) The taxpayer's deductions for interest charged by the lending entity include passive activity deductions.

(2) *General rule*. If any of the taxpayer's deductions for interest charged by the lending entity are allocable to an activity for a taxable year in which this paragraph (d) applies, the passive activity gross income and passive activity deductions from that activity are determined under the following rules—

(i) The applicable percentage of the taxpayer's share for the taxable year of each item of the lending entity's self-charged interest income is treated as passive activity gross income from the activity.

(ii) The applicable percentage of the taxpayer's share for the taxable year of each deduction for interest expense that is properly allocable (within the meaning of paragraph (f) of this section) to the lending entity's self-charged interest income is treated as a passive activity deduction from the activity.

(3) *Applicable percentage*. In applying this paragraph (d) with respect to a taxpayer's interest in a lending entity, the applicable percentage is separately determined for each of the taxpayer's activities. The percentage applicable to an activity for a taxable year is obtained by dividing—

Reg. § 1.469-7(d)(3)

(i) The taxpayer's deductions for the taxable year for interest charged by the lending entity, to the extent treated as passive activity deductions from the activity; by

(ii) The greater of—

(A) The taxpayer's aggregate deductions for all activities for the taxable year for interest charged by the lending entity (regardless of whether these deductions are treated as passive activity deductions); or

(B) The taxpayer's aggregate share for the taxable year of the lending entity's self-charged interest income for all activities of the lending entity.

(e) *Identically-owned passthrough entities*—(1) *Applicability.* Except as provided in paragraph (g) of this section, this paragraph (e) applies with respect to lending transactions between passthrough entities if each owner of the borrowing entity has the same proportionate ownership interest in the lending entity,

(2) *General rule.* To the extent an owner shares in interest income from a loan between passthrough entities described in paragraph (e)(1) of this section, the owner is treated as having made the loan to the borrowing passthrough entity and paragraph (c) of this section applies to determine the applicable percentage of portfolio income or properly allocable interest expense that is recharacterized as passive.

(3) *Example.* The following example illustrates the application of this paragraph (e):

Example. (i) A and B, both calendar year taxpayers, each own a 50-percent interest in the capital and profits of partnerships RS and XY, both calendar year partnerships. Under the partnership agreements of RS and XY, A and B are each entitled to a 50-percent distributive share of each partnership's income, gain, loss, deduction, or credit. RS makes a $20,000 loan to XY and XY pays RS $2,000 of interest for the taxable year. A's distributive share of interest income attributable to this loan is $1,000 (50 percent × $2,000). XY uses all of the proceeds received from RS in a passive activity. A's distributive share of interest expense attributable to the loan is $1,000 (50 percent × $2,000).

(ii) This paragraph (e) applies in determining A's passive activity gross income because RS and XY are identically-owned passthrough entities as described in paragraph (e)(1) of this section. Under paragraph (e)(2) of this section, the RS-to-XY loan is treated as if A made the loan to XY. Therefore, A must apply paragraph (c) of this section to determine the applicable percentage of portfolio income that is recharacterized as passive income.

(iii) Paragraph (c) of this section applies in determining A's passive activity gross income because: XY has deductions for interest charged to XY by RS for the taxable year (XY's self-charged interest deductions); A owns an interest in XY during XY's taxable year and has gross income for the taxable year from interest charged to XY by RS; and A's share of XY's self-charged interest deductions includes passive activity deductions. See paragraph (c)(1) of this section.

(iv) Under paragraph (c)(2)(i) of this section, the applicable percentage of A's interest income is recharacterized as passive activity gross income from the activity. Paragraph (c)(3) of this section provides that the applicable percentage is obtained by dividing A's share for the taxable year of XY's self-charged interest deductions that are treated as passive activity deductions from the activity ($1,000) by the greater of A's share for the taxable year of XY's self-charged interest deductions ($1,000), or A's income for the year from interest charged to XY ($1,000). Thus, A's applicable percentage is 100 percent ($1,000/$1,000), and $1,000 (100 percent × $1,000) of A's income from interest charged to XY is treated as passive activity gross income from the passive activity.

(f) *Identification of properly allocable deductions.* For purposes of this section, interest expense is properly allocable to an item of interest income if the interest expense is allocated under § 1.163-8T to an expenditure that—

(1) Is properly chargeable to capital account with respect to the investment producing the item of interest income; or

(2) May reasonably be taken into account as a cost of producing the item of interest income.

(g) *Election to avoid application of the rules of this section*—(1) *In general.* Paragraphs (c), (d) and (e) of this section shall not apply with respect to any taxpayer's interest in a passthrough entity for a taxable year if the passthrough entity has made, under this paragraph (g), an election that applies to the entity's taxable year.

(2) *Form of election.* A passthrough entity makes an election under this paragraph (g) by attaching to its return (or amended return) a written statement that includes the name, address, and taxpayer identification number of the passthrough entity and a declaration that an election is being made under this paragraph (g).

(3) *Period for which election applies.* An election under this paragraph (g) made with a return (or amended return) for a taxable year applies to that taxable year and all subsequent taxable

Reg. § 1.469-7(e)(1)

years that end before the date on which the election is revoked.

(4) *Revocation.* An election under this paragraph (g) may be revoked only with the consent of the Commissioner.

(h) *Examples.* The following examples illustrate the principles of this section. The examples assume for purposes of simplifying the presentation, that the lending transactions described do not result in foregone interest (within the meaning of section 7872(e)(2)), original issue discount (within the meaning of section 1273), or total unstated interest (within the meaning of section 483(b)).

Example 1. (i) A and B, two calendar year individuals, each own 50-percent interests in the capital, profits and losses of AB, a calendar year partnership. AB is engaged in a single rental activity within the meaning of § 1.469-1T(e)(3). AB borrows $50,000 from A and uses the loan proceeds in the rental activity. AB pays $5,000 of interest to A for the taxable year. A and B each incur $2,500 of interest expense as their distributive share of AB's interest expense.

(ii) AB has self-charged interest deductions for the taxable year (i.e., the deductions for interest charged to AB by A); A owns a direct interest in AB during AB's taxable year and has income for A's taxable year from interest charged to AB; and A's share of AB's self-charged interest deductions includes passive activity deductions. Accordingly, paragraph (c) of this section applies in determining A's passive activity gross income. See paragraph (c)(1) of this section.

(iii) Under paragraph (c)(2)(i) of this section, the applicable percentage of A's interest income is recharacterized as passive activity gross income from AB's rental activity. Paragraph (c)(3) of this section provides that the applicable percentage is obtained by dividing A's share for the taxable year of AB's self-charged interest deductions that are treated as passive activity deductions from the activity ($2,500) by the greater of A's share for the taxable year of AB's self-charged interest deductions ($2,500), or A's income for the taxable year from interest charged to AB ($5,000). Thus, A's applicable percentage is 50 percent ($2,500/$5,000), and $2,500 (50 percent × $5,000) of A's income from interest charged to AB is treated as passive activity gross income from the passive activity A conducts through AB.

(iv) Because B does not have any gross income for the year from interest charged to AB, this section does not apply to B. See paragraph (c)(1)(ii) of this section.

Example 2. (i) C and D, two calendar year taxpayers, each own 50-percent interests in the capital and profits of CD, a calendar year partnership. CD is engaged in a single rental activity, within the meaning of § 1.469-1T(e)(3). C obtains a $10,000 loan from a third-party lender, and pays the lender $900 in interest for the taxable year. C lends the $10,000 to CD, and receives $1,000 of interest income from CD for the taxable year. D lends $20,000 to CD and receives $2,000 of interest income from CD for the taxable year. CD uses all of the proceeds in the rental activity. C and D are each allocated $1,500 (50 percent × $3,000) of interest expense as their distributive share of CD's interest expense for the taxable year.

(ii) CD has self-charged interest deductions for the taxable year (i.e., deductions for interest charged to CD by C and D); C and D each own direct interests in CD during CD's taxable year and have gross income for the taxable year from interest charged to CD; and both C's and D's shares of CD's self-charged interest deductions include passive activity deductions. Accordingly, paragraph (c) of this section applies in determining C's and D's passive activity gross income. See paragraph (c)(1) of this section.

(iii) Under paragraph (c)(2)(i) of this section, the applicable percentage of each partner's interest income is recharacterized as passive activity gross income from CD's rental activity. Paragraph (c)(3) of this section provides that C's applicable percentage is obtained by dividing C's share for the taxable year of CD's self-charged interest deductions that are treated as passive activity deductions from the activity ($1,500) by the greater of C's share for the taxable year of CD's self-charged interest deductions ($1,500), or C's income for the taxable year from interest charged to CD ($1,000). Thus, C's applicable percentage is 100 percent ($1,500/$1,500), and all of C's income from interest charged to CD ($1,000) is treated as passive activity gross income from the passive activity C conducts through CD. Similarly, D's applicable percentage is obtained by dividing D's share for the taxable year of CD's self-charged interest deductions that are treated as passive activity deductions from the activity ($1,500) by the greater of D's share for the taxable year of CD's self-charged interest deductions ($1,500), or D's income for the taxable year from interest charged to CD ($2,000). Thus, D's applicable percentage is 75 percent ($1,500/$2,000), and $1,500 (75 percent × $2,000) of D's income from interest charged to CD is treated as passive activity gross income from the rental activity.

(iv) The $900 of interest expense that C pays to the third-party lender is allocated under § 1.163-8T(c)(1) to an expenditure that is properly chargeable to capital account with respect to

Reg. § 1.469-7(h)

the loan to CD. Thus, the expense is properly allocable to the interest income C receives from CD (see paragraph (f) of this section). Under paragraph (c)(2)(ii) of this section, the applicable percentage of C's deductions for the taxable year for interest expense that is properly allocable to C's income from interest charged to CD is recharacterized as a passive activity deduction from CD's rental activity. Accordingly, all of C's $900 interest deduction is treated as a passive activity deduction from the rental activity.

Example 3. (i) E and F, calendar year taxpayers, each own 50 percent of the stock of X, a calendar year S corporation. E borrows $30,000 from X, and pays X $3,000 of interest for the taxable year. E uses $15,000 of the loan proceeds to make a personal expenditure (as defined in § 1.163-8T(b)(5)), and uses $15,000 of loan proceeds to purchase a trade or business activity in which E does not materially participate (within the meaning of § 1.469-5T) for the taxable year. E and F each receive $1,500 as their pro rata share of X's interest income from the loan for the taxable year.

(ii) X has gross income for X's taxable year from interest charged to E (X's self-charged interest income); E owns a direct interest in X during X's taxable year and has deductions for the taxable year for interest charged by X; and E's deductions for interest charged by X include passive activity deductions. Accordingly, paragraph (d) of this section applies in determining E's passive activity gross income. See paragraph (d)(1) of this section.

(iii) Under the rules in paragraph (d)(2)(i) of this section, the applicable percentage of E's share of X's self-charged interest income is recharacterized as passive activity gross income from the activity. Paragraph (d)(3) of this section provides that the applicable percentage is obtained by dividing E's deductions for the taxable year for interest charged by X, to the extent treated as passive activity deductions from the activity ($1,500), by the greater of E's deductions for the taxable year for interest charged by X, regardless of whether those deductions are treated as passive activity deductions ($3,000), or E's share for the taxable year of X's self-charged interest income ($1,500). Thus, E's applicable percentage is 50 percent ($1,500/$3,000), and $750 (50 percent × $1,500) of E's share of X's self-charged interest income is treated as passive activity gross income.

(iv) Because F does not have any deductions for the taxable year for interest charged by X, this section does not apply to F. See paragraph (d)(1)(ii) of this section.

Example 4. (i) This *Example 4* illustrates the application of this section to a partner that has a different taxable year from the partnership. The facts are the same as in *Example 1* except as follows: Partnership AB has properly adopted a fiscal year ending June 30 for federal tax purposes; AB borrows the $50,000 from A on October 1, 1990; and under the terms of the loan, AB must pay A $5,000 in interest annually, in quarterly installments, for a term of 2 years.

(ii) For A's taxable years from 1990 through 1993 and AB's corresponding entity taxable years (as defined in paragraph (b)(4) of this section) A's interest income and AB's interest deductions from the loan are as follows:

	A's Interest Income	AB's Interest Deductions
1990	$1,250	0
1991	$5,000	$3,750
1992	$3,750	$5,000
1993	0	$1,250

(iii) For A's taxable year ending December 31, 1990, the corresponding entity taxable year is AB's taxable year ending June 30, 1990. Because AB does not have any deductions for the entity taxable year for interest charged to AB by A, paragraph (c) of this section does not apply in determining A's passive activity gross income for 1990 (see paragraph (c)(1)(i) of this section). Accordingly, A reports $1,250 of portfolio income on A's 1990 income tax return.

(iv) For A's taxable year ending December 31, 1991, the corresponding entity taxable year ends on June 30, 1991. AB has $3,750 of deductions for the entity taxable year for interest charged to AB by A (AB's self-charged interest deductions); A owns a direct interest in AB during the entity taxable year and has $5,000 of interest income for A's taxable year from interest charged to AB; and A's share of AB's self-charged interest deductions includes passive activity deductions. Accordingly, paragraph (c) of this section applies in determining A's passive activity gross income.

(v) Under paragraph (c)(2)(i) of this section, the applicable percentage of A's 1991 interest income is recharacterized as passive activity gross income from the activity. Paragraph (c)(3) of this section provides that the applicable percentage is obtained by dividing A's share for A's 1991 taxable year of AB's self-charged interest deductions that are treated as passive activity deductions from the activity (50 percent × $3,750 = $1,875) by the greater of A's share for A's taxable year of

Reg. § 1.469-7(h)

Methods of Accounting

AB's self-charged interest deductions ($1,875), or A's income for A's taxable year from interest charged to AB ($5,000). Thus, A's applicable percentage is 37.5 percent ($1,875/$5,000), and $1,875 (37.5 percent × $5,000) of A's income from interest charged to AB is treated as passive activity gross income from the passive activity A conducts through AB.

(vi) For A's taxable year ending December 31, 1992, the corresponding entity taxable year ends on June 30, 1992. AB has $5,000 of deductions for the entity taxable year for interest charged to AB by A (AB's self-charged interest deductions); A owns a direct interest in AB during the entity taxable year and has $3,750 of gross income for A's taxable year from interest charged to AB; and A's share of AB's self-charged interest deductions includes passive activity deductions. Accordingly, paragraph (c) of this section applies in determining A's passive activity gross income.

(vii) The applicable percentage for 1992 is obtained by dividing A's share for A's 1992 taxable year of AB's self-charged interest deductions that are treated as passive activity deductions from the activity ($2,500) by the greater of A's share for A's taxable year of AB's self-charged interest deductions ($2,500), or A's income for A's taxable year from interest charged to AB ($3,750). Thus, A's applicable percentage is 66 2/3 percent ($2,500/$3,750), and $2,500 (66 2/3 percent × $3,750) of A's income from interest charged to AB is treated as passive activity gross income from the passive activity A conducts through AB.

(viii) Paragraph (c) of this section does not apply in determining A's passive activity gross income for the taxable year ending December 31, 1993, because A has no gross income for the taxable year from interest charged to AB (see paragraph (c)(1)(ii) of this section). A's share of AB's self-charged interest deductions for the entity taxable year ending June 30, 1993 ($625) is taken into account as a passive activity deduction on A's 1993 income tax return.

(ix) Because B does not have any gross income from interest charged to AB for any of the taxable years, this section does not apply to B. See paragraph (c)(1)(ii) of this section.

Example 5. (i) This *Example 5* illustrates the application of the rules of this section in the case of a taxpayer who has an indirect interest in a partnership. G, a calendar year taxpayer, is an 80-percent partner in partnership UTP. UTP owns a 25-percent interest in the capital and profits of partnership LTP. UTP and LTP are both calendar year partnerships. The partners of LTP conduct a single passive activity through LTP. UTP obtains a $10,000 loan from a bank, and pays the bank $1,000 of interest per year. G's distributive share of the interest paid to the bank is $800 (80 percent × $1,000). UTP uses the $10,000 debt proceeds and another $10,000 of cash to make a loan to LTP, and LTP pays UTP $2,000 of interest for the taxable year. G's distributive share of interest income attributable to the UTP-to-LTP loan is $1,600 (80 percent × $2,000). LTP uses all of the proceeds received from UTP in the passive activity. UTP's distributive share of interest expense attributable to the UTP-to-LTP loan is $500 (25 percent × $2,000). G's distributive share of interest expense attributable to the UTP-to-LTP loan is $400 (80 percent × $500).

(ii) LTP has deductions for interest charged to LTP by UTP for the taxable year (LTP's self-charged interest deductions); G owns an indirect interest in LTP during LTP's taxable year and has gross income for the taxable year from interest charged to LTP by a passthrough entity (UTP) through which G owns an interest in LTP; and G's share of LTP's self-charged interest deductions includes passive activity deductions. Accordingly, paragraph (c) of this section applies in determining G's passive activity gross income. See paragraph (c)(1) of this section.

(iii) Under paragraph (c)(2)(i) of this section, the applicable percentage of G's interest income is recharacterized as passive activity gross income from the activity. Paragraph (c)(3) of this section provides that the applicable percentage is obtained by dividing G's share for the taxable year of LTP's self-charged interest deductions that are treated as passive activity deductions from the activity ($400) by the greater of G's share for the taxable year of LTP's self-charged interest deductions ($400), or G's income for the year from interest charged to LTP ($1,600). Thus, G's applicable percentage is 25 percent ($400/$1,600), and $400 (25 percent × $1,600) of G's income from interest charged to LTP is treated as passive activity gross income from the passive activity that G conducts through UTP and LTP.

(iv) G's $800 distributive share of the interest expense that UTP pays to the third-party lender is allocated under § 1.163-8T(c)(1) to an expenditure that is properly chargeable to capital account with respect to the loan to LTP. Thus, the expense is a deduction properly allocable to the interest income that G receives as a result of the UTP-to-LTP loan (see paragraph (f) of this section). Under paragraph (c)(2)(ii) of this section, the applicable percentage of G's deductions for the taxable year for interest expense that is properly allocable to G's income from interest charged by UTP to LTP is recharacterized as a passive

Reg. § 1.469-7(h)

activity deduction from LTP's passive activity. Accordingly, $200 (25 percent × $800) of G's interest deduction is treated as a passive activity deduction from LTP's activity.

Example 6. (i) This *Example 6* illustrates the application of the rules of this section in the case of a taxpayer who conducts two passive activities through a passthrough entity. J, a calendar year taxpayer, is the 100-percent shareholder of Y, a calendar year S corporation. J conducts two passive activities through Y: a rental activity and a trade or business activity in which J does not materially participate. Y borrows $80,000 from J, and uses $60,000 of the loan proceeds in the rental activity and $20,000 of the loan proceeds in the passive trade or business activity. Y pays $8,000 of interest to J for the taxable year, and J incurs $8,000 of interest expense as J's distributive share of Y's interest expense.

(ii) Y has self-charged interest deductions for the taxable year (i.e., the deductions for interest charged to Y by J); J owns a direct interest in Y during Y's taxable year and has gross income for J's taxable year from interest charged to Y; and J's share of Y's self-charged interest deductions includes passive activity deductions. Accordingly, paragraph (c) of this section applies in determining J's passive activity gross income. See paragraph (c)(1) of this section.

(iii) Under paragraph (c)(2)(i) of this section, the applicable percentage of J's interest income is recharacterized as passive activity gross income attributable to the rental activity. Paragraph (c)(3) of this section provides that the applicable percentage is obtained by dividing J's share for the taxable year of Y's self-charged interest deductions that are treated as passive activity deductions from the rental activity ($6,000) by the greater of J's share for the taxable year of Y's self-charged interest deductions ($8,000), or J's income for the taxable year from interest charged to Y ($8,000). Thus, J's applicable percentage is 75 percent ($6,000/$8,000), and $6,000 (75 percent × $8,000) of J's income from interest charged to Y is treated as passive activity gross income from the rental activity J conducts through Y.

(iv) Under paragraph (c)(2)(i) of this section, the applicable percentage of J's interest income is recharacterized as passive activity gross income attributable to the passive trade or business activity. Paragraph (c)(3) of this section provides that the applicable percentage is obtained by dividing J's share for the taxable year of Y's self-charged interest deductions that are treated as passive activity deductions from the passive trade or business activity ($2,000) by the greater of J's share for the taxable year of Y's self-charged interest deductions ($8,000), or J's income for the taxable year from interest charged to Y ($8,000). Thus, J's applicable percentage is 25 percent ($2,000/$8,000), and $2,000 of J's income from interest charged to Y is treated as passive activity gross income from the passive trade or business activity J conducts through Y.

[Reg. § 1.469-7.]

☐ [T.D. 9013, 8-20-2002.]

[Reg. § 1.469-8]

§ 1.469-8. **Application of section 469 and the regulations thereunder to trusts, estates, and their beneficiaries. [Reserved]**

[Reg. § 1.469-9]

§ 1.469-9. **Rules for certain rental real estate activities.**—(a) *Scope and purpose.* This section provides guidance to taxpayers engaged in certain real property trades or businesses on applying section 469(c)(7) to their rental real estate activities.

(b) *Definitions.* The following definitions apply for purposes of this section:

(1) *Trade or business.* A *trade or business* is any trade or business determined by treating the types of activities in § 1.469-4(b)(1) as if they involved the conduct of a trade or business, and any interest in rental real estate, including any interest in rental real estate that gives rise to deductions under section 212.

(2) *Real property trade or business. Real property trade or business* is defined in section 469(c)(7)(C).

(3) *Rental real estate. Rental real estate* is any real property used by customers or held for use by customers in a rental activity within the meaning of § 1.469-1T(e)(3). However, any rental real estate that the taxpayer grouped with a trade or business activity under § 1.469-4(d)(1)(i)(A) or (C) is not an interest in rental real estate for purposes of this section.

(4) *Personal services. Personal services* means any work performed by an individual in connection with a trade or business. However, personal services do not include any work performed by an individual in the individual's capacity as an investor as described in § 1.469-5T(f)(2)(ii).

(5) *Material participation. Material participation* has the same meaning as under § 1.469-5T. Paragraph (f) of this section contains rules applicable to limited partnership interests in rental real estate that a qualifying taxpayer elects to aggregate with other interests in rental real estate of that taxpayer.

Reg. § 1.469-8

(6) *Qualifying taxpayer.* A *qualifying taxpayer* is a taxpayer that owns at least one interest in rental real estate and meets the requirements of paragraph (c) of this section.

(c) *Requirements for qualifying taxpayers*—(1) *In general.* A qualifying taxpayer must meet the requirements of section 469(c)(7)(B).

(2) *Closely held C corporations.* A closely held C corporation meets the requirements of paragraph (c)(1) of this section by satisfying the requirements of section 469(c)(7)(D)(i). For purposes of section 469(c)(7)(D)(i), gross receipts do not include items of portfolio income within the meaning of § 1.469-2T(c)(3).

(3) *Requirement of material participation in the real property trades or businesses.* A taxpayer must materially participate in a real property trade or business in order for the personal services provided by the taxpayer in that real property trade or business to count towards meeting the requirements of paragraph (c)(1) of this section.

(4) *Treatment of spouses.* Spouses filing a joint return are qualifying taxpayers only if one spouse separately satisfies both requirements of section 469(c)(7)(B). In determining the real property trades or businesses in which a married taxpayer materially participates (but not for any other purpose under this paragraph (c)), work performed by the taxpayer's spouse in a trade or business is treated as work performed by the taxpayer under § 1.469-5T(f)(3), regardless of whether the spouses file a joint return for the year.

(5) *Employees in real property trades or businesses.* For purposes of paragraph (c)(1) of this section, personal services performed during a taxable year as an employee generally will be treated as performed in a trade or business but will not be treated as performed in a real property trade or business, unless the taxpayer is a five-percent owner (within the meaning of section 416(i)(1)(B)) in the employer. If an employee is not a five-percent owner in the employer at all times during the taxable year, only the personal services performed by the employee during the period the employee is a five-percent owner in the employer will be treated as performed in a real property trade or business.

(d) *General rule for determining real property trades or businesses*—(1) *Facts and circumstances.* The determination of a taxpayer's real property trades or businesses for purposes of paragraph (c) of this section is based on all of the relevant facts and circumstances. A taxpayer may use any reasonable method of applying the facts and circumstances in determining the real property trades or businesses in which the taxpayer provides personal services. Depending on the facts and circumstances, a real property trade or business consists either of one or more than one trade or business specifically described in section 469(c)(7)(C). A taxpayer's grouping of activities under § 1.469-4 does not control the determination of the taxpayer's real property trades or businesses under this paragraph (d).

(2) *Consistency requirement.* Once a taxpayer determines the real property trades or businesses in which personal services are provided for purposes of paragraph (c) of this section, the taxpayer may not redetermine those real property trades or businesses in subsequent taxable years unless the original determination was clearly inappropriate or there has been a material change in the facts and circumstances that makes the original determination clearly inappropriate.

(e) *Treatment of rental real estate activities of a qualifying taxpayer*—(1) *In general.* Section 469(c)(2) does not apply to any rental real estate activity of a taxpayer for a taxable year in which the taxpayer is a qualifying taxpayer under paragraph (c) of this section. Instead, a rental real estate activity of a qualifying taxpayer is a passive activity under section 469 for the taxable year unless the taxpayer materially participates in the activity. Each interest in rental real estate of a qualifying taxpayer will be treated as a separate rental real estate activity, unless the taxpayer makes an election under paragraph (g) of this section to treat all interests in rental real estate as a single rental real estate activity. Each separate rental real estate activity, or the single combined rental real estate activity if the taxpayer makes an election under paragraph (g), will be an activity of the taxpayer for all purposes of section 469, including the former passive activity rules under section 469(f) and the disposition rules under section 469(g). However, section 469 will continue to be applied separately with respect to each publicly traded partnership, as required under section 469(k), notwithstanding the rules of this section.

(2) *Treatment as a former passive activity.* For any taxable year in which a qualifying taxpayer materially participates in a rental real estate activity, that rental real estate activity will be treated as a former passive activity under section 469(f) if disallowed deductions or credits are allocated to the activity under § 1.469-1(f)(4).

(3) *Grouping rental real estate activities with other activities*—(i) *In general.* For purposes of this section, a qualifying taxpayer may not group a rental real estate activity with any other activity of the taxpayer. For example, if a qualifying taxpayer develops real property, constructs

Reg. § 1.469-9(e)(3)

buildings, and owns an interest in rental real estate, the taxpayer's interest in rental real estate may not be grouped with the taxpayer's development activity or construction activity. Thus, only the participation of the taxpayer with respect to the rental real estate may be used to determine if the taxpayer materially participates in the rental real estate activity under § 1.469-5T.

(ii) *Special rule for certain management activities.* A qualifying taxpayer may participate in a rental real estate activity through participation, within the meaning of §§ 1.469-5(f) and 5T(f), in an activity involving the management of rental real estate (even if this management activity is conducted through a separate entity). In determining whether the taxpayer materially participates in the rental real estate activity, however, work the taxpayer performs in the management activity is taken into account only to the extent it is performed in managing the taxpayer's own rental real estate interests.

(4) *Example.* The following example illustrates the application of this paragraph (e).

Example. (i) Taxpayer B owns interests in three rental buildings, U, V and W. In 1995, B has $30,000 of disallowed passive losses allocable to Building U and $10,000 of disallowed passive losses allocable to Building V under § 1.469-1(f)(4). In 1996, B has $5,000 of net income from building U, $5,000 of net losses from building V, and $10,000 of net income from building W. Also in 1996, B is a qualifying taxpayer within the meaning of paragraph (c) of this section. Each building is treated as a separate activity of B under paragraph (e)(1) of this section, unless B makes the election under paragraph (g) to treat the three buildings as a single rental real estate activity. If the buildings are treated as separate activities, material participation is determined separately with respect to each building. If B makes the election under paragraph (g) to treat the buildings as a single activity, all participation relating to the buildings is aggregated in determining whether B materially participates in the combined activity.

(ii) Effective beginning in 1996, B makes the election under paragraph (g) to treat the three buildings as a single rental real estate activity. B works full-time managing the three buildings and thus materially participates in the combined activity in 1996 (even if B conducts this management function through a separate entity, including a closely held C corporation). Accordingly, the combined activity is not a passive activity of B in 1996. Moreover, as a result of the election under paragraph (g), disallowed passive losses of $40,000 ($30,000 + $10,000) are allocated to the combined activity. B's net income from the activity for 1996 is $10,000 ($5,000 − $5,000 + $10,000). This net income is nonpassive income for purposes of section 469. However, under section 469(f), the net income from a former passive activity may be offset with the disallowed passive losses from the same activity. Because Buildings U, V and W are treated as one activity for all purposes of section 469 due to the election under paragraph (g), and this activity is a former passive activity under section 469(f), B may offset the $10,000 of net income from the buildings with an equal amount of disallowed passive losses allocable to the buildings, regardless of which buildings produced the income or losses. As a result, B has $30,000 ($40,000 − $10,000) of disallowed passive losses remaining from the buildings after 1996.

(f) *Limited partnership interests in rental real estate activities*—(1) *In general.* If a taxpayer elects under paragraph (g) of this section to treat all interests in rental real estate as a single rental real estate activity, and at least one interest in rental real estate is held by the taxpayer as a limited partnership interest (within the meaning of § 1.469-5T(e)(3)), the combined rental real estate activity will be treated as a limited partnership interest of the taxpayer for purposes of determining material participation. Accordingly, the taxpayer will not be treated under this section as materially participating in the combined rental real estate activity unless the taxpayer materially participates in the activity under the tests listed in § 1.469-5T(e)(2) (dealing with the tests for determining the material participation of a limited partner).

(2) *De minimis exception.* If a qualifying taxpayer elects under paragraph (g) of this section to treat all interests in rental real estate as a single rental real estate activity, and the taxpayer's share of gross rental income from all of the taxpayer's limited partnership interests in rental real estate is less than ten percent of the taxpayer's share of gross rental income from all of the taxpayer's interests in rental real estate for the taxable year, paragraph (f)(1) of this section does not apply. Thus the taxpayer may determine material participation under any of the tests listed in § 1.469-5T(a) that apply to rental real estate activities.

(g) *Election to treat all interests in rental real estate as a single rental real estate activity*—(1) *In general.* A qualifying taxpayer may make an election to treat all of the taxpayer's interests in rental real estate as a single rental real estate activity. This election is binding for the taxable year in which it is made and for all future years in

Reg. § 1.469-9(e)(4)

which the taxpayer is a qualifying taxpayer under paragraph (c) of this section, even if there are intervening years in which the taxpayer is not a qualifying taxpayer. The election may be made in any year in which the taxpayer is a qualifying taxpayer, and the failure to make the election in one year does not preclude the taxpayer from making the election in a subsequent year. In years in which the taxpayer is not a qualifying taxpayer, the election will not have effect and the taxpayer's activities will be those determined under § 1.469-4. If there is a material change in the taxpayer's facts and circumstances, the taxpayer may revoke the election using the procedure described in paragraph (g)(3) of this section.

(2) *Certain changes not material.* The fact that an election is less advantageous to the taxpayer in a particular taxable year is not, of itself, a material change in the taxpayer's facts and circumstances. Similarly, a break in the taxpayer's status as a qualifying taxpayer is not, of itself, a material change in the taxpayer's facts and circumstances.

(3) *Filing a statement to make or revoke the election.* A qualifying taxpayer makes the election to treat all interests in rental real estate as a single rental real estate activity by filing a statement with the taxpayer's original income tax return for the taxable year. This statement must contain a declaration that the taxpayer is a qualifying taxpayer for the taxable year and is making the election pursuant to section 469(c)(7)(A). The taxpayer may make this election for any taxable year in which section 469(c)(7) is applicable. A taxpayer may revoke the election only in the taxable year in which a material change in the taxpayer's facts and circumstances occurs or in a subsequent year in which the facts and circumstances remain materially changed from those in the taxable year for which the election was made. To revoke the election, the taxpayer must file a statement with the taxpayer's original income tax return for the year of revocation. This statement must contain a declaration that the taxpayer is revoking the election under section 469(c)(7)(A) and an explanation of the nature of the material change.

(h) *Interests in rental real estate held by certain passthrough entities*—(1) *General rule.* Except as provided in paragraph (h)(2) of this section, a qualifying taxpayer's interest in rental real estate held by a partnership or an S corporation (passthrough entity) is treated as a single interest in rental real estate if the passthrough entity grouped its rental real estate as one rental activity under § 1.469-4(d)(5). If the passthrough entity grouped its rental real estate into separate rental activities under § 1.469-4(d)(5), each rental real estate activity of the passthrough entity will be treated as a separate interest in rental real estate of the qualifying taxpayer. However, the qualifying taxpayer may elect under paragraph (g) of this section to treat all interests in rental real estate, including the rental real estate interests held through passthrough entities, as a single rental real estate activity.

(2) *Special rule if a qualifying taxpayer holds a fifty-percent or greater interest in a passthrough entity.* If a qualifying taxpayer owns, directly or indirectly, a fifty-percent or greater interest in the capital, profits, or losses of a passthrough entity for a taxable year, each interest in rental real estate held by the passthrough entity will be treated as a separate interest in rental real estate of the qualifying taxpayer, regardless of the passthrough entity's grouping of activities under § 1.469-4(d)(5). However, the qualifying taxpayer may elect under paragraph (g) of this section to treat all interests in rental real estate, including the rental real estate interests held through passthrough entities, as a single rental real estate activity.

(3) *Special rule for interests held in tiered passthrough entities.* If a passthrough entity owns a fifty-percent or greater interest in the capital, profits, or losses of another passthrough entity for a taxable year, each interest in rental real estate held by the lower-tier entity will be treated as a separate interest in rental real estate of the upper-tier entity, regardless of the lower-tier entity's grouping of activities under § 1.469-4(d)(5).

(i) [Reserved].

(j) *$25,000 offset for rental real estate activities of qualifying taxpayers*—(1) *In general.* A qualifying taxpayer's passive losses and credits from rental real estate activities (including prior-year disallowed passive activity losses and credits from rental real estate activities in which the taxpayer materially participates) are allowed to the extent permitted under section 469(i). The amount of losses or credits allowable under section 469(i) is determined after the rules of this section are applied. However, losses allowable by reason of this section are not taken into account in determining adjusted gross income for purposes of section 469(i)(3).

(2) *Example.* The following example illustrates the application of this paragraph (j).

Example. (i) Taxpayer A owns building X and building Y, both interests in rental real estate. In 1995, A is a qualifying taxpayer within the meaning of paragraph (c) of this section. A does not elect to treat X and Y as one activity under section 469(c)(7)(A) and paragraph (g) of this section. As a result, X and Y are treated as separate activities pursuant to section 469(c)(7)(A)(ii). A materially participates in X which has $100,000 of passive losses disallowed from prior years and produces $20,000 of losses in 1995. A does not materially participate in Y which produces $40,000 of income in 1995. A also has $50,000 of income from other nonpassive sources in 1995. A otherwise meets the requirements of section 469(i).

(ii) Because X is not a passive activity in 1995, the $20,000 of losses produced by X in 1995 are nonpassive losses that may be used by A to offset part of the $50,000 of nonpassive income. Accordingly, A is left with $30,000 ($50,000 − $20,000) of nonpassive income. In addition, A may use the prior year disallowed passive losses of X to offset any income from X and passive income from other sources. Therefore, A may offset the $40,000 of passive income from Y with $40,000 of passive losses from X.

(iii) Because A has $60,000 ($100,000 − $40,000) of passive losses remaining from X and meets all of the requirements of section 469(i), A may offset up to $25,000 of nonpassive income with passive losses from X pursuant to section 469(i). As a result, A has $5,000 ($30,000 − $25,000) of nonpassive income remaining and disallowed passive losses from X of $35,000 ($60,000 − $25,000) in 1995. [Reg. § 1.469-9.]

☐ [T.D. 8417, 5-11-92. Amended by T.D. 8645, 12-21-95.

[Reg. § 1.469-10]

§ 1.469-10. **Application of section 469 to publicly traded partnerships.**—(a) [Reserved].

(b) *Publicly traded partnership*—(1) *In general.* For purposes of section 469(k), a partnership is a publicly traded partnership only if the partnership is a publicly traded partnership as defined in § 1.7704-1.

(2) *Effective date.* This section applies for taxable years of a partnership beginning on or after December 17, 1998. [Reg. § 1.469-10.]

☐ [T.D. 8799, 12-16-98.]

[Reg. § 1.469-11]

§ 1.469-11. **Effective date and transition rules.**—(a) *Generally applicable effective dates.* Except as otherwise provided in this section—

(1) The rules contained in §§ 1.469-1, 1.469-1T, 1.469-2, 1.469-2T, 1.469-3, 1.469-3T, 1.469-4, 1.469-5, and 1.469-5T apply for taxable years ending after May 10, 1992.

(2) The rules contained in 26 CFR 1.469-1T, 1.469-2T, 1.469-3T, 1.469-4T, 1.469-5T, and 1.469-11T(b) and (c) (as contained in the CFR edition revised as of April 1, 1992) apply for taxable years beginning after December 31, 1986, and ending on or before May 10, 1992;

(3) The rules contained in § 1.469-9 apply for taxable years beginning on or after January 1, 1995, and to elections made under § 1.469-9(g) with returns filed on or after January 1, 1995;

(4) The rules contained in § 1.469-7 apply for taxable years ending after December 31, 1986; and

(5) This section applies for taxable years beginning after December 31, 1986.

(b) *Additional effective dates*—(1) *Application of 1992 amendments for taxable years beginning before October 4, 1994.* Except as provided in paragraph (b)(2) of this section, for taxable years that end after May 10, 1992, and begin before October 4, 1994, a taxpayer may determine tax liability in accordance with Project PS-1-89 published at 1992-1 C.B. 1219 (see § 601.601(d)(2)(ii)(b) of this chapter).

(2) *Additional transition rule for 1992 amendments.* If a taxpayer's first taxable year ending after May 10, 1992, begins on or before that date, the taxpayer may treat the taxable year, for purposes of paragraph (a) of this section, as a taxable year ending on or before May 10, 1992.

(3) *Fresh starts under consistency rules*—(i) *Regrouping when tax liability is first determined under Project PS-1-89.* For the first taxable year in which a taxpayer determines its tax liability under Project PS-1-89, the taxpayer may regroup its activities without regard to the manner in which the activities were grouped in the preceding taxable year and must regroup its activities if the grouping in the preceding taxable year is inconsistent with the rules of Project PS-1-89.

(ii) *Regrouping when tax liability is first determined under § 1.469-4.* For the first taxable year in which a taxpayer determines its tax liability under § 1.469-4, rather than under the rules of Project PS-1-89, the taxpayer may regroup its activities without regard to the manner in which the activities were grouped in the preceding taxable year and must regroup its activities if the grouping in the preceding taxable year is inconsistent with the rules of § 1.469-4.

(iii) *Regrouping when taxpayer is first subject to section 469(c)(7).* For the first taxable year beginning after December 31, 1993, a taxpayer may regroup its activities to the extent necessary or appropriate to avail itself of the provisions of section 469(c)(7) and without regard to the manner in which the activities were grouped in the preceding taxable year.

Reg. § 1.469-10(a)

(4) *Certain investment credit property.*—(i) The rules contained in § 1.469-3(f) apply with respect to property placed in service after December 31, 1990 (other than property described in section 11813(c)(2) of the Omnibus Reconciliation Act of 1990 (P.L. 101-508)).

(ii) The rules contained in 26 CFR 1.469-3T(f) (as contained in the CFR edition revised as of April 1, 1992) apply with respect to property placed in service on or before December 31, 1990, and property described in section 11813(c)(2) of the Omnibus Reconciliation Act of 1990.

(c) *Special rules*—(1) *Application of certain income recharacterization rules and self-charged rules*—(i) *Certain recharacterization rules inapplicable in 1987.* No amount of gross income shall be treated under § 1.469-2T(f)(3) through (7) as income that is not from a passive activity for any taxable year of the taxpayer beginning before January 1, 1988.

(ii) *Property rented to a nonpassive activity.* In applying § 1.469-2(f)(6) or § 1.469-2T(f)(6) to a taxpayer's rental of an item of property, the taxpayer's net rental activity income (within the meaning of § 1.469-2(f)(9)(iv) or § 1.469-2T(f)(9)(iv)) from the property for any taxable year beginning after December 31, 1987, does not include the portion of the income (if any) that is attributable to the rental of that item of property pursuant to a written binding contract entered into before February 19, 1988.

(iii) *Self-charged rules.* For taxable years beginning before June 4, 1991—

(*1*) A taxpayer is not required to apply the rules in § 1.469-7 in computing the taxpayer's passive activity loss and passive activity credit; and

(*2*) A taxpayer that owns an interest in a passthrough entity may use any reasonable method of offsetting items of interest income and interest expense from lending transactions between the passthrough entity and its owners or between identically-owned passthrough entities (as defined in § 1.469-7(e)) to compute the taxpayer's passive activity loss and passive activity credit. Items from nonlending transactions cannot be offset under the self-charged rules.

(2) *Qualified low-income housing projects.* For a transitional rule concerning the application of section 469 to losses form [from] qualified low-income housing projects, see section 502 of the Tax Reform Act of 1986.

(3) *Effect of events occurring in years prior to 1987.* The treatment for a taxable year beginning after December 31, 1986, of any item of income, gain, loss, deduction, or credit as an item of passive activity gross income, passive activity deduction, or credit from a passive activity is determined as if section 469 and the regulations thereunder had been in effect for taxable years beginning before January 1, 1987, but without regard to any passive activity loss or passive activity credit that would have been disallowed for any taxable year beginning before January 1, 1987, if section 469 and the regulations thereunder had been in effect for that year. For example, in determining whether a taxpayer materially participates in an activity under § 1.469-5T(a)(5) (relating to taxpayers who have materially participated in an activity for five of the ten immediately preceding taxable years) for any taxable year beginning after December 31, 1986, the taxpayer's participation in the activity for all prior taxable years (including taxable years beginning before 1987) is taken into account. See § 1.469-5(j) (relating to the determination of material participation for taxable years beginning before January 1, 1987).

(d) *Examples.* The following examples illustrate the application of paragraph (c) of this section:

Example 1. A, a calendar year individual, is a partner in a partnership with a taxable year ending on January 31. During its taxable year ending January 31, 1987, the partnership was engaged in a single activity involving the conduct of a trade or business. In applying section 469 and the regulations thereunder to A for calendar year 1987, A's distributive share of partnership items for the partnership's taxable year ending January 31, 1987, is taken into account. Therefore, under § 1.469-2T(e)(1) and paragraph (c)(3) of this section, A's participation in the activity throughout the partnership's taxable year beginning February 1, 1986, and ending January 31, 1987, is taken into account for purposes of determining the character under section 469 of the items of gross income, deduction, and credit allocated to A for the partnership's taxable year ending January 31, 1987.

Example 2. B, a calendar year individual, is a beneficiary of a trust described in section 651 that has a taxable year ending January 31. The trust conducts a rental activity (within the meaning of § 1.469-1T(e)(3)). Because the trust's taxable year ending January 31, 1987, began before January 1, 1987, section 469 and the regulations thereunder do not apply to the trust for that year. Section 469 and the regulations thereunder do apply, however, to B for B's calendar year 1987. Therefore, income of the trust from the rental activity for the trust's taxable year ending January 31, 1987, that is included in B's gross income for 1987 is

Reg. § 1.469-11(d)

taken into account in applying section 469 to B for 1987. [Reg. § 1.469-11.]

☐ [T.D. 8417, 5-11-92. Amended by T.D. 8565, 10-3-94, T.D. 8645, 12-21-95 and T.D. 9013, 8-20-2002.]

[Reg. § 1.471-1]

§ 1.471-1. Need for inventories.—In order to reflect taxable income correctly, inventories at the beginning and end of each taxable year are necessary in every case in which the production, purchase, or sale of merchandise is an income-producing factor. The inventory should include all finished or partly finished goods and, in the case of raw materials and supplies, only those which have been acquired for sale or which will physically become a part of merchandise intended for sale, in which class fall containers, such as kegs, bottles, and cases, whether returnable or not, if title thereto will pass to the purchaser of the product to be sold therein. Merchandise should be included in the inventory only if title thereto is vested in the taxpayer. Accordingly, the seller should include in his inventory goods under contract for sale but not yet segregated and applied to the contract and goods out upon consignment, but should exclude from inventory goods sold (including containers) title to which has passed to the purchaser. A purchaser should include in inventory merchandise purchased (including containers), title to which has passed to him, although such merchandise is in transit or for other reasons has not been reduced to physical possession, but should not include goods ordered for future delivery, transfer of title to which has not yet been effected. (But see § 1.472-1.) [Reg. § 1.471-1.]

☐ [T.D. 6336, 12-1-58.]

[Reg. § 1.471-2]

§ 1.471-2. Valuation of inventories.—(a) Section 471 provides two tests to which each inventory must conform:

(1) It must conform as nearly as may be to the best accounting practice in the trade or business, and

(2) It must clearly reflect the income.

(b) It follows, therefore, that inventory rules cannot be uniform but must give effect to trade customs which come within the scope of the best accounting practice in the particular trade or business. In order clearly to reflect income, the inventory practice of a taxpayer should be consistent from year to year, and greater weight is to be given to consistency than to any particular method of inventorying or basis of valuation so long as the method or basis used is in accord with §§ 1.471-1 through 1.471-11.

(c) The bases of valuation most commonly used by business concerns and which meet the requirements of section 471 are (1) cost and (2) cost or market, whichever is lower. (For inventories by dealers in securities, see § 1.471-5.) Any goods in an inventory which are unsalable at normal prices or unusable in the normal way because of damage, imperfections, shop wear, changes of style, odd or broken lots, or other similar causes, including secondhand goods taken in exchange, should be valued at bona fide selling prices less direct cost of disposition, whether subparagraph (1) or (2) of this paragraph is used, or if such goods consist of raw materials or partly finished goods held for use or consumption, they shall be valued upon a reasonable basis, taking into consideration the usability and the condition of the goods, but in no case shall such value be less than the scrap value. Bona fide selling price means actual offering of goods during a period ending not later than 30 days after inventory date. The burden of proof will rest upon the taxpayer to show that such exceptional goods as are valued upon such selling basis come within the classifications indicated above, and he shall maintain such records of the disposition of the goods as will enable a verification of the inventory to be made.

(d) In respect of normal goods, whichever method is adopted must be applied with reasonable consistency to the entire inventory of the taxpayer's trade or business except as to those goods inventoried under the last-in, first-out method authorized by section 472 or to animals inventoried under the elective unit-livestock-price-method authorized by § 1.471-6. See paragraph (d) of § 1.446-1 for rules permitting the use of different methods of accounting if the taxpayer has more than one trade or business. Where the taxpayer is engaged in more than one trade or business the Commissioner may require that the method of valuing inventories with respect to goods in one trade or business also be used with respect to similar goods in other trades or businesses if, in the opinion of the Commissioner, the use of such method with respect to such other goods is essential to a clear reflection of income. Taxpayers were given an option to adopt the basis of either (1) cost or (2) cost or market, whichever is lower, for their 1920 inventories. The basis properly adopted for that year or any subsequent year is controlling, and a change can now be made only after permission is secured from the Commissioner. Application for permission to change the basis of valuing inventories shall be made in writing and filed with the Commissioner as provided in paragraph (e) of § 1.446-1. Goods taken in the inventory which have been so intermingled that they cannot be identified with specific invoices will be deemed to be the goods most recently purchased or produced, and the cost thereof will be the actual cost of the goods purchased or produced during the period in which the quantity of goods in the inventory has been acquired. But see section 472 as to last-in, first-out inventories. Where the taxpayer maintains book inventories in accordance with a sound accounting system in which the respective inventory accounts are charged with the actual cost of the goods purchased or produced and credited with the value of goods used, transferred, or sold, calculated upon the basis of the actual cost of the goods acquired during the taxable year (including the inventory at the beginning of the year), the net value as shown by such inventory accounts will be deemed to be the cost of the goods on hand. The balances shown by such book inventories should be verified by physical inventories at reasonable intervals and adjusted to conform therewith.

(e) Inventories should be recorded in a legible manner, properly computed and summarized, and should be preserved as a part of the accounting records of the taxpayer. The inventories of taxpayers on whatever basis taken will be subject to investigation by the district director, and the taxpayer must satisfy the district director of the correctness of the prices adopted.

(f) The following methods, among others, are sometimes used in taking or valuing inventories, but are not in accord with the regulations in this part:

(1) Deducting from the inventory a reserve for price changes, or an estimated depreciation in the value thereof.

(2) Taking work in process, or other parts of the inventory, at a nominal price or at less than its proper value.

(3) Omitting portions of the stock on hand.

(4) Using a constant price or nominal value for so-called normal quantity of materials or goods in stock.

(5) Including stock in transit, shipped either to or from the taxpayer, the title to which is not vested in the taxpayer.

(6) Segregating indirect production costs into fixed and variable production cost classifications (as defined in § 1.471-11(b)(3)(ii)) and allocating only the variable costs to the cost of goods produced while treating fixed costs as period costs which are currently deductible. This method is commonly referred to as the "direct cost" method.

(7) Treating all or substantially all indirect production costs (whether classified as fixed or variable) as period costs which are currently deductible. This method is generally referred to as the "prime cost" method. [Reg. § 1.471-2.]

☐ [T.D. 6336, 12-1-58. *Amended by T.D. 7285, 9-14-73.*]

[Reg. § 1.471-3]

§ 1.471-3. Inventories at cost.—Cost means:

(a) In the case of merchandise on hand at the beginning of the taxable year, the inventory price of such goods.

(b) In the case of merchandise purchased since the beginning of the taxable year, the invoice price less trade or other discounts, except strictly cash discounts approximating a fair interest rate, which may be deducted or not at the option of the taxpayer, provided a consistent course is followed. To this net invoice price should be added transportation or other necessary charges incurred in acquiring possession of the goods. For taxpayers acquiring merchandise for resale that are subject to the provisions of section 263A, see §§ 1.263A-1 and 1.263A-3 for additional amounts that must be included in inventory costs.

(c) In the case of merchandise produced by the taxpayer since the beginning of the taxable year, (1) the cost of raw materials and supplies entering into or consumed in connection with the product, (2) expenditures for direct labor, and (3) indirect production costs incident to and necessary for the production of the particular article, including in such indirect production costs an appropriate portion of management expenses, but not including any cost of selling or return on capital, whether by way of interest or profit. See §§ 1.263A-1 and 1.263A-2 for more specific rules regarding the treatment of production costs.

(d) In any industry in which the usual rules for computation of cost of production are inapplicable, costs may be approximated upon such basis as may be reasonable and in conformity with established trade practice in the particular industry. Among such cases are: (1) Farmers and raisers of livestock (see § 1.471-6); (2) miners and manufacturers who by a single process or uniform series of processes derive a product of two or more kinds, sizes, or grades, the unit cost of which is substantially alike (see § 1.471-7); and (3) retail merchants who use what is known as the "retail method" in ascertaining approximate cost (see § 1.471-8).

Notwithstanding the other rules of this section, cost shall not include an amount which is of a type for which a deduction would be disallowed under section 162(c), (f), or (g) and the regulations thereunder in the case of a business expense. [Reg. § 1.471-3.]

Reg. § 1.471-3(d)

☐ [T.D. 6336, 12-1-58. Amended by T.D. 7285, 9-14-73; T.D. 7345, 2-19-75; T.D. 8131, 3-24-87 and T.D. 8482, 8-6-93.]

[Reg. § 1.471-4]

§ 1.471-4. **Inventories at cost or market, whichever is lower.**—(a) *In general*—(1) *Market definition.* Under ordinary circumstances and for normal goods in an inventory, *market* means the aggregate of the current bid prices prevailing at the date of the inventory of the basic elements of cost reflected in inventories of goods purchased and on hand, goods in process of manufacture, and finished manufactured goods on hand. The basic elements of cost include direct materials, direct labor, and indirect costs required to be included in inventories by the taxpayer (e.g., under section 263A and its underlying regulations for taxpayers subject to that section). For taxpayers to which section 263A applies, for example, the basic elements of cost must reflect all direct costs and all indirect costs properly allocable to goods on hand at the inventory date at the current bid price of those costs, including but not limited to the cost of purchasing, handling, and storage activities conducted by the taxpayer, both prior to and subsequent to acquisition or production of the goods. The determination of the current bid price of the basic elements of costs reflected in goods on hand at the inventory date must be based on the usual volume of particular cost elements purchased (or incurred) by the taxpayer.

(2) *Fixed price contracts.* Paragraph (a)(1) of this section does not apply to any goods on hand or in process of manufacture for delivery upon firm sales contracts (i.e., those not legally subject to cancellation by either party) at fixed prices entered into before the date of the inventory, under which the taxpayer is protected against actual loss. Any such goods must be inventoried at cost.

(3) *Examples.* The valuation principles in paragraph (a)(1) of this section are illustrated by the following examples:

Example 1. (i) Taxpayer A manufactures tractors. A values its inventory using cost or market, whichever is lower, under paragraph (a)(1) of this section. At the end of 1994, the cost of one of A's tractors on hand is determined as follows:

Direct materials	$ 3,000
Direct labor	4,000
Indirect costs under section 263A	3,000
Total section 263A costs (cost)	$10,000

(ii) A determines that the aggregate of the current bid prices of the materials, labor, and overhead required to reproduce the tractor at the end of 1994 are as follows:

Direct materials	$ 3,100
Direct labor	4,100
Indirect costs under section 263A	3,100
Total section 263A costs (market)	$10,300

(iii) In determining the lower of cost or market value of the tractor, A compares the cost of the tractor, $10,000, with the market value of the tractor, $10,300, in accordance with paragraph (c) of this section. Thus, under this section, A values the tractor at $10,000.

Example 2. (i) Taxpayer B purchases and resells several lines of shoes and is subject to section 263A. B values its inventory using cost or market, whichever is lower, under paragraph (a)(1) of this section. At the end of 1994, the cost of one pair of shoes on hand is determined as follows:

Acquisition cost	$200
Indirect costs under section 263A	10
Total section 263A costs (cost)	$210

(ii) B determines the aggregate current bid prices prevailing at the end of 1994 for the elements of cost (both direct costs and indirect costs incurred prior and subsequent to acquisition of the shoes) based on the volume of the elements usually purchased (or incurred) by B as follows:

Acquisition cost	$178
Indirect costs under section 263A	12
Total [section] 263A costs (market)	$190

Reg. § 1.471-4(a)(1)

(iii) In determining the lower of cost or market value of the shoes, B compares the cost of the pair of shoes, $210, with the market value of the shoes, $190, in accordance with paragraph (c) of this section. Thus, under this section, B values the shoes at $190.

(b) *Inactive markets.* Where no open market exists or where quotations are nominal, due to inactive market conditions, the taxpayer must use such evidence of a fair market price at the date or dates nearest the inventory as may be available, such as specific purchases or sales by the taxpayer or others in reasonable volume and made in good faith, or compensation paid for cancellation of contracts for purchase commitments. Where the taxpayer in the regular course of business has offered for sale such merchandise at prices lower than the current price as above defined, the inventory may be valued at such prices less direct cost of disposition, and the correctness of such prices will be determined by reference to the actual sales of the taxpayer for a reasonable period before and after the date of the inventory. Prices which vary materially from the actual prices so ascertained will not be accepted as reflecting the market.

(c) *Comparison of cost and market.* Where the inventory is valued upon the basis of cost or market, whichever is lower, the market value of each article on hand at the inventory date shall be compared with the cost of the article, and the lower of such values shall be taken as the inventory value of the article.

(d) *Effective date.* This section applies to inventory valuations for taxable years beginning after December 31, 1993. For taxable years beginning before January 1, 1994, taxpayers must take reasonable positions on their federal income tax returns with respect to the application of section 263A, and must have otherwise complied with § 1.471-4 (as contained in the 26 CFR part 1 edition revised April 1, 1993). For purposes of this paragraph (d), a reasonable position as to the application of section 263A is a position consistent with the temporary regulations, revenue rulings, revenue procedures, notices, and announcements concerning section 263A applicable in taxable years beginning before January 1, 1994. (See § 601.601(d)(2)(ii)(*b*) of this chapter.) [Reg. § 1.471-4.]

☐ [*T.D. 6336, 12-1-58. Amended by T.D. 8482, 8-6-93.*]

[Reg. § 1.471-5]

§ 1.471-5. Inventories by dealers in securities.—A dealer in securities who in his books of account regularly inventories unsold securities on hand either—

(a) At cost,

(b) At cost or market, whichever is lower, or

(c) At market value,

may make his return upon the basis upon which his accounts are kept, provided that a description of the method employed is included in or attached to the return, that all the securities are inventoried by the same method, and that such method is adhered to in subsequent years, unless another method is authorized by the Commissioner pursuant to a written application therefor filed as provided in paragraph (e) of § 1.446-1. A dealer in securities in whose books of account separate computations of the gain or loss from the sale of the various lots of securities sold are made on the basis of the cost of each lot shall be regarded, for the purposes of this section, as regularly inventorying his securities at cost. For the purposes of this section, a dealer in securities is a merchant of securities, whether an individual, partnership, or corporation, with an established place of business, regularly engaged in the purchase of securities and their resale to customers; that is, one who as a merchant buys securities and sells them to customers with a view to the gains and profits that may be derived therefrom. If such business is simply a branch of the activities carried on by such person, the securities inventoried as provided in this section may include only those held for purposes of resale and not for investment. Taxpayers who buy and sell or hold securities for investment or speculation, irrespective of whether such buying or selling constitutes the carrying on of a trade or business, and officers of corporations and members of partnerships who in their individual capacities buy and sell securities, are not dealers in securities within the meaning of this section. See §§ 1.263A-1 and 1.263A-3 for rules regarding the treatment of costs with respect to property acquired for resale. [Reg. § 1.471-5.]

☐ [*T.D. 6336, 12-1-58. Amended by T.D. 8131, 3-24-87 and T.D. 8482, 8-6-93.*]

[Reg. § 1.471-6]

§ 1.471-6. Inventories of livestock raisers and other farmers.—(a) A farmer may make his return upon an inventory method instead of the cash receipts and disbursements method. It is optional with the taxpayer which of these methods of accounting is used but, having elected one method, the option so exercised will be binding upon the taxpayer for the year for which the option is exercised and for subsequent years unless another method is authorized by the Commissioner as provided in paragraph (e) of § 1.446-1.

(b) In any change of accounting method from the cash receipts and disbursements method to an inventory method, adjustments shall be made as provided in section 481 (relating to adjustments required by change in method of accounting) and the regulations thereunder.

(c) Because of the difficulty of ascertaining actual cost of livestock and other farm products, farmers who render their returns upon an inventory method may value their inventories according to the "farm-price method", and farmers raising livestock may value their inventories of animals according to either the "farm-price method" or the "unit-livestock-price method". In addition, these inventory methods may be used to account for the costs of property produced in a farming business that are required to be capitalized under section 263A regardless of whether the property being produced is otherwise treated as inventory by the taxpayer, and regardless of whether the taxpayer is otherwise using the cash or an accrual method of accounting.

(d) The "farm-price method" provides for the valuation of inventories at market price less direct cost of disposition. If this method of valuation is used, it generally must be applied to all property produced by the taxpayer in the trade or business of farming, except as to livestock accounted for, at the taxpayer's election, under the unit livestock method of accounting. However, see § 1.263A-4(c)(3) for an exception to this rule. If the use of the "farm-price method" of valuing inventories for any taxable year involves a change in method of valuing inventories from that employed in prior years, permission for such change shall first be secured from the Commissioner as provided in paragraph (e) of § 1.446-1.

(e) The "unit-livestock-price method" provides for the valuation of the different classes of animals in the inventory at a standard unit price for each animal within a class. A livestock raiser electing this method of valuing his animals must adopt a reasonable classification of the animals in his inventory with respect to the age and kind included so that the unit prices assigned to the several classes will reasonably account for the normal costs incurred in producing the animals within such classes. Thus, if a cattle raiser determines that it costs approximately $15 to produce a calf, and $7.50 each year to raise the calf to maturity, his classifications and unit prices would be as follows: Calves, $15; yearlings, $22.50; 2-year olds, $30; mature animals, $37.50. The classification selected by the livestock raiser, and the unit prices assigned to the several classes, are subject to approval by the district director upon examination of the taxpayer's return.

(f) A taxpayer that elects to use the "unit-livestock-price method" must apply it to all livestock raised, whether for sale or for draft, breeding, or dairy purposes. The inventoriable costs of animals raised for draft, breeding, or dairy purposes can, at the election of the livestock raiser, be included in inventory or treated as property used in a trade or business subject to depreciation after maturity. See § 1.263A-4 for rules regarding the computation of inventoriable costs for purposes of the unit-livestock-price method. Once established, the methods of accounting used by the taxpayer to determine unit prices and to classify animals must be consistently applied in all subsequent taxable years. A taxpayer that uses the unit-livestock-price method must annually reevaluate its unit prices and adjust the prices either upward to reflect increases, or downward to reflect decreases, in the costs of raising livestock. The consent of the Commissioner is not required to make such upward or downward adjustments. No other changes in the classification of animals or unit prices may be made without the consent of the Commissioner. See § 1.446-1(e) for procedures for obtaining the consent of the Commissioner. The provisions of this paragraph (f) apply to taxable years ending after October 28, 2002.

(g) A livestock raiser who uses the "unit-livestock-price method" must include in his inventory at cost any livestock purchased, except that animals purchased for draft, breeding, or dairy purposes can, at the election of the livestock raiser, be included in inventory or be treated as property used in a trade or business subject to depreciation after maturity. If the animals purchased are not mature at the time of purchase, the cost should be increased at the end of each taxable year in accordance with the established unit prices, except that no increase is to be made in the taxable year of purchase if the animal is acquired during the last six months of that year. If the records maintained permit identification of a purchased animal, the cost of such animal will be eliminated from the closing inventory in the event of its sale or loss. Otherwise, the first-in, first-out method of valuing inventories must be applied.

(h) If a taxpayer using the "farm-price method" desires to adopt the "unit-livestock-price method" in valuing his inventories of livestock, permission for the change shall first be secured from the Commissioner as provided in paragraph (e) of § 1.446-1. However, a taxpayer who has filed returns on the basis of inventories at cost, or cost or market whichever is lower, may adopt the "unit-livestock-price method" for valuing his inventories of livestock without formal application for permission, but the classifications and unit prices selected are subject to approval by the

Reg. § 1.471-6(b)

Methods of Accounting

district director upon examination of the taxpayer's return. A livestock raiser who has adopted a constant unit-price method of valuing livestock inventories and filed returns on that basis will be considered as having elected the "unit-livestock-price method."

(i) If returns have been made in which the taxable income has been computed upon incomplete inventories, the abnormality should be corrected by submitting with the return for the current taxable year a statement for the preceding taxable year. In this statement such adjustments shall be made as are necessary to bring the closing inventory for the preceding taxable year into agreement with the opening complete inventory for the current taxable year. If necessary clearly to reflect income, similar adjustments may be made as at the beginning of the preceding year or years, and the tax, if any be due, shall be assessed and paid at the rate of tax in effect for such year or years. [Reg. § 1.471-6.]

☐ [T.D. 6336, 12-1-58. Amended by T.D. 8131, 3-24-87; T.D. 8729, 8-21-97; T.D. 8897, 8-18-2000 and T.D. 9019, 10-25-2002.]

[Reg. § 1.471-7]

§ 1.471-7. Inventories of miners and manufacturers.—A taxpayer engaged in mining or manufacturing who by a single process or uniform series of processes derives a product of two or more kinds, sizes, or grades, the unit cost of which is substantially alike, and who in conformity to a recognized trade practice allocates an amount of cost to each kind, size, or grade of product, which in the aggregate will absorb the total cost of production, may, with the consent of the Commissioner, use such allocated cost as a basis for pricing inventories, provided such allocation bears a reasonable relation to the respective selling values of the different kinds, sizes, or grades of product. See section 472 as to last-in, first-out inventories. [Reg. § 1.471-7.]

☐ [T.D. 6336, 12-1-58.]

[Reg. § 1.471-8]

§ 1.471-8. Inventories of retail merchants.— (a) Retail merchants who employ what is known as the "retail method" of pricing inventories may make their returns upon that method, provided that the use of such method is designated upon the return, that accurate accounts are kept, and that such method is consistently adhered to unless a change is authorized by the Commissioner as provided in paragraph (e) of § 1.446-1. Under the retail method the total of the retail selling prices of the goods on hand at the end of the year in each department or of each class of goods is reduced to approximate cost by deducting therefrom an amount which bears the same ratio to such total as—

(1) The total of the retail selling prices of the goods included in the opening inventory plus the retail selling prices of the goods purchased during the year, with proper adjustment to such selling prices for all mark-ups and mark-downs, less

(2) The cost of the goods included in the opening inventory plus the cost of the goods purchased during the year, bears to (1).

The result should represent as accurately as may be the amounts added to the cost price of the goods to cover selling and other expenses of doing business and for the margin of profit. See §§ 1.263A-1 and 1.263A-3 for rules regarding the computation of costs with respect to property acquired for resale.

(b) For further adjustments to be made in the case of a retail merchant using the last-in, first-out inventory method authorized by section 472, see paragraph (k) of § 1.472-1.

(c) A taxpayer maintaining more than one department in his store or dealing in classes of goods carrying different percentages of gross profit should not use a percentage of profit based upon an average of his entire business, but should compute and use in valuing his inventory the proper percentages for the respective departments or classes of goods.

(d) A taxpayer (other than one using the last-in, first-out inventory method) who previously has determined inventories in accordance with the retail method, except that, to obtain a basis of approximate cost or market, whichever is lower, has consistently and uniformly followed the practice of adjusting the retail selling prices of the goods included in the opening inventory and purchased during the taxable year for mark-ups but not for mark-downs, may continue such practice subject to the conditions prescribed in this section. The adjustments must be bona fide and consistent and uniform. Where mark-downs are not included in the adjustments, mark-ups made to cancel or correct mark-downs shall not be included; and the mark-ups included must be reduced by the mark-downs made to cancel or correct such mark-ups.

(e) In no event shall mark-downs not based on actual reduction of retail sale prices, such as mark-downs based on depreciation and obsolescence, be recognized in determining the retail selling prices of the goods on hand at the end of the taxable year.

(f) A taxpayer (other than one using the last-in, first-out inventory method) who previously has determined inventories without following the practice of eliminating mark-downs in making adjustments to retail selling prices may adopt such practice, provided permission to do so is obtained in accordance with, and subject to the terms provided by, paragraph (e) of § 1.446-1. A taxpayer filing a first return of income may adopt such practice subject to approval by the district director upon examination of the return.

(g) A taxpayer using the last-in, first-out inventory method in conjunction with retail computations must adjust retail selling prices for markdowns as well as mark-ups, in order that there may be reflected the approximate cost of the goods on hand at the end of the taxable year regardless of market values. [Reg. § 1.471-8.]

☐ [T.D. 6336, 12-1-58. Amended by T.D. 8131, 3-24-87 and T.D. 8482, 8-6-93.]

[Reg. § 1.471-9]

§ 1.471-9. Inventories of acquiring corporations.—For additional rules in the case of certain corporate acquisitions specified in section 381(a), see section 381(c)(5) and the regulations thereunder. [Reg. § 1.471-9.]

☐ [T.D. 6336, 12-1-58.]

[Reg. § 1.471-10]

§ 1.471-10. Applicability of long-term contract methods.—See § 1.460-2 for rules providing for the application of the long-term contract methods to certain manufacturing contracts. [Reg. § 1.471-10.]

☐ [T.D. 7397, 1-14-76. Amended by T.D. 8067, 12-30-85 and T.D. 8929, 1-10-2001.]

[Reg. § 1.471-11]

§ 1.471-11. Inventories of manufacturers.—(a) *Use of full absorption method of inventory costing.* In order to conform as nearly as may be possible to the best accounting practices and to clearly reflect income (as required by section 471 of the Code), both direct and indirect production costs must be taken into account in the computation of inventoriable costs in accordance with the "full absorption" method of inventory costing. Under the full absorption method of inventory costing production costs must be allocated to goods produced during the taxable year, whether sold during the taxable year or in inventory at the close of the taxable year determined in accordance with the taxpayer's method of identifying goods in inventory. Thus, the taxpayer must include as inventoriable costs all direct production costs and, to the extent provided by paragraphs (c) and (d) of this section, all indirect production costs. For purposes of this section, the term "financial reports" means financial reports (including consolidated financial statements) to shareholders, partners, beneficiaries or other proprietors and for credit purposes. See also § 1.263A-1T with respect to the treatment of production costs incurred in taxable years beginning after December 31, 1986, and before January 1, 1994. See also §§ 1.263A-1 and 1.263A-2 with respect to the treatment of production costs incurred in taxable years beginning after December 31, 1993.

(b) *Production costs*—(1) *In general.* Costs are considered to be production costs to the extent that they are incident to and necessary for production or manufacturing operations or processes. Production costs include direct production costs and fixed and variable indirect production costs.

(2) *Direct production costs.* (i) Costs classified as "direct production costs" are generally those costs which are incident to and necessary for production or manufacturing operations or processes and are components of the cost of either direct material or direct labor. Direct material costs include the cost of those materials which become an integral part of the specific product and those materials which are consumed in the ordinary course of manufacturing and can be identified or associated with particular units or groups of units of that product. See § 1.471-3 for the elements of direct material costs. Direct labor costs include the cost of labor which can be identified or associated with particular units or groups of units of a specific product. The elements of direct labor costs include such items as basic compensation, overtime pay, vacation and holiday pay, sick leave pay (other than payments pursuant to a wage continuation plan under section 105(d)), shift differential, payroll taxes and payments to a supplemental unemployment benefit plan paid or incurred on behalf of employees engaged in direct labor. For the treatment of rework labor, scrap, spoilage costs, and any other costs not specifically described as direct production costs see § 1.471-11(c)(2).

(ii) Under the full absorption method, a taxpayer must take into account all items of direct production cost in his inventoriable costs. Nevertheless, a taxpayer will not be treated as using an incorrect method of inventory costing if he treats any direct production costs as indirect production costs, provided such costs are allocated to the taxpayer's ending inventory to the extent provided by paragraph (d) of this section. Thus, for example, a taxpayer may treat direct labor costs as part of indirect production costs (for example, by use of the conversion cost method), provided all such costs are allocated to ending inventory to the extent provided by paragraph (d) of this section.

(3) *Indirect production costs*—(i) *In general.* The term "indirect production costs" includes all

costs which are incident to and necessary for production or manufacturing operations or processes other than direct production costs (as defined in subparagraph (2) of this paragraph). Indirect production costs may be classified as to kind or type in accordance with acceptable accounting principles so as to enable convenient identification with various production or manufacturing activities or functions and to facilitate reasonable groupings of such costs for purposes of determining unit product costs.

(ii) *Fixed and variable classifications.* For purposes of this section, fixed indirect production costs are generally those costs which do not vary significantly with changes in the amount of goods produced at any given level of production capacity. These fixed costs may include, among other costs, rent and property taxes on buildings and machinery incident to and necessary for manufacturing operations or processes. On the other hand, variable indirect production costs are generally those costs which do vary significantly with changes in the amount of goods produced at any given level of production capacity. These variable costs may include, among other costs, indirect materials, factory janitorial supplies, and utilities. Where a particular cost contains both fixed and variable elements, these elements should be segregated into fixed and variable classifications to the extent necessary under the taxpayer's method of allocation, such as for the application of the practical capacity concept (as described in paragraph (d)(4) of this section).

(c) *Certain indirect and production costs*—(1) *General rule.* Except as provided in paragraph (c)(3) of this section and in paragraph (d)(6)(v) of § 1.451-3, in order to determine whether indirect production costs referred to in paragraph (b) of this section must be included in a taxpayer's computation of the amount of inventoriable costs, three categories of costs have been provided in subparagraph (2) of this paragraph. Costs described in subparagraph (2)(i) of this paragraph must be included in the taxpayer's computation of the amount of inventoriable costs, regardless of their treatment by the taxpayer in his financial reports. Costs described in subparagraph (2)(ii) of this paragraph need not enter into the taxpayer's computation of the amount of inventoriable costs, regardless of their treatment by the taxpayer in his financial reports. Costs described in subparagraph (2)(iii) of this paragraph must be included in or excluded from the taxpayer's computation of the amount of inventoriable costs in accordance with the treatment of such costs by the taxpayer in his financial reports and generally accepted accounting principles. For the treatment of indirect production costs described in subparagraph (2) of this paragraph in the case of a taxpayer who is not using comparable methods of accounting for such costs for tax and financial reporting see paragraph (c)(3) of this section. For contracts entered into after December 31, 1982, notwithstanding this section, taxpayers who use an inventory method of accounting for extended period long-term contracts (as defined in paragraph (b)(3) of § 1.451-3) for tax purposes may be required to use the cost allocation rules provided in paragraph (d)(6) of § 1.451-3 rather than the cost allocation rules provided in this section. See paragraph (d)(6)(v) of § 1.451-3. After a taxpayer has determined which costs must be treated as indirect production costs includible in the computation of the amount of inventoriable costs, such costs must be allocated to a taxpayer's ending inventory in a manner prescribed by paragraph (d) of this section.

(2) *Includibility of certain indirect production costs*—(i) *Indirect production costs included in inventoriable costs.* Indirect production costs which must enter into the computation of the amount of inventoriable costs (regardless of their treatment by a taxpayer in his financial reports) include:

(*a*) Repair expenses,

(*b*) Maintenance,

(*c*) Utilities, such as heat, power and light,

(*d*) Rent,

(*e*) Indirect labor and production supervisory wages, including basic compensation, overtime pay, vacation and holiday pay, sick leave pay (other than payments pursuant to a wage continuation plan under section 105(d)), shift differential, payroll taxes and contributions to a supplemental unemployment benefit plan,

(*f*) Indirect materials and supplies,

(*g*) Tools and equipment not capitalized, and

(*h*) Costs of quality control and inspection,

to the extent, and only to the extent, such costs are incident to and necessary for production or manufacturing operations or processes.

(ii) *Costs not included in inventoriable costs.* Costs which are not required to be included for tax purposes in the computation of the amount of inventoriable costs (regardless of their treatment by a taxpayer in his financial reports) include:

(*a*) Marketing expenses,

(*b*) Advertising expenses,

(*c*) Selling expenses,

Reg. § 1.471-11(c)(2)

(d) Other distribution expenses,

(e) Interest,

(f) Research and experimental expenses including engineering and product development expenses,

(g) Losses under section 165 and the regulations thereunder,

(h) Percentage depletion in excess of cost depletion,

(i) Depreciation and amortization reported for Federal income tax purposes in excess of depreciation reported by the taxpayer in his financial reports,

(j) Income taxes attributable to income received on the sale of inventory,

(k) Pension contributions to the extent that they represent past services cost,

(l) General and administrative expenses incident to and necessary for the taxpayer's activities as a whole rather than to production or manufacturing operations or processes, and

(m) Salaries paid to officers attributable to the performance of services which are incident to and necessary for the taxpayer's activities taken as a whole rather than to production or manufacturing operations or processes.

Notwithstanding the preceding sentence, if a taxpayer consistently includes in his computation of the amount of inventoriable costs any of the costs described in the preceding sentence, a change in such method of inclusion shall be considered a change in method of accounting within the meaning of sections 446, 481, and paragraph (e)(4) of this section.

(iii) *Indirect production costs includible in inventoriable costs depending upon treatment in taxpayer's financial reports.* In the case of costs listed in this subdivision, the inclusion or exclusion of such costs from the amount of inventoriable costs for purposes of a taxpayer's financial reports shall determine whether such costs must be included in or excluded from the computation of inventoriable costs for tax purposes, but only if such treatment is not inconsistent with generally accepted accounting principles.

In the case of costs which are not included in subdivision (i) or (ii) of this subparagraph, nor listed in this subdivision, whether such costs must be included in or excluded from the computation of inventoriable costs for tax purposes depends upon the extent to which such costs are similar to costs included in subdivision (i) or (ii), and if such costs are dissimilar to costs in subdivision (i) or (ii), such costs shall be treated as included in or excludable from the amount of inventoriable costs

in accordance with this subdivision. The costs listed in this subdivision are:

(a) *Taxes.* Taxes otherwise allowable as a deduction under section 164 (other than State and local and foreign income taxes) attributable to assets incident to and necessary for production or manufacturing operations or processes. Thus, for example, the cost of State and local property taxes imposed on a factory or other production facility and any State and local taxes imposed on inventory must be included in or excluded from the computation of the amount of inventoriable costs for tax purposes depending upon their treatment by a taxpayer in his financial reports.

(b) *Depreciation and depletion.* Depreciation reported in financial reports and cost depletion on assets incident to and necessary for production or manufacturing operation or processes. In computing cost depletion under this section, the adjusted basis of such assets shall be reduced by cost depletion and not by percentage depletion taken thereon.

(c) *Employee benefits.* Pension and profit-sharing contributions representing current service costs otherwise allowable as a deduction under section 404, and other employee benefits incurred on behalf of labor incident to and necessary for production or manufacturing operations or processes. These other benefits include workmen's compensation expenses, payments under a wage continuation plan described in section 105(d), amounts of a type which would be includible in the gross income of employees under nonqualified pension, profit-sharing and stock bonus plans, premiums on life and health insurance and miscellaneous benefits provided for employees such as safety, medical treatment, cafeteria, recreational facilities, membership dues, etc., which are otherwise allowable as deductions under chapter 1 of the Code.

(d) *Costs attributable to strikes, rework labor, scrap and spoilage.* Costs attributable to rework labor, scrap and spoilage which are incident to and necessary for production or manufacturing operations or processes and costs attributable to strikes incident to production or manufacturing operation or processes.

(e) *Factory administrative expenses.* Administrative costs of production (but not including any cost of selling or any return on capital) incident to and necessary for production or manufacturing operations or processes.

(f) *Officers' salaries.* Salaries paid to officers attributable to services performed incident to and necessary for production or manufacturing operations or processes.

Reg. § 1.471-11(c)(2)

(*g*) *Insurance costs.* Insurance costs incident to and necessary for production or manufacturing operations or processes such as insurance on production machinery and equipment.

A change in the taxpayer's treatment in his financial reports of costs described in this subdivision which results in a change in treatment of such costs for tax purposes shall constitute a change in method of accounting within the meaning of sections 446 and 481 to which paragraph (e) applies.

(3) *Exception.* Except as provided in paragraph (d)(6) of § 1.451-3, in the case of a taxpayer whose method of accounting for production costs in his financial reports is not comparable to his method of accounting for such costs for tax purposes (such as a taxpayer using the prime cost method for purposes of financial reports), the following rules apply:

(i) *Indirect production costs included in inventoriable costs.* Indirect production costs which must enter into the computation of the amount of inventoriable costs (to the extent, and only to the extent, such costs are incident to and necessary for production or manufacturing operations or processes) include:

(*a*) Repair expenses,

(*b*) Maintenance,

(*c*) Utilities, such as heat, power and light,

(*d*) Rent,

(*e*) Indirect labor and production supervisory wages, including basic compensation, overtime pay, vacation and holiday pay, sick leave pay (other than payments pursuant to a wage continuation plan under section 105(d)), shift differential, payroll taxes and contributions to a supplemental unemployment benefit plan,

(*f*) Indirect materials and supplies,

(*g*) Tools and equipment not capitalized,

(*h*) Costs of quality control and inspection,

(*i*) Taxes otherwise allowable as a deduction under section 164 (other than State and local and foreign income taxes),

(*j*) Depreciation and amortization reported for financial purposes and cost depletion,

(*k*) Administrative costs of production (but not including any cost of selling or any return on capital) incident to and necessary for production or manufacturing operations or processes,

(*l*) Salaries paid to officers attributable to services performed incident to and necessary for production or manufacturing operations or processes, and

(*m*) Insurance costs incident to and necessary for production or manufacturing operations or processes such as insurance on production machinery and equipment.

(ii) *Costs not included in inventoriable costs.* Costs which are not required to be included in the computation of the amount of inventoriable costs include:

(*a*) Marketing expenses,

(*b*) Advertising expenses,

(*c*) Selling expenses,

(*d*) Other distribution expenses,

(*e*) Interest,

(*f*) Research and experimental expenses including engineering and product development expenses,

(*g*) Losses under section 165 and the regulations thereunder,

(*h*) Percentage depletion in excess of cost depletion,

(*i*) Depreciation reported for Federal income tax purposes in excess of depreciation reported by the taxpayer in his financial reports,

(*j*) Income taxes attributable to income received on the sale of inventory,

(*k*) Pension and profit-sharing contributions representing either past service costs or representing current service costs otherwise allowable as a deduction under section 404, and other employee benefits incurred on behalf of labor. These other benefits include workmen's compensation expenses, payments under a wage continuation plan described in section 105(d), amounts of a type which would be includible in the gross income of employees under nonqualified pension, profit-sharing and stock bonus plans, premiums on life and health insurance and miscellaneous benefits provided for employees such as safety, medical treatment, cafeteria, recreational facilities, membership dues, etc., which are otherwise allowable as deductions under chapter 1 of the Code,

(*l*) Costs attributable to strikes, rework labor, scrap and spoilage,

(*m*) General and administrative expenses incident to and necessary for the taxpayer's activities as a whole rather than to production or manufacturing operations or processes, and

(*n*) Salaries paid to officers attributable to the performance of services which are incident to and necessary for the taxpayer's activities as a whole rather than to production or manufacturing operations or processes.

Reg. § 1.471-11(c)(3)

(d) *Allocation methods*—(1) *In general.* Indirect production costs required to be included in the computation of the amount of inventoriable costs pursuant to paragraphs (b) and (c) of this paragraph must be allocated to goods in a taxpayer's ending inventory (determined in accordance with the taxpayer's method of identification) by the use of a method of allocation which fairly apportions such costs among the various items produced. Acceptable methods for allocating indirect production costs to the cost of goods in the ending inventory include the manufacturing burden rate method and the standard cost method. In addition, the practical capacity concept can be used in conjunction with either the manufacturing burden rate or standard cost method.

(2) *Manufacturing burden rate method*—(i) *In general.* Manufacturing burden rates may be developed in accordance with acceptable accounting principles and applied in a reasonable manner. In developing a manufacturing burden rate, the factors described in subdivision (ii) of this subparagraph may be taken into account. Furthermore, if the taxpayer chooses, he may allocate different indirect production costs on the basis of different manufacturing burden rates. Thus, for example, the taxpayer may use one burden rate for allocating rent and another burden rate for allocating utilities. The method used by the taxpayer in allocating such costs in his financial reports shall be given great weight in determining whether the taxpayer's method employed for tax purposes fairly allocates indirect production costs to the ending inventory. Any change in a manufacturing burden rate which is merely a periodic adjustment to reflect current operating conditions, such as increases in automation or changes in operation, does not constitute a change in method of accounting under section 446. However, a change in the concept upon which such rates are developed does constitute a change in method of accounting requiring the consent of the Commissioner. The taxpayer shall maintain adequate records and working papers to support all manufacturing burden rate calculations.

(ii) *Development of manufacturing burden rate.* The following factors, among others, may be taken into account in developing manufacturing burden rates:

(*a*) The selection of an appropriate level of activity and period of time upon which to base the calculation of rates which will reflect operating conditions for purposes of the unit costs being determined;

(*b*) The selection of an appropriate statistical base such as direct labor hours, direct labor dollars, or machine hours, or a combination thereof, upon which to apply the overhead rate to determine production costs; and

(*c*) The appropriate budgeting, classification and analysis of expenses (for example, the analysis of fixed and variable costs).

(iii) *Operation of the manufacturing burden rate method.* (*a*) The purpose of the manufacturing burden rate method used in conjunction with the full absorption method of inventory costing is to allocate an appropriate amount of indirect production costs to a taxpayer's goods in ending inventory by the use of predetermined rates intended to approximate the actual amount of indirect production costs incurred. Accordingly, the proper use of the manufacturing burden rate method under this section requires that any net negative or net positive difference between the total predetermined amount of indirect production costs allocated to the goods in ending inventory and the total amount of indirect production costs actually incurred and required to be allocated to such goods (*i.e.*, the under or over-applied burden) must be treated as an adjustment to the taxpayer's ending inventory in the taxable year in which such difference arises. However, if such adjustment is not significant in amount in relation to the taxpayer's total actual indirect production costs for the year then such adjustment need not be allocated to the taxpayer's goods in ending inventory unless such allocation is made in the taxpayer's financial reports. The taxpayer must treat both positive and negative adjustments consistently.

(*b*) Notwithstanding subdivision (*a*), the practical capacity concept may be used to determine the total amount of fixed indirect production costs which must be allocated to goods in ending inventory. See subparagraph (4) of this paragraph.

(3) *Standard cost method*—(i) *In general.* A taxpayer may use the so-called "standard cost" method of allocating inventoriable costs to the goods in ending inventory, provided he treats variances in accordance with the procedures prescribed in subdivision (ii) of this subparagraph. The method used by the taxpayer in allocating such costs in his financial reports shall be given great weight in determining whether the taxpayer's method employed for tax purposes fairly allocates indirect production costs to the ending inventory. For purposes of this subparagraph, a "net positive overhead variance" shall mean the excess of total standard (or estimated) indirect production costs over total actual indirect production costs and a "net negative overhead variance" shall mean the excess of total actual indirect pro-

Reg. § 1.471-11(d)(1)

duction costs over total standard (or estimated) indirect production costs.

(ii) *Treatment of variances.* (*a*) The proper use of the standard cost method pursuant to this subparagraph requires that a taxpayer must reallocate to the goods in ending inventory a pro rata portion of any net negative or net positive overhead variances and any net negative or net positive direct production cost variances. The taxpayer must apportion such variances among his various items in ending inventory. However, if such variances are not significant in amount in relation to the taxpayer's total actual indirect production costs for the year then such variances need not be allocated to the taxpayer's goods in ending inventory unless such allocation is made in the taxpayer's financial reports. The taxpayer must treat both positive and negative variances consistently.

(*b*) Notwithstanding subdivision (*a*), the practical capacity concept may be used to determine the total amount of fixed indirect production costs which must be allocated to goods in ending inventory. See subparagraph (4) of this paragraph.

(4) *Practical capacity concept*—(i) *In general.* Under the practical capacity concept, the percentage of practical capacity represented by actual production (not greater than 100 percent), as calculated under subdivision (ii) of this subparagraph, is used to determine the total amount of fixed indirect production costs which must be included in the taxpayer's computation of the amount of inventoriable costs. The portion of such costs to be included in the taxpayer's computation of the amount of inventoriable costs is then combined with variable indirect production costs and both are allocated to the goods in ending inventory in accordance with this paragraph. See the example in subdivision (ii)(*d*) of this subparagraph. The difference (if any) between the amount of all fixed indirect production costs and the fixed indirect production costs which are included in the computation of the amount of inventoriable costs under the practical capacity concept is allowable as a deduction for the taxable year in which such difference occurs.

(ii) *Calculation of practical capacity*—(*a*) *In general.* Practical capacity and theoretical capacity (as described in (*c*) of this subdivision) may be computed in terms of tons, pounds, yards, labor hours, machine hours, or any other unit of production appropriate to the cost accounting system used by a particular taxpayer. The determination of practical capacity and theoretical capacity should be modified from time to time to reflect a change in underlying facts and conditions such as increased output due to automation or other changes in plant operation. Such a change does not constitute a change in method of accounting under sections 446 and 481.

(*b*) *Based upon taxpayer's experience.* In selecting an appropriate level of production activity upon which to base the calculation of practical capacity, the taxpayer shall establish the production operating conditions expected during the period for which the costs are being determined, assuming that the utilization of production facilities during operations will be approximately at capacity. This level of production activity is frequently described as practical capacity for the period and is ordinarily based upon the historical experience of the taxpayer. For example, a taxpayer operating on a 5-day, 8-hour basis may have a "normal" production of 100,000 units a year based upon three years of experience.

(*c*) *Based upon theoretical capacity.* Practical capacity may also be established by the use of "theoretical" capacity, adjusted for allowances for estimated inability to achieve maximum production, such as machine breakdown, idle time, and other normal work stoppages. Theoretical capacity is the level of production the manufacturer could reach if all machines and departments were operated continuously at peak efficiency.

(*d*) *Example.* The provisions of (*c*) of this subdivision may be illustrated by the following example:

Corporation X operates a stamping plant with a theoretical capacity of 50 units per hour. The plant actually operates 1960 hours per year based on an 8-hour day, 5 day week basis and 15 shut-down days for vacations and holidays. A reasonable allowance for down time (the time allowed for ordinary and necessary repairs and maintenance) is 5 percent of practical capacity before reduction for down time. Assuming no loss of production during starting up, closing down, or employee work breaks, under these facts and circumstances X may properly make a practical capacity computation as follows:

Practical capacity without allowance
 for down time based on theoretical
 capacity per hour is (1960 × 50) 98,000
Reduction for down time (98,000 × 5%) 4,900
Practical capacity 93,100

The 93,100 unit level of activity (*i.e.*, practical capacity) would, therefore, constitute an appropriate base for calculating the amount of fixed indirect production costs to be included in the computation of the amount of inventoriable costs for the period under review. On this basis if only 76,000 units were produced for the period, the

Reg. § 1.471-11(d)(4)

effect would be that approximately 81.6 percent (76,000, the actual number of units produced, divided by 93,100, the maximum number of units producible at practical capacity) of the fixed indirect production costs would be included in the computation of the amount of inventoriable costs during the year. The portion of the fixed indirect production costs not so included in the computation of the amount of inventoriable costs would be deductible in the year in which paid or incurred. Assume further that 7,600 units were on hand at the end of the taxable year and the 7,600 units were in the same proportion to the total units produced. Thus, 10 percent (7,600 units in inventory at the end of the taxable year, divided by 76,000, the actual number of units produced) of the fixed indirect production costs included in the computation of the amount of inventoriable costs (the above-mentioned 81.6 percent) and 10 percent of the variable indirect production costs would be included in the cost of the goods in the ending inventory, in accordance with a method of allocation provided by this paragraph.

(e) *Transition to full absorption method of inventory costing*—(1) *In general*—(i) *Mandatory requirement.* A taxpayer not using the full absorption method of inventory costing, as prescribed by paragraph (a) of this section, must change to that method. Any change to the full absorption method must be made by the taxpayer with respect to all trades or businesses of the taxpayer to which this section applies. A taxpayer not using the full absorption method of inventory costing, as prescribed by paragraph (a) of this section, who makes the special election provided in subdivision (ii) of this subparagraph during the transition period described in subdivision (ii) of this subparagraph need not change to the full absorption method of inventory costing for taxable years prior to the year for which such election is made. In determining whether the taxpayer is changing to a more or a less inclusive method of inventory costing, all positive and negative adjustments for all items and all trades or businesses of the taxpayer shall be aggregated. If the net adjustment is positive, paragraph (e)(3) shall apply, and if the net adjustment is negative, paragraph (e)(4) shall apply to the change. The rules otherwise prescribed in sections 446 and 481 and the regulations thereunder shall apply to any taxpayer who fails to make the special election in subdivision (ii) of this subparagraph. The transition rules of this paragraph are available only to those taxpayers who change their method of inventory costing.

(ii) *Special election during two-year-transition period.* If a taxpayer elects to change to the full absorption method of inventory costing during the transition period provided herein, he may elect on Form 3115 to change to such full absorption method of inventory costing and, in so doing, employ the transition procedures and adopt any of the transition methods prescribed in subparagraph (3) of this paragraph. Such election shall be made during the first 180 days of any taxable year beginning on or after September 19, 1973, and before September 19, 1975 (*i.e.*, the "transition period") and the change in inventory costing method shall be made for the taxable year in which the election is made. Notwithstanding the preceding sentence if the taxpayer's prior returns have been examined by the Service prior to September 19, 1973 and there is a pending issue involving the taxpayer's method of inventory costing, the taxpayer may request the application of this regulation by agreeing and filing a letter to that effect with the district director, within 90 days after September 19, 1973 to change to the full absorption method for the first taxable year of the taxpayer beginning after September 19, 1973 and subsequently filing Form 3115 within the first 180 days of such taxable year of change.

(iii) *Change initiated by the Commissioner.* A taxpayer who properly makes an election under subdivision (ii) of this subparagraph shall be considered to have made a change in method of accounting not initiated by the taxpayer, notwithstanding the provisions of § 1.481-1(c)(5). Thus, any of the taxpayer's "pre-1954 inventory balances" with respect to such inventory shall not be taken into account as an adjustment under section 481. For purposes of this paragraph, a "pre-1954 inventory balance" is the net amount of the adjustments which would have been required if the taxpayer had made such change in his method of accounting with respect to his inventory in his first taxable year which began after December 31, 1953, and ended after August 16, 1954. See section 481(a)(2) and § 1.481-3.

(2) *Procedural rules for change.* If a taxpayer makes an election pursuant to subparagraph (1)(ii) of this paragraph, the Commissioner's consent will be evidenced by a letter of consent to the taxpayer, setting forth the values of inventory, as provided by the taxpayer, determined under the full absorption method of inventory costing, except to the extent that no determination of such values is necessary under subparagraph (3)(ii)(B) of this paragraph (the cut off method), the amount of the adjustments (if any) required to be taken into account by section 481, and the treatment to be accorded to any such adjustments. Such full absorption values shall be subject to verification on examination by the district director. The taxpayer shall preserve at his principal place of business all records, data, and other evi-

Reg. § 1.471-11(e)(1)

dence relating to the full absorption values of inventory.

(3) *Transition methods.* In the case of a taxpayer who properly makes an election under subparagraph (1)(ii) of this paragraph during the transition period—

(i) *10-year adjustment period.* Such taxpayer may elect to take any adjustment required by section 481 with respect to any inventory being revalued under the full absorption method into account ratably over a period designated by the taxpayer at the time of such election, not to exceed the lesser of 10 taxable years commencing with the year of transition or the number of years the taxpayer has been on the inventory method from which he is changing. If the taxpayer dies or ceases to exist in a transaction other than one to which section 381(a) of the Code applies or if the taxpayer's inventory (determined under the full absorption method) on the last day of any taxable year is reduced (by other than a strike or involuntary conversion) by more than an amount equal to 33 1/3 percent of the taxpayer's inventory (determined under the full absorption method) as of the beginning of the year of change, the entire amount of the section 481 adjustment not previously taken into account in computing income shall be taken into account in computing income for the taxable year in which such taxpayer so ceases to exist or such taxpayer's inventory is so reduced.

(ii) *Additional rules for LIFO taxpayers.* A taxpayer who uses the LIFO method of inventory identification may either—

(A) Employ the special transition rules described in subdivision (i) of this subparagraph. Accordingly, all LIFO layers must be revalued under the full absorption method and the section 481 adjustment must be computed for all items in all layers in inventory, but no pre-1954 inventory balances shall be taken into account as adjustments under section 481; or

(B)(*1*) Employ a cut-off method whereby the full absorption method is only applied in costing layers of inventory acquired during all taxable years beginning with the year for which an election is made under subparagraph (e)(1)(ii).

(*2*) In the case of a taxpayer using dollar value LIFO, employ a cut-off method whereby the taxpayer must use, for the year of change, the full absorption method in computing the base year cost and current cost of a dollar value inventory pool for the beginning of such year. The taxpayer shall not be required to recompute his LIFO inventories based on the full absorption method for a taxable year beginning prior to the year of change to the full absorption method. The base cost and layers of increment previously computed shall be retained and treated as if such base cost and layers of increment had been computed under the method authorized by this section. The taxpayer shall use the year of change as the base year in applying the double extension method or other method approved by the Commissioner, instead of the earliest year for which he adopted the LIFO method for any items in the pool.

(4) *Transition to full absorption method of inventory costing from a method more inclusive of indirect production costs*—(i) *Taxpayer has not previously changed to his present method pursuant to subparagraphs (1), (2), and (3) of this paragraph.* If a taxpayer wishes to change to the full absorption method of inventory costing (as prescribed by paragraph (a) of this section) from a method of inventory costing which is more inclusive of indirect production costs and he has not previously changed to his present method by use of the special transition rules provided by subparagraphs (1), (2) and (3) of this paragraph, he may elect on Form 3115 to change to the full absorption method of inventory costing and, in so doing, take into account any resulting section 481 adjustment generally over 10 taxable years commencing with the year of transition. The Commissioner's consent to such election will be evidenced by a letter of consent to the taxpayer setting forth the values of inventory, as provided by the taxpayer determined under the full absorption method of inventory costing, except to the extent that no determination of such values is necessary under subparagraph (3)(ii)(*b*) of this paragraph, the amount of the adjustments (if any) required to be taken into account by section 481, and the treatment to be accorded such adjustments, subject to terms and conditions specified by the Commissioner to prevent distortions of income. Such election must be made within the transition period described in subparagraph (1)(ii) of this paragraph. A change pursuant to this subparagraph shall be a change initiated by the taxpayer as provided by § 1.481-1(c)(5). Thus, any of the taxpayers "pre-1954 inventory balances" will be taken into account as an adjustment under section 481.

(ii) *Taxpayer has previously changed to his present method pursuant to subparagraphs (1), (2) and (3) of this paragraph or would satisfy all the requirements of subdivision (i) of this subparagraph but fails to elect within the transition period.* If a taxpayer wishes to change to the full absorption method of inventory costing (as prescribed by paragraph (a) of this section) from a method of inventory costing which is more inclu-

Reg. § 1.471-11(e)(4)

sive of indirect production costs and he has previously changed to his present method pursuant to subparagraphs (1), (2), and (3) of this paragraph or he would satisfy the requirements of subdivision (i) of this subparagraph but he fails to elect within the transition period, he must secure the consent of the Commissioner prior to making such change. [Reg. § 1.471-11.]

☐ [T.D. 7285, 9-14-73. Amended by T.D. 8067, 12-30-89; T.D. 8131, 3-24-87 and T.D. 8482, 8-6-93.]

[Reg. § 1.472-1]

§ 1.472-1. Last-in, first-out inventories.—(a) Any taxpayer permitted or required to take inventories pursuant to the provisions of section 471, and pursuant to the provisions of §§ 1.471-1 to 1.471-9, inclusive, may elect with respect to those goods specified in his application and properly subject to inventory to compute his opening and closing inventories in accordance with the method provided by section 472, this section, and § 1.472-2. Under this last-in, first-out (LIFO) inventory method, the taxpayer is permitted to treat those goods remaining on hand at the close of the taxable year as being:

(1) Those included in the opening inventory of the taxable year, in the order of acquisition and to the extent thereof, and

(2) Those acquired during the taxable year.

The LIFO inventory method is not dependent upon the character of the business in which the taxpayer is engaged, or upon the identity or want of identity through commingling of any of the goods on hand, and may be adopted by the taxpayer as of the close of any taxable year.

(b) If the LIFO inventory method is used by a taxpayer who regularly and consistently, in a manner similar to hedging on a futures market, matches purchases with sales, then firm purchases and sales contracts (i.e., those not legally subject to cancellation by either party) entered into at fixed prices on or before the date of the inventory may be included in purchases or sales, as the case may be, for the purpose of determining the cost of goods sold and the resulting profit or loss, provided that this practice is regularly and consistently adhered to by the taxpayer and provided that, in the opinion of the Commissioner, income is clearly reflected thereby.

(c) A manufacturer or processor who has adopted the LIFO inventory method as to a class of goods may elect to have such method apply to the raw materials only (including those included in goods in process and in finished goods) expressed in terms of appropriate units. If such method is adopted, the adjustments are confined to costs of the raw material in the inventory and the cost of the raw material in goods in process and in finished goods produced by such manufacturer or processor and reflected in the inventory. The provisions of this paragraph may be illustrated by the following examples:

Example (1). Assume that the opening inventory had 10 units of raw materials, 10 units of goods in process, and 10 units of finished goods, and that the raw material cost was 6 cents a unit, the processing cost 2 cents a unit, and overhead cost 1 cent a unit. For the purposes of this example, it is assumed that the entire amount of goods in process was 50 percent processed.

OPENING INVENTORY

	Raw material	Goods in process	Finished goods
Raw material	$0.60	$0.60	$0.60
Processing cost	...	.10	.20
Overhead	...	.05	.10

In the closing inventory there are 20 units of raw material, 6 units of goods in process, and 8 units of finished goods and the costs were: Raw material 10 cents, processing cost 4 cents, and overhead 1 cent.

CLOSING INVENTORY
[Based on cost and prior to adjustment]

	Raw material	Goods in process	Finished goods
Raw material	$2.00	$0.60	$0.80
Processing costs	...	.12	.32
Overhead	...	.03	.08
Total	$2.00	$ .75	$1.20

There were 30 units of raw material in the opening inventory and 34 units in the closing inventory. The adjustment to the closing inventory would be as follows:

Methods of Accounting

See p. 20,601 for regulations not amended to reflect law changes

CLOSING INVENTORY AS ADJUSTED

	Raw material	Goods in process	Finished goods
Raw material:			
20 at 6 cents	$1.20	...	...
6 at 6 cents	...	$0.36	...
4 at 6 cents	...	...	$0.24
4 at 10 cents[1]	...	...	.40
Processing costs	...	.12	.32
Overhead	...	.03	.08
Total	$1.20	$ .51	$1.04

[1] This excess is subject to determination of price under section 472(b)(1) and § 1.472-2. If the excess falls in goods in process, the same adjustment is applicable.

The only adjustment to the closing inventory is the cost of the raw material; the processing costs and overhead cost are not changed.

Example (2). Assume that the opening inventory had 5 units of raw material, 10 units of goods in process, and 20 units of finshed goods, with the same prices as in example (1), and that the closing inventory had 20 units of raw material, 20 units of goods in process, and 10 units of finished goods, with raw material costs as in the closing inventory in example (1). The adjusted closing inventory would be as follows in so far as the raw material is concerned:

Raw material, 20 at 6 cents	$1.20
Goods in process:	
15 at 6 cents	.90
5 at 10 cents [1]	.50
Finished goods:	
None at 6 cents	.00
10 at 10 cents [1]	1.00

[1] This excess is subject to determination of price under section 472(b)(1) and § 1.472-2.

The 20 units of raw material in the raw state plus 15 units of raw material in goods in process make up the 35 units of raw material that were contained in the opening inventory.

(d) For the purposes of this section, raw material in the opening inventory must be compared with similar raw material in the closing inventory. There may be several types of raw materials, depending upon the character, quality, or price, and each type of raw material in the opening inventory must be compared with a similar type in the closing inventory.

(e) In the cotton textile industry there may be different raw materials depending upon marked differences in length of staple, in color or grade of the cotton. But where different staple lengths or grades of cotton are being used at different times in the same mill to produce the same class of goods, such differences would not necessarily require the classification into different raw materials.

(f) As to the pork packing industry a live hog is considered as being composed of various raw materials, different cuts of a hog varying markedly in price and use. Generally a hog is processed into approximately 10 primal cuts and several miscellaneous articles. However, due to similarity in price and use, these may be grouped into fewer classifications, each group being classed as one raw material.

(g) When the finished product contains two or more different raw materials as in the case of cotton and rayon mixtures, each raw material is treated separately and adjustment made accordingly.

(h) Upon written notice addressed to the Commissioner of Internal Revenue, Attention T:R, Washington 25, D.C., by the taxpayer, a taxpayer who has heretofore adopted the LIFO inventory method in respect of any goods may adopt the method authorized in this section and limit the election to the raw material including raw materials entering into goods in process and in finished goods. If this method is adopted as to any specific goods, it must be used exclusively for such goods for any prior taxable year (not closed by agreement) to which the prior election applies and for all subsequent taxable years, unless permission to change is granted by the Commissioner.

(i) The election may also be limited to that phase in the manufacturing process where a product is produced that is recognized generally as a salable product as, for example, in the textile industry where one phase of the process is the production of yarn. Since yarn is generally recognized as a salable product, the election may be

Reg. § 1.472-1(i)

limited to that portion of the process when yarn is produced. In the case of copper and brass processors, the election may be limited to the production of bars, plates, sheets, etc., although these may be further processed into other products.

(j) The election may also apply to any one raw material, when two or more raw materials enter into the composition of the finished product; for example, in the case of cotton and rayon yarn, the taxpayer may elect to inventory the cotton only. However, a taxpayer who has previously made an election to use the LIFO inventory may not later elect to exclude any raw materials that were covered by such previous election.

(k) If a taxpayer using the retail method of pricing inventories, authorized by § 1.471-8, elects to use in connection therewith the LIFO inventory method authorized by section 472 and this section, the apparent cost of the goods on hand at the end of the year, determined pursuant to § 1.471-8, shall be adjusted to the extent of price changes therein taking place after the close of the preceding taxable year. The amount of any apparent inventory increase or decrease to be eliminated in this adjustment shall be determined by reference to acceptable price indexes established to the satisfaction of the Commissioner. Price indexes prepared by the United States Bureau of Labor Statistics which are applicable to the goods in question will be considered acceptable to the Commissioner. Price indexes which are based upon inadequate records, or which are not subject to complete and detailed audit within the Internal Revenue Service, will not be approved.

(l) If a taxpayer uses consistently the so-called "dollar-value" method of pricing inventories, or any other method of computation established to the satisfaction of the Commissioner as reasonably adaptable to the purpose and intent of section 472 and this section, and if such taxpayer elects under section 472 to use the LIFO inventory method authorized by such section, the taxpayer's opening and closing inventories shall be determined under section 472 by the use of the appropriate adaptation. See § 1.472-8 for rules relating to the use of the dollar-value method. [Reg. § 1.472-1.]

☐ [T.D. 6336, 12-1-58. Amended by T.D. 6539, 1-19-61.]

[Reg. § 1.472-2]

§ 1.472-2. Requirements incident to adoption and use of LIFO inventory method.—Except as otherwise provided in § 1.472-1 with respect to raw material computations, with respect to retail inventory computations, and with respect to other methods of computation established to the satisfaction of the Commissioner as reasonably adapted to the purpose and intent of section 472, and in § 1.472-8 with respect to the "dollar-value" method, the adoption and use of the LIFO inventory method is subject to the following requirements:

(a) The taxpayer shall file an application to use such method specifying with particularity the goods to which it is to be applied.

(b) The inventory shall be taken at cost regardless of market value.

(c) Goods of the specified type included in the opening inventory of the taxable year for which the method is first used shall be considered as having been acquired at the same time and at a unit cost equal to the actual cost of the aggregate divided by the number of units on hand. The actual cost of the aggregate shall be determined pursuant to the inventory method employed by the taxpayer under the regulations applicable to the prior taxable year with the exception that restoration shall be made with respect to any write-down to market values resulting from the pricing of former inventories.

(d) Goods of the specified type on hand as of the close of the taxable year in excess of what were on hand as of the beginning of the taxable year shall be included in the closing inventory, regardless of identification with specific invoices and regardless of specific cost accounting records, at costs determined pursuant to the provisions of subparagraph (1) or (2) of this paragraph, dependent upon the character of the transactions in which the taxpayer is engaged:

(1)(i) In the case of a taxpayer engaged in the purchase and sale of merchandise, such as a retail grocer or druggist, or engaged in the initial production of merchandise and its sale without processing, such as a miner selling his ore output without smelting or refining, such costs shall be determined—

(*a*) By reference to the actual cost of the goods most recently purchased or produced;

(*b*) By reference to the actual cost of the goods purchased or produced during the taxable year in the order of acquisition;

(*c*) By application of an average unit cost equal to the aggregate cost of all of the goods purchased or produced throughout the taxable year divided by the total number of units so purchased or produced, the goods reflected in such inventory increase being considered for the purposes of section 472 as having been acquired all at the same time; or

Reg. § 1.472-2(a)

Methods of Accounting

See p. 20,601 for regulations not amended to reflect law changes

(d) Pursuant to any other proper method which, in the opinion of the Commissioner, clearly reflects income.

(ii) Whichever of the several methods of valuing the inventory increase is adopted by the taxpayer and approved by the Commissioner shall be consistently adhered to in all subsequent taxable years so long as the LIFO inventory method is used by the taxpayer.

(iii) The application of subdivisions (i) and (ii) of this subparagraph may be illustrated by the following examples:

Example (1). Suppose that the taxpayer adopts the LIFO inventory method for the taxable year 1957 with an opening inventory of 10 units at 10 cents per unit, that it makes 1957 purchases of 10 units as follows:

January	1 at $0.11 =	$0.11
April	2 at .12 =	.24
July	3 at .13 =	.39
October	4 at .14 =	.56
Totals	10	$1.30

and that is has a 1957 closing inventory of 15 units. This closing inventory, depending upon the taxpayer's method of valuing inventory increases, will be computed as follows:

(a) Most recent purchases—

10 at $0.10		$1.00
4 at .14	(October)	.56
1 at .13	(July)	.13
Totals 15		$1.69

or

(b) In order of acquisition—

10 at $0.10		$1.00
1 at .11	(January)	.11
2 at .12	(April)	.24
2 at .13	(July)	.26
Totals 15		$1.61

or

(c) At an annual average—

10 at $0.10		$1.00
5 at .13	(130/10)	.65
Totals 15		$1.65

Example (2). Suppose that the taxpayer's closing inventory for 1958, the year following that involved in example (1) of this subdivision, reflects an inventory decrease for the year, and not an increase; suppose that there is, accordingly, a 1958 closing inventory of 13 units. Inasmuch as the decreased closing inventory will be determined wholly by reference to the 15 units reflected in the opening inventory for the year, and will be taken "in the order of acquisition" pursuant to section 472(b)(1), and inasmuch as the character of the taxpayer's opening inventory for 1958 will be dependent upon its method of valuing its 5-unit inventory increase for 1957, the closing inventory for 1958 will be computed as follows:

(a) In case the increase for 1957 was taken by reference to the most recent purchases—

10 at $0.10	(from 1956)	$1.00
1 at .13	(July 1957)	.13
2 at .14	(October 1957)	.28
Totals 13		$1.41

or

(b) In case the increase for 1957 was taken in the order of acquisition—

10 at $0.10	(from 1956)	$1.00
1 at .11	(January 1957)	.11
	(April 1957)	
2 at .12		.24
Totals 13		$1.35

or

(c) In case the increase for 1957 was taken on the basis of an average—

10 at $0.10	(from 1956)	$1.00
3 at .13	(from 1957)	.39
Totals 13		$1.39

(2) In the case of a taxpayer engaged in manufacturing, fabricating, processing, or otherwise producing merchandise, such costs shall be determined:

(i) In the case of raw materials purchased or initially produced by the taxpayer, in the manner elected by the taxpayer under subparagraph (1) of this paragraph to the same extent as if the taxpayer were engaged in purchase and sale transactions; and

(ii) In the case of goods in process, regardless of the stage to which the manufacture, fabricating, or processing may have advanced, and in the case of finished goods, pursuant to any proper method which, in the opinion of the Commissioner, clearly reflects income.

(e) *LIFO conformity requirement* —(1) *In general.* The taxpayer must establish to the satisfaction of the Commissioner that the taxpayer, in ascertaining the income, profit, or loss for the taxable year for which the LIFO inventory method is first used, or for any subsequent taxable year, for credit purposes or for purposes of reports to shareholders, partners, or other proprietors, or to beneficiaries, has not used any inventory method other than that referred to in § 1.472-1 or

Reg. § 1.472-2(e)(1)

at variance with the requirement referred to in § 1.472-2(c). See paragraph (e)(2) of this section for rules relating to the meaning of the term "taxable year" as used in this paragraph. The following are not considered at variance with the requirement of this paragraph:

(i) The taxpayer's use of an inventory method other than LIFO for purposes of ascertaining information reported as a supplement to or explanation of the taxpayer's primary presentation of the taxpayer's income, profit, or loss for a taxable year in credit statements or financial reports (including preliminary and unaudited financial reports). See paragraph (e)(3) of this section for rules relating to the reporting of supplemental and explanatory information ascertained by the use of an inventory method other than LIFO.

(ii) The taxpayer's use of an inventory method other than LIFO to ascertain the value of the taxpayer's inventory of goods on hand for purposes of reporting the value of such inventories as assets. See paragraph (e)(4) of this section for rules relating to such disclosures.

(iii) The taxpayer's use of an inventory method other than LIFO for purposes of ascertaining information reported in internal management reports. See paragraph (e)(5) of this section for rules relating to such reports.

(iv) The taxpayer's use of an inventory method other than LIFO for purposes of issuing reports or credit statements covering a period of operations that is less than the whole of a taxable year for which the LIFO method is used for Federal income tax purposes. See paragraph (e)(6) of this section for rules relating to series of interim reports.

(v) The taxpayer's use of the lower of LIFO cost or market method to value LIFO inventories for purposes of financial reports and credit statements. However, except as provided in paragraph (e)(7) of this section, a taxpayer may not use market value in lieu of cost to value inventories for purposes of financial reports or credit statements.

(vi) The taxpayer's use of a costing method or accounting method to ascertain income, profit, or loss for credit purposes or for purposes of financial reports if such costing method or accounting method is neither inconsistent with the inventory method referred to in § 1.472-1 nor at variance with the requirement referred to in § 1.472-2(c), regardless of whether such costing method or accounting method is used by the taxpayer for Federal income tax purposes. See paragraph (e)(8) of this section for examples of such costing methods and accounting methods.

(vii) For credit purposes or for purposes of financial reports, the taxpayer's treatment of inventories, after such inventories have been acquired in a transaction to which section 351 applies from a transferor that used the LIFO method with respect to such inventories, as if such inventories had the same acquisition dates and costs as in the hands of the transferor.

(viii) For credit purposes or for purposes of financial reports relating to a taxable year, the taxpayer's determination of income, profit, or loss for the taxable year by valuing inventories in accordance with the procedures described in section 472(b)(1) and (3), notwithstanding that such valuation differs from the valuation of inventories for Federal income tax purposes because the taxpayer either—

(A) Adopted such procedures for credit or financial reporting purposes beginning with an accounting period other than the taxable year for which the LIFO method was first used by the taxpayer for Federal income tax purposes, or

(B) With respect to such inventories treated a business combination for credit or financial reporting purposes in a manner different from the treatment of the business combination for Federal income tax purposes.

(2) *One-year periods other than a taxable year.* The rules of this paragraph relating to the determination of income, profit, or loss for a taxable year and credit statements or financial reports that cover a taxable year also apply to the determination of income, profit, or loss for a one-year period other than a taxable year and credit statements or financial reports that cover a one-year period other than a taxable year, but only if the one-year period both begins and ends in a taxable year or years for which the taxpayer uses the LIFO method for Federal income tax purposes. For example, the requirements of paragraph (e)(1) of this section apply to a taxpayer's determination of income for purposes of a credit statement that covers a 52-week fiscal year beginning and ending in a taxable year for which the taxpayer uses the LIFO method for Federal income tax purposes. Similarly, in the case of a calendar year taxpayer, the requirements of paragraph (e)(1) of this section apply to the taxpayer's determination of income for purposes of a credit statement that covers the period October 1, 1981, through September 30, 1982, if the taxpayer uses the LIFO method for Federal income tax purposes in taxable years 1981 and 1982. However, the Commissioner will waive any violation of the requirements of this paragraph in the case of a credit statement or financial report that covers a

Reg. § 1.472-2(e)(2)

one-year period other than a taxable year if the report was issued before January 22, 1981.

(3) *Supplemental and explanatory information*—(i) *Face of the income statement.* Information reported on the face of a taxpayer's financial income statement for a taxable year is not considered a supplement to or explanation of the taxpayer's primary presentation of the taxpayer's income, profit, or loss for the taxable year in credit statements or financial reports. For purposes of paragraph (e)(3) of this section, the face of an income statement does not include notes to the income statement presented on the same page as the income statement, but only if all notes of the financial income statement are presented together.

(ii) *Notes to the income statement.* Information reported in notes to a taxpayer's financial income statement is considered a supplement to or explanation of the taxpayer's primary presentation of income, profit, or loss for the period covered by the income statement if all notes to the financial income statement are presented together and if they accompany the income statement in a single report. If notes to an income statement are issued in a report that does not include the income statement, the question of whether the information reported therein is supplemental or explanatory is determined under the rules in paragraph (e)(3)(iv) of this section.

(iii) *Appendices and supplements to the income statement.* Information reported in an appendix or supplement to a taxpayer's financial income statement is considered a supplement to or explanation of the taxpayer's primary presentation of income, profit, or loss for the period covered by the income statement if the appendix or supplement accompanies the income statement in a single report and the information reported in the appendix or supplement is clearly identified as a supplement to or explanation of the taxpayer's primary presentation of income, profit, or loss as reported on the face of the taxpayer's income statement. If an appendix or supplement to an income statement is issued in a report that does not include the income statement, the question of whether the information reported therein is supplemental or explanatory is determined under the rules in paragraph (e)(3)(iv) of this section. For purposes of paragraph (e)(3)(iii) of this section, an appendix or supplement to an income statement includes written statements, schedules, and reports that are labelled supplements or appendices to the income statement. However, sections of an annual report such as those labelled "President's Letter", "Management's Analysis", "Statement of Changes in Financial Position", "Summary of Key Figures", and similar sections are reports described in paragraph (e)(3)(iv) of this section and are not considered "supplements or appendices to an income statement" within the meaning of paragraph (e)(3)(iii) of this section, regardless of whether such sections are also labelled as supplements or appendices. For purposes of paragraph (e)(3)(iii) of this section, information is considered to be clearly identified as a supplement to or explanation of the taxpayer's primary presentation of income, profit, or loss as reported on the face of the taxpayer's income statement if the information either—

(A) Is reported in an appendix or supplement that contains a general statement identifying all such supplemental or explanatory information;

(B) Is identified specifically as supplemental or explanatory by a statement immediately preceding or following the disclosure of the information;

(C) Is disclosed in the context of making a comparison to corresponding information disclosed both on the face of the taxpayer's income statement and in the supplement or appendix; or

(D) Is a disclosure of the effect on an item reported on the face of the taxpayer's income statement of having used the LIFO method.

For example, a restatement of cost of goods sold based on an inventory method other than LIFO is considered to be clearly identified as supplemental or explanatory information if the supplement or appendix containing the restatement contains a general statement that all information based on such inventory method is reported in the appendix or supplement as a supplement to or explanation of the taxpayer's primary presentation of income, profit, or loss as reported on the face of the taxpayer's income statement.

(iv) *Other reports; in general.* The rules of paragraph (e)(3)(iv), (v), and (vi) of this section apply to the following types of reports: news releases; letters to shareholders, partners, or other proprietors or beneficiaries; oral statements at press conferences, shareholders' meetings or securities analysts' meetings; sections of an annual report such as those labelled "President's Letter", "Management's Analysis", "Statement of Changes in Financial Position", "Summary of Key Figures", and similar sections; and reports other than a taxpayer's income statement or accompanying notes, appendices, or supplements. Information disclosed in such a report is considered a supplement to or explanation of the taxpayer's primary presentation of income, profit, or loss for the period covered by an income state-

Reg. § 1.472-2(e)(3)

ment if the supplemental or explanatory information is clearly identified as a supplement to or explanation of the taxpayer's primary presentation of income, profit, or loss as reported on the face of the taxpayer's income statement and the specific item of information being explained or supplemented, such as the cost of goods sold, net income, or earnings per share ascertained using the LIFO method, is also reported in the other report.

(v) *Other reports; disclosure of non-LIFO income.* For purposes of paragraph (e)(3)(iv) of this section, supplemental or explanatory information is considered to have been clearly identified as such if it would be considered to have been clearly identified as such under the rules of paragraph (e)(3)(iii) of this section, relating to information reported in supplements or appendices to an income statement. For example, if at a securities analysts' meeting the following question is asked, "What would the reported earnings per share for the year have been if the FIFO method had been used to value inventories?", it would be permissible to respond "Reported earnings per share for the year were $6.00. If the company had used the FIFO method to value inventories this year and had computed earnings based upon the following assumptions, earnings per share would have been $8.20. FIFO earnings are based on the following assumptions:

"(A) The use of the same effective tax rate as used in computing LIFO earnings, and

"(B) All other conditions and assumptions remain the same, including—

"(*1*) The use of the LIFO method for Federal income tax purposes and

"(*2*) The investment of the tax savings resulting from such use of the LIFO method, the income from which is included in both LIFO and FIFO earnings."

(vi) *Other reports; disclosure of effect on income.* For purposes of paragraph (e)(3)(iv) of this section, if the only supplement to or explanation of a specific item is the effect on the item of having used LIFO instead of a method other than LIFO to value inventories, it is not necessary to also report the specific item. For example, if at a shareholders' meeting the question is asked, "What was the effect on reported earnings per share of not having used FIFO to value inventories?", it would be permissible to respond "If earnings would have been computed on the basis of the following assumptions, the use of LIFO instead of FIFO to value inventories would have decreased reported earnings per share by $2.20. FIFO earnings are based on the following assumptions:

"(A) The use of the same effective tax rate as used in computing LIFO earnings, and

"(B) All other conditions and assumptions remain the same, including—

"(*1*) The use of the LIFO method for Federal income tax purposes and

"(*2*) The investment of the tax savings resulting from such use of the LIFO method, the income from which is included in both LIFO and FIFO earnings."

(4) *Inventory asset value disclosures.* Under paragraph (e)(1)(ii) of this section, the use of an inventory method other than LIFO to ascertain the value of the taxpayer's inventories for purposes of reporting the value of the inventories as assets is not considered the ascertainment of income, profit, or loss and therefore is not considered at variance with the requirement of paragraph (e)(1) of this section. Therefore, a taxpayer may disclose the value of inventories on a balance sheet using a method other than LIFO to identify the inventories, and such a disclosure will not be considered at variance with the requirement of paragraph (e)(1) of this section. However, the disclosure of income, profit, or loss for a taxable year on a balance sheet issued to creditors, shareholders, partners, other proprietors, or beneficiaries is considered at variance with the requirement of paragraph (e)(1) of this section if such income information is ascertained using an inventory method other than LIFO and such income information is for a taxable year for which the LIFO method is used for Federal income tax purposes. Therefore, a balance sheet that discloses the net worth of a taxpayer, determined as if income had been ascertained using an inventory method other than LIFO, may be at variance with the requirement of paragraph (e)(1) of this section if the disclosure of net worth is made in a manner that also discloses income, profit, or loss for a taxable year. However, a disclosure of income, profit, or loss using an inventory method other than LIFO is not considered at variance with the requirement of paragraph (e)(1) of this section if the disclosure is made in the form of either a footnote to the balance sheet or a parenthetical disclosure on the face of the balance sheet. In addition, an income disclosure is not considered at variance with the requirement of paragraph (e)(1) of this section if the disclosure is made on the face of a supplemental balance sheet labelled as a supplement to the taxpayer's primary presentation of financial position, but only if, consistent with the rules of paragraph (e)(3) of this section, such a disclosure is clearly identified as a supplement to or explanation of the taxpayer's primary presentation of financial income

Reg. § 1.472-2(e)(4)

as reported on the face of the taxpayer's income statement.

(5) *Internal management reports.* [Reserved]

(6) *Series of interim reports.* For purposes of paragraph (e)(1)(iv) of this section, a series of credit statements or financial reports is considered a single statement or report covering a period of operations if the statements or reports in the series are prepared using a single inventory method and can be combined to disclose the income, profit, or loss for the period. However, the Commissioner will waive any violation of the requirement of this paragraph in the case of a series of interim reports issued before February 6, 1978, that cover a taxable year, or a series of interim reports issued before January 22, 1981, that cover a one-year period other than a taxable year.

(7) *Market value.* The Commissioner will waive any violation of the requirement of this paragraph in the case of a taxpayer's use of market value in lieu of cost for a credit statement or financial report issued before January 22, 1981. However, the special rule of this (7) applies only to a taxpayer's use of market value in lieu of cost and does not apply to the use of a method of valuation such as market value in lieu of cost but not more than FIFO cost.

(8) *Use of different methods.* The following are examples of costing methods and accounting methods that are neither inconsistent with the inventory method referred to in § 1.472-1 nor at variance with the requirement of § 1.472-2(c) and which, under paragraph (e)(1)(vi) of this section, may be used to ascertain income, profit, or loss for credit purposes or for purposes of financial reports regardless of whether such method is also used by the taxpayer for Federal income tax purposes:

(i) Any method relating to the determination of which costs are includible in the computation of the cost of inventory under the full absorption inventory method.

(ii) Any method of establishing pools for inventory under the dollar-value LIFO inventory method.

(iii) Any method of determining the LIFO value of a dollar-value inventory pool, such as the double-extension method, the index method, and the link chain method.

(iv) Any method of determining or selecting a price index to be used with the index or link chain method of valuing inventory pools under the dollar-value LIFO inventory method.

(v) Any method permitted under § 1.472-8 for determining the current-year cost of closing inventory for purposes of using the dollar-value LIFO inventory method.

(vi) Any method permitted under § 1.472-2(d) for determining the cost of goods in excess of goods on hand at the beginning of the year for purposes of using a LIFO method other than the dollar-value LIFO method.

(vii) Any method relating to the classification of an item as inventory or a capital asset.

(viii) The use of an accounting period other than the period used for Federal income tax purposes.

(ix) The use of cost estimates.

(x) The use of actual cost of cut timber or the cost determined under section 631(a).

(xi) The use of inventory costs unreduced by any adjustment required by the application of section 108 and section 1017, relating to discharge of indebtedness.

(xii) The determination of the time when sales or purchases are accrued.

(xiii) The use of a method to allocate basis in the case of a business combination other than the method used for Federal income tax purposes.

(xiv) The treatment of transfers of inventory between affiliated corporations in a manner different from that required by § 1.1502-13.

(9) *Reconciliation of LIFO inventory values.* A taxpayer may be required to reconcile differences between the value of inventories maintained for credit or financial reporting purposes and for Federal income tax purposes in order to show that the taxpayer has satisfied the requirements of this paragraph.

(f) Goods of the specified type on hand as of the close of the taxable year preceding the taxable year for which this inventory method is first used shall be included in the taxpayer's closing inventory for such preceding taxable year at cost determined in the manner prescribed in paragraph (c) of this section.

(g) The LIFO inventory method, once adopted by the taxpayer with the approval of the Commissioner, shall be adhered to in all subsequent taxable years unless—

(1) A change to a different method is approved by the Commissioner; or

(2) The Commissioner determines that the taxpayer, in ascertaining income, profit, or loss for the whole of any taxable year subsequent to his adoption of the LIFO inventory method, for credit purposes or for the purpose of reports to shareholders, partners, or other proprietors, or to beneficiaries, has used any inventory method at variance with that referred to in § 1.472-1 and requires of the taxpayer a change to a different

Reg. § 1.472-2(g)(2)

method for such subsequent taxable year or any taxable year thereafter.

(h) The records and accounts employed by the taxpayer in keeping his books shall be maintained in conformity with the inventory method referred to in § 1.472-1; and such supplemental and detailed inventory records shall be maintained as will enable the district director readily to verify the taxpayer's inventory computations as well as his compliance with the requirements of section 472 and §§ 1.472-1 through 1.472-7.

(i) Where the taxpayer is engaged in more than one trade or business, the Commissioner may require that if the LIFO method of valuing inventories is used with respect to goods in one trade or business the same method shall also be used with respect to similar goods in the other trades or businesses if, in the opinion of the Commissioner, the use of such method with respect to such other goods is essential to a clear reflection of income. [Reg. § 1.472-2.]

☐ [T.D. 6336, 12-1-58. Amended by T.D. 6539, 1-19-61 and T.D. 7756, 1-16-81.]

[Reg. § 1.472-3]

§ 1.472-3. Time and manner of making election.—(a) The LIFO inventory method may be adopted and used only if the taxpayer files with his income tax return for the taxable year as of the close of which the method is first to be used a statement of his election to use such inventory method. The statement shall be made on Form 970 pursuant to the instructions printed with respect thereto and to the requirements of this section, or in such other manner as may be acceptable to the Commissioner. Such statement shall be accompanied by an analysis of all inventories of the taxpayer as of the beginning and as of the end of the taxable year for which the LIFO inventory method is proposed first to be used, and also as of the beginning of the prior taxable year. In the case of a manufacturer, this analysis shall show in detail the manner in which costs are computed with respect to raw materials, goods in process, and finished goods, segregating the products (whether in process or finished goods) into natural groups on the basis of either (1) similarity in factory processes through which they pass, or (2) similarity of raw materials used, or (3) similarity in style, shape, or use of finished products. Each group of products shall be clearly described.

(b) The taxpayer shall submit for the consideration of the Commissioner in connection with the taxpayer's adoption or use of the LIFO inventory method such other detailed information with respect to his business or accounting system as may be at any time requested by the Commissioner.

(c) As a condition to the taxpayer's use of the LIFO inventory method, the Commissioner may require that the method be used with respect to goods other than those specified in the taxpayer's statement of election if, in the opinion of the Commissioner, the use of such method with respect to such other goods is essential to a clear reflection of income.

(d) Whether or not the taxpayer's application for the adoption and use of the LIFO inventory method should be approved, and whether or not such method, once adopted, may be continued, and the propriety of all computations incidental to the use of such method, will be determined by the Commissioner in connection with the examination of the taxpayer's income tax returns. [Reg. § 1.472-3.]

☐ [T.D. 6336, 12-1-58. Amended by T.D. 7295, 12-11-73.]

[Reg. § 1.472-4]

§ 1.472-4. Adjustments to be made by taxpayer.—A taxpayer may not change to the LIFO method of taking inventories unless, at the time he files his application for the adoption of such method, he agrees to such adjustments incident to the change to or from such method, or incident to the use of such method, in the inventories of prior taxable years or otherwise, as the district director upon the examination of the taxpayer's returns may deem necessary in order that the true income of the taxpayer will be clearly reflected for the years involved. [Reg. § 1.472-4.]

☐ [T.D. 6336, 12-1-58.]

[Reg. § 1.472-5]

§ 1.472-5. Revocation of election.—An election made to adopt and use the LIFO inventory method is irrevocable, and the method once adopted shall be used in all subsequent taxable years, unless the use of another method is required by the Commissioner, or authorized by him pursuant to a written application therefor filed as provided in paragraph (e) of § 1.446-1. [Reg. § 1.472-5.]

☐ [T.D. 6336, 12-1-58.]

[Reg. § 1.472-6]

§ 1.472-6. Change from LIFO inventory method.—If the taxpayer is granted permission by the Commissioner to discontinue the use of LIFO method of taking inventories, and thereafter to use some other method, or if the taxpayer is required by the Commissioner to discontinue the use of the LIFO method by reason of the taxpayer's failure to conform to the requirements detailed in § 1.472-2, the inventory of the specified goods for the first taxable year affected by the change and for each taxable year thereafter shall be taken—

(a) In conformity with the method used by the taxpayer under section 471 in inventorying goods not included in his LIFO inventory computations; or

(b) If the LIFO inventory method was used by the taxpayer with respect to all of his goods subject to inventory, then in conformity with the inventory method used by the taxpayer prior to his adoption of the LIFO inventory method; or

(c) If the taxpayer had not used inventories prior to his adoption of the LIFO inventory method and had no goods currently subject to inventory by a method other than the LIFO inventory method, then in conformity with such inventory method as may be selected by the taxpayer and approved by the Commissioner as resulting in a clear reflection of income; or

(d) In any event, in conformity with any inventory method to which the taxpayer may change pursuant to application approved by the Commissioner. [Reg. § 1.472-6.]

☐ [*T.D.* 6336, 12-1-58.]

[Reg. § 1.472-7]

§ 1.472-7. Inventories of acquiring corporations.—For additional rules in the case of certain corporate acquisitions specified in section 381(a), see section 381(c)(5) and the regulations thereunder. [Reg. § 1.472-7.]

☐ [*T.D.* 6336, 12-1-58.]

[Reg. § 1.472-8]

§ 1.472-8. Dollar-value method of pricing LIFO inventories.—(a) *Election to use dollar-value method.* Any taxpayer may elect to determine the cost of his LIFO inventories under the so-called "dollar-value" LIFO method, provided such method is used consistently and clearly reflects the income of the taxpayer in accordance with the rules of this section. The dollar-value method of valuing LIFO inventories is a method of determining cost by using "base-year" cost expressed in terms of total dollars rather than the quantity and price of specific goods as the unit of measurement. Under such method the goods contained in the inventory are grouped into a pool or pools as described in paragraphs (b) and (c) of this section. The term "base-year cost" is the aggregate of the cost (determined as of the beginning of the taxable year for which the LIFO method is first adopted, i.e., the base date) of all items in a pool. The taxable year for which the LIFO method is first adopted with respect to any item in the pool is the "base year" for that pool, except as provided in paragraph (g)(3) of this section.

Liquidations and increments of items contained in the pool shall be reflected only in terms of a net liquidation or increment for the pool as a whole. Fluctuations may occur in quantities of various items within the pool, new items which properly fall within the pool may be added, and old items may disappear from the pool, all without necessarily effecting a change in the dollar value of the pool as a whole. An increment in the LIFO inventory occurs when the end of the year inventory for any pool expressed in terms of base-year cost is in excess of the beginning of the year inventory for that pool expressed in terms of base-year cost. In determining the inventory value for a pool, the increment, if any, is adjusted for changing unit costs or values by reference to a percentage, relative to base-year-cost, determined for the pool as a whole. See paragraph (e) of this section. See also paragraph (f) of this section for rules relating to the change to the dollar-value LIFO method from another LIFO method.

(b) *Principles for establishing pools of manufacturers and processors*—(1) *Natural business unit pools.* A pool shall consist of all items entering into the entire inventory investment for a natural business unit of a business enterprise, unless the taxpayer elects to use the multiple pooling method provided in subparagraph (3) of this paragraph. Thus, if a business enterprise is composed of only one natural business unit, one pool shall be used for all of its inventories, including raw materials, goods in process, and finished goods. If, however, a business enterprise is actually composed of more than one natural business unit, more than one pool is required. Where similar types of goods are inventoried in two or more natural business units of the taxpayer, the Commissioner may apportion or allocate such goods among the various natural business units, if he determines that such apportionment or allocation is necessary in order to clearly reflect the income of such taxpayer. Where a manufacturer or processor is also engaged in the wholesaling or retailing of goods purchased from others, any pooling of the LIFO inventory of such purchased goods for the wholesaling or retailing operations shall be determined in accordance with the rules of paragraph (c) of this section.

(2) *Definition of natural business unit.* (i) Whether an enterprise is composed of more than one natural business unit is a matter of fact to be determined from all the circumstances. The natural business divisions adopted by the taxpayer for internal management purposes, the existence of separate and distinct production facilities and processes, and the maintenance of separate profit and loss records with respect to separate operations are important considerations in determining

Reg. § 1.472-8(b)(2)

what is a business unit, unless such divisions, facilities, or accounting records are set up merely because of differences in geographical location. In the case of a manufacturer or processor, a natural business unit ordinarily consists of the entire productive activity of the enterprise within one product line or within two or more related product lines including (to the extent engaged in by the enterprise) the obtaining of materials, the processing of materials, and the selling of manufactured or processed goods. Thus, in the case of a manufacturer or processor, the maintenance and operation of a raw material warehouse does not generally constitute, of itself, a natural business unit. If the taxpayer maintains and operates a supplier unit the production of which is both sold to others and transferred to a different unit of the taxpayer to be used as a component part of another product, the supplier unit will ordinarily constitute a separate and distinct natural business unit. Ordinarily, a processing plant would not in itself be considered a natural business unit if the production of the plant, although saleable at this stage, is not sold to others, but is transferred to another plant of the enterprise, not operated as a separate division, for further processing or incorporation into another product. On the other hand, if the production of a manufacturing or processing plant is transferred to a separate and distinct division of the taxpayer, which constitutes a natural business unit, the supplier unit itself will ordinarily be considered a natural business unit. However, the mere fact that a portion of the production of a manufacturing or processing plant may be sold to others at a certain stage of processing with the remainder of the production being further processed or incorporated into another product will not of itself be determinative that the activities devoted to the production of the portion sold constitute a separate business unit. Where a manufacturer or processor is also engaged in the wholesaling or retailing of goods purchased from others, the wholesaling or retailing operations with respect to such purchased goods shall not be considered a part of any manufacturing or processing unit.

(ii) The rules of this subparagraph may be illustrated by the following examples:

Example (1). A corporation manufactures, in one division, automatic clothes washers and driers of both commercial and domestic grade as well as electric ranges, mangles, and dishwashers. The corporation manufactures, in another division, radios and television sets. The manufacturing facilities and processes used in manufacturing the radios and television sets are distinct from those used in manufacturing the automatic clothes washers, etc. Under these circumstances, the enterprise would consist of two business units and two pools would be appropriate, one consisting of all of the LIFO inventories entering into the manufacture of clothes washers and driers, electric ranges, mangles, and dishwashers and the other consisting of all of the LIFO inventories entering into the production of radio and television sets.

Example (2). A taxpayer produces plastics in one of its plants. Substantial amounts of the production are sold as plastics. The remainder of the production is shipped to a second plant of the taxpayer for the production of plastic toys which are sold to customers. The taxpayer operates his plastics plant and toy plant as separate divisions. Because of the different product lines and the separate divisions the taxpayer has two natural business units.

Example (3). A taxpayer is engaged in the manufacture of paper. At one stage of processing, uncoated paper is produced. Substantial amounts of uncoated paper are sold at this stage of processing. The remainder of the uncoated paper is transferred to the taxpayer's finishing mill where coated paper is produced and sold. This taxpayer has only one natural business unit since coated and uncoated paper are within the same product line.

(3) *Multiple pools*—(i) *Principles for establishing multiple pools.* (a) A taxpayer may elect to establish multiple pools for inventory items which are not within a natural business unit as to which the taxpayer has adopted the natural business unit method of pooling as provided in subparagraph (1) of this paragraph. Each such pool shall ordinarily consist of a group of inventory items which are substantially similar. In determining whether such similarity exists, consideration shall be given to all the facts and circumstances. The formulation of detailed rules for selection of pools applicable to all taxpayers is not feasible. Important considerations to be taken into account include, for example, whether there is substantial similarity in the types of raw materials used or in the processing operations applied; whether the raw materials used are readily interchangeable; whether there is similarity in the use of the products; whether the groupings are consistently followed for purposes of internal accounting and management; and whether the groupings follow customary business practice in the taxpayer's industry. The selection of pools in each case must also take into consideration such factors as the nature of the inventory items subject to the dollar-value LIFO method and the significance of such items to the taxpayer's business operations. Where similar types of goods are inventoried in

Reg. § 1.472-8(b)(3)

natural business units and multiple pools of the taxpayer, the Commissioner may apportion or allocate such goods among the natural business units and the multiple pools, if he determines that such apportionment or allocation is necessary in order to clearly reflect the income of the taxpayer.

(*b*) Raw materials which are substantially similar shall be pooled together in accordance with the principles of this subparagraph. However, inventories of raw or unprocessed materials of an unlike nature may not be placed into one pool, even though such materials become part of otherwise identical finished products.

(*c*) Finished goods and goods-in-process in the inventory shall be placed into pools classified by major classes or types of goods. The same class or type of finished goods and goods-in-process shall ordinarily be included in the same pool. Where the material content of a class of finished goods and goods-in-process included in a pool has been changed, for example, to conform with current trends in an industry, a separate pool of finished goods and goods-in-process will not ordinarily be required unless the change in material content results in a substantial change in the finished goods.

(*d*) The requirement that pools be established by major types of materials or major classes of goods is not to be construed so as to preclude the establishment of a miscellaneous pool. Since a taxpayer may elect the dollar-value LIFO method with respect to all or any designated goods in his inventory, there may be a number of such inventory items covered in the election. A miscellaneous pool shall consist only of items which are relatively insignificant in dollar value by comparison with other inventory items in the particular trade or business and which are not properly includible as part of another pool.

(ii) *Raw materials content pools.* The dollar-value method of pricing LIFO inventories may be used in conjunction with the raw materials content method authorized in § 1.472-1. Raw materials (including the raw material content of finished goods and goods-in-process) which are substantially similar shall be pooled together in accordance with the principles of subdivision (i) of this subparagraph. However, inventories of materials of an unlike nature may not be placed into one pool, even though such materials become part of otherwise identical finished products.

(4) *IPIC method pools.* A manufacturer or processor that elects to use the inventory price index computation method described in paragraph (e)(3) of this section (IPIC method) for a trade or business may elect to establish dollar-value pools for those items accounted for using the IPIC method based on the 2-digit commodity codes (i.e., major commodity groups) in Table 6 (Producer price indexes and percent changes for commodity groupings and individual items, not seasonally adjusted) of the "PPI Detailed Report" published monthly by the United States Bureau of Labor Statistics (available from New Orders, Superintendent of Documents, P.O. Box 371954, Pittsburgh, PA 15250-7954). A taxpayer electing to establish dollar-value pools under this paragraph (b)(4) may combine IPIC pools that comprise less than 5 percent of the total current-year cost of all dollar-value pools to form a single miscellaneous IPIC pool. A taxpayer electing to establish dollar-value pools under this paragraph (b)(4) may combine a miscellaneous IPIC pool that comprises less than 5 percent of the total current-year cost of all dollar-value pools with the largest IPIC pool. Each of these 5 percent rules is a method of accounting. A taxpayer may not change to, or cease using, either 5 percent rule without obtaining the Commissioner's prior consent. Whether a specific IPIC pool or the miscellaneous IPIC pool satisfies the applicable 5 percent rule must be determined in the year of adoption or year of change (whichever is applicable) and redetermined every third taxable year. Any change in pooling required or permitted as a result of a 5 percent rule is a change in method of accounting. A taxpayer must secure the consent of the Commissioner pursuant to § 1.446-1(e) before combining or separating pools and must combine or separate its IPIC pools in accordance with paragraph (g)(2) of this section.

(*c*) *Principles for establishing pools for wholesalers, retailers, etc.*—(1) *In general.* Items of inventory in the hands of wholesalers, retailers, jobbers, and distributors shall be placed into pools by major lines, types, or classes of goods. In determining such groupings, customary business classifications of the particular trade in which the taxpayer is engaged is an important consideration. An example of such customary business classification is the department in the department store. In such case, practices are relatively uniform throughout the trade, and departmental grouping is peculiarly adapted to the customs and needs of the business. However, in appropriate cases, the principles set forth in paragraphs (b)(1) and (2) of this section, relating to pooling by natural business units, may be used, with permission of the Commissioner, by wholesalers, retailers, jobbers, or distributors. Where a wholesaler or retailer is also engaged in the manufacturing or processing of goods, the pooling of the LIFO inventory for the manufacturing or processing operations shall be determined in accordance with the rules of paragraph (b) of this section.

Reg. § 1.472-8(c)(1)

(2) *IPIC method pools.* A retailer that elects to use the inventory price index computation method described in paragraph (e)(3) of this section (IPIC method) for a trade or business may elect to establish dollar-value pools for those items accounted for using the IPIC method based on either the general expenditure categories (i.e., major groups) in Table 3 (Consumer Price Index for all Urban Consumers (CPI-U): U.S. city average, detailed expenditure categories) of the "CPI Detailed Report" or the 2-digit commodity codes (i.e., major commodity groups) in Table 6 (Producer price indexes and percent changes for commodity groupings and individual items, not seasonally adjusted) of the "PPI Detailed Report." A wholesaler, jobber, or distributor that elects to use the IPIC method for a trade or business may elect to establish dollar-value pools for any group of goods accounted for using the IPIC method and included within one of the 2-digit commodity codes (i.e., major commodity groups) in Table 6 (Producer price indexes and percent changes for commodity groupings and individual items, not seasonally adjusted) of the "PPI Detailed Report." The "CPI Detailed Report" and the "PPI Detailed Report" are published monthly by the United States Bureau of Labor Statistics (BLS) (available from New Orders, Superintendent of Documents, P.O. Box 371954, Pittsburgh, PA 15250-7954). A taxpayer electing to establish dollar-value pools under this paragraph (c)(2) may combine IPIC pools that comprise less than 5 percent of the total current-year cost of all dollar-value pools to form a single miscellaneous IPIC pool. A taxpayer electing to establish pools under this paragraph (c)(2) may combine a miscellaneous IPIC pool that comprises less than 5 percent of the total current-year cost of all dollar-value pools with the largest IPIC pool. Each of these 5 percent rules is a method of accounting. Thus, a taxpayer may not change to, or cease using, either 5 percent rule without obtaining the Commissioner's prior consent. Whether a specific IPIC pool or the miscellaneous IPIC pool satisfies the applicable 5 percent rule must be determined in the year of adoption and year of change (whichever is applicable) and redetermined every third taxable year. Any change in pooling required or permitted under a 5 percent rule is a change in method of accounting. A taxpayer must secure the consent of the Commissioner pursuant to section 1.446-1(e) before combining or separating pools and must combine or separate its IPIC pools in accordance with paragraph (g)(2) of this section.

(d) *Determination of appropriateness of pools.* Whether the number and the composition of the pools used by the taxpayer is appropriate, as well as the propriety of all computations incidental to the use of such pools, will be determined in connection with the examination of the taxpayer's income tax returns. Adequate records must be maintained to support the base-year unit cost as well as the current-year unit cost for all items priced on the dollar-value LIFO inventory method, regardless of the method authorized by paragraph (e) of this section which is used in computing the LIFO value of the dollar-value pool. The pool or pools selected must be used for the year of adoption and for all subsequent taxable years unless a change is required by the Commissioner in order to clearly reflect income, or unless permission to change is granted by the Commissioner as provided in paragraph (e) of § 1.446-1. However, see paragraph (h) of this section for authorization to change the method of pooling in certain specified cases.

(e) *Methods of computation of the LIFO value of a dollar-value pool*—(1) *Methods authorized.* A taxpayer may ordinarily use only the so-called "double-extension" method for computing the base-year and current-year cost of a dollar-value inventory pool. Where the use of the double-extension method is impractical, because of technological changes, the extensive variety of items, or extreme fluctuations in the variety of the items, in a dollar-value pool, the taxpayer may use an index method for computing all or part of the LIFO value of the pool. An index may be computed by double-extending a representative portion of the inventory in a pool or by the use of other sound and consistent statistical methods. The index used must be appropriate to the inventory pool to which it is to be applied. The appropriateness of the method of computing the index and the accuracy, reliability, and suitability of the use of such index must be demonstrated to the satisfaction of the district director in connection with the examination of the taxpayer's income tax returns. The use of any so-called "link-chain" method will be approved for taxable years beginning after December 31, 1960, only in those cases where the taxpayer can demonstrate to the satisfaction of the district director that the use of either an index method or the double-extension method would be impractical or unsuitable in view of the nature of the pool. A taxpayer using either an index or link-chain method shall attach to his income tax return for the first taxable year beginning after December 31, 1960, for which the index or link-chain method is used, a statement describing the particular link-chain method or the method used in computing the index. The statement shall be in sufficient detail to facilitate the determination as to whether the method used meets the standards set forth in this subparagraph. In addition, a copy of the statement shall be filed with the Commissioner of Internal Revenue, Attention: T:R, Washington 25, D.C. The taxpayer shall submit such other information as may be requested with respect to such index or link-chain method. Adequate records must be maintained by the taxpayer to support the appropriateness, accuracy, and reliability of an index or link-chain method. A taxpayer may request the Commissioner to approve the appropriateness of an index or link-chain method for the first taxable year beginning after December 31, 1960, for which it is used. Such request must be submitted within 90 days after the beginning of the first taxable year beginning after December 31, 1960, in which the taxpayer desires to use the index or link-chain method, or on or before May 1, 1961, whichever is later. A taxpayer entitled to use the retail method of pricing LIFO inventories authorized by § 1.472-1(k) may use retail price indexes prepared by the United States Bureau of Labor Statistics. Any method of computing the LIFO value of a dollar-value pool must be used for the year of adoption and all subsequent taxable years, unless the taxpayer obtains the consent of the Commissioner in accordance with paragraph (e) of § 1.446-1 to use a different method.

(2) *Double-extension method.* (i) Under the double-extension method the quantity of each item in the inventory pool at the close of the taxable year is extended at both base-year unit cost and current-year unit cost. The respective extensions at the two costs are then each totaled. The first total gives the amount of the current inventory in terms of base-year cost and the second total gives the amount of such inventory in terms of current-year cost.

(ii) The total current-year cost of items making up a pool may be determined—

(*a*) By reference to the actual cost of the goods most recently purchased or produced;

(*b*) By reference to the actual cost of the goods purchased or produced during the taxable year in the order of acquisition;

(*c*) By application of an average unit cost equal to the aggregate cost of all of the goods purchased or produced throughout the taxable year divided by the total number of units so purchased or produced; or

(*d*) Pursuant to any other proper method which, in the opinion of the Commissioner, clearly reflects income.

(iii) Under the double-extension method a base-year unit cost must be ascertained for each item entering a pool for the first time subsequent to the beginning of the base year. In such a case, the base-year unit cost of the entering item shall be the current-year cost of that item unless the taxpayer is able to reconstruct or otherwise establish a different cost. If the entering item is a product or raw material not in existence on the base date, its cost may be reconstructed, that is, the taxpayer using reasonable means may determine what the cost of the item would have been had it been in existence in the base year. If the item was in existence on the base date but not stocked by the taxpayer, he may establish, by using available data or records, what the cost of the item would have been to the taxpayer had he stocked the item. If the base-year unit cost of the entering item is either reconstructed or otherwise established to the satisfaction of the Commissioner, such cost may be used as the base-year unit cost in applying the double-extension method. If the taxpayer does not reconstruct or establish to the satisfaction of the Commissioner a base-year unit cost, but does reconstruct or establish to the satisfaction of the Commissioner the cost of the item at some year subsequent to the base year, he may use the earliest cost which he does reconstruct or establish as the base-year unit cost.

(iv) To determine whether there is an increment or liquidation in a pool for a particular taxable year, the end of the year inventory of the pool expressed in terms of base-year cost is compared with the beginning of the year inventory of the pool expressed in terms of base-year cost. When the end of the year inventory of the pool is in excess of the beginning of the year inventory of the pool, an increment occurs in the pool for that year. If there is an increment for the taxable year, the ratio of the total current-year cost of the pool to the total base-year cost of the pool must be computed. This ratio when multiplied by the amount of the increment measured in terms of base-year cost gives the LIFO value of such increment. The LIFO value of each such increment is hereinafter referred to in this section as the "layer of increment" and must be separately accounted for and a record thereof maintained as a separate layer of the pool, and may not be combined with a layer of increment occurring in a different year. On the other hand, when the end of the year inventory of the pool is less than the beginning of the year inventory of the pool, a liquidation occurs in the pool for that year. Such liquidation is to be reflected by reducing the most recent layer of increment by the excess of the beginning of the year inventory over the end of the year inventory of the pool. However, if the amount of the liquidation exceeds the amount of the most recent layer of increment, the preceding layers of increment in reverse chronological order are to be successively reduced by the amount of such excess until all the

Reg. § 1.472-8(e)(2)

37,142 Methods of Accounting

See p. 20,601 for regulations not amended to reflect law changes

excess is absorbed. The base-year inventory is to be reduced by liquidation only to the extent that the aggregate of all liquidation exceeds the aggregate of all layers of increment.

(v) The following examples illustrate the computation of the LIFO value of inventories under the double-extension method.

Example (1). (a) A taxpayer elects, beginning with the calendar year 1961, to compute his inventories by use of the LIFO inventory method under section 472 and further elects to use the dollar-value method in pricing such inventories as provided in paragraph (a) of this section. He creates Pool No. 1 for items A, B, and C. The composition of the inventory for Pool No. 1 at the base date, January 1, 1961, is as follows:

Items	Units	Unit cost	Total cost
A	1,000	$5	$ 5,000
B	2,000	4	8,000
C	500	2	1,000
Total base-year cost at Jan. 1, 1961			$14,000

(b) The closing inventory of Pool No. 1 at December 31 1961, contains 3,000 units of A, 1,000 units of B, and 500 units of C. The taxpayer computes the current-year cost of the items making up the pool by reference to the actual cost of goods most recently purchased. The most recent purchases of items A, B, and C are as follows:

Item	Purchase date	Quantity purchased	Unit cost
A	Dec. 15, 1961	3,500	$6.00
B	Dec. 10, 1961	2,000	5.00
C	Nov. 1, 1961	500	2.50

(c) The inventory of Pool No. 1 at December 31, 1961, shown at base-year and current-year cost is as follows:

		Dec. 31, 1961, inventory at Jan. 1, 1961, base-year cost		Dec. 31, 1961, inventory at current-year cost	
Item	Quantity	Unit cost	Amount	Unit cost	Amount
A	3,000	$5.00	$15,000	$6.00	$18,000
B	1,000	4.00	4,000	5.00	5,000
C	500	2.00	1,000	2.50	1,250
Totals			$20,000		$24,250

(d) If the amount of the December 31, 1961 inventory at base-year cost were equal to, or less than, the base-year cost of $14,000 at January 1, 1961, such amount would be the closing LIFO inventory at December 31, 1961. However, since the base-year cost of the closing LIFO inventory at December 31, 1961, amounts to $20,000, and is in excess of the $14,000 base-year cost of the opening inventory for that year, there is a $6,000 increment in Pool No. 1 during the year. This increment must be valued at current-year cost, i.e., the ratio of 24,250/20,000, or 121.25 percent. The LIFO value of the inventory at December 31, 1961, is $21,275, computed as follows:

Pool No. 1

	Dec. 31, 1961, inventory at Jan. 1, 1961, base-year cost	Ratio of total current-year cost to total base-year cost Percent	Dec. 31, 1961, inventory at LIFO value
Jan. 1, 1961, base cost	$14,000	100.00	$14,000
Dec. 31, 1961, increment	6,000	121.25	7,275
Totals	$20,000		$21,275

Example (2). (a) Assume the taxpayer in example (1) during the year 1962 completely disposes of item C and purchases item D. Assume further that item D is properly includible in Pool No. 1 under the provisions of this section. The

Reg. § 1.472-8(e)(2)

Methods of Accounting 37,143

See p. 20,601 for regulations not amended to reflect law changes

closing inventory on December 31, 1962, consists of quantities at current-year unit cost, as follows:

Items	Units	Current-year unit cost Dec. 31, 1962
A	2,000	$6.50
B	1,500	6.00
D	1,000	5.00

(b) The taxpayer establishes that the cost of item D, had he acquired it on January 1, 1961, would have been $2.00 per unit. Such cost shall be used as the base-year unit cost for item D, and the LIFO computations at December 31, 1962, are made as follows:

Item	Quantity	Dec. 31, 1962, inventory at Jan. 1, 1961, base-year cost Unit cost	Amount	Dec. 31, 1962, inventory at current-year cost Unit cost	Amount
A	2,000	$5.00	$10,000	$6.50	$13,000
B	1,500	4.00	6,000	6.00	9,000
D	1,000	2.00	2,000	5.00	5,000
Totals			$18,000		$27,000

(c) Since the closing inventory at base-year cost, $18,000, is less than the 1962 opening inventory at base-year cost, $20,000, a liquidation of $2,000 has occurred during 1962. This liquidation is to be reflected by reducing the most recent layer of increment. The LIFO value of the inventory at December 31, 1962, is $18,850, and is summarized as follows:

Pool No. 1

	Dec. 31, 1962, inventory at Jan. 1, 1961, base-year cost	Ratio of total current-year cost to total base-year cost Percent	Dec. 31, 1962, inventory at LIFO value
Jan. 1, 1961, base cost	$14,000	100.00	$14,000
Dec. 31, 1961, increment	4,000	121.25	4,850
Totals	$18,000		$18,850

(3) *Inventory price index computation (IPIC) method*—(i) *In general.* The inventory price index computation method provided by this paragraph (e)(3) (IPIC method) is an elective method of determining the LIFO value of a dollar-value pool using consumer or producer price indexes published by the United States Bureau of Labor Statistics (BLS). A taxpayer using the IPIC method must compute a separate inventory price index (IPI) for each dollar-value pool. This IPI is used to convert the total current-year cost of the items in a dollar-value pool to base-year cost in order to determine whether there is an increment or liquidation in terms of base-year cost and, if there is an increment, to determine the LIFO inventory value of the current year's layer of increment (layer). Using one IPI to compute the base-year cost of a dollar-value pool for the current taxable year and using a different IPI to compute the LIFO inventory value of the current taxable year's layer is not permitted under the IPIC method. The IPIC method will be accepted by the Commissioner as an appropriate method of computing an index, and the use of that index to compute the LIFO value of a dollar-value pool will be accepted as accurate, reliable, and suitable. The appropriateness of a taxpayer's computation of an IPI, which includes all the steps described in paragraph (e)(3)(iii) of this section, will be determined in connection with an examination of the taxpayer's federal income tax return. A taxpayer using the IPIC method may elect to establish dollar-value pools according to the special rules in paragraphs (b)(4) and (c)(2) of this section or the general rules in paragraphs (b) and (c) of this section. Taxpayers eligible to use the IPIC method are described in paragraph (e)(3)(ii) of this section. The manner in which an IPI is computed is described in paragraph (e)(3)(iii) of this section. Rules relating to the adoption of, or change to, the IPIC method are in paragraph (e)(3)(iv) of this section.

(ii) *Eligibility.* Any taxpayer electing to use the dollar-value LIFO method may elect to use the IPIC method. Except as provided in this paragraph (e)(3)(ii) or in other published guid-

Reg. § 1.472-8(e)(3)

ance, a taxpayer that elects to use the IPIC method for a specific trade or business must use that method to account for all items of dollar-value LIFO inventory. A taxpayer that uses the retail price indexes computed by the BLS and published in "Department Store Inventory Price Indexes" (available from the BLS by calling (202) 606-6325 and entering document code 2415) may elect to use the IPIC method for items that do not fall within any of the major groups listed in "Department Store Inventory Price Indexes."

(iii) *Computation of an inventory price index*—(A) *In general.* The computation of an IPI for a dollar-value pool requires the following four steps, which are described in more detail in this paragraph (e)(3)(iii): First, selection of a BLS table and an appropriate month; second, assignment of items in a dollar-value pool to BLS categories (selected BLS categories); third, computation of category inflation indexes for selected BLS categories; and fourth, computation of the IPI. A taxpayer may compute the IPI for each dollar-value pool using either the double-extension method (double-extension IPIC method) or the link-chain method (link-chain IPIC method), without regard to whether the use of a double-extension method is impractical or unsuitable. The use of either the double-extension IPIC method or the link-chain IPIC method is a method of accounting, and the adopted method must be applied consistently to all dollar-value pools within a trade or business accounted for under the IPIC method. A taxpayer that wants to change from the double-extension IPIC method to the link-chain IPIC method, or vice versa, must secure the consent of the Commissioner under § 1.446-1(e). This change must be made with a new base year as described in paragraph (e)(3)(iv)(B)(*1*).

(B) *Selection of BLS table and appropriate month*—(*1*) *In general.* Under the IPIC method, an IPI is computed using the consumer or producer price indexes for certain categories (BLS price indexes and BLS categories, respectively) listed in the selected BLS table of the "CPI Detailed Report" or the "PPI Detailed Report" for the appropriate month.

(*2*) *BLS table selection.* Manufacturers, processors, wholesalers, jobbers, and distributors must select BLS price indexes from Table 6 (Producer price indexes and percent changes for commodity groupings and individual items, not seasonally adjusted) of the "PPI Detailed Report", unless the taxpayer can demonstrate that selecting BLS price indexes from another table of the "PPI Detailed Report" is more appropriate. Retailers may select BLS price indexes from either Table 3 (Consumer Price Index for all Urban Consumers (CPI-U): U.S. city average, detailed expenditure categories) of the "CPI Detailed Report" or from Table 6 (or another more appropriate table) of the "PPI Detailed Report." The selection of a BLS table is a method of accounting and must be used for the taxable year of adoption and all subsequent years, unless the taxpayer obtains the Commissioner's consent under § 1.446-1(e) to change its table selection. A taxpayer that changes its BLS table must establish a new base year in the year of change as described in paragraph (e)(3)(iv)(B) of this section.

(*3*) *Appropriate month.* In the case of a retailer using the retail method, the appropriate month is the last month of the retailer's taxable year. In the case of all other taxpayers, the appropriate month is the month most consistent with the method used to determine the current-year cost of the dollar-value pool under paragraph (e)(2)(ii) of this section and the taxpayer's history of inventory production or purchases during the taxable year. A taxpayer not using the retail method may annually select an appropriate month for each dollar-value pool or make an election on Form 970, "Application to Use LIFO Inventory Method," to use a representative appropriate month (representative month). An election to use a representative month is a method of accounting and the month elected must be used for the taxable year of the election and all subsequent taxable years, unless the taxpayer obtains the Commissioner's consent under § 1.446-1(e) to change or revoke its election.

(*4*) *Examples.* The following examples illustrate the rules of this paragraph (e)(3)(iii)(B)(*3*):

Example 1. Determining an appropriate month. A wholesaler of seasonal goods timely files a Form 970, "Application to Use LIFO Inventory Method," for the taxable year ending December 31, 2001. The taxpayer indicates elections to use the dollar-value LIFO method, to determine the current-year cost using the earliest acquisitions method in accordance with paragraph (e)(2)(ii)(*b*) of this section, and to use the IPIC method under paragraph (e)(3) of this section. Although the taxpayer purchases inventory items regularly throughout the year, the items purchased vary according to the seasons. The seasonal items on hand at December 31, 2001, are purchased between October and December. Thus, based on the taxpayer's use of the earliest acquisitions method of determining current-year cost and its experience with inventory purchases, the appropriate month for the items represented in the ending inventory at December 31, 2001, is October.

Example 2. Electing a representative month. A retailer not using the retail method timely files a Form 970, "Application to Use LIFO Inventory Method," for the taxable year ending December 31, 2001. The taxpayer indicates elections to use the dollar-value LIFO method, the most recent purchases method of determining current-year cost under paragraph (e)(2)(ii)(*a*) of this section, the IPIC method under paragraph (e)(3) of this section, and December as its representative month under paragraph (e)(3)(iii)(B)(*3*) of this section. The items in the taxpayer's ending inventory are purchased fairly uniformly throughout the year, with the first purchases normally occurring in January and the last purchases normally occurring in December. The taxpayer's election to use December as its representative month is permissible because the taxpayer elected to use the most recent purchases method and the taxpayer's last purchases of the taxable year normally occur during December, the last month of the taxpayer's taxable year.

Example 3. Changing representative month. The facts are the same as in *Example 2,* except the taxpayer files a Form 3115, "Application for Change in Accounting Method," requesting permission to change to the earliest acquisitions method of determining current-year cost in accordance with paragraph (e)(2)(ii)(*b*) of this section and to change its representative month from December to January beginning with the taxable year ending December 31, 2003. If the Commissioner consents to the taxpayer's request to change to the earliest acquisitions method, December will no longer be a permissible representative month for this taxpayer because of the absence of a nexus between the earliest acquisitions method, the month of December (the last month of the taxpayer's taxable year), and the taxpayer's experience with inventory purchases during the year. Thus, the Commissioner will permit the taxpayer to change its representative month to January, the first month of the taxpayer's taxable year.

Example 4. Changing representative month. The facts are the same as in *Example 2.* In 2002, the taxpayer changes its annual accounting period to a taxable year ending June 30, which requires the taxpayer to file a return for the short taxable year beginning January 1, 2002, and ending June 30, 2002. As a result, December is no longer a permissible representative month because of the absence of a nexus between the most recent purchases method, the month of December, and the taxpayer's experience with inventory purchases during the year. The taxpayer should file a Form 3115 requesting permission to change its representative month from December to June beginning with the short taxable year ending June 30, 2002. Because the taxpayer's last purchases of the taxable year now will occur in June, the Commissioner will consent to the taxpayer's request to change its representative month to June.

Example 5. Changing representative month. The facts are the same as in *Example 2,* except that the taxpayer elects to use January as its representative month. The taxpayer timely files a Form 3115 requesting permission to change its representative month from January to December beginning with the taxable year ending December 31, 2003. January is not a permissible representative month because of the absence of a nexus between the most recent purchases method, the taxpayer's history of inventory purchases, and the month of January, the first month in the taxpayer's taxable year. Because December is a permissible representative month, the Commissioner will permit the taxpayer to change its representative month to December.

(C) *Assignment of inventory items to BLS categories*—(*1*) *In general.* Except as provided in paragraph (e)(3)(iii)(C)(*2*) of this section, a taxpayer must assign each item in a dollar-value pool to the most-detailed BLS category of the selected BLS table that contains that item. For example, in Table 6 of the "PPI Detailed Report" for a given month, the commodity codes for the various BLS categories run from 2 to 8 digits, with the least-detailed BLS categories having a 2-digit code and the most-detailed BLS categories usually (but not always) having an 8-digit code. For purposes of assigning items to the most-detailed BLS category, manufacturers and processors must assign each raw material item to the most-detailed PPI category that includes that raw material and must assign each finished good item to the most-detailed PPI category that includes that finished good. In addition, manufacturers and processors must assign each work-in-process (WIP) item to the most-detailed PPI category that includes the finished good into which the item will be manufactured or processed. For this purpose, *finished good* means a salable item that the taxpayer regularly sells. For example, a gasoline-engine manufacturer that also manufactures the pistons used in those engines and regularly sells some of the pistons (e.g., to retailers of replacement parts) must assign both finished pistons that have not been affixed to an engine block and piston WIP items to the most-detailed PPI category that includes pistons. Finished pistons that have been affixed to an engine block must be

Reg. § 1.472-8(e)(3)

assigned to the most-detailed PPI category that includes gasoline engines. In contrast, if sales of these pistons occur infrequently, the taxpayer must assign both finished pistons and piston WIP items to the most-detailed PPI category that includes gasoline engines.

(*2*) *10 percent method.* Instead of assigning each item in a dollar-value pool to the most-detailed BLS categories, as described in paragraph (e)(3)(iii)(C)(*1*) of this section, a taxpayer may elect to use the 10 percent method described in this paragraph (e)(3)(iii)(C)(*2*). Under the 10 percent method, items are assigned to BLS categories using a three-step procedure. First, when the current-year cost of a specific item is 10 percent or more of the total current-year cost of the dollar-value pool, the taxpayer must assign that item to the most-detailed BLS category that includes that item (10 percent BLS category). Any other item that is includible in that 10 percent BLS category (other than an item that qualifies for its own 10 percent BLS category under the preceding sentence) must be assigned to that 10 percent BLS category. Second, if one or more items have not been assigned to BLS categories in the first step, the taxpayer must investigate successively less-detailed BLS categories and assign the unassigned item(s) to the first BLS category that contains unassigned items whose current-year cost, in the aggregate, is 10 percent or more of the total current-year cost of the dollar-value pool (also, 10 percent BLS categories). This step must be repeated until all the items in the dollar-value pool have been included in an appropriate 10 percent BLS category, the current-year cost of the unassigned items, in the aggregate, is less than 10 percent of the total current-year cost of the dollar-value pool, or the taxpayer determines that a single BLS category is not appropriate for the aggregate of the unassigned items. Third, if items in a dollar-value pool have not been assigned to a 10 percent BLS category because the current-year cost of those items, in the aggregate, is less than 10 percent of the total current-year cost of the dollar-value pool, the taxpayer must assign those items to the most-detailed BLS category that includes all those items (also, a 10 percent category). On the other hand, if items in a dollar-value pool have not been assigned to a 10 percent BLS category because the taxpayer determines that a single BLS category is not appropriate for the aggregate of those items, the taxpayer must assign each of those items to a single miscellaneous BLS category created by the taxpayer (also, a 10 percent category). In no event may a taxpayer assign items in a dollar-value pool to a BLS category that is less detailed than either the major groups of consumer goods described in Table 3 of the monthly "CPI Detailed Report" or the major commodity groups of producer goods described in Table 6 of the monthly "PPI Detailed Report." Principles similar to those described in paragraph (e)(3)(iii)(C)(*1*) apply for purposes of assigning raw material, work-in-process, and finished good items to the most-detailed BLS category under the 10 percent method.

(*3*) *Change in method of accounting.* The 10 percent method of assigning items in a dollar-value pool to BLS categories is a method of accounting. In addition, a taxpayer's selection of a BLS category for a specific item is a method of accounting. However, the assignment of items to different BLS categories solely as a result of the application of the 10 percent method is a change in underlying facts and not a change in method of accounting. Likewise, the selection of a new BLS category for a specific item as a result of a revision to a BLS table is a change in underlying facts and not a change in method of accounting. A taxpayer that wants to change its method of selecting BLS categories (i.e., to or from the 10-percent method) or of selecting a BLS category for a specific item must secure the Commissioner's consent in accordance with § 1.446-1(e). A taxpayer that voluntarily changes its method of selecting BLS categories or of selecting a BLS category for a specific item must establish a new base year in the year of change as described in paragraph (e)(3)(iv)(B) of this section.

(D) *Computation of a category inflation index*—(*1*) *In general.* As described in more detail in this paragraph (e)(3)(iii)(D), a category inflation index reflects the inflation that occurs in the BLS price indexes for a selected BLS category (or, if applicable, 10 percent BLS category) during the relevant measurement period.

(*2*) *BLS price indexes.* The BLS price indexes are the cumulative indexes published in the selected BLS table for the appropriate month. A taxpayer may elect to use either preliminary or final BLS price indexes for the appropriate month, provided that the selected BLS price indexes are used consistently. However, a taxpayer that elects to use final BLS price indexes for the appropriate month must use preliminary BLS price indexes for any taxable year for which the taxpayer files its original federal income tax return before the BLS publishes final BLS price indexes for the appropriate month. If a BLS price index for a most-detailed or 10 percent BLS category is not otherwise available for the appropriate or representative month (but not because the BLS categories in the BLS table have been revised), the taxpayer must use the BLS price index for the next most-detailed BLS category that includes the

Reg. § 1.472-8(e)(3)

specific item(s) in the most-detailed or 10 percent BLS category. If a BLS price index is not otherwise available for the appropriate or representative month because the BLS categories in the BLS table have been revised, the rules of paragraph (e)(3)(iii)(D)(4) of this section apply.

(3) *Category inflation index.* (*i*) *In general.* Except as provided in paragraph (e)(3)(iii)(D)(4) of this section (concerning compound category inflation indexes) or (e)(3)(iii)(D)(5) of this section (concerning category inflation indexes for certain 10 percent BLS categories), a category inflation index for a selected BLS category (or, if applicable, 10 percent BLS category) is computed under the rules of this paragraph (e)(3)(iii)(D)(3).

(*ii*) *Double-extension IPIC method.* In the case of a taxpayer using the double-extension IPIC method, the category inflation index for a BLS category is the quotient of the BLS price index for the appropriate or representative month of the current year divided by the BLS price index for the appropriate month of the taxable year preceding the base year (base month). However, if the taxpayer did not have an opening inventory in the year that its election to use the dollar-value LIFO method and double-extension IPIC method became effective, the category inflation index for a BLS category is the quotient of the BLS price index for the appropriate or representative month of the current year divided by the BLS price index for the month immediately preceding the month of the taxpayer's first inventory production or purchase.

(*iii*) *Link-chain IPIC method.* In the case of a taxpayer using the link-chain IPIC method, the category inflation index for a BLS category is the quotient of the BLS price index for the appropriate or representative month of the current year divided by the BLS price index for the appropriate month used for the immediately preceding taxable year. However, if the taxpayer did not have an opening inventory in the year that its election to use the dollar-value LIFO method and link-chain IPIC method became effective, the category inflation index for a BLS category for the year of election is the quotient of the BLS price index for the appropriate or representative month of the current year divided by the BLS price index for the month immediately preceding the month of the taxpayer's first inventory production or purchase.

(*iv*) *Special rules concerning representative months.* A taxpayer electing to use a representative month under paragraph (e)(3)(iii)(B)(3) of this section must use an appropriate month, rather than the representative month, to determine category inflation indexes in the circumstances described in this paragraph (e)(3)(iii)(D)(3)(*iv*) and in other similar circumstances. For example, in the case of a short taxable year, the category inflation index should reflect the inflation that occurs from the base month (in the case of the double-extension IPIC method), or the appropriate or representative month used for the preceding taxable year (in the case of the link-chain IPIC method), and the appropriate month for the short taxable year. Similarly, if a taxpayer using the link-chain IPIC method is granted consent to change both its method of determining the current-year cost of a dollar-value pool and its representative month, the category inflation index for the year of change should reflect the inflation that occurs between the old representative month used for the preceding taxable year and the new representative month used for the year of change.

(4) *Compound category inflation index for revised BLS categories or price indexes—*(*i*) *In general.* Periodically, the BLS revises a BLS table to add one or more new BLS categories, eliminate one or more previously reported BLS categories, or reset the base-year BLS price index of one or more BLS categories. If the BLS has revised the applicable BLS table for a taxable year, a taxpayer must compute the category inflation index for each BLS category for which the taxpayer cannot compute a category inflation index in accordance with paragraph (e)(3)(iii)(D)(3) of this section (affected BLS category) using a reasonable method, provided the method is used consistently for all affected BLS categories within a particular taxable year. For example, if the BLS revised the CPI by adding new BLS categories as of January 2001 and eliminating some previously reported BLS categories as of December 2000, January 2002 would be the first month for which it would be possible to compute a category inflation index for a 12-month period using the BLS price indexes for any affected category. The compound category inflation index described in paragraph (e)(3)(iii)(D)(4)(*ii*) of this section is a reasonable method of computing the category inflation index for an affected BLS category.

(*ii*) *Computation of compound category inflation index.* When the applicable BLS table is revised as described in paragraph (e)(3)(iii)(D)(4)(*i*) of this section, a taxpayer may use the procedure described in this paragraph (e)(3)(iii)(D)(4)(*ii*) to compute a compound category inflation index for each affected BLS category represented in the taxpayer's ending inventory. For this purpose, a compound category inflation index is the product of the category inflation index for the "first portion" multiplied

Reg. § 1.472-8(e)(3)

by the corresponding category inflation index for the "second portion." The category inflation index for the first portion must reflect the inflation that occurs between the end of the base month (in the case of the double-extension IPIC method), or the preceding year's appropriate or representative month (in the case of the link-chain IPIC method), and the end of the last month covered by the unrevised BLS table based on the old BLS category. The corresponding category inflation index for the second portion must reflect the inflation that occurs between the beginning of the first month covered by the revised BLS table based on the new BLS category and the end of the current year's appropriate or representative month. First, using the revised BLS table for the current-year's appropriate or representative month, the taxpayer assigns items in the dollar-value pool using its method of assigning items to BLS categories as described in paragraph (e)(3)(iii)(C) of this section. Second, for each affected BLS category represented in the ending inventory, the taxpayer computes the category inflation index for the second portion using this formula: [A / B], where A equals the BLS price index for the current year's appropriate or representative month and B equals the BLS price index for the last month covered by the unrevised BLS table (as published for the first month of the revised BLS table). Third, using the unrevised BLS table for the base month (in the case of the double extension IPIC method) or the preceding year's appropriate or representative month (in the case of the link-chain IPIC method), the taxpayer assigns each of the items in the dollar-value pool using its method of assigning items to BLS categories. Fourth, for each affected BLS category represented in the ending inventory, the taxpayer computes the category inflation index for the first portion using this formula: [C / D], where C equals the BLS price index for the last month covered by the unrevised BLS table (as published for the last month of the unrevised BLS table) and D equals the BLS price index for the base month (in the case of the double-extension IPIC method) or the preceding year's appropriate or representative month (in the case of the link-chain IPIC method). Fifth, for each affected BLS category represented in the ending inventory, the taxpayer computes the compound category inflation index using this formula: [X * Y], where X equals the category inflation index for the second portion, and Y equals the corresponding category inflation index for the first portion. For the purpose of computing the compound category inflation index for each affected BLS category, the corresponding category inflation index for the first portion is the category inflation index for the unrevised BLS category that includes the specific inventory item(s) included in the revised BLS category. If items included in a single revised BLS category had been included in separate BLS categories before the revision of the BLS table, the corresponding category inflation index for the first portion is the weighted harmonic mean of the category inflation indexes for these unrevised BLS categories. See paragraph (e)(3)(iii)(E)(*1*) of this section for a formula of the weighted harmonic mean. When computing this weighted-average category inflation index, a taxpayer must use the current-year costs (or in the case of a retailer using the retail method, the retail selling prices) in ending inventory as the weights.

(*iii*) *New base year.* A taxpayer may establish a new base year in the year following the taxable year for which the taxpayer computed a compound category inflation index under this paragraph (e)(3)(iii)(D)(*4*) for one or more affected BLS categories in a dollar-value pool. See paragraph (e)(3)(iv)(B) of this section for the procedures and computations incident to establishing a new base year.

(*iv*) *Examples.* The following examples illustrate the rules of this paragraph (e)(3)(iii)(D)(*4*):

Example 1. BLS categories eliminated. (i) A retailer, whose taxable year ends January 31, elected to account for its inventories using the dollar-value LIFO method and double-extension IPIC method (based on the CPI), beginning with the taxable year ending January 31, 1997. The taxpayer does not use the retail method, but elected to use January as its representative month. On January 31, 1999, the taxpayer's only dollar-value pool contains only two items—lemons and peaches. The total current-year cost of these items is as follows: lemons, $40, and peaches, $30.

(ii) The CPI was revised in October of 1998 to eliminate the "Citrus fruits" subcategory of "Other fresh fruits." In addition, the base-year BLS price index for "Other fresh fruits" was reset to 100.00 as of October 1, 1998. In relevant part, the January 1999 CPI permits the assignment of both lemons and peaches to "Other fresh fruits." The January 1999 BLS price indexes for "Citrus fruits" and "Other fresh fruits" are 96.6 and 105.6, respectively. In relevant part, the September 1998 CPI permits the assignment of lemons to "Citrus fruits" and peaches to "Other fresh fruits." The September 1998 BLS price indexes for "Citrus fruits" and "Other fresh fruits" are 194.9 and 294.9, respectively, and the January 1997 BLS price indexes for "Citrus fruits"

Reg. § 1.472-8(e)(3)

Methods of Accounting

37,149

See p. 20,601 for regulations not amended to reflect law changes

and "Other fresh fruits" are 190.2 and 290.2, respectively.

(iii) Because the BLS eliminated the category, "Citrus fruits," as of October 1998, it did not publish a BLS price index for that category in the January 1999 CPI. Thus, the taxpayer cannot compute a category inflation index for "Citrus fruits" under the normal procedures, but may compute a compound category inflation index for that affected BLS category using the procedures described in paragraph (e)(3)(iii)(D)(4)(ii) of this section.

(iv) The taxpayer computes a compound category inflation index for the two BLS categories that formerly included lemons and peaches. The taxpayer first assigns lemons and peaches to "Other fresh fruits," the most-detailed index in the January 1999 CPI, and then computes the category inflation index for the second portion as follows:

Item	1999 Category	Jan. 1999 index / Sept. 1998 index (as published in Oct. 1998)	Category inflation index
Lemons & Peaches	Other fresh fruits	105.6 / 100.0	1.0560

(v) The taxpayer assigns the lemons and peaches to the most-detailed BLS categories in the January 1998 CPI as follows: lemons to "Citrus fruits" and peaches to "Other fresh fruits." Then, the taxpayer computes the category inflation index for the first portion as follows:

Item	1998 Category	Sept. 1998 index (as published in Sept. 1998) / Jan. 1997	Category inflation index
Lemons	Citrus fruits	194.9 / 190.2	1.0247
Peaches	Other fresh Fruits	294.9 / 290.2	1.0162

(vi) Because lemons and peaches, which are included together in the revised "Other fresh fruits" category, had been included in separate BLS categories before the BLS table was revised, the taxpayer must compute a single corresponding category inflation index for the affected BLS categories for the first portion. This corresponding category inflation index is the weighted harmonic mean of the separate corresponding category inflation indexes for the first portion using the cost of the items in ending inventory as the weights. The taxpayer computes the corresponding category inflation index for "Other fresh fruits" for the first portion as follows:

Item	(I) Weight (Cost of Item)	(II) Category Inflation Index	(III) Quotient: (I) / (II)
Lemons	$40.00	1.0247	$39.04
Peaches	30.00	1.0162	29.52
Total	$70.00		$68.56

(IV) Sum of Weights	(V) Sum of (Weight / Category Inflation Index)	(VI) Weighted Harmonic Mean of Other Fresh Fruits: (IV) / (V)
$70.00	$68.56	1.0210

(vii) Finally, the taxpayer computes the compound category inflation index for Other fresh fruits as follows:

Item	(I) Category Inflation Index (Second Portion)	(II) Category Inflation Index (First Portion)	(III) Compound Category Inflation Index: (I) * (II)
Other fresh fruits	1.0560	1.0210	1.0782

(viii) The taxpayer may establish a new base year for the taxable year ending January 31, 2000.

Example 2. BLS categories separated. (i) The facts are the same as in *Example 1*, except prior to October 1998, both lemons and peaches were assigned to "Other fresh fruits" and in the October 1998 CPI, the BLS created a new category, "Citrus fruits," for citrus fruits, such as lemons. Moreover, the BLS reset the base-year BLS price index for "Other fresh fruits" to 100.0 as of October 1, 1998. As a result of these changes, the taxpayer may no longer assign lemons to "Other fresh fruits."

Reg. § 1.472-8(e)(3)

(ii) Because "Citrus fruits" is new as of October 1998, the BLS did not publish a BLS price index for this BLS category in the January 1999 CPI. Thus, because the taxpayer cannot compute a category inflation index for "Citrus fruits" under the normal procedures, the taxpayer may compute a compound category inflation index for the affected BLS category using the procedures described in paragraph (e)(3)(iii)(D)(4)(ii) of this section.

(iii) Based on the January 1999 CPI, the taxpayer assigns lemons to "Citrus fruits" and peaches to "Other fresh fruits." Then, the taxpayer computes a compound category inflation index for each of the two BLS categories. The computation of the category inflation index for the second portion is as follows:

Item	1999 Category	Jan. 1999 index / Sept. 1998 index (as published in Oct. 1998)	Category Inflation Index
Lemons	Citrus fruits	96.6 / 100	0.9660
Peaches	Other fresh fruits	105.6 / 100	1.0560

(iv) Then, the taxpayer computes the category inflation index for the first portion as follows:

Item	1998 Category	Sept. 1998 index (as published in Sept. 1998) / Jan. 1997	Category Inflation Index
Lemons & Peaches	Other fresh fruits	294.9 / 290.2	1.0162

(v) Finally, the taxpayer computes the compound category inflation index for "Citrus fruits" and "Other fresh fruits":

Item	(I) Category Inflation Index (Second Portion)	(II) Category Inflation Index (First Portion)	(III) Compound Category Inflation Index: (I) * (II)
Citrus fruits	0.9660	1.0162	0.9816
Other fresh fruits	1.0560	1.0162	1.0731

(vi) The taxpayer may establish a new base year for the taxable year ending January 31, 2000.

(5) *10 percent method.* (*i*) *Applicability.* A taxpayer that elects to use the 10 percent method described in paragraph (e)(3)(iii)(C)(*2*) of this section must compute a category inflation index for a less-detailed 10 percent BLS category as provided in this paragraph (e)(3)(iii)(D)(*5*). A less-detailed 10 percent category is a BLS category that—

(*A*) subsumes two or more BLS categories;

(*B*) does not have a single assigned item whose current-year cost is 10 percent or more of the current-year cost of all the items in the dollar-value pool;

(*C*) has at least one item in at least one of the subsumed BLS categories; and

(*D*) has at least one subsumed BLS category that either does not have any assigned items or is a separate 10 percent BLS category.

(*ii*) *Determination of category inflation index.* If the rules of this paragraph (e)(3)(iii)(D)(*5*) apply, the category inflation index for the less-detailed 10 percent BLS category is equal to the weighted arithmetic mean of the category inflation index (or, compound category inflation index, if applicable) for each of the subsumed BLS categories that have been assigned at least one item from the taxpayer's dollar-value pool (excluding any item that is properly assigned to a separate 10 percent BLS category). [Weighted Arithmetic Mean = Sum of (Weight × Category Inflation Index)] / Sum of Weights]. The appropriate weight for each of the most-detailed BLS categories referenced in the preceding sentence is the corresponding BLS weight. Currently, in January of each year, the BLS publishes the BLS weights determined for December of the preceding year. In the case of a taxpayer using the double-extension IPIC method, the BLS weights for December of the taxable year preceding the base year are to be used for all taxable years. In the case of a taxpayer using the link-chain IPIC method, the BLS weights for December of a given calendar year are to be used for

Reg. § 1.472-8(e)(3)

taxable years that end during the 12-month period that begins on July 1 of the following calendar year. However, if the BLS weights are not published for all of the most-detailed BLS categories referenced above, the taxpayer may use the current-year cost (or in the case of a retailer using the retail method, the retail selling prices) of all items assigned to a specific most-detailed BLS category as the appropriate weight for that category, but must compute a weighted harmonic mean. See paragraph (e)(3)(iii)(E)(*1*) of this section for a formula of the weighted harmonic mean.

(E) *Computation of Inventory Price Index (IPI)*—(*1*) *Double-extension IPIC method.* Under the double-extension IPIC method, the IPI for a dollar-value pool is the weighted harmonic mean of the category inflation indexes (or, if applicable, compound category inflation indexes) determined under paragraph (e)(3)(iii)(D) of this section for each selected BLS category (or, if applicable 10 percent BLS category) represented in the taxpayer's dollar-value pool at the end of the taxable year. The formula for computing the weighted harmonic mean of the category inflation indexes is: [Sum of Weights / Sum of (Weight / Category Inflation Index)]. The weights to be used when computing this weighted harmonic mean are the current-year costs (or, in the case of a retailer using the retail method, the retail selling prices) in each selected BLS category represented in the dollar-value pool at the end of the taxable year.

(*2*) *Link-chain IPIC method.* Under the link-chain IPIC method, the IPI for a dollar-value pool is the product of the weighted harmonic mean of the category inflation indexes (or, if applicable, the compound category inflation indexes) determined under paragraph (e)(3)(iii)(D) of this section for each selected BLS category (or, if applicable, 10 percent BLS category) represented in the taxpayer's dollar-value pool at the end of the taxable year multiplied by the IPI for the immediately preceding taxable year. The formula for computing the weighted harmonic mean of the category inflation indexes is: [Sum of Weights / Sum of (Weight / Category Inflation Index)]. The weights to be used when computing this weighted harmonic mean are the current-year costs (or, in the case of a retailer using the retail method, the retail selling prices) in each selected BLS category represented in the dollar-value pool at the end of the taxable year.

(*3*) *Examples.* The following examples illustrate the rules of this paragraph (e)(3)(iii)(E):

Example 1. Double-extension method. (i) *Introduction.* R is a retail furniture merchant that does not use the retail method. For the taxable year ending December 31, 2000, R used the first-in, first-out method of identifying inventory and valued its inventory at cost. The total cost of R's inventory on December 31, 2000, was $850,000. R elected to use the dollar-value LIFO and double-extension IPIC methods for its taxable year ending December 31, 2001. R does not elect to use the 10 percent method described in paragraph (e)(3)(iii)(C)(*2*) of this section. R determines the current-year cost of the items using the actual cost of the most recently purchased goods. R elected to pool its inventory based on the major groups in Table 6 of the monthly "PPI Detailed Report" in accordance with the special IPIC pooling rules of paragraph (b)(4) of this section. All items in R's inventory fall within the 2-digit commodity code in Table 6 of the monthly "PPI Detailed Report" for "furniture and household durables." Therefore, R will maintain a single dollar-value pool.

(ii) *Select a BLS table and appropriate month for 2001.* R determines that the appropriate month for 2001 is October. R also determines that the appropriate month for 2000 would have been December if R had used the IPIC method for that year.

(iii) *Assign inventory items to BLS categories for 2001.* For 2001, R assigns all items in the dollar-value pool to the most-detailed BLS categories listed in Table 6 of the October 2001 "PPI Detailed Report" that contain those items. The BLS categories and the current-year cost of the items assigned to them are summarized as follows:

Commodity Code	Category	Current-Year Cost
12120101	Living Room Table	$111,924.00
12120211	Dining Room Table	159,578.00
12120216	Dining Room Chairs	98,639.00
12130101	Upholstered Sofas	332,488.00
12130111	Upholstered Chairs	218,751.00
Total		$921,380.00

(iv) *Compute category inflation indexes for 2001.* Because R elected to use the double-extension IPIC method and did not elect the 10 percent method, the category inflation indexes are computed in accordance with paragraph (e)(3)(iii)(D)(*3*)(*ii*) of this section (BLS price indexes for October 2001 divided by BLS

Reg. § 1.472-8(e)(3)

price indexes for December 2000). R computes the category inflation indexes for 2001 as follows:

Category	(I) Oct. 2001 Index:	(II) Dec. 2000 Index	(III) Category Inflation Index: (I) / (II)
Living Room Table	172.4	169.2	1.018913
Dining Room Table	171.9	168.1	1.022606
Dining Room Chairs	172.8	169.7	1.018268
Upholstered Sofas	142.2	140.9	1.009226
Upholstered Chairs	134.1	132.5	1.012075

(v) *Compute IPI for 2001.* R must compute the IPI for 2001, which is the weighted harmonic mean of the category inflation indexes for 2001. The formula for the weighted harmonic mean provided in paragraph (e)(3)(iii)(E)(*1*) of this section is [Sum of Weights / Sum of (Weight / Category Inflation Index)]. The IPI for 2001 is computed as follows:

Category	(I) Weight	(II) Category Inflation Index	(III) Quotient: (I) / (II)
Living Room Table	$111,924.00	1.018913	$109,846.47
Dining Room Table	159,578.00	1.022606	156,050.33
Dining Room Chairs	98,639.00	1.018268	96,869.39
Upholstered Sofas	332,488.00	1.009226	329,448.51
Upholstered Chairs	218,751.00	1.012075	216,141.10
Total	$921,380.00		$908,355.80

(IV) Sum of Weights	(V) Sum of (Weight / Category Inflation Index)	(VI) Inventory Price Index: (IV) / (V)
$921,380.00	$908,355.80	1.01433821

(vi) *Determine the LIFO value of the dollar-value pool for 2001.* For 2001, R determines the total base-year cost of its ending inventory by dividing the total current-year cost of the items in the dollar-value pool by the IPI for 2001. The total base-year cost of R's ending inventory is $908,355.80 ($921,380 / 1.01433821). Comparing the base-year cost of the ending inventory to the base-year cost of the beginning inventory, R determines that the base-year cost of the 2001 increment is $58,355.80 ($908,355.80 − $850,000.00). R multiplies the base-year cost of the 2001 increment by the IPI for 2001 and determines that the LIFO value of the 2001 layer is $59,192.52 ($58,355.80 * 1.01433821). Thus, the LIFO value of R's total inventory at the end of 2001 is $909,192.52 ($850,000.00 (opening inventory) + $59,192.52 (2001 layer)).

(vii) *Select a BLS table and appropriate month for 2002.* For 2002, R must compute a new IPI under the double-extension IPIC method to determine the LIFO value of its dollar-value pool. R determines that the appropriate month for 2002 is November.

(viii) *Assign inventory items to BLS categories for 2002.* For 2002, R assigns all items in the dollar-value pool to the most-detailed BLS categories listed in Table 6 of the November 2002 "PPI Detailed Report" that contain those items. The BLS categories and the current-year cost of the items assigned to them are summarized as follows:

Commodity Code	Category	Current-Year Cost
12120103	Living Room Desks	$125,008.00
12120211	Dining Room Table	136,216.00
12120216	Dining Room Chairs	113,569.00
12130101	Upholstered Sofas	343,900.00
12130111	Upholstered Chairs	233,050.00
Total		$951,743.00

(ix) *Compute category inflation indexes for 2002.* Because R uses the double-extension IPIC method and did not elect the 10 percent method, the category inflation indexes are computed in accordance with paragraph (e)(3)(iii)(D)(*3*)(*ii*) of this section (BLS price indexes for November 2002 divided by BLS price indexes for December 2000). R computes the category inflation indexes for 2002 as follows:

Reg. § 1.472-8(e)(3)

Methods of Accounting

37,153

See p. 20,601 for regulations not amended to reflect law changes

Category	(I) Nov. 2002 Index	(II) Dec. 2000 Index	(III) Category Inflation Index: (I)/(II)
Living Room Desks	172.6	160.3	1.076731
Dining Room Table	174.8	168.1	1.039857
Dining Room Chairs	177.0	169.7	1.043017
Upholstered Sofas	144.9	140.9	1.028389
Upholstered Chairs	136.6	132.5	1.030943

(x) *Compute IPI for 2002.* R must compute the IPI for 2002, which is the weighted harmonic mean [Sum of Weights / Sum of (Weight / Category Inflation Index)] of the category inflation indexes for 2002. The IPI for 2002 is computed as follows:

Category	(I) Weight	(II) Category Inflation Index	(III) Quotient: (I)/(II)
Living Room Desks	$125,008.00	1.076731	$116,099.56
Dining Room Table	136,216.00	1.039857	130,994.93
Dining Room Chairs	113,569.00	1.043017	108,885.09
Upholstered Sofas	343,900.00	1.028389	334,406.53
Upholstered Chairs	233,050.00	1.030943	226,055.17
Total	$951,743.00		$916,441.28

(IV) Sum of Weights	(V) Sum of (Weight / Category Inflation Index)	(VI) Inventory Price Index: (IV)/(V)
$951,743.00	$916,441.28	1.03852044

(xi) *Determine the LIFO value of the pool for 2002.* For 2002, R determines the total base-year cost of its ending inventory by dividing the total current-year cost of the items in the dollar-value pool by the IPI for 2002. The total base-year cost of the ending inventory is $916,441.28 ($951,743.00 / 1.03852044). Comparing the base-year cost of the ending inventory to the base-year cost of the beginning inventory, R determines that the base-year cost of the 2002 increment is $8,085.48 ($916,441.28 − $908,355.80). R multiplies the base-year cost of the 2002 increment by the IPI for 2002 and determines that the LIFO value of the 2002 layer is $8,396.94 ($8,085.48 * 1.03852044). Thus, the LIFO value of R's total inventory at the end of 2002 is $917,589.46 ($850,000.00 (opening inventory) + $59,192.52 (2001 layer) + $8,396.94 (2002 layer)).

Example 2. Link-chain method. (i) *Introduction.* The facts are the same as *Example 1*, except that R uses the link-chain IPIC method. The double-extension IPIC method and the link-chain IPIC method yield the same results for the first taxable year in which the dollar-value LIFO and IPIC methods are used. Therefore, this example illustrates only how R will compute the IPI for, and determine the LIFO value of, its dollar-value pool for 2002.

(ii) *Select a BLS table and appropriate month for 2002.* R determines that the appropriate month for 2002 is November.

(iii) *Assign inventory items to BLS categories for 2002.* For 2002, R assigns all items in the dollar-value pool to the most-detailed BLS categories listed in Table 6 of the November 2002 "PPI Detailed Report" that contain those items. The BLS categories and the current-year cost of the items assigned to them are summarized as follows:

Commodity Code	Category	Current-Year Cost
12120103	Living Room Desks	$125,008.00
12120211	Dining Room Table	136,216.00
12120216	Dining Room Chairs	113,569.00
12130101	Upholstered Sofas	343,900.00
12130111	Upholstered Chairs	233,050.00
Total		$951,743.00

(iv) *Compute category inflation indexes for 2002.* Because R uses the link-chain IPIC method and did not elect the 10 percent method, the category inflation indexes are computed in accordance with paragraph (e)(3)(iii)(D)(*3*)(*iii*) of this section (BLS price indexes for November 2002 divided by BLS price indexes for October 2001). R computes the category inflation indexes for 2002 as follows:

Reg. § 1.472-8(e)(3)

Methods of Accounting

See p. 20,601 for regulations not amended to reflect law changes

Category	(I) Nov. 2002 Index:	(II) Oct. 2001 Index	(III) Category Inflation Index: (I) / (II)
Living Room Desks	172.6	162.0	1.065432
Dining Room Table	174.8	171.9	1.016870
Dining Room Chairs	177.0	172.8	1.024306
Upholstered Sofas	144.9	142.2	1.018987
Upholstered Chairs	136.6	134.1	1.018643

(v) *Compute IPI for 2002.* As provided in paragraph (e)(3)(iii)(E)(*2*) of this section, R must compute the IPI for 2002 by multiplying the weighted harmonic mean of the category inflation indexes for 2002 by the IPI for 2001. The IPI for 2002 is computed as follows:

Category	(I) Weight	(II) Category Inflation Index	(III) Quotient: (I) / (II)
Living Room Desks	$125,008.00	1.065432	$117,330.81
Dining Room Table	136,216.00	1.016870	133,956.16
Dining Room Chairs	113,569.00	1.024306	110,874.09
Upholstered Sofas	343,900.00	1.018987	337,492.04
Upholstered Chairs	233,050.00	1.018643	228,784.77
Total	$951,743.00		$928,437.87

(IV) Sum of Weights	(V) Sum of (Weight / Category Inflation Index)	(VI) Weighted Harmonic Mean of Category Inflation Indexes for 2002: (IV) / (V)	(VII) Inventory Price Index for 2001	(VIII) Inventory Price Index for 2002: (VI) * (VII)
$951,743.00	$928,437.87	1.02510144	1.01433821	1.03979956

(vi) *Determine the LIFO value of the pool for 2002.* R determines the total base-year cost of its ending inventory by dividing the total current-year cost of the items in the dollar-value pool by the IPI for 2002. The total base-year cost of the ending inventory is $915,313.91 ($951,743.00 / 1.03979956). Comparing the base-year cost of the ending inventory to the base-year cost of the beginning inventory, R determines that the base-year cost of the 2002 layer is $6,958.11 ($915,313.91—$908,355.80). R multiplies the base-year cost of the 2002 layer by the IPI for 2002 and determines that the LIFO value of the 2002 layer is $7,235.04 ($6,958.11 * 1.03979956). Thus, the LIFO value of R's total inventory at the end of 2002 is $916,427.56 ($850,000.00 (opening inventory) + $59,192.52 (2001 layer) + $7,235.04 (2002 layer)).

(iv) *Adoption or change of method*—(A) *Adoption or change to IPIC method.* The use of an inventory price index computed under the IPIC method is a method of accounting. A taxpayer permitted to adopt the dollar-value LIFO method without first securing the Commissioner's consent also may adopt the IPIC method without first securing the Commissioner's consent. The IPIC method may be adopted and used, however, only if the taxpayer provides the following information on a Form 970, "Application to Use LIFO Inventory Method," or in another manner as may be acceptable to the Commissioner: A complete list of dollar-value pools (including a description of the items in each dollar-value pool); the BLS table (i.e., CPI or PPI). selected for each dollar-value pool; the representative month, if applicable, elected for each dollar-value pool; the BLS categories to which the items in each dollar-value pool will be assigned; the method of assigning items to BLS categories (e.g., the 10 percent method) for each dollar-value pool; and the method of computing the IPI (i.e., double-extension IPIC method or link-chain IPIC method) for each dollar-value pool. In the case of a taxpayer permitted to adopt the IPIC method without requesting the Commissioner's consent, the Form 970 must be attached to the taxpayer's income tax return for the taxable year of adoption. In all other cases, a taxpayer may change to the IPIC method only after securing the Commissioner's consent as provided in § 1.446-1(e). In these latter cases, the Form 970 containing the information described in this paragraph (e)(3)(iv)(A) must be attached to a Form 3115, "Application for Change in Accounting Method," filed as required by § 1.446-1(e). A taxpayer that simultaneously changes to the dollar-value LIFO and IPIC methods from another LIFO method must apply the rules of paragraph (f)(2) of this section before applying the rules of paragraph (e)(3)(iv)(B)(*1*) of this section. To satisfy the requirements of § 1.472-2(h), taxpayers must maintain adequate books and records, including those concerning the use of the IPIC

Reg. § 1.472-8(e)(3)

method and necessary computations. Notwithstanding the rules in paragraph (e)(1) of this section, a taxpayer that adopts, or changes to, the link-chain IPIC method is not required to demonstrate that the use of any other method of determining the LIFO value of a dollar-value pool is impractical.

(B) *New base year*—(*1*) *Voluntary change*—(*i*) *In general.* In the case of a taxpayer using a non-IPIC method to determine the LIFO value of inventory, the layers previously determined under that method, if any, and the LIFO values of those layers are retained if the taxpayer voluntarily changes to the IPIC method. Instead of using the earliest taxable year for which the taxpayer adopted the LIFO method for any items in the dollar-value pool, the year of change is used as the new base year for the purpose of determining the amount of increments and liquidations, if any, for the year of change and subsequent taxable years. The base-year cost of the layers in a dollar-value pool at the beginning of the year of change must be restated in terms of new base-year cost using the year of change as the new base year and, if applicable, the indexes for the previously determined layers must be recomputed accordingly. The recomputed indexes will be used to determine the LIFO value of subsequent liquidations. For purposes of computing an IPI under paragraph (e)(3)(iii)(E) of this section, the IPI for the immediately preceding year is 1.00. The new total base-year cost of the items in a dollar-value pool for the purpose of determining future increments and liquidations is equal to the total current-year cost of the items in the dollar-value pool (determined using the taxpayer's method of determining the total current-year cost of the items in the dollar-value pool under paragraph (e)(2)(ii) of this section). A taxpayer must allocate this new total base-year cost to each layer based on the ratio of the old base-year cost of the layer to the old total base-year cost of the dollar-value pool.

(*ii*) *Example.* The following example illustrates the rules of this paragraph (e)(3)(iv)(B)(*1*):

Example. (i) In 1990, X elected to use a dollar-value LIFO method (other than the IPIC method) for its single dollar-value pool. X is granted permission to change to the link-chain IPIC method, beginning with the taxable year ending December 31, 2001. X will continue using a single dollar-value pool. X's beginning inventory as of January 1, 2001, computed using its former inventory method, is as follows:

Layer	(I) Base-Year Cost	(II) Inflation Index	(III) LIFO Value: (I) * (II)
Base layer	$135,000	1.00	$135,000
1991 layer	20,000	1.43	28,600
1994 layer	60,000	1.55	93,000
1995 layer	13,000	1.59	20,670
1997 layer	2,000	1.61	3,220
Total	$230,000		$280,490

(ii) Under X's method of determining the current-year cost of items in a dollar-value pool, the current-year cost of the beginning inventory is $391,000. Thus, X's new base-year cost as of January 1, 2001, is $391,000. X allocates this new base-year cost to each layer based on the ratio of old base-year cost of the layer to the total old base-year cost of the dollar-value pool. To recompute the inflation indexes for each of its layers, X divides the LIFO value of each layer by the new base-year cost attributable to the layer. The new base-year cost, recomputed inflation indexes, and LIFO value of X's layers as of January 1, 2001, are as follows:

Layer	(I) Base-Year Cost	(II) Inflation Index	(III) LIFO Value: (I) * (II)
Base layer	$229,500	0.588235	$135,000
1991 layer	34,000	0.841176	28,600
1994 layer	102,000	0.911765	93,000
1995 layer	22,100	0.935294	20,670
1997 layer	3,400	0.947059	3,220
Total	$391,000		$280,490

(iii) In 2001, the current-year cost of X's ending inventory is $430,139. The weighted harmonic mean of the category inflation indexes applicable to X's ending inventory is 1.075347, and in accordance with paragraph (e)(3)(iv)(B)(*1*)(*i*) of this section, the inflation index for the immediately preceding taxable year is 1.00. Thus, X's IPI for 2001 is 1.075347 (1.00 *

Reg. § 1.472-8(e)(3)

37,156   Methods of Accounting

See p. 20,601 for regulations not amended to reflect law changes

1.075347). The total base-year cost of X's ending inventory is $400,000 ($430,139 / 1.075347). The base-year cost, IPI, and LIFO value of X's layers as of December 31, 2001, are as follows:

Layer	(I) Base-Year Cost	(II) Inflation Index	(III) LIFO Value: (I) * (II)
Base layer	$229,500	0.588235	$135,000
1991 layer	34,000	0.841176	28,600
1994 layer	102,000	0.911765	93,000
1995 layer	22,100	0.935294	20,670
1997 layer	3,400	0.947059	3,220
2001 layer	9,000	1.075347	9,678
Total	$400,000		$290,168

(iv) In 2002, the current-year cost of X's ending inventory is $418,000. The weighted harmonic mean of the category inflation indexes applicable to X's ending inventory is 1.02292562, and the IPI for the immediately preceding year is 1.075347. Thus, X's IPI for 2001 is 1.10 (1.075347 * 1.02292562). The total base-year cost of X's ending inventory is $380,000 ($418,000 / 1.10), which results in a liquidation of $20,000 ($400,000 − $380,000) in terms of base-year cost. This liquidation eliminates the 2001 layer ($9,000 base-year cost), the 1997 layer ($3,400 base-year cost), and part of the 1995 layer ($7,600 base-year cost). The base-year cost, indexes, and LIFO value of X's layers as of December 31, 2002, are as follows:

Layer	(I) Base-Year Cost	(II) Inflation Index	(III) LIFO Value: (I) * (II)
Base layer	$229,500	0.588235	$135,000
1991 layer	34,000	0.841176	28,600
1994 layer	102,000	0.911765	93,000
1995 layer	14,500	0.935294	13,562
Total	$380,000		$270,162

(2) *Involuntary change*—(i) *In general.* If a taxpayer uses a non-IPIC method to compute the LIFO value of a dollar-value pool, and if the Commissioner determines that the taxpayer's method does not clearly reflect income, the Commissioner may require the taxpayer to change to the IPIC method. If the Commissioner requires a taxpayer to change to the IPIC method, and the taxpayer does not provide sufficient information from its books and records to compute an adjustment under section 481, the Commissioner may implement the change using the simplified transition method described in paragraph (e)(3)(iv)(B)(*2*)(*ii*) of this section.

(*ii*) *Simplified Transition Method.* Under the simplified transition method, the Commissioner will recompute the LIFO value of each dollar-value pool as of the beginning of the year of change using the double-extension IPIC method or the link-chain IPIC method. The adjustment under section 481 is equal to the difference between the recomputed LIFO value and the LIFO value of the pool determined under the taxpayer's former method. The Commissioner will compute an IPI using the double-extension IPIC method or link-chain IPIC method for each taxable year in which the LIFO method was used by the taxpayer based on the assumptions that the ending inventory of the pool in each taxable year was comprised of items that fall into the same BLS categories as the items in the ending inventory of the year of change and that the relative weights of those BLS categories in all prior years were the same as the relative weights of those BLS categories in the ending inventory of the year of change. The base-year cost of the items in a dollar-value pool at the end of a taxable year will be determined by dividing the IPI computed for the taxable year into the current-year cost of the items in that pool determined in accordance with paragraph (e)(2)(ii) of this section. If the comparison of the base-year cost of the beginning and ending inventory produces a current-year increment, the base-year cost of that increment will be multiplied by the IPI computed for that taxable year to determine the LIFO value of that layer.

(*iii*) *Example.* The following example illustrates the rules of this paragraph (e)(3)(iv)(B)(*2*)(*ii*).

Example. (i) Z began using a dollar-value LIFO method other than the IPIC method in the taxable year ending December 31, 1998, and maintains a single dollar-value pool. Z's beginning inventory as of January 1, 2000, computed using its method of accounting, was as follows:

Reg. § 1.472-8(e)(3)

Methods of Accounting

Layer	(I) Base-Year Cost	(II) Inflation Index	(III) LIFO Value: (I) * (II)
Base layer	$105,000	1.00	$105,000
1998 layer	3,000	1.40	4,200
Total	$108,000		$109,200

(ii) Upon examining Z's federal income tax return for the taxable year ending December 31, 2000, the examining agent determines that Z's dollar-value LIFO method does not clearly reflect income. The examining agent chooses to change Z to the double-extension IPIC method for 2000 and implements the change using the simplified transition method as follows. First, the inventory in Z's dollar-value pool at the end of 2000 is assigned to the most-detailed categories in the CPI or PPI, whichever is appropriate. Assume that 80 percent of the current-year cost of Z's inventory as of December 31, 2000, is assigned to Category 1, 10 percent is assigned to Category 2, and 10 percent is assigned to Category 3. Assume further that the current-year cost of the inventory in Z's dollar-value pool at the end of 1998 and 1999 was $133,000 and $145,000, respectively.

(iii) The category inflation indexes for 1998 computed under the double-extension IPIC method are 1.17 for Category 1, 1.26 for Category 2, and 1.19 for Category 3. The weights to be used in computing the IPI for 1998 are $106,400 ($133,000 * 80 percent) for Category 1, $13,300 ($133,000 * 10 percent) for Category 2, and $13,300 ($133,000 * 10 percent) for Category 3. The IPI for 1998 is computed as follows:

Category	(I) Weight	(II) Category Inflation Index	(III) Quotient: (I)/(II)
1	$106,400	1.17	90,940
2	13,300	1.26	10,556
3	13,300	1.19	11,176
Total	$133,000		$112,672

(IV) Sum of Weights	(V) Sum of (Weight / Category Inflation Index)	(VI) Inventory Price Index: (IV)/(V)
$133,000	$112,672	1.180417

(iv) The base-year cost of the inventory in Z's pool at the end of 1998 is $112,672 ($133,000 / 1.180417), and the base-year cost of the 1998 increment is $7,672 ($112,672 − $105,000). The LIFO value of the 1998 layer is $9,056 ($7,672 * 1.180417).

(v) The category inflation indexes for 1999 computed under the double-extension IPIC method were 1.21 for Category 1, 1.29 for Category 2 and 1.23 for Category 3. The weights to be used in computing the IPI for 1999 are $116,000 ($145,000 * 80 percent) for Category 1, $14,500 ($145,000 * 10 percent) for Category 2, and $14,500 ($145,000 * 10 percent) for Category 3. The IPI for 1999 is computed as follows:

Category	(I) Weight	(II) Category Inflation Index	(III) Quotient: (I)/(II)
1	$116,000	1.21	$ 95,868
2	14,500	1.29	11,240
3	14,500	1.23	11,789
Total	$145,000		$118,897

(IV) Sum of Weights	(V) Sum of (Weight / Category Inflation Index)	(VI) Inventory Price Index: (IV)/(V)
$145,000	$118,897	1.219543

(vi) The base-year cost of the inventory in Z's pool at the end of 1999 is $118,897 ($145,000 / 1.219543), and the base-year cost of the 1999 layer is $6,225 ($118,897 − $112,672). The LIFO value of the 1999 layer is $7,592 ($6,225 * 1.219543).

(vii) The LIFO value of Z's dollar-value pool at the end of 1999 computed under the double-extension IPIC method is as follows:

Reg. § 1.472-8(e)(3)

Layer	(I) Base-Year Cost	(II) Inflation Index	(III) LIFO Value: (I) * (II)
Base layer	$105,000	1.000000	$105,000
1998 layer	7,672	1.180417	9,056
1999 layer	6,225	1.219542	7,592
Total	$118,897		$121,648

(viii) The section 481(a) adjustment is equal to the difference between the LIFO value of the inventory at the beginning of 2000 computed under Z's former method of accounting and recomputed by the examining agent under the double-extension IPIC method, or $12,448 ($121,648 − $109,200).

(ix) Finally, the examining agent will recompute Z's taxable income for 2000 and succeeding taxable years using the double-extension IPIC method.

(v) *Effective date*—(A) *In general.* The rules of this paragraph (e)(3) and paragraphs (b)(4) and (c)(2) of this section are applicable for taxable years ending on or after December 31, 2001.

(B) *Change in method of accounting.* Any change in a taxpayer's method of accounting necessary to comply with this paragraph (e)(3) or with paragraphs (b)(4) or (c)(2) of this section is a change in method of accounting to which the provisions of section 446 and the regulations thereunder apply. For the first or second taxable year ending on or after December 31, 2001, a taxpayer is granted the consent of the Commissioner to change its method of accounting to a method required or permitted by this paragraph (e)(3) and paragraphs (b)(4) and (c)(2) of this section. A taxpayer that wants to change its method of accounting under this paragraph (e)(3)(v) must follow the automatic consent procedures in Rev. Proc. 2002-9 (2002-3 I.R.B. xxx) (see § 601.601(d)(2) of this chapter). However, the scope limitations in section 4.02 of Rev. Proc. 2002-9 do not apply, and the five-year limitation on the readoption of the LIFO method under section 10.01(2) of the Appendix is waived. In addition, if the taxpayer's method of accounting for its LIFO inventories is an issue under consideration at the time the application is filed with the national office, the audit protection of section 7 of Rev. Proc. 2002-9 does not apply. If a taxpayer changing its method of accounting under this paragraph (e)(3)(v)(B) is under examination, before an appeals office, or before a federal court with respect to any income tax issue, the taxpayer must provide a copy of the application to the examining agent(s), appeals officer or counsel for the government, as appropriate, at the same time it files the application with the national office.

Any change under this paragraph (e)(3)(v)(B) must be made using a cut-off method and new base year. See paragraph (e)(3)(iv)(B)(*1*) of this section for an example of this computation. Because a change under this paragraph (e)(3)(v)(B) is made using a cut-off method, a section 481(a) adjustment is not permitted. However, a taxpayer changing its method of accounting under this paragraph (e)(3)(v)(B) must comply with the requirements of section 10.06(3) of the APPENDIX of Rev. Proc. 2002-9 (concerning bargain purchases).

(f) *Change to dollar-value method from another method of pricing LIFO inventories*—(1) *Consent required.* Except as provided in § 1.472-3, in the case of a taxpayer electing to use a LIFO inventory method for the first time, or in the case of a taxpayer changing to the dollar-value method and continuing to use the same pools as were used under another LIFO method, a taxpayer using another LIFO method of pricing inventories may not change to the dollar-value method of pricing such inventories unless he first secures the consent of the Commissioner in accordance with paragraph (e) of § 1.446-1.

(2) *Method of converting inventory.* Where the taxpayer changes from one method of pricing LIFO inventories to the dollar-value method, the ending LIFO inventory for the taxable year immediately preceding the year of change shall be converted to the dollar-value LIFO method. This is done to establish the base-year cost for subsequent calculations. Thus, if the taxpayer was previously valuing LIFO inventories on the specific goods method, these separate values shall be combined into appropriate pools. For this purpose, the base year for the pool shall be the earliest taxable year for which the LIFO inventory method had been adopted for any item in that pool. No change will be made in the overall LIFO value of the opening inventory for that year of change as a result of the conversion, and that inventory will merely be restated in the manner used under the dollar-value method. All layers of increment for such inventory must be retained, except that all layers of increment which occurred in the same taxable year must be combined. The following examples illustrate the provisions of this subparagraph:

Example (1). (i) Assume that the taxpayer has used another LIFO method for finished goods

Reg. § 1.472-8(f)(1)

Methods of Accounting 37,159
See p. 20,601 for regulations not amended to reflect law changes

since 1954 and has complied with all the requirements prerequisite for a change to the dollar-value method. Items A, B, and C, which have previously been inventoried under the specific goods LIFO method may properly be included in a single dollar-value LIFO pool. The LIFO inventory value of items A, B, and C at December 31, 1960, is $12,200, computed as follows:

Year	Base quantity and yearly increments	Unit cost	Dec. 31, 1960, inventory at LIFO value
Item A			
1954 (base year)	$ 100	$ 1	$ 100
1955	200	2	400
1956	100	4	400
1960	100	6	600
Total	500		1,500
Item B			
1954 (base year)	$ 300	$ 6	$ 1,800
1955	100	8	800
1960	50	10	500
Total	450		3,100
Item C			
1954 (base year)	$1,000	$ 4	$ 4,000
1955	200	6	1,200
1956	300	8	2,400
Total	1,500		7,600
LIFO value of items A, B, and C at Dec. 31, 1960			$12,200

There were no increments in the years 1957, 1958, or 1959.

(ii) The computation of the ratio of the total current-year cost to the total base-year cost for the base year and each layer of increment in Pool No. 1 is shown as follows:

Item A	1954 base-year unit cost	Year 1954	1955	Increments 1956	1960
Base-year cost	$1.00	$ 100	$ 200	$ 100	$ 100
LIFO value	...	100	400	400	600
Item B					
Base-year cost	6.00	1,800	600	...	300
LIFO value	...	1,800	800	...	500
Item C					
Base-year cost	4.00	4,000	800	1,200	...
LIFO value	...	4,000	1,200	2,400	...
Total—Base-year cost	...	$ 5,900	$ 1,600	$ 1,300	$ 400
Total—LIFO value	...	5,900	2,400	2,800	1,100
Ratio of total current-year cost to total base-year cost (percent)	...	100.00	150.00	215.38	275.00

(iii) On the basis of the foregoing computations, the LIFO inventory of Pool No. 1, at December 31, 1960, is restated as follows:

	Dec. 31, 1960, inventory at base-year cost	Ratio of total current-year cost to total base-year cost Percent	Dec. 31, 1960, inventory at LIFO value
1954 base cost	$5,900	100.00	$ 5,900
1955 increment	1,600	150.00	2,400
1956 increment	1,300	215.38	2,800
1960 increment	400	275.00	1,100
Total	$9,200		$12,200

Reg. § 1.472-8(f)(2)

Methods of Accounting

Example (2). Assume the same facts as in example (1) and assume further that the base-year cost of Pool No. 1 at December 31, 1961, is $8,350. Since the closing inventory for the taxable year 1961 at base-year cost is less than the opening inventory for that year at base-year cost, a liquidation has occurred during 1961. This liquidation absorbs all of the 1960 layer of increment and part of the 1956 layer of increment. The December 31, 1961, inventory is $10,131, computed as follows:

	Dec. 31, 1961, inventory at base-year cost	Ratio of total current-year cost to total base-year cost Percent	Dec. 31, 1961, inventory at LIFO value
1954 base cost	$5,900	100.00	$ 5,900
1955 increment	1,600	150.00	2,400
1956 increment	850	215.38	1,831
Total	$8,350		$10,131

(g) *Transitional rules*—(1) *Change in method of pooling.* Any method of pooling authorized by this section and used by the taxpayer in computing his LIFO inventories under the dollar-value method shall be treated as a method of accounting. Any method of pooling which is authorized by this section shall be used for the year of adoption and for all subsequent taxable years unless a change is required by the Commissioner in order to clearly reflect income, or unless permission to change is granted by the Commissioner as provided in paragraph (e) of § 1.446-1. Where the taxpayer changes from one method of pooling to another method of pooling permitted by this section, the ending LIFO inventory for the taxable year preceding the year of change shall be restated under the new method of pooling.

(2) *Manner of combining or separating dollar-value pools.* (i) A taxpayer who has been using the dollar-value LIFO method and who is permitted or required to change his method of pooling, shall combine or separate the LIFO value of his inventory for the base year and each yearly layer of increment in order to conform to the new pool or pools. Each yearly layer of increment in the new pool or pools must be separately accounted for and a record thereof maintained, and any liquidation occurring in the new pool or pools subsequent to the formation thereof shall be treated in the same manner as if the new pool or pools had existed from the date the taxpayer first adopted the LIFO inventory method. The combination or separation of the LIFO value of his inventory for the base year and each yearly layer of increment shall be made in accordance with the appropriate method set forth in this subparagraph, unless the use of a different method is approved by the Commissioner.

(ii) Where the taxpayer is permitted or required to separate a pool into more than one pool, the separation shall be made in the following manner: First, each item in the former pool shall be placed in an appropriate new pool. Every item in each new pool is then extended at its base-year unit cost and the extensions are totaled. Each total is the amount of inventory for each new pool expressed in terms of base-year cost. Then a ratio of the total base-year cost of each new pool to the base-year cost of the former pool is computed. The resulting ratio is applied to the amount of inventory for the base year and each yearly layer of increment of the former pool to obtain an allocation to each new pool of the base-year inventory of the former pool and subsequent layers of increment thereof. The foregoing may be illustrated by the following example of a change for the taxable year 1961:

Example. (a) Assume that items A, B, C, and D are all grouped together in one pool prior to December 31, 1960. The LIFO inventory value at December 31, 1960, is computed as follows:

	Dec. 31, 1960, inventory at Jan. 1, 1956, base-year cost	Pool ABCD Ratio of total current-year cost to total base-year cost Percent	Dec. 31, 1960, inventory at LIFO value
Jan. 1, 1956, base cost	$10,000	100	$10,000
Dec. 31, 1956, increment	1,000	110	1,100
Dec. 31, 1958, increment	5,000	120	6,000
Dec. 31, 1960, increment	4,000	125	5,000
Total	$20,000		$22,100

Reg. § 1.472-8(g)(1)

Methods of Accounting

See p. 20,601 for regulations not amended to reflect law changes

(*b*) The extension of the quantity of items A, B, C, and D at respective base-year unit costs is as follows:

Item	Quantity	Base-year unit cost	Amount
A	2,000	$2	$ 4,000
B	1,000	3	3,000
C	1,000	5	5,000
D	4,000	2	8,000
Total			$20,000

(*c*) Under the provisions of this section the taxpayer separates former pool ABCD into two pools, Pool AB and Pool CD. The computation of the ratio of total base-year cost for each of the new pools to the base-year cost of the former pool is as follows:

Item	Total base-year cost		Ratio
Pool AB:			
A	$ 4,000		....
B	3,000		....
	$ 7,000		7,000/20,000
Pool CD:			
C	$ 5,000		....
D	8,000		....
Total for pool ABCD	$13,000	$20,000	13,000/20,000

(*d*) The ratio of the base-year cost of new Pools AB and CD to the base-year cost of former Pool ABCD is 7,000/20,000 and 13,000/20,000, respectively. The allocation of the January 1, 1956 base cost and subsequent yearly layers of increment of former Pool ABCD to new Pools AB and CD is as follows:

	Base-year cost to be allocated	Pool AB	Pool CD
Jan. 1, 1956, base cost	$10,000	$3,500	$6,500
Dec. 31, 1956, increment	1,000	350	650
Dec. 31, 1958, increment	5,000	1,750	3,250
Dec. 31, 1960, increment	4,000	1,400	2,600
Total	$20,000	$7,000	$13,000

(*e*) The LIFO value of new Pools AB and CD at December 31, 1960, as allocated, is as follows:

	Dec. 31, 1960, inventory at Jan. 1, 1956, base-year cost	Ratio of total current-year cost to total base-year cost Percent	Dec. 31, 1960, inventory at LIFO value
Pool AB			
Jan. 1, 1956, base cost	$ 3,500	100	$ 3,500
Dec. 31, 1956, increment	350	110	385
Dec. 31, 1958, increment	1,750	120	2,100
Dec. 31, 1960, increment	1,400	125	1,750
Total	$ 7,000	...	$ 7,735
Pool CD			
Jan. 1, 1956, base cost	$ 6,500	100	$ 6,500
Dec. 31, 1956, increment	650	110	715
Dec. 31, 1958, increment	3,250	120	3,900
Dec. 31, 1960, increment	2,600	125	3,250
Total	$13,000	...	$14,365

Reg. § 1.472-8(g)(2)

Methods of Accounting

(iii) Where the taxpayer is permitted or required to combine two or more pools having the same base year, they shall be combined into one pool in the following manner: The LIFO value of the base-year inventory of each of the former pools is combined to obtain a LIFO value of the base-year inventory for the new pool. Then, any layers of increment in the various pools which occurred in the same taxable year are combined into one total layer of increment for that taxable year. However, layers of increment which occurred in different taxable years may not be combined. In combining the layers of increment a new ratio of current-year cost to base-year cost is computed for each of the combined layers of increment. The foregoing may be illustrated by the following example:

Example. (a) Assume the taxpayer has two pools at December 31, 1960. Under the provisions of this section the taxpayer combines these pools into a single pool as of January 1, 1961. The LIFO inventory value of each pool at December 31, 1960, is shown as follows:

	Dec. 31, 1960, inventory at Jan. 1, 1957, base-year cost	Ratio of total current-year cost to total base-year cost	Dec. 31, 1960, inventory at LIFO value
Pool No. 1		Percent	
Jan. 1, 1957, base cost	$10,000	100	$10,000
Dec. 31, 1957, increment	2,000	110	2,200
Dec. 31, 1960 increment	1,000	120	1,200
Total	$13,000		$13,400
Pool No. 2		Percent	
Jan. 1, 1957, base cost	$ 5,000	100	$ 5,000
Dec. 31, 1960, increment	3,000	140	4,200
Total	$ 8,000		$ 9,200

(b) The computation of the ratio of the total current-year cost to the total base-year cost for the base year and each yearly layer of increment in the new pool is as follows:

Pool	Base year 1957	Increments Dec. 31, 1957	Dec. 31, 1960
No. 1:			
Base-year cost	$10,000	$2,000	$1,000
LIFO value	10,000	2,200	1,200
No. 2:			
Base-year cost	5,000	......	3,000
LIFO value	5,000	......	4,200
Total, base-year cost	$15,000	$2,000	$4,000
Total, LIFO value	15,000	2,200	5,400
Ratio of total current-year cost to total base-year cost (percent)	100	110	135

(c) On the basis of the foregoing computations, the LIFO inventory of the new pool at December 31, 1960, is restated as follows:

	Dec. 31, 1960, inventory at Jan. 1, 1957, base-year cost	Ratio of total current-year cost to total base-year cost	Dec. 31, 1960, inventory at LIFO value
		Percent	
Jan. 1, 1957, base cost	$15,000	100	$15,000
Dec. 31, 1957, increment	2,000	110	2,200
Dec. 31, 1960, increment	4,000	135	5,400
Total	$21,000	...	$22,600

(iv) In combining pools having different base years, the principles set forth in subdivision (iii) of this subparagraph are to be applied, except that all base years subsequent to the earliest base

Reg. § 1.472-8(g)(2)

Methods of Accounting

year shall be treated as increments, and the base-year costs for all pools having a base year subsequent to the earliest base year of any pool shall be redetermined in terms of the base cost for the earliest base year. The foregoing may be illustrated by the following example:

Example. (a) Assume that the taxpayer has two pools at December 31, 1960. Under the provisions of this section the taxpayer combines these pools into a single pool as of January 1, 1961. The LIFO inventory value of each pool at December 31, 1960, is shown as follows:

	Dec. 31, 1960, inventory at Jan. 1, 1956, base-year cost	Ratio of total current-year cost to total base-year cost	Dec. 31, 1960, inventory at LIFO value
Pool No. 1		Percent	
Jan. 1, 1956, base cost	$ 7,000	100	$ 7,000
Dec. 31, 1956, increment	1,000	105	1,050
Dec. 31, 1957, increment	500	110	550
Dec. 31, 1958, increment	500	110	550
Dec. 31, 1960, increment	1,000	120	1,200
Total	$10,000	...	$10,350

	Dec. 31, 1960, inventory at Jan. 1, 1958, base-year cost		
Pool No. 2			
Jan. 1, 1958, base cost	$3,500	100	$ 3,500
Dec. 31, 1958, increment	1,000	110	1,100
Dec. 31, 1959, increment	500	115	575
Total	$5,000	...	$ 5,175

(b) The next step is to redetermine the 1958 base-year cost for Pool No. 2 in terms of 1956 base-year cost. January 1, 1956 base-year unit cost must be reconstructed or established in accordance with paragraph (e)(2) of this section for each item in Pool No. 2. Such costs are assumed to be $9.00 for item A, $20.00 for item B, and $1.80 for item C. A ratio of the 1958 total base-year cost to the 1956 total base-year cost for Pool No. 2 is computed as follows:

Item	Quantity	Jan. 1, 1956, base-year unit cost	Jan. 1, 1956, base-year cost
A	250	$ 9.00	$2,250
B	75	20.00	1,500
C	500	1.80	900
Total			$4,650

Item	Quantity	Jan. 1, 1958, base-year unit cost	Jan. 1, 1958, base-year cost
A	250	$10.00	$2,500
B	75	20.00	1,500
C	500	2.00	1,000
Total			$5,000

(c) The ratio of the 1956 total base-year cost to the 1958 total base-year cost for Pool No. 2 is 4,650/5,000 or 93 percent. The January 1, 1958 base cost and each yearly layer of increment at 1958 base-year cost is multiplied by this ratio. Such computation is as follows:

Reg. § 1.472-8(g)(2)

37,164 Methods of Accounting

See p. 20,601 for regulations not amended to reflect law changes

	Dec. 31, 1960, inventory at Jan. 1, 1958, base-year cost	Ratio Percent	Dec. 31, 1960, inventory restated at Jan. 1, 1956, base-year cost
Jan. 1, 1958, base cost	$3,500	93	$3,255
Dec. 31, 1958, increment	1,000	93	930
Dec. 31, 1959, increment	500	93	465
Total			$4,650

(d) The computation of the ratio of the total current-year cost to the total base-year cost for the base year (1956) and each yearly layer of increment in the new pool is as follows:

	Base year 1956	Dec. 31, 1956	Dec. 31, 1957	Dec. 31, 1958	Dec. 31, 1959	Dec. 31, 1960
Pool No. 1:						
Base-year cost	$7,000	$1,000	$ 500	$ 500	...	$1,000
LIFO value	7,000	1,050	550	550	...	1,200
No. 2:						
Base-year cost as restated	...	...	3,255	930	$ 465	...
LIFO value	...	...	3,500	1,100	575	...
Total, base-year cost	$7,000	$1,000	$3,755	$1,430	$ 465	$1,000
Totals, LIFO value	7,000	1,050	4,050	1,650	575	1,200
Ratio of total current-year cost to total base-year cost (percent)	100.00	105.00	107.86	115.38	123.66	120.00

(e) On the basis of the foregoing computation, the LIFO inventory of the new pool at December 31, 1960, is restated as follows:

	Dec. 31, 1960, inventory at Jan. 1, 1956, base-year cost	Ratio of total current-year cost to total base-year cost Percent	Dec. 31, 1960, inventory at LIFO value
Jan. 1, 1956, base cost	$ 7,000	100.00	$ 7,000
Dec. 31, 1956, increment	1,000	105.00	1,050
Dec. 31, 1957, increment	3,755	107.86	4,050
Dec. 31, 1958, increment	1,430	115.38	1,650
Dec. 31, 1959, increment	465	123.66	575
Dec. 31, 1960, increment	1,000	120.00	1,200
Total	$14,650	...	$15,525

(3) *Change in methods of computation of the LIFO value of a dollar-value pool.* For the first taxable year beginning after December 31, 1960, the taxpayer must use a method authorized by paragraph (e)(1) of this section in computing the base-year cost and current-year cost of a dollar-value inventory pool for the end of such year. If the taxpayer had previously used any methods other than one authorized by paragraph (e)(1) of this section, he shall not be required to recompute his LIFO inventories for taxable years beginning on or before December 31, 1960, under a method authorized by such paragraph. The base cost and layers of increment previously computed by such other method shall be retained and treated as if such base cost and layers of increment had been computed under a method authorized by paragraph (e)(1) of this section. The taxpayer shall use the year of change as the base year in applying the double-extension method or other method approved by the Commissioner, instead of the earliest year for which he adopted the LIFO method for any items in the pool.

(h) *LIFO inventories received in certain nonrecognition transactions*—(1) *In general.* Except as provided in paragraph (h)(3) of this section, if inventory items accounted for under the LIFO method are received in a transaction described in paragraph (h)(2) of this section, then, for the purpose of determining future increments and liquidations, the transferee must use the year of transfer as the base year and must use its current-

Reg. § 1.472-8(g)(3)

year cost (computed under the transferee's method of accounting) of those items as their new base-year cost. If the transferee had opening inventories in the year of transfer, then, for the purpose of determining future increments and liquidations, the transferee must use its current-year cost (computed under the transferee's method of accounting) of those inventories as their new base-year cost. For this purpose, "opening inventory" refers to all items owned by the transferee before the transfer for which the transferee uses, or elects to use, the LIFO method. The total new base-year cost of the transferee's inventory as of the beginning of the year of transfer is equal to the new base-year cost of the inventory received from the transferor and the new base-year cost of the transferee's opening inventory. The index (or, the cumulative index in the case of the link-chain method) for the year immediately preceding the year of transfer is 1.00. The base-year cost of any layers in the dollar-value pool, as determined after the transfer, must be recomputed accordingly. See paragraph (e)(3)(iv)(B)(*1*) of this section for an example of this computation.

(2) *Transactions to which this paragraph (h) applies.* The rules in this paragraph (h) apply to a transaction in which—

(i) The transferee determines its basis in the inventories, in whole or in part, by reference to the basis of the inventories in the hands of the transferor;

(ii) The transferor used the dollar-value LIFO method to account for the transferred inventories;

(iii) The transferee uses the dollar-value LIFO method to account for the inventories in the year of the transfer; and

(iv) The transaction is not described in section 381(a).

(3) *Anti-avoidance rule.* The rules in this paragraph (h) do not apply to a transaction entered into with the principal purpose to avail the transferee of a method of accounting that would be unavailable to the transferor (or would be unavailable to the transferor without securing consent from the Commissioner). In determining the principal purpose of a transfer, consideration will be given to all of the facts and circumstances. However, a transfer is deemed made with the principal purpose to avail the transferee of a method of accounting that would be unavailable to the transferor without securing consent from the Commissioner if the transferor acquired inventory in a bargain purchase within the five taxable years preceding the year of the transfer and used a dollar-value LIFO method to account for that inventory that did not treat the bargain purchase inventory and physically identical inventory acquired at market prices as separate items. Inventory is deemed acquired in a bargain purchase if the actual cost of the inventory (or, if appropriate, the allocated cost of the inventory) was less than or equal to 50 percent of the replacement cost of physically identical inventory. Inventory is not considered acquired in a bargain purchase if the actual cost of the inventory (or, if appropriate, the allocated cost of the inventory) was greater than or equal to 75 percent of the replacement cost of physically identical inventory.

(4) *Effective date.* The rules of this paragraph (h) are applicable for transfers that occur during a taxable year ending on or after December 31, 2001. [Reg. § 1.472-8.]

☐ [*T.D.* 6539, 1-19-61. *Amended by T.D.* 7814, 3-15-82 *and T.D.* 8976, 1-8-2002 (*corrected* 2-1-2002).]

[Reg. § 1.475-0]

§ 1.475-0. Table of contents.—This section lists the major captions in §§ 1.475(a)-3, 1.475(b)-1, 1.475(b)-2, 1.475(b)-4, 1.475(c)-1, 1.475(c)-2, 1.475(d)-1, and 1.475(e)-1.

§ 1.475(a)-1 [Reserved]

§ 1.475(a)-2 [Reserved]

§ 1.475(a)-3 Acquisition by a dealer of a security with a substituted basis.

(a) Scope.

(b) Rules.

§ 1.475(b)-1 Scope of exemptions from mark-to-market requirement.

(a) Securities held for investment or not held for sale.

(b) Securities deemed identified as held for investment.

(1) In general.

(2) Relationships.

(i) General rule.

(ii) Attribution.

(iii) Trusts treated as partnerships.

(3) Securities traded on certain established financial markets.

(4) Changes in status.

(i) Onset of prohibition against marking.

(ii) Termination of prohibition against marking.

(iii) Examples.

(c) Securities deemed not held for investment; dealers in notional principal contracts and derivatives.

(d) Special rule for hedges of another member's risk.

(e) Transitional rules.

Reg. § 1.475-0

Methods of Accounting

See p. 20,601 for regulations not amended to reflect law changes

(1) Stock, partnership, and beneficial ownership interests in certain controlled corporations, partnerships, and trusts before January 23, 1997.
    (i) In general.
    (ii) Control defined.
    (iii) Applicability.
(2) Dealers in notional principal contracts and derivatives acquired before January 23, 1997.
    (i) General rule.
    (ii) Exception for securities not acquired in dealer capacity.
    (iii) Applicability.

§ 1.475(b)-2 Exemptions—identification requirements.
(a) Identification of the basis for exemption.
(b) Time for identifying a security with a substituted basis.
(c) Integrated transactions under § 1.1275-6.
    (1) Definitions.
    (2) Synthetic debt held by a taxpayer as a result of legging in.
    (3) Securities held after legging out.

§ 1.475(b)-3 [Reserved]

§ 1.475(b)-4 Exemptions—transitional issues.
(a) Transitional identification.
    (1) Certain securities previously identified under section 1236.
    (2) Consistency requirement for other securities.
(b) Corrections on or before January 31, 1994.
    (1) Purpose.
    (2) To conform to § 1.475(b)-1(a).
        (i) Added identifications.
        (ii) Limitations.
    (3) To conform to § 1.475(b)-1(c).
(c) Effect of corrections.

§ 1.475(c)-1 Definitions—dealer in securities.
(a) Dealer-customer relationship.
    (1) [Reserved].
    (2) Transactions described in section 475(c)(1)(B).
        (i) In general.
        (ii) Examples.
    (3) Related parties.
        (i) General rule.
        (ii) Special rule for members of a consolidated group.
            (iii) The intragroup-customer election.
                (A) Effect of election.
                (B) Making and revoking the election.
            (iv) Examples.
(b) Sellers of nonfinancial goods and services.

(1) Purchases and sales of customer paper.
(2) Definition of customer paper.
(3) Exceptions.
(4) Election not to be governed by the exception for sellers of nonfinancial goods or services.
    (i) Method of making the election.
        (A) Taxable years ending after December 24, 1996.
        (B) Taxable years ending on or before December 24, 1996.
    (ii) Continued applicability of an election.
(c) Taxpayers that purchase securities from customers but engage in no more than negligible sales of the securities.
    (1) Exemption from dealer status.
        (i) General rule.
        (ii) Election to be treated as a dealer.
    (2) Negligible sales.
    (3) Special rules for members of a consolidated group.
        (i) Intragroup-customer election in effect.
        (ii) Intragroup-customer election not in effect.
    (4) Special rules.
    (5) Example.
(d) Issuance of life insurance products.

§ 1.475(c)-2 Definitions—security.
(a) Items that are not securities.
(b) Synthetic debt that § 1.1275-6(b) treats the taxpayer as holding.
(c) Negative value REMIC residuals acquired before January 4, 1995.
    (1) Description.
    (2) Special rules applicable to negative value REMIC residuals acquired before January 4, 1995.

§ 1.475(d)-1 Character of gain or loss.
(a) Securities never held in connection with the taxpayer's activities as a dealer in securities.
(b) Ordinary treatment for notional principal contracts and derivatives held by dealers in notional principal contracts and derivatives.

§ 1.475(e)-1 Effective dates.
[Reg. § 1.475-0.]
☐ [T.D. 8700, 12-23-96.]

[Reg. § 1.475(a)-3]

§ 1.475(a)-3. Acquisition by a dealer of a security with a substituted basis.—(a) *Scope.* This section applies if—
(1) A dealer in securities acquires a security that is subject to section 475(a) and the dealer's basis in the security is determined, in whole or in part, by reference to the basis of that security in

the hands of the person from whom the security was acquired; or

(2) A dealer in securities acquires a security that is subject to section 475(a) and the dealer's basis in the security is determined, in whole or in part, by reference to other property held at any time by the dealer.

(b) *Rules.* If this section applies to a security—

(1) Section 475(a) applies only to changes in value of the security occurring after the acquisition; and

(2) Any built-in gain or loss with respect to the security (based on the difference between the fair market value of the security on the date the dealer acquired it and its basis to the dealer on that date) is taken into account at the time, and has the character, provided by the sections of the Internal Revenue Code that would apply to the built-in gain or loss if section 475(a) did not apply to the security. [Reg. § 1.475(a)-3.]

☐ [T.D. 8700, 12-23-96.]

[Reg. § 1.475(b)-1]

§ 1.475(b)-1. **Scope of exemptions from mark-to-market requirement.**—(a) *Securities held for investment or not held for sale.* Except as otherwise provided by this section and subject to the identification requirements of section 475(b)(2), a security is held for investment (within the meaning of section 475(b)(1)(A)) or not held for sale (within the meaning of section 475(b)(1)(B)) if it is not held by the taxpayer primarily for sale to customers in the ordinary course of the taxpayer's trade or business.

(b) *Securities deemed identified as held for investment*—(1) *In general.* The following items held by a dealer in securities are per se held for investment within the meaning of section 475(b)(1)(A) and are deemed to be properly identified as such for purposes of section 475(b)(2)—

(i) Except as provided in paragraph (b)(3) of this section, stock in a corporation, or a partnership or beneficial ownership interest in a widely held or publicly traded partnership or trust, to which the taxpayer has a relationship specified in paragraph (b)(2) of this section; or

(ii) A contract that is treated for federal income tax purposes as an annuity, endowment, or life insurance contract (see sections 72, 817, and 7702).

(2) *Relationships*—(i) *General rule.* The relationships specified in this paragraph (b)(2) are—

(A) Those described in section 267(b)(2), (3), (10), (11), or (12); or

(B) Those described in section 707(b)(1)(A) or (B).

(ii) *Attribution.* The relationships described in paragraph (b)(2)(i) of this section are determined taking into account sections 267(c) and 707(b)(3), as appropriate.

(iii) *Trusts treated as partnerships.* For purposes of this paragraph (b)(2), the phrase *partnership or trust* is substituted for the word *partnership* in sections 707(b)(1) and (3), and a reference to beneficial ownership interest is added to each reference to capital interest or profits interest in those sections.

(3) *Securities traded on certain established financial markets.* Paragraph (b)(1)(i) of this section does not apply to a security if—

(i) The security is actively traded within the meaning of § 1.1092(d)-1(a) taking into account only established financial markets identified in § 1.1092(d)-1(b)(1)(i) or (ii) (describing national securities exchanges and interdealer quotation systems);

(ii) Less than 15 percent of all of the outstanding shares or interests in the same class are held by the taxpayer and all persons having a relationship to the taxpayer that is specified in paragraph (b)(2) of this section; and

(iii) If the security was acquired (e.g., on original issue) from a person having a relationship to the taxpayer that is specified in paragraph (b)(2) of this section, then, after the time the security was acquired—

(A) At least one full business day has passed, and

(B) There has been significant trading involving persons not having a relationship to the taxpayer that is specified in paragraph (b)(2) of this section.

(4) *Changes in status*—(i) *Onset of prohibition against marking*—(A) Once paragraph (b)(1) of this section begins to apply to the security and for so long as it continues to apply, section 475(a) does not apply to the security in the hands of the taxpayer.

(B) If a security has not been timely identified under section 475(b)(2) and, after the last day on which such an identification would have been timely, paragraph (b)(1) of this section begins to apply to the security, then the dealer must recognize gain or loss on the security as if it were sold for its fair market value as of the close of business of the last day before paragraph (b)(1) of this section begins to apply to the security, and gain or loss is taken into account at that time.

(ii) *Termination of prohibition against marking.* If a taxpayer did not timely identify a security under section 475(b)(2), and paragraph (b)(1) of this section applies to the security on the last day on which such an identification would have been timely but thereafter ceases to apply—

(A) An identification of the security under section 475(b)(2) is timely if made on or before the close of the day paragraph (b)(1) of this section ceases to apply; and

(B) Unless the taxpayer timely identifies the security under section 475(b)(2) (taking into account the additional time for identification that is provided by paragraph (b)(4)(ii)(A) of this section), section 475(a) applies to changes in value of the security after the cessation in the same manner as under section 475(b)(3).

(iii) *Examples.* These examples illustrate this paragraph (b)(4):

Example 1. Onset of prohibition against marking—(A) *Facts.* Corporation H owns 75 percent of the stock of corporation D, a dealer in securities within the meaning of section 475(c)(1). On December 1, 1995, D acquired less than half of the stock in corporation X. D did not identify the stock for purposes of section 475(b)(2). On July 17, 1996, H acquired from other persons 70 percent of the stock of X. As a result, D and X became related within the meaning of paragraph (b)(2)(i) of this section. The stock of X is not described in paragraph (b)(3) of this section (concerning some securities traded on certain established financial markets).

(B) *Holding.* Under paragraph (b)(4)(i) of this section, D recognizes gain or loss on its X stock as if the stock were sold for its fair market value at the close of business on July 16, 1996, and the gain or loss is taken into account at that time. As with any application of section 475(a), proper adjustment is made in the amount of any gain or loss subsequently realized. After July 16, 1996, section 475(a) does not apply to D's X stock while paragraph (b)(1)(i) of this section (concerning the relationship between X and D) continues to apply.

Example 2. Termination of prohibition against marking; retained securities identified as held for investment—(A) *Facts.* On July 1, 1996, corporation H owned 60 percent of the stock of corporation Y and all of the stock of corporation D, a dealer in securities within the meaning of section 475(c)(1). Thus, D and Y are related within the meaning of paragraph (b)(2)(i) of this section. Also on July 1, 1996, D acquired, as an investment, 10 percent of the stock of Y. The stock of Y is not described in paragraph (b)(3) of this section (concerning some securities traded on certain established financial markets). When D acquired its shares of Y stock, it did not identify them for purposes of section 475(b)(2). On December 24, 1996, D identified its shares of Y stock as held for investment under section 475(b)(2). On December 30, 1996, H sold all of its shares of stock in Y to an unrelated party. As a result, D and Y ceased to be related within the meaning of paragraph (b)(2)(i) of this section.

(B) *Holding.* Under paragraph (b)(4)(ii)(A) of this section, identification of the Y shares is timely if done on or before the close of December 30, 1996. Because D timely identified its Y shares under section 475(b)(2), it continues after December 30, 1996, to refrain from marking to market its Y stock.

Example 3. Termination of prohibition against marking; retained securities not identified as held for investment—(A) *Facts.* The facts are the same as in *Example 2* above, except that D did not identify its stock in Y for purposes of section 475(b)(2) on or before December 30, 1996. Thus, D did not timely identify these securities under section 475(b)(2) (taking into account the additional time for identification provided in paragraph (b)(4)(ii)(A) of this section).

(B) *Holding.* Under paragraph (b)(4)(ii)(B) of this section, section 475(a) applies to changes in value of D's Y stock after December 30, 1996, in the same manner as under section 475(b)(3). Thus, any appreciation or depreciation that occurred while the securities were prohibited from being marked to market is suspended. Further, section 475(a) applies only to those changes occurring after December 30, 1996.

Example 4. Acquisition of actively traded stock from related party—(A) *Facts.* Corporation P is the parent of a consolidated group whose taxable year is the calendar year, and corporation M, a member of that group, is a dealer in securities within the meaning of section 475(c)(1). Corporation M regularly acts as a market maker with respect to common and preferred stock of corporation P. Corporation P has outstanding 2,000,000 shares of series X preferred stock, which are traded on a national securities exchange. During the business day on December 29, 1997, corporation P sold 100,000 shares of series X preferred stock to corporation M for $100 per share. Subsequently, also on December 29, 1997, persons not related to corporation M engaged in significant trading of the series X preferred stock. At the close of business on December 30, 1997, the fair market value of series X stock was $99 per share. At the close of business on December 31, 1997, the fair market value of series X stock was $98.50 per share. Corporation M sold the series X stock on the exchange on January 2, 1998. At all relevant times, corporation M and all persons related to M owned less than 15% of the outstanding series X preferred stock.

(B) *Holding.* The 100,000 shares of series X preferred stock held by corporation M are not subject to mark-to-market treatment under section 475(a) on December 29, 1997, because at that time the stock was held for less than one full business day and is therefore treated as properly identified as held for investment. At the close of business on December 30, 1997, that prohibition on marking ceases to apply, and section 475(b)(3) begins to apply. The built-in loss is suspended, and subsequent appreciation and depreciation are subject to section 475(a). Accordingly, when corporation M marks the series X stock to market at the close of business on December 31, 1997, under section 475(a) it recognizes and takes into account a loss of $.50 per share. Under section 475(b)(3), when corporation M sells the series X stock on January 2, 1998, it takes into account the suspended loss, that is, the difference between the $100 per share it paid corporation P for that stock and the $99-per-share fair market value when section 475(b)(1) ceased to be apply to the stock. No deduction, however, is allowed for that loss. (See § 1.1502-13(f)(6), under which no deduction is allowed to a member of a consolidated group for a loss with respect to a share of stock of the parent of that consolidated group, if the member does not take the gain or loss into account pursuant to section 475(a).)

(c) *Securities deemed not held for investment; dealers in notional principal contracts and derivatives*—(1) Except as otherwise determined by the Commissioner in a revenue ruling, revenue procedure, or letter ruling, section 475(b)(1)(A) (exempting from mark-to-market accounting certain securities that are held for investment) does not apply to a security if—

(i) The security is described in section 475(c)(2)(D) or (E) (describing certain notional principal contracts and derivative securities); and

(ii) The taxpayer is a dealer in such securities.

(2) See § 1.475(d)-1(b) for a rule concerning the character of gain or loss on securities described in this paragraph (c).

(d) *Special rule for hedges of another member's risk.* A taxpayer may identify under section 475(b)(1)(C) (exempting certain hedges from mark-to-market accounting) a security that hedges a position of another member of the taxpayer's consolidated group if the security meets the following requirements—

(1) The security is a hedging transaction within the meaning of § 1.1221-2(b);

(2) The security is timely identified as a hedging transaction under § 1.1221-2(f) (including identification of the hedged item); and

(3) The security hedges a position that is not marked to market under section 475(a).

(e) *Transitional rules*—(1) *Stock, partnership, and beneficial ownership interests in certain controlled corporations, partnerships, and trusts before January 23, 1997*—(i) *In general.* The following items held by a dealer in securities are per se held for investment within the meaning of section 475(b)(1)(A) and are deemed to be properly identified as such for purposes of section 475(b)(2)—

(A) Stock in a corporation that the taxpayer controls (within the meaning of paragraph (e)(1)(ii) of this section); or

(B) A partnership or beneficial ownership interest in a widely held or publicly traded partnership or trust that the taxpayer controls (within the meaning of paragraph (e)(1)(ii) of this section).

(ii) *Control defined.* Control means the ownership, directly or indirectly through persons described in section 267(b) (taking into account section 267(c)), of—

(A) 50 percent or more of the total combined voting power of all classes of stock entitled to vote; or

(B) 50 percent or more of the capital interest, the profits interest, or the beneficial ownership interest in the widely held or publicly traded partnership or trust.

(iii) *Applicability.* The rules of this paragraph (e)(1) apply only before January 23, 1997.

(2) *Dealers in notional principal contracts and derivatives acquired before January 23, 1997*—(i) *General rule.* Section 475(b)(1)(A) (exempting certain securities from mark-to-market accounting) does not apply to a security if—

(A) The security is described in section 475(c)(2)(D) or (E) (describing certain notional principal contracts and derivative securities); and

(B) The taxpayer is a dealer in such securities.

(ii) *Exception for securities not acquired in dealer capacity.* This paragraph (e)(2) does not apply if the taxpayer establishes unambiguously that the security was not acquired in the taxpayer's capacity as a dealer in such securities.

(iii) *Applicability.* The rules of paragraph (e)(2) apply only to securities acquired before January 23, 1997. [Reg. § 1.475(b)-1.]

☐ [*T.D.* 8700, 12-23-96. Amended by T.D. 8985, 3-15-2002.]

Reg. § 1.475(b)-1(e)(2)

[Reg. § 1.475(b)-2]

§ 1.475(b)-2. Exemptions—Identification requirements.—(a) *Identification of the basis for exemption.* An identification of a security as exempt from mark to market does not satisfy section 475(b)(2) if it fails to state whether the security is described in—

(1) Either of the first two subparagraphs of section 475(b)(1) (identifying a security as held for investment or not held for sale); or

(2) The third subparagraph thereof (identifying a security as a hedge).

(b) *Time for identifying a security with a substituted basis.* For purposes of determining the timeliness of an identification under section 475(b)(2), the date that a dealer acquires a security is not affected by whether the dealer's basis in the security is determined, in whole or in part, either by reference to the basis of the security in the hands of the person from whom the security was acquired or by reference to other property held at any time by the dealer. See § 1.475(a)-3 for rules governing how the dealer accounts for such a security if this identification is not made.

(c) *Integrated transactions under § 1.1275-6*—(1) *Definitions.* The following terms are used in this paragraph (c) with the meanings that are given to them by § 1.1275-6: integrated transaction, legging into, legging out, qualifying debt instrument, § 1.1275-6 hedge, and synthetic debt instrument.

(2) *Synthetic debt held by a taxpayer as a result of legging in.* If a taxpayer is treated as the holder of a synthetic debt instrument as the result of legging into an integrated transaction, then, for purposes of the timeliness of an identification under section 475(b)(2), the synthetic debt instrument is treated as having the same acquisition date as the qualifying debt instrument. A pre-leg-in identification of the qualifying debt instrument under section 475(b)(2) applies to the integrated transaction as well.

(3) *Securities held after legging out.* If a taxpayer legs out of an integrated transaction, then, for purposes of the timeliness of an identification under section 475(b)(2), the qualifying debt instrument, or the § 1.1275-6 hedge, that remains in the taxpayer's hands is generally treated as having been acquired, originated, or entered into, as the case may be, immediately after the leg-out. If any loss or deduction determined under § 1.1275-6(d)(2)(ii)(B) is disallowed by § 1.1275-6(d)(2)(ii)(D) (which disallows deductions when a taxpayer legs out of an integrated transaction within 30 days of legging in), then, for purposes of this section and section 475(b)(2), the qualifying debt instrument that remains in the taxpayer's hands is treated as having been acquired on the same date that the synthetic debt instrument was treated as having been acquired. [Reg. § 1.475(b)-2.]

☐ [T.D. 8700, 12-23-96.]

[Reg. § 1.475(b)-4]

§ 1.475(b)-4. Exemptions—Transitional issues.—(a) *Transitional identification*—(1) *Certain securities previously identified under section 1236.* If, as of the close of the last taxable year ending before December 31, 1993, a security was identified under section 1236 as a security held for investment, the security is treated as being identified as held for investment for purposes of section 475(b).

(2) *Consistency requirement for other securities.* In the case of a security (including a security described in section 475(c)(2)(F)) that is not described in paragraph (a)(1) of this section and that was held by the taxpayer as of the close of the last taxable year ending before December 31, 1993, the security is treated as having been properly identified under section 475(b)(2) or 475(c)(2)(F)(iii) if the information contained in the dealer's books and records as of the close of that year supports the identification. If there is any ambiguity in those records, the taxpayer must, no later than January 31, 1994, place in its records a statement resolving this ambiguity and indicating unambiguously which securities are to be treated as properly identified. Any information that supports treating a security as having been properly identified under section 475(b)(2) or (c)(2)(F)(iii) must be applied consistently from one security to another.

(b) *Corrections on or before January 31, 1994*—(1) *Purpose.* This paragraph (b) allows a taxpayer to add or remove certain identifications covered by § 1.475(b)-1.

(2) *To conform to § 1.475(b)-1(a)*—(i) *Added identifications.* To the extent permitted by paragraph (b)(2)(ii) of this section, a taxpayer may identify as being described in section 475(b)(1)(A) or (B)—

(A) A security that was held for immediate sale but was not held primarily for sale to customers in the ordinary course of the taxpayer's trade or business (for example, a trading security); or

(B) An evidence of indebtedness that was not held for sale to customers in the ordinary course of the taxpayer's trade or business and that the taxpayer intended to hold for less than one year.

Reg. § 1.475(b)-2(a)(1)

(ii) *Limitations.* An identification described in paragraph (b)(2)(i) of this section is permitted only if—

(A) Prior to December 28, 1993, the taxpayer did not identify as being described in section 475(b)(1)(A) or (B) any of the securities described in paragraph (b)(2)(i) of this section;

(B) The taxpayer identifies every security described in paragraph (b)(2)(i) of this section for which a timely identification of the security under section 475(b)(2) cannot be made after the date on which the taxpayer makes these added identifications; and

(C) The identification is made on or before January 31, 1994.

(3) *To conform to § 1.475(b)-1(c).* On or before January 31, 1994, a taxpayer described in § 1.475(b)-1(e)(2)(i)(B) may remove an identification under section 475(b)(1)(A) of a security described in § 1.475(b)-1(e)(2)(i)(A).

(c) *Effect of corrections.* An identification added under paragraph (a)(2) or (b)(2) of this section is timely for purposes of section 475(b)(2) or (c)(2)(F)(iii). An identification removed under paragraph (a)(2) or (b)(3) of this section does not subject the taxpayer to the provisions of section 475(d)(2). [Reg. § 1.475(b)-4.]

☐ [T.D. 8700, 12-23-96.]

[Reg. § 1.475(c)-1]

§ 1.475(c)-1. Definitions—Dealer in securities.—(a) *Dealer-customer relationship.* Whether a taxpayer is transacting business with customers is determined on the basis of all of the facts and circumstances.

(1) [Reserved].

(2) *Transactions described in section 475(c)(1)(B)*—(i) *In general.* For purposes of section 475(c)(1)(B), the term *dealer in securities* includes, but is not limited to, a taxpayer that, in the ordinary course of the taxpayer's trade or business, regularly holds itself out as being willing and able to enter into either side of a transaction enumerated in section 475(c)(1)(B).

(ii) *Examples.* The following examples illustrate the rules of this paragraph (a)(2). In the following examples, *B* is a bank and is not a member of a consolidated group:

Example 1. B regularly offers to enter into interest rate swaps with other persons in the ordinary course of its trade or business. *B* is willing to enter into interest rate swaps under which it either pays a fixed interest rate and receives a floating rate or pays a floating rate and receives a fixed rate. *B* is a dealer in securities under section 475(c)(1)(B), and the counterparties are its customers.

Example 2. B, in the ordinary course of its trade or business, regularly holds itself out as being willing and able to enter into either side of positions in a foreign currency with other banks in the interbank market. *B*'s activities in the foreign currency make it a dealer in securities under section 475(c)(1)(B), and the other banks in the interbank market are its customers.

Example 3. B engages in frequent transactions in a foreign currency in the interbank market. Unlike the facts in *Example 2*, however, *B* does not regularly hold itself out as being willing and able to enter into either side of positions in the foreign currency, and all of *B*'s transactions are driven by its internal need to adjust its position in the currency. No other circumstances are present to suggest that *B* is a dealer in securities for purposes of section 475(c)(1)(B). *B*'s activity in the foreign currency does not qualify it as a dealer in securities for purposes of section 475(c)(1)(B), and its transactions in the interbank market are not transactions with customers.

(3) *Related parties*—(i) *General rule.* Except as provided in paragraph (a)(3)(ii) of this section (concerning transactions between members of a consolidated group, as defined in § 1.1502-1(h)), a taxpayer's transactions with related persons may be transactions with customers for purposes of section 475. For example, if a taxpayer, in the ordinary course of the taxpayer's trade or business, regularly holds itself out to its foreign subsidiaries or other related persons as being willing and able to enter into either side of transactions enumerated in section 475(c)(1)(B), the taxpayer is a dealer in securities within the meaning of section 475(c)(1), even if it engages in no other transactions with customers.

(ii) *Special rule for members of a consolidated group.* Solely for purposes of paragraph (c)(1) of section 475 (concerning the definition of dealer in securities) and except as provided in paragraph (a)(3)(iii) of this section, a taxpayer's transactions with other members of its consolidated group are not with customers. Accordingly, notwithstanding paragraph (a)(2) of this section, the fact that a taxpayer regularly holds itself out to other members of its consolidated group as being willing and able to enter into either side of a transaction enumerated in section 475(c)(1)(B) does not cause the taxpayer to be a dealer in securities within the meaning of section 475(c)(1)(B).

(iii) *The intragroup-customer election*—(A) *Effect of election.* If a consolidated group makes the intragroup-customer election, paragraph (a)(3)(ii) of this section (special rule for members of a consolidated group) does not apply to the members of the group. Thus, a member of a group that has made this election may be a dealer in securities within the meaning of section 475(c)(1) even if its only customer transactions are with other members of its consolidated group.

(B) *Making and revoking the election.* Unless the Commissioner otherwise prescribes, the intragroup-customer election is made by filing a statement that says, "[Insert name and employer identification number of common parent] hereby makes the Intragroup-Customer Election (as described in § 1.475(c)-1(a)(3)(iii) of the income tax regulations) for the taxable year ending [describe the last day of the year] and for subsequent taxable years." The statement must be signed by the common parent and attached to the timely filed federal income tax return for the consolidated group for that taxable year. The election applies for that year and continues in effect for subsequent years until revoked. The election may be revoked only with the consent of the Commissioner.

(iv) *Examples.* The following examples illustrate this paragraph (a)(3):

General Facts. HC, a hedging center, provides interest rate hedges to all of the members of its affiliated group (as defined in section 1504(a)(1)). Because of the efficiencies created by having a centralized risk manager, group policy prohibits members other than HC from entering into derivative interest rate positions with outside parties. HC regularly holds itself out as being willing and able to, and in fact does, enter into either side of interest rate swaps with its fellow members. HC periodically computes its aggregate position and hedges the net risk with an unrelated party. HC does not otherwise enter into interest rate positions with persons that are not members of the affiliated group. HC attempts to operate at cost, and the terms of its swaps do not factor in any risk of default by the affiliate. Thus, HC's affiliates receive somewhat more favorable terms then they would receive from an unrelated swaps dealer (a fact that may subject HC and its fellow members to reallocation of income under section 482). No other circumstances are present to suggest that HC is a dealer in securities for purposes of section 475(c)(1)(B).

Example 1. General rule for related persons. In addition to the *General Facts* stated above, assume that HC's affiliated group has not elected under section 1501 to file a consolidated return. Under paragraph (a)(3)(i) of this section, HC's transactions with its affiliates can be transactions with customers for purposes of section 475(c)(1). Thus, under paragraph (a)(2)(i) of this section, HC is a dealer in securities within the meaning of section 475(c)(1)(B), and the members of the group with which it does business are its customers.

Example 2. Special rule for members of a consolidated group. In addition to the *General Facts* stated above, assume that HC's affiliated group has elected to file consolidated returns and has not made the intragroup-customer election. Under paragraph (a)(3)(ii) of this section, HC's interest rate swap transactions with the members of its consolidated group are not transactions with customers for purposes of determining whether HC is a dealer in securities within the meaning of section 475(c)(1). Further, the fact that HC regularly holds itself out to members of its consolidated group as being willing and able to enter into either side of a transaction enumerated in section 475(c)(1)(B) does not cause HC to be a dealer in securities within the meaning of section 475(c)(1)(B). Because no other circumstances are present to suggest that HC is a dealer in securities for purposes of section 475(c)(1)(B), HC is not a dealer in securities.

Example 3. Intragroup-customer election. In addition to the *General Facts* stated above, assume that HC's affiliated group has elected to file a consolidated return but has also made the intragroup-customer election under paragraph (a)(3)(iii) of this section. Thus, the analysis and result are the same as in *Example 1.*

(b) *Sellers of nonfinancial goods and services*—(1) *Purchases and sales of customer paper.* Except as provided in paragraph (b)(3) of this section, if a taxpayer would not be a dealer in securities within the meaning of section 475(c)(1) but for its purchases and sales of debt instruments that, at the time of purchase or sale, are customer paper with respect to either the taxpayer or a corporation that is a member of the same consolidated group (as defined in § 1.1502-1(h)) as the taxpayer, then for purposes of section 475 the taxpayer is not a dealer in securities.

(2) *Definition of customer paper.* A debt instrument is customer paper with respect to a person at a point in time if—

(i) The person's principal activity is selling nonfinancial goods or providing nonfinancial services;

(ii) The debt instrument was issued by a purchaser of the goods or services at the time of the purchase of those goods or services in order to finance the purchase; and

(iii) At all times since the debt instrument was issued, it has been held either by the person selling those goods or services or by a corporation that is a member of the same consolidated group as that person.

(3) *Exceptions.* Paragraph (b)(1) of this section does not apply if—

(i) For purposes of section 471, the taxpayer accounts for any security (as defined in section 475(c)(2)) as inventory;

(ii) The taxpayer is subject to an election under paragraph (b)(4) of this section; or

(iii) The taxpayer is not described in paragraph (b)(2)(i) of this section and one or more debt instruments that are customer paper with respect to a corporation that is a member of the same consolidated group as the taxpayer are accounted for by the taxpayer, or by a corporation that is a member of the same consolidated group as the taxpayer, in a manner that allows recognition of unrealized gains or losses or deductions for additions to a reserve for bad debts.

(4) *Election not to be governed by the exception for sellers of nonfinancial goods or services*—(i) *Method of making the election.* Unless the Commissioner otherwise prescribes, an election under this paragraph (b)(4) must be made in the manner, and at the time, prescribed in this paragraph (b)(4)(i). The taxpayer must file with the Internal Revenue Service a statement that says, "[Insert name and taxpayer identification number of the taxpayer] hereby elects not to be governed by § 1.475(c)-1(b)(1) of the income tax regulations for the taxable year ending [describe the last day of the year] and for subsequent taxable years."

(A) *Taxable years ending after December 24, 1996.* If the first taxable year subject to an election under this paragraph (b)(4) ends after December 24, 1996, the statement must be attached to a timely filed federal income tax return for that taxable year.

(B) *Taxable years ending on or before December 24, 1996.* If the first taxable year subject to an election under this paragraph (b)(4) ends on or before December 24, 1996, and the election changes the taxpayer's taxable income for any taxable year the federal income tax return for which was filed before February 24, 1997, the statement must be attached to an amended return for the earliest such year that is so affected, and that amended return (and an amended return for any other such year that is so affected) must be filed not later than June 23, 1997. If the first taxable year subject to an election under this paragraph (b)(4) ends on or before December 24, 1996, but the taxpayer is not described in the preceding sentence, the statement must be attached to the first federal income tax return that is for a taxable year subject to the election and that is filed on or after February 24, 1997.

(ii) *Continued applicability of an election.* An election under this paragraph (b)(4) continues in effect for subsequent taxable years until revoked. The election may be revoked only with the consent of the Commissioner.

(c) *Taxpayers that purchase securities from customers but engage in no more than negligible sales of the securities*—(1) *Exemption from dealer status*—(i) *General rule.* A taxpayer that regularly purchases securities from customers in the ordinary course of a trade or business (including regularly making loans to customers in the ordinary course of a trade or business of making loans) but engages in no more than negligible sales of the securities so acquired is not a dealer in securities within the meaning of section 475(c)(1) unless the taxpayer elects to be so treated or, for purposes of section 471, the taxpayer accounts for any security (as defined in section 475(c)(2)) as inventory.

(ii) *Election to be treated as a dealer.* A taxpayer described in paragraph (c)(1)(i) of this section elects to be treated as a dealer in securities by filing a federal income tax return reflecting the application of section 475(a) in computing its taxable income.

(2) *Negligible sales.* Solely for purposes of paragraph (c)(1) of this section, a taxpayer engages in negligible sales of debt instruments that it regularly purchases from customers in the ordinary course of its business if, and only if, during the taxable year, either—

(i) The taxpayer sells all or part of fewer than 60 debt instruments, regardless how acquired; or

(ii) The total adjusted basis of the debt instruments (or parts of debt instruments), regardless how acquired, that the taxpayer sells is less than 5 percent of the total basis, immediately after acquisition, of the debt instruments that it acquires in that year.

(3) *Special rules for members of a consolidated group*—(i) *Intragroup-customer election in effect.* If a taxpayer is a member of a consolidated group that has made the intragroup-customer election (described in paragraph (a)(3)(iii) of this section), the negligible sales test in paragraph (c)(2) of this section takes into account all of the taxpayer's sales of debt instruments to other group members.

(ii) *Intragroup-customer election not in effect.* If a taxpayer is a member of a consolidated group that has not made the intragroup-customer election (described in paragraph (a)(3)(iii) of this

Reg. § 1.475(c)-1(c)(3)

section), the taxpayer satisfies the negligible sales test in paragraph (c)(2) of this section if either—

(A) The test is satisfied by the taxpayer, taking into account sales of debt instruments to other group members (as in paragraph (c)(3)(i) of this section); or

(B) The test is satisfied by the group, treating the members of the group as if they were divisions of a single corporation.

(4) *Special rules.* Whether sales of securities are negligible is determined without regard to—

(i) Sales of securities that are necessitated by exceptional circumstances and that are not undertaken as recurring business activities;

(ii) Sales of debt instruments that decline in quality while in the taxpayer's hands and that are sold pursuant to an established policy of the taxpayer to dispose of debt instruments below a certain quality; or

(iii) Acquisitions and sales of debt instruments that are qualitatively different from all debt instruments that the taxpayer purchases from customers in the ordinary course of its business.

(5) *Example.* The following example illustrates paragraph (c)(4)(iii) of this section:

Example. I, an insurance company, regularly makes policy loans to its customers but does not sell them. I, however, actively trades Treasury securities. No other circumstances are present to suggest that I is a dealer in securities for purposes of section 475(c)(1). Since the Treasuries are qualitatively different from the policy loans that I originates, under paragraph (c)(4)(iii) of this section, I disregards the purchases and sales of Treasuries in applying the negligible sales test in paragraph (c)(2) of this section.

(d) *Issuance of life insurance products.* A life insurance company that is not otherwise a dealer in securities within the meaning of section 475(c)(1) does not become a dealer in securities solely because it regularly issues life insurance products to its customers in the ordinary course of a trade or business. For purposes of the preceding sentence, the term *life insurance product* means a contract that is treated for federal income tax purposes as an annuity, endowment, or life insurance contract. See sections 72, 817, and 7702. [Reg. § 1.475(c)-1.]

☐ [T.D. 8700, 12-23-96.]

[Reg. § 1.475(c)-2]

§ 1.475(c)-2. Definitions—Security.—(a) *Items that are not securities.* The following items are not securities within the meaning of section 475(c)(2) with respect to a taxpayer and, therefore, are not subject to section 475—

(1) A security (determined without regard to this paragraph (a)) if section 1032 prevents the taxpayer from recognizing gain or loss with respect to that security;

(2) A debt instrument issued by the taxpayer (including a synthetic debt instrument, within the meaning of § 1.1275-6(b)(4), that § 1.1275-6(b) treats the taxpayer as having issued); or

(3) A REMIC residual interest, or an interest or arrangement that is determined by the Commissioner to have substantially the same economic effect, if the residual interest or the interest or arrangement is acquired on or after January 4, 1995.

(b) *Synthetic debt that § 1.1275-6(b) treats the taxpayer as holding.* If § 1.1275-6 treats a taxpayer as the holder of a synthetic debt instrument (within the meaning of § 1.1275-6(b)(4)), the synthetic debt instrument is a security held by the taxpayer within the meaning of section 475(c)(2)(C).

(c) *Negative value REMIC residuals acquired before January 4, 1995.* A REMIC residual interest that is described in paragraph (c)(1) of this section or an interest or arrangement that is determined by the Commissioner to have substantially the same economic effect is not a security within the meaning of section 475(c)(2).

(1) *Description.* A residual interest in a REMIC is described in this paragraph (c)(1) if, on the date the taxpayer acquires the residual interest, the present value of the anticipated tax liabilities associated with holding the interest exceeds the sum of—

(i) The present value of the expected future distributions on the interest; and

(ii) The present value of the anticipated tax savings associated with holding the interest as the REMIC generates losses.

(2) *Special rules applicable to negative value REMIC residuals acquired before January 4, 1995.* Solely for purposes of this paragraph (c)—

(i) If a transferee taxpayer acquires a residual interest with a basis determined by reference to the transferor's basis, then the transferee is deemed to acquire the interest on the date the transferor acquired it (or is deemed to acquire it under this paragraph (c)(2)(i)).

(ii) Anticipated tax liabilities, expected future distributions, and anticipated tax savings are determined under the rules in § 1.860E-2(a)(3) and without regard to the operation of section 475.

(iii) Present values are determined under the rules in § 1.860E-2(a)(4). [Reg. § 1.475(c)-2.]

☐ [T.D. 8700, 12-23-96.]

[Reg. § 1.475(d)-1]

§ 1.475(d)-1. Character of gain or loss.—(a) *Securities never held in connection with the taxpayer's activities as a dealer in securities.* If a security is never held in connection with the taxpayer's activities as a dealer in securities, section 475(d)(3)(A) does not affect the character of gain or loss from the security, even if the taxpayer fails to identify the security under section 475(b)(2).

(b) *Ordinary treatment for notional principal contracts and derivatives held by dealers in notional principal contracts and derivatives.* Section 475(d)(3)(B)(ii) (concerning the character of gain or loss with respect to a security held by a person other than in connection with its activities as a dealer in securities) does not apply to a security if § 1.475(b)-1(c) and the absence of a determination by the Commissioner prevent section 475(b)(1)(A) from applying to the security. [Reg. § 1.475(d)-1.]

☐ [T.D. 8700, 12-23-96.]

[Reg. § 1.475(e)-1]

§ 1.475(e)-1. Effective dates.—(a) and (b) [Reserved].

(c) Section 1.475(a)-3 (concerning acquisition by a dealer of a security with a substituted basis) applies to securities acquired, originated, or entered into on or after January 4, 1995.

(d) Except as provided elsewhere in this paragraph (d), § 1.475(b)-1 (concerning the scope of exemptions from the mark-to-market requirement) applies to taxable years ending on or after December 31, 1993.

(1) Section 1.475(b)-1(b) applies as follows:

(i) Section 1.475(b)-1(b)(1)(i) (concerning equity interests issued by a related person) applies beginning June 19, 1996. If, on June 18, 1996, a security is subject to mark-to-market accounting and, on June 19, 1996, § 1.475(b)-1(b)(1) begins to apply to the security solely because of the effective dates in this paragraph (d) (rather than because of a change in facts), then the rules of § 1.475(b)-1(b)(4)(i)(A) (concerning the prohibition against marking) apply, but § 1.475(b)-1(b)(4)(i)(B) (imposing a mark to market on the day before the onset of the prohibition) does not apply.

(ii) Section 1.475(b)-1(b)(2) (concerning relevant relationships for purposes of determining whether equity interests in related persons are prohibited from being marked to market) applies beginning June 19, 1996.

(iii) Section 1.475(b)-1(b)(3) (concerning certain actively traded securities) applies beginning June 19, 1996, to securities held on or after that date, except for securities described in § 1.475(b)-1(e)(1)(i) (concerning equity interests issued by controlled entities). If a security is described in § 1.475(b)-1(e)(1)(i), § 1.475(b)-1(b)(3) applies only on or after January 23, 1997, if the security is held on or after that date. If § 1.475(b)-1(b)(1) ceases to apply to a security by virtue of the operation of this paragraph (d)(1)(iii), the rules of § 1.475(b)-1(b)(4)(ii) apply to the cessation.

(iv) Except to the extent provided in paragraph (d)(1) of this section, § 1.475(b)-1(b)(4) (concerning changes in status) applies beginning June 19, 1996.

(2) Section 1.475(b)-1(c) (concerning securities deemed not held for investment by dealers in notional principal contracts and derivatives) applies to securities acquired on or after January 23, 1997.

(3) Section 1.475(b)-1(d) (concerning the special rule for hedges of another member's risk) is effective for securities acquired, originated, or entered into on or after January 23, 1997.

(e) Section 1.475(b)-2 (concerning identification of securities that are exempt from mark to market treatment) applies as follows:

(1) Section 1.475(b)-2(a) (concerning the general rules for identification of basis for exemption from mark to market treatment) applies to identifications made on or after July 1, 1997.

(2) Section 1.475(b)-2(b) (concerning time for identifying a security with a substituted basis) applies to securities acquired, originated, or entered into on or after January 4, 1995.

(3) Section 1.475(b)-2(c) (concerning identification in the context of integrated transactions under § 1.1275-6) applies on and after August 13, 1996 (the effective date of § 1.1275-6).

(f) [Reserved].

(g) Section 1.475(b)-4 (concerning transitional issues relating to exemptions) applies to taxable years ending on or after December 31, 1993.

(h) Section 1.475(c)-1 applies as follows:

(1) Except as otherwise provided in this paragraph (h)(1), § 1.475(c)-1(a) (concerning the dealer-customer relationship) applies to taxable years beginning on or after January 1, 1995.

(i) [Reserved].

(ii) Section 1.475(c)-1(a)(2)(ii) (illustrating rules concerning the dealer-customer relationship) applies to taxable years beginning on or after June 20, 1996.

(iii) (A) Section 1.475(c)-1(a)(3) applies to taxable years beginning on or after June 20, 1996, except for transactions between members of the same consolidated group.

(B) For transactions between members of the same consolidated group, paragraph § 1.475(c)-1(a)(3) applies to taxable years beginning on or after December 24, 1996.

(2) Section 1.475(c)-1(b) (concerning sellers of nonfinancial goods and services) applies to taxable years ending on or after December 31, 1993.

(3) Except as otherwise provided in this paragraph (h)(3), § 1.475(c)-1(c) (concerning taxpayers that purchase securities but engage in no more than negligible sales of the securities) applies to taxable years ending on or after December 31, 1993.

(i) Section 1.475(c)-1(c)(3) (special rules for members of a consolidated group) is effective for taxable years beginning on or after December 24, 1996.

(ii) A taxpayer may rely on the rules set out in § 1.475(c)-1T(b) (as contained in 26 CFR part 1 revised April 1, 1996) for taxable years beginning before January 23, 1997, provided the taxpayer applies that paragraph reasonably and consistently.

(4) Section 1.475(c)-1(d) (concerning the issuance of life insurance products) applies to taxable years beginning on or after January 1, 1995.

(i) Section 1.475(c)-2 (concerning the definition of security) applies to taxable years ending on or after December 31, 1993. By its terms, however, § 1.475(c)-2(a)(3) applies only to residual interests or to interests or arrangements that are acquired on or after January 4, 1995; and the integrated transactions that are referred to in §§ 1.475(c)-2(a)(2) and 1.475(c)-2(b) exist only after August 13, 1996 (the effective date of § 1.1275-6).

(j) Section 1.475(d)-1 (concerning the character of gain or loss) applies to taxable years ending on or after December 31, 1993. [Reg. § 1.475(e)-1.]

☐ [*T.D.* 8700, 12-23-96.]

Adjustments

[Reg. § 1.481-1]

§ 1.481-1. **Adjustments in general.**—(a) (1) Section 481 prescribes the rules to be followed in computing taxable income in cases where the taxable income of the taxpayer is computed under a method of accounting different from that under which the taxable income was previously computed. A change in method of accounting to which section 481 applies includes a change in the overall method of accounting for gross income or deductions, or a change in the treatment of a material item. For rules relating to changes in methods of accounting, see section 446(e) and paragraph (e) of § 1.446-1. In computing taxable income for the taxable year of the change, there shall be taken into account those adjustments which are determined to be necessary solely by reason of such change in order to prevent amounts from being duplicated or omitted. The "year of the change" is the taxable year for which the taxable income of the taxpayer is computed under a method of accounting different from that used for the preceding taxable year.

(2) Unless the adjustments are attributable to a change in method of accounting initiated by the taxpayer, no part of the adjustments required by subparagraph (1) of this paragraph shall be based on amounts which were taken into account in computing income (or which should have been taken into account had the new method of accounting been used) for taxable years beginning before January 1, 1954, or ending before August 17, 1954 (hereinafter referred to as pre-1954 years).

(b) The adjustments specified in section 481(a) and this section shall take into account inventories, accounts receivable, accounts payable, and any other item determined to be necessary in order to prevent amounts from being duplicated or omitted.

(c) (1) The term "adjustments", as used in section 481, has reference to the net amount of the adjustments required by section 481(a) and paragraph (b) of this section. In the case of a change in the over-all method of accounting, such as from the cash receipts and disbursements method to an accrual method, the term "net amount of the adjustments" means the consolidation of adjustments (whether the amounts thereof represent increases or decreases in items of income or deductions) arising with respect to balances in various accounts, such as inventory, accounts receivable, and accounts payable, at the beginning of the taxable year of the change in method of accounting. With respect to the portion of the adjustments attributable to pre-1954 years, it is immaterial that the same items or class of items with respect to which adjustments would have to be made (for the first taxable year to which section 481 applies) do not exist at the time the actual change in method of accounting occurs. For purposes of section 481, only the net dollar bal-

Reg. § 1.481-1(a)(2)

ance is to be taken into account. In the case of a change in the treatment of a single material item, the amount of the adjustment shall be determined with reference only to the net dollar balances in that particular account.

(2) If a change in method of accounting is voluntary (i.e., initiated by the taxpayer), the entire amount of the adjustments required by section 481(a) is generally taken into account in computing taxable income in the taxable year of the change, regardless of whether the adjustments increase or decrease taxable income. See, however, §§ 1.446-1(e)(3) and 1.481-4 which provide that the Commissioner may prescribe the taxable year or years in which the adjustments are taken into account.

(3) If the change in method of accounting is involuntary (i.e., not initiated by the taxpayer), then only the amount of the adjustments required by section 481(a) that is attributable to taxable years beginning after December 31, 1953, and ending after August 16, 1954, (hereinafter referred to as post-1953 years) is taken into account. This amount is generally taken into account in computing taxable income in the taxable year of the change, regardless of whether the adjustments increase or decrease taxable income. See, however, §§ 1.446-1(e)(3) and 1.481-4 which provide that the Commissioner may prescribe the taxable year or years in which the adjustments are taken into account. See also § 1.481-3 for rules relating to adjustments attributable to pre-1954 years.

(4) For any adjustments attributable to post-1953 years that are taken into account entirely in the year of change and that increase taxable income by more than $3,000, the limitations on tax provided in section 481(b)(1) or (2) apply. See § 1.481-2 for rules relating to the limitations on tax provided by sections 481(b)(1) and (2).

(5) A change in the method of accounting initiated by the taxpayer includes not only a change which he originates by securing the consent of the Commissioner, but also a change from one method of accounting to another made without the advance approval of the Commissioner. A change in the taxpayer's method of accounting required as a result of an examination of the taxpayer's income tax return will not be considered as initiated by the taxpayer. On the other hand, a taxpayer who, on his own initiative, changes his method of accounting in order to conform to the requirements of any Federal income tax regulation or ruling shall not, merely because of such fact, be considered to have made an involuntary change.

(d) Any adjustments required under section 481(a) that are taken into account during a taxable year must be properly taken into account for purposes of computing gross income, adjusted gross income, or taxable income in determining the amount of any item of gain, loss, deduction, or credit that depends on gross income, adjusted gross income, or taxable income. [Reg. § 1.481-1.]

☐ [T.D. 6366, 2-19-59. Amended by T.D. 8608, 8-4-95.]

[Reg. § 1.481-2]

§ 1.481-2. Limitation on tax.—(a) *Three-year allocation.* Section 481(b)(1) provides a limitation on the tax under chapter 1 of the Internal Revenue Code for the taxable year of change that is attributable to the adjustments required under section 481(a) and § 1.481-1 if the entire amount of the adjustments is taken into account in the year of change. If such adjustments increase the taxpayer's taxable income for the taxable year of the change by more than $3,000, then the tax for such taxable year that is attributable to the adjustments shall not exceed the lesser of the tax attributable to taking such adjustments into account in computing taxable income for the taxable year of the change under section 481(a) and § 1.481-1, or the aggregate of the increases in tax that would result if the adjustments were included ratably in the taxable year of the change and the two preceding taxable years. For the purpose of computing the limitation on tax under section 481(b)(1), the adjustments shall be allocated ratably to the taxable year of the change and the two preceding taxable years, whether or not the adjustments are in fact attributable in whole or in part to such years. The limitation on the tax provided in this paragraph shall be applicable only if the taxpayer used the method of accounting from which the change was made in computing taxable income for the two taxable years preceding the taxable year of the change.

(b) *Allocation under new method of accounting.* Section 481(b)(2) provides a second alternative limitation on the tax for the taxable year of change under chapter 1 of the Internal Revenue Code that is attributable to the adjustments required under section 481(a) and § 1.481-1 where such adjustments increase taxable income for the taxable year of change by more than $3,000. If the taxpayer establishes from his books of account and other records what his taxable income would have been under the new method of accounting for one or more consecutive taxable years immediately preceding the taxable year of the change, and if the taxpayer in computing taxable income for such years used the method of accounting from which the change was made, then the tax attribu-

Reg. § 1.481-2(b)

table to the adjustments shall not exceed the smallest of the following amounts:

(1) The tax attributable to taking the adjustments into account in computing taxable income for the taxable year of the change under section 481(a) and § 1.481-1;

(2) The tax attributable to such adjustments computed under the 3-year allocation provided in section 481(b)(1), if applicable; or

(3) The net increase in the taxes under chapter 1 (or under corresponding provisions of prior revenue laws) which would result from allocating that portion of the adjustments to the one or more consecutive preceding taxable years to which properly allocable under the new method of accounting and from allocating the balance thereof to the taxable year of the change.

(c) *Rules for computation of tax.* (1) The first step in determining whether either of the limitations described in section 481(b)(1) or (2) applies is to compute the increase in tax for the taxable year of the change that is attributable to the increase in taxable income for such year resulting solely from the adjustments required under section 481(a) and § 1.481-1. This increase in tax is the excess of the tax for the taxable year computed by taking into account such adjustments under section 481(a) over the tax computed for such year without taking the adjustments into account.

(2) The next step is to compute under section 481(b)(1) the tax attributable to the adjustments referred to in paragraph (c)(1) of this section for the taxable year of the change and the two preceding taxable years as if an amount equal to one-third of the net amount of such adjustments had been received or accrued in each of such taxable years. The increase in tax attributable to the adjustments for each such taxable year is the excess of the tax for such year computed with the allocation of one-third of the net adjustments to such taxable year over the tax computed without the allocation of any part of the adjustments to such year. For the purpose of computing the aggregate increase in taxes for such taxable years, there shall be taken into account the increase or decrease in tax for any taxable year preceding the taxable year of the change to which no adjustment is allocated under section 481(b)(1) but which is affected by a net operating loss under section 172 or by a capital loss carryback or carryover under section 1212, determined with reference to taxable years with respect to which adjustments under section 481(b)(1) are allocated.

(3) In the event that the taxpayer satisfies the conditions set forth in section 481(b)(2), the next step is to determine the amount of the net increase in tax attributable to the adjustments referred to in paragraph (c)(1) of this section for:

(i) The taxable year of the change,

(ii) The consecutive taxable year or years immediately preceding the taxable year of the change for which the taxpayer can establish his taxable income under the new method of accounting, and

(iii) Any taxable year preceding the taxable year of the change to which no adjustment is allocated under section 481(b)(2), but which is affected by a net operating loss or by a capital loss carryback or carryover determined with reference to taxable years with respect to which such adjustments are allocated.

(4) The tax for the taxable year of the change shall be the tax for such year, computed without taking any of the adjustments referred to in paragraph (c)(1) of this section into account, increased by the smallest of the following amounts:

(i) The amount of tax for the taxable year of the change attributable solely to taking into account the entire amount of the adjustments required by section 481(a) and § 1.481-1;

(ii) The sum of the increases in tax liability for the taxable year of the change and the two immediately preceding taxable years that would have resulted solely from taking into account one-third of the amount of such adjustments required for each of such years as though such amounts had been properly attributable to such years (computed in accordance with paragraph (c)(2) of this section); or

(iii) The net increase in tax attributable to allocating such adjustments under the new method of accounting (computed in accordance with paragraph (c)(3) of this section).

(5)(i) In the case of a change in method of accounting by a partnership, the adjustments required by section 481 shall be made with respect to the taxable income of the partnership but the limitations on tax under section 481(b) shall apply to the individual partners. Each partner shall take into account his distributive share of the partnership items, as so adjusted, for the taxable year of the change. Section 481(b) applies to a partner whose taxable income is so increased by more than $3,000 as a result of such adjustments to the partnership taxable income. It is not necessary for the partner to have been a member of the partnership for the two taxable years immediately preceding the taxable year of the change of the partnership's accounting method in order to have the limitation provided by section 481(b)(1) apply. Further, a partner may apply section 481(b)(2) even though he was not a member of the

Reg. § 1.481-2(b)(1)

partnership for all the taxable years affected by the computation thereunder.

(ii) In the case of a change in method of accounting by an electing small business corporation under subchapter S, chapter 1 of the Code, the adjustments required by section 481 shall be made with respect to the taxable income of such electing corporation in the year of the change, but the limitations on tax under section 481(b) shall apply to the individual shareholders. Section 481(b) applies to a shareholder of an electing small business corporation whose taxable income is so increased by more than $3,000 as a result of such adjustments to such corporation's taxable income. It is not necessary for the shareholder to have been a member of the electing small business corporation, or for such corporation to have been an electing small business corporation, for the two taxable years immediately preceding the taxable year of the change of the corporation's accounting method in order to have the limitation provided by section 481(b)(1) apply. Further, a shareholder may apply section 481(b)(2), even though he was not a shareholder, or the corporation was not an electing small business corporation, for all the taxable years affected by the computation thereunder.

(6) For the purpose of the successive computations of the limitation on tax under section 481(b)(1) or (2), if the treatment of any item under the provisions of the Internal Revenue Code of 1986 (or corresponding provisions of prior internal revenue laws) depends upon the amount of gross income, adjusted gross income, or taxable income (for example, medical expenses, charitable contributions, or credits against the tax), such item shall be determined for the purpose of each such computation by taking into account the proper portion of the amount of any adjustments required to be taken into account under section 481 in each such computation.

(7) The increase or decrease in the tax for any taxable year for which an assessment of any deficiency, or a credit or refund of any overpayment, is prevented by any law or rule of law, shall be determined by reference to the tax previously determined (within the meaning of section 1314(a) for such year.

(8) In applying section 7807(b)(1), the provisions of chapter 1 (other than subchapter E, relating to tax on self-employment income) and chapter 2 of the Internal Revenue Code of 1939 shall be treated as the corresponding provisions of the Internal Revenue Code of 1939.

(d) *Examples.* The application of section 481(b)(1) and (2) may be illustrated by the following examples. Although the examples in this paragraph are based upon adjustments required in the case of a change in the over-all method of accounting, the principles illustrated would be equally applicable to adjustments required in the case of a change in method of accounting for a particular material item, provided the treatment of such adjustments is not specifically subject to some other provision of the Internal Revenue Code of 1986.

Example (1). An unmarried individual taxpayer using the cash receipts and disbursements method of accounting for the calendar year is required by the Commissioner to change to an accrual method effective with the year 1958. As of January 1, 1958, he had an opening inventory of $11,000. On December 31, 1958, he had a closing inventory of $12,500. Merchandise purchases during the year amounted to $22,500, and net sales were $32,000. Total deductible business expenses were $5,000. There were no receivables or payables at January 1, 1958. The computation of taxable income for 1958, assuming no other adjustments, using the new method of accounting follows:

Net sales		$32,000
Opening inventory	$11,000	
Purchases	22,500	
Total	$33,500	
Less closing inventory	12,500	
Cost of goods sold		$21,000
Gross profit		$11,000
Business expenses		5,000
Business income		$ 6,000
Personal exemption and itemized deductions		$ 1,600
Taxable income		$ 4,400

Under the cash receipts and disbursements method of accounting, only $9,000 of the $11,000 opening inventory had been included in the cost of goods sold and claimed as a deduction for the taxable years 1954 through 1957; the remaining $2,000 had been so accounted for in pre-1954 years. In order to prevent the same item from reducing taxable income twice, an adjustment of $9,000 must be made to the taxable income of 1958 under the provisions of section 481(a) and § 1.481-1. Since the change in method of accounting was not initiated by the taxpayer, the $2,000 of opening inventory which had been included in cost of goods sold in pre-1954 years is not taken into account. Taxable income for 1958 is accordingly increased by $9,000 under section 481(a) to $13,400. Assuming that the tax on $13,400 is $4,002 and that the tax on $4,400 (income with-

Reg. § 1.481-2(d)

37,180 Adjustments

See p. 20,601 for regulations not amended to reflect law changes

out the adjustment) is $944, the increase in tax attributable to the adjustment, if taken into account for the taxable year of the change, would be the difference between the two, or $3,058. Since the adjustment required by section 481(a) and § 1.481-1 ($9,000) increases taxable income by more than $3,000, the increase in tax for the taxable year 1958 attributable to the adjustment of $9,000 (i.e., $3,058) may be limited under the provisions of section 481(b)(1) or (2). See examples (2) and (3).

Example (2). Assume that the taxpayer in example (1) used the cash receipts and disbursements method of accounting in computing taxable income for the years 1956 and 1957 and that the taxable income for these years determined under such method was $4,000 and $6,000, respectively. The section 481(b)(1) limitation on tax with a pro rata three-year allocation of the $9,000 adjustment is computed as follows:

Taxable year	Taxable income before adjustment	Taxable income with adjustment	Assumed total tax	Assumed tax before adjustment	Increase in tax attributable to adjustment
1956	$4,000	$7,000	$1,660	$ 840	$ 820
1957	6,000	9,000	2,300	1,360	940
1958	4,400	7,400	1,780	944	836
Total					$2,596

Since this increase in tax of $2,596 is less than the increase in tax attributable to the inclusion of the entire adjustment in the income for the taxable year of the change ($3,058), the limitation provided by section 481(b)(1) applies, and the total tax for 1958, the taxable year of the change, if section 481(b)(2) does not apply, is determined as follows:

Tax without any portion of adjustment	$ 944
Increase in tax attributable to adjustment computed under section 481(b)(1)	2,596
Total tax for taxable year of the change	$3,540

Example (3). (i) Assume the same facts as in example (1) and, in addition, assume that the taxpayer used the cash receipts and disbursements method of accounting in computing taxable income for the years 1953 through 1957; that he established his taxable income under the new method for the taxable years 1953, 1954, and 1957, but did not have sufficient records to establish his taxable income under such method for the taxable years 1955 and 1956. The original taxable income and taxable income as redetermined are as follows:

Taxable Income

Taxable year	Determined under cash receipts and disbursements method	Established under new method	Increase (or decrease) in taxable income
1953	$5,000	$ 7,000	$2,000
1954	6,000	7,000	1,000
1955	5,500	[1]	.....
1956	4,000	[1]	.....
1957	6,000	10,000	4,000

[1] Undetermined.

As in examples (1) and (2), the total adjustment under section 481(a) is $9,000. Of the $9,000 adjustment, $4,000 may be allocated to 1957, which is the only year consecutively preceding the taxable year of the change for which the taxpayer was able to establish his income under the new method. Since the income cannot be established under the new method for 1956 and 1955, no allocation may be made to 1954 or 1953, even though the taxpayer has established his income for those years under the new method of accounting. The balance of $5,000 ($9,000 minus $4,000) must be allocated to 1958.

(ii) The limitation provided by section 481(b)(2) is computed as follows: The tax for 1957, based on taxable income of $6,000, is assumed to be $1,360. Under the new method, based on taxable income of $10,000, the tax for 1957 is assumed to be $2,640, the increase attributable to $4,000 of the $9,000 section 481(a) adjustment being $1,280, ($2,640 minus $1,360). The tax for 1958, computed on the basis of taxable income of $4,400 (determined under the new method), is assumed to be $944. The tax computed for 1958 on taxable income of $9,400 ($4,400 plus the $5,000 adjustment allocated to 1958) is assumed to be $2,436, leaving a difference of $1,492 ($2,436 minus $944) attributable to the inclusion in 1958 of the portion of the total adjustment to be taken into account which could not be properly

Reg. § 1.481-2(d)

allocated to the taxable year or years consecutively preceding 1958.

(iii) The tax attributable to the adjustment is determined by selecting the smallest of the three following amounts:

Increase in tax attributable to adjustment computed under section 481(b)(2) ($1,280 + $1,492)	$2,772
Increase in tax attributable to adjustment computed under section 481(b)(1) (example (2))	2,596
Increase in tax if the entire adjustment is taken into account in the taxable year of the change (example (1))	3,058

The final tax for 1958 is then $3,540 computed as follows:

Tax before inclusion of any adjustment	944
Increase in tax attributable to adjustments (smallest of $2,772, $2,596 or $3,058)	2,596
Total tax for 1958 (limited in accordance with section 481(b)(1))	$3,540

Example (4). Assume that X Corporation has maintained its books of account and filed its income tax returns using the cash receipts and disbursements method of accounting for the years 1953 through 1957. The corporation secures permission to change to an accrual method of accounting for the calendar year 1958. The following tabulation presents the date with respect to the taxpayer's income for the years involved:

Year	Taxable income under the cash receipts and disbursements method — Before application of net operating loss carryback	Taxable income under the cash receipts and disbursements method — After application of net operating loss carryback	Taxable income established under accrual method	Increase (or decrease) attributable to change	Changes in taxable income due to changes in net operating loss carryback
1953	$ 2,000	0	[1]		$2,000
1954	4,000	$ 1,000	[1]		3,000
1955	(5,000)		$1,000	$6,000	
1956	80,000	80,000	77,000	(3,000)	
1957	90,000	90,000	96,000	6,000	
1958			100,000		

[1] Not established.

As indicated above, taxable income for 1953 and 1954, as determined under the cash receipts and disbursements method of accounting, was $2,000 and $4,000, respectively, and after application of the net operating loss carryback from 1955, the taxable income was reduced to zero in 1953 and to $1,000 in 1954. The taxpayer was unable to establish taxable income for these years under an accrual method of accounting; however, under section 481(b)(3)(A), increases or decreases in the tax for taxable years to which no adjustment is allocated must, nevertheless, be taken into account to the extent the tax for such years would be affected by a net operating loss determined with reference to taxable years to which adjustments are allocated. The total amount of the adjustments required under section 481(a) and attributable to the taxable years 1953 through 1957 in this example is assumed to be $10,000. The redetermination of taxable income established by the taxpayer for the taxable years 1955, 1956, and 1957 appears under the heading "Taxable income established under accrual method" in the above tabulation. The tabulation assumes that the taxpayer has been able to recompute the income for those years so as to establish a net adjustment of $9,000, which leaves a balance of $1,000 unaccounted for. In accordance with the requirements of section 481(b)(2), the $1,000 amount is allocated to 1958, the taxable year of the change. The following computations are necessary in order to determine the tax attributable to the adjustments under section 481(a):

Increase in tax attributable to inclusion in 1958 of the entire $10,000 adjustment

Tax on income of 1958 increased by entire amount of adjustment ($100,000 + $10,000)	$51,700
Tax on income of 1958 without adjustment ($100,000)	46,500
Increase in tax attributable to inclusion of entire adjustment in year of the change	$ 5,200

Reg. § 1.481-2(d)

37,182 Adjustments

See p. 20,601 for regulations not amended to reflect law changes

Increase in tax attributable to adjustment computed under section 481(b)(1)

Year	Amount of adjustment	Tax before adjustment	Tax after adjustment	Increase in tax liability attributable to adjustment
1958	$ 3,334	$ 46,500	$ 48,234	$ 1,734
1957	3,333	41,300	43,033	1,733
1956	3,333	36,100	37,833	1,733

Increase in tax attributable to adjustment computed under section 481(b)(1)............ $ 5,200

Increase in tax attributable to adjustment computed under section 481(b)(2)

Year	Amount of adjustment	Tax before adjustment	Tax after adjustment	Increase (or decrease), in tax liability
1953	$ 2,000 [1]	0	$ 600 [1]	$ 600
1954	3,000 [1]	$ 300	1,200 [1]	900
1955	6,000	0	300	300
1956	(3,000)	36,100	34,540	(1,560)
1957	6,000	41,300	44,420	3,120
1958	1,000 [2]	46,500	47,020 [2]	520

Increase in tax attributable to the adjustment computed under section 481(b)(2) .... $ 3,880

---

[1] Attributable to recomputations of net operating loss carrybacks determined with reference to net operating loss in 1955.
[2] Attributable to the inclusion of $1,000 in the year of thee change which represents the portion of the $10,000 adjustment not allocated to taxable years prior to thee year of change for which taxable income is established under the new method.

Since the limitation under section 481(b)(2) ($3,880) on the amount of tax attributable to the adjustments is applicable, the final tax for the taxable year of the change is computed by adding such amount to the tax for that year computed without the inclusion of any amount attributable to the adjustments, that is, $46,500 plus $3,880, or $50,380. [Reg. § 1.481-2.]

☐ [*T.D. 6366, 2-19-59. Amended by T.D. 6490, 8-30-60; T.D. 7301, 1-3-74 and T.D. 8608, 8-4-95.*]

[Reg. § 1.481-3]

§ 1.481-3. Adjustments attributable to pre-1954 years where change was not initiated by taxpayer.—If the adjustments required by section 481(a) and § 1.481-1 are attributable to a change in method of accounting which was not initiated by the taxpayer, no portion of any adjustments which is attributable to pre-1954 years shall be taken into account in computing taxable income. For example, if the total adjustments in the case of a change in method of accounting which is not initiated by the taxpayer amount to $10,000, of which $4,000 is attributable to pre-1954 years, only $6,000 of the $10,000 total adjustments is required to be taken into account under section 481 in computing taxable income. The portion of the adjustments which is attributable to pre-1954 years is the net amount of the adjustments which would have been required if the taxpayer had changed his method of accounting in his first taxable year which began after December 31, 1953, and ended after August 16, 1954. [Reg. § 1.481-3.]

☐ [*T.D. 6366, 2-19-59. Amended by T.D. 8608, 8-4-95.*]

[Reg. § 1.481-4]

§ 1.481-4. Adjustments taken into account with consent.—(a) In addition to the terms and conditions prescribed by the Commissioner under § 1.446-1(e)(3) for effecting a change in method of accounting, including the taxable year or years in which the amount of the adjustments required by section 481(a) is to be taken into account, or the methods of allocation described in section 481(b), a taxpayer may request approval of an alternative method of allocating the amount of the adjustments under section 481. See section 481(c). Requests for approval of an alternative method of allocation shall set forth in detail the facts and circumstances upon which the taxpayer bases its request. Permission will be granted only if the taxpayer and the Commissioner agree to the terms and conditions under which the allocation is to be effected. See § 1.446-1(e) for the rules regarding how to secure the Commissioner's consent to a change in method of accounting.

(b) An agreement to the terms and conditions of a change in method of accounting under § 1.446-1(e)(3), including the taxable year or years prescribed by the Commissioner under that

Reg. § 1.481-3

Adjustments

section (or an alternative method described in paragraph (a) of this section) for taking the amount of the adjustments under section 481(a) into account, shall be in writing and shall be signed by the Commissioner and the taxpayer. It shall set forth the items to be adjusted, the amount of the adjustments, the taxable year or years for which the adjustments are to be taken into account, and the amount of the adjustments allocable to each year. The agreement shall be binding on the parties except upon a showing of fraud, malfeasance, or misrepresentation of material fact. [Reg. § 1.481-4.]

☐ [T.D. 6366, 2-19-59. Amended by T.D. 8608, 8-4-95.]

[Reg. § 1.481-5]

§ 1.481-5. Effective dates.—Sections 1.481-1, 1.481-2, 1.481-3, and 1.481-4 are effective for Consent Agreements signed on or after December 27, 1994. For Consent Agreements signed before December 27, 1994, see §§ 1.481-1, 1.481-2, 1.481-3, 1.481-4, and 1.481-5 (as contained in the 26 CFR part 1 edition revised as of April 1, 1995). [Reg. § 1.481-5.]

☐ [T.D. 8608, 8-4-95.]

[Reg. § 1.482-0]

§ 1.482-0. Outline of regulations under section 482.—This section contains major captions for §§ 1.482-1 through 1.482-8.

§ 1.482-1. Allocation of income and deductions among taxpayers.

(a) In general.
  (1) Purpose and scope.
  (2) Authority to make allocations.
  (3) Taxpayer's use of section 482.
(b) Arm's length standard.
  (1) In general.
  (2) Arm's length methods.
    (i) Methods.
    (ii) Selection of category of method applicable to transaction.
(c) Best method rule.
  (1) In general.
  (2) Determining the best method.
    (i) Comparability.
    (ii) Data and assumptions.
      (A) Completeness and accuracy of data.
      (B) Reliability of assumptions.
      (C) Sensitivity of results to deficiencies in data and assumptions.
    (iii) Confirmation of results by another method.
(d) Comparability.
  (1) In general.
  (2) Standard of comparability.
  (3) Factors for determining comparability.
    (i) Functional analysis.
    (ii) Contractual terms.
      (A) In general.
      (B) Identifying contractual terms.
        (1) Written agreement.
        (2) No written agreement.
      (C) Examples.
    (iii) Risk.
      (A) Comparability.
      (B) Identification of party that bears risk.
      (C) Examples.
    (iv) Economic conditions.
    (v) Property or services.
  (4) Special circumstances.
    (i) Market share strategy.
    (ii) Different geographic markets.
      (A) In general.
      (B) Example.
      (C) Location savings.
      (D) Example.
    (iii) Transactions ordinarily not accepted as comparables.
      (A) In general.
      (B) Examples.
(e) Arm's length range.
  (1) In general.
  (2) Determination of arm's length range.
    (i) Single method.
    (ii) Selection of comparables.
    (iii) Comparables included in arm's length range.
      (A) In general.
      (B) Adjustment of range to increase reliability.
      (C) Interquartile range.
  (3) Adjustment if taxpayer's results are outside arm's length range.
  (4) Arm's length range not prerequisite to allocation.
  (5) Examples.
(f) Scope of review.
  (1) In general.
    (i) Intent to evade or avoid tax not a prerequisite.

Reg. § 1.482-0

37,184 Adjustments

See p. 20,601 for regulations not amended to reflect law changes

(ii) Realization of income not a prerequisite.
    (A) In general.
    (B) Example.
(iii) Nonrecognition provisions may not bar allocation.
    (A) In general.
    (B) Example.
(iv) Consolidated returns.
(2) Rules relating to determination of true taxable income.
(i) Aggregation of transactions.
    (A) In general.
    (B) Examples.
(ii) Allocation based on taxpayer's actual transactions.
    (A) In general.
    (B) Example.
(iii) Multiple year data.
    (A) In general.
    (B) Circumstances warranting consideration of multiple year data.
    (C) Comparable effect over comparable period.
    (D) Applications of methods using multiple year averages.
    (E) Examples.
(iv) Product lines and statistical techniques.
(v) Allocations apply to results, not methods.
    (A) In general.
    (B) Example.
(g) Collateral adjustments with respect to allocations under section 482.
(1) In general.
(2) Correlative allocations.
    (i) In general.
    (ii) Manner of carrying out correlative allocation.
    (iii) Events triggering correlative allocation.
    (iv) Examples.
(3) Adjustments to conform accounts to reflect section 482 allocations.
    (i) In general.
    (ii) Example.
(4) Setoffs.
    (i) In general.
    (ii) Requirements.

(iii) Examples.
(h) Special rules.
(1) Small taxpayer safe harbor [Reserved].
(2) Effect of foreign legal restrictions.
    (i) In general.
    (ii) Applicable legal restrictions.
    (iii) Requirement for electing the deferred income method of accounting.
    (iv) Deferred income method of accounting.
    (v) Examples.
(3) Coordination with section 936.
    (i) Cost sharing under section 936.
    (ii) Use of terms.
(i) Definitions.
(j) Effective dates.

§ 1.482-2. Determination of taxable income in specific situations.

(a) Loans or advances.
(1) Interest on bona fide indebtedness.
    (i) In general.
    (ii) Application of paragraph (a) of this section.
        (A) Interest on bona fide indebtedness.
        (B) Alleged indebtedness.
    (iii) Period for which interest shall be charged.
        (A) General rule.
        (B) Exception for certain intercompany transactions in the ordinary course of business.
        (C) Exception for trade or business of debtor member located outside the United States.
        (D) Exception for regular trade practice of creditor member or others in creditor's industry.
        (E) Exception for property purchased for resale in a foreign country.
            (*1*) General rule.
            (*2*) Interest-free period.
            (*3*) Average collection period.
            (*4*) Illustration.
    (iv) Payment; book entries.
(2) Arm's length interest rate.
    (i) In general.
    (ii) Funds obtained at situs of borrower.
    (iii) Safe haven interest rates for certain loans and advances made after May 8, 1986.
        (A) Applicability.
            (*1*) General rule.

Reg. § 1.482-0

(2) Grandfather rule for existing loans.

(B) Safe haven interest rate based on applicable Federal rate.

(C) Applicable Federal rate.

(D) Lender in business of making loans.

(E) Foreign currency loans.

(3) Coordination with interest adjustments required under certain other Internal Revenue Code sections.

(4) Examples.

(b) Performance of services for another.

(1) General rule.

(2) Benefit test.

(3) Arm's length charge.

(4) Costs or deductions to be taken into account.

(5) Costs and deductions not to be taken into account.

(6) Methods.

(7) Certain services.

(8) Services rendered in connection with the transfer of property.

(c) Use of tangible property.

(1) General rule.

(2) Arm's length charge.

(i) In general.

(ii) Safe haven rental charge.

(iii) Subleases.

(d) Transfer of property.

§ 1.482-3. Methods to determine taxable income in connection with a transfer of tangible property.

(a) In general.

(b) Comparable uncontrolled price method.

(1) In general.

(2) Comparability and reliability considerations.

(i) In general.

(ii) Comparability.

(A) In general.

(B) Adjustments for differences between controlled and uncontrolled transactions.

(iii) Data and assumptions.

(3) Arm's length range.

(4) Examples.

(5) Indirect evidence of comparable uncontrolled transactions.

(i) In general.

(ii) Limitations.

(iii) Examples.

(c) Resale price method.

(1) In general.

(2) Determination of arm's length price.

(i) In general.

(ii) Applicable resale price.

(iii) Appropriate gross profit.

(iv) Arm's length range.

(3) Comparability and reliability considerations.

(i) In general.

(ii) Comparability.

(A) Functional comparability.

(B) Other comparability factors.

(C) Adjustments for differences between controlled and uncontrolled transactions.

(D) Sales agent.

(iii) Data and assumptions.

(A) In general.

(B) Consistency in accounting.

(4) Examples.

(d) Cost plus method.

(1) In general.

(2) Determination of arm's length price.

(i) In general.

(ii) Appropriate gross profit.

(iii) Arm's length range.

(3) Comparability and reliability considerations.

(i) In general.

(ii) Comparability.

(A) Functional comparability.

(B) Other comparability factors.

(C) Adjustments for differences between controlled and uncontrolled transactions.

(D) Purchasing agent.

(iii) Data and assumptions.

(A) In general.

(B) Consistency in accounting.

(4) Examples.

(e) Unspecified methods.

(1) In general.

(2) Example.

(f) Coordination with intangible property rules.

§ 1.482-4. Methods to determine taxable income in connection with a transfer of intangible property.

(a) In general.

(b) Definition of intangible.

(c) Comparable uncontrolled transaction method.
  (1) In general.
  (2) Comparability and reliability considerations.
    (i) In general.
    (ii) Reliability.
    (iii) Comparability.
      (A) In general.
      (B) Factors to be considered in determining comparability.
        (1) Comparable intangible property.
        (2) Comparable circumstances.
    (iv) Data and assumptions.
  (3) Arm's length range.
  (4) Examples.
(d) Unspecified methods.
  (1) In general.
  (2) Example.
(e) Coordination with tangible property rules.
(f) Special rules for transfers of intangible property.
  (1) Form of consideration.
  (2) Periodic adjustments.
    (i) General rule.
    (ii) Exceptions.
      (A) Transactions involving the same intangible.
      (B) Transactions involving comparable intangible.
      (C) Methods other than comparable uncontrolled transaction.
      (D) Extraordinary events.
      (E) Five-year period.
    (iii) Examples.
  (3) Ownership of intangible property.
    (i) In general.
    (ii) Identification of the owner.
      (A) Legally protected intangible property.
      (B) Intangible property that is not legally protected.
    (iii) Allocations with respect to assistance provided to the owner.
    (iv) Examples.
  (4) Consideration not artificially limited.
  (5) Lump sum payments.
    (i) In general.
    (ii) Exceptions.
    (iii) Example.

§ 1.482-5. Comparable profits method.
(a) In general.
(b) Determination of arm's length result.
  (1) In general.
  (2) Tested party.
    (i) In general.
    (ii) Adjustments for tested party.
  (3) Arm's length range.
  (4) Profit level indicators.
    (i) Rate of return on capital employed.
    (ii) Financial ratios.
    (iii) Other profit level indicators.
(c) Comparability and reliability considerations.
  (1) In general.
  (2) Comparability.
    (i) In general.
    (ii) Functional, risk and resource comparability.
    (iii) Other comparability factors.
    (iv) Adjustments for differences between tested party and the uncontrolled taxpayers.
  (3) Data and assumptions.
    (i) In general.
    (ii) Consistency in accounting.
    (iii) Allocations between the relevant business activity and other activities.
(d) Definitions.
(e) Examples.

§ 1.482-6. Profit split method.
(a) In general.
(b) Appropriate share of profits and losses.
(c) Application.
  (1) In general.
  (2) Comparable profit split.
    (i) In general.
    (ii) Comparability and reliability considerations.
      (A) In general.
      (B) Comparability.
        (1) In general.
        (2) Adjustments for differences between the controlled and uncontrolled taxpayers.
      (C) Data and assumptions.
      (D) Other factors affecting reliability.
  (3) Residual profit split.
    (i) In general.
      (A) Allocate income to routine contributions.

Reg. § 1.482-0

(B) Allocate residual profit.
(ii) Comparability and reliability considerations.
(A) In general.
(B) Comparability.
(C) Data and assumptions.
(D) Other factors affecting reliability.
(iii) Example.

§ 1.482-7. Sharing of costs.
(a) In general.
(1) Scope and application of the rules in this section.
(2) Limitation on allocations.
(3) Cross references.
(b) Qualified cost sharing arrangement.
(c) Participant.
(1) In general.
(2) Treatment of a controlled taxpayer that is not a controlled participant.
(i) In general.
(ii) Example.
(3) Treatment of consolidated group.
(d) Costs.
(1) Intangible development costs.
(2) Examples.
(e) Anticipated benefits.
(1) Benefits.
(2) Reasonably anticipated benefits.
(f) Cost allocations.
(1) In general.
(2) Share of intangible development costs.
(i) In general.
(ii) Example.
(3) Share of reasonably anticipated benefits.
(i) In general.
(ii) Measure of benefits.
(iii) Indirect bases for measuring anticipated benefits.
(A) Units used, produced or sold.
(B) Sales.
(C) Operating profit.
(D) Other bases for measuring anticipated benefits.
(E) Examples.
(iv) Projections used to estimate anticipated benefits.
(A) In general.
(B) Unreliable projections.
(C) Foreign-to-foreign adjustments.

(D) Examples.
(4) Timing of allocations.
(g) Allocations of income, deductions or other tax items to reflect transfers of intangibles (buy-in).
(1) In general.
(2) Pre-existing intangibles.
(3) New controlled participant.
(4) Controlled participant relinquishes interests.
(5) Conduct inconsistent with the terms of a cost sharing arrangement.
(6) Failure to assign interests under a qualified cost sharing arrangement.
(7) Form of consideration.
(i) Lump sum payments.
(ii) Installment payments.
(iii) Royalties.
(8) Examples.
(h) Character of payments made pursuant to a qualified cost sharing arrangement.
(1) In general.
(2) Examples.
(i) Accounting requirements.
(j) Administrative requirements.
(1) In general.
(2) Documentation.
(i) Requirements.
(ii) Coordination with penalty regulation.
(3) Reporting requirements.
(k) Effective date.
(l) Transition rule.

§ 1.482-8. Examples of the best method rule.
(a) In general.
(b) Examples.
[Reg. § 1.482-0.]

☐ [*T.D. 8552, 7-1-94. Amended by T.D. 8632, 12-19-95 and T.D. 8670, 5-9-96.*]

[Reg. § 1.482-1]

§ 1.482-1. Allocation of income and deductions among taxpayers.—(a) *In general*—(1) *Purpose and scope.* The purpose of section 482 is to ensure that taxpayers clearly reflect income attributable to controlled transactions, and to prevent the avoidance of taxes with respect to such transactions. Section 482 places a controlled taxpayer on a tax parity with an uncontrolled taxpayer by determining the true taxable income of the controlled taxpayer. This § 1.482-1 sets forth general principles and guidelines to be followed under section 482. Section 1.482-2 provides rules

Reg. § 1.482-1(a)(1)

for the determination of the true taxable income of controlled taxpayers in specific situations, including controlled transactions involving loans or advances, services, and property. Sections 1.482-3 through 1.482-6 elaborate on the rules that apply to controlled transactions involving property. Section 1.482-7T sets forth the cost sharing provisions. Finally, § 1.482-8 provides examples illustrating the application of the best method rule.

(2) *Authority to make allocations.* The district director may make allocations between or among the members of a controlled group if a controlled taxpayer has not reported its true taxable income. In such case, the district director may allocate income, deductions, credits, allowances, basis, or any other item or element affecting taxable income (referred to as allocations). The appropriate allocation may take the form of an increase or decrease in any relevant amount.

(3) *Taxpayer's use of section 482.* If necessary to reflect an arm's length result, a controlled taxpayer may report on a timely filed U.S. income tax return (including extensions) the results of its controlled transactions based upon prices different from those actually charged. Except as provided in this paragraph, section 482 grants no other right to a controlled taxpayer to apply the provisions of section 482 at will or to compel the district director to apply such provisions. Therefore, no untimely or amended returns will be permitted to decrease taxable income based on allocations or other adjustments with respect to controlled transactions. See § 1.6662-6T(a)(2) or successor regulations.

(b) *Arm's length standard*—(1) *In general.* In determining the true taxable income of a controlled taxpayer, the standard to be applied in every case is that of a taxpayer dealing at arm's length with an uncontrolled taxpayer. A controlled transaction meets the arm's length standard if the results of the transaction are consistent with the results that would have been realized if uncontrolled taxpayers had engaged in the same transaction under the same circumstances (arm's length result). However, because identical transactions can rarely be located, whether a transaction produces an arm's length result generally will be determined by reference to the results of comparable transactions under comparable circumstances. See § 1.482-1(d)(2) (Standard of comparability). Evaluation of whether a controlled transaction produces an arm's length result is made pursuant to a method selected under the best method rule described in § 1.482-1(c).

(2) *Arm's length methods*—(i) *Methods.* Sections 1.482-2 through 1.482-6 provide specific methods to be used to evaluate whether transactions between or among members of the controlled group satisfy the arm's length standard, and if they do not, to determine the arm's length result.

(ii) *Selection of category of method applicable to transaction.* The methods listed in § 1.482-2 apply to different types of transactions, such as transfers of property, services, loans or advances, and rentals. Accordingly, the method or methods most appropriate to the calculation of arm's length results for controlled transactions must be selected, and different methods may be applied to interrelated transactions if such transactions are most reliably evaluated on a separate basis. For example, if services are provided in connection with the transfer of property, it may be appropriate to separately apply the methods applicable to services and property in order to determine an arm's length result. But see § 1.482-1(f)(2)(i) (Aggregation of transactions). In addition, other applicable provisions of the Code may affect the characterization of a transaction, and therefore affect the methods applicable under section 482. See for example section 467.

(c) *Best method rule*—(1) *In general.* The arm's length result of a controlled transaction must be determined under the method that, under the facts and circumstances, provides the most reliable measure of an arm's length result. Thus, there is no strict priority of methods, and no method will invariably be considered to be more reliable than others. An arm's length result may be determined under any method without establishing the inapplicability of another method, but if another method subsequently is shown to produce a more reliable measure of an arm's length result, such other method must be used. Similarly, if two or more applications of a single method provide inconsistent results, the arm's length result must be determined under the application that, under the facts and circumstances, provides the most reliable measure of an arm's length result. See § 1.482-8 for examples of the application of the best method rule.

(2) *Determining the best method.* Data based on the results of transactions between unrelated parties provides the most objective basis for determining whether the results of a controlled transaction are arm's length. Thus, in determining which of two or more available methods (or applications of a single method) provides the most reliable measure of an arm's length result, the two primary factors to take into account are the degree of comparability between the controlled transaction (or taxpayer) and any uncontrolled com-

Reg. § 1.482-1(a)(2)

parables, and the quality of the data and assumptions used in the analysis. In addition, in certain circumstances, it also may be relevant to consider whether the results of an analysis are consistent with the results of an analysis under another method. These factors are explained in paragraphs (c)(2)(i), (ii), and (iii) of this section.

(i) *Comparability.* The relative reliability of a method based on the results of transactions between unrelated parties depends on the degree of comparability between the controlled transaction or taxpayers and the uncontrolled comparables, taking into account the factors described in § 1.482-1(d)(3) (Factors for determining comparability), and after making adjustments for differences, as described in § 1.482-1(d)(2) (Standard of comparability). As the degree of comparability increases, the number and extent of potential differences that could render the analysis inaccurate is reduced. In addition, if adjustments are made to increase the degree of comparability, the number, magnitude, and reliability of those adjustments will affect the reliability of the results of the analysis. Thus, an analysis under the comparable uncontrolled price method will generally be more reliable than analyses obtained under other methods if the analysis is based on closely comparable uncontrolled transactions, because such an analysis can be expected to achieve a higher degree of comparability and be susceptible to fewer differences than analyses under other methods. See § 1.482-3(b)(2)(ii)(A). An analysis will be relatively less reliable, however, as the uncontrolled transactions become less comparable to the controlled transaction.

(ii) *Data and assumptions.* Whether a method provides the most reliable measure of an arm's length result also depends upon the completeness and accuracy of the underlying data, the reliability of the assumptions, and the sensitivity of the results to possible deficiencies in the data and assumptions. Such factors are particularly relevant in evaluating the degree of comparability between the controlled and uncontrolled transactions. These factors are discussed in paragraphs (c)(2)(ii)(A), (B), and (C) of this section.

(A) *Completeness and accuracy of data.* The completeness and accuracy of the data affects the ability to identify and quantify those factors that would affect the result under any particular method. For example, the completeness and accuracy of data will determine the extent to which it is possible to identify differences between the controlled and uncontrolled transactions, and the reliability of adjustments that are made to account for such differences. An analysis will be relatively more reliable as the completeness and accuracy of the data increases.

(B) *Reliability of assumptions.* All methods rely on certain assumptions. The reliability of the results derived from a method depends on the soundness of such assumptions. Some assumptions are relatively reliable. For example, adjustments for differences in payment terms between controlled and uncontrolled transactions may be based on the assumption that at arm's length such differences would lead to price differences that reflect the time value of money. Although selection of the appropriate interest rate to use in making such adjustments involves some judgement, the economic analysis on which the assumption is based is relatively sound. Other assumptions may be less reliable. For example, the residual profit split method may be based on the assumption that capitalized intangible development expenses reflect the relative value of the intangible property contributed by each party. Because the costs of developing an intangible may not be related to its market value, the soundness of this assumption will affect the reliability of the results derived from this method.

(C) *Sensitivity of results to deficiencies in data and assumptions.* Deficiencies in the data used or assumptions made may have a greater effect on some methods than others. In particular, the reliability of some methods is heavily dependent on the similarity of property or services involved in the controlled and uncontrolled transaction. For certain other methods, such as the resale price method, the analysis of the extent to which controlled and uncontrolled taxpayers undertake the same or similar functions, employ similar resources, and bear similar risks is particularly important. Finally, under other methods, such as the profit split method, defining the relevant business activity and appropriate allocation of costs, income, and assets may be of particular importance. Therefore, a difference between the controlled and uncontrolled transactions for which an accurate adjustment cannot be made may have a greater effect on the reliability of the results derived under one method than the results derived under another method. For example, differences in management efficiency may have a greater effect on a comparable profits method analysis than on a comparable uncontrolled price method analysis, while differences in product characteristics will ordinarily have a greater effect on a comparable uncontrolled price method analysis than on a comparable profits method analysis.

(iii) *Confirmation of results by another method.* If two or more methods produce inconsis-

Reg. § 1.482-1(c)(2)

tent results, the best method rule will be applied to select the method that provides the most reliable measure of an arm's length result. If the best method rule does not clearly indicate which method should be selected, an additional factor that may be taken into account in selecting a method is whether any of the competing methods produce results that are consistent with the results obtained from the appropriate application of another method. Further, in evaluating different applications of the same method, the fact that a second method (or another application of the first method) produces results that are consistent with one of the competing applications may be taken into account.

(d) *Comparability*—(1) *In general*. Whether a controlled transaction produces an arm's length result is generally evaluated by comparing the results of that transaction to results realized by uncontrolled taxpayers engaged in comparable transactions under comparable circumstances. For this purpose, the comparability of transactions and circumstances must be evaluated considering all factors that could affect prices or profits in arm's length dealings (comparability factors). While a specific comparability factor may be of particular importance in applying a method, each method requires analysis of all of the factors that affect comparability under that method. Such factors include the following—

(i) Functions;

(ii) Contractual terms;

(iii) Risks;

(iv) Economic conditions; and

(v) Property or services.

(2) *Standard of comparability*. In order to be considered comparable to a controlled transaction, an uncontrolled transaction need not be identical to the controlled transaction, but must be sufficiently similar that it provides a reliable measure of an arm's length result. If there are material differences between the controlled and uncontrolled transactions, adjustments must be made if the effect of such differences on prices or profits can be ascertained with sufficient accuracy to improve the reliability of the results. For purposes of this section, a material difference is one that would materially affect the measure of an arm's length result under the method being applied. If adjustments for material differences cannot be made, the uncontrolled transaction may be used as a measure of an arm's length result, but the reliability of the analysis will be reduced. Generally, such adjustments must be made to the results of the uncontrolled comparable and must be based on commercial practices, economic principles, or statistical analyses. The extent and reliability of any adjustments will affect the relative reliability of the analysis. See § 1.482-1(c)(1) (Best method rule). In any event, unadjusted industry average returns themselves cannot establish arm's length results.

(3) *Factors for determining comparability*. The comparability factors listed in § 1.482-1(d)(1) are discussed in this section. Each of these factors must be considered in determining the degree of comparability between transactions or taxpayers and the extent to which comparability adjustments may be necessary. In addition, in certain cases involving special circumstances, the rules under paragraph (d)(4) of this section must be considered.

(i) *Functional analysis*. Determining the degree of comparability between controlled and uncontrolled transactions requires a comparison of the functions performed, and associated resources employed, by the taxpayers in each transaction. This comparison is based on a functional analysis that identifies and compares the economically significant activities undertaken, or to be undertaken, by the taxpayers in both controlled and uncontrolled transactions. A functional analysis should also include consideration of the resources that are employed, or to be employed, in conjunction with the activities undertaken, including consideration of the type of assets used, such as plant and equipment, or the use of valuable intangibles. A functional analysis is not a pricing method and does not itself determine the arm's length result for the controlled transaction under review. Functions that may need to be accounted for in determining the comparability of two transactions include—

(A) Research and development;

(B) Product design and engineering;

(C) Manufacturing, production and process engineering;

(D) Product fabrication, extraction, and assembly;

(E) Purchasing and materials management;

(F) Marketing and distribution functions, including inventory management, warranty administration, and advertising activities;

(G) Transportation and warehousing; and

(H) Managerial, legal, accounting and finance, credit and collection, training, and personnel management services.

(ii) *Contractual terms*—(A) *In general*. Determining the degree of comparability between the controlled and uncontrolled transactions requires a comparison of the significant contractual terms that could affect the results of the two transactions. These terms include—

(*1*) The form of consideration charged or paid;

(*2*) Sales or purchase volume;

(*3*) The scope and terms of warranties provided;

(*4*) Rights to updates, revisions or modifications;

(*5*) The duration of relevant license, contract or other agreements, and termination or renegotiation rights;

(*6*) Collateral transactions or ongoing business relationships between the buyer and the seller, including arrangements for the provision of ancillary or subsidiary services; and

(*7*) Extension of credit and payment terms. Thus, for example, if the time for payment of the amount charged in a controlled transaction differs from the time for payment of the amount charged in an uncontrolled transaction, an adjustment to reflect the difference in payment terms should be made if such difference would have a material effect on price. Such comparability adjustment is required even if no interest would be allocated or imputed under § 1.482-2(a) or other applicable provisions of the Internal Revenue Code or regulations.

(B) *Identifying contractual terms*—(*1*) *Written agreement.* The contractual terms, including the consequent allocation of risks, that are agreed to in writing before the transactions are entered into will be respected if such terms are consistent with the economic substance of the underlying transactions. In evaluating economic substance, greatest weight will be given to the actual conduct of the parties, and the respective legal rights of the parties (see, for example, § 1.482-4(f)(3) (Ownership of intangible property)). If the contractual terms are inconsistent with the economic substance of the underlying transaction, the district director may disregard such terms and impute terms that are consistent with the economic substance of the transaction.

(*2*) *No written agreement.* In the absence of a written agreement, the district director may impute a contractual agreement between the controlled taxpayers consistent with the economic substance of the transaction. In determining the economic substance of the transaction, greatest weight will be given to the actual conduct of the parties and their respective legal rights (see, for example, § 1.482-4(f)(3) (Ownership of intangible property)). For example, if, without a written agreement, a controlled taxpayer operates at full capacity and regularly sells all of its output to another member of its controlled group, the district director may impute a purchasing contract from the course of conduct of the controlled taxpayers, and determine that the producer bears little risk that the buyer will fail to purchase its full output. Further, if an established industry convention or usage of trade assigns a risk or resolves an issue, that convention or usage will be followed if the conduct of the taxpayers is consistent with it. See UCC § 1-205. For example, unless otherwise agreed, payment generally is due at the time and place at which the buyer is to receive goods. See UCC § 2-310.

(C) *Examples.* The following examples illustrate this paragraph (d)(3)(ii).

Example 1—Differences in volume. USP, a United States agricultural exporter, regularly buys transportation services from FSub, its foreign subsidiary, to ship its products from the United States to overseas markets. Although FSub occasionally provides transportation services to URA, an unrelated domestic corporation, URA accounts for only 10% of the gross revenues of FSub, and the remaining 90% of FSub's gross revenues are attributable to FSub's transactions with USP. In determining the degree of comparability between FSub's uncontrolled transaction with URA and its controlled transaction with USP, the difference in volumes involved in the two transactions and the regularity with which these services are provided must be taken into account if such difference would have a material effect on the price charged. Inability to make reliable adjustments for these differences would affect the reliability of the results derived from the uncontrolled transaction as a measure of the arm's length result.

Example 2—Reliability of adjustment for differences in volume. (i) FS manufactures product XX and sells that product to its parent corporation, P. FS also sells product XX to uncontrolled taxpayers at a price of $100 per unit. Except for the volume of each transaction, the sales to P and to uncontrolled taxpayers take place under substantially the same economic conditions and contractual terms. In uncontrolled transactions, FS offers a 2% discount for quantities of 20 per order, and a 5% discount for quantities of 100 per order. If P purchases product XX in quantities of 60 per order, in the absence of other reliable information, it may reasonably be concluded that the arm's length price to P would be $100, less a discount of 3.5%.

(ii) If P purchases product XX in quantities of 1,000 per order, a reliable estimate of the appropriate volume discount must be based on proper economic or statistical analysis, not neces-

Reg. § 1.482-1(d)(3)

Adjustments

See p. 20,601 for regulations not amended to reflect law changes

sarily a linear extrapolation from the 2% and 5% catalog discounts applicable to sales of 20 and 100 units, respectively.

Example 3—Contractual term imputed from economic substance. (i) USD, a United States corporation, is the exclusive distributor of products manufactured by FP, its foreign parent. The FP products are sold under a tradename that is not known in the United States. USD does not have an agreement with FP for the use of FP's tradename. For Years 1 through 6, USD bears marketing expenses promoting FP's tradename in the United States that are substantially above the level of such expenses incurred by comparable distributors in uncontrolled transactions. FP does not directly or indirectly reimburse USD for its marketing expenses. By Year 7, the FP tradename has become very well known in the market and commands a price premium. At this time, USD becomes a commission agent for FP.

(ii) In determining USD's arm's length result for Year 7, the district director considers the economic substance of the arrangements between USD and FP throughout the course of their relationship. It is unlikely that at arm's length, USD would incur these above-normal expenses without some assurance it could derive a benefit from these expenses. In this case, these expenditures indicate a course of conduct that is consistent with an agreement under which USD received a long-term right to use the FP tradename in the United States. Such conduct is inconsistent with the contractual arrangements between FP and USD under which USD was merely a distributor, and later a commission agent, for FP. Therefore, the district director may impute an agreement between USD and FP under which USD will retain an appropriate portion of the price premium attributable to the FP tradename.

(iii) *Risk*—(A) *Comparability.* Determining the degree of comparability between controlled and uncontrolled transactions requires a comparison of the significant risks that could affect the prices that would be charged or paid, or the profit that would be earned, in the two transactions. Relevant risks to consider include—

(*1*) Market risks, including fluctuations in cost, demand, pricing, and inventory levels;

(*2*) Risks associated with the success or failure of research and development activities;

(*3*) Financial risks, including fluctuations in foreign currency rates of exchange and interest rates;

(*4*) Credit and collection risks;

(*5*) Product liability risks; and

(*6*) General business risks related to the ownership of property, plant, and equipment.

(B) *Identification of taxpayer that bears risk.* In general, the determination of which controlled taxpayer bears a particular risk will be made in accordance with the provisions of § 1.482-1(d)(3)(ii)(B) (Identifying contractual terms). Thus, the allocation of risks specified or implied by the taxpayer's contractual terms will generally be respected if it is consistent with the economic substance of the transaction. An allocation of risk between controlled taxpayers after the outcome of such risk is known or reasonably knowable lacks economic substance. In considering the economic substance of the transaction, the following facts are relevant—

(*1*) Whether the pattern of the controlled taxpayer's conduct over time is consistent with the purported allocation of risk between the controlled taxpayers; or where the pattern is changed, whether the relevant contractual arrangements have been modified accordingly;

(*2*) Whether a controlled taxpayer has the financial capacity to fund losses that might be expected to occur as the result of the assumption of a risk, or whether, at arm's length, another party to the controlled transaction would ultimately suffer the consequences of such losses; and

(*3*) The extent to which each controlled taxpayer exercises managerial or operational control over the business activities that directly influence the amount of income or loss realized. In arm's length dealings, parties ordinarily bear a greater share of those risks over which they have relatively more control.

(C) *Examples.* The following examples illustrate this paragraph (d)(3)(iii).

Example 1. FD, the wholly-owned foreign distributor of USM, a U.S. manufacturer, buys widgets from USM under a written contract. Widgets are a generic electronic appliance. Under the terms of the contract, FD must buy and take title to 20,000 widgets for each of the five years of the contract at a price of $10 per widget. The widgets will be sold under FD's label, and FD must finance any marketing strategies to promote sales in the foreign market. There are no rebate or buy back provisions. FD has adequate financial capacity to fund its obligations under the contract under any circumstances that could reasonably be expected to arise. In Years 1, 2 and 3, FD sold only 10,000 widgets at a price of $11 per unit. In Year 4, FD sold its entire inventory of widgets at a price of $25 per unit. Since the contractual terms allocating market risk were agreed to before

Reg. § 1.482-1(d)(3)

the outcome of such risk was known or reasonably knowable, FD had the financial capacity to bear the market risk that it would be unable to sell all of the widgets it purchased currently, and its conduct was consistent over time, FD will be deemed to bear the risk.

Example 2. The facts are the same as in *Example 1,* except that in Year 1 FD had only $100,000 in total capital, including loans. In subsequent years USM makes no additional contributions to the capital of FD, and FD is unable to obtain any capital through loans from an unrelated party. Nonetheless, USM continues to sell 20,000 widgets annually to FD under the terms of the contract, and USM extends credit to FD to enable it to finance the purchase. FD does not have the financial capacity in Years 1, 2 and 3 to finance the purchase of the widgets given that it could not sell most of the widgets it purchased during those years. Thus, notwithstanding the terms of the contract, USM and not FD assumed the market risk that a substantial portion of the widgets could not be sold, since in that event FD would not be able to pay USM for all of the widgets it purchased.

Example 3. S, a Country X corporation, manufactures small motors that it sells to P, its U.S. parent. P incorporates the motors into various products and sells those products to uncontrolled customers in the United States. The contract price for the motors is expressed in U.S. dollars, effectively allocating the currency risk for these transactions to S for any currency fluctuations between the time the contract is signed and payment is made. As long as S has adequate financial capacity to bear this currency risk (including by hedging all or part of the risk) and the conduct of S and P is consistent with the terms of the contract (i.e., the contract price is not adjusted to reflect exchange rate movements), the agreement of the parties to allocate the exchange risk to S will be respected.

Example 4. USSub is the wholly-owned U.S. subsidiary of FP, a foreign manufacturer. USSub acts as a distributor of goods manufactured by FP. FP and USSub execute an agreement providing that FP will bear any ordinary product liability costs arising from defects in the goods manufactured by FP. In practice, however, when ordinary product liability claims are sustained against USSub and FP, USSub pays the resulting damages. Therefore, the district director disregards the contractual arrangement regarding product liability costs between FP and USSub, and treats the risk as having been assumed by USSub.

(iv) *Economic conditions.* Determining the degree of comparability between controlled and uncontrolled transactions requires a comparison of the significant economic conditions that could affect the prices that would be charged or paid, or the profit that would be earned in each of the transactions. These factors include—

(A) The similarity of geographic markets;

(B) The relative size of each market, and the extent of the overall economic development in each market;

(C) The level of the market (e.g., wholesale, retail, etc.);

(D) The relevant market shares for the products, properties, or services transferred or provided;

(E) The location-specific costs of the factors of production and distribution;

(F) The extent of competition in each market with regard to the property or services under review;

(G) The economic condition of the particular industry, including whether the market is in contraction or expansion; and

(H) The alternatives realistically available to the buyer and seller.

(v) *Property or services.* Evaluating the degree of comparability between controlled and uncontrolled transactions requires a comparison of the property or services transferred in the transactions. This comparison may include any intangibles that are embedded in tangible property or services being transferred. The comparability of the embedded intangibles will be analyzed using the factors listed in § 1.482-4(c)(2)(iii)(B)(*1*) (Comparable intangible property). The relevance of product comparability in evaluating the relative reliability of the results will depend on the method applied. For guidance concerning the specific comparability considerations applicable to transfers of tangible and intangible property, see §§ 1.482-3 through 1.482-6; see also § 1.482-3(f), dealing with the coordination of the intangible and tangible property rules.

(4) *Special circumstances*—(i) *Market share strategy.* In certain circumstances, taxpayers may adopt strategies to enter new markets or to increase a product's share of an existing market (market share strategy). Such a strategy would be reflected by temporarily increased market development expenses or resale prices that are temporarily lower than the prices charged for comparable products in the same market. Whether or not the strategy is reflected in the

Reg. § 1.482-1(d)(4)

transfer price depends on which party to the controlled transaction bears the costs of the pricing strategy. In any case, the effect of a market share strategy on a controlled transaction will be taken into account only if it can be shown that an uncontrolled taxpayer engaged in a comparable strategy under comparable circumstances for a comparable period of time, and the taxpayer provides documentation that substantiates the following—

(A) The costs incurred to implement the market share strategy are borne by the controlled taxpayer that would obtain the future profits that result from the strategy, and there is a reasonable likelihood that the strategy will result in future profits that reflect an appropriate return in relation to the costs incurred to implement it;

(B) The market share strategy is pursued only for a period of time that is reasonable, taking into consideration the industry and product in question; and

(C) The market share strategy, the related costs and expected returns, and any agreement between the controlled taxpayers to share the related costs, were established before the strategy was implemented.

(ii) *Different geographic markets*—(A) *In general.* Uncontrolled comparables ordinarily should be derived from the geographic market in which the controlled taxpayer operates, because there may be significant differences in economic conditions in different markets. If information from the same market is not available, an uncontrolled comparable derived from a different geographic market may be considered if adjustments are made to account for differences between the two markets. If information permitting adjustments for such differences is not available, then information derived from uncontrolled comparables in the most similar market for which reliable data is available may be used, but the extent of such differences may affect the reliability of the method for purposes of the best method rule. For this purpose, a geographic market is any geographic area in which the economic conditions for the relevant product or service are substantially the same, and may include multiple countries, depending on the economic conditions.

(B) *Example.* The following example illustrates this paragraph (d)(4)(ii).

Example. Manuco, a wholly-owned foreign subsidiary of P, a U.S. corporation, manufactures products in Country Z for sale to P. No uncontrolled transactions are located that would provide a reliable measure of the arm's length result under the comparable uncontrolled price method. The district director considers applying the cost plus method or the comparable profits method. Information on uncontrolled taxpayers performing comparable functions under comparable circumstances in the same geographic market is not available. Therefore, adjusted data from uncontrolled manufacturers in other markets may be considered in order to apply the cost plus method. In this case, comparable uncontrolled manufacturers are found in the United States. Accordingly, data from the comparable U.S. uncontrolled manufacturers, as adjusted to account for differences between the United States and Country Z's geographic market, is used to test the arm's length price paid by P to Manuco. However, the use of such data may affect the reliability of the results for purposes of the best method rule. See § 1.482-1(c).

(C) *Location savings.* If an uncontrolled taxpayer operates in a different geographic market than the controlled taxpayer, adjustments may be necessary to account for significant differences in costs attributable to the geographic markets. These adjustments must be based on the effect such differences would have on the consideration charged or paid in the controlled transaction given the relative competitive positions of buyers and sellers in each market. Thus, for example, the fact that the total costs of operating in a controlled manufacturer's geographic market are less than the total costs of operating in other markets ordinarily justifies higher profits to the manufacturer only if the cost differences would increase the profits of comparable uncontrolled manufacturers operating at arm's length, given the competitive positions of buyers and sellers in that market.

(D) *Example.* The following example illustrates the principles of this paragraph (d)(4)(ii)(C).

Example. Couture, a U.S. apparel design corporation, contracts with Sewco, its wholly owned Country Y subsidiary, to manufacture its clothes. Costs of operating in Country Y are significantly lower than the operating costs in the United States. Although clothes with the Couture label sell for a premium price, the actual production of the clothes does not require significant specialized knowledge that could not be acquired by actual or potential competitors to Sewco at reasonable cost. Thus, Sewco's functions could be performed by several actual or potential competitors to Sewco in geographic markets that are similar to Country Y. Thus, the fact that production is less costly in Country Y will not, in and of itself, justify additional profits derived from lower operating costs in Country Y inuring to Sewco, because the competitive positions of the other

Reg. § 1.482-1(d)(4)

actual or potential producers in similar geographic markets capable of performing the same functions at the same low costs indicate that at arm's length such profits would not be retained by Sewco.

(iii) *Transactions ordinarily not accepted as comparables*—(A) *In general.* Transactions ordinarily will not constitute reliable measures of an arm's length result for purposes of this section if—

(*1*) They are not made in the ordinary course of business; or

(*2*) One of the principal purposes of the uncontrolled transaction was to establish an arm's length result with respect to the controlled transaction.

(B) *Examples.* The following examples illustrate the principle of this paragraph (d)(4)(iii).

Example 1—Not in the ordinary course of business. USP, a United States manufacturer of computer software, sells its products to FSub, its foreign distributor in country X. Compco, a United States competitor of USP, also sells its products in X through unrelated distributors. However, in the year under review, Compco is forced into bankruptcy, and Compco liquidates its inventory by selling all of its products to unrelated distributors in X for a liquidation price. Because the sale of its entire inventory was not a sale in the ordinary course of business, Compco's sale cannot be used as an uncontrolled comparable to determine USP's arm's length result from its controlled transaction.

Example 2—Principal purpose of establishing an arm's length result. USP, a United States manufacturer of farm machinery, sells its products to FSub, its wholly-owned distributor in Country Y. USP, operating at nearly full capacity, sells 95% of its inventory to FSub. To make use of its excess capacity, and also to establish a comparable uncontrolled price for its transfer price to FSub, USP increases its production to full capacity. USP sells its excess inventory to Compco, an unrelated foreign distributor in Country X. Country X has approximately the same economic conditions as that of Country Y. Because one of the principal purposes of selling to Compco was to establish an arm's length price for its controlled transactions with FSub, USP's sale to Compco cannot be used as an uncontrolled comparable to determine USP's arm's length result from its controlled transaction.

(e) *Arm's length range*—(1) *In general.* In some cases, application of a pricing method will produce a single result that is the most reliable measure of an arm's length result. In other cases, application of a method may produce a number of results from which a range of reliable results may be derived. A taxpayer will not be subject to adjustment if its results fall within such range (arm's length range).

(2) *Determination of arm's length range*—(i) *Single method.* The arm's length range is ordinarily determined by applying a single pricing method selected under the best method rule to two or more uncontrolled transactions of similar comparability and reliability. Use of more than one method may be appropriate for the purposes described in paragraph (c)(2)(iii) of this section (Best method rule).

(ii) *Selection of comparables.* Uncontrolled comparables must be selected based upon the comparability criteria relevant to the method applied and must be sufficiently similar to the controlled transaction that they provide a reliable measure of an arm's length result. If material differences exist between the controlled and uncontrolled transactions, adjustments must be made to the results of the uncontrolled transaction if the effect of such differences on price or profits can be ascertained with sufficient accuracy to improve the reliability of the results. See § 1.482-1(d)(2) (Standard of comparability). The arm's length range will be derived only from those uncontrolled comparables that have, or through adjustments can be brought to, a similar level of comparability and reliability, and uncontrolled comparables that have a significantly lower level of comparability and reliability will not be used in establishing the arm's length range.

(iii) *Comparables included in arm's length range*—(A) *In general.* The arm's length range will consist of the results of all of the uncontrolled comparables that meet the following conditions: the information on the controlled transaction and the uncontrolled comparables is sufficiently complete that it is likely that all material differences have been identified, each such difference has a definite and reasonably ascertainable effect on price or profit, and an adjustment is made to eliminate the effect of each such difference.

(B) *Adjustment of range to increase reliability.* If there are no uncontrolled comparables described in paragraph (e)(2)(iii)(A) of this section, the arm's length range is derived from the results of all the uncontrolled comparables, selected pursuant to paragraph (e)(2)(ii) of this section, that achieve a similar level of comparability and reliability. In such cases the reliability of the analysis must be increased, where it is possible to do so, by adjusting the range through application of a valid statistical method to the results of all of the uncontrolled comparables so selected.

Reg. § 1.482-1(e)(2)

The reliability of the analysis is increased when statistical methods are used to establish a range of results in which the limits of the range will be determined such that there is a 75 percent probability of a result falling above the lower end of the range and a 75 percent probability of a result falling below the upper end of the range. The interquartile range ordinarily provides an acceptable measure of this range; however a different statistical method may be applied if it provides a more reliable measure.

(C) *Interquartile range.* For purposes of this section, the interquartile range is the range from the 25th to the 75th percentile of the results derived from the uncontrolled comparables. For this purpose, the 25th percentile is the lowest result derived from an uncontrolled comparable such that at least 25 percent of the results are at or below the value of that result. However, if exactly 25 percent of the results are at or below a result, then the 25th percentile is equal to the average of that result and the next higher result derived from the uncontrolled comparables. The 75th percentile is determined analogously.

(3) *Adjustment if taxpayer's results are outside arm's length range.* If the results of a controlled transaction fall outside the arm's length range, the district director may make allocations that adjust the controlled taxpayer's result to any point within the arm's length range. If the interquartile range is used to determine the arm's length range, such adjustment will ordinarily be to the median of all the results. The median is the 50th percentile of the results, which is determined in a manner analogous to that described in paragraph (e)(2)(iii)(C) of this section (Interquartile range). In other cases, an adjustment normally will be made to the arithmetic mean of all the results. See § 1.482-1(f)(2)(iii)(D) for determination of an adjustment when a controlled taxpayer's result for a multiple year period falls outside an arm's length range consisting of the average results of uncontrolled comparables over the same period.

(4) *Arm's length range not prerequisite to allocation.* The rules of this paragraph (e) do not require that the district director establish an arm's length range prior to making an allocation under section 482. Thus, for example, the district director may properly propose an allocation on the basis of a single comparable uncontrolled price if the comparable uncontrolled price method, as described in § 1.482-3(b), has been properly applied. However, if the taxpayer subsequently demonstrates that the results claimed on its income tax return are within the range established by additional equally reliable comparable uncontrolled prices in a manner consistent with the requirements set forth in § 1.482-1(e)(2)(iii), then no allocation will be made.

(5) *Examples.* The following examples illustrate the principles of this paragraph (e).

Example 1—Selection of comparables. (i) To evaluate the arm's length result of a controlled transaction between USSub, the United States taxpayer under review, and FP, its foreign parent, the district director considers applying the resale price method. The district director identifies ten potential uncontrolled transactions. The distributors in all ten uncontrolled transactions purchase and resell similar products and perform similar functions to those of USSub.

(ii) Data with respect to three of the uncontrolled transactions is very limited, and although some material differences can be identified and adjusted for, the level of comparability of these three uncontrolled comparables is significantly lower than that of the other seven. Further, of those seven, adjustments for the identified material differences can be reliably made for only four of the uncontrolled transactions. Therefore, pursuant to § 1.482-1(e)(2)(ii) only these four uncontrolled comparables may be used to establish an arm's length range.

Example 2—Arm's length range consists of all the results. (i) The facts are the same as in *Example 1.* Applying the resale price method to the four uncontrolled comparables, and making adjustments to the uncontrolled comparables pursuant to § 1.482-1(d)(2), the district director derives the following results:

Comparable	Result ($ price)
1	44.00
2	45.00
3	45.00
4	45.50

(ii) The district director determines that data regarding the four uncontrolled transactions is sufficiently complete and accurate so that it is likely that all material differences between the controlled and uncontrolled transactions have been identified, such differences have a definite and reasonably ascertainable effect, and appropriate adjustments were made for such differences. Accordingly, if the resale price method is determined to be the best method pursuant to § 1.482-1(c), the arm's length range for the controlled transaction will consist of the results of all of the uncontrolled comparables, pursuant to paragraph (e)(2)(iii)(A) of this section. Thus, the arm's length range in this case would be the range from $44 to $45.50.

Example 3—Arm's length range limited to interquartile range. (i) The facts are the same as in *Example 2,* except in this case there are some product and functional differences between the four uncontrolled comparables and USSub. However, the data is insufficiently complete to determine the effect of the differences. Applying the resale price method to the four uncontrolled comparables, and making adjustments to the uncontrolled comparables pursuant to § 1.482-1(d)(2), the district director derives the following results:

Uncontrolled Comparable	Result ($ price)
1	42.00
2	44.00
3	45.00
4	47.50

(ii) It cannot be established in this case that all material differences are likely to have been identified and reliable adjustments made for those differences. Accordingly, if the resale price method is determined to be the best method pursuant to § 1.482-1(c), the arm's length range for the controlled transaction must be established pursuant to paragraph (e)(2)(iii)(B) of this section. In this case, the district director uses the interquartile range to determine the arm's length range, which is the range from $43 to $46.25. If USSub's price falls outside this range, the district director may make an allocation. In this case that allocation would be to the median of the results, or $44.50.

Example 4—Arm's length range limited to interquartile range. (i) To evaluate the arm's length result of controlled transactions between USP, a United States manufacturing company, and FSub, its foreign subsidiary, the district director considers applying the comparable profits method. The district director identifies 50 uncontrolled taxpayers within the same industry that potentially could be used to apply the method.

(ii) Further review indicates that only 20 of the uncontrolled manufacturers engage in activities requiring similar capital investments and technical know-how. Data with respect to five of the uncontrolled manufacturers is very limited, and although some material differences can be identified and adjusted for, the level of comparability of these five uncontrolled comparables is significantly lower than that of the other 15. In addition, for those five uncontrolled comparables it is not possible to accurately allocate costs between the business activity associated with the relevant transactions and other business activities. Therefore, pursuant to § 1.482-1(e)(2)(ii) only the other fifteen uncontrolled comparables may be used to establish an arm's length range.

(iii) Although the data for the fifteen remaining uncontrolled comparables is relatively complete and accurate, there is a significant possibility that some material differences may remain. The district director has determined, for example, that it is likely that there are material differences in the level of technical expertise or in management efficiency. Accordingly, if the comparable profits method is determined to be the best method pursuant to § 1.482-1(c), the arm's length range for the controlled transaction may be established only pursuant to paragraph (e)(2)(iii)(B) of this section.

(f) *Scope of review*—(1) *In general.* The authority to determine true taxable income extends to any case in which either by inadvertence or design the taxable income, in whole or in part, of a controlled taxpayer is other than it would have been had the taxpayer, in the conduct of its affairs, been dealing at arm's length with an uncontrolled taxpayer.

(i) *Intent to evade or avoid tax not a prerequisite.* In making allocations under section 482, the district director is not restricted to the case of improper accounting, to the case of a fraudulent, colorable, or sham transaction, or to the case of a device designed to reduce or avoid tax by shifting or distorting income, deductions, credits, or allowances.

(ii) *Realization of income not a prerequisite*—(A) *In general.* The district director may make an allocation under section 482 even if the income ultimately anticipated from a series of transactions has not been or is never realized. For example, if a controlled taxpayer sells a product at less than an arm's length price to a related taxpayer in one taxable year and the second controlled taxpayer resells the product to an unrelated party in the next taxable year, the district director may make an appropriate allocation to reflect an arm's length price for the sale of the product in the first taxable year, even though the second controlled taxpayer had not realized any gross income from the resale of the product in the first year. Similarly, if a controlled taxpayer lends money to a related taxpayer in a taxable year, the district director may make an appropriate allocation to reflect an arm's length charge for interest during such taxable year even if the second controlled taxpayer does not realize income during such year. Finally, even if two controlled taxpayers realize an overall loss that is attributable to a particular controlled transaction, an allocation under section 482 is not precluded.

(B) *Example.* The following example illustrates this paragraph (f)(1)(ii).

Example. USSub is a U.S. subsidiary of FP, a foreign corporation. Parent manufactures product X and sells it to USSub. USSub functions as a distributor of product X to unrelated customers in the United States. The fact that FP may incur a loss on the manufacture and sale of prod-

Reg. § 1.482-1(f)(1)

uct X does not by itself establish that USSub, dealing with FP at arm's length, also would incur a loss. An independent distributor acting at arm's length with its supplier would in many circumstances be expected to earn a profit without regard to the level of profit earned by the supplier.

(iii) *Nonrecognition provisions may not bar allocation*—(A) *In general.* If necessary to prevent the avoidance of taxes or to clearly reflect income, the district director may make an allocation under section 482 with respect to transactions that otherwise qualify for nonrecognition of gain or loss under applicable provisions of the Internal Revenue Code (such as section 351 or 1031).

(B) *Example.* The following example illustrates this paragraph (f)(1)(iii).

Example. (i) In Year 1 USP, a United States corporation, bought 100 shares of UR, an unrelated corporation, for $100,000. In Year 2, when the value of the UR stock had decreased to $40,000, USP contributed all 100 shares of UR stock to its wholly-owned subsidiary in exchange for subsidiary's capital stock. In Year 3, the subsidiary sold all of the UR stock for $40,000 to an unrelated buyer, and on its U.S. income tax return, claimed a loss of $60,000 attributable to the sale of the UR stock. USP and its subsidiary do not file a consolidated return.

(ii) In determining the true taxable income of the subsidiary, the district director may disallow the loss of $60,000 on the ground that the loss was incurred by USP. *National Securities Corp. v. Commissioner,* 137 F.2d 600 (3rd Cir. 1943), cert. denied, 320 U.S. 794 (1943).

(iv) *Consolidated returns.* Section 482 and the regulations thereunder apply to all controlled taxpayers, whether the controlled taxpayer files a separate or consolidated U.S. income tax return. If a controlled taxpayer files a separate return, its true separate taxable income will be determined. If a controlled taxpayer is a party to a consolidated return, the true consolidated taxable income of the affiliated group and the true separate taxable income of the controlled taxpayer must be determined consistently with the principles of a consolidated return.

(2) *Rules relating to determination of true taxable income.* The following rules must be taken into account in determining the true taxable income of a controlled taxpayer.

(i) *Aggregation of transactions*—(A) *In general.* The combined effect of two or more separate transactions (whether before, during, or after the taxable year under review) may be considered, if such transactions, taken as a whole, are so interrelated that consideration of multiple transactions is the most reliable means of determining the arm's length consideration for the controlled transactions. Generally, transactions will be aggregated only when they involve related products or services, as defined in § 1.6038A-3(c)(7)(vii).

(B) *Examples.* The following examples illustrate this paragraph (f)(2)(i).

Example 1. P enters into a license agreement with S1, its subsidiary, that permits S1 to use a proprietary manufacturing process and to sell the output from this process throughout a specified region. S1 uses the manufacturing process and sells its output to S2, another subsidiary of P, which in turn resells the output to uncontrolled parties in the specified region. In evaluating the arm's length character of the royalty paid by S1 to P, it may be appropriate to consider the arm's length character of the transfer prices charged by S1 to S2 and the aggregate profits earned by S1 and S2 from the use of the manufacturing process and the sale to uncontrolled parties of the products produced by S1.

Example 2. S1, S2, and S3 are Country Z subsidiaries of U.S. manufacturer P. S1 is the exclusive Country Z distributor of computers manufactured by P. S2 provides marketing services in connection with sales of P computers in Country Z, and in this regard uses significant marketing intangibles provided by P. S3 administers the warranty program with respect to P computers in Country Z, including maintenance and repair services. In evaluating the arm's length character of the transfer price paid by S1 to P, of the fees paid by S2 to P for the use of P marketing intangibles, and of the service fees earned by S2 and S3, it may be appropriate to consider the combined effects of these separate transactions because they are so interrelated that they are most reliably analyzed on an aggregated basis.

Example 3. The facts are the same as in *Example 2.* In addition, U1, U2, and U3 are uncontrolled taxpayers that carry out functions comparable to those of S1, S2, and S3, respectively, with respect to computers produced by unrelated manufacturers. R1, R2, and R3 are a controlled group of taxpayers (unrelated to the P controlled group) that also carry out functions comparable to those of S1, S2, and S3 with respect to computers produced by their common parent. Prices charged to uncontrolled customers of the R group differ from the prices charged to customers of U1, U2, and U3. In determining whether the transactions of U1, U2, and U3, or the transactions of R1, R2, and R3 would provide a more reliable measure of the arm's length result, it is determined that the interrelated R group transactions are more reliable than the wholly indepen-

Reg. § 1.482-1(f)(2)

dent transactions of U1, U2, and U3, given the interrelationship of the P group transactions.

Example 4. P enters into a license agreement with S1 that permits S1 to use a propriety process for manufacturing product X and to sell product X to uncontrolled parties throughout a specified region. P also sells to S1 product Y which is manufactured by P in the United States, and which is unrelated to product X. Product Y is resold by S1 to uncontrolled parties in the specified region. In evaluating the arm's length character of the royalty paid by S1 to P for the use of the manufacturing process for product X, and the transfer prices charged for unrelated product Y, it would not be appropriate to consider the combined effects of these separate and unrelated transactions.

(ii) *Allocation based on taxpayer's actual transactions*—(A) *In general.* The district director will evaluate the results of a transaction as actually structured by the taxpayer unless its structure lacks economic substance. However, the district director may consider the alternatives available to the taxpayer in determining whether the terms of the controlled transaction would be acceptable to an uncontrolled taxpayer faced with the same alternatives and operating under comparable circumstances. In such cases the district director may adjust the consideration charged in the controlled transaction based on the cost or profit of an alternative as adjusted to account for material differences between the alternative and the controlled transaction, but will not restructure the transaction as if the alternative had been adopted by the taxpayer. See § 1.482-1(d)(3) (Factors for determining comparability, Contractual terms and Risk); §§ 1.482-3(e) and 1.482-4(d) (Unspecified methods).

(B) *Example.* The following example illustrates this paragraph (f)(2)(ii).

Example. P and S are controlled taxpayers. P enters into a license agreement with S that permits S to use a proprietary process for manufacturing product X. Using its sales and marketing employees, S sells product X to related and unrelated customers outside the United States. If the license agreement between P and S has economic substance, the district director ordinarily will not restructure the taxpayer's transaction to treat P as if it had elected to exploit directly the manufacturing process. However, the fact that P could have manufactured product X may be taken into account under § 1.482-4(d) in determining the arm's length consideration for the controlled transaction. For an example of such an analysis, see *Example* in § 1.482-4(d)(2).

(iii) *Multiple year data*—(A) *In general.* The results of a controlled transaction ordinarily will be compared with the results of uncontrolled comparables occurring in the taxable year under review. It may be appropriate, however, to consider data relating to the uncontrolled comparables or the controlled taxpayer for one or more years before or after the year under review. If data relating to uncontrolled comparables from multiple years is used, data relating to the controlled taxpayer for the same years ordinarily must be considered. However, if such data is not available, reliable data from other years, as adjusted under paragraph (d)(2) (Standard of comparability) of this section may be used.

(B) *Circumstances warranting consideration of multiple year data.* The extent to which it is appropriate to consider multiple-year data depends on the method being applied and the issue being addressed. Circumstances that may warrant consideration of data from multiple years include the extent to which complete and accurate data is available for the taxable year under review, the effect of business cycles in the controlled taxpayer's industry, or the effects of life cycles of the product or intangible being examined. Data from one or more years before or after the taxable year under review must ordinarily be considered for purposes of applying the provisions of § 1.482-1(d)(3)(iii) (Risk), § 1.482-1(d)(4)(i) (Market share strategy), § 1.482-4(f)(2) (Periodic adjustments), and § 1.482-5 (Comparable profits method). On the other hand, multiple-year data ordinarily will not be considered for purposes of applying the comparable uncontrolled price method (except to the extent that risk or market share strategy issues are present).

(C) *Comparable effect over comparable period.* Data from multiple years may be considered to determine whether the same economic conditions that caused the controlled taxpayer's results had a comparable effect over a comparable period of time on the uncontrolled comparables that establish the arm's length range. For example, given that uncontrolled taxpayers enter into transactions with the ultimate expectation of earning a profit, persistent losses among controlled taxpayers may be an indication of non-arm's length dealings. Thus, if a controlled taxpayer that realizes a loss with respect to a controlled transaction seeks to demonstrate that the loss is within the arm's length range, the district director may take into account data from taxable years other than the taxable year of the transaction to determine whether the loss was attributable to arm's length dealings. The rule of this paragraph (f)(2)(iii)(C) is illustrated by *Example 3* of paragraph (f)(2)(iii)(E) of this section.

Reg. § 1.482-1(f)(2)

(D) *Applications of methods using multiple year averages.* If a comparison of a controlled taxpayer's average result over a multiple year period with the average results of uncontrolled comparables over the same period would reduce the effect of short-term variations that may be unrelated to transfer pricing, it may be appropriate to establish a range derived from the average results of uncontrolled comparables over a multiple year period to determine if an adjustment should be made. In such a case the district director may make an adjustment if the controlled taxpayer's average result for the multiple year period is not within such range. Such a range must be determined in accordance with § 1.482-1(e) (Arm's length range). An adjustment in such a case ordinarily will be equal to the difference, if any, between the controlled taxpayer's result for the taxable year and the midpoint of the uncontrolled comparables' results for that year. If the interquartile range is used to determine the range of average results for the multiple year period, such adjustment will ordinarily be made to the median of all the results of the uncontrolled comparables for the taxable year. See *Example 2* of § 1.482-5(e). In other cases, the adjustment normally will be made to the arithmetic mean of all the results of the uncontrolled comparables for the taxable year. However, an adjustment will be made only to the extent that it would move the controlled taxpayer's multiple year average closer to the arm's length range for the multiple year period or to any point within such range. In determining a controlled taxpayer's average result for a multiple year period, adjustments made under this section for prior years will be taken into account only if such adjustments have been finally determined, as described in § 1.482-1(g)(2)(iii). See *Example 3* of § 1.482-5(e).

(E) *Examples.* The following examples, in which S and P are controlled taxpayers, illustrate this paragraph (f)(2)(iii). *Examples 1* and *4* also illustrate the principle of the arm's length range of paragraph (e) of this section.

Example 1. P sold product Z to S for $60 per unit in 1995. Applying the resale price method to data from uncontrolled comparables for the same year establishes an arm's length range of prices for the controlled transaction from $52 to $59 per unit. Since the price charged in the controlled transaction falls outside the range, the district director would ordinarily make an allocation under section 482. However, in this case there are cyclical factors that affect the results of the uncontrolled comparables (and that of the controlled transaction) that cannot be adequately accounted for by specific adjustments to the data for 1995. Therefore, the district director considers results over multiple years to account for these factors. Under these circumstances, it is appropriate to average the results of the uncontrolled comparables over the years 1993, 1994, and 1995 to determine an arm's length range. The averaged results establish an arm's length range of $56 to $58 per unit. For consistency, the results of the controlled taxpayers must also be averaged over the same years. The average price in the controlled transaction over the three years is $57. Because the controlled transfer price of product Z falls within the arm's length range, the district director makes no allocation.

Example 2. (i) FP, a Country X corporation, designs and manufactures machinery in Country X. FP's costs are incurred in Country X currency. USSub is the exclusive distributor of FP's machinery in the United States. The price of the machinery sold by FP to USSub is expressed in Country X currency. Thus, USSub bears all of the currency risk associated with fluctuations in the exchange rate between the time the contract is signed and the payment is made. The prices charged by FP to USSub for 1995 are under examination. In that year, the value of the dollar depreciated against the currency of Country X, and as a result, USSub's gross margin was only 8%.

(ii) UD is an uncontrolled distributor of similar machinery that performs distribution functions substantially the same as those performed by USSub, except that UD purchases and resells machinery in transactions where both the purchase and resale prices are denominated in U.S. dollars. Thus, UD had no currency exchange risk. UD's gross margin in 1995 was 10%. UD's average gross margin for the period 1990 to 1998 has been 12%.

(iii) In determining whether the price charged by FP to USSub in 1995 was arm's length, the district director may consider USSub's average gross margin for an appropriate period before and after 1995 to determine whether USSub's average gross margin during the period was sufficiently greater than UD's average gross margin during the same period such that USSub was sufficiently compensated for the currency risk it bore throughout the period. See § 1.482-1(d)(3)(iii) (Risk).

Example 3. FP manufactures product X in Country M and sells it to USSub, which distributes X in the United States. USSub realizes losses with respect to the controlled transactions in each of five consecutive taxable years. In each of the five consecutive years a different uncontrolled comparable realized a loss with respect to comparable transactions equal to or greater than US-Sub's loss. Pursuant to paragraph (f)(3)(iii)(C) of this section, the district director examines whether the uncontrolled comparables realized similar losses over a comparable period of time, and finds that each of the five comparables realized losses in only one of the five years, and their average result over the five-year period was a profit. Based on this data, the district director may conclude that the controlled taxpayer's results are not within the arm's length range over the five year period, since the economic conditions that resulted in the controlled taxpayer's loss did not have a comparable effect over a comparable period of time on the uncontrolled comparables.

Example 4. (i) USP, a U.S. corporation, manufactures product Y in the United States and sells it to FSub, which acts as USP's exclusive distributor of product Y in Country N. The resale price method described in § 1.482-3(c) is used to evaluate whether the transfer price charged by USP to FSub for the 1994 taxable year for product Y was arm's length. For the period 1992 through 1994, FSub had a gross profit margin for each year of 13%. A, B, C and D are uncontrolled distributors of products that compete directly with product Y in country N. After making appropriate adjustments in accordance with §§ 1.482-1(d)(2) and 1.482-3(c), the gross profit margins for A, B, C, and D are as follows:

	1992	1993	1994	Average
A	13	3	8	8.00
B	11	13	2	8.67
C	4	7	13	8.00
D	7	9	6	7.33

(ii) Applying the provisions of § 1.482-1(e), the district director determines that the arm's length range of the average gross profit margins is between 7.33 and 8.67. The district director concludes that FSub's average gross margin of 13% is not within the arm's length range, despite the fact that C's gross profit margin for 1994 was also 13%, since the economic conditions that caused S's result did not have a comparable effect over a comparable period of time on the results of C or the other uncontrolled comparables. In this case, the district director makes an allocation equivalent to adjusting FSub's gross profit margin for 1994 from 13% to the mean of the uncontrolled comparables' results for 1994 (7.25%).

(iv) *Product lines and statistical techniques.* The methods described in §§ 1.482-2 through 1.482-6 are generally stated in terms of individual transactions. However, because a taxpayer may have controlled transactions involving many different products, or many separate transactions involving the same product, it may be impractical to analyze every individual transaction to determine its arm's length price. In such cases, it is permissible to evaluate the arm's length results by applying the appropriate methods to the overall results for product lines or other groupings. In addition, the arm's length results of all related party transactions entered into by a controlled taxpayer may be evaluated by employing sampling and other valid statistical techniques.

(v) *Allocations apply to results, not methods*—(A) *In general.* In evaluating whether the result of a controlled transaction is arm's length, it is not necessary for the district director to determine whether the method or procedure that a controlled taxpayer employs to set the terms for its controlled transactions corresponds to the method or procedure that might have been used by a taxpayer dealing at arm's length with an uncontrolled taxpayer. Rather, the district director will evaluate the result achieved rather than the method the taxpayer used to determine its prices.

(B) *Example.* The following example illustrates this paragraph (f)(2)(v).

Example. (i) FS is a foreign subsidiary of P, a U.S. corporation. P manufactures and sells household appliances. FS operates as P's exclusive distributor in Europe. P annually establishes the price for each of its appliances sold to FS as part of its annual budgeting, production allocation and scheduling, and performance evaluation processes. FS's aggregate gross margin earned in its distribution business is 18%.

(ii) ED is an uncontrolled European distributor of competing household appliances. After adjusting for minor differences in the level of inventory, volume of sales, and warranty programs conducted by FS and ED, ED's aggregate gross margin is also 18%. Thus, the district director may conclude that the aggregate prices charged by P for its appliances sold to FS are arm's length, without determining whether the budgeting, production, and performance evaluation processes of P are similar to such processes used by ED.

(g) *Collateral adjustments with respect to allocations under section 482*—(1) *In general.* The district director will take into account appropriate collateral adjustments with respect to allocations under section 482. Appropriate collateral adjustments may include correlative allocations, conforming adjustments, and setoffs, as described in this paragraph (g).

(2) *Correlative allocations*—(i) *In general.* When the district director makes an allocation under section 482 (referred to in this paragraph

Reg. § 1.482-1(g)(2)

(g)(2) as the primary allocation), appropriate correlative allocations will also be made with respect to any other member of the group affected by the allocation. Thus, if the district director makes an allocation of income, the district director will not only increase the income of one member of the group, but correspondingly decrease the income of the other member. In addition, where appropriate, the district director may make such further correlative allocations as may be required by the initial correlative allocation.

(ii) *Manner of carrying out correlative allocation.* The district director will furnish to the taxpayer with respect to which the primary allocation is made a written statement of the amount and nature of the correlative allocation. The correlative allocation must be reflected in the documentation of the other member of the group that is maintained for U.S. tax purposes, without regard to whether it affects the U.S. income tax liability of the other member for any open year. In some circumstances the allocation will have an immediate U.S. tax effect, by changing the taxable income computation of the other member (or the taxable income computation of a shareholder of the other member, for example, under the provisions of subpart F of the Internal Revenue Code). Alternatively, the correlative allocation may not be reflected on any U.S. tax return until a later year, for example when a dividend is paid.

(iii) *Events triggering correlative allocation.* For purposes of this paragraph (g)(2), a primary allocation will not be considered to have been made (and therefore, correlative allocations are not required to be made) until the date of a final determination with respect to the allocation under section 482. For this purpose, a final determination includes—

(A) Assessment of tax following execution by the taxpayer of a Form 870 (Waiver of Restrictions on Assessment and Collection of Deficiency in Tax and Acceptance of Overassessment) with respect to such allocation;

(B) Acceptance of a Form 870-AD (Offer of Waiver of Restriction on Assessment and Collection of Deficiency in Tax and Acceptance of Overassessment);

(C) Payment of the deficiency;

(D) Stipulation in the Tax Court of the United States; or

(E) Final determination of tax liability by offer-in-compromise, closing agreement, or final resolution (determined under the principles of section 7481) of a judicial proceeding.

(iv) *Examples.* The following examples illustrate this paragraph (g)(2). In each example, X and Y are members of the same group of controlled taxpayers and each regularly computes its income on a calendar year basis.

Example 1. (i) In 1996, Y, a U.S. corporation, rents a building owned by X, also a U.S. corporation. In 1998 the district director determines that Y did not pay an arm's length rental charge. The district director proposes to increase X's income to reflect an arm's length rental charge. X consents to the assessment reflecting such adjustment by executing Form 870, a Waiver of Restrictions on Assessment and Collection of Deficiency in Tax and Acceptance of Overassessment. The assessment of the tax with respect to the adjustment is made in 1998. Thus, the primary allocation, as defined in paragraph (g)(2)(i) of this section, is considered to have been made in 1998.

(ii) The adjustment made to X's income under section 482 requires a correlative allocation with respect to Y's income. The district director notifies X in writing of the amount and nature of the adjustment made with respect to Y. Y had net operating losses in 1993, 1994, 1995, 1996, and 1997. Although a correlative adjustment will not have an effect on Y's U.S. income tax liability for 1996, an adjustment increasing Y's net operating loss for 1996 will be made for purposes of determining Y's U.S. income tax liability for 1998 or a later taxable year to which the increased net operating loss may be carried.

Example 2. (i) In 1995, X, a U.S. construction company, provided engineering services to Y, a U.S. corporation, in the construction of Y's factory. In 1997, the district director determines that the fees paid by Y to X for its services were not arm's length and proposes to make an adjustment to the income of X. X consents to an assessment reflecting such adjustment by executing Form 870. An assessment of the tax with respect to such adjustment is made in 1997. The district director notifies X in writing of the amount and nature of the adjustment to be made with respect to Y.

(ii) The fees paid by Y for X's engineering services properly constitute a capital expenditure. Y does not place the factory into service until 1998. Therefore, a correlative adjustment increasing Y's basis in the factory does not affect Y's U.S. income tax liability for 1997. However, the correlative adjustment must be made in the books and records maintained by Y for its U.S. income tax purposes and such adjustment will be taken into account in computing Y's allowable depreciation or gain or loss on a subsequent disposition of the factory.

Reg. § 1.482-1(g)(2)

Example 3. In 1995, X, a U.S. corporation, makes a loan to Y, its foreign subsidiary not engaged in a U.S. trade or business. In 1997, the district director, upon determining that the interest charged on the loan was not arm's length, proposes to adjust X's income to reflect an arm's length interest rate. X consents to an assessment reflecting such allocation by executing Form 870, and an assessment of the tax with respect to the section 482 allocation is made in 1997. The district director notifies X in writing of the amount and nature of the correlative allocation to be made with respect to Y. Although the correlative adjustment does not have an effect on Y's U.S. income tax liability, the adjustment must be reflected in the documentation of Y that is maintained for U.S. tax purposes. Thus, the adjustment must be reflected in the determination of the amount of Y's earnings and profits for 1995 and subsequent years, and the adjustment must be made to the extent it has an effect on any person's U.S. income tax liability for any taxable year.

(3) *Adjustments to conform accounts to reflect section 482 allocations*—(i) *In general.* Appropriate adjustments must be made to conform a taxpayer's accounts to reflect allocations made under section 482. Such adjustments may include the treatment of an allocated amount as a dividend or a capital contribution (as appropriate), or, in appropriate cases, pursuant to such applicable revenue procedures as may be provided by the Commissioner (see § 601.601(d)(2) of this chapter), repayment of the allocated amount without further income tax consequences.

(ii) *Example.* The following example illustrates the principles of this paragraph (g)(3).

Example—Conforming cash accounts. (i) USD, a United States corporation, buys Product from its foreign parent, FP. In reviewing USD's income tax return, the district director determines that the arm's length price would have increased USD's taxable income by $5 million. The district director accordingly adjusts USD's income to reflect its true taxable income.

(ii) To conform its cash accounts to reflect the section 482 allocation made by the district director, USD applies for relief under Rev. Proc. 65-17, 1965-1 C.B. 833 (see § 601.601(d)(2)(ii)(*b*) of this chapter), to treat the $5 million adjustment as an account receivable from FP, due as of the last day of the year of the transaction, with interest accruing therefrom.

(4) *Setoffs*—(i) *In general.* If an allocation is made under section 482 with respect to a transaction between controlled taxpayers, the district director will also take into account the effect of any other non-arm's length transaction between the same controlled taxpayers in the same taxable year which will result in a setoff against the original section 482 allocation. Such setoff, however, will be taken into account only if the requirements of § 1.482-1(g)(4)(ii) are satisfied. If the effect of the setoff is to change the characterization or source of the income or deductions, or otherwise distort taxable income, in such a manner as to affect the U.S. tax liability of any member, adjustments will be made to reflect the correct amount of each category of income or deductions. For purposes of this setoff provision, the term arm's length refers to the amount defined in paragraph (b) (Arm's length standard) of this section, without regard to the rules in § 1.482-2 under which certain charges are deemed to be equal to arm's length.

(ii) *Requirements.* The district director will take a setoff into account only if the taxpayer—

(A) Establishes that the transaction that is the basis of the setoff was not at arm's length and the amount of the appropriate arm's length charge;

(B) Documents, pursuant to paragraph (g)(2) of this section, all correlative adjustments resulting from the proposed setoff; and

(C) Notifies the district director of the basis of any claimed setoff within 30 days after the earlier of the date of a letter by which the district director transmits an examination report notifying the taxpayer of proposed adjustments or the date of the issuance of the notice of deficiency.

(iii) *Examples.* The following examples illustrate this paragraph (g)(4).

Example 1. P, a U.S. corporation, renders services to S, its foreign subsidiary in Country Y, in connection with the construction of S's factory. An arm's length charge for such services determined under § 1.482-2(b) would be $100,000. During the same taxable year P makes available to S the use of a machine to be used in the construction of the factory, and the arm's length rental value of the machine is $25,000. P bills S $125,000 for the services, but does not charge S for the use of the machine. No allocation will be made with respect to the undercharge for the machine if P notifies the district director of the basis of the claimed setoff within 30 days after the date of the letter from the district director transmitting the examination report notifying P of the proposed adjustment, establishes that the excess amount charged for services was equal to an arm's length charge for the use of the machine and that the taxable income and income tax liabilities of P are not distorted, and documents the

Reg. § 1.482-1(g)(4)

correlative allocations resulting from the proposed setoff.

Example 2. The facts are the same as in Example 1, except that, if P had reported $25,000 as rental income and $25,000 less as service income, it would have been subject to the tax on personal holding companies. Allocations will be made to reflect the correct amounts of rental income and service income.

(h) *Special rules*—(1) *Small taxpayer safe harbor.* [Reserved]

(2) *Effect of foreign legal restrictions*—(i) *In general.* The district director will take into account the effect of a foreign legal restriction to the extent that such restriction affects the results of transactions at arm's length. Thus, a foreign legal restriction will be taken into account only to the extent that it is shown that the restriction affected an uncontrolled taxpayer under comparable circumstances for a comparable period of time. In the absence of evidence indicating the effect of the foreign legal restriction on uncontrolled taxpayers, the restriction will be taken into account only to the extent provided in paragraphs (h)(2)(iii) and (iv) of this section (Deferred income method of accounting).

(ii) *Applicable legal restrictions.* Foreign legal restrictions (whether temporary or permanent) will be taken into account for purposes of this paragraph (h)(2) only if, and so long as, the conditions set forth in paragraphs (h)(2)(ii)(A) through (D) of this section are met.

(A) The restrictions are publicly promulgated, generally applicable to all similarly situated persons (both controlled and uncontrolled), and not imposed as part of a commercial transaction between the taxpayer and the foreign sovereign;

(B) The taxpayer (or other member of the controlled group with respect to which the restrictions apply) has exhausted all remedies prescribed by foreign law or practice for obtaining a waiver of such restrictions (other than remedies that would have a negligible prospect of success if pursued);

(C) The restrictions expressly prevented the payment or receipt, in any form, of part or all of the arm's length amount that would otherwise be required under section 482 (for example, a restriction that applies only to the deductibility of an expense for tax purposes is not a restriction on payment or receipt for this purpose); and

(D) The related parties subject to the restriction did not engage in any arrangement with controlled or uncontrolled parties that had the effect of circumventing the restriction, and have not otherwise violated the restriction in any material respect.

(iii) *Requirement for electing the deferred income method of accounting.* If a foreign legal restriction prevents the payment or receipt of part or all of the arm's length amount that is due with respect to a controlled transaction, the restricted amount may be treated as deferrable if the following requirements are met—

(A) The controlled taxpayer establishes to the satisfaction of the district director that the payment or receipt of the arm's length amount was prevented because of a foreign legal restriction and circumstances described in paragraph (h)(2)(ii) of this section; and

(B) The controlled taxpayer whose U.S. tax liability may be affected by the foreign legal restriction elects the deferred income method of accounting, as described in paragraph (h)(2)(iv) of this section, on a written statement attached to a timely U.S. income tax return (or an amended return) filed before the IRS first contacts any member of the controlled group concerning an examination of the return for the taxable year to which the foreign legal restriction applies. A written statement furnished by a taxpayer subject to the Coordinated Examination Program will be considered an amended return for purposes of this paragraph (h)(2)(iii)(B) if it satisfies the requirements of a qualified amended return for purposes of § 1.6664-2(c)(3) as set forth in those regulations or as the Commissioner may prescribe by applicable revenue procedures. The election statement must identify the affected transactions, the parties to the transactions, and the applicable foreign legal restrictions.

(iv) *Deferred income method of accounting.* If the requirements of paragraph (h)(2)(ii) of this section are satisfied, any portion of the arm's length amount, the payment or receipt of which is prevented because of applicable foreign legal restrictions, will be treated as deferrable until payment or receipt of the relevant item ceases to be prevented by the foreign legal restriction. For purposes of the deferred income method of accounting under this paragraph (h)(2)(iv), deductions (including the cost or other basis of inventory and other assets sold or exchanged) and credits properly chargeable against any amount so deferred, are subject to deferral under the provisions of § 1.461-1(a)(4). In addition, income is deferrable under this deferred income method of accounting only to the extent that it exceeds the related deductions already claimed in open taxable years to which the foreign legal restriction applied.

Reg. § 1.482-1(h)(1)

(v) *Examples.* The following examples, in which Sub is a Country FC subsidiary of U.S. corporation, Parent, illustrate this paragraph (h)(2).

Example 1. Parent licenses an intangible to Sub. FC law generally prohibits payments by any person within FC to recipients outside the country. The FC law meets the requirements of paragraph (h)(2)(ii) of this section. There is no evidence of unrelated parties entering into transactions under comparable circumstances for a comparable period of time, and the foreign legal restrictions will not be taken into account in determining the arm's length amount. The arm's length royalty rate for the use of the intangible property in the absence of the foreign restriction is 10% of Sub's sales in country FC. However, because the requirements of paragraph (h)(2)(ii) of this section are satisfied, Parent can elect the deferred income method of accounting by attaching to its timely filed U.S. income tax return a written statement that satisfies the requirements of paragraph (h)(2)(iii)(B) of this section.

Example 2. (i) The facts are the same as in *Example 1,* except that Sub, although it makes no royalty payment to Parent, arranges with an unrelated intermediary to make payments equal to an arm's length amount on its behalf to Parent.

(ii) The district director makes an allocation of royalty income to Parent, based on the arm's length royalty rate of 10%. Further, the district director determines that because the arrangement with the third party had the effect of circumventing the FC law, the requirements of paragraph (h)(2)(ii)(D) of this section are not satisfied. Thus, Parent could not validly elect the deferred income method of accounting, and the allocation of royalty income cannot be treated as deferrable. In appropriate circumstances, the district director may permit the amount of the distribution to be treated as payment by Sub of the royalty allocated to Parent, under the provisions of § 1.482-1(g) (Collateral adjustments).

Example 3. The facts are the same as in *Example 1,* except that the laws of FC do not prevent distributions from corporations to their shareholders. Sub distributes an amount equal to 8% of its sales in country FC. Because the laws of FC did not expressly prevent all forms of payment from Sub to Parent, Parent cannot validly elect the deferred income method of accounting with respect to any of the arm's length royalty amount. In appropriate circumstances, the district director may permit the 8% that was distributed to be treated as payment by Sub of the royalty allocated to Parent, under the provisions of § 1.482-1(g) (Collateral adjustments).

Example 4. The facts are the same as in *Example 1,* except that Country FC law permits the payment of a royalty, but limits the amount to 5% of sales, and Sub pays the 5% royalty to Parent. Parent demonstrates the existence of a comparable uncontrolled transaction for purposes of the comparable uncontrolled transaction method in which an uncontrolled party accepted a royalty rate of 5%. Given the evidence of the comparable uncontrolled transaction, the 5% royalty rate is determined to be the arm's length royalty rate.

(3) *Coordination with section 936*—(i) *Cost sharing under section 936.* If a possessions corporation makes an election under section 936(h)(5)(C)(i)(I), the corporation must make a section 936 cost sharing payment that is at least equal to the payment that would be required under section 482 if the electing corporation were a foreign corporation. In determining the payment that would be required under section 482 for this purpose, the provisions of §§ 1.482-1 and 1.482-4 will be applied, and to the extent relevant to the valuation of intangibles, §§ 1.482-5 and 1.482-6 will be applied. The provisions of section 936(h)(5)(C)(i)(II) (Effect of Election—electing corporation treated as owner of intangible property) do not apply until the payment that would be required under section 482 has been determined.

(ii) *Use of terms.* A cost sharing payment, for the purposes of section 936(h)(5)(C)(i)(I), is calculated using the provisions of section 936 and the regulations thereunder and the provisions of this paragraph (h)(3). The provisions relating to cost sharing under section 482 do not apply to payments made pursuant to an election under section 936(h)(5)(C)(i)(I). Similarly, a profit split payment, for the purposes of section 936(h)(5)(C)(ii)(I), is calculated using the provisions of section 936 and the regulations thereunder, not section 482 and the regulations thereunder.

(i) *Definitions.* The definitions set forth in paragraphs (i)(1) through (10) of this section apply to §§ 1.482-1 through 1.482-8.

(1) *Organization* includes an organization of any kind, whether a sole proprietorship, a partnership, a trust, an estate, an association, or a corporation (as each is defined or understood in the Internal Revenue Code or the regulations thereunder), irrespective of the place of organization, operation, or conduct of the trade or business, and regardless of whether it is a domestic or foreign organization, whether it is an exempt organization, or whether it is a member of an affiliated group that files a consolidated U.S. income

Reg. § 1.482-1(i)(1)

tax return, or a member of an affiliated group that does not file a consolidated U.S. income tax return.

(2) *Trade or business* includes a trade or business activity of any kind, regardless of whether or where organized, whether owned individually or otherwise, and regardless of the place of operation. Employment for compensation will constitute a separate trade or business from the employing trade or business.

(3) *Taxpayer* means any person, organization, trade or business, whether or not subject to any internal revenue tax.

(4) *Controlled* includes any kind of control, direct or indirect, whether legally enforceable or not, and however exercisable or exercised, including control resulting from the actions of two or more taxpayers acting in concert or with a common goal or purpose. It is the reality of the control that is decisive, not its form or the mode of its exercise. A presumption of control arises if income or deductions have been arbitrarily shifted.

(5) *Controlled taxpayer* means any one of two or more taxpayers owned or controlled directly or indirectly by the same interests, and includes the taxpayer that owns or controls the other taxpayers. *Uncontrolled taxpayer* means any one of two or more taxpayers not owned or controlled directly or indirectly by the same interests.

(6) *Group, controlled group,* and *group of controlled taxpayers* mean the taxpayers owned or controlled directly or indirectly by the same interests.

(7) *Transaction* means any sale, assignment, lease, license, loan, advance, contribution, or any other transfer of any interest in or a right to use any property (whether tangible or intangible, real or personal) or money, however such transaction is effected, and whether or not the terms of such transaction are formally documented. A transaction also includes the performance of any services for the benefit of, or on behalf of, another taxpayer.

(8) *Controlled transaction* or *controlled transfer* means any transaction or transfer between two or more members of the same group of controlled taxpayers. The term *uncontrolled transaction* means any transaction between two or more taxpayers that are not members of the same group of controlled taxpayers.

(9) *True taxable income* means, in the case of a controlled taxpayer, the taxable income that would have resulted had it dealt with the other member or members of the group at arm's length. It does not mean the taxable income resulting to the controlled taxpayer by reason of the particular contract, transaction, or arrangement the controlled taxpayer chose to make (even though such contract, transaction, or arrangement is legally binding upon the parties thereto).

(10) *Uncontrolled comparable* means the uncontrolled transaction or uncontrolled taxpayer that is compared with a controlled transaction or taxpayer under any applicable pricing methodology. Thus, for example, under the comparable profits method, an uncontrolled comparable is any uncontrolled taxpayer from which data is used to establish a comparable operating profit.

(j) *Effective dates*—(1) These regulations are generally effective for taxable years beginning after October 6, 1994.

(2) Taxpayers may elect to apply retroactively all of the provisions of these regulations for any open taxable year. Such election will be effective for the year of the election and all subsequent taxable years.

(3) Although these regulations are generally effective for taxable years as stated, the final sentence of section 482 (requiring that the income with respect to transfers or licenses of intangible property be commensurate with the income attributable to the intangible) is generally effective for taxable years beginning after December 31, 1986. For the period prior to the effective date of these regulations, the final sentence of section 482 must be applied using any reasonable method not inconsistent with the statute. The IRS considers a method that applies these regulations or their general principles to be a reasonable method.

(4) These regulations will not apply with respect to transfers made or licenses granted to foreign persons before November 17, 1985, or before August 17, 1986, for transfers or licenses to others. Nevertheless, they will apply with respect to transfers or licenses before such dates if, with respect to property transferred pursuant to an earlier and continuing transfer agreement, such property was not in existence or owned by the taxpayer on such date. [Reg. § 1.482-1.]

☐ [*T.D.* 8552, 7-1-94.]

[Reg. § 1.482-2]

§ 1.482-2. Determination of taxable income in specific situations.—(a) *Loans or advances*— (1) *Interest on bona fide indebtedness*—(i) *In general.* Where one member of a group of controlled entities makes a loan or advance directly or indirectly to, or otherwise becomes a creditor of, another member of such group and either charges no interest, or charges interest at a rate which is not equal to an arm's length rate of interest (as defined in paragraph (a)(2) of this section) with respect to such loan or advance, the district director may make appropriate allocations to reflect an arm's length rate of interest for the use of such loan or advance.

(ii) *Application of paragraph (a) of this section*—(A) *Interest on bona fide indebtedness.* Paragraph (a) of this section applies only to determine the appropriateness of the rate of interest charged on the principal amount of a bona fide indebtedness between members of a group of controlled entities, including—

(*1*) Loans or advances of money or other consideration (whether or not evidenced by a written instrument); and

(*2*) Indebtedness arising in the ordinary course of business from sales, leases, or the rendition of services by or between members of the group, or any other similar extension of credit.

(B) *Alleged indebtedness.* This paragraph (a) does not apply to so much of an alleged indebtedness which is not in fact a bona fide indebtedness, even if the stated rate of interest thereon would be within the safe haven rates prescribed in paragraph (a)(2)(iii) of this section. For example, paragraph (a) of this section does not apply to payments with respect to all or a portion of such alleged indebtedness where in fact all or a portion of an alleged indebtedness is a contribution to the capital of a corporation or a distribution by a corporation with respect to its shares. Similarly, this paragraph (a) does not apply to payments with respect to an alleged purchase-money debt instrument given in consideration for an alleged sale of property between two controlled entities where in fact the transaction constitutes a lease of the property. Payments made with respect to alleged indebtedness (including alleged stated interest thereon) shall be treated according to their substance. See § 1.482-2(a)(3)(i).

(iii) *Period for which interest shall be charged*—(A) *General rule.* This paragraph (a)(1)(iii) is effective for indebtedness arising after June 30, 1988. See § 1.482-2(a)(3) (26 CFR Part 1 edition revised as of April 1, 1988) for indebtedness arising before July 1, 1988. Except as otherwise provided in paragraphs (a)(1)(iii)(B) through (E) of this section, the period for which interest shall be charged with respect to a bona fide indebtedness between controlled entities begins on the day after the day the indebtedness arises and ends on the day the indebtedness is satisfied (whether by payment, offset, cancellation, or otherwise). Paragraphs (a)(1)(iii)(B) through (E) of this section provide certain alternative periods during which interest is not required to be charged on certain indebtedness.

These exceptions apply only to indebtedness described in paragraph (a)(1)(ii)(A)(*2*) of this section (relating to indebtedness incurred in the ordinary course of business from sales, services, etc., between members of the group) and not evidenced by a written instrument requiring the payment of interest. Such amounts are hereinafter referred to as intercompany trade receivables. The period for which interest is not required to be charged on intercompany trade receivables under this paragraph (a)(1)(iii) is called the interest-free period. In general, an intercompany trade receivable arises at the time economic performance occurs (within the meaning of section 461(h) and the regulations thereunder) with respect to the underlying transaction between controlled entities. For purposes of this paragraph (a)(1)(iii), the term United States includes any possession of the United States, and the term foreign country excludes any possession of the United States.

(B) *Exception for certain intercompany transactions in the ordinary course of business.* Interest is not required to be charged on an intercompany trade receivable until the first day of the third calendar month following the month in which the intercompany trade receivable arises.

(C) *Exception for trade or business of debtor member located outside the United States.* In the case of an intercompany trade receivable arising from a transaction in the ordinary course of a trade or business which is actively conducted outside the United States by the debtor member, interest is not required to be charged until the first day of the fourth calendar month following the month in which such intercompany trade receivable arises.

(D) *Exception for regular trade practice of creditor member or others in creditor's industry.* If the creditor member or unrelated persons in the creditor member's industry, as a regular trade practice, allow unrelated parties a longer period without charging interest than that described in paragraph (a)(1)(iii)(B) or (C) of this section (whichever is applicable) with respect to transactions which are similar to transactions that give rise to intercompany trade receivables, such longer interest-free period shall be allowed with respect to a comparable amount of intercompany trade receivables.

(E) *Exception for property purchased for resale in a foreign country*—(*1*) *General rule.* If in the ordinary course of business one member of the group (related purchaser) purchases property from another member of the group (related seller) for resale to unrelated persons located in a particular foreign country, the related purchaser and the related seller may use as the interest-free

Reg. § 1.482-2(a)(1)

period for the intercompany trade receivables arising during the related seller's taxable year from the purchase of such property within the same product group an interest-free period equal the sum of—

(*i*) The number of days in the related purchaser's average collection period (as determined under paragraph (a)(1)(iii)(E)(*2*) of this section) for sales of property within the same product group sold in the ordinary course of business to unrelated persons located in the same foreign country; plus

(*ii*) Ten (10) calendar days.

(*2*) *Interest-free period.* The interest-free period under this paragraph (a)(1)(iii)(E), however, shall in no event exceed 183 days. The related purchaser does not have to conduct business outside the United States in order to be eligible to use the interest-free period of this paragraph (a)(1)(iii)(E). The interest-free period under this paragraph (a)(1)(iii)(E) shall not apply to intercompany trade receivables attributable to property which is manufactured, produced, or constructed (within the meaning of § 1.954-3(a)(4)) by the related purchaser. For purposes of this paragraph (a)(1)(iii)(E) a product group includes all products within the same three-digit Standard Industrial Classification (SIC) Code (as prepared by the Statistical Policy Division of the Office of Management and Budget, Executive Office of the President.)

(*3*) *Average collection period.* An average collection period for purposes of this paragraph (a)(1)(iii)(E) is determined as follows—

(*i*) *Step 1.* Determine total sales (less returns and allowances) by the related purchaser in the product group to unrelated persons located in the same foreign country during the related purchaser's last taxable year ending on or before the first day of the related seller's taxable year in which the intercompany trade receivable arises.

(*ii*) *Step 2.* Determine the related purchaser's average month-end accounts receivable balance with respect to sales described in paragraph (a)(1)(iii)(E)(*2*)(*i*) of this section for the related purchaser's last taxable year ending on or before the first day of the related seller's taxable year in which the intercompany trade receivable arises.

(*iii*) *Step 3.* Compute a receivables turnover rate by dividing the total sales amount described in paragraph (a)(1)(iii)(E)(*2*)(*i*) of this section by the average receivables balance described in paragraph (a)(1)(iii)(E)(*2*)(*ii*) of this section.

(*iv*) *Step 4.* Divide the receivables turnover rate determined under paragraph (a)(1)(iii)(E)(*2*)(*iii*) of this section into 365, and round the result to the nearest whole number to determine the number of days in the average collection period.

(*v*) *Other considerations.* If the related purchaser makes sales in more than one foreign country, or sells property in more than one product group in any foreign country, separate computations of an average collection period, by product group within each country, are required. If the related purchaser resells fungible property in more than one foreign country and the intercompany trade receivables arising from the related party purchase of such fungible property cannot reasonably be identified with resales in particular foreign countries, then solely for the purpose of assigning an interest-free period to such intercompany trade receivables under this paragraph (a)(1)(iii)(E), an amount of each such intercompany trade receivable shall be treated as allocable to a particular foreign country in the same proportion that the related purchaser's sales of such fungible property in such foreign country during the period described in paragraph (a)(1)(iii)(E)(*2*)(*i*) of this section bears to the related purchaser's sales of all such fungible property in all such foreign countries during such period. An interest-free period under this paragraph (a)(1)(iii)(E) shall not apply to any intercompany trade receivables arising in a taxable year of the related seller if the related purchaser made no sales described in paragraph (a)(1)(iii)(E)(*2*)(*i*) of this section from which the appropriate interest-free period may be determined.

(*4*) *Illustration.* The interest-free period provided under paragraph (a)(1)(iii)(E) of this section may be illustrated by the following example:

Example—(i) *Facts.* X and Y use the calendar year as the taxable year and are members of the same group of controlled entities within the meaning of section 482. For Y's 1988 calendar taxable year X and Y intend to use the interest-free period determined under this paragraph (a)(1)(iii)(E) for intercompany trade receivables attributable to X's purchases of certain products from Y for resale by X in the ordinary course of business to unrelated persons in country Z. For its 1987 calendar taxable year all of X's sales in country Z were of products within a single product group based upon a three-digit SIC code, were not manufactured, produced, or constructed (within the meaning of § 1.954-3(a)(4)) by X, and were sold in the ordinary course of X's trade or

Reg. § 1.482-2(a)(1)

Adjustments

See p. 20,601 for regulations not amended to reflect law changes

business to unrelated persons located only in country Z. These sales and the month-end accounts receivable balances (for such sales and for such sales uncollected from prior months) are as follows:

Month	Sales	Accounts Receivable
January 1987	$ 500,000	$ 2,835,850
February	600,000	2,840,300
March	450,000	2,850,670
April	550,000	2,825,700
May	650,000	2,809,360
June	525,000	2,803,200
July	400,000	2,825,850
August	425,000	2,796,240
September	475,000	2,839,390
October	525,000	2,650,550
November	450,000	2,775,450
December 1987	650,000	2,812,600
TOTALS	$6,200,000	$33,665,160

(ii) *Average collection period.* X's total sales within the same product group to unrelated persons within country Z for the period are $6,200,000. The average receivables balance for the period is $2,805,430 ($33,665,160/12). The average collection period in whole days is determined as follows:

$$\text{Receivables Turnover Rate} = \frac{\$6,200,000}{\$2,805,430} = 2.21$$

$$\text{Average Collection Period days} = \frac{365}{2.21} = 165.16 \text{ days, rounded to the nearest whole day} = 165$$

(iii) *Interest-free period.* Accordingly, for intercompany trade receivables incurred by X during Y's 1988 calendar taxable year attributable to the purchase of property from Y for resale to unrelated persons located in country Z and included in the product group, X may use an interest-free period of 175 days (165 days in the average collection period plus 10 days, but not in excess of a maximum of 183 days). All other intercompany trade receivables incurred by X are subject to the interest-free periods described in paragraphs (a)(1)(iii)(B), (C), or (D), whichever are applicable. If X makes sales in other foreign countries in addition to country Z or makes sales of property in more than one product group in any foreign country, separate computations of X's average collection period, by product group within each country, are required in order for X and Y to determine an interest-free period for such product groups in such foreign countries under this paragraph (a)(1)(iii)(E).

(iv) *Payment; book entries*—(A) Except as otherwise provided in this paragraph (a)(1)(iv), in determining the period of time for which an amount owed by one member of the group to another member is outstanding, payments or other credits to an account are considered to be applied against the earliest amount outstanding, that is, payments or credits are applied against amounts in a first-in, first-out (FIFO) order. Thus, tracing payments to individual intercompany trade receivables is generally not required in order to determine whether a particular intercompany trade receivable has been paid within the applicable interest-free period determined under paragraph (a)(1)(iii) of this section. The application of this paragraph (a)(1)(iv)(A) may be illustrated by the following example:

Example—(i) *Facts.* X and Y are members of a group of controlled entities within the meaning of section 482. Assume that the balance of intercompany trade receivables owed by X to Y on June 1 is $100, and that all of the $100 balance represents amounts incurred by X to Y during the month of May. During the month of June X incurs an additional $200 of intercompany trade receivables to Y. Assume that on July 15, $60 is properly credited against X's intercompany account to Y, and that $240 is properly credited against the intercompany account on August 31. Assume that under paragraph (a)(1)(iii)(B) of this section interest must be charged on X's intercompany trade receivables to Y beginning with the first day of the third calendar month following the month the intercompany trade receivables arise, and that no alternative interest-free period applies. Thus, the interest-free period for intercompany trade receivables incurred during the month of May ends on July 31, and the interest-free period for intercompany trade receivables incurred during the month of June ends on August 31.

Reg. § 1.482-2(a)(1)

(ii) *Application of payments.* Using a FIFO payment order, the aggregate payments of $300 are applied first to the opening June balance, and then to the additional amounts incurred during the month of June. With respect to X's June opening balance of $100, no interest is required to be accrued on $60 of such balance paid by X on July 15, because such portion was paid within its interest-free period. Interest for 31 days, from August 1 to August 31 inclusive, is required to be accrued on the $40 portion of the opening balance not paid until August 31. No interest is required to be accrued on the $200 of intercompany trade receivables X incurred to Y during June because the $240 credited on August 31, after eliminating the $40 of indebtedness remaining from periods before June, also eliminated the $200 incurred by X during June prior to the end of the interest-free period for that amount. The amount of interest incurred by X to Y on the $40 amount during August creates bona fide indebtedness between controlled entities and is subject to the provisions of paragraph (a)(1)(iii)(A) of this section without regard to any of the exceptions contained in paragraphs (a)(1)(iii)(B) through (E).

(B) Notwithstanding the first-in, first-out payment application rule described in paragraph (a)(1)(iv)(A) of this section, the taxpayer may apply payments or credits against amounts owed in some other order on its books in accordance with an agreement or understanding of the related parties if the taxpayer can demonstrate that either it or others in its industry, as a regular trade practice, enter into such agreements or understandings in the case of similar balances with unrelated parties.

(2) *Arm's length interest rate*—(i) *In general.* For purposes of section 482 and paragraph (a) of this section, an arm's length rate of interest shall be a rate of interest which was charged, or would have been charged, at the time the indebtedness arose, in independent transactions with or between unrelated parties under similar circumstances. All relevant factors shall be considered, including the principal amount and duration of the loan, the security involved, the credit standing of the borrower, and the interest rate prevailing at the situs of the lender or creditor for comparable loans between unrelated parties.

(ii) *Funds obtained at situs of borrower.* Notwithstanding the other provisions of paragraph (a)(2) of this section, if the loan or advance represents the proceeds of a loan obtained by the lender at the situs of the borrower, the arm's length rate for any taxable year shall be equal to the rate actually paid by the lender increased by an amount which reflects the costs or deductions incurred by the lender in borrowing such amounts and making such loans, unless the taxpayer establishes a more appropriate rate under the standards set forth in paragraph (a)(2)(i) of this section.

(iii) *Safe haven interest rates for certain loans and advances made after May 8, 1986*—(A) *Applicability*—(*1*) *General rule.* Except as otherwise provided in paragraph (a)(2) of this section, paragraph (a)(2)(iii)(B) applies with respect to the rate of interest charged and to the amount of interest paid or accrued in any taxable year—

(*i*) Under a term loan or advance between members of a group of controlled entities where (except as provided in paragraph (a)(2)(iii)(A)(*2*)(*ii*) of this section) the loan or advance is entered into after May 8, 1986; and

(*ii*) After May 8, 1986 under a demand loan or advance between such controlled entities.

(*2*) *Grandfather rule for existing loans.* The safe haven rates prescribed in paragraph (a)(2)(iii)(B) of this section shall not apply, and the safe haven rates prescribed in § 1.482-2(a)(2)(iii) (26 CFR part 1 edition revised as of April 1, 1985), shall apply to—

(*i*) Term loans or advances made before May 9, 1986; and

(*ii*) Term loans or advances made before August 7, 1986, pursuant to a binding written contract entered into before May 9, 1986.

(B) *Safe haven interest rate based on applicable Federal rate.* Except as otherwise provided in this paragraph (a)(2), in the case of a loan or advance between members of a group of controlled entities, an arm's length rate of interest referred to in paragraph (a)(2)(i) of this section shall be for purposes of chapter 1 of the Internal Revenue Code—

(*1*) The rate of interest actually charged if that rate is—

(*i*) Not less than 100 percent of the applicable Federal rate (lower limit); and

(*ii*) Not greater than 130 percent of the applicable Federal rate (upper limit); or

(*2*) If either no interest is charged or if the rate of interest charged is less than the lower limit, then an arm's length rate of interest shall be equal to the lower limit, compounded semiannually; or

(*3*) If the rate of interest charged is greater than the upper limit, then an arm's length rate of interest shall be equal to the upper limit, compounded semiannually, unless the taxpayer establishes a more appropriate compound rate of

Reg. § 1.482-2(a)(2)

interest under paragraph (a)(2)(i) of this section. However, if the compound rate of interest actually charged is greater than the upper limit and less than the rate determined under paragraph (a)(2)(i) of this section, or if the compound rate actually charged is less than the lower limit and greater than the rate determined under paragraph (a)(2)(i) of this section, then the compound rate actually charged shall be deemed to be an arm's length rate under paragraph (a)(2)(i). In the case of any sale-leaseback described in section 1274(e), the lower limit shall be 110 percent of the applicable Federal rate, compounded semiannually.

(C) *Applicable Federal rate.* For purposes of paragraph (a)(2)(iii)(B) of this section, the term applicable Federal rate means, in the case of a loan or advance to which this section applies and having a term of—

(*1*) Not over 3 years, the Federal short-term rate;

(*2*) Over 3 years but not over 9 years, the Federal mid-term rate; or

(*3*) Over 9 years, the Federal long-term rate,

as determined under section 1274(d) in effect on the date such loan or advance is made. In the case of any sale or exchange between controlled entities, the lower limit shall be the lowest of the applicable Federal rates in effect for any month in the 3-calendar-month period ending with the first calendar month in which there is a binding written contract in effect for such sale or exchange (lowest 3-month rate, as defined in section 1274(d)(2)). In the case of a demand loan or advance to which this section applies, the applicable Federal rate means the Federal short-term rate determined under section 1274(d) (determined without regard to the lowest 3-month short term rate determined under section 1274(d)(2)) in effect for each day on which any amount of such loan or advance (including unpaid accrued interest determined under paragraph (a)(2) of this section) is outstanding.

(D) *Lender in business of making loans.* If the lender in a loan or advance transaction to which paragraph (a)(2) of this section applies is regularly engaged in the trade or business of making loans or advances to unrelated parties, the safe haven rates prescribed in paragraph (a)(2)(iii)(B) of this section shall not apply, and the arm's length interest rate to be used shall be determined under the standards described in paragraph (a)(2)(i) of this section, including reference to the interest rates charged in such trade or business by the lender on loans or advances of a similar type made to unrelated parties at and about the time the loan or advance to which paragraph (a)(2) of this section applies was made.

(E) *Foreign currency loans.* The safe haven interest rates prescribed in paragraph (a)(2)(iii)(B) of this section do not apply to any loan or advance the principal or interest of which is expressed in a currency other than U.S. dollars.

(3) *Coordination with interest adjustments required under certain other Code sections.* If the stated rate of interest on the stated principal amount of a loan or advance between controlled entities is subject to adjustment under section 482 and is also subject to adjustment under any other section of the Internal Revenue Code (for example, section 467, 483, 1274 or 7872), section 482 and paragraph (a) of this section may be applied to such loan or advance in addition to such other Internal Revenue Code section. After the enactment of the Tax Reform Act of 1964, Pub. L. 98-369, and the enactment of Pub. L. 99-121, such other Internal Revenue Code sections include sections 467, 483, 1274 and 7872. The order in which the different provisions shall be applied is as follows—

(i) First, the substance of the transaction shall be determined; for this purpose, all the relevant facts and circumstances shall be considered and any law or rule of law (assignment of income, step transaction, etc.) may apply. Only the rate of interest with respect to the stated principal amount of the bona fide indebtedness (within the meaning of paragraph (a)(1) of this section), if any, shall be subject to adjustment under section 482, paragraph (a) of this section, and any other Internal Revenue Code section.

(ii) Second, the other Internal Revenue Code section shall be applied to the loan or advance to determine whether any amount other than stated interest is to be treated as interest, and if so, to determine such amount according to the provisions of such other Internal Revenue Code section.

(iii) Third, whether or not the other Internal Revenue Code section applies to adjust the amounts treated as interest under such loan or advance, section 482 and paragraph (a) of this section may then be applied by the district director to determine whether the rate of interest charged on the loan or advance, as adjusted by any other Code section, is greater or less than an arm's length rate of interest, and if so, to make appropriate allocations to reflect an arm's length rate of interest.

(iv) Fourth, section 482 and paragraphs (b) through (d) of this section and §§ 1.482-3 through 1.482-7, if applicable, may be applied by the district director to make any appropriate allo-

Reg. § 1.482-2(a)(3)

cations, other than an interest rate adjustment, to reflect an arm's length transaction based upon the principal amount of the loan or advance and the interest rate as adjusted under paragraph (a)(3)(i), (ii) or (iii) of this section. For example, assume that two commonly controlled taxpayers enter into a deferred payment sale of tangible property and no interest is provided, and assume also that section 483 is applied to treat a portion of the stated sales price as interest, thereby reducing the stated sales price. If after this recharacterization of a portion of the stated sales price as interest, the recomputed sales price does not reflect an arm's length sales price under the principles of § 1.482-3, the district director may make other appropriate allocations (other than an interest rate adjustment) to reflect an arm's length sales price.

(4) *Examples.* The principles of paragraph (a)(3) of this section may be illustrated by the following examples:

Example 1. An individual, A, transfers $20,000 to a corporation controlled by A in exchange for the corporation's note which bears adequate stated interest. The district director recharacterizes the transaction as a contribution to the capital of the corporation in exchange for preferred stock. Under paragraph (a)(3)(i) of this section, section 1.482-2(a) does not apply to the transaction because there is no bona fide indebtedness.

Example 2. B, an individual, is an employee of Z corporation, and is also the controlling shareholder of Z. Z makes a term loan of $15,000 to B at a rate of interest that is less than the applicable Federal rate. In this instance the other operative Code section is section 7872. Under section 7872(b), the difference between the amount loaned and the present value of all payments due under the loan using a discount rate equal to 100 percent of the applicable Federal rate is treated as an amount of cash transferred from the corporation to B and the loan is treated as having original issue discount equal to such amount. Under paragraph (a)(3)(iii) of this section, section 482 and paragraph (a) of this section may also be applied by the district director to determine if the rate of interest charged on this $15,000 loan (100 percent of the AFR, compounded semiannually, as adjusted by section 7872) is an arm's length rate of interest. Because the rate of interest on the loan, as adjusted by section 7872, is within the safe haven range of 100-130 percent of the AFR, compounded semiannually, no further interest rate adjustments under section 482 and paragraph (a) of this section will be made to this loan.

Example 3. The facts are the same as in Example 2 except that the amount lent by Z to B is $9,000, and that amount is the aggregate outstanding amount of loans between Z and B. Under the $10,000 de minimis exception of section 7872(c)(3), no adjustment for interest will be made to this $9,000 loan under section 7872. Under paragraph (a)(3)(iii) of this section, the district director may apply section 482 and paragraph (a) of this section to this $9,000 loan to determine whether the rate of interest charged is less than an arm's length rate of interest, and if so, to make appropriate allocations to reflect an arm's length rate of interest.

Example 4. X and Y are commonly controlled taxpayers. At a time when the applicable Federal rate is 12 percent, compounded semiannually, X sells property to Y in exchange for a note with a stated rate of interest of 18 percent, compounded semiannually. Assume that the other applicable Code section to the transaction is section 483. Section 483 does not apply to this transaction because, under section 483(d), there is no total unstated interest under the contract using the test rate of interest equal to 100 percent of the applicable Federal rate. Under paragraph (a)(3)(iii) of this section, section 482 and paragraph (a) of this section may be applied by the district director to determine whether the rate of interest under the note is excessive, that is, to determine whether the 18 percent stated interest rate under the note exceeds an arm's length rate of interest.

Example 5. Assume that A and B are commonly controlled taxpayers and that the applicable Federal rate is 10 percent, compounded semiannually. On June 30, 1986, A sells property to B and receives in exchange B's purchase-money note in the amount of $2,000,000. The stated interest rate on the note is 9%, compounded semiannually, and the stated redemption price at maturity on the note is $2,000,000. Assume that the other applicable Code section to this transaction is section 1274. As provided in section 1274A(a) and (b), the discount rate for purposes of section 1274 will be nine percent, compounded semiannually, because the stated principal amount of B's note does not exceed $2,800,000. Section 1274 does not apply to this transaction because there is adequate stated interest on the debt instrument using a discount rate equal to 9%, compounded semiannually, and the stated redemption price at maturity does not exceed the stated principal amount. Under paragraph (a)(3)(iii) of this section, the district director may apply section 482 and paragraph (a) of this section to this $2,000,000 note to determine whether the 9% rate of interest charged is less than an arm's length rate of interest, and if

Reg. § 1.482-2(a)(4)

so, to make appropriate allocations to reflect an arm's length rate of interest.

(b) *Performance of services for another*—(1) *General rule.* Where one member of a group of controlled entities performs marketing, managerial, administrative, technical, or other services for the benefit of, or on behalf of another member of the group without charge, or at a charge which is not equal to an arm's length charge as defined in paragraph (b)(3) of this section, the district director may make appropriate allocations to reflect an arm's length charge for such services.

(2) *Benefit test*—(i) Allocations may be made to reflect arm's length charges with respect to services undertaken for the joint benefit of the members of a group of controlled entities, as well as with respect to services performed by one member of the group exclusively for the benefit of another member of the group. Any allocations made shall be consistent with the relative benefits intended from the services, based upon the facts known at the time the services were rendered, and shall be made even if the potential benefits anticipated are not realized. No allocations shall be made if the probable benefits to the other members were so indirect or remote that unrelated parties would not have charged for such services. In general, allocations may be made if the service, at the time it was performed, related to the carrying on of an activity by another member or was intended to benefit another member, either in the member's overall operations or in its day-to-day activities. The principles of this paragraph (b)(2)(i) may be illustrated by the following examples in each of which it is assumed that X and Y are corporate members of the same group of controlled entities:

Example 1. X's International Division engages in a wide range of sales promotion activities. Although most of these activities are undertaken exclusively for the benefit of X's international operations, some are intended to jointly benefit both X and Y and others are undertaken exclusively for the benefit of Y. The district director may make an allocation to reflect an arm's length charge with respect to the activities undertaken for the joint benefit of X and Y consistent with the relative benefits intended as well as with respect to the services performed exclusively for the benefit of Y.

Example 2. X operates an international airline, and Y owns and operates hotels in several cities which are serviced by X. X, in conjunction with its advertising of the airline, often pictures Y's hotels and mentions Y's name. Although such advertising was primarily intended to benefit X's airline operations, it was reasonable to anticipate that there would be substantial benefits to Y resulting from patronage by travelers who responded to X's advertising. Since an unrelated hotel operator would have been charged for such advertising, the district director may make an appropriate allocation to reflect an arm's length charge consistent with the relative benefits intended.

Example 3. Assume the same facts as in *Example 2* except that X's advertising neither mentions nor pictures Y's hotels. Although it is reasonable to anticipate that increased air travel attributable to X's advertising will result in some benefit to Y due to increased patronage by air travelers, the district director will not make an allocation with respect to such advertising since the probable benefit to Y was so indirect and remote that an unrelated hotel operator would not have been charged for such advertising.

(ii) Allocations will generally not be made if the service is merely a duplication of a service which the related party has independently performed or is performing for itself. In this connection, the ability to independently perform the service (in terms of qualification and availability of personnel) shall be taken into account. The principles of this paragraph (b)(2)(ii) may be illustrated by the following examples, in each of which it is assumed that X and Y are corporate members of the same group of controlled entities:

Example 1. At the request of Y, the financial staff of X makes an analysis to determine the amount and source of the borrowing needs of Y. Y does not have personnel qualified to make the analysis, and it does not undertake the same analysis. The district director may make an appropriate allocation to reflect an arm's length charge for such analysis.

Example 2. Y, which has a qualified financial staff, makes an analysis to determine the amount and source of its borrowing needs. Its report, recommending a loan from a bank, is submitted to X. X's financial staff reviews the analysis to determine whether X should advise Y to reconsider its plan. No allocation should be made with respect to X's review.

(3) *Arm's length charge.* For the purpose of this paragraph an arm's length charge for services rendered shall be the amount which was charged or would have been charged for the same or similar services in independent transactions with or between unrelated parties under similar circumstances considering all relevant facts. However, except in the case of services which are an integral part of the business activity of either the member rendering the services or the member receiving the benefit of the services (as described

Reg. § 1.482-2(b)(3)

in paragraph (b)(7) of this section) the arm's length charge shall be deemed equal to the costs or deductions incurred with respect to such services by the member or members rendering such services unless the taxpayer establishes a more appropriate charge under the standards set forth in the first sentence of this subparagraph. Where costs or deductions are a factor in applying the provisions of this paragraph adequate books and records must be maintained by taxpayers to permit verification of such costs or deductions by the Internal Revenue Service.

(4) *Costs or deductions to be taken into account*—(i) Where the amount of an arm's length charge for services is determined with reference to the costs or deductions incurred with respect to such services, it is necessary to take into account on some reasonable basis all the costs or deductions which are directly or indirectly related to the service performed.

(ii) Direct costs or deductions are those identified specifically with a particular service. These include, but are not limited to, costs or deductions for compensation, bonuses, and travel expenses attributable to employees directly engaged in performing such services, for material and supplies directly consumed in rendering such services, and for other costs such as the cost of overseas cables in connection with such services.

(iii) Indirect costs or deductions are those which are not specifically identified with a particular activity or service but which relate to the direct costs referred to in paragraph (b)(4)(ii) of this section. Indirect costs or deductions generally include costs or deductions with respect to utilities, occupancy, supervisory and clerical compensation, and other overhead burden of the department incurring the direct costs or deductions referred to in paragraph (b)(4)(ii) of this section. Indirect costs or deductions also generally include an appropriate share of the costs or deductions relating to supporting departments and other applicable general and administrative expenses to the extent reasonably allocable to a particular service or activity. Thus, for example, if a domestic corporation's advertising department performs services for the direct benefit of a foreign subsidiary, in addition to direct costs of such department, such as salaries of employees and fees paid to advertising agencies or consultants, which are attributable to such foreign advertising, indirect costs must be taken into account on some reasonable basis in determining the amount of costs or deductions with respect to which the arm's length charge to the foreign subsidiary is to be determined. These generally include depreciation, rent, property taxes, other costs of occupancy, and other overhead costs of the advertising department itself, and allocations of costs from other departments which service the advertising department, such as the personnel, accounting, payroll, and maintenance departments, and other applicable general and administrative expenses including compensation of top management.

(5) *Costs and deductions not to be taken into account.* Costs or deductions of the member rendering the services which are not to be taken into account in determining the amount of an arm's length charge for services include—

(i) Interest expense on indebtedness not incurred specifically for the benefit of another member of the group;

(ii) Expenses associated with the issuance of stock and maintenance of shareholder relations; and

(iii) Expenses of compliance with regulations or policies imposed upon the member rendering the services by its government which are not directly related to the service in question.

(6) *Methods*—(i) Where an arm's length charge for services rendered is determined with reference to costs or deductions, and a member has allocated and apportioned costs or deductions to reflect arm's length charges by employing in a consistent manner a method of allocation and apportionment which is reasonable and in keeping with sound accounting practice, such method will not be disturbed. If the member has not employed a method of allocation and apportionment which is reasonable and in keeping with sound accounting practice, the method of allocating and apportioning costs or deductions for the purpose of determining the amount of arm's length charges shall be based on the particular circumstances involved.

(ii) The methods of allocation and apportionment referred to in this paragraph (b)(6) are applicable both in allocating and apportioning indirect costs to a particular activity or service (see paragraph (b)(4)(iii) of this section) and in allocating and apportioning the total costs (direct and indirect) of a particular activity or service where such activity or service is undertaken for the joint benefit of two or more members of a group (see paragraph (b)(2)(i) of this section). While the use of one or more bases may be appropriate under the circumstances, in establishing the method of allocation and apportionment, appropriate consideration should be given to all bases and factors, including, for example, total expenses, asset size, sales, manufacturing expenses, payroll, space utilized, and time spent. The costs incurred by supporting departments

Reg. § 1.482-2(b)(4)

may be apportioned to other departments on the basis of reasonable overall estimates, or such costs may be reflected in the other departments' costs by means of application of reasonable departmental overhead rates. Allocations and apportionments of costs or deductions must be made on the basis of the full cost as opposed to the incremental cost. Thus, if an electronic data processing machine, which is rented by the taxpayer, is used for the joint benefit of itself and other members of a controlled group, the determination of the arm's length charge to each member must be made with reference to the full rent and cost of operating the machine by each member, even if the additional use of the machine for the benefit of the other members did not increase the cost to the taxpayer.

(iii) Practices actually employed to apportion costs or expenses in connection with the preparation of statements and analyses for the use of management, creditors, minority shareholders, joint venturers, clients, customers, potential investors, or other parties or agencies in interest shall be considered by the district director. Similarly, in determining the extent to which allocations are to be made to or from foreign members of a controlled group, practices employed by the domestic members of a controlled group in apportioning costs between themselves shall also be considered if the relationships with the foreign members of the group are comparable to the relationships between the domestic members of the group. For example, if, for purposes of reporting to public stockholders or to a governmental agency, a corporation apportions the costs attributable to its executive officers among the domestic members of a controlled group on a reasonable and consistent basis, and such officers exercise comparable control over foreign members of such group, such domestic apportionment practice will be taken into consideration in determining the amount of allocations to be made to the foreign members.

(7) *Certain services.* An arm's length charge shall not be deemed equal to costs or deductions with respect to services which are an integral part of the business activity of either the member rendering the services (referred to in this paragraph (b) as the renderer) or the member receiving the benefit of the services (referred to in this paragraph (b) as the recipient). Paragraphs (b)(7)(i) through (b)(7)(iv) of this section describe those situations in which services shall be considered an integral part of the business activity of a member of a group of controlled entities.

(i) Services are an integral part of the business activity of a member of a controlled group where either the renderer or the recipient is engaged in the trade or business of rendering similar services to one or more unrelated parties.

(ii) (A) Services are an integral part of the business activity of a member of a controlled group where the renderer renders services to one or more related parties as one of its principal activities. Except in the case of services which constitute a manufacturing, production, extraction, or construction activity, it will be presumed that the renderer does not render services to related parties as one of its principal activities if the cost of services of the renderer attributable to the rendition of services for the taxable year to related parties do not exceed 25 percent of the total costs or deductions of the renderer for the taxable year. Where the cost of services rendered to related parties is in excess of 25 percent of the total costs or deductions of the renderer for the taxable year or where the 25-percent test does not apply, the determination of whether the rendition of such services is one of the principal activities of the renderer will be based on the facts and circumstances of each particular case. Such facts and circumstances may include the time devoted to the rendition of the services, the relative cost of the services, the regularity with which the services are rendered, the amount of capital investment, the risk of loss involved, and whether the services are in the nature of supporting services or independent of the other activities of the renderer.

(B) For purposes of the 25-percent test provided in this paragraph (b)(7)(ii), the cost of services rendered to related parties shall include all costs or deductions directly or indirectly related to the rendition of such services including the cost of services which constitute a manufacturing, production, extraction, or construction activity; and the total costs or deductions of the renderer for the taxable year shall exclude amounts properly reflected in the cost of goods sold of the renderer. Where any of the costs or deductions of the renderer do not reflect arm's length consideration and no adjustment is made under any provision of the Internal Revenue Code to reflect arm's length consideration, the 25-percent test will not apply if, had an arm's length charge been made, the costs or deductions attributable to the renderer's rendition of services to related entities would exceed 25 percent of the total costs or deductions of the renderer for the taxable year.

(C) For purposes of the 25-percent test in this paragraph (b)(7)(ii), a consolidated group (as defined in this paragraph (b)(7)(ii)(C)) may, at the option of the taxpayer, be considered as the renderer where one or more members of the con-

Reg. § 1.482-2(b)(7)

solidated group render services for the benefit of or on behalf of a related party which is not a member of the consolidated group. In such case, the cost of services rendered by members of the consolidated group to any related parties not members of the consolidated group, as well as the total costs or deductions of the members of the consolidated group, shall be considered in the aggregate to determine if such services constitute a principal activity of the renderer. Where a consolidated group is considered the renderer in accordance with this paragraph (b)(7)(ii)(C), the costs or deductions referred to in this paragraph (b)(7)(ii) shall not include costs or deductions paid or accrued to any member of the consolidated group. In addition to the preceding provisions of this paragraph (b)(7)(ii)(C), if part or all of the services rendered by a member of a consolidated group to any related party not a member of the consolidated group are similar to services rendered by any other member of the consolidated group to unrelated parties as part of a trade or business, the 25-percent test in this paragraph (b)(7)(ii) shall be applied with respect to such similar services without regard to this paragraph (b)(7)(ii)(C). For purposes of this paragraph (b)(7)(ii)(C), the term consolidated group means all members of a group of controlled entities created or organized within a single country and subjected to an income tax by such country on the basis of their combined income.

(iii) Services are an integral part of the business activity of a member of a controlled group where the renderer is peculiarly capable of rendering the services and such services are a principal element in the operations of the recipient. The renderer is peculiarly capable of rendering the services where the renderer, in connection with the rendition of such services, makes use of a particularly advantageous situation or circumstance such as by utilization of special skills and reputation, utilization of an influential relationship with customers, or utilization of its intangible property (as defined in § 1.482-4(b)). However, the renderer will not be considered peculiarly capable of rendering services unless the value of the services is substantially in excess of the costs or deductions of the renderer attributable to such services.

(iv) Services are an integral part of the business activity of a member of a controlled group where the recipient has received the benefit of a substantial amount of services from one or more related parties during its taxable year. For purposes of this paragraph (b)(7)(iv), services rendered by one or more related parties shall be considered substantial in amount if the total costs or deductions of the related party or parties rendering services to the recipient during its taxable year which are directly or indirectly related to such services exceed an amount equal to 25 percent of the total costs or deductions of the recipient during its taxable year. For purposes of the preceding sentence, the total costs or deductions of the recipient shall include the renderers' costs or deductions directly or indirectly related to the rendition of such services and shall exclude any amounts paid or accrued to the renderers by the recipient for such services and shall also exclude any amounts paid or accrued for materials the cost of which is properly reflected in the cost of goods sold of the recipient. At the option of the taxpayer, where the taxpayer establishes that the amount of the total costs or deductions of a recipient for the recipient's taxable year are abnormally low due to the commencement or cessation of an operation by the recipient, or other unusual circumstances of a nonrecurring nature, the costs or deductions referred to in the preceding two sentences shall be the total of such amount for the 3-year period immediately preceding the close of the taxable year of the recipient (or for the first 3 years of operation of the recipient if the recipient had been in operation for less than 3 years as of the close of the taxable year in which the services in issue were rendered).

(v) The principles of paragraphs (b)(7)(i) through (iv) of this section may be illustrated by the following examples:

Example 1. Y is engaged in the business of selling merchandise and X, an entity related to Y, is a printing company regularly engaged in printing and mailing advertising literature for unrelated parties. X also prints circulars advertising Y's products, mails the circulars to potential customers of Y, and in addition, performs the art work involved in the preparation of the circulars. Since the printing, mailing, and art work services rendered by X to Y are similar to the printing and mailing services rendered by X as X's trade or business, the services rendered to Y are an integral part of the business activity of X as described in paragraph (b)(7)(i) of this section.

Example 2. V, W, X, and Y are members of the same group of controlled entities. Each member of the group files a separate income tax return. X renders wrecking services to V, W, and Y, and, in addition, sells building materials to unrelated parties. The total costs or deductions incurred by X for the taxable year (exclusive of amounts properly reflected in the cost of goods sold of X) are $4 million. The total costs or deductions of X for the taxable year which are directly or indirectly related to the services rendered to V, W, and Y are $650,000. Since $650,000 is less

Reg. § 1.482-2(b)(7)

than 25 percent of the total costs or deductions of X (exclusive of amounts properly reflected in the cost of goods sold of X) for the taxable year ($4,000,000 * 25% = $1,000,000), the services rendered by X to V, W, and Y will not be considered one of X's principal activities within the meaning of paragraph (b)(7)(ii) of this section.

Example 3. Assume the same facts as in *Example 2,* except that the total costs or deductions of X for the taxable year which are directly or indirectly related to the services rendered to V, W, and Y are $1,800,000. Assume in addition, that there is a high risk of loss involved in the rendition of the wrecking services by X, that X has a large investment in the wrecking equipment, and that a substantial amount of X's time is devoted to the rendition of wrecking services to V, W, and Y. Since $1,800,000 is greater than 25 percent of the total costs or deductions of X for the taxable year (exclusive of amounts properly reflected in the cost of goods sold of X), i.e., $1 million, the services rendered by X to V, W, and Y will not be automatically excluded from classification as one of the principal activities of X as in *Example 2,* and consideration must be given to the facts and circumstances of the particular case. Based on the facts and circumstances in this case, X would be considered to render wrecking services to related parties as one of its principal activities. Thus, the wrecking services are an integral part of the business activity of X as described in paragraph (b)(7)(ii) of this section.

Example 4. Z is a domestic corporation and has several foreign subsidiaries. Z and X, a domestic subsidiary of Z, have exercised the privilege granted under section 1501 to file a consolidated return and, therefore, constitute a *consolidated group* within the meaning of paragraph (b)(7)(ii)(C) of this section. Pursuant to paragraph (b)(7)(ii)(C) of this section, the taxpayer treats X and Z as the renderer. The sole function of X is to provide accounting, billing, communication, and travel services to the foreign subsidiaries of Z. Z also provides some other services for the benefit of its foreign subsidiaries. The total costs or deductions of X and Z related to the services rendered for the benefit of the foreign subsidiaries is $750,000. Of that amount, $710,000 represents the costs of X, which are X's total operating costs. The total costs or deductions of X and Z for the taxable year with respect to their operations (exclusive of amounts properly reflected in the cost of goods sold of X and Z) is $6,500,000. Since the total costs or deductions related to the services rendered to the foreign subsidiaries ($750,000) is less than 25 percent of the total costs or deductions of X and Z (exclusive of amounts properly reflected in the costs of goods sold of X or Z) in the aggregate ($6,500,000 * 25% = $1,625,000), the services rendered by X and Z to the foreign subsidiaries will not be considered one of the principal activities of X and Z within the meaning of paragraph (b)(7)(ii) of this section.

Example 5. Assume the same facts as in *Example 4,* except that all the communication services rendered for the benefit of the foreign subsidiaries are rendered by X and that Z renders communication services to unrelated parties as part of its trade or business. X is regularly engaged in rendering communication services to foreign subsidiaries and devotes a substantial amount of its time to this activity. The costs or deductions of X related to the rendition of the communication services to the foreign subsidiaries are $355,000. By application of the paragraph (b)(7)(ii)(C) of this section, the services provided by X and Z to related entities other than the communication services will not be considered one of the principal activities of X and Z. However, since Z renders communication services to unrelated parties as a part of its trade or business, the communication services rendered by X to the foreign subsidiaries will be subject to the provisions of paragraph (b)(7)(ii) of this section without regard to paragraph (b)(7)(ii)(C) of this section. Since the costs or deductions of X related to the rendition of the communication services ($355,000) are in excess of 25 percent of the total costs or deductions of X (exclusive of amounts properly reflected in the cost of goods sold of X) for the taxable year ($710,000 × 25% = $177,500), the determination of whether X renders the communication services as one of its principal activities will depend on the particular facts and circumstances. The given facts and circumstances indicate that X renders the communication services as one of its principal activities.

Example 6. X and Y are members of the same group of controlled entities. Y produces and sells product D. As a part of the production process, Y sends materials to X who converts the materials into component parts. This conversion activity constitutes only a portion of X's operations. X then ships the component parts back to Y who assembles them (along with other components) into the finished product for sale to unrelated parties. Since the services rendered by X to Y constitute a manufacturing activity, the 25-percent test in paragraph (b)(7)(ii) of this section does not apply.

Example 7. X and Y are members of the same group of controlled entities. X manufactures product D for distribution and sale in the United States, Canada, and Mexico. Y manufactures product D for distribution and sale in South and

Central America. Due to a breakdown of machinery, Y is forced to cease its manufacturing operations for a 1-month period. In order to meet demand for product D during the shutdown period, Y sends partially finished goods to X. X, for that period, completes the manufacture of product D for Y and ships the finished product back to Y. The costs or deductions of X related to the manufacturing services rendered to Y are $750,000. The total costs or deductions of X are $24,000,000. Since the services in issue constitute a manufacturing activity, the 25-percent test in paragraph (b)(7)(ii) of this section does not apply. However, under these facts and circumstances, i.e., the insubstantiality of the services rendered to Y in relation to X's total operations, the lack of regularity with which the services are rendered, and the short duration for which the services are rendered, X's rendition of manufacturing services to Y is not considered one of X's principal activities within the meaning of paragraph (b)(7)(ii) of this section.

Example 8. Assume the same facts as in Example 7, except that, instead of temporarily ceasing operations, Y requests assistance from X in correcting the defects in the manufacturing equipment. In response, X sends a team of engineers to discover and correct the defects without the necessity of a shutdown. Although the services performed by the engineers were related to a manufacturing activity, the services are essentially supporting in nature and, therefore, do not constitute a manufacturing, production, extraction, or construction activity. Thus, the 25-percent test in paragraph (b)(7)(ii) of this section applies.

Example 9. X is a domestic manufacturing corporation. Y, a foreign subsidiary of X, has decided to construct a plant in Country A. In connection with the construction of Y's plant, X draws up the architectural plans for the plant, arranges the financing of the construction, negotiates with various Government authorities in Country A, invites bids from unrelated parties for several phases of construction, and negotiates, on Y's behalf, the contracts with unrelated parties who are retained to carry out certain phases of the construction. Although the unrelated parties retained by X for Y perform the physical construction, the aggregate services performed by X for Y are such that they, in themselves, constitute a construction activity. Thus, the 25-percent test in paragraph (b)(7)(ii) of this section does not apply with respect to such services.

Example 10. X and Y are members of the same group of controlled entities. X is a finance company engaged in financing automobile loans. In connection with such loans it requires the borrower to have life insurance in the amount of the loan. Although X's borrowers are not required to take out life insurance from any particular insurance company, at the same time that the loan agreement is being finalized, X's employees suggest that the borrower take out life insurance from Y, which is an agency for life insurance companies. Since there would be a delay in the processing of the loan if some other company were selected by the borrower, almost all of X's borrowers take out life insurance through Y. Because of this utilization of its influential relationship with its borrowers, X is peculiarly capable of rendering selling services to Y and, since a substantial amount of Y's business is derived from X's borrowers, such selling services are a principal element in the operation of Y's insurance business. In addition, the value of the services is substantially in excess of the costs incurred by X. Thus, the selling services rendered by X to Y are an integral part of the business activity of a member of the controlled group as described in paragraph (b)(7)(iii) of this section.

Example 11. X and Y are members of the same group of controlled entities. Y is a manufacturer of product E. In past years product E has not always operated properly because of imperfections present in the finished product. X owns an exclusive patented process by which such imperfections can be detected and removed prior to sale of the product, thereby greatly increasing the marketability of the product. In connection with its manufacturing operations Y sends its products to X for inspection which involves utilization of the patented process. The inspection of Y's products by X is not one of the principal activities of X. However, X is peculiarly capable of rendering the inspection services to Y because of its utilization of the patented process. Since this inspection greatly increases the marketability of product E it is extremely valuable. Such value is substantially in excess of the cost incurred by X in rendition of such services. Because of the impact of the inspection on sales, such services are a principal element in the operations of Y. Thus, the inspection services rendered by X to Y are an integral part of the business activity of a member of the controlled group as described in paragraph (b)(7)(iii) of this section.

Example 12. Assume the same facts as in Example 11 except that Y owns the patented process for detecting the imperfections. Y, however, does not have the facilities to implement the inspection process. Therefore, Y sends its products to X for inspection which involves utilization of the patented process owned by Y. Since Y owns the patent, X is not peculiarly capable of render-

Reg. § 1.482-2(b)(7)

ing the inspection services to Y within the meaning of paragraph (b)(7)(iii) of this section.

Example 13. Assume the same facts as in *Example 12* except that X and Y both own interests in the patented process as a result of having developed the process pursuant to a bona fide cost sharing plan (within the meaning of § 1.482-7T. Since Y owns the requisite interest in the patent, X is not peculiarly capable of rendering the inspection services to Y within the meaning of paragraph (b)(7)(iii) of this section.

Example 14. X and Y are members of the same group of controlled entities. X is a large manufacturing concern. X's accounting department has, for many years, maintained the financial records of Y, a distributor of X's products. Although X is able to render these accounting services more efficiently than others due to its thorough familiarity with the operations of Y, X is not peculiarly capable of rendering the accounting services to Y because such familiarity does not, in and of itself, constitute a particularly advantageous situation or circumstance within the meaning of paragraph (b)(7)(iii) of this section. Furthermore, under these circumstances, the accounting services are supporting in nature and, therefore, do not constitute a principal element in the operations of Y. Thus, the accounting services rendered by X to Y are not an integral part of the business activity of either X or Y within the meaning of paragraph (b)(7)(iii) of this section.

Example 15. (i) Corporations X, Y, and Z are members of the same group of controlled entities. X is a manufacturer, and Y and Z are distributors of X's products. X provides a variety of services to Y including billing, shipping, accounting, and other general and administrative services. During Y's taxable year, on several occasions, Z renders selling and other promotional services to Y. None of the services rendered to Y constitute one of the principal activities of any of the renderers within the meaning of paragraph (b)(7)(ii) of this section. Y's total costs and deductions for Y's taxable year (exclusive of amounts paid to X and Z for services rendered and amounts paid for goods purchased for resale) are $1,600,000. The total direct and indirect costs of X and Z for services rendered to Y during Y's taxable year are as follows:

Services provided by X:	
Billing	$ 50,000
Shipping	250,000
Accounting	150,000
Other	200,000
Services provided by Z:	
Selling	500,000
Total Costs	**$1,150,000**

(ii) Since the total costs or deductions of X and Z related to the rendition of services to Y exceed the amount equal to 25 percent of the total costs or deductions of Y (exclusive of amounts paid to X and Z for the services rendered and amounts paid for goods purchased for resale) plus the total costs or deductions of X and Z related to the rendition of services to Y ($1,150,000 ÷ [$1,600,000 + $1,150,000] = 41.8%), the services rendered by X and Z to Y are substantial within the meaning of paragraph (b)(7)(iv) of this section. Thus, the services rendered by X and Z to Y are an integral part of the business activity of Y as described in paragraph (b)(7)(iv) of this section.

Example 16. Assume the same facts as in *Example 15,* except that the taxpayer establishes that, due to a major change in the operations of Y, Y's total costs or deductions for Y's taxable year were abnormally low. Y has always used the calendar year as its taxable year. Y's total costs and deductions for the 2 years immediately preceding the taxable year in issue (exclusive of amounts paid to X and Z for services rendered and amounts paid for goods purchased for resale) were $6 million and $6,200,000 respectively. The total direct and indirect costs of X and Z for services rendered to Y were $1,150,000 for each of the 3 years. Applying the same formula to the costs or deductions for the 3 years immediately preceding the close of the taxable year in issue, the costs or deductions of X and Z related to the rendition of services to Y (3 × $1,150,000 = $3,450,000) amount to 20 percent of the sum of the total costs or deductions of Y (exclusive of amounts paid to X and Z for the services rendered and amounts paid for goods purchased for resale) plus the total costs or deductions of X and Z related to the rendition of services to Y ($3,450,000 ÷ [$1,600,000 + $6,000,000 + $6,200,000 + $3,450,000] = 20%). If the taxpayer chooses to use the 3-year period, the services rendered by X and Z to Y are not substantial within the meaning of paragraph (b)(7)(iv) of this section. Thus, the services will not be an integral part of the business activity of a member of the controlled group as described in paragraph (b)(7)(iv) of this section.

Reg. § 1.482-2(b)(7)

(8) *Services rendered in connection with the transfer of property.* Where tangible or intangible property is transferred, sold, assigned, loaned, leased, or otherwise made available in any manner by one member of a group to another member of the group and services are rendered by the transferor to the transferee in connection with the transfer, the amount of any allocation that may be appropriate with respect to such transfer shall be determined in accordance with the rules of paragraph (c) of this section, or §§ 1.482-3 or 1.482-4, whichever is appropriate and a separate allocation with respect to such services under this paragraph shall not be made. Services are rendered in connection with the transfer of property where such services are merely ancillary and subsidiary to the transfer of the property or to the commencement of effective use of the property by the transferee. Whether or not services are merely ancillary and subsidiary to a property transfer is a question of fact. Ancillary and subsidiary services could be performed, for example, in promoting the transaction by demonstrating and explaining the use of the property, or by assisting in the effective starting-up of the property transferred, or by performing under a guarantee relating to such effective starting-up. Thus, where an employee of one member of a group, acting under the instructions of his employer, reveals a valuable secret process owned by his employer to a related entity, and at the same time supervises the integration of such process into the manufacturing operation of the related entity, such services could be considered to be rendered in connection with the transfer, and, if so considered, shall not be the basis for a separate allocation. However, if the employee continues to render services to the related entity by supervising the manufacturing operation after the secret process has been effectively integrated into such operation, a separate allocation with respect to such additional services may be made in accordance with the rules of this paragraph.

(c) *Use of tangible property*—(1) *General rule.* Where possession, use, or occupancy of tangible property owned or leased by one member of a group of controlled entities (referred to in this paragraph as the owner) is transferred by lease or other arrangement to another member of such group (referred to in this paragraph as the user) without charge or at a charge which is not equal to an arm's length rental charge (as defined in paragraph (c)(2)(i) of this section) the district director may make appropriate allocations to properly reflect such arm's length charge. Where possession, use, or occupancy of only a portion of such property is transferred, the determination of the arm's length charge and the allocation shall be made with reference to the portion transferred.

(2) *Arm's length charge*—(i) *In general.* For purposes of paragraph (c) of this section, an arm's length rental charge shall be the amount of rent which was charged, or would have been charged for the use of the same or similar property, during the time it was in use, in independent transactions with or between unrelated parties under similar circumstances considering the period and location of the use, the owner's investment in the property or rent paid for the property, expenses of maintaining the property, the type of property involved, its condition, and all other relevant facts.

(ii) *Safe haven rental charge.* See § 1.482-2(c)(2)(ii) (26 CFR Part 1 revised as of April 1, 1985), for the determination of safe haven rental charges in the case of certain leases entered into before May 9, 1986, and for leases entered into before August 7, 1986, pursuant to a binding written contract entered into before May 9, 1986.

(iii) *Subleases*—(A) Except as provided in paragraph (c)(2)(iii)(B) of this section, where possession, use, or occupancy of tangible property, which is leased by the owner (lessee) from an unrelated party is transferred by sublease or other arrangement to the user, an arm's length rental charge shall be considered to be equal to all the deductions claimed by the owner (lessee) which are attributable to the property for the period such property is used by the user. Where only a portion of such property was transferred, any allocations shall be made with reference to the portion transferred. The deductions to be considered include the rent paid or accrued by the owner (lessee) during the period of use and all other deductions directly and indirectly connected with the property paid or accrued by the owner (lessee) during such period. Such deductions include deductions for maintenance and repair, utilities, management and other similar deductions.

(B) The provisions of paragraph (c)(2)(iii)(A) of this section shall not apply if either—

(*1*) The taxpayer establishes a more appropriate rental charge under the general rule set forth in paragraph (c)(2)(i) of this section; or

(*2*) During the taxable year, the owner (lessee) or the user was regularly engaged in the trade or business of renting property of the same general type as the property in question to unrelated persons.

(d) *Transfer of property.* For rules governing allocations under section 482 to reflect an arm's length consideration for controlled transactions

Reg. § 1.482-2(b)(8)

involving the transfer of property, see §§ 1.482-3 through 1.482-6. [Reg. § 1.482-2.]

☐ [*T.D.* 8552, 7-1-94.]

[Reg. § 1.482-3]

§ 1.482-3. Methods to determine taxable income in connection with a transfer of tangible property.—(a) *In general.* The arm's length amount charged in a controlled transfer of tangible property must be determined under one of the six methods listed in this paragraph (a). Each of the methods must be applied in accordance with all of the provisions of § 1.482-1, including the best method rule of § 1.482-1(c), the comparability analysis of § 1.482-1(d), and the arm's length range of § 1.482-1(e). The methods are—

(1) The comparable uncontrolled price method, described in paragraph (b) of this section;

(2) The resale price method, described in paragraph (c) of this section;

(3) The cost plus method, described in paragraph (d) of this section;

(4) The comparable profits method, described in § 1.482-5;

(5) The profit split method, described in § 1.482-6; and

(6) Unspecified methods, described in paragraph (e) of this section.

(b) *Comparable uncontrolled price method*—(1) *In general.* The comparable uncontrolled price method evaluates whether the amount charged in a controlled transaction is arm's length by reference to the amount charged in a comparable uncontrolled transaction.

(2) *Comparability and reliability considerations*—(i) *In general.* Whether results derived from applications of this method are the most reliable measure of the arm's length result must be determined using the factors described under the best method rule in § 1.482-1(c). The application of these factors under the comparable uncontrolled price method is discussed in paragraph (b)(2)(ii) and (iii) of this section.

(ii) *Comparability*—(A) *In general.* The degree of comparability between controlled and uncontrolled transactions is determined by applying the provisions of § 1.482-1(d). Although all of the factors described in § 1.482-1(d)(3) must be considered, similarity of products generally will have the greatest effect on comparability under this method. In addition, because even minor differences in contractual terms or economic conditions could materially affect the amount charged in an uncontrolled transaction, comparability under this method depends on close similarity with respect to these factors, or adjustments to account for any differences. The results derived from applying the comparable uncontrolled price method generally will be the most direct and reliable measure of an arm's length price for the controlled transaction if an uncontrolled transaction has no differences with the controlled transaction that would affect the price, or if there are only minor differences that have a definite and reasonably ascertainable effect on price and for which appropriate adjustments are made. If such adjustments cannot be made, or if there are more than minor differences between the controlled and uncontrolled transactions, the comparable uncontrolled price method may be used, but the reliability of the results as a measure of the arm's length price will be reduced. Further, if there are material product differences for which reliable adjustments cannot be made, this method ordinarily will not provide a reliable measure of an arm's length result.

(B) *Adjustments for differences between controlled and uncontrolled transactions.* If there are differences between the controlled and uncontrolled transactions that would affect price, adjustments should be made to the price of the uncontrolled transaction according to the comparability provisions of § 1.482-1(d)(2). Specific examples of the factors that may be particularly relevant to this method include—

(*1*) Quality of the product;

(*2*) Contractual terms, (e.g., scope and terms of warranties provided, sales or purchase volume, credit terms, transport terms);

(*3*) Level of the market (i.e., wholesale, retail, etc.);

(*4*) Geographic market in which the transaction takes place;

(*5*) Date of the transaction;

(*6*) Intangible property associated with the sale;

(*7*) Foreign currency risks; and

(*8*) Alternatives realistically available to the buyer and seller.

(iii) *Data and assumptions.* The reliability of the results derived from the comparable uncontrolled price method is affected by the completeness and accuracy of the data used and the reliability of the assumptions made to apply the method. See § 1.482-1(c) (Best method rule).

(3) *Arm's length range.* See § 1.482-1(e)(2) for the determination of an arm's length range.

(4) *Examples.* The principles of this paragraph (b) are illustrated by the following examples.

Reg. § 1.482-3(b)(4)

Example 1—Comparable Sales of Same Product. USM, a U.S. manufacturer, sells the same product to both controlled and uncontrolled distributors. The circumstances surrounding the controlled and uncontrolled transactions are substantially the same, except that the controlled sales price is a delivered price and the uncontrolled sales are made f.o.b. USM's factory. Differences in the contractual terms of transportation and insurance generally have a definite and reasonably ascertainable effect on price, and adjustments are made to the results of the uncontrolled transaction to account for such differences. No other material difference has been identified between the controlled and uncontrolled transactions. Because USM sells in both the controlled and uncontrolled transactions, it is likely that all material differences between the two transactions have been identified. In addition, because the comparable uncontrolled price method is applied to an uncontrolled comparable with no product differences, and there are only minor contractual differences that have a definite and reasonably ascertainable effect on price, the results of this application of the comparable uncontrolled price method will provide the most direct and reliable measure of an arm's length result. See § 1.482-3(b)(2)(ii)(A).

Example 2—Effect of Trademark. The facts are the same as in *Example 1*, except that USM affixes its valuable trademark to the property sold in the controlled transactions, but does not affix its trademark to the property sold in the uncontrolled transactions. Under the facts of this case, the effect on price of the trademark is material and cannot be reliably estimated. Because there are material product differences for which reliable adjustments cannot be made, the comparable uncontrolled price method is unlikely to provide a reliable measure of the arm's length result. See § 1.482-3(b)(2)(ii)(A).

Example 3—Minor Product Differences. The facts are the same as in *Example 1*, except that USM, which manufactures business machines, makes minor modifications to the physical properties of the machines to satisfy specific requirements of a customer in controlled sales, but does not make these modifications in uncontrolled sales. If the minor physical differences in the product have a material affect on prices, adjustments to account for these differences must be made to the results of the uncontrolled transactions according to the provisions of § 1.482-1(d)(2), and such adjusted results may be used as a measure of the arm's length result.

Example 4—Effect of Geographic Differences. FM, a foreign specialty radio manufacturer, sells its radios to a controlled U.S. distributor, AM, that serves the West Coast of the United States. FM sells its radios to uncontrolled distributors to serve other regions in the United States. The product in the controlled and uncontrolled transactions is the same, and all other circumstances surrounding the controlled and uncontrolled transactions are substantially the same, other than the geographic differences. If the geographic differences are unlikely to have a material effect on price, or they have definite and reasonably ascertainable effects for which adjustments are made, then the adjusted results of the uncontrolled sales may be used under the comparable uncontrolled price method to establish an arm's length range pursuant to § 1.482-1(e)(2)(iii)(A). If the effects of the geographic differences would be material but cannot be reliably ascertained, then the reliability of the results will be diminished. However, the comparable uncontrolled price method may still provide the most reliable measure of an arm's length result, pursuant to the best method rule of § 1.482-1(c), and, if so, an arm's length range may be established pursuant to § 1.482-1(e)(2)(iii)(B).

(5) *Indirect evidence of comparable uncontrolled transactions*—(i) *In general.* A comparable uncontrolled price may be derived from data from public exchanges or quotation media, but only if the following requirements are met—

(A) The data is widely and routinely used in the ordinary course of business in the industry to negotiate prices for uncontrolled sales;

(B) The data derived from public exchanges or quotation media is used to set prices in the controlled transaction in the same way it is used by uncontrolled taxpayers in the industry; and

(C) The amount charged in the controlled transaction is adjusted to reflect differences in product quality and quantity, contractual terms, transportation costs, market conditions, risks borne, and other factors that affect the price that would be agreed to by uncontrolled taxpayers.

(ii) *Limitation.* Use of data from public exchanges or quotation media may not be appropriate under extraordinary market conditions.

(iii) *Examples.* The following examples illustrate this paragraph (b)(5).

Example 1—Use of Quotation Medium. (i) On June 1, USOil, a United States corporation, enters into a contract to purchase crude oil from its foreign subsidiary, FS, in Country Z. USOil and FS agree to base their sales price on the average of the prices published for that crude in a quotation medium in the five days before August

Reg. § 1.482-3(b)(5)

1, the date set for delivery. USOil and FS agree to adjust the price for the particular circumstances of their transactions, including the quantity of the crude sold, contractual terms, transportation costs, risks borne, and other factors that affect the price.

(ii) The quotation medium used by USOil and FS is widely and routinely used in the ordinary course of business in the industry to establish prices for uncontrolled sales. Because USOil and FS use the data to set their sales price in the same way that unrelated parties use the data from the quotation medium to set their sales prices, and appropriate adjustments were made to account for differences, the price derived from the quotation medium used by USOil and FS to set their transfer prices will be considered evidence of a comparable uncontrolled price.

Example 2—Extraordinary Market Conditions. The facts are the same as in *Example 1,* except that before USOil and FS enter into their contract, war breaks out in Countries X and Y, major oil producing countries, causing significant instability in world petroleum markets. As a result, given the significant instability in the price of oil, the prices listed on the quotation medium may not reflect a reliable measure of an arm's length result. See § 1.482-3(b)(5)(ii).

(c) *Resale price method*—(1) *In general.* The resale price method evaluates whether the amount charged in a controlled transaction is arm's length by reference to the gross profit margin realized in comparable uncontrolled transactions. The resale price method measures the value of functions performed, and is ordinarily used in cases involving the purchase and resale of tangible property in which the reseller has not added substantial value to the tangible goods by physically altering the goods before resale. For this purpose, packaging, repackaging, labelling, or minor assembly do not ordinarily constitute physical alteration. Further the resale price method is not ordinarily used in cases where the controlled taxpayer uses its intangible property to add substantial value to the tangible goods.

(2) *Determination of arm's length price*—(i) *In general.* The resale price method measures an arm's length price by subtracting the appropriate gross profit from the applicable resale price for the property involved in the controlled transaction under review.

(ii) *Applicable resale price.* The applicable resale price is equal to either the resale price of the particular item of property involved or the price at which contemporaneous resales of the same property are made. If the property purchased in the controlled sale is resold to one or more related parties in a series of controlled sales before being resold in an uncontrolled sale, the applicable resale price is the price at which the property is resold to an uncontrolled party, or the price at which contemporaneous resales of the same property are made. In such case, the determination of the appropriate gross profit will take into account the functions of all members of the group participating in the series of controlled sales and final uncontrolled resales, as well as any other relevant factors described in § 1.482-1(d)(3).

(iii) *Appropriate gross profit.* The appropriate gross profit is computed by multiplying the applicable resale price by the gross profit margin (expressed as a percentage of total revenue derived from sales) earned in comparable uncontrolled transactions.

(iv) *Arm's length range.* See § 1.482-1(e)(2) for determination of the arm's length range.

(3) *Comparability and reliability considerations*—(i) *In general.* Whether results derived from applications of this method are the most reliable measure of the arm's length result must be determined using the factors described under the best method rule in § 1.482-1(c). The application of these factors under the resale price method is discussed in paragraphs (c)(3)(ii) and (iii) of this section.

(ii) *Comparability*—(A) *Functional comparability.* The degree of comparability between an uncontrolled transaction and a controlled transaction is determined by applying the comparability provisions of § 1.482-1(d). A reseller's gross profit provides compensation for the performance of resale functions related to the product or products under review, including an operating profit in return for the reseller's investment of capital and the assumption of risks. Therefore, although all of the factors described in § 1.482-1(d)(3) must be considered, comparability under this method is particularly dependent on similarity of functions performed, risks borne, and contractual terms, or adjustments to account for the effects of any such differences. If possible, appropriate gross profit margins should be derived from comparable uncontrolled purchases and resales of the reseller involved in the controlled sale, because similar characteristics are more likely to be found among different resales of property made by the same reseller than among sales made by other resellers. In the absence of comparable uncontrolled transactions involving the same reseller, an appropriate gross profit margin may be derived from comparable uncontrolled transactions of other resellers.

Reg. § 1.482-3(c)(3)

37,224
Adjustments
See p. 20,601 for regulations not amended to reflect law changes

(B) *Other comparability factors.* Comparability under this method is less dependent on close physical similarity between the products transferred than under the comparable uncontrolled price method. For example, distributors of a wide variety of consumer durables might perform comparable distribution functions without regard to the specific durable goods distributed. Substantial differences in the products may, however, indicate significant functional differences between the controlled and uncontrolled taxpayers. Thus, it ordinarily would be expected that the controlled and uncontrolled transactions would involve the distribution of products of the same general type (e.g., consumer electronics). Furthermore, significant differences in the value of the distributed goods due, for example, to the value of a trademark, may also affect the reliability of the comparison. Finally, the reliability of profit measures based on gross profit may be adversely affected by factors that have less effect on prices. For example, gross profit may be affected by a variety of other factors, including cost structures (as reflected, for example, in the age of plant and equipment), business experience (such as whether the business is in a start-up phase or is mature), or management efficiency (as indicated, for example, by expanding or contracting sales or executive compensation over time). Accordingly, if material differences in these factors are identified based on objective evidence, the reliability of the analysis may be affected.

(C) *Adjustments for differences between controlled and uncontrolled transactions.* If there are material differences between the controlled and uncontrolled transactions that would affect the gross profit margin, adjustments should be made to the gross profit margin earned with respect to the uncontrolled transaction according to the comparability provisions of § 1.482-1(d)(2). For this purpose, consideration of operating expenses associated with functions performed and risks assumed may be necessary, because differences in functions performed are often reflected in operating expenses. If there are differences in functions performed, however, the effect on gross profit of such differences is not necessarily equal to the differences in the amount of related operating expenses. Specific examples of the factors that may be particularly relevant to this method include—

(*1*) Inventory levels and turnover rates, and corresponding risks, including any price protection programs offered by the manufacturer;

(*2*) Contractual terms (e.g., scope and terms of warranties provided, sales or purchase volume, credit terms, transport terms);

(*3*) Sales, marketing, advertising programs and services, (including promotional programs, rebates, and co-op advertising);

(*4*) The level of the market (e.g., wholesale, retail, etc.); and

(*5*) Foreign currency risks.

(D) *Sales agent.* If the controlled taxpayer is comparable to a sales agent that does not take title to goods or otherwise assume risks with respect to ownership of such goods, the commission earned by such sales agent, expressed as a percentage of the uncontrolled sales price of the goods involved, may be used as the comparable gross profit margin.

(iii) *Data and assumptions*—(A) *In general.* The reliability of the results derived from the resale price method is affected by the completeness and accuracy of the data used and the reliability of the assumptions made to apply this method. See § 1.482-1(c) (Best method rule).

(B) *Consistency in accounting.* The degree of consistency in accounting practices between the controlled transaction and the uncontrolled comparables that materially affect the gross profit margin affects the reliability of the result. Thus, for example, if differences in inventory and other cost accounting practices would materially affect the gross profit margin, the ability to make reliable adjustments for such differences would affect the reliability of the results. Further, the controlled transaction and the uncontrolled comparable should be consistent in the reporting of items (such as discounts, returns and allowances, rebates, transportation costs, insurance, and packaging) between cost of goods sold and operating expenses.

(4) *Examples.* The following examples illustrate the principles of this paragraph (c).

Example 1. A controlled taxpayer sells property to another member of its controlled group that resells the property in uncontrolled sales. There are no changes in the beginning and ending inventory for the year under review. Information regarding an uncontrolled comparable is sufficiently complete to conclude that it is likely that all material differences between the controlled and uncontrolled transactions have been identified and adjusted for. If the applicable resale price of the property involved in the controlled sale is $100 and the appropriate gross profit margin is 20%, then an arm's length result of the controlled sale is a price of $80 ($100 minus (20% × $100)).

Example 2. (i) S, a U.S. corporation, is the exclusive distributor for FP, its foreign parent. There are no changes in the beginning and ending

Reg. § 1.482-3(c)(4)

inventory for the year under review. S's total reported cost of goods sold is $800, consisting of $600 for property purchased from FP and $200 of other costs of goods sold incurred to unrelated parties. S's applicable resale price and reported gross profit are as follows:

Applicable resale price	$1000
Cost of goods sold	
Cost of purchases from FP	600
Costs incurred to unrelated parties	200
Reported gross profit	$ 200

(ii) The district director determines that the appropriate gross profit margin is 25%. Therefore, S's appropriate gross profit is $250 (i.e., 25% of the applicable resale price of $1000). Because S is incurring costs of sales to unrelated parties, an arm's length price for property purchased from FP must be determined under a two-step process. First, the appropriate gross profit ($250) is subtracted from the applicable resale price ($1000). The resulting amount ($750) is then reduced by the costs of sales incurred to unrelated parties ($200). Therefore, an arm's length price for S's cost of sales of FP's product in this case equals $550 (i.e., $750 minus $200).

Example 3. FP, a foreign manufacturer, sells Product to USSub, its U.S. subsidiary, which in turn sells Product to its domestic affiliate Sister. Sister sells Product to unrelated buyers. In this case, the applicable resale price is the price at which Sister sells Product in uncontrolled transactions. The determination of the appropriate gross profit margin for the sale from FP to USSub will take into account the functions performed by USSub and Sister, as well as other relevant factors described in § 1.482-1(d)(3).

Example 4. USSub, a U.S. corporation, is the exclusive distributor of widgets for its foreign parent. To determine whether the gross profit margin of 25% earned by USSub is an arm's length result, the district director considers applying the resale price method. There are several uncontrolled distributors that perform similar functions under similar circumstances in uncontrolled transactions. However, the uncontrolled distributors treat certain costs such as discounts and insurance as cost of goods sold, while USSub treats such costs as operating expenses. In such cases, accounting reclassifications, pursuant to § 1.482-3(c)(3)(iii)(B), must be made to ensure consistent treatment of such material items. Inability to make such accounting reclassifications will decrease the reliability of the results of the uncontrolled transactions.

Example 5. (i) USP, a U.S. corporation, manufactures Product X, an unbranded widget, and sells it to FSub, its wholly owned foreign subsidiary. FSub acts as a distributor of Product X in country M, and sells it to uncontrolled parties in that country. Uncontrolled distributors A, B, C, D, and E distribute competing products of approximately similar value in country M. All such products are unbranded.

(ii) Relatively complete data is available regarding the functions performed and risks borne by the uncontrolled distributors and the contractual terms under which they operate in the uncontrolled transactions. In addition, data is available to ensure accounting consistency between all of the uncontrolled distributors and FSub. Because the available data is sufficiently complete and accurate to conclude that it is likely that all material differences between the controlled and uncontrolled transactions have been identified, such differences have a definite and reasonably ascertainable effect, and reliable adjustments are made to account for such differences, the results of each of the uncontrolled distributors may be used to establish an arm's length range pursuant to § 1.482-1(e)(2)(iii)(A).

Example 6. The facts are the same as *Example 5,* except that sufficient data is not available to determine whether any of the uncontrolled distributors provide warranties or to determine the payment terms of the contracts. Because differences in these contractual terms could materially affect price or profits, the inability to determine whether these differences exist between the controlled and uncontrolled transactions diminishes the reliability of the results of the uncontrolled comparables. However, the reliability of the results may be enhanced by the application of a statistical method when establishing an arm's length range pursuant to § 1.4821(e)(2)(iii)(B).

Example 7. The facts are the same as in *Example 5,* except that Product X is branded with a valuable trademark that is owned by P. A, B, and C distribute unbranded competing products, while D and E distribute products branded with other trademarks. D and E do not own any rights in the trademarks under which their products are sold. The value of the products that A, B, and C sold are not similar to the value of the products sold by S. The value of products sold by D and E, however, is similar to that of Product X. Although close product similarity is not as important for a reliable application of the resale price method as for the comparable uncontrolled price method, significant differences in the value of the

Reg. § 1.482-3(c)(4)

products involved in the controlled and uncontrolled transactions may affect the reliability of the results. In addition, because in this case it is difficult to determine the effect the trademark will have on price or profits, reliable adjustments for the differences cannot be made. Because D and E have a higher level of comparability than A, B, and C with respect to S, pursuant to § 1.482-1(e)(2)(ii), only D and E may be included in an arm's length range.

(d) *Cost plus method*—(1) *In general.* The cost plus method evaluates whether the amount charged in a controlled transaction is arm's length by reference to the gross profit markup realized in comparable uncontrolled transactions. The cost plus method is ordinarily used in cases involving the manufacture, assembly, or other production of goods that are sold to related parties.

(2) *Determination of arm's length price*—(i) *In general.* The cost plus method measures an arm's length price by adding the appropriate gross profit to the controlled taxpayer's costs of producing the property involved in the controlled transaction.

(ii) *Appropriate gross profit.* The appropriate gross profit is computed by multiplying the controlled taxpayer's cost of producing the transferred property by the gross profit markup, expressed as a percentage of cost, earned in comparable uncontrolled transactions.

(iii) *Arm's length range.* See § 1.482-1(e)(2) for determination of an arm's length range.

(3) *Comparability and reliability considerations*—(i) *In general.* Whether results derived from the application of this method are the most reliable measure of the arm's length result must be determined using the factors described under the best method rule in § 1.482-1(c).

(ii) *Comparability*—(A) *Functional comparability.* The degree of comparability between controlled and uncontrolled transactions is determined by applying the comparability provisions of § 1.482-1(d). A producer's gross profit provides compensation for the performance of the production functions related to the product or products under review, including an operating profit for the producer's investment of capital and assumption of risks. Therefore, although all of the factors described in § 1.482-1(d)(3) must be considered, comparability under this method is particularly dependent on similarity of functions performed, risks borne, and contractual terms, or adjustments to account for the effects of any such differences. If possible, the appropriate gross profit markup should be derived from comparable uncontrolled transactions of the taxpayer involved in the controlled sale, because similar characteristics are more likely to be found among sales of property by the same producer than among sales by other producers. In the absence of such sales, an appropriate gross profit markup may be derived from comparable uncontrolled sales of other producers whether or not such producers are members of the same controlled group.

(B) *Other comparability factors.* Comparability under this method is less dependent on close physical similarity between the products transferred than under the comparable uncontrolled price method. Substantial differences in the products may, however, indicate significant functional differences between the controlled and uncontrolled taxpayers. Thus, it ordinarily would be expected that the controlled and uncontrolled transactions involve the production of goods within the same product categories. Furthermore, significant differences in the value of the products due, for example, to the value of a trademark, may also affect the reliability of the comparison. Finally, the reliability of profit measures based on gross profit may be adversely affected by factors that have less effect on prices. For example, gross profit may be affected by a variety of other factors, including cost structures (as reflected, for example, in the age of plant and equipment), business experience (such as whether the business is in a start-up phase or is mature), or management efficiency (as indicated, for example, by expanding or contracting sales or executive compensation over time). Accordingly, if material differences in these factors are identified based on objective evidence, the reliability of the analysis may be affected.

(C) *Adjustments for differences between controlled and uncontrolled transactions.* If there are material differences between the controlled and uncontrolled transactions that would affect the gross profit markup, adjustments should be made to the gross profit markup earned in the comparable uncontrolled transaction according to the provisions of § 1.482-1(d)(2). For this purpose, consideration of the operating expenses associated with the functions performed and risks assumed may be necessary, because differences in functions performed are often reflected in operating expenses. If there are differences in functions performed, however, the effect on gross profit of such differences is not necessarily equal to the differences in the amount of related operating expenses. Specific examples of the factors that may be particularly relevant to this method include—

(*1*) The complexity of manufacturing or assembly;

Reg. § 1.482-3(d)(1)

(2) Manufacturing, production, and process engineering;

(3) Procurement, purchasing, and inventory control activities;

(4) Testing functions;

(5) Selling, general, and administrative expenses;

(6) Foreign currency risks; and

(7) Contractual terms (e.g., scope and terms of warranties provided, sales or purchase volume, credit terms, transport terms).

(D) *Purchasing agent.* If a controlled taxpayer is comparable to a purchasing agent that does not take title to property or otherwise assume risks with respect to ownership of such goods, the commission earned by such purchasing agent, expressed as a percentage of the purchase price of the goods, may be used as the appropriate gross profit markup.

(iii) *Data and assumptions*—(A) *In general.* The reliability of the results derived from the cost plus method is affected by the completeness and accuracy of the data used and the reliability of the assumptions made to apply this method. See § 1.482-1(c) (Best method rule).

(B) *Consistency in accounting.* The degree of consistency in accounting practices between the controlled transaction and the uncontrolled comparables that materially affect the gross profit markup affects the reliability of the result. Thus, for example, if differences in inventory and other cost accounting practices would materially affect the gross profit markup, the ability to make reliable adjustments for such differences would affect the reliability of the results. Further, the controlled transaction and the comparable uncontrolled transaction should be consistent in the reporting of costs between cost of goods sold and operating expenses. The term *cost of producing* includes the cost of acquiring property that is held for resale.

(4) *Examples.* The following examples illustrate the principles of this paragraph (d).

Example 1. (i) USP, a domestic manufacturer of computer components, sells its products to FS, its foreign distributor. UT1, UT2, and UT3 are domestic computer component manufacturers that sell to uncontrolled foreign purchasers.

(ii) Relatively complete data is available regarding the functions performed and risks borne by UT1, UT2, and UT3, and the contractual terms in the uncontrolled transactions. In addition, data is available to ensure accounting consistency between all of the uncontrolled manufacturers and USP. Because the available data is sufficiently complete to conclude that it is likely that all material differences between the controlled and uncontrolled transactions have been identified, the effect of the differences are definite and reasonably ascertainable, and reliable adjustments are made to account for the differences, an arm's length range can be established pursuant to § 1.482-1(e)(2)(iii)(A).

Example 2. The facts are the same as in *Example 1,* except that USP accounts for supervisory, general, and administrative costs as operating expenses, which are not allocated to its sales to FS. The gross profit markups of UT1, UT2, and UT3, however, reflect supervisory, general, and administrative expenses because they are accounted for as costs of goods sold. Accordingly, the gross profit markups of UT1, UT2, and UT3 must be adjusted as provided in paragraph (d)(3)(iii)(B) of this section to provide accounting consistency. If data is not sufficient to determine whether such accounting differences exist between the controlled and uncontrolled transactions, the reliability of the results will be decreased.

Example 3. The facts are the same as in *Example 1,* except that under its contract with FS, USP uses materials consigned by FS. UT1, UT2, and UT3, on the other hand, purchase their own materials, and their gross profit markups are determined by including the costs of materials. The fact that USP does not carry an inventory risk by purchasing its own materials while the uncontrolled producers carry inventory is a significant difference that may require an adjustment if the difference has a material effect on the gross profit markups of the uncontrolled producers. Inability to reasonably ascertain the effect of the difference on the gross profit markups will affect the reliability of the results of UT1, UT2, and UT3.

Example 4. (i) FS, a foreign corporation, produces apparel for USP, its U.S. parent corporation. FS purchases its materials from unrelated suppliers and produces the apparel according to designs provided by USP. The district director identifies 10 uncontrolled foreign apparel producers that operate in the same geographic market and are similar in many respect to FS.

(ii) Relatively complete data is available regarding the functions performed and risks borne by the uncontrolled producers. In addition, data is sufficiently detailed to permit adjustments for differences in accounting practices. However, sufficient data is not available to determine whether it is likely that all material differences in contractual terms have been identified. For example, it is not possible to determine which parties in the uncontrolled transactions bear currency risks. Because differences in these contractual terms could

Reg. § 1.482-3(d)(4)

materially affect price or profits, the inability to determine whether differences exist between the controlled and uncontrolled transactions will diminish the reliability of these results. Therefore, the reliability of the results of the uncontrolled transactions must be enhanced by the application of a statistical method in establishing an arm's length range pursuant to § 1.482-1(e)(2)(iii)(B).

(e) *Unspecified methods*—(1) *In general.* Methods not specified in paragraphs (a)(1), (2), (3), (4), and (5) of this section may be used to evaluate whether the amount charged in a controlled transaction is arm's length. Any method used under this paragraph (e) must be applied in accordance with the provisions of § 1.482-1. Consistent with the specified methods, an unspecified method should take into account the general principle that uncontrolled taxpayers evaluate the terms of a transaction by considering the realistic alternatives to that transaction, and only enter into a particular transaction if none of the alternatives is preferable to it. For example, the comparable uncontrolled price method compares a controlled transaction to similar uncontrolled transactions to provide a direct estimate of the price to which the parties would have agreed had they resorted directly to a market alternative to the controlled transaction. Therefore, in establishing whether a controlled transaction achieved an arm's length result, an unspecified method should provide information on the prices or profits that the controlled taxpayer could have realized by choosing a realistic alternative to the controlled transaction. As with any method, an unspecified method will not be applied unless it provides the most reliable measure of an arm's length result under the principles of the best method rule. See § 1.482-1(c). Therefore, in accordance with § 1.482-1(d) (Comparability), to the extent that a method relies on internal data rather than uncontrolled comparables, its reliability will be reduced. Similarly, the reliability of a method will be affected by the reliability of the data and assumptions used to apply the method, including any projections used.

(2) *Example.* The following example illustrates an application of the principle of this paragraph (e).

Example. Amcan, a U.S. company, produces unique vessels for storing and transporting toxic waste, toxicans, at its U.S. production facility. Amcan agrees by contract to supply its Canadian subsidiary, Cancan, with 4000 toxicans per year to serve the Canadian market for toxicans. Prior to entering into the contract with Cancan, Amcan had received a bona fide offer from an independent Canadian waste disposal company, Cando, to serve as the Canadian distributor for toxicans and to purchase a similar number of toxicans at a price of $5,000 each. If the circumstances and terms of the Cancan supply contract are sufficiently similar to those of the Cando offer, or sufficiently reliable adjustments can be made for differences between them, then the Cando offer price of $5,000 may provide reliable information indicating that an arm's length consideration under the Cancan contract will not be less than $5,000 per toxican.

(f) *Coordination with intangible property rules.* The value of an item of tangible property may be affected by the value of intangible property, such as a trademark affixed to the tangible property (embedded intangible). Ordinarily, the transfer of tangible property with an embedded intangible will not be considered a transfer of such intangible if the controlled purchaser does not acquire any rights to exploit the intangible property other than rights relating to the resale of the tangible property under normal commercial practices. Pursuant to § 1.482-1(d)(3)(v), however, the embedded intangible must be accounted for in evaluating the comparability of the controlled transaction and uncontrolled comparables. For example, because product comparability has the greatest effect on an application of the comparable uncontrolled price method, trademarked tangible property may be insufficiently comparable to unbranded tangible property to permit a reliable application of the comparable uncontrolled price method. The effect of embedded intangibles on comparability will be determined under the principles of § 1.482-4. If the transfer of tangible property conveys to the recipient a right to exploit an embedded intangible (other than in connection with the resale of that item of tangible property), it may be necessary to determine the arm's length consideration for such intangible separately from the tangible property, applying methods appropriate to determining the arm's length result for a transfer of intangible property under § 1.482-4. For example, if the transfer of a machine conveys the right to exploit a manufacturing process incorporated in the machine, then the arm's length consideration for the transfer of that right must be determined separately under § 1.482-4. [Reg. § 1.482-3.]

☐ [*T.D.* 8552, 7-1-94.]

[Reg. § 1.482-4]

§ 1.482-4. **Methods to determine taxable income in connection with a transfer of intangible property.**—(a) *In general.* The arm's length amount charged in a controlled transfer of intangible property must be determined under one of the four methods listed in this paragraph (a). Each of the methods must be applied in accor-

Adjustments

dance with all of the provisions of § 1.482-1, including the best method rule of § 1.482-1(c), the comparability analysis of § 1.482-1(d), and the arm's length range of § 1.482-1(e). The arm's length consideration for the transfer of an intangible determined under this section must be commensurate with the income attributable to the intangible. See § 1.482-4(f)(2) (Periodic adjustments). The available methods are—

(1) The comparable uncontrolled transaction method, described in paragraph (c) of this section;

(2) The comparable profits method, described in § 1.482-5;

(3) The profit split method, described in § 1.482-6; and

(4) Unspecified methods described in paragraph (d) of this section.

(b) *Definition of intangible.* For purposes of section 482, an intangible is an asset that comprises any of the following items and has substantial value independent of the services of any individual—

(1) Patents, inventions, formulae, processes, designs, patterns, or know-how;

(2) Copyrights and literary, musical, or artistic compositions;

(3) Trademarks, trade names, or brand names;

(4) Franchises, licenses, or contracts;

(5) Methods, programs, systems, procedures, campaigns, surveys, studies, forecasts, estimates, customer lists, or technical data; and

(6) Other similar items. For purposes of section 482, an item is considered similar to those listed in paragraph (b)(1) through (5) of this section if it derives its value not from its physical attributes but from its intellectual content or other intangible properties.

(c) *Comparable uncontrolled transaction method*—(1) *In general.* The comparable uncontrolled transaction method evaluates whether the amount charged for a controlled transfer of intangible property was arm's length by reference to the amount charged in a comparable uncontrolled transaction. The amount determined under this method may be adjusted as required by paragraph (f)(2) of this section (Periodic adjustments).

(2) *Comparability and reliability considerations*—(i) *In general.* Whether results derived from applications of this method are the most reliable measure of an arm's length result is determined using the factors described under the best method rule in § 1.482-1(c). The application of these factors under the comparable uncontrolled transaction method is discussed in paragraphs (c)(2)(ii), (iii), and (iv) of this section.

(ii) *Reliability.* If an uncontrolled transaction involves the transfer of the same intangible under the same, or substantially the same, circumstances as the controlled transaction, the results derived from applying the comparable uncontrolled transaction method will generally be the most direct and reliable measure of the arm's length result for the controlled transfer of an intangible. Circumstances between the controlled and uncontrolled transactions will be considered substantially the same if there are at most only minor differences that have a definite and reasonably ascertainable effect on the amount charged and for which appropriate adjustments are made. If such uncontrolled transactions cannot be identified, uncontrolled transactions that involve the transfer of comparable intangibles under comparable circumstances may be used to apply this method, but the reliability of the analysis will be reduced.

(iii) *Comparability*—(A) *In general.* The degree of comparability between controlled and uncontrolled transactions is determined by applying the comparability provisions of § 1.482-1(d). Although all of the factors described in § 1.482-1(d)(3) must be considered, specific factors may be particularly relevant to this method. In particular, the application of this method requires that the controlled and uncontrolled transactions involve either the same intangible property or comparable intangible property, as defined in paragraph (c)(2)(iii)(B)(*1*) of this section. In addition, because differences in contractual terms, or the economic conditions in which transactions take place, could materially affect the amount charged, comparability under this method also depends on similarity with respect to these factors, or adjustments to account for material differences in such circumstances.

(B) *Factors to be considered in determining comparability*—(*1*) *Comparable intangible property.* In order for the intangible property involved in an uncontrolled transaction to be considered comparable to the intangible property involved in the controlled transaction, both intangibles must—

(*i*) Be used in connection with similar products or processes within the same general industry or market; and

(*ii*) Have similar profit potential. The profit potential of an intangible is most reliably measured by directly calculating the net present value of the benefits to be realized (based on prospective profits to be realized or costs to be saved) through the use or subsequent transfer of

Reg. § 1.482-4(c)(2)

the intangible, considering the capital investment and start-up expenses required, the risks to be assumed, and other relevant considerations. The need to reliably measure profit potential increases in relation to both the total amount of potential profits and the potential rate of return on investment necessary to exploit the intangible. If the information necessary to directly calculate net present value of the benefits to be realized is unavailable, and the need to reliably measure profit potential is reduced because the potential profits are relatively small in terms of total amount and rate of return, comparison of profit potential may be based upon the factors referred to in paragraph (c)(2)(iii)(B)(*2*) of this section. See *Example 3* of § 1.482-4(c)(4). Finally, the reliability of a measure of profit potential is affected by the extent to which the profit attributable to the intangible can be isolated from the profit attributable to other factors, such as functions performed and other resources employed.

(*2*) *Comparable circumstances.* In evaluating the comparability of the circumstances of the controlled and uncontrolled transactions, although all of the factors described in § 1.482-1(d)(3) must be considered, specific factors that may be particularly relevant to this method include the following—

(*i*) The terms of the transfer, including the exploitation rights granted in the intangible, the exclusive or nonexclusive character of any rights granted, any restrictions on use, or any limitations on the geographic area in which the rights may be exploited;

(*ii*) The stage of development of the intangible (including, where appropriate, necessary governmental approvals, authorizations, or licenses) in the market in which the intangible is to be used;

(*iii*) Rights to receive updates, revisions, or modifications of the intangible;

(*iv*) The uniqueness of the property and the period for which it remains unique, including the degree and duration of protection afforded to the property under the laws of the relevant countries;

(*v*) The duration of the license, contract, or other agreement, and any termination or renegotiation rights;

(*vi*) Any economic and product liability risks to be assumed by the transferee;

(*vii*) The existence and extent of any collateral transactions or ongoing business relationships between the transferee and transferor; and

(*viii*) The functions to be performed by the transferor and transferee, including any ancillary or subsidiary services.

(*iv*) *Data and assumptions.* The reliability of the results derived from the comparable uncontrolled transaction method is affected by the completeness and accuracy of the data used and the reliability of the assumptions made to apply this method. See § 1.482-1(c) (Best method rule).

(3) *Arm's length range.* See § 1.482-1(e)(2) for the determination of an arm's length range.

(4) *Examples.* The following examples illustrate the principles of this paragraph (c).

Example 1. (i) USpharm, a U.S. pharmaceutical company, develops a new drug Z that is a safe and effective treatment for the disease zeezee. USpharm has obtained patents covering drug Z in the United States and in various foreign countries. USpharm has also obtained the regulatory authorizations necessary to market drug Z in the United States and in foreign countries.

(ii) USpharm licenses its subsidiary in country X, Xpharm, to produce and sell drug Z in country X. At the same time, it licenses an unrelated company, Ydrug, to produce and sell drug Z in country Y, a neighboring country. Prior to licensing the drug, USpharm had obtained patent protection and regulatory approvals in both countries and both countries provide similar protection for intellectual property rights. Country X and country Y are similar countries in terms of population, per capita income and the incidence of disease zeezee. Consequently, drug Z is expected to sell in similar quantities and at similar prices in both countries. In addition, costs of producing and marketing drug Z in each country are expected to be approximately the same.

(iii) USpharm and Xpharm establish terms for the license of drug Z that are identical in every material respect, including royalty rate, to the terms established between USpharm and Ydrug. In this case the district director determines that the royalty rate established in the Ydrug license agreement is a reliable measure of the arm's length royalty rate for the Xpharm license agreement.

Example 2. The facts are the same as in *Example 1,* except that the incidence of the disease zeezee in Country Y is much higher than in Country X. In this case, the profit potential from exploitation of the right to make and sell drug Z is likely to be much higher in country Y than it is in Country X. Consequently, the Ydrug license agreement is unlikely to provide a reliable measure of the arm's length royalty rate for the Xpharm license.

Reg. § 1.482-4(c)(3)

Example 3. (i) FP is a foreign company that designs, manufactures and sells industrial equipment. FP has developed proprietary components that are incorporated in its products. These components are important in the operation of FP's equipment and some of them have distinctive features, but other companies produce similar components and none of these components by itself accounts for a substantial part of the value of FP's products.

(ii) FP licenses its U.S. subsidiary, USSub, exclusive North American rights to use the patented technology for producing component X, a heat exchanger used for cooling operating mechanisms in industrial equipment. Component X incorporates proven technology that makes it somewhat more efficient than the heat exchangers commonly used in industrial equipment. FP also agrees to provide technical support to help adapt component X to USSub's products and to assist with initial production. Under the terms of the license agreement USSub pays FP a royalty equal to 3 percent of sales of USSub equipment incorporating component X.

(iii) FP does not license unrelated parties to use component X, but many similar components are transferred between uncontrolled taxpayers. Consequently, the district director decides to apply the comparable uncontrolled transaction method to evaluate whether the 3 percent royalty for component X is an arm's length royalty.

(iv) The district director uses a database of company documents filed with the Securities and Exchange Commission (SEC) to identify potentially comparable license agreements between uncontrolled taxpayers that are on file with the SEC. The district director identifies 40 license agreements that were entered into in the same year as the controlled transfer or in the prior or following year, and that relate to transfers of technology associated with industrial equipment that has similar applications to USSub's products. Further review of these uncontrolled agreements indicates that 25 of them involved components that have a similar level of technical sophistication as component X and could be expected to play a similar role in contributing to the total value of the final product.

(v) The district director makes a detailed review of the terms of each of the 25 uncontrolled agreements and finds that 15 of them are similar to the controlled agreement in that they all involve—

(A) The transfer of exclusive rights for the North American market;

(B) Products for which the market could be expected to be of a similar size to the market for the products into which USSub incorporates component X;

(C) The transfer of patented technology;

(D) Continuing technical support;

(E) Access to technical improvements;

(F) Technology of a similar age; and

(G) A similar duration of the agreement.

(vi) Based on these factors and the fact that none of the components to which these license agreements relate accounts for a substantial part of the value of the final products, the district director concludes that these fifteen intangibles have similar profit potential to the component X technology.

(vii) The 15 uncontrolled comparables produce the following royalty rates:

License	Royalty rate (percent)
1	1.0
2	1.0
3	1.25
4	1.25
5	1.5
6	1.5
7	1.75
8	2.0
9	2.0
10	2.0
11	2.25
12	2.5
13	2.5
14	2.75
15	3.0

(viii) Although the uncontrolled comparables are clearly similar to the controlled transaction, it is likely that unidentified material differences exist between the uncontrolled comparables and the controlled transaction. Therefore, an appropriate statistical technique must be used to establish the arm's length range. In this case the district director uses the interquartile range to determine the

Reg. § 1.482-4(c)(4)

arm's length range. Therefore, the arm's length range covers royalty rates from 1.25 to 2.5 percent, and an adjustment is warranted to the 3 percent royalty charged in the controlled transfer. The district director determines that the appropriate adjustment corresponds to a reduction in the royalty rate to 2.0 percent, which is the median of the uncontrolled comparables.

Example 4. (i) USdrug, a U.S. pharmaceutical company, has developed a new drug, Nosplit, that is useful in treating migraine headaches and produces no significant side effects. Nosplit replaces another drug, Lessplit, that USdrug had previously produced and marketed as a treatment for migraine headaches. A number of other drugs for treating migraine headaches are already on the market, but Nosplit can be expected rapidly to dominate the worldwide market for such treatments and to command a premium price since all other treatments produce side effects. Thus, USdrug projects that extraordinary profits will be derived from Nosplit in the U.S. market and other markets.

(ii) USdrug licenses its newly established European subsidiary, Eurodrug, the rights to produce and market Nosplit in the European market. In setting the royalty rate for this license, USdrug considers the royalty that it established previously when it licensed the right to produce and market Lessplit in the European market to an unrelated European pharmaceutical company. In many respects the two license agreements are closely comparable. The drugs were licensed at the same stage in their development and the agreements conveyed identical rights to the licensees. Moreover, there appear to have been no significant changes in the European market for migraine headache treatments since Lessplit was licensed. However, at the time that Lessplit was licensed there were several other similar drugs already on the market to which Lessplit was not in all cases superior. Consequently, the projected and actual Lessplit profits were substantially less than the projected Nosplit profits. Thus, USdrug concludes that the profit potential of Lessplit is not similar to the profit potential of Nosplit, and the Lessplit license agreement consequently is not a comparable uncontrolled transaction for purposes of this paragraph (c) in spite of the other indicia of comparability between the two intangibles.

(d) *Unspecified methods*—(1) *In general.* Methods not specified in paragraphs (a)(1), (2), and (3) of this section may be used to evaluate whether the amount charged in a controlled transaction is arm's length. Any method used under this paragraph (d) must be applied in accordance with the provisions of § 1.482-1. Consistent with the specified methods, an unspecified method should take into account the general principle that uncontrolled taxpayers evaluate the terms of a transaction by considering the realistic alternatives to that transaction, and only enter into a particular transaction if none of the alternatives is preferable to it. For example, the comparable uncontrolled transaction method compares a controlled transaction to similar uncontrolled transactions to provide a direct estimate of the price the parties would have agreed to had they resorted directly to a market alternative to the controlled transaction. Therefore, in establishing whether a controlled transaction achieved an arm's length result, an unspecified method should provide information on the prices or profits that the controlled taxpayer could have realized by choosing a realistic alternative to the controlled transaction. As with any method, an unspecified method will not be applied unless it provides the most reliable measure of an arm's length result under the principles of the best method rule. See § 1.482-1(c). Therefore, in accordance with § 1.482-1(d) (Comparability), to the extent that a method relies on internal data rather than uncontrolled comparables, its reliability will be reduced. Similarly, the reliability of a method will be affected by the reliability of the data and assumptions used to apply the method, including any projections used.

(2) *Example.* The following example illustrates an application of the principle of this paragraph (d).

Example. (i) USbond is a U.S. company that licenses to its foreign subsidiary, Eurobond, a proprietary process that permits the manufacture of Longbond, a long-lasting industrial adhesive, at a substantially lower cost than otherwise would be possible. Using the proprietary process, Eurobond manufactures Longbond and sells it to related and unrelated parties for the market price of $550 per ton. Under the terms of the license agreement, Eurobond pays USbond a royalty of $100 per ton of Longbond sold. USbond also manufactures and markets Longbond in the United States.

(ii) In evaluating whether the consideration paid for the transfer of the proprietary process to Eurobond was arm's length, the district director may consider, subject to the best method rule of § 1.482-1(c), USbond's alternative of producing and selling Longbond itself. Reasonably reliable estimates indicate that if USbond directly supplied Longbond to the European market, a selling price of $300 per ton would cover its costs and provide a reasonable profit for its functions, risks and investment of capital associated with the production of Longbond for the European market.

Reg. § 1.482-4(d)(1)

Given that the market price of Longbond was $550 per ton, by licensing the proprietary process to Eurobond, USbond forgoes $250 per ton of profit over the profit that would be necessary to compensate it for the functions, risks and investment involved in supplying Longbond to the European market itself. Based on these facts, the district director concludes that a royalty of $100 for the proprietary process is not arm's length.

(e) *Coordination with tangible property rules.* See § 1.482-3(f) for the provisions regarding the coordination between the tangible property and intangible property rules.

(f) *Special rules for transfers of intangible property*—(1) *Form of consideration.* If a transferee of an intangible pays nominal or no consideration and the transferor has retained a substantial interest in the property, the arm's length consideration shall be in the form of a royalty, unless a different form is demonstrably more appropriate.

(2) *Periodic adjustments*—(i) *General rule.* If an intangible is transferred under an arrangement that covers more than one year, the consideration charged in each taxable year may be adjusted to ensure that it is commensurate with the income attributable to the intangible. Adjustments made pursuant to this paragraph (f)(2) shall be consistent with the arm's length standard and the provisions of § 1.482-1. In determining whether to make such adjustments in the taxable year under examination, the district director may consider all relevant facts and circumstances throughout the period the intangible is used. The determination in an earlier year that the amount charged for an intangible was an arm's length amount will not preclude the district director in a subsequent taxable year from making an adjustment to the amount charged for the intangible in the subsequent year. A periodic adjustment under the commensurate with income requirement of section 482 may be made in a subsequent taxable year without regard to whether the taxable year of the original transfer remains open for statute of limitation purposes. For exceptions to this rule see paragraph (f)(2)(ii) of this section.

(ii) *Exceptions*—(A) *Transactions involving the same intangible.* If the same intangible was transferred to an uncontrolled taxpayer under substantially the same circumstances as those of the controlled transaction; this transaction serves as the basis for the application of the comparable uncontrolled transaction method in the first taxable year in which substantial periodic consideration was required to be paid; and the amount paid in that year was an arm's length amount, then no allocation in a subsequent year will be made under paragraph (f)(2)(i) of this paragraph for a controlled transfer of intangible property.

(B) *Transactions involving comparable intangible.* If the arm's length result is derived from the application of the comparable uncontrolled transaction method based on the transfer of a comparable intangible under comparable circumstances to those of the controlled transaction, no allocation will be made under paragraph (f)(2)(i) of this section if each of the following facts is established—

(*1*) The controlled taxpayers entered into a written agreement (controlled agreement) that provided for an amount of consideration with respect to each taxable year subject to such agreement, such consideration was an arm's length amount for the first taxable year in which substantial periodic consideration was required to be paid under the agreement, and such agreement remained in effect for the taxable year under review;

(*2*) There is a written agreement setting forth the terms of the comparable uncontrolled transaction relied upon to establish the arm's length consideration (uncontrolled agreement), which contains no provisions that would permit any change to the amount of consideration, a renegotiation, or a termination of the agreement, in circumstances comparable to those of the controlled transaction in the taxable year under review (or that contains provisions permitting only specified, non-contingent, periodic changes to the amount of consideration);

(*3*) The controlled agreement is substantially similar to the uncontrolled agreement, with respect to the time period for which it is effective and the provisions described in paragraph (f)(2)(ii)(B)(*2*) of this section;

(*4*) The controlled agreement limits use of the intangible to a specified field or purpose in a manner that is consistent with industry practice and any such limitation in the uncontrolled agreement;

(*5*) There were no substantial changes in the functions performed by the controlled transferee after the controlled agreement was executed, except changes required by events that were not foreseeable; and

(*6*) The aggregate profits actually earned or the aggregate cost savings actually realized by the controlled taxpayer from the exploitation of the intangible in the year under examination, and all past years, are not less than 80% nor more than 120% of the prospective profits or cost savings that were foreseeable when the comparability of the uncontrolled agreement was established under paragraph (c)(2) of this section.

Reg. § 1.482-4(f)(2)

(C) *Methods other than comparable uncontrolled transaction.* If the arm's length amount was determined under any method other than the comparable uncontrolled transaction method, no allocation will be made under paragraph (f)(2)(i) of this section if each of the following facts is established—

(*1*) The controlled taxpayers entered into a written agreement (controlled agreement) that provided for an amount of consideration with respect to each taxable year subject to such agreement, and such agreement remained in effect for the taxable year under review;

(*2*) The consideration called for in the controlled agreement was an arm's length amount for the first taxable year in which substantial periodic consideration was required to be paid, and relevant supporting documentation was prepared contemporaneously with the execution of the controlled agreement;

(*3*) There have been no substantial changes in the functions performed by the transferee since the controlled agreement was executed, except changes required by events that were not foreseeable; and

(*4*) The total profits actually earned or the total cost savings realized by the controlled transferee from the exploitation of the intangible in the year under examination, and all past years, are not less than 80% nor more than 120% of the prospective profits or cost savings that were foreseeable when the controlled agreement was entered into.

(D) *Extraordinary events.* No allocation will be made under paragraph (f)(2)(i) of this section if the following requirements are met—

(*1*) Due to extraordinary events that were beyond the control of the controlled taxpayers and that could not reasonably have been anticipated at the time the controlled agreement was entered into, the aggregate actual profits or aggregate cost savings realized by the taxpayer are less than 80% or more than 120% of the prospective profits or cost savings; and

(*2*) All of the requirements of paragraph (f)(2)(ii)(B) or (C) of this section are otherwise satisfied.

(E) *Five-year period.* If the requirements of § 1.482-4(f)(2)(ii)(B) or (f)(2)(ii)(C) are met for each year of the five-year period beginning with the first year in which substantial periodic consideration was required to be paid, then no periodic adjustment will be made under paragraph (f)(2)(i) of this section in any subsequent year.

(iii) *Examples.* The following examples illustrate this paragraph (f)(2).

Example 1. (i) USdrug, a U.S. pharmaceutical company, has developed a new drug, Nosplit, that is useful in treating migraine headaches and produces no significant side effects. A number of other drugs for treating migraine headaches are already on the market, but Nosplit can be expected rapidly to dominate the worldwide market for such treatments and to command a premium price since all other treatments produce side effects. Thus, USdrug projects that extraordinary profits will be derived from Nosplit in the U.S. and European markets.

(ii) USdrug licenses its newly established European subsidiary, Eurodrug, the rights to produce and market Nosplit for the European market for 5 years. In setting the royalty rate for this license, USdrug makes projections of the annual sales revenue and the annual profits to be derived from the exploitation of Nosplit by Eurodrug. Based on the projections, a royalty rate of 3.9% is established for the term of the license.

(iii) In Year 1, USdrug evaluates the royalty rate it received from Eurodrug. Given the high profit potential of Nosplit, USdrug is unable to locate any uncontrolled transactions dealing with licenses of comparable intangible property. USdrug therefore determines that the comparable uncontrolled transaction method will not provide a reliable measure of an arm's length royalty. However, applying the comparable profits method to Eurodrug, USdrug determines that a royalty rate of 3.9% will result in Eurodrug earning an arm's length return for its manufacturing and marketing functions.

(iv) In Year 5, the U.S. income tax return for USdrug is examined, and the district director must determine whether the royalty rate between USdrug and Eurodrug is commensurate with the income attributable to Nosplit. In making this determination, the district director considers whether any of the exceptions in § 1.482-4(f)(2)(ii) are applicable. In particular, the district director compares the profit projections attributable to Nosplit made by USdrug against the actual profits realized by Eurodrug. The projected and actual profits are as follows:

Reg. § 1.482-4(f)(2)

Adjustments

	Profit projections	Actual profits
Year 1	200	250
Year 2	250	300
Year 3	500	600
Year 4	350	200
Year 5	100	100
Total	1400	1450

(v) The total profits earned through Year 5 were not less than 80% nor more than 120% of the profits that were projected when the license was entered into. If the district director determines that the other requirements of § 1.482-4(f)(2)(ii)(C) were met, no adjustment will be made to the royalty rate between USdrug and Eurodrug for the license of Nosplit.

Example 2. (i) The facts are the same as in Example 1, except that Eurodrug's actual profits earned were much higher than the projected profits, as follows:

	Profit projections	Actual profits
Year 1	200	250
Year 2	250	500
Year 3	500	800
Year 4	350	700
Year 5	100	600
Total	1400	2850

(ii) In examining USdrug's tax return for Year 5, the district director considers the actual profits realized by Eurodrug in Year 5, and all past years. Accordingly, although Years 1 through 4 may be closed under the statute of limitations, for purposes of determining whether an adjustment should be made with respect to the royalty rate in Year 5 with respect to Nosplit, the district director aggregates the actual profits from those years with the profits of Year 5. However, the district director will make an adjustment, if any, only with respect to Year 5.

Example 3. (i) FP, a foreign corporation, licenses to USS, its U.S. subsidiary, a new air-filtering process that permits manufacturing plants to meet new environmental standards. The license runs for a 10-year period, and the profit derived from the new process is projected to be $15 million per year, for an aggregate profit of $150 million.

(ii) The royalty rate for the license is based on a comparable uncontrolled transaction involving a comparable intangible under comparable circumstances. The requirements of paragraphs (f)(2)(ii)(B)(*1*) through (*5*) of this section have been met. Specifically, FP and USS have entered into a written agreement that provides for a royalty in each year of the license, the royalty rate is considered arm's length for the first taxable year in which a substantial royalty was required to be paid, the license limited the use of the process to a specified field, consistent with industry practice, and there are no substantial changes in the functions performed by USS after the license was entered into.

(iii) In examining Year 4 of the license, the district director determines that the aggregate actual profits earned by USS through Year 4 are $30 million, less than 80% of the projected profits of $60 million. However, USS establishes to the satisfaction of the district director that the aggregate actual profits from the process are less than 80% of the projected profits in Year 3 because an earthquake severely damaged USS's manufacturing plant. Because the difference between the projected profits and actual profits was due to an extraordinary event that was beyond the control of USS, and could not reasonably have been anticipated at the time the license was entered into, the requirement under § 1.482-4(f)(2)(ii)(D) has been met, and no adjustment under this section is made.

(3) *Ownership of intangible property*—(i) *In general.* If the owner of the rights to exploit an intangible transfers such rights to a controlled taxpayer, the owner must receive an amount of consideration with respect to such transfer that is determined in accordance with the provisions of this section. If another controlled taxpayer provides assistance to the owner in connection with the development or enhancement of an intangible, such person may be entitled to receive consideration with respect to such assistance. See § 1.482-4(f)(3)(iii) (Allocations with respect to assistance provided to the owner). Because the right to exploit an intangible can be subdivided in various ways, a single intangible may have multiple owners for purposes of this paragraph (3)(i). Thus, for example, the owner of a trademark may license to another person the exclusive right to use that trademark in a specified geographic area for

Reg. § 1.482-4(f)(3)

a specified period of time (while otherwise retaining the right to use the intangible). In such a case, both the licensee and the licensor will be considered owners for purposes of this paragraph (f)(3)(i), with respect to their respective exploitation rights.

(ii) *Identification of owner*—(A) *Legally protected intangible property.* The legal owner of a right to exploit an intangible ordinarily will be considered the owner for purposes of this section. Legal ownership may be acquired by operation of law or by contract under which the legal owner transfers all or part of its rights to another. Further, the district director may impute an agreement to convey legal ownership if the conduct of the controlled taxpayers indicates the existence in substance of such an agreement. See § 1.482-1(d)(3)(ii)(B) (Identifying contractual terms).

(B) *Intangible property that is not legally protected.* In the case of intangible property that is not legally protected, the developer of the intangible will be considered the owner. Except as provided in § 1.482-7T, if two or more controlled taxpayers jointly develop an intangible, for purposes of section 482, only one of the controlled taxpayers will be regarded as the developer and owner of the intangible, and the other participating members will be regarded as assisters. Ordinarily, the developer is the controlled taxpayer that bore the largest portion of the direct and indirect costs of developing the intangible, including the provision, without adequate compensation, of property or services likely to contribute substantially to developing the intangible. A controlled taxpayer will be presumed not to have borne the costs of development if, pursuant to an agreement entered into before the success of the project is known, another person is obligated to reimburse the controlled taxpayer for its costs. If it cannot be determined which controlled taxpayer bore the largest portion of the costs of development, all other facts and circumstances will be taken into consideration, including the location of the development activities, the capability of each controlled taxpayer to carry on the project independently, the extent to which each controlled taxpayer controls the project, and the conduct of the controlled taxpayers.

(iii) *Allocations with respect to assistance provided to the owner.* Allocations may be made to reflect an arm's length consideration for assistance provided to the owner of an intangible in connection with the development or enhancement of the intangible. Such assistance may include loans, services, or the use of tangible or intangible property. Assistance does not, however, include expenditures of a routine nature that an unrelated party dealing at arm's length would be expected to incur under circumstances similar to those of the controlled taxpayer. The amount of any allocation required with respect to that assistance must be determined in accordance with the applicable rules under section 482.

(iv) *Examples.* The principles of this paragraph are illustrated by the following examples.

Example 1. A, a member of a controlled group, allows B, another member of the controlled group and the owner of an intangible, to use tangible property, such as laboratory equipment, in connection with the development of the intangible. Any allocations with respect to the owner's use of the property will be determined under § 1.482-2(c).

Example 2. FP, a foreign producer of cheese, markets the cheese in countries other than the United States under the tradename Fromage Frere. FP owns all the worldwide rights to this name. The name is widely known and is valuable outside the United States but is not known within the United States. In 1995, FP decides to enter the United States market and incorporates U.S. subsidiary, USSub, to be its U.S. distributor and to supervise the advertising and other marketing efforts that will be required to develop the name Fromage Frere in the United States. USSub incurs expenses that are not reimbursed by FP for developing the U.S. market for Fromage Frere. These expenses are comparable to the levels of expense incurred by independent distributors in the U.S. cheese industry when introducing a product in the U.S. market under a brand name owned by a foreign manufacturer. Since USSub would have been expected to incur these expenses if it were unrelated to FP, no allocation to USSub is made with respect to the market development activities performed by USSub.

Example 3. The facts are the same as in *Example 2,* except that the expenses incurred by USSub are significantly larger than the expenses incurred by independent distributors under similar circumstances. FP does not reimburse USSub for its expenses. The district director concludes based on this evidence that an unrelated party dealing at arm's length under similar circumstances would not have engaged in the same level of activity relating to the development of FP's marketing intangibles. The expenditures in excess of the level incurred by the independent distributors therefore are considered to be a service provided to FP that adds to the value of FP's trademark for Fromage Frere. Accordingly, the district director makes an allocation under section

Reg. § 1.482-4(f)(3)

482 for the fair market value of the services that USSub is considered to have performed for FP.

Example 4. The facts are the same as in *Example 3,* except that FP and USSub conclude a long term agreement under which USSub receives the exclusive right to distribute cheese in the United States under FP's trademark. USSub purchases cheese from FP at an arm's length price. Since USSub is the owner of the trademark under paragraph (f)(3)(ii)(A) of this section, and its conduct is consistent with that status, its activities related to the development of the trademark are not considered to be a service performed for the benefit of FP, and no allocation is made with respect to such activities.

(4) *Consideration not artificially limited.* The arm's length consideration for the controlled transfer of an intangible is not limited by the consideration paid in any uncontrolled transactions that do not meet the requirements of the comparable uncontrolled transaction method described in paragraph (c) of this section. Similarly, the arm's length consideration for an intangible is not limited by the prevailing rates of consideration paid for the use or transfer of intangibles within the same or similar industry.

(5) *Lump sum payments*—(i) *In general.* If an intangible is transferred in a controlled transaction for a lump sum, that amount must be commensurate with the income attributable to the intangible. A lump sum is commensurate with income in a taxable year if the equivalent royalty amount for that taxable year is equal to an arm's length royalty. The equivalent royalty amount for a taxable year is the amount determined by treating the lump sum as an advance payment of a stream of royalties over the useful life of the intangible (or the period covered by an agreement, if shorter), taking into account the projected sales of the licensee as of the date of the transfer. Thus, determining the equivalent royalty amount requires a present value calculation based on the lump sum, an appropriate discount rate, and the projected sales over the relevant period. The equivalent royalty amount is subject to periodic adjustments under § 1.482-4(f)(2)(i) to the same extent as an actual royalty payment pursuant to a license agreement.

(ii) *Exceptions.* No periodic adjustment will be made under paragraph (f)(2)(i) of this section if any of the exceptions to periodic adjustments provided in paragraph (f)(2)(ii) of this section apply.

(iii) *Example.* The following example illustrates the principle of this paragraph (f)(5).

Example. Calculation of the equivalent royalty amount. (i) FSub is the foreign subsidiary of USP, a U.S. company. USP licenses FSub the right to produce and sell the whopperchopper, a patented new kitchen appliance, for the foreign market. The license is for a period of five years, and payment takes the form of a single lump-sum charge of $500,000 that is paid at the beginning of the period.

(ii) The equivalent royalty amount for this license is determined by deriving an equivalent royalty rate equal to the lump-sum payment divided by the present discounted value of FSub's projected sales of whopperchoppers over the life of the license. Based on the riskiness of the whopperchopper business, an appropriate discount rate is determined to be 10 percent. Projected sales of whopperchoppers for each year of the license are as follows:

Year	Projected Sales ($)
1	2,500,000
2	2,600,000
3	2,700,000
4	2,700,000
5	2,750,000

(iii) Based on this information, the present discounted value of the projected whopperchopper sales is approximately $10 million, yielding an equivalent royalty rate of approximately 5%. Thus, the equivalent royalty amounts for each year are as follows:

Year	Projected Sales ($)	Equivalent royalty amount ($)
1	2,500,000	125,000
2	2,600,000	130,000
3	2,700,000	135,000
4	2,700,000	135,000
5	2,750,000	137,500

(iv) If in any of the five taxable years the equivalent royalty amount is determined not to be an arm's length amount, a periodic adjustment may be made pursuant to § 1.482-4(f)(2)(i). The adjustment in such case would be equal to the difference between the equivalent royalty amount and the arm's length royalty in that taxable year. [Reg. § 1.482-4.]

☐ [*T.D.* 8552, 7-1-94.]

[Reg. § 1.482-5]

§ 1.482-5. **Comparable profits method.**—(a) *In general.* The comparable profits method evaluates whether the amount charged in a controlled transaction is arm's length based on objective measures of profitability (profit level indicators) derived from uncontrolled taxpayers that engage in similar business activities under similar circumstances.

(b) *Determination of arm's length result*—(1) *In general.* Under the comparable profits method, the determination of an arm's length result is based on the amount of operating profit that the tested party would have earned on related party transactions if its profit level indicator were equal to that of an uncontrolled comparable (comparable operating profit). Comparable operating profit is calculated by determining a profit level indicator for an uncontrolled comparable, and applying the profit level indicator to the financial data related to the tested party's most narrowly identifiable business activity for which data incorporating the controlled transaction is available (relevant business activity). To the extent possible, profit level indicators should be applied solely to the tested party's financial data that is related to controlled transactions. The tested party's reported operating profit is compared to the comparable operating profits derived from the profit level indicators of uncontrolled comparables to determine whether the reported operating profit represents an arm's length result.

(2) *Tested party*—(i) *In general.* For purposes of this section, the tested party will be the participant in the controlled transaction whose operating profit attributable to the controlled transactions can be verified using the most reliable data and requiring the fewest and most reliable adjustments, and for which reliable data regarding uncontrolled comparables can be located. Consequently, in most cases the tested party will be the least complex of the controlled taxpayers and will not own valuable intangible property or unique assets that distinguish it from potential uncontrolled comparables.

(ii) *Adjustments for tested party.* The tested party's operating profit must first be adjusted to reflect all other allocations under section 482, other than adjustments pursuant to this section.

(3) *Arm's length range.* See § 1.482-1(e)(2) for the determination of the arm's length range. For purposes of the comparable profits method, the arm's length range will be established using comparable operating profits derived from a single profit level indicator.

(4) *Profit level indicators.* Profit level indicators are ratios that measure relationships between profits and costs incurred or resources employed. A variety of profit level indicators can be calculated in any given case. Whether use of a particular profit level indicator is appropriate depends upon a number of factors, including the nature of the activities of the tested party, the reliability of the available data with respect to uncontrolled comparables, and the extent to which the profit level indicator is likely to produce a reliable measure of the income that the tested party would have earned had it dealt with controlled taxpayers at arm's length, taking into account all of the facts and circumstances. The profit level indicators should be derived from a sufficient number of years of data to reasonably measure returns that accrue to uncontrolled comparables. Generally, such a period should encompass at least the taxable year under review and the preceding two taxable years. This analysis must be applied in accordance with § 1.482-1(f)(2)(iii)(D). Profit level indicators that may provide a reliable basis for comparing operating profits of the tested party and uncontrolled comparables include the following—

(i) *Rate of return on capital employed.* The rate of return on capital employed is the ratio of operating profit to operating assets. The reliability of this profit level indicator increases as operating assets play a greater role in generating operating profits for both the tested party and the uncontrolled comparable. In addition, reliability under this profit level indicator depends on the extent to which the composition of the tested party's assets is similar to that of the uncontrolled comparable. Finally, difficulties in properly valuing operating assets will diminish the reliability of this profit level indicator.

(ii) *Financial ratios.* Financial ratios measure relationships between profit and costs or sales revenue. Since functional differences generally have a greater effect on the relationship between profit and costs or sales revenue than the relationship between profit and operating assets, financial ratios are more sensitive to functional differences than the rate of return on capital employed. Therefore, closer functional comparability normally is required under a financial ratio than under the rate of return on capital employed to achieve a similarly reliable measure of an arm's length result. Financial ratios that may be appropriate include the following—

(A) Ratio of operating profit to sales; and

(B) Ratio of gross profit to operating expenses.

Reliability under this profit level indicator also depends on the extent to which the composition of the tested party's operating expenses is similar to that of the uncontrolled comparables.

(iii) *Other profit level indicators.* Other profit level indicators not described in this paragraph (b)(4) may be used if they provide reliable measures of the income that the tested party would have earned had it dealt with controlled taxpayers at arm's length. However, profit level indicators based solely on internal data may not be used under this paragraph (b)(4) because they are not objective measures of profitability derived from operations of uncontrolled taxpayers engaged in similar business activities under similar circumstances.

(c) *Comparability and reliability considerations*—(1) *In general.* Whether results derived from application of this method are the most reliable measure of the arm's length result must be determined using the factors described under the best method rule in § 1.482-1(c).

(2) *Comparability*—(i) *In general.* The degree of comparability between an uncontrolled taxpayer and the tested party is determined by applying the provisions of § 1.482-1(d)(2). The comparable profits method compares the profitability of the tested party, measured by a profit level indicator (generally based on operating profit), to the profitability of uncontrolled taxpayers in similar circumstances. As with all methods that rely on external market benchmarks, the greater the degree of comparability between the tested party and the uncontrolled taxpayer, the more reliable will be the results derived from the application of this method. The determination of the degree of comparability between the tested party and the uncontrolled taxpayer depends upon all the relevant facts and circumstances, including the relevant lines of business, the product or service markets involved, the asset composition employed (including the nature and quantity of tangible assets, intangible assets and working capital), the size and scope of operations, and the stage in a business or product cycle.

(ii) *Functional, risk and resource comparability.* An operating profit represents a return for the investment of resources and assumption of risks. Therefore, although all of the factors described in § 1.482-1(d)(3) must be considered, comparability under this method is particularly dependent on resources employed and risks assumed. Moreover, because resources and risks usually are directly related to functions performed, it is also important to consider functions performed in determining the degree of comparability between the tested party and an uncontrolled taxpayer. The degree of functional comparability required to obtain a reliable result under the comparable profits method, however, is generally less than that required under the resale price or cost plus methods. For example, because differences in functions performed often are reflected in operating expenses, taxpayers performing different functions may have very different gross profit margins but earn similar levels of operating profit.

(iii) *Other comparability factors.* Other factors listed in § 1.482-1(d)(3) also may be particularly relevant under the comparable profits method. Because operating profit usually is less sensitive than gross profit to product differences, reliability under the comparable profits method is not as dependent on product similarity as the resale price or cost plus method. However, the reliability of profitability measures based on operating profit may be adversely affected by factors that have less effect on results under the comparable uncontrolled price, resale price, and cost plus methods. For example, operating profit may be affected by varying cost structures (as reflected, for example, in the age of plant and equipment), differences in business experience (such as whether the business is in a start-up phase or is mature), or differences in management efficiency (as indicated, for example, by objective evidence such as expanding or contracting sales or executive compensation over time). Accordingly, if material differences in these factors are identified based on objective evidence, the reliability of the analysis may be affected.

(iv) *Adjustments for the differences between the tested party and the uncontrolled taxpayers.* If there are differences between the tested party and an uncontrolled comparable that would materially affect the profits determined under the relevant profit level indicator, adjustments should be made according to the comparability provisions of § 1.482-1(d)(2). In some cases, the assets of an uncontrolled comparable may need to be adjusted to achieve greater comparability between the tested party and the uncontrolled comparable. In such cases, the uncontrolled comparable's operating income attributable to those assets must also be adjusted before computing a profit level indicator in order to reflect the income and expense attributable to the adjusted assets. In certain cases it may also be appropriate to adjust the operating profit of the tested party and comparable parties. For example, where there are material differences in accounts payable among the comparable parties and the tested party, it will generally be appropriate to adjust the operating profit of each party by increasing it to reflect an imputed interest charge on each party's accounts payable.

(3) *Data and assumptions*—(i) *In general.* The reliability of the results derived from the comparable profits method is affected by the quality of the data and assumptions used to apply this method.

(ii) *Consistency in accounting.* The degree of consistency in accounting practices between the controlled transaction and the uncontrolled comparables that materially affect operating profit affects the reliability of the result. Thus, for example, if differences in inventory and other cost

Reg. § 1.482-5(c)(3)

accounting practices would materially affect operating profit, the ability to make reliable adjustments for such differences would affect the reliability of the results.

(iii) *Allocations between the relevant business activity and other activities.* The reliability of the allocation of costs, income, and assets between the relevant business activity and other activities of the tested party or an uncontrolled comparable will affect the reliability of the determination of operating profit and profit level indicators. If it is not possible to allocate costs, income, and assets directly based on factual relationships, a reasonable allocation formula may be used. To the extent direct allocations are not made, the reliability of the results derived from the application of this method is reduced relative to the results of a method that requires fewer allocations of costs, income, and assets. Similarly, the reliability of the results derived from the application of this method is affected by the extent to which it is possible to apply the profit level indicator to the tested party's financial data that is related solely to the controlled transactions. For example, if the relevant business activity is the assembly of components purchased from both controlled and uncontrolled suppliers, it may not be possible to apply the profit level indicator solely to financial data related to the controlled transactions. In such a case, the reliability of the results derived from the application of this method will be reduced.

(d) *Definitions.* The definitions set forth in paragraphs (d)(1) through (6) of this section apply for purposes of this section.

(1) *Sales revenue* means the amount of the total receipts from sale of goods and provision of services, less returns and allowances. Accounting principles and conventions that are generally accepted in the trade or industry of the controlled taxpayer under review must be used.

(2) *Gross profit* means sales revenue less cost of goods sold.

(3) *Operating expenses* includes all expenses not included in cost of goods sold except for interest expense, foreign income taxes (as defined in § 1.901-2(a)), domestic income taxes, and any other expenses not related to the operation of the relevant business activity. Operating expenses ordinarily include expenses associated with advertising, promotion, sales, marketing, warehousing and distribution, administration, and a reasonable allowance for depreciation and amortization.

(4) *Operating profit* means gross profit less operating expenses. Operating profit includes all income derived from the business activity being evaluated by the comparable profits method, but does not include interest and dividends, income derived from activities not being tested by this method, or extraordinary gains and losses that do not relate to the continuing operations of the tested party.

(5) *Reported operating profit* means the operating profit of the tested party reflected on a timely filed U.S. income tax return. If the tested party files a U.S. income tax return, its operating profit is considered reflected on a U.S. income tax return if the calculation of taxable income on its return for the taxable year takes into account the income attributable to the controlled transaction under review. If the tested party does not file a U.S. income tax return, its operating profit is considered reflected on a U.S. income tax return in any taxable year for which income attributable to the controlled transaction under review affects the calculation of the U.S. taxable income of any other member of the same controlled group. If the comparable operating profit of the tested party is determined from profit level indicators derived from financial statements or other accounting records and reports of comparable parties, adjustments may be made to the reported operating profit of the tested party in order to account for material differences between the tested party's operating profit reported for U.S. income tax purposes and the tested party's operating profit for financial statement purposes. In addition, in accordance with § 1.482-1(f)(2)(iii)(D), adjustments under section 482 that are finally determined may be taken into account in determining reported operating profit.

(6) *Operating assets.* The term operating assets means the value of all assets used in the relevant business activity of the tested party, including fixed assets and current assets (such as cash, cash equivalents, accounts receivable, and inventories). The term does not include investments in subsidiaries, excess cash, and portfolio investments. Operating assets may be measured by their net book value or by their fair market value, provided that the same method is consistently applied to the tested party and the comparable parties, and consistently applied from year to year. In addition, it may be necessary to take into account recent acquisitions, leased assets, intangibles, currency fluctuations, and other items that may not be explicitly recorded in the financial statements of the tested party or uncontrolled comparable. Finally, operating assets must be measured by the average of the values for the beginning of the year and the end of the year, unless substantial fluctuations in the value of operating assets during the year make this an inaccurate measure of the average value over the year. In such a case, a more accurate measure of

Reg. § 1.482-5(d)(1)

Adjustments

See p. 20,601 for regulations not amended to reflect law changes

the average value of operating assets must be applied.

(e) *Examples.* The following examples illustrate the application of this section.

Example 1—Transfer of tangible property resulting in no adjustment. (i) FP is a publicly traded foreign corporation with a U.S. subsidiary, USSub, that is under audit for its 1996 taxable year. FP manufactures a consumer product for worldwide distribution. USSub imports the assembled product and distributes it within the United States at the wholesale level under the FP name.

(ii) FP does not allow uncontrolled taxpayers to distribute the product. Similar products are produced by other companies but none of them is sold to uncontrolled taxpayers or to uncontrolled distributors.

(iii) Based on all the facts and circumstances, the district director determines that the comparable profits method will provide the most reliable measure of an arm's length result. USSub is selected as the tested party because it engages in activities that are less complex than those undertaken by FP. There is data from a number of independent operators of wholesale distribution businesses. These potential comparables are further narrowed to select companies in the same industry segment that perform similar functions and bear similar risks to USSub. An analysis of the information available on these taxpayers shows that the ratio of operating profit to sales is the most appropriate profit level indicator, and this ratio is relatively stable where at least three years are included in the average. For the taxable years 1994 through 1996, USSub shows the following results:

	1994	1995	1996	Average
Sales	500,000	560,000	500,000	520,000
Cost of Goods Sold	393,000	412,400	400,000	401,800
Operating Expenses	80,000	110,000	104,600	98,200
Operating Profit	27,000	37,600	(4,600)	20,000

(iv) After adjustments have been made to account for identified material differences between USSub and the uncontrolled distributors, the average ratio of operating profit to sales is calculated for each of the uncontrolled distributors. Applying each ratio to USSub would lead to the following comparable operating profit (COP) for USSub:

Uncontrolled Distributor	OP/S	USSub COP
A	1.7%	$ 8,840
B	3.1%	16,120
C	3.8%	19,760
D	4.5%	23,400
E	4.7%	24,440
F	4.8%	24,960
G	4.9%	25,480
H	6.7%	34,840
I	9.9%	51,480
J	10.5%	54,600

(v) The data is not sufficiently complete to conclude that it is likely that all material differences between USSub and the uncontrolled distributors have been identified. Therefore, an arm's length range can be established only pursuant to § 1.482-1(e)(2)(iii)(B). The district director measures the arm's length range by the interquartile range of results, which consists of the results ranging from $19,760 to $34,840. Although USSub's operating income for 1996 shows a loss of $4,600, the district director determines that no allocation should be made, because USSub's average reported operating profit of $20,000 is within this range.

Example 2—Transfer of tangible property resulting in adjustment. (i) The facts are the same as in *Example 1* except that USSub reported the following income and expenses:

	1994	1995	1996	Average
Sales	500,000	560,000	500,000	520,000
Cost of Goods Sold	370,000	460,000	400,000	410,000
Operating Expenses	110,000	110,000	110,000	110,000
Operating Profit	20,000	(10,000)	(10,000)	0

(ii) The interquartile range of comparable operating profits remains the same as derived in *Example 1*: $19,760 to $34,840. USSub's average operating profit for the years 1994 through 1996

Reg. § 1.482-5(e)

($0) falls outside this range. Therefore, the district director determines that an allocation may be appropriate.

(iii) To determine the amount, if any, of the allocation, the district director compares USSub's reported operating profit for 1996 to comparable operating profits derived from the uncontrolled distributors' results for 1996. The ratio of operating profit to sales in 1996 is calculated for each of the uncontrolled comparables and applied to USSub's 1996 sales to derive the following results:

Uncontrolled Distributor	OP/S	USSub COP
C	0.5%	$ 2,500
D	1.5%	7,500
E	2.0%	10,000
A	1.6%	13,000
F	2.8%	14,000
B	2.9%	14,500
J	3.0%	15,000
I	4.4%	22,000
H	6.9%	34,500
G	7.4%	37,000

(iv) Based on these results, the median of the comparable operating profits for 1996 is $14,250. Therefore, USSub's income for 1996 is increased by $24,250, the difference between USSub's reported operating profit for 1996 and the median of the comparable operating profits for 1996.

Example 3—Multiple year analysis. (i) The facts are the same as in *Example 2*. In addition, the district director examines the taxpayer's results for the 1997 taxable year. As in *Example 2*, the district director increases USSub's income for the 1996 taxable year by $24,250. The results for the 1997 taxable year, together with the 1995 and 1996 taxable years, are as follows:

	1995	1996	1997	Average
Sales	560,000	500,000	530,000	530,000
Cost of Goods Sold	460,000	400,000	430,000	430,000
Operating Expenses	110,000	110,000	110,000	110,000
Operating Profit	(10,000)	(10,000)	(10,000)	(10,000)

(ii) The interquartile range of comparable operating profits, based on average results from the uncontrolled comparables and average sales for USSub for the years 1995 through 1997, ranges from $15,500 to $30,000. In determining whether an allocation for the 1997 taxable year may be made, the district director compares USSub's average reported operating profit for the years 1995 through 1997 to the interquartile range of average comparable operating profits over this period. USSub's average reported operating profit is determined without regard to the adjustment made with respect to the 1996 taxable year. See § 1.482-1(f)(2)(iii)(D). Therefore, USSub's average reported operating profit for the years 1995 through 1997 is ($10,000). Because this amount of income falls outside the interquartile range, the district director determines that an allocation may be appropriate.

(iii) To determine the amount, if any, of the allocation for the 1997 taxable year, the district director compares USSub's reported operating profit for 1997 to the median of the comparable operating profits derived from the uncontrolled distributors' results for 1997. The median of the comparable operating profits derived from the uncontrolled comparables results for the 1997 taxable year is $12,000. Based on this comparison, the district director increases USSub's 1997 taxable income by $22,000, the difference between median of the comparable operating profits for the 1997 taxable year and USSub's reported operating profit of ($10,000) for the 1997 taxable year.

Example 4—Transfer of intangible to offshore manufacturer. (i) DevCo is a U.S. developer, producer and marketer of widgets. DevCo develops a new "high tech widget" (htw) that is manufactured by its foreign subsidiary ManuCo located in Country H. ManuCo sells the htw to MarkCo (a U.S. subsidiary of DevCo) for distribution and marketing in the United States. The taxable year 1996 is under audit, and the district director examines whether the royalty rate of 5 percent paid by ManuCo to DevCo is an arm's length consideration for the htw technology.

(ii) Based on all the facts and circumstances, the district director determines that the comparable profits method will provide the most reliable measure of an arm's length result. ManuCo is selected as the tested party because it engages in relatively routine manufacturing activities, while DevCo engages in a variety of complex activities

Reg. § 1.482-5(e)

using unique and valuable intangibles. Finally, because ManuCo engages in manufacturing activities, it is determined that the ratio of operating profit to operating assets is an appropriate profit level indicator.

(iii) Uncontrolled taxpayers performing similar functions cannot be found in country H. It is determined that data available in countries M and N provides the best match of companies in a similar market performing similar functions and bearing similar risks. Such data is sufficiently complete to identify many of the material differences between ManuCo and the uncontrolled comparables, and to make adjustments to account for such differences. However, data is not sufficiently complete so that it is likely that no material differences remain. In particular, the differences in geographic markets might have materially affected the results of the various companies.

(iv) In a separate analysis, it is determined that the price that ManuCo charged to MarkCo for the htw's is an arm's length price under § 1.482-3(b). Therefore, ManuCo's financial data derived from its sales to MarkCo are reliable. ManuCo's financial data from 1994-1996 is as follows:

	1994	1995	1996	Average
Assets	$24,000	$25,000	$26,000	$ 25,000
Sales to MarkCo	25,000	30,000	35,000	30,000
Cost of Goods Sold	6,250	7,500	8,750	7,500
Royalty to DevCo (5%)	1,250	1,500	1,750	1,500
Other	5,000	6,000	7,000	6,000
Operating Expenses	1,000	1,000	1,000	1,000
Operating Profit	17,750	21,500	25,250	21,500

(v) Applying the ratios of average operating profit to operating assets for the 1994 through 1996 taxable years derived from a group of similar uncontrolled comparables located in country M and N to Manuco's average operating assets for the same period provides a set of comparable operating profits. The interquartile range for these average comparable operating profits is $3,000 to $4,500. ManuCo's average reported operating profit for the years 1994 through 1996 ($21,500) falls outside this range. Therefore, the district director determines that an allocation may be appropriate for the 1996 taxable year.

(vi) To determine the amount, if any, of the allocation for the 1996 taxable year, the district director compares ManuCo's reported operating profit for 1996 to the median of the comparable operating profits derived from the uncontrolled distributors' results for 1996. The median result for the uncontrolled comparables for 1996 is $3,750. Based on this comparison, the district director increases royalties that ManuCo paid by $21,500 (the difference between $25,250 and the median of the comparable operating profits, $3,750).

Example 5—Adjusting operating assets and operating profit for differences in accounts receivable. (i) USM is a U.S. company that manufactures parts for industrial equipment and sells them to its foreign parent corporation. For purposes of applying the comparable profits method, 15 uncontrolled manufacturers that are similar to USM have been identified.

(ii) USM has a significantly lower level of accounts receivable than the uncontrolled manufacturers. Since the rate of return on capital employed is to be used as the profit level indicator, both operating assets and operating profits must be adjusted to account for this difference. Each uncontrolled comparable's operating assets is reduced by the amount (relative to sales) by which they exceed USM's accounts receivable. Each uncontrolled comparable's operating profit is adjusted by deducting imputed interest income on the excess accounts receivable. This imputed interest income is calculated by multiplying the uncontrolled comparable's excess accounts receivable by an interest rate appropriate for short-term debt.

Example 6—Adjusting operating profit for differences in accounts payable. (i) USD is the U.S. subsidiary of a foreign corporation. USD purchases goods from its foreign parent and sells them in the U.S. market. For purposes of applying the comparable profits method, 10 uncontrolled distributors that are similar to USD have been identified.

(ii) There are significant differences in the level of accounts payable among the uncontrolled distributors and USD. To adjust for these differences, the district director increases the operating profit of the uncontrolled distributors and USD to reflect interest expense imputed to the accounts payable. The imputed interest expense for each company is calculated by multiplying the company's accounts payable by an interest rate appropriate for its short-term debt. [Reg. § 1.482-5.]

☐ [*T.D.* 8552, 7-1-94.]

[Reg. § 1.482-6]

§ 1.482-6. **Profit split method.**—(a) *In general.* The profit split method evaluates whether

Reg. § 1.482-6(a)

the allocation of the combined operating profit or loss attributable to one or more controlled transactions is arm's length by reference to the relative value of each controlled taxpayer's contribution to that combined operating profit or loss. The combined operating profit or loss must be derived from the most narrowly identifiable business activity of the controlled taxpayers for which data is available that includes the controlled transactions (relevant business activity).

(b) *Appropriate share of profits and losses.* The relative value of each controlled taxpayer's contribution to the success of the relevant business activity must be determined in a manner that reflects the functions performed, risks assumed, and resources employed by each participant in the relevant business activity, consistent with the comparability provisions of § 1.482-1(d)(3). Such an allocation is intended to correspond to the division of profit or loss that would result from an arrangement between uncontrolled taxpayers, each performing functions similar to those of the various controlled taxpayers engaged in the relevant business activity. The profit allocated to any particular member of a controlled group is not necessarily limited to the total operating profit of the group from the relevant business activity. For example, in a given year, one member of the group may earn a profit while another member incurs a loss. In addition, it may not be assumed that the combined operating profit or loss from the relevant business activity should be shared equally, or in any other arbitrary proportion. The specific method of allocation must be determined under paragraph (c) of this section.

(c) *Application*—(1) *In general.* The allocation of profit or loss under the profit split method must be made in accordance with one of the following allocation methods—

(i) The comparable profit split, described in paragraph (c)(2) of this section; or

(ii) The residual profit split, described in paragraph (c)(3) of this section.

(2) *Comparable profit split*—(i) *In general.* A comparable profit split is derived from the combined operating profit of uncontrolled taxpayers whose transactions and activities are similar to those of the controlled taxpayers in the relevant business activity. Under this method, each uncontrolled taxpayer's percentage of the combined operating profit or loss is used to allocate the combined operating profit or loss of the relevant business activity.

(ii) *Comparability and reliability considerations*—(A) *In general.* Whether results derived from application of this method are the most reliable measure of the arm's length result is determined using the factors described under the best method rule in § 1.482-1(c).

(B) *Comparability*—(*1*) *In general.* The degree of comparability between the controlled and uncontrolled taxpayers is determined by applying the comparability provisions of § 1.482-1(d). The comparable profit split compares the division of operating profits among the controlled taxpayers to the division of operating profits among uncontrolled taxpayers engaged in similar activities under similar circumstances. Although all of the factors described in § 1.482-1(d)(3) must be considered, comparability under this method is particularly dependent on the considerations described under the comparable profits method in § 1.482-5(c)(2), because this method is based on a comparison of the operating profit of the controlled and uncontrolled taxpayers. In addition, because the contractual terms of the relationship among the participants in the relevant business activity will be a principal determinant of the allocation of functions and risks among them, comparability under this method also depends particularly on the degree of similarity of the contractual terms of the controlled and uncontrolled taxpayers. Finally, the comparable profit split may not be used if the combined operating profit (as a percentage of the combined assets) of the uncontrolled comparables varies significantly from that earned by the controlled taxpayers.

(*2*) *Adjustments for differences between the controlled and uncontrolled taxpayers.* If there are differences between the controlled and uncontrolled taxpayers that would materially affect the division of operating profit, adjustments must be made according to the provisions of § 1.482-1(d)(2).

(C) *Data and assumptions.* The reliability of the results derived from the comparable profit split is affected by the quality of the data and assumptions used to apply this method. In particular, the following factors must be considered—

(*1*) The reliability of the allocation of costs, income, and assets between the relevant business activity and the participants' other activities will affect the accuracy of the determination of combined operating profit and its allocation among the participants. If it is not possible to allocate costs, income, and assets directly based on factual relationships, a reasonable allocation formula may be used. To the extent direct allocations are not made, the reliability of the results derived from the application of this method is reduced relative to the results of a method that requires fewer allocations of costs,

Reg. § 1.482-6(b)

income, and assets. Similarly, the reliability of the results derived from the application of this method is affected by the extent to which it is possible to apply the method to the parties' financial data that is related solely to the controlled transactions. For example, if the relevant business activity is the assembly of components purchased from both controlled and uncontrolled suppliers, it may not be possible to apply the method solely to financial data related to the controlled transactions. In such a case, the reliability of the results derived from the application of this method will be reduced.

(*2*) The degree of consistency between the controlled and uncontrolled taxpayers in accounting practices that materially affect the items that determine the amount and allocation of operating profit affects the reliability of the result. Thus, for example, if differences in inventory and other cost accounting practices would materially affect operating profit, the ability to make reliable adjustments for such differences would affect the reliability of the results. Further, accounting consistency among the participants in the controlled transaction is required to ensure that the items determining the amount and allocation of operating profit are measured on a consistent basis.

(D) *Other factors affecting reliability.* Like the methods described in §§ 1.482-3, 1.482-4, and 1.482-5, the comparable profit split relies exclusively on external market benchmarks. As indicated in § 1.482-1(c)(2)(i), as the degree of comparability between the controlled and uncontrolled transactions increases, the relative weight accorded the analysis under this method will increase. In addition, the reliability of the analysis under this method may be enhanced by the fact that all parties to the controlled transaction are evaluated under the comparable profit split. However, the reliability of the results of an analysis based on information from all parties to a transaction is affected by the reliability of the data and the assumptions pertaining to each party to the controlled transaction. Thus, if the data and assumptions are significantly more reliable with respect to one of the parties than with respect to the others, a different method, focusing solely on the results of that party, may yield more reliable results.

(3) *Residual profit split*—(i) *In general.* Under this method, the combined operating profit or loss from the relevant business activity is allocated between the controlled taxpayers following the two-step process set forth in paragraphs (c)(3)(i)(A) and (B) of this section.

(A) *Allocate income to routine contributions.* The first step allocates operating income to each party to the controlled transactions to provide a market return for its routine contributions to the relevant business activity. Routine contributions are contributions of the same or a similar kind to those made by uncontrolled taxpayers involved in similar business activities for which it is possible to identify market returns. Routine contributions ordinarily include contributions of tangible property, services and intangibles that are generally owned by uncontrolled taxpayers engaged in similar activities. A functional analysis is required to identify these contributions according to the functions performed, risks assumed, and resources employed by each of the controlled taxpayers. Market returns for the routine contributions should be determined by reference to the returns achieved by uncontrolled taxpayers engaged in similar activities, consistent with the methods described in §§ 1.482-3, 1.482-4 and 1.482-5.

(B) *Allocate residual profit.* The allocation of income to the controlled taxpayers' routine contributions will not reflect profits attributable to the controlled group's valuable intangible property where similar property is not owned by the uncontrolled taxpayers from which the market returns are derived. Thus, in cases where such intangibles are present there normally will be an unallocated residual profit after the allocation of income described in paragraph (c)(3)(i)(A) of this section. Under this second step, the residual profit generally should be divided among the controlled taxpayers based upon the relative value of their contributions of intangible property to the relevant business activity that was not accounted for as a routine contribution. The relative value of the intangible property contributed by each taxpayer may be measured by external market benchmarks that reflect the fair market value of such intangible property. Alternatively, the relative value of intangible contributions may be estimated by the capitalized cost of developing the intangibles and all related improvements and updates, less an appropriate amount of amortization based on the useful life of each intangible. Finally, if the intangible development expenditures of the parties are relatively constant over time and the useful life of the intangible property of all parties is approximately the same, the amount of actual expenditures in recent years may be used to estimate the relative value of intangible contributions. If the intangible property contributed by one of the controlled taxpayers is also used in other business activities (such as transactions with other controlled taxpayers), an appropriate allocation of the value of the intangibles must be

Reg. § 1.482-6(c)(3)

made among all the business activities in which it is used.

(ii) *Comparability and reliability considerations*—(A) *In general.* Whether results derived from this method are the most reliable measure of the arm's length result is determined using the factors described under the best method rule in § 1.482-1(c). Thus, comparability and the quality of data and assumptions must be considered in determining whether this method provides the most reliable measure of an arm's length result. The application of these factors to the residual profit split is discussed in paragraph (c)(3)(ii)(B), (C), and (D) of this section.

(B) *Comparability.* The first step of the residual profit split relies on market benchmarks of profitability. Thus, the comparability considerations that are relevant for the first step of the residual profit split are those that are relevant for the methods that are used to determine market returns for the routine contributions. The second step of the residual profit split, however, may not rely so directly on market benchmarks. Thus, the reliability of the results under this method is reduced to the extent that the allocation of profits in the second step does not rely on market benchmarks.

(C) *Data and assumptions.* The reliability of the results derived from the residual profit split is affected by the quality of the data and assumptions used to apply this method. In particular, the following factors must be considered—

(*1*) The reliability of the allocation of costs, income, and assets as described in paragraph (c)(2)(ii)(C)(*1*) of this section;

(*2*) Accounting consistency as described in paragraph (c)(2)(ii)(C)(*2*) of this section;

(*3*) The reliability of the data used and the assumptions made in valuing the intangible property contributed by the participants. In particular, if capitalized costs of development are used to estimate the value of intangible property, the reliability of the results is reduced relative to the reliability of other methods that do not require such an estimate, for the following reasons. First, in any given case, the costs of developing the intangible may not be related to its market value. Second, the calculation of the capitalized costs of development may require the allocation of indirect costs between the relevant business activity and the controlled taxpayer's other activities, which may affect the reliability of the analysis. Finally, the calculation of costs may require assumptions regarding the useful life of the intangible property.

(D) *Other factors affecting reliability.* Like the methods described in §§ 1.482-3, 1.482-4, and 1.482-5, the first step of the residual profit split relies exclusively on external market benchmarks. As indicated in § 1.482-1(c)(2)(i), as the degree of comparability between the controlled and uncontrolled transactions increases, the relative weight accorded the analysis under this method will increase. In addition, to the extent the allocation of profits in the second step is not based on external market benchmarks, the reliability of the analysis will be decreased in relation to an analysis under a method that relies on market benchmarks. Finally, the reliability of the analysis under this method may be enhanced by the fact that all parties to the controlled transaction are evaluated under the residual profit split. However, the reliability of the results of an analysis based on information from all parties to a transaction is affected by the reliability of the data and the assumptions pertaining to each party to the controlled transaction. Thus, if the data and assumptions are significantly more reliable with respect to one of the parties than with respect to the others, a different method, focusing solely on the results of that party, may yield more reliable results.

(iii) *Example.* The provisions of this paragraph (c)(3) are illustrated by the following example.

Example—Application of Residual Profit Split. (i) XYZ is a U.S. corporation that develops, manufactures and markets a line of products for police use in the United States. XYZ's research unit developed a bulletproof material for use in protective clothing and headgear (Nulon). XYZ obtains patent protection for the chemical formula for Nulon. Since its introduction in the U.S., Nulon has captured a substantial share of the U.S. market for bulletproof material.

(ii) XYZ licensed its European subsidiary, XYZ-Europe, to manufacture and market Nulon in Europe. XYZ-Europe is a well-established company that manufactures and markets XYZ products in Europe. XYZ-Europe has a research unit that adapts XYZ products for the defense market, as well as a well-developed marketing network that employs brand names that it developed.

(iii) XYZ-Europe's research unit alters Nulon to adapt it to military specifications and develops a high-intensity marketing campaign directed at the defense industry in several European countries. Beginning with the 1995 taxable year, XYZ-Europe manufactures and sells Nulon in Europe through its marketing network under one of its brand names.

Reg. § 1.482-6(c)(3)

(iv) For the 1995 taxable year, XYZ has no direct expenses associated with the license of Nulon to XYZ-Europe and incurs no expenses related to the marketing of Nulon in Europe. For the 1995 taxable year, XYZ-Europe's Nulon sales and pre-royalty expenses are $500 million and $300 million, respectively, resulting in net pre-royalty profit of $200 million related to the Nulon business. The operating assets employed in XYZ-Europe's Nulon business are $200 million. Given the facts and circumstances, the district director determines under the best method rule that a residual profit split will provide the most reliable measure of an arm's length result. Based on an examination of a sample of European companies performing functions similar to those of XYZ-Europe, the district director determines that an average market return on XYZ-Europe's operating assets in the Nulon business is 10 percent, resulting in a market return of $20 million (10% × $200 million) for XYZ-Europe's Nulon business, and a residual profit of $180 million.

(v) Since the first stage of the residual profit split allocated profits to XYZ-Europe's contributions other than those attributable to highly valuable intangible property, it is assumed that the residual profit of $180 million is attributable to the valuable intangibles related to Nulon, i.e., the European brand name for Nulon and the Nulon formula (including XYZ-Europe's modifications). To estimate the relative values of these intangibles, the district director compares the ratios of the capitalized value of expenditures as of 1995 on Nulon-related research and development and marketing over the 1995 sales related to such expenditures.

(vi) Because XYZ's protective product research and development expenses support the worldwide protective product sales of the XYZ group, it is necessary to allocate such expenses among the worldwide business activities to which they relate. The district director determines that it is reasonable to allocate the value of these expenses based on worldwide protective product sales. Using information on the average useful life of its investments in protective product research and development, the district director capitalizes and amortizes XYZ's protective product research and development expenses. This analysis indicates that the capitalized research and development expenditures have a value of $0.20 per dollar of global protective product sales in 1995.

(vii) XYZ-Europe's expenditures on Nulon research and development and marketing support only its sales in Europe. Using information on the average useful life of XYZ-Europe's investments in marketing and research and development, the district director capitalizes and amortizes XYZ-Europe's expenditures and determines that they have a value in 1995 of $0.40 per dollar of XYZ-Europe's Nulon sales.

(viii) Thus, XYZ and XYZ-Europe together contributed $0.60 in capitalized intangible development expenses for each dollar of XYZ-Europe's protective product sales for 1995, of which XYZ contributed one-third (or $0.20 per dollar of sales). Accordingly, the district director determines that an arm's length royalty for the Nulon license for the 1995 taxable year is $60 million, i.e., one-third of XYZ-Europe's $180 million in residual Nulon profit. [Reg. § 1.482-6.]

☐ [T.D. 8552, 7-1-94.]

[Reg. § 1.482-7]

§ 1.482-7. Sharing of costs.—(a) *In general*—(1) *Scope and application of the rules in this section*. A cost sharing arrangement is an agreement under which the parties agree to share the costs of development of one or more intangibles in proportion to their shares of reasonably anticipated benefits from their individual exploitation of the interests in the intangibles assigned to them under the arrangement. A taxpayer may claim that a cost sharing arrangement is a qualified cost sharing arrangement only if the agreement meets the requirements of paragraph (b) of this section. Consistent with the rules of § 1.482-1(d)(3)(ii)(B) (Identifying contractual terms), the district director may apply the rules of this section to any arrangement that in substance constitutes a cost sharing arrangement, notwithstanding a failure to comply with any requirement of this section. A qualified cost sharing arrangement, or an arrangement to which the district director applies the rules of this section, will not be treated as a partnership to which the rules of subchapter K apply. See § 301.7701-3(e) of this chapter. Furthermore, a participant that is a foreign corporation or nonresident alien individual will not be treated as engaged in trade or business within the United States solely by reason of its participation in such an arrangement. See generally § 1.864-2(a).

(2) *Limitation on allocations*. The district director shall not make allocations with respect to a qualified cost sharing arrangement except to the extent necessary to make each controlled participant's share of the costs (as determined under paragraph (d) of this section) of intangible development under the qualified cost sharing arrangement equal to its share of reasonably anticipated benefits attributable to such development, under the rules of this section. If a controlled taxpayer acquires an interest in intangible property from another controlled taxpayer (other than in consid-

Reg. § 1.482-7(a)(2)

eration for bearing a share of the costs of the intangible's development), then the district director may make appropriate allocations to reflect an arm's length consideration for the acquisition of the interest in such intangible under the rules of §§ 1.482-1 and 1.482-4 through 1.482-6. See paragraph (g) of this section. An interest in an intangible includes any commercially transferable interest, the benefits of which are susceptible of valuation. See § 1.482-4(b) for the definition of an intangible.

(3) *Cross references.* Paragraph (c) of this section defines participant. Paragraph (d) of this section defines the costs of intangible development. Paragraph (e) of this section defines the anticipated benefits of intangible development. Paragraph (f) of this section provides rules governing cost allocations. Paragraph (g) of this section provides rules governing transfers of intangibles other than in consideration for bearing a share of the costs of the intangible's development. Rules governing the character of payments made pursuant to a qualified cost sharing arrangement are provided in paragraph (h) of this section. Paragraph (i) of this section provides accounting requirements. Paragraph (j) of this section provides administrative requirements. Paragraph (k) of this section provides an effective date. Paragraph (l) provides a transition rule.

(b) *Qualified cost sharing arrangement.* A qualified cost sharing arrangement must—

(1) Include two or more participants;

(2) Provide a method to calculate each controlled participant's share of intangible development costs, based on factors that can reasonably be expected to reflect that participant's share of anticipated benefits;

(3) Provide for adjustment to the controlled participants' shares of intangible development costs to account for changes in economic conditions, the business operations and practices of the participants, and the ongoing development of intangibles under the arrangement; and

(4) Be recorded in a document that is contemporaneous with the formation (and any revision) of the cost sharing arrangement and that includes—

(i) A list of the arrangement's participants, and any other member of the controlled group that will benefit from the use of intangibles developed under the cost sharing arrangement;

(ii) The information described in paragraphs (b)(2) and (b)(3) of this section;

(iii) A description of the scope of the research and development to be undertaken, including the intangible or class of intangibles intended to be developed;

(iv) A description of each participant's interest in any covered intangibles. A covered intangible is any intangible property that is developed as a result of the research and development undertaken under the cost sharing arrangement (intangible development area);

(v) The duration of the arrangement; and

(vi) The conditions under which the arrangement may be modified or terminated and the consequences of such modification or termination, such as the interest that each participant will receive in any covered intangibles.

(c) *Participant*—(1) *In general.* For purposes of this section, a participant is a controlled taxpayer that meets the requirements of this paragraph (c)(1) (controlled participant) or an uncontrolled taxpayer that is a party to the cost sharing arrangement (uncontrolled participant). See § 1.482-1(i)(5) for the definitions of controlled and uncontrolled taxpayers. A controlled taxpayer may be a controlled participant only if it—

(i) Reasonably anticipates that it will derive benefits from the use of covered intangibles;

(ii) Substantially complies with the accounting requirements described in paragraph (i) of this section; and

(iii) Substantially complies with the administrative requirements described in paragraph (j) of this section.

(iv) The following example illustrates paragraph (c)(1)(i) of this section:

Example. Foreign Parent (FP) is a foreign corporation engaged in the extraction of a natural resource. FP has a U.S. subsidiary (USS) to which FP sells supplies of this resource for sale in the United States. FP enters into a cost sharing arrangement with USS to develop a new machine to extract the natural resource. The machine uses a new extraction process that will be patented in the United States and in other countries. The cost sharing arrangement provides that USS will receive the rights to use the machine in the extraction of the natural resource in the United States, and FP will receive the rights in the rest of the world. This resource does not, however, exist in the United States. Despite the fact that USS has received the right to use this process in the United States, USS is not a qualified participant because it will not derive a benefit from the use of the intangible developed under the cost sharing arrangement.

(2) *Treatment of a controlled taxpayer that is not a controlled participant*—(i) *In general.* If a controlled taxpayer that is not a controlled par-

Reg. § 1.482-7(a)(3)

ticipant (within the meaning of this paragraph (c)) provides assistance in relation to the research and development undertaken in the intangible development area, it must receive consideration from the controlled participants under the rules of § 1.482-4(f)(3)(iii) (Allocations with respect to assistance provided to the owner). For purposes of paragraph (d) of this section, such consideration is treated as an operating expense and each controlled participant must be treated as incurring a share of such consideration equal to its share of reasonably anticipated benefits (as defined in paragraph (f)(3) of this section).

(ii) *Example.* The following example illustrates this paragraph (c)(2):

Example. (i) U.S. Parent (USP), one foreign subsidiary (FS), and a second foreign subsidiary constituting the group's research arm (R+D) enter into a cost sharing agreement to develop manufacturing intangibles for a new product line A. USP and FS are assigned the exclusive rights to exploit the intangibles respectively in the United States and the rest of the world, where each presently manufactures and sells various existing product lines. R+D is not assigned any rights to exploit the intangibles. R+D's activity consists solely in carrying out research for the group. It is reliably projected that the shares of reasonably anticipated benefits of USP and FS will be 66⅔% and 33⅓%, respectively, and the parties' agreement provides that USP and FS will reimburse 66⅔% and 33⅓%, respectively, of the intangible development costs incurred by R+D with respect to the new intangible.

(ii) R+D does not qualify as a controlled participant within the meaning of paragraph (c) of this section, because it will not derive any benefits from the use of covered intangibles. Therefore, R+D is treated as a service provider for purposes of this section and must receive arm's length consideration for the assistance it is deemed to provide to USP and FS, under the rules of § 1.482-4(f)(3)(iii). Such consideration must be treated as intangible development costs incurred by USP and FS in proportion to their shares of reasonably anticipated benefits (i.e., 66⅔% and 33⅓%, respectively). R+D will not be considered to bear any share of the intangible development costs under the arrangement.

(3) *Treatment of consolidated group.* For purposes of this section, all members of the same affiliated group (within the meaning of section 1504(a)) that join in the filing of a consolidated return for the taxable year under section 1501 shall be treated as one taxpayer.

(d) *Costs*—(1) *Intangible development costs.* For purposes of this section, a controlled participant's costs of developing intangibles for a taxable year mean all of the costs incurred by that participant related to the intangible development area, plus all of the cost sharing payments it makes to other controlled and uncontrolled participants, minus all of the cost sharing payments it receives from other controlled and uncontrolled participants. Costs incurred related to the intangible development area consist of the following items: operating expenses as defined in § 1.482-5(d)(3), other than depreciation or amortization expense, plus (to the extent not included in such operating expenses, as defined in § 1.482-5(d)(3)) the charge for the use of any tangible property made available to the qualified cost sharing arrangement. If tangible property is made available to the qualified cost sharing arrangement by a controlled participant, the determination of the appropriate charge will be governed by the rules of § 1.482-2(c) (Use of tangible property). Intangible development costs do not include the consideration for the use of any intangible property made available to the qualified cost sharing arrangement. See paragraph (g)(2) of this section. If a particular cost contributes to the intangible development area and other areas or other business activities, the cost must be allocated between the intangible development area and the other areas or business activities on a reasonable basis. In such a case, it is necessary to estimate the total benefits attributable to the cost incurred. The share of such cost allocated to the intangible development area must correspond to covered intangibles' share of the total benefits. Costs that do not contribute to the intangible development area are not taken into account.

(2) *Examples.* The following examples illustrate this paragraph (d):

Example 1. Foreign Parent (FP) and U.S. Subsidiary (USS) enter into a qualified cost sharing arrangement to develop a better mousetrap. USS and FP share the costs of FP's research and development facility that will be exclusively dedicated to this research, the salaries of the researchers, and reasonable overhead costs attributable to the project. They also share the cost of a conference facility that is at the disposal of the senior executive management of each company but does not contribute to the research and development activities in any measurable way. In this case, the cost of the conference facility must be excluded from the amount of intangible development costs.

Example 2. U.S. Parent (USP) and Foreign Subsidiary (FS) enter into a qualified cost sharing arrangement to develop a new device. USP and FS share the costs of a research and development facility, the salaries of researchers, and reasonable

Reg. § 1.482-7(d)(2)

overhead costs attributable to the project. USP also incurs costs related to field testing of the device, but does not include them in the amount of intangible development costs of the cost sharing arrangement. The district director may determine that the field testing costs are intangible development costs that must be shared.

(e) *Anticipated benefits*—(1) *Benefits.* Benefits are additional income generated or costs saved by the use of covered intangibles.

(2) *Reasonably anticipated benefits.* For purposes of this section, a controlled participant's reasonably anticipated benefits are the aggregate benefits that it reasonably anticipates that it will derive from covered intangibles.

(f) *Cost allocations*—(1) *In general.* For purposes of determining whether a cost allocation authorized by paragraph (a)(2) of this section is appropriate for a taxable year, a controlled participant's share of intangible development costs for the taxable year under a qualified cost sharing arrangement must be compared to its share of reasonably anticipated benefits under the arrangement. A controlled participant's share of intangible development costs is determined under paragraph (f)(2) of this section. A controlled participant's share of reasonably anticipated benefits under the arrangement is determined under paragraph (f)(3) of this section. In determining whether benefits were reasonably anticipated, it may be appropriate to compare actual benefits to anticipated benefits, as described in paragraph (f)(3)(iv) of this section.

(2) *Share of intangible development costs*—(i) *In general.* A controlled participant's share of intangible development costs for a taxable year is equal to its intangible development costs for the taxable year (as defined in paragraph (d) of this section), divided by the sum of the intangible development costs for the taxable year (as defined in paragraph (d) of this section) of all the controlled participants.

(ii) *Example.* The following example illustrates this paragraph (f)(2):

Example. (i) U.S. Parent (USP), Foreign Subsidiary (FS), and Unrelated Third Party (UTP) enter into a cost sharing arrangement to develop new audio technology. In the first year of the arrangement, the controlled participants incur $2,250,000 in the intangible development area, all of which is incurred directly by USP. In the first year, UTP makes a $250,000 cost sharing payment to USP, and FS makes a $800,000 cost sharing payment to USP, under the terms of the arrangement. For that year, the intangible development costs borne by USP are $1,200,000 (its $2,250,000 intangible development costs directly incurred, minus the cost sharing payments it receives of $250,000 from UTP and $800,000 from FS); the intangible development costs borne by FS are $800,000 (its cost sharing payment); and the intangible development costs borne by all of the controlled participants are $2,000,000 (the sum of the intangible development costs borne by USP and FS of $1,200,000 and $800,000, respectively). Thus, for the first year, USP's share of intangible development costs is 60% ($1,200,000 divided by $2,000,000), and FS's share of intangible development costs is 40% ($800,000 divided by $2,000,000).

(ii) For purposes of determining whether a cost allocation authorized by paragraph § 1.482-7(a)(2) is appropriate for the first year, the district director must compare USP's and FS's shares of intangible development costs for that year to their shares of reasonably anticipated benefits. See paragraph (f)(3) of this section.

(3) *Share of reasonably anticipated benefits*—(i) *In general.* A controlled participant's share of reasonably anticipated benefits under a qualified cost sharing arrangement is equal to its reasonably anticipated benefits (as defined in paragraph (e)(2) of this section), divided by the sum of the reasonably anticipated benefits (as defined in paragraph (e)(2) of this section) of all the controlled participants. The anticipated benefits of an uncontrolled participant will not be included for purposes of determining each controlled participant's share of anticipated benefits. A controlled participant's share of reasonably anticipated benefits will be determined using the most reliable estimate of reasonably anticipated benefits. In determining which of two or more available estimates is most reliable, the quality of the data and assumptions used in the analysis must be taken into account, consistent with § 1.482-1(c)(2)(ii) (Data and assumptions). Thus, the reliability of an estimate will depend largely on the completeness and accuracy of the data, the soundness of the assumptions, and the relative effects of particular deficiencies in data or assumptions on different estimates. If two estimates are equally reliable, no adjustment should be made based on differences in the results. The following factors will be particularly relevant in determining the reliability of an estimate of anticipated benefits—

(A) The reliability of the basis used for measuring benefits, as described in paragraph (f)(3)(ii) of this section; and

(B) The reliability of the projections used to estimate benefits, as described in paragraph (f)(3)(iv) of this section.

Reg. § 1.482-7(e)(1)

(ii) *Measure of benefits.* In order to estimate a controlled participant's share of anticipated benefits from covered intangibles, the amount of benefits that each of the controlled participants is reasonably anticipated to derive from covered intangibles must be measured on a basis that is consistent for all such participants. See paragraph (f)(3)(iii)(E), *Example 8,* of this section. If a controlled participant transfers covered intangibles to another controlled taxpayer, such participant's benefits from the transferred intangibles must be measured by reference to the transferee's benefits, disregarding any consideration paid by the transferee to the controlled participant (such as a royalty pursuant to a license agreement). Anticipated benefits are measured either on a direct basis, by reference to estimated additional income to be generated or costs to be saved by the use of covered intangibles, or on an indirect basis, by reference to certain measurements that reasonably can be assumed to be related to income generated or costs saved. Such indirect bases of measurement of anticipated benefits are described in paragraph (f)(3)(iii) of this section. A controlled participant's anticipated benefits must be measured on the most reliable basis, whether direct or indirect. In determining which of two bases of measurement of reasonably anticipated benefits is most reliable, the factors set forth in § 1.482-1(c)(2)(ii) (Data and assumptions) must be taken into account. It normally will be expected that the basis that provided the most reliable estimate for a particular year will continue to provide the most reliable estimate in subsequent years, absent a material change in the factors that affect the reliability of the estimate. Regardless of whether a direct or indirect basis of measurement is used, adjustments may be required to account for material differences in the activities that controlled participants undertake to exploit their interests in covered intangibles. See *Example 6* of paragraph (f)(3)(iii)(E) of this section.

(iii) *Indirect bases for measuring anticipated benefits.* Indirect bases for measuring anticipated benefits from participation in a qualified cost sharing arrangement include the following:

(A) *Units used, produced or sold.* Units of items used, produced or sold by each controlled participant in the business activities in which covered intangibles are exploited may be used as an indirect basis for measuring its anticipated benefits. This basis of measurement will be more reliable to the extent that each controlled participant is expected to have a similar increase in net profit or decrease in net loss attributable to the covered intangibles per unit of the item or items used, produced or sold. This circumstance is most likely to arise when the covered intangibles are exploited by the controlled participants in the use, production or sale of substantially uniform items under similar economic conditions.

(B) *Sales.* Sales by each controlled participant in the business activities in which covered intangibles are exploited may be used as an indirect basis for measuring its anticipated benefits. This basis of measurement will be more reliable to the extent that each controlled participant is expected to have a similar increase in net profit or decrease in net loss attributable to covered intangibles per dollar of sales. This circumstance is most likely to arise if the costs of exploiting covered intangibles are not substantial relative to the revenues generated, or if the principal effect of using covered intangibles is to increase the controlled participants' revenues (e.g., through a price premium on the products they sell) without affecting their costs substantially. Sales by each controlled participant are unlikely to provide a reliable basis for measuring benefits unless each controlled participant operates at the same market level (e.g., manufacturing, distribution, etc.).

(C) *Operating profit.* Operating profit of each controlled participant from the activities in which covered intangibles are exploited may be used as an indirect basis for measuring its anticipated benefits. This basis of measurement will be more reliable to the extent that such profit is largely attributable to the use of covered intangibles, or if the share of profits attributable to the use of covered intangibles is expected to be similar for each controlled participant. This circumstance is most likely to arise when covered intangibles are integral to the activity that generates the profit and the activity could not be carried on or would generate little profit without use of those intangibles.

(D) *Other bases for measuring anticipated benefits.* Other bases for measuring anticipated benefits may, in some circumstances, be appropriate, but only to the extent that there is expected to be a reasonably identifiable relationship between the basis of measurement used and additional income generated or costs saved by the use of covered intangibles. For example, a division of costs based on employee compensation would be considered unreliable unless there were a relationship between the amount of compensation and the expected income of the controlled participants from the use of covered intangibles.

(E) *Examples.* The following examples illustrate this paragraph (f)(3)(iii):

Example 1. Foreign Parent (FP) and U.S. Subsidiary (USS) both produce a feedstock for the manufacture of various high-performance

Reg. § 1.482-7(f)(3)

plastic products. Producing the feedstock requires large amounts of electricity, which accounts for a significant portion of its production cost. FP and USS enter into a cost sharing arrangement to develop a new process that will reduce the amount of electricity required to produce a unit of the feedstock. FP and USS currently both incur an electricity cost of X% of its other production costs and rates for each are expected to remain similar in the future. How much the new process, if it is successful, will reduce the amount of electricity required to produce a unit of the feedstock is uncertain, but it will be about the same amount for both companies. Therefore, the cost savings each company is expected to achieve after implementing the new process are similar relative to the total amount of the feedstock produced. Under the cost sharing arrangement FP and USS divide the costs of developing the new process based on the units of the feedstock each is anticipated to produce in the future. In this case, units produced is the most reliable basis for measuring benefits and dividing the intangible development costs because each participant is expected to have a similar decrease in costs per unit of the feedstock produced.

Example 2. The facts are the same as in Example 1, except that USS pays X% of its other production costs for electricity while FP pays 2X% of its other production costs. In this case, units produced is not the most reliable basis for measuring benefits and dividing the intangible development costs because the participants do not expect to have a similar decrease in costs per unit of the feedstock produced. The district director determines that the most reliable measure of benefit shares may be based on units of the feedstock produced if FP's units are weighted relative to USS' units by a factor of 2. This reflects the fact that FP pays twice as much as USS as a percentage of its other production costs for electricity and, therefore, FP's savings per unit of the feedstock would be twice USS's savings from any new process eventually developed.

Example 3. The facts are the same as in Example 2, except that to supply the particular needs of the U.S. market USS manufactures the feedstock with somewhat different properties than FP's feedstock. This requires USS to employ a somewhat different production process than does FP. Because of this difference, it will be more costly for USS to adopt any new process that may be developed under the cost sharing agreement. In this case, units produced is not the most reliable basis for measuring benefit shares. In order to reliably determine benefit shares, the district director offsets the reasonably anticipated costs of adopting the new process against the reasonably anticipated total savings in electricity costs.

Example 4. U.S. Parent (USP) and Foreign Subsidiary (FS) enter into a cost sharing arrangement to develop new anesthetic drugs. USP obtains the right to use any resulting patent in the U.S. market, and FS obtains the right to use the patent in the European market. USP and FS divide costs on the basis of anticipated operating profit from each patent under development. USP anticipates that it will receive a much higher profit than FS per unit sold because drug prices are uncontrolled in the U.S., whereas drug prices are regulated in many European countries. In this case, the controlled taxpayers' basis for measuring benefits is the most reliable.

Example 5. (i) Foreign Parent (FP) and U.S. Subsidiary (USS) both manufacture and sell fertilizers. They enter into a cost sharing arrangement to develop a new pellet form of a common agricultural fertilizer that is currently available only in powder form. Under the cost sharing arrangement, USS obtains the rights to produce and sell the new form of fertilizer for the U.S. market while FP obtains the rights to produce and sell the fertilizer for the rest of the world. The costs of developing the new form of fertilizer are divided on the basis of the anticipated sales of fertilizer in the participants' respective markets.

(ii) If the research and development is successful the pellet form will deliver the fertilizer more efficiently to crops and less fertilizer will be required to achieve the same effect on crop growth. The pellet form of fertilizer can be expected to sell at a price premium over the powder form of fertilizer based on the savings in the amount of fertilizer that needs to be used. If the research and development is successful, the costs of producing pellet fertilizer are expected to be approximately the same as the costs of producing powder fertilizer and the same for both FP and USS. Both FP and USS operate at approximately the same market levels, selling their fertilizers largely to independent distributors.

(iii) In this case, the controlled taxpayers' basis for measuring benefits is the most reliable.

Example 6. The facts are the same as in Example 5, except that FP distributes its fertilizers directly while USS sells to independent distributors. In this case, sales of USS and FP are not the most reliable basis for measuring benefits unless adjustments are made to account for the difference in market levels at which the sales occur.

Example 7. Foreign Parent (FP) and U.S. Subsidiary (USS) enter into a cost sharing arrangement to develop materials that will be

Reg. § 1.482-7(f)(3)

used to train all new entry-level employees. FP and USS determine that the new materials will save approximately ten hours of training time per employee. Because their entry-level employees are paid on differing wage scales, FP and USS decide that they should not divide costs based on the number of entry-level employees hired by each. Rather, they divide costs based on compensation paid to the entry-level employees hired by each. In this case, the basis used for measuring benefits is the most reliable because there is a direct relationship between compensation paid to new entry-level employees and costs saved by FP and USS from the use of the new training materials.

Example 8. U.S. Parent (USP), Foreign Subsidiary 1 (FS1) and Foreign Subsidiary 2 (FS2) enter into a cost sharing arrangement to develop computer software that each will market and install on customers' computer systems. The participants divide costs on the basis of projected sales by USP, FS1, and FS2 of the software in their respective geographic areas. However, FS1 plans not only to sell but also to license the software to unrelated customers, and FS1's licensing income (which is a percentage of the licensees' sales) is not counted in the projected benefits. In this case, the basis used for measuring the benefits of each participant is not the most reliable because all of the benefits received by participants are not taken into account. In order to reliably determine benefit shares, FS1's projected benefits from licensing must be included in the measurement on a basis that is the same as that used to measure its own and the other participants' projected benefits from sales (e.g., all participants might measure their benefits on the basis of operating profit).

(iv) *Projections used to estimate anticipated benefits*—(A) *In general.* The reliability of an estimate of anticipated benefits also depends upon the reliability of projections used in making the estimate. Projections required for this purpose generally include a determination of the time period between the inception of the research and development and the receipt of benefits, a projection of the time over which benefits will be received, and a projection of the benefits anticipated for each year in which it is anticipated that the intangible will generate benefits. A projection of the relevant basis for measuring anticipated benefits may require a projection of the factors that underlie it. For example, a projection of operating profits may require a projection of sales, cost of sales, operating expenses, and other factors that affect operating profits. If it is anticipated that there will be significant variation among controlled participants in the timing of their receipt of benefits, and consequently benefit shares are expected to vary significantly over the years in which benefits will be received, it may be necessary to use the present discounted value of the projected benefits to reliably determine each controlled participant's share of those benefits. If it is not anticipated that benefit shares will significantly change over time, current annual benefit shares may provide a reliable projection of anticipated benefit shares. This circumstance is most likely to occur when the cost sharing arrangement is a long-term arrangement, the arrangement covers a wide variety of intangibles, the composition of the covered intangibles is unlikely to change, the covered intangibles are unlikely to generate unusual profits, and each controlled participant's share of the market is stable.

(B) *Unreliable projections.* A significant divergence between projected benefit shares and actual benefit shares may indicate that the projections were not reliable. In such a case, the district director may use actual benefits as the most reliable measure of anticipated benefits. If benefits are projected over a period of years, and the projections for initial years of the period prove to be unreliable, this may indicate that the projections for the remaining years of the period are also unreliable and thus should be adjusted. Projections will not be considered unreliable based on a divergence between a controlled participant's projected benefit share and actual benefit share if the amount of such divergence for every controlled participant is less than or equal to 20% of the participant's projected benefit share. Further, the district director will not make an allocation based on such divergence if the difference is due to an extraordinary event, beyond the control of the participants, that could not reasonably have been anticipated at the time that costs were shared. For purposes of this paragraph, all controlled participants that are not U.S. persons will be treated as a single controlled participant. Therefore, an adjustment based on an unreliable projection will be made to the cost shares of foreign controlled participants only if there is a matching adjustment to the cost shares of controlled participants that are U.S. persons. Nothing in this paragraph (f)(3)(iv)(B) will prevent the district director from making an allocation if the taxpayer did not use the most reliable basis for measuring anticipated benefits. For example, if the taxpayer measures anticipated benefits based on units sold, and the district director determines that another basis is more reliable for measuring anticipated benefits, then the fact that actual units sold were within 20% of the projected unit sales will not preclude an allocation under this section.

(C) *Foreign-to-foreign adjustments.* Notwithstanding the limitations on adjustments pro-

Reg. § 1.482-7(f)(3)

vided in paragraph (f)(3)(iv)(B) of this section, adjustments to cost shares based on an unreliable projection also may be made solely among foreign controlled participants if the variation between actual and projected benefits has the effect of substantially reducing U.S. tax.

(D) *Examples.* The following examples illustrate this paragraph (f)(3)(iv):

Example 1. (i) Foreign Parent (FP) and U.S. Subsidiary (USS) enter into a cost sharing arrangement to develop a new car model. The participants plan to spend four years developing the new model and four years producing and selling the new model. USS and FP project total sales of $4 billion and $2 billion, respectively, over the planned four years of exploitation of the new model. Cost shares are divided for each year based on projected total sales. Therefore, USS bears 66 2/3% of each year's intangible development costs and FP bears 33 1/3% of such costs.

(ii) USS typically begins producing and selling new car models a year after FP begins producing and selling new car models. The district director determines that in order to reflect USS' one-year lag in introducing new car models, a more reliable projection of each participant's share of benefits would be based on a projection of all four years of sales for each participant, discounted to present value.

Example 2. U.S. Parent (USP) and Foreign Subsidiary (FS) enter into a cost sharing arrangement to develop new and improved household cleaning products. Both participants have sold household cleaning products for many years and have stable market shares. The products under development are unlikely to produce unusual profits for either participant. The participants divide costs on the basis of each participant's current sales of household cleaning products. In this case, the participants' future benefit shares are reliably projected by current sales of cleaning products.

Example 3. The facts are the same as in *Example 2*, except that FS's market share is rapidly expanding because of the business failure of a competitor in its geographic area. The district director determines that the participants' future benefit shares are not reliably projected by current sales of cleaning products and that FS's benefit projections should take into account its growth in sales.

Example 4. Foreign Parent (FP) and U.S. Subsidiary (USS) enter into a cost sharing arrangement to develop synthetic fertilizers and insecticides. FP and USS share costs on the basis of each participant's current sales of fertilizers and insecticides. The market shares of the participants have been stable for fertilizers, but FP's market share for insecticides has been expanding. The district director determines that the participants' projections of benefit shares are reliable with regard to fertilizers, but not reliable with regard to insecticides; a more reliable projection of benefit shares would take into account the expanding market share for insecticides.

Example 5. U.S. Parent (USP) and Foreign Subsidiary (FS) enter into a cost sharing arrangement to develop new food products, dividing costs on the basis of projected sales two years in the future. In year 1, USP and FS project that their sales in year 3 will be equal, and they divide costs accordingly. In year 3, the district director examines the participants' method for dividing costs. USP and FS actually accounted for 42% and 58% of total sales, respectively. The district director agrees that sales two years in the future provide a reliable basis for estimating benefit shares. Because the differences between USP's and FS's actual and projected benefit shares are less than 20% of their projected benefit shares, the projection of future benefits for year 3 is reliable.

Example 6. The facts are the same as in *Example 5*, except that the in year 3 USP and FS actually accounted for 35% and 65% of total sales, respectively. The divergence between USP's projected and actual benefit shares is greater than 20% of USP's projected benefit share and is not due to an extraordinary event beyond the control of the participants. The district director concludes that the projection of anticipated benefit shares was unreliable, and uses actual benefits as the basis for an adjustment to the cost shares borne by USP and FS.

Example 7. U.S. Parent (USP), a U.S. corporation, and its foreign subsidiary (FS) enter a cost sharing arrangement in year 1. They project that they will begin to receive benefits from covered intangibles in years 4 through 6, and that USP will receive 60% of total benefits and FS 40% of total benefits. In years 4 through 6, USP and FS actually receive 50% each of the total benefits. In evaluating the reliability of the participants' projections, the district director compares these actual benefit shares to the projected benefit shares. Although USP's actual benefit share (50%) is within 20% of its projected benefit share (60%), FS's actual benefit share (50%) is not within 20% of its projected benefit share (40%). Based on this discrepancy, the district director may conclude that the participants' projections were not reliable and may use actual benefit shares as the basis for an adjustment to the cost shares borne by USP and FS.

Reg. § 1.482-7(f)(3)

Adjustments

Example 8. Three controlled taxpayers, USP, FS1 and FS2 enter into a cost sharing arrangement. FS1 and FS2 are foreign. USP is a United States corporation that controls all the stock of FS1 and FS2. The participants project that they will share the total benefits of the covered intangibles in the following percentages: USP 50%; FS1 30%; and FS2 20%. Actual benefit shares are as follows: USP 45%; FS1 25%; and FS2 30%. In evaluating the reliability of the participants' projections, the district director compares these actual benefit shares to the projected benefit shares. For this purpose, FS1 and FS2 are treated as a single participant. The actual benefit share received by USP (45%) is within 20% of its projected benefit share (50%). In addition, the non-US participants' actual benefit share (55%) is also within 20% of their projected benefit share (50%). Therefore, the district director concludes that the participants' projections of future benefits were reliable, despite the fact that FS2's actual benefit share (30%) is not within 20% of its projected benefit share (20%).

Example 9. The facts are the same as in *Example 8.* In addition, the district director determines that FS2 has significant operating losses and has no earnings and profits, and that FS1 is profitable and has earnings and profits. Based on all the evidence, the district director concludes that the participants arranged that FS1 would bear a larger cost share than appropriate in order to reduce FS1's earnings and profits and thereby reduce inclusions USP otherwise would be deemed to have on account of FS1 under subpart F. Pursuant to § 1.482-7 (f)(3)(iv)(C), the district director may make an adjustment solely to the cost shares borne by FS1 and FS2 because FS2's projection of future benefits was unreliable and the variation between actual and projected benefits had the effect of substantially reducing USP's U.S. income tax liability (on account of FS1 subpart F income).

Example 10. (i) (A) Foreign Parent (FP) and U.S. Subsidiary (USS) enter into a cost sharing arrangement in 1996 to develop a new treatment for baldness. USS's interest in any treatment developed is the right to produce and sell the treatment in the U.S. market while FP retains rights to produce and sell the treatment in the rest of the world. USS and FP measure their anticipated benefits from the cost sharing arrangement based on their respective projected future sales of the baldness treatment. The following sales projections are used:

Sales ($ millions)

Year	USS	FP
1997	5	10
1998	20	20
1999	30	30
2000	40	40
2001	40	40
2002	40	40
2003	40	40
2004	20	20
2005	10	10
2006	5	5

(B) In 1997, the first year of sales, USS is projected to have lower sales than FP due to lags in U.S. regulatory approval for the baldness treatment. In each subsequent year USS and FP are projected to have equal sales. Sales are projected to build over the first three years of the period, level off for several years, and then decline over the final years of the period as new and improved baldness treatments reach the market.

(ii) To account for USS's lag in sales in the first year, the present discounted value of sales over the period is used as the basis for measuring benefits. Based on the risk associated with this venture, a discount rate of 10 percent is selected. The present discounted value of projected sales is determined to be approximately $154.4 million for USS and $158.9 million for FP. On this basis USS and FP are projected to obtain approximately 49.3% and 50.7% of the benefit, respectively, and the costs of developing the baldness treatment are shared accordingly.

(iii) (A) In the year 2002 the district director examines the cost sharing arrangement. USS and FP have obtained the following sales results through the year 2001:

Sales ($ millions)

Year	USS	FP
1997	0	17
1998	17	35
1999	25	41
2000	38	41
2001	39	41

Reg. § 1.482-7(f)(3)

(B) USS's sales initially grew more slowly than projected while FP's sales grew more quickly. In each of the first three years of the period the share of total sales of at least one of the parties diverged by over 20% from its projected share of sales. However, by the year 2001 both parties' sales had leveled off at approximately their projected values. Taking into account this leveling off of sales and all the facts and circumstances, the district director determines that it is appropriate to use the original projections for the remaining years of sales. Combining the actual results through the year 2001 with the projections for subsequent years, and using a discount rate of 10%, the present discounted value of sales is approximately $141.6 million for USS and $187.3 million for FP. This result implies that USS and FP obtain approximately 43.1% and 56.9%, respectively, of the anticipated benefits from the baldness treatment. Because these benefit shares are within 20% of the benefit shares calculated based on the original sales projections, the district director determines that, based on the difference between actual and projected benefit shares, the original projections were not unreliable. No adjustment is made based on the difference between actual and projected benefit shares.

Example 11. (i) The facts are the same as in *Example 10*, except that the actual sales results through the year 2001 are as follows:

Sales ($ millions)

Year	USS	FP
1997	0	17
1998	17	35
1999	25	44
2000	34	54
2001	36	55

(ii) Based on the discrepancy between the projections and the actual results and on consideration of all the facts, the district director determines that for the remaining years the following sales projections are more reliable than the original projections:

Sales ($ millions)

Year	USS	FP
2002	36	55
2003	36	55
2004	18	28
2005	9	14
2006	4.5	7

(iii) Combining the actual results through the year 2001 with the projections for subsequent years, and using a discount rate of 10%, the present discounted value of sales is approximately $131.2 million for USS and $229.4 million for FP. This result implies that USS and FP obtain approximately 35.4% and 63.6%, respectively, of the anticipated benefits from the baldness treatment. These benefit shares diverge by greater than 20% from the benefit shares calculated based on the original sales projections, and the district director determines that, based on the difference between actual and projected benefit shares, the original projections were unreliable. The district director adjusts costs shares for each of the taxable years under examination to conform them to the recalculated shares of anticipated benefits.

(4) *Timing of allocations.* If the district director reallocates costs under the provisions of this paragraph (f), the allocation must be reflected for tax purposes in the year in which the costs were incurred. When a cost sharing payment is owed by one member of a qualified cost sharing arrangement to another member, the district director may make appropriate allocations to reflect an arm's length rate of interest for the time value of money, consistent with the provisions of § 1.482-2(a) (Loans or advances).

(g) *Allocations of income, deductions or other tax items to reflect transfers of intangibles (buy-in)*—(1) *In general.* A controlled participant that makes intangible property available to a qualified cost sharing arrangement will be treated as having transferred interests in such property to the other controlled participants, and such other controlled participants must make buy-in payments to it, as provided in paragraph (g)(2) of this section. If the other controlled participants fail to make such payments, the district director may make appropriate allocations, under the provisions of §§ 1.482-1 and 1.482-4 through 1.482-6, to reflect an arm's length consideration for the transferred intangible property. Further, if a group of controlled taxpayers participates in a qualified cost sharing arrangement, any change in the controlled participants' interests in covered intangibles, whether by reason of entry of a new participant or otherwise by reason of transfers (including deemed transfers) of interests among existing participants, is a transfer of intangible property, and the district director may make ap-

Reg. § 1.482-7(f)(4)

propriate allocations, under the provisions of §§ 1.482-1 and 1.482-4 through 1.482-6, to reflect an arm's length consideration for the transfer. See paragraphs (g)(3), (4), and (5) of this section. Paragraph (g)(6) of this section provides rules for assigning unassigned interests under a qualified cost sharing arrangement.

(2) *Pre-existing intangibles.* If a controlled participant makes pre-existing intangible property in which it owns an interest available to other controlled participants for purposes of research in the intangible development area under a qualified cost sharing arrangement, then each such other controlled participant must make a buy-in payment to the owner. The buy-in payment by each such other controlled participant is the arm's length charge for the use of the intangible under the rules of §§ 1.482-1 and 1.482-4 through 1.482-6, multiplied by the controlled participant's share of reasonably anticipated benefits (as defined in paragraph (f)(3) of this section). A controlled participant's payment required under this paragraph (g)(2) is deemed to be reduced to the extent of any payments owed to it under this paragraph (g)(2) from other controlled participants. Each payment received by a payee will be treated as coming pro rata out of payments made by all payors. See paragraph (g)(8), *Example 4*, of this section. Such payments will be treated as consideration for a transfer of an interest in the intangible property made available to the qualified cost sharing arrangement by the payee. Any payment to or from an uncontrolled participant in consideration for intangible property made available to the qualified cost sharing arrangement will be shared by the controlled participants in accordance with their shares of reasonably anticipated benefits (as defined in paragraph (f)(3) of this section). A controlled participant's payment required under this paragraph (g)(2) is deemed to be reduced by such a share of payments owed from an uncontrolled participant to the same extent as by any payments owed from other controlled participants under this paragraph (g)(2). See paragraph (g)(8), *Example 5*, of this section.

(3) *New controlled participant.* If a new controlled participant enters a qualified cost sharing arrangement and acquires any interest in the covered intangibles, then the new participant must pay an arm's length consideration, under the provisions of §§ 1.482-1 and 1.482-4 through 1.482-6, for such interest to each controlled participant from whom such interest was acquired.

(4) *Controlled participant relinquishes interests.* A controlled participant in a qualified cost sharing arrangement may be deemed to have acquired an interest in one or more covered intangibles if another controlled participant transfers, abandons, or otherwise relinquishes an interest under the arrangement, to the benefit of the first participant. If such a relinquishment occurs, the participant relinquishing the interest must receive an arm's length consideration, under the provisions of §§ 1.482-1 and 1.482-4 through 1.482-6, for its interest. If the controlled participant that has relinquished its interest subsequently uses that interest, then that participant must pay an arm's length consideration, under the provisions of §§ 1.482-1 and 1.482-4 through 1.482-6, to the controlled participant that acquired the interest.

(5) *Conduct inconsistent with the terms of a cost sharing arrangement.* If, after any cost allocations authorized by paragraph (a)(2) of this section, a controlled participant bears costs of intangible development that over a period of years are consistently and materially greater or lesser than its share of reasonably anticipated benefits, then the district director may conclude that the economic substance of the arrangement between the controlled participants is inconsistent with the terms of the cost sharing arrangement. In such a case, the district director may disregard such terms and impute an agreement consistent with the controlled participants' course of conduct, under which a controlled participant that bore a disproportionately greater share of costs received additional interests in covered intangibles. See § 1.482-1(d)(3)(ii)(B) (Identifying contractual terms) and § 1.482-4(f)(3)(ii) (Identification of owner). Accordingly, that participant must receive an arm's length payment from any controlled participant whose share of the intangible development costs is less than its share of reasonably anticipated benefits over time, under the provisions of §§ 1.482-1 and 1.482-4 through 1.482-6.

(6) *Failure to assign interests under a qualified cost sharing arrangement.* If a qualified cost sharing arrangement fails to assign an interest in a covered intangible, then each controlled participant will be deemed to hold a share in such interest equal to its share of the costs of developing such intangible. For this purpose, if cost shares have varied materially over the period during which such intangible was developed, then the costs of developing the intangible must be measured by their present discounted value as of the date when the first such costs were incurred.

(7) *Form of consideration.* The consideration for an acquisition described in this paragraph (g) may take any of the following forms:

Reg. § 1.482-7(g)(7)

(i) *Lump sum payments.* For the treatment of lump sum payments, see § 1.482-4(f)(5) (Lump sum payments);

(ii) *Installment payments.* Installment payments spread over the period of use of the intangible by the transferee, with interest calculated in accordance with § 1.482-2(a) (Loans or advances); and

(iii) *Royalties.* Royalties or other payments contingent on the use of the intangible by the transferee.

(8) *Examples.* The following examples illustrate allocations described in this paragraph (g):

Example 1. In year one, four members of a controlled group enter into a cost sharing arrangement to develop a commercially feasible process for capturing energy from nuclear fusion. Based on a reliable projection of their future benefits, each cost sharing participant bears an equal share of the costs. The cost of developing intangibles for each participant with respect to the project is approximately $1 million per year. In year ten, a fifth member of the controlled group joins the cost sharing group and agrees to bear one-fifth of the future costs in exchange for part of the fourth member's territory reasonably anticipated to yield benefits amounting to one-fifth of the total benefits. The fair market value of intangible property within the arrangement at the time the fifth company joins the arrangement is $45 million. The new member must pay one-fifth of that amount (that is, $9 million total) to the fourth member from whom it acquired its interest in covered intangibles.

Example 2. U.S. Subsidiary (USS), Foreign Subsidiary (FS) and Foreign Parent (FP) enter into a cost sharing arrangement to develop new products within the Group X product line. USS manufactures and sells Group X products in North America, FS manufactures and sells Group X products in South America, and FP manufactures and sells Group X products in the rest of the world. USS, FS and FP project that each will manufacture and sell a third of the Group X products under development, and they share costs on the basis of projected sales of manufactured products. When the new Group X products are developed, however, USS ceases to manufacture Group X products, and FP sells its Group X products to USS for resale in the North American market. USS earns a return on its resale activity that is appropriate given its function as a distributor, but does not earn a return attributable to exploiting covered intangibles. The district director determines that USS' share of the costs (one-third) was greater than its share of reasonably anticipated benefits (zero) and that it has transferred an interest in the intangibles for which it should receive a payment from FP, whose share of the intangible development costs (one-third) was less than its share of reasonably anticipated benefits over time (two-thirds). An allocation is made under §§ 1.482-1 and 1.482-4 through 1.482-6 from FP to USS to recognize USS' one-third interest in the intangibles. No allocation is made from FS to USS because FS did not exploit USS' interest in covered intangibles.

Example 3. U.S. Parent (USP), Foreign Subsidiary 1 (FS1), and Foreign Subsidiary 2 (FS2) enter into a cost sharing arrangement to develop a cure for the common cold. Costs are shared USP-50%, FS1-40% and FS2-10% on the basis of projected units of cold medicine to be produced by each. After ten years of research and development, FS1 withdraws from the arrangement, transferring its interests in the intangibles under development to USP in exchange for a lump sum payment of $10 million. The district director may review this lump sum payment, under the provisions of § 1.482-4(f)(5), to ensure that the amount is commensurate with the income attributable to the intangibles.

Example 4. (i) Four members A, B, C, and D of a controlled group form a cost sharing arrangement to develop the next generation technology for their business. Based on a reliable projection of their future benefits, the participants agree to bear shares of the costs incurred during the term of the agreement in the following percentages: A 40%; B 15%; C 25%; and D 20%. The arm's length charges, under the rules of §§ 1.482-1 and 1.482-4 through 1.482-6, for the use of the existing intangible property they respectively make available to the cost sharing arrangement are in the following amounts for the taxable year: A 80X; B 40X; C 30X; and D 30X. The provisional (before offsets) and final buy-in payments/receipts among A, B, C, and D are shown in the table as follows:

(All amounts stated in X's)

	A	B	C	D
Payments	<40>	<21>	<37.5>	<30>
Receipts	48	34	22.5	24
Final	8	13	<15>	<6>

Reg. § 1.482-7(g)(8)

(ii) The first row/first column shows A's provisional buy-in payment equal to the product of 100X (sum of 40X, 30X, and 30X) and A's share of anticipated benefits of 40%. The second row/first column shows A's provisional buy-in receipts equal to the sum of the products of 80X and B's, C's, and D's anticipated benefits shares (15%, 25%, and 20%, respectively). The other entries in the first two rows of the table are similarly computed. The last row shows the final buy-in receipts/payments after offsets. Thus, for the taxable year, A and B are treated as receiving the 8X and 13X, respectively, pro rata out of payments by C and D of 15X and 6X, respectively.

Example 5. A and B, two members of a controlled group form a cost sharing arrangement with an unrelated third party C to develop a new technology useable in their respective businesses. Based on a reliable projection of their future benefits, A and B agree to bear shares of 60% and 40%, respectively, of the costs incurred during the term of the agreement. A also makes available its existing technology for purposes of the research to be undertaken. The arm's length charge, under the rules of §§ 1.482-1 and 1.482-4 through 1.482-6, for the use of the existing technology is 100X for the taxable year. Under its agreement with A and B, C must make a specified cost sharing payment as well as a payment of 50X for the taxable year on account of the pre-existing intangible property made available to the cost sharing arrangement. B's provisional buy-in payment (before offsets) to A for the taxable year is 40X (the product of 100X and B's anticipated benefits share of 40%). C's payment of 50X is shared provisionally between A and B in accordance with their shares of reasonably anticipated benefits, 30X (50X times 60%) to A and 20X (50X times 40%) to B. B's final buy-in payment (after offsets) is 20X (40X less 20X). A is treated as receiving the 70X total provisional payments (40X plus 30X) pro rata out of the final payments by B and C of 20X and 50X, respectively.

(h) *Character of payments made pursuant to a qualified cost sharing arrangement*—(1) *In general.* Payments made pursuant to a qualified cost sharing arrangement (other than payments described in paragraph (g) of this section) generally will be considered costs of developing intangibles of the payor and reimbursements of the same kind of costs of developing intangibles of the payee. For purposes of this paragraph (h), a controlled participant's payment required under a qualified cost sharing arrangement is deemed to be reduced to the extent of any payments owed to it under the arrangement from other controlled or uncontrolled participants. Each payment received by a payee will be treated as coming pro rata out of payments made by all payors. Such payments will be applied pro rata against deductions for the taxable year that the payee is allowed in connection with the qualified cost sharing arrangement. Payments received in excess of such deductions will be treated as in consideration for use of the tangible property made available to the qualified cost sharing arrangement by the payee. For purposes of the research credit determined under section 41, cost sharing payments among controlled participants will be treated as provided for intra-group transactions in § 1.41-6(e). Any payment made or received by a taxpayer pursuant to an arrangement that the district director determines not to be a qualified cost sharing arrangement, or a payment made or received pursuant to paragraph (g) of this section, will be subject to the provisions of §§ 1.482-1 and 1.482-4 through 1.482-6. Any payment that in substance constitutes a cost sharing payment will be treated as such for purposes of this section, regardless of its characterization under foreign law.

(2) *Examples.* The following examples illustrate this paragraph (h):

Example 1. U.S. Parent (USP) and its wholly owned Foreign Subsidiary (FS) form a cost sharing arrangement to develop a miniature widget, the Small R. Based on a reliable projection of their future benefits, USP agrees to bear 40% and FS to bear 60% of the costs incurred during the term of the agreement. The principal costs in the intangible development area are operating expenses incurred by FS in Country Z of 100X annually, and operating expenses incurred by USP in the United States also of 100X annually. Of the total costs of 200X, USP's share is 80X and FS's share is 120X, so that FS must make a payment to USP of 20X. This payment will be treated as a reimbursement of 20X of USP's operating expenses in the United States. Accordingly, USP's Form 1120 will reflect an 80X deduction on account of activities performed in the United States for purposes of allocation and apportionment of the deduction to source. The Form 5471 for FS will reflect a 100X deduction on account of activities performed in Country Z, and a 20X deduction on account of activities performed in the United States.

Example 2. The facts are the same as in *Example 1*, except that the 100X of costs borne by USP consist of 5X of operating expenses incurred by USP in the United States and 95X of fair market value rental cost for a facility in the United States. The depreciation deduction attributable to the U.S. facility is 7X. The 20X net payment by FS to USP will first be applied in reduction pro rata of the 5X deduction for operating expenses and the 7X depreciation deduction

Reg. § 1.482-7(h)(2)

attributable to the U.S. facility. The 8X remainder will be treated as rent for the U.S. facility.

(i) *Accounting requirements.* The accounting requirements of this paragraph are that the controlled participants in a qualified cost sharing arrangement must use a consistent method of accounting to measure costs and benefits, and must translate foreign currencies on a consistent basis.

(j) *Administrative requirements*—(1) *In general.* The administrative requirements of this paragraph consist of the documentation requirements of paragraph (j)(2) of this section and the reporting requirements of paragraph (j)(3) of this section.

(2) *Documentation*—(i) *Requirements.* A controlled participant must maintain sufficient documentation to establish that the requirements of paragraphs (b)(4) and (c)(1) of this section have been met, as well as the additional documentation specified in this paragraph (j)(2)(i), and must provide any such documentation to the Internal Revenue Service within 30 days of a request (unless an extension is granted by the district director). Documents necessary to establish the following must also be maintained—

(A) The total amount of costs incurred pursuant to the arrangement;

(B) The costs borne by each controlled participant;

(C) A description of the method used to determine each controlled participant's share of the intangible development costs, including the projections used to estimate benefits, and an explanation of why that method was selected;

(D) The accounting method used to determine the costs and benefits of the intangible development (including the method used to translate foreign currencies), and, to the extent that the method materially differs from U.S. generally accepted accounting principles, an explanation of such material differences; and

(E) Prior research, if any, undertaken in the intangible development area, any tangible or intangible property made available for use in the arrangement, by each controlled participant, and any information used to establish the value of pre-existing and covered intangibles.

(ii) *Coordination with penalty regulation.* The documents described in paragraph (j)(2)(i) of this section will satisfy the principal documents requirement under § 1.6662-6(d)(2)(iii)(B) with respect to a qualified cost sharing arrangement.

(3) *Reporting requirements.* A controlled participant must attach to its U.S. income tax return a statement indicating that it is a participant in a qualified cost sharing arrangement, and listing the other controlled participants in the arrangement. A controlled participant that is not required to file a U.S. income tax return must ensure that such a statement is attached to Schedule M of any Form 5471 or to any Form 5472 filed with respect to that participant.

(k) *Effective date.* This section is effective for taxable years beginning on or after January 1, 1996.

(l) *Transition rule.* A cost sharing arrangement will be considered a qualified cost sharing arrangement, within the meaning of this section, if, prior to January 1, 1996, the arrangement was a bona fide cost sharing arrangement under the provisions of § 1.482-7T (as contained in the 26 CFR part 1 edition revised as of April 1, 1995), but only if the arrangement is amended, if necessary, to conform with the provisions of this section by December 31, 1996. [Reg. § 1.482-7.]

☐ [*T.D.* 8632, 12-19-95. *Amended by T.D.* 8670, 5-9-96 *and T.D.* 8930, 12-27-2000.]

[Reg. § 1.482-8]

§ 1.482-8. **Examples of the best method rule.**—In accordance with the best method rule of § 1.482-1(c), a method may be applied in a particular case only if the comparability, quality of data, and reliability of assumptions under that method make it more reliable than any other available measure of the arm's length result. The following examples illustrate the comparative analysis required to apply this rule. As with all of the examples in these regulations, these examples are based on simplified facts, are provided solely for purposes of illustrating the type of analysis required under the relevant rule, and do not provide rules of general application. Thus, conclusions reached in these examples as to the relative reliability of methods are based on the assumed facts of the examples, and are not general conclusions concerning the relative reliability of any method.

Example 1—Preference for comparable uncontrolled price method. Company A is the U.S. distribution subsidiary of Company B, a foreign manufacturer of consumer electrical appliances. Company A purchases toaster ovens from Company B for resale in the U.S. market. To exploit other outlets for its toaster ovens, Company B also sells its toaster ovens to Company C, an unrelated U.S. distributor of toaster ovens. The products sold to Company A and Company C are identical in every respect and there are no material differences between the transactions. In this case application of the CUP method, using the sales of toaster ovens to Company C, generally will provide a more reliable measure of an arm's length result for the controlled sale of toaster ovens to

Reg. § 1.482-8

Company A than the application of any other method. See §§ 1.482-1(c)(2)(i) and -3(b)(2)(ii)(A).

Example 2—Resale price method preferred to comparable uncontrolled price method. The facts are the same as in *Example 1*, except that the toaster ovens sold to Company A are of substantially higher quality than those sold to Company C and the effect on price of such quality differences cannot be accurately determined. In addition, in order to round out its line of consumer appliances Company A purchases blenders from unrelated parties for resale in the United States. The blenders are resold to substantially the same customers as the toaster ovens, have a similar resale value to the toaster ovens, and are purchased under similar terms and in similar volumes. The distribution functions performed by Company A appear to be similar for toaster ovens and blenders. Given the product differences between the toaster ovens, application of the resale price method using the purchases and resales of blenders as the uncontrolled comparables is likely to provide a more reliable measure of an arm's length result than application of the comparable uncontrolled price method using Company B's sales of toaster ovens to Company C.

Example 3—Resale price method preferred to comparable profits method. (i) The facts are the same as in *Example 2* except that Company A purchases all its products from Company B and Company B makes no uncontrolled sales into the United States. However, six uncontrolled U.S. distributors are identified that purchase a similar line of products from unrelated parties. The uncontrolled distributors purchase toaster ovens from unrelated parties, but there are significant differences in the characteristics of the toaster ovens, including the brandnames under which they are sold.

(ii) Under the facts of this case, reliable adjustments for the effect of the different brandnames cannot be made. Except for some differences in payment terms and inventory levels, the purchases and resales of toaster ovens by the three uncontrolled distributors are closely similar to the controlled purchases in terms of the markets in which they occur, the volume of the transactions, the marketing activities undertaken by the distributor, inventory levels, warranties, allocation of currency risk, and other relevant functions and risks. Reliable adjustments can be made for the differences in payment terms and inventory levels. In addition, sufficiently detailed accounting information is available to permit adjustments to be made for differences in accounting methods or in reporting of costs between cost of goods sold and operating expenses. There are no other material differences between the controlled and uncontrolled transactions.

(iii) Because reliable adjustments for the differences between the toaster ovens, including the trademarks under which they are sold, cannot be made, these uncontrolled transactions will not serve as reliable measures of an arm's length result under the comparable uncontrolled price method. There is, however, close functional similarity between the controlled and uncontrolled transactions and reliable adjustments have been made for material differences that would be likely to affect gross profit. Under these circumstances, the gross profit margins derived under the resale price method are less likely to be susceptible to any unidentified differences than the operating profit measures used under the comparable profits method. Therefore, given the close functional comparability between the controlled and uncontrolled transactions, and the high quality of the data, the resale price method achieves a higher degree of comparability and will provide a more reliable measure of an arm's length result. See § 1.482-1(c) (Best method rule).

Example 4—Comparable profits method preferred to resale price method. The facts are the same as in *Example 3*, except that the accounting information available for the uncontrolled comparables is not sufficiently detailed to ensure consistent reporting between cost of goods sold and operating expenses of material items such as discounts, insurance, warranty costs, and supervisory, general and administrative expenses. These expenses are significant in amount. Therefore, whether these expenses are treated as costs of goods sold or operating expenses would have a significant effect on gross margins. Because in this case reliable adjustments can not be made for such accounting differences, the reliability of the resale price method is significantly reduced. There is, however, close functional similarity between the controlled and uncontrolled transactions and reliable adjustments have been made for all material differences other than the potential accounting differences. Because the comparable profits method is not adversely affected by the potential accounting differences, under these circumstances the comparable profits method is likely to produce a more reliable measure of an arm's length result than the resale price method. See § 1.482-1(c) (Best method rule).

Example 5—Cost plus method preferred to comparable profits method. (i) USS is a U.S. company that manufactures machine tool parts and sells them to its foreign parent corporation, FP. Four U.S. companies are identified that also manufacture various types of machine tool parts but sell them to uncontrolled purchasers.

Reg. § 1.482-8

(ii) Except for some differences in payment terms, the manufacture and sales of machine tool parts by the four uncontrolled companies are closely similar to the controlled transactions in terms of the functions performed and risks assumed. Reliable adjustments can be made for the differences in payment terms. In addition, sufficiently detailed accounting information is available to permit adjustments to be made for differences between the controlled transaction and the uncontrolled comparables in accounting methods and in the reporting of costs between cost of goods sold and operating expenses.

(iii) There is close functional similarity between the controlled and uncontrolled transactions and reliable adjustments can be made for material differences that would be likely to affect gross profit. Under these circumstances, the gross profit markups derived under the cost plus method are less likely to be susceptible to any unidentified differences than the operating profit measures used under the comparable profits method. Therefore, given the close functional comparability between the controlled and uncontrolled transactions, and the high quality of the data, the cost plus method achieves a higher degree of comparability and will provide a more reliable measure of an arm's length result. See § 1.482-1(c) (Best method rule).

Example 6—Comparable profits method preferred to cost plus method. The facts are the same as in *Example 5*, except that there are significant differences between the controlled and uncontrolled transactions in terms of the types of parts and components manufactured and the complexity of the manufacturing process. The resulting functional differences are likely to materially affect gross profit margins, but it is not possible to identify the specific differences and reliably adjust for their effect on gross profit. Because these functional differences would be reflected in differences in operating expenses, the operating profit measures used under the comparable profits method implicitly reflect to some extent these functional differences. Therefore, because in this case the comparable profits method is less sensitive than the cost plus method to the potentially significant functional differences between the controlled and uncontrolled transactions, the comparable profits method is likely to produce a more reliable measure of an arm's length result than the cost plus method. See § 1.482-1(c) (Best method rule).

Example 7—Preference for comparable uncontrolled transaction method. (i) USpharm, a U.S. pharmaceutical company, develops a new drug Z that is a safe and effective treatment for the disease zeezee. USpharm has obtained patents covering drug Z in the United States and in various foreign countries. USpharm has also obtained the regulatory authorizations necessary to market drug Z in the United States and in foreign countries.

(ii) USpharm licenses its subsidiary in country X, Xpharm, to produce and sell drug Z in country X. At the same time, it licenses an unrelated company, Ydrug, to produce and sell drug Z in country Y, a neighboring country. Prior to licensing the drug, USpharm had obtained patent protection and regulatory approvals in both countries and both countries provide similar protection for intellectual property rights. Country X and country Y are similar countries in terms of population, per capita income and the incidence of disease zeezee. Consequently, drug Z is expected to sell in similar quantities and at similar prices in both countries. In addition, costs of producing drug Z in each country are expected to be approximately the same.

(iii) USpharm and Xpharm establish terms for the license of drug Z that are identical in every material respect, including royalty rate, to the terms established between USpharm and Ydrug. In this case the district director determines that the royalty rate established in the Ydrug license agreement is a reliable measure of the arm's length royalty rate for the Xpharm license agreement. Given that the same property is transferred in the controlled and uncontrolled transactions, and that the circumstances under which the transactions occurred are substantially the same, in this case the comparable uncontrolled transaction method is likely to provide a more reliable measure of an arm's length result than any other method. See § 1.482-4(c)(2)(ii).

Example 8—Residual profit split method preferred to other methods. (i) USC is a U.S. company that develops, manufactures and sells communications equipment. EC is the European subsidiary of USC. EC is an established company that carries out extensive research and development activities and develops, manufactures and sells communications equipment in Europe. There are extensive transactions between USC and EC. USC licenses valuable technology it has developed to EC for use in the European market but EC also licenses valuable technology it has developed to USC. Each company uses components manufactured by the other in some of its products and purchases products from the other for resale in its own market.

(ii) Detailed accounting information is available for both USC and EC and adjustments can be made to achieve a high degree of consistency in accounting practices between them. Relatively reliable allocations of costs, income and assets can

Reg. § 1.482-8

be made between the business activities that are related to the controlled transactions and those that are not. Relevant marketing and research and development expenditures can be identified and reasonable estimates of the useful life of the related intangibles are available so that the capitalized value of the intangible development expenses of USC and EC can be calculated. In this case there is no reason to believe that the relative value of these capitalized expenses is substantially different from the relative value of the intangible property of USC and EC. Furthermore, comparables are identified that could be used to estimate a market return for the routine contributions of USC and EC. Based on these facts, the residual profit split could provide a reliable measure of an arm's length result.

(iii) There are no uncontrolled transactions involving property that is sufficiently comparable to much of the tangible and intangible property transferred between USC and EC to permit use of the comparable uncontrolled price method or the comparable uncontrolled transaction method. Uncontrolled companies are identified in Europe and the United States that perform somewhat similar activities to USC and EC; however, the activities of none of these companies are as complex as those of USC and EC and they do not use similar levels of highly valuable intangible property that they have developed themselves. Under these circumstances, the uncontrolled companies may be useful in determining a market return for the routine contributions of USC and EC, but that return would not reflect the value of the intangible property employed by USC and EC. Thus, none of the uncontrolled companies is sufficiently similar so that reliable results would be obtained using the resale price, cost plus, or comparable profits methods. Moreover, no uncontrolled companies can be identified that engaged in sufficiently similar activities and transactions with each other to employ the comparable profit split method.

(iv) Given the difficulties in applying the other methods, the reliability of the internal data on USC and EC, and the fact that acceptable comparables are available for deriving a market return for the routine contributions of USC and EC, the residual profit split method is likely to provide the most reliable measure of an arm's length result in this case.

Example 9—Comparable profits method preferred to profit split. (i) Company X is a large, complex U.S. company that carries out extensive research and development activities and manufactures and markets a variety of products. Company X has developed a new process by which compact disks can be fabricated at a fraction of the cost previously required. The process is expected to prove highly profitable, since there is a large market for compact disks. Company X establishes a new foreign subsidiary, Company Y, and licenses it the rights to use the process to fabricate compact disks for the foreign market as well as continuing technical support and improvements to the process. Company Y uses the process to fabricate compact disks which it supplies to related and unrelated parties.

(ii) The process licensed to Company Y is unique and highly valuable and no uncontrolled transfers of intangible property can be found that are sufficiently comparable to permit reliable application of the comparable uncontrolled transaction method. Company X is a large, complex company engaged in a variety of activities that owns unique and highly valuable intangible property. Consequently, no uncontrolled companies can be found that are similar to Company X. Furthermore, application of the profit split method in this case would involve the difficult and problematic tasks of allocating Company X's costs and assets between the relevant business activity and other activities and assigning a value to Company X's intangible contributions. On the other hand, Company Y performs relatively routine manufacturing and marketing activities and there are a number of similar uncontrolled companies. Thus, application of the comparable profits method using Company Y as the tested party is likely to produce a more reliable measure of an arm's length result than a profit split in this case. [Reg. § 1.482-8.]

☐ [*T.D.* 8552, 7-1-94.]

→ *Caution: Reg. § 1.482-1A applies for tax years beginning on or before April 21, 1993.*←

[Reg. § 1.482-1A]

§ 1.482-1A. Allocation of income and deductions among taxpayers.—(a) *Definitions.* When used in this section and in § 1.482-2—

(1) The term "organization" includes any organization of any kind, whether it be a sole proprietorship, a partnership, a trust, an estate, an association, or a corporation (as each is defined or understood in the Internal Revenue Code or the regulations thereunder), irrespective of the place where organized, where operated, or where its trade or business is conducted, and regardless of whether domestic or foreign, whether exempt, whether affiliated, or whether a party to a consolidated return.

Reg. § 1.482-1A(a)(1)

→ *Caution: Reg. § 1.482-1A applies for tax years beginning on or before April 21, 1993.*←

(2) The term "trade" or "business" includes any trade or business activity of any kind, regardless of whether or where organized, whether owned individually or otherwise, and regardless of the place where carried on.

(3) The term "controlled" includes any kind of control, direct or indirect, whether legally enforceable, and however exercisable or exercised. It is the reality of the control which is decisive, not its form or the mode of its exercise. A presumption of control arises if income or deductions have been arbitrarily shifted.

(4) The term "controlled taxpayer" means any one of two or more organizations, trades, or businesses owned or controlled directly or indirectly by the same interests.

(5) The terms "group" and "group of controlled taxpayers" mean the organizations, trades, or businesses owned or controlled by the same interests.

(6) The term "true taxable income" means, in the case of a controlled taxpayer, the taxable income (or, as the case may be, any item or element affecting taxable income) which would have resulted to the controlled taxpayer, had it in the conduct of its affairs (or, as the case may be, in the particular contract, transaction, arrangement, or other act) dealt with the other member or members of the group at arm's length. It does not mean the income, the deductions, the credits, the allowances, or the item or element of income, deductions, credits, or allowances, resulting to the controlled taxpayer by reason of the particular contract, transaction, or arrangement, the controlled taxpayer, or the interests controlling it, chose to make (even though such contract, transaction, or arrangement be legally binding upon the parties thereto).

(b) *Scope and purpose.* (1) The purpose of section 482 is to place a controlled taxpayer on a tax parity with an uncontrolled taxpayer, by determining, according to the standard of an uncontrolled taxpayer, the true taxable income from the property and business of a controlled taxpayer. The interests controlling a group of controlled taxpayers are assumed to have complete power to cause each controlled taxpayer so to conduct its affairs that its transactions and accounting records truly reflect the taxable income from the property and business of each of the controlled taxpayers. If, however, this has not been done, and the taxable incomes are thereby understated, the district director shall intervene, and, by making such distributions, apportionments, or allocations as he may deem necessary of gross income, deductions, credits, or allowances, or of any item or element affecting taxable income, between or among the controlled taxpayers constituting the group, shall determine the true taxable income of each controlled taxpayer. The standard to be applied in every case is that of an uncontrolled taxpayer dealing at arm's length with another uncontrolled taxpayer.

(2) Section 482 and this section apply to the case of any controlled taxpayer, whether such taxpayer makes a separate or a consolidated return. If a controlled taxpayer makes a separate return, the determination is of its true separate taxable income. If a controlled taxpayer is a party to a consolidated return, the true consolidated taxable income of the affiliated group and the true separate taxable income of the controlled taxpayer are determined consistently with the principles of a consolidated return.

(3) Section 482 grants no right to a controlled taxpayer to apply its provisions at will, nor does it grant any right to compel the district director to apply such provisions. It is not intended (except in the case of the computation of consolidated taxable income under a consolidated return) to effect in any case such a distribution, apportionment, or allocation of gross income, deductions, credits, or allowances, or any item of gross income, deductions, credits, or allowances, as would produce a result equivalent to a computation of consolidated taxable income under subchapter A, chapter 6 of the Code.

(c) *Application.* Transactions between one controlled taxpayer and another will be subjected to special scrutiny to ascertain whether the common control is being used to reduce, avoid, or escape taxes. In determining the true taxable income of a controlled taxpayer, the district director is not restricted to the case of improper accounting, to the case of a fraudulent, colorable, or sham transaction, or to the case of a device designed to reduce or avoid tax by shifting or distorting income, deductions, credits, or allowances. The authority to determine true taxable income extends to any case in which either by inadvertence or design the taxable income, in whole or in part, of a controlled taxpayer, is other than it would have been had the taxpayer in the conduct of his affairs been an uncontrolled taxpayer dealing at arm's length with another uncontrolled taxpayer.

(d) *Method of allocation.* (1) The method of allocating, apportioning, or distributing income, deductions, credits, and allowances to be used by the district director in any case, including the form of the adjustments and the character and

→ **Caution: Reg. § 1.482-1A applies for tax years beginning on or before April 21, 1993.** ←

source of amounts allocated, shall be determined with reference to the substance of the particular transactions or arrangements which result in the avoidance of taxes or the failure to clearly reflect income. The appropriate adjustments may take the form of an increase or decrease in gross income, increase or decrease in deductions (including depreciation), increase or decrease in basis of assets (including inventory), or any other adjustment which may be appropriate under the circumstances. See § 1.482-2 for specific rules relating to methods of allocation in the case of several types of business transactions.

(2) Whenever the district director makes adjustments to the income of one member of a group of controlled taxpayers (such adjustments being referred to in this paragraph as "primary" adjustments) he shall also make appropriate correlative adjustments to the income of any other member of the group involved in the allocation. The correlative adjustment shall actually be made if the U.S. income tax liability of the other member would be affected for any pending taxable year. Thus, if the district director makes an allocation of income, he shall not only increase the income of one member of the group, but shall decrease the income of the other member if such adjustment would have an effect on the U.S. income tax liability of the other member for any pending taxable year. For the purposes of this subparagraph, a "pending taxable year" is any taxable year with respect to which the U.S. income tax return of the other member has been filed by the time the allocation is made, and with respect to which a credit or refund is not barred by the operation of any law or rule of law. If a correlative adjustment is not actually made because it would have no effect on the U.S. income tax liability of the other member involved in the allocation for any pending taxable year, such adjustment shall nevertheless be deemed to have been made for the purpose of determining the U.S. income tax liability of such member for a later taxable year, or for the purposes of determining the U.S. income tax liability of any person for any taxable year. The district director shall furnish to the taxpayer with respect to which the primary adjustment is made a written statement of the amount and nature of the correlative adjustment which is deemed to have been made. For purposes of this subparagraph, a primary adjustment shall not be considered to have been made (and therefore a correlative adjustment is not required to be made) until the first occurring of the following events with respect to the primary adjustment:

(i) The date of assessment of the tax following execution by the taxpayer of a Form 870 (Waiver of Restrictions on Assessment and Collection of Deficiency in Tax and Acceptance of Overassessment) with respect to such adjustment,

(ii) Acceptance of a Form 870-AD (Offer of Waiver of Restriction on Assessment and Collection of Deficiency in Tax and Acceptance of Overassessment),

(iii) Payment of the deficiency,

(iv) Stipulation in the Tax Court of the United States, or

(v) Final determination of tax liability by offer-in-compromise, closing agreement, or court action.

The principles of this subparagraph may be illustrated by the following examples in each of which it is assumed that X and Y are members of the same group of controlled entities and that they regularly compute their incomes on the basis of a calendar year:

Example (1). Assume that in 1968 the district director proposes to adjust X's income for 1966 to reflect an arm's length rental charge for Y's use of X's tangible property in 1966; that X consents to an assessment reflecting such adjustment by executing a Waiver, Form 870; and that an assessment of the tax with respect to such adjustment is made in 1968. The primary adjustment is therefore considered to have been made in 1968. Assume further that both X and Y are United States corporations and that Y had net operating losses in 1963, 1964, 1965, 1966, and 1967. Although a correlative adjustment would not have an effect on Y's U.S. income tax liability for any pending taxable year, an adjustment increasing Y's net operating loss for 1966 shall be deemed to have been made for the purposes of determining Y's U.S. income tax liability for 1968 or a later taxable year to which the increased operating loss may be carried. The district director shall notify X in writing of the amount and nature of the adjustment which is deemed to have been made to Y.

Example (2). Assume that X and Y are United States corporations; that X is in the business of rendering engineering services; that in 1968 the district director proposes to adjust X's income for 1966 to reflect an arm's length fee for the rendition of engineering services by X in 1966 relating to the construction of Y's factory; that X consents to an assessment reflecting such adjustment by executing a Waiver, Form 870; and that an assessment of the tax with respect to such adjustment is made in 1968. Assume further that fees for such services would properly constitute a capital expenditure by Y, and that Y does not

Reg. § 1.482-1A(d)(2)

→ *Caution: Reg. § 1.482-1A applies for tax years beginning on or before April 21, 1993.*←

place the factory in service until 1969. Although a correlative adjustment (increase in basis) would not have an effect on Y's U.S. income tax liability for a pending taxable year, an adjustment increasing the basis of Y's assets for 1966 shall be deemed to have been made in 1968 for the purpose of computing allowable depreciation or gain or loss on disposition for 1969 and any future taxable year. The district director shall notify X in writing of the amount and nature of the adjustment which is deemed to have been made to Y.

Example (3). Assume that X is a U.S. taxpayer and Y is a foreign taxpayer not engaged in a trade or business in the United States; that in 1968 the district director proposes to adjust X's income for 1966 to reflect an arm's length interest charge on a loan made to Y; that X consents to an assessment reflecting such allocation by executing a Waiver, Form 870; and that an assessment of the tax with respect to such adjustment is made in 1968. Although a correlative adjustment would not have an effect on Y's U.S. income tax liability, an adjustment in Y's income for 1966 shall be deemed to have been made in 1968 for the purposes of determining the amount of Y's earnings and profits for 1966 and subsequent years, and of any other effect it may have on any person's U.S. income tax liability for any taxable year. The district director shall notify X in writing of the amount and nature of the allocation which is deemed to have been made to Y.

(3) In making distributions, apportionments, or allocations between two members of a group of controlled entities with respect to particular transactions, the district director shall consider the effect upon such members of an arrangement between them for reimbursement within a reasonable period before or after the taxable year if the taxpayer can establish that such an arrangement in fact existed during the taxable year under consideration. The district director shall also consider the effect of any other nonarm's length transaction between them in the taxable year which, if taken into account, would result in a setoff against any allocation which would otherwise be made, provided the taxpayer is able to establish with reasonable specificity that the transaction was not at arm's length and the amount of the appropriate arm's length charge. For purposes of the preceding sentence, the term arm's length refers to the amount which was charged or would have been charged in independent transactions with unrelated parties under the same or similar circumstances considering all the relevant facts and without regard to the rules found in § 1.482-2 by which certain charges are deemed to be equal to arm's length. For example, assume that one member of a group performs services which benefit a second member, which would in itself require an allocation to reflect an arm's length charge for the performance of such services. Assume further that the first member can establish that during the same taxable year the second member engages in other nonarm's length transactions which benefit the first member, such as by selling products to the first member at a discount, or purchasing products from the first member at a premium, or paying royalties to the first member in an excessive amount. In such case, the value of the benefits received by the first member as a result of the other activities will be set off against the allocation which would otherwise be made. If the effect of the set-off is to change the characterization or source of the income or deductions, or otherwise distort taxable income, in such a manner as to affect the United States tax liability of any member, allocations will be made to reflect the correct amount of each category of income or deductions. In order to establish that a set-off to the adjustments proposed by the district director is appropriate, the taxpayer must notify the district director of the basis of any claimed set-off at any time before the expiration of the period ending 30 days after the date of a letter by which the district director transmits an examination report notifying the taxpayer of proposed adjustments or before July 16, 1968, whichever is later. The principles of this subparagraph may be illustrated by the following examples, in each of which it is assumed that P and S are calendar year corporations and are both members of the same group of controlled entities:

Example (1). P performs services in 1966 for the benefit of S in connection with S's manufacture and sale of a product. S does not pay P for such services in 1966, but in consideration for such services, agrees in 1966 to pay P a percentage of the amount of sales of the product in 1966 through 1970. In 1966 it appeared this agreement would provide adequate consideration for the services. No allocation will be made with respect to the services performed by P.

Example (2). P renders services to S in connection with the construction of S's factory. An arm's length charge for such services, determined under paragraph (b) of § 1.482-2, would be $100,000. During the same taxable year P makes available to S a machine to be used in such construction. P bills S $125,000 for the services, but does not bill for the use of the machine. No allocation will be made with respect to the excessive charge for services or the undercharge for the

Reg. § 1.482-1A(d)(3)

→ **Caution: Reg. § 1.482-1A applies for tax years beginning on or before April 21, 1993.** ←

machine if P can establish that the excessive charge for services was equal to an arm's length charge for the use of the machine, and if the taxable income and income tax liabilities of P and S are not distorted.

Example (3). Assume the same facts as in example (2), except that, if P had reported $25,000 as rental income and $25,000 less service income, it would have been subject to the tax on personal holding companies. Allocations will be made to reflect the correct amounts of rental income and service income.

(4) If the members of a group of controlled taxpayers engage in transactions with one another, the district director may distribute, apportion, or allocate income, deductions, credits, or allowances to reflect the true taxable income of the individual members under the standards set forth in this section and in § 1.482-2 notwithstanding the fact that the ultimate income anticipated from a series of transactions may not be realized or is realized during a later period. For example, if one member of a controlled group sells a product at less than an arm's length price to a second member of the group in one taxable year and the second member resells the product to an unrelated party in the next taxable year, the district director may make an appropriate allocation to reflect an arm's length price for the sale of the product in the first taxable year, notwithstanding that the second member of the group had not realized any gross income from the resale of the product in the first year. Similarly, if one member of a group lends money to a second member of the group in a taxable year, the district director may make an appropriate allocation to reflect an arm's length charge for interest during such taxable year even if the second member does not realize income during such year. The provisions of this subparagraph apply even if the gross income contemplated from a series of transactions is never, in fact, realized by the other members.

(5) Section 482 may, when necessary to prevent the avoidance of taxes or to clearly reflect income, be applied in circumstances described in sections of the Code (such as section 351) providing for nonrecognition of gain or loss. See, for example, *National Securities Corporation v. Commissioner of Internal Revenue,* 137 F. 2d 600 (3rd Cir. 1943), cert. denied, 320 U.S. 794 (1943).

(6) If payment or reimbursement for the sale, exchange, or use of property, the rendition of services, or the advance of other consideration among members of a group of controlled entities was prevented, or would have been prevented, at the time of the transaction because of currency or other restrictions imposed under the laws of any foreign country, any distributions, apportionments, or allocations which may be made under section 482 with respect to such transactions may be treated as deferrable income or deductions, providing the taxpayer has, for the year to which the distributions, apportionments, or allocations relate, elected to use a method of accounting in which the reporting of deferrable income is deferred until the income ceases to be deferrable income. Under such method of accounting, referred to in this section as the deferred income method of accounting, any payments or reimbursements which were prevented or would have been prevented, and any deductions attributable directly or indirectly to such payments or reimbursements, shall be deferred until they cease to be deferrable under such method of accounting. If such method of accounting has not been elected with respect to the taxable year to which the allocations under section 482 relate, the taxpayer may elect such method with respect to such allocations (but not with respect to other deferrable income) at any time before the first occurring of the following events with respect to the allocations:

(i) Execution by the taxpayer of Form 870 (Waiver of Restrictions on Assessment and Collection of Deficiency in Tax and Acceptance of Overassessment);

(ii) Expiration of the period ending 30 days after the date of a letter by which the district director transmits an examination report notifying the taxpayer of the proposed adjustments reflecting such allocations or before July 16, 1968, whichever is later; or

(iii) Execution of a closing agreement or offer-in-compromise. The principles of this subparagraph may be illustrated by the following example in which it is assumed that X, a domestic corporation, and Y, a foreign corporation, are members of the same group of controlled entities:

Example. X, which is in the business of rendering a certain type of service to unrelated parties, renders such services for the benefit of Y in 1965. The direct and indirect costs allocable to such services are $60,000, and an arm's length charge for such services is $100,000. Assume that the district director proposes to increase X's income by $100,000, but that the country in which Y is located would have blocked payment in 1965 for such services. If, prior to the first occurring of the events described in subdivisions (i), (ii), or (iii) of this subparagraph, X elects to use the deferred

Reg. § 1.482-1A(d)(6)

→ **Caution: Reg. § 1.482-1A applies for tax years beginning on or before April 21, 1993.** ←

income method of accounting with respect to such allocation, the $100,000 allocation and the $60,000 of costs are deferrable until such amounts cease to be deferrable under X's method of accounting. [Reg. § 1.482-1A.]

☐ [T.D. 6595, 4-13-62. Amended by T.D. 6952, 4-15-68 and T.D. 8470, 1-13-93.]

→ **Caution: Reg. § 1.482-2A applies for tax years beginning on or before April 21, 1993.** ←

[Reg. § 1.482-2A]

§ 1.482-2A. **Determination of taxable income in specific situations.**—(a)-(c) For applicable rules, see § 1.482-2T(a) through (c).

(d) *Transfer or use of intangible property*—(1) *In general.* (i) Except as otherwise provided in subparagraph (4) of this paragraph, where intangible property or an interest therein is transferred, sold, assigned, loaned, or otherwise made available in any manner by one member of a group of controlled entities (referred to in this paragraph as the transferor) to another member of the group (referred to in this paragraph as the transferee) for other than an arm's length consideration, the district director may make appropriate allocations to reflect an arm's length consideration for such property or its use. Subparagraph (2) of this paragraph provides rules for determining the form an amount of an appropriate allocation, subparagraph (3) of this paragraph provides a definition of "intangible property", and subparagraph (4) of this paragraph provides rules with respect to certain cost-sharing arrangements in connection with the development of intangible property. For purposes of this paragraph, an interest in intangible property may take the form of the right to use such property.

(ii)(a) In the absence of a bona fide cost-sharing arrangement (as defined in subparagraph (4) of this paragraph), where one member of a group of related entities undertakes the development of intangible property as a developer within the meaning of (c) of this subdivision, no allocation with respect to such development activity shall be made under the rules of this paragraph or any other paragraph of this section (except as provided in subdivision (b) of this division) until such time as any property developed, or any interest therein, is or is deemed to be transferred, sold, assigned, loaned, or otherwise made available in any manner by the developer to a related entity in a transfer subject to the rules of this paragraph. Where a member of the group other than the developer acquires an interest in the property developed by virtue of obtaining a patent or copyright, or by any other means, the developer shall be deemed to have transferred such interest in such property to the acquiring member in a transaction subject to the rules of this paragraph. For example, if one member of a group (the developer) undertakes to develop a new patentable product and the costs of development are incurred by that entity over a period of 3 years, no allocation with respect to that entity's activity shall be made during such period. The amount of any allocation that may be appropriate at the expiration of such development period when, for example, the patent on the product is transferred, or deemed transferred, to a related entity for other than an arm's length consideration, shall be determined in accordance with the rules of this paragraph.

(b) Where one member of a group renders assistance in the form of loans, services, or the use of tangible or intangible property to a developer in connection with an attempt to develop intangible property, the amount of any allocation that may be appropriate with respect to such assistance shall be determined in accordance with the rules of the appropriate paragraph or paragraphs of this section. Thus, where one entity allows a related entity, which is the developer, to use tangible property, such as laboratory equipment, in connection with the development of intangible property, the amount of any allocation that may be appropriate with respect to such use shall be determined in accordance with the rules of paragraph (c) of this section. In the event that the district director does not exercise his discretion to make allocations with respect to the assistance rendered to the developer, the value of the assistance shall be allowed as a set-off against any allocation that the district director may make under this paragraph as a result of the transfer of the intangible property to the entity rendering the assistance.

(c) The determination as to which member of a group of related entities is a developer and which members of the group are rendering assistance to the developer in connection with its development activities shall be based upon all the facts and circumstances of the individual case. Of all the facts and circumstances to be taken into account in making this determination, greatest weight shall be given to the relative amounts of all the direct and indirect costs of development

Adjustments

See p. 20,601 for regulations not amended to reflect law changes

37,269

→ *Caution: Reg. § 1.482-2A applies for tax years beginning on or before April 21, 1993.* ←

and the corresponding risks of development borne by the various members of the group, and the relative values of the use of any intangible property of members of the group which is made available without adequate consideration for use in connection with the development activity, which property is likely to contribute to a substantial extent in the production of intangible property. For this purpose, the risk to be borne with respect to development activity is the possibility that such activity will not result in the production of intangible property or that the intangible property produced will not be of sufficient value to allow for the recovery of the costs of developing it. A member will not be considered to have borne the costs and corresponding risks of development unless such member is committed to bearing such costs in advance of, or contemporaneously with, their incurrence and without regard to the success of the project. Other factors that may be relevant in determining which member of the group is the developer include the location of the development activity, the capabilities of the various members to carry on the project independently, and the degree of control over the project exercised by the various members.

(d) The principles of this subdivision (ii) may be illustrated by the following examples in which it is assumed that X and Y are corporate members of the same group:

Example (1). X, at the request of Y, undertakes to develop a new machine which will function effectively in the climate in which Y's factory is located. Y agrees to bear all the direct and indirect costs of the project whether or not X successfully develops the machine. Assume that X does not make any of its own intangible property available for use in connection with the project. The machine is successfully developed and Y obtains possession of the intangible property necessary to produce such machine. Based on the facts and circumstances as stated, Y shall be considered to be the developer of the intangible property and, therefore, Y shall not be treated as having obtained the property in a transfer subject to the rules of this paragraph. Any amount which may be allocable with respect to the assistance rendered by X shall be determined in accordance with the rules of (b) of this subdivision.

Example (2). Assume the same facts as in example (1) except that Y agrees to reimburse X for its costs only in the event that the property is successfully developed. In such case X is the developer and Y is deemed to have received the property in a transfer subject to the rules of this paragraph. Therefore, the district director may make an allocation to reflect an arm's length consideration for such property.

Example (3). In 1967 X undertakes to develop product M in its research and development department. X incurs direct and indirect costs of $1,000,000 per year in connection with the project in 1967, 1968, and 1969. In connection with the project, X employs the formula for compound N, which it owns, and which is likely to contribute substantially to the success of the project. The value of the use of the formula for compound N in connection with this project is $750,000. In 1968, 4 chemists employed by Y spend 6 months working on the project in X's laboratory. The salary and other expenses connected with the chemists' employment for that period ($100,000) are paid by Y, for which no charge is made to X. In 1969, product M is perfected and Y obtains patents thereon. X is considered to be the developer of product M since, among other things, it bore the greatest relative share of the costs and risks incurred in connection with this project and made available intangible property (formula for compound N) which was likely to contribute substantially in the development of product M. Accordingly, no allocation with respect to X's development activity should be made before 1969. The property is deemed to have been transferred to Y at that time by virtue of the fact that Y obtained the patent rights to product M. In such case the district director may make an allocation to reflect an arm's length consideration for such transfer. In the event that the district director makes such an allocation and he has not made or does not make an allocation for 1968 with respect to the services of the chemists in accordance with the principles of paragraph (b) of this section, the value of the assistance shall be allowed as a set-off against the amount of the allocation reflecting an arm's length consideration for the transfer of the intangible property.

(2) *Arm's length consideration.* (i) An arm's length consideration shall be in a form which is consistent with the form which would be adopted in transactions between unrelated parties under the same circumstances. To the extent appropriate, an arm's length consideration may take any one or more of the following forms: *(a)* royalties based on the transferee's output, sales, profits, or any other measure; *(b)* lump-sum payments; or *(c)* any other form, including reciprocal licensing rights, which might reasonably have been adopted by unrelated parties under the circumstances, provided that the parties can establish that such form was adopted pursuant to an arrangement

Reg. § 1.482-2A(d)(2)

→ **Caution: Reg. § 1.482-2A applies for tax years beginning on or before April 21, 1993.**

which in fact existed between them. However, where the transferee pays nominal or no consideration for the property or interest therein and where the transferor has retained a substantial interest in the property, an allocation shall be presumed not to take the form of a lump-sum payment.

(ii) In determining the amount of an arm's length consideration, the standard to be applied is the amount that would have been paid by an unrelated party for the same intangible property under the same circumstances. Where there have been transfers by the transferor to unrelated parties involving the same or similar intangible property under the same or similar circumstances the amount of the consideration for such transfers shall generally be the best indication of an arm's length consideration.

(iii) Where a sufficiently similar transaction involving an unrelated party cannot be found, the following factors, to the extent appropriate (depending upon the type of intangible property and the form of the transfer), may be considered in arriving at the amount of the arm's length consideration:

(a) The prevailing rates in the same industry or for similar property,

(b) The offers of competing transferors or the bids of competing transferees,

(c) The terms of the transfer, including limitations on the geographic area covered and the exclusive or nonexclusive character of any rights granted,

(d) The uniqueness of the property and the period for which it is likely to remain unique,

(e) The degree and duration of protection afforded to the property under the laws of the relevant countries,

(f) Value of services rendered by the transferor to the transferee in connection with the transfer within the meaning of paragraph (b)(8) of this section,

(g) Prospective profits to be realized or costs to be saved by the transferee through its use or subsequent transfer of the property,

(h) The capital investment and starting up expenses required of the transferee,

(i) The next subdivision is (j),

(j) The availability of substitutes for the property transferred,

(k) The arm's length rates and prices paid by unrelated parties where the property is resold or sublicensed to such parties,

(l) The costs incurred by the transferor in developing the property, and

(m) Any other fact or circumstance which unrelated parties would have been likely to consider in determining the amount of an arm's length consideration for the property.

(3) *Definition of intangible property.* (i) Solely for the purposes of this section, intangible property shall consist of the items described in subdivision (ii) of this subparagraph, provided that such items have substantial value independent of the services of individual persons.

(ii) The items referred to in subdivision (i) of this subparagraph are as follows:

(a) Patents, inventions, formulas, processes, designs, patterns, and other similar items;

(b) Copyrights, literary, musical, or artistic compositions, and other similar items;

(c) Trademarks, trade names, brand names, and other similar items;

(d) Franchises, licenses, contracts, and other similar items;

(e) Methods, programs, systems, procedures, campaigns, surveys, studies, forecasts, estimates, customer lists, technical data, and other similar items.

(4) *Sharing of costs and risks.* Where a member of a group of controlled entities acquires an interest in intangible property as a participating party in a bona fide cost sharing arrangement with respect to the development of such intangible property, the district director shall not make allocations with respect to such acquisition except as may be appropriate to reflect each participant's arm's length share of the costs and risks of developing the property. A bona fide cost sharing arrangement is an agreement, in writing, between two or more members of a group of controlled entities providing for the sharing of the costs and risks of developing intangible property in return for a specified interest in the intangible property that may be produced. In order for the arrangement to qualify as a bona fide arrangement, it must reflect an effort in good faith by the participating members to bear their respective shares of all the costs and risks of development on an arm's length basis. In order for the sharing of costs and risks to be considered on an arm's length basis, the terms and conditions must be comparable to those which would have been adopted by unrelated parties similarly situated had they entered into such an arrangement. If an oral cost sharing arrangement, entered into prior to April 16, 1968, and

Reg. § 1.482-2A(d)(3)

→ **Caution: Reg. § 1.482-2A applies for tax years beginning on or before April 21, 1993.**←

continued in effect after that date, is otherwise in compliance with the standards prescribed in this subparagraph, it shall constitute a bona fide cost sharing arrangement if it is reduced to writing prior to January 1, 1969.

(e) *Sales of tangible property*—(1) *In general.* (i) Where one member of a group of controlled entities (referred to in this paragraph as the "seller") sells or otherwise disposes of tangible property to another member of such group (referred to in this paragraph as the "buyer") at other than an arm's length price (such a sale being referred to in this paragraph as a "controlled sale"), the district director may make appropriate allocations between the seller and the buyer to reflect an arm's length price for such sale or disposition. An arm's length price is the price that an unrelated party would have paid under the same circumstances for the property involved in the controlled sale. Since unrelated parties normally sell products at a profit, an arm's length price normally involves a profit to the seller.

(ii) Subparagraphs (2), (3), and (4) of this paragraph describe three methods of determining an arm's length price and the standards for applying each method. They are, respectively, the comparable uncontrolled price method, the resale price method, and the cost plus method. In addition, a special rule is provided in subdivision (v) of this subparagraph for use (notwithstanding any other provision of this subdivision) in determining an arm's length price for an ore or mineral. If there are comparable uncontrolled sales as defined in subparagraph (2) of this paragraph, the comparable uncontrolled price method must be utilized because it is the method likely to result in the most accurate estimate of an arm's length price (for the reason that it is based upon the price actually paid by unrelated parties for the same or similar products). If there are no comparable uncontrolled sales, then the resale price method must be utilized if the standards for its application are met because it is the method likely to result in the next most accurate estimate in such instances (for the reason that, in such instances, the arm's length price determined under such method is based more directly upon actual arm's length transactions than is the cost plus method). A typical situation where the resale price method may be required is where a manufacturer sells products to a related distributor which, without further processing, resells the products in uncontrolled transactions. If all the standards for the mandatory application of the resale price method are not satisfied, then, as provided in subparagraph (3)(iii) of this paragraph, either that method or the cost plus method may be used, depending upon which method is more feasible and is likely to result in a more accurate estimate of an arm's length price. A typical situation where the cost plus method may be appropriate is where a manufacturer sells products to a related entity which performs substantial manufacturing, assembly, or other processing of the product or adds significant value by reason of its utilization of its intangible property prior to resale in uncontrolled transactions.

(iii) Where the standards for applying one of the three methods of pricing described in subdivision (ii) of this subparagraph are met, such method must, for the purposes of this paragraph, be utilized unless the taxpayer can establish that, considering all the facts and circumstances, some method of pricing other than those described in subdivision (ii) of this subparagraph is clearly more appropriate. Where none of the three methods of pricing described in subdivision (ii) of this subparagraph can reasonably be applied under the facts and circumstances as they exist in a particular case, some appropriate method of pricing other than those described in subdivision (ii) of this subparagraph, or variations on such methods, can be used.

(iv) The methods of determining arm's length prices described in this section are stated in terms of their application to individual sales of property. However, because of the possibility that a taxpayer may make controlled sales of many different products, or many separate sales of the same product, it may be impractical to analyze every sale for the purposes of determining the arm's length price. It is therefore permissible to determine or verify arm's length prices by applying the appropriate methods of pricing to product lines or other groupings where it is impractical to ascertain an arm's length price for each product or sale. In addition, the district director may determine or verify the arm's length price of all sales to a related entity by employing reasonable statistical sampling techniques.

(v) The price for a mineral product which is sold at the stage at which mining or extraction ends shall be determined under the provisions of §§ 1.613-3 and 1.613-4.

(2) *Comparable uncontrolled price method.* (i) Under the method of pricing described as the "comparable uncontrolled price method", the arm's length price of a controlled sale is equal to the price paid in comparable uncontrolled sales, adjusted as provided in subdivision (ii) of this subparagraph.

Reg. § 1.482-2A(e)(2)

→ **Caution: Reg. § 1.482-2A applies for tax years beginning on or before April 21, 1993.** ←

(ii) "Uncontrolled sales" are sales in which the seller and the buyers are not members of the same controlled group. These include (a) sales made by a member of the controlled group to an unrelated party, (b) sales made to a member of the controlled group by an unrelated party, and (c) sales made in which the parties are not members of the controlled group and are not related to each other. However, uncontrolled sales do not include sales at unrealistic prices, as for example where a member makes uncontrolled sales in small quantities at a price designed to justify a nonarm's length price on a large volume of controlled sales. Uncontrolled sales are considered comparable to controlled sales if the physical property and circumstances involved in the uncontrolled sales are identical to the physical property and circumstances involved in the controlled sales, or if such properties and circumstances are so nearly identical that any differences either have no effect on price, or such differences can be reflected by a reasonable number of adjustments to the price of uncontrolled sales. For this purpose, differences can be reflected by adjusting prices only where such differences have a definite and reasonably ascertainable effect on price. If the differences can be reflected by such adjustment, then the price of the uncontrolled sale as adjusted constitutes the comparable uncontrolled sale price. Some of the differences which may affect the price of property are differences in the quality of the product, terms of sale, intangible property associated with the sale, time of sale, and the level of the market and the geographic market in which the sale takes place. Whether and to what extent differences in the various properties and circumstances affect price, and whether differences render sales noncomparable, depends upon the particular circumstances and property involved. The principles of this subdivision may be illustrated by the following examples, in each of which it is assumed that X makes both controlled and uncontrolled sales of the identical property:

Example (1). Assume that the circumstances surrounding the controlled and the uncontrolled sales are identical, except for the fact that the controlled sales price is a delivered price and the uncontrolled sales are made f.o.b. X's factory. Since differences in terms of transportation and insurance generally have a definite and reasonably ascertainable effect on price, such differences do not normally render the uncontrolled sales noncomparable to the controlled sales.

Example (2). Assume that the circumstances surrounding the controlled and uncontrolled sales are identical, except for the fact that X affixes its valuable trademark in the controlled sales, and does not affix its trademark in uncontrolled sales. Since the effects on price of differences in intangible property associated with the sale of tangible property, such as trademarks, are normally not reasonably ascertainable, such differences would normally render the uncontrolled sales noncomparable.

Example (3). Assume that the circumstances surrounding the controlled and uncontrolled sales are identical except for the fact that X, a manufacturer of business machines, makes certain minor modifications in the physical properties of the machines to satisfy safety specifications or other specific requirements of a customer in controlled sales, and does not make these modifications in uncontrolled sales. Since minor physical differences in the product generally have a definite and reasonably ascertainable effect on prices, such differences do not normally render the uncontrolled sales noncomparable to the controlled sales.

(iii) Where there are two or more comparable uncontrolled sales susceptible of adjustment as defined in subdivision (ii) of this subparagraph, the comparable uncontrolled sale or sales requiring the fewest and simplest adjustments provided in subdivision (ii) of this subparagraph should generally be selected. Thus, for example, if a taxpayer makes comparable uncontrolled sales of a particular product which differ from the controlled sale only with respect to the terms of delivery, and makes other comparable uncontrolled sales of the product which differ from the controlled sale with respect to both terms of delivery and terms of payment, the comparable uncontrolled sales differing only with respect to terms of delivery should be selected as the comparable uncontrolled sale.

(iv) One of the circumstances which may affect the price of property is the fact that the seller may desire to make sales at less than a normal profit for the primary purpose of establishing or maintaining a market for his products. Thus, a seller may be willing to reduce the price of a product, for a time, in order to introduce his product into an area or in order to meet competition. However, controlled sales may be priced in such a manner only if such price would have been charged in an uncontrolled sale under comparable circumstances. Such fact may be demonstrated by showing that the buyer in the controlled sale made corresponding reductions in the resale price to uncontrolled purchasers, or that such buyer engaged in substantially greater sales promotion

Reg. § 1.482-2A(e)(2)

Adjustments 37,273

See p. 20,601 for regulations not amended to reflect law changes

→ *Caution: Reg. § 1.482-2A applies for tax years beginning on or before April 21, 1993.*←

activities with respect to the product involved in the controlled sale than with respect to other products. For example, assume X, a manufacturer of batteries, commences to sell car batteries to Y, a subsidiary of X, for resale in a new market. In its existing markets X's batteries sell to independent retailers at $20 per unit, and X sells them to wholesalers at $17 per unit. Y also sells X's batteries to independent retailers at $20 per unit. X's batteries are not known in the new market in which Y is operating. In order to engage competitively in the new market Y incurs selling and advertising costs substantially higher than those incurred for its sales of other products. Under these circumstances X may sell to Y, for a time, at less than $17 to take into account the increased selling and advertising activities of Y in penetrating and establishing the new market. This may be done even though it may result in a transfer price from X to Y which is below X's full costs of manufacturing the product.

(3) *Resale price method.* (i) Under the pricing method described as the "resale price method", the arm's length price of a controlled sale is equal to the applicable resale price (as defined in subdivision (iv) or (v) of this subparagraph), reduced by an appropriate markup, and adjusted as provided in subdivision (ix) of this subparagraph. An appropriate markup is computed by multiplying the applicable resale price by the appropriate markup percentage as defined in subdivision (vi) of this subparagraph. Thus, where one member of a group of controlled entities sells property to another member which resells the property in uncontrolled sales, if the applicable resale price of the property involved in the uncontrolled sale is $100 and the appropriate markup percentage for resales by the buyer is 20 percent, the arm's length price of the controlled sale is $80 ($100 minus 20 percent × $100), adjusted as provided in subdivision (ix) of this subparagraph.

(ii) The resale price method must be used to compute an arm's length price of a controlled sale if all the following circumstances exist:

(a) There are no comparable uncontrolled sales as defined in subparagraph (2) of this paragraph.

(b) An applicable resale price, as defined in subdivision (iv) or (v) of this subparagraph, is available with respect to resales made within a reasonable time before or after the time of the controlled sale.

(c) The buyer (reseller) has not added more than an insubstantial amount to the value of the property by physically altering the product before resale. For this purpose packaging, repacking, labeling, or minor assembly of property does not constitute physical alteration.

(d) The buyer (reseller) has not added more than an insubstantial amount to the value of the property by the use of intangible property. See § 1.482-2(d)(3) for the definition of intangible property.

(iii) Notwithstanding the fact that one or both of the requirements of subdivision (ii)(c) or (d) of this subparagraph may not be met, the resale price method may be used if such method is more feasible and is likely to result in a more accurate determination of an arm's length price than the use of the cost plus method. Thus, even though one of the requirements of such subdivision is not satisfied, the resale price method may nevertheless be more appropriate than the cost plus method because the computations and evaluations required under the former method may be fewer and easier to make than under the latter method. In general, the resale price method is more appropriate when the functions performed by the seller are more extensive and more difficult to evaluate than the functions performed by the buyer (reseller).

The principle of this subdivision may be illustrated by the following examples in each of which it is assumed that corporation X developed a valuable patent covering product M which it manufactures and sells to corporation Y in a controlled sale, and for which there is no comparable uncontrolled sale:

Example (1). Corporation Y adds a component to product M and resells the assembled product in an uncontrolled sale within a reasonable time after the controlled sale of product M. Assume further that the addition of the component added more than an insubstantial amount to the value of product M, but that Y's function in purchasing the component and assembling the product prior to sale was subject to reasonably precise valuation. Although the controlled sale and resale does not meet the requirements of subdivision (ii)(c) of this subparagraph, the resale price method may be used under the circumstances because that method involves computations and evaluations which are fewer and easier to make than under the cost plus method. This is because X's use of a patent may be more difficult to evaluate in determining an appropriate gross profit percentage under the cost plus method, than is evaluation of Y's assembling function in

Reg. § 1.482-2A(e)(3)

→ **Caution:** *Reg. § 1.482-2A applies for tax years beginning on or before April 21, 1993.* ←

determining the appropriate markup percentage under the resale price method.

Example (2). Corporation Y resells product M in an uncontrolled sale within a reasonable time after the controlled sale after attaching its valuable trademark to it. Assume further that it can be demonstrated through comparison with other uncontrolled sales of Y that the addition of Y's trademark to a product usually adds 25 percent to the markup on its sales. On the other hand, the effect of X's use of its patent is difficult to evaluate in applying the cost plus method because no reasonable standard of comparison is available. Although the controlled sale and resale does not meet the requirements of subdivision (ii)(d) of this subparagraph, the resale price method may be used because that method involves computations and evaluations which are fewer and easier to make than under the cost plus method. This is because, under the circumstances, X's use of a patent is more difficult to evaluate in determining an appropriate gross profit percentage under the cost plus method, than is evaluation of the use of Y's trademark in determining the appropriate markup percentage under the resale price method.

(iv) For the purposes of this subparagraph the "applicable resale price" is the price at which it is anticipated that property purchased in the controlled sale will be resold by the buyer in an uncontrolled sale. The "applicable resale price" will generally be equal to either the price at which current resales of the same property are being made or the resale price of the particular item of property involved.

(v) Where the property purchased in the controlled sale is resold in another controlled sale, the "applicable resale price" is the price at which such property is finally resold in an uncontrolled sale, providing that the series of sales as a whole meets all the requirements of subdivision (ii) of this subparagraph or that the resale price method is used pursuant to subdivision (iii) of this subparagraph. In such case, the determination of the appropriate markup percentage shall take into account the function or functions performed by all members of the group participating in the series of sales and resales. Thus, if X sells a product to Y in a controlled sale, Y sells the product to Z in a controlled sale, and Z sells the product in an uncontrolled sale, the resale price method must be used if Y and Z together have not added more than an insubstantial amount to the value of the product through physical alteration or the application of intangible property, and the final resale occurs within a reasonable time of the sale from X to Y. In such case, the applicable resale price is the price at which Z sells the product in the uncontrolled sale, and the appropriate markup percentage shall take into account the functions performed by both Y and Z.

(vi) For the purposes of this subparagraph, the appropriate markup percentage is equal to the percentage of gross profit (expressed as a percentage of sales) earned by the buyer (reseller) or another party on the resale of property which is both purchased and resold in an uncontrolled transaction, which resale is most similar to the applicable resale of the property involved in the controlled sale. The following are the most important characteristics to be considered in determining the similarity of resales:

(a) The type of property involved in the sales. For example: machine tools, men's furnishings, small household appliances.

(b) The functions performed by the reseller with respect to the property. For example: packaging, labeling, delivering, maintenance of inventory, minor assembly, advertising, selling at wholesale, selling at retail, billing, maintenance of accounts receivable, and servicing.

(c) The effect on price of any intangible property utilized by the reseller in connection with the property resold. For example: patents, trademarks, trade names.

(d) The geographic market in which the functions are performed by the reseller.

In general, the similarity to be sought relates to the probable effect upon the markup percentage of any differences in such characteristics between the uncontrolled purchases and resales on the one hand and the controlled purchases and resales on the other hand. Thus, close physical similarity of the property involved in the sales compared is not required under the resale price method since a lack of close physical similarity is not necessarily indicative of dissimilar markup percentages.

(vii) Whenever possible, markup percentages should be derived from uncontrolled purchases and resales of the buyer (reseller) involved in the controlled sale, because similar characteristics are more likely to be found among different resales of property made by the same reseller than among sales made by other resellers. In the absence of resales by the same buyer (reseller) which meet the standards of subdivision (vi) of this subparagraph, evidence of an appropriate markup percentage may be derived from resales by other resellers selling in the same or a similar market in which the controlled buyer (reseller) is selling, providing such resellers perform

Reg. § 1.482-2A(e)(3)

→ **Caution:** Reg. § 1.482-2A applies for tax years beginning on or before April 21, 1993. ←

comparable functions. Where the function performed by the reseller is similar to the function performed by a sales agent which does not take title, such sales agent will be considered a reseller for the purpose of determining an appropriate markup percentage under this subparagraph and the commission earned by such sales agent, expressed as a percentage of the sales price of the goods, may constitute the appropriate markup percentage. If the controlled buyer (reseller) is located in a foreign country and information on resales by other resellers in the same foreign market is not available, then markup percentages earned by United States resellers performing comparable functions may be used. In the absence of data on markup percentages of particular sales or groups of sales, the prevailing markup percentage in the particular industry involved may be appropriate.

(viii) In calculating the markup percentage earned on uncontrolled purchases and resales, and in applying such percentage to the applicable resale price to determine the appropriate markup, the same elements which enter into the computation of the sales price and the costs of goods sold of the property involved in the comparable uncontrolled purchases and resales should enter into such computation in the case of the property involved in the controlled purchases and resales. Thus, if freight-in and packaging expense are elements of the cost of goods sold in comparable uncontrolled purchases, then such elements should also be taken into account in computing the cost of goods sold of the controlled purchase. Similarly, if the comparable markup percentage is based upon net sales (after reduction for returns and allowances) of uncontrolled resellers, such percentage must be applied to net sales of the buyer (reseller).

(ix) In determining an arm's length price appropriate adjustment must be made to reflect any material differences between the uncontrolled purchases and resales used as the basis for the calculation of the appropriate markup percentage and the resales of property involved in the controlled sale. The differences referred to in this subdivision are those differences in functions or circumstances which have a definite and reasonably ascertainable effect on price. The principles of this subdivision may be illustrated by the following example:

Example. Assume that X and Y are members of the same group of controlled entities and that Y purchases electric mixers from X and electric toasters from uncontrolled entities. Y performs substantially similar functions with respect to resales of both the mixers and the toasters, except that it does not warrant the toasters, but does provide a 90-day warranty for the mixers. Y normally earns a gross profit on toasters of 20 percent of gross selling price. The 20-percent gross profit on the resale of toasters is an appropriate markup percentage, but the price of the controlled sale computed with reference to such rate must be adjusted to reflect the difference in terms (the warranty).

(4) *Cost plus method.* (i) Under the pricing method described as the "cost plus method", the arm's length price of a controlled sale of property shall be computed by adding to the cost of producing such property (as computed in subdivision (ii) of this subparagraph), an amount which is equal to such cost multiplied by the appropriate gross profit percentage (as computed in subdivision (iii) of this subparagraph), plus or minus any adjustments as provided in subdivision (v) of this subparagraph.

(ii) For the purposes of this subparagraph, the cost of producing the property involved in the controlled sale, and the costs which enter into the computation of the appropriate gross profit percentage shall be computed in a consistent manner in accordance with sound accounting practices for allocating or apportioning costs, which neither favors nor burdens controlled sales in comparison with uncontrolled sales. Thus, if the costs used in computing the appropriate gross profit percentage are comprised of the full cost of goods sold, including direct and indirect costs, then the cost of producing the property involved in the controlled sales must be comprised of the full cost of goods sold, including direct and indirect costs. On the other hand, if the costs used in computing the appropriate gross profit percentage are comprised only of direct costs, the cost of producing the property involved in the controlled sale must be comprised only of direct costs. The term "cost of producing", as used in this subparagraph, includes the cost of acquiring property which is held for resale.

(iii) For the purposes of this subparagraph, the appropriate gross profit percentage is equal to the gross profit percentage (expressed as a percentage of cost) earned by the seller or another party on the uncontrolled sale or sales of property which are most similar to the controlled sale in question. The following are the most important characteristics to be considered in determining the similarity of the uncontrolled sale or sales:

Reg. § 1.482-2A(e)(4)

Adjustments

See p. 20,601 for regulations not amended to reflect law changes

→ **Caution: Reg. § 1.482-2A applies for tax years beginning on or before April 21, 1993.**←

(a) The type of property involved in the sales. For example: machine tools, men's furnishings, small household appliances.

(b) The functions performed by the seller with respect to the property sold. For example: contract manufacturing, product assembly, selling activity, processing, servicing, delivering.

(c) The effect of any intangible property used by the seller in connection with the property sold. For example: patents, trademarks, trade names.

(d) The geographic market in which the functions are performed by the seller. In general, the similarity to be sought relates to the probable effect upon the margin of gross profit of any differences in such characteristics between the uncontrolled sales and the controlled sale. Thus, close physical similarity of the property involved in the sales compared is not required under the cost plus method since a lack of close physical similarity is not necessarily indicative of dissimilar profit margins. See subparagraph (2)(iv) of this paragraph, relating to sales made at less than a normal profit for the primary purpose of establishing or maintaining a market.

(iv) Whenever possible, gross profit percentages should be derived from uncontrolled sales made by the seller involved in the controlled sale, because similar characteristics are more likely to be found among sales of property made by the same seller than among sales made by other sellers. In the absence of such sales, evidence of an appropriate gross profit percentage may be derived from similar uncontrolled sales by other sellers whether or not such sellers are members of the controlled group. Where the function performed by the seller is similar to the function performed by a purchasing agent which does not take title, such purchasing agent will be considered a seller for the purpose of determining an appropriate gross profit percentage under this subparagraph and the commission earned by such purchasing agent, expressed as a percentage of the purchase price of the goods, may constitute the appropriate gross profit percentage. In the absence of data on gross profit percentages of particular sales or groups of sales which are similar to the controlled sale, the prevailing gross profit percentages in the particular industry involved may be appropriate.

(v) Where the most similar sale or sales from which the appropriate gross profit percentage is derived differ in any material respect from the controlled sale, the arm's length price which is computed by applying such percentage must be adjusted to reflect such differences to the extent such differences would warrant an adjustment of price in uncontrolled transactions. The differences referred to in this subdivision are those differences which have a definite and reasonably ascertainable effect on price. [Reg. § 1.482-2A.]

☐ [T.D. 6952, 4-15-68. Amended by T.D. 6964, 7-24-68; T.D. 6998, 1-17-69; T.D. 7170, 3-10-72; T.D. 7394, 12-31-75; T.D. 7747, 12-29-80; T.D. 7781, 7-1-81; T.D. 7920, 11-2-83; T.D. 8204, 5-20-88 and T.D. 8470, 1-13-93.]

[Reg. § 1.483-1]

§ 1.483-1. **Interest on certain deferred payments.**—(a) *Amount constituting interest in certain deferred payment transactions*—(1) *In general.* Except as provided in paragraph (c) of this section, section 483 applies to a contract for the sale or exchange of property if the contract provides for one or more payments due more than 1 year after the date of the sale or exchange, and the contract does not provide for adequate stated interest. In general, a contract has adequate stated interest if the contract provides for a stated rate of interest that is at least equal to the test rate (determined under § 1.483-3) and the interest is paid or compounded at least annually. Section 483 may apply to a contract whether the contract is express (written or oral) or implied. For purposes of section 483, a sale or exchange is any transaction treated as a sale or exchange for tax purposes. In addition, for purposes of section 483, property includes debt instruments and investment units, but does not include money, services, or the right to use property. For the treatment of certain obligations given in exchange for services or the use of property, see sections 404 and 467. For purposes of this paragraph (a), money includes functional currency and, in certain circumstances, nonfunctional currency. See § 1.988-2(b)(2) for circumstances when nonfunctional currency is treated as money rather than as property.

(2) *Treatment of contracts to which section 483 applies*—(i) *Treatment of unstated interest.* If section 483 applies to a contract, unstated interest under the contract is treated as interest for tax purposes. Thus, for example, unstated interest is not treated as part of the amount realized from the sale or exchange of property (in the case of the seller), and is not included in the purchaser's basis in the property acquired in the sale or exchange.

(ii) *Method of accounting for interest on contracts subject to section 483.* Any stated or

Reg. § 1.483-1(a)(1)

unstated interest on a contract subject to section 483 is taken into account by a taxpayer under the taxpayer's regular method of accounting (e.g., an accrual method or the cash receipts and disbursements method). See §§ 1.446-1, 1.451-1, and 1.461-1. For purposes of the preceding sentence, the amount of interest (including unstated interest) allocable to a payment under a contract to which section 483 applies is determined under § 1.446-2(e).

(b) *Definitions*—(1) *Deferred payments.* For purposes of the regulations under section 483, a deferred payment means any payment that constitutes all or a part of the sales price (as defined in paragraph (b)(2) of this section), and that is due more than 6 months after the date of the sale or exchange. Except as provided in section 483(c)(2) (relating to the treatment of a debt instrument of the purchaser), a payment may be made in the form of cash, stock or securities, or other property.

(2) *Sales price.* For purposes of section 483, the sales price for any sale or exchange is the sum of the amount due under the contract (other than stated interest) and the amount of any liability included in the amount realized from the sale or exchange. See § 1.1001-2. Thus, the sales price for any sale or exchange includes any amount of unstated interest under the contract.

(c) *Exceptions to and limitations on the application of section 483*—(1) *In general.* Sections 483(d), 1274(c)(4), and 1275(b) contain exceptions to and limitations on the application of section 483.

(2) *Sales price of $3,000 or less.* Section 483(d)(2) applies only if it can be determined at the time of the sale or exchange that the sales price cannot exceed $3,000, regardless of whether the sales price eventually paid for the property is less than $3,000.

(3) *Other exceptions and limitations*—(i) *Certain transfers subject to section 1041.* Section 483 does not apply to any transfer of property subject to section 1041 (relating to transfers of property between spouses or incident to divorce).

(ii) *Treatment of certain obligees.* Section 483 does not apply to an obligee under a contract for the sale or exchange of personal use property (within the meaning of section 1275(b)(3)) in the hands of the obligor and that evidences a below-market loan described in section 7872(c)(1).

(iii) *Transactions involving certain demand loans.* Section 483 does not apply to any payment under a contract that evidences a demand loan that is a below-market loan described in section 7872(c)(1).

(iv) *Transactions involving certain annuity contracts.* Section 483 does not apply to any payment under an annuity contract described in section 1275(a)(1)(B) (relating to annuity contracts excluded from the definition of debt instrument).

(v) *Options.* Section 483 does not apply to any payment under an option to buy or sell property.

(d) *Assumptions.* If a debt instrument is assumed, or property is taken subject to a debt instrument, in connection with a sale or exchange of property, the debt instrument is treated for purposes of section 483 in a manner consistent with the rules of § 1.1274-5.

(e) *Aggregation rule.* For purposes of section 483, all sales or exchanges that are part of the same transaction (or a series of related transactions) are treated as a single sale or exchange and all contracts calling for deferred payments arising from the same transaction (or a series of related transactions) are treated as a single contract. This rule, however, generally only applies to contracts and to sales or exchanges involving a single buyer and a single seller.

(f) *Effective date.* This section applies to sales and exchanges that occur on or after [INSERT DATE THAT IS 60 DAYS AFTER PUBLICATION OF THIS DOCUMENT IN THE FEDERAL REGISTER]. Taxpayers, however, may rely on this section for sales and exchanges that occur after December 21, 1992, and before [INSERT DATE THAT IS 60 DAYS AFTER PUBLICATION OF THIS DOCUMENT IN THE FEDERAL REGISTER]. [Reg. § 1.483-1.]

☐ [*T.D.* 6873, 1-24-66. *Amended by T.D.* 7154, 12-27-71; *T.D.* 7394, 12-31-75; *T.D.* 7781, 7-1-81 and *T.D.* 8517, 1-27-94.]

[Reg. § 1.483-2]

§ 1.483-2. **Unstated interest.**—(a) *In general*—(1) *Adequate stated interest.* For purposes of section 483, a contract has unstated interest if the contract does not provide for adequate stated interest. A contract does not provide for adequate stated interest if the sum of the deferred payments exceeds—

(i) The sum of the present values of the deferred payments and the present values of any stated interest payments due under the contract; or

(ii) In the case of a cash method debt instrument (within the meaning of section 1274A(c)(2)) received in exchange for property in a potentially abusive situation (as defined in § 1.1274-3), the fair market value of the property reduced by the fair market value of any consideration other than the debt instrument, and reduced by the sum of all principal payments that are not deferred payments.

(2) *Amount of unstated interest.* For purposes of section 483, unstated interest means an amount equal to the excess of the sum of the deferred payments over the amount described in paragraph (a)(1)(i) or (a)(1)(ii) of this section, whichever is applicable.

(b) *Operational rules*—(1) *In general.* For purposes of paragraph (a) of this section, rules similar to those in § 1.1274-2 apply to determine whether a contract has adequate stated interest and the amount of unstated interest, if any, on the contract.

(2) *Present value.* For purposes of paragraph (a) of this section, the present value of any deferred payment or interest payment is determined by discounting the payment from the date it becomes due to the date of the sale or exchange at the test rate of interest applicable to the contract in accordance with § 1.483-3.

(c) *Examples.* The following examples illustrate the rules of this section.

Example 1. Contract that does not have adequate stated interest. On January 1, 1995, A sells B nonpublicly traded property under a contract that calls for a $100,000 payment of principal on January 1, 2005, and 10 annual interest payments of $9,000 on January 1 of each year, beginning on January 1, 1996. Assume that the test rate of interest is 9.2 percent, compounded annually. The contract does not provide for adequate stated interest because it does not provide for interest equal to 9.2 percent, compounded annually. The present value of the deferred payments is $98,727.69. As a result, the contract has unstated interest of $1,272.31 ($100,000 − $98,727.69)

Example 2. Contract that does not have adequate stated interest; no interest for initial short period. On May 1, 1996, A sells B nonpublicly traded property under a contract that calls for B to make a principal payment of $200,000 on December 31, 1998, and semiannual interest payments of $9,000, payable on June 30 and December 31 of each year, beginning on December 31, 1996. Assume that the test rate of interest is 9 percent, compounded semiannually. Even though the contract calls for a stated rate of interest no lower than the test rate of interest, the contract does not provide for adequate stated interest because the stated rate of interest does not apply for the short period from May 1, 1996, through June 30, 1996.

Example 3. Potentially abusive situation—(i) *Facts.* In a potentially abusive situation, a contract for the sale of nonpublicly traded personal property calls for the issuance of a cash method debt instrument (as defined in section 1274A(c)(2)) with a stated principal amount of $700,000, payable in 5 years. No other consideration is given. The debt instrument calls for annual payments of interest over its entire term at a rate of 9.2 percent, compounded annually (the test rate of interest applicable to the debt instrument). Thus, the present value of the deferred payment and the interest payments is $700,000. Assume that the fair market value of the properly is $500,000.

(ii) *Amount of unstated interest.* A cash method debt instrument received in exchange for property in a potentially abusive situation provides for adequate stated interest only if the sum of the deferred payments under the instrument does not exceed the fair market value of the property. Because the deferred payment ($700,000) exceeds the fair market value of the property ($500,000), the debt instrument does not provide for adequate stated interest. Therefore, the debt instrument has unstated interest of $200,000.

Example 4. Variable rate debt instrument with adequate stated interest; variable rate as of the issue date greater than the test rate—(i) *Facts.* A contract for the sale of nonpublicly traded property calls for the issuance of a debt instrument in the principal amount of $75,000 due in 10 years. The debt instrument calls for interest payable semiannually at a rate of 3 percentage points above the yield on 6-month Treasury bills at the mid-point of the semiannual period immediately preceding each interest payment date. Assume that the interest rate is a qualified floating rate and that the debt instrument is a variable rate debt instrument within the meaning of § 1.1275-5.

(ii) *Adequate stated interest.* Under paragraph (b)(1) of this section, rules similar to those in § 1.1274-2(f) apply to determine whether the debt instrument has adequate stated interest. Assume that the test rate of interest applicable to the debt instrument is 9 percent, compounded semiannually. Assume also that the yield on 6-month Treasury bills on the date of the sale is 8.89 percent, which is greater than the yield on 6-month Treasury bills on the first date on which there is a binding written contract that substantially sets forth the terms under which the sale is consummated. Under § 1.1274-2(f), the debt instrument is tested for adequate stated interest as if it provided for a stated rate of interest of 11.89 percent (3 percent plus 8.89 percent), compounded semiannually, payable over its entire term. Because the test rate of interest is 9 percent, compounded semiannually, and the debt instrument is treated as providing for stated interest of 11.89 percent,

Reg. § 1.483-2(a)(2)

compounded semiannually, the debt instrument provides for adequate stated interest.

(d) *Effective date.* This section applies to sales and exchanges that occur on or after April 4, 1994. Taxpayers, however, may rely on this section for sales and exchanges that occur after December 21, 1992, and before April 4, 1994. [Reg. § 1.483-2.]

☐ [T.D. 6873, 1-24-66. Amended by T.D. 8517, 1-27-94.]

[Reg. § 1.483-3]

§ 1.483-3. **Test rate of interest applicable to a contract.**—(a) *General rule.* For purposes of section 483, the test rate of interest for a contract is the same as the test rate that would apply under § 1.1274-4 if the contract were a debt instrument. Paragraph (b) of this section, however, provides for a lower test rate in the case of certain sales or exchanges of land between related individuals.

(b) *Lower rate for certain sales or exchanges of land between related individuals*—(1) *Test rate.* In the case of a qualified sale or exchange of land between related individuals (described in section 483(e)), the test rate is not greater than 6 percent, compounded semiannually, or an equivalent rate based on an appropriate compounding period.

(2) *Special rules.* The following rules and definitions apply in determining whether a sale or exchange is a qualified sale under section 483(e):

(i) *Definition of family members.* The members of an individual's family are determined as of the date of the sale or exchange. The members of an individual's family include those individuals described in section 267(c)(4) and the spouses of those individuals. In addition, for purposes of section 267(c)(4), full effect is given to a legal adoption, ancestor means parents and grandparents, and lineal descendants means children and grandchildren.

(ii) *$500,000 limitation.* Section 483(e) does not apply to the extent that the stated principal amount of the debt instrument issued in the sale or exchange, when added to the aggregate stated principal amount of any other debt instruments to which section 483(e) applies that were issued in prior qualified sales between the same two individuals during the same calendar year, exceeds $500,000. See *Example 3* of paragraph (b)(3) of this section.

(iii) *Other limitations.* Section 483(e) does not apply if the parties to a contract include persons other than the related individuals and the parties enter into the contract with an intent to circumvent the purposes of section 483(e). In addition, if the property sold or exchanged includes any property other than land, section 483(e) applies only to the extent that the stated principal amount of the debt instrument issued in the sale or exchange is attributable to the land (based on the relative fair market values of the land and the other property).

(3) *Examples.* The following examples illustrate the rules of this paragraph (b).

Example 1. On January 1, 1995, A sells land to B, A's child, for $650,000. The contract for sale calls for B to make a $250,000 down payment and issue a debt instrument with a stated principal amount of $400,000. Because the stated principal amount of the debt instrument is less than $500,000, the sale is a qualified sale and section 483(e) applies to the debt instrument.

Example 2. The facts are the same as in *Example 1* of paragraph (b)(3) of this section, except that on June 1, 1995, A sells additional land to B under a contract that calls for B to issue a debt instrument with a stated principal amount of $100,000. The stated principal amount of this debt instrument ($100,000) when added to the stated principal amount of the prior debt instrument ($400,000) does not exceed $500,000. Thus, section 483(e) applies to both debt instruments.

Example 3. The facts are the same as in *Example 1* of paragraph (b)(3) of this section, except that on June 1, 1995, A sells additional land to B under a contract that calls for B to issue a debt instrument with a stated principal amount of $150,000. The stated principal amount of this debt instrument when added to the stated principal amount of the prior debt instrument ($400,000) exceeds $500,000. Thus, for purposes of section 483(e), the debt instrument issued in the sale of June 1, 1995, is treated as two separate debt instruments: a $100,000 debt instrument (to which section 483(e) applies) and a $50,000 debt instrument (to which section 1274, if otherwise applicable, applies).

(c) *Effective date.* This section applies to sales and exchanges that occur on or after April 4, 1994. Taxpayers, however, may rely on this section for sales and exchanges that occur after December 21, 1992, and before April 4, 1994. [Reg. § 1.483-3.]

☐ [T.D. 8517, 1-27-94.]

[Reg. § 1.483-4]

§ 1.483-4. **Contingent payments.**—(a) *In general.* This section applies to a contract for the sale or exchange of property (the overall contract) if the contract provides for one or more contingent payments and the contract is subject to section 483. This section applies even if the contract provides for adequate stated interest under § 1.483-2. If this section applies to a contract, interest under the contract is generally computed and accounted for using rules similar to those that would apply if the contract were a debt instrument subject to § 1.1275-4(c). Consequently, all noncontingent payments under the overall contract are treated as if made under a separate contract, and interest accruals on this separate contract are computed under rules similar to those contained in § 1.1275-4(c)(3). Each contingent payment under the overall contract is characterized as principal and interest under rules similar to those contained in § 1.1275-4(c)(4). However, any interest, or amount treated as interest, on a contract subject to this section is taken into account by a taxpayer under the taxpayer's regular method of accounting (e.g., an accrual method or the cash receipts and disbursements method).

(b) *Examples.* The following examples illustrate the provisions of paragraph (a) of this section:

Example 1. Deferred payment sale with contingent interest— (i) *Facts.* On December 31, 1996, A sells depreciable personal property to B. As consideration for the sale, B issues to A a debt instrument with a maturity date of December 31, 2001. The debt instrument provides for a principal payment of $200,000 on the maturity date, and a payment of interest on December 31 of each year, beginning in 1997, equal to a percentage of the total gross income derived from the property in that year. However, the total interest payable on the debt instrument over its entire term is limited to a maximum of $50,000. Assume that on December 31, 1996, the short-term applicable Federal rate is 4 percent, compounded annually, and the mid-term applicable Federal rate is 5 percent, compounded annually.

(ii) *Treatment of noncontingent payment as separate contract.* Each payment of interest is a contingent payment. Accordingly, under paragraph (a) of this section, for purposes of applying section 483 to the debt instrument, the right to the noncontingent payment of $200,000 is treated as a separate contract. The amount of unstated interest on this separate contract is equal to $43,295, which is the amount by which the payment ($200,000) exceeds the present value of the payment ($156,705), calculated using the test rate of 5 percent, compounded annually. The $200,000 payment is thus treated as consisting of a payment of interest of $43,295 and a payment of principal of $156,705. The interest is includible in A's gross income, and deductible by B, under their respective methods of accounting.

(iii) *Treatment of contingent payments.* Assume that the amount of the contingent payment that is paid on December 31, 1997, is $20,000. Under paragraph (a) of this section, the $20,000 payment is treated as a payment of principal of $19,231 (the present value, as of the date of sale, of the $20,000 payment, calculated using a test rate equal to 4 percent, compounded annually) and a payment of interest of $769. The $769 interest payment is includible in A's gross income, and deductible by B, in their respective taxable years in which the payment occurs. The amount treated as principal gives B additional basis in the property on December 31, 1997. The remaining contingent payments on the debt instrument are accounted for similarly, using a test rate of 4 percent, compounded annually, for the payments made on December 31, 1998, and December 31, 1999, and a test rate of 5 percent, compounded annually, for the payments made on December 31, 2000, and December 31, 2001.

Example 2. Contingent stock payout—(i) *Facts.* M Corporation and N Corporation each owns one-half of the stock of O Corporation. On December 31, 1996, pursuant to a reorganization qualifying under section 368(a)(1)(B), M acquires the one-half interest of O held by N in exchange for 30,000 shares of M voting stock and a nonassignable right to receive up to 10,000 additional shares of M's voting stock during the next 3 years, provided the net profits of O exceed certain amounts specified in the contract. No interest is provided for in the contract. No additional shares are received in 1997 or in 1998. In 1999, the annual earnings of O exceed the specified amount, and, on December 31, 1999, an additional 3,000 M voting shares are transferred to N. The fair market value of the 3,000 shares on December 31, 1999, is $300,000. Assume that on December 31, 1996, the short-term applicable Federal rate is 4 percent, compounded annually. M and N are calendar year taxpayers.

(ii) *Allocation of interest.* Section 1274 does not apply to the right to receive the additional shares because the right is not a debt instrument for federal income tax purposes. As a result, the transfer of the 3,000 M voting shares to N is a deferred payment subject to section 483 and a portion of the shares is treated as unstated interest under that section. The amount of interest allocable to the shares is equal to the excess of $300,000 (the fair market value of the shares on December 31, 1999) over $266,699 (the present value of $300,000, determined by discounting the payment at the test rate of 4 percent, compounded annually, from December 31, 1999, to December 31, 1996). As a result, the amount of interest allocable to the payment of the shares is $33,301 ($300,000 − $266,699). Both M and N take the interest into account in 1999.

(c) *Effective date.* This section applies to sales and exchanges that occur on or after August 13, 1996. [Reg. § 1.483-4.]

☐ [T.D. 8674, 6-11-96.]

[The next page is 39,011.]

EXEMPT ORGANIZATIONS

General Rule

[Reg. § 1.501(a)-1]

§ 1.501(a)-1. Exemption from taxation.—(a) *In general; proof of exemption.* (1) Section 501(a) provides an exemption from income taxes for organizations which are described in section 501(c) or (d) and section 401(a), unless such organization is a "feeder organization" (see section 502), or unless it engages in a transaction described in section 503. However, the exemption does not extend to "unrelated business taxable income" of such an organization (see part III (Section 511 and following), subchapter F, chapter 1 of the Code).

(2) An organization, other than an employees' trust described in section 401(a), is not exempt from tax merely because it is not organized and operated for profit. In order to establish its exemption, it is necessary that every such organization claiming exemption file an application form as set forth below with the district director for the internal revenue district in which is located the principal place of business or principal office of the organization. Subject only to the Commissioner's inherent power to revoke rulings because of a change in the law or regulations or for other good cause, an organization that has been determined by the Commissioner or the district director to be exempt under section 501(a) or the corresponding provision of prior law may rely upon such determination so long as there are no substantial changes in the organization's character, purposes, or methods of operation. An organization which has been determined to be exempt under the provisions of the Internal Revenue Code of 1939 or prior law is not required to secure a new determination of exemption merely because of the enactment of the Internal Revenue Code of 1954 unless affected by substantive changes in law made by such Code.

(3) An organization claiming exemption under section 501(a) and described in any paragraph of section 501(c) (other than section 501(c)(1)) shall file the form of application prescribed by the Commissioner and shall include thereon such information as required by such form and the instructions issued with respect thereto. For rules relating to the obtaining of a determination of exempt status by an employees' trust described in section 401(a), see the regulations under section 401.

(b) *Additional proof by particular classes of organizations.* (1) Organizations mentioned below shall submit with and as a part of their applications the following information:

(i) Mutual insurance companies shall submit copies of the policies or certificates of membership issued by them.

(ii) In the case of title holding companies described in section 501(c)(2), if the organization for which title is held has not been specifically notified in writing by the Internal Revenue Service that it is held to be exempt under section 501(a), the title holding company shall submit the information indicated herein as necessary for a determination of the status of the organization for which title is held.

(iii) An organization described in section 501(c)(3) shall submit with, and as a part of, an application filed after July 26, 1959, a detailed statement of its proposed activities.

(2) In addition to the information specifically called for by this section, the Commissioner may require any additional information deemed necessary for a proper determination of whether a particular organization is exempt under section 501(a), and when deemed advisable in the interest of an efficient administration of the internal revenue laws, he may in the cases of particular types of organizations prescribe the form in which the proof of exemption shall be furnished.

(3) An organization claiming to be specifically exempted by section 6033(a) from filing annual returns shall submit with and as a part of its application a statement of all the facts on which it bases its claim.

(c) *"Private shareholder or individual" defined.* The words "private shareholder or individual" in section 501 refer to persons having a personal and private interest in the activities of the organization.

(d) *Requirement of annual returns.* For the annual return requirements of organizations exempt under section 501(a), see section 6033 and § 1.6033-1.

(e) *Certain Puerto Rican pension, etc., trusts.* Effective for taxable years beginning after December 31, 1973, section 1022(i)(1) of the Employee Retirement Income Security Act of 1974 (ERISA) (88 Stat. 942) provides that trusts under certain Puerto Rican pension, etc., plans (as defined under P.R. Laws Ann. tit. 13, § 3165, and the articles thereunder), all of the participants of which are residents of the Commonwealth of Puerto Rico, are to be treated only for purposes of section 501(a) as trusts described in section

Reg. § 1.501(a)-1(e)

401(a). The practical effect of section 1022(i)(1) is to exempt these trusts from U.S. income tax on income from their U.S. investments. For purposes of section 1022(i)(1), the term "residents of the Commonwealth of Puerto Rico" means bona fide residents of Puerto Rico, and persons who perform labor or services primarily within the Commonwealth of Puerto Rico, regardless of residence for other purposes, and the term "participants" is restricted to current employees who are not excluded under the eligibility provisions of the plan. [Reg. § 1.501(a)-1.]

☐ [T.D. 6301, 7-8-58. Amended by T.D. 6391, 6-25-59, by T.D. 6972, 9-11-68, by T.D. 7428, 8-13-76, and by T.D. 7859, 12-1-82.]

[Reg. § 1.501(c)(2)-1]

§ 1.501(c)(2)-1. **Corporations organized to hold title to property for exempt organizations.**—(a) A corporation described in section 501(c)(2) and otherwise exempt from tax under section 501(a) is taxable upon its unrelated business taxable income. For taxable years beginning before January 1, 1970, see § 1.511-2(c)(4). Since a corporation described in section 501(c)(2) cannot be exempt under section 501(a) if it engages in any business other than that of holding title to property and collecting income therefrom, it cannot have unrelated business taxable income as defined in section 512 other than income which is treated as unrelated business taxable income solely because of the applicability of section 512(a)(3)(C); or debt financed income which is treated as unrelated business taxable income solely because of section 514; or certain interest, annuities, royalties, or rents which are treated as unrelated business taxable income solely because of section 512(b)(3)(B)(ii) or (13). Similarly, exempt status under section 501(c)(2) shall not be affected where certain rents from personal property leased with real property are treated as unrelated business taxable income under section 512(b)(3)(A)(ii) solely because such rents attributable to such personal property are more than incidental when compared to the total rents received or accrued under the lease, or under section 512(b)(3)(B)(i) solely because such rents attributable to such personal property exceed 50 percent of the total rents received or accrued under the lease.

(b) A corporation described in section 501(c)(2) cannot accumulate income and retain its exemption, but it must turn over the entire amount of such income, less expenses, to an organization which is itself exempt from tax under section 501(a). [Reg. § 1.501(c)(2)-1.]

☐ [T.D. 6301, 7-8-58. Amended by T.D. 7698, 5-20-80.]

[Reg. § 1.501(c)(3)-1]

§ 1.501(c)(3)-1. **Organizations organized and operated for religious, charitable, scientific, testing for public safety, literary, or educational purposes, or for the prevention of cruelty to children or animals.**—(a) *Organizational and operational tests.* (1) In order to be exempt as an organization described in section 501(c)(3), an organization must be both organized and operated exclusively for one or more of the purposes specified in such section. If an organization fails to meet either the organizational test or the operational test, it is not exempt.

(2) The term "exempt purpose or purposes", as used in this section, means any purpose or purposes specified in section 501(c)(3), as defined and elaborated in paragraph (d) of this section.

(b) *Organizational test* —(1) *In general.* (i) An organization is organized exclusively for one or more exempt purposes only if its articles of organization (referred to in this section as its "articles") as defined in subparagraph (2) of this paragraph:

(*a*) Limit the purposes of such organization to one or more exempt purposes; and

(*b*) Do not expressly empower the organization to engage, otherwise than as an insubstantial part of its activities, in activities which in themselves are not in furtherance of one or more exempt purposes.

(ii) In meeting the organizational test, the organization's purposes, as stated in its articles, may be as broad as, or more specific than, the purposes stated in section 501(c)(3). Therefore, an organization which, by the terms of its articles, is formed "for literary and scientific purposes within the meaning of section 501(c)(3) of the Code shall, if it otherwise meets the requirements in this paragraph, be considered to have met the organizational test. Similarly, articles stating that the organization is created solely "to receive contributions and pay them over to organizations which are described in section 501(c)(3) and exempt from taxation under section 501(a)" are sufficient for purposes of the organizational test. Moreover, it is sufficient if the articles set forth the purpose of the organization to be the operation of a school for adult education and describe in detail the manner of the operation of such school. In addition, if the articles state that the organization is formed for "charitable purposes", such articles ordinarily shall be sufficient for purposes of the organizational test (see subparagraph (5) of this paragraph for rules relating to construction of terms).

(iii) An organization is not organized exclusively for one or more exempt purposes if its articles expressly empower it to carry on, otherwise than as an insubstantial part of its activities, activities which are not in furtherance of one or more exempt purposes, even though such organization is, by the terms of such articles, created for a purpose that is no broader than the purposes specified in section 501(c)(3). Thus, an organization that is empowered by its articles "to engage in a manufacturing business", or "to engage in the operation of a social club" does not meet the organizational test regardless of the fact that its articles may state that such organization is created "for charitable purposes within the meaning of section 501(c)(3) of the Code."

(iv) In no case shall an organization be considered to be organized exclusively for one or more exempt purposes, if, by the terms of its articles, the purposes for which such organization is created are broader than the purposes specified in section 501(c)(3). The fact that the actual operations of such an organization have been exclusively in furtherance of one or more exempt purposes shall not be sufficient to permit the organization to meet the organizational test. Similarly, such an organization will not meet the organizational test as a result of statements or other evidence that the members thereof intend to operate only in furtherance of one or more exempt purposes.

(v) An organization must, in order to establish its exemption, submit a detailed statement of its proposed activities with and as a part of its application for exemption (see paragraph (b) of § 1.501(a)-1).

(2) *Articles of organization.* For purposes of this section, the term "articles of organization" or "articles" includes the trust instrument, the corporate charter, the articles of association, or any other written instrument by which an organization is created.

(3) *Authorization of legislative or political activities.* An organization is not organized exclusively for one or more exempt purposes if its articles expressly empower it—

(i) To devote more than an insubstantial part of its activities to attempting to influence legislation by propaganda or otherwise; or

(ii) Directly or indirectly to participate in, or intervene in (including the publishing or distributing of statements), any political campaign on behalf of or in opposition to any candidate for public office; or

(iii) To have objectives and to engage in activities which characterize it as an "action" organization as defined in paragraph (c)(3) of this section.

The terms used in subdivisions (i), (ii), and (iii) of this subparagraph shall have the meanings provided in paragraph (c)(3) of this section. An organization's articles will not violate the provisions of paragraph (b)(3)(i) of this section even though the organization's articles expressly empower it to make the election provided for in section 501(h) with respect to influencing legislation and, only if it so elects, to make lobbying or grass roots expenditures that do not normally exceed the ceiling amounts prescribed by section 501(h)(2)(B) and (D).

(4) *Distribution of assets on dissolution.* An organization is not organized exclusively for one or more exempt purposes unless its assets are dedicated to an exempt purpose. An organization's assets will be considered dedicated to an exempt purpose, for example, if, upon dissolution, such assets would, by reason of a provision in the organization's articles or by operation of law, be distributed for one or more exempt purposes, or to the Federal government, or to a State or local government, for a public purpose, or would be distributed by a court to another organization to be used in such manner as in the judgment of the court will best accomplish the general purposes for which the dissolved organization was organized. However, an organization does not meet the organizational test if its articles or the law of the State in which it was created provide that its assets would, upon dissolution, be distributed to its members or shareholders.

(5) *Construction of terms.* The law of the State in which an organization is created shall be controlling in construing the terms of its articles. However, any organization which contends that such terms have under State law a different meaning from their generally accepted meaning must establish such special meaning by clear and convincing reference to relevant court decisions, opinions of the State attorney-general, or other evidence of applicable State law.

(6) *Applicability of the organizational test.* A determination by the Commissioner or a district director that an organization is described in section 501(c)(3) and exempt under section 501(a) will not be granted after July 26, 1959 (regardless of when the application is filed), unless such organization meets the organizational test prescribed by this paragraph. If, before July 27, 1959, an organization has been determined by the Commissioner or district director to be exempt as an organization described in section 501(c)(3) or in a corresponding provision of prior law and such determination has not been revoked before such date, the fact that such organization does not meet the organizational test prescribed by this

Reg. § 1.501(c)(3)-1(b)(6)

paragraph shall not be a basis for revoking such determination. Accordingly, an organization which has been determined to be exempt before July 27, 1959, and which does not seek a new determination of exemption is not required to amend its articles of organization to conform to the rules of this paragraph, but any organization which seeks a determination of exemption after July 26, 1959, must have articles of organization which meet the rules of this paragraph. For the rules relating to whether an organization determined to be exempt before July 27, 1959, is organized exclusively for one or more exempt purposes, see 26 CFR (1939) 39.101(6)-1 (Regulation 118) as made applicable to the Code by Treasury Decision 6091, approved August 16, 1954 (19 F.R. 5167; C.B. 1954-2, 47).

(c) *Operational test* —(1) *Primary activities.* An organization will be regarded as "operated exclusively" for one or more exempt purposes only if it engages primarily in activities which accomplish one or more of such exempt purposes specified in section 501(c)(3). An organization will not be so regarded if more than an insubstantial part of its activities is not in furtherance of an exempt purpose.

(2) *Distribution of earnings.* An organization is not operated exclusively for one or more exempt purposes if its net earnings inure in whole or in part to the benefit of private shareholders or individuals. For the definition of the words "private shareholder or individual", see paragraph (c) of § 1.501(a)-1.

(3) *"Action" organizations.* (i) An organization is not operated exclusively for one or more exempt purposes if it is an "action" organization as defined in subdivisions (ii), (iii), or (iv) of this subparagraph.

(ii) An organization is an "action" organization if a substantial part of its activities is attempting to influence legislation by propaganda or otherwise. For this purpose, an organization will be regarded as attempting to influence legislation if the organization—

(*a*) Contacts, or urges the public to contact, members of a legislative body for the purpose of proposing, supporting, or opposing legislation; or

(*b*) Advocates the adoption or rejection of legislation.

The term "legislation", as used in this subdivision, includes action by the Congress, by any State legislature, by any local council or similar governing body, or by the public in a referendum, initiative, constitutional amendment, or similar procedure. An organization will not fail to meet the operational test merely because it advocates, as an insubstantial part of its activities, the adoption or rejection of legislation. An organization for which the expenditure test election of section 501(h) is in effect for a taxable year will not be considered an "action" organization by reason of this paragraph (c)(3)(ii) for that year if it is not denied exemption from taxation under section 501(a) by reason of section 501(h).

(iii) An organization is an "action" organization if it participates or intervenes, directly or indirectly, in any political campaign on behalf of or in opposition to any candidate for public office. The term "candidate for public office" means an individual who offers himself, or is proposed by others, as a contestant for an elective public office, whether such office be national, State, or local. Activities which constitute participation or intervention in a political campaign on behalf of or in opposition to a candidate include, but are not limited to, the publication or distribution of written or printed statements or the making of oral statements on behalf of or in opposition to such a candidate.

(iv) An organization is an "action" organization if it has the following two characteristics: (*a*) Its main or primary objective or objectives (as distinguished from its incidental or secondary objectives) may be attained only by legislation or a defeat of proposed legislation; and (*b*) it advocates, or campaigns for, the attainment of such main or primary objective or objectives as distinguished from engaging in nonpartisan analysis, study, or research and making the results thereof available to the public. In determining whether an organization has such characteristics, all the surrounding facts and circumstances, including the articles and all activities of the organization, are to be considered.

(v) An "action" organization, described in subdivisions (ii) or (iv) of this subparagraph, though it cannot qualify under section 501(c)(3), may nevertheless qualify as a social welfare organization under section 501(c)(4) if it meets the requirements set out in paragraph (a) of § 1.501(c)(4)-1.

(d) *Exempt purposes*—(1) *In general.* (i) An organization may be exempt as an organization described in section 501(c)(3) if it is organized and operated exclusively for one or more of the following purposes:

(*a*) Religious,

(*b*) Charitable,

(*c*) Scientific,

(*d*) Testing for public safety,

(*e*) Literary,

(*f*) Educational, or

Reg. § 1.501(c)(3)-1(c)(1)

General Rule

39,015

See p. 20,601 for regulations not amended to reflect law changes

(*g*) Prevention of cruelty to children or animals.

(ii) An organization is not organized or operated exclusively for one or more of the purposes specified in subdivision (i) of this subparagraph unless it serves a public rather than a private interest. Thus, to meet the requirement of this subdivision, it is necessary for an organization to establish that it is not organized or operated for the benefit of private interests such as designated individuals, the creator or his family, shareholders of the organization, or persons controlled, directly or indirectly, by such private interests.

(iii) Since each of the purposes specified in subdivision (i) of this subparagraph is an exempt purpose in itself, an organization may be exempt if it is organized and operated exclusively for any one or more of such purposes. If, in fact, an organization is organized and operated exclusively for an exempt purpose or purposes, exemption will be granted to such an organization regardless of the purpose or purposes specified in its application for exemption. For example, if an organization claims exemption on the ground that it is "educational", exemption will not be denied if, in fact, it is "charitable".

(2) *Charitable defined.* The term "charitable" is used in section 501(c)(3) in its generally accepted legal sense and is, therefore, not to be construed as limited by the separate enumeration in section 501(c)(3) of other tax-exempt purposes which may fall within the broad outlines of "charity" as developed by judicial decisions. Such terms include: Relief of the poor and distressed or of the underprivileged; advancement of religion; advancement of education or science; erection or maintenance of public buildings, monuments, or works; lessening of the burdens of Government; and promotion of social welfare by organizations designed to accomplish any of the above purposes, or (i) to lessen neighborhood tensions; (ii) to eliminate prejudice and discrimination; (iii) to defend human and civil rights secured by law; or (iv) to combat community deterioration and juvenile delinquency. The fact that an organization which is organized and operated for the relief of indigent persons may receive voluntary contributions from the persons intended to be relieved will not necessarily prevent such organization from being exempt as an organization organized and operated exclusively for charitable purposes. The fact that an organization, in carrying out its primary purpose, advocates social or civic changes or presents opinion on controversial issues with the intention of molding public opinion or creating public sentiment to an acceptance of its views does not preclude such organization from qualifying under section 501(c)(3) so long as it is not an "action" organization of any one of the types described in paragraph (c)(3) of this section.

(3) *Educational defined*—(i) *In general.* The term "educational", as used in section 501(c)(3), relates to—

(*a*) The instruction or training of the individual for the purpose of improving or developing his capabilities; or

(*b*) The instruction of the public on subjects useful to the individual and beneficial to the community.

An organization may be educational even though it advocates a particular position or viewpoint so long as it presents a sufficiently full and fair exposition of the pertinent facts as to permit an individual or the public to form an independent opinion or conclusion. On the other hand, an organization is not educational if its principal function is the mere presentation of unsupported opinion.

(ii) *Examples of educational organizations.* The following are examples of organizations which, if they otherwise meet the requirements of this section, are educational:

Example (1). An organization, such as a primary or secondary school, a college, or a professional or trade school, which has a regularly scheduled curriculum, a regular faculty, and a regularly enrolled body of students in attendance at a place where the educational activities are regularly carried on.

Example (2). An organization whose activities consist of presenting public discussion groups, forums, panels, lectures, or other similar programs. Such programs may be on radio or television.

Example (3). An organization which presents a course of instruction by means of correspondence or through the utilization of television or radio.

Example (4). Museums, zoos, planetariums, symphony orchestras, and other similar organizations.

(4) *Testing for public safety defined.* The term "testing for public safety", as used in section 501(c)(3), includes the testing of consumer products, such as electrical products, to determine whether they are safe for use by the general public.

(5) *Scientific defined.* (i) Since an organization may meet the requirements of section 501(c)(3) only if it serves a public rather than a private interest, a "scientific" organization must be organized and operated in the public interest

Reg. § 1.501(c)(3)-1(d)(5)

(see subparagraph (1)(ii) of this paragraph). Therefore, the term "scientific", as used in section 501(c)(3), includes the carrying on of scientific research in the public interest. Research when taken alone is a word with various meanings; it is not synonymous with "scientific"; and the nature of particular research depends upon the purpose which it serves. For research to be "scientific", within the meaning of section 501(c)(3), it must be carried on in furtherance of a "scientific" purpose. The determination as to whether research is "scientific" does not depend on whether such research is classified as "fundamental" or "basic" as contrasted with "applied" or "practical". On the other hand, for purposes of the exclusion from unrelated business taxable income provided by section 512(b)(9), it is necessary to determine whether the organization is operated primarily for purposes of carrying on "fundamental", as contrasted with "applied", research.

(ii) Scientific research does not include activities of a type ordinarily carried on as an incident to commercial or industrial operations, as, for example, the ordinary testing or inspection of materials or products or the designing or construction of equipment, buildings, etc.

(iii) Scientific research will be regarded as carried on in the public interest—

(a) If the results of such research (including any patents, copyrights, processes, or formulae resulting from such research) are made available to the public on a nondiscriminatory basis;

(b) If such research is performed for the United States, or any of its agencies or instrumentalities, or for a State or political subdivision thereof; or

(c) If such research is directed toward benefiting the public. The following are examples of scientific research which will be considered as directed toward benefiting the public, and, therefore, which will be regarded as carried on in the public interest:

(1) Scientific research carried on for the purpose of aiding in the scientific education of college or university students;

(2) scientific research carried on for the purpose of obtaining scientific information, which is published in a treatise, thesis, trade publication, or in any other form that is available to the interested public;

(3) scientific research carried on for the purpose of discovering a cure for a disease; or

(4) scientific research carried on for the purpose of aiding a community or geographical area by attracting new industry to the community or area or by encouraging the development of, or retention of, an industry in the community or area. Scientific research described in this subdivision (c) will be regarded as carried on in the public interest even though such research is performed pursuant to a contract or agreement under which the sponsor or sponsors of the research have the right to obtain ownership or control of any patents, copyrights, processes, or formulae resulting from such research.

(iv) An organization will not be regarded as organized and operated for the purpose of carrying on scientific research in the public interest and, consequently, will not qualify under section 501(c)(3) as a "scientific" organization, if—

(a) Such organization will perform research only for persons which are (directly or indirectly) its creators and which are not described in section 501(c)(3), or

(b) Such organization retains (directly or indirectly) the ownership or control of more than an insubstantial portion of the patents, copyrights, processes, or formulae resulting from its research and does not make such patents, copyrights, processes, or formulae available to the public. For purposes of this subdivision, a patent, copyright, process, or formula shall be considered as made available to the public if such patent, copyright, process, or formula is made available to the public on a nondiscriminatory basis. In addition, although one person is granted the exclusive right to the use of a patent, copyright, process, or formula, such patent, copyright, process, or formula shall be considered as made available to the public if the granting of such exclusive right is the only practicable manner in which the patent, copyright, process, or formula can be utilized to benefit the public. In such a case, however, the research from which the patent, copyright, process, or formula resulted will be regarded as carried on in the public interest (within the meaning of subdivision (iii) of this subparagraph) only if it is carried on for a person described in subdivision (iii)(b) of this subparagraph or if it is scientific research described in subdivision (iii)(c) of this subparagraph.

(v) The fact that any organization (including a college, university, or hospital) carries on research which is not in furtherance of an exempt purpose described in section 501(c)(3) will not preclude such organization from meeting the requirements of section 501(c)(3) so long as the organization meets the organizational test and is not operated for the primary purpose of carrying on such research (see paragraph (e) of this section, relating to organizations carrying on a trade or business). See paragraph (a)(5) of § 1.513-2, with respect to research which constitutes an unrelated trade or business, and section 512(b)(7), (8), and (9), with respect to income derived from research which is excludable from the tax on unrelated business income.

(vi) The regulations in this subparagraph are applicable with respect to taxable years beginning after December 31, 1960.

(e) *Organizations carrying on trade or business*—(1) *In general.* An organization may meet the requirements of section 501(c)(3) although it operates a trade or business as a substantial part of its activities, if the operation of such trade or business is in furtherance of the organization's exempt purpose or purposes and if the organization is not organized or operated for the primary purpose of carrying on an unrelated trade or business, as defined in section 513. In determining the existence or nonexistence of such primary purpose, all the circumstances must be considered, including the size and extent of the trade or business and the size and extent of the activities which are in furtherance of one or more exempt purposes. An organization which is organized and operated for the primary purpose of carrying on an unrelated trade or business is not exempt under section 501(c)(3) even though it has certain religious purposes, its property is held in common, and its profits do not inure to the benefit of individual members of the organization. See, however, section 501(d) and § 1.501(d)-1, relating to religious and apostolic organizations.

(2) *Taxation of unrelated business income.* For provisions relating to the taxation of unrelated business income of certain organizations described in section 501(c)(3), see sections 511 to 515, inclusive, and the regulations thereunder.

(f) *Applicability of regulations in this section.* The regulations in this section are, except as otherwise expressly provided, applicable with respect to taxable years beginning after July 26, 1959. For the rules applicable with respect to taxable years beginning before July 27, 1959, see 26 CFR (1939) 39.101(6)-1 (Regulations 118) as made applicable to the Code by Treasury Decision 6091, approved August 16, 1954 (19 F.R. 5167; C.B. 1954-2, 47). [Reg. § 1.501(c)(3)-1.]

☐ [T.D. 6391, 6-25-59. Amended by T.D. 6525, 1-10-61; T.D. 6939, 12-11-67; T.D. 7428, 8-13-76 and T.D. 8308, 8-30-90.]

[Reg. § 1.501(c)(4)-1]

§ 1.501(c)(4)-1. **Civic organizations and local associations of employees.**—(a) *Civic organizations*—(1) *In general.* A civic league or organization may be exempt as an organization described in section 501(c)(4) if:

(i) It is not organized or operated for profit; and

(ii) It is operated exclusively for the promotion of social welfare.

(2) *Promotion of social welfare*—(i) *In general.* An organization is operated exclusively for the promotion of social welfare if it is primarily engaged in promoting in some way the common good and general welfare of the people of the community. An organization embraced within this section is one which is operated primarily for the purpose of bringing about civic betterments and social improvements. A "social welfare" organization will qualify for exemption as a charitable organization if it falls within the definition of "charitable" set forth in paragraph (d)(2) of § 1.501(c)(3)-1 and is not an "action" organization as set forth in paragraph (c)(3) of § 1.501(c)(3)-1.

(ii) *Political or social activities.* The promotion of social welfare does not include direct or indirect participation or intervention in political campaigns on behalf of or in opposition to any candidate for public office. Nor is an organization operated primarily for the promotion of social welfare if its primary activity is operating a social club for the benefit, pleasure, or recreation of its members, or is carrying on a business with the general public in a manner similar to organizations which are operated for profit. See, however, section 501(c)(6) and § 1.501(c)(6)-1, relating to business leagues and similar organizations. A social welfare organization that is not, at any time after October 4, 1976, exempt from taxation as an organization described in section 501(c)(3) may qualify under section 501(c)(4) even though it is an "action" organization described in § 1.501(c)(3)-1(c)(3)(ii) or (iv), if it otherwise qualifies under this section. For rules relating to an organization that is, after October 4, 1976, exempt from taxation as an organization described in section 501(c)(3), see section 504 and § 1.504-1.

(b) *Local associations of employees.* Local associations of employees described in section 501(c)(4) are expressly entitled to exemption under section 501(a). As conditions to exemption, it is required (1) that the membership of such an association be limited to the employees of a designated person or persons in a particular municipality, and (2) that the net earnings of the association be devoted exclusively to charitable, educational, or recreational purposes. The word "local" is defined in paragraph (b) of § 1.501(c)(12)-1. See paragraph (d)(2) and (3) of § 1.501(c)(3)-1 with reference to the meaning of "charitable" and "educational" as used in this section. [Reg. § 1.501(c)(4)-1.]

☐ [T.D. 6391, 6-25-59. Amended by T.D. 8308, 8-30-90.]

[Reg. § 1.501(c)(5)-1]

§ 1.501(c)(5)-1. **Labor, agricultural, and horticultural organizations.**—(a) The organizations contemplated by section 501(c)(5) as entitled to exemption from income taxation are those which:

(1) Have no net earnings inuring to the benefit of any member, and

(2) Have as their objects the betterment of the conditions of those engaged in such pursuits, the improvement of the grade of their products, and the development of a higher degree of efficiency in their respective occupations.

(b)(1) *General rule.* An organization is not a organization described in section 501(c)(5) if the principal activity of the organization is to receive, hold, invest, disburse or otherwise manage funds associated with savings or investment plans or programs, including pension or other retirement savings plans or programs.

(2) *Exception.* Paragraph (b)(1) of this section shall not apply to an organization which—

(i) Is established and maintained by another labor organization described in section 501(c)(5), (determined without regard to this paragraph (b)(2));

(ii) Is not directly or indirectly established or maintained in whole or in part by one or more—

(A) Employers;

(B) Governments or agencies or instrumentalities thereof; or

(C) Government controlled entities;

(iii) Is funded by membership dues from members of the labor organization described in this paragraph (b)(2) and earnings thereon; and

(iv) Has not at any time after September 2, 1974 (the date of enactment of the Employee Retirement Income Security Act of 1974, Pub. L. 93-406, 88 Stat. 829) provided for, permitted or accepted employer contributions.

(3) *Example.* The principles of this paragraph (b) are illustrated by the following example:

Example. Trust A is organized in accordance with a collective bargaining agreement between labor union K and multiple employers. Trust A forms part of a plan that is established and maintained pursuant to the agreement and which covers employees of the signatory employers who are members of K. Representatives of both the employers and K serve as trustees. A receives contributions from the employers who are subject to the agreement. Retirement benefits paid to K's members as specified in the agreement are funded exclusively by the employers' contributions and accumulated earnings. A also provides information to union members about their retirement benefits and assists them with administrative tasks associated with the benefits. Most of A's activities are devoted to these functions. From time to time, A also participates in the renegotiation of the collective bargaining agreement. A's principal activity is to receive, hold, invest, disburse, or otherwise manage funds associated with a retirement savings plan. In addition, A does not satisfy all the requirements of the exception described in paragraph (b)(2) of this section. (For example, A accepts contributions from employers). Therefore, A is not a labor organization described in section 501(c)(5).

(c) Organizations described in section 501(c)(5) and otherwise exempt from tax under section 501(a) are taxable upon their unrelated business taxable income. See part II section 511 (and following), subchapter F, chapter 1 of the Code, and the regulations thereunder. [Reg. § 1.501(c)(5)-1.]

☐ [T.D. 6301, 7-8-58. Amended by T.D. 8726, 7-28-97.]

[Reg. § 1.501(c)(6)-1]

§ 1.501(c)(6)-1. **Business leagues, chambers of commerce, real estate boards, and boards of trade.**—A business league is an association of persons having some common business interest, the purpose of which is to promote such common interest and not to engage in a regular business of a kind ordinarily carried on for profit. It is an organization of the same general class as a chamber of commerce or board of trade. Thus, its activities should be directed to the improvement of business conditions of one or more lines of business as distinguished from the performance of particular services for individual persons. An organization whose purpose is to engage in a regular business of a kind ordinarily carried on for profit, even though the business is conducted on a cooperative basis or produces only suffcient income to be self sustaining, is not a business league. An association engaged in furnishing information to prospective investors, to enable them to make sound investments, is not a business league, since its activities do not further any common business interest, even though all of its income is devoted to the purpose stated. A stock or commodity exchange is not a business league, a chamber of commerce, or a board of trade within the meaning of section 501(c)(6) and is not exempt from tax. Organizations otherwise exempt from tax under this section are taxable upon their unrelated business taxable income. See part II (section 511 and following), subchapter F, chapter 1 of the Code, and the regulations thereunder. [Reg.§ 1.501(c)(6)-1.]

☐ [*T.D.* 6301, 7-8-58.]

[Reg. § 1.501(c)(7)-1]

§ 1.501(c)(7)-1. **Social clubs.**—(a) The exemption provided by section 501(a) for organizations described in section 501(c)(7) applies only to clubs which are organized and operated exclusively for pleasure, recreation, and other nonprofitable purposes, but does not apply to any club if any part of its net earnings inures to the benefit of any private shareholder. In general, this exemption extends to social and recreation clubs which are supported solely by membership fees, dues, and assessments. However, a club otherwise entitled to exemption will not be disqualified because it raises revenue from members through the use of club facilities or in connection with club activities.

(b) A club which engages in business, such as making its social and recreational facilities available to the general public or by selling real estate, timber, or other products, is not organized and operated exclusively for pleasure, recreation, and other nonprofitable purposes, and is not exempt under section 501(a). Solicitation by advertisement or otherwise for public patronage of its facilities is prima facie evidence that the club is engaging in business and is not being operated exclusively for pleasure, recreation, or social purposes. However, an incidental sale of property will not deprive a club of its exemption. [Reg. § 1.501(c)(7)-1.]

☐ [*T.D.* 6301, 7-8-58.]

[Reg. § 1.501(c)(8)-1]

§ 1.501(c)(8)-1. **Fraternal beneficiary societies.**—(a) A fraternal beneficiary society is exempt from tax only if operated under the "lodge system" or for the exclusive benefit of the members so operating. "Operating under the lodge system" means carrying on its activities under a form of organization that comprises local branches, chartered by a parent organization and largely self-governing, called lodges, chapters, or the like. In order to be exempt it is also necessary that the society have an established system for the payment to its members or their dependents of life, sick, accident, or other benefits.

(b) [Revoked.]

[Reg. § 1.501(c)(8)-1.]

☐ [*T.D.* 6301, 7-8-58. *Amended by T.D.* 7061, 9-22-70.]

[Reg. § 1.501(c)(9)-1]

§ 1.501(c)(9)-1. **Voluntary employees' beneficiary associations, in general.**—To be described in section 501(c)(9) an organization must meet all of the following requirements:

(a) The organization is an employees' association,

(b) Membership in the association is voluntary,

(c) The organization provides for the payment of life, sick, accident, or other benefits to its members or their dependents or designated beneficiaries, and substantially all of its operations are in furtherance of providing such benefits, and

(d) No part of the net earnings of the organization inures, other than by payment of the benefits referred to in paragraph (c) of this section, to the benefit of any private shareholder or individual. [Reg. § 1.501(c)(9)-1.]

☐ [*T.D.* 7750, 12-30-80.]

[Reg. § 1.501(c)(9)-2]

§ 1.501(c)(9)-2. **Membership in a voluntary employees' beneficiary association; employees; voluntary association of employees.**—(a) *Membership*—(1) *In general.* The membership of an organization described in section 501(c)(9) must consist of individuals who become entitled to participate by reason of their being employees and whose eligibility for membership is defined by reference to objective standards that constitute an employment-related common bond among such individuals. Typically, those eligible for membership in an organization described in section 501(c)(9) are defined by reference to a common employer (or affiliated employers), to coverage under one or more collective bargaining agreements (with respect to benefits provided by reason of such agreement(s)), to membership in a labor union, or to membership in one or more locals of a national or international labor union. For example, membership in an association might be open to all employees of a particular employer, or to employees in specified job classifications working for certain employers at specified locations and who are entitled to benefits by reason of one or more collective bargaining agreements. In addition, employees of one or more employers engaged in the same line of business in the same geographic locale will be considered to share an employment-related bond for purposes of an organization through which their employers provide benefits. Employees of a labor union also will be considered to share an employment-related com-

Reg. § 1.501(c)(9)-2(a)(1)

mon bond with members of the union, and employees of an association will be considered to share an employment-related common bond with members of the association. Whether a group of individuals is defined by reference to a permissible standard or standards is a question to be determined with regard to all the facts and circumstances, taking into account the guidelines set forth in this paragraph. Exemption will not be denied merely because the membership of an association includes some individuals who are not employees (within the meaning of paragraph (b) of this section), provided that such individuals share an employment-related bond with the employee-members. Such individuals may include, for example, the proprietor of a business whose employees are members of the association. For purposes of the preceding two sentences, an association will be considered to be composed of employees if 90 percent of the total membership of the association on one day of each quarter of the association's taxable year consists of employees (within the meaning of paragraph (b) of this section).

(2) *Restrictions*—(i) *In general*. Eligibility for membership may be restricted by geographic proximity, or by objective conditions or limitations reasonably related to employment, such as a limitation to a reasonable classification of workers, a limitation based on a reasonable minimum period of service, a limitation based on maximum compensation, or a requirement that a member be employed on a full-time basis. Similarly, eligibility for benefits may be restricted by objective conditions relating to the type or amount of benefits offered. Any objective criteria used to restrict eligibility for membership or benefits may not, however, be selected or administered in a manner that limits membership or benefits to officers, shareholders, or highly compensated employees of an employer contributing to or otherwise funding the employees' association. Similarly, eligibility for benefits may not be subject to conditions or limitations that have the effect of entitling officers, shareholders, or highly compensated employees of an employer contributing to or otherwise funding the employees' association to benefits that are disproportionate in relation to benefits to which other members of the association are entitled. See § 1.501(c)(9)-4(b). Whether the selection or administration of objective conditions has the effect of providing disproportionate benefits to officers, shareholders, or highly compensated employees generally is to be determined on the basis of all the facts and circumstances.

(ii) *Generally permissible restrictions or conditions*. In general the following restrictions will not be considered to be inconsistent with § 1.501(c)(9)-2(a)(2)(i) or § 1.501(c)(9)-4(b):

(A) In the case of an employer-funded organization, a provision that excludes or has the effect of excluding from membership in the organization or participation in a particular benefit plan employees who are members of another organization or covered by a different plan, funded or contributed to by the employer, to the extent that such other organization or plan offers similar benefits on comparable terms to the excluded employees.

(B) In the case of an employer-funded organization, a provision that excludes from membership, or limits the type or amount of benefits provided to, individuals who are included in a unit of employees covered by an agreement which the Secretary of Labor finds to be a collective bargaining agreement between employee representatives and one or more employers, if there is evidence that the benefit or benefits provided by the organization were the subject of good faith bargaining between such employee representatives and such employer or employers.

(C) Restrictions or conditions on eligibility for membership or benefits that are determined through collective bargaining, by trustees designated pursuant to a collective bargaining agreement, or by the collective bargaining agents of the members of an association or trustees named by such agent or agents.

(D) The allowance of benefits only on condition that a member or recipient contribute to the cost of such benefits, or the allowance of different benefits based solely on differences in contributions, provided that those making equal contributions are entitled to comparable benefits.

(E) A requirement that a member (or a member's dependents) meet a reasonable health standard related to eligibility for a particular benefit.

(F) The provision of life benefits in amounts that are a uniform percentage of the compensation received by the individual whose life is covered.

(G) The provision of benefits in the nature of wage replacement in the event of disability in amounts that are a uniform percentage of the compensation of the covered individuals (either before or after taking into account any disability benefits provided through social security or any similar plan providing for wage replacement in the event of disability).

(3) *Examples*. The provisions of this section may be illustrated by the following examples:

Example (1). Pursuant to a collective bargaining agreement entered into by X Corporation and W, a labor union which represents all of X

Reg. § 1.501(c)(9)-2(a)(2)

Corporation's hourly-paid employees, the X Corporation Union Benefit Plan is established to provide life insurance benefits to employees of X represented by W. The Plan is funded by contributions from X, and is jointly administered by X and W. In order to provide its non-unionized employees with comparable life insurance benefits, X also establishes and funds the X Corporation Life Insurance Trust. The Trust will not be ineligible for exemption as an organization described in section 501(c)(9) solely because membership is restricted to those employees of X who are not members of W.

Example (2). The facts are the same as in Example (1) except that the life insurance benefit provided to the non-unionized employees of X differs from the life insurance benefit provided to the unionized employees of X pursuant to the collective bargaining agreement. The trust will not be ineligible for exemption as an organization described in section 501(c)(9) solely because the life insurance benefit provided to X's nonunionized employees is not the same as the life insurance benefit provided to X's unionized employees.

Example (3). S corporation established a plan to provide health benefits to all its employees. In accordance with the provisions of the plan each employee may secure insurance coverage by making an election under which the employee agrees to contribute periodically to the plan an amount which is determined solely by whether the employee elects a high option coverage or a low option coverage and on whether the employee is unmarried or has a family. As an alternative, the employee may elect high or low options, self only or self and family, coverage through a local prepaid group medical plan. The contributions required of those electing the prepaid group medical plan also vary with the type of coverage selected, and differ from those required of employees electing insurance. The difference between the amount contributed by employees electing the various coverages and the actual cost of purchasing the coverage is made up through contributions by S to the plan, and under the plan, S provides approximately the same proportion of the cost for each coverage. To fund the plan, S established an arrangement in the nature of a trust under applicable local law and contributes all employee contributions, and all amounts which by the terms of the plan it is required to contribute, to the trust. The terms of the plan do not provide for disproportionate benefits to the employees of S and will not be considered inconsistent with § 1.501(c)(9)-2(a)(2)(i).

Example (4). The facts are the same as in Example (3) except that, for those employees or former employees covered by Medicare, the plan provides a distinct coverage which supplements Medicare benefits. Eligibility for Medicare is an objective condition relating to a type of benefit offered, and the provision of separate coverage for those eligible for Medicare will not be considered inconsistent with § 1.501(c)(9)-2(a)(2)(i).

(b) *Meaning of "employee".* Whether an individual is an "employee" is determined by reference to the legal and bona fide relationship of employer and employee. The term "employee" includes the following:

(1) An individual who is considered an employee:

(i) For employment tax purposes under Subtitle C of the Internal Revenue Code and the regulations thereunder, or

(ii) For purposes of a collective bargaining agreement, whether or not the individual could qualify as an employee under applicable common law rules. This would include any person who is considered an employee for purposes of the Labor Management Relations Act of 1947, 61 Stat. 136, as amended, 29 U.S.C. 141 (1979).

(2) An individual who became entitled to membership in the association by reason of being or having been an employee. Thus, an individual who would otherwise qualify under this paragraph will continue to qualify as an employee even though such individual is on leave of absence, works temporarily for another employer or as an independent contractor, or has been terminated by reason of retirement, disability or layoff. For example, an individual who in the normal course of employment is employed intermittently by more than one employer in an industry characterized by short-term employment by several different employers will not, by reason of temporary unemployment, cease to be an employee within the meaning of this paragraph.

(3) The surviving spouse and dependents of an employee (if, for purposes of the 90-percent test of § 1.501(c)(9)-2(a)(1) they are considered to be members of the association).

(c) *Description of voluntary association of employees*—(1) *Association.* To be described in section 501(c)(9) and this section there must be an entity, such as a corporation or trust established under applicable local law, having an existence independent of the member-employees or their employer.

(2) *Voluntary.* Generally, membership in an association is voluntary if an affirmative act is required on the part of an employee to become a member rather than the designation as a member due to employee status. However, an association

Reg. § 1.501(c)(9)-2(c)(2)

shall be considered voluntary although membership is required of all employees, provided that the employees do not incur a detriment (for example, in the form of deductions from pay) as the result of membership in the association. An employer is not deemed to have imposed involuntary membership on the employee if membership is required as the result of a collective bargaining agreement or as an incident of membership in a labor organization.

(3) *Of employees.* To be described in this section, an organization must be controlled—

(i) By its membership,

(ii) By independent trustee(s) (such as a bank), or

(iii) By trustees or other fiduciaries at least some of whom are designated by, or on behalf of, the membership. Whether control by or on behalf of the membership exists is a question to be determined with regard to all of the facts and circumstances, but generally such control will be deemed to be present when the membership (either directly or through its representative) elects, appoints or otherwise designates a person or persons to serve as chief operating officer(s), administrator(s), or trustee(s) of the organization. For purposes of this paragraph an organization will be considered to be controlled by independent trustees if it is an "employee welfare benefit plan", as defined in section 3(1) of the Employee Retirement Income Security Act of 1974 (ERISA), and, as such, is subject to the requirements of Parts 1 and 4 of Subtitle B, Title I of ERISA. Similarly, a plan will be considered to be controlled by its membership if it is controlled by one or more trustees designated pursuant to a collective bargaining agreement (whether or not the bargaining agent of the represented employees bargained for and obtained the right to participate in selecting the trustees).

(4) *Examples.* The provisions of this section may be illustrated by the following examples:

Example (1). X, a labor union, represents all the hourly-paid employees of Y Corporation. A health insurance benefit plan was established by X and Y as the result of a collective bargaining agreement entered into by them. The plan established the terms and conditions of membership in, and the benefits to be provided by, the plan. In accordance with the terms of the agreement, Y Corporation is obligated to establish a trust fund and make contributions thereto at specified rates. The trustees, some of whom are designated by X and some by Y, are authorized to hold and invest the assets of the trust and to make payments on instructions issued by Y Corporation in accordance with the conditions contained in the plan. The interdependent benefit plan agreement and trust indenture together create a voluntary employees' beneficiary association over which the employees possess the requisite control through the trustees designated by their representative, X.

Example (2). Z Corporation unilaterally established an educational benefit plan for its employees. The purpose of the plan is to provide payments for job-related educational or training courses, such as apprenticeship training programs, for Z Corporation employees, according to objective criteria set forth in the plan. Z establishes a separate bank account which it uses to fund payments to the plan. Contributions to the account are to be made at the discretion of and solely by Z Corporation, which also administers the plan and retains control over the assets in the fund. Z Corporation's educational benefit plan and the related account do not constitute an association having an existence independent of Z Corporation and therefore do not constitute a voluntary employees' beneficiary association.

Example (3). A, an individual, is the incorporator and chief operating officer of Lawyers' Beneficiary Association (LBA). LBA is engaged in the business of providing medical benefits to members of the Association and their families. Membership is open only to practicing lawyers located in a particular metropolitan area who are neither self-employed nor partners in a law firm. Membership in LBA is solicited by insurance agents under the control of X Corporation (owned by A) which, by contract with LBA, is the exclusive sales agent. Medical benefits are paid from a trust account containing periodic "contributions" paid by the members, together with proceeds from the investment of those contributions. Contribution and benefit levels are set by LBA. The "members" of LBA do not hold meetings, have no right to elect officers or directors of the Association, and no right to replace trustees. Collectively, the subscribers for medical benefits from LBA cannot be said to control the association and membership is neither more than nor different from the purchase of an insurance policy from a stock insurance company. LBA is not a voluntary employees' beneficiary association.

Example (4). U corporation unilaterally established a plan to provide health benefits to its employees. In accordance with the provisions of the plan, each employee may secure insurance or benefit coverage by making an election under which the employee agrees to contribute to the plan an amount which is determined solely by whether the employee elects a high option coverage or a low option coverage and on whether the employee elects self only or self and family cover-

Reg. § 1.501(c)(9)-2(c)(3)

age. The difference between the amount contributed by employees electing the various coverages and the actual cost of the coverage is made up through contributions by U to the plan. To fund the plan, U established an arrangement in the nature of a trust under applicable local law and contributed all employee contributions, and all amounts which by the term of the plan it was required to provide to the plan, to the trust. The trust constitutes an "employee welfare benefit plan" within the meaning of, and subject to relevant requirements of, ERISA. It will be considered to meet the requirements of § 1.501(c)(9)-2(c)(3). [Reg. § 1.501(c)(9)-2]

☐ [T.D. 7750, 12-30-80.]

[Reg. § 1.501(c)(9)-3]

§ 1.501(c)(9)-3. **Voluntary employees' beneficiary associations; life, sick, accident, or other benefits.**—(a) *In general.* The life, sick, accident, or other benefits provided by a voluntary employee's beneficiary association must be payable to its members, their dependents, or their designated beneficiaries. For purposes of section 501(c)(9), "dependent" means the member's spouse; any child of the member or the member's spouse who is a minor or a student (within the meaning of section 151(e)(4)); any other minor child residing with the member; and any other individual who an association, relying on information furnished to it by a member, in good faith believes is a person described in section 152(a). Life, sick, accident, or other benefits may take the form of cash or noncash benefits. A voluntary employees' beneficiary association is not operated for the purpose of providing life, sick, accident, or other benefits unless substantially all of its operations are in furtherance of the provision of such benefits. Further, an organization is not described in this section if it systematically and knowingly provides benefits (of more than a *de minimis* amount) that are not permitted by paragraph (b), (c), (d), or (e) of this section.

(b) *Life benefits.* The term "life benefit" means a benefit (including a burial benefit or a wreath) payable by reason of the death of a member or dependent. A "life benefit" may be provided directly or through insurance. It generally must consist of current protection, but also may include a right to convert to individual coverage on termination of eligibility for coverage through the association, or a permanent benefit as defined in, and subject to the conditions in, the regulations under section 79. A "life benefit" also includes the benefit provided under any life insurance contract purchased directly from an employee-funded association by a member or provided by such an association to a member. The term "life benefit" does not include a pension, annuity or similar benefit, except that a benefit payable by reason of the death of an insured may be settled in the form of an annuity to the beneficiary in lieu of a lump-sum death benefit (whether or not the contract provides for settlement in a lump sum).

(c) *Sick and accident benefits.* The term "sick and accident benefits" means amounts furnished to or on behalf of a member or a member's dependents in the event of illness or personal injury to a member or dependent. Such benefits may be provided through reimbursement to a member or a member's dependents for amounts expended because of illness or personal injury, or through the payment of premiums to a medical benefit or health insurance program. Similarly, a sick and accident benefit includes an amount paid to a member in lieu of income during a period in which the member is unable to work due to sickness or injury. Sick benefits also include benefits designed to safeguard or improve the health of members and their dependents. Sick and accident benefits may be provided directly by an association to or on behalf of members and their dependents, or may be provided indirectly by an association through the payment of premiums or fees to an insurance company, medical clinic, or other program under which members and their dependents are [is] entitled to medical services or to other sick and accident benefits. Sick and accident benefits may also be furnished in noncash form, such as, for example, benefits in the nature of clinical care services by visiting nurses, and transportation furnished for medical care.

(d) *Other benefits.* The term "other benefits" includes only benefits that are similar to life, sick, or accident benefits. A benefit is similar to a life, sick, or accident benefit if—

(1) It is intended to safeguard or improve the health of a member or a member's dependents, or

(2) It protects against a contingency that interrupts or impairs a member's earning power.

(e) *Examples of "other benefits".* Paying vacation benefits, providing vacation facilities, reimbursing vacation expenses, and subsidizing recreational activities such as athletic leagues are considered "other benefits". The provision of child-care facilities for preschool and school-age dependents is also considered "other benefits". The provision of job readjustment allowances, income maintenance payments in the event of economic dislocation, temporary living expense loans and grants at times of disaster (such as fire or flood), supplemental unemployment compensation benefits (as defined in section 501(c)(17)(D)(i) of the Code), severance benefits (under a severance pay plan within the meaning

Reg. § 1.501(c)(9)-3(e)

of 29 CFR § 2510.3-2(b)) and education or training benefits or courses (such as apprentice training programs) for members, are considered "other benefits" because they protect against a contingency that interrupts earning power. Personal legal service benefits which consist of payments or credits to one or more organizations or trusts described in section 501(c)(20) are considered "other benefits". Except to the extent otherwise provided in these regulations, as amended from time to time, "other benefits" also include any benefit provided in the manner permitted by paragraphs (5) et seq. of section 302(c) of the Labor Management Relations Act of 1947, 61 Stat. 136, as amended, 29 U.S.C. 186(c) (1979).

(f) *Examples of nonqualifying benefits.* Benefits that are not described in paragraphs (d) or (e) of this section are not "other benefits". Thus, "other benefits" do not include the payment of commuting expenses, such as bridge tolls or train fares, the provision of accident or homeowner's insurance benefits for damage to property, the provision of malpractice insurance, or the provision of loans to members except in times of distress (as permitted by § 1.501(c)(9)-3(e)). "Other benefits" also do not include the provision of savings facilities for members. The term "other benefits" does not include any benefit that is similar to a pension or annuity payable at the time of mandatory or voluntary retirement, or a benefit that is similar to the benefit provided under a stock bonus or profit-sharing plan. For purposes of section 501(c)(9) and these regulations, a benefit will be considered similar to that provided under a pension, annuity, stock bonus or profit-sharing plan if it provides for deferred compensation that becomes payable by reason of the passage of time, rather than as the result of an unanticipated event. Thus, for example, supplemental unemployment benefits, which generally become payable by reason of unanticipated layoff, are not, for purposes of these regulations, considered similar to the benefit provided under a pension, annuity, stock bonus or profit-sharing plan.

(g) *Examples.* The provisions of this section may be further illustrated by the following examples:

Example (1). V was organized in connection with a vacation plan created pursuant to a collective bargaining agreement between M, a labor union, which represents certain hourly paid employees of T corporation, and T. The agreement calls for the payment by T to V of a specified sum per hour worked by T employees who are covered by the collective bargaining agreement. T includes the amounts in the covered employees' wages and withholds income and FICA taxes. The amounts are paid by T to V to provide vacation benefits provided under the collective bargaining agreement. Generally, each covered employee receives a check in payment of his or her vacation benefit during the year following the year in which contributions were made by T to V. The amount of the vacation benefit is determined by reference to the contributions during the prior year to V by T on behalf of each employee, and is distributed in cash to each such employee. If the earnings on investments by V during the year preceding distribution are sufficient after deducting the expenses of administering the plan, each recipient of a vacation benefit is paid an amount, in addition to the contributions on his or her behalf, equal to his/her ratable share of the net earnings of V during such year. The plan provides a vacation benefit that constitutes an eligible "other benefit" described in section 501(c)(9) and § 1.501(c)(9)-3(e).

Example (2). The facts are the same as in Example 1, except that each covered employee of T is entitled, at his or her discretion, to contribute up to an additional $1,000 each year to V, which agrees in respect of such sum to pay interest at a stated rate from the time of contribution until the time at which the contributing employee's vacation benefit is distributed. In addition, each employee may elect to leave all or a portion of his/her distributable benefit on deposit past the time of distribution, in which case interest will continue to accrue. Because the plan more closely resembles a savings arrangement than a vacation plan, the benefit payable to the covered employees of T is not a "vacation benefit" and is not an eligible "other benefit" described in section 501(c)(9) and § 1.501(c)(9)-3(d) or (e). [Reg. § 1.501(c)(9)-3.]

☐ [*T.D.* 7750, 12-30-80.]

[Reg. § 1.501(c)(9)-4]

§ 1.501(c)(9)-4. **Voluntary employees' beneficiary associations; inurement.**—(a) *General rule.* No part of the net earnings of an employees' association may inure to the benefit of any private shareholder or individual other than through the payment of benefits permitted by § 1.501(c)(9)-3. The disposition of property to, or the performance of services for, a person for less than the greater of fair market value or cost (including indirect costs) to the association, other than as a life, sick, accident or other permissible benefit, constitutes prohibited inurement. Generally, the payment of unreasonable compensation to the trustees or employees of the association, or the purchase of insurance or services for amounts in excess of their fair market value from a company in which one or more of the association's trustees, officers or fiduciaries has an interest, will constitute prohibited inurement. Whether prohibited inurement has occurred is a question to be determined with regard to all of the facts and circumstances, taking into account the guidelines set forth in this section. The guidelines and examples contained in this section are not an exhaustive list of the activities that may constitute prohibited inurement, or the persons to whom the association's earnings could impermissibly inure. See § 1.501(a)-1(c).

(b) *Disproportionate benefits.* For purposes of subsection (a), the payment to any member of disproportionate benefits, where such payment is not pursuant to objective and nondiscriminatory standards, will not be considered a benefit within the meaning of § 1.501(c)(9)-3 even though the benefit otherwise is one of the type permitted by that section. For example, the payment to highly compensated personnel of benefits that are disproportionate in relation to benefits received by other members of the association will constitute prohibited inurement. Also, the payment to similarly situated employees of benefits that differ in kind or amount will constitute prohibited inurement unless the difference can be justified on the basis of objective and reasonable standards adopted by the association or on the basis of standards adopted pursuant to the terms of a collective bargaining agreement. In general, benefits paid pursuant to standards or subject to conditions that do not provide for disproportionate benefits to officers, shareholders, or highly compensated employees will not be considered disproportionate. See § 1.501(c)(9)-2(a)(2) and (3).

(c) *Rebates.* The rebate of excess insurance premiums, based on the mortality or morbidity experience of the insurer to which the premiums were paid, to the person or persons whose contributions were applied to such premiums, does not constitute prohibited inurement. A voluntary employees' beneficiary association may also make administrative adjustments strictly incidental to the provision of benefits to its members.

(d) *Termination of plan or dissolution of association.* It will not constitute prohibited inurement if, on termination of a plan established by an employer and funded through an association described in section 501(c)(9), any assets remaining in the association, after satisfaction of all liabilities to existing beneficiaries of the plan, are applied to provide, either directly or through the purchase of insurance, life, sick, accident or other benefits within the meaning of § 1.501(c)(9)-3 pursuant to criteria that do not provide for disproportionate benefits to officers, shareholders, or highly compensated employees of the employer.

See § 1.501(c)(9)-2(a)(2). Similarly, a distribution to members upon the dissolution of the association will not constitute prohibited inurement if the amount distributed to members are [is] determined pursuant to the terms of a collective bargaining agreement or on the basis of objective and reasonable standards which do not result in either unequal payments to similarly situated members or in disproportionate payments to officers, shareholders, or highly compensated employees of an employer contributing to or otherwise funding the employees' association. Except as otherwise provided in the first sentence of this paragraph, if the association's corporate charter, articles of association, trust instrument, or other written instrument by which the association was created, as amended from time to time, provides that on dissolution its assets will be distributed to its members' contributing employers, or if in the absence of such provision the law of the state in which the association was created provides for such distribution to the contributing employers, the association is not described in section 501(c)(9).

(e) *Example.* The provisions of this section may be illustrated by the following example:

Example. Employees A, B and C, members of the X voluntary employees' beneficiary association, are unemployed. They receive unemployment benefits from X. Those to A include an amount in addition to those provided to B and C, to provide for A's retraining. B has been found pursuant to objective and reasonable standards not to qualify for the retraining program. C, although eligible for retraining benefits has declined. X's additional payment to A for retraining does not constitute prohibited inurement. [Reg. § 1.501(c)(9)-4.]

☐ [*T.D. 7750, 12-30-80.*]

[Reg. § 1.501(c)(9)-5]

§ 1.501(c)(9)-5. **Voluntary employees' beneficiary associations; recordkeeping requirements.**—(a) *Records.* In addition to such other records which may be required (for example, by section 512(a)(3) and the regulations thereunder) every organization described in section 501(c)(9) must maintain records indicating the amount contributed by each member and contributing employer, and the amount and type of benefits paid by the organization to or on behalf of each member.

(b) *Cross reference.* For provisions relating to annual information returns with respect to payments, see section 6041 and the regulations thereunder. [Reg. § 1.501(c)(9)-5.]

☐ [*T.D. 7750, 12-30-80.*]

Reg. § 1.501(c)(9)-5(b)

39,026

General Rule

See p. 20,601 for regulations not amended to reflect law changes

[Reg. § 1.501(c)(9)-6]

§ 1.501(c)(9)-6. **Voluntary employees' beneficiary associations; benefits includible in gross income.**—(a) *In general.* Cash and noncash benefits realized by a person on account of the activities of an organization described in section 501(c)(9) shall be included in gross income to the extent provided in the Internal Revenue Code of 1954, including, but not limited to, sections 61, 72, 101, 104 and 105 of the Code and regulations thereunder.

(b) *Availability of statutory exclusions from gross income.* The availability of any statutory exclusion from gross income with respect to contributions to, or the payment of benefits from, an organization described in section 501(c)(9) is determined by the statutory provision conferring the exclusion, and the regulations and rulings thereunder, not by whether an individual is eligible for membership in the organization or by the permissibility of the benefit paid. Thus, for example, if a benefit is paid by an employer-funded organization described in section 501(c)(9) to a member who is not an "employee", a statutory exclusion from gross income that is available only for "employees" would be unavailable in the case of a benefit paid to such individual. Similarly, the fact that, for example, under some circumstances educational benefits constitute "other benefits" does not of itself mean that such benefits are eligible for the exclusion of either section 117 or section 127 of the Code. [Reg. § 1.501(c)(9)-6.]

☐ [*T.D.* 7750, 12-30-80.]

[Reg. § 1.501(c)(9)-7]

§ 1.501(c)(9)-7. **Voluntary employees' beneficiary associations; section 3(4) of ERISA.**—The term "voluntary employees' beneficiary association" in section 501(c)(9) of the Internal Revenue Code is not necessarily coextensive with the term "employees' beneficiary association" as used in section 3(4) of the Employee Retirement Income Security Act of 1974 (ERISA), 29 U.S.C. 1002(4), and the requirements which an organization must meet to be an "employees' beneficiary association" within the meaning of section 3(4) of ERISA are not necessarily identical to the requirements that an organization must meet in order to be a "voluntary employees' beneficiary association" within the meaning of section 501(c)(9) of the Code. [Reg. § 1.501(c)(9)-7.]

☐ [*T.D.* 7750, 12-30-80.]

[Reg. § 1.501(c)(9)-8]

§ 1.501(c)(9)-8. **Voluntary employees' beneficiary associations; effective date.**—(a) *General rule.* Except as otherwise provided in this section, the provisions of §§ 1.501(c)(9)-1 through 7 shall apply with respect to taxable years beginning after December 31, 1954.

(b) *Pre-1970 taxable years.* For taxable years beginning before January 1, 1970, section 501(c)(9)(B) (relating to the requirement that 85 percent or more of the association's income consist of amounts collected from members and contributed by employers), as in effect for such years, shall apply.

(c) *Existing associations.* Except as otherwise provided in paragraph (d), the provisions of §§ 1.501(c)(9)-2(a)(1) and (c)(3) shall apply with respect to taxable years beginning after December 31, 1980.

(d) *Collectively-bargained plans.* In the case of a voluntary employees' beneficiary association which receives contributions from one or more employers pursuant to one or more collective bargaining agreements in effect on December 31, 1980, the provisions of §§ 1.501(c)(9)-1 through 5 shall apply with respect to taxable years beginning after the date on which the agreement terminates (determined without regard to any extension thereof agreed to after December 31, 1980).

(e) *Election.* Notwithstanding paragraphs (c) and (d) of this section, an organization may choose to be subject to all or a portion of one or more of the provisions of these regulations for any taxable year beginning after December 31, 1954. [Reg. § 1.501(c)(9)-8.]

☐ [*T.D.*7750, 12-30-80.]

[Reg. § 1.501(c)(10)-1]

§ 1.501(c)(10)-1. **Certain fraternal beneficiary societies.**—(a) For taxable years beginning after Dec. 31, 1969, an organization will qualify for exemption under section 501(c)(10) if it—

(1) is a domestic fraternal beneficiary society order, or association, described in section 501(c)(8) and the regulations thereunder except that it does not provide for the payment of life, sick, accident, or other benefits to its members, and

(2) devotes its net earnings exclusively to religious, charitable, scientific, literary, educational, and fraternal purposes.

Any organization described in section 501(c)(7), such as, for example, a national college fraternity, is not described in section 501(c)(10) and this section. [Reg. § 1.501(c)(10)-1.]

☐ [*T.D.* 7172, 3-16-72.]

Reg. § 1.501(c)(9)-6(a)

[Reg. § 1.501(c)(12)-1]

§ 1.501(c)(12)-1. **Local benevolent life insurance associations, mutual irrigation and telephone companies, and like organizations.**—(a) An organization described in section 501(c)(12) must receive at least 85 percent of its income from amounts collected from members for the sole purpose of meeting losses and expenses. If an organization issues policies for stipulated cash premiums, or if it requires advance deposits to cover the cost of the insurance and maintains investments from which more than 15 percent of its income is derived, it is not entitled to exemption. On the other hand, an organization may be entitled to exemption, although it makes advance assessments for the sole purpose of meeting future losses and expenses, provided that the balance of such assessments remaining on hand at the end of the year is retained to meet losses and expenses or is returned to members.

(b) The phrase "of a purely local character" applies to benevolent life insurance associations, and not to the other organizations specified in section 501(c)(12). It also applies to any organization seeking exemption on the ground that it is an organization similar to a benevolent life insurance association. An organization of a purely local character is one whose business activities are confined to a particular community, place, or district, irrespective, however, of political subdivisions. If the activities of an organization are limited only by the borders of a State it cannot be considered to be purely local in character.

(c) For taxable years of a mutual or cooperative telephone company beginning after December 31, 1974, the 85 percent member-income test described in paragraph (a) of this section is applied without taking into account income received or accrued from another telephone company for the performance of communication services involving the completion of long distance calls to, from, or between members of the mutual or cooperative telephone company. For example, if, in one year, a cooperative telephone company receives $85x from its members for telephone calls, $15x as interest income, and $20x as credits under long distance interconnection agreements with other telephone companies for the performance of communication services involving the completion of long distance calls to, from, or between the cooperative's members (whether or not the credits may be offset, in whole or in part, by amounts due the other companies under the interconnection agreements), the member-income fraction is calculated without taking into account, either in the numerator or denominator, the $20x credits received from the other telephone companies. In this example, the 85 percent member-income test is satisfied because at least 85 percent

$$\frac{\text{member income}}{\text{total income}} = \frac{85x}{85x + 15x} = \frac{85}{100} = 85\%$$

of the cooperative's total income is derived from member income. [Reg. § 1.501(c)(12)-1.]

☐ [T.D. 6301, 7-8-58. Amended by T.D. 7648, 10-15-79.]

[Reg. § 1.501(c)(13)-1]

§ 1.501(c)(13)-1. **Cemetery companies and crematoria.**—(a) *Nonprofit mutual cemetery companies.* A nonprofit cemetery company may be entitled to exemption if it is owned by and operated exclusively for the benefit of its lot owners who hold such lots for bona fide burial purposes and not for the purpose of resale. A mutual cemetery company which also engages in charitable activities, such as the burial of paupers, will be regarded as operating in conformity with this standard. Further, the fact that a mutual cemetery company limits its membership to a particular class of individuals, such as members of a family, will not affect its status as mutual so long as all the other requirements of section 501(c)(13) are met.

(b) *Nonprofit cemetery companies and crematoria.* Any nonprofit corporation, chartered solely for the purpose of the burial, or (for taxable years beginning after December 31, 1970) the cremation of bodies, and not permitted by its charter to engage in any business not necessarily incident to that purpose, is exempt from income tax, provided that no part of its net earnings inures to the benefit of any private shareholder or individual.

(c) *Preferred stock*—(1) *In general.* Except as provided in subparagraph (3) of this paragraph, a cemetery company or crematorium is not described in section 501(c)(13) if it issues preferred stock on or after November 28, 1978.

(2) *Transitional rule for preferred stock issued prior to November 28, 1978.* In the case of preferred stock issued prior to November 28, 1978, a cemetery company or crematorium which issued such stock shall not fail to be exempt from income tax solely because it issued preferred stock which entitled the holders to dividends at a fixed rate, not exceeding the legal rate of interest in the State of incorporation or 8 percent per annum, whichever is greater, on the value of the consideration for which the stock was issued, if its articles of incorporation require:

Reg. § 1.501(c)(13)-1(c)(2)

(i) That the preferred stock be retired at par as rapidly as funds therefor become available from operations, and

(ii) That all funds not required for the payment of dividends upon or for the retirement of preferred stock be used by the company for the care and improvement of the Cemetery property.

The term "legal rate of interest" shall mean the rate of interest prescribed by law in the State of incorporation which prevails in the absence of an agreement between contracting parties fixing a rate.

(3) *Transitional rule for preferred stock issued on or after November 28, 1978.* In the case of preferred stock issued on or after November 28, 1978, a cemetery company or crematorium shall not fail to be exempt from income tax if its articles of incorporation and the preferred stock meet the requirements of subparagraph (2) and if such stock is issued pursuant to a plan which has been reduced to writing and adopted prior to November 28, 1978. The adoption of the plan must be shown by the acts of the duly constituted responsible officers and appear upon the official records of the cemetery company or crematorium.

(d) *Sales to exempt cemetery companies and crematoria.* Except as provided in paragraph (c)(2) or (c)(3) of this section (relating to transitional rules for preferred stock), no person may have any interest in the net earnings of a tax-exempt cemetery company or crematorium. Thus, a cemetery company or crematorium is not exempt from tax if property is transferred to such organization in exchange for an interest in the net earnings of the organization so long as such interest remains outstanding. An interest in a cemetery company or crematorium that constitutes an equity interest within the meaning of section 385 will be considered an interest in the net earnings of the cemetery. However, an interest in a cemetery company or crematorium that does not constitute an equity interest within the meaning of section 385 may nevertheless constitute an interest in the net earnings of the organization. Thus, for example, a bond or other evidence of indebtedness issued by a cemetery company or crematorium which provides for a fixed rate of interest but which, in addition, provides for additional interest payments contingent upon the revenues or income of the organization is considered an interest in the net earnings of the organization. Similarly, a convertible debt obligation issued by a cemetery company or crematorium after July 7, 1975, is considered an interest in the net earnings of the organization. [Reg. § 1.501(c)(13)-1.]

☐ [T.D. 6301, 7-8-58. Amended by T.D. 7698, 5-20-80.]

Reg. § 1.501(c)(14)-1(a)

[Reg. § 1.501(c)(14)-1]

§ 1.501(c)(14)-1. **Credit unions and mutual insurance funds.**—Credit unions (other than Federal credit unions described in section 501(c)(1)) without capital stock, organized and operated for mutual purposes and without profit, are exempt from tax under section 501(a). Corporations or associations without capital stock organized before September 1, 1951, and operated for mutual purposes and without profit for the purpose of providing reserve funds for, and insurance of, shares or deposits in:

(a) Domestic building and loan associations as defined in section 7701(a)(19),

(b) Cooperative banks without capital stock organized and operated for mutual purposes and without profit, or

(c) Mutual savings banks not having capital stock represented by shares,

are also exempt from tax under section 501(a). In addition, corporations or associations of the type described in the preceding sentence which were organized on or after September 1, 1951, but before September 1, 1957, are exempt from tax under section 501(a) for taxable years beginning after December 31, 1959. [Reg. § 1.501(c)(14)-1.]

☐ [T.D. 6301, 7-8-58. Amended by T.D. 6493, 9-26-60.]

[Reg. § 1.501(c)(15)-1]

§ 1.501(c)(15)-1. **Mutual insurance companies or associations.**—(a) *Taxable years beginning after December 31, 1962.* An insurance company or association described in section 501(c)(15) is exempt under section 501(a) if it is a mutual company or association (other than life or marine) or if it is a mutual interinsurer or reciprocal underwriter (other than life or marine) and if the gross amount received during the taxable year from the sum of the following items does not exceed $150,000.

(1) The gross amount of income during the taxable year from—

(i) Interest (including tax-exempt interest and partially tax-exempt interest), as described in § 1.61-7. Interest shall be adjusted for amortization of premium and accrual of discount in accordance with the rules prescribed in section 822(d)(2) and the regulations thereunder.

(ii) Dividends, as described in § 1.61-9.

(iii) Rents and royalties, as described in § 1.61-8.

(iv) The entering into of any lease, mortgage, or other instrument or agreement from which the company may derive interest, rents, or royalties.

General Rule
See p. 20,601 for regulations not amended to reflect law changes

(v) The alteration or termination of any instrument or agreement described in subdivision (iv) of this subparagraph.

(2) The gross income from any trade or business (other than an insurance business) carried on by the company or association, or by a partnership of which the company or association is a partner.

(3) Premiums (including deposits and assessments).

(b) *Taxable years beginning after December 31, 1954, and before January 1, 1963.* An insurance company or association described in section 501(c)(15) and paragraph (a) of this section is exempt under section 501(a) if the gross amount received during the taxable year from the sum of the items described in paragraph (a)(1), (2), and (3) of this section does not exceed $75,000.

(c) *No double inclusion of income.* In computing the gross income from any trade or business (other than an insurance business) carried on by the company or asociation, or by a partnership of which the company or association is a partner, any item described in section 822(b)(1)(A), (B), or (C) and paragraph (a)(1) of this section shall not be considered as gross income arising from the conduct of such trade or business, but shall be taken into account under section 822(b)(1)(A), (B), or (C) and paragraph (a)(1) of this section.

(d) *Taxable years beginning after December 31, 1953, and before January 1, 1955.* An insurance company or association described in section 501(c)(15) is exempt under section 501(a) if it is a mutual company or association (other than life or marine) or if it is a mutual interinsurer or reciprocal underwriter (other than life or marine) and if the gross amount received during the taxable year from the sum of the following items does not exceed $75,000:

(1) The gross amount of income during the taxable year from—

(i) Interest (including tax-exempt interest and partially tax-exempt interest), as described in § 1.61-7. Interest shall be adjusted for amortization of premium and accrual of discount in accordance with the rules prescribed in section 822(d)(2) and § 1.822-3.

(ii) Dividends, as described in § 1.61-9.

(iii) Rents (but excluding royalties), as described in § 1.61-8.

(2) Premiums (including deposits and assessments).

(e) *Exclusion of capital gains.* Gains from sales or exchanges of capital assets to the extent provided in subchapter P (section 1201 and following, relating to capital gains and losses), chapter 1 of the Code, shall be excluded from the amounts described in this section. [Reg. § 1.501(c)(15)-1.]

☐ [*T.D.* 6301, 7-8-58. Amended by *T.D.* 6662, 7-8-63.]

[Reg. § 1.501(c)(16)-1]

§ 1.501(c)(16)-1. **Corporations organized to finance crop operations.**—A corporation organized by a farmers' cooperative marketing or purchasing association, or the members thereof, for the purpose of financing the ordinary crop operations of such members or other producers is exempt, provided the marketing or purchasing association is exempt under section 521 and the financing corporation is operated in conjunction with the marketing or purchasing association. The provisions of § 1.521-1 relating to a reserve or surplus and to capital stock shall also apply to corporations coming under this section. [Reg. § 1.501(c)(16)-1.]

☐ [*T.D.* 6301, 7-8-58.]

[Reg. § 1.501(c)(17)-1]

§ 1.501(c)(17)-1. **Supplemental unemployment benefit trusts.**—(a) *Requirements for qualification.*—(1) A supplemental unemployment benefit trust may be exempt as an organization described in section 501(c)(17) if the requirements of subparagraph (2) through (6) of this paragraph are satisfied.

(2) The trust is a valid, existing trust under local law and is evidenced by an executed written document.

(3) The trust is part of a written plan established and maintained by an employer, his employees, or both the employer and his employees, solely for the purpose of providing supplemental unemployment compensation benefits (as defined in section 501(c)(17)(D) and paragraph (b)(1) of § 1.501(c)(17)-1).

(4) The trust is part of a plan which provides that the corpus and income of the trust cannot (in the taxable year, and at any time thereafter, before the satisfaction of all liabilities to employees covered by the plan) be used for, or diverted to, any purpose other than the providing of supplemental unemployment compensation benefits. Thus, if the plan provides for the payment of any benefits other than supplemental unemployment compensation benefits as defined in paragraph (b) of this section, the trust will not be entitled to exemption as an organization described in section 501(c)(17). However, the payment of any necessary or appropriate expenses in connection with the administration of a plan providing supplemental unemployment compensation benefits shall be considered a payment to provide such

Reg. § 1.501(c)(17)-1(a)(4)

benefits and shall not affect the qualification of the trust.

(5) The trust is part of a plan whose eligibility conditions and benefits do not discriminate in favor of employees who are officers, shareholders, persons whose principal duties consist of supervising the work of other employees, or highly compensated employees. See sections 401(a)(3)(B) and 401(a)(4) and §§ 1.401-3 and 1.401-4. However, a plan is not discriminatory within the meaning of section 501(c)(17)(A)(iii), relating to the requirement that the benefits paid under the plan be nondiscriminatory, merely because the benefits received under the plan bear a uniform relationship to the total compensation, or the basic or regular rate of compensation, of the employees covered by the plan. Accordingly, the benefits provided for highly paid employees may be greater than the benefits provided for lower paid employees if the benefits are determined by reference to their compensation; but, in such a case, the plan will not qualify if the benefits paid to the higher paid employees bear a larger ratio to their compensation than the benefits paid to the lower paid employees bear to their compensation. In addition, section 501(c)(17)(B) sets forth certain other instances in which a plan will not be considered discriminatory (see paragraph (c) of § 1.501(c)(17)-2).

(6) The trust is part of a plan which requires that benefits are to be determined according to objective standards. Thus, a plan may provide similarly situated employees with benefits which differ in kind and amount, but may not permit such benefits to be determined solely in the discretion of the trustees.

(b) *Meaning of terms.* The following terms are defined for purposes of section 501(c)(17):

(1) *Supplemental unemployment compensation benefits.* The term supplemental unemployment compensation benefits means only—

(i) Benefits paid to an employee because of his involuntary separation from the employment of the employer, whether or not such separation is temporary, but only when such separation is one resulting directly from a reduction in force, the discontinuance of a plant or operation, or other similar conditions; and

(ii) Sick and accident benefits subordinate to the benefits described in subdivision (i) of this subparagraph.

(2) *Employee.* The term "employee" means an individual whose status is that of an employee under the usual common-law rules applicable in determining the employer-employee relationship. The term "employee" also includes an individual who qualifies as an "employee" under the State or Federal unemployment compensation law covering his employment, whether or not such an individual could qualify as an employee under such common-law rules.

(3) *Involuntary separation from the employment of the employer.* Whether a "separation from the employment of the employer" occurs is a question to be decided with regard to all the facts and circumstances. However, for purposes of section 501(c)(17), the term "separation" includes both a temporary separation and a permanent severance of the employment relationship. Thus, for example, an employee may be separated from the employment of his employer even though at the time of separation it is believed that he will be re-employed by the same employer. Whether or not an employee is "involuntarily" separated from the employment of the employer is a question of fact. However, normally, an employee will not be deemed to have separated himself voluntarily from the employment of his employer merely because his collective bargaining agreement provides for the termination of his services upon the happening of a condition subsequent and that condition does in fact occur. For example, if the collective bargaining agreement provides that the employer may automate a given department and thereby dislocate several employees, the fact that the employees' collective bargaining agent has consented to such a condition will not render any employee's subsequent unemployment for such cause voluntary.

(4) *Other similar conditions.* Involuntary separation directly resulting from "other similar conditions" includes, for example, involuntary separation from the employment of the employer resulting from cyclical, seasonal, or technological causes. Some causes of involuntary separation from the employment of the employer which are not similar to those enumerated in section 501(c)(17)(D)(i) are separation for disciplinary reasons or separation because of age.

(5) *Subordinate sick and accident benefits.* In general, a sick and accident benefit payment is an amount paid to an employee in the event of his illness of personal injury (whether or not such illness or injury results in the employee's separation from the service of his employer). In addition, the phrase "sick and accident benefits" includes amounts provided under the plan to reimburse an employee for amounts he expends because of the illness or injury of his spouse or a dependent (as defined in section 152). Sick and accident benefits may be paid by a trust described in section 501(c)(17) only if such benefits are subordinate to the separation payments provided under the plan of which the trust forms a part. Whether the sick

Reg. § 1.501(c)(17)-1(a)(5)

and accident benefits provided under a supplemental unemployment compensation benefit plan are subordinate to the separation benefits provided under such plan is a question to be decided with regard to all the facts and circumstances. [Reg. § 1.501(c)(17)-1.]

☐ [T.D. 6972, 9-11-68.]

[Reg. § 1.501(c)(17)-2]

§ 1.501(c)(17)-2. General rules.—(a) *Supplemental unemployment compensation benefits.* Supplemental unemployment compensation benefits as defined in section 501(c)(17)(D) and paragraph (b)(1) of § 1.501(c)(17)-1 may be paid in a lump sum or installments. Such benefits may be paid to an employee who has, subsequent to his separation from the employment of the employer, obtained other part-time, temporary, or permanent employment. Furthermore, such payments may be made in cash, services, or property. Thus, supplemental unemployment compensation benefits provided to involuntarily separated employees may include, for example, the following: furnishing of medical care at an established clinic, furnishing of food, job training and schooling, and job counseling. If such benefits are furnished in services or property, the fair market value of the benefits must satisfy the requirements of section 501(c)(17)(A)(iii), relating to nondiscrimination as to benefits. However, supplemental unemployment compensation benefits may be provided only to an employee and only under circumstances described in paragraph (b)(1) of § 1.501(c)(17)-1. Thus, a trust described in section 501(c)(17) may not provide, for example, for the payment of a death, vacation, or retirement benefit.

(b) *Sick and accident benefits.* If a trust described in section 501(c)(17) provides for the payment of sick and accident benefits, such benefits may only be provided for employees who are eligible for receipt of separation benefits under the plan of which the trust is a part. However, the sick and accident benefits need not be provided for all the employees who are eligible for receipt of separation benefits, so long as the plan does not discriminate in favor of persons with respect to whom discrimination is proscribed in section 501(c)(17)(A)(ii) and (iii). Furthermore, the portion of the plan which provides for the payment of sick and accident benefits must satisfy the nondiscrimination requirements of section 501(c)(17)(A)(ii) and (iii) without regard to the portion of the plan which provides for the payment of benefits because of involuntary separation.

(c) *Correlation with other plans.* (1) In determining whether a plan meets the requirements of section 501(c)(17)(A)(ii) and (iii), any benefits provided under any other plan shall not be taken into consideration except in the particular instances enumerated in section 501(c)(17)(B)(i), (ii) and (iii). In general, these three exceptions permit a plan providing for the payment of supplemental unemployment compensation benefits to satisfy the nondiscrimination requirements in section 501(c)(17)(A)(ii) and (iii) if the plan is able to satisfy such requirements when it is correlated with one or more of the plans described in section 501(c)(17)(B).

(2) Under section 501(c)(17)(B)(i), a plan will not be considered discriminatory merely because the benefits under the plan which are first determined in a nondiscriminatory manner (within the meaning of section 501(c)(17)(A)) are then reduced by any sick, accident, or unemployment compensation benefits received under State or Federal law, or are reduced by a portion of these benefits if determined in a nondiscriminatory manner. Under this exception, a plan may, for example, satisfy the requirements of section 501(c)(17)(A)(iii) if it provides for the payment of an unemployment benefit and the amount of such benefit is determined as a percentage of the employee's compensation which is then reduced by any unemployment benefit which the employee receives under a State plan. In addition, a plan could provide for the reduction of such a plan benefit by a percentage of the State benefit. Furthermore, a plan may also satisfy the requirements of section 501 (c)(17)(A) if it provides for the payment to an employee of an amount which when added to any State unemployment benefit equals a percentage of the employee's compensation.

(3) Under section 501(c)(17)(B)(ii), a plan will not be considered discriminatory merely because the plan provides benefits only for employees who are not eligible to receive sick, accident, or unemployment compensation benefits under State or Federal law. In such a case, however, the benefits provided under the plan seeking to satisfy the requirements of section 501(c)(17) must be the same benefits, or a portion of the same benefits if determined in a nondiscriminatory manner, which such ineligible employees would receive under State or Federal law if they were eligible for such benefits. Under this exception, for example, an employer may establish a plan only for employees who have exhausted their benefits under the State law, and, if the plan provides for such employees the same benefits which they would receive under the State plan, the State plan and the plan of the employer will be considered as one plan in determining whether the requirements relating to nondiscrimination in section 501(c)(17)(A) are satisfied. Furthermore, such a

Reg. § 1.501(c)(17)-2(c)(3)

plan could also qualify even though it does not provide all of the benefits provided under the State plan. Thus, a plan could provide for the payment of a reduced amount of the benefits, or for the payment of only certain of the types of benefits, provided by the State plan. For example, if the State plan provides for the payment of sick, accident, and separation benefits, the plan of the employer may provide for the payment of only separation benefits, or for the payment of an amount equal to only one-half of the State provided benefit. However, if a plan provides benefits for employees who are not eligible to receive the benefits provided under a State plan and such benefits are greater or of a different type than those under the State plan, the plan of the employer must satisfy the requirements of section 501(c)(17)(A) without regard to the benefits and coverage provided by the State plan.

(4) Under section 501(c)(17)(B)(iii), a plan is not considered discriminatory merely because the plan provides benefits only for employees who are not eligible to receive benefits under another plan which satisfies the requirements of section 501(c)(17)(A) and which is funded solely by contributions of the employer. In such a case, the plan seeking to qualify under section 501(c)(17) must provide the same benefits, or a portion of such benefits if determined in a nondiscriminatory manner, as are provided for the employees under the plan funded solely by employer contributions. Furthermore, this exception only applies if the employees eligible to receive benefits under both plans would satisfy the requirements in section 501(c)(17)(A)(ii), relating to nondiscrimination as to coverage. The plan of the employer which is being correlated with the plan seeking to satisfy the requirements of section 501(c)(17) may be a plan which forms part of a voluntary employees' beneficiary association described in section 501(c)(9), if such plan satisfies all the requirements of section 501(c)(17)(A). Under this exception, for example, if an employer has established a plan providing for the payment of supplemental unemployment compensation benefits for his hourly-wage employees and such plan satisfies the requirements of section 501(c)(17)(A) (even though the plan forms part of a voluntary employees' beneficiary association described in section 501(c)(9)), the salaried employees of such employer may establish a plan for themselves, and, if such plan provides for the same benefits as the plan covering hourly-wage employees, both plans may be considered as one plan in determining whether the plan covering the salaried employees satisfies the requirement that it be nondiscriminatory as to coverage. The foregoing example would also be applicable if the benefits provided for the salaried employees were funded solely or in part by employer contributions.

(d) *Permanency of the plan.* A plan providing for the payment of supplemental unemployment compensation benefits contemplates a permanent as distinguished from a temporary program. Thus, although there may be reserved the right to change or terminate the plan, and to discontinue contributions thereunder, the abandonment of the plan for any reason other than business necessity within a few years after it has taken effect will be evidence that the plan from its inception was not a bona fide program for the purpose of providing supplemental unemployment compensation benefits to employees. Whether or not a particular plan constitutes a permanent arrangement will be determined by all of the surrounding facts and circumstances. However, merely because a collective bargaining agreement provides that a plan may be modified at the termination of such agreement, or that particular provisions of the plan are subject to renegotiation during the duration of such agreement, does not necessarily imply that the plan is not a permanent arrangement. Moreover, the fact that the plan provides that the assets remaining in the trust after the satisfaction of all liabilities (including contingent liabilities) under the plan may be returned to the employer does not imply that the plan is not a permanent arrangement nor preclude the trust from qualifying under section 501(c)(17).

(e) *Portions of years.* A plan must satisfy the requirements of section 501(c)(17) throughout the entire taxable year of the trust in order for the trust to be exempt for such year. However, section 501(c)(17)(C) provides that a plan will satisfy the nondiscrimination requirements of section 501(c)(17)(A) if on at least one day in each quarter of the taxable year of the trust it satisfies such requirements.

(f) *Several trusts constituting one plan.* Several trusts may be designated as constituting part of one plan which is intended to satisfy the requirements of section 501(c)(17), in which case all of such trusts taken as a whole must meet the requirements of such section. The fact that a combination of trusts fails to satisfy the requirements of section 501(c)(17) as one plan does not prevent such of the trusts as satisfy the requirements of section 501(c)(17) from qualifying for exemption under that section.

(g) *Plan of several employers.* A trust forming part of a plan of several employers, or the employees of several employers, will be a supplemental unemployment benefit trust described in section 501(c)(17) if all the requirements of that section are otherwise satisfied.

Reg. § 1.501(c)(17)-2(c)(4)

(h) *Investment of trust funds.* No specific limitations are provided in section 501(c)(17) with respect to investments which may be made by the trustees of a trust qualifying under that section. Generally, the contributions may be used by the trustees to purchase any investments permitted by the trust agreement to the extent allowed by local law. However, the tax-exempt status of the trust will be forfeited if the investments made by the trustees constitute "prohibited transactions" within the meaning of section 503. See section 503 and the regulations thereunder. In addition, such a trust will be subject to tax under section 511 with respect to any "unrelated business taxable income" (as defined in section 512) realized by it from its investments. See section 511 to 515, inclusive, and the regulations thereunder.

(i) *Allocations.* If a plan which provides sick and accident benefits is financed solely by employer contributions to the trust, and such sick and accident benefits are funded by payment of premiums on an accident or health insurance policy (whether on a group or individual basis) or by contributions to a separate fund which pays such sick and accident benefits, the plan must specify that portion of the contributions to be used to fund such benefits. If a plan which is financed in whole or in part by employee contributions provides sick and accident benefits, the plan must specify the portion, if any, of employee contributions allocated to the cost of funding such benefits, and must allocate the cost of funding such benefits between employer contributions and employee contributions.

(j) *Required records and returns.* Every trust described in section 501(c)(17) must maintain records indicating the amount of separation benefits and sick and accident benefits which have been provided to each employee. If a plan is financed, in whole or in part, by employee contributions to the trust, the trust must maintain records indicating the amount of each employee's total contributions allocable to separation benefits. In addition, every trust described in section 501(c)(17) which makes one or more payments totaling $600 or more in 1 year to an individual must file an annual information return in the manner described in paragraph (b)(1) of § 1.6401-2. However, if the payments from such trust are subject to income tax withholding under section 3402(o) and the regulations thereunder, the trust must file, in lieu of such annual information return, the returns of income tax withheld from wages required by section 6011 and the regulations thereunder. In such circumstances, the trust must also furnish the statements to the recipients of trust distributions required by section 6051 and the regulations thereunder. [Reg. § 1.501(c)(17)-2.]

☐ [T.D. 6972, 9-11-68. Amended by T.D. 7068, 11-10-70.]

[Reg. § 1.501(c)(17)-3]

§ 1.501(c)(17)-3. **Relation to other sections of the Code.**—(a) *Taxability of benefit distributions*—(1) *Separation benefits.* If the separation benefits described in section 501(c)(17)(D)(i) are funded entirely by employer contributions, then the full amount of any separation benefit payment received by an employee is includible in his gross income under section 61(a). If any such separation benefit is funded by both employer and employee contributions, or solely by employee contributions, the amount of any separation benefit payment which is includible in the gross income of the employee is the amount by which such distribution and any prior distributions of such separation payments exceeds the employee's total contributions to fund such separation benefits.

(2) *Sick and accident benefits.* Any benefit payment received from the trust under the part of the plan, if any, which provides for the payment of sick and accident benefits must be included in gross income under section 61(a), unless specifically excluded under section 104 or 105 and the regulations thereunder. See section 105(b) and § 1.105-2 for benefit payments expended for medical care, benefit payments in excess of actual medical expenses, and benefit payments which an employee is entitled to receive irrespective of whether or not he incurs expenses for medical care. See section 213 and § 1.213-1(g) for benefit payments representing reimbursement for medical expenses paid in prior years. See § 1.501(c)(17)-2(i) for the requirement that a trust described in section 501(c)(17) which receives employee contributions must be part of a written plan which provides for the allocation of the cost of funding sick and accident benefits.

(b) *Exemption as a voluntary employees' beneficiary association.* Section 501(c)(17)(E) contemplates that a trust forming part of a plan providing for the payment of supplemental unemployment compensation benefits may, if it qualifies, apply for exemption from income tax under section 501(a) either as a voluntary employees' beneficiary association described in section 501(c)(9) or as a trust described in section 501(c)(17).

(c) *Returns.* A trust which is described in section 501(c)(17) and which is exempt from tax under section 501(a) must file a return in accordance with section 6033 and the regulations thereunder. If such a trust realizes any unrelated business taxable income, as defined in section 512, the trust is also required to file a return with respect to such income.

(d) *Effective date.* Section 501(c)(17) shall apply to taxable years beginning after December 31, 1959, and shall apply to supplemental unemployment benefit trusts regardless of when created or organized. [Reg. § 1.501(c)(17)-3.]

☐ [*T.D. 6972, 9-11-68.*]

[Reg. § 1.501(c)(18)-1]

§ 1.501(c)(18)-1. **Certain funded pension trusts.**—(a) *In general.* Organizations described in section 501(c)(18) are trusts created before June 25, 1959, forming part of a plan for the payment of benefits under a pension plan funded only by contributions of employees. In order to be exempt, such trusts must also meet the requirements set forth in section 501(c)(18)(A), (B) and (C), and in paragraph (b) of this section.

(b) *Requirements for qualification.* A trust described in section 501(c)(18) must meet the following requirements—

(1) *Local law.* The trust must be a valid, existing trust under local law, and must be evidenced by an executed written document.

(2) *Funding.* The trust must be funded solely from contributions of employees who are members of the plan. For purposes of this section, the term "contributions of employees" shall include earnings on, and gains derived from, the assets of the trust which were contributed by employees.

(3) *Creation before June 25, 1959*—(i) *In general.* The trust must have been created before June 25, 1959. A trust created before June 25, 1959 is described in section 501(c)(18) and this section even though changes in the makeup of the trust have occurred since that time so long as these are not fundamental changes in the character of the trust or in the character of the beneficiaries of the trust. Increases in the beneficiaries of the trust by the addition of employees in the same or related industries, whether such additions are of individuals or of units (such as local units of a union) will generally not be considered a fundamental change in the character of the trust. A merger of a trust created after June 25, 1959 into a trust created before such date is not in itself a fundamental change in the character of the latter trust if the two trusts are for the benefit of employees of the same or related industries.

(ii) *Examples.* The provisions of this subparagraph may be illustrated by the following examples:

Example (1). Assume that trust C, for the benefit of members of participating locals of National Union X, was established in 1950 and adopted by 29 locals before June 25, 1959. The subsequent adoption of trust C by additional locals of National Union X in 1962 will not constitute a fundamental change in the character of trust C, since such subsequent adoption is by employees in a related industry.

Example (2). Assume the facts as stated in example (1), except that in 1965 National Union X merged with National Union Y, whose members are engaged in trades related to those engaged in by X's members. Assume further that trust D, the employee funded pension plan and fund for employees of Y, was subsequently merged into trust C. The merger of trust D into trust C would in itself constitute a fundamental change in the character of trust C, since both C and D are for the benefit of employees of related industries.

(4) *Payment of benefits.* The trust must provide solely for the payment of pension or retirement benefits to its beneficiaries. For purposes of this section, the term "retirement benefits" is intended to include customary and incidental benefits, such as death benefits within the limits permissible under section 401.

(5) *Diversion.* The trust must be part of a plan which provides that, before the satisfaction of all liabilities to employees covered by the plan, the corpus and income of the trust cannot (within the taxable year and at any time thereafter) be used for, or diverted to, any purpose other than the providing of pension or retirement benefits. Payment of expenses in connection with the administration of a plan providing pension or retirement benefits shall be considered a payment to provide such benefits and shall not affect the qualification of the trust.

(6) *Discrimination.* The trust must be part of a plan whose eligibility conditions and benefits do not discriminate in favor of employees who are officers, shareholders, persons whose principal duties consist of supervising the work of other employees, or highly compensated employees. See sections 401(a)(3)(B) and 401(a)(4) and §§ 1.401-3 and 1.401-4. However, a plan is not discriminatory within the meaning of section 501(c)(18) merely because the benefits received under the plan bear a uniform relationship to the total compensation, or the basic or regular rate of compensation, of the employees covered by the plan. Accordingly, the benefits provided for highly paid employees may be greater than the benefits provided for lower paid employees if the benefits are determined by reference to their compensation; but, in such a case, the plan will not qualify

Reg. § 1.501(c)(18)-1(a)

if the benefits paid to the higher paid employees are a larger portion of compensation than the benefits paid to lower paid employees.

(7) *Objective standards.* The trust must be part of a plan which requires that benefits be determined according to objective standards. Thus, while a plan may provide similarly situated employees with benefits which differ in kind and amount, these benefits may not be determined solely in the discretion of the trustees.

(c) *Effective date.* The provisions of section 501(c)(18) and this section shall apply with respect to taxable years beginning after December 31, 1969. [Reg. § 1.501(c)(18)-1.]

☐ [T.D. 7172, 3-16-72.]

[Reg. § 1.501(c)(19)-1]

§ 1.501(c)(19)-1. **War veterans organizations.**—(a) *In general.* (1) For taxable years beginning after December 31, 1969, a veterans post or organization which is organized in the United States or any of its possessions may exempt as an organization described in section 501(c)(19) if the requirements of paragraphs (b) and (c) of this section are met and if no part of its net earnings inures to the benefit of any private shareholder or individual. Paragraph (b) of this section contains the membership requirements such a post or organization must meet in order to qualify under section 501(c)(19). Paragraph (c) of this section outlines the purposes, at least one of which such a post or organization must have in order to so qualify.

(2) In addition, an auxiliary unit or society described in paragraph (d) of this section of such a veterans post or organization and a trust or foundation described in paragraph (e) of this section for such post or organization may be exempt as an organization described in section 501(c)(19).

(b) *Membership requirements.* (1) In order to be described in section 501(c)(19) under paragraph (a)(1) of this section, an organization must meet the membership requirements of section 501(c)(19)(B) and this paragraph. There are two requirements that must be met under this paragraph. The first requirement is that at least 75 percent of the members of the organization must be war veterans. For purposes of this section the term "war veterans" means persons, whether or not present members of the United States Armed Forces, who have served in the Armed Forces of the United States during a period of war (including the Korean and Vietnam conflicts).

(2) The second requirement of this paragraph is that at least 97.5 percent of all members of the organization must be described in one or more of the following categories:

(i) War veterans,

(ii) Present or former members of the United States Armed Forces,

(iii) Cadets (including only students in college or university ROTC programs or at Armed Services academies), or

(iv) Spouses, widows, or widowers of individuals referred to in paragraph (b)(2)(i), (ii) or (iii) of this section.

(c) *Exempt purposes.* In addition to the requirements of paragraphs (a)(1) and (b) of this section, in order to be described in section 501(c)(19) under paragraph (a)(1) of this section an organization must be operated exclusively for one or more of the following purposes:

(1) To promote the social welfare of the community as defined in § 1.501(c)(4)-1(a)(2),

(2) To assist disabled and needy war veterans and members of the United States Armed Forces and their dependents, and the widows and orphans of deceased veterans,

(3) to provide entertainment, care, and assistance to hospitalized veterans or members of the Armed Forces of the United States,

(4) To carry on programs to perpetuate the memory of deceased veterans and members of the Armed Forces and to comfort their survivors,

(5) To conduct programs for religious, charitable, scientific, literary, or educational purposes,

(6) To sponsor or participate in activities of a patriotic nature,

(7) To provide insurance benefits for their members or dependents of their members or both, or

(8) To provide social and recreational activities for their members.

(d) *Auxiliary units or societies for war veterans organizations.* A unit or society may be exempt as an organization described in section 501(c)(19) and paragraph (a)(2) of this section if it is an auxiliary unit or society of a post or organization of war veterans described in paragraph (a)(1) of this section. A unit or society is an auxiliary unit or society of such a post or organization if it meets the following requirements:

(1) It is affiliated with, and organized in accordance with, the bylaws and regulations formulated by an organization described in paragraph (a)(1) of this section,

(2) At least 75 percent of its members are either war veterans, or spouses of war veterans, or are related to a war veteran within two degrees of consanguinity (i.e., grandparent, brother, sister, grandchild represent the most distant allowable relationships),

Reg. § 1.501(c)(19)-1(d)(2)

(3) All of its members are either members of an organization described in paragraph (a)(1) of this section, or spouses of a member of such an organization or are related to a member of such an organization, within two degrees of consanguinity, and

(4) No part of its net earnings inures to the benefit of any private shareholder or individual.

(e) *Trusts or foundations.* A trust or foundation may be exempt as an organization described in section 501(c)(19) and paragraph (a)(2) of this section if it is a trust or foundation for a post or organization of war veterans described in paragraph (a)(1) of this section. A trust or foundation is a trust or foundation for such a post or organization if it meets the following requirements:

(1) The trust or foundation is in existence under local law and, if organized for charitable purposes, has a dissolution provision described in § 1.501(c)(3)-1(b)(4);

(2) The corpus or income cannot be diverted or used other than for the funding of a post or organization of war veterans described in paragraph (a)(1) of this section, for section 170(c)(4) purposes, or as an insurance set aside (as defined in § 1.512(a)-4(b)),

(3) The trust income is not unreasonably accumulated and, if the trust or foundation is not an insurance set aside, a substantial portion of the income is in fact distributed to such post or organization or for section 170(c)(4) charitable purposes, and

(4) It is organized exclusively for one or more of those purposes enumerated in paragraph (c) of this section. [Reg. § 1.501(c)(19)-1.]

☐ [T.D. 7438, 10-7-76.]

[Reg. § 1.501(c)(21)-1]

§ 1.501(c)(21)-1. **Black lung trusts—certain terms.**—(a) *Created or organized in the United States.* A trust is not "created or organized in the United States" unless it is maintained at all times as a domestic trust in the United States. For this purpose, section 7701(a)(9) limits the term "United States" to the District of Columbia and States of the United States.

(b) *Insurance company.* The term "insurance company" means an insurance, surety, bonding or other company whose liability for the kinds of claims to which section 501(c)(21)(A)(i) applies is as an insurer or guarantor of the liabilities of another.

(c) *Black Lung Acts.* The term "Black Lung Acts" includes any State law providing compensation for disability or death due to pneumoconiosis even though the State law compensates for other kinds of injuries. In such a case, section 501(c)(21) applies only to the extent that the liability is attributable to disability or death due to pneumoconiosis. For this purpose, the term "pneumoconiosis" has the same meaning as it has under federal law. See 30 U.S.C. 902.

(d) *Insurance exclusively covering such liability.* The term "insurance exclusively covering such liability" includes insurance that covers risk for liabilities in addition to the liabilities to which section 501(c)(21)(A)(i) applies. In such a case, payment for premiums may be made from the trust only to the extent of that portion of the premiums that has been separately allocated and stated by the insurer as attributable solely to coverage of the liabilities to which section 501(c)(21)(A)(i) applies.

(e) *Administrative and other incidental expenses.* The term "administrative and other incidental expenses" means expenditures that are appropriate and helpful to the trust making them in carrying out the purposes for which its assets may be used under section 501(c)(21)(B). The term includes any excise tax imposed on the trust under section 4952 (relating to taxes on taxable expenditures) and reasonable expenses, such as legal expenses, incurred by the trust in connection with an assertion against the trust of liability for a taxable expenditure. The term does not include an excise tax imposed on the trustee or on other disqualified persons under section 4951 (relating to taxes on self-dealing or under section 4953 (relating to tax on excess contributions to black lung benefit trusts) or any expenses incurred in connection with the assertion of these taxes other than expenses that are treated as part of reasonable compensation under section 4951(d)(2)(C). See §§ 53.4941(d)-2(f)(3) and (d)-3(c) for interpretations of similar provisions under section 4941(d)(2)(E), relating to reasonable compensation for private foundation disqualified persons.

(f) *Public debt securities of the United States.* The term "public debt securities of the United States" means obligations that are taken into consideration for purposes of the public debt limit. See, for example, 31 U.S.C. 757b.

(g) *Obligations of a State or local government.* The term "obligations of a State or local government" means the obligations of a State or local governmental unit the interest on which is exempt from tax under section 103(a). See § 1.103-1(a).

(h) *Time or demand deposits.* The term "time or demand deposits" includes checking accounts, savings accounts, certificates of deposit or other time or demand deposits. The term does not include common or collective trust funds such as a common trust fund as defined in section 584. [Reg. § 1.501(c)(21)-1.]

☐ [T.D. 7644, 9-6-79.]

[Reg. § 1.501(c)(21)-2]

§ 1.501(c)(21)-2. **Trust instrument.**—A trust does not meet the requirements of section 501(c)(21) if it is not established and maintained pursuant to a written instrument. The trust instrument must definitely and affirmatively prohibit a diversion or use of trust assets that is not permitted under section 501(c)(21)(B) or section 4953(c), whether by operation or natural termination of the trust, by power of revocation or amendment, by the happening of a contingency, by collateral arrangement, or by any other means. No particular form for the trust instrument is required. A trust may meet the requirements of section 501(c)(21) although the trust instrument fails to contain provisions the effects of which are to prohibit acts that are subject to section 4951 (relating to taxes on self-dealing), section 4952 (relating to taxes on taxable expenditures) or the retention of contributions subject to section 4953 (relating to tax on excess contributions to black lung benefit trusts). [Reg. § 1.501(c)(21)-2.]

☐ [T.D. 7644, 9-6-79.]

[Reg. § 1.501(d)-1]

§ 1.501(d)-1. **Religious and apostolic associations or corporations.**—(a) Religious or apostolic associations or corporations are described in section 501(d) and are exempt from taxation under section 501(a) if they have a common treasury or community treasury, even though they engage in business for the common benefit of the members, provided each of the members includes (at the time of filing his return) in his gross income his entire pro rata share, whether distributed or not, of the net income of the association or corporation for the taxable year of the association or corporation ending with or during his taxable year. Any amount so included in the gross income of a member shall be treated as a dividend received.

(b) For annual return requirements of organizations described in section 501(d), see section 6033 and paragraph (a)(5) of § 1.6033-1. [Reg. § 1.501(d)-1.]

☐ [T.D. 6301, 7-8-58.]

[Reg. § 1.501(e)-1]

§ 1.501(e)-1. **Cooperative hospital service organizations.**—(a) *General rule.* Section 501(e) is the exclusive and controlling section under which a cooperative hospital service organization can qualify as a charitable organization. A cooperative hospital service organization which meets the requirements of section 501(e) and this section shall be treated as an organization described in section 501(c)(3), exempt from taxation under section 501(a), and referred to in section 170(b)(1)(A)(iii) (relating to percentage limitations on charitable contributions). In order to qualify for tax exempt status, a cooperative hospital service organization must—

(1) Be organized and operated on a cooperative basis,

(2) Perform, on a centralized basis, only one or more specifically enumerated services which, if performed directly by a tax exempt hospital, would constitute activities in the exercise or performance of the purpose or function constituting the basis for its exemption, and

(3) Perform such service or services solely for two or more patron-hospitals as described in paragraph (d) of this section.

(b) *Organized and operated on a cooperative basis*—(1) *In general.* In order to meet the requirements of section 501(e), the organization must be organized and operated on a cooperative basis (whether or not under a specific statute on cooperatives) and must allocate or pay all of its net earnings within 8½ months after the close of the taxable year to its patron-hospitals on the basis of the percentage of its services performed for each patron. To "allocate" its net earnings to its patron-hospitals, the organization must make appropriate bookkeeping entries and provide timely written notice to each patron-hospital disclosing to the patron-hospital the amount allocated to it on the books of the organization. For the recordkeeping requirements of a section 501(e) organization, see § 1.521-1(a)(1).

(2) *Percentage of services defined.* The percentage of services performed for each patron-hospital may be determined on the basis of either the value or the quantity of the services provided by the organization to the patron-hospital, provided such basis is realistic in terms of the actual cost of the services to the organization.

(3) *Retention of net earnings.* Exemption will not be denied a cooperative hospital service organization solely because the organization, instead of paying all net earnings to its patron-hospitals, retains an amount for such purposes as retiring indebtedness, expanding the services of the organization, or for any other necessary purpose and allocates such amounts to its patrons. However, such funds may not be accumulated beyond the reasonably anticipated needs of the organization. See § 1.537-1(b). Whether there is an improper accumulation of funds depends upon the particular circumstances of each case. Moreover, where an organization retains net earnings for necessary

Reg. § 1.501(e)-1(b)(3)

purposes, the organization's records must show each patron's rights and interests in the funds retained. For purposes of this paragraph, the term "net earnings" does not include capital contributions to the organization and such contributions need not satisfy the allocation or payment requirements.

(4) *Nonpatronage and other income.* An organization described in section 501(e) may, in addition to net earnings, receive membership dues and related membership assessment fees, gifts, grants and income from nonpatronage sources such as investment of retained earnings. However, such an organization cannot be exempt if it engages in any business other than that of providing the specified services, described in paragraph (c), for the specified patron-hospitals, described in paragraph (d). Thus, an organization described in section 501(e) generally cannot have unrelated business taxable income as defined in section 512, although it may earn certain interest, annuities, royalties, and rents which are excluded from unrelated business taxable income because of the modifications contained in sections 512(b)(1), (2) or (3). An organization described in section 501(e) may, however, have debt-financed income which is treated as unrelated business taxable income solely because of the applicability of section 514. In addition, exempt status under section 501(e) will not be affected where rent from personal property leased with real property is treated as unrelated business taxable income under section 512(b)(3)(A)(ii) solely because the rent attributable to the personal property is more than incidental or under section 512(b)(3)(B)(i) solely because the rent attributable to the personal property exceeds 50 percent of the total rent received or accrued under the lease. Exemption will not be affected solely because the determination of the amount of rent depends in whole or in part on the income or profits derived from the property leased. See, section 512(b)(3)(B)(ii). An organization described in section 501(e) may also derive nonpatronage income from sources that are incidental to the conduct of its exempt purposes or functions. For example, income derived from the operation of a cafeteria or vending machines primarily for the convenience of its employees or the disposition of by-products in substantially the same state they were in on completion of the exempt function (e.g., the sale of silver waste produced in the processing of x-ray film) will not be considered unrelated business taxable income. See, section 513(a)(2) and § 1.513-1(d)(4)(ii). The nonpatronage and other income permitted under this subparagraph (4) must be allocated or paid as provided in subparagraph (1) or retained as provided in subparagraph (3).

(5) *Stock ownership*—(i) *Capital stock of organization.* An organization does not meet the requirements of section 501(e) unless all of the organization's outstanding capital stock, if there is such stock, is held solely by its patron-hospitals. However, no amount may be paid as dividends on the capital stock of the organization. For purposes of the preceding sentence, the term "capital stock" includes common stock (whether voting or nonvoting), preferred stock, or any other form evidencing a proprietary interest in the organization.

(ii) *Stock ownership as a condition for obtaining credit.* If by statutory requirement a cooperative hospital service organization must be a shareholder in a United States or state chartered corporation as a condition for obtaining credit from that corporate-lender, the ownership of shares and the payment of dividends thereon will not for such reason be a basis for the denial of exemption to the organization. See, e.g., National Consumer Cooperative Bank, 12 USC § 3001 et seq.

(c) *Scope of services*—(1) *Permissible services.* An organization meets the requirements of section 501(e) only if the organization performs, on a centralized basis, one or more of the following services and only such services: data processing, purchasing (including the purchasing and dispensing of drugs and pharmaceuticals to patron-hospitals), warehousing, billing and collection, food, clinical (including radiology), industrial engineering (including the installation, maintenance and repair of biomedical and similar equipment), laboratory, printing, communications, record center, and personnel (including recruitment, selection, testing, training, education and placement of personnel) services. An organization is not described in section 501(e) if, in addition to or instead of one or more of these specified services, the organization performs any other service (other than services referred to under paragraph (b)(4) that are incidental to the conduct of exempt purposes or functions).

(2) *Illustration.* The provisions of this subparagraph may be illustrated by the following example.

Example. An organization performs industrial engineering services on a cooperative basis solely for patron-hospitals each of which is an organization described in section 501(c)(3) and exempt from taxation under section 501(a). However, in addition to this service, the organization operates laundry services for its patron-hospitals. This cooperative organization does not meet the requirements of this paragraph because it per-

Reg. § 1.501(e)-1(b)(4)

forms laundry services not specified in this paragraph.

(d) *Patron-hospitals*—(1) *Defined.* Section 501(e) only applies if the organization performs its services solely for two or more patron-hospitals each of which is—

(i) An organization described in section 501(c)(3) which is exempt from taxation under section 501(a),

(ii) A constituent part of an organization described in section 501(c)(3) which is exempt from taxation under section 501(a) and which, if organized and operated as a separate entity, would constitute an organization described in section 501(c)(3), or

(iii) Owned and operated by the United States, a State, the District of Columbia, or a possession of the United States, or a political subdivision or an agency or instrumentality of any of the foregoing.

(2) *Business with nonvoting patron-hospitals.* Exemption will not be denied a cooperative hospital service organization solely because the organization (whether organized on a stock or membership basis) transacts business with patron-hospitals which do not have voting rights in the organization and therefore do not participate in the decisions affecting the operation of the organization. Where the organization has both patron-hospitals with voting rights and patron-hospitals without such rights, the organization must provide at least 50 percent of its services to patron-hospitals with voting rights in the organization. Thus, the percentage of services provided to nonvoting patrons may not exceed the percentage of such services provided to voting patrons. A patron-hospital will be deemed to have voting rights in the cooperative hospital service organization if the patron-hospital may vote directly on matters affecting the operation of the organization or if the patron-hospital may vote in the election of cooperative board members. Notwithstanding that an organization may have both voting and nonvoting patron-hospitals, patronage refunds must nevertheless be allocated or paid to all patron-hospitals solely on the basis specified in paragraph (b) of this section.

(3) *Services to other organizations.* An organization does not meet the requirements of section 501(e) if, in addition to performing services for patron-hospitals (entities described in subdivisions (i), (ii) or (iii) of subparagraph (1)), the organization performs any service for any other organization. For example, a cooperative hospital service organization is not exempt if it performs services for convalescent homes for children or the aged, vocational training facilities for the handicapped, educational institutions which do not provide hospital care in their facilities, and proprietary hospitals. However, the provision of the specified services between or among cooperative hospital service organizations meeting the requirements of section 501(e) and this section is permissible. Also permissible is the provision of the specified services to entities which are not patron-hospitals, but only if such services are de minimis and are mandated by a governmental unit as, for example, a condition for licensing.

(e) *Effective dates.* An organization, other than an organization performing clinical services, may meet the requirements of section 501(e) and be a tax exempt organization for taxable years ending after June 28, 1968. An organization performing clinical services may meet the requirements of section 501(e) and be a tax exempt organization for taxable years ending after December 31, 1976. However, pursuant to the authority contained in section 7805(b) of the Internal Revenue Code, these regulations shall not become effective with respect to an organization which has received a ruling or determination letter from the Internal Revenue Service recognizing its exemption under section 501(e) until January 2, 1987. [Reg. § 1.501(e)-1.]

☐ [*T.D.* 8100, 9-4-86.]

[Reg. § 1.501(h)-1]

§ 1.501(h)-1. **Application of the "expenditure test" to expenditures to influence legislation; introduction.**—(a) *Scope*—(1) There are certain requirements an organization must meet in order to be a "charity" described in section 501(c)(3). Among other things, section 501(c)(3) states that "no substantial part of the activities of [a charity may consist of] carrying on propaganda, or otherwise attempting to influence legislation, (except as otherwise provided in subsection (h))." This requirement is called the "substantial part test."

(2) Under section 501(h), many public charities may elect the "expenditure test" as a substitute for the substantial part test. The expenditure test is described in section 501(h) and this § 1.501(h)[-1]. A public charity is any charity that is not a private foundation under section 509(a). (Unlike a public charity, a private foundation may not make any lobbying expenditures: if a private foundation does make a lobbying expenditure, it is subject to an excise tax under section 4945). Section 1.501(h)-2 lists which public charities are eligible to make the expenditure test election. Section 1.501(h)-2 also provides information about how a public charity makes and revokes the election to be covered by the expenditure test.

Reg. § 1.501(h)-1(a)(2)

(3) A public charity that makes the election may make lobbying expenditures within specified dollar limits. If an electing public charity's lobbying expenditures are within the dollar limits determined under section 4911(c), the electing public charity will not owe tax under section 4911 nor will it lose its tax exempt status as a charity by virtue of section 501(h). If, however, that electing public charity's lobbying expenditures exceed its section 4911 lobbying limit, the organization is subject to an excise tax on the excess lobbying expenditures. Further, under section 501(h), if an electing public charity's lobbying expenditures normally are more than 150 percent of its section 4911 lobbying limit, the organization will cease to be a charity described in section 501(c)(3).

(4) A public charity that elects the expenditure test may nevertheless lose its tax exempt status if it is an action organization under § 1.501(c)(3)-1(c)(3)(iii) or (iv). A public charity that does not elect the expenditure test remains subject to the substantial part test. The substantial part test is applied without regard to the provisions of section[s] 501(h) and 4911 and the related regulations.

(b) *Effective date.* The provisions of § 1.501(h)-1 through § 1.501(h)-3, are effective for taxable years beginning after August 31, 1990. An election made before August 31, 1990, under the provisions of § 7.0(c)(4) or the instructions to Form 5768, will be effective under these regulations without again filing Form 5768. [Reg. § 1.501(h)-1.]

☐ [T.D. 8308, 8-30-90.]

[Reg. § 1.501(h)-2]

§ 1.501(h)-2. **Electing the expenditure test.**—(a) *In general.* The election to be governed by section 501(h) may be made by an eligible organization (as described in paragraph (b) of this section) for any taxable year of the organization beginning after December 31, 1976, other than the first taxable year for which a voluntary revocation of the election is effective (see paragraph (d) of this section). The election is made by filing a completed Form 5768, Election/Revocation of Election by an Eligible Section 501(c)(3) Organization to Make Expenditures to Influence Legislation, with the appropriate Internal Revenue Service Center listed on that form. Under section 501(h)(6), the election is effective with the beginning of the taxable year in which the form is filed. For example, if an eligible organization whose taxable year is the calendar year files Form 5768 on December 31, 1979, the organization is governed by section 501(h) for its taxable year beginning January 1, 1979. Once made, the expenditure test election is effective (without again filing Form 5768) for each succeeding taxable year for which the organization is an eligible organization and which begins before a notice of revocation is filed under paragraph (d) of this section.

(b) *Organizations eligible to elect the expenditure test*—(1) *In general.* For purposes of section 501(h) and the regulations thereunder, an organization is an eligible organization for a taxable year if, for that taxable year, it is—

(i) Described in section 501(c)(3) (determined, in any year for which an election is in effect, without regard to the substantial part test of section 501(c)(3)),

(ii) Described in section 501(h)(4) and paragraph (b)(2) of this section, and

(iii) Not a disqualified organization described in section 501(h)(5) and paragraph (b)(3) of this section.

(2) *Certain organizations listed.* An organization is described in section 501(h)(4) and this paragraph (b)(2) if it is an organization described in—

(i) Section 170(b)(1)(A)(ii) (relating to educational institutions),

(ii) Section 170(b)(1)(A)(iii) (relating to hospitals and medical research organizations),

(iii) Section 170(b)(1)(A)(iv) (relating to organizations supporting government schools),

(iv) Section 170(b)(1)(A)(vi) (relating to organizations publicly supported by charitable contributions),

(v) Section 509(a)(2) (relating to organizations publicly supported by admissions, sales, etc.), or

(vi) Section 509(a)(3) (relating to organizations supporting public charities), except that for purposes of this paragraph (b)(2), section 509(a)(3) shall be applied without regard to the last sentence of section 509(a).

(3) *Disqualified organizations.* An organization is a disqualified organization described in section 501(h)(5) and this paragraph (b)(3) if the organization is—

(i) Described in section 170(b)(1)(A)(i) (relating to churches),

(ii) An integrated auxiliary of a church or of a convention or association of churches (see § 1.6033-2(g)(5)), or

(iii) Described in section 501(c)(3) and affiliated (within the meaning of § 56.4911-7) with one or more organizations described in paragraph (b)(3)(i) or (ii) of this section.

(4) *Other organizations ineligible to elect.* Under section 501(h)(4), certain organizations, although not disqualified organizations, are not eli-

gible to elect the expenditure test. For example, organizations described in section 509(a)(4) are not listed in section 501(h)(4) and therefore are not eligible to elect. Similarly, private foundations (within the meaning of section 509(a)) are not eligible to elect. For the treatment of expenditures by a private foundation for the purpose of carrying on propaganda, or otherwise attempting, to influence legislation, see § 53.4945-2.

(c) *New organizations.* A newly created organization may submit Form 5768 to elect the expenditure test under section 501(h) before it is determined to be an eligible organization and may submit Form 5768 at the time it submits its application for recognition of exemption (Form 1023). If the newly created organization is determined to be an eligible organization, the election will be effective under the provisions of paragraph (a) of this section, that is, with the beginning of the taxable year in which the Form 5768 is filed by the eligible organization. However, if a newly created organization is determined by the Service not to be an eligible organization, the organization's election will not be effective and the substantial part test will apply from the effective date of its section 501(c)(3) classification.

(d) *Voluntary revocation of expenditure test election*—(1) *Revocation effective.* An organization may voluntarily revoke an expenditure test election by filing a notice of voluntary revocation with the appropriate Internal Revenue Service Center listed on Form 5768. Under section 501(h)(6)(B), a voluntary revocation is effective with the beginning of the first taxable year after the taxable year in which the notice is filed. If an organization voluntarily revokes its election, the substantial part test of section 501(c)(3) will apply with respect to the organization's activities in attempting to influence legislation beginning with the taxable year for which the voluntary revocation is effective.

(2) *Re-election of expenditure test.* If an organization's expenditure test election is voluntarily revoked, the organization may again make the expenditure test election, effective no earlier than for the taxable year following the first taxable year for which the revocation is effective.

(3) *Example.* X, an organization whose taxable year is the calendar year, plans to voluntarily revoke its expenditure test election effective beginning with its taxable year 1985. X must file its notice of voluntary revocation on Form 5768 after December 31, 1983, and before January 1, 1985. If X files a notice of voluntary revocation on December 31, 1984, the revocation is effective beginning with its taxable year 1985. The organization may again elect the expenditure test by filing Form 5768. Under paragraph (d)(2) of this section, the election may not be made for taxable year 1985. Under paragraph (a) of this section, a new expenditure test election will be effective for taxable years beginning with taxable year 1986, if the Form 5768 is filed after December 31, 1985, and before January 1, 1987.

(e) *Involuntary revocation of expenditure test election.* If, while an election by an eligible organization is in effect, the organization ceases to be an eligible organization, its election is automatically revoked. The revocation is effective with the beginning of the first full taxable year for which it is determined that the organization is not an eligible organization. If an organization's expenditure test election is involuntarily revoked under this paragraph (e) but the organization continues to be described in section 501(c)(3), the substantial part test of section 501(c)(3) will apply with respect to the organization's activities in attempting to influence legislation beginning with the first taxable year for which the involuntary revocation is effective.

(f) *Supersession.* This section supersedes § 7.0(c)(4) of the Temporary Income Tax Regulations under the Tax Reform Act of 1976, effective August 31, 1990. [Reg. § 1.501(h)-2.]

☐ [T.D. 8308, 8-30-90.]

[Reg. § 1.501(h)-3]

§ 1.501(h)-3. Lobbying or grass roots expenditures normally in excess of ceiling amount.—(a) *Scope.* This section provides rules under section 501(h) for determining whether an organization that has elected the expenditure test and that is not a member of an affiliated group of organizations (as defined in § 56.4911-7(e)) either normally makes lobbying expenditures in excess of its lobbying ceiling amount or normally makes grass roots expenditures in excess of its grass roots ceiling amount. Under section 501(h) and this section, an organization that has elected the expenditure test and that normally makes expenditures in excess of the corresponding ceiling amount will cease to be exempt from tax under section 501(a) as an organization described in section 501(c)(3). For similar rules relating to members of an affiliated group of organizations, see § 56.4911-9.

(b) *Loss of exemption*—(1) *In general.* Under section 501(h)(1), an organization that has elected the expenditure test shall be denied exemption from taxation under section 501(a) as an organization described in section 501(c)(3) for the taxable year following a determination year if—

(i) The sum of the organization's lobbying expenditures for the base years exceeds 150 per-

Reg. § 1.501(h)-3(b)(1)

cent of the sum of its lobbying nontaxable amounts for the base years, or

(ii) The sum of the organization's grass roots expenditures for its base years exceeds 150 percent of the sum of its grass roots nontaxable amounts for the base years.

The organization thereafter shall not be exempt from tax under section 501(a) as an organization described in section 501(c)(3) unless, pursuant to paragraph (d) of this section, the organization reapplies for recognition of exemption and is recognized as exempt.

(2) *Special exception for organization's first election.* For the first, second, or third consecutive determination year for which an organization's first expenditure test election is in effect, no determination is required under paragraph (b)(1) of this section, and the organization will not be denied exemption from tax by reason of section 501(h) and this section if, taking into account as base years only those years for which the expenditure test election is in effect—

(i) The sum of the organization's lobbying expenditures for such base years does not exceed 150 percent of the sum of its lobbying nontaxable amounts for the same base years, and

(ii) The sum of the organization's grass roots expenditure for those base years does not exceed 150 percent of the sum of its grass roots nontaxable amounts for such base years. If an organization does not satisfy the requirements of this paragraph (b)(2), paragraph (b)(1) of this section will apply.

(c) *Definitions.* For purposes of this section—

(1) The term "lobbying expenditures" means lobbying expenditures as defined in section 4911(c)(1) or section 4911(f)(4)(A) and § 56.4911-2(a).

(2) The term "lobbying nontaxable amount" is defined in § 56.4911-1(c)(1).

(3) An organization's "lobbying ceiling amount" is 150 percent of the organization's lobbying nontaxable amount for a taxable year.

(4) The term "grass roots expenditures" means expenditures for grass roots lobbying communications as defined in section 4911(c)(3) or section 4911(f)(4)(A) and § § 56.4911-2 and 3.

(5) The term "grass roots nontaxable amount" is defined in § 56.4911-1(c)(2).

(6) An organization's "grass roots ceiling amount" is 150 percent of the organization's grass roots nontaxable amount for a taxable year.

(7) In general, the term "base years" means the determination year and the three taxable years immediately preceding the determination year. The base years, however, do not include any taxable year preceding the taxable year for which the organization is first treated as described in section 501(c)(3).

(8) A taxable year is a "determination year" if it is a year for which the expenditure test election is in effect, other than the taxable year for which the organization is first treated as described in section 501(c)(3).

(d) *Reapplication for recognition of exemption*—(1) *Time of application.* An organization that is denied exemption from taxation under section 501(a) by reason of section 501(h) and this section may apply on Form 1023 for recognition of exemption as an organization described in section 501(c)(3) for any taxable year following the first taxable year for which exemption is so denied. See paragraphs (d)(2) and (d)(3) of this section for material to be included with an application described in the preceding sentence.

(2) *Section 501(h) calculation.* An application described in paragraph (d)(1) of this section must demonstrate that the organization would not be denied exemption from taxation under section 501(a) by reason of section 501(h) if the expenditure test election had been in effect for all of its last taxable year ending before the application is made by providing the calculations, described either in paragraph (b)(1)(i) and (ii) of this section or in § 56.4911-9(b), that would have applied to the organization for that year.

(3) *Operations not disqualifying.* An application described in paragraph (d)(1) of this section must include information that demonstrates to the satisfaction of the Commissioner that the organization will not knowingly operate in a manner that would disqualify the organization for tax exemption under section 501(c)(3) by reason of attempting to influence legislation.

(4) *Reelection of expenditure test.* If an organization is denied exemption from tax for a taxable year by reason of section 501(h) and this section, and thereafter is again recognized as an organization described in section 501(c)(3) pursuant to this paragraph (d), it may again elect the expenditure test under section 501(h) in accordance with § 1.501(h)-2(a).

(e) *Examples.* The provisions of this section are illustrated by the following examples, which also illustrate the operation of the tax imposed by section 4911.

Example (1). (1) The following table contains information used in this example concerning organization X.

Reg. § 1.501(h)-3(b)(2)

General Rule

See p. 20,601 for regulations not amended to reflect law changes

Year	Exempt Purpose Expenditures (EPE)	Calculation	Lobbying Nontaxable Amount (LNTA)	Lobbying Expenditures (LE)
1979	$ 400,000	(20% of $400,000 =)	$ 80,000	$100,000
1980	300,000	(20% of $300,000 =)	60,000	100,000
1981	600,000	(20% of $500,000 + 15% of $100,000 =)	115,000	120,000
1982	500,000	(20% of $500,000 =)	100,000	100,000
Totals:	$1,800,000		$355,000	$420,000

(2) Organization X, whose taxable year is the calendar year, was organized in 1971. X first made the expenditure test election under section 501(h) effective for taxable years beginning with 1979 and has not revoked the election. None of X's lobbying expenditures for its taxable years 1979 through 1982 are grass roots expenditures. Under section 4911(a) and § 56.4911-1(a), X must determine for each year for which the expenditure test election is effective whether it is liable for the 25 percent excise tax imposed by section 4911(a) on excess lobbying expenditures. X is liable for this tax for each of its taxable years 1979, 1980, and 1981, because in each year its lobbying expenditures exceeded its lobbying nontaxable amount for the year. For 1979, the tax imposed by section 4911(a) is $5,000 (25% × ($100,000 − $80,000) = $5,000). For 1980, the tax is $10,000. For 1981, the tax is $1,250.

(3) The taxable years 1979 through 1981 are all determination years under paragraph (c)(8) of this section. On its annual return for determination year 1979, the first year of its first election, X can demonstrate, under paragraph (b)(2) of this section, that its lobbying expenditures during 1979 ($100,000) do not exceed 150 percent of its lobbying nontaxable amount for 1979 ($120,000). For determination year 1980, under paragraph (b)(2), X can demonstrate that the sum of its lobbying expenditures for 1979 and 1980 ($200,000) does not exceed 150 percent of the sum of its lobbying nontaxable amounts for 1979 and 1980 ($210,000). For 1981, under paragraph (b)(2), X can demonstrate that the sum of its lobbying expenditures for 1979, 1980, and 1981 ($320,000) does not exceed 150 percent of the sum of its lobbying nontaxable amounts for 1979, 1980, and 1981 ($382,500). For each of the determination years 1979, 1980, and 1981, the first three years of its first election, X satisfies the requirements of paragraph (b)(2). Accordingly, no determination under paragraph (b)(1) of this section is required for those years, and X is not denied tax exemption by reason of section 501(h).

(4) Under paragraph (b)(1) of this section, X must determine for its determination year 1982 whether it has normally made lobbying expenditures in excess of the lobbying ceiling amount. This determination takes into account expenditures in base years 1979 through 1982. The sum of X's lobbying expenditures for the base years ($420,000) does not exceed 150% of the sum of the lobbying nontaxable amounts for the base years (150% × $355,000 = $532,500). Accordingly, X is not denied tax exemption by reason of section 501(h).

Example (2). (1) The following table contains information used in this example concerning W.

[Taxable] Year	Exempt Purpose Expenditures (EPE)	Calculation	Lobbying Nontaxable Amount (LNTA)	Lobbying Expenditures (LE)	Gross Roots Nontaxable Amount (25% of LNTA)	Grass Roots Expenditures
1979	$ 700,000	(20% of $500,000 + 15% of $200,000 =)	$130,000	$120,000	$ 32,500	$ 30,000
1980	$ 800,000	(20% of $500,000 + 15% of $300,000 =)	$145,000	$100,000	$ 36,250	$ 60,000
1981	$ 800,000	(20% of $500,000 + 15% of $300,000 =)	$145,000	$100,000	$ 36,250	$ 65,000
1982	$ 900,000	(20% of $500,000 + 15% of $400,000 =)	$160,000	$150,000	$ 40,000	$ 65,000
Totals:	$3,200,000		$580,000	$470,000	$145,000	$220,000

(2) Organization W, whose taxable year is the calendar year, made the expenditure test election under section 501(h) effective for taxable years beginning with 1979 and has not revoked the election. W has been treated as an organization described in section 501(c)(3) for each of its taxable years beginning with its taxable year 1974.

(3) Under section 4911(a) and § 56.4911-1(a), W must determine for each year for which the expenditure test election is effective whether it is liable for the 25 percent excise tax imposed by section 4911(a) on excess lobbying expenditures. In 1980, 1981, and 1982, W has excess lobbying expenditures because its grass roots expenditures

Reg. § 1.501(h)-3(e)

General Rule

See p. 20,601 for regulations not amended to reflect law changes

in each of those years exceeded its grass roots nontaxable amount for the year. Therefore, W is liable for the excise tax under section 4911(a) for those years. The tax imposed by section 4911(a) for 1980 is $5,937.50 (25% × ($60,000 − $36,250) = $5,937.50). For 1981, the tax is $7,187.50. For 1982, the tax is $6,250.

(4) On its annual return for its determination years 1979, 1980, and 1981, the first three years of its first election, W demonstrates that it satisfies the requirements of paragraph (b)(2) of this section. Accordingly, no determination under paragraph (b)(1) of this section is required for those years, and W is not denied tax exemption by reason of section 501(h).

(5) On its annual return for its determination year 1982, W must determine under paragraph (b)(1) whether it has normally made lobbying expenditures or grass roots expenditures in excess of the corresponding ceiling amount. This determination takes into account expenditures in base years 1979 through 1982. The sum of W's lobbying expenditures for the base years ($470,000) does not exceed 150% of the sum of W's lobbying nontaxable amounts for those years (150% × $580,000 = $870,000). However, the sum of W's grass roots expenditures for the base years ($220,000) does exceed 150% of the sum of W's grass roots nontaxable amounts for those years (150% × $145,000 = $217,500). Under section 501(h), W is denied tax exemption under section 501(a) as an organization described in section 501(c)(3) for its taxable year 1983. For its taxable year 1984 and any taxable year thereafter, W is exempt from tax as an organization described in section 501(c)(3) only if W applies for recognition of its exempt status under paragraph (d) of this section and is recognized as exempt from tax.

Example (3). (1) The following table contains information used in this example concerning organization Y.

Taxable Year	Exempt Purpose Expenditures (EPE)	Calculation	Lobbying Nontaxable Amount (LNTA)	Lobbying Expenditures (LE)	Gross Roots Nontaxable Amount (25% of LNTA)	Grass Roots Expenditures
1977	$ 700,000	(20% of $500,000 + 15% of $200,000 =)	$130,000	$182,000	$ 32,500	$ 30,000
1978	$ 800,000	(20% of $500,000 + 15% of $300,000 =)	$145,000	$224,750	$ 36,250	$ 35,000
Subtotal	$1,500,000		$275,000	$406,750	$ 68,750	$ 65,000
1979	$ 900,000	(20% of $500,000 + 15% of $400,000 =)	$160,000	$264,000	$ 40,000	$ 50,000
Totals:	$2,400,000		$435,000	$670,750	$108,750	$115,000

(2) Organization Y, whose taxable year is the calendar year, was first treated as an organization described in section 501(c)(3) on February 1, 1977. Y made the expenditure test election under section 501(h) effective for taxable years beginning with 1977 and has not revoked the election.

(3) For 1977, Y has excess lobbying expenditures of $52,000 because its lobbying expenditures ($182,000) exceed its lobbying nontaxable amount ($130,000) for the taxable year. Accordingly, Y is liable for the 25 percent excise tax imposed by section 4911(a). The amount of the tax is $13,000 (25% × ($182,000 − $130,000) = $13,000).

(4) For 1978, Y again has excess lobbying expenditures and is again liable for the 25 percent excise tax imposed by section 4911(a). The amount of the tax is $19,937.50 (25% × ($224,750 − $145,000) = $19,937.50).

(5) For 1979, Y's lobbying expenditures ($264,000) exceed its lobbying nontaxable amount ($160,000) by $104,000, and its grass roots expenditures ($50,000) exceed its grass roots nontaxable amount ($40,000) by $10,000. Under § 56.4911-1(b), Y's excess lobbying expenditures are the greater of $104,000 or $10,000. The amount of the tax, therefore, is $26,000 (25% × $104,000 = $26,000).

(6) Under paragraph (c)(8) of this section, 1977 is not a determination year because it is the first year for which the organization is treated as described in section 501(c)(3). For 1977, Y need not determine whether it has normally made lobbying expenditures or grass roots expenditures in excess of the corresponding ceiling amount for purposes of determining whether it is denied exemption under section 501(h) for its taxable year 1978.

(7) For determination year 1978, Y must determine whether it has normally made lobbying or grass roots expenditures in excess of the corresponding ceiling amount, taking into account expenditures for the base years 1977 and 1978. For Y, the determination under paragraph (b)(2) of this section considers the same base years as the determination under paragraph (b)(1) of this section and is, therefore, redundant. Accordingly, Y proceeds to determine, under (b)(1), whether it is denied exemption. Y's grass roots expenditures for 1977 and 1978 ($65,000) did not exceed 150 per-

Reg. § 1.501(h)-3(e)

cent of the sum of its grass roots nontaxable amounts for those years ($103,125). Y's lobbying expenditures for 1977 and 1978 ($406,750) did not exceed 150% of its lobbying nontaxable amount for those years (150% × $275,000 = $412,500). Therefore, Y is not denied tax exemption under section 501(h) for its taxable year 1979.

(8) For determination year 1979, the sum of Y's grass roots expenditures in base years 1977, 1978, and 1979 does not exceed 150 percent of its grass roots nontaxable amount (calculation omitted). However, the sum of Y's lobbying expenditures for the base years ($670,750) does exceed 150% of the sum of the lobbying nontaxable amounts for those years (150% × $435,000 = $652,500). Since Y was not described in section 501(c)(3) prior to 1977, only the years 1977, 1978, and 1979 may be considered in determining whether Y has normally made lobbying expenditures in excess of its lobbying ceiling. Therefore, Y determines that it has normally made lobbying expenditures in excess of its lobbying ceiling. Under section 501(h), Y is denied tax exemption under section 501(a) as an organization described in section 501(c)(3) for its taxable year 1980. For its taxable year 1981, and any taxable year thereafter, Y is exempt from tax as an organization described in section 501(c)(3) only if Y applies for recognition of its exempt status under paragraph (d) of this section and is recognized as exempt from tax.

Example (4). Organization M made the expenditure test election under section 501(h) effective for taxable years beginning with 1977 and has not revoked the election. M has $500,000 of exempt purpose expenditures during each of the years 1981 through 1984. In addition, during each of those years, M spends $75,000 for direct lobbying and $25,000 for grass roots lobbying. Since the amount expended for M's lobbying (both total lobbying and grass roots lobbying) is within the respective nontaxable expenditure limitations, M is not liable for the 25 percent excise tax imposed under section 4911(a) upon excess lobbying expenditures, nor is M denied tax-exempt status by reason of section 501(h).

Example (5). Assume the same facts as in Example (4), except that, on behalf of M, numerous unpaid volunteers conduct substantial lobbying activities with no reimbursement. Since the substantial lobbying activities of the unpaid volunteers are not counted towards the expenditure limitations and the amount expended for M's lobbying is within the respective nontaxable expenditure limitations, M is not liable for the 25 percent excise tax under section 4911, nor is M denied tax-exempt status by reason of section 501(h). [Reg. § 1.501(h)-3.]

☐ [*T.D. 8308, 8-30-90.*]

[Reg. § 1.501(k)-1]

§ 1.501(k)-1. **Communist-controlled organizations.**—Under section 11(b) of the Internal Security Act of 1950 (50 U.S.C. 790(b)), as amended, which is made applicable to the Code by section 7852(b) of that Code, no organization is entitled to exemption under section 501(a) or 521(a) for any taxable year if at any time during such year such organization is registered under section 7 of such Act or if there is in effect a final order of the Subversive Activities Control Board established by section 12 of such Act requiring such organization to register under section 7 of such Act, or determining that it is a Communist-infiltrated organization. [Reg. § 1.501(k)-1.]

☐ [*T.D. 6301, 7-8-58. Amended by T.D. 8100, 9-4-86.*]

[Reg. § 1.502-1]

§ 1.502-1. **Feeder organizations.**—(a) In the case of an organization operated for the primary purpose of carrying on a trade or business for profit, exemption is not allowed under section 501 on the ground that all the profits of such organization are payable to one or more organizations exempt from taxation under section 501. In determining the primary purpose of an organization, all the circumstances must be considered, including the size and extent of the trade or business and the size and extent of those activities of such organization which are specified in the applicable paragraph of section 501.

(b) If a subsidiary organization of a tax-exempt organization would itself be exempt on the ground that its activities are an integral part of the exempt activities of the parent organization, its exemption will not be lost because, as a matter of accounting between the two organizations, the subsidiary derives a profit from its dealings with its parent organization, for example, a subsidiary organization which is operated for the sole purpose of furnishing electric power used by its parent organization, a tax-exempt educational organization, in carrying on its educational activities. However, the subsidiary organization is not exempt from tax if it is operated for the primary purpose of carrying on a trade or business which would be an unrelated trade or business (that is, unrelated to exempt activities) if regularly carried on by the parent organization. For example, if a subsidiary organization is operated primarily for the purpose of furnishing electric power to consumers other than its parent organization (and the parent's tax-exempt subsidiary organizations),

Reg. § 1.502-1(b)

it is not exempt since such business would be an unrelated trade or business if regularly carried on by the parent organization. Similarly, if the organization is owned by several unrelated exempt organizations, and is operated for the purpose of furnishing electric power to each of them, it is not exempt since such business would be an unrelated trade or business if regularly carried on by any one of the tax-exempt organizations. For purposes of this paragraph, organizations are related only if they consist of—

(1) A parent organization and one or more of its subsidiary organizations; or

(2) Subsidiary organizations having a common parent organization. An exempt organization is not related to another exempt organization merely because they both engage in the same type of exempt activities.

(c) In certain cases an organization which carries on a trade or business for profit but is not operated for the primary purpose of carrying on such trade or business is subject to the tax imposed under section 511 on its unrelated business taxable income.

(d) *Exception*—(1) *Taxable years beginning before January 1, 1970.* For purposes of section 502 and this section, for taxable years beginning before January 1, 1970, the term "trade or business" does not include the rental by an organization of its real property (including personal property leased with the real property).

(2) *Taxable years beginning after December 31, 1969.* For purposes of section 502 and this section, for taxable years beginning after December 31, 1969, the term "trade or business" does not include—

(i) the deriving of rents described in section 512(b)(3)(A),

(ii) any trade or business in which substantially all the work in carrying on such trade or business is performed for the organization without compensation, or

(iii) any trade or business (such as a "thrift shop") which consists of the selling of merchandise, substantially all of which has been received by the organization as gifts or contributions.

For purposes of the exception described in subdivision (i) of this subparagraph, if the rents derived by an organization would not be excluded from unrelated business income pursuant to section 512(b)(3) and the regulations thereunder, the deriving of such rents shall be considered a "trade or business".

(3) *Cross references and special rules.* (i) For determination of when rents are excluded from the tax on unrelated business income see section 512(b)(3) and the regulations thereunder.

(ii) The rules contained in § 1.513-1(e)(1) shall apply in determining whether a trade or business is described in section 502(b)(2) and subparagraph (2)(ii) of this paragraph.

(iii) The rules contained in § 1.513-1(e)(3) shall apply in determining whether a trade or business is described in section 502(b)(3) and subparagraph (2)(iii) of this paragraph. [Reg. § 1.502-1.]

☐ [T.D. 6301, 7-8-58. *Amended by* T.D. 6662, 7-8-63, *and by* T.D. 7083, 12-30-70.]

[Reg. § 1.503(a)-1]

§ 1.503(a)-1. **Denial of exemption to certain organizations engaged in prohibited transactions.**—(a)(1) Prior to January 1, 1970 section 503 applies to those organizations described in sections 501(c)(3), 501(c)(17), and section 401(a) except—(i) A religious organization (other than a trust);

(ii) An educational organization which normally maintains a regular faculty and curriculum and normally has a regularly enrolled body of pupils or students in attendance at the place where its educational activities are regularly carried on;

(iii) An organization which normally receives a substantial part of its support (exclusive of income received in the exercise or performance by such organization of its charitable, educational, or other purpose or function constituting the basis for its exemption under section 501(a)) from the United States or any State or political subdivision thereof or from direct or indirect contributions from the general public;

(iv) An organization which is operated, supervised, controlled or principally supported by a religious organization (other than a trust) which is itself not subject to the provisions of this section; and

(v) An organization the principal purposes or functions of which are the providing of medical or hospital care or medical education or medical research or agricultural research.

(2) Effective January 1, 1970, and prior to January 1, 1975, section 503 shall apply only to organizations described in section 501(c)(17) or (18) or section 401(a).

(3) Effective January 1, 1975, section 503 shall apply only to organizations described in section 501(c)(17) or (18) or described in section 401(a) and referred to in section 4975(g)(2) or (3).

(b) The prohibited transactions enumerated in section 503(b) are in addition to and not in limitation of the restrictions contained in section 501(c)(3), (17), or (18) or section 401(a). Even though an organization has not engaged in any of the prohibited transactions referred to in section 503(b), it still may not qualify for tax exemptions in view of the general provisions of section 501(c)(3), (17), or (18) or section 401(a). Thus, if a trustee or other fiduciary of the organization (whether or not he is also a creator or [of] such organization) enters into a transaction with the organization, such transaction will be closely scrutinized in the light of the fiduciary principle requiring undivided loyalty to ascertain whether the organization is in fact being operated for the stated exempt purpose.

(c) An organization—(1) Described in section 501(c)(3) which after July 1, 1950, but before January 1, 1970, has engaged in any prohibited transaction as defined in section 503(b), unless it is excepted by the provisions of paragraph (a)(1) of this section;

(2) Described in section 401(a) and referred to in section 4975(g)(2) or (3) which after March 1, 1954, has engaged in any prohibited transaction as defined in section 503(b);

(3) Described in section 401(a) and not referred to in section 4975(g)(2) or (3) which after March 1, 1954, but before January 1, 1975, has engaged in any prohibited transaction as defined in section 503(b) or which after December 31, 1962, but before January 1, 1975, has engaged in any prohibited transaction as defined in section 503(g) prior to its repeal by section 2003(b)(5) of the Employee Retirement Income Security Act of 1974 (88 Stat. 978);

(4) Described in section 501(c)(17) which after December 31, 1959, has engaged in any prohibited transaction as defined in section 503(b); or

(5) Described in section 501(c)(18) which after December 31, 1969, has engaged in any prohibited transaction described in section 503(b);

shall not be exempt from taxation under section 501(a) for any taxable year subsequent to the taxable year in which there is mailed to it a notice in writing by the Commissioner that it has engaged in such prohibited transactions. Such notification by the Commissioner shall be by registered or certified mail to the last known name and address of the organization. However, notwithstanding the requirement of notification by the Commissioner, the exemption shall be denied with respect to any taxable year if such organization during or prior to such taxable year commenced the prohibited transaction with the purpose of diverting income or corpus from its exempt purposes and such transaction involved a substantial part of the income or corpus of such organization.

For the purpose of this section, the term "taxable year" means the established annual accounting period of the organization; or, if the organization has no such established annual accounting period, the "taxable year" of the organizations means a calendar year. See 26 CFR § 1.503(j)-1 (rev. as of Apr. 1, 1974) for provisions relating to the definition of prohibited transactions in the case of trusts benefiting certain owner-employees after December 31, 1962, but prior to January 1, 1975. See also section 2003(c)(1)(B) of the Employee Retirement Income Security Act of 1974 (88 Stat. 978) in the case of an organization described in section 401(a) with respect to which a disqualified person elects to pay a tax in the amount and manner provided with respect to the tax imposed by section 4975 of the Code so that the organization may avoid denial of exemption under section 503. For further guidance regarding the definition of last known address, see § 301.6212-2 of this chapter.

(d) The application of section 503(b) may be illustrated by the following examples:

Example (1). A creates a foundation in 1954 ostensibly for educational purposes. B, a trustee, accumulates the foundation's income from 1957 until 1959 and then uses a substantial part of this accumulated income to send A's children to college. The foundation would lose its exemption for the taxable years 1957 through 1959 and for subsequent taxable years until it regains its exempt status.

Example (2). If under the facts in example (1) such private benefit was the purpose of the foundation from its inception, such foundation is not exempt by reason of the general provisions of section 501(c)(3), without regard to the provisions of section 503, for all years since its inception, that is, for the taxable years 1954 through 1959 and subsequent taxable years, since under section 501(c)(3) the organization must be organized and operated exclusively for exempt purposes. See § 1.501(c)(3)-1. [Reg. § 1.503(a)-1.]

☐ [T.D. 6301, 7-8-58. Amended by T.D. 6722, 4-13-64; T.D. 6972, 9-11-68; T.D. 7428, 8-13-76 and T.D. 8939, 1-11-2001.]

[Reg. § 1.503(b)-1]

§ 1.503(b)-1. Prohibited transactions.—(a) *In general.* The term "prohibited transaction" means any transaction set forth in section 503(b) engaged in by any organization described in paragraph (a) of § 1.503(a)-1. Whether a transaction is a prohibited transaction depends on the facts and circumstances of the particular case. This section is intended to deny tax-exempt status to such organizations which engage in certain transactions which inure to the private advantage of (1) the creator of such organization (if it is a trust); (2) any substantial contributor to such organization; (3) a member of the family (as defined in section 267(c)(4)) of an individual who is such creator of or such substantial contributor to such organization; or (4) a corporation controlled as set forth in section 503(b), by such creator or substantial contributor.

(b) *Loans as prohibited transactions under section 503(b)(1)* — (1) *Adequate security.* For the purposes of section 503(b)(1), which treats as prohibited transactions certain loans by an organization without receipt of adequate security and a reasonable rate of interest, the term "adequate security" means something in addition to and supporting a promise to pay, which is so pledged to the organization that it may be sold, foreclosed upon, or otherwise disposed of in default of repayment of the loan, the value and liquidity of which security is such that it may reasonably be anticipated that loss of principal or interest will not result from the loan. Mortgages or liens on property, accommodation endorsements of those financially capable of meeting the indebtedness, and stock or securities issued by corporations other than the borrower may constitute security for a loan to the persons or organizations described in section 503(b). Stock of a borrowing corporation does not constitute adequate security. A borrower's evidence of indebtedness, irrespective of its name, is itself not security for a loan, whether or not it was issued directly to the exempt organization. However, if any such evidence of indebtedness provides for security that may be sold, foreclosed upon, or otherwise disposed of in default of repayment of the loan, there may be adequate security for such loan. If an organization subject to section 503(b) purchases debentures issued by a person specified in section 503(b), the purchase is considered, for purposes of section 503(b)(1), as a loan made by the purchaser to the issuer on the date of such purchase. For example, if an exempt organization subject to section 503(b) makes a purchase through a registered security exchange of debentures issued by a person described in section 503(b), and owned by an unknown third party, the purchase will be considered as a loan to the issuer by the purchaser. For rules relating to loan of funds to, or investment of funds in stock or securities of, persons described in section 503(b) by an organization described in section 401(a), see paragraph (b)(5) of § 1.401-1.

(2) *Effective dates.* The effective dates for the application of the definition of adequate security in paragraph (b)(1) of this paragraph are:

(i) March 15, 1956, for loans (other than debentures) made after March 15, 1956;

(ii) January 31, 1957, for loans (other than debentures) made before March 16, 1956, and continued after January 31, 1957;

(iii) November 8, 1956, for debentures which were purchased after November 8, 1956;

(iv) December 1, 1958, for debentures which were purchased before November 9, 1956, and held after December 1, 1958;

(v) If an employees' pension, stock bonus, or profit-sharing trust described in section 401(a) made a loan before March 1, 1954, repayable by its terms after December 31, 1955, and which would constitute a prohibited transaction if made on or after March 1, 1954, the loan shall not constitute a prohibited transaction if held until maturity (determined without regard to any extension or renewal thereof);

(vi) January 1, 1960, for loans (including the purchase of debentures) made by supplemental unemployment benefit trusts, described in section 501(c)(17);

(vii) January 1, 1970, for loans (including the purchase of debentures) made by employees' contribution pension plan trusts described in section 501(c)(18).

(3) *Certain exceptions to section 503(b)(1).* See section 503(e) and §§ 1.503(e)-1, 1.503(e)-2, and 1.503(e)-3 for special rules providing that certain obligations acquired by trusts described in section 401(a) or section 501(c)(17) or (18) shall not be treated as loans made without the receipt of adequate security for purposes of section 503(b)(1). See section 503(f) and § 1.503(f)-1 for an exception to the application of section 503(b)(1) for certain loans made by employees' trusts described in section 401(a).

(c) *Examples.* The principles of this section are illustrated by the following examples: (Assume that section 503(e) and (f) are not applicable.)

Example (1). A, creator of an exempt trust subject to section 503, borrows $100,000 from such trust in 1960, giving his unsecured promissory note. The net worth of A is $1,000,000. The net worth of A is not "security" for such loan and the transaction is a prohibited transaction. If, however, the note is secured by a mortgage on property of sufficient value, or is accompanied by acceptable collateral of sufficient value, or carries with it the secondary promise of repayment by an accommodation endorser financially capable of meeting the indebtedness, it may be adequately secured. However, subordinated debenture bonds of a partnership which are guaranteed by the general partners are not adequately secured since

Reg. § 1.503(b)-1(b)(1)

the general partners are liable for the firm's debt and their guaranty adds no additional security.

Example (2). Assume the same facts as in example (1) except that A's promissory note in the amount of $100,000 to the trust is secured by property which has a fair market value of $75,000. A's promissory note secured to the extent of $75,000 is not adequately secured within the meaning of section 503(b)(1) since the security at the time of the transaction must be sufficient to repay the indebtedness, interest, and charges which may pertain thereto.

Example (3). Corporation M, a substantial contributor to an exempt organization subject to section 503, borrows $150,000 from such organization in 1960, giving its promissory note accompanied by stock of the borrowing corporation with a fair market value of $200,000. Since promissory notes and debentures have priority over stock in the event of liquidation of the corporation, stock of a borrowing corporation is not adequate security. Likewise, debenture bonds which are convertible on default into voting stock of the issuing corporation do not constitute "adequate security" under section 503(b)(1).

Example (4). B, creator of an exempt trust subject to section 503, borrows $100,000 from such trust in 1960, giving his secured promissory note at the rate of 3 percent interest. The prevailing rate of interest charged by financial institutions in the community where the transaction takes place is 5 percent for a loan of the same duration and similarly secured. The loan by the trust to the grantor is a prohibited transaction since section 503(b)(1) requires both adequate security and a reasonable rate of interest. Further, a promise to repay the loan plus a percentage of future profits which may be greater than the prevailing rate of interests [interest] does not meet the reasonable rate of interest requirement.

Example (5). N Corporation, a substantial contributor to an exempt organization subject to section 503 borrows $50,000 on or after March 16, 1956, from the organization. If the loan is not adequately secured, the organization has committed a prohibited transaction at the time the loan was made. If the loan had been made on or before March 15, 1956, and is continued after January 31, 1957, it must be adequately secured on February 1, 1957, or it will be considered a prohibited transaction on that date. However, if the exempt organization were an employees' trust, described in section 401(a), and the loan were made before March 1, 1954, repayable by its terms after December 31, 1955, it would not have to be adequately secured on February 1, 1957. Moreover, if the exempt organization were a supplemental unemployment benefit trust, described in section 501(c)(17), and the loan were made before January 1, 1960, repayable by its terms after December 31, 1959, it would not have to be adequately secured on January 1, 1960.

Example (6). An exempt organization subject to section 503 purchases a debenture issued by O Corporation, which is a substantial contributor to the organization. The organization purchases the debenture in an arm's length transaction from a third person on or after November 9, 1956. The purchase is considered as a loan by the organization to O Corporation. The loan must be adequately secured when it is made, or it is considered as a prohibited transaction at that time. If the organization purchased the debenture before November 9, 1956, and holds it after December 1, 1958, the debenture must be adequately secured on December 2, 1958, or it will then be considered as a prohibited transaction. However, if the organization were an employees' trust described in section 401(a), and if the debenture were purchased before March 1, 1954, and its maturity date is after December 31, 1955, the debenture does not have to be adequately secured. Moreover, if the organization were an employees' contribution pension plan trust described in section 501(c)(18), and if the debenture were purchased before January 1, 1970, and its maturity date is after December 31, 1969, the debenture does not have to be adequately secured. [Reg. § 1.503(b)-1.]

☐ [T.D. 6301, 7-8-58. *Amended by* T.D. 6493, 9-26-60, *by* T.D. 6722, 4-13-64, *by* T.D. 6972, 9-11-68, *and by* T.D. 7428, 8-13-76.]

[Reg. § 1.503(c)-1]

§ 1.503(c)-1. Future status of organizations denied exemption.—(a) Any organization described in section 501(c)(3), (17), or (18), or an employees' trust described in section 401(a), which is denied exemption under section 501(a) by reason of the provisions of section 503(a), may file, in any taxable year following the taxable year in which notice of denial was issued, a claim for exemption. In the case of organizations described in section 501(c)(3), (17), or (18), the appropriate exemption application shall be used for this purpose, and shall be filed with the district director. In the case of an employees' trust described in section 401(a), the information described in § 1.404(a)-2 shall be submitted with a letter claiming exemption. An employees' trust described in section 401(a) shall submit this information to the district director with whom a request for a determination as to its qualification under section 401 and exemption under section 501 may be submitted under paragraph (s) of

Reg. § 1.503(c)-1(a)

§ 601.201 of this chapter (Statement of Procedural Rules). A claim for exemption must contain or have attached to it, in addition to the information generally required as such an organization claiming exemption as an organization described in section 501(c)(17), or (18), or section 401(a) (or section 501(c)(3) prior to January 1, 1970), a written declaration made under the penalties of perjury by a principal officer of such organization authorized to make such declaration that the organization will not knowingly again engage in a prohibited transaction, (as defined in section 503(b) (or 4975(c) if such section applies to such organization)). In the case of section 501(c)(3) organizations which have lost their exemption after December 31, 1969, pursuant to section 503, a claim for exemption must contain or have attached to it a written agreement made under penalties of perjury by a principal officer of such organization authorized to make such agreement that the organization will not violate the provisions of chapter 42. In addition, such organization must comply with the rules for governing instruments as prescribed in § 1.508-3. See § 1.501(a)-1 for proof of exemption requirements in general.

(b) If the Commissioner is satisfied that such organization will not knowingly again engage in a prohibited transaction (as defined under section 503(b) or 4975(c), as applicable to such organization) or in the case of a section 501(c)(3) organization, will not violate the provisions of chapter 42, and the organization also satisfied all the other requirements under section 501(c)(3), (17), or (18), or section 401(a), the organization will be so notified in writing. In such case the organization will be exempt (subject to the provisions of section 501(c)(3), or sections 501(c)(17), (18) or 401(a), and 503, and 504 when applicable) with respect to the taxable years subsequent to the taxable year in which the claim described in section 503(c) is filed. Section 503 contemplates that an organization denied exemption because of the terms of such section will be subject to taxation for at least one full taxable year. For the purpose of this section, the term "taxable year" means the established annual accounting period of the organization; or, if the organization has no such established annual accounting period, the "taxable year" of the organization means the calendar year.

(c) For taxable years beginning after December 31, 1969, the denial of an exemption pursuant to this section, for a taxable year prior to January 1, 1970, of an organization described in section 501(c)(3) shall not cause such organization to cease to be described in section 501(c)(3) for purposes of part II of subchapter F, chapter 1 and for purposes of the application of chapter 42 taxes.

(d) In the case of an organization described in section 501(c)(3), which has lost its exemption pursuant to section 503, and which has not notified the Commissioner that it is applying for recognition of its exempt status under section 508(a) and this section, no gift or contribution made after December 31, 1969, which would otherwise be deductible under section 170, 642(c), or 545(b)(2) shall be allowed as a deduction. For rules relating to the denial of deductions with respect to gifts or contributions made before January 1, 1970, see § 1.503(e)-4. [Reg. § 1.503(c)-1.]

☐ [*T.D.* 6301, 7-8-58. *Amended by T.D.* 6972, 9-11-88, *by T.D.* 7428, 8-13-76, *and by T.D.* 7896, 5-26-83.]

[Reg. § 1.503(d)-1]

§ 1.503(d)-1. Cross references.—For provisions relating to loans described in section 503(b)(1) by a trust described in section 401(a), see § 1.503(b)-1 and section 503(e) and (f) and the regulations thereunder. [Reg. § 1.503(d)-1.]

☐ [*T.D.* 6301, 7-8-58. *Amended by T.D.* 6493, 9-26-60, *by T.D.* 6722, 4-13-63, *and by T.D.* 7428, 8-13-76.]

[Reg. § 1.503(e)-1]

§ 1.503(e)-1. Special rules.—(a) *In general.* (1) Section 503(e) provides that for purposes of section 503(b)(1) (relating to loans made without the receipt of adequate security and a reasonable rate of interest) the acquisition of a bond, debenture, note, or certificate or other evidence of indebtedness shall not be treated as a loan made without the receipt of adequate security if certain requirements are met. Those requirements are described in § 1.503(e)-2.

(2) Section 503(e) does not affect the requirement in section 503(b)(1) of a reasonable rate of interest. Thus, although the acquisition of a certificate of indebtedness which meets all of the requirements of section 503(e) and of § 1.503(e)-2 will not be considered as a loan made without the receipt of adequate security, the acquisition of such an indebtedness does constitute a prohibited transaction if the indebtedness does not bear a reasonable rate of interest.

(3) The provisions of section 503(e) do not limit the effect of section 401(a) and § 1.401-2, section 501(c)(17)(A)(i), or section 501(c)(18)(A), all relating to the use or diversion of corpus or income of the respective employee trusts. Furthermore, the provisions of section 503(e) do not limit the effect of any of the provisions of section 503 other than section 503(b)(1). Thus, for example, although a loan made by an employees' trust described in section 503(a)(1)(B) meets all the

General Rule

See p. 20,601 for regulations not amended to reflect law changes

requirements of section 503(e) and therefore is not treated as a loan made without the receipt of adequate security, such an employees' trust making such a loan will lose its exempt status if the loan is not considered as made for the exclusive benefit of the employees or their beneficiaries. Similarly, a loan which meets the requirements of section 503(e) will constitute a prohibited transaction within the meaning of section 503(b)(6) if it results in a substantial diversion of the trust's income or corpus to a person described in section 503(b).

(b) *Definitions.* For purposes of section 503(e):

(1) The term "obligation" means bond, debenture, note, or certificate or other evidence of indebtedness.

(2) The term "issuer" includes any person described in section 503(b) who issues an obligation.

(3) (i) The term "person independent of the issuer" means a person who is not related to the issuer by blood, by marriage, or by reason of any substantial business interests. Persons who will be considered not to be independent of the issuer include but are not limited to:

(*a*) The spouse, ancestor, lineal descendant, or brother or sister (whether by whole or half blood) of an individual who is the issuer of an obligation;

(*b*) A corporation controlled directly or indirectly by an individual who is the issuer, or directly or indirectly by the spouse, ancestor, lineal descendant, or brother or sister (whether by whole or half blood) of an individual who is the issuer;

(*c*) A corporation which directly or indirectly controls, or is controlled by, a corporate issuer;

(*d*) A controlling shareholder of a corporation which is the issuer, or which controls the issuer;

(*e*) An officer, director, or other employee of the issuer, of a corporation controlled by the issuer, or of a corporation which controls the issuer;

(*f*) A fiduciary of any trust created by the issuer, by a corporation which controls the issuer, or by a corporation which is controlled by the issuer; or

(*g*) A corporation controlled by a person who controls a corporate issuer.

(ii) For purposes of paragraph (b)(3)(i) of this section, the term "control" means, with respect to a corporation, direct or indirect ownership of 50 percent or more of the total combined voting power of all voting stock or 50 percent or more of the total value of shares of all classes of stock. If the aggregate amount of stock in a corporation owned by an individual and by the spouse, ancestors, lineal descendants, brothers, and sisters (whether by whole or half blood) of the individual is 50 percent or more of the total combined voting power of all voting stock or is 50 percent or more of the total value of all classes of stock, then each of these persons shall be considered as the controlling shareholder of the corporation.

(iii) In determining family relationships for purposes of paragraph (b)(3)(i) of this subparagraph, a legally adopted child of an individual shall be treated as a child of such individual by blood.

(4) The term "issue" means all the obligations of an issuer which are offered for sale on substantially the same terms. Obligations shall be considered offered for sale on substantially the same terms if such obligation would, at the same time and under the same circumstances, be traded on the market at the same price. On the other hand, if the terms on which obligations are offered for sale differ in such manner as would cause such obligations to be traded on the market at different prices, then such obligations are not part of the same issue. The following are examples of terms which, if different, would cause obligations to be traded on the market at different prices: (i) Interest rate; (ii) Maturity date; (iii) Collateral; and (iv) Conversion provisions.

The fact that obligations are offered for sale on different dates will not preclude such obligations from being part of the same issue if they all mature on the same date and if the terms on which they are offered for sale are otherwise the same, since such obligations would, at the same time and under the same conditions, be traded on the market at the same price. Obligations shall not be considered part of the same issue merely because they are part of the same authorization or because they are registered as part of the same issue with the Securities and Exchange Commission. [Reg. § 1.503(e)-1.]

☐ [T.D. 6493, 9-26-60. *Amended by T.D.* 6972, 9-11-68 *and by T.D.* 7428, 8-13-76.]

[Reg. § 1.503(e)-2]

§ 1.503(e)-2. **Requirements.**—(a) *In general.* The requirements which must be met under section 503(e) for an obligation not to be treated as a loan made without the receipt of adequate security for purposes of section 503(b)(1) are described in paragraphs (b), (c), and (d) of this section. For purposes of this section, the term "employee trust" shall mean any of the three kinds of organizations described in section 503(a)(1).

Reg. § 1.503(e)-2(a)

General Rule

(b) *Methods of acquisition*—(1) *In general.* The employee trust must acquire the obligation on the market, by purchase from an underwriter, or by purchase from the issuer, in the manner described in subparagraph (2), (3), or (4) of this paragraph.

(2) *On the market.* (i) An obligation is acquired on the market when it is purchased through a national securities exchange which is registered with the Securities and Exchange Commission, or when it is purchased in an over-the-counter transaction. For purposes of the preceding sentence, securities purchased through an exchange which is not a national securities exchange registered with the Securities and Exchange Commission shall be treated as securities purchased in an over-the-counter transaction.

(ii)(*a*) If the obligation is listed on a national securities exchange registered with the Securities and Exchange Commission, it must be purchased through such an exchange or in an over-the-counter transaction at a price not greater than the price of the obligation prevailing on such an exchange at the time of the purchase by the employee trust.

(*b*) For purposes of section 503(e), the price of the obligation prevailing at the time of the purchase means the price which accurately reflects the market value of the obligation. In the case of an obligation purchased through a national securities exchange which is registered with the Securities and Exchange Commission, the price paid for the obligation will be considered the prevailing price of the obligation. In the case of an obligation purchased in an over-the-counter transaction, the prevailing price may be the price at which the last sale of the obligation was affected on such national securities exchange immediately before the employee trust's purchase of such obligation on the same day or may be the mean between the highest and lowest prices at which sales were effected on such exchange on the same day or on the immediately preceding day or on the last day during which there were sales of such obligation or may be a price determined by any other method which accurately reflects the market value of the obligation.

(iii)(*a*) If the obligation is not listed on a national securities exchange which is registered with the Securities and Exchange Commission, it must be purchased in an over-the-counter transaction at a price not greater than the offering price for the obligation as established by current bid and asked prices quoted by persons independent of the issuer.

(*b*) For purposes of section 503(e) the offering price for the obligation at the time of the purchase means the price which accurately reflects the market value of the obligation. The offering price may be the price at which the last sale of the obligation to a person independent of the issuer was effected immediately before the employee trust's purchase of such obligation on the same day or may be the mean between the highest and lowest prices at which sales to persons independent of the issuer were effected on the same day or on the immediately preceding day or on the last day during which there were sales of such obligation or may be a price determined by any other method which accurately reflects the market value of the obligation. The offering price for an obligation must be a valid price for the amount of the obligations which the trust is purchasing. For example, if an employee's trust described in section 503(a)(1)(B) purchases 1,000 bonds of the employer corporation at the offering price established by current prices for a lot of 10 such bonds, such offering price may not be a valid price for 1,000 bonds and the purchase may therefore not meet the requirements of this subdivision. For a purchase of an obligation to qualify under this subdivision, there must be sufficient current prices quoted by persons independent of the issuer to establish accurately the current value of the obligation. Thus, if there are no current prices quoted by persons independent of the issuer, an over-the-counter transaction will not qualify under this subparagraph even though the obligation was purchased in an arm's length transaction from a person independent of the issuer.

(iv) For purposes of this section, an over-the-counter transaction is one not executed on a national securities exchange which is registered with the Securities and Exchange Commission. An over-the-counter transaction may be made through a dealer or an exchange which is not such a national securities exchange or may be made directly from the seller to the purchaser.

(3) *From an underwriter.* An obligation may be purchased from an underwriter if it is purchased at a price not greater than:

(i) The public offering price for the obligation as set forth in a prospectus or offering circular filed with the Securities and Exchange Commission, or

(ii) The price at which a substantial portion of the issue including such obligation is acquired by persons independent of the issuer, whichever is the lesser price. For purposes of this subparagraph, a portion of the issue will be considered substantial if the purchasers of such portion by persons independent of the issuer are sufficient to establish that fair market value of the obligations included in such issue. In determining whether the purchases are sufficient to

Reg. § 1.503(e)-2(b)(1)

establish the fair market value, all the surrounding facts and circumstances will be considered, including the number of independent purchasers, the aggregate amount purchased by each such independent purchaser, and the number of transactions. In the case of a large issue, purchases of a small percentage of the outstanding obligations may be considered purchases of a substantial portion of the issue; whereas, in the case of a small issue, purchases of a larger percentage of the outstanding obligations will ordinarily be required. The requirement in paragraph (b)(3)(ii) of this section contemplates purchase of the obligations by persons independent of the issuer contemporaneously with the purchase by the employee trust.

If a substantial portion has been purchased at different prices, the price of the portion may be based on the average of such prices, and if several substantial portions have been sold to persons independent of the issuer, the price of any of the substantial portions may be used for purposes of this subparagraph.

(4) *From the issuer.* An obligation may be purchased directly from the issuer at a price not greater than the price paid currently for a substantial portion of the same issue by persons independent of the issuer. This requirement contemplates purchase of a substantial portion of the same issue by persons independent of the issuer contemporaneously with the purchase by the employee trust. For purposes of this subparagraph, a portion of the issue will be considered substantial if the purchases of such portion by persons independent of the issuer are sufficient to establish the fair market value of the obligations included in such issue. In determining whether the purchases are sufficient to establish the fair market value, all the surrounding facts and circumstances will be considered, including the number of independent purchasers, the aggregate amount purchased by each such independent purchaser, and the number of transactions. In the case of a large issue, purchases of a small percentage of the outstanding obligations may be considered purchases of a substantial portion of the issue; whereas, in the case of a small issue, purchases of a larger percentage of the outstanding obligations will ordinarily be required. The price paid for a substantial portion of the issue may be determined in the manner provided in paragraph (b)(3) of this section.

(c) *Limitations on holdings of obligations.* (1) Immediately following acquisition of the obligation by the employee trust:

(i) Not more than 25 percent of the aggregate amount of the obligations issued in such issue and outstanding immediately after acquisition by the trust may be held by the trust, and

(ii) At least 50 percent of such aggregate amount must be held by persons independent of the issuer.

(2)(i) For purposes of paragraph (c)(1) of this section, an obligation is not considered as outstanding if it is held by the issuer. For example, if an obligation which has been issued and outstanding is repurchased and held by the issuer, without cancellation or retirement, such an obligation is not considered outstanding.

(ii) For purposes of paragraph (c)(1) of this section, the amounts of the obligations held by the trust and by persons independent of the issuer shall be computed on the basis of the face amount of the obligations.

(d) *Limitation on amount invested in obligations.* (1)(i) Immediately following acquisition of the obligation, not more than 25 percent of the assets of the employee trust may be invested in all obligations of all persons described in section 503(b). For purposes of determining the amount of the trust's assets which are invested in obligations of persons described in section 503(b) immediately following acquisition of the obligation, those obligations shall be valued as follows:

(*a*) Those obligations included in the acquisition in respect of which the percentage test in the first sentence of this subdivision is being applied shall be valued at their adjusted basis, as provided in section 1011, relating to adjusted basis for determining gain or loss; and

(*b*) All other obligations of persons described in section 503(b) which were part of the trust's assets immediately before the acquisition of the obligations described in (d)(1)(i)(*a*) of this section shall be valued at their fair market value on the day that the obligations described in (d)(1)(i)(*a*) of this section were acquired. For purposes of determining the total amount of the assets of the trust (including obligations of persons described in section 503(b)), there shall be used the fair market value of those assets on the day the obligation is acquired.

(ii) The application of the rules in paragraph (d)(1)(i) of this section may be illustrated by the following example:

Example. On February 1, 1960, an exempt employees' trust described in section 401(a) purchases unsecured debentures issued by the employer corporation for $1,000. At the time of this purchase, such debentures have a fair market value of $1,200. Immediately after the purchase of such unsecured debentures, the assets of the trust consist of the following:

Reg. § 1.503(e)-2(d)

General Rule

See p. 20,601 for regulations not amended to reflect law changes

	Cost	Fair market value on Feb. 1, 1960
(a) Assets other than obligations of persons described in sec. 503(b)	$5,000	$7,800
(b) Obligations of persons described in sec. 503(b) acquired before Feb. 1, 1960	$ 500	$1,000
(c) Unsecured debentures of employer purchased on Feb. 1, 1960	1,000	1,200

Immediately following acquisition of the unsecured debentures by the trust, the percent of the assets of the trust that are invested in all obligations of all persons described in section 503(b) is computed as follows:

(1) Obligations of persons described in section 503(b) acquired before Feb. 1, 1960 (valued at fair market value) .... $ 1,000

(2) Unsecured debentures of employer purchased on Feb. 1, 1960 (valued at cost)... 1,000

(3) Total amount of trust's assets invested in obligations of persons described in section 503(b) ((1) plus (2)).................... $ 2,000

(4) Assets of the trust other than obligations of persons described in section 503(b) (valued at fair market value on Feb. 1, 1960).................... $ 7,800

(5) Obligations of persons described in section 503(b) acquired before Feb. 1, 1960 (valued at fair market value on Feb. 1, 1960).................... 1,000

(6) Unsecured debentures of employer purchased on Feb. 1, 1960 (valued at fair market value on Feb. 1, 1960).................... 1,200

(7) Total assets of the trust valued at fair market value on Feb. 1, 1960 (sum of (4), (5), and (6)).................... $10,000

(8) Percent of assets of the trust invested in all obligations of all persons described in section 503(b) immediately following purchase of unsecured debentures on Feb. 1, 1960 ((3) ÷ (7), that is, $2,000 ÷ $10,000).................... 20%

(2) In determining for purposes of subparagraph (1) of this paragraph the amount invested in obligations of persons described in section 503(b), there shall be included amounts invested in any obligations issued by any such person, irrespective of whether the obligation is secured, and irrespective of whether the obligation meets the conditions of section 503(e) or section 503(f). Obligations of persons described in section 503(b) other than the issuer of the obligation to which section 503(e) applies are also included within the 25 percent limitation. For example, if on February 19, 1959, an exempt employees' trust described in section 401(a) purchases unsecured debentures issued by the employer corporation in a transaction effected on the New York Stock Exchange, and if immediately after the purchase 10 percent of the trust's assets is invested in such debentures and 20 percent of its assets is invested in a loan made with adequate security on January 12, 1959, to the wholly-owned subsidiary of the employer corporation, then the purchase of the employer's debentures will not qualify under section 503(e) since 30 percent of the trust's assets are then invested in obligations of persons described in section 503(b).

(e) *Change of terms of an obligation.* A change in terms of an obligation is considered as the acquisition of a new obligation. If such new obligation is not adequately secured, the requirements of section 503(e) must be met at the time the terms of the obligation are changed for such section to be applicable to such new loan. [Reg. § 1.503(e)-2.]

☐ [*T.D. 6493, 9-26-60. Amended by T.D. 6972, 9-11-68, and by T.D. 7428, 8-13-76.*]

[Reg. § 1.503(e)-3]

§ 1.503(e)-3. **Effective dates.**—(a) Section 503(e) and §§ 1.503(e)-1 and 1.503(e)-3 are effective in the case of an employee's trust described in section 401(a) for taxable years ending after March 15, 1956. Thus, if during a taxable year ending before March 16, 1956, an employee's trust made a loan which meets the requirements of section 503(e), such loan will not be treated as made without the receipt of adequate security and will not cause the loss of exemption for taxable years ending after March 15, 1956, although

Reg. § 1.503(e)-3(a)

General Rule

such loan was not considered adequately secured when made. (However, section 503 does not apply to organizations described in section 401(a) not referred to in section 4975(g)(2) or (3) for transactions occurring after December 31, 1974.)

(b)(1) In the case of obligations acquired by an employees' trust described in section 401(a) before September 2, 1958, which were held on that date, the requirements described in paragraphs (c) and (d) of § 1.503(e)-2 which were not satisfied immediately following the acquisition shall be treated as satisfied at that time if those requirements would have been satisfied had the obligations been acquired on September 2, 1958. For example, on January 3, 1955, an employees' trust described in section 401(a) purchased through the New York Stock Exchange unsecured debentures issued by the employer corporation. Under section 503(e) the acquisition of such debentures by the trust will not be treated for taxable years ending after March 15, 1956, as a loan made without receipt of adequate security if the debentures were held by the employees' trust on September 2, 1958, and if the requirements of paragraphs (c) and (d) of § 1.503(e)-2 which were not met on January 3, 1955, were met on September 2, 1958, as if that date were the date of acquisition.

(2) In the case of obligations acquired before September 2, 1958, which were not held by the employees' trust described in section 401(a) on that date, only the requirements described in paragraph (b) of § 1.503(e)-2 must be satisfied for section 503(e) to be applicable to such acquisition. For example, if on December 5, 1956, an employees' trust lent money to the employer corporation by purchasing a debenture issued by the employer and if the trust sold the debenture on August 1, 1958, such loan would not be treated as made without the receipt of adequate security if the requirement described in paragraph (b) of § 1.503(e)-2 was met on December 5, 1956.

(c) Section 503(e) and §§ 1.503(e)-1 and 1.503(e)-2 are effective in the case of trusts described in section 501(c)(17) with respect to loans made, renewed, or, in the case of demand loans, continued after December 31, 1959, and in the case of trusts described in section 501(c)(18) with respect to loans made, renewed or, in the case of demand loans, continued after December 31, 1969.

(d) See paragraph (b)(2) of § 1.503(b)-1 for effective dates for the application of the definition of adequate security. [Reg. § 1.503(e)-3.]

☐ [*T.D. 6493, 9-26-60. Amended by T.D. 6972, 9-11-68, and by T.D. 7428, 8-13-76.*]

[Reg. § 1.503(f)-1]

§ 1.503(f)-1. **Loans by employers who are prohibited from pledging assets.**—(a) *In general.* (1) Section 503(f) provides that section 503(b)(1) shall not apply to a loan made to the employer by an employees' trust described in section 401(a) if the loan bears a reasonable rate of interest and certain conditions are met. Section 503(f) also applies to the renewal of loans to the employer and, in the case of demand loans, to the continuation of such loans.

(2) The provisions of section 503(f) do not limit the effect of section 401(a) and § 1.401-2, relating to use or diversion of corpus or income of an employees' trust, or the effect of any of the provisions of section 503 other than section 503(b)(1). Consequently, although a loan made by an employees' trust described in section 503(a)(1)(B) meets all the requirements of section 503(f) and therefore is not treated as a loan made without the receipt of adequate security, an employees' trust making such a loan will lose its exempt status if the loan is not considered as made for the exclusive benefit of the employees or their beneficiaries. Similarly, a loan which meets the requirements of section 503(f) will constitute a prohibited transaction within the meaning of section 503(b)(6) if it results in a substantial diversion of the trust's income or corpus to a person described in section 503(b).

(b) *Conditions.* (1) Section 503(f) applies to a loan only if, with respect to the making or renewal of the loan, the conditions described in paragraphs (b)(2), (3), and (4) of this section are met. For purpose of this paragraph, the mere continuance of a demand loan is not considered as the making or renewal of such a loan.

(2) The employer must be prohibited (at the time of the making or renewal of the loan) by any law of the United States or regulations thereunder from directly or indirectly pledging, as security for such a loan, a particular class or classes of his assets the value of which (at such time) represents more than one-half of the value of all his assets. If a loan is made or renewed when the employer is prohibited by a law of the United States (or the regulations thereunder) from pledging a class of his assets, the qualification of such a loan under section 503(f) will not be affected by a subsequent change in such law or regulations permitting the employer to pledge such assets, unless such loan is renewed after such change. See section 8(a) of the Securities Exchange Act of 1934, as amended (15 U.S.C. 78h(a)), which prohibits certain persons from pledging a class of assets as security for loans, and 12 CFR 220.5(a) (credit by brokers,

Reg. § 1.503(f)-1(b)(2)

dealers, and members of national securities exchanges).

(3) The making or renewal, as the case may be, must be approved in writing as an investment which is consistent with the exempt purposes of the trust by a trustee who is independent of the employer, and such written approval must not have been previously refused by any other such trustee. A trustee is independent of the employer, for purposes of this subparagraph, if he is entirely free of influence or control by the employer. For example, if the employer is a partnership, then a partner in such partnership, or a member of a partner's family would not be considered independent of the employer. Similarly, an employee of the employer would not be considered independent of the employer. For purposes of this subparagraph, the term "trustee" means, with respect to any trust for which there are two trustees who are independent of the employer, both of such trustees and, with respect to any trust for which there are more than two such independent trustees, a majority of the trustees independent of the employer.

(4)(i) Immediately following the making or renewal, as the case may be, the aggregate amount lent by the trust to the employer, without the receipt of adequate security, must not exceed 25 percent of the value of all the assets of the trust.

(ii) For purposes of paragraph (b)(4)(i) of this section, the determination as to whether any amount lent by the trust to the employer is a loan made without the receipt of adequate security shall be made without regard to section 503(e). Thus, if an employees' trust makes a loan on January 2, 1959, to the employer without adequate security (but which loan is not considered as made without adequate security under section 503(e)), and if immediately after making such loan 10 percent of the value of all its assets is invested in such loan, then the trust may on that day invest not more than an additional 15 percent of its assets in a loan which would be considered made without adequate security if it were not for the provisions of section 503(f).

(iii) For purposes of paragraph (b)(4)(i) of this section, in determining the value of all the assets of the trust, there shall be used the fair market value of those assets on the day of the making or renewal.

(c) *Reasonable rate of interest.* Section 503(f) only applies if, in addition to meeting the conditions described in paragraph (b) of this section, the loan bears a reasonable rate of interest when it is made, renewed, or, in the case of demand loans, during the period of its existence.

(d) *Change of terms of loan.* A change in the terms of a loan (including a reduction in the security for a loan) is considered as the making of a new loan.

If such a new loan is not adequately secured, the requirements of section 503(f) must be met at the time the terms of the loan are changed for such section to be applicable to such new loan.

(e) *Effective date.* (1) This section and section 503(f) are effective for taxable years ending after September 2, 1958, but only with respect to periods after such date. Thus, if a loan was made on or before September 2, 1958, without the receipt of adequate security and if, when such loan was made, it met all of the requirements of section 503(f) and this section, then the loan is not subject to section 503(b)(1) after September 2, 1958, and would not constitute a prohibited transaction after that date because of a lack of adequate security.

(2) See paragraph (b)(2) of § 1.503(b)-1 for the effective dates for application of the definition of adequate security. [Reg. § 1.503(f)-1.]

☐ [*T.D.* 6493, 9-26-60. Amended by *T.D.* 7428, 8-13-76.]

[Reg. § 1.504-1]

§ 1.504-1. **Attempts to influence legislation; certain organizations formerly described in section 501(c)(3) denied exemption.**—Section 504(a) and this section apply to an organization that is exempt from taxation at any time after October 4, 1976, as an organization described in section 501(c)(3), and that ceases to be described in that section because it—

(a) Is an "action" organization within the meaning of § 1.501(c)(3)-1(c)(3)(ii) or (iv), on account of activities occurring after October 4, 1976, or

(b) Is denied exemption under the provisions of section 501(h) (see § 1.501(h)-3 or § 56.4911-9).

This section does not apply, however, to an organization that was described in section 501(h)(5) and § 1.501(h)-2(b)(3) (relating generally to churches) for its taxable year immediately preceding the first taxable year for which it is no longer an organization described in section 501(c)(3). An organization to which section 504(a) and this section apply shall not be treated as described in section 501(c)(4) at any time after the organization ceases to be described in section 501(c)(3). Further, an organization denied treatment as an organization described in section 501(c)(4) under this section may not be treated as an organization described in section 501(c) other than as an organization described in section 501(c)(3). For rules relating to recognition of exemption after exemp-

Reg. § 1.504-1(a)

tion is denied under section 501(h), see § 1.501(h)-3(d). [Reg. § 1.504-1.]

☐ [*T.D.* 8308, 8-30-90.]

[Reg. § 1.504-2]

§ 1.504-2. **Certain transfers made to avoid section 504(a).**—(a) *Scope.* Under section 504(b), a transfer described in paragraph (b) or (c) of this section to an organization exempt from tax under section 501(a) may result in loss of exemption by the transferee unless the Commissioner determines, under paragraph (e) of this section, that the original transfer did not effect an avoidance of section 504(a). For purposes of this section, the term "transfer" includes any use by, or for the benefit of, the recipient of the transfer, but does not include any transfer made for adequate and full consideration.

(b) *Transferor and transferee commonly controlled*—(1) *Loss of exemption.* A transfer is described in this paragraph (b) if it is described in paragraphs (b)(2) through (b)(6). The transferee of a transfer described in this paragraph will cease to be exempt from tax under section 501(a), unless the provisions of paragraph (e) of this section apply.

(2) *Transferor organization.* A transfer is described in this paragraph (b)(2) only if it is from an organization that—

(i) Is or was described in section 501(c)(3), but not in section 501(h)(5), and

(ii) Is determined to be an "action" organization (as defined in § 1.501(c)(3)-1(c)(3)(ii) or (iv)), or is denied exemption from tax by reason of section 501(h) and either § 1.501(h)-3 or § 56.4911-9.

(3) *Transferor and transferee commonly controlled.* A transfer is described in this paragraph (b)(3) only if, at the time of the transfer or at any time during the transferee's ten taxable years following the year in which the transfer was made, the transferee is controlled (directly or indirectly), as defined in paragraph (f) of this section, by the same person or persons who control the transferor.

(4) *Time of transfer.* A transfer is described in this paragraph (b)(4) only if the transfer is made—

(i) After the date that is 24 months before the earliest of the effective date of the determination under section 501(h) that the transferor is not exempt, the effective date of the Commissioner's determination that the transferor is an "action" organization (as defined in § 1.501(c)(3)(ii) or (iv)), or the date on which the Commissioner proposes to treat it as no longer described in section 501(c)(3), and

(ii) Before the transferor again is recognized as an organization described in section 501(c)(3).

(5) *Transferee.* A transfer is described in this paragraph (b)(5) only if the transferee is exempt from tax under section 501(a) but the transferee is neither—

(i) An organization described in section 501(c)(3), nor

(ii) An organization described in section 401(a) to which the transferor contributes as an employer.

(6) *Amount of transfer.* A transfer is described in this paragraph (b)(6) only if the amount of the transfer exceeds the lesser of 30 percent of the net fair market value of the transferor's assets or 50 percent of the net fair market value of the transferee's assets, computed immediately before the transfer. For purposes of this paragraph (b)(6)—

(i) The amount of a transfer by a transferor is the sum of the amounts transferred to any number of transferees in any number of transfers, all of which are described in paragraphs (b)(2) through (b)(5) of this section, and the time of the transfer is the time of the first transfer so taken into account; and

(ii) The amount of a transfer to a transferee is the sum of the amounts transferred by a transferor to the transferee in any number of transfers, all of which are described in paragraphs (b)(2) through (b)(5) of this section, and the time of the transfer is the time of the first transfer so taken into account.

(c) *Other transfers*—(1) *Transfers included.* A transfer is described in this paragraph (c) if it would be described in paragraph (b) of this section except that either—

(i) The amount of the transfer is less than the amount determined in paragraph (b)(6) of this section, or

(ii) The transferor and transferee are not commonly controlled as described in paragraph (b)(3) of this section, or

(iii) The transferee is an organization described in sections 501(c)(3) and 501(h)(4).

(2) *Loss of exemption.* The transferee of a transfer described in this paragraph (c) will cease to be exempt under section 501(a) if the Commissioner determines on all the facts and circumstances that the transfer effected an avoidance of section 504(a). In determining whether a transfer effected an avoidance of section 504(a), the Commissioner may consider whether the transferee engages, or has engaged, in attempts to influence

legislation and may also consider any factors enumerated in paragraph (e) of this section.

(d) *Date of loss of exempt status.* A transferee of a transfer described in paragraph (b), (c)(1)(ii), or (c)(1)(iii) of this section will cease to be exempt from tax under section 501(a) on the date that all requirements of paragraph (b), (c)(1)(ii), or (c)(1)(iii) (other than the determination by the Commissioner) are satisfied. A transferee of a transfer described in paragraph (c)(1)(i) of this section will cease to be exempt from tax under section 501(a) on the date of the last transfer preceding notification of the transferee that the Commissioner proposes to treat the transferee as other than an exempt organization.

(e) *Transfers not in avoidance of section 504(a).* Notwithstanding paragraph (b) of this section, if, based on all the facts and circumstances, the Commissioner determines that a transfer described in paragraph (b) did not effect an avoidance of section 504(a), the transferee will not be denied exemption from tax by reason of section 504(b) and this section. In making the determination called for in the preceding sentence, the Commissioner may consider all relevant factors including:

(1) Whether enforceable and effective conditions on the transfer preclude use of any of the transferred assets for any purpose that, if it were a substantial part of an organization's activities, would be inconsistent with exemption as an organization described in section 501(c)(3);

(2) In the absence of conditions described in paragraph (e)(1) of this section, whether the transferred assets are used exclusively for purposes that are consistent with the transferor's exemption as an organization described in section 501(c)(3);

(3) Whether the assets transferred would be described in § 53.4942(a)-2(c)(3) before, as well as after, the transfer if both the transferor and transferee were private foundations;

(4) Whether and to what extent the transfer would satisfy the provisions of § 1.507-2(a)(7) and (8) if the transferor were a private foundation;

(5) Whether all of the transferred assets have been expended during a period when the transferee was not controlled (directly or indirectly) by the same person or persons who controlled the transferor; and

(6) Whether the entire amount of the transferred assets were in turn transferred, before the close of the transferee's taxable year following the taxable year in which the transferred assets were received, to one or more organizations described in section 507(b)(1)(A) none of which are controlled (directly or indirectly) by the same persons who control either the original transferor or transferee.

(f) *Control.* For purposes of section 504 and the regulations thereunder—

(1) The transferor will be presumed to control any organization with which it is affiliated within the meaning of § 56.4911-7(a), or would be if both organizations were described in section 501(c)(3), and

(2) The transferee will be treated as controlled (directly or indirectly) by the same person or persons who control the transferor if the transferee would be treated as controlled under § 53.4942(a)-3(a)(3), for which purpose the transferor shall be treated as a private foundation. [Reg. § 1.504-2.]

☐ [*T.D.* 8308, 8-30-90.]

[Reg. § 1.505(c)-1T]

§ 1.505(c)-1T. **Questions and Answers Relating to the Notification Requirement for Recognition of Exemption Under Paragraphs (9), (17) and (20) of Section 501(c) (Temporary).**

Q-1: What does section 505(c) of the Internal Revenue Code provide?

A-1: Section 505(c) provides that an organization will not be recognized as exempt under section 501(c)(9) as a voluntary employee's beneficiary association, under section 501(c)(17) as a trust forming part of a plan providing for the payment of supplemental unemployment compensation benefits, or under section 501(c)(20) as a trust forming part of a qualified group legal services plan unless notification is given to the Internal Revenue Service. The notification required of a trust created pursuant to section 501(c)(20) and forming part of a qualified group legal services plan is set forth in Q&A-2. The notification required of an organization organized after July 18, 1984, and applying for exempt status as an organization described in section 501(c)(9) or (17) is set forth in Q&A-3 through Q&A-8. The notification required of an organization organized on or before July 18, 1984, and claiming exemption as an organization described in section 501(c)(9) or (17) is set forth in Q&A-9 through Q&A-11. However, an organization that has previously notified the Internal Revenue Service of its claim to exemption under section 501(c)(9), (17) or (20) or its claim to exemption under those sections pursuant to another provision of the Code, is not required, under section 505(c), to submit a renotification (See Q&A-2 and Q&A-12).

Reg. § 1.505(c)-1T

SECTION 501(c)(20) TRUSTS

Q-2: What is the notice required of a trust created pursuant to section 501(c)(20) and forming part of a qualified group legal services plan under section 120?

A-2: (a) A trust claiming exemption as an organization described in section 501(c)(20) will be recognized as exempt if the exclusive function of the trust is to form part of a qualified group legal services plan or plans. Exemption of the trust under section 501(c)(20) will generally be dependent upon and coextensive with recognition of the plan as a qualified group legal services plan. Therefore, a trust organized pursuant to section 501(c)(20) after July 18, 1984, need not file a separate notice with the Internal Revenue Service of its claim to exemption because the notice required by section 120(c)(4) will suffice for purposes of section 505(c), provided a copy of the trust instrument is filed with the Form 1024 submitted by the group legal services plan. If the trust instrument has not been filed with the Form 1024 submitted by the group legal services plan, the trust must comply with (and exemption will be dependent upon) the filing applicable to a trust organized on or before July 18, 1984. For the notice required and effective dates of exemption of a qualified group legal services plan under section 120, see § 1.120-3.

(b) A trust organized on or before July 18, 1984, that claims exempt status as a trust described in section 501(c)(20) and that forms part of a qualified group legal services plan which has been recognized as exempt under section 120, must file a copy of its trust instrument with the Internal Revenue Service before February 4, 1987. If a copy of the trust instrument is filed within the time provided, the trust's exemption will be recognized retroactively to the date the qualified group legal services plan was recognized as exempt under section 120. However, if a copy of the trust instrument is filed after the time provided, exemption will be recognized only for the period after the copy of the trust instrument is filed with the Internal Revenue Service. See Q&A 7 for a further discussion of "date of filing." A trust that has previously filed a copy of its trust instrument with the Service need not refile that document.

SECTION 501(c)(9) and (17) ORGANIZATIONS ORGANIZED AFTER JULY 18, 1984

Q-3: What is the notice required of an organization or trust, organized after July 18, 1984, that is applying for recognition of tax exempt status under section 501(c)(9) or (17)?

A-3: An organization or trust that is organized after July 18, 1984, will not be treated as described in paragraphs (9) or (17) of section 501(c), unless the organization notifies the Internal Revenue Service that it is applying for recognition of exemption. In addition, unless the required notice is given in the manner and within the time prescribed by these regulations, an organization will not be treated as exempt for any period before the giving of the required notice. The notice is filed by submitting a properly completed and executed Form 1024, "Application for Recognition of Exemption Under Section 501(a) or for Determination Under Section 120" together with the additional information required under Q&A-4 and Q&A-5. The notice is filed with the district director for the key district in which the organization's principal place of business or principal office is located. The notice may be filed by either the plan administrator (as defined in section 414(g)) or the trustee. The Internal Revenue Service will not accept a Form 1024 for any organization or trust before such entity has been organized.

Q-4: What information, in addition to the information required by Form 1024, must be submitted by an organization or trust seeking recognition of exemption under section 501(c)(9) or (17)?

A-4: A notice will not be considered complete unless, in addition to a properly completed and executed Form 1024, the organization or trust submits a full description of the benefits available to participants under section 501(c)(9) or (17). Moreover, both the terms and conditions of eligibility for membership and the terms and conditions of eligibility for benefits must be set forth. This information may be contained in a separate document, such as a "plan document," or it may be contained in the creating document of the entit). For benefits provided through a policy or policies of insurance, all such policies must be included with the notice. Where individual policies of insurance are provided to the participants, single exemplar copies, typical of policies generally issued to participants, are acceptable, provided they adequately describe all forms of insurance available to participants. In providing a full description of the benefits available, the benefits provided must be sufficiently described so that each benefit is definitely determinable. A benefit is definitely determinable if the amount of the benefit, its duration, and the persons eligible to receive it are ascertainable from the plan document or other instrument. Thus, a benefit is not definitely determinable if the rules governing either its amount, its duration, or its recipients are not ascertainable from the plan document or other instrument but are instead subject to the discretion of a person or committee. Likewise, a benefit is not definitely determinable if the amount for any individual is based upon a percentage share

Reg. § 1.505(c)-1T

of any item that is within the discretion of the employer. However, a disability benefit will not fail to be considered definitely determinable merely because the determination of whether an individual is disabled is made under established guidelines by an authorized person or committee.

Q-5: What is the notice required of collectively bargained plans?

A-5: If an organization or trust claiming exemption under section 501(c)(9) or (17) is organized and maintained pursuant to a collective bargaining agreement between employee representatives and one or more employers, only one Form 1024 is required to be filed for the organization or trust, regardless of the number of employers originally participating in the agreement. Moreover, once a Form 1024 is filed pursuant to a collective bargaining agreement, an additional Form 1024 is not required to be filed by an employer who thereafter participates in that agreement. When benefits are provided pursuant to a collective bargaining agreement, the notice will not be considered complete unless, in addition to a properly completed and executed Form 1024, a copy of the collective bargaining agreement is also submitted together with the additional information delineated in Q&A-4.

Q-6: When must the required notice be filed by an organization or trust, organized after July 18, 1984, that seeks recognition of exemption under section 501(c)(9) or (17)?

A-6: An organization or trust applying for exemption must file the required notice by the later of February 4, 1987, or 15 months from the end of the month in which the organization or trust was organized. An extension of time for filing the required notice may be granted by the district director if the request is submitted before the end of the applicable period and it is demonstrated that additional time is needed.

Q-7: What is the effective date of exemption for a new organization or trust, organized after July 18, 1984, that has submitted the required notice?

A-7: If the required notice is filed within the time provided by these regulations, the organization's exemption will be recognized retroactively to the date the organization was organized, provided its purpose, organization and operation (including compliance with the applicable nondiscrimination requirements) during the period prior to the date of the determination letter are in accordance with the applicable law. However, if the required notice is filed after the time provided by these regulations, exemption will be recognized only for the period after the application is filed with the Internal Revenue Service. The date of filing is the date of the United States postmark on the cover in which an exemption application is mailed or, if no postmark appears on the cover, the date the application is stamped as received by the Service. If an extension for filing the required notice has been granted to the organization, a notice filed on or before the last day specified in the extension will be considered timely and not the otherwise applicable date under Q&A-6.

Q-8: What is the effect on exemption of the filing of an incomplete notice?

A-8: Although a properly completed and executed Form 1024 together with the required additional information (See Q&A-4 and Q&A-5) must be submitted to satisfy the notice required by section 505(c), the failure to file, within the time specified, all of the information necessary to complete such notice will not alone be sufficient to deny recognition of exemption from the date of organization to the date the completed information is submitted to the Service. If the notice which is filed with the Service within the required time is substantially complete, and the organization supplies the necessary additional information requested by the Service within the additional time allowed, the original notice will be considered timely. However, if the notice is not substantially complete or the additional information is not provided within the additional time allowed, exemption will be recognized only from the date of filing of the additional information.

SECTION 501(c)(9) and (17) ORGANIZATIONS ORGANIZED ON OR BEFORE JULY 18, 1984

Q-9: What is the notice required of an organization or trust organized on or before July 18, 1984, that claims exempt status as an organization described in section 501(c)(9) or (17)?

A-9: Section 505(c) provides a special rule for existing organizations and trusts organized on or before July 18, 1984. Such an organization or trust will not be treated as described in paragraphs (9) or (17) of section 501(c) unless the organization or trust notifies the Internal Revenue Service in the manner and within the time prescribed in these regulations that it is claiming exemption under the particular section. The type of notice, the manner for filing that notice, and the additional information required is the same as that set forth in Q&A-3 through Q&A-5 for new organizations.

Q-10: When must the required notice be filed by an organization or trust organized on or before July 18, 1984?

A-10: An organization or trust organized on or before July 18, 1984, that claims exempt status as an organization described in section 501(c)(9) or

Reg. § 1.505(c)-1T

Private Foundations

(17), must file the required notice before February 4, 1987. An extension of time for filing the required notice may be granted by the district director if the request is submitted before the due date of the notice and it is demonstrated that additional time is needed.

Q-11: What is the effective date of exemption for an organization or trust organized on or before July 18, 1984, that has submitted the required notice?

A-11: If the required notice is filed within the time provided by these regulations, the organization's exemption will be recognized retroactively to the date the organization was organized, provided its purpose, organization and operation (including compliance with the applicable nondiscrimination requirements) during the period prior to the date of the determination letter are in accordance with the applicable law. If, on the other hand, the required notice is filed after the time provided by these regulations, exemption will be recognized only for the period after the notice is received by the Internal Revenue Service. See Q&A-7 for a further discussion of "date of filing." See also Q&A-8 for the effect on exemption of a notice that has been timely filed but is incomplete.

EXCEPTIONS TO NOTICE REQUIREMENT

Q-12: Are any organizations or trusts claiming recognition of exemption as an organization described in section 501(c)(9) or (17) excepted from the notice requirement of section 505(c)?

A-12: An organization or trust that has previously notified the Internal Revenue Service of its claim to exemption by filing Form 1024 is not required, under section 505(c), to renotify the Service. Thus, an organization that has filed a Form 1024 that is pending with the Service need not refile that form. Also, an organization that has received a ruling or determination letter from the Service recognizing its exemption from taxation need not submit the notification required by section 505(c). [Temporary Reg. § 1.505(c)-1T.]

☐ [T.D. 8073, 1-29-86.]

Private Foundations

[Reg. § 1.507-1]

§ 1.507-1. General rule.—(a) *In general.* Except as provided in § 1.507-2, the status of any organization as a private foundation shall be terminated only if—

(1) Such organization notifies the district director of its intent to accomplish such termination, or

(2)(i) With respect to such organization, there have been either willful repeated acts (or failures to act), or a willful and flagrant act (or failure to act), giving rise to liability for tax under chapter 42, and

(ii) The Commissioner notifies such organization that, by reason of subdivision (i) of this subparagraph, such organization is liable for the tax imposed by section 507(c),

and either such organization pays the tax imposed by section 507(c) (or any portion not abated under section 507(g)) or the entire amount of such tax is abated under section 507(g).

(b) *Termination under section 507(a)(1).* (1) In order to terminate its private foundation status under paragraph (a)(1) of this section, an organization must submit a statement to the district director of its intent to terminate its private foundation status under section 507(a)(1). Such statement must set forth in detail the computation and amount of tax imposed under section 507(c). Unless the organization requests abatement of such tax pursuant to section 507(g), full payment of such tax must be made at the time the statement is filed under section 507(a)(1). An organization may request the abatement of all of the tax imposed under section 507(c) or may pay any part thereof and request abatement of the unpaid portion of the amount of tax assessed. If the organization requests abatement of the tax imposed under section 507(c) and such request is denied, the organization must pay such tax in full upon notification by the Internal Revenue Service that such tax will not be abated. For purposes of subtitle F of the Code, the statement described in this subparagraph, once filed, shall be treated as a return.

(2) Termination of private foundation status under section 507(a)(1) does not relieve a private foundation, or any disqualified person with respect thereto, of liability for tax under chapter 42 with respect to acts or failures to act prior to termination or for any additional taxes imposed for failure to correct such acts or failures to act. See subparagraph (8) of this paragraph as to the possible imposition of transferee liability in cases not involving termination of private foundation status.

(3) In the case of an organization which has terminated its private foundation status under section 507(a) and continues in operation thereafter, if such organization wishes to be treated as described in section 501(c)(3), then pursuant to section 509(c) and § 1.509(c)-1 such organization must apply for recognition of exemption as an

Reg. § 1.507-1(b)(3)

organization described in section 501(c)(3) in accordance with the provisions of section 508(a).

(4) See § 53.4947-1(c)(7) as to the application of section 507(a) to certain split-interest trusts.

(5) For purposes of section 508(d)(1), the Internal Revenue Service shall make notice to the public (such as by publication in the Internal Revenue Bulletin) of any notice received from a private foundation pursuant to section 507(a)(1) or of any notice given to a private foundation pursuant to section 507(a)(2).

(6) If a private foundation transfers all or part of its assets to one or more other private foundations (or one or more private foundations and one or more section 509(a)(1), (2), (3), or (4) organizations) pursuant to a transfer described in section 507(b)(2) and § 1.507-3(c), such transferor foundation will not have terminated its private foundation status under section 507(a)(1). See § 1.507-3, however, for the special rules applicable to private foundations participating in section 507(b)(2) transfers.

(7) Neither a transfer of all of the assets of a private foundation nor a significant disposition of assets (as defined in § 1.507-3(c)(2)) by a private foundation (whether or not any portion of such significant disposition of assets is made to another private foundation) shall be deemed to result in a termination of the transferor private foundation under section 507(a) unless the transferor private foundation elects to terminate pursuant to section 507(a)(1) or section 507(a)(2) is applicable. Thus, if a private foundation transfers all of its assets to one or more persons, but less than all of its net assets to one or more organizations described in section 509(a)(1) which have been in existence and so described for a continuous period of 60 calendar months, for purposes of this paragraph such transferor foundation will not be deemed by reason of such transfer to have terminated its private foundation status under section 507(a) or (b) unless section 507(a)(2) is applicable. Such foundation will continue to be treated as a private foundation for all purposes. For example, if a private foundation transfers all of its net assets to a section 509(a)(2) organization in 1971 and receives a bequest in 1973, the bequest will be regarded as having been made to a private foundation and the foundation will be subject to the provisions of chapter 42 with respect to such funds. If a private foundation makes a transfer of all of its net assets to a section 509(a)(2) or (3) organization, for example, it must retain sufficient income or assets to pay the tax imposed under section 4940 for that portion of its taxable year prior to such transfer. For additional rules applicable to a transfer by a private foundation of all of its net assets to a section 509(a)(1) organization which has not been in existence and so described for a continuous period of 60 calendar months, see § 1.507-3(e).

(8) If a private foundation makes a transfer described in subparagraph (7) of this paragraph and prior to, or in connection with, such transfer, liability for any tax under chapter 42 is incurred by the transferor foundation, transferee liability may be applied against the transferee organization for payment of such taxes. For purposes of this subparagraph, liablility for any tax imposed under chapter 42 for failure to correct any act or failure to act shall be deemed incurred on the date on which the act or failure to act giving rise to the initial tax liability occurred.

(9) A private foundation which transfers all of its net assets is required to file the annual information return required by section 6033, and the foundation managers are required to file the annual report of a private foundation required by section 6056, for the taxable year in which such transfer occurs. However, neither such foundation nor its foundation managers will be required to file such returns for any taxable year following the taxable year in which the last of any such transfers occurred, if at no time during the subsequent taxable years in question the foundation has either legal or equitable title to any assets or engages in any activity.

(c) *Involuntary termination under section 507(a)(2).* (1) For purposes of section 507(a)(2)(A), the term "willful repeated acts (or failures to act)" means at least two acts or failures to act both of which are voluntary, conscious, and intentional.

(2) For purposes of section 507(a)(2)(A), a "willful and flagrant act (or failure to act)" is one which is voluntarily, consciously, and knowingly committed in violation of any provision of chapter 42 (other than section 4940 or 4948(a)) and which appears to a reasonable man to be a gross violation of any such provision.

(3) An act (or failure to act) may be treated as an act (or failure to act) by the private foundation for purposes of section 507(a)(2) even though tax is imposed upon one or more foundation managers rather than upon the foundation itself.

(4) For purposes of section 507(a)(2), the failure to correct the act or acts (or failure or failures to act) which gave rise to liability for tax under any section of chapter 42 by the close of the correction period for such section may be a willful and flagrant act (or failure to act).

(5) No motive to avoid the restrictions of the law or the incurrence of any tax is necessary to make an act (or failure to act) willful. However, a

Reg. § 1.507-1(b)(4)

foundation's act (or failure to act) is not willful if the foundation (or a foundation manager, if applicable) does not know that it is an act of self-dealing, a taxable expenditure, or other act (or failure to act) to which chapter 42 applies. Rules similar to the regulations under chapter 42 (see, for example, § 53.4945-1(a)(2)(iii) of this chapter) shall apply in determining whether a foundation or a foundation manager "knows" that an act (or failure to act) is an act of self-dealing, a taxable expenditure or other such act (or failure to act). [Reg. § 1.507-1.]

☐ [T.D. 7233, 12-20-72. Amended by T.D. 7290, 11-16-73.]

[Reg. § 1.507-2]

§ 1.507-2. Special rules; transfer to, or operation as, public charity.—(a) *Transfer to public charities*—(1) *General rule.* Under section 507(b)(1)(A) a private foundation, with respect to which there have not been either willful repeated acts (or failures to act) or a willful and flagrant act (or failure to act) giving rise to liability for tax under chapter 42, may terminate its private foundation status by distributing all of its net assets to one or more organizations described in section 170(b)(1)(A) (other than in clauses (vii) and (viii)) each of which has been in existence and so described for a continuous period of at least 60 calendar months immediately preceding such distribution. Since section 507(a) does not apply to such a termination, a private foundation which makes such a termination is not required to give the notification described in section 507(a)(1). A private foundation which terminates its private foundation status under section 507(b)(1)(A) does not incur tax under section 507(c) and, therefore, no abatement of such tax under section 507(g) is required.

(2) *Effect of current ruling*—(i) *Distributions before final regulations.* With respect to distributions made before December 30, 1972, an organization to which a distribution of net assets is made will qualify as an organization "described in section 170(b)(1)(A) (other than clauses (vii) and (viii))" for purposes of meeting the requirements of section 507(b)(1)(A) without a further showing if such distributee organization:

(a) Has been in existence for a continuous period of at least 60 calendar months preceding the distribution described in subparagraph (1) of this paragraph;

(b) Has received a ruling or determination letter that it is an organization described in clause (i), (ii), (iii), (iv), (v), or (vi) of section 170(b)(1)(A);

(c) The facts and circumstances forming the basis for the issuance of the ruling have not substantially changed during the 60-month period referred to in (a) of this subdivision; and

(d) The ruling or determination letter referred to in (b) of this subdivision has not been revoked expressly or by a subsequent change of the law or regulations under which the ruling was issued.

(ii) *Distributions after final regulations.* With respect to distributions made after December 29, 1972, a private foundation seeking to terminate its private foundation status pursuant to section 507(b)(1)(A) may rely on a ruling or determination letter issued to a potential distributee organization that such distributee organization is an organization described in clause (i), (ii), (iii), (iv), (v), or (vi) of section 170(b)(1)(A) in accordance with the provisions of § 1.509(a)-7.

(3) *Organizations described in more than one clause of section 170(b)(1)(A).* For purposes of this paragraph and section 507(b)(1)(A), the parenthetical term "other than in clauses (vii) and (viii)" shall refer only to an organization which is described only in section 170(b)(1)(A)(vii) or (viii). Thus, an organization described in clause (i), (ii), (iii), (iv), (v), or (vi) of section 170(b)(1)(A) will not be precluded from being a distributee described in section 507(b)(1)(A) merely because it also appears to meet the description of an organization described in section 170(b)(1)(A)(vii) or (viii).

(4) *Applicability of chapter 42 to foundations terminating under section 507(b)(1)(A).* Except as provided in subparagraph (5) of this paragraph, an organization which terminates its private foundation status pursuant to section 507(b)(1)(A) will remain subject to the provisions of chapter 42 until the distribution of all of its net assets to distributee organizations described in section 507(b)(1)(A) has been completed.

(5) *Special transitional rule.* (i) Section 4940(a) imposes a tax upon private foundations with respect to the carrying on of activities for each taxable year. For purposes of section 4940, an organization which terminates its private foundation status under section 507(b)(1)(A) by the end of the period described in subdivision (ii) of this subparagraph will not be considered as carrying on activities within the meaning of section 4940 during such period. Such organization will therefore not be subject to the tax imposed under section 4940(a) for such period.

(ii) The period referred to in subdivision (i) of this subparagraph is the 12-month period beginning with the first day of the organization's first taxable year which begins after December

31, 1969, but such period shall not be treated as ending before February 20, 1973. In the case of a private foundation distributing assets pursuant to section 507(b)(1)(A) to a medical research organization or a community trust (or in the case of a private foundation seeking to terminate into such an organization or trust pursuant to section 507(b)(1)(B)), the period described in this subdivision shall be treated as not ending before—

(A) In the case of distribution to a medical research organization, March 29, 1976; or

(B) In the case of a community trust, May 11, 1977.

(iii) If the period described in subdivision (ii) of this subparagraph has not expired prior to the due date for the organization's annual return required to be filed by section 6033 or 6012 (determined with regard to any extension of time for filing the return) for its first taxable year which begins after December 31, 1969 (or for any other taxable year ending before the expiration of the period referred to in subdivision (ii) of this subparagraph), and if the organization has not terminated its private foundation status under section 507(b)(1)(A) by such date, then notwithstanding the provisions of subdivision (ii) of this subparagraph, the organization must take either of the following courses of action:

(a) Complete and file its annual return, including the line relating to excise taxes on investment income, by such date, and pay the tax on investment income imposed under section 4940 at the time it files its annual return. If such organization subsequently terminates its private foundation status under section 507(b)(1)(A) within the period specified in subdivision (ii) of this subparagraph, it may file a claim for refund of the tax paid under section 4940; or

(b) Complete and file its annual return, except for the line relating to excise taxes on investment income, by such date, and, in lieu of paying the tax on investment income imposed under section 4940, file a statement with its annual return which establishes that the organization has taken affirmative action by such date to terminate its private foundation status under section 507(b)(1)(A). Such statement must indicate the type of affirmative action taken and explain how such action will result in the termination of its private foundation status under section 507(b)(1)(A). Such affirmative action may include making application to the appropriate State court for approval of the distribution of all net assets pursuant to section 507(b)(1)(A) in the case of a charitable trust, or the passage of a resolution by the organization's governing body directing the distribution of all net assets pursuant to section 507(b)(1)(A) in the case of a not-for-profit corporation. A written commitment or letter of agreement by the trustee or governing body to one or more section 509(a)(1) distributees indicating an intent to distribute all of the organization's net assets to such distributees will also constitute appropriate affirmative action for purposes of this subdivision. An organization may take such affirmative action and may terminate its private foundation status under section 507(b)(1)(A) in reliance upon 26 CFR § 13.12 (rev. as of January 1, 1972) and upon the provisions of the notices of proposed rule making under sections 170(b)(1)(A), 507(b)(1), and 509. Thus, if a distributee organization meets the requirements of the provisions of the notices of proposed rule making under sections 170(b)(1)(A), 507, or 509 as a distributee under section 507(b)(1)(A), the distributor organization may terminate its private foundation status under section 507(b)(1)(A) in reliance upon such provisions prior to the expiration of the period described in subdivision (ii) of this subparagraph. If such organization, however, fails to terminate its private foundation status under section 507(b)(1)(A) within the period specified in subdivision (ii) of this subparagraph by failing to meet the requirements of either the notices of proposed rule making under section 170(b)(1)(A), 507(b)(1), or 509 or the final regulations published under these Code sections, the tax imposed under section 4940 shall be treated as if due from the due date for its annual return (determined without regard to any extension of time for filing its return).

The provisions of this subdivision are applicable only to an organization terminating its private foundation status under section 507(b)(1)(A) and may not be relied upon by any other organization with respect to its own classification under section 509(a)(1) (except as to its liability as a transferee for the tax imposed by section 4940).

(6) *Return required from organizations terminating private foundation status under section 507(b)(1)(A)*. (i) An organization which terminates its private foundation status under section 507(b)(1)(A) is required to file a return under the provisions of section 6043(b), rather than under the provisions of section 6050.

(ii) An organization which terminates its private foundation status under section 507(b)(1)(A) is not required to comply with section 6104(d) for the taxable year in which such termination occurs. For purposes of this subdivision, the term "taxable year" shall include the period described in subparagraph (5)(ii) of this paragraph.

Reg. § 1.507-2(a)(6)

(7) *Distribution of net assets.* A private foundation will meet the requirement that it "distribute all of its net assets" within the meaning of section 507(b)(1)(A) only if it transfers all of its right, title, and interest in and to all of its net assets to one or more organizations referred to in section 507(b)(1)(A).

(8) *Effect of restrictions and conditions upon distributions of net assets*—(i) *In general.* In order to effectuate a transfer of "all of its right, title, and interest in and to all of its net assets" within the meaning of paragraph (a)(7) of this section, a transferor private foundation may not impose any material restriction or condition that prevents the transferee organization referred to in section 507(b)(1)(A) (herein sometimes referred to as the "public charity") from freely and effectively employing the transferred assets, or the income derived therefrom, in furtherance of its exempt purposes. Whether or not a particular condition or restriction imposed upon a transfer of assets is "material" (within the meaning of paragraph (a)(8) of this section) must be determined from all of the facts and circumstances of the transfer. Some of the more significant facts and circumstances to be considered in making such a determination are:

(A) Whether the public charity (including a participating trustee, custodian, or agent in the case of a community trust) is the owner in fee of the assets it receives from the private foundation;

(B) Whether such assets are to be held and administered by the public charity in a manner consistent with one or more of its exempt purposes;

(C) Whether the governing body of the public charity has the ultimate authority and control over such assets, and the income derived therefrom; and

(D) Whether, and to what extent, the governing body of the public charity is organized and operated so as to be independent from the transferor.

(ii) *Independent governing body.* As provided in paragraph (a)(8)(i)(D) of this section, one of the more significant facts and circumstances to be considered in making the determination whether a particular condition or restriction imposed upon a transfer of assets is "material" within the meaning of paragraph (a)(8) of this section is whether, and the extent to which, the governing body is organized and operated so as to be independent from the transferor. In turn, the determination as to such factor must be determined from all of the facts and circumstances. Some of the more significant facts and circumstances to be considered in making such a determination are:

(A) Whether, and to what extent, members of the governing body are comprised of persons selected by the transferor private foundation or disqualified persons with respect thereto, or are themselves such disqualified persons;

(B) Whether, and to what extent, members of the governing body are selected by public officials acting in their capacities as such; and

(C) How long a period of time each member of the governing body may serve as such. In the case of a transfer that is a community trust, the community trust shall meet paragraph (a)(8)(ii)(C) of this section if it meets the requirements of § 1.170A-9(e)(13)(iv) (other than § 1.170A-9(e)(13)(iv)(C) or (D)), relating to rules for governing body.

(iii) *Factors not adversely affecting determination.* The presence of some or all of the following factors will not be considered as preventing the transferee "from freely and effectively employing the transferred assets, or the income derived therefrom, in furtherance of its exempt purposes" (within the meaning of paragraph (a)(8)(i) of this section):

(A) *Name.* The fund is given a name or other designation which is the same as or similar to that of the transferor private foundation or otherwise memorializes the creator of the foundation or his family.

(B) *Purpose.* The income and assets of the fund are to be used for a designated purpose or for one or more particular section 509(a)(1), (2), or (3) organizations, and such use is consistent with the charitable, educational, or other basis for the exempt status of the public charity under section 501(c)(3).

(C) *Administration.* The transferred assets are administered in an identifiable or separate fund, some or all of the principal of which is not to be distributed for a specified period, if the public charity (including a participating trustee, custodian, or agent in the case of a community trust) is the legal and equitable owner of the fund and the governing body exercises ultimate and direct authority and control over such fund, as, for example, a fund to endow a chair at a university or a medical research fund at a hospital. In the case of a community trust, the transferred assets must be administered in or as a component part of the community trust within the meaning of § 1.170A-9(e)(11).

(D) *Restrictions on disposition.* The transferor private foundation transfers property the continued retention of which by the transferee

Reg. § 1.507-2(a)(8)

is required by the transferor if such retention is important to the achievement of charitable or other similar purposes in the community because of the peculiar features of such property, as, for example, where a private foundation transfers a woodland preserve which is to be maintained by the public charity as an arboretum for the benefit of the community. Such a restriction does not include a restriction on the disposition of an investment asset or the distribution of income.

(iv) *Adverse factors.* The presence of any of the following factors will be considered as preventing the transferee "from freely and effectively employing the transferred assets, or the income derived therefrom, in furtherance of its exempt purposes" (within the meaning of paragraph (a)(8)(i) of this section):

(A) *Distributions. (1)* With respect to distributions made after April 19, 1977, the transferor private foundation, a disqualified person with respect thereto, or any person or committee designated by, or pursuant to the terms of an agreement with, such a person (hereinafter referred to as "donor"), reserves the right, directly or indirectly, to name (other than by designation in the instrument of transfer of particular section 509(a)(1), (2), or (3) organizations) the persons to which the transferee public charity must distribute, or to direct the timing of such distributions (other than by direction in the instrument of transfer that some or all of the principal, as opposed to specific assets, not be distributed for a specified period) as, for example, by a power of appointment. The Internal Revenue Service will examine carefully whether the seeking of advice by the transferee from, or the giving of advice by, any donor after the assets have been transferred to the transferee constitutes an indirect reservation of a right to direct such distributions. In any such case, the reservation of such a right will be considered to exist where the only criterion considered by the public charity in making a distribution of income or principal from a donor's fund is advice offered by the donor. Whether there is a reservation of such a right will be determined from all of the facts and circumstances, including, but not limited to, the facts contained in paragraph (a)(8)(iv)(A)(*2*) and (*3*) of this section.

(*2*) The presence of some or all of the following factors will indicate that the reservation of such a right does not exist:

(i) There has been an independent investigation by the staff of the public charity evaluating whether the donor's advice is consistent with specific charitable needs most deserving of support by the public charity (as determined by the public charity);

(ii) The public charity has promulgated guidelines enumerating specific charitable needs consistent with the charitable purposes of the public charity and the donor's advice is consistent with such guidelines;

(iii) The public charity has instituted an educational program publicizing to donors and other persons the guidelines enumerating specific charitable needs consistent with the charitable purposes of the public charity;

(iv) The public charity distributes funds in excess of amounts distributed from the donor's fund to the same or similar types of organizations or charitable needs as those recommended by the donor; and

(v) The public charity's solicitations (written or oral) for funds specifically state that such public charity will not be bound by advice offered by the donor.

(3) The presence of some or all of the following factors will indicate the reservation of such a right does exist:

(i) The solicitations (written or oral) of funds by the public charity state or imply, or a pattern of conduct on the part of the public charity creates an expectation, that the donor's advice will be followed;

(ii) The advice of a donor (whether or not restricted to a distribution of income or principal from the donor's trust or fund) is limited to distributions of amounts from the donor's fund, and the factors described in paragraph (a)(8)(iv)(A)(*2*)(*i*) or (*ii*) of this section are not present;

(iii) Only the advice of the donor as to distributions of such donor's fund is solicited by the public charity and no procedure is provided for considering advice from persons other than the donor with respect to such fund; and

(iv) For the taxable year and all prior taxable years the public charity follows the advice of all donors with respect to their funds substantially all of the time.

(B) *Other action or withholding of action.* The terms of the transfer agreement, or any expressed or implied understanding, require the public charity to take or withhold action with respect to the transferred assets which is not designed to further one or more of the exempt purposes of the public charity, and such action or withholding of action would, if performed by the transferor private foundation with respect to such assets, have subjected the transferor to tax under chapter 42 (other than with respect to the minimum investment return requirement of section 4942(e)).

Reg. § 1.507-2(a)(8)

(C) *Assumption of leases, etc.* The public charity assumes leases, contractual obligations, or liabilities of the transferor private foundation, or takes the assets thereof subject to such liabilities (including obligations under commitments or pledges to donees of the transferor private foundation), for purposes inconsistent with the purposes or best interests of the public charity, other than the payment of the transferor's chapter 42 taxes incurred prior to the transfer to the public charity to the extent of the value of the assets transferred.

(D) *Retention of investment assets.* The transferee public charity is required by any restriction or agreement (other than a restriction or agreement imposed or required by law or regulatory authority), express or implied, to retain any securities or other investment assets transferred to it by the private foundation. In a case where such transferred assets consistently produce a low annual return of income, the Internal Revenue Service will examine carefully whether the transferee is required by any such restriction or agreement to retain such assets.

(E) *Right of first refusal.* An agreement is entered into in connection with the transfer of securities or other property which grants directly or indirectly to the transferor private foundation or any disqualified person with respect thereto a right of first refusal with respect to the transferred securities or other property when and if disposed of by the public charity, unless such securities or other property was acquired by the transferor private foundation subject to such right of first refusal prior to October 9, 1969.

(F) *Relationships.* An agreement is entered into between the transferor private foundation and the transferee public charity which establishes irrevocable relationships with respect to the maintenance or management of assets transferred to the public charity, such as continuing relationships with banks, brokerage firms, investment counselors, or other advisors with regard to the investments or other property transferred to the public charity (other than a relationship with a trustee, custodian, or agent for a community trust acting as such). The transfer of property to a public charity subject to contractual obligations which were established prior to November 11, 1976 between the transferor private foundation and persons other than disqualified persons with respect to such foundation will not be treated as prohibited under the preceding sentence, but only if such contractual obligations were not entered into pursuant to a plan to terminate the private foundation status of the transferor under section 507(b)(1)(A) and if the continuation of such contractual obligations is in the best interests of the public charity.

(G) *Other conditions.* Any other condition is imposed on action by the public charity which prevents it from exercising ultimate control over the assets received from the transferor private foundation for purposes consistent with its exempt purposes.

(v) *Examples.* The provisions of paragraph (a)(8) of this section may be illustrated by the following examples:

Example (1). The M Private Foundation transferred all of its net assets to the V Cancer Institute, a public charity described in section 170(b)(1)(A)(iii). Prior to the transfer, M's activities consisted of making grants to hospitals and universities to further research into the causes of cancer. Under the terms of the transfer, V is required to keep M's assets in a separate fund and use the income and principal to further cancer research. Although the assets may be used only for a limited purpose, this purpose is consistent with and in furtherance of V's exempt purposes, and does not prevent the transfer from being a distribution for purposes of section 507(b)(1)(A).

Example (2). The N Private Foundation transferred all of its assets to W University, a public charity described in section 170(b)(1)(A)(ii). Under the terms of the transfer, W is required to use the income and principal to endow a chair at the university to be known as the "John J. Doe Memorial Professorship", named after N's creator. Although the transferred assets are to be used for a specified purpose by W, this purpose is in furtherance of W's exempt educational purposes, and there are no conditions on investment or reinvestment of the principal or income. The use of the name of the foundation's creator for the chair is not a restriction which would prevent the transfer from being a distribution for purposes of section 507(b)(1)(A).

Example (3). The O Private Foundation transferred all of its net assets to X Bank as trustee for the P Community Trust, a community trust which is a public charity described in section 170(b)(1)(A)(vi). Under the terms of the transfer, X is to hold the assets in trust for P and is directed to distribute the income annually to the Y Church, a public charity described in Section 170(b)(1)(A)(i). The distribution of income to Y Church is consistent with P's exempt purposes. If the trust created by this transfer otherwise meets the requirements of § 1.170A-9(e)(11) as a component part of P Community Trust, the assets transferred by O to X will be treated as distributed to one or more public charities within the meaning of section 507(b)(1)(A). The direction to distribute

Reg. § 1.507-2(a)(8)

the income to Y Church meets the conditions of paragraph (a)(8)(iii)(B) of this section and will therefore not disqualify the transfer under section 507(b)(1)(A).

Example (4). The U Private Foundation transferred all of its net assets to Z Bank as trustee for the R Community Trust, a community trust which is a public charity described in section 170(b)(1)(A)(vi). Under the terms of the transfer, Z is to hold the assets in trust for R and distribute the income to those public charities described in section 170(b)(1)(A)(i) through (vi) that are designated by B, the creator of U. R's governing body has no authority during B's lifetime to vary B's direction. Under the terms of the transfer, it is intended that Z retain the transferred assets in their present form for a period of 20 years, or until the date of B's death if it occurs before the expiration of such period. Upon the death of B, R will have the power to distribute the income to such public charities as it selects and may dispose of the corpus as it sees fit.

Under paragraph (a)(8)(iv)(A) or (D) of this section, as a result of the restrictions imposed with respect to the transferred assets, there has been no distribution of all U's net assets within the meaning of section 507(b)(1)(A) at the time of the transfer. In addition, U has not transferred its net assets to a component part of R Community Trust, but rather to a separate trust described in § 1.170A-9(e)(14).

(vi) *Transitional rule.* If the governing instrument of the public charity (or an instrument of transfer) lacks the factors described in paragraph (a)(8)(i)(D) or (ii) of this section, but with respect to gifts or bequests acquired before January 1, 1982, the public charity changes its governing instrument (or instrument of transfer) by the later of November 11, 1977, or one year after the gift or bequest is acquired, in order to conform such instrument to such provisions, then such an instrument shall be treated as consistent with such provisions for taxable years beginning prior to the date of change. In addition, if prior to the later of such dates, the organization has instituted court proceedings in order to conform such an instrument, then it may apply (prior to the later of such dates) for an extension of the period to conform such instrument to such provisions. Such application shall be made to the Commissioner of Internal Revenue, Attention E:EO, Washington, D.C. 20224. The Commissioner, at the Commissioner's discretion, may grant such an extension, if in the Commissioner's opinion such a change will conform the instrument to such provisions, and the change will be made within a reasonable time.

(b) *Operation as a public charity.*—(1) *In general.* Under section 507(b)(1)(B) an organization can terminate its private foundation status if the organization:

(i) Meets the requirements of section 509(a)(1), (2), or (3) by the end of the 12-month period (as extended by paragraph (c)(3)(i) of this section) beginning with its first taxable year which begins after December 31, 1969, or for a continuous period of 60 calendar months beginning with the first day of any taxable year which begins after December 31, 1969;

(ii) In compliance with section 507(b)(1)(B)(ii) and subparagraph (3) of this paragraph, properly notifies the district director before the commencement of such 12-month or 60-month period or before March 29, 1973, that it is terminating its private foundation status; and

(iii) Properly establishes immediately after the expiration of such 12-month or 60-month period that such organization has complied with the requirements of section 509(a)(1), (2) or (3) by the end of the 12-month period or during the 60-month period, as the case may be, in the manner described in subparagraph (4) of this paragraph.

(2) *Relationship of section 507(b)(1)(B) to section 507(a), (c), and (g).* Since section 507(a) does not apply to a termination described in section 507(b)(1)(B), a private foundation's notification that it is commencing a termination pursuant to section 507(b)(1)(B) will not be treated as a notification described in section 507(a) even if the private foundation does not successfully terminate its private foundation status pursuant to section 507(b)(1)(B). A private foundation which terminates its private foundation status under section 507(b)(1)(B) does not incur tax under section 507(c) and, therefore, no abatement of such tax under section 507(g) is required.

(3) *Notification of termination.* In order to comply with the requirements under section 507(b)(1)(B)(ii), an organization shall before the commencement of the 12-month or 60-month period under section 507(b)(1)(B)(i) (or before March 29, 1973) or, in the case of the 12-month period) for a community trust, before May 11, 1977, notify the district director of its intention to terminate its private foundation status. Such notification shall contain the following information:

(i) The name and address of the private foundation;

(ii) Its intention to terminate its private foundation status;

(iii) Whether the 12-month or 60-month period shall apply;

Reg. § 1.507-2(b)(1)

(iv) The Code section under which it seeks classification (section 509(a)(1), (2), or (3));

(v) If section 509(a)(1) is applicable, the clause of section 170(b)(1)(A) involved;

(vi) The date its regular taxable year begins; and

(vii) The date of commencement of the 12-month or 60-month period.

(4) *Establishment of termination.* In order to comply with the requirements under section 507(b)(1)(B)(iii), an organization shall within 90 days after the expiration of the 12-month or 60-month period, file such information with the district director as is necessary to make a determination as to the organization's status as an organization described under section 509(a)(1), (2), or (3) and the regulations thereunder. See paragraphs (c) and (d) of this section as to the information required to be submitted under this subparagraph.

(5) *Incomplete information; 12- and 60-month terminations.* The failure to supply, within the required time, all of the information required by subparagraph (3) or (4) of this paragraph is not alone sufficient to constitute a failure to satisfy the requirements of section 507(b)(1)(B). If the information which is submitted within the required time is incomplete and the organization supplies the necessary additional information at the request of the Commissioner within the additional time period allowed by him, the original submission will be considered timely.

(6) *Application of special rules and filing requirements.* An organization which has terminated its private foundation status under section 507(b)(1)(B) is not required to comply with the special rules set forth in section 508(a) and (b). Such organization is also not required to file a return under the provisions of section 6043(b) or 6050 by reason of termination of its private foundation status under the provisions of section 507(b)(1)(B).

(7) *Extension of time to assess deficiencies.* If a private foundation files a notification (described in subparagraph (3) of this paragraph) that it intends to begin a 60-month termination pursuant to section 507(b)(1)(B) and does not file a request for an advance ruling pursuant to paragraph (e) of this section, such private foundation may file with the notification described in subparagraph (3) of this paragraph a consent under section 6501(c)(4) to the effect that the period of limitation upon assessment under section 4940 for any taxable year within the 60-month termination period shall not expire prior to one year after the date of the expiration of the time prescribed by law for the assessment of a deficiency for the last taxable year within the 60-month period. Such consents, if filed, will ordinarily be accepted by the Commissioner. See paragraph (f)(3) of this section for an illustration of the procedure required to obtain a refund of the tax imposed by section 4940 in a case where such a consent is not in effect.

(c) *Twelve-month terminations*—(1) *Method of determining normal sources of support*—(i) *In general.* The 12-month termination provisions of section 507(b)(1)(B) permit a private foundation to terminate its private foundation status by changing its organizational structure, its operations, the sources of its support, or any combination thereof, in order to conform to the requirements of section 509(a)(1), (2), or (3) by the end of the 12-month period.

(ii) *Support requirements for twelve-month termination under section 170(b)(1)(A)(vi).* A private foundation attempting to meet the requirements of section 509(a)(1) as an organization described in section 170(b)(1)(A)(vi) will be considered "normally" to receive a substantial part of its support from governmental units or direct or indirect contributions from the general public if it can establish that it has changed the sources of its support before the close of the 12-month period to those of an organization described in section 170(b)(1)(A)(vi) and it can reasonably be expected to maintain its publicly supported status for subsequent years. In order to establish these facts, an organization shall submit all information sufficient to make a determination under § 1.170A-9(e) as if such provisions applied, including a description of all organizational and operational changes which have occurred during the 12-month period. It shall also submit detailed information with respect to its sources of support for the 12-month period, as well as for the four taxable years immediately preceding the 12-month period. In applying the tests contained in § 1.170A-9(e), however, data from periods preceding the 12-month period shall be disregarded except for purposes of determining whether the organization has effectively changed its sources of support and whether it can reasonably be expected to maintain such publicly supported status for subsequent years. Thus, for example, in applying the mathematical tests of § 1.170A-9(e) only data for the 12-month period may enter into the computation.

(iii) *Support requirements for twelve-month terminations under section 170(b)(1)(A)(iv).* Section 170(b)(1)(A)(iv) describes an organization which "normally" receives a substantial part of its support (exclusive of

Reg. § 1.507-2(c)(1)

income from related activities) from the United States or any state or political subdivision thereof, or from the general public, and which is organized and operated exclusively to receive, hold, invest, and administer property and to make expenditures to or for the benefit of certain colleges or universities. For purposes of the 12-month termination period, the rule set forth in subdivision (ii) of this subparagraph with respect to section 170(b)(1)(A)(vi) organizations shall be applicable in determining whether an organization "normally" receives a substantial part of its support from the sources required under section 170(b)(1)(A)(iv).

(iv) *Support requirements for twelve-month terminations under section 509(a)(2)*. An organization attempting to terminate its private foundation status under section 507(b)(1)(B) by meeting the requirements of section 509(a)(2) by the end of the 12-month period will be considered as "normally" receiving its support in compliance with the one-third support requirements of section 509(a)(2) if:

(*a*) For the 12-month period under section 507(b)(1)(B), the organization receives more than one-third of its support from gifts, grants, contributions, membership fees, and gross receipts from related activities (as limited by section 509(a)(2)(A)(ii)) and not more than one-third of its support from items described in section 509(a)(2)(B), and

(*b*) The organization can establish that it can reasonably be expected to maintain its continued public support for subsequent years. In order to establish a reasonable expectation of continued public support, an organization shall submit a detailed statement describing its past and current operations, any organizational or operational changes and when such changes have occurred, and any changes in its foundation managers (as defined in section 4946(b)(1)). Duplicate copies of its governing instrument and bylaws, with an indication of any amendments made, and detailed information with respect to its sources of support for the four taxable years immediately preceding the 12-month period shall also be submitted as part of the evidence that the organization can reasonably be expected to maintain its publicly supported status.

(2) *Organizational and operational tests*—(i) *Section 509(a)(3) organizations*—(*a*) *In general.* An organization attempting to terminate its private foundation status under section 507(b)(1)(B) by meeting the requirements of section 509(a)(3) by the end of the 12-month period is required to meet the organizational and operational test of section 509(a)(3)(A), in addition to the requirements of section 509(a)(3)(B) and (C), by the end of the 12-month period beginning with its first taxable year which begins after December 31, 1969. An organization may qualify under section 509(a)(3)(A) even though its original governing instrument did not limit its purposes to those set forth in section 509(a)(3)(A) and even though it operated for some other purpose before the end of the 12-month period, if it has amended its governing instrument and changed its operations to conform to the requirements of section 509(a)(3) by the end of the 12-month period.

(*b*) *Proof of changed status.* In order to establish that an organization described in (*a*) of this subdivision will continue to be operated exclusively for the required purposes in years subsequent to the end of the 12-month period, such organization shall submit a detailed statement describing its past and current operations, any organizational or operational changes and when such changes have occurred, any changes in foundation managers (as defined in section 4946(b)(1)), and duplicate copies of its governing instrument and bylaws, with an indication of any amendments made. A detailed statement of the relationship between such organization and the specified organizations described in section 509(a)(1) or (2) (as required by section 509(a)(3)(A) and (B)) and all pertinent information to establish that the organization does not violate the control requirements of section 509(a)(3)(C) shall also be submitted.

(ii) *Section 509(a)(1) organizations other than those described in section 170(b)(1)(A)((vi)*—(*a*) *In general.* An organization attempting to terminate its private foundation status under section 507(b)(1)(B) by meeting the requirements of section 170(b)(1)(A)(i), (ii), (iii), (iv), or (v) by the end of the 12-month period is required to be operated as an organization described in clauses (i), (ii), (iii), (iv), or (v) of section 170(b)(1)(A) by the end of the 12-month period beginning with its first taxable year which begins after December 31, 1969.

(*b*) *Proof of changed status.* In order to establish that it will continue to be operated as an organization described in section 509(a)(1) in years subsequent to the end of the 12-month period, the organization shall submit a detailed statement describing its past and current operations, any organizational or operational changes and when such changes have occurred, and any changes in its foundation managers (as defined in section 4946(b)(1)). Duplicate copies of its governing instrument and bylaws, with an indication of any amendments made, and its financial statements for the 4 taxable years immediately preceding the 12-month period shall also be submitted as evidence that the organization can reasonably be expected to maintain its status as an organization described in section 170(b)(1)(A)(i), (ii), (iii), (iv), or (v).

(3) *Extensions of the 12-month period.* (i) For purposes of this section, an organization may accomplish a 12-month termination if it meets the requirements of section 507(b)(1)(B) and this paragraph for such a termination with respect to any of the following periods:

(*a*) The 12-month period beginning with the organization's first taxable year which begins after December 31, 1969;

(*b*) The period described in paragraph (a)(5)(ii) of this section; or

(*c*) Any period consisting of two or more taxable years beginning with the organization's first taxable year beginning after December 31, 1969, and ending with any taxable year ending before the end of the period described in paragraph (a)(5)(ii) of this section.

(ii) An organization will be considered as "normally" meeting the requirements of section 170(b)(1)(A)(iv) or (vi) or 509(a)(2), as the case may be, if it meets the requirements of such provision with respect to any period described in subdivision (i) (*a*), (*b*), or (*c*) of this subparagraph. Thus, for example, an organization on a calendar year basis which seeks to convert to a section 509(a)(2) organization under section 507(b)(1)(B) may meet the one-third support requirement based on the aggregate support received during a period described in subdivision (i) (*a*), (*b*), or (*c*) of this subparagraph, for purposes of subparagraph (1)(iv) of this paragraph.

(4) *Status of organization subsequent to the 12-month period.* For purposes of sections 507 through 509, an organization, the status of which as a private foundation is terminated under section 507(b)(1), shall (except as provided in paragraph (b)(6) of this section) be treated as an organization created on the day after the date of such termination. However, termination of private foundation status under the provisions of section 507(b)(1)(B) is based upon an organization's submission of information establishing compliance by the end of the 12-month period with the requirements of subparagraph (1) or (2) of this paragraph. Therefore, if in the four taxable years immediately following the end of the 12-month period, the sources of support or the methods of operation of the organization are materially different from the facts and circumstances presented during the 12-month period upon which the determination under section 507(b)(1)(B)(iii) was made (and such material difference adversely affects such determination), the organization will be deemed not to have satisfied the requirements of section 507(b)(1)(B). Under such circumstances, section 509(c) will not apply and the organization will continue to remain subject to the provisions of section 507. However, the status of grants and contributions under sections 170, 4942, and 4945 will not be affected until the Internal Revenue Service makes notice to the public (such as by publication in the Internal Revenue Bulletin) that the organization has been deleted from classification as an organization described in section 509(a)(1), (2), or (3) unless the donor (1) was in part responsible for, or was aware of, the act or failure to act that resulted in the organization's inability to satisfy the requirements of section 507(b)(1)(B), or (2) had knowledge that such organization would be deleted from classification as an organization described in section 509(a)(1), (2) or (3). Prior to the making of any grant or contribution which allegedly will not result in the grantee's loss of classification under section 509(a)(1), (2), or (3), a potential grantee organization may request a ruling whether such grant or contribution may be made without such loss of classification. A request for such ruling may be filed by the grantee organization with the district director. The issuance of such ruling will be at the sole discretion of the Commissioner.

(d) *Sixty-month terminations*—(1) *Method of determining normal sources of support.* (i) In order to meet the requirements of section 507(b)(1)(B) for the 60-month termination period as a section 509(a)(1) or (2) organization, an organization must meet the requirements of section 509(a)(1) or (2), as the case may be, for a continuous period of at least 60 calendar months. In determining whether an organization seeking status under section 509(a)(1) as an organization described in section 170(b)(1)(A)(iv) or (vi) or under section 509(a)(2) "normally" meets the requirements set forth under such sections, support received in taxable years prior to the commencement of the 60-month period shall not be taken into consideration, except as otherwise provided in this section. Therefore, in such cases rules similar to the rules applicable to new organizations would apply.

(ii) For purposes of section 507(b)(1)(B), an organization will be considered to be a section 509(a)(1) organization described in section 170(b)(1)(A)(vi) for a continuous period of 60 calendar months only if the organization satisfies the provisions of § 1.170A-9(e) based upon aggregate data for such entire period, rather than for any shorter period set forth in § 1.170A-9(e). Except for the substitution of such 60-month period for the periods described in § 1.170A-9(e), all

Reg. § 1.507-2(d)(1)

other provisions of such regulations pertinent to determining an organization's normal sources of support shall remain applicable.

(iii) For purposes of section 507(b)(1)(B), an organization will be considered to be a section 509(a)(2) organization only if such organization meets the support requirements set forth in section 509(a)(2)(A) and (B) for the continuous period of 60 calendar months prescribed under section 507(b)(1)(B), rather than for any shorter period set forth in the regulations under section 509(a)(2). Except for the substitution of such 60-month period for the periods described in the regulations under section 509(a)(2), all other provisions of such regulations pertinent to determining an organization's normal sources of support shall remain applicable.

(2) *Organizational and operational tests.* In order to meet the requirements of section 507(b)(1)(B) for the 60-month termination period as an organization described in section 170(b)(1)(A)(i), (ii), (iii), (iv), or (v) or section 509(a)(3), as the case may be, an organization must meet the requirements of the applicable provisions for a continuous period of at least 60 calendar months. For purposes of section 507(b)(1)(B), an organization will be considered to be such an organization only if it satisfies the requirements of the applicable provision (including with respect to section 509(a)(3), the organizational and operational test set forth in subparagraph (A) thereof) at the commencement of such 60-month period and continuously thereafter during such period.

(e) *Advance rulings for 60-month terminations*—(1) *In general.* An organization which files the notification required by section 507(b)(1)(B)(ii) that it is commencing a 60-month termination may obtain an advance ruling from the Commissioner that it can be expected to satisfy the requirements of section 507(b)(1)(B)(i) during the 60-month period. Such an advance ruling may be issued if the organization can reasonably be expected to meet the requirements of section 507(b)(1)(B)(i) during the 60-month period. The issuance of a ruling will be discretionary with the Commissioner.

(2) *Basic consideration.* In determining whether an organization can reasonably be expected (within the meaning of subparagraph (1) of this paragraph) to meet the requirements of section 507(b)(1)(B)(i) for the 60-month period, the basic consideration is whether its organizational structure (taking into account any revisions made prior to the beginning of the 60-month period), proposed programs or activities, intended method of operation, and projected sources of support are such as to indicate that the organization is likely to satisfy the requirements of section 509(a)(1), (2), or (3) and paragraph (d) of this section during the 60-month period. In making such a determination, all pertinent facts and circumstances shall be considered.

(3) *Reliance by grantors and contributors.* For purposes of sections 170, 545(b)(2), 556(b)(2), 642(c), 4942, 4945, 2055, 2106(a)(2), and 2522, grants or contributions to an organization which has obtained a ruling referred to in this paragraph will be treated as made to an organization described in section 509(a)(1), (2), or (3), as the case may be, until notice that such advance ruling is being revoked is made to the public (such as by publication in the Internal Revenue Bulletin). The preceding sentence shall not apply, however, if the grantor or contributor was responsible for, or aware of, the act or failure to act that resulted in the organization's failure to meet the requirements of section 509(a)(1), (2), or (3) or acquired knowledge that the Internal Revenue Service had given notice to such organization that its advance ruling would be revoked. Prior to the making of any grant or contribution which allegedly will not result in the grantee's failure to meet the requirements of section 509(a)(1), (2), or (3), a potential grantee organization may request a ruling whether such grant or contribution may be made without such failure. A request for such ruling may be filed by the grantee organization with the district director. The issuance of such ruling will be at the sole discretion of the Commissioner. The organization must submit all information necessary to make a determination on the factors referred to in subparagraph (2) of this paragraph. If a favorable ruling is issued, such ruling may be relied upon by the grantor or contributor of the particular contribution in question for purposes of sections 170, 507, 545(b)(2), 556(b)(2), 642(c), 4942, 4945, 2055, 2106(a)(2), and 2522.

(4) *Reliance by organization.* An organization obtaining an advance ruling pursuant to this paragraph can not rely on such a ruling. Consequently, if the organization does not pay the tax imposed by section 4940 for any taxable year or years during the 60-month period, and it is subsequently determined that such tax is due for such year or years (because the organization did not in fact complete a successful termination pursuant to section 507(b)(1)(B) and was not treated as an organization described in section 509(a)(1), (2), or (3) for such year or years), the organization is liable for interest in accordance with section 6601 if any amount of tax under section 4940 has not been paid on or before the last date prescribed for payment. However, since any failure to pay such tax during the 60-month period (or prior to the

Reg. § 1.507-2(d)(2)

revocation of such ruling) is due to reasonable cause, the penalty under section 6651 with respect to the tax imposed by section 4940 shall not apply.

(5) *Extension of time to assess deficiencies.* The advance ruling described in subparagraph (1) of this paragraph shall be issued only if such organization's request for an advance ruling is filed with a consent under section 6501(c)(4) to the effect that the period of limitation upon assessment under section 4940 for any taxable year within the advance ruling period shall not expire prior to one year after the date of the expiration of the time prescribed by law for the assessment of a deficiency for the last taxable year within the 60-month period.

(f) *Effect on grantors or contributors and on the organization itself*—(1) *Effect of satisfaction of requirements for termination*—(i) *Treatment during the termination period.* In the event that an organization satisfies the requirements of section 507(b)(1)(B) for termination of its private foundation status by the end of the 12-month period or during the continuous 60-month period, such organization shall be treated for such entire 12-month or 60-month period in the same manner as an organization described in section 509(a)(1), (2), or (3).

(ii) *Twelve-month terminations by fiscal-year organizations.* In the case of an organization which operates on a fiscal year basis and terminates its private foundation status by the end of the 12-month period beginning with its first taxable year which begins after December 31, 1969, such 12-month period shall, for purposes of this paragraph, be treated as including the period between January 1, 1970, and the last day of the taxable year immediately preceding its first taxable year which begins after December 31, 1969, so long as the requirements of section 507(b)(1)(B) and paragraph (c) of this section are met by the end of the 12-month period (including such additional period).

(2) *Failure to meet termination requirements*—(i) *In general.* Except as otherwise provided in subdivision (ii) of this subparagraph and paragraph (e) of this section, any organization which fails to satisfy the requirements of section 507(b)(1)(B) for termination of its private foundation status by the end of the 12-month period or during the continuous 60-month period shall be treated as a private foundation for the entire 12-month or 60-month period, for purposes of sections 507 through 509 and chapter 42, and grants or contributions to such an organization shall be treated as made to a private foundation for purposes of sections 170, 507(b)(1)(A), 4942, and 4945.

(ii) *Certain 60-month terminations.* Notwithstanding subdivision (i) of this subparagraph, if an organization fails to satisfy the requirements of section 509(a)(1), (2), or (3) for the continuous 60-month period but does satisfy the requirements of section 509(a)(1), (2), or (3), as the case may be, for any taxable year or years during such 60-month period, the organization shall be treated as a section 509(a)(1), (2), or (3) organization for such taxable year or years and grants or contributions made during such taxable year or years shall be treated as made to an organization described in section 509(a)(1), (2), or (3). In addition, sections 507 through 509 and chapter 42 shall not apply to such organization for any taxable year within such 60-month period for which it does meet such requirements. For purposes of determining whether an organization satisfies the requirements of section 509(a)(1), (2), or (3) for any taxable year in the 60-month period, the organization shall be treated as if it were a new organization with its first taxable year beginning on the date of the commencement of the 60-month period. Thus, for example, if an organization were attempting to terminate its private foundation status under section 507(b)(1)(B) by meeting the requirements of section 170(b)(1)(A)(vi), the rules under § 1.170A-9(e) relating to the initial determination of status of a new organization would apply.

(iii) *Aggregate tax benefit.* For purposes of section 507(d), the organization's aggregate tax benefit resulting from the organization's section 501(c)(3) status shall continue to be computed from the date from which such computation would have been made, but for the notice filed under section 507(b)(1)(B)(ii), except that any taxable year within such 60-month period for which such organization meets the requirements of section 509(a)(1), (2), or (3) shall be excluded from such computations.

(iv) *Excess business holdings.* See section 4943 and the regulations thereunder for rules relating to decreases in a private foundation's holdings in a business enterprise which are caused by the foundation's failure to terminate its private foundation status after giving the notification for termination under section 507(b)(1)(B)(ii).

(3) *Example.* The provisions of this paragraph may be illustrated by the following example:

Example. Y, a calendar year private foundation, notifies the district director that it intends to terminate its private foundation status by converting into a publicly supported organization

Reg. § 1.507-2(f)(3)

described in section 170(b)(1)(A)(vi) and that its 60-month termination period will commence on January 1, 1974. Y does not obtain a ruling described in paragraph (e) of this section. Based upon its support for 1974 Y does not qualify as a publicly supported organization within the meaning of § 1.170A-9(e) and this paragraph. Consequently, in order to avoid the risks of penalties and interest if Y fails to terminate within the 60-month period, Y files its return as a private foundation and pays the tax imposed by section 4940. Similarly, based upon its support for the period 1974 through 1975, Y fails to qualify as such a publicly supported organization and files its return and pays the tax imposed by section 4940 for both 1975 and 1976. Since a consent (described in paragraph (b)(7) of this section) which would prevent the period of limitation from expiring is not in effect, in order to be able to file a claim for refund, Y and the district director agree to extend the period of limitation for all taxes imposed under chapter 42. However, based upon its support for the period 1974 through 1976 Y does qualify as a publicly supported organization, and therefore shall not be treated as a private foundation for either 1977 or 1978 even if it fails to terminate within the 60-month period. However, based upon the aggregate data for the entire 60-month period (1974 through 1978), Y does qualify as an organization described in section 170(b)(1)(A)(vi). Consequently, pursuant to this paragraph, Y is treated as if it had been a publicly-supported organization for the entire 60-month period. Y files claim for refund for the taxes paid under section 4940 for the years 1974, 1975 and 1976, and such taxes are refunded.

(g) *Special transitional rules for organizations operating as public charities.* Section 4940 imposes a tax upon private foundations with respect to the carrying on of activities for each taxable year. For purposes of section 4940, an organization which terminates its private foundation status under section 507(b)(1)(B) by the end of the period described in paragraph (a)(5)(ii) of this section will not be considered as carrying on activities within the meaning of section 4940 during such period. Such organization will therefore not be subject to the tax imposed under section 4940 for such period. Consequently, in the case of an organization seeking to terminate its private foundation status under section 507(b)(1)(B), if the period described in paragraph (a)(5)(ii) of this section has not expired prior to the due date for the organization's annual return required to be filed under section 6033 or 6012 (determined with regard to any extension of time for filing the return) for its first taxable year which begins after December 31, 1969 (or any other taxable year ending before the expiration of the period described in paragraph (a)(5)(ii) of this paragraph) and if the organization has not terminated its private foundation status under section 507(b)(1)(B) by such date, then notwithstanding the provisions of paragraph (f) of this section, the organization must take either of the following courses of action:

(1) Complete and file its annual return including the line relating to excise taxes on investment income, by such date, and pay the tax on investment income imposed under section 4940 at the time it files its annual return. If such organization subsequently terminates its private foundation status under section 507(b)(1)(B) within a period specified in paragraph (c)(3)(i) of this section, it may file a claim for refund of the tax paid under section 4940; or

(2) Complete and file its annual return, except for the line relating to excise taxes on investment income, by such date, and in lieu of paying the tax on investment income imposed under section 4940, file a statement with its annual return which establishes that the organization has taken affirmative action by such date to terminate its private foundation status under section 507(b)(1)(B). Such statement must indicate the type of affirmative action taken and explain how such action will result in the termination of its private foundation status under section 507(b)(1)(B). Such affirmative action may include making application to the appropriate State court for approval to amend the provisions of the organization's trust instrument to limit payments to specified section 509(a)(1) or (2) beneficiaries pursuant to section 509(a)(3) in the case of a charitable trust; commencing a fund-raising drive among the general public in the case of an organization seeking to become a section 170(b)(1)(A)(vi) or 509(a)(2) organization; or the passage of a resolution by the organization's governing body or the filing of an amendment to the organization's articles of incorporation permitting a change in the operations of the organization to enable it to conform to the provisions of section 509(a)(1), (2), or (3) in the case of a not-for-profit corporation. An organization may take such affirmative action and may terminate its private foundation status under section 507(b)(1)(B) in reliance upon 26 CFR § 13.12 (rev. as of 1/1/72) and upon the provisions of the notices of proposed rule making under sections 170(b)(1)(A), 507(b)(1), and 509. Thus, if an organization meets the requirements of the provisions of the notice of proposed rule making as a section 509(a)(3) organization, such organization may terminate its private foundation status under section 507(b)(1)(B) in reliance upon such provisions prior to the expiration of the

Reg. § 1.507-2(g)(1)

period described in paragraph (a)(5)(ii) of this section. If such organization, however, fails to terminate its private foundation status under section 507(b)(1)(B) within the period specified in paragraph (a)(5)(ii) of this section by failing to meet the requirements of either the notices of proposed rule making under section 170(b)(1)(A), 507(b)(1), or 509 or the final regulations published under these code sections, the tax imposed under section 4940 shall be treated as if due from the due date for its annual return (determined without regard to any extension of time for filing its return).

While an organization can terminate its private foundation status under section 507(b)(1)(B) by operation as a section 509(a)(1), (2) or (3) organization in reliance upon the provisions of this paragraph, it will retain its status as a section 509(a)(1), (2) or (3) organization after the publication of final regulations under sections 170(b)(1)(A), 507, and 509 only if it meets the requirements of such final regulations. [Reg. § 1.507-2.]

☐ [T.D. 7248, 12-29-72. Amended by T.D. 7290, 11-16-73, by T.D. 7440, 11-11-76, by T.D. 7465, 1-9-77, and by T.D. 7784, 7-22-81.]

[Reg. § 1.507-3]

§ 1.507-3. Special rules; transferee foundations.—(a) *General rule.* (1) For purposes of Part II, subchapter F, chapter 1 of the Code, in the case of a transfer of assets of any private foundation to another private foundation pursuant to any liquidation, merger, redemption, recapitalization, or other adjustment, organization, or reorganization, the transferee organization shall not be treated as a newly created organization. Thus, in the case of a significant disposition of assets to one or more private foundations within the meaning of paragraph (c) of this section, the transferee organization shall not be treated as a newly created organization. A transferee organization to which this paragraph applies shall be treated as possessing those attributes and characteristics of the transferor organization which are described in subparagraphs (2), (3) and (4) of this paragraph.

(2)(i) A transferee organization to which this paragraph applies shall succeed to the aggregate tax benefit of the transferor organization in an amount determined as follows: Such amount shall be an amount equal to the amount of such aggregate tax benefit multiplied by a fraction the numerator of which is the fair market value of the assets (less encumbrances) transferred to such transferee and the denominator of which is the fair market value of the assets of the transferor (less encumbrances) immediately before the transfer. Fair market value shall be determined as of the time of the transfer.

(ii) Notwithstanding subdivision (i) of this subparagraph, a transferee organization which is not effectively controlled (within the meaning of § 1.482-1(a)(3)), directly or indirectly, by the same person or persons who effectively control the transferor organization shall not succeed to an aggregate tax benefit in excess of the fair market value of the assets transferred at the time of the transfer.

(iii) This subparagraph may be illustrated by the following examples:

Example (1). Pursuant to a transfer described in section 507(b)(2), F, a private foundation, transfers to G, a private foundation, all of its assets, which have a fair market value of $400,000. Immediately before the transfer F's aggregate tax benefit was $200,000, and G's aggregate tax benefit was $300,000. After the transfer G's aggregate tax benefit is $500,000 ($200,000 + $300,000).

Example (2). Pursuant to a transfer described in section 507(b)(2), M, a private foundation, transfers all of its assets, which immediately prior to the transfer have a fair market value of $100,000. The assets were transferred to the following organizations at the following fair market values (determined at the time of transfer) $40,000 to N, a private foundation, $30,000 to O, a private foundation, and $30,000 to P, an organization described in section 170(b)(1)(A)(vi). Immediately before the transfer M's aggregate tax benefit was $50,000. Therefore, N succeeds to M's aggregate tax benefit to the extent of $20,000 ($50,000 × $40,000/$100,000) and O succeeds to M's aggregate tax benefit to the extent of $15,000 ($50,000 × $30,000/$100,000). The remaining $15,000 of M's aggregate tax benefit is retained by M as M has not terminated under section 507.

Example (3). Assume the same facts as in Example (2) except that the transfers were made as follows: M transferred $30,000 to N on January 1, 1972, $40,000 to P on July 1, 1972 and $30,000 to O on December 31, 1972. Further, assume that the fair market value of the assets and the aggregate tax benefit do not change during 1972 and that O is not effectively controlled (directly or indirectly) by the same person or persons who effectively control M. N succeeds to M's aggregate tax benefit to the extent of $15,000 ($50,000 × $30,000/$100,000). However, since $40,000 of the remaining $70,000 ($100,000 − $30,000) of assets of M was transferred to P on July 1, 1972, immediately before the transfer to O, the fair market value of the assets held by M is $30,000 ($70,000 − $40,000). On the other hand, because

P is not a private foundation, M's aggregate tax benefit immediately before the transfer to O remains $35,000 ($50,000 − $15,000). Therefore, before applying subdivision (ii) of this subparagraph, O would succeed to $35,000 ($35,000 × $30,000/$30,000) of M's aggregate tax benefit. However, applying subdivision (ii) of this subparagraph since M transferred only $30,000 to O, O shall succeed to only $30,000 of M's aggregate tax benefit. The remaining $5,000 ($35,000 − $30,000) of M's aggregate tax benefit is retained by M as M has not terminated under section 507.

(3) For purposes of section 507(d)(2), in the event of a transfer of assets described in section 507(b)(2), any person who is a "substantial contributor" (within the meaning of section 507(d)(2)) with respect to the transferor foundation shall be treated as a "substantial contributor" with respect to the transferee foundation, regardless of whether such person meets the $5,000-two percent test with respect to the transferee organization at any time. If a private foundation makes a transfer described in section 507(b)(2) to two or more transferee private foundations, any person who is a "substantial contributor" with respect to the transferor foundation prior to such transfer shall be considered a "substantial contributor" with respect to each transferee private foundation.

(4) If a private foundation incurs liability for one or more of the taxes imposed under chapter 42 (or any penalty resulting therefrom) prior to, or as a result of, making a transfer of assets described in section 507(b)(2) to one or more private foundations, in any case where transferee liability applies each transferee foundation shall be treated as receiving the transferred assets subject to such liability to the extent that the transferor foundation does not satisfy such liability.

(5) Except as provided in subparagraph (9) of this paragraph, a private foundation is required to meet the distribution requirements of section 4942 for any taxable year in which it makes a section 507(b)(2) transfer of all or part of its net assets to another private foundation. Such transfer shall itself be counted toward satisfaction of such requirements to the extent the amount transferred meets the requirements of section 4942(g). However, where the transferor has disposed of all of its assets, the record-keeping requirements of section 4942(g)(3)(B) shall not apply during any period in which it has no assets. Such requirements are applicable for any taxable year other than a taxable year during which the transferor has no assets.

(6) For purposes of section 4943(c)(4), (5), and (6), whenever a private foundation makes a section 507(b)(2) transfer of all or part of its net assets to another private foundation, the applicable period of time described in section 4943(c)(4), (5), or (6) shall include both the period during which the transferor foundation held such assets and the period during which the transferee foundation holds such assets.

(7) Except as provided in subparagraph (9) of this paragraph, where the transferor has disposed of all of its assets, during any period in which the transferor has no assets, section 4945(d)(4) and (h) shall not apply to the transferee or the transferor with respect to any "expenditure responsibility" grants made by the transferor. However, the exception contained in this subparagraph shall not apply with respect to any information reporting requirements imposed by section 4945 and the regulations thereunder for any year in which any such transfer is made.

(8)(i) Except as provided in subdivision (ii) of this subparagraph or subparagraph (6) or (9) of this paragraph, whenever a private foundation makes a transfer of assets described in section 507(b)(2) to one or more private foundations, the transferee foundation:

(a) Will not be treated as being in existence prior to January 1, 1970 with respect to any transferred assets;

(b) will not be treated as holding the transferred assets prior to January 1, 1970; and

(c) Will not be treated as having engaged in, or become subject to, any transaction, lease, contract, or other obligation with respect to the transferred assets prior to January 1, 1970.

(ii) Notwithstanding subdivision (i) of this subparagraph, the provisions enumerated in (a) through (g) of this subdivision shall apply to the transferee foundation with respect to the assets transferred to the same extent and in the same manner that they would have applied to the transferor foundation had the transfer described in section 507(b)(2) not been effected:

(a) Section 4940(c)(4)(B) and the regulations thereunder with respect to basis of property,

(b) Section 4942(f)(4) and the regulations thereunder with respect to distributions of income,

(c) Section 101(l)(2) of the Tax Reform Act of 1969 (83 Stat. 533), as amended by sections 1301 and 1309 of the Tax Reform Act of 1976 (90 Stat. 1713, 1729), with respect to the provisions of section 4941.

(d) Section 101(l)(3)(A) of the Tax Reform Act of 1969 (83 Stat. 534) with respect to the provisions of section 4942, but only if the transferor qualified for the application of such

Reg. § 1.507-3(a)(3)

section immediately before the transfer, and at least 85 percent of the fair market value of the net assets of the transferee immediately after the transfer was received pursuant to the transfer,

(e) Section 101(l)(3)(B) through (E) of the Tax Reform Act of 1969 (83 Stat. 534) with respect to the provisions of section 4942,

(f) Section 101(l)(5) of the Tax Reform Act of 1969 (83 Stat. 535) with respect to the provisions of section 4945, and

(g) Section 101(l)(6) of the Tax Reform Act of 1969 (83 Stat. 535) with respect to the provisions of section 508(e).

(9)(i) If a private foundation transfers all of its net assets to one or more private foundations which are effectively controlled (within the meaning of § 1.482-1(a)(3)), directly or indirectly, by the same person or persons which effectively controlled the transferor private foundation, for purposes of chapter 42 (sections 4940 et seq.) and part II of subchapter F of chapter 1 of the Code (sections 507 through 509) such a transferee private foundation shall be treated as if it were the transferor. However, where proportionality is appropriate, such a transferee private foundation shall be treated as if it were the transferor in the proportion which the fair market value of the assets (less encumbrances) transferred to such transferee bears to the fair market value of the assets (less encumbrances) of the transferor immediately before the transfer.

(ii) Subdivision (i) of this subparagraph shall not apply to the requirements under sections 6033, 6056, and 6104 which must be complied with by the transferor private foundation, nor to the requirement under section 6043 that the transferor file a return with respect to its liquidation, dissolution, or termination.

(iii) This subparagraph may be illustrated by the following examples:

Example (1). The trustees of X charitable trust, a private foundation, form the Y charitable corporation, also a private foundation, in order to facilitate the conduct of their activities. The trustees of X are also the directors of Y. Y has the same charitable purposes as X. All of the assets of X are transferred to Y, and Y continues to carry on X's charitable activities. Under such circumstances, Y shall be treated as if it were X for the purposes of subdivision (i) of this subparagraph. Thus, for example, Y will be permitted to take advantage of any special rules or savings provisions with respect to chapter 42 to the same extent as X could have if X had continued in existence.

Example (2). A and B are the trustees of the P charitable trust, a private foundation, and are the only substantial contributors to P. On July 1, 1973, in order to facilitate accomplishment of diverse charitable purposes, A and B create and control the R Foundation, the S Foundation and the T Foundation and transfer the net assets of P to R, S, and T. As of the end of 1973, P has an outstanding grant to Foundation W and has been required to exercise expenditure responsibility with respect to this grant under sections 4945(d)(4) and (h). Under these circumstances, R, S, and T shall each be treated as if they are P in the proportion the fair market value of the assets transferred to each bears to the fair market value of the assets of P immediately before the transfer. Since R, S, and T are treated as P, absent a specific provision for exercising expenditure responsibility with respect to the grant to W, each of them is required to exercise expenditure responsibility with respect to such grant. If, as a part of the transfer to R, P assigned, and R assumed, P's duties with respect to the expenditure responsibility grant to W, only R would be required to exercise expenditure responsibility with respect to the grant to W. Since R, S, and T are treated as P rather than as recipients of "expenditure responsibility" grants, there are no expenditure responsibility requirements which must be exercised under sections 4945(d)(4) and (h) with respect to the transfers of assets to R, S, and T.

(10) For certain rules relating to filing requirements where a private foundation has transferred all its net assets, see § 1.507-1(b)(9).

(b) *Status of transferee organization under section 507(b)(2).* Since a transfer of assets pursuant to any liquidation, merger, redemption, recapitalization, or other adjustment, organization or reorganization to an organization not described in section 501(c)(3) (other than an organization described in section 509(a)(4) or 4947 is a taxable expenditure under section 4945(d)(5), in order for such a transfer of assets not to be a taxable expenditure, it must be to an organization described in section 501(c)(3) (other than an organization described in section 509(a)(4)) or treated as described in section 501(c)(3) under section 4947. See § 53.4945-6(c)(3). Consequently, unless such a transferee is an organization described in section 509(a)(1), (2) or (3), the transferee is a private foundation and the rules of section 507(b)(2) and paragraph (a) of this section apply. On the other hand, if such a transfer of assets is made to a transferee organization which is not described in either section 501(c)(3) (other than an organization described in section 509(a)(4)) or 4947, and in order to correct the making of a taxable expenditure, such assets are transferred to a private

Reg. § 1.507-3(b)

foundation, section 507(b)(2) and paragraph (a) of this section shall apply as if the transfer of assets had been made directly to such private foundation.

(c) *Section 507(b)(2) transfers.* (1) A transfer of assets is described in section 507(b)(2) if it is made by a private foundation to another private foundation pursuant to any liquidation, merger, redemption, recapitalization, or other adjustment, organization, or reorganization. This shall include any organization or reorganization described in subchapter C of chapter 1. For purposes of section 507(b)(2), the terms "other adjustment, organization, or reorganization" shall include any partial liquidation or any other significant disposition of assets to one or more private foundations, other than transfers for full and adequate consideration or distributions out of current income. For purposes of this paragraph, a distribution out of current income shall include any distribution described in section 4942(h)(1)(A) and (B).

(2) The term "significant disposition of assets to one or more private foundations" shall include any disposition for a taxable year where the aggregate of:

(i) The dispositions to one or more private foundations for the taxable year, and

(ii) Where any disposition to one or more private foundations for the taxable year is part of a series of related dispositions made during prior taxable years, the total of the related dispositions made during such prior taxable years,

is 25 percent or more of the fair market value of the net assets of the foundation at the beginning of the taxable year (in the case of subdivision (i) of this subparagraph) or at the beginning of the first taxable year in which any of the series of related dispositions was made (in the case of subdivision (ii) of this subparagraph). A "significant disposition of assets" may occur in a single taxable year (as in subdivision (i) of this subparagraph) or over the course of two or more taxable years (as in subdivision (ii) of this subparagraph). The determination whether a significant disposition has occurred through a series of related distributions (within the meaning of subdivision (ii) of this subparagraph) will be made on the basis of all the facts and circumstances of the particular case. However, if one or more persons who are disqualified persons (within the meaning of section 4946) with respect to the transferor private foundation are also disqualified persons with respect to any of the transferee private foundation, such fact shall be *evidence that the transfer is* part of a series of related dispositions (within the meaning of subdivision (ii) of this subparagraph). In the case of a series of related dispositions described in subdivi-

sion (ii) of this subparagraph, each transferee private foundation shall (on any date) be subject to the provisions of section 507(b)(2) (with respect to all such dispositions made to it on or before such date) to the extent described in paragraphs (a) and (b) of this section.

(3) A private foundation which fails to meet the requirements of section 507(b)(1)(A) for a taxable year may be required to file a return under section 6043(b) by reason of a transfer of assets to one or more section 509(a)(1), (2), or (3) organizations. Hence, such filing does not necessarily mean that a section 507(b)(2) transfer has occurred. See § 1.6043-3(f)(1).

(4) This paragraph applies to any section 507(b)(2) transfer made by a private foundation referred to in section 170(b)(1)(E)(i), (ii), or (iii).

(5) The provisions of this paragraph may be illustrated by the following examples:

Example (1). M is a private foundation on the calendar year basis. It has net assets worth $100,000 as of January 1, 1971. In 1971, in addition to distributions out of current income, M transfers $10,000 to N, $10,000 to O, and $10,000 to P. N, O, and P are all private foundations. Under subparagraph (2)(i) of this paragraph, M has made a significant disposition of its assets in 1971 since M has disposed of more than 25 percent of its net assets (with respect to the fair market value of such assets as of January 1, 1971). M has therefore made section 507(b)(2) transfers within the meaning of this paragraph, and section 507(b)(2) applies to the transfers made to N, O, and P.

Example (2). U, a tax-exempt private foundation on the calendar year basis, has net assets worth $100,000 as of January 1, 1971. As part of a series of related dispositions in 1971 and 1972, U transfers in 1971, in addition to distributions out of current income, $10,000 to private Foundation X and $10,000 to private Foundation Y, and in 1972, in addition to distributions out of current income, U transfers $10,000 to private Foundation Z. Under subparagraph (2)(ii) of this paragraph, U is treated as having made a series of related dispositions in 1971 and 1972. The aggregate of the 1972 disposition (under subparagraph (2)(i) of this paragraph) and the series of related dispositions (under subparagraph (2)(ii) of this paragraph) is $30,000, which is more than 25 percent of the fair market value of U's net assets as of the beginning of 1971 ($100,000), the first year in which any such disposition was made. Thus, U has made a significant disposition of its assets and has made transfers described in section 507(b)(2). The provisions of paragraphs (a) and

Reg. § 1.507-3(c)(2)

(b) of this section apply to each of the transferees as of the date on which it received assets from U.

(d) *Inapplicability of section 507(a) to section 507(b)(2) transfers.* Unless a private foundation voluntarily gives notice pursuant to section 507(a)(1), a transfer of assets described in section 507(b)(2) will not constitute a termination of the transferor's private foundation status under section 507(a)(1). Such transfer must, nevertheless, satisfy the requirements of any pertinent provisions of chapter 42. See subparagraphs (5) through (7) of paragraph (a) of this section. However, if such transfer constitutes an act or failure to act which is described in section 507(a)(2)(A), then such transfer will be subject to the provisions of section 507(a)(2) rather than section 507(b)(2). For example, X, a private nonoperating foundation, transfers all of its net assets to Y, a private operating foundation, in 1971. X does not file the notice referred to in section 507(a)(1) and the transfer does not constitute either a willful and flagrant act (or failure to act), or one of a series of willful repeated acts (or failures to act), giving rise to liability for tax under chapter 42. Under these circumstances, the transfer is described in section 507(b)(2) and the provisions of paragraph (a) of this section apply with respect to Y. The private foundation status of X has not been terminated under section 507(a).

(e) *Transfers to certain section 509(a)(1), (2), or (3) organizations.* If a private foundation transfers all or part of its assets to one or more organizations described in section 509(a)(1), (2), or (3) and, within a period of three years from the date of such transfers, one or more of the transferee organizations lose their section 509(a)(1), (2), or (3) status and become private foundations, then for purposes of this section, a transfer of assets within the meaning of paragraph (c) of this section to such an organization which becomes a private foundation will be treated as a transfer described in section 507(b)(2), and the provisions of paragraph (a) of this section shall be treated as applying to such a transferee organization from the date on which any such transfer was made to it.

(f) *Certain transfers made during section 507(b)(1)(B) terminations.* If—

(1) During the course of the 12-month or 60-month period described in section 507(b)(1)(B), a private foundation makes one or more transfers to one or more private foundations;

(2) Such transfers are described in § 1.507-3(c)(1); and

(3) Even though the transferor foundation thereafter meets the requirements of section 507(b)(1)(B),

then for purposes of this section, the provisions of § 1.507-2(e) shall not apply with respect to such transfers, and such transfers will be treated as transfers described in section 507(b)(2) and § 1.507-3 rather than as transfers from an organization described in section 509(a)(1), (2), or (3). [Reg. § 1.507-3.]

☐ [T.D. 7233, 12-20-72. Amended by T.D. 7678, 2-25-80.]

[Reg. § 1.507-4]

§ 1.507-4. **Imposition of tax.**—(a) *General rule.* Section 507(c) imposes on each organization the private foundation status of which is terminated under section 507(a) a tax equal to the lower of:

(1) The amount which such organization substantiates by adequate records (or other corroborating evidence which may be required by the Commissioner) as the aggregate tax benefit (as defined in section 507(d)) resulting from the section 501(c)(3) status of such organization, or

(2) The value of the net assets of such organization.

(b) *Transfers not subject to section 507(c).* Private foundations which make transfers described in section 507(b)(1)(A) or (2) are not subject to the tax imposed under section 507(c) with respect to such transfers unless the provisions of section 507(a) become applicable. See § 1.507-1(b), § 1.507-2(a)(6) and § 1.507-3(d). [Reg. § 1.507-4.]

☐ [T.D. 7233, 12-20-72.]

[Reg. § 1.507-5]

§ 1.507-5. **Aggregate tax benefit; in general.**—(a) *General rule.* For purposes of section 507(c)(1), the aggregate tax benefit resulting from the section 501(c)(3) status of any private foundation is the sum of:

(1) The aggregate increases in tax under chapters 1, 11, and 12 (or the corresponding provisions of prior law) which would have been imposed with respect to all substantial contributors to the foundation if deductions for all contributions made by such contributors to the foundation after February 28, 1913, had been disallowed,

(2) The aggregate increases in tax under chapter 1 (or the corresponding provisions of prior law) which would have been imposed with respect to the income of the private foundation for taxable years beginning after December 31, 1912, if (i) it had not been exempt from tax under section 501(a) (or the corresponding provisions of prior law), and (ii) in the case of a trust, deductions under section 642(c) (or the corresponding provisions of prior law) had been limited to 20 percent of the taxable income of the trust (computed

Reg. § 1.507-5(a)(2)

without the benefit of section 642(c) but with the benefit of section 170(b)(1)(A)),

(3) The amount succeeded to from transferors under § 1.507-3(a) and section 507(b)(2), and

(4) Interest on the increases in tax determined under subparagraphs (1), (2), and (3) of this paragraph from the first date on which each such increase would have been due and payable to the date on which the organization ceases to be a private foundation.

(b) *Contributions.* In computing the amount of the aggregate increases in tax under subparagraph (1) of this paragraph, all deductions attributable to a particular contribution shall be included. For example, if a substantial contributor has taken deductions under sections 170 and 2522 (or the corresponding provisions of prior law) with respect to the same contribution, the amount of each deduction shall be included in the computations under section 507(d)(1)(A). Accordingly, the aggregate tax benefit may exceed the fair market value of the property transferred. [Reg. § 1.507-5.]

☐ [T.D. 7233, 12-20-72.]

[Reg. § 1.507-6]

§ 1.507-6. **Substantial contributor defined.**—(a) *Definition*—(1) *In general.* Except as provided in subparagraph (2) of this paragraph, the term "substantial contributor" means, with respect to a private foundation, any person (within the meaning of section 7701(a)(1)), whether or not exempt from taxation under section 501(a), who contributed or bequeathed an aggregate amount of more than $5,000 to the private foundation, if such amount is more than 2 percent of the total contributions and bequests received by the private foundation before the close of the taxable year of the private foundation in which a contribution or bequest is received by the foundation from such person. In the case of a trust, the term "substantial contributor" also means the creator of the trust. Such term does not include a governmental unit described in section 170(c)(1).

(2) *Special rules.* For purposes of sections 170(b)(1)(E)(iii), 507(d)(1), 508(d), 509(a)(1) and (3), and chapter 42, the term "substantial contributor" shall not include an organization which is described in section 509(a)(1), (2), or (3) or any other organization which is wholly owned by such section 509(a)(1), (2), or (3) organization. Furthermore, taking section 4941 (relating to taxes on self-dealing) in context, it would unduly restrict the activities of a private foundation if the term "substantial contributor" were to include any section 501(c)(3) organizations. It was not intended, for example, that a large grant for charitable purposes from one private foundation to another would forever preclude the latter from making any grants to, or otherwise dealing with the former. Accordingly, for purposes of section 4941 only, the term "substantial contributor" shall not include any organization which is described in section 501(c)(3) (other than an organization described in section 509(a)(4)).

(b) *Determination of substantial contributor*—(1) *In general.* In determining under paragraph (a) of this section whether the aggregate of contributions and bequests from a person exceeds 2 percent of the total contributions and bequests received by a private foundation, both the total of such amounts received by the private foundation, and the aggregate of such amounts contributed and bequeathed by such person, shall be determined as of the last day of each taxable year commencing with the first taxable year ending after October 9, 1969. Generally, under section 507(d)(2) and this section, except for purposes of valuation under section 507(d)(2)(B)(i), all contributions and bequests made before October 9, 1969, are deemed to have been made on October 9, 1969. For purposes of section 509(a)(2) and the support test described in § 1.509(a)-3(c), contributions and bequests before October 9, 1969, will be taken into account in the year when actually made. For example, in the case of a contribution or bequest of $6,000 in 1967, such contribution or bequest shall be treated as made by a substantial contributor in 1967 for purposes of section 509(a)(2) and § 1.509(a)-3(c) if such person met the $5,000—2 percent test as of December 31, 1967 and December 31, 1969 (in the case of a calendar year accounting period). Although the determination of the percentage of total contributions and bequests represented by a given donor's contributions and bequests is not made until the end of the foundation's taxable year, a donor is a substantial contributor as of the first date when the foundation received from him an amount sufficient to make him a substantial contributor. Except as otherwise provided in this subparagraph, such amount is treated for all purposes as made by a substantial contributor. Thus, the total contributions and bequests received by the private foundation from all persons, and the aggregate contributions and bequests made by a particular person, are to be determined as of December 31, 1969 (in the case of a calendar year organization which was in existence on that date), and the amounts included in each respective total would be all contributions and bequests received by the organization on or before that date, and all contributions and bequests made by the person on or before that date. Thereafter, a similar determination is to be made with respect to such private

Reg. § 1.507-6(a)(1)

foundation as of the end of each of its succeeding taxable years. Status as a substantial contributor, however, will date from the time when the donor first met the $5,000 and 2 percent test. Once a person is a substantial contributor with respect to a private foundation, he remains a substantial contributor even though he might not be so classified if a determination were first made at some later date. For instance, even though the aggregate contributions and bequests of a person become less than 2 percent of the total received by a private foundation (for example, because of subsequent contributions and bequests by other persons), such person remains a substantial contributor with respect to the foundation.

(2) *Examples.* The provisions of paragraph (a) of this section and this paragraph (b) may be illustrated by the following examples:

Example (1). On January 1, 1968, A, an individual, gave $4,500 to M, a private foundation on a calendar year basis. On June 1, 1969, A gave M the further sum of $1,500. Throughout its existence, through December 31, 1969, M has received $250,000 in contributions and bequests from all sources. As of June 1, 1969, A is a substantial contributor to M for purposes of section 509(a)(2).

Example (2). On September 9, 1966, B, an individual, gave $3,500 to N, a private foundation on a calendar year basis. On March 15, 1970 B gave N the further sum of $3,500. Throughout its existence, through December 31, 1970, N has received $200,000 in contributions and bequests from all sources. B is a substantial contributor to N as of March 15, 1970, since that is the first date on which his contributions met the 2 percent-$5,000 test.

Example (3). On July 21, 1964, X, a corporation, gave $2,000 to O, a private foundation on a calendar year basis. As of December 31, 1969, O had received $150,000 from all sources. On September 17, 1970, X gave O the further sum of $3,100. Through September 17, 1970, O had received $245,000 from all sources as total contributions and bequests. Between September 17, 1970, and December 31, 1970, however, O received $50,000 in contributions and bequests from others. X is not a substantial contributor to O, since X's contributions to O were not more than 2 percent of the total contributions and bequests received by O by December 31, 1970, the end of O's taxable year, even though X's contributions met that test at one point during the year.

Example (4). On September 16, 1970, C, an individual, gave $10,000 to P, a private foundation on a calendar year basis. Throughout its existence, and through December 31, 1970, the close of its taxable year, P had received a total of $100,000 in contributions and bequests. On January 3, 1971 P received a bequest of $1,000,000. C is a substantial contributor to P since he was a substantial contributor as of September 16, 1970, and therefore remains one even though he no longer meets the 2 percent test on a later date after the end of the taxable year of the foundation in which he first became a substantial contributor.

(c) *Special rules*—(1) *Contributions defined.* The term "contribution" shall, for purposes of section 507(d)(2), have the same meaning as such term has under section 170(c) and also include bequests, legacies, devises, and transfers within the meaning of section 2055 or 2106(a)(2). Thus, for purposes of section 507(d)(2), any payment of money or transfer of property without adequate consideration shall be considered a "contribution". Where payment is made or property transferred as consideration for admissions, sales of merchandise, performance of services, or furnishing of facilities to the donor, the qualification of all or any part of such payment or transfer as a "contribution" under section 170(c) shall determine whether and to what extent such payment or transfer constitutes a "contribution" under section 507(d)(2).

(2) *Valuation of contributions and bequests.* Each contribution or bequest to a private foundation shall be valued at fair market value when actually received by the private foundation.

(3) *Contributions and bequests by a spouse.* An individual shall be considered, for purposes of this section, to have made all contributions and bequests made by his spouse during the period of their marriage. Thus, for example, where W contributed $500,000 to P, a private foundation, in 1941 and that amount exceeded 2 percent of the total contributions received by P as of the end of P's first taxable year ending after October 9, 1969, H (W's spouse at the time of the 1941 gift) is considered to have made such contribution (even if W died prior to October 9, 1969, or their marriage was otherwise terminated prior to such date). Similarly, any bequest or devise shall be treated as having been made by the decedent's surviving spouse. [Reg. § 1.507-6.]

☐ [T.D. 7241, 12-28-72.]

[Reg. § 1.507-7]

§ 1.507-7. **Value of assets.**—(a) *In general.* For purposes of section 507(c), the value of the net assets shall be determined at whichever time such value is higher:

Reg. § 1.507-7(a)

(1) The first day on which action is taken by the organization which culminates in its ceasing to be a private foundation, or

(2) The date on which it ceases to be a private foundation.

(b) *Valuation dates.* (1) In the case of a termination under section 507(a)(1), the date referred to in paragraph (a)(1) of this section shall be the date on which the terminating foundation gives the notification described in section 507(a)(1).

(2) In the case of a termination under section 507(a)(2), the date referred to in paragraph (a)(1) of this section shall be the date of occurrence of the willful and flagrant act (or failure to act) or the first of the series of willful repeated acts (or failures to act) giving rise to liability for tax under chapter 42 and the imposition of tax under section 507(a)(2).

(c) *Fair market value.* For purposes of this section, fair market value shall be determined pursuant to the provisions of § 53.4942(a)-2(c)(4) of this chapter.

(d) *Net assets.* For purposes of section 507 and the regulations thereunder, the term "net assets" shall mean the gross assets of a private foundation reduced by all liabilities of the foundation, including appropriate estimated and contingent liabilities. Thus, a determination of net assets may reflect reductions for any liability or contingent liability for tax imposed upon the private foundation under chapter 42 with respect to acts or failures to act prior to termination, for any liability or contingent liability for failures to correct such acts or failures to act, or for any liability or estimated or contingent liability with respect to expenses associated with winding up the organization. If a private foundation's determination of net assets reflects any reduction for any estimated or contingent liability, such private foundation must establish, to the satisfaction of the Commissioner, the reasonableness of such reduction. If the amount of net assets reflects a reduction for any estimated or contingent liability, at the earlier of the final determination of the contingency or the termination of a reasonable time, any excess of the amount by which the gross assets was reduced over the amount of the liability shall be treated in the same manner as if such excess had been considered part of the net assets. [Reg. § 1.507-7.]

☐ [*T.D. 7233, 12-20-72.*]

[Reg. § 1.507-8]

§ 1.507-8. **Liability in case of transfers.**—For purposes of determining liability for the tax imposed under section 507(c) in the case of assets transferred by the private foundation, such tax shall be deemed to have been imposed on the first day on which action is taken by the organization which culminates in its ceasing to be a private foundation. If an organization's private foundation status is terminated under section 507(a)(2), the first day on which action is taken which culminates in its ceasing to be a private foundation (within the meaning of section 507(f)) shall be the date described in § 1.507-7(b)(2). If an organization terminates its private foundation status under section 507(a)(1), the first day on which action is taken which culminates in its ceasing to be a private foundation (within the meaning of section 507(f)) shall be the date described in § 1.507-7(b)(1). [Reg. § 1.507-8.]

☐ [*T.D. 7233, 12-20-72.*]

[Reg. § 1.507-9]

§ 1.507-9. **Abatement of taxes.**—(a) *General rule.* The Commissioner may at his discretion abate the unpaid portion of the assessment of any tax imposed by section 507(c), or any liability in respect thereof, if:

(1) The private foundation distributes all of its net assets to one or more organizations described in section 170(b)(1)(A) (other than in clauses (vii) or (viii)) each of which has been in existence and so described for a continuous period of at least 60 calendar months, or

(2) Effective assurance is given to the Commissioner in accordance with paragraphs (b) and (c) of this section that the assets of the organization which are dedicated to charitable purposes will, in fact, be used for charitable purposes.

The provisions of § 1.507-2(a)(2), (3), and (7) shall apply to distributions under subparagraph (1) of this paragraph. Since section 507(g) provides only for the abatement of tax imposed under section 507(c), no tax imposed under any provision of chapter 42 shall be abated under section 507(g). Where the taxpayer files a petition with the Tax Court with respect to a notice of deficiency regarding any tax under section 507(c), such tax shall be treated as having been assessed for the purposes of abatement of such tax under section 507(g) and the regulations thereunder.

(b) *State proceedings.* (1) The Commissioner may at his discretion abate the unpaid portion of the assessment of any tax imposed by section 507(c), or any liability in respect thereof, under the procedures outlined in subparagraphs (2) and (3) of this paragraph. Such tax may not be abated by the Commissioner unless he determines that corrective action as defined in paragraph (c) of this section has been taken. The Commissioner may not abate by reason of section 507(g) any amount of such tax which has already been collected since only the unpaid portion thereof can be abated.

(2) The appropriate State officer shall have 1 year from the date of notification prescribed in section 6104(c) that a notice of deficiency of tax imposed under section 507(c) has been issued with respect to a foundation, to advise the Commissioner that corrective action has been initiated pursuant to State law as may be ordered or approved by a court of competent jurisdiction. Corrective action may be initiated either by the appropriate State officer or by an organization described in section 509(a)(1), (2), or (3) which is a beneficiary of the private foundation and has enforceable rights against such foundation under State law. Copies of all pleadings and other documents filed with the court at the initial stages of the proceedings shall be attached to the notification made by the State officer to the Commissioner. Prior to notification by the appropriate State officer that corrective action has been initiated, the Commissioner shall follow those procedures which would apply with respect to the assessment and collection of the tax imposed under section 507(c) without regard to section 507(g)(2). Subsequent to notification by the appropriate State officer that corrective action has been initiated, the Commissioner shall suspend action with respect to the assessment or collection of tax imposed under section 507(c) until notified of the final determination of such corrective action, as long as any such resulting delay does not jeopardize the collection of such tax and does not cause collection to be barred by operation of law or any rule of law. In any case where collection of such tax is about to be barred by operation of section 6502 and the Commissioner has not been advised of the final determination of corrective action, the Commissioner should make every effort to obtain appropriate agreements with the foundation subject to such tax to extend the period of limitations under section 6502(a)(2). Where such agreements are obtained, action with respect to the assessment and collection of such tax may be suspended to the extent not inconsistent with this subparagraph.

(3) Upon receipt of certification from the appropriate State officer that action has been ordered or approved by a court of competent jurisdiction, the Commissioner may abate the unpaid portion of the assessment of tax imposed by section 507(c), or any liability in respect thereof, if in his judgment such action is corrective action within the meaning of paragraph (c) of this section. In the event that such action is not corrective action, the Commissioner may in his discretion again suspend action on the assessment and collection of such tax until corrective action is obtained, or if in his judgment corrective action cannot be obtained, he may resume the assessment and collection of such tax.

(c) *Corrective action.* The term "corrective action" referred to in paragraph (b) of this section means vigorous enforcement of State laws sufficient to assure implementation of the provisions of chapter 42 and insure that the assets of such private foundation are preserved for such charitable or other purposes specified in section 501(c)(3). Except where assets of the terminated private foundation are transferred to an organization described in section 509(a)(1) through (4) the State is required to take such action to assure that the provisions of section 508(e)(1)(A) and (B) are applicable to the terminated foundation (or any transferee) with respect to such assets as if such organization were a private foundation. Thus, the governing instrument of such organization must include provisions with respect to such assets—

(1) Requiring its income therefrom for each taxable year to be distributed at such time and in such manner as not to subject such organization to tax under section 4942 (as if the organization were a private foundation),

(2) Prohibiting such organization from engaging in any act of self-dealing (as defined in section 4941(d) as if the organization were a private foundation),

(3) Prohibiting such organization from retaining any excess business holdings (as defined in section 4943(c) as if the organization were a private foundation),

(4) Prohibiting such organization from making any investments in such manner as to subject such organization to tax under section 4944 (as if the organization were a private foundation), and

(5) Prohibiting such organization from making any taxable expenditures (as defined in section 4945(d) as if the organization were a private foundation).

Consequently, in cases where the preceding sentence applies, although the private foundation status of an organization is terminated for tax purposes, it is contemplated that its status under State law would remain unchanged, because the tax under section 507(c) has been abated solely because the Commissioner has been given effective assurance that there is vigorous enforcement of State laws sufficient to assure implementation of the provisions of chapter 42. Therefore, in such a case while chapter 42 will not apply to acts occurring subsequent to termination which previously would have resulted in the imposition of tax under chapter 42, it is contemplated that there will be vigorous enforcement of State laws (including laws made applicable by the provisions in the governing instrument) with respect to such acts. Notwithstanding the preceding three sentences, no amendment to the organization's governing instrument is necessary where there are provisions of State law which have the effect of requiring a terminated private foundation to which the rules of subparagraphs (1) through (5) of this paragraph apply to be subject to such rules whether or not there are such provisions in such terminated private foundation's governing instrument. [Reg. § 1.507-9.]

☐ [T.D. 7233, 12-20-72.]

[Reg. § 1.508-1]

§ 1.508-1. Notices.—(a) *New organizations must notify the Commissioner that they are applying for recognition of section 501(c)(3) status*—(1) *In general.* Except as provided in subparagraph (3) of this paragraph, an organization that is organized after October 9, 1969, will not be treated as described in section 501(c)(3)—

(i) Unless such organization has given the Commissioner notice in the manner prescribed in subparagraph (2) of this paragraph; or

(ii) For any period before the giving of such notice, unless such notice is given in the manner and within the time prescribed in subparagraph (2) of this paragraph.

No organization shall be exempt from taxation under section 501(a) by reason of being described in section 501(c)(3) whenever such organization is not treated as described in section 501(c)(3) by reason of section 508(a) and this paragraph. See section 508(d)(2)(B) and § 1.508-2(b) regarding the deductibility of charitable contributions to an organization during the period such organization is not exempt under section 501(a) as an organization described in section 501(c)(3) by reason of failing to file a notice under section 508(a) and this subparagraph. See also § 1.508-2(b)(1)(viii) regarding the deductibility of charitable contributions to trusts described in section 4947(a)(1).

(2) *Filing of notice.* (i) For purposes of subparagraph (1) of this paragraph, except as provided in subparagraph (3) of this paragraph, an organization seeking exemption under section 501(c)(3) must file the notice described in section 508(a) within 15 months from the end of the month in which the organization was organized, or before March 22, 1973, whichever comes later. Such notice is filed by submitting a properly completed and executed Form 1023, Exemption Application. Notice should be filed with the district director. A request for extension of time for the filing of such notice should be submitted to such district director. Such request may be granted if it demonstrates that additional time is required.

(ii) Although the information required by Form 1023 must be submitted to satisfy the notice required by this section, the failure to supply, within the required time, all of the information required to complete such form is not alone sufficient to deny exemption from the date of organization to the date such complete information is submitted by the organization. If the information which is submitted within the required time is incomplete, and the organization supplies the necessary additional information at the request of the Commissioner within the additional time period allowed by him, the original notice will be considered timely.

(iii) For purposes of subdivision (i) of this subparagraph and paragraph (b)(2)(i) of this section, an organization shall be considered "organized" on the date it becomes an organization described in section 501(c)(3) (determined without regard to section 508(a)).

(iv) Since a trust described in section 4947(a)(2) is not an organization described in section 501(c)(3), it is not required to file a notice described in section 508(a).

(v) For the treatment of community trusts, and the trusts or funds comprising them, under section 508, see the special rules under § 1.170A-9(e).

(vi) A foreign organization shall, for purposes of section 508, be treated in the same manner as a domestic organization, except that section 508 shall not apply to a foreign organization which is described in section 4948(b).

(3) *Exceptions from notice.* (i) Paragraphs (a)(1) and (2) of this section are inapplicable to the following organizations:

(*a*) Churches, interchurch organizations of local units of a church, conventions or associations of churches, or integrated auxiliaries of a church. See § 1.6033-2(h) regarding the definition of integrated auxiliary of a church;

(*b*) Any organization which is not a private foundation (as defined in section 509(a)) and the gross receipts of which in each taxable year are normally not more than $5,000 (as described in subdivision (ii) of this subparagraph);

(*c*) Subordinate organizations (other than private foundations) covered by a group exemption letter;

(*d*) Solely for purposes of sections 507, 508(d)(1), 508(d)(2)(A) and 508(d)(3), 508(e), 509 and chapter 42, a trust described in section 4947(a)(1). (However, a trust described in section 501(c)(3) which was organized after October 9, 1969, shall be exempt under section 501(a) by reason of being described in section 501(c)(3) only if it files such notice); and

(e) Any other class of organization that the Commissioner from time to time excludes from the requirement of filing notice under section 508(a).

(ii) For purposes of subdivision (i)(b) of this subparagraph and paragraph (b)(7)(ii) of this section, the gross receipts (as defined in subdivision (iii) of this subparagraph) of an organization are normally not more than $5,000 if—

(a) During the first taxable year of the organization the organization has received gross receipts of $7,500 or less;

(b) During its first two taxable years the aggregate gross receipts received by the organization are $12,000 or less; and

(c) In the case of an organization which has been in existence for at least three taxable years, the aggregate gross receipts received by the organization during the immediately preceding two taxable years, plus the current year are $15,000 or less.

If an organization fails to meet the requirements of (a), (b), or (c) of this subdivision, then with respect to the organization, such organization shall be required to file the notices described in section 508(a) and (b) within 90 days after the end of the period described in (a), (b), or (c) of this subdivision or before March 22, 1973, whichever is later, in lieu of the period prescribed in subparagraph (2)(i) of this paragraph. Thus, for example, if an organization meets the $7,500 requirement of (a) of this subdivision for its first taxable year, but fails to meet the $12,000 requirement of (b) of this subdivision for the period ending with its second taxable year, then such organization shall meet the notification requirements of section 508(a)(1) and 508(b) and subparagraph (2)(i) of this paragraph if it files such notification within 90 days after the close of its second taxable year. If an organization which has been in existence at least three taxable years meets the requirements of (a), (b), and (c) with respect to all prior taxable years, but fails to meet the requirements of (c) of this subdivision with respect to the current taxable year, then even if the organization fails to make such notification within 90 days after the close of the current taxable year, section 508(a)(1) and 508(b) shall not apply with respect to its prior years. In such a case, the organization shall not be treated as described in section 501(c)(3) for a period beginning with such current taxable year and ending when such notice is given under section 508(a)(2).

(iii) For a definition of "gross receipts" for purposes of subdivision (i)(b) of this subparagraph and paragraph (b)(7)(ii) of this section, see § 1.6033-2(g)(4).

(4) *Voluntary filings by new organizations excepted from filing notice.* Any organization excepted from the requirement of filing notice under section 508(a) will be exempt from taxation under section 501(c)(3) if it meets the requirements of that section, whether or not it files such notice. However, in order to establish its exemption with the Internal Revenue Service and receive a ruling or determination letter recognizing its exempt status, an organization excepted from the notice requirement by reason of subparagraph (3) of this paragraph should file proof of its exemption in the manner prescribed in § 1.501(a)-1.

(b) *Presumption that old and new organizations are private foundations*—(1) *In general.* Except as provided in subparagraph (7) of this paragraph, any organization (including an organization in existence on October 9, 1969) which is described in section 501(c)(3), and which does not notify the Commissioner within the time and in the manner prescribed in subparagraph (2) that it is not a private foundation, will be presumed to be a private foundation.

(2) *Filing of notice.* (i) Except as provided in subparagraph (7) of this paragraph, an organization must file the notice described in section 508(b) and subparagraph (1) of this paragraph within 15 months from the end of the month in which such organization was organized, or before March 22, 1973, whichever comes later. See paragraph (a)(2)(iii) of this section, for rules pertaining to when an organization is "organized".

(ii) Any organization filing notice under this paragraph that has received a ruling or determination letter from the Internal Revenue Service dated on or before July 13, 1970, recognizing its exemption from taxation under section 501(c)(3) (or the corresponding provisions of prior law), shall file the notice described in section 508(b) by submitting a properly completed and executed Form 4653, Notification Concerning Foundation Status.

(iii) The financial schedule on Form 4653 need be completed only if the organization is, or thinks it might be, described in section 170(b)(1)(A)(iv) or (vi) or section 509(a)(2).

(iv) Any organization filing notice under this paragraph that has not received a ruling or determination letter from the Internal Revenue Service dated on or before July 13, 1970, recognizing its exemption from taxation under section 501(c)(3) (or the corresponding provisions of prior law), shall file its notice by submitting a properly completed and executed Form 1023 and providing information that it is not a private foundation.

Reg. § 1.508-1(b)(2)

The organization shall also submit all information required by the regulations under section 170 or 509 (whichever is applicable) necessary to establish recognition of its classification as an organization described in section 509(a)(1), (2), (3), or (4). A Form 1023 submitted prior to July 14, 1970, will satisfy this requirement if the organization submits an additional statement that it is not a private foundation together with all pertinent additional information required. Any statement filed under this subdivision shall be accompanied by a written declaration by the principal officer, manager or authorized trustee that there is a reasonable basis in law and in fact for the statement that the organization so filing is not a private foundation, and that to the best of the knowledge and belief of such officer, manager or trustee, the information submitted is complete and correct.

(v) The notice filed under subdivision (ii) of this subparagraph should be filed in accordance with the instructions applicable to Form 4653. The notice required by subdivision (iv) of this subparagraph should be filed with the district director. An extension of time for the filing of such notice may be granted by the director of the Internal Revenue Service Center or district director upon timely request by the organization to such person, if the organization demonstrates that additional time is required.

(3) *Effect of notice upon the filing organization.* (i) The notice filed under this paragraph may not be relied upon by the organization so filing unless and until the Internal Revenue Service notifies the organization that it is an organization described in paragraph (1), (2), (3) or (4) of section 509(a). For purposes of the preceding sentence, an organization that has filed notice under section 508(b), and has previously received a ruling that it is an organization described in section 170(b)(1)(A) (other than clauses (vii) and (viii) thereof), will be considered to have been notified by the Internal Revenue Service that it is an organization described in paragraph (1) of section 509(a) if (*a*) the facts and circumstances forming the basis for the issuance of such ruling have not substantially changed, and (*b*) the ruling issued under that section has not been revoked expressly or by a subsequent change of the law or regulations under which the ruling was issued.

(ii) If an organization has filed a notice under section 508(b) stating that it is not a private foundation and designating only one paragraph of section 509(a) under which it claims recognition of its classification (such as an organization described in section 509(a)(2)), and if it has received a ruling or determination letter which recognizes that it is not a private foundation but which fails to designate the paragraph under section 509(a) in which it is described, then such organization will be treated as described under the paragraph designated by it, until such ruling or determination letter is modified or revoked. The rule in the preceding sentence shall not apply to an organization which indicated that it does not know its status under section 509(a) or which claimed recognition of its status under more than one paragraph of section 509(a).

(4) *Effect of notice upon grantors or contributors to the filing organization.* In the case of grants, contributions, or distributions made prior to—

(i) In the case of community trusts, 6 months after the date on which corrective and clarifying regulations designated as § 1.170A-9(e)(10) become final;

(ii) In the case of medical research organizations, 6 months after the date on which corrective and clarifying regulations designated as § 1.170A-9(b)(2), become final, and

(iii) In all other cases, January 1, 1976, any organization which has properly filed the notice described in section 508(b) prior to March 22, 1973 will not be treated as a private foundation for purposes of making any determination under the internal revenue laws with respect to a grantor, contributor or distributor (as for example, a private foundation distributing all of its net assets pursuant to a section 507(b)(1)(A) termination) thereto, unless the organization is controlled directly or indirectly by such grantor, contributor or distributor, if by the 30th day after the day on which such notice is filed, the organization has not been notified by the Commissioner that the notice filed by such organization has failed to establish that such organization is not a private foundation. See subparagraph (6) of this paragraph for the effect of an adverse notice by the Internal Revenue Service. For purposes of this subparagraph, an organization which has properly filed the notice described in section 508(b) prior to March 22, 1973, and which has claimed recognition of its status under only one paragraph of section 509(a) in such notice, will be treated only for purposes of grantors, contributors or distributors as having the classification claimed in the notice if the provisions of this subparagraph are otherwise satisfied.

(5) *Statement that old and new organizations are operating foundations.* (i) Any organization (including an organization in existence on October 9, 1969) which is described in section 501(c)(3) may submit a statement, in the form and manner provided for notice in subparagraph (2) of this

Reg. § 1.508-1(b)(3)

paragraph, that it is an operating foundation (as defined in section 4942(j)(3)) and include in such statement:

(a) Necessary supporting information as required by the regulations under section 4942(j)(3) to confirm such determination (including a statement identifying the clause of section 4942(j)(3)(B) that is applicable); and

(b) A written declaration by the principal officer, manager or authorized trustee that there is a reasonable basis in law and in fact that the organization so filing is an operating foundation, and that to the best of the knowledge and belief of such officer, manager or trustee, the information submitted is complete and correct.

(ii) The statement filed under this subparagraph may not be relied upon by the organization so filing unless and until the Internal Revenue Service notifies the organization that it is an operating foundation described in section 4942(j)(3).

(iii) In the case of grants, contributions or distributions made prior to March 22, 1973, any organization which has properly filed the statement described in this subparagraph prior to such date will be treated as an operating foundation for purposes of making any determination under the internal revenue laws with respect to a grantor, contributor or distributor thereto, unless the organization is controlled directly or indirectly by such grantor, contributor or distributor, if by the 30th day after the day on which such statement is filed, the organization has not been notified by the Commissioner or his delegate that its statement has failed to establish that such organization is an operating foundation. See subparagraph (6) of this paragraph for the effect of an adverse notice by the Internal Revenue Service.

(6) *Effect of notice by Internal Revenue Service concerning organization's notice or statement.* Subparagraph (4) and subdivision (iii) of subparagraph (5) of this paragraph shall have no effect:

(i) With respect to a grantor, contributor, or distributor to any organization for any period after the date on which the Internal Revenue Service makes notice to the public (such as by publication in the Internal Revenue Bulletin) that a grantor, contributor, or distributor to such organization can no longer rely upon the notice or statement submitted by such organization; and

(ii) Upon any grant, contribution, or distribution made to an organization on or after the date on which a grantor, contributor, or distributor acquired knowledge that the Internal Revenue Service has given notice to such organization that its notice or statement has failed to establish that

such organization either is not a private foundation, or is an operating foundation, as the case may be.

(7) *Exceptions from notice.* Subparagraphs (1) and (2) of this paragraph are inapplicable to the following organizations:

(i) Churches, interchurch organizations of local units of a church, conventions or associations of churches, or integrated auxiliaries of a church, such as a men's or women's organization, religious school, mission society, or youth group;

(ii) Any organization which is not a private foundation (as defined in section 509(a)) and the gross receipts of which in each taxable year are normally not more than $5,000 (as determined under paragraph (a)(3)(ii) of this section);

(iii) Subordinate organizations (other than private foundations) covered by a group exemption letter but only if the parent or supervisory organization submits a notice covering the subordinates;

(iv) Trusts described in section 4947(a)(1); and

(v) Any other class of organization that the Commissioner from time to time excludes from the notification requirements of section 508(b).

(8) *Voluntary filings by organizations excepted from filing notice.* Any organization excepted from the requirement of filing notice under section 508(b) by reason of subdivisions (i), (ii), and (v) of subparagraph (7) of this paragraph may receive the benefits of subparagraph (4) of this paragraph by filing such notice. [Reg. § 1.508-1.]

☐ [T.D. 7232, 12-21-72. Amended by T.D. 7258, 2-9-73, by T.D. 7300, 12-26-73, by T.D. 7342, 1-6-75, T.D. 7395, 1-5-76 and T.D. 8640, 12-19-95.]

[Reg. § 1.508-2]

§ 1.508-2. **Disallowance of certain charitable, etc., deductions.**—(a) *Gift or bequest to organizations subject to section 507(c) tax*—(1) *General rule.* No gift or bequest made to an organization upon which the tax provided by section 507(c) has been imposed shall be allowed as a deduction under section 170, 545(b)(2), 556(b)(2), 642(c), 2055, 2106(a)(2), or 2522, if such gift or bequest is made:

(i) By any person after notification has been made by the organization under section 507(a)(1) or after notification has been made by the Commissioner under section 507(a)(2)(B), or

(ii) By a substantial contributor (as defined in section 507(d)(2)) in his taxable year which includes the first day on which action is taken by such organization which culminates in the imposition of tax under section 507(c) and any subsequent taxable year.

For purposes of subdivision (ii) of this subparagraph, the first day on which action is taken by an organization which culminates in the imposition of tax under section 507(c) shall be determined under the rules set forth in § 1.507-7(b)(1) and (2).

(2) *Exception.* Subparagraph (1) of this paragraph shall not apply if the entire amount of the unpaid portion of the tax imposed by section 507(c) is abated by the Commissioner under section 507(g).

(b) *Gift or bequest to taxable private foundation, section 4947 trust, etc.*—(1) *General rule.* (i) Except as provided in subparagraph (2) of this paragraph, no gift or bequest made to an organization shall be allowed as a deduction under section 170, 545(b)(2), 556(b)(2), 642(c), 2055, 2106(a)(2), or 2522, if such gift or bequest is made:

(*a*) To a private foundation or a trust described in section 4947(a)(2) in a taxable year for which it fails to meet the requirements of section 508(e) (determined without regard to section 508(e)(2)(B) and (C)), or

(*b*) To any organization in a period for which it is not treated as an organization described in section 501(c)(3) by reason of section 508(a).

(ii) For purposes of subdivision (i)(*a*) of this subparagraph the term "taxable year" refers to the taxable year of the donee or beneficiary organization. In the event a bequest is made to a private foundation or trust described in section 4947(a)(2) which is not in existence at the date of the testator's death (but which is created under the terms of the testator's will), the term "taxable year" shall mean the first taxable year of the private foundation or trust.

(iii) For purposes of subdivision (i)(*a*) of this subparagraph, an organization does not fail to meet the requirements of section 508(e) for a taxable year, unless it fails to meet such requirements for the entire year. Therefore, even if a donee organization fails to meet the requirements of section 508(e) on the date it receives a grant from a donor, the donor's grant will not be disallowed by operation of section 508(d)(2)(A) and subdivision (i)(*a*) of this subparagraph, if the organization meets the requirements of section 508(e) (determined without regard to section 508(e)(2)(B) or (C)) by the end of its taxable year.

(iv) No deduction will be disallowed under section 508(d)(2)(A) with respect to a deduction under section 170, 545(b)(2), 556(b)(2), 642(c), 2055, 2106(a)(2), or 2522 if during the taxable year in question, the private foundation or trust described in section 4947(a)(2) has instituted a judicial proceeding which is necessary to reform its governing instrument or other instrument in order to meet the requirements of section 508(e)(1). This subdivision shall not apply unless within a reasonable time such judicial proceedings succeed in so reforming such instrument.

(v) No deduction will be disallowed under section 508(d)(2)(A) and subdivision (i)(*a*) of this subparagraph for any taxable year beginning before January 1, 1972 with respect to a private foundation or trust described in section 4947 organized before January 1, 1970. See also § 1.508-3(g) regarding transitional rules for extending compliance with section 508(e)(1).

(vi)(*a*) In the case of a contribution or bequest to a trust described in section 4947(a)(2) other than to a trust to which subdivision (vii) of this subparagraph applies, no deduction shall be disallowed by reason of section 508(d)(2)(A) on the grounds that such trust's governing instrument contains no provisions with respect to section 4942. Similarly, if for a taxable year such trust is also a trust described in section 4947(b)(3), no deduction for such year shall be so disallowed on the grounds that the governing instrument contains no provision with respect to section 4943 or 4944.

(*b*) This subdivision may be illustrated by the following example:

Example. H executes a will on January 1, 1977 establishing a charitable remainder trust (as described in section 664) with income payable to W, his wife, for life, remainder to X university, an organization described in section 170(b)(1)(A)(ii). The will provides that the trust is prohibited from engaging in activities which would subject itself, its foundation manager or a disqualified person to taxes under section 4941 or 4945 of the Code. The will is silent as to sections 4942, 4943, and 4944. H dies February 12, 1978. Section 508(d)(2)(A) will not operate to disallow any deduction to H's estate under section 2055 with respect to such trust.

(vii)(*a*) In the case of a trust described in section 4947(a)(2) which by its terms will become a trust described in section 4947(a)(1) and the governing instrument of which is executed after March 22, 1973, the governing instrument shall not meet the requirements of section 508(e)(1) if it does not contain provisions to the effect that the trust must comply with the provisions of sec-

Reg. § 1.508-2(a)(2)

tion 4942, or sections 4942, 4943, and 4944 (as the case may be) to the extent such section or sections shall become applicable to such trust.

(b) This subdivision may be illustrated by the following example:

Example. H executes a will on January 1, 1977, establishing a charitable remainder trust (as described in section 664) with income payable to W, his wife, for life, remainder in trust in perpetuity for the benefit of an organization described in section 170(c). By its terms the trust will become a trust described in section 4947(a)(1), and will become a private foundation. The will provides that the trust is prohibited from engaging in activities which would subject itself, its foundation manager or a disqualified person to taxes under sections 4941 or 4945 of the Code. The will is silent as to sections 4942, 4943 and 4944. H dies February 12, 1978. Unless the trust's governing instrument is amended prior to the end of the trust's first taxable year, or judicial proceedings have been instituted under subdivision (iv) of this subparagraph, section 508(d)(2)(A) will operate to disallow any deduction to H's estate under section 2055 with respect to such trust.

(viii) Since a charitable trust described in section 4947(a)(1) is not required to file a notice under section 508(a), section 508(d)(2)(B) and subdivision (i)(*b*) of this subparagraph are not applicable to such a trust.

(2) *Transitional rules.* Any deduction which would otherwise be allowable under section 642(c)(2), 2106(a)(2) or 2055 shall not be disallowed under section 508(d)(2)(A) if such deduction is attributable to:

(i) Property passing under the terms of a will executed on or before October 9, 1969,

(*a*) If the decedent dies after October 9, 1969, but before October 9, 1972, without having amended any dispositive provision of the will after October 9, 1969, by codicil or otherwise,

(*b*) If the decedent dies after October 9, 1969, and at no time after that date had the right to change the portions of the will which pertains to the passing of property to, or for the use of, an organization described in section 170(c)(2)(B) or 2055(a), or

(*c*) If no dispositive provision of the will is amended by the decedent, by codicil or otherwise, before October 9, 1972, and the decedent is on October 9, 1972, and at all times thereafter under a mental disability (as defined in § 1.642(c)-2(b)(3)(ii)) to amend the will by codicil or otherwise, or

(ii) Property transferred in trust on or before October 9, 1969,

(*a*) If the grantor dies after October 9, 1969, but before October 9, 1972, without having amended, after October 9, 1969, any dispositive provision of the instrument governing the disposition of the property,

(*b*) If the property transferred was an irrevocable interest to, or for the use of, an organization described in section 170(c)(2)(B) or 2055(a),

(*c*) In the case of a deduction under section 2106(a)(2) or 2055; if no dispositive provision of the instrument governing the disposition of the property is amended by the grantor before October 9, 1972, and the grantor is on October 9, 1972, and at all times thereafter under a mental disability (as defined in § 1.642(c)-2(b)(3)(ii)) to change the disposition of the property, or

(*d*) In the case of a deduction under section 642(c)(2)(A), if the grantor is at all times after October 9, 1969, and up to, and including, the last day of the taxable year for which the deduction under such section is claimed, under a mental disability (as defined in § 1.642(c)-2(b)(3)(ii)) to change the terms of the trust.

See also § 1.508-3(g) regarding the extension of time for compliance with section 508(e), § 1.664-1(f)(3)(ii) and (g) regarding the special transitional rules for charitable remainder annuity and unitrusts described in section 664 which were created prior to December 31, 1972, and § 20.2055-2(e)(4) of this chapter regarding the rules for determining if the dispositive provisions have been amended. [Reg. § 1.508-2.]

☐ [*T.D. 7232, 12-21-72.*]

[Reg. § 1.508-3]

§ 1.508-3. Governing instruments.—(a) *General rule.* A private foundation shall not be exempt from taxation under section 501(a) for a taxable year unless by the end of such taxable year its governing instrument includes provisions the effects of which are:

(1) To require distributions at such times and in such manner as not to subject the foundation to tax under section 4942, and

(2) To prohibit the foundation from engaging in any act of self-dealing (as defined in section 4941(d)), from retaining any excess business holdings (as defined in section 4943(c)), from making any investments in such manner as to subject the foundation to tax under section 4944, and from making any taxable expenditures (as defined in section 4945(d)).

(b) *Effect and nature of governing instrument* —(1) *In general.* Except as provided in paragraph (d) of this section, the provisions of a

Reg. § 1.508-3(b)(1)

foundation's governing instrument must require or prohibit, as the case may be, the foundation to act or refrain from acting so that the foundation, and any foundation managers or other disqualified persons with respect thereto, shall not be liable for any of the taxes imposed by sections 4941, 4942, 4943, 4944 and 4945 of the Code or, in the case of a split-interest trust described in section 4947(a)(2), any of the taxes imposed by those sections of chapter 42 made applicable under section 4947. Specific reference to these sections of the Code will generally be required to be included in the governing instrument, unless equivalent language is used which is deemed by the Commissioner to have the same full force and effect. However, a governing instrument which contains only language sufficient to satisfy the requirements of the organizational test under § 1.501(c)(3)-1(b) will not be considered as meeting the requirements of this subparagraph regardless of the interpretation placed on such language as a matter of law by a State court in a particular jurisdiction, unless the requirements of paragraph (d) of this section are satisfied.

(2) *Corpus.* A governing instrument does not meet the requirements of paragraph (a)(1) of this section if it expressly prohibits the distribution of capital or corpus.

(3) *Savings provisions.* For purposes of section 508(d)(2)(A) and (e), a governing instrument need not include any provision which is inconsistent with section 101(1)(2), (3), (4) or (5) of the Tax Reform Act of 1969 (83 Stat. 533), as amended by sections 1301 and 1309 of the Tax Reform Act of 1976 (90 Stat. 1713, 1729), with respect to the organization. Accordingly, a governing instrument complying with the requirements of subparagraph (1) of this paragraph may incorporate any savings provision contained in section 101(1)(2), (3), (4) or (5) of the Tax Reform Act of 1969, as amended by sections 1301 and 1309 of the Tax Reform Act of 1976, as a specific exception to the general provisions of paragraph (a) of this section. In addition, in the absence of any express provisions to the contrary, the exceptions contained in such savings provisions will generally be regarded as contained in a governing instrument meeting the requirements of subparagraph (1) of this paragraph.

(4) *Excess holdings.* For purposes of paragraph (a)(2) of this section, the prohibition against "retaining any excess business holdings (as defined in section 4943(c))" shall be deemed only to prohibit the foundation from retaining any excess business holdings when such holdings would subject the foundation to tax under section 4943(a).

(5) *Revoked ruling on status.* In the case of an organization which—

(i) Has been classified as an organization described in section 509(a)(1), (2), (3), or (4), and

(ii) Subsequently receives a ruling or determination letter stating that it is no longer described in section 509(a)(1), (2), (3), or (4), but is a private foundation within the meaning of section 509,

such organization shall have one year from the date of receipt of such ruling or determination letter, or the final ruling or determination letter if a protest is filed to an earlier one, to meet the requirements of section 508(e). Section 508(d)(2)(A) shall not be applicable with respect to gifts and bequests made during this one-year period if such requirements are met within the one-year period.

(6) *Judicial proceeding.* For purposes of paragraphs (a), (b)(5), (d)(2), and (e)(3) of this section, an organization shall be deemed to have met the requirements of section 508(e) within a year, if a judicial proceeding which is necessary to reform its governing instrument or other instrument is instituted within the year and within a reasonable time the organization, in fact, meets the requirements of section 508(e). For purposes only of paragraphs (b)(5), (d)(2), and (e)(3) of this section, if an organization organized before January 1, 1970, institutes such a judicial proceeding within such one-year period, section 508(e)(2)(C) shall be applied as if such proceeding had been instituted prior to January 1, 1972.

(c) *Meaning of governing instrument.* For purposes of section 508(e), the term "governing instrument" shall have the same meaning as the term "articles of organization" under § 1.501(c)(3)-1(b)(2). The by-laws of an organization shall not constitute its governing instrument for purposes of section 508(e).

(d) *Effect of State law*—(1) *In general.* A private foundation's governing instrument shall be deemed to conform with the requirements of paragraph (a) of this section if valid provisions of State law have been enacted which:

(i) Require it to act or refrain from acting so as not to subject the foundation to the taxes imposed by section 4941 (relating to taxes on self-dealing), 4942 (relating to taxes on failure to distribute income), 4943 (relating to taxes on excess business holdings), 4944 (relating to taxes on investments which jeopardize charitable purpose), and 4945 (relating to taxable expenditures); or

(ii) Treat the required provisions as contained in the foundation's governing instrument.

Reg. § 1.508-3(b)(2)

(2) *Validity.* (i) Any provision of State law described in subparagraph (1) of this paragraph shall be presumed valid as enacted, and in the absence of State provisions to the contrary, to apply with respect to any foundation that does not specifically disclaim coverage under State law (either by notification to the appropriate State official or by commencement of judicial proceedings) except as provided in subdivisions (ii) and (iii) of this subparagraph.

(ii) If such provision is declared invalid or inapplicable with respect to a class of foundations by the highest appellate court of the State or by the Supreme Court of the United States, the foundations covered by the determination must meet the requirements of section 508(e) within one year from the date on which the time for perfecting an application for review by the Supreme Court expires. If such application is filed, the requirements of section 508(e) must be met within a year from the date on which the Supreme Court disposes of the case, whether by denial of the application for review or decision on the merits.

(iii) In addition, if such provision of State law is declared invalid or inapplicable with respect to a class of foundations by any court of competent jurisdiction which decision is not reviewed by a court referred to in subdivision (ii) of this subparagraph, and the Commissioner makes notice to the general public (such as by publication in the Internal Revenue Bulletin) that such provision has been so declared invalid or inapplicable, then all foundations in such state must meet the requirements of section 508(e), without reliance upon such statute to the extent declared invalid or inapplicable by such decision, within one year from the date such notice is made public.

(iv) This subparagraph shall not apply to any foundation that is subject to a final judgment entered by a court of competent jurisdiction, holding the law invalid or inapplicable with respect to such foundation. See paragraph (b)(6) of this section for the effect of certain judicial proceedings that are brought within one year.

(3) *Conflicting instrument.* For taxable years beginning after March 22, 1973, in order for a private foundation or trust described in section 4947(a)(2) to receive the benefit of coverage under any State statute which makes applicable the requirements of section 508(e)(1)(A) and (B), where the statute by its terms does not apply to a governing instrument which contains a mandatory direction conflicting with any of such requirements, such organization must indicate on its annual return required to be filed under section 6033 (or section 6012 in the case of a trust described in section 4947(a)) that its governing instrument contains no mandatory directions which conflict with the requirements of section 508(e)(1)(A) or (B), as incorporated by the State statute. General language in a governing instrument empowering the trustee to make investments without being limited to those investments authorized by law will not be regarded as a mandatory conflicting direction.

(4) *Exclusion from statute.* (i) For any taxable year beginning after March 22, 1973, in the case of a private foundation or trust described in section 4947(a)(2) subject to a State statute which makes applicable the requirements of section 508(e)(1)(A) and (B) to the governing instruments of such organizations, other than those which take action to be excluded therefrom (such as by filing a notice of exclusion or by instituting appropriate judicial proceedings), an organization will receive the benefit of such State statute only if it indicates on its annual return required to be filed under section 6033 (or section 6012 in the case of a trust described in section 4947(a)) that it has not so taken action to be excluded.

(ii) This paragraph permits certain organizations that are subject to the provisions of such a State law, to avoid changing their governing instruments in order to meet the requirements of section 508(e)(1). Since an organization which avoids the application of a provision or provisions of State law, such as by filing a notice of exclusion, is not entitled to the benefits of this paragraph, such an organization must meet the requirements of section 508(e)(1) without regard to this paragraph and except as provided in section 508(e)(2)(C) or paragraph (g)(1)(iii) of this section must change its governing instrument to the extent inconsistent with section 508(e)(1).

(5) *Treatment of prevailing conflicting clause.* If provisions of State law are inapplicable to a clause in a governing instrument which is contrary to the provisions of section 508(e)(1), the requirements of section 508(e)(2)(C) and paragraph (g)(1)(iii) of this section are not satisfied by a provision of State law which purports to eliminate the need for litigation under such circumstances. Therefore, except as otherwise provided in this section unless the governing instrument is changed or litigation is commenced pursuant to section 508(e)(2)(B) by an organization organized before January 1, 1970, or pursuant to paragraph (g)(1)(ii) of this section, to amend the nonconforming provision to meet the requirements of section 508(e)(1)(A) and (B), then pursuant to section 508(e), such organization will not be exempt from taxation.

(6) *Retroactive application to grants or bequests.* If valid provisions of such a State law

Reg. § 1.508-3(d)(6)

apply retroactively to a taxable year within which an organization has received a grant or bequest, section 508(d)(2)(A) shall not apply so as to disallow such grant or bequest, but only if such valid provisions of State law are enacted within two years of such grant or bequest.

(e) *Effect of section 508(e) upon section 4947 trusts*—(1) *Section 4947(a)(1) trusts.* A charitable trust described in section 4947(a)(1) (unless also described in a paragraph of section 509(a)) is subject to all the provisions of paragraph (a) of this section.

(2) *Section 4947(a)(2) trusts.* A split-interest trust described in section 4947(a)(2), as long as it is so described, is subject to the provisions of paragraph (a)(2) of this section, except to the extent that section 4947 makes any such provisions inapplicable to certain trusts and certain amounts in trust. The governing instrument of a trust described in section 4947(a)(2) may except amounts described in section 4947(a)(2)(A), (B) and (C) from the requirements of paragraph (a)(2) of this section. In the case of a trust having amounts transferred to it both before May 27, 1969, and after May 26, 1969, its governing instrument may except from the provisions of paragraph (a)(2) of this section only those segregated amounts excluded from the application of section 4947(a)(2) by reason of section 4947(a)(2)(C) and the regulations thereunder. Also, the governing instrument of such a trust may exclude the application of sections 4943 and 4944 for any period during which such trust is described in section 4947(b)(3)(A) or (B). See § 53.4947-1(c) of this chapter for rules relating to the applicability of section 4947 to split-interest trusts and § 1.508-2(b)(1)(vi) and (vii) for rules relating to the deductibility of grants or bequests to such trusts.

(3) *A section 4947(a)(2) trust becoming a section 4947(a)(1) trust.* If the governing instrument of a trust described in section 4947(a)(2) meets the applicable requirements of paragraph (a)(2) of this section and such trust ceases to be so described and becomes instead a trust described in section 4947(a)(1), then such governing instrument must meet, prior to the end of 12 months from the date such trust first becomes described in section 4947(a)(1) (except as otherwise provided in this section) all the requirements of paragraph (a) of this section in order to comply with section 508(e).

(f) *Special rules for existing private foundations.* (1) Pursuant to section 508(e)(2), section 508(e)(1) and paragraph (a) of this section shall not apply in the case of any organization whose governing instrument was executed before January 1, 1970:

(i) To any taxable year beginning before January 1, 1972;

(ii) To any period after December 31, 1971, during the pendency of any judicial proceeding begun before January 1, 1972, by the private foundation which is necessary to reform, or to excuse such foundation from compliance with, its governing instrument or any other instrument in order to meet the requirements of section 508(e)(1); and

(iii) To any period after the termination of any judicial proceeding described in subdivision (ii) of this subparagraph during which its governing instrument or any other instrument does not permit it to meet the requirements of section 508(e)(1).

(2) For purposes of subparagraph (1) of this paragraph, and § 1.508-2(b)(1)(vi)(*a*), a governing instrument will not be treated as executed before the applicable date, if, after such date the dispositive provisions of the instrument are amended (determined under rules similar to the rules set forth in § 20.2055-2(e)(4) of this chapter).

(3) For purposes of subparagraph (1)(ii) and (iii) of this paragraph, a private foundation will be treated as meeting the requirements of section 508(e)(2)(B) and (C) if it has commenced a necessary and timely proceeding in an appropriate court of original jurisdiction and such court has ruled that the foundation's governing instrument or any other instrument does not permit it to meet the requirements of section 508(e)(1). Such foundation is not required to commence proceedings in any court of appellate jurisdiction in order to comply with section 508(e)(2)(C). See also § 1.508-2(b)(2).

(g) *Extension of time for compliance with section 508(e)*—(1) Except as provided in subparagraph (2) of this paragraph, section 508(e)(1) shall not apply to any private foundation (regardless of when organized) with respect—

(i) To any taxable year beginning before the transitional date,

(ii) To any period on or after the transitional date during the pendency of any judicial proceeding begun before the transitional date by the private foundation which is necessary to reform, or to excuse such foundation from compliance with, its governing instrument or any other instrument in order to meet the requirements of section 508(e)(1), and

(iii) To any period after the termination of any judicial proceeding described in subdivision (ii) of this subparagraph during which its gov-

Reg. § 1.508-3(e)(1)

erning instrument or any other instrument does not permit it to meet the requirements of section 508(e)(1).

(2) Subparagraph (1) of this paragraph shall apply only to gifts or bequests referred to in section 508(d)(2)(A) that are made before the transitional date.

(3) For purposes of this paragraph the term "transitional dates" means the earlier of the following dates:

(i) In the case of a medical research organization, May 21, 1976 or in the case of a community trust February 10, 1977, or

(ii) The 91st day after the date an organization receives a final ruling or determination letter that it is a private foundation under section 509(a). [Reg. § 1.508-3.]

☐ [T.D. 7232, 12-21-72. Amended by T.D. 7440, 11-11-76 and T.D. 7678, 2-25-80.]

[Reg. § 1.508-4]

§ 1.508-4. Effective date.—Except as otherwise provided, §§ 1.508-1 through 1.508-3 shall take effect on January 1, 1970. [Reg. § 1.508-4.]

☐ [T.D. 7232, 12-21-72.]

[Reg. § 1.509(a)-1]

§ 1.509(a)-1. Definition of private foundation.—In general. Section 509(a) defines the term "private foundation" to mean any domestic or foreign organization described in section 501(c)(3) other than an organization described in section 509(a)(1), (2), (3) or (4). Organizations which fall into the categories excluded from the definition of "private foundation" are generally those which either have broad public support or actively function in a supporting relationship to such organizations. Organizations which test for public safety are also excluded. [Reg. § 1.509(a)-1.]

☐ [T.D. 7212, 10-16-72.]

[Reg. § 1.509(a)-2]

§ 1.509(a)-2. Exclusion for certain organizations described in section 170(b)(1)(A).—(a) General rule. Organizations described in section 170(b)(1)(A) (other than in clauses (vii) and (viii)) are excluded from the definition of "private foundation" by section 509(a)(1). For the requirements to be met by organizations described in section 170(b)(1)(A)(i) through (vi), see § 1.170A-9(a) through (e) and paragraph (b) of this section. For purposes of this section, the parenthetical language "other than in clauses (vii) and (viii)" used in section 509(a)(1) means "other than an organization which is described only in clause (vii) or (viii)." For purposes of this section, an organization may qualify as a section 509(a)(1) organization regardless of the fact that it does not satisfy section 170(c)(2) because:

(1) Its funds are not used within the United States or its possessions, or

(2) It was created or organized other than in, or under the law of, the United States, any State or territory, the District of Columbia, or any possession of the United States.

(b) *Medical research organizations.* In order to qualify under section 509(a)(1) as a medical research organization described in section 170(b)(1)(A)(iii), an organization must meet the requirements of section 170(b)(1)(A)(iii) and § 1.170A-9(c)(2), except that, solely for purposes of classification as a section 509(a)(1) organization, such organization need not be committed to spend every contribution for medical research before January 1 of the fifth calendar year which begins after the date such contribution is made. [Reg. § 1.509(a)-2.]

☐ [T.D. 7212, 10-16-72.]

[Reg. § 1.509(a)-3]

§ 1.509(a)-3. Broadly, publicly supported organizations.—(a) *In general.* (1) *General rule*—Section 509(a)(2) excludes certain types of broadly, publicly supported organizations from private foundation status. An organization will be excluded under section 509(a)(2) if it meets the one-third support test under section 509(a)(2)(A) and the not-more-than-one-third support test under section 509(a)(2)(B).

(2) *One-third support test*—An organization will meet the one-third support test if it normally (within the meaning of paragraph (c), (d) or (e) of this section) receives more than one-third of its support in each taxable year from any combination of:

(i) Gifts, grants, contributions, or membership fees, and

(ii) Gross receipts from admissions, sales of merchandise, performance of services, or furnishing of facilities, in an activity which is not an unrelated trade or business (within the meaning of section 513), subject to certain limitations described in paragraph (b) of this section, from permitted sources. For purposes of this section, governmental units, organizations described in section 509(a)(1) and persons other than disqualified persons with respect to the organization shall be referred to as permitted sources. For purposes of this section, the amount of support received from the sources described in subdivisions (i) and (ii) of this subparagraph (subject to the limitations referred to in this subparagraph) will be referred to as the numerator of the one-third support fraction, and the total amount of support

Reg. § 1.509(a)-3(a)(2)

received (as defined in section 509(d)) will be referred to as the denominator of the one-third support fraction. For purposes of section 509(a)(2), paragraph (f) of this section distinguishes gifts and contributions from gross receipts; paragraph (g) of this section distinguishes grants from gross receipts; paragraph (h) of this section defines membership fees; paragraph (i) of this section defines "any bureau or similar agency of a governmental unit"; paragraph (j) of this section describes the treatment of certain indirect forms of support; paragraph (k) of this section describes the method of accounting for support; paragraph (l) of this section describes the treatment of gross receipts from section 513(a)(1), (2), or (3) activities; and paragraph (m) of this section distinguishes gross receipts from gross investment income.

(3) *Not-more-than-one-third support test* — (i) *In general.* An organization will meet the not-more-than-one-third support test under section 509(a)(2)(B) if it normally (within the meaning of paragraph (c), (d), or (e) of this section) receives not more than one-third of its support in each taxable year from the sum of its gross investment income (as defined in section 509(e)) and the excess (if any) of the amount of its unrelated business taxable income (as defined in section 512) derived from trades or businesses which were acquired by the organization after June 30, 1975, over the amount of tax imposed on such income by section 511. For purposes of this section the amount of support received from items described in section 509(a)(2)(B) will be referred to as the numerator of the not-more-than-one-third support fraction, and the total amount of support (as defined in section 509(d)) will be referred to as the denominator of the not-more-than-one-third support fraction. For purposes of section 509(a)(2), paragraph (m) of this section distinguishes gross receipts from gross investment income. For purposes of section 509(e), gross investment income included the items of investment income described in § 1.512(b)-1(a).

(ii) *Trade or business.* For purposes of section 509(a)(2)(B)(ii), a trade or business acquired after June 30, 1975, by an organization shall include, in addition to other trades or businesses:

(A) A trade or business acquired after such date from, or as a result of the liquidation of, an organization's subsidiary which is described in section 502 whether or not the subsidiary was held on June 30, 1975.

(B) A new trade or business commenced by an organization after such date.

(iii) *Allocation of deduction between businesses acquired before, and businesses acquired after, June 30, 1975.* Deductions which are allowable under section 512 but are not directly connected to a particular trade or business, such as deductions referred to in paragraphs (10) and (12) of section 512(b), shall be allocated in the proportion that the unrelated trade or business taxable income derived from trades or businesses acquired after June 30, 1975, bears to the organization's total unrelated business taxable income, both amounts being determined without regard to such deductions.

(iv) *Allocation of tax.* The tax imposed by section 511 shall be allocated in the same proportion as in paragraph (a)(3)(iii) of this section.

(4) *Purposes*—The one-third support test and the not-more-than-one-third support test are designed to insure that an organization which is excluded from private foundation status under section 509(a)(2) is responsive to the general public, rather than to the private interests of a limited number of donors or other persons.

(b) *Limitation on gross receipts*—(1) *General rule.* In computing the amount of support received from gross receipts under section 509(a)(2)(A)(ii) for purposes of the one-third support test of section 509(a)(2)(A), gross receipts from related activities received from any person, or from any bureau or similar agency of a governmental unit, are includible in any taxable year only to the extent that such receipts do not exceed the greater of $5,000 or one percent of the organization's support in such taxable year.

(2) *Examples.* The application of this paragraph may be illustrated by the examples set forth below. For purposes of these examples, the term "general public" is defined as persons other than disqualified persons and other than persons from whom the foundation receives gross receipts in excess of the greater of $5,000 or 1 percent of its support in any taxable year, and the term "gross receipts" is limited to receipts from activities which are not unrelated trade or business (within the meaning of section 513).

Example (1). For the taxable year 1970, X, an organization described in section 501(c)(3), received support of $100,000 from the following sources:

Bureau M (a governmental bureau from which X received gross receipts for services rendered)	$ 25,000
Bureau N (a governmental bureau from which X received gross receipts for services rendered)	25,000

Reg. § 1.509(a)-3(a)(3)

General public (gross receipts for services rendered)	20,000
Gross investment income	15,000
Contributions from individual substantial contributors (defined as disqualified persons under section 4946(a)(2))	15,000
Total support	$100,000

Since the $25,000 received from each bureau amounts to more than the greater of $5,000 or one percent of X's support for 1970 (1% of $100,000 = $1,000) under section 509(a)(2)(A)(ii), each amount is includible in the numerator of the one-third support fraction only to the extent of $5,000. Thus, for the taxable year 1970, X received support from sources which are taken into account in meeting the one-third support test of section 509(a)(2)(A) computed as follows:

Bureau M	$ 5,000
Bureau N	5,000
General public	20,000
Total	$30,000

Therefore, in making the computations required under paragraph (c), (d), or (e) of this section, only $30,000 is includible in the aggregate numerator and $100,000 is includible in the aggregate denominator of the support fraction.

Example (2). For the taxable year 1970, Y, an organization described in section 501(c)(3), received support of $600,000 from the following sources:

Bureau O (gross receipts for services rendered)	$ 10,000
Bureau P (gross receipts for services rendered)	10,000
General public (gross receipts for services rendered)	150,000
General public (contributions)	40,000
Gross investment income	150,000
Contributions from substantial contributors	$240,000
Total support	$600,000

Since the $10,000 received from each bureau amounts to more than the greater of $5,000 or one percent of Y's support for 1970 (1% of $600,000 = $6,000), each amount is includible in the numerator of the one-third support fraction only to the extent of $6,000. Thus, for the taxable year 1970, Y received support from sources required to meet the one-third support test of section 509(a)(2)(A) computed as follows:

Bureau O	$ 6,000
Bureau P	6,000
General public (gross receipts)	150,000
General public (contributions)	40,000
	$202,000

Therefore, in making the computations required under paragraph (c), (d), or (e) of this section, $202,000 is includible in the aggregate numerator and $600,000 is includible in the aggregate denominator of the support fraction.

(c) *"Normally"*—(1) *In general*—(i) *Definition.* The support tests set forth in section 509(a)(2) are to be computed on the basis of the nature of the organization's "normal" sources of support. An organization will be considered as "normally" receiving one-third of its support from any combination of gifts, grants, contributions, membership fees, and gross receipts from permitted sources (subject to the limitations described in paragraph (b) of this section) and not more than one-third of its support from items described in section 509(a)(2)(B) for its current taxable year and the taxable year immediately succeeding its current year, if, for the four taxable years immediately preceding the current taxable year, the aggregate amount of the support received during the applicable period from gifts, grants, contributions, membership fees, and gross receipts from permitted sources (subject to the limitations described in paragraph (b) of this section) is more than one-third and the aggregate amount of the support received from items described in section 509(a)(2)(B) is not more than one-third, of the total support of the organization for such four year period.

(ii) *Exception for material changes in sources of support.* If for the current taxable year there are substantial and material changes in an organization's sources of support other than changes arising from unusual grants excluded under subparagraph (3) of this paragraph, then in applying subdivision (i) of this subparagraph, neither the 4-year computation period applicable to such year as an immediately succeeding taxable year, nor the 4-year computation period appli-

Reg. § 1.509(a)-3(c)(1)

cable to such year as a current taxable year shall apply, and in lieu of such computation periods there shall be applied a computation period consisting of the taxable year of substantial and material changes and the 4 taxable years immediately preceding such year. Thus, for example, if there are substantial and material changes in an organization's sources of support for taxable year 1976, then even though such organization meets the requirements of subdivision (i) of this subparagraph based on a computation period of taxable years 1971 through 1974 or 1972 through 1975, such an organization will not meet the requirements of section 509(a)(2) unless it meets the requirements of subdivision (i) of this subparagraph for a computation period of the taxable years 1972 through 1976. See example (3) in subparagraph (6) of this paragraph for an illustration of this subdivision. An example of a substantial and material change is the receipt of an unusually large contribution or bequest which does not qualify as an unusual grant under subparagraph (3) of this paragraph. See subparagraph (5)(ii) of this paragraph as to the procedure for obtaining a ruling whether an unusually large grant may be excluded as an unusual grant.

(iii) *Status of grantors and contributors.* (a) If as a result of subdivision (ii) of this subparagraph, an organization is not able to meet the requirements of either the one-third support test described in paragraph (a)(2) of this section or the not-more-than-one-third support test described in paragraph (a)(3) of this section for its current taxable year, its status (with respect to a grantor or contributor under sections 170, 507, 545(b)(2), 556(b)(2), 642(c), 4942, 4945, 2055, 2106(a)(2), and 2522) will not be affected until notice of change of status under section 509(a)(2) is made to the public (such as by publication in the Internal Revenue Bulletin). The preceding sentence shall not apply, however, if the grantor or contributor was responsible for, or was aware of, the substantial and material change referred to in subdivision (ii) of this subparagraph, or acquired knowledge that the Internal Revenue Service had given notice to such organization that it would be deleted from classification as section 509(a)(2) organization.

(b) A grantor or contributor (other than one of the organization's founders, creators, or foundation managers (within the meaning of section 4946(b)) will not be considered to be responsible for, or aware of, the substantial and material change referred to in subdivision (ii) of this subparagraph if such grantor or contributor has made such grant or contribution in reliance upon a written statement by the grantee organization that such grant or contribution will not result in the loss of such organization's classification as not a private foundation under section 509(a). Such statement must be signed by a responsible officer of the grantee organization and must set forth sufficient information, including a summary of the pertinent financial data for the four preceding years, to assure a reasonably prudent man that his grant or contribution will not result in the loss of the grantee organization's classification as not a private foundation under section 509(a). If a reasonable doubt exists as to the effect of such grant or contribution, or if the grantor or contributor is one of the organizations' founders, creators, or foundation managers, the procedure set forth in subparagraph (5)(ii) of this paragraph may be followed by the grantee organization for the protection of the grantor or contributor.

(iv) *Special rule for new organizations.* If an organization has been in existence for at least one taxable year consisting of at least 8 months, but for fewer than 5 taxable years, the number of years for which the organization has been in existence immediately preceding each current taxable year being tested will be substituted for the 4-year period described in subdivision (i) of this subparagraph to determine whether the organization "normally" meets the requirements of paragraph (a) of this section. However, if subdivision (ii) of this subparagraph applies, then the period consisting of the number of years for which the organization has been in existence (up to and including the current year) will be substituted for the 4-year period described in subdivision (i) of this subparagraph. An organization which has been in existence for at least one taxable year, consif it "normally" meets the requirements of paragraph (a) of this section for the number of years described in this subdivision. Such an organization may apply for a ruling or determination letter under the provisions of this paragraph, rather than under the provisions of paragraph (d) of this section. The issuance of a ruling or determination letter will be discretionary with the Commissioner. See paragraph (e)(4) of this section as to the initial determination of the status of a newly created organization. This subdivision shall not apply to those organizations receiving an extended advance ruling under paragraph (d)(4) of this section.

(2) *Terminations under section 507(b)(1)(B).* For the special rules applicable to the term "normally" as applied to private foundations which elect to terminate their private foundation status pursuant to the 12-month or 60-month procedure provided in section 507(b)(1)(B), see the regulations under such section.

Reg. § 1.509(a)-3(c)(2)

(3) *Exclusion of unusual grants.* For purposes of applying the 4-year aggregation test for support set forth in subparagraph (1) of this paragraph, one or more contributions (including contributions made prior to January 1, 1970) may be excluded from the numerator of the one-third support fraction and from the denominator of both the one-third support and not-more-than-one-third support fractions only if such a contribution meets the requirements of this subparagraph. The exclusion provided by this subparagraph is generally intended to apply to substantial contributions and bequests from disinterested parties, which contributions or bequests:

(i) Are attracted by reason of the publicly supported nature of the organization;

(ii) Are unusual or unexpected with respect to the amount thereof; and

(iii) Would by reason of their size, adversely affect the status of the organization as normally meeting the one-third support test for any of the applicable periods described in paragraph (c), (d), or (e) of this section. In the case of a grant (as defined in paragraph (g) of this section) which meets the requirements of this subparagraph, if the terms of the granting instrument (whether executed before or after 1969) require that the funds be paid to the recipient organization over a period of years, the amount received by the organization each year pursuant to the terms of such grant may be excluded for such year. However, no item described in section 509(a)(2)(B) may be excluded under this subparagraph. The provisions of this subparagraph shall apply to exclude unusual grants made during any of the applicable periods described in paragraph (c), (d), or (e) of this section. See subparagraph (5)(ii) of this paragraph as to reliance by a grantee organization upon an unusual grant ruling under this subparagraph.

(4) *Determining factors.* In determining whether a particular contribution may be excluded under subparagraph (3) of this paragraph, all pertinent facts and circumstances will be taken into consideration. No single factor will necessarily be determinative. Among the factors to be considered are:

(i) Whether the contribution was made by any person (or persons standing in a relationship to such person which is described in section 4946(a)(1)(C) through (G)) who created the organization, previously contributed a substantial part of its support or endowment, or stood in a position of authority, such as a foundation manager (within the meaning of section 4946(b)), with respect to the organization. A contribution made by a person other than those persons described in this subdivision will ordinarily be given more favorable consideration than a contribution made by a person described in this subdivision.

(ii) Whether the contribution was a bequest or an inter vivos transfer. A bequest will ordinarily be given more favorable consideration than an inter vivos transfer.

(iii) Whether the contribution was in the form of cash, readily marketable securities, or assets which further the exempt purposes of the organization, such as a gift of a painting to a museum.

(iv) Except in the case of a new organization, whether, prior to the receipt of the particular contribution, the organization (*a*) has carried on an actual program of public solicitation and exempt activities and (*b*) has been able to attract a significant amount of public support.

(v) Whether the organization may reasonably be expected to attract a significant amount of public support subsequent to the particular contribution. In this connection, continued reliance on unusual grants to fund an organization's current operating expenses (as opposed to providing new endowment funds) may be evidence that the organization cannot reasonably be expected to attract future support from the general public.

(vi) Whether, prior to the year in which the particular contribution was received, the organization met the one-third support test described in subparagraph (1) of this paragraph without the benefit of any exclusions of unusual grants pursuant to subparagraph (3) of this paragraph;

(vii) Whether neither the contributor nor any person standing in a relationship to such contributor which is described in section 4946(a)(1)(C) through (G) continues directly or indirectly to exercise control over the organization;

(viii) Whether the organization has a representative governing body as described in § 1.509(a)-3(d)(3)(i); and

(ix) Whether material restrictions or conditions (within the meaning of § 1.507-2(a)(8)) have been imposed by the transferor upon the transferee in connection with such transfer.

(5) *Grantors and contributors.* (i) As to the status of grants and contributions which result in substantial and material changes in the organization (as described in subparagraph (1)(ii) of this paragraph) and which fail to meet the requirements for exclusion under subparagraph (3) of this paragraph, see the rules prescribed in subparagraph (1)(iii) of this paragraph.

Reg. § 1.509(a)-3(c)(5)

(ii) Prior to the making of any grant or contribution which will allegedly meet the requirements for exclusion under subparagraph (3) of this paragraph, a potential grantee organization may request a ruling whether such grant or contribution may be so excluded. Requests for such ruling may be filed by the grantee organization with the district director. The issuance of such ruling will be at the sole discretion of the Commissioner. The organization must submit all information necessary to make a determination of the applicability of subparagraph (3) of this paragraph, including all information relating to the factors described in subparagraph (4) of this paragraph. If a favorable ruling is issued, such ruling may be relied upon by the grantor or contributor of the particular contribution in question for purposes of sections 170, 507, 545(b)(2), 556(b)(2), 642(c), 4942, 4945, 2055, 2106(a)(2), and 2522 and by the grantee organization for purposes of subparagraph (3) of this paragraph.

(6) *Examples*. The application of the principles set forth in this paragraph is illustrated by the examples set forth below. For purposes of these examples, the term "general public" is defined as persons other than disqualified persons and other than persons from whom the foundation received gross receipts in excess of the greater of $5,000 or 1 percent of its support in any taxable year, the term "gross investment income" is as defined in section 509(e), and the term "gross receipts" is limited to receipts from activities which are not unrelated trade or business (within the meaning of section 513).

Example (1). For the years 1970 through 1973, X, an organization exempt under section 501(c)(3) which makes scholarship grants to needy students of a particular city, received support from the following sources:

1970
Gross receipts (General public)	$ 35,000
Contributions (Substantial contributors)	36,000
Gross investment income	29,000
Total Support	$100,000

1971
Gross receipts (General public)	$ 34,000
Contributions (Substantial contributors)	35,000
Gross Investment Income	31,000
Total Support	$100,000

1972
Gross receipts (General public)	$ 35,000
Contributions (Substantial contributors)	30,000
Gross Investment Income	35,000
Total Support	$100,000

1973
Gross receipts (General public)	$ 30,000
Contributions (Substantial contributors)	39,000
Gross Investment Income	31,000
Total Support	$100,000

In applying section 509(a)(2) to the taxable year 1974 on the basis of subparagraph (1)(i) of this paragraph, the total amount of support from gross receipts from the general public ($134,000) for the period 1970 through 1973 was more than one-third, and the total amount of support from gross investment income ($126,000) was less than one-third of its total support for the same period ($400,000). For the taxable years 1974 and 1975, X is therefore considered "normally" to receive more than one-third of its support from the public sources described in section 509(a)(2)(A) and less than one-third of its support from items described in section 509(a)(2)(B) since due to the pattern of X's support, there are no substantial and material changes in the sources of the organization's support in these years. The fact that X received less than one-third of its support from section 509(a)(2)(A) sources in 1973 and more than one-third of its support from items described in section 509(a)(2)(B) in 1972 does not affect its status since it met the "normally" test over a 4-year period.

Example (2). Assume the same facts as in example (1) except that in 1973 X also received an unexpected bequest of $50,000 from A, an elderly widow who was interested in encouraging the work of X, but had no other relationship to it. Solely by reason of the bequest, A became a disqualified person. X used the bequest to create five new scholarships. Its operations otherwise remained the same. Under these circumstances X

Reg. § 1.509(a)-3(c)(6)

could not meet the 4-year support test since the total amount received from gross receipts from the general public ($134,000) would not be more than one-third of its total support for the 4-year period ($450,000). Since A is a disqualified person, her bequest cannot be included in the numerator of the one-third support test under section 509(a)(2)(A). However, based on the factors set forth in subparagraph (4) of this paragraph, A's bequest may be excluded as an unusual grant under subparagraph (3) of this paragraph. Therefore, X will be considered to have met the support test for the taxable years 1974 and 1975.

Example (3). In 1970, Y, an organization described in section 501(c)(3), was created by A, the holder of all the common stock in M corporation, B, A's wife, and C, A's business associate. Each of the three creators made small cash contributions to Y to enable it to begin operations. The purpose of Y was to sponsor and equip athletic teams for underprivileged children in the community. Between 1970 and 1973, Y was able to raise small amounts of contributions through fund raising drives and selling admission to some of the sponsored sporting events. For its first year of operations, it was determined that Y was excluded from the definition of "private foundation" under the provisions of section 509(a)(2). A made small contributions to Y from time to time. At all times, the operations of Y were carried out on a small scale, usually being restricted to the sponsorship of two to four baseball teams of underprivileged children. In 1974, M recapitalized and created a first and second class of 6 percent nonvoting preferred stock, most of which was held by A and B. A then contributed 49 percent of his common stock in M to Y. A, B, and C continued to be active participants in the affairs of Y from its creation through 1974. A's contribution of M's common stock was substantial and constituted 90 percent of Y's total support for 1974. Although Y could satisfy the one-third support test on the basis of the four taxable years prior to 1974, a combination of the facts and circumstances described in subparagraph (4) of this paragraph preclude A's contribution of M's common stock in 1974 from being excluded as an unusual grant under subparagraph (3) of this paragraph. A's contribution in 1974 constituted a substantial and material change in Y's sources of support within the meaning of subparagraph (1)(ii) of this paragraph and on the basis of the 5-year period prescribed in subparagraph (1)(ii) of this paragraph (1970 to 1974), Y would not be considered as "normally" meeting the one-third support test described in paragraph (a)(2) of this section for the taxable years 1974 (the current taxable year) and 1975 (the immediately succeeding taxable year).

Example (4). M, an organization described in section 501(c)(3), was organized in 1971 to promote the appreciation of ballet in a particular region of the United States. Its principal activities will consist of erecting a theater for the performance of ballet and the organization and operation of a ballet company. The governing body of M consists of 9 prominent unrelated citizens residing in the region who have either an expertise in ballet or a strong interest in encouraging appreciation of the art form. In order to provide sufficient capital for M to commence its activities, X, a private foundation, makes a grant of $500,000 in cash to M. Although A, the creator of X, is one of the 9 members of M's governing body, was one of M's original founders, and continues to lend his prestige to M's activities and fund raising efforts, A does not, directly or indirectly, exercise any control over M. By the close of its first taxable year, M has also received a significant amount of support from a number of smaller contributions and pledges from other members of the general public. Upon the opening of its first season of ballet performances, M expects to charge admission to the general public. Under the above circumstances, the grant by X to M may be excluded as an unusual grant under subparagraph (3) of this paragraph for purposes of determining whether M meets the one-third support test under section 509(a)(2). Although A was a founder and member of the governing body of M, X's grant may be excluded.

Example (5). Assume the same facts as example (4). In 1974, during M's third season of operations, B, a widow, passed away and bequeathed $4,000,000 to M. During 1971 through 1973, B had made small contributions to M, none exceeding $10,000 in any year. During 1971 through 1974, M had received approximately $550,000 from receipts for admissions and contributions from the general public. At the time of B's death, no person standing in a relationship to B described in section 4946(a)(1)(C) through (G) was a member of M's governing body. B's bequest was in the form of cash and readily marketable securities. The only condition placed upon the bequest was that it be used by M to advance the art of ballet. Under the above circumstances, the bequest of B to M may be excluded as an unusual grant under subparagraph (3) of this paragraph for purposes of determining whether M meets the one-third support test under section 509(a)(2).

Example (6). O is a research organization described in section 501(c)(3). O was created by A in 1971 for the purpose of carrying on economic

Reg. § 1.509(a)-3(c)(6)

studies primarily through persons receiving grants from O and engaging in the sale of economic publications. O's five member governing body consists of A, A's sons, B and C, and two unrelated economists. In 1971, A made a contribution to O of $100,000 to help establish the organization. During 1971 through 1974 A made annual contributions to O averaging $20,000 a year. During the same period, O received annual contributions from members of the general public averaging $15,000 per year and receipts from the sale of its publications averaging $50,000 per year. In 1974, B made an inter vivos contribution to O of $600,000 in cash and readily marketable securities. Under the above circumstances, B's contribution cannot be excluded as an unusual grant under subparagraph (3) of this paragraph for purposes of determining whether O meets the one-third support test.

Example (7). P is an educational organization described in section 501(c)(3). P was created in 1971. The governing body of P has 9 members, consisting of A, a prominent civic leader and 8 other unrelated civic leaders and educators in the community, who also participated in the creation of P. During 1971 through 1974, the principal source of income for P has been receipts from the sale of its educational periodicals. These sales have amounted to $200,000 for this period. Small contributions amounting to $50,000 have also been received during the same period from members of the governing body, including A, as well as other members of the general public. In 1974 A contributed $750,000 of the nonvoting stock of Y, a closely held corporation. A retained a substantial portion of the voting stock of Y. By a majority vote, the governing body decided to retain the Y stock for a period of at least 5 years. Under the above circumstances, A's contribution of the Y stock cannot be excluded as an unusual grant under subparagraph (3) of this paragraph for purposes of determining whether P meets the one-third support test.

(d) *Advance rulings to newly created organizations*—(1) *In general.* A ruling or determination letter that an organization is described in section 509(a)(2) will not be issued to a newly created organization prior to the close of its first taxable year consisting of at least 8 months. However, such organization may request a ruling or determination letter that it will be treated as a section 509(a)(2) organization for its first 2 taxable years (or its first 3 taxable years, if its first taxable year consists of less than 8 months). For purposes of this section such 2- or 3-year period, whichever is applicable, shall be referred to as the advance ruling period. Such an advance ruling or determination letter may be issued if the organization can reasonably be expected to meet the requirements of paragraph (a) of this section during the advance ruling period. The issuance of a ruling or determination letter will be discretionary with the Commissioner.

(2) *Basic consideration.* In determining whether an organization "can reasonably be expected" (within the meaning of subparagraph (1) of this paragraph) to meet the one-third support test under section 509(a)(2)(A) and the not-more-than-one-third support test under section 509(a)(2)(B) described in paragraph (a) of this section for its advance ruling period or extended advance ruling period as provided in subparagraph (4) of this paragraph, if applicable, the basic consideration is whether its organizational structure, proposed programs or activities, and intended method of operation are such as to attract the type of broadly based support from the general public, public charities, and governmental units which is necessary to meet such tests. While the factors which are relevant to this determination, and the weight accorded to each of them, may differ from case to case, depending on the nature and functions of the organization, a favorable determination will not be made where the facts indicate that an organization is likely during its advance or extended advance ruling period to receive less than one-third of its support from permitted sources (subject to the limitations of paragraph (b) of this section) or to receive more than one-third of its support from items described in section 509(a)(2)(B).

(3) *Factors taken into account.* All pertinent facts and circumstances shall be taken into account under subparagraph (2) of this paragraph in determining whether the organizational structure, programs or activities, and method of operation of an organization are such as to enable it to meet the tests under section 509(a)(2) for its advance or extended advance ruling period. Some of the pertinent factors are:

(i) Whether the organization has or will have a governing body which is comprised of public officials, or individuals chosen by public officials acting in their capacity as such, of persons having special knowledge in the particular field or discipline in which the organization is operating, of community leaders, such as elected officials, clergymen, and educators, or, in the case of a membership organization, of individuals elected pursuant to the organization's governing instrument or bylaws by a broadly based membership. This characteristic does not exist if the membership of the organization's governing body is such as to indicate that it represents the personal or private interests of disqualified persons, rather than the interests of the community or the general public.

(ii) Whether a substantial portion of the organization's initial funding is to be provided by the general public, by public charities, or by government grants, rather than by a limited number of grantors or contributors who are disqualified persons with respect to the organization. The fact that the organization plans to limit its activities to a particular community or region or to a special field which can be expected to appeal to a limited number of persons will be taken into consideration in determining whether those persons providing the initial support for the organization are representative of the general public. On the other hand, the subsequent sources of funding which the organization can reasonably expect to receive after it has become established and fully operational will also be taken into account.

(iii) Whether a substantial proportion of the organization's initial funds are placed, or will remain, in an endowment, and whether the investment of such funds is unlikely to result in more than one-third of its total support being received from items described in section 509(a)(2)(B).

(iv) In the case of an organization which carries on fund-raising activities, whether the organization has developed a concrete plan for solicitation of funds from the general public on a community or area-wide basis; whether any steps have been taken to implement such plan; whether any firm commitments of financial or other support have been made to the organization by civic, religious, charitable, or similar groups within the community; and whether the organization has made any commitments to, or established any working relationships with, those organizations or classes of persons intended as the future recipients of its funds.

(v) In the case of an organization which carries on community services, such as slum clearance and employment opportunities, whether the organization has a concrete program to carry out its work in the community; whether any steps have been taken to implement that program; whether it will receive any part of its funds from a public charity or governmental agency to which it is in some way held accountable as a condition of the grant or contribution; and whether it has enlisted the sponsorship or support of other civic or community leaders involved in community service programs similar to those of the organization.

(vi) In the case of an organization which carries on educational or other exempt activities for, or on behalf of, members, whether the solicitation for dues-paying members is designed to enroll a substantial number of persons in the community, area, profession, or field of special interest (depending on the size of the area and the nature of the organization's activities); whether membership dues for individual (rather than institutional) members have been fixed at rates designed to make membership available to a broad cross-section of the public rather than to restrict membership to a limited number of persons; and whether the activities of the organization will be likely to appeal to persons having some broad common interest or purpose, such as educational activities in the case of alumni associations, musical activities in the case of symphony societies, or civic affairs in the case of parent-teacher associations.

(vii) In the case of an organization which provides goods, services, or facilities, whether the organization is or will be required to make its services, facilities, performances or products available (regardless of whether a fee is charged) to the general public, public charities, or governmental units, rather than to a limited number of persons or organizations; whether the organization will avoid executing contracts to perform services for a limited number of firms or governmental agencies or bureaus; and whether the service to be provided is one which can be expected to meet a special or general need among a substantial portion of the general public.

(4) *Extension of advance ruling period.* (i) The advance ruling period described in subparagraph (1) of this paragraph shall be extended for a period of three taxable years after the close of the unextended advance ruling period if the organization so requests, but only if such organization's request accompanies its request for an advance ruling and is filed with a consent under section 6501(c)(4) to the effect that the period of limitation upon assessment under section 4940 for any taxable year within the extended advance ruling period shall not expire prior to 1 year after the date of the expiration of the time prescribed by law for the assessment of a deficiency for the last taxable year within the extended advance ruling period. An organization's extended advance ruling period is 5 taxable years if its first taxable year consists of at least 8 months, or is 6 taxable years if its first taxable year is less than 8 months.

(ii) Notwithstanding subdivision (i) of this subparagraph, an organization which has received or applied for an advance ruling prior to October 16, 1972, may file its request for the three-year extension within 90 days from such date, but only if it files the consents required in this section.

(iii) See paragraph (e)(4)(i)(*d*) of this section for the effect upon the initial determination of status of an organization which receives an

Reg. § 1.509(a)-3(d)(4)

advance ruling for an extended advance ruling period.

(e) *Status of newly created organizations*—(1) *Advance or extended advance ruling.* This subparagraph shall apply to a newly created organization which has received a ruling or determination letter under paragraph (d) of this section that it be treated as a section 509(a)(2) organization for its advance or extended advance ruling period. So long as such an organization's ruling or determination letter has not been terminated by the Commissioner before the expiration of the advance or extended advance ruling period, then whether or not such organization has satisfied the requirements of paragraph (a) of this section during such advance or extended advance ruling period, such an organization will be treated as an organization described in section 509(a)(2) in accordance with subparagraphs (2) and (3) of this paragraph, both for purposes of the organization and any grantor or contributor to such organization.

(2) *Reliance period.* Except as provided in subparagraphs (1) and (3) of this paragraph, an organization described in subparagraph (1) of this paragraph will be treated as an organization described in section 509(a)(2) for all purposes other than section 507(d) and 4940 for the period beginning with its inception and ending 90 days after its advance or extended advance ruling period. Such period will be extended until a final determination is made of such an organization's status only if the organization submits, within the 90-day period, information needed to determine whether it meets the requirements of paragraph (a) of this section for its advance or extended advance ruling period (even if such organization fails to meet the requirements of such paragraph (a)). However, since this subparagraph does not apply to section 4940, if it is subsequently determined that the organization was a private foundation from its inception, then the tax imposed by section 4940 shall be due without regard to the advance ruling or determination letter. Consequently, if any amount of tax under section 4940 in such a case is not paid on or before the last date prescribed for payment, the organization is liable for interest in accordance with section 6601. However, since any failure to pay such tax during the period referred to in this subparagraph is due to reasonable cause, the penalty under section 6651 with respect to the tax imposed by section 4940 shall not apply.

(3) *Grantors or contributors.* If a ruling or determination letter is terminated by the Commissioner prior to the expiration of the period described in subparagraph (2) of this paragraph, for purposes of sections 170, 507, 545(b)(2), 556(b)(2), 642(c), 4942, 4945, 2055, 2106(a)(2), and 2522 the status of grants or contributions with respect to grantors or contributors to such organizations will not be affected until notice of change of status of such organization is made to the public (such as by publication of the Internal Revenue Bulletin).

The preceding sentence shall not apply, however, if the grantor or contributor was responsible for, or aware of, the act or failure to act that resulted in the organization's loss of classification under section 509(a)(2) or acquired knowledge that the Internal Revenue Service had given notice to such organization that it would be deleted from such classification. See, however, § 1.509(a)-3(c)(5)(ii) for the procedures to be followed to protect the grantor or contributor from being considered responsible for, or aware of, the act or failure to act resulting in the grantee's loss of classification under section 509(a)(2).

(4) *Initial determination of status*—

(i) *New organizations.*

(*a*) The initial determination of status of a newly created organization is the first determination (other than by issuance of an advance ruling or determination letter under paragraph (d) of this section) that the organization will be considered as "normally" meeting the requirements of paragraph (a) of this section for a period beginning with its first taxable year.

(*b*) In the case of a new organization whose first taxable year is at least eight months, except as provided for in subdivision (i)(*d*) of this subparagraph, the initial determination of status shall be based on a computation period of either the first taxable year or the first and second taxable years.

(*c*) In the case of a new organization whose first taxable year is less than eight months, except as provided for in subdivision (i)(*d*) of this subparagraph, the initial determination of status shall be based on a computation period of either the first and second taxable years or the first, second and third taxable years.

(*d*) In the case of an organization which has received a ruling or determination letter for an extended advance ruling period under paragraph (d)(4) of this section, the initial determination of status shall be based on a computation period of all of the taxable years in the extended advance ruling period. However, where the ruling or determination letter for an extended advance ruling period under paragraph (d)(4) of this section is terminated by the Commissioner prior to the expiration of the period described in subparagraph (2) of this paragraph, the initial determination of status shall be based on a computation

Reg. § 1.509(a)-3(e)(1)

period of the period provided for in (*b*) or (*c*) of this subdivision or, if greater, the number of years to which the advance ruling applies.

(*e*) An initial determination that an organization will be considered as "normally" meeting the requirements of paragraph (a) of this section shall be effective for each taxable year in the computation period plus (except as provided by paragraph (c)(1)(ii) of this section relating to material changes in sources of support) the two taxable years immediately succeeding the computation period. Therefore, in the case of an organization referred to in (*b*) of this subdivision to which paragraph (c)(1)(ii) of this section does not apply, with respect to its first, second, and third taxable years, such an organization shall be described in section 509(a)(2) if it meets the requirements of paragraph (a) of this section for either its first taxable year or for its first and second taxable years on an aggregate basis. In addition, if it meets the requirements of paragraph (a) of this section for its first and second taxable years it shall be described in section 509(a)(2) for its fourth taxable year. Once an organization is considered as "normally" meeting the requirements of paragraph (a) for a period specified under this subdivision, paragraph (c)(1)(i), (ii), or (iv) of this section shall apply.

(*f*) The provisions of this subdivision may be illustrated by the following examples:

Example (1). X, a calendar year organization described in section 501(c)(3), is created in February 1972 for the purpose of displaying African art. The support X received from the public in 1972 satisfies the one-third support and not-more-than-one-third support tests described in section 509(a)(2) for its first taxable year, 1972. X may therefore get an initial determination that it meets the requirements of paragraph (a) of this section for its first taxable year beginning in February 1972 and ending on December 31, 1972. This determination will be effective for taxable years 1972, 1973 and 1974.

Example (2). Assume the same facts as in example (1) except that X also receives a substantial contribution from one individual in 1972 which is not excluded from the denominator of the one-third support fraction described in section 509(a)(2) by reason of the unusual grant provision of subparagraph (c)(3) of this section. Because of this substantial contribution, X fails to satisfy the one-third support test over its first taxable year, 1972. However, the support received from the public over X's first and second taxable years in the aggregate satisfies the one-third support and not-more-than-one-third support tests. X may therefore get an initial determination that it meets the requirements of paragraph (a) of this section for its first and second taxable years in the aggregate beginning in February 1972 and ending on December 31, 1973. This determination will be effective for taxable years 1972, 1973, 1974 and 1975.

Example (3). Y, a calendar year organization described in section 501(c)(3), is created in July 1972 for the encouragement of the musical arts. Y requests and receives an extended advance ruling period of five full taxable years plus its initial short taxable year of six months under subparagraph (d)(4) of this section. The extended advance ruling period begins in July 1972 and ends on December 31, 1977. The support received from the public over Y's first through sixth taxable years in the aggregate will satisfy the one-third support and not-more-than-one-third support tests described in section 509(a)(2). Therefore, Y in 1978 may get an initial determination that it meets the requirements of paragraph (a) of this section in the aggregate over all the taxable years in its extended advance ruling period beginning in July 1972 and ending on December 31, 1977. This determination will be effective for taxable years 1972 through 1979.

Example (4). Assume the same facts as in example (3) except that the ruling for the extended advance ruling period is terminated prospectively at the end of 1975, so that Y may not rely upon such ruling for 1976 or any succeeding year. The support received from the public over Y's first through fourth taxable years (1972 through 1975) will not satisfy the one-third support and not-more-than-one-third support tests described in section 509(a)(2). Because the ruling was terminated, the computation period for Y's initial determination of status is the period 1972 through 1975. Since Y has not met the requirements of paragraph (a) of this section for such computation period, Y is not described in section 509(a)(2) for purposes of its initial determination of status. If Y is not described in section 509(a)(1), (3), or (4), then Y is a private foundation. As of 1976, Y shall be treated as a private foundation for all purposes (except as provided in subparagraph (3) of this paragraph with respect to grantors and contributors), and as of July 1972 for purposes of the tax imposed by section 4940 and for purposes of section 507(d) (relating to aggregate tax benefit).

(ii) *Advance rulings.* Unless a newly created organization has obtained a ruling or determination letter under paragraph (d) of this section that it be treated as a section 509(a)(2) organization for its advance or extended advance ruling period, it can not rely upon the possibility

Reg. § 1.509(a)-3(e)(4)

it will meet the requirements of paragraph (a) of this section for a taxable year which begins before the close of either applicable computation period provided for in subdivision (i)(*b*) or (c) of this subparagraph. Therefore, an organization which has not obtained such a ruling or determination letter, in order to avoid the risks associated with subsequently being determined to be a private foundation, may comply with the rules applicable to private foundations, and may pay, for example, the tax imposed by section 4940. In that event, if the organization subsequently meets the requirements of paragraph (a) for either applicable computation period, it shall be treated as a section 509(a)(2) organization from its inception, and, therefore, any tax imposed under chapter 42 shall be refunded and section 509(b) shall not apply.

(iii) *Penalties.* If a newly created organization fails to obtain a ruling or determination letter under paragraph (d) of this section, and fails to meet the requirements of paragraph (a) of this section for the first applicable computation period provided for in subdivision (i)(*b*) or (c) of this subparagraph, see section 6651 for penalty for failure to file return and pay tax.

(iv) *Examples.* This subparagraph may be illustrated by the following examples:

Example (1). On January 1, 1972, A contributes $100,000 to X, an organization described in section 501(c)(3) which he created on such date. X is not described in section 509(a)(1), (3) or (4). X's governing instrument does not contain the provisions referred to in section 508(e).

Therefore, A is not entitled to a deduction under section 170 for the $100,000 contribution by reason of section 508(d)(2)(A) unless X is described in section 509(a)(2). If X meets the requirements of section 509(a)(2) for 1972 and 1973 on an aggregate basis, then whether or not X met the requirements of section 509(a)(2) for 1972 based on the support received in 1972, X would not have to meet the governing instrument requirements of section 508(e), and section 508(d)(2)(A) would not prevent A from claiming the deduction under section 170 for 1972. If X fails to meet the requirements of section 509(a)(2) for both 1972 and, on an aggregate basis, 1972 and 1973, X would lose its exempt status under section 508(e) for both 1972 and 1973, and A would be barred by section 508(d)(2)(A) from claiming a deduction for the $100,000 contribution to X.

Example (2). Assume the same facts as in example (1) except that X's governing instrument contains provisions which meet the requirements of section 508(e) in the event X is a private foundation, but do not apply to X in the event X is not a private foundation. Whether or not X meets the requirements of section 509(a)(2) for 1972 based on the support received in 1972 or 1972 and 1973 on an aggregate basis, since X meets the requirements of section 508(e), section 508(d)(2)(A) would not bar A from claiming a deduction under section 170 for 1972 for the contribution to X.

(f) *Gifts and contributions distinguished from gross receipts*—(1) *In general.* In determining whether an organization normally receives more than one-third of its support from permitted sources, all "gifts" and "contributions" (within the meaning of section 509(a)(2)(A)(i)) received from permitted sources, are includible in the numerator of the support fraction in each taxable year. However, "gross receipts" (within the meaning of section 509(a)(2)(A)(ii)) from admissions, sales of merchandise, performance of services, or furnishing of facilities, in an activity which is not an unrelated trade or business, are includible in the numerator of the support fraction in any taxable year only to the extent that such gross receipts do not exceed the limitation with respect to the greater of $5,000 or 1 percent of support which is described in paragraph (b) of this section. The terms "gifts" and "contributions" shall, for purposes of section 509(a)(2), have the same meaning as such terms have under section 170(c) and also include bequests, legacies, devises, and transfers within the meaning of section 2055 or 2106(a)(2). Thus, for purposes of section 509(a)(2)(A), any payment of money or transfer of property without adequate consideration shall be considered a "gift" or "contribution". Where payment is made or property transferred as consideration for admissions, sales of merchandise, performance of services, or furnishing of facilities to the donor, the status of the payment or transfer under section 170(c) shall determine whether and to what extent such payment or transfer constitutes a "gift" or "contribution" under section 509(a)(2)(A)(i) as distinguished from "gross receipts" from related activities under section 509(a)(2)(A)(ii). For purposes of section 509(a)(2), the term *contributions* includes qualified sponsorship payments (as defined in § 1.513-4) in the form of money or property (but not services).

(2) *Valuation of property.* For purposes of section 509(a)(2), the amount includible in computing support with respect to gifts, grants or contributions of property or use of such property shall be the fair market or rental value of such property at the date of such gift or contribution.

(3) *Examples.* The provisions of this paragraph (f) may be illustrated by the following examples:

Reg. § 1.509(a)-3(f)(1)

Example 1. P is a local agricultural club described in section 501(c)(3). In order to encourage interest and proficiency by young people in farming and raising livestock, it makes awards at its annual fair for outstanding specimens of produce and livestock. Most of these awards are cash or other property donated by local businessmen. When the awards are made, the donors are given recognition for their donations by being identified as the donor of the award. The recognition given to donors is merely incidental to the making of the award to worthy youngsters. For these reasons, the donations will constitute "contributions" for purposes of section 509(a)(2)(A)(i). The amount includible in computing support with respect to such contributions is equal to the cash contributed or the fair market value of other property on the dates contributed.

Example 2. Q, a performing arts center, enters into a contract with a large company to be the exclusive sponsor of the center's theatrical events. The company makes a payment of cash and products in the amount of $100,000 to Q, and in return, Q agrees to make a broadcast announcement thanking the company before each show and to provide $2,000 of advertising in the show's program (2% of $100,000 is $2,000). The announcement constitutes use or acknowledgment pursuant to section 513(i)(2). Because the value of the advertising does not exceed 2% of the total payment, the entire $100,000 is a qualified sponsorship payment under section 513(i), and $100,000 is treated as a contribution for purposes of section 509(a)(2)(A)(i).

Example 3. R, a charity, enters into a contract with a law firm to be the exclusive sponsor of the charity's outreach program. Instead of making a cash payment, the law firm agrees to perform $100,000 of legal services for the charity. In return, R agrees to acknowledge the law firm in all its informational materials. The total fair market value of the legal services, or $100,000, is a qualified sponsorship payment under section 513(i), but no amount is treated as a contribution under section 509(a)(2)(A)(i) because the contribution is of services.

(g) *Grants distinguished from gross receipts*— (1) *In general.* In determining whether an organization normally receives more than one-third of its support from public sources, all "grants" (within the meaning of section 509(a)(2)(A)(i)) received from permitted sources are includible in full in the numerator of the support fraction in each taxable year. However, "gross receipts" (within the meaning of section 509(a)(2)(A)(ii)) from admissions, sales of merchandise, performance of services, or furnishing of facilities, in an activity which is not an unrelated trade or business, are includible in the numerator of the support fraction in any taxable year only to the extent that such gross receipts do not exceed the limitation with respect to the greater of $5,000 or 1 percent of support which is described in paragraph (b) of this section. A grant is normally made to encourage the grantee organization to carry on certain programs or activities in furtherance of its exempt purposes. It may contain certain terms and conditions imposed by the grantor to insure that the grantee's programs or activities are conducted in a manner compatible with the grantor's own programs and policies and beneficial to the public. The grantee may also perform a service or produce a work product which incidentally benefits the grantor. Because of the imposition of terms and conditions, the frequent similarity of public purposes of grantor and grantee, and the possibility of benefit resulting to the grantor, amounts received as grants "for" the carrying on of exempt activities are sometimes difficult to distinguish from amounts received as gross receipts "from" the carrying on of exempt activities. The fact that the agreement, pursuant to which payment is made, is designated a "contract" or a "grant" is not controlling for purposes of classifying the payment under section 509(a)(2).

(2) *Distinguishing factors.* For purposes of Section 509(a)(2)(A)(ii), in distinguishing the term "gross receipts" from the term "grants", the term "gross receipts" means amounts received from an activity which is not an unrelated trade or business, if a specific service, facility, or product is provided to serve the direct and immediate needs of the payor, rather than primarily to confer a direct benefit upon the general public. In general, payments made primarily to enable the payor to realize or receive some economic or physical benefit as a result of the service, facility, or product obtained will be treated as "gross receipts" with respect to the payee. The fact that a profit-making organization would, primarily for its own economic or physical betterment, contract with a nonprofit organization for the rendition of a comparable service, facility or product from such organization constitutes evidence that any payments received by the nonprofit payee organization (whether from a governmental unit, a nonprofit or a profit-making organization) for such services, facilites or products are primarily for the economic or physical benefit of the payor and would therefore be considered "gross receipts," rather than "grants" with respect to the payee organization. For example, if a nonprofit hospital described in section 170(b)(1)(A)(iii) engages an exempt research and development organization to

Reg. § 1.509(a)-3(g)(2)

develop a more economical system of preparing food for its own patients and personnel, and it can be established that a hospital operated for profit might engage the services of such an organization to perform a similar benefit for its economic betterment, such fact would constitute evidence that the payments received by the research and development organization constitute "gross receipts", rather than "grants". Research leading to the development of tangible products for the use or benefit of the payor will generally be treated as a service provided to serve the direct and immediate needs of the payor, while basic research or studies carried on in the physical or social sciences will generally be treated as primarily to confer a direct benefit upon the general public.

(3) *Examples.* The application of this paragraph may be illustrated by the following examples:

Example (1). M, a nonprofit research organization described in section 501(c)(3), engages in some contract research. It receives funds from the government to develop a specific electronic device needed to perfect articles of space equipment. The initiative for the project came solely from the government. Furthermore, the government could have contracted with profit-making research organizations which carry on similar activities. The funds received from the government for this project are gross receipts and do not constitute "grants" within the meaning of section 509(a)(2)(A)(i). M provided a specific product at the government's request and thus was serving the direct and immediate needs of the payor within the meaning of subparagraph (2) of this paragraph.

Example (2). N is a nonprofit educational organization described in section 501(c)(3). Its principal activity is to operate institutes to train employees of various industries in the principles of management and administration. The government pays N to set up a special institute for certain government employees and to train them over a two-year period. Management training is also provided by profit-making organizations. The funds received are included as "gross receipts." The particular services rendered were to serve the direct and immediate needs of the government in the training of its employees within the meaning of subparagraph (2) of this paragraph.

Example (3). The Office of Economic Opportunity makes a Community Action Program Grant to O, an organization described in section 509(a)(1). O serves as a "delegate agency" of OEO for purposes of financing a local community action program. As part of this program, O signs an agreement with X, an educational and charitable organization described in section 501(c)(3), to carry out a housing program for the benefit of poor families. Pursuant to this agreement, O pays X out of the funds provided by OEO to build or rehabilitate low income housing and to provide advisory services to other nonprofit organizations in order for them to meet similar housing objectives, all on a nonprofit basis. Payments made from O to X constitute "grants" for purposes of section 509(a)(2)(A) because such program is carried on primarily for the direct benefit of the community.

Example (4). P is an educational institute described in section 501(c)(3). It carries on studies and seminars to assist institutions of higher learning. It receives funds from the government to research and develop a program of black studies for institutions of higher learning. The performance of such a service confers a direct benefit upon the public. Because such program is carried on primarily for the direct benefit of the public, the funds are considered a "grant."

Example (5). Q is an organization described in section 501(c)(3) which carries on medical research. Its efforts have primarily been directed toward cancer research. Q sought funds from the government for a particular project being contemplated in connection with its work. In order to encourage its activities, the government gives Q the sum of $25,000. The research project sponsored by government funds is primarily to provide direct benefit to the general public, rather than to serve the direct and immediate needs of the government. The funds are therefore considered a "grant."

Example (6). R is a public service organization described in section 501(c)(3) and composed of state and local officials involved in public works activities. The Bureau of Solid Waste Management of the Department of Health, Education, and Welfare paid R to study the feasibility of a particular system for disposal of solid waste. Upon completion of the study, R was required to prepare a final report setting forth its findings and conclusions. Although R is providing the Bureau of Solid Waste Management with a final report, such report is the result of basic research and study in the physical sciences and is primarily to provide direct benefit to the general public by serving to further the general functions of government, rather than a direct and immediate governmental need. The funds paid to R are therefore a "grant" within the meaning of section 509(a)(2).

Example (7). R is the public service organization referred to in example (6). W, a municipality described in section 170(c)(1), decides to construct a sewage disposal plant. W pays R to

Reg. § 1.509(a)-3(g)(3)

study a number of possible locations for such plant and to make recommendations to W, based upon a number of factors, as to the best location. W instructed R that in making its recommendation, primary consideration should be given to minimizing the costs of the project to W. Since the study commissioned by W was primarily directed towards producing an economic benefit to W in the form of minimizing the costs of its project, the services rendered are treated as serving W's direct and immediate needs and are includible as "gross receipts" by R.

Example (8). S is an organization described in section 501(c)(3). It was organized and is operated to further African development and strengthen understanding between the United States and Africa. To further these purposes, S receives funds from the Agency for International Development and the Department of State under which S is required to carry out the following programs: selection, transportation, orientation, counseling, and language training of African students admitted to American institutions of higher learning; payment of tuition, other fees, and maintenance of such students; and operation of schools and vocational training programs in underdeveloped countries for residents of those countries. Since the programs carried on by S are primarily to provide direct benefit to the general public, all of the funds received by S from the federal agencies are considered "grants" within the meaning of section 509(a)(2).

(h) *Definition of membership fees*—(1) *General rule.* For purposes of section 509(a)(2), the fact that a membership organization provides services, admissions, facilities, or merchandise to its members as part of its overall activities will not, in itself, result in the classification of fees received from members as "gross receipts" rather than "membership fees". If an organization uses membership fees as a means of selling admissions, merchandise, services, or the use of facilities to members of the general public who have no common goal or interest (other than the desire to purchase such admissions, merchandise, services, or use of facilities), then the income received from such fees shall not constitute "membership fees" under section 509(a)(2)(A)(i), but shall, if from a related activity, constitute "gross receipts" under section 509(a)(2)(A)(ii). On the other hand, to the extent the basic purpose for making the payment is to provide support for the organization rather than to purchase admissions, merchandise, services, or the use of facilities, the income received from such payment shall constitute "membership fees".

(2) *Examples.* The provisions of this paragraph may be illustrated by the following examples:

Example (1). M is a symphony society described in section 501(c)(3). Its primary purpose is to support the local symphony orchestra. The organization has three classes of membership. Contributing members pay annual dues of $10, sustaining members pay $25, and honorary members pay $100. The dues are placed in a maintenance fund which is used to provide financial assistance in underwriting the orchestra's annual deficit. Members have the privilege of purchasing subscriptions to the concerts before they go on sale to the general public, but must pay the same price as any other member of the public. They also are entitled to attend a number of rehearsals each season without charge. Under these circumstances, M's receipts from members constitute "membership fees" for purposes of section 509(a)(2)(A)(i).

Example (2). N is a theater association described in section 501(c)(3). Its purpose is to support a repertory company in the community in order to make live theatrical performances available to the public. The organization sponsors six plays each year. Members of the organization are entitled to a season subscription to the plays. The fee paid as dues approximates the retail price of the six plays, less a ten percent discount. Tickets to each performance are also sold directly to the general public. The organization also holds a series of lectures on the theater which members may attend. Under these circumstances, the fees paid by members as dues will be considered "gross receipts" from a related activity. Although the fees are designated as membership fees, they are actually admissions to a series of plays.

(i) *"Bureau" defined* —(1) *In general.* The term "any bureau or similar agency of a governmental unit" (within the meaning of section 509(a)(2)(A)(ii)), refers to a specialized operating unit of the executive, judicial or legislative branch of government where business is conducted under certain rules and regulations. Since the term "bureau" refers to a unit functioning at the operating, as distinct from the policy-making, level of government, it is normally descriptive of a subdivision of a department of government. The term "bureau", for purposes of section 509(a)(2)(A)(ii), would therefore not usually include those levels of government which are basically policy-making or administrative, such as the office of the Secretary or Assistant Secretary of a department, but would consist of the highest operational level under such policy-making or administrative levels. Each subdivision of a larger unit within the Federal gov-

Reg. § 1.509(a)-3(i)(1)

ernment, which is headed by a Presidential appointee holding a position at or above Level V of the Executive Schedule under 5 U.S.C. 5316, will normally be considered an administrative or policy-making, rather than an operating, unit. Amounts received from a unit functioning at the policy-making or administrative level of government will be treated as received from one bureau or similar agency of such unit. Units of a governmental agency above the operating level shall be aggregated and considered a separate bureau for this purpose. Thus, an organization receiving gross receipts from both a policy-making or administrative unit and an operational unit of a department will be treated as receiving gross receipts from two "bureaus" within the meaning of section 509(a)(2)(A)(ii). For purposes of this subparagraph, the Departments of Air Force, Army, and Navy are separate departments and each is considered as having its own policy-making, administrative, and operating units.

(2) *Examples.* The provisions of this paragraph may be illustrated by the following examples:

Example (1). The Bureau of Health Insurance is considered a "bureau" within the meaning of section 509(a)(2)(A)(ii). It is a part of the Department of Health, Education and Welfare, whose Secretary performs a policy-making function, and is under the Social Security Administration, which is basically an administrative unit. The Bureau of Health Insurance is in the first operating level within the Social Security Administration. Similarly, the National Cancer Institute would be considered a "bureau", as it is an operating part of the National Institutes of Health within the Department of Health, Education, and Welfare.

Example (2). The Bureau for Africa and the Bureau for Latin America are considered "bureaus" within the meaning of section 509(a)(2)(A)(ii). Both are separate operating units under the Administrator of the Agency for International Development, a policy-making official. If an organization received gross receipts from both of these bureaus, the amount of gross receipts received from each would be subject to the greater of $5,000 or 1 percent limitation under section 509(a)(2)(A)(ii).

Example (3). The Bureau of International Affairs of the Civil Aeronautics Board is considered a "bureau" within the meaning of section 509(a)(2)(A)(ii). It is an operating unit under the administrative office of the Executive Director. The subdivisions of the Bureau of International Affairs are Geographic Areas and Project Development Staff. If an organization received gross receipts from these subdivisions, the total gross receipts from these subdivisions would be considered gross receipts from the same "bureau", the Bureau of International Affairs, and would be subject to the greater of $5,000 or 1 percent limitation under section 509(a)(2)(A)(ii).

Example (4). The Department of Mental Health, a state agency which is an operational part of State X's Department of Public Health, is considered a "bureau." The Department of Public Health is basically an administrative agency and the Department of Mental Health is at the first operational level within it.

Example (5). The Aeronautical Systems Division of the Air Force Systems Command, and other units on the same level, are considered separate "bureaus" within the meaning of section 509(a)(2)(A)(ii). They are part of the Department of the Air Force which is a separate department for this purpose, as are the Army and Navy. The Secretary and the Under Secretary of the Air Force perform the policy-making function, the Chief of Staff and the Air Force Systems Command are basically administrative, having a comprehensive complement of staff functions to provide administration for the various divisions. The Aeronautical Systems division and other units on the same level are thus the first operating level, as evidenced by the fact that they are the units that let contracts and perform the various operating functions.

Example (6). The Division of Space Nuclear Systems, the Division of Biology and Medicine, and other units on the same level within the Atomic Energy Commission are each separate "bureaus" within the meaning of section 509(a)(2)(A)(ii). The Commissioners (which make up the Commission) are the policy-makers. The General Manager and the various Assistant General Managers perform the administrative function. The various Divisions perform the operating function as evidenced by the fact that each has separate programs to pursue and contracts specifically for these various programs.

(j) *Grants from public charities*—(1) *General rule.* For purposes of the one-third support test in section 509(a)(2)(A), grants (as defined in paragraph (g) of this section) received from an organization described in section 509(a)(1) (hereinafter referred to in this subparagraph as a "public charity") are generally includible in full in computing the numerator of the recipient's support fraction for the taxable year in question. It is sometimes necessary to determine whether the recipient of a grant from a public charity has received such support from the public charity as a grant, or whether the recipient has in fact re-

Reg. § 1.509(a)-3(i)(2)

ceived such support as an indirect contribution from a donor to the public charity. If the amount received is considered a grant from the public charity, it is fully includible in the numerator of the support fraction under section 509(a)(2)(A). However, if the amount received is considered to be an indirect contribution from one of the public charity's donors which has passed through the public charity to the recipient organization, such amount will retain its character as a contribution from such donor and, if, for example, the donor is a substantial contributor (as defined in section 507(d)(2)) with respect to the ultimate recipient, such amount shall be excluded from the numerator of the support fraction under section 509(a)(2). If a public charity makes both an indirect contribution from its donor and an additional grant to the ultimate recipient, the indirect contribution shall be treated as made first.

(2) *Indirect contributions.* For purposes of subparagraph (1) of this paragraph, an indirect contribution is one which is expressly or impliedly earmarked by the donor as being for, or for the benefit of, a particular recipient (rather than for a particular purpose).

(3) *Examples.* The provisions of this paragraph may be illustrated by the following examples:

Example (1). M, a national foundation for the encouragement of the musical arts, is an organization described in section 170(b)(1)(A)(vi). A gives M a donation of $5,000 without imposing any restrictions or conditions upon the gift. M subsequently makes a $5,000 grant to X, an organization devoted to giving public performances of chamber music. Since the grant to X is treated as being received from M, it is fully includible in the numerator of X's support fraction for the taxable year of receipt.

Example (2). Assume M is the same organization described in example (1). B gives M a donation of $10,000, but requires that M spend the money for the purpose of supporting organizations devoted to the advancement of contemporary American music. M has complete discretion as to the organizations of the type described to which it will make a grant. M decides to make grants of $5,000 each to Y and Z, both being organizations described in section 501(c)(3) and devoted to furthering contemporary American music. Since the grants to Y and Z are treated as being received from M, Y and Z may each include one of the $5,000 grants in the numerator of its support fraction for purposes of section 509(a)(2)(A). Although the donation to M was conditioned upon the use of the funds for a particular purpose, M was free to select the ultimate recipient.

Example (3). N is a national foundation for the encouragement of art and is an organization described in section 170(b)(1)(A)(vi). Grants to N are permitted to be earmarked for particular purposes. O, which is an art workshop devoted to training young artists and claiming status under section 509(a)(2), persuades C, a private foundation, to make a grant of $25,000 to N. C is a disqualified person with respect to O. C made the grant to N with the understanding that N would be bound to make a grant to O in the sum of $25,000, in addition to a matching grant of N's funds to O in the sum of $25,000. Only the $25,000 received directly from N is considered a grant from N. The other $25,000 is deemed an indirect contribution from C to O and is to be excluded from the numerator of O's support fraction.

(k) *Method of accounting.* For purposes of section 509(a)(2), an organization's support will be determined solely on the cash receipts and disbursement method of accounting described in section 446(c)(1). For example, if a grantor makes a grant to an organization payable over a term of years, such grant will be includible in the support fraction of the grantee organization only when and to the extent amounts payble under the grant are received by the grantee.

(l) *Gross receipts from section 513(a)(1), (2), or (3) activities.* For purposes of section 509(a)(2)(A)(ii), gross receipts from activities described in section 513(a)(1), (2), or (3) will be considered gross receipts from activities which are not unrelated trade or business.

(m) *Gross receipts distinguished from gross investment income.* (1) For purposes of section 509(a)(2), where the charitable purpose of an organization described in section 501(c)(3) is accomplished through the furnishing of facilities for a rental fee or loans to a particular class of persons, such as aged, sick or needy persons, the support received from such persons will be considered "gross receipts" (within the meaning of section 509(d)(2)) from an activity which is not an unrelated trade or business, rather than "gross investment income". However, if such organization also furnishes facilities or loans to persons who are not members of such class and such furnishing does not contribute importantly to the accomplishment of such organization's exempt purposes (aside from the need of such organization for income or funds or the use it makes of the profits derived), the support received from such furnishing will be considered "rents" or "interest" and therefore will be treated as "gross investment income" within

Reg. § 1.509(a)-3(m)

the meaning of section 509(d)(4), unless such income is included in computing the tax imposed by section 511.

(2) The provisions of this paragraph may be illustrated by the following example:

Example. X, an organization described in section 501(c)(3), is organized and operated to provide living facilities for needy widows of deceased servicemen. X charges such widows a small rental fee for the use of such facilities. Since X is accomplishing its exempt purpose through the rental of such facilities, the support received from the widows is considered "gross receipts" within the meaning of section 509(d)(2). However, if X rents part of its facilities to persons having no relationship to X's exempt purpose, the support received from such rentals will be considered "gross investment income" within the meaning of section 509(d)(4), unless such income is included in computing the tax imposed by section 511. [Reg. § 1.509(a)-3.]

☐ [T.D. 7212, 10-16-72. Amended by T.D. 7784, 7-22-81; T.D. 8423, 7-28-92 and T.D. 8991, 4-24-2002.]

[Reg. § 1.509(a)-4]

§ 1.509(a)-4. Supporting organizations.—(a) *In general.* (1) Section 509(a)(3) excludes from the definition of "private foundation" those organizations which meet the requirements of subparagraphs (A), (B), and (C) thereof.

(2) Section 509(a)(3)(A) provides that a section 509(a)(3) organization must be organized, and at all times thereafter operated, exclusively for the benefit of, to perform the functions of, or to carry out the purposes of one or more specified organizations described in section 509(a)(1) or (2). Section 509(a)(3)(A) describes the nature of the support or benefit which a section 509(a)(3) organization must provide to one or more section 509(a)(1) or (2) organizations. For purposes of section 509(a)(3)(A), paragraph (b) of this section generally describes the organizational and operational tests; paragraph (c) of this section describes permissible purposes under the organizational test; paragraph (d) of this section describes the requirement of supporting or benefiting one or more "specified" publicly supported organizations; and paragraph (e) of this section describes permissible beneficiaries and activities under the operational test.

(3) Section 509(a)(3)(B) provides that a section 509(a)(3) organization must be operated, supervised, or controlled by or in connection with one or more organizations described in section 509(a)(1) or (2). Section 509(a)(3)(B) and paragraph (f) of this section describe the nature of the relationship which must exist between the section 509(a)(3) and section 509(a)(1) or (2) organizations. For purposes of section 509(a)(3)(B), paragraph (g) of this section defines "operated, supervised, or controlled by"; paragraph (h) of this section defines "supervised or controlled in connection with"; and paragraph (i) of this section defines "operated in connection with".

(4) Section 509(a)(3)(C) provides that a section 509(a)(3) organization must not be controlled directly or indirectly by disqualified persons (other than foundation managers or organizations described in section 509(a)(1) or (2)). Section 509(a)(3)(C) and paragraph (j) of this section prescribe a limitation on the control over the section 509(a)(3) organization.

(5) For purposes of this section, the term "supporting organization" means either an organization described in section 509(a)(3) or an organization seeking section 509(a)(3) status, depending upon its context. For purposes of this section, the term "publicly supported organization" means an organization described in section 509(a)(1) or (2).

(b) *Organizational and operational tests.* (1) Under subparagraph (A) of section 509(a)(3), in order to qualify as a supporting organization, an organization must be both organized and operated exclusively "for the benefit of, to perform the functions of, or to carry out the purposes of" (hereinafter referred to in this section as being organized and operated "to support or benefit") one or more specified publicly supported organizations. If an organization fails to meet either the organizational or the operational test, it cannot qualify as a supporting organization.

(2) In the case of supporting organizations created prior to January 1, 1970, the organizational and operational tests shall apply as of January 1, 1970. Therefore, even though the original articles of organization did not limit its purposes to those required under section 509(a)(3)(A) and even though it operated before January 1, 1970, for some purpose other than those required under section 509(a)(3)(A), an organization will satisfy the organizational and operational tests if, on January 1, 1970, and at all times thereafter, it is so constituted as to comply with these tests.

For the special rules pertaining to the application of the organizational and operational tests to organizations terminating their private foundation status under the 12-month or 60-month termination period provided under section 507(b)(1)(B) by becoming "public" under section 509(a)(3), see the regulations under section 507(b).

(c) *Organizational test*—(1) *In general.* An organization is organized exclusively for one or more of the purposes specified in section 509(a)(3)(A) only if its articles of organization (as defined in § 1.501(c)(3)-1(b)(2)):

(i) Limit the purposes of such organization to one or more of the purposes set forth in section 509(a)(3)(A);

(ii) Do not expressly empower the organization to engage in activities which are not in furtherance of the purposes referred to in subdivision (i) of this subparagraph;

(iii) State the specified publicly supported organizations on whose behalf such organization is to be operated (within the meaning of paragraph (d) of this section); and

(iv) Do not expressly empower the organization to operate to support or benefit any organization other than the specified publicly supported organizations referred to in subdivision (iii) of this subparagraph.

(2) *Purposes.* In meeting the organizational test, the organization's purposes, as stated in its articles, may be as broad as, or more specific than, the purposes set forth in section 509(a)(3)(A). Therefore, an organization which, by the terms of its articles, is formed "for the benefit of" one or more specified publicly supported organizations shall, if it otherwise meets the other requirements of this paragraph, be considered to have met the organizational test. Similarly, articles which state that an organization is formed "to perform the publishing functions" of a specified university are sufficient to comply with the organizational test. An organization which is "operated, supervised, or controlled by" (within the meaning of paragraph (g) of this section) or "supervised or controlled in connection with" (within the meaning of paragraph (h) of this section) one or more section 509(a)(1) or (2) organizations to carry out the purposes of such organizations, will be considered as meeting the requirements of this paragraph if the purposes set forth in its articles are similar to, but no broader than, the purposes set forth in the articles of its controlling section 509(a)(1) or (2) organizations. If, however, the organization by which it is operated, supervised, or controlled is a publicly supported section 501(c)(4), (5) or (6) organization (deemed to be a section 509(a)(2) organization for purposes of section 509(a)(3) under the provisions of section 509(a)), the supporting organization will be considered as meeting the requirements of this paragraph if its articles require it to carry on charitable, etc., activities within the meaning of section 170(c)(2).

(3) *Limitations.* An organization is not organized exclusively for the purposes set forth in section 509(a)(3)(A) if its articles expressly permit it to operate to support or benefit any organization other than those specified publicly supported organizations referred to in subparagraph (1)(iii) of this paragraph. Thus, for example, an organization will not meet the organizational test under section 509(a)(3)(A) if its articles expressly empower it to pay over any part of its income to, or perform any service for, any organization other than those publicly supported organizations specified in its articles (within the meaning of paragraph (d) of this section). The fact that the actual operations of such organization have been exclusively for the benefit of the specified publicly supported organizations shall not be sufficient to permit it to meet the organizational test.

(d) *Specified organizations*—(1) *In general.* In order to meet the requirements of section 509(a)(3)(A), an organization must be organized and operated exclusively to support or benefit one or more "specified" publicly supported organizations. The manner in which the publicly supported organizations must be "specified" in the articles for purposes of section 509(a)(3)(A) will depend upon whether the supporting organization is "operated, supervised, or controlled by" or "supervised or controlled in connection with" (within the meaning of paragraph (g) and (h) of this section) such organizations or whether it is "operated in connection with" (within the meaning of paragraph (i) of this section) such organizations.

(2) *Nondesignated publicly supported organizations; requirements.* (i) Except as provided in subdivision (iv) of this subparagraph, in order to meet the requirements of subparagraph (1) of this paragraph, the articles of the supporting organization must designate each of the "specified" organizations by name unless:

(a) The supporting organization is operated, supervised, or controlled by (within the meaning of paragraph (g) of this section), or is supervised or controlled in connection with (within the meaning of paragraph (h) of this section) one or more publicly supported organizations; and

(b) The articles of organization of the supporting organization require that it be operated to support or benefit one or more beneficiary organizations which are designated by class or purpose and which include:

(1) The publicly supported organizations referred to in subdivision (i)*(a)* of this subparagraph (without designating such organization by name); or

(2) Publicly supported organizations which are closely related in purpose or function to those publicly supported organizations referred to in subdivision (i)*(a)* or this subparagraph (without designating such organization by name).

Reg. § 1.509(a)-4(d)(2)

(ii) If a supporting organization is described in subdivision (i)(a) of this subparagraph, it will not be considered as failing to meet the requirements of subparagraph (1) of this paragraph that the publicly supported organizations be specified merely because its articles of organization permit the conditions described in subparagraphs (3)(i), (ii), and (iii) and (4)(i)(a) and (b) of this paragraph.

(iii) This subparagraph may be illustrated by the following examples:

Example (1). X is an organization described in section 501(c)(3) which operates for the benefit of institutions of higher learning in the state of Y. X is controlled by these institutions (within the meaning of paragraph (g) of this section) and such institutions are all section 509(a)(1) organizations. X's articles will meet the organizational test if they require X to operate for the benefit of institutions of higher learning or educational organizations in the state of Y (without naming each institution). X's articles would also meet the organizational test if they provided for the giving of scholarships to enable students to attend institutions of higher learning but only in the state of Y.

Example (2). M is an organization described in section 501(c)(3) which was organized and operated by representatives of N church to run a home for the aged. M is controlled (within the meaning of paragraph (g) of this section) by N church, a section 509(a)(1) organization. The care of the sick and the aged are long standing temporal functions and purposes of organized religion. By operating a home for the aged, M is operating to support or benefit N church in carrying out one of its temporal purposes. Thus M's articles will meet the organizational test if they require M to care for the aged since M is operating to support one of N church's purposes (without designating N church by name).

(iv) A supporting organization will meet the requirements of subparagraph (1) of this paragraph even though its articles do not designate each of the "specified" organizations by name if:

(a) There has been an historic and continuing relationship between the supporting organization and the section 509(a)(1) or (2) organizations, and

(b) By reason of such relationship, there has developed a substantial identity of interests between such organizations.

(3) *Nondesignated publicly supported organizations; scope of rule.* If the requirements of subparagraph (2)(i)(a) of this paragraph are met, a supporting organization will not be considered as failing the test of being organized for the benefit of "specified" organizations solely because its articles:

(i) Permit the substitution of one publicly supported organization within a designated class for another publicly supported organization either in the same or a different class designated in the articles;

(ii) Permit the supporting organization to operate for the benefit of new or additional publicly supported organizations of the same or a different class designated in the articles; or

(iii) Permit the supporting organization to vary the amount of its support among different publicly supported organizations within the class or classes of organizations designated by the articles.

For example, X is an organization which operates for the benefit of private colleges in the state of Y. If X is controlled by these colleges (within the meaning of paragraph (g) of this section) and such colleges are all section 509(a)(1) organizations, X's articles will meet the organizational test even if they permit X to operate for the benefit of any new colleges created in state Y in addition to the existing colleges or in lieu of one which has ceased to operate, or if they permit X to vary its support by paying more to one college than to another in a particular year.

(4) *Designated publicly supported organizations.* (i) If an organization is organized and operated to support one or more publicly supported organizations and it is "operated in connection with" such organization or organizations, then, except as provided in subparagraph (2)(iv) of this paragraph, its articles of organization must, for purposes of satisfying the organizational test under section 509(a)(3)(A), designate the "specified" organizations by name. Under the circumstances described in this subparagraph, a supporting organization which has one or more "specified" organizations designated by name in its articles, will not be considered as failing the test of being organized for the benefit of "specified" organizations solely because its articles:

(a) Permit a publicly supported organization which is designated by class or purpose, rather than by name, to be substituted for the publicly supported organization or organizations designated by name in the articles, but only if such substitution is conditioned upon the occurrence of an event which is beyond the control of the supporting organization, such as loss of exemption, substantial failure or abandonment of operations, or dissolution of the publicly supported organization or organizations designated in the articles;

Reg. § 1.509(a)-4(d)(3)

(b) Permit the supporting organization to operate for the benefit of a beneficiary organization which is not a publicly supported organization, but only if such supporting organization is currently operating for the benefit of a publicly supported organization and the possibility of its operating for the benefit of other than a publicly supported organization is a remote contingency; or

(c) Permit the supporting organization to vary the amount of its support between different designated organizations, so long as it meets the requirements of the integral part test set forth in paragraph (i)(3) of this section with respect to at least one beneficiary organization.

(ii) If the beneficiary organization referred to in subdivision (i)(b) of this subparagraph is not a publicly supported organization, the supporting organization will not then meet the operational test of paragraph (e)(1) of this section. Therefore, if a supporting organization substituted in accordance with such subdivision (i)(b) a beneficiary other than a publicly supported organization and operated in support of such beneficiary organization, the supporting organization would not be described in section 509(a)(3).

(iii) This subparagraph may be illustrated by the following example:

Example. X is a charitable trust described in section 4947 (a)(1) organized in 1968. Under the terms of its trust instrument, X's trustees are required to pay over all of X's annual income to M University Medical School for urological research. If M University Medical School is unable or unwilling to devote these funds to urological research, the trustees are required to pay all of such income to N University Medical School. However if N University Medical School is also unable or unwilling to devote these funds to urological research, X's trustees are directed to choose a similar organization willing to apply X's funds for urological research. From 1968 to 1973, X pays all of its net income to M University Medical School pursuant to the terms of the trust. M and N are publicly supported organizations. Although the contingent remainderman may not be a publicly supported organization, the possibility that X may operate for the benefit of other than a publicly supported organization is, in 1973, a remote possibility, and X will be considered as operating for the benefit of a "specified" publicly supported organization under subdivision (i)(b) of this subparagraph. However, if, at some future date, X actually substituted a non-publicly supported organization as beneficiary, X would fail the requirements of the operational test set forth in paragraph (e)(1) of this section.

(e) *Operational test* —(1) *Permissible beneficiaries.* A supporting organization will be regarded as "operated exclusively" to support one or more specified publicly supported organizations (hereinafter referred to as the "operational test") only if it engages solely in activities which support or benefit the specified publicly supported organizations. Such activities may include making payments to or for the use of, or providing services or facilities for, individual members of the charitable class benefited by the specified publicly supported organization. A supporting organization may also, for example, make a payment indirectly through another unrelated organization to a member of a charitable class benefited by a specified publicly supported organization, but only if such a payment constitutes a grant to an individual rather than a grant to an organization. In determining whether a grant is indirectly to an individual rather than to an organization the same standard shall be applied as in § 53.4945-4(a)(4) of this chapter. Similarly, an organization will be regarded as "operated exclusively" to support or benefit one or more specified publicly supported organizations even if it supports or benefits an organization, other than a private foundation, which is described in section 501(c)(3) and is operated, supervised, or controlled directly by or in connection with such publicly supported organizations, or which is described in section 511(a)(2)(B). However, an organization will not be regarded as operated exclusively if any part of its activities is in furtherance of a purpose other than supporting or benefiting one or more specified publicly supported organizations.

(2) *Permissible activities.* A supporting organization is not required to pay over its income to the puublicly supported organizations in order to meet the operational test. It may satisfy the test by using its income to carry on an independent activity or program which supports or benefits the specified publicly supported organizations. All such support must, however, be limited to permissible beneficiaries in accordance with subparagraph (1) of this paragraph. The supporting organization may also engage in fund raising activities, such as solicitations, fund raising dinners, and unrelated trade or business to raise funds for the publicly supported organizations, or for the permissible beneficiaries.

(3) *Examples.* The provisions of this paragraph may be illustrated by the following examples:

Example (1). M is a separately incorporated alumni association of X University and is an organization described in section 501(c)(3). X

Reg. § 1.509(a)-4(e)(3)

University is designated in M's articles as the sole beneficiary of its support. M uses all of its dues and income to support its own program of educational activities for alumni, faculty, and students of X University and to encourage alumni to maintain a close relationship with the university and to make contributions to it. M does not distribute any of its income directly to X for the latter's general purposes. M pays no part of its funds to, or for the benefit of, any organization other than X. Under these circumstances, M is considered as operated exclusively to perform the functions and carry out the purposes of X. Although it does not pay over any of its funds to X, it carries on a program which both supports and benefits X.

Example (2). N is a separately incorporated religious and educational organization described in section 501(c)(3). It was formed and is operated by Y Church to provide religious training for the members of the church. While it does not maintain a regular faculty, N conducts a Sunday school, weekly adult education lectures on religious subjects, and other similar activities for the benefit of the church members. All of its funds are disbursed in furtherance of such activities and no part of its funds is paid to, or for the benefit of, any organization other than Y Church. N is considered as operated exclusively to perform the educational functions of Y Church and to carry out its religious purposes by providing various forms of religious instruction.

Example (3). P is an organization described in section 501(c)(3). Its primary activity is providing financial assistance to S, a publicly supported organization which aids underdeveloped nations in Central America. P's articles of organization designate S as the principal recipient of F's assistance. However, P also makes a small annual general purpose grant to T, a private foundation engaged in work similar to that carried on by S. T performs a particular function that assists in the overall aid program carried on by S. Even though P is operating primarily for the benefit of S, a specified publicly supported organization, it is not considered as operated exclusively for the purposes set forth in section 509(a)(3)(A). The grant to T, a private foundation, prevents it from complying with the operational test under section 509(a)(3)(A).

Example (4). Assume the same facts as Example (3), except that T is a section 501(c)(3) organization other than a private foundation and is operated in connection with S. Under these circumstances, P will be considered as operated exclusively to support S within the meaning of Section 509(a)(3)(A).

Example (5). Assume the same facts as example (3) except that instead of the annual general purpose grant made to T, each grant made by P to T is specifically earmarked for the training of social workers and teachers, designated by name, from Central America. Under these circumstances, P's grants to T would be treated as grants to the individual social workers and teachers under section 4945(d)(3) and § 53.4945-4(a)(4), rather than as grants to T under section 4945(d)(4). These social workers and teachers are part of the charitable class benefitted by S. P would thus be considered as operating exclusively to support S within the meaning of section 509(a)(3)(A).

(f) *Nature of relationship required between organizations*—(1) *In general.* Section 509(a)(3)(B) describes the nature of the relationship required between a section 501(c)(3) organization and one or more publicly supported organizations in order for such section 501(c)(3) organization to qualify under the provisions of section 509(a)(3). To meet the requirements of section 509(a)(3), an organization must be operated, supervised, or controlled by or in connection with one or more publicly supported organizations. If an organization does not stand in one of such relationships (as provided in this paragraph) to one or more publicly supported organizations, it is not an organization described in section 509(a)(3).

(2) *Types of relationships.* Section 509(a)(3)(B) sets forth three different types of relationships, one of which must be met in order to meet the requirements of subparagraph (1) of this paragraph. Thus, a supporting organization may be:

(i) Operated, supervised, or controlled by,

(ii) Supervised or controlled in connection with, or

(iii) Operated in connection with, one or more publicly supported organizations.

(3) *Requirements of relationships.* Although more than one type of relationship may exist in any one case, any relationship described in section 509(a)(3)(B) must insure that:

(i) The supporting organization will be responsive to the needs or demands of one or more publicly supported organizations; and

(ii) The supporting organization will constitute an integral part of, or maintain a significant involvement in, the operations of one or more publicly supported organizations.

(4) *General description of relationships.* In the case of supporting organizations which are "operated, supervised, or controlled by" one or more publicly supported organizations, the distin-

Reg. § 1.509(a)-4(f)(1)

guishing feature of this type of relationship is the presence of a substantial degree of direction by the publicly supported organizations over the conduct of the supporting organization, as described in paragraph (g) of this section. In the case of supporting organizations which are "supervised or controlled in connection with" one or more publicly supported organizations, the distinguishing feature is the presence of common supervision or control among the governing bodies of all organizations involved, such as the presence of common directors, as described in paragraph (h) of this section. In the case of a supporting organization which is "operated in connection with" one or more publicly supported organizations, the distinguishing feature is that the supporting organization is responsive to, and significantly involved in the operations of, the publicly supported organization, as described in paragraph (i) of this section.

(g) *Meaning of "operated, supervised, or controlled by".* (1)(i) Each of the items "operated by", "supervised by", and "controlled by", as used in section 509(a)(3)(B), presupposes a substantial degree of direction over the policies, programs, and activities of a supporting organization by one or more publicly supported organizations. The relationship required under any one of these terms is comparable to that of a parent and subsidiary, where the subsidiary is under the direction of, and accountable or responsible to, the parent organization. This relationship is established by the fact that a majority of the officers, directors, or trustees of the supporting organization are appointed or elected by the governing body, members of the governing body, officers acting in their official capacity, or the membership of one or more publicly supported organizations.

(ii) A supporting organization may be "operated, supervised or controlled by" one or more publicly supported organizations within the meaning of section 509(a)(3)(B) even though its governing body is not comprised of representatives of the specified publicly supported organizations for whose benefit it is operated within the meaning of section 509(a)(3)(A). A supporting organization may be "operated, supervised, or controlled by" one or more publicly supported organizations (within the meaning of section 509(a)(3)(B)) and be operated "for the benefit of" one or more different publicly supported organizations (within the meaning of section 509(a)(3)(A)) only if it can be demonstrated that the purposes of the former organizations are carried out by benefiting the latter organizations.

(2) The provisions of this paragraph may be illustrated by the following examples:

Example (1). X is a university press which is organized and operated as a nonstock educational corporation to perform the publishing and printing for M University, a publicly supported organization. Control of X is vested in a Board of Governors appointed by the Board of Trustees of M University upon the recommendation of the president of the university. X is considered to be operated, supervised, or controlled by M University within the meaning of section 509(a)(3)(B).

Example (2). Y Council was organized under the joint sponsorship of seven independent publicly supported organizations, each of which is dedicated to the advancement of knowledge in a particular field of social science. The sponsoring organizations organized Y Council as a means of pooling their ideas and resources for the attainment of common objectives, including the conducting of scholarly studies and formal discussions in various fields of social science. Under Y Council's by-laws, each of the seven sponsoring organizations elects three members to Y's board of trustees for three-year terms. Y's board also includes the president of Y Council and eight other individuals elected at large by the board. Pursuant to policies established or approved by the board, Y Council engages in research, planning, and evaluation in the social sciences and sponsors or arranges conferences, seminars, and similar programs for scholars and social scientists. It carries out these activities through its own full-time professional staff, through a part-time committee of scholars, and through grant recipients. Under the above circumstances, Y Council is subject to a substantial degree of direction by the sponsoring publicly supported organizations. It is therefore considered to be operated, supervised, or controlled by such sponsoring organizations within the meaning of section 509(a)(3)(B).

Example (3). Z is a charitable trust created by A in 1972. It has 3 trustees, all of whom are appointed by M University, a publicly supported organization. The trust was organized and is operated to pay over all of its net income for medical research to N, O and P, each of which is specified in the trust, is a hospital described in section 509(a)(1), and is located in the same city as M. Members of M's biology department are permitted to use the research of N, O and P. Under subparagraph (1)(ii) of this paragraph, Z is considered to be operated, supervised, or controlled by M within the meaning of section 509(a)(3)(B), even though it is operated for the benefit of N, O, and P within the meaning of section 509(a)(3)(A).

Reg. § 1.509(a)-4(g)(2)

(h) *Meaning of "supervised or controlled in connection with."* (1) In order for a supporting organization to be "supervised or controlled in connection with" one or more publicly supported organizations, there must be common supervision or control by the persons supervising or controlling both the supporting organization and the publicly supported organizations to insure that the supporting organization will be responsive to the needs and requirements of the publicly supported organizations. Therefore, in order to meet such requirement, the control or management of the supporting organization must be vested in the same persons that control or manage the publicly supported organizations.

(2) A supporting organization will not be considered to be "supervised or controlled in connection with" one or more publicly supported organizations if such organization merely makes payments (mandatory or discretionary) to one or more named publicly supported organizations, even if the obligation to make payments to the named beneficiaries is enforceable under state law by such beneficiaries and the supporting organization's governing instrument contains provisions whose effect is described in section 508(e)(1)(A) and (B). Such arrangements do not provide a sufficient "connection" between the payor organization and the needs and requirements of the publicly supported organization to constitute supervisions or control in connection with such organizations.

(3) The provisions of this paragraph may be illustrated by the following examples:

Example (1). A, a philanthropist, founded X school for orphan boys (a publicly supported organization). At the same time A founded X school, he also established Y trust into which he transferred all of the operating assets of the school, together with a substantial endowment for it. Under the provisions of the trust instrument, the same persons who control and manage the school also control and manage the trust. The sole function of Y trust is to hold legal title to X school's operating and endowment assets, to invest the endowment assets and to apply the income from the endowment to the benefit of the school in accordance with direction from the school's governing body. Under these circumstances, Y trust is organized and operated "for the benefit of" X school and is "supervised or controlled in connection with" such organization within the meaning of section 509(a)(3). The fact that the same persons control both X and Y insures Y's responsiveness to X's needs.

Example (2). In 1972, B, a philanthropist, created P, a charitable trust for the benefit of Z, a symphony orchestra described in section 509(a)(2). B transferred 100 shares of common stock to P. Under the terms of the trust instrument, the trustees (none of whom is under the control of B) were required to pay over all of the income produced by the trust assets to Z. The governing instrument of P contains certain provisions whose effect is described in section 508(e)(1)(A) and (B). Under applicable state law, Z can enforce the provisions of the trust instrument and compel payment to Z in a court of equity. There is no relationship between the trustees of P and the governing body of Z. Under these circumstances P is not supervised or controlled in connection with a publicly supported organization. Because of the lack of any common supervision or control by the trustees of P and the governing body of Z, P is not supervised or controlled in connection with Z within the meaning of section 509(a)(3)(B).

Example (3). T is a charitable trust described in section 501(c)(3) and created under the will of D. Prior to his death, D was a leader and very active in C Church, a publicly supported organization. D created T to perpetuate his interest in, and assistance to, C. The sole purpose of T was to provide financial support for C and its related institutions. All of the original named trustees of T are members of C, are leaders in C, and hold important offices in one or more of C's related institutions. Successor trustees of T are by the terms of the charitable trust instrument to be chosen by the remaining trustees and are also to be members of C. All of the original trustees have represented that any successor trustee will be a leader in C and will hold an important office in one or more of C's related institutions. By reason of the foregoing relationship T and its trustees are responsive to the needs and requirements of C and its related institutions. Under these circumstances, T trust is organized and operated "for the benefit of" C and is "supervised or controlled in connection with" C and its related institutions within the meaning of section 509(a)(3)(B).

(i) *Meaning of "operated in connection with"* —(1) *General rule.* (i) Except as provided in subdivisions (ii) and (iii) of this subparagraph and subparagraph (4) of this paragraph, a supporting organization will be considered as being operated in connection with one or more publicly supported organizations only if it meets the "responsiveness test" which is defined in subparagraph (2) of this paragraph and the "integral part test" which is defined in subparagraph (3) of this paragraph.

(ii) In the case of an organization which was supporting or benefiting one or more publicly

Reg. § 1.509(a)-4(h)(2)

supported organizations before November 20, 1970, additional facts and circumstances, such as a historic and continuing relationship between organizations, may be taken into account, in addition to the factors described in subparagraph (2) of this paragraph, to establish compliance with the responsiveness test.

(iii) If—

(a) A supporting organization can establish that it has met the integral part test set forth in subparagraph (3)(iii) of this paragraph for any five-year period,

(b) Such organization cannot meet the requirements of such test for its current taxable year solely because the amount received by one or more of the publicly supported beneficiary organizations from such supporting organization is no longer sufficient, with respect to such beneficiary organizations, to satisfy subparagraph (3) (iii) of this paragraph, and

(c) There has been a historic and continuing relationship of support between such organizations between the end of such five-year period and the taxable year in question,

then such supporting organization will be considered as meeting the requirements of the integral part test in subparagraph (3)(iii) of this paragraph for such taxable year.

(2) *Responsiveness test.* (i) For purposes of this paragraph, a supporting organization will be considered to meet the "responsiveness test" if the organization is responsive to the needs or demands of the publicly supported organizations within the meaning of this subparagraph. In order to meet this test, either subdivision (ii) or subdivision (iii) of this subparagraph must be satisfied.

(ii)(a) One or more officers, directors, or trustees of the supporting organization are elected or appointed by the officers, directors, trustees, or membership of the publicly supported organizations;

(b) One or more members of the governing bodies of the publicly supported organizations are also officers, directors or trustees of, or hold other important offices in, the suupporting organizations; or

(c) The officers, directors or trustees of the supporting organization maintain a close and continuous working relationship with the officers, directors or trustees of the publicly supported organizations; and

(d) By reason of (a), (b), or (c) of this subdivision, the officers, directors or trustees of the publicly supported organizations have a significant voice in the investment policies of the supporting organization, the timing of grants, the manner of making them, and the selection of recipients of such supporting organization, and in otherwise directing the use of the income or assets of such supporting organization.

(iii)(a) The supporting organization is a charitable trust under State law;

(b) Each specified publicly supported organization is a named beneficiary under such charitable trust's governing instrument; and

(c) The beneficiary organization has the power to enforce the trust and compel an accounting under State law.

(3) *Integral part test; general rule.* (i) For purposes of this paragraph, a supporting organization will be considered to meet the "integral part test" if it maintains a significant involvement in the operations of one or more publicly supported organizations and such publicly supported organizations are in turn dependent upon the supporting organization for the type of support which it provides. In order to meet this test, either subdivision (ii) or subdivision (iii) of this subparagraph must be satisfied.

(ii) The activities engaged in for or on behalf of the publicly supported organizations are activities to perform the functions of, or to carry out the purposes of, such organizations, and, but for the involvement of the supporting organization, would normally be engaged in by the publicly supported organizations themselves.

(iii)(a) The supporting organization makes payments of substantially all of its income to or for the use of one or more publicly supported organizations, and the amount of support received by one or more of such publicly supported organizations is sufficient to insure the attentiveness of such organizations to the operations of the supporting organization. In addition, a substantial amount of the total support of the supporting organization must go to those publicly supported organizations which meet the attentiveness requirement of this subdivision with respect to such supporting organization. Except as provided in (b) of this subdivision, the amount of support received by a publicly supported organization must represent a sufficient part of the organization's total support so as to insure such attentiveness. In applying the preceding sentence, if such supporting organization makes payments to, or for the use of, a particular department or school of a university, hospital or church, the total support of the department or school shall be substituted for the total support of the beneficiary organization.

(b) Even where the amount of support received by a publicly supported beneficiary organization does not represent a sufficient part of

Reg. § 1.509(a)-4(i)(3)

the beneficiary organization's total support, the amount of support received from a supporting organization may be sufficient to meet the requirements of this subdivision if it can be demonstrated that in order to avoid the interruption of the carrying on of a particular function or activity, the beneficiary organization will be sufficiently attentive to the operations of the supporting organization. This may be the case where either the supporting organization or the beneficiary organization earmarks the support received from the supporting organization for a particular program or activity, even if such program or activity is not the beneficiary organization's primary program or activity so long as such program or activity is a substantial one.

(c) This subdivision may be illustrated by the following examples:

Example (1). X, an organization described in section 501(c)(3) pays over all of its annual net income to Y, a museum described in section 509(a)(2). X meets the responsiveness test described in subparagraph (2) of this paragraph. In recent years, Y has earmarked the income received from X to underwrite the cost of carrying on a chamber music series consisting of 12 performances a year which are performed for the general public free of charge at its premises. Because of the expense involved in carrying on these recitals, Y is dependent upon the income from X for their continuation. Under these circumstances, X will be treated as providing Y with a sufficient portion of Y's total support to assure Y's attentiveness to X's operations, even though the chamber music series is not the primary part of Y's activities.

Example (2). M, an organization described in section 501(c)(3), pays over all of its annual net income to the Law School of N University, a publicly supported organization. M meets the responsiveness test described in subparagraph (2) of this paragraph. M has earmarked the income paid over to N's Law School to endow a chair in its Department of International Law. Without M's continued support, N might not continue to maintain this chair. Under these circumstances, M will be treated as providing N with a sufficient portion of N's total support to assure N's attentiveness to M's operations.

(d) All pertinent factors, including the number of beneficiaries, the length and nature of the relationship between the beneficiary and supporting organization and the purpose to which the funds are put (as illustrated by subdivision (iii)*(b)* and *(c)* of this subparagraph), will be considered in determining whether the amount of support received by a publicly supported beneficiary organization is sufficient to insure the attentiveness of such organization to the operations of the supporting organization. Normally the attentiveness of a beneficiary organization is motivated by reason of the amounts received from the supporting organization. Thus, the more substantial the amount involved, in terms of a percentage of the publicly supported organization's total support the greater the likelihood that the required degree of attentiveness will be present. However, in determining whether the amount received from the supporting organization is sufficient to insure the attentiveness of the beneficiary organization to the operations of the supporting organization (including attentiveness to the nature and yield of such supporting organization's investments), evidence of actual attentiveness by the beneficiary organization is of almost equal importance. An example of acceptable evidence of actual attentiveness is the imposition of a requirement that the supporting organization furnish reports at least annually for taxable years beginning after December 31, 1971, to the beneficiary organization to assist such beneficiary organization in insuring that the supporting organization has invested its endowment in assets productive of a reasonable rate of return (taking appreciation into account) and has not engaged in any activity which would give rise to liability for a tax imposed under sections 4941, 4943, 4944, or 4945 if such organization were a private foundation. The imposition of such requirement within 120 days after October 16, 1972, will be deemed to have retroactive effect to January 1, 1970, for purposes of determining whether a supporting organization has met the requirements of this subdivision for its first two taxable years beginning after December 31, 1969. The imposition of such requirement is, however, merely one of the factors in determining whether a supporting organization is complying with this subdivision and the absence of such requirement will not preclude an organization from classification as a supporting organization based on other factors.

(e) However, where none of the beneficiary organizations is dependent upon the supporting organization for a sufficient amount of the beneficiary organization's support within the meaning of this subdivision, the requirements of this subparagraph will not be satisfied, even though such beneficiary organizations have enforceable rights against such organization under State law.

(4) *Integral part test; transitional rule.* (i) A trust (whether or not exempt from taxation under section 501(a)) which on November 20, 1970, has met and continues to meet the requirements of subdivisions (ii) through (vi) of this subparagraph

Reg. § 1.509(a)-4(i)(4)

shall be treated as meeting the requirements of the integral part test (whether or not it meets the requirements of subparagraph (3)(ii) or (iii) of this paragraph) if for taxable years beginning after October 16, 1972, the trustee of such trust makes annual written reports to all of the beneficiary publicly supported organizations with respect to such trust setting forth a description of the assets of the trust, including a detailed list of the assets and the income produced by such assets. A trust organization which meets the requirements of this subparagraph may request a ruling that it is described in section 509(a)(3) in such manner as the Commissioner may prescribe.

(ii) All the unexpired interests in the trust are devoted to one or more purposes decribed in section 170(c)(1) or (2)(B) and a deduction was allowed with respect to such interests under section 170, 545(b)(2), 556(b)(2), 642(c), 2055, 2106(a)(2), 2522, or corresponding provisions of prior law (or would have been allowed such a deduction if the trust had not been created before 1913).

(iii) The trust was created prior to November 20, 1970, and did not receive any grant, contribution, bequest or other transfer on or after such date. For purposes of this subdivision, a split-interest trust described in section 4947(a)(2) which was created prior to November 20, 1970, which was irrevocable on such date, and which becomes a charitable trust described in section 4947(a)(1) after such date shall be treated as having been created prior to such date;

(iv) The trust is required by its governing instrument to distribute all of its net income currently to a designated publicly supported beneficiary organization. Where more than one publicly supported beneficiary organization is designated in the governing instrument of a trust, all of the net income must be distributable and must be distributed currently to each of such beneficiary organizations in fixed shares pursuant to such governing instrument. For purposes of this subdivision, the governing instrument of a charitable trust shall be treated as requiring distribution to a designated beneficiary organization where the trust instrument describes the charitable purpose of the trust so completely that such description can apply to only one existing beneficiary organization and is of sufficient particularity as to vest in such organization rights against the trust enforceable in a court possessing equitable powers;

(v) The trustee of the trust does not have discretion to vary either the beneficiaries or the amounts payable to the beneficiaries. For purposes of this subdivision, a trustee shall not be treated as having such discretion where the trustee has discretion to make payments of principal to the single section 509(a)(1) or (2) organization that is currently entitled to receive all of the trust's income or where the trust instrument provides that the trustee may cease making income payments to a particular charitable beneficiary in the event of certain specific occurrences, such as the loss of exemption under section 501(c)(3) or classification under section 509(a)(1) or (2) by the beneficiary or the failure of the beneficiary to carry out its charitable purpose properly;

(vi) None of the trustees would be disqualified persons within the meaning of section 4946(a) (other than foundation managers under 4946(a)(1)(B)) with respect to the trust if such trust were treated as a private foundation.

(5) *Examples.* The provisions of this paragraph may be illustrated by the following examples:

Example (1). N is a nonprofit publishing organization described in section 501(c)(3). It does all of the publishing and printing for the churches of a particular denomination (which are publicly supported organizations).

Control of the organization is vested in a five-man Board of Directors, which includes one church official and four lay members of the congregations of that denomination. N does no other printing or publishing. It publishes all of the churches' religious as well as secular tracts and materials. Under these circumstances, N is considered as being "operated in connection with" a number of publicly supported organizations. Publishing religious literature is an integral part of the churches' activities; it is carried on by N on behalf of the churches, and there is sufficient direction over N's activities by the churches to insure responsiveness by N to their needs.

Example (2). O, an alumni association described in section 501(c)(3), was formed to promote a spirit of loyalty among graduates of Y University, a publicly supported organization, and to effect united action in promoting the general welfare of the university. A special committee of Y's governing board meets with O and makes recommendations as to the allocation of O's program of gifts and scholarships to the university and its students. O also provides certain functions which would otherwise be part of Y's functions, such as maintaining records of alumni. O publishes a bulletin to keep alumni aware of the activities of the university. Under these circumstances O is considered to be operated in connection with Y within the meaning of section 509(a)(3)(B).

Example (3). P is a trust created under the will of A for the purpose of furthering musical

Reg. § 1.509(a)-4(i)(5)

education. As a means of accomplishing its purposes P founded X, a school of music described in section 509(a)(1). The trust instrument is thereafter amended to name X specifically as the beneficiary of the trust. X can enforce its equitable rights as trust beneficiary under State law. Members of the governing body of X form a minority of the foundation managers of P. For many years the organizations have been operated in close association with each other. P provides the principal endowment fund for the operation of X. In addition, while the governing body of X concerns itself with artistic policies, the foundation managers of P handle the budgetary concerns of X. X's annual budget is prepared with the assistance of P's foundation managers and is approved by P. Under these circumstances, P is considered to be operated in connection with X within the meaning of section 509(a)(3)(B).

Example (4). Q is a charitable trust described in section 501(c)(3) and created under the will of C. Prior to his death, C built H Hospital and deeded it to I University for use as a training and clinical facility for I's medical school. Both H and I are publicly supported organizations. C created Q to perpetuate his interest in, and assistance to, H Hospital. The sole purpose of Q was to provide financial support for H, the beneficiary organization named in C's will. H can enforce its equitable rights as trust beneficiary under State law. After the death of C, Q continued to provide substantial support for H. It was primarily responsible for the erecting of a new hospital building, as well as the construction of other facilities for the hospital. In addition, each medical department of H indicates during the year what its greatest needs are. Once these requests are approved by the medical director of I University's Medical School, they are presented to Q, and subject to the amount of Q's income (all of which is applied to H), these requests are honored and the new equipment of facility is supplied through Q's funds. The governing body of Q and those of H and I are completely independent. However, based on the above facts, Q is responsive to the needs of H, Q maintains a substantial involvement in the conduct of H, and H is substantially dependent upon the receipt of support from Q. Accordingly, Q is operated in connection with one or more section 509(a)(1) organizations within the meaning of section 509(a)(3)(B).

Example (5). R is a charitable trust created under the will of B, who died in 1971. Its purpose is to hold assets as an endowment for S, a hospital, T, a university, and U, a national medical research organization (all being publicly supported organizations and specifically named in the trust instrument), and to distribute all of the income each year in equal shares among the three named beneficiaries. S, T, and U have certain enforceable rights against R under State law, including the right to compel an accounting. Except for making these annual payments, the trustees of R have no further contacts or relationships with S, T, or U. The payments by R to such organizations do not comprise a sufficient amount of support to meet the requirements of subparagraph (3) of this paragraph for any of these organizations. Although R meets the responsiveness test described in subparagraph (2) of this paragraph, it does not meet the integral part test described in subparagraph (3) of this paragraph. R is not, therefore, considered as operated in connection with one or more publicly supported organizations within the meaning of section 509(a)(3)(B). However, if B had died prior to November 20, 1970, R could, upon meeting all of the requirements of subparagraph (4) of this paragraph, be considered as operated in connection with one or more of publicly supported organizations within the meaning of section 509(a)(3)(B).

Example (6). S is a charitable trust described in section 501(c)(3). S was created under the will of C in 1910 for the purpose of providing aged and indigent women with care and shelter. Prior to his death in 1910, C helped to create T, a home for aged women, through a substantial inter vivos contribution. Although T is not specifically named in C's will, the trustees of S (who are completely independent of T) have paid over all of S's income to T in furtherance of the trust's purposes since the death of C. S establishes that between 1910 and 1955, the amount of support received by T from S was sufficient support to satisfy the provisions of § 1.509(a)-4(i)(3)(iii). In 1956, T merged with U, a home for aged and indigent men, and V, a nursing home. S continued to pay all its income to W, the organization resulting from the merger of T, U, and V. However, as a result of the merger and certain changes in the methods of financing the operations, the payments made by S after 1955 no longer were sufficient to satisfy the integral part test of § 1.509(a)-4(i)(3)(iii). W qualifies as an organization described in section 509(a)(2). For the taxable year 1971, S meets the responsiveness test under § 1.509(a)-4(i)(2)(ii). Although W is not a named beneficiary under S's governing instrument, pursuant to § 1.509(a)-4(i)(1)(ii) the historic and continuing relationship between the organizations will be taken into account to establish compliance with the responsiveness test. Furthermore, pursuant to § 1.509(a)-4(i)(1)(iii), under the facts set forth above, the integral part test under § 1.509(a)-(4)(i)(3)(iii) will be considered as being satisfied for the taxable year 1971.

Reg. § 1.509(a)-4(i)(5)

Thus S will be considered as "operated in connection with" W for the taxable year 1971.

(j) *Control by disqualified persons*—(1) *In general.* Under the provisions of section 509(a)(3)(C) a supporting organization may not be controlled directly or indirectly by one or more disqualified persons (as defined in section 4946) other than foundation managers and other than one or more publicly supported organizations. If a person who is a disqualified person with respect to a supporting organization, such as a substantial contributor to the supporting organization, is appointed or designated as a foundation manager of the supporting organization by a publicly supported beneficiary organization to serve as the representative of such publicly supported organization, then for purposes of this pargraph such person will be regarded as a disqualified person, rather than as a representative of the publicly supported organization. An organization will be considered "controlled", for purposes of section 509(a)(3)(C), if the disqualified persons, by aggregating their votes or positions of authority, may require such organization to perform any act which significantly affects its operations or may prevent such organization from performing such act. This includes, but is not limited to, the right of any substantial contributor or his spouse to designate annually the recipients, from among the publicly supported organizations of the income attributable to his contribution to the supporting organization. Except as provided in subparagraph (2) of this paragraph, a supporting organization will be considered to be controlled directly or indirectly by one or more disqualified persons if the voting power of such persons is 50 percent or more of the total voting power of the organization's governing body or if one or more of the total voting power of the organization's governing body or if one or more of such persons have the right to exercise veto power over the actions of the organization. Thus, if the governing body of a foundation is composed of five trustees, none of whom has a veto power over the actions of the foundation, and no more than two trustees are at any time disqualified persons, such foundation will not be considered to be controlled directly or indirectly by one or more disqualified persons by reason of this fact alone. However, all pertinent facts and circumstances including the nature, diversity, and income yield of an organization's holdings, the length of time particular stocks, securities, or other assets are retained, and its manner of exercising its voting rights with respect to stocks in which members of its governing body also have some interest, will be taken into consideration in determining whether a disqualified person does in fact indirectly control an organization.

(2) *Proof of independent control.* Notwithstanding subparagraph (1) of this paragraph, an organization shall be permitted to establish to the satisfaction of the Commissioner that disqualified persons do not directly or indirectly control it. For example, in the case of a religious organization operated in connection with a church, the fact that the majority of the organization's governing body is composed of lay persons who are substantial contributors to the organization will not disqualify the organization under section 509(a)(3)(C) if a representative of the church, such as a bishop or other official, has control over the policies and decisions of the organization.

(k) *Organizations operated in conjunction with certain section 501(c)(4), (5), or (6) organizations.* (1) For purposes of section 509(a)(3), an organization which is operated in conjunction with an organization described in section 501(c)(4), (5), or (6) (such as a social welfare organization, labor or agricultural organization, business league, or real estate board) shall, if it otherwise meets the requirements of section 509(a)(3), be considered an organization described in section 509(a)(3) if such section 501(c)(4), (5), or (6) organization would be described in section 509(a)(2) if it were an organization described in section 501(c)(3). The section 501(c)(4), (5), or (6) organization which the supporting organization is operating in conjunction with, must therefore meet the one-third tests of a publicly supported organization set forth in section 509(a)(2).

(2) This paragraph may be illustrated by the following example:

Example. X medical association, described in section 501(c)(6), is supported by membership dues and funds resulting from the performance of its exempt activities. This support, which is entirely from permitted sources, constitutes more than one-third of X's support. X does not normally receive more than one-third of its support from items described in section 509(a)(2)(B). X organized and operated an endowment fund for the sole purpose of furthering medical education. The fund is an organization described in section 501(c)(3). Since more than one-third of X's support is derived from membership dues and from funds resulting from the performance of exempt purposes (all of which are from permitted sources) and not more than one-third of its support is from items described in section 509(a)(2)(B), it would be a publicly supported organization described in section 509(a)(2) if it were described in section 501(c)(3) rather than section 501(c)(6). Accordingly, if the fund otherwise meets the requirements of section 509(a)(3) with respect to X, it

Reg. § 1.509(a)-4(k)(2)

will be considered an organization described in section 509(a)(3). [Reg. § 1.509(a)-4.]

☐ [T.D. 7212, 10-16-72. Amended by T.D. 7784, 7-22-81.]

[Reg. § 1.509(a)-5]

§ 1.509(a)-5. Special rules of attribution.—(a) *Retained character of gross investment income.* (1) For purposes of determining whether an organization meets the not-more-than-one-third support test set forth in section 509(a)(2)(B), amounts received by such organization from:

(i) An organization which seeks to be described in section 509(a)(3) by reason of its support of such organization; or

(ii) A charitable trust, corporation, fund, or association described in section 501(c)(3) (including a charitable trust described in section 4947(a)(1) or a split interest trust described in section 4947(a)(2), which is required by its governing instrument or otherwise to distribute, or which normally does distribute, at least 25 percent of its adjusted net income (within the meaning of section 4942(f)) to such organization, and such distribution normally comprises at least 5 percent of such distributee organization's adjusted net income,

will retain their character as gross investment income (rather than gifts or contributions) to the extent that such amounts are characterized as gross investment income in the possession of the distributing organization described in subdivision (i) or (ii) of this subparagraph or, if the distributing organization is a split interest trust described in section 4947(a)(2), to the extent that such amounts would be characterized as gross investment income attributable to transfers in trust after May 26, 1969, if such trust were a private foundation. For purposes of this section, all income which is characterized as gross investment income in the possession of the distributing organization shall be deemed to be distributed first by such organization and shall retain its character as such in the possession of the recipient of amounts described in this paragraph. If an organization described in subdivision (i) or (ii) of this subparagraph makes distributions to more than one organization, the amount of gross investment income deemed distributed shall be proated among the distributees.

(2) For purpose of subparagraph (1) of this paragraph, amounts paid by an organization to provide goods, services, or facilities for the direct benefit of an organization seeking section 509(a)(2) status (rather than for the direct benefit of the general public) shall be treated in the same manner as amounts received by the latter organization. Such amounts will be treated as gross investment income to the extent that such amounts are characterized as gross investment income in the possession of the organization spending such amounts. For example, X is an organization described in subparagraph (1)(i) of this paragraph. It uses part of its funds to provide Y, an organization seeking section 509(a)(2) status, with certain services which Y would otherwise be required to purchase on its own. To the extent that the funds used by X to provide such services for Y are characterized as gross investment income in the possession of X, such funds will be treated as gross investment income received by Y.

(3) An organization seeking section 509(a)(2) status shall file a separate statement with its return required by section 6033, setting forth all amounts received from organizations described in subparagraph (1)(i) or (ii) of this paragraph.

(b) *Relationships created for avoidance purposes.* (1) If a relationship between an organization seeking section 509(a)(3) status and an organization seeking section 509(a)(2) status:

(i) Is established or availed of after October 9, 1969, and

(ii) One of the purposes of establishing or utilizing such relationship is to avoid classification as a private foundation with respect to either organization,

the character and amount of support received by the section 509(a)(3) organization will be attributed to the section 509(a)(2) organization for purposes of determining whether the latter meets the one-third support test and the not-more-than-one-third support test under section 509(a)(2). If a relationship described in this subparagraph is established or utilized by an organization seeking section 509(a)(3) status and two or more organizations seeking section 509(a)(2) status, the amount of support received by the former organization will be prorated among the latter organizations and the character of each class of support (as defined in section 509(d)) will be attributed pro rata to each such organization. The provisions of this paragraph and of paragraph (a) of this section are not mutually exclusive.

(2) In determining whether a relationship between one or more organizations seeking section 509(a)(2) status (hereinafter referred to as "beneficiary organizations") and an organization seeking section 509(a)(3) status (hereinafter referred to as the "supporting organization") has been established or availed of to avoid classification as a private foundation (within the meaning of subparagraph (1) of this paragraph), all pertinent facts and circumstances, including the following,

Reg. § 1.509(a)-5(a)(2)

shall be taken into account as evidence that a relationship was not established or availed of to avoid classification as a private foundation:

(i) The supporting organization is operated to support or benefit several specified beneficiary organizations.

(ii) The beneficiary organization has a substantial number of dues-paying members (in relation to the public it serves and the nature of its activities) and such members have an effective voice in the management of both the supporting and beneficiary organizations.

(iii) The beneficiary organization is composed of several membership organizations, each of which has a substantial number of members (in relation to the public it serves and the nature of its activities), and such membership organization have an effective voice in the management of the supporting and beneficiary organizations.

(iv) The beneficiary organization receives a substantial amount of support from the general public, public charities or governmental grants.

(v) The supporting organization uses its funds to carry on a meaningful program of activities to support or benefit the beneficiary organization and such use would, if such supporting organization were a private foundation, be sufficient to avoid the imposition of any tax upon such organization under section 4942.

(vi) The supporting organization is not able to exercise substantial control or influence over the beneficiary organization by reason of the former's receiving support or holding assets which are disproportionately large in comparison with the support received or the assets held by the latter.

(vii) Different persons manage the operations of the beneficiary and supporting organizations and each organization performs a different function.

(3) The provisions of this paragraph may be illustrated by the following examples:

Example (1). M, an organization described in section 509(a)(2), is a council composed of ten learned societies. Each member society has a large membership of scholars interested in a particular academic area. In 1970 M established N, an organization seeking section 509(a)(3) status, for the purpose of carrying on research and study projects of interest to the member societies. The principal source of funds for N's activities is from foundation and government grants and contracts. The principal source of funds for M's activities after the creation of N is membership dues. M continued to maintain a wide variety of activities for its members, such as publishing periodicals and carrying on seminars and conferences. N is subject to complete control by the governing body of M. Under these circumstances, the relationship between these organizations is not one which is described in subparagraph (1) of this paragraph.

Example (2). Q is a local medical research organization described in section 509(a)(2). Its fixed assets are negligible and it carries on research activities on a limited scale. It also makes a limited number of grants to scientists and doctors who are engaged in medical research of interest to Q. It receives support through small government grants and a few research contracts from private foundations. R is an organization described in section 501(c)(3). As of January 1, 1970, R was classified as a private foundation under section 509. It has a substantial endowment which it uses to make grants to various charitable and scientific organizations described in section 501(c)(3). During 1970, R agrees to subsidize the research activities of Q. R amends its governing instrument to provide specifically that all of R's support will be used for research activities which are approved and supervised by Q. R also amends its bylaws to permit a minority of Q's board of directors to be members of R's governing body. R then gives timely notification under section 507(b)(1)(B)(ii) that R is terminating its private foundation status by meeting the requirements of section 509(a)(3) by the end of the 12-month period described in section 507(b)(1)(B)(i). For purposes of determining whether R has met the requirements of section 509(a)(3) by the end of the 12-month period, as well as determining Q's status under section 509(a)(2), the character and amount of support received by R will be attributed to Q.

(c) *Effect on organizations claiming section 509(a)(3) status.* If an organization claiming section 509(a)(2) status fails to meet either the one-third support test or the not-more-than-one-third support test under section 509(a)(2) by reason of the application of the provisions of paragraph (a) or (b) of this section, and such organization is one of the specified organizations (within the meaning of section 509(a)(3)(A)) for whose support or benefit an organization claiming section 509(a)(3) status is operated, the organization claiming section 509(a)(3) status will not be considered to be operated exclusively to support or benefit one or more section 509(a)(1) or (2) organizations. [Reg. § 1.509(a)-5.]

☐ [*T.D.* 7212, 10-16-72. *Amended by T.D.* 7290, 11-16-73 *and by T.D.* 7784, 7-22-81.]

[Reg. § 1.509(a)-6]

§ 1.509(a)-6. **Classification under section 509(a).**—If an organization is described in section

509(a)(1) and also in another paragraph of section 509(a), it will be treated as described in section 509(a)(1). For purposes of this section, the parenthetical language "other than in clauses (vii) and (viii)" used in section 509(a)(1) shall be construed to mean "other than an organization which is described only in clause (vii) or (viii)." For example, X is an organization which is described in section 170(b)(1)(A)(vi), but could also meet the description of section 170(b)(1)(A)(viii) as an organization described in section 509(a)(2). For purposes of the one-third support test in section 509(a)(2)(A), contributions from X to other organizations will be treated as support from an organization described in section 170(b)(1)(A)(vi) rather than from an organization described in section 170(b)(1)(A)(viii). [Reg. § 1.509(a)-6.]

☐ [T.D. 7212, 10-16-72.]

[Reg. § 1.509(a)-7]

§ 1.509(a)-7. **Reliance by grantors and contributors to section 509(a)(1), (2) and (3) organizations.**—(a) *General rule.* Once an organization has received a final ruling or determination letter classifying it as an organization described in section 509(a)(1), (2), or (3), the treatment of grants and contributions and the status of grantors and contributors to such organization under sections 170, 507, 545(b)(2), 556(b)(2), 642(c), 4942, 4945, 2055, 2106(a)(2), and 2522 will not be affected by reason of a subsequent revocation by the Service of the organization's classification as described in section 509(a)(1), (2), or (3) until the date on which notice of change of status is made to the public (such as by publication in the Internal Revenue Bulletin) or another applicable date, if any, specified in such public notice. In appropriate cases, however, the treatment of grants and contributions and the status of grantors and contributors to an organization described in section 509(a)(1), (2), or (3) may be affected pending verification of the continued classification of such organization under section 509(a)(1), (2), or (3). Notice to this effect will be made in a public announcement by the Service. In such cases the effect of grants and contributions made after the date of the announcement will depend upon the statutory qualification of the organization as an organization described in section 509(a)(1), (2), or (3).

(b) *Exceptions.* (1) Paragraph (a) of this section shall not apply if the grantor or contributor:

(i) Had knowledge of the revocation of the ruling or determination letter classifying the organization as an organization described in section 509(a)(1), (2), or (3), or

(ii) Was in part responsible for, or was aware of, the act, the failure to act, or the substantial and material change on the part of the organization which gave rise to the revocation of the ruling or determination letter classifying the organization as an organization described in section 509(a)(1), (2), or (3),

(2) Paragraph (a) of this section shall not apply where a different rule is otherwise expressly provided in the regulations under sections 170(b)(1)(A), 507(b)(1)(B), or 509. [Reg. § 1.509(a)-7.]

☐ [T.D. 7212, 10-16-72.]

[Reg. § 1.509(b)-1]

§ 1.509(b)-1. **Continuation of private foundation status.**—(a) *In general.* If an organization is a private foundation (within the meaning of section 509(a)) on October 9, 1969, or becomes a private foundation on any subsequent date, such organization shall be treated as a private foundation for all periods after October 9, 1969, or after such subsequent date, unless its status as such is terminated under section 507. Therefore, if an organization was described in section 501(c)(3) and was a private foundation within the meaning of section 509(a) on October 9, 1969, it shall be treated as a private foundation for all periods thereafter, even though it may also satisfy the requirements of an organization described in some other paragraph of section 501(c). For example, if on October 9, 1969, an organization was described in section 501(c)(3), but because of its activities, it could also have qualified as an organization described in section 501(c)(4), such organization will continue to be treated as a private foundation, if it was a private foundation within the meaning of section 509(a) on October 9, 1969.

(b) *Taxable private foundations.* If an organization is a private foundation on October 9, 1969, and it is determined that it is not exempt under section 501(a) as an organization described in section 501(c)(3) as of any date after October 9, 1969, such organization, even though it may operate thereafter as a taxable entity, will continue to be treated as a private foundation unless its status as such is terminated under section 507. For example, X organization is a private foundation on October 9, 1969. It is subsequently determined that, as of July 1, 1972, X is no longer exempt under section 501(a) as an organization described in section 501(c)(3) because, for example, it has not conformed its governing instrument pursuant to section 508(e). X will continue to be treated as a private foundation after July 1, 1972, unless its status as such is terminated under section 507. However, if an organization is not exempt under section 501(a) as an organization described in

Reg. § 1.509(a)-7(a)

section 501(c)(3) on October 9, 1969, then it will not be treated as a private foundation within the meaning of section 509(a) by reason of section 509(b), unless it becomes a private foundation on a subsequent date. [Reg. § 1.509(b)-1.]

☐ [T.D. 7212, 10-16-72.]

[Reg. § 1.509(c)-1]

§ 1.509(c)-1. **Status of organization after termination of private foundation status.**—(a) *In general.* For purposes of Part II of Subchapter F of this chapter, an organization whose status as a private foundation is terminated under section 507 shall be treated as an organization created on the day after the date of such termination. An organization whose private foundation status has been terminated under the provisions of section 507(a) will, if it continues to operate, be treated as a new organization and must, if it desires to be classified under section 501(c)(3), give notification that it is applying for recognition of section 501(c)(3) status pursuant to the provisions of section 508(a).

(b) *Effect upon section 507(d)(1).* If the private foundation status of an organization has been terminated under section 507(b)(1)(B) and the regulations thereunder, and:

(1) Such organization does not continue at all times thereafter to meet the requirements of section 509(a)(1), (2), or (3) (and is therefore no longer excluded from the definition of a private foundation); and

(2) The status of such organization as a private foundation is thereafter terminated under section 507(a),

then the tax imposed under section 507(c)(1) upon the aggregate tax benefit (described in section 507(d)(1)) resulting from section 501(c)(3) status shall be computed only upon the aggregate tax benefit resulting after the date on which the organization again becomes a private foundation under subparagraph (1) of this paragraph. [Reg. § 1.509(c)-1.]

☐ [T.D. 7212, 10-16-72.]

[Reg. § 1.509(d)-1]

§ 1.509(d)-1. **Definition of support.**—For purposes of section 509(a)(2), the term "support" does not include amounts received in repayment of the principal of a loan or other indebtedness. See, however, section 509(e) as to amounts received as interest on a loan or other indebtedness. [Reg. § 1.509(d)-1.]

☐ [T.D. 7212, 10-16-72.]

[Reg. § 1.509(e)-1]

§ 1.509(e)-1. **Definition of gross investment income.**—For the distinction between gross receipts and gross investment income, see § 1.509(a)-3(m). [Reg. § 1.509(e)-1.]

☐ [T.D. 7212, 10-16-72.]

Unrelated Business Income

[Reg. § 1.511-1]

§ 1.511-1. **Imposition and rates of tax.**—Section 511(a) imposes a tax upon the unrelated business taxable income of certain organizations otherwise exempt from Federal income tax. Under section 511(a)(1), organizations described in section 511(a)(2)(A) and in paragraph (a) of § 1.511-2 and organizations described in section 511(a)(2)(B) are subject to normal tax and surtax at the corporate rates provided by section 11. Under section 511(b)(1), trusts described in section 511(b)(2) are subject to tax at the individual rates prescribed in section 1(d) of the Code as amended by the Tax Reform Act of 1969 (section 1 for taxable years ending before January 1, 1971). The deduction for personal exemption provided in section 642(b) in the case of a trust taxable under subchapter J, chapter 1 of the Code, is not allowed in computing unrelated business taxable income. [Reg. § 1.511-1.]

☐ [T.D. 6301, 7-8-58. Amended by T.D. 7117, 5-24-71.]

[Reg. § 1.511-2]

§ 1.511-2. **Organizations subject to tax.**—(a) *Organizations other than trusts and title holding companies.*—(1)(i) The taxes imposed by section 511(a)(1) apply in the case of any organization (other than a trust described in section 511(b)(2) or an organization described in section 501(c)(1)) which is exempt from taxation under section 501(a) (except as provided in sections 507 through 515). For special rules concerning corporations described in section 501(c)(2), see paragraph (c) of this section.

(ii) In the case of an organization described in section 501(c)(4), (7), (8), (9), (10), (11), (12), (13), (14)(A), (15), (16) or (18), the taxes imposed by section 511(a)(1) apply only for taxable years beginning after December 31, 1969. In the case of an organization described in section 501(c)(14)(B) or (C), the taxes imposed by section 511(a)(1) apply only for taxable years beginning after February 2, 1966.

(2) The taxes imposed by section 511(a) apply in the case of any college or university which

Reg. § 1.511-2(a)(2)

is an agency or instrumentality of any government or any political subdivision thereof, or which is owned or operated by a government or any political subdivision thereof or by any agency or instrumentality of any one or more governments or political subdivisions. Such taxes also apply in the case of any corporation wholly owned by one or more such colleges or universities. As here used, the word "government" includes any foreign government (to the extent not contrary to any treaty obligation of the United States) and all domestic governments (the United States and any of its Territories or possessions, any State, and the District of Columbia). Elementary and secondary schools operated by such governments are not subject to the tax on unrelated business income.

(3)(i) For taxable years beginning before January 1, 1970, churches and associations or conventions of churches are exempt from the taxes imposed by section 511. The exemption is applicable only to an organization which itself is a church or an association or convention of churches. Subject to the provisions of subdivision (ii) of this subparagraph, religious organizations, including religious orders, if not themselves churches or associations or conventions of churches, and all other organizations which are organized or operated under church auspices, are subject to the tax imposed by section 511, whether or not they engage in religious, educational, or charitable activities approved by a church.

(ii) The term "church" includes a religious order or a religious organization if such order or organization (a) is an integral part of a church, and (b) is engaged in carrying out the functions of a church, whether as a civil law corporation or otherwise. In determining whether a religious order or organization is an integral part of a church, consideration will be given to the degree to which it is connected with, and controlled by, such church. A religious order or organization shall be considered to be engaged in carrying out the functions of a church if its duties include the ministration of sacerdotal functions and the conduct of religious worship. If a religious order or organization is not an integral part of a church, or if such an order or organization is not authorized to carry out the functions of a church (ministration of sacerdotal functions and conduct of religious worship) then it is subject to the tax imposed by section 511 whether or not it engages in religious, educational, or charitable activities approved by a church. What constitutes the conduct of religious worship or the ministration of sacerdotal functions depends on the tenets and practices of a particular religious body constituting a church. If a religious order or organization can fully meet the requirements stated in this subdivision, exemption from the tax imposed by section 511 will apply to all its activities, including those which it conducts through a separate corporation (other than a corporation described in section 501(c)(2)) or other separate entity which it wholly owns and which is not operated for the primary purpose of carrying on a trade or business for profit. Such exemption from tax will also apply to activities conducted through a separate corporation (other than a corporation described in section 501(c)(2)) or other separate entity which is wholly owned by more than one religious order or organization, if all such orders or organizations fully meet the requirements stated in this subdivision and if such corporation or other entity is not operated for the primary purpose of carrying on a trade or business for profit.

(iii) For taxable years beginning after December 31, 1969, churches and conventions or associations of churches are subject to the taxes imposed by section 511, unless otherwise entitled to the benefit of the transitional rules of section 512(b)(14) and § 1.512(b)-1(i).

(b) *Trusts*—(1) *In general.* The taxes imposed by section 511(b) apply in the case of any trust which is exempt from taxation under section 501(a) (except as provided in sections 507 through 515), and which, if it were not for such exemption, would be subject to the provisions of subchapter J, Chapter 1, of the Code. An organization which is considered as "trustee" of a stock bonus, pension, or profit-sharing plan described in section 401(a), a supplemental unemployment benefit trust described in section 501(c)(17), or a pension plan described in section 501(c)(18) (regardless of the form of such organization) is subject to the taxes imposed by section 511(b)(1) on its unrelated business income. However, if such an organization conducts a business which is a separate taxable entity on the basis of all the facts and circumstances, for example, an association taxable as a corporation, the business will be taxable as a feeder organization described in section 502.

(2) *Effective dates.* In the case of a trust described in section 501(c)(3), the taxes imposed by section 511(b) apply for taxable years beginning after December 31, 1953. In the case of a trust described in section 401(a), the taxes imposed by section 511(b) apply for taxable years beginning after June 30, 1954. In the case of a trust described in section 501(c)(17), the taxes imposed by section 511(b) apply for taxable years beginning after December 31, 1959. In the case of any other trust described in subparagraph (1) of this paragraph, the taxes imposed by section 511(b) apply for taxable years beginning after December 31, 1969.

Reg. § 1.511-2(a)(3)

(c) *Title holding companies*—(1) *In general.* If a corporation described in section 501(c)(2) pays any amount of its net income to an organization exempt from taxation under section 501(a) (or would pay such an amount but for the fact that the expenses of collecting its income exceed its income), and if such corporation and such organization file a consolidated income tax return for such taxable year, then such corporation shall be treated, for purposes of the tax imposed by section 511(a), as being organized and operated for the same purposes as such organization, as well as for its title-holding purpose. Therefore, if an item of income of the section 501(c)(2) corporation is derived from a source which is related to the exempt function of the exempt organization to which such income is payable and with which such corporation files a consolidated return, such item is, together with all deductions directly connected therewith, excluded from the determination of unrelated business taxable income under section 512 and shall not be subject to the tax imposed by section 511(a). If, however, such item of income is derived from a source which is not so related, then such item, less all deductions directly connected therewith, is, subject to the modifications provided in section 512(b), unrelated business taxable income subject to the tax imposed by section 511(a).

(2) The provisions of subparagraph (1) of this paragraph may be illustrated by the following example:

Example. The income of X, a section 501(c)(2) corporation, is required to be distributed to exempt organization A. During the taxable year X realizes net income of $900,000 from source M and $100,000 from source N. Source M is related to A's exempt function, while source N is not so related. X and A file a consolidated return for such taxable year. X has net unrelated business income of $100,000, subject to the modifications in section 512(b).

(3) *Cross reference.* For rules relating generally to the filing of consolidated returns by certain organizations exempt from taxation under section 501(a), see section 1504(e) of the Code and § 1.1502-100.

(4) *Effective dates.* Subparagraphs (1) through (3) of this paragraph apply with respect to taxable years beginning after December 31, 1969. For taxable years beginning before January 1, 1970, a corporation described in section 501(c)(2) and otherwise exempt from taxation under section 501(a) is taxable upon is unrelated business taxable income enly if such income is payable either—

(i) To a church or convention or association of churches, or

(ii) To any organization subject, for taxable years beginning before January 1, 1970, to the tax imposed by section 511(a)(1).

(d) The fact that any class of organizations exempt from taxation under section 501(a) is subject to the unrelated business income tax under section 511 and this section does not in any way enlarge the permissible scope of business activities of such class for purposes of the continued qualification of such class under section 501(a). [Reg. § 1.511-2.]

☐ [T.D. 6301, 7-8-58. Amended by T.D. 6972, 9-11-68; T.D. 7183, 4-20-72 and T.D. 7632, 7-19-79.]

[Reg. § 1.511-3]

§ 1.511-3. Provisions generally applicable to the tax on unrelated business income.—(a) *Assessment and collections.* Since the taxes imposed by section 511 are taxes imposed by subtitle A of the Internal Revenue Code of 1954, all provisions of law and of the regulations applicable to the taxes imposed by subtitle A are applicable to the assessment and collection of the taxes imposed by section 511. Organizations subject to the tax imposed by section 511(a)(1) are subject to the same provisions, including penalties, as are provided in the case of the income tax of other corporations. In the case of a trust subject to the tax imposed by section 511(b)(1), the fiduciaries for such trust are subject to the same provisions, including penalties, as are applicable to fiduciaries in the case of the income tax of other trusts. See sections 6151, et seq., and the regulations prescribed thereunder, for provisions relating to payment of tax.

(b) *Returns.* For requirements of filing annual returns with respect to unrelated business taxable income by organizations subject to the tax on such income, see section 6012, paragraph (e) of § 1.6012-2, and paragraph (a)(5) of § 1.6012-3.

(c) *Taxable years, method of accounting, etc.* The taxable year (fiscal year or calendar year, as the case may be) of an organization shall be determined without regard to the fact that such organization may have been exempt from tax during any prior period. See sections 441 and 446, and the regulations thereunder in this part, and section 7701 and the regulations in Part 301 of this chapter (Regulations on Procedure and Administration). Similarly, in computing unrelated business taxable income, the determination of the taxable year for which an item of income or expense is taken into account shall be made under the provisions of sections 441, 446, 451, and 461,

Reg. § 1.511-3(c)

and the regulations thereunder, whether or not the item arose during a taxable year beginning before, on, or after the effective date of the provisions imposing a tax upon unrelated business taxable income. If a method for treating bad debts was selected in a return of income (other than an information return) for a previous taxable year, the taxpayer must follow such method in its returns under section 511, unless such method is changed in accordance with the provisions of § 1.166-1. A taxpayer which has not previously selected a method for treating bad debts may, in its first return under section 511, exercise the option granted in § 1.166-1.

(d) *Foreign tax credit.* See section 515 for provisions applicable to the credit for foreign taxes provided in section 901. [Reg. § 1.511-3.]

☐ [T.D. 6301, 7-8-58.]

[Reg. § 1.511-4]

§ 1.511-4. Minimum tax for tax preferences.—The tax imposed by section 56 applies to an organization subject to tax under section 511 with respect to items of tax preference which enter into the computation of unrelated business taxable income. For this purpose, only those items of income and those deductions entering into the determination of the tax imposed by this section are considered in the determination of the items of tax preference under section 57. For rules relating to the minimum tax for tax preferences, see sections 56 through 58 and the regulations thereunder. [Reg. § 1.511-4.]

☐ [T.D. 7564, 9-11-78.]

[Reg. § 1.512(a)-1]

§ 1.512(a)-1. Definition.—(a) *In general.* Except as otherwise provided in § 1.512(a)-3, § 1.512(a)-4, or paragraph (f) of this section, section 512(a)(1) defines "unrelated business taxable income" as the gross income derived from any unrelated trade or business regularly carried on, less those deductions allowed by chapter 1 of the Code which are directly connected with the carrying on of such trade or business, subject to certain modifications referred to in § 1.512(b)-1. To be deductible in computing unrelated business taxable income, therefore, expenses, depreciation, and similar items not only must qualify as deductions allowed by chapter 1 of the Code, but also must be directly connected with the carrying on of unrelated trade or business. Except as provided in paragraph (d)(2) of this section, to be "directly connected with" the conduct of unrelated business for purposes of section 512, an item of deduction must have proximate and primary relationship to the carrying on of that business. In the case of an organization which derives gross income from the regular conduct of two or more unrelated business activities, unrelated business taxable income is the aggregate of gross income from all such unrelated business activities less the aggregate of the deductions allowed with respect to all such unrelated business activities. For the treatment of amounts of income or loss of common trust funds, see § 1.584-2(c)(3).

(b) *Expenses attributable solely to unrelated business activities.* Expenses, depreciation and similar items attributable solely to the conduct of unrelated business activities are proximately and primarily related to that business activity, and therefore qualify for deduction to the extent that they meet the requirements of section 162, section 167 or other relevant provisions of the Code. Thus, for example, salaries of personnel employed full-time in carrying on unrelated business activities are directly connected with the conduct of that activity and are deductible in computing unrelated business taxable income if they otherwise qualify for deduction under the requirements of section 162. Similarly, depreciation of a building used entirely in the conduct of unrelated business activities would be an allowable deduction to the extent otherwise permitted by section 167.

(c) *Dual use of facilities or personnel.* Where facilities are used both to carry on exempt activities and to conduct unrelated trade or business activities, expenses, depreciation and similar items attributable to such facilities (as, for example, items of overhead) shall be allocated between the two uses on a reasonable basis. Similarly, where personnel are used both to carry on exempt activities and to conduct unrelated trade or business activities, expenses and similar items attributable to such personnel (as, for example, items of salary) shall be allocated between the two uses on a reasonable basis. The portion of any such item so allocated to the unrelated trade or business activity is proximately and primarily related to that business activity, and shall be allowable as a deduction in computing unrelated business taxable income in the manner and to the extent permitted by section 162, section 167 or other relevant provisions of the Code. Thus, for example, assume that X, an exempt organization subject to the provisions of section 511, pays its president a salary of $20,000 a year. X derives gross income from the conduct of unrelated trade or business activities. The president devotes approximately 10 percent of his time during the year to the unrelated business activity. For purposes of computing X's unrelated business taxable income, a deduction of $2,000 (10 percent of $20,000) would be allowable for the salary paid to its president.

Reg. § 1.511-4

(d) *Exploitation of exempt activities*—(1) *In general.* In certain cases, gross income is derived from an unrelated trade or business activity which exploits an exempt activity. One example of such exploitation is the sale of advertising in a periodical of an exempt organization which contains editorial material related to the accomplishment of the organization's exempt purpose. Except as specified in subparagraph (2) of this paragraph and paragraph (f) of this section, in such cases, expenses, depreciation and similar items attributable to the conduct of the exempt activities are not deductible in computing unrelated business taxable income. Since such items are incident to an activity which is carried on in furtherance of the exempt purpose of the organization, they do not possess the necessary proximate and primary relationship to the unrelated trade or business activity and are therefore not directly connected with that business activity.

(2) *Allowable deductions.* Where an unrelated trade or business activity is of a kind carried on for profit by taxable organizations and where the exempt activity exploited by the business is a type of activity normally conducted by taxable organizations in pursuance of such business, expenses, depreciation and similar items which are attributable to the exempt activity qualify as directly connected with the carrying on of the unrelated trade or business activity to the extent that:

(i) The aggregate of such items exceeds the income (if any) derived from or attributable to the exempt activity; and

(ii) The allocation of such excess to the unrelated trade or business activity does not result in a loss from such unrelated trade or business activity.

Under the rule of the preceding sentence, expenses, depreciation and similar items paid or incurred in the performance of an exempt activity must be allocated first to the exempt activity to the extent of the income derived from or attributable to the performance of that activity. Furthermore, such items are in no event allocable to the unrelated trade or business activity exploiting such exempt activity to the extent that their deduction would result in a loss carryover or carryback with respect to that trade or business activity. Similarly, they may not be taken into account in computing unrelated business taxable income attributable to any unrelated trade or business activity not exploiting the same exempt activity. See paragraph (f) of this section for the application of these rules to periodicals published by exempt organizations.

(e) *Examples.* This section is illustrated by the following examples:

Example 1. W is an exempt business league with a large membership. Under an arrangement with an advertising agency W regularly mails brochures, pamphlets and other advertising materials to its members, charging the agency an agreed amount per enclosure. The distribution of the advertising materials does not contribute importantly to the accomplishment of the purpose for which W is granted exemption. Accordingly, the payments made to W by the advertising agency constitute gross income from an unrelated trade or business activity. In computing W's unrelated business taxable income, the expenses attributable solely to the conduct of the business, or allocable to such business under the rule of paragraph (c) of this section, are allowable as deductions in accordance with the provisions of section 162. Such deductions include the costs of handling and mailing, the salaries of personnel used full-time in the unrelated business activity and an allocable portion of the salaries of personnel used both to carry on exempt activities and to conduct the unrelated business activity. However, costs of developing W's membership and carrying on its exempt activities are not deductible. Those costs are necessary to the maintenance of the intangible asset exploited in the unrelated business activity—W's membership—but are incurred primarily in connection with W's fundamental purpose as an exempt organization. As a consequence, they do not have proximate and primary relationship to the conduct of the unrelated business activity and do not qualify as directly connected with it.

Example 2. (i) P, a manufacturer of photographic equipment, underwrites a photography exhibition organized by M, an art museum described in section 501(c)(3). In return for a payment of $100,000, M agrees that the exhibition catalog sold by M in connection with the exhibit will advertise P's product. The exhibition catalog will also include educational material, such as copies of photographs included in the exhibition, interviews with photographers, and an essay by the curator of M's department of photography. For purposes of this example, assume that none of the $100,000 is a qualified sponsorship payment within the meaning of section 513(i) and § 1.513-4, that M's advertising activity is regularly carried on, and that the entire amount of the payment is unrelated business taxable income to M. Expenses directly connected with generating the unrelated business taxable income (i.e., direct advertising costs) total $25,000. Expenses directly connected with the preparation and publication of the exhibition catalog (other than direct advertis-

Reg. § 1.512(a)-1(e)

ing costs) total $110,000. M receives $60,000 of gross revenue from sales of the exhibition catalog. Expenses directly connected with the conduct of the exhibition total $500,000.

(ii) The computation of unrelated business taxable income is as follows:

(A) Unrelated trade or business (sale of advertising):

Income	$100,000	
Directly-connected expenses	(25,000)	
Subtotal	75,000	$75,000

(B) Exempt function (publication of exhibition catalog):

Income (from catalog sales)	60,000
Directly-connected expenses	(110,000)

Net exempt function income (loss)	(50,000)	(50,000)
Unrelated business taxable income		25,000

(iii) Expenses related to publication of the exhibition catalog exceed revenues by $50,000. Because the unrelated business activity (the sale of advertising) exploits an exempt activity (the publication of the exhibition catalog), and because the publication of editorial material is an activity normally conducted by taxable entities that sell advertising, the net loss from the exempt publication activity is allowed as a deduction from unrelated business income under paragraph (d)(2) of this section. In contrast, the presentation of an exhibition is not an activity normally conducted by taxable entities engaged in advertising and publication activity for purposes of paragraph (d)(2) of this section. Consequently, the $500,000 cost of presenting the exhibition is not directly connected with the conduct of the unrelated advertising activity and does not have a proximate and primary relationship to that activity. Accordingly, M has unrelated business taxable income of $25,000.

(f) *Determination of unrelated business taxable income derived from sale of advertising in exempt organization periodicals*—(1) *In general.* Under section 513 (relating to the definition of unrelated trade or business) and § 1.513-1, amounts realized by an exempt organization from the sale of advertising in a periodical constitute gross income from an unrelated trade or business activity involving the exploitation of an exempt activity, namely, the circulation and readership of the periodical developed through the production and distribution of the readership content of the periodical. Paragraph (d) of this section provides for the allowance of deductions attributable to the production and distribution of the readership content of the periodical. Thus, subject to the limitations of paragraph (d)(2) of this section, where the circulation and readership of an exempt organization periodical are utilized in connection with the sale of advertising in the periodical, expenses, depreciation and similar items of deductions attributable to the production and distribution of the editorial or readership content of the periodical shall qualify as items of deductions directly connected with the unrelated advertising activity. Subparagraphs (2) through (6) of this paragraph provide rules for determining the amount of unrelated business taxable income attributable to the sale of advertising in exempt organization periodicals. Subparagraph (7) of this paragraph provides rules for determining when the unrelated business taxable income of two or more exempt organization periodicals may be determined on a consolidated basis.

(2) *Computation of unrelated business taxable income attributable to sale of advertising*—(i) *Excess advertising costs.* If the direct advertising costs of an exempt organization periodical (determined under subparagraph (6)(ii) of this paragraph) exceed gross advertising income (determined under subparagraph (3)(ii) of this paragraph), such excess shall be allowable as a deduction in determining unrelated business taxable income from any unrelated trade or business activity carried on by the organization.

(ii) *Excess advertising income.* If the gross advertising income of an exempt organization periodical exceeds direct advertising costs, paragraph (d)(2) of this section provides that items of deduction attributable to the production and distribution of the readership content of an exempt organization periodical shall qualify as items of deduction directly connected with unrelated advertising activity in computing the amount of unrelated business taxable income derived from the advertising activity to the extent that such items exceed the income derived from or attributable to such production and distribution, but only to the extent that such items do not result in a loss from such advertising activity. Furthermore, such items of deduction shall not qualify as directly connected with such advertising activity to the extent that their deduction would result in a loss carryback or carryover with respect to such advertising activity. Similarly, such items of deduction shall not be taken into account in computing unrelated business taxable income attributable to any unrelated trade or business activity other than such advertising activity. Thus—

(a) If the circulation income of the periodical (determined under subparagraph (3) (iii) of

Reg. § 1.512(a)-1(f)(2)

this paragraph) equals or exceeds the readership costs of such periodical (determined under subparagraph (6)(iii) of this paragraph), the unrelated business taxable income attributable to the periodical is the excess of the gross advertising income of the periodical over direct advertising costs; but

(b) If the readership costs of an exempt organization periodical exceed the circulation income of the periodical, the unrelated business taxable income is the excess, if any, of the total income attributable to the periodical (determined under subparagraph (3) of this paragraph) over the total periodical costs (as defined in subparagraph (6)(i) of this paragraph).

See subparagraph (7) of this paragraph for rules relating to the consolidation of two or more periodicals.

(iii) *Examples.* The application of this paragraph may be illustrated by the following examples. For purposes of these examples it is assumed that the production and distribution of the readership content of the periodical is related to the organization's exempt purpose.

Example (1). X, an exempt trade association, publishes a single periodical which carries advertising. During 1971, X realizes a total of $40,000 from the sale of advertising in the periodical (gross advertising income) and $60,000 from sales of the periodical to members and nonmembers (circulation income). The total periodical costs are $90,000, of which $50,000 is directly connected with the sale and publication of advertising (direct advertising costs) and $40,000 is attributable to the production and distribution of the readership content (readership costs). Since the direct advertising costs of the periodical ($50,000) exceed gross advertising income ($40,000), pursuant to subdivision (i) of this subparagraph, the unrelated business taxable income attributable to advertising is determined solely on the basis of the income and deductions directly connected with the production and sale of the advertising:

Gross Advertising Revenue...	$40,000
Direct Advertising Costs.....	(50,000)
Loss attributable to advertising	($10,000)

X has realized a loss of $10,000 from its advertising activity. This loss is an allowable deduction in computing X's unrelated business taxable income derived from any other unrelated trade or business activity.

Example (2). Assume the facts as stated in example (1), except that the circulation income of X periodical is $100,000 instead of $60,000, and that of the total periodical costs, $25,000 are direct advertising costs, and $65,000 are readership costs. Since the circulation income ($100,000) exceeds the total readership costs ($65,000), pursuant to subdivision (ii)(a) of this subparagraph the unrelated business taxable income attributable to the advertising activity is $15,000, the excess of gross advertising income ($40,000) over direct advertising costs ($25,000).

Example (3). Assume the facts as stated in example (1), except that of the total periodical costs, $20,000 are direct advertising costs and $70,000 are readership costs. Since the readership costs of the periodical ($70,000) exceed the circulation income ($60,000), pursuant to subdivision (ii)(b) of this subparagraph, the unrelated business taxable income attributable to advertising is the excess of the total income attributable to the periodical over the total periodical cost. Thus, X has unrelated business taxable income attributable to the advertising activity of $10,000 ($100,000 total income attributable to the periodical less $90,000 total periodical costs).

Example (4). Assume the facts as stated in example (1), except that the total periodical costs are $120,000 of which $30,000 are direct advertising costs and $90,000 are readership costs. Since the readership costs of the periodical ($90,000) exceed the circulation income ($60,000), pursuant to subdivision (ii)(b) of this subparagraph, the unrelated business taxable income attributable to advertising is the excess, if any, of the total income attributable to the periodical over the total periodical costs. Since the total income of the periodical ($100,000) does not exceed the total periodical costs ($120,000), X has not derived any unrelated business taxable income from the advertising activity. Further, only $70,000 of the $90,000 of readership costs may be deducted in computing unrelated business taxable income since, as provided in subdivision (ii) of this subparagraph, such costs may be deducted, to the extent they exceed circulation income only to the extent they do not result in a loss from the advertising activity. Thus, there is no loss from such activity, and no amount may be deducted on this account in computing X's unrelated trade or business income derived from any other unrelated trade or business activity.

(3) *Income attributable to exempt organization periodicals*—(i) *In general.* For purposes of this paragraph the total income attributable to an exempt organization periodical is the sum of its gross advertising income and its circulation income.

(ii) *Gross advertising income.* The term "gross advertising income" means all amounts derived from the unrelated advertising activities

Reg. § 1.512(a)-1(f)(3)

of an exempt organization periodical (or for purposes of this paragraph in the case of a taxable organization, all amounts derived from the advertising activities of the taxable organization).

(iii) *Circulation income.* The term "circulation income" means the income attributable to the production, distribution or circulation of a periodical (other than gross advertising income) including all amounts realized from or attributable to the sale or distribution of the readership content of the periodical, such as amounts realized from charges made for reprinting or republishing articles and special items in the periodical and amounts realized from sales of back issues. Where the right to receive an exempt organization periodical is associated with membership or similar status in such organization for which dues, fees or other charges are received (hereinafter referred to as "membership receipts"), circulation income includes the portion of such membership receipts allocable to the periodical (hereinafter referred to as "allocable membership receipts"). Allocable membership receipts is the amount which would have been charged and paid if—

(a) The periodical was that of a taxable organization,

(b) The periodical was published for profit, and

(c) The member was an unrelated party dealing with the taxable organization at arm's length.

See subparagraph (4) of this paragraph for a discussion of the factors to be considered in determining allocable membership receipts of an exempt organization periodical under the standard described in the preceding sentence.

(4) *Allocable membership receipts.* The allocable membership receipts of an exempt organization periodical shall be determined in accordance with the following rules:

(i) *Subscription price charged to nonmembers.* If 20 percent or more of the total circulation of a periodical consist of sales to nonmembers, the subscription price charged to such nonmembers shall determine the price of the periodical for purposes of allocating membership receipts to the periodical.

(ii) *Subscription price to nonmembers.* If paragraph (f)(4)(i) of this section does not apply and if the membership dues from 20 percent or more of the members of an exempt organization are less than those received from the other members because the former members do not receive the periodical, the amount of the reduction in membership dues for a member not receiving the periodical shall determine the price of the periodical for purposes of allocating membership receipts to the periodical.

(iii) *Pro rata allocation of membership receipts.* Since it may generally be assumed that membership receipts and gross advertising income are equally available for all the exempt activities (including the periodical) of the organization, the share of membership receipts allocated to the periodical, where paragraphs (f)(4)(i) and (ii) of this section do not apply, shall be an amount equal to the organization's membership receipts multiplied by a fraction the numerator of which is the total periodical costs and denominator of which is such costs plus the cost of other exempt activities of the organization. For example, assume that an exempt organization has total periodical costs of $30,000 and other exempt costs of $70,000. Further assume that the membership receipts of the organization are $60,000 and that paragraphs (f)(4)(i) and (ii) of this section do not apply. Under these circumstances $18,000 ($60,000 times $30,000/$100,000) is allocated to the periodical's circulation income.

(5) *Examples.* The rules set forth in paragraph (f)(4) of this section may be illustrated by the following examples. For purposes of these examples it is assumed that the exempt organization periodical contains advertising, and that the production and distribution of the readership content of the periodical is related to the organization's exempt purpose.

Example (1). U is an exempt scientific organization with 10,000 members who pay annual dues of $15 per year. One of U's activities is the publication of a monthly periodical which is distributed to all of its members. U also distributes 5,000 additional copies of its periodical to nonmember subscribers at a cost of $10 per year. Pursuant to paragraph (f)(4)(i) of this section, since the nonmember circulation of U's periodical represents 33 1/3 percent of its total circulation the subscription price charged to nonmembers will be used to determine the portion of U's membership receipts allocable to the periodical. Thus, U's allocable membership receipts will be $100,000 ($10 times 10,000 members), and U's total circulation income for the periodical will be $150,000 ($100,000 from members plus $50,000 from sales to nonmembers).

Example (2). Assume the facts as stated in example (1), except that U sells only 500 copies of its periodical to nonmembers, at a price of $10 per year. Assume further that U's members may elect not to receive the periodical, in which case their annual dues are reduced from $15 per year to $6 per year, and that only 3,000 members elect to receive the periodical and pay the full dues of $15

Reg. § 1.512(a)-1(f)(4)

per year. U's stated subscription price to members of $9 consistently results in an excess of total income (including gross advertising income) attributable to the periodical over total costs of the periodical. Since the 500 copies of the periodical distributed to nonmembers represents only 14 percent of the 3,500 copies distributed, pursuant to paragraph (f)(4)(i) of this section the $10 subscription price charged to nonmembers will not be used in determining the portion of membership receipts allocable to the periodical. On the other hand, since 70 percent of the members elect not to receive the periodical and pay $9 less per year in dues, pursuant to paragraph (f)(4)(ii) of this section, such $9 price will be used in determining the subscription price charged to members. Thus, the allocable membership receipts will be $9 per member, or $27,000 ($9 times 3,000 copies) and U's total circulation income will be $32,000 ($27,000 plus $5,000).

Example (3). (a) W, an exempt trade association, has 800 members who pay annual dues of $50 per year. W publishes a monthly journal the editorial content and advertising of which are directed to the business interests of its own members. The journal is distributed to all of W's members and no receipts are derived from nonmembers.

(b) W has total receipts of $100,000 of which $40,000 ($50 × 800) are membership receipts and $60,000 are gross advertising income. W's total costs for the journal and other exempt activities is $100,000. W has total periodical costs of $76,000 of which $41,000 are direct advertising costs and $35,000 are readership costs.

(c) Paragraph (f)(4)(i) of this section will not apply since no copies are available to nonmembers. Therefore, the allocation of membership receipts shall be made in accordance with paragraph (f)(4)(iii) of this section. Based upon pro rata allocation of membership receipts (40,000) by a fraction the numerator of which is total periodical costs ($76,000) and the denominator of which is the total costs of the journal and the other exempt activities ($100,000), $30,400 ($76,000/$100,000 times $40,000) of membership receipts is circulation income.

(6) *Deductions attributable to exempt organization periodicals*—(i) *In general.* For purposes of this paragraph the term "total periodical costs" means the total deductions attributable to the periodical. For purposes of this paragraph the total periodical costs of an exempt organization periodical are the sum of the direct advertising costs of the periodical (determined under subdivision (ii) of this subparagraph) and the readership costs of the periodical (determined under subdivision (iii) of this subparagraph). Items of deduction properly attributable to exempt activities other than the publication of an exempt organization periodical may not be allocated to such periodical. Where items are attributable both to an exempt organization periodical and to other activities of an exempt organization, the allocation of such items must be made on a reasonable basis which fairly reflects the portion of such item properly attributable to each such activity. The method of allocation will vary with the nature of the item, but once adopted, a reasonable method of allocation with respect to an item must be used consistently. Thus, for example, salaries may generally be allocated among various activities on the basis of the time devoted to each activity; occupancy costs such as rent, heat and electricity may be allocated on the basis of the portion of space devoted to each activity; and depreciation may be allocated on the basis of space occupied and the portion of the particular asset utilized in each activity. Allocations based on dollar receipts from various exempt activities will generally not be reasonable since such receipts are usually not an accurate reflection of the costs associated with activities carried on by exempt organizations.

(ii) *Direct advertising costs.* (*a*) The direct advertising costs of an exempt organization periodical include all expenses, depreciation and similar items of deduction which are directly connected with the sale and publication of advertising as determined in accordance with paragraphs (a), (b) and (c) of this section. These items are allowable as deductions in the computation of unrelated business income of the organization for the taxable year to the extent they meet the requirements of section 162, section 167 or other relevant provisions of the Code. The items allowable as deductions under this subdivision do not include any items of deduction attributable to the production or distribution or the readership content of the periodical.

(*b*). The items allowable deductions under this subdivision would include agency commissions and other direct selling costs, such as transportation and travel expenses, office salaries, promotion and research expenses, and direct office overhead directly connected with the sale of advertising lineage in the periodical. Also included would be other items of deduction commonly classified as advertising costs under standard account classification, such as art work and copy preparation, telephone, telegraph, postage and similar costs directly connected with advertising.

(*c*) In addition to the items of deduction normally included in standard account classifications relating to advertising costs, it is also neces-

Reg. § 1.512(a)-1(f)(6)

sary to ascertain the portion of mechanical and distribution costs attributable to advertising lineage. For this purpose, the general account classifications of items includible in mechanical and distribution costs ordinarily employed in business-paper and consumer publication accounting provide a guide for the computation. Thus, the mechanical and distribution costs in such cases would include the portion of the costs and other expenses of composition, press work, binding, mailing (including paper and wrappers used for mailing) and the bulk postage attributable to the advertising lineage of the publication. The portion of mechanical and distribution costs attributable to advertising lineage of the periodical will be determined on the basis of the ratio of advertising lineage to total lineage of the periodical and the application of that ratio to the total mechanical and distribution costs of the periodical, where records are not kept in such a manner as to reflect more accurately the allocation of mechanical and distributions costs to advertising lineage of the periodical, and where there is no factor in the character of the periodical to indicate that such an allocation would be unreasonable.

(iii) *Readership costs.* The "readership costs" of an exempt organization periodical include expenses, depreciation or similar items which are directly connected with the production and distribution of the readership content of the periodical and which would otherwise be allowed as deductions in determining unrelated business taxable income under section 512 and the regulations thereunder if such production and distribution constituted an unrelated trade or business activity. Thus, readership costs include all the items of deduction attributable to an exempt organization periodical which are not allocated to direct advertising costs under subdivision (ii) of this subparagraph, including the portion of such items attributable to the readership content of the periodical, as opposed to the advertising content, and the portion of mechanical and distribution costs which is not attributable to advertising lineage in the periodical.

(7) *Consolidation*—(i) *In general.* Where an exempt organization subject to unrelated business income tax under section 511 publishes two or more periodicals for the production of income, it may treat the gross income from all (but not less than all) of such periodicals and the items of deduction directly connected with such periodicals (including readership costs of such periodicals) on a consolidated basis as if such periodicals were one periodical in determining the amount of unrelated business taxable income derived from the sale of advertising in such periodical. Such treatment must, however, be followed consistently and once adopted shall be binding unless the consent of the Commissioner, as provided in section 446(e) and § 1.446-1(e), is obtained.

(ii) *Production of income.* For purposes of this subparagraph, an exempt organization periodical is "published for the production of income" if—

(*a*) The organization generally receives gross advertising income from the periodical equal to at least 25 percent of the readership costs of such periodical, and

(*b*) The publication of such periodical is an activity engaged in for profit.

For purposes of the preceding sentence, the determination whether the publication of a periodical is an activity engaged in for profit is to be made by reference to objective standards taking into account all the facts and circumstances involved in each case. The facts and circumstances must indicate that the organization carries on the activity with the objective that the publication of the periodical will result in economic profit (without regard to tax consequences), although not necessarily in a particular year. Thus, an exempt organization periodical may be treated as having been published with such an objective even though in a particular year its total periodical costs exceed its total income. Similarly, if an exempt organization begins publishing a new periodical, the fact that the total periodical costs exceed the total income for the start-up years because of a lack of advertising sales does not mean that the periodical was published without an objective of economic profit. The organization may establish that the activity was carried on with such an objective. This might be established by showing, for example, that there is a reasonable expectation that the total income, by reason of an increase in advertising sales, will exceed costs within a reasonable time. See § 1.183-2 for additional factors bearing on this determination.

(iii) *Example.* This subparagraph may be illustrated by the following example:

Example. Y, an exempt trade association, publishes three periodicals which it distributes to its members: a weekly newsletter, a monthly magazine, and [a] quarterly journal. Both the monthly magazine and the quarterly journal contain advertising which accounts for gross advertising income equal to more than 25 percent of their respective readership costs. Similarly, the total income attributable to each such periodical has exceeded the total deductions attributable to each such periodical for substantially all the years they have been published. The newsletter carries no advertising and its annual subscription price is not intended to cover the cost of publication. The

Reg. § 1.512(a)-1(f)(7)

newsletter is a service of Y distributed to all of its members in an effort to keep them informed of changes occurring in the business world and is not engaged in for profit. Under these circumstances, Y may consolidate the income and deductions from the monthly and quarterly journals in computing its unrelated business taxable income, but may not consolidate the income and deductions attributable to the publication of the newsletter with the income and deductions of its other periodicals since the newsletter is not published for the production of income.

(g) *Foreign organizations*—(1) *In general.* The unrelated business taxable income of a foreign organization exempt from taxation under section 501(a) consists of:

(i) The organization's unrelated business taxable income which is derived from sources within the United States but which is not effectively connected with the conduct of a trade or business within the United States, plus

(ii) The organization's unrelated business taxable income effectively connected with the conduct of a trade or business within the United States (whether or not such income is derived from sources within the United States).

To determine whether income realized by a foreign organization is derived from sources within the United States or is effectively connected with the conduct of a trade or business within the United States, see part 1, subchapter N, chapter 1 of the Code (section 861 and following) and the regulations thereunder.

(2) *Effective dates.* Subparagraph (1) of this paragraph applies to taxable years beginning after December 31, 1969. For taxable years beginning on or before December 31, 1969, the unrelated business taxable income of a foreign organization exempt from taxation under section 501(a) consists of the organization's unrelated business taxable income which—

(i) For taxable years beginning after December 31, 1966, is effective connected with the conduct of a trade or business within the United States, whether or not such income is derived from sources within the United States;

(ii) For taxable years beginning on or before December 31, 1966, is derived from sources within the United States.

(h) *Effective date.* Paragraphs (a) through (f) of this section are applicable with respect to taxable years beginning after December 12, 1967. However, if a taxpayer wishes to rely on the rules stated therein for taxable years beginning before December 13, 1967, it may do so. [Reg. § 1.512(a)-1.]

☐ [*T.D.* 6939, 12-11-67. *Amended by T.D.* 7183, 4-20-72; *T.D.* 7392, 12-17-75; *T.D.* 7438, 10-7-76; *T.D.* 7935, 1-12-84 *and T.D.* 8991, 4-24-2002.]

[Reg. § 1.512(a)-4]

§ 1.512(a)-4. **Special rules applicable to war veterans organizations.**—(a) *In general.* For taxable years beginning after December 31, 1969, this section provides special rules for the determination of the unrelated business taxable income of an organization described in section 501(c)(19). In general, the rules contained in sections 511 through 514 which are applicable to any organization listed in section 501(c) apply in determining the unrelated business taxable income of an organization described in section 501(c)(19). However, that amount which is paid by members to the organization for the purpose described in paragraph (b)(1) of this section, if set aside from other organizational monies and accounts in an insurance set aside, may be excluded from the unrelated business taxable income of the organization. The insurance set aside shall be used exclusively for providing insurance benefits, for the purposes specified in section 170(c)(4) of the Code, for the reasonable cost of administering the insurance program that are directly related to such set aside, or for the reasonable costs of distributing funds for section 170(c)(4) purposes. If an amount so set aside is used for any purposes other than those described in the preceding sentence, it shall be included in unrelated business taxable income without regard to any modifications provided by section 512(b), in the taxable year in which it is withdrawn from such set aside. Amounts will be considered to have been withdrawn from an insurance set aside if they are used in any manner inconsistent with providing insurance benefits, paying the reasonable costs of administering the insurance program, for section 170(c)(4) purposes, and for costs of distributing funds for section 170(c)(4) purposes. An example of a use of funds which would be considered a withdrawal would be the use of such funds as security for a loan.

(b) *Insurance set aside.* (1) *Purpose of payments by members.* Payments by members (including commissions on such payments earned by the set aside as agent for an insurance company) into an insurance set aside must be for the sole purpose of obtaining life, sick, accident or health insurance benefits from the organization or for the reasonable costs of administration of the insurance program, except that such purpose is not violated when excess funds from an experience gain are utilized for those purposes specified in section 170(c)(4) or the reasonable costs of distrib-

Reg. § 1.512(a)-4(b)

uting funds for such purposes. Funds for any other purpose may not be set aside in the insurance set aside.

(2) *Income from set aside.* In addition to the payments by members described in paragraph (b)(1) of this section, only income from amounts in the insurance set aside (including commissions earned as agent for an insurance company) may be so set aside. Moreover, unless such income is used for providing insurance benefits, for those purposes specified in section 170(c)(4), or for reasonable costs of administration, such income must be set aside within the period described in paragraph (b)(3) of this section in order to avoid being included as an item of unrelated business taxable income under section 512(a)(4).

(3) *Time within which income must be set aside.* Income from amounts in the insurance set aside generally must be set aside in the taxable year in which it would be includible in gross income but for this section. However, income set aside on or before the date prescribed for filing the organization's return of unrelated business taxable income (whether or not it had such income) for the taxable year (including any extension of time) may, at the election of the organization, be treated as having been set aside in such taxable year.

(4) *Computation of income from set aside.* Income from amounts in the insurance set aside shall consist solely of items of investment income from, and certain gains derived from dealings in, property in the set aside. The deductions allowed against such items of income or other gains are those amounts which are related to the production of such income or other gains. Only the amounts of income or other gain which are in excess of such deductions may be set aside in the insurance set aside.

(5) *Requirements for set aside.* An amount is not properly set aside if the organization commingles it with any amount which is not to be set aside. However, adequate records describing the amount set aside and indicating that it is to be used for the designated purpose are sufficient. Amounts that are set aside need not be permanently committed to such use either under state law or by contract. Thus, for example, it is not necessary that the organization place these funds in an irrevocable trust. Although set aside income may be accumulated, any accumulation which is unreasonable in amount or duration is evidence that the income was not accumulated for the purposes set forth. For purposes of the preceding sentence, accumulations which are reasonably necessary for the purpose of providing life, sick, health, or accident insurance benefits on the basis of recognized mortality or morbidity tables and assumed rates of interest under an actuarially acceptable method would not be unreasonable even though such accumulations are quite large and the time between the receipt by the organization of such amounts and the date of payment of the benefits is quite long. For example, an accumulation of income for 20 years or longer which is determined to be reasonably necessary to pay life insurance benefits to members, their dependents or designated beneficiaries, generally would not be an unreasonable accumulation. Income which has been set aside may be invested, pending the action contemplated by the set aside, without being regarded as having been used for other purposes. [Reg. § 1.512(a)-4.]

☐ [*T.D.* 7438, 10-7-76.]

[Reg. § 1.512(a)-5T]

§ 1.512(a)-5T. Questions and answers relating to the unrelated business taxable income of organizations described in paragraph (9), (17) or (20) of section 501(c) (Temporary).

Q-1: What does section 512(a)(3), as amended by the Tax Reform Act of 1984 (Act), provide with respect to organizations described in paragraphs (9), (17) or (20) of section 501(c)?

A-1: In general, section 512(a)(3), as amended by section 511 of the Act, extends the rules for determining the unrelated business income tax of voluntary employees' beneficiary associations (VEBAs) to supplemental unemployment compensation benefit trusts (SUBs) and group legal service organizations (GLSOs). The section also restricts the amount of income that may be set aside by such organizations for exempt purposes.

Q-2: What is the effective date of the amendments to section 512(a)(3)?

A-2: The amendments to section 512(a)(3) will apply to income earned by VEBAs, SUBs or GLSOs after December 31, 1985, in the taxable years of such organizations ending after such date. For purposes of applying section 512(a)(3) to the first taxable year of such an organization ending after December 31, 1985, the income of the VEBA, SUB or GLSO earned after December 31, 1985, will be determined by allocating the total income earned for such taxable year on the basis of the calendar year 1985 and 1986 months in such taxable year. However, if a VEBA, SUB or GLSO is part of a plan that is maintained pursuant to one or more collective bargaining agreements (i) between employee representatives and one or more employers, and (ii) which are in effect on July 1, 1985 (or ratified on or before that date), the amendments do not apply to income earned in a taxable year of a VEBA, SUB or GLSO begin-

Reg. § 1.512(a)-5T

ning before the termination of the last of the collective bargaining agreements pursuant to which the plan is maintained (determined without regard to any extension of the contract agreed to after July 1, 1985). For purposes of the preceding sentence, any plan amendment made pursuant to a collective bargaining agreement relating to the plan which amends the plan solely to conform to any requirement added under section 511 of the Tax Reform Act 1984 (i.e., requirements under sections 419, 419A, 512(a)(3)(E), and 4976) shall not be treated as a termination of such collective bargaining agreement.

Q-3: What amount of income may a VEBA, SUB or GLSO set aside for exempt purposes?

A-3: (a) Pursuant to section 512 (a)(3)(E)(i), the amounts set aside in a VEBA, SUB, or GLSO (including a VEBA, SUB, or GLSO that is part of a 10 or more employer plan, as defined in section 419A(f)(6)(B)) as of the close of a taxable year of such VEBA, SUB, or GLSO to provide for the payment of life, sick, accident, or other benefits may not be taken into account for purposes of determining "exempt function income" to the extent that such amounts exceed the qualified asset account limit, determined under sections 419A(c) and 419A(f)(7), for such taxable year of the VEBA, SUB, or GLSO. In calculating the qualified asset account limit for this purpose, a reserve for post-retirement medical benefits under section 419A(c)(2)(A) is not to be taken into account.

(b) The exempt function income of a VEBA, SUB, or GLSO for a taxable year of such an organization, under section 512(a)(3)(B), includes: (1) certain amounts paid by members of the VEBA, SUB, or GLSO within the meaning of the first sentence of section 512(a)(3)(B) ("member contributions"); and (2) other income of the VEBA, SUB, or GLSO (including earnings on member contributions) that is set aside for the payment of life, sick, accident, or other benefits to the extent that the total amount set aside in the VEBA, SUB or GLSO as of the close of the taxable year for any purpose (including member contributions and other income set aside in the VEBA, SUB, or GLSO as of the close of the year) does not exceed the qualified asset account limit for such taxable year of the organization. For purposes of section 512(c)(3)(B), member contributions include both employee contributions and employer contributions to the VEBA, SUB or GLSO. In calculating the total amount set aside in a VEBA, SUB, or GLSO as of the close of a taxable year, certain assets with useful lives extending substantially beyond the end of the taxable year (e.g., buildings, and licenses) are not to be taken into account to the extent they are used in the provision of life, sick, accident, or other benefits. For example, cash and securities (and similar investments) held by a VEBA, SUB, or GLSO are not disregarded in calculating the total amount set aside for this purpose because they are used to pay welfare benefits, rather than merely used in the provision of such benefits. Accordingly, the unrelated business taxable income of a VEBA, SUB, or GLSO for a taxable year of such an organization generally will equal the lesser of two amounts: the income of the VEBA, SUB, or GLSO for the taxable year (excluding member contributions); or, the excess of the total amount set aside as of the close of the taxable year (including member contributions, and excluding certain assets with a useful life extending substantially beyond the end of the taxable year to the extent they are used in the provision of welfare benefits) over the qualified asset account limit (calculated without regard to the otherwise permitted reserve for post-retirement medical benefits) for the taxable year. See § 1.419A-2T for special rules relating to collectively bargained welfare benefit funds.

(c) The income of a VEBA, SUB, or GLSO for any taxable year includes gain realized by the organization on the sale or disposition of any asset during such year. The gain realized by a VEBA, SUB, or GLSO on the sale or disposition of an asset is equal to the amount realized by the organization over the basis of such asset (in the hands of the organization), reduced by any qualified direct costs attributable to such asset (under paragraphs (b), (c) and (d) of Q&A-6 of § 1.419-1T).

Q-4: What transition rules apply to "existing reserves for post-retirement medical or life insurance benefits"?

A-4: (a) Section 512(a)(3)(E)(iii)(I) provides that income that is either directly or indirectly attributable to "existing reserves for post-retirement medical or life insurance benefits" will not be treated as unrelated business taxable income. An "existing reserve for post-retirement medical or life insurance benefits" (as defined in section 512(a)(3)(E)(iii)(II)) is the total amount of assets actually set aside in a VEBA, SUB, or GLSO on July 18, 1984 (calculated in the manner set forth in Q&A-3 of this regulation, and adjusted under paragraph (c) of Q&A-11 of § 1.419-1T), reduced by employer contributions to the fund on or before such date to the extent such contributions are not deductible for the taxable year of the employer containing July 18, 1984, and for any prior taxable year of the employer, for purposes of providing such post-retirement benefits. For purposes of the preceding sentence only, an amount that was not actually set aside on July 18, 1984, will be treated

Reg. § 1.512(a)-5T

as having been actually set aside on such date if (1) such amount was incurred by the employer (without regard to section 461(h)) as of the close of the last taxable year of the VEBA, SUB, or GLSO ending before July 18, 1984, and (2) such amount was actually contributed to the VEBA, SUB, or GLSO within 8½ months following the close of such taxable year.

(b) In addition, section 512(a)(3)(E)(iii)(I) applies to existing reserves for such post-retirement benefits only to the extent that such "existing reserves" do not exceed the amount that could be accumulated under the principles set forth in Revenue Rulings 69-382, 1969-2 C.B. 28; 69-478, 1969-2 C.B. 29; and 73-599, 1973-2 C.B. 40. Thus, amounts attributable to such excess "existing reserves" are not within this transition rule even though they were actually set aside on July 18, 1984.

(c) All post-retirement medical or life insurance benefits (or other benefits to the extent paid with amounts set aside to provide post-retirement medical or life insurance benefits) provided after July 18, 1984 (whether or not the employer has maintained a reserve or fund for such benefits) are to be charged, first, against the "existing reserves" within this transition rule (including amounts attributable to "existing reserves" within this transition rule) for post-retirement medical benefits or for post-retirement life insurance benefits (as the case may be) and, second, against all other amounts. For this purpose, the qualified direct cost of an asset with a useful life extending substantially beyond the end of the taxable year (as determined under Q&A-6 of § 1.419-1T) will be treated as a benefit provided and thus charged against the "existing reserve" based on the extent to which such asset is used in the provision of post-retirement medical benefits or post-retirement life insurance benefits (as the case may be). All plans of an employer providing post-retirement medical benefits are to be treated as one plan for purposes of section 512(a)(3)(E)(iii)(III), and all plans of an employer providing post-retirement life insurance benefits are to be treated as one plan for purposes of section 512(a)(3)(E)(iii)(III).

(d) In calculating the unrelated business taxable income of a VEBA, SUB, or GLSO for a taxable year of such organization, the total income of the VEBA, SUB, or GLSO for the taxable year is reduced by the income attributable to "existing reserves" within the transition rule before such income is compared to the excess of the total amount set aside as of the close of the taxable year over the qualified asset account limit for the taxable year. Thus, for example, assume that the total income of a VEBA for a taxable year is $1,000, and that the excess of the total amount of the VEBA set aside as of the close of the taxable year over the applicable qualified asset account limit is $600. Assume also that of the $1,000 of total income, $500 is attributable to "existing reserves" within the transition rule of section 512(a)(3)(E)(iii)(I). The unrelated business income of this VEBA for the taxable year is equal to the lesser of the following two amounts: (1) the total income of the VEBA for the taxable year ($1,000), reduced to the extent that such income is attributable to "existing reserves" within the transition rule ($500); or (2) the excess of the total amount set aside as of the close of the taxable year over the applicable qualified asset account limit ($600). Thus, the unrelated business income of this VEBA for the taxable year is $500. [Temporary Reg. § 1.512(a)-5T.]

☐ [T.D. 8073, 1-29-86.]

[Reg. § 1.512(b)-1]

§ 1.512(b)-1. Modifications.—Whether a particular item of income falls within any of the modifications provided in section 512(b) shall be determined by all the facts and circumstances of each case. For example, if a payment termed "rent" by the parties is in fact a return of profits by a person operating the property for the benefit of the tax-exempt organization or is a share of the profits retained by such organization as a partner or joint venturer, such payment is not within the modification for rents. The modifications provided in section 512(b) are as follows:

(a) Certain Investment Income—(1) In general. Dividends, interest, payments with respect to securities loans (as defined in section 512(a)(5)), annuities, income from notional principal contracts (as defined in Treasury Regulations 26 CFR 1.863-7 or regulations issued under section 446), other substantially similar income from ordinary and routine investments to the extent determined by the Commissioner, and all deductions directly connected with any of the foregoing items of income shall be excluded in computing unrelated business taxable income.

(2) Limitations. The exclusions under paragraph (a)(1) of this section do not apply to income derived from and deductions in connection with debt-financed property (as defined in section 514(b)). Moreover, the exclusions under paragraph (a)(1) of this section do not apply to gains or losses from the sale, exchange, or other disposition of any property, or to gains or losses from the lapse or termination of options to buy or sell securities. For rules regarding the treatment of these gains and losses, see section 512(b)(5) and § 1.512(b)-1(d). Furthermore, the exclusions under

paragraph (a)(1) of this section do not apply to interest and annuities derived from and deductions in connection with controlled organizations. For rules regarding the treatment of such amounts, see section 512(b)(13) and § 1.512(b)-1(l). Finally, the exclusions under paragraph (a)(1) of this section of income from notional principal contracts and income that the Commissioner determines to be substantially similar income from ordinary and routine investments do not apply to income earned by brokers or dealers (including organizations that make a market in derivative financial products, as described in Treasury Regulations 26 CFR 1.954-2T(a)(4)(iii)(B)).

(3) *Effective dates.* The effective dates of the rules of paragraphs (a)(1) and (a)(2) of this section that were in effect prior to August 30, 1991, remain the same. The exclusion under paragraph (a)(1) of this section of income from notional principal contracts is effective for amounts received after August 30, 1991. However, an organization may apply the exclusion under paragraph (a)(1) of this section of income from notional principal contracts prior to that date, provided that such amounts are treated consistently for all open taxable years. Unless otherwise provided by the Commissioner, the exclusion under paragraph (a)(1) of this section of income that the Commissioner determines to be substantially similar income from ordinary and routine investments is effective for amounts received after the date of the Commissioner's determination.

(b) *Royalties.* Royalties, including overriding royalties, and all deductions directly connected with such income shall be excluded in computing unrelated business taxable income. However, for taxable years beginning after December 31, 1969, certain royalties from and certain deductions in connection with either debt-financed property (as defined in Sec. 514(b)) or controlled organizations (as defined in paragraph (1) of this section) shall be included in computing unrelated business taxable income. Mineral royalties shall be excluded whether measured by production or by gross or taxable income from the mineral property. However, where an organization owns a working interest in a mineral property, and is not relieved of its share of the development costs by the terms of any agreement with an operator, income received from such an interest shall not be excluded. To the extent not treated as a loan under section 636, payments in discharge of mineral production payments shall be treated in the same manner as royalty payments for the purpose of computing unrelated business taxable income. To the extent treated as a loan under section 636, the amount of any payments in discharge of a production payment which is the equivalent of interest shall be treated as interest for purposes of section 512(b)(1) and paragraph (a) of this section.

(c) *Rents*—(1) *Taxable years beginning before January 1, 1970.* For taxable years beginning before January 1, 1970, rents from real property (including personal property leased with the real property) and the deductions directly connected therewith shall be excluded in computing unrelated business taxable income, except that certain rents from, and certain deductions in connection with, a business lease (as defined in section 514(f)) shall be included in computing unrelated business taxable income. See subparagraph (5) of this paragraph for rules governing amounts received for the rendering of services.

(2) *Taxable years beginning after December 31, 1969* —(i) *In general.* For taxable years beginning after December 31, 1969, except as provided in subdivision (iii) of this subparagraph, rents from property described in subdivision (ii) of this subparagraph, and the deductions directly connected therewith, shall be excluded in computing unrelated business taxable income. However, notwithstanding subdivision (ii) of this subparagraph, certain rents from and certain deductions in connection with either debt-financed property (as defined in section 514 (b)) or property rented to controlled organizations (as defined in paragraph (1) of this section) shall be included in computing unrelated business taxable income.

(ii) *Excluded rents.* The rents which are excluded from unrelated business income under section 512(b)(3)(A) and this paragraph are—

(a) *Real property.* All rents from real property; and

(b) *Personal property.* All rents from personal property leased with real property if the rents attributable to such personal property are an incidental amount of the total rents received or accrued under the lease, determined at the time the personal property is first placed in service by the lessee.

For purposes of the preceding sentence, rents attributable to personal property generally are not an incidental amount of the total rents if such rents exceed 10 percent of the total rents from all the property leased. For example, if the rents attributable to the personal property leased are determined to be $3,000 per year, and the total rents from all property leased are $10,000 per year, then such $3,000 amount is not to be excluded from the computation of unrelated business taxable income by operation of section 512(b)(3)(A)(ii) and this paragraph, since such amount is not an incidental portion of the total rents.

Reg. § 1.512(b)-1(c)(2)

(iii) *Exception.* Subdivision (ii) of this subparagraph shall not apply, if either—

(a) *Excess personal property rentals.* More than 50 percent of the total rents are attributable to personal property, determined at the time such personal property is first placed in service by the lessee; or

(b) *Net profits.* The determination of the amount of such rents depends in whole or in part on the income or profits derived by any person from the property leased, other than an amount based on a fixed percentage or percentages of the gross receipts or sales. For purposes of the preceding sentence, the rules contained in paragraph (b)(3) and (6) (other than paragraph (b)(6)(ii)) of § 1.856-4 shall apply.

(iv) *Illustration.* This subparagraph may be illustrated by the following example:

Example. A, an exempt organization, owns a printing factory which consists of a building housing two printing presses and other equipment necessary for printing. On January 1, 1971, A rents the building and the printing equipment to B for $10,000 a year. The lease states that $9,000 of such rent is for the building and $1,000 for the printing equipment. However, if it is determined that notwithstanding the terms of the lease $4,000, or 40 percent ($4,000/$10,000), of the rent is actually attributable to the printing equipment. During 1971, A has $3,000 of deductions, all of which are properly allocable to the land and building. Under these circumstances, A shall not take into account in computing its unrelated business taxable income the $6,000 of rent attributable to the building and the $3,000 of deductions directly connected with such rent. However, the $4,000 of rent attributable to the printing equipment is not excluded from the computation of A's unrelated business taxable income by operation of section 512(b)(3)(A)(ii) or this paragraph since such rent represents more than an incidental portion of the total rents.

(3) *Definitions and special rules.* For purposes of subparagraph (2) of this paragraph—

(i) *Real property defined.* The term "real property" means all real property, including any property described in sections 1245(a)(3)(C) and 1250(c) and the regulations thereunder.

(ii) *Personal property defined.* The term "personal property" means all personal property, including any property described in section 1245(a)(3)(B) and the regulations thereunder.

(iii) *Multiple leases.* If separate leases are entered into with respect to real and personal property, and such properties have an integrated use (*e.g.,* one or more leases for real property and another lease or leases for personal property to be used upon such real property), all such leases shall be considered as one lease.

(iv) *Placed in service.* Property is "placed in service" by the lessee when it is first subject to his use in accordance with the terms of the lease. For example, property subject to a lease entered into on November 1, 1971, for a term commencing on January 1, 1972, shall be considered as placed in service on January 1, 1972, regardless of when the property is first actually used by the lessee.

(v) *Changes in rent charged or personal property rented.* If—

(a) By reason of the placing of additional or substitute personal property in service, there is an increase of 100 percent or more in the rent attributable to all the personal property leased, or

(b) There is a modification of the lease by which there is a change in the rent charged (whether or not there is a change in the amount of personal property rented),

the rent attributable to personal property shall be recomputed to determine whether the exclusion under subparagraph (2)(ii)(b) of this paragraph or the exception under subparagraph (2)(iii)(a) of this paragraph applies. Any change in the treatment of rents, attributable to a recomputation under this subdivision, shall be effective only with respect to rents for the period beginning with the event which occasioned the recomputation.

(4) *Examples.* Subparagraphs (2) and (3) of this paragraph may be illustrated by the following examples:

Example (1). On January 1, 1971, A, an exempt organization, executes two leases with B. One is for the rental of a computer, with a stated annual rental of $750. The other is for the rental of office space in which to use the computer, at a stated annual rent of $7,250. The total annual rent under both leases for 1971 is $8,000. At the time the computer is first placed in service, however, taking both leases into consideration, it is determined that notwithstanding the terms of the leases $3,000, or 37.5 percent ($3,000/$8,000), of the rent is actually attributable to the computer. Therefore, for 1971, only the $5,000 ($8,000 − $3,000) attributable to the rental of the office space is excluded from the computation of A's unrelated business taxable income by the operation of section 512(b)(3).

Example (2). Assume the facts as stated in example (1). Assume further that the leases to which the computer and office space are subject in example (1) provide that the rent may be increased or decreased, depending upon the pre-

Reg. § 1.512(b)-1(c)(3)

vailing rental value for similar computers and office space. On January 1, 1972, the total annual rent is increased in the computer lease to $2,000, and in the office space lease to $9,000. For 1972, it is determined that notwithstanding the terms of the leases $6,000, or 54.5 percent ($6,000/$11,000), of the total rent is actually attributable to the computer as of that time. Even though the rent attributable to personal property now exceeds 50 percent of the total rent, the rent attributable to real property continues to be excluded, since there was no modification of the terms of the leases and since the increase in the rent was not attributable to the placing of new personal property in service. See subparagraph (3)(v) of this paragraph. Thus, for 1972 the $5,000 of the rent attributable to the office space continues to be excluded from the computation of A's unrelated business taxable income by operation of section 512(b)(3).

Example (3). Assume the facts as stated in example (1), except that on January 1, 1973, B rents a second computer from A, which is placed in service on that date. The total rent is increased to $2,000 for the computer lease and to $10,000 for the office space lease. It is determined at the time the second computer is first placed in service that notwithstanding the terms of the leases $7,000 of the rent is actually attributable to the computers. Since the rent attributable to personal property has increased by more than 100 percent ($4,000/$3,000 = 133%), a redetermination must be made pursuant to subparagraph (3)(v)(*a*) of this paragraph. As a result, 58.3 percent ($7,000/$12,000) of the total rent is determined to be attributable to personal property. Accordingly, since more than 50 percent of the total rent A receives is attributable to personal property leased, this exceeds 50 percent of the total rent received by A, none of the rents are excluded from the computation of A's unrelated business taxable income by operation of section 512(b)(3).

Example (4). Assume the facts as stated in example (3), except that on June 30, 1975, the lease between B and A is modified. The total rent for the computer lease is reduced to $1,500 and the total rent for the office space lease is reduced to $7,500. Pursuant to subdivision (3)(v)(*b*) of this paragraph, a redetermination is made as of June 30, 1975. As of the modification date, it is determined that notwithstanding the terms of the leases, the rent actually attributable to the computers is $4,000, or 44.4 percent ($4,000/$9,000), of the total rent. Since less than 50 percent of the total rent is now attributable to personal property, the rent attributable to real property ($5,000), for periods after June 30, 1975, is excluded from the computation of A's unrelated business taxable income by operation of section 512(b)(3). However, the rent attributable to personal property ($4,000) is not excluded from unrelated business taxable income for such periods by operation of section 512(b)(3), since it represents more than an incidental portion of the total rent.

(5) *Rendering of services.* For purposes of this paragraph, payments for the use or occupancy of rooms and other space where services are also rendered to the occupant, such as for the use or occupancy of rooms or other quarters in hotels, boarding houses, or apartment houses furnishing hotel services, or in tourist camps or tourist homes, motor courts or motels, or for the use or occupancy of space in parking lots, warehouses, or storage garages, do not constitute rent from real property. Generally, services are considered rendered to the occupant if they are primarily for his convenience and are other than those usually or customarily rendered in connection with the rental of rooms or other space for occupancy only. The supplying of maid service, for example, constitutes such service; whereas the furnishing of heat and light, the cleaning of public entrances, exits, stairways, and lobbies, the collection of trash, etc., are not considered as services rendered to the occupant. Payments for the use or occupancy of entire private residences or living quarters in duplex or multiple housing units, of offices in any office building, etc., are generally rent from real property.

(d) *Gains and losses from the sale, etc. of property.* (1) There shall also be excluded from the computation of unrelated business taxable income gains or losses from the sale, exchange, or other disposition of property other than (1) stock in trade or other property of a kind which would properly be included in the inventory of the organization if on hand at the close of the taxable year, or (2) property held primarily for sale to customers in the ordinary course of the trade or business. This exclusion does not apply with respect to the cutting of timber which is considered, upon the application of section 631(a), as a sale or exchange of such timber. In addition, for taxable years beginning after December 31, 1969, this exclusion does not apply to the gain derived from the sale or other disposition of debt-financed property (as defined in section 514(b)). Otherwise, the exclusion under section 512(b)(5) applies with respect to gains and losses from involuntary conversions, casualties, etc.

(2) There shall be excluded from the computation of unrelated business taxable income any gain from the lapse or termination after December 31, 1975, of options to buy or sell securities (as that term is defined in section 1236(c)). An option

Reg. § 1.512(b)-1(d)(2)

is considered terminated when the organization's obligation under the option ceases by any means other than by reason of the exercise or lapse of such option. If the exclusion is otherwise available it will apply whether or not the organization owns the securities upon which the option is written, that is, whether or not the option is "covered." However, income from the lapse or termination of an option is excludable only if the option is written in connection with the organization's investment activities. Thus, for example, if the securities upon which the options are written are held by the organization as inventory or for sale to customers in the ordinary course of a trade or business, the income from the lapse or termination will not be excludable under the provisions of this paragraph. Similarly, if an organization is engaged in the trade or business of writing options (whether or not such options are covered) the exclusion will not be available.

(e) *Net operating losses.* (1) The net operating loss deduction provided in section 172 shall be allowed in computing unrelated business taxable income. However, the net operating loss carryback or carryover (from a taxable year for which the taxpayer is subject to the provisions of section 511) shall be determined under section 172 without taking into account any amount of income or deduction which is not included under section 511 in computing unrelated business taxable income. For example, a loss attributable to an unrelated trade or business shall not be diminished by reason of the receipt of dividend income.

(2) For the purpose of computing the net operating loss deduction provided by section 172, any prior taxable year for which an organization was not subject to the provisions of section 511, or a corresponding provision of prior law, shall not be taken into account. Thus, if the organization was not subject to the provisions of section 511 or Supplement U of the Internal Revenue Code of 1939 for a preceding taxable year, the net operating loss is not a carryback to such preceding taxable year, and the net operating loss carryover to succeeding taxable years is not reduced by the taxable income for such preceding taxable year.

(3) A net operating loss carryback or carryover shall be allowed only from a taxable year for which the taxpayer is subject to the provisions of section 511, or a corresponding provision of prior law.

(4) In determining the span of years for which a net operating loss may be carried for purposes of section 172, taxable years in which an organization was not subject to the provisions of section 511 or a corresponding provision of prior law shall be taken into account. Thus, for example, if an organization is subject to the provisions of section 511 for the taxable year 1955 and has a net operating loss for that year, the last taxable year to which any part thereof may be carried over is the year 1960 regardless of whether the organization is subject to the provisions of section 511 in any of the intervening taxable years.

(f) *Research.* (1) Income derived from research for the United States or any of its agencies or instrumentalities or a State or political subdivision thereof, and all deductions directly connected with such income, shall be excluded in computing unrelated business taxable income.

(2) In the case of a college, university, or hospital, all income derived from research performed for any person and all deductions directly connected with such income, shall be excluded in computing unrelated business taxable income.

(3) In the case of an organization operated primarily for the purpose of carrying on fundamental research (as distinguished from applied research) the results of which are freely available to the general public, all income derived from research performed for any person and all deductons directly connected with such income shall be excluded in computing unrelated business taxable income.

(4) For the purpose of §§ 1.512(a)-1, 1.512(a)-2, and this section, the term "research" does not include activities of a type ordinarily carried on as an incident to commercial or industrial operations, for example, the ordinary testing or inspection of materials or products or the designing or construction of equipment, buildings, etc. The term "fundamental research" does not include research carried on for the primary purpose of commercial or industrial application.

(g) *Charitable, etc., contributions.*—(1) In computing the unrelated business taxable income of an organization described in section 511(a)(2) the deduction from gross income allowed by section 170 (relating to charitable contributions and gifts) shall be allowed, whether or not the contribution is directly connected with the carrying on of the trade or business. Section 512(b)(10) provides that this deduction shall not exceed 5 percent of the organization's unrelated business taxable income computed without regard to that deduction. The provisions of section 170(b)(2) are not applicable to contributions by the organizations described in section 511(a)(2).

(2) In computing the unrelated business taxable income of a trust described in section 511(b)(2), the deduction allowed by section 170 (relating to charitable contributions and gifts) shall be allowed whether or not the contribution is directly connected with the carrying on of the

Reg. § 1.512(b)-1(e)(2)

trade or business. The deduction is limited as provided in section 170(b)(1)(A) and (B), except that the amounts so allowed are determined on the basis of unrelated business taxable income computed without regard to this deduction (rather than on the basis of adjusted gross income). For purposes of this deduction, a distribution by a trust described in section 511(b)(2) made pursuant to the trust instrument to a beneficiary described in section 170 shall be treated in the same manner as gifts or contributions.

(3) The contribution, whether made by a trust or other exempt organization, must be paid to another organization to be allowable. For example, a university described in section 501(c)(3) which is exempt from tax and which operates as unrelated business, shall be allowed a deduction, not in excess of 5 percent of its unrelated business taxable income, for gifts or contributions to another university described in section 501(c)(3) for educational work but shall not be allowed any deduction for amounts expended in administering its own educational program.

(h) *Specific deduction*—(1) *In general.* In computing unrelated business taxable income a specific deduction from gross income of $1000 is allowed. However, for taxable years beginning after December 31, 1969, such specific deduction is not allowed in computing the net operating loss under section 172 and paragraph (6) of section 512(b).

(2) *Special rule for a diocese, province of a religious order, or a convention or association of churches.* (i) In the case of a diocese, province of a religious order, or a convention or association of churches, there shall be allowed with respect to each parish, individual church, district, or other local unit a specific deduction equal to the lower of $1000 or the gross income derived from any unrelated trade or business regularly conducted by such local unit. However, a diocese, province of a religious order, or a convention or association of churches shall not be entitled to a specific deduction for a local unit which, for a taxable year, files a separate return. In the case of a local unit which, for a taxable year, files a separate return, such local unit may claim a specific deduction equal to the lower of $1000 or the gross income derived from any unrelated trade or business which it regularly conducts.

(ii) The provisions of this subparagraph may be illustrated by the following example:

Example. X is an association of churches on the calendar year basis. X is divided into local units A, B, C, and D. During 1973, A, B, C, and D derive gross income of, respectively, $1200, $800, $1500, and $700 from unrelated businesses which they regularly conduct. Furthermore, for such taxable year, D files a separate return. X may claim a specific deduction of $1000 with respect to A, $800 with respect to B, and $1000 with respect to C. X may not claim a specific deduction with respect to D. D, however, may claim a specific deduction of $700 on its return.

(i) *Transitional period for churches.*—(1)(i) In the case of an unrelated trade or business (as defined in section 513) carried on before May 27, 1969 by a church or convention or association of churches (as defined in § 1.511-2(a)(3)(ii)), or by the predecessor of a church or convention or association of churches which predecessor was itself a church or convention or association of churches, all gross income derived from such unrelated trade or business and all deductions directly connected with the carrying on of such unrelated trade or business shall be excluded from the determination of unrelated business taxable income under section 512(a) for all taxable years beginning before January 1, 1976. Notwithstanding the preceding sentence, in the case of income from debt-financed property (and the deductions attributable thereto), as defined in section 514, of a church or convention or association of churches or by the predecessor of a church or convention or association of churches, the provisions of paragraphs (a) through (e) of section 514 and paragraph (4) of section 512(b) shall apply for taxable years beginning after December 31, 1969.

(ii) The provisions of subdivision (i) may be illustrated by the following example:

Example. X, a church as defined in § 1.511-2(a)(3)(ii), realizes gross income from an unrelated business (as defined in section 513) of $100,000 for calendar year 1972. X's predecessor church, Y, began conducting such unrelated business on January 1, 1968. Of the $100,000 realized for calendar year 1972, $40,000 is attributable to debt-financed property (as defined in section 514). Since the unrelated business was conducted by Y prior to May 27, 1969, and since X's taxable year begins before January 1, 1976, that amount of the income realized from such business (and all deductions directly connected therewith) which is not attributable to debt-financed property shall be excluded from the determination of unrelated business taxable income under section 512(a). Therefore, of the $100,000 realized, $60,000 ($100,000 less $40,000 attributable to debt-financed property), and all deductions directly connected therewith shall be excluded from the determination of such unrelated business taxable income for purposes of imposition of the tax under section 511(a). The remaining $40,000 and the deductions attributable thereto shall be subject to

Reg. § 1.512(b)-1(i)(1)

the provisions of paragraphs (a) through (e) of section 514 and paragraph (4) of section 512(b).

(2) This paragraph shall not apply in the case of income from property, or deductions directly connected with such income, if title to the property is held by a corporation described in section 501(c)(2) for a church or convention or association of churches. Thus, if such income is derived from an unrelated trade or business, the corporation shall be liable for the tax imposed by section 511(a) on such income.

(j) *Special rule for certain unrelated trades or businesses carried on by a religious order or by an educational institution maintained by such order.* (1) Except as provided in subparagraph (2) of this paragraph, gross income realized by a religious order (or an educational organization described in section 170(b)(1)(A)(ii) maintained by such order) from an unrelated trade or business, together with all deductions directly connected therewith, shall be excluded from the determination of unrelated business taxable income under section 512(a), if—

(i) The trade or business has been operated by such order or by such institution since before May 27, 1959,

(ii) The trade or business consists of providing services under a license issued by a Federal regulatory agency,

(iii) More than 90 percent of the net income from the business is, for each taxable year for which gross income from such business is so excluded by reason of section 512(b)(15) and this paragraph, devoted to religious, charitable, or educational purposes, and

(iv) It is established to the satisfaction of an officer no lower than the Regional Commissioner that the rates or other charges for such services are fully competitive with rates or other charges charged for such services by persons not exempt from taxation. Rates or other charges for such services shall be considered as fully competitive with rates or other charges charged for such services by persons not exempt from taxation if the rates charged by such unrelated trade or business are neither materially higher nor materially lower than the rates charged by similar businesses operating in the same general area.

(2) The provisions of this paragraph shall not apply with respect to income from debt-financed property (as defined in section 514) and the deductions attributable thereto. For taxable years beginning after December 31, 1969, such income and deductions are subject to the provisions of paragraphs (a) through (e) of section 514 and paragraph (4) of section 512(b).

(k) Income and deductions from debt-financed property. For taxable years beginning after December 31, 1969, in the case of debt-financed property (as defined in section 514(b)), there shall be included in the unrelated business taxable income of an exempt organization, as an item of gross income derived from an unrelated trade or business, the amount of unrelated debt-financed income determined under section 514(a)(1) and § 1.514(a)-1(a), and there shall be allowed, as a deduction with respect to such income, the amount determined under section 514(a)(2) and § 1.514(a)-1(b).

(l) *Interest, annuities, royalties and rents from controlled organizations*—(1) *In general.* For taxable years beginning after December 31, 1969, if an exempt organization (hereinafter referred to as the "controlling organization") has control (as defined in subparagraph (4) of this paragraph) of another organization (hereinafter referred to as the "controlled organization"), the controlling organization shall include as an item of gross income in computing its unrelated business taxable income, the amount of interest, annuities, royalties, and rents derived from the controlled organization determined under subparagraph (2) or (3) of this paragraph. The preceding sentence shall apply whether or not the activity conducted by the controlling organization to derive such amounts represents a trade or business or is regularly carried on. Thus, amounts received by a controlling organization from the rental of its real property to a controlled organization may be included in the unrelated business taxable income of the controlling organization, even though the rental of such property is not an activity regularly carried on by the controlling organization.

(2) *Exempt controlled organization*—(i) *In general.* If the controlled organization is exempt from taxation under section 501(a), the amount referred to in subparagraph (1) of this paragraph is an amount which bears the same ratio to the interest, annuities, royalties, and rents received by the controlling organization from the controlled organization as the unrelated business taxable income of the controlled organization bears to whichever of the following amounts is the greater—

(*a*) The taxable income of the controlled organization, computed as though the controlled organization were not exempt from taxation under section 501(a), or

(*b*) The unrelated business taxable income of the controlled organization,

both determined without regard to any amounts paid directly or indirectly to the controlling organization. The controlling organization shall be

Reg. § 1.512(b)-1(i)(2)

Unrelated Business Income

See p. 20,601 for regulations not amended to reflect law changes

allowed all deductions directly connected with amounts included in gross income under the preceding sentence.

(ii) *Examples.* This subparagraph may be illustrated by the following examples:

Example (1). A, an exempt scientific organization described in section 501(c)(3), owns all the stock of B, another exempt scientific organization described in section 501(c)(3). During 1971, A rents space for a laboratory to B for $15,000 a year. A's total deductions for 1971 with respect to the leased property are $3,000: $1,000 for maintenance and $2,000 for depreciation. If B were not an exempt organization, its total taxable income would be $300,000, disregarding rent paid to A. B's unrelated business taxable income, disregarding rent paid to A, is $100,000. Under these circumstances, $4,000 of the rent paid by B will be included by A as net rental income in determining its unrelated business taxable income, computed as follows:

B's unrelated business taxable income (disregarding rent paid to A)	$100,000
B's taxable income (computed as though B were not exempt and disregarding rent paid to A)	$300,000
Ratio ($100,000/$300,000)	1/3
Total rent	$ 15,000
Total deductions	$ 3,000
Rental income treated as gross income from an unrelated trade or business (1/3 of $15,000)	$ 5,000
Less deductions directly connected with such income (1/3 of $3,000)	$ 1,000
Net rental income included by A in computing its unrelated business taxable income	$ 4,000

Example (2). Assume the facts as stated in example (1), except that B's taxable income is $90,000 (computed as though B were not an exempt organization, and disregarding rents paid to A). B's unrelated business taxable income ($100,000) is therefore greater than its taxable income ($90,000). Thus, the ratio used to determine the portion of the rent received by A which is to be taken into account is one since both the numerator and denominator of such ratio is B's unrelated business taxable income. Consequently, all the rent received by A from B ($15,000), and the deductions directly connected therewith ($3,000), are included by A in computing its unrelated business taxable income.

(3) *Nonexempt controlled organization*—(i) *In general.* If the controlled organization is not exempt from taxation under section 501(a), the amount referred to in subparagraph (1) of this paragraph is an amount which bears the same ratio to the interest, annuities, royalties, and rents received by the controlling organization from the controlled organization as the "excess taxable income" (as defined in subdivision (ii) of this subparagraph) of the controlled organization bears to whichever of the following amounts is the greater—

(*a*) The taxable income of the controlled organization, or

(*b*) The excess taxable income of the controlled organization,

both determined without regard to any amount paid directly or indirectly to the controlling organization. The controlling organization shall be allowed all deductions which are directly connected with amounts included in gross income under the preceding sentence.

(ii) *Excess taxable income.* For purposes of this paragraph, the term "excess taxable income" means the excess of the controlled organization's taxable income over the amount of such taxable income which, if derived directly by the controlling organization, would not be unrelated business taxable income.

(iii) *Examples.* This subparagraph may be illustrated by the following examples:

Example (1). A, an exempt university described in section 501(c)(3), owns all the stock of M, a nonexempt organization. During 1971, M leases a factory and a dormitory from A for a total annual rent of $100,000. During the taxable year, M has $500,000 of taxable income, disregarding the rent paid to A: $150,000 from a dormitory for students of A university, and $350,000 from the operation of a factory which is a business unrelated to A's exempt purpose. A's deductions for 1961 with respect to the leased property are $4,000 for the dormitory and $16,000 for the factory. Under these circumstances, $56,000 of the rent paid by M will be included by A as net rental income in determining its unrelated business taxable income, computed as follows:

M's taxable income (disregarding rent paid to A)	$500,000
Less taxable income from dormitory	150,000
Excess taxable income	350,000
Ratio ($350,000/$500,000)	7/10

Reg. § 1.512(b)-1(l)(3)

Total rent paid to A	$100,000
Total deductions ($4,000 + $16,000)	20,000
Rental income treated as gross income from an unrelated trade or business (7/10 of $100,000)	$ 70,000
Less deductions directly connected with such income (7/10 of $20,000)	14,000
Net rental income included by A in computing its unrelated business taxable income	$ 56,000

Example (2). Assume the facts as stated in example (1), except that M's taxable income (disregarding rent paid to A) is $300,000, consisting of $350,000 from the operation of the factory and a $50,000 loss from the operation of the dormitory. Thus, M's "excess taxable income" is also $300,000, since none of M's taxable income would be excluded from the computation of A's unrelated business taxable income if received directly by A. The ratio of M's "excess taxable income" to its taxable income is therefore one ($300,000/$300,000). Thus, all the rent received by A from M ($100,000), and all the deductions directly connected therewith ($20,000), are included in the computation of A's unrelated business taxable income.

(4) *Control*—(i) *In general.* For purposes of this paragraph—

(a) *Stock corporation.* In the case of an organization which is a stock corporation, the term "control" means ownership by an exempt organization of stock possessing at least 80 percent of the total combined voting power of all classes of stock entitled to vote and at least 80 percent of the total number of shares of all other classes of stock of such corporation.

(b) *Non-stock organization.* In the case of a non-stock organization, the term "control" means that at least 80 percent of the directors or trustees of such organization are either representatives of or directly or indirectly controlled by an exempt organization. A trustee or director is a representative of an exempt organization if he is a trustee, director, agent, or employee of such exempt organization. A trustee or director is controlled by an exempt organization if such organization has the power to remove such trustee or director and designate a new trustee or director.

(ii) *Gain or loss of control.* If control of an organization (as defined in subdivision (i) of this subparagraph) is acquired or relinquished during the taxable year, only the interest, annuities, royalties, and rents paid or accrued to the controlling organization in accordance with its method of accounting for that portion of the taxable year it has control shall be subject to the tax on unrelated business income.

(5) *Amounts taxable under other provisions of the Code*—(i) *In general.* Section 512(b)(13) and this paragraph do not apply to amounts which are included in the computation of unrelated business income by operation of any other provision of the Code. However, amounts which are not included in unrelated business taxable income by operation of section 512(a)(1), or which are excluded by operation of section 512(b)(1), (2), or (3), may be included in unrelated business taxable income by operation of section 512(b)(13) and this paragraph.

(ii) *Debt-financed property.* Rents derived from the lease of debt-financed property by a controlling organization to a controlled organization are subject to the rules contained in section 512(b)(13) and this paragraph. Thus, if a controlling organization leases debt-financed property to a controlled organization, the amount of rents includible in the controlling organization's unrelated business taxable income shall first be determined under section 512(b)(13) and this paragraph, and only the portion of such rents not taken into account by operation of section 512(b)(13) are taken into account by operation of section 514. See example (3) of § 1.514(b)-1(b)(3). [Reg. § 1.512(b)-1.]

☐ [*T.D. 6301, 7-8-58. Amended by T.D. 6939, 12-11-67; T.D. 7177, 4-7-72; T.D. 7183, 4-20-72; T.D. 7229, 12-20-72; T.D. 7261, 2-26-73 and 3-8-73; T.D. 7632, 7-17-79; T.D. 7767, 2-3-81; and T.D. 8423, 7-28-92.*]

[Reg. § 1.512(c)-1]

§ 1.512(c)-1. **Special rules applicable to partnerships; in general.**—In the event an organization to which section 511 applies is a member of a partnership regularly engaged in a trade or business which is an unrelated trade or business with respect to such organization, the organization shall include in computing its unrelated business taxable income so much of its share (whether or not distributed) of the partnership gross income as is derived from that unrelated business and its share of the deductions attributable thereto. For this purpose, both the gross income and the deductions shall be computed with the necessary adjustments for the exceptions, additions, and limitations referred to in section 512(b) and in § 1.512(b)-1. For example, if an exempt educational institution is a partner in a partnership which operates a factory and if such partnership also holds stock in a corporation, the exempt organization shall include in computing its unrelated business taxable income its share of the gross income from the operation of the factory, but not its share of any dividends received by the partnership from the corporation. If the taxable year of the organization differs from that of the partnership, the amounts included or deducted in computing unrelated business taxable income shall be based upon the income and deductions of the partnership for each taxable year of the partnership ending within or with the taxable year of the organization. [Reg. § 1.512(c)-1.]

☐ [T.D. 6301, 7-8-58.]

[Reg. § 1.513-1]

§ 1.513-1. **Definition of unrelated trade or business.**—(a) *In general.* As used in section 512 the term "unrelated business taxable income" means the gross income derived by an organization from any unrelated trade or business regularly carried on by it, less the deductions and subject to the modifications provided in section 512. Section 513 specifies with certain exceptions that the phrase "unrelated trade or business" means, in the case of an organization subject to the tax imposed by section 511, any trade or business the conduct of which is not substantially related (aside from the need of such organization for income or funds or the use it makes of the profits derived) to the exercise or performance by such organization of its charitable, educational or other purpose or function constituting the basis for its exemption under section 501 (or, in the case of an organization described in section 511(a)(2)(B), to the exercise or performance of any purpose or function described in section 501(c)(3)). (For certain exceptions from this definition, see paragraph (e) of this section. For a special definition of "unrelated trade or business" applicable to certain trusts, see section 513(b).) Therefore, unless one of the specific exceptions of section 512 or 513 is applicable, gross income of an exempt organization subject to the tax imposed by section 511 is includible in the computation of unrelated business taxable income if (1) it is income from trade or business, (2) such trade or business is regularly carried on by the organization, and (3) the conduct of such trade or business is not substantially related (other than through the production of funds) to the organization's performance of its exempt functions.

(b) *Trade or business.* The primary objective of adoption of the unrelated business income tax was to eliminate a source of unfair competition by placing the unrelated business activities of certain exempt organizations upon the same tax basis as the nonexempt business endeavors with which they compete. On the other hand, where an activity does not possess the characteristics of a trade or business within the meaning of section 162, such as when an organization sends out low cost articles incidental to the solicitation of charitable contribution, the unrelated business income tax does not apply since the organization is not in competition with taxable organizations. However, in general, any activity of a section 511 organization which is carried on for the production of income and which otherwise possesses the characteristics required to constitute "trade or business" within the meaning of section 162—and which, in addition, is not substantially related to the performance of exempt functions—presents sufficient likelihood of unfair competition to be within the policy of the tax. Accordingly, for purposes of section 513 the term "trade or business" has the same meaning it has in section 162, and generally includes any activity carried on for the production of income from the sale of goods or performance of services. Thus, the term "trade or business" in section 513 is not limited to integrated aggregates of assets, activities and good will which comprise businesses for the purposes of certain other provisions of the Internal Revenue Code. Activities of producing or distributing goods or performing services from which a particular amount of gross income is derived do not lose identity as trade or business merely because they are carried on within a larger aggregate of similar activities or within a larger complex of other endeavors which may, or may not, be related to the exempt purposes of the organization. Thus, for example, the regular sale of pharmaceutical supplies to the general public by a hospital pharmacy does not lose identity as trade or business merely because the pharmacy also furnishes supplies to the hospital and patients of the hospital in accordance with its exempt purposes or in compliance with the terms of section 513(a)(2). Similarly, activities of soliciting, selling, and publishing commercial advertising do not lose identity as a trade or business even though the advertising is published in an exempt organization periodical which contains editorial matter related to the exempt purposes of the organization. However, where an activity carried on for the production of income constitutes an unrelated trade or business, no part of such trade or business shall be excluded from such classification merely because it does not result in profit.

(c) *Regularly carried on*—(1) *General principles.* In determining whether trade or business from which a particular amount of gross income derives is "regularly carried on," within the meaning of section 512, regard must be had to the frequency and continuity with which the activities productive of the income are conducted and the manner in which they are pursued. This requirement must be applied in light of the purpose of the unrelated business income tax to place exempt organization business activities upon the same tax basis as the nonexempt business endeavors with which they compete. Hence, for example, specific business activities of an exempt organization will ordinarily be deemed to be "regularly carried on" if they manifest a frequency and continuity, and are pursued in a manner, generally similar to comparable commercial activities of nonexempt organizations.

(2) *Application of principles in certain cases*—(i) *Normal time span of activities.* Where income producing activities are of a kind normally conducted by nonexempt commercial organizations on a year-round basis, the conduct of such activities by an exempt organization over a period of only a few weeks does not constitute the regular carrying on of trade or business. For example, the operation of a sandwich stand by a hospital auxiliary for only two weeks at a state fair would not be the regular conduct of trade or business. However, the conduct of year-round business activities for one day each week would constitute the regular carrying on of trade or business. Thus, the operation of a commercial parking lot on Saturday of each week would be the regular conduct of trade or business. Where income producing activities are of a kind normally undertaken by nonexempt commercial organizations only on a seasonal basis, the conduct of such activities by an exempt organization during a significant portion of the season ordinarily constitutes the regular conduct of trade or business. For example, the operation of a track for horse racing for several weeks of a year would be considered the regular conduct of trade or business because it is usual to carry on such trade or business only during a particular season.

(ii) *Intermittent activities; in general.* In determining whether or not intermittently conducted activities are regularly carried on, the manner of conduct of the activities must be compared with the manner in which commercial activities are normally pursued by nonexempt organizations. In general, exempt organization business activities which are engaged in only discontinuously or periodically will not be considered regularly carried on if they are conducted without the competitive and promotional efforts typical of commercial endeavors. For example, the publication of advertising in programs for sports events or music or drama performances will not ordinarily be deemed to be the regular carrying on of business. Similarly, where an organization sells certain types of goods or services to a particular class of persons in pursuance of its exempt functions or "primarily for the convenience" of such persons within the meaning of section 513(a)(2) (as, for example, the sale of books by a college bookstore to students or the sale of pharmaceutical supplies by a hospital pharmacy to patients of the hospital), casual sales in the course of such activity which do not qualify as related to the exempt function involved or as described in section 513(a)(2) will not be treated as regular. On the other hand, where the nonqualifying sales are not merely casual, but are systematically and consistently promoted and carried on by the organization, they meet the section 512 requirement of regularity.

(iii) *Intermittent activities; special rule in certain cases of infrequent conduct.* Certain intermittent income producing activities occur so infrequently that neither their recurrence nor the manner of their conduct will cause them to be regarded as trade or business regularly carried on. For example, income producing or fund raising activities lasting only a short period of time will not ordinarily be treated as regularly carried on if they recur only occasionally or sporadically. Furthermore, such activities will not be regarded as regularly carried on merely because they are conducted on an annually recurrent basis. Accordingly, income derived from the conduct of an annual dance or similar fund raising event for charity would not be income from trade or business regularly carried on.

(d) *Substantially related*—(1) *In general.* Gross income derives from "unrelated trade or business," within the meaning of section 513(a), if the conduct of the trade or business which produces the income is not substantially related (other than through the production of funds) to the purposes for which exemption is granted. The presence of this requirement necessitates an examination of the relationship between the business activities which generate the particular income in question—the activities, that is, of producing or distributing the goods or performing the services involved—and the accomplishment of the organization's exempt purposes.

(2) *Type of relationship required.* Trade or business is "related" to exempt purposes, in the relevant sense, only where the conduct of the business activities has causal relationship to the achievement of exempt purposes (other than through the production of income); and it is "substantially related," for purposes of section 513, only if the causal relationship is a substantial one. Thus, for the conduct of trade or business from which a particular amount of gross income is derived to be substantially related to purposes for which exemption is granted, the production or distribution of the goods or the performance of the services from which the gross income is derived

Reg. § 1.513-1(c)(2)

must contribute importantly to the accomplishment of those purposes. Where the production or distribution of the goods or the performance of the services does not contribute importantly to the accomplishment of the exempt purposes of an organization, the income from the sale of the goods or the performance of the services does not derive from the conduct of related trade or business. Whether activities productive of gross income contribute importantly to the accomplishment of any purpose for which an organization is granted exemption depends in each case upon the facts and circumstances involved.

(3) *Size and extent of activities.* In determining whether activities contribute importantly to the accomplishment of an exempt purpose, the size and extent of the activities involved must be considered in relation to the nature and extent of the exempt function which they purport to serve. Thus, where income is realized by an exempt organization from activities which are in part related to the performance of its exempt functions, but which are conducted on a larger scale than is reasonably necessary for performance of such functions, the gross income attributable to that portion of the activities in excess of the needs of exempt functions constitutes gross income from the conduct of unrelated trade or business. Such income is not derived from the production or distribution of goods or the performance of services which contribute importantly to the accomplishment of any exempt purpose of the organization.

(4) *Application of principles*—(i) *Income from performance of exempt functions.* Gross income derived from charges for the performance of exempt functions does not constitute gross income from the conduct of unrelated trade or business. The following examples illustrate the application of this principle:

Example (1). M, an organization described in section 501(c)(3), operates a school for training children in the performing arts, such as acting, singing, and dancing. It presents performances by its students and derives gross income from admission charges for the performances. The students' participation in performances before audiences is an essential part of their training. Since the income realized from the performances derives from activities which contribute importantly to the accomplishment of M's exempt purposes, it does not constitute gross income from unrelated trade or business. (For specific exclusion applicable in certain cases of contributed services, see section 513(a)(1) and paragraph (e)(1) of this section.)

Example (2). N is a trade union qualified for exemption under section 501(c)(5). To improve the trade skills of its members, N conducts refresher training courses and supplies handbooks and technical manuals. N receives payments from its members for these services and materials. However, the development and improvement of the skills of its members is one of the purposes for which exemption is granted N; and the activities described contribute importantly to that purpose. Therefore, the income derived from these activities does not constitute gross income from unrelated trade or business.

Example (3). O is an industry trade association qualified for exemption under section 501(c)(6). It presents a trade show in which members of its industry join in an exhibition of industry products. O derives income from charges made to exhibitors for exhibit space and admission fees charged patrons or viewers of the show. The show is not a sales facility for individual exhibitors; its purpose is the promotion and stimulation of interest in, and demand for, the industry's products in general, and it is conducted in a manner reasonably calculated to achieve that purpose. The stimulation of demand for the industry's products in general is one of the purposes for which exemption is granted O. Consequently, the activities productive of O's gross income from the show—that is, the promotion, organization and conduct of the exhibition—contribute importantly to the achievement of an exempt purpose, and the income does not constitute gross income from unrelated trade or business. See also section 513(d) and regulations thereunder regarding sales activity.

(ii) *Disposition of product of exempt functions.* Ordinarily, gross income from the sale of products which result from the performance of exempt functions does not constitute gross income from the conduct of unrelated trade or business if the product is sold in substantially the same state it is in on completion of the exempt functions. Thus, in the case of an organization described in section 501(c)(3) and engaged in a program of rehabilitation of handicapped persons, income from sale of articles made by such persons as a part of their rehabilitation training would not be gross income from conduct of unrelated trade or business. The income in such case would be from sale of products, the production of which contributed importantly to the accomplishment of purposes for which exemption is granted the organization—namely, rehabilitation of the handicapped. On the other hand, if a product resulting from an exempt function is utilized or exploited in further business endeavor beyond that reasonably appropriate or necessary for disposition in the state it is in upon completion of exempt functions, the gross income derived therefrom would be from

Reg. § 1.513-1(d)(4)

conduct of unrelated trade or business. Thus, in the case of an experimental dairy herd maintained for scientific purposes by an organization described in section 501(c)(3), income from sale of milk and cream produced in the ordinary course of operation of the project would not be gross income from conduct of unrelated trade or business. On the other hand, if the organization were to utilize the milk and cream in the further manufacture of food items such as ice cream, pastries, etc., the gross income from the sale of such products would be from the conduct of unrelated trade or business unless the manufacturing activities themselves contribute importantly to the accomplishment of an exempt purpose of the organization.

(iii) *Dual use of assets or facilities.* In certain cases, an asset or facility necessary to the conduct of exempt functions may also be employed in a commercial endeavor. In such cases, the mere fact of the use of the asset or facility in exempt functions does not, by itself, make the income from the commercial endeavor gross income from related trade or business. The test, instead, is whether the activities productive of the income in question contribute importantly to the accomplishment of exempt purposes. Assume, for example, that a museum exempt under section 501(c)(3) has a theater auditorium which is specially designed and equipped for showing of educational films in connection with its program of public education in the arts and sciences. The theater is a principal feature of the museum and is in continuous operation during the hours the museum is open to the public. If the organization were to operate the theater as an ordinary motion picture theater for public entertainment during the evening hours when the museum was closed, gross income from such operation would be gross income from conduct of unrelated trade or business.

(iv) *Exploitation of exempt functions.* In certain cases, activities carried on by an organization in the performance of exempt functions may generate good will or other intangibles which are capable of being exploited in commercial endeavors. Where an organization exploits such an intangible in commercial activities, the mere fact that the resultant income depends in part upon an exempt function of the organization does not make it gross income from related trade or business. In such cases, unless the commercial activities themselves contribute importantly to the accomplishment of an exempt purpose, the income which they produce is gross income from the conduct of unrelated trade or business. The application of this subdivision is illustrated in the following examples:

Example (1). U, an exempt scientific organization, enjoys an excellent reputation in the field of biological research. It exploits this reputation regularly by selling endorsements of various items of laboratory equipment to manufacturers. The endorsing of laboratory equipment does not contribute importantly to the accomplishment of any purpose for which exemption is granted U. Accordingly, the income derived from the sale of endorsements is gross income from unrelated trade or business.

Example (2). V, an exempt university, has a regular faculty and a regularly enrolled student body. During the school year, V sponsors the appearance of professional theater companies and symphony orchestras which present drama and musical performances for the students and faculty members. Members of the general public are also admitted. V advertises these performances and supervises advance ticket sales at various places, including such university facilities as the cafeteria and the university bookstore. V derives gross income from the conduct of the performances. However, while the presentation of the performances makes use of an intangible generated by V's exempt educational functions—the presence of the student body and faculty—the presentation of such drama and music events contributes importantly to the overall educational and cultural function of the university. Therefore, the income which V receives does not constitute gross income from the conduct of unrelated trade or business.

Example (3). W is an exempt business league with a large membership. Under an arrangement with an advertising agency, W regularly mails brochures, pamphlets and other commercial advertising materials to its members, for which service W charges the agency an agreed amount per enclosure. The distribution of the advertising materials does not contribute importantly to the accomplishment of any purpose for which W is granted exemption. Accordingly, the payments made to W by the advertising agency constitute gross income from unrelated trade or business.

Example (4). X, an exempt organization for the advancement of public interest in classical music, owns a radio station and operates it in a manner which contributes importantly to the accomplishment of the purposes for which the organization is granted exemption. However, in the course of the operation of the station the organization derives gross income from the regular sale of advertising time and services to commercial advertisers in the manner of an ordinary commercial station. Neither the sale of such time nor the performance of such services contributes impor-

Reg. § 1.513-1(d)(4)

tantly to the accomplishment of any purpose for which the organization is granted exemption. Notwithstanding the fact that the production of the advertising income depends upon the existence of the listening audience resulting from performance of exempt functions, such income is gross income from unrelated trade or business.

Example (5). Y, an exempt university, provides facilities, instruction and faculty supervision for a campus newspaper operated by its students. In addition to news items and editorial commentary, the newspaper publishes paid advertising. The solicitation, sale, and publication of the advertising are conducted by students, under the supervision and instruction of the university. Although the services rendered to advertisers are of a commercial character, the advertising business contributes importantly to the university's educational program through the training of the students involved. Hence, none of the income derived from publication of the newspaper constitutes gross income from unrelated trade or business. The same result would follow even though the newspaper is published by a separately incorporated section 501(c)(3) organization, qualified under the university rules for recognition of student activities, and even though such organization utilizes its own facilities and is independent of faculty supervision, but carries out its educational purposes by means of student instruction of other students in the editorial and advertising activities and student participation in those activities.

Example (6). Z is an association exempt under section 501(c)(6), formed to advance the interests of a particular profession and drawing its membership from the members of that profession. Z publishes a monthly journal containing articles and other editorial material which contribute importantly to the accomplishment of purposes for which exemption is granted the organization. Income from the sale of subscriptions to members and others in accordance with the organization's exempt purposes, therefore, does not constitute gross income from unrelated trade or business. In connection with the publication of the journal, Z also derives income from the regular sale of space and services for general consumer advertising, including advertising of such products as soft drinks, automobiles, articles of apparel, and home appliances. Neither the publication of such advertisements nor the performance of services for such commercial advertisers contributes importantly to the accomplishment of any purpose for which exemption is granted. Therefore, notwithstanding the fact that the production of income from advertising utilizes the circulation developed and maintained in performance of exempt functions, such income is gross income from unrelated trade or business.

Example (7). The facts are as described in the preceding example, except that the advertising in Z's journal promotes only products which are within the general area of professional interest of its members. Following a practice common among taxable magazines which publish advertising, Z requires its advertising to comply with certain general standards of taste, fairness, and accuracy; but within those limits the form, content, and manner of presentation of the advertising messages are governed by the basic objective of the advertisers to promote the sale of the advertised products. While the advertisements contain certain information, the informational function of the advertising is incidental to the controlling aim of stimulating demand for the advertised products and differs in no essential respect from the informational function of any commercial advertising. Like taxable publishers of advertising, Z accepts advertising only from those who are willing to pay its prescribed rates. Although continuing education of its members in matters pertaining to their profession is one of the purposes for which Z is granted exemption, the publication of advertising designed and selected in the manner of ordinary commercial advertising is not an educational activity of the kind contemplated by the exemption statute; it differs fundamentally from such an activity both in its governing objective and in its method. Accordingly, Z's publication of advertising does not contribute importantly to the accomplishment of its exempt purposes; and the income which it derives from advertising constitutes gross income from unrelated trade or business.

(e) *Exceptions.* Section 513(a) specifically states that the term "unrelated trade or business" does not include—

(1) Any trade or business in which substantially all the work in carrying on such trade or business is performed for the organization without compensation; or

(2) Any trade or business carried on by an organization described in section 501(c)(3) or by a governmental college or university described in section 511(a)(2)(B), primarily for the convenience of its members, students, patients, officers, or employees; or, any trade or business carried on by a local association of employees described in section 501(c)(4) organized before May 27, 1969, which consists of the selling by the organization of items of work-related clothes and equipment and items normally sold through vending machines, through food dispensing facilities, or by snack bars, for the convenience of its members at their usual places of employment; or

Reg. § 1.513-1(e)(2)

(3) Any trade or business which consists of selling merchandise, substantially all of which has been received by the organization as gifts or contributions.

An example of the operation of the first of the exceptions mentioned above would be an exempt orphanage operating a retail store and selling to the general public, where substantially all the work in carrying on such business is performed for the organization by volunteers without compensation. An example of the first part of the second exception, relating to an organization described in section 501(c)(3) or a governmental college or university described in section 511(a)(2)(B), would be a laundry operated by a college for the purpose of laundering dormitory linens and the clothing of students. The latter part of the second exception, dealing with certain sales by local employee associations, will not apply to sales of these items at locations other than the usual place of employment of the employees; therefore sales at such other locations will continue to be treated as unrelated trade or business. The third exception applies to so-called "thrift shops" operated by a tax-exempt organization where those desiring to benefit such organization contribute old clothes, books, furniture, etc., to be sold to the general public with the proceeds going to the exempt organization.

(f) *Special rule respecting publishing businesses prior to 1970.* For a special rule for taxable years beginning before January 1, 1970, with respect to publishing businesses carried on by an organization, see section 513(c) of the Code prior to its amendment by section 121(c) of the Tax Reform Act of 1969 (83 Stat. 542).

(g) *Effective date.* This section is applicable with respect to taxable years beginning after December 12, 1967. However, if a taxpayer wishes to rely on the rules stated in this section for taxable years beginning before December 13, 1967, it may do so. [Reg. § 1.513-1.]

☐ [T.D. 6939, 12-11-67. Amended by T.D. 7107, 4-2-71, *by* T.D. 7392, 12-17-75, *and by* T.D. 7896, 5-26-83.]

[Reg. § 1.513-3]

§ 1.513-3. **Qualified convention and trade show activity.**—(a) *Introduction*—(1) *In general.* Section 513(d) and § 1.513-3(b) provide that convention and trade show activities carried on by a qualifying organization in connection with a qualified convention or trade show will not be treated as unrelated trade or business. Consequently, income from qualified convention and trade show activities, derived by a qualifying organization that sponsors the qualified convention or trade show, will not be subject to the tax imposed by section 511. Section 1.513-3(c) defines qualifying organizations and qualified conventions or trade shows. Section 1.513-3(d) concerns the treatment of income derived from certain activities, including rental of exhibition space at a qualified convention or trade show where sales activity is permitted, and the treatment of supplier exhibits at qualified conventions and trade shows.

(2) *Effective date.* This section is effective for taxable years beginning after October 4, 1976.

(b) *Qualified activities not unrelated.* A convention or trade show activity, as defined in section 513(d)(3)(A) and § 1.513-3(c)(4), will not be considered unrelated trade or business if it is conducted by a qualifying organization described in section 513(d)(3)(C) and § 1.513-3(c)(1), in conjunction with a qualified convention or trade show, as defined in section 513(d)(3)(B) and § 1.513-3(c)(2), sponsored by the qualifying organization. Such an activity is a qualified convention or trade show activity. A convention or trade show activity which is conducted by an organization described in section 501(c)(5) or (6), but which otherwise is not so qualified under this section, will be considered unrelated trade or business.

(c) *Definitions*—(1) *Qualifying organization.* Under section 513(d)(3)(C), a qualifying organization is one which—

(i) Is described in either section 501(c)(5) or (6), and

(ii) Regularly conducts as one of its substantial exempt purposes a qualified convention or trade show.

(2) *Qualified convention or trade show.* For purposes of this section, the term "qualified convention or trade show" means a show that meets the following requirements:

(i) It is conducted by a qualifying organization described in section 513(d)(3)(C);

(ii) At least one purpose of the sponsoring organization in conducting the show is the education of its members, or the promotion and stimulation of interest in, and demand for, the products or services of the industry (or segment thereof) of the members of the qualifying organization; and

(iii) The show is designed to achieve that purpose through the character of a significant portion of the exhibits or the character of conferences and seminars held at a convention or meeting.

(3) *Show.* For purposes of this section, the term "show" includes an international, national,

Reg. § 1.513-3(a)(1)

state, regional, or local convention, annual meeting or show.

(4) *Convention and trade show activity.* For purposes of this section, convention and trade show activity means any activity of a kind traditionally carried on at shows. It includes, but is not limited to—

    (i) Activities designed to attract to the show members of the sponsoring organization, members of an industry in general, and members of the public, to view industry products or services and to stimulate interest in, and demand for such products or services;

    (ii) Activities designed to educate persons in the industry about new products or services or about new rules and regulations affecting the industry; and

    (iii) Incidental activities, such as furnishing refreshments, of a kind traditionally carried on at such shows.

(d) *Certain activities*—(1) *Rental or exhibition space.* The rental of display space to exhibitors (including exhibitors who are suppliers) at a qualified trade show or at a qualified convention and trade show will not be considered unrelated trade or business even though the exhibitors who rent the space are permitted to sell or solicit orders.

(2) *Suppliers defined.* For purposes of subparagraph (1), a supplier's exhibit is one in which the exhibitor displays goods or services that are supplied to, rather than by, the members of the qualifying organization in the conduct of such members' own trades or businesses.

(e) *Examples.* The provisions of this section may be illustrated by the following examples:

Example 1. X, an organization described in section 501(c)(6), was formed to promote the construction industry. Its membership is made up of manufacturers of heavy construction machinery many of whom own, rent, or lease one or more digital computers produced by various computer manufacturers. X is a qualifying organization under section 513(d)(3)(C) that regularly holds an annual meeting. At this meeting a national industry sales campaign and methods of consumer financing for heavy construction machinery are discussed. In addition, new construction machinery developed for use in the industry is on display with representatives of the various manufacturers present to promote their machinery. Both members and nonmembers attend this portion of the conference. In addition, manufacturers of computers are present to educate X's members. While this aspect of the conference is a supplier exhibit (as defined in paragraph (d) of this section), income earned from such activity by X will not constitute unrelated business taxable income to X because the activity is conducted as part of a qualified trade show described in § 1.513-3(c).

Example 2. Assume the same facts as in Example 1, but the only goods or services displayed are those of suppliers, the computer manufacturers. Selling and order taking are permitted. No member exhibits are maintained. Standing alone, this supplier exhibit (as defined in paragraph (d)(2) of this section) would constitute a supplier show and not a qualified convention or trade show. In this situation, however, the rental of exhibition space to suppliers is not unrelated trade or business. It is conducted by a qualifying organization in conjunction with a qualified convention or trade show. The show (the annual meeting) is a qualified convention or trade show because one of its purposes is the promotion and stimulation of interest in, and demand for, the products or services of the industry through the character of the annual meeting.

Example 3. Y is an organization described in section 501(c)(6). The organization conducts an annual show at which its members exhibit their products and services in order to promote public interest in the line of business. Potential customers are invited to the show, and sales and order taking are permitted. The organization secures the exhibition facility, undertakes the planning and direction of the show, and maintains exhibits designed to promote the line of business in general. The show is a qualified convention or trade show described in paragraph (c)(2) of this section. The provision of exhibition space to individual members is a qualified trade show activity, and is not unrelated trade or business.

Example 4. Z is an organization described in section 501(c)(6) that sponsors an annual show. As the sole activity at the show, suppliers to the members of Z exhibit their products and services for the purpose of stimulating the sale of their products. Selling and order taking are permitted. The show is a supplier show and does not meet the definition of a qualified convention show as it does not satisfy any of the three alternative bases for qualification. First, the show does not stimulate interest in the members' products through the character of product exhibits as the only products exhibited are those of suppliers rather than members. Second, the show does not stimulate interest in members' products through conferences or seminars as no such conferences are held at the show. Third, the show does not meet the definition of a qualified show on the basis of educational activities as the exhibition of suppliers' products is designed primarily to stimulate interest in, and sale of, suppliers' products. Thus, the organiza-

Reg. § 1.513-3(e)

tion's provision of exhibition space is not a qualified convention or trade show activity. Income derived from rentals of exhibition space to suppliers will be unrelated business taxable income under section 512. [Reg. § 1.513-3.]

☐ [*T.D.* 7896, 5-26-83.]

[Reg. § 1.513-4]

§ 1.513-4. Certain sponsorship not unrelated trade or business.—(a) *In general.* Under section 513(i), the receipt of qualified sponsorship payments by an exempt organization which is subject to the tax imposed by section 511 does not constitute receipt of income from an unrelated trade or business.

(b) *Exception.* The provisions of this section do not apply with respect to payments made in connection with qualified convention and trade show activities. For rules governing qualified convention and trade show activity, see § 1.513-3. The provisions of this section also do not apply to income derived from the sale of advertising or acknowledgments in exempt organization periodicals. For this purpose, the term *periodical* means regularly scheduled and printed material published by or on behalf of the exempt organization that is not related to and primarily distributed in connection with a specific event conducted by the exempt organization. For this purpose, printed material includes material that is published electronically. For rules governing the sale of advertising in exempt organization periodicals, see § 1.512(a)-1(f).

(c) *Qualified sponsorship payment*—(1) *Definition.* The term *qualified sponsorship payment* means any payment by any person engaged in a trade or business with respect to which there is no arrangement or expectation that the person will receive any substantial return benefit. In determining whether a payment is a qualified sponsorship payment, it is irrelevant whether the sponsored activity is related or unrelated to the recipient organization's exempt purpose. It is also irrelevant whether the sponsored activity is temporary or permanent. For purposes of this section, payment means the payment of money, transfer of property, or performance of services.

(2) *Substantial return benefit*—(i) *In general.* For purposes of this section, a *substantial return benefit* means any benefit other than a use or acknowledgment described in paragraph (c)(2)(iv) of this section, or disregarded benefits described in paragraph (c)(2)(ii) of this section.

(ii) *Certain benefits disregarded.* For purposes of paragraph (c)(2)(i) of this section, benefits are disregarded if the aggregate fair market value of all the benefits provided to the payor or persons designated by the payor in connection with the payment during the organization's taxable year is not more than 2% of the amount of the payment. If the aggregate fair market value of the benefits exceeds 2% of the amount of the payment, then (except as provided in paragraph (c)(2)(iv) of this section) the entire fair market value of such benefits, not merely the excess amount, is a substantial return benefit. Fair market value is determined as provided in paragraph (d)(1) of this section.

(iii) *Benefits defined.* For purposes of this section, benefits provided to the payor or persons designated by the payor may include:

(A) Advertising as defined in paragraph (c)(2)(v) of this section.

(B) Exclusive provider arrangements as defined in paragraph (c)(2)(vi)(B) of this section.

(C) Goods, facilities, services or other privileges.

(D) Exclusive or nonexclusive rights to use an intangible asset (e.g., trademark, patent, logo, or designation) of the exempt organization.

(iv) *Use or acknowledgment.* For purposes of this section, a substantial return benefit does not include the use or acknowledgment of the name or logo (or product lines) of the payor's trade or business in connection with the activities of the exempt organization. Use or acknowledgment does not include advertising as described in paragraph (c)(2)(v) of this section, but may include the following: exclusive sponsorship arrangements; logos and slogans that do not contain qualitative or comparative descriptions of the payor's products, services, facilities or company; a list of the payor's locations, telephone numbers, or Internet address; value-neutral descriptions, including displays or visual depictions, of the payor's product-line or services; and the payor's brand or trade names and product or service listings. Logos or slogans that are an established part of a payor's identity are not considered to contain qualitative or comparative descriptions. Mere display or distribution, whether for free or remuneration, of a payor's product by the payor or the exempt organization to the general public at the sponsored activity is not considered an inducement to purchase, sell or use the payor's product for purposes of this section and, thus, will not affect the determination of whether a payment is a qualified sponsorship payment.

(v) *Advertising.* For purposes of this section, the term *advertising* means any message or other programming material which is broadcast or otherwise transmitted, published, displayed or distributed, and which promotes or markets any trade or business, or any service, facility or product. Advertising includes messages containing qualitative or comparative language, price information or other indications of savings or value, an endorsement, or an inducement to purchase, sell, or use any company, service, facility or product. A single message that contains both advertising and an acknowledgment is advertising. This section does not apply to activities conducted by a payor on its own. For example, if a payor purchases broadcast time from a television station to advertise its product during commercial breaks in a sponsored program, the exempt organization's activities are not thereby converted to advertising.

(vi) *Exclusivity arrangements*—(A) *Exclusive sponsor.* An arrangement that acknowledges the payor as the exclusive sponsor of an exempt organization's activity, or the exclusive sponsor representing a particular trade, business or industry, generally does not, by itself, result in a substantial return benefit. For example, if in exchange for a payment, an organization announces that its event is sponsored exclusively by the payor (and does not provide any advertising or other substantial return benefit to the payor), the payor has not received a substantial return benefit.

(B) *Exclusive provider.* An arrangement that limits the sale, distribution, availability, or use of competing products, services, or facilities in connection with an exempt organization's activity generally results in a substantial return benefit. For example, if in exchange for a payment, the exempt organization agrees to allow only the payor's products to be sold in connection with an activity, the payor has received a substantial return benefit.

(d) *Allocation of payment*—(1) *In general.* If there is an arrangement or expectation that the payor will receive a substantial return benefit with respect to any payment, then only the portion, if any, of the payment that exceeds the fair market value of the substantial return benefit is a qualified sponsorship payment. However, if the exempt organization does not establish that the payment exceeds the fair market value of any substantial return benefit, then no portion of the payment constitutes a qualified sponsorship payment.

(i) *Treatment of payments other than qualified sponsorship payments.* The unrelated business income tax (UBIT) treatment of any payment (or portion thereof) that is not a qualified sponsorship payment is determined by application of sections 512, 513 and 514. For example, payments related to an exempt organization's providing facilities, services, or other privileges to the payor or persons designated by the payor,

advertising, exclusive provider arrangements described in paragraph (c)(2)(vi)(B) of this section, a license to use intangible assets of the exempt organization, or other substantial return benefits, are evaluated separately in determining whether the exempt organization realizes unrelated business taxable income.

(ii) *Fair market value.* The fair market value of any substantial return benefit provided as part of a sponsorship arrangement is the price at which the benefit would be provided between a willing recipient and a willing provider of the benefit, neither being under any compulsion to enter into the arrangement and both having reasonable knowledge of relevant facts, and without regard to any other aspect of the sponsorship arrangement.

(iii) *Valuation date.* In general, the fair market value of the substantial return benefit is determined when the benefit is provided. However, if the parties enter into a binding, written sponsorship contract, the fair market value of any substantial return benefit provided pursuant to that contract is determined on the date the parties enter into the sponsorship contract. If the parties make a material change to a sponsorship contract, it is treated as a new sponsorship contract as of the date the material change is effective. A material change includes an extension or renewal of the contract, or a more than incidental change to any amount payable (or other consideration) pursuant to the contract.

(iv) *Examples.* The following examples illustrate the provisions of this section:

Example 1. On June 30, 2001, a national corporation and Z, a charitable organization, enter into a five-year binding, written contract effective for years 2002 through 2007. The contract provides that the corporation will make an annual payment of $5,000 to Z, and in return the corporation will receive no benefit other than advertising. On June 30, 2001, the fair market value of the advertising to be provided to the corporation in each year of the agreement is $75, which is less than the disregarded benefit amount provided for in paragraph (c)(2)(ii) of this section (2% of $5,000 is $100). In 2002, pursuant to the sponsorship contract, the corporation makes a payment to Z of $5,000, and receives the specified benefit (advertising). As of January 1, 2002, the fair market value of the advertising to be provided by Z each year has increased to $110. However, for purposes of this section, the fair market value of the advertising benefit is determined on June 30, 2001, the date the parties entered into the sponsorship contract. Therefore, the entire $5,000 pay-

Reg. § 1.513-4(d)(1)

ment received in 2002 is a qualified sponsorship payment.

Example 2. The facts are the same as Example 1, except that the contract provides for an initial payment by the corporation to Z of $5,000 in 2002, followed by annual payments of $1,000 during each of years 2003-2007. In 2003, pursuant to the sponsorship contract, the corporation makes a payment to Z of $1,000, and receives the specified advertising benefit. In 2003, the fair market value of the benefit provided ($75, as determined on June 30, 2001) exceeds 2% of the total payment received (2% of $1,000 is $20). Therefore, only $925 of the $1,000 payment received in 2003 is a qualified sponsorship payment.

(2) *Anti-abuse provision.* To the extent necessary to prevent avoidance of the rule stated in paragraphs (d)(1) and (c)(2) of this section, where the exempt organization fails to make a reasonable and good faith valuation of any substantial return benefit, the Commissioner (or the Commissioner's delegate) may determine the portion of a payment allocable to such substantial return benefit and may treat two or more related payments as a single payment.

(e) *Special rules*—(1) *Written agreements.* The existence of a written sponsorship agreement does not, in itself, cause a payment to fail to be a qualified sponsorship payment. The terms of the agreement, not its existence or degree of detail, are relevant to the determination of whether a payment is a qualified sponsorship payment. Similarly, the terms of the agreement and not the title or responsibilities of the individuals negotiating the agreement determine whether a payment (or any portion thereof) made pursuant to the agreement is a qualified sponsorship payment.

(2) *Contingent payments.* The term *qualified sponsorship payment* does not include any payment the amount of which is contingent, by contract or otherwise, upon the level of attendance at one or more events, broadcast ratings, or other factors indicating the degree of public exposure to the sponsored activity. The fact that a payment is contingent upon sponsored events or activities actually being conducted does not, by itself, cause the payment to fail to be a qualified sponsorship payment.

(3) *Determining public support.* Qualified sponsorship payments in the form of money or property (but not services) are treated as contributions received by the exempt organization for purposes of determining public support to the organization under section 170(b)(1)(A)(vi) or 509(a)(2). See §§ 1.509(a)-3(f)(1) and 1.170A-9(e)(6)(i). The fact that a payment is a qualified sponsorship payment that is treated as a contribution to the payee organization does not determine whether the payment is deductible by the payor under section 162 or 170.

(f) *Examples.* The provisions of this section are illustrated by the following examples. The tax treatment of any payment (or portion of a payment) that does not constitute a qualified sponsorship payment is governed by general UBIT principles. In these examples, the recipients of the payments at issue are section 501(c) organizations. The expectations or arrangements of the parties are those specifically indicated in the example. The examples are as follows:

Example 1. M, a local charity, organizes a marathon and walkathon at which it serves to participants drinks and other refreshments provided free of charge by a national corporation. The corporation also gives M prizes to be awarded to winners of the event. M recognizes the assistance of the corporation by listing the corporation's name in promotional fliers, in newspaper advertisements of the event and on T-shirts worn by participants. M changes the name of its event to include the name of the corporation. M's activities constitute acknowledgment of the sponsorship. The drinks, refreshments and prizes provided by the corporation are a qualified sponsorship payment, which is not income from an unrelated trade or business.

Example 2. N, an art museum, organizes an exhibition and receives a large payment from a corporation to help fund the exhibition. N recognizes the corporation's support by using the corporate name and established logo in materials publicizing the exhibition, which include banners, posters, brochures and public service announcements. N also hosts a dinner for the corporation's executives. The fair market value of the dinner exceeds 2% of the total payment. N's use of the corporate name and logo in connection with the exhibition constitutes acknowledgment of the sponsorship. However, because the fair market value of the dinner exceeds 2% of the total payment, the dinner is a substantial return benefit. Only that portion of the payment, if any, that N can demonstrate exceeds the fair market value of the dinner is a qualified sponsorship payment.

Example 3. O coordinates sports tournaments for local charities. An auto manufacturer agrees to underwrite the expenses of the tournaments. O recognizes the auto manufacturer by including the manufacturer's name and established logo in the title of each tournament as well as on signs, scoreboards and other printed material. The auto manufacturer receives complimentary admission passes and pro-am playing spots for each tournament that have a combined fair market value in

Reg. § 1.513-4(d)(2)

excess of 2% of the total payment. Additionally, O displays the latest models of the manufacturer's premier luxury cars at each tournament. O's use of the manufacturer's name and logo and display of cars in the tournament area constitute acknowledgment of the sponsorship. However, the admission passes and pro-am playing spots are a substantial return benefit. Only that portion of the payment, if any, that O can demonstrate exceeds the fair market value of the admission passes and pro-am playing spots is a qualified sponsorship payment.

Example 4. P conducts an annual college football bowl game. P sells to commercial broadcasters the right to broadcast the bowl game on television and radio. A major corporation agrees to be the exclusive sponsor of the bowl game. The detailed contract between P and the corporation provides that in exchange for a $1,000,000 payment, the name of the bowl game will include the name of the corporation. In addition, the contract provides that the corporation's name and established logo will appear on player's helmets and uniforms, on the scoreboard and stadium signs, on the playing field, on cups used to serve drinks at the game, and on all related printed material distributed in connection with the game. P also agrees to give the corporation a block of game passes for its employees and to provide advertising in the bowl game program book. The fair market value of the passes is $6,000, and the fair market value of the program advertising is $10,000. The agreement is contingent upon the game being broadcast on television and radio, but the amount of the payment is not contingent upon the number of people attending the game or the television ratings. The contract provides that television cameras will focus on the corporation's name and logo on the field at certain intervals during the game. P's use of the corporation's name and logo in connection with the bowl game constitutes acknowledgment of the sponsorship. The exclusive sponsorship arrangement is not a substantial return benefit. Because the fair market value of the game passes and program advertising ($16,000) does not exceed 2% of the total payment (2% of $1,000,000 is $20,000), these benefits are disregarded and the entire payment is a qualified sponsorship payment, which is not income from an unrelated trade or business.

Example 5. Q organizes an amateur sports team. A major pizza chain gives uniforms to players on Q's team, and also pays some of the team's operational expenses. The uniforms bear the name and established logo of the pizza chain. During the final tournament series, Q distributes free of charge souvenir flags bearing Q's name to employees of the pizza chain who come out to support the team. The flags are valued at less than 2% of the combined fair market value of the uniforms and operational expenses paid. Q's use of the name and logo of the pizza chain in connection with the tournament constitutes acknowledgment of the sponsorship. Because the fair market value of the flags does not exceed 2% of the total payment, the entire amount of the funding and supplied uniforms are a qualified sponsorship payment, which is not income from an unrelated trade or business.

Example 6. R is a liberal arts college. A soft drink manufacturer enters into a binding, written contract with R that provides for a large payment to be made to the college's English department in exchange for R agreeing to name a writing competition after the soft drink manufacturer. The contract also provides that R will allow the soft drink manufacturer to be the exclusive provider of all soft drink sales on campus. The fair market value of the exclusive provider component of the contract exceeds 2% of the total payment. R's use of the manufacturer's name in the writing competition constitutes acknowledgment of the sponsorship. However, the exclusive provider arrangement is a substantial return benefit. Only that portion of the payment, if any, that R can demonstrate exceeds the fair market value of the exclusive provider arrangement is a qualified sponsorship payment.

Example 7. S is a noncommercial broadcast station that airs a program funded by a local music store. In exchange for the funding, S broadcasts the following message: "This program has been brought to you by the Music Shop, located at 123 Main Street. For your music needs, give them a call today at 555-1234. This station is proud to have the Music Shop as a sponsor." Because this single broadcast message contains both advertising and an acknowledgment, the entire message is advertising. The fair market value of the advertising exceeds 2% of the total payment. Thus, the advertising is a substantial return benefit. Unless S establishes that the amount of the payment exceeds the fair market value of the advertising, none of the payment is a qualified sponsorship payment.

Example 8. T, a symphony orchestra, performs a series of concerts. A program guide that contains notes on guest conductors and other information concerning the evening's program is distributed by T at each concert. The Music Shop makes a $1,000 payment to T in support of the concert series. As a supporter of the event, the Music Shop receives complimentary concert tickets with a fair market value of $85, and is recognized in the program guide and on a poster in the

Reg. § 1.513-4(f)

lobby of the concert hall. The lobby poster states that, "The T concert is sponsored by the Music Shop, located at 123 Main Street, telephone number 555-1234." The program guide contains the same information and also states, "Visit the Music Shop today for the finest selection of music CDs and cassette tapes." The fair market value of the advertisement in the program guide is $15. T's use of the Music Shop's name, address and telephone number in the lobby poster constitutes acknowledgment of the sponsorship. However, the combined fair market value of the advertisement in the program guide and complimentary tickets is $100 ($15 + $85), which exceeds 2% of the total payment (2% of $1,000 is $20). The fair market value of the advertising and complimentary tickets, therefore, constitutes a substantial return benefit and only that portion of the payment, or $900, that exceeds the fair market value of the substantial return benefit is a qualified sponsorship payment.

Example 9. U, a national charity dedicated to promoting health, organizes a campaign to inform the public about potential cures to fight a serious disease. As part of the campaign, U sends representatives to community health fairs around the country to answer questions about the disease and inform the public about recent developments in the search for a cure. A pharmaceutical company makes a payment to U to fund U's booth at a health fair. U places a sign in the booth displaying the pharmaceutical company's name and slogan, "Better Research, Better Health," which is an established part of the company's identity. In addition, U grants the pharmaceutical company a license to use U's logo in marketing its products to health care providers around the country. The fair market value of the license exceeds 2% of the total payment received from the company. U's display of the pharmaceutical company's name and slogan constitutes acknowledgment of the sponsorship. However, the license granted to the pharmaceutical company to use U's logo is a substantial return benefit. Only that portion of the payment, if any, that U can demonstrate exceeds the fair market value of the license granted to the pharmaceutical company is a qualified sponsorship payment.

Example 10. V, a trade association, publishes a monthly scientific magazine for its members containing information about current issues and developments in the field. A textbook publisher makes a large payment to V to have its name displayed on the inside cover of the magazine each month. Because the monthly magazine is a periodical within the meaning of paragraph (b) of this section, the section 513(i) safe harbor does not apply. See § 1.512(a)-1(f).

Example 11. W, a symphony orchestra, maintains a website containing pertinent information and its performance schedule. The Music Shop makes a payment to W to fund a concert series, and W posts a list of its sponsors on its website, including the Music Shop's name and Internet address. W's website does not promote the Music Shop or advertise its merchandise. The Music Shop's Internet address appears as a hyperlink from W's website to the Music Shop's website. W's posting of the Music Shop's name and Internet address on its website constitutes acknowledgment of the sponsorship. The entire payment is a qualified sponsorship payment, which is not income from an unrelated trade or business.

Example 12. X, a health-based charity, sponsors a year-long initiative to educate the public about a particular medical condition. A large pharmaceutical company manufactures a drug that is used in treating the medical condition, and provides funding for the initiative that helps X produce educational materials for distribution and post information on X's website. X's website contains a hyperlink to the pharmaceutical company's website. On the pharmaceutical company's website, the statement appears, "X endorses the use of our drug, and suggests that you ask your doctor for a prescription if you have this medical condition." X reviewed the endorsement before it was posted on the pharmaceutical company's website and gave permission for the endorsement to appear. The endorsement is advertising. The fair market value of the advertising exceeds 2% of the total payment received from the pharmaceutical company. Therefore, only the portion of the payment, if any, that X can demonstrate exceeds the fair market value of the advertising on the pharmaceutical company's website is a qualified sponsorship payment. [Reg. § 1.513-4.]

☐ [T.D. 8991, 4-24-2002.]

[Reg. § 1.513-5]

§ 1.513-5. Certain bingo games not unrelated trade or business.—(a) *In general*. Under section 513(f), and subject to the limitations in paragraph (c) of this section, in the case of an organization subject to the tax imposed by section 511, the term "unrelated trade or business" does not include any trade or business that consists of conducting bingo games (as defined in paragraph (d) of this section).

(b) *Exception*. The provisions of this section shall not apply with respect to any bingo game otherwise excluded from the term "unrelated trade or business" by reason of section 513(a)(1) and § 1.513-1(e)(1) (relating to trades or businesses in which substantially all the work is performed without compensation).

(c) *Limitations*—(1) *Bingo games must be legal.* Paragraph (a) of this section shall not apply with respect to any bingo game conducted in violation of State or local law.

(2) *No commercial competition.* Paragraph (a) of this section shall not apply with respect to any bingo game conducted in a jurisdiction in which bingo games are ordinarily carried out on a commercial basis. Bingo games are "ordinarily carried out on a commercial basis" within a jurisdiction if they are regularly carried on (within the meaning of § 1.513-1(c)) by for-profit organizations in any part of that jurisdiction. Normally, the entire State will constitute the appropriate jurisdiction for determining whether bingo games are ordinarily carried out on a commercial basis. However, if State law permits local jurisdictions to determine whether bingo games may be conducted by for-profit organizations, or if State law limits or confines the conduct of bingo games by for-profit organizations to specific local jurisdictions, then the local jurisdiction will constitute the appropriate jurisdiction for determining whether bingo games are ordinarily carried out on a commercial basis.

(3) *Examples.* The application of this paragraph is illustrated by the examples that follow. In each example, it is assumed that the bingo games referred to are operated by individuals who are compensated for their services. Accordingly, none of the bingo games would be excluded from the term "unrelated trade or business" under section 513(a)(1).

Example (1). Church Z, a tax-exempt organization, conducts weekly bingo games in State O. State and local laws in State O expressly provide that bingo games may be conducted by tax-exempt organizations. Bingo games are not conducted in State O by any for-profit businesses. Since Z's bingo games are not conducted in violation of State or local law and are not the type of activity ordinarily carried out on a commercial basis in State O, Z's bingo games do not constitute unrelated trade or business.

Example (2). Rescue Squad X, a tax-exempt organization, conducts weekly bingo games in State M. State M has a statutory provision that prohibits all forms of gambling including bingo games. However, that law generally is not enforced by State officials against local charitable organizations such as X that conduct bingo games to raise funds. Since bingo games are illegal under State law, X's bingo games constitute unrelated trade or business regardless of the degree to which the State law is enforced.

Example (3). Veterans' organizations Y and X, both tax-exempt organizations, are organized under the laws of State N. State N has a statutory provision that permits bingo games to be conducted by tax-exempt organizations. In addition, State N permits bingo games to be conducted by for-profit organizations in city S, a resort community located in county R. Several for-profit organizations conduct nightly bingo games in city S. Y conducts weekly bingo games in city S. X conducts weekly bingo games in county R. Since State law confines the conduct of bingo games by for-profit organizations to city S, and since bingo games are regularly carried on there by those organizations, Y's bingo games conducted in city S constitute unrelated trade or business. However, X's bingo games conducted in county R outside of city S do not constitute unrelated trade or business.

(d) *Bingo game defined.* A bingo game is a game of chance played with cards that are generally printed with five rows of five squares each. Participants place markers over randomly called numbers on the cards in an attempt to form a preselected pattern such as a horizontal, vertical, or diagonal line, or all four corners. The first participant to form the preselected pattern wins the game. As used in this section, the term "bingo game" means any game of bingo of the type described above in which wagers are placed, winners are determined, and prizes or other property is distributed in the presence of all persons placing wagers in that game. The term "bingo game" does not refer to any game of chance (including, but not limited to, keno games, dice games, card games, and lotteries) other than the type of game described in this paragraph.

(e) *Effective date.* Section 513(f) and this section apply to taxable years beginning after December 31, 1969. [Reg. § 1.513-5.]

☐ [*T.D.* 7699, 5-20-80.]

[Reg. § 1.513-6]

§ 1.513-6. Certain hospital services not unrelated trade or business.—(a) *In general.* Under section 513(e), the furnishing of a service listed in section 501(e)(1)(A) by a hospital to one or more other hospitals will not constitute unrelated trade or business if—

(1) The service is provided solely to hospitals that have facilities to serve not more than 100 inpatients,

(2) The service would, if performed by the recipient hospital, constitute an activity consistent with that hospital's exempt purposes, and

(3) The service is provided at a fee not in excess of actual cost, including straight line depreciation and a reasonable rate of return on the capital goods used to provide the service. For

Reg. § 1.513-6(a)(3)

purposes of this section, a rate of return on capital goods will be considered "reasonable" provided that it does not exceed, on an annual basis, the percentage described below which is based on the average of the rates of interest on special issues of public debt obligations issued to the Federal Hospital Insurance Trust Fund for each of the months included in the taxable year of the hospital during which the capital goods are used in providing the service. Determinations as to the cost of services and the applicable rate of return should be made as prescribed by 42 U.S.C. § 1395x(v)(1)(A) and (B) and the regulations thereunder (permitting a health care facility to be reimbursed under the Medicare program for the "reasonable cost of [its] services," including, in the case of certain proprietary facilities, a "reasonable return on equity capital"). For taxable years beginning on or before May 14, 1986 the rate of return shall be one and one-half times the average of the rates of interest on public debt obligations described above which were in effect on or before April 20, 1983.

(b) *Hospital defined.* As used in this section the word "hospital" means a hospital described in section 170(b)(1)(A)(iii).

(c) *Example.* The provisions of this section are illustrated by the following example:

Example. A large metropolitan hospital provides various services to other hospitals. The hospital furnishes a purchasing service to hospitals N and O, a data processing service to hospitals R and S, and a food service to hospitals X and Y. All the hospitals are described in section 170(b)(1)(A)(iii). All the hospitals have facilities to serve not more than 100 inpatients except hospital N. The services are furnished at cost to all hospitals except that hospital R is charged a fee in excess of cost for its use of the data processing service. The purchasing service constitutes unrelated trade or business because it is not provided solely to hospitals having facilities to serve not more than 100 inpatients.

The data processing service constitutes unrelated trade or business because it is provided at a fee in excess of cost. The food service satisfies all three requirements of paragraph (a) of this section and does not constitute unrelated trade or business.

(d) *Effective date.* Section 513(e) and this section apply to taxable years beginning after December 31, 1953. [Reg. § 1.513-6.]

☐ [T.D. 8075, 2-12-86.]

[Reg. § 1.513-7]

§ 1.513-7. Travel and tour activities of tax exempt organizations.—(a) Travel tour activities that constitute a trade or business, as defined in § 1.513-1(b), and that are not substantially related to the purposes for which exemption has been granted to the organization constitute an unrelated trade or business with respect to that organization. Whether travel tour activities conducted by an organization are substantially related to the organization's exempt purpose is determined by looking at all relevant facts and circumstances, including, but not limited to, how a travel tour is developed, promoted and operated. Section 513(c) and § 1.513-1(b) also apply to travel tour activity. Application of the rules of section 513(c) and § 1.513-1(b) may result in different treatment for individual tours within an organization's travel tour program.

(b) *Examples.* The provisions of this section are illustrated by the following examples. In all of these examples, the travel tours are priced to produce a profit for the exempt organization. The examples are as follows:

Example 1. O, a university alumni association, is exempt from federal income tax under section 501(a) as an educational organization described in section 501(c)(3). As part of its activities, O operates a travel tour program. The program is open to all current members of O and their guests. O works with travel agencies to schedule approximately 10 tours annually to various destinations around the world. Members of O pay $x to the organizing travel agency to participate in a tour. The travel agency pays O a per person fee for each participant. Although the literature advertising the tours encourages O's members to continue their lifelong learning by joining the tours, and a faculty member of O's related university frequently joins the tour as a guest of the alumni association, none of the tours includes any scheduled instruction or curriculum related to the destinations being visited. The travel tours made available to O's members do not contribute importantly to the accomplishment of O's educational purpose. Rather, O's program is designed to generate revenues for O by regularly offering its members travel services. Accordingly, O's tour program is an unrelated trade or business within the meaning of section 513(a).

Example 2. N is an organization formed for the purpose of educating individuals about the geography and culture of the United States. It is exempt from federal income tax under section 501(a) as an educational and cultural organization described in section 501(c)(3). N engages in a number of activities to accomplish its purposes, including offering courses and publishing periodicals and books. As one of its activities, N conducts study tours to national parks and other locations within the United States. The study tours are conducted by teachers and other personnel certified by the Board of Education of the State of P. The tours are directed toward students enrolled in degree programs at educational institutions in P, as reflected in the promotional materials, but are open to all who agree to participate in the required study program. Each tour's study program consists of instruction on subjects related to the location being visited on the tour. During the tour, five or six hours per day are devoted to organized study, preparation of reports, lectures, instruction and recitation by the students. Each tour group brings along a library of material related to the subject being studied on the tour. Examinations are given at the end of each tour and the P State Board of Education awards academic credit for tour participation. Because the tours offered by N include a substantial amount of required study, lectures, report preparation, examinations and qualify for academic credit, the tours are substantially related to N's educational purpose. Accordingly, N's tour program is not an unrelated trade or business within the meaning of section 513(a).

Example 3. R is a section 501(c)(4) social welfare organization devoted to advocacy on a particular issue. On a regular basis throughout the year, R organizes travel tours for its members to Washington, DC. While in Washington, the members follow a schedule according to which they spend substantially all of their time during normal business hours over several days attending meetings with legislators and government officials and receiving briefings on policy developments related to the issue that is R's focus. Members do have some time on their own in the evenings to engage in recreational or social activities of their own choosing. Bringing members to Washington to participate in advocacy on behalf of the organization and learn about developments relating to the organization's principal focus is substantially related to R's social welfare purpose. Therefore, R's operation of the travel tours does not constitute an unrelated trade or business within the meaning of section 513(a).

Example 4. S is a membership organization formed to foster cultural unity and to educate X Americans about X, their country of origin. It is exempt from federal income tax under section 501(a) and is described in section 501(c)(3) as an educational and cultural organization. Membership in S is open to all Americans interested in the X heritage. As part of its activities, S sponsors a program of travel tours to X. The tours are divided into two categories. Category A tours are trips to X that are designed to immerse participants in the X history, culture and language. Substantially all of the daily itinerary includes scheduled instruction on the X language, history and cultural heritage, and visits to destinations selected because of their historical or cultural significance or because of instructional resources they offer. Category B tours are also trips to X, but rather than offering scheduled instruction, participants are given the option of taking guided tours of various X locations included in their itinerary. Other than the optional guided tours, Category B tours offer no instruction or curriculum. Destinations of principally recreational interest, rather than historical or cultural interest, are regularly included on Category B tour itineraries. Based on the facts and circumstances, sponsoring Category A tours is an activity substantially related to S's exempt purposes, and does not constitute an unrelated trade or business within the meaning of section 513(a). However, sponsoring Category B tours does not contribute importantly to S's accomplishment of its exempt purposes and, thus, constitutes an unrelated trade or business within the meaning of section 513(a).

Example 5. T is a scientific organization engaged in environmental research. T is exempt from federal income tax under section 501(a) as an organization described in section 501(c)(3). T is engaged in a long-term study of how agricultural pesticide and fertilizer use affects the populations of various bird species. T collects data at several bases located in an important agricultural region of country U. The minutes of a meeting of T's Board of Directors state that, after study, the Board has determined that non-scientists can reliably perform needed data collection in the field, under supervision of T's biologists. The Board minutes reflect that the Board approved offering one-week trips to T's bases in U, where participants will assist T's biologists in collecting data for the study. Tour participants collect data during the same hours as T's biologists. Normally, data collection occurs during the early morning and evening hours, although the work schedule varies by season. Each base has rustic accommodations and few amenities, but country U is renowned for its beautiful scenery and abundant wildlife. T promotes the trips in its newsletter and on its Internet site and through various conservation organizations. The promotional materials describe the work schedule and emphasize the valuable contribution made by trip participants to T's research activities. Based on the facts and circumstances, sponsoring trips to T's bases in country U is an activity substantially related to T's exempt purpose, and, thus, does not constitute an unrelated trade or business within the meaning of section 513(a).

Example 6. V is an educational organization devoted to the study of ancient history and cul-

Reg. § 1.513-7(b)

tures and is exempt from federal income tax under section 501(a) as an organization described in section 501(c)(3). In connection with its educational activities, V conducts archaeological expeditions around the world, including in the Y region of country Z. In cooperation with the National Museum of Z, V recently presented an exhibit on ancient civilizations of the Y region of Z, including artifacts from the collection of the Z National Museum. V instituted a program of travel tours to V's archaeological sites located in the Y region. The tours were initially proposed by V staff members as a means of educating the public about ongoing field research conducted by V. V engaged a travel agency to handle logistics such as accommodations and transportation arrangements. In preparation for the tours, V developed educational materials relating to each archaeological site to be visited on the tour, describing in detail the layout of the site, the methods used by V's researchers in exploring the site, the discoveries made at the site, and their historical significance. V also arranged special guided tours of its exhibit on the Y region for individuals registered for the travel tours. Two archaeologists from V (both of whom had participated in prior archaeological expeditions in the Y region) accompanied the tours. These experts led guided tours of each site and explained the significance of the sites to tour participants. At several of the sites, tour participants also met with a working team of archaeologists from V and the National Museum of Z, who shared their experiences. V prepared promotional materials describing the educational nature of the tours, including the daily trips to V's archaeological sites and the educational background of the tour leaders, and providing a recommended reading list. The promotional materials do not refer to any particular recreational or sightseeing activities. Based on the facts and circumstances, sponsoring trips to the Y region is an activity substantially related to V's exempt purposes. The scheduled activities, which include tours of archaeological sites led by experts, are part of a coordinated educational program designed to educate tour participants about the ancient history of the Y region of Z and V's ongoing field research. Therefore, V's tour program does not constitute an unrelated trade or business within the meaning of section 513(a).

Example 7. W is an educational organization devoted to the study of the performing arts and is exempt from federal income tax under section 501(a) as an organization described in section 501(c)(3). In connection with its educational activities, W presents public performances of musical and theatrical works. Individuals become members of W by making an annual contribution to W of $q. Each year, W offers members an opportunity to travel as a group to one or more major cities in the United States or abroad. In each city, tour participants are provided tickets to attend a public performance of a play, concert or dance program each evening. W also arranges a sightseeing tour of each city and provides evening receptions for tour participants. W views its tour program as an important means to develop and strengthen bonds between W and its members, and to increase their financial and volunteer support of W. W engaged a travel agency to handle logistics such as accommodations and transportation arrangements. No educational materials are prepared by W or provided to tour participants in connection with the tours. Apart from attendance at the evening cultural events, the tours offer no scheduled instruction, organized study or group discussion. Although several members of W's administrative staff accompany each tour group, their role is to facilitate member interaction. The staff members have no special expertise in the performing arts and play no educational role in the tours. W prepared promotional materials describing the sightseeing opportunities on the tours and emphasizing the opportunity for members to socialize informally and interact with one another and with W staff members, while pursuing shared interests. Although W's tour program may foster goodwill among W members, it does not contribute importantly to W's educational purposes. W's tour program is primarily social and recreational in nature. The scheduled activities, which include sightseeing and attendance at various cultural events, are not part of a coordinated educational program. Therefore, W's tour program is an unrelated trade or business within the meaning of section 513(a).

[Reg. § 1.513-7.]

☐ [T.D. 8874, 2-4-2000 (corrected 3-24-2000).]

[Reg. § 1.514(a)-1]

§ 1.514(a)-1. Unrelated debt-financed income and deductions.—(a) *Income includible in gross income—*

(1) *Percentage of income taken into account* —(i) *In general.* For taxable years beginning after December 31, 1969, there shall be included with respect to each debt-financed property (as defined in section 514 and § 1.514(b)-1) as an item of gross income derived from an unrelated trade or business, the amount of unrelated debt-financed income (as defined in subdivision (ii) of this subparagraph). See paragraph (a)(5) of § 1.514(c)-1 for special rules regarding indebtedness incurred before June 28, 1966, applicable for taxable years beginning before January 1, 1972,

Reg. § 1.514(a)-1(a)(1)

and for special rules applicable to churches or conventions or associations of churches.

(ii) *Unrelated debt-financed income.* The "unrelated debt-financed income" with respect to each debt-financed property is an amount which is the same percentage (but not in excess of 100 percent) of the total gross income derived during the taxable year from or on account of such property as—

(*a*) The average acquisition indebtedness (as defined in subparagraph (3) of this paragraph) with respect to the property is of

(*b*) The average adjusted basis of such property (as defined in subparagraph (2) of this paragraph).

(iii) *Debt/basis percentage.* The percentage determined under subdivision (ii) of this subparagraph is hereinafter referred to as the "debt/basis percentage."

(iv) *Example.* Subdivisions (i), (ii), and (iii) of this subparagraph are illustrated by the following example. For purposes of this example it is assumed that the property is debt-financed property.

Example. X, an exempt trade association, owns an office building which in 1971 produces $10,000 of gross rental income. The average adjusted basis of the building for 1971 is $100,000, and the average acquisition indebtedness with respect to the building for 1971 is $50,000. Accordingly, the debt/basis percentage for 1971 is 50 percent (the ratio of $50,000 to $100,000). Therefore, the unrelated debt-financed income with respect to the building for 1971 is $5,000 (50% of $10,000).

(v) *Gain from sale or other disposition.* If debt-financed property is sold or otherwise disposed of, there shall be included in computing unrelated business taxable income an amount with respect to such gain (or loss) which is the same percentage (but not in excess of 100 percent) of the total gain (or loss) derived from such sale or other disposition as—

(*a*) The highest acquisition indebtedness with respect to such property during the 12-month period, preceding the date of disposition, is of

(*b*) The average adjusted basis of such property.

The tax on the amount of gain (or loss) included in unrelated business taxable income pursuant to the preceding sentence shall be determined in accordance with the rules set forth in subchapter P, chapter 1 of the Code (relating to capital gains and losses). See also section 511(d) and the regulations thereunder (relating to the minimum tax for tax preferences).

(2) *Average adjusted basis*—(i) *In general.* The "average adjusted basis" of debt-financed property is the average amount of the adjusted basis of such property during that portion of the taxable year it is held by the organization. This amount is the average of:

(*a*) The adjusted basis of such property as of the first day during the taxable year that the organization holds the property and

(*b*) The adjusted basis of such property as of the last day during the taxable year that the organization holds the property.

See section 1011 and the regulations thereunder for determination of the adjusted basis of property.

(ii) *Adjustments for prior taxable years.* For purposes of subdivision (i) of this subparagraph, the determination of the average adjusted basis of debt-financed property is not affected by the fact that the organization was exempt from taxation for prior taxable years. Proper adjustment must be made under section 1011 for the entire period since the acquisition of the property. For example, adjustment must be made for depreciation for all prior taxable years whether or not the organization was exempt from taxation for any such years. Similarly, the fact that only a portion of the depreciation allowance may be taken into account in computing the percentage of deductions allowable under section 514(a)(2) does not affect the amount of the adjustment for depreciation which is used in determining average adjusted basis.

(iii) *Cross reference.* For the determination of the basis of debt-financed property acquired in a complete or partial liquidation of a corporation in exchange for its stock, see § 1.514(d)-1.

(iv) *Example.* This subparagraph may be illustrated by the following example. For purposes of this example it is assumed that the property is debt-financed property.

Example. On July 10, 1970, X, an exempt educational organization, purchased an office building for $510,000, using $300,000 of borrowed funds. During 1970 the only adjustment to basis is $20,000 for depreciation. As of December 31, 1970, the adjusted basis of the building is $490,000 and the indebtedness is still $300,000. X files its return on a calendar year basis. Under these circumstances, the debt/basis percentage for 1970 is 60 percent, calculated in the following manner:

Reg. § 1.514(a)-1(a)(2)

39,164   Unrelated Business Income

See p. 20,601 for regulations not amended to reflect law changes

	Basis
As of July 10, 1970 (acquisition date)	$ 510,000
As of December 31, 1970	490,000
	$1,000,000

Average adjusted basis:
$1,000,000 ÷ 2 = ... $ 500,000

Debt/basis percentage:
$$\frac{\text{Average acquisition indebtedness}}{\text{Average adjusted basis}} = \frac{\$300,000}{\$500,000} = 60 \text{ percent}$$

For an illustration of the determination of the debt/basis percentage as changes in the acquisition indebtedness occur, see example (1) of subparagraph (3)(iii) of this paragraph.

(3) *Average acquisition indebtedness*—(i) *In general.* The "average acquisition indebtedness" with respect to debt-financed property is the average amount of the outstanding principal indebtedness during that portion of the taxable year the property is held by the organization.

(ii) *Computation.* The average acquisition indebtedness is computed by determining the amount of the outstanding principal indebtedness on the first day in each calendar month during the taxable year that the organization holds the property, adding these amounts together, and then dividing this sum by the total number of months during the taxable year that the organization held such property. A fractional part of a month shall be treated as a full month in computing average acquisition indebtedness.

(iii) *Examples.* The application of this subparagraph may be illustrated by the following examples. For purposes of these examples it is assumed that the property is debt-financed property.

Example (1). Assume the facts as stated in the example in subparagraph (2)(iv) of this paragraph, except that beginning July 20, 1970, the organization makes payments of $21,000 a month ($20,000 of which is attributable to principal and $1,000 to interest). In this situation, the average acquisition indebtedness for 1970 is $250,000. Thus, the debt/basis percentage for 1970 is 50 percent, calculated in the following manner:

Month	Indebtedness on the first day in each calendar month that the property is held
July	$ 300,000
August	280,000
September	260,000
October	240,000
November	220,000
December	200,000
	$1,500,000

Average acquisition indebtedness:
$1,500,000 ÷ 6 months = ... $250,000

Debt/basis percentage:
$$\frac{\text{Average acquisition indebtedness}}{\text{Average adjusted basis}} = \frac{\$250,000}{\$500,000} = 50 \text{ percent}$$

Example (2). Y, an exempt organization, owns stock in a corporation which it does not control. At the beginning of the year, Y has an outstanding principal indebtedness with respect to such stock of $12,000. Such indebtedness is paid off at the rate of $2,000 per month beginning January 30, so that it is retired at the end of six months. The average acquisition indebtedness for the taxable year is $3,500, calculated in the following manner:

Month	Indebtedness on the first day in each calendar month that the property is held
January	$12,000
February	10,000

Reg. § 1.514(a)-1(a)(3)

Unrelated Business Income

See p. 20,601 for regulations not amended to reflect law changes

March	8,000
April	6,000
May	4,000
June	2,000
July thru December	0
Average acquisition indebtedness:	$42,000
$42,000 ÷ 12 months =	$ 3,500

(4) *Indeterminate price*—(i) *In general.* If an exempt organization acquires (or improves) property for an indeterminate price, the initial acquisition indebtedness and the unadjusted basis shall be determined in accordance with subdivisions (ii) and (iii) of this paragraph, unless the organization has obtained the consent of the Commissioner to use another method to compute such amounts.

(ii) *Unadjusted basis.* For purposes of this subparagraph, the unadjusted basis of property (or of an improvement) is the fair market value of the property (or improvement) on the date of acquisition (or the date of completion of the improvement). The average adjusted basis of such property shall be determined in accordance with paragraph (a)(2) of this section.

(iii) *Initial acquisition indebtedness.* For purposes of this subparagraph, the initial acquisition indebtedness is the fair market value of the property (or improvement) on the date of acquisition (or the date of completion of the improvement) less any down payment or other initial payment applied to the principal indebtedness. The average acquisition indebtedness with respect to such property shall be computed in accordance with paragraph (a)(3) of this section.

(iv) *Example.* The application of this subparagraph may be illustrated by the following example. For purposes of this example it is assumed that the property is debt-financed property.

Example. On January 1, 1971, X, an exempt trade association, acquires an office building for a down payment of $310,000 and an agreement to pay 10 percent of the income generated by the building for 10 years. Neither the sales price nor the amount which X is obligated to pay in the future is certain. The fair market value of the building on the date of acquisition is $600,000. The depreciation allowance for 1971 is $40,000. Unless X obtains the consent of the Commissioner to use another method, the unadjusted basis of the property is $600,000 (the fair market value of the property on the date of acquisition), and the initial acquisition indebtedness is $290,000 (fair market value of $600,000 less initial payment of $310,000). Under these circumstances, the average adjusted basis of the property for 1971 is $580,000, calculated as follows:

$$\frac{\text{initial fair market value} + (\text{initial fair market value} - \text{depreciation})}{2} = \frac{\$600,000 + (\$600,000 - \$40,000)}{2} = \$580,000$$

If no payment other than the initial payment is made in 1971, the average acquisition indebtedness for 1971 is $290,000. Thus, the debt/basis percentage for 1971 is 50 percent, calculated as follows:

$$\frac{\text{average acquisition indebtedness}}{\text{average adjusted basis}} = \frac{\$290,000}{\$580,000} = 50 \text{ percent}$$

(b) *Deductions*—(1) *Percentage of deductions taken into account.* Except as provided in subparagraphs (4) and (5) of this paragraph, there shall be allowed as a deduction with respect to each debt-financed property an amount determined by applying the debt/basis percentage to the sum of the deductions allowable under subparagraph (2) of this paragraph.

(2) *Deductions allowable.* The deductions allowable are those items allowed as deductions by chapter 1 of the Code which are directly connected with the debt-financed property or the income therefrom (including the dividends received deductions allowed by sections 243, 244, and 245), except that—

(i) The allowable deductions are subject to the modifications provided by section 512(b) on computation of the unrelated business taxable income, and

(ii) If the debt-financed property is of a character which is subject to the allowance for depreciation provided in section 167, such allowance shall be computed only by use of the straight-line method of depreciation.

(3) *Directly connected with.* To be "directly connected with" debt-financed property or the income therefrom, an item of deduction must

Reg. § 1.514(a)-1(b)(3)

have proximate and primary relationship to such property or the income therefrom. Expenses, depreciation, and similar items attributable solely to such property are proximately and primarily related to such property or the income therefrom, and therefore qualify for deduction, to the extent they meet the requirements of subparagraph (2) of this paragraph. Thus, for example, if the straight-line depreciation allowance for an office building is $10,000 a year, an organization would be allowed a deduction for depreciation of $10,000 if the entire building were debt-financed property. However, if only one-half of the building were treated as debt-financed property, then the depreciation allowed as a deduction would be $5,000. (See example (2) of § 1.514(b)-1(b)(1)(iii).)

(4) *Capital losses*—(i) *In general.* If the sale or exchange of debt-financed property results in a capital loss, the amount of such loss taken into account in the taxable year in which the loss arises shall be computed in accordance with paragraph (a)(1)(v) of this section. If, however, any portion of such capital loss not taken into account in such year may be carried back or carried over to another taxable year, the debt/basis percentage is not applied to determine what portion of such capital loss may be taken as a deduction in the year to which such capital loss is carried.

(ii) *Example.* This subparagraph is illustrated by the following example. For purposes of this example it is assumed that the property is debt-financed property.

Example. X, an exempt educational organization, owns securities which are capital assets and which it has held for more than six months. In 1972 X sells the securities at a loss of $20,000. The debt/basis percentage with respect to computing the gain (or loss) derived from the sale of the securities is 40 percent. Thus, X has sustained a capital loss of $8,000 (40% of $20,000) with respect to the sale of the securities. For 1972 and the preceding three taxable years X has no other capital transactions. Under these circumstances, the $8,000 of capital loss may be carried over to the succeeding five taxable years without further application of the debt/basis percentage.

(5) *Net operating loss*—(i) *In general.* If, after applying the debt/basis percentage to the income derived from debt-financed property and the deductions directly connected with such income, such deductions exceed such income, the organization has sustained a net operating loss for the taxable year. This amount may be carried back or carried over to other taxable years in accordance with section 512(b)(6). However, the debt/basis percentage shall not be applied in such

other years to determine the amounts that may be taken as a deduction in those years.

(ii) *Example.* This subparagraph may be illustrated by the following example. For purposes of this example it is assumed that the property is debt-financed property.

Example. During 1974, Y, an exempt organization, receives $20,000 of rent from a building which it owns. Y has no other unrelated business taxable income for 1974. For 1974 the deductions directly connected with this building are property taxes of $5,000, interest of $5,000 on the acquisition indebtedness, and salary of $15,000 to the manager of the building. The debt/basis percentage for 1974 with respect to the building is 50 percent. Under these circumstances, Y shall take into account in computing its unrelated business taxable income for 1974, $10,000 of income (50% of $20,000) and $12,500 (50% of $25,000) of the deductions directly connected with such income. Thus, for 1974 Y has sustained a net operating loss of $2,500 ($10,000 of income less $12,500 of deductions) which may be carried back or carried over to other taxable years without further application of the debt/basis percentage. [Reg. § 1.514(a)-1.]

☐ [T.D. 6301, 7-8-58. Amended by T.D. 7229, 12-20-72.]

[Reg. § 1.514(b)-1]

§ 1.514(b)-1. **Definition of debt-financed property.**—(a) *In general.* For purposes of section 514 and the regulations thereunder, the term "debt-financed property" means any property which is held to produce income (*e.g.*, rental real estate, tangible personal property, and corporate stock), and with respect to which there is an acquisition indebtedness (determined without regard to whether the property is debt-financed property) at any time during the taxable year. The term "income" is not limited to recurring income but applies as well to gains from the disposition of property. Consequently, when any property held to produce income by an organization which is not used in a manner described in section 514(b)(1)(A), (B), (C), or (D) is disposed of at a gain during the taxable year and there was an acquisition indebtedness outstanding with respect to such property at any time during the 12-month period preceding the date of disposition (even though such period covers more than one taxable year), such property is "debt-financed property". For example, assume that on June 1, 1972, an organization is given mortgaged, unimproved property which it does not use in a manner described in section 514(b)(1)(A), (B), (C), or (D) and that the organization assumes payment of the mortgage on such property. On July 15, 1972, the organization sells such property for a gain. Such property is "debt-financed property" and such gain is taxable as unrelated debt-financed income. See paragraph (a) of § 1.514(a)-1 for rules determining the amount of income or gain from debt-financed property which is treated as unrelated debt-financed income. See section 514(c) and § 1.514(c)-1 for rules relating to when there is acquisition indebtedness with respect to property.

(b) *Exceptions*—(1) *Property related to certain exempt purposes.* (i) To the extent that the use of any property is substantially related (aside from the need of the organization for income or funds or the use it makes of the profits derived) to the exercise or performance by an organization of its charitable, educational, or other purpose or function constituting its basis for exemption under section 501 (or, in the case of an organization described in section 511(a)(2)(B), to the exercise or performance of any purpose or function designated in section 501(c)(3)) such property shall not be treated as "debt-financed property." See § 1.513-1 for principles applicable in determining whether there is a substantial relationship to the exempt purpose of the organization.

(ii) If substantially all of any property is used in a manner described in subdivision (i) of this subparagraph, such property shall not be treated as "debt-financed property." In general the preceding sentence shall apply if 85 percent or more of the use of such property is devoted to the organization's exempt purpose. The extent to which property is used for a particular purpose shall be determined on the basis of all the facts and circumstances. These may include (where appropriate)—

(*a*) A comparison of the portion of time such property is used for exempt purposes with the total time such property is used,

(*b*) A comparison of the portion of such property that is used for exempt purposes with the portion of such property that is used for all purposes, or

(*c*) Both the comparisons described in (*a*) and (*b*) of this subdivision.

(iii) This subparagraph may be illustrated by the following examples. For purposes of these examples it is assumed that the indebtedness is acquisition indebtedness.

Example (1). W, an exempt organization, owns a computer with respect to which there is an outstanding principal indebtedness and which is used by W in the performance of its exempt purpose. W sells time for the use of the computer to M corporation on occasions when the computer is not in full-time use by W. W uses the computer in furtherance of its exempt purpose more than 85 percent of the time it is in use and M uses the computer less than 15 percent of the total operating time the computer is in use. In this situation, substantially all the use of the computer is related to the performance of W's exempt purpose. Therefore, no portion of the computer is treated as debt-financed property.

Example (2). X, an exempt college, owns a four story office building which has been purchased with borrowed funds. In 1971, the lower two stories of the building are used to house computers which are used by X for administrative purposes. The top two stories are rented to the public for purposes not described in section 514(b)(1)(A), (B), (C), or (D). The gross income derived by X from the building is $6,000, all of which is attributable to the rents paid by tenants. There are $2,000 of expenses, allocable equally to each use of the building. The average adjusted basis of the building for 1971 is $100,000, and the outstanding principal indebtedness throughout 1971 is $60,000. Thus, the average acquisition indebtedness for 1971 is $60,000. In accordance with subdivision (i) of this subparagraph, only the upper half of the building is debt-financed property. Consequently, only the rental income and the deductions directly connected with such income are to be taken into account in computing unrelated business taxable income. The portion of such amounts to be taken into account is determined by multiplying the $6,000 of rental income and $1,000 of deductions directly connected with such rental income by the debt/basis percentage. The debt/basis percentage is the ratio which the allocable part of the average acquisition indebtedness is of the allocable part of the average adjusted basis of the property, that is, the ratio which $30,000 (one-half of $60,000) bears to $50,000 (one-half of $100,000). Thus, the debt/basis percentage for 1971 is 60 percent (the ratio of $30,000 to $50,000). Under these circumstances, X shall include net rental income of $3,000 in its unrelated business taxable income for 1971, computed as follows:

Total rental income	$6,000
Deductions directly connected with rental income	1,000
Debt/basis percentage ($30,000/$50,000)	60 percent
Rental income treated as gross income from an unrelated trade or business (60 percent of $6,000)	$3,600

Reg. § 1.514(b)-1(b)(1)

Less the allowable portion of deductions directly connected with such income (60 percent of $1,000)	$ 600
Net rental income included by X in computing its unrelated business taxable income pursuant to section 514	$3,000

Example (3). Assume the facts as stated in example (2) except that on December 31, 1971, X sells the building and realizes a long-term capital gain of $10,000. This is X's only capital transaction for 1971. An allocable portion of this gain is subject to tax. This amount is determined by multiplying the gain related to the nonexempt use, $5,000 (one-half of $10,000), by the ratio which the allocable part of the highest acquisition indebtedness for the 12-month period preceding the date of sale, $30,000 (one-half of $60,000), is of the allocable part of the average adjusted basis, $50,000 (one- half of $100,000). Thus, the debt/basis percentage with respect to computing the gain (or loss) derived from the sale of the building is 60 percent (the ratio of $30,000 to $50,000). Consequently, $3,000 (60 percent of $5,000) is a net section 1201 gain (net capital gain for taxable years beginning after December 31, 1976). The portion of such gain which is taxable shall be determined in accordance with rules contained in subchapter P, chapter 1 of the Code (relating to capital gains and losses). See also section 511(d) and the regulations thereunder (relating to the minimum tax for tax preferences).

(2) *Property used in an unrelated trade or business*—(i) *In general.* To the extent that the gross income from any property is treated as income from the conduct of an unrelated trade or business, such property shall not be treated as "debt-financed property." However, any gain on the disposition of such property which is not included in the income of an unrelated trade or business by reason of section 512(b)(5) is includible as gross income derived "from or on account of debt-financed property" under paragraph (a)(1) of § 1.514(a)-1.

(ii) *Amounts specifically taxable under other provisions of the Code.* Section 514 does not apply to amounts which are otherwise included in the computation of unrelated business taxable income, such as rents from personal property includible pursuant to section 512(b)(3) or rents and interest from controlled organizations includible pursuant to section 512(b)(13). See paragraph (1)(5) of § 1.512(b)-1 for the rules determining the manner in which amounts are taken into account where such amounts may be included in the computation of unrelated business taxable income by operation of more than one provision of the Code.

(3) *Examples.* Subparagraphs (1) and (2) of this paragraph may be illustrated by the following examples. For purposes of these examples it is assumed that the indebtedness is acquisition indebtedness.

Example (1). X, an exempt scientific organization, owns a 10-story office building. During 1972, four stories are occupied by X's administrative offices, and the remaining six stories are rented to the public for purposes not described in section 514(b)(1)(A), (B), (C), or (D). On December 31, 1972, the building is sold and X realizes a long-term capital gain of $100,000. This is X's only capital transaction for 1972. The debt/basis percentage with respect to computing the gain (or loss) derived from the sale of the building is 30 percent. Since 40 percent of the building was used for X's exempt purpose, only 60 percent of the building is debt-financed property. Thus, only $60,000 of the gain (60 percent of $100,000) is subject to this section. Consequently, the amount of gain treated as unrelated debt-financed income is $18,000 ($60,000 multiplied by the debt/basis percentage of 30 percent). The portion of such $18,000 which is taxable shall be determined in accordance with the rules contained in subchapter P, chapter 1 of the Code. See also section 511(d) and the regulations thereunder (relating to the minimum tax for tax preferences).

Example (2). Y, an exempt organization, owns two properties, a restaurant and an office building. In 1972, all the space in the office building, except for the portion utilized by Y to house the administrative offices of the restaurant, is rented to the public for purposes not described in section 514(b)(1)(A), (B), (C), or (D). The average adjusted basis of the office building for 1972 is $2 million. The outstanding principal indebtedness throughout 1972 is $1 million. Thus, the highest acquisition indebtedness in the calendar year of 1972 is $1 million. It is determined that 30 percent of the space in the office building is used for the administrative functions engaged in by the employees of the organization with respect to the restaurant. Since the income attributable to the restaurant is attributable to the conduct of an unrelated trade or business, only 70 percent of the building is treated as debt-financed property for purposes of determining the portion of the rental income which is unrelated debt-financed income. On December 31, 1972, the office building is sold and Y realizes a long-term capital gain of $250,000. This is Y's only capital transaction for 1972. In accordance with subparagraph (2)(i) of this paragraph, all the gain derived from this sale is taken into account in computing the amount of such gain subject to tax. The portion of such gain which is taxable is determined by multiplying the $250,000 gain by the debt/basis percentage. The debt/basis percentage is the ratio which the highest acquisition indebtedness for the 12-month period preceding the date of sale, $1 million, is of the average adjusted basis, $2 million. Thus, the debt/basis percentage with respect to computing the gain (or loss) derived from the sale of the building is 50 percent (the ratio of $1 million to $2 million). Consequently, $125,000 (50 percent of $250,000) is a net section 1201 gain (net capital gain for taxable years beginning before December 31, 1976). The amount of such gain which is taxable shall be determined in accordance with the rules contained in subchapter P, chapter 1 of the Code. See also section 511(d) and the regulations thereunder.

Example (3). (a) Z, an exempt university, owns all the stock of M, a nonexempt corporation. During 1971 M leases from Z university a factory unrelated to Z's exempt purpose and a dormitory for the students of Z, for a total annual rent of $100,000: $80,000 for the factory and $20,000 for the dormitory. During 1971, M has $500,000 of taxable income, disregarding the rent paid to Z: $150,000 from the dormitory and $350,000 from the factory. The factory is subject to a mortgage of $150,000. Its average adjusted basis for 1971 is determined to be $300,000. Z's deductions for 1971 with respect to the leased property are $4,000 for the dormitory and $16,000 for the factory. In accordance with subdivision (ii) of this subparagraph, section 514 applies only to that portion of the rent which is excluded from the computation of unrelated business taxable income by operation of section 512(b)(3) and not included in such computation pursuant to section 512(b)(13). Since all the rent received by Z is derived from real property, section 512(b)(3) would exclude all such rent from computation of Z's unrelated business taxable income. However, 70 percent of the rent paid to Z with respect to the factory and 70 percent of the deductions directly connected with such rent shall be taken into account by Z in determining its unrelated business taxable income pursuant to section 512(b)(13), computed as follows:

M's taxable income (disregarding rent paid to Z)	$500,000
Less taxable income from dormitory	150,000
Excess taxable income	$350,000
Ratio ($350,000/$500,000)	7/10
Total rent paid to Z	$100,000
Total deductions ($4,000 + $16,000)	$ 20,000
Rental income treated under section 512(b)(13) as gross income from an unrelated trade or business (7/10 of $100,000)	$ 70,000
Less deductions directly connected with such income (7/10 of $20,000)	$ 14,000
Net rental income included by Z in computing its unrelated business taxable income pursuant to section 512(b)(13)	$ 56,000

(b) Since only that portion of the rent derived from the factory and the deductions directly connected with such rent not taken into account pursuant to section 512(b)(13) may be included in computing unrelated business taxable income by operation of section 514, only $10,000 ($80,000 minus $70,000) of rent and $2,000 ($16,000 minus $14,000) of deductions are so taken into account. The portion of such amounts to be taken into account is determined by multiplying the $10,000 of income and $2,000 of deductions by the debt/basis percentage. The debt/basis percentage is the ratio which the average acquisition indebtedness ($150,000) is of the average adjusted basis of the property ($300,000). Thus, the debt basis percentage for 1971 is 50 percent (the ratio of $150,000 to $300,000). Under these circumstances, Z shall include net rental income of $4,000 on its unrelated business taxable income for 1971, computed as follows:

Total rents	$ 10,000
Deductions directly connected with such rents	2,000
Debt/basis percentage ($150,000/$300,000)	50 percent
Rental income treated as gross income from an unrelated trade or business (50% of $10,000)	$ 5,000
Less the allowable portion of deductions directly connected with such income (50% of $2,000)	$ 1,000
Net rental income included by Z in computing its unrelated business taxable income pursuant to section 514	$ 4,000

Reg. § 1.514(b)-1(b)(3)

(4) *Property related to research activities.* To the extent that the gross income from any property is derived from research activities excluded from the tax on unrelated business income by paragraph (7), (8), or (9) of section 512(b), such property shall not be treated as "debt-financed property".

(5) *Property used in "thrift shops", etc.* To the extent that property is used in any trade or business which is excepted from the definition of "unrelated trade or business" by paragraph (1), (2), or (3) of section 513(a), such property shall not be treated as "debt-financed property".

(6) *Use by a related organization.* For purposes of subparagraphs (1), (4), or (5) of this paragraph, use of property by a related exempt organization (as defined in paragraph (c)(2)(ii) of this section) for a purpose described in such subparagraphs shall be taken into account in order to determine the extent to which such property is used for a purpose described in such subparagraphs.

(c) *Special rules*—(1) *Medical clinic.* Property is not debt-financed property if it is real property subject to a lease to a medical clinic, and the lease is entered into primarily for purposes which are substantially related (aside from the need of such organization for income or funds or the use it makes of the rents derived) to the exercise or performance by the lessor of its charitable, educational, or other purpose or function constituting the basis for its exemption under section 501. For example, assume that an exempt hospital leases all of its clinic space to an unincorporated association of physicians and surgeons who, by the provisions of the lease, agree to provide all of the hospital's out-patient medical and surgical services and to train all of the hospital's residents and interns. In this situation, the rents received by the hospital from this clinic are not to be trained as unrelated debt-financed income.

(2) *Related exempt uses*—(i) *In general.* Property owned by an exempt organization and used by a related exempt organization or by an exempt organization related to such related exempt organization shall not be treated as "debt-financed property" to the extent such property is used by either organization in furtherance of the purpose constituting the basis for its exemption under section 501. Furthermore, property shall not be treated as "debt-financed property" to the extent such property is used by a related exempt organization for a purpose described in paragraph (b)(4) or (5) of this section.

(ii) *Related organizations.* For purposes of subdivision (i) of this subparagraph, an exempt organization is related to another exempt organization only if—

(a) One organization is an exempt holding company described in section 501(c)(2) and the other organization receives the profits derived by such exempt holding company,

(b) One organization has control of the other organization within the meaning of paragraph (l)(4) of § 1.512(b)-1,

(c) More than 50 percent of the members of one organization are members of the other organization, or

(d) Each organization is a local organization which is directly affiliated with a common state, national, or international organization which is also exempt.

(iii) *Examples.* This subparagraph may be illustrated by the following examples. For purposes of these examples it is assumed that the indebtedness is acquisition indebtedness.

Example (1). M, an exempt trade association described in section 501(c)(6), leases 70 percent of the space of an office building for furtherance of its exempt purpose. The title to such building is held by N, an exempt holding company described in section 501(c)(2), which acquired title to the building with borrowed funds. The other 30 percent of the space in this office building is leased to L, a non-stock exempt trade association described in section 501(c)(6). L uses such office space in furtherance of its exempt purpose. The members of L's Board of Trustees serves for fixed terms and M's Board of Directors has the power to select all such members. N pays over to M all the profits it derives from the leasing of space in this building to M and L. Accordingly, M is "related" to N (as such term is defined in subdivision (ii)(a) of this subparagraph) and L is "related" to M (as such term is defined in subdivision (ii)(b) of this subparagraph). Under these circumstances, since all the available space in the building is leased to either an exempt organization related to the exempt organization holding title to the building or an exempt organization related to such related exempt organization, no portion of the building is treated as debt-financed property.

Example (2). W, an exempt labor union described in section 501(c)(5), owns a ten-story office building which has been purchased with borrowed funds. Five floors of the building are used by W in furtherance of its exempt purpose. Four of the other floors are rented to X which is an exempt voluntary employees' beneficiary association described in section 501(c)(9), operated for the benefit of W's members. X uses such office space in furtherance of its exempt purpose. 70

percent of the members of W are also members of X. Accordingly, X is "related" to W (as such term is defined in subdivision (ii)(c) of this subparagraph). The remaining floor of the building is rented to the general public for purposes not described in section 514(b)(1)(A), (B), (C), or (D). Under these circumstances, no portion of this building is treated as debt-financed property since more than 85 percent of the office space available in this building is used either by W or X, an exempt organization related to W, in furtherance of their respective exempt purpose. See paragraph (b)(1) of this section for rules relating to the use of property substantially related to an exempt purpose. See paragraph (b)(6) of this section for rules relating to uses by related exempt organizations.

Example (3). Assume the same facts as in example (2), except that W and X are each exempt local labor unions described in section 501(c)(5) having no common membership and are each affiliated with N, an exempt international labor union described in section 501(c)(5). Under these circumstances, no portion of this building is treated as debt-financed property since more than 85 percent of the office space available in this building is used either by W or X, an exempt organization related to W, in furtherance of their respective exempt purpose.

Example (4). Assume the same facts as in example (3), except that W and X are directly affiliated with different exempt international labor unions and that W and X are not otherwise affiliated with, or members of, a common exempt organization, other than an association of international labor unions. Under these circumstances, the portions of this building which are rented to X and to the general public are treated as debt-financed property since X is not related to W and W uses less than 85 percent of the building for its exempt purpose.

(3) *Life income contracts.* (i) Property shall not be treated as "debt-financed property" when—

(a) An individual transfers property to a trust or a fund subject to a contract providing that the income is to be paid to him or other individuals or both for a period of time not to exceed the life of such individual or individuals in a transaction in which the payments to the individual or individuals do not constitute the proceeds of a sale or exchange of the property so transferred, and

(b) The remainder interest is payable to an exempt organization described in section 501(c)(3).

(ii) Subdivision (i) of this subparagraph is illustrated by the following example.

Example. On January 1, 1967, A transfers property to X, an exempt organization described in section 501(c)(3), which immediately places the property in a fund. On January 1, 1971, A transfers additional property to X, which property is also placed in the fund. In exchange for each transfer, A receives income participation fund certificates which entitle him to a proportionate part of the fund's income for his life and for the life of another individual. None of the payments made by X are treated by the recipients as the proceeds of a sale or exchange of the property transferred. In this situation, none of the property received by X from A is treated as debt-financed property.

(d) *Property acquired for prospective exempt use*—(1) *Neighborhood land*—(i) *In general.* If an organization acquires real property for the principal purpose of using the land in the exercise or performance of its exempt purpose, commencing within 10 years of the time of acquisition, such property will not be treated as debt-financed property, so long as (a) such property is in the neighborhood of other property owned by the organization which is used in the performance of its exempt purpose, and (b) the organization does not abandon its intent to use the land in such a manner within the 10-year period. The rule expressed in this subdivision is hereinafter referred to as the "neighborhood land rule".

(ii) *"Neighborhood" defined.* Property shall be considered in the "neighborhood" of property owned and used by the organization in the performance of its exempt purpose if the acquired property is contiguous with the exempt purpose property or would be contiguous with such property except for the interposition of a road, street, railroad, stream, or similar property. If the acquired property is not contiguous with exempt function property, it may still be in the "neighborhood" of such property, but only if it is within one mile of such property and the facts and circumstances of the particular situation make the acquisition of contiguous property unreasonable. Some of the criteria to consider in determining this question include the availability of land and the intended future use of the land. For example, a university attempts to purchase land contiguous to its present campus but cannot do so because the owners either refuse to sell or ask unreasonable prices. The nearest land of sufficient size and utility is a block away from the campus. The university purchases such land. Under these circumstances, the contiguity requirement is unreasonable and the land purchased would be considered "neighborhood land".

Reg. § 1.514(b)-1(d)(1)

(iii) *Exception.* The neighborhood land rule shall not apply to any property after the expiration of 10 years from the date of acquisition. Further, the neighborhood land rule shall apply after the first 5 years of the 10-year period only if the organization establishes to the satisfaction of the Commissioner that future use of the acquired land in furtherance of the organization's exempt purpose before the expiration of the 10-year period is reasonably certain. In order to satisfy the Commissioner, the organization does not necessarily have to show binding contracts. However, it must at least have a definite plan detailing a specific improvement and a completion date, and some affirmative action toward the fulfillment of such a plan. This information shall be forwarded to the Commissioner of Internal Revenue, Washington, D.C. 20224, for a ruling at least ninety days before the end of the fifth year after acquisition of the land.

(2) *Actual use.* If the neighborhood land rule is inapplicable because—

(i) The acquired land is not in the neighborhood of other property used by the organization in performance of its exempt purpose, or

(ii) The organization (for the period after the first 5 years of the 10-year period) is unable to establish to the satisfaction of the Commissioner that the use of the acquired land for its exempt purposes within the 10-year period is reasonably certain,

but the land is actually used by the organization in furtherance of its exempt purpose within the 10-year period, such property (subject to the provisions of subparagraph (4) of this paragraph) shall not be treated as debt-financed property for any period prior to such conversion.

(3) *Limitations*—(i) *Demolition or removal required.* (*a*) Subparagraphs (1) and (2) of this paragraph shall apply with respect to any structure on the land when acquired by the organization, or to the land occupied by the structure, only so long as the intended future use of the land in furtherance of the organization's exempt purpose requires that the structure be demolished or removed in order to use the land in such a manner. Thus, during the first five years after acquisition (and for subsequent years if there is a favorable ruling in accordance with subparagraph (1)(iii) of this paragraph) improved property is not debt-financed so long as the organization does not abandon its intent to demolish the existing structures and use the land in furtherance of its exempt purpose. Furthermore, if there is an actual demolition of such structures, the use made of the land need not be the one originally intended. Therefore, the actual use requirement of this subdivision may be satisfied by using the land in any manner which furthers the exempt purpose of the organization.

(*b*) Subdivision (i)(*a*) of this subparagraph may be illustrated by the following examples. For purposes of the following examples it is assumed that but for the application of the neighborhood land rule such property would be debt-financed property.

Example (1). An exempt university acquires a contiguous tract of land on which there is an apartment building. The university intends to demolish the apartment building and build classrooms and does not abandon this intent during the first four years after acquisition. In the fifth year after acquisition it abandons the intent to demolish and sells the apartment building. Under these circumstances, such property is not debt-financed property for the first four years after acquisition even though there was no eventual demolition or use made of such land in furtherance of the university's exempt purpose. However, such property is debt-financed property as of the time in the fifth year that the intent to demolish the building is abandoned and any gain on the sale of the property is subject to section 514.

Example (2). Assume the facts as stated in Example (1) except that the university did not abandon its intent to demolish the existing building and construct a classroom building until the eighth year after acquisition when it sells the property. Assume further that the university did not receive a favorable ruling in accordance with subparagraph (1)(iii) of this paragraph. Under these circumstances, the building is debt-financed property for the sixth, seventh, and eighth years. It is not, however, treated as debt-financed property for the first five years after acquisition.

Example (3). Assume the facts as stated in Example (2) except that the university received a favorable ruling in accordance with subparagraph (1)(iii) of this paragraph. Under these circumstances, the building is not debt-financed property for the first seven years after acquisition. It only becomes debt-financed property as of the time in the eighth year when the university abandoned its intent to demolish the existing structure.

Example (4). (*1*) Assume that a university acquired a contiguous tract of land containing an office building for the principal purpose of demolishing the office building and building a modern dormitory. Five years later the dormitory has not been constructed, and the university has failed to satisfy the Commissioner that the office building will be demolished and the land will be used in furtherance of its exempt purpose (and

Reg. § 1.514(b)-1(d)(2)

consequently has failed to obtain a favorable ruling under subparagraph (1)(iii) of this paragraph). In the ninth taxable year after acquisition the university converts the office building into an administration building. Under these circumstances, during the sixth, seventh, and eighth years after acquisition, the office building is treated as debt-financed property because the office building was not demolished or removed. Therefore, the income derived from such property during these years shall be subject to the tax on unrelated business income.

(*2*) Assume that instead of converting the office building to an administration building, the university demolishes the office building in the ninth taxable year after acquisition and then constructs a new administration building. Under these circumstances, the land would not be considered debt-financed property for any period following the acquisition, and the university would be entitled to a refund of taxes paid on the income derived from such property for the sixth through eighth taxable years after the acquisition in accordance with subparagraph (4) of this paragraph.

(ii) *Subsequent construction.* Subparagraphs (1) and (2) of this paragraph do not apply to structures erected on the land after the acquisition of the land.

(iii) *Property subject to business lease.* Subparagraphs (1) and (2) of this paragraph do not apply to property subject to a lease which is a business lease (as defined in § 1.514(f)-1) whether the organization acquired the property subject to the lease or whether it executed the lease subsequent to acquisition. If only a portion of the real property is subject to a lease, paragraph (c) of § 1.514(f)-1 applies in determining whether such lease is a business lease.

(4) *Refund of taxes.* (i) If an organization has not satisfied the actual use condition of subparagraph (2) of this paragraph or paragraph (e)(3) of this section before the date prescribed by law (including extensions) for filing the return for the taxable year, the tax for such year shall be computed without regard to the application of such actual use condition. However, if—

(*a*) A credit or refund of any overpayment of taxes is allowable for a prior taxable year as a result of the satisfaction of such actual use condition, and

(*b*) Such credit or refund is prevented by the operation of any law or rule of law (other than chapter 74, relating to closing agreements and compromises), such credit or refund may nevertheless be allowed or made, if a claim is filed within 1 year after the close of the taxable year in which such actual use condition is satisfied. For a special rule with respect to the payment of interest at the rate of 4 percent per annum, see section 514(b)(3)(D), prior to its amendment by section 7(b) of the Act of January 3, 1975 (Pub. L. 93-625, 88 Stat. 2115).

(ii) This subparagraph may be illustrated by the following example. For purposes of this example it is assumed that but for the neighborhood land rule such property would be debt-financed property.

Example. Y, a calendar year exempt organization, acquires real property in January 1970, which is contiguous with all the property used by Y in furtherance of its exempt purpose. However, Y does not satisfy the Commissioner by January 1975, that the existing structure will be demolished and the land will be used in furtherance of its exempt purpose. In accordance with this subparagraph, from 1975 until the property is converted to an exempt use, the income derived from such property shall be subject to the tax on unrelated business income. During July 1979, Y demolishes the existing structure on the land and begins using the land in furtherance of its exempt purpose. At this time Y may file claims for refund for the open years 1976 through 1978. Further, in accordance with this subparagraph, Y may also file a claim for refund for 1975, even though a claim for such taxable year may be barred by the statute of limitations, provided such claim is filed before the close of 1980.

(e) *Churches*—(1) *In general.* If a church or association or convention of churches acquires real property, for the principal purpose of using the land in the exercise or performance of its exempt purpose, commencing within 15 years of the time of acquisition, such property shall not be treated as debt-financed property so long as the organization does not abandon its intent to use the land in such a manner within the 15-year period.

(2) *Exception.* This paragraph shall not apply to any property after the expiration of the 15-year period. Further, this paragraph shall apply after the first 5 years of the 15-year period only if the church or association or convention of churches establishes to the satisfaction of the Commissioner that use of the acquired land in furtherance of the organization's exempt purpose before the expiration of the 15-year period is reasonably certain. For purposes of the preceding sentence, the rules contained in paragraph (d)(1)(iii) of this section with respect to satisfying the Commissioner that the exempt organization intends to use the land within the prescribed time in furtherance of its exempt purpose shall apply.

(3) *Actual use.* If the church or association or convention of churches for the period after the

first 5 years of the 15-year period is unable to establish to the satisfaction of the Commissioner that the use of the acquired land for its exempt purpose within the 15-year period is reasonably certain, but such land is in fact converted to an exempt use within the 15-year period, the land (subject to the provisions of paragraph (d)(4) of this section) shall not be treated as debt-financed property for any period prior to such conversion.

(4) *Limitations.* The limitations stated in paragraph (d)(3)(i) and (ii) of this section shall similarly apply to the rules contained in this paragraph. [Reg. § 1.514(b)-1.]

☐ [T.D. 6301, 7-8-58. Amended by T.D. 7229, 12-20-72, by T.D. 7384, 10-21-75, by T.D. 7632, 7-17-79, and by T.D. 7728, 10-31-80.]

[Reg. § 1.514(c)-1]

§ 1.514(c)-1. **Acquisition indebtedness.**—(a) *In general*—(1) *Definition of acquisition indebtedness.* For purposes of section 514 and the regulations thereunder, the term "acquisition indebtedness" means, with respect to any debt-financed property, the outstanding amount of—

(i) The principal indebtedness incurred by the organization in acquiring or improving such property;

(ii) The principal indebtedness incurred before the acquisition or improvement of such property if such indebtedness would not have been incurred but for such acquisition or improvement; and

(iii) The principal indebtedness incurred after the acquisition or improvement of such property if such indebtedness would not have been incurred but for such acquisition or improvement and the incurrence of such indebtedness was reasonably foreseeable at the time of such acquisition or improvement.

Whether the incurrence of an indebtedness is reasonably foreseeable depends upon the facts and circumstances of each situation. The fact that an organization did not actually foresee the need for the incurrence of an indebtedness prior to the acquisition or improvement does not necessarily mean that the subsequent incurrence of indebtedness was not reasonably foreseeable.

(2) *Examples.* The application of subparagraph (1) of this paragraph may be illustrated by the following examples:

Example (1). X, an exempt organization, pledges some of its investment securities with a bank for a loan and uses the proceeds of such loan to purchase an office building which it leases to the public for purposes other than those described in section 514(b)(1)(A), (B), (C), or (D). The outstanding principal indebtedness with respect to the loan constitutes acquisition indebtedness incurred prior to the acquisition which would not have been incurred but for such acquisition.

Example (2). Y, an exempt scientific organization, mortgages its laboratory to replace working capital used in remodeling an office building which Y rents to an insurance company for purposes not described in section 514(b)(1)(A), (B), (C), or (D). The indebtedness is "acquisition indebtedness" since such indebtedness, though incurred subsequent to the improvement of the office building, would not have been incurred but for such improvement, and the indebtedness was reasonably foreseeable when, to make such improvement, Y reduced its working capital below the amount necessary to continue current operations.

Example (3). (a) U, an exempt private preparatory school, as its sole educational facility owns a classroom building which no longer meets the needs of U's students. In 1971, U sells this building for $3 million to Y, a corporation which it does not control. U receives $1 million as a down payment from Y and takes back a purchase money mortgage of $2 million which bears interest at 10 percent per annum. At the time U became the mortgagee of the $2 million purchase money mortgage, U realized that it would have to construct a new classroom building and knew that it would have to incur an indebtedness in the construction of the new classroom building. In 1972, U builds a new classroom building for a cost of $4 million. In connection with the construction of this building, U borrows $2.5 million from X Bank pursuant to a deed of trust bearing interest at 6 percent per annum. Under these circumstances, $2 million of the $2.5 million borrowed to finance construction of the new classroom building would not have been borrowed but for the retention of the $2 million purchase money mortgage. Since such indebtedness was reasonably foreseeable, $2 million of the $2.5 million borrowed to finance the construction of the new classroom building is acquisition indebtedness with respect to the purchase money mortgage and the purchase money mortgage is debt-financed property.

(*b*) In 1972, U receives $200,000 in interest from Y (10% of $2 million) and makes a $150,000 interest payment to X (6% of $2.5 million). In addition, assume that for 1972 the debt/basis percentage is 100 percent ($2 million/$2 million). Accordingly, all the interest and all the deductions directly connected with such interest income are to be taken into account in computing unrelated business taxable income. Thus, $200,000 of interest income and $120,000 ($150,000 × $2 million/$2.5 million) of deductions directly connected with such interest income (6% of the $2 million of the deed of trust treated as acquisition indebtedness) are taken into account. Under these circumstances, U shall include net interest income of $80,000 ($200,000 of income less $120,000 of deductions directly connected with such income) in its unrelated business taxable income for 1972.

Example (4). In 1972 X, an exempt organization, forms a partnership with A and B. The partnership agreement provides that all three partners shall share equally in the profits of the partnership, shall each invest $3 million, and that X shall be a limited partner. X invests $1 million of its own funds in the partnership and $2 million of borrowed funds. The partnership purchases as its sole asset an office building which is leased to the general public for purposes other than those described in section 514(b)(1)(A), (B), (C), or (D). The office building cost the partnership $24 million of which $15 million is borrowed from Y Bank. This loan is secured by a mortgage on the entire office building. By agreement with Y Bank, X is held not to be personally liable for payment of such mortgage. By reason of section 702(b) the character of any item realized by the partnership and included in the partner's distributive share shall be determined as if the partner realized such item directly from the source from which it was realized by the partnership and in the same manner. Therefore, a portion of X's income from the building is debt-financed income. Under these circumstances, since both the $2 million indebtedness incurred by X in acquiring its partnership interest and $5 million, the allocable portion of the partnership's indebtedness incurred with respect to acquiring the office building which is attributable to X in computing the debt/basis percentage (one-third of $15 million), were incurred in acquiring income-producing property, X has acquisition indebtedness of $7 million ($2 million plus $5 million). Similarly, the allocable portion of the partnership's adjusted basis in the office building which is attributable to X in computing the debt/basis percentage is $8 million (one-third of $24 million). Assuming no payment with respect to either indebtedness and no adjustments to basis in 1972, X's average acquisition indebtedness is $7 million and X's average adjusted basis is $8 million for such year. Therefore, X's debt/basis percentage with respect to its share of the partnership income for 1972 is 87.5% ($7 million/$8 million).

(3) *Changes in use of property.* Since property used in a manner described in section 514(b)(1)(A), (B), (C), and (D) is not considered debt-financed property, indebtedness with respect to such property is not acquisition indebtedness. However, if an organization converts such property to a use which is not described in section 514(b)(1)(A), (B), (C), or (D) and such property is otherwise treated as debt-financed property, the outstanding principal indebtedness with respect to such property will thereafter be treated as "acquisition indebtedness". For example, assume that in 1971 a university borrows funds to acquire an apartment building as housing for married students. In 1974, the university rents the apartment building to the public for purposes not described in section 514(b)(1)(A), (B), (C), or (D). The outstanding principal indebtedness is "acquisition indebtedness" as of the time in 1974 when the building is first rented to the public.

(4) *Continued indebtedness.* If—

(i) An organization sells or exchanges property, subject to an indebtedness (incurred in a manner described in subparagraph (1) of this paragraph),

(ii) Acquires another property without retiring the indebtedness, and

(iii) The newly acquired property is otherwise treated as debt-financed property, the outstanding principal indebtedness with respect to the acquired property is "acquisition indebtedness", even though the original property was not debt-financed property. For example, to house its administrative offices, an exempt organization purchases a building with $600,000 of its own funds and $400,000 of borrowed funds secured by a pledge of its securities. It later sells the building for $1,000,000 without redeeming the pledge. It uses these proceeds to purchase an apartment building which it rents to the public for purposes not described in section 514(b)(1)(A), (B), (C), or (D). The indebtedness of $400,000 is "acquisition indebtedness" with respect to the apartment building even though the office building was not debt-financed property.

(5) *Indebtedness incurred before June 28, 1966.* For taxable years beginning before January 1, 1972, "acquisition indebtedness" does not include any indebtedness incurred before June 28, 1966, unless such indebtedness was incurred on rental real property subject to a business lease and such indebtedness constituted business lease indebtedness. Furthermore, in the case of a church or convention or association of churches, the preceding sentence applies without regard to whether the indebtedness incurred before June 28, 1966, constituted business lease indebtedness.

(b) *Property acquired subject to lien*—(1) *Mortgages.* Except as provided in subparagraphs (3) and (4) of this paragraph, whenever property is acquired subject to a mortgage, the amount of

Reg. § 1.514(c)-1(b)(1)

the outstanding principal indebtedness secured by such mortgage is treated as "acquisition indebtedness" with respect to such property even though the organization did not assume or agree to pay such indebtedness. The preceding sentence applies whether property is acquired by purchase, gift, devise, bequest, or any other means. Thus, for example, assume that an exempt organization pays $50,000 for real property valued at $150,000 and subject to a $100,000 mortgage. The $100,000 of outstanding principal indebtedness is "acquisition indebtedness" just as though the organization had borrowed $100,000 to buy the property.

(2) *Other liens.* For purposes of this paragraph, liens similar to mortgages shall be treated as mortgages. A lien is similar to a mortgage if title to property is encumbered by the lien for the benefit of a creditor. However, in the case where State law provides that a tax lien attaches to property prior to the time when such lien becomes due and payable, such lien shall not be treated as similar to a mortgage until after it has become due and payable and the organization has had an opportunity to pay such lien in accordance with State law. Liens similar to mortgages include (but are not limited to):

(i) Deeds of trust,

(ii) Conditional sales contracts,

(iii) Chattel mortgages,

(iv) Security interests under the Uniform Commercial Code,

(v) Pledges,

(vi) Agreements to hold title in escrow, and

(vii) Tax liens (other than those described in the third sentence of this subparagraph).

(3) *Certain encumbered property acquired by gift, bequest or devise*—(i) *Bequest or devise.* Where property subject to a mortgage is acquired by an organization by bequest or devise, the outstanding principal indebtedness secured by such mortgage is not to be treated as "acquisition indebtedness" during the 10-year period following the date of acquisition. For purposes of the preceding sentence, the date of acquisition is the date the organization receives the property.

(ii) *Gifts.* If an organization acquires property by gift subject to a mortgage, the outstanding principal indebtedness secured by such mortgage shall not be treated as "acquisition indebtedness" during the 10-year period following the date of such gift, so long as—

(a) The mortgage was placed on the property more than 5 years before the date of the gift, and

(b) The property was held by the donor for more than 5 years before the date of the gift.

For purposes of the preceding sentence, the date of the gift is the date the organization receives the property.

(iii) *Limitation.* Subdivisions (i) and (ii) of this subparagraph shall not apply if—

(a) The organization assumes and agrees to pay all or any part of the indebtedness secured by the mortgage, or

(b) The organization makes any payment for the equity owned by the decedent or the donor in the property (other than a payment pursuant to an annuity excluded from the definition of "acquisition indebtedness" by paragraph (e) of this section).

Whether an organization has assumed and agreed to pay all or any part of an indebtedness in order to acquire the property shall be determined by the facts and circumstances of each situation.

(iv) *Examples.* The application of this subparagraph may be illustrated by the following examples:

Example (1). A dies on January 1, 1971. His will devises an office building subject to a mortgage to U, an exempt organization described in section 501(c)(3). U does not at any time assume the mortgage. For the period 1971 through 1980, the outstanding principal indebtedness secured by the mortgage is not acquisition indebtedness. However, after December 31, 1980, the outstanding principal indebtedness secured by the mortgage is acquisition indebtedness if the building is otherwise treated as debt-financed property.

Example (2). Assume the facts as stated in example (1) except that on January 1, 1975, U assumes the mortgage. After January 1, 1975, the outstanding principal indebtedness secured by the mortgage is acquisition indebtedness if the building is otherwise treated as debt-financed property.

(4) *Bargain sale before October 9, 1969.* Where property subject to a mortgage is acquired by an organization before October 9, 1969, the outstanding principal indebtedness secured by such mortgage is not to be treated as "acquisition indebtedness" during the 10-year period following the date of acquisition if—

(i) The mortgage was placed on the property more than 5 years before the purchase, and

(ii) The organization paid the seller a total amount no greater than the amount of the seller's cost (including attorney's fees) directly related to the transfer of such property to the organization, but in any event no more than 10 percent of the value of the seller's equity in the property transferred.

Reg. § 1.514(c)-1(b)(2)

(c) *Extension of obligations*—(1) *In general.* An extension, renewal, or refinancing of an obligation evidencing a pre-existing indebtedness is considered as a continuation of the old indebtedness to the extent the outstanding principal amount thereof is not increased. Where the principal amount of the modified obligation exceeds the outstanding principal amount of the pre-existing indebtedness, the excess shall be treated as a separate indebtedness for purposes of section 514 and the regulations thereunder. For example, if the interest rate on an obligation incurred prior to June 28, 1966, by an exempt university is modified subsequent to such date, the modified obligation shall be deemed to have been incurred prior to June 28, 1966. Thus, such an indebtedness will not be treated as acquisition indebtedness for taxable years beginning before January 1, 1972, unless the original indebtedness was business lease indebtedness (as defined in § 1.514(g)-1).

(2) *Extension or renewal.* In general, any modification or substitution of the terms of an obligation by the organization shall be an extension or renewal of the original obligation, rather than the creation of a new indebtedness to the extent that the outstanding principal amount of the indebtedness is not increased. The following are examples of acts which result in the extension or renewal of an obligation:

(i) Substitution of liens to secure the obligation;

(ii) Substitution of obligees, whether or not with the consent of the organization;

(iii) Renewal, extension or acceleration of the payment terms of the obligation; and

(iv) Addition, deletion, or substitution of sureties or other primary or secondary obligors.

(3) *Allocation.* In cases where the outstanding principal amount of the modified obligation exceeds the outstanding principal amount of the unmodified obligation and only a portion of such refinanced indebtedness is to be treated as acquisition indebtedness, payments on the amount of the refinanced indebtedness shall be apportioned pro-rata between the amount of the pre-existing indebtedness and the excess amount. For example, assume that an organization has an outstanding principal indebtedness of $500,000 which is treated as acquisition indebtedness. It borrows another $100,000 which is not acquisition indebtedness, from the same lending institution and gives the lender a $600,000 note for its total obligation. In this situation, a payment of $60,000 on the amount of the total obligation would reduce the acquisition indebtedness by $50,000 and the excess indebtedness by $10,000.

(d) *Indebtedness incurred in performing exempt purpose.* "Acquisition indebtedness" does not include the incurrence of an indebtedness inherent in the performance or exercise of the purpose or function constituting the basis of the organization's exemption. Thus, "acquisition indebtedness" does not include the indebtedness incurred by an exempt credit union in accepting deposits from its members or the obligation incurred by an exempt organization in accepting payments from its members to provide such members with insurance, retirement or other similar benefits.

(e) *Annuities*—(1) *Requirements.* The obligation to make payment of an annuity is not "acquisition indebtedness" if the annuity meets all the following requirements—

(i) It must be the sole consideration (other than a mortgage to which paragraph (b)(3) of this section applies) issued in exchange for the property acquired;

(ii) At the time of the exchange, the present value of the annuity (determined in accordance with subparagraph (2) of this paragraph) must be less than 90 percent of the value of the prior owner's equity in the property received in the exchange;

(iii) The annuity must be payable over the life of one individual in being at the time the annuity is issued, or over the lives of two individuals in being at such time; and

(iv) The annuity must be payable under a contract which—

(*a*) Does not guarantee a minimum number of payments or specify a maximum number of payments, and

(*b*) Does not provide for any adjustment of the amount of the annuity payments by reference to the income received from the transferred property or any other property.

(2) *Valuation.* For purposes of this paragraph, the value of an annuity at the time of exchange shall be computed in accordance with section 1011(b), § 1.1011-2(e)(1)(iii)(*b*)(*2*), and section 3 of Rev. Rul. 62-216, C.B. 1962-2, 30.

(3) *Examples.* The application of this paragraph may be illustrated by the following examples. For purposes of these examples it is assumed that the property transferred is used for purposes other than those described in section 514(b)(1)(A), (B), (C), or (D).

Example (1). On January 1, 1971, X, an exempt organization, receives property valued at $100,000 from donor A, a male aged 60. In return X promises to pay A $6,000 a year for the rest of A's life, with neither a minimum nor maximum

Reg. § 1.514(c)-1(e)(3)

number of payments specified. The annuity is payable on December 31 of each year. The amounts paid under the annuity are not dependent on the income derived from the property transferred to X. The present value of this annuity is $81,156, determined in accordance with Table A of Rev. Rul. 62-216. Since the value of the annuity is less than 90 percent of A's equity in the property transferred and the annuity meets all the other requirements of subparagraph (1) of this paragraph, the obligation to make annuity payments is not acquisition indebtedness.

Example (2). On January 1, 1971, B transfers an office building to Y, an exempt university, subject to a mortgage. In return Y agrees to pay B $5,000 a year for the rest of his life, with neither a minimum nor maximum number of payments specified. The amounts paid under the annuity are not dependent on the income derived from the property transferred to Y. It is determined that the actual value of the annuity is less than 90 percent of the value of B's equity in the property transferred. Y does not assume the mortgage. For the taxable years 1971 through 1980, the outstanding principal indebtedness secured by the mortgage is not treated as acquisition indebtedness. Further, Y's obligation to make annuity payments to B never constitutes acquisition indebtedness.

(f) *Certain federal financing.* "Acquisition indebtedness" does not include an obligation to finance the purchase, rehabilitation, or construction of housing for low and moderate income persons to the extent that it is insured by the Federal Housing Administration. Thus, for example, to the extent that an obligation is insured by the Federal Housing Administration under section 221(d)(3) (12 U.S.C. 17151(d)(3)) or section 236 (12 U.S.C. 1715z-1) of title II of the National Housing Act, as amended, the obligation is not "acquisition indebtedness".

(g) *Certain obligations of charitable remainder trusts.* For purposes of section 664(c) and § 1.664-1(c), a charitable remainder trust (as defined in § 1.664-1(a)(1)(iii)(*a*)) does not incur "acquisition indebtedness" when the sole consideration it is required to pay in exchange for unencumbered property is an "annuity amount" or a "unitrust amount" (as defined in § 1.664-1(a)(1)(iii)(*b*) and (*c*)). [Reg. § 1.514(c)-1.]

□ [*T.D.* 6301, 7-8-58. Amended by *T.D.* 6972, 9-11-68; *T.D.* 7229, 12-20-72 and *T.D.* 7698, 5-20-80.]

[Reg. § 1.514(c)-2]

§ 1.514(c)-2. Permitted allocations under section 514(c)(9)(E).—(a) *Table of contents.* This paragraph contains a listing of the major headings of this § 1.514(c)-2.

(a) Table of contents.

(b) Application of section 514(c)(9)(E), relating to debt-financed real property held by partnerships.

(1) In general.

(i) The fractions rule.

(ii) Substantial economic effect.

(2) Manner in which fractions rule is applied.

(i) In general.

(ii) Subsequent changes.

(c) General definitions.

(1) Overall partnership income and loss.

(i) Items taken into account in determining overall partnership income and loss.

(ii) Guaranteed payments to qualified organizations.

(2) Fractions rule percentage.

(3) Definitions of certain terms by cross reference to partnership regulations.

(4) Example.

(d) Exclusion of reasonable preferred returns and guaranteed payments.

(1) Overview.

(2) Preferred returns.

(3) Guaranteed payments.

(4) Reasonable amount.

(i) In general.

(ii) Safe harbor.

(5) Unreturned capital.

(i) In general.

(ii) Return of capital.

(6) Timing rules.

(i) Limitation on allocations of income with respect to reasonable preferred returns for capital.

(ii) Reasonable guaranteed payments may be deducted only when paid in cash.

(7) Examples.

(e) Chargebacks and offsets.

(1) In general.

(2) Disproportionate allocations.

(i) In general.

(ii) Limitation on chargebacks of partial allocations.

(3) Minimum gain chargebacks attributable to nonrecourse deductions.

(4) Minimum gain chargebacks attributable to distribution of nonrecourse debt proceeds.

(i) Chargebacks disregarded until allocations made.

(ii) Certain minimum gain chargebacks related to returns of capital.

(5) Examples.

(f) Exclusion of reasonable partner-specific items of deduction or loss.

(g) Exclusion of unlikely losses and deductions.

(h) Provisions preventing deficit capital account balances.

(i) [Reserved].

(j) Exception for partner nonrecourse deductions.

(1) Partner nonrecourse deductions disregarded until actually allocated.

(2) Disproportionate allocation of partner nonrecourse deductions to a qualified organization.

(k) Special rules.

(1) Changes in partnership allocations arising from a change in the partners' interests.

(2) De minimis interest rule.

(i) In general.

(ii) Example.

(3) De minimis allocations disregarded.

(4) Anti-abuse rule.

(l) [Reserved].

(m) Tiered partnerships.

(1) In general.

(2) Examples.

(n) Effective date.

(1) In general.

(2) General effective date of the regulations.

(3) Periods after June 24, 1990, and prior to December 30, 1992.

(4) Periods prior to the issuance of Notice 90-41.

(5) Material modifications to partnership agreements.

(b) *Application of section 514(c)(9)(E), relating to debt-financed real property held by partnerships*—(1) *In general.* This § 1.514(c)-2 provides rules governing the application of section 514(c)(9)(E). To comply with section 514(c)(9)(E), the following two requirements must be met:

(i) *The fractions rule.* The allocation of items to a partner that is a qualified organization cannot result in that partner having a percentage share of overall partnership income for any partnership taxable year greater than that partner's fractions rule percentage (as defined in paragraph (c)(2) of this section).

(ii) *Substantial economic effect.* Each partnership allocation must have substantial economic effect. However, allocations that cannot have economic effect must be deemed to be in accordance with the partners' interests in the partnership pursuant to § 1.704-1(b)(4), or (if § 1.704-1(b)(4) does not provide a method for deeming the allocations to be in accordance with the partners' interests in the partnership) must otherwise comply with the requirements of § 1.704-1(b)(4). Allocations attributable to nonrecourse liabilities or partner nonrecourse debt must comply with the requirements of § 1.704-2(e) or § 1.704-2(i).

(2) *Manner in which fractions rule is applied*—(i) *In general.* A partnership must satisfy the fractions rule both on a prospective basis and on an actual basis for each taxable year of the partnership, commencing with the first taxable year of the partnership in which the partnership holds debt-financed real property and has a qualified organization as a partner. Generally, a partnership does not qualify for the unrelated business income tax exception provided by section 514(c)(9)(A) for any taxable year of its existence unless it satisfies the fractions rule for every year the fractions rule applies. However, if an actual allocation described in paragraph (e)(4), (h), (j)(2), or (m)(1)(ii) of this section (regarding certain allocations that are disregarded or not taken into account for purposes of the fractions rule until an actual allocation is made) causes the partnership to violate the fractions rule, the partnership ordinarily is treated as violating the fractions rule only for the taxable year of the actual allocation and subsequent taxable years. For purposes of applying the fractions rule, the term *partnership agreement* is defined in accordance with § 1.704-1(b)(2)(ii)(h), and informal understandings are considered part of the partnership agreement in appropriate circumstances. See paragraph (k) of this section for rules relating to changes in the partners' interests and *de minimis* exceptions to the fractions rule.

(ii) *Subsequent changes.* A subsequent change to a partnership agreement that causes the partnership to violate the fractions rule ordinarily causes the partnership's income to fail the exception provided by section 514(c)(9)(A) only for the taxable year of the change and subsequent taxable years.

Reg. § 1.514(c)-2(b)(2)

(c) *General definitions*—(1) *Overall partnership income and loss.* Overall partnership income is the amount by which the aggregate items of partnership income and gain for the taxable year exceed the aggregate items of partnership loss and deduction for the year. Overall partnership loss is the amount by which the aggregate items of partnership loss and deduction for the taxable year exceed the aggregate items of partnership income and gain for the year.

(i) *Items taken into account in determining overall partnership income and loss.* Except as otherwise provided in this section, the partnership items that are included in computing overall partnership income or loss are those items of income, gain, loss, and deduction (including expenditures described in section 705(a)(2)(B)) that increase or decrease the partners' capital accounts under § 1.704-1(b)(2)(iv). Tax items allocable pursuant to section 704(c) or § 1.704-1(b)(2)(iv)(*f*)(*4*) are not included in computing overall partnership income or loss. Nonetheless, allocations pursuant to section 704(c) or § 1.704-1(b)(2)(iv)(*f*)(*4*) may be relevant in determining that this section is being applied in a manner that is inconsistent with the fractions rule. See paragraph (k)(4) of this section.

(ii) *Guaranteed payments to qualified organizations.* Except to the extent otherwise provided in paragraph (d) of this section—

(A) A guaranteed payment to a qualified organization is not treated as an item of partnership loss or deduction in computing overall partnership income or loss; and

(B) Income that a qualified organization may receive or accrue with respect to a guaranteed payment is treated as an allocable share of overall partnership income or loss for purposes of the fractions rule.

(2) *Fractions rule percentage.* A qualified organization's fractions rule percentage is that partner's percentage share of overall partnership loss for the partnership taxable year for which that partner's percentage share of overall partnership loss will be the smallest.

(3) *Definitions of certain terms by cross reference to partnership regulations. Minimum gain chargeback, nonrecourse deduction, nonrecourse liability, partner nonrecourse debt, partner nonrecourse debt minimum gain, partner nonrecourse debt minimum gain chargeback, partner nonrecourse deduction,* and *partnership minimum gain* have the meanings provided in § 1.704-2.

(4) *Example.* The following example illustrates the provisions of this paragraph (c).

Example. Computation of overall partnership income and loss for a taxable year. (i) Taxable corporation TP and qualified organization QO form a partnership to own and operate encumbered real property. Under the partnership agreement, all items of income, gain, loss, deduction, and credit are allocated 50 percent to TP and 50 percent to QO. Neither partner is entitled to a preferred return. However, the partnership agreement provides for a $900 guaranteed payment for services to QO in each of the partnership's first two taxable years. No part of the guaranteed payments qualify as a reasonable guaranteed payment under paragraph (d) of this section.

(ii) The partnership violates the fractions rule. Due to the existence of the guaranteed payment, QO's percentage share of any overall partnership income in the first two years will exceed QO's fractions rule percentage. For example, the partnership might have bottom-line net income of $5,100 in its first taxable year that is comprised of $10,000 of rental income, $4,000 of salary expense, and the $900 guaranteed payment to QO. The guaranteed payment would not be treated as an item of deduction in computing overall partnership income or loss because it does not qualify as a reasonable guaranteed payment. See paragraph (c)(1)(ii)(A) of this section. Accordingly, overall partnership income for the year would be $6,000, which would consist of $10,000 of rental income less $4,000 of salary expense. See paragraph (c)(1)(i) of this section. The $900 QO would include in income with respect to the guaranteed payment would be treated as an allocable share of the $6,000 of overall partnership income. See paragraph (c)(1)(ii)(B) of this section. Therefore, QO's allocable share of the overall partnership income for the year would be $3,450, which would be comprised of the $900 of income pertaining to QO's guaranteed payment, plus QO's $2,550 allocable share of the partnership's net income for the year (50 percent of $5,100). QO's $3,450 allocable share of overall partnership income would equal 58 percent of the $6,000 of overall partnership income and would exceed QO's fractions rule percentage, which is less than 50 percent. (If there were no guaranteed payment, QO's fractions rule percentage would be 50 percent. However, the existence of the guaranteed payment to QO that is not disregarded for purposes of the fractions rule pursuant to paragraph (d) of this section means that QO's fractions rule percentage is less than 50 percent.)

(d) *Exclusion of reasonable preferred returns and guaranteed payments*—(1) *Overview.* This paragraph (d) sets forth requirements for disregarding reasonable preferred returns for capital and reasonable guaranteed payments for capital or services for purposes of the fractions rule. To qualify, the preferred return or guaranteed pay-

Reg. § 1.514(c)-2(c)(1)

ment must be set forth in a binding, written partnership agreement.

(2) *Preferred returns.* Items of income (including gross income) and gain that may be allocated to a partner with respect to a current or cumulative reasonable preferred return for capital (including allocations of minimum gain attributable to nonrecourse liability (or partner nonrecourse debt) proceeds distributed to the partner as a reasonable preferred return) are disregarded in computing overall partnership income or loss for purposes of the fractions rule. Similarly, if a partnership agreement effects a reasonable preferred return with an allocation of what would otherwise be overall partnership income, those items comprising that allocation are disregarded in computing overall partnership income for purposes of the fractions rule.

(3) *Guaranteed payments.* A current or cumulative reasonable guaranteed payment to a qualified organization for capital or services is treated as an item of deduction in computing overall partnership income or loss, and the income that the qualified organization may receive or accrue from the current or cumulative reasonable guaranteed payment is not treated as an allocable share of overall partnership income or loss. The treatment of a guaranteed payment as reasonable for purposes of section 514(c)(9)(E) does not affect its possible characterization as unrelated business taxable income under other provisions of the Internal Revenue Code.

(4) *Reasonable amount*—(i) *In general.* A guaranteed payment for services is reasonable only to the extent the amount of the payment is reasonable under § 1.162-7 (relating to the deduction of compensation for personal services). A preferred return or guaranteed payment for capital is reasonable only to the extent it is computed, with respect to unreturned capital, at a rate that is commercially reasonable based on the relevant facts and circumstances.

(ii) *Safe harbor.* For purposes of this paragraph (d)(4), a rate is deemed to be commercially reasonable if it is no greater than four percentage points more than, or if it is no greater than 150 percent of, the highest long-term applicable federal rate (AFR) within the meaning of section 1274(d), for the month the partner's right to a preferred return or guaranteed payment is first established or for any month in the partnership taxable year for which the return or payment on capital is computed. A rate in excess of the rates described in the preceding sentence may be commercially reasonable, based on the relevant facts and circumstances.

(5) *Unreturned capital*—(i) *In general.* Unreturned capital is computed on a weighted-average basis and equals the excess of—

(A) The amount of money and the fair market value of property contributed by the partner to the partnership (net of liabilities assumed, or taken subject to, by the partnership); over

(B) The amount of money and the fair market value of property (net of liabilities assumed, or taken subject to, by the partner) distributed by the partnership to the partner as a return of capital.

(ii) *Return of capital.* In determining whether a distribution constitutes a return of capital, all relevant facts and circumstances are taken into account. However, the designation of distributions in a written partnership agreement generally will be respected in determining whether a distribution constitutes a return of capital, so long as the designation is economically reasonable.

(6) *Timing rules*—(i) *Limitation on allocations of income with respect to reasonable preferred returns for capital.* Items of income and gain (or part of what would otherwise be overall partnership income) that may be allocated to a partner in a taxable year with respect to a reasonable preferred return for capital are disregarded for purposes of the fractions rule only to the extent the allocable amount will not exceed—

(A) The aggregate of the amount that has been distributed to the partner as a reasonable preferred return for the taxable year of the allocation and prior taxable years, on or before the due date (not including extensions) for filing the partnership's return for the taxable year of the allocation; minus

(B) The aggregate amount of corresponding income and gain (and what would otherwise be overall partnership income) allocated to the partner in all prior years.

(ii) *Reasonable guaranteed payments may be deducted only when paid in cash.* If a partnership that avails itself of paragraph (d)(3) of this section would otherwise be required (by virtue of its method of accounting) to deduct a reasonable guaranteed payment to a qualified organization earlier than the taxable year in which it is paid in cash, the partnership must delay the deduction of the guaranteed payment until the taxable year it is paid in cash. For purposes of this paragraph (d)(6)(ii), a guaranteed payment that is paid in cash on or before the due date (not including extensions) for filing the partnership's return for a taxable year may be treated as paid in that prior taxable year.

Reg. § 1.514(c)-2(d)(6)

Unrelated Business Income

See p. 20,601 for regulations not amended to reflect law changes

(7) *Examples.* The following examples illustrate the provisions of this paragraph (d).

Facts. Qualified organization QO and taxable corporation TP form a partnership. QO contributes $9,000 to the partnership and TP contributes $1,000. The partnership borrows $50,000 from a third party lender and purchases an office building for $55,000. At all relevant times the safe harbor rate described in paragraph (d)(4)(ii) of this section equals 10 percent.

Example 1. Allocations made with respect to preferred returns. (i) The partnership agreement provides that in each taxable year the partnership's *distributable cash* is first to be distributed to QO as a 10 percent preferred return on its unreturned capital. To the extent the partnership has insufficient cash to pay QO its preferred return in any taxable year, the preferred return is compounded (at 10 percent) and is to be paid in future years to the extent the partnership has distributable cash. The partnership agreement first allocates gross income and gain 100 percent to QO, to the extent cash has been distributed to QO as a preferred return. All remaining profit or loss is allocated 50 percent to QO and 50 percent to TP.

(ii) The partnership satisfies the fractions rule. Items of income and gain that may be specially allocated to QO with respect to its preferred return are disregarded in computing overall partnership income or loss for purposes of the fractions rule because the requirements of paragraph (d) of this section are satisfied. After disregarding those allocations, QO's fractions rule percentage is 50 percent (see paragraph (c)(2) of this section), and under the partnership agreement QO may not be allocated more than 50 percent of overall partnership income in any taxable year.

(iii) The facts are the same as in paragraph (i) of this *Example 1*, except that QO's preferred return is computed on unreturned capital at a rate that exceeds a commercially reasonable rate. The partnership violates the fractions rule. The income and gain that may be specially allocated to QO with respect to the preferred return is not disregarded in computing overall partnership income or loss to the extent it exceeds a commercially reasonable rate. See paragraph (d) of this section. As a result, QO's fractions rule percentage is less than 50 percent (see paragraph (c)(2) of this section), and allocations of income and gain to QO with respect to its preferred return could result in QO being allocated more than 50 percent of the overall partnership income in a taxable year.

Example 2. Guaranteed payments and the computation of overall partnership income or loss.

(i) The partnership agreement allocates all bottom-line partnership income and loss 50 percent to QO and 50 percent to TP throughout the life of the partnership. The partnership agreement provides that QO is entitled each year to a 10 percent guaranteed payment on unreturned capital. To the extent the partnership is unable to make a guaranteed payment in any taxable year, the unpaid amount is compounded at 10 percent and is to be paid in future years.

(ii) Assuming the requirements of paragraph (d)(6)(ii) of this section are met, the partnership satisfies the fractions rule. The guaranteed payment is disregarded for purposes of the fractions rule because it is computed with respect to unreturned capital at the safe harbor rate described in paragraph (d)(4)(ii) of this section. Therefore, the guaranteed payment is treated as an item of deduction in computing overall partnership income or loss, and the corresponding income that QO may receive or accrue with respect to the guaranteed payment is not treated as an allocable share of overall partnership income or loss. See paragraph (d)(3) of this section. Accordingly, QO's fractions rule percentage is 50 percent (see paragraph (c)(2) of this section), and under the partnership agreement QO may not be allocated more than 50 percent of overall partnership income in any taxable year.

(e) *Chargebacks and offsets*—(1) *In general.* The following allocations are disregarded in computing overall partnership income or loss for purposes of the fractions rule—

(i) Allocations of what would otherwise be overall partnership income that may be made to chargeback (i. e., reverse) prior disproportionately large allocations of overall partnership loss (or part of the overall partnership loss) to a qualified organization, and allocations of what would otherwise be overall partnership loss that may be made to chargeback prior disproportionately small allocations of overall partnership income (or part of the overall partnership income) to a qualified organization;

(ii) Allocations of income or gain that may be made to a partner pursuant to a minimum gain chargeback attributable to prior allocations of nonrecourse deductions to the partner;

(iii) Allocations of income or gain that may be made to a partner pursuant to a minimum gain chargeback attributable to prior allocations of partner nonrecourse deductions to the partner and allocations of income or gain that may be made to other partners to chargeback compensating allocations of other losses, deductions, or section 705(a)(2)(B) expenditures to the other partners; and

Reg. § 1.514(c)-2(d)(7)

(iv) Allocations of items of income or gain that may be made to a partner pursuant to a qualified income offset, within the meaning of § 1.704-1(b)(2)(ii)(*d*).

(v) Allocations made in taxable years beginning on or after January 1, 2002, that are mandated by statute or regulation other than subchapter K of chapter 1 of the Internal Revenue Code and the regulations thereunder.

(2) *Disproportionate allocations*—(i) *In general.* To qualify under paragraph (e)(1)(i) of this section, prior disproportionate allocations may be reversed in full or in part, and in any order, but must be reversed in the same ratio as originally made. A prior allocation is disproportionately large if the qualified organization's percentage share of that allocation exceeds its fractions rule percentage. A prior allocation is disproportionately small if the qualified organization's percentage share of that allocation is less than its fractions rule percentage. However, a prior allocation (or allocations) is not considered disproportionate unless the balance of the overall partnership income or loss for the taxable year of the allocation is allocated in a manner that would independently satisfy the fractions rule.

(ii) *Limitation on chargebacks of partial allocations.* Except in the case of a chargeback allocation pursuant to paragraph (e)(4) of this section, and except as otherwise provided by the Internal Revenue Service by revenue ruling, revenue procedure, or, on a case-by-case basis, by letter ruling, paragraph (e)(1)(i) of this section applies to a chargeback of an allocation of part of the overall partnership income or loss only if that part consists of a pro rata portion of each item of partnership income, gain, loss, and deduction (other than nonrecourse deductions, as well as partner nonrecourse deductions and compensating allocations) that is included in computing overall partnership income or loss.

(3) *Minimum gain chargebacks attributable to nonrecourse deductions.* Commencing with the first taxable year of the partnership in which a minimum gain chargeback (or partner nonrecourse debt minimum gain chargeback) occurs, a chargeback to a partner is attributable to nonrecourse deductions (or separately, on a debt-by-debt basis, to partner nonrecourse deductions) in the same proportion that the partner's percentage share of the partnership minimum gain (or separately, on a debt-by-debt basis, the partner nonrecourse debt minimum gain) at the end of the immediately preceding taxable year is attributable to nonrecourse deductions (or partner nonrecourse deductions). The partnership must determine the extent to which a partner's percentage share of the partnership minimum gain (or partner nonrecourse debt minimum gain) is attributable to deductions in a reasonable and consistent manner. For example, in those cases in which none of the exceptions contained in § 1.704-2(f)(2) through (5) are relevant, a partner's percentage share of the partnership minimum gain generally is attributable to nonrecourse deductions in the same ratio that—

(i) The aggregate amount of the nonrecourse deductions previously allocated to the partner but not charged back in prior taxable years; bears to

(ii) The sum of the amount described in paragraph (e)(3)(i) of this section, plus the aggregate amount of distributions previously made to the partner of proceeds of a nonrecourse liability allocable to an increase in partnership minimum gain but not charged back in prior taxable years.

(4) *Minimum gain chargebacks attributable to distribution of nonrecourse debt proceeds*—(i) *Chargebacks disregarded until allocations made.* Allocations of items of income and gain that may be made pursuant to a provision in the partnership agreement that charges back minimum gain attributable to the distribution of proceeds of a nonrecourse liability (or a partner nonrecourse debt) are taken into account for purposes of the fractions rule only to the extent an allocation is made. (See paragraph (d)(2) of this section, pursuant to which there is permanently excluded chargeback allocations of minimum gain that are attributable to proceeds distributed as a reasonable preferred return.)

(ii) *Certain minimum gain chargebacks related to returns of capital.* Allocations of items of income or gain that (in accordance with § 1.704-2(f)(1)) may be made to a partner pursuant to a minimum gain chargeback attributable to the distribution of proceeds of a nonrecourse liability are disregarded in computing overall partnership income or loss for purposes of the fractions rule to the extent that the allocations (subject to the requirements of paragraph (e)(2) of this section) also charge back prior disproportionately large allocations of overall partnership loss (or part of the overall partnership loss) to a qualified organization. This exception applies only to the extent the disproportionately large allocation consisted of depreciation from real property (other than items of nonrecourse deduction or partner nonrecourse deduction) that subsequently was used to secure the nonrecourse liability providing the distributed proceeds, and only if those proceeds were distributed as a return of capital and in the same proportion as the disproportionately large allocation.

Reg. § 1.514(c)-2(e)(4)

(5) *Examples.* The following examples illustrate the provisions of this paragraph (e).

Example 1. Chargebacks of disproportionately large allocations of overall partnership loss. (i) Qualified organization QO and taxable corporation TP form a partnership. QO contributes $900 to the partnership and TP contributes $100. The partnership agreement allocates overall partnership loss 50 percent to QO and 50 percent to TP until TP's capital account is reduced to zero; then 100 percent to QO until QO's capital account is reduced to zero; and thereafter 50 percent to QO and 50 percent to TP. *Overall partnership income* is allocated first 100 percent to QO to chargeback overall partnership loss allocated 100 percent to QO, and thereafter 50 percent to QO and 50 percent to TP.

(ii) The partnership satisfies the fractions rule. QO's fractions rule percentage is 50 percent. See paragraph (c)(2) of this section. Therefore, the 100 percent allocation of overall partnership loss to QO is disproportionately large. See paragraph (e)(2)(i) of this section. Accordingly, the 100 percent allocation to QO of what would otherwise be overall partnership income (if it were not disregarded), which charges back the disproportionately large allocation of overall partnership loss, is disregarded in computing overall partnership income and loss for purposes of the fractions rule. The 100 percent allocation is in the same ratio as the disproportionately large loss allocation, and the rest of the allocations for the taxable year of the disproportionately large loss allocation will independently satisfy the fractions rule. See paragraph (e)(2)(i) of this section. After disregarding the chargeback allocation of 100 percent of what would otherwise be overall partnership income, QO will not be allocated a percentage share of overall partnership income in excess of its fractions rule percentage for any taxable year.

Example 2. Chargebacks of disproportionately small allocations of overall partnership income. (i) Qualified organization QO and taxable corporation TP form a partnership. QO contributes $900 to the partnership and TP contributes $100. The partnership purchases real property with money contributed by its partners and with money borrowed by the partnership on a recourse basis. In any year, the partnership agreement allocates the first $500 of overall partnership income 50 percent to QO and 50 percent to TP; the next $100 of overall partnership income 100 percent to TP (as an incentive for TP to achieve significant profitability in managing the partnership's operations); and all remaining overall partnership income 50 percent to QO and 50 percent to TP. *Overall partnership loss* is allocated first 100 percent to TP to chargeback overall partnership income allocated 100 percent to TP at any time in the prior three years and not reversed; and thereafter 50 percent to QO and 50 percent to TP.

(ii) The partnership satisfies the fractions rule. QO's fractions rule percentage is 50 percent because qualifying chargebacks are disregarded pursuant to paragraph (e)(1)(i) in computing overall partnership income or loss. See paragraph (c)(2) of this section. The zero percent allocation to QO of what would otherwise be overall partnership loss is a qualifying chargeback that is disregarded because it is in the same ratio as the income allocation it charges back, because the rest of the allocations for the taxable year of that income allocation will independently satisfy the fractions rule (see paragraph (e)(2)(i) of this section), and because it charges back an allocation of zero overall partnership income to QO, which is proportionately smaller (i.e., disproportionately small) than QO's 50 percent fractions rule percentage. After disregarding the chargeback allocation of 100 percent of what would otherwise be overall partnership loss, QO will not be allocated a percentage share of overall partnership income in excess of its fractions rule percentage for any taxable year.

Example 3. Chargebacks of partner nonrecourse deductions and compensating allocations of other items. (i) Qualified organization QO and taxable corporation TP form a partnership to own and operate encumbered real property. QO and TP each contribute $500 to the partnership. In addition, QO makes a $300 nonrecourse loan to the partnership. The partnership agreement contains a partner nonrecourse debt minimum gain chargeback provision and a provision that allocates partner nonrecourse deductions to the partner who bears the economic burden of the deductions in accordance with § 1.704-2. The partnership agreement also provides that to the extent partner nonrecourse deductions are allocated to QO in any taxable year, other compensating items of partnership loss or deduction (and, if appropriate, section 705(a)(2)(B) expenditures) will first be allocated 100 percent to TP. In addition, to the extent items of income or gain are allocated to QO in any taxable year pursuant to a partner nonrecourse debt minimum gain chargeback of deductions, items of partnership income and gain will first be allocated 100 percent to TP. The partnership agreement allocates all other overall partnership income or loss 50 percent to QO and 50 percent to TP.

(ii) The partnership satisfies the fractions rule on a prospective basis. The allocations of the

Reg. § 1.514(c)-2(e)(5)

partner nonrecourse deductions and the compensating allocation of other items of loss, deduction, and expenditure that may be made to TP (but which will not be made unless there is an allocation of partner nonrecourse deductions to QO) are not taken into account for purposes of the fractions rule until a taxable year in which an allocation is made. See paragraph (j)(1) of this section. In addition, partner nonrecourse debt minimum gain chargebacks of deductions and allocations of income or gain to other partners that chargeback compensating allocations of other deductions are disregarded in computing overall partnership income or loss for purposes of the fractions rule. See paragraph (e)(1)(iii) of this section. Since all other overall partnership income and loss is allocated 50 percent to QO and 50 percent to TP, QO's fractions rule percentage is 50 percent (see paragraph (c)(2) of this section), and QO will not be allocated a percentage share of overall partnership income in excess of its fractions rule percentage for any taxable year.

(iii) The facts are the same as in paragraph (i) of this *Example 3*, except that the partnership agreement provides that compensating allocations of loss or deduction (and section 705(a)(2)(B) expenditures) to TP will not be charged back until year 10. The partners expect $300 of partner nonrecourse deductions to be allocated to QO in year 1 and $300 of income or gain to be allocated to QO in year 2 pursuant to the partner nonrecourse debt minimum gain chargeback provision.

(iv) The partnership fails to satisfy the fractions rule on a prospective basis under the anti-abuse rule of paragraph (k)(4) of this section. If the partners' expectations prove correct, at the end of year 2, QO will have been allocated $300 of partner nonrecourse deductions and an offsetting $300 of partner nonrecourse debt minimum gain. However, the $300 of compensating deductions and losses that may be allocated to TP will not be charged back until year 10. Thus, during the period beginning at the end of year 2 and ending eight years later, there may be $300 more of unreversed deductions and losses allocated to TP than to QO, which would be inconsistent with the purpose of the fractions rule.

Example 4. Minimum gain chargeback attributable to distributions of nonrecourse debt proceeds. (i) Qualified organization QO and taxable corporation TP form a partnership. QO contributes $900 to the partnership and TP contributes $100. The partnership agreement generally allocates overall partnership income and loss 90 percent to QO and 10 percent to TP. However, the partnership agreement contains a minimum gain chargeback provision, and also provides that in any partnership taxable year in which there is a chargeback of partnership minimum gain to QO attributable to distributions of proceeds of nonrecourse liabilities, all other items comprising overall partnership income or loss will be allocated in a manner such that QO is not allocated more than 90 percent of the overall partnership income for the year.

(ii) The partnership satisfies the fractions rule on a prospective basis. QO's fractions rule percentage is 90 percent. See paragraph (c)(2) of this section. The chargeback that may be made to QO of minimum gain attributable to distributions of nonrecourse liability proceeds is taken into account for purposes of the fractions rule only to the extent an allocation is made. See paragraph (e)(4) of this section. Accordingly, that potential allocation to QO is disregarded in applying the fractions rule on a prospective basis (see paragraph (b)(2) of this section), and QO is treated as not being allocated a percentage share of overall partnership income in excess of its fractions rule percentage in any taxable year. (Similarly, QO is treated as not being allocated items of income or gain in a taxable year when the partnership has an overall partnership loss.)

(iii) In year 3, the partnership borrows $400 on a nonrecourse basis and distributes it to QO as a return of capital. In year 8, the partnership has $400 of gross income and cash flow and $300 of overall partnership income, and the partnership repays the $400 nonrecourse borrowing.

(iv) The partnership violates the fractions rule for year 8 and all future years. Pursuant to the minimum gain chargeback provision, the entire $400 of partnership gross income is allocated to QO. Accordingly, notwithstanding the curative provision in the partnership agreement that would allocate to TP the next $44 (($400 + .9) × 10%) of income and gain included in computing overall partnership income, the partnership has no other items of income and gain to allocate to QO. Because the $400 of gross income actually allocated to QO is taken into account for purposes of the fractions rule in the year an allocation is made (see paragraph (e)(4) of this section), QO's percentage share of overall partnership income in year 8 is greater than 100 percent. Since this exceeds QO's fractions rule percentage (i.e., 90 percent), the partnership violates the fractions rule for year 8 and all subsequent taxable years. See paragraph (b)(2) of this section.

(f) *Exclusion of reasonable partner-specific items of deduction or loss.* Provided that the expenditures are allocated to the partners to whom they are attributable, the following partner-specific expenditures are disregarded in computing

Reg. § 1.514(c)-2(f)

overall partnership income or loss for purposes of the fractions rule—

(1) Expenditures for additional record-keeping and accounting incurred in connection with the transfer of a partnership interest (including expenditures incurred in computing basis adjustments under section 743(b));

(2) Additional administrative costs that result from having a foreign partner;

(3) State and local taxes or expenditures relating to those taxes; and

(4) Expenditures designated by the Internal Revenue Service by revenue ruling or revenue procedure, or, on a case-by-case basis, by letter ruling. (See § 601.601(d)(2)(ii)(*b*) of this chapter).

(g) *Exclusion of unlikely losses and deductions.* Unlikely losses or deductions (other than items of nonrecourse deduction) that may be specially allocated to partners that bear the economic burden of those losses or deductions are disregarded in computing overall partnership income or loss for purposes of the fractions rule, so long as a principal purpose of the allocation is not tax avoidance. To be excluded under this paragraph (g), a loss or deduction must have a low likelihood of occurring, taking into account all relevant facts, circumstances, and information available to the partners (including bona fide financial projections). The types of events that may give rise to unlikely losses or deductions, depending on the facts and circumstances, include tort and other third-party litigation that give rise to unforeseen liabilities in excess of reasonable insurance coverage; unanticipated labor strikes; unusual delays in securing required permits or licenses; abnormal weather conditions (considering the season and the job site); significant delays in leasing property due to an unanticipated severe economic downturn in the geographic area; unanticipated cost overruns; and the discovery of environmental conditions that require remediation. No inference is drawn as to whether a loss or deduction is unlikely from the fact that the partnership agreement includes a provision for allocating that loss or deduction.

(h) *Provisions preventing deficit capital account balances.* A provision in the partnership agreement that allocates items of loss or deduction away from a qualified organization in instances where allocating those items to the qualified organization would cause or increase a deficit balance in its capital account that the qualified organization is not obligated to restore (within the meaning of § 1.704-1(b)(2)(ii)(*b*) or (*d*)), is disregarded for purposes of the fractions rule in taxable years of the partnership in which no such allocations are made pursuant to the provision. However, this exception applies only if, at the time the provision becomes part of the partnership agreement, all relevant facts, circumstances, and information (including bona fide financial projections) available to the partners reasonably indicate that it is unlikely that an allocation will be made pursuant to the provision during the life of the partnership.

(i) [Reserved].

(j) *Exception for partner nonrecourse deductions*—(1) *Partner nonrecourse deductions disregarded until actually allocated.* Items of partner nonrecourse deduction that may be allocated to a partner pursuant to § 1.704-2, and compensating allocations of other items of loss, deduction, and section 705(a)(2)(B) expenditures that may be allocated to other partners, are not taken into account for purposes of the fractions rule until the taxable years in which they are allocated.

(2) *Disproportionate allocation of partner nonrecourse deductions to a qualified organization.* A violation of the fractions rule will be disregarded if it arises because an allocation of partner nonrecourse deductions to a qualified organization that is not motivated by tax avoidance reduces another qualified organization's fractions rule percentage below what it would have been absent the allocation of the partner nonrecourse deductions.

(k) *Special rules*—(1) *Changes in partnership allocations arising from a change in the partners' interests.* A qualified organization that acquires a partnership interest from another qualified organization is treated as a continuation of the prior qualified organization partner (to the extent of that acquired interest) for purposes of applying the fractions rule. Changes in partnership allocations that result from other transfers or shifts of partnership interests will be closely scrutinized (to determine whether the transfer or shift stems from a prior agreement, understanding, or plan or could otherwise be expected given the structure of the transaction), but generally will be taken into account only in determining whether the partnership satisfies the fractions rule in the taxable year of the change and subsequent taxable years.

(2) *De minimis interest rule*—(i) *In general.* Section 514(c)(9)(B)(vi) does not apply to a partnership otherwise subject to that section if—

(A) Qualified organizations do not hold, in the aggregate, interests of greater than five percent in the capital or profits of the partnership; and

(B) Taxable partners own substantial interests in the partnership through which they participate in the partnership on substantially the same terms as the qualified organization partners.

Reg. § 1.514(c)-2(f)(1)

(ii) *Example.* Partnership *PRS* has two types of limited partnership interests that participate in partnership profits and losses on different terms. Qualified organizations (QOs) only own one type of limited partnership interest and own no general partnership interests. In the aggregate, the QOs own less than five percent of the capital and profits of *PRS*. Taxable partners also own the same type of limited partnership interest that the QOs own. These limited partnership interests owned by the taxable partners are 30 percent of the capital and profits of *PRS*. Thirty percent is a substantial interest in the partnership. Therefore, *PRS* satisfies paragraph (k)(2) of this section and section 514(c)(9)(B)(vi) does not apply.

(3) *De minimis allocations disregarded.* A qualified organization's fractions rule percentage of the partnership's items of loss and deduction, other than nonrecourse and partner nonrecourse deductions, that are allocated away from the qualified organization and to other partners in any taxable year are treated as having been allocated to the qualified organization for purposes of the fractions rule if—

(i) The allocation was neither planned nor motivated by tax avoidance; and

(ii) The total amount of those items of partnership loss or deduction is less than both—

(A) One percent of the partnership's aggregate items of gross loss and deduction for the taxable year; and

(B) $50,000.

(4) *Anti-abuse rule.* The purpose of the fractions rule is to prevent tax avoidance by limiting the permanent or temporary transfer of tax benefits from tax-exempt partners to taxable partners, whether by directing income or gain to tax-exempt partners, by directing losses, deductions, or credits to taxable partners, or by some other similar manner. This section may not be applied in a manner that is inconsistent with the purpose of the fractions rule.

(l) [Reserved].

(m) *Tiered partnerships*—(1) *In general.* If a qualified organization holds an indirect interest in real property through one or more tiers of partnerships (a chain), the fractions rule is satisfied only if—

(i) The avoidance of tax is not a principal purpose for using the tiered-ownership structure (investing in separate real properties through separate chains of partnerships so that section 514(c)(9)(E) is, effectively, applied on a property-by-property basis is not, in and of itself, a tax avoidance purpose); and

(ii) The relevant partnerships can demonstrate under any reasonable method that the relevant chains satisfy the requirements of paragraphs (b)(2) through (k) of this section. For purposes of applying § 1.704-2(k) under the independent chain approach described in Example 3 of paragraph (m)(2) of this section, allocations of items of income or gain that may be made pursuant to a provision in the partnership agreement that charges back minimum gain are taken into account for purposes of the fractions rule only to the extent an allocation is made.

(2) *Examples.* The following examples illustrate the provisions of this paragraph (m).

Example 1. Tiered partnerships—collapsing approach. (i) Qualified organization QO3 and taxable individual TP3 form upper-tier partnership P2. The P2 partnership agreement allocates overall partnership income 20 percent to QO3 and 80 percent to TP3. Overall partnership loss is allocated 30 percent to QO3 and 70 percent to TP3. P2 and taxable individual TP2 form lower-tier partnership P1. The P1 partnership agreement allocates overall partnership income 60 percent to P2 and 40 percent to TP2. Overall partnership loss is allocated 40 percent to P2 and 60 percent to TP2. The only asset of P2 (which has no outstanding debt) is its interest in P1. P1 purchases real property with money contributed by its partners and with borrowed money. There is no tax avoidance purpose for the use of the tiered-ownership structure, which is illustrated by the following diagram.

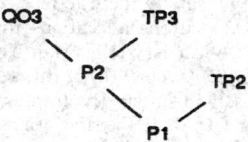

(ii) P2 can demonstrate that the P2/P1 chain satisfies the requirements of paragraphs (b)(2) through (k) of this section by collapsing the tiered-partnership structure. On a collapsed basis, QO3's fractions rule percentage is 12 percent (30 percent of 40 percent). See paragraph (c)(2) of this section. P2 satisfies the fractions rule because QO3 may not be allocated more than 12 percent (20 percent of 60 percent) of overall partnership income in any taxable year.

Example 2. Tiered partnerships—entity-by-entity approach. (i) Qualified organization QO3A is a partner with taxable individual TP3A in upper-tier partnership P2A. Qualified organization QO3B is a partner with taxable individual TP3B in upper-tier partnership P2B. P2A, P2B, and taxable individual TP2 are partners in lower-tier partnership P1, which owns encumbered real estate. None of QO3A, QO3B, TP3A, TP3B or TP2 has a direct or indirect ownership interest in each other. P2A has been established for the purpose of investing in numerous real estate properties independently of P2B and its partners. P2B has been established for the purpose of investing in numerous real estate properties independently of P2A and its partners. Neither P2A nor P2B has outstanding debt. There is no tax avoidance purpose for the use of the tiered-ownership structure, which is illustrated by the following diagram.

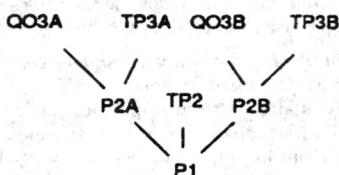

(ii) The P2A/P1 chain (Chain A) will satisfy the fractions rule if P1 and P2A can demonstrate in a reasonable manner that they satisfy the requirements of paragraphs (b)(2) through (k) of this section. The P2B/P1 chain (Chain B) will satisfy the fractions rule if P1 and P2B can demonstrate in a reasonable manner that they satisfy the requirements of paragraphs (b)(2) through (k) of this section. To meet its burden, P1 treats P2A and P2B as qualified organizations. Provided that the allocations that may be made by P1 would satisfy the fractions rule if P2A and P2B were direct qualified organization partners in P1, Chain A will satisfy the fractions rule (for the benefit of QO3A) if the allocations that may be made by P2A satisfy the requirements of paragraphs (b)(2) through (k) of this section. Similarly, Chain B will satisfy the fractions rule (for the benefit of QO3B) if the allocations that may be made by P2B satisfy the requirements of paragraphs (b)(2) through (k) of this section. Under these facts, QO3A does not have to know how income and loss may be allocated by P2B, and QO3B does not have to know how income and loss may be allocated by P2A. QO3A's and QO3B's burden would not change even if TP2 were not a partner in P1.

Example 3. Tiered partnerships—independent chain approach. (i) Qualified organization QO3 and taxable corporation TP3 form upper-tier partnership P2. P2 and taxable corporation TP2 form lower-tier partnership P1A. P2 and qualified organization QO2 form lower-tier partnership P1B. P2 has no outstanding debt. P1A and P1B each purchase real property with money contributed by their respective partners and with borrowed money. Each partnership's real property is completely unrelated to the real property owned by the other partnership. P1B's allocations do not satisfy the requirements of paragraphs (b)(2) through (k) of this section because of allocations that may be made to QO2. However, if P2's interest in P1B were completely disregarded, the P2/P1A chain would satisfy the requirements of paragraphs (b)(2) through (k) of this section. There is no tax avoidance purpose for the use of the tiered-ownership structure, which is illustrated by the following diagram.

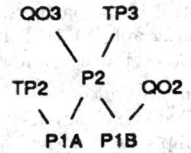

(ii) P2 satisfies the fractions rule with respect to the P2/P1A chain, but only if the P2 partnership agreement allocates those items allocated to P2 by P1A separately from those items allocated to P2 by P1B. For this purpose, allocations of items of income or gain that may be made pursuant to a provision in the partnership agreement that charges back minimum gain, are taken into account for purposes of the fractions rule only to the extent an allocation is made. See paragraph (m)(1)(ii) of this section. P2 does not satisfy the fractions rule with respect to the P2/P1B chain.

(n) *Effective date*—(1) *In general.* Section 514(c)(9)(E), as amended by sections 2004(h)(1) and (2) of the Technical and Miscellaneous Revenue Act of 1988, Pub. L. 100-647, applies generally with respect to property acquired by partnerships after October 13, 1987, and to partnership interests acquired after October 13, 1987.

(2) *General effective date of the regulations.* Section 1.514(c)-2(a) through (m) applies with respect to partnership agreements entered into after December 30, 1992, property acquired by partnerships after December 30, 1992, and partnership interests acquired by qualified organizations after December 30, 1992 (other than a partnership interest that at all times after October 13, 1987, and prior to the acquisition was held by a qualified organization). For this purpose, paragraphs (a) through (m) of this section will be treated as satisfied with respect to partnership agreements entered into on or before May 13, 1994, property acquired by partnerships on or before May 13, 1994, and partnership interests acquired by qualified organizations on or before May 13, 1994, if the guidance set forth in (paragraphs (a) through (m) of § 1.514(c)-2 of) PS-56-90, published at 1993-5 I.R.B. 42, February

Reg. § 1.514(c)-2(n)(1)

1, 1993, is satisfied. (See § 601.601(d)(2)(ii)(b) of this chapter).

(3) *Periods after June 24, 1990, and prior to December 30, 1992.* To satisfy the requirements of section 514(c)(9)(E) with respect to partnership agreements entered into after June 24, 1990, property acquired by partnerships after June 24, 1990, and partnership interests acquired by qualified organizations after June 24, 1990, (other than a partnership interest that at all times after October 13, 1987, and prior to the acquisition was held by a qualified organization) to which paragraph (n)(2) of this section does not apply, paragraphs (a) through (m) of this section must be satisfied as of the first day that section 514(c)(9)(E) applies with respect to the partnership, property, or acquired interest. For this purpose, paragraphs (a) through (m) of this section will be treated as satisfied if the guidance in sections I through VI of Notice 90-41, 90-1 C.B. 350, (see § 601.601(d)(2)(ii)(b) of this chapter) has been followed.

(4) *Periods prior to the issuance of Notice 90-41.* With respect to partnerships commencing after October 13, 1987, property acquired by partnerships after October 13, 1987, and partnership interests acquired by qualified organizations after October 13, 1987, to which neither paragraph (n)(2) nor (n)(3) of this section applies, the Internal Revenue Service will not challenge an interpretation of section 514(c)(9)(E) that is reasonable in light of the underlying purposes of section 514(c)(9)(E) (as reflected in its legislative history) and that is consistently applied as of the first day that section 514(c)(9)(E) applies with respect to the partnership, property, or acquired interest. A reasonable interpretation includes an interpretation that substantially follows the guidance in either sections I through VI of Notice 90-41, (see § 601.601(d)(2)(ii)(b) of this chapter) or paragraphs (a) through (m) of this section.

(5) *Material modifications to partnership agreements.* A material modification will cause a partnership agreement to be treated as a new partnership agreement in appropriate circumstances for purposes of this paragraph (n). [Reg. § 1.514(c)-2.]

☐ [T.D. 8539, 5-11-94. Amended by T.D. 9047, 3-13-2003.]

[Reg. § 1.514(d)-1]

§ 1.514(d)-1. **Basis of debt-financed property acquired in corporate liquidation.**—(a) If debt-financed property is acquired by an exempt organization in a complete or partial liquidation of a corporation in exchange for its stock, the organization's basis in such property shall be the same as it would be in the hands of the transferor corporation, increased by the amount of gain recognized to the transferor corporation upon such distribution and by the amount of any gain which is includible, on account of such distribution, in the gross income of the organization as unrelated debt-financed income.

(b) The application of this section may be illustrated by the following example:

Example. On July 1, 1970, T, an exempt trust, exchanges $15,000 of borrowed funds for 50 percent of the shares of M Corporation's stock. M uses $35,000 of borrowed funds in acquiring depreciable assets which are not used at any time for purposes described in section 514(b)(1)(A), (B), (C), or (D). On July 1, 1978, and for the 12-month period preceding this date, T's acquisition indebtedness with respect to M's stock has been $3,000. On this date, there is a complete liquidation of M Corporation to which section 331(a)(1) applies. In the liquidation T receives a distribution in kind of depreciable assets and assumes $7,000 of M's indebtedness which remains unpaid with respect to the depreciable assets. On this date, M's adjusted basis of these depreciable assets is $9,000, and such assets have a fair market value of $47,000. M recognizes gain of $6,000 with respect to this liquidation pursuant to sections 1245 and 1250. T realizes a gain of $25,000 (the difference between the excess of fair market value of the property received over the indebtedness assumed, $40,000 ($47,000 − $7,000) and T's basis in M's stock, $15,000). A portion of this gain is to be treated as unrelated debt-financed income. This amount is determined by multiplying T's gain of $25,000 by the debt/basis percentage. The debt/basis percentage is 20 percent, the ratio which the average acquisition indebtedness ($3,000) is of the average adjusted basis ($15,000). Thus, $5,000 (20% of $25,000) is unrelated debt-financed income. This amount and the gain recognized pursuant to sections 1245 and 1250 are added to M's basis to determine T's basis in the property received. Consequently, T's basis in the property received from M Corporation is $20,000, determined as follows:

39,190 Farmers' Cooperatives

See p. 20,601 for regulations not amended to reflect law changes

M Corporation's adjusted basis	$9,000
Gain recognized by M Corporation on the distribution	6,000
Unrelated debt-financed income recognized by T with respect to the distribution	5,000
T's transferred basis	$20,000

[Reg. § 1.514(d)-1.]

☐ [T.D. 7229, 12-20-72.]

[Reg. § 1.514(e)-1]

§ 1.514(e)-1. **Allocation rules.**—Where only a portion of property is debt-financed property, proper allocation of the basis, indebtedness, income, and deductions with respect to such property must be made to determine the amount of income or gain derived from such property which is to be treated as unrelated debt-financed income. See examples (2) and (3) of paragraph (b)(1)(iii) of § 1.514(b)-1 and examples (1), (2), and (3) of paragraph (b)(3) of § 1.514(b)-1 for illustrations of proper allocation. [Reg. § 1.514(e)-1.]

☐ [T.D. 7229, 12-20-72.]

Farmers' Cooperatives

[Reg. § 1.521-1]

§ 1.521-1. **Farmers' cooperative marketing and purchasing associations; requirements for exemption under section 521.**—(a)(1) Cooperative associations engaged in the marketing of farm products for farmers, fruit growers, livestock growers, dairymen, etc., and turning back to the producers the proceeds of the sales of their products, less the necessary operating expenses, on the basis of either the quantity or the value of the products furnished by them, are exempt from income tax except as otherwise provided in section 522, or part I, subchapter T, chapter 1 of the Code, and the regulations thereunder. For instance, cooperative dairy companies which are engaged in collecting milk and disposing of it or the products thereof and distributing the proceeds, less necessary operating expenses, among the producers upon the basis of either the quantity or the value of milk or of butterfat in the milk furnished by such producers, are exempt from the tax. If the proceeds of the business are distributed in any other way than on such a proportionate basis, the association does not meet the requirements of the Code and is not exempt. In other words, nonmember patrons must be treated the same as members insofar as the distribution of patronage dividends is concerned. Thus, if products are marketed for nonmember producers, the proceeds of the sale, less necessary operating expenses, must be returned to the patrons from the sale of whose goods such proceeds result, whether or not such patrons are members of the association. In order to show its cooperative nature and to establish compliance with the requirement of the Code that the proceeds of sales, less necessary expenses, be turned back to all producers on the basis of either the quantity or the value of the products furnished by them, it is necessary for such an association to keep permanent records of the business done both with members and nonmembers. The Code does not require, however, that the association keep ledger accounts with each producer selling through the association. Any permanent records which show that the association was operating during the taxable year on a cooperative basis in the distribution of patronage dividends to all producers will suffice. While under the Code patronage dividends must be paid to all producers on the same basis, this requirement is complied with if an association instead of paying patronage dividends to nonmember producers in cash, keeps permanent records from which the proportionate shares of the patronage dividends due to nonmember producers can be determined, and such shares are made applicable toward the purchase price of a share of stock or of a membership in the association. See, however, paragraph (c)(1) of § 1.1388-1 for the meaning of "payment in money" for purposes of qualifying a written notice of allocation.

(2) An association which has capital stock will not for such reason be denied exemption (i) if the dividend rate of such stock is fixed at not to exceed the legal rate of interest in the State of incorporation or 8 percent per annum, whichever is greater, on the value of the consideration for which the stock was issued, and (ii) if substantially all of such stock (with the exception noted below) is owned by producers who market their products or purchase their supplies and equipment through the association. Any ownership of stock by others than such actual producers must be satisfactorily explained in the association's application for exemption. The association will be required to show that the ownership of its capital stock has been restricted as far as possible to such actual producers. If by statutory requirement all officers of an association must be shareholders, the ownership of a share of stock by a nonproducer to qualify him as an officer will not destroy the association's exemption. Likewise, if a shareholder for any reason ceases to be a producer and the association is unable, because of a constitu-

Reg. § 1.514(e)-1

tional restriction or prohibition or other reason beyond the control of the association, to purchase or retire the stock of such nonproducer, the fact that under such circumstances a small amount of the outstanding capital stock is owned by shareholders who are no longer producers will not destroy the exemption. The restriction placed on the ownership of capital stock of an exempt cooperative association shall not apply to nonvoting preferred stock, provided the owners of such stock are not entitled or permitted to participate, directly or indirectly, in the profits of the association, upon dissolution or otherwise, beyond the fixed dividends.

(3) The accumulation and maintenance of a reserve required by State statute, or the accumulation and maintenance of a reasonable reserve or surplus for any necessary purpose, such as to provide for the erection of buildings and facilities required in business or for the purchase and installation of machinery and equipment or to retire indebtedness incurred for such purposes, will not destroy the exemption. An association will not be denied exemption because it markets the products of nonmembers, provided the value of the products marketed for nonmembers does not exceed the value of the products marketed for members. Anyone who shares in the profits of a farmers' cooperative marketing association, and is entitled to participate in the management of the association, must be regarded as a member of such association within the meaning of section 521.

(b) Cooperative associations engaged in the purchasing of supplies and equipment for farmers, fruit growers, livestock growers, dairymen, etc., and turning over such supplies and equipment to them at actual cost, plus the necessary operating expenses, are exempt. The term "supplies and equipment" as used in section 521 includes groceries and all other goods and merchandise used by farmers in the operation and maintenance of a farm or farmer's household. The provisions of paragraph (a) of this section relating to a reserve or surplus and to capital stock shall apply to associations coming under this paragraph. An association which purchases supplies and equipment for nonmembers will not for such reason be denied exemption, provided the value of the purchases for nonmembers does not exceed the value of the supplies and equipment purchased for members, and provided the value of the purchases made for nonmembers who are not producers does not exceed 15 percent of the value of all its purchases.

(c) In order to be exempt under either paragraph (a) or (b) of this section an association must establish that it has no taxable income for its own account other than that reflected in a reserve or surplus authorized in paragraph (a) of this section. An association engaged both in marketing farm products and in purchasing supplies and equipment is exempt if as to each of its functions it meets the requirements of the Code. Business done for the United States or any of its agencies shall be disregarded in determining the right to exemption under section 521 and this section. An association to be entitled to exemption must not only be organized but actually operated in the manner and for the purposes specified in section 521.

(d) Cooperative organizations engaged in occupations dissimilar from those of farmers, fruit growers, and the like, are not exempt.

(e) An organization is not exempt from taxation under this section merely because it claims that it complies with the requirements prescribed therein. In order to establish its exemption every organization claiming exemption under section 521 is required to file a Form 1028. The Form 1028, executed in accordance with the instructions on the form or issued therewith, should be filed with the district director for the internal revenue district in which is located the principal place of business or principal office of the organization. However, an organization which has been granted exemption under the provisions of the Internal Revenue Code of 1939 or prior law may rely on that ruling, unless affected by substantive changes in the Internal Revenue Code of 1954 or any changes in the character, purposes, or methods of operation of the organization, and it is not necessary in such case for the organization to request a new determination as to its exempt status.

(f) A cooperative association will not be denied exemption merely because it makes payments solely in nonqualified written notices of allocation to those patrons who do not consent as provided in section 1388 and § 1.1388–1, but makes payments of 20 percent in cash and the remainder in qualified written notices of allocation to those patrons who do so consent. Nor will such an association be denied exemption merely because, in the case of patrons who have so consented, payments of less than $5 are made solely in nonqualified written notices of allocation while payments of $5 or more are made in the form of 20 percent in cash and the remainder in qualified written notices of allocation. In addition, a cooperative association will not be denied exemption if it pays a smaller amount of interest or dividends on nonqualified written notices of allocation held by persons who have not consented as provided in section 1388 and § 1.1388–1 (or on per-unit retain certificates issued to patrons who are not qualifying patrons

Reg. § 1.521–1(f)

with respect thereto within the meaning of § 1.61-5(d)(2)) than it pays on qualified written notices of allocation held by persons who have so consented (or on per-unit retain certificates issued to patrons who are qualifying patrons with respect thereto) provided that the amount of the interest or dividend reduction is reasonable in relation to the fact that the association receives no tax benefit with respect to such nonqualified written notices of allocation (or such certificates issued to nonqualifying patrons) until redeemed. However, such an association will be denied exemption if it otherwise treats patrons who have not consented (or are not qualifying patrons) differently from patrons who have consented (or are qualifying patrons), either with regard to the original payment or allocation or with regard to the redemption of written notices of allocation or per-unit retain certificates. For example, if such an association pays patronage dividends in the form of written notices of allocation accompanied by qualified checks, and provides that any patron who does not cash his check within a specified time will forfeit the portion of the patronage dividend represented by such check, then the cooperative association will be denied exemption under this section as it does not treat all patrons alike. [Reg. § 1.521-1.]

☐ [T.D. 6301, 7-8-58. Amended by T.D. 6643, 4-1-63, and by T.D. 6855, 10-14-65.]

Political Organizations

[Reg. § 1.527-1]

§ 1.527-1. Political organizations; Generally.—Section 527 provides that a political organization is considered an organization exempt from income taxes for the purpose of any law which refers to organizations exempt from income taxes. A political organization is subject to tax only to the extent provided in section 527. In general, a political organization is an organization that is organized and operated primarily for an exempt function as defined in § 1.527-2(c). Section 527 provides that a political organization is taxed on its political organization taxable income (see § 1.527-4) which, in general, does not include the exempt function income (see § 1.527-3) of the political organization. Furthermore, section 527 provides that an exempt organization, other than a political organization, may be subject to tax under section 527 when it expends an amount for an exempt function, see § 1.527-6. The taxation of newsletter funds is provided under section 527(g) and § 1.527-7. A special rule for principal campaign committees is provided under section 527(h) and § 1.527-9. [Reg. § 1.527-1.]

☐ [T.D. 7744, 12-29-80. Amended by T.D. 8041, 7-29-85.]

[Reg. § 1.527-2]

§ 1.527-2. Definitions.—For purposes of section 527 and these regulations—

(a) *Political organization*—(1) *In general.* A "political organization" is a party, committee, association, fund, or other organization (whether or not incorporated) organized and operated primarily for the purpose of directly or indirectly accepting contributions or making expenditures for an exempt function activity (as defined in paragraph (c) of this section). Accordingly, a political organization may include a committee or other group which accepts contributions or makes expenditures for the purpose of promoting the nomination of an individual for an elective public office in a primary election, or in a meeting or caucus of a political party. A segregated fund (as defined in paragraph (b) of this section) established and maintained by an individual may qualify as a political organization.

(2) *Organizational test.* A political organization meets the organizational test if its articles of organization provide that the primary purpose of the organization is to carry on one or more exempt functions. A political organization is not required to be formally chartered or established as a corporation, trust, or association. If an organization has no formal articles of organization, consideration is given to statements of the members of the organization at the time the organization is formed that they intend to operate the organization primarily to carry on one or more exempt functions.

(3) *Operational test.* A political organization does not have to engage exclusively in activities that are an exempt function. For example, a political organization may—

(i) Sponsor nonpartisan educational workshops which are not intended to influence or attempt to influence the selection, nomination, election, or appointment of any individual for public office,

(ii) Pay an incumbent's office expenses, or

(iii) Carry on social activities which are unrelated to its exempt function, provided these are not the organization's primary activities. However, expenditures for purposes described in the preceding sentence are not for an exempt function. See § 1.527-2(c) and (d). Furthermore, it is not necessary that a political organization operate in accordance with normal corporate formalities as ordinarily established in bylaws or under state law.

(b) *Segregated fund*—(1) *General rule.* A "segregated fund" is a fund which is established and maintained by a political organization or an individual separate from the assets of the organization or the personal assets of the individual. The purpose of such a fund must be to receive and segregate exempt function income (and earnings on such income) for use only for an exempt function or for an activity necessary to fulfill an exempt function. Accordingly, the amounts in the fund must be dedicated for use only for an exempt function. Thus, expenditures for the establishment of administration of a political organization or the solicitation of political contributions may be made from the segregated fund, if necessary to fulfill an exempt function. The fund must be clearly identified and established for the purposes intended. A savings or checking account into which only contributions to the political organization are placed and from which only expenditures for exempt functions are made may be a segregated fund. If an organization that had designated a fund to be a segregated fund for purposes of segregating amounts referred to in section 527(c)(3)(A) through (D), expends more than an insubstantial amount from the segregated fund for activities that are not for an exempt function during a taxable year, the fund will not be treated as a segregated fund for such year. In such a case amounts referred to in section 527(c)(3)(A)-(D), segregated in such fund will not be exempt function income. Further, if more than insubstantial amounts segregated for an exempt function in prior years are expended for other than an exempt function the facts and circumstances may indicate that the fund was never a segregated fund as defined in this paragraph.

(2) *Record keeping.* The organization or individual maintaining a segregated fund must keep records that are adequate to verify receipts and disbursements of the fund and identify the exempt function activity for which each expenditure is made.

(c) *Exempt function*—(1) *Directly related expenses.* An "exempt function", as defined in section 527(e)(2), includes all activities that are directly related to and support the process of influencing or attempting to influence the selection, nomination, election, or appointment of any individual to public office or office in a political organization (the selection process). Whether an expenditure is for an exempt function depends upon all the facts and circumstances. Generally, where an organization supports an individual's campaign for public office, the organization's activities and expenditures in furtherance of the individual's election or appointment to that office are for an exempt function of the organization. The individual does not have to be an announced candidate for the office. Furthermore, the fact that an individual never becomes a candidate is not crucial in determining whether an organization is engaging in an exempt function. An activity engaged in between elections which is directly related to, and supports, the process of selection, nomination, or election of an individual in the next applicable political campaign is an exempt function activity.

(2) *Indirect expenses.* Expenditures that are not directly related to influencing or attempting to influence the selection process may also be an expenditure for an exempt function by a political organization. These are expenses which are necessary to support the directly related activities of the political organization. Activities which support the directly related activities are those which must be engaged in to allow the political organization to carry out the activity of influencing or attempting to influence the selection process. For example, expenses for overhead and record keeping are necessary to allow the political organization to be established and to engage in political activities. Similarly, expenses incurred in soliciting contributions to the political organization are necessary to support the activities of the political organization.

(3) *Terminating activities.* An exempt function includes an activity which is in furtherance of the process of terminating a political organization's existence. For example, where a political organization is established for a single campaign, payment of campaign debts after the conclusion of the campaign is an exempt function activity.

(4) *Illegal expenditures.* Expenditures which are illegal or are for a judicially determined illegal activity are not considered expenditures in furtherance of an exempt function, even though such expenditures are made in connection with the selection process.

(5) *Examples.* The following examples illustrate the principles of paragraph (c) of this section. The term "exempt function" when used in the following examples means exempt function within the meaning of section 527(e)(2).

(i) *Example (1).* A wants to run for election to public office in State X. A is not a candidate. A travels throughout X in order to rally support for A's intended candidacy. While in X, A attends a convention of an organization for the purpose of attempting to solicit its support. The amount expended for travel, lodging, food, and similar expenses are for an exempt function.

(ii) *Example (2).* B, a member of the United States House of Representatives, is a candidate for reelection. B travels with B's spouse to

Reg. § 1.527-2(c)(5)

the district B represents. B feels it is important for B's reelection that B's spouse accompany B. While in the district, B makes speeches and appearances for the purpose of persuading voters to reelect B. The travel expenses of B and B's spouse are for an exempt function.

(iii) *Example (3)*. C is a candidate for public office. In connection with C's campaign, C takes voice and speech lessons to improve C's skills. The expenses for these lessons are for an exempt function.

(iv) *Example (4)*. D, an officeholder and candidate for reelection, purchases tickets to a testimonial dinner. D's attendance at the dinner is intended to aid D's reelection. Such expenditures are for an exempt function.

(v) *Example (5)*. E, an officeholder, expends amounts for periodicals of general circulation in order to keep informed on national and local issues. Such expenditures are not for an exempt function.

(vi) *Example (6)*. N is an organization described in section 501(c) and is exempt from taxation under section 501(a). F is employed as president of N. F, as a representative of N, testifies in response to a written request from a Congressional committee in support of the confirmation of an individual to a cabinet position. The expenditures of N that are directly related to F's testimony are not for an exempt function.

(vii) *Example (7)*. P is a political organization described in section 527(e)(2). Between elections P does not support any particular individual for public office. However, P does train staff members for the next election, drafts party rules, implements party reform proposals, and sponsors a party convention. The expenditures for these activities are for an exempt function.

(viii) *Example (8)*. Q is a political organization described in section 527(e)(2). Q finances seminars and conferences which are intended to influence persons who attend to support individuals to public office whose political philosophy is in harmony with the political philosophy of Q. The expenditures for these activities are for an exempt function.

(d) *Public office*. The facts and circumstances of each case will determine whether a particular Federal, State, or local office is a "public office." Principles consistent with those found under § 53.4946-1(g)(2) (relating to the definition of public office) will be applied.

(e) *Principal campaign committee*. A "principal campaign committee" is the political committee designated by a candidate for Congress as his or her principal campaign committee for purposes of section 302(e) of the Federal Election Campaign Act of 1971 (2 U.S.C. section 432(e)), as amended, and section 527(h) and § 1.527-x. [Reg. § 1.527-2.]

☐ [T.D. 7744, 12-29-80. Amended by T.D. 8041, 7-29-85.]

[Reg. § 1.527-3]

§ 1.527-3. **Exempt function income.**—(a) *General rule*—(1) For purposes of section 527, exempt function income consists solely of amounts received as—

(i) Contributions of money or other property,

(ii) Membership dues, fees, or assessments from a member of a political organization, or

(iii) Proceeds from a political fund raising or entertainment event, or proceeds from the sale of political campaign materials, which are not received in the ordinary course of any trade or business, but only to the extent such income is segregated for use only for exempt functions of the political organization.

(2) Income will be considered segregated for use only for an exempt function only if it is received into and disbursed from a segregated fund as defined in § 1.527-2(b).

(b) *Contributions*. The rules of section 271(b)(2) apply in determining whether the transfer of money or other property constitutes a contribution. Generally, money or other property, whether solicited personally, by mail, or through advertising, qualifies as a contribution. In addition, to the extent a political organization receives Federal, State, or local funds under the $1 "checkoff" provision (sections 9001-9013), or any other provision for financing of campaigns, such amounts are to be treated as contributions.

(c) *Dues, fees, and assessments*. Amounts received as membership fees and assessments from members of a political organization may constitute exempt function income to the political organization. Membership fees and assessments received in consideration for services, goods, or other items of value do not constitute exempt function income. However, filing fees paid by an individual directly or indirectly to a political party in order that the individual may run as a candidate in a primary election of the party (or run in a general election as a candidate of that party) are to be treated as exempt function income. For example, some States provide that a certain percentage of the first year's salary of the office sought must be paid to the State as a filing (or "qualifying") fee and party assessment. The State then transfers part of this fee to the candidate's party. In such a case, the entire amount transferred to the party is to be treated as exempt function income. Furthermore, amounts paid by an individual directly to the party as a qualification fee are treated similarly.

(d) *Fund raising events*—(1) *In general.* Amounts received from fund raising and entertainment events are eligible for treatment as exempt function income if the events are political in nature and are not carried on in the ordinary course of a trade or business. Whether an event is "political" in nature depends on all facts and circumstances. One factor that indicates an event is a political event is the extent to which the event is related to a political activity aside from the need of the organization for income or funds. For example, an event that is intended to rally and encourage support for an individual for public office would be a political fund raising event. Examples of political events can include dinners, breakfasts, receptions, picnics, dances, and athletic exhibitions.

(2) *Ordinary course of any trade or business.* Whether an activity is in the ordinary course of a trade or business depends on the facts and circumstances of each case. Generally, proceeds from casual, sporadic fund raising or entertainment events are not in the ordinary course of a trade or business. Factors to be taken into account in determining whether an activity is a trade or business include the frequency of the activity, the manner in which the activity is conducted, and the span of time over which the activity is carried on.

(e) *Sale of campaign materials.* Amounts received from the sale of campaign materials are eligible for treatment as exempt function income if the sale is not carried on in the ordinary course of a trade or business (as defined in paragraph (d)(2) of this section), and is related to a political activity of the organization aside from the need of such organization for income or funds. Proceeds from the sale of political memorabilia, bumper stickers, campaign buttons, hats, shirts, political posters, stationery, jewelry, or cookbooks are related to such a political activity where such items can be identified as relating to distributing political literature or organizing voters to vote for a candidate for public office. [Reg. § 1.527-3.]

☐ [T.D. 7744, 12-29-80.]

[Reg. § 1.527-4]

§ 1.527-4. **Special rules for computation of political organization taxable income.**—(a) *In general.* Political organization taxable income is determined according to the provisions of section 527(b) and the rules set forth in this section.

(b) *Limitation on capital losses.* If for any taxable year a political organization has a net capital loss, the rules of sections 1211(a) and 1212(a) apply.

(c) *Allowable deductions*—(1) *In general.* To be deductible in computing political organization taxable income, expenses, depreciation, and similar items must not only qualify as deductions allowed by chapter 1 of the Code, but must also be directly connected with the production of political organization taxable income.

(2) *"Directly connected with" defined.* To be "directly connected with" the production of political organization taxable income, an item of deduction must have a proximate and primary relationship to the production of such income and have been incurred in the production of such income. Items of deduction attributable solely to items of political organization taxable income are proximately and primarily related to such income. Whether an item of deduction is incurred in the production of political organization taxable income is determined on the basis of all the facts and circumstances of each case.

(3) *Dual use of facilities or personnel.* Expenses, depreciation, and similar items that are attributable to the production of exempt function income and political organization taxable income shall be allocated between the two on a reasonable and consistent basis. For example, where facilities are used both for an exempt function of the organization and for the production of political organization taxable income, expenses, depreciation, and similar items attributable to such facilities (for example, items of overhead) shall be allocated between the two uses on a reasonable and consistent basis. Similarly, where personnel are employed both for an exempt function and for the production of political organization taxable income, expenses and similar items attributable to such personnel (for example, items of salary) shall be allocated between the activities on a reasonable and consistent basis. The portion of any such item so allocated to the production of political organization taxable income is directly connected with such income and is allowable as a deduction in computing political organization taxable income to the extent that it qualifies as an item of deduction allowed by chapter 1 of the Code. Thus, for example, assume that X, a political organization, pays its manager a salary of $10,000 a year and that it derives political organization taxable income. If 10 percent of the manager's time during the year is devoted to deriving X's gross income (other than exempt function income), a deduction of $1,000 (10 percent of $10,000) would generally be allowable for purposes of computing

Reg. § 1.527-4(c)(3)

X's political organization taxable income. [Reg. § 1.527-4.]

☐ [T.D. 7744, 12-29-80.]

[Reg. § 1.527-5]

§ 1.527-5. Activities resulting in gross income to an individual or political organization.—(a) *In general*—(1) *General rule.* Amounts expended by a political organization for an exempt function are not income to the individual or individuals on whose behalf such expenditures are made. However, where a political organization expends any other amount for the personal use of any individual, the individual on whose behalf the amount is expended will be in receipt of income. Amounts are expended for the personal use of an individual where a direct or indirect financial benefit accrues to such individual. For example, if a political organization pays a personal legal obligation of a candidate for public office, such as the candidate's federal income tax liability, the amount paid is includible in such candidate's gross income. Similarly, if a political organization expends any amount of its exempt function income for other than an exempt function, and the expenditure results in a direct or indirect financial benefit to the political organization, it must include the amount of such expenditure in its gross income. For example, if a political organization expends exempt function income for making an improvement or addition to its facilities, or for equipment, which is not necessary for or used in carrying out an exempt function, the amount of the expenditure will be included in the political organization's gross income. However, if a political organization expends exempt function income to make ordinary and necessary repairs on the facilities the political organization uses in conducting its exempt function, such amounts will not be included in the political organization's gross income.

(2) *Expenditure for an illegal activity.* Expenditures by a political organization that are illegal or for an activity that is judicially determined to be illegal are treated as amounts not segregated for use only for the exempt function and shall be included in the political organization's taxable income. However, expenses incurred in defense of civil or criminal suits against the organization are not treated as taxable to the organization. Similarly, voluntary reimbursement to the participants in the illegal activity for similar expenses incurred by them are not taxable to the organization if the organization can demonstrate that such payments do not constitute a part of the inducement to engage in the illegal activity or part of the agreed upon compensation therefor. However, if the organization entered into an agreement with the participants to defray such expenses as part of the inducement, such payments would be treated as an expenditure for an illegal activity. Except where necessary to prevent the period of limitation for assessment and collection of a tax from expiring, a notice of deficiency will not generally be issued until after there has been a final determination of illegality by an appropriate court in a criminal proceeding.

(b) *Certain uses not treated as income to a candidate.* Except as otherwise provided in paragraph (a) of this section, if a political organization—

(1) Contributes any amount to or for the use of any political organization described in section 527(e)(1) or newsletter fund described in section 527(g),

(2) Contributes any amount to or for the use of any organization described in paragraph (1) or (2) of section 509(a) which is exempt from taxation under section 501(a), or

(3) Deposits any amount in the general fund of the U.S. Treasury or in the general fund of any State or local government,

such amount shall not be treated as an amount expended for the personal use of a candidate or other person. No deduction shall be allowed under the Internal Revenue Code of 1954 for the contribution or deposit described in the preceding sentence.

(c) *Excess funds*—(1) *General rule.* Generally, funds controlled by a political organization or other person after a campaign or election are excess funds and are treated as expended for the personal use of the person having control over the ultimate use of such funds. However, such funds will not be treated as excess funds to the extent they are—

(i) Transferred within a reasonable period of time by the person controlling the funds in accordance with paragraph (b) of this section, or

(ii) Held in reasonable anticipation of being used by the political organization for future exempt functions.

(2) *Excess funds transferred at death.* Where excess funds are held by an individual who dies, and these funds go to the individual's estate or any other person (other than an organization or fund described in paragraph (b) of this section), the funds are income of the decedent and will be included in the decedent's gross estate unless the estate or other person receiving such funds transfers the funds within a reasonable period of time in accordance with paragraph (b) of this section.

This paragraph (c)(2) will not apply where the individual who dies provides that the funds be transferred to an organization or fund described in paragraph (b) of this section. [Reg. § 1.527-5.]

☐ [T.D. 7744, 12-29-80.]

[Reg. § 1.527-6]

§ 1.527-6. **Inclusion of certain amounts in the gross income of an exempt organization which is not a political organization.**—(a) *Exempt organizations—General rule.* If an organization described in section 501(c) which is exempt from tax under section 501(a) expends any amount for an exempt function, it may be subject to tax. There is included in the gross income of such organization for the taxable year an amount equal to the lesser of—

(1) The net investment income of such organization for the taxable year, or

(2) The aggregate amount expended during the taxable year for an exempt function.

The amount included will be treated as political organization taxable income.

(b) *Exempt function expenditures*—(1) *Directly related expenses*—(i) Except as provided in this section, the term "exempt function" will generally have the same meaning it has in § 1.527-2(c). Thus, expenditures which are directly related to the selection process as defined in § 1.527-2(c)(1) are expenditures for an exempt function. Expenditures for indirect expenses as defined in § 1.527-2(c)(2), when made by a section 501(c) organization are for an exempt function only to the extent provided in paragraph (b)(2) of this section. Expenditures of a section 501(c) organization which are otherwise allowable under the Federal Election Campaign Act or similar State statute are for an exempt function only to the extent provided in paragraph (b)(3) of this section.

(ii) An expenditure may be made for an exempt function directly or through another organization. A section 501(c) organization will not be absolutely liable under section 527(f)(1) for amounts transferred to an individual or organization. A section 501(c) organization is, however, required to take reasonable steps to ensure that the transferee does not use such amounts for an exempt function.

(2) *Indirect expenses.* [Reserved].

(3) *Expenditures allowed by Federal Election Campaign Act.* [Reserved].

(4) *Appointments or confirmations.* Where an organization described in paragraph (a) of this section appears before any legislative body in response to a written request by such body for the purpose of influencing the appointment or confirmation of an individual to a public office, any expenditure directly related to such appearance is not treated as an expenditure for an exempt function.

(5) *Nonpartisan activity.* Expenditures for nonpartisan activities by an organization to which paragraph (a) of this section applies are not expenditures for an exempt function. Nonpartisan activities include voter registration and "get-out-the-vote" campaigns. To be nonpartisan voter registration and "get-out-the-vote" campaigns must not be specifically identified by the organization with any candidate or political party.

(c) *Character of items included in gross income*—(1) *General rule.* The items of income included in the gross income of an organization under paragraph (a) of this section retain their character as ordinary income or capital gain.

(2) *Special rule in determining character of item.* If the amount included in gross income is determined under paragraph (a)(2)(ii) of this section, the character of the items of income is determined by multiplying the total amount included in gross income under such paragraph by a fraction, the numerator of which is the portion of the organization's net investment income that is gain from the sale or exchange of a capital asset, and the denominator of which is the organization's net investment income. For example, if $5,000 is included in the gross income of an organization under paragraph (a)(2) of this section, and the organization had $100,000 of net investment income of which $10,000 is long term capital gain, then $500 would be treated as long term capital gain:

Capital gain net investment income	×	Amount expended on an exempt function	=	Portion of income subject to tax under section 1201
$\dfrac{\$10,000}{\$100,000}$	×	$5,000	=	$500

(d) *Modifications.* The modifications described in section 527(c)(2) apply in computing the tax under paragraph (a)(2) of this section. Thus, no net operating loss is allowed under section 172 nor is any deduction allowed under part VIII of subchapter B. However, there is allowed a specific deduction of $100.

(e) *Transfer not treated as exempt function expenditures.* Provided the provisions of this paragraph (e) are met, a transfer of political contributions or dues collected by a section 501(c) organization to a separate segregated fund as defined in paragraph (f) of this section is not treated as an expenditure for an exempt function (within the meaning of § 1.527-2(c)). Such transfers must be made promptly after the receipt of such

Reg. § 1.527-6(e)

amounts by the section 501(c) organization, and must be made directly to the separate segregated fund. A transfer is considered promptly and directly made if:

(1) The procedures followed by the section 501(c) organization satisfy the requirements of applicable Federal or State campaign law and regulations;

(2) The section 501(c) organization maintains adequate records to demonstrate that amounts transferred in fact consist of political contributions or dues, rather than investment income; and

(3) The political contributions or dues transferred were not used to earn investment income for the section 501(c) organization.

(f) *Separate segregated fund.* An organization or fund described in section 527(f)(3) is a separate segregated fund. To avoid the application of paragraph (a) of this section, an organization described in section 501(c) that is exempt from taxation under section 501(a) may, if it is consistent with its exempt status, establish and maintain such a separate segregated fund to receive contributions and make expenditures in a political campaign. If such a fund meets the requirements of § 1.527-2(a) (relating to the definition of a political organization), it shall be treated as a political organization subject to the provisions of section 527. A segregated fund established under the Federal Election Campaign Act will continue to be treated as a segregated fund when it engages in exempt function activities as defined in § 1.527-2(c), relating to State campaigns.

(g) *Effect of expenditures on exempt status.* Section 527(f) and this section do not sanction the intervention in any political campaign by an organization described in section 501(c) if such activity is inconsistent with its exempt status under section 501(c). For example, an organization described in section 501(c)(3) is precluded from engaging in any political campaign activities. The fact that section 527 imposes a tax on the exempt function (as defined in § 1.527-2(c)) expenditures of section 501(c) organizations and permits such organizations to establish separate segregated funds to engage in campaign activities does not sanction the participation in these activities by section 501(c)(3) organizations. [Reg. § 1.527-6.]

☐ [T.D. 7744, 12-29-80.]

[Reg. § 1.527-7]

§ 1.527-7. Newsletter funds.—(a) *In general.* For purposes of this section, a fund established and maintained by an individual who holds, has been elected to, or is a candidate (within the meaning of section 41(c)(2)) for nomination or election to, any Federal, State, or local elective public office for the use by such individual exclusively for an exempt function, as defined in paragraph (c) of this section, shall be a newsletter fund. If assets of a newsletter fund are used for any purpose other than the exempt function of the newsletter fund as defined in paragraph (c) of this section, such amount shall be treated as expended for the personal use of the individual who established and maintained such fund. In addition, future contributions to such fund are treated as income to the individual who established and maintained the fund. In such a case, the facts and circumstances may indicate that the fund was never established and maintained exclusively for an exempt function as defined in paragraph (c) of this section.

(b) *Determination of taxable income.* A newsletter fund shall be treated as if it were a political organization for purposes of determining its taxable income. However, the specific $100 deduction provided by section 527(c)(2)(A) shall not be allowed.

(c) *Exempt function.* For purposes of this section, the exempt function of a newsletter fund consists solely of the preparation and circulation of the newsletter. Among the expenditures treated as preparation and circulation expenditures of the newsletter are—

(1) Secretarial services,

(2) Printing,

(3) Addressing, and

(4) Mailing.

(d) *Nonexempt function purposes.* Newsletter fund assets may not be used for campaign activities. Therefore, an exempt function of a newsletter fund does not include—

(1) Expenditures for an exempt function as defined in § 1.527-2(c) or

(2) Transfers of unexpended amounts to a political organization described in section 527(e)(1).

(e) *Excess funds.* Excess funds held by a newsletter fund which has ceased to engage in the preparation and circulation of the newsletter are treated as expended for the personal use of the individual who established and maintained such fund. However, to the extent such excess funds are within a reasonable period of time—

(1) Contributed to or for the use of any organization described in paragraph (1) or (2) of section 509(a) which is exempt from taxation under section 501(a),

(2) Deposited in the general fund of the U.S. Treasury or in the general fund of any State or

local government (including the District of Columbia), or

(3) Contributed to any other newsletter fund as described in paragraph (a) of this section, the excess funds are not treated as expended for the personal use of such individual. In such a case the individual is not allowed a deduction under the Internal Revenue Code of 1954 for such contribution or deposit. [Reg. § 1.527-7.]

☐ [T.D. 7744, 12-29-80.]

[Reg. § 1.527-8]

§ 1.527-8. Effective date; filing requirements; and miscellaneous provisions.—(a) *Assessment and collections.* Since the taxes imposed by section 527 are taxes imposed by subtitle A of the Code, all provisions of law and of the regulations applicable to the taxes imposed by subtitle A are applicable to the assessment and collection of the taxes imposed by section 527. Organizations subject to the tax imposed by section 527 are subject to the same provisions, including penalties, as are provided for corporations, in general, except that the requirements of section 6154 concerning the payment of estimated tax do not apply. See, generally, sections 6151, et seq., and the regulations prescribed thereunder, for provisions relating to payment of tax.

(b) *Returns.* For requirements of filing annual returns with respect to political organization taxable income, see section 6012(a)(6) and the applicable regulations.

(c) *Taxable years, method of accounting, etc.* The taxable year (fiscal year or calendar year, as the case may be) of a political organization is determined without regard to the fact that such organization may have been exempt from tax during any prior period. See sections 441 and 446, and the regulations thereunder in this part, and section 7701 and the regulations in Part 301 of this chapter (Regulations on Procedure and Administration). Similarly, in computing political organization taxable income, the determination of the taxable year for which an item of income or expense is taken into account is made under the provisions of sections 441, 446, 451, 461, and the regulations thereunder, whether or not the item arose during a taxable year beginning before, on, or after the effective date of the provisions imposing a tax upon political organization taxable income. If a method for treating bad debts was selected in a return of income (other than an information return) for a previous taxable year, the taxpayer must follow such method in its returns under section 527, unless such method is changed in accordance with the provisions of § 1.166-1. A taxpayer who has not previously selected a method for treating bad debts may, in its first return under section 6012(a)(6), exercise the option granted in § 1.166-1.

(d) *Effective date.* Except as provided in paragraph (b)(2) of § 1.527-6 and in paragraph (a) of § 1.527-9, the regulations under section 527 apply to taxable years beginning after December 31, 1974. [Reg. § 1.527-8.]

☐ [T.D. 7744, 12-29-80. *Amended by* T.D. 8041, 7-29-85.]

[Reg. § 1.527-9]

§ 1.527-9. Special rule for principal campaign committees.—(a) *In general.* Effective with respect to taxable years beginning after December 31, 1981, the tax imposed by section 527(b) on the political organization taxable income of a principal campaign committee shall be computed by multiplying the political organization taxable income by the appropriate rates of tax specified in section 11(b). The political organization taxable income of a campaign committee not a principal campaign committee is taxed at the highest rate of tax specified in section 11(b). A candidate for Congress may designate one political committee to serve as his or her principal campaign committee for purposes of section 527(h)(1). If a designation is made, it shall be made in accordance with the requirements of paragraph (b) of this section. A candidate for Congress may have only one designation in effect at any time. Under 11 CFR § 102.12, no political committee may be designated as the principal campaign committee of more than one candidate for Congress. Further, no political committee that supports or has supported more than one candidate for Congress may be designated as a principal campaign committee. No designation need be made where there is only one political campaign committee with respect to a candidate.

(b) *Manner of designation.* If a candidate for Congress elects to make a designation under section 527(h) and this section, he or she shall designate his or her principal campaign committee by appending a copy of his or her Statement of Candidacy (that is, the Federal Election Commission Form 2 or equivalent statement that the candidate filed with the Federal Election Commission under 11 CFR § 101.1(a)), to the Form 1120-POL filed by the principal campaign committee for each taxable year for which the designation is effective. This designation may also be made by appending to the Form 1120-POL a statement containing the following information: the name and address of the candidate for Congress; his or her taxpayer identification number; his or her party affiliation and the office sought; the district and State in which the office is sought; and the name and address of the principal campaign committee. This designation shall be made on or before the due date (as extended) for filing Form 1120-POL. Only a candidate for Congress may make a designation in accordance with this paragraph.

(c) *Manner of revoking designation.* A designation of a principal campaign committee that has been filed in accordance with this section may be revoked only with the consent of the Commissioner. In general, the Commissioner will grant such consent in every case where the candidate for Congress has revoked his or her designation in compliance with the requirements of the Federal Election Commission by filing an amended Statement of Organization or its equivalent pursuant to 11 CFR § 102.2(a)(2). In the case of the revocation of the designation of a principal campaign committee by a candidate followed by the designation of another principal campaign committee by such candidate, for purposes of determining the appropriate rate of tax under section 11(b) for a taxable year, the political organization taxable income of the first principal campaign committee shall be treated as that of the subsequent principal campaign committee. In a case where consent to revoke a designation of a principal campaign committee is granted and a new designation is filed, the Commissioner may condition his consent upon the agreement of the candidate for Congress to insure compliance with the preceding sentence. [Reg. § 1.527-9.]

☐ [T.D. 8041, 7-29-85.]

Certain Homeowners Associations

[Reg. § 1.528-1]

§ 1.528-1. **Homeowners associations.**—(a) *In general.* Section 528 only applies to taxable years of homeowners associations beginning after December 31, 1973. To qualify as a homeowners association an organization must either be a condominium management association or a residential real estate management association. For the purposes of section 528 and the regulations under that section, the term "homeowners association" shall refer only to an organization described in section 528. Cooperative housing corporations and organizations based on a similar form of ownership are not eligible to be taxed as homeowners associations. As a general rule, membership in either a condominium management association or a residential real estate management association is confined to the developers and the owners of the units, residences, or lots. Furthermore, membership in either type of association is normally required as a condition of such ownership. However, if the membership of an organization consists of other homeowners associations, the owners of units, residences, or lots who are members of such other homeowners associations will be treated as the members of the organization for the purposes of the regulations under section 528.

(b) *Condominium.* The term "condominium" means an interest in real property consisting of an undivided interest in common in a portion of a parcel of real property (which may be a fee simple estate or an estate for years, such as a leasehold or subleasehold) together with a separate interest in space in a building located on such property. An interest in property is not a condominium unless the undivided interests in the common elements are vested in the unit holders. In addition, a condominium must meet the requirements of applicable state or local law relating to condominiums or horizontal property regimes.

(c) *Residential real estate management association.* Residential real estate management associations are normally composed of owners of single-family residential units located in a subdivision, development, or similar area. However, they may also include as members owners of multiple-family dwelling units located in such area. They are commonly formed to administer and enforce covenants relating to the architecture and appearance of the real estate development as well as to perform certain maintenance duties relating to common areas.

(d) *Tenants.* Tenants will not be considered members for purposes of meeting the source of income test under section 528(c)(1)(B) and § 1.528-5. However, the fact that tenants of members of a homeowners association are permitted to be members of the association will not disqualify an association under section 528(c)(1) if it otherwise meets the requirements of section 528(c) and these regulations. [Reg. § 1.528-1.]

☐ [T.D. 7692, 4-17-80.]

[Reg. § 1.528-2]

§ 1.528-2. **Organized and operated to provide for the acquisition, construction, management, maintenance and care of association property.**—(a) *Organized and operated*—(1) *Organized.* To be treated as a homeowners association an organization must be organized and operated primarily for the purpose of carrying on one or more of the exempt functions of a homeowners association. For the purposes of section 528 and these regulations, the exempt functions of a homeowners association are the acquisition, construction, management, maintenance, and care of

Reg. § 1.528-1(a)

association property. In determining whether an organization is organized and operated primarily to carry on one or more exempt functions, all the facts and circumstances of each case shall be considered. For example, when an organization provides in its articles of organization that its sole purpose is to carry on one or more exempt functions, in the absence of other relevant factors it will be considered to have met the organizational test. (The term "articles of organization" means the organization's corporate charter, trust instruments, articles of association or other instrument by which it is created.)

(2) *Operated.* An organization will be treated as being operated for the purpose of carrying on one or more of the exempt functions of a homeowners association if it meets the provisions of § 1.528-5 and § 1.528-6.

(b) *Terms to be interpreted according to common meaning and usage.* As used in section 528 and these regulations, the terms acquisition, construction, management, maintenance, and care are to be interpreted according to their common meaning and usage. For example, maintenance of association property includes the painting and repairing of such property as well as the gardening and janitorial services associated with its upkeep. Similarly, the term "construction" of association property includes covenants or other rules for preserving the architectural and general appearance of the area. The term also includes regulations relating to the location, color and allowable building materials to be used in all structures. (For the definition of association property see § 1.528-3). [Reg. § 1.528-2.]

☐ [*T.D.* 7692, 4-17-80.]

[Reg. § 1.528-3]

§ 1.528-3. **Association property.**—(a) *Property owned by the organization.* "Association property" includes real and personal property owned by the organization or owned as tenants in common by the members of the organization. Such property must be available for the common benefit of all members of the organization and must be of a nature that tends to enhance the beneficial enjoyment of the private residences by their owners. If two or more facilities or items of property of a similar nature are owned by a homeowners association, and if the use of any particular facility or item is restricted to fewer than all association members, such facilities or items nevertheless will be considered association property if all association members are treated equitably and have similar rights with respect to comparable items or facilities. Among the types of property that ordinarily will be considered association property are swimming pools and tennis courts. On the other hand, facilities or areas set aside for the use of nonmembers, or in fact used primarily by nonmembers, are not association property for the purposes of this section. For example, property owned by an organization for the purpose of leasing it to groups consisting primarily of nonmembers to be used as a meeting place or a retreat will not be considered association property.

(b) *Property normally owned by a governmental unit.* "Association property" also includes areas and facilities traditionally recognized and accepted as being of direct governmental concern in the exercise of the powers and duties entrusted to governments to regulate community health, safety and welfare. Such areas and facilities would normally include roadways, parklands, sidewalks, streetlights and firehouses. Property described in this paragraph will be considered association property regardless of whether it is owned by the organization itself, by its members as tenants in common or by a governmental unit and used for the benefit of the residents of such unit including the members of the organization.

(c) *Privately owned property.* "Association property" may also include property owned privately by members of the organization. However, to be so included the condition of such property must affect the overall appearance or structure of the residential units which make up the organization. Such property may include the exterior walls and roofs of privately owned residences as well as the lawn and shrubbery on privately owned land and any other privately owned property the appearance of which may directly affect the appearance of the entire organization. However, privately owned property will not be considered association property unless—

(1) There is a covenant or similar requirement relating to exterior appearance or maintenance that applies on the same basis to all such property (or to a reasonable classification of such property);

(2) There is a pro rata mandatory assessment (at least once a year) on all members of the association for maintaining such property; and

(3) Membership in the organization is a condition of ownership of such property. [Reg. § 1.528-3.]

☐ [*T.D.* 7692, 4-17-80.]

[Reg. § 1.528-4]

§ 1.528-4. **Substantially test.**—(a) *In general.* In order for an organization to be considered a condominium management association or a residential real estate management association (and therefore in order for it to be considered a homeowners association), substantially all of its units, lots or buildings must be used by individuals for residences. For the purposes of applying paragraph (b) or (c) of this section, an organization which has attributes of both a condominium management association and a residential real estate management association shall be considered that association which, based on all the facts and circumstances, it more closely resembles. In addition, those paragraphs shall be applied based on conditions existing on the last day of the organization's taxable year.

(b) *Condominium management associations.* Substantially all of the units of a condominium management association will be considered as used by individuals for residences if at least 85% of the total square footage of all units within the project is used by individuals for residential purposes. If a completed unit has never been occupied, it will nonetheless be considered as used for residential purposes if, based on all the facts and circumstances, it appears to have been constructed for use as a residence. Similarly, a unit which is not occupied but which has been in the past will be considered as used for residential purposes if, based on all the facts and circumstances, it appears that it was constructed for use as a residence, and the last individual to occupy it did in fact use it as a residence. Units which are used for purposes auxiliary to residential use (such as laundry areas, swimming pools, tennis courts, storage rooms and areas used by maintenance personnel) shall be considered used for residential purposes.

(c) *Residential Real Estate Management Associations.* Substantially all of the lots or buildings of a residential real estate management association (including unimproved lots) will be considered as used by individuals as residences if at least 85% of the lots are zoned for residential purposes. Lots shall be treated as zoned for residential purposes even if under such zoning lots may be used for parking spaces, swimming pools, tennis courts, schools, fire stations, libraries, churches and other similar purposes which are auxiliary to residential use. However, commercial shopping areas (and their auxiliary parking areas) are not lots zoned for residential purposes.

(d) *Exception.* Notwithstanding any other provision of this section, a unit, or building will not be considered used for residential purposes, if for more than one-half the days in the association's taxable year, such unit, or building is occupied by a person or series of persons, each of whom so occupies such unit, or building for less than 30 days. [Reg. § 1.528-4.]

☐ [*T.D.* 7692, 4-17-80.]

Reg. § 1.528-5

[Reg. § 1.528-5]

§ 1.528-5. Source of income test.—An organization cannot qualify as a homeowners association under section 528 for a taxable year unless 60 percent or more of its gross income for such taxable year is exempt function income as defined in § 1.528-9. The determination of whether an organization meets the provisions of this section shall be made after the close of the organization's taxable year. [Reg. § 1.528-5.]

☐ [*T.D.* 7692, 4-17-80.]

[Reg. § 1.528-6]

§ 1.528-6. Expenditure test.—(a) *In general.* An organization cannot qualify as a homeowners association under section 528 for a taxable year unless 90 percent or more of its expenditures for such taxable year are qualifying expenditures as defined in paragraphs (b) and (c) of this section. The determination of whether an organization meets the provisions of this section shall be made after the close of the organization's taxable year. Investments or transfers of funds to be held to meet future costs shall not be taken into account as expenditures. For example, transfers to a sinking fund account for the replacement of a roof would not be considered an expenditure for the purposes of this section even if the roof is association property. In addition, excess assessments which are either rebated to members or applied against the members' following year's assessments will not be considered an expenditure for the purposes of this section.

(b) *Qualifying expenditures.* Qualifying expenditures are expenditures by an organization for the acquisition, construction, management, maintenance, and care of the organization's association property. They include both current operating and capital expenditures on association property. Qualifying expenditures include expenditures on association property despite the fact that such property may produce income which is not exempt function income. Thus expenditures on a swimming pool are qualifying expenditures despite the fact that fees from guests of members using the pool are not exempt function income. Where expenditures by an organization are used both for association property as well as other property, an allocation shall be made between the two uses on a reasonable basis. Only that portion of the expenditure which is properly allocable to the acquisition, construction, management, maintenance or care of association property, shall constitute qualifying expenditures.

(c) *Examples of qualifying expenditures.* Qualifying expenditures may include (but are not limited to) expenditures for—

(1) Salaries of an association manager and secretary;

(2) Paving of streets;

(3) Street signs;

(4) Security personnel;

(5) Legal fees;

(6) Upkeep of tennis courts;

(7) Swimming pools;

(8) Recreation rooms and halls;

(9) Replacement of common buildings, facilities, air conditioning, etc.,

(10) Insurance premiums on association property;

(11) Accountant's fees;

(12) Improvement of private property to the extent it is association property; and

(13) Real estate and personal property taxes imposed on association property by a State or local government. [Reg. § 1.528-6.]

☐ [T.D. 7692, 4-17-80.]

[Reg. § 1.528-7]

§ 1.528-7. Inurement.—An organization is not a homeowners association if any part of its net earnings inures (other than as a direct result of its engaging in one or more exempt functions) to the benefit of any private person. Thus, to the extent that members receive a benefit from the general maintenance, etc. of association property, this benefit generally would not constitute inurement. If an organization pays rebates from amounts other than exempt function income, such rebates will constitute inurement. In general, in determining whether an organization is in violation of this section, the principles used in making similar determinations under section 501(c) will be applied. [Reg. § 1.528-7.]

☐ [T.D. 7692, 4-17-80.]

[Reg. § 1.528-8]

§ 1.528-8. Election to be treated as a homeowners association.—(a) *General rule.* An organization wishing to be treated as a homeowners association under section 528 and this section for a taxable year must elect to be so treated. Except as otherwise provided in this section such election shall be made by the filing of a properly completed Form 1120-H (or such other form as the Secretary may prescribe). A separate election must be made for each taxable year.

(b) *Taxable years ending after December 30, 1976.* For taxable years ending after December 30, 1976, the election must be made not later than the time, including extensions, for filing an income tax return for the year in which the election is to apply.

(c) *Taxable years ending before December 31, 1976, for which a return was filed before January 31, 1977.* For taxable years ending before December 31, 1976, for which a return was filed before January 31, 1977, the election must be made not later than the time provided by law for filing a claim for credit or refund of overpayment of taxes for the year in which the election is to apply. Such an election shall be made by filing an amended return on Form 1120-H (or such other form as the Secretary may prescribe).

(d) *Taxable years ending before December 31, 1976, for which a return was not filed before January 31, 1977.* For taxable years ending before December 31, 1976, for which a return has not been filed before January 31, 1977, the election must be made by October 20, 1980. Instead of making such an election in the manner described in paragraph (a) of this section, such an election may be made by a statement attached to the applicable income tax return or amended return for the year in which the election is made. The statement should identify the election being made, the period for which it applies and the taxpayer's basis for making the election.

(e) *Revocation of exempt status.* If an organization is notified after the close of a taxable year that its exemption for such taxable year under section 501(a) is being revoked retroactively, it may make a timely election under section 528 for such taxable year. Notwithstanding any other provisions of this section, such an election will be considered timely if it is made within 6 months after the date of revocation. The preceding sentence shall apply to revocations made after April 18, 1980. If the revocation was made on or before April 18, 1980, the election will be considered timely if it is made before the expiration of the period for filing a claim for credit or refund for the taxable year for which it is to apply.

(f) *Effect of election*—(1) *Revocation.* An election to be treated as an organization described in section 528 is binding on the organization for the taxable year and may not be revoked without the consent of the Commissioner.

(2) *Exception.* Notwithstanding paragraph (f)(1) of this section, an election under this section may be revoked prior to July 18, 1980. Such a revocation shall be made by filing a statement with the director of the Internal Revenue Service Center with whom the return of the organization for the year in which the revocation is to apply was filed. The statement shall include the following information.

(i) The name of the organization.

(ii) The fact that it is revoking an election made under section 528.

(iii) The taxable year for which the revocation is to apply.

[Reg. § 1.528-8.]

☐ [T.D. 7692, 4-17-80.]

[Reg. § 1.528-9]

§ 1.528-9. Exempt function income.—(a) *General rule.* For the purposes of section 528 exempt function income consists solely of income which is attributable to membership dues, fees, or assessments of owners of residential units or residential lots. It is not necessary that the source of income be labeled as membership dues, fees, or assessments. What is important is that such income be derived from owners of residential units or residential lots in their capacity as owner-members rather than in some other capacity such as customers for services. Generally, for the membership dues, fees, or assessments with respect to a residential unit or lot to be exempt function income, the unit must be used for (or the unit or lot must be expected to be used for) residential purposes. However, dues, fees, or assessments paid to an organization by a developer with respect to unfinished or finished but unsold units or lots shall be exempt function income even though the developer does not use the units or lots. If an assessment is more in the nature of a fee for the provision of services in the course of a trade or business than a fee for a common activity undertaken by a collective group of owners for the purpose of enhancing or maintaining the value of their residences, the assessment will not be considered exempt function income to the organization. Furthermore, income attributable to dues, fees, or assessments will not be considered exempt function income unless each member's liability for payment arises solely from membership in the association. Dues, fees, or assessments that are based on the extent, if any, to which a member avails him or herself of a facility or facilities are not exempt function income. For the purposes of section 528, dues, fees, or assessments which are based on the assessed value or size of property will be considered as arising solely as a result of membership in the organization. Regardless of the organization's method of accounting, excess assessments during a taxable year which are either rebated to the members or applied to their future assessments are not considered gross income and therefore will not be considered exempt function income for such taxable year. However, if such excess assessments are applied to a future year's assessments, they will be considered gross income and exempt function income for that future year. In addition, assessments in a taxable year, such as an assessment for a capital improvement, which are not treated as gross income do not enter into the determination of whether the organization meets the source of income test for that taxable year.

(b) *Examples of exempt function income.* Assessments which are considered more in the nature of a fee for common activity than for the providing of services and which will therefore generally be considered exempt function income include assessments made for the purpose of—

(1) Paying the principal and interest on debts incurred for the acquisition of association property;

(2) Paying real estate taxes on association property;

(3) Maintaining association property;

(4) Removing snow from public areas; and

(5) Removing trash.

(c) *Examples of receipts which are not exempt function income.* Exempt function income does not include—

(1) Amounts which are not includible in the organization's gross income other than by reason of section 528 (for example, tax-exempt interest);

(2) Amounts received from persons who are not members of the association;

(3) Amounts received from members for special use of the organization's facilities, the use of which is not available to all members as a result of having paid the dues, fees or assessments required to be paid by all members;

(4) Interest earned on amounts set aside in a sinking fund;

(5) Amounts received for work done on privately owned property which is not association property; or

(6) Amounts received from members in return for their transportation to or from shopping areas, work location, etc.

(d) *Special rule.* Notwithstanding paragraphs (a) and (c)(3) of this section, amounts received from members or from tenants of residential units owned by members (notwithstanding § 1.528-1(d)) for special use of an association's facilities will be considered exempt function income if—

(1) The amounts paid by the members are not paid more than once in any 12 month period; and

(2) The privilege obtained from the payment of such amounts lasts for the entire 12 month period or portion thereof in which the facility is commonly in use.

Reg. § 1.528-9(a)

Thus, amounts received as the result of payments by members of a yearly fee for use of tennis courts or a swimming pool shall be considered exempt function income. However, amounts received for the use of a building for an evening, weekend, week, etc. shall not be considered exempt function income. [Reg. § 1.528-9.]

☐ [T.D. 7692, 4-17-80.]

[Reg. § 1.528-10]

§ 1.528-10. Special rules for computation of homeowners association taxable income and tax.—(a) *In general.* Homeowners association taxable income shall be determined according to the provisions of section 528(d) and the rules set forth in this section.

(b) *Limitation on capital losses.* If for any taxable year a homeowners association has a net capital loss, the rules of sections 1211(a) and 1212(a) shall apply.

(c) *Allowable deductions*—(1) *In general.* To be deductible in computing the unrelated business taxable income of a homeowners association, expenses, depreciation and similar items must not only qualify as items of deduction allowed by chapter 1 of the Code but must also be directly connected with the production of gross income (excluding exempt function income). To be "directly connected with" the production of gross income (excluding exempt function income), an item of deduction must have both proximate and primary relationship to the production of such income. Items of deduction attributable solely to items of gross income (excluding exempt function income) are proximately and primarily related to such income. Whether an item of deduction is incurred in the production of gross income (excluding exempt function income) is determined on the basis of all the facts and circumstances involved in each case.

(2) *Dual use of facilities or personnel.* Where facilities are used both for exempt functions of the organization and for the production of gross income (excluding exempt function income), expenses, depreciation and similar items attributable to such facilities (for example, items of overhead) shall be allocated between the two uses on a reasonable basis. Similarly, where personnel are employed both for exempt functions and for the production of gross income (excluding exempt function income), expenses and similar items attributable to such personnel (for example, items of salary) shall be allocated between the two activities on a reasonable basis. The portion of any such item so allocated to the production of gross income (excluding exempt function income) is directly connected with such income and shall be allowable as a deduction in computing homeowners association taxable income to the extent that it qualifies as an item of deduction allowed by chapter 1 of the Code. Thus, for example, assume that X, a homeowners association, pays its manager a salary of $10,000 a year and that it derives gross income other than exempt function income. If 10 percent of the manager's time during the year is devoted to deriving X's gross income (other than exempt function income), a deduction of $1,000 (10 percent of $10,000) would generally be allowable for purposes of computing X's homeowners association taxable income.

(d) *Investment credit.* A homeowners association is not entitled to an investment credit.

(e) *Cross reference.* For the definition of exempt function income, see § 1.528-9. [Reg. § 1.528-10.]

☐ [T.D. 7692, 4-17-80.]

CORPORATIONS USED TO AVOID INCOME TAX ON SHAREHOLDERS

Corporations Improperly Accumulating Surplus

[Reg. § 1.531-1]

§ 1.531-1. Imposition of tax.—Section 531 imposes (in addition to the other taxes imposed upon corporations by chapter 1 of the Code) a graduated tax on the accumulated taxable income of every corporation described in section 532 and § 1.532-1. In the case of an affiliated group which makes or is required to make a consolidated return see § 1.1502-43. All of the taxes on corporations under chapter 1 of the Code are treated as one tax for purposes of assessment, collection, payment, period of limitations, etc. See section 535 and §§ 1.535-1, 1.535-2, and 1.535-3 for the definition and determination of accumulated taxable income. [Reg. § 1.531-1.]

☐ [T.D. 6377, 5-12-59. Amended by T.D. 7244, 12-29-72 and by T.D. 7937, 1-26-84.]

[Reg. § 1.532-1]

§ 1.532-1. Corporations subject to accumulated earnings tax.—(a) *General rule.* (1) The tax imposed by section 531 applies to any domestic or foreign corporation (not specifically excepted under section 532(b) and paragraph (b) of this section) formed or availed of to avoid or prevent the imposition of the individual income tax on its shareholders, or on the shareholders of

Reg. § 1.532-1(a)

Corporations Improperly Accumulating Surplus

See p. 20,601 for regulations not amended to reflect law changes

any other corporation, by permitting earnings and profits to accumulate instead of dividing or distributing them. See section 533 and § 1.533-1, relating to evidence of purpose to avoid income tax with respect to shareholders.

(2) The tax imposed by section 531 may apply if the avoidance is accomplished through the formation or use of one corporation or a chain of corporations. For example, if the capital stock of the M Corporation is held by the N Corporation, the earnings and profits of the M Corporation would not be returned as income subject to the individual income tax until such earnings and profits of the M Corporation were distributed to the N Corporation and distributed in turn by the N Corporation to its shareholders. If either the M Corporation or the N Corporation was formed or is availed of for the purpose of avoiding or preventing the imposition of the individual income tax upon the shareholders of the N Corporation, the accumulated taxable income of the corporation so formed or availed of (M or N, as the case may be) is subject to the tax imposed by section 531.

(b) *Exceptions.* The accumulated earnings tax imposed by section 531 does not apply to a personal holding company (as defined in section 542), to a foreign personal holding company (as defined in section 552), or to a corporation exempt from tax under subchapter F, of chapter 1 of the Code.

(c) *Foreign corporations.* Section 531 is applicable to any foreign corporation, whether resident or nonresident, with respect to any income derived from sources within the United States, if any of its shareholders are subject to income tax on the distributions of the corporation by reason of being (1) citizens or residents of the United States, or (2) nonresident alien individuals to whom section 871 is applicable, or (3) foreign corporations if a beneficial interest therein is owned directly or indirectly by any shareholder specified in subparagraph (1) or (2) of this paragraph. [Reg. § 1.532-1.]

☐ [T.D. 6377, 5-12-59.]

[Reg. § 1.533-1]

§ 1.533-1. **Evidence of purpose to avoid income tax.**—(a) *In general.* (1) The Commissioner's determination that a corporation was formed or availed of for the purpose of avoiding income tax with respect to shareholders is subject to disproof by competent evidence. Section 533(a) provides that the fact that earnings and profits of a corporation are permitted to accumulate beyond the reasonable needs of the business shall be determinative of the purpose to avoid the income tax with respect to shareholders unless the corporation, by the preponderance of the evidence, shall prove to the contrary. The burden of proving that earnings and profits have been permitted to accumulate beyond the reasonable needs of the business may be shifted to the Commissioner under section 534. See §§ 1.534-1 through 1.534-4. Section 533(b) provides that the fact that the taxpayer is a mere holding or investment company shall be prima facie evidence of the purpose to avoid income tax with respect to shareholders.

(2) The existence or nonexistence of the purpose to avoid income tax with respect to shareholders may be indicated by circumstances other than the conditions specified in Section 533. Whether or not such purpose was present depends upon the particular circumstances of each case. All circumstances which might be construed as evidence of the purpose to avoid income tax with respect to shareholders cannot be outlined, but among other things, the following will be considered:

(i) Dealings between the corporation and its shareholders, such as withdrawals by the shareholders as personal loans or the expenditure of funds by the corporation for the personal benefit of the shareholders,

(ii) The investment by the corporation of undistributed earnings in assets having no reasonable connection with the business of the corporation (see § 1.537-3), and

(iii) the extent to which the corporation has distributed its earnings and profits.

The fact that a corporation is a mere holding or investment company or has an accumulation of earnings and profits in excess of the reasonable needs of the business is not absolutely conclusive against it if the taxpayer satisfies the Commissioner that the corporation was neither formed nor availed of for the purpose of avoiding income tax with respect to shareholders.

(b) *General burden of proof and statutory presumptions.* The Commissioner may determine that the taxpayer was formed or availed of to avoid income tax with respect to shareholders through the medium of permitting earnings and profits to accumulate. In the case of litigation involving any such determination (except where the burden of proof is on the Commissioner under section 534), the burden of proving such determination wrong by a preponderance of the evidence, together with the corresponding burden of first going forward with the evidence, is on the taxpayer under principles applicable to income tax cases generally. For the burden of proof in a proceeding before the Tax Court with respect to the allegation that earnings and profits have been permitted to accumulate beyond the reasonable

Reg. § 1.533-1(a)(2)

needs of the business, see section 534 and § 1.534-2 through 1.534-4. For a definition of a holding or investment company, see paragraph (c) of this section. For determination of the reasonable needs of the business, see section 537 and §§ 1.537-1 through 1.537-3. If the taxpayer is a mere holding or investment company, and the Commissioner therefore determines that the corporation was formed or availed of for the purpose of avoidng income tax with respect to shareholders, then section 533(b) gives further weight to the presumption of correctness already arising from the Commissioner's determination by expressly providing an additional presumption of the existence of a purpose to avoid income tax with respect to shareholders. Further, if it is established (after complying with section 534 where applicable) that earnings and profits were permitted to accumulate beyond the reasonable needs of the business and the Commissioner has therefore determined that the corporation was formed or availed of for the purpose of avoiding income tax with respect to shareholders, then section 533(a) adds still more weight to the Commissioner's determination. Under such circumstances, the existence of such an accumulation is made determinative of the purpose to avoid income tax with respect to shareholders unless the taxpayer proves to the contrary by the preponderance of the evidence.

(c) *Holding or investment company.* A corporation having practically no activities except holding property and collecting the income therefrom or investing therein shall be considered a holding company within the meaning of section 533(b). If the activities further include, or consist substantially of, buying and selling stocks, securities, real estate, or other investment property (whether upon an outright or marginal basis) so that the income is derived not only from the investment yield but also from profits upon market fluctuations, the corporation shall be considered an investment company within the meaning of section 533(b).

(d) *Small business investment companies.* A corporation which is licensed to operate as a small business investment company under the Small Business Investment Act of 1958 (15 U.S.C. ch. 14B) and the regulations thereunder (13 CFR Part 107) will generally be considered to be a "mere holding or investment company" within the meaning of section 533(b). However, the presumption of the existence of the purpose to avoid income tax with respect to shareholders which results from the fact that such a company is a "mere holding or investment company" will be considered overcome so long as such company:

(1) Complies with all the provisions of the Small Business Investment Act of 1958 and the regulations thereunder; and

(2) Actively engages in the business of providing funds to small business concerns through investment in the equity capital of, or through the disbursement of long-term loans to, such concerns in such manner and under such terms as the company may fix in accordance with regulations promulgated by the Small Business Administration (see secs. 304 and 305 of the Small Business Investment Act of 1958, as amended (15 U.S.C. 684, 685)). On the other hand, if such a company violates or fails to comply with any of the provisions of the Small Business Investment Act of 1958, as amended, or the regulations thereunder, or ceases to be actively engaged in the business of providing funds to small business concerns in the manner provided in subparagraph (2) of this paragraph, it will not be considered to have overcome the presumption by reason of any rules provided in this paragraph. [Reg. § 1.533-1.]

☐ [*T.D. 6377, 5-12-59. Amended by T.D. 6449, 1-27-60 and by T.D. 6652, 5-13-63.*]

[Reg. § 1.533-2]

§ 1.533-2. **Statement required.**—The corporation may be required to furnish a statement of its accumulated earnings and profits, the payment of dividends, the name and address of, and number of shares held by, each of its shareholders, the amounts that would be payable to each of the shareholders if the income of the corporation were distributed, and other information required under section 6042. [Reg. § 1.533-2.]

☐ [*T.D. 6377, 5-12-59.*]

[Reg. § 1.534-1]

§ 1.534-1. **Burden of proof as to unreasonable accumulations generally.**—For purposes of applying the presumption provided for in section 533(a) and in determining the extent of the accumulated earnings credit under section 535(c)(1), the burden of proof with respect to an allegation by the Commissioner that all or any part of the earnings and profits of the corporation have been permitted to accumulate beyond the reasonable needs of the business may vary under section 534 as between litigation in the Tax Court and that in any other court. In case of a proceeding in a court other than the Tax Court, see paragraph (b) of § 1.533-1. [Reg. § 1.534-1.]

☐ [*T.D. 6377, 5-12-59.*]

[Reg. § 1.534-2]

§ 1.534-2. **Burden of proof as to unreasonable accumulations in cases before the Tax Court**—(a) *Burden of proof on Commissioner.*

Reg. § 1.534-2(a)

Under the general rule provided in section 534(a), in any proceeding before the Tax Court involving a notice of deficiency based in whole or in part on the allegation that all or any part of the earnings and profits have been permitted to accumulate beyond the reasonable needs of the business, the burden of proof with respect to such allegation is upon the Commissioner if—

(1) A notification, as provided for in section 534(b) and paragraph (c) of this section, has not been sent to the taxpayer; or

(2) A notification, as provided for in section 534(b) and paragraph (c) of this section, has been sent to the taxpayer and, in response to such notification, the taxpayer has submitted a statement, as provided in section 534(c) and paragraph (d) of this section, setting forth the ground or grounds (together with facts sufficient to show the basis thereof) on which it relies to establish that all or any part of its earnings and profits have not been permitted to accumulate beyond the reasonable needs of the business. However, the burden of proof in the latter case is upon the Commissioner only with respect to the relevant ground or grounds set forth in the statement submitted by the taxpayer, and only if such ground or grounds are supported by facts (contained in the statement) sufficient to show the basis therof.

(b) *Burden of proof on the taxpayer.* The burden of proof in a Tax Court proceeding with respect to an allegation that all or any part of the earnings and profits have been permitted to accumulate beyond the reasonable needs of the business is upon the taxpayer if—

(1) A notification, as provided for in section 534(b) and paragraph (c) of this section, has been sent to the taxpayer and the taxpayer has not submitted a statement, in response to such notification, as provided in section 534(c) and paragraph (d) of this section; or

(2) A statement has been submitted by the taxpayer in response to such notification, but the ground or grounds on which the taxpayer relies are not relevant to the allegation or, if relevant, the statement does not contain facts sufficient to show the basis thereof.

(c) *Notification to the taxpayer.* Under section 534(b) a notification informing the taxpayer that the proposed notice of deficiency includes an amount with respect to the accumulated earnings tax imposed by section 531 may be sent by registered mail (or by certified or registered mail, if the notification is mailed after September 2, 1958) to the taxpayer at any time before the mailing of the notice of deficiency in the case of a taxable year beginning after December 31, 1953, and ending after August 16, 1954. See § 1.534-4 for rules relating to taxable years subject to the Internal Revenue Code of 1939. See section 534(d) and § 1.534-3 with respect to a notification in the case of a jeopardy assessment.

(d) *Statement by taxpayer.* (1) A taxpayer who has received a notification, as provided in section 534(b) and paragraph (c) of this section, that the proposed notice of deficiency includes an amount with respect to the accumulated earnings tax imposed by section 531, may, under section 534(c), submit a statement that all or any part of the earnings and profits of the corporation have not been permitted to accumulate beyond the reasonable needs of the business. Such statement shall set forth the ground or grounds (together with facts sufficient to show the basis thereof) on which the taxpayer relies to establish that there has been no accumulation of earnings and profits beyond the reasonable needs of the business. See paragraphs (a) and (b) of this section for rules concerning the effect of the statement with respect to burden of proof. See §§ 1.537-1 to 1.537-3, inclusive, relating to reasonable needs of the business.

(2) The taxpayer's statement, under section 534(c) and this paragraph, must be submitted to the Internal Revenue office which issued the notification (referred to in section 534(b) and paragraph (c) of this section) within 60 days after the mailing of such notification. If the taxpayer is unable, for good cause, to submit the statement within such 60-day period, an additional period not exceeding 30 days may be granted upon receipt in the Internal Revenue office concerned (before the expiration of the 60-day period provided herein) of a request from the taxpayer, setting forth the reasons for such request. See section 534(d) and § 1.534-3 with respect to a statement in the case of a jeopardy assessment. [Reg. § 1.534-2.]

☐ [*T.D.* 6377, 5-12-59.]

[Reg. § 1.534-3]

§ 1.534-3. **Jeopardy assessments in Tax Court cases.**—In the case of a jeopardy assessment, a notice of deficiency is required to be sent to the taxpayer by registered mail (or by certified or registered mail, if the notice is mailed after September 2, 1958) within 60 days after the making of the assessment. See section 6861. If a jeopardy assessment is made before the mailing of the deficiency notice, then in the case of a proceeding in the Tax Court, if the deficiency notice informs the taxpayer that an amount of accumulated earnings tax is included in the deficiency, such notice shall constitute the notification provided for in section 534(b) and paragraph (c) of § 1.534-2. Under such circumstances the statement described in section 534(c) and paragraph (d) of § 1.534-2 shall instead be included in the taxpayer's petition to the Tax Court, if the taxpayer desires to submit such statement. See paragraph (b) of § 1.534-2, relating to burden of proof on the taxpayer. [Reg. § 1.534-3.]

☐ [T.D. 6377, 5-12-59.]

[Reg. § 1.535-1]

§ 1.535-1. Definition.—(a) The accumulated earnings tax is imposed by section 531 on the accumulated taxable income. Accumulated taxable income is the taxable income of the corporation with the adjustments prescribed by section 535(b) and § 1.535-2, minus the sum of the dividends paid deduction and the accumulated earnings credit. See section 561 and the regulations thereunder, relating to the definition of the deduction for dividends paid, and section 535(c) and § 1.535-3, relating to the accumulated earnings credit.

(b) In the case of a foreign corporation, whether resident or nonresident, which files or causes to be filed a return, the accumulated taxable income shall be the taxable income from sources within the United States with the adjustments prescribed by section 535(b) and § 1.535-2 minus the sum of the dividends paid deduction and the accumulated earnings credit. In the case of a foreign corporation which files no return, the accumulated taxable income shall be the gross income from sources within the United States without allowance of any deductions (including the accumulated earnings credit). [Reg. § 1.535-1.]

☐ [T.D. 6377, 5-12-59. Amended by T.D. 7244, 12-29-72.]

[Reg. § 1.535-2]

§ 1.535-2. Adjustments to taxable income.—(a) *Taxes*—(1) *United States taxes.* In computing accumulated taxable income for any taxable year, there shall be allowed as a deduction the amount by which Federal income and excess profits taxes accrued during the taxable year exceed the credit provided by section 33 (relating to taxes of foreign countries and possessions of the United States), except that no deduction shall be allowed for (i) the accumulated earnings tax impose by section 531 (or a corresponding section of a prior law), (ii) the personal holding company tax imposed by section 541 (or a corresponding section of a prior law), and (iii) the excess profits tax imposed by subchapter E, chapter 2 of the Internal Revenue Code of 1939, for taxable years beginning after December 31, 1940. The deduction is for taxes accrued during the taxable year, regardless of whether the corporation uses an accrual method of accounting, the cash receipts and disbursements method, or any other allowable method of accounting. In computing the amount of taxes accrued, an unpaid tax which is being contested is not considered accrued until the contest is resolved.

(2) *Taxes of foreign countries and United States possessions.* In determining accumulated taxable income for any taxable year, if the taxpayer chooses the benefits of section 901 for such taxable year, a deduction shall be allowed for—

(i) The income, war profits, and excess profits taxes imposed by foreign countries or possessions of the United States and accrued during such taxable year, and

(ii) In the case of a domestic corporation, the foreign income taxes deemed to be paid for such taxable year under section 902(a) in accordance with §§ 1.902-1 and 1.902-2 or section 960(a)(1) in accordance with § 1.960-7. In no event shall the amount under subdivision (ii) of this subparagraph exceed the amount includible in gross income with respect to such taxes under section 78 and § 1.78-1. The credit for such taxes provided by section 901 shall not be allowed against the accumulated earnings tax imposed by section 531. See section 901(a).

(b) *Charitable contributions.* Section 535(b)(2) provides that, in computing the accumulated taxable income of a corporation, the deduction for charitable contributions shall be computed without regard to section 170(b)(2). Thus, the amount of charitable contributions made during the taxable year not allowable as a deduction under section 170 by reason of the limitations imposed by section 170(b)(2) shall be allowed as a deduction in computing accumulated taxable income for the taxable year. However, any excess of the amount of the charitable contributions made in a prior taxable year over the amount allowed as a deduction under section 170 for such year shall not be allowed as a deduction from taxable income in computing accumulated taxable income for the taxable year.

(c) *Special deductions disallowed.* Sections 241 through 248 provide for the allowance of special deductions for such items as partially tax-exempt interest, certain dividends received, dividends paid on certain preferred stock of public utilities, and organizational expenses. Such special deductions, except the deduction provided by section 248 (relating to organizational expenses) shall be disallowed in computing accumulated taxable income.

(d) *Net operating loss.* The net operating loss deduction provided in section 172 is not allowed for purposes of computing accumulated taxable income.

Reg. § 1.535-2(d)

39,210   Corporations Improperly Accumulating Surplus
See p. 20,601 for regulations not amended to reflect law changes

(e) *Capital losses.* (1) Losses from sales or exchanges of capital assets during the taxable year, which are disallowed as deductions under section 1211(a) in computing taxable income, shall be allowed as deductions in computing accumulated taxable income.

(2) The computation of the capital losses allowable as a deduction in computing accumulated taxable income may be illustrated by the following example:

Example: X Corporation has capital losses of $30,000 which are disallowed under section 1211(a) for the taxable year ended December 31, 1956. This amount represents a loss of $25,000 from the sale or exchange of capital assets during the taxable year ended December 31, 1956, plus a $5,000 capital loss carryover resulting from the sale or exchange of capital assets during the taxable year ended December 31, 1955. In computing accumulated taxable income for the taxable year ended December 31, 1956, only the loss of $25,000 arising from the sale or exchange of capital assets during that taxable year will be allowed as a deduction.

(f) *Long-term capital gains.* (1) There is allowed as a deduction in computing accumulated taxable income, the excess of the net long-term capital gain for the taxable year over the net short-term capital loss for such year (determined without regard to the capital loss carryover provided in section 1212) minus the taxes attributable to such excess as provided by section 535(b)(6). The tax attributable to such excess is the difference between—

(i) The taxes (except the accumulated earnings tax) imposed by subtitle A of the Code for such year, and

(ii) The taxes (except the accumulated earnings tax) imposed by subtitle A computed for such year as if taxable income were reduced by the excess of the net long-term capital gain over net short-term capital loss (including the capital loss carryover to such year).

Where the tax (except the accumulated earnings tax) imposed by subtitle A includes an amount computed under section 1201(a)(2), the tax attributable to such excess is such amount computed under section 1201(a)(2).

(2) The application of the rule in subparagraph (1) of this paragraph may be illustrated by the following example:

Example. Assume that D Corporation, for the taxable year ended December 31, 1956, has taxable income of $103,000 of which $3,000 is the excess of net long-term capital gain of $12,000 over a net short-term capital loss of $9,000. The $9,000 net short-term capital loss includes a capital loss carryover of $5,000. The amount allowable as a deduction under section 535(b)(6) and subparagraph (1) of this paragraph is $7,250, computed as follows: Net long-term capital gain less net short-term capital loss (computed without regard to the capital loss carryover) is $8,000 (that is, $12,000 net long-term capital gain less $4,000 net short-term capital loss computed without regard to the capital loss carryover of $5,000). The tax attributable to the excess of net long-term capital gain over net short-term capital loss (computed by taking the capital loss carryover into account) is $750, that is, 25 percent of such excess of $3,000, computed under section 1201(a)(2). The difference of $7,250 ($8,000 less $750) is the amount allowable as a deduction in computing accumulated taxable income.

(3) Section 631(c) (relating to gain or loss in the case of disposal of coal or domestic iron ore) shall have no application in determining the amount of the deduction allowable under section 535(b)(6).

(g) *Capital loss carrybacks and carryovers.* Capital losses carried to a taxable year under section 1212(a) shall have no application for purposes of computing accumulated taxable income for such year.

(h) *Bank affiliates.* There is allowed the deduction provided by section 601 in the case of bank affiliates (as defined in section 2 of the Banking Act of 1933; 12 U.S.C. 221a(c)). [Reg. § 1.535-2.]

☐ [*T.D. 6377, 5-12-59. Amended by T.D. 6805, 3-8-65, by T.D. 6841, 7-26-65, by T.D. 7301, 1-3-74, and by T.D. 7649, 10-17-79.*]

[Reg. § 1.535-3]

§ 1.535-3. Accumulated earnings credit.—(a) *In general.* As provided in section 535(a) and § 1.535-1, the accumulated earnings credit, provided by section 535(c), reduces taxable income in computing accumulated taxable income. In the case of a corporation, not a mere holding or investment company, the accumulated earnings credit is determined as provided in paragraph (b) of this section and, in the case of a holding or investment company, as provided in paragraph (c) of this section.

(b) *Corporation which is not a mere holding or investment company*—(1) *General rule.* (i) In the case of a corporation, not a mere holding or investment company, the accumulated earnings credit is the amount equal to such part of the earnings and profits of the taxable year which is retained for the reasonable needs of the business, minus the deduction allowed by section 535(b)(6) (see paragraph (f) of § 1.535-2, relating to the deduction

Reg. § 1.535-3(a)

for long-term capital gains). In no event shall the accumulated earnings credit be less than the minimum credit provided for in section 535(c)(2) and subparagraph (2) of this paragraph. The amount of the earnings and profits for the taxable year retained is the amount by which the earnings and profits for the taxable year exceed the dividends paid deduction for such taxable year. See section 561 and §§ 1.561-1 and 1.561-2, relating to the deduction for dividends paid.

(ii) In determining whether any amount of the earnings and profits of the taxable year has been retained for the reasonable needs of the business, the accumulated earnings and profits of prior years will be taken into consideration. Thus, for example, if such accumulated earnings and profits of prior years are sufficient for the reasonable needs of the business, then any earnings and profits of the current taxable year which are retained will not be considered to be retained for the reasonable needs of the business. See section 537 and §§ 1.537-1 and 1.537-2.

(2) *Minimum credit.* Section 535(c)(2) provides for the allowance of a minimum accumulated earnings credit in the case of a corporation which is not a mere holding or investment company. Except as otherwise provided in section 243(b)(3) and § 1.243-5 (relating to effect of 100-percent dividends received deduction under section 243(b)) and sections 1561, 1562, and 1564 (relating to limitations on certain tax benefits in the case of certain controlled corporations), in the case of such a corporation, this minimum credit shall in no case be less than the amount by which $150,000 ($100,000 in the case of taxable years beginning before January 1, 1975) exceeds the accumulated earnings and profits of the corporation at the close of the preceding taxable year. See paragraph (d) of this section for the effect of dividends paid after the close of the taxable year in determining accumulated earnings and profits at the close of the preceding taxable year. In determining the amount of the minimum credit allowable under section 535(c)(2), the needs of the business are not taken into consideration. If the taxpayer has accumulated earnings and profits at the close of the preceding taxable year equal to or in excess of $150,000 ($100,000 in the case of taxable years beginning before January 1, 1975), the credit, if any, is determined without regard to section 535(c)(2). It is not intended that the provision for the minimum credit shall in any way create an inference that an accumulation in excess of $150,000 ($100,000 in the case of taxable years beginning before January 1, 1975) is unreasonable. The reasonable needs of the business may require the accumulation of more or less than $150,000 ($100,000 in the case of taxable years beginning before January 1, 1975), depending upon the circumstances in the case, but such needs shall not be taken into consideration to any extent in cases where the minimum accumulated earnings credit is applicable. For a discussion of the reasonable needs of the business, see section 537 and §§ 1.537-1, 1.537-2, and 1.537-3.

(3) *Illustrations of accumulated earnings credit.* The computation of the accumulated earnings credit provided by section 535(c) may be illustrated by the following examples:

Example (1). The X Corporation, which is not a mere holding or investment company, has accumulated earnings and profits in the amount of $125,000 as of December 31, 1974. Thus, the minimum credit provided by section 535(c)(2) exceeds the accumulated earnings and profits of X by $25,000. It has earnings and profits for the taxable year ended December 31, 1975, in the amount of $100,000 and has a dividends paid deduction under section 561 in the amount of $30,000 so that the earnings and profits for the taxable year which are retained in the business amount to $70,000. Assume that it has been determined that the earnings and profits for the taxable year which may be retained for the reasonable needs of the business amount to $55,000 and that a deduction has been allowed under section 535(b)(6) in the amount of $5,000. Since the amount by which $150,000 exceeds the accumulated earnings and profits at the close of the preceding taxable year is less than $50,000 ($55,000 − $5,000), the minimum credit provided by section 535(c)(2) will not apply and the accumulated earnings credit must be computed under section 535(c)(1) on the basis of the reasonable needs of the business. In this case, the accumulated earnings credit for the taxable year ended December 31, 1975, will be $50,000, computed as follows:

Earnings and profits of the taxable year determined to be retained for the reasonable needs of the business . $55,000
Less: The deduction for long-term capital gains (less applicable tax) allowed under section 535(c)(6) 5,000

Accumulated earnings credit allowable under section 535(c)(1) $50,000

Example (2). The Z Corporation, which is not a mere holding or investment company, has accumulated earnings and profits in the amount of $45,000 as of December 31, 1974; it has earnings and profits for the taxable year ended December 31, 1975, in the amount of $115,000 and has a dividends paid deduction under section 561 in the amount of $10,000, so that the earnings and prof-

Reg. § 1.535-3(b)(3)

its for the taxable year which are retained amount to $105,000. Assume that it has been determined that the accumulated earnings and profits of the taxable year which may be retained for the reasonable needs of the business amount to $20,000 and that no deduction is allowable for long-term capital gains under section 535(b)(6). The accumulated earnings credit allowable under section 535(c)(1) on the basis of the reasonable needs of the business is determined to be only $20,000. However, since the amount by which $150,000 exceeds the accumulated earnings and profits at the close of the preceding taxable year is more than $20,000, the minimum accumulated earnings credit provided by section 535(c)(2) is applicable. The allowable credit will be the amount by which $150,000 exceeds the accumulated earnings and profits at the close of the preceding taxable year (i.e., $105,000, $150,000 less $45,000 of accumulated earnings and profits at the close of the preceding taxable year).

(c) *Holding and investment companies.* Section 535(c)(3) provides that, in the case of a mere holding or investment company, the accumulated earnings credit shall be the amount, if any, by which $150,000 ($100,000 in the case of taxable years beginning before January 1, 1975) exceeds the accumulated earnings and profits of the corporation at the close of the preceding taxable year. Thus, if such a corporation has accumulated earnings equal to or in excess of $150,000 ($100,000 in the case of taxable years beginning before January 1, 1975) at the close of its preceding taxable year, no accumulated earnings credit is allowable in computing the accumulated taxable income. See paragraph (c) of § 1.533-1 for a definition of a holding or investment company. For the accumulated earnings credit of a mere holding or investment company which is a member of an affiliated group which has elected the 100-percent dividends received deduction under section 243(b), see section 243(b)(3) and § 1.243-5. For the accumulated earnings credit of a mere holding or investment company which is a component member of a controlled group of corporations (as defined in section 1563), see sections 1561, 1562, and 1564.

(d) *Accumulated earnings and profits.* For the purposes of determining the minimum credit provided by section 535(c)(2) and paragraph (b)(2) of this section, and the credit provided by section 535(c)(3) and paragraph (c) of this section, dividends paid after the close of any taxable year which are considered paid during such taxable year, shall be deducted from the earnings and profits accumulated at the close of such taxable year. See section 563 and §§ 1.563-1 and 1.563-3, relating to dividends paid after the close of the taxable year. [Reg. § 1.535-3.]

☐ [*T.D.* 6377, 5-12-59. Amended by *T.D.* 6992, 1-17-69, by *T.D.* 7181, 4-25-72, by *T.D.* 7244, 12-29-72, by *T.D.* 7376, 9-15-75, and by *T.D.* 7528, 12-27-77.]

[Reg. § 1.536-1]

§ 1.536-1. Short taxable years.—Accumulated taxable income for a taxable year consisting of a period of less than 12 months shall not be placed on an annual basis for the purpose of the accumulated earnings tax imposed by section 531. In such cases accumulated taxable income shall be computed on the basis of the taxable income for such period of less than 12 months, adjusted in the manner provided by section 535(b) and § 1.535-2. [Reg. § 1.536-1.]

☐ [*T.D.* 6377, 5-12-59.]

[Reg. § 1.537-1]

§ 1.537-1. Reasonable needs of the business.—(a) *In general.* The term "reasonable needs of the business" includes (1) the reasonable anticipated needs of the business (including product liability loss reserves, as defined in paragraph (f) of this section), (2) the section 303 redemption needs of the business, as defined in paragraph (c) of this section, and (3) the excess business holdings redemption needs of the business as described in paragraph (d) of this section. See paragraph (e) of this section for additional rules relating to the section 303 redemption needs and the excess business holdings redemption needs of the business. An accumulation of the earnings and profits (including the undistributed earnings and profits of prior years) is in excess of the reasonable needs of the business if it exceeds the amount that a prudent businessman would consider appropriate for the present business purposes and for the reasonably anticipated future needs of the business. The need to retain earnings and profits must be directly connected with the needs of the corporation itself and must be for bona fide business purposes. For purposes of this paragraph the section 303 redemption needs of the business and the excess business holdings redemption needs of the business are deemed to be directly connected with the needs of the business and for a bona fide business purpose. See § 1.537-3 for a discussion of what constitutes the business of the corporation. The extent to which earnings and profits have been distributed by the corporation may be taken into account in determining whether or not retained earnings and profits exceed the reasonable needs of the business. See § 1.537-2, relating to grounds for accumulation of earnings and profits.

(b) *Reasonably anticipated needs.* (1) In order for a corporation to justify an accumulation of earnings and profits for reasonably anticipated

Reg. § 1.536-1

future needs, there must be an indication that the future needs of the business require such accumulation, and the corporation must have specific, definite, and feasible plans for the use of such accumulation. Such an accumulation need not be used immediately, nor must the plans for its use be consummated within a short period after the close of the taxable year, provided that such accumulation will be used within a reasonable time depending upon all the facts and circumstances relating to the future needs of the business. Where the future needs of the business are uncertain or vague, where the plans for the future use of an accumulation are not specific, definite, and feasible, or where the execution of such a plan is postponed indefinitely, an accumulation cannot be justified on the grounds of reasonably anticipated needs of the business.

(2) Consideration shall be given to reasonably anticipated needs as they exist on the basis of the facts at the close of the taxable year. Thus, subsequent events shall not be used for the purpose of showing that the retention of earnings or profits was unreasonable at the close of the taxable year if all the elements of reasonable anticipation are present at the close of such taxable year. However, subsequent events may be considered to determine whether the taxpayer actually intended to consummate or has actually consummated the plans for which the earnings and profits were accumulated. In this connection, projected expansion or investment plans shall be reviewed in the light of the facts during each year and as they exist as of the close of the taxable year. If a corporation has justified an accumulation for future needs by plans never consummated, the amount of such an accumulation shall be taken into account in determining the reasonableness of subsequent accumulations.

(c) *Section 303 redemption needs of the business.* (1) The term "section 303 redemption needs" means, with respect to the taxable year of the corporation in which a shareholder of the corporation died or any taxable year thereafter, the amount needed (or reasonably anticipated to be needed) to redeem stock included in the gross estate of such shareholder but not in excess of the amount necessary to effect a distribution to which section 303 applies. For purposes of this paragraph, the term "shareholder" includes an individual in whose gross estate stock of the corporation is includable upon his death for Federal estate tax purposes.

(2) This paragraph applies to a corporation to which section 303(c) would apply if a distribution described therein were made.

(3) If stock included in the gross estate of a decedent is stock of two or more corporations described in section 303(b)(2)(B), the amount needed by each such corporation for section 303 redemption purposes under this section shall, unless the particular facts and circumstances indicate otherwise, be that amount which bears the same ratio to the amount described in section 303(a) as the fair market value of such corporation's stock included in the gross estate of such decedent bears to the fair market value of all of the stock of such corporations included in the gross estate. For example, facts and circumstances indicating that the allocation prescribed by this subparagraph is not required would include notice given to the corporations by the executor or administrator of the decedent's estate that he intends to request the redemption of stock of only one of such corporations or the redemption of stock of such corporations in a ratio which is unrelated to the respective fair market values of the stock of the corporations included in the decedent's gross estate.

(4) The provisions of this paragraph apply only to taxable years ending after May 26, 1969.

(d) *Excess business holdings redemption needs.* (1) The term "excess business holdings redemption needs" means, with respect to taxable years of the corporation ending after May 26, 1969, the amount needed (or reasonably anticipated to be needed) to redeem from a private foundation stock which—

(i) Such foundation held on May 26, 1969 (or which was received by such foundation pursuant to a will or irrevocable trust to which section 4943(c)(5) applies), and either

(ii) Constituted excess business holdings on such date or would have constituted excess business holdings as of that date if there were taken into account (*a*) stock received pursuant to a will or trust described in subdivision (i) of this subparagraph and (*b*) the reduction in the total outstanding stock of the corporation which would have resulted solely from the redemption of stock held by the private foundation, or

(iii) Constituted stock redemption of which before January 1, 1975, or after October 4, 1976, and before January 1, 1977, is, by reason of section 101(1)(2)(B) of the Tax Reform Act of 1969, as amended by section 1309 of the Tax Reform Act of 1976, and § 53.4941(d)-4(b), permitted without imposition of tax under section 4941, but only to the extent such stock is to be redeemed before January 1, 1975 or after October 4, 1976, and before January 1, 1977, or is to be redeemed thereafter pursuant to the terms of a binding contract entered into on or before such date to

Reg. § 1.537-1(d)

redeem all of the stock of the corporation held by the private foundation on such date.

(2) The purpose of subparagraph (1) of this paragraph is to facilitate a private foundation's disposition of certain excess business holdings, in order for the private foundation not to be liable for tax under section 4943. See section 4943(c) and the regulations thereunder for the definition of excess business holdings. For purposes of section 537(b)(2) and this paragraph, however, any determination of the existence of excess business holdings shall be made without taking into account the provisions of section 4943(c)(4) which treat certain excess business holdings as held by a disqualified person (rather than by the private foundation), except that the periods described in section 4943(c)(4)(B), (C), and (D), if applicable, shall be taken into account in determining the period during which an excess business holdings redemption need may be deemed to exist. Thus, an excess business holdings redemption need may, depending upon the facts and circumstances, be deemed to exist for a part or all of the 20-year, 15-year, or 10-year period specified in section 4943(c)(4)(B) during which the interest in the corporation held by the private foundation is treated as held by a disqualified person rather than by the private foundation, and, if applicable, (i) any suspension of such 20-year, 15-year, or 10-year period as provided by section 4943(c)(4)(C) and (ii) the 15-year "second phase" specified in section 4943(c)(4)(D). The foregoing sentence is not to be construed to prevent an accumulation of earnings and profits for the purpose of effecting a redemption of excess business holdings at a time or times prior to expiration of the periods described in such sentence. This subparagraph is not to be construed to prevent an accumulation of earnings and profits for the purpose of effecting a redemption described in subdivision (iii) of subparagraph (1) of this paragraph.

(3) The extent of an excess business holdings redemption need cannot exceed the total number of shares of stock so held or received by the private foundation (i) redemption of which alone would sufficiently reduce such private foundation's proportionate share of the corporation's total outstanding stock in order for the private foundation not be liable for tax under section 4943, or (ii) redemption of which is, by reason of § 53.4941(d)-4(b), permitted without imposition of tax under section 4941 provided that such redemption is accomplished within the period and in the manner prescribed in subdivision (iii) of subparagraph (1) of this paragraph. Thus, excess business holdings of a private foundation attributable to an increase in the private foundation's proportionate share of the corporation's total outstanding stock by reason of a redemption of stock after May 26, 1969, from any person other than the private foundation do not give rise to an excess business holdings redemption need.

(4) For purposes of subdivision (ii) of subparagraph (1) of this paragraph, an excess business holdings redemption need can arise with respect to shares of the corporation's stock under section 537(a)(3) only following actual acquisition by the private foundation of such shares and their characterization as an excess business holding. Thus, this paragraph does not apply to an accumulation of earnings and profits in one taxable year in anticipation of a redemption of excess business holdings to be acquired by a private foundation in a subsequent year pursuant to a will or irrevocable trust to which section 4943(c)(5) applies or in anticipation of shares held becoming excess business holdings of the private foundation in a subsequent year by reason of additional shares to be received by the private foundation in such subsequent year pursuant to a will or irrevocable trust to which section 4943(c)(5) applies. Once having arisen, however, an excess business holdings redemption need may continue until redemption of the private foundation's excess business holdings described in this paragraph or other disposition of such excess business holdings by the private foundation.

(5) Notwithstanding any other provision of this paragraph, an excess business holdings redemption need will not be deemed to exist with respect to stock held by a private foundation the redemption of which would subject any person to tax under section 4941.

(6) For purposes of subdivision (ii) of subparagraph (1) of this paragraph, the number of shares of stock held by a private foundation on May 26, 1969 (or received pursuant to a will or irrevocable trust to which section 4943(c)(5) applies), redemption of which alone would sufficiently reduce such foundation's proportionate share of a corporation's total outstanding stock in order for the foundation not to be liable for tax under section 4943 may be determined by application of the following formula:

$$X = \frac{PH - (Y \times SO)}{1 - Y}$$

X = Number of shares to be redeemed.
Y = Maximum percentage of outstanding stock which private foundation can hold without being liable for tax under section 4943.
PH = Number of shares of stock held by private foundation on May 26, 1969, or received pursuant to a will or irrevocable trust to which section 4943(c)(5) applies.

Reg. § 1.537-1(d)(2)

SO = Total number of shares of stock outstanding unreduced by any redemption from a person other than the private foundation.

(7) The provisions of this paragraph may be illustrated by the following example:

Example. (i) On May 26, 1969, Private Foundation A holds 60 of the 100 outstanding shares of the capital stock of corporation X, which is not a disqualified person with respect to A. None of the remaining 40 shares is owned by a disqualified person within the meaning of section 4946(a). On June 1, 1975, X redeems 10 shares of its stock from individual B, thus reducing its outstanding stock to 90 shares. On June 1, 1976, A receives 20 additional shares of X stock by bequest under a will to which section 4943(c)(5) applies. As of June 1, 1976, then, A holds 80 of the 90 outstanding shares of X. Solely for purposes of this example and to illustrate the application of this paragraph, it will be assumed that in order not to be liable for the initial tax under section 4943, A must, before the close of the "second phase" described in section 4943(c)(4)(D), reduce its proportionate stock interest in X to 35 percent. A requests X to redeem from it a sufficient number of its shares to so reduce its proportionate stock interest in X to 35 percent, and X agrees to effect such a redemption.

(ii) As of May 26, 1969, A's excess business holdings are 25 shares of X, the number of shares which A would be required to dispose of to a person other than X in order to reduce its proportionate holdings in X to no more than 35 percent. If the disposition is to be by means of a redemption, however, A's excess business holdings on May 26, 1969, for purposes of determining X's excess business holdings redemption needs, are 39 shares, *i.e.*, the number of shares X would be required to redeem in order to reduce A's proportionate stock interest to 35 percent. Although the redemption of 10 shares from B on June 1, 1975, creates additional excess business holdings of A because it effectively increases A's proportionate stock interest in X, this increase does not create an additional excess business holdings redemption need because it resulted from a redemption from a person other than A. The bequest of 20 shares of X received by A on June 1, 1976, creates a further excess business holdings redemption need as of that date in the amount needed (or reasonably anticipated to be needed) to redeem an additional 31 shares from A, i.e., the number of shares which, when added to the excess business holdings of A on May 26, 1969, would have to be redeemed to reduce A's proportionate stock interest in X to 35 percent without taking the earlier redemption from B into account.

(e)(1) A determination whether and to what extent an amount is needed (or reasonably anticipated to be needed) for the purpose described in subparagraph (1) of paragraph (c) or (d) of this section is dependent upon the particular circumstances of the case, including the total amount of earnings and profits accumulated in prior years which may be available for such purpose and the existence of a reasonable expectation that a redemption described in paragraph (c) or (d) of this section will in fact be effected. Although paragraph (c) or (d) of this section may apply even though no redemption of stock is in fact effected, the failure to effect such redemption may be taken into account in determining whether the accumulation was needed (or reasonably anticipated to be needed) for a purpose described in paragraph (c) or (d).

(2) In applying subparagraph (1) of paragraph (c) or (d) of this section, the discharge of an obligation incurred to make a redemption shall be treated as the making of the redemption.

(3) In determining whether an accumulation is in excess of the reasonable needs of the business for a particular year, the fact that one of the exceptions specified in paragraph (c) or (d) of this section applies in a subsequent year is not to give rise to an inference that the accumulation would not have been for the reasonable needs of the business in the prior year. Also, no inference is to be drawn from the enactment of section 537(a)(2) and (3) that accumulations in any prior year would not have been for the reasonable needs of the business in the absence of such provisions. Thus, the reasonableness of accumulations in years prior to a year in which one of the exceptions specified in paragraph (c) or (d) of this section applies is to be determined solely upon the facts and circumstances existing at the times the accumulations occur.

(f) *Product liability loss reserves.* (1) The term "product liability loss reserve" means, with respect to taxable years beginning after September 30, 1979, reasonable amounts accumulated for the payment of reasonably anticipated product liability losses, as defined in section 172(j) and § 1.172-13(b)(1).

(2) For purposes of this paragraph, whether an accumulation for anticipated product liability losses is reasonable in amount and whether such anticipated product liability losses are likely to occur shall be determined in light of all facts and circumstances of the taxpayer making such accumulation. Some of the factors to be considered in determining the reasonableness of the accumulation include the taxpayer's previous product liability experience, the extent of the taxpayer's

Reg. § 1.537-1(f)(2)

coverage by commercial product liability insurance, the income tax consequences of the taxpayer's ability to deduct product liability losses and related expenses, and the taxpayer's potential future liability due to defective products in light of the taxpayer's plans to expand the production of products currently being manufactured, provided such plans are specific, definite and feasible. Additionally, a factor to be considered in determining whether the accumulation is reasonable in amount is whether the taxpayer, in accounting for its potential future liability, took into account the reasonably estimated present value of the potential future liability.

(3) Only those accumulations made with respect to products that have been manufactured, leased, or sold shall be considered as accumulations made under this paragraph. Thus, for example, accumulations with respect to a product which has not progressed beyond the development stage are not reasonable accumulations under this paragraph. [Reg. § 1.537-1.]

☐ [T.D. 6377, 5-12-59. Amended by T.D. 7165, 3-8-72, by T.D. 7678, 2-25-80, and by T.D. 8096, 8-27-86.]

[Reg. § 1.537-2]

§ 1.537-2. Grounds for accumulation of earnings and profits.—(a) *In general.* Whether a particular ground or grounds for the accumulation of earnings and profits indicate that the earnings and profits have been accumulated for the reasonable needs of the business or beyond such needs is dependent upon the particular circumstances of the case. Listed below in paragraphs (b) and (c) of this section are some of the grounds which may be used as guides under ordinary circumstances.

(b) *Reasonable accumulation of earnings and profits.* Although the following grounds are not exclusive, one or more of such grounds, if supported by sufficient facts, may indicate that the earnings and profits of a corporation are being accumulated for the reasonable needs of the business provided the general requirements under §§ 1.537-1 and 1.537-3 are satisfied:

(1) To provide for bona fide expansion of business or replacement of plant;

(2) To acquire a business enterprise through purchasing stock or assets;

(3) To provide for the retirement of bona fide indebtedness created in connection with the trade or business, such as the establishment of a sinking fund for the purpose of retiring bonds issued by the corporation in accordance with contract obligations incurred on issue;

(4) To provide necessary working capital for the business, such as, for the procurement of inventories;

(5) To provide for investments or loans to suppliers or customers if necessary in order to maintain the business of the corporation; or

(6) To provide for the payment of reasonably anticipated product liability losses, as defined in section 172(j), § 1.172-13(b)(1), and § 1.537-1(f).

(c) *Unreasonable accumulations of earnings and profits.* Although the following purposes are not exclusive, accumulations of earnings and profits to meet any one of such objectives may indicate that the earnings and profits of a corporation are being accumulated beyond the reasonable needs of the business:

(1) Loans to shareholders, or the expenditure of funds of the corporation for the personal benefit of the shareholders;

(2) Loans having no reasonable relation to the conduct of the business made to relatives or friends of shareholders, or to other persons;

(3) Loans to another corporation, the business of which is not that of the taxpayer corporation, if the capital stock of such other corporation is owned, directly or indirectly, by the shareholder or shareholders of the taxpayer corporation and such shareholder or shareholders are in control of both corporations;

(4) Investments in properties, or securities which are unrelated to the activities of the business of the taxpayer corporation; or

(5) Retention of earnings and profits to provide against unrealistic hazards. [Reg. § 1.537-2.]

☐ [T.D. 6377, 5-12-59. Amended by T.D. 8096, 8-26-86.]

[Reg. § 1.537-3]

§ 1.537-3. Business of the corporation.—(a) The business of a corporation is not merely that which it has previously carried on but includes, in general, any line of business which it may undertake.

(b) If one corporation owns the stock of another corporation and, in effect, operates the other corporation, the business of the latter corporation may be considered in substance, although not in legal form, the business of the first corporation. However, investment by a corporation of its earnings and profits in stock and securities of another corporation is not, of itself, to be regarded as employment of the earnings and profits in its business. Earnings and profits of the first corporation put into the second corporation through the purchase of stock or securities or otherwise, may, if a subsidiary relationship is established, consti-

Reg. § 1.537-2(a)

Personal Holding Companies

See p. 20,601 for regulations not amended to reflect law changes

tute employment of the earnings and profits in its own business. Thus, the business of one corporation may be regarded as including the business of another corporation if such other corporation is a mere instrumentality of the first corporation; that may be established by showing that the first corporation owns at least 80 percent of the voting stock of the second corporation. If the taxpayer's ownership of stock is less than 80 percent in the other corporation, the determination of whether the funds are employed in a business operated by the taxpayer will depend upon the particular circumstances of the case. Moreover, the business of one corporation does not include the business of another corporation if such other corporation is a personal holding company, an investment company, or a corporation not engaged in the active conduct of a trade or business. [Reg. § 1.537-3.]

☐ [T.D. 6377, 5-12-59.]

Personal Holding Companies

[Reg. § 1.541-1]

§ 1.541-1. Imposition of tax.—(a) Section 541 imposes a graduated tax upon corporations classified as personal holding companies under section 542. This tax, if applicable, is in addition to the tax imposed upon corporations generally under section 11. Unless specifically excepted under section 542(c) the tax applies to domestic and foreign corporations and, to the extent provided by section 542(b), to an affiliated group of corporations filing a consolidated return. Corporations classified as personal holding companies are exempt from the accumulated earnings tax imposed under section 531 but are not exempt from other income taxes imposed upon corporations, generally, under any other provisions of the Code. Unlike the accumulated earnings tax imposed under section 531, the personal holding company tax imposed by section 541 applies to all personal holding companies as defined in section 542, whether or not they were formed or availed of to avoid income tax upon shareholders. See section 6501(f) and § 301.6501(f)-1 of this chapter (Regulations on Procedure and Administration) with respect to the period of limitation on assessment of personal holding company tax upon failure to file a schedule of personal holding company income.

(b) A foreign corporation, whether resident or nonresident, which is classified as a personal holding company is subject to the tax imposed under section 541 with respect to its income from sources within the United States, even though such income is not fixed or determinable annual or periodical income specified in section 881. A foreign corporation is not classified as a personal holding company subject to tax under section 541 if it is a foreign personal holding company as defined in section 552 or if it meets the requirements of the exception provided in section 542(c)(10). [Reg. § 1.541-1.]

☐ [T.D. 6308, 9-9-58.]

[Reg. § 1.542-1]

§ 1.542-1. General rule.—A personal holding company is any corporation (other than one specifically excepted under section 542(c)) which, for the taxable year, meets—

(a) The gross income requirement specified in section 542(a)(1) and § 1.542-2, and

(b) The stock ownership requirement specified in section 542(a)(2) and § 1.542-3.

Both requirements must be satisfied with respect to each taxable year. [Reg. § 1.542-1.]

☐ [T.D. 6308, 9-9-58.]

[Reg. § 1.542-2]

§ 1.542-2. Gross income requirement.—To meet the gross income requirement it is necessary that at least 80 percent of the total gross income of the corporation for the taxable year be personal holding company income as defined in section 543 and §§ 1.543-1 and 1.543-2. For the definition of "gross income" see section 61 and §§ 1.61-1 through 1.61-14. Under such provisions gross income is not necessarily synonymous with gross receipts. Further, in the case of transactions in stocks and securities and in commodities transactions, gross income for personal holding company tax purposes shall include only the excess of gains over losses from such transactions. See section 543(b), paragraph (b)(5) and (6) of § 1.543-1, and § 1.543-2. For determining the character of the amount includible in gross income under section 951(a), see paragraph (a) of § 1.951-1. [Reg. § 1.542-2.]

☐ [T.D. 6308, 9-9-58. Amended by T.D. 6795, 1-28-65.]

[Reg. § 1.542-3]

§ 1.542-3. Stock ownership requirement.—(a) General rule. To meet the stock ownership requirement, it is necessary that at sometime during the last half of the taxable year more than 50 percent in value of the outstanding stock of the corporation be owned, directly or indirectly, by or for not more than 5 individuals. Any organization or trust to which subparagraph (1) of this paragraph applies shall be considered as one individual for purposes of this stock ownership requirement subject, however, to the exception in subparagraph (2) of this paragraph which is applicable only to taxable years beginning after December 31, 1954. Thus, if an organization or trust which is considered as an individual owns 51 percent in value of the outstanding stock of the corporation at any time during the last half of the taxable year, the stock ownership requirement will be met by ownership of the required percentage by one individual. See section 544 and § 1.544-1 through § 1.544-7 for the determination of stock ownership.

(1) *An organization or trust considered as an individual.* Any of the following organizations or trusts shall be considered as an individual:

(i) An organization to which section 503 applies, namely, any organization described in section 501(c)(3) (relating to charitable, etc., organizations) or section 401(a) (relating to employees' pension trust, etc.) other than an organization excepted from the application of section 503 by paragraphs (1) to (5) of section 503(b). Therefore, a religious organization (other than a trust) excepted under section 503(b)(1) is not considered an individual for purposes of the stock ownership requirement of section 542(a)(2).

(ii) A portion of a trust permanently set aside or to be used exclusively for the purposes described in section 642(c), relating to amounts set aside for charitable purposes, or described in a corresponding provision of the prior income tax law (such as section 162(a), Internal Revenue Code of 1939).

(2) *Exception.* For taxable years beginning after December 31, 1954, an organization or trust to which subparagraph (1) of this paragraph applies shall not be considered an individual if all of the following conditions are met:

(i) It was organized or created before July 1, 1950,

(ii) At all times on or after July 1, 1950, and before the close of the taxable year, it owned all of the common stock and at least 80 percent of the total number of shares of all other classes of stock of the corporation, and

(iii) (*a*) For the taxable year it is not denied exemption under section 504(a) or the unlimited charitable deduction under section 681(c). In determining whether, for the purpose of section 542(a)(2), exemption is not denied under section 504(a) or the unlimited charitable deduction is not denied under section 681(c) all the income of the corporation which is available for distribution as dividends to its shareholders shall be deemed to have been distributed at the close of the taxable year whether or not any portion of such income was in fact distributed. If the amounts described in section 504(a) or section 681(c), increased by the income of the corporation deemed distributed pursuant to the preceding sentence, would be sufficient to deny exemption or the unlimited charitable deduction, the organization or trust will be considered to be an individual for the purpose of section 542(a)(2). For the purpose of this subdivision the restrictions in sections 504(a)(1) and 681(c)(1) against unreasonable accumulations will not apply to income attributable to property of a decedent dying before January 1, 1951, which was transferred during his lifetime to a trust or property that was transferred under his will to such trust.

(iv) This subparagraph is illustrated by the following example:

Example. The X Charitable Foundation (an organization described in section 501(c)(3) to which section 503 is applicable) has owned all of the stock of the Y Corporation since Y's organization in 1949. Both X and Y are calendar year corporations. At the end of the year 1955, X has accumulated $100,000 out of income and has actually paid out only $75,000 of this amount, leaving a balance of $25,000 on December 31, 1955. X was not denied an exemption under section 504(a) for the year 1955. Y, during the calendar year 1955, has $400,000 taxable income of which $200,000 is available for distribution as dividends at the end of the year. X will be considered to have accumulated out of income during the calendar year 1955 the amount of $225,000 for the purpose of determining whether it would have been denied an exemption under section 504(a)(1). If X would have been denied an exemption under section 504(a)(1) by reason of having been deemed to have accumulated $225,000, the stock ownership requirement of section 542(a)(2) and this section will have been satisfied. If Y Corporation also satisfies the gross income requirement of section 542(a)(1) and § 1.542-2 it will be a personal holding company.

(b) *Changes in stock outstanding.* It is necessary to consider any change in the stock outstanding during the last half of the taxable year, whether in the number of shares or classes of stock, or in the ownership thereof. Stock subscribed and paid for will be considered as stock outstanding, whether or not such stock is evidenced by issued certificates. Treasury stock shall not be considered as stock outstanding.

(c) *Value of stock outstanding.* The value of the stock outstanding shall be determined in the light of all the circumstances. The value may be determined upon the basis of the company's net worth, earning and dividend paying capacity, appreciation of assets, together with such other factors as have a bearing upon the value of the stock. If the

Reg. § 1.542-3(a)(1)

value of the stock is greatly at variance with that reflected by the corporate books, the evidence of such value should be filed with the return. In any case where there are two or more classes of stock outstanding, the total value of all the stock should be allocated among the different classes according to the relative value of each class. [Reg. § 1.542-3.]

☐ [T.D. 6308, 9-9-58. Amended by T.D. 6739, 6-16-64.]

[Reg. § 1.542-4]

§ 1.542-4. **Corporations filing consolidated returns.**—(a) *General rule.* A consolidated return under section 1501 shall determine the application of the personal holding company tax to the group and to any member thereof on the basis of the consolidated gross income and consolidated personal holding company income of the group, as determined under the regulations prescribed pursuant to section 1502 (relating to consolidated returns); however, this rule shall not apply to either (1) an ineligible affiliated group as defined in section 542(b)(2) and paragraph (b) of this section, or (2) an affiliated group of corporations a member of which is excluded from the definition of a personal holding company under section 542(c) and paragraph (c) of this section. Thus, in the latter two instances the gross income requirement provided in section 542(a)(1) and § 1.542-2 shall apply to each individual member of the affiliated group of corporations.

(b) *Ineligible affiliated group.* (1) Except for certain affiliated railroad corporations, as provided in subparagraph (2) of this paragraph, an affiliated group of corporations is an ineligible affiliated group and therefore may not use its consolidated gross income and consolidated personal holding company income to determine the liability of the group or any member thereof for personal holding company tax (as provided in paragraph (a) of this section), if (i) any member of such group, including the common parent, derived gross income from sources outside the affiliated group for the taxable year in an amount equal to 10 percent or more of its gross income from all sources for that year and (ii) 80 percent or more of the gross income from sources outside the affiliated group consists of personal holding company income as defined in section 543 and §§ 1.543-1 and 1.543-2. For purposes of subdivision (i) of this subparagraph gross income shall not include certain dividend income received by a common parent from a corporation not a member of the affiliated group which qualifies under section 542(b)(4) and paragraph (d) of this section. See particularly the examples contained in paragraph (d)(2) of this section. Intercorporate dividends received by members of the affiliated group (including the common parent) are to be included in the gross income from all sources for purposes of the test in subdivision (i) of this subparagraph. For purposes of subdivision (ii) of this subparagraph, section 543 and paragraph (a) of § 1.543-1 shall be applied as if the amount of gross income derived from sources outside the affiliated group by a corporation which is a member of such group is the gross income of such corporation.

(2) An affiliated group of railroad corporations shall not be considered to be an ineligible affiliated group, notwithstanding any other provisions of section 542(b)(2) and this paragraph, if the common parent of such group would be eligible to file a consolidated return under section 141 of the Internal Revenue Code of 1939 prior to its amendment by the Revenue Act of 1942 (56 Stat. 798).

(3) See section 562(d) and § 1.562-3 for dividends paid deduction in the case of a distribution by a member of an ineligible affiliated group.

(4) The determination of whether an affiliated group of corporations is an ineligible group under section 542(b)(2) and this paragraph, may be illustrated by the following examples:

Example (1). Corporations X, Y, and Z constitute an affiliated group of corporations which files a consolidated return for the calendar year 1954; Corporations Y and Z are wholly-owned subsidiaries of Corporation X and derive no gross income from sources outside the affiliated group; Corporation X, the common parent, has gross income in the amount of $250,000 for the taxable year 1954. $200,000 of such gross income consists of dividends received from Corporations Y and Z. The remaining $50,000 was derived from sources outside the affiliated group, $40,000 of which represents personal holding company income as defined in section 543. The $50,000 included in the gross income of Corporation X and derived from sources outside the affiliated group is more than 10 percent of X's gross income ($50,000/250,000) and the $40,000 which represents personal holding company income is 80 percent of $50,000 (the amount considered to be the gross income of Corporation X). Accordingly, Corporations X, Y, and Z would be an ineligible affiliated group and the gross income requirement under section 542(a)(1) and § 1.542-2 would be applied to each corporation individually.

Example (2). If, in the above example, only $30,000 of the $50,000 derived from sources outside the affiliated group by Corporation X represented personal holding company income, this group of affiliated corporations would not be an ineligible affiliated group. Although the

$50,000 representing the gross income of Corporation X from sources outside the affiliated group is more than 10 percent of its total gross income, the amount of $30,000 representing personal holding company income is not 80 percent or more of the amount considered to be gross income for the purpose of this test. Under section 542(b)(2) and subparagraph (1) of this paragraph both the gross income and the personal holding company income requirements must be satisfied in determining that an affiliated group constitutes an ineligible group. Since both of these requirements have not been satisfied in this example this group of affiliated corporations would not be an ineligible group.

(c) *Excluded corporations.* The general rule for determining liability of an affiliated group under paragraph (a) of this section shall not apply if any member thereof is a corporation which is excluded, under section 542(c), from the definition of a personal holding company.

(d) *Certain dividend income received by a common parent.* (1) Dividends received by the common parent of an affiliated group from a corporation which is not a member of the affiliated group shall not be included in gross income or personal holding company income, for the purpose of the test under section 542(b)(2), (i) if such common parent owned, directly or indirectly, more than 50 percent of the outstanding voting stock of the dividend paying corporation at the time such common parent became entitled to the dividend and (ii) if the dividend paying corporation is not a personal holding company for the taxable year in which the dividends are paid. Thus, if the tests in subdivision (i) and (ii) of this subparagraph are met, the dividend income received by the common parent from such other corporation will not be considered gross income for purposes of the test in section 542(b)(2)(A) (paragraph (b) of this section), that is, either to determine gross income from sources outside the affiliated group or to determine gross income from all sources.

(2) The application of subparagraph (1) of this paragraph may be illustrated by the following examples:

Example (1). Corporation X is the common parent of Corporation Y and Corporation Z and together they constitute an affiliated group which files a consolidated return under section 1501. Corporation Y and Corporation Z derived no income from sources outside the affiliated group. Corporation X, the common parent, had gross income of $100,000 for the calendar year 1954 of which amount $20,000 represented a dividend received from Corporation W, and $4,000 represented interest from Corporation T. The remaining gross income of X, $76,000, was received from Corporations Y and Z. Corporation X, for its entire taxable year, owned 60 percent of the voting stock of Corporation W which was not a personal holding company for the calendar year 1954. For the purpose of the gross income and personal holding company income test under section 542(b)(2) and paragraph (b) of this section, the $20,000 dividend received from Corporation W would not be included in the gross income or personal holding company income of Corporation X. The affiliated group would not be an ineligible group under section 542(b)(2) because 10 percent or more of its gross income was not from sources outside the affiliated group as required by section 542(b)(2)(A). Inasmuch as the $20,000 dividend from Corporation W is not included in the gross income of Corporation X for purposes of section 542(b)(2) Corporation X only has $4,000 gross income from sources outside the affiliated group which is only 5 percent of its gross income from all sources, $80,000.

Example (2). If, in example (1), Corporation X owned 50 percent or less of the voting stock of Corporation W at the time X became entitled to the dividend, or if Corporation W had been a personal holding company for the taxable year in which the dividends were paid, the $20,000 dividends received by Corporation X would be included in gross income and personal holding company income of Corporation X for the purpose of the test under section 542(b)(2) and paragraph (b) of this section. Thus, the affiliated group would be an ineligible affiliated group under section 542(b)(2) because 24 percent of its gross income was from sources outside the affiliated group ($24,000/$100,000) and 100 percent of this $24,000 was personal holding company income. [Reg. § 1.542-4.]

☐ [*T.D.* 6308, 9-9-58.]

[Reg. § 1.543-1]

§ 1.543-1. **Personal holding company income.**—(a) *General rule.* The term "personal holding company income" means the portion of the gross income which consists of the classes of gross income described in paragraph (b) of this section. See section 543(b) and § 1.543-2 for special limitations on gross income and personal holding company income in cases of gains from stocks', securities', and commodities' transactions.

(b) *Definitions*—(1) *Dividends.* The term "dividends" includes dividends as defined in section 316 and amounts required to be included in gross income under section 551 and §§ 1.551-1—

Reg. § 1.543-1(a)

1.551-2 (relating to foreign personal holding company income taxed to United States shareholders).

(2) *Interest.* The term "interest" means any amounts, includible in gross income, received for the use of money loaned. However, (i) interest which constitutes "rent" shall not be classified as interest but shall be classified as "rents" (see subparagraph (10) of this paragraph) and (ii) interest on amounts set aside in a reserve fund under section 511 or 607 of the Merchant Marine Act, 1936 (46 U.S.C. 1161 or 1177), shall not be included in personal holding company income.

(3) *Royalties (other than mineral, oil, or gas royalties or certain copyright royalties).* The term "royalties" (other than mineral, oil, or gas royalties or certain copyright royalties) includes amounts received for the privilege of using patents, copyrights, secret processes and formulas, good will, trade marks, trade brands, franchises, and other like property. It does not, however, include rents. For rules relating to rents see section 543(a)(7) and subparagraph (10) of this paragraph. For rules relating to mineral, oil, or gas royalties, see section 543(a)(8) and subparagraph (11) of this paragraph. For rules relating to certain copyright royalties for taxable years beginning after December 31, 1959, see section 543(a)(9) and subparagraph (12) of this paragraph.

(4) *Annuities.* The term "annuities" includes annuities only to the extent includible in the computation of gross income. See section 72 and §§ 1.72-1—1.72-14 for rules relating to the inclusion of annuities in gross income.

(5) *Gains from the sale or exchange of stock or securities.* (i) Except in the case of regular dealers in stocks or securities as provided in subdivision (ii) of this subparagraph, gross income and personal holding company income include the amount by which the gains exceed the losses from the sale or exchange of stock or securities. See section 543(b)(1) and § 1.543-2 for provisions relating to this limitation. For this purpose, there shall be taken into account all those gains includible in gross income (including gains from liquidating dividends and other distributions from capital) and all those losses deductible from gross income which are considered under chapter 1 of the Code to be gains or losses from the sale or exchange of stock or securities. The term "stock or securities" as used in section 543(a)(2) and this subparagraph includes shares or certificates of stock, stock rights or warrants, or interest in any corporation (including any joint stock company, insurance company, association, or other organization classified as a corporation by the Code), certificates of interest or participation in any profit-sharing agreement, or in any oil, gas, or other mineral property, or lease, collateral trust certificates, voting trust certificates, bonds, debentures, certificates of indebtedness, notes, car trust certificates, bills of exchange, obligations issued by or on behalf of a State, Territory, or political subdivision thereof.

(ii) In the case of "regular dealers in stock or securities" there shall not be included gains or losses derived from the sale or exchange of stock or securities made in the normal course of business. The term "regular dealer in stock or securities" means a corporation with an established place of business regularly engaged in the purchase of stock or securities and their resale to customers. However, such corporations shall not be considered as regular dealers with respect to stock or securities which are held for investment. See section 1236 and § 1.1236-1.

(6) *Gains from futures transactions in commodities.* Gross income and personal holding company income include the amount by which the gains exceed the losses from futures transactions in any commodity on or subject to the rules of a board of trade or commodity exchange. See § 1.543-2 for provisions relating to this limitation. In general, for the purpose of determining such excess, there are included all gains and losses on futures contracts which are speculative. However, for the purpose of determining such excess, there shall not be included gains or losses from cash transactions, or gains or losses by a producer, processor, merchant, or handler of the commodity, which arise out of bona fide hedging transactions reasonably necessary to the conduct of its business in the manner in which such business is customarily and usually conducted by others. See section 1233 and § 1.1233-1.

(7) *Estates and trusts.* Under section 543(a)(4) personal holding company income includes amounts includible in computing the taxable income of the corporation under part I, subchapter J, chapter 1 of the Code (relating to estates, trusts, and beneficiaries); and any gain derived by the corporation from the sale or other disposition of any interest in an estate or trust.

(8) *Personal service contracts.* (i) Under section 543(a)(5) amounts received under a contract under which the corporation is to furnish personal services, as well as amounts received from the sale or other disposition of such contract, shall be included as personal holding company income if—

(*a*) Some person other than the corporation has the right to designate (by name or by description) the individual who is to perform the services, or if the individual who is to perform the

Reg. § 1.543-1(b)(8)

services is designated (by name or by description) in the contract; and

(b) At any time during the taxable year 25 percent or more in value of the outstanding stock of the corporation is owned, directly or indirectly, by or for the individual who has performed, is to perform, or may be designated (by name or by description) as the one to perform, such services. For this purpose, the amount of stock outstanding and its value shall be determined in accordance with the rules set forth in the last two sentences of paragraph (b) and in paragraph (c) of § 1.542-3. It should be noted that the stock ownership requirement of section 543(a)(5) and this subparagraph relates to the stock ownership at any time during the taxable year. For rules relating to the determination of stock ownership, see section 544 and §§ 1.544-1 through 1.544-7.

(ii) If the contract, in addition to requiring the performance of services by a 25-percent stockholder who is designated or who could be designated (as specified in section 543(a)(5) and subdivision (i) of this subparagraph), requires the performance of services by other persons which are important and essential, then only that portion of the amount received under such contract which is attributable to the personal services of the 25-percent stockholder shall constitute personal holding company income. Incidental personal services of other persons employed by the corporation to facilitate the performance of the services by the 25-percent stockholder, however, shall not constitute important or essential services. Under section 482 gross income, deductions, credits, or allowances between or among organizations, trades, or businesses may be allocated if it is determined that allocation is necessary in order to prevent evasion of taxes or clearly to reflect the income of any such organizations, trades, or businesses.

(iii) The application of section 543(a)(5) and this subparagraph may be illustrated by the following examples:

Example (1). A, whose profession is that of an actor, owns all of the outstanding capital stock of the M Corporation. The M Corporation entered into a contract with A under which A was to perform personal services for the person or persons whom the M Corporation might designate, in consideration of which A was to receive $10,000 a year from the M Corporation. The M Corporation entered into a contract with the O Corporation in which A was designated to perform personal services for the O Corporation in consideration of which the O Corporation was to pay the M Corporation $500,000 a year. The $500,000 received by the M Corporation from the O Corporation constitutes personal holding company income.

Example (2). Assume the same facts as in example (1), except that, in addition to A's contract with the M Corporation, B, whose profession is that of a dancer and C, whose profession is that of a singer, were also under contract to the M Corporation to perform personal services for the person or persons whom the M Corporation might designate, in consideration of which they were each to receive $25,000 a year from the M Corporation. Neither B nor C were stockholders of the M Corporation. The contract entered into by the M Corporation with the O Corporation, in addition to designating that A was to perform personal services for the O Corporation, designated that B and C were also to perform personal services for the O Corporation. Although the O Corporation particularly desired the services of A for an entertainment program it planned, it also desired the services of B and C, who were prominent in their fields, to provide a good supporting cast for the program. The services of B and C required under the contract are determined to be important and essential; therefore, only that portion of the $500,000 received by the M Corporation which is attributable to the personal services of A constitutes personal holding company income. The same result would obtain although the dancer and the singer required by the contract were not designated by name but the contract gave the M Corporation discretion to select and provide the services of a singer and a dancer for the program and such services were provided.

Example (3). The N Corporation is engaged in engineering. Its entire outstanding capital stock is owned by four individuals. The N Corporation entered into a contract with the R Corporation to perform engineering services in consideration of which the R Corporation was to pay the N Corporation $50,000. The individual who was to perform the services was not designated (by name or by description) in the contract and no one but the N Corporation had the right to designate (by name or by description) such individual. The $50,000 received by the N Corporation from the R Corporation does not constitute personal holding company income.

(9) *Compensation for use of property.* Under section 543(a)(6) amounts received as compensation for the use of, or right to use, property of the corporation shall be included as personal holding company income if, at any time during the taxable year, 25 percent or more in value of the outstanding stock of the corporation is owned, directly or indirectly, by or for an individual entitled to the use of the property. Thus, if a

Reg. § 1.543-1(b)(9)

shareholder who meets the stock ownership requirement of section 543(a)(6) and this subparagraph uses, or has the right to use, a yacht, residence, or other property owned by the corporation, the compensation to the corporation for such use, or right to use, the property constitutes personal holding company income. This is true even though the shareholder may acquire the use of, or the right to use, the property by means of a sublease or under any other arrangement involving parties other than the corporation and the shareholder. However, if the personal holding company income of the corporation (after excluding any such income described in section 543(a)(6) and this subparagraph, relating to compensation for use of property, and after excluding any such income described in section 543(a)(7) and subparagraph (10) of this paragraph, relating to rents) is not more than 10 percent of its gross income, compensation for the use of property shall not constitute personal holding company income. For purposes of the preceding sentence, in determining whether personal holding company income is more than 10 percent of gross income, copyright royalties constitute personal holding company income, regardless of whether such copyright royalties are excluded from personal holding company income under section 543(a)(9) and subparagraph (12)(ii) of this paragraph. For purposes of applying section 543(a)(6) and this subparagraph, the amount of stock outstanding and its value shall be determined in accordance with the rules set forth in the last two sentences of paragraph (b) and in paragraph (c) of § 1.542-3. It should be noted that the stock ownership requirement of section 543(a)(6) and this subparagraph relates to the stock outstanding at any time during the entire taxable year. For rules relating to the determination of stock ownership, see section 544 and §§ 1.544-1 through 1.544-7.

(10) *Rents (including interest constituting rents).* Rents which are to be included as personal holding company income consist of compensation (however designated) for the use, or right to use, property of the corporation. The term "rents" does not include amounts includible in personal holding company income under section 543(a)(6) and subparagraph (9) of this paragraph. The amounts considered as rents include charter fees, etc., for the use of, or the right to use, property, as well as interest on debts owed to the corporation (to the extent such debts represent the price for which real property held primarily for sale to customers in the ordinary course of the corporation's trade or business was sold or exchanged by the corporation). However, if the amount of the rents includible under section 543(a)(7) and this subparagraph constitutes 50 percent or more of the gross income of the corporation, such rents shall not be considered to be personal holding company income.

(11) *Mineral, oil, or gas royalties.* (i) The income from mineral, oil, or gas royalties is to be included as personal holding company income, unless (*a*) the aggregate amount of such royalties constitutes 50 percent or more of the gross income of the corporation for the taxable year and (*b*) the aggregate amount of deductions allowable under section 162 (other than compensation for personal services rendered by the shareholders of the corporation) equals 15 percent or more of the gross income of the corporation for the taxable year.

(ii) The term "mineral, oil, or gas royalties" means all royalties, including overriding royalties and, to the extent not treated as loans under section 636, mineral production payments, received from any interest in mineral, oil, or gas properties. The term "mineral" includes those minerals which are included within the meaning of the term "minerals" in the regulations under section 611.

(iii) The first sentence of subdivision (ii) of this subparagraph shall apply to overriding royalties received from the sublessee by the operating company which originally leased and developed the natural resource property in respect of which such overriding royalties are paid, and to mineral, oil, or gas production payments, only with respect to amounts received after September 30, 1958.

(12) *Copyright royalties*—(i) *In general.* The income from copyright royalties constitutes, generally, personal holding company income. However, for taxable years beginning after December 31, 1959, those copyright royalties which come within the definition of "copyright royalties" in section 543(a)(9) and subdivision (iv) of this subparagraph shall be excluded from personal holding company income only if the conditions set forth in subdivision (ii) of this subparagraph are satisfied.

(ii) *Exclusion from personal holding company income.* For taxable years beginning after December 31, 1959, copyright royalties (as defined in section 543(a)(9) and subdivision (iv) of this subparagraph) shall be excluded from personal holding company income only if the conditions set forth in (*a*), (*b*), and (*c*) of this subdivision are met.

(*a*) Such copyright royalties for the taxable year must constitute 50 percent or more of the corporation's gross income. For this purpose, copyright royalties shall be computed by excluding royalties received for the use of, or the right to use, copyrights or interests in copyrights in works created, in whole or in part, by any person who, at

Reg. § 1.543-1(b)(12)

any time during the corporation's taxable year, is a shareholder.

(*b*) Personal holding company income for the taxable year must be 10 percent or less of the corporation's gross income. For this purpose, personal holding company income shall be computed by excluding (*1*) copyright royalties (except that there shall be included royalties received for the use of, or the right to use, copyrights or interests in copyrights in works created, in whole or in part, by any shareholder owning, at any time during the corporation's taxable year, more than 10 percent in value of the outstanding stock of the corporation), and (*2*) dividends from any corporation in which the taxpayer owns, on the date the taxpayer becomes entitled to the dividends, at least 50 percent of all classes of stock entitled to vote and at least 50 percent of the total value of all classes of stock, provided the corporation which pays the dividends meets the requirements of subparagraphs (A), (B), and (C) of section 543(a)(9).

(*c*) The aggregate amount of the deductions allowable under section 162 must constitute 50 percent or more of the corporation's gross income for the taxable year. For this purpose, the deductions allowable under section 162 shall be computed by excluding deductions for compensation for personal services rendered by, and deductions for copyright and other royalties to, shareholders of the corporation.

(iii) *Determination of stock value and stock ownership.* For purposes of section 543(a)(9) and this subparagraph, the following rules shall apply:

(*a*) The amount and value of the outstanding stock of a corporation shall be determined in accordance with the rules set forth in the last two sentences of paragraph (b) and in paragraph (c) of § 1.542-3.

(*b*) The ownership of stock shall be determined in accordance with the rules set forth in section 544 and §§ 1.544-1 through 1.544-7.

(*c*) Any person who is considered to own stock within the meaning of section 544 and §§ 1.544-1 through 1.544-7 shall be a shareholder.

(iv) *Copyright royalties defined.* For purposes of section 543(a)(9) and this subparagraph, the term "copyright royalties" means compensation, however designated, for the use of, or the right to use, copyrights in works protected by copyright issued under Title 17 of the United States Code (other than by reason of section 2 or 6 thereof), and to which copyright protection is also extended by the laws of any foreign country as a result of any international treaty, convention, or agreement to which the United States is a signatory. Thus, "copyright royalties" includes not only royalties from sources within the United States under protection of United States laws relating to statutory copyrights but also royalties from sources within a foreign country with respect to United States statutory copyrights protected in such foreign country by any international treaty, convention, or agreement to which the United States is a signatory. The term "copyright royalties" includes compensation for the use of, or right to use, an interest in any such copyrighted works as well as payments from any person for performing rights in any such copyrighted works.

(v) *Compensation which is rent.* Section 543(a)(9) and subdivisions (i) through (iv) of this subparagraph shall not apply to compensation which is "rent" within the meaning of the second sentence of section 543(a)(7). [Reg. § 1.543-1.]

☐ [*T.D.* 6308, 9-9-58. Amended by T.D. 6739, 6-16-64 and T.D. 7261, 2-26-73.]

[Reg. § 1.543-2]

§ 1.543-2. **Limitation on gross income and personal holding company income in transactions involving stocks, securities and commodities.**—(a) Under section 543(b)(1) the gains which are to be included in gross income, and in personal holding company income with respect to transactions described in section 543(a)(2) of paragraph (b)(5) of § 1.543-1, shall be the net gains from the sale or exchange of stock or securities. If there is an excess of losses over gains from such transactions, such excess (or net loss) shall not be used to reduce gross income or personal holding company income for purposes of the personal holding company tax. Similarly, under section 543(b)(2) the gains which are to be included in gross income, and in personal holding company income with respect to transactions described in section 543(a)(3) and paragraph (b)(6) of § 1.543-1, shall be the net gains from commodity transactions which reflect personal holding company income. Any excess of losses over gains from such transactions (resulting in a net loss) shall not be used to reduce gross income or personal holding company income. The capital loss carryover under section 1212 shall not be taken into account.

(b) The application of section 543(b) may be illustrated by the following examples:

Example (1). The P Corporation, not a regular dealer in stocks and securities, received rentals of $250,000 for its property from a 25-percent shareholder, and also had gains of $50,000 during the taxable year from the sale of stocks and securities. It also had losses on the sale of stocks and securities in the amount of $30,000. Accordingly, P Corporation had gross income during the taxable year of $270,000 ($250,000 plus $20,000 net gain from the sales of stocks and securities). It had personal holding company income of $20,000. (The rentals of $250,000 would not be personal holding company income under section 543(a)(6) since the personal holding company income of the corporation, $20,000 (after excluding any such income described in section 543(a)(6)), is not more than 10 percent of its gross income.)

Example (2). The R Corporation, not a regular dealer in stocks or securities, realized total gains during the taxable year of $900,000 from commodity futures transactions and $200,000 from the sales of stocks and securities. It also sustained total losses of $1,000,000 on such commodity futures transactions, resulting in a net gain for the taxable year of $100,000. None of the commodity futures transactions are hedging or other types of futures transactions excluded from the application of section 543(a)(3). No part of the loss on commodity futures transactions is to be taken into account in determining personal holding company income and gross income for personal holding company tax purposes for the taxable year. The full amount of the $200,000 in gains from the sales of stocks and securities is to be included in personal holding company income and in gross income for personal holding company tax purposes for the taxable year. [Reg. § 1.543-2.]

☐ [*T.D.* 6308, 9-9-58.]

[Reg. § 1.544-1]

§ 1.544-1. **Constructive ownership.**—(a) Rules relating to the constructive ownership of stock are provided by section 544 for the purpose of determining whether the stock ownership requirements of the following sections are satisfied:

(1) Section 542(a)(2), relating to ownership of stock by five or fewer individuals.

(2) Section 543(a)(5), relating to personal holding company income derived from personal service contracts.

(3) Section 543(a)(6), relating to personal holding company income derived from property used by shareholders.

(4) Section 543(a)(9), relating to personal holding company income derived from copyright royalties.

(b) Section 544 provides four general rules with respect to constructive ownership. These rules are:

(1) Constructive ownership by reason of indirect ownership. See section 544(a)(1) and § 1.544-2.

(2) Constructive ownership by reason of family and partnership ownership. See section 544(a)(2), (4), (5), and (6), and §§ 1.544-3, 1.544-6, and 1.544-7.

(3) Constructive ownership by reason of ownership of options. See section 544(a)(3), (4), (5), and (6), and §§ 1.544-4, 1.544-6, and 1.544-7.

(4) Constructive ownership by reason of ownership of convertible securities. See section 544(b) and § 1.544-5.

Each of the rules referred to in subparagraphs (2), (3), and (4) of this paragraph is applicable only if it has the effect of satisfying the stock ownership requirement of the section to which applicable; that is, when applied to section 542(a)(2), its effect is to make the corporation a personal holding company, or when applied to section 543(a)(5), section 543(a)(6), or section 543(a)(9), its effect is to make the amounts described in such provisions includible as personal holding company income.

(c) All forms and classes of stock, however denominated, which represent the interests of shareholders, members, or beneficiaries in the corporation shall be taken into consideration in applying the constructive ownership rules of section 544.

(d) For rules applicable in treating constructive ownership, determined by one application of section 544, as actual ownership for purposes of a second application of section 544, see section 544(a)(5) and § 1.544-6. [Reg. § 1.544-1.]

☐ [*T.D.* 6308, 9-9-58. Amended by *T.D.* 6739, 6-16-64.]

[Reg. § 1.544-2]

§ 1.544-2. **Constructive ownership by reason of indirect ownership.**—The following example illustrates the application of section 544(a)(1), relating to constructive ownership by reason of indirect ownership:

Example. A and B, two individuals, are the exclusive and equal beneficiaries of a trust or estate which owns the entire capital stock of the M Corporation. The M Corporation in turn owns the entire capital stock of the N Corporation. Under such circumstances the entire capital stock of both the M Corporation and the N Corporation shall be considered as being owned equally by A and B as the individuals owning the beneficial interest therein. [Reg. § 1.544-2.]

☐ [*T.D.* 6308, 9-9-58.]

[Reg. § 1.544-3]

§ 1.544-3. **Constructive ownership by reason of family and partnership ownership.**—(a) The following example illustrates the application of section 544(a)(2), relating to constructive owner-

Reg. § 1.544-3(a)

Personal Holding Companies

See p. 20,601 for regulations not amended to reflect law changes

ship by reason of family and partnership ownership.

Example. The M Corporation at some time during the last half of the taxable year, had 1,800 shares of outstanding stock, 450 of which were held by various individuals having no relationship to one another and none of whom were partners, and the remaining 1,350 were held by 51 shareholders as follows:

Relationships		Shares		Shares		Shares		Shares		Shares
An individual	A	100	B	20	C	20	D	20	E	20
His father	AF	10	BF	10	CF	10	DF	10	EF	10
His wife	AW	10	BW	40	CW	40	DW	40	EW	40
His brother	AB	10	BB	10	CB	10	DB	10	EB	10
His son	AS	10	BS	40	CS	40	DS	40	ES	40
His daughter by former marriage (son's half-sister)	ASHS	10	BSHS	40	CSHS	40	DSHS	40	ESHS	40
His brother's wife	ABW	10	BBW	10	CBW	10	DBW	160	EBW	10
His wife's father	AWF	10	BWF	10	CWF	110	DWF	10	EWF	10
His wife's brother	AWB	10	BWB	10	CWB	10	DWB	10	EWB	10
His wife's brother's wife	AWBW	10	BWBW	10	CWBW	10	DWBW	10	EWBW	110
Individual's partner	AP	10								

By applying the statutory rule provided in section 544(a)(2) five individuals own more than 50 percent of the outstanding stock as follows:

```
A (including AF, AW, AB, AS, ASHS, AP) .......................... 160
B (including BF, BW, BB, BS, BSHS) ............................... 160
CW (including C, CS, CWF, CWB) ................................. 220
DB (including D, DF, DBW) ....................................... 200
EWB (including EW, EWF, EWBW) ................................. 170
            Total, or more than 50 percent ............................ 910
```

Individual A represents the obvious case where the head of the family owns the bulk of the family stock and naturally is the head of the group. A's partner owns 10 shares of the stock. Individual B represents the case where he is still head of the group because of the ownership of stock by his immediate family. Individuals C and D represent cases where the individuals fall in groups headed in C's case by his wife and in D's case by his brother because of the preponderance of holdings on the part of relatives by marriage. Individual E represents the case where the preponderant holdings of others eliminate that individual from the group.

(b) For the restriction on the applicability of the family and partnership rules of this section, see paragraph (b) of § 1.544-1. For rules relating to constructive ownership as actual ownership, see § 1.544-6. [Reg. § 1.544-3.]

☐ [T.D. 6308, 9-9-58.]

[Reg. § 1.544-4]

§ 1.544-4. Options.—The shares of stock which may be acquired by reason of an option shall be considered to be constructively owned by the individual having the option to acquire such stock. For example: If C, an individual, on March 1, 1955, purchases an option, or otherwise comes into possession of an option, to acquire 100 shares of the capital stock of M Corporation, such 100 shares of stock shall be considered to be constructively owned by C as if C had actually acquired the stock on that date. If C has an option on an option (or one of a series of options) to acquire such stock, he shall also be considered to have constructive ownership of the stock which may be acquired by reason of the option (or the series of options). Under such circumstances, C shall be considered to have acquired constructive ownership of the stock on the date he acquired his option. For the restriction on the applicability of the rule of this section, see paragraph (b) of § 1.544-1. [Reg. § 1.544-4.]

☐ [T.D. 6308, 9-9-58.]

[Reg. § 1.544-5]

§ 1.544-5. Convertible securities.—Under section 544(b) outstanding securities of a corporation such as bonds, debentures, or other corporate obligations, convertible into stock of the corporation (whether or not convertible during the taxable year) shall be considered as outstanding stock of the corporation. The consideration of convertible securities as outstanding stock is subject to the exception that, if some of the outstanding securities are convertible only after a later date than in the case of others, the class having the earlier conversion date may be considered as outstanding stock although the others are not so considered, but no convertible securities shall be considered as outstanding stock unless all outstanding securities having a prior conversion date are also so considered. For example, if outstanding securities are convertible in 1954, 1955 and 1956, those convertible in 1954 can be properly considered as outstanding stock without so considering those convertible in 1955 or 1956, and those convertible in 1954 and 1955 can be properly considered as outstanding stock without so considering those convertible in 1956. However, the securities convertible in 1955 could not be properly considered as outstanding stock without so considering those convertible in 1954 and the securities convertible in 1956 could not be properly considered as outstanding stock without so considering those convertible in 1954 and 1955. For the restriction on the applicability of the rule of this section, see paragraph (b) of § 1.544-1(b). [Reg. § 1.544-5.]

☐ [T.D. 6308, 9-9-58.]

[Reg. § 1.544-6]

§ 1.544-6. **Constructive ownership as actual ownership.**—(a) *General rules.* (1) Stock constructively owned by a person by reason of the application of the rule provided in section 544(a)(1), relating to stock not owned by an individual, shall be considered as actually owned by such person for the purpose of again applying such rule or of applying the family and partnership rule provided in section 544(a)(2), in order to make another person the constructive owner of such stock, and

(2) Stock constructively owned by a person by reason of the application of the option rule provided in section 544(a)(3) shall be considered as actually owned by such person for the purpose of applying either the rule provided in section 544(a)(1), relating to stock not owned by an individual, or the family and partnership rule provided in section 544(a)(2) in order to make another person the constructive owner of such stock, but

(3) Stock constructively owned by an individual by reason of the application of the family and partnership rule provided in section 544(a)(2) shall not be considered as actually owned by such individual for the purpose of again applying such rule in order to make another individual the constructive owner of such stock.

(b) *Examples.* The application of this section may be illustrated by the following examples:

Example (1). A's wife, AW, owns all the stock of the M Corporation, which in turn owns all the stock of the O Corporation. The O Corporation in turn owns all the stock of the P Corporation. Under the rule provided in section 544(a)(1), relating to stock not owned by an individual, the stock in the P Corporation owned by the O Corporation is considered to be owned constructively by the M Corporation, the sole shareholder of the O Corporation. Such constructive ownership of the stock of the M Corporation is considered as actual ownership for the purpose of again applying such rule in order to make AW, the sole shareholder of the M Corporation, the constructive owner of the stock of the P Corporation. Similarly, the constructive ownership of the stock by AW is considered as actual ownership for the purpose of applying the family and partnership rule provided in section 544(a)(2) in order to make A the constructive owner of the stock of the P Corporation, if such application is necessary for any of the purposes set forth in paragraph (b) of § 1.544-1. But the stock thus constructively owned by A may not be considered as actual ownership for the purpose of again applying the family and partnership rule in order to make another member of A's family, for example, A's father, the constructive owner of the stock of the P Corporation.

Example (2). B, an individual, owns all the stock of the R Corporation which has an option to acquire all the stock of the S Corporation, owned by C, an individual, who is not related to B. Under the option rule provided in section 544(a)(3) the R Corporation may be considered as owning constructively the stock of the S Corporation owned by C. Such constructive ownership of the stock by the R Corporation is considered as actual ownership for the purpose of applying the rule provided in section 544(a)(1), relating to stock not owned by an individual, in order to make B, the sole shareholder of the R Corporation, the constructive owner of the stock of the S Corporation. The stock thus constructively owned by B by reason of the application of the rule provided in section 544(a)(1) likewise is considered as actual ownership for the purpose, if necessary, of applying the family and partnership rule provided in section 544(a)(2), in order to make another member of B's family, for example, B's wife, BW, the constructive owner of the stock of the S Corporation. However, the family and partnership rule could not again be applied so as to make still another individual the constructive owner of the stock of the S Corporation, that is, the stock constructively owned by BW could not be considered as actually owned by her in order to make BW's father the constructive owner of such stock by a second application of the family and partnership rule. [Reg. § 1.544-6.]

☐ [T.D. 6308, 9-9-58.]

[Reg. § 1.544-7]

§ 1.544-7. **Option rule in lieu of family and partnership rule.**—(a) If, in determining the ownership of stock, such stock may be considered as constructively owned by an individual by an

Reg. § 1.544-7(a)

application of either the family and partnership rule (section 544(a)(2)) or the option rule (section 544(a)(3)), such stock shall be considered as owned constructively by the individual by reason of the application of the option rule.

(b) The application of this section may be illustrated by the following example:

Example. Two brothers, A and B, each own 10 percent of the stock of the M Corporation, and A's wife, AW, also owns 10 percent of the stock of such corporation. AW's husband, A, has an option to acquire the stock owned by her at any time. It becomes necessary, for one of the purposes stated in section 544(a)(4), to determine the stock ownership of B in the M Corporation. If the family and partnership rule were the only rule that applied in the case, B would be considered, under that rule, as owning 20 percent of the stock of the M Corporation, namely, his own stock plus the stock owned by his brother. In that event, B could not be considered as owning the stock held by AW since (1) AW is not a member of B's family and (2) the constructive ownership of such stock by A through the application of the family and partnership rule in his case is not considered as actual ownership so as to make B the constructive owner by a second application of the same rule with respect to the ownership of the stock. However, there is more than the family and partnership rule involved in this example. As the holder of an option upon the stock, A may be considered the constructive owner of his wife's stock by the application of the option rule and without reference to the family relationship between A and AW. If A is considered as owning the stock of his wife by application of the option rule, then such constructive ownership by A is regarded as actual ownership for the purpose of applying the family and partnership rule so as to make another member of A's family, for example, B, the constructive owner of the stock. Hence, since A may be considered as owning his wife's stock by applying either the family-partnership rule or the option rule, the provisions of section 544(a)(6) apply and accordingly A must be considered the constructive owner of his wife's stock under the option rule rather than the family-partnership rule. B thus becomes the constructive owner of 30 percent of the stock of the M Corporation, namely, his own 10 percent, A's 10 percent, and AW's 10 percent constructively owned by A as the holder of an option on the stock. [Reg. § 1.544-7.]

☐ [*T.D. 6308, 9-9-58.*]

[Reg. § 1.545-1]

§ 1.545-1. **Definition.**—(a) Undistributed personal holding company income is the amount which is subject to the personal holding company tax imposed under section 541. Undistributed personal holding company income is the taxable income of the corporation adjusted in the manner described in section 545(b) and § 1.545-2, and section 545(c) and § 1.545-3, less the deduction for dividends paid. See part IV (section 561 and following), subchapter G, chapter 1 of the Code, and the regulations thereunder, relating to the dividends paid deduction.

(b) For purposes of the imposition of the personal holding company tax on a foreign corporation, resident or nonresident, which files or causes to be filed a return, the undistributed personal holding company income shall be computed on the basis of the taxable income from sources within the United States, and such income shall be adjusted in accordance with the principles of section 545(b) and § 1.545-2, and section 545(c) and § 1.545-3. For purposes of the imposition of such tax on a foreign corporation, resident or nonresident, which files no return, the undistributed personal holding company income shall be computed on the basis of the gross income from sources within the United States without allowance of any deductions. For purposes of this paragraph, a nonresident foreign corporation will be considered to have filed a return for any taxable year ending before September 9, 1958, if the return for any such taxable year is filed on or before February 5, 1960. [Reg. § 1.545-1.]

☐ [*T.D. 6308, 9-9-58. Amended by T.D. 6427, 12-2-59, and by T.D. 6949, 4-8-68.*]

[Reg. § 1.545-2]

§ 1.545-2. **Adjustments to taxable income.**—(a) *Taxes*—(1) *General rule.* (i) In computing undistributed personal holding company income for any taxable year, there shall be allowed as a deduction the amount by which Federal income and excess profits taxes accrued during the taxable year exceed the credit provided by section 33 (relating to taxes of foreign countries and possessions of the United States), and the income, war profits, and excess profits taxes of foreign countries and possessions of the United States accrued during the taxable year (to the extent provided by subparagraph (3) of this paragraph), except that no deduction shall be allowed for *(a)* the accumulated earnings tax imposed by section 531 (or a corresponding section of a prior law), *(b)* the personal holding company tax imposed by section 541 (or a corresponding section of a prior law), and *(c)* the excess profits tax imposed by subchapter E, chapter 2 of the Internal Revenue Code of 1939, for taxable years beginning after December 31, 1940. The deduction is for taxes for the taxable year, determined under the accrual method of accounting, regardless of whether the

Reg. § 1.545-1(a)

corporation uses an accrual method of accounting, the cash receipts and disbursement method, or any other allowable method of accounting. In computing the amount of taxes accrued, an unpaid tax which is being contested is not considered accrued until the contest is resolved.

(ii) However, the taxpayer shall deduct taxes paid, rather than taxes accrued, if it used that method with respect to Federal taxes for each taxable year for which it was subject to the tax imposed by section 500 of the Internal Revenue Code of 1939, unless an election is made under subparagraph (2) of this paragraph to deduct taxes accrued.

(2) *Election by taxpayer which deducted taxes paid.* (i) If the corporation was subject to the personal holding company tax imposed by section 500 of the Internal Revenue Code of 1939 and, for the purpose of that tax, deducted Federal taxes paid rather than such taxes accrued for each taxable year for which it was subject to such taxes, the corporation may elect for any taxable year ending after June 30, 1954, to deduct taxes accrued, including taxes of foreign countries and possessions of the United States, rather than taxes paid, for the purposes of the tax imposed by section 541 of the Internal Revenue Code of 1954. The election shall be made by deducting such taxes accrued on Schedule PH, Form 1120, to be filed with the return. The schedule shall, in addition, contain a statement that the corporation has made such election and shall set forth the year to which such election was first applicable. The deduction of taxes accrued in the year of election precludes the deduction of taxes paid during such year. The election, if made, shall be irrevocable and the deduction for taxes accrued shall be allowed for the year of election and for all subsequent taxable years.

(ii) Pursuant to section 7851(a)(1)(C), the election provided for in subdivision (i) of this subparagraph may be made with respect to a taxable year ending after June 30, 1954, even though such taxable year is subject to the Internal Revenue Code of 1939.

(3) *Taxes of foreign countries and United States possessions.* In determining undistributed personal holding company income for any taxable year, if the taxpayer chooses the benefit of section 901 for such taxable year, a deduction shall be allowed for—

(i) The income, war profits, and excess profits taxes imposed by foreign countries or possessions of the United States and accrued (or paid, if required under subparagraph (1)(ii) of this paragraph) during such taxable year, and

(ii) In the case of a domestic corporation, the foreign income taxes deemed to be paid for such taxable year under section 902(a) in accordance with §§ 1.902-1 and 1.902-2 or section 960(a)(1) in accordance with § 1.960-7.

In no event shall the amount under subdivision (ii) of this subparagraph exceed the amount includible in gross income with respect to such taxes under section 78 and § 1.78-1. The credit for such taxes provided by section 901 shall not be allowed against the personal holding company tax imposed by section 541. See section 901(a).

(b) *Charitable contributions*—(1) *Taxable years beginning before January 1, 1970.* (i) Section 545(b)(2) provides that, in computing the deduction for charitable contributions for purposes of determining undistributed personal holding company income of a corporation for taxable years beginning before January 1, 1970, the limitations in section 170(b)(1)(A) and (B), relating to charitable contributions by individuals, shall apply and section 170(b)(2) and (5), relating to charitable contributions by corporations and carryover of certain excess charitable contributions made by individuals, respectively, shall not apply.

(ii) Although the limitations of section 170(b)(1)(A) and (B) are 10 and 20 percent, respectively, of the individual's adjusted gross income, the limitations are applied for purposes of section 545(b)(2) by using 10 and 20 percent, respectively, of the corporation's taxable income as adjusted for purposes of section 170(b)(2), that is, the same amount of taxable income to which the 5-percent limitation applied. Thus, the term "adjusted gross income" when used in section 170(b)(1) means the corporation's taxable income computed with the adjustment, other than the 5-percent limitation, provided in the first sentence of section 170(b)(2). However, a further adjustment for this purpose is that the taxable income shall also be computed without the deduction of the amount disallowed under section 545(b)(8), relating to expenses and depreciation applicable to property of the taxpayer. The carryover of charitable contributions made in a prior year, otherwise allowable as a deduction in computing taxable income to the extent provided in section 170(b)(2) and, with respect to contributions paid in taxable years beginning after December 31, 1963, in section 170(b)(5), shall not be allowed as a deduction in computing undistributed personal holding company income for any taxable year.

(iii) See § 1.170-2 with respect to the charitable contributions to which the 10-percent limitation is applicable and the charitable contributions to which the 20-percent limitation is applicable.

(2) *Taxable years beginning after December 31, 1969.* (i) Section 545(b)(2) provides that, in computing the deduction allowable for charitable contributions for purposes of determining undistributed personal holding company income of a corporation for taxable years beginning after December 31, 1969, the limitations in section 170(b)(1)(A), (B), and (D)(i) (relating to charitable contributions by individuals) shall apply, and section 170(b)(1)(D)(ii) (relating to excess charitable contributions by individuals of certain capital gain property), section 170(b)(2) (relating to the 5-percent limitation on charitable contributions by corporations), and section 170(d) (relating to carryovers of excess contributions of individuals and corporations) shall not apply.

(ii) Although the limitations of section 170(b)(1)(A), (B), and (D)(i) are 50, 20, and 30 percent, respectively, of an individual's contribution base, these limitations are applied for purposes of section 545(b)(2) by using 50, 20, and 30 percent, respectively, of the corporation's taxable income as adjusted for purposes of section 170(b)(2), that is, the same amount of taxable income to which the 5-percent limitation applies. Thus, the term "contribution base" when used in section 170(b)(1) means the corporation's taxable income computed with the adjustments, other than the 5-percent limitation, provided in section 170(b)(2). However, a further adjustment for this purpose is that the taxable income shall also be computed without the deduction of the amount disallowed under section 545(b)(8), relating to expenses and depreciation applicable to property of the taxpayer. The carryover of charitable contributions made in a prior year, otherwise allowable as a deduction in computing taxable income to the extent provided in section 170(b)(1)(D)(ii) and (d), shall not be allowed as a deduction in computing undistributed personal holding company income for any taxable year.

(iii) See § 1.170A-8 for the rules with respect to the charitable contributions to which the 50-, 20-, and 30-percent limitations apply.

(c) *Special deductions disallowed.* Part VIII, subchapter B, chapter 1 allows corporations, in computing taxable income, special deductions for such matters as partially tax-exempt interest, certain dividends received, dividends paid on certain preferred stock of public utilities, organizational expenses, etc. See section 241. Such special deductions, except the deduction provided by section 248 (relating to organizational expenses) shall be disallowed in computing undistributed personal holding company income.

(d) *Net operating loss.* The net operating loss deduction provided in section 172 is not allowed for purposes of the computation of undistributed personal holding company income. For purposes of such a computation, however, there is allowed as a deduction the amount of the net operating loss (as defined in section 172(c)) for the preceding taxable year, except that, in computing undistributed personal holding company income for a taxable year beginning after December 31, 1957, the amount of such net operating loss shall be computed without the deductions provided in part VIII (section 241 and following, except section 248), subchapter B of chapter 1 of the Code.

(e) *Long-term capital gains.* (1) There is allowed as a deduction the excess of the net long-term capital gain for the taxable year over the net short-term capital loss for such year, minus the taxes attributable to such excess, as provided in section 545(b)(5).

(2) Section 631(c) (relating to gain or loss in the case of disposal of coal or domestic iron ore) shall have no application.

(f) *Bank affiliates.* There is allowed the deduction provided by section 601 in the case of bank affiliates (as defined in section 2 of the Banking Act of 1933; 12 U.S.C. 221a(c)).

(g) *Payment of indebtedness incurred prior to January 1, 1934*—(1) *General rule.* In computing undistributed personal holding company income, section 545(b)(7) provides that there shall be allowed as deduction amounts used or irrevocably set aside to pay or to retire indebtedness of any kind incurred before January 1, 1934, if such amounts are reasonable with reference to the size and terms of such indebtedness. See § 1.545-3 for the deduction in computing undistributed personal holding company income of amounts used or irrevocably set aside to pay or retire qualified indebtedness (as defined in paragraph (d) of § 1.545-3).

(2) *Indebtedness.* The term "indebtedness" means an obligation absolute and not contingent, to pay on demand or within a given time, in cash or other medium, a fixed amount. The term "indebtedness" does not include the obligation of a corporation on its capital stock. The indebtedness must have been incurred (or, if incurred by assumption, assumed) by the taxpayer before January 1, 1934. An indebtedness evidenced by bonds, notes, or other obligations issued by a corporation is ordinarily incurred as of the date such obligations are issued and the amount of such indebtedness is the amount represented by the face value of the obligations. In the case of refunding, renewal, or other change in the form of an indebtedness, the giving of a new promise to pay by the

Reg. § 1.545-2(b)(2)

taxpayer will not have the effect of changing the date the indebtedness was incurred.

(3) *Amounts used or irrevocably set aside.* The deduction is allowable, in any taxable year, only for amounts used or irrevocably set aside in that year. The use or irrevocable setting aside must be to effect the extinguishment or discharge of indebtedness. In the case of refunding, renewal, or other change in the form of an indebtedness, the mere giving of a new promise to pay by the taxpayer will not result in an allowable deduction. If amounts are set aside in one year, no deduction is allowable for such amounts for a later year in which actually paid. As long as all other conditions are satisfied, the aggregate amount allowable as a deduction for any taxable year includes all amounts (from whatever source) used and all amounts (from whatever source) irrevocably set aside, irrespective of whether in cash or other medium. Double deductions shall not be allowed.

(4) *Reasonableness of the amounts with reference to the size and terms of the indebtedness.* (i) The reasonableness of the amounts used or irrevocably set aside must be determined by reference to the size and terms of the particular indebtedness. Hence, all the facts and circumstances with respect to the nature, scope, conditions, amount, maturity, and other terms of the particular indebtedness must be shown in each case.

(ii) Ordinarily an amount used to pay or retire an indebtedness, in whole or in part, at or prior to the maturity and in accordance with the terms thereof will be considered reasonable and may be allowable as a deduction for the year in which so used. However, if an amount has been set aside in a prior year for payment or retirement of the same indebtedness, the amount so set aside shall not be allowed as a deduction in the year of the payment.

(iii) All amounts irrevocably set aside for the payment or retirement of an indebtedness in accordance with and pursuant to the terms of the obligation, for example, the annual contribution to trustees required by the provisions of a mandatory sinking fund agreement, will be considered as complying with the requirement of reasonableness. To be considered reasonable, it is not necessary that the plan of retirement provide for a retroactive setting aside of amounts for years prior to that in which the plan is adopted. However, if a voluntary plan was adopted before 1934, no adjustment is allowable in respect of the amounts set aside in the years prior to 1934.

(5) *Burden of proof.* The burden of proof will rest upon the taxpayer to sustain the deduction claimed. Therefore, the taxpayer must furnish the information required by the return, and such other information as the district director may require in substantiation of the deduction claimed.

(6) *Allowance to a successor corporation.* For allowance of deduction for pre-1934 indebtedness to a successor corporation, see section 381(c)(15).

(h) *Expenses and depreciation applicable to property of the taxpayer.* (1) In computing undistributed personal holding company income in the case of a personal holding company which owns or operates property, section 545(b)(8) provides a specific limitation with respect to the allowance of deductions for trade or business expenses and depreciation allocable to the operation or maintenance of such property. Under this limitation, these deductions shall not be allowed in an amount in excess of the aggregate amount of the rent or other compensation received for the use of, or the right to use, the property, unless it is established to the satisfaction of the Commissioner—

(i) That the rent or other compensation received was the highest obtainable, or if none was received, that none was obtainable;

(ii) That the property was held in the course of a business carried on bona fide for profit: and

(iii) Either that there was reasonable expectation that the operation of the property would result in a profit, or that the property was necessary to the conduct of the business.

(2) The burden of proof will rest upon the taxpayer to sustain the deduction claimed. If, in computing undistributed personal holding company income, a personal holding company claims deductions for expenses and depreciation allocable to the operation and maintenance of property owned or operated by the company, in an aggregate amount in excess of the rent or other compensation received for the use of, or the right to use, the property, it shall attach to its income tax return a statement setting forth its claim for allowance of the additional deductions, together with a complete statement of the facts and circumstances pertinent to its claim and the arguments on which it relies. Such statement shall set forth:

(i) A description of the property;

(ii) The cost or other basis to the corporation and the nature and value of the consideration paid for the property;

(iii) The name and address of the person from whom the property was acquired and the date the property was acquired;

Reg. § 1.545-2(h)(2)

(iv) The name and address of the person to whom the property is leased or rented, or the person permitted to use the property, and the number of shares of stock, if any, held by such person and the members of his family;

(v) The nature and gross amount of the rent or other compensation received for the use of, or the right to use, the property during the taxable year and for each of the five preceding years and the amount of the expenses incurred with respect to, and the depreciation sustained on, the property for such years;

(vi) Evidence that the rent or other compensation was the highest obtainable or, if none was received, a statement of the reasons therefor;

(vii) A copy of the contract, lease or rental agreement;

(viii) The purpose for which the property was used;

(ix) The business, carried on by the corporation, with respect to which the property was held and the gross income, expenses, and taxable income derived from the conduct of such business for the taxable year and for each of the five preceding years;

(x) A statement of any reasons which existed for expectation that the operation of the property would be profitable, or a statement of the necessity for the use of the property in the business of the corporation, and the reasons why the property was acquired; and

(xi) Any other information pertinent to the taxpayer's claim.

(i) *Amount of a lien in favor of the United States.* (1) If notices of lien are filed in the manner provided in section 6323(f), the amount of the liability to the United States outstanding at the close of the taxable year, and secured by such liens which are in effect at that time, shall be allowed as a deduction in computing undistributed personal holding company income. However, the amount of such deduction which may be allowed for any taxable year shall not exceed the taxable income (as adjusted for purposes of determining the undistributed personal holding company income, but without regard to the deduction under section 545(b)(9)) for such year. The fact that the amount of, or any part of, the outstanding obligation to the United States was deducted for one taxable year does not prevent its deduction for a subsequent taxable year to the extent the obligation is still outstanding at the close of the subsequent taxable year and is secured by a lien, notice of which has been filed.

(2) Subparagraph (1) of this paragraph may be illustrated by the following example:

Example. If the taxpayer (on the calendar year basis) is subject to a lien (notice of which has been properly filed) in the amount of $500,000 at the close of the calendar year 1954 and has taxable income of $400,000 for such taxable year, the deduction allowable by reason of the lien for the calendar year 1954 is $400,000. If, at the close of the taxable year ending December 31, 1955, the taxpayer is still subject to the same lien of $500,000 and it has taxable income of $450,000, a deduction is allowed by reason of such lien in the amount of $450,000.

(3) When the obligation secured by the lien in favor of the United States has been satisfied or released, the sum of the amounts which have been allowed as deductions under section 545(b)(9) in respect of such obligation shall be restored to taxable income for the year in which such lien is satisfied or released. If only a part of the obligation secured by the lien has been satisfied, the sum of the amounts which have been allowed as deductions under section 545(b)(9) in respect of such part shall be included in taxable income for the year of the satisfaction for the purpose of determining undistributed personal holding company income. It should be noted, however, that only the sum of the amounts which have been allowed as deductions under section 545(b)(9) and subparagraph (1) of this paragraph shall be included in taxable income. Thus, any amounts which were allowed as deductions under section 504(e) of the Internal Revenue Code of 1939 shall not be included as taxable income for any taxable year under section 545(b)(9) and subparagraph (1) of this paragraph.

(4) The application of subparagraph (3) of this paragraph may be illustrated by the following example:

Example. Assume the same facts as in the example in subparagraph (2) of this paragraph, and assume further that the corporation has $100,000 taxable income both for 1956 (before including the $400,000 described below) and for 1957. In 1956, the corporation pays $200,000 of the obligation, thereby reducing its liability from $500,000 to $300,000. In such case, $400,000 is included in taxable income in computing its undistributed personal holding company income for 1956, that is, the sum of the $200,000 deduction for 1954 and the $200,000 deduction for 1955 in respect of the liability which is paid in 1956. In 1957, property of the corporation is discharged from the lien by reason of the fact that the value of the remaining property of the corporation exceeds double the outstanding liability. (See section 6325(b)(1).) Since this was not a release or satisfaction of the lien, no amount is added to taxable

Reg. § 1.545-2(i)(2)

income for 1957 with respect to the property discharged from the lien. In 1958, the remaining property is released from the lien by reason of a bond being accepted under section 6325(a)(2). There is added to taxable income in computing undistributed personal holding company income for 1958, $850,000, that is, the sum of the deductions allowed for 1954, 1955, 1956, and 1957 in respect of the $300,000 liability, the lien for which was released in 1958. This amount of $850,000, is computed as follows:

Year	Outstanding Liability	Taxable Income	Deduction As Limited By Taxable Income	Amount Attributable to Part Payment of $200,000 in 1956	Amount Attributable to Release of Lien in 1958
1954	$500,000	$400,000	$400,000	$200,000	$200,000
1955	500,000	450,000	450,000	200,000	250,000
1956	300,000	500,000	300,000	—	300,000
1957	300,000	100,000	100,000	—	100,000
Total					$850,000

(5)(i) If an amount has been included in undistributed personal holding company income of the personal holding company by reason of section 545(b)(9), any shareholder of the company may elect to compute his income tax with respect to such of his dividends as are attributable to such amount as though such dividends were received ratably over the period the lien was in effect.

(ii) For purposes of section 545(b)(9), the dividends paid during the taxable year of the personal holding company (computed as of the close of such year) shall be deemed attributable first to undistributed personal holding company income by reason of section 545(b)(9) (computed as of the close of the taxable year of the personal holding company). If the period over which the lien was in effect consists of several taxable years of the personal holding company, the dividend deemed received for any taxable year shall be deemed received on the last day of such taxable year of the personal holding company.

(iii) Such election shall be made in a statement showing the amount of the deduction under section 545(b)(9) for each taxable year of the period in which the lien was in effect, the amount of such deduction, if any, which was added to undistributed personal holding company income in a later year or years as a result of partial satisfaction or release of such lien, and the details thereof, the taxable year or years to which such dividends are allocable, and a computation of tax, on the basis of the election, for all taxable years affected by such ratable allocation of the dividends. Further, the statement shall show the district director's office in which the returns, for the years to which the dividends are allocable, were filed, the kind of returns which were filed (separate returns or joint returns), and the name and address under which the returns were filed. The statement shall be attached to the shareholder's return for the taxable year for which the dividend would be reported but for such election.

(iv) The operation of this subparagraph may be illustrated as follows: If, in the example under subparagraph (4) of this paragraph, shareholder A owns 75 percent in value of the outstanding stock of the personal holding company, and receives a dividend of $540,000 from such company during 1958 (the total dividend distribution being $720,000) he may elect to compute his income tax with respect to the $540,000 in dividends for 1958 as if he had received $127,058.82 of such dividends for 1954 ($200,000/850,000 of $540,000), $158,823.53 of such dividends for 1955 ($250,000/850,000 of $540,000), $190,588.23 of such dividends for 1956 ($300,000/850,000 of $540,000), and $63,529.41 of such dividends for 1957 ($100,000/850,000 of $540,000). Accordingly, the tax computed for 1958 with respect to such dividends shall be the aggregate of the taxes attributable to such amounts had they been distributed in the respective years. [Reg. § 1.545-2.]

☐ [T.D. 6308, 9-9-58. Amended by T.D. 6376, 5-6-59, by T.D. 6805, 3-8-65, by T.D. 6841, 7-26-65, by T.D. 6900, 11-16-66, by T.D. 6949, 4-8-68, by T.D. 7207, 10-3-72, by T.D. 7429, 8-20-76, and by T.D. 7649, 10-17-79.]

[Reg. § 1.545-3]

§ 1.545-3. Special adjustment to taxable income.—(a) *In general.* In computing undistributed personal holding company income for any taxable year beginning after December 31, 1963, section 545(c)(1) provides that, except as otherwise provided in section 545(c), there shall be allowed as a deduction amounts used or amounts irrevocably set aside (to the extent reasonable with reference to the size and terms of the indebtedness) during such year to pay or retire qualified indebtedness (as defined in section 545(c)(3) and paragraph (d) of this section). The reasonableness of amounts irrevocably set aside shall be determined under the rules of paragraph (g)(4) of § 1.545-2.

(b) *Amounts used or irrevocably set aside*—(1) *In general.* The deduction is allowable, in any taxable year, only for amounts used or irrevocably set aside in that year to extinguish or discharge qualified indebtedness. If amounts are set aside in one year, no deduction is allowable for a later year in which such amounts are actually paid. As long as all other conditions are satisfied, the aggregate amount allowable as a deduction for any taxable year includes all amounts (from whatever source) used and all amounts (from whatever source) irrevocably set aside, irrespective of whether in cash or other medium. The same item shall not be deducted more than once.

(2) *Refunding, etc., of qualified indebtedness.* (i) A refunding, renewal, or mere change in the form of a qualified indebtedness which does not involve a substantial change in the economic terms of the indebtedness will not result in an allowable deduction whether or not funds are obtained from such refunding, renewal, or change in form, and whether or not such funds are applied on the prior obligation, and will not constitute a reduction in the amount of such qualified indebtedness. For purposes of this section, if, in connection with a refunding, renewal, or other change in the form of an indebtedness, the rate of interest or principal amount of such debt, or the date when payment is due with respect to such debt are significantly changed, or if, after the refunding, renewal, or other change in the form of such debt, the creditor to whom such debt is owed is neither the creditor to whom such debt was owed before such refunding, renewal, or other change, nor a person standing in a relationship to such creditor described in section 267(b), then a substantial change in the economic terms of such indebtedness will normally have occurred.

(ii) The application of this subparagraph may be illustrated by the following examples:

Example (1). On December 31, 1963, M owes $10,000 to X represented by a 6-percent, 90-day note payable on January 31, 1964. On January 31, 1964, M renews the debt, giving X a new 6-percent, 90-day note (payable on Apr. 30, 1964) and paying the accrued interest on the old note. Since the date when payment is due has been significantly changed, a substantial change in the economic terms of the indebtedness has occurred.

Example (2). On December 31, 1963, S owes $5,000 to T represented by a 6-percent note payable on January 1, 1965. On December 23, 1964, S liquidates the note, giving T a new note for $5,000 due on January 2, 1965, and bearing interest at 6 percent. Since the transaction does not involve a substantial change in the economic terms of the indebtedness, the transaction will not result in an allowable deduction, and the amount of the qualified indebtedness will not be reduced.

Example (3). (i) On December 31, 1963, Q owes $45,000 to R represented by a demand note. On July 1, 1964, Q renews $30,000 of the indebtedness by issuing a new demand note to R and liquidates $15,000 of the debt. Since the principal amount of the debt has been significantly changed, there has been a substantial change in the economic terms of the indebtedness.

(ii) If Q has issued renewal notes for $44,000 and had paid only $1,000 of the total indebtedness, then a significant change in the principal amount of the debt would not have occurred and Q would have been entitled to only a $1,000 deduction (the amount actually paid during the taxable year). In addition, the amount of qualified indebtedness would have been reduced to $44,000.

(c) *Corporations to which applicable.* Section 545(c)(2) describes the corporations to which section 545(c) applies. In order to qualify under section 545(c)(2), the corporation must be one:

(1) Which for at least one of its two most recent taxable years ending before February 26, 1964, was not a personal holding company under section 542, but which would have been a personal holding company under section 542 for such taxable year if the law applicable for the first taxable year beginning after December 31, 1963, had been applicable to such taxable year; or

(2) Which is an acquiring corporation treated as a corporation described in subparagraph (1) of this paragraph by reason of section 381(c)(15) (relating to the carryover of certain indebtedness in corporate acquisitions), but only to the extent of the qualified indebtedness to which it has succeeded under section 381(c)(15) and the indebtedness referred to in paragraph (d)(1)(ii) of this section incurred to replace qualified indebtedness to which it has succeeded under section 381(c)(15).

The law applicable for the first taxable year beginning after December 31, 1963, for purposes of this paragraph means part II (section 541 and following), subchapter G, chapter 1 of the Code as applicable to such year but does not include amendments to other parts of the Code first applicable with respect to such year. For an example of a corporation described in subparagraph (1) of this paragraph see paragraph (f)(1) of § 1.333-5.

(d) *Qualified indebtedness*—(1) *General definition.* Except as provided in subparagraphs (2), (3), and (4) of this paragraph the term "qualified indebtedness" means:

(i) The outstanding indebtedness (as defined in subparagraph (6) of this paragraph) incurred after December 31, 1933, and before January 1, 1964, by the taxpayer (or to which the taxpayer succeeded in a transaction to which section 381(c)(15) applies), and

(ii) The outstanding indebtedness (as defined in subparagraph (6) of this paragraph) incurred after December 31, 1963, by the taxpayer (or to which the taxpayer succeeded in a transaction to which section 381(c)(15) applies) for the purpose of making a payment or set-aside referred to in paragraph (a) of this section in the same taxable year of the debtor in which such indebtedness was incurred. An indebtedness shall be deemed not to have been incurred for the purpose of making a payment or set-aside referred to in paragraph (a) of this section when such indebtedness is a consequence of a refunding, renewal, or mere change in the form of a qualified indebtedness which does not involve a substantial change in the economic terms of the qualified indebtedness. (See paragraph (b)(2) of this section for the meaning of "substantial change in the economic terms of the indebtedness".) In the case of such a payment or set-aside which is made on or after the first day of the first taxable year beginning after December 31, 1963, such indebtedness incurred after December 31, 1963, is treated as qualified indebtedness only to the extent that the deduction from taxable income otherwise allowed by section 545(c)(1) with respect to such payment or set-aside is treated as non-deductible by reason of the election referred to in paragraph (e) of this section.

(2) *Exception for indebtedness owed to certain shareholders.* For purposes of subparagraph (1) of this paragraph, qualified indebtedness does not include any amounts which were, at any time after December 31, 1963, and before the payment or set-aside to which this section applies, owed directly or indirectly to a person who at such time owned more than 10 percent in value of the taxpayer's outstanding stock. The rules of section 318(a) and the regulations thereunder apply for the purpose of determining ownership under this subparagraph. Amounts which cease to be qualified indebtedness by reason of this subparagraph may not subsequently become qualified indebtedness as a result of any change in the facts (for example, a subsequent sale of stock by the person to whom the amounts are directly or indirectly owed).

(3) *Reduction for amounts irrevocably set aside.* For purposes of subparagraph (1) of this paragraph, qualified indebtedness with respect to a particular contract is reduced when and to the extent that amounts are irrevocably set aside to pay or retire such indebtedness. An amount is not considered to be irrevocably set aside if any person could use such amount for any purpose other than the retirement of the qualified indebtedness with respect to which it was set aside. No deduction is allowed under section 545(c)(1) and this section for payments out of amounts previously set aside. Thus, for example, if a corporation, which is a June 30 fiscal year taxpayer, incurs indebtedness of $1 million on February 1, 1962, and, in accordance with its contract of indebtedness, irrevocably sets aside $50,000 in a sinking fund on February 1, of each of the years 1963, 1964, and 1965, then its qualified indebtedness on January 1, 1964, is $950,000 ($1 million less one set-aside of $50,000 in 1963). The corporation is not allowed a deduction under section 545(c)(1) for the set-aside of $50,000 made during its taxable year ending on June 30, 1964, since section 545(c) is applicable only to taxable years beginning after December 31, 1963, but the qualified indebtedness is nevertheless reduced by such amount. The corporation is allowed a deduction of $50,000 for its taxable year ending June 30, 1965, as a result of the set-aside made during such taxable year, and qualified indebtedness on July 1, 1965, is $850,000. No deduction is allowed to the corporation for a payment in any subsequent taxable year from the amounts so set aside.

(4) *Reduction on disposition of certain property.* (i) Section 545(c)(6) provides that the total amount of the taxpayer's qualified indebtedness (as determined under subdivision (ii) of this subparagraph) shall be reduced if property of a character subject to the allowance for exhaustion, wear and tear, obsolescence, amortization, or depletion is disposed of after December 31, 1963. The reduction is made pro rata (in accordance with subdivision (iii) of this subparagraph) for the taxable year of such disposition and is equal in total amount to the excess, if any, of:

(*a*) The adjusted basis of the property disposed of (determined under section 1011 and the regulations thereunder) immediately before such disposition; over

(*b*) The amount of qualified indebtedness which ceased to be qualified indebtedness with respect to the taxpayer by reason of the assumption of indebtedness by the transferee of the property disposed of (whether or not such indebtedness was incurred by the taxpayer in connection with the property disposed of).

Reg. § 1.545-3(d)(4)

For purposes of (b) of this subdivision, the transferee will be treated as having assumed qualified indebtedness if such transferee acquires real estate of which the taxpayer is the legal or equitable owner immediately before the transfer and which is subject to indebtedness that, with respect to the taxpayer, is qualified indebtedness immediately before the transfer, provided the taxpayer shows to the satisfaction of the Commissioner that under all the facts and circumstances it no longer bears the burden of discharging such indebtedness.

(ii) The indebtedness reduced under the rule of this subparagraph is the qualified indebtedness which is outstanding with respect to the taxpayer immediately after the disposition referred to in subdivision (i) of this subparagraph.

(iii) The reduction with respect to any particular contract of indebtedness under the rules of this subparagraph shall be determined by multiplying the total reduction (determined under subdivision (i) of this subparagraph) by the ratio which the amount of the qualified indebtedness owed with respect to such contract by the taxpayer on the date referred to in subdivision (ii) of this subparagraph bears to the aggregate qualified indebtedness owed by the taxpayer with respect to all contracts on such date.

(5) *Total debt consisting of both qualified and nonqualified indebtedness.* In any case where, with respect to a particular contract of indebtedness, a part of the total indebtedness owed with respect to such contract is qualified indebtedness and the other part is indebtedness which is not qualified indebtedness, then, any amount paid or irrevocably set aside with respect to such contract shall be allocated between both such parts pro rata unless the taxpayer clearly indicates in its return the part of the payment or set-aside which shall be allocated to the qualified indebtedness.

(6) *Outstanding indebtedness.* For purposes of determining qualified indebtedness, the term "indebtedness" has the same meaning that it has under section 545(b)(7) and paragraph (g)(2) of § 1.545-2. Indebtedness ceases to be outstanding when the taxpayer no longer has an obligation absolute and not contingent with respect to the payment of such debt. An indebtedness evidenced by bonds, notes, or other obligations issued by a corporation is ordinarily incurred as of the date such obligations are issued, and the amount of such indebtedness is the amount represented by the face value of the obligations. However, a refunding, renewal, or mere change in the form of an indebtedness which does not involve a substantial change in the economic terms of the indebtedness will not have the effect of changing the date the indebtedness was incurred. (See paragraph (b)(2) of this section for the meaning of "substantial change in the economic terms of the indebtedness".) For purposes of this section, the outstanding indebtedness of a taxpayer includes a mortgage or other security interest on real estate of which such taxpayer is the legal or equitable owner (even though the taxpayer is not directly liable on the underlying evidence of indebtedness secured by such mortgage or security interest) provided such taxpayer shows to the satisfaction of the Commissioner that under all of the facts and circumstances it bears the burden of discharging such indebtedness. Thus, for example, if X acquires from Y property which is subject to a mortgage (X not assuming the indebtedness underlying such mortgage) and if X actually bears the burden of discharging the indebtedness, then, after the date of acquisition, such underlying indebtedness is outstanding indebtedness with respect to X, and since Y's obligation to pay is in fact contingent upon X failing to discharge the indebtedness, such indebtedness is not outstanding indebtedness with respect to Y.

(7) *Examples.* The application of this paragraph may be illustrated by the following examples:

Example (1). M Corporation, a calendar year taxpayer, has $600,000 of indebtedness outstanding on December 31, 1963 (which was incurred after 1933), represented by three demand notes. Individuals A and B (who are not shareholders) each hold one of M Corporation's notes in the amount of $150,000 and N Corporation (which is not a shareholder) holds M Corporation's note in the amount of $300,000. The note held by N Corporation is secured by a mortgage on certain depreciable real estate owned by M Corporation which has an adjusted basis to it on July 1, 1964, of $500,000. On July 1, 1964, M Corporation sells the depreciable real estate to O Corporation in consideration for $200,000 in cash and the assumption by O Corporation of the indebtedness on the note held by N Corporation. M Corporation borrows $200,000 on September 30, 1964, of which amount $150,000 is simultaneously applied to liquidate the note held by B. M Corporation's qualified indebtedness is reduced on July 1, 1964, by $300,000, the qualified indebtedness which ceased to be outstanding by reason of the transfer. In addition, the reduction (computed under section 545(c)(6) and subparagraph (4) of this paragraph) of M Corporation's qualified indebtedness by reason of the disposition of depreciable property on July 1, 1964, is as follows:

Personal Holding Companies

See p. 20,601 for regulations not amended to reflect law changes

39,237

Outstanding qualified indebtedness after reduction of qualified indebtedness which ceased to be outstanding by reason of the transfer but before the sec. 545(c)(6) reduction	$300,000
Reduced by—	
The excess of the adjusted basis of depreciable real estate disposed of on July 1, 1964 ($500,000), over the amount of qualified indebtedness assumed by O Corporation ($300,000)	200,000
Qualified indebtedness after reductions from transfer and assumption of indebtedness	$100,000

The pro-rata share of the reduction with respect to each debt is computed as follows:

Note held by A

Qualified indebtedness owed by taxpayer on the note held by A before the disposition of depreciable property	$150,000
Less the pro-rata share of the total reduction computed under subparagraph (4) of this paragraph allocable to such note	
$200,000 \times \dfrac{\$150,000}{\$300,000}$	$100,000
Qualified indebtedness owed on the note held by A after the transfer ...	$50,000

Note held by B

Qualified indebtedness owed by taxpayer on the note held by B before the transfer of depreciable property	$150,000
Less the pro-rata share of the total reduction computed under subparagraph (4) of this paragraph allocable to such note	
$200,000 \times \dfrac{\$150,000}{\$300,000}$	100,000
Qualified indebtedness owed on the note held by B after the transfer	$50,000

Of the $150,000 paid by M Corporation on September 30, 1964, to retire the note held by B only $50,000 qualified as a use of an amount to pay or retire qualified indebtedness and, thus, only $50,000 is allowable as a deduction for purposes of computing undistributed personal holding company income for 1964.

Example (2). The facts are the same as in example (1) except that M Corporation elects in accordance with paragraph (e) of this section not to deduct $25,000 of the $50,000 amount otherwise deductible. Then $25,000 of the $200,000 of new indebtedness incurred by M Corporation is qualified indebtedness. If the payment on the note held by B had not been made until January 1, 1965, then the new indebtedness would not be qualified indebtedness since the payment was not made in the taxable year in which the new indebtedness was incurred. If M Corporation pays $40,000 on April 1 and July 1, 1965, on the indebtedness incurred September 30, 1964, then (unless M indicates otherwise in its return for 1965 in accordance with subparagraph (5) of this paragraph) the payments made on such dates must be allocated between qualified and nonqualified indebtedness in the following manner:

			Qualified	Non-qualified
April 1 payment				
$40,000 \times \dfrac{\$ 25,000 \text{ (qualified)}}{\$200,000 \text{ (total indebtedness)}}$		=	$5,000	
$40,000 \times \dfrac{\$175,000 \text{ (nonqualified)}}{\$200,000 \text{ (total indebtedness)}}$		=		$35,000
July 1 payment				
$40,000 \times \dfrac{\$ 20,000 \text{ (nonqualified)}}{\$160,000 \text{ (total indebtedness)}}$		=	$5,000	
$40,000 \times \dfrac{\$140,000 \text{ (nonqualified)}}{\$160,000 \text{ (total indebtedness)}}$		=		$35,000
Total			$10,000	$70,000

Reg. § 1.545-3(d)(7)

Thus, a total of $10,000 of the two payments would be considered used to pay or retire qualified indebtedness. The results in examples (1) and (2) would be the same if O Corporation purchased the real estate subject to the indebtedness (not assuming the indebtedness) on the note held by N Corporation, provided M Corporation does not bear the burden of discharging such indebtedness after July 1, 1964.

Example (3). C owns all of the 1000 shares of outstanding capital stock of P Corporation. On December 31, 1963, P Corporation, a calendar year taxpayer, owes $200,000 of outstanding indebtedness to D and $500,000 of outstanding indebtedness to E. These debts were incurred after 1933. On January 15, 1964, P Corporation pays $100,000 in partial liquidation of the $500,000 indebtedness. On March 15, 1964, P Corporation pays $50,000 into a sinking fund with respect to the $200,000 indebtedness owed to D. On April 15, 1964, D purchases one-half of the shares owned by C, constituting 50 percent in value of P Corporation's outstanding stock. P Corporation, on June 15, 1964, pays $50,000 into a sinking fund with respect to the indebtedness owed to D. For purposes of the March 15, 1964, set-aside, the indebtedness owed to D ($200,000) is qualified indebtedness. However, the indebtedness owed to D is not qualified indebtedness for purposes of the June set-aside with respect to such indebtedness since D is a person who after December 31, 1963, and before the June set-aside, owned more than 10 percent in value of P Corporation's outstanding stock. Moreover, any subsequent set-asides made with respect to the indebtedness owed to D will not be made with respect to qualified indebtedness even if the shares owned by D are subsequently sold. Assuming no payments or set-asides are made by P Corporation after June 15, 1964, the P Corporation is entitled to a deduction of $150,000 under section 545(c)(1) for the calendar year 1964 for amounts paid and for amounts irrevocably set aside to pay or retire qualified indebtedness, and the total qualified indebtedness at the end of 1964 is $400,000. No additional deduction is allowed in subsequent taxable years for amounts paid out of the amounts set aside in 1964.

(e) *Election not to deduct* —(1) *In general.* Section 545(c)(4) provides that a taxpayer may elect to treat as nondeductible amounts otherwise deductible under section 545(c)(1) for the taxable year. The election shall be in the form of a statement of election filed on or before the 15th day of the third month following the close of the taxable year with respect to which the election applies. The election shall be irrevocable after such date.

(2) *Statement of election.* The statement of election referred to in subparagraph (1) of this paragraph shall be attached to the taxpayer's Schedule PH (Form 1120) for the year with respect to which such election applies, if such schedule is filed on or before the date referred to in subparagraph (1) of this paragraph. If the taxpayer's Schedule PH (Form 1120) is not filed on or before such date, then the statement of election shall clearly set forth the taxpayer's name, address, and employer identification number, shall be signed by an officer of the taxpayer who is authorized to sign a return of the taxpayer with respect to income, and shall be filed with the district director for the internal revenue district in which the taxpayer's income tax return (for the year with respect to which the election is applicable) would be filed. The following information shall be included in the statement of election:

(i) A statement that the taxpayer wishes to elect in accordance with section 545(c)(4);

(ii) The amounts paid or set aside which are to be treated as nondeductible under section 545(c)(4) and this section;

(iii) All information necessary to identify the qualified indebtedness with respect to which such amounts were paid or set aside;

(iv) The date on which such payments or set-asides were made; and

(v) All information necessary to identify the indebtedness (referred to in section 545(c)(3)(A)(ii) and paragraph (d)(1)(ii) of this section) incurred for the purpose of making the payments or set-asides which the taxpayer elects to treat as nondeductible, including:

(*a*) The date on which such indebtedness was incurred;

(*b*) The amount of such indebtedness;

(*c*) The person or persons to whom such indebtedness is owed; and

(*d*) A statement that such person or persons do not own more than 10 percent in value of the taxpayer's outstanding stock.

(f) *Limitation on deduction*—(1) *In general.* Section 545(c)(5) provides certain limitations on the deduction otherwise allowed by section 545(c)(1). Such deduction is reduced by the sum of the following amounts:

(i) The amount, if any, by which—

(*a*) The deductions allowed for the taxable year and all preceding taxable years beginning after December 31, 1963, for exhaustion, wear and tear, obsolescence, amortization, or depletion (other than such deductions which are disallowed in computing undistributed personal holding com-

Reg. § 1.545-3(e)(1)

pany income under the rule of paragraph (h) of § 1.545-2), exceed

(b) Any reduction, by reason of section 545(c)(5)(A) and this subdivision (i), of the deductions otherwise allowed by section 545(c)(1) for such preceding years; and

(ii) The amount, if any, by which—

(a) The deductions allowed under section 545(b)(5) (relating to long-term capital gain deduction) in computing undistributed personal holding company income for the taxable year and all preceding taxable years beginning after December 31, 1963, exceed

(b) Any reduction, by reason of section 545(c)(5)(B) and this subdivision (ii), of the deductions otherwise allowed by section 545(c)(1) for such preceding years.

(2) *Allocation of reduction.* If the total reduction required by subparagraph (1) of this paragraph is greater than the amount of the payment or set-aside made in respect of qualified indebtedness in a taxable year, then the portion of the reduction which is attributable to either section 545(c)(5)(A) or section 545(c)(5)(B), as the case may be, is that portion which bears the same ratio to the total reduction as the total reduction available under either section 545(c)(5)(A) or section 545(c)(5)(B), respectively, bears to the total reduction available under both such sections.

$$\left(\frac{\$\,50{,}000}{\$100{,}000} \times \$50{,}000\right),$$

and the reduction by reason of section 545(c)(5)(B) and subparagraph (1)(ii) of this paragraph (capital gain) is $25,000

$$\left(\frac{\$\,50{,}000}{\$100{,}000} \times \$50{,}000\right)$$

(iii) For 1966, Q Corporation is allowed a deduction for payment of qualified indebtedness of $100,000 computed as follows:

(3) *Example.* The provisions of this paragraph may be illustrated by the following example:

Example. (i) Q Corporation, a calendar year taxpayer, has qualified indebtedness of $400,000 on January 1, 1964, with respect to which payments of $50,000 are made on April 15, 1964, and 1965, and $300,000 on April 15, 1966. In the years 1964 and 1966, Q Corporation is allowed a deduction under section 545(b)(5) of $50,000 for the excess of its net long-term capital gain over its net short-term capital loss, minus the taxes attributable to such excess. Q Corporation is allowed a depreciation deduction of $50,000 for each of its taxable years 1964 through 1966. Q Corporation is a personal holding company with taxable income of $200,000 in each of the years 1964 and 1966.

(ii) For 1964, in computing undistributed personal holding company income, Q Corporation's taxable income is reduced by $50,000 by reason of the deduction under section 545(b)(5). No part of the depreciation deduction is disallowed under the rule of paragraph (h) of § 1.545-2. Q Corporation's deduction for payment of qualified indebtedness otherwise allowable under section 545(c)(1) and this section is reduced to zero by reason of the depreciation deduction and the capital gains deduction. The reduction by reason of section 545(c)(5)(A) and subparagraph (1)(i) of this paragraph (depreciation) is $25,000

Amount paid in 1966 to retire qualified indebtedness			$300,000
Less the sum of:			
(a) Depreciation deductions allowed for 1964 through 1966 (3 times $50,000)	$150,000		
Reduction of deductions in preceding taxable years (1964)	25,000		
		$125,000	
(b) Deduction allowed under section 545(b)(5) (relating to long-term capital gains) for 1964 through 1966	$100,000		
Reduction of deductions in preceding taxable years (1964)	25,000		
		75,000	
			$200,000
Deduction after reduction			$100,000

(iv) If, in the year 1966, Q Corporation's depreciation deduction had been limited for purposes of computing undistributed personal holding company income to $25,000 by reason of section

Reg. § 1.545-3(f)(3)

545(b)(8), then Q Corporation's deduction for payment of qualified indebtedness would be $125,000, computed as follows:

Amounts paid in 1966 to retire qualified indebtedness		$300,000
Less the sum of:		
(a) Depreciation deductions allowed for 1964 through 1966	$125,000	
Reduction of deductions in preceding taxable year (1964)	$ 25,000	
	$100,000	
(b) Deduction allowed under section 545(b)(5) (relating to long-term capital gains) for 1964 through 1966	$100,000	
Reduction of deductions in preceding taxable years (1964)	25,000	
	$ 75,000	
		$175,000
Deduction after reduction		$125,000

(g) *Burden of proof.* The burden of proof rests upon the taxpayer to sustain the deduction claimed under this section. In addition to any information required by this section, the taxpayer must furnish the information required by the return, and such other information as the district director may require in substantiation of the deduction claimed.

(h) *Application of section 381(c)(15).* Under section 381(c)(15), if an acquiring corporation assumes liability for qualified indebtedness in a transaction to which section 381(a) applies, then the acquiring corporation is considered to be the distributor or transferor corporation for purposes of section 545(c). Paragraph (c)(2) of this section reflects the application of section 381(c)(15) by including an acquiring corporation within the definition of corporation to which this section applies. Thus, the acquiring corporation is not required to meet the requirements of paragraph (c)(1) or paragraph (d)(1) of this section with respect to such acquired qualified indebtedness to which section 381(c)(15) is applicable. All the other provisions of this section apply in full to the acquiring corporation with respect to such acquired indebtedness. [Reg. § 1.545-3.]

☐ [*T.D.* 6949, 4-8-68.]

[Reg. § 1.547-1]

§ 1.547-1. **General rule.**—Section 547 provides a method under which, by virtue of dividend distributions, a corporation may be relieved from the payment of a deficiency in the personal holding company tax imposed by section 541 (or by a corresponding provision of a prior income tax law), or may be entitled to a credit or refund of a part or all of any such deficiency which has been paid. The method provided by section 547 is to allow an additional deduction for a dividend distribution (which meets the requirements of this section) in computing undistributed personal holding company income for the taxable year for which a deficiency in personal holding company tax is determined. The additional deduction for deficiency dividends will not, however, be allowed for the purpose of determining interest, additional amounts, or assessable penalties, computed with respect to the personal holding company tax prior to the allowance of the additional deduction for deficiency dividends. Such amounts remain payable as if section 547 had not been enacted. [Reg. § 1.547-1.]

☐ [*T.D.* 6308, 9-9-58.]

[Reg. § 1.547-2]

§ 1.547-2. **Requirements for deficiency dividends.**—(a) *In general.* There are certain requirements which must be fulfilled before a deduction is allowed for a deficiency dividend under section 547 and this section. These are—

(1) The taxpayer's liability for personal holding company tax shall be determined only in the manner provided in section 547(c) and paragraph (b) of this section.

(2) The deficiency dividend shall be paid by the corporation on, or within 90 days after, the date of such determination and prior to the filing of a claim under section 547(e) and paragraph (b)(2) of this section for deduction for deficiency dividends. This claim must be filed within 120 days after such determination.

(3) The deficiency dividend must be of such a nature as would have permitted its inclusion in the computation of a deduction for dividends paid under section 561 for the taxable year with respect to which the liability for personal holding company tax exists, if it had been distributed during such year. See section 562 and §§ 1.562-1 through 1.562-3. In this connection, it should be noted that under section 316(b)(2), the term "dividend" means (in addition to the usual meaning under section 316(a)) any distribution of property (whether or not a dividend as defined in section 316(a)) made by a corporation to its shareholders,

to the extent of its undistributed personal holding company income (determined under section 545 and §§ 1.545-1 and 1.545-2 without regard to section 316(b)(2)) for the taxable year in respect of which the distribution is made.

(b) *Special rules*—(1) *Nature and details of determination.* (i) A determination of a taxpayer's liability for personal holding company tax shall, for the purposes of section 547, be established in the manner specified in section 547(c) and this subparagraph.

(ii) The date of determination by a decision of the Tax Court of the United States is the date upon which such decision becomes final, as prescribed in section 7481.

(iii) The date upon which a judgment of a court becomes final, which is the date of the determination in such cases, must be determined upon the basis of the facts in the particular case. Ordinarily, a judgment of a United States district court becomes final upon the expiration of the time allowed for taking an appeal, if no such appeal is duly taken within such time; and a judgment of the United States Court of Claims becomes final upon the expiration of the time allowed for filing a petition for certiorari if no such petition is duly filed within such time.

(iv) The date of determination by a closing agreement, made under section 7121, is the date such agreement is approved by the Commissioner.

(v) A determination under section 547(c)(3) may be made by an agreement signed by the district director or such other official to whom authority to sign the agreement is delegated, and by or on behalf of the taxpayer. The agreement shall set forth the total amount of the liability for personal holding company tax for the taxable year or years. An agreement under this subdivision which is signed by the district director (or such other official to whom authority to sign the agreement is delegated) on or after July 15, 1963, shall be sent to the taxpayer at his last known address by either registered or certified mail. For further guidance regarding the definition of last known address, see § 301.6212-2 of this chapter. If registered mail is used for such purpose, the date of registration shall be treated as the date of determination; if certified mail is used for such purpose, the date of the postmark on the sender's receipt for such mail shall be treated as the date of determination. However, if a dividend is paid by the corporation before such registration or postmark date but on or after the date such agreement is signed by the district director or such other official to whom authority to sign the agreement is delegated, the date of determination shall be such date of signing. The date of determination with respect to an agreement which is signed by the district director (or such other official to whom authority to sign the agreement is delegated) before July 15, 1963, shall be the date of the postmark on the cover envelope in which such agreement is sent by ordinary mail, except that if a dividend is paid by the corporation before such postmark date but on or after the date such agreement is signed by the district director or such other official to whom authority to sign the agreement is delegated, the date of determination shall be such date of signing.

(2) *Claim for deduction*—(i) *Contents of claim.* A claim for deduction for a deficiency dividend shall be made, with the requisite declaration, on Form 976 and shall contain the following information:

(a) The name and address of the corporation;

(b) The place and date of incorporation;

(c) The amount of the deficiency determined with respect to the tax imposed by section 541 (or a corresponding provision of a prior income tax law) and the taxable year or years involved; the amount of the unpaid deficiency or, if the deficiency has been paid in whole or in part, the date of payment and the amount thereof; a statement as to how the deficiency was established, if unpaid; or if paid in whole or in part, how it was established that any portion of the amount paid was a deficiency at the time when paid and, in either case whether it was by an agreement under section 547(c)(3), by a closing agreement under section 7121, or by a decision of the Tax Court or court judgment and the date thereof; if established by a final judgment in a suit against the United States for refund, the date of payment of the deficiency, the date the claim for refund was filed, and the date the suit was brought; if established by a Tax Court decision or court judgment, a copy thereof shall be attached, together with an explanation of how the decision became final; if established by an agreement under section 547(c)(3), a copy of such agreement shall be attached;

(d) The amount and date of payment of the dividend with respect to which the claim for the deduction for deficiency dividends is filed;

(e) A statement setting forth the various classes of stock outstanding, the name and address of each shareholder, the class and number of shares held by each on the date of payment of the dividend with respect to which the claim is filed, and the amount of such dividend paid to each shareholder;

(f) The amount claimed as a deduction for deficiency dividends; and

Reg. § 1.547-2(b)(2)

(g) Such other information as may be required by the claim form.

(ii) *Filing of claim and corporate resolution.* The claim together with a certified copy of the resolution of the board of directors or other authority, authorizing the payment of the dividend with respect to which the claim is filed, shall be filed with the district director of internal revenue for the district in which the return is filed.

(iii) *Carryover of deficiency dividends paid by acquiring corporation.* In the case of the acquisition of assets of a corporation by another corporation in a distribution or transfer described in section 381(a), the distributor or transferor corporation shall be entitled to a deduction for any deficiency dividends (as defined in section 547(d)) paid by the acquiring corporation with respect to such distributor or transferor corporation. See section 381(c)(17). [Reg. § 1.547-2.]

☐ [*T.D.* 6308, 9-9-58. Amended by *T.D.* 6657, 6-11-63; *T.D.* 7604, 3-28-79 and *T.D.* 8939, 1-11-2001.]

[Reg. § 1.547-3]

§ 1.547-3. **Claim for credit or refund.**—(a) If a deficiency in personal holding company tax is asserted for any taxable year, and the corporation has paid any portion of such asserted deficiency, it is entitled to a credit or refund of such payment to the extent that such payment constitutes an overpayment as the result of a deduction for a deficiency dividend as provided in section 547 and §§ 1.547-1 through 1.547-7. It should be noted that a "determination" under section 547(c) and paragraph (b)(1) of § 1.547-2, of taxpayer's liability for personal holding company tax may take place subsequent to the time the deficiency was paid. To secure credit or refund of such overpayment, the taxpayer must file a claim on Form 843 in addition to the claim for the deduction for deficiency dividends required under section 547(e) and paragraph (b)(2) of § 1.547-2.

(b) No interest shall be allowed on such credit or refund.

(c) Such credit or refund will be allowed as if, on the date of the determination under section 547(c) and paragraph (b)(1) of § 1.547-2, two years remained before the expiration of the period of limitation on the filing of claim for refund for the taxable year to which the overpayment relates. [Reg. § 1.547-3.]

☐ [*T.D.* 6308, 9-9-58.]

[Reg. § 1.547-4]

§ 1.547-4. **Effect on dividends paid deduction.**—The deficiency dividends deduction shall be allowed as of the date the claim is filed. No duplication of deductions with respect to any deficiency dividends is permitted. If a corporation claims and receives the benefit of the provisions of section 547 (or the corresponding section 506 of the Internal Revenue Code of 1939, or section 407 of the Revenue Act of 1938 (52 Stat. 447)), based upon a distribution of deficiency dividends, that distribution does not become a part of the dividends paid deduction under section 561. Likewise, it will not be made the basis of a dividends paid deduction under section 561 by reason of the application of section 563(b), relating to dividends paid after the close of the taxable year and on or before the 15th day of the third month following the close of such taxable year. [Reg. § 1.547-4.]

☐ [*T.D.* 6308, 9-9-58.]

[Reg. § 1.547-5]

§ 1.547-5. **Deduction denied in case of fraud or wilful failure to file timely return.**—No deduction for deficiency dividends shall be allowed under section 547(a) if the determination contains a finding that any part of the deficiency is due to fraud with intent to evade tax, or to wilful failure to file an income tax return within the time prescribed by law or prescribed by the Secretary or his delegate in pursuance of law. See § 1.547-7 for effective date. [Reg. § 1.547-5.]

☐ [*T.D.* 6308, 9-9-58.]

[Reg. § 1.547-6]

§ 1.547-6. **Suspension of statute of limitations and stay of collection.**—(a) *Statute of limitations.* If the corporation files a claim for a deduction for deficiency dividends under section 547(e) and paragraph (b)(2) of § 1.547-2, the running of the statute of limitations upon assessment, distraint, and collection in court in respect of the deficiency, and all interest, additional amounts, or assessable penalties, shall be suspended for a period of two years after the date of the determination under section 547(c) and paragraph (b)(1) of § 1.547-2.

(b) *Stay of collection.* If a deficiency in personal holding company tax is established by a determination under section 547(c) and paragraph (b)(1) of § 1.547-2, collection by distraint or court proceeding (except in case of jeopardy), of the deficiency and all interest, additional amounts, and assessable penalties, shall be stayed for a period of 120 days after the date of such determination, and, to the extent any part of such deficiency remains after deduction for deficiency dividends, for an additional period until the date the claim is disallowed. After such claim is allowed or rejected, either in whole or in part, the amount of the deficiency which was not eliminated by the appli-

Foreign Personal Holding Companies

See p. 20,601 for regulations not amended to reflect law changes

cation of section 547, together with interest, additional amounts and assessable penalties, will be assessed and collected in the usual manner. [Reg. § 1.547-6.]

☐ [T.D. 6308, 9-9-58.]

[Reg. § 1.547-7]

§ 1.547-7. **Effective date.**—The deduction for deficiency dividends, in computing personal holding company tax for any taxable year, is allowable only with respect to determinations under section 547(c) made after November 14, 1954 (the date falling 90 days after the date of enactment of the Internal Revenue Code of 1954). If the taxable year with respect to which the deficiency is asserted began before January 1, 1954, the deficiency dividends deduction shall include only the amounts which would have been includible in the computation of the basic surtax credit for such taxable year under the Internal Revenue Code of 1939. Section 547(g), relating to the denial of a deficiency dividends deduction if the determination contains a finding that any part of the deficiency is due to fraud, etc., shall apply only if the taxable year with respect to which the deficiency is asserted begins after December 31, 1953. [Reg. § 1.547-7.]

☐ [T.D. 6308, 9-9-58.]

Foreign Personal Holding Companies

[Reg. § 1.551-1]

§ 1.551-1. **General rule.**—Part III (section 55 and following), subchapter G, chapter 1 of the Code does not impose a tax on foreign personal holding companies. The undistributed foreign personal holding company income of such companies, however, must be included in the manner and to the extent set forth in section 551, in the gross income of their "United States shareholders," that is, the shareholders who are individual citizens or residents of the United States, domestic corporations, domestic partnerships, and estates or trusts other than estates or trusts the gross income of which under subtitle A of the Code includes only income from sources within the United States. [Reg. § 1.551-1.]

☐ [T.D. 6308, 9-9-58.]

[Reg. § 1.551-2]

§ 1.551-2. **Amount included in gross income.**—(a) The undistributed foreign personal holding company income is included only in the gross income of the United States shareholders who were shareholders in the company on the last day of its taxable year on which a United States group (as defined in section 552(a)(2)) existed with respect to the company. Such United States shareholders, accordingly, are determined by the stock holdings as of such specified time. This rule applies to every United States shareholder who was a shareholder in the company at the specified time regardless of whether the United States shareholder is included within the United States group. For example, a domestic corporation which is a United States shareholder at the specified time must return its distributive share in the undistributed foreign personal holding company income even though the domestic corporation cannot be included within the United States group since, under section 554, the stock it owns in the foreign corporation is considered as being owned proportionately by its shareholders for the purpose of determining whether the foreign corporation is a foreign personal holding company.

(b) The United States shareholders must include in their gross income their distributive shares of that proportion of the undistributed foreign personal holding company income for the taxable year of the company which is equal in ratio to that which the portion of the taxable year up to and including the last day on which the United States group with respect to the company existed bears to the entire taxable year. Thus, if the last day in the taxable year on which the required United States group existed was also the end of the taxable year, the portion of the taxable year up to and including such last day would be equal to 100 percent and, in such case, the United States shareholders would be required to return their distributive shares in the entire undistributed foreign personal holding company income. But if the last day on which the required United States group existed was September 30, and the taxable year was a calendar year, the portion of the taxable year up to and including such last day would be equal to nine-twelfths and, in that case, the United States shareholders would be required to return their distributive shares in only nine-twelfths of the undistributed foreign personal holding company income.

(c) The amount which each United States shareholder must return is that amount which he would have received as a dividend if the above-specified portion of the undistributed foreign personal holding company income had in fact been distributed by the foreign personal holding company as a dividend on the last day of its taxable year on which the required United States group existed. Such amount is determined, therefore, by the interest of the United States shareholder in the foreign personal holding company, that is, by the number of shares of stock owned by the

Reg. § 1.551-2(c)

United States shareholder and the relative rights of his class of stock, if there are several classes of stock outstanding. Thus, if a foreign personal holding company has both common and preferred stock outstanding and the preferred shareholders are entitled to a specified dividend before any distribution may be made to the common shareholders, then the assumed distribution of the stated portion of the undistributed foreign personal holding company income must first be treated as a payment of the specified dividend on the preferred stock before any part may be allocated as a dividend on the common stock.

(d) The assumed distribution of the required portion of the undistributed foreign personal holding company income must be returned as dividend income by the United States shareholders for their respective taxable years in which or with which the taxable year of the foreign personal holding company ends. For example, if the M Corporation, whose taxable year is the calendar year, is a foreign personal holding company for 1954 and if A, one of its United States shareholders, makes returns on a calendar year basis, while B, another United States shareholder, makes returns on the basis of a fiscal year ending November 30, A must return his assumed dividend as income for the taxable year 1954 and B must return his distributive share as income for the fiscal year ending November 30, 1955. In applying this rule, the date as of which the United States group last existed with respect to the company is immaterial. Thus, in the foregoing example, if September 30, 1954, was the last day on which the United States group with respect to the M Corporation existed, B would still be required to return his assumed dividend as income for the fiscal year ending November 30, 1955, even though September 30, 1954, the date as of which the distribution is assumed to have been made, does not fall within such fiscal year.

(e) For the treatment of gain on the sale of certain stock, see section 306(f) and paragraph (h) of § 1.306-3. [Reg. § 1.551-2.]

☐ [*T.D.* 6308, 9-9-58.]

[Reg. § 1.551-3]

§ **1.551-3. Deduction for obligations of the United States and its instrumentalities.**—(a) Each United States shareholder required to return his distributive share of undistributed foreign personal holding company income for any taxable year shall take into account in computing the credit against tax under section 35, or the deduction under section 242, whichever is allowable to such shareholder, his proportionate share of whatever interest on obligations of the United States or its instrumentalities (as specified in section 35 or 242, as the case may be) may be included in the gross income of the company for such taxable year, with the exception of any such interest as may be so included by reason of the application of the provisions of section 555. For reduction of credit for such interest on account of amortizable bond premium, see section 171 and the regulations thereunder.

(b) The rule set forth in paragraph (a) of this section may be illustrated by the following example:

Example. The M Corporation is a foreign personal holding company which owns all the stock of the N Corporation, another foreign personal holding company. Both companies receive interest on obligations of the United States or its instrumentalities as specified in section 35. In determining the amount of the credit allowable under section 35 (if the shareholder is an individual) or the deduction allowable under section 242 (if the shareholder is a corporation), the United States shareholder of the M Corporation would be entitled to a credit or a deduction, as the case may be, only for his proportionate share of the interest received by that Company and not for any part of the interest received by the N Corporation, regardless of whether the interest received by the N Corporation is included in the gross income of the M Corporation as an actual dividend or as a constructive dividend under section 555. [Reg. § 1.551-3.]

☐ [*T.D.* 6308, 9-9-58.]

[Reg. § 1.551-4]

§ **1.551-4. Information in return.**—The information required by section 551(d) in the returns of certain United States shareholders relates only to the taxable year of a foreign personal holding company for which any part of such corporation's undistributed foreign personal holding company income must be included in gross income by the United States shareholder of whom the information is required. The information shall be submitted as a part of the income tax return in the form of a statement attached to the return. [Reg. § 1.551-4.]

☐ [*T.D.* 6308, 9-9-58.]

[Reg. § 1.551-5]

§ **1.551-5. Effect on capital account of foreign personal holding company and basis of stock in hands of shareholders.**—(a) Sections 551(e) and 551(f) are designed to prevent double taxation with respect to the undistributed foreign personal holding company income.

Foreign Personal Holding Companies

See p. 20,601 for regulations not amended to reflect law changes

(b) The application of sections 551(e) and 551(f) may be illustrated by the following examples:

Example (1). The M Corporation is a foreign personal holding company. Seventy-five percent in value of its capital stock is owned by A, a citizen of the United States, and the remainder, or 25 percent, of its stock is owned by B, a nonresident alien individual. For the calendar year 1954 the M Corporation has an undistributed foreign personal holding company income of $100,000. A is required to include $75,000 of such income in gross income as a dividend in his return for the calendar year 1954. The $100,000 is treated as paid-in surplus or as a contribution to the capital of the M Corporation and its accumulated earnings and profits as of the close of the calendar year 1954 are correspondingly reduced. If after treating such $100,000 as paid-in surplus or as a contribution to capital, the M Corporation has no accumulated earnings and profits at the close of 1954, and if for the calendar year 1955, the M Corporation had no earnings and profits, but distributed $40,000, the amount so distributed would be a nontaxable distribution and would not be included in the gross income of either A or B for the calendar year 1955. If, however, after treating the $100,000 as paid-in surplus or as a contribution to capital, the M Corporation had accumulated earnings and profits of $100,000 at the close of 1954, the facts otherwise being the same, the distributions in 1955 would be taxable to A as a dividend, and the taxability of such distributions to B would depend upon the application of section 861(a)(2), relating to the treatment of dividends from a foreign corporation as income from sources within or without the United States.

Example (2). In example (1) assume the basis of A's stock to be $300,000. If A includes in gross income in his return for the calendar year 1954, $75,000 as a dividend from the M Corporation, the basis of his stock would be $375,000. After the nontaxable distribution of $30,000 to A by the M Corporation in 1955 (75 percent of the $40,000 distribution) the basis of A's stock, assuming no other changes, would be $345,000. If A failed to include the $75,000 as a dividend in gross income in his return for 1954 and his failure was not discovered until after the 6-year period of limitations had expired, the application of the rule would not increase the basis of A's stock. The subsequent nontaxable distribution of $30,000 to A in 1955 would reduce his basis of $300,000 to $270,000, thus tending to compensate for his failure to include the amount of $75,000 as a dividend in his gross income for 1954. If the undistributed foreign personal holding company income of the M Corporation is readjusted within the statutory period of limitations, thus increasing or decreasing the amount A would have to include in his gross income, proper adjustment is required to be made to the basis of A's stock on account of such readjustment. [Reg. § 1.551-5.]

☐ [T.D. 6308, 9-9-58.]

[Reg. § 1.552-1]

§ 1.552-1. Definition of foreign personal holding company.—(a) A foreign personal holding company is any foreign corporation, other than a corporation exempt from taxation under subchapter F (section 501 and following) and other than certain banking institutions which satisfy the requirements of section 552(b)(2) and paragraph (b) of § 1.552-4 which for the taxable year meets (1) the gross income requirement specified in section 552(a)(1); and (2) the stock ownership requirement specified in section 552(a)(2). Both requirements must be satisfied with respect to each taxable year.

(b) A foreign corporation which comes within the classification of a foreign personal holding company is not subject to taxation either under section 531 or section 541. See sections 532(b)(2) and 542(c)(5). The fact that a foreign corporation is a foreign personal holding company does not relieve the corporation from liability for the taxes imposed generally upon foreign corporations, such as the taxes imposed by sections 881 and 882, since such taxes apply regardless of the classification of the foreign corporation as a foreign personal holding company. [Reg. § 1.552-1.]

☐ [T.D. 6308, 9-9-58.]

[Reg. § 1.552-2]

§ 1.552-2. Gross income requirement.—(a) To meet the gross income requirement, it is necessary that either of the following percentages of gross income of the corporation for the taxable year (including the additions to gross income provided in section 555(b) as required by section 555(c)(2)) be foreign personal holding company income as defined in section 553:

(1) 60 percent or more; or

(2) 50 percent or more if the foreign corporation has been classified as a foreign personal holding company for any taxable year ending after August 26, 1937, unless—

(i) A taxable year has intervened since the last taxable year for which it was so classified, during no part of which the stock ownership requirement specified in section 552(a)(2) exists; or

(ii) Three consecutive years have intervened since the last taxable year for which it was so classified, during each of which its foreign per-

Reg. § 1.552-2(a)(2)

sonal holding company income was less than 50 percent of its gross income.

(b) In determining whether the foreign personal holding company income is equal to the required percentage of the total gross income, the determination must not be made upon the basis of gross receipts, since gross income is not synonymous with gross receipts. For meaning of gross income in this part, see section 555 and § 1.555-1. [Reg. § 1.552-2.]

☐ [T.D. 6308, 9-9-58.]

[Reg. § 1.552-3]

§ 1.552-3. Stock ownership requirement.—(a) To meet the stock ownership requirement, it is necessary that at sometime in the taxable year more than 50 percent in value of the outstanding stock of the foreign corporation be owned, directly or indirectly, by or for not more than five individuals who are citizens or residents of the United States, herein referred to as "United States group." For the purpose of the requirement under section 552(a)(2), section 554 provides that the ownership of the stock must be determined under the rules prescribed by section 544 (relating to rules for determining stock ownership in the case of personal holding companies generally). Accordingly, section 544 and §§ 1.544-1 through 1.544-7 are applicable for purposes of section 552(a)(2) and this section as if each reference in section 544 and §§ 1.544-1 through 1.544-7 to a personal holding company or to part II (sections 541 and following), subchapter G, chapter 1 of the Code, was a reference to a foreign personal holding company or to part III (section 551) of subchapter G, chapter 1 of the 1954 Code, as the case may be.

(b) It is necessary to consider any change in the stock outstanding during the taxable year, whether in the number of shares or classes of stock, or in the ownership thereof, since a corporation comes within the classification if the statutory conditions with respect to stock ownership are present at any time during the taxable year.

(c) In determining whether the statutory conditions with respect to stock ownership are present at any time during the taxable year, the phrase "in value" shall, in the light of all the circumstances, be deemed the value of the corporate stock outstanding at such time (not including treasury stock). This value may be determined upon the basis of the company's net worth, earning and dividend paying capacity, appreciation of assets, together with such other factors as having a bearing upon the value of the stock. If the value of the stock which is used is greatly at variance with that reflected by the corporate books, the evidence of such value should be filed with the return. In any case where there are two or more classes of stock outstanding, the total value of all the stock should be allocated among the different classes according to the relative value of each class therein. [Reg. § 1.552-3.]

☐ [T.D. 6308, 9-9-58.]

[Reg. § 1.552-4]

§ 1.552-4. Certain excluded banks.—(a) A corporation is excluded from the definition of "foreign personal holding company" if it is organized and doing business under the banking and credit laws of a foreign country and if it establishes to the satisfaction of the Commissioner that it was not formed or availed of for the purpose of evading or avoiding United States income taxes which would otherwise be imposed on its shareholders. If this is established, the Commissioner, or such other official to whom authority may be delegated, will certify, by letter to the corporation, that it is not a foreign personal holding company.

(b) An application for certification under section 552(b)(2) shall be made in writing to the Commissioner of Internal Revenue, Washington 25, D.C., Attention: Director of International Operations. A separate application shall be filed for each taxable year for which certification is requested and the application shall be accompanied by a completed Form 958 for the taxable year. See section 6035. The following information shall be set forth in, or submitted with, the application:

(1) A complete reference to the banking or credit laws of the foreign country under which the corporation operates;

(2) A statement as to the extent of the corporation's business in receiving deposits and making loans and discounts and similar banking and credit operations;

(3) A statement as to the extent of the operations of the corporation other than such banking and credit operations;

(4) A statement as to whether the banking and credit operations of the corporation are customary for it;

(5) A statement setting forth the degree and manner of supervision exercised over it by the foreign government under its banking and credit laws; a copy (in English) of the corporation's last annual financial statement, as submitted to the Government authority having jurisdiction over it, shall be submitted with the application;

(6) A statement setting forth the business reasons of the corporation for not distributing the amount which would be its undistributed foreign personal holding company income if the corporation were not excluded under section 552(b);

Reg. § 1.552-3(a)

(7) A statement setting forth the extent of the corporation's profits which must be retained as reserves under the foreign law;

(8) A statement setting forth the date or dates when the corporation reasonably expects to distribute its undistributed foreign personal holding company income for the taxable year;

(9) A statement setting forth the name and address of each of the individuals described in section 552(a)(2), the extent of their stock ownership in the corporation, and the amount of distributions or other payments to such stockholders, including, but not limited to, dividends, compensation, interest, and rents; and

(10) Any other facts or information the corporation may wish to submit to show that it was not formed or availed of for the purpose of evading or avoiding United States income taxes which would otherwise be imposed on its shareholders.

The corporation shall also furnish such other information requested as necessary by the Director of International Operations. The application for certification, together with the information required by this paragraph, should be filed within 60 days after the close of the taxable year of the corporation or before November 9, 1958, whichever is later. However, if the corporation is unable, for good cause, to submit the application for certification within such 60-day period, additional time may be granted by the Director of International Operations upon receipt of a request from the corporation setting forth the reasons for such request. [Reg. § 1.552-4.]

☐ [T.D. 6308, 9-9-58.]

[Reg. § 1.552-5]

§ 1.552-5. United States shareholder of excluded bank.—A copy of the certification issued to an excluded bank under section 552(b)(2) and § 1.552-4 shall be filed with, and made a part of, the income tax return for the taxable year of each United States shareholder of such foreign corporation, if he has been a shareholder of such corporation for any part of such year. If the certificate has not been issued at the time the return of the United States shareholder is filed, the shareholder shall compute the tax on his return by treating the bank as a foreign personal holding company. If a certificate is issued after the return is filed, the United States shareholder may file a claim for refund or an amended return, and shall attach thereto a copy of the certification. [Reg. § 1.552-5.]

☐ [T.D. 6308, 9-9-58.]

[Reg. § 1.553-1]

§ 1.553-1. Foreign personal holding company income.—Foreign personal holding company income shall consist of the items defined under section 543 and §§ 1.543-1 and 1.543-2, relating to personal holding company income, with the following exceptions:

(a) The entire amount received as "interest," whether or not treated as rent, shall be considered to be foreign personal holding company income. Thus, the exception in the second sentence of section 543(a)(1) and paragraph (b)(2) of § 1.543-1 (relating to interest treated as rent under section 543(a)(7) and paragraph (b)(10) of § 1.543-1), is inapplicable for the purpose of determining foreign personal holding company income. Similarly, section 543(a)(7) and paragraph (b)(10) of § 1.543-1 are applied for this purpose without regard to the interest described in that section.

(b)(1) The entire amount received as "royalties", whether or not mineral, oil, or gas royalties, or copyright royalties, shall be considered to be foreign personal holding company income. Thus, subparagraphs (A) and (B) of section 543(a)(8) and paragraph (b)(11)(i) (*a*) and (*b*) of § 1.543-1 (relating to mineral, oil, or gas royalties), and subparagraphs (A), (B), and (C) of section 543(a)(9) and paragraph (b)(12)(ii) of § 1.543-1 (relating to copyright royalties), are inapplicable for the purpose of determining foreign personal holding income.

(2) In computing foreign personal holding company income, the first sentence of paragraph (b)(11)(ii) of § 1.543-1 shall apply to overriding royalties received from the sublessee by the operating company which originally leased and developed the natural resource property in respect of which such overriding royalties are paid, and to mineral, oil, or gas production payments, only with respect to amounts received after September 30, 1958. [Reg. § 1.553-1.]

☐ [T.D. 6038, 9-9-58. Amended by T.D. 6739, 6-16-64.]

[Reg. § 1.554-1]

§ 1.554-1. Stock ownership.—For regulations under section 554, see § 1.552-3. [Reg. § 1.554-1.]

☐ [T.D. 6308, 9-9-58.]

[Reg. § 1.555-1]

§ 1.555-1. General rule.—The gross income of a foreign corporation which is a foreign personal holding company is computed the same as if the foreign corporation were a domestic corporation which is a personal holding company. See section 542(a)(1) and § 1.542-2. The gross income of a foreign personal holding company thus includes income from all sources, whether within or without the United States, which is not specifically excluded from gross income under any other provisions of the Code. For example, the gross income of a foreign personal holding company includes all income from sources outside the United States even though the foreign personal holding company is a foreign corporation not engaged in trade or business within the United States. However, the gross income of a foreign corporation which is a foreign personal holding company shall not include, with respect to a United States shareholder described in section 951(b), dividends received by such corporation which are excluded under section 959(b) from the income of such corporation with respect to such shareholder. [Reg. § 1.555-1.]

☐ [T.D. 6308, 9-9-58. Amended by T.D. 6795, 1-28-65.]

[Reg. § 1.555-2]

§ 1.555-2. Additions to gross income.—(a) If, for any taxable year—

(1) A foreign corporation meets the stock ownership requirement specified in section 552(a)(2) and § 1.552-3, regardless of whatever day in its taxable year is the last day on which the required United States group exists, and

(2) Such foreign corporation is a shareholder in a foreign personal holding company on any day of a taxable year of the second company which ends with or within the taxable year of the first company and such day is the last day in the taxable year of the second company in which the United States group exists with respect to the second company, then for the purpose of—

(i) Determining whether the first company meets the specified gross income requirement so as to come within the classification of a foreign personal holding company, and

(ii) Determining the undistributed foreign personal holding company income of the first company which (in the event the first company is a foreign personal holding company) is to be included, in whole or in part, in the gross income of its shareholders, whether United States shareholders or other foreign personal holding companies,

there shall be included as a dividend in the gross income of the first company for the taxable year in which or with which the taxable year of the second company ends, the amount the first company would have received as a dividend, if on the last day referred to in this subparagraph there had been distributed by the second company, and received by the shareholders, an amount which bears the same ratio to the undistributed foreign personal holding company income of the second company for its taxable year as the portion of

such taxable year up to and including such last day bears to the entire taxable year. The foregoing rules apply to any chain of foreign corporations regardless of the number of corporations included in the chain.

(b) The application of section 555(b) may be illustrated by the following examples:

Example (1). The X Corporation is a foreign corporation whose stock is owned by A, a United States citizen. The X Corporation owns the entire stock of the Y Corporation, another foreign corporation. The taxable year of the X Corporation is the calendar year and the taxable year of the Y Corporation is the fiscal year ending June 30. For the fiscal year ending June 30, 1955, more than the required percentage of the Y Corporation's gross income consists of foreign personal holding company income and no part of the earnings for such year is distributed as dividends. On the basis of these facts the Y Corporation is a foreign personal holding company for the fiscal year ending June 30, 1955. The X Corporation meets the stock ownership requirement and constitutes a foreign personal holding company for 1955, if it also meets the gross income requirement. For the purpose of determining whether the X Corporation meets the gross income requirement, the entire undistributed foreign personal holding company income of the Y Corporation for the fiscal year ending June 30, 1955, must be included as a dividend in the gross income of the X Corporation for 1955, since—

(1) The X Corporation was a shareholder in the Y Corporation on a day (June 30, 1955) in the taxable year of the Y Corporation ending with or within the taxable year of the X Corporation, which day was the last day in the taxable year of the Y Corporation on which the United States group required with respect to the Y Corporation existed,

(2) Such last day was also the end of the Y Corporation's taxable year so that the portion of the taxable year of the Y Corporation up to and including such last day is equal to 100 percent of the taxable year of the Y Corporation, and, therefore, the portion of the undistributed foreign personal holding company income of the Y Corporation includible in the gross income of its shareholders is likewise equal to 100 percent, and

(3) The X Corporation being the sole shareholder of the Y Corporation must include such portion in its gross income for 1955, the taxable year in which or with which the taxable year of the Y Corporation ends. If, after the inclusion of the presumptive dividend in its gross income, the X Corporation is a foreign personal holding company for 1955, then the undistributed foreign

personal holding company income of the Y Corporation must also be included as a dividend in the gross income of the X Corporation in determining its undistributed foreign personal holding company income which is to be included in the gross income of A, the sole shareholder in the X Corporation. On the other hand, if, after including such presumptive dividend, the X Corporation does not constitute a foreign personal holding company, the undistributed foreign personal holding company income of the Y Corporation is not includible in the gross income of the X Corporation.

Example (2). The X Corporation referred to in example (1) sold the stock in the Y Corporation to other interests on September 30, 1955, so that after that date no United States group existed with respect to the Y Corporation. For the fiscal year ending June 30, 1956, more than the required percentage of the gross income of the Y Corporation consists of foreign personal holding company income. The taxable income of the Y Corporation for such fiscal year amounts to $1,000,000, of which $900,000 is distributed in dividends after September 30, 1955. The undistributed foreign personal holding company income of the Y Corporation for such fiscal amounts to $100,000. Upon the basis of these facts the Y Corporation is a foreign personal holding company for the fiscal year ending June 30, 1956, since at one time in such fiscal year, or from July 1 to and including September 30, 1955, it meets the stock ownership requirement, and the gross income requirement is also satisfied. In determining whether the X Corporation constitutes a foreign personal holding company for 1956, a portion of the undistributed foreign personal holding company income of the Y Corporation for the fiscal year ending June 30, 1956 (three-twelfths of $100,000, or $25,000), must be included as a dividend in the gross income of the X Corporation, since—

(1) The X Corporation was a shareholder in the Y Corporation on September 30, 1955, or on a day in the taxable year of the Y Corporation ending with or within the taxable year of the X Corporation which day was the last day in the Y Corporation's taxable year on which the United States group required with respect to the Y Corporation existed.

(2) The portion of the taxable year of the Y Corporation up to and including such day is three-twelfths of the entire taxable year of the Y Corporation and, therefore, the portion of the undistributed foreign personal holding company income of the Y Corporation includible in the gross income of its shareholders also is equal to three-twelfths, and

(3) The X Corporation, being the sole shareholder of the Y Corporation at the time the United States group with respect to the Y Corporation last existed, must include all of such portion in its gross income for 1956, the taxable year of the X Corporation in which or with which the taxable year of Y Corporation ends.

It is to be observed that three-twelfths of the undistributed foreign personal holding company income of the Y Corporation for the entire taxable year and not the earnings realized by the Y Corporation up to and including September 30, 1955, the last day on which the United States group with respect to the Y Corporation existed, must be included in the gross income of the X Corporation.

Example (3). The X Corporation referred to in example (1) sold the stock in the Y Corporation to other interests on September 30, 1955, so that after that date a different United States group existed with respect to the Y Corporation. Assuming that the Y Corporation is a foreign personal holding company for the fiscal year ending June 30, 1956, no part of the undistributed foreign personal holding company income of the Y Corporation for such fiscal year would, in this instance, be includible in the gross income of the X Corporation for the year 1956, in determining whether the X Corporation is a foreign personal holding company for that year. In such case, the undistributed foreign personal holding company income of the Y Corporation is includible in the gross income of the other foreign personal holding companies, if any, and of the United States shareholders who are shareholders in the Y Corporation the day after September 30, 1955, which was the last day in the taxable year of the Y Corporation on which the United States group with respect to the Y Corporation existed. If, however, the X Corporation sells 90 percent of its stock in the Y Corporation and thus is a minority shareholder in the Y Corporation on the last day of the taxable year of the Y Corporation on which the United States group with respect to the Y Corporation exists, the portion of the undistributed foreign personal holding company income allocable to the minority interest of the X Corporation would be includible in the gross income of the X Corporation, even though on such last day the United States group is not the same with respect to both corporations.

Example (4). If the Y Corporation in example (1) owns all of the stock of the Z Corporation, another foreign corporation, there would be a chain of three foreign corporations. In such case, assuming that the Z Corporation is a foreign personal holding company for a taxable year ending with or within the taxable year of the Y Corporation, the undistributed foreign personal holding

Reg. § 1.555-2(b)

company income of the Z Corporation would be included in the gross income of the Y Corporation for the purpose of determining whether the Y Corporation comes within the classification of a foreign personal holding company. If, after the inclusion of such presumptive dividend, the Y Corporation is a foreign personal holding company, the undistributed foreign personal holding company income of the Z Corporation would be includible in the gross income of the Y Corporation in determining the undistributed foreign personal holding company income of the Y Corporation which is includible in the gross income of its shareholder, the X Corporation. The same process would be repeated with respect to determining whether the X Corporation is a foreign personal holding company and in determining its undistributed foreign personal holding company income. If all three corporations are foreign personal holding companies, the undistributed foreign personal holding company income of each would, in this manner, be reflected as a dividend in the gross income of A, the ultimate beneficial shareholder of the chain. In the event that after the inclusion of the undistributed foreign personal holding company income of the Z Corporation in the gross income of the Y Corporation, the Y Corporation is not a foreign personal holding company, then no part of the income of either the Z Corporation or the Y Corporation would be includible in the gross income of the X Corporation. In that event, whether the X Corporation is a foreign personal holding company, and its undistributed foreign personal holding company income, would be determined independently of the income of the Y Corporation and the Z Corporation. [Reg. § 1.555-2.]

☐ [T.D. 6308, 9-9-58.]

[Reg. § 1.556-1]

§ 1.556-1. Definition.—Undistributed foreign personal holding company income is the amount which is to be included in the gross income of the United States shareholders under section 551(b) and § 1.551-2. Undistributed foreign personal holding company income is the taxable income of the foreign personal holding company, as defined in section 63(a) (computed without regard to subchapter N, chapter 1 of the Code), and adjusted in the manner described in section 556(b) and § 1.556-2, less the deduction for dividends paid (§§ 1.561-1 through 1.565-6). See § 1.556-3 for an illustration of the computation of undistributed foreign personal holding company income. [Reg. § 1.556-1.]

☐ [T.D. 6308, 9-9-58.]

[Reg. § 1.556-2]

§ 1.556-2. Adjustments to taxable income.—(a) *Taxes*—(1) *General rule.* (i) In computing undistributed foreign personal holding company income for any taxable year, there shall be allowed as a deduction the Federal income and excess profits taxes accrued during the taxable year except that no deduction shall be allowed for (*a*) the accumulated earnings tax imposed by section 531 (or a corresponding section of a prior law). (*b*) the personal holding company tax imposed by section 541 (or a corresponding section of a prior law), and (*c*) the excess profits tax imposed by subchapter E, chapter 2 of the Internal Revenue Code of 1939 for taxable years beginning after December 31, 1940. The deduction is for taxes for the taxable year determined under the accrual method of accounting, regardless of whether the corporation uses an accrual method of accounting, the cash receipts and disbursements method, or any other allowable method of accounting. In computing the amount of taxes accrued, an unpaid tax which is being contested is not considered accrued until the contest is resolved.

(ii) However, the corporation shall deduct taxes paid, rather than taxes accrued, if it used that method with respect to Federal taxes for each taxable year for which it was subject to the provisions of supplement P, subchapter C, chapter 1 of the Internal Revenue Code of 1939, unless an election is made under subparagraph (2) of this paragraph to deduct taxes accrued.

(2) *Election by corporation which deducted taxes paid.* (i) If the corporation was subject to supplement P, subchapter C, chapter 1 of the Internal Revenue Code of 1939, and, for the purpose of computing undistributed supplement P net income under such Code, deducted Federal taxes paid, rather than such taxes accrued, for each taxable year for which it was subject to supplement P of the 1939 Code, the corporation may elect for any taxable year ending after August 16, 1954, to deduct taxes accrued, rather than taxes paid, for the purpose of computing its undistributed foreign personal holding company income. The election shall be made by deducting such taxes accrued in the return (Form 958) required to be filed for such taxable year. The return shall, in addition, contain a statement that the corporation has made such election and shall set forth the year to which such election was first applicable. The deduction of taxes accrued in the year of election precludes the deduction of taxes paid during such year. The election, if made, shall be irrevocable and the deduction for taxes accrued shall be allowed for the year of election and for all subsequent taxable years. See section 6035 and

the regulations thereunder for rules relative to the filing of returns of officers, directors, and shareholders of foreign personal holding companies.

(ii) Pursuant to section 7851(a)(1)(C), the election provided for in subdivision (i) of this subparagraph may be made with respect to a taxable year ending after August 16, 1954, even though such taxable year is subject to the Internal Revenue Code of 1939.

(3) *Taxes of foreign countries and United States possessions.* In computing taxable income, a foreign personal holding company is allowed a deduction under section 164 for income, war profits, and excess-profits taxes paid or accrued during the taxable year to foreign countries or possessions of the United States, but is not allowed the foreign tax credit under section 901. Therefore, in computing undistributed foreign personal holding company income for any taxable year, no adjustment under section 556(b)(1) is allowed for such taxes.

(b) *Charitable contributions*—(1) *Taxable years beginning before January 1, 1970.* (i) Section 556(b)(2) provides that, in computing the deduction for charitable contributions for purposes of determining the undistributed foreign personal holding company income of a corporation for taxable years beginning before January 1, 1970, the limitations in section 170(b)(1)(A) and (B), relating to charitable contributions by individuals, shall apply and section 170(b)(2) and (5), relating to charitable contributions by corporations and carryover of certain excess charitable contributions made by individuals, respectively, shall not apply.

(ii) Although the limitations of section 170(b)(1)(A) and (B) are 10 and 20 percent, respectively, of the individual's adjusted gross income, the limitations are applied for purposes of section 556(b)(2) by using 10 and 20 percent, respectively, of the corporation's taxable income as adjusted for purposes of section 170(b)(2), that is, the same amount of taxable income to which the 5-percent limitation applied. Thus, the term "adjusted gross income" when used in section 170(b)(1) means the corporation's taxable income computed with the adjustments, other than the 5-percent limitation, provided in the first sentence of section 170(b)(2). However, a further adjustment for this purpose is that the taxable income shall also be computed without the deduction of the amount disallowed under section 556(b)(5), relating to expenses and depreciation applicable to property of the taxpayer, and section 556(b)(6), relating to taxes and contributions to pension trusts, and without the inclusion of the amounts includible as dividends under section 555(b), relating to the inclusion in gross income of a foreign personal holding company of its distributive share of the undistributed foreign personal holding company income of another company in which it is a shareholder. The carryover of charitable contributions made in a prior year, otherwise allowable as a deduction in computing taxable income to the extent provided in section 170(b)(2) and, with respect to contributions paid in taxable years beginning after December 31, 1963, in section 170(b)(5), shall not be allowed as a deduction in computing undistributed foreign personal holding company income for any taxable year.

(iii) See § 1.170-2 with respect to the charitable contributions to which the 10-percent limitation is applicable and the charitable contributions to which the 20-percent limitation is applicable.

(2) *Taxable years beginning after December 31, 1969.* (i) Section 556(b)(2) provides that, in computing the deduction allowable for charitable contributions for purposes of determining the undistributed foreign personal holding company income of a corporation for taxable years beginning after December 31, 1969, the limitations in section 170(b)(1)(A), (B), and (D)(i) (relating to charitable contributions by individuals) shall apply, and section 170(b)(1)(D)(ii) (relating to excess charitable contributions by individuals of certain capital gain property), section 170(b)(2) (relating to the 5-percent limitation on charitable contributions by corporations), and section 170(d) (relating to carryovers of excess contributions of individuals and corporations) shall not apply.

(ii) Although the limitations of section 170(b)(1)(A), (B), and (D)(i) are 50, 20, and 30 percent, respectively, of an individual's contribution base, these limitations are applied for purposes of section 556(b)(2) by using 50, 20, and 30 percent, respectively, of the corporation's taxable income as adjusted for purposes of section 170(b)(2), that is, the same amount of taxable income to which the 5-percent limitation applies. Thus, the term "contribution base" when used in section 170(b)(1) means the corporation's taxable income computed with the adjustments, other than the 5-percent limitation, provided in section 170(b)(2). However, a further adjustment for this purpose is that the taxable income shall also be computed without the deduction of the amount disallowed under section 556(b)(5), relating to expenses and depreciation applicable to property of the taxpayer, and section 556(b)(6), relating to taxes and contributions to pension trusts, and without the inclusion of the amounts includible as dividends under section 555(b), relating to the inclusion in gross income of a foreign personal holding company of its distributive share of the undistributed foreign personal holding company income of another company in which it is a shareholder. The carryover of charitable contributions made in a prior year, otherwise allowable as a deduction in computing taxable income to the extent provided in section 170(b)(1)(D)(ii) and (d), shall not be allowed as a deduction in computing undistributed foreign personal holding company income for any taxable year.

(iii) See § 1.170A-8 for the rules with respect to the charitable contributions to which the 50-, 20-, and 30-percent limitations apply.

(c) *Special deductions disallowed.* Part VIII, subchapter B, chapter 1 of the Code allows corporations special deductions in computing taxable income for such matters as partially tax-exempt interest, certain dividends received, dividends paid on certain preferred stock of public utilities, organizational expenses, etc. See section 241. For purposes of computing undistributed foreign personal holding company income, such special deductions, except the deduction provided by section 248 (relating to organizational expenditures) and, with respect to such a computation for a taxable year ending before January 1, 1958, the deduction provided by section 242 (relating to partially tax-exempt interest), shall be disallowed.

(d) *Net operating loss.* The net operating loss deduction provided in section 172 is not allowed for purposes of the computation of undistributed foreign personal holding company income. For purposes of such a computation, however, there is allowed as a deduction the amount of the net operating loss (as defined in section 172(c)) for the preceding taxable year, except that, in computing undistributed foreign personal holding company income for a taxable year ending after December 31, 1957, the amount of such net operating loss shall be computed without the deductions provided in part VIII (section 241 and following) except section 248, relating to organizational expenditures, subchapter B, chapter 1 of the Code.

(e) *Expenses and depreciation applicable to property of the corporation.* (1) Section 556(b)(5) provides a specific limitation in computing undistributed foreign personal holding company income, with respect to the allowance of deductions for trade or business expenses and depreciation which are allocable to the operation and maintenance of property owned or operated by a foreign personal holding company. Under this limitation these deductions shall not be allowed in excess of the aggregate amount of the rent or other compensation received for the use of, or the right to use, the property, unless it is established to the satisfaction of the Commissioner—

(i) That the rent or other compensation received was the highest obtainable, or if none was received, that none was obtainable;

(ii) That the property was held in the course of a business carried on bona fide for profit; and

(iii) Either that there was reasonable expectation that the operation of the property would result in a profit, or that the property was necessary to the conduct of the business.

(2) The burden of proof will rest upon the taxpayer to sustain the deduction claimed. If a United States shareholder, in computing his distributive share of undistributed foreign personal holding company income to be included in gross income in his individual return (see section 551, and §§ 1.551-1 and 1.551-2), claims deductions for expenses and depreciation allocable to the operation and maintenance of property owned or operated by the company, in an aggregate amount in excess of the rent or other compensation received for the use of, or the right to use, the property, he shall attach to his income tax return a statement setting forth his claim for allowance of the additional deductions, together with a complete statement of the facts and circumstances pertinent to his claim and the arguments on which he relies. Such statement shall set forth—

(i) A description of the property;

(ii) The cost or other basis to the corporation and the nature and value of the consideration paid for the property;

(iii) The name and address of the person from whom the property was acquired and the date the property was acquired;

(iv) The name and address of the person to whom the property is leased or rented, or the person permitted to use the property, and the number of shares of stock, if any, held by such person and the members of his family;

(v) The nature and gross amount of the rent or other compensation received for the use of, or the right to use, the property during the taxable year and for each of the five preceding years and the amount of the expenses incurred with respect to, and the depreciation sustained on, the property for such years;

(vi) Evidence that the rent or other compensation was the highest obtainable, or, if none was received, a statement of the reasons therefor;

(vii) A copy of the contract, lease or rental agreement;

(viii) The purpose for which the property was used;

Reg. § 1.556-2(c)

(ix) The business carried on by the corporation with respect to which the property was held and the gross income, expenses, and taxable income derived from the conduct of such business for the taxable year and for each of the five preceding years;

(x) A statement of any reasons which existed for expectation that the operation of the property would be profitable, or a statement of the necessity for the use of the property in the business of the corporation, and the reasons why the property was acquired; and

(xi) Any other information pertinent to the taxpayer's claim.

(f) *Taxes and contributions to pension trusts.* Section 164(e) provides for deductions by a corporation for taxes of a shareholder paid by it; section 404 provides for deduction by an employer for its contributions on an employees' trust, etc. For the purpose of computing undistributed foreign personal holding company income, neither of these deductions is allowable. [Reg. § 1.556-2.]

☐ [T.D. 6308, 9-9-58. *Amended by* T.D. 6376, 5-6-59, *by* T.D. 6900, 11-16-66, *and by* T.D. 7207, 10-3-72.]

[Reg. § 1.556-3]

§ 1.556-3. **Illustration of computation of undistributed foreign personal holding company income.**—The method of computation of the undistributed foreign personal holding company income may be illustrated by the following example:

Example. (a) The following facts exist with respect to the M Corporation, a foreign personal holding company, for the calendar year 1954:

(1) The gross income of the corporation as defined in section 555 amounts to $300,000, of which $85,000 represents its distributive share of the undistributed foreign personal holding company income of another foreign personal holding company in which it is a shareholder, $200,000 consists of dividends, $10,000 consists of fully taxable interest, and the remainder ($5,000) consists of rent received from the principal shareholder of the corporation for the use of property owned by the corporation.

(2) The expenses of the corporation amount to $85,000, of which $75,000 is allocable to the maintenance and operation of the property used by the principal shareholder and $10,000 consists of ordinary and necessary office expenses allowble as a deduction. The claim for deduction for the expenses of, and depreciation on, the rented property in excess of the rent received for its use is not established as provided in section 556(b)(5). The yearly depreciation on the rented property amounts to $30,000.

(3) Federal income tax withheld at the source on the income of the corporation from sources within the United States amounts to $59,125.

(4) No gain from the sale or exchange of stock or securities is realized during the taxable year, but losses in the amount of $10,000 are sustained from the sale of stock or securities which constitute capital assets. Such losses are not allowed as a deduction in any amount. See section 1211(a).

(5) Contributions, payment of which is made to or for the use of donees described in section 170(b)(1)(A) for the purposes therein specified, amount to $15,000, of which $5,000 is deductible in computing taxable income under section 63.

(6) Dividends paid by the corporation to its shareholders during the taxable year amount to $50,000.

(b) The taxable income of the corporation (including the distributive share of the undistributed foreign personal holding company income of the other foreign personal holding company) is $180,000, computed as follows (assuming for the purposes of this example only that the expenses of, and depreciation on, the rental property are deductible under sections 162 and 167):

INCOME (SECTION 61)

Dividends	$200,000
Interest	10,000
Rent	5,000
Gross income as defined in section 61	215,000
Add: Distributive share of undistributed income of the other foreign personal holding company (considered as a dividend)	85,000
Gross income as defined in section 555	300,000

Reg. § 1.556-3

39,254 **Deduction for Dividends Paid**

See p. 20,601 for regulations not amended to reflect law changes

DEDUCTIONS (SECTION 161)

Expenses allocable to operation of the rented property	$ 75,000	
Depreciation of the rented property	30,000	
Ordinary and necessary expenses (office)	10,000	
Contributions (within the 5-percent limitation specified in section 170(b)(2))	5,000	
		$120,000
Taxable income for purposes of computing undistributed foreign personal holding company income		$180,000

(c) The undistributed foreign personal holding company income of the corporation is $160,875, computed as follows:

Taxable income for purposes of computing undistributed foreign personal holding company income		$180,000
Add (see section 556(b)):		
Contributions deductible in computing taxable income under section 63	$ 5,000	
Excess property expenses and depreciation over amount of rent received for use of property ($105,000 − $5,000)	100,000	
Total	105,000	
Deduct (see section 556(b)):		
Federal income taxes	$ 59,125	
Contributions (within the percentage limitations specified in section 170(b)(1)(A) and (B), determined under the rules provided in section 556(b)(2))	15,000	
Total	74,125	
Net additions under section 556(b)		$ 30,875
Taxable income, as adjusted under section 556(b)		$210,875
Less:		
Deduction for dividends paid (see section 561)		50,000
Undistributed foreign personal holding company income		$160,875

[Reg. § 1.556-3.]   ☐ [T.D. 6308, 9-9-58.]

Deduction for Dividends Paid

[Reg. § 1.561-1]

§ 1.561-1. **Deduction for dividends paid.**—(a) The deduction for dividends paid is applicable in determining accumulated taxable income under section 535, undistributed personal holding company income under section 545, undistributed foreign personal holding company income under section 556, investment company taxable income under section 852, and real estate investment trust taxable income under section 857. The deduction for dividends paid includes—

(1) The dividends paid during the taxable year;

(2) The consent dividends for the taxable year, determined as provided in section 565; and

(3) In the case of a personal holding company, the dividend carryover computed as provided in section 564.

(b) For dividends for which the dividends paid deduction is allowable, see section 562 and

§ 1.562-1. As to when dividends are considered paid, see § 1.561-2. [Reg. § 1.561-1.]

☐ [T.D. 6308, 9-9-58. Amended by T.D. 6598, 4-25-62.]

[Reg. § 1.561-2]

§ 1.561-2. **When dividends are considered paid.**—(a) *In general.* (1) A dividend will be considered as paid when it is received by the shareholder. A deduction for dividends paid during the taxable year will not be permitted unless the shareholder receives the dividend during the taxable year for which the deduction is claimed. See section 563 for special rule with respect to dividends paid after the close of the taxable year.

(2) If a dividend is paid by check and the check bearing a date within the taxable year is deposited in the mails, in a cover properly stamped and addressed to the shareholder at his last known address, at such time that in the ordinary handling of the mails the check would be

Reg. § 1.561-1(a)(1)

received by the shareholder within the taxable year, a presumption arises that the dividend was paid to the shareholder in such year.

(3) The payment of a dividend during the taxable year to the authorized agent of the shareholder will be deemed payment of the dividend to the shareholder during such year.

(4) If a corporation, instead of paying the dividend directly to the shareholder, credits the account of the shareholder on the books of the corporation with the amount of the dividend, the deduction for a dividend paid will not be permitted unless it be shown to the satisfaction of the Commissioner that such crediting constituted payment of the dividend of the shareholder.

(5) A deduction will not be permitted for the amount of a dividend credited during the taxable year upon an obligation of the shareholder to the corporation unless it is shown to the satisfaction of the Commissioner that such crediting constituted payment of the dividend to the shareholder within the taxable year.

(6) If the dividend is payable in obligations of the corporation, they should be entered or registered in the taxable year on the books of the corporation, in the name of the shareholder (or his nominee or transferee), and, in the case of obligations payable to bearer, should be received in the taxable year by the shareholder (or his nominee or transferee) to constitute payment of the dividend within the taxable year.

(7) In the case of a dividend from which the tax has been deducted and withheld as required by chapter 3 (section 1441 and following), of the Code the dividend is considered as paid when such deducting and withholding occur.

(b) *Methods of accounting.* The determination of whether a dividend has been paid to the shareholder by the corporation during its taxable year is in no way dependent upon the method of accounting regularly employed by the corporation in keeping its books or upon the method of accounting upon the basis of which the taxable income of the corporation is computed.

(c) *Records.* Every corporation claiming a deduction for dividends paid shall keep such permanent records as are necessary (1) to establish that the dividends with respect to which such deduction is claimed were actually paid during the taxable year and (2) to supply the information required to be filed with the income tax return of the corporation. Such corporation shall file with its return (i) a copy of the dividend resolution; and (ii) a concise statement of the pertinent facts relating to the payment of the dividend, clearly specifying (*a*) the medium of payment and (*b*) if not paid in money, the fair market value and adjusted basis (or face value, if paid in its own obligations) on the date of distribution of the property distributed and the manner in which such fair market value and adjusted basis were determined. Canceled dividend checks and receipts obtained from shareholders acknowledging payment of dividends paid otherwise than by check need not be filed with the return but shall be kept by the corporation as a part of its records. [Reg. § 1.561-2.]

☐ [*T.D.* 6308, 9-9-58.]

[Reg. § 1.562-1]

§ 1.562-1. **Dividends for which dividends paid deduction is allowable.**—(a) *General rule.* Except as otherwise provided in section 562(b) and (d), the term "dividend", for purposes of determining dividends eligible for the dividends paid deduction, refers only to a dividend described in section 316 (relating to definition of dividends for purposes of corporate distributions). No distribution, however, which is preferential within the meaning of section 562(c) and § 1.562-2 shall be eligible for the dividends paid deduction. Moreover, when computing the dividends paid deduction with respect to a United States person (as defined in section 957(d)), no distribution which is excluded from the gross income of a foreign corporation under section 959(b) with respect to such person or from the gross income of such person under section 959(a) shall be eligible for such deduction. Further, for purposes of the dividends paid deduction, the term "dividend" does not include a distribution in liquidation unless the distribution is treated as a dividend under section 316(b)(2) and paragraph (b)(2) of § 1.316-1, or under section 333(e)(1) and paragraph (c) of § 1.333-4 or paragraph (c)(2), (d)(1)(ii), or (d)(2) of § 1.333-5, or qualifies under section 562(b) and paragraph (b) of this section. If a dividend is paid in property (other than money) the amount of the dividends paid deduction with respect to such property shall be the adjusted basis of the property in the hands of the distributing corporation at the time of the distribution. See paragraph (b)(2) of this section for special rules with respect to liquidating distributions by personal holding companies occurring during a taxable year of the distributing corporation beginning after December 31, 1963. Also see section 563 for special rules with respect to dividends paid after the close of the taxable year.

(b) *Distributions in liquidation*—(1) *General rule*—(i) *In general.* In the case of amounts distributed in liquidation by any corporation during a taxable year of such corporation beginning before January 1, 1964, or by a corporation other than a personal holding company (as defined in

Reg. § 1.562-1(b)(1)

section 542) or a foreign personal holding company (as defined in section 552) during a taxable year of such a corporation beginning after December 31, 1963, section 562(b) makes an exception to the general rule that a deduction for dividends paid is permitted only with respect to dividends described in section 316. In order to qualify under that exception, the distribution must be one either in complete or partial liquidation of a corporation pursuant to sections 331, 332, or 333. See subparagraph (2) of this paragraph for rules relating to the treatment of distributions in complete liquidation made by a corporation which is a personal holding company to corporate shareholders during a taxable year of such distributing corporation beginning after December 31, 1963. As provided by section 346(a), for the purpose of section 562(b), a partial liquidation includes a redemption of stock to which section 302 applies. Amounts distributed in liquidation in a transaction which is preceded, or followed, by a transfer to another corporation of all or part of the assets of the liquidating corporation, may not be eligible for the dividends paid deduction.

(ii) *Amount of dividends paid deduction allowable*—(a) *General rule.* In the case of distributions in liquidation with respect to which a deduction for dividends paid is permissible under subdivision (i) of this subparagraph, the amount of the deduction is equal to the part of such distribution which is properly chargeable to the earnings and profits accumulated after February 28, 1913. To determine the amount properly chargeable to the earnings and profits accumulated after February 28, 1913, there must be deducted from the amount of the distribution that part allocable to capital account. The capital account, for the purposes of this subdivision, includes not only amounts representing the par or stated value of the stock with respect to which the liquidation distribution is made, but also that stock's proper share of the paid-in surplus, and such other corporate items, if any, which, for purposes of income taxation, are treated like capital in that they are not taxable dividends when distributed but are applied against and reduce the basis of the stock. The remainder of the distribution in liquidation is, ordinarily, properly chargeable to the earnings and profits accumulated after February 28, 1913. Thus, if there is a deficit in earnings and profits on the first day of a taxable year, and the earnings and profits for such taxable year do not exceed such deficit, no dividends paid deduction would be allowed for such taxable year with respect to a distribution in liquidation; if the earnings and profits for such taxable year exceed the deficit in earnings and profits which existed on the first day of such taxable year, then a dividends paid deduction would be allowed to the extent of such excess.

(b) *Special rule.* Section 562(b)(1)(B) provides that in the case of a complete liquidation occurring within 24 months after the adoption of a plan of liquidation the amount of the deduction is equal to the earnings and profits for each taxable year in which distributions are made. Thus, if there is a distribution in liquidation pursuant to section 333, or a distribution in complete liquidation pursuant to section 331(a)(1) or 332 which occurs within a 24-month period after the adoption of a plan of liquidation, a dividends paid deduction will be allowable to the extent of the current earnings and profits for the taxable year or years even though there was a deficit in earnings and profits on the first day of such taxable year or years. In computing the earnings and profits for the taxable year in which the distributions are made, computation shall be made with the inclusion of capital gains and without any deduction for capital losses.

(c) *Examples.* The application of this subparagraph may be illustrated by the following examples:

Example (1). The Y Corporation, which makes its income tax returns on the calendar year basis, was organized on January 1, 1910, with an authorized and outstanding capital stock of 2,000 shares of common stock of a par value of $100 each and 1,000 shares of participating preferred stock of a par value of $100 each. The preferred stock was to receive annual dividends of $7 per share and $100 per share on complete liquidation of the corporation in priority to any payments on common stock, and was to participate equally with the common stock in either instance after the common stock had received a similar amount. However, the preferred stock was redeemable in whole or in part at the option of the board of directors at any time at $106 per share plus its proportion of the earnings of the company at the time of such redemption. In 1910 the preferred stock was issued at $106 per share, for a total of $106,000 and the common stock was issued, at $100 per share, for a total of $200,000. On July 15, 1954, the company had a paid-in surplus of $6,000, consisting of the premium received on the preferred stock; earnings and profits of $30,000 accumulated prior to March 1, 1913; and earnings and profits accumulated since February 28, 1913, of $75,000. On July 15, 1954, the option with respect to the preferred stock was exercised and the entire amount of such stock was redeemed at $141 per share or a total of $141,000 in a transaction upon which gain or loss to the distributees resulting from the exchange was determined and

Reg. § 1.562-1(b)(1)

recognized under section 302(a). The amount of the distribution allocable to capital account was $116,000 ($100,000 attributable to par value, $6,000 attributable to paid-in surplus, and $10,000 attributable to earnings and profits accumulated prior to March 1, 1913). The remainder, $25,000 ($141,000, the amount of the distribution, less $116,000, the amount allocable to capital account) is properly chargeable to the earnings and profits accumulated since February 28, 1913, and is deductible as dividends paid.

Example (2). The M Corporation, a calendar year taxpayer, is completely liquidated on November 1, 1955, pursuant to a plan of liquidation adopted April 1, 1955. On January 1, 1955, the M Corporation has a deficit in earnings and profits of $100,000. During the period January 1, 1955, to the date of liquidation, November 1, 1955, it has earnings and profits of $10,000. The M Corporation is entitled to a dividends paid deduction in the amount of $10,000 as a result of its distribution in complete liquidation on November 1, 1955.

Example (3). The N Corporation, a calendar year taxpayer, is completely liquidated on July 1, 1958, pursuant to a plan of liquidation adopted February 1, 1955. No distributions in liquidation were made pursuant to the plan of liquidation adopted February 1, 1955, until the distribution in complete liquidation on July 1, 1958. On January 1, 1958, N Corporation had a deficit in earnings and profits of $30,000. During the period January 1, 1958, to the date of liquidation, July 1, 1958, the N Corporation has earnings and profits of $5,000. The N Corporation is not entitled to any deduction for dividends paid as a result of the distribution in complete liquidation on July 1, 1958. If the earnings and profits for the period January 1, 1958, to July 1, 1958, had been $32,000, the N Corporation would have been entitled to a deduction for dividends paid in the amount of $2,000.

(2) *Special rule*—(i) *Distributions to corporate shareholders.* In the case of amounts distributed in complete liquidation of a personal holding company (as defined in section 542) within 24 months after the adoption of a plan of liquidation, section 562(b)(2) makes a further exception to the general rule that a deduction for dividends paid is permitted only with respect to dividends described in section 316. The exception referred to in the preceding sentence applies only to distributions made in any taxable year of the distributing corporation beginning after December 31, 1963. Under the exception, the amount of any distribution within the 24-month period pursuant to the plan shall be treated as a dividend for purposes of computing the dividends paid deduction, but:

(*a*) Only to the extent that such amount is distributed to corporate distributees, and

(*b*) Only to the extent that such amount represents such corporate distributees' allocable share of undistributed personal holding company income for the taxable year of such distribution (computed without regard to section 316(b)(2)(B) and section 562(b)(2)).

Amounts distributed in liquidation in a transaction which is preceded, or followed, by a transfer to another corporation of all or part of the assets of the liquidating corporation, may not be eligible for the dividends paid deduction.

(ii) *Corporate distributees' allocable share.* For purposes of subdivision (i)(*b*) of this subparagraph—

(*a*) Except as provided in (*b*) of this subdivision, the corporate distributees' allocable share of undistributed personal holding company income for the taxable year of the distribution (computed without regard to sections 316(b)(2)(B) and 562(b)(2)) shall be determined by multiplying such undistributed personal holding company income by the ratio which the aggregate value of the stock held by all corporate shareholders immediately before the record date of the last liquidating distribution in such year bears to the total value of all stock outstanding on such date. For rules applicable in a case where the distributing corporation has more than one class of stock, see (*c*) of this subdivision (ii).

(*b*) If more than one liquidating distribution was made during the year, and if, after the record date of the first distribution but before the record date of the last distribution, there was a change in the relative shareholdings as between corporate shareholders and noncorporate shareholders, then the corporate distributees' allocable share of undistributed personal holding company income for the taxable year of the distributions (computed without regard to sections 316(b)(2)(B) and 562(b)(2)) shall be determined as follows:

(*1*) First, allocate the corporation's undistributed personal holding company income for the taxable year among the distributions made during such year by reference to the ratio which the aggregate amount of each distribution bears to the total amount of all distributions during such year;

(*2*) Second, determine the corporate distributees' allocable share of the corporation's undistributed personal holding company income for each distribution by multiplying the amount

Reg. § 1.562-1(b)(2)

determined under (*1*) of this subdivision (*b*) for each distribution by the ratio which the aggregate value of the stock held by all corporate shareholders immediately before the record date of such distribution bears to the total value of all stock outstanding on such date; and

(*3*) Last, determine the sum of the corporate distributees' allocable share of the corporation's undistributed personal holding company income for all such distributions.

For rules applicable in a case where the distributing corporation has more than one class of stock, see (*c*) of this subdivision (ii).

(*c*) *Where the distributing corporation has more than one class of stock*—

(*1*) The undistributed personal holding company income for the taxable year in which, or in respect of which, the distribution was made shall be treated as a fund from which dividends may properly be paid and shall be allocated between or among the classes of stock in a manner consistent with the dividend rights of such classes under local law and the pertinent governing instruments, such as, for example, the distributing corporation's articles or certificate of incorporation and by-laws;

(*2*) The corporate distributees' allocable share of the undistributed personal holding company income for each class of stock shall be determined separately in accordance with the rules set forth in (*a*) and (*b*) of this subdivision (ii) as if each class of stock were the only class of stock outstanding; and

(*3*) The sum of the corporate distributees' allocable share of the undistributed personal holding company income for the taxable year in which, or in respect of which, the distribution was made shall be the sum of the corporate distributees' allocable share of the undistributed personal holding company income for all classes of stock.

(*d*) For purposes of this subdivision (ii), in any case where the record date of a liquidating distribution cannot be ascertained, the record date of the distribution shall be the date on which the liquidating distribution was actually made.

(iii) *Example*. The application of this subparagraph may be illustrated by the following example:

Example. O Corporation, a calendar year taxpayer is completely liquidated on December 31, 1964, pursuant to a plan of liquidation adopted July 1, 1964. No distributions in liquidation were made pursuant to the plan of liquidation adopted July 1, 1964, until the distribution in complete liquidation on December 31, 1964. O Corporation has undistributed personal holding company income of $300,000 for the year 1964 (computed without regard to section 316(b)(2)(B) and section 562(b)(2)). On December 31, 1964, immediately before the record date of the distribution in complete liquidation, P Corporation owns 100 shares of O Corporation's outstanding stock and individual A owns the remaining 200 shares. All shares are equal in value. The amount which represents P Corporation's allocable share of undistributed personal holding company income is $100,000

$$\left(\frac{100 \text{ shares}}{300 \text{ shares}} \times \$300,000\right),$$

and for purposes of computing the dividends paid deduction, such amount is treated as a dividend under section 562(b)(2) provided that the liquidating distribution to P Corporation equals or exceeds $100,000. P Corporation does not treat the $100,000 distributed to it as a dividend to which section 301 applies. For an example of the treatment of the distribution to individual A see example (5) of paragraph (e) of § 1.316-1.

(iv) *Distributions to noncorporate shareholders*. For the rules for determining the extent to which distributions in complete liquidation made to noncorporate shareholders by a personal holding company are dividends within the meaning of section 562(a), see section 316(b)(2)(B) and paragraph (b)(2) of § 1.316-1.

(c) *Special definition of dividend for nonliquidating distributions by personal holding companies*. Section 316(b)(2)(A) provides that in the case of a corporation which, under the law applicable to the taxable year in which or in respect of which a distribution is made, is a personal holding company, the term "dividend" (in addition to the general meaning set forth in section 316(a)) also means a nonliquidating distribution to its shareholders to the extent of the corporation's undistributed personal holding company income (determined under section 545 without regard to such distributions) for the taxable year in which or in respect of which the distribution is made. See paragraph (b)(1) of § 1.316-1. [Reg. § 1.562-1.]

☐ [*T.D. 6308, 9-9-58. Amended by T.D. 6795, 1-28-65, by T.D. 6949, 4-8-68, and by T.D. 7767, 2-3-81.*]

[Reg. § 1.562-2]

§ 1.562-2. **Preferential dividends**.—(a) Section 562(c) imposes a limitation upon the general rule that a corporation is entitled to a deduction for dividends paid with respect to all dividends which it actually pays during the taxable year. Before a corporation may be entitled to any such deduction with respect to a distribution regardless of the medium in which the distribution is made, every shareholder of the class of stock with respect to which the distribution is made must be treated the same as every other shareholder of that class, and no class of stock may be treated otherwise than in accordance with its dividend rights as a class. The limitation imposed by section 562(c) is unqualified, except in the case of an actual distribution made in connection with a consent distribution (see section 565), if the entire distribution composed of such actual distribution and consent distribution is not preferential. The existence of a preference is sufficient to prohibit the deduction regardless of the fact (1) that such preference is authorized by all the shareholders of the corporation or (2) that the part of the distribution received by the shareholder benefited by the preference is taxable to him as a dividend. A corporation will not be entitled to a deduction for dividends paid with respect to any distribution upon a class of stock if there is distributed to any shareholder of such class (in proportion to the number of shares held by him) more or less than his pro rata part of the distribution as compared with the distribution made to any other shareholder of the same class. Nor will a corporation be entitled to a deduction for dividends paid in the case of any distribution upon a class of stock if there is distributed upon such class of stock more or less than the amount to which it is entitled as compared with any other class of stock. A preference exists if any rights to preference inherent in any class of stock are violated. The disallowance, where any preference in fact exists, extends to the entire amount of the distribution and not merely to a part of such distribution. As used in this section, the term "distribution" includes a dividend as defined in subchapter C, chapter 1 of the Code and a distribution in liquidation referred to in section 562(b).

(b) The application of the provisions of section 562(c) may be illustrated by the following examples:

Example (1). A, B, C, and D are the owners of all the shares of class A common stock in the M Corporation, which makes its income tax returns on a calendar year basis. With the consent of all the shareholders, the M Corporation on July 15, 1954, declared a dividend of $5 a share payable in cash on August 1, 1954, to A. On September 15, 1954, it declared a dividend of $5 a share payable in cash on October 1, 1954, to B, C, and D. No allowance for dividends paid for the taxable year 1954 is permitted to the M Corporation with respect to any part of the dividends paid on August 1, 1954, and October 1, 1954.

Example (2). The N Corporation, which makes its income tax returns on the calendar year basis, has a capital of $100,000 (consisting of 1,000 shares of common stock of a par value of $100) and earnings or profits accumulated after February 28, 1913, in the amount of $50,000. In the year 1954, the N Corporation distributes $7,500 in cancellation of 50 shares of the stock owned by three of the four shareholders of the corporation. No deduction for dividends paid is permissible under section 562(c) and paragraph (a) of this section with respect to such distribution.

Example (3). The P Corporation has two classes of stock outstanding, 10 shares of cumulative preferred, owned by E, entitled to $5 per share and on which no dividends have been paid for two years, and 10 shares of common, owned by F. On December 31, 1954, the corporation distributes a dividend of $125, $50 to E, and $75 to F. The corporation is entitled to no deduction for any part of such dividend paid, since there has been a preference to F. If, however, the corporation had distributed $100 to E and $25 to F, it would have been entitled to include $125 as a dividend paid deduction. [Reg. § 1.562-2.]

☐ [*T.D.* 6308, 11-16-56.]

[Reg. § 1.562-3]

§ 1.562-3. Distributions by a member of an affiliated group.—A personal holding company which files or is required to file a consolidated return with other members of an affiliated group may be required to file a separate personal holding company schedule by reason of the limitations and exceptions provided in section 542(b) and § 1.542-4. Section 562(d) provides that in such case the dividends paid deduction shall be allowed to the personal holding company, with respect to a distribution made to any member of the affiliated group, if such distribution would constitute a dividend if it were made to a shareholder which is not a member of the affiliated group. [Reg. § 1.562-3.]

☐ [*T.D.* 6308, 9-9-58.]

[Reg. § 1.563-1]

§ 1.563-1. Accumulated earnings tax.—In the determination of the dividends paid deduction for purposes of the accumulated earnings tax imposed by section 531, a dividend paid after the close of any taxable year and on or before the 15th day of the third month following the close of such taxable year shall be considered as paid during such taxable year, and shall not be included in the computation of the dividends paid deduction for the year of payment. However, the rule provided in section 563(a) is not applicable to dividends paid during the first two and one-half months of

Reg. § 1.563-1

Deduction for Dividends Paid

See p. 20,601 for regulations not amended to reflect law changes

the first taxable year of the corporation subject to tax under chapter 1 of the Internal Revenue Code of 1954. [Reg. § 1.563-1.]

☐ [T.D. 6308, 9-9-58.]

[Reg. § 1.563-2]

§ 1.563-2. **Personal holding company tax.**—In the case of a personal holding company subject to the provisions of section 541, dividends paid after the close of the taxable year and before the 15th day of the third month thereafter shall be included in the computation of the dividends paid deduction for the taxable year only if the taxpayer so elects in its return for such taxable year. The election shall be made by including such dividends in computing its dividends paid deduction. The amount of such dividends which may be included in computing the dividends paid deduction for the taxable year shall not exceed either—

(a) The undistributed personal holding company income of the corporation for the taxable year, computed without regard to this section, or

(b) In the case of a taxable year beginning after December 31, 1969, 20 percent (10 percent, in the case of a taxable year beginning before January 1, 1970) of the sum of the dividends paid during the taxable year (not including consent dividends), computed without regard to this section.

In computing the amount of the dividends paid deduction allowable for any taxable year, the amount allowed by reason of section 563(b) for any preceding taxable year is considered a dividend paid in such preceding taxable year and not in the year of actual distribution. Thus, a double deduction is not allowable. [Reg. § 1.563-2.]

☐ [T.D. 6308, 9-9-58. Amended by T.D. 7079, 12-7-70.]

[Reg. § 1.563-3]

§ 1.563-3. **Dividends considered as paid on last day of taxable year.**—(a) *General rule.* Where a distribution made after the close of the taxable year is considered as paid during such taxable year, for purposes of applying section 562(a) the distribution shall be considered as made on the last day of such taxable year.

(b) *Personal holding company tax.* In the case of a corporation which under the law applicable to the taxable year in respect of which a distribution is made under section 563(b) and § 1.563-2 is a personal holding company under the law applicable to such taxable year, section 316(b)(2) provides that the term dividend means (in addition to the general rule under section 316(a)) any distribution to the extent of the corporation's undistributed personal holding company income (determined under section 545 without regard to distributions under section 316(b)(2)) for such year. See paragraph (b) of § 1.316-1.

(c) *Dividends paid on or before December 15, 1955.* The Act of June 15, 1955 (Public Law 74, 84th Congress, 69 Stat. 136), repealed sections 452 and 462 of the Code, relating to prepaid income and reserve for estimated expenses. Under section 4(c)(4) of that Act, dividends paid after the 15th day of the third month following the close of the taxable year and on or before December 15, 1955, may be treated as having been paid on the last day of the taxable year for purposes of the accumulated earnings tax or the personal holding company tax and in the case of regulated investment companies, but only to the extent that such dividends are attributable to an increase in taxable income for the taxable year by reason of the repeal of sections 452 and 462. See paragraph (b) of § 1.9000-8, relating to treatment of certain dividends, prescribed pursuant to section 4(c)(4) of the Act of June 15, 1955. [Reg. § 1.563-3.]

☐ [T.D. 6308, 9-9-58.]

[Reg. § 1.564-1]

§ 1.564-1. **Dividend carryover.**—(a) *General rule.* The dividend carryover from the two preceding years, allowable only to personal holding companies, is includible in the dividends paid deduction under section 561. It is computed as follows:

(1) If, for each of the preceding two years, the deduction for dividends paid under section 561 (determined without regard to the dividend carryover to each such year) exceeds the taxable income (adjusted as provided in section 545 for purposes of determining undistributed personal holding company income) then the dividend carryover to the taxable year is the sum of both such excess amounts.

(2) If the deduction for dividends paid under section 561 for the second preceding year (determined without regard to the dividend carryover to such year) exceeds the taxable income for such year (adjusted as provided in section 545), and if the taxable income for the first preceding year (as so adjusted) exceeds the dividends paid deduction for such first preceding year (as so determined), then the dividend carryover to the taxable year shall be such excess amount for the second preceding year, less such excess amount for the first preceding year.

(3) If for the first preceding year the deduction for dividends paid under section 561 (determined without regard to the dividend carryover to such year) exceeds the taxable income (adjusted as provided in section 545) for such year, and such excess is not present in the second preceding year,

Reg. § 1.563-2(a)

Deduction for Dividends Paid 39,261
See p. 20,601 for regulations not amended to reflect law changes

then the dividend carryover to the taxable year shall be such excess amount for the first preceding year.

(b) *Dividend carryover from year in which taxpayer was not a personal holding company.* In computing the dividend carryover, the taxable income as adjusted under section 545 of any preceding taxable year shall be determined as if the corporation was, under the law applicable to such taxable year, a personal holding company.

(c) *Dividend carryover from year in which taxpayer was subject to 1939 Code.* In a case where the first or the second preceding taxable year began before the taxpayer's first taxable year under the Internal Revenue Code of 1954, the amount of the dividend carryover shall be determined under the Internal Revenue Code of 1939.

(d) *Statement to be filed with return.* Every corporation claiming a dividend carryover for any taxable year shall file with its return for such year a concise statement setting forth the amount of the dividend carryover claimed and all material and pertinent facts relative thereto, including a detailed schedule showing the computation of the dividend carryover claimed.

(e) *Computation of dividend carryover.* The computation of the dividend carryover may be illustrated by the following examples:

Example (1). The X Corporation, which files its income tax returns on the calendar year basis, has taxable income, adjusted as required by section 545, in the amount of $110,000 and has a dividends paid deduction of $150,000 for the year 1954. For 1955, its taxable income, adjusted as required by section 545, is $200,000 and its dividends paid deduction is $300,000. The dividend carryover to the year 1956 is $140,000, computed as follows:

Dividends paid deduction for 1954	$150,000
Taxable income for 1954	110,000
Dividend carryover from 1954	$ 40,000
Dividends paid deduction for 1955	$300,000
Taxable income for 1955	200,000
Dividend carryover from 1955	$100,000
Dividend carryover for two preceding taxable years, allowable as a deduction for the year 1956	$140,000

Example (2). The Y Corporation, which files its income tax returns on the calendar year basis, has taxable income, adjusted as required by section 545, in the amount of $100,000 and has a dividends paid deduction of $150,000 for the year 1954. For 1955, its taxable income, adjusted as required by section 545, is $200,000 and its dividends paid deduction is $170,000. The dividend carryover to the year 1956 is $20,000, computed as follows:

Dividends paid deduction for 1954	$150,000
Taxable income for 1954	100,000
Dividend carryover from 1954	$ 50,000
Taxable income for 1955	$200,000
Dividends paid deduction for 1955	170,000
Excess of taxable income over dividends paid deduction	$ 30,000
Dividend carryover for second preceding taxable year, allowable as a deduction for the year 1956	$ 20,000

[Reg. § 1.564-1.]
☐ [T.D. 6308, 9-9-58.]

[Reg. § 1.565-1]

§ 1.565-1. **General rule.**—(a) *Consent dividends.* The dividends paid deduction, as defined in section 561, includes the consent dividends for the taxable year. A consent dividend is a hypothetical distribution (as distinguished from an actual distribution) made by:

(1) A corporation that has a reasonable basis to believe that it is subject to the accumulated earnings tax imposed in part I of subchapter G, chapter 1 of the Code, or

(2) A corporation described in part II (personal holding companies or a corporation with adjusted income from rents described in section 543(a)(2)(A) which utilizes the consent dividends described in section 543(a)(2)(B)(iii) to avoid personal holding company status) or part III (foreign personal holding companies) of subchapter G or in part I (regulated investment companies) or part II (real estate investment trusts) of subchapter M, chapter 1 of the Code.

Reg. § 1.565-1(a)(2)

A consent dividend may be made by a corporation described in this paragraph to any person who owns consent stock on the last day of the taxable year of such corporation and who agrees to treat the hypothetical distribution as an actual dividend, subject to the limitations in section 565, § 1.565-2, and paragraph (c)(2) of this section, by filing a consent at the time and in the manner specified in paragraph (b) of this section.

(b) *Making and filing of consents.* (1) A consent shall be made on Form 972 in accordance with this section and the instructions on the form issued therewith. It may be made only by or on behalf of a person who was the actual owner on the last day of the corporation's taxable year of any class of consent stock, that is, the person who would have been required to include in gross income any dividends on such stock actually distributed on the last day of such year. Form 972 shall contain or be verified by a written declaration that it is made under the penalties of perjury. In the consent such person must agree to include in gross income for his taxable year in which or with which the taxable year of the corporation ends a specific amount as a taxable dividend.

(2) See paragraph (c) of this section and § 1.565-2 for the rules as to when all or a portion of the amount so specified will be disregarded for tax purposes.

(3) A consent may be filed at any time not later than the due date of the corporation's income tax return for the taxable year for which the dividends paid deduction is claimed. With such return, and not later than the due date thereof, the corporation must file Forms 972 duly executed by each consenting shareholder, and a return on Form 973 showing by classes the stock outstanding on the first and last days of the taxable year, the dividend rights of such stock, distributions made during the taxable year to shareholders, and giving all the other information required by the form. Form 973 shall contain or be verified by a written declaration that is made under the penalties of perjury.

(c) *Taxability of amounts specified in consents.* (1) The filing of a consent is irrevocable, and except as otherwise provided in section 565(b), § 1.565-2, and paragraph (c)(2) of this section, the full amount specified in a consent filed by a shareholder of a corporation described in paragraph (a) of this section shall be included in the gross income of the shareholder as a taxable dividend. Where the shareholder is taxable on a dividend only if received from sources within the United States, the amount specified in the consent of the shareholder shall be treated as a dividend from sources within the United States in the same manner as if the dividend had been paid in money to the shareholder on the last day of the corporation's taxable year. See paragraph (b) of this section relating to the making and filing of consents, and section 565(e) and § 1.565-5, with respect to the payment requirement in the case of nonresident aliens and foreign corporations.

(2) To the extent that the Commissioner determines that the corporation making a consent dividend is not a corporation described in paragraph (a) of this section, the amount specified in the consent is not a consent dividend and the amount specified in the consent will not be included in the gross income of the shareholder. In addition, where a corporation is described in paragraph (a)(1) but not paragraph (a)(2) of this section, to the extent that the Commissioner determines that the amount specified in a consent is larger than the amount of earnings subject to the accumulated earnings tax imposed by part I of subchapter G, such excess is not a consent dividend under paragraph (a) of this section and will not be included in the gross income of the shareholder.

(3) Except as provided in section 565(b), § 1.565-2 and paragraph (c)(2) of this section, once a shareholder's consent is filed, the full amount specified in such consent must be included in the shareholder's gross income as a taxable dividend, and the ground upon which a deduction for consent dividends is denied the corporation does not affect the taxability of a shareholder whose consent has been filed for the amount specified in the consent. For example, although described in part I, II, or III of subchapter G, or part I or II of subchapter M, chapter I of the Code, the corporation's taxable income (as adjusted under section 535(b), 545(b), 556(b), 852(b)(2), or 857(b)(2), as appropriate) may be less than the total of the consent dividends.

(4) A shareholder who is a nonresident alien or a foreign corporation is taxable on the full amount of the consent dividend that otherwise qualifies under this section even though that payment has not been made as required by section 565(e) and § 1.565-5.

(5) Income of a foreign corporation is not subject to the tax on accumulated earnings under part I of subchapter G, chapter 1 of the Code except to the extent of U.S. source income, adjusted as permitted under section 535. See section 535(b) and (d) and § 1.535-1(b). Therefore, foreign source earnings (other than those distributions subject to resourcing under section 535(d)) of a foreign corporation that is not described in paragraph (a)(2) of this section cannot qualify for consent dividend treatment. Accordingly, a con-

Reg. § 1.565-1(b)(2)

sent dividend made by a foreign corporation described in paragraph (a)(1) of this section shall not be effective with respect to all of the corporation's earnings, but shall relate solely to earnings which would have been, in the absence of the consent dividend, subject to the accumulated earnings tax. [Reg. § 1.565-1.]

☐ [T.D. 8244, 3-13-89.]

[Reg. § 1.565-2]

§ 1.565-2. Limitations.—(a) *General rule.* Amounts specified in consents filed by shareholders or other beneficial owners of a corporation described in § 1.565-1(a) are not treated as consent dividends to the extent that—

(1) They would constitute a preferential dividend or

(2) They would not constitute a dividend (as defined in section 316),

if distributed in money to shareholders on the last day of the taxable year of the corporation. If any portion of any amount specified in a consent filed by a shareholder of a corporation described in the preceding sentence is not treated as a consent dividend under section 565(b) and this section, it is disregarded for all tax purposes. For example, it is not taxable to the consenting shareholder, and paragraph (c) of § 1.565-1 is not applicable to this portion of the amount specified in the consent.

(b) *Preferential distribution.* (1) A preferential distribution is an actual distribution, or a consent distribution, or a combination of the two, which involves a preference to one or more shares of stock as compared with other shares of the same class or to one class of stock as compared with any other class of stock. See section 562(c) and § 1.562-2.

(2) The application of section 565(b)(1) and § 1.565-2(b) may be illustrated by the following examples:

Example (1). The X Corporation, a personal holding company, which makes its income tax returns on the calendar year basis, has 200 shares of stock outstanding, owned by A and B in equal amounts. On December 15, 1987, the corporation distributes $600 to B and $100 to A. As a part of the same distribution, A executes a consent to include $500 in his gross income as a taxable dividend although such amount is not distributed to him. The X Corporation, assuming the other requirements of section 565 have been complied with, is entitled to a consent dividends deduction of $500. Although the consent dividend is deemed to have been paid on December 31, 1987, the last day of the taxable year of the corporation, the total amount of all distributions constitutes a single nonpreferential distribution of $1,200.

Example (2). The Y Corporation, a personal holding company, which makes its income tax returns on the calendar year basis, has one class of consent stock outstanding, owned in equal amounts by A, B, and C. If A and B each receive a distribution in cash of $5,000 and C consents to include $3,000 in gross income as a taxable dividend, the combined actual and consent distribution of $13,000 is preferential. See section 562(c) and § 1.562-2(a). Similarly, if no one receives a distribution in cash, but A and B each consent to include $5,000 as a taxable dividend in gross income and C agrees to include only $3,000, the entire consent distribution is preferential.

Example (3). The Z Corporation, which makes its income tax returns on the calendar year basis and is subject, for the taxable year in question, to the accumulated earnings tax, has only two classes of stock outstanding, each class being consent stock and consisting of 500 shares. Class A, with a par value of $40 per share, is entitled to two-thirds of any distribution of earnings and profits. Class B, with a par value of $20 per share, is entitled to one-third of any distribution of earnings and profits. On December 15, 1987, there is distributed on the class B stock $2 per share, or $1,000, and shareholders of the class A stock consent to include in gross income amounts equal to $2 per share, or $1,000. The entire distribution of $2,000 is preferential, inasmuch as the class B stock has received more than its pro rata share of the combined amounts of the actual distributions and the consent distributions.

(c) *Section 316 limitation.* (1) An additional limitation under section 565(b) is that the amounts specified in consents which may be treated as consent dividends cannot exceed the amounts which would constitute a dividend (as defined in section 316) if the corporation had distributed the total specified amounts in money to shareholders on the last day of the taxable year of the corporation. If only a portion of such total would constitute a dividend, then only a corresponding portion of each specified amount is treated as a consent dividend.

(2) The application of section 565(b)(2) and § 1.565-2(c) may be illustrated by the following example:

Example. The X Corporation, a corporation described in § 1.565-2(a)(1) or (2), which makes its income tax returns on the calendar year basis, has only one class of stock outstanding, owned in equal amounts by A and B. It makes no distributions during the taxable year 1987. Its earnings and profits for the calendar year 1987 amount to $8,000, there being at the beginning of such year no accumulated earnings or profits. A and B execute proper consents to include $5,000 each in their gross income as a dividend received by them on December 31, 1987. The sum of the amounts specified in the consents executed by A and B is $10,000, but if $10,000 had actually been distributed by the X Corporation on December 31, 1987, only $8,000 would have constituted a dividend under section 316(a). The amount which could be considered as consent dividends in computing the dividends paid deduction for purposes of the accumulated earnings tax is limited to $8,000, or $4,000 of the $5,000 specified in each consent. The remaining $1,000 in each consent is disregarded for all tax purposes. (In the case of a personal holding company, see also the example in § 1.565-3(b).) [Reg. § 1.565-2.]

☐ [T.D. 8244, 3-13-89.]

[Reg. § 1.565-3]

§ 1.565-3. **Effect of consent.**—(a) *General Rule.* The amount of the consent dividend that is described in paragraph (a) of § 1.565-1 shall be considered, for all purposes of the Code, as if it were distributed in money by the corporation to the shareholder on the last day of the taxable year of the corporation, received by the shareholder on such day, and immediately contributed by the shareholder as paid-in capital to the corporation on such day. Thus, the amount of the consent dividend will be treated by the shareholder as a dividend. The shareholder will be entitled to the dividends received deduction under section 243 or 245 with respect to such consent dividend. The basis of the shareholder's consent stock in a corporation will be increased by the amount thus treated in his hands as a dividend which he is considered as having contributed to the corporation as paid-in capital. The amount of the current dividend will also be treated as a dividend received from sources within the United States in the same manner as if the dividend had been paid in money to the shareholders. Among other effects of the consent dividend, the earnings and profits of the corporation will be decreased by the amount of the consent dividends. Moreover, if the shareholder is a corporation, its accumulated earnings and profits will be increased by the amount of the consent dividend with respect to which it makes a consent.

(b) *Example.* The application of section 565(c) may be illustrated by the following example:

Example. Corporation A, a personal holding company and a calendar year taxpayer, has one shareholder, individual B, whose consent to include $10,000 in his gross income for the calendar year 1987 has been timely filed. A has $8,000 of earnings and profits at the beginning of 1987. A has $10,000 of undistributed personal holding company income (determined without regard to distributions under section 316(b)(2)) for 1987. B must include $10,000 in his gross income as a taxable income and is treated as having immediately contributed $10,000 to A as paid-in capital. See section 316(b)(2). [Reg. § 1.565-3.]

☐ [T.D. 8244, 3-13-89.]

[Reg. § 1.565-4]

§ 1.565-4. **Consent dividends and other distributions.**—Section 565(d) provides a rule applicable where a distribution is made in part in consent dividends and in part in money or other property. With respect to such a distribution the entire amount specified in the consents and the amount of such money or other property shall be considered together. Thus, if as a part of the same distribution consents are filed by some of the shareholders and cash is distributed to other shareholders, for example, those who may be unwilling to sign consents, the total amount of the cash and the amounts specified in the consents will be viewed as a single distribution to determine the tax effects of such distribution. For example, the total of such amounts must be considered to determine whether the distribution (including the amounts specified in the consents) is preferential and whether any part of such distribution would not be dividends if the total amounts specified in the consents were distributed in cash. See paragraph (b)(2) of § 1.565-2 for examples illustrating the treatment of distributions which consist in part of consent dividends and in part of other property. [Reg. § 1.565-4.]

☐ [T.D. 6308, 9-9-58.]

[Reg. § 1.565-5]

§ 1.565-5. **Nonresident aliens and foreign corporations.**—(a) *Withholding.* In the event that a corporation makes a consent dividend, as described in § 1.565-1(a), to a shareholder that is subject to a withholding tax under section 1441 or 1442 on a distribution of cash or other property, the corporation must remit an amount of tax equal to the withholding tax that would be imposed under section 1441 or 1442 if an actual cash distribution equal to the consent dividend had been paid to the shareholder on the last day of the corporation's taxable year. Such payment must be in one of the following forms:

(1) Cash,

(2) United States postal money order,

(3) Certified check drawn on a domestic bank, provided that the law of the place where the bank is located does not permit the certification to be rescinded prior to presentation,

(4) A cashier's check of a domestic bank, or

Rules of General Application to Banking Institutions 39,265
See p. 20,601 for regulations not amended to reflect law changes

(5) A draft on a domestic bank or a foreign bank maintaining a United States agency or branch and payable in United States funds.

The amount of such payment shall be credited against the tax imposed on the shareholder. [Reg. § 1.565-5.]

☐ [T.D. 8244, 3-13-89.]

[Reg. § 1.565-6]

§ 1.565-6. Definitions.—(a) *Consent stock.* (1) The term "consent stock" includes what is generally known as common stock. It also includes participating preferred stock, the participation rights of which are unlimited.

(2) The definition of consent stock may be illustrated by the following example:

Example. If in the case of the X Corporation, a personal holding company, there is only one class of stock outstanding, it would all be consent stock. If, on the other hand, there were two classes of stock, class A and class B, and class A was entitled to 6 percent before any distribution could be made on class B, but class B was entitled to everything distributed after class A had received its 6 percent, only class B stock would be consent stock. Similarly, if class A, after receiving its 6 percent, was to participate equally or in some fixed proportion with class B until it had received a second 6 percent, after which class B alone was entitled to any further distributions, only class B stock would be consent stock. The same result would follow if the order of preferences were class A 6 percent, then class B 6 percent, then class A a second 6 percent, either alone or in conjunction with class B, then class B the remainder. If, however, class A stock is entitled to ultimate participation without limit as to amount, then it, too, may be consent stock. For example, if class A is to receive 3 percent and then share equally or in some fixed proportion with class B in the remainder of the earnings or profits distributed, both class A stock and class B stock are consent stock.

(b) *Preferred dividends.* (1) The term "preferred dividends" includes all fixed amounts (whether determined by percentage of par value, a stated return expressed in a certain number of dollars per share, or otherwise) the distribution of which on any class of stock is a condition precedent to a further distribution of earnings or profits (not including a distribution in partial or complete liquidation). A distribution, though expressed in terms of a fixed amount, is not a preferred dividend, however, unless it is preferred over a subsequent distribution within the taxable year upon some class or classes of stock other than one on which it is payable.

(2) The definition of preferred dividends may be illustrated by the following example:

Example. If, in the case of the X Corporation, there are only two classes of stock outstanding, class A and class B, and class A is entitled to a distribution of 6 percent of par, after which the balance of the earnings and profits are distributable on class B exclusively, class A's 6 percent is a preferred dividend. If the order of preferences is class A $6 per share, class B $6 per share, then class A and class B in fixed proportions until class A receives $3 more per share, then class B the remainder, all of class A's $9 per share and $6 per share of the amount distributable on class B are preferred dividends. The amount which class B is entitled to receive in conjunction with the payment to class A of its last $3 per share is not a preferred dividend, because the payment of such amount is preferred over no subsequent distribution except one made on class B itself. Finally, if a distribution must be $6 on class A, $6 on class B, then on class A and class B share and share alike, the distribution on class A of $6 and the distribution on class B of $6 are both preferred dividends. [Reg. § 1.565-6.]

☐ [T.D. 8244, 3-13-89.]

BANKING INSTITUTIONS

Rules of General Application to Banking Institutions

[Reg. § 1.581-1]

§ 1.581-1. Banks.—(a) In order to be a bank as defined in section 581, an institution must be a corporation for federal tax purposes. See § 301.7701-2(b) of this chapter for the definition of a corporation.

(b) This section is effective as of January 1, 1997. [Reg. § 1.581-1.]

☐ [T.D. 6188, 7-5-56. Amended by T.D. 8697, 12-17-96.]

[Reg. § 1.581-2]

§ 1.581-2. **Mutual savings banks, building and loan associations, and cooperative banks.**—(a) While the general principles for determining the taxable income of a corporation are applicable to a mutual savings bank, a building and loan association, or a cooperative bank not having capital stock represented by shares, there are certain exceptions and special rules governing the computation in the case of such institutions. See section 593 for special rules concerning

Reg. § 1.581-2(a)

reserves for bad debts. See section 591 and § 1.591-1, relating to dividends paid by banking corporations, for special rules concerning deductions for amounts paid to, or credited to the accounts of, depositors or holders of withdrawable accounts as dividends. See also section 594 and § 1.594-1 for special rules governing the taxation of a mutual savings bank conducting a life insurance business.

(b) For the purpose of computing the net operating loss deduction provided in section 172, any taxable year for which a mutual savings bank, building and loan association, or a cooperative bank not having capital stock represented by shares was exempt from tax shall be disregarded. Thus, no net operating loss carryover shall be allowed from a taxable year beginning before January 1, 1952, and, in the case of any taxable year beginning after December 31, 1951, the amount of the net operating loss carryback or carryover from such year shall not be reduced by reference to the income of any taxable year beginning before January 1, 1952. [Reg. § 1.581-2.]

☐ [T.D. 6188, 7-5-56. Amended by T.D. 8697, 12-17-96.]

[Reg. § 1.581-3]

§ 1.581-3. **Definition of bank prior to September 28, 1962.**—Prior to September 28, 1962, for purposes of sections 582 and 584, the term "bank" means a bank or trust company incorporated and doing business under the laws of the United States (including laws relating to the District of Columbia), of any State, or of any Territory, a substantial part of the business of which consists of receiving deposits and making loans and discounts, or of exercising fiduciary powers similar to those permitted to national banks under section 11(k) of the Federal Reserve Act (38 Stat. 262; 12 U.S.C. 248(k)), and which is subject by law to supervision and examination by State, Territorial, or Federal authority having supervision over banking institutions. Such term also means a domestic building and loan association. [Reg. § 1.581-3.]

☐ [T.D. 6651, 5-16-63.]

[Reg. § 1.582-1]

§ 1.582-1. **Bad debts, losses, and gains with respect to securities held by financial institutions.**—(a) *Bad debt deduction for banks.* A bank, as defined in section 581, is allowed a deduction for bad debts to the extent and in the manner provided by subsections (a), (b), and (c) of section 166 with respect to a debt which has become worthless in whole or in part and which is evidenced by a security (a bond, debenture, note, certificate, or other evidence of indebtedness to pay a fixed or determinable sum of money) issued by any corporation (including governments and their political subdivisions), with interest coupons or in registered form.

(b) *Worthless stock in affiliated bank.* For purposes of section 165(g)(1), relating to the deduction for losses involving worthless securities, if the taxpayer is a bank (as defined in section 581) and owns directly at least 80 percent of each class of stock of another bank, stock in such other bank shall not be treated as a capital asset.

(c) *Pre-1970 sales and exchanges of bonds, etc., by banks.* For taxable years beginning before July 12, 1969, with respect to the taxation under subtitle A of the Code of a bank (as defined in section 581), if the losses of the taxable year from sales or exchanges of bonds, debentures, notes, or certificates, or other evidences of indebtedness, issued by any corporation (including one issued by a government or political subdivision thereof), exceed the gains of the taxable year from such sales or exchanges, no such sale or exchange shall be considered a sale or exchange of a capital asset.

(d) *Post-1969 sales and exchanges of securities by financial institutions.* For taxable years beginning after July 11, 1969, the sale or exchange of a security is not considered the sale or exchange of a capital asset if such sale or exchange is made by a financial institution to which any of the following sections applies: Section 585 (relating to banks), 586 (relating to small business investment companies and business development corporations), or 593 (relating to mutual savings banks, domestic building and loan associations, and cooperative banks). This paragraph shall apply to determine the character of gain or loss from the sale or exchange of a security notwithstanding any other provision of subtitle A of the Code, such as section 1233 (relating to short sales). However, this paragraph shall have no effect in the determination of whether a security is a capital asset under section 1221 for purposes of applying any other provision of the Code, such as section 1232 (relating to original issue discount). For purposes of this paragraph, a security is a bond, debenture, note, or certificate or other evidence of indebtedness, issued by any person. See paragraphs (e) and (f) of this section for special transitional rules applicable, respectively, to banks and to small business investment companies and business development corporations.

(e) *Transition rule for qualifying securities held by banks*—(1) *In general.* Notwithstanding the provisions of paragraph (d) of this section, if the net long-term capital gain from sales and exchanges of qualifying securities exceeds the net short-term capital loss from such sales and exchanges in any taxable year beginning after July 11, 1969, such excess shall be treated as long-term capital gain, but in an amount not to exceed the net gain from sales and exchange of securities in such year. For purposes of computing such net gain, a capital loss carried to the taxable year under section 1212 shall not be taken into account. See section 1222 and the regulations thereunder for definitions of the terms "net long-term capital gain" and "net short-term capital loss". For purposes of this paragraph:

(i) The term "security" means a security within the meaning of paragraph (d) of this section.

(ii) The term "qualifying security" means a security which is held by the bank on July 11, 1969, and continuously thereafter until it is first sold or exchanged by the bank.

See also subparagraph (4) of this paragraph for rules under which the time certain securities are held is deemed to include a period of time determined under section 1223(1) and (2) with respect to such security.

(2) *Computation of capital gain or loss.* For purposes of this paragraph, the amount of gain or loss from the sale or exchange of a qualifying security treated as capital gain or loss is determined by multiplying the amount of gain or loss recognized from such sale or exchange by a fraction the numerator of which is the number of days before July 12, 1969, that such security was held by the bank and the denominator of which is the sum of the number of days included in the numerator and the number of days the security was held by the bank after July 11, 1969.

(3) *Special rules.* For purposes of subparagraphs (1) and (2) of this paragraph, the following items are not taken into account:

(i) Any amount treated as original issue discount under section 1232, and

(ii) Any amount which, without regard to section 582(c) and this section, would be treated as gain or loss from the sale or exchange of property which is not a capital asset, such as an amount which is realized from the sale or exchange of a security which is held by a bank as a dealer in securities.

(4) *Holding period in certain cases.* For purposes of this paragraph—

(i) The time a security received in an exchange is deemed to have been held by a bank includes a period of time determined under section 1223(1) with respect to such security.

(ii) The time a security transferred to a bank from another bank is deemed to have been held by the transferee bank includes a period of time determined under section 1223(2) with respect to such security.

For example, if a bank on December 3, 1972, surrendered an obligation of the United States which it held as a capital asset on July 11, 1969, in a transaction to which section 1037 applied, the time during which the newly received obligation is deemed to have been held includes the time during which the surrendered obligation was deemed to have been held by the bank. Because the surrendered obligation was held on July 11, 1969, the newly acquired obligation is deemed to have been held on that date and is a qualifying security. The period during which the surrendered obligation is deemed to have been held is taken into account in computing the fraction determined under subparagraph (2) of this paragraph with respect to the newly received obligation.

(5) *Examples.* The provisions of this paragraph may be illustrated by the following examples:

Example (1). Bank A, a calendar year taxpayer, purchased a qualifying security on July 14, 1968, and held it to maturity on August 20, 1970, when it was redeemed. The redemption resulted in a taxable gain of $10,000. The security was held by the bank for 363 days before July 12, 1969, and for a total of 768 days. During the taxable year, the bank had no other gains and no losses from sales or exchanges of qualifying securities, but had a net loss of $4,000 from sales of securities other than qualifying securities. The portion of the gain from the redemption of the qualifying security treated as capital gain under subparagraph (2) of this paragraph is $4,726.56 ($363/768 \times $10,000$). Because the net gain of the taxable year from sales and exchanges of securities, $6,000 ($10,000 − $4,000), exceeds the portion of the gain on the sale of the qualifying security treated as capital gain under this paragraph, $4,726.56 is treated as long-term capital gain on the sale of the qualifying security for the taxable year.

Example (2). Assume the same facts as in example (1), except that the bank's net loss of the taxable year from the sale of securities other than qualifying securities was $7,000. The amount considered as long-term capital gain under this paragraph is limited by the amount of gain on the sale of securities to $3,000 ($10,000 − $7,000).

(f) *Small business investment companies and business development corporations*—(1) *Election.* In the case of a small business investment company or a business development corporation, described in section 586(a), section 582(c) does not apply for taxable years beginning after July 11, 1969, and before July 11, 1974, unless the tax-

Reg. § 1.582-1(f)(1)

payer elects that such section shall apply. In the case of a small business investment company, see paragraph (a)(1) of § 1.1243-1 if such an election is made, but see paragraph (a)(2) of § 1.1243-1 if such an election is not made. Such election applies to all such taxable years and, except as provided in subparagraph (3) of this paragraph, is irrevocable. Such election must be made not later than (i) the time, including extensions thereof, prescribed by law for filing the taxpayer's income tax return for its first taxable year beginning after July 11, 1969, or (ii) June 8, 1970, whichever is later.

(2) *Manner of making election.* An election pursuant to the provisions of this paragraph is made by the taxpayer by a written statement attached to the taxpayer's income tax return (or an amended return) for its first taxable year beginning after July 11, 1969. Such statement shall indicate that the election is made pursuant to section 433(d) of the Tax Reform Act of 1969 (83 Stat. 624). The taxpayer shall attach to its income tax return for each subsequent taxable year to which such election is applicable a statement indicating that the election has been made and the amount to which it applies for such year.

(3) *Revocation of election.* An election made pursuant to subparagraph (2) of this paragraph shall be irrevocable unless—

(i) A written application for consent to revoke the election, setting forth the reasons therefor, is filed with the Commissioner within 90 days after the permanent regulations relating to section 433(d)(2) of the Tax Reform Act of 1969 (83 Stat. 624) are filed with the Office of the Federal Register, and

(ii) The Commissioner consents to the revocation.

The revocation is effective for all taxable years to which the election applied. [Reg. § 1.582-1.]

☐ [T.D. 6188, 7-5-56. Amended by T.D. 6362, 2-16-59 and by T.D. 7171, 3-16-72.]

[Reg. § 1.584-1]

§ 1.584-1. **Common trust funds.**—(a) *Method of taxation.* A common trust fund maintained by a bank is not subject to taxation under this chapter and is not considered a corporation. Its participants are taxed on their proportionate share of income from the common trust fund.

(b) *Conditions for qualification.*—(1) For a fund to be qualified as a common trust fund it must be maintained by a bank (as defined in section 581) in conformity with the rules and regulations of the Comptroller of the Currency, exclusively for the collective investment and reinvestment of contributions to the fund by the bank. The bank may either act alone or with one or more other fiduciaries, but it must act solely in its capacity as one or a combination of the following: (i) As a trustee of a trust created by will, deed, agreement, declaration of trust, or order of court; (ii) as an executor of a will or as an administrator of an estate; (iii) as a guardian (by whatever name known under local law) of the estate of an infant, of an incompetent individual, or of an absent individual; or (iv) on or after October 3, 1976, as a custodian of a Uniform Gifts to Minors account. A Uniform Gifts to Minors account is an account established pursuant to a State law substantially similar to the Uniform Gifts to Minors Act. (*See* the Uniform Gifts to Minors Act of 1956 or the Uniform Gifts to Minors Act of 1966, as published by the National Conference of Commissioners on Uniform State Laws.) The Commissioner will publish a list of the States whose laws he determines to be substantially similar to such uniform acts. A bank that maintains a Uniform Gifts to Minors Act account must establish, to the satisfaction of the Commissioner or his delegate, that with respect to the account the bank has duties and responsibilities similar to the duties and responsibilities of a trustee or guardian.

(2) A common trust fund may be a participant in another common trust fund.

(c) *Affiliated groups.* For taxable years beginning after December 31, 1975, two or more banks that are members of the same affiliated group (within the meaning of section 1504) are treated, for purposes of section 584, as one bank for the period of their affiliation. A common trust fund may be maintained by one or by more than one member of an affiliated group. Any member of the group may, but need not, contribute to the fund. Further, for purposes of this paragraph, members of an affiliated group may be, but need not be, co-trustees of the common trust fund. [Reg. § 1.584-1.]

☐ [T.D. 6188, 7-5-56. Amended by T.D. 6651, 5-16-63, and by T.D. 7935, 12-12-83.]

[Reg. § 1.584-2]

§ 1.584-2. **Income of participants in common trust fund.**—(a) Each participant in a common trust fund is required to include in computing its taxable income for its taxable year within which or with which the taxable year of the fund ends, whether or not distributed and whether or not distributable:

(1) Its proportionate share of short-term capital gains and losses, computed as provided in § 1.584-3;

Reg. § 1.584-1(a)

Rules of General Application to Banking Institutions

(2) Its proportionate share of long-term capital gains and losses, computed as provided in § 1.584-3; and

(3) Its proportionate share of the ordinary taxable income or the ordinary net loss of the common trust fund, computed as provided in § 1.584-3.

(b) Any tax withheld at the source from income of the fund (*e.g.*, under section 1441) is deemed to have been withheld proportionately from the participants to whom such income is allocated.

(c)(1) The proportionate share of each participant's short-term capital gains and losses, long-term capital gains and losses, ordinary taxable income or ordinary net loss, dividends and interest received, and tax withheld at the source shall be determined under the method of accounting adopted by the bank in accordance with the written plan by which the common trust fund is established and administered, provided such method clearly reflects the income of each participant.

(2) Items of income and deductions shall be allocated to the periods between valuation dates established by the plan within the taxable year in which they were realized. Ordinary taxable income or ordinary net loss, short-term capital gains and losses, long-term capital gains and losses, and tax withheld at the source shall be computed for each period. The participants' proportionate shares of income and losses for each period shall then be determined.

(3) For taxable years beginning on or after September 22, 1980, any amount of income or loss of the common trust fund which is included in the computation of a participant's taxable income for the taxable year shall be treated as income or loss from an unrelated trade or business to the extent that such amount would have been income or loss from an unrelated trade or business if such participant had made directly the investments of the common trust fund.

(4) The provisions of this paragraph may be illustrated by the following example:

Example. (i) The plan of a common trust fund provides for quarterly valuation dates and for the computation and the distribution of the income upon a quarterly basis, except that there shall be no distribution of capital gains. The participants are as follows: Trusts A, B, C, and D for the first quarter; Trusts A, B, C, and E for the second quarter; and Trusts A, B, F, and G for the third and fourth quarters, the participants having equal participating interests. As computed upon the quarterly basis, the ordinary taxable income, the short-term capital gain, and the long-term capital loss for the taxable year were as follows:

	First Quarter	Second Quarter	Third Quarter	Fourth Quarter	Total
Short-term capital gain	200	100	200	100	600
Long-term capital loss	100	200	100	200	600

(ii) The participants' shares of ordinary taxable income are as follows:

PARTICIPANTS' SHARES OF ORDINARY TAXABLE INCOME

Participant	First Quarter	Second Quarter	Third Quarter	Fourth Quarter	Total
A	$ 50	$ 75	$ 50	$100	$ 275
B	50	75	50	100	275
C	50	75	...	...	125
D	50	...	...	...	50
E	...	75	...	...	75
F	...	...	50	100	150
G	...	...	50	100	150
Total	$200	$300	$200	$400	$1,100

(iii) The participants' shares of the short-term capital gain are as follows:

PARTICIPANTS' SHARES OF SHORT-TERM CAPITAL GAIN

Participant	First Quarter	Second Quarter	Third Quarter	Fourth Quarter	Total
A	$ 50	$ 25	$ 50	$ 25	$ 150
B	50	25	50	25	150
C	50	25	...	...	75
D	50	...	...	...	50
E	...	25	...	...	25
F	...	...	50	25	75
G	...	...	50	25	75
Total	$200	$100	$200	$100	$ 600

Reg. § 1.584-2(c)(4)

39,270 Rules of General Application to Banking Institutions
See p. 20,601 for regulations not amended to reflect law changes

(iv) The participants' shares of the long-term capital loss are as follows:

PARTICIPANTS' SHARES OF LONG-TERM CAPITAL LOSS

Participant	First Quarter	Second Quarter	Third Quarter	Fourth Quarter	Total
A	$ 25	$ 50	$ 25	$ 50	$ 150
B	25	50	25	50	150
C	25	50	...	...	75
D	25	...	...	...	25
E	...	50	...	...	50
F	...	...	25	50	75
G	...	...	25	50	75
Total	$100	$200	$100	$200	$ 600

(v) If in the above example the common trust fund also had short-term capital losses and long-term capital gains, the treatment of such gains or losses would be similar to that accorded to the short-term capital gains and long-term capital losses in the above example.

(vi) Assume in the above example that participant Trust A qualified as a trust forming part of a pension, profit sharing, or stock bonus plan under section 401(a). Assume further that 20 percent of the ordinary taxable income of the common trust fund would be unrelated business taxable income (as defined under section 512(a)(1)) if received directly by Trust A. Under paragraph (c)(3), participant Trust A, for purposes of computing its taxable income, must treat its proportionate share of the common trust fund's ordinary taxable income as income from an unrelated trade or business to the extent such amount would have been income from an unrelated trade or business if Trust A had directly made the investments of the common trust fund. Therefore, participant Trust A must take into account 20 percent of its proportionate share of the common trust fund's ordinary taxable income as income from an unrelated trade or business.

(d) The provisions of part I, subchapter J, chapter 1 of the Code, or, as the case may be, the provisions of subchapters D, F, or H of chapter 1 of the Code, are applicable in determining the extent to which each participant's proportionate share of any income or loss of the common trust fund is taxable to the participant, or to a person other than the participant. [Reg. § 1.584-2.]

☐ [T.D. 6188, 7-5-56. Amended by T.D. 6777, 12-15-64; T.D. 7935, 1-12-84 and T.D. 8662, 5-1-96.]

[Reg. § 1.584-3]

§ 1.584-3. **Computation of common trust fund income.**—The taxable income of the common trust fund shall be computed in the same manner and on the same basis as in the case of an individual, except that—

(a) No deduction shall be allowed under section 170 (relating to charitable, etc., contributions and gifts);

(b) The gains and losses from sales or exchanges of capital assets of the common trust fund are required to be segregated. A common trust fund is not allowed the benefit of the capital loss carryover provided by section 1212; and

(c) The ordinary taxable income (the excess of the gross income over deductions) or the ordinary net loss (the excess of the deductions over the gross income) shall be computed after excluding all items of gain and loss from sales or exchanges of capital assets. [Reg. § 1.584-3.]

☐ [T.D. 6188, 7-5-56. Amended by T.D. 7935, 1-12-84.]

[Reg. § 1.584-4]

§ 1.584-4. **Admission and withdrawal of participants in the common trust fund.**—(a) *Gain or loss.* For taxable years of participants ending after April 7, 1976, and for transfers occurring after that date, the transfer of property by a participant to a common trust fund is treated as a sale or exchange of the property transferred. The common trust fund realizes no gain or loss by the admission or withdrawal of a participant, and the basis of the assets and the period for which they are deemed to have been held by the common trust fund for the purposes of section 1202 are unaffected by such an admission or withdrawal. If a participant withdraws the whole or any part of its participating interest from the common trust fund, such withdrawal shall be treated as a sale or exchange by the participant of the participating interest or portion thereof which is so withdrawn. A participant is not deemed to have withdrawn any part of its participating interest in the common trust fund so as to have completed a closed transaction by reason of the segregation and administration of an investment of the fund, pursuant to the provisions of 12 CFR 9.18(b)(7) (or, for periods before September 28, 1962, 12 CFR 206.17(c)(7)), for the benefit of all the then participants in the common trust fund. Such segregated investment shall be considered as held by,

Reg. § 1.584-3(a)

or on behalf of, the common trust fund for the benefit ratably of all participants in the common trust fund at the time of segregation, and any income or loss arising from its administration and liquidation shall constitute income or loss to the common trust fund apportionable among the participants for whose benefit the investment was segregated. When a participating interest is transferred by a bank, or by two or more banks that are members of the same affiliated group (within the meaning of section 1504), as a result of the combination of two or more common trust funds or the division of a single common trust fund, the transfer to the surviving or divided fund is not considered to be an admission or a withdrawal if the combining, dividing, and resulting common trust funds have diversified portfolios. For purposes of this paragraph (a), a common trust fund has a diversified portfolio if it satisfies the 25 and 50-percent tests of section 368(a)(2)(F)(ii), applying the relevant provisions of section 368(a)(2)(F). However, Government securities are included in total assets for purposes of the denominator of the 25 and 50-percent tests (unless the Government securities are acquired to meet the 25 and 50-percent tests), but are not treated as securities of an issuer for purposes of the numerator of the 25 and 50-percent tests. In addition, for a transfer of a participating interest in a division of a common trust fund not to be considered an admission or withdrawal, each participant's pro rata interest in each of the resulting common trust funds must be substantially the same as was the participant's pro rata interest in the dividing fund. However, in the case of the division of a common trust fund maintained by two or more banks that are members of the same affiliated group resulting from the termination of such affiliation, the division will be treated as meeting the requirements of the preceding sentence if the written plans of operation of the resulting common trust funds are substantially identical to the plan of operation of the dividing common trust fund, each of the assets of the dividing common trust fund are distributed substantially pro rata to each of the resulting common trust funds, and each participant's aggregate interest in the assets of the resulting common trust funds of which he or she is a participant is substantially the same as was the participant's pro rata interest in the assets of the dividing common trust fund. The plan of operation of a resulting common trust fund will not be considered to be substantially identical to that of the dividing common trust fund where, for example, the plan of operation of the resulting common trust fund contains restrictions as to the types of participant's that may invest in the common trust fund where such restrictions were not present in the plan of operation of the dividing common trust fund.

(b) *Basis for gain or loss upon withdrawal.* The participant's gain or loss upon withdrawal of its participating interest or portion thereof shall be measured by the difference between the amount received upon such withdrawal and the adjusted basis of the participating interest or portion thereof withdrawn plus the additions prescribed in paragraph (c) of this section and minus the reductions prescribed in paragraph (d) of this section. The amount received by the participant shall be the sum of any money plus the fair market value of property (other than money) received upon such withdrawal. The basis of the participating interest or portion thereof withdrawn shall be the sum of any money plus the fair market value of any property (other than money) contributed by the participant to the common trust fund to acquire the participating interest or portion thereof withdrawn. Such basis shall not be reduced on account of the segregation of any investment in the common trust fund pursuant to the provisions of 12 CFR 9.18(b)(7) (or, for periods before September 28, 1962, 12 CFR 206.17(c)(7)). For the purpose of making the adjustments, additions, and reductions with respect to basis as prescribed in this paragraph, the ward, rather than the guardian, shall be deemed to be the participant; and the grantor, rather than the trust, shall be deemed to be the participant, to the extent that the income of the trust is taxable to the grantor under subpart E (section 671 and following), part I, subchapter J, chapter 1 of the Code.

(c) *Additions to basis.* As prescribed in paragraph (b) of this section, in computing the gain or loss upon the withdrawal of a participating interest or portion thereof, there shall be added to the basis of the participating interest or portion thereof withdrawn an amount equal to the aggregate of the following items (to the extent that they were properly allocated to the participant for a taxable year of the common trust fund and were not distributed to the participant prior to withdrawal):

(1) Wholly exempt income of the common trust fund for any taxable year,

(2) Net income of the common trust fund for the taxable years beginning after December 31, 1935, and prior to January 1, 1938,

(3) Net short-term capital gain of the common trust fund for each taxable year beginning after December 31, 1937,

(4) The excess of the gains over the losses recognized to the common trust fund upon sales or exchanges of capital assets held (i) for more than 18 months for taxable years beginning after December 31, 1937, and before January 1, 1942, (ii) for more than 6 months for taxable years beginning after December 31, 1941, and before January 1, 1977, (iii) for more than 9 months for taxable years beginning 1977, and (iv) for more than 1 year for taxable years beginning after December 31, 1977, and

(5) Ordinary net or taxable income of the common trust fund for each taxable year beginning after December 31, 1937.

(d) *Reductions in basis.* As prescribed in paragraph (b) of this section, in computing the gain or loss upon the withdrawal of a participating interest or portion thereof, the basis of the participating interest or portion thereof withdrawn shall be reduced by such portions of the following items as were allocable to the participant with respect to the participating interest or portion thereof withdrawn:

(1) The amount of the excess of the allowable deductions of the common trust fund over its gross income for the taxable years beginning after December 31, 1935, and before January 1, 1938, and

(2) The amount of the net short-term capital loss, net long-term capital loss, and ordinary net loss of the common trust fund for each taxable year beginning after December 31, 1937.

(e) *Effective date.* The eighth sentence of paragraph (a) of this section is effective for combinations and divisions of common trust funds completed on or after May 2, 1996. [Reg. § 1.584-4.]

☐ [T.D. 6188, 7-5-56. Amended by T.D. 6651, 5-16-63; T.D. 7935, 1-12-84 and T.D. 8662, 5-1-96.]

[Reg. § 1.584-5]

§ 1.584-5. **Returns of banks with respect to common trust funds.**—For rules applicable to filing returns of common trust funds, see section 6032 and the regulations thereunder. [Reg. § 1.584-5.]

☐ [T.D. 6188, 7-5-56.]

[Reg. § 1.584-6]

§ 1.584-6. **Net operating loss deduction.**—The net operating loss deduction is not allowed to a common trust fund. Each participant in a common trust fund, however, will be allowed the benefits of such deduction. In the computation of such deduction, a participant in a common trust fund shall take into account its pro rata share of items of income, gain, loss, deduction, or credit of the common trust fund. The character of any such item shall be determined as if the participant had realized such item directly from the source from which realized by the common trust fund, or incurred such item in the same manner as incurred by the common trust fund. [Reg. § 1.584-6.]

☐ [T.D. 6188, 7-5-56.]

[Reg. § 1.585-1]

§ 1.585-1. **Reserve for losses on loans of banks.**—(a) *General rule.* As an alternative to a deduction from gross income under section 166(a) for specific debts which become worthless in whole or in part, a financial institution to which section 585 and this section apply shall be allowed a deduction under section 585(a) (or, for taxable years beginning before January 1, 1987, section 166(c)) for a reasonable addition to a reserve for bad debts provided such financial institution has adopted or adopts the reserve method of treating bad debts in accordance with paragraph (b) of § 1.166-1. In the case of such a taxpayer the amount of the reasonable addition to such reserve for a taxable year beginning after July 11, 1969, shall be an amount determined by the taxpayer which does not exceed the amount computed under § 1.585-2. Such reasonable addition for the taxable year shall be an amount at least equal to the amount provided by § 1.585-2(a)(2). For each taxable year the taxpayer must include in its income tax return (or amended return) for that year a computation of the amount of the addition determined under this section showing the method used to determine that amount. The use of a particular method in the return for a taxable year is not a binding election by the taxpayer to apply such method either for such taxable year or for subsequent taxable years. A financial institution to which section 585 and this section apply which adopts the reserve method is not entitled to charge off any bad debts pursuant to section 166(a) with respect to a loan (as defined in § 1.585-2(e)(2)). Except as provided by § 1.585-3, the reserve for bad debts of a financial institution to which section 585 and this section apply shall be established and maintained in the same manner as is provided by section 585 (or, for taxable years beginning before January 1, 1987, section 166(c)) and the regulations under section 166 with respect to reserves for bad debts. Except as provided by this section, no deduction is allowable for an addition to a reserve for losses on loans as defined in § 1.585-2(e)(2) of a financial institution to which section 585 and this section apply. For rules relating to deduction with respect to debts

Reg. § 1.584-5

which are not loans (as defined in § 1.585-2(e)(2)), see section 166(a) and the regulations thereunder. For rules relating to a debt evidenced by a security (as defined in section 165(g)(2)(c)), see sections 166 and 582(a) and the regulations thereunder. For the definition of certain terms, see paragraph (e) of § 1.585-2. For rules relating to a transaction to which section 381(a) applies, see § 1.585-4. For rules relating to large banks, see §§ 1.585-5 through 1.585-8.

(b) *Application of section*—(1) *In general.* Except as provided in paragraph (b)(2) of this section, section 585 and this section apply to the following financial institutions—

(i) Any bank (as defined in section 581 and the regulations thereunder) other than a mutual savings bank, domestic building and loan association, or cooperative bank, to which section 593 applies; and

(ii) Any corporation to which paragraph (b)(1)(i) of this section would apply except for the fact that it is a foreign corporation and in the case of any such foreign corporation, the rules provided by section 585(a) and (b), this section, §§ 1.585-2, 1.585-3, and 1.585-4 apply only with respect to loans outstanding the interest on which is effectively connected with the conduct of a banking business within the United States.

(2) *Exception.* For taxable years beginning after December 31, 1986, section 585(a) and (b) and this section do not apply to any large bank (as defined in § 1.585-5(b)). For these years, a large bank may not deduct any amount under section 585 or any other section for an addition to a reserve for bad debts. [Reg. § 1.585-1.]

☐ [T.D. 7532, 1-18-78. Amended by T.D. 8513, 12-28-93.]

[Reg. § 1.585-2]

§ 1.585-2. **Addition to reserve.**—(a) *In general*—(1) *Maximum addition.* For taxable years beginning before January 1, 1988, the maximum reasonable addition to the reserve for losses on loans as defined in paragraph (e)(2) of this section is the amount allowable under the percentage method provided by paragraph (b) of this section or the experience method provided by paragraph (c) of this section, whichever is greater. For taxable years beginning after December 31, 1987, the maximum reasonable addition to the reserve for losses on loans is the amount determined under the experience method provided by paragraph (c) of this section.

(2) *Minimum addition.* For taxable years beginning after December 31, 1976, and before January 1, 1988, a taxpayer to which this section applies shall make a minimum addition to the reserve for losses on loans as defined in paragraph (e)(2) of this section. For purposes of this subparagraph, the term "minimum addition" means an addition to the reserve for losses on loans in an amount equal to the lesser of (i) the amount allowable under section 585(b)(3)(A) and paragraph (c)(1)(ii) of this section, or (ii) the maximum amount allowable under section 585(b)(2) and paragraph (b) of this section. For taxable years beginning after December 31, 1987, a taxpayer to which this section applies shall make a minimum addition to the reserve for losses on loans for each taxable year in an amount equal to the amount allowable under section 585(b)(3)(A) and paragraph (c)(1)(ii) of this section.

(b) *Percentage method*—(1) *In general*—(i) *Maximum addition.* Except as limited under subparagraph (2) of this paragraph, the maximum reasonable addition to the reserve for losses on loans under the percentage method for a taxable year is the amount determined under paragraph (b)(1)(ii), (iii), or (iv), whichever is applicable. For purposes of this paragraph, the term "allowable percentage" means 1.8 percent for taxable years beginning before 1976; 1.2 percent for taxable years beginning after 1975 but before 1982; 1.0 percent for taxable years beginning in 1982; and 0.6 percent for taxable years beginning after 1982 and before 1988. This paragraph does not apply for taxable years beginning after 1987.

(ii) *Reserve less than allowable percentage of eligible loans.* (A) If the reserve for losses on loans as of the close of the base year is less than the allowable percentage for the taxable year multiplied by the eligible loans outstanding at the close of the base year, the amount determined under this subdivision for the taxable year is the amount necessary to increase the balance of the reserve for losses on loans as of the close of the taxable year to an amount equal to the allowable percentage for the taxable year multiplied by the eligible loans outstanding at the close of that year, except that the amount determined with respect to the reserve deficiency shall not exceed one-fifth of the reserve deficiency. For purposes of this section, the term "reserve deficiency" means the excess of the allowable percentage for the taxable year multiplied by the eligible loans outstanding at the close of the base year over the reserve for losses on loans as of the close of the base year. Where a taxpayer has recoveries of bad debts for a taxable year which exceed the bad debts sustained for such year, the taxpayer is not required to reduce its otherwise permissible current addition by the amount of the net recovery. A reasonable addition attributable to an increase in eligible loans outstanding at the close of the taxable year over eligible loans outstanding at the close of the

Reg. § 1.585-2(b)(1)

39,274 Rules of General Application to Banking Institutions

See p. 20,601 for regulations not amended to reflect law changes

base year may be made only for the portion of such increase which does not exceed the excess of eligible loans outstanding at the close of the taxable year over the sum of the amount of eligible loans outstanding at the close of the base year and the amount of previous increases in such loans for which an addition was made in taxable years ending after the close of the base year. For purposes of this subdivision, the order in which the factors which make up the annual reserve addition shall be claimed is:

(1) An amount equal to one-fifth of the reserve deficiency;

(2) Net bad debts charged to the reserve; and

(3) An amount attributable to an increase in the amount of eligible loans outstanding.

(B) For its first taxable year, a newly organized financial institution to which § 1.585-1 and this section apply shall be considered to have no reserve deficiency. For example, a new financial institution would compute its annual reserve addition by including in such addition an amount not in excess of the sum of (1) the amount of its net bad debts charged to the reserve for the taxable year, and (2) the allowable percentage of the increase in its eligible loans outstanding at the close of the taxable year over the amount of its loans outstanding (zero) at the end of the year preceding its first taxable year. Such amount would be subject to the 0.6 percent limitations provided in subparagraph (2) of this paragraph.

(C) The application of the rules provided by this subdivision may be illustrated by the following example:

Example. The X Bank is a commercial bank which has a calendar year as its taxable year. X adopted the reserve method of accounting for bad debts in 1950. On December 31, 1969, X has $1,000,000 of outstanding eligible loans and a balance of $13,000 in its reserve for losses on loans. The base year is 1969 and, consequently, X has a reserve deficiency of $5,000 (1.8% × $1,000,000) − $13,000).

(a) During 1970, X has net bad debts of $1,000 charged to the reserve for losses on loans. On December 31, 1970, X has $1,050,000 of outstanding eligible loans. The maximum reasonable addition under the percentage method is $2,900 which consists of $1,000 of reserve deficiency (1/5 × $5,000), the $1,000 in net bad debts charged to the reserve for losses on loans, and $900 attributable to the increase in the balance of eligible loans (1.8% × $1,050,000 − $1,000,000). Assuming that X makes an addition to the reserve for losses on loans of $2,900 for the year, the balance of the reserve as of December 31, 1970 is $14,900 ($13,000 − $1,000 + $2,900).

(b) During 1971, X has net bad debts of $1,000 charged to the reserve for losses on loans. On December 31, 1971, X has $800,000 of outstanding eligible loans. The allowable percentage of eligible loans is $14,400 (1.8% × $800,000). The maximum reasonable addition under the percentage method is $500 which is a portion of one-fifth of the reserve deficiency. Assuming that X makes an addition to the reserve for losses on loans of $500 for the year, the balance of the reserve as of December 31, 1971, is $14,400 ($14,900 − $1,000 + $500).

(c) During 1972, X has net bad debts of $600 charged to the reserve for losses on loans. On December 31, 1972, X has $850,000 of outstanding eligible loans. The allowable percentage of eligible loans is $15,300 (1.8% × $850,000). The maximum reasonable addition under the percentage method is $1,500 which consists of $1,000 of reserve deficiency (1/5 × $5,000) and $500 of the net bad debts charged to the reserve for losses on loans in 1971. Even though the full addition with respect to the reserve deficiency in 1971 was not made, the amount of the addition that can be made in 1972 with respect to the reserve deficiency is limited to one-fifth of such deficiency. Assuming that X makes an addition to the reserve for losses on loans of $1,500 for the year, the balance of the reserve as of December 31, 1972, is $15,300 ($14,400 − $600 + $1,500).

(d) During 1973, X did not have any net bad debts charged to the reserve for losses on loans. On December 31, 1973, X has $1,000,000 of outstanding eligible loans. The allowable percentage of eligible loans is $18,000 (1.8% × $1,000,000). The maximum reasonable addition under the percentage method is $2,100 which consists of $1,000 of reserve deficiency (1/5 × $5,000), $500 of net bad debts charged to the reserve for losses in 1971, and $600 of net bad debts charged to the reserve in 1972. Although outstanding eligible loans increased from $850,000 in 1972 to $1,000,000 in 1973, no addition is permitted with respect to the increase because the amount of eligible loans outstanding at the close of 1973 ($1,000,000) does not exceed the sum of the amount of such loans at the close of the base year ($1,000,000) and the amount of previous increases in such loans for which an addition was made in taxable years ending after the close of the base year ($50,000 loan increase in 1970). Assuming that X makes an addition to the reserve for losses on loans of $2,100, the balance of the reserve as of December 31, 1973, is $17,400 ($15,300 + $2,100).

Reg. § 1.585-2(b)(1)

(iii) *Reserve equal to or greater than allowable percentage and eligible loans have not declined.* If the reserve for losses on loans as of the close of the base year is equal to or greater than the allowable percentage for the taxable year multiplied by the eligible loans outstanding at the close of the base year and if the amount of eligible loans outstanding at the close of the taxable year is equal to or greater than the amount of eligible loans outstanding at the close of the base year, the amount determined under this subdivision is the amount necessary to increase the reserve to the greater of (A) the allowable percentage for the taxable year multiplied by the eligible loans outstanding at the close of the year, or (B) the balance of the reserve as of the close of the base year. The application of the rule provided by this subdivision may be illustrated by the following example:

Example. The M Bank is a commercial bank which has a calendar year as its taxable year. M adopted the reserve method of accounting for bad debts in 1950. On December 31, 1969, M has $1,000,000 of outstanding eligible loans and a balance of $20,000 in its reserve for losses on loans.

(a) During 1970, M has net bad debts of $1,000 charged to the reserve for losses on loans. On December 31, 1970, M has $1,100,000 of outstanding eligible loans. The allowable percentage of eligible loans is $19,800 (1.8% × $1,100,000). The maximum reasonable addition under the percentage method is $1,000 which is the amount sufficient to increase the balance of the reserve as of the close of the taxable year to the balance of the reserve as of the close of the 1969 base year ($20,000). Assuming that M makes an addition to the reserve for losses on loans of $1,000 for the year, the balance of the reserve as of December 31, 1970, is $20,000 ($20,000 − $1,000 + $1,000).

(b) During 1971, M has net bad debts of $1,000 charged to the reserve for losses on loans. On December 31, 1971, M has $1,300,000 of outstanding eligible loans. The allowable percentage of eligible loans is $23,400 (1.8% × $1,300,000). The maximum reasonable addition under the percentage method is $4,400 which is the amount sufficient to increase the balance of the reserve to the allowable percentage of eligible loans outstanding at the close of the taxable year. Assuming that M makes an addition to the reserve for losses on loans of $4,400 for the year, the balance of the reserve as of December 31, 1971, is $23,400 ($20,000 − $1,000 + $4,400).

(c) During 1972, M has net bad debts of $1,000 charged to the reserve for losses on loans. On December 31, 1972, M has $1,200,000 of outstanding eligible loans. The allowable percentage of eligible loans is $21,600 (1.8% × $1,200,000). No reasonable addition may be made under the percentage method because the reserve for losses on loans ($22,400, *i.e.,* $23,400 − $1,000) is greater than the allowable percentage of eligible loans outstanding at the close of the taxable year ($21,600) and the balance of the reserve as of the close of the base year ($20,000). Assuming that no amount is added under the experience method provided by paragraph (c) of this section, the balance of the reserve for losses on loans as of December 31, 1972, is $22,400 ($23,400 − $1,000).

(d) During 1973, M has net bad debts of $1,000 charged to the reserve for losses on loans. On December 31, 1973, M has $1,200,000 of outstanding eligible loans. The allowable percentage of eligible loans is $21,600 (1.8% × $1,200,000). The maximum reasonable addition under the percentage method is $200 which is the amount sufficient to increase the reserve for losses on loans to the allowable percentage of eligible loans outstanding at the close of the taxable year. Assuming that M makes an addition to the reserve for losses on loans of $200 for the year, the balance of the reserve as of December 31, 1973, is $21,600 ($22,400 − 1,000 + $200).

(iv) *Reserve greater than allowable percentage and eligible loans have declined.* If the reserve for losses on loans as of the close of the base year is equal to or greater than the allowable percentage of eligible loans outstanding at such time and if the amount of eligible loans at the close of the taxable year is less than the amount of eligible loans outstanding at the close of the base year, the amount determined under this subdivision is the amount necessary to increase the balance of the reserve to the amount which bears the same ratio to eligible loans outstanding at the close of the taxable year as the balance of the reserve as of the close of the base year bears to the amount of eligible loans outstanding at the close of the base year. The application of the rule provided by this subdivision may be illustrated by the following example:

Example. The N Bank is a commercial bank which has a calendar year as its taxable year. N adopted the reserve method of accounting for bad debts in 1950. On December 31, 1969, N has $1,000,000 of outstanding eligible loans and a balance of $20,000 in its reserve for losses on loans.

(a) During 1970, N has net bad debts of $3,000 charged to the reserve for losses on loans. On December 31, 1970, N has $900,000 of out-

Reg. § 1.585-2(b)(1)

39,276 Rules of General Application to Banking Institutions
See p. 20,601 for regulations not amended to reflect law changes

standing eligible loans. The maximum reasonable addition under the percentage method is $1,000, which is the amount necessary to increase the balance of the reserve to the amount ($18,000) which bears the same ratio to eligible loans outstanding at the close of the taxable year ($900,000) as the balance of the reserve as of the close of the base year ($20,000) bears to the amount of the eligible loans outstanding at the close of the base year ($1,000,000). Assuming that N makes an addition to the reserve for losses on loans of $1,000 for the year, the balance of the reserve as of December 31, 1970, is $18,000 ($20,000 − $3,000 + $1,000).

(b) During 1971, N has net bad debts of $1,000 charged to the reserve for losses on loans. On December 31, 1971, N has $1,100,000 of outstanding eligible loans. The maximum reasonable addition under the percentage method, determined under subdivision (111) of this subparagraph, is $3,000 which is the amount necessary to increase the balance of the reserve to the greater of the allowable percentage of eligible loans outstanding at the close of the taxable year ($19,800) or the balance of the reserve at the close of the base year ($20,000). Assuming that N makes an addition to the reserve for losses on loans of $3,000 for the year, the balance of the reserve as of December 31, 1971, is $20,000 ($18,000 − $1,000 + $3,000).

(2) *Limitations.* Notwithstanding any other provision of this paragraph, the maximum reasonable addition to the reserve for losses on loans under the percentage method shall not exceed the greater of—

(i) Six-tenths of 1 percent of the eligible loans outstanding at the close of the taxable year, or

(ii) An amount sufficient to increase the reserve for losses on loans at the close of the taxable year to six-tenths of 1 percent of the eligible loans outstanding at the close of the taxable year.

The application of the rules provided by this subparagraph may be illustrated by the following example:

Example. The Y Bank begins business as a commercial bank on July 1, 1974. Y adopts the calendar year as its taxable year and the reserve method of accounting for bad debts.

(a) During 1974, Y has net bad debts of $1,000. On December 31, 1974, Y has $1,000,000 of outstanding eligible loans. Under subparagraph (1)(ii)(B) of this paragraph, because Y is a newly-organized financial institution, there is no reserve deficiency. Except for the limitations of this subparagraph, the maximum reasonable addition under subparagraph (1)(ii)(A) of this paragraph would be the amount of net bad debts charged to the reserve for losses ($1,000) plus the allowable percentage of outstanding eligible loans at the close of the taxable year $18,000 (1.8% × $1,000,000). However, because of the limitations of this subparagraph, the maximum reasonable addition to the reserve for losses on loans under the percentage method is an amount sufficient to increase the balance of the reserve for losses on loans to $6,000 which is 0.6 percent of the eligible loans outstanding at the close of the taxable year. Assuming that Y makes an addition to the reserve for losses on loans of $7,000 for the year, the balance of the reserve as of December 31, 1974, is $6,000 ($7,000 − $1,000). The $7,000 consists of the $1,000 in net bad debts and $6,000 attributable to the increase in eligible loans outstanding.

(b) During 1975, Y has net bad debts of $1,000 charged to the reserve for losses on loans. On December 31, 1975, Y has $1,000,000 of outstanding eligible loans. Except for the limitations of this subparagraph, the maximum reasonable addition under subparagraph (1)(ii)(A) of this paragraph would be the amount of net bad debts charged to the reserve for losses ($1,000) plus an amount attributable to the increase in the amount of eligible loans outstanding with respect to which no reasonable addition was allowed in 1974 ($12,000, *i.e.,* $18,000 − $6,000). However, because of the limitations of this paragraph, the maximum reasonable addition to the reserve for losses on loans under the percentage method is $6,000 which is an amount equal to 0.6 percent of the eligible loans outstanding at the close of the taxable year. This amount consists of net bad debts of $1,000 and $5,000 attributable to a portion of the increase in eligible loans in 1974 with respect to which no reasonable addition was allowable for 1974. Assuming that Y makes an addition to the reserve for losses on loans of $6,000 for the year, the balance of the reserve as of December 31, 1975, is $11,000 ($6,000 − $1,000 + $6,000).

(c) During 1976, Y has net bad debts charged to the reserve for losses on loans of $1,000. On December 31, 1976, Y has $1,000,000 in outstanding eligible loans. At the close of 1975 (Y's base year for 1976), the amount of outstanding eligible loans was also $1,000,000. Consequently, there is a reserve deficiency of $1,000 ((1.2% × $1,000,000) − $11,000). The maximum reasonable addition to the reserve for losses under subparagraph (1)(ii)(A) of this paragraph is $1,200 which consists of one-fifth of the reserve deficiency ($1,000 × 1/5 = $200) and the net bad debts charged to the reserve for losses on loans for the year ($1,000). Because that amount is less than 0.6 percent of the eligible loans outstanding

Reg. § 1.585-2(b)(2)

at the close of the taxable year (0.6% × $1,000,000 = $6,000), the limitations of this subparagraph do not apply. Assuming that Y makes an addition to the reserve for losses on loans of $1,200 for the year, the balance of the reserve as of December 31, 1976, is $11,200 ($11,000 − $1,000 + $1,200).

(c) *Experience method*—(1) *In general*—(i) *Maximum addition.* The amount determined under this paragraph for a taxable year is the amount necessary to increase the balance of the reserve for losses on loans (as of the close of the taxable year) to the greater of the amount determined under subdivision (ii) or (iii) of this subparagraph. For special rules for a new financial institution, see subparagraph (2) of this paragraph.

(ii) *Six-year moving average amount.* The amount determined under this subdivision is the amount which bears the same ratio to loans outstanding at the close of the taxable year as (A) the total bad debts sustained during the taxable year and the 5 preceding taxable years (or, with the approval of the Commissioner, a shorter period), adjusted for recoveries of bad debts during such period, bears to (B) the sum of the loans outstanding at the close of such 6 (or fewer) taxable years. For purposes of applying this subdivision, a period shorter than 6 years generally would be appropriate only where there is a change in the type of a substantial portion of the loans outstanding such that the risk of loss is substantially increased. For example, if the major portion of a bank's portfolio of loans changes from agricultural loans to industrial loans which results in a substantial increase in the risk of loss, a period shorter than 6 years may be appropriate. Similarly, a bank which has recently altered its lending practices to include in its portfolio of loans consumer-installment loans, when it had previously made only commercial loans, may also qualify to use a period shorter than six years. A decline in the general economic conditions in the area, which substantially increase the risk of loss, is a relevant factor which may be considered. In any case, however, approval to use a shorter period will not be granted unless the taxpayer supplies specific evidence that the loans outstanding at the close of the taxable years for the shorter period requested are not comparable in nature and risk to loans outstanding at the close of the six taxable years. The fact that a bank's bad debt experience has shown a substantial increase is not, by itself, sufficient to justify use of a shorter period. If approval is granted to use a shorter period, the experience for those taxable years which are excluded shall not be used for any subsequent year. A request for approval to exclude the experience of a prior taxable year shall not be considered unless it is sent to the Commissioner at least 30 days before the close of the first taxable year for which such approval is requested.

(iii) *Base year amount.* The amount determined under this subdivision is the lower of (A) the balance of the reserve as of the close of the base year, or (B) if the amount of loans outstanding at the close of the taxable year is less than the amount of loans outstanding at the close of the base year, the amount which bears the same ratio to loans outstanding at the close of the taxable year as the balance of the reserve as of the close of the base year bears to the amount of loans outstanding at the close of the base year.

(2) *Special rules for new financial institutions*—(i) *In general.* In the case of any taxable year preceded by less than 5 authorization years (as defined in paragraph (e)(5) of this section), subparagraph (1) of this paragraph shall be applied with the adjustments provided by subdivision (ii) of this subparagraph.

(ii) *Adjustments.* (A) The total bad debts for the 6-year period computed under subparagraph (1)(ii)(A) of this paragraph shall be the sum of:

(*1*) The bad debts sustained by the taxpayer during its authorization years, adjusted for recoveries of bad debts for such years, and

(*2*) That fraction of the total bad debts sustained by a comparable bank (as defined in paragraph (e)(7) of this section) during the comparison years (as defined in paragraph (e)(6) of this section), adjusted for recoveries of bad debts for such years, which bears the same ratio to such total as the average loans outstanding of the taxpayer during the authorization years bears to the average loans outstanding of the comparable bank during the comparison years.

(B) The total amount of loans outstanding during the 6-year period computed under subparagraph (1)(ii)(B) of this paragraph shall be six times the average loans outstanding of the taxpayer during the authorization years.

(d) *Change in accounting method from specific charge-off method to reserve method of treating bad debts*—(1) *In general.* If a bank is granted permission in accordance with § 1.446-1(e)(3) to change its method of accounting for bad debts from a method under which specific bad debt items are deducted to the reserve method of treating bad debts, the taxpayer shall effect the change as provided in subparagraphs (2) and (3) of this paragraph.

(2) *Initial balance of the reserve.* The initial balance of the reserve at the close of the year of

Reg. § 1.585-2(d)(2)

39,278 Rules of General Application to Banking Institutions

See p. 20,601 for regulations not amended to reflect law changes

change shall be no less than the minimum addition as described in paragraph (a)(2) of this section and shall be no larger than the greater of—

(i) The allowable percentage of eligible loans outstanding at the close of the taxable year of change, or

(ii) The amount which bears the same ratio to loans outstanding at the close of the taxable year as the total bad debts sustained during the taxable year and the 5 preceding taxable years (or, with the approval of the Commissioner, a shorter period), adjusted for recoveries of bad debts during such period, bears to the sum of the loans outstanding at the close of such 6 or fewer taxable years.

In the case of taxable years beginning after 1987, the initial balance of the reserve at the end of the year of change shall be the amount specified in subdivision (ii) of this subparagraph.

(3) *Deduction with respect to initial balance.* The deduction with respect to the initial balance of the reserve at the close of the taxable year of change, determined under subparagraph (2) of this paragraph, is allowed ratably over a period of 10 years commencing with the taxable year of change (or a shorter period as may be approved by the Commissioner). Thus, the bad debt deduction under section 166 for the taxable year of change will consist of the amount of debts determined to be wholly or partially worthless and charged-off during such taxable year plus one-tenth (if a 10-year period is used) of the amount of the reserve determined under subparagraph (2) of this paragraph. For each of the 9 taxable years following the taxable year of change, the bad debt deduction will consist of the reasonable addition to the reserve for bad debts for each such year as provided by section 585, as otherwise determined, plus one-tenth of the amount determined to be the initial balance of the reserve under subparagraph (2) of this paragraph. The amount established as a bad debt reserve for the taxable year of change under subparagraph (2) of this paragraph shall be considered as the balance of the reserve for purposes of determining the amount of subsequent additions to such reserve, even though the entire amount of the reserve may not have been deducted under section 585(a)(1) or former section 166(c) because of the requirement that it be deducted over a number of years.

(e) *Definitions*—(1) *Base year*—(i) *Percentage method.* For purposes of paragraph (b) of this section (relating to the percentage method), the term "base year" means: For years beginning before 1976, the last taxable year beginning on or before July 11, 1969; for taxable years beginning after 1975 but before 1983, the last taxable year beginning before 1976; and, for taxable years beginning after 1982, the last taxable year beginning before 1983. However, for purposes of section 585(b)(2)(A) the term "base year" means the last taxable year before the most recent adoption of the percentage method, if later than the base year as determined under the preceding sentence.

(ii) *Experience method.* For purposes of paragraph (c) of this section (relating to the experience method), the term "base year" means (A) the last taxable year before the most recent adoption of the experience method, or (B) the last taxable year beginning on or before July 11, 1969, whichever is later; and for taxable years beginning after 1987, the last taxable year beginning before 1988.

(iii) *Example.* The application of the rules provided by this subparagraph may be illustrated by the following example:

Example. The T Bank is a commercial bank which has a calendar year as its taxable year. T adopted the reserve method of accounting for bad debts in 1950. On December 31, 1969, T has $1,000,000 of outstanding eligible loans and a balance of $19,300 in its reserve for losses on loans.

(a) During 1970, T has net bad debts of $1,000 charged to the reserve for losses on loans. On December 31, 1970, T has $1,050,000 of outstanding eligible loans. T elects the percentage method. The base year is 1969. The maximum reasonable addition under the percentage method is $1,000 which is the amount sufficient to increase the balance of the reserve as of the close of the taxable year to the balance of the reserve as of the close of the base year 1969 ($19,300). Assuming that T makes an addition to the reserve for losses on loans of $1,000 for the year, the balance of the reserve for losses on loans as of December 31, 1970, is $19,300 ($19,300 − $1,000 + $1,000).

(b) During 1971, T has net bad debts of $8,000 charged to the reserve for losses on loans. On December 31, 1971, T has $1,100,000 of outstanding eligible loans. T elects the experience method. The base year is 1970. The maximum reasonable addition under the experience method is $8,000 which is the amount sufficient to increase the balance of the reserve as of the close of the taxable year to the balance of the reserve as of the close of the 1970 base year ($19,300). Assuming that T makes an addition to the reserve for losses on loans of $8,000 for the year, the balance of the reserve for losses on loans as of December 31, 1971, is $19,300 ($19,300 − $8,000 + $8,000).

Reg. § 1.585-2(d)(3)

Rules of General Application to Banking Institutions

(c) During 1972, T has net bad debts of $1,000 charged to the reserve for losses on loans. On December 31, 1972, T has $1,200,000 of outstanding eligible loans. T elects the percentage method. The base year is 1971 and there is a reserve deficiency of $500 ((1.8% × $1,100,000) − $19,300). The maximum reasonable addition under the percentage method is $2,900 which consists of $100 of reserve deficiency (1/5 × $500), the $1,000 in net bad debts charged to the reserve for losses on loans, and $1,800 attributable to the increase in the balance of eligible loans (1.8% × ($1,200,000 − $1,100,000)). Assuming that T makes an addition to the reserve for losses on loans of $2,900 for the year, the balance of the reserve for losses on loans as of December 31, 1972, is $21,200 ($19,300 − $1,000 + $2,900).

(2) *Loan*—(i) *General rule.* For purposes of this section and §§ 1.585-1, 1.585-3, and 1.585-4, the term "loan" means debt as the term "debt" is used in section 166 and the regulations thereunder. The term "loan" includes (but is not limited to) the following items:

(A) An overdraft in one or more deposit accounts by a customer in good faith whether or not other deposit accounts of the same customer have balances in excess of the overdraft;

(B) A bankers acceptance purchased or discounted by a bank; and

(C) A loan participation to the extent that the taxpayer bears a risk of loss.

For purposes of (B) of this subdivision (i), a bankers acceptance shall be considered as a loan made by the bank which purchased or discounted the bankers acceptance and not a loan made by the originating bank.

(ii) *Exceptions.* Notwithstanding the provisions of subdivision (i) of this subparagraph, the term "loan" does not include the following items:

(A) Discount or interest receivable reflected in the face amount of an outstanding loan, which discount or interest has not been included in gross income;

(B) For taxable years beginning after December 31, 1976, commercial paper, however acquired by the bank, including, for example, short-term promissory notes which may be purchased on the open market;

(C) For taxable years beginning after December 31, 1976, a debt evidenced by a security (as defined in section 165(g)(2)(C) and the regulations thereunder);

(D) Any loan which is entered into or acquired for the primary purpose of enlarging the otherwise available bad debt deduction;

(E) Loans which have been contractually committed to the extent that funds have not been disbursed to the borrower or disbursed on behalf of the borrower; and

(F) Any transaction which is in violation of a Federal or State statute that governs the activities of the financial institution.

(3) *Eligible loan*—(i) *General rule.* For purposes of this section and §§ 1.585-3 and 1.585-4, the term "eligible loan" means a loan (as defined in subparagraph (2) of this paragraph) which is incurred in the course of the normal customer loan activities of a financial institution and which is not a loan described in subdivision (ii) of this subparagraph. Nothing within the preceding sentence will be construed to exclude from the term "eligible loan" a bona fide loan in a new market or under a novel repayment arrangement if the likelihood of nonrepayment is at least as great as that of other customer loans of the financial institution.

(ii) *Exceptions.* Loans which do not constitute eligible loans include:

(A) A loan to a bank (as defined in section 581 and the regulations thereunder) or to a domestic branch of a foreign corporation to which § 1.585-1 applies, including a repurchase transaction or other similar transaction;

(B) Bank funds on deposit in any bank (foreign or domestic) such as a deposit represented by a certificate of deposit or any other form of instrument evidencing the deposit of a sum of money with the issuing bank that will be available on or after a stated date or period of time;

(C) A sale or loan of Federal funds irrespective of the purchaser or borrower;

(D) A loan, to the extent that it is directly or indirectly made to, guaranteed by, or insured by the United States, a possession or instrumentality thereof, or a State or political subdivision thereof; and

(E) A loan which is secured by a deposit in the lending financial institution or in a bank as defined in section 581 or a domestic branch of a foreign corporation which this section applies to the extent that the financial institution has control over withdrawal of such deposit.

(iii) *Definition of loan which is secured by a deposit.* For purposes of subdivision (ii)(E) of this subparagraph—

(A) A loan is considered secured if the loan is on the security of any instrument which makes the deposit specific security for the payment of the loan, provided that such instrument is of such a nature that in the event of default the

Reg. § 1.585-2(e)(3)

39,280 Rules of General Application to Banking Institutions

See p. 20,601 for regulations not amended to reflect law changes

deposit could be subjected to the satisfaction of the loan;

(B) A deposit includes a guarantee deposit in the form of a "holdback", pledged collateral that has been reduced to cash, and loan payments that are maintained in a separate account; and

(C) Control over the withdrawal of a deposit is evidenced by possession of a passbook, certificate of deposit, note, or other similar instrument the possession of which is normally required to permit withdrawal. The lending financial institution does not have control over withdrawal of the deposit if the deposit can be withdrawn without consent of the lending financial institution. Thus, the lending financial institution normally does not have control over the withdrawal of a deposit in an account merely because the borrower agrees to maintain a minimum, average, or compensating balance.

(4) *Predecessor.* For purposes of this section, the term "predecessor" means (i) any taxpayer which transferred more than 50 percent of the total amount of its assets to the taxpayer and is described in § 1.585-1, or (i) any predecessor of such predecessor.

(5) *Authorization years.* For purposes of this section, the term "authorization years" means the number of years, containing 12 complete months, between (i) the first day of the first full taxable year of the taxpayer for which it (or any predecessor) was authorized to do business as a financial institution described in § 1.585-1, and (ii) the taxable year.

(6) *Comparison years.* For purposes of this section, the term "comparison years" means those consecutive taxable years containing 12 complete months of a comparable bank, the last of which ends within 12 months immediately preceding the beginning of the first taxable year of the taxpayer, which are equal in number to six minus the number of authorization years of the taxpayer.

(7) *Comparable bank.* For purposes of this section, the term "comparable bank" means all the financial institutions described in § 1.585-1 located within the same Federal Reserve district.

(8) *Average loans outstanding.* For purposes of this section, the term "average loans outstanding" means the sum of the loans outstanding at the close of each taxable year of a period divided by the number of taxable years in such period.

(9) *Adjusted for recoveries of bad debts.* For purposes of this section, the term "adjusted for recoveries of bad debts" means any adjustment for the full amount recovered with respect to bad debts previously charged to the reserve during any of the applicable taxable years. [Reg. § 1.585-2.]

☐ [T.D. 7532, 1-18-78. Amended by T.D. 7835, 9-24-82 and T.D. 8513, 12-28-93.]

[Reg. § 1.585-3]

§ 1.585-3. **Special rules.**—(a) *Treatment of reserve.* For taxable years beginning after July 11, 1969, if a financial institution to which section 585 and § 1.585-1 apply establishes a reserve pursuant to section 585(a) (or, for taxable years beginning before January 1, 1987, section 166(c)), any bad debt in respect of a loan (whether or not such loan is an eligible loan) must be charged to the reserve for losses on loans provided for by § 1.585-1 for the taxable year in which the bad debt occurs. For such a year, any recovery of a bad debt previously charged to the reserve account in respect of a loan (whether or not such loan is an eligible loan) must be credited to such reserve in the taxable year of recovery regardless of whether such credit causes the reserve to exceed the permissible amount. If, as a result of net recoveries during the taxable year, the reserve balance exceeds the permissible amount, a taxpayer is not required to report the excess as taxable income. In such a case, the excess over the otherwise permissible amount in the reserve account precludes current reasonable additions to the reserve and may affect future reasonable additions. Recoveries of bad debts which were not charged to the reserve shall not be credited to such reserve, but shall be treated as taxable income subject to the provisions of section II.I No item other than a loan as defined in § 1.585-2(e)(2) shall be charged to the reserve for losses on loans.

(b) *Accounting for reserve.* A financial institution to which section 585 and § 1.585-1 apply which establishes a reserve pursuant to section 585(a) (or, for taxable years beginning before January 1, 1987, section 166(c)) shall establish and maintain a permanent record of such reserve. Copies of Federal income tax returns and amended returns with attached schedules satisfy the requirements of this paragraph provided that such returns are permanently maintained by the financial institution and the balance of the reserve for losses on loans established pursuant to section 585(a) (or former section 166(c)) can be readily reconciled with the reserve for losses on loans maintained by the financial institution for financial statement purposes. The requirements of this paragraph would also be satisfied if a financial institution establishes and maintains a permanent subsidiary ledger reflecting an account for the reserve for losses on loans established pursuant to section 585(a) (or former section 166(c))

Reg. § 1.585-3(a)

provided the balance in such account can be readily reconciled with the balance of the reserve for losses on loans for financial statement purposes maintained in any other ledger. The permanent records maintained pursuant to this section must reflect any changes in the amount initially added to the reserve for losses on loans and the amount finally determined by the taxpayer to be a reasonable addition to the reserve for losses on loans. [Reg. § 1.585-3.]

☐ [*T.D. 7532, 1-18-78. Amended by T.D. 8513, 12-28-93.*]

[Reg. § 1.585-4]

§ 1.585-4. Reorganizations and asset acquisitions.—(a) *In general.* In computing a reasonable addition to the reserve for losses on loans for the first taxable year ending after a transaction to which section 381(a) applies and for subsequent taxable years, the separate reserves for losses on loans, the amount of loans outstanding, the total bad debts sustained (adjusted for recoveries), and the amount of eligible loans outstanding of the distributor or transferor corporation and the acquiring corporation (or, in the case of a consolidation, the transferor corporations) shall be combined for all applicable years. Thus, for example, in applying § 1.585-2(c)(1)(i) for the first taxable year ending after the distribution or transfer, the total bad debts sustained during the 5 preceding taxable years are the sum of the bad debts sustained by the acquiring corporation for the 5 preceding taxable years and bad debts sustained by the distributor or transferor corporation for the taxable year ending on the date of distribution or transfer and the 4 preceding taxable years.

(b) *Base year and base year amounts of acquiring corporation*—(1) *Base year.* For transactions to which section 381(a) applies, the base year of the acquiring corporation for the first taxable year ending after the date of distribution or transfer shall be the last taxable year ending on or before the date of distribution or transfer. The balance of the reserve, the amount of loans outstanding, and the amount of eligible loans outstanding at the close of such base year shall be determined in accordance with the provisions of subparagraph (2)(i) of this paragraph. For taxable years subsequent to the first taxable year ending after the date of distribution or transfer, the base year of the acquiring corporation shall be the more recent of the base year provided by the first sentence of this subparagraph or the base year provided by § 1.585-2(e)(1). If § 1.585-2(e)(1) provides the more recent base year, the balance of the reserve for losses on loans, the amount of loans outstanding, and the amount of eligible loans outstanding shall be determined at the close of such base year without regard to this paragraph.

(2) *Base year amounts*—(i) *Method of determination.* The balance of the reserve for losses on loans, the amount of loans outstanding, and the amount of eligible loans outstanding at the close of the base year provided by the first sentence of subparagraph (1) of this paragraph shall be the total of such amounts of the distributor or transferor corporation and the acquiring corporation (or, in the case of a consolidation, the transferor corporations) at the close of what would have been their respective base years determined under § 1.585-2(e)(1) if the distribution or transfer to which section 381(a) applies had not occurred, except that the method (experience or percentage) used or adopted by the acquiring corporation to determine its reasonable addition to a reserve for losses on loans for the first taxable year ending after the date of the distribution or transfer shall be considered to be the method that the distributor or transferor corporation (or, in the case of a consolidation, that the transferor corporations) would have used or adopted for its first taxable year ending after the date of distribution or transfer if the distribution or transfer had not occurred.

(ii) *Examples.* The application of the rule provided by this subparagraph may be illustrated by the following examples:

Example (1). The X Corporation and the Y Corporation are commercial banks both of which have a calendar year as a taxable year. Both X and Y adopted the reserve method of accounting for bad debts prior to July 11, 1969. For the taxable years 1970 through 1973, X and Y determined their reasonable additions to a reserve for losses on loans as defined in § 1.585-2(e)(2) under the percentage method. On June 30, 1974, the X Bank is merged into the Y Bank; for its short taxable year ending on June 30, 1974, X determines its reasonable addition under the percentage method. If, for the taxable year ending on December 31, 1974 (the first taxable year ending after the date of distribution or transfer) Y determines its reasonable addition to a reserve for losses on loans under the percentage method, then at the close of the base year the reserve balance, the amount of outstanding loans, and the amount of eligible loans outstanding are the sum of X's and Y's respective amounts at the close of the taxable year ending December 31, 1969 (the base year of both X and Y determined under § 1.585-2(e)(1) as if the distribution or transfer had not taken place). If, instead of the above, Y adopts the experience method of determining its reasonable addition to a reserve for losses for the taxable year 1974, than at the close of the base

39,282 Rules of General Application to Banking Institutions
See p. 20,601 for regulations not amended to reflect law changes

year (1973) the reserve balances, the amount of loans outstanding, and the amount of eligible loans outstanding are the sum of X's respective amounts at the close of its short taxable year ending on June 30, 1974 (X's last taxable year before its (Y's) most recent adoption of the experience method) and of Y's respective amounts at the close of its taxable year 1973 (Y's last taxable year before its most recent adoption of the experience method).

Example (2). The M Corporation and the N Corporation are commercial banks. M has a fiscal year ending September 30, as its taxable year and N has a calendar year as its taxable year. Both M and N adopted the reserve method of accounting for bad debts prior to July 11, 1969. For the taxable years ending in 1970, 1971, and 1972, M determined its reasonable addition to a reserve for losses under the percentage method; for the taxable year ending in 1973 M adopted the experience method. For the taxable years 1970 through 1973 N determined its reasonable addition under the percentage method. M is merged into N on June 30, 1974, and for its short taxable year ending on June 30, 1974, M determines its reasonable addition under the experience method. If, for the taxable year ending on December 31, 1974 (the first taxable year ending after the date of distribution or transfer), N determines its reasonable addition to a reserve for losses under the percentage method, then at the close of the base year (1973) the reserve balance, the amount of loans outstanding, and the amount of eligible loans outstanding are the sum of M's respective amounts at the close of (a) if M had a reserve deficiency as of June 30, 1974, its short taxable year ending on June 30, 1974 (M's last taxable year before its (N's) most recent adoption of the percentage method) or (b) if M did not have a reserve deficiency, the taxable year ending on September 30, 1969, and N's respective amounts at the close of its taxable year 1969. If, instead of the above, N adopts the experience method for the taxable year 1974, then at the close of the base year the reserve balance, the amount of outstanding loans, and the amount of eligible loans outstanding are the sum of M's respective amounts at the close of its taxable year ending on September 30, 1972 (the last taxable year before M's most recent adoption of the experience method) and N's respective amounts at the close of the taxable year 1973 (the last taxable year ending before N's most recent adoption of the experience method). [Reg. § 1.585-4.]

☐ [T.D. 7532, 1-18-78.]

Reg. § 1.585-5(a)

[Reg. § 1.585-5]

§ 1.585-5. **Denial of bad debt reserves for large banks.**—(a) *General rule.* For taxable years beginning after December 31, 1986, a large bank (as defined in paragraph (b) of this section) may not deduct any amount under section 585 or any other section for an addition to a reserve for bad debts. However, for these years, except as provided in § 1.585-7, a large bank may deduct amounts allowed under section 166(a) for specific debts that become worthless in whole or in part. Any large bank that maintained a reserve for bad debts under section 585 for the taxable year immediately preceding its disqualification year (as defined in paragraph (d)(1) of this section) must follow the rules prescribed by § 1.585-6 or § 1.585-7 for changing from the reserve method of accounting for bad debts that is allowed by section 585, to the specific charge-off method of accounting for bad debts, in its disqualification year. However, except as may be provided otherwise in regulations prescribed under section 593, the rules prescribed by §§ 1.585-6 and 1.585-7 do not apply to a large bank that maintained a reserve for bad debts under section 593 for the taxable year immediately preceding its disqualification year.

(b) *Large bank*—(1) *General definition.* For purposes of this section, a large bank is any institution described in § 1.585-1(b)(1)(i) or (ii) if, for the taxable year (or for any preceding taxable year beginning after December 31, 1986)—

(i) The average total assets of the institution (determined under paragraph (c) of this section) exceed $500,000,000; or

(ii) The institution is a member of a parent-subsidiary controlled group (as defined in paragraph (d)(2) of this section) and the average total assets of the group exceed $500,000,000.

(2) *Large bank resulting from transfer by large bank*—(i) *In general.* If a corporation acquires the assets of a large bank (as defined in this paragraph (b)) in an acquisition to which paragraph (b)(2)(ii), (iii) or (iv) of this section applies, the acquiring corporation (the acquiror) is treated as a large bank for any taxable year ending after the date of the acquisition in which it is an institution described in § 1.585-1(b)(1)(i) or (ii).

(ii) *Transfer of significant portion of assets where control is retained.* This paragraph (b)(2)(ii) applies to any direct or indirect acquisition of a significant portion of a large bank's assets if, after the acquisition, the transferor large bank owns more than 50 percent (by vote or value) of the outstanding stock of the acquiror. For this purpose, stock of an acquiror is considered owned by a transferor bank if the stock is owned by any member of a parent-subsidiary controlled group (as defined in paragraph (d)(2) of this section) of which the bank is a member, by any related party within the meaning of section 267(b) or 707(b), or by any person that received the stock in a transaction to which section 355 applies.

(iii) *Transfer to which section 381 applies.* This paragraph (b)(2)(iii) applies to any acquisition to which section 381(a) applies if, immediately after the acquisition, the acquiror's principal method of accounting for bad debts (determined under § 1.381(c)(4)-1(c)(2)) with respect to its banking business is the specific charge-off method. In applying § 1.381(c)(4)-1(c)(2) for this purpose, the following rules apply: a transferor large bank is considered to use the specific charge-off method for all of its loans immediately before the acquisition; an acquiror is considered to use a reserve method for all of its loans immediately before the acquisition; and all banking businesses of the acquiror immediately after the acquisition are treated as one integrated business. See §§ 1.585-6(c)(3) and 1.585-7(d)(2) for rules on the treatment of assets acquired from large banks in section 381(a) transactions.

(iv) *Transfer of substantially all assets to related party.* This paragraph (b)(2)(iv) applies to any direct or indirect acquisition of substantially all of a large bank's assets if the transferor large bank and the acquiror are related parties before or after the acquisition and a principal purpose of the acquisition is to avoid treating the acquired assets as those of a large bank. A transferor bank and an acquiror are considered to be related parties for this purpose if they are members of the same parent-subsidiary controlled group (as defined in paragraph (d)(2) of this section) or related parties within the meaning of section 267(b) or 707(b).

(3) *Examples.* The following examples illustrate the principles of this paragraph (b):

Example 1. Bank M, a calendar year taxpayer, is an institution described in § 1.585-1(b)(1)(i). For its taxable year beginning on January 1, 1987, M has average total assets of $600 million. Since M's average total assets for 1987 exceed $500 million, M is a large bank for that year. Pursuant to § 1.585-5(d)(1), 1987 is M's disqualification year. If M maintained a bad debt reserve under section 585 for its immediately preceding taxable year (1986), M must change in 1987 to the specific charge-off method of accounting for bad debts, in accordance with § 1.585-6 or § 1.585-7.

Example 2. Assume the same facts as in Example 1. Also assume that in 1988 M disposes of a portion of its assets and, as a result, M's average total assets for taxable year 1988 fall to $400 million. M remains a large bank for taxable year 1988 and succeeding taxable years, since its average total assets for a preceding taxable year (1987) beginning after December 31, 1986, exceeded $500 million.

Example 3. Bank P, a calendar year taxpayer, is an institution described in § 1.585-1(b)(1)(i). P has average total assets of $300 million for its taxable year beginning on January 1, 1988. For the same year, P is a member of a parent-subsidiary controlled group (within the meaning of § 1.585-5(d)(2)) that has average total assets of $800 million. In February 1989, the group sells its stock in P to several individual investors. P is a large bank for taxable year 1988 because it is a member of a group described in § 1.585-5(b)(1)(ii) for that year. P also is a large bank for taxable year 1989 and succeeding taxable years because it was a member of a group described in § 1.585-5(b)(1)(ii) for a preceding taxable year (1988) beginning after December 31, 1986.

Example 4. Assume the same facts as in Example 3, except that P's stock is purchased by a corporation that is not a large bank under § 1.585-5(b). Also assume that the purchasing corporation elects under section 338 to treat the stock purchase as an asset acquisition. Under section 338, P is considered to have sold all of its assets on the purchase date and is treated as a new corporation that purchased these assets on the next day. Since P is treated as a new corporation, its prior membership in a group described in § 1.585-5(b)(1)(ii) does not cause it to be treated as a large bank for taxable years ending after the date of its sale by the group. However, P may be treated as a large bank because of new membership in such a group or pursuant to § 1.585-5(b)(1)(i) or (b)(2).

Example 5. Bank Q is a large bank, within the meaning of § 1.585-5(b)(1), for its taxable year beginning on January 1, 1988, and hence for all later years. On March 1, 1989, Q transfers $200 million of its $600 million of assets to Bank R, a newly created subsidiary, in a transaction to which section 351 applies; these assets are R's only assets. On the same day, Q then spins off R in a transaction to which section 355 applies. After these transactions, the shareholders of Q own more than 50 percent of R's outstanding stock. Although R's average total assets do not exceed $500 million, R becomes a large bank on March 1, 1989, pursuant to § 1.585-5(b)(2)(ii). These transactions do not affect Q's status as a large bank.

39,284   Rules of General Application to Banking Institutions
See p. 20,601 for regulations not amended to reflect law changes

Example 6. Bank S is a large bank, within the meaning of § 1.585-5(b)(1)(ii), for its taxable year beginning on January 1, 1987. As a result, S changes to the specific charge-off method of accounting for bad debts in that year. Bank T, which is not a large bank under § 1.585-5(b), uses the reserve method of accounting for bad debts. On June 30, 1988, T acquires substantially all of S's assets in a transaction to which section 381(a) applies. Immediately before the acquisition, S's banking business has total assets of $200 million, and T's has total assets of $250 million. To determine whether T is a large bank under § 1.585-5(b)(2)(iii) for taxable years ending after the acquisition, it is necessary to determine T's principal method of accounting for bad debts with respect to its banking business immediately after the acquisition. This determination requires an application of § 1.381(c)(4)-1(c)(2). For this purpose, T's original and acquired banking businesses are treated as an integrated business. Applying § 1.381(c)(4)-1(c)(2), it is determined that the business's principal method of accounting for bad debts immediately after the acquisition is the reserve method. Hence, the acquisition does not cause T to become a large bank under § 1.585-5(b)(2)(iii).

(c) *Average total assets*—(1) *In general.* For purposes of paragraph (b)(1) of this section, and except as otherwise provided in paragraph (c)(3)(ii) of this section, the average total assets of an institution or group for any taxable year are determined by—

(i) Computing, for each report date (as defined in paragraph (c)(2) of this section) within the taxable year, the amount of total assets (as defined in paragraph (c)(3) of this section) held by the institution or group as of the close of business on the report date;

(ii) Adding these amounts; and

(iii) Dividing the sum of these amounts by the number of report dates within the taxable year.

(2) *Report date*—(i) *Institutions*—(A) *In general.* A report date for an institution generally is the last day of the regular period for which the institution must report to its primary Federal regulatory agency. However, an institution that is required to report to its primary Federal regulatory agency more frequently than quarterly may choose the last day of the calendar quarter as its report date, and an institution that is required to report to its primary Federal regulatory agency less frequently than quarterly must choose the last day of the calendar quarter as its report date. If an institution does not have a Federal regulatory agency, its primary State regulatory agency is considered its primary Federal regulatory agency for purposes of this paragraph (c)(2)(i)(A). In the case of a short taxable year that does not otherwise include a report date, the first or last day of the taxable year is the institution's report date for the year.

(B) *Alternative report date.* In lieu of the report date prescribed by paragraph (c)(2)(i)(A) of this section, for any taxable year an institution may choose as its report date the last day of any regular interval in the taxable year that is more frequent than quarterly (such as bi-monthly, monthly, weekly, or daily).

(ii) *Groups.* If all members of a parent-subsidiary controlled group have the same taxable year, a report date for the group is the report date, determined under paragraph (c)(2)(i) of this section, for any one member of the group that is an institution described in § 1.585-1(b)(1)(i) or (ii). The same report date must be used in applying paragraph (b)(1)(ii) of this section to all members of the group for a taxable year. If all members of a parent-subsidiary controlled group do not have the same taxable year, a report date for the group must be determined under similar principles.

(iii) *Member of group for only part of taxable year.* If an institution is a member of a parent-subsidiary controlled group for only part of a taxable year, paragraph (b)(1)(ii) of this section is applied to the institution for that year on the basis of the group's average total assets for the portion of the year that the institution is a member of the group. Thus, only the group's report dates (as determined under paragraph (c)(2)(ii) of this section) that are included in that portion of the year are taken into account in determining the group's average total assets for purposes of applying paragraph (b)(1)(ii) of this section to the institution. If no report date of the group is included in that portion of the year, the first or last day of that portion of the year must be treated as the group's report date for purposes of this paragraph (c)(2)(iii).

(3) *Total assets*—(i) *All corporations.* The amount of total assets held by an institution or group is the amount of cash, plus the sum of the adjusted bases of all other assets, held by the institution or group. For this purpose, the adjusted basis of an asset generally is its basis for Federal income tax purposes, determined under sections 1012, 1016 and other applicable sections of the Internal Revenue Code. In determining the amount of total assets held by a group, any asset of a member of the group that is an interest in another member of the group is not to be counted.

Reg. § 1.585-5(c)(1)

(ii) *Foreign corporations.* In determining the amount of total assets held by a foreign corporation, all of the corporation's assets are taken into account, including those that are not effectively connected with the conduct of a banking business within the United States. In the case of a foreign corporation that is not engaged in a trade or business in the United States, the adjusted basis of an asset must be determined substantially in accordance with United States tax principles as provided in regulations under section 964. In the case of a foreign corporation that is engaged in a trade or business in the United States, the amount of its average total assets for a taxable year (within the meaning of paragraph (c)(1) of this section) is the amount of the corporation's average worldwide assets used for purposes of computing the interest expense deduction allowable under section 882 and § 1.882-5 for the taxable year.

(4) *Estimated adjusted tax bases*—(i) *In general.* The amount of the adjusted Federal income tax bases (tax bases) of assets held on a report date may be estimated, for purposes of applying paragraph (c)(3) of this section. This estimate must be based on the adjusted bases of the assets on that date as determined by reference to the asset holder's books and records maintained for financial reporting purposes (book bases). The estimate must reflect any change in the ratio between the asset holder's tax and book bases of assets that occurs during the taxable year, and the estimate must assume that this change occurs ratably. If an institution or group member estimates the tax bases of assets held on any report date during a taxable year, it must do so for all assets (other than cash) held on that report date, and it must do so for all other report dates during the year. However, the tax bases of assets may not be estimated for any report date that is the first or last day of the taxable year or that is determined under paragraph (c)(2)(i)(B) of this section.

(ii) *Formulas.* The estimated amount of the tax bases of assets held on any report date during a taxable year is based on the following variables: the total book bases of the assets on the report date (B); the asset holder's *tax/book ratio* as of the close of the preceding taxable year (R); and the result (whether positive or negative) obtained when R is subtracted from the asset holder's *tax/book ratio* as of the close of the current taxable year (Y). For purposes of determining R and Y, an asset holder's *tax/book ratio* is the ratio of the total tax bases of all of the holder's assets (other than cash), to the total book bases of those assets. If an asset holder's taxable year is the calendar year and its report date is the last day of the calendar quarter, its estimated tax bases of assets held on the first three report dates of the year are determined under the following formulas:

1st Report Date = B × (R + ¼Y)
2nd Report Date = B × (R + ½Y)
3rd Report Date = B × (R + ¾Y)

(5) *Examples.* The following examples illustrate the principles of this paragraph (c):

Example 1. Bank U is a fiscal year taxpayer, and its fiscal year ends on January 31. U reports to its primary Federal regulatory agency as of the last day of the calendar quarter. U does not choose under § 1.585-5(c)(2)(i)(B) a report date more frequent than quarterly. Thus, U's report dates under § 1.585-5(c)(2)(i)(A) are March 31, June 30, September 30, and December 31. For its taxable year beginning on February 1, 1987, U has total assets (within the meaning of § 1.585-5(c)(3)) of $480 million on March 31, $490 million on June 30, $510 million on September 30, and $540 million on December 31. Thus, pursuant to § 1.585-5(c)(1), U's average total assets for its taxable year beginning on February 1, 1987, are $505 million.

Example 2. Bank W is a calendar year taxpayer, and its report date (within the meaning of § 1.585-5(c)(2)(i)(A)) is the last day of the calendar quarter. Pursuant to § 1.585-5(c)(4), W chooses to estimate the tax bases of its assets for 1990. Therefore, W must estimate the tax bases of all of its assets (other than cash) for its first three report dates in 1990. Since W's fourth report date (December 31) is the last day of its taxable year, the tax bases of its assets may not be estimated for this date. The adjusted tax bases of all of W's assets (other than cash) are $450z on December 31, 1989, and $480z on December 31, 1990. The book bases of those assets are $500z on December 31, 1989; $520z on March 31, 1990; $540z on June 30, 1990; $560z on September 30, 1990; and $600z on December 31, 1990. Applying the formulas provided in § 1.585-5(c)(4)(ii), W's tax/book ratio as of the close of 1989(R), is 0.9 (450z/500z). W's tax/book ratio as of the close of 1990 is 0.8 (480z/600z). Thus, Y is −0.1. The estimated adjusted tax bases of all of W's assets (other than cash) on the first three report dates of 1990 are as follows:

1st = B × (R + ¼Y)
    = $520z × [0.9 + ¼(−0.1)]
    = $455z

2nd = B × (R + ½Y)
    = $540z × [0.9 + ½(−0.1)]
    = $459z

3rd = B × (R + ¾Y)
    = $560z × [0.9 + ¾(−0.1)]
    = $462z

Reg. § 1.585-5(c)(5)

39,286 Rules of General Application to Banking Institutions

See p. 20,601 for regulations not amended to reflect law changes

(d) *Definitions.* The following definitions apply for purposes of this section and §§ 1.585-6, 1.585-7 and 1.585-8:

(1) *Disqualification year.* A bank's disqualification year is its first taxable year beginning after December 31, 1986, for which the bank is a large bank within the meaning of paragraph (b) of this section.

(2) *Parent-subsidiary controlled group.* A parent-subsidiary controlled group includes all of the members of a controlled group of corporations described in section 1563(a)(1). The members of such a group are determined without regard to whether any member is an *excluded member* described in section 1563(b)(2), a foreign entity, or a commercial bank.

(3) *Example.* The following example illustrates the principles of this paragraph (d):

Example. Bank X is a large bank within the meaning of § 1.585-5(b)(1)(i). Bank Y is not a large bank under § 1.585-5(b), and it maintains a bad debt reserve under section 585. In 1988, X purchases all of the stock of Y. If the acquisition causes Y to become a member of a parent-subsidiary controlled group described in § 1.585-5(b)(1)(ii), Y is a large bank beginning in its first taxable year that ends after the date of the acquisition. Pursuant to § 1.585-5(d)(1), this year is Y's disqualification year. Y must change in this year to the specific charge-off method of accounting for bad debts, in accordance with § 1.585-6 or § 1.585-7. [Reg. § 1.585-5.]

☐ [T.D. 8513, 12-28-93.]

[Reg. § 1.585-6]

§ 1.585-6. **Recapture method of changing from the reserve method of section 585.**—(a) *General rule.* This section applies to any large bank (as defined in § 1.585-5(b)) that maintained a reserve for bad debts under section 585 for the taxable year immediately preceding its disqualification year (as defined in § 1.585-5(d)(1)) and that does not elect the cut-off method set forth in § 1.585-7. Except as otherwise provided in paragraphs (c) and (d) of this section, any bank to which this section applies must include in income the amount of its net section 481(a) adjustment (as defined in paragraph (b)(3) of this section) over the four-year period beginning with the bank's disqualification year. If a bank follows the rules prescribed by this section, its change to the specific charge-off method of accounting for bad debts in its disqualification year will be treated as a change in accounting method that is made with the consent of the Commissioner. Paragraph (b) of this section specifies the portion of the net section 481(a) adjustment to be included in income in each year of the recapture period; paragraph (c) of this section provides rules on the effect of disposing of loans; and paragraph (d) of this section provides rules on the suspension of recapture by financially troubled banks.

(b) *Four-year spread of net section 481(a) adjustment*—(1) *In general.* If a bank to which this section applies does not make the election allowed by paragraph (b)(2) of this section, the bank must include in income the following portions of its net section 481(a) adjustment in each year of the four-year recapture period: 10 percent in the bank's disqualification year; 20 percent in its first taxable year after its disqualification year; 30 percent in its second taxable year after its disqualification year; and 40 percent in its third taxable year after its disqualification year.

(2) *Election to include more than 10 percent in disqualification year.* A bank to which this section applies may elect to include in income, in its disqualification year, any percentage of its net section 481(a) adjustment that is larger than 10 percent. Any such election must be made at the time and in the manner prescribed by § 1.585-8. If a bank makes such an election, the bank must include in income the remainder, if any, of its net section 481(a) adjustment in the following portions: 2/9 of the remainder in the bank's first taxable year after its disqualification year; 1/3 of the remainder in its second taxable year after its disqualification year; and 4/9 of the remainder in its third taxable year after its disqualification year. For this purpose, the remainder of a bank's net section 481(a) adjustment is any portion of the adjustment that the bank does not elect to include in income in its disqualification year.

(3) *Net section 481(a) adjustment.* For purposes of this section, the amount of a bank's net section 481(a) adjustment is the amount of the bank's reserve for bad debts as of the close of the taxable year immediately preceding its disqualification year. Since the change from the reserve method of section 585 is initiated by the taxpayer, the amount of the bank's bad debt reserve for this purpose is not reduced by amounts attributable to taxable years beginning before 1954.

(4) *Examples.* The following examples illustrate the principles of this paragraph (b):

Example 1. Bank M is a large bank within the meaning of § 1.585-5(b). M's disqualification year is its taxable year beginning on January 1, 1989, and M maintained a bad debt reserve under section 585 for the preceding taxable year. Pursuant to § 1.585-5(a), M must change from the reserve method of accounting for bad debts to the

Reg. § 1.585-6(a)

specific charge-off method in its disqualification year. M does not elect the cut-off method set forth in § 1.585-7. Thus, M must follow the recapture method set forth in this § 1.585-6. M's net section 481(a) adjustment, as defined in § 1.585-6(b)(3), is $2 million. M does not make the election allowed by § 1.585-6(b)(2). Pursuant to § 1.585-6(b)(1), M must include the following amounts in income: $200,000 in taxable year 1989; $400,000 in 1990; $600,000 in 1991; and $800,000 in 1992.

Example 2. Assume the same facts as in *Example 1*, except that M elects under § 1.585-6(b)(2) to recapture 55 percent of its net section 481(a) adjustment in its disqualification year. Pursuant to § 1.585-6(b)(2), M must include the following amounts in income: $1,100,000 in taxable year 1989; $200,000 in 1990; $300,000 in 1991; and $400,000 in 1992.

(c) *Effect of disposing of loans*—(1) *In general.* Except as provided in paragraphs (c)(2) and (c)(3) of this section, if a bank to which this section applies sells or otherwise disposes of any of its outstanding loans on or after the first day of its disqualification year, the disposition does not affect the bank's obligation under this section to include in income the amount of its net section 481(a) adjustment, and the disposition does not affect the amount of this adjustment.

(2) *Cessation of banking business*—(i) *In general.* If a bank to which this section applies ceases to engage in the business of banking before it is otherwise required to include in income the full amount of its net section 481(a) adjustment, the bank must include in income the remaining amount of the adjustment in the taxable year in which it ceases to engage in the business of banking. For this purpose, and except as provided in paragraph (c)(2)(ii) of this section, whether a bank ceases to engage in the business of banking is determined under the principles of § 1.446-1(e)(3)(ii) and its administrative procedures.

(ii) *Transition rule.* A bank that ceases to engage in the business of banking as the result of a transaction to which section 381(a) applies is not treated as ceasing to engage in the business of banking if, on or before March 29, 1994, either the transaction occurs or the bank enters into a binding written agreement to carry out the transaction.

(3) *Certain section 381 transactions.* This paragraph (c)(3) applies if a bank to which this section applies transfers outstanding loans to another corporation on or after the first day of the bank's disqualification year (and before it has included in income the full amount of its net section 481(a) adjustment) in a transaction to which section 381(a) applies, and under paragraph (c)(2)(i) or (ii) of this section the transferor bank is not treated as ceasing to engage in the business of banking as a result of the transaction. If this paragraph (c)(3) applies, the acquiring corporation (the acquiror) steps into the shoes of the transferor with respect to using the recapture method prescribed by this section and assumes all of the transferor's rights and obligations under paragraph (b) of this section. The unrecaptured balance of the transferor's net section 481(a) adjustment carries over in the transaction to the acquiror, and the acquiror must complete the four-year recapture procedure begun by the transferor. In applying this procedure, the transferor's taxable year that ends on or includes the date of the acquisition and the acquiror's first taxable year ending after the date of the acquisition represent two consecutive taxable years within the four-year recapture period.

(4) *Examples.* The following examples illustrate the principles of this paragraph (c):

Example 1. Bank P is a bank to which this § 1.585-6 applies. P's disqualification year is its taxable year beginning on January 1, 1989, and P recaptures 10 percent of its net section 481(a) adjustment in that year pursuant to § 1.585-6(b)(1). In July 1990 P disposes of a portion of its loan portfolio in a transaction to which section 381(a) does not apply, and P continues to engage in the business of banking. Pursuant to § 1.585-6(c)(1), the disposition does not affect P's obligation under § 1.585-6(b)(1) to recapture the remainder of its net section 481(a) adjustment in 1990, 1991 and 1992. Nor does the disposition affect the amount of the adjustment.

Example 2. Assume the same facts as in *Example 1*, except that P ceases to engage in the business of banking in 1990, as determined under the principles of § 1.446-1(e)(3)(ii) and its administrative procedures. Pursuant to § 1.585-6(c)(2)(i), in 1990 P must include in income the remaining 90 percent of its net section 481(a) adjustment.

Example 3. Assume the same facts as in *Example 1*, except that P's 1990 disposition of loans is a transaction to which section 381(a) applies, P ceases to engage in the business of banking as a result of the transaction, and P's taxable year ends on the date of the transaction. Thus, in the transaction, P transfers substantially all of its loans to an acquiring corporation (Q). Q is a calendar year taxpayer. Because the transaction occurred before March 29, 1994, the transition rule of § 1.585-6(c)(2)(ii) applies, and P is not treated as ceasing to engage in the business of

Reg. § 1.585-6(c)(4)

banking. Pursuant to § 1.585-6(c)(3), Q steps into P's shoes with respect to using the recapture method prescribed by § 1.585-6. The unrecaptured balance of P's net section 481(a) adjustment carries over to Q in the section 381(a) transaction, and Q must complete the four-year recapture procedure begun by P. Pursuant to §§ 1.585-6(b) and 1.585-6(c)(3), P includes 20 percent of its net section 481(a) adjustment in income in its taxable year ending on the date of the section 381(a) transaction, and Q includes 30 percent of the adjustment in income in 1990 and 40 percent in 1991.

Example 4. Assume the same facts as in Example 3. Assume also that Q becomes a large bank under § 1.585-5(b) as a result of the transaction and maintained a bad debt reserve immediately before the transaction. Q must change to the specific charge-off method for all of its loans in the first taxable year that it is a large bank. Thus, Q not only completes the recapture procedure begun by P but also follows the rules prescribed by § 1.585-6 or § 1.585-7 with respect to its own reserve.

Example 5. Assume the same facts as in Example 3. Assume also that Q is not a large bank after the transaction and properly establishes a bad debt reserve for the loans it receives in the transaction. This establishment of the reserve results in a new negative section 481(a) adjustment. Thus, Q not only completes the recapture procedure begun by P but also takes into account the new negative adjustment as required under section 381.

(d) *Suspension of recapture by financially troubled banks*—(1) *In general.* Except as provided in paragraph (d)(2) of this section, a bank that is financially troubled (within the meaning of paragraph (d)(3) of this section) for any taxable year must not include any amount in income under paragraphs (a) and (b) of this section for that taxable year and must disregard that taxable year in applying paragraphs (a) and (b) of this section to other taxable years. See paragraph (d)(4) of this section for rules on determining estimated tax payments of financially troubled banks, and see paragraph (d)(5) of this section for examples illustrating this paragraph (d).

(2) *Election to recapture.* A bank that is financially troubled (within the meaning of paragraph (d)(3) of this section) for its disqualification year may elect to include in income, in one taxable year, any percentage of its net section 481(a) adjustment that is greater than 10 percent. This election may be made for the bank's disqualification year, for the first taxable year after the disqualification year in which the bank is not financially troubled (within the meaning of paragraph (d)(3) of this section), or for any intervening taxable year. Any such election must be made at the time and in the manner prescribed by § 1.585-8. A bank that makes this election must include an amount in income under paragraphs (a) and (b) of this section in the year for which the election is made (election year) and must not disregard this year in applying paragraphs (a) and (b) of this section to other taxable years. Such a bank must follow the rules of paragraph (b)(2) of this section in applying paragraph (b) of this section to later taxable years, treating the election year as the disqualification year for purposes of applying paragraph (b)(2) of this section. However, if the bank is financially troubled for any year after its election year, the bank must not include any amount in income under paragraphs (a) and (b) of this section for the later year and must disregard the later year in applying paragraphs (a) and (b) of this section to other taxable years.

(3) *Definition of financially troubled*—(i) *In general.* For purposes of this section, a bank is considered financially troubled for any taxable year if the bank's nonperforming loan percentage for that year exceeds 75 percent. For this purpose, a bank's nonperforming loan percentage is the percentage determined by dividing the sum of the outstanding balances of the bank's nonperforming loans (as defined in paragraph (d)(3)(iii) of this section) as of the close of each quarter of the taxable year, by the sum of the amounts of the bank's equity (as defined in paragraph (d)(3)(iv) of this section) as of the close of each such quarter. The quarters for a short taxable year of at least 3 months are the same as those of the bank's annual accounting period, except that quarters ending before or after the short year are disregarded. If a taxable year consists of less than 3 months, the first or last day of the taxable year is treated as the last day of its only quarter. In lieu of determining its nonperforming loan percentage on the basis of loans and equity as of the close of each quarter of the taxable year, a bank may, for all years, determine this percentage on the basis of loans and equity as of the close of each report date (as defined in § 1.585-5(c)(2), without regard to § 1.585-5(c)(2)(i)(B)). In the case of a bank that is a foreign corporation, all nonperforming loans and equity of the bank are taken into account, including loans and equity that are not effectively connected with the conduct of a banking business within the United States.

(ii) *Parent-subsidiary controlled groups*—(A) *In general.* If a bank is a member of a parent-subsidiary controlled group (as defined in § 1.585-5(d)(2)) for the taxable year, the nonperforming loans and the equity of all members of the bank's financial group (as determined under paragraph (d)(3)(ii)(B) of this section) are treated as the nonperforming loans and the equity of the bank for purposes of paragraph (d)(3)(i) of this section. However, any equity interest that a member of a bank's financial group holds in another member of this group is not to be counted in determining equity. Similarly, any loan that a member of a bank's financial group makes to another member of the group is not to be counted in determining nonperforming loans. All banks that are members of the same parent-subsidiary controlled group must (for all taxable years that they are members of this group) determine their nonperforming loan percentage on the basis of the close of each quarter of the taxable year, or all must (for all such taxable years) determine this percentage on the basis of the close of each report date (as determined under § 1.585-5(c)(2)(ii), applied without regard to § 1.585-5(c)(2)(i)(B)).

(B) *Financial group*—(*1*) *In general.* All banks that are members of the same parent-subsidiary controlled group must (for all taxable years that they are members of this group) determine their financial group under paragraph (d)(3)(ii)(B)(*2*) of this section, or all must (for all such taxable years) determine their financial group under paragraph (d)(3)(ii)(B)(*3*) of this section.

(*2*) *Financial institution members of parent-subsidiary controlled group.* A bank's financial group, determined under this paragraph (d)(3)(ii)(B)(*2*), consists of all financial institutions within the meaning of section 265(b)(5) (and comparable foreign financial institutions) that are members of the parent-subsidiary controlled group of which the bank is a member.

(*3*) *All members of parent-subsidiary controlled group.* A bank's financial group, determined under this paragraph (d)(3)(ii)(B)(*3*), consists of all members of the parent-subsidiary controlled group of which the bank is a member.

(iii) *Nonperforming loan*—(A) *In general.* For purposes of this section, a nonperforming loan is any loan (as defined in paragraph (d)(3)(iii)(B) of this section) that is considered to be nonperforming by the holder's primary Federal regulatory agency. Nonperforming loans include the following types of loans as defined by the Federal Financial Institutions Examination Council: loans that are past due 90 days or more and still accruing; loans that are in nonaccrual status; and loans that are restructured troubled debt. A loan is not considered to be nonperforming merely because it is past due, if it is past due less than 90 days. The outstanding balances of nonperforming loans are determined on the basis of amounts that are required to be reported to the holder's primary Federal regulatory agency. For purposes of this paragraph (d)(3)(iii)(A), a holder that does not have a Federal regulatory agency is treated as Federally regulated under the standards prescribed by the Federal Financial Institutions Examination Council.

(B) *Loan.* For purposes of paragraph (d)(3)(iii)(A) of this section, a loan is any extension of credit that is defined and treated as a loan under the standards prescribed by the Federal Financial Institutions Examination Council. (Accordingly, a troubled debt restructuring that is in substance a foreclosure or repossession is not considered a loan.) In addition, a debt evidenced by a security issued by a foreign government is treated as a loan if the security is issued as an integral part of a restructuring of one or more troubled loans to the foreign government (or an agency or instrumentality thereof). Similarly, a deposit with the central bank of a foreign country is treated as a loan if the deposit is made under a deposit facility agreement that is entered into as an integral part of a restructuring of one or more troubled loans to the foreign country's government (or an agency or instrumentality thereof).

(iv) *Equity.* For purposes of this section, the equity of a bank or other financial institution is its equity (i.e., assets minus liabilities) as required to be reported to the institution's primary Federal regulatory agency (or, if the institution does not have a Federal regulatory agency, as required under the standards prescribed by the Federal Financial Institutions Examination Council). The balance in a reserve for bad debts is not treated as equity.

(4) *Estimated tax payments of financially troubled banks.* For purposes of applying section 6655(e)(2)(A)(i) with respect to any installment of estimated tax, a bank that is financially troubled as of the due date of the installment is treated as if no amount will be included in income under paragraphs (a) and (b) of this section for the taxable year. For this purpose, a bank is considered financially troubled as of the due date of an installment of estimated tax only if its nonperforming loan percentage (computed under paragraph (d)(3) of this section) would exceed 75 percent for a short taxable year ending on that date. For purposes of computing this nonperforming loan percentage, the ending of such a short taxable year would not cause the last day of that year to be treated as the last day of a quarter of the taxable year.

(5) *Examples.* The following examples illustrate the principles of this paragraph (d):

Reg. § 1.585-6(d)(5)

Example 1. Bank R is a bank to which this § 1.585-6 applies. R's disqualification year is its taxable year beginning on January 1, 1987. R is not financially troubled (within the meaning of § 1.585-6(d)(3)) for taxable year 1987 or for any taxable year after 1989, but it is financially troubled for taxable years 1988 and 1989. Since R is not financially troubled for its disqualification year, R must include an amount in income under § 1.585-6(a) and (b) for that year (taxable year 1987). R may make the election allowed by § 1.585-6(b)(2) for that year. Since R is financially troubled for taxable years 1988 and 1989, pursuant to § 1.585-6(d)(1) R does not include any amount in income under § 1.585-6(a) and (b) for these years, and it treats taxable years 1990, 1991 and 1992 as the first, second and third taxable years after its disqualification year for purposes of applying § 1.585-6(a) and (b).

Example 2. Assume the same facts as in *Example 1*, except that R is financially troubled for taxable year 1987 (its disqualification year). R may make the election allowed by § 1.585-6(b)(2) for 1987 (the disqualification year) and for 1990 (the first year after the disqualification year in which R is not financially troubled), or for 1988 or 1989 (the intervening years). R elects to include 60 percent of its net section 481(a) adjustment in income in 1987. Thus, the remainder of the adjustment, for purposes of applying the rules of § 1.585-6(b)(2), is 40 percent. R must include in income 2/9 of the remainder in 1990, 1/3 of the remainder in 1991, and 4/9 of the remainder in 1992.

Example 3. Bank S, which is not a member of a parent-subsidiary controlled group, is a bank to which this § 1.585-6 applies. S's disqualification year is its taxable year beginning on January 1, 1987. S determines its nonperforming loan percentage under § 1.585-6(d)(3) on a quarterly basis. S is not financially troubled for taxable year 1987 and includes 10 percent of its net section 481(a) adjustment in income in that year. S's outstanding balance of nonperforming loans (as defined in § 1.585-6(d)(3)(iii)) is $80 million on March 31, 1988; $68 million on June 30, 1988; and $59 million on September 30, 1988. The amount of S's equity (as defined in § 1.585-6(d)(3)(iv)) is $100 million on each of these three dates. Thus, S's nonperforming loan percentage, computed under § 1.585-6(d)(3), would be 80 percent (80/100) for a short taxable year ending on April 15 or June 15, 74 percent [(80+68) ÷ 200] for a short taxable year ending on September 15, and 69 percent [(80 + 68 + 59) ÷ 300] for a short taxable year ending on December 15. Since S's nonperforming loan percentage for a short taxable year ending on April 15 or June 15 would exceed 75 percent, pursuant to § 1.585-6(d)(4) S is considered financially troubled as of these dates. Thus, S is treated as if no amount will be included in income under § 1.585-6(a) and (b) for the year for purposes of applying section 6655(e)(2)(A)(i) with respect to the installments of estimated tax that are due on April 15, 1988, and June 15, 1988. However, since S's nonperforming loan percentage for a short taxable year ending on September 15 or December 15 would not exceed 75 percent, S is not considered financially troubled as of these dates. Thus, S is treated as if 20 percent of its net section 481(a) adjustment will be included in income under § 1.585-6(a) and (b) for the year for purposes of applying section 6655(e)(2)(A)(i) with respect to the installments of estimated tax that are due on September 15, 1988, and December 15, 1988. [Reg. § 1.585-6.]

☐ [T.D. 8513, 12-28-93.]

[Reg. § 1.585-7]

§ 1.585-7. **Elective cut-off method of changing from the reserve method of section 585.**— (a) *General rule.* Any large bank (as defined in § 1.585-5(b)) that maintained a reserve for bad debts under section 585 for the taxable year immediately preceding its disqualification year (as defined in § 1.585-5(d)(1)) may elect to use the cut-off method set forth in this section. Any such election must be made at the time and in the manner prescribed by § 1.585-8. If a bank makes this election, the bank must maintain its bad debt reserve for its pre-disqualification loans, as prescribed in paragraph (b) of this section, and the bank must include in income any excess balance in this reserve, as required by paragraph (c) of this section. The bank may not deduct, for its disqualification year or any subsequent taxable year, any amount allowed under section 166(a) for pre-disqualification loans (as defined in paragraph (b)(2) of this section) that become worthless in whole or in part, except as allowed by paragraph (b)(1) of this section. However, except as provided in paragraph (d)(3) of this section, the bank may deduct, for its disqualification year or any subsequent taxable year, amounts allowed under section 166(a) for loans that the bank originates or acquires on or after the first day of its disqualification year and that become worthless in whole or in part. If a bank makes the election allowed by this paragraph (a), its change to the specific charge-off method of accounting for bad debts in its disqualification year does not give rise to a section 481(a) adjustment.

(b) *Maintaining reserve for pre-disqualification loans*—(1) *In general.* A bank that makes the election allowed by paragraph (a) of this section

Reg. § 1.585-7(a)

must maintain its bad debt reserve for its pre-disqualification loans (as defined in paragraph (b)(2) of this section). Except as provided in paragraph (d)(3) of this section, the bank must charge against the reserve the amount of any losses resulting from these loans (including losses resulting from the sale or other disposition of these loans), and the bank must add to the reserve the amount of recoveries with respect to these loans. In general, the reserve must be maintained in the manner provided by former section 166(c) of the Internal Revenue Code and the regulations thereunder. However, after the balance in the reserve is reduced to zero, the bank is to account for any losses and recoveries with respect to outstanding pre-disqualification loans under the specific charge-off method of accounting for bad debts, as if the bank always had accounted for these loans under this method.

(2) *Definition of pre-disqualification loans.* For purposes of this section, a pre-disqualification loan of a bank is any loan that the bank held on the last day of its taxable year immediately preceding its disqualification year (as defined in § 1.585-5(d)(1)). If the amount of a pre-disqualification loan is increased during or after the disqualification year, the amount of the increase is not treated as a pre-disqualification loan.

(c) *Amount to be included in income when reserve balance exceeds loan balance.* If, as of the close of any taxable year, the balance in a bank's reserve that is maintained under paragraph (b) of this section exceeds the balance of the bank's outstanding pre-disqualification loans, the bank must include in income the amount of the excess for the taxable year. The balance in the reserve is then reduced by the amount of this excess. See paragraph (d) of this section for rules on the application of this paragraph (c) when a bank disposes of loans.

(d) *Effect of disposing of loans*—(1) *In general.* Except as provided in paragraphs (d)(2) and (d)(3) of this section, if a bank that makes the election allowed by paragraph (a) of this section sells or otherwise disposes of any of its outstanding pre-disqualification loans, the bank is to reduce the balance of its outstanding pre-disqualification loans by the amount of the loans disposed of, for purposes of applying paragraph (c) of this section.

(2) *Section 381 transactions.* If a bank that makes the election allowed by paragraph (a) of this section transfers outstanding pre-disqualification loans to another corporation in a transaction to which section 381(a) applies, the acquiring corporation (the acquiror) must follow the rules of paragraph (d)(2)(i) or (ii) of this section.

(i) *Acquiror completes cut-off method of change.* Except as provided in paragraph (d)(2)(ii) of this section, the acquiror steps into the shoes of the transferor in the section 381(a) transaction with respect to using the cut-off method of change. Thus, the transferor's bad debt reserve immediately before the section 381(a) transaction carries over to the acquiror, and the acquiror must complete the cut-off method begun by the transferor. For purposes of completing the transferor's cut-off method, the acquiror's balance of outstanding pre-disqualification loans immediately after the section 381(a) transaction is the balance of these loans that it receives in the transaction, and the acquiror assumes all of the transferor's rights and obligations under this section.

(ii) *Acquiror uses reserve method.* If the acquiror is not a large bank (within the meaning of § 1.585-5(b)) immediately after the section 381(a) transaction and uses a reserve method of accounting for bad debts attributable to the pre-disqualification loans (and any other loans) received in the transaction, the acquiror does not step into the shoes of the transferor with respect to using the cut-off method of change. The transferor's bad debt reserve immediately before the section 381(a) transaction carries over to the acquiror, but the acquiror does not continue the cut-off method begun by the transferor. If the six-year moving average amount (as defined in § 1.585-2(c)(1)(ii)) for all of the loans received in the transaction exceeds the balance of the reserve that carries over to the acquiror, the acquiror increases this balance by the amount of the excess. Any such increase in the reserve results in a negative section 481(a) adjustment that is taken into account as required under section 381.

(3) *Dispositions intended to change the status of pre-disqualification loans.* This paragraph (d)(3) applies if a bank that makes the election allowed by paragraph (a) of this section sells, exchanges, or otherwise disposes of a significant amount of its pre-disqualification loans (as defined in paragraph (b)(2) of this section) and a principal purpose of the transaction is to avoid the provisions of this section by increasing the amount of loans for which deductions are allowable under the specific charge-off method. If this paragraph (d)(3) applies, the District Director may disregard the disposition for purposes of paragraphs (b)(1) and (d)(1) of this section or treat the replacement loans as pre-disqualification loans. If loans are so treated as pre-disqualification loans, no deductions are allowable under the specific charge-off method for the loans, except as provided in paragraph (b)(1) of this section, and the disposition that causes the loans to

be so treated may be disregarded for purposes of paragraphs (b)(1) and (d)(1) of this section. If a bank sells pre-disqualification loans and uses the proceeds of the sale to originate new loans, this paragraph (d)(3) does not apply to the transaction.

(e) *Examples.* The following examples illustrate the principles of this section:

Example 1. Bank M is a bank that properly elects to use the cut-off method set forth in this § 1.585-7. M's disqualification year is its taxable year beginning on January 1, 1987. On December 31, 1986, M had outstanding loans of $700 million (pre-disqualification loans), and the balance in its bad debt reserve was $10 million. M must maintain its reserve for its pre-disqualification loans in accordance with § 1.585-7(b), and it may not deduct any addition to this reserve for taxable year 1987 or any later year. For these years, M may deduct amounts allowed under section 166(a) for loans that it originates or acquires after December 31, 1986, and that become worthless in whole or in part.

Example 2. Assume the same facts as in *Example 1.* Also assume that in 1987 M collects $150 million of its pre-disqualification loans, M determines that $2 million of its pre-disqualification loans are worthless, and M recovers $1 million of pre-disqualification loans that it had previously charged against the reserve as worthless. On December 31, 1987, the balance in M's bad debt reserve is $9 million ($10 million − $2 million + $1 million), and the balance of its outstanding pre-disqualification loans is $548 million ($700 million − $150 million − $2 million).

Example 3. Assume the same facts as in *Examples 1* and *2.* Also assume that on December 31, 1990, the balance in M's bad debt reserve is $5 million and the balance of its outstanding pre-disqualification loans is $25 million. In 1991 M collects $21 million of its outstanding pre-disqualification loans and determines that $1 million of its outstanding pre-disqualification loans are worthless. Thus, on December 31, 1991, the balance in M's bad debt reserve is $4 million ($5 million − $1 million), and the balance of its outstanding pre-disqualification loans is $3 million ($25 million − $21 million − $1 million). Accordingly, M must include $1 million ($4 million − $3 million) in income in taxable year 1991, pursuant to § 1.585-7(c). On January 1, 1992, the balance in M's reserve is $3 million ($4 million − $1 million).

Example 4. Assume the same facts as in *Examples 1* through *3.* Also assume that in 1992 M transfers substantially all of its assets to another corporation (N) in a transaction to which section 381(a) applies, and N is treated as a large bank under § 1.585-5(b)(2) for taxable years ending after the date of the transaction. Pursuant to § 1.585-7(d)(2)(i), N steps into M's shoes with respect to using the cut-off method. M's bad debt reserve immediately before the section 381(a) transaction carries over to N, and N must complete the cut-off procedure begun by M. For this purpose, N's balance of outstanding pre-disqualification loans immediately after the section 381(a) transaction is the balance of these loans that it receives from M.

Example 5. Assume the same facts as in *Examples 1* through *4,* except that N is not treated as a large bank after the section 381(a) transaction. Also assume that N uses the reserve method of section 585 and plans to use this method for all of the loans it acquires from M (including loans that were not pre-disqualification loans). Pursuant to § 1.585-7(d)(2)(ii), M's bad debt reserve immediately before the section 381(a) transaction carries over to N in the transaction; however, N does not continue the cut-off procedure begun by M and does not treat any loan as a pre-disqualification loan. If the six-year moving average amount (as defined in § 1.585-2(c)(1)(ii)) for all of N's newly acquired loans exceeds the balance of the reserve that carries over to N, N increases this balance by the amount of the excess. Any such increase in the reserve results in a negative section 481(a) adjustment that is taken into account as required under section 381. [Reg. § 1.585-7.]

☐ [*T.D.* 8513, 12-28-93.]

[Reg. § 1.585-8]

§ 1.585-8. **Rules for making and revoking elections under §§ 1.585-6 and 1.585-7.**—(a) *Time of making elections*—(1) *In general.* Any election under § 1.585-6(b)(2), § 1.585-6(d)(2) or § 1.585-7(a) must be made on or before the later of—

(i) February 28, 1994; or

(ii) The due date (taking extensions into account) of the electing bank's original tax return for its disqualification year (as defined in § 1.585-5(d)(1)) or, for elections under § 1.585-6(d)(2), the year for which the election is made.

(2) *No extension of time for payment.* Payments of tax due must be made in accordance with chapter 62 of the Internal Revenue Code. However, if an election under § 1.585-6(b)(2), § 1.585-6(d)(2) or § 1.585-7(a) is made or revoked on or before February 28, 1994 and the making or revoking of the election results in an underpayment of estimated tax (within the meaning of section 6655(a)) with respect to an installment of

estimated tax due on or before the date the election was so made or revoked, no addition to tax will be imposed under section 6655(a) with respect to the amount of the underpayment attributable to the making or revoking of the election.

(b) *Manner of making elections*—(1) *In general.* Except as provided in paragraph (b)(2) of this section, an electing bank must make any election under § 1.585-6(b)(2), § 1.585-6(d)(2) or § 1.585-7(a) by attaching a statement to its tax return (or amended return) for its disqualification year or, for elections under § 1.585-6(d)(2), the year for which the election is made. This statement must contain the following information:

(i) The name, address and taxpayer identification number of the electing bank;

(ii) The nature of the election being made (i.e., whether the election is to include in income more than 10 percent of the bank's net section 481(a) adjustment under § 1.585-6(b)(2) or (d)(2) or to use the cut-off method under § 1.585-7); and

(iii) If the election is under § 1.585-6(b)(2) or (d)(2), the percentage being elected.

(2) *Certain tax returns filed before* December 29, 1993. A bank is deemed to have made an election under § 1.585-6(b)(2) or (d)(2) if the bank evidences its intent to make an election under section 585(c)(3)(A)(iii)(I) or section 585(c)(3)(B)(ii) for its disqualification year (or, for elections under § 1.585-6(d)(2), the election year), by designating a specific recapture amount on its tax return or amended return for that year (or attaching a statement in accordance with § 301.9100-7T(a)(3)(i) of this chapter), and the return is filed before December 29, 1993. A bank is deemed to have made an election under § 1.585-7(a) if the bank evidences its intent to make an election under section 585(c)(4) for its disqualification year by attaching a statement in accordance with § 301.9100-7T(a)(3)(i) of this chapter to its tax return or amended return for that year, and the return is filed before December 29, 1993.

(c) *Revocation of elections*—(1) *On or before final date for making election.* An election under § 1.585-6(b)(2), § 1.585-6(d)(2) or § 1.585-7(a) may be revoked without the consent of the Commissioner on or before the final date prescribed by paragraph (a)(1) of this section for making the election. To do so, the bank that made the election must file an amended tax return for its disqualification year (or, for elections under § 1.585-6(d)(2), the year for which the election was made) and attach a statement that—

(i) Includes the bank's name, address and taxpayer identification number;

(ii) Identifies and withdraws the previous election; and

(iii) If the bank is making a new election under § 1.585-6(b)(2), § 1.585-6(d)(2) or § 1.585-7(a), contains the information described in paragraphs (b)(1)(ii) and (b)(1)(iii) of this section.

(2) *After final date for making election.* An election under § 1.585-6(b)(2), § 1.585-6(d)(2) or § 1.585-7(a) may be revoked only with the consent of the Commissioner after the final date prescribed by paragraph (a)(1) of this section for making the election. The Commissioner will grant this consent only in extraordinary circumstances.

(d) *Elections by banks that are members of parent-subsidiary controlled groups.* In the case of a bank that is a member of a parent-subsidiary controlled group (as defined in § 1.585-5(d)(2)), any election under § 1.585-6(b)(2), § 1.585-6(d)(2) or § 1.585-7(a) with respect to the bank is to be made separately by the bank. An election made by one member of such a group is not binding on any other member of the group.

(e) *Elections made or revoked by amended return on or before* February 28, 1994. This paragraph (e) applies to any election that a bank seeks to make under paragraph (b) of this section, or revoke under paragraph (c) of this section, by means of an amended return that is filed on or before February 28, 1994. To make or revoke an election to which this paragraph (e) applies, a bank must file (before expiration of each applicable period of limitations under section 6501) this amended return and amended returns for all taxable years after the taxable year for which the election is made or revoked by amended return, to any extent necessary to report the bank's tax liability in a manner consistent with the making or revoking of the election by amended return. [Reg. § 1.585-8.]

☐ [*T.D.* 8513, 12-28-93.]

[Reg. § 1.586-1]

§ 1.586-1. **Reserve for losses on loans of small business investment companies, etc.**—(a) *General rule.* As an alternative to a deduction from gross income under section 166(a) for specific debts which become worthless in whole or in part, a taxpayer which is a financial institution to which section 586 and this section apply is allowed a deduction under section 166(c) for a reasonable addition to a reserve for bad debts provided such financial insitution has adopted or adopts the reserve method of treating bad debts in accordance with paragraph (b) of § 1.166-1. In the case of such a taxpayer, the amount of the reasonable addition to such reserve for a taxable year beginning after July 11, 1969, shall be an amount determined by the taxpayer which does not exceed the amount computed under § 1.586-2. A financial institution to which section 586 and this section apply which adopts the reserve method is not entitled to charge-off any bad debts pursuant to section 166(a) with respect to a loan (as defined in § 1.586-2(c)(2)). Except as provided by § 1.586-2, regarding the manner of computation of the addition to the reserve for bad debts, the reserve for bad debts of a financial institution to which this section applies shall be maintained in the same manner as is provided by section 166(c) and the regulations thereunder with respect to reserves for bad debts. Except as provided by this section, no deduction is allowable for an addition to a reserve for bad debts of a financial institution to which section 586 and this section apply. For rules relating to deduction with respect to debts which are not loans (as defined in § 1.586-2(c)(2)), see section 166(a) and the regulations thereunder.

(b) *Application of section.* Section 586 and this section shall apply only to the following financial institutions—

(1) Any small business investment company operating under the Small Business Investment Act of 1958 as amended and supplemented (72 Stat. 689), and

(2) Any business development corporation, which for purposes of this section, means a corporation which was created by or pursuant to an act of a State legislature for purposes of promoting, maintaining, and assisting the economy and industry within such State on a regional or state-wide basis by making loans which would generally not be made by banks (as defined in section 581 and the regulations thereunder) within such region or State in the ordinary course of their business (except on the basis of a partial participation), and which is operated primarily for such purposes. [Reg. § 1.586-1.]

☐ [T.D. 7444, 12-7-76.]

[Reg. § 1.586-2]

§ 1.586-2. **Addition to reserve.**—(a) *General rule.* Except as provided by paragraph (b) of this section, the amount computed under this section is the amount necessary to increase the balance of the reserve for bad debts (as of the close of the taxable year) to the greater of—

(1) The amount which bears the same ratio to loans outstanding at the close of the taxable year as (i) the total bad debts sustained during the taxable year and the 5 preceding taxable years (or, with the approval of the Commissioner, a shorter period), adjusted for recoveries of bad debts during such period, bears to (ii) the sum of the loans outstanding at the close of such 6 or fewer taxable years, or

(2) The lower of—

(i) The balance of the reserve as of the close of the base year, or

(ii) If the amount of loans outstanding at the close of the taxable year is less than the amount of loans outstanding at the close of the base year, the amount which bears the same ratio to loans outstanding at the close of the taxable year as the balance of the reserve as of the close of the base year bears to the amount of loans outstanding at the close of the base year.

For purposes of subparagraph (2) of this paragraph, the term "base year" means the last taxable year beginning on or before July 11, 1969. For purposes of applying this paragraph, a period shorter than the 6 years generally would be appropriate only where there is a change in the type of a substantial portion of the loans outstanding such that the risk of loss is substantially increased. For example, if the major portion of a business development corporation's portfolio of loans changes from agricultural loans to industrial loans which results in a substantial increase in the risk of loss, a period shorter than the 6 years may be appropriate. If approval is granted to use a shorter period, the experience for those taxable years which are excluded shall not be used for any subsequent year. A request for approval to exclude the experience of a prior taxable year shall not be considered unless it is sent to the Commissioner at least 30 days before the close of the current taxable year. The request shall include a statement of the reasons such experience should be excluded.

(b) *New financial institutions*—(1) *Small business investment companies.* In the case of a new financial institution which is a small business investment company to which section 586 applies, the amount computed under this section is the greater of the amount computed under paragraph (a) of this section or the amount necessary to increase the balance of the reserve for bad debts as of the close of the taxable year to the amount which bears the same ratio to loans outstanding at the close of the taxable year as—

(i) The total bad debts (as determined by the Commissioner) sustained by all such small business investment companies during the 12-month period ending on March 31 that ends with or within the taxpayer's previous taxable year, and during the five 12-month periods ending on March 31 that precede such 12-month period, adjusted for recoveries of bad debts during such periods (as determined by the Commissioner), bears to

Reg. § 1.586-2(a)(1)

Mutual Savings Banks, Etc.

(ii) The sum of the loans outstanding (as determined by the Commissioner) by all such small business investment companies at the close of each of such six 12-month periods ending on March 31.

(2) *Business development corporations.* In the case of a new financial institution which is a business development corporation to which section 586 applies, the amount computed under this section is the greater of the amount computed under paragraph (a) of this section or the amount necessary to increase the balance of the reserve for bad debts as of the close of the taxable year to the amount which bears the same ratio to loans outstanding at the close of the taxable year as—

(i) The total bad debts (as determined by the Commissioner) sustained by all such business development corporations during the calendar year ending with or within the taxpayer's previous taxable year and during the 5 calendar years preceding such calendar year, adjusted for recoveries of bad debts during such period (as determined by the Commissioner), bears to

(ii) The sum of the loans outstanding (as determined by the Commissioner) by all such business development corporations at the close of each of such 6 calendar years.

(c) *Definitions.* For purposes of this section—

(1) *New financial institution.* A financial institution is a new financial institution for any taxable year beginning less than 10 years after the day on which it (or any predecessor) was authorized to do business as a financial institution described in the applicable subparagraph of § 1.586-1(b). For this purpose, the term "predecessor" means (i) any taxpayer which transferred more than 50 percent of the total amount of its assets to the taxpayer and is described in the same subparagraph of § 1.586-1(b) which describes the taxpayer, or (ii) any predecessor of such predecessor.

(2) *Loan.* (i) The term "loan" means debt, as the term "debt" is used in section 166 and the regulations thereunder.

(ii) The term "loan" does not include the following items:

(A) Discount or interest receivable reflected in the face amount of an outstanding loan, which discount or interest has not been included in gross income;

(B) A debt evidenced by a security (as defined in section 165(g)(2)(C) and the regulations thereunder); and

(C) Any loan which is entered into or acquired for the primary purpose of enlarging the otherwise available bad debt deduction. [Reg. § 1.586-2.]

☐ [T.D. 7444, 12-6-76.]

Mutual Savings Banks, Etc.
[Reg. § 1.591-1]

§ 1.591-1. **Deduction for dividends paid on deposits.**—(a) *In general.* (1) In the case of a taxpayer described in paragraph (c)(1) or (2) of this section, whichever is applicable, there are allowed as deductions from gross income amounts which during the taxable year are paid to, or credited to the accounts of, depositors or holders of accounts as dividends or interest on their deposits or withdrawable accounts, if such amounts paid or credited are withdrawable on demand subject only to customary notice of intention to withdraw.

(2) The deduction provided in section 591 is applicable to the taxable year in which amounts credited as dividends or interest become withdrawable by the depositor or holder of an account subject only to customary notice of intention to withdraw. Thus, amounts which, as of the last day of the taxable year, are credited as dividends or interest, but which are not withdrawable by depositors or holders of accounts until the following business day, are deductible under section 591 in the year subsequent to the taxable year in which they were so credited. A deduction under this section will not be denied by reason of the fact that the amounts credited as dividends or interest, otherwise deductible under section 591, are subject to the terms of a pledge agreement between the taxpayer and the depositor or holder of an account. In the case of a domestic building and loan association having nonwithdrawable capital stock represented by shares, no deduction is allowable under this section for amounts paid or credited as dividends on such shares. In the case of a taxable year ending after December 31, 1962, for special rules governing the treatment of dividends or interest paid or credited for periods representing more than 12 months, see section 461(e).

(b) *Serial associations, bonus plans, etc.* If a taxpayer described in paragraph (c)(1) or (2) of this section, whichever is applicable, operates in whole or in part as a serial association, maintains a bonus plan, or issues shares, or accepts deposits, subject to fines, penalties, forfeitures, or other withdrawal fees, it may deduct under section 591 the total amount credited as dividends or interest upon such shares or deposits, credited to a bonus account for such shares or deposits, or allocated to a series of shares for the taxable year, notwithstanding that as a customary condition of withdrawal:

(1) Amounts invested in, and earnings credited to, series shares must be withdrawn in multiples of even shares, or

(2) Such taxpayer has the right, pursuant to bylaw, contract, or otherwise, to retain or recover a portion of the total amount invested in, or credited as earnings upon, such shares or deposits, such bonus account, or series of shares, as a fine, penalty, forfeiture, or other withdrawal fee.

In any taxable year in which the right referred to in subparagraph (2) of this paragraph is exercised, there is includible in the gross income of such taxpayer for such taxable year amounts retained or recovered by the taxpayer pursuant to the exercise of such right. If the provisions of paragraph (a) of § 1.163-4 (relating to deductions for original issue discount) apply to deposits made with respect to a certificate of deposit, time deposit, bonus plan or other deposit arrangement, the provisions of this paragraph shall not apply.

(c) *Effective date.* The provisions of paragraphs (a) and (b) of this section shall apply to—

(1) Dividends or interest paid or credited after October 16, 1962, by any taxpayer which (at the time of such payment or credit) qualifies as (i) a mutual savings bank not having capital stock represented by shares, (ii) a domestic building and loan association (as defined in section 7701(a)(19)), (iii) a cooperative bank (as defined in section 7701(a)(32)), or (iv) any other savings institution chartered and supervised as a savings and loan or similar association under Federal or State law; and

(2) Dividends paid or credited before October 17, 1962, by any taxpayer which (at the time of such payment or credit) qualifies as (i) a mutual savings bank not having capital stock represented by shares, (ii) a cooperative bank without capital stock organized and operated for mutual purposes and without profit, or (iii) a domestic building and loan association (as defined in section 7701(a)(19) before amendment by section 6(c) of the Revenue Act of 1962 (76 Stat. 982)). [Reg. § 1.591-1.]

☐ [*T.D.* 6188, 7-5-56. *Amended by T.D.* 6728, 5-4-64, *and by T.D.* 7154, 12-27-71.]

[Reg. § 1.593-1]

§ 1.593-1. **Additions to reserve for bad debts.**—(a) *In general.* A mutual savings bank not having capital stock represented by shares, a domestic building and loan association, and a cooperative bank without capital stock organized and operated for mutual purposes and without profit may, as an alternative to a deduction from gross income under section 166(a) for specific debts which become worthless in whole or in part, deduct amounts credited to a reserve for bad debts in the manner and under the circumstances prescribed in this section and § 1.593-2. In the case of such an institution, the selection of either of the alternative methods for treating bad debts may be made by the taxpayer in the return for its first taxable year beginning after December 31, 1951. The method selected shall be subject to the approval of the Commissioner upon examination of the return. If the method selected is approved, it must be followed in returns for subsequent years, unless permission is granted by the Commissioner to change to another method. Application for permission to change the method of treating bad debts shall be made at least 30 days prior to the close of the taxable year for which the change is to be effective.

(b) *Addition to reserve.* Except as otherwise provided in § 1.593-2, the reasonable addition to a reserve for bad debts shall be any amount determined by the taxpayer which does not exceed the lesser of—

(1) The amount of its taxable income for the taxable year, computed without regard to section 593 and without regard to any section providing for a deduction the amount of which is dependent upon the amount of taxable income (such as section 170, relating to charitable, etc., contributions and gifts), or

(2) The amount by which 12 percent of the total deposits or withdrawable accounts of its depositors at the close of such year exceeds the sum of its surplus, undivided profits, and reserves at the beginning of the taxable year.

(c) *Adjustments to reserve.* Bad debt losses sustained during the taxable year shall be charged against the bad debt reserve. Recoveries of debts charged against the bad debt reserve during a prior taxable year in which the institution was subject to tax under chapter 1 of the Internal Revenue Code of 1954 or under chapter 1 of the Internal Revenue Code of 1939 shall be credited to the bad debt reserve. The establishment of such reserve and all adjustments made thereto must be reflected on the regular books of account of the institution at the close of the taxable year, or as soon as practicable thereafter. Minimum amounts credited in compliance with Federal or State statutes, regulations, or supervisory orders to reserve or similar accounts, or additional amounts credited to such reserve or similar accounts and permissive under such statutes, regulations, or orders, against which charges may be made for the purpose of absorbing losses sustained by an institution, will be deemed to have been credited to the bad debt reserve.

(d) *Definitions.* When used in this section and in § 1.593-2:

(1) *Institution.* The term "institution" means either a mutual savings bank not having capital stock represented by shares, a domestic building and loan association as defined in section 7701(a)(19), or a cooperative bank without capital stock organized and operated for mutual purposes and without profit.

(2) *Surplus, undivided profits, and reserves.* (i) The phrase "surplus, undivided profits, and reserves" means the amount by which the total assets of an institution exceed the amount of the total liabilities of such an institution.

(ii) For this purpose the term "total assets" means the sum of money, plus the aggregate of the adjusted basis of the property other than money, held by an institution. Such adjusted basis for any asset is its adjusted basis for determining gain upon sale or exchange for Federal income tax purposes. (See sections 1011 through 1022, and the regulations thereunder. For special rules with respect to adjustments to basis for prior taxable years during which the institution was exempt from tax, see section 1016(a)(3) and the regulations thereunder.) The determination of the total assets of any taxpayer shall conform to the method of accounting employed by such taxpayer in determining taxable income and to the rules applicable in determining its earnings and profits.

(iii) The term "total liabilities" means all liabilities of the taxpayer, which are fixed and determined, absolute and not contingent, and includes those items which constitute liabilities in the sense of debts or obligations. The total deposits or withdrawable accounts, as defined in subparagraph (3) of this paragraph, shall be considered a liability. In the case of a building and loan association having permanent nonwithdrawable capital stock represented by shares, the paid-in amount of such stock shall also be considered a liability. Reserves for contingencies and other reserves, however, which are mere appropriations of surplus, are not liabilities.

(3) *Total deposits or withdrawable accounts.* The phrase "total deposits or withdrawable accounts" means the aggregate of (i) amounts placed with an institution for deposit or investment and (ii) earnings outstanding on the books of account of the institution at the close of the taxable year which have been credited as dividends upon such accounts prior to the close of the taxable year, except that such term, in the case of a building and loan association, does not include permanent nonwithdrawable capital stock represented by shares, or earnings credited thereon.

(e) *Examples.* The provisions of this section may be illustrated by the following examples:

Example (1). (i) Institution X, which keeps its books on the basis of the calendar year, has surplus, reserves, and undivided profits of $800,000 as of January 1, 1955, and total deposits or withdrawable accounts of $10,000,000 as of December 31, 1955. During 1955 the institution credits $30,000, as required by a Federal agency, to a Federal insurance reserve for the sole purpose of absorbing losses. Likewise, it credits $25,000, as permitted by State statute, to another reserve fund for the purpose of absorbing losses. In 1955 Institution X charges $5,000 against its bad debt reserve for losses sustained during the taxable year.

(ii) The taxable income of Institution X for the taxable year 1955, computed without regard to section 593 and without regard to any section providing for a deduction the amount of which is dependent upon the amount of taxable income, is $200,000.

(iii) Upon the basis of the facts as stated in subdivision (i) of this example, the amount by which 12 percent of the total deposits or withdrawable accounts of Institution X at the close of taxable year 1955 exceeds the sum of such institution's surplus, undivided profits, and reserves at the beginning of the taxable year is $400,000 (12% of $10,000,000, minus $800,000).

(iv) Institution X, therefore, may deduct, for the taxable year 1955, as an addition to a reserve for bad debts, any amount it may determine that does not exceed the lesser of the amounts determined in subdivision (ii) or (iii) of this example. That amount is $200,000 (as determined in subdivision (ii) of this example). Since under paragraph (c) of this section, the $30,000 credited to the reserve as required by the Federal agency and the $25,000 credited to the reserve as permitted by the State statute are regarded as amounts credited to a reserve for bad debts account, Institution X can credit an additional $145,000 ($200,000 minus $55,000) to a general reserve for bad debts account at any time during the taxable year.

(v) The loss of $5,000 charged to the bad debt reserve during the taxable year does not affect the amount of the addition to the bad debt reserve provided for in paragraph (b) of this section. It is of significance only in determining the surplus, undivided profits and reserves of Institution X as of January 1, 1956.

Example (2). The taxable income of Institution Y for the taxable year 1955, computed without

Reg. § 1.593-1(e)

regard to the deduction under section 593 and without regard to any section providing for a deduction the amount of which is dependent upon the amount of taxable income, is determined to be $250,000. The amount by which 12 percent of the total deposits or withdrawable accounts of Institution Y at the close of the taxable year exceeds the sum of such institution's surplus, undivided profits, and reserves at the beginning of the taxable year is $500,000. Institution Y credits $250,000 to its bad debt reserve in 1955. In 1957, it is determined that the correct taxable income of Institution Y for 1955, computed without regard to any deduction under section 593 and without regard to any section providing for a deduction the amount of which is dependent upon the amount of taxable income, is $275,000 and not $250,000. Assuming that Institution Y credits the additional $25,000 to its bad debt reserve, $275,000 is allowable as a deduction from gross income for such institution for the taxable year 1955. [Reg. § 1.593-1.]

☐ [T.D. 6188, 7-5-56.]

[Reg. § 1.593-2]

§ 1.593-2. **Additions to reserve for bad debts where surplus, reserves, and undivided profits equal or exceed 12 percent of deposits or withdrawable accounts.**—Where 12 percent of the total deposits or withdrawable accounts of an institution at the close of the taxable year is equal to or less than the sum of such institution's surplus, undivided profits, and reserves at the beginning of the taxable year, a reasonable addition to the reserve for bad debts as determined under the general provisions of section 166(c) may be allowable as a deduction from gross income. In making such determination, there shall be taken into account (a) surplus or bad debts reserves existing at the close of December 31, 1951 (i.e., the amount of surplus, undivided profits, and reserves accumulated prior to January 1, 1952, and in existence at the close of December 31, 1951), and (b) changes in the surplus, undivided profits, and reserves of the institution from December 31, 1951, until the beginning of the taxable year. A deduction for an addition to the reserve for bad debts pursuant to this section will be authorized only in those cases where the institution proves to the satisfaction of the Commissioner that the bad debt experience of the institution warrants an addition to the reserve for bad debts in excess of that provided in paragraph (b) of § 1.593-1. For definitions, see paragraph (d) of § 1.593-1. [Reg. § 1.593-2].

☐ [T.D. 6188, 7-5-56.]

[Reg. § 1.593-3]

§ 1.593-3. **Taxable years affected.**—Sections 1.593-1 and 1.593-2 apply only to taxable years beginning after December 31, 1953, and ending after August 16, 1954, but before January 1, 1963, and all references to sections of the Code are to the Internal Revenue Code of 1954 before amendment by the Revenue Act of 1962. Sections 1.593-4 through 1.593-11 apply only to taxable years ending after December 31, 1962, and all references to sections of the Code are to the Internal Revenue Code of 1954 after amendment by the Revenue Act of 1962. [Reg. § 1.593-3.]

☐ [T.D. 6728, 5-4-64.]

[Reg. § 1.593-4]

§ 1.593-4. **Organizations to which section 593 applies.**—The provisions of section 593 and §§ 1.593-5 through 1.593-11 (except subsection (f) of section 593 and § 1.593-10) apply to any mutual savings bank not having capital stock represented by shares, any domestic building and loan association, and any cooperative bank without capital stock organized and operated for mutual purposes and without profit. The term "thrift institution", as used in this section and §§ 1.593-5 through 1.593-11, refers to any such financial institution. For definition of the terms "domestic building and loan association" and "cooperative bank", see paragraphs (19) and (32), respectively, of section 7701(a). [Reg. § 1.593-4.]

☐ [T.D. 6728, 5-17-78.]

[Reg. § 1.593-5]

§ 1.593-5. **Addition to reserves for bad debts.**—(a) *Amount of addition.* As an alternative to a deduction from gross income under section 166(a) for specific debts which become worthless in whole or in part, a thrift institution is allowed a deduction under section 166(c) for a reasonable addition to a reserve for bad debts. In the case of a thrift institution, the amount of the reasonable addition to such reserve for a taxable year may not exceed:

(1) For taxable years beginning after July 11, 1969, the sum of (i) the amount determined to be the reasonable addition to the reserve for losses on nonqualifying loans, determined in the same manner as is provided with respect to additions to the reserve for losses on qualifying real property loans under paragraph (d) of § 1.593-6A (relating to the experience method), and (ii) the amount determined under § 1.593-6A to be the reasonable addition to the reserve for losses on qualifying real property loans, or

(2) For taxable years beginning before July 12, 1969, the sum of (i) the amount determined

under § 1.166-4 to be the reasonable addition to the reserve for losses on nonqualifying loans, and (ii) the amount determined under § 1.593-6 to be the reasonable addition to the reserve for losses on qualifying real property loans.

(b) *Crediting to reserves required*—(1) *In general.* The amounts referred to in paragraph (a)(1) and (2) of this section must be credited, respectively, to the reserve for losses on nonqualifying loans and to the reserve for losses on qualifying real property loans by the close of the taxable year, or as soon as practicable thereafter. For rules with respect to accounting for such reserves, see paragraph (a)(2) of § 1.593-7.

(2) *Subsequent adjustments.* If an adjustment with respect to the income tax return for a taxable year is made, and if such adjustment (whether initiated by the taxpayer or the Commissioner) has the effect of permitting an increase, or requiring a reduction, in the amount claimed on such return as an addition to the reserve for losses on nonqualifying loans or to the reserve for losses on qualifying real property loans, then the amount initially credited to such reserve for such year pursuant to subparagraph (1) of this paragraph may have to be increased or decreased, as the case may be, to the extent necessary to reflect such adjustment.

(c) *Transition year.* For rules governing the computation of taxable income in the case of a taxable year beginning in 1962 and ending in 1963, see § 1.593-9. [Reg. § 1.593-5.]

☐ [T.D. 6728, 5-4-64. Amended by T.D. 7549, 5-17-78.]

[Reg. § 1.593-6]

§ 1.593-6. Pre-1970 addition to reserve for losses on qualifying real property loans.—(a) *In general.* For purposes of paragraph (a)(2)(ii) of § 1.593-5, the amount of the addition to the reserve for losses on qualifying real property loans for any taxable year beginning before July 12, 1969, is the amount which the taxpayer determines to constitute a reasonable addition to such reserve for such year. However, the amount so determined for such year—

(1) Cannot exceed the largest of the amounts computed under one of the three methods described in paragraph (b), (c), or (d) of this section (relating, respectively, to the percentage of taxable income method, the percentage of real property loans method, and the experience method),

(2) Cannot exceed the maximum permissible addition described in paragraph (e) of this section (if applicable), and

(3) Shall be determined without regard to any amount charged for any taxable year against the reserve for losses on qualifying real property loans pursuant to § 1.593-10 (relating to certain distributions to shareholders by a domestic building and loan association).

For each taxable year the taxpayer must include in its income tax return for such year a computation of the addition under this section. The use of a particular method in the return for a taxable year is not a binding election by the taxpayer to apply such method either for such taxable year or for subsequent taxable years. Thus, in the case of a subsequent adjustment described in paragraph (b)(2) of § 1.593-5 which has the effect of permitting an increase, or requiring a reduction, in the amount claimed in the return for a taxable year as an addition to the reserve for losses on qualifying real property loans, the amount of such addition may be recomputed under whichever method the taxpayer selects for the purposes of such recomputation, irrespective of the method initially applied for such taxable year. However, a taxpayer may not subsequently reduce the amount claimed in the return for a taxable year for the purpose of obtaining a larger deduction in a later year.

(b) *Percentage of taxable income method*—(1) *In general.* The amount determined under the percentage of taxable income method for any taxable year is an amount equal to 60 percent of the taxable income for such year, minus the amount determined under § 1.166-4 as a reasonable addition for such year to the reserve for losses on nonqualifying loans. However, the amount determined under such method shall not exceed the amount necessary to increase the balance (as of the close of the taxable year) of the reserve for losses on qualifying real property loans to an amount equal to 6 percent of such loans outstanding at such time.

(2) *Taxable income defined.* For purposes of this paragraph, taxable income shall be computed—

(i) By excluding from gross income any amount included therein by reason of the application of § 1.593-10 (relating to certain distributions to shareholders by a domestic building and loan association);

(ii) Without regard to any deduction allowable under section 166(c) for an addition to a reserve for bad debts;

(iii) Without regard to any section providing for a deduction the amount of which is dependent upon the amount of taxable income (such as section 170, relating to charitable, etc., contributions and gifts), other than section 243, 244, and 245 (relating to deductions for dividends received); and

(iv) Without regard to any net operating loss carryback to such year under section 172.

In computing the deductions under sections 243, 244, and 245, section 246(b) (relating to limitation on aggregate amount of deduction) shall not apply. For purposes of subdivision (iii) of this subparagraph, a net operating loss deduction under section 172 is not a deduction the amount of which is dependent upon the amount of taxable income.

(c) *Percentage of real property loans method.—* (1) *General rule.* The amount determined under the percentage of real property loans method for any taxable year is the amount necessary to increase the balance (as of the close of such year) of the reserve for losses on qualifying real property loans to—

(i) An amount equal to 3 percent of such loans outstanding at such time, plus

(ii) In the case of a taxpayer described in subparagraph (2) of this paragraph, an amount equal to—

(a) The lesser of 2 percent of such loans outstanding at such time, or $80,000, reduced (but not below zero) by

(b) The balance as of the close of such year, if any, of such taxpayer's supplemental reserve for losses on loans.

(2) *Certain new companies.* (i) Subparagraph (1)(ii) of this paragraph applies only in the case of a taxpayer which is a new company, and which does not have capital stock with respect to which distributions of property (as defined in section 317(a)) are not allowable as a deduction under section 591.

(ii) For purposes of this subparagraph, a taxpayer is a new company for any taxable year only if such year begins not more than 10 calendar years after the first day on which such taxpayer, or any predecessor of such taxpayer, was authorized by Federal or State law to do business as (a) a mutual savings bank not having capital stock represented by shares, (b) a domestic building and loan association, (c) a cooperative bank without capital stock organized and operated for mutual purposes and without profit, or (d) any other savings institution chartered and supervised as a savings and loan or similar association under Federal or State law.

(iii) As used in subdivision (ii) of this subparagraph, the term "calendar year" has the meaning assigned to such term in section 441 (relating to the period for computation of taxable income); and the term "predecessor" means any organization which transferred more than 50 percent of the total amount of its assets to the taxpayer, and which, prior to the time of such transfer, was (a) authorized by Federal or State law to do business as a mutual savings bank not having capital stock represented by shares, a domestic building and loan association, or a cooperative bank without capital stock organized and operated for mutual purposes and without profit, or (b) any other savings institution chartered and supervised as a savings and loan or similar association under Federal or State law. The term "predecessor" also means any predecessor of such predecessor.

(d) *Experience method.* The amount determined under the experience method for any taxable year is the amount determined under § 1.166-4 to be a reasonable addition for such year to the reserve for losses on qualifying real property loans.

(e) *Maximum permissible addition where percentage of taxable income method or percentage of real property loans method is applied.—*(1) *12 percent of deposits limitation.* If, for the taxable year, the taxpayer uses either the percentage of taxable income method described in paragraph (b) of this section or the percentage of real property loans method described in paragraph (c) of this section, then (unless subparagraph (2) of this paragraph applies) the maximum permissible addition for such year is equal to the lesser of—

(i) The amount determined under such paragraph (b) or (c), or

(ii) An amount which, when added to the amount determined under § 1.166-4 as an addition for such year to the reserve for losses on nonqualifying loans, equals the amount by which 12 percent of the total deposits or withdrawable accounts of depositors of the taxpayer at the close of such year exceeds the sum of the taxpayer's surplus, undivided profits, and reserves at the beginning of such year (taking into account any portion thereof which is attributable to the period before the first taxable year beginning after December 31, 1951).

For definition of the terms "surplus, undivided profits, and reserves" and "total deposits or withdrawable accounts", see paragraph (f) of this section.

(2) *Special rule where a domestic building and loan association or cooperative bank exceeds certain assets limitations.* If, for the taxable year, the taxpayer uses either the percentage of taxable income method described in paragraph (b) of this section or the percentage of real property loans method described in paragraph (c) of this section, and if for such year such taxpayer qualifies as a domestic building and loan association under the first sentence of paragraph (19) of section 7701(a)

Reg. § 1.593-6(c)(1)

Mutual Savings Banks, Etc.

39,301

See p. 20,601 for regulations not amended to reflect law changes

(or as a cooperative bank under paragraph (32) thereof) solely by reason of the application of the second sentence of such paragraph (19) (that is, solely by reason of the fact that for such year more than 36 percent, but not more than 41 percent, of the amount of the total assets of such association or bank consists of assets other than assets described in section 7701(a)(19)(D)(ii), then the maximum permissible addition for such year is equal to the amount determined under subparagraph (1) of this paragraph, reduced in accordance with the following table:

If the percentage of the taxpayer's assets which are not assets described in section 7701 (a) (19) (D) (ii) exceeds—	but does not exceed—	the reduction shall be the following proportion of the amount determined under such subparagraph (1)—
36 percent	37 percent	1/12
37 percent	38 percent	1/6
38 percent	39 percent	1/4
39 percent	40 percent	1/3
40 percent	41 percent	5/12

(f) *Definitions.* For purposes of this section—

(1) *Surplus, undivided profits, and reserves.* The term "surplus, undivided profits, and reserves" means the amount by which the total assets of the taxpayer exceed its total liabilities. The determination of such total assets and total liabilities shall conform to the method of accounting employed by the taxpayer in determining taxable income and to the rules applicable in determining its earnings and profits. Total deposits or withdrawable accounts (as defined in subparagraph (3) of this paragraph but determined as of the beginning of the taxable year) shall be considered a liability. In the case of a domestic building and loan association having permanent nonwithdrawable capital stock represented by shares, the paid-in amount of such stock shall also be considered a liability. However, reserves for contingencies and other reserves which are mere appropriations of surplus are not liabilities for purposes of this section.

(2) *Total assets.* The term "total assets" means the sum of money (including time or demand deposits with, or withdrawable accounts in, any financial institution), plus the aggregate of the adjusted basis (determined under § 1.1011-1) of the property other than money held by the taxpayer. For special rules with respect to adjustments to basis in the case of property acquired by the taxpayer in a transaction described in section 595(a), see section 595.

(3) *Total deposits or withdrawable accounts.* The term "total deposits or withdrawable accounts" means the total of the amounts placed with the taxpayer for deposit or investment. Such term also includes earnings outstanding on the books of account of the taxpayer at the close of the taxable year which have been credited as dividends or interest upon such deposits or withdrawable accounts prior to the close of such taxable year, and which are withdrawable on demand subject only to customary notice of intention to withdraw. In the case of a domestic building and loan association, however, such phrase does not include permanent nonwithdrawable capital stock represented by shares, or earnings credited thereon.

(g) *Examples.* The provisions of this section may be illustrated by the following examples:

Example (1)—(i) *Facts.* X is a domestic building and loan association which was organized in 1947 and which makes its returns on the basis of the calendar year and the reserve method of accounting for bad debts. X's accounts contain the following entries:

Account	Balance as of Jan. 1, 1965	Dec. 31, 1965
Total deposits or withdrawable accounts	$1,000,000	$1,200,000
Nonqualifying loans	50,000	60,000
Qualifying real property loans	900,000	940,000
Reserve for losses on nonqualifying loans	200	160*
Reserve for losses on qualifying real property loans	24,000	21,000*
Supplemental reserve for losses on loans	60,800	60,800
Surplus, undivided profits, and other reserves	15,000	18,040

* Computed before any addition for 1965 under section 166(c).

Reg. § 1.593-6(g)

X's taxable income for 1965 (before any deductible addition to a reserve for bad debts and without regard to charitable contributions of $200) is $20,000, computed as follows:

Interest and other income	$19,940
Dividends received from Y Corporation, a domestic corporation subject to taxation under chapter 1 of the Code	400
	$20,340
Deduction for 85 percent of dividends received computed without regard to the limitation of section 246(b)	340
Taxable income	$20,000

It is assumed that under § 1.166-4 X's addition for 1965 to its reserve for losses on nonqualifying loans is $80.

(ii) *Computation of addition to reserve for losses on qualifying real property loans*—(a) *In general*. X determines that the reasonable addition for 1965 to its reserve for losses on qualifying real property loans is $11,920. Such amount, computed under the percentage of taxable income method, is the largest of the amounts determined under (b), (c) and (d) of this subdivision, and does not exceed the 12 percent of deposits limitation computed under (e) of this subdivision.

(b) *Percentage of taxable income method.* The amount determined under the percentage of taxable income method is $11,920, that is, 60 percent of the taxable income for 1965, or $12,000 (60 percent of $20,000), minus $80, the addition for such year to the reserve for losses on nonqualifying loans. This amount is not subject to reduction under the 6 percent of qualifying real property loans limitation described in paragraph (b)(1) of this section since the addition of $11,920 to the $21,000 balance of the reserve for losses on qualifying real property loans at the close of 1965 will not increase such balance to an amount in excess of $56,400, that is, 6 percent of such loans of $940,000 outstanding at such time.

(c) *Percentage of real property loans method.* Since X is not a new company within the meaning of paragraph (c)(2) of this section, the amount determined under the percentage of real property loans method is $7,200, that is, the amount necessary to increase the balance of the reserve for losses on qualifying real property loans at the close of 1965 from $21,000 to an amount equal to 3 percent of such loans outstanding at such time, or $28,200 (3 percent of $940,000).

(d) *Experience method.* The amount determined under the experience method is zero since it is assumed that the $21,000 balance of the reserve for losses on qualifying real property loans at the close of 1965 before any addition for such year exceeds the maximum amount to which such reserve could be increased under such method.

(e) *12 percent of deposits limitation.* The amount determined under the 12 percent of deposits limitation is $43,920, that is, $44,000 (the excess of 12 percent of $1,200,000 of deposits at the close of 1965, or $144,000, over the $100,000 of surplus, undivided profits, and reserves at the beginning of such year), minus $80, the addition for such year to the reserve for losses on nonqualifying loans. Since such $43,920 is greater than $11,920 (the amount determined under (b) of this subdivision), the 12 percent of deposits limitation does not apply for 1965.

(iii) *Computation of taxable income for 1965.* X's taxable income for 1965, after deducting the additions for such year to its reserves for losses on nonqualifying loans and on qualifying real property loans, after deducting the charitable contributions which were not taken into account in computing taxable income for purposes of the addition to the reserve for losses on qualifying real property loans, after including in taxable income dividends received from Y Corporation, and after taking into account the deduction for dividends received under section 243 (subject to the limitation in section 246(b)), is $7,800, computed as follows:

Interest and other income		$19,940	
Dividends received from Y Corporation		400	$20,340
Less:			
Deduction for charitable contributions	$ 200		
85 percent of dividends received from Y Corporation	340		
Additions to reserves for bad debts	12,000		12,540
Taxable income			$ 7,800

Example (2). Assume the same facts as in example (1), except that X Corporation was organized in 1957, and qualifies for the taxable year 1965 as a new company within the meaning of

Reg. § 1.593-6(g)

paragraph (c)(2) of this section. The maximum permissible addition for 1965 to X's reserve for losses on qualifying real property loans is $18,000, the amount computed under the percentage of real property loans method, since such amount is greater than (i) $11,920, the amount computed under the percentage of taxable income method, or (ii) zero, the amount computed under the experience method. The $18,000 amount (as computed under the percentage of real property loans method) is the amount necessary to increase the reserve for losses on qualifying real property loans from the $21,000 closing balance to $39,000, computed as follows:

3 percent of $940,000 of qualifying real property loans at close of 1965		$28,200
Plus:		
Lesser of $80,000 or $18,800 (2 percent of such loans of $940,000)	$18,800	
Reduced by the balance of supplemental reserve for losses on loans	8,000	10,800
		$39,000

Example (3). Assume the same facts as in example (1), except that for 1965, 38.4 percent of X's total assets consist of assets other than the assets described in section 7701(a)(19)(D)(ii). In such case, the maximum permissible addition of $11,920 for such year to the reserve for losses on qualifying real property loans (as determined under subdivision (ii) of example (1)) would be reduced by $2,980 (¼ of $11,920) to $8,940. [Reg. § 1.593-6.]

☐ [T.D. 6728, 5-4-64. Amended by T.D. 7549, 5-17-78.]

[Reg. § 1.593-6A]

§ 1.593-6A. Post-1969 addition to reserve for losses on qualifying real property loans.—(a) *In general.*—(1) *Amount of addition determined for the taxable year.* For purposes of paragraph (a)(1)(ii) of § 1.593-5, the amount of the addition to the reserve for losses on qualifying real property loans for any taxable year beginning after July 11, 1969, is the amount which the taxpayer determines to constitute a reasonable addition to such reserve for such year. However, the amount so determined for such year—

(i) Cannot exceed the largest of the amount determined under section 593(b)(2), (3), or (4) (relating, respectively, to the percentage of taxable income method, the percentage method, and the experience method), and

(ii) Shall be determined without regard to any amount charged for any taxable year against the reserve for losses on qualifying real property loans pursuant to § 1.593-10 (relating to certain distributions to shareholders by a domestic building and loan association).

For each taxable year the taxpayer must include in its income tax return for such year a computation of the amount of the addition determined under this section. The use of a particular method in the return for a taxable year is not a binding election by the taxpayer to apply such method either for such taxable year or for subsequent taxable years. Thus, in the case of a subsequent adjustment described in paragraph (b)(2) of § 1.593-5 which has the effect of permitting an increase, or requiring a reduction, in the amount claimed in the return for a taxable year as an addition to the reserve for losses on qualifying real property loans, the amount of such addition may be recomputed under whichever method the taxpayer selects for the purpose of such recomputation, irrespective of the method initially applied for such taxable year.

(2) *Method of determination.* For purposes of this section and § 1.596-1 (relating to limitation on dividends received deduction), a thrift institution is deemed to have determined the addition to its reserve for losses on qualifying real property loans for the taxable year under the percentage of taxable income method provided by section 593(b)(2) and paragraph (b) of this section if the amount finally determined to be a reasonable addition for such year to such reserve exceeds the amount determined for such year under section 593(b)(3) (relating to the percentage method) and exceeds the amount determined for such year under section 593(b)(4) (relating to the experience method).

(b) *Percentage of taxable income method.*—(1) *In general.* Subject to the limitations described in subparagraph (4) of this paragraph and in paragraph (e) of this section, the amount determined under section 593(b)(2) and this paragraph for the taxable year, if such section and paragraph are applicable, is an amount equal to the applicable percentage of the taxable income for such year, reduced by the amount determined under subparagraph (3) of this paragraph. For this purpose, taxable income is computed as provided in subparagraph (5) of this paragraph, and the applicable percentage (except as reduced under subparagraph (2) of this paragraph) is determined under the following table:

For a taxable year beginning in—	The applicable percentage under this subparagraph is—
1969	60 percent
1970	57 percent

Reg. § 1.593-6A(b)(1)

Mutual Savings Banks, Etc.

See p. 20,601 for regulations not amended to reflect law changes

Year	Percent
1971	54 percent
1972	51 percent
1973	49 percent
1974	47 percent
1975	45 percent
1976	43 percent
1977	42 percent
1978	41 percent
1979 or thereafter	40 percent

(2) *Reduction of applicable percentage in certain cases*—(i) *General rule.* If for the taxable year the percentage of the assets of a thrift institution, which are assets described in section 7701(a)(19)(C) (relating to assets of a domestic building and loan association) is less than—

(a) 82 percent of the total assets in the case of a thrift institution other than a mutual savings bank, the applicable percentage for such year provided by subparagraph (1) of this paragraph is reduced by 3/4 of 1 percentage point for each 1 percentage point of such difference; or

(b) 72 percent of the total assets in the case of a thrift institution which is a mutual savings bank, the applicable percentage for such year provided by subparagraph (1) of this paragraph is reduced by 1 1/2 percentage points for each 1 percentage point of such difference.

If such percentage is less than 60 percent of the total assets in the case of any thrift institution (less than 50 percent of the total assets for a taxable year beginning before 1973 in the case of a thrift institution which is a mutual savings bank), section 593(b)(2) and this paragraph are not applicable. The percentage of total assets specified in this subparagraph is computed as of the close of the taxable year or, at the option of the taxpayer, may be computed on the basis of the average assets outstanding during the taxable year. Such average is determined by computing such percentage either as of the close of each month, as of the close of each quarter, or as of the close of each semiannual period during the taxable year and by using the yearly average of the monthly, quarterly, or semiannual percentages. A thrift institution which is a mutual savings bank and which determines the amount of the reasonable addition for the taxable year to the reserve for losses on qualifying real property loans under this paragraph shall file for such taxable year a statement which shall show the amount of assets defined in paragraph (e) of § 402.1-2 (Temporary Regulations On Procedure and Administration under Tax Reform Act of 1969) as of the close of the taxable year and a brief description and the amount of all other assets, together with a description of the method used in determining such amounts. If the percentage specified in this subparagraph is computed by such thrift institution on the basis of the average assets outstanding during the taxable year, the statement shall also show such information as of the end of each month, each quarter, or each semiannual period and the manner of calculating the average.

(ii) *Example.* The provisions of this subparagraph may be illustrated by the following example:

Example. M is a cooperative bank to which section 593 applies. For its taxable year beginning in 1970, 80.4 percent of M's assets (computed as of the close of such year) constitute assets described in section 7701(a)(19)(C). M's assets which are assets described in section 7701(a)(19)(C), when computed on semiannual, quarterly, and monthly bases, constitute 79.8, 79.6 and 79.5 percent, respectively, of its total assets computed on the corresponding bases. M's applicable percentage for 1970 is 56.25 percent, determined as follows:

Percentage of total assets specified in (a) of subdivision (i) of this subparagraph	82.0 percent
Percentage of total assets constituting assets described in section 7701(a)(19)(C)	80.4 percent
Difference	1.6 percent
Applicable percentage determined under table in subparagraph (1) of this paragraph	57.0 percent
Reduction of applicable percentage required by (a) of subdivision (i) of this subparagraph (3/4 of 1 percentage point for each full percentage point of difference)	.75 percent
Applicable percentage	56.25 percent

(3) *Reduction for addition to reserve for nonqualifying loans*—(i) *General rule.* Subparagraph (1) of this paragraph provides that, subject to certain limitations, the amount determined under the percentage of taxable income method provided by section 593(b)(2) and this paragraph for the taxable year is an amount equal to the applicable percentage of the taxable income for such year, reduced by the amount determined under this subparagraph. In the case of a thrift institution other than a mutual savings bank, the amount determined under this subparagraph is an amount equal to the amount determined under paragraph (a)(1)(i) of § 1.593-5 to be a reasonable addition for the taxable year to the reserve for

Reg. § 1.593-6A(b)(2)

losses on nonqualifying loans multiplied by a fraction—

  (a) The numerator of which is 18 percent, and

  (b) The denominator of which is the percentage (in no case less than 18 percent) of the assets of the taxpayer for such year which are not assets defined in paragraph (e) of § 402.1-2 of this chapter.

In the case of a thrift institution which is a mutual savings bank, the amount determined under this subparagraph is an amount determined in the manner described in the preceding sentence, except that the numerator of the fraction described therein is 28 percent, and the denominator of such fraction shall not be less than 28 percent. For purposes of this subparagraph, the percentage of assets for a taxable year which are not assets defined in paragraph (e) of § 402.1-2 is determined upon the same annual or average basis as is used in determining the percentage specified in subparagraph (2) of this paragraph.

  (ii) *Examples.* The provisions of this subparagraph may be illustrated by the following examples:

  Example (1). K is a domestic building and loan association to which section 593 applies. The amount determined under subparagraph (1) of this paragraph (before reduction by the amount determined under this subparagraph) to be the reasonable addition for the taxable year to K's reserve for losses on qualifying real property loans is $100,000. The amount determined under paragraph (a)(1)(i) of § 1.593-5 as the reasonable addition for the taxable year to the association's reserve for losses on nonqualifying loans is $10,000. The percentage of K's assets which are not assets defined in paragraph (e) of § 402.1-2 is 24 percent. The amount determined under subparagraph (1) of this paragraph ($100,000) must be reduced by $7,500

$$\left(\$10,000 \times \frac{18 \text{ percent}}{24 \text{ percent}}\right)$$

Therefore, subject to the limitations described in subparagraph (4) of this paragraph and in paragraph (e) of this section, the amount determined under this paragraph to be the reasonable addition for the taxable year to K's reserve for losses on qualifying real property loans is $92,500 ($100,000 less $7,500).

  Example (2). The facts are the same as in Example (1), except that the percentage of K's assets which are not assets defined in paragraph (e) of § 402.1-2 is 12 percent. The amount determined under subparagraph (1) of this paragraph (before reduction by the amount determined under this subparagraph) to be the reasonable addition for the taxable year to K's reserve for losses on qualifying real property loans must be reduced by $10,000

$$\left(\$10,000 \times \frac{18 \text{ percent}}{18 \text{ percent}}\right)$$

Because the denominator of the fraction may not be less than 18 percent, the fraction used in determining the amount of such reduction is equal to 1.

  (4) *Overall limitation.* The amount determined under this paragraph shall not exceed the amount necessary to increase the balance (as of the close of the taxable year) of the reserve for losses on qualifying real property loans to 6 percent of such loans outstanding at such time.

  (5) *Computation of taxable income.* For purposes of this paragraph, taxable income is computed—

  (i) By excluding from gross income any amount included therein by reason of the application of section 593(e) and § 1.593-10 (relating to certain distributions to shareholders by a domestic building and loan association).

  (ii) Without regard to any deduction allowable under section 166(c) (whether or not determined under section 593) and the regulations thereunder for an addition to a reserve for bad debts.

  (iii)(a) By excluding from gross income an amount equal to the excess (if any) of (*1*) the total gains of the taxable year arising from sales and exchanges at a gain of (*i*) obligations the interest on which is excludable from gross income under section 103, and (*ii*) corporate stock, over (*2*) the total losses of such year arising from sales and exchanges at a loss of such obligations and stock.

  (b) The provisions of this subdivision (iii) may be illustrated by the following example:

  Example. For its taxable year beginning in 1971, the gains and losses of a domestic building and loan association from sales of stock and securities (all of which were made on December 31, 1971) were as follows:

	Gain	Loss
Municipal bonds acquired July 1, 1969, the interest on which is excludable from income under section 103	$25,000	.....
Stock of Corporation A, acquired July 14, 1971	......	$6,000
Stock of Corporation B, acquired December 22, 1970	$3,000	.....

Reg. § 1.593-6A(b)(5)

For purposes of this paragraph, the association's taxable income for 1971 is computed by excluding $22,000 ($25,000 + $3,000 − $6,000) from its gross income.

(iv) By excluding from gross income an amount equal to the lesser of (a) 3/8 of the net long-term capital gain for the taxable year or (b) 3/8 of the net long-term capital gain for the taxable year from the sale or exchange of property other than property described in subdivision (iii) of this subparagraph.

(v)(a) By excluding from gross income so much of the amount of dividends with respect to which a deduction is allowable under part VIII, subchapter B, chapter 1, subtitle A of the Code (section 241 and following) as is in excess of the applicable percentage (determined under subparagraphs (1) and (2) of this paragraph) of the dividends received deduction (determined under part VIII, subchapter B, chapter 1, subtitle A of the Code, without regard to section 596) for the taxable year.

(b) The provisions of this subdivision (v) may be illustrated by the following example:

Example. For its taxable year beginning in 1977, a domestic building and loan association receives dividends of $100 with respect to which a dividends received deduction of $85 is allowable under section 243(a)(1). The association receives no other dividends for the taxable year. The association's applicable percentage for the taxable year, as determined under subparagraphs (1) and (2) of this paragraph, is 42 percent. For purposes of this paragraph, the association's taxable income is computed by excluding from gross income the excess of the amount of dividends received ($100) over the applicable percentage of the allowable dividends received deduction (42 percent of $85, or $35.70), computed without regard to section 596. Thus, for purposes of this paragraph, $64.30 ($100 less $35.70) is excluded from gross income. See section 596 and § 1.596-1 with respect to the computation of the dividends received deduction for purposes of determining taxable income under section 63(a).

(vi) For taxable years beginning before January 1, 1978, without regard to any deduction the amount of which is computed upon, or may be subject to a limitation computed upon, the amount of taxable income, and without regard to any net operating loss carryback to such year from a taxable year beginning before January 1, 1979. (For purposes of this subparagraph, a net operating loss deduction under section 172 is not a deduction the amount of which may be subject to a limitation computed upon the amount of taxable income.)

(vii) For taxable years beginning after December 31, 1977, by taking into account any deduction the amount of which is computed upon or may be subject to a limitation computed upon the amount of taxable income, and any other deduction or loss allowed under subtitle A of the Code, such as any deduction allowable under section 172 or any loss allowable under section 1212(a), unless otherwise provided in this subparagraph.

(c) *Percentage method.* [Reserved]

(d) *Experience method.* [Reserved]

(e) *Percentage of deposits limitation where percentage of taxable income method or percentage method is applied.* If the amount determined by the taxpayer to constitute a reasonable addition for the taxable year to the reserve for losses on qualifying real property loans is greater than the amount determined under paragraph (d) of this section (relating to the experience method), the amount so determined cannot exceed an amount which, when added to the amount determined under paragraph (a)(1)(i) of § 1.593-5 to be a reasonable addition for such year to the reserve for losses on nonqualifying loans, equals the amount by which 12 percent of the total deposits or withdrawable accounts of depositors of the taxpayer at the close of such year exceeds the sum of the taxpayer's surplus, undivided profits, and reserves at the beginning of such year (taking into account any portion thereof which is attributable to the period before the first taxable year beginning after December 31, 1951). The terms "surplus, undivided profits, and reserves" and "total deposits or withdrawable accounts" have the same meanings as are assigned to them in paragraph (f) of § 1.593-6. [Reg. § 1.593-6A.]

☐ [T.D. 7549, 5-17-78. Amended by T.D. 7629, 5-30-79.]

[Reg. § 1.593-7]

§ 1.593-7. **Establishment and treatment of reserves for bad debts.**—(a) *Establishment of reserves*—(1) *In general.* A taxpayer described in § 1.593-4 shall establish and maintain a reserve for losses on nonqualifying loans, a reserve for losses on qualifying real property loans, and, if required under paragraph (b)(4) or (c)(3)(i)(c) of this section, a supplemental reserve for losses on loans. For rules governing the crediting of additions to the reserve for losses on nonqualifying loans and the reserve for losses on qualifying real property loans, see paragraph (b) of § 1.593-5.

(2) *Accounting for reserves.* (i) The taxpayer shall establish and maintain as a permanent part of its regular books of account an account for each of the reserves established pursuant to subpara-

graph (1) of this paragraph. For purposes of the preceding sentence, a taxpayer may establish and maintain a permanent subsidiary ledger containing an account for each of such reserves. If a taxpayer maintains such a permanent subsidiary ledger, the total of the reserve accounts in such ledger, and the total of the reserve accounts in any other ledger, must be reconciled.

(ii) Any credit or charge to a reserve established pursuant to subparagraph (1) of this paragraph must be made to such reserve irrespective of whether the amount thereof is also credited or charged to any surplus, reserve, or other account which the taxpayer may be required or permitted to maintain pursuant to any Federal or State statute, regulation, or supervisory order. Minimum amounts credited in compliance with such Federal or State statutes, regulations, or supervisory orders to reserve or similar accounts, or additional amounts credited to such reserve or similar accounts and permissible under such statutes, regulations, or orders, against which charges may be made for the purpose of absorbing losses sustained by the taxpayer, may also be credited to the reserve for losses on nonqualifying loans or the reserve for losses on qualifying real property loans, provided that the total of the amounts so credited to the reserve for losses on nonqualifying loans, or to the reserve for losses on qualifying real property loans, for any taxable years does not exceed the amount described in subparagraph (1) or (2) of § 1.593-5(a) (whichever applies) as the addition to such reserve for such year.

(b) *Allocation of pre-1963 reserves*—(1) *In general.* In the case of a taxpayer described in § 1.593-4, the pre-1963 reserves, if any, of such taxpayer shall be allocated to (and constitute the opening balance of) the reserve for losses on nonqualifying loans, the reserve for losses on qualifying real property loans, and, if required under subparagraph (4) of this paragraph, the supplemental reserve for losses on loans. The term "pre-1963 reserves" means the net amount (determined as of the close of December 31, 1962) accumulated for taxable years beginning after December 31, 1951, in the taxpayer's reserve for bad debts pursuant to section 166(c) of the Internal Revenue Code of 1954 and section 23(k)(1) of the Internal Revenue Code of 1939 (including the amount of any bad debt reserves acquired from another taxpayer). For purposes of the preceding sentence in the case of a taxable year beginning before January 1, 1963, and ending after December 31, 1962, the part of such year occurring before January 1, 1963, shall be treated as a taxable year. Thus, the pre-1963 reserves of the taxpayer shall be an amount equal to—

(i) The sum of the amounts allowed as deductions for additions to a reserve for bad debts for taxable years beginning after December 31, 1951, and ending before January 1, 1963, plus

(ii) In the case of a taxable year beginning before January 1, 1963, and ending after December 31, 1962, the amount (determined under § 1.593-1 or 1.593-2) which would be allowable under section 166(c) as a deduction for an addition to a reserve for bad debts for the part of such year occurring before January 1, 1963, if such part year constituted a taxable year, minus

(iii) The total amount of bad debts charged against a reserve for bad debts during the period which begins with the opening of the first taxable year beginning after December 31, 1951, and which ends at the close of December 31, 1962, plus

(iv) The total amount of recoveries, during the period described in subdivision (iii) of this subparagraph, on bad debts charged against a reserve for bad debts in a taxable year beginning after December 31, 1951.

(2) *Allocation to opening balance of reserve for losses on nonqualifying loans.* (i) As of the close of December 31, 1962, the pre-1963 reserves shall first be allocated to (and constitute the opening balance of) the reserve for losses on nonqualifying loans in an amount equal to the lesser of (*a*) the amount of such pre-1963 reserves, or (*b*) the amount determined under subdivision (ii) of this subparagraph.

(ii) The amount referred to in subdivision (i)(*b*) of this subparagraph shall be the amount which would constitute a reasonable addition to the reserve for losses on nonqualifying loans under § 1.166-4 for a period in which the taxpayer's nonqualifying loans increased from zero to the amount thereof outstanding at the close of December 31, 1962.

(3) *Allocation to opening balance of reserve for losses on qualifying real property loans.* (i) Any portion of the pre-1963 reserves remaining after the allocation provided in subparagraph (2) of this paragraph shall, as of the close of December 31, 1962, be allocated to (and constitute the opening balance of) the reserve for losses on qualifying real property loans in an amount equal to the lesser of (*a*) the amount of such remaining portion, or (*b*) the amount determined under subdivision (ii) of this subparagraph. If the amount described in (*a*) of the preceding sentence is less than the amount described in (*b*) thereof, see § 1.593-8 for allocation of pre-1952 surplus, if any, to the opening balance of such reserve.

Reg. § 1.593-7(b)(3)

(ii) The amount referred to in subdivision (i)(b) of this subparagraph shall be an amount equal to the greater of—

(a) 3 percent of the taxpayer's qualifying real property loans outstanding at the close of December 31, 1962, or

(b) The amount which would constitute a reasonable addition to the reserve for losses on such loans under § 1.166-4 for a period in which the amount of such loans increased from zero to the amount thereof outstanding at the close of December 31, 1962.

(4) *Allocation to supplemental reserve for losses on loans.* Any portion of the pre-1963 reserves remaining after the allocations provided in subparagraphs (2) and (3) of this paragraph shall be allocated in its entirety to the supplemental reserve for losses on loans.

(5) *Examples.* This paragraph may be illustrated by the following examples:

Example (1)—(i) *Facts.* X Corporation, a domestic building and loan association organized on April 1, 1954, makes its returns on the basis of a taxable year ending March 31 and the reserve method of accounting for bad debts. For its taxable years ending March 31, 1955, through March 31, 1962, X was allowed a total of $750,000 as deductible additions to its reserve for bad debts under section 166(c). For its taxable year ending March 31, 1963, X was allowed a deduction under section 166(c) for an addition to a reserve for bad debts. Of such deduction $46,000 was determined under § 1.593-1 (relating to additions to reserve for bad debts) by reference to § 1.593-9 (relating to taxable income for taxable years beginning in 1962 and ending in 1963) as the amount which would be allowable for the period April 1 through December 31, 1962, if such period constituted a taxable year. During the taxable years ending March 31, 1955, through March 31, 1963, X charged bad debts of $55,000 against its reserve for bad debts and made recoveries on such debts of $10,000. Of such bad debt charges and recoveries, $50,000 was charged off and $9,000 was recovered prior to January 1, 1963. At the close of December 31, 1962, X had outstanding nonqualifying loans of $500,000 and outstanding qualifying real property loans of $10 million. It is assumed that, under § 1.166-4, $2,000 would constitute a reasonable addition to the reserve for losses on nonqualifying loans for a period in which such loans increased from zero to $500,000 and $20,000 would constitute a reasonable addition to the reserve for losses on qualifying real property loans for a period in which such loans increased from zero to $10 million.

(ii) *Pre-1963 reserves determined.* X's pre-1963 reserves are $755,000, computed as follows:

Deductible additions to reserve for bad debts:
  Years ending March 31, 1955 through March 31, 1962 .... $750,000
  Period April 1 through December 31, 1962 .... 46,000 $796,000

Less:
  Net bad debt losses for period April 1, 1954 through December 31, 1962:
    Bad debts .... $ 50,000
    Recoveries .... (9,000)   41,000
                                                                          _____
                                                                          $755,000

(iii) *Allocation to opening balance of reserve for losses on nonqualifying loans.* The portion of the $755,000 of pre-1963 reserves to be allocated to the reserve for losses on nonqualifying loans as the opening balance thereof is $2,000 since such amount would constitute a reasonable addition to the reserve for losses on nonqualifying loans under § 1.166-4 for a period in which the amount of such loans increased from zero to $500,000.

(iv) *Allocation to opening balance of reserve for losses on qualifying real property loans.* Of the $753,000 ($755,000 minus $2,000) of pre-1963 reserves remaining after the allocation described in subdivision (iii) of this example, $300,000 (3 percent of $10 million, the total amount of qualifying real property loans outstanding at the close of December 31, 1962) is allocated to the opening balance of the reserve for losses on qualifying real property loans, since such amount is greater than $20,000, the amount which would constitute a reasonable addition to the reserve for losses on such loans under § 1.166-4 for a period in which the amount of such loans increased from zero to $10 million.

(v) *Allocation to supplemental reserve for losses on loans.* The balance of the pre-1963 reserves, or $453,000 ($755,000 minus the sum of $2,000 and $300,000), is allocated in its entirety to the supplemental reserve for losses on loans.

Example (2). Assume the same facts as in example (1), except that X was organized in 1936, and on December 31, 1962, had pre-1963 reserves of only $15,000 (rather than $755,000). In such

Reg. § 1.593-7(b)(4)

case, $2,000 of such pre-1963 reserves would be allocated to, and constitute the opening balance of, the reserve for losses on nonqualifying loans, and $13,000 ($15,000 minus $2,000) would be allocated to and constitute part of the opening balance of the reserve for losses on qualifying real property loans. However, since such $13,000 is less than $300,000 (3 percent of $10 million), the opening balance of the reserve for losses on qualifying real property loans must be increased by so much of the taxpayer's pre-1952 surplus as is necessary to increase such opening balance to $300,000. For rules on the allocation of pre-1952 surplus to the opening balance of the reserve for losses on qualifying real property loans, see § 1.593-8.

(c) *Treatment of reserves*—(1) *In general.* Except as provided in paragraph (d) of § 1.593-8 (relating to the allocation of pre-1952 surplus), each of the reserves established pursuant to paragraph (a) of this section shall be treated, for purposes of subtitle A of the Code, as a reserve for bad debts, except that no deduction shall be allowed under section 166 for any addition to the supplemental reserve for losses on loans. Accordingly, if in any taxable year the taxpayer charges any of the reserves established pursuant to paragraph (a) of this section for an item other than a bad debt, gross income for such year shall be increased by the amount of such charge. For special rules in case of certain nondeductible distributions to shareholders by a domestic building and loan association, see § 1.593-10.

(2) *Bad debt losses.* Any bad debt in respect of a nonqualifying loan shall be charged against the reserve for losses on nonqualifying loans, and any bad debt in respect of a qualifying real property loan shall be charged against the reserve for losses on qualifying real property loans. At the option of the taxpayer, however, any bad debt in respect of either class of loans may be charged in whole or in part against the supplemental reserve for losses on loans.

(3) *Recoveries of bad debts.* Any amount recovered after December 31, 1962, in respect of a bad debt shall be credited to the reserves established pursuant to paragraph (a) of this section in the following manner:

(i) If the recovery is in respect of a bad debt which was charged prior to January 1, 1963, against a reserve for bad debts established pursuant to section 166(c) of the Internal Revenue Code of 1954, or section 23(k)(1) of the Internal Revenue Code of 1939, then the amount recovered shall be credited—

(a) First, to the reserve for losses on nonqualifying loans in an amount equal to the amount, if any, by which the amount determined under subdivision (ii) of paragraph (b)(2) of this section exceeds the opening balance of such reserve (determined under such paragraph (b)(2)),

(b) Second, to the reserve for losses on qualifying real property loans in an amount equal to the amount, if any, by which the amount determined under subdivision (ii) of paragraph (b)(3) of this section exceeds the opening balance of such reserve (determined under such paragraph (b)(3)), and

(c) Finally, to the supplemental reserve for losses on loans. For purposes of determining the amounts of the credits under (a) and (b) of this subdivision, the opening balances of the reserve for losses on nonqualifying loans and the reserve for losses on qualifying real property loans shall be deemed to include the sum of the amounts of any prior credits made to such reserves pursuant to this subdivision.

(ii) If the recovery is in respect of a bad debt which is charged after December 31, 1962, against only one of the reserves established pursuant to paragraph (a) of this section, the entire amount recovered shall be credited to the reserve so charged.

(iii) If the recovery is in respect of a bad debt which is charged after December 31, 1962, against more than one of the reserves established pursuant to paragraph (a) of this section, then the amount recovered shall be credited to each of the reserves so charged in the ratio which the amount of the bad debt charged against such reserve bears to the total amount of such bad debt charged against both such reserves.

(iv) Subdivision (i) of this subparagraph may be illustrated by the following example:

Example. In 1962, the taxpayer sustained a bad debt of $10,000, which was charged against a reserve for bad debts established pursuant to section 166(c). As of the close of December 31, 1962, the balance of the taxpayer's reserve for losses on nonqualifying loans was $2,000, the amount determined under paragraph (b)(2)(ii) of this section. As of the same time, the balance of the taxpayer's reserve for losses on qualifying real property loans was $100,000, but the amount determined under paragraph (b)(3)(ii) of this section was $106,000. In 1963, the taxpayer recovers $8,000 of the $10,000 charged off in 1962. Of the $8,000 recovered in 1963, $6,000 ($106,000 minus $100,000) is credited to the reserve for losses on qualifying real property loans, and the balance of $2,000 is credited to the supplemental reserve for losses on loans. [Reg. § 1.593-7.]

☐ [T.D. 6728, 5-4-64. *Amended by T.D.* 7549, 5-17-78.]

Reg. § 1.593-7(c)(3)

[Reg. § 1.593-8]

§ 1.593-8. Allocation of pre-1952 surplus to opening balance of reserve for losses on qualifying real property loans.—(a) *General rule.* In the case of a taxpayer described in § 1.593-4, if the amount of pre-1963 reserves allocated (under paragraph (b)(3)(i) of § 1.593-7) to the opening balance of the reserve for losses on qualifying real property loans is less than an amount equal to the greater of—

(1) The total amount of qualifying real property loans outstanding at the close of December 31, 1962, multiplied by 3 percent, or

(2) The amount which would constitute a reasonable addition to the reserve for losses on such loans under § 1.166-4 for a period in which the amount of such loans increased from zero to the amount thereof outstanding at the close of December 31, 1962,

then such opening balance shall be increased by an amount equal to so much of the "pre-1952 surplus" of the taxpayer as is necessary to increase such opening balance to the greater of the amounts described in subparagraph (1) or (2) of this paragraph. The amount of such increase shall be deemed to be included in such opening balance solely for the limited purpose described in paragraph (d) of this section.

(b) *Pre-1952 surplus defined*—(1) *In general.* For purposes of this section and § 1.593-7, the term "pre-1952 surplus" means an amount equal to—

(i) The sum of the taxpayer's surplus, undivided profits, and reserves determined (under the principles of paragraph (d)(2) of § 1.593-1) as of the close of the taxpayer's last taxable year beginning before January 1, 1952 (including any amount acquired from another taxpayer), minus

(ii) The amount of any impairments of such sum (as determined under paragraph (c) of this section).

(2) *Reduction for certain excludable interest.* (i) The amount otherwise determined under subparagraph (1) of this paragraph may, at the option of the taxpayer, be reduced by the portion, if any, of such amount which is attributable to interest which would have been excludable from gross income of such taxpayer under section 22(b)(4) of the Internal Revenue Code of 1939 (relating to interest on governmental obligations) or the corresponding provisions of prior revenue laws, had such taxpayer been subject, when such interest was received or accrued, to the income tax imposed by such Code or prior revenue laws.

(ii) For purposes of subdivision (i) of this subparagraph, the portion of the amount otherwise determined under subparagraph (1) of this paragraph which is attributable to interest which would have been excludable from gross income shall be determined by multiplying such amount by the ratio which—

(*a*) The total amount of such excludable interest for the period before the taxpayer's first taxable year beginning after December 31, 1951, bears to

(*b*) The total amount of the taxpayer's gross income, plus the total amount of such excludable interest, for such period.

If the amount determined under subparagraph (1)(i) of this paragraph includes any amount acquired from another taxpayer, then the gross income and excludable interest of the taxpayer for the period before its first taxable year beginning after December 31, 1951, shall include the gross income and excludable interest (for the same period) of such other taxpayer.

(c) *Impairment of surplus, undivided profits, and reserves*—(1) *General rule.* In the case of a taxable year beginning after December 31, 1951, and ending before January 1, 1963, if for such year—

(i) The amount described in paragraph (b)(1)(i) of this section (as decreased under subparagraph (3)(i) of this paragraph), exceeds

(ii) The sum of the taxpayer's surplus, undivided profits, and reserves (excluding the amount of any pre-1963 reserves) determined as of the close of such year under the principles of paragraph (d)(2) of § 1.593-1, then the amount described in paragraph (b)(1)(i) of this section may, at the option of the taxpayer, be reduced by the amount of such excess.

(2) *Transition year.* In the case of a taxable year beginning before January 1, 1963, and ending after December 31, 1962, the part of such year which occurs before January 1, 1963, shall be considered to be a taxable year for purposes of subparagraph (1) of this paragraph.

(3) *Rules for applying subparagraph (1).* (i) For purposes of subparagraph (1)(i) of this paragraph, the amount described in paragraph (b)(1)(i) of this section shall be decreased by the total of any reductions under subparagraph (1) of this paragraph for prior taxable years; and

(ii) For purposes of subparagraph (1)(ii) of this paragraph, the term "pre-1963 reserves" means the amount determined under the principles of paragraph (b)(1) of § 1.593-7 for the period which begins with the first day of the first taxable year beginning after December 31, 1951, and which ends at the close of the taxable year with respect to which the computation under subparagraph (1) is being made.

(d) *Treatment of pre-1952 surplus.* Any portion of the taxpayer's pre-1952 surplus which, pursuant to paragraph (a) of this section, is deemed to

Mutual Savings Banks, Etc.

See p. 20,601 for regulations not amended to reflect law changes

be included in the opening balance of the reserve for losses on qualifying real property loans shall not be treated as a reserve for bad debts for any purpose other than computing for any taxable year the amount determined under the method described in paragraph (b), (c), or (d) of § 1.593-6 (relating, respectively, to the percentage of taxable income method, the percentage of real property loans method, and the experience method) or paragraph (b), (c), or (d) of § 1.593-6A (relating, respectively, to the percentage of taxable income method, the percentage method, and the experience method). For such limited purpose, such portion shall be deemed to remain in, and constitute a part of, the reserve for losses on qualifying real property loans. For all other purposes, such portion will retain its character as part of the taxpayer's pre-1952 surplus.

(e) *Example.* The provisions of this section may be illustrated by the following example:

Example. (1) *Facts.* X Corporation, a mutual savings bank organized in 1934, makes its returns on the basis of the calendar year and the reserve method of accounting for bad debts. For the taxable years 1934 through 1951, X's gross income was $2.7 million, in addition to which X received $300,000 of interest which would have been excludable from gross income under section 22(b)(4) of the Internal Revenue Code of 1939, or the corresponding provisions of prior revenue laws, if X had been subject to the income tax imposed by such Code or prior revenue laws when such interest was received. At the close of 1951, the sum of X's surplus, undivided profits, and reserves was $650,000. At the close of 1954, X had pre-1963 reserves of $10,000, and surplus, undivided profits, and reserves of $630,000. At the close of 1955, X had pre-1963 reserves of $15,000, and surplus, undivided profits, and reserves of $625,000. At the close of 1962, X had pre-1963 reserves of $55,000, nonqualifying loans of $4 million, and qualifying real property loans of $10 million. It is assumed that, under § 1.166-4, $16,000 would constitute a reasonable addition to the reserve for losses on nonqualifying loans for a period in which such loans increased from zero to $4 million and $20,000 would constitute a reasonable addition to the reserve for losses on qualifying real property loans for a period in which such loans increased from zero to $10 million.

(2) *Impairment of surplus, undivided profits, and reserves for 1954.* The sum of X's surplus, undivided profits, and reserves at the close of 1951 was impaired during 1954 by $30,000, computed as follows:

Sum of surplus, undivided profits, and reserves at close of 1951	$650,000
Less:	
Sum of surplus, undivided profits, and reserves at close of 1954, excluding pre-1963 reserves at close of such year ($630,000 minus $10,000)	620,000
	$ 30,000

(3) *Impairment of surplus, undivided profits, and reserves for 1955.* The sum of X's surplus, undivided profits, and reserves at the close of 1951 was further impaired during 1955 by $10,000, computed as follows:

Sum of surplus, undivided profits, and reserves at close of 1951, decreased by amount of 1954 impairment ($650,000 minus $30,000)	$620,000
Less:	
Sum of surplus, undivided profits, and reserves at close of 1955, excluding pre-1963 reserves at close of such year ($625,000 minus $15,000)	610,000
	$ 10,000

(4) *Pre-1952 surplus.* X's pre-1952 surplus is $549,000, computed as follows:

Sum of surplus, undivided profit, and reserves at close of 1951	$650,000	
Less:		
Sum of impairments for 1954 and 1955 ($30,000 plus $10,000)	40,000	$610,000
Less:		
Portion of such $610,000 which is attributable to excludable interest ($610,000 multiplied by $300,000/$3 million)		$ 61,000
		$549,000

Reg. § 1.593-8(e)

(5) *Allocation of pre-1963 reserves to reserve for losses on nonqualifying loans and to reserve for losses on qualifying real property loans.* Of the $55,000 of pre-1963 reserves at the close of 1962, $16,000 (the amount which would constitute a reasonable addition to the reserve for losses on nonqualifying loans for a period in which such loans increased from zero to $4 million) shall be allocated to, and constitute the opening balance of, the reserve for losses on nonqualifying loans, and the balance of $39,000 ($55,000 minus $16,000) shall be allocated to, and constitute a part of the opening balance of, the reserve for losses on qualifying real property loans.

(6) *Allocation of pre-1952 surplus to reserve for losses on qualifying real property loans.* X's pre-1963 reserves are not sufficient to bring the opening balance of the reserve for losses on qualifying real property loans to $300,000, which is an amount equal to the greater of—

(i) $300,000 (*i.e.*, $10 million of qualifying real property loans outstanding at the close of 1962, multiplied by 3 percent), or

(ii) $20,000 (the amount which would constitute a reasonable addition to the reserve for losses on such loans under § 1.166-4 for a period in which the amount of such loans increased from zero to the $10 million).

Therefore, $261,000 ($300,000 minus $39,000) of X's pre-1952 surplus of $549,000 shall be deemed to be included in the opening balance of such reserve in order to increase such opening balance to $300,000. [Reg. § 1.593-8.]

☐ [T.D. 6728, 5-4-64. Amended by T.D. 7549, 5-17-78.]

[Reg. § 1.593-10]

§ 1.593-10. Certain distributions to shareholders by a domestic building and loan association.—(a) *In general.* Section 593(f) provides that if a domestic building and loan association (as defined in section 7701(a)(19) and the regulations thereunder) distributes property after December 31, 1962, to a shareholder with respect to its stock and if the amount of such distribution is not allowable to the association as a deduction under section 591 (relating to deduction for dividends paid on deposits), then, notwithstanding any other provision of the Code, the distribution shall be treated as provided in paragraphs (b) and (c) of this section. For purposes of the preceding sentence, the term "distribution" includes any distribution in redemption of stock to which section 302(a) or 303 applies, or in partial or complete liquidation of the association, as well as any other distribution which the association may make to a shareholder with respect to its stock. For definition of the term "property", see section 317(a). For determination of the amount of a distribution, see section 301(b). For taxable years beginning after July 11, 1969, this paragraph is not applicable to any transaction to which section 381 (relating to carryovers in certain corporate acquisitions) and the regulations thereunder apply.

(b) *Distributions out of certain reserves*—(1) *Distributions not in exchange for stock.* If the distribution is not in a redemption to which section 302(a) or 303 applies or in partial or complete liquidation of the association, then to the extent that the distribution is not out of earnings and profits of the taxable year (within the meaning of section 316(a)(2)) or out of earnings and profits accumulated in taxable years beginning after December 31, 1951, the distribution shall be treated as made out of—

(i) First, the reserve for losses on qualifying real property loans (determined under subparagraph (3) of this paragraph), to the extent thereof,

(ii) Second, the supplemental reserve for losses on loans, to the extent thereof, and

(iii) Finally, such other accounts as may be proper.

(2) *Distributions in redemption of stock or in liquidation.* If the distribution is a redemption to which section 302(a) or 303 applies, or in partial or complete liquidation of the association, the distribution shall be treated as made out of—

(i) First, the reserve for losses on qualifying real property loans (as determined under subparagraph (3) of this paragraph), to the extent thereof,

(ii) Second, the supplemental reserve for losses on loans, to the extent thereof,

(iii) Third, earnings and profits of the taxable year (within the meaning of section 316(a)(2)),

(iv) Fourth, earnings and profits accumulated in taxable years beginning after December 31, 1951, and

(v) Finally, such other accounts as may be proper.

(3) *Special rule.* For purposes of subparagraphs (1)(i) and (2)(i) of this paragraph, the reserve for losses on qualifying real property loans shall be an amount equal to—

(i) The balance of such reserve determined as of the close of the taxable year after all adjustments for such year have been made (including the addition for such year determined under § 1.593-6 or § 1.593-6A (whichever is applicable)), minus

(ii) The sum of—

(a) The amount which would have constituted the opening balance of such reserve (at the close of December 31, 1962) if such opening balance had been determined under the experience method described in paragraph (b)(3)(ii)(b) of § 1.593-7 (relating to allocation of pre-1963 reserves to the opening balance of the reserve for losses on qualifying real property loans), and

(b) The total amount of the annual additions which would have been made to such reserve under section 166(c) for taxable years ending after December 31, 1962, if each such addition had been determined under the experience method described in paragraph (d) of § 1.593-6 or paragraph (d) of § 1.593-6A, whichever is applicable for the taxable year of such addition.

For purposes of subdivision (i) of this subparagraph, the balance of the reserve for losses on qualifying real property loans shall include the total amount of any pre-1963 reserves allocated thereto under paragraph (b) (3) of § 1.593-7, but shall not include any pre-1952 surplus which is deemed to be included therein under paragraph (a) of § 1.593-8 (relating to allocation of pre-1952 surplus to the opening balance of the reserve for losses on qualifying real property loans).

(c) *Amount charged against reserve and included in gross income*—(1) *In general.* If a distribution is treated under paragraph (b) (1) or (2) of this section as having been made out of the reserve for losses on qualifying real property loans or out of the supplemental reserve for losses on loans, such reserves shall be charged with, and gross income for the taxable year shall be increased by, an amount equal to the lesser of—

(i) The amount of such reserves, or

(ii) The amount which, when reduced by the amount of income tax imposed by chapter 1 of the Code and attributable to the inclusion of such amount in gross income, is equal to the amount of such distribution.

(2) *Special rule.* For purposes of subparagraph (1)(ii) of this paragraph, in determining the income tax attributable to the inclusion of an amount in gross income, taxable income shall be determined without regard to any net operating loss carryback to the taxable year under section 172.

(d) *Examples.* This section may be illustrated by the following examples:

Example (1)—(i) *Facts.* X Corporation, a domestic building and loan association having non-withdrawable capital stock represented by shares, was organized in 1946, and makes its returns on the basis of the calendar year and the reserve method of accounting for bad debts. As of the close of December 31, 1962, X had $6,900 of earnings and profits accumulated in taxable years beginning after December 31, 1951. X's taxable income for 1963 is $30,000 (computed prior to the inclusion of any amount in gross income for such year under section 593(f)) and during such year X received tax-exempt interest of $500. X's earnings and profits for 1963 (computed at the close of the taxable year without diminution by reason of any distributions made during the taxable year) is $20,400. The opening balance of X's reserve for losses on qualifying real property loans as of the close of December 31, 1962 (determined under paragraph (b)(3)(ii)(a) of § 1.593-7) was $24,500. Pre-1963 reserves of $22,500 were included in such opening balance, but it is assumed that pre-1963 reserves of only $2,500 would have been included in the opening balance if the opening balance had been determined under the experience method described in paragraph (b)(3)(ii)(b) of § 1.593-7. Pre-1952 surplus of $2,000 was deemed included in such opening balance under paragraph (a) of § 1.593-8. The deductible addition to such reserve for 1963 is $47,000. It is assumed that the addition to such reserve for 1963 would have been $2,200 if such addition had been computed under the experience method described in paragraph (d) of § 1.593-6. On each of four dates during 1963 (January 1, April 1, July 1, and October 1), X made a $12,000 distribution (which was not a redemption to which section 302(a) or 303 applied or in partial or complete liquidation of X) to its shareholders with respect to its stock.

(ii) *Reserve for losses on qualifying real property loans.* For purposes of paragraph (b)(1)(i) of this section, X's reserve for losses on qualifying real property loans is $64,800, computed as follows:

Reg. § 1.593-10(d)

Closing balance of reserve for losses on qualifying real property loans after addition for 1963 ($24,500 opening balance plus $47,000 addition)		$71,500
Minus:		
Amount of pre-1963 reserves which would have been included in opening balance under experience method	$2,500	
Total additions which would have been made under experience method	2,200	
Pre-1952 surplus included in opening balance	2,000	6,700
		$64,800

(iii) *Treatment of distributions.* On each $12,000 quarterly distribution, $5,100 ($20,400 earnings and profits of the taxable year divided by 4) is out of X's earnings and profits of the taxable year (within the meaning of section 316(a)(2)); the remainder of the January 1 distribution, $6,900 ($12,000 minus $5,100), is out of X's earnings and profits accumulated in taxable years beginning after December 31, 1951. Since $20,700 ($6,900 multiplied by 3) is not out of X's earnings and profits, such amount shall be treated as made out of X's reserve for losses on qualifying real property loans (as determined under subdivision (ii) of this example).

(iv) *Amount charged against reserve for losses on qualifying real property loans and included in gross income.* The reserve for losses on qualifying real property loans is charged with, and X's gross income for 1963 is increased by, $43,124, which is the lesser of—

(a) $64,800 (the reserve as of December 31, 1963, as determined under subdivision (ii) of this example), or

(b) $43,124, i.e., the amount which, when reduced by the amount of income tax attributable to the inclusion of such amount in gross income, $22,424 ($43,124 multiplied by a tax rate of 52 percent), is equal to the amount of such distribution, $20,700.

Example (2) —(i) *Facts.* Assume the same facts as in example (1) and the following additional facts: X's taxable income for 1964 is $6,000. The deductible addition to the reserve for losses on qualifying real property loans for 1964 is $11,000, but it is assumed that only $2,676 would have been the addition to such reserve for 1964 if such addition had been computed under the experience method described in paragraph (d) of § 1.593–6. On December 31, 1964, X makes a $10,000 distribution in a redemption to which section 302(a) applies.

(ii) *Reserve for losses on qualifying real property loans.* For purposes of paragraph (b)(2)(i) of this section, X's reserve for losses on qualifying real property loans is $30,000, computed as follows:

Closing balance of reserve for losses on qualifying real property loans after addition for 1964 ($71,500 opening balance plus $11,000 addition)		$82,500
Minus:		
Amount of pre-1963 reserves which would have been included in opening balance under the experience method	$2,500	
Total additions which would have been made under the experience method ($2,200 for 1963 plus $2,676 for 1964)	4,876	
Pre-1952 surplus included in opening balance	2,000	$ 9,376
		$73,124
Less charge against reserve under subdivision (iv) of example (1) for 1963 distribution		43,124
		$30,000

(iii) *Treatment of distribution.* The $10,000 distribution in a redemption to which section 302(a) applies shall be treated as made out of X's reserve for losses on qualifying real property loans (as determined under subdivision (ii) of this example).

(iv) *Amount charged against reserve for losses on qualifying real property loans and included in gross income.* The reserve for losses on qualifying real property loans is charged with, and X's gross income for 1964 is increased by, $12,820, which is the lesser of—

(a) $30,000 (the reserve as of December 31, 1964, as determined under subdivision (ii) of this example), or

(b) $12,820, i.e., the amount which, when reduced by the amount of income tax attributable to the inclusion of such amount in gross income, $2,820 ($12,820 multiplied by a tax rate of 22 percent), is equal to the amount of such distribution, $10,000.

Example (3) —(i) *Facts.* X Corporation, a domestic building and loan association having nonwithdrawable capital stock represented by shares, was organized in 1946, and makes its returns on

Reg. § 1.593–10(d)

the basis of the calendar year and the reserve method of accounting for bad debts. As of the close of December 31, 1962, X had $6,900 of earnings and profits accumulated in taxable years beginning after December 31, 1951. X's taxable income for 1963 is $30,000 (computed prior to the inclusion of any amount in gross income for such year under section 593(f)) and during such year X received tax-exempt interest of $500. X's earnings and profits for 1963 (computed at the close of the taxable year without diminution by reason of any distributions made during the taxable year) is $20,400. The opening balance of X's reserve for losses on qualifying real property loans as of the close of December 31, 1962 (determined under paragraph (b)(3)(ii)(a) of § 1.593-7) was $24,500. Pre-1963 reserves of $24,500 were included in such opening balance, but it is assumed that pre-1963 reserves of only $4,500 would have been included in the opening balance if the opening balance had been determined under the experience method described in paragraph (b)(3)(ii)(b) of § 1.593-7. The deductible addition to such reserve for 1963 is $500. It is assumed that the addition to such reserve for 1963 would have been $100 if such addition had been computed under the experience method described in paragraph (d) of § 1.593-6. As of December 31, 1963, the balance of X's supplemental reserve for losses on loans is $30,000. On each of four dates during 1963 (January 1, April 1, July 1, and October 1), X made a $12,000 distribution (which was not a redemption to which section 302(a) or 303 applied or in partial or complete liquidation of X) to its shareholders with respect to its stock.

(ii) *Reserve for losses on qualifying real property loans.* For purposes of paragraph (b)(1)(i) of this section, X's reserve for losses on qualifying real property loans is $20,400, computed as follows:

Closing balance of reserve for losses on qualifying real property loans after addition for 1963 ($24,500 opening balance plus $500 addition)		$25,000
Minus:		
Amount of pre-1963 reserves which would have been included in opening balance under experience method	$4,500	
Total additions which would have been made under experience method	100	4,600
		$20,400

(iii) *Treatment of distributions.* Of each $12,000 quarterly distribution, $5,100 ($20,400 earnings and profits of the taxable year divided by 4) is out of X's earnings and profits of the taxable year (within the meaning of section 316(a)(2)); the remainder of the January 1 distribution, $6,900 ($12,000 minus $5,100), is out of X's earnings and profits accumulated in taxable years beginning after December 31, 1951. Since $20,700 ($6,900 multiplied by 3) is not out of X's earnings and profits, $20,400 of such amount shall be treated as made out of X's reserve for losses on qualifying real property loans (as determined under subdivision (ii) of this example) and $300 ($20,700 minus $20,400) shall be treated as made out of X's supplemental reserve for losses on loans.

(iv) *Amount included in gross income.* X's gross income for 1963 is increased by $43,124, which is the lesser of—

(a) $50,400 ($20,400, the reserve for losses on qualifying real property loans, as determined under subdivision (ii) of this example, plus $30,000, the supplemental reserve for losses on loans), or

(b) $43,124, *i.e.*, the amount which, when reduced by the amount of income tax attributable to the inclusion of such amount in gross income, $22,424 ($43,124 multiplied by a tax rate of 52 percent), is equal to the amount of such distribution, $20,700.

(v) *Amount charged against reserve for losses on qualifying real property loans and supplemental reserve for losses on loans.* The reserve for losses on qualifying real property loans is charged with $20,400 (the balance of the reserve as of December 31, 1963, as determined under subdivision (ii) of this example), and the supplemental reserve for losses on loans is charged with $22,724 ($43,124, the amount included in gross income under subdivision (iv) of this example, minus $20,400). [Reg. § 1.593-10.]

□ [T.D. 6728, 5-4-64. Amended by T.D. 7549, 5-17-78.]

[Reg. § 1.593-11]

§ 1.593-11. **Qualifying real property loan and nonqualifying loan defined.**—(a) *Loan defined.* For purposes of this section, the term "loan" means debt, as the term "debt" is used in section 166 and the regulations thereunder. The term "loan" also includes a redeemable ground rent (as defined in section 1055(c)) which is owned by the taxpayer, and any property acquired by the taxpayer in a transaction described in section 595(a). For determination of the amount of a loan, see paragraph (d) of this section.

(b) *Qualifying real property loan defined* —(1) *General rule.* For purposes of §§ 1.593-4 through 1.593-10, the term "qualifying real property loan" means any loan (other than a loan described in subparagraph (5) of this paragraph) which is secured by an interest in qualifying real property. For purposes of this section, the term "real property" means any property which, under the law of the jurisdiction in which such property is situated, constitutes real property. The term "real property" also includes a mobile unit which is permanently fixed to real property. The determination of whether a mobile unit is permanently fixed to real property shall be made on the basis of facts and circumstances in each particular case. For example, a mobile unit is permanently fixed to real property during a taxable year if, except for a brief period during which the unit is transported to a site, such unit was placed upon a foundation at a site with wheels and axles removed, affixed to the ground by means of straps, and connected to water, sewer, gas, and electric facilities. See paragraph (e) of this section for the treatment of a REMIC interest as a qualifying real property loan.

(2) *Meaning of "secured"*. A loan will be considered as "secured" only if the loan is on the security of any instrument (such as a mortgage, deed of trust, or land contract) which makes the interest of the debtor in the property described therein specific security for the payment of the loan, provided that such instrument is of such a nature that, in the event of default, the property could be subjected to the satisfaction of the loan with the same priority as a mortgage or deed of trust in the jurisdiction in which the property is situated.

(3) *Meaning of "interest"*. The word "interest" means an interest in real property which, under the law of the jurisdiction in which such property is situated, constitutes either (i) an interest in fee in such property (or in the case of a mobile unit, an ownership interest), (ii) a leasehold interest in such property extending or renewable automatically for a period of at least 30 years, or at least 10 years beyond the date scheduled for the final payment on the loan secured by such interest, (iii) a leasehold interest in improved residential real property consisting of a structure or structures containing, in the aggregate, no more than four family units extending for a period of at least 2 years beyond the date scheduled for the final payment on the loan secured by such interest, or (iv) a leasehold interest in such property held subject to a redeemable ground rent defined in section 1055(c).

(4) *Meaning of "qualifying real property"*. The term "qualifying real property" means any real property which is improved real property, or which from the proceeds of the loan will become improved real property. As used in the preceding sentence, the term "improved real property" means—

(i) Land on which is located any building of a permanent nature (such as a house, mobile unit, apartment house, office building, hospital, shopping center, warehouse, garage, or other similar permanent structure), provided that the value of such building is substantial in relation to the value of such land,

(ii) Any building lot or site which, by reason of installations and improvements that have been completed in keeping with applicable governmental requirements and with general practice in the community, is a building lot or site ready for the construction of any building of a permanent nature within the meaning of paragraph (G)(4)(i) of this section, or

(iii) Real property which, because of its state of improvement, produces sufficient income to maintain such real property and retire the loan in accordance with the terms thereof, or

(iv) A mobile unit which is permanently fixed to real property.

(5) *Loans not included*. The term "qualifying real property loan" does not include—

(i) Any loan evidenced by a security as defined in section 165(g)(2)(C),

(ii) Any loan (whether or not evidenced by a security as so defined) the primary obligor on which is (*a*) a government or a political subdivision or instrumentality thereof, (*b*) a bank (as defined in section 581), or (*c*) another member of the same affiliated group,

(iii) Any loan to the extent such loan is secured by a deposit in or share of the taxpayer (including a share of nonwithdrawable capital stock), determined as of the close of the taxable year, and

(iv) Any loan which (within a 60-day period beginning in one taxable year of the taxpayer and ending in the next taxable year of such taxpayer) is made or acquired, and then repaid or disposed of, unless both the transaction by which the loan is made or acquired and the transaction by which the loan is repaid or disposed of are established to the satisfaction of the district director to be for bona fide business purposes.

As used in subdivision (ii)(*c*) of this subparagraph, the term "affiliated group" shall have the meaning assigned to such term by section 1504(a) (relating to the definition of an affiliated group), except that the phrase "more than 50 percent" shall be substituted for the phrase "at least 80 percent" each place the latter phrase appears in section 1504(a), and all corporations shall be

Reg. § 1.593-11(b)(2)

treated as includible corporations (without regard to any of the exclusions provided in section 1504(b)).

(c) *Nonqualifying loan defined.* For purposes of §§ 1.593-4 through 1.593-9, the term "nonqualifying loan" means any loan which is not a qualifying real property loan.

(d) *Amount of loan determined*—(1) *General rule.* Except as provided in subparagraph (2) of this paragraph, the amount of any qualifying real property loan or nonqualifying loan, for purposes of section 593, is the adjusted basis of such loan as determined under § 1.1011-1. However, the adjusted basis, determined under § 1.1011-1, of any "loan in process" does not include the unadvanced portion of such loan. For the basis of a redeemable ground rent reserved or created by the taxpayer before April 11, 1963, see section 1055(b)(3); and for the basis of a loan represented by property acquired by the taxpayer in a transaction described in section 595(a), see section 595(c).

(2) *Limitation.* If the total amount advanced on any loan exceeds the loan value of any interest in qualifying real property which secures such loan, then the portion of such loan which, as of the close of any taxable year, will be considered as a qualifying real property loan shall be determined under the principles of section 7701(a)(19) and the regulations thereunder.

(e) *Treatment of REMIC interests as qualifying real property loans*—(1) *In general.* For purposes of section 593 and §§ 1.593-4 through 1.593-10, if, for any calendar quarter, at least 95 percent of a REMIC's assets (as determined in accordance with § 1.860F-4(e)(1)(ii) or § 1.6049-7(f)(3)) are qualifying real property loans (as defined in paragraph (b) of this section), then, for that calendar quarter, all the regular and residual interests in that REMIC are treated as qualifying real property loans. If less than 95 percent of a REMIC's assets are qualifying real property loans, then a percentage of each regular or residual interest is treated as a qualifying real property loan. The percentage equals the percentage of the REMIC's assets that are qualifying real property loans. See § 1.860F-4(e)(1)(ii)(B) and § 1.6049-7(f)(3) for information required to be provided to regular and residual interest holders if the 95-percent test is not met.

(2) *Treatment of REMIC assets for section 593 purposes*—(i) *Manufactured housing treated as qualifying real property.* For purposes of paragraph (e)(1) of this section, the term "qualifying real property" includes manufactured housing treated as a single family residence under section 25(e)(10).

(ii) *Status of cash flow investments.* For purposes of paragraph (e)(1) of this section, cash flow investments (as defined in section 860G(a)(6) and § 1.860G-2(g)(1)) are treated as qualifying real property loans. [Reg. § 1.593-11.]

☐ [*T.D.* 6728, 5-4-64. *Amended by T.D.* 7549, 5-17-78 *and T.D.* 8458, 12-23-92.]

[Reg. § 1.594-1]

§ 1.594-1. **Mutual savings banks conducting life insurance business.**—(a) *Scope of application.* Section 594 applies to the case of a mutual savings bank not having capital stock represented by shares which conducts a life insurance business, if:

(1) The conduct of the life insurance business is authorized under State law,

(2) The life insurance business is carried on in a separate department of the bank,

(3) The books of account of the life insurance business are maintained separately from other departments of the bank, and

(4) The life insurance department of the bank would, if it were treated as a separate corporation, qualify as a life insurance company under section 801.

(b) *Computation of tax.* In the case of a mutual savings bank conducting a life insurance business to which section 594 is applicable, the tax upon such bank consists of the sum of the following:

(1) A partial tax computed under section 11 upon the taxable income of the bank determined without regard to any items of income or deduction properly allocable to the life insurance department, and

(2) A partial tax computed on the income (or, in the case of taxable years beginning before January 1, 1955, the taxable income (as defined in section 803)) of the life insurance department determined without regard to any items of income or deduction not properly allocable to such department, at the rates and in the manner provided in subchapter L (section 801 and following), chapter 1 of the Code, with respect to life insurance companies. [Reg. § 1.594-1.]

☐ [*T.D.* 6188, 7-5-56.]

[Reg. § 1.595-1]

§ 1.595-1. **Treatment of foreclosed property by certain creditors.**—(a) *Nonrecognition of gain or loss on the acquisition of security property by certain creditors*—(1) *In general.* Section 595(a) provides that in the case of a creditor which is an organization described in section 593(a) (that is, a mutual savings bank not having capital stock represented by shares, a domestic building and loan association, or a cooperative bank without capital stock organized and operated for mutual purposes and without profit), no gain or loss shall be recognized, and no debt shall be considered as becoming worthless or partially worthless for purposes of section 166 (relating to bad debts), as the result of a transaction by which such creditor bids in at foreclosure, or reduces to ownership or possession by agreement or process of law, any property (whether real or personal, tangible or intangible) which was security for the payment of any indebtedness (whether or not a qualifying real property loan as defined in section 593(e)(1)). The treatment provided by section 595(a) is mandatory (regardless of whether such creditor utilizes the specific deduction or reserve method of accounting for bad debts) if, for the taxable year in which the property is bid in at foreclosure, or reduced to ownership or possession by agreement or process of law, the creditor is an organization described in section 593(a), even though the creditor subsequently becomes an organization not described in section 593(a). For definition of the terms "domestic building and loan association" and "cooperative bank" for taxable years beginning after October 16, 1962, see paragraphs (19) and (32), respectively, of section 7701(a).

(2) *Effective date.* Section 595 applies to any transaction (described in subparagraph (1) of this paragraph) occurring after December 31, 1962, except that such section does not apply to any such transaction in which the taxable event determined without regard to section 595 (that is, the sale or exchange to the creditor of the security property by reason of the default or anticipated default of the debtor) occurred before January 1, 1963.

(b) *Rules for determining when security property is reduced to ownership or possession by agreement or process of law*—(1) *Ownership or possession.* For purposes of this section, security property shall be considered as reduced to ownership or possession by agreement or process of law on the earliest date on which the creditor, by reason of the default or anticipated default of the debtor,—

(i) Acquires, by agreement or process of law, a title to, or a right or interest in, the security property which under local law is indefeasible and which the creditor can validly dispose of apart from the indebtedness which the property secures, or

(ii) Acquires, by agreement or process of law, an enforceable right to direct the use to which the security property shall be put, including, in the case of real property, whether or not the property shall continue to be occupied by the debtor who has defaulted (regardless of whether such creditor has obtained indefeasible title to the property), or

(iii) Sells or otherwise disposes of the security property or any interest therein.

(2) *Agreement or process of law.* The reduction of security property to ownership or possession by agreement includes, where valid under local law, such methods as voluntary conveyance from the debtor (including a conveyance directly to the Federal Housing Commissioner) and abandonment to the creditor. The reduction of security property to ownership or possession by process of law includes foreclosure proceedings in which a competitive bid is entered, such as foreclosure by judicial sale or by power of sale contained in the loan agreement without recourse to the courts, as well as those types of foreclosure proceedings in which a competitive bid is not entered, such as strict foreclosure and foreclosure by entry and possession, by writ of entry, or by publication or notice.

(c) *Examples.* The provisions of paragraphs (a) and (b) of this section may be illustrated by the following examples:

Example (1). On January 31, 1963, X, a creditor which is an organization described in section 593(a), purchases at a foreclosure sale residential real property which was security for a debt owing to X, and with respect to which the debtor has defaulted. Under local law, there is a 1-year statutory redemption period (during which period the debtor is entitled to remain in possession) so that X must wait until February 1, 1964, to obtain indefeasible title to the property. No gain or loss is recognized by reason of the purchase at the foreclosure sale on January 31, 1963. However, the date on which the security property is considered as reduced to ownership or possession by agreement or process of law is February 1, 1964. If, under local law, there were no statutory redemption period so that X obtained indefeasible title to the security property at the foreclosure sale, the date on which the security property would be considered as so reduced is January 31, 1963. Furthermore, with respect to either of the preceding situations, if the foreclosure sale had occurred on November 1, 1962 (instead of on January 31, 1963), section 595 would not apply to the transaction since the taxable event in respect of such transaction occurred prior to January 1, 1963.

Example (2). The facts are the same as in example (1), except that instead of purchasing the property at a foreclosure sale, X, pursuant to the provisions of local law, enters upon the security property on January 31, 1963, and acquires an

Reg. § 1.595-1(a)(2)

enforceable right to direct whether the property shall continue to be occupied by the debtor. X does not obtain indefeasible title to the property until February 1, 1964. The date on which the security property is considered as reduced to ownership or possession by agreement or process of law is January 31, 1963.

(d) *Basis of acquired property.* Section 595(c) provides that the basis of any property to which section 595(a) applies (hereinafter referred to as "acquired property") shall be the adjusted basis of the indebtedness for which such property was security, determined as of the date of acquisition of such property, properly increased for costs of acquisition. The date of acquisition is the date, determined under paragraph (b) of this section, on which the security property is reduced to ownership or possession by agreement or process of law. Costs of acquisition are expenditures incurred by the creditor (for example, fees for an attorney, master, trustee, auctioneer, for publication, acquiring title, clearing liens, filing and recording, and court costs) which are directly related to the foreclosure sale or proceeding, or to the other process used to reduce the security property to ownership or possession, or both, by agreement or process of law. For purposes of determining the adjusted basis of the indebtedness for which the acquired property was security, there shall be included the amount of any unpaid interest with respect to such indebtedness, but only to the extent that it has been included in gross income. The basis of the acquired property, as determined under this paragraph, shall be adjusted in accordance with the rules provided in paragraph (e) of this section.

(e) *Characteristics of acquired property*—(1) *Depreciation; decline in fair market value.* Section 595(b) provides, in part, that for purposes of section 166 (relating to bad debts) acquired property shall be considered as property having the same characteristics as the indebtedness for which such property was security. Thus, no deduction for exhaustion, wear and tear, obsolescence, amortization, or depletion shall be allowed to a creditor with respect to acquired property. However, if, at any time, the adjusted basis of the acquired property exceeds the fair market value of such property (determined by proper appraisal and without regard to any outstanding right of redemption), and the creditor can establish (in the same manner as worthlessness in whole or in part is established for purposes of section 166) that an amount equal to any portion of such excess will not be collected with respect to the indebtedness for which such property was security, the creditor may treat such portion, under the provisions of section 166, as a worthless debt. In such case, the basis of the acquired property shall be reduced by the amount treated as a worthless debt.

(2) *Example.* The provisions of subparagraph (1) of this paragraph may be illustrated by the following example:

Example. X Corporation, a creditor which is an organization described in section 593(a), makes its returns on the basis of the calendar year and the reserve method of accounting for bad debts. In 1963, A defaults in his payments on a debt owed to X which is secured by residential real property. X reduces the property to ownership or possession by agreement or process of law by bidding it in at a foreclosure sale for $23,000. The adjusted basis of the indebtedness at the date of acquisition of the property (increased for costs of acquisition) is $25,000, and this amount becomes the basis of the acquired property. X obtains a deficiency judgment against A for $2,000. Later in 1963, a proper appraisal enables X to establish that the fair market value of the property is $18,000. X is also able to establish (under the rules of section 166 and the regulations thereunder) that due to A's poor financial condition only $1,000 can be collected on the outstanding deficiency judgment. For the year 1963, X may charge its bad debt reserve for $6,000, computed as follows:

Basis of acquired property	$25,000
Less: Fair market value of acquired property	18,000
Excess	$ 7,000
Less: Collectible portion of deficiency judgment	1,000
Portion of excess treated as worthless debt	$ 6,000

(3) *Capital improvements made after date of acquisition not treated as acquired property.* Except as provided in subparagraph (4) of this paragraph, the term "acquired property" does not include capital improvements made after the date of acquisition (within the meaning of paragraph (d) of this section) of the property. Thus, the applicable deduction for exhaustion, wear and tear, obsolescence, amortization, or depletion shall be allowed, if otherwise allowable, for improvements which are made by the creditor with respect to acquired property and which are properly chargeable to the capital account. If the creditor sells or otherwise disposes of the acquired property with such capital improvements, any amount realized by reason of such sale or other disposition

Reg. § 1.595-1(e)(3)

shall be allocated in proportion to the respective fair market values of the acquired property and such capital improvements. The portion of the amount realized which is allocable to the acquired property shall be treated in accordance with the rules prescribed in subparagraph (6) of this paragraph. The portion of the amount realized which is allocable to such capital improvements shall be treated under the applicable rules governing the sale or other disposition of such property and without regard to section 595.

(4) *Treatment of minor capital improvements as acquired property.* A creditor may treat any minor capital improvements which it makes to a particular acquired property after the date of acquisition (within the meaning of paragraph (d) of this section) in the same manner as the acquired property, provided such creditor treats all minor capital improvements with respect to that particular acquired property in such manner. For purposes of section 595, a capital improvement shall be considered as "minor" only if the cost of such improvement does not exceed $3,000.

(5) *Records for capital improvements.* For purposes of subparagraphs (3) and (4) of this paragraph, the creditor must maintain such records as are necessary to clearly reflect, with respect to each particular acquired property, the cost of each capital improvement and whether the taxpayer treated minor capital improvements with respect to such property in the same manner as the acquired property.

(6) *Amounts realized with respect to acquired property.* Section 595(b) provides, in part, that any amount realized with respect to acquired property shall be treated as a payment on account of the indebtedness for which such property was security, and any loss with respect thereto shall be treated as a bad debt to which the provisions of section 166 (relating to bad debts) apply. An amount realized with respect to acquired property means an amount representing a recovery of capital, such as proceeds from the sale or other disposition of the property, payments on the original indebtedness made by or on behalf of the debtor (including amounts received under an insurance contract with the Federal Housing Administration or a guarantee by the Veterans' Administration), and collections on a deficiency judgment obtained against the debtor (other than amounts treated as interest under applicable local law). Amounts realized with respect to acquired property include amounts which otherwise would be treated in the manner prescribed in section 351 (relating to transfer to a corporation controlled by transferor), section 354 (relating to exchanges of stock and securities in certain reorganizations), section 453 (relating to installment method), section 1031 (relating to exchange of property held for productive use or for investment), or section 1033 (relating to involuntary conversions). For purposes of section 595(b), if a corporation distributes acquired property in a distribution to which section 311 (relating to taxability of corporation on distribution) or section 336 (relating to nonrecognition of gain or loss to a corporation on distribution of its property in partial or complete liquidation) applies, the fair market value of the acquired property at the time of the distribution shall be treated as an amount realized with respect to such property. However, no amount shall be considered realized by reason of the distribution or transfer of acquired property in a transaction to which section 381(a) (relating to carryovers in certain corporate acquisitions) applies, and in the case of such a distribution or transfer the acquired property shall be treated by the distributee or transferee as having the same characteristics as it had in the hands of the distributor or transferor at the time of such distribution or transfer. The following rules shall apply to amounts realized with respect to acquired property:

(i) Any amount realized shall be applied against and reduce the adjusted basis of the acquired property, and to the extent that such amount exceeds the adjusted basis, it shall, in the case of a creditor using the specific deduction method of accounting for bad debts, be included in gross income as ordinary income, or, in the case of a creditor using the reserve method of accounting for bad debts, be credited to the appropriate bad debt reserve (that is, the reserve for losses on qualifying real property loans or the reserve for losses on nonqualifying loans). Any amounts credited during the taxable year to a reserve for bad debts pursuant to this subdivision shall not be considered as a part of the addition under section 593 for such year, but shall be included in the balance of the reserve for purposes of computing such addition to the reserve for such taxable year. Thus, for example, an amount credited to the reserve for losses on qualifying real property loans during a taxable year shall not be considered as a part of the addition to such reserve computed under the percentage of taxable income method. However, the amount of such credit shall be included in the balance of such reserve for the purpose of determining the amount necessary to increase the balance of such reserve (as of the close of such taxable year) to an amount equal to 3 percent of qualifying real property loans and for the purpose of determining whether such balance exceeds 6 percent of such loans.

(ii) If an amount realized on the sale or other disposition of the acquired property is insufficient to restore to the creditor the adjusted basis of the property, the difference between such adjusted basis and such amount realized shall be treated as a bad debt to which the provisions of section 166 apply. If the creditor subsequently realizes an additional amount with respect to the original indebtedness or the acquired property, such additional amount shall be treated as the recovery of a bad debt.

(7) *Treatment of rents, similar amounts, and expenses.* Section 595 does not change the treatment of rents, royalties, dividends, interest, or similar amounts received or accrued by the creditor with respect to acquired property, nor does it change the treatment of expenses incurred with respect to such property. (See, however, subparagraph (1) of this paragraph for treatment of depreciation, etc.) Thus, for example, if the acquired property is a governmental obligation within the meaning of section 103 (relating to interest on certain governmental obligations), interest payments received by the creditor with respect to such obligation would not be included in gross income.

(8) *Examples.* The provisions of subparagraphs (6) and (7) of this paragraph may be illustrated by the following examples:

Example (1)—(i) *Facts.* X Corporation, a creditor which is an organization described in section 593(a), uses the reserve method of accounting for bad debts. On May 1, 1964, X reduces to ownership or possession by agreement or process of law improved real property which is security for an indebtedness of A which is in default. On the date of acquisition there remains unpaid on the indebtedness $20,000 principal and $700 interest. X has previously included the $700 interest in gross income. Subsequent to acquisition, X incurs expenses totaling $500 for maintenance, and during the period June 1 through September 30, 1964, rents the property for a total rental of $400. Under local law, X is accountable to A for the rents received and A is accountable to X for the expenses incurred. There are no other receipts or expenses until October 1, 1964, at which time X sells the acquired property for $22,000. Under local law, A is not entitled to any portion of the sales proceeds.

(ii) *Treatment of rents, expenses, and sales proceeds.* X would treat rents, expenses, and sales proceeds in the following manner:

Basis of acquired property at aquisition (adjusted basis of indebtedness, *i.e.*, $20,000 principal plus $700 interest)	$20,700
Plus: Expenses charged to debtor	500
	$21,200
Less: Rents credited to debtor	$ 400
Adjusted basis of acquired property at sale	$20,800
Less: Portion of $22,000 sales proceeds applied in reduction of adjusted basis of acquired property	20,800
	0
Portion of sales proceeds credited to reserve for losses on qualifying real property loans ($22,000 minus $20,800)	$ 1,200

(iii) *Creditor using specific deduction method.* If instead of using the reserve method of accounting for bad debts X used the specific deduction method, the $1,200 portion of the sales proceeds would be treated as ordinary income.

Example (2)—(i) *Facts.* The facts are the same as in example (1) except that under local law X is not accountable to A for any portion of the rents received and A is not accountable to X for the expenses incurred by X.

(ii) *Treatment of rents and expenses.* X includes in gross income the total rent receipts of $400 and deducts (if otherwise allowable) the expenses of $500.

(iii) *Treatment of sales proceeds.* As the result of the sale of the acquired property, X credits $1,300 to the reserve for losses on qualifying real property loans, computed as follows:

Basis of acquired property at acquisition and at date of sale (adjusted basis of indebtedness, *i.e.*, $20,000 principal plus $700 interest)	$20,700
Less: Portion of $22,000 sales proceeds applied in reduction of adjusted basis of acquired property	20,700
	0
Portion of sales proceeds credited to reserve for losses on qualifying real property loans ($22,000 minus $20,700)	$ 1,300

Reg. § 1.595-1(e)(8)

Mutual Savings Banks, Etc.

See p. 20,601 for regulations not amended to reflect law changes

(iv) *Creditor using specific deduction method.* If instead of using the reserve method of accounting for bad debts X used the specific deduction method, the $1,300 portion of the sales proceeds would be treated as ordinary income.

Example (3)—(i) *Facts.* The facts are the same as in example (1) except that X sells the acquired property for $15,000.

Basis of acquired property at acquisition (adjusted basis of indebtedness, i.e., $20,000 principal plus $700 interest)	$20,700
Plus: Expenses charged to debtor	500
	$21,200
Less: Rents credited to debtor	$ 400
Adjusted basis of acquired property at sale	$20,800
Less: Portion of $15,000 sales proceeds applied in reduction of adjusted basis of acquired property	15,000
Amount charged to reserve for losses on qualifying real property loans	$ 5,800

(iii) *Creditor using specific deduction method.* If instead of using the reserve method of accounting for bad debts X used the specific deduction method, the excess of $5,800 would be allowed as a specific bad debt deduction. [Reg. § 1.595-1.]

☐ [T.D. 6814, 4-6-64.]

[Reg. § 1.596-1]

§ 1.596-1. Limitation on dividends received deduction.—(a) *In general.* For taxable years beginning after July 11, 1969, in the case of mutual savings banks, domestic building and loan associations, and cooperative banks, if the addition to the reserve for losses on qualifying real property loans for the taxable year is determined under section 593(b)(2) (relating to the percentage of taxable income method), the total amount allowed as a deduction with respect to dividends received under part VIII, subchapter B, chapter 1, subtitle A of the Code (section 241 et seq.) (determined without regard to section 596 and this section) for such taxable year is reduced as provided by this section. In such case, the dividends received deduction otherwise determined under part VIII, subchapter B, chapter 1, subtitle A of the Code, is reduced by an amount equal to the applicable percentage for such year (determined solely under subparagraphs (A) and (B) of section 593(b)(2) and the regulations thereunder) of such total amount. For the rule under which a mutual savings bank, domestic building and loan association, or cooperative bank is deemed to have determined the addition to its reserve for losses on qualifying real property loans for the taxable year under section 593(b)(2), see § 1.593-6A(a)(2).

(b) *Example.* The provisions of this section may be illustrated by the following example:

(ii) *Treatment of rents, expenses, and sales proceeds.* X would treat rents, expenses, and sales proceeds in the following manner:

Example. X Corporation, a domestic building and loan association, determined the addition to its reserve for losses on qualifying real property loans under section 593(b)(2) for its taxable year beginning in 1971. During that taxable year, X Corporation received a total of $100,000 as dividends from domestic corporations subject to tax under chapter 1 of the Code. X Corporation received no other dividends during the taxable year. Under part VIII, subchapter B, chapter 1, subtitle A of the Code, a deduction, determined without regard to section 596 and this section, of $85,000 would be allowed with respect to the dividends. For the taxable year, the applicable percentage, determined under subparagraphs (A) and (B) of section 593(b)(2), is 54 percent. Under section 596 and this section, the amount allowed as a deduction under section 243 and the regulations thereunder is reduced by $45,900 (54 percent of $85,000) to $39,100 ($85,000 less $45,900).

(c) *Dividends received by members of a controlled group.* If a thrift institution that computes a deduction under section 593(b)(2) is a member of a controlled group of corporations (within the meaning of section 1563(a), determined by substituting "50 percent" for "80 percent" each place it appears therein) and if the thrift institution, without a bona fide business purpose, transfers stock, directly or indirectly, to another member of the group, the Commissioner may allocate any dividends with respect to the stock to the thrift institution. If the Commissioner allocates a dividend to a thrift institution under this paragraph (c), the Commissioner will also make appropriate correlative adjustments to the income of any other member of the group involved in the allocation, at a time and in a manner consistent with the procedures of § 1.482-1(d)(2). This paragraph (c) ap-

Reg. § 1.596-1(a)

plies to taxable years ending on or after August 30, 1975. [Reg. § 1.596-1.]

☐ [T.D. 7149, 11-1-71. Amended by T.D. 7631, 7-10-79.]

[Reg. § 1.597-1]

§ 1.597-1. Definitions.—For purposes of the regulations under section 597—

(a) Unless the context otherwise requires, the terms *consolidated group*, *member* and *subsidiary* have the meanings provided in § 1.1502-1; and

(b) The following terms have the meanings provided below—

Acquiring. The term *Acquiring* means a corporation that is a transferee in a Taxable Transfer, other than a deemed transferee in a Taxable Transfer described in § 1.597-5(b).

Agency. The term *Agency* means the Resolution Trust Corporation, the Federal Deposit Insurance Corporation, any similar instrumentality of the United States government, and any predecessor or successor of the foregoing (including the Federal Savings and Loan Insurance Corporation).

Agency Control. An Institution or entity is under *Agency Control* if Agency is conservator or receiver of the Institution or entity, or if Agency has the right to appoint any of the Institution's or entity's directors.

Agency Obligation. The term *Agency Obligation* means a debt instrument that Agency issues to an Institution or to a direct or indirect owner of an Institution.

Bridge Bank. The term *Bridge Bank* means an Institution that is organized by Agency to hold assets and liabilities of another Institution and that continues the operation of the other Institution's business pending its acquisition or liquidation, and that is any of the following—

(1) A national bank chartered by the Comptroller of the Currency under section 11(n) of the Federal Deposit Insurance Act (12 U.S.C. 1821(n)) or section 21A(b)(10)(A) of the Federal Home Loan Bank Act (12 U.S.C. 1441a(b)(10)(A)) or any successor sections;

(2) A Federal savings association chartered by the Director of the Office of Thrift Supervision under section 21A(b)(10)(A) of the Federal Home Loan Bank Act (12 U.S.C. 1441a(b)(10)(A)) or any successor section; or

(3) A similar Institution chartered under any other statutory provisions.

Consolidated Subsidiary. The term *Consolidated Subsidiary* means a member of the consolidated group of which an Institution is a member that bears the same relationship to the Institution that the members of a consolidated group bear to their common parent under section 1504(a)(1).

Continuing Equity. An Institution has *Continuing Equity* for any taxable year if, on the last day of the taxable year, the Institution is not (1) a Bridge Bank, (2) in Agency receivership, or (3) treated as a New Entity.

Controlled Entity. The term *Controlled Entity* means an entity under Agency Control.

Federal Financial Assistance (FFA). The term *Federal Financial Assistance* (FFA), as defined by section 597(c), means any money or property provided by Agency to an Institution or to a direct or indirect owner of stock in an Institution under section 406(f) of the National Housing Act (12 U.S.C. 1729(f)), section 21A(b)(4) of the Federal Home Loan Bank Act (12 U.S.C. 1441a(b)(4)), section 11(f) or 13(c) of the Federal Deposit Insurance Act (12 U.S.C. 1821(f), 1823(c)), or under any similar provision of law. Any such money or property is FFA, regardless of whether the Institution or any of its affiliates issues Agency a note or other obligation, stock, warrants, or other rights to acquire stock in connection with Agency's provision of the money or property. FFA includes Net Worth Assistance, Loss Guarantee payments, yield maintenance payments, cost to carry or cost of funds reimbursement payments, expense reimbursement or indemnity payments, and interest (including original issue discount) on an Agency Obligation.

Institution. The term *Institution* means an entity that is, or immediately before being placed under Agency Control was, a bank or domestic building and loan association within the meaning of section 597 (including a Bridge Bank). Except as otherwise provided in the regulations under section 597, the term *Institution* includes a New Entity or Acquiring that is a bank or domestic building and loan association within the meaning of section 597.

Loss Guarantee. The term *Loss Guarantee* means an agreement pursuant to which Agency or a Controlled Entity guarantees or agrees to pay an Institution a specified amount upon the disposition or charge-off (in whole or in part) of specific assets, an agreement pursuant to which an Institution has a right to put assets to Agency or a Controlled Entity at a specified price, or a similar arrangement.

Net Worth Assistance. The term *Net Worth Assistance* means money or property (ilcluding an Agency Obligation to the extent it has a fixed principal amount) that Agency provides as an integral part of a Taxable Transfer, other than FFA that accrues after the date of the Taxable Transfer. For example, Net Worth Assistance does not include Loss Guarantee payments, yield maintenance payments, cost to carry or cost of funds reimbursement payments, or expense reimbursement or indemnity payments. An Agency Obligation is considered to have a fixed principal amount notwithstanding an agreement providing for its adjustment after issuance to reflect a more accurate determination of the condition of the Institution at the time of the acquisition.

New Entity. The term *New Entity* means the new corporation that is treated as purchasing all of the assets of an Old Entity in a Taxable Transfer described in § 1.597-5(b).

Old Entity. The term *Old Entity* means the Institution or Consolidated Subsidiary that is treated as selling all of its assets in a Taxable Transfer described in § 1.597-5(b).

Residual Entity. The term *Residual Entity* means the entity that remains after an Institution transfers deposit liabilities to a Bridge Bank.

Taxable Transfer. The term *Taxable Transfer* has the meaning provided in § 1.597-5(a)(1). [Reg. § 1.597-1.]

☐ [*T.D.* 8641, 12-20-95.]

[Reg. § 1.597-2]

§ 1.597-2. Taxation of federal financial assistance.—(a) *Inclusion in income*—(1) *In general.* Except as otherwise provided in the regulations under section 597, all FFA is includible as ordinary income to the recipient at the time the FFA is received or accrued in accordance with the recipient's method of accounting. The amount of FFA received or accrued is the amount of any money, the fair market value of any property (other than an Agency Obligation), and the issue price of any Agency Obligation (determined under § 1.597-3(c)(2)). An Institution (and not the nominal recipient) is treated as receiving directly any FFA that Agency provides in a taxable year to a direct or indirect shareholder of the Institution, to the extent money or property is transferred to the Institution pursuant to an agreement with Agency.

(2) *Cross references.* See paragraph (c) of this section for rules regarding the timing of inclusion of certain FFA. See paragraph (d) of this section for additional rules regarding the treatment of FFA received in connection with transfers of money or property to Agency or a Controlled Entity, or paid pursuant to a Loss Guarantee. See § 1.597-5(c)(1) for additional rules regarding the inclusion of Net Worth Assistance in the income of an Institution.

(b) *Basis of property that is FFA.* If FFA consists of property, the Institution's basis in the property equals the fair market value of the property (other than an Agency Obligation) or the issue price of the Agency Obligation, as determined under § 1.597-3(c)(2).

(c) *Timing of inclusion of certain FFA*—(1) *Scope.* This paragraph (c) limits the amount of FFA an Institution must include in income currently under certain circumstances and provides rules for the deferred inclusion in income of amounts in excess of those limits. This paragraph (c) does not apply to a New Entity or Acquiring.

(2) *Amount currently included in income by an Institution without Continuing Equity.* The amount of FFA an Institution without Continuing Equity must include in income in a taxable year under paragraph (a)(1) of this section is limited to the sum of—

(i) The excess at the beginning of the taxable year of the Institution's liabilities over the adjusted bases of the Institution's assets; and

(ii) The amount by which the excess for the taxable year of the Institution's deductions allowed by chapter 1 of the Internal Revenue Code (other than net operating and capital loss carryovers) over its gross income (determined without regard to FFA) is greater than the excess at the beginning of the taxable year of the adjusted bases of the Institution's assets over the Institution's liabilities.

(3) *Amount currently included in income by an Institution with Continuing Equity.* The amount of FFA an Institution with Continuing Equity must include in income in a taxable year under paragraph (a)(1) of this section is limited to the sum of—

(i) The excess at the beginning of the taxable year of the Institution's liabilities over the adjusted bases of the Institution's assets;

(ii) The greater of—

(A) The excess for the taxable year of the Institution's deductions allowed by chapter 1 of the Internal Revenue Code (other than net operating and capital loss carryovers) over its gross income (determined without regard to FFA); or

(B) The excess for the taxable year of the deductions allowed by chapter 1 of the Internal Revenue Code (other than net operating and capital loss carryovers) of the consolidated group of which the Institution is a member on the last day of the Institution's taxable year over the group's gross income (determined without regard to FFA); and

(iii) The excess of the amount of any net operating loss carryover of the Institution (or in the case of a carryover from a consolidated return year of the Institution's current consolidated group, the net operating loss carryover of the group) to the taxable year over the amount described in paragraph (c)(3)(i) of this section.

(4) *Deferred FFA*—(i) *Maintenance of account.* An Institution must establish a deferred FFA account commencing in the first taxable year in which it receives FFA that is not currently included in income under paragraph (c)(2) or (c)(3) of this section, and must maintain that account in accordance with the requirements of this paragraph (c)(4). The Institution must add the amount of any FFA that is not currently included in income under paragraph (c)(2) or (c)(3) of this section to its deferred FFA account. The Institution must decrease the balance of its deferred FFA account by the amount of deferred FFA included in income under paragraphs (c)(4)(ii), (iv) and (v) of this section. (See also paragraph (d)(5)(i)(B) of this section for other adjustments that decrease the deferred FFA account.) If, under paragraph (c)(3) of this section, FFA is not currently included in income in a taxable year, the Institution thereafter must maintain its deferred FFA account on a FIFO (first in, first out) basis (e.g., for purposes of the first sentence of paragraph (c)(4)(iv) of this section).

(ii) *Deferred FFA recapture.* In any taxable year in which an Institution has a balance in its deferred FFA account, it must include in income an amount equal to the lesser of the amount described in paragraph (c)(4)(iii) of this section or the balance in its deferred FFA account.

(iii) *Annual recapture amount*—(A) *Institutions without Continuing Equity*—(*1*) *In general.* In the case of an Institution without Continuing Equity, the amount described in this paragraph (c)(4)(iii) is the amount by which—

(*i*) The excess for the taxable year of the Institution's deductions allowed by chapter 1 of the Internal Revenue Code (other than net operating and capital loss carryovers) over its gross income (taking into account FFA included in income under paragraph (c)(2) of this section); is greater than

(*ii*) The Institution's remaining equity as of the beginning of the taxable year.

(*2*) *Remaining equity.* The Institution's remaining equity is—

(*i*) The amount at the beginning of the taxable year in which the deferred FFA account was established equal to the adjusted bases of the Institution's assets minus the Institution's liabilities (which amount may be positive or negative); plus

(*ii*) The Institution's taxable income (computed without regard to any carryover from any other year) in any subsequent taxable year or years; minus

(*iii*) The excess in any subsequent taxable year or years of the Institution's deductions allowed by chapter 1 of the Internal Revenue Code (other than net operating and capital loss carryovers) over its gross income.

(B) *Institutions with Continuing Equity.* In the case of an Institution with Continuing Equity, the amount described in this paragraph (c)(4)(iii) is the amount by which the Institution's deductions allowed by chapter 1 of the Internal Revenue Code (other than net operating and capital loss carryovers) exceed its gross income (taking into account FFA included in income under paragraph (c)(3) of this section).

(iv) *Additional deferred FFA recapture by an Institution with Continuing Equity.* To the extent that, as of the end of a taxable year, the cumulative amount of FFA deferred under paragraph (c)(3) of this section that an Institution with Continuing Equity has recaptured under this paragraph (c)(4) is less than the cumulative amount of FFA deferred under paragraph (c)(3) of this section that the Institution would have recaptured if that FFA had been included in income ratably over the six taxable years immediately following the taxable year of deferral, the Institution must include that difference in income for the taxable year. An Institution with Continuing Equity must include in income the balance of its deferred FFA account in the taxable year in which it liquidates, ceases to do business, transfers (other than to a Bridge Bank) substantially all of its assets and liabilities, or is deemed to transfer all of its assets under § 1.597-5(b).

(v) *Optional accelerated recapture of deferred FFA.* An Institution that has a deferred FFA account may include in income the balance of its deferred FFA account on its timely filed (including extensions) original income tax return for any taxable year that it is not under Agency Control. The balance of its deferred FFA account is income on the last day of that year.

(5) *Exceptions to limitations on use of losses.* In computing an Institution's taxable income or alternative minimum taxable income for a taxable year, sections 56(d)(1), 382 and 383 and §§ 1.1502-15, 1.1502-21 and 1.1502-22 (or §§ 1.1502-15A, 1.1502-21A, and 1.1502-22A, as appropriate) do not limit the use of the attributes of the Institution to the extent, if any, that the inclusion of FFA (including recaptured FFA) in income results in taxable income or alternative minimum taxable income (determined without re-

Reg. § 1.597-2(c)(5)

gard to this paragraph (c)(5)) for the taxable year. This paragraph (c)(5) does not apply to any limitation under section 382 or 383 or § 1.1502-15, 1.1502-21 or 1.1502-22 (or §§ 1.1502-15A, 1.1502-21A or 1.1502-22A, as appropriate) that arose in connection with or prior to a corporation becoming a Consolidated Subsidiary of the Institution.

(6) *Operating rules*—(i) *Bad debt reserves.* For purposes of paragraphs (c)(2), (c)(3) and (c)(4) of this section, the adjusted bases of an Institution's assets are reduced by the amount of the Institution's reserves for bad debts under section 585 or 593, other than supplemental reserves under section 593.

(ii) *Aggregation of Consolidated Subsidiaries.* For purposes of this paragraph (c), an Institution is treated as a single entity that includes the income, expenses, assets, liabilities, and attributes of its Consolidated Subsidiaries, with appropriate adjustments to prevent duplication.

(iii) *Alternative minimum tax.* To compute the alternative minimum taxable income attributable to FFA of an Institution for any taxable year under section 55, the rules of this section, and related rules, are applied by using alternative minimum tax basis, deductions, and all other items required to be taken into account. All other alternative minimum tax provisions continue to apply.

(7) *Earnings and profits.* FFA that is not currently included in income under this paragraph (c) is included in earnings and profits for all purposes of the Internal Revenue Code to the extent and at the time it is included in income under this paragraph (c).

(d) *Transfers of money or property to Agency, and property subject to a Loss Guarantee*—(1) *Transfers of property to Agency.* The transfer of property to Agency or a Controlled Entity is a taxable sale or exchange in which the Institution is treated as realizing an amount equal to—

(i) The property's fair market value; or

(ii) For property subject to a Loss Guarantee, the greater of the property's fair market value or the guaranteed value or price at which the property can be put at the time of transfer.

(2) *FFA with respect to property covered by a Loss Guarantee other than on transfer to Agency.* (i) FFA provided pursuant to a Loss Guarantee with respect to covered property is included in the amount realized with respect to the property to the extent the total amount realized does not exceed the greater of—

(A) The property's fair market value; or

(B) The guaranteed value or price at which the property can be put at the time of transfer.

(ii) For the purposes of this paragraph (d)(2), references to an amount realized include amounts obtained in whole or partial satisfaction of loans, amounts obtained by virtue of charging off or marking to market covered property, and other amounts similarly related to property, whether or not disposed of.

(3) *Treatment of FFA received in exchange for property.* FFA included in the amount realized for property under this paragraph (d) is not includible in income under paragraph (a)(1) of this section. The amount realized is treated in the same manner as if realized from a person other than Agency or a Controlled Entity. For example, gain attributable to FFA received with respect to a capital asset retains its character as capital gain. Similarly, FFA received with respect to property that has been charged off for income tax purposes is treated as a recovery to the extent of the amount previously charged off. Any FFA provided in excess of the amount realized under this paragraph (d) is includible in income under paragraph (a)(1) of this section.

(4) *Adjustment to FFA*—(i) *In general.* If an Institution pays or transfers money or property to Agency or a Controlled Entity, the amount of money and fair market value of the property is an adjustment to its FFA to the extent the amount paid and transferred exceeds the amount of money and fair market value of property Agency or a Controlled Entity provides in exchange.

(ii) *Deposit insurance.* This paragraph (d)(4) does not apply to amounts paid to Agency with respect to deposit insurance.

(iii) *Treatment of an interest held by Agency or a Controlled Entity*—(A) *In general.* For purposes of this paragraph (d), an interest described in § 1.597-3(b) is not treated as property when transferred by the issuer to Agency or a Controlled Entity nor when acquired from Agency or a Controlled Entity by the issuer.

(B) *Dispositions to persons other than issuer.* On the date Agency or a Controlled Entity transfers an interest described in § 1.597-3(b) to a holder other than the issuer, Agency or a Controlled Entity, the issuer is treated for purposes of this paragraph (d)(4) as having transferred to Agency an amount of money equal to the sum of the amount of money and the fair market value of property that was paid by the new holder as consideration for the interest.

(iv) *Consolidated groups.* For purposes of this paragraph (d), an Institution will be treated as having made any transfer to Agency or a Con-

Reg. § 1.597-2(c)(6)

trolled Entity that was made by any other member of its consolidated group. The consolidated group must make appropriate investment basis adjustments to the extent the member transferring money or other property is not the member that received FFA.

(5) *Manner of making adjustments to FFA*—(i) *Reduction of FFA and deferred FFA.* An Institution adjusts its FFA under paragraph (d)(4) of this section by reducing in the following order and in an aggregate amount not greater than the adjustment—

(A) The amount of any FFA that is otherwise includible in income for the taxable year (before application of paragraph (c) of this section); and

(B) The balance (but not below zero) in the deferred FFA account, if any, maintained under paragraph (c)(4) of this section.

(ii) *Deduction of excess amounts.* If the amount of the adjustment exceeds the sum of the amounts described in paragraph (d)(5)(i) of this section, the Institution may deduct the excess to the extent the deduction does not exceed the amount of FFA included in income for prior taxable years reduced by the amount of deductions allowable under this paragraph (d)(5)(ii) in prior taxable years.

(iii) *Additional adjustments.* Any adjustment to FFA in excess of the sum of the amounts described in paragraphs (d)(5)(i) and (ii) of this section is treated—

(A) By an Institution other than a New Entity or Acquiring, as a deduction of the amount in excess of FFA received that is required to be transferred to Agency under section 11(g) of the Federal Deposit Insurance Act (12 U.S.C. 1821(g)); or

(B) By a New Entity or Acquiring, as an adjustment to the purchase price paid in the Taxable Transfer (see § 1.338-7).

(e) *Examples.* The following examples illustrate the provisions of this section:

Example 1. Timing of inclusion of FFA in income. (i) Institution M, a calendar year taxpayer without Continuing Equity because it is in Agency receivership, is not a member of a consolidated group and has not been acquired in a Taxable Transfer. On January 1, 1997, M has assets with a total adjusted basis of $100 million and total liabilities of $120 million. M's deductions do not exceed its gross income (determined without regard to FFA) for 1997. Agency provides $30 million of FFA to M in 1997. The amount of this FFA that M must include in income in 1997 is limited by § 1.597-2(c)(2) to $20 million, the amount by which M's liabilities ($120 million) exceed the total adjusted basis of its assets ($100 million) at the beginning of the taxable year. Pursuant to § 1.597-2(c)(4)(i), M must establish a deferred FFA account for the remaining $10 million.

(ii) If Agency instead lends M the $30 million, M's indebtedness to Agency is disregarded and the results are the same as in paragraph (i) of this *Example 1.* Section 597(c); §§ 1.597-1(b) (defining FFA) and 1.597-3(b).

Example 2. Transfer of property to Agency. (i) Institution M, a calendar year taxpayer without Continuing Equity because it is in Agency receivership, is not a member of a consolidated group and has not been acquired in a Taxable Transfer. At the beginning of 1998, M's remaining equity is $0 and M has a deferred FFA account of $10 million. Agency does not provide any FFA to M in 1998. During the year, M transfers property not covered by a Loss Guarantee to Agency and does not receive any consideration. The property has an adjusted basis of $5 million and a fair market value of $1 million at the time of the transfer. M has no other taxable income or loss in 1998.

(ii) Under § 1.597-2(d)(1), M is treated as selling the property for $1 million, its fair market value, thus recognizing a $4 million loss ($5 million − $1 million). In addition, because M did not receive any consideration from Agency, under § 1.597-2(d)(4) M has an adjustment to FFA of $1 million, the amount by which the fair market value of the transferred property ($1 million) exceeds the consideration M received from Agency ($0). Because no FFA is provided to M in 1998, this adjustment reduces the balance of M's deferred FFA account to $9 million ($10 million − $1 million). Section 1.597-2(d)(5)(i)(B). Because M's $4 million loss causes M's deductions to exceed its gross income by $4 million in 1998 and M has no remaining equity, under § 1.597-2(c)(4)(iii)(A) M must include $4 million of deferred FFA in income, and must decrease the remaining $9 million balance of its deferred FFA account by the same amount, leaving a balance of $5 million.

Example 3. Loss Guarantee. Institution Q, a calendar year taxpayer, sells an asset covered by a Loss Guarantee to an unrelated third party for $4,000. Q's adjusted basis in the asset at the time of sale and the asset's guaranteed value are both $10,000. Pursuant to the Loss Guarantee, Agency pays Q $6,000 ($10,000 − $4,000). Q's amount realized from the sale of the asset is $10,000 ($4,000 from the third party and $6,000 from Agency). Section 1.597-2(d)(2). Q realizes no gain or loss on the sale ($10,000 − $10,000 = $0), and

Reg. § 1.597-2(e)

therefore includes none of the $6,000 of FFA it receives pursuant to the Loss Guarantee in income. Section 1.597-2(d)(3). [Reg. § 1.597-2.]

☐ [T.D. 8641, 12-20-95. Amended by T.D. 8677, 6-26-96; T.D. 8823, 6-25-99; T.D. 8858, 1-5-2000 and T.D. 8940, 2-12-2001.]

[Reg. § 1.597-3]

§ 1.597-3. Other rules.—(a) *Ownership of assets.* For all income tax purposes, an Institution is treated as the owner of all assets covered by a Loss Guarantee, yield maintenance agreement, or cost to carry or cost of funds reimbursement agreement, regardless of whether Agency (or a Controlled Entity) otherwise would be treated as the owner under general principles of income taxation.

(b) *Debt and equity interests received by Agency.* Debt instruments, stock, warrants, or other rights to acquire stock of an Institution (or any of its affiliates) that Agency or a Controlled Entity receives in connection with a transaction in which FFA is provided are not treated as debt, stock or other equity interests of or in the issuer for any purpose of the Internal Revenue Code while held by Agency or a Controlled Entity. On the date Agency or a Controlled Entity transfers an interest described in this paragraph (b) to a holder other than Agency or a Controlled Entity, the interest is treated as having been newly issued by the issuer to the holder with an issue price equal to the sum of the amount of money and the fair market value of property paid by the new holder in exchange for the interest.

(c) *Agency Obligations*—(1) *In general.* Except as otherwise provided in this paragraph (c), the original issue discount rules of sections 1271 et seq. apply to Agency Obligations.

(2) *Issue price of Agency Obligations provided as Net Worth Assistance.* The issue price of an Agency Obligation that is provided as Net Worth Assistance and that bears interest at either a single fixed rate or a qualified floating rate (and provides for no contingent payments) is the lesser of the sum of the present values of all payments due under the obligation, discounted at a rate equal to the applicable federal rate (within the meaning of section 1274(d)(1) and (3)) in effect for the date of issuance, or the stated principal amount of the obligation. The issue price of an Agency Obligation that bears a qualified floating rate of interest (within the meaning of § 1.1275-5(b)) is determined by treating the obligation as bearing a fixed rate of interest equal to the rate in effect on the date of issuance under the obligation.

(3) *Adjustments to principal amount.* Except as provided in § 1.597-5(d)(2)(iv), this paragraph (c)(3) applies if Agency modifies or exchanges an Agency Obligation provided as Net Worth Assistance (or a successor obligation). The issue price of the modified or new Agency Obligation is determined under paragraphs (c)(1) and (2) of this section. If the issue price is greater than the adjusted issue price of the existing Agency Obligation, the difference is treated as FFA. If the issue price is less than the adjusted issue price of the existing Agency Obligation, the difference is treated as an adjustment to FFA under § 1.597-2(d)(4).

(d) *Successors.* To the extent necessary to effectuate the purposes of the regulations under section 597, an entity's treatment under the regulations applies to its successor. A successor includes a transferee in a transaction to which section 381(a) applies or a Bridge Bank to which another Bridge Bank transfers deposit liabilities.

(e) [Reserved].

(f) *Losses and deductions with respect to covered assets.* Prior to the disposition of an asset covered by a Loss Guarantee, the asset cannot be charged off, marked to a market value, depreciated, amortized, or otherwise treated in a manner that supposes an actual or possible diminution of value below the greater of the asset's highest guaranteed value or the highest price at which the asset can be put.

(g) *Anti-abuse rule.* The regulations under section 597 must be applied in a manner consistent with the purposes of section 597. Accordingly, if, in structuring or engaging in any transaction, a principal purpose is to achieve a tax result that is inconsistent with the purposes of section 597 and the regulations thereunder, the Commissioner can make appropriate adjustments to income, deductions and other items that would be consistent with those purposes. [Reg. § 1.597-3.]

☐ [T.D. 8641, 12-20-95. Amended by T.D. 9048, 3-11-2003.]

[Reg. § 1.597-4]

§ 1.597-4. Bridge banks and agency control.—(a) *Scope.* This section provides rules that apply to a Bridge Bank or other Institution under Agency Control and to transactions in which an Institution transfers deposit liabilities (whether or not the Institution also transfers assets) to a Bridge Bank.

(b) *Status as taxpayer.* A Bridge Bank or other Institution under Agency Control is a corporation within the meaning of section 7701(a)(3) for all purposes of the Internal Revenue Code and is subject to all Internal Revenue Code provisions

Reg. § 1.597-3(a)

that generally apply to corporations, including those relating to methods of accounting and to requirements for filing returns, even if Agency owns stock of the Institution.

(c) *No section 382 ownership change.* The imposition of Agency Control, the cancellation of Institution stock by Agency, a transaction in which an Institution transfers deposit liabilities to a Bridge Bank, and an election under paragraph (g) of this section are disregarded in determining whether an ownership change has occurred within the meaning of section 382(g).

(d) *Transfers to Bridge Banks*—(1) *In general.* Except as otherwise provided in paragraph (g) of this section, the rules of this paragraph (d) apply to transfers to Bridge Banks. In general, a Bridge Bank and its associated Residual Entity are together treated as the successor entity to the transferring Institution. If an Institution transfers deposit liabilities to a Bridge Bank (whether or not it also transfers assets), the Institution recognizes no gain or loss on the transfer and the Bridge Bank succeeds to the transferring Institution's basis in any transferred assets. The associated Residual Entity retains its basis in any assets it continues to hold. Immediately after the transfer, the Bridge Bank succeeds to and takes into account the transferring Institution's items described in section 381(c) (subject to the conditions and limitations specified in section 381(c)), taxpayer identification number ("TIN"), deferred FFA account, and account receivable for future FFA as described in paragraph (g)(4)(ii) of this section. The Bridge Bank also succeeds to and continues the transferring Institution's taxable year.

(2) *Transfers to a Bridge Bank from multiple Institutions.* If two or more Institutions transfer deposit liabilities to the same Bridge Bank, the rules in paragraph (d)(1) of this section are modified to the extent provided in this paragraph (d)(2). The Bridge Bank succeeds to the TIN and continues the taxable year of the Institution that transfers the largest amount of deposits. The taxable years of the other transferring Institutions close at the time of the transfer. If all the transferor Institutions are members of the same consolidated group, the Bridge Bank's carryback of losses to the Institution that transfers the largest amount of deposits is not limited by section 381(b)(3). The limitations of section 381(b)(3) do apply to the Bridge Bank's carrybacks of losses to all other transferor Institutions. If the transferor Institutions are not all members of the same consolidated group, the limitations of section 381(b)(3) apply with respect to all transferor Institutions. See paragraph (g)(6)(ii) of this section for additional rules that apply if two or more Institutions that are not members of the same consolidated group transfer deposit liabilities to the same Bridge Bank.

(e) *Treatment of Bridge Bank and Residual Entity as a single entity.* A Bridge Bank and its associated Residual Entity or Entities are treated as a single entity for income tax purposes and must file a single combined income tax return. The Bridge Bank is responsible for filing all income tax returns and statements for this single entity and is the agent of each associated Residual Entity to the same extent as if the Bridge Bank were the common parent of a consolidated group including the Residual Entity. The term *Institution* includes a Residual Entity that files a combined return with its associated Bridge Bank.

(f) *Rules applicable to members of consolidated groups*—(1) *Status as members.* Unless an election is made under paragraph (g) of this section, Agency Control of an Institution does not terminate the Institution's membership in a consolidated group. Stock of a subsidiary that is canceled by Agency is treated as held by the members of the consolidated group that held the stock prior to its cancellation. If an Institution is a member of a consolidated group immediately before it transfers deposit liabilities to a Bridge Bank, the Bridge Bank succeeds to the Institution's status as the common parent or, unless an election is made under paragraph (g) of this section, as a subsidiary of the group. If a Bridge Bank succeeds to an Institution's status as a subsidiary, its stock is treated as held by the shareholders of the transferring Institution, and the stock basis or excess loss account of the Institution carries over to the Bridge Bank. A Bridge Bank is treated as owning stock owned by its associated Residual Entities, including for purposes of determining membership in an affiliated group.

(2) *No 30-day election to be excluded from consolidated group.* Neither an Institution nor any of its Consolidated Subsidiaries may be excluded from a consolidated group for a taxable year under § 1.1502-76(b)(5)(ii), as contained in 26 CFR part 1 edition revised April 1, 1994, if the Institution is under Agency Control at any time during the year.

(3) *Coordination with consolidated return regulations.* The provisions of the regulations under section 597 take precedence over conflicting provisions in the regulations under section 1502.

(g) *Elective disaffiliation*—(1) *In general.* A consolidated group of which an Institution is a subsidiary may elect irrevocably not to include

Reg. § 1.597-4(g)(1)

the Institution in its affiliated group if the Institution is placed in Agency receivership (whether or not assets or deposit liabilities of the Institution are transferred to a Bridge Bank). See paragraph (g)(6) of this section for circumstances under which a consolidated group is deemed to make this election.

(2) *Consequences of election.* If the election under this paragraph (g) is made with respect to an Institution, the following consequences occur immediately before the subsidiary Institution to which the election applies is placed in Agency receivership (or, in the case of a deemed election under paragraph (g)(6) of this section, immediately before the consolidated group is deemed to make the election) and in the following order—

(i) All adjustments of the Institution and its Consolidated Subsidiaries under section 481 are accelerated;

(ii) Deferred intercompany gains and losses with respect to the Institution and its Consolidated Subsidiaries are taken into account and the Institution and its Consolidated Subsidiaries take into account any other items required under the regulations under section 1502 for members that become nonmembers within the meaning of § 1.1502-32(d)(4);

(iii) The taxable year of the Institution and its Consolidated Subsidiaries closes and the Institution includes the amount described in paragraph (g)(3) of this section in income as ordinary income as its last item for that taxable year;

(iv) The members of the consolidated group owning the common stock of the Institution include in income any excess loss account with respect to the Institution's stock under § 1.1502-19 and any other items required under the regulations under section 1502 for members that own stock of corporations that become nonmembers within the meaning of § 1.1502-32(d)(4); and

(v) If the Institution's liabilities exceed the aggregate fair market value of its assets on the date the Institution is placed in Agency receivership (or, in the case of a deemed election under paragraph (g)(6) of this section, on the date the consolidated group is deemed to make the election), the members of the consolidated group treat their stock in the Institution as worthless. (See §§ 1.337(d)-2T and 1.1502-35T(f) for rules applicable when a member of a consolidated group is entitled to a worthless stock deduction with respect to stock of another member of the group.) In all other cases, the consolidated group will be treated as owning stock of a nonmember corporation until such stock is disposed of or becomes worthless under rules otherwise applicable.

(3) *Toll charge.* The amount described in this paragraph (g)(3) is the excess of the Institution's liabilities over the adjusted bases of its assets immediately before the Institution is placed in Agency receivership (or, in the case of a deemed election under paragraph (g)(6) of this section, immediately before the consolidated group is deemed to make the election). In computing this amount, the adjusted bases of an Institution's assets are reduced by the amount of the Institution's reserves for bad debts under section 585 or 593, other than supplemental reserves under section 593. For purposes of this paragraph (g)(3), an Institution is treated as a single entity that includes the assets and liabilities of its Consolidated Subsidiaries, with appropriate adjustments to prevent duplication. The amount described in this paragraph (g)(3) for alternative minimum tax purposes is determined using alternative minimum tax basis, deductions, and all other items required to be taken into account. In computing the increase in the group's taxable income or alternative minimum taxable income, sections 56(d)(1), 382 and 383 and §§ 1.1502-15, 1.1502-21 and 1.1502-22 (or §§ 1.1502-15A, 1.1502-21A and 1.1502-22A, as appropriate) do not limit the use of the attributes of the Institution and its Consolidated Subsidiaries to the extent, if any, that the inclusion of the amount described in this paragraph (g)(3) in income would result in the group having taxable income or alternative minimum taxable income (determined without regard to this section) for the taxable year. The preceding sentence does not apply to any limitation under section 382 or 383 or §§ 1.1502-15, 1.1502-21, or 1.1502-22 (or §§ 1.1502-15A, 1.1502-21A, or 1.1502-22A, as appropriate) that arose in connection with or prior to a corporation becoming a Consolidated Subsidiary of the Institution.

(4) *Treatment of Institutions after disaffiliation*—(i) *In general.* If the election under this paragraph (g) is made with respect to an Institution, immediately after the Institution is placed in Agency receivership (or, in the case of a deemed election under paragraph (g)(6) of this section, immediately after the consolidated group is deemed to make the election), the Institution and each of its Consolidated Subsidiaries are treated for income tax purposes as new corporations that are not members of the electing group's affiliated group. Each new corporation retains the TIN of the corresponding disaffiliated corporation and is treated as having received the assets and liabilities of the corresponding disaffiliated corporation in a transaction to which section 351 applies (and in which no gain was recognized under section 357(c) or otherwise). Thus, the new corpo-

Reg. § 1.597-4(g)(2)

ration has no net operating or capital loss carryforwards. An election under this paragraph (g) does not terminate the single entity treatment of a Bridge Bank and its Residual Entities provided in paragraph (e) of this section.

(ii) *FFA.* A new Institution is treated as having a non-interest bearing, nontransferable account receivable for future FFA with a basis equal to the amount described in paragraph (g)(3) of this section. If a disaffiliated Institution has a deferred FFA account at the time of its disaffiliation, the corresponding new Institution succeeds to and takes into account that deferred FFA account.

(iii) *Filing of consolidated returns.* If a disaffiliated Institution has Consolidated Subsidiaries at the time of its disaffiliation, the corresponding new Institution is required to file a consolidated income tax return with the subsidiaries in accordance with the regulations under section 1502.

(iv) *Status as Institution.* If an Institution is disaffiliated under this paragraph (g), the resulting new corporation is treated as an Institution for purposes of the regulations under section 597 regardless of whether it is a bank or domestic building and loan association within the meaning of section 597.

(v) *Loss carrybacks.* To the extent a carryback of losses would result in a refund being paid to a fiduciary under section 6402(i), an Institution or Consolidated Subsidiary with respect to which an election under this paragraph (g) (other than under paragraph (g)(6)(ii) of this section) applies is allowed to carry back losses as if the Institution or Consolidated Subsidiary had continued to be a member of the consolidated group that made the election.

(5) *Affirmative election*—(i) *Original Institution*—(A) *Manner of making election.* Except as otherwise provided in paragraph (g)(6) of this section, a consolidated group makes the election provided by this paragraph (g) by sending a written statement by certified mail to the affected Institution on or before the later of 120 days after its placement in Agency receivership or May 31, 1996. The statement must contain the following legend at the top of the page: "THIS IS AN ELECTION UNDER § 1.597-4(g) TO EXCLUDE THE BELOW-REFERENCED INSTITUTION AND CONSOLIDATED SUBSIDIARIES FROM THE AFFILIATED GROUP," and must include the names and taxpayer identification numbers of the common parent and of the Institution and Consolidated Subsidiaries to which the election applies, and the date on which the Institution was placed in Agency receivership. The consolidated group must send a similar statement to all subsidiary Institutions placed in Agency receivership during the consistency period described in paragraph (g)(5)(ii) of this section. (Failure to satisfy the requirement in the preceding sentence, however, does not invalidate the election with respect to any subsidiary Institution placed in Agency receivership during the consistency period described in paragraph (g)(5)(ii) of this section.) The consolidated group must include a copy of any election statement and accompanying certified mail receipt as part of its first income tax return filed after the due date under this paragraph (g)(5) for such statement. A statement must be attached to this return indicating that the individual who signed the election was authorized to do so on behalf of the consolidated group. Agency cannot make this election under the authority of section 6402(i) or otherwise.

(B) *Consistency limitation on affirmative elections.* A consolidated group may make an affirmative election under this paragraph (g)(5) with respect to a subsidiary Institution placed in Agency receivership only if the group made, or is deemed to have made, the election under this paragraph (g) with respect to every subsidiary Institution of the group placed in Agency receivership on or after May 10, 1989 and within five years preceding the date the subject Institution was placed in Agency receivership.

(ii) *Effect on Institutions placed in receivership simultaneously or subsequently.* An election under this paragraph (g), other than under paragraph (g)(6)(ii) of this section, applies to the Institution with respect to which the election is made or deemed made (the original Institution) and each subsidiary Institution of the group placed in Agency receivership or deconsolidated in contemplation of Agency Control or the receipt of FFA simultaneously with the original Institution or within five years thereafter.

(6) *Deemed Election*—(i) *Deconsolidations in contemplation.* If one or more members of a consolidated group deconsolidate (within the meaning of § 1.1502-19(c)(1)(ii)(B)) a subsidiary Institution in contemplation of Agency Control or the receipt of FFA, the consolidated group is deemed to make the election described in this paragraph (g) with respect to the Institution on the date the deconsolidation occurs. A subsidiary Institution is conclusively presumed to have been deconsolidated in contemplation of Agency Control or the receipt of FFA if either event occurs within six months after the deconsolidation.

(ii) *Transfers to a Bridge Bank from multiple groups.* On the day an Institution's transfer of deposit liabilities to a Bridge Bank results in the Bridge Bank holding deposit liabilities from both a subsidiary Institution and an Institution not included in the subsidiary Institution's consolidated group, each consolidated group of which a transferring Institution or the Bridge Bank is a subsidiary is deemed to make the election described in this paragraph (g) with respect to its subsidiary Institution. If deposit liabilities of another Institution that is a subsidiary member of any consolidated group subsequently are transferred to the Bridge Bank, the consolidated group of which the Institution is a subsidiary is deemed to make the election described in this paragraph (g) with respect to that Institution at the time of the subsequent transfer.

(h) *Examples.* The following examples illustrate the provisions of this section:

Facts. Corporation X, the common parent of a consolidated group, owns all the stock (with a basis of $4 million) of Institution M, an insolvent Institution with no Consolidated Subsidiaries. At the close of business on April 30, 1996, M has $4 million of deposit liabilities, $1 million of other liabilities, and assets with an adjusted basis of $4 million and a fair market value of $3 million.

Example 1. Effect of receivership on consolidation. On May 1, 1996, Agency places M in receivership and begins liquidating M. X does not make an election under § 1.597-4(g). M remains a member of the X consolidated group after May 1, 1996. Section 1.597-4(f)(1).

Example 2. Effect of Bridge Bank on consolidation—(i) *Additional facts.* On May 1, 1996, Agency places M in receivership and causes M to transfer all of its assets and deposit liabilities to Bridge Bank MB.

(ii) *Consequences without an election to disaffiliate.* M recognizes no gain or loss from the transfer and MB succeeds to M's basis in the transferred assets, M's items described in section 381(c) (subject to the conditions and limitations specified in section 381(c)) and TIN. Section 1.597-4(d)(1). (If M had a deferred FFA account, MB would also succeed to that account. Section 1.597-4(d)(1).) MB continues M's taxable year and succeeds to M's status as a member of the X consolidated group after May 1, 1996. Section 1.597-4(d)(1) and (f). MB and M are treated as a single entity for income tax purposes. Section 1.597-4(e).

(iii) *Consequences with an election to disaffiliate.* If, on July 1, 1996, X makes an election under § 1.597-4(g) with respect to M, the following consequences are treated as occurring immediately before M was placed in Agency receivership. M must include $1 million ($5 million of liabilities − $4 million of adjusted basis) in income as of May 1, 1996. Section 1.597-4(g)(2) and (3). M is then treated as a new corporation that is not a member of the X consolidated group and that has assets (including a $1 million account receivable for future FFA) with a basis of $5 million and $5 million of liabilities received from disaffiliated corporation M in a section 351 transaction. New corporation M retains the TIN of disaffiliated corporation M. Section 1.597-4(g)(4). Immediately after the disaffiliation, new corporation M is treated as transferring its assets and deposit liabilities to Bridge Bank MB. New corporation M recognizes no gain or loss from the transfer and MB succeeds to M's TIN and taxable year. Section 1.597-4(d)(1). Bridge Bank MB is treated as a single entity that includes M and has $5 million of liabilities, an account receivable for future FFA with a basis of $1 million, and other assets with a basis of $4 million. Section 1.597-4(d)(1). [Reg. § 1.597-4.]

☐ [*T.D.* 8641, 12-20-95. Amended by *T.D.* 8677, 6-26-96; *T.D.* 8823, 6-25-99 and *T.D.* 9048, 3-11-2003.]

[Reg. § 1.597-5]

§ 1.597-5. **Taxable transfers.**—(a) *Taxable Transfers*—(1) *Defined.* The term *Taxable Transfer* means—

(i) A transaction in which an entity transfers to a transferee other than a Bridge Bank—

(A) Any deposit liability (whether or not the Institution also transfers assets), if FFA is provided in connection with the transaction; or

(B) Any asset for which Agency or a Controlled Entity has any financial obligation (e.g., pursuant to a Loss Guarantee or Agency Obligation); or

(ii) A deemed transfer of assets described in paragraph (b) of this section.

(2) *Scope.* This section provides rules governing Taxable Transfers. Rules applicable to both actual and deemed asset acquisitions are provided in paragraphs (c) and (d) of this section. Special rules applicable only to deemed asset acquisitions are provided in paragraph (e) of this section.

(b) *Deemed asset acquisitions upon stock purchase*—(1) *In general.* In a deemed transfer of assets under this paragraph (b), an Institution (including a Bridge Bank or a Residual Entity) or a Consolidated Subsidiary of the Institution (the Old Entity) is treated as selling all of its assets in a single transaction and is treated as a new corporation (the New Entity) that purchases all of the Old Entity's assets at the close of the day immediately preceding the occurrence of an event described in paragraph (b)(2) of this section. However, such an event results in a deemed transfer of assets under this paragraph (b) only if it occurs—

(i) In connection with a transaction in which FFA is provided;

(ii) While the Old Entity is a Bridge Bank;

(iii) While the Old Entity has a positive balance in a deferred FFA account (see § 1.597-2(c)(4)(v) regarding the optional accelerated recapture of deferred FFA); or

(iv) With respect to a Consolidated Subsidiary, while the Institution of which it is a Consolidated Subsidiary is under Agency Control.

(2) *Events*. A deemed transfer of assets under this paragraph (b) results if the Old Entity—

(i) Becomes a non-member within the meaning of § 1.1502-32(d)(4) of its consolidated group (other than pursuant to an election under § 1.597-4(g));

(ii) Becomes a member of an affiliated group of which it was not previously a member (other than pursuant to an election under § 1.597-4(g)); or

(iii) Issues stock such that the stock that was outstanding before the imposition of Agency Control or the occurrence of any transaction in connection with the provision of FFA represents 50 percent or less of the vote or value of its outstanding stock (disregarding stock described in section 1504(a)(4) and stock owned by Agency or a Controlled Entity).

(3) *Bridge Banks and Residual Entities*. If a Bridge Bank is treated as selling all of its assets to a New Entity under this paragraph (b), each associated Residual Entity is treated as simultaneously selling its assets to a New Entity in a Taxable Transfer described in this paragraph (b).

(c) *Treatment of transferor*—(1) *FFA in connection with a Taxable Transfer*. A transferor in a Taxable Transfer is treated as having directly received immediately before a Taxable Transfer any Net Worth Assistance that Agency provides to the New Entity or Acquiring in connection with the transfer. (See § 1.597-2(a) and (c) for rules regarding the inclusion of FFA in income and § 1.597-2(a)(1) for related rules regarding FFA provided to shareholders.) The Net Worth Assistance is treated as an asset of the transferor that is sold to the New Entity or Acquiring in the Taxable Transfer.

(2) *Amount realized in a Taxable Transfer*. In a Taxable Transfer described in paragraph (a)(1)(i) of this section, the amount realized is determined under section 1001(b) by reference to the consideration paid for the assets. In a Taxable Transfer described in paragraph (a)(1)(ii) of this section, the amount realized is the sum of the grossed-up basis of the stock acquired in connection with the Taxable Transfer (excluding stock acquired from the Old or New Entity), plus the amount of liabilities assumed or taken subject to in the deemed transfer, plus other relevant items. The grossed-up basis of the acquired stock equals the acquirors' basis in the acquired stock divided by the percentage of the Old Entity's stock (by value) attributable to the acquired stock.

(3) *Allocation of amount realized*—(i) *In general*. The amount realized under paragraph (c)(2) of this section is allocated among the assets transferred in the Taxable Transfer in the same manner as amounts are allocated among assets under § 1.338-6(b), (c)(1) and (2).

(ii) *Modifications to general rule*. This paragraph (c)(3)(ii) modifies certain of the allocation rules of paragraph (c)(3)(i) of this section. Agency Obligations and assets covered by Loss Guarantees in the hands of the New Entity or Acquiring are treated as Class II assets. Stock of a Consolidated Subsidiary is treated as a Class II asset to the extent the fair market value of the Consolidated Subsidiary's Class I and Class II assets exceeds the amount of its liabilities. The fair market value of an Agency Obligation is deemed to equal its adjusted issue price immediately before the Taxable Transfer. The fair market value of an asset covered by a Loss Guarantee immediately after the Taxable Transfer is deemed to be not less than the greater of the asset's highest guaranteed value or the highest price at which the asset can be put.

(d) *Treatment of a New Entity and Acquiring*—(1) *Purchase price*. The purchase price for assets acquired in a Taxable Transfer described in paragraph (a)(1)(i) of this section is the cost of the assets acquired. See § 1.1060-1T(c)(1). The purchase price for assets acquired in a Taxable Transfer described in paragraph (a)(1)(ii) of this section is the sum of the grossed-up basis of the stock acquired in connection with the Taxable Transfer (excluding stock acquired from the Old or New Entity), plus the amount of liabilities assumed or taken subject to in the deemed transfer, plus other relevant items. The grossed-up basis of the acquired stock equals the acquirors' basis in the acquired stock divided by the percentage of the Old Entity's stock (by value) attributable to the acquired stock. FFA provided in connection with a Taxable Transfer is not included in the New Entity's or Acquiring's purchase price for the acquired assets. Any Net Worth Assistance so provided is treated as an

Reg. § 1.597-5(d)(1)

asset of the transferor sold to the New Entity or Acquiring in the Taxable Transfer.

(2) *Allocation of basis*—(i) *In general.* Except as otherwise provided in this paragraph (d)(2), the purchase price determined under paragraph (d)(1) of this section is allocated among the assets transferred in the Taxable Transfer in the same manner as amounts are allocated among assets under § 1.338-6(b), (c)(1) and (2).

(ii) *Modifications to general rule.* The allocation rules contained in paragraph (c)(3)(ii) of this section apply to the allocation of basis among assets acquired in a Taxable Transfer. No basis is allocable to Agency's agreement to provide Loss Guarantees, yield maintenance payments, cost to carry or cost of funds reimbursement payments, or expense reimbursement or indemnity payments. A New Entity's basis in assets it receives from its shareholders is determined under general principles of income taxation and is not governed by this paragraph (d).

(iii) *Allowance and recapture of additional basis in certain cases.* If the fair market value of the Class I and Class II assets acquired in a Taxable Transfer is greater than the New Entity's or Acquiring's purchase price for the acquired assets, the basis of the Class I and Class II assets equals their fair market value. The amount by which the fair market value of the Class I and Class II assets exceeds the purchase price is included ratably as ordinary income by the New Entity or Acquiring over a period of six taxable years beginning in the year of the Taxable Transfer. The New Entity or Acquiring must include as ordinary income the entire amount remaining to be recaptured under the preceding sentence in the taxable year in which an event occurs that would accelerate inclusion of an adjustment under section 481.

(iv) *Certain post-transfer adjustments*—(A) *Agency Obligations.* If an adjustment to the principal amount of an Agency Obligation or cash payment to reflect a more accurate determination of the condition of the Institution at the time of the Taxable Transfer is made before the earlier of the date the New Entity or Acquiring files its first post-transfer income tax return or the due date of that return (including extensions), the New Entity or Acquiring must adjust its basis in its acquired assets to reflect the adjustment. In making adjustments to the New Entity's or Acquiring's basis in its acquired assets, paragraph (c)(3)(ii) of this section is applied by treating an adjustment to the principal amount of an Agency Obligation pursuant to the first sentence of this paragraph (d)(2)(iv)(A) as occurring immediately before the Taxable Transfer. (See § 1.597-3(c)(3) for rules regarding other adjustments to the principal amount of an Agency Obligation.)

(B) *Assets covered by a Loss Guarantee.* If, immediately after a Taxable Transfer, an asset is not covered by a Loss Guarantee but the New Entity or Acquiring has the right to designate specific assets that will be covered by a Loss Guarantee, the New Entity or Acquiring must treat any asset so designated as having been subject to the Loss Guarantee at the time of the Taxable Transfer. The New Entity or Acquiring must adjust its basis in the covered assets and in its other acquired assets to reflect the designation in the manner provided by paragraph (d)(2) of this section. The New Entity or Acquiring must make appropriate adjustments in subsequent taxable years if the designation is made after the New Entity or Acquiring files its first post-transfer income tax return or the due date of that return (including extensions) has passed.

(e) *Special rules applicable to Taxable Transfers that are deemed asset acquisitions*—(1) *Taxpayer identification numbers.* Except as provided in paragraph (e)(3) of this section, a New Entity succeeds to the TIN of the transferor in a deemed sale under paragraph (b) of this section.

(2) *Consolidated Subsidiaries*—(i) *In general.* A Consolidated Subsidiary that is treated as selling its assets in a Taxable Transfer under paragraph (b) of this section is treated as engaging immediately thereafter in a complete liquidation to which section 332 applies. The consolidated group of which the Consolidated Subsidiary is a member does not take into account gain or loss on the sale, exchange, or cancellation of stock of the Consolidated Subsidiary in connection with the Taxable Transfer.

(ii) *Certain minority shareholders.* Shareholders of the Consolidated Subsidiary that are not members of the consolidated group that includes the Institution do not recognize gain or loss with respect to shares of Consolidated Subsidiary stock retained by the shareholder. The shareholder's basis for that stock is not affected by the Taxable Transfer.

(3) *Bridge Banks and Residual Entities*—(i) *In general.* A Bridge Bank or Residual Entity's sale of assets to a New Entity under paragraph (b) of this section is treated as made by a single entity under § 1.597-4(e). The New Entity deemed to acquire the assets of a Residual Entity under paragraph (b) of this section is not treated as a single entity with the Bridge Bank (or with the New Entity acquiring the Bridge Bank's assets) and must obtain a new TIN.

(ii) *Treatment of consolidated groups.* At the time of a Taxable Transfer described in para-

Reg. § 1.597-5(d)(2)

graph (a)(1)(ii) of this section, treatment of a Bridge Bank as a subsidiary member of a consolidated group under § 1.597-4(f)(1) ceases. However, the New Entity deemed to acquire the assets of a Residual Entity is a member of the selling consolidated group after the deemed sale. The group's basis or excess loss account in the stock of the New Entity that is deemed to acquire the assets of the Residual Entity is the group's basis or excess loss account in the stock of the Bridge Bank immediately before the deemed sale, as adjusted for the results of the sale.

(4) *Certain returns.* If an Old Entity without Continuing Equity is not a subsidiary of a consolidated group at the time of the Taxable Transfer, the controlling Agency must file all income tax returns for the Old Entity for periods ending on or prior to the date of the deemed sale described in paragraph (b) of this section that are not filed as of that date.

(5) *Basis limited to fair market value.* If all of the stock of the corporation is not acquired on the date of the Taxable Transfer, the Commissioner may make appropriate adjustments under paragraphs (c) and (d) of this section to the extent using a grossed-up basis of the stock of a corporation results in an aggregate amount realized for, or basis in, the assets other than the aggregate fair market value of the assets.

(f) *Examples.* The following examples illustrate the provisions of this section:

Example 1. Branch sale resulting in Taxable Transfer. (i) Institution M is a calendar year taxpayer in Agency receivership. M is not a member of a consolidated group. On January 1, 1997, M has $200 million of liabilities (including deposit liabilities) and assets with an adjusted basis of $100 million. M has no income or loss for 1997 and, except as described below, receives no FFA. On September 30, 1997, Agency causes M to transfer six branches (with assets having an adjusted basis of $1 million) together with $120 million of deposit liabilities to N. In connection with the transfer, Agency provides $121 million in cash to N.

(ii) The transaction is a Taxable Transfer in which M receives $121 million of Net Worth Assistance. Section 1.597-5(a)(1). (M is treated as directly receiving the $121 million of Net Worth Assistance immediately before the Taxable Transfer. Section 1.597-5(c)(1).) M transfers branches having a basis of $1 million and is treated as transferring $121 million in cash (the Net Worth Assistance) to N in exchange for N's assumption of $120 million of liabilities. Thus, M realizes a loss of $2 million on the transfer. The amount of the FFA M must include in its income in 1997 is limited by § 1.597-2(c) to $102 million, which is the sum of the $100 million excess of M's liabilities ($200 million) over the total adjusted basis of its assets ($100 million) at the beginning of 1997, plus the $2 million excess for the taxable year, which results from the Taxable Transfer, of M's deductions (other than carryovers) over its gross income other than FFA. M must establish a deferred FFA account for the remaining $19 million of FFA. Section 1.597-2(c)(4).

(iii) N, as Acquiring, must allocate its $120 million purchase price for the assets acquired from M among those assets. Cash is a Class I asset. The branch assets are in Classes III and IV. N's adjusted basis in the cash is its amount, i.e., $121 million. Section 1.597-5(d)(2). Because this amount exceeds N's purchase price for all of the acquired assets by $1 million, N allocates no basis to the other acquired assets and, under § 1.597-5(d)(2), must recapture the $1 million excess at an annual rate of $166,667 in the six consecutive taxable years beginning with 1997 (subject to acceleration for certain events).

Example 2. Stock issuance by Bridge Bank causing Taxable Transfer. (i) On April 1, 1996, Institution P is placed in receivership and caused to transfer assets and liabilities to Bridge Bank PB. On August 31, 1996, the assets of PB consist of $20 million in cash, loans outstanding with an adjusted basis of $50 million and a fair market value of $40 million, and other non-financial assets (primarily branch assets and equipment) with an adjusted basis of $5 million. PB has deposit liabilities of $95 million and other liabilities of $5 million. P, the Residual Entity, holds real estate with an adjusted basis of $10 million and claims in litigation having a zero basis. P retains no deposit liabilities and has no other liabilities (except its liability to Agency for having caused its deposit liabilities to be satisfied).

(ii) On September 1, 1996, Agency causes PB to issue 100 percent of its common stock for $2 million cash to X. On the same day, Agency issues a $25 million note to PB. The note bears a fixed rate of interest in excess of the applicable federal rate in effect for September 1, 1996. Agency provides Loss Guarantees guaranteeing PB a value of $50 million for PB's loans outstanding.

(iii) The stock issuance is a Taxable Transfer in which PB is treated as selling all of its assets to a new corporation, New PB. Section 1.597-5(b)(1). PB is treated as directly receiving $25 million of Net Worth Assistance (the issue price of the Agency Obligation) immediately before the Taxable Transfer. Section 1.597-3(c)(2); § 1.597-5(c)(1). The amount of FFA PB must include in income is determined under § 1.597-2(a)

Reg. § 1.597-5(f)

and (c). PB in turn is deemed to transfer the note to New PB in the Taxable Transfer, together with $20 million of cash, all its loans outstanding (with a basis of $50 million) and its other non-financial assets (with a basis of $5 million). The amount realized by PB from the sale is $100 million, the amount of PB's liabilities deemed to be assumed by New PB. This amount realized equals PB's basis in its assets and thus, PB realizes no gain or loss on the transfer to New PB.

(iv) Residual Entity P also is treated as selling all its assets (consisting of real estate and claims in litigation) for $0 (the amount of consideration received by P) to a new corporation (New P) in a Taxable Transfer. Section 1.597-5(b)(3). (P's only liability is to Agency and a liability to Agency is not treated as a debt under § 1.597-3(b).) Thus, P realizes a $10 million loss on the transfer to New P. The combined return filed by PB and P for 1996 will reflect a total loss on the Taxable Transfer of $10 million ($0 for PB and $10 million for P). Section 1.597-5(e)(3). That return also will reflect FFA income from the Net Worth Assistance, determined under § 1.597-2(a) and (c).

(v) New PB is treated as having acquired the assets it acquired from PB for $100 million, the amount of liabilities assumed. In allocating basis among these assets, New PB treats the Agency note and the loans outstanding (which are covered by Loss Guarantees) as Class II assets. For the purpose of allocating basis, the fair market value of the Agency note is deemed to equal its adjusted issue price immediately before the transfer, $25 million. The fair market value of the loans is deemed not to be less than the guaranteed value of $50 million.

(vi) New P is treated as having acquired its assets for no consideration. Thus its basis in its assets immediately after the transfer is zero. New PB and New P are not treated as a single entity. Section 1.597-5(e)(3).

Example 3. Taxable Transfer of previously disaffiliated Institution. (i) Corporation X, the common parent of a consolidated group, owns all the stock of Institution M, an insolvent Institution with no Consolidated Subsidiaries. On April 30, 1996, M has $4 million of deposit liabilities, $1 million of other liabilities, and assets with an adjusted basis of $4 million and a fair market value of $3 million. On May 1, 1996, Agency places M in receivership. X elects under § 1.597-4(g) to disaffiliate M. Accordingly, as of May 1, 1996, new corporation M is not a member of the X consolidated group. On May 1, 1996, Agency causes M to transfer all of its assets and liabilities to Bridge Bank MB. Under § 1.597-4(e), MB and M are thereafter treated as a single entity which has $5 million of liabilities, an account receivable for future FFA with a basis of $1 million, and other assets with a basis of $4 million. Section 1.597-4(g)(4).

(ii) During May 1996, MB earns $25,000 of interest income and accrues $20,000 of interest expense on depositor accounts and there is no net change in deposits other than the additional $20,000 of interest expense accrued on depositor accounts. MB pays $5,000 of wage expenses and has no other items of income or expense.

(iii) On June 1, 1996, Agency causes MB to issue 100 percent of its stock to corporation Y. In connection with the stock issuance, Agency provides an Agency Obligation for $2 million and no other FFA.

(iv) The stock issuance results in a Taxable Transfer. Section 1.597-5(b). MB is treated as receiving the Agency Obligation immediately prior to the Taxable Transfer. Section 1.597-5(c)(1). MB has $1 million of basis in its account receivable for FFA. This receivable is treated as satisfied, offsetting $1 million of the $2 million of FFA provided by Agency in connection with the Taxable Transfer. The status of the remaining $1 million of FFA as includible income is determined as of the end of the taxable year under § 1.597-2(c). However, under § 1.597-2(b), MB obtains a $2 million basis in the Agency Obligation received as FFA.

(v) Under § 1.597-5(c)(2), in the Taxable Transfer, Old Entity MB is treated as selling, to New Entity MB, all of Old Entity MB's assets, having a basis of $6,020,000 (the original $4 million of asset basis as of April 30, 1996, plus $20,000 net cash from May 1996 activities, plus $2 million in the Agency Obligation received as FFA), for $5,020,000, the amount of Old Entity MB's liabilities assumed by New Entity MB pursuant to the Taxable Transfer. Therefore, Old Entity MB recognizes, in the aggregate, a loss of $1 million from the Taxable Transfer.

(vi) Because this $1 million loss causes Old Entity MB's deductions to exceed its gross income (determined without regard to FFA) by $1 million, Old Entity MB must include in its income the $1 million of FFA not offset by the FFA receivable. Section 1.597-2(c). (As of May 1, 1996, Old Entity MB's liabilities ($5,000,000) did not exceed MB's $5 million adjusted basis of its assets. For the taxable year, MB's deductions of $1,025,000 ($1,000,000 loss from the Taxable Transfer, $20,000 interest expense and $5,000 of wage expense) exceeded its gross income (disregarding FFA) of $25,000 (interest income) by $1,000,000. Thus, under § 1.597-2(c), MB includes in income the entire $1,000,000 of FFA not offset by the FFA receivable.)

(vii) Therefore, Old Entity MB's taxable income for the taxable year ending on the date of the Taxable Transfer is $0.

(viii) Residual Entity M is also deemed to engage in a deemed sale of its assets to New Entity M under § 1.597-5(b)(3), but there are no tax consequences as M has no assets or liabilities at the time of the deemed sale.

(ix) Under § 1.597-5(d)(1), New Entity MB is treated as purchasing Old Entity MB's assets for $5,020,000, the amount of New Entity MB's liabilities. Of this, $2,000,000 is allocated to the $2 million Agency Obligation, and $3,020,000 is allocated to the other assets New Entity MB is treated as purchasing in the Taxable Transfer.

Example 4. Loss Sharing. Institution N acquires assets and assumes liabilities of another Institution in a Taxable Transfer. Among the assets transferred are three parcels of real estate. In the hands of the transferring Institution, these assets had book values of $100,000 each. In connection with the Taxable Transfer, Agency agrees to reimburse Institution N for 80 percent of any loss (based on the original book value) realized on the disposition or charge-off of the three properties. This arrangement constitutes a Loss Guarantee. Thus, in allocating basis, Institution N treats the three parcels as Class II assets. By virtue of the arrangement with the Agency, Institution N is assured that the parcels will not be worth less to it than $80,000 each, because even if the properties are worthless, Agency will reimburse 80 percent of the loss. Although Institution could obtain payments under the Loss Guarantee if the properties are worth more, it is not guaranteed that it will realize more than $80,000. Accordingly, $80,000 is the highest guaranteed value of the three parcels. Institution N will allocate basis to the Class II assets up to their fair market value. For this purpose, the fair market value of the three parcels is not less than $80,000 each. Section 1.597-5(d)(2)(ii); § 1.597-5(c)(3)(ii). [Reg. § 1.597-5.]

☐ [T.D. 8641, 12-20-95. Amended by T.D. 8858, 1-5-2000 and T.D. 8940, 2-12-2001.]

[Reg. § 1.597-6]

§ 1.597-6. Limitation on collection of income tax.—(a) *Limitation on collection where tax is borne by Agency.* If an Institution without Continuing Equity (or any of its Consolidated Subsidiaries) is liable for income tax that is attributable to the inclusion in income of FFA or gain from a Taxable Transfer, the tax will not be collected if it would be borne by Agency. The final determination of whether the tax would be borne by Agency is within the sole discretion of the Commissioner. In determining whether tax would be borne by Agency, the Commissioner will disregard indemnity, tax-sharing, or similar obligations of Agency, an Institution, or its Consolidated Subsidiaries. Collection of the several income tax liability under § 1.1502-6 from members of an Institution's consolidated group other than the Institution or its Consolidated Subsidiaries is not affected by this section. Income tax will continue to be subject to collection except as specifically limited in this section. This section does not apply to taxes other than income taxes.

(b) *Amount of tax attributable to FFA or gain on a Taxable Transfer.* For purposes of paragraph (a) of this section, the amount of income tax in a taxable year attributable to the inclusion of FFA or gain from a Taxable Transfer in the income of an Institution (or a Consolidated Subsidiary) is the excess of the actual income tax liability of the Institution (or the consolidated group in which the Institution is a member) over the income tax liability of the Institution (or the consolidated group in which the Institution is a member) determined without regard to FFA or gain or loss on the Taxable Transfer.

(c) *Reporting of uncollected tax.* A taxpayer must specify on the front page of Form 1120 (U.S. Corporate Income Tax Return), to the left of the space provided for "Total Tax," the amount of income tax for the taxable year that is potentially not subject to collection under this section. If an Institution is a subsidiary member of a consolidated group, the amount specified as not subject to collection is zero.

(d) *Assessments of tax to offset refunds.* Income tax that is not collected under this section will be assessed and, thus, used to offset any claim for refund made by or on behalf of the Institution, the Consolidated Subsidiary or any other corporation with several liability for the tax.

(e) *Collection of taxes from Acquiring or a New Entity*—(1) *Acquiring.* No income tax liability (including the several liability for taxes under § 1.1502-6) of a transferor in a Taxable Transfer will be collected from Acquiring.

(2) *New Entity.* Income tax liability (including the several liability for taxes under § 1.1502-6) of a transferor in a Taxable Transfer will be collected from a New Entity only if stock that was outstanding in the Old Entity remains outstanding as stock in the New Entity or is reacquired or exchanged for consideration.

(f) *Effect on section 7507.* This section supersedes the application of section 7507, and the regulations thereunder, for the assessment and collection of income tax attributable to FFA. [Reg. § 1.597-6.]

☐ [T.D. 8641, 12-20-95.]

[Reg. § 1.597-7]

§ 1.597-7. Effective date.—(a) *FIRREA effective date.* Section 597, as amended by section 1401 of the Financial Institutions Reform, Recovery, and Enforcement Act of 1989 (FIRREA), Public Law 101-73, is generally effective for any FFA received or accrued by an Institution on or after May 10, 1989, and for any transaction in connection with which such FFA is provided, unless the FFA is provided in connection with an acquisition occurring prior to May 10, 1989. See § 1.597-8 for rules regarding FFA received or accrued on or after May 10, 1989, that relates to an acquisition that occurred before May 10, 1989.

(b) *Effective date of regulations.* Except as otherwise provided in this section, §§ 1.597-1 through 1.597-6 apply to taxable years ending on or after April 22, 1992. However, the provisions of §§ 1.597-1 through 1.597-6 do not apply to FFA received or accrued for taxable years ending on or after April 22, 1992, in connection with an Agency assisted acquisition within the meaning of Notice 89-102 (1989-2 C.B. 436; see § 601.601(d)(2)) (which does not include a transfer to a Bridge Bank), that occurs before April 22, 1992. Taxpayers not subject to §§ 1.597-1 through 1.597-6 must comply with an interpretation of the statute that is reasonable in light of the legislative history and applicable administrative pronouncements. For this purpose, the rules contained in Notice 89-102 apply to the extent provided in the Notice.

(c) *Elective application to prior years and transactions* —(1) *In general.* Except as limited in this paragraph (c), an election is available to apply §§ 1.597-1 through 1.597-6 to taxable years prior to the general effective date of these regulations. A consolidated group may elect to apply §§ 1.597-1 through 1.597-6 for all members of the group in all taxable years to which section 597, as amended by FIRREA, applies. The common parent makes the election for the group. An entity that is not a member of a consolidated group may elect to apply §§ 1.597-1 through 1.597-6 to all taxable years to which section 597, as amended by FIRREA, applies for which it is not a member of a consolidated group. The election is irrevocable.

(2) *Election unavailable in certain cases*—(i) *Statute of limitations closed.* The election cannot be made if the period for assessment and collection of tax has expired under the rules of section 6501 for any taxable year in which §§ 1.597-1 through 1.597-6 would affect the determination of the electing entity's or group's income, deductions, gain, loss, basis, or other items.

(ii) *No section 338 election under Notice 89-102.* The election cannot be made with respect to an Institution if, under Notice 89-102, it was a Target with respect to which a qualified stock purchase was made, a timely election under section 338 was not made, and on April 22, 1992, a timely election under section 338 could not be made.

(iii) *Inconsistent treatment of Institution that would be New Entity.* If, under § 1.597-5(b), an Institution would become a New Entity before April 22, 1992, the election cannot be made with respect to that Institution unless elections are made by all relevant persons such that §§ 1.597-1 through § 1.597-6 apply both before and after the deemed sale under § 1.597-5. However, this requirement does not apply if, under §§ 1.597-1 through § 1.597-6, the Institution would not have Continuing Equity prior to the deemed sale.

(3) *Expense reimbursements.* Notice 89-102, 1989-2 C.B. 436, provides that reimbursements paid or accrued pursuant to an expense reimbursement or indemnity arrangement are not included in income but the taxpayer may not deduct, or otherwise take into account, the item of cost or expense to which the reimbursement or indemnity payment relates. With respect to an Agency assisted acquisition within the meaning of Notice 89-102 that occurs before April 22, 1992, a taxpayer that elects to apply these regulations retroactively under this paragraph (c) may continue to account for these items under the rules of Notice 89-102.

(4) *Procedural rules*—(i) *Manner of making election.* An Institution or consolidated group makes the election provided by this paragraph (c) by attaching a written statement to, and including it as a part of, the taxpayer's or consolidated group's first annual income tax return filed on or after March 15, 1996. The statement must contain the following legend at the top of the page: "THIS IS AN ELECTION UNDER § 1.597-7(c)," and must contain the name, address and employer identification number of the taxpayer or common parent making the election. The statement must include a declaration that "TAXPAYER AGREES TO EXTEND THE STATUTE OF LIMITATIONS ON ASSESSMENT FOR THREE YEARS FROM THE DATE OF THE FILING OF THIS ELECTION UNDER § 1.597-7(c), IF THE LIMITATIONS PERIOD WOULD EXPIRE EARLIER WITHOUT SUCH EXTENSION, FOR ANY ITEMS AFFECTED IN ANY TAXABLE YEAR BY THE FILING OF THIS ELECTION," and a declaration that

either "AMENDED RETURNS WILL BE FILED FOR ALL TAXABLE YEARS AFFECTED BY THE FILING OF THIS ELECTION WITHIN 180 DAYS OF MAKING THIS STATEMENT, UNLESS SUCH REQUIREMENT IS WAIVED IN WRITING BY THE DISTRICT DIRECTOR OR HIS DELEGATE" or "ALL RETURNS PREVIOUSLY FILED ARE CONSISTENT WITH THE PROVISIONS OF §§ 1.597-1 THROUGH 1.597-6," and be signed by an individual who is authorized to make the election under this paragraph (c) on behalf of the taxpayer. An election with respect to a consolidated group must be made by the common parent of the group, not Agency, and applies to all members of the group.

(ii) *Effect of elective disaffiliation.* To make the affirmative election described in § 1.597-4(g)(5) for an Institution placed in Agency receivership in a taxable year ending before April 22, 1992, the consolidated group must send the affected Institution the statement described in § 1.597-4(g)(5) on or before May 31, 1996. Notwithstanding the requirements of paragraph (c)(4)(i) of this section, a consolidated group sending such a statement is deemed to make the election described in, and to agree to the conditions contained in, this paragraph (c). The consolidated group must nevertheless attach the statement described in paragraph (c)(4)(i) of this section to its first annual income tax return filed on or after March 15, 1996.

(d) *Reliance on prior guidance*—(1) *Notice 89-102.* Taxpayers may rely on Notice 89-102, 1989-2 C.B. 436, to the extent they acted in reliance on that Notice prior to April 22, 1992. Such reliance must be reasonable and transactions with respect to which taxpayers rely must be consistent with the overriding policies of section 597, as expressed in the legislative history.

(2) *Notice FI-46-89*—(i) *In general.* Notice FI-46-89 was published in the **Federal Register** on April 23, 1992 (57 FR 14804). Taxpayers may rely on the provisions of §§ 1.597-1 through 1.597-6 of that notice to the extent they acted in reliance on those provisions prior to December 21, 1995. Such reliance must be reasonable and transactions with respect to which taxpayers rely must be consistent with the overriding policies of section 597, as expressed in the legislative history, as well as the overriding policies of notice FI-46-89.

(ii) *Taxable Transfers.* Any taxpayer described in this paragraph (d) that, under notice FI-46-89, would be a New Entity or Acquiring with respect to a Taxable Transfer on or after April 22, 1992, and before December 21, 1995,

may apply the rules of that notice with respect to such transaction. [Reg. § 1.597-7.]

☐ [*T.D.* 8641, 12-20-95.]

[Reg. § 1.597-8]

§ 1.597-8. **Transitional rules for Federal financial assistance.**—(a) *Scope.* This section provides transitional rules for the tax consequences of Federal financial assistance received or accrued on or after May 10, 1989, if the assistance payment relates to an acquisition that occurred before that date.

(b) *Transitional rules.* The tax consequences of any payment of Federal financial assistance received or accrued on or after May 10, 1989, are governed by the applicable provisions of section 597 that were in effect prior to the Financial Institutions Reform, Recovery, and Enforcement Act of 1989 ("FIRREA") if either—

(1) The payment—

(i) Is pursuant to an acquisition of a bank or domestic building and loan association before May 10, 1989,

(ii) Is provided pursuant to an assistance agreement executed before May 10, 1989,

(iii) Is provided to a party to that agreement or to such other party as the Commissioner may determine appropriate by letter ruling or other written guidance, and

(iv) Would, if provided before May 10, 1989, have been governed by applicable provisions of section 597 that were in effect prior to FIRREA; or

(2) The payment—

(i) Represents a prepayment of (or a payment in lieu of) a fixed or contingent right to Federal financial assistance that would have satisfied the conditions of paragraphs (b)(1)(i), (ii) and (iv) of this section, and

(ii) Is provided to a party described in paragraph (b)(1)(iii) of this section.

(c) *Definition of Federal financial assistance.* Federal financial assistance for purposes of this section has the meaning prescribed by section 597(c) as amended by FIRREA.

(d) *Examples.* The following examples illustrate the provisions of this section:

Example 1. X corporation acquired Y, a domestic building and loan association on September 10, 1988. Pursuant to a written agreement executed at the time of the acquisition, Y received Federal financial assistance that included a note bearing a market rate of interest, the right to future payments if certain assets were sold at a loss, and the right to future payments if the income produced by certain assets was less than an agreed upon amount. On December 1, 1991, an agreement was executed in which Y relinquished its rights to Federal financial assistance under the September 10, 1988 agreement in return for a lump sum payment. The lump sum payment represented a prepayment of the principal and accrued but unpaid interest for the note, and the rights to the contingent future loss and income payments. The entire prepayment is excluded from the income of Y because it is a prepayment of Federal financial assistance and the assistance (i) would have been provided pursuant to an acquisition that occurred before May 10, 1989, would have been provided pursuant to an assistance agreement executed before May 10, 1989, and would, if it had been provided prior to May 10, 1989, have been governed by a pre-FIRREA version of section 597; and (ii) the prepayment is paid to a party to the assistance agreement.

Example 2. The facts are the same as those in *Example 1,* except that the note bears an above market rate of interest and part of the lump sum represents a premium payment for the note. The portion of the lump sum allocable to the premium payment is also excluded from the income of Y because the payment represents the present value of the right to future Federal financial assistance in the form of interest.

Example 3. The facts are the same as those in *Example 1,* except that a portion of the lump sum payment represents compensation for additional expenses Y may incur in the future because of termination of the September 10, 1988 agreement. The portion of the lump sum payment allocable to the compensation for additional expenses must be included in the income of Y because it is not a prepayment of Federal financial assistance provided for by a written agreement entered into prior to May 10, 1989.

Example 4. The facts are the same as those in *Example 1,* except that instead of a new assistance agreement, the September 10, 1988 assistance agreement was modified on December 1, 1991. The modified agreement provided new Federal financial assistance in addition to the amounts previously agreed to. None of the new Federal financial assistance is governed by this regulation because the new assistance was not provided for by a written agreement entered into prior to May 10, 1989. The modification does not, however, affect the tax treatment of assistance provided for by the agreement prior to its modification.

(e) *Effective Date.* This section is effective April 23, 1992 for assistance received or accrued on or after May 10, 1989 in connection with acquisitions before that date. [Reg. § 1.597-8.]

☐ [*T.D. 8406, 4-22-92. Redesignated by T.D. 8471, 4-7-93.*]

NATURAL RESOURCES

Deductions

[Reg. § 1.611-0]

§ 1.611-0. **Regulatory authority.**—Sections 1.611-1 through 1.614-8, inclusive, are prescribed under the authority granted the Secretary or his delegate by section 611(a) of the Code to prescribe regulations under which a reasonable allowance for depletion and depreciation of improvements shall be allowed, according to the peculiar conditions in each case, in the case of mines, oil and gas wells, other natural deposits and timber. [Reg. § 1.611-0.]

☐ [*T.D. 6965, 7-25-68.*]

[Reg. § 1.611-1]

§ 1.611-1. **Allowance of deduction for depletion.**—(a) *Depletion of mines, oil and gas wells, other natural deposits, and timber*—(1) *In general.* Section 611 provides that there shall be allowed as a deduction in computing taxable income in the case of mines, oil and gas wells, other natural deposits, and timber, a reasonable allowance for depletion. In the case of standing timber, the depletion allowance shall be computed solely upon the adjusted basis of the property. In the case of other exhaustible natural resources the allowance for depletion shall be computed upon either the adjusted depletion basis of the property (see section 612, relating to cost depletion) or upon a percentage of gross income from the property (see section 613, relating to percentage depletion), whichever results in the greater allowance for depletion for any taxable year. In no case will depletion based upon discovery value be allowed.

(2) See § 1.611-5 for methods of depreciation relating to improvements connected with mineral or timber properties.

(3) See paragraph (d) of this section for definition of terms.

(b) *Economic interest.* (1) Annual depletion deductions are allowed only to the owner of an economic interest in mineral deposits or standing timber. An economic interest is possessed in every case in which the taxpayer has acquired by investment any interest in mineral in place or standing timber and secures, by any form of legal relationship, income derived from the extraction of the mineral or severance of the timber, to which he must look for a return of his capital. For an exception in the case of certain mineral production payments, see section 636 and the regulations thereunder. A person who has no capital investment in the mineral deposit or standing timber does not possess an economic interest merely because through a contractual relation he possesses a mere economic or pecuniary advantage derived from production. For example, an agreement between the owner of an economic interest and another entitling the latter to purchase or process the product upon production or entitling the latter to compensation for extraction or cutting does not convey a depletable economic interest. Further, depletion deductions with respect to an economic interest of a corporation are allowed to the corporation and not to its shareholders.

(2) No depletion deduction shall be allowed the owner with respect to any timber, coal, or domestic iron ore that such owner has disposed of under any form of contract by virtue of which he retains an economic interest in such timber, coal, or iron ore, if such disposal is considered a sale of timber, coal, or domestic iron ore under section 631(b) or (c).

(c) *Special rules*—(1) *In general.* For the purpose of the equitable apportionment of depletion among the several owners of economic interests in a mineral deposit or standing timber, if the value of any mineral or timber must be ascertained as of any specific date for the determination of the basis for depletion, the values of such several interests therein may be determined separately, but, when determined as of the same date, shall together never exceed the value at that date of the mineral or timber as a whole.

(2) *Leases.* In the case of a lease, the deduction for depletion under section 611 shall be equitably apportioned between the lessor and lessee. In the case of a lease or other contract providing for the sharing of economic interest in a mineral deposit or standing timber, such deduction shall be computed by each taxpayer by reference to the adjusted basis of his property determined in accordance with sections 611 and 612, or computed in accordance with section 613, if applicable, and the regulations thereunder.

(3) *Life tenant and remainderman.* In the case of property held by one person for life with remainder to another person, the deduction for depletion under section 611 shall be computed as if the life tenant were the absolute owner of the property so that he will be entitled to the deduction during his life, and thereafter the deduction, if any, shall be allowed to the remainderman.

(4) *Mineral or timber property held in trust.* If a mineral property or timber property is held in trust, the allowable deduction for depletion is to be apportioned between the income beneficiaries and the trustee on the basis of the trust income from such property allocable to each, unless the governing instrument (or local law) requires or permits the trustee to maintain a reserve for depletion in any amount. In the latter case, the deduction is first allocated to the trustee to the extent that income is set aside for a depletion reserve, and any part of the deduction in excess of the income set aside for the reserve shall be apportioned between the income beneficiaries and the trustee on the basis of the trust income (in excess of the income set aside for the reserve) allocable to each. For example:

(i) If under the trust instrument or local law the income of a trust computed without regard to depletion is to be distributed to a named beneficiary, the beneficiary is entitled to the deduction to the exclusion of the trustee.

(ii) If under the trust instrument or local law the income of a trust is to be distributed to a named beneficiary, but the trustee is directed to maintain a reserve for depletion in any amount, the deduction is allowed to the trustee (except to the extent that income set aside for the reserve is less than the allowable deduction). The same result would follow if the trustee sets aside income for a depletion reserve pursuant to discretionary authority to do so in the governing instrument.

No effect shall be given to any allocation of the depletion deduction which gives any beneficiary or the trustee a share of such deduction greater than his pro rata share of the trust income, irrespective of any provisions in the trust instrument, except as otherwise provided in this paragraph when the trust instrument or local law requires or permits the trustee to maintain a reserve for depletion.

(5) *Mineral or timber property held by estate.* In the case of mineral property or timber property held by an estate, the deduction for depletion under section 611 shall be apportioned between the estate and the heirs, legatees, and devisees on the basis of income of the estate from such property which is allocable to each.

(d) *Definitions.* As used in this part, and the regulations thereunder, the term—

(1) "Property" means—(i) in the case of minerals, each separate economic interest owned in each mineral deposit in each separate tract or parcel of land or an aggregation or combination of such mineral interests permitted under section

Reg. § 1.611-1(d)(1)

614(b), (c), (d), or (e); and (ii) in the case of timber, an economic interest in standing timber in each tract or block representing a separate timber account (see paragraph (d) of § 1.611-3). For rules with respect to waste or residue of prior mining, see paragraph (c) of § 1.614-1. When, in the regulations under this part, either the word "mineral" or "timber" precedes the word "property", such adjectives are used only to classify the type of "property" involved. For further explanation of the term "property", see section 614 and the regulations thereunder.

(2) "Fair market value" of a property is that amount which would induce a willing seller to sell and a willing buyer to purchase.

(3) "Mineral enterprise" is the mineral deposit or deposits and improvements, if any, used in mining or in the production of oil and gas and only so much of the surface of the land as is necessary for purposes of mineral extraction. The value of the mineral enterprise is the combined value of its component parts.

(4) "Mineral deposit" refers to minerals in place. When a mineral enterprise is acquired as a unit, the cost of any interest in the mineral deposit or deposits is that proportion of the total cost of the mineral enterprise which the value of the interest in the deposit bears to the value of the entire enterprise at the time of its acquisition.

(5) "Minerals" includes ores of the metals, coal, oil, gas, and all other natural metallic and nonmetallic deposits, except minerals derived from sea water, the air, or from similar inexhaustible sources. It includes but is not limited to all of the minerals and other natural deposits subject to depletion based upon a percentage of gross income from the property under section 613 and the regulations thereunder. [Reg. § 1.611-1.]

☐ [T.D. 6446, 1-20-60. Amended by T.D. 6841, 7-26-65 and by T.D. 7261, 2-26-73.]

[Reg. § 1.611-2]

§ 1.611-2. Rules applicable to mines, oil and gas wells, and other natural deposits.—(a) *Computation of cost depletion of mines, oil and gas wells, and other natural deposits.* (1) The basis upon which cost depletion is to be allowed in respect of any mineral property is the basis provided for in section 612 and the regulations thereunder. After the amount of such basis applicable to the mineral property has been determined for the taxable year, the cost depletion for that year shall be computed by dividing such amount by the number of units of mineral remaining as of the taxable year (see subparagraph (3) of this paragraph), and by multiplying the depletion unit, so determined, by the number of units of mineral sold within the taxable year (see subparagraph (2) of this paragraph). In the selection of a unit of mineral for depletion, preference shall be given to the principal or customary unit or units paid for in the products sold, such as tons of ore, barrels of oil, or thousands of cubic feet of natural gas.

(2) As used in this paragraph the phrase "number of units sold within the taxable year"—

(i) In the case of a taxpayer reporting income on the cash receipts and disbursements method, includes units for which payments were received within the taxable year although produced or sold prior to the taxable year, and excludes units sold but not paid for in the taxable year, and

(ii) In the case of a taxpayer reporting income on the accrual method, shall be determined from the taxpayer's inventories kept in physical quantities and in a manner consistent with his method of inventory accounting under section 471 or 472.

The phrase does not include units with respect to which depletion deductions were allowed or allowable prior to the taxable year.

(3) "The number of units of mineral remaining as of the taxable year" is the number of units of mineral remaining at the end of the period to be recovered from the property (including units recovered but not sold) plus the "number of units sold within the taxable year" as defined in this section.

(4) In the case of a natural gas well where the annual production is not metered and is not capable of being estimated with reasonable accuracy, the taxpayer may compute the cost depletion allowance in respect of such property for the taxable year by multiplying the adjusted basis of the property by a fraction, the numerator of which is equal to the decline in rock pressure during the taxable year and the denominator of which is equal to the expected total decline in rock pressure from the beginning of the taxable year to the economic limit of production. Taxpayers computing depletion by this method must keep accurate records of periodical pressure determinations.

(5) If an aggregation of two or more separate mineral properties is made during a taxable year under section 614, cost depletion for each such property shall be computed separately for that portion of the taxable year ending immediately before the effective date of the aggregation. Cost depletion with respect to the aggregated property shall be computed for that portion of the taxable year beginning on such effective date. The allowance for cost depletion for the taxable year shall be the sum of such cost depletion computations.

For purposes of this paragraph, each such portion of the taxable year shall be considered as a taxable year. Similar rules shall be applied where a separate mineral property is properly removed from an existing aggregation during a taxable year. See section 614 and the regulations thereunder for rules relating to the effective date of an aggregation of mineral interests and for rules relating to the adjusted basis of an aggregation.

(6) The apportionment of the deduction among the several owners of economic interests in the mineral deposit or deposits will be made as provided in paragraph (c) of § 1.611-1.

(b) *Depletion account of mineral property.* (1) Every taxpayer claiming and making a deduction for depletion of mineral property shall keep a separate account in which shall be accurately recorded the cost or other basis provided by section 1012, of such property together with subsequent allowable capital additions to each account and all the other adjustments required by section 1016.

(2) Mineral property accounts shall thereafter be credited annually with amounts of the depletion computed in accordance with section 611 or 613 and the regulations thereunder; or the amounts of the depletion so computed shall be credited to depletion reserve accounts. No further deductions for cost depletion shall be allowed when the sum of the credits for depletion equals the cost or other basis of the property, plus allowable capital additions. However, depletion deductions may be allowable thereafter computed upon a percentage of gross income from the property. See section 613 and the regulations thereunder. In no event shall percentage depletion in excess of cost or other basis of the property be credited to the improvements account or the depreciation reserve account.

(c) *Determination of mineral contents of deposits.* (1) If it is necessary to estimate or determine with respect to any mineral deposit as of any specific date the total recoverable units (tons, pounds, ounces, barrels, thousands of cubic feet, or other measure) of mineral products reasonably known, or on good evidence believed, to have existed in place as of that date, the estimate or determination must be made according to the method current in the industry and in the light of the most accurate and reliable information obtainable. In the selection of a unit of estimate, preference shall be given to the principal unit (or units) paid for in the product marketed. The estimate of the recoverable units of the mineral products in the deposit for the purposes of valuation and depletion shall include as to both quantity and grade:

(i) The ores and minerals "in sight", "blocked out", "developed", or "assured", in the usual or conventional meaning of these terms with respect to the type of the deposits, and

(ii) "Probable" or "prospective" ores or minerals (in the corresponding sense), that is, ores or minerals that are believed to exist on the basis of good evidence although not actually known to occur on the basis of existing development. Such "probable" or "prospective" ores or minerals may be estimated:

(*a*) As to quantity, only in case they are extensions of known deposits or are new bodies or masses whose existence is indicated by geological surveys or other evidence to a high degree of probability, and

(*b*) As to grade, only in accordance with the best indications available as to richness.

(2) If the number of recoverable units of mineral in the deposit has been previously estimated for the prior year or years, and if there has been no known change in the facts upon which the prior estimate was based, the number of recoverable units of mineral in the deposit as of the taxable year will be the number remaining from the prior estimate. However, for any taxable year for which it is ascertained either by the taxpayer or the district director from any source, such as operations or development work prior to the close of the taxable year, that the remaining recoverable mineral units as of the taxable year are materially greater or less than the number remaining from the prior estimate, then the estimate of the remaining recoverable units shall be revised, and the annual cost depletion allowance with respect to the property for the taxable year and for subsequent taxable years will be based upon the revised estimate until a change in the facts requires another revision. Such revised estimate will not, however, change the adjusted basis for depletion.

(d) *Determination of fair market value of mineral properties, and improvements, if any.* (1) If the fair market value of the mineral property and improvements at a specified date is to be determined for the purpose of ascertaining the basis, such value must be determined, subject to approval or revision by the district director, by the owner of such property and improvements in the light of the conditions and circumstances known at that date, regardless of later discoveries or developments or subsequent improvements in methods of extraction and treatment of the mineral product. The district director will give due weight and consideration to any and all factors and evidence having a bearing on the market value, such as cost, actual sales and transfer of

Reg. § 1.611-2(d)

similar properties and improvements, bona fide offers, market value of stock or shares, royalties and rentals, valuation for local or State taxation, partnership accountings, records of litigation in which the value of the property and improvements was in question, the amount at which the property and improvements may have been inventoried or appraised in probate or similar proceedings, and disinterested appraisals by approved methods.

(2) If the fair market value must be ascertained as of a certain date, analytical appraisal methods of valuation, such as the present value method will not be used:

(i) If the value of a mineral property and improvements, if any, can be determined upon the basis of cost or comparative values and replacement value of equipment, or

(ii) If the fair market value can reasonably be determined by any other method.

(e) *Determination of the fair market value of mineral property by the present value method.* (1) To determine the fair market value of a mineral property and improvements by the present value method, the essential factors must be determined for each mineral deposit. The essential factors in determining the fair market value of mineral deposits are:

(i) The total quantity of mineral in terms of the principal or customary unit (or units) paid for in the product marketed,

(ii) The quantity of mineral expected to be recovered during each operating period,

(iii) The average quality or grade of the mineral reserves,

(iv) The allocation of the total expected profit to the several processes or operations necessary for the preparation of the mineral for market,

(v) The probable operating life of the deposit in years,

(vi) The development cost,

(vii) The operating cost,

(viii) The total expected profit,

(ix) The rate at which this profit will be obtained, and

(x) The rate of interest commensurate with the risk for the particular deposit.

(2) If the mineral deposit has been sufficiently developed the valuation factors specified in subparagraph (1) of this paragraph may be determined from past operating experience. In the application of factors derived from past experience, full allowance should be made for probable future variations in the rate of exhaustion, quality or grade of the mineral, percentage of recovery, cost of development, production, interest rate, and selling price of the product marketed during the expected operating life of the mineral deposit. Mineral deposits for which these factors cannot be determined with reasonable accuracy from past operating experience may also be valued by the present value method; but the factors must be deduced from concurrent evidence, such as the general type of the deposit, the characteristics of the district in which it occurs, the habit of the mineral deposits, the intensity of mineralization, the oil-gas ratio, the rate at which additional mineral has been disclosed by exploitation, the stage of the operating life of the deposit, and any other evidence tending to establish a reasonable estimate of the required factors.

(3) Mineral deposits of different grades, locations, and probable dates of extraction should be valued separately. The mineral content of a deposit shall be determined in accordance with paragraph (c) of this section. In estimating the average grade of the developed and prospective mineral, account should be taken of probable increases or decreases as indicated by the operating history. The rate of exhaustion of a mineral deposit should be determined with due regard to the limitations imposed by plant capacity, by the character of the deposit, by the ability to market the mineral product, by labor conditions, and by the operating program in force or reasonably to be expected for future operations. The operating life of a mineral deposit is that number of years necessary for the exhaustion of both the developed and prospective mineral content at the rate determined as above. The operating life of oil and gas wells is also influenced by the natural decline in pressure and flow, and by voluntary or enforced curtailment of production. The operating cost includes all current expense of producing, preparing, and marketing the mineral product sold (due consideration being given to taxes) exclusive of allowable capital additions, as described in §§ 1.612-2 and 1.612-4, and deductions for depreciation and depletion, but including cost of repairs. This cost of repairs is not to be confused with the depreciation deduction by which the cost of improvements is returned to the taxpayer free from tax. In general, no estimates of these factors will be approved by the district director which are not supported by the operating experience of the property or which are derived from different and arbitrarily selected periods.

(4) The value of each mineral deposit is measured by the expected gross income (the number of units of mineral recoverable in marketable form multiplied by the estimated market price per unit) less the estimated operating cost, reduced to

a present value as of the date for which the valuation is made at the rate of interest commensurate with the risk for the operating life, and further reduced by the value at that date of the improvements and of the capital additions, if any, necessary to realize the profits. The degree of risk is generally lowest in cases where the factors of valuation are fully supported by the operating record of the mineral enterprise before the date for which the valuation is made. On the other hand, higher risks ordinarily attach to appraisals upon any other basis.

(f) *Revaluation of mineral property not allowed.* No revaluation of a mineral property whose value as of any specific date has been determined and approved will be made or allowed during the continuance of the ownership under which the value was so determined and approved, except in the case of misrepresentation or fraud or gross error as to any facts known on the date as of which the valuation was made. Revaluation on account of misrepresentation or fraud or such gross error will be made only with the written approval of the Commissioner.

(g) *Statement to be attached to return when valuation, depletion, or depreciation of mineral property or improvements are claimed.* (1) For the first taxable year ending before December 31, 1967, for which a taxpayer asserts a value for any mineral property or improvement as of a specific date or claims a deduction for depletion, or depreciation, there shall be attached to the return of the taxpayer for such taxable year a statement setting forth, in complete, summary form, the pertinent information required by this paragraph with respect to each such mineral property or improvement (including oil and gas properties or improvements). The summary statement shall be deemed a part of the income tax return to which it relates. In addition to such summary statement, the taxpayer must assemble, segregate and have readily available at his principal place of business, all the supporting data (listed in subparagraphs (2), (3) and (4) of this paragraph) which is used in compiling the summary statement. For taxable years after such first taxable year, and ending before December 31, 1967, the taxpayer need attach to his return only an explanation of the changes, if any, in the information previously furnished. For example, when a taxpayer has filed adequate maps with the district director he may be relieved of filing further maps of the same area, if all additional information necessary for keeping the maps up-to-date is filed each year. In any case in which any of the information required by this paragraph has been previously filed by the taxpayer (including information furnished in accordance with corresponding provisions of prior regulations), such information need not be filed again, but a statement should be attached to the return of the taxpayer indicating clearly when and in what form such information was previously filed. For provisions relating to the data which shall be submitted with returns for taxable years ending on or after December 31, 1967, see subparagraph (5) of this paragraph.

(2) The information referred to in subparagraph (1) is as follows:

(i) An adequate map showing the name, description, location, date of surveys, and identification of the deposit or deposits;

(ii) A description of the character of the taxpayer's property, accompanied by a copy of the instrument or instruments by which it was acquired;

(iii) The date of acquisition of the property, the exact terms and dates of expiration of all leases involved, and if terminated, the reasons therefor;

(iv) The cost of the mineral property and improvements, stating the amount paid to each vendor, with his name and address;

(v) The date as of which the mineral property and improvements are valued, if a valuation is necessary to establish the basis as provided by section 1012;

(vi) The value of the mineral property and improvements on that date with a statement of the precise method by which it was determined;

(vii) An allocation of the cost or value among the mineral property, improvements and the surface of the land for purposes other than mineral production;

(viii) The estimated number of units of each kind of mineral at the end of the taxable year, and also at the date of acquisition, if acquired during the taxable year or at the date as of which any valuation is made, together with an explanation of the method used in the estimation, the name and address of the person making the estimate, and an average analysis which will indicate the quality of the mineral valued, including the grade or gravity in the case of oil;

(ix) The number of units sold and the number of units for which payment was received or accrued during the year for which the return is made (in the case of newly developed oil and gas deposits it is desirable that this information be furnished by months);

(x) The gross amount received from the sale of mineral;

(xi) The amount of depreciation for the taxable year and the amount of cost depletion for the taxable year;

Reg. § 1.611-2(g)(2)

(xii) The amounts of depletion and depreciation, if any, stated separately, which for each and every prior year:

(a) Were allowed (see section 1016(a)(2)),

(b) Were allowable, and

(c) Would have been allowable without reference to percentage or discovery depletion;

(xiii) The fractions (however measured) of gross production from the deposit or deposits to which the taxpayer and other persons are entitled together with the names and addresses of such other persons; and

(xiv) Any other data which will be helpful in determining the reasonableness of the valuation asserted or of the deductions claimed.

(3) In the case of oil and gas properties, the following information with respect to each property is required in addition to that information set forth in subparagraph (2) of this paragraph:

(i) The number of acres of producing oil or gas land and, if additional acreage is claimed to be proven, the amount of such acreage and the reasons for believing it to be proven;

(ii) The number of wells producing at the beginning and end of the taxable year;

(iii) The date of completion of each well finished during the taxable year;

(iv) The date of abandonment of each well abandoned during the taxable year;

(v) Maps showing the location of the tracts or leases and of the producing and abandoned wells, dry holes, and proven oil and gas lands (the maps should show depth, initial production, and date of completion of each well, etc., to the extent that these data are available);

(vi) The number of pay sands and average thickness of each pay sand or zone;

(vii) The average depth to the top of each of the different pay sands;

(viii) The annual production of the deposit or of the individual wells, if the latter information is available, from the beginning of its productivity to the end of the taxable year, the average number of wells producing during each year, and the initial daily production of each well (the extent to which oil or gas is used for fuel on the premises should be stated with reasonable accuracy);

(ix) All available data regarding change in operating conditions, such as unit operation, proration, flooding, use of air-gas lift, vacuum, shooting, and similar information, which have a direct effect on the production of the deposit; and

(x) Available geological information having a probable bearing on the oil and gas content;

information with respect to edge water, water drive, bottom hold pressures, oil-gas ratio, porosity of reservoir rock, percentage of recovery, expected date of cessation of natural flow, decline in estimated potential, and characteristics similar to characteristics of other known fields.

(4) For rules relating to an additional statement to be attached to the return when the depletion deduction is computed upon a percentage of gross income from the property, see § 1.613-6.

(5) A taxpayer who claims a total deduction of more than $200 for depletion of mines, oil and gas wells, or other natural deposits for the taxable year ending on or after December 31, 1967, and before December 31, 1968, shall submit with his return for such taxable year a filled-out Form M (Mines and Other Natural Deposits—Depletion Data) or Form O (Oil and Gas Depletion Data). See section 6011(a). For the purpose of this subparagraph, the determination under section 631(c) of gain or loss upon the disposition of coal or domestic iron ore with a retained economic interest shall not be regarded as the claiming of a deduction for depletion. Such forms shall be filed for any subsequent taxable year if the Commissioner determines that the forms are required for such year. Where appropriate, both Form M and Form O shall be filed. Forms M and O shall be deemed to be part of the return to which they relate. If a taxpayer mines more than one mineral, a separate Form M shall be filed for each such mineral. If a taxpayer has both domestic and foreign properties, separate forms shall be filed for each country in which a taxpayer's properties are located. All data relating to a taxpayer's domestic oil and gas properties shall be summarized on a single Form O, and data relating to a taxpayer's domestic mineral properties (other than oil and gas properties) shall be summarized on a single Form M for each mineral. Similarly, all data relating to a taxpayer's oil and gas properties in a specific foreign country shall be summarized on a single Form O, and data relating to a taxpayer's mineral properties (other than oil and gas properties) in a specific foreign country shall be summarized on a single Form M for each mineral. In addition, the taxpayer shall assemble, segregate, and have readily available at his principal place of business, the data listed in subparagraphs (2), (3), and (4) of this paragraph. [Reg. § 1.611-2.]

☐ [T.D. 6446, 1-20-60. Amended by T.D. 6938, 12-6-67 and by T.D. 7170, 3-10-72.]

[Reg. § 1.611-3]

§ 1.611-3. Rules applicable to timber.—(a) Capital recoverable through depletion allowance in case of timber. In general, the capital remaining in any year recoverable through depletion allowances is the basis provided by section 612 and the regulations thereunder. For the method of determining fair market value and quantity of timber, see paragraphs (d), (e), and (f) of this section. For capitalization of carrying charges, see section 1016(a)(1)(A). Amounts paid or incurred in connection with the planting of timber (including planting for Christmas tree purposes) shall be capitalized and recoverable through depletion allowances. Such amounts include, for example, expenditures made for the preparation of the timber site for planting or for natural seeding and the cost of seedlings. The apportionment of deductions between the several owners of economic interests in standing timber will be made as provided in paragraph (c) of § 1.611-1.

(b) *Computation of allowance for depletion of timber for taxable year.* (1) The depletion of timber takes place at the time timber is cut, but the amount of depletion allowable with respect to timber that has been cut may be computed when the quantity of cut timber is first accurately measured in the process of exploitation. To the extent that depletion is allowable in a particular taxable year with respect to timber the products of which are not sold during such year, the depletion so allowable shall be included as an item of cost in the closing inventory of such products for such year.

(2) The depletion unit of the timber for a given timber account in a given year shall be the quotient obtained by dividing (i) the basis provided by section 1012 and adjusted as provided by section 1016, of the timber on hand at the beginning of the year plus the cost of the number of units of timber acquired during the year plus proper additions to capital, by (ii) the total number of units of timber on hand in the given account at the beginning of the year plus the number of units acquired during the year plus (or minus) the number of units required to be added (or deducted) by way of correcting the estimate of the number of units remaining available in the account. The number of units of timber of a given timber account cut during any taxable year multiplied by the depletion unit of that timber account applicable to such year shall be the amount of depletion allowable for the taxable year. Those taxpayers who keep their accounts on a monthly basis may, at their option, keep their depletion accounts on such basis, in which case the amount allowable on account of depletion for a given month will be determined in the manner outlined herein for a given year. The total amount of the allowance for depletion in any taxable year shall be the sum of the amounts allowable for the several timber accounts. For a description of timber accounts, see paragraphs (c) and (d) of this section.

(3) When a taxpayer has elected to treat the cutting of timber as a sale or exchange of such timber under the provisions of section 631(a), he shall reduce the timber account containing such timber by an amount equal to the adjusted depletion basis of such timber. In computing any further gain or loss on such timber, see paragraph (e) of § 1.631-1.

(c) *Timber depletion accounts on books.* (1) Every taxpayer claiming or expecting to claim a deduction for depletion of timber property shall keep accurate ledger accounts in which shall be recorded the cost or other basis provided by section 1012 of the property and land together with subsequent allowable capital additions in each account and all other adjustments provided by section 1016 and the regulations thereunder.

(2) In such accounts there shall be set up separately the quantity of timber, the quantity of land, and the quantity of other resources, if any, and a proper part of the total cost or value shall be allocated to each after proper provision for immature timber growth. See paragraph (d) of this section. The timber accounts shall be credited each year with the amount of the charges to the depletion accounts computed in accordance with paragraph (b) of this section or the amount of the charges to the depletion accounts shall be credited to depletion reserve accounts. When the sum of the credits for depletion equals the cost or other basis of the timber property, plus subsequent allowable capital additions, no further deduction for depletion will be allowed.

(d) *Aggregating timber and land for purposes of valuation and accounting.* (1) With a view to logical and reasonable valuation of timber, the taxpayer shall include his timber in one or more accounts. In general, each such account shall include all of the taxpayer's timber which is located in one "block". A block may be an operation unit which includes all the taxpayer's timber which would logically go to a single given point of manufacture. In those cases in which the point of manufacture is at a considerable distance, or in which the logs or other products will probably be sold in a log or other market, the block may be a logging unit which includes all of the taxpayer's timber which would logically be removed by a single logging development. Blocks may also be established by geographical or political boundaries or by logical management areas. Timber acquired under cutting contracts should be carried in separate accounts and shall not constitute part of any block. In exceptional cases, provided there are good and substantial reasons, and subject to ap-

Reg. § 1.611-3(d)

proval or revision by the district director on audit, the taxpayer may divide the timber in a given block into two or more accounts. For example, timber owned on February 28, 1913, and that purchased subsequently may be kept in separate accounts, or timber owned on February 28, 1913, and the timber purchased since that date in several distinct transactions may be kept in several distinct accounts. Individual tree species or groups of tree species may be carried in distinct accounts, or special timber products may be carried in distinct accounts. Blocks may be divided into two or more accounts based on the character of the timber or its accessibility, or scattered tracts may be included in separate accounts. If such a division is made, a proper portion of the total value or cost, as the case may be, shall be allocated to each account.

(2) The timber accounts mentioned in subparagraph (1) of this paragraph shall not include any part of the value or cost, as the case may be, of the land. In a manner similar to that prescribed in subparagraph (1) of this paragraph, the land in a given "block" may be carried in a single land account or may be divided into two or more accounts on the basis of its character or accessibility. When such a division is made, a proper portion of the total value or cost, as the case may be, shall be allocated to each account.

(3) The total value or total cost, as the case may be, of land and timber shall be equitably allocated to the timber and land accounts, respectively. In cases in which immature timber growth is a factor, a reasonable portion of the total value or cost shall be allocated to such immature timber, and when the timber becomes merchantable such value or cost shall be recoverable through depletion allowances.

(4) Each of the several land and timber accounts carried on the books of the taxpayer shall be definitely described as to their location on the ground either by maps or by legal descriptions.

(5) For good and substantial reasons satisfactory to the district director, or as required by the district director on audit, the timber or the land accounts may be readjusted by dividing individual accounts, by combining two or more accounts, or by dividing and recombining accounts.

(e) *Determination of quantity of timber.* Each taxpayer claiming or expecting to claim a deduction for depletion is required to estimate with respect to each separate timber account the total units (feet board measure, log scale, cords, or other units) of timber reasonably known, or on good evidence believed, to have existed on the ground on March 1, 1913, or on the date of acquisition of the property, whichever date is applicable in determining the basis for cost depletion. This estimate shall state as nearly as possible the number of units which would have been found present by careful estimate made on the specified date with the object of determining 100 percent of the quantity of timber which the area covered by the specific account would have produced on that date if all of the merchantable timber had been cut and utilized in accordance with the standards of utilization prevailing in that region at that time. If subsequently during the ownership of the taxpayer making the return, as the result of the growth of the timber, of changes in standards of utilization, of losses not otherwise accounted for, of abandonment of timber, or of operations or development work, it is ascertained either by the taxpayer or the district director that there remain on the ground, available for utilization, more or less units of timber at the close of the taxable year (or at the close of the month if the taxpayer keeps his depletion accounts on a monthly basis) than remain in the timber account or accounts on the basis of the original estimate, then the original estimate (but not the basis for depletion) shall be revised. The depletion unit shall be changed when such revision has been made. The annual charge to the depletion account with respect to the property shall be computed by using such revised unit for the taxable year for which the revision is made and all subsequent taxable years until a change in facts requires another revision.

(f) *Determination of fair market value of timber property.* (1) If the fair market value of the property at a specified date is the basis for depletion deductions, such value shall be determined, subject to approval or revision by the district director upon audit, by the owner of the property in the light of the most reliable and accurate information available with reference to the condition of the property as it existed at that date, regardless of all subsequent changes, such as changes in surrounding circumstances, and methods of exploitation, in degree of utilization, etc. Such factors as the following will be given due consideration:

(i) Character and quality of the timber as determined by species, age, size, condition, etc.;

(ii) The quantity of timber per acre, the total quantity under consideration, and the location of the timber in question with reference to other timber;

(iii) Accessibility of the timber (location with reference to distance from a common carrier, the topography and other features of the ground upon which the timber stands and over which it must be transported in process of exploitation, the probable cost of exploitation and the climate and

Reg. § 1.611-3(d)(2)

the state of industrial development of the locality); and

 (iv) The freight rates by common carrier to important markets.

 (2) The timber in each particular case will be valued on its own merits and not on the basis of general averages for regions; however, the value placed upon it, taking into consideration such factors as those mentioned in this paragraph, will be consistent with that of other similar timber in the region. The district director will give weight and consideration to any and all facts and evidence having a bearing on the market value, such as cost, actual sales and transfers of similar properties, the margin between the cost of production and the price realized for timber products, market value of stock or shares, royalties and rentals, valuation for local or State taxation, partnership accountings, records of litigation in which the value of the property has been involved, the amount at which the property may have been inventoried or appraised in probate or similar proceedings, disinterested appraisals by approved methods, and other factors.

 (g) *Revaluation of timber property not allowed.* No revaluation of a timber property whose value as of any specific date has been determined and approved will be made or allowed during the continuance of the ownership under which the value was so determined and approved, except in the case of misrepresentation or fraud or gross error as to any facts known on the date as of which the valuation was made. Revaluation on account of misrepresentation or fraud or such gross error will be made only with the written approval of the Commissioner. The depletion unit shall be revised when such a revaluation of a timber property has been made and the annual charge to the depletion account with respect to the property shall be computed by using such revised unit for the taxable year for which such revision is made and for all subsequent taxable years.

 (h) *Reporting and recordkeeping requirements*—(1) *Taxable years beginning before January 1, 2002.* A taxpayer claiming a deduction for depletion of timber for a taxable year beginning before January 1, 2002, shall attach to the income tax return of the taxpayer a filled-out Form T (Timber) for the taxable year covered by the income tax return, including the following information—

 (i) A map where necessary to show clearly timber and land acquired, timber cut, and timber and land sold;

 (ii) Description of, cost of, and terms of purchase of timberland or timber, or cutting rights, including timber or timber rights acquired under any type of contract;

 (iii) Profit or loss from sale of land, or timber, or both;

 (iv) Description of timber with respect to which claim for loss, if any, is made;

 (v) Record of timber cut;

 (vi) Changes in each timber account as a result of purchase, sale, cutting, reestimate, or loss;

 (vii) Changes in improvements accounts as the result of additions to or deductions from capital and depreciation, and computation of profit or loss on sale or other disposition of such improvements;

 (viii) Operation data with respect to raw and finished material handled and inventoried;

 (ix) Statement as to application of the election under section 631(a) and pertinent information in support of the fair market value claimed thereunder;

 (x) Information with respect to land ownership and capital investment in timberland; and

 (xi) Any other data which will be helpful in determining the reasonableness of the depletion or depreciation deductions claimed in the return.

 (2) *Taxable years beginning after December 31, 2001.* A taxpayer claiming a deduction for depletion of timber on a return filed for a taxable year beginning after December 31, 2001, shall attach to the income tax return of the taxpayer a filled-out Form T (Timber) for the taxable year covered by the income tax return. In addition, the taxpayer must retain records sufficient to substantiate the right of the taxpayer to claim the deduction, including a map, where necessary, to show clearly timber and land acquired, timber cut, and timber and land sold for as long as their contents may become material in the administration of any internal revenue law. [Reg. § 1.611-3.]

 ☐ [*T.D.* 6446, 1-20-60. Amended by *T.D.* 8989, 4-23-2002 and *T.D.* 9040, 1-30-2003.]

[Reg. § 1.611-4]

§ 1.611-4. Depletion as a factor in computing earnings and profits for dividend purposes.—For rules with respect to computation of earnings and profits where depletion is a factor in the case of corporations, see paragraph (c)(1) of § 1.312-6. [Reg. § 1.611-4.]

 ☐ [*T.D.* 6446, 1-20-60.]

[Reg. § 1.611-5]

§ 1.611-5. Depreciation of improvements.—(a) *In general.* Section 611 provides in the case of mines, oil and gas wells, other natural deposits, and timber that there shall be allowed as a deduction a reasonable allowance for depreciation of improvements. Such allowance shall include exhaustion, wear and tear, and obsolescence. The deduction allowed under section 611 shall be determined under the provisions of section 167 and the regulations thereunder. For purposes of section 167 the unit of production method may, under appropriate circumstances, be considered a reasonable method under section 167(a), and therefore, not subject to the limitations prescribed by section 167(b).

(b) *Special rules for mines, oil and gas wells, other natural deposits and timber.* (1) For principles governing the apportioning of depreciation allowances under sections 611 and 167 in the case of property held by one person for life with remainder to another or in the case of property held in trust or by an estate, see § 1.167(h)-1.

(2) A reasonable allowance for depreciation on account of obsolescence or decay shall be required in an appropriate case during periods when the improvement is not used in production or is used in producing at a rate below its normal capacity. This rule is applicable whether or not the taxpayer uses the unit of production method.

(3) See sections 615 and 616 and the regulations thereunder for special rules for treatment of allowances for depreciation of improvements with respect to the exploration and development of a mine or other natural deposit (other than oil or gas).

(4) In the case of operating oil or gas properties, the deduction for depreciation shall be allowed for those costs of improvements such as machinery, tools, equipment, pipes and other similar items and the costs of installation which are not treated as a deductible expense under section 263(c). See § 1.612-4.

(c) *Accounting and record keeping.* See § 1.167(a)-7 for accounting and record keeping requirements for taxpayers claiming deductions under section 611 and this section. [Reg. § 1.611-5.]

☐ [T.D. 6446, 1-20-60. Amended by T.D. 6712, 3-23-64 and by T.D. 6836, 7-14-65.]

[Reg. § 1.612-1]

§ **1.612-1. Basis for allowance of cost depletion.**—(a) *In general.* The basis upon which the deduction for cost depletion under section 611 is to be allowed in respect of any mineral or timber property is the adjusted basis provided in section 1011 for the purpose of determining gain upon the sale or other disposition of such property except as provided in paragraph (b) of this section. The adjusted basis of such property is the cost or other basis determined under section 1012, relating to the basis of property, adjusted as provided in section 1016, relating to adjustments to basis, and the regulations under such sections. In the case of the sale of a part of such property, the unrecovered basis thereof shall be allocated to the part sold and the part retained.

(b) *Special rules.* (1) The basis for cost depletion of mineral or timber property does not include:

(i) Amounts recoverable through depreciation deductions, through deferred expenses, and through deductions other than depletion, and

(ii) The residual value of land and improvements at the end of operations.

In the case of any mineral property the basis for cost depletion does not include amounts representing the cost or value of land for purposes other than mineral production. Furthermore, in the case of certain mineral properties, such basis does not include exploration or development expenditures which are treated under section 615(b) or 616(b) as deferred expenses to be taken into account as deductions on a ratable basis as the units of minerals benefited thereby are produced and sold. However, there shall be included in the basis for cost depletion of oil and gas property the amounts of capitalized drilling and development costs which, as provided in § 1.612-4, are recoverable through depletion deductions. In the case of timber property, the basis for cost depletion does not include amounts representing the cost or value of land.

(2) Where a taxpayer elects to treat the cutting of timber as a sale or exchange of such timber, the basis for cost depletion shall be the fair market value of such timber as of the first day of the taxable year in which such timber is cut and such value shall be considered for such taxable year and all subsequent taxable years as the cost of such timber for all purposes for which such cost is a necessary factor. See section 631(a).

(c) *Cross references.* In cases where the valuation, revaluation, or mineral content of deposits is a factor, see paragraphs (c), (d), (e), and (f) of § 1.611-2. In cases where the valuation, revaluation, or quantity of timber is a factor, see paragraphs (e), (f), and (g) of § 1.611-3. For definitions of the terms "property", "fair market value", "mineral enterprise", "mineral deposit", and "minerals", see paragraph (d) of § 1.611-1. For rules with respect to treatment of depletion accounts on taxpayer's books, see paragraph (b) of § 1.611-2 in the case of mineral property, and paragraph (c) of § 1.611-3 in the case of timber property. [Reg. § 1.612-1.]

☐ [T.D. 6446, 1-20-60.]

Reg. § 1.612-1(a)

Deductions

39,351

See p. 20,601 for regulations not amended to reflect law changes

[Reg. § 1.612-2]

§ 1.612-2. Allowable capital additions in case of mines.—(a) *In general.* Expenditures for improvements and for replacements, not including expenditures for ordinary and necessary maintenance and repairs, shall ordinarily be charged to capital account recoverable through depreciation deductions. Expenditures for equipment (including its installation and housing) and for replacements thereof, which are necessary to maintain the normal output solely because of the recession of the working faces of the mine and which—

(1) Do not increase the value of the mine, or

(2) Do not decrease the cost of production of mineral units, or

(3) Do not represent an amount expended in restoring property or in making good the exhaustion thereof for which an allowance is or has been made

shall be deducted as ordinary and necessary business expenses.

(b) *Special rule.* For special provisions applicable to treatment of expenditures for certain exploration and development costs (other than for the acquisition, restoration, or betterment of improvements) with respect to minerals other than oil or gas, see sections 615 and 616 and the regulations thereunder. [Reg. § 1.612-2.]

☐ [T.D. 6446, 1-20-60.]

[Reg. § 1.612-3]

§ 1.612-3. Depletion; treatment of bonus and advanced royalty.—(a) *Bonus.* (1) If a bonus in addition to royalties is received upon the grant of an economic interest in a mineral deposit, or standing timber, there shall be allowed to the payee as a cost depletion deduction in respect of the bonus an amount equal to that proportion of his basis for depletion as provided in section 612 and § 1.612-1 which the amount of the bonus bears to the sum of the bonus and the royalties expected to be received. Such allowance shall be deducted from the payee's basis for depletion and the remainder of the basis is recoverable through depletion deductions as the royalties are thereafter received. (But see paragraph (e) of this section.) For example, a taxpayer leases mineral property to another reserving a one-eighth royalty and in addition receives a bonus of $10,000. Assuming that the taxpayer's basis with respect to the mineral property is $21,000 and that the royalties expected to be received are estimated to total $20,000, the depletion on the bonus would be $7,000

$$\left(\frac{\$21,000 \text{ (basis)} \times \$10,000 \text{ (bonus)}}{\$30,000 \text{ (bonus plus estimated royalties)}} \right)$$

The remaining $14,000 of basis will be recovered through depletion as the royalties are received.

(2) If the grant of an economic interest in a mineral deposit or standing timber with respect to which a bonus was received expires, terminates, or is abandoned before there has been any income derived from the extraction of mineral or cutting of timber, the payee shall adjust his capital account by restoring thereto the depletion deduction taken on the bonus and a corresponding amount must be returned as income in the year of such expiration, termination, or abandonment.

(3) In the case of the payor, payment of the bonus constitutes a capital investment made for the acquisition of an economic interest in a mineral deposit or standing timber recoverable through the depletion allowance. See paragraph (c)(5)(ii) of § 1.613-2 in cases in which percentage depletion is used.

(b) *Advanced royalties.* (1) If the owner of an operating interest in a mineral deposit or standing timber is required to pay royalties on a specified number of units of such mineral or timber annually whether or not extracted or cut within the year, and may apply any amounts paid on account of units not extracted or cut within the year against the royalty on the mineral or timber thereafter extracted or cut, the payee shall compute cost depletion on the number of units so paid for in advance of extraction or cutting and shall treat the amount so determined as an allowable deduction for depletion from the gross income of the year in which such payment or payments are made. No deduction for depletion by such payee shall be claimed or allowed in any subsequent year on account of the extraction or cutting in such year of any mineral or timber so paid for in advance and for which deduction has once been made. (But see paragraph (e) of this section.)

(2) If the right to extract minerals or to cut timber against which the advanced royalties may be applied expires, terminates, or is abandoned before all such minerals or timber have been extracted or cut, the payee shall adjust his capital account by restoring thereto the depletion deductions made in prior years on account of any units of mineral or timber paid for in advance but not extracted or cut, and a corresponding amount must be returned as income for the year of such expiration, termination or abandonment. (But see paragraph (e) of this section.)

(3) The payor shall treat the advanced royalties paid or accrued in connection with mineral property as deductions from gross income for the year the mineral product, in respect of which the advanced royalties were paid or accrued, is sold. For purposes of the preceding sentence, in the

Reg. § 1.612-3(b)(3)

Deductions

See p. 20,601 for regulations not amended to reflect law changes

case of mineral sold before production the mineral product is considered to be sold when the mineral is produced (*i.e.*, when a mineral product first exists). However, in the case of advanced mineral royalties paid or accrued in connection with mineral property as a result of a minimum royalty provision, the payor, at his option, may instead treat the advanced royalties as deductions from gross income for the year in which the advanced royalties are paid or accrued. See section 446 (relating to general rule for methods of accounting) and the regulations thereunder. For purposes of this paragraph, a minimum royalty provision requires that a substantially uniform amount of royalties be paid at least annually either over the life of the lease or for a period of at least 20 years, in the absence of mineral production requiring payment of aggregate royalties in a greater amount. For purposes of the preceding sentence, in the case of a lease which is subject to renewal or extension, the period for which it can be renewed or extended shall be treated as part of the term of the original lease. For special rules applicable when the payor is a sublessor of coal or domestic iron ore, see paragraph (b)(3) of § 1.631-3. Every taxpayer who pays or accrues advanced royalties resulting from a minimum royalty provision must make an election as to the treatment of all such advanced royalties in his return for the first taxable year ending after December 31, 1939, in which the advanced royalties are paid or accrued. The taxpayer's treatment of the advanced royalties for the first year shall be deemed to be the exercise of the election. Accordingly, a failure to deduct the advanced royalties for that year will constitute an election to have all the advanced royalties treated as deductions for the year of the sale of the mineral product in respect of which the advanced royalties are paid or accrued. See section 7807(b)(2). For additional rules relating to elections in the case of partners and partnerships, see section 703(b) and the regulations thereunder. The provisions of this subparagraph do not allow as deductions from gross income amounts disallowed as deductions under other provisions of the Code, such as section 461 (relating to general rule for taxable year of deduction), section 465 (relating to deductions limited to amount at risk in case of certain activities), or section 704(d) (relating to limitation on allowance to partners of partnership losses).

(4) The application of subparagraphs (2) and (3) of this paragraph may be illustrated by the following examples:

Example (1). B leased certain mineral lands from A under a lease in which A reserved a royalty of 10 cents a ton on minerals mined and sold by B. The lease also provided that B had to pay an annual minimum royalty of $10,000 representing the amount due on 100,000 tons of the particular mineral whether or not B mined and sold that amount. It was further provided that, if B did not mine and sell 100,000 tons in any year, he could mine and sell in any subsequent year the amount of mineral on which he had paid the royalty without the payment of any additional royalty. However, this right of recoupment was limited to minerals mined and sold in any later year in excess of the 100,000 tons represented by the $10,000 minimum royalty required to be paid for that later year. Assume that in 1956 B paid A the minimum royalty of $10,000, but mined and sold only 60,000 tons of the mineral and that in 1957 he abandoned the lease without any further production. Since the $10,000 represents royalties on 100,000 tons of mineral and only 60,000 tons were mined and sold, A must restore in 1957 to his capital account the depletion deductions taken in 1956 on $4,000 on account of the 40,000 tons paid for in advance but not mined and sold, and must also return the corresponding amount as income in 1957.

Example (2). Assume that B, under the lease in example (1), paid the $10,000 minimum royalty and mined no minerals in 1956 but that in 1957 B mined and sold 200,000 tons of mineral. If this is B's first such expenditure, B has an option, for the purpose of computing taxable income under section 63, to deduct in 1956 the $10,000 paid in that year although no mineral was mined, or to take the deduction in 1957 when the mineral, for which the $10,000 was paid in 1956, was mined and sold. (For treatment under percentage depletion, see example in paragraph (c)(5)(iii) of § 1.613-2.)

(c) *Delay rental.* (1) A delay rental is an amount paid for the privilege of deferring development of the property and which could have been avoided by abandonment of the lease, or by commencement of development operations, or by obtaining production.

(2) Since a delay rental is in the nature of rent it is ordinary income to the payee and not subject to depletion. The payor may at his election deduct such amount as an expense, or under section 266 and the regulations thereunder, charge it to depletable capital account.

(d) *Percentage depletion deduction with respect to bonus and advanced royalty.* In lieu of the allowance based on cost depletion computed under paragraphs (a) and (b) of this section, the payees referred to therein may be allowed a depletion deduction in respect of any bonus or advanced royalty for the taxable year in an amount computed on the basis of the percentage of gross

Reg. § 1.612-3(b)(4)

Deductions

See p. 20,601 for regulations not amended to reflect law changes

income from the property as provided in section 613 and the regulations thereunder. However, for special rules applicable to certain bonuses and advanced royalties received in connection with oil or gas properties, see paragraph (j) of § 1.613A-3.

(e) *Cross reference.* In the case of bonuses and advanced royalties received in connection with a contract of disposal of timber covered by section 631(b) or coal or iron ore covered by section 631(c), see that section and the regulations thereunder. [Reg. § 1.612-3.]

☐ [T.D. 6446, 1-20-60. Amended by T.D. 6841, 7-26-65; by T.D. 7523, 12-14-77 and T.D. 8348, 5-10-91.]

[Reg. § 1.612-4]

§ **1.612-4. Charges to capital and to expense in case of oil and gas wells.**—(a) *Option with respect to intangible drilling and development costs.* In accordance with the provisions of section 263(c), intangible drilling and development costs incurred by an operator (one who holds a working or operating interest in any tract or parcel of land either as a fee owner or under a lease or any other form of contract granting working or operating rights) in the development of oil and gas properties may at his option be chargeable to capital or to expense. This option applies to all expenditures made by an operator for wages, fuel, repairs, hauling, supplies, etc., incident to and necessary for the drilling of wells and the preparation of wells for the production of oil or gas. Such expenditures have for convenience been termed intangible drilling and development costs. They include the cost to operators of any drilling or development work (excluding amounts payable only out of production or gross or net proceeds from production, if such amounts are depletable income to the recipient, and amounts properly allocable to cost of depreciable property) done for them by contractors under any form of contract, including turnkey contracts. Examples of items to which this option applies are, all amounts paid for labor, fuel, repairs, hauling, and supplies, or any of them, which are used—

(1) In the drilling, shooting, and cleaning of wells,

(2) In such clearing of ground, draining, road making, surveying, and geological works as are necessary in preparation for the drilling of wells, and

(3) In the construction of such derricks, tanks, pipelines, and other physical structures as are necessary for the drilling of wells and the preparation of wells for the production of oil or gas.

In general, this option applies only to expenditures for those drilling and developing items which in themselves do not have a salvage value. For the purpose of this option, labor, fuel, repairs, hauling, supplies, etc., are not considered as having a salvage value, even though used in connection with the installation of physical property which has a salvage value. Included in this option are all costs of drilling and development undertaken (directly or through a contract) by an operator of an oil and gas property whether incurred by him prior or subsequent to the formal grant or assignment to him of operating rights (a leasehold interest, or other form of operating rights, or working interest); except that in any case where any drilling or development project is undertaken for the grant or assignment of a fraction of the operating rights, only that part of the costs thereof which is attributable to such fractional interest is within this option. In the excepted cases, costs of the project undertaken, including depreciable equipment furnished, to the extent allocable to fractions of the operating rights held by others, must be capitalized as the depletable capital cost of the fractional interest thus acquired.

(b) *Recovery of optional items, if capitalized.* (1) Items returnable through depletion: If the taxpayer charges such expenditures as fall within the option to capital account, the amounts so capitalized and not deducted as a loss are returnable through depletion insofar as they are not represented by physical property. For the purposes of this section the expenditures for clearing ground, draining, road making, surveying, geological work, excavation, grading, and the drilling, shooting, and cleaning of wells, are considered not to be represented by physical property, and when charged to capital account are returnable through depletion.

(2) Items returnable through depreciation: If the taxpayer charges such expenditures as fall within the option to capital account, the amounts so capitalized and not deducted as a loss are returnable through depreciation insofar as they are represented by physical property. Such expenditures are amounts paid for wages, fuel, repairs, hauling, supplies, etc., used in the installation of casing and equipment and in the construction on the property of derricks and other physical structures.

(3) In the case of capitalized intangible drilling and development costs incurred under a contract, such costs shall be allocated between the foregoing classes of items specified in subparagraphs (1) and (2) for the purpose of determining the depletion and depreciation allowances.

Reg. § 1.612-4(b)(3)

Deductions

See p. 20,601 for regulations not amended to reflect law changes

(4) *Option with respect to cost of nonproductive wells:* If the operator has elected to capitalize intangible drilling and development costs, then an additional option is accorded with respect to intangible drilling and development costs incurred in drilling a nonproductive well. Such costs incurred in drilling a nonproductive well may be deducted by the taxpayer as an ordinary loss provided a proper election is made in the return for the first taxable year beginning after December 31, 1942, in which such a nonproductive well is completed. Such election with respect to intangible drilling and development costs of nonproductive wells is a new election, and, when made, shall be binding for all subsequent years. Any taxpayer who incurs optional drilling and development costs in drilling a nonproductive well must make a clear statement of election under this option in the return for the first taxable year beginning after December 31, 1942, in which such nonproductive well is completed. The absence of a clear indication in such return of an election to deduct as ordinary losses intangible drilling and development costs of nonproductive wells shall be deemed to be an election to recover such costs through depletion to the extent that they are not represented by physical property, and through depreciation to the extent that they are represented by physical property.

(c) *Nonoptional items distinguished.* (1) Capital items: The option with respect to intangible drilling and development costs does not apply to expenditures by which the taxpayer acquires tangible property ordinarily considered as having a salvage value. Examples of such items are the costs of the actual materials in those structures which are constructed in the wells and on the property, and the cost of drilling tools, pipe, casing, tubing, tanks, engines, boilers, machines, etc. The option does not apply to any expenditure for wages, fuel, repairs, hauling, supplies, etc., in connection with equipment, facilities, or structures, not incident to or necessary for the drilling of wells, such as structures for storing or treating oil or gas. These are capital items and are returnable through depreciation.

(2) Expense items: Expenditures which must be charged off as expense, regardless of the option provided by this section, are those for labor, fuel, repairs, hauling, supplies, etc., in connection with the operation of the wells and of other facilities on the property for the production of oil or gas.

(d) *Manner of making election.* The option granted in paragraph (a) of this section to charge intangible drilling and development costs to expense may be exercised by claiming intangible drilling and development costs as a deduction on the taxpayer's return for the first taxable year in which the taxpayer pays or incurs such costs; no formal statement is necessary. If the taxpayer fails to deduct such costs as expenses in such return, he shall be deemed to have elected to recover such costs through depletion to the extent that they are not represented by physical property, and through depreciation to the extent that they are represented by physical property.

(e) *Effect of option and election.* This section does not grant a new option under paragraph (a) of this section or new election under paragraph (b) of this section. Section 3 of the Act of October 23, 1962 (Public Law 87-863, 76 Stat. 1142) granted any taxpayer who had exercised an option to capitalize intangible drilling and development costs under Regulations 111, § 29.23(m)-16 (1939 Code) or Regulations 118, § 39.23(m)-16 (1939 Code) a new option for the first taxable year ending after October 22, 1962, to deduct such costs as expenses. Unless he has exercised the new option granted by such Act, any taxpayer who exercised an option or made an election under the regulations described in the preceding sentence is, by such option or election, bound with respect to all intangible drilling and development costs (whether made before January 1, 1954, or after December 31, 1953) in connection with oil and gas properties. See section 7807(b)(2). Any taxpayer who has not made intangible drilling and development expenditures in any taxable year beginning after December 31, 1942, prior to his first taxable year beginning after December 31, 1953, and ending after August 16, 1954, must exercise the option granted in paragraph (a) of this section in the return for the first taxable year in which the taxpayer pays or incurs such expenditures. If such return is required by law (including extensions thereof) to be filed before November 1, 1965, the option under paragraph (a) of this section, or the election under paragraph (b) of this section, may be exercised or changed not later than November 1, 1965. The exercise of or change in such option or election shall be effective with respect to the earliest taxable year to which the option or election is applicable in respect of which assessment of a deficiency or credit or refund of an overpayment, as the case may be, resulting from such exercise or exchange is not prevented by any law or rule of law on the date such option is exercised or such election is made. Any such option or election shall be binding upon the taxpayer for the first taxable year for which it is effective and for all subsequent taxable years. [Reg. § 1.612-4.]

☐ [*T.D.* 6836, 7-14-65.]

Reg. § 1.612-4(b)(4)

[Reg. § 1.612-5]

§ 1.612-5. Charges to capital and to expense in case of geothermal wells.—(a) *Option with respect to intangible drilling and development costs.* In accordance with the provisions of section 263(c), intangible drilling and development costs incurred by an operator (one who holds a working or operating interest in any tract or parcel of land either as a fee owner or under a lease or any other form of contract granting working or operating rights) in the development of a geothermal deposit (as defined in section 613(e)(3) and the regulations thereunder) may at the operator's option be chargeable to capital or to expense. This option applies to all expenditures made by an operator for wages, fuel, repairs, hauling, supplies, etc., incident to and necessary for the drilling of wells and the preparation of wells for the production of geothermal steam or hot water. Such expenditures have for convenience been termed intangible drilling and development costs. They include the cost to operators of any drilling or development work (excluding amounts payable only out of production or gross or net proceeds from production, if such amounts are depletable income to the recipient, and amounts properly allocable to cost of depreciable property) done for them by contractors under any form of contract, including turnkey contracts. Examples of items to which this option applies are all amounts paid for labor, fuel, repairs, hauling, and supplies, or any of them, which are used—

(1) In the drilling, shooting, and cleaning of wells,

(2) In such clearing of ground, draining, road making, surveying, and geological work as are necessary in preparation for the drilling of wells, and

(3) In the construction of such derricks, tanks, pipelines, and other physical structures as are necessary for the drilling of wells and the preparation of wells for the production of geothermal steam or hot water. In general, this option applies only to expenditures for those drilling and developing items which in themselves do *not* have a salvage value. For the purpose of *this* option, labor, fuel, repairs, hauling, supplies, etc. are not considered as having a salvage value, even though used in connection with the installation of physical property which has a salvage value. Included in this option are all costs of drilling and development undertaken (directly or through a contract) by an operator of a geothermal property whether incurred by the operator prior or subsequent to the formal grant or assignment of operating rights (a leasehold interest, or other form of operating rights, or working interest): except that in any case where any drilling or development project is undertaken for the grant or assignment of a fraction of the operating rights, only that part of the costs thereof which is attributable to such fractional interest is within this option. In the excepted cases, costs of the project undertaken, including depreciable equipment furnished, to the extent allocable to fractions of the operating rights held by others, must be capitalized as the depletable capital cost of the fractional interest thus acquired.

(b) *Recovery of optional items, if capitalized.* (1) Items recoverable through depletion: If the taxpayer charges such expenditures as fall within the option to capital account, the amounts so capitalized and not deducted as a loss are recoverable through depletion insofar as they are not represented by physical property. For the purposes of this section the expenditures for clearing ground, draining, road making, surveying, geological work, excavation, grading, and the drilling, shooting, and cleaning of wells, are considered not to be represented by physical property, and when charged to capital account are recoverable through depletion.

(2) Items recoverable through depreciation: If the taxpayer charges such expenditures as fall within the option to capital account, the amounts so capitalized and not deducted as a loss are recoverable through depreciation insofar as they are represented by physical property. Such expenditures are amounts paid for wages, fuel, repairs, hauling, supplies, etc. used in the installation of casing and equipment and in the construction on the property of derricks and other physical structures.

(3) In the case of capitalized intangible drilling and development costs incurred under a contract, such costs shall be allocated between the foregoing classes of items specified in paragraphs (b)(1) and (2) of this section for the purpose of determining the depletion and depreciation allowances.

(4) Option with respect to cost of nonproductive wells: If the operator has elected to capitalize intangible drilling and development costs; then an additional option is accorded with respect to intangible drilling and development costs incurred in drilling a nonproductive well. Such costs incurred in drilling a nonproductive well may be deducted by the taxpayer as an ordinary loss provided a proper election is made in the taxpayer's original or amended return for the first taxable year ending on or after October 1, 1978, in which such a nonproductive well is completed. The taxpayer must make a clear statement of election under this option in the return or

Reg. § 1.612-5(b)(4)

amended return. The election may be revoked by the filing of an amended return that does not contain such a statement. The absence of a clear indication in such return of an election to deduct as ordinary losses intangible drilling and development costs of nonproductive wells shall be deemed to be an election to recover such costs through depletion to the extent that they are not represented by physical property, and through depreciation to the extent that they are represented by physical property. Upon the expiration of the time for filing a claim for credit or refund of any overpayment of tax imposed by chapter 1 of the Code with respect to the first taxable year ending on or after October 1, 1978 in which a nonproductive well is completed, the taxpayer is bound for all subsequent years by his exercise of the option to deduct intangible drilling and development costs of nonproductive wells as an ordinary loss or his deemed election to recover such costs through depletion or depreciation.

(c) *Nonoptional items distinguished.* (1) *Capital items:* The option with respect to intangible drilling and development costs does not apply to expenditures by which the taxpayer acquires tangible property ordinarily considered as having a salvage value. Examples of such items are the costs of the actual materials in those structures which are constructed in the wells and on the property, and the cost of drilling tools, pipe, casing, tubing, tanks, engines, boilers, machines, etc. The option does not apply to any expenditure for wages, fuel, repairs, hauling, supplies, etc., in connection with equipment, facilities, or structures, not incident to or necessary for the drilling of wells, such as structures for treating geothermal steam or hot water. These are capital items and are recoverable through depreciation.

(2) *Expense items:* Expenditures which must be charged off as expense, regardless of the option provided by this section, are those for labor, fuel, repairs, hauling, supplies, etc., in connection with the operation of the wells and of other facilities on the property for the production of geothermal steam or hot water.

(d) *Manner of making election.* The option granted in paragraph (a) of this section to charge intangible drilling and development costs to expense may be exercised by claiming intangible drilling and development costs as a deduction on the taxpayer's original or amended return for the first taxable year ending on or after October 1, 1978, in which the taxpayer pays or incurs such costs with respect to a geothermal well commenced on or after that date. No formal statement is necessary. The exercise of the option may be revoked by the filing of an amended return that does not claim such a deduction. If the taxpayer fails to deduct such costs as expenses in any such return, he shall be deemed to have elected to recover such costs through depletion to the extent that they are not represented by physical property, and through depreciation to the extent that they are represented by physical property. Upon the expiration of the time for filing a claim for credit or refund of any overpayment of tax imposed by chapter 1 of the Code with respect to the first taxable year ending on or after October 1, 1978, in which the taxpayer pays or incurs intangible drilling and development costs with respect to a geothermal well commenced on or after that date, the taxpayer is bound by his exercise of the option to charge such costs to expense or his deemed election to recover such costs through depletion or depreciation for that year and for all subsequent years.

(e) *Effective date.* The option granted by paragraph (a) of this section is available only for taxable years ending on or after October 1, 1978, with respect to geothermal wells commenced on or after that date. [Reg. § 1.612-5.]

☐ [T.D. 7806, 1-27-82.]

[Reg. § 1.613-1]

§ 1.613-1. **Percentage depletion; general rule.**—(a) *In general.* In the case of a taxpayer computing the deduction for depletion under section 611 with respect to minerals on the basis of a percentage of gross income from the property, as defined in section 613(c) and §§ 1.613-3 and 1.613-4, the deduction shall be the percentage of the gross income as specified in section 613(b) and § 1.613-2. The deduction shall not exceed 50 percent (100 percent in the case of oil and gas properties for taxable years beginning after December 31, 1990) of the taxpayer's taxable income from the property (computed without regard to allowance for depletion). The taxable income shall be computed in accordance with § 1.613-5. In no case shall the deduction for depletion computed under this section be less than the deduction computed upon the cost or other basis of the property provided in section 612 and the regulations thereunder. The apportionment of the deduction between the several owners of economic interests in a mineral deposit will be made as provided in paragraph (c) of § 1.611-1. For rules with respect to "gross income from the property" and for definition of the term "mining," see §§ 1.613-3 and 1.613-4. For definitions of the terms "property," "mineral deposit," and "minerals," see paragraph (d) of § 1.611-1.

(b) *Denial of percentage depletion in case of oil and gas wells.* Except as otherwise provided in section 613A and the regulations thereunder, in

Deductions

the case of oil or gas which is produced after December 31, 1974, and to which gross income is attributable after that date, the allowance for depletion shall be computed without regard to section 613. [Reg. § 1.613-1.]

☐ [*T.D.* 6446, 1-20-60. *Amended by T.D.* 7170, 3-10-72; *T.D.* 8348, 5-10-91 *and T.D.* 8437, 9-22-92.]

[Reg. § 1.613-2]

§ 1.613-2. **Percentage depletion rates.**—(a) *In general.* Subject to the provisions of paragraph (b) of this section and as provided in section 613(b), in the case of mines, wells, or other natural deposits, a taxpayer may deduct as an allowance for depletion under section 611 the percentages of gross income from the property as set forth in subparagraphs (1), (2), and (3) of this paragraph.

(1) *Without regard to situs of deposits.* The following rates are applicable to the minerals listed in this subparagraph regardless of the situs of the deposits from which the minerals are produced:

(i) 27½ percent—Gas wells, oil wells.

(ii) 23 percent—Sulfur, uranium.

(iii) 15 percent—Ball clay, bentonite, china clay, metal mines,[1] sagger clay, rock asphalt, vermiculite.

(iv) 10 percent—Asbestos,[1] brucite, coal, lignite, perlite, sodium chloride, wollastonite.

(v) 5 percent—Brick and tile clay, gravel, mollusk shells (including clam shells and oyster shells), peat, pumice, sand, scoria, shale, stone (except dimension or ornamental stone). If from brine wells—Bromine, calcium chloride, magnesium chloride.

(2) *Production from United States deposits.* A rate of 23 percent is applicable to the minerals listed in this subparagraph if produced from deposits within the United States:

Anorthosite.[2]
Asbestos.
Bauxite.
Beryl.[3]
Celestite.
Chromite.
Corundum.
Fluorspar.
Graphite.
Ilmenite.
Kyanite.
Mica.
Olivine.
Quartz crystals (radio grade).
Rutile.
Block steatite talc.
Zircon.

Ores of the following metals—
Antimony.
Beryllium.[4]
Bismuth.
Cadmium.
Cobalt.
Columbium.
Lead.
Lithium.
Manganese.
Mercury.
Nickel.
Platinum.
Platinum group metals.
Tantalum.
Thorium.
Tin.
Titanium.
Tungsten.
Vanadium.
Zinc.

(3) *Other minerals.* A rate of 15 percent is applicable to the minerals listed in this subparagraph regardless of the situs of the deposits from which the minerals are produced, provided the minerals are not used or sold for use by the mine owner or operator as rip rap, ballast, road material, rubble, concrete aggregates, or for similar purposes. If, however, such minerals are sold or used for the purposes described in the preceding sentence, a rate of 5 percent is applicable to any of such minerals unless sold on bid in direct competition with a bona fide bid to sell any of the minerals listed in subdivision (iii) of subparagraph (1) of this paragraph, in which case the rate is 15 percent. In addition, the provisions of this subparagraph are not applicable with respect to

---

[1] Not applicable if the rate prescribed in subparagraph (2) of this paragraph is applicable.

[2] The rate prescribed in this subparagraph does not apply except to the extent that alumina and aluminum compounds are extracted therefrom.

[3] Applicable only for taxable years beginning before January 1, 1964.

[4] Applicable only for taxable years beginning after December 31, 1963.

Reg. § 1.613-2(a)(3)

39,358   Deductions

See p. 20,601 for regulations not amended to reflect law changes

any of the minerals listed herein if the rate prescribed in subparagraph (2) of this paragraph is applicable:

Aplite.
Barite.
Bauxite.
Beryl.[5]
Borax.
Calcium carbonates.
Clay, refractory and fire.[6]
Diatomaceous earth.
Dolomite.
Feldspar.
Flake graphite.
Flourspar.
Fullers earth.
Garnet.
Gilsonite.
Granite.
Lepidolite.
Limestone.
Magnesite.
Magnesium carbonates.
Marble.
Mica.
Phosphate rock.
Potash.
Quartzite.
Slate.
Soapstone.
Spodumene.
Stone (dimension or ornamental).[7]
Talc (including pyrophyllite).
Thenardite.
Tripoli.
Trona.
All other minerals.

(b) *Definitions of terms.* (1) For purposes of this section, the minerals indicated below shall have the following meanings:

(i) Clay, brick and tile—Clay used or sold for use in the manufacture of common brick, drain and roofing tile, sewer pipe, flower pots, and kindred products (other than clay specifically identified as a clay for which a 15 percent rate of percentage allowance is provided).

(ii) Clay, refractory and fire—Clay which has a pyrometric cone equivalent of 19 or higher.

(iii) Pumice—All pumice including pumicite.

(iv) Scoria—Only scoria produced from natural deposits.

(2) For purposes of this section, the term "United States" means the States and the District of Columbia. See section 7701(a)(9).

(3) For purposes of this section, the term "dimension stone" means blocks and slabs of natural stone, subsequently cut to definite shapes and sizes and used or sold for such uses as building stone (excluding rubble), monumental stone, paving blocks, curbing and flagging. For purposes of this section, "ornamental stone" means blocks and slabs of natural stone, subsequently cut to definite shapes and sizes and used or sold for use for making ornaments or statues.

(4) For purposes of this section, the term "all other minerals" does not include (i) soil, sod, dirt, turf, water, or mosses; or (ii) minerals from sea water, the air, or similar inexhaustible sources. However, the term "all other minerals" is not limited in meaning to the minerals listed in section 613(b), but includes all other minerals (except those to which a specific percentage rate applies under subparagraphs (1), (2), (3), (4), and (5) of section 613(b)): For example, gypsum, novaculite, natural mineral pigments, quartz sand and quartz pebbles, graphite and kyanite (if section 613(b)(2)(B) does not apply), and anorthosite to the extent that alumina and aluminum compounds are not extracted therefrom. The 15-percent rate applies to such "all other minerals" when used or sold for use by the mine owner or operator for purposes other than as rip rap, ballast, road material, rubble, concrete aggregates, or for similar purposes. When any such minerals are used or sold for use by the mine owner or operator as rip rap, ballast, road material, rubble, concrete aggregates, or for similar purposes, the 5-percent rate applies except that, when sold for such use by the mine owner or operator on a bid in direct competition with a bona fide bid to sell a mineral listed in section 613(b)(3), the 15-percent rate applies. For example, limestone sold on a bid in direct competition with a bona fide bid to sell rock asphalt for road building purposes may be entitled to a 15-percent rate. In every case the taxpayer must establish to the satisfaction of the district director that there was a bona fide bid to

---

[5] Applicable only for taxable years beginning before January 1, 1964.

[6] Not applicable for taxable years beginning after December 31, 1960.

[7] The 15-percent rate is applicable only to stone used or sold for use by the mine owner or operator as dimension stone or ornamental stone.

Reg. § 1.613-2(b)(2)

Deductions

sell a mineral listed under section 613(b)(3) by a person other than the taxpayer, and that the mineral sold by the taxpayer was sold on a bid in direct competition with such bona fide bid to sell such other material.

(c) *Rules for application of paragraph (a) of this section.* (1) In no case may the allowance for depletion computed upon the basis of a percentage of gross income from the property exceed 50 percent of the taxpayer's taxable income from the property (computed without allowance for depletion). For rules relating to the computation of such taxable income, see § 1.613-5.

(2) In cases in which there are produced from a mineral property two or more minerals, each entitled to a different percentage depletion rate under section 613(b) and this section or any of which is entitled to cost depletion only, the percentage depletion allowance is the sum of the results obtained by applying the percentage applicable to each mineral (zero, if not entitled to percentage depletion) to the "gross income from the property" attributable to such mineral. The sum so computed is subject to the limitation provided in section 613(a) and § 1.613-1, that is, 50 percent of the taxpayer's taxable income from the property (computed without allowance for depletion). Such taxable income (computed in accordance with § 1.613-4) is the total taxable income resulting from the sale of all minerals produced from the mineral property (as defined in section 614 and the regulations thereunder). The provisions of this subparagraph may be illustrated by the following examples:

Example (1). Pyrite, an iron sulfide, may be sold for either its sulphur content or its iron content, or both. Sulphur is entitled to a percentage depletion deduction based on 23 percent of gross income from the property whereas the percentage depletion deduction for iron is based on 15 percent of such gross income. Therefore, in the case of a taxpayer who sells pyrite for both its sulphur and iron content, 23 percent of his gross income from sulphur plus 15 percent of his gross income from iron would be his maximum allowable percentage depletion deduction. However, this maximum deduction would be subject to the limitation provided for in section 613(a), i.e., 50 percent of "taxable income from the property (computed without allowance for depletion)", such taxable income being the overall taxable income resulting from the sale of both minerals contained in the deposit.

Example (2). Oil and gas are produced from a single mineral property of a taxpayer who operates a retail outlet for the sale of oil products within the meaning of section 613A(d)(2). The taxpayer is not entitled to percentage depletion on the gross income attributable to the oil, but is entitled to percentage depletion on the gross income attributable to gas which is regulated gas under section 613(b)(2)(B). Accordingly, the taxpayer's maximum allowable percentage depletion deduction would be zero percent of gross income from the property with respect to oil, plus 22 percent (see section 613A(b)(1)) of gross income from the property with respect to gas. This maximum deduction would be subject to the limitation provided for in section 613(a), *i.e.*, 50 percent of "taxable income from the property (computed without allowance for depletion)," such taxable income being the overall taxable income resulting from the sale of both oil and gas. However, in the case of oil or gas production which qualifies for percentage depletion under section 613A(c), see the special allocation rules contained in section 613A(c)(7)(C) and (E) and § 1.613A-4.

(3) Except as provided in section 613(d) and the regulations thereunder relating to special rules for determining rates of depletion for taxable years ending after December 31, 1953, to which the Internal Revenue Code of 1939 applies—

(i) The percentage rates set forth in this section are applicable only for taxable years beginning after December 31, 1953, and ending after August 16, 1954; and

(ii) The percentage rates set forth in 26 CFR (1939) 39.23(m)-5 (Regulations 118) are applicable for taxable years beginning before January 1, 1954, or ending before August 17, 1954.

(4) Percentage depletion is not allowable with respect to the income from a disposal of coal (including lignite) or domestic iron ore (as defined in paragraph (e) of § 1.631-3) with a retained economic interest to the extent that such income is treated as from a sale of coal or iron ore under section 631(c) and § 1.631-3. Rents or royalties paid or incurred by a taxpayer with respect to coal (including lignite) or domestic iron ore shall be excluded by such taxpayer in determining "gross income from the property" without regard to the treatment under section 631(c) of such rents and royalties in the hands of the recipient.

(5)(i) In all cases there shall be excluded in determining the "gross income from the property" an amount equal to any rents or royalties (which are depletable income to the payee) which are paid or incurred by the taxpayer in respect of the property and are not otherwise excluded from "gross income from the property". The following example illustrates this rule:

Example. A leases coal-bearing lands to B on condition that B will annually pay a royalty of 25 cents a ton on coal mined and sold by B.

Reg. § 1.613-2(c)(5)

During the year 1956, B mines and sells f.o.b. mine 100,000 tons of coal for $600,000. In computing "gross income from the property" for the year 1956, B will exclude $25,000 (100,000 tons × $0.25) in computing his allowable percentage depletion deduction. B's allowable percentage depletion deduction (without reference to the limitation based on taxable income from the property) for the year 1956 will be $57,500 (($600,000 − $25,000) × 10 percent).

(ii) If bonus payments have been paid in respect of the property in any taxable year or any prior taxable years, there shall be excluded in determining the "gross income from the property", an amount equal to that part of such payments which is allocable to the product sold (or otherwise giving rise to gross income) for the taxable year. For purposes of the preceding sentence, bonus payments include payments by the lessee with respect to a production payment which is treated as a bonus under section 636(c). Such a production payment is equally allocable to all mineral from the mineral property burdened thereby. The following examples illustrate the provisions of this subdivision:

Example (1). In 1956, A leases oil bearing lands to B, receiving $200,000 as a bonus and reserving a royalty of one-eighth of the proceeds of all oil produced and sold. It is estimated at the time the lease is entered into that there are 1,000,000 barrels of oil recoverable. In 1956, B produces and sells 100,000 barrels for $240,000. In computing his "gross income from the property" for the year 1956, B will exclude $30,000 (1/8 of $240,000), the royalty paid to A, and $20,000 (100,000 bbls. sold/1,000,000 bbls. estimated to be available × $200,000 bonus), the portion of the bonus allocable to the oil produced and sold during the year. However, in computing B's taxable income under section 63, the $20,000 attributable to the bonus payment shall not be either excluded or deducted from B's gross income computed under section 61 (See paragraph (a)(3) of § 1.612-3.)

Example (2). In 1971, C leases to D oil bearing lands estimated to contain 1,000,000 barrels of oil, reserving a royalty of one-eighth of the proceeds of all oil produced and sold and a $500,000 production payment payable out of 50 percent of the first oil produced and sold attributable to the seven-eighths operating interest. In 1972, D produces and sells 100,000 barrels of oil. In computing his "gross income from the property" for the year 1972, D will exclude, in addition to the royalty paid to C, $50,000 (100,000 bbls. sold/1,000,000 bbls. estimated to be available × $500,000 treated under section 636(c) as a bonus), the portion of the production payment allocable to the oil produced and sold during the taxable year. However, in computing D's taxable income under section 63, the $50,000 attributable to the retained production payment shall not be either excluded or deducted from D's gross income computed under section 61.

(iii) If advanced royalties have been paid in respect of the property in any taxable year the amount excluded from "gross income from the property" of the payor for the current taxable year on account of such payment shall be an amount equal to the deduction for such taxable year taken on account of such payment pursuant to paragraph (b)(3) of § 1.612-3.

Example. If B in example (2) in paragraph (b)(4) of § 1.612-3, elects to deduct in 1956 the $10,000 paid to A in that year, he must exclude the same amount from "gross income from the property" in 1956; however, if B elects to defer the deduction until 1957 when he mined and sold the mineral, he must exclude the $10,000 from "gross income from the property" in 1957. [Reg. § 1.613-2.]

☐ [*T.D.* 6446, 1-20-60. *Amended by T.D.* 6841, 7-26-65; *T.D.* 7170, 3-10-72; *T.D.* 7261, 2-26-73 and *T.D.* 7487, 5-12-77.]

[Reg. § 1.613-3]

§ 1.613-3. **Gross income from the property.**—*Oil and gas wells.* In the case of oil and gas wells, "gross income from the property", as used in section 613(c)(1), means the amount for which the taxpayer sells the oil or gas in the immediate vicinity of the well. If the oil or gas is not sold on the premises but is manufactured or converted into a refined product prior to sale, or is transported from the premises prior to sale, the gross income from the property shall be assumed to be equivalent to the representative market or field price of the oil or gas before conversion or transportation. [Reg. § 1.613-3.]

☐ [*T.D.* 6446, 1-20-60. *Amended by T.D.* 6965, 7-25-68 and *T.D.* 8474, 4-26-93.]

[Reg. § 1.613-4]

§ 1.613-4. **Gross income from the property in the case of minerals other than oil and gas.**—(a) *In general.* The rules contained in this section are applicable to the determination of gross income from the property in the case of minerals other than oil and gas and the rules contained in § 1.613-3 are not applicable to such determination, notwithstanding provisions to the contrary in § 1.613-3. The term "gross income from the property," as used in section 613(c)(1), means, in the case of a mineral property other than an oil or

Reg. § 1.613-3

gas property, gross income from mining. "Gross income from mining" is that amount of income which is attributable to the extraction of the ores or minerals from the ground and the application of mining processes, including mining transportation. For the purpose of this section, "ordinary treatment processes" (applicable to the taxable years beginning before January 1, 1961) and "treatment processes considered as mining" (applicable to the taxable years beginning after December 31, 1960) will be referred to as "mining processes." Processes, including packaging and transportation, which do not qualify as mining will be referred to as "nonmining processes." Also for the purpose of this section, transportation which qualifies as "mining" will be referred to as "mining transportation" and transportation which does not qualify as "mining" will be referred to as nonmining transportation." See paragraph (f) of this section for the definition of the term "mining" and paragraph (g) of this section for the rules relating to nonmining processes.

(b) *Sales prior to the application of nonmining processes including nonmining transportation.* (1) Subject to the adjustments required by paragraph (e)(1) of this section, gross income from mining means (except as provided in subparagraph (2) of this paragraph) the actual amount for which the ore or mineral is sold if the taxpayer sells the ore or mineral—

(i) As it emerges from the mine, prior to the application of any process other than a mining process or any transportation, or

(ii) After application of only mining processes, including mining transportation, and before any nonmining transportation.

If the taxpayer sells his ore or mineral in more than one form, and if only mining processes are applied to the ore or mineral, gross income from mining is the actual amount for which the various forms of the ore or mineral are sold, after any adjustments required by paragraph (e)(1) of this section. For example, if, at his mine or quarry, a taxpayer sells several sizes of crushed gypsum and also sells gypsum fines produced as an incidental by-product of his crushing operations, without applying any nonmining processes, gross income from mining will ordinarily be the total amount for which such crushed gypsum and fines are actually sold. See paragraphs (f) and (g) of this section for provisions defining mining and nonmining processes for various minerals.

(2) In the case of sales between members of a controlled group (including sales as to which the district director exercises his authority under section 482 and the regulations thereunder), the prices for such sales (which shall be deemed to be the actual amounts for which the ore or mineral is sold) shall be determined, if possible, by use of the representative market or field price method, as described in paragraph (c) of this section; otherwise such prices shall be determined by the appropriate pricing method as provided in subparagraph (d)(1) of this section. For the definitions of the terms "controlled" and "group", see paragraph (j)(1) and (2) of this section.

(c) *Cases where a representative market or field price for the taxpayer's ore or mineral can be ascertained*—(1) *General rule.* If the taxpayer processes the ore or mineral before sale by the application of nonmining processes (including nonmining transportation), or uses it in his operations, gross income from mining shall be computed by use of the representative market or field price of an ore or mineral of like kind and grade as the taxpayer's ore or mineral after the application of the mining processes actually applied (if any), including mining transportation (if any), and before any nonmining transportation, subject to any adjustments required by paragraph (e)(1) of this section. See paragraph (e)(2)(i) of this section for certain other situations in which this paragraph shall apply. The objective in computing gross income from mining by the representative market or field price method is to ascertain, on the basis of an analysis of actual competitive sales by the taxpayer or others, the dollar figure or amount which most nearly represents the approximate price at which the taxpayer, in light of market conditions, could have sold his ores or minerals if, prior to the application of nonmining processes, the taxpayer had sold the quantities and types of ores and minerals to which he applied nonmining processes. If it is possible to determine a market or field price under the provisions of this paragraph, and if that price is determined to be representative, the taxpayer's gross income from mining shall be determined on the basis of that price and not under the provisions of paragraph (d) of this section. The taxpayer's own actual sales prices for ores or minerals of like kind and grade shall be taken into account when establishing market or field prices, provided that those sales are determined to be representative.

(2) *Criteria for determining whether an ore or mineral is of like kind and grade as the taxpayer's ore or mineral.* An ore or mineral will be considered to be of like kind and grade as the taxpayer's ore or mineral if, in common commercial practice, it is sufficiently similar in chemical, mineralogical, or physical characteristics to the taxpayer's ore or mineral that it is used, or is commercially suitable for use, for essentially the same purposes as the uses to which the taxpayer's

Reg. § 1.613-4(c)(2)

ore or mineral is put. Whether an ore or mineral is of like kind and grade as the taxpayer's ore or mineral will generally be determined by reference to industrial or commercial specifications and by consideration of chemical and physical data relating to the minerals and deposits in question. The fact that the taxpayer applies slightly different size reduction processes, or the fact that the taxpayer uses slightly different beneficiation processes, or the fact that the taxpayer sells his ore or mineral for different purposes, will not, in itself, prevent another person's ore or mineral from being considered to be of like kind and grade as the taxpayer's ore or mineral. On the other hand, the fact that the taxpayer's ore or mineral is suitable for the same general commercial use as another person's ore or mineral will not cause the two ores or minerals to be considered to be of like kind and grade if the desirable natural constituents of the two ores or minerals are markedly different substances. For example, anthracite coal will not be considered to be of like kind as bituminous coal merely because both types of coal can be used as fuel. Similarly, bituminous coal which does not possess coking qualities will not be considered to be of like grade as bituminous coking coal. However, in the case of a taxpayer who mines and uses his bituminous coal in the production of coke, all bituminous coals in the same marketing area will be considered to be of like kind, and all such bituminous coals having the same or similar coking quality suitable for commercial use by coke producers will be considered to be of like grade as the coal mined and used by the taxpayer. Fine distinctions between various grades of minerals are to be avoided unless those distinctions are clearly shown to have genuine commercial significance.

(3) *Factors to be considered in determining the representative market or field price for the taxpayer's ore or mineral.* In determining the representative market or field price for the taxpayer's ore or mineral, consideration shall be given only to prices of ores or minerals of like kind and grade as the taxpayer's ore or mineral and with which, under commercially accepted standards, the taxpayer's ore or mineral would be considered to be in competition if it were sold under the conditions described in paragraph (b)(1) of this section. A weighted average of the competitive selling prices of ores or minerals of like kind and grade as the taxpayer's, beneficiated only by mining processes, if any, in the relevant markets, although not determinative of the representative market or field price, is an important factor in the determination of that price. The taxpayer's own competitive sales prices for minerals which have been subjected only to mining processes shall be taken into account in computing such a weighted average. For purposes of the preceding sentence, if the district director has exercised his authority under section 482 and the regulations thereunder and has determined the appropriate price with respect to specific sales transactions by the taxpayer, that price shall be deemed to be a competitive sales price for those transactions. Sales or purchases, including the taxpayer's, of ores or minerals of like kind and grade as the taxpayer's, will be taken into consideration in determining the representative market or field price for the taxpayer's ore or mineral only if those sales or purchases are the result of competitive transactions. The identity of the taxpayer's relevant markets (including their accessibility to the taxpayer), and the representative market or field price within those markets, are necessarily factual determinations to be made on the basis of the facts and circumstances of each individual case. For the purpose of determining the representative market or field price for the taxpayer's ore or mineral, exceptional, insignificant, unusual, tie-in, or accommodation sales shall be disregarded. Except as provided above, representative market or field prices shall not be determined by reference to prices established between members of a controlled group. See paragraph (j) of this section for the definitions of the terms "controlled" and "group."

(4) *Use of prices of mineral of different grade.* If there is no representative market or field price for a mineral of like kind and grade as the taxpayer's, representative market or field prices for an ore or mineral which is of like kind but which is not of like grade as his ore or mineral may be used, with appropriate adjustments for differences in mineral content. Representative market or field prices of an ore or mineral of like kind but not of like grade may be used only if such adjustments are readily ascertainable. For example, it may be appropriate in a particular case to establish the representative market or field price for an ore having 50 percent X mineral content by reference to the representative market or field price for the same kind of ore having 60 percent X mineral content with an appropriate adjustment for the differences in the valuable mineral content of the two ores, any differences in processing costs attributable to impurities, and any other relevant factors.

(5) *Information to be furnished by a taxpayer computing gross income from mining by use of a representative market or field price.* A taxpayer who computes his gross income from mining pursuant to the provisions of this paragraph shall attach to his return a summary statement indicating the prices used by him in computing gross

Reg. § 1.613-4(c)(3)

income from mining under this paragraph and the source of his information as to those prices, and the relevant supporting data shall be assembled, segregated, and made readily available at the taxpayer's principal place of business.

(6) *Limitation on gross income from mining computed under the provisions of this paragraph.* It shall be presumed that a price is not a representative market or field price for the taxpayer's ore or mineral if the sum of such price plus the total of all costs of the nonmining processes (including nonmining transportation) which the taxpayer applies to his ore or mineral regularly exceeds the taxpayer's actual sales price of his product. For example, if on a regular basis the total of all costs of nonmining processes applied by the taxpayer to coal for the purpose of making coke is $12.00 per ton, and if the taxpayer's actual sale price for such coke is $18.00 per ton, a price of $7.00 per ton would not be a representative market or field price for the taxpayer's coal which is used for making coke. In order to rebut the presumption set forth in the first sentence of this subparagraph, it must be established that the loss on nonmining operations is directly attributable to unusual, peculiar, and nonrecurring factors rather than to the use of a market or field price which is not representative. For example, the first sentence of this subparagraph shall not apply if the taxpayer establishes in an appropriate case that the loss on nonmining operations is directly attributable to an event such as a fire, flood, explosion, earthquake, or strike.

(d) *Cases where a representative market or field price cannot be ascertained*—(1) *General rule.* (i) If it is impossible to determine a representative market or field price as described in paragraph (c) of this section then, except as provided in subdivision (ii) of this subparagraph, gross income from mining shall be computed by use of the proportionate profits method as set forth in subparagraph (4) of this paragraph. A method of computing gross income from mining under the provisions of this paragraph shall not be deemed to be a method of accounting for purposes of paragraph (e) of § 1.446-1.

(ii)*(a)* The Office of the Assistant Commissioner (Technical) may determine that a method of computation is more appropriate than the proportionate profits method or the method being used by the taxpayer. The taxpayer may request such a determination (see *(d)* of this subdivision (ii)). If the taxpayer is using a method of computation which has been determined by the Office of Assistant Commissioner (Technical) to be more appropriate than the proportionate profits method, such method shall continue to be used until it is determined by the Office of Assistant Commissioner (Technical) that either the proportionate profits method or another method is more appropriate.

(b) The proportionate profits method is more appropriate than the method being used under *(a)* if, under the particular facts and circumstances, the method being used under *(a)* consistently fails to clearly reflect gross income from mining and the proportionate profits method more clearly reflects gross income from mining for the taxable year.

(c) An alternative method (a method other than the method being used under *(a)* (if any) and the proportionate profits method) is more appropriate than the method being used under *(a)* (if any) and the proportionate profits method if, under the particular facts and circumstances, the latter methods consistently fail to clearly reflect gross income from mining, and the alternative method being considered more clearly reflects gross income from mining on a consistent basis than the method being used under *(a)* (if any and the proportionate profits method. When determining whether a method of computation clearly reflects gross income from mining, it is relevant to compare the gross income from mining produced by such method with the gross income from mining, on an equivalent amount of production, which results from the computation methods used by competitors. When determining the acceptability of proposed alternative methods, primary consideration will be given to computation methods based upon representative charges for ores, minerals, products, or services. See paragraph (c) of this section for principles determining the representative character of a charge.

(d) Application for permission to compute gross income from mining by use of an alternative method shall be made by submitting a request to the Commissioner of Internal Revenue, Attention: Assistant Commissioner (Technical), Washington, D.C. 20224.

(e) Among the alternative methods of computation to which consideration will be given, provided that the requirements of this subdivision (ii) are met, are the methods listed in subparagraphs (5), (6), and (7) of this paragraph. The order in which these methods are listed is not significant, and the listing of these methods does not preclude a request to make use of a method which is not listed.

(iii) Approval and continued use of any method of computation under this paragraph depends upon all the facts and circumstances in each case, and shall be subject to such terms and conditions as may be necessary in the opinion of

Reg. § 1.613-4(d)(1)

the Commissioner to reflect clearly the gross income from mining. Accordingly, the use of such a method for any taxable year shall be subject to review and change.

(2) *Costs to be used in computing gross income from mining by use of methods based on the taxpayer's costs.* In determining the taxpayer's gross income from mining by use of methods based on the taxpayer's costs, only costs actually paid or incurred shall be taken into consideration. In general, if the taxpayer has consistently employed a reasonable method of determining the costs of the various individual phases of his mining and nonmining processes (such as extraction, loading for shipment, calcining, packaging, etc.), such method shall not be disturbed. The amount of any particular item to be taken into account shall, for taxable years beginning after November 30, 1968, be the amount used in determining the taxpayer's income for tax purposes. For example, the depreciation lives, methods, and records used for tax purposes, if different from those used for book purposes, shall be the basis for determining the amount of depreciation to be used. However, a taxpayer may continue to use a reasonable method for determining those costs on the basis of the amounts computed for cost control or similar financial or accounting books and records if that method has been used consistently and is applied to the determination of all those costs.

(3) *Treatment of particular items in computing gross income from the mining by use of methods based on the taxpayer's costs.* (i) Except as specifically provided elsewhere in this section, when determining gross income from mining by use of methods based on the taxpayer's costs, the costs attributable to mining transportation shall be treated as mining costs, and the costs attributable to nonmining transportation shall be treated as nonmining costs. Accordingly, except as specifically provided elsewhere in this section, all profits attributable to mining transportation shall be treated as mining profits, and all profits attributable to nonmining transportation shall be treated as nonmining profits. For this purpose, mining transportation means so much of the transportation of ores or minerals (whether or not by common carrier) from the point of extraction from the ground to plants or mills in which other mining processes are applied thereto as is not in excess of 50 miles or, if the taxpayer files an application pursuant to paragraph (h) of this section and the Commissioner finds that both the physical and other requirements are such that the ores or minerals must be transported a greater distance to such plants or mills, the transportation over the greater distance. Further, for this purpose, nonmining transportation includes the transportation (whether or not by common carrier) of ores, minerals, or the products produced therefrom, from the point of extraction from the ground to nonmining facilities, or from a mining facility to a nonmining facility, or from one nonmining facility to another, or from a nonmining facility to the customers who purchase the taxpayer's first marketable product or group of products. See paragraph (e)(2) of this section for provisions relating to purchased transportation to the customer and paragraph (g)(3) of this section for provisions relating to transportation the primary purpose of which is marketing or distribution. In the absence of other methods which clearly reflect the costs of the various phases of transportation, the cost attributable to nonmining transportation shall be an amount which is in the same ratio to the costs incurred for the total transportation as the distance of the nonmining transportation is to the distance of the total transportation. As an example, where the plants or mills in which mining processes are applied to ores or minerals are in excess of 50 miles from the point of extraction from the ground (or in excess of a greater distance approved by the Commissioner), the costs incurred for transportation to those plants or mills in excess of 50 miles (or of that greater distance) shall be treated as nonmining costs in determining gross income from mining. Accordingly, all profits attributable to that excess transportation are treated as nonmining profits. However, except in the case of transportation performed in conveyances owned or leased by the taxpayer, the preceding sentence shall apply only to taxable years beginning after November 30, 1968.

(ii) In determining gross income from mining by use of methods based on the taxpayer's costs, a process shall not be considered as a mining process to the extent it is applied to ores, minerals, or other materials with respect to which the taxpayer is not entitled to a deduction for depletion under section 611. The costs of such nondepletable ores, minerals, or materials; the costs of the processes (including blending, size reduction, etc.) applied thereto; and the transportation costs thereof, if any, shall be considered as nonmining costs in determining gross income from mining. If a mining process is applied to an admixture of depletable and nondepletable material, the cost of the process and the cost of transportation, if any, attributable to the nondepletable material shall be considered as nonmining costs in determining gross income from mining. Accordingly, all profits attributable thereto are treated as nonmining profits. In the absence of other methods which clearly reflect the cost attributable to the processing and transportation, if any, of the nondepletable admixed mate-

Reg. § 1.613-4(d)(2)

rial, that cost shall be deemed to be that proportion of the costs which the tonnage of nondepletable material bears to the total tonnage of both depletable and nondepletable material.

(iii) In determining gross income from mining by use of methods based on the taxpayer's costs—

(a) The costs attributable to containers, bags, packages, pallets, and similar items as well as the costs of materials and labor attributable to bagging, packaging, palletizing, or similar operations shall be considered as nonmining costs.

(b) The costs attributable to the bulk loading of manufactured products shall be considered as nonmining costs.

(c) The costs attributable to the operation of warehouses or distribution terminals for manufactured products shall be considered as nonmining costs.

Accordingly, all profits attributable thereto are treated as nonmining profits.

(iv) In computing gross income from mining by the use of methods based on the taxpayer's costs, the principles set forth in paragraph (c) of § 1.613-5 shall apply when determining whether selling expenses and trade association dues are to be treated, in whole or in part, as mining costs or as nonmining costs. To the extent that selling expenses and trade association dues are treated as nonmining costs, all profits attributable thereto are treated as nonmining profits.

(v) See paragraph (e)(1) of this section for provisions excluding certain allowances from the taxpayer's gross sales and costs of his first marketable product or group of products.

(4) *Proportionate profits method.* (i) The objective of the "proportionate profits method" of computation is to ascertain gross income from mining by applying the principle that each dollar of the total costs paid or incurred to produce, sell, and transport the first marketable product or group of products (as defined in subdivision (iv) of this subparagraph) earns the same percentage of profit. Accordingly, in the proportionate profits method no ranking of costs is permissible which results in excluding or minimizing the effect of any costs incurred to produce, sell, and transport the first marketable product or group of products. For purposes of this subparagraph, members of a controlled group shall be treated as divisions of a single taxpayer. See paragraph (j) of this section for the definitions of the terms "controlled" and "group."

(ii) The proportionate profits method of computation is applied by multiplying the taxpayer's gross sales (actual or constructive) of his first marketable product or group of products (after making the adjustments required by paragraph (e) of this section) by a fraction whose numerator is the sum of all the costs allocable to those mining processes which are applied to produce, sell, and transport the first marketable product or group of products, and whose denominator is the total of all the mining and nonmining costs paid or incurred to produce, sell, and transport the first marketable product or group of products (after making the adjustments required by this paragraph and paragraph (e) of this section). The method as described herein is merely a restatement of the method formerly set forth in the second sentence of Regulations 118, § 39.23(m)-1(e)(3) (1939 Code). The proportionate profits method of computation may be illustrated by the following equation:

$$\frac{\text{Mining Costs}}{\text{Total Costs}} \times \text{Gross Sales} = \text{Gross Income from Mining}$$

(iii) Those costs which are paid or incurred by the taxpayer to produce, sell, and transport the first marketable product or group of products, and which are not directly identifiable with either a particular mining process or a particular nonmining process shall, in the absence of a specific provision of this section providing an apportionment method, be apportioned to mining and to nonmining by use of a method which is reasonable under the circumstances. One method which may be reasonable in a particular case is an allocation based on the proportion that the direct costs of mining processes and the direct costs of nonmining processes bear to each other. For example, the salary of a corporate officer engaged in overseeing all of the taxpayer's processes is an expense which may reasonably be apportioned on the basis of the ratio between the direct costs of mining and nonmining processes. On the other hand, an expense such as workmen's compensation premiums would normally be apportioned on the basis of direct labor costs. For the rule relating to selling expenses, see paragraph (c)(4) of § 1.613-5.

(iv) As used in this section, the term "first marketable product or group of products" means the product (or group of essentially the same products) produced by the taxpayer as a result of the application of nonmining processes, in the form or condition in which such product or products are first marketed in significant quantities by the taxpayer or by others in the taxpayer's marketing area. For this purpose, bulk and pack-

Reg. § 1.613-4(d)(4)

aged products are considered to be essentially the same product. Sales between members of a controlled group (as defined in paragraph (j) of this section) shall not be considered in making a determination under this subdivision. The first marketable product or group of products does not include any product which results from additional manufacturing or other nonmining processes applied to the product or products first marketed in significant quantities by the taxpayer or others in the taxpayer's marketing area. For example, if a cement manufacturer sells his own finished cement in bulk and bags and also sells concrete blocks or dry ready-mix aggregates containing additives, the finished cement, in bulk and bags, constitutes the first marketable product or group of products produced by him. Similarly, if an integrated iron ore and steel producer sells both pig iron in various sizes and rolled sheet iron or shapes, his first marketable product is the pig iron in its various sizes. Further if an integrated clay and brick producer sells both unglazed bricks and tiles of various shapes and sizes and additionally manufactured bricks and tiles which are specially glazed, the unglazed products, both packaged and unpackaged, constitute his first marketable product or group of products.

(v)(a) As used in this subparagraph, the term "gross sales (actual or constructive)" means the total of the taxpayer's actual competitive sales to others of the first marketable product or group of products, plus the taxpayer's constructive sales of the first marketable product or group of products used or retained for use in his own subsequent operations, subject to the adjustments required by paragraph (e) of this section. See (b) of this subdivision in the case of actual sales between members of controlled groups and in the case of constructive sales. A "constructive sale" occurs when a miner-manufacturer is deemed, for percentage depletion purposes, to be selling the first marketable product or group of products to himself.

(b) In the case of sales between members of a controlled group as to which the district director has exercised his authority under section 482 and the regulations thereunder and has determined the appropriate price with respect to specific sales transactions, that price shall be deemed, for those transactions, to be the actual amount for which the first marketable product or group of products is sold for purposes of this subdivision (v). In the case of all other sales between members of a controlled group, and in the case of constructive sales, the prices for such sales shall be determined by use of the principles set forth in paragraph (c) of this section, subject to the adjustments required by paragraph (e) of this section. In the case of constructive sales, see paragraph (c)(4) of this section for rules relating to information to be furnished by the taxpayer.

(vi) The provisions of this subparagraph may be illustrated by the following example:

Example (1).—(a) *Facts.* A is engaged in the mining of a mineral to which section 613 applies and in the application thereto of nonmining processes. During 1968, A incurred extraction costs of $35,000; other mining costs of $56,000; $150,000 for manufacturing costs; $46,000 for other nonmining processes; and $14,000 for the company president's salary and similar costs resulting from both nonmining and mining processes. During that year, A produced and sold 70,000 tons of his first marketable product for an actual gross sales price of $420,000, after the adjustments required by paragraph (e) of this section. A representative market or field price for A's mineral before the application of nonmining processes cannot be established.

(b) *Computation.* (1) The computation of A's gross income from mining by use of the proportionate profits method involves two steps. The first step is to apportion A's costs to mining and to nonmining. A apportions the company president's salary and similar costs to mining and to nonmining in the manner described in the second and third sentences of subdivision (iii) of this subparagraph, and apportions his remaining costs as follows:

Cost	Mining	Nonmining	Total
Extraction	$35,000	....	$ 35,000
Other Mining Processes	56,000	....	56,000
Manufacturing	....	$150,000	150,000
Other Nonmining Processes	....	46,000	46,000
Subtotal	$91,000	$196,000	$287,000
President's Salary and similar costs	4,439	9,561	14,000
Total Costs	$95,439	$205,561	$301,000

(2) The second step is to apply the proportionate profits fraction so as to compute A's gross income from mining. To do this, A first computes his gross sales of his first marketable group of products, in this case $420,000. A multiplies his actual gross sales of $420,000 by the proportionate profits fraction, whose numerator consists of his total mining costs ($95,439) and

Reg. § 1.613-4(d)(4)

whose denominator consists of his total costs ($301,000). Thus, A's gross income from mining is $133,170 (i.e., 95,439/301,000ths of A's actual gross sales of $420,000).

Example (2). B, who leases a mineral property from C, is engaged in the mining of a mineral to which section 613 applies and in the application thereto of nonmining processes. Pursuant to the terms of the lease, B is required to pay C ten cents for each ton of mineral which B mines. During 1971, B extracted 100,000 tons of mineral. He sold his first marketable product for an actual gross sales price of $225,000 after the adjustments required by paragraph (e) of this section. A representative market or field price for B's mineral before the application of nonmining processes cannot be established. During 1971, with respect to the 100,000 tons of mineral extracted, B incurred mining costs of $50,000 and nonmining costs of $100,000, and paid $10,000 to C as C's royalty. Since the royalty payment is considered to be C's share of the gross income from mining under section 613(a), it is not considered to be either a mining cost or a nonmining cost of B. B's gross income from mining is $65,000 under the proportionate profits method, determined as follows: The $225,000 gross receipts must be multiplied by the proportionate profits fraction which is $50,000 mining costs over $150,000 total costs ($50,000 + $100,000 nonmining costs). Since the resulting $75,000 is the total gross income from mining with respect to the property, it must be allocated between B's lease interest and C's royalty interest. The $10,000 paid to C must be subtracted from the $75,000 leaving $65,000 which represents B's gross income from mining. C's gross income from mining is the royalty he received for $10,000.

(5) *Representative schedule method.* The "representative schedule method" is a pricing formula which uses representative finished product prices, penalties, charges and adjustments, established in arms-length transactions between unrelated parties, to determine the market or field price for a crude mineral product. The representative character of a price, penalty, charge, or adjustment shall be determined by applying the principles set forth in paragraph (c) of this section. The representative schedule method is principally intended for use in those industries in which such a schedule-type pricing method is in general use to determine the price paid to unintegrated mineral producers for their crude mineral product. For example, if unintegrated producers of copper concentrate in a particular field or market customarily sell their product at prices which are determined in accordance with a schedule-type pricing formula, consideration will be given to the determination of concentrate prices for integrated copper producers in accordance with the same pricing formula. The representative schedule method shall not be used if it is impossible to determine one or more of the elements in the representative schedule formula by reference to prices, penalties, charges, or adjustments established in representative transactions between unrelated parties. See paragraph (c) of this section for principles determining the representative character of a charge.

(6) *Method using prices outside the taxpayer's market.* Under the "other market method" the taxpayer uses representative market or field prices established outside his markets, provided that conditions there are substantially the same as in his markets. For example, it may be appropriate in a particular case to establish the representative market or field price for pellets containing 60 percent iron which are produced and used in market area X by reference to the representative market or field price for pellets containing 60 percent iron which are produced and sold in adjacent market area Y, provided that conditions in the two marketing areas are shown to be substantially the same.

(7) *Rate of return on investment method.* [Reserved]

(e) *Reductions of sales price in computing gross income from mining*—(1) *Discounts.* If a taxpayer computes gross income from mining under the provisions of paragraph (b)(1) of this section, trade discounts and, for taxable years beginning after November 30, 1968, cash discounts actually allowed by the taxpayer shall be subtracted from the sale price of the taxpayer's ore or mineral. If a taxpayer computes gross income from mining under the provisions of paragraph (c) of this section, any such discounts actually allowed (if not otherwise taken into account) by the person or persons making the sales on the basis of which the representative market or field price for the taxpayer's ore or mineral is to be determined shall be subtracted from the sale price in computing such representative market or field price. If a taxpayer computes gross income from mining under the provisions of paragraph (d) of this section, such discounts actually allowed (if not otherwise taken into account) shall be subtracted from the gross sales (actual or constructive), and shall not be considered a cost, of the first marketable product or group of products. The provisions of this subparagraph shall apply to arrangements which have the same effect as trade or cash discounts, regardless of the form of the arrangements.

(2) *Purchased transportation to the customer.* (i) A taxpayer who computes gross income

Reg. § 1.613-4(e)(2)

from mining under the provisions of paragraph (c) of this section and who sells his ore or mineral after the application of only mining processes but after nonmining transportation shall use as the representative market or field price his delivered price (if otherwise representative) reduced by costs paid or incurred by him for purchased transportation to the customer as defined in subdivision (iii) of this subparagraph. If the transportation by the taxpayer is not purchased transportation to the customer, or if the taxpayer does not sell the ore or mineral until after the application of nonmining processes and if other producers in the taxpayer's marketing area sell significant quantities of an ore or mineral of like kind and grade after the application of only mining processes but after purchased transportation to the customer, the representative delivered price at which the ore or mineral is sold by those other producers reduced by representative costs of purchased transportation to the customer paid or incurred by those producers shall be used by the taxpayer as the representative market or field price for his ore or mineral in applying paragraph (c) of this section. Furthermore, appropriate adjustments shall be made to take into account differences in mode of transportation and distance. When applying this subdivision, the representative market or field price so computed shall not exceed the taxpayer's delivered price less his actual costs of transportation to the customer. For purposes of this subdivision, any delivered price shall be adjusted as provided in subparagraph (1) of this paragraph.

(ii) If a taxpayer computes gross income from mining under the provisions of paragraph (d) of this section, the cost of purchased transportation to the customer (as defined in subdivision (iii) of this subparagraph) shall be excluded from the gross sales of his first marketable product or group of products (after any adjustments required by subparagraph (1) of this paragraph), and from the denominator of the proportionate profits fraction, so as not to attribute profits to the cost of that transportation. Similar transportation cost adjustments may be made, if appropriate, in the case of other methods of computation which are based on the taxpayer's costs. For the treatment of costs and profits attributable to transportation which is not purchased transportation to the customer as defined in subdivision (iii) of this subparagraph, see paragraph (d)(3)(i) of this section.

(iii) For purposes of this section, the term "purchased transportation to the customer" means, in general, nonmining transportation of the taxpayer's minerals or mineral products to the customer—

(a) Which is not performed in conveyances owned or leased directly or indirectly, in whole or in part, by the taxpayer,

(b) Which is performed solely to deliver the taxpayer's minerals or mineral products to the customer, rather than to transport such minerals or products for packaging or other additional processing by the taxpayer (other than incidental storage or handling), and

(c) With respect to which the taxpayer ordinarily does not earn any profit.

For purposes of the preceding sentence, transportation which is performed by a person controlling or controlled by the taxpayer (within the meaning of paragraph (j)(1) of this section) shall be deemed to have been performed in conveyances owned or leased by the taxpayer unless it is established by the taxpayer that the price charged by the controlling or controlled person for such transportation constitutes an arm's-length charge (under the standard described in paragraph (b)(1) of § 1.482-1). The term "purchased transportation to the customer" includes transportation to a warehouse, terminal, or distribution facility owned or operated by the taxpayer, provided that such transportation is performed under the conditions described in the first sentence of this subdivision. A taxpayer will not be deemed ordinarily to earn a profit on transportation merely because charges for the transportation are included in the stated selling price, rather than being separately stated or segregated from other billing. A taxpayer will not be deemed ordinarily to earn a profit on transportation if the rates for the transportation constitute an arm's-length charge ordinarily paid by shippers of the same product in similar circumstances. If a taxpayer computes gross income from mining under the provisions of paragraph (d) of this section, the term "purchased transportation to the customer" refers to transportation which conforms to the other requirements of this subdivision and which is performed to transport the taxpayer's first marketable product or group of products (as defined in paragraph (d)(4)(iv) of this section) rather than to transport minerals or mineral products which do not yet constitute the taxpayer's first marketable product or group of products.

(iv) The provisions of this subparagraph may be illustrated by the following examples:

Example (1). A is engaged in the mining of an ore of mineral M and in the production and sale of M concentrate. A retains a portion of his concentrate for use in his own nonmining operations. During 1968, A sold 100,000 tons of M concentrate of ore mined and processed by him, which sales constituted a significant portion of his

Reg. § 1.613-4(e)(2)

total production. Eighty thousand tons of that concentrate were sold by A on the basis of a representative price (after adjustments required by subparagraph (1) of this paragraph) of $30.00 per ton f.o.b. mine or plant, resulting in gross income from mining of $2,400,000. The remaining 20,000 tons were sold by A, both directly and through terminals, on the basis of a delivered price (after adjustments required by subparagraph (1) of this paragraph) at City X of $40.00 per ton. The delivered price included $15.00 per ton cost of purchased transportation from the mine or plant to customers in City X. The representative market or field price of the concentrate sold by A on the basis of a delivered price is $25.00 per ton, determined by subtracting the cost of the purchased transportation to the customer ($15.00 per ton) from the delivered price for the concentrate ($40.00 per ton). Accordingly, A's gross income from mining with respect to the 20,000 tons of M concentrate sold on a delivered basis is $500,000. The representative market or field price for the concentrate retained by A and used in his own nonmining operations may be computed by reference to the weighted average price for both A's f.o.b. mine and A's delivered sales of concentrate, with the delivered sales prices reduced in the manner described above. On this basis, the representative market or field price for the retained concentrate is $29.00 per ton.

Example (2). B is engaged in the mining of an ore of mineral N and in the production of N concentrate. B retained all but an insignificant amount of his concentrate for use in his own nonmining operations. Other producers in B's marketing area sell significant amounts of N concentrate of like kind and grade, both on an f.o.b. mine or plant basis and on a delivered basis. In this case, the prices for both the f.o.b. and the delivered sales made by other producers (after any adjustments required by subparagraph (1) of this paragraph), after reduction of the delivered prices by the cost of purchased transportation to the customer, shall, if such prices are otherwise representative, be taken into account in establishing the representative market or field price for the N concentrate produced and used by B.

(f) *Definition of mining*—(1) *In general.* The term "mining" includes only—

(i) The extraction of ores or minerals from the ground;

(ii) Mining processes, as described in subparagraphs (2) through (6) of this paragraph; and

(iii) So much of the transportation (whether or not by common carrier) of ores or minerals from the point of extraction of the ores or minerals from the ground to the plants or mills in which the processes referred to in subdivision (ii) of this subparagraph are applied thereto as is not in excess of 50 miles, and, if the Commissioner finds that both the physical and other requirements are such that the ores or minerals must be transported a greater distance to such plants or mills, the transportation over such greater distance as the Commissioner authorizes. See paragraph (h) of this section for rules relating to the filing of applications to treat as mining any transportation in excess of 50 miles.

(2) *Definition of mining processes.* (i) As used in subparagraph (1)(ii) of this paragraph, the term "mining processes" means, for taxable years beginning before January 1, 1961, the ordinary treatment processes normally applied by mine owners or operators in order to obtain the commercially marketable mineral product or products, including the following processes (and the processes necessary or incidental thereto), and, for taxable years beginning after December 31, 1960, the following processes (and the processes necessary or incidental thereto):

(*a*) In the case of coal—cleaning, breaking, sizing, dust allaying, treating to prevent freezing, and loading for shipment;

(*b*) In the case of sulfur recovered by the Frasch process—cleaning, pumping to vats, cooling, breaking, and loading for shipment;

(*c*) In the case of iron ore, bauxite, ball and sagger clay, rock asphalt, and ores or minerals which are customarily sold in the form of a crude mineral product (as defined in subparagraph (3)(iv) of this paragraph)—

(*1*) Where applied for the purpose of bringing to shipping grade and form (as defined in subparagraph (3)(iii) of this paragraph)—sorting, concentrating, sintering, and substantially equivalent processes, and

(*2*) Loading for shipment.

(*d*) In the case of lead, zinc, copper, gold, silver, uranium, or fluospar ores, potash, and ores or minerals which are not customarily sold in the form of the crude mineral product—crushing, grinding, and beneficiation by concentration (gravity, flotation, amalgamation, electrostatic, or magnetic), cyanidation, leaching, crystallization, precipitation (but not including electrolytic deposition, roasting, thermal or electric smelting, or refining), or by substantially equivalent processes or combination of processes used in the separation or extraction of the product or products from the ore or the mineral or minerals from other material from the mine or other natural deposit; and

(*e*) In the case of the following ores or minerals—

Reg. § 1.613-4(f)(2)

(1) The furnacing of quicksilver ores,

(2) The pulverization of talc,

(3) The burning of magnesite, and

(4) The sintering and nodulizing of phosphate rock.

(ii) The term "mining processes" also includes the following processes (and, except as otherwise provided in this subdivision, the processes necessary or incidental thereto):

(a) For taxable years beginning after December 31, 1960, in the case of calcium carbonates and other minerals when used in making cement—all processes (other than preheating the kiln feed) applied prior to the introduction of the kiln feed into the kiln, but not including any subsequent process;

(b) For taxable years beginning after December 31, 1960, and before November 14, 1966, in the case of clay to which former section 613(b)(5)(B) applied, and for taxable years beginning after November 13, 1966, in the case of clay to which section 613(b)(5) or (6)(B) applies—crushing, grinding, and separating the clay from waste, but not including any subsequent process;

(c) For taxable years beginning after October 9, 1969, in the case of minerals (other than sodium chloride) extracted from brines pumped from a saline perennial lake (as defined in paragraph (b) of § 1.613-2)—the extraction of such minerals from the brines, but in no case including any further processing or refining of such extracted minerals; and

(d) For taxable years beginning after December 30, 1969, in the case of oil shale (as defined in paragraph (b) of § 1.613-2)—extraction from the ground, crushing, loading into the retort, and retorting, but in no case hydrogenation, refining, or any other process subsequent to retorting.

(iii) A process is "necessary" to another related process if it is prerequisite to the performance of the other process. For example, if the concentrating of low-grade iron ores to bring to shipping grade and form cannot be effectively accomplished without fine pulverization, such pulverization shall be treated as a process which is "necessary" to the concentration process. Accordingly, because concentration is a mining process, such pulverization is also a mining process. Furthermore, if mining processes cannot be effectively applied to a mineral without storage of the mineral while awaiting the application of such processes, such storage shall be treated as a process which is "necessary" to the accomplishment of such mining processes. A process is "incidental" to another related process if the cost thereof is insubstantial in relation to the cost of the other process, or if the process is merely the coincidental result of the application of the other process. For example, the sprinkling of coal, prior to loading for shipment, with dots of paper to identify the coal for trade name purposes will be considered incidental to the loading where the cost of that sprinkling is insubstantial in relation to the cost of the loading process. Also, where crushing of a crude mineral is treated as a mining process, the production of fines as a by-product is ordinarily the coincidental result of the application of a mining process. If a taxpayer demonstrates that, as a factual matter, a particular process is necessary or incidental to a process named as a mining process in section 613(c)(4) or this paragraph, the necessary or incidental process will also be considered a mining process.

(iv) The term "mining" does not include purchasing minerals from another. Accordingly, the processes listed in this paragraph shall be considered as mining processes only to the extent that they are applied by a mine owner or operator to an ore or mineral in respect of which he is entitled to a deduction for depletion under section 611. The application of these processes to purchased ores, minerals, or materials does not constitute mining.

(3) *Processes recognized as mining for ores or minerals covered by section 613(c)(4)(C).* (i) As used in section 613(c)(4)(C) and subparagraph (2)(i)(c) of this paragraph, the terms "sorting" and "concentrating" mean the process of eliminating substantial amounts of impurities or foreign matter associated with the ores or minerals in their natural state, or of separating two or more valuable minerals or ores, without changing the physical or chemical identity of the ores or minerals. Examples of sorting and concentrating processes are hand or mechanical sorting, magnetic separation, gravity concentration, jigging, the use of shaking or concentrating tables, the use of spiral concentrators, the use of sluices or sluice boxes, sink-and-float processes, classifiers, hydrotators and flotation processes. Under section 613(c)(4)(C), sorting and concentration will be considered mining processes only where they are applied to bring an ore or mineral to shipping grade and form.

(ii) As used in section 613(c)(4)(C) and subparagraph (2)(i)(c) of this paragraph, the term "sintering" means the agglomeration of fine particles by heating to a temperature at which incipient, but not complete, fusion occurs. Sintering will be considered a mining process only where it is applied to an ore or mineral, or a concentrate of an ore or mineral, as an auxiliary process necessary to bring the ore or mineral to shipping form.

Reg. § 1.613-4(f)(3)

A thermal action which is applied in the manufacture of a finished product will not be considered to be a mining process even though such thermal action may cause the agglomeration of fine particles by incipient fusion, and even though such action does not cause a chemical change in the agglomerated particles. For example, the sintering of finely ground iron ore concentrate, prior to shipment from the concentration plant, for the purpose of preventing the risk of loss of the finely divided particles during shipment is considered a mining process. On the other hand, for example, a heating process applied to expand or harden clay, shale, perlite, vermiculite, or other materials in the course of the manufacture of lightweight aggregate or other building materials is not considered to be a mining process.

(iii) As used in section 613(c)(4)(C) and this section, to "bring to shipping grade and form" means, with respect to taxable years beginning after December 31, 1960, to bring (by the application of mining processes at the mine or concentration plant) the quality or size of an ore or mineral to the stage or stages at which the ore or mineral is shipped to a customer or used in a nonmining process (as defined in paragraph (g) of this section) by the taxpayer.

(iv) An ore or mineral is "customarily sold in the form of a crude mineral product," within the meaning of section 613(c)(4)(C), if a significant portion of the production thereof is sold or used in a nonmining process prior to the alteration of its inherent mineral content by some form of beneficiation, concentration, or ore dressing. An ore or mineral does not lose its classification as a crude mineral product by reason of the fact that, before sale or use in a nonmining process, the ore or mineral may be crushed or subjected to other processes which do not alter its inherent mineral content. Whether the portion of production sold or used in the form of a crude mineral product is a significant portion of the total production of an ore or mineral is a question of fact.

(4) *Type of processes recognized as mining for ores or minerals covered by section 613(c)(4)(D).* Cyanidation, leaching, crystallization, and precipitation, which are listed in section 613(c)(4)(D) as treatment processes considered as mining, and the processes (or combination of processes) which are substantially equivalent thereto, will be recognized as mining only to the extent that they are applied to the taxpayer's ore or mineral for the purpose of separation or extraction of the valuable mineral product or products from the ore, or for the purpose of separation or extraction of the mineral or minerals from other material extracted from the mine or other natural deposit. A process, no matter how denominated, will not be recognized as mining if the process beneficiates the ore or mineral to the degree that such process, in effect, constitutes smelting, refining, or any other nonmining process within the meaning of paragraph (g) of this section. As used in section 613(c)(4)(D) and subparagraph (2)(i)(*d*) of this paragraph, the term "concentration" has the meaning set forth in the first two sentences of subparagraph (3)(i) of this paragraph.

(5) *Processes recognized as mining under section 613(c)(4)(I).* Under the authority granted the Secretary or his delegate in section 613(c)(4)(I), the processes which are described in subdivisions (i) through (iv) of this subparagraph, and the processes necessary or incidental thereto, are recognized as mining processes for taxable years beginning after December 31, 1960. The processes described in subdivisions (i) through (iv) of this subparagraph are in addition to the specific processes recognized as mining under section 613(c)(4). Such additional processes are:

(i) Crushing and grinding, but not fine pulverization (as defined in paragraph (g)(6)(v) of this section);

(ii) Size classification processes applied to the products of an allowable mining process;

(iii) Drying to remove free water, provided that such drying does not change the physical or chemical identity or composition of the mineral; and

(iv) Washing or cleaning the surface of mineral particles (including the washing of sand and gravel and the treatment of kaolin particles to remove surface stains), provided that such washing or cleaning does not activate or otherwise change the physical or chemical structure of the mineral particles.

(6) In the case of a process applied subsequent to a nonmining process, see paragraph (g)(2) of this section.

(g) *Nonmining processes*—(1) *General rule.* Unless they are otherwise provided for in paragraph (f) of this section as mining processes (or are necessary or incidental to processes listed therein), the following processes are not considered to be mining processes—electrolytic deposition, roasting, calcining, thermal or electric smelting, refining, polishing, fine pulverization, blending with other materials, treatment effecting a chemical change, thermal action, and molding or shaping. See subparagraph (6) of this paragraph for definitions of certain of these terms.

(2) *Processes subsequent to nonmining processes.* Notwithstanding any other provision of

Reg. § 1.613-4(g)(2)

this section, a process applied subsequent to a nonmining process (other than nonmining transportation) shall also be considered to be a nonmining process. Exceptions to this rule shall be made, however, in those instances in which the rule would discriminate between similarly situated producers of the same mineral. For example, roasting is specifically designated in subparagraph (1) of this paragraph as a nonmining process, but in the case of minerals referred to in section 613(c)(4)(C) sintering is recognized as a mining process. If certain impurities in an ore can only be removed by roasting in order to bring it to the same shipping grade and form as a competitive sintered ore of the same kind which requires no roasting, the subsequent sintering of the roasted ore will be treated as a mining process. In that case, however, the roasting of the ore will nonetheless continue to be treated as a nonmining process.

(3) *Transportation for the purpose of marketing or distribution; storage.* Transportation the primary purpose of which is marketing, distribution, or delivery for the application of only nonmining processes shall not be considered as mining. Nor shall transportation be considered as mining merely because, during the course of such transportation, some extraneous matter is removed from the ore or mineral by the operation of forces of nature, such as evaporation, drainage, or gravity flow. Similarly, storage or warehousing of manufactured products shall not be considered as mining. The preceding sentence shall apply even though, during the course of such storage or warehousing, some extraneous matter is removed from the ore or mineral by the operation of forces of nature, such as evaporation, drainage, or gravity flow.

(4) *Manufacturing, etc.* The production, packaging, distribution, and marketing of manufactured products, and the processes necessary or incidental thereto, are nonmining processes.

(5) *Transformation processes.* Processes which effect a substantial physical or chemical change in a crude mineral product, or which transform a crude mineral product into new or different mineral products, or into refined or manufactured products, are nonmining processes except to the extent that such processes are specifically allowed as mining processes in section 613(c) or under paragraph (f) of this section.

(6) *Definitions.* As used in section 613(c)(5) and this section—

(i) The term "calcining" refers to processes used to expel the volatile portions of a mineral by the application of heat, as, for example, the burning of carbonate rock to produce lime, the heating of gypsum to produce calcined gypsum or plaster of Paris, or the heating of clays to reduce water of crystallization.

(ii) The term "thermal smelting" refers to processes which reduce, separate, or remove impurities from ores or minerals by the application of heat, as, for example, the furnacing of copper concentrates, the heating of iron ores, concentrates, or pellets in a blast furnace to produce pig iron, or the heating of iron ores or concentrates in a direct reduction kiln to produce a feed for direct conversion into steel.

(iii) The term "refining" refers to processes (other than mining processes designated in section 613(c)(4) or this section) used to eliminate impurities or foreign matter from smelted or partially processed metallic and nonmetallic ores and minerals, as, for example, the refining of blister copper. In general, a refining process is designed to achieve a high degree of purity by removing relatively small amounts of impurities or foreign matter from smelted or partially processed ores or minerals.

(iv) The term "polishing" refers to processes used to smooth the surface of minerals, as, for example, sawing applied to finish rough cut blocks of stone, sand finishing, buffing, or otherwise smoothing blocks of stone.

(v) The term "fine pulverization" refers to any grinding or other size reduction process applied to reduce the normal topsize of a mineral product to less than .0331 inches, which is the size opening in a No. 20 Screen (U.S. Standard Sieve Series). A mineral product will be considered to have a normal topsize of .0331 inches if at least 98 percent of the product will pass through a No. 20 Screen (U.S. Standard Sieve Series), provided that at least 5 percent of the product is retained on a No. 45 Screen (U.S. Standard Sieve Series). Compliance with the normal topsize test may also be demonstrated by other tests which are shown to be reasonable in the circumstances. The normal topsize test shall be applied to the product of the operation of each separate and distinct piece of size reduction equipment utilized (such as a roller mill), rather than to the final products for sale. Fine pulverization includes the repeated recirculation of material through crushing or grinding equipment to accomplish fine pulverization. Separating or screening the product of a fine pulverization process (including separation by air or water flotation) shall be treated as a nonmining process.

(vi) The term "blending with other materials" refers to processes used to blend different kinds of minerals with one another, as, for exam-

Reg. § 1.613-4(g)(3)

ple, blending iodine with common salt for the purpose of producing iodized table salt.

(vii) The term "treatment effecting a chemical change" refers to processes which transform or modify the chemical composition of a crude mineral, as, for example, the coking of coal. The term does not include the use of chemicals to clean the surface of mineral particles provided that such cleaning does not make any change in the physical or chemical structure of the mineral particles.

(viii) The term "thermal action" refers to processes which involve the application of artificial heat to ores or minerals, such as, for example, the burning of bricks, the coking of coal, the expansion or popping of perlite, the exfoliation of vermiculite, the heat treatment of garnet, and the heating of shale, clay, or slate to produce lightweight aggregates. The term does not include drying to remove free water.

(h) *Application to treat, as mining, transportation in excess of 50 miles.* If a taxpayer desires to include in the computation of his gross income from mining transportation in excess of 50 miles from the point of extraction of the minerals from the ground, he shall file an original and one copy of an application for the inclusion of such greater distance with the Commissioner of Internal Revenue, Washington, D.C. 20224. The application must include a statement setting forth in detail the facts concerning the physical and other requirements which prevented the construction and operation of the plant (in which mining processes, as defined in paragraph (f) of this section, are applied) at a place nearer to the point of extraction from the ground. These facts must be sufficient to apprise the Commissioner of the exact basis of the application. If the taxpayer's return is filed prior to receipt of notice of the Commissioner's action upon the application, a copy of such application shall be attached to the return. If, after an application is approved by the Commissioner, there is a material change in any of the facts relied upon in such application, a new application must be submitted by the taxpayer.

(i) *Extraction from waste or residue.* "Extraction of ores or minerals from the ground" means not only the extraction of ores or minerals from a deposit, but also the extraction by mine owners or operators of ores or minerals from waste or residue of their prior mining. It is immaterial whether the waste or residue results from the process of extraction from the ground or from application of mining processes as defined in paragraph (f) of this section. However, extraction of ores or minerals from waste or residue which results from processes which are not allowable as mining processes is not treated as mining. "Extraction of ores or minerals from the ground" does not include extraction of ores or minerals by the purchaser of waste or residue or the purchaser of the rights to extract ores or minerals from waste or residue. The term "purchaser" does not apply to any person who acquires a mineral property, including waste or residue, in a tax-free exchange, such as a corporate reorganization, from a person who was entitled to a depletion allowance upon ores or minerals produced from such waste or residue, or from a person who would have been entitled to such depletion allowance had section 613(c)(3) been in effect at the time of the transfer. The term "purchaser" also does not apply to a lessee who has renewed a mineral lease if the lessee was entitled to a depletion allowance (or would have been so entitled had section 613(c)(3) been in effect at the time of the renewal) upon ores or minerals produced from waste or residue before renewal of the lease. It is not necessary, for purposes of the preceding sentence, that the mineral lease contain an option for renewal. The term "purchaser" does include a person who acquires waste or residue in a taxable transaction, even though such waste or residue is acquired merely as an incidental part of the entire mineral enterprise. For special rules with respect to certain corporate acquisitions referred to in section 381(a), see section 381(c)(18) and the regulations thereunder.

(j) *Definition of controlled group.* When used in this section—

(1) The term "controlled" includes any kind of control, direct or indirect, whether or not legally enforceable, and however exercisable or exercised. It is the reality of the control which is decisive, not its form or the mode of its exercise. A presumption of control arises if income or deductions have been arbitrarily shifted.

(2) The term "group" means the organizations, trades, or businesses owned or controlled by the same interests. [Reg. § 1.613-4.]

☐ [*T.D.* 7170, 3-10-72.]

[Reg. § 1.613-5]

§ 1.613-5. **Taxable income from the property.**—(a) *General rule.* The term "taxable income from the property (computed without allowance for depletion)," as used in section 613 and this part, means "gross income from the property" as defined in section 613(c) and §§ 1.613-3 and 1.613-4, less all allowable deductions (excluding any deduction for depletion) which are attributable to mining processes, including mining transportation, with respect to which depletion is claimed. These deductible items include operating expenses, certain selling expenses, administrative and financial overhead, depreciation, taxes deductible under section 162 or 164, losses sustained, intangible drilling and development costs, exploration and development expenditures, etc. See paragraph (c) of this section for special rules relating to discounts and to certain of these deductible items. Expenditures which may be attributable both to the mineral property upon which depletion is claimed and to other activities shall be properly apportioned to the mineral property and to such other activities. Furthermore, where a taxpayer has more than one mineral property, deductions which are not directly attributable to a specific mineral property shall be properly apportioned among the several properties. In determining the taxpayer's taxable income from the property, the amount of any particular item to be taken into account shall be determined in accordance with the principles set forth in paragraph (d)(2) and (3) of § 1.613-4.

(b) *Special rule; decrease in mining expenses resulting from gain recognized under section 1245(a)(1).* (1) If during any taxable year beginning after December 31, 1962, the taxpayer disposes of an item of section 1245 property (as defined in section 1245(a)(3)) which has been used in connection with a mineral property, then for the purpose of computing the taxable income from such mineral property for such taxable year, the allowable deductions taken into account with respect to expenses of mining (that is, expenses attributable to a mineral property other than an oil and gas property) shall be decreased by an amount equal to the portion of any gain recognized under section 1245(a)(1) (relating to treatment of gain from dispositions of certain depreciable property as ordinary income) which is properly allocable to such mineral property in respect of which the taxable income is being computed. The portion of such gain which is properly allocable to such mineral property shall bear the same ratio to the total of such gain as—

(i) The portion of the "adjustments reflected in the adjusted basis" (as such term is defined in paragraph (a)(2) of § 1.1245-2, relating to definition of recomputed basis) of such section 1245 property, which were allowable as deductions from the "gross income from the property" (as defined in section 613(c) and § 1.613-3) in computing the taxable income from such mineral property, bears to

(ii) The total of the "adjustments reflected in the adjusted basis" of such section 1245 property.

(2) For the purposes of this paragraph, the adjustments reflected in the adjusted basis of the section 1245 property disposed of shall be deemed to have been taken into account in computing the taxable income from the mineral property for any taxable year notwithstanding that for the taxable year the allowance for depletion was determined without reference to percentage depletion under section 613.

(3) If the amount of gain described in subparagraph (1) of this paragraph allocable to a mineral property for a taxable year exceeds the allowable deductions otherwise taken into account in computing the taxable income from the mineral property for the taxable year, the excess may not be taken into account in computing the taxable income from the mineral property for any other taxable year.

(4) To the extent that the adjustments reflected in the adjusted basis of the section 1245 property are allocable to mineral property which the taxpayer no longer owns in the taxable year in which he disposes of the section 1245 property, the gain recognized under section 1245(a)(1) does not result in any tax benefit to the taxpayer under this paragraph since he has no taxable income from the mineral property for such year. However, if a taxpayer has, in the taxable year in which he disposes of an item of section 1245 property, only a portion of the original mineral property to which gain described in subparagraph (1) of this paragraph with respect to the section 1245 property is properly allocable, the entire amount of that gain shall nevertheless be taken into account in computing the taxable income of the remaining portion of the mineral property. Furthermore, the fact that a mineral property to which section 1245 gain is properly allocable is (in the taxable year in which the taxpayer disposes of an item of section 1245 property) no longer in existence merely because the mineral property has been made a part of an aggregation or has been deaggregated will not result in the loss of tax benefits under this section. Accordingly,

(i) If a taxpayer has made an aggregation of mineral properties (see section 614 and the regulations thereunder), the amount of any gain described in subparagraph (1) of this paragraph which is properly allocable to the aggregation shall include the portion of any gain which would be properly allocable to the mineral properties which existed separately prior to the aggregation and of which the aggregation is or was composed, if the prior mineral properties had not been aggregated; and

(ii) If a taxpayer has deaggregated a mineral property, the amount of any gain described in subparagraph (1) of this paragraph which is properly allocable to each of the resulting mineral

Reg. § 1.613-5(b)(2)

properties shall include a part of the portion of any gain which would be properly allocable to the prior aggregation if the aggregation had not been deaggregated, the part properly allocable to each of the resulting properties being determined by allocating the gain between the resulting properties in the same manner as basis is allocated between them for tax purposes (see paragraph (a)(2) of § 1.614-6 and example (5) of subparagraph (7) of this paragraph).

(5) In any case in which it is necessary to determine the portion of any gain recognized under section 1245(a)(1) which is properly allocable to the mineral property in respect of which the taxable income is being computed, the taxpayer shall have available permanent records of all the facts necessary to determine with reasonable accuracy the amount of such portion. In the absence of such records, none of the gain recognized under section 1245(a)(1) shall be allocable to such mineral property.

(6) As used in this paragraph, the term "mineral property" has the meaning assigned to it by section 614 and § 1.614-1.

(7) The provisions of this paragraph may be illustrated by the following examples:

Example (1). A, who uses the calendar year as his taxable year, operated and treated as separate properties mines Nos. 1 and 2. On January 1, 1963, A acquired a truck which was section 1245 property. During 1963 and 1964 the truck was used 25 percent of the time at mine No. 1 and 75 percent of the time at mine No. 2. For each such year the depreciation adjustments allowed in respect of the truck were $800 (the amount allowable). In computing the taxable income from mines Nos. 1 and 2 for each such year, $200 (25 percent of $800) of the depreciation adjustments was allocated by A to mine No. 1 and $600 (75 percent of $800) to mine No. 2. Thus, for the 2 years, the total of the depreciation adjustments on the truck was $1,600, of which $400 was allocated to mine No. 1 and $1,200 to mine No. 2. On January 1, 1965, A recognized upon sale of the truck a gain of $500 to which section 1245(a)(1) applied. During 1965, A did not recognize any other gain to which section 1245(a)(1) applied. In computing taxable income from the mines for 1965, the expenses otherwise required to be taken into account are reduced by $125 (that is $400/$1,600 of $500) for mine No. 1 and by $375 (that is $1,200/$1,600 of $500) for mine No. 2.

Example (2). This situation is the same as in example (1), except that the truck in question is used 25 percent of the time at mine No. 1, and 75 percent of the time in a nonmining business owned by A. Accordingly, in computing taxable income from A's mines for 1965, the expenses for mine No. 1 otherwise required to be taken into account are reduced by $125 (that is $400/$1600 of $500), but no reduction is made in the expenses for mine No. 2, since the truck in question was not used in connection with that mineral property.

Example (3). That situation is the same as in example (1), except that the truck in question was used exclusively at mine No. 1 in 1963. On January 1, 1964, the truck was transferred to mine No. 2, and was used exclusively at mine No. 2 during the remaining period prior to its sale. However, A continued to own and operate mine No. 1. For the 2 years 1963 and 1964, the total of the depreciation adjustments on the truck was $1600 of which $800 was allocated to mine No. 1 and $800 to mine No. 2. In computing taxable income from A's mines for 1965, the expenses for mines Nos. 1 and 2 otherwise required to be taken into account are reduced by $250 each (that is $800/$1600 of $500). If A had sold mine No. 1 on January 1, 1964, no reduction in expenses would be allowable as a result of the operation of the truck at mine No. 1, since A would no longer have owned mine No. 1 in the year in which the truck was sold.

Example (4). On January 1, 1963, B, who uses the calendar year as his taxable year and who normally allocates depreciation costs to mines according to the percentage of time which the depreciable asset is used with respect to the mines, acquired a truck which was section 1245 property. During 1963 the truck was used exclusively on mine No. 1, which B operated and treated as a separate property. The depreciation adjustments allowed in respect of the truck for 1963 were $1,000 (the amount allowable), which amount was allocated to mine No. 1 in computing the taxable income therefrom. On January 1, 1964, B acquired and began operating mine No. 2 and elected under section 614(c) to aggregate and treat as one property mines Nos. 1 and 2. During 1964 B used the truck 60 percent of the time for mine No. 1 and 40 percent of the time for mine No. 2. For 1964 the depreciation adjustments allowed in respect of the truck were $1,000 (the amount allowable), which amount was allocated to the aggregation of mines Nos. 1 and 2 in computing the taxable income therefrom. On December 31, 1964, B sold mine No. 2. For 1965 the depreciation adjustments allowed in respect of the truck were $1,000 (the amount allowable), which amount was allocated to mine No. 1 in computing the taxable income therefrom. On January 1, 1966, B recognized gain upon sale of the truck of $600 to which section 1245(a)(1) applied. In computing the taxable income from mine No. 1 for 1966, the expenses otherwise required to be taken into account are reduced by $600, since all the

Reg. § 1.613-5(b)(7)

depreciation adjustments allowed with respect to the truck, including those allowed with respect to the use of the truck at mine No. 2 ($400 for 1964), relate to the same mineral property from which B had taxable income in 1966, the taxable year in which he sold the truck.

Example (5). On January 1, 1962, A who uses the calendar year as his taxable year, elected under section 614(c) to aggregate and treat as one mineral property his operating mineral interests in mines Nos. 1 and 2. On January 1, 1963, A acquired a truck which was section 1245 property, to be used at both mine No. 1 and mine No. 2. A later elected (with the consent of the Commissioner) to deaggregate mines Nos. 1 and 2, and this deaggregation became effective on January 1, 1964. At the time of deaggregation, half of the tax basis of the aggregated property was allocated to mine No. 1, and the other half to mine No. 2. During each of the years 1963 and 1964, the truck was used 25 percent of the time on mine No. 1 and 75 percent of the time on mine No. 2, and the depreciation adjustments allowed in respect of the truck were $800 (the amount allowable). On January 1, 1965, A recognized upon sale of the truck a gain of $500 to which section 1245(a)(1) applied. In computing taxable income from A's mines for 1965, the expenses otherwise required to be taken into account are reduced by $187.50 (that is half of $250 for 1963 and $200/$800 of $250 for 1964) for mine No. 1 and by $312.50 (that is half of $250 for 1963 and $600/$800 of $250 for 1964) for mine No. 2.

(c) *Treatment of particular items in computing taxable income from the property.* In determining taxable income from the property under the provisions of paragraph (a) of this section—

(1) Trade or cash discounts (or allowances determined to have the same effect as trade or cash discounts) which are actually allowed to the taxpayer in connection with the acquisition of property, supplies, or services shall not be included in the cost of such property, supplies, or services.

(2) Intangible drilling and development costs which are deducted under section 263(c) and § 1.612-4 shall be subtracted from the gross income from the property.

(3) Exploration and development expenditures which are deducted for the taxable year under sections 615, 616, or 617 shall be subtracted from the gross income from the property.

(4)(i) Selling expenses, if any, paid or incurred with respect to a raw mineral product shall be subtracted from gross income from the property. See subdivision (iii) of this subparagraph for the definition of the term "raw mineral product." For example, the selling expenses paid or incurred by a producer of raw mineral products with respect to products such as crude oil, raw gas, coal, iron ore, or crushed dolomite shall be subtracted from gross income from the property.

(ii) A reasonable portion of the expenses of selling a refined, manufactured, or fabricated product shall be subtracted from gross income from the property. Such reasonable portion shall be equivalent to the typical selling expenses which are incurred by unintegrated miners or producers in the same mineral industry so as to maintain equality in the tax treatment of unintegrated miners or producers in comparison with integrated miner-manufacturers or producer-manufacturers. If unintegrated miners or producers in the same mineral industry do not typically incur any selling expenses, then no portion of the expenses of selling a refined, manufactured, or fabricated product shall be subtracted from gross income from the property when determining the taxpayer's taxable income from the property.

(iii) For purposes of this subparagraph, a product will be considered to be a raw mineral product if (in the case of oil and gas) it is sold in the immediate vicinity of the well or if (in the case of minerals other than oil and gas) it is sold under the conditions described in paragraph (b)(1) of § 1.613-4. In addition, a product will be considered to be a raw mineral product if only insubstantial value is added to the product by nonmining processes (or, in the case of oil and gas, by conversion or transportation processes). For example, in the case of a producer of crushed granite poultry grit, both bulk and bagged grit will be deemed to be a raw mineral product for purposes of the selling expense rule set forth in this subparagraph.

(iv) The term "selling expenses", for purposes of this subparagraph, includes sales management salaries, rent of sales offices, sales clerical expenses, salesmen's salaries, sales commissions and bonuses, advertising expenses, sales traveling expenses, and similar expenses, together with an allocable share of the costs of supporting services, but the term does not include delivery expenses.

(5) Taxes which are taken as a credit rather than as a deduction or which are capitalized shall not be subtracted from the gross income from the property.

(6) Trade association dues paid or incurred by a producer of crude oil or gas or a raw mineral product shall be subtracted from the gross income from the property. See subparagraph (4)(iii) of this paragraph for the definition of the term "raw mineral product". In addition, a reasonable por-

Reg. § 1.613-5(c)(1)

Deductions

See p. 20,601 for regulations not amended to reflect law changes

tion of the trade association dues incurred by a producer of a refined, manufactured, or fabricated product shall also be subtracted from gross income from the property if the activities of the association relate to production, treatment and marketing of the crude oil or gas or raw mineral product. One reasonable method of allocating the trade association dues described in the preceding sentence is an allocation based on the proportion that the direct costs of mining processes and the direct costs of nonmining processes (or, in the case of oil and gas, conversion and transportation processes) bear to each other. The foregoing rules shall apply even though one of the principal purposes of an association is to advise, promote, or assist in the production, marketing, or sale of refined, manufactured, or fabricated products. For example, a reasonable portion of the trade association dues paid to an association which promotes the sale of cement, refined petroleum, or copper products shall be subtracted from gross income from the property. [Reg. § 1.613-5.]

☐ [*T.D. 6446, 1-20-60. Amended by T.D. 6836, 7-14-65, by T.D. 6955, 5-8-68, and by T.D. 7170, 3-10-72.*]

[Reg. § 1.613-6]

§ 1.613-6. Statement to be attached to return when depletion is claimed on percentage basis.—In addition to the requirements set forth in paragraph (g) of § 1.611-2, a taxpayer who claims the percentage depletion deduction under section 613 for any taxable year shall attach to his return for such year a statement setting forth in complete, summary form, with respect to each property for which such deduction is allowable, the following information:

(a) All data necessary for the determination of the "gross income from the property", as defined in §§ 1.613-3 and 1.613-4, including—

(1) Amounts paid as rents or royalties including amounts which the recipient treats under section 631(c),

(2) Proportion and amount of bonus excluded, and

(3) Amounts paid to holders of other interests in the mineral deposit.

(b) All additional data necessary for the determination of the "taxable income from the property (computed without the allowance for depletion)", as defined in § 1.613-5. [Reg. § 1.613-6.]

☐ [*T.D. 6446, 1-20-60. Amended by T.D. 7170, 3-10-72.*]

[Reg. § 1.613A-0]

§ 1.613A-0. Limitations on percentage depletion in the case of oil and gas wells; table of contents.

This section lists the paragraphs contained in §§ 1.613A-0 through 1.613A-7.

§ 1.613A-1. Post-1974 limitations on percentage depletion in case of oil and gas wells; general rule.

§ 1.613A-2. Exemption for certain domestic gas wells.

§ 1.613A-3. Exemption for independent producers and royalty owners.

(a) General rules.

(b) Phase-out table.

(c) Applicable percentage.

(d) Production in excess of depletable quantity.

(1) Primary production.

(2) Secondary or tertiary production.

(3) Taxable income from the property.

(4) Examples.

(e) Partnerships.

(1) General rule.

(2) Initial allocation of adjusted basis of oil or gas property among partners.

(i) General rule.

(ii) Allocation methods.

(3) Adjustments by partnership to allocated adjusted bases.

(i) Capital expenditures by partnership.

(ii) Admission of a new partner or increase in partner's interest.

(A) In general.

(B) Allocation of basis to contributing partner.

(C) Reduction of existing partners' bases.

(iii) Determination of aggregate of partners' adjusted bases in the property.

(A) In general.

(B) Written data.

(C) Assumptions.

(iv) Withdrawal of partner or decrease in partner's interest.

(A) In general.

(B) Special rule for determining a withdrawing partner's basis in the property.

(v) Effective date.

(4) Determination of a partner's interest in partnership capital or income.

(5) Special rules on allocation of adjusted basis to partners.

Reg. § 1.613A-0

(6) Miscellaneous rules.

(7) Examples.

(f) S corporations.

(g) Trusts and estates.

(h) Businesses under common control; members of the same family.

(1) Component members of a controlled group.

(2) Aggregation of business entities under common control.

(3) Allocation among members of the same family.

(4) Special rules.

(5) Examples.

(i) Transfer of oil or gas property.

(1) General rule.

(i) In general.

(ii) Examples.

(2) Transfers after October 11, 1990.

(i) General rule.

(ii) Transfer.

(iii) Transferee.

(iv) Effective date.

(v) Examples.

(j) Percentage depletion with respect to bonuses and advanced royalties.

(1) Amounts received or accrued after August 16, 1986.

(2) Amounts received or accrued before August 17, 1986.

(k) Special rules for fiscal year taxpayers.

(l) Information furnished by partnerships, trusts, estates, and operators.

§ 1.613A-4. Limitations on application of § 1.613A-3 exemption.

(a) Limitation based on taxable income.

(b) Retailers excluded.

(c) Certain refiners excluded.

§ 1.613A-5. Election under section 613A (c)(4).

§ 1.613A-6. Recordkeeping requirements.

(a) Principal value of property demonstrated.

(b) Production from secondary or tertiary processes.

(c) Retention of records.

§ 1.613A-7. Definitions.

(a) Domestic.

(b) Natural gas.

(c) Regulated natural gas.

(d) Natural gas sold under fixed contract.

Reg. § 1.613A-0

(e) Qualified natural gas from geopressured brine.

(f) Average daily production.

(g) Crude oil.

(h) Depletable oil quantity.

(i) Depletable natural gas quantity.

(j) Barrel.

(k) Secondary or tertiary production.

(l) Controlled group of corporations.

(m) Related person.

(n) Transfer.

(o) Transferee.

(p) Interest in proven oil or gas property.

(q) Amount disallowed.

(r) Retailer.

(s) Refiner.

[Reg. § 1.613A-0.]

☐ [T.D. 8348, 5-10-91. *Amended by* T.D. 8437, 9-22-92.]

[Reg. § 1.613A-1]

§ 1.613A-1. Post-1974 limitations on percentage depletion in case of oil and gas wells; general rule.—Except as otherwise provided in section 613A and the regulations thereunder, in the case of oil or gas which is produced after December 31, 1974, and to which gross income from the property is attributable after such year, the allowance for depletion under section 611 with respect to any oil or gas well shall be computed without regard to section 613. In the case of a taxable year beginning before January 1, 1975, and ending after that date, the percentage depletion allowance (but not the cost depletion allowance) with respect to oil and gas wells for such taxable year shall be determined by treating the portion thereof in 1974 as if it were a short taxable year for purposes of section 613 and the portion thereof in 1975 as if it were a short taxable year for purposes of section 613A. [Reg. § 1.613A-1.]

☐ [T.D. 7487, 5-12-77.]

[Reg. § 1.613A-2]

§ 1.613A-2. Exemption for certain domestic gas wells.—(a) The allowance for depletion under section 611 shall be computed in accordance with section 613 with respect to:

(1) Regulated natural gas (as defined in paragraph (c) of § 1.613A-7),

(2) Natural gas sold under a fixed contract (as defined in paragraph (d) of § 1.613A-7), and

(3) Any geothermal deposit in the United States or in a possession of the United States that

is determined to be a gas well within the meaning of former section 613(b)(1)(A) (as in effect before enactment of the Tax Reduction Act of 1975) for taxable years ending after December 31, 1974, and before October 1, 1978 (see section 613(e) for depletion on geothermal deposits thereafter),

and 22 percent shall be deemed to be specified in section 613(b) for purposes of section 613(a).

(b) For taxable years ending after September 30, 1978, the allowance for depletion under section 611 shall be computed in accordance with section 613 with respect to any qualified natural gas from geopressured brine (as defined in paragraph (e) of § 1.613A-7), and 10 percent shall be deemed to be specified in section 613(b) for purposes of section 613(a).

(c) For special rules applicable to partnerships, S corporations, trusts, and estates, see paragraphs (e), (f), and (g) of § 1.613A-3.

(d) The provisions of this section may be illustrated by the following examples:

Example 1. A is a producer of natural gas which is sold by A under a contract in effect on February 1, 1975. The contract provides for an increase in the price of the gas sold under the contract to the highest price paid to a producer for natural gas in the area. The gas sold by A qualifies under section 613A(b)(1)(B) for percentage depletion as gas sold under a fixed contract until its price increases, but is presumed not to qualify thereafter unless A demonstrates by clear and convincing evidence that the price increase in no event takes increases in tax liabilities into account.

Example 2. B is a producer of natural gas which is sold by B under a contract in effect on February 1, 1975. The contract provides that beginning January 1, 1980, the price of the gas may be renegotiated. Such a provision does not disqualify gas from qualifying for the exemption under section 613A(b)(1)(B) with respect to the gas sold prior to January 1, 1980. However, gas sold on or after January 1, 1980, does not qualify for the exemption whether or not the price of the gas is renegotiated. [Reg. § 1.613A-2.]

☐ [*T.D.* 8348, 5-10-91. Amended by *T.D.* 8437, 9-22-92.]

[Reg. § 1.613A-3]

§ 1.613A-3. Exemption for independent producers and royalty owners.—(a) *General rules.*

(1) Except as provided in section 613A(d) and § 1.613A-4, the allowance for depletion under section 611 with respect to oil or gas which is produced after December 31, 1974, and to which gross income from the property is attributable after that date, shall be computed in accordance with section 613 with respect to:

(i) So much of the taxpayer's average daily production (as defined in paragraph (f) of § 1.613A-7) of domestic crude oil (as defined in paragraphs (a) and (g) of § 1.613A-7) as does not exceed the taxpayer's depletable oil quantity (as defined in paragraph (h) of § 1.613A-7), and

(ii) So much of the taxpayer's average daily production of domestic natural gas (as defined in paragraphs (a) and (b) of § 1.613A-7) as does not exceed the taxpayer's depletable natural gas quantity (as defined in paragraph (i) of § 1.613A-7), and the applicable percentage (determined in accordance with the table in paragraph (c) of this section shall be deemed to be specified in section 613(b) for purposes of section 613(a).

(2) Except as provided in section 613A(d) and § 1.613A-4, the allowance for depletion under section 611 with respect to oil or gas which is produced after December 31, 1974, and to which gross income from the property is attributable after that date and before January 1, 1984, shall be computed in accordance with section 613 with respect to:

(i) So much of the taxpayer's average daily secondary or tertiary production (as defined in paragraph (k) of § 1.613A-7) of domestic crude oil as does not exceed the taxpayer's depletable oil quantity (determined without regard to section 613A(c)(3)(A)(ii), as in effect prior to the Revenue Reconciliation Act of 1990), and

(ii) So much of the taxpayer's average daily secondary or tertiary production of domestic natural gas as does not exceed the taxpayer's depletable natural gas quantity (determined without regard to section 613A(c)(3)(A)(ii), as in effect prior to the Revenue Reconciliation Act of 1990), and 22 percent shall be deemed to be specified in section 613(b) for purposes of section 613(a).

(3) For purposes of this section, there shall not be taken into account any production with respect to which percentage depletion is allowed pursuant to section 613A(b) or is not allowable by reason of section 613A(c)(9), as in effect prior to the Revenue Reconciliation Act of 1990.

(4) The provisions of this paragraph may be illustrated by the following examples:

Example 1. A, a calendar year taxpayer, owns an oil producing property with 100,000 barrels of production to which income was attributable for 1975 and a gas producing property with 1,200,000,000 cubic feet of production to which income was attributable for 1975. Under section 613A(c)(4), the oil equivalent of 1,200,000,000 cubic feet of gas is 200,000 barrels, bringing A's total production of oil and gas to which income was attributable for 1975 to the equivalent of 300,000 barrels of oil. A's average daily production was 821.92 barrels (300,000 barrels ÷ 365 days) which is less than the depletable oil quantity (2,000 barrels) before reduction for any election by A under section 613A(c)(4). Accordingly, A may make an election with respect to A's entire gas production and thereby be entitled to percentage depletion with respect to A's entire 1975 income from production of oil and gas. A's allowable depletion pursuant to section 613A(c) for A's oil and gas properties would be the amount determined under section 613(a) computed at the 22 percent rate specified in section 613A(c)(5), as in effect prior to the Revenue Reconciliation Act 1990, for 1975.

Example 2. B, a calendar year taxpayer, owns oil producing properties with 365,000 barrels of production to which income was attributable for 1975. B was a retailer of oil and gas for only the last 3 months of 1975. B's average daily production for 1975 was 1,000 barrels (365,000 barrels ÷ 365 days).

Example 3. C, a calendar year taxpayer, owns property X with 500,000 barrels of primary production to which income was attributable for 1975 and property Y with 200,000 barrels of primary production to which income was attributable for 1975. Property Y had been transferred to C on January 1, 1975, on which date it was a proven property. Therefore, the exemption under section 613A(c)(1) does not apply to C with respect to production from property Y. In determining C's depletable oil quantity for the year, the production from property Y is not taken into account. Thus, C's average daily production for 1975 was 1,369.86 barrels (500,000 barrels ÷ 375).

Example 4. D owns an oil property with producing wells X and Y on it. In 1975 D converts well X into an injection well. Prior to the application of the secondary process, it is estimated that without the application of the process the annual production from well X would have been 50x barrels of oil and from well Y would have been 100x barrels of oil. For the taxable year in which injection is commenced production from well X is 10x barrels and from well Y is 180x barrels. Forty x barrels of oil [190x barrels of oil (actual production from the property) —150x barrels (estimate of primary production from the property)] qualify as secondary production.

Example 5. E, a calendar year taxpayer, owns a domestic oil well which produced 100,000 barrels of oil in 1980. The proceeds from the sale of 15,000 barrels of that production are not includible in E's income until 1981. The 15,000 barrels produced in 1980 are included in E's average daily production for 1981 and excluded from such production for 1980. The tentative quantity and the percentage depletion rate for 1981 are applicable to the 15,000 barrels of oil.

(b) *Phase-out table.* For purposes of section 613A(c)(3)(A)(i) and § 1.613A-7(h) (relating to depletable oil quantity)—

In the case of production after 1974 and to which gross income from the property is attributable for the calendar year:	The tentative quantity in barrels per day is:
1975	2,000
1976	1,800
1977	1,600
1978	1,400
1979	1,200
1980 and thereafter	1,000

(c) *Applicable percentage.* For purposes of section 613A(c)(1) and paragraph (a) of this section—

In the case of production after 1974 and to which gross income from the property is attributable for the calendar year:	The applicable percentage is:
1975	22
1976	22
1977	22
1978	22
1979	22
1980	22
1981	20
1982	18
1983	16
1984 and thereafter	15

Reg. § 1.613A-3(b)

(d) *Production in excess of depletable quantity*—(1) *Primary production.*

(i) If the taxpayer's average daily production of domestic crude oil exceeds his depletable oil quantity, the allowance for depletion pursuant to section 613A(c)(1)(A) and paragraph (a)(1)(i) of this section with respect to oil produced during the taxable year from each property in the United States shall be that amount which bears the same ratio to the amount of depletion which would have been allowable under section 613(a) for all of the taxpayer's oil produced from the property during the taxable year (computed as if section 613 applied to all of the production at the rate specified in paragraph (c) of this section) as the amount of his depletable oil quantity bears to the aggregate number of barrels representing the average daily production of domestic crude oil of the taxpayer for such year.

(ii) If the taxpayer's average daily production of domestic natural gas exceeds his depletable natural gas quantity, the allowance for depletion pursuant to section 613A(c)(1)(B) and paragraph (a)(1)(ii) of this section with respect to natural gas produced during the taxable year from each property in the United States shall be that amount which bears the same ratio to the amount of depletion which would have been allowable pursuant to section 613(a) for all of the taxpayer's natural gas produced from the property during the taxable year (computed as if section 613 applied to all of the production at the rate specified in paragraph (c) of this section) as the amount of his depletable natural gas quantity in cubic feet bears to the aggregate number of cubic feet representing the average daily production of domestic natural gas of the taxpayer for such year.

(2) *Secondary or tertiary production.*

(i) If the taxpayer's average daily secondary or tertiary production of domestic crude oil exceeds his depletable oil quantity (determined without regard to section 613A(c)(3)(A)(ii), as in effect prior to the Revenue Reconciliation Act of 1990), the allowance for depletion pursuant to section 613A(c)(6)(A)(i), as in effect prior to the Revenue Reconciliation Act of 1990, and paragraph (a)(2)(i) of this section with respect to oil produced during the taxable year from each property in the United States shall be that amount which bears the same ratio to the amount of depletion which would have been allowable pursuant to section 613(a) for all of the taxpayer's secondary or tertiary production of oil from the property during the taxable year (computed as if section 613 applied to all of the production at the rate specified in paragraph (a)(2) of this section) as the amount of his depletable oil quantity (determined without regard to section 613A(c)(3)(A)(ii), as in effect prior to the Revenue Reconciliation Act of 1990) bears to the aggregate number of barrels representing the average daily secondary or tertiary production of domestic crude oil of the taxpayer for such year.

(ii) If the taxpayer's average daily secondary or tertiary production of domestic natural gas exceeds his depletable natural gas quantity (determined without regard to section 613A(c)(3)(A)(ii), as in effect prior to the Revenue Reconciliation Act of 1990), the allowance for depletion pursuant to section 613A(c)(6)(A)(ii), as in effect prior to the Revenue Reconciliation Act of 1990, and paragraph (a)(2)(ii) of this section with respect to natural gas produced during the taxable year from each property in the United States shall be that amount which bears the same ratio to the amount of depletion which would have been allowable pursuant to section 613(a) for all of the taxpayer's secondary or tertiary production of natural gas from the property during the taxable year (computed as if section 613 applied to all of the production at the rate specified in paragraph (a)(2) of this section) as the amount of his depletable natural gas quantity in cubic feet (determined without regard to section 613A(c)(3)(A)(ii), as in effect prior to the Revenue Reconciliation Act of 1990) bears to the aggregate number of cubic feet representing the average daily secondary or tertiary production of domestic natural gas of the taxpayer for such year.

(iii) This paragraph (d)(2) shall not apply after December 31, 1983.

(3) *Taxable income from the property.* If both oil and gas are produced from the property during the taxable year, then for purposes of section 613A(c)(7)(A) and (B) and paragraph (d) of this section the taxable income from the property, in applying the taxable income limitation in section 613(a), shall be allocated between the oil production and the gas production in proportion to the gross income from the property during the taxable year from each. If both gas with respect to which section 613A(b) and § 1.613A-2 apply and oil or gas with respect to which section 613A(c) and this section apply are produced from the property during the taxable year, then for purposes of section 613A(d)(1) and paragraph (a) of § 1.613A-4 the taxable income from the property, in applying the taxable income limitation in section 613(a), shall also be so allocated. In addition, if both primary production and secondary or tertiary production (to which gross income from the property is attributable before January 1, 1984)

Reg. § 1.613A-3(d)(3)

are produced from the property during the taxable year and the total amount of production is in excess of the depletable quantity, then for purposes of paragraph (d) of this section the taxable income from the property, in applying the taxable income limitation in section 613(a), shall also be so allocated.

(4) *Examples.* The application of this paragraph may be illustrated by the following examples:

Example 1. A owns Y and Z oil producing properties. With respect to properties Y and Z, the percentage depletion allowable pursuant to section 613(a) (computed as if section 613 applied to all of the production at the rate specified in section 613A(c)(5)) for 1975 was $100x and $200x, respectively. A's average daily production for 1975 was 4,000 barrels. A's allowable depletion pursuant to section 613A(c) with respect to property Y was $50x: [$100x depletion (2,000 depletable oil quantity/ 4,000 average daily production)]. A's allowable depletion pursuant to section 613A(c) with respect to property Z was $100x ($200x depletion × 2,000 depletable oil quantity/ 4,000 average daily production).

Example 2. B owns gas producing properties which had secondary gas production for 1975 of 3,285,000,000 cubic feet, which under section 613A(c)(4) is equivalent to 547,500 barrels of oil. B's average daily secondary production of gas for 1975 was equivalent to 1,500 barrels (547,500 barrels ÷ 365). B elected to have section 613A(c)(4) apply to the gas production. With respect to the production, the percentage depletion allowable pursuant to section 613(a) (computed at the rate specified in section 613A(c)(6)(A), as in effect prior to the Revenue Reconciliation Act of 1990) was $150x. B also owns an oil producing property which had primary oil production for 1975 of 365,000 barrels. B's average daily production of oil for 1975 was 1,000 barrels (365,000 ÷ 365). With respect to the oil property, the percentage depletion allowable pursuant to section 613(a) (computed as if section 613 applied to all of the production at the rate specified in section 613A(c)(5), as in effect prior to the Revenue Reconciliation Act of 1990) was $100x. B's depletable oil quantity for 1975 was 500 barrels (2,000 barrels tentative quantity—1,500 barrels average daily secondary production). B's allowable depletion pursuant to section 613A (c) with respect to the oil property was $50x ($100x depletion × 500 depletable oil quantity/ 1,000 average daily production).

Example 3. Assume the same facts as in *Example 2* except that B's primary production was 6,000,000 cubic feet of natural gas daily rather than its equivalent under section 613A(c)(4) of 1,000 barrels of oil and that B elected to have that section apply to such gas. B's allowable depletion pursuant to section 613A(c) with respect to B's primary production is $50x, the same as in example (2).

Example 4. C is a partner with a one-third interest in Partnerships CDE and CFG with each partnership owning a single oil property. C's percentage depletion allowable under section 613(a) (computed as if section 613 applied to all of the production at the rate specified in section 613A(c)(5), as in effect prior to the Revenue Reconciliation Act of 1990) for 1975 was $20x with respect to 495,000 barrels (his allocable share of Partnership CDE production) and $40x with respect to 600,000 barrels (his allocable share of Partnership CFG production). C's average daily production is 3,000 barrels (1,095,000 total production ÷ 365 days). C's allowable depletion pursuant to section 613A(c) with respect to C's share of the production of Partnership CDE is $13.33x ($20x depletion × 2,000 depletable oil quantity/3,000 average daily production). C's allowable depletion pursuant to section 613A(c) with respect to C's share of the production of Partnership CFG is $26.67x ($40x depletion × 2,000 depletable oil quantity/3,000 average daily production). See § 1.613A-3(e) for the rules on computing depletion in the case of a partnership.

Example 5. H owns a property which, during H's fiscal year which began on June 1, 1975, and ended on May 31, 1976, produced gas qualifying under section 613A (b) and oil qualifying under section 613A(c). For the fiscal year H's gross income from the property was $400x, of which $100x was from gas and $300x was from oil. For the oil his gross income from the property for the period beginning June 1, 1975, and ending December 31, 1975, was $100x and for the 1976 portion of the fiscal year was $200x. The percentage depletion allowance (before applying the 50 percent limitation of section 613(a) or the 65 percent limitation of section 613A(d)(1)) was $22x for the gas, $22x for the oil in 1975, and $44x for the oil in 1976. H's taxable income from the property for the fiscal year was $100x. In accordance with paragraph (d)(3) of this section, the taxable income from the property is allocated $25x to the gas:

Reg. § 1.613A-3(d)(4)

$$\left[\$100x \text{ taxable income from the property} \left(\frac{\$100x \text{ gross income from gas from the property}}{\$400x \text{ total gross income from the property}}\right)\right],$$

$25x to the 1975 oil:

$$\left[\$100x \text{ taxable income from the property} \left(\frac{\$100x \text{ gross income from 1975 oil from the property}}{\$400x \text{ total gross income from the property}}\right)\right],$$

and $50x to the 1976 oil:

$$\left[\$100x \text{ taxable income from the property} \left(\frac{\$200x \text{ gross income from 1976 oil from the property}}{\$400x \text{ total gross income from the property}}\right)\right].$$

With the application of the 50 percent of taxable income from the property limitation, the allowable percentage depletion (computed without reference to section 613A) is limited to $12.50x for the gas, $12.50x for the oil in 1975, and $25x for the oil in 1976.

(e) *Partnerships*—(1) *General rule.* In the case of a partnership, the depletion allowance under section 611 with respect to production from domestic oil and gas properties shall be computed separately by the partners and not by the partnership. The determination of whether cost or percentage depletion is applicable is to be made at the partner level. The partnership must allocate to each partner the partner's proportionate share of the adjusted basis of each partnership oil or gas property in accordance with the provisions of paragraphs (e)(2) through (e)(6) of this section. This allocation of the adjusted basis of oil or gas property does not affect a partner's adjusted basis in his or her partnership interest.

(2) *Initial allocation of adjusted basis of oil or gas property among partners*—(i) *General rule.* Each partner shall be allocated his or her proportionate share of the adjusted basis of each partnership domestic oil or gas property. The initial allocation of adjusted basis is to be made as of the later of the date of acquisition of the oil or gas property by the partnership or January 1, 1975.

(ii) *Allocation methods.* Except as otherwise provided in paragraph (e)(5) of this section, the provisions of this paragraph (e)(2)(ii) govern the determination under paragraph (e)(2)(i) of this section of a partner's proportionate share of the adjusted basis of oil or gas property. Each partner's proportionate share is determined in accordance with the partner's proportionate interest in partnership capital at the time of the allocation unless both—

(A) The partnership agreement provides that a partner's share of the adjusted basis of one or more properties is determined in accordance with his or her proportionate interest in partnership income; and

(B) At the time of allocation under the partnership agreement the share of each partner in partnership income is reasonably expected to be substantially unchanged throughout the life of the partnership, other than changes merely to reflect the admission of a new partner, an increase in a partner's interest in consideration for money, property, or services, or a partial or complete withdrawal of an existing partner.

If the requirements of paragraph (e)(2)(ii)(A) and (B) of this section are met, a partner's proportionate share is determined in accordance with his or her proportionate interest in partnership income. The partners' shares of adjusted basis are determined on a property-by-property basis. Accordingly, the basis of one property may be allocated in proportion to capital and the basis of another property may be allocated in proportion to income. See §§ 1.613A-3(e)(5) and 1.704-1(b)(4)(v) for special rules concerning allocation of the adjusted basis of oil and gas properties.

(3) *Adjustments by partnership to allocated adjusted bases*—(i) *Capital expenditures by partnership.* Appropriate adjustments shall be made to the partners' adjusted bases in any domestic oil and gas property for any partnership capital expenditures relating to such property that are made after the initial allocation. These adjustments shall be allocated among the partners in accordance with the principles set forth in paragraph (e)(2)(ii) of this section.

(ii) *Admission of a new partner or increase in partner's interest*—(A) *In general.* Upon a contribution of money, other property, or services to the partnership by a new or existing partner ("contributing partner") as consideration for an interest in the partnership, the partnership shall allocate, in accordance with paragraph (e)(3)(ii)(B) of this section, a share of the partnership's basis in each existing oil and gas property

Reg. § 1.613A-3(e)(3)

to the contributing partner, and each existing partner shall reduce, in accordance with paragraph (e)(3)(ii)(C) of this section, his or her share of the partnership's basis in such property.

(B) *Allocation of basis to contributing partner.* The partnership shall allocate to a contributing partner his or her proportionate share (determined under paragraph (e)(2)(ii) of this section in accordance with the partner's proportionate interest in partnership capital or income) of the partnership's adjusted basis in each existing partnership oil or gas property. For purposes of this allocation, the partnership's adjusted basis in such property equals the aggregate of its partners' adjusted bases in the property, as determined under paragraph (e)(3)(iii) of this section.

(C) *Reduction of existing partners' bases.* Each existing partner's basis in each existing partnership oil or gas property is reduced by the percentage of the partnership's aggregate basis in the property that is allocated to the contributing partner. Thus, if one third of the partnership's aggregate basis in a property is allocated to a contributing partner because the contributing partner has a one-third interest in partnership capital, after the admission of the contributing partner each existing partner's basis (including the contributing partner's pre-existing basis if such partner is also an existing partner) in each property equals the partner's basis (prior to the admission) reduced by one-third.

(iii) *Determination of aggregate of partners' adjusted bases in the property*—(A) *In general.* To determine the aggregate of its partners' adjusted bases for purposes of this paragraph (e)(3), the partnership must determine each partner's adjusted basis under either paragraph (e)(3)(iii)(B) (written data) or paragraph (e)(3)(iii)(C) (assumptions) of this section. The partnership is permitted to determine the bases of some partners under paragraph (e)(3)(iii)(B) of this section and of others under paragraph (e)(3)(iii)(C) of this section. For this purpose, a partner's basis in an oil or gas property does not include any basis adjustment under section 743(b).

(B) *Written data.* A partnership may determine a partner's basis in an oil or gas property by using written data provided by a partner stating the amount of the partner's adjusted basis or depletion deductions with respect to the property unless the partnership knows or has reason to know that the written data is inaccurate. In determining depletion deductions, a partner must treat as actually deducted any amount disallowed and carried over as a result of the 65 percent-of-income limitation of section 613A(d)(1). If a partnership does not receive written data upon which it may rely, the partnership must use the assumptions provided in paragraph (e)(3)(iii)(C) of this section in determining a partner's adjusted basis in an oil or gas property.

(C) *Assumptions.* Except as provided in paragraph (e)(3)(iv)(B) of this section, a partnership that does not use written data pursuant to paragraph (e)(3)(iii)(B) of this section to determine a partner's basis must use the following assumptions to determine the partner's adjusted basis in an oil or gas property:

(*1*) The partner deducted his or her share of deductions under section 263(c) in the first year in which the partner could claim a deduction for such amounts, unless the partnership elected to capitalize such amounts;

(*2*) The partner was not subject to the 65 percent-of-income limitation of section 613A(d)(1) with respect to the partner's depletion allowance under section 611; and

(*3*) The partner was not subject to the following limitations, with respect to the partner's depletion allowance under section 611, except to the extent a limitation applied at the partnership level: the taxable income limitation of section 613(a); the depletable quantity limitations of section 613A(c); the prohibition against claiming percentage depletion on transferred proven property under section 613A(c)(9), prior to its repeal; or the limitations of section 613A(d)(2), (3), and (4) (exclusion of retailers and refiners).

(iv) *Withdrawal of partner or decrease in partner's interest*—(A) *In general.* Upon a distribution of money or other property to a withdrawing partner as consideration for an interest in the partnership, the withdrawing partner's adjusted basis in each domestic oil or gas property that continues to be held by the partnership is allocated to the remaining partners in proportion to their proportionate interest in partnership capital or income after taking into account any increase or decrease as a result of the event giving rise to the reallocation. A similar rule shall apply in the case of a diminution of a continuing partner's interest in the partnership.

(B) *Special rule for determining a withdrawing partner's basis in the property.* If a partnership is required to determine a withdrawing partner's adjusted basis using the assumptions under paragraph (e)(3)(iii)(C) of this section, the partnership may rebut the assumption in paragraph (e)(3)(iii)(C)(*3*) of this section that the withdrawing partner was not subject to the limitations of sections 613A(d)(2), (3), and (4) (exclusion of retailers and refiners) by demonstrating

Reg. § 1.613A-3(e)(3)

that the withdrawing partner was subject to the limitations of sections 613A(d)(2), (3), or (4).

(v) *Effective date.* The provisions of § 1.613A-3(e)(3)(i) through (iv) are effective for taxable years beginning after May 13, 1991. However, a partnership may elect to apply these provisions to taxable years beginning on or before May 13, 1991.

(4) *Determination of a partner's interest in partnership capital or income.* For purposes of this paragraph (e), a partner's interest in partnership capital or income is determined by taking into account all facts and circumstances relating to the economic arrangement of the partners. See the factors listed in § 1.704-1(b)(3)(ii).

(5) *Special rules on allocation of adjusted basis to partners.* An allocation or reallocation of the adjusted basis of oil or gas property is pursuant to this paragraph (e) of this section deemed to be in accordance with the partner's proportionate interest in partnership capital or income for purposes of this paragraph (e) where so provided in § 1.704-1(b)(4)(v). In addition, in connection with a revaluation described in § 1.704-1(b)(2)(iv)(*f*), the basis of an oil or gas property is allocated among the partners based on the principles used under § 1.704-1(b)(4)(i) of allocating tax items to take into account variations between the adjusted basis of the property and its fair market value. In the case of an oil or gas property contributed to a partnership by a partner, section 704(c) is taken into account in determining the partner's share of the adjusted basis.

(6) *Miscellaneous rules*—(i) Each partner must separately keep records of his or her share of the adjusted basis in each domestic oil or gas property of the partnership, adjust his or her share of such basis pursuant to section 1016 (including adjustments for any depletion allowed or allowable with respect to such property), and use that adjusted basis each year in the computation of his or her cost depletion or in the computation of his or her gain or loss on the disposition (including abandonment) of the property by the partnership.

(ii) The adjusted basis of a partner's interest in a partnership is decreased (but not below zero) pursuant to section 705(a)(3) by the amount of the depletion deduction allowed or allowable to the partner with respect to a domestic oil or gas property to the extent such deduction does not exceed the proportionate share of the adjusted basis of such property allocated to the partner under section 613A(c)(7)(D), as adjusted by the partner after the initial allocation. Section 705(a)(1)(C) does not apply to depletion deductions that are not included in a partner's distributive share under section 702. Accordingly, the adjusted basis of a partner's interest in a partnership is not increased under section 705(a)(1)(C) with respect to depletion of oil or gas properties. See § 1.705-1(a)(2)(iii).

(iii) Upon the disposition of an oil or gas property by the partnership, each partner must subtract the partner's adjusted basis in the property from his or her allocable portion of the amount realized from the sale of the property to determine gain or loss. The partner's allocable portion of amount realized must, except to the extent governed by section 704(c) (or related principles under § 1.704-1(b)(4)(i)), be determined in accordance with § 1.704-1(b)(4)(v). Except as otherwise provided (*e.g.,* section 751), the sale of a partnership interest is not treated as a sale of an oil and gas property.

(iv) In the case of a transfer of an interest in a partnership, the transferor partner's adjusted basis in each partnership oil or gas property carries over to the transferee partner. If an election under section 754 (relating to optional adjustment to the basis of partnership property) is in effect, such basis is adjusted in accordance with section 743.

(v) For purposes of section 732 (relating to basis of distributed property other than money) and section 734(b) (relating to optional adjustment to basis of partnership property), the partnership's adjusted basis in oil and gas property is an amount equal to the aggregate of its partners' adjusted bases in the property as determined under the rules provided in paragraph (e)(3) of this section.

(7) *Examples.* The provisions of this paragraph may be illustrated by the following examples:

Example 1. A, B, and C have equal interests in capital in Partnership ABC. On January 1, 1992, the partnership acquired a producing domestic oil property. The partnership's basis in the property was $90x. The partnership allocated the adjusted basis of the property to each partner in proportion to the partner's interest in partnership capital. Accordingly, each partner was allocated an adjusted basis of $30x. Each partner must separately compute his or her depletion allowance. The amount of percentage depletion allowable for each partner for 1992 was $10x. On January 1, 1993, each partner's adjusted basis in the property was $20x ($30x minus $10x). On January 1, 1993, the oil property was sold for $150x. Each partner's gain was $30x ($50x allocable share of amount realized minus the partner's adjusted basis of $20x). Each partner must adjust the partner's adjusted basis in his or her partnership interest to reflect the gain.

Example 2. The facts are the same as in *Example 1* except that on January 1, 1993, the property was not sold but transferred by the partnership to partner A. A's basis in the property was $60x (the sum of A's, B's, and C's adjusted bases in the property).

Example 3. The facts are the same as in *Example 1* with the exception that in 1992 C was a retailer of oil and gas and was only entitled to a cost depletion deduction of $5x. C's gain from the sale of the mineral property on January 1, 1993, was $25x ($50x allocable share of amount realized minus C's adjusted basis of $25x ($30x minus $5x)).

Example 4. D, a calendar year taxpayer, is a partner in Partnership DEF which owns a domestic producing oil property. On January 1, 1993, the partnership's adjusted basis in the property was $900x. On January 1, 1993, D's adjusted basis in D's partnership interest was $300x and D's adjusted basis in the partnership's oil property was $300x. D's allowable percentage depletion for 1993 with respect to production from the oil property was $50x. On January 1, 1994, D's adjusted basis in D's partnership interest was $250x and D's adjusted basis in the partnership's oil property was $250x ($300x minus $50x).

Example 5. On January 1, 1990, G has an adjusted basis of $5x in partnership GH's proven domestic oil property, which is the sole asset of the partnership. On January 1, 1990 G sells G's partnership interest to I for $100x when the election under section 754 is in effect. I has a special basis adjustment for the oil property of $95x (the difference between I's basis, $100x, and I's share of the basis of the partnership property, $5x). I is not entitled to percentage depletion with respect to I's distributive share of the oil property income because I is a transferee of an interest in a proven oil property. However, I is entitled to cost depletion and for this purpose I's interest in the oil property has an adjusted basis to I of $100x ($5x, plus I's special basis adjustment of $95x).

Example 6. On January 1, 1960, Partnership JK acquired a domestic producing oil property. On January 1, 1990, the partnership's adjusted basis in the property was zero. On January 1, 1990, L is admitted as a partner to the partnership. Since the partnership's adjusted basis in the oil property is zero, L's proportionate share of the basis in the property is also zero. L is not entitled to percentage depletion because L is a transferee of a proven oil property (see paragraph (g) of this section). Since the property's basis is zero, L is also not entitled to any cost depletion with respect to production from the property.

Example 7. (i) O and P have equal interests in capital in Partnership OP. On January 1, 1991, the partnership acquired an unproven domestic oil property X the basis of which is $200x to the partnership. The partnership allocates $100x of the basis of the property to each partner in accordance with each partner's proportionate interest in partnership capital. For the 1991 taxable year, O has a $10x cost depletion allowance and P has a $25x percentage depletion allowance. Accordingly, at the end of the 1991 taxable year, O's adjusted basis in the property is $90x, and P's adjusted basis in the property is $75x. On January 1, 1992, Q is admitted as an equal partner. The partnership does not use written data from the partners and must therefore assume that each partner was entitled to $25x depletion based on the assumptions provided in § 1.613A-3(e)(3)(iii). This would result in a $50x combined depletion allowance for the partners and an aggregate adjusted basis in the oil property of $150x. Accordingly, the partnership allocates $50x of the basis of the property to Q, one-third of the aggregate adjusted basis determined by the partnership. O and P must each reduce their basis in the property by one-third. Accordingly, after the admission of Q, O's adjusted basis in the property is $60x ($90x minus $30x), and P's adjusted basis in the property is $50x ($75x minus $25x).

(ii) Assume the same facts as in paragraph (i) of this *Example 7* except that O informs the partnership that its adjusted basis in the property is $90x (determined without regard to section 613A(d)(1)). The partnership uses the written data provided by O and determines the aggregate adjusted basis in the property to be $165x ($90x + $75x). Accordingly, the partnership allocates $55x (1/3 of $165x) of the basis of the property to Q, and O and P must each reduce their adjusted basis in the property by one-third, as in paragraph (i) of this *Example 7.* Thus, after the admission of Q, O's adjusted basis in the property is $60x and P's adjusted basis in the property is $50x.

(f) *S corporations.* For purposes of section 613A(c)(13), adjustments to shareholders' adjusted bases in any domestic oil or gas property to reflect capital expenditures by S corporations, the addition of a new shareholder or an increase in a shareholder's interest by reason of a contribution to the S corporation, the redemption of a shareholder's interest, or other appropriate transaction shall be made in accordance with principles similar to the principles under § 1.613A-3(e) applicable to the entry or withdrawal of a partner.

Reg. § 1.613A-3(f)

(g) *Trusts and estates.*

(1) In the case of production from domestic oil and gas properties held by a trust or estate, the depletion allowance under section 611 shall be computed initially by the trust or estate. The determination of whether cost or percentage depletion is applicable shall be made at the trust or estate level, but such determination shall not result in the disallowance of cost depletion to a beneficiary of a trust or estate for whom cost depletion exceeds percentage depletion. The limitations contained in section 613A(c) and (d), other than section 613A(d)(1), shall be applied at the trust or estate level in its computation of percentage depletion pursuant to section 613A and shall also be applied by a beneficiary with respect to any percentage depletion apportioned to the beneficiary by the trust or estate. The limitation of section 613A(d)(1) shall be applied by each taxpayer (*i.e.*, trust, estate or beneficiary) only with respect to its allocable share of percentage depletion under section 611(b)(3) or (4). For purposes of adjustments to the basis of oil or gas properties held by a trust or estate, in the absence of clear and convincing evidence to the contrary, it shall be presumed that no beneficiary is affected by any section 613A(d) limitations or by the rules contained in section 613A(c)(8) and (9) (relating to businesses under common control and members of the same family and to transfers, respectively), as in effect prior to the Revenue Reconciliation Act of 1990, or has any oil or gas production from sources other than the trust or estate.

(2) The provisions of this paragraph may be illustrated by the following examples.

Example 1. A is the income beneficiary of a trust the only asset of which is a domestic producing oil property. The trust instrument requires that an amount which equals 10 percent of the gross income from the property be set aside annually as a reserve for depletion. In 1975 the property had production of 1,095,000 barrels of oil. The trust's gross income from the property in 1975 was $30,000x. In that year, after setting aside $3,000x of income for the reserve for depletion, the trustee distributed the remaining income to A which represented 80 percent of the trust's net income. The percentage depletion computed by the trust with respect to the production (computed as if section 613 applied to all of the production at the rate specified in section 613A(c)(5), as in effect prior to the Revenue Reconciliation Act of 1990) for 1975 was $6,600x. The trust's average daily production for 1975 was 3,000 barrels (1,095,000 ÷ 365 days). The trust's allowable depletion pursuant to section 613A(c) with respect to the production was $4,400x:

$$\left[\$6{,}600x \text{ depletion} \left(\frac{2{,}000 \text{ depletable oil quantity}}{3{,}000 \text{ average daily production}} \right) \right]$$

Pursuant to § 1.611-1(c)(4)(ii), the percentage depletion of $4,400x was apportioned between the trustee and A so that the trustee received $3,000x (an amount equal to the amount of income set aside for the reserve for depletion) and A received $1,400x of the depletion deduction. The $1,400x depletion received by A is attributable to 80 percent of the trust's depletable oil quantity, *i.e.*, 1,600 barrels per day.

Example 2. B, a retailer of oil and gas, is the income beneficiary of a trust the only asset of which is a domestic producing oil property. In 1975 the trustee distributed one-half of the trust's net income and accumulated the other one-half for the benefit of the remainderman. One-half of the percentage depletion computed by the trust with respect to the production from the property was apportioned to B. Since B is a retailer of oil and gas, B is not entitled to deduct any of the percentage depletion apportioned to B. However, B is entitled to take cost depletion with respect to one-half of the production from the oil property, notwithstanding the fact that depletion was computed at the trust level on the basis of percentage depletion.

(h) *Businesses under common control; members of the same family*—(1) *Component members of a controlled group.* For purposes of only the depletable quantity limitations contained in section 613A(c) and this section, component members of a controlled group of corporations (as defined in paragraph (1) of § 1.613A-7) shall be treated as one taxpayer. Accordingly, the group shares the depletable oil (or natural gas) quantity prescribed for a taxpayer for the taxable year and the secondary production (to which gross income from the property is attributable before January 1, 1984) of a member of the group will reduce the other members' share of the group's depletable quantity.

(2) *Aggregation of business entities under common control.* If 50 percent or more of the beneficial interest in any two or more entities (*i.e.*, corporations, trusts, or estates) is owned by the same or related persons (taking into account only each person who owns at least 5 percent of the beneficial interest in an entity and with respect to such person his or her entire interest) as defined in paragraph (m)(2) of § 1.613A-7, the tentative quantity determined under the table in section 613A(c)(3)(B) (as in effect prior to the Revenue

Reg. § 1.613A-3(h)(2)

Reconciliation Act of 1990) for a taxpayer for the taxable year shall be allocated among all such entities in proportion to their respective production. This paragraph (h)(2) shall not apply to component members of a controlled group of corporations (as defined in § 1.613A-7(1)). For purposes of determining ownership interest, an interest owned by or for a corporation, partnership, trust, or estate shall be considered as owned directly both by itself and proportionately by its shareholders, partners, or beneficiaries, as the case may be.

(3) *Allocation among members of the same family.* In the case of individuals who are members of the same family, the tentative quantity determined under the table in section 613A(c)(3)(B) (as in effect prior to the Revenue Reconciliation Act of 1990) for a taxpayer for the taxable year shall be allocated among such individuals in proportion to the respective production of barrels of domestic crude oil (and the equivalent in barrels to the cubic feet of natural gas determined under paragraph (h)(4)(ii) of this section) during the period in question by such individuals.

(4) *Special rules.* For purposes of section 613A(c)(8) and this section—

(i) The family of an individual includes only his spouse and minor children, and

(ii) Each 6,000 cubic feet of domestic natural gas shall be treated as 1 barrel of domestic crude oil.

(5) *Examples.* The application of this paragraph may be illustrated by the following examples:

Example 1. A owns 50 percent of the stock of Corporation M and 50 percent of the stock of Corporation N. Both corporations are calendar year taxpayers. For 1975 Corporation M's production of domestic crude oil was 8,000,000 barrels (365,000 of which was secondary production) and Corporation N's was 2,000,000 barrels (all of which was primary production). The tentative quantity (2,000 barrels per day) determined under the table in section 613A(c)(3)(B) (as in effect prior to the Revenue Reconciliation Act of 1990) must be allocated between the two corporations in proportion to their respective barrels of production of domestic crude oil during the taxable year. Corporation M's allocable share of the tentative quantity is 1,600 barrels:

$$\left[2{,}000 \left(\frac{8{,}000{,}000}{10{,}000{,}000} \right) \right]$$

and Corporation N's allocable share is 400 barrels:

$$\left[2{,}000 \left(\frac{2{,}000{,}000}{10{,}000{,}000} \right) \right]$$

With respect to M's primary production, M's depletable oil quantity is 600 barrels (1,600 barrels − 1,000 barrels [365,000 secondary production ÷ 365 days]). N's depletable oil quantity, unaffected by M's secondary production, is 400 barrels.

Example 2. Assume the same facts as in Example 1 except that Corporation M is a retailer and Corporation N is not selling its oil through Corporation M. Because Corporation M is a retailer, no portion of the tentative quantity is allocated to Corporation M. Accordingly, Corporation N's depletable oil quantity is the entire 2,000 barrels per day because section 613A(c), which contains the allocation requirements, is inapplicable to retailers.

Example 3. Corporations O and P are members of a controlled group and are treated as one taxpayer as provided in paragraph (h)(1) of this section. Corporation O owns oil properties A and B. Property A had primary production for 1975 of 800,000 barrels of oil. Property B had secondary production for 1975 of 365,000 barrels of oil. Corporation P owns oil property C which had primary production of 660,000 barrels for 1975. The allowable percentage depletion with respect to property B's secondary production was $360x. The controlled group's average daily production was 4,000 barrels [(800,000 + 660,000) ÷ 365]. The controlled group's depletable oil quantity was 1,000 barrels [2,000 tentative quantity − 1,000 average daily secondary production (365,000 ÷ 365)]. The allowable percentage depletion pursuant to section 613(a)(computed as if section 613 applied to all of the production at the rate specified in section 613A(c)(5), as in effect prior to the Revenue Reconciliation Act of 1990) was $800x with respect to production from property A and $660x with respect to production from property C. Corporation O's allowable depletion pursuant to section 613A(c) with respect to property B's secondary production (for which depletion is allowable before primary production) for 1975 was $360x. Corporation O's allowable depletion pursu-

Reg. § 1.613A-3(h)(3)

ant to section 613A(c) with respect to property A was $200x:

$$\left[\$800x \text{ depletion} \left(\frac{1{,}000 \text{ depletable oil quantity}}{4{,}000 \text{ average daily production}}\right)\right]$$

Therefore, Corporation O's allowable depletion pursuant to section 613A(c) was $560x ($360x relating to property B plus $200x relating to property A). Corporation P's allowable depletion pursuant to section 613A(c) with respect to property C was $165x:

$$\left[\$660x \text{ depletion} \left(\frac{1{,}000 \text{ depletable oil quantity}}{4{,}000 \text{ average daily production}}\right)\right]$$

(i) *Transfer of oil or gas property.*

(1) *General rule*—(i) *In general.* Except as provided in paragraph (i)(2) of this section, in the case of a transfer (as defined in paragraph (n) of § 1.613A-7) of an interest in any proven oil or gas property (as defined in paragraph (p) of § 1.613A-7), paragraph (a)(1) of this section shall not apply to a transferee (as defined in paragraph (o) of § 1.613A-7) with respect to production of crude oil or natural gas attributable to such interest, and such production shall not be taken into account for any computation by the transferee under this section.

(ii) *Examples.* The provisions of this subparagraph may be illustrated by the following examples:

Example 1. On January 1, 1975, Individual A transfers proven oil properties to Corporation M in an exchange to which section 351 applies for shares of its stock. Since there is no allocation requirement pursuant to section 613A(c)(8) between A (the transferor) and Corporation M (the transferee), the transfer of the proven properties by A is a transfer for purposes of section 613A(c)(9)(as in effect prior to the Revenue Reconciliation Act of 1990) and percentage depletion is not allowable to Corporation M with respect to such properties.

Example 2. On January 1, 1975, Corporation N sells proven oil property to Corporation O, its wholly-owned subsidiary. Because the transfer was made between corporations which are members of the same controlled group of corporations, Corporation O is entitled to percentage depletion with respect to production from the property so long as the tentative oil quantity is allocated between the two corporations. If Corporation N were a retailer, the tentative oil quantity would not be required to be allocated between the two corporations (see example (2) of § 1.613A-3(h)(5)), and Corporation O would not be entitled to percentage depletion on the production from the property.

Example 3. B, owner of a proven oil property, died on January 1, 1975. Pursuant to the provisions of B's will, B's estate transferred the oil property on April 1, 1975, into a trust. On July 1, 1976, pursuant to a requirement in B's will, the trustee distributed the oil property to C. The transfer of the oil property by the estate to the trust and the later distribution of the property by the trust to C are transfers at death. Therefore, the trust was entitled to compute percentage depletion with respect to the production from the oil property when the property was owned by the trust and C is entitled to percentage depletion with respect to production from the oil property after the trust distributes the property to C.

Example 4. On January 1, 1975, property which produces oil resulting from secondary processes was transferred to D. The exemption under section 613A(c) applies to D because section 613A(c)(9)(relating to transfers of oil or gas property), as in effect in 1975, does not apply with respect to secondary production. In addition, even if at the time of the transfer the production from the property was primary and D applied secondary processes to the property transferred and obtained secondary production, D would be entitled to percentage depletion with respect to the secondary production.

Example 5. On July 1, 1975, E and F entered into a contract whereby F is given the privilege of drilling a well on E's unproven property, and if F does so F is to own the entire working interest in the property until F has recovered all the costs of drilling, equipping, and operating the well. Thereafter, 50 percent of the working interest would revert to E. In accordance with the contract, 50 percent of the working interest reverted to E on July 1, 1976. F is entitled to percentage depletion because the transfer of the working interest to F occurred when the property was unproven on July 1, 1975, which is the date of the contract establishing F's right to the working interest. E is entitled to percentage depletion with respect to this working interest since the reversion of such interest with respect to which E was eligible for percentage depletion is not a transfer. However, if on the date of the contract E's property was proven (although not proven when E acquired the property), F would not be entitled to claim percentage depletion with respect to any of

Reg. § 1.613A-3(i)(1)

the working interest income. Nonetheless, E would still be entitled to percentage depletion with respect to E's working interest since the reversion of the interest is not a transfer.

Example 6. On January 1, 1975, G subleased an oil property to H, retaining a 1/8 royalty interest with the option to convert G's royalty into a 50 percent working interest. On July 1, 1975, the property was proven and on July 1, 1976, G exercised G's option. G is entitled to claim percentage depletion with respect to G's working interest since the conversion of the royalty interest which is eligible for percentage depletion pursuant to section 613A(c) into an interest which constituted part of an interest previously owned by G is not a transfer pursuant to § 1.613A-7(n)(8).

Example 7. I and J (both of whom are minors) are beneficiaries of a trust which owned a proven oil property. The oil property was transferred to the trust on January 1, 1975, by the father of I and J. For 1975, the trustee allocated all the income from the oil property to I. For 1976, the trustee allocated all the income from such property to J. On January 1, 1977, the trustee distributed the property to I and J as equal tenants in common. Since I, J, and their father are members of the same family within the meaning of section 613A(c)(8)(C), the transfer of the property to the trust by the father, the shifting of income between I and J, and the distribution of the oil property by the trust to I and J are not transfers for purposes of section 613A(c)(9)(as in effect prior to the Revenue Reconciliation Act of 1990). However, the distribution of the oil property will constitute a transfer to each distributee on the date on which the distributee reaches majority under state law.

Example 8. In 1975, K transferred a proven oil property productive at 5,000 feet to L. Subsequent to the transfer, L drilled new wells on the property finding another reservoir at 10,000 feet. The two zones were combined under section 614 as a single property. L is not entitled to percentage depletion on the gross income attributable to the production from the productive zone at 5,000 feet, but is entitled to percentage depletion on the gross income attributable to the production from the productive zone at 10,000 feet because that zone was not part of the proven property until the date of development expenses by L, which is after the date of the transfer. Accordingly, L's maximum allowable percentage depletion deduction for 1975 would be zero percent of gross income from the property with respect to the production from 5,000 feet, plus 22 percent of gross income from the property with respect to the production from 10,000 feet. This maximum deduction would be subject to the limitation provided for in section 613(a), *i.e.*, 50 percent of "taxable income from the property (computed without allowance for depletion)," such taxable income being the overall taxable income resulting from the sale of production from both zones, and would also be subject to the limitations provided in section 613A. The production from the productive zone at 5,000 feet is not taken into account in determining K's depletable oil quantity for the year.

Example 9. On July 1, 1975, M transferred an oil property with a fair market value of $100x to N. On February 1, 1976, N commenced production of oil from the property. The fair market value of the property on February 1, 1976, as reduced by actual costs incurred by N for equipment and intangible drilling and development costs, was $300x. Because the value of the property on transfer was not 50 percent or more of the value on February 1, 1976, the property transferred to N was not a proven property (see § 1.613A-7(p)). However, if there had been only marginal production from the property so that the fair market value of the property on February 1, 1976, was $40x rather than $300x, the property transferred to N would have been a proven property provided the other requirements of a proven property were met.

Example 10. O is the owner of a remainder interest in a trust created January 1, 1970. On that date, the trust held oil and gas properties. On January 1, 1976, O's interest for the first time entitled O to the trust's income from oil and gas production from the properties. The reversion of the remainder interest to O is not a transfer (see § 1.613A-7(n)(7)). Accordingly, the transfer of the interest in oil and gas property to O is deemed to have occurred on January 1, 1970, the date O's interest was created.

Example 11. On January 1, 1976, P, Q, and R entered into a partnership for the acquisition of oil and gas leases. It was agreed that the sharing of income will be divided equally among P, Q, and R. However, it was further agreed that with respect to the first production obtained from each property acquired P will receive 80 percent thereof and Q and R each will receive 10 percent thereof until $100x has been received by P. Assume these allocations have substantial economic effect under section 704 of the Code and the regulations thereunder. On February 1, 1976, Partnership PQR acquired an unproven property and production therefrom was shared pursuant to the partnership agreement. P is entitled to percentage depletion with respect to the production allocated to him since the transfer of right to the production is deemed to have been made on the date the partnership agreement became applicable to the specific property, at which time the property was unproven. See § 1.613A-7(n) for rules relating to the definition of transfer. Similarly, when $100x has been obtained and Q and R each commence receiving 33⅓ percent of the revenue, Q and R are entitled to percentage depletion with respect to their entire interests. However, if the property had been proven when acquired by the partnership, P, Q, and R would not be entitled to claim any percentage depletion with respect to production from the property.

Example 12. On December 30, 1960, S placed producing oil property in trust for the benefit of S's nephew, T, and executed a trust agreement which required the trustee of the trust to transfer the oil property to T on January 1, 1975. The trustee's transfer of the oil property to T on January 1, 1975, is deemed to have occurred on December 30, 1960 (see § 1.613A-7(n)). Since the transfer is deemed to have occurred before January 1, 1975, section 613A(c) applies with respect to the production from the oil property. Moreover, if the trustee was not required to transfer the oil property on a specific date but was given discretion to select the date of transfer, the transfer of such property would still be deemed to have occurred on December 30, 1960. However, the result would be different if the trust agreement had provided that the trustee, at the trustee's discretion, may transfer the oil property to T on January 1, 1975, but is not under any obligation to transfer the property to T on January 1, 1975, or on any other date. Since the transfer was discretionary, the date of the actual transfer governs.

Example 13. On January 1, 1974, U acquired an oil property. On February 1, 1974, U granted V an option to purchase the oil property. V exercised V's option on March 2, 1975, and subsequently the oil property was conveyed to V. The date of the transfer was March 2, 1975, the day V exercised V's option (on which date both parties were bound).

Example 14. On July 1, 1974, W executed a deed conveying oil and gas property to X. W delivered the deed to X on January 1, 1975. Under state law, the mere execution of the deed without delivery did not give X any rights in the property. Title to the oil property passed to X on the date of delivery. Therefore, the date of transfer was January 1, 1975.

Example 15. Y, owner of a proven oil property, transferred Y's interest therein on July 25, 1975, to a revocable trust of which Y is treated as the owner under section 676. Y is not deemed a transferee and section 613A(c) applies to Y because immediately preceding the transfer Y was entitled to percentage depletion on the production from the property.

Example 16. On January 1, 1975, a proven oil property was transferred to Z; therefore, section 613A(c)(1) did not apply with respect to the production from such property. After Z's death, neither Z's estate nor its beneficiaries are entitled to percentage depletion with respect to the decedent's oil property since Z was a transferee of proven property.

Example 17. Partnership ABC, owner of proven oil and gas properties, admitted D as a partner in 1975 in consideration of cash. The shares of Partners A, B, and C of the partnership income were proportionately reduced so that D had a 25 percent interest in the income. D is not entitled to percentage depletion with respect to D's share of partnership oil and gas income because D is a transferee for purposes of section 613A(c)(9) (as in effect prior to the Revenue Reconciliation Act of 1990). See § 1.613A-7(n).

Example 18. On January 1, 1975, E and F formed Partnership EF to which E contributed proven oil property. For 1975, pursuant to the partnership agreement 70 percent of the mineral income from the property was allocated to E and 30 percent of the mineral income from the property was allocated F. F is not entitled to percentage depletion with respect to production from the property because F is a transferee of an interest in proven property. However, E is not a transferee of an interest in proven property because E was entitled to percentage depletion on the oil produced with respect to the property immediately before the transfer. Therefore, E is entitled to percentage depletion with respect to the income allocated to E. However, if in 1976 the partnership agreement were revised so that E's interest in the income was increased by 10 percent, E would not be entitled to percentage depletion with respect to the additional 10 percent interest because E is a transferee with respect thereto.

Example 19. G is the owner of a ⅓ interest in a partnership owning a proven oil property, and as such is entitled to ⅓ of the income from the property. G received a distribution on July 1, 1975, from the partnership of a ⅓ interest in the proven oil property. Although the transfer of such interest is a transfer for purposes of section 613A(c)(9) (as in effect prior to the Revenue Reconciliation Act of 1990), G is still entitled to percentage depletion with respect to the ⅓ interest in the oil production from the property since G was entitled to percentage depletion on such pro-

Reg. § 1.613A-3(i)(1)

duction with respect to such property immediately before the transfer. If the entire property were distributed to G, G's percentage depletion allowance would still be based on only 1/3 of the oil produced.

Example 20. H and I contributed property X and property Y respectively to Partnership HI. The partnership agreement provides that all the gross income from property X is to be allocated to H and all the gross income from property Y is to be allocated to I. Assume these allocations have substantial economic effect under section 704 of the Code and the regulations thereunder. For 1975 H and I each received 100x gross income. Although the contributions of the properties by H and I are transfers for purposes of section 613A(c)(9) (as in effect prior to the Revenue Reconciliation Act of 1990), both H and I are entitled to percentage depletion with respect to the $100x income received since each was entitled to a percentage depletion allowance with respect to the property contributed immediately before the transfer. However, if no special allocation of income were made but H and I are to share equally in the income from both properties, each would be entitled to a depletion allowance based on only one-half of the production with respect to the property he had contributed. If property X produces $100x of gross income from the property and property Y produces $200x of gross income from the property, H would be entitled to percentage depletion but only with respect to $50x (50 percent of $100x) of gross income from the property and I would be entitled to percentage depletion with respect to $100x (50 percent of $200x) of gross income from the property.

(2) *Transfers after October 11, 1990*—(i) *General rule.* Section 613A(c)(9) and (10), as in effect prior to the Revenue Reconciliation Act of 1990 (relating to prohibition of percentage depletion on transferred proven properties) has been repealed effective for transfers after October 11, 1990. Accordingly, a transferee of a proven oil or gas property transferred after October 11, 1990 is permitted to claim percentage depletion with respect to production from the property. For purposes of transfers of property occurring before October 12, 1990 under section 613A(c)(10), prior to its repeal, the disposition of stock after October 11, 1990 by a transferor will not result in a reduction in the depletable quantity of the transferee corporation under section 613A(c)(10)(F).

(ii) *Transfer.* The term "transfer" has the same meaning as under § 1.613A-7(n).

(iii) *Transferee.* A person shall not be treated as a transferee with respect to a transferred property to the extent that such person held an interest in the property but was not entitled to a percentage depletion allowance on mineral produced with respect to the property immediately before the transfer. Thus, for example, if a taxpayer who is not entitled to claim percentage depletion on a proven property transfers the property to a partnership for an interest in the partnership, the taxpayer is not a transferee with respect to the property in the hands of the partnership.

(iv) *Effective date.* The provisions of paragraph (i)(2) of § 1.613A-3 are effective for transfers occurring after May 13, 1991. However, a taxpayer may elect to apply these provisions to transfers occurring after October 11, 1990 and on or before May 13, 1991.

(v) *Examples.* The examples below illustrate the provisions of this subparagraph. The examples ignore the application of any restriction on percentage depletion other than the proven property transfer rule.

Example 1. On December 31, 1991, A transfers a proven oil property to B. B may claim percentage depletion with respect to production from the property regardless of whether production from the property was eligible for percentage depletion in A's hands (even if A were a retailer or refiner of oil or gas).

Example 2. On October 10, 1990, A transfers a proven oil property to B. B may not claim percentage depletion with respect to production from the property.

Example 3. On January 1, 1990, C purchases a proven oil property. Because C is a transferee of a proven property, production from the property is not eligible for percentage depletion in C's hands. On December 31, 1991, C contributes the property to Corporation M, an S corporation in which C owns 100 percent of the stock. The contribution of the property is a transfer, but C is not a transferee with respect to the property in the hands of the corporation. Accordingly, C may not claim percentage depletion with respect to production from the property. However, if prior to the contribution C had been entitled to claim percentage depletion with respect to production from the property, C would be entitled to claim percentage depletion with respect to production from the property after the contribution.

Example 4. On December 31, 1991, C contributes a proven oil property (with respect to which C is not entitled to claim percentage depletion) to Corporation N, an S corporation in which C owns 30 percent and D owns 70 percent of the stock. The contribution of the property is a transfer, but C is not a transferee with respect to the

Reg. § 1.613A-3(i)(2)

property in the hands of the corporation. Accordingly, C may not claim percentage depletion with respect to C's share of the production from the property. D is a transferee with respect to the property in the hands of Corporation N, and may claim percentage depletion with respect to D's share of production from the property.

Example 5. On December 31, 1991, D transfers a proven oil property (with respect to which D is not entitled to claim percentage depletion) to DE, an equal partnership between D and E. E is a transferee with respect to the property and may claim percentage depletion with respect to production from the property allocated to D under the DE partnership agreement. D is not a transferee with respect to the property, and may not claim percentage depletion with respect to production from the property allocated to E under the DE partnership agreement. However, if D had been entitled to claim percentage depletion with respect to production from the property, then D would be entitled to claim percentage depletion with respect to production from the property in the hands of DE.

Example 6. On January 1, 1990, Corporation P contributes a proven property to Corporation O, its wholly owned subsidiary. Under § 1.613A-7(n)(4), the contribution is not treated as a transfer, but only for so long as the tentative quantity is required under section 613A(c)(8) to be allocated between P and O. On December 31, 1991, P sells 90% of the O stock to an unrelated person; accordingly, the tentative quantity is no longer required under section 613A(c)(8) to be allocated between P and O. After the sale of O stock, production from the property in O's hands is eligible for percentage depletion because a transfer of a proven property is deemed to occur upon the transfer of the stock.

Example 7. On October 10, 1990, G transfers a proven oil property to his minor son, H. G had been entitled to claim percentage depletion with respect to production from the property. Under § 1.613A-7(n)(5), H is permitted to claim percentage depletion for so long as G and H are related persons under section 613A(c)(8)(C). On December 31, 1991, H reaches majority and is no longer related to G under section 613A(c)(8)(C). H is entitled to continue to claim percentage depletion on production from the property because the property is treated as being transferred to H on December 31, 1991.

Example 8. On December 31, 1991, I sells a proven property to J, her husband. I had not been entitled to claim percentage depletion with respect to production from the property. Under § 1.613A-7(n)(5), the sale is not a transfer because it is made between persons related under section 613A(c)(8). Accordingly, J may not claim percentage depletion with respect to production from the property. If, however, I had been entitled to claim percentage depletion with respect to production from the property, J would be entitled to claim percentage depletion with respect to production from the property.

Example 9. On December 31, 1991, L inherits a proven property from K. K had not been entitled to claim percentage depletion with respect to production from the property. Under § 1.613A-7(n)(1), the inheritance is not a transfer. Accordingly, L may not claim percentage depletion with respect to production from the property. If, however, K had been entitled to claim percentage depletion with respect to production from the property, L would be entitled to claim percentage depletion with respect to production from the property.

Example 10. On December 31, 1991, Corporation R, a calendar year taxpayer, made an S election effective for the taxable year beginning January 1, 1992 and succeeding taxable years. Since Corporation R is deemed to have transferred its oil and gas properties on January 1, 1992, the shareholders of Corporation R are eligible to claim percentage depletion with respect to the production from the properties.

Example 11. Assume the same facts as in *Example 10* except that Corporation R makes the S election on December 31, 1989, effective for the taxable year beginning January 1, 1990 and succeeding taxable years. Since Corporation R is deemed to have transferred its oil and gas properties on January 1, 1990, the shareholders of Corporation R are not eligible to claim percentage depletion with respect to the production from the properties.

(j) *Percentage depletion with respect to bonuses and advanced royalties*—(1) *Amounts received or accrued after August 16, 1986.* In computing the percentage depletion allowance pursuant to section 613A(c) with respect to amounts received or accrued after August 16, 1986, there shall not be taken into account any advance royalty (to the extent that actual production during the taxable year is insufficient to earn such royalty), lease bonus, or other amount payable without regard to production, even though the amount may be taken into account for purposes of sections 61 and 612 (relating to definitions of gross income and cost depletion, respectively).

(2) *Amounts received or accrued before August 17, 1986.* (i) A lease bonus or advanced royalty received or accrued before August 17, 1986, with respect to oil or gas property shall be

Reg. § 1.613A-3(j)(2)

taken into account for purposes of percentage depletion in the taxable year such payment is includible in income. Percentage depletion shall be determined according to the depletion rate and depletable oil and natural gas limitations of section 613A(c)(1) and § 1.613A-3(a) applicable on the date of such inclusion. The payee of the bonus or advanced royalty shall apply the depletable oil and natural gas quantity limitations by attributing a specific number of barrels of oil or cubic feet of natural gas to the lease bonus or advanced royalty. The determination of the number of barrels of oil or cubic feet of natural gas shall be based on the average price of oil or gas produced from the property during the taxable year. If oil or gas is not produced from the property during that year, or if the oil or gas is not sold before conversion or transportation from the premises, the number of barrels of oil or cubic feet of gas shall be based on a price (as of the date of the bonus or advanced royalty) determined under the constructive pricing principles applicable under section 613(a), generally the representative market or field price. In the case where no oil or gas has been produced in such year, the constructive price applicable to the type of production expected to be produced from the property shall apply. However, if the first actual production from the property in a later year is different from the type of production upon which the conversion of the bonus or advanced royalty into barrels of oil or cubic feet of gas was based and the period of limitations on assessment has not expired (see section 6501) for the year in which the lease bonus or advanced royalty is includible in income, the taxpayer should promptly file an amended return, if necessary. In the amended return the conversion shall be recomputed taking into account the pricing applicable to the actual production. For purposes of paragraph (f) of § 1.613A-7, the number of barrels of oil or cubic feet of natural gas attributed to a lease bonus or advanced royalty is deemed to have been extracted on the date the bonus or advanced royalty is includible in the payee's income.

(ii) For purposes of applying the depletable oil and natural gas quantity limitations in taxable years after the year in which the advanced royalty payment is included in income, the payee of an advanced royalty which is recouped out of future production shall not include production which recoups the advanced royalty in such later years. The payor of a bonus or advanced royalty that is not recouped from future production may reduce the production to be taken into account for purposes of applying the depletable quantity limitations in each year in which the payor's gross income from the property is adjusted under § 1.613-2(c)(5)(ii) to reflect the bonus paid by an amount determined by dividing the portion of the bonus required to be excluded from the payor's gross income from the property by the price of oil or gas applicable to the payee for converting the bonus into barrels of oil or cubic feet of gas.

(iii) See § 1.612-3(a)(2) and (b)(2) for rules relating to the requirement that certain depletion deductions allowed with respect to lease bonuses and advanced royalties be restored to income.

(k) *Special rules for fiscal year taxpayers.* In applying this section to a taxable year which is not a calendar year, each portion of such taxable year which occurs during a single calendar year shall be treated as if it were a short taxable year.

(l) *Information furnished by partnerships, trusts, estates, and operators.* Each partnership, trust, or estate producing domestic crude oil or natural gas, and each operator of a well from which domestic crude oil or natural gas was produced, shall provide each partner, beneficiary, or person holding a nonoperating interest, as the case may be, with all information in its possession necessary to determine the amount of his depletion deduction allowable with respect to such crude oil or natural gas. For example, for each property a partnership is required to provide each partner with partnership information relating to the partner's allocable share of gross income from the property, the partner's allocable share of operating expenses, the partner's allocable share of depreciation, the partner's share of allocated overhead, the partner's share of estimated reserves, the partner's share of production in barrels or cubic feet for the taxable year, the partner's original share of the partnership adjusted basis of properties producing domestic crude oil or domestic natural gas, the partner's allocable share of any adjustments made to the basis of such properties by the partnership, and the percentage by which existing partners must reduce their bases in a partnership oil or gas property upon entry of a partner by contribution. In addition, upon the disposition of an oil or gas property by the partnership, the partnership shall inform each partner of his allocable portion of the amount realized from the sale of the property. [Reg. § 1.613A-3.]

☐ [T.D. 8348, 5-10-91. Amended by T.D. 8437, 9-22-92.]

[Reg. § 1.613A-4]

§ 1.613A-4. **Limitations on application of § 1.613A-3 exemption.**—(a) *Limitation based on taxable income.*

(1) The aggregate amount of a taxpayer's deductions allowed pursuant to section 613A(c)

for the taxable year shall not exceed 65 percent of the taxpayer's taxable income (reduced in the case of an individual by the zero bracket amount for taxable years beginning after December 31, 1976, and before January 1, 1987) for the year, adjusted to eliminate the effects of:

(i) Any depletion with respect to an oil or gas property (other than a gas property with respect to which the depletion allowance for all production is determined pursuant to section 613A(b)) for which percentage depletion would exceed cost depletion in the absence of the depletable quantity limitations contained in section 613A(c)(1) and (6) (as in effect prior to the Revenue Reconciliation Act of 1990) or the taxable income limitation contained in section 613A(d)(1);

(ii) Any net operating loss carryback to the taxable year under section 172;

(iii) Any capital loss carryback to the taxable year under section 1212; and

(iv) In the case of a trust, any distributions to its beneficiaries, except in the case of any trust where any beneficiary of such trust is a member of the family (as defined in section 267(c)(4)) of a settlor who created inter vivos and testamentary trusts for members of the family and such settlor died within the last 6 days of the 5th month in 1970, and the law in the jurisdiction in which such trust was created requires all or a portion of the gross or net proceeds of any royalty or other interest in oil, gas, or other mineral representing any percentage depletion allowance to be allocated to the principal of the trust.

The amount disallowed (as defined in paragraph (q) of § 1.613A-7) shall be carried over to the succeeding year and treated as an amount allowable as a deduction pursuant to section 613A(c) for such succeeding year, subject to the 65-percent limitation of section 613A(d)(1). For rules relating to corporations filing a consolidated return, see the regulations under section 1502. With respect to fiscal year taxpayers, except as provided in § 1.613A-1 for taxable years beginning before January 1, 1975, and ending after that date, the limitation shall be calculated on the entire fiscal year and not applied with respect to each short period included in a fiscal year. For purposes of basis adjustments and determining whether cost depletion exceeds percentage depletion with respect to the production from a property, any amount disallowed as a deduction after the application of this paragraph shall be allocated to the respective properties from which the oil or gas was produced in proportion to the percentage depletion otherwise allowable to such properties pursuant to section 613A(c). Accordingly, the maximum amount which may be allowable as a deduction pursuant to section 613A(c) after application of this paragraph (65 percent × adjusted taxable income) shall be allocated to properties for which percentage depletion pursuant to section 613A(c) would be allowed in the absence of the limitation contained in section 613A(d)(1) by application of the same proportion. However, once it is determined that after application of this paragraph cost depletion exceeds percentage depletion with respect to a property, the maximum amount determined under the preceding sentence shall be reallocated among the remaining properties, and the portion of the amount disallowed which is allocable to such property shall be the amount by which percentage depletion pursuant to section 613A(c) before application of this paragraph exceeds cost depletion. See *Example 1* of paragraph (a)(2) of this section. If the taxpayer becomes entitled to the deduction in a later year (*i.e.*, because the disallowed depletion does not exceed 65 percent of the taxpayer's taxable income for that year after taking account of any percentage depletion deduction otherwise allowable for that year), then the basis of the taxpayer's properties must be adjusted downward (but not below zero) by the amount of the deduction in proportion to the portion of the amount disallowed to the respective properties in the year of the disallowance. However, if the property in question was disposed of by the taxpayer prior to the beginning of such later year, the amount of the deduction in such later year shall be reduced by the difference between the taxpayer's adjusted basis in the property at the time it is disposed of and the adjusted basis which the taxpayer would have had in the property in the absence of the 65-percent limitation.

(2) The application of this paragraph may be illustrated by the following examples:

Example 1. A owns producing oil properties M, N, and O. With respect to property M, the depletion allowable pursuant to section 613A(c) for 1975 without regard to section 613A(d)(1) was $60x (cost depletion would have been $40x). With respect to property N, the depletion allowable pursuant to section 613A(c) for 1975 without regard to section 613A(d)(1) was $90x (cost depletion would have been zero). With respect to property O, the depletion pursuant to section 613A(c) for 1975 without regard to section 613A(d)(1) was $50x (cost depletion would have been $10x). A's taxable income (as adjusted under § 1.613A-4(a)(1)) for 1975 was $100x; accordingly, A's percentage depletion pursuant to section 613A(c) for 1975 must be reduced from $200x to $65x (65 percent × $100x taxable income). Of that amount, $19.5x:

Reg. § 1.613A-4(a)(2)

$$\left[65x \text{ dollars} \left(\frac{\$60x}{\$60x + \$90x + \$50x}\right)\right] \text{ is tentatively allocated}$$

to property M, $29.25x:

$$\left[65x \text{ dollars} \left(\frac{\$90x}{\$90x + \$60x + \$50x}\right)\right] \text{ is tentatively allocated}$$

to property N, and $16.25x:

$$\left[65x \text{ dollars} \left(\frac{\$50x}{\$50x + \$90x + \$60x}\right)\right] \text{ is tentatively allocated}$$

to property O. Since cost depletion of $40x with respect to property M exceeded the percentage depletion of $19.5x allowable on such property, A claimed the cost depletion. Accordingly, the only percentage depletion deduction allowable to A pursuant to section 613A(c) for 1975 is with respect to properties N and O. Therefore, the $65x ceiling applies to the percentage depletion allowable on properties N and O. Of that amount, $41.79x:

$$\left[65x \text{ dollars} \left(\frac{\$90x}{\$90x + \$50x}\right)\right] \text{ is allocated to}$$

property N, and $23.21x:

$$\left[65x \text{ dollars} \left(\frac{\$50x}{\$50x + \$90x}\right)\right] \text{ is allocated}$$

to property O. Accordingly, A is allowed a total depletion deduction of $105x ($40x cost depletion on property M + $41.79x percentage depletion on property N + $23.21x percentage depletion on property O). The amount disallowed to A under section 613A(d)(1) is $95x ($200x aggregate depletion allowable before application of section 613A(d)(1) − $105x [$40x cost depletion allowable on property M + $41.79x percentage depletion allowable on property N after application of section 613A(d)(1) + $23.21x depletion allowable on property O after application of section 613A(d)(1)]). For purposes of basis adjustments, $20x ($60x percentage depletion before limitation − $40x cost depletion allowed) of the amount disallowed is allocated to property M. The balance of the amount disallowed of $75x is allocated $48.21x:

$$\left[75x \text{ dollars} \left(\frac{\$90x}{\$90x + \$50x}\right)\right] \text{ to property N, and}$$

$26.79x:

$$\left[75x \text{ dollars} \left(\frac{\$50x}{\$50x + \$90x}\right)\right] \text{ to property O.}$$

Example 2. The amount disallowed to B as a deduction under this paragraph is $50x for 1975 and $125x for 1976 (including the $50x carried over from 1975). B may carry forward the $125x as a deduction to 1977 and subsequent years.

Example 3. C is a fiscal year taxpayer whose fiscal year ended on May 31, 1975. For purposes of applying the 65 percent of taxable income limitation, the period beginning January 1, 1975, and ending May 31, 1975, is treated as a short taxable year. The depletion allowable pursuant to section 613A(c) without regard to section 613A(d)(1) for such short taxable year was $80x and A's taxable income (as adjusted under § 1.613A-4(a)(1)) during such short taxable year was $100x. Only $65x (65 percent × $100x adjusted taxable income) of the deduction pursuant to section 613A(c) was deductible for such portion of 1975, in addition to any percentage depletion allowable for June 1, 1974, through December 31, 1974. With respect to the taxable year commencing June 1, 1975, and ending May 31, 1976, the 65 percent limitation is applied to the taxable income for the entire taxable year.

Example 4. Under the trust law of State X, a trustee is required to allocate 22 percent of gross mineral income to the principal of a trust for purposes of maintaining a reserve for depletion and the depletion deduction is entirely allocated to the trustee. In 1975 the gross income of a trust in State X the only assets of which were oil properties was $1,000. The trust's allowable percentage depletion pursuant to section 613A(c) without regard to section 613A(d)(1) was $220. The trust incurred expenses of $150 for the taxable year and made distributions to beneficiaries (who are not described in the exception for family members set forth in paragraph (a)(1)(iv) of this

Reg. § 1.613A-4(a)(2)

section) of $630 ($1,000 gross income − $220 allocated to principal − $150 expenses). The trust's deduction for personal exemption under section 642(b) is $300. For purposes of applying the 65 percent limitation, the trust's taxable income was $550 ($1,000 gross income − $150 expenses − $300 exemption). The limitation under section 613A(d)(1) was $357.50 (65% × $550 taxable income). Accordingly, the trust's percentage depletion allowance was unaffected by the 65 percent limitation.

Example 5. In 1980 the gross income of the estate of D was $1,000. The only assets of the estate were oil properties. The estate's adjusted basis in the oil properties was $0. The estate's allowable percentage depletion pursuant to section 613A(c) without regard to section 613A(d)(1) was $220. The estate incurred expenses of $150 for the taxable year and made distributions to beneficiaries of $425. The distributions thus equaled one half of the net income of the estate (ignoring depletion). Under section 611(b)(4), the percentage depletion is apportioned equally between the estate and its beneficiary. The distribution amount of $425 is deductible under section 661(a) in computing the taxable income of the estate. For purposes of applying the 65 percent limitation to the percentage depletion apportioned to the estate, the estate's taxable income was $0 ($1,000 gross income − $150 expenses − $425 distribution − $600 exemption). The limitation under section 613A(d)(1) was therefore also $0 (65% × $0 taxable income). Accordingly, the $110 amount is disallowed to the estate for the taxable year but may be carried forward by the estate as a deduction to 1981 and subsequent years. The beneficiaries shall apply the 65 percent limitation to the $110 percentage depletion apportioned to them based on their respective taxable incomes.

Example 6. In 1975 E sold an oil property for which E's adjusted basis was $20x. The amount disallowed for 1975 to E under section 613A(d) was $10x. The amount of the carryover under that section to 1976 was $0 ($10x disallowed amount − $10x [$20x adjusted basis of property on sale − $10x adjusted basis which taxpayer would have had in the property in the absence of the 65-percent limitation]). However, if the adjusted basis of the property on disposition had been $0, the amount of the carryover to 1976 would have been $10x ($10x disallowed amount − $0 adjusted basis of property on sale).

Example 7. In 1975 F owned producing properties M, N, O, P, Q, and R. With respect to property M, the allowable cost depletion was $100x (the allowable percentage depletion pursuant to section 613A(c) without regard to the depletable quantity and taxable income limitations contained in section 613A(c)(1), (6) and (d)(1) would have been $90x). With respect to property N, the allowable percentage depletion pursuant to section 613A(c) before applying section 613A(d)(1) was $80x (cost depletion would have been $0). With respect to property O, the allowable cost depletion was $60x (the allowable percentage depletion pursuant to section 613A(c) would have been $70x, except that the application of section 613A(d)(1) reduced allowable percentage depletion to less than $60x). With respect to property P, the allowable percentage depletion pursuant to section 613A(b) was $55x (cost depletion would have been $40x). With respect to property Q, which produces both gas subject to section 613A(b)(1)(B) and oil subject to section 613A(c), the allowable percentage depletion was $45x (cost depletion would have been $40x). With respect to property R, the allowable cost depletion was $40x (the allowable percentage depletion pursuant to section 613A(c) would have been $50x, except that the application of section 613A(c)(7)(A) reduced allowable percentage depletion to less than $40x). Under paragraph (a)(1)(i) of this section, for purposes of applying the 65 percent limitation under section 613A(d)(1), F's taxable income must be reduced by the allowable depletion with respect to property M (for which cost depletion exceeded percentage depletion even in the absence of section 613A(c)(1), (6), and (d)) and property P (for which all depletion is determined pursuant to section 613A(b)), but shall not be reduced by the allowable depletion with respect to properties N, O, Q, and R.

(b) *Retailers excluded.* (1) Section 613A(c) and § 1.613A-3 shall not apply in the case of any taxpayer who is a retailer as defined in paragraph (r) of § 1.613A-7.

(2) The application of this paragraph may be illustrated by the following examples (those that involve sales through retail outlets assume, unless otherwise stated, that the $5,000,000 gross receipts requirement of section 613A(d)(2) is met):

Example 1. A, owner of producing oil and gas properties, also owns 5 percent in value of the stock of Corporation M, a retailer of oil and gas. None of A's production is sold through Corporation M. Since A may benefit from Corporation M's sales of oil and gas through A's ownership interest in Corporation M, A is considered to be selling oil or natural gas through Corporation M, a related person. Accordingly, the exemption under section 613A(c) does not apply to A, even though none of A's production is sold through Corporation M.

Reg. § 1.613A-4(b)(2)

Example 2. Assume the same facts as in *Example 1* except that A has gross receipts of $2 million from sales of oil for the taxable year from A's retail outlets and Corporation M has gross receipts of $4 million from sales of oil for the taxable year from its retail outlets. For purposes of the $5 million gross receipts requirement of section 613A(d)(2), A is treated as having gross receipts of $6 million. Accordingly, the exemption under section 613A(c) does not apply to A.

Example 3. Corporation N, a retailer of oil and gas, owns 5 percent in value of the stock of Corporation O, owner of producing oil and gas properties. None of Corporation O's production is sold through Corporation N. Since Corporation O has no direct or indirect ownership interest in Corporation N, and therefore does not benefit from Corporation N's sales of oil and gas, and since none of Corporation O's production is sold through Corporation N, the exemption under section 613A(c) applies to Corporation O.

Example 4. Corporation P, a producer of oil, owns 70 percent in value of the stock of Corporation Q. Corporation Q owns 30 percent in value of the stock of Corporation R. Corporation R owns 30 percent in value of the stock of Corporation S, a retailer of oil and gas. P indirectly owns 6.3 percent (70 percent × 30 percent × 30 percent) in value of the stock of Corporation S. Since P may benefit from Corporation S's sales of oil and gas through P's indirect ownership interest in Corporation S, P is not entitled to percentage depletion.

Example 5. B is the owner of certain oil and gas properties in Texas and is also the owner of a service station in Washington, D. C., which B leases to Corporation T. None of B's production is sold to Corporation T. The exemption under section 613A(c) applies to B. However, if sales of B's production were made to Corporation T and the gross receipts from such sales of B's production to Corporation T exceed 5 million dollars, the exemption under section 613A(c) would not apply to B because B is selling oil or natural gas to a person given authority to occupy a retail outlet leased by the taxpayer, B.

Example 6. C has a 1/8 royalty interest and Corporation U has a 7/8 working interest in an oil property. Corporation V, a retailer of oil, owns 5 percent in value of the stock of Corporation U. C has no interest in either corporation. All of the production from the property is sold through Corporation V, C receiving from Corporation U 1/8 of its receipts therefrom. The exemption under section 613A(c) does not apply to Corporation U because Corporation U is selling oil or natural gas through Corporation V, a related person that is a retailer. However, the exemption applies to C because C, as owner of a nonoperating mineral interest, is not treated as an operator of a retail outlet merely because C's oil or gas is sold on C's behalf through a retail outlet operated by an unrelated person.

Example 7. D owns and operates retail grocery stores where refined oil may be purchased. D also owns oil and gas producing properties. If the sales of refined oil at each store location constitute less than 5 percent of the gross receipts from all sales made at that store, D is not considered a retailer by reason of such sales.

Example 8. Lessee E sells natural gas to lessor F directly from a wellhead gathering pipeline system for F's local agricultural use, in transactions incidental to the acquisition of a natural gas lease. The sales of natural gas to F are not sales through a retail outlet.

Example 9. Corporation W produces natural gas, some of which it sells at retail. For purposes of determining whether Corporation W is a retailer selling gas through a retail outlet within the meaning of § 1.613A-7(r), the business office of Corporation W where a purchaser would normally contact the corporation with respect to its sales to the purchaser is considered the place at which those sales of natural gas are made.

Example 10. G, husband, is the sole owner and operator of a retail outlet which sells oil and gas. H, wife, owns producing oil and gas properties. G is not related to H for purposes of section 613A(d).

Example 11. I, husband, and J, wife, are community property owners of 10 percent in value of the stock of Corporation X which is a retailer of oil and gas. I and J are each treated as owning 5 percent of Corporation X. Therefore, neither I nor J qualify for the exemption under section 613A(c).

Example 12. Corporation Y, an electing small business corporation as defined in section 1371 (as in effect prior to the enactment of the Subchapter S Revision Act of 1982), owns producing oil and gas properties. K, a retailer of oil and gas, is a 50 percent interest shareholder of Corporation Y. None of Corporation Y's production is sold through K. Corporation Y is eligible for percentage depletion.

Example 13. Corporation Z, a producer of natural gas, makes bulk sales of natural gas to industrial users. For purposes of determining whether Corporation Z is a retailer under § 1.613A-7 (r), the bulk sales are disregarded.

Example 14. L, a calendar year taxpayer, is the owner of a producing oil property. On September 1, 1976, L purchased a chain of gasoline

Reg. § 1.613A-4(b)(2)

Deductions

See p. 20,601 for regulations not amended to reflect law changes

service stations. Therefore, L was a retailer of oil and gas for the last 122 days of 1976. L's gross income from the oil property for the taxable year was $150x and L's taxable income from the property was $30x. L is treated as a retailer with respect to $50x of gross income from the property ($150x × 122/366) and $10x of taxable income from the property ($30x × 122/366). Therefore, L is entitled to percentage depletion with respect to $100x of gross income from the property ($150x minus $50x). However, the allowable percentage depletion is limited by the 50 percent of taxable income from the property limitation to $10x (50 percent times $20x taxable income ($30x minus $10x)).

Example 15. Corporation M is a partner in Partnership MNO which is the owner of an operating interest in a producing oil property. Corporation P, a retailer of oil and gas, owns 5 percent in value of the stock of Corporation M. Partnership MNO sells its production to Corporation P. Corporation M is retailing oil through Corporation P, a related person, because its share of the oil is being sold on its behalf by the partnership through a retail outlet operated by a person related to Corporation M. Therefore, the exemption under section 613A(c) does not apply to Corporation M.

Example 16. AA and BB are beneficiaries of a trust which is a retailer of oil and gas. AA has an interest in the income of the trust for AA's lifetime which, actuarially determined, represents more than 5 percent of the beneficial interests in the trust. BB's interest in the trust, which entitles BB to 5 percent of the corpus of the trust 5 years after AA's death, represents less than 5 percent of the beneficial interests in the trust prior to AA's death and represents more than 5 percent after AA's death. The trust is a related person of AA but not BB while AA is alive. Accordingly, during AA's lifetime BB is not disqualified from the exemption provided by section 613A(c), but AA is.

Example 17. Assume the same facts as in Example 16, except that AA's interest in the income of the trust represents 4 percent of the beneficial interests in the trust. AA is disqualified from the exemption provided by section 613A(c) with respect to the income from the trust but not with respect to income from other sources.

(c) *Certain refiners excluded.* (1) Section 613A(c) and § 1.613A-3 shall not apply in the case of any taxpayer who is a refiner as defined in paragraph(s) of § 1.613A-7.

(2) The provisions of this paragraph may be illustrated by the following examples:

Example 1. Corporation M owns a refinery which has refinery runs in excess of 50,000 barrels on at least one day during the taxable year. Corporation M also owns a 5 percent interest in Corporation N, owner of producing oil and gas properties. None of Corporation N's production is sold to Corporation M. The exemption under section 613A(c) does not apply to Corporation N because Corporation M, a related person of Corporation N, engages in the refining of crude oil.

Example 2. A and B are equal partners in Partnership AB, which owns oil and gas producing properties. A owns a refinery which has refinery runs in excess of 50,000 barrels on at least one day during the taxable year and which buys all of Partnership AB's production. B has no ownership interest in any refinery. B is not a refiner. [Reg. § 1.613A-4.]

☐ [T.D. 8348, 5-10-91.]

[Reg. § 1.613A-5]

§ 1.613A-5. **Election under section 613A(c)(4).**—The election under section 613A(c)(4) is an annual election which the taxpayer may make by claiming percentage depletion deductions for the taxable year based upon such election. The election may be made, on an original or amended tax return or a claim for credit or refund, at any time prior to the expiration of the statutory period (including any extensions thereof) for the filing of a claim for credit or refund by the taxpayer. The election may be changed by the taxpayer by filing an amended return or a claim for credit or refund. The election allows the taxpayer to treat as his depletable natural gas quantity an amount equal to 6,000 cubic feet multiplied by the number of barrels of the taxpayer's depletable oil quantity to which the election applies. The election applies to secondary or tertiary production, as well as primary production, but in determining the taxpayer's depletable natural gas quantity with respect to secondary or tertiary production the taxpayer's depletable oil quantity shall be determined without regard to section 613A(c)(3)(A)(ii) with respect to production from secondary or tertiary processes. [Reg. § 1.613A-5.]

☐ [T.D. 7487, 5-12-77.]

[Reg. § 1.613A-6]

§ 1.613A-6. **Recordkeeping requirements.**—(a) *Principal value of property demonstrated.* In the case of a transfer (as defined in § 1.613A-7(n)) after December 31, 1974, of an interest in an oil or gas property (as defined in § 1.613A-7(p)), the transferee (as defined in section 1.613A-7(o)) shall keep records showing the terms of the transfer, any geological and geophysical data in the possession of the transferee or other exploratory data with respect to the property transferred, and any

Reg. § 1.613A-6(a)

other information which bears upon the question of whether at the time of the transfer the principal value of the property transferred had been demonstrated by prospecting, exploration, and discovery work.

(b) *Production from secondary or tertiary processes.* Every taxpayer who claims depletion with respect to oil or gas produced by secondary or tertiary processes (as defined in § 1.613A-7(k)) shall keep records of the secondary and tertiary processes applied and maintain records of the amount of production so resulting.

(c) *Retention of records.* The records required by this section shall be kept at all times available for inspection by authorized Internal Revenue officers or employees, and shall be retained so long as the contents thereof may become material in the administration of any Internal Revenue law. [Reg. § 1.613A-6.]

☐ [T.D. 7487, 5-12-77.]

[Reg. § 1.613A-7]

§ 1.613A-7. **Definitions.**—For purposes of section 613A and the regulations thereunder—

(a) *Domestic.* The term "domestic," as applied to oil and gas wells (or to production from such wells), refers to wells located in the United States or in a possession of the United States, as defined in section 638 and the regulations thereunder.

(b) *Natural gas.* The term "natural gas" means any product (other than crude oil as defined in paragraph (g) of this section) of an oil or gas well if a deduction for depletion is allowable under section 611 with respect to such product.

(c) *Regulated natural gas.* Natural gas is considered to be "regulated" only if all of the following requirements are met:

(1) The gas must be domestic gas produced and sold by the producer (whether for himself or on behalf of another person) before July 1, 1976,

(2) The price for which the gas is sold by the producer must not be adjusted to reflect to any extent the increase in liability of the seller for tax under chapter 1 of the Code by reason of the repeal of percentage depletion for gas,

(3) The sale of the gas must have been subject to the jurisdiction of the Federal Power Commission for regulatory purposes,

(4) An order or certificate of the Federal Power Commission must be in effect (or a proceeding to obtain such an order or certificate must have been instituted), and

(5) The price at which the gas is sold must be taken into account, directly or indirectly, in the issuance of the order or certificate by the Federal Power Commission. Price increases after February 1, 1975, are presumed to take increases in tax liabilities into account unless the taxpayer demonstrates to the contrary by clear and convincing evidence that the increases are wholly attributable to a purpose or purposes unrelated to the repeal of percentage depletion for gas (*e.g.*, where the record of the Federal Power Commission clearly establishes that the Commission did not take the repeal into account). Increases to reflect additional State and local real property or severance taxes, increases for additional operating costs (such as costs of secondary or tertiary processes), adjustments for inflation, increases for additional drilling and related costs, or increases to reflect changes in the quality of gas sold, are some examples of increases that are not attributable to the repeal of percentage depletion for gas. In the absence of a statement in writing by the Federal Power Commission that the price of the gas in question was not in fact regulated, the requirement of paragraph (c)(5) of this section is deemed to have been met in any case in which the Federal Power Commission issued an order or certificate approving the sale to an interstate pipeline company or, in a case in which it is established by the taxpayer that the Federal Power Commission has influenced the price of such gas, an order or certificate permitting the interstate transportation of such gas. In addition, an "emergency" sale of natural gas to an interstate pipeline, which, pursuant to the authority contained in 18 CFR 2.68, 2.70, 157.22, and 157.29, may be made without prior order approving the sale, is deemed to have met the requirements of paragraph (c)(3), (4), and (5) of this section. For purposes of meeting the requirements under this paragraph, it is not necessary that the total gas production from a property qualify as "regulated natural gas." The determination of whether mineral production is "regulated natural gas" shall be made with respect to each sale of the mineral or minerals produced.

(d) *Natural gas sold under a fixed contract.* The term "natural gas sold under a fixed contract" means domestic natural gas sold by the producer (whether for himself or on behalf of another person) under a contract, in effect on February 1, 1975, and at all times thereafter before such sale, under which the price for the gas during such period cannot be adjusted to reflect to any extent the increase in liabilities of the seller for tax under chapter 1 of the Code by reason of the repeal of percentage depletion for gas. The term may include gas sold under a fixed contract even though production sold under the contract had previously been treated as regulated natural gas. Price increases after February 1, 1975, are presumed to take increases in tax liabilities into account unless

Reg. § 1.613A-7(a)

the taxpayer demonstrates to the contrary by clear and convincing evidence. Paragraph (c) of this section provides examples of increases which do not take increases in tax liabilities into account. However, if an adjustment provided for in the contract permits the possible increase in federal income tax liability of the seller to be taken into account to any extent, the gas sold under the contract after such an increase becomes permissible is not gas sold under a fixed contract. If the adjustment provided for in the contract provides for an increase in the price of the contract to the highest price paid to a producer for natural gas in the area, or if the price may be renegotiated, then gas sold under the contract after such an increase becomes permissible is presumed not to be sold under a fixed contract unless the taxpayer demonstrates by clear and convincing evidence that the price increase in no event takes increases in tax liabilities into account. For purposes of meeting the requirements of this paragraph, it is not necessary that the total gas production from a property qualify as "natural gas sold under a fixed contract," for the determination of "natural gas sold under a fixed contract" is to be made with respect to each sale of each type of natural gas sold pursuant to each contract.

(e) *Qualified natural gas from geopressured brine.* The term "qualified natural gas from geopressured brine" means any natural gas which is determined in accordance with section 503 of the Natural Gas Policy Act of 1978 to be produced from geopressured brine and which is produced from any well the drilling of which began after September 30, 1978, and before January 1, 1984.

(f) *Average daily production.*

(1) The term "average daily production" means the taxpayer's aggregate production of domestic crude oil or natural gas, as the case may be, which is extracted after December 31, 1974, and to which gross income from the property is attributable during the taxable year divided by the number of days in such year. As used in the preceding sentence the term "taxpayer" includes a small business corporation as defined in section 1371 (as in effect prior to the enactment of the Subchapter S Revision Act of 1982) and the regulations thereunder. Notwithstanding the provisions of § 1.612-3 and except as provided in § 1.613A-3(j)(2), in computing the average daily production for a taxable year only oil or gas which has been actually produced by the close of such taxable year is taken into account. Average daily production does not include production resulting from secondary or tertiary processes to which gross income from the property is attributable before January 1, 1984.

(2) In the case of a fiscal-year taxpayer, paragraph (f)(1) of this section shall be applied separately to each short taxable year under section 613A(c)(11), as in effect prior to the Revenue Reconciliation Act of 1990.

(3) In the case of a taxpayer holding a partial interest in the production from any property (including an interest of a partner in property of a partnership or a net profits interest) such taxpayer's production shall be considered to be that amount of such production determined by multiplying the total production (which is produced after December 31, 1974, and to which gross income from the property is attributable during the taxable year) of the property by the taxpayer's percentage participation in the gross revenues from the property during the year. However, the portion of trust (or estate) production allocable to a beneficiary shall not exceed that amount of the trust's (or estate's) depletable oil quantity determined by multiplying such quantity by the beneficiary's percentage interest in the trust's (or estate's) gross income from the property.

(g) *Crude oil.* For purposes of section 613A and the regulations thereunder, the term "crude oil" means—

(1) A mixture of hydrocarbons which existed in the liquid phase in natural underground reservoirs and which remains liquid at atmospheric pressure after passing through surface separating facilities,

(2) Hydrocarbons which existed in the gaseous phase in natural underground reservoirs but which are liquid at atmospheric pressure after being recovered from oil well (casinghead) gas in lease separators, and

(3) Natural gas liquid recovered from gas well effluent in lease separators or field facilities before any conversion process has been applied to such production.

(h) *Depletable oil quantity.* The taxpayer's depletable oil quantity, within the meaning of section 613A(c)(1)(A), shall be equal to the tentative quantity determined under the table contained in section 613A(c)(3)(B) and paragraph (b) of § 1.613A-3 (except that, in the case of determinations with respect to days prior to January 1, 1984, such quantity shall be reduced (but not below zero) by the taxpayer's average daily secondary or tertiary production for the taxable year).

(i) *Depletable natural gas quantity.* The taxpayer's depletable natural gas quantity, within the meaning of section 613A(c)(1)(B), shall be equal to 6,000 cubic feet multiplied by the number of barrels of the taxpayer's depletable oil quantity to which the taxpayer elects to have section 613A(c)(4) apply. The taxpayer's deplet-

39,402 Deductions

See p. 20,601 for regulations not amended to reflect law changes

able oil quantity for any taxable year shall be reduced (in addition to any reduction required to be made under paragraph (h) of this section) by the number of barrels with respect to which an election under section 613A(c)(4) for natural gas has been made. See § 1.613A-5.

(j) *Barrel.* The term "barrel" means 42 United States gallons.

(k) *Secondary or tertiary production.* For purposes of section 613A the term "secondary or tertiary production" means the increased production of domestic crude oil or natural gas from a property at any time after the application of a secondary or tertiary process. The increased production is the excess of actual production over the maximum primary production which would have resulted during the taxable year if the secondary or tertiary process had not been applied. The increased production may be due to an increase in either the rate or the duration of recovery. A secondary or tertiary process is a process applied for the recovery of hydrocarbons in which liquids, gases, or other matter is injected into the reservoir to supplement or augment the natural forces required to move the hydrocarbons through the reservoir. However, no process which must be introduced early in the productive life of the mineral property in order to be reasonably effective (such as cycling of gas in the case of a gas-condensate reservoir) is a secondary or tertiary process. A process (such as fire flooding or miscible fluid injection) introduced early in the productive life of the mineral property will not be disqualified as a secondary or tertiary process if a later introduction of the process in the property would still have been reasonably effective.

(l) *Controlled group of corporations.* The term "controlled group of corporations" has the meaning given to such term by section 1563(a), except that section 1563(b)(2) shall not apply and except that "more than 50 percent" shall be substituted for "at least 80 percent" each place it appears in section 1563(a).

(m) *Related person.*

(1) A person is a "related person" to another person, within the meaning of section 613A(d)(2) and (4), paragraphs (b) and (c) of § 1.613A-4, and paragraphs (r) and (s) of this section, if either a significant ownership interest in such person is held by the other, or a third person has a significant ownership interest in both such persons. For purposes of determining a significant ownership interest, an interest owned by or for a corporation, partnership, trust, or estate shall be considered as owned directly both by itself and proportionately by its shareholders, partners, or beneficiaries, as the case may be. The term "significant ownership" means—

(i) With respect to any corporation, direct or indirect ownership of 5 percent or more in value of the outstanding stock of such corporation,

(ii) With respect to a partnership, direct or indirect ownership of 5 percent or more interest in the profits or capital of such partnership, and

(iii) With respect to an estate or trust, direct or indirect ownership of 5 percent or more of the beneficial interests in such estate or trust. The relative percentage ownership of beneficiaries of an estate or trust in the beneficial interests therein shall be determined under actuarial principles.

(2) A person is a "related person" to another person, within the meaning of section 613A(c)(8)(B) and paragraph (h)(2) of § 1.613A-3, if such persons are members of the same controlled group of corporations or if the relationship between such persons would result in a disallowance of losses under section 267 or 707 (b), except that for this purpose the family of an individual includes only the individual's spouse and minor children.

(n) *Transfer.* The term "transfer" means any change in ownership for federal tax purposes after December 31, 1974, by sale, exchange, gift, lease, sublease, assignment, contract, or other disposition (including any contribution to or any distribution by a corporation, partnership, or trust), any change in the membership of a partnership or the beneficiaries of a trust, or any other change by which a taxpayer's proportionate share of the income subject to depletion of an oil or gas property is increased. For taxable years beginning after 1982, the term "transfer" includes an election by a C corporation to be an S corporation (properties deemed transferred by the C corporation on the day the election first becomes effective) and a termination of an S election (each shareholder's pro rata share of assets of S corporation deemed transferred to C corporation on the day that the termination first becomes effective). However, the term does not include—

(1) A transfer of property at death (including a distribution by an estate, whether or not a pro rata distribution),

(2) An exchange to which section 351 applies,

(3) A change of beneficiaries of a trust by reason of the death, birth, or adoption of any vested beneficiary if the transferee was a beneficiary of the trust or is a lineal descendant of the settlor or any other vested beneficiary of the trust, except in the case of any trust where any beneficiary of the trust is a member of the family

Reg. § 1.613A-7(j)

(as defined in section 267(c)(4)) of a settlor who created inter vivos and testamentary trusts for members of the family and the settlor died within the last six days of the fifth month in 1970, and the law in the jurisdiction in which the trust was created requires all or a portion of the gross or net proceeds of any royalty or other interest in oil, gas, or other mineral representing any percentage depletion allowance to be allocated to the principal of the trust,

(4) A transfer of property between corporations which are members of the same controlled group of corporations (as defined in section 613A(c)(8)(D)(i)),

(5) A transfer of property between business entities which are under common control (within the meaning of section 613A(c)(8)(B)) or between related persons in the same family (within the meaning of section 613A(c)(8)(C)),

(6) A transfer of property between a trust and members of the same family (within the meaning of section 613A(c)(8)(C)) to the extent that both (i) the beneficiaries of the trust are and continue to be members of the family that transferred the property, and (ii) the tentative oil quantity is allocated among the members of such family,

(7) A reversion of all or part of an interest with respect to which the taxpayer was eligible for percentage depletion pursuant to section 613A(c), or

(8) A conversion of a retained interest which is eligible for such depletion into an interest which constituted all or part of an interest previously owned by the taxpayer also eligible for such depletion.

However, paragraph (n)(2), (4), and (5) of this section shall apply only so long as the tentative quantity determined under the table contained in section 613A(c)(3)(B) (as in effect prior to the Revenue Reconciliation Act of 1990) is required to be allocated under section 613A(c)(8) between the transferor and transferee, or among members of a controlled group of corporations. In the case of an individual transferor, the allocation test of the preceding sentence shall not be failed merely because of the death of the transferor. For purposes of paragraph (n)(3) and (6), an individual adopted by a beneficiary is a lineal descendant of that beneficiary. For purposes of paragraph (n)(7) and (8), a taxpayer previously ineligible for percentage depletion solely by reason of section 613A(d)(2) or (4) will be considered to have been eligible for such depletion. A transfer is deemed to occur on the day on which a contract or other commitment to transfer the property becomes binding upon both the transferor and transferee, or, if no such contract or commitment is made, on the day on which ownership of the interest in oil or gas property passes to the transferee.

(o) *Transferee.* The term "transferee," as used in section 613A(c)(9), paragraph (i)(1) of § 1.613A-3, and this section includes the original transferee of proven property and his or her successors in interest (excluding successors in interest of proven property transferred after October 11, 1990). A person shall not be treated as a transferee of an interest in a proven oil or gas property to the extent that such person was entitled to a percentage depletion allowance on mineral produced with respect to the property immediately before the transfer. However, a person shall be treated as a transferee of an interest in a proven property to the extent that the interest such person receives is greater than the interest in the property the person held immediately before the transfer. For example, where the owner of a proven oil property transfers his or her entire interest therein to a partnership of which he or she is a member and, as a consequence, becomes entitled to a depletion allowance based on only one-third of the oil produced with respect to that property, the owner (the transferor) is not denied percentage depletion with respect to the one-third interest in oil production which the owner still possesses. If the partnership agreement had made an effective allocation (under section 704 and § 1.704.1) of all the income in respect of such property to the transferor partner, that partner would be entitled to percentage depletion on the entire oil production from that property. For this purpose, a person who has transferred oil or gas property pursuant to a unitization or pooling agreement shall be treated as having been entitled to a depletion allowance immediately before the transfer to that person of the interest in the unit or pool with respect to all of the mineral in respect of which the person receives gross income from the property pursuant to the unitization or pooling agreement, except to the extent such income is attributable to consideration paid by that person for such interest in addition to that person's contribution of the oil or gas property and equipment affixed thereto.

(p) *Interest in proven oil or gas property.* The term "interest in an oil or gas property" means an economic interest in oil or gas property. An economic interest includes working or operating interests, royalties, overriding royalties, net profits interests, and, to the extent not treated as loans under section 636, production payments from oil or gas properties. The term also includes an interest in a partnership, S corporation, small business corporation, or trust holding an economic interest in oil or gas property but does not include shares

Reg. § 1.613A-7(p)

of stock in a corporation (other than an S corporation and small business corporation) owning such an interest. An oil or gas property is "proven" if its principal value has been demonstrated by prospecting, exploration, or discovery work. The principal value of the property has been demonstrated by prospecting, exploration, or discovery work only if at the time of the transfer—

(1) Any oil or gas has been produced from a deposit, whether or not produced by the taxpayer or from the property transferred;

(2) Prospecting, exploration, or discovery work indicate that it is probable that the property will have gross income from oil or gas from the deposit sufficient to justify development of the property; and

(3) The fair market value of the property is 50 percent or more of the fair market value of the property, minus actual expenses of the transferee for equipment and intangible drilling and development costs, at the time of the first production from the property subsequent to the transfer and before the transferee transfers his or her interest. For purposes of this paragraph, the property is to be determined by applying section 614 and the regulations thereunder to the transferee at the time of the transfer. If the transfer is of an interest in a partnership, S corporation, small business corporation, or trust, the determination shall be made with respect to each property owned by the partnership, S corporation, small business corporation, or trust. The term "prospecting, exploration, or discovery work" includes activities which produce information relating to the existence, location, extent, or quality of any deposit of oil or gas, such as seismograph surveys and drilling activities (whether for exploration or for the production of oil or gas).

(q) *Amount disallowed.* The amount disallowed, within the meaning of section 613A(d)(1) and paragraph (a) of § 1.613A-4, is the excess of the amount of the aggregate of the taxpayer's allowable depletion deductions (whether based upon cost or percentage depletion) computed without regard to section 613A(d)(1) over the amount of the aggregate of such deductions computed with regard to such section. The disallowed amount shall be carried over to the succeeding year and treated as an amount allowable as a deduction pursuant to section 613A(c) for the succeeding year, subject to the 65-percent limitation of section 613A(d)(1) and the rules contained in § 1.613A-4(a).

(r) *Retailer.* (1) Except as otherwise provided in paragraph (r)(2) of this section, the term "retailer" means any taxpayer who directly, or through a related person (as defined in paragraph (m)(1) of this section), sells oil or natural gas, or any product derived from oil or natural gas—

    (i) Through any retail outlet operated by the taxpayer or a related person, or

    (ii) To any person—

        (A) Obligated under an agreement or contract with the taxpayer or a related person to use a trademark, trade name, or service mark or name owned by such taxpayer or a related person, in marketing or distributing oil or natural gas or any product derived from oil or natural gas, or

        (B) Given authority, pursuant to an agreement or contract with the taxpayer or a related person, to occupy any retail outlet owned, leased, or in any way controlled by the taxpayer or a related person.

For purposes of the preceding sentence, bulk sales (*i.e.*, sales in very large quantities) of oil or natural gas (but not bulk sales of any product derived from oil or natural gas) to commercial or industrial users shall be disregarded. Bulk sales made after September 18, 1982, of aviation fuels to the Department of Defense shall be also disregarded. In addition, sales of oil or natural gas (whether or not produced by the taxpayer), or of any product derived from oil or natural gas, which are made outside the United States shall be disregarded if no domestic production of oil, natural gas (or products derived therefrom) of the taxpayer or a related person is exported during the taxable year or the immediately preceding taxable year.

(2) Notwithstanding paragraph (r)(1) of this section, the taxpayer shall not be considered a retailer in any case where, during the taxable year of the taxpayer, the combined gross receipts from sales (excluding sales for resale) of oil or natural gas, or products derived therefrom, of all retail outlets taken into account under paragraph (r)(1) of this section (including sales through a retail outlet of oil, natural gas, or a product derived from oil or natural gas which had previously been the subject of a sale described in paragraph (r)(1)(ii) of this section) do not exceed $5 million. If the taxpayer's combined gross receipts for the taxable year exceed $5 million, the taxpayer will be treated as a retailer as of the first day in which a retail sale was made. For purposes of paragraph (r)(1) of this section, a taxpayer shall be deemed to be selling oil or natural gas (or a product derived therefrom) through a related person in any case in which any sale of oil or natural gas (or a derivative product) by the related person produces gross income from which the taxpayer may benefit by reason of the taxpayer's direct or indirect ownership interest in the related person. In such cases (and in any other case in which the taxpayer is selling through a retail outlet referred

to in section 613A(d)(2)(A) or is selling such items to a person described in section 613A(d)(2)(B)), it is immaterial whether the oil or natural gas which is sold, or from which is derived a product which is sold, was produced by the taxpayer. A taxpayer shall be deemed to be selling oil or natural gas (or a derivative product) through a retail outlet operated by a related person in any case in which a related person who operates a retail outlet acquires for resale oil or natural gas (or a derivative product) which the taxpayer produced or caused to be made available for acquisition by the related person pursuant to an arrangement whereby some or all of the taxpayer's production is marketed. An owner of a nonoperating mineral interest (such as a royalty) shall not be treated as an operator of a retail outlet merely because the owner's oil or gas is sold on the owner's behalf through a retail outlet operated by an unrelated person. In addition, the mere fact that a member of a partnership is a retailer shall not result in characterization of the remaining partners as retailers. However, any partner of a partnership who has a 5 percent or more interest in any entity actually engaging in retail activities (including the partnership or another entity to which the partnership is related) is treated as a retailer. See paragraph (m)(1) of this section for rules on the ownership interest by partners in an entity related to a partnership. Similarly, if a trust or estate is a retailer, only its beneficiaries having a 5 percent or more current income interest from the trust or estate are treated as retailers. A person who is a retailer during a portion of the taxable year shall be treated as a retailer with respect to a fraction of that person's gross and taxable income from oil or gas properties for the taxable year, the numerator of which is the number of days during the taxable year in which the taxpayer is a retailer and the denominator of which is the total number of days during the taxable year; except that a person who ceases to be a retailer during the taxable year before the first production of oil or gas during such year shall not be treated as a retailer for any portion of such year.

(3) For purposes of this paragraph (r), the term "any product derived from oil or natural gas" means gasoline, kerosene, Number 2 fuel oil, refined lubricating oils, diesel fuel, butane, propane, and similar products which are recovered from petroleum refineries or extracted from natural gas in field facilities or natural gas processing plants. The term "retail outlet" means any place where sales of oil or natural gas (excluding bulk sales of such items to commercial or industrial users), or a product of oil or natural gas (excluding bulk sales of aviation fuels to the Department of Defense), accounting for more than 5 percent of the gross receipts from all sales made at such place during the taxpayer's taxable year, are systematically made for any purpose other than for resale. For this purpose, sales of oil or natural gas, or any product derived from oil or natural gas, to a person for refining are considered as sales made for resale.

(s) *Refiner.* A person is a refiner if such person or a related person (as defined in paragraph (m)(1) of this section) engages in the refining of crude oil (whether or not owned by such person or related person) and if the total refinery runs of such person and any related persons exceed 50,000 barrels on any day during the taxable year. A refinery run is the volume of inputs of crude oil (excluding any product derived from oil) into the refining stream. For purposes of this paragraph, crude oil refined outside the United States shall be taken into account. Refining is any operation by which the physical or chemical characteristics of crude oil are changed, exclusive of such operations as passing crude oil through separators to remove gas, placing crude oil in settling tanks to recover basic sediment and water, dehydrating crude oil, and blending of crude oil products. [Reg. § 1.613A-7.]

☐ [*T.D.* 8348, 5-10-91. *Amended by T.D.* 8437, 9-22-92.]

[Reg. § 1.614-0]

§ 1.614-0. Introduction.—Section 614 relates to the definition of property and to the various special rules by means of which taxpayers are permitted to aggregate or combine separate properties or to treat such properties as separate. These rules are set forth in detail in §§ 1.614-1 through 1.614-8. Section 1.614-1 sets forth rules under section 614(a) relating to the definition of the term "property". Section 1.614-2 contains the rules relating to the election under section 614(b), as it existed prior to its amendment by section 226(a) of the Revenue Act of 1964, to aggregate operating mineral interests. In the case of mines, the rules contained in § 1.614-2 are applicable only to taxable years beginning before January 1, 1958, to which the Internal Revenue Code of 1954 applies. In the case of oil and gas wells, the rules contained in § 1.614-2 are applicable only to taxable years beginning before January 1, 1964, to which the Internal Revenue Code of 1954 applies. In the case of oil and gas wells, the taxpayer may, however, for taxable years beginning before January 1, 1964, treat any operating mineral interests as if section 614(a) and (b) (as it existed prior to its amendment by section 226(a) of the Revenue Act of 1964) had not been enacted. If any operating mineral interests are so treated, the rules

Reg. § 1.614-0

contained in § 1.614-2 are not applicable to such interests and such interests are, in respect of taxable years beginning before January 1, 1964, subject to the rules set forth in § 1.614-4 relating to the Internal Revenue Code of 1939 treatment of separate operating mineral interests in the case of oil and gas wells. Section 1.614-3 prescribes the rules relating to the election under section 614(c)(1) permitting the aggregation of operating mineral interests in the cases of mines for taxable years beginning after December 31, 1957. Section 1.614-3 also sets forth rules relating to the election under section 614(c)(2) in the case of mines by means of which a taxpayer is permitted to treat a single operating mineral interest as more than one such interest for taxable years beginning after December 31, 1957. At the election of the taxpayer with respect to an operating unit, the rules contained in § 1.614-3 are also applicable to taxable years beginning before January 1, 1958, to which the Internal Revenue Code of 1954 applies. If the taxpayer makes such an election, the rules contained in § 1.614-2 are not applicable to any of the operating mineral interests which are part of the operating unit with respect to which the election described in § 1.614-3 is made. Section 1.614-5 sets forth the rules relating to the aggregation of nonoperating mineral interests. Section 1.614-6 contains the rules relating to basis, holding period, and abandonment and casualty losses where properties have been aggregated or combined. Section 1.614-7 relates to the extension of time for performing certain acts. Section 1.614-8 contains the rules relating to the elections under section 614(b) as amended by section 226(a) of the Revenue Act of 1964 to treat separate operating mineral interests in the case of oil and gas wells as separate properties or in combination for taxable years beginning after December 31, 1963. [Reg. § 1.614-0.]

☐ [*T.D. 6524, 1-9-61. Amended by T.D. 6859, 10-27-65.*]

[Reg. § 1.614-1]

§ 1.614-1. Definition of property.—(a) *General rule.* (1) For purposes of subtitle A of the Internal Revenue Code of 1954, in the case of mines, wells, and other natural deposits, the term "property" means each separate interest owned by the taxpayer in each mineral deposit in each separate tract or parcel of land.

(2) The term "interest" means an economic interest in a mineral deposit. See paragraph (b) of § 1.611-1. The term includes working or operating interests, royalties, overriding royalties, net profits interests, and, to the extent not treated as loans under section 636, production payments.

(3) The term "tract or parcel of land" is merely descriptive of the physical scope of the land to which the taxpayer's interest relates. It is not descriptive of the nature of his rights or interests in the land. All contiguous areas (even though separately described) included in a single conveyance or grant or in separate conveyances or grants at the same time from the same owner constitute a single separate tract or parcel of land. Areas included in separate conveyances or grants (whether or not at the same time) from separate owners are separate tracts or parcels of land even though the areas described may be contiguous. If the taxpayer's rights or interests within the same tract or parcel of land are dissimilar, then each such dissimilar interest constitutes a separate property. If the taxpayer's rights or interests (whether or not dissimilar) within the same tract or parcel of land relate to more than one separate mineral deposit, then his interest with respect to each such separate deposit is a separate property.

(4) Upon the transfer of a "property" in any transaction in which the basis of such property in the hands of the transferee is determined by reference to the basis of such property in the hands of the transferor, such property shall, notwithstanding the provisions of subparagraph (3) of this paragraph, retain the same status and identity in the hands of the transferee as it had in the hands of the transferor. See paragraph (c) of § 1.614-6 if the transferor has made a binding election to treat a separate mineral interest as a separate property, to treat a separate mineral interest as more than one property under section 614(c), or to treat two or more separate mineral interests as an aggregated or combined property under section 614(b) (as it existed either before or after its amendment by section 226(a) of the Revenue Act of 1964), (c), or (e).

(5) The provisions of this paragraph may be illustrated by the following examples:

Example (1). A taxpayer owns one tract of land under which lie three separate and distinct seams of coal. Therefore, the taxpayer owns three separate mineral interests each of which constitutes a separate property.

Example (2). A taxpayer conducts mining operations on eight tracts of land as a single unit. He acquired his interests in each of the eight tracts from separate owners. Even if each tract of land contains part of the same mineral deposit, the taxpayer owns eight separate mineral interests each of which constitutes a separate property.

Example (3). A taxpayer owns a tract of land under which lies one mineral deposit. The taxpayer operates a well on part of the tract and leases to another operator the mineral rights in the remainder retaining a royalty interest therein. The taxpayer thereafter owns two separate mineral interests each of which constitutes a separate property.

Example (4). In 1954 a taxpayer acquires from a single owner in a single deed, three noncontiguous tracts of mineral land for a single consideration. Even if each tract contains part of the same mineral deposit, the taxpayer owns three separate mineral interests each of which constitutes a separate property.

Example (5). In 1954, taxpayer A simultaneously acquires in fee two contiguous tracts of mineral land from two separate owners. The same mineral deposit underlies both tracts. Thereafter, taxpayer A owns two separate mineral interests each of which constitutes a separate property.

Example (6). Assume that in 1955, taxpayer A, in example (5), leases the two contiguous tracts of mineral land that he acquired in 1954 to taxpayer B by means of a single lease. Thereafter, taxpayer B owns one mineral interest which constitutes a separate property for such time as the lease continues in existence.

Example (7). Assume that in 1955, taxpayer A, in example (5), transfers all the mineral land he acquired in 1954 to taxpayer B. Thereafter, taxpayer B owns one mineral interest which constitutes a separate property. If taxpayer B acquires the mineral land in a transaction in which the basis of such mineral land in his hands is determined by reference to the basis of such mineral land in the hands of taxpayer A, then taxpayer B owns two separate mineral interests each of which constitutes a separate property.

Example (8). In 1954, taxpayer A simultaneously acquires two contiguous leasehold interests from two separate owners. The same mineral deposit underlies both tracts. Thereafter, taxpayer A owns two separate mineral interests each of which constitutes a separate property.

Example (9). In 1955, taxpayer A, in example (8) simultaneously assigns the two leases to taxpayer B. Thereafter, taxpayer B owns two separate mineral interests each of which constitutes a separate property.

(b) *Separation of interests treated as "single property" under prior regulations.* Each separate mineral interest which, in accordance with paragraph (a) of this section, is a separate property shall be so treated, notwithstanding the fact that the taxpayer under paragraph (i) of § 39.23(m)-1 of this chapter (Regulations 118) and corresponding provisions of prior regulations may have treated more than one of such interests as a "single property." The basis of each such separate property must be established by a reasonable method. See, however, section 614(b) and (d) (as they existed prior to amendment by section 226 of the Revenue Act of 1964), section 614(c) and (e), and §§ 1.614-2, 1.614-3, 1.614-4, and 1.614-5 for special rules relating to the treatment of two or more separate mineral interests as a single property.

(c) *Treatment of a waste bank or residue.* A waste bank or residue of prior mining, the extraction of ores or minerals from which is treated as mining under section 613(c)(3), shall not be considered to be a separate mineral deposit but is a part of the mineral deposit from which it was extracted. However, if the owner of such waste bank or residue has disposed of the deposit from which the waste bank or residue was accumulated, or if the waste bank or residue cannot practicably be attributed to a particular deposit of the owner, the waste bank or residue will be regarded as a separate deposit. [Reg. § 1.614-1.]

☐ [*T.D.* 6524, 1-9-61. *Amended by T.D.* 6859, 10-27-65, *and by T.D.* 7261, 2-26-73.]

[Reg. § 1.614-2]

§ 1.614-2. **Election to aggregate separate operating mineral interests under section 614(b) prior to its amendment by Revenue Act of 1964.**—(a) *General rule.* (1) The provisions of this section relate to the election, under section 614(b) prior to its amendment by section 226(a) of the Revenue Act of 1964, to aggregate separate operating mineral interests, and, unless otherwise indicated, all references in this section to section 614(b) or any paragraph or subparagraph thereof are references to section 614(b) or a paragraph or subparagraph thereof as it existed prior to such amendment. Notwithstanding the preceding sentence, the definitions contained in paragraphs (b) and (c) of this section shall apply both before and after such amendment. All references in this section to section 614(d) are references to section 614(d) as it existed prior to its amendment by section 226(b)(3) of the Revenue Act of 1964.

(2) A taxpayer who owns two or more separate operating mineral interests, which constitute part or all of an operating unit, may elect under section 614(b) and this section to form one aggregation of any two or more of such operating mineral interests and to treat such aggregation as one property. Any operating mineral interest which the taxpayer does not elect to include within the aggregation within the time prescribed in paragraph (d) of this section shall be treated as a separate property. The aggregation of separate properties which results from exercising the election shall be considered as one property for all purposes of subtitle A of the Code. The preceding sentence does not preclude the use of more than

one account under a single method of computing depreciation or the use of more than one method of computing depreciation under section 167, if otherwise proper. Any reasonable and consistently applied method or methods of computing depreciation of the improvements made with respect to the separate properties aggregated may be continued in accordance with section 167 and the regulations thereunder. Operating interests in different minerals which comprise part or all of the same operating unit may be included in the aggregation. It is not necessary for purposes of the aggregation that the separate operating mineral interests be included in a single tract or parcel of land or in contiguous tracts or parcels of land so long as such interests are a part of the same operating unit. Under section 614(b), a taxpayer cannot elect to form more than one aggregation of separate operating mineral interests within one operating unit. For definitions of "operating mineral interest" and "operating unit" see respectively paragraphs (b) and (c) of this section.

(b) *Operating mineral interest defined.* The term "operating mineral interest" means a separate mineral interest as described in section 614(a), in respect of which the costs of production are required to be taken into account by the taxpayer for purposes of computing the limitation of 50 percent of the taxable income from the property in determining the deduction for percentage depletion computed under section 613, or such costs would be so required to be taken into account if the mine, well, or other natural deposit were in the production stage. The term does not include royalty interests or similar interests, such as production payments or net profits interests. For the purpose of determining whether a mineral interest is an operating mineral interest, "costs of production" do not include intangible drilling and development costs, exploration expenditures under section 615, or development expenditures under section 616. Taxes, such as production taxes, payable by holders of nonoperating interests are not considered costs of production for this purpose. A taxpayer may not aggregate operating mineral interests and nonoperating mineral interests such as royalty interests.

(c) *Operating unit defined.* (1) The term "operating unit" refers to the operating mineral interests which are operated together for the purpose of producing minerals. An "operating unit" of a particular taxpayer must be determined on the basis of his own operations. It is recognized that operating units may not be uniform in the various natural resources industries or in any one of the natural resources industries, such as coal, oil and gas, and the like. As to a particular taxpayer, business reasons may require the formation of operating units that vary in size and content. The term "operating unit" refers to a producing unit, and not to an administrative or sales organization. Among the factors which indicate that mineral interests are operated together as a unit are—

(i) Common field or operating personnel,

(ii) Common supply and maintenance facilities,

(iii) Common processing or treatment plants, and

(iv) Common storage facilities.

However, operating mineral interests which are geographically widespread may not be treated as parts of the same operating unit merely because a single set of accounting records, a single executive organization, or a single sales force is maintained by the taxpayer with respect to such interests, or merely because the products of such interests are processed at the same treatment plant.

(2) If aggregated, an undeveloped operating mineral interest shall be aggregated only with those interests with which it will be operated as a unit when it reaches the production stage.

(3) While a taxpayer may operate an operating mineral interest through an agent, a coowner may aggregate only his operating mineral interests that are actually operated as a unit. For example, if A owned and actually operated the entire working interest in lease X and also owned an undivided fraction of lease Y in which B owned the remaining interest and which B actually operated as a unit with lease Z, A may not aggregate his interest in lease X with his undivided interest in lease Y, since they are not actually operated as a unit.

(4) The determination of the taxpayer as to what constitutes an operating unit is to be accepted unless there is a clear and convincing basis for a change in such determination.

(d) *Manner and scope of election*—(1) *Election; when made.* (i) Except as provided in subparagraph (2)(ii) of this paragraph, the election under section 614(b) and paragraph (a) of this section to treat an operating mineral interest as part of an aggregation shall be made not later than the time prescribed by law for filing the taxpayer's income tax return (including extensions thereof), for whichever of the following taxable years is the later:

(*a*) The first taxable year beginning after December 31, 1953, and ending after August 16, 1954, or

(*b*) The first taxable year in which any expenditure for exploration, development, or operation in respect of the separate operating mineral

Reg. § 1.614-2(b)

interest is made by the taxpayer after the acquisition of such interest.

See, however, paragraph (c) of § 1.614-6 as to the binding effect of an election where the basis of a separate operating mineral interest in the hands of the taxpayer is determined by reference to the basis in the hands of a transferor. The election under section 614(b) may not be made with respect to any taxable year beginning after December 31, 1957, except in the case of oil and gas wells. See paragraph (e) of this section for rules with respect to the termination of the election under section 614(b) except in the case of oil and gas wells. If an expenditure has been made in respect of a separate operating mineral interest, it is immaterial whether or not any proven deposit has been discovered with respect to such interest when such expenditure has been made. The provisions of this subdivision may be illustrated by the following example:

Example. Taxpayer A is producing from an oil and gas horizon and in 1958 he drills for the purpose of locating a deeper horizon which will be operated in the same operating unit as the upper producing horizon. At the end of the taxable year 1958 he has expended $50,000 drilling for the purpose of locating a deeper horizon although at such time there is no assurance that such a horizon will be found. If taxpayer A desires to aggregate the deeper horizon, if found, with the upper horizon under section 614(b), he must elect to do so in his return for 1958. If the election to aggregate the upper and lower horizons as one property is made, the drilling expenditures with respect to the prospective lower horizon must be taken into account along with the income and expenses with respect to the upper producing horizon in computing the depletion allowance on the aggregated property.

However, where expenditures for development of, or production from, a particular mineral deposit result in the discovery of another mineral deposit, the election with respect to such other deposit shall be made for the taxable year in which it is discovered and not for the taxable year in which the expenditures were first made which resulted in such discovery.

(ii) Except in the case of oil and gas wells, if a taxpayer fails to make an election under section 614(b) to aggregate a particular operating mineral interest on or before the time prescribed for the making of such election, such interest will be treated as if an election had been made under section 614(b) to treat it as a separate property and it cannot be included in any aggregation within the operating unit of which it is a part unless the taxpayer obtains the consent of the Commissioner. However, where the taxpayer owns more than one property within an operating unit, but has elected to treat such properties separately and one or more additional operating mineral interests are subsequently acquired, any one or more of the latter may be aggregated with one of the existing separate properties within the operating unit but not with more than one of them since they cannot be validly aggregated with each other.

(iii) In the case of oil and gas wells, if the taxpayer fails to make an election under section 614(b) with respect to a particular operating mineral interest on or before the time prescribed for the making of such election, the taxpayer shall be deemed to have treated such interest under the provisions of section 614(d). See section 614(d) and § 1.614-4.

(iv) For purposes of section 614(b), the acquisition of an option to acquire an economic interest in minerals in place does not constitute the acquisition of a mineral interest. Thus, a taxpayer who makes expenditures for the exploration of minerals on a particular tract under an option to acquire an economic interest in minerals in place is not required to make an election with respect to such interest at that time. Furthermore, the election need not be made in the taxable year in which payments are made for the acquisition of a lease, such as the payment of a bonus, unless exploratory, development, or operation expenditures are made thereafter with respect to the property in that year.

(2) *Election—how made.* (i) The election under section 614(b) must be made by a statement attached to the income tax return of the taxpayer for the first taxable year for which the election is made. This statement shall indicate that the taxpayer is making an aggregation of separate operating mineral interests within an operating unit under section 614(b) and shall contain a description of the aggregation and describe the operating mineral interests within the operating unit which are to be treated as separate properties apart from the aggregation. A general description accompanied by maps appropriately marked, which accurately circumscribes the scope of the aggregation and identifies the properties which are to be treated separately will be sufficient. The statement shall also contain a description of the operating unit in sufficient detail to show that the aggregated operating mineral interests are properly within a single operating unit. See paragraph (c) of this section. The taxpayer shall maintain adequate records and maps in support of the above information. In the event expenditures are first made on an operating mineral

Reg. § 1.614-2(d)(2)

interest within an operating unit after an election with respect to the aggregation of interests in that operating unit has been made, the taxpayer shall furnish only information describing such operating mineral interest, its location in the operating unit, and whether it is to be included within the aggregation.

(ii) If the taxpayer made or did not make the election under section 614(b) with respect to a particular operating mineral interest and the last day prescribed by law for filing the return (including extensions of time therefor) on which the election was required to be made falls on or before the first day of the first month which begins more than 90 days after the regulations under section 614 are published in the Federal Register as a Treasury decision, consent is hereby given to the taxpayer to make or change the election not later than the first day of such first month. Any such election or change of such election shall be effective with respect to the earliest taxable year to which the election is applicable in respect of which assessment of a deficiency or credit or refund of an overpayment, as the case may be, resulting from such election or change is not prevented by any law or rule of law on the date such election or change is made. An election or change of election made pursuant to this subdivision shall be binding upon the taxpayer for the first taxable year for which it is effective and for all subsequent taxable years unless consent to a different treatment is obtained from the Commissioner. (See, however, paragraph (e) of this section for rules relating to the termination and nonapplicability of the election under section 614(b) except in the case of oil and gas wells.) Such election or change shall be made in the form of a statement setting forth the nature of the election or change, including information substantially the same as that required by subdivision (i) of this subparagraph, and shall be accompanied by an amended return or returns if necessary or, if appropriate, a claim for refund or credit. The appropriate documents must be filed on or before the first day of such first month with the district director for the district in which the original return was filed.

(3) *Election—when effective.* If a taxpayer has elected to aggregate an operating mineral interest, the date on which the aggregation becomes effective is the earliest date within the taxable year affected, on which the taxpayer incurred any expenditure for exploration, development, or operation of such interest. The application of this rule may be illustrated by the following examples:

Example (1). In 1953, a taxpayer owned and operated mineral interests Nos. 1, 2, and 3. All three interests form one operating unit. The taxpayer, who files his return on a calendar year basis, continued to own and operate these interests during the year 1954, and in his return for that year, filed on April 15, 1955, elected to aggregate these three interests. As the result of this election, the aggregation was effective for all purposes of subtitle A of the Internal Revenue Code of 1954 as of January 1, 1954.

Example (2). Assume that, on March 1, 1955, the taxpayer described in example (1) acquired operating mineral interest No. 4 which was also a part of the operating unit composed of operating mineral interests Nos. 1, 2, and 3, that he made his first expenditure for exploration with respect to operating mineral interest No. 4 on September 1, 1955, and that, in his return filed on April 15, 1956, he elected to aggregate operating mineral interest No. 4 with the aggregation consisting of Nos. 1, 2, and 3. As the result of that election, operating mineral interest No. 4 became a part of the aggregation for all purposes of subtitle A of the Internal Revenue Code of 1954 on September 1, 1955.

(4) *Election—binding effect.* A valid election made under section 614(b) and this section shall be binding upon the taxpayer for the taxable year for which made and all subsequent taxable years unless consent to make a change is obtained from the Commissioner. However, see paragraph (e) of this section for rules with respect to the termination of the election under section 614(b) except in the case of oil and gas wells. For rules relating to the binding effect of an election where the basis of a separate or an aggregated property in the hands of the transferee is determined by reference to the basis in the hands of the transferor, see paragraph (c) of § 1.614-6. A taxpayer can neither include within the aggregation a separate operating mineral interest which he had previously elected to treat separately, nor exclude from the aggregation a separate operating mineral interest previously included therein unless consent to do so is obtained from the Commissioner. A change in tax consequences alone is not sufficient to obtain consent to change the treatment of an operating mineral interest. However, consent may be appropriate where, for example, there has been a substantial change in the taxpayer's operations so that a major part of an aggregation becomes a part of another operating unit. Applications for consent shall be made in writing to the Commissioner of Internal Revenue, Attention: Special Technical Services Division, Engineering and Valuation Branch, Washington 25, D.C. The application must be accompanied by a statement indicating the reason or reasons for the change and furnishing the information required under

Reg. § 1.614-2(d)(3)

subdivision (i) of subparagraph (2) of this paragraph, unless such information has been previously filed and is current.

(5) *Invalid aggregations*—(i) *In general.* In addition to aggregations which are invalid under section 614(b) because of the failure to make timely elections, aggregations may be invalid under such section in situations which may be divided into two general categories. The first category involves basic aggregations which were timely but otherwise initially invalid. The second category involves invalid additions of operating mineral interests to basic aggregations which additions became subject to the election in years subsequent to the year in which the initial basic aggregation or aggregations were formed.

(ii) *Invalid basic aggregations.* The term "invalid basic aggregations" refers to those aggregations which were initially invalid. Generally, such basic aggregations will be invalid because more than one aggregation has been formed within an operating unit or because operating mineral interests in two or more operating units have been improperly aggregated. For any year in which an invalid basic aggregation exists, each operating mineral interest included in such aggregation shall be treated for all purposes as a separate property unless consent is obtained from the Commissioner to treat any such interest in a different manner. Consent will be granted in appropriate cases as, for example, where the taxpayer demonstrates that he inadvertently formed an invalid basic aggregation. The provisions of this subdivision may be illustrated by the following examples:

Example (1). In 1953, taxpayer A owned six operating mineral interests, designated No. 1 through No. 6, and he continued to own and operate such interests during 1954. He acquired no other operating mineral interests during such year. All six of these operating mineral interests form one operating unit. Assume that A elected under section 614(b) to aggregate operating mineral interests Nos. 1 through 3 into one aggregation and Nos. 4 through 6 into another aggregation. Since A has formed two aggregations in one operating unit, they are invalid basic aggregations. Therefore, interests Nos. 1 through 6 must be treated as separate properties for 1954 and all subsequent taxable years unless consent is obtained from the Commissioner to treat any of such interests in a different manner.

Example (2). Assume the same facts as in example (1) and assume also that, in his return for 1954, A correctly elected to aggregate all six operating mineral interests into one aggregation under section 614(b). Assume further that all these operating mineral interests continued to be in one operating unit for the years 1954, 1955, and 1956 but that, because of changes in the facts and circumstances of A's operations, in 1957 operating mineral interests Nos. 1, 2, and 3 became a part of one operating unit and Nos. 4, 5, and 6 became a part of another operating unit. Notwithstanding the change in operations, the election made by A shall continue to be binding unless consent to change such election is obtained from the Commissioner.

(iii) *Invalid additions.* The term "additions" refers to the additions that a taxpayer makes by electing to aggregate an operating mineral interest with an aggregation formed in a previous year. Such additions will be invalid where the taxpayer either elected to aggregate an operating mineral interest with an invalid basic aggregation or elected to aggregate an operating mineral interest which is part of one operating unit with an aggregation of operating mineral interests which is a part of another operating unit. An operating mineral interest which is invalidly added to either a valid basic aggregation or to an invalid basic aggregation shall be considered as a separate property unless consent is obtained from the Commissioner to treat such interest in a different manner. The following are examples of invalid additions:

Example (1). In 1953, taxpayer A owned six operating mineral interests designated No. 1 through No. 6 and he continued to own and operate such interests during 1954. He acquired no other operating mineral interests during that year. Nos. 1 through 3 formed one operating unit and Nos. 4 through 6 formed another operating unit. In his return for 1954, A incorrectly elected to aggregate all six operating mineral interests into one aggregation under section 614(b). In 1955, A acquired and commenced development of operating mineral interest No. 7 which is correctly a part of the operating unit of which operating mineral interests Nos. 1, 2, and 3 are a part. A elected under section 614(b), for the year 1955, to aggregate operating mineral interest No. 7 with the invalid basic aggregation composed of Nos. 1 through 6. Since operating mineral interest No. 7 was aggregated with an invalid basic aggregation, it is an invalid addition and must be treated as a separate property unless consent is obtained from the Commissioner to treat it in a different manner.

Example (2). In 1953, taxpayer A owned nine operating mineral interests designated No. 1 through No. 9. During 1954, he continued to own and operate such interests and acquired no other operating mineral interest. Interests No. 1

Reg. § 1.614-2(d)(5)

Deductions

See p. 20,601 for regulations not amended to reflect law changes

through No. 3 form one operating unit, Nos. 4 through 6 form another operating unit, and Nos. 7 through 9 form a third operating unit. For the year 1954, A elected under section 614(b) to aggregate operating mineral interests Nos. 1, 2, 3, and 4 into one aggregation, to treat Nos. 5 and 6 as separate properties, and to aggregate Nos. 7, 8, and 9 into another aggregation. Assume that in 1955 A acquired and commenced development of operating mineral interest No. 10 which was a part of the operating unit composed of Nos. 1, 2, and 3. Assume further that he elected under section 614(b) to aggregate No. 10 with the aggregation composed of Nos. 7, 8, and 9. This would be an invalid addition to a valid basic aggregation since operating mineral interest No. 10 was not properly a part of the operating unit formed by Nos. 7, 8, and 9. Therefore, interest No. 10 must be treated as a separate property for 1955 and all subsequent taxable years unless consent is obtained from the Commissioner to treat it in a different manner. However, the valid basic aggregation composed of interests Nos. 7 through 9 is not affected by the invalid addition of interest No. 10.

Example (3). Assume the same facts as in example (2) except that A elected under section 614(b) in 1955 to aggregate No. 10 with the aggregation of Nos. 1 through 4. This would also be an invalid addition because the aggregation composed of Nos. 1 through 4 is an invalid basic aggregation since operating mineral interest No. 4 is not a part of the operating unit consisting of Nos. 1, 2, and 3. Therefore, interest No. 10 must be treated as a separate property for 1955 and all subsequent taxable years unless consent is obtained from the Commissioner to treat such interest in a different manner.

(e) *Termination of election*—(1) *Taxable years beginning after December 31, 1963, in the case of oil and gas wells.* In the case of oil and gas wells, the election provided for under section 614(b) and paragraph (a) of this section to form an aggregation of separate operating mineral interests shall not apply with respect to any taxable year beginning after December 31, 1963. In addition, if a taxpayer treated certain separate operating mineral interests in a single tract or parcel of land as separate rather than as an aggregation and decides to continue such treatment for taxable years beginning after December 31, 1963, he must make an appropriate election under section 614(b) as amended by the Revenue Act of 1964. See § 1.614-8.

(2) *Taxable years beginning after December 31, 1957, in the case of mines.* Except in the case of oil and gas wells, the election provided for under section 614(b) and paragraph (a) of this section to form an aggregation of separate operating mineral interests shall not apply with respect to any taxable year beginning after December 31, 1957. Thus, if a taxpayer makes a binding election under section 614(b) to form an aggregation of separate operating mineral interests within an operating unit for taxable years beginning before January 1, 1958, he must make a new election for the first taxable year beginning after December 31, 1957, under section 614(c) within the time prescribed in § 1.614-3 if he wishes to aggregate any separate operating mineral interests within such operating unit. A new election must be made under section 614(c) notwithstanding the fact that the aggregation formed under section 614(b) would constitute a valid aggregation under section 614(c). Failure to make such an election within the time prescribed shall constitute an election to treat each separate operating mineral interest within the operating unit as a separate property for taxable years beginning after December 31, 1957.

(3) *Taxable years beginning before January 1, 1958, in the case of mines.* An election made under section 614(b) and paragraph (a) of this section to form an aggregation of separate operating mineral interests within a particular operating unit shall not apply with respect to any taxable year beginning prior to January 1, 1958, for which the taxpayer makes an election under section 614(c)(3)(B) and paragraph (f)(2) of § 1.614-3 which is applicable to any separate operating mineral interest within the same operating unit. The provisions of this subparagraph may be illustrated by the following examples:

Example (1). In 1953, taxpayer A owned six separate operating mineral interests, designated No. 1 through No. 6, which he operated as a unit. Operating mineral interests Nos. 1 through 5 comprise a mine, and operating mineral interest No. 6 represents one mineral deposit in a single tract of land which is being extracted by means of two mines. Taxpayer A previously made a binding election under section 614(b) to aggregate operating mineral interests Nos. 1 through 5 and to treat operating mineral interest No. 6 as a separate property. Under section 614(c)(2) and (3)(B) taxpayer A makes an election which is applicable for the taxable year 1954 and all subsequent taxable years to treat operating mineral interest No. 6 as two separate operating mineral interests. Therefore, the previous election of taxpayer A to aggregate operating mineral interests Nos. 1 through 5 under section 614(b) does not apply. Unless taxpayer A also makes an election to aggregate operating mineral interests Nos. 1 through 5 as one property under section 614(c)(1)

Reg. § 1.614-2(e)(1)

and (3)(B) within the time prescribed in paragraph (f)(2) of § 1.614-3, he shall be deemed to have made an election to treat each of such interests as a separate property for 1954 and all subsequent taxable years.

Example (2). In 1953, taxpayer B owned six separate operating mineral interests, designated No. 1 through No. 6, which he operated as a unit. Operating mineral interests Nos. 1 through 3 comprise a mine and Nos. 4 through 6 comprise a second mine. Taxpayer B previously made a binding election under section 614(b) to aggregate operating mineral interests Nos. 1 through 3 and to treat Nos. 4 through 6 as separate properties. Under section 614(c)(1) and (3)(B) taxpayer B makes an election which is applicable for the taxable year 1954 and all subsequent taxable years to aggregate operating mineral interests Nos. 4 through 6 as one property. The previous election of the taxpayer under section 614(b) to aggregate operating mineral interests Nos. 1 through 3 does not apply even though such aggregation would constitute a valid aggregation if formed under section 614(c)(1). Therefore, if taxpayer B wishes to continue to treat operating mineral interests Nos. 1 through 3 as one property, he must also make an election to do so under section 614(c)(1) and (3)(B) within the time prescribed in paragraph (f)(2) of § 1.614-3.

(4) *Bases of separate operating mineral interests.* If an aggregation formed under section 614(b) is terminated by reason of the provisions of section 614(b)(4)(A), is terminated under section 614(b)(4)(B) for any taxable year after the first taxable year to which the election under section 614(b) applies, or is terminated by reason of the provisions of section 614(b) as amended by the Revenue Act of 1964, the bases of the separate operating mineral interests (and combinations thereof) included in such aggregation shall be determined in accordance with the rules contained in paragraph (a)(2) of § 1.614-6 as of the first day of the first taxable year for which the termination is effective. However, if by reason of the provisions of section 614(b)(4)(B), an election to aggregate under section 614(b) does not apply for any taxable year for which such election was made, the bases of the separate operating mineral interests included in the aggregation formed under section 614(b) shall be determined without regard to the election under section 614(b).

(f) *Alternative treatment of separate operating mineral interests in the case of oil and gas wells.* For rules relating to an alternative treatment of separate operating mineral interests in the case of oil and gas wells, see § 1.614-4. [Reg. § 1.614-2.]

☐ [*T.D. 6524, 1-9-61. Amended by T.D. 6859, 10-27-65.*]

[Reg. § 1.614-3]

§ 1.614-3. Rules relating to separate operating mineral interests in the case of mines.—(a) *Election to aggregate separate operating mineral interests*—(1) *General rule.* Except in the case of oil and gas wells, a taxpayer who owns two or more separate operating mineral interests, which constitute part or all of the same operating unit, may elect under section 614(c)(1) and this paragraph to form an aggregation of all such operating mineral interests which comprise any one mine or any two or more mines and to treat such aggregation as one property. The aggregated property which results from the exercise of such election shall be considered as one property for all purposes of subtitle A of the Internal Revenue Code of 1954. The preceding sentence does not preclude the use of more than one account under a single method of computing depreciation or the use of more than one method of computing depreciation under section 167, if otherwise proper. Any reasonable and consistently applied method or methods of computing depreciation of the improvements made with respect to the separate properties aggregated may be continued in accordance with section 167 and the regulations thereunder. It is not necessary for purposes of the aggregation that the separate operating mineral interests be included in a single tract or parcel of land or in contiguous tracts or parcels of land so long as such interests constitute part or all of the same operating unit. A taxpayer may elect to form more than one aggregation of separate operating mineral interests within one operating unit so long as each aggregation consists of all the separate operating mineral interests which comprise any one mine or any two or more mines. Thus, no aggregation may include any separate operating mineral interest which is a part of a mine without including all of the separate operating mineral interests which comprise such mine in the first taxable year for which the election to aggregate is effective. Any separate operating mineral interest which becomes a part of such mine in a subsequent taxable year must also be included in such aggregation as of the taxable year that such interest becomes a part of such mine. The taxable year in which such interest becomes a part of such mine shall be determined upon the basis of the facts and circumstances of the particular case. If a taxpayer fails to make an election under this paragraph to aggregate a particular operating mineral interest (other than an interest which becomes a part of a mine with respect to which the interests have been aggre-

Reg. § 1.614-3(a)(1)

gated in a prior taxable year) on or before the last day prescribed for making such an election, such interest shall be treated as if an election had been made to treat it as a separate property. A taxpayer may not aggregate operating mineral interests and nonoperating mineral interests such as royalty interests. For definitions of the terms "operating mineral interests", "operating unit", and "mine," see respectively paragraphs (c), (d), and (e) of this section.

(2) *Aggregation in subsequent taxable years.* If the taxpayer has made an election under section 614(c)(1) for a particular taxable year with respect to any operating mineral interest or interests within a particular operating unit, and if, for a subsequent taxable year, the taxpayer desires to make an election with respect to an additional operating mineral interest within the same operating unit, then whether or not the taxpayer may elect to include such additional interest in an aggregation or treat it as a separate property depends upon the nature of such additional interest and of the taxpayer's previous elections. If the additional interest is a part of a mine with respect to which the other interests have been aggregated, the additional interest must be included in such aggregation. If the additional interest is a part of a mine with respect to which the other interests have been treated as separate properties, the additional interest must be treated as a separate property. If the additional interest is part of a mine which previously consisted of only a single interest which has not been aggregated with any other mine, such additional interest may be aggregated or treated as a separate property. If the additional interest is an entire mine, it may, at the election of the taxpayer, (i) be added to any aggregation within the same operating unit, (ii) be aggregated with any other single interest which is an entire mine provided both interests are within the same operating unit even though such single interest has previously been treated as a separate property, or (iii) be treated as a separate property.

(b) *Election to treat a single operating mineral interest as more than one property*—(1) *General rule.* Except in the case of oil and gas wells, a taxpayer who owns a separate operating mineral interest in a mineral deposit in a single tract or parcel of land may elect under section 614(c)(2) and this paragraph to treat such interest as two or more separate operating mineral interests if such mineral deposit is being developed or extracted by means of two or more mines. In order for this election to be applicable, there must be at least two mines with respect to each of which an expenditure for development or operation has been made by the taxpayer. The election under section 614(c)(2) may also be made with respect to a separate operating mineral interest formed by a previous election under section 614(c)(2) at such time as the mineral deposit previously allocated to such interest is being developed or extracted by means of two or more mines. If there is more than one mineral deposit in a single tract or parcel of land, an election under section 614(c)(2) with respect to any one of such mineral deposits has no application to the other mineral deposits. The election under section 614(c)(2) may not be made with respect to an aggregated property or with respect to any operating mineral interest which is a part of any aggregation formed by the taxpayer unless the taxpayer obtains consent from the Commissioner. Such consent will not be granted where the principal purpose for the request to make the election is based on tax consequences. Application for such consent shall be made in writing to the Commissioner of Internal Revenue, Washington 25, D.C. The application must be accompanied by a statement setting forth in detail the reason or reasons for the request to exercise the election with respect to an aggregated property.

(2) *Allocation of mineral deposit.* If the taxpayer elects to treat a separate operating mineral interest in a mineral deposit in a single tract or parcel of land as more than one separate operating mineral interest, then all of such mineral deposit therein and all of the portion of the tract or parcel of land allocated thereto must be allocated to the newly formed separate operating mineral interests. A portion of such mineral deposit and such tract or parcel of land must be allocated to each such newly formed separate operating mineral interest. There must be at least one mine, with respect to which an expenditure for development or operation has been made by the taxpayer, with respect to each such portion. The extent of the portion to be allocated to each newly formed separate operating mineral interest is to be determined upon the basis of the facts and circumstances of the particular case.

(3) *Basis of newly formed separate operating mineral interests.* The adjusted basis of each of the separate operating mineral interests formed by the making of the election under section 614(c)(2) shall be determined by apportioning the adjusted basis of the separate operating mineral interest with respect to which such election as made between (or among) the newly formed separate operating mineral interests in the same proportion as the fair market value of each such newly formed interest (as of the date on which the election becomes effective) bears to the total fair market value of the interest with respect to which the election was made as of such date.

Reg. § 1.614-3(a)(2)

(4) *Aggregation of newly formed separate operating mineral interests.* Any separate operating mineral interest formed by the making of the election under section 614(c)(2) may be included as a part of an aggregation subject to the requirements of paragraph (a) of this section, provided that the time for making the election under section 614(c)(1) to include such separate operating mineral interest in such aggregation has not expired. See paragraph (f) of this section. The provisions of this subparagraph may be illustrated by the following example:

Example. In 1958, taxpayer A acquired two separate operating mineral interests designated No. 1 and 2. Each is an interest in a single mineral deposit in a single tract of land. In the same year, taxpayer A made his first development expenditure with respect to a mine on operating mineral interest No. 1 and a mine on operating mineral interest No. 2. Operating mineral interests Nos. 1 and 2 are operated as a unit. Taxpayer A did not elect to aggregate operating mineral interests Nos. 1 and 2 under section 614(c)(1) within the time prescribed for making such an election. In 1960 taxpayer A made his first development expenditure with respect to a second mine on operating mineral interest No. 2. Taxpayer A elected under section 614(c)(2) to treat operating mineral interest No. 2 as two separate operating mineral interests, designated as Nos. 2(a) and 2(b), for the taxable year 1960 and all subsequent taxable years. No. 2(a) contained the mine for which the first development expenditure was made in 1958, and No. 2(b) contained the mine for which the first development expenditure was made in 1960. If taxpayer A wishes to do so, he may elect to aggregate mineral interests Nos. 1 and 2(b) under section 614(c)(1) for the taxable year 1960 and all subsequent taxable years since the first development expenditure with respect to the mine on operating mineral interest No. 2(b) was made during the taxable year 1960. Taxpayer A may not elect to aggregate mineral interests Nos. 1 and 2(a) under such section since the time for making such an election has expired.

(c) *Operating mineral interest defined.* For the definition of the term "operating mineral interest" as used in this section, see paragraph (b) of § 1.614-2.

(d) *Operating unit defined.* For the definition of the term "operating unit" as used in this section, see paragraph (c) of § 1.614-2.

(e) *Mine defined.* For purposes of this section, the term "mine" means any excavation or other workings or series of related excavations or related workings, as the case may be, for the purpose of extracting any known mineral deposit except oil and gas deposits. For the purpose of the preceding sentence, the term "excavations" or "workings" includes quarries, pits, shafts, and wells (except oil and gas wells). The number of excavations or workings that constitute a mine is to be determined upon the basis of the facts and circumstances of the particular case such as the nature and position of the mineral deposit or deposits, the method of mining the mineral, the location of the excavations or other workings in relation to the mineral deposit or deposits, and the topography of the area. The determination of the taxpayer as to the composition of a mine is to be accepted unless there is a clear and convincing basis for a change in such determination.

(f) *Manner and scope of election*—(1) *Election to apply section 614(c)(1) and (2) for taxable years beginning after December 31, 1957.* Except as provided in subparagraphs (2) and (3) of this paragraph, the election under section 614(c)(1) and paragraph (a) of this section to treat an operating mineral interest as part of an aggregation shall be made under section 614(c)(3)(A) not later than the time prescribed by law for filing the taxpayer's income tax return (including extensions thereof) for whichever of the following taxable years is the later:

(i) The first taxable year beginning after December 31, 1957, or

(ii) The first taxable year in which any expenditure for development or operation in respect of the separate operating mineral interest is made by the taxpayer after the acquisition of such interest.

Except as provided in subparagraphs (2) and (3) of this paragraph, the election under section 614(c)(2) and paragraph (b) of this section to treat a single operating mineral interest as more than one operating mineral interest shall be made under section 614(c)(3)(A) not later than the time prescribed by law for filing the taxpayer's income tax return (including extensions thereof) for whichever of the following taxable years is the later:

(iii) The first taxable year beginning after December 31, 1957, or

(iv) The first taxable year in which expenditures for development or operation of more than one mine in respect of the separate operating mineral interest are made by the taxpayer after the acquisition of such interest.

However, if the latest time at which an election may be made under this subparagraph falls on or before the first day of the first month which begins more than 90 days after the regulations under section 614 are published in the Federal Register as a Treasury decision, such election may

Reg. § 1.614-3(f)(1)

be made or modified at any time on or before the first day of such first month. See paragraph (c) of § 1.614-6 as to the binding effect of an election where the basis of a separate operating mineral interest in the hands of the taxpayer is determined by reference to the basis in the hands of a transferor.

(2) *Election to apply section 614(c)(1) and (2) for taxable years beginning before January 1, 1958.* In accordance with section 614(c)(3)(B), the election under section 614(c)(1) and paragraph (a) of this section to treat an operating mineral interest as part of an aggregation may, at the election of the taxpayer, be made not later than the time prescribed by law for filing the taxpayer's income tax return (including extensions thereof) for whichever of the following taxable years is the later:

(i) The first taxable year beginning after December 31, 1953, and ending after August 16, 1954, for which assessment of a deficiency or credit or refund of an overpayment, as the case may be, resulting from an election under section 614(c)(1), is not prevented on September 2, 1958, by the operation of any law or rule of law, or

(ii) The first taxable year in which any expenditure for development or operation in respect of the separate operating mineral interest is made by the taxpayer after the acquisition of such interest.

In accordance with section 614(c)(3)(B), the election under section 614(c)(2) and paragraph (b) of this section to treat an operating mineral interest as more than one operating mineral interest may, at the election of the taxpayer, be made not later than the time prescribed by law for filing the taxpayer's income tax return (including extensions thereof) for whichever of the following taxable years is the later:

(iii) The first taxable year beginning after December 31, 1953, and ending after August 16, 1954, for which assessment of a deficiency or credit or refund of an overpayment, as the case may be, resulting from an election under section 614(c)(2), is not prevented on September 2, 1958, by the operation of any law or rule of law, or

(iv) The first taxable year in which expenditures for development or operation of more than one mine in respect of the separate operating mineral interest are made by the taxpayer after the acquisition of such interest. However, if the latest time at which an election may be made under this subparagraph falls on or before the first day of the first month which begins more than 90 days after the regulations under section 614 are published in the Federal Register as a Treasury decision, such election may be made or modified at any time on or before the first day of such first month. See paragraph (c) of § 1.614-6 as to the binding effect of an election where the basis of a separate operating mineral interest in the hands of the taxpayer is determined by reference to the basis in the hands of a transferor.

(3) *Limitation.* If the taxpayer makes an election under section 614(c)(1) or (2) in accordance with section 614(c)(3)(B) and subparagraph (2) of this paragraph with respect to any operating mineral interest which constitutes part or all of an operating unit, such taxpayer may not make any election under section 614(c)(1) or (2) in accordance with section 614(c)(3)(A) and subparagraph (1) of this paragraph with respect to any operating mineral interest which constitutes part or all of such operating unit. The provisions of this subparagraph may be illustrated by the following example:

Example: In 1953, taxpayer A owned six separate operating mineral interests, designated No. 1 through No. 6, which he operated as a unit. Operating mineral interests Nos. 1 through 5 comprise a mine, and operating mineral interest No. 6 represents one mineral deposit in a single tract of land which is being extracted by means of two mines. In accordance with section 614(c)(3)(B) and subparagraph (2) of this paragraph, taxpayer A elects under section 614(c)(2) to treat operating mineral interest No. 6 as two separate operating mineral interests for the taxable year 1954 and all subsequent taxable years. Unless taxpayer A also makes an election under section 614(c)(1) to aggregate operating mineral interests Nos. 1 through 5 for the taxable year 1954 and all subsequent taxable years in accordance with section 614(c)(3)(B) and subparagraph (2) of this paragraph, he shall be deemed to have made an election to treat each of such interests as a separate property. Taxpayer A may not elect, under section 614(c)(1) and (3)(A), to aggregate operating mineral interests Nos. 1 through 5 for the taxable year 1958 or any subsequent taxable year.

(4) *Statute of limitations.* If the taxpayer makes any election in accordance with section 614(c)(3)(B) and subparagraph (2) of this paragraph and if assessment of any deficiency for any taxable year resulting from such election is prevented on the first day of the first month which begins more than 90 days after the regulations under section 614 are published in the Federal Register as a Treasury decision, or at any time within one year after such first day, by the operation of any law or rule of law, such assessment may, nevertheless, be made within one year after such first day. Any election by a taxpayer in accordance with section 614(c)(3)(B) shall consti-

Reg. § 1.614-3(f)(2)

tute consent to the assessment of any deficiency resulting from any such election. If refund or credit of any overpayment of income tax resulting from any election made in accordance with section 614(c)(3)(B) is prevented on such first day, or at any time within one year after such first day, by the operation of any law or rule of law, refund or credit of such overpayment may, nevertheless, be made or allowed but only if claim therefor is filed within one year after such first day. This subparagraph shall not apply with respect to any taxable year of a taxpayer for which an assessment of a deficiency resulting from an election made in accordance with section 614(c)(3)(B) or a refund or credit of an overpayment resulting from any such election, as the case may be, is prevented by the operation of any law or rule of law on September 2, 1958.

(5) *Elections—how made*—(i) *General rule.* Except as provided in subdivision (ii) of this subparagraph, an election under section 614(c)(1) or (2) and paragraph (a) or (b) of this section must be made by a statement attached to the income tax return of the taxpayer for the first taxable year for which the election is made. The statement shall contain the following information:

(*a*) Whether the taxpayer is making an election or elections with respect to the operating unit in accordance with section 614(c)(3)(A) or (B);

(*b*) A description of the operating unit of the taxpayer in sufficient detail to identify the operating mineral interests which are included within such operating unit;

(*c*) A description of each aggregation to be formed within the operating unit in sufficient detail to show that each aggregation consists of all the separate operating mineral interests which comprise any one mine or any two or more mines;

(*d*) A description of each separate operating mineral interest within the operating unit which is to be treated as a separate property in sufficient detail to show that such interest is not a part of any mine for which an election to aggregate has been made;

(*e*) The taxable year in which the first expenditure for development or operation was made by the taxpayer with respect to each separate operating mineral interest within the operating unit, but if the first expenditure for development or operation has not been made with respect to a separate operating mineral interest before the close of the taxable year for which the election under this section is made, such information should also be included;

(*f*) A description of each separate operating mineral interest within the operating unit which the taxpayer elects to treat as more than one such interest under section 614(c)(2) in sufficient detail to show that the separate operating mineral interest was not a part of an aggregation formed by the taxpayer under section 614(c)(1) for any taxable year prior to the taxable year for which the election under section 614(c)(2) is made, and to show that the mineral deposit representing the separate operating mineral interest is being developed or extracted by means of two or more mines;

(*g*) The taxable year in which the first expenditure for development or operation was made by the taxpayer with respect to each mine on the separate operating mineral interest that the taxpayer is electing to treat as more than one such interest; and

(*h*) The allocation of the mineral deposit representing the separate operating mineral interest between (or among) the newly formed interests and the method by which such allocation was made.

For the purpose of applying subdivisions (*e*) and (*g*) of this subdivision, if the first expenditure for development or operation with respect to a separate operating mineral interest or a mine was made prior to the first taxable year for which the election with respect to such interest or mine is applicable, the taxpayer may state that such is the case in lieu of identifying the exact taxable year in which such first expenditure was made. In any case where part of the information required under this subdivision can be adequately supplied by means of appropriately marked maps, the statement may be accompanied by such maps and may omit the required descriptive material to the extent replaced by the maps. The taxpayer shall maintain adequate records and maps in support of the above information. In the event that the first expenditure for development or operation with respect to a separate operating mineral interest is made by the taxpayer in a taxable year subsequent to the taxable year for which an election under this section has been made with respect to the operating unit of which such interest is a part, the taxpayer shall furnish information describing such interest in sufficient detail to identify it as a part of such operating unit, to show whether it is a part of a mine with respect to which the interests have previously been aggregated or have previously been treated as separate properties, and to indicate whether it is to be included within an aggregation.

(ii) *Special rule.* If the last day prescribed by law for filing the taxpayer's income tax return (including extensions thereof) for the first taxable year for which an election under section 614(c)(1)

Reg. § 1.614-3(f)(5)

or (2) is made falls before the first day of the first month which begins more than 90 days after the regulations under 614 are published in the Federal Register as a Treasury decision, the statement of election or modification thereof for such taxable year must be filed on or before the first day of such first month with the district director for the district in which such return was filed. The statement must contain the information as required in subdivision (i) of this subparagraph, must indicate the first taxable year for which the election contained therein is made, and shall be accompanied by an amended return or returns if necessary or, if appropriate, a claim for refund or credit.

(6) *Elections—when effective.* If the taxpayer has elected to form an aggregation under section 614(c)(1) and this section, the date on which the aggregation becomes effective is the first day of the first taxable year for which the election is made; except that if any separate operating mineral interest included in such aggregation was acquired after such first day, the date on which the inclusion of such interest in such aggregation becomes effective is the date of its acquisition. If the taxpayer elects to add another operating mineral interest to such aggregation for a subsequent taxable year, the date on which aggregation of the additional interest becomes effective is the first day of such subsequent taxable year or the date of acquisition of such interest, whichever is later. If an operating mineral interest is required to be included in the aggregation for a subsequent taxable year because such interest becomes a part of a mine which the taxpayer has previously elected to aggregate, the date on which the inclusion of such interest in the aggregation becomes effective is the first day of the subsequent taxable year or the date of acquisition of such interest, whichever is later. If the taxpayer has elected to treat a separate operating mineral interest as more than one such interest, the date on which the election becomes effective is the first day of the first taxable year for which the election is made or the earliest date on which the first expenditure for development or operation has been made by the taxpayer with respect to a mine on each newly formed separate operating mineral interest, whichever is later.

(7) *Elections—binding effect.* A valid election under section 614(c)(1) or (2) whether made in accordance with section 614(c)(3)(A) or (B) shall be binding upon the taxpayer for the taxable year for which made and for all subsequent taxable years unless consent to change the treatment of an operating mineral interest with respect to which an election has been made is obtained from the Commissioner. For rules relating to the binding effect of an election where the basis of a separate or an aggregated property in the hands of the transferee is determined by reference to the basis in the hands of the transferor, see paragraph (c) of § 1.614-6. A taxpayer can neither include within an aggregation a separate operating mineral interest which he has previously elected to treat as a separate property, nor exclude from an aggregation a separate operating mineral interest which he has properly elected to include within such aggregation unless consent to do so is obtained from the Commissioner. A change in tax consequences alone is not sufficient to obtain consent to change the treatment of an operating mineral interest. However, consent may be appropriate where, for example, there has been a substantial change in the taxpayer's operations so that a major part of an aggregation becomes a part of another operating unit. Applications for consent shall be made in writing to the Commissioner of Internal Revenue, Washington 25, D.C. The application must be accompanied by a statement indicating the reason or reasons for the change and furnishing the information required in subparagraph (5)(i) of this paragraph, unless such information has been previously filed and is current.

(8) *Invalid aggregations*—(i) *General rule.* In addition to aggregations which are invalid under this section because of the failure to make timely elections, aggregations may be invalid under this section in situations which may be divided into two general categories. The first category involves invalid basic aggregations. The second category involves invalid additions to basic aggregations.

(ii) *Invalid basic aggregations.* The term "invalid basic aggregations" refers to aggregations which are initially invalid. Generally, a basic aggregation is initially invalid because it does not include all the separate operating mineral interests which comprise a complete mine or mines or because it includes separate operating mineral interests which are not part of the same operating unit. If the taxpayer makes an invalid basic aggregation, each of the separate operating mineral interests included in such aggregation shall be treated as a separate property for the first taxable year for which the election is made and for all subsequent taxable years unless consent is obtained from the Commissioner to treat any such interest in a different manner. Consent will be granted in appropriate cases. For example, assume that the taxpayer elects to form an aggregation of the operating mineral interests which comprise one or more complete mines. If the taxpayer demonstrates that he inadvertently failed to include a minor part of one of the aggregated mines or inadvertently included a minor part of

Reg. § 1.614-3(f)(6)

another mine that is not a part of the aggregation, consent will ordinarily be granted to maintain the aggregation by including the part omitted or by excluding the part included. The provisions of this subdivision may be illustrated by the following examples.

Example (1). In 1958, taxpayer A owned ten operating mineral interests, designated No. 1 through No. 10, which he operated as a unit. Interests Nos. 1 through 5 comprised mine X, and interests Nos. 6 through 10 comprised mine Y. Taxpayer A had made his first development expenditure with respect to each of the ten interests before January 1, 1958. Taxpayer A elected under section 614(c)(1) and (3)(A) to aggregate interests Nos. 1 through 8 for 1958 and all subsequent taxable years. The aggregation formed by taxpayer A is an invalid basic aggregation because it does not include all the operating mineral interests which comprise a complete mine or mines. Therefore, interests Nos. 1 through 8 must be treated as separate properties for 1958 and all subsequent taxable years unless consent is obtained from the Commissioner to treat any of such interests in a different manner.

Example (2). In 1958, taxpayer B owned ten operating mineral interests designated No. 1 through No. 10. Interests Nos. 1 through 5 comprised mine X, and interests Nos. 6 through 10 comprised mine Y. Taxpayer B had made his first development expenditure with respect to each of the ten interests before January 1, 1958. Taxpayer B elected under section 614(c)(1) and (3)(A) to aggregate interests Nos. 1 through 10 for 1958 and all subsequent taxable years. Upon audit, it was determined that mines X and Y were in two separate operating units. Therefore, the aggregation formed by taxpayer B is invalid, and interests Nos. 1 through 10 must be treated as separate properties for 1958 and all subsequent taxable years unless consent is obtained from the Commissioner to treat any such interests in a different manner.

(iii) *Invalid additions.* The term "invalid addition" refers to an operating mineral interest which is invalidly aggregated with an existing aggregation. Generally, an addition is invalid because it is a part of a mine and is aggregated with an aggregation which does not include other interests which are parts of the same mine, or because it is in one operating unit and is included as part of an aggregation which is in another operating unit. If an invalid addition is properly a part of a mine with respect to which other interests have been validly aggregated for a taxable year prior to the first taxable year for which the election to aggregate the invalid addition is made, then the invalid addition shall be included in the aggregation of which it is properly a part of such first taxable year and all subsequent taxable years. Any other invalid addition shall be treated as a separate property for the first taxable year for which the election to aggregate such addition is made and for all subsequent taxable years unless consent is obtained from the Commissioner to treat any such interest in a different manner. The provisions of this subdivision may be illustrated by the following examples:

Example (1). In 1958, taxpayer A owned six operating mineral interests, designated No. 1 through No. 6, who he operated as a unit. Interests Nos. 1 through 3 comprised mine X, and interests Nos. 4 through 6 comprised mine Y. Taxpayer A had made his first development expenditure with respect to each of the six interests before January 1, 1958. Taxpayer A elected under section 614(c)(1) and (3)(A) to aggregate interests Nos. 1 through 3 for 1958 and all subsequent taxable years. He elected to treat interests Nos. 4 through 6 as separate properties for 1958 and all subsequent taxable years. In 1959, taxpayer A acquired and made his first development expenditure with respect to interest No. 7. Interest No. 7 was a part of the mine composed of interests Nos. 4 through 6. Taxpayer A elected under section 614(c)(1) and (3)(A) to aggregate interest No. 7 with the aggregation of interests Nos. 1 through 3 for 1959 and all subsequent taxable years. Interest No. 7 is an invalid addition and must be treated as a separate property for 1959 and all subsequent taxable years. It cannot be aggregated with interests Nos. 4 through 6 since taxpayer A has previously elected to treat such interests as separate properties. However, the valid basic aggregation composed of interests Nos. 1 through 3 is not affected by the invalid addition of interest No. 7.

Example (2). Assume the same facts as in example (1) except that taxpayer A elected under section 614(c)(1) and (3)(A) to aggregate interests Nos. 1 through 3 as one aggregation and interests Nos. 4 through 6 as another aggregation for 1958 and all subsequent taxable years. The aggregation of interest No. 7 with the aggregation consisting of interests Nos. 1 through 3 constitutes an invalid addition. Interest No. 7 must be included in the aggregation consisting of interests Nos. 4 through 6 for 1959 and all subsequent taxable years.

Example (3). In 1958, taxpayer B owned three operating mineral interests, designated No. 1 through No. 3, which comprised mine X. Taxpayer B had made his first development expenditure with respect to each of the three interests

Reg. § 1.614-3(f)(8)

before January 1, 1958. Taxpayer B elected under section 614(c)(1) and (3)(A) to aggregate interests Nos. 1 through 3 for 1958 and all subsequent taxable years. In 1959, taxpayer B acquired interests Nos. 4 through 7 which comprised mine Y. Taxpayer B made his first development expenditure with respect to each of the four interests during 1959. Taxpayer B elected under section 614(c)(1) and (3)(A) to aggregate interests Nos. 4 through 6 and to aggregate interest No. 7 with the aggregation consisting of interests Nos. 1 through 3 for 1959 and all subsequent taxable years. The aggregation consisting of interests Nos. 4 through 6 is an invalid basis aggregation, and the aggregation of interest No. 7 is an invalid addition. Interests Nos. 4 through 7 must be treated as separate properties for 1959 and all subsequent taxable years unless consent is obtained from the Commissioner to treat such interests in a different manner.

(g) *Special rule as to deductions under section 615(a) prior to aggregation*—(1) *General rule.* If an aggregation of operating mineral interests under section 614(c)(1) and paragraph (a) of this section includes any interest or interests in respect of which exploration expenditures, paid or incurred after the acquisition of such interest or interests, were deducted by the taxpayer under section 615(a) for any taxable year which precedes the date on which such aggregation becomes effective, then the tax imposed by chapter 1 of the Internal Revenue Code of 1954 for the taxable year or years in which such exploration expenditures were so deducted shall be recomputed in accordance with the rules contained in this paragraph. If an operating mineral interest is added to such aggregation for a subsequent taxable year and exploration expenditures made with respect to such interest after its acquisition were deducted by the taxpayer under section 615(a) for any taxable year which precedes the date on which the aggregation of such additional interest becomes effective, then the tax imposed by chapter 1 of the Internal Revenue Code of 1954 for the taxable year or years in which such exploration expenditures were so deducted shall be recomputed. For purposes of this paragraph, such taxable year or years shall be referred to as the taxable year or years for which a recomputation is required to be made. See paragraph (f)(6) of this section for rules relating to the date on which an aggregation becomes effective or the date on which the aggregation of an additional interest to an aggregation becomes effective. See subparagraph (3) of this paragraph for rules relating to the method of recomputation of tax. The provisions of this subparagraph may be illustrated by the following examples:

Example (1). In 1954, taxpayer A owned two operating mineral interests designated Nos. 1 and 2. Interest No. 1 was in the production stage prior to 1954. The first exploration expenditures with respect to interest No. 2 were made by taxpayer A in 1954 and were deducted under section 615(a) on his return for that year. In 1955, taxpayer A made his first development expenditure with respect to interest No. 2, and thereafter it was operated with interest No. 1 as a unit. Taxpayer A elected under section 614(c)(1) and (3)(B) to form an aggregation of interests Nos. 1 and 2 for 1955 and all subsequent taxable years. Taxpayer A must recompute his tax for 1954 in accordance with this paragraph.

Example (2). Assume the same facts as in example (1) except that, in 1957, taxpayer A acquired another operating mineral interest, designated No. 3, made his first exploration expenditures with respect to such interest in that year, and deducted such expenditures under section 615(a) on his return for that year. In 1958, taxpayer A made his first development expenditure with respect to interest No. 3. Interest No. 3 was part of the same operating unit as interests Nos. 1 and 2. Taxpayer A elected under section 614(c)(1) and (3)(B) to add interest No. 3 to his aggregation of interests Nos. 1 and 2 for 1958 and all subsequent taxable years. Taxpayer A must recompute his tax for 1957 in accordance with this paragraph.

(2) *Exceptions*—(i) *Taxable years beginning before January 1, 1958.* In the case of exploration expenditures deducted by the taxpayer with respect to an operating mineral interest for any taxable year beginning before January 1, 1958, subparagraph (1) of this paragraph shall apply only if the taxpayer has made an election under section 614(c)(1) or (2) with respect to the operating unit of which such interest is a part and such election applies to the taxable year for which such exploration expenditures were deducted. Thus, if the taxpayer does not make an election with respect to the operating unit under section 614(c)(1) or (2) and (3)(B), subparagraph (1) of this paragraph does not apply in the case of exploration expenditures deducted with respect to any operating mineral interest which is a part of such operating unit for any taxable year beginning before January 1, 1958. The provisions of this subdivision may be illustrated by the following examples:

Example (1). In 1956, taxpayer A acquired two operating mineral interests designated Nos. 1 and 2. Interest No. 1 was in the production stage at that time. Taxpayer A made his first exploration expenditures with respect to interest No. 2 in 1956, 1957, and 1958 and deducted such expendi-

Reg. § 1.614-3(g)(1)

tures under section 615(a) on his returns for such years. In 1959, taxpayer A made his first development expenditure with respect to interest No. 2. Interests Nos. 1 and 2 were operated as a unit. Taxpayer A elected under section 614(c)(1) taxable years. Only the exploration expenditures deducted by the taxpayer and (3)(A) to aggregate interests Nos. 1 and 2 for 1959 and all subsequent for 1958 must be taken into account for purposes of applying subparagraph (1) of this paragraph.

Example (2). In 1954, taxpayer B owned two operating mineral interests, designated Nos. 1 and 2, which he operated as a unit. Interest No. 1 was in the production stage at that time, and interest No. 2 represented one mineral deposit in a single tract of land which was being extracted by means of two mines. Under section 614(c)(2) and (3)(B), taxpayer B elects to treat interest No. 2 as two separate operating mineral interests, designated as Nos. 2(a) and 2(b), for 1954 and all subsequent taxable years. In 1955, taxpayer B acquired operating mineral interest No. 3. He made his first exploration expenditures with respect to interest No. 3 in 1955, 1956, and 1957 and deducted such expenditures under section 615(a) on his returns for such years. In 1958, taxpayer B made his first development expenditure with respect to interest No. 3, and thereafter it was operated with interests No. 1, 2(a), and 2(b) as a unit. Taxpayer B elects under section 614(c)(1) and (3)(B) to aggregate interests Nos. 1 and 3 for 1958 and all subsequent taxable years. The exploration expenditures deducted by the taxpayer for 1955, 1956, and 1957 must be taken into account for purposes of applying subparagraph (1) of this paragraph since the taxpayer has made an election under section 614(c)(2) with respect to the operating unit of which interest No. 3 is a part and such election applies to the taxable years 1955, 1956, and 1957.

(ii) *Interests formed pursuant to an election under section 614(c)(2).* In the case of exploration expenditures deducted with respect to an operating mineral interest which the taxpayer elects to treat as more than one such interest under section 614(c)(2) and paragraph (b) of this section, subparagraph (1) of this paragraph shall not apply. Thus, if the taxpayer deducts exploration expenditures with respect to an operating mineral interest, subsequently elects to treat such interest as more than one interest under section 614(c)(2), and includes one of the newly formed interests in an aggregation under section 614(c)(1), subparagraph (1) of this paragraph does not apply in the case of the exploration expenditures deducted with respect to the interest which the taxpayer elected to treat as more than one interest. The provisions of this subdivision may be illustrated by the following examples:

Example (1). In 1958, taxpayer A acquired two operating mineral interests, designated Nos. 1 and 2, which he operated as a unit. Each interest was an interest in a single mineral deposit in a single tract or parcel of land. There was a mine in the production stage on each of the two interests at that time. Taxpayer A elected under section 614(c)(1)(B) to treat interests Nos. 1 and 2 as separate properties. In 1959 and 1960, taxpayer A made exploration expenditures with respect to interest No. 2 for the purpose of extracting the mineral by means of a second mine, and he deducted such expenditures on his returns for such years. In 1961, taxpayer A made his first development expenditure with respect to a second mine on interest No. 2. Taxpayer A elected under section 614(c)(2) to treat interest No. 2 as two separate operating mineral interests, designated as Nos. 2(a) and 2(b), for 1961 and all subsequent taxable years. Interest No. 2(a) contained the producing mine and interest No. 2(b) contained the subsequently developed mine.

In his return for 1961, taxpayer A also elected under section 614(c)(1)(A) to aggregate interests Nos. 1 and 2(b) for 1961 and all subsequent taxable years. The exploration expenditures deducted with respect to interest No. 2 prior to the effective date of the formation of interests Nos. 2(a) and 2(b) need not be taken into account for purposes of applying subparagraph (1) of this paragraph.

Example (2). In 1954, taxpayer B owned two operating mineral interests designated Nos. 1 and 2. Interest No. 1 was an interest in a single mineral deposit in a single tract of land which was being extracted by means of two mines. Taxpayer B elected under section 614(c)(2) and (3)(B) to treat interest No. 1 as two separate operating mineral interests, designated as Nos. 1(a) and 1(b), for 1954 and all subsequent taxable years. In 1955, 1956, and 1957, taxpayer B made exploration expenditures with respect to interest No. 2 and deducted such expenditures on his returns for such years. In 1958, taxpayer B made his first development expenditure with respect to interest No. 2, and, on his return for that year, taxpayer B elected to aggregate interests Nos. 1(a) and 2 under section 614(c)(1) for 1958 and all subsequent taxable years. The exploration expenditures deducted with respect to interest No. 2 for 1955, 1956, and 1957 shall be taken into account for purposes of applying subparagraph (1) of this paragraph since such exploration expenditures were deducted with respect to an interest to which this subdivision does not apply.

Reg. § 1.614-3(g)(2)

(3) *Recomputation of tax*—(i) *General rule.* In the case of an aggregation formed under section 614(c)(1) and paragraph (a) of this section in respect of which a recomputation of tax is required to be made under the provisions of subparagraphs (1) and (2) of this paragraph for any taxable year or years, the tax imposed by chapter 1 of the Internal Revenue Code of 1954 shall be recomputed for each such taxable year as if—

(a) The taxpayer had elected to form an aggregation for the taxable year for which the recomputation is required to be made, and

(b) Such aggregation had included all the interests included in the aggregation formed under section 614(c)(1) except those interests which the taxpayer did not own during the taxable year for which the recomputation is required to be made and those interests in respect of which the taxpayer had made no expenditures for exploration, development, or operation before or during the taxable year for which the recomputation is required to be made.

If a recomputation of tax is required to be made for any taxable year in the case of the aggregation of an additional interest to an existing aggregation under section 614(c)(1), such recomputation shall be made as if—

(c) The taxpayer had elected to form an aggregation for the taxable year for which the recomputation is required to be made, and

(d) Such aggregation had included all the interests included in the aggregation formed under section 614(c)(1) (including any interest which the taxpayer had disposed of prior to the date on which the aggregation of the additional interest becomes effective) except those interests which the taxpayer did not own during the taxable year for which the recomputation is required to be made and those interests in respect of which the taxpayer had made no expenditures for exploration, development, or operation before or during the taxable year for which the recomputation is required to be made.

For purposes of this paragraph, any aggregation which is treated as having been formed under subdivisions *(a)* and *(b)* or under subdivisions *(c)* and *(d)* shall be referred to as the "constructed aggregated property".

(ii) *Recomputation of depletion allowance.* The taxpayer shall compute the depletion allowance with respect to the constructed aggregated property for the taxable year for which the recomputation is required to be made. In making this computation, cost depletion for such taxable year shall be computed with reference to the depletion unit for the constructed aggregated property. See paragraph (a) of § 1.611-2. Percentage depletion for such taxable year shall not exceed 50 percent of the taxable income from the constructed aggregated property computed in accordance with § 1.613-5. If a recomputation is required to be made for the same taxable year with respect to any other aggregation or aggregations formed by the taxpayer under section 614(c)(1), the depletion allowance with respect to the other constructed aggregated property or properties shall be similarly computed. If, for a taxable year in respect of which a recomputation is required, the sum of the depletion allowance or allowances as computed under this subdivision is less than the sum of the depletion allowance or allowances actually deducted for such taxable year with respect to all the properties required to be taken into account in making the computation under this subdivision, then the total depletion allowance deducted by the taxpayer for such taxable year shall be reduced by the difference. The taxable income or net operating loss of the taxpayer for such taxable year shall be adjusted to reflect such reduction for purposes of the recomputation of tax. However, if for a taxable year in respect of which a recomputation is required, the sum of the depletion allowance or allowances as computed under this subdivision exceeds the sum of the depletion allowance or allowances actually deducted for such taxable year with respect to all the properties required to be taken into account in making the computation under this subdivision, the recomputation of tax for such taxable year is disregarded for purposes of applying section 614(c)(4)(B), (C), and (D).

(iii) *Effect of recomputation with respect to items based on amount of income.* In making the recomputation of tax under this subparagraph for any taxable year, any deduction, credit, or other allowance which is based upon the adjusted gross income or taxable income of the taxpayer for such year shall be recomputed taking into account the adjustment required under subdivision (ii) of this subparagraph. For example, if a corporate taxpayer's taxable income is increased under the provisions of such subdivision, then the amount of charitable contributions which may be deducted under the limitation contained in section 170(b)(2) shall be correspondingly increased for purposes of the recomputation. Moreover, the effect that the recomputation of any deduction, credit, or other allowance for a taxable year has on the tax imposed for any other taxable year shall also be taken into account for purposes of the recomputation of tax under this subparagraph. Any change in items of tax preferences (as defined in section 57 and the regulations thereunder) must also be taken into account for purposes of the recomputation under this subparagraph.

Reg. § 1.614-3(g)(3)

(iv) *Effect of recomputation with respect to a net operating loss and a net operating loss deduction.* If the recomputation of tax under this subparagraph for the taxable year for which the recomputation is required to be made results in a reduction of a net operating loss for such year, then the taxpayer shall take into account the effect of such reduction on the tax imposed by chapter 1 of the Internal Revenue Code of 1954 (or by corresponding provisions of the Internal Revenue Code of 1939) for any taxable year affected by such reduction. If the recomputation of tax for the taxable year for which the recomputation is required to be made results in an increase in taxable income as defined in section 172(b)(2) for such year, then the taxpayer shall take into account the effect of such increase on the tax imposed by chapter 1 of the Internal Revenue Code of 1954 (or by corresponding provisions of the Internal Revenue Code of 1939) for any taxable year affected by such increase. Furthermore in making the recomputation of tax for any taxable year for which the recomputation is required to be made, the taxpayer shall take into account any change in the net operating loss deduction for such year resulting from the recomputation of tax for any other taxable year for which a recomputation is required to be made. For provisions relating to the net operating loss deduction, see section 172 and the regulations thereunder. For rules relating to the effect of the net operating loss deduction on the minimum tax for tax preferences see section 56 and the regulations thereunder and § 1.58-7.

(v) *Determination of increase in tax.* If the taxpayer elects to form an aggregation or aggregations for a taxable year under section 614(c)(1) and if a recomputation of tax is required to be made under this paragraph for any prior taxable year or years, then the taxpayer shall compute the difference between the tax, including the tax imposed by section 56 (relating to the minimum tax for tax preferences), as recomputed under this subparagraph for such prior taxable year or years (and other taxable years affected by the recomputation) and the tax liability previously determined (computed without regard to section 614(c)(4)) with respect to such prior taxable year or years (and other taxable years affected by the recomputation). If the taxpayer is subsequently required to make a recomputation with respect to any taxable year or years for which he has previously made a recomputation, then the taxpayer shall compute the difference between the tax as subsequently recomputed for such taxable year or years (and other taxable years affected by the subsequent recomputation) and the tax as previously recomputed for such taxable year or years (and other taxable years affected by the subsequent recomputation). For treatment of the increase in tax resulted from the recomputation of tax under this subparagraph, see subparagraph (4) of this paragraph.

(4) *Treatment of increase in tax*—(i) *General rule.* If the taxpayer elects to form an aggregation or aggregations for a taxable year under section 614(c)(1) and if a recomputation of tax is required to be made for any prior taxable year or years, then the total increase in tax resulting from such recomputation determined under subparagraph (3)(v) of this paragraph shall be taken into account in the first taxable year to which the election to form such aggregation or aggregations is applicable and in each succeeding taxable year until the full amount of such total increase in tax has been taken into account. The number of taxable years over which such total increase shall be taken into account shall be equal to the number of taxable years for which such recomputation results in a reduction of the taxpayer's depletion of this paragraph as limited by subparagraph (2) of this paragraph and for which a recomputation of tax is required to be made under subparagraph (1) allowance under subparagraph (3)(ii) of this paragraph. The amount of the increase in tax which is to be taken into account in a taxable year is determined by dividing the total increase in tax by the number of taxable years over which such total increase is to be taken into account. The tax imposed by chapter 1 of the Internal Revenue Code of 1954 for each of the taxable years over which the total increase in tax is to be taken into account shall be increased by the amount determined in accordance with the preceding sentence. However, such increase in tax for each of such taxable years shall have no effect upon the determination of the amount of any credit against the tax for any of such taxable years. For example, the amount of such increase shall not affect the computation of the limitation on the foreign tax credit under section 904. The amount of the increase in tax which is required to be taken into account by the taxpayer in a particular taxable year under section 614(c)(4)(C) shall be treated as a tax imposed with respect to such taxable years even though, without regard to section 614(c)(4) and this paragraph, such taxpayer would otherwise have no tax liability for such taxable year.

(ii) *Increase in tax not determinable as of first taxable year of aggregation.* If the recomputation of tax under subparagraph (3) of this paragraph, for any taxable year or years prior to the first taxable year to which the election to form an aggregation or aggregations under section 614(c)(1) applies, results in a reduction of any net operating loss carryover to a taxable year subse-

Reg. § 1.614-3(g)(4)

quent to such first taxable year, then the total increase in tax resulting from the recomputation is not determinable as of such first taxable year. In such case, the total increase in tax shall be taken into account in equal installments in the first taxable year for which such total increase is determinable and in each succeeding taxable year for which a portion of the increase in tax would have been taken into account under subdivision (i) of this subparagraph if the total increase had been determinable as of the first taxable year to which the election to form the aggregation or aggregations under section 614(c)(1) applies. The provisions of this subdivision may be illustrated by the following example:

Example. Assume that taxpayer A elects under section 614(c)(1) to form an aggregation for 1960 and all subsequent taxable years. Assume further that taxpayer A is required to recompute his tax for four prior taxable years under subparagraphs (1) and (2) of this paragraph and that the recomputation for each of such taxable years results in a reduction of taxpayer A's depletion allowance. Under subdivision (i) of this subparagraph, the total increase in tax resulting from the recomputation is to be taken into account in equal installments in 1960, 1961, 1962, and 1963. However, if the total increase in tax is not determinable until 1961 because the recomputation for the prior taxable years results in the reduction of a net operating loss carryover to 1961, then the total increase shall be taken into account in equal installments in 1961, 1962, and 1963. In like manner, if the total increase in tax is not determinable until 1962, it shall be taken into account in equal installments in 1962 and 1963.

(iii) *Death or cessation of existence of taxpayer.* If the taxpayer dies or ceases to exist, the portion of the increase in tax determined under subparagraph (3)(v) of this paragraph which has not been taken into account under subdivision (i) or (ii) of this subparagraph for taxable years prior to the taxable year of the occurrence of such death or such cessation of existence, as the case may be, shall be taken into account for the taxable year in which such death or such cessation of existence, as the case may be, occurs.

(5) *Adjustments to basis of aggregated property.* If the taxpayer elects to form an aggregated property or properties under section 614(c)(1) for a taxable year and if a recomputation of tax is required to be made for any taxable year which results in reduction of the depletion allowance previously deducted by the taxpayer for such year, then proper adjustments shall be made with respect to the adjusted basis of such aggregated property or properties. In such a case—

(i) If the sum of the depletion allowances actually deducted with respect to the interests included in a constructed aggregated property exceeds the depletion allowance computed under subparagraph (3)(ii) of this paragraph with respect to such constructed aggregated property, the adjusted basis of the aggregated property formed under section 614(c)(1) shall be increased by such excess, and

(ii) If the depletion allowance computed under subparagraph (3)(ii) of this paragraph with respect to a constructed aggregated property exceeds the sum of the depletion allowances actually deducted with respect to the interests included in such constructed aggregated property, the adjusted basis of the aggregated property formed under section 614(c)(1) shall be reduced (but not below zero) by such excess.

However, the adjusted basis of an aggregated property formed under section 614(c)(1) may be increased only to the extent such excess would have resulted in an increase in such adjusted basis if taken into account under paragraph (a) of § 1.614-6. Thus, if depletion previously allowed with respect to the separate operating mineral interests included in the aggregation formed under section 614(c)(1) exceeds the total of the unadjusted bases of such interests by $5,000, and if the recomputation of tax required to be made under this paragraph results in a depletion allowance which is $7,000 less than the depletion actually deducted with respect to such interests, then the adjusted basis of such aggregation may be increased by only $2,000. If, with respect to the same aggregated property formed under section 614(c)(1), adjustments to adjusted basis are required under this subparagraph as a result of recomputation of tax for two or more taxable years, the total or net amount of such adjustments shall be taken into account. Any adjustment to the adjusted basis of an aggregation required by this subparagraph shall be taken into account as of the effective date of the election to form such aggregation under section 614(c)(1) and shall be effective for all purposes of subtitle A of the Internal Revenue Code of 1954. For other rules relating to the determination of the adjusted basis of an aggregated property, see paragraph (a) of § 1.614-6. [Reg. § 1.614-3.]

☐ [*T.D.* 6524, 1-19-61. *Amended by T.D.* 7170, 3-10-72 *and by T.D.* 7564, 9-11-78.]

[Reg. § 1.614-4]

§ 1.614-4. Treatment under the Internal Revenue Code of 1939 with respect to separate operating mineral interests for taxable years beginning before January 1, 1964, in the case of oil and gas wells.—[The text of Reg.

Reg. § 1.614-4

§ 1.614-4, relating to the treatment of separate operating mineral interests for tax years beginning before 1964, is no longer reproduced by CCH. For post-1963 regulations, see Reg. § 1.614-8.]

[Reg. § 1.614-5]

§ 1.614-5. **Special rules as to aggregating nonoperating mineral interests.**—(a) *Aggregating nonoperating mineral interests for taxable years beginning before January 1, 1958.* Upon proper showing to the Commissioner, a taxpayer who owns two or more separate nonoperating mineral interests in a single tract or parcel of land, or in two or more contiguous tracts or parcels of land, shall be permitted to aggregate all such interests in each separate kind of mineral deposit and treat them as one property. Permission will be granted by the Commissioner only if the taxpayer establishes that he will sustain an undue hardship if such nonoperating mineral interests are not treated as one property. Such hardship may exist, for example, if it is impossible for the taxpayer to determine the boundaries, source, or costs of the separate interests, or if a taxpayer who owns a single royalty interest, production payment, or net profits interest cannot determine the separate deposits from which his payments will be derived. In no event shall undue hardship be deemed to exist solely by reason of tax disadvantage. The treatment of such interests as one property shall be applicable for all purposes of subtitle A of the Internal Revenue Code of 1954. In no event may nonoperating mineral interests in tracts or parcels of land which are not contiguous be treated as one property. The term "two or more contiguous tracts or parcels of land" means tracts or parcels of land which have common boundaries. Common boundaries include survey lines, public roads, or similar easements for the use of land without the existence of an intervening mineral right between the tracts or parcels of land. Tracts or parcels of land which touch only at a common corner are not contiguous. For the definition of "nonoperating mineral interests," see paragraph (g) of this section.

(b) *Manner and scope of election*—(1) *Time for filing application for permission to aggregate separate nonoperating mineral interests under paragraph (a) of this section.* The application for permission to aggregate separate nonoperating mineral interests under paragraph (a) of this section shall be filed at any time on or before the first day of the first month which begins more than 90 days after the regulations under section 614 are published in the Federal Register as a Treasury decision. Such application shall indicate the first taxable year for which the aggregation is to be formed. If, prior to such publication of the regulations under section 614, an application has been filed, the taxpayer need file only a supplemental application containing such additional information as is necessary to comply with the requirements of subparagraph (2) of this paragraph.

(2) *Contents of application and returns under permission.* The application for permission to aggregate nonoperating mineral interests under paragraph (a) of this section shall include a complete statement of the facts upon which the taxpayer relies to show the undue hardship which would result if such an aggregation were not permitted. Such application shall also include a description of all the nonoperating mineral interests owned by the taxpayer within the tract or tracts of land involved. A general description, accompanied by maps appropriately marked, which accurately circumscribes the scope of the aggregation and shows that the taxpayer is aggregating all the nonoperating mineral interests in a particular kind of mineral deposit within the tract or tracts of land involved will be sufficient. If the Commissioner grants permission, a copy of the letter granting such permission shall be filed with the district director for the district in which the taxpayer's income tax return was filed for the first taxable year for which such permission applies, and shall be accompanied by an amended return or returns if necessary.

(3) *Election—binding effect.* The election to aggregate separate nonoperating mineral interests under paragraph (a) of this section shall be binding upon the taxpayer for the first taxable year for which made and all subsequent taxable years beginning before January 1, 1958, unless consent to make a change is obtained from the Commissioner. The application for consent to make a change must set forth in detail the reason or reasons for such change. Consent to a different treatment shall not be granted where the principal purpose for such change is due to tax consequences. For rules relating to the binding effect of an election where the basis of an aggregated property in the hands of the transferee is determined by reference to the basis in the hands of the transferor, see paragraph (c) of § 1.614-6.

(4) *Aggregations under the 1939 Code.* An application for permission to aggregate nonoperating mineral interests under paragraph (a) of this section shall be submitted in accordance with the requirements of this paragraph notwithstanding the fact that the taxpayer may have aggregated such interests for taxable years to which the Internal Revenue Code of 1939 is applicable. If such interests were aggregated for taxable years to which the Internal Revenue Code of 1939 applies and the aggregation was approved by the

Reg. § 1.614-5(b)(4)

Internal Revenue Service for such years after full consideration thereof on its merits, such approval will generally be accepted as evidence that undue hardship would result if the aggregation were not permitted.

(c) *Termination of aggregation of nonoperating mineral interests.*—(1) *General rule.* Any aggregation of nonoperating mineral interests formed under paragraphs (a) and (b) of this section shall not apply with respect to any taxable year beginning after December 31, 1957. Thus, if a taxpayer makes a binding election to form such an aggregation for taxable years beginning before January 1, 1958, then in order to form an aggregation with respect to any taxable year beginning after December 31, 1957, he must obtain permission in accordance with the rules prescribed in paragraphs (d) and (e) of this section.

(2) *Bases of separate nonoperating mineral interests.* If a taxpayer forms an aggregation of nonoperating mineral interests under paragraphs (a) and (b) of this section which is terminated under subparagraph (1) of this paragraph, the adjusted bases of the separate nonoperating mineral interests included in such aggregation shall be determined in accordance with paragraph (a)(2) of § 1.614-6.

(d) *Aggregating nonoperating mineral interests for taxable years beginning after December 31, 1957, or for earlier taxable years.* Upon proper showing to the Commissioner, a taxpayer who owns two or more separate nonoperating mineral interests in a single tract or parcel of land, or in two or more adjacent tracts or parcels of land, shall be permitted, under section 614(e), to form an aggregation of all of such interests in each separate kind of mineral deposit and treat such aggregation as one property. Permission shall be granted by the Commissioner only if the taxpayer establishes that a principal purpose in forming the aggregation is not the avoidance of tax. The fact that the aggregation of nonoperating mineral interests will result in a substantial reduction in tax is evidence that avoidance of tax is a principal purpose of the taxpayer. An aggregation formed under the provisions of this paragraph shall be considered as one property for all purposes of the Internal Revenue Code of 1954. In no event may nonoperating mineral interests in tracts or parcels of land which are not adjacent be aggregated and treated as one property. The term "two or more adjacent tracts or parcels of land" means tracts or parcels of land that are in reasonably close proximity to each other depending on the facts and circumstances of each case. Adjacent tracts or parcels of land do not necessarily have any common boundaries, and may be separated by intervening mineral rights. For the definition of "nonoperating mineral interests," see paragraph (g) of this section.

(e) *Manner and scope of election*—(1) *Time for filing application for permission to aggregate separate nonoperating mineral interests under section 614(e).* The application for permission to aggregate separate nonoperating mineral interests under section 614(e) and paragraph (d) of this section shall be made in writing to the Commissioner of Internal Revenue, Washington 25, D.C. Such application shall be filed within 90 days after the beginning of the first taxable year beginning after December 31, 1957, for which aggregation is desired or within 90 days after the acquisition of one of the nonoperating mineral interests which is to be included in the aggregation, whichever is later. However, if the last day on which the application may be filed under this paragraph falls before the first day of the first month which begins more than 90 days after the regulations under section 614 are published in the Federal Register as a Treasury decision, such application may be filed at any time on or before the first day of such first month. If, prior to such publication of the regulations under section 614, an application has been filed, the taxpayer need file only a supplemental application containing such additional information as is necessary to comply with subparagraph (4) of this paragraph.

(2) *Election to apply section 614(e) retroactively.* The application for permission to aggregate separate nonoperating mineral interests under section 614(e) and paragraph (d) of this section may be filed, at the election of the taxpayer, for any taxable year beginning before January 1, 1958, to which the Internal Revenue Code of 1954 is applicable. In such case, the application may be filed at any time on or before the first day of the first month which begins more than 90 days after the regulations under section 614 are published in the Federal Register as a Treasury decision. Such application shall designate the first taxable year for which the aggregation is to be formed. If, prior to such publication of regulations under section 614, an application has been filed, the taxpayer need file only a supplemental application containing such additional information as is necessary to comply with the requirements of subparagraph (4) of this paragraph.

(3) *Limitation.* If the taxpayer forms any aggregation of nonoperating mineral interests under subparagraph (2) of this paragraph, then any aggregation of nonoperating mineral interests formed under paragraphs (a) and (b) of this section shall not apply for any taxable year. The

Reg. § 1.614-5(c)(1)

provisions of this subparagraph may be illustrated by the following example:

Example. In 1954, taxpayer A owns six separate nonoperating mineral interests designated No. 1 through No. 6. Interests Nos. 1 through 3 are royalty interests in contiguous tracts of land. Interests Nos. 4 through 6, which are located in an entirely different area from interests Nos. 1 through 3, are royalty interests in tracts of land which are not contiguous but which are adjacent to each other. In 1959 taxpayer A obtains permission and elects under section 614(e) and subparagraph (2) of this paragraph to form an aggregation of interests Nos. 4 through 6 for 1956 and all subsequent taxable years. Taxpayer A may not elect to form an aggregation of interests Nos. 1 through 3 under paragraphs (a) and (b) of this section for 1954 or any subsequent taxable year. If taxpayer A wishes to form an aggregation of interests Nos. 1 through 3, he must obtain permission under paragraph (d) of this section and this paragraph.

(4) *Contents of application and returns under permission.* The application for permission to aggregate nonoperating mineral interests under section 614(e) and paragraph (d) of this section shall include a complete statement of the facts upon which the taxpayer relies to show that avoidance of tax is not a principal purpose of forming the aggregation. Such application shall also include a description of the nonoperating mineral interests within the tract or tracts of land involved. A general description, accompanied by maps appropriately marked, which accurately circumscribes the scope of the aggregation and shows that the taxpayer is aggregating all the nonoperating mineral interests in a particular kind of mineral deposit within the tract or tracts of land involved will be sufficient. If the Commissioner grants permission, a copy of the letter granting such permission shall be attached to the taxpayer's income tax return for the first taxable year for which such permission applies. If the taxpayer has already filed such return, a copy of the letter of permission shall be filed with the district director for the district in which such return was filed and shall be accompanied by an amended return or returns if necessary or, if appropriate, a claim for credit or refund.

(5) *Election—binding effect.* The election to aggregate separate nonoperating mineral interests under section 614(e) and paragraph (d) of this section shall be binding upon the taxpayer for the first taxable year for which made and for all subsequent taxable years unless consent to make a change is obtained from the Commissioner. The application for consent to make a change must set forth in detail the reason or reasons for such change. Consent to a different treatment shall not be granted where the principal purpose for such change is due to tax consequences. For rules relating to the binding effect of an election where the basis of an aggregated property in the hands of the transferee is determined by reference to the basis in the hands of the transferor, see paragraph (c) of § 1.614-6.

(6) *Aggregations under the 1939 Code.* An application for permission to aggregate nonoperating mineral interests under section 614(e) and paragraph (d) of this section shall be submitted in accordance with the requirements of this paragraph notwithstanding the fact that the taxpayer may have aggregated such interests for taxable years to which the Internal Revenue Code of 1939 is applicable. If such interests were aggregated for taxable years to which the Internal Revenue Code of 1939 applies and the aggregation was approved by the Internal Revenue Service for such years after full consideration thereof on its merits, such approval will generally be accepted as evidence that avoidance of tax is not a principal purpose of forming the aggregation.

(f) *Elections—when effective.* If the taxpayer has elected to form an aggregation under either paragraph (a) or paragraph (d) of this section, the date on which the aggregation becomes effective is the first day of the first taxable year for which the election is made; except that if any separate nonoperating mineral interest included in such aggregation was acquired after such first day, the date on which the inclusion of such interest in such aggregation becomes effective is the date of its acquisition.

(g) *Definition of nonoperating mineral interests.* For purposes of this section, "nonoperating mineral interests" includes only those interests described in section 614(a) which are not operating mineral interests within the meaning of paragraph (b) of § 1.614-2. The taxpayer who holds the operating or working rights in a mineral deposit, but is not actually conducting operations with respect to such deposit, does not have a nonoperating mineral interest in such deposit notwithstanding the fact that he intends to transfer such operating rights at a later time. [Reg. § 1.614-5.]

☐ [*T.D.* 6524, 1-9-61.]

[Reg. § 1.614-6]

§ 1.614-6. Rules applicable to basis, holding period, and abandonment losses where mineral interests have been aggregated or combined.—(a) *Basis of property resulting from aggregation or combination*—(1) *General rule.* (i) When a taxpayer has aggregated as one property

Reg. § 1.614-6(a)

two or more interests under section 614(b) (prior to its amendment by section 226(a) of the Revenue Act of 1964), (c), or (e), the unadjusted basis of such aggregated property shall be the sum of the unadjusted bases of the various mineral interests aggregated. The adjusted basis of the aggregated property on the effective date of the aggregation shall be the unadjusted basis of the aggregated property, adjusted by the total of all adjustments to the bases of the several mineral interests aggregated as required by section 1016 to the effective date of aggregation. Thereafter, the adjustments to basis required by section 1016 shall apply to the total adjusted basis of the aggregated property for all purposes of subtitle A of the Code.

(ii) When a taxpayer has combined as one property two or more interests under section 614(b) (as amended by section 226(a) of the Revenue Act of 1964), the adjusted basis of such combined property shall be the sum of—

(a) The unadjusted bases of all such interests which have never been included in an aggregation; and

(b) The adjusted bases of all such interests which at some time have been included in an aggregation, as of the date on which they ceased to participate in an aggregation;

adjusted by the total of all adjustments to the bases of the several mineral interests combined, as required by section 1016,

(c) In the case of interests described in (a), for the entire period of the taxpayer's ownership of such interest; and

(d) In the case of interests described in (b), for the period, if any, between the time of deaggregation and the time of combination.

Thereafter, the adjustments to basis required by section 1016 shall apply to the total adjusted basis of the combined property for all purposes of subtitle A of the Code.

(2) *Bases upon disposition of part of, or termination of, or change in, an aggregated or combined property*—(i) *In general.* (a) When a taxpayer has aggregated or combined two or more separate mineral interests as one property under section 614(b) (either before or after its amendment by section 226(a) of the Revenue Act of 1964), (c), or (e) and thereafter sells, exchanges, or otherwise disposes of part of such property, the total adjusted basis of the property as of the date of sale, exchange, or other disposition shall be apportioned to determine the adjusted basis of the part disposed of and the part retained for purposes of computing gain or loss, depletion, and for all other purposes of subtitle A of the Code. Such adjusted basis shall be determined by apportioning the total adjusted basis of the property between the part of the property disposed of and the part retained in the same proportion as the fair market value of each part (as of the date of sale, exchange, or other disposition) bears to the total fair market value of the property as of such date. For determining gain or loss on the sale or exchange of any part of the aggregated or combined property, the adjusted basis of the aggregated or combined property (from which the adjusted basis of the part is determined) shall not be reduced below zero.

(b) If, for any taxable year after the first taxable year for which an aggregation under section 614(b) (prior to its amendment by section 226(a) of the Revenue Act of 1964), (c), or (e) is effective—

(1) Any such aggregation is terminated for any reason other than the expiration of an aggregation by reason of section 614(b) as amended by section 226(a) of the Revenue Act of 1964 (see subdivision (ii) of this subparagraph), or

(2) The treatment of any mineral interests in any such aggregation is changed after obtaining the consent of the Commissioner,

then the adjusted basis of the aggregated property as of the first day of the first taxable year for which such termination or change is effective shall be apportioned to determine the adjusted bases of the resultant separate mineral interests, as of such first day, for purposes of computing gain or loss, depletion, and for all other purposes of subtitle A of the Code. The adjusted bases of such separate mineral interests shall be determined by apportioning the adjusted basis of the aggregated property (as of the first day of the first taxable year for which such termination or change is effective) between or among such interests in the same proportion as the fair market value of each such interest (as of such first day) bears to the total fair market value of the aggregated property as of such first day. For the purpose of determining the adjusted bases of the separate mineral interests, the adjusted bases of the aggregated property (from which the adjusted basis of each separate mineral interest is determined) shall not be reduced below zero.

(ii) *Allocation of basis of aggregation of operating mineral interests in oil and gas wells as of the first day of the first taxable year beginning after December 31, 1963*—(a) *Fair market value method.* Unless the taxpayer elects to use the allocation of adjustments method of determining basis provided in (b) of this subdivision (ii), the adjusted basis as of the first day of the first taxable year beginning after December 31, 1963,

Reg. § 1.614-6(a)(2)

of each interest which was participating in an aggregation of operating mineral interests on the day preceding such first day shall be determined by multiplying the adjusted basis of the aggregation by a fraction the numerator of which is the fair market value of such interest and the denominator of which is the fair market value of such aggregation. For purposes of this subdivision (a), the adjusted basis and the fair market value of the aggregation, and the fair market value of such interest, shall be determined as of the day preceding the first day of the first taxable year which begins after December 31, 1963. Unless the taxpayer elects to use the allocation of adjustments method, he shall obtain accurate and reliable information, and keep records with respect thereto, establishing all facts necessary for making the computation prescribed in this subdivision (a). See example (5) of subparagraph (3) of this paragraph.

(b) *Allocation of adjustments method.* (i) The taxpayer may elect to determine basis by an allocation of adjustments in lieu of the fair market value method prescribed in (a) of this subdivision (ii). In such a case, the adjusted basis (as of the first day of the first taxable year beginning after December 31, 1963) of each interest which was participating in an aggregation of operating mineral interests on the day preceding such first day is the unadjusted basis of such interest immediately after its acquisition by the taxpayer, adjusted by the total of all adjustments to its basis as required by section 1016 to the effective date of aggregation, and by that portion of those section 1016 adjustments to the basis of the aggregation which is reasonably attributable to such interest. For this purpose, two or more interests which are being combined upon deaggregation shall be treated as one interest. An adjustment to the basis of the aggregation is reasonably attributable to such interest to the extent that the adjustment thereto resulted from inclusion of the interest in the aggregation, even though such interest would not have been entitled to the adjustment to the same extent if such interest had been treated separately because of the 50 percent of taxable income limitation or for any other reason. In a case in which the amount of a percentage depletion deduction which was allowed with respect to an aggregation was limited by the 50 percent of taxable income limitation of section 613(a), the portion of such amount which is attributable to each of the interests in the aggregation shall be determined by multiplying such amount by a fraction, the numerator of which is the gross income from such interest and the denominator of which is the gross income from the aggregation. The determination as to which property a particular adjustment is attributable may be based upon records of production or any other facts which establish the reasonableness of the determination. See example (6) of subparagraph (3) of this paragraph.

(ii) If, under the adjustment described in (i) of this subdivision (b), the total of the adjusted bases of the interest which were included in the aggregation exceeds the adjusted basis of the aggregation, the adjusted bases of the interests shall be further adjusted so that the total of the adjusted bases of the interests equals the adjusted basis of the aggregation. This further adjustment shall be made by reducing the basis of each interest (other than an interest having a basis of zero) by an amount which is determined by multiplying such excess by a fraction, the numerator of which is the adjusted basis of such interest after making the adjustment described in (i) of this subdivision (b) and the denominator of which is the total of the adjusted bases of all such interests after making the adjustment described in (i) of this subdivision (b). See example (6) of subparagraph (3) of this paragraph.

(iii) The election provided for in this subdivision (b) shall be made not later than the time prescribed by law for filing the taxpayer's income tax return (including extensions thereof) for the first taxable year beginning after December 31, 1963, and shall be made in a statement attached to such return.

(3) The application of subparagraphs (1) and (2) of this paragraph may be illustrated by the following examples:

Example (1). A taxpayer owning three operating mineral interests, designated Nos. 1, 2, and 3, within a single operating unit, properly elects to aggregate such properties under section 614(b) for the calendar year 1954 in his income tax return filed on April 15, 1955. The unadjusted bases and adjustments under section 1016 for depletion through December 31, 1953, in respect of such properties are as follows:

	Unadjusted basis	Adjustments under Section 1016
No. 1	$25,000	$27,000
No. 2	18,000	10,000
No. 3	15,000	4,000
Total	$58,000	$41,000

Reg. § 1.614-6(a)(3)

The adjusted basis of the aggregated property as of January 1, 1954, is $17,000 ($58,000 − $41,000).

Example (2). Assume the same facts as in example (1), except that a portion of the aggregated property is sold on June 1, 1956, for $15,000 which is also the fair market value of such portion on the date of sale. In order to determine the gain or loss from this sale as well as the adjusted basis of the retained property, an apportionment must be made. The aggregated property had a fair market value of $25,000 on the date of sale. From January 1, 1954, through May 31, 1956, $10,000 of depletion has been allowed with respect to the aggregated property. The adjusted basis of the portion sold is determined as follows:

$$\$7,000 \text{ (adjusted basis of aggregated property)} \times \frac{\$15,000}{\$25,000} = \$4,200 \text{ (adjusted basis of portion sold)}$$

Therefore, the gain on this sale of the portion sold is $10,800 ($15,000 − $4,200). The adjusted basis of the property retained is $2,800 ($7,000 − $4,200).

Example (3). Assume the same facts as in example (2), except that instead of selling, the taxpayer subleases one of the leases making up the aggregated property, retaining a one-eighth royalty interest therein. The fair market value of such lease is $15,000 on the date of the sublease. The adjusted basis of such royalty interest is $4,200 which is computed as follows:

$$\$7,000 \text{ (adjusted basis of aggregated property)} \times \frac{\$15,000 \text{ (FMV of portion transferred)}}{\$25,000 \text{ (FMV of aggregated property)}}$$

Example (4). In 1953, a taxpayer owned mineral interests Nos. 1, 2, and 3 which he operated as a unit. He owned no other operating interests during that year. The unadjusted bases of these properties were $10,000, $15,000, and $20,000, respectively, and depletion allowed through December 31, 1953, was $5,000 with respect to each property. The taxpayer operated these properties during the year 1954 and, in addition, operated as part of the unit mineral interest No. 4 which he acquired on July 1, 1954, on which date he made the first exploration expenditure with respect thereto. He paid $20,000 for No. 4. In his return for the calendar year 1954, the taxpayer elected under section 614(b) to aggregate all of these mineral interests. The taxpayer must compute cost depletion for the calendar year 1954 on the basis of an aggregated property with an adjusted basis of $30,000 ($45,000 − $15,000) for the period from January 1 to June 30, and with an adjusted basis of $50,000 (less depletion for the first six months) for the period from July 1 to December 31. If applicable, the taxpayer must compute percentage depletion on the basis of gross income and taxable income from the aggregated property for the entire year, including the gross income and deductions with respect to operating mineral interest No. 4 for the period from July 1 to December 31. If a portion of the aggregated property is sold during the first six months, its adjusted basis must be determined at the time of sale with an adjustment for depletion to the date of sale. If percentage depletion is applicable, it must be allocated on an equitable basis to the periods prior and subsequent to the date of sale in order to determine the adjustment for depletion to the date of sale.

Example (5). A taxpayer owns two operating mineral interests in oil wells, designated Nos. 1 and 2, in tract A, and another such interest, designated No. 3, in tract B. All three interests are in the same operating unit (as defined in paragraph (c) of § 1.614-2). The taxpayer, who is on a calendar year basis, has properly elected under § 1.614-2 to aggregate such interests for the calendar years 1954 through 1963. The unadjusted bases and adjustments under section 1016 for depletion through December 31, 1953, in respect of such interests are as follows:

	Unadjusted basis	Adjustments under section 1016
No. 1	$42,000	$11,000
No. 2	37,000	4,000
No. 3	19,000	23,000
Total	$98,000	$38,000

The adjusted basis of the aggregated property as of January 1, 1954, is therefore $60,000 ($98,000 minus $38,000). The taxpayer properly elects under section 614(b) and § 1.614-8 to treat Nos. 1 and 2 as separate properties for the calendar year 1964 and thereafter and does not elect to use the allocation of adjustments method of determining basis provided in subparagraph (2)(ii)(*b*) of this paragraph. No. 3 will be treated as a separate property, also, because it is in a different tract than the taxpayer's other interests. From January 1, 1954, through December 31, 1963, $50,000 of

Reg. § 1.614-6(a)(3)

depletion has been allowed with respect to the aggregated property, leaving an adjusted basis of $10,000 ($60,000 minus $50,000) on January 1, 1964. On December 31, 1963, the aggregated property has a fair market value of $40,000. Nos. 1, 2, and 3 have fair market values of $16,000, $22,000, and $2,000, respectively. Accordingly, the adjusted bases of Nos. 1, 2, and 3 on January 1, 1964, are $4,000

($10,000 (adjusted basis of aggregated property) × $\frac{16,000}{40,000}$), $5,500 ($10,000 × $\frac{22,000}{40,000}$), and $500 ($10,000 × $\frac{2,000}{40,000}$), respectively.

Example (6). A taxpayer owns four operating mineral interests in oil wells, designated Nos 1, 2, 3, and 4. All four interests are in the same operating unit and the same tract or parcel of land. The taxpayer, who is on a calendar year basis, has properly elected under § 1.614-2 to aggregate such interests for the calendar years 1954 through 1963. The taxpayer properly elects under section 614(b) and paragraph (a) of § 1.614-8 to treat Nos. 1 and 2 as separate properties for the calendar year 1964 and thereafter. The taxpayer also properly elects to use the allocation of adjustments method of determining basis as provided in subparagraph (2)(ii)(*b*) of this paragraph. The unadjusted bases of Nos. 1, 2, and combined 3 and 4, the adjustments attributable to each, and the deaggregated basis of each (prior to further adjustment as provided in subparagraph (2)(ii)(*b*)(*ii*) of this paragraph) are as follows:

	Basis upon acquisition	Adjustments to time of aggregation	Attributable adjustments during aggregation	Basis upon deaggregation after first adjustment
No. 1	$ 35,000	$ 1,000	$16,000	$18,000
No. 2	30,000	11,000	23,000	0
No. 3	25,000	3,000	5,000⎫	
No. 4	10,000	12,000	9,000⎭	6,000
	$100,000	$27,000	$53,000	$24,000

The total of the adjusted bases (prior to further adjustment) of the interests which were included in the aggregation is $24,000 while the adjusted basis of the aggregation is $20,000 ($100,000 minus the sum of $27,000 and $53,000). Therefore,

($4,000 × $\frac{18,000}{24,000}$)

to $15,000. Similarly, the adjusted basis of combined Nos. 3 and 4 of $6,000 is further reduced by $1,000

($4,000 × $\frac{6,000}{24,000}$)

to $5,000. Assume further that the taxpayer also owns interest No. 5 in the same tract or parcel of land, that such interest was not a part of any aggregation, that such interest had a basis of $15,000 upon acquisition and had subsequent adjustments in reduction of basis totalling $17,000, and that the taxpayer does not elect to treat such interest as a separate property. In such case, Nos. 3, 4, and 5 will be combined. The combination will have an adjusted basis of $3,000, determined by adding the unadjusted basis of No. 5 ($15,000) and the adjusted bases of combined Nos. 3 and 4 the adjusted bases of the interests are further reduced by $4,000 ($24,000 minus $20,000). The adjusted basis of No. 1 of $18,000 is further reduced by $3,000

upon deaggregation ($5,000), and subtracting from the total thereof ($20,000) the adjustments to No. 5 ($17,000).

(4) *Basis for gain and loss where mineral interests acquired before March 1, 1913, are included in an aggregation.* Where mineral interests acquired before March 1, 1913, are included in an aggregation under section 614(b), (c), or (e), the aggregated property has two bases, one for the determination of gain and another for the determination of loss upon the disposition of the whole or a part of the aggregated property. For the

Reg. § 1.614-6(a)(4)

purpose of determining gain, the adjusted basis of the aggregated property on the effective date of aggregation shall be the sum of—

(i) The unadjusted bases of those mineral interests acquired on or after March 1, 1913, plus

(ii) The cost of any interest acquired before March 1, 1913 (adjusted for the period before March 1, 1913), or the fair market value of such interest as of March 1, 1913, whichever is greater,

and such sum shall be adjusted by the total of all adjustments to the bases of the several mineral interests aggregated as required by section 1016 to the effective date of aggregation. For the purpose of determining loss, the adjusted basis of the aggregated property on the effective date of aggregation shall be the sum of—

(iii) The unadjusted bases of those mineral interests acquired on or after March 1, 1913, plus

(iv) The cost of those interests acquired before March 1, 1913, adjusted for the period before March 1, 1913,

and such sum shall be adjusted by the total of all adjustments to the bases of the several mineral interests aggregated as required by section 1016 to the effective date of aggregation. Thereafter, the adjustments to basis required by section 1016 shall apply to the total adjusted basis of the aggregated property for all purposes of the Internal Revenue Code of 1954. Upon disposition of a part of the aggregated property or upon termination of the aggregation for any reason, or upon change in the treatment of any mineral interests in the aggregation with consent of the Commissioner, the adjusted basis for determining gain and the adjusted basis for determining loss with respect to each resultant part of the aggregated property shall be determined in accordance with subparagraph (2) of this paragraph. The provisions of this subparagraph may be illustrated by the following examples:

Example (1). At the close of 1953 a taxpayer owned two operating mineral interests designated as Nos. 1 and 2 in the same operating unit. Operating mineral interest No. 1 was acquired by the taxpayer before March 1, 1913, and on such date its basis with reference to its fair market value was $50,000 and its adjusted basis with reference to its cost was $44,000. The unadjusted basis of operating mineral interest No. 2, acquired after March 1, 1913, was $30,000. Adjustments under section 1016 for depletion from March 1, 1913, through December 31, 1953, were $37,000 for operating mineral interest No. 1 and $20,000 for operating mineral interest No. 2. Assume that the taxpayer elected for the taxable year 1954 to aggregate operating mineral interests Nos. 1 and 2. The adjusted basis of the aggregated property as of January 1, 1954, for the purpose of determining gain would be $23,000 ($50,000 plus $30,000) minus ($37,000 plus $20,000). For the purpose of determining loss, the adjusted basis would be $17,000 ($44,000 plus $30,000) minus ($37,000 plus $20,000).

Example (2). Assume the same facts as in example (1) and further assume that for the taxable years 1954 and 1955, the taxpayer was allowed $5,000 of depletion on the aggregated property, that on January 1, 1954, he sold a portion of the aggregated property for $20,000, and that, as of January 1, 1956, the aggregated property had a fair market value of $24,000. At the time of sale, the adjusted basis of the aggregated property for the purpose of determining gain was $18,000 ($23,000 − $5,000): and the adjusted basis for the purpose of determining loss was $12,000 ($17,000 − $5,000). The adjusted basis of the portion sold would be computed as follows:

$$\frac{\$20,000 \text{ (FMV of portion sold)}}{\$24,000 \text{ (FMV of aggregated property)}} \times \$18,000 \text{ (adjusted basis for gain)} = \$15,000 \text{ (adjusted basis of portion sold)}$$

Taxpayer's gain would then be computed as follows:

$20,000 amount received for portion sold
Less: 15,000 adjusted basis of portion sold
$ 5,000 gain on portion sold

The adjusted basis of the portion retained as of January 1, 1956, for the purpose of determining gain is $3,000 ($18,000 − $15,000). For the purpose of determining loss, the adjusted basis is $2,000 ($12,000 − $10,000).

Example (3). Assume the same facts as in example (2), except that a portion of the aggregated property was sold for $5,000 and that the fair market value of the aggregated property at the time of sale was $10,000. The adjusted basis of the portion sold would be computed as follows:

Reg. § 1.614-6(a)(4)

$$\frac{\$5{,}000 \text{ (FMV of portion sold)}}{\$10{,}000 \text{ (FMV of aggregated property)}} \times \$12{,}000 \text{ (adjusted basis for loss)} = \$6{,}000 \text{ (adjusted basis of portion sold)}$$

Taxpayer's loss would then be computed as follows:

$5,000 amount received for portion sold
Less: 6,000 adjusted basis of portion sold
($1,000) loss on portion sold

(5) *Basis for gain and loss where mineral interests acquired before March 1, 1913, are included in a combination and one or more of such interests have not previously been included in an aggregation.* Where mineral interests acquired before March 1, 1913, are included in a combination under section 614(b) and § 1.614-8 and one or more of such interests have not previously been included in an aggregation, the combined property has two bases, one for the determination of gain and another for the determination of loss upon the disposition of the whole or a part of the combined property. For the purpose of determining gain, the adjusted basis of the combined property on the effective date of combination shall be the sum of—

(i) The adjusted bases at the time of deaggregation, as determined under subparagraph (2) of this paragraph, of all interests which have previously been included in an aggregation,

(ii) The unadjusted bases of other mineral interests acquired on or after March 1, 1913, and

(iii) The cost of each other interest acquired before March 1, 1913 (adjusted for the period before March 1, 1913), or the fair market value of such interest as of March 1, 1913, whichever is greater,

and such sum shall be adjusted by the total of all adjustments to the bases of the mineral interests as required by section 1016 to the effective date of combination. For the purpose of determining loss, the adjusted basis of the combined property on the effective date of combination shall be the sum of—

(iv) The adjusted bases at the time of deaggregation, as determined under subparagraph (2) of this paragraph, of all interests which have previously been included in an aggregation,

(v) The unadjusted bases of other mineral interests acquired on or after March 1, 1913, and

(vi) The cost of other mineral interests acquired before March 1, 1913, adjusted for the period before March 1, 1913,

and such sum shall be adjusted by the total of all adjustments to the bases of the mineral interests as required by section 1016 to the effective date of combination. Thereafter, the adjustments to basis required by section 1016 shall apply to the total adjusted basis of the combined property for all purposes of the Code. Upon disposition of a part of the combined property, the adjusted basis for determining gain and the adjusted basis for determining loss with respect to each resultant part of the combined property shall be determined in accordance with subparagraph (2) of this paragraph.

(b) *Holding period of aggregated or combined properties.* Where a taxpayer sells or exchanges either a part or all of an aggregated or combined property which includes part or all of a mineral interest which the taxpayer has held for 1 year (6 months for taxable years beginning before 1977; 9 months for taxable years beginning in 1977) or less, the sales price and adjusted basis attributable to the interest sold must be apportioned in proportion to the relative fair market values as of the date of sale to determine the amount of income represented by the sale of property held for 1 year (6 months for taxable years beginning before 1977; 9 months for taxable years beginning in 1977) or less. The application of this rule may be illustrated by the following example:

Example. Taxpayer A owns operating mineral interests Nos. 1, 2, and 3. He acquired interests Nos. 1 and 2 in 1953 but purchased and made development expenditures on interest No. 3 on December 1, 1954. In his return for the taxable year 1954, taxpayer A elects to aggregate interests Nos. 1, 2, and 3 which are operated as a unit. On May 1, 1955, taxpayer A sells the north half of the aggregated property which includes portions of interests Nos. 1, 2, and 3. The sales price of the north half was $80,000; the adjusted basis of the aggregated property as of the date of sale was $20,000; and the fair market value of the aggregated property as of the date of sale was $100,000. The adjusted basis applicable to the north half is computed as follows:

Reg. § 1.614-6(b)

$$\frac{\$80{,}000 \text{ (FMV of portion sold)}}{\$100{,}000 \text{ (FMV of aggregated property)}} \times$$

$20,000 (adjusted basis of aggregated property) = $16,000 (adjusted basis of portion sold)

The total gain on the sale is $64,000 ($80,000 − $16,000).

The gain attributable to the sale of the portion held for six months or less is computed as follows (assuming that the fair market value of the portion of No. 3 included in the sale as of the date of sale was $30,000):

$$\frac{\$30{,}000 \text{ (FMV of portion of No. 3 sold)}}{\$80{,}000 \text{ (FMV of north half)}} \times$$

$16,000 (adjusted basis of north half) = $6,000 (adjusted basis of portion of No. 3 sold)

The gain on the portion of No. 3 sold is $24,000 ($30,000 − $6,000).

(c) *Acquisition of property with transferor's basis.* If a separate property or an aggregated or combined property is acquired in a transaction in which the basis of such property in the hands of the taxpayer is determined by reference to the basis of such property in the hands of a transferor, then the election of such transferor as to the treatment of such separate, aggregated, or combined property shall be binding upon the taxpayer for all taxable years ending after the transfer unless, in the case of an aggregation, the aggregation terminates or consent to make a change is obtained under paragraph (d)(4) of § 1.614-2, paragraph (f)(7) of § 1.614-3, or paragraph (b)(3) or (e)(5) of § 1.614-5, whichever is applicable.

(d) *Abandonment and casualty losses.* In the case of mineral interests which are aggregated or combined as one property, no losses resulting from worthlessness or abandonment are allowable until all the mineral rights in the entire aggregated or combined property are proven to be worthless or until the entire aggregated or combined property is disposed of or abandoned. Casualty losses are allowable in accordance with the rules applicable to casualty losses in general. For rules applicable to losses in general, see section 165 and the regulations thereunder. [Reg. § 1.614-6.]

☐ [*T.D.* 6524, 1-19-61. Amended by *T.D.* 6859, 10-27-65 and by *T.D.* 7728, 10-31-80.]

[Reg. § 1.614-7]

§ 1.614-7. **Extension of time for performing certain acts.**—Sections 1.614-2 to 1.614-5, inclusive, require certain acts to be performed on or before May 1, 1961 (the first day of the first month which begins more than 90 days after the regulations under section 614 were published in the Federal Register as a Treasury decision). The district director may, upon good cause shown, extend for a period not exceeding 6 months the period within which such acts are to be performed, and shall, if the interests of the Government would otherwise be jeopardized thereby, grant such an extension only if the taxpayer and the district director agree in writing to a corresponding or greater extension of the period prescribed for the assessment of the tax, or in the case of taxable years described in section 614(c)(3)(E), the assessment of the tax resulting from the exercise or change in an election. [Reg. § 1.614-7.]

☐ [*T.D.* 6561, 4-24-61.]

[Reg. § 1.614-8]

§ 1.614-8. **Elections with respect to separate operating mineral interests for taxable years beginning after December 31, 1963, in the case of oil and gas wells.**—(a) *Election to treat separate operating mineral interests as separate properties*—(1) *General rule.* If a taxpayer has more than one operating mineral interest in oil and gas wells in one tract or parcel of land, he may elect to treat one or more of such interests as separate properties for taxable years beginning after December 31, 1963. Any such interests with respect to which the taxpayer does not so elect shall be combined and treated as one property. Nonoperating mineral interests may not be included in such combination. There may be only one such combination in one tract or parcel. Any such combination of interests shall be considered as one property for all purposes of subtitle A of the Code for the period to which the election applies. The preceding sentence does not preclude the use of more than one account under a single method of computing depreciation or the use of more than one method of computing depreciation under section 167, if otherwise proper. Any reasonable and consistently applied method or methods of computing depreciation of the improvements made with respect to the separate interests which are combined may be continued in accordance with section 167 and the regulations thereunder. Except as provided in paragraph (b) of this section, such an interest in one tract or parcel may not be combined with such an interest in another tract or parcel. For rules with respect to the allocation of the basis of an aggregation of separate operating mineral interests under this section among such interests as of the first day of the first taxable year beginning after December 31, 1963, see paragraph (a)(2)(ii) of § 1.614-6. For the definition of "operating mineral interest" see paragraph (b) of § 1.614-2.

(2) *Election in respect of newly discovered or acquired interest or interest ceasing to participate in cooperative or unit plan of operation.* (i) If the taxpayer makes an election under this paragraph in respect of an operating mineral interest in a tract or parcel of land and, after the taxable year for which such election is made, an additional operating mineral interest in the same tract or parcel is discovered or acquired by the taxpayer or is the subject of an election under this paragraph because it ceases to participate in a cooperative or unit plan of operation to which paragraph (b) of this section applies, the additional operating mineral interest shall be treated—

(*a*) If there is no combination of interests in such tract or parcel, as a separate property unless the taxpayer elects to combine it with another interest, or

(*b*) If there is a combination of interests in such tract or parcel, as part of such combination unless the taxpayer elects to treat it as a separate property.

(ii) The application of this subparagraph may be illustrated by the following example:

Example. Prior to 1964 a taxpayer acquired, and incurred development expenditures with respect to, three operating mineral interests in oil, designated Nos. 1, 2, and 3. All three interests are in the same tract or parcel of land. For the taxable year 1964, the taxpayer elects to treat such interests as three separate properties. During the taxable year 1965, the taxpayer discovers and incurs development costs with respect to a fourth operating mineral interest, No. 4, in the same tract of land. During the taxable year 1966, the taxpayer discovers and incurs development costs with respect to a fifth operating mineral interest, No. 5, in the same tract of land. If the taxpayer makes no election relative to No. 4 for 1965, such interest will thereafter be treated as a separate property. Alternatively, the taxpayer may make an election for 1965 to combine No. 4 with any one (and only one) of the three other interests and to treat such combination as one property. If, for example, he elects to combine No. 4 with No. 3, then in 1966, No. 5 will automatically become part of the combination of Nos. 3 and 4 if no election is made to treat it as a separate property. After the combination of Nos. 3 and 4 is formed, Nos. 1 and 2, which were acquired or discovered prior to the formation of the combination and which were not included in such combination within the time prescribed, may not be included in that or any other combination. However, see subparagraph (3)(iv) of this paragraph.

(3) *Manner and scope of election*—(i) *Election; when made.* Except as provided hereafter in this subdivision (i), any election under subparagraph (1) or (2) of this paragraph shall be made for each operating mineral interest not later than the time prescribed by law for filing the income tax return (including extensions thereof) for whichever of the following taxable years is later:

(*a*) The first taxable year beginning after December 31, 1963; or

(*b*) The first taxable year in which any expenditure for development or operation in respect of such operating mineral interest is made by the taxpayer after his acquisition of such interest.

Notwithstanding the provisions of (*a*) and (*b*), if it is determined that the operating mineral interest in respect of which the election is to be made was, during what would otherwise be the entire effective period of the election insofar as it would apply to the appropriate taxable year determined under (*a*) and (*b*), participating in a cooperative or unit plan of operation to which section 614(b)(3) applies, the election shall be made not later than the time prescribed by law for filing the income tax return (including extensions thereof) for the taxable year in which the interest ceases to participate in the cooperative or unit plan. See subdivision (iii) of this subparagraph for provisions relating to the effective date of an election and paragraph (b) of this section for provisions relating to certain unitization or pooling arrangements. For purposes of this subparagraph, expenditures for development include any intangible drilling or development costs within the purview of section 263(c). Delay rentals are not considered as expenditures for development. For purposes of this subparagraph, the acquisition of an option to acquire an economic interest in minerals in place does not constitute the acquisition of a mineral interest.

(ii) *Election; how made.* Any election under this paragraph shall be made by a statement attached to the income tax return of the taxpayer for the first taxable year for which the election is made. This statement shall identify by name, code number, or other means the operating mineral interests within the same tract or parcel of land which the taxpayer is electing to treat as separate properties or in combination, as the case may be. The statement shall also identify by name, code number, or other means the tract or parcel and shall set forth the facts upon which its treatment as a single and entire tract or parcel is based. See paragraph (a)(3) of § 1.614-1. However, if the taxpayer is electing to treat all of his operating mineral interests in a tract or parcel as separate properties, a blanket election with re-

Reg. § 1.614-8(a)(3)

spect to all of such interests in that tract or parcel which are owned by the taxpayer at the time the election is made will suffice and only the tract or parcel itself need be so identified. The taxpayer shall maintain and have available records and maps sufficient to clearly define the tract or parcel and all of the taxpayer's operating mineral interests therein.

(iii) *Election; when combination effective.* (*a*) If, by reason of the exercise or nonexercise of an election under this paragraph, a combination is formed of two or more operating mineral interests, all of which are owned and operated by a taxpayer on the first day of the first taxable year beginning after December 31, 1963, and are not participating in a cooperative or unit plan of operation to which paragraph (b) of this section applies on such first day, the combination is effective on such first day.

(*b*) If, by reason of the exercise or nonexercise of an election under this paragraph, a combination of operating mineral interests not described in (*a*) of this subdivision (including a combination described in (*a*) to which another operating mineral interest is added) is formed, the date on which each operating mineral interest which is being combined by the taxpayer for the first time enters into the combination is the later of (*1*) the earliest date within the taxable year affected on which the taxpayer incurred any expenditure for development or operation of such interest at a time when such interest was not participating in a cooperative or unit plan of operation to which paragraph (b) of this section applies, or (*2*) the earliest date on which the taxpayer incurred any expenditure for development or operation of any other interest with which such interest is to be combined at a time when such other interest was not participating in a cooperative or unit plan of operation to which paragraph (b) of this section applies.

(*c*) The application of these provisions may be illustrated by the following examples:

Example (1). In 1963, a taxpayer owned and operated mineral interests Nos. 1 and 2, both of which are in the same tract or parcel of land. Neither No. 1 nor No. 2 participates in a cooperative or unit plan of operation. The taxpayer, who is on a calendar year basis, continued to own and operate these interests during the year 1964, and made no election with respect to such interests in his income tax return for that year. As a result, Nos. 1 and 2 are combined as of January 1, 1964.

Example (2). Assume that the taxpayer described in example (1) discovered operating mineral interests Nos. 3 and 4 in the same tract or parcel of land as Nos. 1 and 2, that he made his first expenditures for development of No. 3 on June 1, 1964, and of No. 4 on September 1, 1964, and that, in a timely return for 1964, he elected to treat No. 3 as a separate property and made no election with respect to No. 4. As a result, No. 3 is treated as a separate property and No. 4 joins the combination of Nos. 1 and 2 as of September 1, 1964.

Example (3). On March 1, 1964, a taxpayer acquired a tract or parcel of land containing operating mineral interests Nos. 1 and 2. The taxpayer made his first operating expenditures on No. 1 on April 1, 1964. On October 1, 1964, the taxpayer made his first development expenditures with respect to operating mineral interest No. 2. The taxpayer made no election with respect to these interests. As a result, Nos. 1 and 2 enter into a combination as of October 1, 1964.

(iv) *Election; binding effect.* A valid election made under section 614(b) and this subparagraph shall be binding upon the taxpayer for the first taxable year for which made and for all subsequent taxable years. However, notwithstanding the preceding sentence, an election to treat one or more operating mineral interests as separate properties shall not prevent the making of a later election to combine a newly discovered or acquired operating mineral interest with one of such interests, if no other combination exists in the tract or parcel of land on the date when the later election would become effective under subdivision (iii) of this subparagraph. Nor will an election to treat an operating mineral interest as a separate property prevent its treatment with another interest as a single property under paragraph (b) of this section if such interest later participates in a cooperative or unit plan of operation to which paragraph (b) applies. For rules relating to the binding effect of an election in certain cases in which the basis of a separate or combined property in the hands of the transferee is determined by reference to the basis in the hands of the transferor, see paragraph (c) of § 1.614-6.

(b) *Certain unitization or pooling arrangements.* (1) Except as provided in this paragraph, if one or more of the taxpayer's operating mineral interests, or a part or parts thereof, participate, under a voluntary or compulsory unitization or pooling agreement as defined in subparagraph (6) of this paragraph, in a single cooperative or unit plan of operation, then for the period of such participation in taxable years beginning after December 31, 1963, such interest or interests, and part or parts thereof, included in such unit, shall be treated for purposes of subtitle A of the Code as one property, separate from the interest or interests, or part or parts thereof, not included in such unit.

Reg. § 1.614-8(b)

(2) Subparagraph (1) of this paragraph shall apply to a voluntary agreement only if all the operating mineral interests covered by the agreement are in the same deposit or are in two or more deposits, the joint development or production of which is logical, without taking tax benefits into account, from the standpoint of geology, convenience, economy, or conservation, and which are in tracts or parcels of land which are contiguous or in close proximity. Operating mineral interests under a voluntary agreement to which subparagraph (1) does not apply are subject to the rules contained in paragraph (a) of this section. For purposes of this paragraph an agreement is voluntary unless required by the laws or rulings of any State or any agency of any State.

(3) Notwithstanding the provisions of subparagraph (1) of this paragraph, if the taxpayer, for the last taxable year beginning before January 1, 1964, treated as separate properties two or more operating mineral interests which participate, under a voluntary or compulsory unitization or pooling agreement entered into in any taxable year beginning before January 1, 1964, in a single cooperative or unit plan of operation, and if it is determined that such treatment was proper under the law applicable to such taxable year, the taxpayer may continue to treat all such interests in a consistent manner for the period of such participation. If it is determined that such treatment was not proper under the law applicable to such taxable year, or if the taxpayer does not continue to treat all such interests in a manner consistent with the treatment of them for the last taxable year beginning before January 1, 1964, the treatment of the interests shall be in accordance with the provisions of subparagraph (1).

(4) If only a part of an operating mineral interest, which interest is not being treated under paragraph (a) of this section as part of a combination of interests, participates in a unit or pool, such part shall, for the period of its participation in the unit or pool, be treated for purposes of this section as being separate from the nonparticipating portion of the operating mineral interest of which it is a part. A portion of the adjusted basis and of the units of mineral of such operating mineral interest remaining at the beginning of the period described in the preceding sentence shall be allocated to the participating part in accordance with the principles contained in paragraph (a)(2)(i)(a) of § 1.614-6 as if such participating part had been sold. If participation in the unit or pool ends, the separate status of the participating part shall immediately terminate. At such time the adjusted basis of such part and the units of mineral with respect to such part remaining at the time of termination shall be added to the adjusted basis and to the remaining units of mineral of the nonparticipating portion of the operating mineral interest. During the period of participation in the unit or pool such participating part shall not be treated separately from the nonparticipating portion of the operating mineral interest in applying section 165.

(5) Where an operating mineral interest which is being treated under paragraph (a) of this section as part of a combination of interests begins participation in a unit or pool, the combination shall remain in force but the treatment of such participating interest as a part of the combination shall be suspended for the period of its participation in the unit or pool. If, for example, a taxpayer owns operating mineral interests Nos. 1, 2, and 3 in a single tract or parcel of land, elects to treat No. 1 as a separate property (with mineral interests Nos. 2 and 3 thus being combined), is later required by an agency of a State to place No. 2 in a unit, and subsequently discovers operating mineral interest No. 4 in the same tract or parcel of land, then under paragraph (a)(2)(i)(b) of this section No. 4 will automatically be combined with No. 3 unless the taxpayer elects to treat it as a separate property. Under this subparagraph, an interest may be treated as part of a combination for a portion of a taxable year and as part of a unit or pool for a portion of a taxable year. At the commencement of participation in the unit or pool, a portion of the adjusted basis of the combination and a portion of the units of mineral with respect to the combination remaining at that time shall be allocated to such participating interest in accordance with the principles contained in paragraph (a)(2)(i)(a) of § 1.614-6 as if such interest had been sold. During the period of participation in the unit or pool such participating interest is nevertheless treated as a part of the combination for purposes of paragraph (d) of § 1.614-6. If participation in the unit or pool ends, the treatment of such interest as participating in the unit or pool shall immediately terminate. At such time, the adjusted basis of the participating interest and the units of mineral with respect to such interest remaining at the time of termination shall be added to the adjusted basis and to the remaining units of mineral of the nonparticipating portion of the combination. In determining the adjusted basis of the participating interest at the time of termination there shall be taken into account any section 1016 adjustments attributable to such interest for the period of its participation in the unit or pool. If two or more operating mineral interests of the taxpayer participate in a unit or pool and are treated as one property under subparagraph (1) of this paragraph, and if participation by such interests in the unit or pool termi-

Reg. § 1.614-8(b)(5)

nates, the adjusted basis of each such interest at the time of termination shall be separately determined. If the total of the adjusted bases of such interests upon termination of their participation in the unit or pool exceeds the adjusted basis of such one property, then the adjusted bases of such interests shall be further adjusted by applying the principles contained in paragraph (a)(2)(ii)(*b*)(*ii*) of § 1.614-6 so that the total of the adjusted bases of such interests equals the adjusted basis of such one property. In addition, the units of oil and gas estimated to be attributable to a participating interest at the time of termination of participation shall be restored to the units of oil and gas of the combination of which it is a part. The rules stated in this subparagraph with respect to an operating mineral interest which is being treated under paragraph (a) of this section as part of a combination and which begins participation in a unit or pool shall also apply to a portion of an operating mineral interest which is being treated under paragraph (a) as part of a combination if such portion begins participation in a unit or pool.

(6) As used in this paragraph, the term "unitization or pooling agreement" means an agreement under which two or more persons owning operating mineral interests agree to have the interests operated on a unified basis and further agree to share in production on a stipulated percentage or fractional basis regardless of from which interest or interests the oil or gas is produced. In addition, in a situation in which one person owns operating mineral interests in several leases, an agreement of such person with his several royalty owners to determine the royalties payable to each on a stipulated percentage basis regardless of from which lease or leases oil or gas is obtained is also considered to be a unitization or pooling agreement. No formal cross-conveyance of properties is necessary. An agreement between co-owners of a tract or parcel of land or a part thereof for the development of the property by one of such co-owners for the account of all is not a unitization or pooling agreement, provided that the agreement does not affect ownership of minerals or entitle any such co-owner to share in production from any operating mineral interests other than his own.

(c) *Operating mineral interest defined.* For the definition of the term "operating mineral interest" as used in this section, see paragraph (b) of § 1.614-2.

(d) *Alternative treatment under Internal Revenue Code of 1939.* If, on the day preceding the first day of the first taxable year beginning after December 31, 1963, the taxpayer has any operating mineral interests which he treats under section 614(d) (as in effect before the amendments made by the Revenue Act of 1964) and § 1.614-4, such treatment shall be continued and shall be deemed to have been adopted pursuant to the provisions of section 614(b) and paragraph (a) of this section. Accordingly, a taxpayer, who has four operating mineral interests in a single tract or parcel of land, and who has treated two of such interests as one property and two of such interests as separate properties under section 614(d) prior to the first day of the first taxable year beginning after December 31, 1963, is deemed to have adopted such treatment pursuant to the provisions of section 614(b) and paragraph (a) of this section. Hence, in the absence of an election to the contrary, a fifth operating mineral interest in the same tract or parcel acquired by the taxpayer in a taxable year beginning after December 31, 1963, will after an expenditure for development or operation, be combined with the combination of two interests made under section 614(d). Furthermore, an election which was made for a taxable year beginning before January 1, 1964, under section 614(d) as then in effect will be binding for all taxable years beginning after December 31, 1963, even though the time for making an election under section 614(b) and paragraph (a) of this section has not elapsed. [Reg. § 1.614-8.]

☐ [*T.D.* 6859, 10-27-65.]

[Reg. § 1.616-1]

§ 1.616-1. *Development expenditures.*—(a) *General rule.* Section 616 prescribes rules for treating expenditures paid or incurred during the taxable year by the taxpayer for the development of a mine or other natural deposit (other than an oil or gas well). Development expenditures under section 616 are those which are made after such time when, in consideration of all the facts and circumstances (including actions of the taxpayer), deposits of ore or other mineral are shown to exist in sufficient quantity and quality to reasonably justify commercial exploitation by the taxpayer. Under section 616(a), a taxpayer is allowed a deduction for development expenditures whether or not such expenditures are made in the development or production stage of the mine or other natural deposit. Under section 616(b), the taxpayer may elect to defer development expenditures made in the development or producing stage and to deduct such expenditures ratably as the minerals or ores benefited are sold. While the mine or other natural deposit is in the development stage, the election applies only to that portion of the development expenditures which is in excess of net receipts from the mine or other natural deposit. See § 1.616-2 for rules with respect to the election to defer. It is not necessary that the taxpayer incur the development costs directly. He may engage a contractor to make the expenditures on his behalf.

(b) *Expenditures to which section 616 is not applicable.* (1) Section 616 is not applicable to development expenditures which are deductible for the taxable year under any other provision of the internal revenue laws.

(2) Section 616 is not applicable to expenditures which are reflected in improvements subject to allowances for depreciation under sections 167 and 611. However, allowances for depreciation of such improvements which are used in the development of ores or minerals are considered development expenditures under section 616. If such improvements are used only in part for development during a taxable year, an allocable portion of the allowance for depreciation shall be treated as a development expenditure.

(3) Section 616 is applicable to development expenditures paid or incurred by a taxpayer in connection with the acquisition of a fractional share of the working or operating interest to the extent of the fractional interest so acquired. The expenditure attributable to the remaining fractional share shall be considered as part of the cost of his acquired interest and shall be capitalized and recovered through depletion allowances. For example, taxpayer A owns mineral leases on undeveloped mineral lands. A agrees to convey an undivided three-fourths (3/4) interest in such leases to B, provided B will pay all of the expenditures incurred during the development stage of the deposits on these leases. B may deduct three-fourths (3/4) of such amount under section 616, but shall treat one-fourth of such amount as part of the cost of his interest, recoverable through depletion.

(4) The provisions of section 616 do not apply to costs of development paid or incurred by a prior owner which are reflected in the amount which the taxpayer paid or incurred to acquire the property. Such provisions apply only to costs paid or incurred by the taxpayer for development undertaken directly or through contract by the taxpayer. See, however, sections 381(a) and 381(c)(10) for special rules with respect to deferred development expenditures in certain corporate acquisitions.

(c) *Mine or other natural deposit.* Section 616 has reference to expenditures made for the development of a mine or other natural deposit. Within an aggregated property, as that term is defined in section 614(b) and (c), or within a single tract or parcel of land, there may be more than one mine or other natural deposit. Where a property, as determined under section 614, contains more than one mine or other natural deposit, the taxpayer may deduct under section 616(a) the development expenditures made with respect to one of such mines or deposits, and may defer under section 616(b) the development expenditures made with respect to another of such mines or deposits. Where there is more than one mine with respect to a single underlying deposit, the taxpayer may deduct under section 616(a) the development expenditures made with respect to one of such mines, and may defer under section 616(b) the development expenditures made with respect to another of such mines. The taxpayer must treat consistently all development expenditures with respect to each such mine or other natural deposit in a taxable year. The taxpayer must make a separate determination of the units of minerals or ores benefited in a mine or other natural deposit (regardless of the computation of the depletion allowance) in order that deferred expenditures with respect to such mine or deposit may be deducted on a ratable basis. See paragraph (f) of § 1.616-2. [Reg. § 1.616-1.]

☐ [*T.D.* 6446, 1-20-60.]

[Reg. § 1.616-2]

§ 1.616-2. **Election to defer.**—(a) *General rule.* In lieu of taking a deduction under section 616(a), in the taxable year when the development expenditures are paid or incurred, a taxpayer may elect under section 616(b) to treat such expenditures with respect to each mine or other natural deposit as deferred expenses to be deducted ratably as the units of the produced ore or minerals benefited by such expenditures are sold. Section 616(b) is applicable to development expenditures paid or incurred both in the development and producing stage of the mine or other natural deposit. However, in the case of such expenditures made in the development stage, this election is applicable only to the excess of the amount of such expenditures over the net receipts from the ore or minerals from such mine or deposit received or accrued during the development stage and in the same taxable year as the expenditures were paid or incurred. Such development expenditures not in excess of such net receipts shall be subject to the provisions of section 616(a).

(b) *Producing stage; definition of.* The mine or other natural deposit will be considered to be in a producing stage when the major portion of the mineral production is obtained from workings other than those opened for the purpose of development, or when the principal activity of the mine or other natural deposit is the production of developed ores or minerals rather than the development of additional ores or minerals for mining.

Reg. § 1.616-2(b)

(c) *Expenditures made by the owner who retains a nonoperating interest.* (1) A taxpayer who elects to defer development expenditures and thereafter transfers his interest in the mine or other natural deposit, retaining an economic interest therein, shall deduct an amount attributable to such interest on a pro rata basis as the interest pays out. For example, a taxpayer who defers development expenditures and then leases his deposit, retaining a royalty interest therein, shall deduct the deferred expenditures ratably as he receives the royalties. If the taxpayer receives a bonus or advanced royalties in connection with the transfer of his interest, he shall deduct the deferred expenditures allocable to such bonus or advanced royalties in an amount which is in the same proportion to the total of such costs as the bonus or advanced royalties bears to the bonus and total royalties expected to be received. Also, in the case of a transfer of a mine or other natural deposit by a taxpayer who retains a production payment therein, he may deduct the development expenditures ratably over the payments expected to be received.

(2) Where a taxpayer receives an amount, in addition to retaining an economic interest, which amount is treated as from the sale or exchange of a capital asset or property treated under section 1231 (except coal or iron ore to which section 631(c) applies), the deferred development expenditures shall be allocated between the interest sold and the interest retained in proportion to the fair market value of each interest as of the date of sale. The amount allocated to the interest sold may not be deducted, but shall be a part of the basis of such interest for the purpose of determining gain or loss upon the sale thereof.

(d) *Losses from abandonment.* Section 165 and the regulations thereunder contain general rules relating to the treatment of losses resulting from abandonment.

(e) *Effect of election.* (1) The election to defer development expenditures shall apply only to expenditures for the taxable year for which made. However, once made, the election shall be binding with respect to the expenditures for that taxable year. Thus, a taxpayer cannot revoke his election for any reason whatsoever.

(2) The election shall be made for each mine or other natural deposit by a clear indication on the return or by a statement filed with the district director with whom the return is filed, not later than the time prescribed by law for filing such return (including extensions thereof) for the taxable year to which such election is applicable.

(f) *Computation of amount of deduction.* The amount of the deduction allowable during the taxable year is an amount A, which bears the same ratio to B (the total deferred development expenditures for a particular mine or other natural deposit reduced by the amount of such expenditures deducted in prior taxable years) as C (the number of units of the ore or mineral benefited by such expenditures sold during the taxable year) bears to D (the number of units of ore or mineral benefited by such expenditures remaining as of the taxable year). For the purposes of this proportion, the "number of units of ore or mineral benefited by such expenditure remaining as of the taxable year" is the number of units of ore or mineral benefited by the deferred development expenditures remaining at the end of the year to be recovered from the mine or other natural deposit (including units benefited by such expenditures recovered but not sold) plus the number of units benefited by such expenditures sold within the taxable year. The principles outlined in § 1.611-2 are applicable in estimating the number of units remaining as of the taxable year and the number of units sold during that taxable year. The estimate is subject to revision in accordance with that section in the event it is ascertained, from any source, such as operations or development work, that the remaining units are materially greater or less than the number of units remaining from a prior estimate. [Reg. § 1.616-2.]

☐ [*T.D.* 6446, 1-20-60. *Amended by T.D.* 6841, 7-26-65.]

[Reg. § 1.616-3]

§ 1.616-3. **Time for making election with respect to returns due on or before May 2, 1960.**—In the case of any taxable year beginning after December 31, 1953, and ending after August 16, 1954, the income tax return for which is due not later than May 2, 1960, the time to deduct or defer development expenditures for such a year under section 616(a) or (b) shall expire on May 2, 1960. [Reg. § 1.616-3.]

☐ [*T.D.* 6446, 1-20-60.]

[Reg. § 1.617-1]

§ 1.617-1. **Exploration expenditures.**—(a) *General rule.* Section 617 prescribes rules for the treatment of expenditures paid or incurred after September 12, 1966, for ascertaining the existence, location, extent, or quality of any deposit of ore or other mineral for which a deduction for depletion is allowable under section 613 (other than oil or gas) paid or incurred by the taxpayer before the beginning of the development stage of the mine or other natural deposit. Such expenditures hereinafter in the regulations under section 617 will be referred to as exploration expenditures. The development stage of the mine or other natural deposit will be deemed to begin at the time when, in consideration of all the facts and circumstances (including the actions of the taxpayer), deposits of ore or other mineral are disclosed in sufficient quantity and quality to reasonably justify commercial exploitation by the taxpayer. For example, core drilling expenditures paid or incurred by the taxpayer to ascertain the existence of commercially marketable ore are exploration expenditures within the meaning of this section. Also, expenditures for exploratory drilling from within a producing mine to ascertain the existence of what appears (on the basis of all of the facts and circumstances known at the time of the expenditure) to be a different ore deposit are exploration expenditures within the meaning of this section. Expenditures paid or incurred in connection with core drilling to further delineate the extent and location of an existing commercially marketable deposit to facilitate its development are development expenditures. Under section 617(a), a taxpayer may deduct exploration expenditures paid or incurred for the exploration of any deposit of ore or other mineral subject to the limitation of section 617(h). Under section 617(b), a taxpayer shall recapture the exploration expenditures previously deducted under section 617(a) either through including in income an amount equal to the amount of the adjusted exploration expenditures (as defined in section 617(f)) or through disallowance of the deduction for depletion under section 611. Certain rules are provided in section 617(c) for recapture of exploration expenditures made with respect to property for which the taxpayer later receives a bonus or royalty. Under section 617(d), gain from dispositions of mining property, with respect to which exploration expenditures have been previously deducted, is to be recognized notwithstanding certain other provisions of the Code.

(b) *Expenditures to which section 617 is not applicable.* (1) Section 617 is not applicable to expenditures which would be allowed as deductions for the taxable year without regard to section 617.

(2) Section 617 is not applicable to expenditures which are reflected in improvements subject to allowances for depreciation under sections 167 and 611. However, allowances for depreciation of such improvements which are used in the exploration of ores or minerals are considered exploration expenditures under section 617. If such improvements are used only in part for exploration during the taxable year, an allocable portion of the allowance for depreciation shall be treated as an exploration expenditure.

(3) Section 617 is applicable to exploration expenditures paid or incurred by a taxpayer in connection with the acquisition of a fractional share of the working or operating interest to the extent of the fractional interest so acquired by the taxpayer. The expenditures attributable to the remaining fractional share shall be considered as the cost of his acquired interest and shall be recovered through depletion allowances. For example, taxpayer A owns mineral leases on unexplored mineral lands and agrees to convey an undivided three-fourths (3/4) interest in such leases to taxpayer B provided B will pay all of the expenses for ascertaining the existence, location, extent, or quality of any deposit of ore or other mineral which will be incurred before the beginning of the development stage. B may elect to treat three-fourths of such amount under section 617. B must treat one-fourth of such amount as part of the cost of his interest, recoverable through depletion.

(4) Section 617 is not applicable to costs of exploration which are reflected in the amount which the taxpayer paid or incurred to acquire the property. Section 617 applies only to costs paid or incurred by the taxpayer for exploration undertaken directly or through a contract by the taxpayer. See, however, sections 381(a) and 381(c)(10) for special rules with respect to deferred exploration expenditures in certain corporate acquisitions.

(5) Section 617 is not applicable to amounts paid or incurred for the purpose of ascertaining the existence, location, extent, or quality of any deposit of oil or gas or of any mineral with respect to which a deduction for percentage depletion is not allowable under section 613. The purpose of the expenditure shall be determined by reference to the facts and circumstances at the time the expenditure is paid or incurred.

(c) *Elections*—(1) *Election to deduct under section 617(a).* (i) The election to deduct exploration expenditures under section 617(a) may be made by deducting such expenditures in the taxpayer's income tax return for his first taxable year ending after September 12, 1966, for which the taxpayer desires to deduct exploration expenditures which are paid or incurred by him during such taxable year and after September 12, 1966. This election may be exercised by deducting such exploration expenditures either in the taxpayer's return for such taxable year or in an amended return filed before the expiration of the period for filing a claim for credit or refund of income tax for such taxable year. Where the election is made in an amended return for a taxable year prior to the most recent year for which the taxpayer has filed

Reg. § 1.617-1(c)(1)

a return, the taxpayer shall file amended income tax returns, reflecting any increase or decrease in tax attributable to the election, for all subsequent taxable years affected by the election for which he has filed income tax returns before making the election. See section 617(a)(2)(C) and subparagraph (4) of this paragraph for provisions relating to extension of the period of limitations for the assessment of any deficiency for any taxable year to the extent the deficiency is attributable to an election or revocation of an election under section 617(a). In applying the election to the years affected, there shall be taken into account the effect that any adjustments resulting from the election shall have on other items affected thereby (such as the deduction for charitable contributions, the foreign tax credit, net operating loss, and other deductions or credits the amount of which is limited by the taxpayer's income) and the effect that adjustments of any such items have on items of other taxable years. Amended returns filed for taxable years subsequent to the taxable year for which the election under section 617(a) is made by amended return shall, where appropriate, apply the recapture rules of subsection (b), (c), and (d) of section 617. See §§ 1.617-3 and 1.617-4.

(ii) A taxpayer who makes or has made an election under section 617(a) shall state clearly on his income tax return for each taxable year for which he deducts exploration expenditures the amount of the deduction claimed under section 617(a) with respect to each property or mine. Such property or mine shall be identified by a description adequate to permit application of the recapture rules of section 617(b), (c), and (d).

(iii) A taxpayer who has made an election under section 617(a) may not make an election under section 615(e) unless, within the period set forth in section 615(e), he revokes his election under section 617(a). A taxpayer who has made and has not revoked an election under section 617(a) may not, in his return for the taxable year for which the election is made or for any subsequent year, charge to capital account any exploration expenditures which are deductible by him under section 617(a); and he must deduct all such expenditures as expenses in computing adjusted gross income. Any exploration expenditures paid or incurred after December 31, 1969, which are not deductible by the taxpayer under section 617(a) solely because of the application of section 617(h) shall be charged to capital account.

(2) *Time for making elections.* The election under section 617(a) may be made at any time before the expiration of the period prescribed for filing a claim for credit or refund of the tax imposed by chapter 1 for the first taxable year for which the taxpayer desires to deduct exploration expenditures under section 617(a).

(3) *Revocation of election to deduct.* (i) A taxpayer may revoke an election made by him under section 617(a) by filing with the Internal Revenue service center with which the taxpayer's income tax return is required to be filed, within the period set forth in subdivision (ii) of this subparagraph, a statement, signed by the taxpayer or his authorized representative, which sets forth that the taxpayer is revoking the section 617(a) election previously made by him and states with whom and where the document making the election was filed. A taxpayer revoking a section 617(a) election shall file amended income tax returns which reflect any increase or decrease in tax attributable to the revocation of election for all taxable years affected by the revocation of election for which he has filed income tax returns before revoking the election. See section 617(a)(2)(C) and subparagraph (4) of this paragraph for provisions relating to extension of the period of limitations for the assessment of any deficiency attributable to an election or revocation of an election under section 617(a). In applying the revocation of election to the years affected, there shall be taken into account the effect that any adjustments resulting from the revocation of election shall have on other items affected thereby (such as the deduction for charitable contributions, the foreign tax credit, net operating loss, and other deductions or credits the amount of which is limited by the taxpayer's income) and the effect that adjustments of any such items have on items of other taxable years.

(ii) An election under section 617(a) may be revoked before the expiration of the last day of the third month following the month in which the final regulations under section 617(a) are published in the Federal Register.

After the expiration of this period, a taxpayer who has made an election under section 617(a) may not revoke that election unless he obtains the prior consent of the Commissioner of Internal Revenue. Consent will not be granted where a principal purpose for the revocation of the election is to circumvent the recapture provisions of section 617(b), (c), or (d). The request for consent shall be made in writing to the Commissioner of Internal Revenue, Attention T:I:E, Washington, D.C. 20224. The request shall include in detail:

(*a*) The reason or reasons for the revocation of election under section 617(a);

(*b*) An itemization of the taxpayer's deductions under section 617(a);

(*c*) A description of all properties and detailed information of the exploration activities

Reg. § 1.617-1(c)(2)

with respect to which the taxpayer has taken deductions under section 617(a);

(d) A description of any development or production activities on all properties with respect to which exploration expenditures were deducted under section 617(a); and

(e) A recomputation of the tax for each prior taxable year affected by the revocation. A letter setting forth the Commissioner's determination will be mailed to the taxpayer. If consent is granted, a copy of the letter granting such consent shall be filed with the director of the Internal Revenue service center with which the taxpayer's income tax return is required to be filed and shall be accompanied by an amended return or returns, if necessary.

(iii) If, before revoking his election, the taxpayer has transferred any mineral property with respect to which he deducted exploration expenditures under section 617(a), to another person in a transaction as a result of which the basis of such property in the hands of the transferee is determined in whole or in part by reference to the basis in the hands of the transferor, the statement submitted pursuant to subdivision (i) of this paragraph shall state that such property has been so transferred, shall identify the transferee, the property transferred, the date of the transfer, and shall indicate the amount of the adjusted exploration expenditures with respect to such property on such date.

(4) *Deficiency attributable to election or revocation of election.* The statutory period for the assessment of any deficiency for any taxable year, to the extent such deficiency is attributable to an election or revocation of an election under section 617(a), shall not expire before the last day of the 2-year period which begins on the day after the date on which such election or revocation of election is made; and such deficiency may be assessed at any time before the expiration of such 2-year period, notwithstanding any law or rule which would otherwise prevent such assessment. [Reg. § 1.617-1.]

☐ [T.D. 7192, 6-29-72.]

[Reg. § 1.617-2]

§ 1.617-2. **Limitation on amount deductible.**—(a) *Expenditures paid or incurred before January 1, 1970.* In the case of expenditures paid or incurred before January 1, 1970, a taxpayer may deduct exploration expenditures paid or incurred during the taxable year with respect to any deposit of ore or other mineral for which a deduction for percentage depletion is allowable under section 613 (other than oil or gas) in the United States or on the Outer Continental Shelf (within the meaning of section 2 of the Outer Continental Shelf Lands Act, as amended and supplemented; 43 U.S.C. 1331).

(b) *Expenditures paid or incurred after December 31, 1969.* In the case of exploration expenditures paid or incurred after December 31, 1969, with respect to any deposit of ore or other mineral for which a deduction for percentage depletion is allowable under section 613 (other than oil or gas), a taxpayer may deduct—

(1) The amount of such expenditures paid or incurred during the taxable year with respect to any such deposit in the United States (as defined in section 638 and the regulations thereunder), and

(2) With respect to any such deposit located outside the United States (as defined in section 638 and the regulations thereunder) the lesser of:

(i) The amount of the exploration expenditures paid or incurred with respect to such deposits during the taxable year, or

(ii) $400,000 minus the sum of the amount to be deducted under subparagraph (1) of this paragraph for the taxable year and all amounts deducted or treated as deferred expenses during all preceding taxable years under section 617 and section 615 of the Internal Revenue Code of 1954 and section 23(ff) of the Internal Revenue Code of 1939. See paragraph (d) of this section for application of the limitation in the case of a transferee of a mining property.

(c) *Examples.* The application of the provisions of paragraphs (a) and (b) of this section may be illustrated by the following examples:

Example (1). A, a calendar-year taxpayer who has claimed the benefits of section 615, expended $100,000 for exploration expenditures during the year 1966. For each of the years 1967, 1968, 1969, and 1970 A had exploration costs of $80,000 all with respect to coal deposits located within the United States. A deducted or deferred the maximum amounts allowable for each of the years 1966 ($100,000), 1967 ($80,000), 1968 ($80,000), and 1969 ($80,000). The $80,000 of exploration expenditures for 1970 may be deducted under section 617 by A.

Example (2). B, a calendar-year taxpayer claimed deductions of $100,000 per year under section 615 for the years 1968 and 1969. In 1970, B deducted $150,000 under section 617 for exploration conducted with respect to coal deposits in the United States. In 1971, B paid $150,000 with respect to exploration of tin deposits outside the United States. The maximum amount B may deduct with respect to the foreign exploration in 1971 is $50,000 computed as follows:

Reg. § 1.617-2(c)

Deductions

(a) Add all amounts deducted or deferred for exploration expenditures by B for all years:

Year:	Expenditures	Deducted or deferred
1968	$100,000	$100,000
1969	100,000	100,000
1970	150,000	150,000
Total		$350,000

(b) Subtract from $400,000 (the maximum amount allowable to B for deduction of foreign exploration expenditures) the sum of the amounts obtained in (a) $350,000:

Maximum amount allowable to taxpayer	$400,000
Sum of amounts obtained in (a)	350,000
	$ 50,000

Example (3). Assume the same facts as in example (2) except that in 1971 in addition to the $150,000 paid with respect to exploration outside the United States, B paid $100,000 with respect to exploration within the United States. As the following computation indicates, B may not deduct any amount with respect to the foreign exploration:

(a) Add all amounts deducted or deferred for exploration expenditures in prior years and the exploration expenditures with respect to exploration in the United States to be deducted in 1971:

Year:	Expenditures	Deducted or deferred	
1968	$100,000	$100,000	
1969	100,000	100,000	
1970	150,000	150,000	
1971	250,000	100,000	(domestic)
Total		$450,000	

(b) Because the sum of the amounts obtained in (a), $450,000, exceeds $400,000 no deduction would be allowable to B with respect to foreign exploration expenditures for 1971.

(d) *Transferee of mineral property.* (1) Where an individual or corporation transfers any mining property to the taxpayer, the taxpayer shall take into account for purposes of the $400,000 limitation described in paragraph (b)(ii) of this section all amounts deducted and amounts treated as deferred expenses by the transferor if—

(i) The taxpayer acquired any mineral property from the transferor in a transaction described in section 23(ff)(3) of the Internal Revenue Code of 1939, excluding the reference therein to section 113(a)(13),

(ii) The taxpayer acquired any mineral property by reason of the acquisition of assets of a corporation in a transaction described in section 381(a) as a result of which the taxpayer succeeds to and takes into account the items described in section 381(c),

(iii) The taxpayer acquired any mineral property under circumstances which make applicable any of the following sections of the Internal Revenue Code:

(a) Section 334(b)(1), relating to the liquidation of a subsidiary where the basis of the property in the hands of the distributee is the same as it would be in the hands of the transferor.

(b) Section 362(a) and (b), relating to property acquired by a corporation as paid-in surplus or as a contribution to capital, or in connection with a transaction to which section 351 applies.

(c) Section 372(a), relating to reorganization in certain receiverships and bankruptcy proceedings.

(d) Section 374(b)(1), relating to property of a railroad corporation acquired in certain bankruptcy or receivership proceedings.

(e) Section 1051, relating to property acquired by a corporation that is a member of an affiliated group.

(f) Section 1082, relating to property acquired pursuant to a Securities Exchange Commission order.

(2) For purposes of applying the limitations imposed by section 617(h):

(i) The partner, and not the partnership, shall be considered as the taxpayer (see paragraph (a)(8)(iii) of § 1.702-1), and

(ii) An electing small business corporation, as defined in section 1371(b), and not its shareholders, shall be considered as the taxpayer.

(3) For purposes of subparagraph (1)(iii)(b) of this paragraph, relating to a transaction to which section 362(a) and (b) applies or to which section 351 applies:

(i) If mineral property is acquired from a partnership, the transfer shall be considered as having been made by the individual partners, so that the amounts which each partner has deducted or deferred under sections 615 and 617 of the Internal Revenue Code of 1954 and section 23(ff) of the Internal Revenue Code of 1939 shall be taken into account, or

(ii) If an interest in a partnership having mineral property is transferred, the transfer shall be considered as a transfer of mineral property by the partner or partners relinquishing an interest, so that the amounts which each such partner has deducted or deferred under sections 615 and 617 of the Internal Revenue Code of 1954 and section

Reg. § 1.617-2(d)(2)

23(ff) of the Internal Revenue Code of 1939 shall be taken into account.

(e) *Examples.* The application of the provisions of this section may be illustrated by the following examples:

Example (1). A calendar year taxpayer (who has never claimed the benefits of section 617) received in 1970 a mineral deposit from X Corporation upon a distribution in complete liquidation of the latter under conditions which make the provisions of section 334(b)(1) applicable in determining the basis of the property in the hands of the taxpayer. During the year 1969, X Corporation expended $60,000 for exploration expenditures which it elected to treat under section 615(b) as deferred expenses. Subsequent to the transfer the taxpayer made similar expenditures for domestic exploration of $250,000 and $140,000, for the years 1970, and 1971, respectively, which the taxpayer elected to deduct. In 1972, the taxpayer made expenditures for domestic exploration of $100,000 and for foreign exploration of $50,000. The taxpayer may deduct the $100,000 domestic exploration expenditures but may not deduct any portion of the $50,000 of foreign exploration expenditures because the $400,000 limitation of section 617(h) applies.

Example (2). In 1971, A and B transfer assets to a corporation in a transfer to which section 351 applied. Among the assets transferred by A is a mineral lease with respect to certain coal lands. A has deducted exploration expenditures under section 615 for the years 1968 and 1969 in the amounts of $50,000 and $100,000, respectively, made with respect to other deposits not included in the transfer to the corporation. The corporation is required to take into account the deductions previously made by A for purposes of applying the $400,000 limitation on deduction of foreign exploration expenditures. Thus, if in 1970 the corporation incurred $400,000 of foreign exploration expenditures, the maximum which it could deduct under section 617(a) is $250,000. [Reg. § 1.617-2.]

☐ [*T.D. 7192, 6-29-72.*]

[Reg. § 1.617-3]

§ 1.617-3. Recapture of exploration expenditures.—(a) *In general.* (1) (i) Except as provided in subparagraphs (2) and (3) of this paragraph, if in any taxable year any mine (as defined in paragraph (c) of this section) with respect to which deductions have been allowed under section 617(a) reaches the producing stage (as defined in paragraph (c) of this section) the deduction for depletion under section 611 (whether determined under § 1.611-2 or under section 613) with respect to the property shall be disallowed for the taxable year and each subsequent taxable year until the aggregate amount of depletion which would be allowable but for section 617(b)(1)(B) and this subparagraph equals the amount of the adjusted exploration expenditures (determined under section 617(f)(1) and paragraph (d) of this section) attributable to the mine. The preceding sentence shall apply notwithstanding the fact that such mine is not in the producing stage at the close of such taxable year. In the case of a taxpayer who owns more than one property in a mine with respect to which he has been allowed deductions under section 617(a), the depletion deduction described in the second preceding sentence shall be disallowed with respect to all of the properties until the aggregate amount of depletion disallowed under section 617(b)(1)(B) is equal to the adjusted exploration expenditures with respect to the mine. In the case of a taxpayer who elects under section 614(c)(1) to aggregate a mine, with respect to which he has been allowed deductions under section 617(a), with another mine, no deduction for depletion will be allowable under section 611 with respect to the aggregated property until the amount of depletion disallowed under section 617(b)(1)(B) equals the adjusted exploration expenditures attributable to all of the producing mines included in the aggregated property.

(ii) If a taxpayer who has made an election under section 617(a) receives or accrues a bonus or royalty with respect to a mining property with respect to which deductions have been allowed under section 617(a), the deduction for depletion under section 611 with respect to such bonus or royalty (whether determined under § 1.611-2 or under section 613) shall be disallowed for the taxable year of receipt or accrual and each subsequent taxable year until the aggregate amount of the depletion disallowed under section 617(c) and this section equals the amount of the adjusted exploration expenditures with respect to the property to which the bonus or royalty relates. The preceding sentence shall not apply if the bonus or royalty is paid with respect to a mineral for which a deduction is not allowable under section 617(a). In the case of a disposal of coal or domestic iron ore with a retained economic interest, see paragraph (a)(2) of § 1.617-4.

(2) If the taxpayer so elects with respect to all mines as to which deductions have been allowed under section 617(a) and which reach the producing stage during the taxable year, he shall include in gross income (but not "gross income from the property" for purposes of section 613) for such taxable year an amount equal to the adjusted exploration expenditures (determined under section 617(f)(1) and paragraph (d) of this section) with respect to all of such mines. The

amount so included in income shall be treated for purposes of subtitle A of the Internal Revenue Code as expenditures which are paid or incurred on the respective dates on which the mines reach the producing stage and which are properly chargeable to capital account. The fact that a taxpayer does not make the election described in this subparagraph for a taxable year during which mines with respect to which deductions have been allowed under section 617(a) reach the producing stage shall not preclude the taxpayer from making the election with respect to other mines which reach the producing stage during subsequent taxable years. However, the election described in this subparagraph may not be made for any taxable year with respect to any mines which reached the producing stage during a preceding taxable year.

(3) The provisions of section 617(b)(1) of subparagraphs (1) and (2) of this paragraph do not apply in the case of any deposit of oil or gas. For example, A in exploring for sulphur incurred $500,000 of exploration expenditures which he deducted under section 617(a). In the following year, A did not find sulphur but on the same mineral property located commercially marketable quantities of oil and gas. In computing the depletion allowance with respect to the oil and gas, no depletion would be disallowed because of section 617(b)(1).

(4) In the case of exploration expenditures which are paid or incurred with respect to a mining property which contains more than one mine, the provisions of subparagraphs (1) and (2) of this paragraph shall apply only to the amount of the adjusted exploration expenditures properly chargeable to the mine or mines which reach the producing stage during the taxable year. For example, A owns a mining property which contains mines X, Y, and Z. For 1970, A deducted under section 617(a), $250,000 with respect to X, $100,000 with respect to Y and $70,000 with respect to Z. In 1971, mine X reaches the producing stage. At that time, A will only have to recapture the $250,000 attributable to mine X.

(b) *Manner and time for making election.* (1) A taxpayer will be deemed not to have elected pursuant to section 617(b)(1)(A) and paragraph (a)(2) of this section unless he clearly indicates such election on his income tax return for the taxable year in which the mine with respect to which deductions were allowed under section 617(a) reaches the producing stage.

(2) The election described in paragraph (a)(2) of this section may be made (or changed) not later than the time prescribed by law for filing the return (including extensions thereof) for the taxable year in which the mine with respect to which deductions were allowed under section 617(a) reaches the producing stage.

(c) *Definitions.* (1) *Mine.* The term "mine" includes all quarries, pits, shafts and wells, and any other excavations or workings for the purpose of extracting any known deposit of ore or other mineral.

(2) *Producing stage.* A mine will be considered to have reached the producing stage when (i) the major portion of the mineral production is obtained from workings other than those opened for the purpose of development, or (ii) the principal activity of the mine is the production of developed ores or minerals rather than the development of additional ores or minerals for mining.

(3) *Mining property.* The term "mining property" means any property (as the term is defined in section 614(a) after the application of subsections (c) and (e) thereof) with respect to which any expenditures allowed as deductions under section 617(a) are properly chargeable.

(d) *Adjusted exploration expenditures*—(1) *In general.* The term "adjusted exploration expenditures" means, with respect to any property or mine—

(i) the aggregate amount of the expenditures allowed as deductions under section 617(a) for the taxable year and all preceding taxable years to the taxpayer or any other person which are properly chargeable to such property or mine and which (but for the election under section 617(a)) would be reflected in the adjusted basis of such property or mine, reduced by

(ii) the excess, if any, of the amount which would have been allowable for all taxable years under section 613 but for the deduction of such expenditures over the amount allowable for depletion under section 611 (determined without regard to section 617(b)(1)(B)). The amount determined under the preceding sentence shall be reduced by the aggregate of the amounts included in gross income for the taxable year and all preceding taxable years under section 617(b) or (c) and the amount treated under section 617(d) as gain from the sale or exchange of the property which is neither a capital asset nor property described in section 1231.

(iii) If a taxpayer pays or incurs exploration expenditures on a property which contains a producing mine and if such taxpayer deducts any portion of such expenditures under section 617(a), an amount equal to the amount so deducted shall be taken into account in computing the taxpayer's "taxable income from the property" for the purposes of the limitation on the percentage depletion deduction under section 613(a) and the regulations thereunder. The amount of the adjusted exploration expenditures with respect to the producing mine shall be reduced by an amount equal to the amount by which the taxpayer's deduction under 617(a) (described in the preceding sentence) reduces the taxpayer's deduction for depletion for the taxable year. See example (1) in subparagraph (6) of this paragraph.

(iv) For purposes of § 1.617-4, the aggregate amount of adjusted exploration expenditures with respect to a mining property includes the aggregate amount of adjusted exploration expenditures properly allocable to all mines on such property.

(v) (*a*) For purposes of paragraph (a)(1) of this section, the aggregate amount of the adjusted exploration expenditures is determined as of the close of the taxpayer's taxable year.

(*b*) For purposes of § 1.617-4, the aggregate amount of the adjusted exploration expenditures is determined as of the date of the disposition of the mining property or portion thereof.

(2) *Adjustments for certain expenditures of other taxpayers or in respect of other property.* (i) For purposes of subparagraph (1) of this paragraph, the exploration expenditures which must be taken into account in determining the adjusted exploration expenditures with respect to any property or mine are not limited to those expenditures with respect to the property disposed of or which entered the production stage nor are such expenditures limited to those deducted by the taxpayer. For the manner of determining the amount of adjusted exploration expenditures immediately after certain dispositions, see subparagraph (4) of this paragraph.

(ii) If a transferee who at the time of the transfer has not made an election under section 617(a) (including a transferee who has made an election under section 615(e)) receives mineral property in a transaction in which the basis of such property in his hands is determined in whole or in part by reference to its basis in the hands of the transferor and with respect to such property the transferor has deducted exploration expenditures under section 617(a), the adjusted exploration expenditures immediately after such transfer shall be treated as exploration expenditures allowed as deductions under section 617(a) to the transferee.

(iii) If a transferee who makes an election under section 617(a) receives mineral property in a transaction in which the basis of such property in his hands is determined in whole or in part by reference to the basis of such property in the hands of the transferor and the transferor had in effect at the time of the transfer an election under section 615(e), an amount equal to the total of the amounts allowed as deductions to the transferor under section 615 with respect to the transferred property shall be treated as expenditures allowed as deductions under section 617(a) to the transferee. The preceding sentence shall not apply to expenditures which could not have been reflected in the basis of the property in the hands of the transferee had the transferor not made the section 615(e) election.

(iv) The provisions of this subparagraph may be illustrated by the following examples:

Example (1). On July 14, 1969, A purchased mineral property Z for $10,000. After deducting exploration expenditures of $20,000 under section 617(a), A transferred the property to his son as a gift on July 9, 1970. Since the exception for gifts in section 617(d)(3) (by incorporation by reference of the provisions of section 1245(b)(1)) applies, A does not recognize gain under section 617(d). On September 30, 1972, after deducting exploration expenditures of $150,000 under section 617(a), the son transfers the mineral property to corporation X in a transaction under which no gain is recognized by the son under section 351. Since the exception of section 617(d)(3) (by incorporation by reference of the provisions of section 1245(b)(3)) applies, the son does not recognize gain under section 617(d). On November 14, 1972, corporation X sells the mineral property. No deductions for exploration expenditures were taken by corporation X. The amount of the adjusted exploration expenditures with respect to mineral property Z to be recaptured by corporation X upon such sale is $170,000 (the total amount deducted by A and the son).

Example (2). Assume the same facts as in example (1) except that A deducted the $20,000 of exploration expenditures under section 615(a). The amount of the adjusted exploration expenditures with respect to mineral property Z in corporation X's hands is $170,000 (the $20,000 deducted under section 615(a) by A plus the $150,000 deducted under section 617(a) by the son).

(3) *Allocation of certain expenditures.* A project area consists of that territory which the taxpayer has determined by analysis of certain variables (the size and topography of the area to be explored, existing information with respect to that area and nearby areas, and the quantity of equipment, men, and money available) can be explored advantageously as a single integrated operation. If exploration expenditures are paid or incurred with respect to a project area and one or more areas of interest are identified within such

Reg. § 1.617-3(d)(3)

project area, the entire amount of such expenditures shall be allocated equally to each such area of interest. If an area of interest contains one or more mines or deposits the expenditures allocable to such area of interest shall be allocated (i) if only one mine or deposit is located or identified, entirely to such mine or deposit, or (ii) if more than one mine or deposit is located or identified, equally among the various mines or deposits located. For purposes of this subparagraph, the term "area of interest" means each separable, noncontiguous portion of the project area which is identified as possessing sufficient material-producing potential to merit further exploration. The provisions of this subparagraph may be illustrated by the following example: A pays $100,000 for the exploration of a project area which results in the identification of two areas of interest. A pays an additional $60,000 for the exploration of one of the areas of interest in which he locates mineral deposit X and mineral deposit Y. With respect to the exploration of deposit X he incurs an additional $100,000 of expenses and with respect to deposit Y he incurs an additional $200,000 of expenses. The exploration expenditures properly attributable to deposit X would be $155,000 ($100,000 plus 1/2 of $50,000 plus 1/2 of $60,000) and the exploration expenditures properly attributable to deposit Y would be $255,000 ($200,000 plus 1/2 of $50,000 plus 1/2 of $60,000).

(4) *Partnership distributions.* The adjusted exploration expenditures with respect to any property or mine received by a taxpayer in a distribution with respect to all or part of his interest in a partnership (i) include the adjusted exploration expenditures (not otherwise included under section 617(f)(1)) with respect to such property or mine immediately prior to such distribution and (ii) shall be reduced by the amount of gain to which section 751(b) applies realized by the partnership (as constituted after the distribution) on the distribution of such property or mine. In the case of any property or mine held by a partnership after a distribution to a partner to which section 751(b) applies, the adjusted exploration expenditures with respect to such property or mine shall be reduced by the amount of gain (if any) to which section 751(b) applies realized by such partner with respect to such distribution on account of such property or mine.

(5) *Amounts of transferee's adjusted exploration expenditures immediately after certain acquisitions*—(i) *Transactions in which basis is determined by reference to the cost or fair market value of the property transferred.*

(*a*) If on the date a person acquires mining property his basis for the property is determined solely by reference to its cost (within the meaning of section 1012), then on such date the amount of the adjusted exploration expenditures for the mining property in such person's hands is zero.

(*b*) If on the date a person acquires mining property his basis for the property is determined solely by reason of the application of section 301(d) (relating to basis of property received in corporate distribution) or section 334(a) (relating to basis of property received in a liquidation in which gain or loss is recognized), then on such date the amount of the adjusted exploration expenditures for the mining property in such person's hands is zero.

(*c*) If on the date a person acquires mining property his basis for the property is determined solely under the provisions of section 334(b)(2) or (c) (relating to basis of property received in certain corporate liquidations), then on such date the amount of the adjusted exploration expenditures for the mining property in such person's hands is zero.

(*d*) If on the date a person acquires mining property from a decedent such person's basis is determined, by reason of the application of section 1014(a), solely by reference to the fair market value of the property on the date of the decedent's death or on the applicable date provided in section 2032 (relating to alternate valuation date), then on the date of acquisition the amount of the adjusted exploration expenditures for the mining property in such person's hands is zero.

(ii) *Gifts and certain tax-free transactions.* (*a*) If mining property is disposed of in a transaction described in subdivision (*b*) of this subdivision (ii), then the amount of the adjusted exploration expenditures for the mining property in the hands of a transferee immediately after the disposition shall be an amount equal to—

(*1*) The amount of the adjusted exploration expenditures with respect to the mining property in the hands of the transferor immediately before the disposition, minus

(*2*) The amount of any gain taken into account under section 617(d) by the transferor upon the disposition.

(*b*) The transactions referred to in subdivision (*a*) of this subdivision (ii) are—

(*1*) A disposition which is in part a sale or exchange and in part a gift, or

(*2*) A disposition which is described in section 617(d) through the incorporation by reference of the provisions of section 1245(b)(3) (relating to certain tax free transactions).

Reg. § 1.617-3(d)(4)

(iii) *Property acquired from a decedent.* If mining property is acquired in a transfer at death to which section 617(d) applies through incorporation by reference of the provisions of section 1245(b)(2), the amount of the adjusted exploration expenditures with respect to the mining property in the hands of the transferee immediately after the transfer shall include the amount, if any, of the exploration expenditures deducted by the transferee before the decedent's death, to the extent that the basis of the mining property (determined under section 1014(a)) is required to be reduced under the second sentence of section 1014(b)(9) (relating to adjustments to basis where the property is acquired from a decedent prior to his death).

(6) *Examples.* The provisions of this paragraph may be illustrated by the following examples:

Example (1). A owns the working interest in a large tract of land located in the United States. A's interest in the entire tract of land constitutes one property for purposes of section 614. In the northwest corner of this tract is an operating mine, X, producing an ore of beryllium, which is entitled to a percentage depletion rate of 22 percent under section 613(b)(2)(B). During 1971, A conducts an exploration program in the southeast corner of this same tract of land, and he incurs $400,000 of expenditures to which section 617(a)(1) applies in connection with this exploration program. A elects to deduct this amount as expenses under section 617(a). During 1971, A's "gross income from the property" computed under section 613 was $1 million, with respect to the property encompassing mine X and the area in which exploration was conducted. A's "taxable income from the property" computed under section 613, before adjustment to reflect the deductions taken with respect to the property during the year under section 617, was $400,000. The cost depletion deduction allowable and deducted with respect to the property during 1971 was $50,000. The amount of adjusted exploration expenditures chargeable to the exploratory mine (hereinafter referred to as mine Y) at the close of 1971 is $250,000, computed as follows:

Expenditures allowed as deductions under sec. 617(a)	$400,000
Gross income from the property	$1,000,000
22 percent thereof	220,000
Taxable income from the property, before adjustment to reflect deductions allowed under sec. 617 during year ..	400,000
50 percent thereof—tentative deduction	200,000
Taxable income from the property after adjustment to reflect deductions allowed under sec. 617 during year ($400,000 minus $400,000)	0
Cost depletion allowed for year	50,000
Amount by which allowance for depletion under section 611 was reduced on account of deductions under sec. 617 ($200,000 minus $50,000)	150,000
Adjusted exploration expenditures at end of 1971	$250,000

Example (2). Assume the same facts as in example 1. Assume further that mine Y, with respect to which exploration expenditures were deducted in 1971, enters the producing stage in 1972, and that no deductions were taken under section 617 with respect to that mine after 1971. A does not make an election under section 617(b)(1)(A) during 1972. Assume that the depletion deduction which would be allowable for 1972 with respect to the property (which includes both mines) but for the application of section 617(b)(1)(B) is $100,000. Pursuant to section 617(b)(1)(B), this depletion deduction is disallowed. Therefore, the amount of adjusted exploration expenditures with respect to mine Y at the end of 1972 is $150,000 ($250,000 less $100,000). [Reg. § 1.617-3.]

☐ [T.D. 7192, 6-29-72.]

[Reg. § 1.617-4]

§ 1.617-4. Treatment of gain from disposition of certain mining property.—(a) *In general.*—(1) Section 617(d)(1) provides that, upon a disposition of mining property, the lower of (i) the "adjusted exploration expenditures" (as defined in section 617(f)(1) and paragraph (d) of § 1.617-3) with respect to the property, or (ii) the amount, if any, by which the amount realized on the sale, exchange, or involuntary conversion (or the fair market value of the property on any other disposition), exceeds the adjusted basis of the property, shall be treated as gain from the sale or exchange of property which is neither a capital asset nor property described in section 1231 (that is, shall be recognized as ordinary income). However, any amount recognized under the preceding sentence shall not be included by the taxpayer in his "gross income from the property" for purposes of section 613. Generally, the ordinary income treatment applies even though in the absence of section 617(d) no gain would be recognized under any

Reg. § 1.617-4(a)(1)

other provision of the Code. For example, if a corporation distributes mining property as a dividend, gain may be recognized as ordinary income to the corporation even though, in the absence of section 617, section 311(a) would preclude any recognition of gain to the corporation. For an exception to the recognition of gain with respect to dispositions which involve mineral production payments, see section 636 and the regulations thereunder. For the definition of the term "mining property," see section 617(f)(2) and paragraph (c)(3), of § 1.617-3. For exceptions and limitations to the application of section 617(d)(1), see section 617(d)(3) and paragraph (c) of this section.

(2) In the case of a sale, exchange, or involuntary conversion of mining property, the gain to which section 617(d)(1) applies is the lower of the adjusted exploration expenditures with respect to such property or the excess of the amount realized upon the disposition of the property over the adjusted basis of the property. In the case of a disposition of mining property other than by a manner described in the preceding sentence, the gain to which section 617(d)(1) applies is the lower of the adjusted exploration expenditures with respect to such property or the excess of the fair market value of the property on the date of disposition over the adjusted basis of the property. In the case of a disposal of coal or domestic iron ore subject to a retained economic interest to which section 631(c) applies, the excess of the amount realized over the adjusted basis of the mining property shall be treated as equal to the gain, if any, referred to in section 631(c). For determination of the amount realized upon a disposition of mining property and non-mining property, see paragraph (c)(3)(i) of this section.

(3) The provisions of this paragraph may be illustrated by the following examples:

Example (1). On July 14, 1970, A purchased undeveloped mining property for $100,000. During 1970, A incurred with respect to the property, $50,000 of exploration expenditures which he deducts under section 617(a). In 1971, A incurred $150,000 of exploration expenditures with respect to the property which he deducts on his income tax return. On January 2, 1972, A sells the mining property to B for $250,000. A's gain on the sale is $150,000 ($250,000 amount realized minus $100,000 basis). Since the excess of the amount realized over the adjusted basis of the mining property is less than the adjusted exploration expenditures with respect to the property ($200,000), the entire gain is treated as ordinary income under section 617(d)(1).

Example (2). Assume the same facts as in example (1) except that A sells the mining property to B for $400,000, thereby realizing gain of $300,000 ($400,000 minus $100,000 basis). Since the amount of adjusted exploration expenditures with respect to the mining property ($200,000) is less than the amount realized upon its disposition ($300,000), an amount equal to the amount of adjusted exploration expenditures is treated as ordinary income under section 617(d)(1). The remaining $100,000 is treated by A without regard to section 617(d)(1).

(4) Section 617(d) does not apply to losses. Thus, section 617(d) does not apply if a loss is realized upon a sale, exchange, or involuntary conversion of mining property, nor does section 617(d) apply to a disposition of mining property other than by way of sale, exchange, or involuntary conversion if at the time of the disposition the fair market value of such property is not greater than its adjusted basis.

(b) *Disposition of portion of mining property.* (1) For purposes of section 617(d)(1) and paragraph (a) of this section, except as provided in subparagraph (3) of this paragraph, in the case of the disposition of a portion of a mining property (other than an undivided interest), the entire amount of the adjusted exploration expenditures with respect to such property shall be treated as attributable to such portion to the extent of the amount of the gain to which section 617(d)(1) applies. If the amount of the gain to which section 617(d)(1) applies is less than the amount of the adjusted exploration expenditures with respect to the property, the balance of the adjusted exploration expenditures shall remain subject to recapture in the hands of the taxpayer under the provisions of section 617(b), (c), and (d). The disposition of a portion of a mining property (other than an undivided interest) includes the disposition of a geographical portion of a mining property. For example, assume that A owns an 80-acre tract of land with respect to which he has deducted exploration expenditures under section 617(a). If A were to sell the north 40 acres, the entire amount of the adjusted exploration expenditures with respect to the 80-acre tract would be treated as attributable to the 40 acre portion sold (to the extent of the amount of the gain to which section 617(d)(1) applies).

(2) For purposes of section 617(d)(1), except as provided in subparagraph (3) of this paragraph, in the case of the disposition of an undivided interest in a mining property (or portion thereof) a proportionate part of the adjusted exploration expenditures with respect to such property shall be treated as attributable to such

undivided interest to the extent of the amount of the gain to which section 617(d)(1) applies. For example, assume that A owns an 80-acre tract of land with respect to which he has deducted exploration expenditures under section 617(a). If A were to sell an undivided 40 percent interest in such tract, 40 percent of the adjusted exploration expenditures with respect to the 80-acre tract would be treated as attributable to the 40 percent of the 80-acre tract disposed of (to the extent of the amount of the gain to which section 617(d)(1) applies).

(3) Section 617(d)(2) and subparagraphs (1) and (2) of this paragraph shall not apply to any expenditure to the extent that such expenditure relates neither to the portion (or interest therein) disposed of nor to any mine, in the property held by the taxpayer before the disposition, which has reached the producing stage. In any case where a taxpayer disposes of a mining property (or interest therein) and treats adjusted exploration expenditures with respect to the mining property as if they relate neither to the portion (or interest therein) disposed of nor to any mine, in the property held by the taxpayer before the disposition, which has reached the producing stage, the taxpayer shall attach to its return for the taxable year in which the disposition occurred, a statement which includes:

(i) A description of the portion (or interest therein) disposed of;

(ii) A description of the mineral property which included the portion (or interest therein) disposed of;

(iii) An itemization of all expenditures deducted under sections 617 and 615 with respect to such mineral property; and

(iv) A description of the location of all producing mines on such mineral property.

(c) *Exceptions.* (1)(i) Section 617(d)(3) provides, through incorporation by reference of the provisions of section 1245(b)(1), that no gain shall be recognized under section 617(d) upon a disposition by gift of mining property. For purposes of this subparagraph, the term "gift" means, except to the extent that subdivision (ii) of this subparagraph applies, a transfer of mining property which, in the hands of the transferee, has a basis determined under the provisions of section 1015(a) or (d) (relating to basis of property acquired by gift). For reduction in amount of the charitable contribution in case of a gift of section 617 property, see section 170(e) and paragraph (c)(3) of § 1.170-1.

(ii) Where a disposition of mining property is in part a sale or exchange and in part a gift, the gain to which section 617(d) applies is the lower of the adjusted exploration expenditures with respect to such property or the excess of the amount realized upon the disposition of the property over the adjusted basis of such property.

(2) Section 617(d)(3) provides, through incorporation by reference of the provisions of section 1245(b)(2), that, except as provided in section 691 (relating to income in respect to a decedent), no gain shall be recognized under section 617(d) upon a transfer at death. For purposes of this paragraph, the term "transfer at death" means a transfer of mining property which property, in the hands of the transferee, has a basis determined under the provisions of section 1014(a) (relating to basis of property acquired from a decedent) because of the death of the transferor.

(3)(i) Section 617(d) provides, through incorporation by reference of the provisions of section 1245(b)(3), that upon a transfer of property described in subdivision (ii) of this subparagraph, the amount of gain taken into account by the transferor under section 617(d) shall not exceed the amount of gain recognized to the transferor on the transfer (determined without regard to section 617). For purposes of this subdivision, in case of a transfer of mining property and non-mining property in one transaction, the amount realized from the disposition of the mining property shall be deemed to be equal to the amount which bears the same ratio to the total amount realized as the fair market value of the mining property bears to the aggregate fair market value of all of the property transferred. The preceding sentence shall be applied solely for purposes of computing the portion of the total gain (determined without regard to section 617) which shall be recognized as ordinary income under section 617(d). Section 617(d)(3) does not apply to a disposition of mining property to an organization (other than a cooperative described in section 521) which is exempt from the tax imposed by chapter 1 of the Code.

(ii) The transfers referred to in subdivision (i) of this subparagraph are transfers of mining property in which the basis of the mining property in the hands of the transferee is determined by reference to its basis in the hands of the transferor by reason of the application of any of the following provisions:

(*a*) Section 332 (relating to distributions in complete liquidation of an 80-percent-or-more controlled subsidiary corporation). See subdivision (iii) of this subparagraph.

(*b*) Section 351 (relating to transfer to a corporation controlled by transferor).

(*c*) Section 361 (relating to exchanges pursuant to certain corporate reorganizations).

Reg. § 1.617-4(c)(3)

(d) Section 371(a) (relating to exchanges pursuant to certain receivership and bankruptcy proceedings).

(e) Section 374(a) (relating to exchanges pursuant to certain railroad reorganizations).

(f) Section 721 (relating to transfers to a partnership in exchange for a partnership interest).

(g) Section 731 (relating to distributions by a partnership to a partner).

(iii) In the case of a distribution in complete liquidation of an 80-percent-or-more controlled subsidiary to which section 332 applies, the limitation provided in section 617(d)(3), through incorporation by reference of the provisions of section 1245(b)(3), is confined to instances in which the basis of the mining property in the hands of the transferee is determined under section 334(b)(1), by reference to its basis in the hands of the transferor. Thus, for example, the limitation may apply in respect of a liquidating distribution of mining property by an 80-percent-or-more controlled corporation to the parent corporation, but does not apply in respect of a liquidating distribution of mining property to a minority shareholder. Section 617(d)(3) does not apply to a liquidating distribution of property by an 80-percent-or-more controlled subsidiary to its parent if the parent's basis for the property is determined under section 334(b)(2), by reference to its basis in the stock of the subsidiary. [Reg. § 1.617-4.]

☐ [T.D. 7192, 6-29-72.]

Exclusions

[Reg. § 1.621-1]

§ 1.621-1. **Payments to encourage exploration, development, and mining for defense purposes.**—(a) *General rule.* (1) Under section 621, a taxpayer shall exclude from gross income amounts which are paid to him:

(i) By the United States or by an agency or instrumentality of the United States,

(ii) As a grant, gift, bounty, bonus, premium, incentive, subsidy, loan, or advance,

(iii) For the encouragement of exploration for, or development or mining of, a critical and strategic mineral or metal,

(iv) Pursuant to or in connection with an undertaking by the taxpayer to explore for, or develop or produce, such mineral or metal and to expend or use any amounts so received for the purpose and in accordance with the terms and conditions upon which such amounts are paid, which undertaking has been approved by the United States or by an agency or instrumentality of the United States, and

(v) For which the taxpayer has accounted, or is required to account, to an appropriate agency of the United States Government for the expenditure or use thereof for the purpose and in accordance with the terms and conditions upon which such amounts are paid.

In order for section 621 to apply, such amount must qualify under each of the foregoing subdivisions of this paragraph. Under section 621, there shall also be excluded from gross income any income attributable to the forgiveness or discharge of any indebtedness arising from amounts to which such section applies.

(2) Section 621 is applicable whether or not the payee is obligated to repay to the United States any portion or all of the amount so received. However, such section is not applicable to any loan or advance for the repayment of which the borrower's liability is unconditional and legally enforceable.

(3) Except as provided in paragraph (d) of this section any expenditure attributable to an amount received by a taxpayer to which section 621 applies shall not be deductible by the taxpayer as an expense under subtitle A of the Code, nor shall any such expenditure increase the basis of the taxpayer's property either for determining gain or loss on sale, exchange, or other disposition, or for computing depletion or depreciation (including amortization under section 168).

(b) *Allowance as part of purchase price.* (1) Section 621 is not applicable to any part of the purchase price of a critical and strategic mineral or metal which amount is received, whether before, on, or after delivery from the United States or any agency or instrumentality thereof, and irrespective of whether such purchase price is below, at, or above the currently prevailing market price.

(2) However, a payment of a separate and specific amount for the encouragement of exploration for, or development or mining of, a critical and strategic mineral or metal shall not be considered to be a part of the purchase price of such mineral or metal merely because such payment is added to, or included with, the payment of such purchase price.

(c) *Payments for expenditures previously deducted or capitalized.* (1) Where amounts described in section 621 and this section are paid to a taxpayer in reimbursement for expenditures previously allowed as a deduction, the taxpayer shall include in gross income that portion of such amounts which is equivalent to the deduction for such expenditures allowed to the taxpayer and which deduction resulted in a reduction for any taxable year of the taxpayer's taxes under subtitle A of the Code (other than chapter 2, relating to tax on self-employment income), or prior income, war-profits, or excess-profits tax laws.

(2) Where amounts described in section 621 and this section are paid to the taxpayer in reimbursement for expenditures which have been deferred under sections 615 and 616 (relating to exploration and development expenditures) the taxpayer shall include in gross income that portion of such amounts which is equivalent to any deduction for such expenditures allowed to the taxpayer and which deduction resulted in a reduction for any taxable year of the taxpayer's taxes under subtitle A of the Code (other than chapter 2, relating to tax on self-employment income), or prior income, war-profits, or excess-profits tax laws. The portion of such amounts, equivalent to expenditures which are reflected in the adjusted basis of the assets to which charged, shall be excluded from gross income, and such adjusted basis shall be decreased by the amount of such exclusion.

(3) Where amounts described in section 621 and this section are paid to the taxpayer in reimbursement for expenditures which have been charged to capital account (either to a depletable or depreciable account), there shall be included in the taxpayer's gross income that portion of such amounts which is equivalent to such capital expenditures that have been recovered through cost depletion or depreciation deductions and which deductions have resulted in a reduction of the taxpayer's taxes for any taxable year under subtitle A of the Code (other than chapter 2, relating to tax on self-employment income), or prior income, war-profits, or excess-profits tax laws. The portion of such amounts which is equivalent to the expenditures which are reflected in the adjusted basis of the asset to which charged shall be excluded from gross income. The adjusted basis of such assets shall be reduced by the amount of such exclusion from gross income.

(4) Where amounts described in section 621 and this section are paid to the taxpayer in reimbursement for expenditures which have been charged to a depletable capital account, such amounts shall be excluded to the extent such expenditures are recovered through depletion deductions computed under section 613 (relating to percentage depletion).

(5) The amount of reimbursed expenditures charged to an account (depletable or depreciable) and recovered through depletion or depreciation deductions for any taxable year shall be that proportion of the total deductions allowed with respect to such account that such reimbursed expenditures bear to the total amount in the account. For example, in 1956 A incurs exploration expenditures of $12,000 which he charges to a depletable capital account. This brings the total amount in this account to $36,000 which is the adjusted basis of the property on January 1, 1957. In 1957, A is allowed a deduction for cost depletion of $9,000 which resulted in a reduction of A's income taxes. One-third of this deduction is attributable to the $12,000 of exploration expenditures since they were a third of the total in the capital account on January 1, 1957. Therefore, on January 1, 1958, these exploration expenditures make up $9,000 of the remaining $27,000 in the account. If on January 1, 1958, A receives $12,000, which qualifies under section 621, in reimbursement for these exploration expenditures, he must report $3,000 as income and reduce the capital account by $9,000.

(d) *Definition.* As used in section 621 and this section, the term "critical and strategic minerals or metals" means minerals and metals which are considered by those departments, agencies, and instrumentalities of the United States charged with the encouragement of exploration for, and development and mining of, critical and strategic minerals and metals, to constitute critical and strategic minerals and metals for defense purposes. See, for example, 30 CFR 301.3 (Regulations for Obtaining Federal Assistance in Financing Explorations for Mineral Reserves, excluding Organic Fields, in the United States, its Territories and Possessions).

(e) *Repayments of amounts excluded under section 621.* Upon the repayment by the taxpayer of any portion of any amount to which section 621 applies and which portion has been expended for the purpose and in accordance with the terms and conditions upon which it was paid to the taxpayer, any expenditures attributable to such amount made by the taxpayer shall be treated as if such expenditures had been made at the time of such repayment. Such expenditures shall to the extent of the repayment be expensed or capitalized, as the case may be, in the order in which they were actually made or in such other manner as may be adopted by the taxpayer with the approval of the Commissioner. [Reg. § 1.621-1.]

☐ [*T.D.* 6446, 1-20-60.]

Reg. § 1.621-1(e)

Sales and Exchanges

See p. 20,601 for regulations not amended to reflect law changes

Sales and Exchanges

[Reg. § 1.631-1]

§ 1.631-1. Election to consider cutting as sale or exchange.—(a) *Effect of election.* (1) Section 631(a) provides an election to certain taxpayers to treat the difference between the actual cost or other basis of certain timber cut during the taxable year and its fair market value as standing timber on the first day of such year as gain or loss from a sale or exchange under section 1231. Thereafter, any subsequent gain or loss shall be determined in accordance with paragraph (e) of this section.

(2) For the purposes of section 631(a) and this section, timber shall be considered cut at the time when in the ordinary course of business the quantity of timber felled is first definitely determined.

(3) The election may be made with respect to any taxable year even though such election was not made with respect to a previous taxable year. If an election has been made under the provisions of section 631(a), or corresponding provisions of prior internal revenue laws, such election shall be binding upon the taxpayer not only for the taxable year for which the election is made but also for all subsequent taxable years, unless the Commissioner on showing by the taxpayer of undue hardship permits the taxpayer to revoke his election for such subsequent taxable years. If the taxpayer has revoked a previous election, such revocation shall preclude any further elections unless the taxpayer obtains the consent of the Commissioner.

(4) Such election shall apply with respect to all timber which the taxpayer has owned, or has had a contract right to cut, for a period of more than 1 year (6 months for taxable years beginning before 1977; 9 months for taxable years beginning in 1977) prior to when such timber is cut for sale or for use in the taxpayer's trade or business, irrespective of whether such timber or contract right was acquired before or after the election. (For purposes of the preceding sentence, the rules with respect to the holding period of property contained in section 1223 shall be applicable.) However, timber which is not cut for sale or for use in the taxpayer's trade or business (for example, firewood cut for the taxpayer's own household consumption) shall not be considered to have been sold or exchanged upon the cutting thereof.

(b) *Who may make election.* (1) A taxpayer who has owned, or has held a contract right to cut, timber for a period of more than 1 year (6 months for taxable years beginning before 1977; 9 months for taxable years beginning in 1977) prior to when the timber is cut may elect under section 631(a) to consider the cutting of such timber during such year for sale or for use in the taxpayer's trade or business as a sale or exchange of the timber so cut. In order to have a "contract right to cut timber" within the meaning of section 631(a) and this section, a taxpayer must have a right to sell the timber cut under the contract on his own account or to use such cut timber in his trade or business.

(2) For purposes of section 631(a) and this section, the term "timber" includes evergreen trees which are more than six years old at the time severed from their roots and are sold for ornamental purposes, such as Christmas decorations. Section 631(a) is not applicable to evergreen trees which are sold in a live state, whether or not for ornamental purposes. Tops and other parts of standing timber are not considered as evergreen trees within the meaning of section 631(a). The term "evergreen trees" is used in its commonly accepted sense and includes pine, spruce, fir, hemlock, cedar, and other coniferous trees.

(c) *Manner of making election.* The election under section 631(a) must be made by the taxpayer in his income tax return for the taxable year for which the election is applicable, and such election cannot be made in an amended return for such year. The election in the return shall take the form of a computation under the provisions of section 631(a) and section 1231.

(d) *Computation of gain or loss under the election.* (1) If the cutting of timber is considered as a sale or exchange pursuant to an election made under section 631(a), gain or loss shall be recognized to the taxpayer in an amount equal to the difference between the adjusted basis for depletion in the hands of the taxpayer of the timber which has been cut during the taxable year and the fair market value of such timber as of the first day of the taxable year in which such timber is cut. The adjusted basis for depletion of the cut timber shall be based upon the number of units of timber cut during the taxable year which are considered to be sold or exchanged and upon the depletion unit of the timber in the timber account or accounts pertaining to the timber cut, and shall be computed in the same manner as is provided in section 611 and the regulations thereunder with respect to the computation of the allowance for depletion.

(2) The fair market value of the timber as of the first day of the taxable year in which such timber is cut shall be determined, subject to approval or revision by the district director upon examination of the taxpayer's return, by the taxpayer in the light of the most reliable and accurate information available with reference to the

Reg. § 1.631-1(a)(2)

condition of the property as it existed at that date, regardless of all subsequent changes, such as changes in surrounding circumstances, methods of exploitation, degree of utilization, etc. The value sought will be the selling price, assuming a transfer between a willing seller and a willing buyer as of that particular day. Due consideration will be given to the factors and the principles involved in the determination of the fair market value of timber as described in the regulations under section 611.

(3) The fair market value as of the beginning of the taxable year of the standing timber cut during the year shall be considered to be the cost of such timber, in lieu of the actual cost or other basis of such timber, for all purposes for which such cost is a necessary factor. See paragraph (e) of this section.

(4) For any taxable year for which the cutting of timber is considered to be a sale or exchange of such timber under section 631(a), the timber so cut shall be considered as property used in the trade or business for the purposes of section 1231, along with other property of the taxpayer used in the trade or business as defined in section 1231(b), regardless of whether such timber is property of a kind which would properly be includible in the inventory of the taxpayer if on hand at the close of the taxable year or property held by the taxpayer primarily for sale to customers in the ordinary course of his trade or business. Whether the gain or loss considered to have resulted from the cutting of the timber will be considered to be gain or loss resulting from the sale or exchange of capital assets held for more than 1 year (6 months for taxable years beginning before 1977; 9 months for taxable years beginning in 1977) depends upon the application of section 1231 to the taxpayer for the taxable year. See section 1231 and the regulations thereunder.

(e) *Computation of subsequent gain or loss.* (1) In case the products of the timber are sold after cutting, either in the form of logs or lumber or in the form of manufactured products, the income from such actual sales shall be considered ordinary income. When the election under section 631(a) is in effect, the cost of standing timber cut during the taxable year is determined as if the taxpayer had purchased such timber on the first day of the taxable year. Thus, in determining the cost of the products so sold, the cost of the timber shall be the fair market value on the first day of the taxable year in which the standing timber was cut, in lieu of the actual cost or other basis of such timber.

(2) This is also the rule in case the products of the timber cut during one taxable year, with respect to which an election has been made under section 631(a), are sold during a subsequent taxable year, whether or not the election provided in section 631(a) is applicable with respect to such subsequent year. If the products of the timber cut during a taxable year with respect to which an election under section 631(a) was made were not sold during such year and are included in inventory at the close of such year, the fair market value as of the beginning of the year of the timber cut during the year shall be used in lieu of the actual cost of such timber in computing the closing inventory for such year and the opening inventory for the succeeding year. With respect to the costs applicable in the determination of the amount of such inventories, there shall be included the fair market value of the timber cut, the costs of cutting, logging, and all other expenses incident to the cost of converting the standing timber into the products in inventory. See section 471 and the regulations thereunder. The fact that the fair market value as of the first day of the taxable year in which the timber is cut is deemed to be the cost of such timber shall not preclude the taxpayer from computing its inventories upon the basis of cost or market, whichever is lower, if such is the method used by the taxpayer. Nor shall it preclude the taxpayer from computing its inventories under the last-in-first-out inventory method provided by section 472 if such section is applicable to, and has been elected by, the taxpayer. [Reg. § 1.631-1.]

☐ [*T.D.* 6281, 12-20-57. *Amended by T.D.* 7728, 10-31-80.]

[Reg. § 1.631-2]

§ 1.631-2. **Gain or loss upon the disposal of timber under cutting contract.**—(a) *In general.* (1) If an owner disposes of timber held for more than 1 year (6 months for taxable years beginning before 1977; 9 months for taxable years beginning in 1977) before such disposal, under any form or type of contract whereby he retains an economic interest in such timber, the disposal shall be considered to be a sale of such timber. The difference between the amounts realized from disposal of such timber in any taxable year and the adjusted basis for depletion thereof shall be considered to be a gain or loss upon the sale of such timber for such year. Such adjusted basis shall be computed in the same manner as provided in section 611 and the regulations thereunder with respect to the allowance for depletion. See paragraph (e)(2) of this section for definition of "owner". For the purpose of determining whether or not the timber disposed of was held for more than 1 year (6 months for taxable years beginning before 1977; 9 months for taxable years beginning in 1977)

Reg. § 1.631-2(a)

39,456 Sales and Exchanges

See p. 20,601 for regulations not amended to reflect law changes

before such disposal the rules with respect to the holding period of property contained in section 1223 shall be applicable.

(2) In the case of such a disposal, the provisions of section 1231 apply and such timber shall be considered to be property used in the trade or business for the taxable year in which it is considered to have been sold, along with other property of the taxpayer used in the trade or business as defined in section 1231(b), regardless of whether such timber is property held by the taxpayer primarily for sale to customers in the ordinary course of his trade or business. Whether gain or loss resulting from the disposition of the timber which is considered to have been sold will be deemed to be gain or loss resulting from a sale of a capital asset held for more than 1 year (6 months for taxable years beginning before 1977; 9 months for taxable years beginning in 1977) will depend upon the application of section 1231 to the taxpayer for the taxable year.

(b) *Determination of date of disposal.* (1) For purposes of section 631(b) and this section, the date of disposal of timber shall be deemed to be the date such timber is cut. However, if payment is made to the owner under the contract for timber before such timber is cut the owner may elect to treat the date of payment as the date of disposal of such timber. Such election shall be effective only for purposes of determining the holding period of such timber. Neither section 631(b) nor the election thereunder has any effect on the time of reporting gain or loss. See subchapter E, chapter 1 of the Code and the regulations thereunder. See paragraph (c)(2) of this section for the effect of exercising the election with respect to the payment for timber held for 1 year (6 months for taxable years beginning before 1977; 9 months for taxable years beginning in 1977) or less. See paragraph (d) of this section for the treatment of payments received in advance of cutting.

(2) For purposes of section 631(b) and this section, the "date such timber is cut" means the date when in the ordinary course of business the quantity of timber felled is first definitely determined.

(c) *Manner and effect of election to treat date of payment as the date of disposal.* (1) The election to treat the date of payment as the date of disposal of timber shall be evidenced by a statement attached to the taxpayer's income tax return filed on or before the due date (including extensions thereof) for the taxable year in which the payment is received. The statement shall specify the advance payments which are subject to the election and shall identify the contract under which the payments are made. However, in no case shall the time for making the election under section 631(b) expire before the close of March 21, 1958.

(2) Where the election to treat the date of payment as the date of disposal is made with respect to a payment made in advance of cutting, and such payment is made 1 year (6 months for taxable years beginning before 1977; 9 months for taxable years beginning in 1977) or less from the date the timber disposed of was acquired, section 631(b) shall not apply to such payment, irrespective of the date such timber is cut, since the timber was not held for more than 1 year (6 months for taxable years beginning before 1977; 9 months for taxable years beginning in 1977) prior to disposal.

(d) *Payments received in advance of cutting.* (1) Where the conditions of paragraph (a) of this section are met, amounts received or accrued prior to cutting (such as advance royalty payments or minimum royalty payments) shall be treated under section 631(b) as realized from the sale of timber if the contract of disposal provides that such amounts are to be applied as payment for timber subsequently cut. Such amounts will be so treated irrespective of whether or not an election has been made under paragraph (c) of this section to treat the date of payment as the date of disposal. For example, if no election has been made under paragraph (c) of this section, amounts received or accrued prior to cutting will be treated as realized from the sale of timber, provided the timber paid for is cut more than 1 year (6 months for taxable years beginning before 1977; 9 months for taxable years beginning in 1977) after the date of acquisition of such timber.

(2) However, if the right to cut timber under the contract expires, terminates, or is abandoned before the timber which has been paid for is cut, the taxpayer shall treat payments attributable to the uncut timber as ordinary income and not as received from the sale of timber under section 631(b). Accordingly, the taxpayer shall recompute his tax liability for the taxable year in which such payments were received or accrued. The recomputation shall be made in the form of an amended return where necessary.

(3)(i) Bonuses received or accrued by an owner in connection with the grant of a contract of disposal shall be treated under section 631(b) as amounts realized from the sale of timber to the extent attributable to timber held for more than 1 year (6 months for taxable years beginning before 1977; 9 months for taxable years beginning in 1977).

(ii) The adjusted depletion basis attributable to the bonus shall be determined under the

Reg. § 1.631-2(a)(2)

provisions of section 612 and the regulations thereunder. This subdivision may be illustrated as follows:

Example. Taxpayer A has held timber having a depletion basis of $90,000 for two months when he enters into a contract of disposal with B. B pays A a bonus of $5,000 upon the execution of the contract and agrees to pay X dollars per unit of timber to A as the timber is cut. A does not exercise the election to treat the date of payment as the date of disposal. It is estimated that there are 50,000 units of timber subject to the contract and that the total estimated royalties to be paid to A will be $95,000. A must report the bonus in the taxable year it is received or accrued by him. The portion of the basis of the timber attributable to the bonus is determined by the following formula:

$$\frac{\text{Bonus}}{\text{Bonus} + \text{amount of expected royalties}} \times \text{Basis of timber} = \text{Basis attributable to bonus}$$

$$\frac{\$5,000}{\$100,000} \times \$90,000 = \$4,500$$

(iii) To the extent attributable to timber not held for more than 1 year (6 months for taxable years beginning before 1977; 9 months for taxable years beginning in 1977), such bonuses shall be treated as ordinary income subject to depletion. In order to determine the amount of the bonus allocable to timber not held for more than 1 year (6 months for taxable years beginning before 1977; 9 months for taxable years beginning in 1977), the bonus shall be apportioned ratably over the estimated number of units of timber covered by the contract of disposal. This subdivision may be illustrated as follows:

Example. Assume under the facts stated in the example in subdivision (ii) of this subparagraph that B cuts 10,000 units of timber that have been held by A for 1 year (6 months for taxable years beginning before 1977; 9 months for taxable years beginning in 1977) or less. The amount of the bonus (as well as the royalties) attributable to these units must be reported as ordinary income subject to depletion. The amount of the bonus attributable to these units is determined by the following formula:

$$\frac{\text{Number of units cut held for 1 year (6 months for taxable years beginning before 1977; 9 months for taxable years beginning in 1977) or less}}{\text{Total units covered by the contract}} \times \text{Amount of bonus} = \text{Amount of bonus treated as ordinary income subject to depletion}$$

$$\frac{\$10,000}{\$50,000} \times \$5,000 = \$1,000$$

The amount of the depletion attributable to the portion of the bonus received for timber held for 1 year (6 months for taxable years beginning before 1977); 9 months for taxable years beginning in 1977) or less is determined by the following formula:

$$\frac{\text{Amount of bonus attributable to timber held for 1 year (6 months for taxable years beginning before 1977; 9 months for taxable years beginning in 1977) or less}}{\text{Total bonus}} \times \frac{\text{Adjusted basis for depletion of bonus}}{} = \text{Depletion allowance on timber held for 1 year (6 months for taxable years beginning before 1977; 9 months for taxable years beginning in 1977) or less}$$

$$\frac{\$1,000}{\$5,000} \times \$4,500 = \$900$$

(iv) If the right to cut timber under the contract of disposal expires, terminates, or is abandoned before any timber is cut, the taxpayer shall treat the bonus received under such contract as ordinary income, not subject to depletion. Accordingly, the taxpayer shall recompute his tax liability for the taxable year in which such bonus

Reg. § 1.631-2(d)(3)

was received. The recomputation shall be made in the form of an amended return where necessary.

(e) *Other rules for application of section.* (1) Amounts paid by the lessee for timber or the acquisition of timber cutting rights, whether designated as such or as a rental, royalty, or bonus, shall be treated as the cost of timber and constitute part of the lessee's depletable basis of the timber, irrespective of the treatment accorded such payment in the hands of the lessor.

(2) The provisions of section 631(b) apply only to an owner of timber. An owner of timber means any person who owns an interest in timber, including a sublessor and a holder of a contract to cut timber. Such owner of timber must have a right to cut timber for sale on his own account or for use in his trade or business in order to own an interest in timber within the meaning of section 631(b).

(3) For purposes of section 631(b) and this section, the term "timber" includes evergreen trees which are more than 6 years old at the time severed from their roots and are sold for ornamental purposes such as Christmas decorations. Tops and other parts of standing timber are not considered as evergreen trees within the meaning of section 631(b). The term "evergreen trees" is used in its commonly accepted sense and includes pine, spruce, fir, hemlock, cedar, and other coniferous trees. [Reg. § 1.631-2.]

☐ [T.D. 6281, 12-20-57. Amended by T.D. 7728, 10-31-80.]

[Reg. § 1.631-3]

§ 1.631-3. **Gain or loss upon the disposal of coal or domestic iron ore with a retained economic interest.**—(a) *In general.* (1) The provisions of section 631(c) apply to an owner who disposes of coal (including lignite), or iron ore mined in the United States, held for more than 1 year (6 months for taxable years beginning before 1977; 9 months for taxable years beginning in 1977) before such disposal under any form or type of contract whereby he retains an economic interest in such coal or iron ore. The difference between the amount realized from disposal of the coal or iron ore in any taxable year, and the adjusted depletion basis thereof plus the deductions disallowed for the taxable year under section 272, shall be gain or loss upon the sale of the coal or iron ore. See paragraph (b)(4) of this section for the definition of "owner." See paragraph (e) of this section for special rules relating to iron ore.

(2) In the case of such a disposal, the provisions of section 1231 apply, and the coal or iron ore shall be considered to be property used in the trade or business for the taxable year in which it is considered to have been sold, along with other property of the taxpayer used in the trade or business as defined in section 1231(b), regardless of whether the coal or iron ore is property held by the taxpayer primarily for sale to customers in the ordinary course of his trade or business. Whether gain or loss resulting from the disposition of the coal or iron ore which is considered to have been sold will be deemed to be gain or loss resulting from a sale of a capital asset held for more than 1 year (6 months for taxable years beginning before 1977; 9 months for taxable years beginning in 1977) will depend on the application of section 1231 to the taxpayer for the taxable year; *i.e.*, if the gains do not exceed the losses, they shall not be considered as gains and losses from sales or exchanges of capital assets but shall be treated as ordinary gains and losses.

(b) *Rules for application of section.* (1) For purposes of section 631(c) and this section, the date of disposal of the coal or iron ore shall be deemed to be the date the coal or iron ore is mined. If the coal or iron ore has been held for more than 1 year (6 months for taxable years beginning before 1977; 9 months for taxable years beginning in 1977) on the date it is mined, it is immaterial that it had not been held for more than 1 year (6 months for taxable years beginning before 1977; 9 months for taxable years beginning in 1977) on the date of the contract. There shall be no allowance for percentage depletion provided in section 613 with respect to amounts which are considered to be realized from the sale of coal or iron ore under section 631(c).

(2) The term "adjusted depletion basis" as used in section 631(c) and this section means the basis for allowance of cost depletion provided in section 612 and the regulations thereunder. Such "adjusted depletion basis" shall include exploration or development expenditures treated as deferred expenses under section 615(b) or 616(b), or corresponding provisions of prior income tax laws, and be reduced by adjustments under section 1016(a)(9) and (10), or corresponding provisions of prior income tax laws, relating to deductions of deferred expenses for exploration or development expenditures in the taxable year or any prior taxable years. The depletion unit of the coal or iron ore disposed of shall be determined under the rules provided in the regulations under section 611, relating to cost depletion.

(3)(i) In determining the gross income, the adjusted gross income, or the taxable income of the lessee, the deductions allowable with respect to rents and royalties (except rents and royalties paid by a lessee with respect to coal or iron ore disposed of by the lessee as an "owner" under section 631(c)) shall be determined without regard to the provisions of section 631(c). Thus, the amounts of rents and royalties paid or incurred by a lessee with respect to coal or iron ore shall be excluded from the lessee's gross income from the property for the purpose of determining his percentage depletion without regard to the treatment of such rents or royalties in the hands of the recipient under this section. See section 613 and the regulations thereunder.

(ii) (a) However, a lessee who is also a sublessor may dispose of coal or iron ore as an "owner" under section 631(c). Rents and royalties paid with respect to coal or iron ore disposed of by such a lessee under section 631(c) shall increase the adjusted depletion basis of the coal or iron ore and are not otherwise deductible.

(b) The provisions of this subdivision may be illustrated by the following example:

Example. B is a sublessor of a coal lease; A is the lessor; and C is the sublessee. B pays A a royalty of 50 cents per ton. C pays B a royalty of 60 cents per ton. The amount realized by B under section 631(c) is 60 cents per ton and will be reduced by the adjusted depletion basis of 50 cents per ton, leaving a gain of 10 cents per ton taxable under section 631(c).

(4)(i) The provisions of this section apply only to an owner who has disposed of coal or iron ore and retained an economic interest. For the purposes of section 631(c) and this section, the word "owner" means any person who owns an economic interest in coal or iron ore in place, including a sublessor thereof. A person who merely acquires an economic interest and has not disposed of coal or iron ore under a contract retaining an economic interest does not qualify under section 631(c). A successor to the interest of a person who has disposed of coal or iron ore under a contract by virtue of which he retained an economic interest in such coal or iron ore is also entitled to the benefits of this section. Section 631(c) and this section shall not apply with respect to any income realized by any owner as co-adventurer, partner, or principal in the mining of such coal or iron ore.

(ii) The provisions of this subparagraph may be illustrated by the following examples:

Example (1). A owns a tract of coal land in fee. A leases to B the right to mine all the coal in this tract in return for a royalty of 30 cents per ton. B subleases his right to mine coal in this tract to C, who agrees to pay A 30 cents per ton and to pay to B an additional royalty of 10 cents per ton. Section 631(c) applies to the royalties of both A and B, if the other requisites of the section have been met.

Example (2). Assume the same facts as in example (1), except that A dies leaving his royalty interest to D. D has an economic interest in the coal in place and qualifies for section 631(c) treatment with respect to his share of the royalties since he is a successor in title to A.

Example (3). Assume the same facts as in example (1), except that E agrees to pay a sum of money to C in return for 10 cents per ton on the coal mined by C. E has an economic interest, since he must look solely to the extraction of the coal for the return of his investment. However, E has not made a disposal of coal under a contract wherein he retains an economic interest, and, therefore, does not qualify under section 631(c). E is entitled to depletion on his royalties.

(c) *Payments received in advance of mining.* (1)(i) Where the conditions of paragraph (a) of this section are met, amounts received or accrued prior to mining shall be treated under section 631(c) as received from the sale of coal or iron ore if the contract of disposal provides that such amounts are to be applied as payment for coal or iron ore subsequently mined. For example, advance royalty payments or minimum royalty payments received by an owner of coal or iron ore qualify under section 631(c) where the contract of disposal grants the lessee the right to apply such royalties in payment of coal or iron ore mined at a later time.

(ii) The provisions of this subparagraph may be illustrated by the following example:

Example. A acquires coal rights on January 1. On January 30, A enters into a contract of disposal providing that mining shall begin July 2, and mining actually begins no earlier. Any advance payments which A receives qualify under section 631(c).

(2) However, if the right to mine coal or iron ore under the contract expires, terminates, or is abandoned before the coal or iron ore which had been paid for is mined, the taxpayer shall treat payments attributable to the unmined coal or iron ore as ordinary income and not as received from the sale of coal or iron ore under section 631(c). Accordingly, the taxpayer shall recompute his tax liability for the taxable year in which such payments were received. The recomputation shall be made in the form of an amended return where necessary.

(3) Bonuses received or accrued by an owner in connection with the grant of a contract of disposal shall be treated under section 631(c) as received from the sale of coal or iron ore to the extent attributable to coal or iron ore held for more than 1 year (6 months for taxable years beginning before 1977; 9 months for taxable years

Reg. § 1.631-3(c)(3)

beginning in 1977). The rules contained in paragraph (d) of § 1.631-2 relating to bonuses in the case of contracts for the disposal of timber shall be equally applicable in the case of bonuses received for the grant of a contract of disposal of coal or iron ore under this section.

(d) *Nonapplication of section.* Section 631(c) shall not affect the application of the provisions of subchapter G, chapter 1 of the Code, relating to corporations used to avoid income tax on shareholders. For example, for the purposes of applying section 543 (relating to personal holding companies), the amounts received from a disposal of coal or iron ore subject to section 631(c) shall be considered as mineral royalties. The determination of whether an amount received under a contract to which section 631(c) applies is "personal holding company income" shall be made in accordance with section 543 and the regulations thereunder, without regard to section 631(c) or this section. See also paragraph (e) of § 1.272-1.

(e) *Special rules with regard to iron ore.* (1) With regard to iron ore, section 631(c) and this section apply only to amounts received or accrued in taxable years beginning after December 31, 1963, attributable to iron ore mined in such taxable years.

(2) Section 631(c) and this section apply only to disposals of iron ore mined in the United States.

(3) For the purposes of section 631(c) and this section, iron ore is any ore which is used as a source of iron, including but not limited to taconite and jaspilite.

(4) Section 631(c) shall not apply to any disposal of iron ore to a person whose relationship to the person disposing of such iron ore would result in the disallowance of losses under section 267 or 707(b).

(5) Section 631(c)(2) results in the denial of section 631(c) treatment in the case of a contract for disposal of iron ore entered into with a person owned or controlled, directly or indirectly, by the same interests which own or control the person disposing of the iron ore, even though section 631(c) treatment would not be denied under the provisions of section 631(c)(1). For example, section 631(c) treatment is denied in the case of a contract for disposal of iron ore entered into between two "brother and sister" corporations, or a parent corporation and its subsidiary. The presence or absence of control shall be determined by applying the same standards as are applied under section 482 (relating to the allocation of income and deductions between taxpayers). [Reg. § 1.631-3.]

☐ [T.D. 6281, 12-20-57. *Amended by T.D. 6841, 7-26-65 and by T.D. 7728, 10-31-80.*]

Mineral Production Payments
[Reg. § 1.636-1]

§ 1.636-1. **Treatment of production payments as loans.**—(a) In general. (1)(i) For purposes of subtitle A of the Internal Revenue Code of 1954, a production payment (as defined in paragraph (a) of § 1.636-3) to which this section applies shall be treated as a loan on the mineral property (or properties) burdened thereby and not as an economic interest in mineral in place, except to the extent that § 1.636-2 or paragraph (b) of this section applies. See paragraph (b) of § 1.611-1. A production payment carved out of mineral property which remains in the hands of the person carving out the production payment immediately after the transfer of such production payment shall be treated as a mortgage loan on the mineral property burdened thereby. A production payment created and retained upon the transfer of the mineral property burdened by such production payment shall be treated as a purchase money mortgage loan on the mineral property burdened thereby. Such production payments will be referred to hereinafter in the regulations under section 636 as carved-out production payments and retained production payments, respectively. Moreover, in the case of a transaction involving a production payment treated as a loan pursuant to this section, the production payment shall constitute an item of income (not subject to depletion), consideration for a sale or exchange, a contribution to capital, or a gift if in the transaction a debt obligation used in lieu of the production payment would constitute such an item of income, consideration, contribution to capital, or gift, as the case may be. For the definition of the term "transfer" see paragraph (c) of § 1.636-3.

(ii) The payer of a production payment treated as a loan pursuant to this section shall include the proceeds from (or, if paid in kind, the value of) the mineral produced and applied to the satisfaction of the production payment in his gross income and "gross income from the property" (see section 613(a)) for the taxable year so applied. The payee shall include in his gross income (but not "gross income from the property") amounts received with respect to such production payment to the extent that such amounts would be includible in gross income if such production payment were a loan. The payer and payee shall determine their allowable deductions as if such production payment were a loan. See section 483, relating to interest on certain deferred payments

Reg. § 1.636-1(a)

Mineral Production Payments

See p. 20,601 for regulations not amended to reflect law changes

in the case of a production payment created and retained upon the transfer of the mineral property burdened thereby, or in the case of a production payment transferred in exchange for property. See section 1232 in the case of a production payment which is originally transferred by the corporation at a discount and is a capital asset in the hands of the payee. In the case of a carved-out production payment treated as a mortgage loan pursuant to this section, the consideration received for such production payment by the taxpayer who created it is not included in either gross income or "gross income from the property" by such taxpayer.

(2) If a production payment is treated as a loan pursuant to this section, no transfer of such production payment or any property burdened thereby (other than a transfer between the payer and payee of the production payment which, if the production payment were a loan, would extinguish the loan) shall cause it to cease to be so treated. For example, A sells operating mineral interest X to P for $100,000, subject to a $500,000 retained production payment payable out of X. Subsequently, A sells the production payment to C, and B sells X to D. C and D must treat the production payment as a purchase money mortgage loan.

(3) The provisions of this paragraph may be illustrated by the following examples:

Example (1). On December 22, 1972, A, a cash-basis calendar-year taxpayer who owns operating mineral interest X, carves out of X a production payment in favor of B for $300,000 plus interest, payable out of 50 percent of the first oil produced and sold from X. In 1972, A treats the $300,000 received from B for the production payment as the proceeds of a mortgage loan on X. In 1973, A produces and sells 125,000 barrels of oil for $373,500. A pays B $186,750 with respect to the production payment, $168,750 being principal and $18,000 being interest. In computing his gross income and "gross income from the property" for the year 1973, A includes the $373,500 and takes as deductions the allowable expenses paid in production of such mineral. A also takes a deduction under section 163 for the $18,000 interest paid with respect to the production payment. For 1973, B would treat $18,000 as ordinary income not subject to the allowance for depletion under section 611.

Example (2). Assume the same facts as in example (1) except that the principal amount of the production payment is to be increased by the amount of the ad valorem tax on the mineral attributable to the production payment which is paid by B. Under State law, the ad valorem tax with respect to the mineral attributable to the production payment is a liability of the owner of the production payment. For 1973, B includes the amount received with respect to such taxes as income and takes a deduction under section 164 for the taxes paid by him. Since the ad valorem taxes paid by B are his liability under State law, A may not take a deduction under section 164 for such taxes.

Example (3). On December 31, 1974, C, a calendar-year taxpayer and owner of the operating mineral interest Y, sells Y to D for $10,000 cash and retains a $40,000 production payment payable out of Y. At the time D acquires the property, it is estimated that 500,000 tons of mineral are recoverable from the property. In 1975, D produces a total of 50,000 tons from the property. D's cost depletion for 1975 is $5,000 determined as follows:

Basis in property: $50,000
Total recoverable units: 500,000

Rate of depletion per ton: $.10 $\left(\dfrac{\$\ 50,000}{500,000}\right)$

Cost depletion for year: $5,000 ($.10 × 50,000)

(b) *Exception.* (1) A production payment carved out of a mineral property (or properties) for exploration or development of such property (or properties) shall not be treated as a mortgage loan under section 636(a) and this section to the extent "gross income from the property" (for purposes of section 613) would not be realized by the taxpayer creating such production payment, under the law existing at the time of the creation of such production payment, in the absence of section 636(a). See section 83 and the regulations thereunder, relating to property transferred in connection with the performance of services. For purposes of section 636(a) and this paragraph, an expenditure is for exploration or development to the extent that it is necessary for ascertaining the existence, location, extent, or quality of any deposit of mineral or is incident to and necessary for the preparation of a deposit for the production of mineral. However, an expenditure which relates primarily to the production of mineral (as, for example, in the case of a pilot water flood program with respect to the secondary recovery of oil) is not for exploration or development as those terms are used in section 636(a) and this paragraph. Whether or not a production payment is carved out for exploration or development shall be determined in light of all relevant facts and circumstances, including any prior production of mineral from the mineral deposit burdened by the production payment. However, a production payment shall not be treated as carved out for explo-

Reg. § 1.636-1(b)

ration or development to the extent that the consideration for the production payment—

(i) Is not pledged for use in the future exploration or development of the mineral property (or properties) which is burdened by the production payment;

(ii) May be used for the exploration or development of any other property, or for any other purpose than that described in subdivision (i) of this subparagraph;

(iii) Does not consist of a binding obligation of the payee of the production payment to pay expenses of the exploration or development described in subdivision (i) of this subparagraph; or

(iv) Does not consist of a binding obligation of the payee of the production payment to provide services, materials, supplies, or equipment for the exploration or development described in subdivision (i) of this subparagraph.

(2) In the case of a carved-out production payment only a portion of which is subject to the exception provided in this paragraph, the rules contained in paragraph (a) of this section with respect to the treatment of income and deductions where a production payment is treated as a loan shall apply to the portion of the taxpayer's income or expenses attributable to the production payment which bears the same ratio to the total amount of such income or expenses, as the case may be, as the amount of the consideration for the production payment which would have been realized as income in the absence of section 636(a), by the taxpayer creating such production payment, bears to the total consideration to the taxpayer for the production payment. For example, A, owner of a mineral property, carves out a production payment in favor of B for $600,000 plus interest in return for $600,000 cash. A pledges to use $400,000 for the development of the burdened mineral property. In each of the payout years loan treatment applies to one-third of the income and expenses of A and B attributable to the production payment.

(c) *Treatment upon disposition or termination of mineral property burdened by production payment.* (1)(i) In the case of a sale or other disposition of the mineral property burdened by a production payment treated as a loan pursuant to this section, there shall be included in determining the amount realized upon such disposition an amount equal to the outstanding principal balance of such production payment on the date of such disposition. However, if such a production payment is created in connection with the disposition, the amount to be so included shall be the fair market value of the production payment, rather than its principal amount, if the fair market value is established by clear and convincing evidence to be an amount which differs from the principal amount. See section 1001 and the regulations thereunder. In determining the cost of the transferred mineral property to the transferee for purposes of section 1012, the outstanding principal balance of the production payment shall be included in the cost.

(ii) The provisions of this subparagraph may be illustrated by the following examples:

Example (1). A, the owner of mineral property X which is burdened by a carved-out production payment to which section 636(a) applies having an outstanding principal balance of $10,000, sells property X to B, an individual, for $100,000 cash. The amount realized by A on the sale of property X is $110,000. B's basis in property X for cost depletion and other purposes is also $110,000.

Example (2). Assume the same facts as in example (1) except that the production payment is retained by A in connection with the sale of property X to B, that section 636(b) applies to the production payment, that the production payment includes, in addition to the $10,000 principal amount, an additional amount equivalent to interest at a rate which precludes application of section 483, and that the fair market value of the production payment is $9,000. The amount realized by A on the sale of property X is $109,000. B's basis in property X for cost depletion and other purposes is $110,000. A's basis in the retained production payment is $9,000. If the production payment is paid in full, A realizes income of $1,000 plus the amount equivalent to interest, which income is includible in A's gross income at the time when such amounts would be so includible if such production payment were a loan.

Example (3). C, the owner of mineral property Y, sells the mineral property to D for $500,000 cash. Property Y is burdened by a carved-out production payment with an outstanding principal balance of $600,000, 40 percent of the consideration for which was pledged for the development of property Y. The amount realized by C on the sale is $860,000 ($500,000 plus $600,000 × .60). D's basis in property Y for cost depletion and other purposes is $860,000.

(2) In the case of the expiration, termination, or abandonment of a mineral property burdened by a production payment treated as a loan pursuant to this section, for purposes of determining the amount of any loss under section 165 with respect to the burdened mineral property the adjusted basis of such property shall be reduced (but not below zero) by an amount equal to the outstand-

ing principal balance of such production payment on the date of such expiration, termination, or abandonment. Thus, in example (2) in subparagraph (1)(ii) of this paragraph, if B abandons the mineral property at a time when $5,000 of the principal amount of the production payment remains unsatisfied, B's adjusted basis immediately before the abandonment would be reduced by $5,000 for determining his loss on abandonment under section 165.

(3) In the case of a transfer of a portion of the mineral property burdened by a production payment treated as a loan pursuant to this section, such production payment shall be apportioned between the transferred portion and the retained portion by allocating to such transferred portion that part of the outstanding principal balance of the production payment which bears the same ratio to such balance as the value of such transferred portion (exclusive of any value not related to the burdened mineral) bears to the total value of the burdened mineral property (exclusive of any value not related to the burdened mineral).

(4) In general, the entire amount of gain or loss realized pursuant to this paragraph shall be recognized in the taxable year of such realization. See section 1211 for limitation on capital losses. This subparagraph shall not affect the applicability of rules providing exceptions to the recognition of gain or loss which has been realized (e.g., a transfer to which section 351 or 1031 applies). However, see section 357(c) with respect to the assumption of liabilities in excess of basis in certain tax-free exchanges. Furthermore, in the case of a transaction which otherwise qualifies, gain realized on a transfer of a mineral property to which section 636(b) applies may be returned on the installment method under section 453. [Reg. § 1.636-1.]

☐ [T.D. 7261, 2-26-73.]

[Reg. § 1.636-2]

§ 1.636-2. Production payments retained in leasing transactions.—(a) *Treatment by lessee.* In the case of a production payment (as defined in paragraph (a) of § 1.636-3) which is retained by the lessor in a leasing transaction (including a sublease or the exercise of an option to acquire a lease or sublease), the lessee (or his successors in interest) shall treat the retained production payment for purposes of subtitle A of the Code as if it were a bonus granted by the lessee to the lessor payable in installments. Accordingly, the lessee shall include the proceeds from (or, if paid in kind, the value of) the mineral produced and applied to the satisfaction of the production payment in his gross income for the taxable year so applied. The lessee shall capitalize each payment (including any interest and any amounts added on to the production payment other than amounts for which the lessee would be liable in the absence of the production payment) paid or incurred with respect to such production payment. See paragraph (c)(5)(ii) of § 1.613-2 for rules relating to computation of percentage depletion with respect to a mineral property burdened by a production payment treated as a bonus under section 636(c) and this section.

(b) *Treatment by lessor.* The lessor who retains a production payment in a leasing transaction (or his successors in interest) shall treat the production payment without regard to the provisions of section 636 and § 1.636-1. Thus, the production payment will be treated as an economic interest in the mineral in place in the hands of the lessor (or his successors in interest) and the receipts in discharge of the production payment will constitute ordinary income subject to depletion.

(c) *Example.* The provisions of this section may be illustrated by the following example:

Example. In 1971, A leases a mineral property to B reserving a one-eighth royalty and a production payment (as defined in § 1.636-3(a)) with a principal amount of $300,000 plus an amount equivalent to interest. In 1972, B pays to A $60,000 with respect to the principal amount of the production payment plus $16,350 equivalent to interest. The adjusted basis of the property in the hands of B for cost depletion and other purposes for 1972 and subsequent years will include (subject to proper adjustment under section 1016) the $76,350 paid to A. In 1973, B pays to A $60,000 with respect to the principal amount of the production payment plus $12,750 equivalent to interest. The adjusted basis of the property in the hands of B for cost depletion and other purposes for 1973 and subsequent years will include (subject to proper adjustment under section 1016) the $72,750 paid to A. The $76,350 received by A in 1972, and the $72,750 received by A in 1973, will constitute ordinary income subject to depletion in the hands of A in the years of receipt of such amounts by A. [Reg. § 1.636-2.]

☐ [T.D. 7261, 2-26-73.]

[Reg. § 1.636-3]

§ 1.636-3. Definitions.—For purposes of section 636 and the regulations thereunder—

(a) *Production payment.* (1) The term "production payment" means, in general, a right to a specified share of the production from mineral in place (if, as, and when produced), or the proceeds from such production. Such right must be an economic interest in such mineral in place. It may burden more than one mineral property, and the burdened mineral property need not be an operating mineral interest. Such right must have an expected economic life (at the time of its creation) of shorter duration than the economic life of one or more of the mineral properties burdened thereby. A right to mineral in place which can be required to be satisfied by other than the production of mineral from the burdened mineral property is not an economic interest in mineral in place. A production payment may be limited by a dollar amount, a quantum of mineral, or a period of time. A right to mineral in place has an economic life of shorter duration than the economic life of a mineral property burdened thereby only if such right may not reasonably be expected to extend in substantial amounts over the entire productive life of such mineral property. The term "production payment" includes payments which are commonly referred to as "in-oil payments", "gas payments", or "mineral payments".

(2) A right which is in substance economically equivalent to a production payment shall be treated as a production payment for purposes of section 636 and the regulations thereunder, regardless of the language used to describe such right, the method of creation of such right, or the form in which such right is cast (even though such form is that of an operating mineral interest). Whether or not a right is in substance economically equivalent to a production payment shall be determined from all the facts and circumstances. An example of an interest which is to be treated as a production payment under this subparagraph is that portion of a "royalty" which is attributable to so much of the rate of the royalty which exceeds the lowest possible rate of the royalty at any subsequent time (disregarding any reductions in the rate of the royalty which are based solely upon changes in volume of production within a specified period of no more than 1 year). For example, assume that A creates a royalty with respect to a mineral property owned by A equal to 5 percent for 5 years and thereafter equal to 4 percent for the balance of the life of the property. An amount equal to 1 percent for 5 years shall be treated as a production payment. On the other hand, if A leases a coal mine to B in return for a royalty of 30 cents per ton on the first 500,000 tons of coal produced from the mine in each year and 20 cents per ton on all coal in excess of 500,000 tons produced from the mine in each year, the fact that the royalty may decline to 20 cents per ton on some of the coal in each year does not result in a production payment of 10 cents per ton of coal on the first 500,000 tons in any year. Another example of an interest which is to be treated as a production payment under this subparagraph is the interest in a partnership engaged in operating oil properties of a partner who provides capital for the partnership if such interest is subject to a right of another person or persons to acquire or terminate it upon terms which merely provide for such partner's recovery of his capital investment and a reasonable return thereon.

(b) *Property.* The term "property" has the meaning assigned to it in section 614(a), without the application of section 614(b), (c), or (e).

(c) *Transfer.* The term "transfer" means any sale, exchange, gift, bequest, devise, or other disposition (including a distribution by an estate or a contribution to or distribution by a corporation, partnership, or trust). [Reg. § 1.636-3.]

☐ [*T.D.* 7261, 2-26-73.]

[Reg. § 1.636-4]

§ 1.636-4. Effective dates of section 636.—(a) *In general.* Except as provided hereinafter in this section, section 636 and §§ 1.636-1, 1.636-2, and 1.636-3 apply to production payments created on or after August 7, 1969, other than production payments created before January 1, 1971, pursuant to a binding contract entered into before August 7, 1969.

(b) *Election.* Under section 503(c)(2) of the Tax Reform Act of 1969, if the taxpayer so elects, section 636(a) of the Code and §§ 1.636-1 and 1.636-3 apply to all production payments carved out by him after the beginning of his last taxable year ending before August 7, 1969, including such production payments created after such date pursuant to a binding contract entered into before such date. No interest shall be allowed on any refund or credit of any overpayment of tax resulting from an election under section 503(c)(2) for any taxable year ending before August 7, 1969. The provisions of this paragraph may be illustrated by the following example:

Example. A, a fiscal-year taxpayer whose taxable year ends on October 31, carved out and sold (from a producing property) production payments on October 1, 1967, and on July 9, 1969. On August 1, 1969, A entered into a binding contract to create another carved-out production payment (from a different producing property) and the production payment was carved out on December 22, 1969. If A elects under section 503(c)(2), the production payments carved out on July 9, 1969, and December 22, 1969, are treated as mortgage loans under section 636(a). The production payment carved-out on October 1, 1967, is not treated as a mortgage loan under section 636(a) because it was carved out before the beginning of A's last taxable year ending before August 7, 1969.

Reg. § 1.636-4(a)

(c) *Time and manner of making election.* (1) Any election under section 503(c)(2) of the Tax Reform Act of 1969 must be made not later than the ninetieth day after the date on which permanent regulations under section 636(a) are published in the Federal Register.

(2) An election under section 503(c)(2) shall be made by a statement attached to the taxpayer's income tax return (or amended return) for the first taxable year in which the taxpayer created a production payment (i) to which the election applies, and (ii) which, in the absence of section 636, would not have been treated as a loan. A statement shall also be attached to an amended return for each subsequent taxable year for which he has filed his income tax return before making the election, but only if his tax liability for such year is affected by the election. Each such statement shall indicate the taxpayer's election under section 503(c)(2), and shall identify by date, amount, parties, and burdened mineral properties all production payments described in subdivisions (i) and (ii) of this subparagraph which have been created by the date on which the statement is filed. However, a taxpayer who, prior to the date on which permanent regulations under this section are published in the Federal Register, made a valid election under section 503(c)(2) pursuant to §§ 301.9100-17T and 301.9100-18T of this chapter are [is] not required to amend statements previously furnished which meet the requirements of § 301.9100-17T(b)(1)(ii) of this chapter unless requested to do so by the district director. In applying the election to the taxable years affected, there shall be taken into account the effect that any adjustments resulting therefrom have on other items affected thereby and the effect that adjustments of any such items have on other taxable years. In the case of a member of a consolidated return group (as defined in paragraph (a) of § 1.1502-1), section 503(c)(2) and paragraphs (b), (c), and (d) of this section shall be applied as if such member filed a separate return.

(d) *Revocation of election.* A valid election under section 503(c)(2) shall be binding upon the taxpayer unless consent to revoke the election is obtained from the Commissioner. The application to revoke such election must be made in writing to the Commissioner of Internal Revenue, Washington, D.C. 20224, not later than the ninetieth day after the date on which permanent regulations under section 636(a) are published in the Federal Register. Such application must set forth the reasons therefor and a recomputation of the tax reflecting such revocation for each prior taxable year affected by the revocation, whether or not the period of limitations for credit or refund or assessment and collection has expired with respect to such taxable year. Consent shall not be given in any case in which the revocation would result in an increase in the taxpayer's tax liability for a taxable year for which such period of limitations has expired unless the taxpayer waives his right to assert the statute of limitations.

(e) *Special rule.* (1) Except as provided in subparagraph (2) of this paragraph, in the case of a taxpayer who does not make the election provided in section 503(c)(2) of the Tax Reform Act of 1969, section 636 of the Code applies to production payments carved out during the taxable year which includes August 7, 1969, as provided in paragraph (a) of this section only to the extent that the aggregate amount of such production payments exceeds the lesser of—

(i) The excess of—

(a) The aggregate amount of production payments carved out and sold by the taxpayer during the 12-month period immediately preceding his taxable year which includes August 7, 1969, over

(b) The aggregate amount of production payments carved out and sold before August 7, 1969, by the taxpayer during his taxable year which includes such date, or

(ii) The amount necessary to increase the amount of the taxpayer's gross income within the meaning of chapter 1 of subtitle A of the Code, for his taxable year which includes August 7, 1969, to an amount equal to the amount of his deductions (other than any deduction under section 172) allowable for such year under such chapter.

In applying the preceding sentence, production payments carved out for exploration or development are to be taken into account only to the extent, if any, that "gross income from the property" (for purposes of section 613) would have been realized by the taxpayer creating such production payment under the law existing at the time of the creation of such production payment, in the absence of section 636(a).

(2) Subparagraph (1) of this paragraph shall not apply for any taxable year for purposes of determining the amount of any deduction for cost or percentage depletion allowable under section 611 or the limitation on any foreign tax credit under section 904.

(3) The application of this paragraph may be illustrated by the following examples:

Example (1). (a) A, a calendar-year taxpayer who does not make the election provided in section 503(c)(2) of the Tax Reform Act of 1969, carves out and sells on December 31, 1968, a $500,000 production payment. Further, A carves out and sells on March 4, 1969, a $300,000 production payment, and on November 14, 1969, a $150,000 production payment. None of the production payments are carved out for exploration or development. During 1969, A has gross income of $600,000 (determined initially for this purpose by treating the $150,000 production payment carved out on November 14, 1969, as a loan) and allowable deductions of $700,000.

(b) The provisions of section 636 do not apply to a portion of the November 14, 1969, production payment for purposes other than section 611 and section 904 of the Code, determined as follows:

(1) Amount of production payment carved out in 1969 on or after August 7, 1969 .... $150,000

(2) Amount of production payment carved out during 1968 .... $500,000

(3) Amount of production payment carved out during 1969 taxable year before August 7, 1969 300,000

(4) Item (2) minus (3) $200,000

(5) Excess of allowable deductions over gross income for 1969 .... $100,000

(6) Amount of production payment carved out in 1969 on or after August 7, 1969, to which section 636 does not apply (lesser of items (1), (4) and (5)) $100,000

Thus, A will not treat $100,000 of the consideration received for the production payment carved out on November 14, 1969, as a loan and as a result his gross income for 1969 will be $700,000. However, in computing percentage depletion, A will not include the $100,000 in "gross income from property" and in computing cost depletion A will not include the mineral units attributable thereto. Nor, will A include the $100,000 in determining the limitation on foreign tax credit under section 904.

Example (2). Assume the same facts as in example (1) except that for taxable year 1969 A's gross income (determined initially for this purpose by treating the November 14, 1969, production payment as a loan) exceeds the amount of his allowable deductions under chapter 1 of subtitle A of the Code. The entire amount of the November 14, 1969, production payment is treated as a mortgage loan under section 636(a). [Reg. § 1.636-4.]

☐ [T.D. 7261, 2-26-73. Amended by T.D. 8435, 9-18-92.]

Continental Shelf Areas

[Reg. § 1.638-1]

§ 1.638-1. **Continental shelf areas.**—(a) *General rule.* For purposes of applying any provision of chapter 1, 2, 3, or 24 (including section 861(a)(3), 862(a)(3), 1441, 3402, or other provisions dealing with the performance of personal services), with respect to mines, oil and gas wells, and other natural deposits—

(1) *United States and possession of the United States.* The terms "United States" and "possession of the United States" when used in a geographical sense include the seabed and subsoil of those submarine areas which are adjacent to the territorial waters of the United States or such possession and over which the United States has exclusive rights, in accordance with international law, with respect to the exploration for, and exploitation of, natural resources. The terms "continental shelf of the United States" and "continental shelf of a possession of the United States", as used in this section, refer to the seabed and subsoil included, respectively, in the terms "United States" and "possession of the United States", as provided in the preceding sentence.

(2) *Foreign country.* The term "foreign country" when used in a geographical sense includes the seabed and subsoil of those submarine areas which are adjacent to the territorial waters of the foreign country and over which such foreign country has exclusive rights, in accordance with international law, with respect to the exploration for, and exploitation of, natural resources, but this sentence applies only if such foreign country exercises, directly or indirectly, taxing jurisdiction with respect to such exploration or exploitation. The term "foreign continental shelf", as used in this section, refers to the seabed and subsoil described in the preceding sentence. A foreign country is not to be treated as a country contiguous to the United States by reason of the application of section 638 and this section.

(b) *Exercise of taxing jurisdiction.* For purposes of paragraph (a)(2) of this section, the exercise, directly or indirectly, of taxing jurisdiction with respect to the exploration for, or exploitation of,

Reg. § 1.638-1(a)(1)

natural resources is deemed to include (but is not limited to) those cases in which a foreign country—

(1) Imposes a tax upon assets, equipment, or other property connected with or income derived from such exploration or exploitation, or

(2) Requires natural resources referred to in paragraph (a)(2) of this section to be transported to points within its landward boundaries and then levies a tax upon such natural resources or upon the income derived from the sale thereof.

A foreign country which, for purposes of paragraph (a)(2) of this section, exercises taxing jurisdiction by the imposition of tax upon any person, property, or activity engaged in or related to the exploration for, or exploitation of, natural resources in the seabed or subsoil referred to in paragraph (a)(2) of this section, or the income therefrom of any taxpayer, is deemed to exercise taxing jurisdiction over all such persons, property, and activities and over all income therefrom of all such taxpayers; thus, for example, a foreign country which imposes tax upon a person engaged in exploitation of oil and gas wells in its seabed and subsoil referred to in paragraph (a)(2) of this section is deemed to exercise taxing jurisdiction over property related to exploration for other natural deposits in such seabed and subsoil. A foreign country is deemed to be imposing tax upon a person, property, activity, or income described in the preceding sentence if such foreign country exempts all persons, property, activity, or income from tax for a period not in excess of 10 years from the commencement of such exploration or exploitation. Except in the case of a foreign country which is deemed under the preceding sentence to impose tax by virtue of an exemption for a period not in excess of 10 years, a foreign country which exempts all persons, property, and activities engaged in or related to the exploration for, or exploitation of, natural resources in the seabed or subsoil referred to in paragraph (a)(2) of this section and the income therefrom, from taxation is deemed not to be exercising, directly or indirectly, taxing jurisdiction for purposes of paragraph (a)(2) of this section. For purposes of paragraph (a)(2) of this section, the exercise of taxing jurisdiction with respect to any type of tax constitutes the exercise of taxing jurisdiction with respect to all types of taxes. However, a royalty or other charge (whether payable in a lump sum or over a period of time or in amounts dependent upon the volume of production of natural resources) for the right to explore for or exploit natural resources does not constitute a tax.

(c) *Scope.* (1) For purposes of applying this section, persons, property, or activities which are engaged in or related to the exploration for, or exploitation of, mines, oil and gas wells, or other natural deposits need not be physically upon, connected, or attached to the seabed or subsoil referred to in subparagraph (1) or (2) of paragraph (a) of this section to be deemed to be within the United States, a possession of the United States, or a foreign country, as the case may be, to the extent provided in subparagraph (2) or (3) and subparagraph (4) of this paragraph.

(2) Persons, property, or activities which are not a foreign country (determined without regard to section 638 or this section), and which are engaged in or related to the exploration for, or exploitation of, mines, oil and gas wells, or other natural deposits of the seabed or subsoil referred to in paragraph (a)(1) of this section, are generally within the United States or a possession of the United States, as the case may be, unless such persons, property, or activities are solely involved in or constitute transportation to (or from) the site of exploration or exploitation from (or to) a foreign country, other than transportation on a regular basis from (or to) a base of operations.

(3) Persons, property, or activities which are not in the United States or in a third country (determined in each case without regard to section 638 or this section), and which are engaged in or related to the exploration for, or exploitation of, mines, oil and gas wells, or other natural deposits of the seabed or subsoil of a foreign country referred to in paragraph (a)(2) of this section, are generally within such foreign country, unless such persons, property, or activities are solely involved in or constitute transportation to (or from) the site of exploration or exploitation from (or to) the United States or a possession of the United States or a third country, as the case may be, other than transportation on a regular basis from (or to) a base of operations.

(4) Persons, property, or activities are within the United States, a possession of the United States, or a foreign country, as the case may be, pursuant to this paragraph, only to the extent such persons, property, or activities are engaged in or related to the exploration for, or exploitation of, mines, oil and gas wells, or other natural deposits.

(d) *Natural deposits and natural resources.* For purposes of this section, the terms "natural deposits" and "natural resources" mean nonliving resources to which section 611(a) applies. Such terms do not include sedentary species (organisms which, at the harvestable stage, either are immovable on or under the seabed or are unable to move except in constant physical contact with the seabed or subsoil), fish or other animal or plant life.

Reg. § 1.638-1(d)

(e) *Rights under international law.* Nothing in this section shall prejudice or affect the freedoms of the high seas and other rights under international law or the exercise of such freedoms and rights by the United States or foreign countries.

(f) *Examples.* The application of the provisions of section 638 and this section may be illustrated by the following examples:

Example (1). A, a citizen of the United States employed as an engineer, is engaged in the exploitation of oil and is physically present on an offshore oil drilling platform operated by employees of L Corporation. Such platform is affixed to the foreign continental shelf of foreign country X. Assuming that foreign country X exercises taxing jurisdiction as provided in paragraph (b) of this section, A is to be treated as being employed in foreign country X with respect to compensation for his employment for purposes of chapters 1 and 24.

Example (2). The facts are the same as in example (1) except that B, a citizen of the United States engaged in the private practice of law, is physically present on such platform for the sole purpose of interviewing his client, A, whom he represents in a domestic relations matter. Since B is not engaged in activities related to the exploration for, or exploitation of, natural deposits, he is not to be treated as being in foreign country X for purposes of chapters 1 and 2.

Example (3). The facts are the same as in example (1) except that C, a citizen of the United States engaged in the private practice of medicine, is physically present on such platform for the purpose of making routine physical examinations of L Corporation's employees who are engaged in the exploitation of oil on the platform. C is paid by L Corporation to give such examinations on the platform at regular intervals in order to determine whether the state of any employee's health is such that he should not continue work on the platform. The balance of C's medical practice is conducted at his office on the United States mainland. Since C is engaged in activities related to the exploitation of oil, he is treated as being in foreign country X under section 638 and this section while making physical examinations on L Corporation's platform, provided that foreign country X exercises taxing jurisdiction as provided in paragraph (b) of this section. For purposes of chapters 1 and 2, amounts paid by L Corporation to C are treated as derived from sources within foreign country X.

Example (4). C, a nonresident alien individual employed as an engineer in a foreign country, designs equipment for use on oil drilling platforms affixed to the continental shelf of the United States and engaged in the exploitation of oil. Although C's activities in this respect are related to the exploitation of oil, C is not treated as being in the United States under section 638 and this section by reason of such activities.

Example (5). M Corporation, a domestic corporation, chartered a ship from N Corporation, also a domestic corporation, under a time charter under which N Corporation's personnel continued to navigate and manage the ship. M Corporation equipped the ship with special oil exploration equipment and furnished its personnel to operate the equipment. The ship then commenced to explore for oil in the foreign continental shelf of foreign country Y. Foreign country Y exercises taxing jurisdiction as provided in paragraph (b) of this section. The ship is treated as being within foreign country Y under section 638 and this section for the period it was engaged in the exploration for oil in such foreign continental shelf. Thus, the entire income derived during such period by N Corporation from the charter is income derived from sources within foreign country Y, since N Corporation had property and employees engaged in the exploration for oil in such foreign continental shelf.

Example (6). The facts are the same as in example (5) except that C, a citizen of the United States, was employed by N Corporation as a cook and was physically present on the ship. C's sole duties consisted of cooking meals for personnel aboard such ship. In such case, as C's activities are related to the exploration for oil, C is to be treated as being in foreign country Y under section 638 and this section for the period he was aboard such ship while it was engaged in activities relating to the exploration for oil in the foreign continental shelf referred to in example (5). For purposes of chapters 1 and 24, C's compensation as a cook for such period is treated as derived from sources without the United States.

Example (7). Z Corporation, a foreign corporation, entered into a contract with Y Corporation, a United States corporation, to engage in exploratory oil drilling activities on a leasehold held by Y Corporation. Such leasehold was located in the continental shelf of the United States. Since Z Corporation is engaged in and has property and activities which are engaged in the exploration for oil, such property and activities are to be treated as being in the United States under section 638 and this section for the period such property and activities were engaged in or related to the exploration for oil in the continental shelf of the United States and were not in a foreign country. For purposes of chapters 1 and 3, amounts paid to Z

Reg. § 1.638-1(e)

Corporation pursuant to the contract are treated as derived from sources within the United States.

Example (8). M Corporation is a controlled foreign corporation (within the meaning of section 957(b)) for its entire taxable year beginning in 1972. During such taxable year, M Corporation issues a policy of insurance relating to fire damage to an offshore oil drilling platform, owned by N Corporation (a foreign corporation), which is attached to the continental shelf of the United States. The income attributable to the issuing of such policy would be taxed under subchapter L, chapter 1, subtitle A of the Code (as modified, for this purpose, by section 953(b)(1), (2), and (3)) if such income were the income of a domestic insurance corporation. Since N Corporation's oil drilling platform is located within the United States under section 638 and this section, M Corporation's income attributable to the issuing of the insurance in connection with such platform is income derived from the insurance of United States risks, within the meaning of section 953(a)(1)(A). [Reg. § 1.638-1.]

☐ [*T.D. 7277, 5-14-73.*]

[Reg. § 1.638-2]

§ 1.638-2. Effective date.—The specific requirements and limitations of § 1.638-1 apply on and after December 30, 1969. [Reg. § 1.638-2.]

☐ [*T.D. 7277, 5-14-73.*]

[The next page is 43,201.]

ESTATES, TRUSTS, BENEFICIARIES, AND DECEDENTS

Estates, Trusts, and Beneficiaries

[Reg. § 1.641(a)-0]

§ 1.641(a)-0. **Scope of subchapter J.**—(a) *In general.* Subchapter J (sections 641 and following), chapter 1 of the Code, deals with the taxation of income of estates and trusts and their beneficiaries, and of income in respect of decedents. Part I of subchapter J contains general rules for taxation of estates and trusts (subpart A), specific rules relating to trusts which distribute current income only (subpart B), estates and trusts which may accumulate income or which distribute corpus (subpart C), treatment of excess distributions by trusts (subpart D), grantors and other persons treated as substantial owners (subpart E), and miscellaneous provisions relating to limitations on charitable deductions, income of an estate or trust in case of divorce, and taxable years to which the provisions of subchapter J are applicable (subpart F). Part I has no application to any organization which is not to be classified for tax purposes as a trust under the classification rules of §§ 301.7701-2, 301.7701-3 and 301.7701-4 of this chapter (Regulations on Procedure and Administration). Part II of subchapter J relates to the treatment of income in respect of decedents. However, the provisions of subchapter J do not apply to employee trusts subject to subchapters D and F, chapter 1 of the Code, and common trust funds subject to subchapter H, chapter 1 of the Code.

(b) *Scope of Subparts A, B, C, and D.* Subparts A, B, C, and D (sections 641 and following), part I, subchapter J, chapter 1 of the Code, relate to the taxation of estates and trusts and their beneficiaries. These subparts have no application to any portion of the corpus or income of a trust which is to be regarded, within the meaning of the Code, as that of the grantor or others treated as its substantial owners. See subpart E (sections 671 and following), part I, subchapter J, chapter 1 of the Code, and the regulations thereunder for rules for the treatment of any portion of a trust where the grantor (or another person) is treated as the substantial owner. So-called alimony trusts are treated under subparts A, B, C, and D, except to the extent otherwise provided in section 71 or section 682. These subparts have no application to beneficiaries of nonexempt employees' trusts. See section 402(b) and the regulations thereunder.

(c) *Multiple trusts.* Multiple trusts that have—

(1) No substantially independent purposes (such as independent dispositive purposes),

(2) The same grantor and substantially the same beneficiary, and

(3) The avoidance or mitigation of *(a)* the progressive rates of tax (including mitigation as a result of deferral of tax) or *(b)* the minimum tax for tax preferences imposed by section 56 as their principal purpose, shall be consolidated and treated as one trust for the purposes of subchapter J. [Reg. § 1.641(a)-0.]

☐ [*T.D.* 6217, 12-19-56. *Amended by* T.D. 6989, 1-16-69 *and by* T.D. 7204, 8-24-72.]

[Reg. § 1.641(a)-1]

§ 1.641(a)-1. **Imposition of tax; application of tax.**—For taxable years beginning after December 31, 1970, section 641 prescribes that the taxes imposed by section 1(d), as amended by the Tax Reform Act of 1969, shall apply to the income of estates or of any kind of property held in trust. For taxable years ending before January 1, 1971, section 641 prescribes that the taxes imposed upon individuals by chapter 1 of the Code apply to the income of estates or of any kind of property held in trust. The rates of tax, the statutory provisions respecting gross income, and, with certain exceptions, the deductions and credits allowed to individuals apply also to estates and trusts. [Reg. § 1.641(a)-1.]

☐ [*T.D.* 6217, 12-19-56. *Amended by* T.D. 7117, 5-24-71.]

[Reg. § 1.641(a)-2]

§ 1.641(a)-2. **Gross income of estates and trusts.**—The gross income of an estate or trust is determined in the same manner as that of an individual. Thus, the gross income of an estate or trust consists of all items of gross income received during the taxable year, including:

(a) Income accumulated in trust for the benefit of unborn or unascertained persons or persons with contingent interests;

(b) Income accumulated or held for future distribution under the terms of the will or trust;

(c) Income which is to be distributed currently by the fiduciary to the beneficiaries, and income collected by a guardian of an infant which is to be held or distributed as the court may direct;

(d) Income received by estates of deceased persons during the period of administration or settlement of the estate; and

(e) Income which, in the discretion of the fiduciary, may be either distributed to the beneficiaries or accumulated.

Reg. § 1.641(a)-2(e)

The several classes of income enumerated in this section do not exclude others which also may come within the general purposes of section 641. [Reg. § 1.641(a)-2.]

☐ [T.D. 6217, 12-19-56.]

[Reg. § 1.641(b)-1]

§ 1.641(b)-1. Computation and payment of tax; deductions and credits of estates and trusts.—Generally, the deductions and credits allowed to individuals are also allowed to estates and trusts. However, there are special rules for the computation of certain deductions and for the allocation between the estate or trust and the beneficiaries of certain credits and deductions. See section 642 and the regulations thereunder. In addition, an estate or trust is allowed to deduct, in computing its taxable income, the deductions provided by sections 651 and 661 and regulations thereunder, relating to distributions to beneficiaries. [Reg.§ 1.641(b)-1.]

☐ [T.D. 6217, 12-19-56.]

[Reg. § 1.641(b)-2]

§ 1.641(b)-2. Filing of returns and payment of the tax.—(a) The fiduciary is required to make and file the return and pay the tax on the taxable income of an estate or of a trust. Liability for the payment of the tax on the taxable income of an estate attaches to the person of the executor or administrator up to and after his discharge if, prior to distribution and discharge, he had notice of his tax obligations or failed to exercise due diligence in ascertaining whether or not such obligations existed. For the extent of such liability, see section 3467 of the Revised Statutes, as amended by section 518 of the Revenue Act of 1934 (31 U.S.C. 192). Liability for the tax also follows the assets of the estate distributed to heirs, devisees, legatees, and distributees, who may be required to discharge the amount of the tax due and unpaid to the extent of the distributive shares received by them. See section 6901. The same considerations apply to trusts.

(b) The estate of an infant, incompetent, or other person under a disability, or, in general, of an individual or corporation in receivership or a corporation in bankruptcy is not a taxable entity separate from the person for whom the fiduciary is acting, in that respect differing from the estate of a deceased person or of a trust. See section 6012(b)(2) and (3) for provisions relating to the obligation of the fiduciary with respect to returns of such persons. [Reg. § 1.641(b)-2.]

☐ [T.D. 6217, 12-19-56. Amended by T.D. 6580, 12-4-61.]

[Reg. § 1.641(b)-3]

§ 1.641(b)-3. Termination of estates and trusts.—(a) The income of an estate of a deceased person is that which is received by the estate during the period of administration or settlement. The period of administration or settlement is the period actually required by the administrator or executor to perform the ordinary duties of administration, such as the collection of assets and the payment of debts, taxes, legacies, and bequests, whether the period required is longer or shorter than the period specified under the applicable local law for the settlement of estates. For example, where an executor who is also named as trustee under a will fails to obtain his discharge as executor, the period of administration continues only until the duties of administration are complete and he actually assumes his duties as trustee, whether or not pursuant to a court order. However, the period of administration of an estate cannot be unduly prolonged. If the administration of an estate is unreasonably prolonged, the estate is considered terminated for Federal income tax purposes after the expiration of a reasonable period for the performance by the executor of all the duties of administration. Further, an estate will be considered as terminated when all the assets have been distributed except for a reasonable amount which is set aside in good faith for the payment of unascertained or contingent liabilities and expenses (not including a claim by a beneficiary in the capacity of beneficiary). Notwithstanding the above, if the estate has joined in making a valid election under section 645 to treat a qualified revocable trust, as defined under section 645(b)(1), as part of the estate, the estate shall not terminate under this paragraph prior to the termination of the section 645 election period. See section 645 and the regulations thereunder for rules regarding the termination of the section 645 election period.

(b) Generally, the determination of whether a trust has terminated depends upon whether the property held in trust has been distributed to the persons entitled to succeed to the property upon termination of the trust rather than upon the technicality of whether or not the trustee has rendered his final accounting. A trust does not automatically terminate upon the happening of the event by which the duration of the trust is measured. A reasonable time is permitted after such event for the trustee to perform the duties necessary to complete the administration of the trust. Thus, if under the terms of the governing instrument, the trust is to terminate upon the death of the life beneficiary and the corpus is to be distributed to the remainderman, the trust continues after the death of the life beneficiary for a period reasonably necessary to a proper winding up of the affairs of the trust. However, the winding up of a trust cannot be unduly postponed and if the distribution of the trust corpus is unreasonably delayed, the trust is considered terminated for Federal income tax purposes after the expiration of a reasonable period for the trustee to complete the administration of the trust. Further, a trust will be considered as terminated when all the assets have been distributed except for a reasonable amount which is set aside in good faith for the payment of unascertained or contingent liabilities and expenses (not including a claim by a beneficiary in the capacity of beneficiary).

(c)(1) Except as provided in subparagraph (2) of this paragraph, during the period between the occurrence of an event which causes a trust to terminate and the time when the trust is considered as terminated under this section, whether or not the income and the excess of capital gains over capital losses of the trust are to be considered as amounts required to be distributed currently to the ultimate distributee for the year in which they are received depends upon the principles stated in § 1.651(a)-2. See § 1.663 et seq. for application of the separate share rule.

(2)(i) Except in cases to which the last sentence of this subdivision applies, for taxable years of a trust ending before September 1, 1957, subparagraph (1) of this paragraph shall not apply and the rule of subdivision (ii) of this subparagraph shall apply unless the trustee elects to have subparagraph (1) of this paragraph apply. Such election shall be made by the trustee in a statement filed on or before April 15, 1959, with the district director with whom such trust's return for any such taxable year was filed. The election provided by this subdivision shall not be available if the treatment given the income and the excess of capital gains over capital losses for taxable years for which returns have been filed was consistent with the provisions of subparagraph (1) of this paragraph.

(ii) The rule referred to in subdivision (i) of this subparagraph is as follows: During the period between the occurrence of an event which causes a trust to terminate and the time when a trust is considered as terminated under this section, the income and the excess of capital gains over capital losses of the trust are in general considered as amounts required to be distributed for the year in which they are received. For example, a trust instrument provides for the payment of income to A during her life, and upon her death for the payment of the corpus to B. The trust reports on the basis of the calendar year. A dies on November 1, 1955, but no distribution is made to B until January 15, 1956. The income of the trust and the excess of capital gains over capital losses for the entire year 1955, to the extent not paid, credited, or required to be distributed to A or A's estate, are treated under sections 661 and 662 as amounts required to be distributed to B for the year 1955.

(d) If a trust or the administration or settlement of an estate is considered terminated under this section for Federal income tax purposes (as for instance, because administration has been unduly prolonged), the gross income, deductions, and credits of the estate or trust are, subsequent to the termination, considered the gross income, deductions, and credits of the person or persons succeeding to the property of the estate or trust. [Reg. § 1.641(b)-3.]

☐ [T.D. 6217, 12-19-56. Amended by T.D. 6353, 1-13-59; T.D. 6462, 5-5-60 and T.D. 9032, 12-23-2002.]

[Reg. § 1.641(c)-0]

§ 1.641(c)-0. Table of contents.—This section lists the major captions contained in § 1.641(c)-1.

§ 1.641(c)-1 Electing small business trust.

(a) In general.

(b) Definitions.

(1) Grantor portion.

(2) S portion.

(3) Non-S portion.

(c) Taxation of grantor portion.

(d) Taxation of S portion.

(1) In general.

(2) Section 1366 amounts.

(3) Gains and losses on disposition of S stock.

(4) State and local income taxes and administrative expenses.

(e) Tax rates and exemption of S portion.

(1) Income tax rate.

(2) Alternative minimum tax exemption.

(f) Adjustments to basis of stock in the S portion under section 1367.

(g) Taxation of non-S portion.

(1) In general.

(2) Dividend income under section 1368(c)(2).

(3) Interest on installment obligations.

(4) Charitable deduction.

(h) Allocation of state and local income taxes and administration expenses.

(i) Treatment of distributions from the trust.

(j) Termination or revocation of ESBT election.

(k) Effective date.

(l) Examples.

[Reg. § 1.641(c)-0.]

☐ [T.D. 8994, 5-13-2002.]

[Reg. § 1.641(c)-1]

§ 1.641(c)-1. **Electing small business trust.**—(a) *In general.* An electing small business trust (ESBT) within the meaning of section 1361(e) is treated as two separate trusts for purposes of chapter 1 of the Internal Revenue Code. The portion of an ESBT that consists of stock in one or more S corporations is treated as one trust. The portion of an ESBT that consists of all the other assets in the trust is treated as a separate trust. The grantor or another person may be treated as the owner of all or a portion of either or both such trusts under subpart E, part I, subchapter J, chapter 1 of the Internal Revenue Code. The ESBT is treated as a single trust for administrative purposes, such as having one taxpayer identification number and filing one tax return. See § 1.1361-1(m).

(b) *Definitions*—(1) *Grantor portion.* The grantor portion of an ESBT is the portion of the trust that is treated as owned by the grantor or another person under subpart E.

(2) *S portion.* The S portion of an ESBT is the portion of the trust that consists of S corporation stock and that is not treated as owned by the grantor or another person under subpart E.

(3) *Non-S portion.* The non-S portion of an ESBT is the portion of the trust that consists of all assets other than S corporation stock and that is not treated as owned by the grantor or another person under subpart E.

(c) *Taxation of grantor portion.* The grantor or another person who is treated as the owner of a portion of the ESBT includes in computing taxable income items of income, deductions, and credits against tax attributable to that portion of the ESBT under section 671.

(d) *Taxation of S portion*—(1) *In general.* The taxable income of the S portion is determined by taking into account only the items of income, loss, deduction, or credit specified in paragraphs (d)(2), (3), and (4) of this section, to the extent not attributable to the grantor portion.

(2) *Section 1366 amounts*—(i) *In general.* The S portion takes into account the items of income, loss, deduction, or credit that are taken into account by an S corporation shareholder pursuant to section 1366 and the regulations thereunder. Rules otherwise applicable to trusts apply in determining the extent to which any loss, deduction, or credit may be taken into account in determining the taxable income of the S portion. See § 1.1361-1(m)(3)(iv) for allocation of those items in the taxable year of the S corporation in which the trust is an ESBT for part of the year and an eligible shareholder under section 1361(a)(2)(A)(i) through (iv) for the rest of the year.

(ii) *Special rule for charitable contributions.* If a deduction described in paragraph (d)(2)(i) of this section is attributable to an amount of the S corporation's gross income that is paid by the S corporation for a charitable purpose specified in section 170(c) (without regard to section 170(c)(2)(A)), the contribution will be deemed to be paid by the S portion pursuant to the terms of the trust's governing instrument within the meaning of section 642(c)(1). The limitations of section 681, regarding unrelated business income, apply in determining whether the contribution is deductible in computing the taxable income of the S portion.

(iii) *Multiple S corporations.* If an ESBT owns stock in more than one S corporation, items of income, loss, deduction, or credit from all the S corporations are aggregated for purposes of determining the S portion's taxable income.

(3) *Gains and losses on disposition of S stock*—(i) *In general.* The S portion takes into account any gain or loss from the disposition of S corporation stock. No deduction is allowed under section 1211(b)(1) and (2) for capital losses that exceed capital gains.

(ii) *Installment method.* If income from the sale or disposition of stock in an S corporation is reported by the trust on the installment method, the income recognized under this method is taken into account by the S portion. See paragraph (g)(3) of this section for the treatment of interest on the installment obligation. See § 1.1361-1(m)(5)(ii) regarding treatment of a trust as an ESBT upon the sale of all S corporation stock using the installment method.

(iii) *Distributions in excess of basis.* Gain recognized under section 1368(b)(2) from distributions in excess of the ESBT's basis in its S corporation stock is taken into account by the S portion.

(4) *State and local income taxes and administrative expenses*—(i) *In general.* State and local income taxes and administrative expenses directly related to the S portion and those allocated to that portion in accordance with paragraph (h) are taken into account by the S portion.

(ii) *Special rule for certain interest.* Interest paid by the trust on money borrowed by the trust to purchase stock in an S corporation is allocated to the S portion but is not a deductible administrative expense for purposes of determining the taxable income of the S portion.

(e) *Tax rates and exemption of S portion*—(1) *Income tax rate.* Except for capital gains, the highest marginal trust rate provided in section 1(e) is applied to the taxable income of the S portion. See section 1(h) for the rates that apply to the S portion's net capital gain.

(2) *Alternative minimum tax exemption.* The exemption amount of the S portion under section 55(d) is zero.

(f) *Adjustments to basis of stock in the S portion under section 1367.* The basis of S corporation stock in the S portion must be adjusted in accordance with section 1367 and the regulations thereunder. If the ESBT owns stock in more than one S corporation, the adjustments to the basis in the S corporation stock of each S corporation must be determined separately with respect to each S corporation. Accordingly, items of income, loss, deduction, or credit of an S corporation that are taken into account by the ESBT under section 1366 can only result in an adjustment to the basis of the stock of that S corporation and cannot affect the basis in the stock of the other S corporations held by the ESBT.

(g) *Taxation of non-S portion*—(1) *In general.* The taxable income of the non-S portion is determined by taking into account all items of income, deduction, and credit to the extent not taken into account by either the grantor portion or the S portion. The items attributable to the non-S portion are taxed under subparts A through D of part I, subchapter J, chapter 1 of the Internal Revenue Code. The non-S portion may consist of more than one share pursuant to section 663(c).

(2) *Dividend income under section 1368(c)(2).* Any dividend income within the meaning of section 1368(c)(2) is includible in the gross income of the non-S portion.

(3) *Interest on installment obligations.* If income from the sale or disposition of stock in an S corporation is reported by the trust on the installment method, the interest on the installment obligation is includible in the gross income of the non-S portion. See paragraph (d)(3)(ii) of this section for the treatment of income from such a sale or disposition.

(4) *Charitable deduction.* For purposes of applying section 642(c)(1) to payments made by the trust for a charitable purpose, the amount of gross income of the trust is limited to the gross income of the non-S portion. See paragraph (d)(2)(ii) of this section for special rules concerning charitable contributions paid by the S corporation that are deemed to be paid by the S portion.

(h) *Allocation of state and local income taxes and administration expenses.* Whenever state and local income taxes or administration expenses relate to more than one portion of an ESBT, they must be allocated between or among the portions to which they relate. These items may be allocated in any manner that is reasonable in light of all the circumstances, including the terms of the governing instrument, applicable local law, and the practice of the trustee with respect to the trust if it is reasonable and consistent. The taxes and expenses apportioned to each portion of the ESBT are taken into account by that portion.

(i) *Treatment of distributions from the trust.* Distributions to beneficiaries from the S portion or the non-S portion, including distributions of the S corporation stock, are deductible under section 651 or 661 in determining the taxable income of the non-S portion, and are includible in the gross income of the beneficiaries under section 652 or 662. However, the amount of the deduction or inclusion cannot exceed the amount of the distributable net income of the non-S portion. Items of income, loss, deduction, or credit taken into account by the grantor portion or the S portion are excluded for purposes of determining the distributable net income of the non-S portion of the trust.

(j) *Termination or revocation of ESBT election.* If the ESBT election of the trust terminates pursuant to § 1.1361-1(m)(5) or the ESBT election is revoked pursuant to § 1.1361-1(m)(6), the rules contained in this section are thereafter not applicable to the trust. If, upon termination or revocation, the S portion has a net operating loss under section 172; a capital loss carryover under section 1212; or deductions in excess of gross income; then any such loss, carryover, or excess deductions shall be allowed as a deduction, in accordance with the regulations under section 642(h), to the trust, or to the beneficiaries succeeding to the property of the trust if the entire trust terminates.

(k) *Effective date.* This section generally is applicable for taxable years of ESBTs beginning on and after May 14, 2002. However, paragraphs (a), (b), (c), and (l) *Example 1* of this section are applicable for taxable years of ESBTs that end on and after December 29, 2000. ESBTs may apply paragraphs (d)(4) and (h) of this section for taxable years of ESBTs beginning after December 31, 1996.

(l) *Examples.* The following examples illustrate the rules of this section:

Example 1. Comprehensive example. (i) Trust has a valid ESBT election in effect. Under section 678, B is treated as the owner of a portion of Trust consisting of a 10% undivided fractional interest in Trust. No other person is treated as the owner of any other portion of Trust under subpart E. Trust owns stock in X, an S corporation, and in Y,

Reg. § 1.641(c)-1(l)

a C corporation. During 2000, Trust receives a distribution from X of $5,100, of which $5,000 is applied against Trust's adjusted basis in the X stock in accordance with section 1368(c)(1) and $100 is a dividend under section 1368(c)(2). Trust makes no distributions to its beneficiaries during the year.

(ii) For 2000, Trust has the following items of income and deduction:

Ordinary income attributable to X under section 1366	$5,000
Dividend income from Y	$ 900
Dividend from X representing C corporation earnings and profits	$ 100
Total trust income	$6,000

Charitable contributions attributable to X under section 1366	$ 300
Trustee fees	$ 200
State and local income taxes	$ 100

(iii) Trust's items of income and deduction are divided into a grantor portion, an S portion, and a non-S portion for purposes of determining the taxation of those items. Income is allocated to each portion as follows:

B must take into account the items of income attributable to the grantor portion, that is, 10% of each item, as follows:

Ordinary income from X	$ 500
Dividend income from Y	$ 90
Dividend income from X	$ 10
Total grantor portion income	$ 600

The total income of the S portion is $4,500, determined as follows:

Ordinary income from X	$5,000
Less: Grantor portion	($ 500)
Total S portion income	$4,500

The total income of the non-S portion is $900 determined as follows:

Dividend income from Y (less grantor portion)	$ 810
Dividend income from X (less grantor portion)	$ 90
Total non-S portion income	$ 900

(iv) The administrative expenses and the state and local income taxes relate to all three portions and under state law would be allocated ratably to the $6,000 of trust income. Thus, these items would be allocated 10% (600/6000) to the grantor portion, 75% (4500/6000) to the S portion and 15% (900/6000) to the non-S portion.

(v) B must take into account the following deductions attributable to the grantor portion of the trust:

Charitable contributions from X	$ 30
Trustee fees	$ 20
State and local income taxes	$ 10

(vi) The taxable income of the S portion is $4,005, determined as follows:

Ordinary income from X	$4,500
Less: Charitable contributions from X (less grantor portion)	($ 270)
75% of trustee fees	($ 150)
75% of state and local income taxes	($ 75)
Taxable income of S portion	$4,005

(vii) The taxable income of the non-S portion is $755, determined as follows:

Dividend income from Y	$ 810
Dividend income from X	$ 90
Total non-S portion income	$ 900
Less: 15% of trustee fees	($ 30)

Reg. § 1.641(c)-1(l)

15% state and local income taxes .... ($ 15)
Personal exemption .... ($ 100)
Taxable income of non-S portion .... $ 755

Example 2. Sale of S stock. Trust has a valid ESBT election in effect and owns stock in X, an S corporation. No person is treated as the owner of any portion of Trust under subpart E. In 2003, Trust sells all of its stock in X to a person who is unrelated to Trust and its beneficiaries and realizes a capital gain of $5,000. This gain is taken into account by the S portion and is taxed using the appropriate capital gain rate found in section 1(h).

Example 3. (i) *Sale of S stock for an installment note.* Assume the same facts as in *Example 2*, except that Trust sells its stock in X for a $400,000 installment note payable with stated interest over ten years. After the sale, Trust does not own any S corporation stock.

(ii) *Loss on installment sale.* Assume Trust's basis in its X stock was $500,000. Therefore, Trust sustains a capital loss of $100,000 on the sale. Upon the sale, the S portion terminates and the excess loss, after being netted against the other items taken into account by the S portion, is made available to the entire trust as provided in section 641(c)(4).

(iii) *Gain on installment sale.* Assume Trust's basis in its X stock was $300,000 and that the $100,000 gain will be recognized under the installment method of section 453. Interest income will be recognized annually as part of the installment payments. The portion of the $100,000 gain recognized annually is taken into account by the S portion. However, the annual interest income is includible in the gross income of the non-S portion.

Example 4. Charitable lead annuity trust. Trust is a charitable lead annuity trust which is not treated as owned by the grantor or another person under subpart E. Trust acquires stock in X, an S corporation, and elects to be an ESBT. During the taxable year, pursuant to its terms, Trust pays $10,000 to a charitable organization described in section 170(c)(2). The non-S portion of Trust receives an income tax deduction for the charitable contribution under section 642(c) only to the extent the amount is paid out of the gross income of the non-S portion. To the extent the amount is paid from the S portion by distributing S corporation stock, no charitable deduction is available to the S portion.

Example 5. ESBT distributions. (i) As of January 1, 2002, Trust owns stock in X, a C corporation. No portion of Trust is treated as owned by the grantor or another person under subpart E. X elects to be an S corporation effective January 1, 2003, and Trust elects to be an ESBT effective January 1, 2003. On February 1, 2003, X makes an $8,000 distribution to Trust, of which $3,000 is treated as a dividend from accumulated earnings and profits under section 1368(c)(2) and the remainder is applied against Trust's basis in the X stock under section 1368(b). The trustee of Trust makes a distribution of $4,000 to Beneficiary during 2003. For 2003, Trust's share of X's section 1366 items is $5,000 of ordinary income. For the year, Trust has no other income and no expenses or state or local taxes.

(ii) For 2003, Trust has $5,000 of taxable income in the S portion. This income is taxed to Trust at the maximum rate provided in section 1(e). Trust also has $3,000 of distributable net income (DNI) in the non-S portion. The non-S portion of Trust receives a distribution deduction under section 661(a) of $3,000, which represents the amount distributed to Beneficiary during the year ($4,000), not to exceed the amount of DNI ($3,000). Beneficiary must include this amount in gross income under section 662(a). As a result, the non-S portion has no taxable income.
[Reg. § 1.641(c)-1.]

☐ [*T.D.* 8994, 5-13-2002.]

[Reg. § 1.642(a)(1)-1]

§ 1.642(a)(1)-1. Partially tax-exempt interest.—An estate or trust is allowed the credit against tax for partially tax-exempt interest provided by section 35 only to the extent that the credit does not relate to interest properly allocable to a beneficiary under section 652 or 662 and the regulations thereunder. A beneficiary of an estate or trust is allowed the credit against tax for partially tax-exempt interest provided by section 35 only to the extent that the credit relates to interest properly allocable to him under section 652 or 662 and the regulations thereunder. If an estate or trust holds partially tax-exempt bonds and elects under section 171 to treat the premium on the bonds as amortizable, the credit allowable under section 35, with respect to the bond interest (whether allowable to the estate or trust or to the beneficiary), is reduced under section 171(a)(3) by reducing the shares of the interest allocable, respectively, to the estate or trust and its beneficiary by the portion of the amortization deduction attributable to the shares. [Reg. § 1.642(a)(1)-1.]

☐ [*T.D.* 6217, 12-19-56.]

[Reg. § 1.642(a)(2)-1]

§ 1.642(a)(2)-1. Foreign taxes.—An estate or trust is allowed the credit against tax for taxes imposed by foreign countries and possessions of the United States to the extent allowed by section 901 only for so much of those taxes as are not properly allocable under that section to the beneficiaries. See section 901(b)(4). For purposes of section 901(b)(4), the term "beneficiaries" includes charitable beneficiaries. [Reg. § 1.642(a)(2)-1.]

☐ [T.D. 6217, 12-19-56.]

[Reg. § 1.642(a)(3)-1]

§ 1.642(a)(3)-1. **Dividends received by an estate or trust.**—An estate or trust is allowed a credit against the tax for dividends received on or before December 31, 1964 (see section 34), only for so much of the dividends as are not properly allocable to any beneficiary under section 652 or 662. Section 642(a)(3), and this section do not apply to amounts received as dividends after December 31, 1964. For treatment of the credit in the hands of the beneficiary see § 1.652(b)-1. [Reg. § 1.642(a)(3)-1.]

☐ [T.D. 6217, 12-19-56. Amended by T.D. 6777, 12-15-64.]

[Reg. § 1.642(a)(3)-2]

§ 1.642(a)(3)-2. **Time of receipt of dividends by beneficiary.**—In general, dividends are deemed received by a beneficiary in the taxable year in which they are includible in his gross income under section 652 or 662. For example, a simple trust, reporting on the basis of a fiscal year ending October 30, receives quarterly dividends on November 3, 1954, and February 3, May 3, and August 3, 1955. These dividends are all allocable to beneficiary A, reporting on a calendar year basis, under section 652 and are deemed received by A in 1955. See section 652(c). Accordingly, A may take all these dividends into account in determining his credit for dividends received under section 34 and his dividends exclusion under section 116. However, solely for purposes of determining whether dividends deemed received by individuals from trusts or estates qualify under the time limitations of section 34(a) or section 116(a), section 642(a)(3) provides that the time of receipt of the dividends by the trust or estate is also considered the time of receipt by the beneficiary. For example, a simple trust reporting on the basis of a fiscal year ending October 30 receives quarterly dividends on December 3, 1953, and March 3, June 3, and September 3, 1954. These dividends are all allocable to beneficiary A, reporting on the calendar year basis, under section 652 and are includible in his income for 1954. However, for purposes of section 34(a) or section 116(a), these dividends are deemed received by A on the same dates that the trust received them. Accordingly, A may take into account in determining the credit under section 34 only those dividends received by the trust on September 3, 1954, since the dividend received credit is not allowed under section 34 for dividends received before August 1, 1954 (or after December 31, 1964). Section 642(a)(3) and this section do not apply to amounts received by an estate or trust as dividends after December 31, 1964. However, the rules in this section relating to time of receipt of dividends by a beneficiary are applicable to dividends received by an estate or trust prior to January 1, 1965, and accordingly, such dividends are deemed to be received by the beneficiary (even though received after December 31, 1964) on the same dates that the estate or trust received them for purposes of determining the credit under section 34 or the exclusion under section 116. [Reg. § 1.642(a)(3)-2.]

☐ [T.D. 6217, 12-19-56. Amended by T.D. 6777, 12-15-64.]

[Reg. § 1.642(a)(3)-3]

§ 1.642(a)(3)-3. **Cross reference.**—See § 1.683-2(c) for examples relating to the treatment of dividends received by an estate or trust during a fiscal year beginning in 1953 and ending in 1954. [Reg. § 1.642(a)(3)-3.]

☐ [T.D. 6217, 12-19-56.]

[Reg. § 1.642(b)-1]

§ 1.642(b)-1. **Deduction for personal exemption.**—In lieu of the deduction for personal exemptions provided by section 151:

(a) An estate is allowed a deduction of $600,

(b) A trust which, under its governing instrument, is required to distribute currently all of its income for the taxable year is allowed a deduction of $300, and

(c) All other trusts are allowed a deduction of $100.

A trust which, under its governing instrument, is required to distribute all of its income currently is allowed a deduction of $300, even though it also distributes amounts other than income in the taxable year and even though it may be required to make distributions which would qualify for the charitable contributions deduction under section 642(c) (and therefore does not qualify as a "simple trust" under sections 651-652). A trust for the payment of an annuity is allowed a deduction of $300 in a taxable year in which the amount of the annuity required to be paid equals or exceeds all the income of the trust for the taxable year. For the meaning of the term "income required to be distributed currently", see § 1.651(a)-2. [Reg. § 1.642(b)-1.]

☐ [T.D. 6217, 12-19-56.]

Estates, Trusts, and Beneficiaries

See p. 20,601 for regulations not amended to reflect law changes

[Reg. § 1.642(c)-0]

§ 1.642(c)-0. Effective dates.—The provisions of section 642(c) (other than section 642(c)(5)) and of §§ 1.642(c)-1 through 1.642(c)-4 apply to amounts paid, permanently set aside, or to be used for a charitable purpose in taxable years beginning after December 31, 1969. The provisions of section 642(c)(5) and of §§ 1.642(c)-5 through 1.642(c)-7 apply to transfers in trust made after July 31, 1969. For provisions relating to amounts paid, permanently set aside, or to be used for a charitable purpose in taxable years beginning before January 1, 1970, see 26 CFR 1.642(c) through 1.642(c)-4 (Rev. as of Jan. 1, 1971). [Reg. § 1.642(c)-0.]

☐ [T.D. 7357, 5-30-75.]

[Reg. § 1.642(c)-1]

§ 1.642(c)-1. Unlimited deduction for amounts paid for a charitable purpose.—(a) *In general*—(1) Any part of the gross income of an estate or trust which, pursuant to the terms of the governing instrument, is paid (or treated under paragraph (b) of this section as paid) during the taxable year for a purpose specified in section 170(c) shall be allowed as a deduction to such estate or trust in lieu of the limited charitable contributions deduction authorized by section 170(a). In applying this paragraph without reference to paragraph (b) of this section, a deduction shall be allowed for an amount paid during the taxable year in respect of gross income received in a previous taxable year, but only if no deduction was allowed for any previous taxable year to the estate or trust, or in the case of a section 645 election, to a related estate, as defined under § 1.645-1(b), for the amount so paid.

(2) In determining whether an amount is paid for a purpose specified in section 170(c)(2) the provisions of section 170(c)(2)(A) shall not be taken into account. Thus, an amount paid to a corporation, trust, or community chest, fund, or foundation otherwise described in section 170(c)(2) shall be considered paid for a purpose specified in section 170(c) even though the corporation, trust, or community chest, fund, or foundation is not created or organized in the United States, any State, the District of Columbia, or any possession of the United States.

(3) See section 642(c)(6) and § 1.642(c)-4 for disallowance of a deduction under this section to a trust which is, or is treated under section 4947(a)(1) as though it were, a private foundation (as defined in section 509(a) and the regulations thereunder) and not exempt from taxation under section 501(a).

(b) *Election to treat contributions as paid in preceding taxable year*—(1) *In general*. For purposes of determining the deduction allowed under paragraph (a) of this section, the fiduciary (as defined in section 7701(a)(6)) of an estate or trust may elect under section 642(c)(1) to treat as paid during the taxable year (whether or not such year begins before January 1, 1970) any amount of gross income received during such taxable year or any preceding taxable year which is otherwise deductible under such paragraph and which is paid after the close of such taxable year but on or before the last day of the next succeeding taxable year of the estate or trust. The preceding sentence applies only in the case of payments actually made in a taxable year which is a taxable year beginning after December 31, 1969. No election shall be made, however, in respect of any amount which was deducted for any previous taxable year or which is deducted for the taxable year in which such amount is paid.

(2) *Time for making election*. The election under subparagraph (1) of this paragraph shall be made not later than the time, including extensions thereof, prescribed by law for filing the income tax return for the succeeding taxable year. Such election shall, except as provided in subparagraph (4) of this paragraph, become irrevocable after the last day prescribed for making it. Having made the election for any taxable year, the fiduciary may, within the time prescribed for making it, revoke the election without the consent of the Commissioner.

(3) *Manner of making the election*. The election shall be made by filing with the income tax return (or an amended return) for the taxable year in which the contribution is treated as paid a statement which—

(i) States the name and address of the fiduciary,

(ii) Identifies the estate or trust for which the fiduciary is acting,

(iii) Indicates that the fiduciary is making an election under section 642(c)(1) in respect of contributions treated as paid during such taxable year,

(iv) Gives the name and address of each organization to which any such contribution is paid, and

(v) States the amount of each contribution and date of actual payment or, if applicable, the total amount of contributions paid to each organization during the succeeding taxable year, to be treated as paid in the preceding taxable year.

(4) *Revocation of certain elections with consent*. An application to revoke with the consent of

the Commissioner any election made on or before June 8, 1970, must be in writing and must be filed not later than September 2, 1975. No consent will be granted to revoke an election for any taxable year for which the assessment of a deficiency is prevented by the operation of any law or rule of law. If consent to revoke the election is granted, the fiduciary must attach a copy of the consent to the return (or amended return) for each taxable year affected by the revocation. The application must be addressed to the Commissioner of Internal Revenue, Washington, D.C. 20224, and must indicate—

(i) The name and address of the fiduciary and the estate or trust for which he was acting,

(ii) The taxable year for which the election was made,

(iii) The office of the district director, or the service center, where the return (or amended return) for the year of election was filed, and

(iv) The reason for revoking the election.

[Reg. § 1.642(c)-1.]

☐ [T.D. 6217, 12-19-56. Amended by T.D. 7357, 5-30-75 and T.D. 9032, 12-23-2002.]

[Reg. § 1.642(c)-2]

§ 1.642(c)-2. **Unlimited deduction for amounts permanently set aside for a charitable purpose.**—(a) *Estates.* Any part of the gross income of an estate which pursuant to the terms of the will—

(1) Is permanently set aside during the taxable year for a purpose specified in section 170(c), or

(2) Is to be used (within or without the United States or any of its possessions) exclusively for religious, charitable, scientific, literary, or educational purposes, or for the prevention of cruelty to children or animals, or for the establishment, acquisition, maintenance, or operation of a public cemetery not operated for profit,

shall be allowed as a deduction to the estate in lieu of the limited charitable contributions deduction authorized by section 170(a).

(b) *Certain trusts*—(1) *In general.* Any part of the gross income of a trust to which either subparagraph (3) or (4) of this paragraph applies, that by the terms of the governing instrument—

(i) Is permanently set aside during the taxable year for a purpose specified in section 170(c), or

(ii) Is to be used (within or without the United States or any of its possessions) exclusively for religious, charitable, scientific, literary, or educational purposes, or for the prevention of cruelty to children or animals, or for the establishment, acquisition, maintenance, or operation of a public cemetery not operated for profit,

shall be allowed, subject to the limitation provided in subparagraph (2) of this paragraph, as a deduction to the trust in lieu of the limited charitable contributions deduction authorized by section 170(a). The preceding sentence applies only to a trust which is required by the terms of its governing instrument to set amounts aside. See section 642(c)(6) and § 1.642(c)-4 for disallowance of a deduction under this section to a trust which is, or is treated under section 4947(a)(1) as though it were, a private foundation (as defined in section 509(a) and the regulations thereunder) that is not exempt from taxation under section 501(a).

(2) *Limitation of deduction.* Subparagraph (1) of this paragraph applies only to the gross income earned by a trust with respect to amounts transferred to the trust under a will executed on or before October 9, 1969, and satisfying the requirements of subparagraph (4) of this paragraph or transferred to the trust on or before October 9, 1969. For such purposes, any income, gains, or losses, which are derived at any time from the amounts so transferred to the trust shall also be taken into account in applying subparagraph (1) of this paragraph. If any such amount so transferred to the trust is invested or reinvested at any time, any asset received by the trust upon such investment or reinvestment shall also be treated as an amount which was so transferred to the trust. In the case of a trust to which this paragraph applies which contains (i) amounts transferred pursuant to transfers described in the first sentence of this subparagraph and (ii) amounts transferred pursuant to transfers not so described, subparagraph (1) of this paragraph shall apply only if the amounts described in subdivision (i) of this subparagraph, together with all income, gains, and losses derived therefrom, are separately accounted for from the amounts described in subdivision (ii) of this subparagraph, together with all income, gains, and losses derived therefrom. Such separate accounting shall be carried out consistently with the principles of paragraph (c)(4) of § 53.4947-1 of this chapter (Foundation Excise Tax Regulations), relating to accounting for segregated amounts of split-interest trusts.

(3) *Trusts created on or before October 9, 1969.* A trust to which this subparagraph applies is a trust, testamentary or otherwise, which was created on or before October 9, 1969, and which qualifies under either subdivision (i) or (ii) of this subparagraph.

(i) *Transfer of irrevocable remainder interest to charity.* To qualify under this subdivision the trust must have been created under the terms of an instrument granting an irrevocable remainder interest in such trust to or for the use of an organization described in section 170(c). If the instrument granted a revocable remainder interest but the power to revoke such interest terminated on or before October 9, 1969, without the remainder interest having been revoked, the remainder interest will be treated as irrevocable for purposes of the preceding sentence.

(ii) *Grantor under a mental disability to change terms of trust.* (A) To qualify under this subdivision (ii) the trust must have been created by a grantor who was at all times after October 9, 1969, under a mental disability to change the terms of the trust. The term "mental disability" for this purpose means mental incompetence to change the terms of the trust, whether or not there has been an adjudication of mental incompetence and whether or not there has been an appointment of a committee, guardian, fiduciary, or other person charged with the care of the person or property of the grantor.

(B) If the grantor has not been adjudged mentally incompetent, the trustee must obtain from a qualified physician a certificate stating that the grantor of the trust has been mentally incompetent at all times after October 9, 1969, and that there is no reasonable probability that the grantor's mental capacity will ever improve to the extent that he will be mentally competent to change the terms of the trust. A copy of this certification must be filed with the first return on which a deduction is claimed by reason of this subdivision (ii) and subparagraph (1) of this paragraph. Thereafter, a statement referring to such medical opinion must be attached to any return for a taxable year for which such a deduction is claimed and during which the grantor's mental incompetence continues. The original certificate must be retained by the trustee of the trust.

(C) If the grantor has been adjudged mentally incompetent, a copy of the judgment or decree, and any modification thereof, must be filed with the first return on which a deduction is claimed by reason of this subdivision (ii) and subparagraph (1) of this paragraph. Thereafter, a statement referring to such judgment or decree must be attached to any return for a taxable year for which such a deduction is claimed and during which the grantor's mental incompetence continues. A copy of such judgment or decree must also be retained by the trustee of the trust.

(D) This subdivision (ii) applies even though a person charged with the care of the person or property of the grantor has the power to change the terms of the trust.

(4) *Testamentary trust established by will executed on or before October 9, 1969.* A trust to which this subparagraph applies is a trust which was established by will executed on or before October 9, 1969, and which qualifies under either subdivision (i), (ii), or (iii) of this subparagraph. This subparagraph does not apply, however, to that portion of any trust, not established by a will executed on or before October 9, 1969, which was transferred to such trust by a will executed on or before October 9, 1969. Nor does it apply to that portion of any trust, not established by a will executed on or before October 9, 1969, which was subject to a testamentary power of appointment that fails by reason of the testator's nonexercise of the power in a will executed on or before October 9, 1969.

(i) *Testator dying within 3 years without republishing his will.* To qualify under this subdivision the trust must have been established by the will of a testator who died after October 9, 1969, but before October 9, 1972, without having amended any dispositive provision of the will after October 9, 1969, by codicil or otherwise.

(ii) *Testator having no right to change his will.* To qualify under this subdivision the trust must have been established by the will of a testator who died after October 9, 1969, and who at no time after that date had the right to change any portion of such will pertaining to such trust. This subdivision could apply, for example, where a contract has been entered into for the execution of wills containing reciprocal provisions as well as provisions for the benefit of an organization described in section 170(c) and under applicable local law the surviving testator is prohibited from revoking his will because he has accepted the benefit of the provisions of the will of the other contracting party.

(iii) *Testator under a mental disability to republish his will.* To qualify under this subdivision the trust must have been established by the will of a testator who died after October 8, 1972, without having amended any dispositive provision of such will after October 9, 1969, and before October 9, 1972, by codicil or otherwise, and who is under a mental disability at all times after October 8, 1972, to amend such will, by codicil or otherwise. The provisions of subparagraph (3)(ii) of this paragraph with respect to mental incompetence apply for purposes of this subdivision.

(iv) *Amendment of dispositive provisions.* The provisions of paragraph (e)(4) and (5) of § 20.2055-2 of this chapter (Estate Tax Regulations) are to be applied under subdivisions (i) and (iii) of this subparagraph in determining whether

Reg. § 1.642(c)-2(b)(4)

there has been an amendment of a dispositive provision of a will.

(c) *Pooled income funds.* Any part of the gross income of a pooled income fund to which § 1.642(c)-5 applies for the taxable year that is attributable to net long-term capital gain (as defined in section 1222(7)) which, pursuant to the terms of the governing instrument, is permanently set aside during the taxable year for a purpose specified in section 170(c) shall be allowed as a deduction to the fund in lieu of the limited charitable contributions deduction authorized by section 170(a). No deduction shall be allowed under this paragraph for any portion of the gross income of such fund which is (1) attributable to income other than net long-term capital gain or (2) earned with respect to amounts transferred to such fund before August 1, 1969. However, see paragraph (b) of this section for a deduction (subject to the limitations of such paragraph) for amounts permanently set aside by a pooled income fund which meets the requirements of that paragraph. The principles of paragraph (b)(2) of this section with respect to investment, reinvestment, and separate accounting shall apply under this paragraph in the case of amounts transferred to the fund after July 31, 1969.

(d) *Disallowance of deduction for certain amounts not deemed to be permanently set aside for charitable purposes.* No amount will be considered to be permanently set aside, or to be used, for a purpose described in paragraph (a) or (b)(1) of this section unless under the terms of the government instrument and the circumstances of the particular case the possibility that the amount set aside, or to be used, will not be devoted to such purpose or use is so remote as to be negligible. Thus, for example, where there is possibility of the invasion of the corpus of a charitable remainder trust, as defined in § 1.664-1(a)(1)(ii), in order to make payment of the annuity amount or unitrust amount, no deduction will be allowed under paragraph (a) of this section in respect of any amount set aside by an estate for distribution to such a charitable remainder trust.

For treatment of distributions by an estate to a charitable remainder trust, see paragraph (a)(5)(iii) of § 1.664-1. [Reg. § 1.642(c)-2.]

☐ [T.D. 6217, 12-19-56. Amended by T.D. 7357, 5-30-75.]

[Reg. § 1.642(c)-3]

§ 1.642(c)-3. Adjustments and other special rules for determining unlimited charitable contributions deduction.—(a) *Income in respect of a decedent.* For purposes of §§ 1.642(c)-1 and 1.642(c)-2, an amount received by an estate or trust which is includible in its gross income under section 691(a)(1) as income in respect of a decedent shall be included in the gross income of the estate or trust.

(b) *Reduction of charitable contributions deduction by amounts not included in gross income.* (1) If an estate, pooled income fund, or other trust pays, permanently sets aside, or uses any amount of its income for a purpose specified in section 642(c)(1), (2), or (3) and that amount includes any items of estate or trust income not entering into the gross income of the estate or trust, the deduction allowable under § 1.642(c)-1 or § 1.642(c)-2 is limited to the gross income so paid, permanently set aside, or used. In the case of a pooled income fund for which a deduction is allowable under paragraph (c) of § 1.642(c)-2 for amounts permanently set aside, only the gross income of the fund which is attributable to net long-term capital gain (as defined in section 1222(7)) shall be taken into account.

(2) In determining whether the amounts of income so paid, permanently set aside, or used for a purpose specified in section 642(c)(1), (2), or (3) include particular items of income of an estate or trust not included in gross income, the specific provision controls if the governing instrument specifically provides as to the source out of which amounts are to be paid, permanently set aside, or used for such a purpose. In the absence of specific provisions in the governing instrument, an amount to which section 642(c)(1), (2), (3) applies is deemed to consist of the same proportion of each class of the items of income of the estate or trust as the total of each class bears to the total of all classes. See paragraph (b) of § 1.643(a)-5 for the method of determining the allocable portion of exempt income and foreign income.

(3) For examples showing the determination of the character of an amount deductible under § 1.642(c)-1 or § 1.642(c)-2, see examples (1) and (2) in § 1.662(b)-2 and paragraph (e) of the example in § 1.662(c)-4.

(4) For the purpose of this paragraph, the provisions of section 116 are not to be taken into account.

(c) *Capital gains included in charitable contribution.* Where any amount of the income paid, permanently set aside, or used for a purpose specified in section 642(c)(1), (2), or (3) is attributable to net long-term capital gain (as defined in section 1222(7)), the amount of the deduction otherwise allowable under § 1.642(c)-1 or § 1.642(c)-2 must be adjusted for any deduction provided in section 1202 of 50 percent of the excess, if any, of the net long-term capital gain over the net short-term capital loss. For determination of the extent to which the contribution to which § 1.642(c)-1 or § 1.642(c)-2 applies is deemed to consist of net long-term capital gains, see paragraph (b) of this section. The application of this paragraph may be illustrated by the following examples:

Example (1). Under the terms of the trust instrument, the income of a trust described in § 1.642(c)-2(b)(3)(i) is currently distributable to A during his life and capital gains are allocable to corpus. No provision is made in the trust instrument for the invasion of corpus for the benefit of A. Upon A's death the corpus of the trust is to be distributed to M University, an organization described in section 501(c)(3) which is exempt from taxation under section 501(a). During the taxable year ending December 31, 1970, the trust has long-term capital gains of $100,000 from property transferred to it on or before October 9, 1969, which are permanently set aside for charitable purposes. The trust includes $100,000 in gross income but is allowed a deduction of $50,000 under section 1202 for the long-term capital gains and a charitable contributions deduction of $50,000 under section 642(c)(2) ($100,000 permanently set aside for charitable purposes less $50,000 allowed as a deduction under section 1202 with respect to such $100,000).

Example (2). Under the terms of the will, $200,000 of the income (including $100,000 capital gains) for the taxable year 1972 of an estate is distributed, one-quarter to each of two individual beneficiaries and one-half to N University, an organization described in section 501(c)(3) which is exempt from taxation under section 501(a). During 1972 the estate has ordinary income of $200,000, long-term capital gains of $100,000, and no capital losses. It is assumed that for 1972 the estate has no other items of income or any deductions other than those discussed herein. The entire capital gains of $100,000 are included in the gross income of the estate for 1972, and N University receives $100,000 from the estate in such year. However, the amount allowable to the estate under section 642(c)(1) is subject to appropriate adjustment for the deduction allowable under section 1202. In view of the distributions of $25,000 of capital gains to each of the individual beneficiaries, the deduction allowable to the estate under section 1202 is limited by such section to $25,000 [($100,000 capital gains less $50,000 capital gains includible in income of individual beneficiaries under section 662) × 50%]. Since the whole of this $25,000 deduction under section 1202 is attributable to the distribution of $50,000 of capital gains to N University, the deduction allowable to the estate in 1972 under section 642(c)(1) is $75,000 [$100,000 (distributed to N) less $25,000 (proper adjustment for section 1202 deduction)].

Example (3). Under the terms of the trust instrument, 30 percent of the gross income (exclusive of capital gains) of a trust described in § 1.642(c)-2(b)(3)(i) is currently distributed to B, the sole income beneficiary. Net capital gains (capital gain net income for taxable years beginning after December 31, 1976) and undistributed ordinary income are allocable to corpus. No provision is made in the trust instrument for the invasion of corpus for the benefit of B. Upon B's death the remainder of the trust is to be distributed to M Church. During the taxable year 1972, the trust has ordinary income of $100,000, long-term capital gains of $15,000, short-term capital gains of $1,000, long-term capital losses of $5,000, and short-term capital losses of $2,500. It is assumed that the trust has no other items of income or any deductions other than those discussed herein. All the ordinary income and capital gains and losses are attributable to amounts transferred to the trust before October 9, 1969. The trust includes in gross income for 1972 the total amount of $116,000 [$100,000 (ordinary income) + $16,000 (total capital gains determined without regard to capital losses)]. Pursuant to the terms of the governing instrument the trust distributes to B in 1972 the amount of $30,000 ($100,000 × 30%). The balance of $78,500 [($116,000 less $7,500 capital losses) − $30,000 distribution] is available for the set-aside for charitable purposes. In determining taxable income for 1972 the capital losses of $7,500 ($5,000 + $2,500) are allowable in full under section 1211(b)(1). The net capital gain (capital gain net income for taxable years beginning after December 31, 1976) of $8,500 ($16,000 less $7,500) is the excess of the net long-term capital gain of $10,000 ($15,000 less $5,000) over the net short-term capital loss of $1,500 ($2,500 less $1,000). The deduction under section 1202 is $4,250 ($8,500 × 50%), all of which is attributable to the set-aside for charitable purposes. Accordingly, for 1972 the deduction allowable to the trust under section 642(c)(2) is $74,250 [$78,500 (set-aside for M) less $4,250 (proper adjustment for section 1202 deduction)].

Example (4). During the taxable year a pooled income fund, as defined in § 1.642(c)-5, has in addition to ordinary income long-term capital gains of $150,000, short-term capital gains of $15,000, long-term capital losses of $100,000, and short-term capital losses of $10,000. Under the Declaration of Trust and pursuant to State law net long-term capital gain is allocable to corpus and net short-term capital gain is to be distributed to the income beneficiaries of the fund. All the capital gains and losses are attributable to

Reg. § 1.642(c)-3(c)

amounts transferred to the fund after July 31, 1969. In view of the distribution of the net short-term capital gain of $5,000 ($15,000 less $10,000) to the income beneficiaries, the deduction allowed to the fund under section 1202 is limited by such section to $25,000 [($150,000 (long-term capital gains) less $100,000 (long-term capital losses)) × 50%]. Since the whole of this deduction under section 1202 is attributable to the set-aside for charitable purposes, the deduction of $50,000 ($150,000 less $100,000) otherwise allowable under section 642(c)(3) is subject to appropriate adjustment under section 642(c)(4) for the deduction allowable under section 1202. Accordingly, the amount of the set-aside deduction is $25,000 [$50,000 (set-aside for public charity) less $25,000 (proper adjustment for section 1202 deduction)].

Example (5). The facts are the same as in example (4) except that under the Declaration of Trust and pursuant to State law all the net capital gain (capital gain net income for taxable years beginning after December 31, 1976) for the taxable year is allocable to corpus of the fund. The fund would thus include in gross income total capital gains of $165,000 ($150,000 + $15,000). In determining taxable income for the taxable year the capital losses of $110,000 ($100,000 + $10,000) are allowable in full under section 1211(b)(1). The net capital gain (capital gain net income for taxable years beginning after December 31, 1976) of $55,000 ($165,000 less $110,000) is available for the set-aside for charitable purposes under section 642(c)(3) only in the amount of the net long-term capital gain of $50,000 ($150,000 long-term gains less $100,000 long-term losses). The deduction under section 1202 is $25,000 ($50,000 × 50%), all of which is attributable to the set-aside for charitable purposes. Accordingly, the deduction allowable to the fund under section 642(c)(3) is $25,000 [$50,000 (set-aside for public charity) less $25,000 (proper adjustment for section 1202 deduction)]. The $5,000 balance of net capital gain (capital gain net income for taxable years beginning after December 31, 1976) is taken into account in determining taxable income of the pooled income fund for the taxable year.

(d) *Disallowance of deduction for amounts allocable to unrelated business income.* In the case of a trust, the deduction otherwise allowable under § 1.642(c)-1 or § 1.642(c)-2 is disallowed to the extent of amounts allocable to the trust's unrelated business income. See section 681(a) and the regulations thereunder.

(e) *Disallowance of deduction in certain cases.* For disallowance of certain deductions otherwise allowable under section 642(c)(1), (2), or (3), see sections 508(d) and 4948(c)(4).

(f) *Information returns.* For rules applicable to the annual information return that must be filed by trusts claiming a deduction under section 642(c) for the taxable year, see section 6034 and the regulations thereunder. [Reg. § 1.642(c)-3.]

☐ [T.D. 6217, 12-19-56. Amended by T.D. 7357, 5-30-75 and T.D. 7728, 10-31-80.]

[Reg. § 1.642(c)-4]

§ 1.642(c)-4. **Nonexempt private foundations.**—In the case of a trust which is, or is treated under section 4947(a)(1) as though it were, a private foundation (as defined in section 509(a) and the regulations thereunder) that is not exempt from taxation under section 501(a) for the taxable year, a deduction for amounts paid or permanently set aside, or used for a purpose specified in section 642(c)(1) or (2) shall not be allowed under § 1.642(c)-1 or § 1.642(c)-2, but such trust shall, subject to the provisions applicable to individuals, be allowed a deduction under section 170 for charitable contributions paid during the taxable year. Section 642(c)(6) and this section do not apply to a trust described in section 4947(a)(1) unless such trust fails to meet the requirements of section 508(e). However, if on October 9, 1969, or at any time thereafter, a trust is recognized as being exempt from taxation under section 501(a) as an organization described in section 501(c)(3), if at such time such trust is a private foundation, and if at any time thereafter such trust is determined not to be exempt from taxation under section 501(a) as an organization described in section 501(c)(3), section 642(c)(6) and this section will apply to such trust. See § 1.509(b)-1(b). [Reg. § 1.642(c)-4.]

☐ [T.D. 6217, 12-19-56. Amended by T.D. 7357, 5-30-75.]

[Reg. § 1.642(c)-5]

§ 1.642(c)-5. **Definition of pooled income fund.**—(a) *In general*—(1) *Application of provisions.* Section 642(c)(5) prescribed certain rules for the valuation of contributions involving transfers to certain funds described in that section as pooled income funds. This section sets forth the requirements for qualifying as a pooled income fund and provides for the manner of allocating the income of the fund to the beneficiaries. Section 1.642(c)-6 provides for the valuation of a remainder interest in property transferred to a pooled income fund. Section 1.642(c)-7 provides transitional rules under which certain funds may be amended so as to qualify as pooled income funds in respect to transfers of property occurring after July 31, 1969.

(2) *Tax status of fund and its beneficiaries.* Notwithstanding any other provision of this chapter, a fund which meets the requirements of a pooled income fund, as defined in section 642(c)(5) and paragraph (b) of this section, shall not be treated as an association within the meaning of section 7701(a)(3). Such a fund, which need not be a trust under local law, and its beneficiaries shall be taxable under part I, subchapter J, chapter 1 of the Code, but the provisions of subpart E (relating to grantors and others treated as substantial owners) of such part shall not apply to such fund.

(3) *Recognition of gain or loss on transfer to fund.* No gain or loss shall be recognized to the donor on the transfer of property to a pooled income fund. In such case, the fund's basis and holding period with respect to property transferred to the fund by a donor shall be determined as provided in sections 1015(b) and 1223(2). If, however, a donor transfers property to a pooled income fund and, in addition to creating or retaining a life income interest therein, receives property from the fund, or transfers property to the fund which is subject to an indebtedness, this subparagraph shall not apply to the gain realized by reason of (i) the receipt of such property or (ii) the amount of such indebtedness, whether or not assumed by the pooled income fund, which is required to be treated as an amount realized on the transfer.

For applicability of the bargain sale rules, see section 1011(b) and the regulations thereunder.

(4) *Charitable contributions deduction.* A charitable contributions deduction for the value of the remainder interest, as determined under § 1.642(c)-6, may be allowed under section 170, 2055, 2106, or 2522, where there is a transfer of property to a pooled income fund. For a special rule relating to the reduction of the amount of a charitable contribution of certain ordinary income property or capital gain property, see section 170(e)(1)(A) or (B)(i) and the regulations thereunder.

(5) *Definitions.* For purposes of this section, § 1.642(c)-6, and § 1.642(c)-7—

(i) The term "income" has the same meaning as it does under section 643(b) and the regulations thereunder.

(ii) The term "donor" includes a decedent who makes a testamentary transfer of property to a pooled income fund.

(iii) The term "governing instrument" means either the governing plan under which the pooled income fund is established and administered or the instrument of transfer, as the context requires.

(iv) The term "public charity" means an organization described in clauses (i) to (vi) of section 170(b)(1)(A). If an organization is described in clauses (i) to (vi) of section 170(b)(1)(A) and is also described in clause (viii) of such section, it shall be treated as a public charity.

(v) The term "fair market value," when used with respect to property, means its value in excess of the indebtedness or charges against such property.

(vi) The term "determination date" means each day within the taxable year of a pooled income fund on which a valuation is made of the property in the fund. The property in the fund shall be valued on the first day of the taxable year of the fund and on at least 3 other days within the taxable year. The period between any two consecutive determination dates within the taxable year shall not be greater than 3 calendar months. In the case of a taxable year of less than 12 months, the property in the fund shall be valued on the first day of such taxable year and on such other days within such year as occur at successive intervals of no greater than 3 calendar months. Where a valuation date falls on a Saturday, Sunday, or legal holiday (as defined in section 7503 and the regulations thereunder), the valuation may be made on either the next preceding day which is not a Saturday, Sunday, or legal holiday or the next succeeding day which is not a Saturday, Sunday, or legal holiday, so long as the next such preceding day or next such succeeding day is consistently used where the valuation date falls on a Saturday, Sunday, or legal holiday.

(6) *Cross references.* (i) See section 4947(a)(2) and section 4947(b)(3)(B) for the application to pooled income funds of the provisions relating to private foundations and section 508(e) for rules relating to provisions required in the governing instrument prohibiting certain activities specified in section 4947(a)(2).

(ii) For rules postponing the time for deduction of a charitable contribution of a future interest in tangible personal property, see section 170(a)(3) and the regulations thereunder.

(b) *Requirements for qualification as a pooled income fund.* A pooled income fund to which this section applies must satisfy all of the following requirements:

(1) *Contribution of remainder interest to charity.* Each donor must transfer property to the fund and contribute an irrevocable remainder interest in such property to or for the use of a public charity, retaining for himself, or creating for another beneficiary or beneficiaries, a life income interest in the transferred property. A contingent remainder interest shall not be treated as an ir-

Reg. § 1.642(c)-5(b)(1)

revocable remainder interest for purposes of this subparagraph.

(2) *Creation of life income interest.* Each donor must retain for himself for life an income interest in the property transferred to such fund, or create an income interest in such property for the life of one or more beneficiaries, each of whom must be living at the time of the transfer of the property to the fund by the donor. The term "one or more beneficiaries" includes those members of a named class who are alive and can be ascertained at the time of the transfer of the property to the fund. In the event more than one beneficiary of the income interest is designated, such beneficiaries may enjoy their shares of income concurrently, consecutively, or both concurrently and consecutively. The donor may retain the power exercisable only by will to revoke or terminate the income interest of any designated beneficiary other than the public charity. The governing instrument must specify at the time of the transfer the particular beneficiary or beneficiaries to whom the income is payable and the share of income distributable to each person so specified. The public charity to or for the use of which the remainder interest is contributed may also be designated as one of the beneficiaries of an income interest. The donor need not retain or create a life interest in all the income from the property transferred to the fund provided any income not payable under the terms of the governing instrument to an income beneficiary is contributed to, and within the taxable year in which it is received is paid to, the same public charity to or for the use of which the remainder interest is contributed. No charitable contributions deduction shall be allowed to the donor for the value of such income interest of the public charity or for the amount of any such income paid to such organization.

(3) *Commingling of property required.* The property transferred to the fund by each donor must be commingled with, and invested or reinvested with, other property transferred to the fund by other donors satisfying the requirements of subparagraphs (1) and (2) of this paragraph. The governing instrument of the pooled income fund must contain a provision requiring compliance with the preceding sentence. The public charity to or for the use of which the remainder interest is contributed may maintain more than one pooled income fund, provided that each such fund is maintained by the organization and is not a device to permit a group of donors to create a fund which may be subject to their manipulation. The fund must not include property transferred under arrangements other than those specified in section 642(c)(5) and this paragraph. However, a fund shall not be disqualified as a pooled income fund under this paragraph because any portion of its properties is invested or reinvested jointly with other properties, not a part of the pooled income fund, which are held by, or for the use of, the public charity which maintains the fund, as, for example, with securities in the general endowment fund of the public charity to or for the use of which the remainder interest is contributed. Where such joint investment or reinvestment of properties occurs, records must be maintained which sufficiently identify the portion of the total fund which is owned by the pooled income fund and the income earned by, and attributable to, such portion. Such a joint investment or reinvestment of properties shall not be treated as an association or partnership for purposes of the Code. A bank which serves as trustee of more than one pooled income fund may maintain a common trust fund to which section 584 applies for the collective investment and reinvestment of moneys of such funds.

(4) *Prohibition against exempt securities.* The property transferred to the fund by any donor must not include any securities the income from which is exempt from tax under subtitle A of the Code, and the fund must not invest in such securities. The governing instrument of the fund must contain specific prohibitions against accepting or investing in such securities.

(5) *Maintenance by charitable organization required.* The fund must be maintained by the same public charity to or for the use of which the irrevocable remainder interest is contributed. The requirement of maintenance will be satisfied where the public charity exercises control directly or indirectly over the fund. For example, this requirement of control shall ordinarily be met when the public charity has the power to remove the trustee or trustees of the fund and designate a new trustee or trustees. A national organization which carries out its purposes through local organizations, chapters, or auxiliary bodies with which it has an identity of aims and purposes may maintain a pooled income fund (otherwise satisfying the requirements of this paragraph) in which one or more local organizations, chapters, or auxiliary bodies which are public charities have been named as recipients of the remainder interests. For example, a national church body may maintain a pooled income fund where donors have transferred property to such fund and contributed an irrevocable remainder interest therein to or for the use of various local churches or educational institutions of such body. The fact that such local organizations or chapters have been separately incorporated from the national organization is immaterial.

Reg. § 1.642(c)-5(b)(2)

(6) *Prohibition against donor or beneficiary serving as trustee.* The fund must not have, and the governing instrument must prohibit the fund from having, as a trustee a donor to the fund or a beneficiary (other than the public charity to or for the use of which the remainder interest is contributed) of an income interest in any property transferred to such fund. Thus, if a donor or beneficiary (other than such public charity) directly or indirectly has general responsibilities with respect to the fund which are ordinarily exercised by a trustee, such fund does not meet the requirements of section 642(c)(5) and this paragraph. The fact that a donor of property to the fund, or a beneficiary of the fund, is a trustee, officer, director, or other official of the public charity to or for the use of which the remainder interest is contributed ordinarily will not prevent the fund from meeting the requirements of section 642(c)(5) and this paragraph.

(7) *Income of beneficiary to be based on rate of return of fund.* Each beneficiary entitled to income of any taxable year of the fund must receive such income in an amount determined by the rate of return earned by the fund for such taxable year with respect to his income interest, computed as provided in paragraph (c) of this section. The governing instrument of the fund shall direct the trustee to distribute income currently or within the first 65 days following the close of the taxable year in which the income is earned. Any such payment made after the close of the taxable year shall be treated as paid on the last day of the taxable year. A statement shall be attached to the return of the pooled income fund indicating the date and amount of such payments after the close of the taxable year. Subject to the provisions of part I, subchapter J, chapter 1 of the Code, the beneficiary shall include in his gross income all amounts properly paid, credited, or required to be distributed to the beneficiary during the taxable year or years of the fund ending within or with his taxable year. The governing instrument shall provide that the income interest of any designated beneficiary shall either terminate with the last regular payment which was made before the death of the beneficiary or be prorated to the date of his death.

(8) *Termination of life income interest.* Upon the termination of the income interest retained or created by any donor, the trustee shall sever from the fund an amount equal to the value of the remainder interest in the property upon which the income interest is based. The value of the remainder interest for such purpose may be either (i) its value as of the determination date next succeeding the termination of the income interest or (ii) its value as of the date on which the last regular payment was made before the death of the beneficiary if the income interest is terminated on such payment date. The amount so severed from the fund must either be paid to, or retained for the use of, the designated public charity, as provided in the governing instrument. However, see subparagraph (3) of this paragraph for rules relating to commingling of property.

(c) *Allocation of income to beneficiary*—(1) *In general.* Every income interest retained or created in property transferred to a pooled income fund shall be assigned a proportionate share of the annual income earned by the fund, such share, or unit of participation, being based on the fair market value of such property on the date of transfer, as provided in this paragraph.

(2) *Units of participation*—(i) *Unit plan.* (*a*) On each transfer of property by a donor to a pooled income fund, one or more units of participation in the fund shall be assigned to the beneficiary or beneficiaries of the income interest retained or created in such property, the number of units of participation being equal to the number obtained by dividing the fair market value of the property by the fair market value of a unit in the fund at the time of the transfer.

(*b*) The fair market value of a unit in the fund at the time of the transfer shall be determined by dividing the fair market value of all property in the fund at such time by the number of units then in the fund. The initial fair market value of a unit in a pooled income fund shall be the fair market value of the property transferred to the fund divided by the number of units assigned to the income interest in that property. The value of each unit of participation will fluctuate with each new transfer of property to the fund in relation to the appreciation or depreciation in the fair market value of the property in the fund, but all units in the fund will always have equal value.

(*c*) The share of income allocated to each unit of participation shall be determined by dividing the income of the fund for the taxable year by the outstanding number of units in the fund at the end of such year, except that, consistently with paragraph (b)(7) of this section, income shall be allocated to units outstanding during only part of such year by taking into consideration the period of time such units are outstanding. For this purpose the actual income of such part of the taxable year, or a prorated portion of the annual income, may be used, after making such adjustments as are reasonably necessary to reflect fluctuations during the year in the fair market value of the property in the fund.

Reg. § 1.642(c)-5(c)(2)

(ii) *Other plans.* The governing instrument of the fund may provide any other reasonable method not described in subdivision (i) of this subparagraph for assigning units of participation in the fund and allocating income to such units which reaches a result reasonably consistent with the provisions of such subdivision.

(iii) *Transfers between determination dates.* For purposes of subdivisions (i) and (ii) of this subparagraph, if a transfer of property to the fund by a donor occurs on other than a determination date, the number of units of participation assigned to the income interest in such property may be determined by using the fair market value of the property in the fund on the determination date immediately preceding the date of transfer (determined without regard to the property so transferred), subject, however, to appropriate adjustments on the next succeeding determination date. Such adjustments may be made by any reasonable method, including the use of a method whereby the fair market value of the property in the fund at the time of the transfer is deemed to be the average of the fair market values of the property in the fund on the determination dates immediately preceding and succeeding the date of transfer. For purposes of determining such average any property transferred to the fund between such preceding and succeeding dates, or on such succeeding date, shall be excluded. The application of this subdivision may be illustrated by the following example:

Example. The determination dates of a pooled income fund are the first day of each calendar month. On April 1, 1971, the fair market value of the property in the fund is $100,000, at which time 1,000 units of participation are outstanding with a value of $100 each. On April 15, 1971, B transfers property with a fair market value of $50,000 to the fund, retaining for himself for life an income interest in such property. No other property is transferred to the fund after April 1, 1971. On May 1, 1971, the fair market value of the property in the fund, including the property transferred by B, is $160,000. The average of the fair market values of the property in the fund (excluding the property transferred by B) on April 1 and May 1, 1971, is $105,000 ($100,000 + [$160,000 − $50,000] ÷ 2). Accordingly, the fair market value of a unit of participation in the fund on April 15, 1971, at the time of B's transfer may be deemed to be $105 ($105,000/1,000 units), and B is assigned 476.19 units of participation in the fund ($50,000/$105).

(3) *Special rule for partial allocation of income to charity.* Notwithstanding subparagraph (2) of this paragraph, the governing instrument may provide that a unit of participation is entitled to share in the income of a fund in a lesser amount than would otherwise be determined under such subparagraph, provided that the income otherwise allocable to the unit under such subparagraph is paid within the taxable year in which it is received to the public charity to or for the use of which the remainder interest is contributed under the governing instrument.

(4) *Illustrations.* The application of this paragraph may be illustrated by the following examples:

Example (1). On July 1, 1970, A and B transfer separate properties with a fair market value of $20,000 and $10,000, respectively, to a newly created pooled income fund which is maintained by Y University and uses as its taxable year the fiscal year ending June 30. A and B each retain in themselves for life an income interest in such property, the remainder interest being contributed to Y University. The pooled income fund assigns an initial value of $100 to each unit of participation in the fund, and under the governing instruments A receives 200 units, and B receives 100 units, in the fund. On October 1, 1970, which is a determination date, C transfers property to the fund with a fair market value of $12,000, retaining in himself for life an income interest in such property and contributing the remainder interest to Y University. The fair market value of the property in the fund at the time of C's transfer is $36,000. The fair market value of A's and B's units at the time of such transfer is $120 each ($36,000/300). By reason of his transfer of property C is assigned 100 units of participation in the fund ($12,000/$120).

Example (2). Assume that the pooled income fund in example (1) earns $2,600 for its taxable year ending June 30, 1971, and there are no further contributions of property to the fund in such year. Further assume $300 is earned in the first quarter ending September 30, 1970. Therefore, the fund earns $1 per unit for the first quarter ($300 divided by 300 units outstanding) and $5.75 per unit for the remainder of the taxable year ([$2,600 − $300] divided by 400 units outstanding). If the fund distributes its income for the year based on its actual earnings per quarter, the income must be distributed as follows:

Beneficiary	Share of Income
A	$1,350 ([200 × $1] + [200 × $5.75])
B	675 ([100 × $1] + [100 × $5.75])
C	575 (100 × $5.75)

Example (3). (a) On July 1, 1970, A and B transfer separate properties with a fair market value of $10,000 and $20,000, respectively, to a newly created pooled income fund which is main-

Reg. § 1.642(c)-5(c)(3)

tained by X University and uses as its taxable year the fiscal year ending June 30. A and B each retain in themselves an income interest for life in such property, the remainder interest being contributed to X University. The governing instrument provides that each unit of participation in the fund shall have a value of not more than its initial fair market value; the instrument also provides that the income allocable to appreciation in the fair market value of such unit (to the extent in excess of its initial fair market value) at the end of each quarter of the fiscal year is to be distributed currently to X University. On October 1, 1970, which is a determination date, C contributes to the fund property with a fair market value of $60,000 and retains in himself an income interest for life in such property, the remainder interest being contributed to X University. The initial fair market value of the units assigned to A, B, and C is $100. A, B, and C's units of participation are as follows:

Beneficiary	Units of Participation
A	100 ($10,000 divided by $100)
B	200 ($20,000 divided by $100)
C	600 ($60,000 divided by $100)

(b) The fair market value of the property in the fund at the time of C's contribution is $40,000. Assuming the fair market value of the property in the fund is $100,000 on December 31, 1970, and that the income of the fund for the second quarter ending December 31, 1970, is $2,000, the income is shared by the income beneficiaries and X University as follows:

Beneficiary	Allocation of Income
A, B, and C	90% ($90,000 divided by $100,000)
X University	10% ($10,000 divided by $100,000)

(c) For the quarter ending December 31, 1970, each unit of participation is allocated $2 (90% × $2,000 divided by 900) of the income earned for that quarter. A, B, C and X University share in the income as follows:

Beneficiary	Share of Income
A	$ 200 (100 × $2)
B	400 (200 × $2)
C	1,200 (600 × $2)
X University	200 (10% × $2,000)

[Reg. § 1.642(c)-5.]

☐ [T.D. 7105, 4-5-71. Amended by T.D. 7125, 6-7-71, by T.D. 7357, 5-30-75, and by T.D. 7633, 7-17-79.]

[Reg. § 1.642(c)-6]

§ 1.642(c)-6. Valuation of a remainder interest in property transferred to a pooled income fund.—(a) *In general.*—(1) For purposes of sections 170, 2055, 2106, and 2522, the fair market value of a remainder interest in property transferred to a pooled income fund is its present value determined under paragraph (d) of this section.

(2) The present value of a remainder interest at the time of the transfer of property to the pooled income fund is determined by computing the present value (at the time of the transfer) of the life income interest and subtracting that value from the fair market value of the transferred property on the valuation date. The fact that the income beneficiary may not receive the last income payment, as provided in paragraph (b)(7) of § 1.642(c)-5, is not taken into account for purposes of determining the value of the life income interest. For purposes of this section, the valuation date is the date on which property is transferred to the fund by the donor except that, for purposes of section 2055 or 2106, it is the alternate valuation date, if elected, under the provisions and limitations set forth in section 2032 and the regulations thereunder.

(3) Any claim for a deduction on any return for the value of the remainder interest in property transferred to a pooled income fund must be supported by a statement attached to the return showing the computation of the present value of the interest.

(b) *Actuarial computations by the Internal Revenue Service.* The regulations in this and in related sections provide tables of actuarial factors and examples that illustrate the use of the tables in determining the value of remainder interests in property. Section 1.7520-1(c)(2) refers to government publications that provide additional tables of factors and examples of computations for more complex situations. If the computation requires the use of a factor that is not provided in this section, the Commissioner may supply the factor upon a request for a ruling. A request for a ruling must be accompanied by a recitation of the facts including the pooled income fund's highest yearly rate of return for the 3 taxable years immediately preceding the date of transfer, the date of birth of each measuring life, and copies of the relevant documents. A request for a ruling must comply with the instructions for requesting a ruling published periodically in the Internal Revenue Bulletin (see §§ 601.201 and 601.601(d)(2)(ii)(b) of this chapter) and include payment of the required user fee. If the Commissioner furnishes the factor, a copy of the letter supplying the factor should be attached to the tax return in which the deduction is claimed. If the Commissioner does not furnish the factor, the taxpayer must furnish a factor computed in accordance with the principles set forth in this section.

(c) *Computation of pooled income fund's yearly rate of return.* (1) For purposes of determining the present value of the life income interest, the yearly rate of return earned by a pooled income fund for a taxable year is the percentage obtained by dividing the amount of income earned by the pooled income fund for the taxable year by an amount equal to—

    (i) The average fair market value of the property in such fund for that taxable year; less

    (ii) The corrective term adjustment.

(2) The average fair market value of the property in a pooled income fund for a taxable year shall be the sum of the amounts of the fair market value of all property held by the pooled income fund on each determination date, as defined in paragraph (a)(5)(vi) of § 1.642(c)-5, of such taxable year divided by the number of determination dates in such taxable year. For such purposes the fair market value of property held by the fund shall be determined without including any income earned by the fund.

(3)(i) The corrective term adjustment shall be the sum of the products obtained by multiplying each income payment made by the pooled income fund within its taxable year by the percentage set forth in column (2) of the following table opposite the period within such year, set forth in column (1), which includes the date on which that payment is made:

Table

(1) Payment Period	(2) Percentage of Payment
Last week of 4th quarter	Zero
Balance of 4th quarter	25
Last week of 3rd quarter	25
Balance of 3rd quarter	50
Last week of 2nd quarter	50
Balance of 2nd quarter	75
Last week of 1st quarter	75
Balance of 1st quarter	100

    (ii) If the taxable year of the fund consists of less than 12 months, the corrective term adjustment shall be the sum of the products obtained by multiplying each income payment made by the pooled income fund within such taxable year by the percentage obtained by subtracting from 1 a fraction the numerator of which is the number of days from the first day of such taxable year to the date of such income payment and the denominator of which is 365.

(4) A pooled income fund's method of calculating its yearly rate of return must be supported by a full statement attached to the income tax return of the pooled income fund for each taxable year.

(5) The application of this paragraph may be illustrated by the following examples:

Example (1). (a) The pooled income fund maintained by W University has established determination dates on the first day of each calendar quarter. The pooled income fund is on a calendar-year basis. The pooled income fund earned $5,000 of income during 1971. The fair market value of its property (determined without including any income earned by the fund), and the income paid out, on the first day of each calendar quarter in 1971 are as follows:

Date	Fair Market Value of Property	Income Payment
Jan. 1	$100,000	$1,200
April 1	105,000	1,200
July 1	95,000	1,200
Oct. 1	100,000	1,400
	400,000	5,000

(b) The average fair market value of the property in the fund for 1971 is $100,000 ($400,000 divided by 4).

(c) The corrective term adjustment for 1971 is $3,050, determined by applying the percentages obtained in column (2) of the table in subparagraph (3) of this paragraph:

Multiplication	Product
100% × $1,200	$1,200
75% × 1,200	900
50% × 1,200	600

Reg. § 1.642(c)-6(c)(2)

Estates, Trusts, and Beneficiaries

See p. 20,601 for regulations not amended to reflect law changes

25% × 1,400	350
Sum of Products	3,050

(d) The pooled income fund's yearly rate of return for 1971 is 5.157 percent, determined as follows:

$$\frac{\$5,000}{\$100,000 - \$3,050} = .05157$$

Example (2). (a) The pooled income fund maintained by X University has established determination dates on the first day of each calendar quarter. The pooled income fund is on a calendar-year basis. The pooled income fund earned $5,000 of income during 1971 and paid out $3,000 on December 15, 1971, and $2,000 on January 15, 1972, the last amount being treated under paragraph (b)(7) of § 1.642(c)-5 as paid on December 31, 1971. The fair market value of its property (determined without including any income earned by the fund) on the determination dates in 1971 and the income paid out during 1971 are as follows:

Date	Fair Market Value of Property	Income Payment
Jan. 1	$125,000	.....
April 1	125,000	.....
July 1	75,000	.....
Oct. 1	75,000	.....
Dec. 15	......	$3,000
Dec. 31	......	2,000
	400,000	5,000

(b) The average fair market value of the property in the fund for 1971 is $100,000 ($400,000 divided by 4).

(c) The corrective term adjustment for 1971 is $750, determined by applying the percentages obtained in column (2) of the table in subparagraph (3) of this paragraph:

Multiplication	Product
0% × $2,000	$...
25% × 3,000	750
Sum of Products	750

(d) *Valuation.* The present value of the remainder interest in property transferred to a pooled income fund after April 30, 1999, is determined under paragraph (e) of this section. The present value of the remainder interest in property transferred to a pooled income fund for which the valuation date is before May 1, 1999, is determined under the following sections:

Valuation Dates		
After	Before	Applicable Regulations
	01-01-52	1.642(c)-6A(a)
12-31-51	01-01-71	1.642(c)-6A(b)
12-31-70	12-01-83	1.642(c)-6A(c)
11-30-83	05-01-89	1.642(c)-6A(d)
04-30-89	05-01-99	1.642(c)-6A(e)

(e) *Present value of the remainder interest in the case of transfers to pooled income funds for which the valuation date is after April 30, 1999*—(1) *In general.* In the case of transfers to pooled income funds for which the valuation date is after April 30, 1999, the present value of a remainder interest is determined under this section. See, however, § 1.7520-3(b) (relating to exceptions to the use of prescribed tables under certain circumstances). The present value of a remainder interest that is dependent on the termination of the life of one individual is computed by the use of Table S in paragraph (e)(6) of this section. For purposes of the computations under this section, the age of an individual is the age at the individual's nearest birthday.

(2) *Transitional rules for valuation of transfers to pooled income funds*—(i) For purposes of sections 2055, 2106, or 2624, if on May 1, 1999, the decedent was mentally incompetent so that the disposition of the property could not be changed, and the decedent died after April 30, 1999, without having regained competency to dispose of the decedent's property, or the decedent died within 90 days of the date that the decedent first regained competency after April 30, 1999,

Reg. § 1.642(c)-6(e)(2)

the present value of a remainder interest is determined as if the valuation date with respect to the decedent's gross estate is either before May 1, 1999, or after April 30, 1999, at the option of the decedent's executor.

(ii) For purposes of sections 170, 2055, 2106, 2522, or 2624, in the case of transfers to a pooled income fund for which the valuation date is after April 30, 1999, and before July 1, 1999, the present value of the remainder interest under this section is determined by use of the section 7520 interest rate for the month in which the valuation date occurs (see §§ 1.7520-1(b) and 1.7520-2(a)(2)) and the appropriate actuarial tables under either paragraph (e)(6) of this section or § 1.642(c)-6A(e)(5), at the option of the donor or the decedent's executor, as the case may be.

(iii) For purposes of paragraphs (e)(2)(i) and (ii) of this section, where the donor or decedent's executor is given the option to use the appropriate actuarial tables under either paragraph (e)(6) of this section or § 1.642(c)-6A(e)(5), the donor or decedent's executor must use the same actuarial table with respect to each individual transaction and with respect to all transfers occurring on the valuation date (for example, gift and income tax charitable deductions with respect to the same transfer must be determined based on the same tables, and all assets includible in the gross estate and/or estate tax deductions claimed must be valued based on the same tables).

(3) *Present value of a remainder interest.* The present value of a remainder interest in property transferred to a pooled income fund is computed on the basis of—

(i) Life contingencies determined from the values of *lx* that are set forth in Table 90CM in § 20.2031-7(d)(7) of this chapter (see § 20.2031-7A of this chapter for certain prior periods); and

(ii) Discount at a rate of interest, compounded annually, equal to the highest yearly rate of return of the pooled income fund for the 3 taxable years immediately preceding its taxable year in which the transfer of property to the fund is made. For purposes of this paragraph (e), the yearly rate of return of a pooled income fund is determined as provided in paragraph (c) of this section unless the highest rate of return is deemed to be the rate described in paragraph (e)(4) of this section for funds in existence less than 3 taxable years. For purposes of this paragraph (e)(3)(ii), the first taxable year of a pooled income fund is considered a taxable year even though the taxable year consists of less than 12 months. However, appropriate adjustments must be made to annualize the rate of return earned by the fund for that period. Where it appears from the facts and circumstances that the highest yearly rate of return of the fund for the 3 taxable years immediately preceding the taxable year in which the transfer of property is made has been purposely manipulated to be substantially less than the rate of return that would otherwise be reasonably anticipated with the purpose of obtaining an excessive charitable deduction, that rate of return may not be used. In that case, the highest yearly rate of return of the fund is determined by treating the fund as a pooled income fund that has been in existence for less than 3 preceding taxable years.

(4) *Pooled income funds in existence less than 3 taxable years.* If a pooled income fund has been in existence less than 3 taxable years immediately preceding the taxable year in which the transfer is made to the fund and the transfer to the fund is made after April 30, 1989, the highest rate of return is deemed to be the interest rate (rounded to the nearest two-tenths of one percent) that is 1 percent less than the highest annual average of the monthly section 7520 rates for the 3 calendar years immediately preceding the calendar year in which the transfer to the pooled income fund is made. The deemed rate of return for transfers to new pooled income funds is recomputed each calendar year using the monthly section 7520 rates for the 3-year period immediately preceding the calendar year in which each transfer to the fund is made until the fund has been in existence for 3 taxable years and can compute its highest rate of return for the 3 taxable years immediately preceding the taxable year in which the transfer of property to the fund is made in accordance with the rules set forth in the first sentence of paragraph (e)(3)(ii) of this section.

(5) *Computation of value of remainder interest.* The factor that is used in determining the present value of a remainder interest that is dependent on the termination of the life of one individual is the factor from Table S in paragraph (e)(6) of this section under the appropriate yearly rate of return opposite the number that corresponds to the age of the individual upon whose life the value of the remainder interest is based (see § 1.642(c)-6A for certain prior periods). The tables in paragraph (e)(6) of this section include factors for yearly rates of return from 4.2 to 14 percent. Many actuarial factors not contained in the tables in paragraph (e)(6) of this section are contained in Table S in Internal Revenue Service Publication 1457, "Actuarial Values, Book Aleph," (7-1999). A copy of this publication is available for purchase from the Superintendent of Documents, United States Government Printing Office, Washington, DC 20402. For other situations, see paragraph (b) of this section. If the yearly rate of

Estates, Trusts, and Beneficiaries 43,223
See p. 20,601 for regulations not amended to reflect law changes

return is a percentage that is between the yearly rates of return for which factors are provided, a linear interpolation must be made. The present value of the remainder interest is determined by multiplying the fair market value of the property on the valuation date by the appropriate remainder factor. This paragraph (e)(5) may be illustrated by the following example:

Example. A, who is 54 years and 8 months, transfers $100,000 to a pooled income fund, and retains a life income interest in the property. The highest yearly rate of return earned by the fund for its 3 preceding taxable years is 9.47 percent. In Table S, the remainder factor opposite 55 years under 9.4 percent is .17449 and under 9.6 percent is .17001. The present value of the remainder interest is $17,292.00, computed as follows:

Factor at 9.4 percent for age 55 17449
Factor at 9.6 percent for age 55 17001
Difference 00448

Interpolation adjustment:

$$\frac{9.47\% - 9.4\%}{0.2\%} = \frac{x}{.00448}$$

$$x = .00157$$

Factor at 9.4 percent for age 55 17449
Less: Interpolation adjustment 00157
Interpolated factor 17292

Present value of remainder interest:

($100,000 × .17292) $17,292.00

(6) *Actuarial tables.* In the case of transfers for which the valuation date is after April 30, 1999, the present value of a remainder interest dependent on the termination of one life in the case of a transfer to a pooled income fund is determined by use of the following Table S:

TABLE S
BASED ON LIFE TABLE 90CM
SINGLE LIFE REMAINDER FACTORS
APPLICABLE AFTER APRIL 30, 1999
INTEREST RATE

AGE	4.2%	4.4%	4.6%	4.8%	5.0%	5.2%	5.4%	5.6%	5.8%	6.0%
0	.06752	.06130	.05586	.05109	.04691	.04322	.03998	.03711	.03458	.03233
1	.06137	.05495	.04932	.04438	.04003	.03620	.03283	.02985	.02721	.02487
2	.06325	.05667	.05088	.04580	.04132	.03737	.03388	.03079	.02806	.02563
3	.06545	.05869	.05275	.04752	.04291	.03883	.03523	.03203	.02920	.02668
4	.06784	.06092	.05482	.04944	.04469	.04048	.03676	.03346	.03052	.02791
5	.07040	.06331	.05705	.05152	.04662	.04229	.03845	.03503	.03199	.02928
6	.07310	.06583	.05941	.05372	.04869	.04422	.04025	.03672	.03357	.03076
7	.07594	.06849	.06191	.05607	.05089	.04628	.04219	.03854	.03528	.03236
8	.07891	.07129	.06453	.05853	.05321	.04846	.04424	.04046	.03709	.03407
9	.08203	.07423	.06731	.06115	.05567	.05079	.04643	.04253	.03904	.03592
10	.08532	.07734	.07024	.06392	.05829	.05326	.04877	.04474	.04114	.03790
11	.08875	.08059	.07331	.06683	.06104	.05587	.05124	.04709	.04336	.04002
12	.09233	.08398	.07653	.06989	.06394	.05862	.05385	.04957	.04572	.04226
13	.09601	.08748	.07985	.07304	.06693	.06146	.05655	.05214	.04816	.04458
14	.09974	.09102	.08322	.07624	.06997	.06435	.05929	.05474	.05064	.04694
15	.10350	.09460	.08661	.07946	.07303	.06725	.06204	.05735	.05312	.04930
16	.10728	.09818	.09001	.08268	.07608	.07014	.06479	.05996	.05559	.05164
17	.11108	.10179	.09344	.08592	.07916	.07306	.06755	.06257	.05807	.05399
18	.11494	.10545	.09691	.08921	.08227	.07601	.07034	.06521	.06057	.05636
19	.11889	.10921	.10047	.09259	.08548	.07904	.07322	.06794	.06315	.05880
20	.12298	.11310	.10417	.09610	.08881	.08220	.07622	.07078	.06584	.06135
21	.12722	.11713	.10801	.09976	.09228	.08550	.07935	.07375	.06866	.06403
22	.13159	.12130	.11199	.10354	.09588	.08893	.08260	.07685	.07160	.06682
23	.13613	.12563	.11612	.10748	.09964	.09250	.08601	.08009	.07468	.06975
24	.14084	.13014	.12043	.11160	.10357	.09625	.08958	.08349	.07793	.07284
25	.14574	.13484	.12493	.11591	.10768	.10018	.09334	.08708	.08135	.07611
26	.15084	.13974	.12963	.12041	.11199	.10431	.09728	.09085	.08496	.07956
27	.15615	.14485	.13454	.12513	.11652	.10865	.10144	.09484	.08878	.08322
28	.16166	.15016	.13965	.13004	.12124	.11319	.10580	.09901	.09279	.08706
29	.16737	.15567	.14497	.13516	.12617	.11792	.11035	.10339	.09699	.09109
30	.17328	.16138	.15048	.14047	.13129	.12286	.11510	.10796	.10138	.09532
31	.17938	.16728	.15618	.14599	.13661	.12799	.12004	.11272	.10597	.09974
32	.18568	.17339	.16210	.15171	.14214	.13333	.12520	.11769	.11076	.10435
33	.19220	.17972	.16824	.15766	.14790	.13889	.13058	.12289	.11578	.10920

Reg. § 1.642(c)-6(e)(6)

TABLE S
BASED ON LIFE TABLE 90CM
SINGLE LIFE REMAINDER FACTORS
APPLICABLE AFTER APRIL 30, 1999

INTEREST RATE

AGE	4.2%	4.4%	4.6%	4.8%	5.0%	5.2%	5.4%	5.6%	5.8%	6.0%
34	.19894	.18627	.17460	.16383	.15388	.14468	.13618	.12831	.12102	.11426
35	.20592	.19307	.18121	.17025	.16011	.15073	.14204	.13399	.12652	.11958
36	.21312	.20010	.18805	.17691	.16658	.15701	.14814	.13990	.13225	.12514
37	.22057	.20737	.19514	.18382	.17331	.16356	.15450	.14608	.13825	.13096
38	.22827	.21490	.20251	.19100	.18031	.17038	.16113	.15253	.14452	.13705
39	.23623	.22270	.21013	.19845	.18759	.17747	.16805	.15927	.15108	.14344
40	.24446	.23078	.21805	.20620	.19516	.18487	.17527	.16631	.15795	.15013
41	.25298	.23915	.22626	.21425	.20305	.19259	.18282	.17368	.16514	.15715
42	.26178	.24782	.23478	.22262	.21125	.20062	.19069	.18138	.17267	.16450
43	.27087	.25678	.24360	.23129	.21977	.20898	.19888	.18941	.18053	.17220
44	.28025	.26603	.25273	.24027	.22860	.21766	.20740	.19777	.18873	.18023
45	.28987	.27555	.26212	.24953	.23772	.22664	.21622	.20644	.19724	.18858
46	.29976	.28533	.27179	.25908	.24714	.23591	.22536	.21542	.20606	.19725
47	.30987	.29535	.28171	.26889	.25682	.24546	.23476	.22468	.21518	.20621
48	.32023	.30563	.29190	.27897	.26678	.25530	.24447	.23425	.22460	.21549
49	.33082	.31615	.30234	.28931	.27702	.26543	.25447	.24412	.23434	.22509
50	.34166	.32694	.31306	.29995	.28756	.27586	.26479	.25432	.24441	.23502
51	.35274	.33798	.32404	.31085	.29838	.28658	.27541	.26482	.25479	.24528
52	.36402	.34924	.33525	.32200	.30946	.29757	.28630	.27561	.26547	.25584
53	.37550	.36070	.34668	.33339	.32078	.30882	.29746	.28667	.27643	.26669
54	.38717	.37237	.35833	.34500	.33234	.32031	.30888	.29801	.28766	.27782
55	.39903	.38424	.37019	.35683	.34413	.33205	.32056	.30961	.29918	.28925
56	.41108	.39631	.38227	.36890	.35617	.34405	.33250	.32149	.31099	.30097
57	.42330	.40857	.39455	.38118	.36844	.35629	.34469	.33363	.32306	.31297
58	.43566	.42098	.40699	.39364	.38089	.36873	.35710	.34600	.33538	.32522
59	.44811	.43351	.41956	.40623	.39350	.38133	.36968	.35855	.34789	.33768
60	.46066	.44613	.43224	.41896	.40624	.39408	.38243	.37127	.36058	.35033
61	.47330	.45887	.44505	.43182	.41914	.40699	.39535	.38418	.37347	.36318
62	.48608	.47175	.45802	.44485	.43223	.42011	.40848	.39732	.38660	.37629
63	.49898	.48478	.47115	.45807	.44550	.43343	.42184	.41069	.39997	.38966
64	.51200	.49793	.48442	.47143	.45895	.44694	.43539	.42427	.41357	.40326
65	.52512	.51121	.49782	.48495	.47255	.46062	.44912	.43805	.42738	.41709
66	.53835	.52461	.51137	.49862	.48634	.47449	.46307	.45206	.44143	.43118
67	.55174	.53818	.52511	.51250	.50034	.48860	.47727	.46633	.45576	.44556
68	.56524	.55188	.53899	.52654	.51452	.50291	.49168	.48083	.47034	.46020
69	.57882	.56568	.55299	.54071	.52885	.51737	.50627	.49552	.48513	.47506
70	.59242	.57951	.56703	.55495	.54325	.53193	.52096	.51034	.50004	.49007
71	.60598	.59332	.58106	.56918	.55767	.54651	.53569	.52520	.51503	.50516
72	.61948	.60707	.59504	.58338	.57206	.56108	.55043	.54009	.53004	.52029
73	.63287	.62073	.60895	.59751	.58640	.57561	.56513	.55495	.54505	.53543
74	.64621	.63435	.62282	.61162	.60073	.59015	.57985	.56984	.56009	.55061
75	.65953	.64796	.63671	.62575	.61510	.60473	.59463	.58480	.57523	.56591
76	.67287	.66160	.65063	.63995	.62954	.61940	.60952	.59989	.59050	.58135
77	.68622	.67526	.66459	.65419	.64404	.63415	.62450	.61509	.60590	.59694
78	.69954	.68892	.67856	.66845	.65858	.64895	.63955	.63036	.62140	.61264
79	.71278	.70250	.69246	.68265	.67308	.66372	.65457	.64563	.63690	.62836
80	.72581	.71588	.70618	.69668	.68740	.67833	.66945	.66077	.65227	.64396
81	.73857	.72899	.71962	.71045	.70147	.69268	.68408	.67566	.66741	.65933
82	.75101	.74178	.73274	.72389	.71522	.70672	.69840	.69024	.68225	.67441
83	.76311	.75423	.74553	.73700	.72864	.72044	.71240	.70451	.69678	.68919
84	.77497	.76645	.75809	.74988	.74183	.73393	.72618	.71857	.71110	.70377
85	.78665	.77848	.77047	.76260	.75487	.74728	.73982	.73250	.72530	.71823
86	.79805	.79025	.78258	.77504	.76764	.76036	.75320	.74617	.73925	.73245
87	.80904	.80159	.79427	.78706	.77998	.77301	.76615	.75940	.75277	.74624
88	.81962	.81251	.80552	.79865	.79188	.78521	.77865	.77220	.76584	.75958
89	.82978	.82302	.81636	.80980	.80335	.79699	.79072	.78455	.77847	.77248
90	.83952	.83309	.82676	.82052	.81437	.80831	.80234	.79645	.79064	.78492
91	.84870	.84260	.83658	.83064	.82479	.81902	.81332	.80771	.80217	.79671

Reg. § 1.642(c)-6(e)(6)

Estates, Trusts, and Beneficiaries 43,225

See p. 20,601 for regulations not amended to reflect law changes

TABLE S
BASED ON LIFE TABLE 90CM
SINGLE LIFE REMAINDER FACTORS
APPLICABLE AFTER APRIL 30, 1999

INTEREST RATE

AGE	4.2%	4.4%	4.6%	4.8%	5.0%	5.2%	5.4%	5.6%	5.8%	6.0%
92	.85716	.85136	.84563	.83998	.83441	.82891	.82348	.81812	.81283	.80761
93	.86494	.85942	.85396	.84858	.84326	.83801	.83283	.82771	.82266	.81767
94	.87216	.86690	.86170	.85657	.85149	.84648	.84153	.83664	.83181	.82704
95	.87898	.87397	.86902	.86412	.85928	.85450	.84977	.84510	.84049	.83592
96	.88537	.88060	.87587	.87121	.86659	.86203	.85751	.85305	.84864	.84427
97	.89127	.88672	.88221	.87775	.87335	.86898	.86467	.86040	.85618	.85200
98	.89680	.89245	.88815	.88389	.87968	.87551	.87138	.86730	.86326	.85926
99	.90217	.89803	.89393	.88987	.88585	.88187	.87793	.87402	.87016	.86633
100	.90738	.90344	.89953	.89567	.89183	.88804	.88428	.88056	.87687	.87322
101	.91250	.90876	.90504	.90137	.89772	.89412	.89054	.88699	.88348	.88000
102	.91751	.91396	.91045	.90696	.90350	.90007	.89668	.89331	.88997	.88666
103	.92247	.91912	.91579	.91249	.90922	.90598	.90276	.89957	.89640	.89326
104	.92775	.92460	.92148	.91839	.91532	.91227	.90924	.90624	.90326	.90031
105	.93290	.92996	.92704	.92415	.92127	.91841	.91558	.91276	.90997	.90719
106	.93948	.93680	.93415	.93151	.92889	.92628	.92370	.92113	.91857	.91604
107	.94739	.94504	.94271	.94039	.93808	.93579	.93351	.93124	.92899	.92675
108	.95950	.95767	.95585	.95404	.95224	.95045	.94867	.94689	.94512	.94336
109	.97985	.97893	.97801	.97710	.97619	.97529	.97438	.97348	.97259	.97170

TABLE S
BASED ON LIFE TABLE 90CM
SINGLE LIFE REMAINDER FACTORS
APPLICABLE AFTER APRIL 30, 1999

INTEREST RATE

AGE	6.2%	6.4%	6.6%	6.8%	7.0%	7.2%	7.4%	7.6%	7.8%	8.0%
0	.03034	.02857	.02700	.02559	.02433	.02321	.02220	.02129	.02047	.01973
1	.02279	.02094	.01929	.01782	.01650	.01533	.01427	.01331	.01246	.01168
2	.02347	.02155	.01983	.01829	.01692	.01569	.01458	.01358	.01268	.01187
3	.02444	.02243	.02065	.01905	.01761	.01632	.01516	.01412	.01317	.01232
4	.02558	.02349	.02163	.01996	.01846	.01712	.01590	.01481	.01382	.01292
5	.02686	.02469	.02275	.02101	.01945	.01804	.01677	.01562	.01458	.01364
6	.02825	.02600	.02398	.02217	.02053	.01906	.01773	.01653	.01544	.01445
7	.02976	.02742	.02532	.02343	.02172	.02019	.01880	.01754	.01640	.01536
8	.03137	.02894	.02675	.02479	.02301	.02140	.01995	.01864	.01744	.01635
9	.03311	.03059	.02832	.02627	.02442	.02274	.02122	.01985	.01859	.01745
10	.03499	.03237	.03001	.02788	.02595	.02420	.02262	.02118	.01987	.01867
11	.03700	.03428	.03183	.02961	.02760	.02578	.02413	.02262	.02125	.02000
12	.03913	.03632	.03377	.03146	.02937	.02748	.02575	.02418	.02275	.02144
13	.04135	.03843	.03579	.03339	.03122	.02924	.02744	.02580	.02431	.02294
14	.04359	.04057	.03783	.03534	.03308	.03102	.02915	.02744	.02587	.02444
15	.04584	.04270	.03986	.03728	.03493	.03279	.03083	.02905	.02742	.02593
16	.04806	.04482	.04187	.03919	.03674	.03452	.03248	.03063	.02892	.02736
17	.05029	.04692	.04387	.04108	.03855	.03623	.03411	.03218	.03040	.02877
18	.05253	.04905	.04588	.04299	.04036	.03795	.03574	.03373	.03187	.03017
19	.05484	.05124	.04796	.04496	.04222	.03972	.03742	.03532	.03339	.03161
20	.05726	.05354	.05013	.04702	.04418	.04158	.03919	.03700	.03498	.03313
21	.05980	.05595	.05242	.04920	.04625	.04354	.04105	.03877	.03667	.03473
22	.06246	.05847	.05482	.05147	.04841	.04559	.04301	.04063	.03844	.03642
23	.06524	.06112	.05734	.05387	.05069	.04777	.04508	.04260	.04032	.03821
24	.06819	.06392	.06001	.05642	.05312	.05008	.04728	.04470	.04232	.04012
25	.07131	.06690	.06285	.05913	.05570	.05255	.04964	.04695	.04447	.04218
26	.07460	.07005	.06586	.06200	.05845	.05518	.05215	.04936	.04677	.04438
27	.07810	.07340	.06907	.06508	.06140	.05800	.05485	.05195	.04925	.04676
28	.08179	.07693	.07246	.06833	.06451	.06098	.05772	.05469	.05189	.04929
29	.08566	.08065	.07603	.07176	.06780	.06414	.06075	.05761	.05469	.05198
30	.08973	.08456	.07978	.07536	.07127	.06748	.06396	.06069	.05766	.05483
31	.09398	.08865	.08372	.07915	.07491	.07098	.06733	.06394	.06078	.05785

Reg. § 1.642(c)-6(e)(6)

43,226 Estates, Trusts, and Beneficiaries

See p. 20,601 for regulations not amended to reflect law changes

TABLE S
BASED ON LIFE TABLE 90CM
SINGLE LIFE REMAINDER FACTORS
APPLICABLE AFTER APRIL 30, 1999

INTEREST RATE

AGE	6.2%	6.4%	6.6%	6.8%	7.0%	7.2%	7.4%	7.6%	7.8%	8.0%
32	.09843	.09294	.08785	.08313	.07875	.07468	.07089	.06737	.06409	.06103
33	.10310	.09745	.09220	.08732	.08279	.07858	.07466	.07100	.06759	.06441
34	.10799	.10217	.09676	.09173	.08705	.08269	.07862	.07483	.07129	.06798
35	.11314	.10715	.10157	.09638	.09155	.08704	.08283	.07890	.07522	.07179
36	.11852	.11236	.10662	.10127	.09628	.09162	.08726	.08319	.07938	.07581
37	.12416	.11783	.11193	.10641	.10126	.09645	.09194	.08772	.08377	.08006
38	.13009	.12359	.11751	.11183	.10652	.10155	.09689	.09253	.08843	.08459
39	.13629	.12962	.12338	.11753	.11206	.10693	.10212	.09761	.09337	.08938
40	.14281	.13597	.12955	.12355	.11791	.11262	.10766	.10299	.09860	.09447
41	.14966	.14264	.13606	.12989	.12409	.11864	.11352	.10870	.10417	.09989
42	.15685	.14966	.14291	.13657	.13061	.12500	.11972	.11475	.11006	.10564
43	.16437	.15702	.15010	.14360	.13747	.13171	.12627	.12115	.11631	.11174
44	.17224	.16472	.15764	.15098	.14469	.13876	.13317	.12789	.12290	.11819
45	.18042	.17274	.16550	.15867	.15223	.14615	.14040	.13496	.12982	.12496
46	.18893	.18110	.17370	.16671	.16011	.15387	.14796	.14238	.13708	.13207
47	.19775	.18975	.18220	.17505	.16830	.16190	.15584	.15010	.14466	.13950
48	.20688	.19873	.19102	.18373	.17682	.17027	.16406	.15817	.15258	.14727
49	.21633	.20804	.20018	.19274	.18568	.17898	.17262	.16658	.16084	.15539
50	.22612	.21769	.20969	.20210	.19490	.18805	.18155	.17536	.16948	.16388
51	.23625	.22769	.21955	.21182	.20448	.19749	.19084	.18452	.17849	.17275
52	.24669	.23799	.22973	.22186	.21438	.20726	.20047	.19400	.18784	.18196
53	.25742	.24861	.24022	.23222	.22461	.21735	.21043	.20383	.19753	.19151
54	.26845	.25952	.25101	.24290	.23516	.22777	.22072	.21399	.20756	.20140
55	.27978	.27074	.26212	.25389	.24604	.23853	.23136	.22450	.21793	.21166
56	.29140	.28227	.27355	.26522	.25725	.24963	.24233	.23535	.22867	.22227
57	.30333	.29411	.28529	.27686	.26879	.26106	.25365	.24656	.23976	.23324
58	.31551	.30621	.29731	.28878	.28061	.27278	.26528	.25807	.25116	.24453
59	.32790	.31854	.30956	.30095	.29269	.28477	.27716	.26986	.26284	.25610
60	.34050	.33107	.32202	.31334	.30500	.29699	.28929	.28190	.27478	.26794
61	.35331	.34384	.33473	.32598	.31757	.30948	.30170	.29422	.28701	.28007
62	.36639	.35688	.34772	.33892	.33044	.32229	.31443	.30687	.29958	.29255
63	.37974	.37020	.36101	.35216	.34363	.33542	.32750	.31986	.31250	.30539
64	.39334	.38378	.37456	.36568	.35711	.34884	.34087	.33317	.32574	.31857
65	.40718	.39761	.38838	.37947	.37087	.36257	.35455	.34681	.33932	.33208
66	.42128	.41172	.40249	.39357	.38496	.37663	.36858	.36079	.35326	.34597
67	.43569	.42616	.41694	.40803	.39941	.39107	.38299	.37518	.36761	.36028
68	.45038	.44089	.43170	.42281	.41419	.40585	.39777	.38994	.38235	.37499
69	.46531	.45587	.44672	.43786	.42927	.42094	.41286	.40503	.39743	.39006
70	.48040	.47103	.46194	.45312	.44456	.43626	.42820	.42038	.41278	.40540
71	.49558	.48629	.47727	.46851	.46000	.45174	.44371	.43591	.42832	.42095
72	.51082	.50162	.49268	.48399	.47554	.46733	.45934	.45157	.44401	.43666
73	.52607	.51697	.50813	.49952	.49114	.48299	.47506	.46733	.45981	.45249
74	.54139	.53241	.52367	.51515	.50686	.49879	.49092	.48325	.47578	.46849
75	.55683	.54798	.53936	.53095	.52276	.51477	.50698	.49938	.49197	.48474
76	.57243	.56373	.55524	.54696	.53888	.53100	.52330	.51579	.50846	.50130
77	.58819	.57965	.57132	.56318	.55523	.54747	.53988	.53247	.52523	.51815
78	.60408	.59572	.58755	.57957	.57177	.56414	.55668	.54939	.54225	.53527
79	.62001	.61184	.60385	.59604	.58840	.58092	.57360	.56644	.55943	.55256
80	.63582	.62786	.62007	.61244	.60497	.59765	.59048	.58347	.57659	.56985
81	.65142	.64367	.63608	.62864	.62135	.61421	.60721	.60034	.59361	.58701
82	.66673	.65920	.65182	.64458	.63748	.63052	.62368	.61698	.61041	.60395
83	.68175	.67444	.66728	.66024	.65334	.64656	.63991	.63338	.62696	.62066
84	.69657	.68950	.68256	.67574	.66904	.66246	.65599	.64964	.64340	.63727
85	.71128	.70446	.69775	.69116	.68467	.67830	.67204	.66587	.65982	.65386
86	.72576	.71919	.71272	.70636	.70010	.69394	.68789	.68193	.67606	.67029
87	.73981	.73349	.72726	.72114	.71511	.70917	.70333	.69757	.69190	.68632
88	.75342	.74735	.74137	.73548	.72968	.72396	.71833	.71279	.70732	.70194
89	.76658	.76076	.75503	.74938	.74381	.73832	.73290	.72757	.72231	.71712
90	.77928	.77371	.76823	.76281	.75748	.75221	.74702	.74190	.73684	.73186

Reg. § 1.642(c)-6(e)(6)

Estates, Trusts, and Beneficiaries   **43,227**

See p. 20,601 for regulations not amended to reflect law changes

TABLE S
BASED ON LIFE TABLE 90CM
SINGLE LIFE REMAINDER FACTORS
APPLICABLE AFTER APRIL 30, 1999

INTEREST RATE

AGE	6.2%	6.4%	6.6%	6.8%	7.0%	7.2%	7.4%	7.6%	7.8%	8.0%
91	.79131	.78600	.78075	.77557	.77046	.76542	.76044	.75553	.75068	.74589
92	.80246	.79737	.79235	.78740	.78250	.77767	.77290	.76818	.76353	.75893
93	.81274	.80788	.80307	.79832	.79363	.78899	.78441	.77989	.77542	.77100
94	.82232	.81766	.81306	.80850	.80401	.79956	.79517	.79082	.78653	.78228
95	.83141	.82695	.82254	.81818	.81387	.80961	.80539	.80122	.79710	.79302
96	.83996	.83569	.83147	.82729	.82316	.81907	.81503	.81103	.80707	.80315
97	.84787	.84378	.83973	.83573	.83176	.82784	.82396	.82012	.81632	.81255
98	.85530	.85138	.84750	.84366	.83985	.83609	.83236	.82867	.82502	.82140
99	.86255	.85880	.85508	.85140	.84776	.84415	.84057	.83703	.83353	.83005
100	.86960	.86601	.86246	.85894	.85546	.85200	.84858	.84519	.84183	.83849
101	.87655	.87313	.86974	.86638	.86305	.85975	.85648	.85324	.85003	.84684
102	.88338	.88012	.87689	.87369	.87052	.86738	.86426	.86116	.85809	.85505
103	.89015	.88706	.88399	.88095	.87793	.87494	.87197	.86903	.86611	.86321
104	.89737	.89446	.89157	.88871	.88586	.88304	.88024	.87745	.87469	.87195
105	.90443	.90170	.89898	.89628	.89360	.89094	.88830	.88568	.88307	.88049
106	.91351	.91101	.90852	.90605	.90359	.90115	.89873	.89632	.89392	.89154
107	.92452	.92230	.92010	.91791	.91573	.91356	.91141	.90927	.90714	.90502
108	.94161	.93987	.93814	.93641	.93469	.93298	.93128	.92958	.92790	.92622
109	.97081	.96992	.96904	.96816	.96729	.96642	.96555	.96468	.96382	.96296

TABLE S
BASED ON LIFE TABLE 90CM
SINGLE LIFE REMAINDER FACTORS
APPLICABLE AFTER APRIL 30, 1999

INTEREST RATE

AGE	8.2%	8.4%	8.6%	8.8%	9.0%	9.2%	9.4%	9.6%	9.8%	10.0%
0	.01906	.01845	.01790	.01740	.01694	.01652	.01613	.01578	.01546	.01516
1	.01098	.01034	.00977	.00924	.00876	.00833	.00793	.00756	.00722	.00691
2	.01113	.01046	.00986	.00930	.00880	.00834	.00791	.00753	.00717	.00684
3	.01155	.01084	.01020	.00962	.00909	.00860	.00816	.00775	.00737	.00702
4	.01211	.01137	.01069	.01008	.00952	.00900	.00853	.00810	.00770	.00733
5	.01279	.01201	.01130	.01065	.01006	.00952	.00902	.00856	.00814	.00775
6	.01356	.01274	.01199	.01131	.01068	.01011	.00959	.00910	.00865	.00824
7	.01442	.01356	.01277	.01205	.01140	.01079	.01023	.00972	.00925	.00881
8	.01536	.01446	.01363	.01287	.01218	.01154	.01096	.01041	.00991	.00945
9	.01641	.01546	.01460	.01380	.01307	.01240	.01178	.01120	.01068	.01019
10	.01758	.01659	.01567	.01484	.01407	.01336	.01270	.01210	.01154	.01103
11	.01886	.01781	.01686	.01598	.01517	.01442	.01373	.01310	.01251	.01196
12	.02024	.01915	.01814	.01721	.01636	.01558	.01485	.01419	.01357	.01299
13	.02168	.02054	.01948	.01851	.01762	.01679	.01603	.01533	.01467	.01407
14	.02313	.02193	.02083	.01981	.01887	.01801	.01721	.01646	.01578	.01514
15	.02456	.02330	.02214	.02107	.02009	.01918	.01834	.01756	.01684	.01617
16	.02593	.02462	.02340	.02229	.02126	.02030	.01942	.01860	.01785	.01714
17	.02728	.02590	.02463	.02346	.02238	.02138	.02046	.01960	.01880	.01806
18	.02861	.02717	.02584	.02462	.02348	.02243	.02146	.02056	.01972	.01894
19	.02998	.02847	.02708	.02580	.02461	.02351	.02249	.02154	.02066	.01984
20	.03142	.02984	.02839	.02704	.02580	.02465	.02357	.02258	.02165	.02079
21	.03295	.03130	.02978	.02837	.02706	.02585	.02473	.02368	.02271	.02180
22	.03455	.03283	.03124	.02976	.02839	.02712	.02594	.02484	.02382	.02286
23	.03626	.03446	.03279	.03124	.02981	.02847	.02723	.02608	.02500	.02400
24	.03809	.03620	.03446	.03283	.03133	.02993	.02863	.02741	.02628	.02522
25	.04005	.03808	.03625	.03456	.03298	.03151	.03014	.02887	.02768	.02656
26	.04216	.04010	.03819	.03641	.03476	.03322	.03178	.03044	.02919	.02802
27	.04444	.04229	.04029	.03843	.03670	.03508	.03357	.03217	.03085	.02962
28	.04687	.04463	.04254	.04059	.03877	.03708	.03550	.03402	.03263	.03133
29	.04946	.04712	.04493	.04289	.04099	.03922	.03756	.03600	.03455	.03318
30	.05221	.04976	.04748	.04534	.04335	.04149	.03975	.03812	.03659	.03515

Reg. § 1.642(c)-6(e)(6)

43,228 Estates, Trusts, and Beneficiaries

See p. 20,601 for regulations not amended to reflect law changes

TABLE S
BASED ON LIFE TABLE 90CM
SINGLE LIFE REMAINDER FACTORS
APPLICABLE AFTER APRIL 30, 1999

INTEREST RATE

AGE	8.2%	8.4%	8.6%	8.8%	9.0%	9.2%	9.4%	9.6%	9.8%	10.0%
31	.05511	.05255	.05017	.04794	.04585	.04390	.04208	.04037	.03876	.03725
32	.05818	.05551	.05302	.05069	.04851	.04647	.04455	.04276	.04107	.03948
33	.06144	.05866	.05606	.05363	.05135	.04921	.04720	.04532	.04355	.04188
34	.06489	.06200	.05928	.05674	.05436	.05212	.05002	.04805	.04619	.04444
35	.06857	.06555	.06273	.06007	.05758	.05524	.05304	.05097	.04902	.04718
36	.07246	.06932	.06638	.06361	.06101	.05856	.05626	.05409	.05205	.05012
37	.07659	.07332	.07025	.06737	.06466	.06210	.05969	.05742	.05528	.05325
38	.08098	.07758	.07439	.07138	.06855	.06588	.06336	.06099	.05874	.05662
39	.08563	.08210	.07878	.07565	.07270	.06992	.06729	.06480	.06245	.06023
40	.09059	.08692	.08347	.08021	.07714	.07423	.07149	.06889	.06643	.06411
41	.09586	.09206	.08848	.08509	.08189	.07886	.07600	.07329	.07072	.06828
42	.10147	.09753	.09381	.09029	.08696	.08381	.08083	.07800	.07531	.07277
43	.10742	.10334	.09948	.09583	.09237	.08909	.08598	.08304	.08024	.07758
44	.11373	.10950	.10551	.10172	.09813	.09472	.09148	.08841	.08549	.08272
45	.12035	.11599	.11185	.10792	.10420	.10066	.09730	.09410	.09106	.08817
46	.12732	.12281	.11853	.11447	.11061	.10694	.10345	.10013	.09696	.09395
47	.13460	.12995	.12553	.12133	.11733	.11353	.10991	.10646	.10317	.10004
48	.14223	.13743	.13287	.12853	.12439	.12046	.11671	.11313	.10972	.10646
49	.15020	.14526	.14056	.13608	.13181	.12774	.12385	.12015	.11661	.11322
50	.15855	.15347	.14862	.14401	.13960	.13540	.13138	.12754	.12388	.12037
51	.16727	.16205	.15707	.15232	.14777	.14344	.13929	.13532	.13153	.12789
52	.17634	.17098	.16587	.16097	.15630	.15183	.14755	.14345	.13953	.13577
53	.18576	.18027	.17501	.16999	.16518	.16057	.15616	.15194	.14789	.14400
54	.19552	.18990	.18451	.17935	.17441	.16968	.16514	.16078	.15661	.15260
55	.20564	.19989	.19437	.18908	.18402	.17915	.17449	.17001	.16571	.16157
56	.21613	.21025	.20461	.19919	.19400	.18901	.18422	.17962	.17519	.17093
57	.22698	.22098	.21522	.20968	.20436	.19925	.19434	.18961	.18507	.18069
58	.23816	.23204	.22616	.22051	.21507	.20984	.20481	.19996	.19530	.19080
59	.24962	.24339	.23740	.23163	.22608	.22073	.21558	.21062	.20584	.20123
60	.26136	.25502	.24892	.24304	.23738	.23192	.22666	.22158	.21669	.21196
61	.27339	.26695	.26075	.25477	.24900	.24343	.23806	.23288	.22787	.22304
62	.28578	.27925	.27295	.26687	.26100	.25533	.24985	.24456	.23945	.23451
63	.29854	.29192	.28553	.27935	.27339	.26762	.26205	.25666	.25145	.24641
64	.31164	.30494	.29846	.29221	.28615	.28030	.27463	.26915	.26384	.25870
65	.32508	.31831	.31177	.30543	.29930	.29336	.28761	.28203	.27663	.27140
66	.33891	.33208	.32547	.31906	.31285	.30684	.30101	.29536	.28987	.28456
67	.35318	.34630	.33963	.33316	.32689	.32081	.31491	.30918	.30363	.29823
68	.36785	.36093	.35422	.34770	.34138	.33524	.32928	.32349	.31787	.31240
69	.38290	.37595	.36920	.36265	.35628	.35009	.34408	.33824	.33256	.32703
70	.39823	.39127	.38450	.37791	.37151	.36529	.35924	.35335	.34762	.34204
71	.41378	.40681	.40003	.39343	.38701	.38076	.37467	.36875	.36298	.35736
72	.42950	.42253	.41575	.40914	.40271	.39644	.39034	.38438	.37858	.37293
73	.44535	.43840	.43162	.42502	.41858	.41231	.40619	.40022	.39440	.38872
74	.46139	.45446	.44771	.44112	.43469	.42842	.42230	.41632	.41049	.40479
75	.47769	.47080	.46408	.45752	.45111	.44485	.43874	.43277	.42693	.42123
76	.49430	.48747	.48079	.47427	.46790	.46167	.45558	.44963	.44380	.43811
77	.51123	.50447	.49786	.49139	.48506	.47888	.47282	.46690	.46111	.45543
78	.52845	.52177	.51523	.50884	.50257	.49645	.49044	.48457	.47881	.47317
79	.54584	.53926	.53282	.52650	.52032	.51426	.50833	.50251	.49681	.49122
80	.56325	.55678	.55044	.54423	.53813	.53216	.52630	.52056	.51492	.50939
81	.58054	.57419	.56797	.56186	.55587	.54999	.54422	.53856	.53300	.52754
82	.59762	.59140	.58530	.57931	.57343	.56766	.56198	.55641	.55094	.54557
83	.61448	.60840	.60243	.59657	.59081	.58515	.57958	.57411	.56874	.56346
84	.63124	.62531	.61949	.61376	.60813	.60259	.59715	.59179	.58652	.58134
85	.64800	.64224	.63657	.63099	.62550	.62010	.61478	.60955	.60441	.59934
86	.66461	.65902	.65351	.64810	.64276	.63751	.63233	.62724	.62222	.61728
87	.68083	.67541	.67008	.66483	.65965	.65455	.64953	.64458	.63970	.63489
88	.69663	.69140	.68624	.68116	.67615	.67121	.66634	.66154	.65680	.65213
89	.71201	.70696	.70199	.69708	.69224	.68747	.68276	.67811	.67353	.66900

Reg. § 1.642(c)-6(e)(6)

Estates, Trusts, and Beneficiaries

See p. 20,601 for regulations not amended to reflect law changes

TABLE S
BASED ON LIFE TABLE 90CM
SINGLE LIFE REMAINDER FACTORS
APPLICABLE AFTER APRIL 30, 1999

INTEREST RATE

AGE	8.2%	8.4%	8.6%	8.8%	9.0%	9.2%	9.4%	9.6%	9.8%	10.0%
90	.72694	.72209	.71730	.71257	.70791	.70330	.69876	.69427	.68984	.68547
91	.74117	.73650	.73190	.72735	.72286	.71842	.71404	.70972	.70545	.70123
92	.75439	.74991	.74548	.74110	.73678	.73251	.72829	.72412	.72000	.71593
93	.76664	.76233	.75806	.75385	.74969	.74557	.74150	.73748	.73350	.72957
94	.77809	.77394	.76983	.76578	.76177	.75780	.75388	.75000	.74616	.74237
95	.78899	.78500	.78106	.77715	.77329	.76947	.76569	.76195	.75826	.75460
96	.79928	.79544	.79165	.78790	.78418	.78050	.77686	.77326	.76970	.76617
97	.80883	.80514	.80149	.79787	.79430	.79075	.78725	.78377	.78033	.77693
98	.81781	.81427	.81075	.80727	.80382	.80041	.79703	.79368	.79036	.78708
99	.82661	.82320	.81982	.81648	.81316	.80988	.80662	.80340	.80020	.79704
100	.83519	.83192	.82868	.82547	.82228	.81913	.81600	.81290	.80982	.80678
101	.84368	.84055	.83744	.83437	.83131	.82829	.82529	.82231	.81936	.81643
102	.85203	.84904	.84607	.84313	.84021	.83731	.83444	.83159	.82876	.82596
103	.86034	.85748	.85465	.85184	.84906	.84629	.84355	.84082	.83812	.83544
104	.86923	.86653	.86385	.86119	.85855	.85593	.85333	.85074	.84818	.84563
105	.87792	.87537	.87283	.87032	.86782	.86534	.86287	.86042	.85799	.85557
106	.88918	.88683	.88450	.88218	.87987	.87758	.87530	.87304	.87079	.86855
107	.90291	.90082	.89873	.89666	.89460	.89255	.89051	.88849	.88647	.88447
108	.92455	.92288	.92123	.91958	.91794	.91630	.91468	.91306	.91145	.90984
109	.96211	.96125	.96041	.95956	.95872	.95788	.95704	.95620	.95537	.95455

TABLE S
BASED ON LIFE TABLE 90CM
SINGLE LIFE REMAINDER FACTORS
APPLICABLE AFTER APRIL 30, 1999

INTEREST RATE

AGE	10.2%	10.4%	10.6%	10.8%	11.0%	11.2%	11.4%	11.6%	11.8%	12.0%
0	.01488	.01463	.01439	.01417	.01396	.01377	.01359	.01343	.01327	.01312
1	.00662	.00636	.00612	.00589	.00568	.00548	.00530	.00513	.00497	.00482
2	.00654	.00626	.00600	.00576	.00554	.00533	.00514	.00496	.00479	.00463
3	.00670	.00641	.00613	.00588	.00564	.00542	.00522	.00502	.00484	.00468
4	.00699	.00668	.00639	.00612	.00587	.00563	.00542	.00521	.00502	.00484
5	.00739	.00706	.00675	.00646	.00620	.00595	.00571	.00550	.00529	.00510
6	.00786	.00751	.00718	.00687	.00659	.00633	.00608	.00585	.00563	.00543
7	.00841	.00803	.00769	.00736	.00706	.00678	.00652	.00627	.00604	.00582
8	.00902	.00863	.00826	.00791	.00759	.00730	.00702	.00675	.00651	.00628
9	.00973	.00931	.00892	.00856	.00822	.00790	.00760	.00733	.00706	.00682
10	.01055	.01010	.00969	.00930	.00894	.00861	.00829	.00799	.00772	.00746
11	.01146	.01099	.01055	.01014	.00976	.00940	.00907	.00875	.00846	.00818
12	.01246	.01196	.01150	.01106	.01066	.01028	.00993	.00960	.00928	.00899
13	.01351	.01298	.01249	.01204	.01161	.01121	.01084	.01049	.01016	.00985
14	.01455	.01400	.01348	.01300	.01255	.01213	.01173	.01136	.01102	.01069
15	.01555	.01497	.01443	.01392	.01345	.01300	.01259	.01220	.01183	.01148
16	.01648	.01587	.01530	.01477	.01427	.01380	.01336	.01295	.01257	.01220
17	.01737	.01673	.01612	.01556	.01504	.01455	.01408	.01365	.01324	.01286
18	.01822	.01754	.01691	.01632	.01576	.01525	.01476	.01430	.01387	.01347
19	.01908	.01837	.01770	.01708	.01650	.01595	.01544	.01495	.01450	.01407
20	.01999	.01924	.01854	.01788	.01726	.01669	.01615	.01564	.01516	.01471
21	.02096	.02017	.01943	.01874	.01809	.01748	.01691	.01637	.01586	.01539
22	.02197	.02114	.02036	.01963	.01895	.01830	.01770	.01713	.01660	.01610
23	.02306	.02218	.02136	.02059	.01987	.01919	.01855	.01795	.01739	.01686
24	.02424	.02331	.02245	.02163	.02087	.02016	.01948	.01885	.01825	.01769
25	.02552	.02455	.02364	.02278	.02197	.02122	.02051	.01984	.01920	.01861
26	.02692	.02589	.02493	.02403	.02318	.02238	.02162	.02091	.02025	.01961
27	.02846	.02738	.02636	.02541	.02451	.02367	.02287	.02212	.02141	.02074
28	.03012	.02898	.02791	.02690	.02595	.02506	.02422	.02342	.02267	.02196
29	.03190	.03070	.02957	.02851	.02751	.02656	.02567	.02483	.02404	.02329

Reg. § 1.642(c)-6(e)(6)

43,230 Estates, Trusts, and Beneficiaries

See p. 20,601 for regulations not amended to reflect law changes

TABLE S
BASED ON LIFE TABLE 90CM
SINGLE LIFE REMAINDER FACTORS
APPLICABLE AFTER APRIL 30, 1999

INTEREST RATE

AGE	10.2%	10.4%	10.6%	10.8%	11.0%	11.2%	11.4%	11.6%	11.8%	12.0%
30	.03381	.03254	.03135	.03023	.02917	.02817	.02723	.02634	.02551	.02471
31	.03583	.03450	.03324	.03206	.03094	.02989	.02890	.02796	.02707	.02623
32	.03799	.03659	.03527	.03402	.03284	.03173	.03068	.02968	.02874	.02785
33	.04031	.03883	.03744	.03612	.03488	.03371	.03260	.03155	.03055	.02961
34	.04279	.04123	.03976	.03838	.03707	.03583	.03465	.03354	.03249	.03149
35	.04545	.04382	.04227	.04081	.03943	.03812	.03688	.03571	.03459	.03354
36	.04830	.04658	.04495	.04341	.04196	.04058	.03927	.03803	.03685	.03573
37	.05134	.04953	.04782	.04620	.04467	.04321	.04183	.04052	.03928	.03809
38	.05462	.05272	.05092	.04921	.04760	.04606	.04461	.04322	.04191	.04066
39	.05812	.05613	.05424	.05245	.05075	.04913	.04760	.04614	.04475	.04343
40	.06190	.05981	.05782	.05594	.05415	.05245	.05083	.04929	.04783	.04643
41	.06597	.06378	.06170	.05972	.05784	.05605	.05435	.05272	.05118	.04970
42	.07035	.06806	.06587	.06380	.06182	.05994	.05815	.05644	.05481	.05326
43	.07505	.07265	.07036	.06818	.06611	.06414	.06225	.06045	.05874	.05710
44	.08008	.07757	.07518	.07290	.07072	.06865	.06667	.06478	.06298	.06125
45	.08542	.08279	.08029	.07791	.07563	.07346	.07138	.06940	.06750	.06569
46	.09108	.08834	.08573	.08324	.08085	.07858	.07640	.07432	.07233	.07043
47	.09705	.09419	.09147	.08886	.08637	.08399	.08172	.07954	.07745	.07545
48	.10335	.10038	.09754	.09482	.09222	.08973	.08735	.08507	.08288	.08078
49	.10999	.10690	.10394	.10111	.09840	.09581	.09332	.09093	.08864	.08644
50	.11701	.11380	.11073	.10778	.10496	.10225	.09965	.09716	.09477	.09247
51	.12441	.12108	.11789	.11482	.11189	.10907	.10636	.10376	.10126	.09886
52	.13217	.12871	.12540	.12222	.11916	.11623	.11341	.11071	.10810	.10560
53	.14028	.13670	.13327	.12997	.12680	.12375	.12082	.11801	.11529	.11268
54	.14875	.14505	.14150	.13808	.13480	.13163	.12859	.12566	.12284	.12012
55	.15760	.15378	.15011	.14657	.14317	.13989	.13674	.13370	.13077	.12794
56	.16684	.16290	.15911	.15546	.15194	.14855	.14528	.14213	.13909	.13615
57	.17648	.17242	.16851	.16474	.16111	.15760	.15422	.15096	.14781	.14477
58	.18647	.18229	.17827	.17438	.17064	.16702	.16353	.16015	.15689	.15374
59	.19678	.19249	.18835	.18435	.18049	.17676	.17316	.16968	.16631	.16305
60	.20740	.20300	.19875	.19464	.19066	.18682	.18311	.17952	.17604	.17268
61	.21837	.21385	.20949	.20527	.20119	.19724	.19341	.18971	.18613	.18266
62	.22973	.22511	.22064	.21631	.21212	.20807	.20414	.20033	.19664	.19306
63	.24152	.23680	.23222	.22779	.22350	.21934	.21530	.21139	.20760	.20392
64	.25372	.24890	.24422	.23969	.23529	.23103	.22690	.22289	.21899	.21521
65	.26633	.26141	.25664	.25201	.24752	.24316	.23893	.23482	.23083	.22695
66	.27940	.27439	.26953	.26481	.26023	.25577	.25145	.24724	.24316	.23918
67	.29299	.28790	.28296	.27815	.27348	.26894	.26453	.26024	.25606	.25200
68	.30709	.30193	.29691	.29202	.28728	.28265	.27816	.27378	.26952	.26537
69	.32166	.31643	.31134	.30639	.30157	.29687	.29230	.28785	.28351	.27928
70	.33661	.33133	.32618	.32116	.31628	.31152	.30688	.30235	.29794	.29364
71	.35188	.34654	.34134	.33627	.33133	.32651	.32181	.31722	.31275	.30838
72	.36742	.36204	.35679	.35168	.34668	.34181	.33706	.33241	.32788	.32345
73	.38317	.37776	.37248	.36733	.36229	.35738	.35257	.34788	.34330	.33882
74	.39923	.39380	.38849	.38330	.37823	.37328	.36844	.36370	.35908	.35455
75	.41566	.41021	.40489	.39968	.39459	.38961	.38474	.37997	.37531	.37074
76	.43254	.42709	.42176	.41655	.41144	.40645	.40156	.39677	.39208	.38749
77	.44988	.44444	.43912	.43391	.42880	.42380	.41891	.41411	.40940	.40479
78	.46765	.46224	.45694	.45174	.44665	.44166	.43677	.43197	.42726	.42265
79	.48574	.48037	.47510	.46993	.46487	.45990	.45502	.45024	.44554	.44094
80	.50397	.49865	.49343	.48830	.48327	.47834	.47349	.46873	.46406	.45947
81	.52219	.51693	.51176	.50669	.50171	.49682	.49201	.48729	.48265	.47809
82	.54029	.53510	.53000	.52499	.52007	.51523	.51047	.50580	.50120	.49667
83	.55826	.55315	.54813	.54319	.53834	.53356	.52886	.52424	.51969	.51522
84	.57624	.57123	.56629	.56144	.55666	.55195	.54732	.54277	.53828	.53386
85	.59435	.58944	.58460	.57984	.57516	.57054	.56599	.56151	.55710	.55275
86	.61241	.60762	.60289	.59824	.59365	.58913	.58468	.58029	.57596	.57170
87	.63015	.62548	.62087	.61633	.61185	.60744	.60309	.59880	.59456	.59039
88	.64753	.64299	.63851	.63409	.62973	.62543	.62118	.61700	.61287	.60879

Reg. § 1.642(c)-6(e)(6)

Estates, Trusts, and Beneficiaries

See p. 20,601 for regulations not amended to reflect law changes

43,231

TABLE S
BASED ON LIFE TABLE 90CM
SINGLE LIFE REMAINDER FACTORS
APPLICABLE AFTER APRIL 30, 1999

INTEREST RATE

AGE	10.2%	10.4%	10.6%	10.8%	11.0%	11.2%	11.4%	11.6%	11.8%	12.0%
89	.66454	.66013	.65579	.65150	.64726	.64308	.63895	.63488	.63086	.62689
90	.68115	.67689	.67268	.66853	.66442	.66037	.65637	.65241	.64851	.64465
91	.69706	.69294	.68887	.68486	.68089	.67696	.67309	.66925	.66547	.66173
92	.71190	.70792	.70399	.70011	.69627	.69247	.68872	.68501	.68134	.67771
93	.72569	.72184	.71804	.71429	.71057	.70689	.70326	.69967	.69611	.69259
94	.73861	.73490	.73123	.72759	.72400	.72044	.71692	.71344	.71000	.70659
95	.75097	.74739	.74384	.74033	.73686	.73342	.73002	.72665	.72331	.72001
96	.76267	.75922	.75579	.75240	.74905	.74572	.74243	.73917	.73595	.73275
97	.77356	.77022	.76691	.76363	.76039	.75718	.75399	.75084	.74772	.74463
98	.78382	.78059	.77740	.77423	.77110	.76799	.76491	.76186	.75884	.75584
99	.79390	.79079	.78771	.78465	.78162	.77862	.77565	.77270	.76978	.76688
100	.80376	.80076	.79779	.79485	.79193	.78904	.78617	.78333	.78051	.77771
101	.81353	.81066	.80780	.80497	.80217	.79938	.79662	.79388	.79117	.78847
102	.82318	.82042	.81768	.81496	.81227	.80960	.80694	.80431	.80170	.79911
103	.83278	.83014	.82752	.82491	.82233	.81977	.81723	.81470	.81220	.80971
104	.84310	.84059	.83810	.83563	.83317	.83073	.82831	.82591	.82352	.82115
105	.85318	.85079	.84843	.84607	.84374	.84142	.83911	.83682	.83455	.83229
106	.86633	.86413	.86193	.85975	.85758	.85543	.85329	.85116	.84904	.84694
107	.88247	.88049	.87852	.87656	.87460	.87266	.87073	.86881	.86690	.86500
108	.90825	.90666	.90507	.90350	.90193	.90037	.89881	.89727	.89572	.89419
109	.95372	.95290	.95208	.95126	.95045	.94964	.94883	.94803	.94723	.94643

TABLE S
BASED ON LIFE TABLE 90CM
SINGLE LIFE REMAINDER FACTORS
APPLICABLE AFTER APRIL 30, 1999

INTEREST RATE

AGE	12.2%	12.4%	12.6%	12.8%	13.0%	13.2%	13.4%	13.6%	13.8%	14.0%
0	.01298	.01285	.01273	.01261	.01250	.01240	.01230	.01221	.01212	.01203
1	.00468	.00455	.00443	.00431	.00420	.00410	.00400	.00391	.00382	.00374
2	.00448	.00435	.00421	.00409	.00398	.00387	.00376	.00366	.00357	.00348
3	.00452	.00437	.00423	.00410	.00398	.00386	.00375	.00365	.00355	.00345
4	.00468	.00452	.00437	.00423	.00410	.00397	.00386	.00375	.00364	.00354
5	.00493	.00476	.00460	.00445	.00431	.00418	.00405	.00393	.00382	.00371
6	.00524	.00506	.00489	.00473	.00458	.00444	.00430	.00418	.00406	.00394
7	.00562	.00543	.00525	.00508	.00492	.00477	.00462	.00449	.00436	.00423
8	.00606	.00586	.00566	.00548	.00531	.00515	.00499	.00485	.00471	.00458
9	.00659	.00637	.00616	.00597	.00579	.00561	.00545	.00529	.00514	.00500
10	.00721	.00698	.00676	.00655	.00636	.00617	.00600	.00583	.00567	.00552
11	.00792	.00767	.00744	.00722	.00701	.00682	.00663	.00645	.00628	.00612
12	.00871	.00845	.00820	.00797	.00775	.00754	.00735	.00716	.00698	.00681
13	.00955	.00928	.00902	.00877	.00854	.00831	.00810	.00790	.00771	.00753
14	.01038	.01009	.00981	.00955	.00930	.00907	.00885	.00864	.00843	.00824
15	.01116	.01085	.01056	.01028	.01002	.00977	.00954	.00932	.00910	.00890
16	.01186	.01153	.01123	.01094	.01066	.01040	.01015	.00992	.00969	.00948
17	.01250	.01215	.01183	.01152	.01124	.01096	.01070	.01045	.01022	.00999
18	.01308	.01272	.01238	.01206	.01175	.01147	.01119	.01093	.01068	.01044
19	.01367	.01329	.01293	.01259	.01227	.01196	.01167	.01140	.01113	.01088
20	.01428	.01388	.01350	.01314	.01280	.01248	.01217	.01188	.01161	.01134
21	.01494	.01451	.01411	.01373	.01337	.01303	.01271	.01240	.01211	.01183
22	.01562	.01517	.01475	.01435	.01397	.01361	.01326	.01294	.01263	.01233
23	.01635	.01588	.01543	.01501	.01460	.01422	.01386	.01351	.01319	.01287
24	.01716	.01665	.01618	.01573	.01530	.01489	.01451	.01415	.01380	.01347
25	.01804	.01751	.01701	.01653	.01608	.01565	.01524	.01485	.01448	.01413
26	.01902	.01845	.01792	.01741	.01693	.01648	.01604	.01563	.01524	.01487
27	.02011	.01951	.01895	.01841	.01790	.01742	.01696	.01652	.01610	.01571
28	.02129	.02066	.02006	.01949	.01895	.01844	.01795	.01748	.01704	.01662

Reg. § 1.642(c)-6(e)(6)

43,232   Estates, Trusts, and Beneficiaries

See p. 20,601 for regulations not amended to reflect law changes

TABLE S
BASED ON LIFE TABLE 90CM
SINGLE LIFE REMAINDER FACTORS
APPLICABLE AFTER APRIL 30, 1999

INTEREST RATE

AGE	12.2%	12.4%	12.6%	12.8%	13.0%	13.2%	13.4%	13.6%	13.8%	14.0%
29	.02258	.02191	.02127	.02067	.02009	.01955	.01903	.01853	.01806	.01762
30	.02396	.02325	.02257	.02193	.02132	.02074	.02019	.01966	.01916	.01869
31	.02543	.02467	.02396	.02328	.02263	.02201	.02143	.02087	.02034	.01983
32	.02701	.02621	.02545	.02472	.02404	.02338	.02276	.02217	.02160	.02106
33	.02871	.02786	.02706	.02629	.02556	.02487	.02420	.02357	.02297	.02240
34	.03054	.02964	.02879	.02797	.02720	.02646	.02576	.02509	.02445	.02383
35	.03253	.03158	.03067	.02981	.02898	.02820	.02745	.02674	.02606	.02541
36	.03467	.03366	.03269	.03178	.03090	.03007	.02928	.02852	.02779	.02710
37	.03697	.03590	.03488	.03391	.03298	.03209	.03125	.03044	.02967	.02893
38	.03947	.03833	.03725	.03622	.03524	.03430	.03340	.03254	.03172	.03094
39	.04217	.04096	.03982	.03873	.03768	.03669	.03573	.03482	.03395	.03312
40	.04510	.04383	.04262	.04146	.04035	.03930	.03828	.03732	.03639	.03550
41	.04830	.04695	.04567	.04445	.04327	.04215	.04108	.04005	.03907	.03812
42	.05177	.05035	.04900	.04770	.04646	.04527	.04413	.04304	.04200	.04100
43	.05553	.05404	.05261	.05123	.04992	.04866	.04746	.04630	.04520	.04413
44	.05960	.05802	.05651	.05506	.05368	.05235	.05107	.04985	.04867	.04754
45	.06395	.06229	.06069	.05917	.05770	.05630	.05495	.05365	.05241	.05121
46	.06860	.06685	.06517	.06356	.06202	.06053	.05911	.05774	.05643	.05516
47	.07353	.07169	.06992	.06823	.06660	.06504	.06353	.06209	.06070	.05936
48	.07877	.07684	.07498	.07320	.07149	.06984	.06826	.06673	.06527	.06385
49	.08433	.08231	.08036	.07849	.07669	.07495	.07329	.07168	.07013	.06864
50	.09026	.08814	.08609	.08413	.08224	.08042	.07867	.07698	.07535	.07378
51	.09655	.09433	.09219	.09013	.08815	.08624	.08440	.08262	.08091	.07926
52	.10318	.10086	.09863	.09647	.09439	.09239	.09046	.08860	.08680	.08506
53	.11017	.10774	.10541	.10315	.10098	.09888	.09686	.09491	.09302	.09120
54	.11750	.11498	.11254	.11019	.10792	.10572	.10361	.10156	.09958	.09767
55	.12522	.12258	.12005	.11759	.11522	.11294	.11072	.10859	.10652	.10451
56	.13332	.13059	.12794	.12539	.12292	.12054	.11823	.11599	.11383	.11174
57	.14183	.13899	.13624	.13359	.13102	.12853	.12613	.12380	.12154	.11936
58	.15070	.14775	.14490	.14215	.13948	.13689	.13439	.13197	.12962	.12734
59	.15990	.15685	.15389	.15103	.14826	.14558	.14298	.14046	.13801	.13564
60	.16942	.16626	.16321	.16024	.15737	.15459	.15189	.14927	.14673	.14426
61	.17929	.17603	.17287	.16981	.16684	.16395	.16115	.15844	.15580	.15324
62	.18960	.18623	.18297	.17980	.17673	.17375	.17085	.16803	.16530	.16264
63	.20035	.19688	.19352	.19025	.18708	.18400	.18100	.17809	.17525	.17250
64	.21154	.20797	.20451	.20114	.19787	.19469	.19159	.18859	.18566	.18281
65	.22318	.21951	.21595	.21249	.20912	.20584	.20265	.19955	.19652	.19358
66	.23532	.23156	.22790	.22434	.22088	.21751	.21422	.21102	.20791	.20487
67	.24804	.24419	.24044	.23679	.23324	.22977	.22640	.22311	.21990	.21678
68	.26133	.25740	.25356	.24983	.24618	.24263	.23917	.23579	.23250	.22929
69	.27516	.27114	.26723	.26341	.25969	.25605	.25251	.24905	.24567	.24237
70	.28945	.28536	.28137	.27747	.27367	.26996	.26633	.26279	.25934	.25596
71	.30412	.29996	.29590	.29193	.28806	.28427	.28057	.27696	.27343	.26998
72	.31913	.31491	.31078	.30675	.30281	.29895	.29519	.29150	.28790	.28438
73	.33444	.33016	.32597	.32188	.31788	.31396	.31013	.30638	.30271	.29913
74	.35012	.34579	.34155	.33741	.33335	.32938	.32549	.32168	.31795	.31430
75	.36628	.36190	.35762	.35343	.34932	.34530	.34136	.33750	.33372	.33001
76	.38299	.37858	.37427	.37004	.36589	.36183	.35784	.35394	.35011	.34636
77	.40028	.39585	.39151	.38725	.38307	.37898	.37496	.37103	.36716	.36337
78	.41812	.41368	.40933	.40506	.40086	.39675	.39271	.38874	.38485	.38103
79	.43641	.43198	.42762	.42334	.41914	.41502	.41096	.40698	.40308	.39924
80	.45496	.45054	.44619	.44192	.43772	.43360	.42954	.42556	.42164	.41779
81	.47360	.46920	.46487	.46061	.45643	.45231	.44827	.44429	.44038	.43653
82	.49223	.48785	.48355	.47932	.47516	.47106	.46703	.46307	.45916	.45532
83	.51081	.50648	.50221	.49802	.49388	.48982	.48581	.48187	.47799	.47416
84	.52951	.52523	.52101	.51686	.51277	.50874	.50477	.50086	.49701	.49321
85	.54847	.54425	.54009	.53600	.53196	.52798	.52406	.52019	.51638	.51262
86	.56749	.56335	.55926	.55523	.55126	.54734	.54348	.53966	.53591	.53220
87	.58627	.58221	.57820	.57425	.57035	.56650	.56270	.55895	.55526	.55161

Reg. § 1.642(c)-6(e)(6)

TABLE S
BASED ON LIFE TABLE 90CM
SINGLE LIFE REMAINDER FACTORS
APPLICABLE AFTER APRIL 30, 1999
INTEREST RATE

AGE	12.2%	12.4%	12.6%	12.8%	13.0%	13.2%	13.4%	13.6%	13.8%	14.0%
88	.60477	.60079	.59688	.59301	.58919	.58542	.58170	.57802	.57439	.57081
89	.62297	.61909	.61527	.61149	.60776	.60408	.60044	.59685	.59330	.58979
90	.64084	.63707	.63335	.62968	.62604	.62246	.61891	.61540	.61194	.60851
91	.65803	.65437	.65076	.64719	.64366	.64017	.63672	.63330	.62993	.62659
92	.67412	.67058	.66707	.66360	.66017	.65678	.65342	.65010	.64682	.64357
93	.68911	.68567	.68227	.67890	.67557	.67227	.66901	.66578	.66258	.65942
94	.70321	.69988	.69657	.69330	.69006	.68686	.68369	.68055	.67744	.67437
95	.71674	.71351	.71031	.70713	.70399	.70088	.69781	.69476	.69174	.68875
96	.72959	.72646	.72335	.72028	.71724	.71422	.71123	.70828	.70534	.70244
97	.74156	.73853	.73552	.73254	.72959	.72666	.72376	.72089	.71804	.71522
98	.75287	.74993	.74702	.74413	.74126	.73842	.73561	.73282	.73006	.72732
99	.76401	.76117	.75834	.75555	.75277	.75002	.74730	.74459	.74191	.73926
100	.77494	.77219	.76946	.76676	.76408	.76142	.75878	.75616	.75357	.75099
101	.78580	.78315	.78052	.77791	.77532	.77275	.77021	.76768	.76517	.76268
102	.79654	.79399	.79146	.78894	.78645	.78397	.78152	.77908	.77666	.77426
103	.80724	.80479	.80236	.79994	.79755	.79517	.79280	.79046	.78813	.78582
104	.81879	.81646	.81413	.81183	.80954	.80726	.80501	.80276	.80054	.79832
105	.83005	.82782	.82560	.82340	.82121	.81904	.81688	.81474	.81260	.81049
106	.84485	.84277	.84071	.83866	.83662	.83459	.83257	.83057	.82857	.82659
107	.86311	.86124	.85937	.85751	.85566	.85382	.85199	.85017	.84835	.84655
108	.89266	.89114	.88963	.88812	.88662	.88513	.88364	.88216	.88068	.87922
109	.94563	.94484	.94405	.94326	.94248	.94170	.94092	.94014	.93937	.93860

(f) *Effective dates.* This section applies after April 30, 1999. [Reg. § 1.642(c)-6.]

☐ [*T.D.* 7105, 4-5-71. *Amended by T.D.* 7955, 5-10-84; *T.D. 8540,* 6-9-94; *T.D.* 8819, 4-29-99 *and T.D.* 8886, 6-9-2000.]

[Reg. § 1.642(c)-6A]

§ 1.642(c)-6A. **Valuation of charitable remainder interests for which the valuation date is before May 1, 1999.**—(a) *Valuation of charitable remainder interests for which the valuation date is before January 1, 1952.* There was no provision for the qualification of pooled income funds under section 642 until 1969. See § 20.2031-7A(a) of this chapter (Estate Tax Regulations) for the determination of the present value of a charitable remainder interest created before January 1, 1952.

(b) *Valuation of charitable remainder interests for which the valuation date is after December 31, 1951, and before January 1, 1971.* No charitable deduction is allowable for a transfer to a pooled income fund for which the valuation date is after the effective dates of the Tax Reform Act of 1969 unless the pooled income fund meets the requirements of section 642(c)(5). See § 20.2031-7A(b) of this chapter (Estate Tax Regulations) for the determination of the present value of a charitable remainder interest for which the valuation date is after December 31, 1951, and before January 1, 1971.

(c) *Present value of remainder interest in the case of transfers to pooled income funds for which the valuation date is after December 31, 1970, and before December 1, 1983.* For the determination of the present value of a remainder interest in property transferred to a pooled income fund for which the valuation date is after December 31, 1970, and before December 1, 1983, see § 20.2031-7A(c) of this chapter (Estate Tax Regulations) and former § 1.642(c)-6(e) (as contained in the 26 CFR Part 1 edition revised as of April 1, 1994).

(d) *Present value of remainder interest dependent on the termination of one life in the case of transfers to pooled income funds made after November 30, 1983, for which the valuation date is before May 1, 1989*—(1) *In general.* For transfers to pooled income funds made after November 30, 1983, for which the valuation date is before May 1, 1989, the present value of the remainder interest at the time of the transfer of property to the fund is determined by computing the present value (at the time of the transfer) of the life income interest in the transferred property (as determined under paragraph (d)(2) of this section) and subtracting that value from the fair market value of the transferred property on the valuation date. The present value of a remainder interest that is dependent on the termination of the life of one individual is computed by use of Table G in paragraph (d)(4) of this section. For purposes of the computation under this section, the age of an individual is to be taken as the age of the individual at the individual's nearest birthday.

(2) *Present value of life income interest.* The present value of the life income interest in property transferred to a pooled income fund shall be computed on the basis of:

(i) Life contingencies determined from the values of l_x that are set forth in Table LN of § 20.2031-7A(d)(6) of this chapter (Estate Tax Regulations); and

(ii) Discount at a rate of interest, compounded annually, equal to the highest yearly rate of return of the pooled income fund for the 3 taxable years immediately preceding its taxable year in which the transfer of property to the fund is made. For purposes of this paragraph (d)(2), the yearly rate of return of a pooled income fund is determined as provided in § 1.642(c)-6(c) unless the highest yearly rate of return is deemed to be 9 percent. For purposes of this paragraph (d)(2), the first taxable year of a pooled income fund is considered a taxable year even though the taxable year consists of less than 12 months. However, appropriate adjustments must be made to annualize the rate of return earned by the fund for that period. Where it appears from the facts and circumstances that the highest yearly rate of return for the 3 taxable years immediately preceding the taxable year in which the transfer of property is made has been purposely manipulated to be substantially less than the rate of return that would otherwise be reasonably anticipated with the purpose of obtaining an excessive charitable deduction, that rate of return may not be used. In that case, the highest yearly rate of return of the fund is determined by treating the fund as a pooled income fund that has been in existence for less than 3 preceding taxable years. If a pooled income fund has been in existence less than 3 taxable years immediately preceding the taxable year in which the transfer of property to the fund is made, the highest yearly rate of return is deemed to be 9 percent.

(3) *Computation of value of remainder interest.* The factor which is used in determining the present value of the remainder interest is the factor under the appropriate yearly rate of return in column (2) of Table G opposite the number in column (1) which corresponds to the age of the individual upon whose life the value of the remainder interest is based. If the yearly rate of return is a percentage which is between yearly rates of return for which factors are provided in Table G, a linear interpolation must be made. The present value of the remainder interest is determined by multiplying, by the factor determined

under this paragraph (d)(3), the fair market value on the appropriate valuation date. If the yearly rate of return is below 2.2 percent or above 14 percent, see § 1.642(c)—6(b). This paragraph (d)(3) may be illustrated by the following example:

Example. A, who will be 50 years old on April 15, 1985, transfers $100,000 to a pooled income fund on January 1, 1985, and retains a life income interest in such property. The highest yearly rate of return earned by the fund for its 3 preceding taxable years is 9.9 percent. In Table G the figure in column (2) opposite 50 years under 9.8 percent is .15653 and under 10 percent is .15257. The present value of the remainder interest is $15,455, computed as follows:

Factor at 9.8 percent for person aged 50	.15653
Factor at 10 percent for person aged 50	.15257
Difference	.00396

Interpolation adjustment:

$$\frac{9.9\% - 9.8\%}{.2\%} = \frac{x}{.00396.2\%}$$
$$x = .00198$$

Factor at 9.8 percent for person aged 50	0.15653
Less:	
Interpolation adjustment	.00198
Interpolated factor	.15455
Present value of remainder interest ($100,000 × .15455)	$15,455

(4) *Actuarial tables.* The following tables shall be used in the application of the provisions of this section.

43,236 Estates, Trusts, and Beneficiaries

See p. 20,601 for regulations not amended to reflect law changes

Table G—Single Life, Unisex—Table Showing the Present Worth of the Remainder Interest in Property Transferred to a Pooled Income Fund Having the Yearly Rate of Return Shown—Applicable for Transfers After November 30, 1983, and Before May 1, 1989

(1) Age	(2) Yearly Rate of Return									
	2.2%	2.4%	2.6%	2.8%	3.0%	3.2%	3.4%	3.6%	3.8%	4.0%
0	.23930	.21334	.19077	.17112	.15401	.13908	.12603	.11461	.10461	.09583
1	.22891	.20224	.17903	.15880	.14114	.12570	.11220	.10036	.08998	.08086
2	.23297	.20610	.18265	.16218	.14429	.12862	.11489	.10284	.09225	.08293
3	.23744	.21035	.18669	.16600	.14787	.13198	.11802	.10576	.09496	.08544
4	.24212	.21485	.19098	.17006	.15171	.13559	.12141	.10893	.09793	.08821
5	.24701	.21955	.19547	.17434	.15577	.13943	.12503	.11234	.10112	.09121
6	.25207	.22442	.20015	.17880	.16001	.14345	.12884	.11593	.10451	.09439
7	.25726	.22944	.20497	.18342	.16441	.14763	.13280	.11968	.10805	.09773
8	.26259	.23461	.20995	.18820	.16898	.15198	.13694	.12360	.11176	.10125
9	.26809	.23995	.21511	.19315	.17373	.15652	.14126	.12771	.11567	.10495
10	.27373	.24544	.22043	.29828	.17865	.16123	.14576	.13200	.11975	.10883
11	.27953	.25110	.22592	.20358	.18375	.16613	.15045	.13648	.12402	.11290
12	.28546	.25690	.23156	.20904	.18902	.17119	.15531	.14113	.12847	.11715
13	.29149	.26280	.23731	.21462	.19440	.17638	.16029	.14591	.13304	.12152
14	.29757	.26877	.24312	.22026	.19986	.18164	.16535	.15076	.13769	.12597
15	.30368	.27476	.24896	.22593	.20535	.18693	.17044	.15565	.14238	.13045
16	.30978	.28075	.25481	.23161	.21085	.19224	.17554	.16055	.14707	.13494
17	.31589	.28676	.26068	.23732	.21637	.19756	.18066	.16547	.15178	.13945
18	.32204	.29280	.26659	.24306	.22193	.20294	.18584	.17044	.15655	.14401
19	.32825	.29892	.27257	.24889	.22759	.20840	.19110	.17550	.16140	.14866
20	.33457	.30514	.27867	.25484	.23336	.21399	.19650	.18069	.16639	.15344
21	.34099	.31148	.28489	.26092	.23927	.21972	.20203	.18602	.17152	.15836
22	.34751	.31794	.29124	.26712	.24532	.22559	.20771	.19151	.17680	.16344
23	.35416	.32452	.29773	.27348	.25152	.23162	.21356	.19716	.18225	.16869
24	.36096	.33127	.30439	.28002	.25791	.23784	.21960	.20301	.18791	.17414
25	.36793	.33821	.31124	.28676	.26452	.24429	.22588	.20910	.19380	.17984
26	.37509	.34535	.31832	.29374	.27136	.25098	.23240	.21545	.19996	.18581
27	.38244	.35269	.32560	.30093	.27844	.25792	.23918	.22206	.20639	.19205
28	.38998	.36023	.33311	.30836	.28577	.26512	.24623	.22894	.21310	.19858
29	.39767	.36795	.34080	.31599	.29330	.27253	.25350	.23605	.22004	.20534
30	.40553	.37584	.34868	.32382	.30104	.28016	.26100	.24341	.22724	.21236
31	.41352	.38388	.35672	.33182	.30897	.28799	.26871	.25097	.23464	.21961
32	.42165	.39208	.36494	.34001	.31710	.29603	.27664	.25877	.24230	.22710
33	.42993	.40044	.37333	.34839	.32543	.30428	.28478	.26679	.25018	.23484
34	.43834	.40894	.38188	.35694	.33395	.31273	.29314	.27504	.25830	.24280
35	.44689	.41760	.39060	.36567	.34266	.32139	.30172	.28351	.26665	.25102
36	.45556	.42640	.39947	.37458	.35156	.33024	.31050	.29220	.27523	.25948
37	.46435	.43534	.40850	.38365	.36063	.33929	.31949	.30111	.28404	.26816
38	.47325	.44440	.41767	.39288	.36987	.34851	.32867	.31022	.29305	.27707
39	.48226	.45358	.42696	.40225	.37927	.35791	.33804	.31953	.30228	.28620
40	.49136	.46288	.43640	.41177	.38884	.36749	.34759	.32904	.31172	.29555
41	.50056	.47228	.44596	.42143	.39856	.37724	.35733	.33874	.32137	.30512
42	.50988	.48182	.45566	.43125	.40846	.38717	.36727	.34866	.33124	.31493
43	.51927	.49145	.46547	.44120	.41850	.39727	.37739	.35877	.34132	.32495
44	.52874	.50118	.47540	.45128	.42869	.40752	.38768	.36906	.35159	.33518
45	.53828	.51099	.48543	.46146	.43899	.41791	.39811	.37952	.36204	.34560
46	.54788	.52088	.49554	.47176	.44943	.42844	.40871	.39014	.37267	.35621
47	.55754	.53083	.50574	.48216	.45998	.43910	.41944	.40092	.38347	.36701
48	.56726	.54087	.51604	.49267	.47065	.44990	.43034	.41188	.39446	.37801
49	.57703	.55097	.52652	.50327	.48144	.46083	.44137	.42299	.40562	.38929
50	.58685	.56114	.53677	.51398	.49234	.47189	.45256	.43427	.41695	.40056
51	.59670	.57136	.54740	.52476	.50333	.48306	.46386	.44567	.42844	.41209
52	.60658	.58161	.55798	.53560	.51441	.49432	.47528	.45721	.44006	.42378
53	.61647	.59189	.56859	.54651	.52556	.50567	.48679	.46886	.45182	.43562
54	.62635	.60217	.57923	.55744	.53675	.51708	.49838	.48060	.46367	.44756

Reg. § 1.642(c)-6A(d)(4)

Estates, Trusts, and Beneficiaries

Table G—Continued (1) Table G—Single Life, Unisex—Table Showing the Present Worth of the Remainder Interest in Property Transferred to a Pooled Income Fund Having the Yearly Rate of Return Shown—Applicable for Transfers After November 30, 1983, and Before May 1, 1989

(1) Age	2.2%	2.4%	2.6%	2.8%	3.0%	3.2%	3.4%	3.6%	3.8%	4.0%
55	.63622	.61246	.58987	.56840	.54798	.52854	.51004	.49242	.47563	.45962
56	.64606	.62273	.60052	.57937	.55923	.54004	.52175	.50430	.48766	.47177
57	.65589	.63299	.61117	.59037	.57052	.55159	.53352	.51626	.49978	.48402
58	.66569	.64324	.62181	.60136	.58183	.56316	.54533	.52827	.51196	.49636
59	.67546	.65347	.63246	.61237	.59316	.57478	.55719	.54036	.52424	.50879
60	.68521	.66368	.64309	.62338	.60450	.58643	.56910	.55250	.53658	.52131
61	.69492	.67388	.65372	.63440	.61587	.59811	.58107	.56471	.54901	.53393
62	.70461	.68406	.66434	.64542	.62726	.60982	.59307	.57697	.56150	.54662
63	.71425	.69420	.67494	.65643	.63865	.62155	.60510	.58928	.57405	.55940
64	.72384	.70430	.68550	.66742	.65002	.63327	.61714	.60161	.58664	.57222
65	.73336	.71434	.69602	.67837	.66137	.64498	.62918	.61395	.59926	.58508
66	.74281	.72431	.70647	.68926	.67267	.65666	.64120	.62628	.61188	.59796
67	.75216	.73419	.71684	.70009	.68391	.66829	.65319	.63859	.62448	.61083
68	.76143	.74399	.72714	.71085	.69509	.67986	.66512	.65086	.63706	.62370
69	.77060	.75370	.73735	.72153	.70622	.69139	.67702	.66311	.64963	.63656
70	.77969	.76334	.74750	.73215	.71728	.70286	.68888	.67533	.66218	.64942
71	.78870	.77290	.75758	.74272	.72830	.71431	.70073	.68754	.67474	.66231
72	.79764	.78240	.76760	.75323	.73928	.72572	.71255	.69974	.68730	.67520
73	.80646	.79178	.77751	.76364	.75016	.73704	.72429	.71188	.69980	.68805
74	.81511	.80099	.78725	.77387	.76086	.74819	.73586	.72384	.71214	.70075
75	.82353	.80995	.79674	.78386	.77132	.75909	.74718	.73557	.72424	.71320
76	.83169	.81866	.80596	.79357	.78149	.76971	.75822	.74700	.73606	.72538
77	.83960	.82710	.81491	.80301	.79139	.78004	.76897	.75815	.74758	.73726
78	.84727	.83530	.82360	.81218	.80101	.79010	.77944	.76902	.75883	.74886
79	.85473	.84328	.83207	.82112	.81041	.79993	.78968	.77965	.76984	.76023
80	.86201	.85106	.84034	.82986	.81960	.80955	.79971	.79008	.78064	.77140
81	.86905	.85861	.84837	.83835	.82853	.81891	.80948	.80024	.79118	.78230
82	.87585	.86589	.85612	.84655	.83717	.82796	.81894	.81009	.80140	.79288
83	.88239	.87291	.86360	.85447	.84552	.83672	.82810	.81962	.81131	.80314
84	.88873	.87971	.87085	.86216	.85362	.84524	.83700	.82891	.82096	.81314
85	.89487	.88630	.87789	.86963	.86150	.85352	.84567	.83795	.83037	.82291
86	.90070	.89258	.88459	.87674	.86901	.86141	.85394	.84659	.83936	.83224
87	.90609	.89838	.89079	.88332	.87597	.86874	.86162	.85461	.84771	.84092
88	.91106	.90372	.89650	.88939	.88234	.87549	.86870	.86201	.85542	.84893
89	.91570	.90872	.90184	.89507	.88839	.88182	.87534	.86895	.86266	.85645
90	.92014	.91350	.90696	.90051	.89416	.88789	.88171	.87562	.86961	.86369
91	.92435	.91804	.91182	.90569	.89964	.89367	.88779	.88198	.87625	.87059
92	.92822	.92222	.91630	.91045	.90469	.89900	.89338	.88784	.88237	.87697
93	.93170	.92597	.92032	.91474	.90923	.90379	.89842	.89312	.88788	.88271
94	.93477	.92929	.92387	.91853	.91325	.90803	.90288	.89780	.89277	.88781
95	.93743	.93216	.92695	.92181	.91673	.91171	.90675	.90185	.89701	.89223
96	.93967	.93458	.92955	.92458	.91966	.91481	.91001	.90527	.90058	.89594
97	.94167	.93674	.93186	.92704	.92228	.91757	.91291	.90831	.90376	.89926
98	.94342	.93863	.93389	.92921	.92457	.91999	.91546	.91098	.90655	.90217
99	.94508	.94041	.93580	.93124	.92673	.92227	.91786	.91349	.90917	.90490
100	.94672	.94218	.93770	.93326	.92887	.92453	.92023	.91598	.91177	.90761
101	.94819	.94377	.93940	.93508	.93080	.92656	.92236	.91821	.91410	.91003
102	.94979	.94550	.94125	.93704	.93288	.92875	.92467	.92063	.91662	.91266
103	.95180	.94766	.94357	.93952	.93550	.93152	.92758	.92367	.91980	.91597
104	.95377	.94979	.94585	.94194	.93806	.93423	.93042	.92665	.92291	.91920
105	.95663	.95288	.94916	.94547	.94181	.93818	.93458	.93101	.92747	.92395
106	.96101	.95762	.95425	.95091	.94760	.94430	.94104	.93779	.93457	.93137
107	.96688	.96398	.96110	.95824	.95539	.95256	.94975	.94696	.94418	.94143
108	.97569	.97354	.97141	.96928	.96717	.96507	.96298	.96090	.95883	.95676
109	.98924	.98828	.98733	.98638	.98544	.98450	.98356	.98263	.98170	.98077

Reg. § 1.642(c)-6A(d)(4)

43,238 Estates, Trusts, and Beneficiaries

See p. 20,601 for regulations not amended to reflect law changes

Table G—Continued (2) Table G—Single Life, Unisex—Table Showing the Present Worth of the Remainder Interest in Property Transferred to a Pooled Income Fund Having the Yearly Rate of Return Shown—Applicable for Transfers After November 30, 1983, and Before May 1, 1989

(1) Age	(2) Yearly Rate of Return									
	4.2%	4.4%	4.6%	4.8%	5.0%	5.2%	5.4%	5.6%	5.8%	6.0%
0	.08811	.08132	.07534	.07006	.06539	.06126	.05759	.05433	.05143	.04884
1	.07283	.06576	.05952	.05400	.04912	.04480	.04096	.03754	.03450	.03179
2	.07471	.06746	.06106	.05539	.05037	.04591	.04194	.03841	.03527	.03246
3	.07704	.06962	.06304	.05722	.05205	.04745	.04336	.03972	.03646	.03355
4	.07962	.07202	.06528	.05930	.05398	.04924	.04502	.04125	.03789	.03487
5	.08243	.07464	.06773	.06159	.05612	.05124	.04689	.04300	.03952	.03639
6	.08542	.07745	.07037	.06406	.05844	.05342	.04893	.04492	.04131	.03808
7	.08857	.08042	.07316	.06669	.06091	.05574	.05112	.04697	.04324	.03990
8	.09189	.08355	.07612	.06948	.06354	.05822	.05346	.04918	.04533	.04186
9	.09540	.08687	.07926	.07245	.06635	.06089	.05598	.05156	.04759	.04400
10	.09908	.09037	.08258	.07560	.06934	.06372	.05866	.05411	.05000	.04630
11	.10296	.09406	.08609	.07894	.07251	.06673	.06153	.05684	.05260	.04877
12	.10701	.09793	.08977	.08245	.07586	.06992	.06457	.05973	.05536	.05141
13	.11119	.10191	.09358	.08608	.07932	.07322	.06772	.06274	.05824	.05415
14	.11544	.10597	.09745	.08978	.08285	.07659	.07093	.06581	.06117	.05695
15	.11972	.11007	.10136	.09350	.08640	.07998	.07417	.06890	.06411	.05976
16	.12402	.11416	.10527	.09723	.08995	.08337	.07739	.07197	.06704	.06255
17	.12832	.11827	.10919	.10096	.09351	.08675	.08062	.07504	.06996	.06533
18	.13268	.12243	.11315	.10474	.09711	.09018	.08387	.07813	.07290	.06813
19	.13712	.12667	.11720	.10860	.10078	.09367	.08720	.08130	.07591	.07099
20	.14170	.13105	.12138	.11259	.10459	.09730	.09065	.08458	.07904	.07397
21	.14642	.13557	.12570	.11671	.10853	.10106	.09423	.08800	.08229	.07707
22	.15129	.14024	.13017	.12099	.11261	.10496	.09796	.09155	.08568	.08030
23	.15634	.14508	.13481	.12544	.11687	.10903	.10185	.09526	.08923	.08368
24	.16159	.15013	.13967	.13009	.12133	.11330	.10594	.09918	.09297	.08726
25	.16709	.15543	.14477	.13500	.12604	.11782	.11028	.10334	.09696	.09108
26	.17286	.16101	.15014	.14018	.13103	.12262	.11489	.10778	.10122	.09518
27	.17891	.16686	.15580	.14564	.13630	.12771	.11979	.11249	.10576	.09955
28	.18525	.17301	.16175	.15140	.14187	.13309	.12499	.11751	.11060	.10421
29	.19183	.17940	.16796	.15742	.14700	.13873	.13044	.12278	.11570	.10914
30	.19867	.18606	.17443	.16370	.15380	.14464	.13617	.12833	.12107	.11433
31	.20574	.19295	.18114	.17023	.16013	.15079	.14214	.13412	.12668	.11977
32	.21307	.20010	.18811	.17702	.16674	.15722	.14838	.14018	.13256	.12548
33	.22064	.20751	.19535	.18407	.17362	.16391	.15490	.14652	.13873	.13147
34	.22846	.21516	.20283	.19138	.18075	.17087	.16168	.15312	.14515	.13772
35	.23653	.22307	.21058	.19896	.18816	.17811	.16874	.16001	.15186	.14426
36	.24484	.23124	.21859	.20681	.19584	.18562	.17608	.16717	.15886	.15108
37	.25340	.23966	.22685	.21492	.20379	.19340	.18369	.17462	.16613	.15819
38	.26219	.24831	.23536	.22328	.21199	.20144	.19157	.18233	.17368	.16557
39	.27120	.25720	.24411	.23188	.22044	.20974	.19971	.19031	.18149	.17322
40	.28045	.26633	.25311	.24075	.22916	.21830	.20812	.19856	.18959	.18115
41	.28992	.27569	.26236	.24986	.23814	.22714	.21681	.20710	.19797	.18938
42	.29965	.28532	.27188	.25926	.24741	.23627	.22579	.21594	.20665	.19791
43	.30960	.29518	.28163	.26890	.25693	.24566	.23606	.22505	.21562	.20673
44	.31977	.30527	.29164	.27880	.26671	.25532	.24458	.23445	.22488	.21585
45	.33013	.31557	.30185	.28892	.27673	.26522	.25436	.24410	.23440	.22523
46	.34071	.32609	.31230	.29929	.28700	.27538	.26441	.25402	.24420	.23490
47	.35148	.33681	.32296	.30988	.29750	.28579	.27471	.26421	.25427	.24484
48	.36246	.34777	.33387	.32072	.30826	.29647	.28529	.27469	.26463	.25508
49	.37364	.35893	.34499	.33179	.31927	.30739	.29613	.28543	.27527	.26562
50	.38503	.37030	.35634	.34310	.33053	.31859	.30724	.29646	.28620	.27645
51	.39659	.38187	.36790	.35462	.34201	.33001	.31860	.30774	.29740	.28755
52	.40832	.39362	.37965	.36636	.35371	.34167	.33020	.31928	.30886	.29893
53	.42021	.40554	.39158	.37829	.36562	.35355	.34204	.33105	.32057	.31056
54	.43222	.41760	.40367	.39039	.37771	.36562	.35407	.34304	.33250	.32243

Reg. § 1.642(c)-6A(d)(4)

Estates, Trusts, and Beneficiaries 43,239
See p. 20,601 for regulations not amended to reflect law changes

Table G——Continued (3) Table G—Single Life, Unisex—Table Showing the Present Worth of the Remainder Interest in Property Transferred to a Pooled Income Fund Having the Yearly Rate of Return Shown—Applicable for Transfers After November 30, 1983, and Before May 1, 1989

(1) Age	(2) Yearly Rate of Return									
	4.2%	4.4%	4.6%	4.8%	5.0%	5.2%	5.4%	5.6%	5.8%	6.0%
55	.44436	.42980	.41591	.41264	.38997	.37787	.36630	.35523	.34465	.33452
56	.45660	.44212	.42828	.41504	.40239	.39029	.37870	.36761	.35699	.34682
57	.46897	.45456	.44079	.42760	.41498	.40289	.39130	.38020	.36956	.35935
58	.48142	.46712	.45342	.44030	.42771	.41565	.40408	.39297	.38231	.37208
59	.49399	.47980	.46620	.45314	.44062	.42859	.41704	.40595	.39529	.38504
60	.50666	.49260	.47910	.46613	.45367	.44170	.43019	.41912	.40847	.39822
61	.51944	.50552	.49214	.47927	.46690	.45499	.44353	.43250	.42187	.41164
62	.53232	.51856	.50531	.49256	.48028	.46845	.45706	.44607	.43548	.42527
63	.54529	.53169	.51860	.50598	.49381	.48208	.47076	.45984	.44930	.43913
64	.55832	.54491	.53198	.51950	.50746	.49583	.48461	.47377	.46329	.45317
65	.57140	.55819	.54544	.53312	.52121	.50971	.49859	.48784	.47744	.46738
66	.58451	.57152	.55895	.54681	.53506	.52369	.51269	.50204	.49173	.48175
67	.59763	.58486	.57251	.56054	.54896	.53774	.52688	.51635	.50614	.49625
68	.61076	.59823	.58609	.57432	.56292	.55187	.54115	.53075	.52066	.51088
69	.62390	.61162	.59971	.58816	.57695	.56607	.55551	.54526	.53530	.52563
70	.63705	.62503	.61337	.60204	.59104	.58035	.56997	.55987	.55006	.54053
71	.65023	.63849	.62709	.61600	.60522	.59474	.58455	.57463	.56498	.55559
72	.66344	.65199	.64086	.63003	.61949	.60923	.59924	.58952	.58004	.57082
73	.67661	.66547	.65463	.64407	.63378	.62375	.61398	.60446	.59518	.58613
74	.68964	.67882	.66827	.65798	.64796	.63818	.62864	.61933	.61026	.60140
75	.70243	.69193	.68168	.67168	.66192	.65240	.64310	.63402	.62515	.61649
76	.71495	.70477	.69482	.68411	.67563	.66636	.65731	.64836	.63981	.63135
77	.72717	.71731	.70768	.69826	.68905	.68005	.67124	.66263	.65420	.64596
78	.73912	.72959	.72026	.71114	.70221	.69347	.68492	.67655	.66836	.66033
79	.75083	.74163	.73262	.72379	.71515	.70669	.69840	.69028	.68232	.67452
80	.76235	.75348	.74479	.73627	.72792	.71973	.71171	.70384	.69613	.68856
81	.77360	.76506	.75669	.74848	.74043	.73252	.72377	.71717	.70970	.70237
82	.78452	.77632	.76827	.76036	.75260	.74499	.73751	.73016	.72295	.71587
83	.79513	.78725	.77952	.77192	.76446	.75713	.74992	.74284	.73589	.72905
84	.80547	.79792	.79051	.78322	.77606	.76901	.76208	.75527	.74857	.74198
85	.81557	.80836	.80126	.79429	.78742	.78067	.77402	.76748	.76104	.75471
86	.82524	.81835	.81157	.80489	.79832	.79185	.78548	.77921	.77304	.76695
87	.83423	.82764	.82115	.81477	.80847	.80228	.79617	.79015	.78423	.77838
88	.84253	.83623	.83002	.82390	.81787	.81193	.80607	.80029	.79460	.78899
89	.85033	.84430	.83836	.83250	.82672	.82102	.81540	.80985	.80438	.79899
90	.85784	.85208	.84639	.84079	.83525	.82979	.82441	.81909	.81384	.80867
91	.86502	.85951	.85408	.84871	.84342	.83820	.83304	.82795	.82292	.81796
92	.87164	.86638	.86118	.85605	.85098	.84598	.84104	.83616	.83134	.82657
93	.87761	.87257	.86759	.86267	.85781	.85300	.84826	.84357	.83894	.83437
94	.88290	.87806	.87327	.86854	.86386	.85924	.85468	.85017	.84570	.84130
95	.88750	.88282	.87820	.87364	.86913	.86466	.86025	.85589	.85158	.84732
96	.89136	.88683	.88236	.87793	.87355	.86922	.86494	.86071	.85652	.85238
97	.89481	.89041	.88606	.88176	.87750	.87329	.86913	.86501	.86093	.85690
98	.89783	.89354	.88930	.88511	.88096	.87685	.87279	.86877	.86479	.86085
99	.90067	.89649	.89235	.88826	.88420	.88019	.87622	.87230	.86814	.86456
100	.90349	.89941	.89538	.89138	.88743	.88351	.87964	.87580	.87200	.86824
101	.90600	.90202	.89807	.89416	.89029	.88646	.88267	.87891	.87519	.87150
102	.90873	.90484	.90099	.89717	.89339	.88965	.88594	.88227	.87863	.87503
103	.91217	.90841	.90468	.90099	.89733	.89370	.89011	.88654	.88301	.87952
104	.91553	.91188	.90827	.90469	.90114	.89763	.89414	.89068	.88725	.88385
105	.92047	.91701	.91358	.91018	.90680	.90345	.90013	.89683	.89356	.89032
106	.92819	.92504	.92191	.91880	.91571	.91265	.90961	.90658	.90358	.90060
107	.93868	.93596	.93325	.93056	.92788	.92522	.92258	.91995	.91734	.91474
108	.95471	.95267	.95064	.94862	.94661	.94461	.94262	.94063	.93866	.93670
109	.97985	.97893	.97801	.97710	.97619	.97529	.97438	.97348	.97259	.97170

Reg. § 1.642(c)-6A(d)(4)

43,240 Estates, Trusts, and Beneficiaries

See p. 20,601 for regulations not amended to reflect law changes

Table G—Continued (4) Table G—Single Life, Unisex—Table Showing the Present Worth of the Remainder Interest in Property Transferred to a Pooled Income Fund Having the Yearly Rate of Return Shown—Applicable for Transfers After November 30, 1983, and Before May 1, 1989

(1) Age	(2) Yearly Rate of Return									
	6.2%	6.4%	6.6%	6.8%	7.0%	7.2%	7.4%	7.6%	7.8%	8.0%
0	.04653	.04447	.04262	.04095	.03946	.03811	.03689	.03579	.03479	.03388
1	.02937	.02720	.02525	.02351	.02194	.02052	.01924	.01809	.01704	.01609
2	.02994	.02769	.02567	.02385	.02221	.02074	.01940	.01819	.01710	.01611
3	.03094	.02860	.02650	.02460	.02290	.02136	.01996	.01870	.01756	.01652
4	.03216	.02973	.02755	.02558	.02380	.02219	.02074	.01942	.01822	.01713
5	.03359	.03106	.02879	.02674	.02488	.02321	.02169	.02031	.01905	.01791
6	.03517	.03255	.03019	.02805	.02612	.02437	.02278	.02134	.02003	.01883
7	.93688	.03416	.03171	.02949	.02747	.02565	.02399	.02248	.02111	.01986
8	.03874	.03592	.03337	.03106	.02896	.02706	.02533	.02376	.02232	.02101
9	.04077	.03784	.03519	.03279	.03061	.02863	.02682	.02518	.02367	.02230
10	.04295	.03992	.03717	.03467	.03240	.03034	.02846	.02674	.02517	.02373
11	.04531	.04217	.03931	.03672	.03436	.03221	.03025	.02846	.02682	.02532
12	.04782	.04457	.04161	.03892	.03647	.03424	.03219	.03032	.02861	.02704
13	.05045	.04708	.04402	.04122	.03868	.03635	.03422	.03228	.03049	.02885
14	.05312	.04964	.04646	.04357	.04093	.03851	.03630	.03427	.03240	.03069
15	.05581	.05220	.04891	.04591	.04317	.04066	.03836	.03624	.03430	.03252
16	.05847	.05474	.05134	.04822	.04538	.04277	.04037	.03817	.03615	.03429
17	.06111	.05726	.05374	.05051	.04756	.04485	.04236	.04007	.03796	.03602
18	.06378	.05979	.05615	.05280	.04974	.04693	.04434	.04196	.03976	.03773
19	.06650	.06238	.05861	.05514	.05196	.04904	.04635	.04387	.04159	.03947
20	.06933	.06507	.06117	.05758	.05429	.05125	.04845	.04588	.04349	.04129
21	.07228	.06788	.06384	.06013	.05671	.05356	.05065	.04797	.04549	.04319
22	.07535	.07081	.06664	.06279	.05925	.05597	.05295	.05016	.04758	.04519
23	.07858	.07389	.06958	.06559	.06192	.05853	.05539	.05248	.04979	.04730
24	.08201	.07717	.07270	.06858	.06477	.06125	.05799	.05497	.05217	.04957
25	.08567	.08067	.07606	.07179	.06785	.06420	.06081	.05767	.05475	.05205
26	.08960	.08444	.07968	.07527	.07118	.06739	.06388	.06062	.05758	.05476
27	.09380	.08849	.08357	.07901	.07478	.07086	.06721	.06382	.06067	.05773
28	.09830	.09283	.08775	.08304	.07867	.07460	.07082	.06730	.06402	.06097
29	.10306	.09742	.09218	.08732	.08280	.07859	.07467	.07102	.06762	.06444
30	.10808	.10228	.09688	.09187	.08720	.08284	.07879	.07500	.07146	.06815
31	.11335	.10738	.10182	.09665	.09182	.08733	.08312	.07920	.07553	.07209
32	.11889	.11275	.10704	.10170	.09672	.09207	.08773	.08366	.07986	.07629
33	.12471	.11840	.11252	.10703	.10189	.09709	.09260	.08829	.08445	.08075
34	.13079	.12432	.11827	.11261	.10732	.10237	.09773	.09338	.08929	.08546
35	.13716	.13052	.12431	.11849	.11305	.10794	.10315	.09865	.09442	.09045
36	.14381	.13701	.13063	.12465	.11905	.11379	.10884	.10420	.09983	.09572
37	.15075	.14378	.13724	.13110	.12534	.11992	.11483	.11003	.10552	.10126
38	.15796	.15083	.14412	.13782	.13190	.12633	.12108	.11614	.11148	.10708
39	.16545	.15815	.15129	.14483	.13875	.13302	.12762	.12253	.11772	.11318
40	.17322	.16576	.15874	.15212	.14589	.14000	.13445	.12921	.12425	.11957
41	.18129	.17367	.16649	.15971	.15332	.14728	.14158	.13619	.13109	.12626
42	.18967	.18190	.17456	.16763	.16108	.15490	.14904	.14350	.13825	.13328
43	.19834	.19041	.18293	.17585	.16915	.16281	.15680	.15111	.14572	.14060
44	.20731	.19924	.19160	.18437	.17753	.17104	.16488	.15905	.15351	.14825
45	.21655	.20834	.20055	.19318	.18619	.17955	.17326	.16727	.16159	.15619
46	.22608	.21773	.20981	.20229	.19516	.18838	.18194	.17582	.16999	.16445
47	.23690	.22741	.21935	.21170	.20443	.19751	.19093	.18467	.17870	.17302
48	.24602	.23741	.22922	.22144	.21403	.20698	.20026	.19386	.18776	.18194
49	.25644	.24770	.23939	.23148	.22394	.21676	.20991	.20338	.19715	.19119
50	.26716	.25831	.24989	.24185	.23419	.22689	.21991	.21325	.20689	.20080
51	.27816	.26921	.26068	.25253	.24475	.23732	.23023	.22344	.21695	.21074
52	.28945	.28040	.27176	.26351	.25562	.24808	.24086	.23396	.22735	.22102
53	.30100	.29187	.28313	.27478	.26679	.25914	.25181	.24479	.23807	.23162
54	.31279	.30357	.29475	.28631	.27822	.27047	.26304	.25591	.24908	.24252

Reg. § 1.642(c)-6A(d)(4)

Estates, Trusts, and Beneficiaries

Table G—Continued (5) Table G, Single Life, Unisex—Table Showing the Present Worth of the Remainder Interest in Property Transferred to a Pooled Income Fund Having the Yearly Rate of Return Shown—Applicable for Transfers After November 30, 1983, and Before May 1, 1989

(1) Age	6.2%	6.4%	6.6%	6.8%	7.0%	7.2%	7.4%	7.6%	7.8%	8.0%
55	.32482	.31553	.30663	.29810	.28992	.28208	.27455	.26733	.26039	.25372
56	.33707	.32771	.31875	.31014	.30188	.29395	.28633	.27901	.27197	.26521
57	.34955	.34015	.33112	.32244	.31411	.30610	.29840	.29099	.28386	.27700
58	.36225	.35280	.34372	.33499	.32659	.31851	.31074	.30325	.29604	.28909
59	.37519	.36571	.35659	.34781	.33936	.33122	.32337	.31581	.30853	.30150
60	.38836	.37886	.36971	.36089	.35239	.34420	.33630	.32867	.32132	.31422
61	.41077	.39226	.38309	.37425	.36572	.35748	.34953	.34185	.33444	.32727
62	.41542	.40591	.39674	.38788	.37932	.37106	.36307	.35535	.34788	.34066
63	.42930	.41981	.41064	.40178	.39321	.38492	.37691	.36915	.36165	.35438
64	.44338	.43392	.42477	.41591	.40734	.39905	.39102	.38324	.37571	.36841
65	.45765	.44823	.43910	.43027	.42171	.41342	.40539	.39760	.39005	.38272
66	.47208	.46271	.45364	.44483	.43630	.42803	.42000	.41221	.40465	.39731
67	.48666	.47736	.46834	.45958	.45108	.44283	.43483	.42705	.41949	.41215
68	.50138	.49215	.48320	.47450	.46605	.45784	.44987	.44211	.43457	.42724
69	.51624	.50711	.49824	.48961	.48122	.47307	.46513	.45741	.44990	.44259
70	.53125	.52223	.51345	.50491	.49660	.48851	.48063	.47296	.46549	.45821
71	.54645	.53755	.52899	.52045	.51223	.50422	.49641	.48880	.48139	.47416
72	.56183	.55307	.54453	.53621	.52809	.52018	.51246	.50493	.49758	.49042
73	.57731	.56870	.56030	.55211	.54412	.53631	.52870	.52126	.51400	.50691
74	.59275	.58431	.57606	.56801	.56015	.55247	.54497	.53764	.53048	.52347
75	.60803	.59976	.59168	.58379	.57607	.56852	.56115	.55393	.54687	.53997
76	.62308	.61500	.60709	.59936	.59179	.58439	.57714	.57005	.56311	.55632
77	.63789	.63000	.62227	.61470	.60730	.60005	.59294	.58599	.57917	.57249
78	.65247	.64477	.63723	.62984	.62261	.61551	.60856	.60174	.59506	.58851
79	.66687	.65938	.65203	.64483	.63777	.63084	.62405	.61739	.61085	.60443
80	.68114	.67386	.66672	.65971	.65284	.64609	.63946	.63296	.62657	.62030
81	.69518	.68812	.68119	.67438	.66770	.66114	.65469	.64836	.64213	.63602
82	.70891	.70207	.69535	.68875	.68227	.67589	.66963	.66347	.65742	.65146
83	.72232	.71572	.70922	.70283	.69655	.69037	.68429	.67831	.67342	.66664
84	.73550	.72913	.72285	.71668	.71061	.70463	.69875	.69296	.68726	.68165
85	.74847	.74234	.73630	.73035	.72449	.71872	.71304	.70745	.70194	.69654
86	.76096	.75506	.74925	.74353	.73789	.73233	.72685	.72146	.71614	.71089
87	.77263	.76696	.76137	.75585	.75042	.74507	.73978	.73458	.72944	.72438
88	.78345	.77799	.77261	.76730	.76207	.75691	.75181	.74679	.74183	.73694
89	.79367	.78842	.78323	.77812	.77308	.76810	.76319	.75834	.75355	.74883
90	.80356	.79851	.79353	.78862	.78376	.77897	.77424	.76957	.76496	.76040
91	.81306	.80821	.80344	.79871	.79405	.78945	.78490	.78040	.77596	.77158
92	.82187	.81722	.81263	.80810	.80361	.79919	.79481	.79048	.78621	.78198
93	.82984	.82538	.82096	.81659	.81228	.80801	.80380	.79963	.79550	.79143
94	.83694	.83263	.82837	.83416	.81999	.81587	.81180	.80777	.80379	.79985
95	.84310	.83893	.83481	.83073	.82670	.82271	.81877	.81487	.81100	.80719
96	.84829	.84424	.84023	.83626	.83234	.82846	.82462	.82083	.81707	.81335
97	.85291	.84897	.84506	.84120	.83738	.83360	.82985	.82615	.82248	.81885
98	.85696	.85310	.84929	.84551	.84177	.83808	.83441	.83079	.82720	.82365
99	.86075	.85698	.85325	.84956	.84590	.84228	.83869	.83514	.83163	.82815
100	.86452	.86084	.85719	.85357	.85000	.84645	.84294	.83947	.83603	.83262
101	.86785	.86424	.86066	.85711	.85360	.85012	.84668	.84327	.83988	.83653
102	.87146	.86792	.86442	.86094	.85750	.85409	.85072	.84737	.84405	.84077
103	.87605	.87261	.86921	.86583	.86248	.85917	.85588	.85262	.84939	.84619
104	.88047	.87713	.87382	.87053	.86727	.86403	.86083	.85765	.85449	.85136
105	.88710	.88390	.88073	.87758	.87446	.87136	.86829	.86524	.86221	.85921
106	.89764	.89471	.89179	.88889	.88601	.88315	.88032	.87750	.87470	.87192
107	.91216	.90960	.90705	.90451	.90199	.89949	.89700	.89452	.89206	.88961
108	.93474	.93280	.93086	.92894	.92702	.92511	.92321	.92132	.91944	.91757
109	.97081	.96992	.96904	.96816	.96729	.96642	.96555	.96468	.96382	.96296

Reg. § 1.642(c)-6A(d)(4)

43,242   Estates, Trusts, and Beneficiaries

See p. 20,601 for regulations not amended to reflect law changes

Table G—Continued (6) Table G, Single Life, Unisex—Table Showing the Present Worth of the Remainder Interest in Property Transferred to a Pooled Income Fund Having the Yearly Rate of Return Shown—Applicable for Transfers After November 30, 1983, and Before May 1, 1989

(1) Age	(2) Yearly Rate of Return									
	8.2%	8.4%	8.6%	8.8%	9.0%	9.2%	9.4%	9.6%	9.8%	10.0%
0	.03305	.03230	.03161	.03098	.03040	.02987	.02938	.02893	.02851	.02812
1	.01523	.01444	.01372	.01307	.01247	.01192	.01141	.01094	.01051	.01012
2	.01520	.01438	.01362	.01294	.01230	.01173	.01119	.01070	.01025	.00983
3	.01557	.01470	.01391	.01319	.01253	.01192	.01136	.01084	.01036	.00992
4	.01613	.01522	.01439	.01363	.01294	.01229	.01170	.01116	.01066	.01019
5	.01687	.01591	.01504	.01424	.01351	.01283	.01221	.01164	.01111	.01062
6	.01774	.01674	.01582	.01498	.01421	.01350	.01284	.01224	.01168	.01116
7	.01871	.01766	.01670	.01581	.01500	.01425	.01356	.01292	.01233	.01178
8	.01980	.01870	.01769	.01676	.01591	.01512	.01439	.01372	.01309	.01252
9	.02104	.01989	.01883	.01785	.01695	.01612	.01535	.01464	.01398	.01337
10	.02241	.02120	.02009	.01906	.01812	.01724	.01644	.01569	.01499	.01435
11	.02394	.02267	.02150	.02042	.01943	.01851	.01766	.01688	.01615	.01547
12	.02560	.02427	.02305	.02192	.02088	.01991	.01902	.01819	.01742	.01671
13	.02734	.02595	.02467	.02349	.02240	.02139	.02045	.01958	.01877	.01802
14	.02912	.02766	.02632	.02509	.02394	.02288	.02190	.02098	.02013	.01934
15	.03087	.02935	.02795	.02666	.02546	.02435	.02331	.02235	.02146	.02063
16	.03257	.03099	.02952	.02817	.02691	.02575	.02466	.02366	.02272	.02185
17	.03423	.03257	.03104	.02962	.02831	.02709	.02595	.02490	.02391	.02300
18	.03586	.03414	.03253	.03105	.02967	.02839	.02721	.02610	.02507	.02410
19	.03752	.03572	.03414	.03249	.03105	.02971	.02846	.02730	.02621	.02520
20	.03925	.03737	.03562	.03399	.03248	.03108	.02977	.02855	.02741	.02635
21	.04107	.03910	.03727	.03557	.03398	.03251	.03114	.02986	.02866	.02755
22	.04297	.04091	.03899	.03722	.03556	.03402	.03258	.03123	.02998	.02880
23	.04498	.04283	.04083	.03897	.03723	.03562	.03410	.03269	.03137	.03014
24	.04715	.04491	.04282	.04087	.03905	.03735	.03577	.03428	.03290	.03159
25	.04953	.04718	.04499	.04295	.04105	.03927	.03761	.03605	.03459	.03322
26	.05213	.04968	.04740	.04527	.04327	.04141	.03966	.03803	.03649	.03505
27	.05499	.05243	.05005	.04782	.04573	.04377	.04194	.04023	.03861	.03710
28	.05811	.05545	.05295	.05062	.04844	.04639	.04447	.04267	.04098	.03938
29	.06146	.05868	.05608	.05365	.05136	.04922	.04721	.04532	.04354	.04187
30	.06506	.06217	.05945	.05691	.05452	.05228	.05017	.04819	.04633	.04457
31	.06888	.06586	.06303	.06038	.05789	.05554	.05334	.05126	.04930	.04746
32	.07295	.06981	.06687	.06410	.06149	.05904	.05674	.05456	.05251	.05058
33	.07728	.07401	.07095	.06806	.06535	.06279	.06038	.05810	.05595	.05392
34	.08185	.07846	.07527	.07227	.06944	.06677	.06425	.06187	.05962	.05750
35	.08671	.08319	.07988	.07675	.07380	.07102	.06839	.06590	.06355	.06132
36	.09184	.08819	.08475	.08150	.07843	.07553	.07278	.07019	.06773	.06540
37	.09725	.09347	.08989	.08652	.08332	.08030	.07745	.07474	.07217	.06974
38	.10293	.09901	.09531	.09180	.08848	.08534	.08237	.07955	.07687	.07433
39	.10889	.10483	.10099	.09736	.09391	.09065	.08755	.08462	.08182	.07917
40	.11514	.11094	.10697	.10320	.09963	.09624	.09302	.08996	.08706	.08429
41	.12168	.11735	.11324	.10934	.10564	.10212	.09878	.09560	.09258	.08970
42	.12856	.12409	.11984	.11581	.11197	.10833	.10486	.10156	.09842	.09543
43	.13574	.13113	.12675	.12258	.11862	.11484	.11125	.10783	.10456	.10145
44	.14325	.13850	.13398	.12967	.12558	.12167	.11795	.11441	.11102	.10779
45	.15105	.14616	.14150	.13706	.13283	.12880	.12495	.12128	.11777	.11442
46	.15917	.15414	.14935	.14478	.14041	.13625	.13227	.12847	.12484	.12137
47	.16760	.16244	.15751	.15280	.14831	.14402	.13991	.13599	.13223	.12863
48	.17639	.17109	.16602	.16119	.15656	.15214	.14791	.14385	.13997	.13626
49	.18551	.18007	.17488	.16991	.16516	.16060	.15625	.15207	.14806	.14422
50	.19499	.18942	.18410	.17900	.17412	.16944	.16496	.16065	.15653	.15257
51	.20480	.19911	.19366	.18844	.18343	.17862	.17401	.16959	.16534	.16126
52	.21495	.20914	.20357	.19822	.19309	.18816	.18343	.17888	.17451	.17031
53	.22544	.21951	.21381	.20835	.20309	.19805	.19320	.18853	.18404	.17972
54	.23622	.23018	.22437	.21878	.21341	.20825	.20328	.19850	.19390	.18946

Reg. § 1.642(c)-6A(d)(4)

Estates, Trusts, and Beneficiaries

Table G—Continued (7) Table G—Single Life, Unisex—Table Showing the Present Worth of the Remainder Interest in Property Transferred to a Pooled Income Fund Having the Yearly Rate of Return Shown—Applicable for Transfers After November 30, 1983, and Before May 1, 1989

(1) Age	(2) Yearly Rate of Return									
	8.2%	8.4%	8.6%	8.8%	9.0%	9.2%	9.4%	9.6%	9.8%	10.0%
55	.24732	.24116	.23524	.22954	.22406	.21878	.21370	.20881	.20409	.19954
56	.25870	.25244	.24641	.24060	.23501	.22963	.22443	.21943	.21460	.20994
57	.27040	.26404	.25791	.25200	.24630	.24081	.23551	.23040	.22546	.22069
58	.28239	.27594	.26971	.26370	.25791	.25231	.24691	.24170	.23665	.23178
59	.29472	.28817	.28186	.27576	.26987	.26418	.25868	.25336	.24822	.24325
60	.30736	.30074	.29434	.28816	.28218	.27640	.27081	.26540	.26016	.25509
61	.32035	.31365	.30718	.30092	.29486	.28899	.28332	.27782	.27249	.26733
62	.33368	.32692	.32038	.31405	.30791	.30197	.29622	.29064	.28523	.27998
63	.34735	.34054	.33394	.32754	.32134	.31533	.30950	.30385	.29836	.29304
64	.36133	.35448	.34783	.34138	.33612	.32905	.32316	.31743	.31188	.30648
65	.37562	.36873	.36204	.35554	.34924	.34311	.33716	.33138	.32576	.32030
66	.39019	.38327	.37655	.37002	.36367	.35751	.35151	.34568	.34001	.33449
67	.40502	.39809	.39134	.38479	.37841	.37221	.36618	.36030	.35459	.34902
68	.42011	.41317	.40642	.39985	.39345	.38723	.38116	.37526	.36950	.36390
69	.43547	.42854	.42179	.41522	.40882	.40257	.39649	.39056	.38478	.37914
70	.45112	.44421	.43748	.43091	.42451	.41826	.41217	.40623	.40043	.39478
71	.46711	.46023	.45352	.44698	.44059	.43435	.42827	.42233	.41642	.41086
72	.48342	.47659	.46992	.46341	.45705	.45084	.44478	.43885	.43305	.42739
73	.49998	.49321	.48660	.48014	.47382	.46765	.46161	.45571	.44994	.44429
74	.51663	.50994	.50339	.49699	.49073	.48460	.47861	.47274	.46700	.46138
75	.53322	.52661	.52014	.51381	.50762	.50155	.49561	.48979	.48409	.47851
76	.54967	.54315	.53678	.53053	.52440	.51841	.41253	.50677	.50112	.49559
77	.56595	.55954	.55326	.54710	.54106	.53514	.52934	.52364	.51806	.51258
78	.58209	.57579	.56961	.56355	.55761	.55177	.54605	.54043	.53492	.52951
79	.59814	.59196	.58590	.57995	.57410	.56837	.56273	.55720	.55177	.54643
80	.61415	.60810	.60217	.59633	.59060	.58497	.57944	.57401	.56866	.56341
81	.63001	.62410	.61830	.61260	.60699	.60148	.59606	.59073	.58548	.58033
82	.64561	.63985	.63419	.62862	.62314	.61775	.61245	.60723	.60210	.59705
83	.66095	.65535	.64983	.64441	.63907	.63381	.62863	.62354	.61852	.61358
84	.67612	.67068	.66533	.66005	.65486	.64974	.64470	.63973	.63484	.63002
85	.69116	.68589	.68070	.67559	.67055	.66558	.66068	.65586	.65110	.64641
86	.70573	.70063	.69561	.69066	.68578	.68096	.67622	.67154	.66692	.66236
87	.71939	.71466	.70961	.70481	.70009	.69542	.69082	.68628	.68180	.67738
88	.73211	.72735	.72265	.71801	.71343	.70891	.70445	.70005	.69570	.69141
89	.74417	.73956	.73501	.73053	.72609	.72172	.71739	.71312	.70891	.70474
90	.75590	.75146	.74707	.74273	.73845	.73422	.73004	.72591	.72182	.71779
91	.76724	.76296	.75873	.75454	.75041	.74632	.74229	.73829	.73435	.73045
92	.77781	.77368	.76960	.76556	.76158	.75763	.75373	.74988	.74606	.74229
93	.78740	.78342	.77948	.77558	.77173	.76791	.76414	.76042	.75673	.75308
94	.79596	.79210	.78829	.78452	.78079	.77710	.77345	.76983	.76626	.76272
95	.80341	.79967	.79597	.79231	.78869	.78510	.78155	.77304	.77457	.77113
96	.80967	.80603	.80242	.79885	.79532	.79183	.78837	.78494	.78155	.77819
97	.81526	.81170	.80818	.80470	.80125	.79783	.79445	.79110	.78779	.78450
98	.82013	.81665	.81320	.80979	.80641	.80306	.79975	.79647	.79322	.79000
99	.82470	.82129	.81791	.81456	.81125	.80797	.80471	.80149	.79830	.79514
100	.82924	.82590	.82258	.81930	.81605	.81283	.80964	.80648	.80335	.80025
101	.83322	.82993	.82667	.82344	.82024	.81708	.81394	.81082	.80774	.80468
102	.83751	.83428	.83108	.82791	.82477	.82165	.81856	.81550	.81247	.80946
103	.84301	.83986	.83674	.83365	.83058	.82754	.82452	.82153	.81857	.81563
104	.84826	.84518	.84213	.83910	.83610	.83312	.83017	.82723	.82433	.82144
105	.85623	.85327	.85033	.84741	.84452	.84164	.83880	.83597	.83316	.83038
106	.86915	.86641	.86369	.86098	.85829	.85562	.85297	.85034	.84772	.84512
107	.88718	.88476	.88236	.87997	.87759	.87523	.87288	.87054	.86822	.86591
108	.91571	.91385	.91201	.91017	.90834	.90652	.90471	.90291	.90111	.89932
109	.96211	.96125	.96041	.95966	.95872	.95788	.95704	.95620	.95537	.95455

Reg. § 1.642(c)-6A(d)(4)

43,244 Estates, Trusts, and Beneficiaries

See p. 20,601 for regulations not amended to reflect law changes

Table G—Continued (8) Table G—Single Life, Unisex—Table Showing the Present Worth of the Remainder Interest in Property Transferred to a Pooled Income Fund Having the Yearly Rate of Return Shown—Applicable for Transfers After November 30, 1983, and Before May 1, 1989

(1) Age	(2) Yearly Rate of Return									
	10.2%	10.4%	10.6%	10.8%	11.0%	11.2%	11.4%	11.6%	11.8%	12.0%
0	.02776	.02743	.02712	.02682	.02655	.02630	.02606	.02583	.02562	.02542
1	.00975	.00941	.00909	.00880	.00852	.00827	.00803	.00780	.00759	.00739
2	.00945	.00909	.00875	.00844	.00816	.00789	.00763	.00740	.00718	.00697
3	.00952	.00914	.00879	.00846	.00815	.00787	.00760	.00736	.00712	.00690
4	.00976	.00936	.00899	.00865	.00832	.00802	.00774	.00748	.00723	.00700
5	.01016	.00974	.00935	.00898	.00864	.00832	.00802	.00774	.00748	.00724
6	.01068	.01023	.00981	.00943	.00907	.00873	.00841	.00812	.00784	.00758
7	.01128	.01080	.01036	.00995	.00957	.00921	.00888	.00856	.00827	.00799
8	.01198	.01148	.01101	.01058	.01017	.00979	.00944	.00910	.00879	.00850
9	.01281	.01228	.01179	.01133	.01090	.01049	.01012	.00976	.00943	.00912
10	.01375	.01319	.01267	.01219	.01173	.01131	.01091	.01053	.01018	.00985
11	.01483	.01425	.01370	.01318	.01270	.01225	.01183	.01143	.01106	.01070
12	.01604	.01542	.01484	.01430	.01379	.01331	.01286	.01244	.01205	.01168
13	.01732	.01666	.01605	.01548	.01494	.01444	.01397	.01352	.01311	.01271
14	.01860	.01792	.01727	.01667	.01610	.01558	.01508	.01461	.01417	.01375
15	.01986	.01913	.01845	.01782	.01723	.01667	.01614	.01565	.01519	.01475
16	.02103	.02027	.01956	.01889	.01827	.01768	.01713	.01661	.01612	.01566
17	.02214	.02134	.02059	.01989	.01923	.01862	.01803	.01749	.01697	.01649
18	.02320	.02236	.02157	.02084	.02014	.01949	.01888	.01831	.01776	.01725
19	.02426	.02337	.02254	.02177	.02104	.02035	.01971	.01910	.01853	.01799
20	.02536	.02442	.02355	.02273	.02197	.02124	.02056	.01992	.01932	.01875
21	.02650	.02552	.02460	.02374	.02293	.02217	.02145	.02078	.02014	.01954
22	.02770	.02667	.02570	.02479	.02394	.02313	.02238	.02166	.02099	.02035
23	.02898	.02789	.02687	.02591	.02501	.02416	.02336	.02261	.02190	.02122
24	.03037	.02923	.02815	.02714	.02619	.02529	.02445	.02365	.02290	.02218
25	.03194	.03073	.02960	.02853	.02752	.02657	.02568	.02484	.02404	.02328
26	.03370	.03243	.03123	.03010	.02904	.02804	.02710	.02620	.02536	.02456
27	.05688	.03434	.03307	.03188	.03076	.02970	.02870	.02776	.02686	.02601
28	.03789	.03647	.03614	.03389	.03271	.03159	.03053	.02953	.02858	.02768
29	.04029	.03880	.03740	.03608	.03483	.03365	.03253	.03147	.03047	.02951
30	.04291	.04135	.03987	.03848	.03716	.03591	.03473	.03361	.03255	.03154
31	.04572	.04407	.04252	.04105	.03966	.03834	.03709	.03591	.03478	.03372
32	.04875	.04702	.04538	.04384	.04237	.04098	.03966	.03841	.03722	.03610
33	.05200	.05019	.04847	.04684	.04530	.04383	.04244	.04112	.03987	.03867
34	.05548	.05358	.05177	.05006	.04843	.04689	.04543	.04403	.04271	.04145
35	.05921	.05722	.05532	.05352	.05181	.05019	.04865	.04718	.04578	.04445
36	.06319	.06110	.05911	.05722	.05543	.05372	.05210	.05055	.04907	.04767
37	.06743	.06524	.06315	.06117	.05929	.05749	.05578	.05416	.05260	.05112
38	.07191	.06962	.06744	.06536	.06338	.06150	.05970	.05799	.05636	.05480
39	.07665	.07425	.07197	.06980	.06773	.06575	.06387	.06207	.06035	.05871
40	.08166	.07916	.07677	.07450	.07233	.07026	.06828	.06639	.06459	.06286
41	.08696	.08434	.08185	.07947	.07721	.07504	.07297	.07099	.06909	.06728
42	.09257	.08985	.08725	.08477	.08239	.08018	.07796	.07589	.07390	.07200
43	.09848	.09564	.09293	.09034	.08787	.08550	.08323	.08106	.07898	.07699
44	.10470	.10175	.09893	.09623	.09365	.09118	.08881	.08654	.08437	.08228
45	.11121	.10815	.10522	.10241	.09972	.09714	.09467	.09230	.09003	.08784
46	.11805	.11486	.11182	.10890	.10610	.10341	.10084	.09837	.09599	.09371
47	.12519	.12189	.11873	.11569	.11279	.10999	.10731	.10473	.10226	.09988
48	.13269	.12927	.12600	.12285	.11983	.11693	.11414	.11145	.10888	.10639
49	.14054	.13700	.13361	.13035	.12721	.12721	.12130	.11852	.11583	.11325
50	.14876	.14511	.14160	.13822	.13497	.13185	.12884	.12595	.12316	.12047
51	.15734	.15356	.14994	.14645	.14309	.13985	.13674	.13373	.13084	.12805
52	.16627	.16238	.15864	.15504	.15156	.14822	.14499	.14188	.13888	.13598
53	.17557	.17156	.16770	.16399	.16040	.15695	.15361	.15039	.14729	.14428
54	.18519	.18107	.17710	.17327	.16957	.16601	.16256	.15924	.15602	.15292

Reg. § 1.642(c)-6A(d)(4)

Estates, Trusts, and Beneficiaries

Table G—Continued (9) Table G—Single Life, Unisex—Table Showing the Present Worth of the Remainder Interest in Property Transferred to a Pooled Income Fund Having The Yearly Rate Of Return Shown—Applicable for Transfers After November 30, 1983, and Before May 1, 1989

(1) Age	\(2\) Yearly Rate of Return									
	10.2%	10.4%	10.6%	10.8%	11.0%	11.2%	11.4%	11.6%	11.8%	12.0%
55	.19515	.19092	.18684	.18290	.17909	.17542	.17186	.16843	.16511	.16190
56	.20544	.20110	.19691	.19286	.18894	.18516	.18150	.17796	.17454	.17122
57	.21609	.21164	.20734	.20318	.19916	.19527	.19150	.18786	.18733	.18091
58	.22707	.22252	.21811	.21385	.20972	.20573	.20186	.19811	.19448	.19096
59	.23844	.23378	.22928	.22491	.22068	.21659	.21262	.20877	.20504	.20142
60	.25018	.24543	.24082	.23636	.23203	.22784	.22377	.21982	.21599	.21227
61	.26233	.25749	.25279	.24823	.24381	.23952	.23535	.23131	.22738	.22357
62	.27490	.26996	.26517	.26052	.25601	.25163	.24737	.24324	.23922	.23531
63	.28787	.28286	.27798	.27325	.26865	.26418	.25984	.25561	.25151	.24751
64	.30124	.29615	.29120	.28639	.28171	.27716	.27273	.26842	.26423	.26015
65	.31500	.30983	.30481	.29993	.29517	.29054	.28604	.28165	.27738	.27322
66	.32912	.32390	.31881	.31386	.30904	.30434	.29976	.29530	.29096	.28672
67	.34360	.33832	.33318	.32817	.32328	.31852	.31388	.30935	.30494	.30063
68	.35843	.35311	.34791	.34285	.33791	.33310	.32840	.32381	.31933	.31496
69	.37365	.36828	.36305	.35794	.35296	.34809	.34334	.33870	.33417	.32975
70	.38925	.38386	.37860	.37346	.36844	.36353	.35874	.35405	.34948	.34500
71	.40532	.39991	.39463	.38945	.38442	.37948	.37466	.36994	.36532	.36081
72	.42185	.41644	.41115	.40597	.40091	.39595	.39111	.38636	.38172	.37718
73	.43876	.43336	.42807	.42289	.41782	.41286	.40801	.40325	.39859	.39403
74	.45588	.45050	.44522	.44005	.43499	.43004	.42518	.42042	.41575	.41118
75	.47304	.46769	.46244	.45729	.45225	.44730	.44245	.43770	.43304	.42846
76	.49016	.48485	.47963	.47451	.46949	.46457	.45974	.45500	.45035	.44579
77	.50721	.50193	.49676	.49168	.48670	.48181	.47700	.47229	.46766	.46311
78	.52419	.51898	.51385	.50882	.50388	.49903	.49426	.48958	.48497	.48045
79	.54119	.53604	.54097	.52600	.52111	.51631	.51159	.50694	.50238	.49789
80	.55825	.55318	.54819	.54328	.53846	.53371	.52905	.52446	.51994	.51550
81	.57526	.57027	.56536	.56053	.55578	.55110	.54650	.54197	.53752	.53313
82	.59208	.58718	.58236	.57762	.57295	.56835	.56382	.55937	.55497	.55065
83	.60871	.60392	.59920	.59455	.58997	.58546	.58101	.57663	.57231	.56806
84	.62527	.62959	.62597	.61143	.60695	.60253	.59817	.59388	.58965	.58547
85	.64179	.63723	.63273	.62830	.62393	.61961	.61536	.61116	.60703	.60294
86	.65787	.65344	.64907	.64475	.64050	.63630	.63215	.62806	.62402	.62004
87	.67302	.66871	.66446	.66026	.65612	.65203	.64800	.64401	.64007	.63619
88	.68717	.68298	.67885	.67477	.67074	.66676	.66282	.65894	.65510	.65131
89	.70063	.69656	.69255	.68858	.68466	.68079	.67696	.67318	.66944	.66574
90	.71380	.70986	.70597	.70212	.69831	.69455	.69084	.68716	.68353	.67993
91	.72659	.72278	.71901	.71528	.71160	.70795	.70435	.70078	.69726	.69377
92	.73856	.73488	.73123	.72762	.72405	.72052	.71703	.71357	.71015	.70677
93	.74947	.74590	.74236	.73887	.73541	.73198	.72860	.72524	.72192	.71864
94	.75922	.75575	.75233	.74893	.74557	.74225	.73896	.73570	.73248	.72928
95	.76773	.76436	.76102	.75772	.75445	.75121	.74801	.74483	.74169	.73858
96	.77487	.77158	.76832	.76510	.76190	.75874	.75561	.75250	.74943	.74639
97	.78125	.77803	.77485	.77169	.76856	.76546	.76240	.75936	.75635	.75336
98	.78681	.78365	.78052	.77742	.77435	.77131	.76830	.76531	.76235	.75942
99	.79201	.78891	.78583	.78279	.77977	.77678	.77382	.77088	.76798	.76509
100	.79717	.79412	.79111	.78811	.78515	.78221	.77930	.77642	.77356	.77072
101	.80165	.79865	.79568	.79273	.78981	.78691	.78404	.78119	.77837	.77557
102	.80648	.80353	.80060	.79769	.79481	.79196	.78912	.78632	.78353	.78077
103	.81271	.80982	.80695	.80411	.80129	.79849	.79572	.79297	.79024	.78753
104	.81858	.81574	.81292	.81013	.80736	.80460	.80188	.79917	.79648	.79381
105	.82761	.82487	.82214	.81943	.81675	.81408	.81143	.80881	.80620	.80361
106	.84254	.83998	.83743	.83490	.83238	.82989	.82740	.82494	.82249	.82006
107	.86362	.86133	.85906	.85681	.85456	.85233	.85012	.84791	.84572	.84353
108	.89755	.89577	.89401	.89226	.89051	.88877	.88704	.88532	.88361	.88190
109	.95372	.95290	.95208	.95126	.95045	.94964	.94883	.94803	.94723	.94643

Reg. § 1.642(c)-6A(d)(4)

43,246 Estates, Trusts, and Beneficiaries

See p. 20,601 for regulations not amended to reflect law changes

Table G—Continued (10) Table G—Single Life, Unisex—Table Showing the Present Worth of the Remainder Interest in Property Transferred to a Pooled Income Fund Having the Yearly Rate of Return Shown—Applicable for Transfers After November 30, 1983, and Before May 1, 1989

(1) Age	(2) Yearly Rate of Return									
	12.2%	12.4%	12.6%	12.8%	13.0%	13.2%	13.4%	13.6%	13.8%	14.0%
0	.02523	.02505	.02488	.02472	.02456	.02442	.02428	.02414	.02402	.02389
1	.00721	.00703	.00687	.00671	.00657	.00643	.00629	.00617	.00605	.00594
2	.00678	.00659	.00642	.00626	.00610	.00596	.00582	.00569	.00556	.00544
3	.00670	.00650	.00632	.00615	.00599	.00583	.00569	.00555	.00542	.00529
4	.00678	.00658	.00638	.00620	.00603	.00586	.00571	.00556	.00542	.00529
5	.00701	.00679	.00658	.00639	.00620	.00603	.00587	.00571	.00556	.00542
6	.00733	.00710	.00688	.00668	.00648	.00630	.00612	.00595	.00580	.00565
7	.00773	.00748	.00725	.00703	.00682	.00663	.00644	.00626	.00610	.00594
8	.00822	.00796	.00771	.00748	.00726	.00705	.00685	.00666	.00648	.00631
9	.00882	.00854	.00828	.00803	.00780	.00757	.00736	.00716	.00697	.00679
10	.00953	.00924	.00896	.00869	.00844	.00821	.00798	.00777	.00756	.00737
11	.01037	.01006	.00976	.00948	.00922	.00896	.00872	.00850	.00828	.00807
12	.01132	.01099	.01068	.01038	.01010	.00983	.00958	.00934	.00911	.00889
13	.01234	.01199	.01166	.01134	.01104	.01076	.01049	.01024	.00999	.00976
14	.01336	.01299	.01264	.01231	.01199	.01170	.01141	.01114	.01088	.01064
15	.01434	.01395	.01358	.01323	.01289	.01258	.01228	.01200	.01172	.01147
16	.01552	.01481	.01442	.01405	.01371	.01337	.01306	.01275	.01247	.01220
17	.01603	.01559	.01518	.01480	.01443	.01408	.01375	.01343	.01313	.01284
18	.01677	.01631	.01588	.01547	.01508	.01471	.01436	.01403	.01371	.01341
19	.01748	.01700	.01654	.01611	.01570	.01531	.01494	.01459	.01426	.01394
20	.01821	.01770	.01722	.01677	.01633	.01592	.01553	.01516	.01481	.01447
21	.01897	.01843	.01792	.01744	.01698	.01655	.01614	.01574	.01537	.01502
22	.01975	.01918	.01864	.01813	.01765	.01719	.01675	.01634	.01594	.01557
23	.02059	.01998	.01941	.01887	.01836	.01787	.01741	.01697	.01655	.01615
24	.02151	.02087	.02027	.01970	.01915	.01863	.01814	.01768	.01723	.01681
25	.02257	.02189	.02125	.02064	.02006	.01952	.01899	.01850	.01802	.01757
26	.02380	.02308	.02240	.02175	.02114	.02056	.02000	.01947	.01897	.01849
27	.02521	.02445	.02373	.02304	.02239	.02177	.02118	.02061	.02008	.01956
28	.02683	.02602	.02525	.02452	.02382	.02317	.02254	.02194	.02137	.02082
29	.02861	.02775	.02694	.02616	.02543	.02472	.02405	.02342	.02281	.02223
30	.03058	.02967	.02881	.02798	.02720	.02645	.02574	.02506	.02441	.02379
31	.03270	.03174	.03082	.02995	.02911	.02832	.02756	.02684	.02615	.02549
32	.03502	.03400	.03303	.03210	.03122	.03037	.02957	.02880	.02806	.02736
33	.03754	.03646	.03543	.03444	.03350	.03261	.03175	.03093	.03015	.02940
34	.04025	.03910	.03801	.03697	.03597	.03502	.03411	.03324	.03241	.03162
35	.04318	.04197	.04081	.03971	.03865	.03764	.03668	.03576	.03488	.03403
36	.04633	.04505	.04383	.04266	.04154	.04048	.03945	.03847	.03754	.03664
37	.04971	.04836	.04707	.04583	.04465	.04352	.04244	.04140	.04040	.03945
38	.05331	.05188	.05052	.04922	.04797	.04677	.04563	.04453	.04347	.04246
39	.05714	.05564	.05420	.05282	.05150	.05024	.04903	.04787	.04675	.04568
40	.06121	.05963	.05812	.05667	.05528	.05394	.05266	.05143	.05025	.04912
41	.06554	.06388	.06229	.06076	.05929	.05789	.05653	.05524	.05399	.05279
42	.07018	.06843	.06675	.06514	.06360	.06212	.06069	.05932	.05800	.05674
43	.07508	.07324	.07148	.06979	.06817	.06661	.06511	.06366	.06227	.06093
44	.08028	.07835	.07651	.07473	.07303	.07138	.06980	.06828	.06682	.06541
45	.08575	.08373	.08180	.07993	.07814	.07642	.07476	.07316	.07162	.07013
46	.09152	.08941	.08738	.08543	.08355	.08174	.08000	.07832	.07670	.07514
47	.09759	.09539	.09326	.09122	.08926	.08736	.08553	.08377	.08207	.08042
48	.10410	.10171	.09949	.09735	.09530	.09331	.09140	.08955	.08776	.08604
49	.11076	.10836	.10605	.10382	.10167	.09959	.09759	.09565	.09378	.09198
50	.11788	.11538	.11297	.11065	.10840	.10624	.10414	.10212	.10016	.09827
51	.12535	.12276	.12025	.11782	.11548	.11322	.11104	.10892	.10688	.10490
52	.13319	.13049	.12788	.12536	.12292	.12057	.11829	.11608	.11395	.11188
53	.14139	.13858	.13588	.13326	.13072	.12827	.12590	.12360	.12138	.11922
54	.14992	.14701	.14420	.14149	.13885	.13631	.13384	.13145	.12913	.12689

Reg. § 1.642(c)-6A(d)(4)

Estates, Trusts, and Beneficiaries

See p. 20,601 for regulations not amended to reflect law changes

43,247

Table G—Continued (11) Table G—Single Life, Unisex—Table Showing the Present Worth of the Remainder Interest in Property Transferred to a Pooled Income Fund Having the Yearly Rate of Return Shown—Applicable for Transfers After November 30, 1983, and Before May 1, 1989

(1) Age	(2) Yearly Rate of Return								
	12.2%	12.4%	12.6%	12.8%	13.0%	13.2%	13.4%	13.6%	13.8%	14.0%
55	.15880	.15579	.15288	.15006	.14733	.14469	.14213	.13964	.13724	.13490
56	.16801	.16491	.16190	.15898	.15615	.15341	.15075	.14817	.14567	.14324
57	.17760	.17439	.17128	.16827	.16534	.16250	.15975	.15708	.15448	.15196
58	.18755	.18424	.18103	.17792	.17489	.17196	.16911	.16634	.16365	.16104
59	.19790	.19450	.19119	.18798	.18486	.18183	.17888	.17602	.17324	.17053
60	.20866	.20516	.20175	.19844	.19523	.19210	.18906	.18611	.18323	.18043
61	.21986	.21626	.21276	.20936	.20695	.20283	.19970	.19665	.19368	.19079
62	.23151	.22782	.22423	.22073	.21733	.21402	.21079	.20766	.20460	.20162
63	.24362	.23984	.23616	.23257	.22908	.22568	.22237	.21914	.21600	.21293
64	.25617	.25231	.24854	.24487	.24129	.23780	.23440	.23109	.22786	.22471
65	.26917	.26522	.26137	.25761	.25395	.25038	.24690	.24350	.24019	.23695
66	.28259	.27857	.27464	.27081	.26707	.26342	.25986	.25638	.25298	.24967
67	.29643	.29233	.28833	.28443	.28061	.27689	.27325	.26970	.26623	.26284
68	.31070	.30653	.30246	.29849	.29461	.29081	.28711	.28348	.27994	.27647
69	.32542	.32120	.31707	.31303	.30908	.30523	.30145	.29776	.29415	.29062
70	.34063	.33635	.33217	.32807	.32407	.32015	.31632	.31257	.30890	.30530
71	.35639	.35207	.34784	.34370	.33965	.33568	.33179	.32799	.32426	.32061
72	.37273	.36837	.36410	.35993	.35583	.35182	.34789	.34404	.34027	.33657
73	.38955	.38517	.38088	.37667	.37255	.36815	.36455	.36066	.35685	.35311
74	.40670	.40230	.39799	.39377	.38962	.38555	.38156	.37765	.37381	.37004
75	.42398	.41958	.41526	.41102	.40686	.40278	.39877	.39484	.39098	.38719
76	.44131	.43691	.43259	.42835	.42419	.42010	.41608	.41213	.40826	.40445
77	.45864	.45425	.44994	.44571	.44155	.43746	.43344	.42949	.42561	.42179
78	.47601	.47164	.46734	.46312	.45897	.45489	.45088	.44693	.44305	.43923
79	.49348	.48914	.48487	.48067	.47654	.47248	.46848	.46454	.46067	.45686
80	.51112	.50682	.50259	.49842	.49432	.49028	.48631	.48240	.47854	.47475
81	.52881	.52455	.52036	.51624	.51218	.50818	.50423	.50035	.49653	.49276
82	.54639	.54219	.53805	.53398	.52996	.52600	.52210	.51826	.51447	.51074
83	.56386	.55973	.55566	.55164	.54768	.54377	.53992	.53613	.53238	.52869
84	.58136	.57730	.57329	.56934	.56545	.56160	.55781	.55407	.55038	.54674
85	.59891	.59494	.59102	.58715	.58333	.57956	.57584	.57216	.56854	.56496
86	.61610	.61222	.60839	.60460	.60086	.59717	.59353	.58993	.58638	.58287
87	.63235	.62856	.62481	.62111	.61746	.61385	.61028	.61676	.60328	.59984
88	.64757	.64386	.64021	.63659	.63302	.62950	.62601	.62256	.61915	.61578
89	.66209	.65848	.65491	.65149	.64790	.64445	.64104	.63767	.63434	.63105
90	.67638	.67387	.66939	.66596	.66256	.65920	.65588	.65259	.64934	.64612
91	.69032	.68691	.68353	.68019	.67689	.67362	.67039	.66719	.66402	.66089
92	.70342	.70011	.69683	.69359	.69038	.68720	.68405	.68094	.67786	.67481
93	.71539	.71217	.70899	.70584	.70271	.69962	.69657	.69354	.69054	.68757
94	.72612	.72299	.71989	.71683	.71379	.71078	.70780	.70485	.70193	.69903
95	.73550	.73245	.73943	.72643	.72347	.72053	.71763	.71475	.71189	.70906
96	.74337	.74039	.73743	.73450	.73160	.73872	.72587	.72305	.72026	.71748
97	.75041	.74748	.74458	.74171	.73886	.73604	.73325	.73048	.72773	.72501
98	.75652	.75364	.75079	.74797	.74517	.74329	.73964	.73692	.73422	.73154
99	.76224	.75941	.75660	.75882	.75106	.74833	.74562	.74294	.74028	.73764
100	.76791	.76521	.76237	.75963	.75692	.75423	.75156	.74892	.74630	.74370
101	.77280	.77005	.75732	.76462	.76194	.75928	.75664	.75403	.75144	.74887
102	.77804	.77532	.77263	.76996	.76732	.76469	.76209	.75950	.75694	.75440
103	.78485	.78218	.77954	.77692	.77432	.77174	.76918	.76664	.76413	.76163
104	.79117	.78854	.78594	.78335	.78078	.77824	.77571	.77320	.77071	.76824
105	.80103	.79848	.79595	.79343	.79093	.78845	.78599	.78354	.78111	.77870
106	.81764	.81524	.81285	.81048	.80813	.80579	.80346	.80115	.79885	.79657
107	.84137	.83921	.83706	.83493	.83281	.83070	.82860	.82652	.82444	.82238
108	.88020	.87851	.87682	.87515	.87348	.87182	.87016	.86852	.86688	.86525
109	.94563	.94484	.94405	.94326	.94248	.94170	.94092	.94014	.93937	.93860

Reg. § 1.642(c)-6A(d)(4)

(e) *Present value of the remainder interest in the case of transfers to pooled income funds for which the valuation date is after April 30, 1989, and before May 1, 1999*—(1) *In general.* In the case of transfers to pooled income funds for which the valuation date is after April 30, 1989, and before May 1, 1999, the present value of a remainder interest is determined under this section. See, however, § 1.7520-3(b) (relating to exceptions to the use of prescribed tables under certain circumstances). The present value of a remainder interest that is dependent on the termination of the life of one individual is computed by the use of Table S in paragraph (e)(5) of this section. For purposes of the computations under this section, the age of an individual is the age at the individual's nearest birthday. If the valuation date of a transfer to a pooled income fund is after April 30, 1989, and before June 10, 1994, a transferor can rely on Notice 89-24, 1989-1 C.B. 660, or Notice 89-60, 1989-1 C.B. 700, in valuing the transferred interest. (See § 601.601(d)(2)(ii)(*b*) of this chapter.)

(2) *Present value of a remainder interest.* The present value of a remainder interest in property transferred to a pooled income fund is computed on the basis of—

(i) Life contingencies determined from the values of l_x that are set forth in Table 80CNSMT in § 20.2031-7A(e)(4) of this chapter (Estate Tax Regulations); and

(ii) Discount at a rate of interest, compounded annually, equal to the highest yearly rate of return of the pooled income fund for the 3 taxable years immediately preceding its taxable year in which the transfer of property to the fund is made. The provisions of § 1.642(c)-6(c) apply for determining the yearly rate of return. However, where the taxable year is less than 12 months, the provisions of § 1.642(c)-6(e)(3)(ii) apply for the determining the yearly rate of return.

(3) *Pooled income funds in existence less than 3 taxable years.* The provisions of § 1.642(c)-6(e)(4) apply for determining the highest yearly rate of return when the pooled income fund has been in existence less than three taxable years.

(4) *Computation of value of remainder interest.* The factor that is used in determining the present value of a remainder interest that is dependent on the termination of the life of one individual is the factor from Table S in paragraph (e)(5) of this section under the appropriate yearly rate of return opposite the number that corresponds to the age of the individual upon whose life the value of the remainder interest is based. Table S in paragraph (e)(5) of this section includes factors for yearly rates of return from 4.2 to 14 percent. Many actuarial factors not contained in Table S in paragraph (e)(5) of this section are contained in Table S in Internal Revenue Service Publication 1457, "Actuarial Values, Alpha Volume," (8-89). Publication 1457 is no longer available for purchase from the Superintendent of Documents, United States Government Printing Office, Washington, DC 20402. However, pertinent factors in this publication may be obtained by a written request to: CC:DOM:CORP:R (IRS Publication 1457), room 5226,Internal Revenue Service, POB 7604, Ben Franklin Station, Washington, DC 20044. For other situations, see § 1.642(c)-6(b). If the yearly rate of return is a percentage that is between the yearly rates of return for which factors are provided, a linear interpolation must be made. The present value of the remainder interest is determined by multiplying the fair market value of the property on the valuation date by the appropriate remainder factor. For an example of a computation of the present value of a remainder interest requiring a linear interpolation adjustment, see § 1.642(c)-6(e)(5).

(5) *Actuarial tables.* In the case of transfers for which the valuation date is after April 30, 1989, and before May 1, 1999, the present value of a remainder interest dependent on the termination of one life in the case of a transfer to a pooled income fund is determined by use of the following tables:

Estates, Trusts, and Beneficiaries 43,249

See p. 20,601 for regulations not amended to reflect law changes

TABLE S
BASED ON LIFE TABLE 80CNSMT
SINGLE LIFE REMAINDER FACTORS
APPLICABLE AFTER APRIL 30, 1989,
AND BEFORE MAY 1, 1999

INTEREST RATE

AGE	4.2%	4.4%	4.6%	4.8%	5.0%	5.2%	5.4%	5.6%	5.8%	6.0%
0	.07389	.06749	.06188	.05695	.05261	.04879	.04541	.04243	.03978	.03744
1	.06494	.05832	.05250	.04738	.04287	.03889	.03537	.03226	.02950	.02705
2	.06678	.05999	.05401	.04874	.04410	.03999	.03636	.03314	.03028	.02773
3	.06897	.06200	.05587	.05045	.04567	.04143	.03768	.03435	.03139	.02875
4	.07139	.06425	.05796	.05239	.04746	.04310	.03922	.03578	.03271	.02998
5	.07401	.06669	.06023	.05451	.04944	.04494	.04094	.03738	.03421	.03137
6	.07677	.06928	.06265	.05677	.05156	.04692	.04279	.03911	.03583	.03289
7	.07968	.07201	.06521	.05918	.05381	.04903	.04477	.04097	.03757	.03453
8	.08274	.07489	.06792	.06172	.05621	.05129	.04689	.04297	.03945	.03630
9	.08597	.07794	.07079	.06443	.05876	.05370	.04917	.04511	.04148	.03821
10	.08936	.08115	.07383	.06730	.06147	.05626	.05159	.04741	.04365	.04027
11	.09293	.08453	.07704	.07035	.06436	.05900	.05419	.04988	.04599	.04250
12	.09666	.08807	.08040	.07354	.06739	.06188	.05693	.05248	.04847	.04486
13	.10049	.09172	.08387	.07684	.07053	.06487	.05977	.05518	.05104	.04731
14	.10437	.09541	.08738	.08017	.07370	.06788	.06263	.05791	.05364	.04978
15	.10827	.09912	.09090	.08352	.07688	.07090	.06551	.06064	.05623	.05225
16	.11220	.10285	.09445	.08689	.08008	.07394	.06839	.06337	.05883	.05472
17	.11615	.10661	.09802	.09028	.08330	.07699	.07129	.06612	.06144	.05719
18	.12017	.11043	.10165	.09373	.08656	.08009	.07422	.06890	.06408	.05969
19	.12428	.11434	.10537	.09726	.08992	.08327	.07724	.07177	.06679	.06226
20	.12850	.11836	.10919	.10089	.09337	.08654	.08035	.07471	.06959	.06492
21	.13282	.12248	.11311	.10462	.09692	.08991	.08355	.07775	.07247	.06765
22	.13728	.12673	.11717	.10848	.10059	.09341	.08686	.08090	.07546	.07049
23	.14188	.13113	.12136	.11248	.10440	.09703	.09032	.08418	.07858	.07345
24	.14667	.13572	.12575	.11667	.10839	.10084	.09395	.08764	.08187	.07659
25	.15167	.14051	.13034	.12106	.11259	.10486	.09778	.09130	.08536	.07991
26	.15690	.14554	.13517	.12569	.11703	.10910	.10184	.09518	.08907	.08346
27	.16237	.15081	.14024	.13056	.12171	.11359	.10614	.09930	.09302	.08724
28	.16808	.15632	.14555	.13567	.12662	.11831	.11068	.10366	.09720	.09125
29	.17404	.16208	.15110	.14104	.13179	.12329	.11547	.10827	.10163	.09551
30	.18025	.16808	.15692	.14665	.13721	.12852	.12051	.11313	.10631	.10002
31	.18672	.17436	.16300	.15255	.14291	.13403	.12584	.11827	.11127	.10480
32	.19344	.18090	.16935	.15870	.14888	.13980	.13142	.12367	.11650	.10985
33	.20044	.18772	.17598	.16514	.15513	.14587	.13730	.12936	.12201	.11519
34	.20770	.19480	.18287	.17185	.16165	.15221	.14345	.13533	.12780	.12080
35	.21522	.20215	.19005	.17884	.16846	.15883	.14989	.14159	.13388	.12670
36	.22299	.20974	.19747	.18609	.17552	.16571	.15660	.14812	.14022	.13287
37	.23101	.21760	.20516	.19360	.18286	.17288	.16358	.15492	.14685	.13933
38	.23928	.22572	.21311	.20139	.19048	.18032	.17085	.16201	.15377	.14607
39	.24780	.23409	.22133	.20945	.19837	.18804	.17840	.16939	.16097	.15310
40	.25658	.24273	.22982	.21778	.20654	.19605	.18624	.17706	.16847	.16043
41	.26560	.25163	.23858	.22639	.21499	.20434	.19436	.18502	.17627	.16806
42	.27486	.26076	.24758	.23525	.22370	.21289	.20276	.19326	.18434	.17597
43	.28435	.27013	.25683	.24436	.23268	.22172	.21143	.20177	.19270	.18416
44	.29407	.27975	.26633	.25373	.24191	.23081	.22038	.21057	.20134	.19265
45	.30402	.28961	.27608	.26337	.25142	.24019	.22962	.21966	.21028	.20144
46	.31420	.29970	.28608	.27326	.26120	.24983	.23913	.22904	.21951	.21053
47	.32460	.31004	.29632	.28341	.27123	.25975	.24892	.23870	.22904	.21991
48	.33521	.32058	.30679	.29379	.28151	.26992	.25897	.24862	.23883	.22957
49	.34599	.33132	.31746	.30438	.29201	.28032	.26926	.25879	.24888	.23949
50	.35695	.34224	.32833	.31518	.30273	.29094	.27978	.26921	.25918	.24966
51	.36809	.35335	.33940	.32619	.31367	.30180	.29055	.27987	.26973	.26010
52	.37944	.36468	.35070	.33744	.32486	.31292	.30158	.29081	.28057	.27083
53	.39098	.37622	.36222	.34892	.33629	.32429	.31288	.30203	.29170	.28186
54	.40269	.38794	.37393	.36062	.34795	.33590	.32442	.31349	.30308	.29316
55	.41457	.39985	.38585	.37252	.35983	.34774	.33621	.32522	.31474	.30473
56	.42662	.41194	.39796	.38464	.37193	.35981	.34824	.33720	.32666	.31658
57	.43884	.42422	.41028	.39697	.38426	.37213	.36053	.34945	.33885	.32872

Reg. § 1.642(c)-6A(e)(5)

43,250   Estates, Trusts, and Beneficiaries

See p. 20,601 for regulations not amended to reflect law changes

AGE	4.2%	4.4%	4.6%	4.8%	5.0%	5.2%	5.4%	5.6%	5.8%	6.0%
58	.45123	.43668	.42279	.40951	.39682	.38468	.37307	.36196	.35132	.34114
59	.46377	.44931	.43547	.42224	.40958	.39745	.38584	.37471	.36405	.35383
60	.47643	.46206	.44830	.43513	.42250	.41040	.39880	.38767	.37699	.36674
61	.48916	.47491	.46124	.44814	.43556	.42350	.41192	.40080	.39012	.37985
62	.50196	.48783	.47427	.46124	.44874	.43672	.42518	.41408	.40340	.39314
63	.51480	.50081	.48736	.47444	.46201	.45006	.43856	.42749	.41684	.40658
64	.52770	.51386	.50054	.48773	.47540	.46352	.45208	.44105	.43043	.42019
65	.54069	.52701	.51384	.50115	.48892	.47713	.46577	.45480	.44422	.43401
66	.55378	.54029	.52727	.51472	.50262	.49093	.47965	.46876	.45824	.44808
67	.56697	.55368	.54084	.52845	.51648	.50491	.49373	.48293	.47248	.46238
68	.58026	.56717	.55453	.54231	.53049	.51905	.50800	.49729	.48694	.47691
69	.59358	.58072	.56828	.55624	.54459	.53330	.52238	.51179	.50154	.49160
70	.60689	.59427	.58205	.57021	.55874	.54762	.53683	.52638	.51624	.50641
71	.62014	.60778	.59578	.58415	.57287	.56193	.55131	.54100	.53099	.52126
72	.63334	.62123	.60948	.59808	.58700	.57624	.56579	.55563	.54577	.53617
73	.64648	.63465	.62315	.61198	.60112	.59056	.58029	.57030	.56059	.55113
74	.65961	.64806	.63682	.62590	.61527	.60492	.59485	.58504	.57550	.56620
75	.67274	.66149	.65054	.63987	.62948	.61936	.60950	.59990	.59053	.58140
76	.68589	.67495	.66429	.65390	.64377	.63390	.62427	.61487	.60570	.59676
77	.69903	.68841	.67806	.66796	.65811	.64849	.63910	.62993	.62097	.61223
78	.71209	.70182	.69179	.68199	.67242	.66307	.65393	.64501	.63628	.62775
79	.72500	.71507	.70537	.69588	.68660	.67754	.66867	.65999	.65151	.64321
80	.73768	.72809	.71872	.70955	.70058	.69180	.68320	.67479	.66655	.65849
81	.75001	.74077	.73173	.72288	.71422	.70573	.69741	.68926	.68128	.67345
82	.76195	.75306	.74435	.73582	.72746	.71926	.71123	.70335	.69562	.68804
83	.77346	.76491	.75654	.74832	.74026	.73236	.72460	.71699	.70952	.70219
84	.78456	.77636	.76831	.76041	.75265	.74503	.73756	.73021	.72300	.71592
85	.79530	.78743	.77971	.77212	.76466	.75733	.75014	.74306	.73611	.72928
86	.80560	.79806	.79065	.78337	.77621	.76917	.76225	.75544	.74875	.74216
87	.81535	.80813	.80103	.79404	.78717	.78041	.77375	.76720	.76076	.75442
88	.82462	.81771	.81090	.80420	.79760	.79111	.78472	.77842	.77223	.76612
89	.83356	.82694	.82043	.81401	.80769	.80147	.79533	.78929	.78334	.77747
90	.84225	.83593	.82971	.82357	.81753	.81157	.80570	.79991	.79420	.78857
91	.85058	.84455	.83861	.83276	.82698	.82129	.81567	.81013	.80466	.79927
92	.85838	.85263	.84696	.84137	.83585	.83040	.82503	.81973	.81449	.80933
93	.86557	.86009	.85467	.84932	.84405	.83884	.83370	.82862	.82360	.81865
94	.87212	.86687	.86169	.85657	.85152	.84653	.84160	.83673	.83192	.82717
95	.87801	.87298	.86801	.86310	.85825	.85345	.84872	.84404	.83941	.83484
96	.88322	.87838	.87360	.86888	.86420	.85959	.85502	.85051	.84605	.84165
97	.88795	.88328	.87867	.87411	.86961	.86515	.86074	.85639	.85208	.84782
98	.89220	.88769	.88323	.87883	.87447	.87016	.86589	.86167	.85750	.85337
99	.89612	.89176	.88745	.88318	.87895	.87478	.87064	.86656	.86251	.85850
100	.89977	.89555	.89136	.88722	.88313	.87908	.87506	.87109	.86716	.86327
101	.90326	.89917	.89511	.89110	.88712	.88318	.87929	.87543	.87161	.86783
102	.90690	.90294	.89901	.89513	.89128	.88746	.88369	.87995	.87624	.87257
103	.91076	.90694	.90315	.89940	.89569	.89200	.88835	.88474	.88116	.87760
104	.91504	.91138	.90775	.90415	.90058	.89704	.89354	.89006	.88661	.88319
105	.92027	.91681	.91337	.90996	.90658	.90322	.89989	.89659	.89331	.89006
106	.92763	.92445	.92130	.91816	.91506	.91197	.90890	.90586	.90284	.89983
107	.93799	.93523	.93249	.92977	.92707	.92438	.92170	.91905	.91641	.91378
108	.95429	.95223	.95018	.94814	.94611	.94409	.94208	.94008	.93809	.93611
109	.97985	.97893	.97801	.97710	.97619	.97529	.97438	.97348	.97259	.97170

Reg. § 1.642(c)-6A(e)(5)

Estates, Trusts, and Beneficiaries   43,251

See p. 20,601 for regulations not amended to reflect law changes

TABLE S
BASED ON LIFE TABLE 80CNSMT
SINGLE LIFE REMAINDER FACTORS
APPLICABLE AFTER APRIL 30, 1989,
AND BEFORE MAY 1, 1999

INTEREST RATE

AGE	6.2%	6.4%	6.6%	6.8%	7.0%	7.2%	7.4%	7.6%	7.8%	8.0%
0	.03535	.03349	.03183	.03035	.02902	.02783	.02676	.02579	.02492	.02413
1	.02486	.02292	.02119	.01963	.01824	.01699	.01587	.01486	.01395	.01312
2	.02547	.02345	.02164	.02002	.01857	.01727	.01609	.01504	.01408	.01321
3	.02640	.02429	.02241	.02073	.01921	.01785	.01662	.01552	.01451	.01361
4	.02753	.02535	.02339	.02163	.02005	.01863	.01735	.01619	.01514	.01418
5	.02883	.02656	.02453	.02269	.02105	.01956	.01822	.01700	.01590	.01490
6	.03026	.02790	.02578	.02387	.02215	.02060	.01919	.01792	.01677	.01572
7	.03180	.02935	.02714	.02515	.02336	.02174	.02027	.01894	.01773	.01664
8	.03347	.03092	.02863	.02656	.02469	.02300	.02146	.02007	.01881	.01766
9	.03528	.03263	.03025	.02810	.02615	.02438	.02278	.02133	.02000	.01880
10	.03723	.03449	.03201	.02977	.02774	.02590	.02423	.02271	.02133	.02006
11	.03935	.03650	.03393	.03160	.02949	.02757	.02583	.02424	.02279	.02147
12	.04160	.03865	.03598	.03356	.03136	.02936	.02755	.02589	.02438	.02299
13	.04394	.04088	.03811	.03560	.03331	.03123	.02934	.02761	.02603	.02458
14	.04629	.04312	.04025	.03764	.03527	.03311	.03113	.02933	.02768	.02617
15	.04864	.04536	.04238	.03968	.03721	.03496	.03290	.03103	.02930	.02773
16	.05099	.04759	.04451	.04170	.03913	.03679	.03466	.03270	.03090	.02926
17	.05333	.04982	.04662	.04370	.04104	.03861	.03638	.03434	.03247	.03075
18	.05570	.05207	.04875	.04573	.04296	.04044	.03812	.03599	.03404	.03225
19	.05814	.05438	.05095	.04781	.04494	.04231	.03990	.03769	.03565	.03378
20	.06065	.05677	.05321	.04996	.04698	.04424	.04173	.03943	.03731	.03535
21	.06325	.05922	.05554	.05217	.04907	.04623	.04362	.04122	.03901	.03697
22	.06594	.06178	.05797	.05447	.05126	.04831	.04559	.04309	.04078	.03865
23	.06876	.06446	.06051	.05688	.05355	.05048	.04766	.04505	.04265	.04042
24	.07174	.06729	.06321	.05945	.05599	.05281	.04987	.04715	.04465	.04233
25	.07491	.07031	.06609	.06219	.05861	.05530	.05224	.04941	.04680	.04438
26	.07830	.07355	.06918	.06515	.06142	.05799	.05481	.05187	.04915	.04662
27	.08192	.07702	.07250	.06832	.06446	.06090	.05759	.05454	.05170	.04906
28	.08577	.08071	.07603	.07171	.06772	.06402	.06059	.05740	.05445	.05170
29	.08986	.08464	.07981	.07534	.07120	.06736	.06380	.06049	.05742	.05456
30	.09420	.08882	.08383	.07921	.07492	.07095	.06725	.06381	.06061	.05763
31	.09881	.09327	.08812	.08335	.07891	.07479	.07095	.06738	.06405	.06095
32	.10369	.09797	.09267	.08774	.08315	.07888	.07491	.07120	.06774	.06451
33	.10885	.10297	.09750	.09241	.08767	.08325	.07913	.07529	.07170	.06834
34	.11430	.10824	.10261	.09736	.09246	.08790	.08363	.07964	.07592	.07243
35	.12002	.11380	.10800	.10259	.09754	.09282	.08841	.08428	.08041	.07679
36	.12602	.11963	.11366	.10809	.10288	.09800	.09344	.08917	.08516	.08140
37	.13230	.12574	.11961	.11387	.10850	.10347	.09876	.09433	.09018	.08628
38	.13887	.13214	.12584	.11994	.11441	.10922	.10436	.09978	.09549	.09145
39	.14573	.13883	.13237	.12630	.12061	.11527	.11025	.10553	.10109	.09690
40	.15290	.14583	.13920	.13297	.12712	.12162	.11644	.11157	.10698	.10266
41	.16036	.15312	.14633	.13994	.13393	.12827	.12294	.11792	.11318	.10871
42	.16810	.16071	.15375	.14720	.14103	.13522	.12973	.12456	.11967	.11505
43	.17614	.16858	.16146	.15475	.14842	.14245	.13682	.13149	.12645	.12169
44	.18447	.17675	.16948	.16261	.15613	.15000	.14421	.13873	.13355	.12864
45	.19310	.18524	.17780	.17078	.16414	.15787	.15192	.14630	.14096	.13591
46	.20204	.19402	.18644	.17926	.17247	.16604	.15995	.15418	.14870	.14350
47	.21128	.20311	.19538	.18806	.18112	.17454	.16830	.16238	.15676	.15141
48	.22080	.21249	.20462	.19716	.19007	.18335	.17696	.17090	.16513	.15964
49	.23059	.22214	.21413	.20653	.19930	.19244	.18591	.17970	.17379	.16816
50	.24063	.23206	.22391	.21617	.20881	.20180	.19514	.18879	.18274	.17697
51	.25095	.24225	.23398	.22610	.21861	.21147	.20466	.19818	.19199	.18609
52	.26157	.25275	.24436	.23636	.22874	.22147	.21453	.20791	.20159	.19556
53	.27249	.26357	.25505	.24694	.23919	.23180	.22474	.21799	.21154	.20537
54	.28369	.27466	.26604	.25782	.24995	.24244	.23526	.22839	.22181	.21552
55	.29518	.28605	.27734	.26900	.26103	.25341	.24611	.23912	.23243	.22601
56	.30695	.29774	.28893	.28050	.27242	.26469	.25728	.25019	.24338	.23685
57	.31902	.30973	.30084	.29232	.28415	.27632	.26881	.26161	.25469	.24805

Reg. § 1.642(c)-6A(e)(5)

43,252 Estates, Trusts, and Beneficiaries

See p. 20,601 for regulations not amended to reflect law changes

AGE	6.2%	6.4%	6.6%	6.8%	7.0%	7.2%	7.4%	7.6%	7.8%	8.0%
58	.33138	.32203	.31306	.30446	.29621	.28829	.28069	.27339	.26637	.25962
59	.34402	.33461	.32558	.31691	.30859	.30059	.29290	.28550	.27839	.27155
60	.35690	.34745	.33836	.32963	.32124	.31317	.30540	.29792	.29073	.28379
61	.36999	.36050	.35137	.34259	.33414	.32601	.31817	.31062	.30334	.29633
62	.38325	.37374	.36458	.35576	.34726	.33907	.33117	.32356	.31621	.30912
63	.39669	.38717	.37799	.36913	.36060	.35236	.34441	.33674	.32933	.32217
64	.41031	.40078	.39159	.38272	.37415	.36588	.35789	.35016	.34270	.33548
65	.42416	.41464	.40545	.39656	.38798	.37968	.37166	.36390	.35639	.34912
66	.43825	.42876	.41958	.41070	.40211	.39380	.38576	.37797	.37043	.36312
67	.45260	.44315	.43399	.42513	.41655	.40824	.40019	.39238	.38482	.37749
68	.46720	.45779	.44868	.43985	.43129	.42299	.41494	.40713	.39956	.39221
69	.48197	.47263	.46357	.45478	.44625	.43798	.42995	.42215	.41458	.40722
70	.49686	.48760	.47861	.46988	.46140	.45316	.44516	.43738	.42983	.42248
71	.51182	.50265	.49374	.48508	.47666	.46847	.46051	.45276	.44523	.43790
72	.52685	.51778	.50896	.50038	.49203	.48390	.47599	.46829	.46079	.45349
73	.54194	.53298	.52426	.51578	.50751	.49946	.49161	.48397	.47652	.46926
74	.55714	.54832	.53972	.53134	.52317	.51520	.50744	.49986	.49247	.48527
75	.57250	.56382	.55536	.54710	.53904	.53118	.52351	.51601	.50870	.50156
76	.58803	.57951	.57120	.56308	.55515	.54740	.53984	.53245	.52522	.51817
77	.60369	.59535	.58720	.57923	.57144	.56383	.55639	.54912	.54200	.53504
78	.61942	.61126	.60329	.59549	.58787	.58040	.57310	.56596	.55896	.55212
79	.63508	.62713	.61935	.61174	.60428	.59698	.58983	.58283	.57597	.56925
80	.65059	.64285	.63527	.62785	.62058	.61345	.60646	.59961	.59290	.58632
81	.66579	.65827	.65090	.64368	.63659	.62965	.62283	.61615	.60959	.60316
82	.68061	.67332	.66616	.65914	.65226	.64550	.63886	.63235	.62595	.61968
83	.69499	.68793	.68099	.67418	.66749	.66092	.65447	.64813	.64191	.63579
84	.70896	.70213	.69541	.68881	.68233	.67595	.66969	.66353	.65748	.65153
85	.72256	.71596	.70947	.70308	.69681	.69063	.68456	.67859	.67271	.66693
86	.73569	.72931	.72305	.71688	.71081	.70484	.69896	.69318	.68748	.68188
87	.74818	.74204	.73599	.73003	.72417	.71839	.71271	.70711	.70159	.69616
88	.76011	.75419	.74836	.74261	.73695	.73137	.72588	.72046	.71512	.70986
89	.77169	.76599	.76037	.75484	.74938	.74400	.73870	.73347	.72831	.72323
90	.78302	.77755	.77215	.76683	.76158	.75640	.75129	.74625	.74128	.73638
91	.79395	.78870	.78352	.77842	.77337	.76840	.76349	.75864	.75385	.74913
92	.80423	.79920	.79423	.78933	.78449	.77971	.77499	.77033	.76572	.76118
93	.81377	.80894	.80417	.79946	.79481	.79022	.78568	.78120	.77677	.77239
94	.82247	.81784	.81325	.80873	.80425	.79983	.79547	.79115	.78688	.78266
95	.83033	.82586	.82145	.81709	.81278	.80852	.80431	.80014	.79602	.79195
96	.83729	.83298	.82872	.82451	.82034	.81622	.81215	.80812	.80414	.80019
97	.84361	.83944	.83532	.83124	.82721	.82322	.81927	.81537	.81151	.80769
98	.84929	.84525	.84126	.83730	.83339	.82952	.82569	.82190	.81815	.81443
99	.85454	.85062	.84674	.84290	.83910	.83534	.83161	.82792	.82427	.82066
100	.85942	.85561	.85184	.84810	.84440	.84074	.83711	.83352	.82997	.82644
101	.86408	.86037	.85670	.85306	.84946	.84589	.84236	.83886	.83539	.83196
102	.86894	.86534	.86177	.85823	.85473	.85126	.84782	.84442	.84104	.83770
103	.87408	.87060	.86714	.86371	.86032	.85695	.85362	.85031	.84703	.84378
104	.87980	.87644	.87311	.86980	.86653	.86328	.86005	.85686	.85369	.85054
105	.88684	.88363	.88046	.87731	.87418	.87108	.86800	.86494	.86191	.85890
106	.89685	.89389	.89095	.88804	.88514	.88226	.87940	.87656	.87374	.87094
107	.91117	.90858	.90600	.90344	.90089	.89836	.89584	.89334	.89085	.88838
108	.93414	.93217	.93022	.92828	.92634	.92442	.92250	.92060	.91870	.91681
109	.97081	.96992	.96904	.96816	.96729	.96642	.96555	.96468	.96382	.96296

Reg. § 1.642(c)-6A(e)(5)

Estates, Trusts, and Beneficiaries   43,253

See p. 20,601 for regulations not amended to reflect law changes

TABLE S
BASED ON LIFE TABLE 80CNSMT
SINGLE LIFE REMAINDER FACTORS
APPLICABLE AFTER APRIL 30, 1989,
AND BEFORE MAY 1, 1999

INTEREST RATE

AGE	8.2%	8.4%	8.6%	8.8%	9.0%	9.2%	9.4%	9.6%	9.8%	10.0%
0	.02341	.02276	.02217	.02163	.02114	.02069	.02027	.01989	.01954	.01922
1	.01237	.01170	.01108	.01052	.01000	.00953	.00910	.00871	.00834	.00801
2	.01243	.01172	.01107	.01048	.00994	.00944	.00899	.00857	.00819	.00784
3	.01278	.01203	.01135	.01073	.01016	.00964	.00916	.00872	.00832	.00795
4	.01332	.01253	.01182	.01116	.01056	.01001	.00951	.00904	.00862	.00822
5	.01400	.01317	.01241	.01172	.01109	.01051	.00998	.00949	.00904	.00862
6	.01477	.01390	.01310	.01238	.01171	.01110	.01054	.01002	.00954	.00910
7	.01563	.01472	.01389	.01312	.01242	.01178	.01118	.01064	.01013	.00966
8	.01660	.01564	.01477	.01396	.01322	.01254	.01192	.01134	.01081	.01031
9	.01770	.01669	.01577	.01492	.01414	.01342	.01276	.01216	.01159	.01107
10	.01891	.01785	.01688	.01599	.01517	.01442	.01372	.01308	.01249	.01194
11	.02026	.01915	.01814	.01720	.01634	.01555	.01481	.01414	.01351	.01293
12	.02173	.02056	.01950	.01852	.01761	.01678	.01601	.01529	.01463	.01402
13	.02326	.02204	.02092	.01989	.01895	.01807	.01726	.01651	.01582	.01517
14	.02478	.02351	.02234	.02126	.02027	.01935	.01850	.01771	.01698	.01630
15	.02628	.02495	.02372	.02259	.02155	.02058	.01969	.01886	.01810	.01738
16	.02774	.02635	.02507	.02388	.02279	.02178	.02084	.01997	.01917	.01842
17	.02917	.02772	.02637	.02513	.02399	.02293	.02194	.02103	.02018	.01940
18	.03059	.02907	.02767	.02637	.02517	.02406	.02302	.02207	.02118	.02035
19	.03205	.03046	.02899	.02763	.02637	.02521	.02412	.02312	.02218	.02131
20	.03355	.03188	.03035	.02892	.02760	.02638	.02524	.02419	.02320	.02229
21	.03509	.03334	.03173	.03024	.02886	.02758	.02638	.02527	.02424	.02328
22	.03669	.03487	.03318	.03162	.03017	.02882	.02757	.02640	.02532	.02430
23	.03837	.03646	.03470	.03306	.03154	.03013	.02881	.02759	.02644	.02538
24	.04018	.03819	.03634	.03463	.03303	.03155	.03016	.02888	.02767	.02655
25	.04214	.04006	.03812	.03633	.03465	.03309	.03164	.03029	.02902	.02784
26	.04428	.04210	.04008	.03820	.03644	.03481	.03328	.03186	.03052	.02928
27	.04662	.04434	.04223	.04025	.03841	.03670	.03509	.03360	.03219	.03088
28	.04915	.04677	.04456	.04249	.04056	.03876	.03708	.03550	.03403	.03264
29	.05189	.04941	.04709	.04493	.04291	.04102	.03925	.03760	.03604	.03458
30	.05485	.05226	.04984	.04757	.04546	.04348	.04162	.03988	.03825	.03671
31	.05805	.05535	.05282	.05045	.04824	.04616	.04421	.04238	.04067	.03905
32	.06149	.05867	.05603	.05356	.05124	.04906	.04702	.04510	.04329	.04160
33	.06520	.06226	.05950	.05692	.05449	.05221	.05007	.04806	.04616	.04438
34	.06916	.06609	.06322	.06052	.05799	.05560	.05336	.05125	.04926	.04738
35	.07339	.07020	.06720	.06439	.06174	.05925	.05690	.05469	.05260	.05063
36	.07787	.07455	.07143	.06850	.06573	.06313	.06068	.05836	.05617	.05411
37	.08262	.07917	.07593	.07287	.06999	.06727	.06470	.06228	.05999	.05783
38	.08765	.08407	.08069	.07751	.07451	.07167	.06899	.06646	.06407	.06180
39	.09296	.08925	.08574	.08243	.07931	.07635	.07356	.07092	.06841	.06604
40	.09858	.09472	.09109	.08765	.08440	.08132	.07841	.07565	.07303	.07055
41	.10449	.10050	.09673	.09316	.08978	.08658	.08355	.08067	.07794	.07535
42	.11069	.10656	.10265	.09895	.09544	.09212	.08896	.08596	.08312	.08041
43	.11718	.11291	.10887	.10503	.10140	.09794	.09466	.09154	.08858	.08576
44	.12399	.11958	.11540	.11143	.10766	.10407	.10067	.09743	.09434	.09141
45	.13111	.12656	.12224	.11814	.11423	.11052	.10699	.10362	.10042	.09736
46	.13856	.13387	.12941	.12516	.12113	.11728	.11362	.11013	.10680	.10363
47	.14633	.14150	.13690	.13252	.12835	.12438	.12059	.11697	.11352	.11022
48	.15442	.14945	.14471	.14020	.13589	.13179	.12787	.12412	.12055	.11713
49	.16280	.15769	.15281	.14816	.14373	.13949	.13544	.13157	.12787	.12433
50	.17147	.16622	.16121	.15643	.15186	.14749	.14331	.13931	.13548	.13182
51	.18045	.17507	.16993	.16501	.16030	.15580	.15150	.14737	.14342	.13963
52	.18979	.18427	.17899	.17394	.16911	.16448	.16004	.15579	.15172	.14780
53	.19947	.19383	.18842	.18324	.17828	.17352	.16896	.16458	.16038	.15635
54	.20950	.20372	.19819	.19288	.18779	.18291	.17822	.17372	.16940	.16524
55	.21986	.21397	.20831	.20288	.19767	.19266	.18785	.18322	.17878	.17450
56	.23058	.22457	.21879	.21324	.20791	.20278	.19785	.19310	.18854	.18414
57	.24167	.23554	.22965	.22399	.21854	.21329	.20824	.20338	.19870	.19419

Reg. § 1.642(c)-6A(e)(5)

AGE	8.2%	8.4%	8.6%	8.8%	9.0%	9.2%	9.4%	9.6%	9.8%	10.0%
58	.25314	.24690	.24090	.23512	.22956	.22420	.21904	.21407	.20927	.20464
59	.26497	.25863	.25252	.24664	.24097	.23550	.23023	.22515	.22024	.21551
60	.27712	.27068	.26448	.25849	.25272	.24716	.24178	.23659	.23158	.22674
61	.28956	.28304	.27674	.27067	.26480	.25913	.25366	.24837	.24325	.23831
62	.30228	.29567	.28929	.28312	.27717	.27141	.26584	.26045	.25524	.25020
63	.31525	.30857	.30211	.29586	.28982	.28397	.27832	.27284	.26754	.26240
64	.32851	.32176	.31522	.30890	.30278	.29685	.29111	.28555	.28016	.27493
65	.34209	.33528	.32868	.32229	.31610	.31010	.30429	.29865	.29317	.28787
66	.35604	.34918	.34253	.33609	.32983	.32377	.31788	.31217	.30663	.30124
67	.37037	.36347	.35678	.35028	.34398	.33786	.33191	.32614	.32053	.31508
68	.38508	.37815	.37142	.36489	.35854	.35237	.34638	.34055	.33488	.32937
69	.40008	.39313	.38638	.37982	.37344	.36724	.36120	.35533	.34961	.34405
70	.41533	.40838	.40162	.39504	.38864	.38241	.37634	.37043	.36468	.35907
71	.43076	.42382	.41705	.41047	.40405	.39780	.39171	.38578	.38000	.37436
72	.44638	.43945	.43269	.42611	.41969	.41344	.40733	.40138	.39558	.38991
73	.46218	.45527	.44854	.44197	.43556	.42931	.42321	.41725	.41143	.40575
74	.47823	.47137	.46466	.45812	.45173	.44549	.43940	.43345	.42763	.42195
75	.49459	.48777	.48112	.47462	.46826	.46205	.45598	.45004	.44424	.43856
76	.51127	.50452	.49793	.49148	.48517	.47900	.47297	.46706	.46129	.45563
77	.52823	.52157	.51505	.50867	.50243	.49632	.49033	.48447	.47873	.47311
78	.54541	.53885	.53242	.52613	.51996	.51392	.50800	.50220	.49652	.49094
79	.56267	.55621	.54989	.54369	.53762	.53166	.52582	.52009	.51448	.50897
80	.57987	.57354	.56733	.56125	.55527	.54941	.54366	.53802	.53248	.52705
81	.59685	.59065	.58457	.57860	.57274	.56699	.56134	.55579	.55035	.54499
82	.61351	.60746	.60151	.59567	.58993	.58429	.57875	.57331	.56796	.56270
83	.62978	.62387	.61806	.61236	.60675	.60123	.59581	.59047	.58523	.58007
84	.64567	.63992	.63426	.62869	.62321	.61783	.61253	.60731	.60218	.59713
85	.66125	.65565	.65014	.64472	.63938	.63413	.62896	.62387	.61886	.61392
86	.67636	.67092	.66557	.66030	.65511	.65000	.64496	.64000	.63511	.63030
87	.69081	.68554	.68034	.67522	.67018	.66520	.66031	.65548	.65071	.64602
88	.70468	.69957	.69453	.68956	.68466	.67983	.67507	.67037	.66574	.66117
89	.71821	.71326	.70838	.70357	.69882	.69414	.68952	.68495	.68045	.67601
90	.73153	.72676	.72204	.71739	.71280	.70827	.70379	.69938	.69502	.69071
91	.74447	.73986	.73532	.73083	.72640	.72202	.71770	.71343	.70921	.70504
92	.75669	.75225	.74787	.74354	.73927	.73504	.73087	.72674	.72267	.71864
93	.76807	.76379	.75957	.75540	.75127	.74719	.74317	.73918	.73524	.73135
94	.77849	.77437	.77030	.76627	.76229	.75835	.75446	.75061	.74680	.74303
95	.78792	.78394	.78001	.77611	.77226	.76845	.76468	.76096	.75727	.75362
96	.79630	.79244	.78863	.78485	.78112	.77742	.77377	.77015	.76657	.76303
97	.80391	.80016	.79646	.79280	.78917	.78559	.78203	.77852	.77504	.77160
98	.81076	.80712	.80352	.79996	.79643	.79294	.78948	.78606	.78267	.77931
99	.81709	.81354	.81004	.80657	.80313	.79972	.79635	.79302	.78971	.78644
100	.82296	.81950	.81609	.81270	.80934	.80602	.80273	.79947	.79624	.79304
101	.82855	.82518	.82185	.81854	.81526	.81201	.80880	.80561	.80245	.79932
102	.83438	.83110	.82785	.82462	.82142	.81826	.81512	.81200	.80892	.80586
103	.84056	.83737	.83420	.83106	.82795	.82487	.82181	.81878	.81577	.81279
104	.84743	.84433	.84127	.83822	.83521	.83221	.82924	.82630	.82338	.82048
105	.85591	.85295	.85001	.84709	.84419	.84132	.83846	.83563	.83282	.83003
106	.86816	.86540	.86266	.85993	.85723	.85454	.85187	.84922	.84659	.84397
107	.88592	.88348	.88105	.87863	.87623	.87384	.87147	.86911	.86676	.86443
108	.91493	.91306	.91119	.90934	.90749	.90566	.90383	.90201	.90020	.89840
109	.96211	.96125	.96041	.95956	.95872	.95788	.95704	.95620	.95537	.95455

Reg. § 1.642(c)-6A(e)(5)

Estates, Trusts, and Beneficiaries 43,255

See p. 20,601 for regulations not amended to reflect law changes

TABLE S
BASED ON LIFE TABLE 80CNSMT
SINGLE LIFE REMAINDER FACTORS
APPLICABLE AFTER APRIL 30, 1989,
AND BEFORE MAY 1, 1999

INTEREST RATE

AGE	10.2%	10.4%	10.6%	10.8%	11.0%	11.2%	11.4%	11.6%	11.8%	12.0%
0	.01891	.01864	.01838	.01814	.01791	.01770	.01750	.01732	.01715	.01698
1	.00770	.00741	.00715	.00690	.00667	.00646	.00626	.00608	.00590	.00574
2	.00751	.00721	.00693	.00667	.00643	.00620	.00600	.00580	.00562	.00544
3	.00760	.00728	.00699	.00671	.00646	.00622	.00600	.00579	.00560	.00541
4	.00786	.00752	.00721	.00692	.00665	.00639	.00616	.00594	.00573	.00554
5	.00824	.00788	.00755	.00724	.00695	.00668	.00643	.00620	.00598	.00578
6	.00869	.00832	.00796	.00764	.00733	.00705	.00678	.00654	.00630	.00608
7	.00923	.00883	.00846	.00811	.00779	.00749	.00720	.00694	.00669	.00646
8	.00986	.00943	.00904	.00867	.00833	.00801	.00771	.00743	.00716	.00692
9	.01059	.01014	.00972	.00933	.00897	.00863	.00831	.00801	.00773	.00747
10	.01142	.01095	.01051	.01009	.00971	.00935	.00901	.00869	.00840	.00812
11	.01239	.01189	.01142	.01098	.01057	.01019	.00983	.00950	.00918	.00889
12	.01345	.01292	.01243	.01197	.01154	.01113	.01075	.01040	.01007	.00975
13	.01457	.01401	.01349	.01300	.01255	.01212	.01172	.01135	.01100	.01067
14	.01567	.01508	.01453	.01402	.01354	.01309	.01267	.01227	.01190	.01155
15	.01672	.01610	.01552	.01498	.01448	.01400	.01356	.01314	.01275	.01238
16	.01772	.01707	.01646	.01589	.01536	.01486	.01439	.01396	.01354	.01315
17	.01866	.01798	.01734	.01674	.01618	.01566	.01516	.01470	.01427	.01386
18	.01958	.01886	.01818	.01755	.01697	.01641	.01590	.01541	.01495	.01452
19	.02050	.01974	.01903	.01837	.01775	.01717	.01662	.01611	.01563	.01517
20	.02143	.02064	.01989	.01919	.01854	.01793	.01735	.01681	.01630	.01582
21	.02238	.02154	.02075	.02002	.01933	.01868	.01807	.01750	.01696	.01646
22	.02336	.02247	.02164	.02087	.02014	.01946	.01882	.01821	.01764	.01711
23	.02438	.02345	.02257	.02176	.02099	.02027	.01959	.01895	.01835	.01778
24	.02550	.02451	.02359	.02273	.02192	.02115	.02044	.01976	.01913	.01853
25	.02673	.02569	.02472	.02381	.02295	.02214	.02138	.02067	.01999	.01936
26	.02811	.02701	.02598	.02502	.02411	.02326	.02246	.02170	.02098	.02031
27	.02965	.02849	.02741	.02639	.02543	.02452	.02367	.02287	.02211	.02140
28	.03134	.03013	.02898	.02790	.02689	.02593	.02503	.02418	.02338	.02262
29	.03322	.03193	.03072	.02958	.02851	.02750	.02654	.02564	.02479	.02398
30	.03527	.03391	.03264	.03143	.03030	.02923	.02821	.02726	.02635	.02550
31	.03753	.03610	.03475	.03348	.03228	.03115	.03008	.02907	.02811	.02720
32	.04000	.03849	.03707	.03573	.03446	.03326	.03213	.03105	.03004	.02907
33	.04269	.04111	.03961	.03819	.03685	.03558	.03438	.03325	.03217	.03115
34	.04561	.04394	.04236	.04087	.03946	.03812	.03685	.03565	.03451	.03342
35	.04877	.04702	.04535	.04378	.04229	.04087	.03953	.03826	.03706	.03591
36	.05215	.05031	.04856	.04690	.04533	.04384	.04242	.04108	.03980	.03859
37	.05578	.05384	.05200	.05025	.04860	.04703	.04553	.04411	.04276	.04148
38	.05965	.05761	.05568	.05385	.05211	.05045	.04888	.04738	.04595	.04460
39	.06379	.06165	.05962	.05770	.05587	.05412	.05247	.05089	.04939	.04795
40	.06820	.06596	.06383	.06181	.05989	.05806	.05631	.05465	.05307	.05155
41	.07288	.07054	.06832	.06620	.06418	.06226	.06042	.05868	.05701	.05541
42	.07784	.07539	.07306	.07085	.06873	.06671	.06479	.06295	.06119	.05952
43	.08308	.08052	.07808	.07576	.07355	.07143	.06941	.06748	.06564	.06387
44	.08861	.08594	.08340	.08097	.07865	.07644	.07432	.07230	.07036	.06851
45	.09445	.09167	.08901	.08648	.08406	.08174	.07953	.07741	.07538	.07343
46	.10060	.09770	.09494	.09230	.08977	.08735	.08503	.08281	.08068	.07865
47	.10707	.10406	.10119	.09843	.09579	.09327	.09085	.08853	.08630	.08417
48	.11386	.11073	.10774	.10487	.10213	.09949	.09697	.09455	.09222	.08999
49	.12094	.11769	.11458	.11160	.10874	.10600	.10337	.10084	.09842	.09609
50	.12831	.12494	.12172	.11862	.11565	.11280	.11006	.10743	.10490	.10247
51	.13600	.13251	.12917	.12596	.12288	.11991	.11706	.11432	.11169	.10915
52	.14405	.14044	.13698	.13366	.13046	.12738	.12442	.12157	.11883	.11619
53	.15247	.14875	.14517	.14172	.13841	.13522	.13215	.12919	.12635	.12360
54	.16124	.15740	.15370	.15014	.14671	.14341	.14023	.13717	.13421	.13136
55	.17039	.16642	.16261	.15893	.15539	.15198	.14868	.14551	.14244	.13948
56	.17991	.17583	.17190	.16811	.16445	.16092	.15752	.15423	.15106	.14799
57	.18984	.18564	.18160	.17769	.17392	.17029	.16677	.16338	.16010	.15692

Reg. § 1.642(c)-6A(e)(5)

43,256   Estates, Trusts, and Beneficiaries
See p. 20,601 for regulations not amended to reflect law changes

AGE	10.2%	10.4%	10.6%	10.8%	11.0%	11.2%	11.4%	11.6%	11.8%	12.0%
58	.20018	.19587	.19172	.18770	.18382	.18007	.17645	.17295	.16956	.16628
59	.21093	.20652	.20225	.19812	.19414	.19028	.18655	.18294	.17945	.17606
60	.22206	.21753	.21316	.20893	.20483	.20087	.19703	.19332	.18972	.18624
61	.23353	.22890	.22442	.22009	.21589	.21182	.20788	.20407	.20037	.19678
62	.24532	.24059	.23601	.23158	.22728	.22311	.21907	.21515	.21135	.20767
63	.25742	.25260	.24793	.24339	.23900	.23473	.23060	.22658	.22268	.21890
64	.26987	.26495	.26019	.25556	.25107	.24671	.24248	.23837	.23438	.23050
65	.28271	.27771	.27286	.26815	.26357	.25912	.25480	.25059	.24651	.24254
66	.29601	.29093	.28600	.28120	.27654	.27200	.26760	.26331	.25913	.25507
67	.30978	.30462	.29961	.29474	.29000	.28539	.28090	.27653	.27227	.26813
68	.32401	.31879	.31371	.30877	.30396	.29927	.29471	.29027	.28593	.28171
69	.33863	.33336	.32822	.32322	.31835	.31359	.30896	.30445	.30005	.29576
70	.35361	.34829	.34310	.33804	.33311	.32830	.32361	.31903	.31457	.31021
71	.36886	.36349	.35826	.35316	.34818	.34332	.33858	.33394	.32942	.32500
72	.38439	.37899	.37373	.36858	.36356	.35866	.35387	.34919	.34461	.34015
73	.40021	.39479	.38950	.38432	.37927	.37433	.36950	.36478	.36016	.35565
74	.41639	.41096	.40565	.40046	.39538	.39042	.38556	.38081	.37616	.37161
75	.43301	.42758	.42226	.41706	.41198	.40699	.40212	.39734	.39267	.38809
76	.45009	.44467	.43937	.43417	.42908	.42410	.41921	.41443	.40974	.40514
77	.46761	.46221	.45693	.45175	.44667	.44170	.43682	.43203	.42734	.42274
78	.48548	.48013	.47488	.46973	.46468	.45972	.45486	.45009	.44541	.44082
79	.50356	.49826	.49306	.48795	.48294	.47802	.47319	.46845	.46379	.45922
80	.52171	.51647	.51133	.50628	.50132	.49644	.49166	.48695	.48233	.47779
81	.53974	.53457	.52950	.52451	.51961	.51479	.51006	.50541	.50083	.49633
82	.55753	.55245	.54745	.54254	.53771	.53296	.52828	.52369	.51917	.51472
83	.57500	.57001	.56510	.56026	.55551	.55083	.54623	.54170	.53724	.53285
84	.59216	.58726	.58245	.57770	.57304	.56844	.56391	.55945	.55506	.55074
85	.60906	.60428	.59956	.59492	.59034	.58583	.58139	.57702	.57270	.56845
86	.62555	.62088	.61627	.61173	.60725	.60284	.59849	.59420	.58997	.58580
87	.64139	.63683	.63233	.62790	.62352	.61921	.61495	.61076	.60661	.60253
88	.65666	.65221	.64783	.64350	.63923	.63502	.63086	.62675	.62270	.61871
89	.67163	.66730	.66304	.65882	.65466	.65055	.64650	.64249	.63854	.63463
90	.68646	.68226	.67812	.67402	.66998	.66599	.66204	.65814	.65430	.65049
91	.70093	.69686	.69285	.68888	.68496	.68108	.67725	.67347	.66973	.66604
92	.71466	.71073	.70684	.70300	.69920	.69545	.69173	.68806	.68444	.68085
93	.72750	.72370	.71994	.71622	.71254	.70890	.70530	.70174	.69822	.69474
94	.73931	.73562	.73198	.72838	.72481	.72129	.71780	.71434	.71093	.70755
95	.75001	.74644	.74291	.73941	.73595	.73253	.72914	.72579	.72247	.71919
96	.75953	.75606	.75262	.74923	.74586	.74253	.73924	.73598	.73275	.72955
97	.76819	.76481	.76147	.75816	.75489	.75165	.74844	.74526	.74211	.73899
98	.77599	.77270	.76944	.76621	.76302	.75986	.75672	.75362	.75054	.74750
99	.78319	.77998	.77680	.77365	.77053	.76744	.76437	.76134	.75833	.75535
100	.78987	.78673	.78362	.78054	.77748	.77446	.77146	.76849	.76555	.76263
101	.79622	.79315	.79010	.78708	.78409	.78113	.77819	.77528	.77239	.76953
102	.80283	.79983	.79685	.79390	.79097	.78807	.78519	.78234	.77951	.77671
103	.80983	.80690	.80399	.80111	.79825	.79541	.79260	.78981	.78705	.78430
104	.81760	.81475	.81192	.80912	.80633	.80357	.80083	.79810	.79541	.79273
105	.82726	.82451	.82178	.81907	.81638	.81371	.81106	.80843	.80582	.80322
106	.84137	.83879	.83623	.83368	.83115	.82863	.82614	.82366	.82119	.81874
107	.86211	.85981	.85751	.85523	.85297	.85071	.84847	.84624	.84403	.84182
108	.89660	.89481	.89304	.89127	.88950	.88775	.88601	.88427	.88254	.88081
109	.95372	.95290	.95208	.95126	.95045	.94964	.94883	.94803	.94723	.94643

Reg. § 1.642(c)-6A(e)(5)

Estates, Trusts, and Beneficiaries   **43,257**

See p. 20,601 for regulations not amended to reflect law changes

TABLE S
BASED ON LIFE TABLE 80CNSMT
SINGLE LIFE REMAINDER FACTORS
APPLICABLE AFTER APRIL 30, 1989,
AND BEFORE MAY 1, 1999

INTEREST RATE

AGE	12.2%	12.4%	12.6%	12.8%	13.0%	13.2%	13.4%	13.6%	13.8%	14.0%
0	.01683	.01669	.01655	.01642	.01630	.01618	.01607	.01596	.01586	.01576
1	.00559	.00544	.00531	.00518	.00506	.00494	.00484	.00473	.00464	.00454
2	.00528	.00513	.00499	.00485	.00473	.00461	.00449	.00439	.00428	.00419
3	.00524	.00508	.00493	.00479	.00465	.00453	.00441	.00429	.00419	.00408
4	.00536	.00519	.00503	.00488	.00473	.00460	.00447	.00435	.00423	.00412
5	.00558	.00540	.00523	.00507	.00492	.00477	.00464	.00451	.00439	.00427
6	.00588	.00569	.00550	.00533	.00517	.00502	.00487	.00473	.00460	.00448
7	.00624	.00604	.00584	.00566	.00549	.00532	.00517	.00502	.00488	.00475
8	.00668	.00646	.00626	.00606	.00588	.00570	.00554	.00538	.00523	.00509
9	.00722	.00699	.00677	.00656	.00636	.00617	.00600	.00583	.00567	.00552
10	.00785	.00761	.00737	.00715	.00694	.00674	.00655	.00637	.00620	.00604
11	.00861	.00835	.00810	.00786	.00764	.00743	.00723	.00704	.00686	.00668
12	.00946	.00918	.00891	.00866	.00843	.00820	.00799	.00779	.00760	.00741
13	.01035	.01006	.00978	.00951	.00927	.00903	.00880	.00859	.00839	.00819
14	.01122	.01091	.01061	.01034	.01007	.00982	.00958	.00936	.00914	.00894
15	.01203	.01171	.01140	.01110	.01082	.01056	.01031	.01007	.00985	.00963
16	.01279	.01244	.01211	.01181	.01151	.01123	.01097	.01072	.01048	.01025
17	.01347	.01311	.01276	.01244	.01213	.01184	.01156	.01130	.01104	.01081
18	.01411	.01373	.01336	.01302	.01270	.01239	.01210	.01182	.01155	.01130
19	.01474	.01434	.01396	.01359	.01325	.01293	.01262	.01233	.01205	.01178
20	.01537	.01494	.01454	.01415	.01379	.01345	.01313	.01282	.01252	.01224
21	.01598	.01553	.01510	.01470	.01432	.01396	.01361	.01329	.01298	.01268
22	.01660	.01613	.01568	.01525	.01485	.01446	.01410	.01375	.01343	.01312
23	.01725	.01674	.01627	.01581	.01539	.01498	.01460	.01423	.01388	.01355
24	.01796	.01742	.01692	.01644	.01599	.01556	.01515	.01476	.01439	.01404
25	.01876	.01819	.01765	.01714	.01666	.01621	.01577	.01536	.01497	.01460
26	.01967	.01907	.01850	.01796	.01745	.01696	.01650	.01606	.01565	.01525
27	.02072	.02008	.01948	.01890	.01836	.01784	.01735	.01688	.01644	.01601
28	.02190	.02122	.02057	.01996	.01938	.01883	.01831	.01781	.01734	.01689
29	.02322	.02249	.02181	.02116	.02054	.01996	.01940	.01887	.01836	.01788
30	.02469	.02392	.02319	.02250	.02184	.02122	.02062	.02006	.01952	.01900
31	.02634	.02552	.02475	.02401	.02331	.02264	.02201	.02140	.02083	.02028
32	.02816	.02729	.02647	.02568	.02494	.02423	.02355	.02291	.02229	.02170
33	.03018	.02926	.02838	.02755	.02675	.02600	.02528	.02459	.02393	.02331
34	.03239	.03142	.03048	.02960	.02875	.02795	.02718	.02645	.02575	.02508
35	.03482	.03378	.03279	.03185	.03095	.03009	.02928	.02850	.02775	.02704
36	.03743	.03633	.03528	.03428	.03333	.03242	.03155	.03072	.02992	.02916
37	.04026	.03909	.03798	.03692	.03591	.03494	.03401	.03313	.03228	.03147
38	.04330	.04207	.04089	.03977	.03869	.03767	.03668	.03574	.03484	.03398
39	.04658	.04528	.04403	.04284	.04170	.04061	.03957	.03857	.03762	.03670
40	.05011	.04873	.04741	.04615	.04495	.04379	.04269	.04163	.04061	.03964
41	.05389	.05244	.05104	.04971	.04844	.04721	.04604	.04492	.04384	.04281
42	.05791	.05638	.05491	.05350	.05216	.05086	.04962	.04844	.04729	.04620
43	.06219	.06057	.05902	.05754	.05612	.05475	.05344	.05218	.05098	.04981
44	.06673	.06503	.06340	.06184	.06034	.05890	.05752	.05619	.05491	.05368
45	.07157	.06978	.06806	.06642	.06484	.06332	.06186	.06046	.05911	.05781
46	.07669	.07481	.07301	.07128	.06962	.06802	.06649	.06501	.06358	.06221
47	.08212	.08015	.07826	.07645	.07470	.07302	.07140	.06984	.06834	.06690
48	.08784	.08578	.08380	.08190	.08006	.07830	.07660	.07496	.07338	.07186
49	.09384	.09169	.08961	.08762	.08570	.08384	.08206	.08034	.07868	.07708
50	.10013	.09787	.09570	.09361	.09160	.08966	.08779	.08598	.08424	.08256
51	.10671	.10436	.10209	.09991	.09780	.09577	.09381	.09192	.09009	.08832
52	.11365	.11120	.10883	.10655	.10435	.10222	.10017	.09819	.09628	.09442
53	.12095	.11840	.11593	.11355	.11126	.10904	.10689	.10482	.10282	.10088
54	.12860	.12595	.12338	.12090	.11851	.11619	.11396	.11179	.10970	.10767
55	.13663	.13386	.13120	.12862	.12613	.12372	.12138	.11912	.11694	.11482
56	.14503	.14217	.13940	.13672	.13413	.13162	.12919	.12683	.12456	.12235
57	.15385	.15089	.14801	.14523	.14254	.13994	.13741	.13496	.13259	.13029

Reg. § 1.642(c)-6A(e)(5)

43,258 Estates, Trusts, and Beneficiaries

See p. 20,601 for regulations not amended to reflect law changes

AGE	12.2%	12.4%	12.6%	12.8%	13.0%	13.2%	13.4%	13.6%	13.8%	14.0%
58	.16311	.16004	.15706	.15418	.15139	.14868	.14606	.14352	.14105	.13866
59	.17279	.16961	.16654	.16355	.16066	.15786	.15514	.15250	.14994	.14745
60	.18286	.17958	.17640	.17332	.17033	.16743	.16462	.16188	.15922	.15664
61	.19330	.18992	.18665	.18347	.18038	.17738	.17447	.17164	.16889	.16622
62	.20409	.20061	.19724	.19396	.19078	.18768	.18467	.18175	.17891	.17614
63	.21522	.21165	.20818	.20480	.20152	.19833	.19523	.19221	.18928	.18642
64	.22672	.22306	.21949	.21602	.21265	.20937	.20617	.20306	.20003	.19708
65	.23867	.23491	.23125	.22769	.22423	.22085	.21757	.21437	.21125	.20821
66	.25112	.24727	.24353	.23988	.23632	.23286	.22948	.22619	.22299	.21986
67	.26409	.26016	.25633	.25260	.24896	.24541	.24195	.23857	.23528	.23206
68	.27760	.27359	.26968	.26586	.26214	.25851	.25497	.25151	.24814	.24484
69	.29157	.28748	.28350	.27961	.27581	.27211	.26849	.26495	.26150	.25812
70	.30596	.30181	.29775	.29379	.28992	.28614	.28245	.27884	.27532	.27187
71	.32069	.31648	.31236	.30833	.30440	.30055	.29679	.29312	.28952	.28600
72	.33578	.33151	.32733	.32325	.31925	.31535	.31152	.30778	.30412	.30054
73	.35123	.34691	.34269	.33855	.33450	.33054	.32666	.32286	.31914	.31550
74	.36715	.36279	.35852	.35434	.35024	.34623	.34230	.33845	.33468	.33098
75	.38360	.37921	.37491	.37069	.36656	.36250	.35853	.35464	.35082	.34708
76	.40064	.39623	.39190	.38765	.38349	.37941	.37540	.37148	.36762	.36384
77	.41823	.41381	.40947	.40521	.40103	.39692	.39290	.38895	.38507	.38126
78	.43632	.43189	.42755	.42329	.41910	.41499	.41095	.40698	.40309	.39926
79	.45473	.45032	.44599	.44173	.43755	.43344	.42940	.42543	.42153	.41770
80	.47333	.46894	.46463	.46040	.45623	.45213	.44811	.44414	.44025	.43642
81	.49191	.48755	.48328	.47907	.47493	.47085	.46684	.46290	.45902	.45520
82	.51034	.50603	.50179	.49762	.49351	.48947	.48549	.48157	.47772	.47392
83	.52852	.52427	.52008	.51595	.51189	.50788	.50394	.50006	.49623	.49246
84	.54648	.54228	.53815	.53407	.53006	.52610	.52221	.51836	.51458	.51084
85	.56426	.56013	.55606	.55205	.54810	.54420	.54035	.53656	.53282	.52913
86	.58169	.57764	.57364	.56970	.56581	.56197	.55818	.55445	.55076	.54713
87	.59850	.59452	.59060	.58673	.58291	.57913	.57541	.57174	.56811	.56453
88	.61476	.61086	.60702	.60322	.59947	.59577	.59212	.58851	.58494	.58142
89	.63078	.62697	.62321	.61950	.61583	.61220	.60862	.60508	.60159	.59813
90	.64674	.64302	.63935	.63573	.63215	.62861	.62511	.62165	.61823	.61485
91	.66238	.65877	.65520	.65167	.64819	.64474	.64133	.63795	.63462	.63132
92	.67730	.67379	.67032	.66689	.66350	.66014	.65682	.65354	.65029	.64708
93	.69130	.68789	.68452	.68119	.67789	.67463	.67140	.66820	.66504	.66191
94	.70421	.70090	.69762	.69438	.69118	.68800	.68486	.68175	.67867	.67563
95	.71594	.71272	.70954	.70639	.70326	.70017	.69712	.69409	.69109	.68812
96	.72638	.72325	.72014	.71707	.71403	.71101	.70803	.70507	.70215	.69925
97	.73590	.73285	.72982	.72682	.72385	.72090	.71799	.71510	.71224	.70941
98	.74448	.74149	.73853	.73560	.73269	.72981	.72696	.72414	.72134	.71856
99	.75240	.74948	.74658	.74371	.74086	.73805	.73525	.73248	.72974	.72702
100	.75974	.75687	.75403	.75121	.74842	.74566	.74292	.74020	.73751	.73484
101	.76669	.76388	.76109	.75833	.75559	.75287	.75018	.74751	.74486	.74223
102	.77393	.77117	.76844	.76573	.76304	.76037	.75773	.75511	.75251	.74993
103	.78158	.77888	.77620	.77355	.77091	.76830	.76571	.76313	.76058	.75805
104	.79007	.78743	.78482	.78222	.77964	.77709	.77455	.77203	.76953	.76705
105	.80065	.79809	.79556	.79304	.79054	.78805	.78559	.78314	.78071	.77829
106	.81631	.81389	.81149	.80911	.80674	.80438	.80204	.79972	.79741	.79511
107	.83963	.83745	.83529	.83313	.83099	.82886	.82674	.82463	.82254	.82045
108	.87910	.87739	.87569	.87400	.87232	.87064	.86897	.86731	.86566	.86401
109	.94563	.94484	.94405	.94326	.94248	.94170	.94092	.94014	.93937	.93860

[Reg. § 1.642(c)-6A.]

☐ [T.D. 8540, 6-9-94. Amended by T.D. 8819, 4-29-99 and T.D. 8886, 6-9-2000.]

[Reg. § 1.642(c)-7]

§ 1.642(c)-7. Transitional rules with respect to pooled income funds.—(a) *In general*—(1) *Amendment of certain funds.* A fund created before May 7, 1971, and not otherwise qualifying as a pooled income fund may be treated as a pooled income fund to which § 1.642(c)-5 applies if on July 31, 1969, or on each date of transfer of property to the fund occurring after July 31, 1969, it possessed the initial characteristics described in paragraph (b) of this section and is amended, in the time and manner provided in paragraph (c) of this section, to meet all the requirements of section 642(c)(5) and § 1.642(c)-5. If a fund to which this subparagraph applies is amended in the time and manner provided in paragraph (c) of this section it shall be treated as provided in paragraph (d) of this sec-

Reg. § 1.642(c)-7(a)(1)

tion for the period beginning on August 1, 1969, or, if later, on the date of its creation and ending the day before the date on which it meets the requirements of section 642(c)(5) and § 1.642(c)-5.

(2) *Severance of a portion of a fund.* Any portion of a fund created before May 7, 1971, which consists of property transferred to such fund after July 31, 1969, may be severed from such fund consistently with the principles of paragraph (c)(2) of this section and established before January 1, 1972, as a separate pooled income fund, provided that on and after the date of severance the severed fund meets all the requirements of section 642(c)(5) and § 1.642(c)-5. A separate fund which is established pursuant to this subparagraph shall be treated as provided in paragraph (d) of this section for the period beginning on the day of the first transfer of property which becomes part of the separate fund and ending the day before the day on which the separate fund meets the requirements of section 642(c)(5) and § 1.642(c)-5.

(b) *Initial characteristics required.* A fund described in paragraph (a)(1) of this section shall not be treated as a pooled income fund to which section 642(c)(5) applies, even though it is amended as provided in paragraph (c) of this section, unless it possessed the following characteristics on July 31, 1969, or on each date of transfer of property to the fund occurring after July 31, 1969:

(1) It satisfied the requirements of section 642(c)(5)(A) other than that the fund be a trust;

(2) It was constituted in a way to attract and contain commingled properties transferred to the fund by more than one donor satisfying such requirements; and

(3) Each beneficiary of a life income interest which was retained or created in any property transferred to the fund was entitled to receive, but not less often than annually, a proportional share of the annual income earned by the fund, such share being based on the fair market value of the property in which such life interest was retained or created.

(c) *Amendment requirements.* (1) A fund described in paragraph (a)(1) of this section and possessing the initial characteristics described in paragraph (b) of this section on the date prescribed therein shall be treated as a pooled income fund if it is amended to meet all the requirements of section 642(c)(5) and § 1.642(c)-5 before January 1, 1972, or if later, on or before the 30th day after the date on which any judicial proceedings commenced before January 1, 1972, which are required to amend its governing instrument or any other instrument which does not permit it to meet such requirements, become final. However, see paragraph (d) of this section for limitation on the period in which a claim for credit or refund may be filed.

(2) In addition, if the transferred property described in paragraph (b)(2) of this section is commingled with other property, the transferred property must be separated on or before the date specified in subparagraph (1) of this paragraph from the other property and allocated to the fund in accordance with the transferred property's percentage share of the fair market value of the total commingled property on the date of separation. The percentage share shall be the ratio which the fair market value of the transferred property on the date of separation bears to the fair market value of the total commingled property on that date and shall be computed in a manner consistent with paragraph (c) of § 1.642(c)-5. The property which is so allocated to the fund shall be treated as property received from transfers which meet the requirements of section 642(c)(5), and such transfers shall be treated as made on the dates on which the properties giving rise to such allocation were transferred to the fund by the respective donors. The property so allocated to the fund must be representative of all the commingled property other than securities the income from which is exempt from tax under subtitle A of the Code; compensating increases in other commingled property allocated to the fund shall be made where such tax-exempt securities are not allocated to the fund. The application of this subparagraph may be illustrated by the following example:

Example. (a) The trustees of X fund are in the process of amending it in order to qualify as a pooled income fund. The property transferred to the X fund was commingled with other property transferred to the organization by which the fund was established. After taking into account the various transfers and the appreciation in the fair market value of all the properties, the fair market value of the property allocated to the fund on the various transfer dates is set forth in the following schedule and determined in the manner indicated:

Reg. § 1.642(c)-7(c)(2)

Estates, Trusts, and Beneficiaries

See p. 20,601 for regulations not amended to reflect law changes

Date of Transfer	Transfers Value of All Property Before Transfer (1)	Trust Property (2)	Other Property (3)	Value of All Property After Transfer (4)	Property Allocated to Fund (5)
1/ 1/68	......	$100,000	$100,000	$200,000	$100,000 [1]
9/30/68	$300,000	100,000	......	400,000	250,000 [2]
1/15/69	480,000	60,000	......	540,000	360,000 [3]
11/11/69	600,000	200,000	......	800,000	600,000 [4]

[1] $100,000 = (the amount in column (2))
[2] 250,000 = ([$100,000/$200,000 × $300,000] + $100,000)
[3] 360,000 = ([$250,000/$400,000 × $480,000] + $ 60,000)
[4] 600,000 = ([$360,000/$540,000 × $600,000] + $200,000)

(b) On September 30, 1970, the trustees decide to separate the property of X fund from the other property. The fair market value of all the commingled property is $1,000,000 on September 30, 1970, and there were no additional transfers to the fund after November 11, 1969. Accordingly, the fair market value of the property required to be allocated to X fund must be $750,000 ($600,000/$800,000 × $1,000,000), and X fund's percentage share of the commingled property is 75 percent ($750,000/$1,000,000). Accordingly, assuming that the commingled property consists of Y stock with a fair market value of $800,000 and Z bonds with a fair market value of $200,000, there must be allocated to X fund at the close of September 30, 1970, Y stock with a value of $600,000 ($800,000 × 75%) and Z bonds with a value of $150,000 ($200,000 × 75%).

(d) *Transactions before amendment of or severance from fund.* (1) A fund which is amended pursuant to paragraph (c) of this section, or is severed from a fund pursuant to paragraph (a)(2) of this section, shall be treated for all purposes, including the allowance of a deduction for any charitable contribution, as if it were before its amendment or severance a pooled income fund to which section 642(c)(5) and § 1.642(c)-5 apply. Thus, for example, where a donor transferred property in trust to such an amended or severed fund on August 1, 1969, but before its amendment or severance under this section, a charitable contributions deduction for the value of the remainder interest may be allowed under section 170, 2055, 2106, or 2522. The deduction may not be allowed, however, until the fund is amended or severed pursuant to this section and shall be allowed only if a claim for credit or refund is filed within the period of limitation prescribed by section 6511(a).

(2) For purposes of determining under § 1.642(c)-6 the highest yearly rate of return earned by a fund (which is amended pursuant to paragraph (c) of this section) for the 3 preceding taxable years, taxable years of the fund preceding its taxable year in which the fund is so amended and qualifies as a pooled income fund under this section shall be used provided that the fund did not at any time during such preceding years hold any investments in securities the income from which is exempt from tax under subtitle A of the Code. If any such tax-exempt securities were held during such period by such amended fund, or if the fund consists of a portion of a fund which is severed pursuant to paragraph (a)(2) of this section, the highest yearly rate of return under § 1.642(c)-6 shall be determined by treating the fund as a pooled income fund which has been in existence for less than 3 taxable years preceding the taxable year in which the transfer of property to the fund is made.

(3) Property transferred to a fund before its amendment pursuant to paragraph (c) of this section, or before its severance under paragraph (a)(2) of this section, shall be treated as property received from transfers which meet the requirements of section 642(c)(5). [Reg. § 1.642(c)-7.]

☐ [T.D. 7105, 4-5-71. Amended by T.D. 7125, 6-7-71, and by T.D. 8540, 6-9-94.]

[Reg. § 1.642(d)-1]

§ 1.642(d)-1. **Net operating loss deduction.**—The net operating loss deduction allowed by section 172 is available to estates and trusts generally, with the following exceptions and limitations:

(a) In computing gross income and deductions for the purposes of section 172, a trust shall exclude that portion of the income and deductions attributable to the grantor or another person under sections 671 through 678 (relating to grantors and others treated as substantial owners).

(b) An estate or trust shall not, for the purposes of section 172, avail itself of the deductions allowed by section 642(c) (relating to charitable contributions deductions) and sections 651 and 661 (relating to deductions for distributions). [Reg. § 1.642(d)-1.]

☐ [T.D. 6217, 12-19-56.]

[Reg. § 1.642(e)-1]

§ 1.642(e)-1. **Depreciation and depletion.**—An estate or trust is allowed the deductions for depreciation and depletion, but only to the extent

Reg. § 1.642(d)-1(a)

the deductions are not apportioned to beneficiaries under sections 167(h) and 611(b). For purposes of sections 167(h) and 611(b), the term "beneficiaries" includes charitable beneficiaries. See the regulations under those sections. [Reg. § 1.642(e)-1.]

☐ [*T.D. 6217,* 12-19-56. *Amended by T.D. 6712,* 3-23-64.]

[Reg. § 1.642(f)-1]

§ 1.642(f)-1. Amortization deductions.—An estate or trust is allowed amortization deductions with respect to an emergency facility as defined in section 168(d), with respect to a certified pollution control facility as defined in section 169(d), with respect to qualified railroad rolling stock as defined in section 184(d), with respect to certified coal mine safety equipment as defined in section 187(d), with respect to on-the-job training and child-care facilities as defined in section 188(b), and with respect to certain rehabilitations of certified historic structures as defined in section 191, in the same manner and to the same extent as in the case of an individual. However, the principles governing the apportionment of the deductions for depreciation and depletion between fiduciaries and the beneficiaries of an estate or trust (see sections 167(h) and 611(b) and the regulations thereunder) shall be applicable with respect to such amortization deductions. [Reg. § 1.642(f)-1.]

☐ [*T.D. 6217,* 12-19-56. *Amended by T.D. 6712,* 3-23-64, *by T.D. 7116,* 5-17-71, *by T.D. 7599,* 3-12-79, *and by T.D. 7700,* 6-4-80.]

[Reg. § 1.642(g)-1]

§ 1.642(g)-1. Disallowance of double deduction; in general.—Amounts allowable under section 2053(a)(2) (relating to administration expenses) or under section 2054 (relating to losses during administration) as deductions in computing the taxable estate of a decedent are not allowed as deductions in computing the taxable income of the estate unless there is filed a statement, in duplicate, to the effect that the items have not been allowed as deductions from the gross estate of the decedent under section 2053 or 2054 and that all rights to have such items allowed at any time as deductions under section 2053 or 2054 are waived. The statement should be filed with the return for the year for which the items are claimed as deductions or with the district director of internal revenue for the internal revenue district in which the return was filed, for association with the return. The statement may be filed at any time before the expiration of the statutory period of limitation applicable to the taxable year for which the deduction is sought. Allowance of a deduction in computing an estate's taxable income is not precluded by claiming a deduction in the estate tax return, so long as the estate tax deduction is not finally allowed and the statement is filed. However, after a statement is filed under section 642(g) with respect to a particular item or portion of an item, the item cannot thereafter be allowed as a deduction for estate tax purposes since the waiver operates as a relinquishment of the right to have the deduction allowed at any time under section 2053 or 2054. [Reg. § 1.642(g)-1.]

☐ [*T.D. 6217,* 12-19-56.]

[Reg. § 1.642(g)-2]

§ 1.642(g)-2. Deductions included.—It is not required that the total deductions, or the total amount of any deduction, to which section 642(g) is applicable be treated in the same way. One deduction or portion of a deduction may be allowed for income tax purposes if the appropriate statement is filed, while another deduction or portion is allowed for estate tax purposes. Section 642(g) has no application to deductions for taxes, interest, business expenses, and other items accrued at the date of a decedent's death so that they are allowable as a deduction under section 2053(a)(3) for estate tax purposes as claims against the estate, and are also allowable under section 691(b) as deductions in respect of a decedent for income tax purposes. However, section 642(g) is applicable to deductions for interest, business expenses, and other items not accrued at the date of the decedent's death so that they are allowable as deductions for estate tax purposes only as administration expenses under section 2053(a)(2). Although deductible under section 2053(a)(3) in determining the value of the taxable estate of a decedent, medical, dental, etc., expenses of a decedent which are paid by the estate of the decedent are not deductible in computing the taxable income of the estate. See section 213(d) and the regulations thereunder for rules relating to the deductibility of such expenses in computing the taxable income of the decedent. [Reg. § 1.642(g)-2.]

☐ [*T.D. 6217,* 12-19-56.]

[Reg. § 1.642(h)-1]

§ 1.642(h)-1. Unused loss carryovers on termination of an estate or trust.—(a) If, on the final termination of an estate or trust, a net operating loss carryover under section 172 or a capital loss carryover under section 1212 would be allowable to the estate or trust in a taxable year subsequent to the taxable year of termination but for the termination, the carryover or carryovers are allowed under section 642(h)(1) to the beneficiaries succeeding to the property of the estate or trust. See § 1.641(b)-3 for the determination of when an estate or trust terminates.

Reg. § 1.642(h)-1(a)

(b) The net operating loss carryover and the capital loss carryover are the same in the hands of a beneficiary as in the estate or trust, except that the capital loss carryover in the hands of a beneficiary which is a corporation is a short-term loss irrespective of whether it would have been a long-term or short-term capital loss in the hands of the estate or trust. The net operating loss carryover and the capital loss carryover are taken into account in computing taxable income, adjusted gross income, and the tax imposed by section 56 (relating to the minimum tax for tax preferences). The first taxable year of the beneficiary to which the loss shall be carried over is the taxable year of the beneficiary in which or with which the estate or trust terminates. However, for purposes of determining the number of years to which a net operating loss, or a capital loss under paragraph (a) of § 1.1212-1, may be carried over by a beneficiary, the last taxable year of the estate or trust (whether or not a short taxable year) and the first taxable year of the beneficiary to which a loss is carried over each constitute a taxable year, and, in the case of a beneficiary of an estate or trust that is a corporation, capital losses carried over by the estate or trust to any taxable year of the estate or trust beginning after December 31, 1963, shall be treated as if they were incurred in the last taxable year of the estate or trust (whether or not a short taxable year). For the treatment of the net operating loss carryover when the last taxable year of the estate or trust is the last taxable year to which such loss can be carried over, see § 1.642(h)-2.

(c) The application of this section may be illustrated by the following examples:

Example (1). A trust distributes all of its assets to A, the sole remainderman, and terminates on December 31, 1954, when it has a capital loss carryover of $10,000 attributable to transactions during the taxable year 1952. A, who reports on the calendar year basis, otherwise has ordinary income of $10,000 and capital gains of $4,000 for the taxable year 1954. A would offset his capital gains of $4,000 against the capital loss of the trust and, in addition, deduct under section 1211(b) $1,000 on his return for the taxable year 1954. The balance of the capital loss carryover of $5,000 may be carried over only to the years 1955 and 1956, in accordance with paragraph (a) of § 1.1212-1 and the rules of this section.

Example (2). A trust distributes all of its assets, one-half to A, an individual, and one-half to X, a corporation, who are the sole remaindermen, and terminates on December 31, 1966, when it has a short-term capital loss carryover of $20,000 attributable to short-term transactions during the taxable years 1964, 1965 and 1966, and a long-term capital loss carryover of $12,000 attributable to long-term transactions during such years. A, who reports on the calendar year basis, otherwise has ordinary income of $15,000, short-term capital gains of $4,000 and long-term capital gains of $6,000, for the taxable year 1966. A would offset his short-term capital gains of $4,000 against his share of the short-term capital loss carryover of the trust, $10,000 (one-half of $20,000), and, in addition deduct under section 1211(b) $1,000 (treated as a short-term gain for purposes of computing capital loss carryovers) on his return for the taxable year 1966. A would also offset his long-term capital gains of $6,000 against his share of the long-term capital loss carryover of the trust, $6,000 (one-half of 12,000). The balance of A's share of the short-term capital loss carryover, $5,000, may be carried over as a short-term capital loss carryover to the succeeding taxable year and treated as a short-term capital loss incurred in such succeeding taxable year in accordance with paragraph (b) of § 1.1212-1. X, which also reports on the calendar year basis, otherwise has capital gains of $4,000 for the taxable year 1966. X would offset its capital gains of $4,000 against its share of the capital loss carryovers of the trust, $16,000 (the sum of one-half of each the short-term carryover and the long-term carryover of the trust), on its return for the taxable year 1966. The balance of X's share, $12,000, may be carried over as a short-term capital loss only to the years 1967, 1968, 1969, and 1970, in accordance with paragraph (a) of § 1.1212-1 and the rules of this section. [Reg. § 1.642(h)-1.]

☐ [*T.D.* 6217, 12-19-56. *Amended by T.D.* 6828, 6-16-65 *and by T.D.* 7564, 9-11-78.]

[Reg. § 1.642(h)-2]

§ 1.642(h)-2. Excess deductions on termination of an estate or trust.—(a) If, on the termination of an estate or trust, the estate or trust has for its last taxable year deductions (other than the deductions allowed under section 642(b) (relating to personal exemption) or section 642(c) (relating to charitable contributions)) in excess of gross income, the excess is allowed under section 642(h)(2) as a deduction to the beneficiaries succeeding to the property of the estate or trust. The deduction is allowed only in computing taxable income and must be taken into account in computing the items of tax preference of the beneficiary; it is not allowed in computing adjusted gross income. The deduction is allowable only in the taxable year of the beneficiary in which or with which the estate or trust terminates, whether the year of termination of the estate or trust is of normal duration or is a short taxable year. For

Estates, Trusts, and Beneficiaries

example: Assume that a trust distributes all of its assets to B and terminates on December 31, 1954. As of that date it has excess deductions, for example, because of corpus commissions on termination, of $18,000. B, who reported on the calendar year basis, could claim the $18,000 as a deduction for the taxable year 1954. However, if the deduction (when added to his other deductions) exceeds his gross income, the excess may not be carried over to the year 1955 or subsequent years.

(b) A deduction based upon a net operating loss carryover will never be allowed to beneficiaries under both paragraphs (1) and (2) of section 642(h). Accordingly, a net operating loss deduction which is allowable to beneficiaries succeeding to the property of the estate or trust under the provisions of paragraph (1) of section 642(h) cannot also be considered a deduction for purposes of paragraph (2) of section 642(h) and paragraph (a) of this section. However, if the last taxable year of the estate or trust is the last year in which a deduction on account of a net operating loss may be taken, the deduction, to the extent not absorbed in that taxable year by the estate or trust, is considered an "excess deduction" under section 642(h)(2) and paragraph (a) of this section.

(c) Any item of income or deduction, or any part thereof, which is taken into account in determining the net operating loss or capital loss carryover of the estate or trust for its last taxable year shall not be taken into account again in determining excess deductions on termination of the trust or estate within the meaning of section 642(h)(2) and paragraph (a) of this section (see example in § 1.642(h)-5). [Reg. § 1.642(h)-2.]

☐ *[T.D. 6217, 12-19-56. Amended by T.D. 7564, 9-11-78.]*

[Reg. § 1.642(h)-3]

§ 1.642(h)-3. Meaning of "beneficiaries succeeding to the property of the estate or trust".—(a) The phrase "beneficiaries succeeding to the property of the estate or trust" means those beneficiaries upon termination of the estate or trust who bear the burden of any loss for which a carryover is allowed, or of any excess of deductions over gross income for which a deduction is allowed, under section 642(h).

(b) With reference to an intestate estate, the phrase means the heirs and next of kin to whom the estate is distributed, or if the estate is insolvent, to whom it would have been distributed if it had not been insolvent. If a decedent's spouse is entitled to a specified dollar amount of property before any distribution to other heirs and next of kin, and if the estate is less than that amount, the spouse is the beneficiary succeeding to the property of the estate or trust to the extent of the deficiency in amount.

(c) In the case of a testate estate, the phrase normally means the residuary beneficiaries (including a residuary trust), and not specific legatees or devisees, pecuniary legatees, or other nonresiduary beneficiaries. However, the phrase does not include the recipient of a specific sum of money even though it is payable out of the residue, except to the extent that it is not payable in full. On the other hand, the phrase includes a beneficiary (including a trust) who is not strictly a residuary beneficiary but whose devise or bequest is determined by the value of the decedent's estate as reduced by the loss or deductions in question. Thus the phrase includes:

(1) A beneficiary of a fraction of a decedent's net estate after payment of debts, expenses, etc.;

(2) A nonresiduary legatee or devisee, to the extent of any deficiency in his legacy or devise resulting from the insufficiency of the estate to satisfy it in full;

(3) A surviving spouse receiving a fractional share of an estate in fee under a statutory right of election, to the extent that the loss or deductions are taken into account in determining the share. However, the phrase does not include a recipient of dower or curtesy, or any income beneficiary of the estate or trust from which the loss or excess deduction is carried over.

(d) The principles discussed in paragraph (c) of this section are equally applicable to trust beneficiaries. A remainderman who receives all or a fractional share of the property of a trust as a result of the final termination of the trust is a beneficiary succeeding to the property of the trust. For example, if property is transferred to pay the income to A for life and then to pay $10,000 to B and distribute the balance of the trust corpus to C, C and not B is considered to be the succeeding beneficiary except to the extent that the trust corpus is insufficient to pay B $10,000. [Reg. § 1.642(h)-3.]

☐ *[T.D. 6217, 12-19-56.]*

[Reg. § 1.642(h)-4]

§ 1.642(h)-4. Allocation.—The carryovers and excess deductions to which section 642(h) applies are allocated among the beneficiaries succeeding to the property of an estate or trust (see § 1.642(h)-3) proportionately according to the share of each in the burden of the loss or deductions. A person who qualified as a beneficiary succeeding to the property of an estate or trust with respect to one amount and does not qualify with respect to another amount is a beneficiary succeeding to the property of the estate or trust as

Reg. § 1.642(h)-4

to the amount with respect to which he qualifies. The application of this section may be illustrated by the following example:

Example. A decedent's will leaves $100,000 to A, and the residue of his estate equally to B and C. His estate is sufficient to pay only $90,000 to A, and nothing to B and C. There is an excess of deductions over gross income for the last taxable year of the estate or trust of $5,000, and a capital loss carryover of $15,000, to both of which section 642(h) applies. A is a beneficiary succeeding to the property of the estate to the extent of $10,000, and since the total of the excess of deductions and the loss carryover is $20,000, A is entitled to the benefit of one half of each item, and the remaining half is divided equally between B and C. [Reg. § 1.642(h)-4.]

☐ [T.D. 6217, 12-19-56.]

[Reg. § 1.642(h)-5]

§ 1.642(h)-5. **Example.**—The application of section 642(h) may be illustrated by the following example:

Example. (a) A decedent dies January 31, 1954, leaving a will which provides for distributing all her estate equally to A and an existing trust for B. The period of administration of the estate terminates on December 31, 1954, at which time all the property of the estate is distributed to A and the trust. A reports his income for tax purposes on a calendar year basis, and the trust reports its income on the basis of a fiscal year ending August 31. During the period of the administration, the estate has the following items of income and deductions:

Taxable interest	$ 2,500
Business income	3,000
Total	5,500
Business expenses (including administrative expense allocable to business income)	5,000
Administrative expenses and corpus commissions not allocable to business income	9,800
Total deductions	14,800

It also has a capital loss of $5,000.

(b) Under section 642(h)(1), an unused net operating loss carryover of the estate on termination of $2,000 will be allowable to: A to the extent of $1,000 for his taxable year 1954 and the next four taxable years in accordance with section 172; and to the trust to the extent of $1,000 for its taxable year ending August 31, 1955, and its next four taxable years. The amount of the net operating loss carryover is computed as follows:

Deductions of estate for 1954	$14,800
Less adjustment under section 172(d)(4) (deductions not attributable to a trade or business ($9,800) allowable only to extent of gross income not derived from such trade or business ($2,500))	7,300
Deductions as adjusted	7,500
Gross income of estate for 1954	5,500
Net operating loss of estate for 1954	$ 2,000
(No deduction for capital loss of $5,000 under section 172(d)(2))	

Neither A nor the trust will be allowed to carry back any part of the net operating loss made available to them under section 642(h)(1).

(c) Under section 642(h)(2), excess deductions of the estate of $7,300 will be allowed as a deduction to A to the extent of $3,650 for the calendar year 1954 and to the trust to the extent of $3,650 for the taxable year ending August 31, 1955. The deduction of $7,300 for administrative expenses and corpus commissions is the only amount which was not taken into account in determining the net operating loss of the estate ($9,800 of such expenses less $2,500 taken into account).

(d) Under section 642(h)(1), there will be allowable to A a capital loss carryover of $2,500 for his taxable year 1954 and for his next four taxable years in accordance with paragraph (a) of § 1.1212-1. There will be allowable to the trust a similar capital loss carryover of $2,500 for its taxable year ending August 31, 1955, and its next four taxable years (but see paragraph (b) of § 1.643(a)-3), (for taxable years beginning after December 31, 1963, net capital losses may be carried over indefinitely by beneficiaries other than corporations, in accordance with § 1.642(h)-1 and paragraph (b) of § 1.1212-1).

Reg. § 1.642(h)-5(d)

(e) The carryovers and excess deductions are not allowable directly to B, the trust beneficiary, but to the extent the distributable net income of the trust is reduced by the carryovers and excess deductions B may receive indirect benefit. [Reg. § 1.642(h)-5.]

☐ [T.D. 6217, 12-19-56. Amended by T.D. 6828, 6-16-65.]

[Reg. § 1.642(i)-1]

§ 1.642(i)-1. **Certain distributions by cemetery perpetual care funds.**—(a) *In general.* Section 642(i) provides that amounts distributed during taxable years ending after December 31, 1963 by a cemetery perpetual care fund trust for the care and maintenance of gravesites shall be treated as distributions solely for purposes of sections 651 and 661. The deduction for such a distribution is allowable only if the fund is taxable as a trust. In addition, the fund must have been created pursuant to local law by a taxable cemetery corporation (as defined in § 1.642(i)-2(a)) expressly for the care and maintenance of cemetery property. A care fund will be treated as having been created by a taxable cemetery corporation ("cemetery") if the distributee cemetery is taxable, even though the care fund was created by the distributee cemetery in a year that it was tax-exempt or by a predecessor of such distributee cemetery which was tax-exempt in the year the fund was established. The deduction is the amount of the distributions during the fund's taxable year to the cemetery corporation for such care and maintenance that would be otherwise allowable under section 651 or 661, but in no event is to exceed the limitations described in paragraphs (b) and (c) of this section. The provisions of this paragraph shall not have the effect of extending the period of limitations under section 6511.

(b) *Limitation on amount of deduction.* The deduction in any taxable year may not exceed the product of $5 multiplied by the aggregate number of gravesites sold by the cemetery corporation before the beginning of the taxable year of the trust. In general, the aggregate number of gravesites sold shall be the aggregate number of interment rights sold by a cemetery corporation (including gravesites sold by the cemetery before a care fund trust law was enacted). In addition, the number of gravesites sold shall include gravesites used to make welfare burials. Welfare burials and pre-trust fund law gravesites shall be included only to the extent that the cemetery cares for and maintains such gravesites. For purposes of this section, a gravesite is sold as of the date on which the purchaser acquires interment rights enforceable under local law. The aggregate number of gravesites includes only those gravesites with respect to which the fund or taxable cemetery corporation has an obligation for care and maintenance.

(c) *Requirements for deductibility of distributions for care and maintenance.* (1) *Obligation for care and maintenance.* A deduction is allowed only for distributions for the care and maintenance of gravesites with respect to which the fund or taxable cemetery corporation has an obligation for care and maintenance. Such obligation may be established by the trust instrument, by local law, or by the cemetery's practice of caring for and maintaining gravesites, such as welfare burial plots or gravesites sold before the enactment of a care fund trust law.

(2) *Distribution actually used for care and maintenance.* The amount of a deduction otherwise allowable for care fund distributions in any taxable year shall not exceed the portion of such distributions expended by the distributee cemetery corporation for the care and maintenance of gravesites before the end of the fund's taxable year following the taxable year in which it makes the distributions. A 6-month extension of time for filing the trust's return may be obtained upon request under section 6081. The failure of a cemetery to expend the care fund's distributions within a reasonable time before the due date for filing the return will be considered reasonable grounds for granting a 6-month extension of time for section 6081. For purposes of this paragraph, any amount expended by the care fund directly for the care and maintenance of gravesites shall be treated as an additional care fund distribution which is expended on the day of distribution by the cemetery corporation. The fund shall be allowed a deduction for such direct expenditure in the fund's taxable year during which the expenditure is made.

(3) *Example.* The application of paragraph (c)(2) of this section is illustrated by the following example:

A, a calendar-year perpetual care fund trust meeting the requirements of section 642(i), makes a $10,000 distribution on December 1, 1978 to X, a taxable cemetery corporation operating on a May 31 fiscal year. From this $10,000 distribution, the cemetery makes the following expenditures for the care and maintenance of gravesites: $2,000 on December 20, 1978; $4,000 on June 1, 1979; $2,000 on October 1, 1979; and $1,000 on April 1, 1980. In addition, as authorized by the trust instrument, A itself makes a direct $1,000 payment to a contractor on September 1, 1979 for qualifying care and maintenance work performed. As a result of these transactions, A will be allowed an $8,000 deduction for its 1978 taxable year attributable to the cemetery's expenditures, and a $1,000 deduction for its 1979 taxable year attributable to the fund's direct payment. A will not be allowed a deduction for its 1978 taxable year for the cemetery's expenditure of either the $1,000 expended on April 1, 1980 or the remaining unspent portion of the original $10,000 distribution. The trustee may request a 6-month extension in order to allow the fund until October 15, 1979 to file its return for 1978.

(d) *Certified statement made by cemetery officials to fund trustees.* A trustee of a cemetery perpetual care fund shall not be held personally liable for civil or criminal penalties resulting from false statements on the trust's tax return to the extent that such false statements resulted from the trustee's reliance on a certified statement made by the cemetery specifying the number of interments sold by the cemetery or the amount of the cemetery's expenditures for care and maintenance. The statement must indicate the basis upon which the cemetery determined what portion of its expenditures were made for the care and maintenance of gravesites. The statement must be certified by an officer or employee of the cemetery who has the responsibility to make or account for expenditures for care and maintenance. A copy of this statement shall be retained by the trustee along with the trust's return and shall be made available for inspection upon request by the Secretary. This paragraph does not relieve the care fund trust of its liability to pay the proper amount of tax due and to maintain adequate records to substantiate each of its deductions, including the deduction provided in section 642(i) and this section. [Reg. § 1.642(i)-1.]

☐ [T.D. 7651, 10-25-79.]

[Reg. § 1.642(i)-2]

§ 1.642(i)-2. **Definitions.**—(a) *Taxable cemetery corporation.* For purposes of section 642(i) and this section, the meaning of the term "taxable cemetery corporation" is limited to a corporation (within the meaning of section 7701(a)(3)) engaged in the business of owning and operating a cemetery that either (1) is not exempt from Federal tax, or (2) is subject to tax under section 511 with respect to its cemetery activities.

(b) *Pursuant to local law.* A cemetery perpetual care fund is created pursuant to local law if:

(1) The governing law of the relevant jurisdiction (State, district, county, parish, etc.) requires or expressly permits the creation of such a fund, or

(2) The legally enforceable bylaws or contracts of a taxable cemetery corporation require a perpetual care fund.

(c) *Gravesite.* A gravesite is any type of interment right that has been sold by a cemetery, including, but not limited to, a burial lot, mausoleum, lawn crypt, niche, or scattering ground. For purposes of § 1.642(i)-1, the term "gravesites" includes only those gravesites with respect to which the care fund or cemetery has an obligation for care and maintenance within the meaning of § 1.642(i)-1(c)(1).

(d) *Care and maintenance.* For purposes of section 642(i) and this section, the term "care and maintenance of gravesites" shall be generally defined in accordance with the definition of such term under the local law pursuant to which the cemetery perpetual care fund is created. If the applicable local law contains no definition, care and maintenance of gravesites may include the upkeep, repair and preservation of those portions of cemetery property in which gravesites (as defined in paragraph (c) of this section) have been sold; including gardening, road maintenance, water line and drain repair and other activities reasonably necessary to the preservation of cemetery property. The costs for care and maintenance include, but are not limited to, expenditures for the maintenance, repair and replacement of machinery, tools, and equipment, compensation of employees performing such work, insurance premiums, reasonable payments for employees' pension and other benefit plans, and the costs of maintaining necessary records of lot ownership, transfers and burials. However, if some of the expenditures of the cemetery corporation, such as officers' salaries, are for both care and maintenance and for other purposes, the expenditures must be properly allocated between care and maintenance of gravesites and the other purposes. Only those expenditures that are properly allocable to those portions of cemetery property in which gravesites have been sold qualify as expenditures for care and maintenance of gravesites. [Reg. § 1.642(i)-2.]

☐ [T.D. 7651, 10-25-79.]

[Reg. § 1.643(a)-0]

§ 1.643(a)-0. **Distributable net income; deduction for distributions; in general.**—The term "distributable net income" has no application except in the taxation of estates and trusts and their beneficiaries. It limits the deductions allowable to estates and trusts for amounts paid, credited, or required to be distributed to beneficiaries and is used to determine how much of an amount paid, credited, or required to be distrib-

Reg. § 1.642(i)-2(a)

uted to a beneficiary will be includible in his gross income. It is also used to determine the character of distributions to the beneficiaries. Distributable net income means for any taxable year, the taxable income (as defined in section 63) of the estate or trust, computed with the modifications set forth in §§ 1.643(a)-1 through 1.643(a)-7. [Reg. § 1.643(a)-0.]

☐ [T.D. 6217, 12-19-56.]

[Reg. § 1.643(a)-1]

§ 1.643(a)-1. Deduction for distributions.—The deduction allowable to a trust under section 651 and to an estate or trust under section 661 for amounts paid, credited, or required to be distributed to beneficiaries is not allowed in the computation of distributable net income [Reg. § 1.643(a)-1.]

☐ [T.D. 6217, 12-19-56.]

[Reg. § 1.643(a)-2]

§ 1.643(a)-2. Deduction for personal exemption.—The deduction for personal exemption under section 642(b) is not allowed in the computation of distributable net income. [Reg. § 1.643(a)-2.]

☐ [T.D. 6217, 12-19-56.]

[Reg. § 1.643(a)-3]

§ 1.643(a)-3. Capital gains and losses.—(a) Except as provided in § 1.643(a)-6, gains from the sale or exchange of capital assets are ordinarily excluded from distributable net income and are not ordinarily considered as paid, credited, or required to be distributed to any beneficiary unless they are:

(1) Allocated to income under the terms of the governing instrument or local law by the fiduciary on its books or by notice to the beneficiary,

(2) Allocated to corpus and actually distributed to beneficiaries during the taxable year, or

(3) Utilized (pursuant to the terms of the governing instrument or the practice followed by the fiduciary) in determining the amount which is distributed or required to be distributed.

However, if capital gains are paid, permanently set aside, or to be used for the purposes specified in section 642(c), so that a charitable deduction is allowed under that section in respect of the gains, they must be included in the computation of distributable net income.

(b) Losses from the sale or exchange of capital assets are excluded in computing distributable net income except to the extent that they enter into the determination of any capital gains that are paid, credited, or required to be distributed to any beneficiary during the taxable year (but see § 1.642(h)-1 with respect to capital loss carryovers in the year of final termination of an estate or trust).

(c) The deduction under section 1202 (relating to capital gains) is taken into account in computing distributable net income to the extent that it is allocable to capital gains which are paid, permanently set aside, or to be used for the purposes specified in section 642(c). See the regulations under section 642(c) to determine the extent to which the amount so paid, permanently set aside, or to be used consists of capital gains. The deduction for capital gains provided in section 1202 insofar as it is allocable to the remainder of the capital gains is not taken into account.

(d) The application of this section may be illustrated by the following examples:

Example (1). A trust is created to pay the income to A for life, with a discretionary power in the trustee to invade principal for A's benefit. In the taxable year, $10,000 is realized from the sale of securities at a profit, and $10,000 in excess of income is distributed to A. The capital gain is not allocated to A by the trustee. During the taxable year the trustee received and paid out $5,000 of dividends. No other cash was received or on hand during the taxable year. The capital gain will not ordinarily be included in distributable net income. However, if the trustee follows a regular practice of distributing the exact net proceeds of the sale of trust property, capital gains will be included in distributable net income.

Example (2). The result in example (1) would have been the same if the trustee had been directed to pay an annuity of $15,000 a year to A (instead of being directed to pay the income to A with a discretionary power to distribute principal).

Example (3). The trustee of a trust containing Blackacre and other property is directed to hold Blackacre for ten years, and then sell it and distribute its proceeds to A. Any capital gain realized from the sale of Blackacre will be included in distributable net income.

Example (4). A trust instrument directs that the income shall be paid to A, and that the principal shall be distributed to A when he reaches age 35. All capital gains realized in the year of termination will be included in distributable net income. (See § 1.641(b)-3 for the determination of the year of final termination and the taxability of capital gains realized after the terminating event and before final distribution.)

Example (5). If in example (4) the trustee had been directed to distribute half of the principal to A when he reached 35, the capital gain would be included in distributable net income (and in the

Reg. § 1.643(a)-3(d)

distribution to A) to the extent the capital gain is allocable to A under the governing instrument and local law. Thus, if the trust assets consisted entirely of 100 shares of corporation M stock and the trustee sold half the shares and distributed the proceeds to A, the entire capital gain would normally be considered as allocated to A. On the other hand, if the trustee sold all the shares and distributed half the proceeds to A, half the capital gain would be considered as allocable to A.

Example (6). If in example (4) the trustee had been directed to pay $10,000 to B before making distribution to A, no portion of the capital gains would be allocable to B since the distribution to B is a gift of a specific sum of money within the meaning of section 663(a)(1). [Reg. § 1.643(a)-3.]

☐ [T.D. 6217, 12-19-56. Amended by T.D. 6989, 1-16-69 and by T.D. 7357, 5-30-75.]

[Reg. § 1.643(a)-4]

§ 1.643(a)-4. Extraordinary dividends and taxable stock dividends.—In the case solely of a trust which qualifies under subpart B (section 651 and following) as a "simple trust", there are excluded from distributable net income extraordinary dividends (whether paid in cash or in kind) or taxable stock dividends which are not distributed or credited to a beneficiary because the fiduciary in good faith determines that under the terms of the governing instrument and applicable local law such dividends are allocable to corpus. See section 665(e), paragraph (b) of § 1.665(e)-1 and paragraph (b) of § 1.665(e)-1A for the treatment of such dividends upon subsequent distribution. [Reg. § 1.643(a)-4.]

☐ [T.D. 6217, 12-19-56. Amended by T.D. 6989, 1-16-69 and by T.D. 7204, 8-24-72.]

[Reg. § 1.643(a)-5]

§ 1.643(a)-5. Tax-exempt interest.—(a) There is included in distributable net income any tax-exempt interest excluded from gross income under section 103, reduced by disbursements allocable to such interest which would have been deductible under section 212 but for the provisions of section 265 (relating to disallowance of deductions allocable to tax-exempt income).

(b) If the estate or trust is allowed a charitable contributions deduction under section 642(c), the amounts specified in paragraph (a) of this section and § 1.643(a)-6 are reduced by the portion deemed to be included in income paid, permanently set aside, or to be used for the purposes specified in section 642(c). If the governing instrument specifically provides as to the source out of which amounts are paid, permanently set aside, or to be used for such charitable purposes, the specific provisions control. In the absence of specific provisions in the governing instrument, an amount to which section 642(c) applies is deemed to consist of the same proportion of each class of the items of income of the estate or trust as the total of each class bears to the total of all classes. For illustrations showing the determination of the character of an amount deductible under section 642(c), see examples (1) and (2) of § 1.662(b)-2 and paragraph (e) of § 1.662(c)-4. [Reg. § 1.643(a)-5.]

☐ [T.D. 6217, 12-19-56.]

[Reg. § 1.643(a)-6]

§ 1.643(a)-6. Income of foreign trust.—(a) *Distributable net income of a foreign trust.* In the case of a foreign trust (see section 7701(a)(31)), the determination of distributable net income is subject to the following rules:

(1) There is included in distributable net income the amounts of gross income from sources without the United States, reduced by disbursements allocable to such foreign income which would have been deductible but for the provisions of section 265 (relating to disallowance of deductions allocable to tax-exempt income). See paragraph (b) of § 1.643(a)-5 for rules applicable when an estate or trust is allowed a charitable contributions deduction under section 642(c).

(2) In the case of a distribution made by a trust before January 1, 1963, for purposes of determining the distributable net income of the trust for the taxable year in which the distribution is made, or for any prior taxable year,

(i) Gross income from sources within the United States is determined by taking into account the provisions of section 894 (relating to income exempt under treaty); and

(ii) Distributable net income is determined by taking into account the provisions of section 643(a)(3) (relating to exclusion of certain gains from the sale or exchange of capital assets).

(3) In the case of a distribution made by a trust after December 31, 1962, for purposes of determining the distributable net income of the trust for any taxable year, whether ending before January 1, 1963, or after December 31, 1962,

(i) Gross income (for the entire foreign trust) from sources within the United States is determined without regard to the provisions of section 894 (relating to income exempt under treaty);

(ii) In respect of a foreign trust created by a United States person (whether such trust constitutes the whole or only a portion of the entire foreign trust) (see section 643(d) and

Reg. § 1.643(a)-4

§ 1.643(d)-1), there shall be included in gross income gains from the sale or exchange of capital assets reduced by losses from such sales or exchanges to the extent such losses do not exceed gains from such sales or exchanges, and the deduction under section 1202 (relating to deduction for capital gains) shall not be taken into account; and

(iii) In respect of a foreign trust created by a person other than a United States person (whether such trust constitutes the whole or only a portion of the entire foreign trust) (see section 643(d) and § 1.643(d)-1), distributable net income is determined by taking into account all of the provisions of section 643 except section 643(a)(6)(C) (relating to gains from the sale or exchange of capital assets by a foreign trust created by a United States person).

(b) The application of this section, showing the computation of distributable net income for one of the taxable years for which such a computation must be made, may be illustrated by the following examples:

Example (1). (1) A trust is created in 1952 under the laws of Country X by the transfer to a trustee in Country X of money and property by a United States person. The entire trust constitutes a foreign trust created by a United States person. The income from the trust corpus is to be accumulated until the beneficiary, a resident citizen of the United States who was born in 1944, reaches the age of 21 years, and upon his reaching that age, the corpus and accumulated income are to be distributed to him. The trust instrument provides that capital gains are to be allocated to corpus and are not to be paid, credited, or required to be distributed to any beneficiary during the taxable year or paid, permanently set aside, or to be used for the purposes specified in section 642(c). Under the terms of a tax convention between the United States and Country X, interest income received by the trust from United States sources is exempt from United States taxation. In 1965 the corpus and accumulated income are distributed to the beneficiary. During the taxable year 1964, the trust has the following items of income, loss, and expense:

Interest on bonds of a United States corporation	$10,000
Net long-term capital gain from United States sources	30,000
Gross income from investments in Country X	40,000
Net short-term capital loss from United States sources	5,000
Expenses allocable to gross income from investments in Country X	5,000

(2) The distributable net income for the taxable year 1964 of the foreign trust created by a United States person, determined under section 643(a), is $70,000, computed as follows:

Interest on bonds of a United States corporation		$10,000
Gross income from investments in Country X		40,000
Net long-term capital gain from United States sources	$30,000	
Less: Net short-term capital loss from United States sources	5,000	
Excess of net long-term capital gain over net short-term capital loss		25,000
Total		$75,000
Less: Expenses allocable to income from investments in Country X		5,000
Distributable net income		$70,000

(3) In determining the distributable net income of $70,000, the taxable income of the trust is computed with the following modifications: No deduction is allowed for the personal exemption of the trust (section 643(a)(2)); the interest received on bonds of a United States corporation is included in the trust gross income despite the fact that such interest is exempt from United States tax under the provisions of the tax treaty between Country X and the United States (section 643(a)(6)(B)); the excess of net long-term capital gain over net short-term capital loss allocable to corpus is included in distributable net income, but such excess is not subject to the deduction under section 1202 (section 643(a)(6)(C)); and the amount representing gross income from investments in Country X is included, but such amount is reduced by the amount of the disbursements allocable to such income (section 643(a)(6)(A)).

Example (2). (1) The facts are the same as in example (1) except that money or property has also been transferred to the trust by a person other than a United States person and, pursuant to the provisions of § 1.643(d)-1, during 1964 only 60 percent of the entire trust constitutes a foreign trust created by a United States person.

(2) The distributable net income for the taxable year 1964 of the foreign trust created by a United States person, determined under section 643(a), is $42,000 computed as follows:

Reg. § 1.643(a)-6(b)

43,270   **Estates, Trusts, and Beneficiaries**

See p. 20,601 for regulations not amended to reflect law changes

Interest on bonds of a United States corporation (60% of $10,000)		$ 6,000
Gross income from investments in County X (60% of $40,000)		24,000
Net long-term capital gain from United States sources (60% of $30,000)	$18,000	
Less: Net short-term capital loss from United States sources (60% of $5,000)	$ 3,000	
Total		$45,000
Less: Expenses allocable to income from investments in Country X (60% of $5,000)		$ 3,000
Distributable net income		$42,000

(3) The distributable net income for the taxable year 1964 of the portion of the entire foreign trust which does not constitute a foreign trust created by a United States person, determined under section 643(a), is $18,000, computed as follows:

Interest on bonds of a United States corporation (40% of $10,000)	$ 4,000
Gross income from investments in Country X (40% of $40,000)	16,000
Total	$20,000
Less: Expenses allocable to income from investments in Country X (40% of $5,000)	2,000

(4) The distributable net income of the entire foreign trust for the taxable year 1964 is $60,000, computed as follows:

Distributable net income of the foreign trust created by a United States person	$42,000
Distributable net income of that portion of the entire foreign trust which does not constitute a foreign trust created by a United States person	18,000
Distributable net income of the entire foreign trust	$60,000

It should be noted that the difference between the $70,000 distributable net income of the foreign trust in example (1) and the $60,000 distributable net income of the entire foreign trust in this example is due to the $10,000 (40% of $25,000) net capital gain (capital gain net income for taxable years beginning after December 31, 1976) which under section 643(a)(3) is excluded from the distributable net income of that portion of the foreign trust in example (2) which does not constitute a foreign trust created by a United States person. [Reg. § 1.643(a)-6.]

☐ [T.D. 6217, 12-19-56. Amended by T.D. 6989, 1-16-69 and by T.D. 7728, 10-31-80.]

[Reg. § 1.643(a)-7]

§ 1.643(a)-7. **Dividends.**—Dividends excluded from gross income under section 116 (relating to partial exclusion of dividends received) are included in distributable net income. For this purpose, adjustments similar to those required by § 1.643(a)-5 with respect to expenses allocable to tax-exempt income and to income included in amounts paid or set aside for charitable purposes are not made. See the regulations under section 642(c). [Reg. § 1.643(a)-7.]

☐ [T.D. 6217, 12-19-56. Amended by T.D. 7357, 5-30-75.]

[Reg. § 1.643(a)-8]

§ 1.643(a)-8. **Certain distributions by charitable remainder trusts.**—(a) *Purpose and scope.* This section is intended to prevent the avoidance of the purposes of the charitable remainder trust rules regarding the characterizations of distributions from those trusts in the hands of the recipients and should be interpreted in a manner consistent with this purpose. This section applies to all charitable remainder trusts described in section 664 and the beneficiaries of such trusts.

(b) *Deemed sale by trust*—(1) For purposes of section 664(b), a charitable remainder trust shall be treated as having sold, in the year in which a distribution of an annuity or unitrust amount is made from the trust, a pro rata portion of the trust assets to the extent that the distribution of the annuity or unitrust amount would (but for the application of this paragraph (b)) be characterized in the hands of the recipient as being from the category described in section 664(b)(4) and exceeds the amount of the previously undistributed

(i) Cash contributed to the trust (with respect to which a deduction was allowable under section 170, 2055, 2106, or 2522); plus

(ii) Basis in any contributed property (with respect to which a deduction was allowable under section 170, 2055, 2106; or 2522) that was sold by the trust.

(2) Any transaction that has the purpose or effect of circumventing the rules in this paragraph (b) shall be disregarded.

(3) For purposes of paragraph (b)(1) of this section, trust assets do not include cash or assets purchased with the proceeds of a trust borrowing, forward sale, or similar transaction.

(4) Proper adjustment shall be made to any gain or loss subsequently realized for gain or loss

Reg. § 1.643(a)-7

taken into account under paragraph (b)(1) of this section.

(c) *Examples.* The following examples illustrate the rules of paragraph (b) of this section:

Example 1. Deemed sale by trust. Donor contributes stock having a fair market value of $2 million to a charitable remainder unitrust with a unitrust amount of 50 percent of the net fair market value of the trust assets and a two-year term. The stock has a total adjusted basis of $400,000. In Year 1, the trust receives dividend income of $20,000. As of the valuation date, the trust's assets have a net fair market value of $2,020,000 ($2 million in stock, plus $20,000 in cash). To obtain additional cash to pay the unitrust amount to the noncharitable beneficiary, the trustee borrows $990,000 against the value of the stock. The trust then distributes $1,010,000 to the beneficiary before the end of Year 1. Under section 664(b)(1), $20,000 of the distribution is characterized in the hands of the beneficiary as dividend income. The rest of the distribution, $990,000, is attributable to an amount received by the trust that did not represent either cash contributed to the trust or a return of basis in any contributed asset sold by the trust during Year 1. Under paragraph (b)(3) of this section, the stock is a trust asset because it was not purchased with the proceeds of the borrowing. Therefore, in Year 1, under paragraph (b)(1) of this section, the trust is treated as having sold $990,000 of stock and as having realized $792,000 of capital gain (the trust's basis in the shares deemed sold is $198,000). Thus, in the hands of the beneficiary, $792,000 of the distribution is characterized as capital gain under section 664(b)(2) and $198,000 is characterized as a tax-free return of corpus under section 664(b)(4). No part of the $990,000 loan is treated as acquisition indebtedness under section 514(c) because the entire loan has been recharacterized as a deemed sale.

Example 2. Adjustment to trust's basis in assets deemed sold. The facts are the same as in *Example 1.* During Year 2, the trust sells the stock for $2,100,000. The trustee uses a portion of the proceeds of the sale to repay the outstanding loan, plus accrued interest. Under paragraph (b)(4) of this section, the trust's adjusted basis in the stock is $1,192,000 ($400,000 plus the $792,000 of gain recognized in Year 1). Therefore, the trust recognizes capital gain (as described in section 664(b)(2)) in Year 2 of $908,000.

Example 3. Distribution of cash contributions. Upon the death of D, the proceeds of a life insurance policy on D's life are payable to T, a charitable remainder annuity trust. The terms of the trust provide that, for a period of three years commencing upon D's death, the trust shall pay an annuity amount equal to $x annually to A, the child of D. After the expiration of such three-year period, the remainder interest in the trust is to be transferred to charity Z. In Year 1, the trust receives payment of the life insurance proceeds and pays the appropriate pro rata portion of the $x annuity to A from the insurance proceeds. During Year 1, the trust has no income. Because the entire distribution is attributable to a cash contribution (the insurance proceeds) to the trust for which a charitable deduction was allowable under section 2055 with respect to the present value of the remainder interest passing to charity, the trust will not be treated as selling a pro rata portion of the trust assets under paragraph (b)(1) of this section. Thus, the distribution is characterized in A's hands as a tax-free return of corpus under section 664(b)(4).

(d) *Effective date.* This section is applicable to distributions made by a charitable remainder trust after October 18, 1999. [Reg. § 1.643(a)-8.]

☐ [T.D. 8926, 1-4-2001.]

[Reg. § 1.643(b)-1]

§ 1.643(b)-1. **Definition of "income".**—For purposes of subparts A through D, part I, subchapter J, chapter 1 of the Code, the term "income", when not preceded by the words "taxable", "distributable net", "undistributed net", or "gross", means the amount of income of an estate or trust for the taxable year determined under the terms of its governing instrument and applicable local law. Trust provisions which depart fundamentally from concepts of local law in the determination of what constitutes income are not recognized for this purpose. For example, if a trust instrument directs that all the trust income shall be paid to A, but defines ordinary dividends and interest as corpus, the trust will not be considered one which under its governing instrument is required to distribute all its income currently for purposes of section 642(b) (relating to the personal exemption) and section 651 (relating to "simple" trusts). [Reg. § 1.643(b)-1.]

☐ [T.D. 6217, 12-19-56.]

[Reg. § 1.643(b)-2]

§ 1.643(b)-2. **Dividends allocated to corpus.**—Extraordinary dividends or taxable stock dividends which the fiduciary, acting in good faith, determines to be allocable to corpus under the terms of the governing instrument and applicable local law are not considered "income" for purposes of subpart A, B, C, or D, part I, subchapter J, chapter 1 of the Code. See section 643(a)(4), § 1.643(a)-4, § 1.643(d)-2, section 665(e), paragraph (b) of § 1.665(e)-1 and paragraph (b) of § 1.665(e)-1A for the treatment of such items in the computation of distributable net income. [Reg. § 1.643(b)-2.]

☐ [T.D. 6217, 12-19-56. *Amended by T.D. 6989, 1-16-69 and by T.D. 7204, 8-24-72.*]

[Reg. § 1.643(c)-1]

§ 1.643(c)-1. **Definition of "beneficiary".**—An heir, legatee, or devisee (including an estate or trust) is a beneficiary. A trust created under a decedent's will is a beneficiary of the decedent's estate. The following persons are treated as beneficiaries:

(a) Any person with respect to an amount used to discharge or satisfy that person's legal obligation as that term is used in § 1.662(a)-4.

(b) The grantor of a trust with respect to an amount applied or distributed for the support of a dependent under the circumstances specified in section 677(b) out of corpus or out of other than income for the taxable year of the trust.

(c) The trustee or cotrustee of a trust with respect to an amount applied or distributed for the support of a dependent under the circumstances specified in section 678(c) out of corpus or out of other than income for the taxable year of the trust. [Reg. § 1.643(c)-1.]

☐ [T.D. 6217, 12-19-56.]

[Reg. § 1.643(d)-1]

§ 1.643(d)-1. **Definition of "foreign trust created by a United States person".**—(a) *In general.* For the purpose of Part I, subchapter J, chapter 1 of the Internal Revenue Code, the term "foreign trust created by a United States person" means that portion of a foreign trust (as defined in section 7701(a)(31)) attributable to money or property (including all accumulated earnings, profits, or gains attributable to such money or property) of a United States person (as defined in Sec. 7701(a)(30)) transferred directly or indirectly, or under the will of a decedent who at the date of his death was a United States citizen or resident, to the foreign trust. A foreign trust created by a person who is not a United States person, to which a United States person transfers his money or property, is a foreign trust created by a United States person to the extent that the fair market value of the entire foreign trust is attributable to money or property of the United States person transferred to the foreign trust. The transfer of money or property to the foreign trust may be made either directly or indirectly by a United States person. Transfers of money or property to a foreign trust do not include transfers of money or property pursuant to a sale or exchange which is made for a full and adequate considera-tion. Transfers to which section 643(d) and this section apply are transfers of money or property which establish or increase the corpus of a foreign trust. The rules set forth in this section with respect to transfers by a United States person to a foreign trust also are applicable with respect to transfers under the will of a decedent who at the date of his death was a United States citizen or resident. For provisions relating to the information returns which are required to be filed with respect to the creation of or transfers to foreign trusts, see section 6048 and § 16.3-1 of this chapter (Temporary Regulations under the Revenue Act of 1962).

(b) *Determination of a foreign trust created by a United States person*—(1) *Transfers of money or property only by a United States person.* If all the items of money or property constituting the corpus of a foreign trust are transferred to the trust by a United States person, the entire foreign trust is a foreign trust created by a United States person.

(2) *Transfers of money or property by both a United States person and a person other than a United States person; transfers required to be treated as separate funds.* Where there are transfers of money or property by both a United States person and a person other than a United States person to a foreign trust, and it is necessary, either by reason of the provisions of the governing instrument of the trust or by reason of some other requirement such as local law, that the trustee treat the entire foreign trust as composed of two separate funds, one consisting of the money or property (including all accumulated earnings, profits, or gains attributable to such money or property) transferred by the United States person and the other consisting of the money or property (including all accumulated earnings, profits, or gains attributable to such money or property) transferred by the person other than the United States person, the foreign trust created by a United States person shall be the fund consisting of the money or property transferred by the United States person. See example (1) in paragraph (c) of this section.

(3) *Transfers of money or property by both a United States person and a person other than a United States person; transfers not required to be treated as separate funds.* Where the corpus of a foreign trust consists of money or property transferred to the trust (simultaneously or at different times) by a United States person and by a person who is not a United States person, the foreign trust created by a United States person within the meaning of section 643(d) is that portion of the entire foreign trust which, immediately after any

Reg. § 1.643(c)-1(a)

Estates, Trusts, and Beneficiaries

See p. 20,601 for regulations not amended to reflect law changes

transfer of money or property to the trust, the fair market value of money or property (including all accumulated earnings, profits, or gains attributable to such money or property) transferred to the foreign trust by the United States person bears to the fair market value of the corpus (including all accumulated earnings, profits, or gains attributable to the corpus) of the entire foreign trust.

(c) The provisions of paragraph (b) of this section may be illustrated by the following examples. Example (1) illustrates the application of paragraph (b)(2) of this section. Example (2) illustrates the application of paragraph (b)(3) of this section in a case where there is no provision in the governing instrument of the trust or elsewhere which would require the trustee to treat the corpus of the trust as composed of more than one fund.

Example (1). On January 1, 1964, the date of the creation of a foreign trust, a United States person transfers to it stock of a United States corporation with a fair market value of $50,000. On the same day, a person other than a United States person transfers to the trust Country X bonds with a fair market value of $25,000. The governing instrument of the trust provides that the income from the stock of the United States corporation is to be accumulated until A, a United States beneficiary, reaches the age of 21 years, and upon his reaching that age, the stock and income accumulated thereon are to be distributed to him. The governing instrument of the trust further provides that the income from the Country X bonds is to be accumulated until B, a United States beneficiary, reaches the age of 21 years, and upon his reaching that age, the bonds and income accumulated thereon are to be distributed to him. To comply with the provisions of the governing instrument of the trust that the income from the stock of the United States corporation be accumulated and distributed to A and that the income from the Country X bonds be accumulated and distributed to B, it is necessary that the trustee treat the transfers as two separate funds. The fund consisting of the stock of the United States corporation is a foreign trust created by a United States person.

Example (2). On January 1, 1964, the date of the creation of a foreign trust, a United States person transfers to it property having a fair market value of $60,000 and a person other than a United States person transfers to it property having a fair market value of $40,000. Immediately after these transfers, the foreign trust created by a United States person is 60 percent of the entire foreign trust, determined as follows:

$$\frac{\$60,000 \text{ (Value of property transferred by U.S. person)}}{\$100,000 \text{ (Value of entire property transferred to trust)}} = 60 \text{ percent}$$

The undistributed net income for the calendar years 1964 and 1965 is $20,000 which increases the value of the entire foreign trust to $120,000 ($100,000 plus $20,000). Accordingly, as of December 31, 1965, the portion of the foreign trust created by the United States person is $72,000 (60% of $120,000). On January 1, 1966, the United States person transfers property having a fair market value of $40,000 increasing the value of the entire foreign trust to $160,000 ($120,000 plus $40,000) and increasing the value of the portion of the foreign trust created by the United States person to $112,000 ($72,000 plus $40,000). Immediately after this transfer, the foreign trust created by the United States person is 70 percent of the entire foreign trust, determined as follows:

$$\frac{\$112,000 \text{ (Value of property transferred by U.S. person)}}{\$160,000 \text{ (Value of entire property transferred to the trust)}} = 70 \text{ percent}$$

[Reg. § 1.643(d)-1.]

☐ [T.D. 6989, 1-16-69.]

[Reg. § 1.643(d)-2]

§ 1.643(d)-2. Illustration of the provisions of section 643.—(a) The provisions of section 643 may be illustrated by the following example:

Example. (1) Under the terms of the trust instrument, the income of a trust is required to be currently distributed to W during her life. Capital gains are allocable to corpus and all expenses are charges against corpus. During the taxable year the trust has the following items of income and expenses:

Dividends for domestic corporations	$30,000
Extraordinary dividends allocated to corpus by the trustee in good faith	20,000
Taxable interest	10,000
Tax-exempt interest	10,000
Long-term capital gains	10,000
Trustee's commissions and miscellaneous expenses allocable to corpus	5,000

(2) The "income" of the trust determined under section 643(b) which is currently distributable to W is $50,000, consisting of dividends of $30,000, taxable interest of $10,000 and tax-exempt interest of $10,000. The trustee's commissions and miscellaneous expenses allocable to tax-exempt in-

Reg. § 1.643(d)-2(a)

terest amount to $1,000 (10,000/50,000 × $5,000).

(3) The "distributable net income" determined under section 643(a) amounts to $45,000, computed as follows:

Dividends from domestic corporations		$30,000
Taxable interest		10,000
Nontaxable interest	$10,000	
Less: Expenses allocable thereto	1,000	9,000
Total		$49,000
Less: Expenses ($5,000 less $1,000 allocable to tax-exempt interest)		$ 4,000
Distributable net income		$45,000

In determining the distributable net income of $45,000, the taxable income of the trust is computed with the following modifications: No deductions are allowed for distributions to W and for personal exemption of the trust (section 643(a)(1) and (2)); capital gains allocable to corpus are excluded and the deduction allowable under section 1202 is not taken into account (section 643(a)(3)); the extraordinary dividends allocated to corpus by the trustee in good faith are excluded (section 643(a)(4)); and the tax-exempt interest (as adjusted for expenses) and the dividend exclusion of $50 are included (section 643(a)(5) and (7)).

(b) See paragraph (c) of the example in § 1.661(c)-2 for the computation of distributable net income where there is a charitable contributions deduction. [Reg. § 1.643(d)-2.]

☐ [T.D. 6217, 12-19-56. Amended by T.D. 6989, 1-16-69.]

[Reg. § 1.643(h)-1]

§ 1.643(h)-1. **Distributions by certain foreign trusts through intermediaries.**—(a) *In general*—(1) *Principal purpose of tax avoidance.* Except as provided in paragraph (b) of this section, for purposes of part I of subchapter j, chapter 1 of the Internal Revenue Code, and section 6048, any property (within the meaning of paragraph (f) of this section) that is transferred to a United States person by another person (an intermediary) who has received property from a foreign trust will be treated as property transferred directly by the foreign trust to the United States person if the intermediary received the property from the foreign trust pursuant to a plan one of the principal purposes of which was the avoidance of United States tax.

(2) *Principal purpose of tax avoidance deemed to exist.* For purposes of paragraph (a)(1) of this section, a transfer will be deemed to have been made pursuant to a plan one of the principal purposes of which was the avoidance of United States tax if the United States person—

(i) Is related (within the meaning of paragraph (e) of this section) to a grantor of the foreign trust, or has another relationship with a grantor of the foreign trust that establishes a reasonable basis for concluding that the grantor of the foreign trust would make a gratuitous transfer (within the meaning of § 1.671-2(e)(2)) to the United States person;

(ii) Receives from the intermediary, within the period beginning twenty-four months before and ending twenty-four months after the intermediary's receipt of property from the foreign trust, either the property the intermediary received from the foreign trust, proceeds from such property, or property in substitution for such property; and

(iii) Cannot demonstrate to the satisfaction of the Commissioner that—

(A) The intermediary has a relationship with the United States person that establishes a reasonable basis for concluding that the intermediary would make a gratuitous transfer to the United States person;

(B) The intermediary acted independently of the grantor and the trustee of the foreign trust;

(C) The intermediary is not an agent of the United States person under generally applicable United States agency principles; and

(D) The United States person timely complied with the reporting requirements of section 6039F, if applicable, if the intermediary is a foreign person.

(b) *Exceptions*—(1) *Nongratuitous transfers.* Paragraph (a) of this section does not apply to the extent that either the transfer from the foreign trust to the intermediary or the transfer from the intermediary to the United States person is a transfer that is not a gratuitous transfer within the meaning of § 1.671-2(e)(2).

(2) *Grantor as intermediary.* Paragraph (a) of this section does not apply if the intermediary is the grantor of the portion of the trust from

Reg. § 1.643(h)-1(a)(1)

which the property that is transferred is derived. For the definition of *grantor*, see § 1.671-2(e).

(c) *Effect of disregarding intermediary*—(1) *General rule.* Except as provided in paragraph (c)(2) of this section, the intermediary is treated as an agent of the foreign trust, and the property is treated as transferred to the United States person in the year the property is transferred, or made available, by the intermediary to the United States person. The fair market value of the property transferred is determined as of the date of the transfer by the intermediary to the United States person. For purposes of section 665(d)(2), the term *taxes imposed on the trust* includes any income, war profits, and excess profits taxes imposed by any foreign country or possession of the United States on the intermediary with respect to the property transferred.

(2) *Exception.* If the Commissioner determines, or if the taxpayer can demonstrate to the satisfaction of the Commissioner, that the intermediary is an agent of the United States person under generally applicable United States agency principles, the property will be treated as transferred to the United States person in the year the intermediary receives the property from the foreign trust. The fair market value of the property transferred will be determined as of the date of the transfer by the foreign trust to the intermediary. For purposes of section 901(b), any income, war profits, and excess profits taxes imposed by any foreign country or possession of the United States on the intermediary with respect to the property transferred will be treated as having been imposed on the United States person.

(3) *Computation of gross income of intermediary.* If property is treated as transferred directly by the foreign trust to a United States person pursuant to this section, the fair market value of such property is not taken into account in computing the gross income of the intermediary (if otherwise required to be taken into account by the intermediary but for paragraph (a) of this section).

(d) *Transfers not in excess of $10,000.* This section does not apply if, during the taxable year of the United States person, the aggregate fair market value of all property transferred to such person from all foreign trusts either directly or through one or more intermediaries does not exceed $10,000.

(e) *Related parties.* For purposes of this section, a United States person is treated as related to a grantor of a foreign trust if the United States person and the grantor are related for purposes of section 643(i)(2)(B), with the following modifications—

(1) For purposes of applying section 267 (other than section 267(f),) and section 707(b)(1), "at least 10 percent" is used instead of "more than 50 percent" each place it appears; and

(2) The principles of section 267(b)(10), using "at least 10 percent" instead of "more than 50 percent," apply to determine whether two corporations are related.

(f) *Definition of property.* For purposes of this section, the term *property* includes cash.

(g) *Examples.* The following examples illustrate the rules of this section. In each example, FT is an irrevocable foreign trust that is not treated as owned by any other person and the fair market value of the property that is transferred exceeds $10,000. The examples are as follows:

Example 1. Principal purpose of tax avoidance. FT was created in 1980 by A, a nonresident alien, for the benefit of his children and their descendants. FT's trustee, T, determines that 1000X of accumulated income should be distributed to A's granddaughter, B, who is a resident alien. Pursuant to a plan with a principal purpose of avoiding the interest charge that would be imposed by section 668, T causes FT to make a gratuitous transfer (within the meaning of § 1.671-2(e)(2)) of 1000X to I, a foreign person. I subsequently makes a gratuitous transfer of 1000X to B. Under paragraph (a)(1) of this section, FT is deemed to have made an accumulation distribution of 1000X directly to B.

Example 2. United States person unable to demonstrate that intermediary acted independently. GM and her daughter, M, are both nonresident aliens. M's daughter, D, is a resident alien. GM creates and funds FT for the benefit of her children. On July 1, 2001, FT makes a gratuitous transfer of XYZ stock to M. M immediately sells the XYZ stock and uses the proceeds to purchase ABC stock. On January 1, 2002, M makes a gratuitous transfer of the ABC stock to D. D is unable to demonstrate that M acted independently of GM and the trustee of FT in making the transfer to D. Under paragraph (a)(2) of this section, FT is deemed to have distributed the ABC stock to D. Under paragraph (c)(1) of this section, M is treated as an agent of FT, and the distribution is deemed to have been made on January 1, 2002.

Example 3. United States person demonstrates that specified conditions are satisfied. Assume the same facts as in *Example 2*, except that M receives 1000X cash from FT instead of XYZ stock. M gives 1000X cash to D on January 1, 2002. Also assume that M receives annual income of 5000X from her own investments and that M has given D 1000X at the beginning of each year for the past ten years. Based on this and additional infor-

Reg. § 1.643(h)-1(g)

mation provided by D, D demonstrates to the satisfaction of the Commissioner that M has a relationship with D that establishes a reasonable basis for concluding that M would make a gratuitous transfer to D, that M acted independently of GM and the trustee of FT, that M is not an agent of D under generally applicable United States agency principles, and that D timely complied with the reporting requirements of section 6039F. FT will not be deemed under paragraph (a)(2) of this section to have made a distribution to D.

Example 4. Transfer to United States person less than 24 months before transfer to intermediary. Several years ago, A, a nonresident alien, created and funded FT for the benefit of his children and their descendants. A has a close friend, C, who also is a nonresident alien. A's granddaughter, B, is a resident alien. On December 31, 2001, C makes a gratuitous transfer of 1000X to B. On January 15, 2002, FT makes a gratuitous transfer of 1000X to C. B is unable to demonstrate that C has a relationship with B that would establish a reasonable basis for concluding that C would make a gratuitous transfer to B or that C acted independently of A and the trustee of FT in making the transfer to B. Under paragraph (a)(2) of this section, FT is deemed to have distributed 1000X directly to B. Under paragraph (c)(1) of this section, C is treated as an agent of FT, and the distribution is deemed to have been made on December 31, 2001.

Example 5. United States person receives property in substitution for property transferred to intermediary. GM and her son, S, are both nonresident aliens. S's daughter, GD, is a resident alien. GM creates and funds FT for the benefit of her children and their descendants. On July 1, 2001, FT makes a gratuitous transfer of ABC stock with a fair market value of approximately 1000X to S. On January 1, 2002, S makes a gratuitous transfer of DEP stock with a fair market value of approximately 1000X to GD. GD is unable to demonstrate that S acted independently of GM and the trustee of FT in transferring the DEF stock to GD. Under paragraph (a)(2) of this section, FT is deemed to have distributed the DEF stock to GD. Under paragraph (c)(1) of this section, S is treated as an agent of FT, and the distribution is deemed to have been made on January 1, 2002.

Example 6. United States person receives indirect loan from foreign trust. Several years ago, A, a nonresident alien, created and funded FT for the benefit of her children and their descendants. A's daughter, B, is a resident alien. B needs funds temporarily while she is starting up her own business. If FT were to loan money directly to B, section 643(i) would apply. FT deposits 500X with FB, a foreign bank, on June 30, 2001. On July 1, 2001, FB loans 400X to B. Repayment of the loan is guaranteed by FT's 500X deposit. B is unable to demonstrate to the satisfaction of the Commissioner that FB has a relationship with B that establishes a reasonable basis for concluding that FB would make a loan to B or that FB acted independently of A and the trustee of FT in making the loan. Under paragraph (a)(2) of this section, FT is deemed to have loaned 400X directly to B on July 1, 2001. Under paragraph (c)(1) of this section, FB is treated as an agent of FT. For the treatment of loans from foreign trusts, see section 643(i).

Example 7. United States person demonstrates that specified conditions are satisfied. GM, a nonresident alien, created and funded FT for the benefit of her children and their descendants. One of GM's children is M, who is a resident alien. During the year 2001, FT makes a gratuitous transfer of 500X to M. M reports the 500X on Form 3520 as a distribution received from a foreign trust. During the year 2002, M makes a gratuitous transfer of 400X to her son, S, who also is a resident alien. M files a Form 709 treating the gratuitous transfer to S as a gift. Based on this and additional information provided by S, S demonstrates to the satisfaction of the Commissioner that M has a relationship with S that establishes a reasonable basis for concluding that M would make a gratuitous transfer to S, that M acted independently of GM and the trustee of FT, and that M is not an agent of S under generally applicable United States agency principles. FT will not be deemed under paragraph (a)(2) of this section to have made a distribution to S.

Example 8. Intermediary as agent of trust; increase in FMV. A, a nonresident alien, created and funded FT for the benefit of his children and their descendants. On December 1, 2001, FT makes a gratuitous transfer of XYZ stock with a fair market value of 85X to B, a nonresident alien. On November 1, 2002, B sells the XYZ stock to a third party in an arm's length transaction for 100X in cash. On November 1, 2002, B makes a gratuitous transfer of 98X to A's grandson, C, a resident alien. C is unable to demonstrate to the satisfaction of the Commissioner that B acted independently of A and the trustee of FT in making the transfer. Under paragraph (a)(2) of this section, FT is deemed to have made a distribution directly to C. Under paragraph (c)(1) of this section, B is treated as an agent of FT, and FT is deemed to have distributed 98X to C on November 1, 2002.

Example 9. Intermediary as agent of United States person; increase in FMV. Assume the same facts as in *Example 8*, except that the Commissioner determines that B is an agent of C under generally applicable United States agency principles. Under paragraph (c)(2) of this section, FT is deemed to have distributed 85X to C on December 1, 2001. C must take the gain of 15X into account in the year 2002.

Example 10. Intermediary as agent of trust; decrease in FMV. Assume the same facts as in *Example 8*, except that the value of the XYZ stock on November 1, 2002, is only 80X. Instead of selling the XYZ stock to a third party and transferring cash to C, B transfers the XYZ stock to C in a gratuitous transfer. Under paragraph (c)(1) of this section, FT is deemed to have distributed XYZ stock with a value of 80X to C on November 1, 2002.

Example 11. Intermediary as agent of United States person; decrease in FMV. Assume the same facts as in *Example 10*, except that the Commissioner determines that B is an agent of C under generally applicable United States agency principles. Under paragraph (c)(2) of this section, FT is deemed to have distributed XYZ stock with a value of 85X to C on December 1, 2001.

(h) *Effective date.* The rules of this section are applicable to transfers made to United States persons after August 10, 1999. [Reg. § 1.643(h)-1.]

☐ [*T.D.* 8831, 8-5-99. *Amended by T.D.* 8890, 7-3-2000.]

[Reg. § 1.645-1]

§ 1.645-1. **Election by certain revocable trusts to be treated as part of estate.**—(a) *In general.* If an election is filed for a qualified revocable trust, as defined in paragraph (b)(1) of this section, in accordance with the rules set forth in paragraph (c) of this section, the qualified revocable trust is treated and taxed for purposes of subtitle A of the Internal Revenue Code as part of its related estate, as defined in paragraph (b)(5) of this section (and not as a separate trust) during the election period, as defined in paragraph (b)(6) of this section. Rules regarding the use of taxpayer identification numbers (TINs) and the filing of a Form 1041, "U.S. Income Tax Return for Estates and Trusts," for a qualified revocable trust are in paragraph (d) of this section. Rules regarding the tax treatment of an electing trust and related estate and the general filing requirements for the combined entity during the election period are in paragraph (e)(2) of this section. Rules regarding the tax treatment of an electing trust and its filing requirements during the election period if no executor, as defined in paragraph (b)(4) of this section, is appointed for a related estate are in paragraph (e)(3) of this section. Rules for determining the duration of the section 645 election period are in paragraph (f) of this section. Rules regarding the tax effects of the termination of the election are in paragraph (h) of this section. Rules regarding the tax consequences of the appointment of an executor after a trustee has made a section 645 election believing that an executor would not be appointed for a related estate are in paragraph (g) of this section.

(b) *Definitions.* For purposes of this section:

(1) *Qualified revocable trust.* A *qualified revocable trust* (QRT) is any trust (or portion thereof) that on the date of death of the decedent was treated as owned by the decedent under section 676 by reason of a power held by the decedent (determined without regard to section 672(e)). A trust that was treated as owned by the decedent under section 676 by reason of a power that was exercisable by the decedent only with the approval or consent of a nonadverse party or with the approval or consent of the decedent's spouse is a QRT. A trust that was treated as owned by the decedent under section 676 solely by reason of a power held by a nonadverse party or by reason of a power held by the decedent's spouse is not a QRT.

(2) *Electing trust.* An *electing trust* is a QRT for which a valid section 645 election has been made. Once a section 645 election has been made for the trust, the trust shall be treated as an electing trust throughout the entire election period.

(3) *Decedent.* The *decedent* is the individual who was treated as the owner of the QRT under section 676 on the date of that individual's death.

(4) *Executor.* An *executor* is an executor, personal representative, or administrator that has obtained letters of appointment to administer the decedent's estate through formal or informal appointment procedures. Solely for purposes of this paragraph (b)(4), an executor does not include a person that has actual or constructive possession of property of the decedent unless that person is also appointed or qualified as an executor, administrator, or personal representative of the decedent's estate. If more that one jurisdiction has appointed an executor, the executor appointed in the domiciliary or primary proceeding is the executor of the related estate for purposes of this paragraph (b)(4).

(5) *Related estate.* A *related estate* is the estate of the decedent who was treated as the owner of the QRT on the date of the decedent's death.

(6) *Election period.* The *election period* is the period of time during which an electing trust is

treated and taxed as part of its related estate. The rules for determining the duration of the election period are in paragraph (f) of this section.

(c) *The election*—(1) *Filing the election if there is an executor*—(i) *Time and manner for filing the election.* If there is an executor of the related estate, the trustees of each QRT joining in the election and the executor of the related estate make an election under section 645 and this section to treat each QRT joining in the election as part of the related estate for purposes of subtitle A of the Internal Revenue Code by filing a form provided by the IRS for making the election (election form) properly completed and signed under penalties of perjury, or in any other manner prescribed after December 24, 2002 by forms provided by the Internal Revenue Service (IRS), or by other published guidance for making the election. For the election to be valid, the election form must be filed not later than the time prescribed under section 6072 for filing the Form 1041 for the first taxable year of the related estate (regardless of whether there is sufficient income to require the filing of that return). If an extension is granted for the filing of the Form 1041 for the first taxable year of the related estate, the election form will be timely filed if it is filed by the time prescribed for filing the Form 1041 including the extension granted with respect to the Form 1041.

(ii) *Conditions to election.* In addition to providing the information required by the election form, as a condition to a valid section 645 election, the trustee of each QRT joining in the election and the executor of the related estate agree, by signing the election form under penalties of perjury, that:

(A) With respect to a trustee—

(*1*) The trustee agrees to the election;

(*2*) The trustee is responsible for timely providing the executor of the related estate with all the trust information necessary to permit the executor to file a complete, accurate, and timely Form 1041 for the combined electing trust(s) and related estate for each taxable year during the election period;

(*3*) The trustee of each QRT joining the election and the executor of the related estate have agreed to allocate the tax burden of the combined electing trust(s) and related estate for each taxable year during the election period in a manner that reasonably reflects the tax obligations of each electing trust and the related estate; and

(*4*) The trustee is responsible for insuring that the electing trust's share of the tax obligations of the combined electing trust(s) and related estate is timely paid to the Secretary.

(B) With respect to the executor—

(*1*) The executor agrees to the election;

(*2*) The executor is responsible for filing a complete, accurate, and timely Form 1041 for the combined electing trust(s) and related estate for each taxable year during the election period;

(*3*) The executor and the trustee of each QRT joining in the election have agreed to allocate the tax burden of the combined electing trust(s) and related estate for each taxable year during the election period in a manner that reasonably reflects the tax obligations of each electing trust and the related estate;

(*4*) The executor is responsible for insuring that the related estate's share of the tax obligations of the combined electing trust(s) and related estate is timely paid to the Secretary.

(2) *Filing the election if there is no executor*—(i) *Time and manner for filing the election.* If there is no executor for a related estate, an election to treat one or more QRTs of the decedent as an estate for purposes of subtitle A of the Internal Revenue Code is made by the trustees of each QRT joining in the election, by filing a properly completed election form, or in any other manner prescribed after December 24, 2002 by forms provided by the IRS, or by other published guidance for making the election. For the election to be valid, the election form must be filed not later than the time prescribed under section 6072 for filing the Form 1041 for the first taxable year of the trust, taking into account the trustee's election to treat the trust as an estate under section 645 (regardless of whether there is sufficient income to require the filing of that return). If an extension is granted for the filing of the Form 1041 for the first taxable year of the electing trust, the election form will be timely filed if it is filed by the time prescribed for filing the Form 1041 including the extension granted with respect to the filing of the Form 1041.

(ii) *Conditions to election.* In addition to providing the information required by the election form, as a condition to a valid section 645 election, the trustee of each QRT joining in the election agrees, by signing the election form under penalties of perjury, that—

(A) The trustee agrees to the election;

(B) If there is more than one QRT joining in the election, the trustees of each QRT joining in the election have appointed one trustee to be responsible for filing the Form 1041 for the

Reg. § 1.645-1(c)(1)

combined electing trusts for each taxable year during the election period (filing trustee) and the filing trustee has agreed to accept that responsibility;

(C) If there is more than one QRT, the trustees of each QRT joining in the election have agreed to allocate the tax liability of the combined electing trusts for each taxable year during the election period in a manner that reasonably reflects the tax obligations of each electing trust;

(D) The trustee agrees to:

(*1*) Timely file a Form 1041 for the electing trust(s) for each taxable year during the election period; or

(*2*) If there is more than one QRT and the trustee is not the filing trustee, timely provide the filing trustee with all of the electing trust's information necessary to permit the filing trustee to file a complete, accurate, and timely Form 1041 for the combined electing trusts for each taxable year during the election period;

(*3*) Insure that the electing trust's share of the tax burden is timely paid to the Secretary;

(E) There is no executor and, to the knowledge and belief of the trustee, one will not be appointed; and

(F) If an executor is appointed after the filing of the election form and the executor agrees to the section 645 election, the trustee will complete and file a revised election form with the executor.

(3) *Election for more than one QRT.* If there is more than one QRT, the election may be made for some or all of the QRTs. If there is no executor, one trustee must be appointed by the trustees of the electing trusts to file Forms 1041 for the combined electing trusts filing as an estate during the election period.

(d) *TIN and filing requirements for a QRT*—(1) *Obtaining a TIN.* Regardless of whether there is an executor for a related estate and regardless of whether a section 645 election will be made for the QRT, a TIN must be obtained for the QRT following the death of the decedent. See § 301.6109-1(a)(3) of this chapter. The trustee must furnish this TIN to the payors of the QRT. See § 301.6109-1(a)(5) of this chapter for the definition of payor.

(2) *Filing a Form 1041 for a QRT*—(i) *Option not to file a Form 1041 for a QRT for which a section 645 election will be made.* If a section 645 election will be made for a QRT, the executor of the related estate, if any, and the trustee of the QRT may treat the QRT as an electing trust from the decedent's date of death until the due date for the section 645 election. Accordingly, the trustee of the QRT is not required to file a Form 1041 for the QRT for the short taxable year beginning with the decedent's date of death and ending December 31 of that year. However, if a QRT is treated as an electing trust under this paragraph from the decedent's date of death until the due date for the section 645 election but a valid section 645 election is not made for the QRT, the QRT will be subject to penalties and interest for failing to timely file a Form 1041 and pay the tax due thereon.

(ii) *Requirement to file a Form 1041 for a QRT if paragraph (d)(2)(i) of this section does not apply*—(A) *Requirement to file Form 1041.* If the trustee of the QRT and the executor of the related estate, if any, do not treat the QRT as an electing trust as provided under paragraph (d)(2)(i) of this section, or if the trustee of the electing trust and the executor, if any, are uncertain whether a section 645 election will be made for a QRT, the trustee of the QRT must file a Form 1041 for the short taxable year beginning with the decedent's death and ending December 31 of that year (unless the QRT is not required to file a Form 1041 under section 6012 for this period).

(B) *Requirement to amend Form 1041 if a section 645 election is made*—(*1*) *If there is an executor.* If there is an executor and a valid section 645 election is made for a QRT after a Form 1041 has been filed for the QRT as a trust (see paragraph (d)(2)(ii)(A) of this section), the trustee must amend the Form 1041. The QRT's items of income, deduction, and credit must be excluded from the amended Form 1041 filed under this paragraph and must be included on the Form 1041 filed for the first taxable year of the combined electing trust and related estate under paragraph (e)(2)(ii)(A) of this section.

(*2*) *If there is no executor.* If there is no executor and a valid section 645 election is made for a QRT after a Form 1041 has been filed for the QRT as a trust (see paragraph (d)(2)(ii)(A) of this section) for the short taxable year beginning with the decedent's death and ending December 31 of that year, the trustee must file an amended return for the QRT. The amended return must be filed consistent with paragraph (e)(3) of this section and must be filed by the due date of the Form 1041 for the QRT, taking into account the trustee's election under section 645.

(e) *Tax treatment and general filing requirements of electing trust and related estate during the election period*—(1) *Effect of election.* The section 645 election once made is irrevocable.

(2) *If there is an executor*—(i) *Tax treatment of the combined electing trust and related estate.*

Reg. § 1.645-1(e)(2)

If there is an executor, the electing trust is treated, during the election period, as part of the related estate for all purposes of subtitle A of the Internal Revenue Code. Thus, for example, the electing trust is treated as part of the related estate for purposes of the set-aside deduction under section 642(c)(2), the subchapter S shareholder requirements of section 1361(b)(1), and the special offset for rental real estate activities in section 469(i)(4).

(ii) *Filing requirements*—(A) *Filing the Form 1041 for the combined electing trust and related estate during the election period.* If there is an executor, the executor files a single income tax return annually (assuming a return is required under section 6012) under the name and TIN of the related estate for the combined electing trust and the related estate. Information regarding the name and TIN of each electing trust must be provided on the Form 1041 as required by the instructions to that form. The period of limitations provided in section 6501 for assessments with respect to an electing trust and the related estate starts with the filing of the return required under this paragraph. Except as required under the separate share rules of section 663(c), for purposes of filing the Form 1041 under this paragraph and computing the tax, the items of income, deduction, and credit of the electing trust and related estate are combined. One personal exemption in the amount of $600 is permitted under section 642(b), and the tax is computed under section 1(e), taking into account section 1(h), for the combined taxable income.

(B) *Filing a Form 1041 for the electing trust is not required.* Except for any final Form 1041 required to be filed under paragraph (h)(2)(i)(B) of this section, if there is an executor, the trustee of the electing trust does not file a Form 1041 for the electing trust during the election period. Although the trustee is not required to file a Form 1041 for the electing trust, the trustee of the electing trust must timely provide the executor of the related estate with all the trust information necessary to permit the executor to file a complete, accurate and timely Form 1041 for the combined electing trust and related estate. The trustee must also insure that the electing trust's share of the tax obligations of the combined electing trust and related estate is timely paid to the Secretary. In certain situations, the trustee of a QRT may be required to file a Form 1041 for the QRT's short taxable year beginning with the date of the decedent's death and ending December 31 of that year. See paragraph (d)(2) of this section.

(iii) *Application of the separate share rules*—(A) *Distributions to beneficiaries (other than to a share (or shares) of the combined electing trust and related estate).* Under the separate share rules of section 663(c), the electing trust and related estate are treated as separate shares for purposes of computing distributable net income (DNI) and applying the distribution provisions of sections 661 and 662. Further, the electing trust share or the related estate share may each contain two or more shares. Thus, if during the taxable year, a distribution is made by the electing trust or the related estate, the DNI of the share making the distribution must be determined and the distribution provisions of sections 661 and 662 must be applied using the separately determined DNI applicable to the distributing share.

(B) *Adjustments to the DNI of the separate shares for distributions between shares to which sections 661 and 662 would apply.* A distribution from one share to another share to which sections 661 and 662 would apply if made to a beneficiary other than another share of the combined electing trust and related estate affects the computation of the DNI of the share making the distribution and the share receiving the distribution. The share making the distribution reduces its DNI by the amount of the distribution deduction that it would be entitled to under section 661 (determined without regard to section 661(c)), had the distribution been made to another beneficiary, and, solely for purposes of calculating DNI, the share receiving the distribution increases its gross income by the same amount. The distribution has the same character in the hands of the recipient share as in the hands of the distributing share. The following example illustrates the provisions of this paragraph (e)(2)(iii)(B):

Example. (i) A's will provides that, after the payment of debts, expenses, and taxes, the residue of A's estate is to be distributed to Trust, an electing trust. The sole beneficiary of Trust is C. The estate share has $15,000 of gross income, $5,000 of deductions, and $10,000 of taxable income and DNI for the taxable year based on the assets held in A's estate. During the taxable year, A's estate distributes $15,000 to Trust. The distribution reduces the DNI of the estate share by $10,000.

(ii) For the same taxable year, the trust share has $25,000 of gross income and $5,000 of deductions. None of the modifications provided for under section 643(a) apply. In calculating the DNI for the trust share, the gross income of the trust share is increased by $10,000, the amount of the reduction in the DNI of the estate share as a

Reg. § 1.645-1(e)(2)

result of the distribution to Trust. Thus, solely for purposes of calculating DNI, the trust share has gross income of $35,000, and taxable income of $30,000. Therefore, the trust share has $30,000 of DNI for the taxable year.

(iii) During the same taxable year, Trust distributes $35,000 to C. The distribution deduction reported on the Form 1041 filed for A's estate and Trust is $30,000. As a result of the distribution by Trust to C, C must include $30,000 in gross income for the taxable year. The gross income reported on the Form 1041 filed for A's estate and Trust is $40,000.

(iv) *Application of the governing instrument requirement of section 642(c).* A deduction is allowed in computing the taxable income of the combined electing trust and related estate to the extent permitted under section 642(c) for—

(A) Any amount of the gross income of the related estate that is paid or set aside during the taxable year pursuant to the terms of the governing instrument of the related estate for a purpose specified in section 170(c); and

(B) Any amount of gross income of the electing trust that is paid or set aside during the taxable year pursuant to the terms of the governing instrument of the electing trust for a purpose specified in section 170(c).

(3) *If there is no executor*—(i) *Tax treatment of the electing trust.* If there is no executor, the trustee treats the electing trust, during the election period, as an estate for all purposes of subtitle A of the Internal Revenue Code. Thus, for example, an electing trust is treated as an estate for purposes of the set-aside deduction under section 642(c)(2), the subchapter S shareholder requirements of section 1361(b)(1), and the special offset for rental real estate activities under section 469(i)(4). The trustee may also adopt a taxable year other than a calendar year.

(ii) *Filing the Form 1041 for the electing trust.* If there is no executor, the trustee of the electing trust must, during the election period, file a Form 1041, under the TIN obtained by the trustee under § 301.6109-1(a)(3) of this chapter upon the death of the decedent, treating the trust as an estate. If there is more than one electing trust, the Form 1041 must be filed by the filing trustee (see paragraph (c)(2)(ii)(B) of this section) under the name and TIN of the electing trust of the filing trustee. Information regarding the names and TINs of the other electing trusts must be provided on the Form 1041 as required by the instructions to that form. Any return filed in accordance with this paragraph shall be treated as a return filed for the electing trust (or trusts, if there is more than one electing trust) and not as a return filed for any subsequently discovered related estate. Accordingly, the period of limitations provided in section 6501 for assessments with respect to a subsequently discovered related estate does not start until a return is filed with respect to the related estate. See paragraph (g) of this section.

(4) *Application of the section 6654(l)(2) to the electing trust.* Each electing trust and related estate (if any) is treated as a separate taxpayer for all purposes of subtitle F of the Internal Revenue Code, including, without limitation, the application of section 6654. The provisions of section 6654(l)(2)(A) relating to the two year exception to an estate's obligation to make estimated tax payments, however, will apply to each electing trust for which a section 645 election has been made.

(f) *Duration of election period*—(1) *In general.* The election period begins on the date of the decedent's death and terminates on the earlier of the day on which both the electing trust and related estate, if any, have distributed all of their assets, or the day before the applicable date. The election does not apply to successor trusts (trusts that are distributees under the trust instrument).

(2) *Definition of applicable date*—(i) *Applicable date if no Form 706 "United States Estate (and Generation Skipping Transfer) Tax Return" is required to be filed.* If a Form 706 is not required to be filed as a result of the decedent's death, the applicable date is the day which is 2 years after the date of the decedent's death.

(ii) *Applicable date if a Form 706 is required to be filed.* If a Form 706 is required to be filed as a result of the decedent's death, the applicable date is the later of the day that is 2 years after the date of the decedent's death, or the day that is 6 months after the date of final determination of liability for estate tax. Solely for purposes of determining the applicable date under section 645, the date of final determination of liability is the earliest of the following—

(A) The date that is six months after the issuance by the Internal Revenue Service of an estate tax closing letter, unless a claim for refund with respect to the estate tax is filed within twelve months after the issuance of the letter;

(B) The date of a final disposition of a claim for refund, as defined in paragraph (f)(2)(iii) of this section, that resolves the liability for the estate tax, unless suit is instituted within six months after a final disposition of the claim;

(C) The date of execution of a settlement agreement with the Internal Revenue Service that determines the liability for the estate tax;

Reg. § 1.645-1(f)(2)

(D) The date of issuance of a decision, judgment, decree, or other order by a court of competent jurisdiction resolving the liability for the estate tax unless a notice of appeal or a petition for certiorari is filed within 90 days after the issuance of a decision, judgment, decree, or other order of a court; or

(E) The date of expiration of the period of limitations for assessment of the estate tax provided in section 6501.

(iii) *Definition of final disposition of claim for refund.* For purposes of paragraph (f)(2)(ii)(B) of this section, a claim for refund shall be deemed finally disposed of by the Secretary when all items have been either allowed or disallowed. If a waiver of notification with respect to disallowance is filed with respect to a claim for refund prior to disallowance of the claim, the claim for refund will be treated as disallowed on the date the waiver is filed.

(iv) *Examples.* The application of this paragraph (f)(2) is illustrated by the following examples:

Example 1. A died on October 20, 2002. The executor of A's estate and the trustee of Trust, an electing trust, made a section 645 election. A Form 706 is not required to be filed as a result of A's death. The applicable date is October 20, 2004, the day that is two years after A's date of death. The last day of the election period is October 19, 2004. Beginning October 20, 2004, Trust will no longer be treated and taxed as part of A's estate.

Example 2. Assume the same facts as *Example 1*, except that a Form 706 is required to be filed as the result of A's death. The Internal Revenue Service issues an estate tax closing letter accepting the Form 706 as filed on March 15, 2005. The estate does not file a claim for refund by March 15, 2006, the day that is twelve months after the date of issuance of the estate tax closing letter. The date of final determination of liability is September 15, 2005, and the applicable date is March 15, 2006. The last day of the election period is March 14, 2006. Beginning March 15, 2006, Trust will no longer be treated and taxed as part of A's estate.

Example 3. Assume the same facts as *Example 1*, except that a Form 706 is required to be filed as the result of A's death. The Form 706 is audited, and a notice of deficiency authorized under section 6212 is mailed to the executor of A's estate as a result of the audit. The executor files a petition in Tax Court. The Tax Court issues a decision resolving the liability for estate tax on December 14, 2005, and neither party appeals within 90 days after the issuance of the decision. The date of final determination of liability is December 14, 2005. The applicable date is June 14, 2006, the day that is six months after the date of final determination of liability. The last day of the election period is June 13, 2006. Beginning June 14, 2006, Trust will no longer be treated and taxed as part of A's estate.

(g) *Executor appointed after the section 645 election is made*—(1) *Effect on the election.* If an executor for the related estate is not appointed until after the trustee has made a valid section 645 election, the executor must agree to the trustee's election, and the IRS must be notified of that agreement by the filing of a revised election form (completed as required by the instructions to that form) within 90 days of the appointment of the executor, for the election period to continue past the date of appointment of the executor. If the executor does not agree to the election or a revised election form is not timely filed as required by this paragraph, the election period terminates the day before the appointment of the executor. If the IRS issues other guidance after December 24, 2002 for notifying the IRS of the executor's agreement to the election, the IRS must be notified in the manner provided in that guidance for the election period to continue.

(2) *Continuation of election period*—(i) *Correction of returns filed before executor appointed.* If the election period continues under paragraph (g)(1) of this section, the executor of the related estate and the trustee of each electing trust must file amended Forms 1041 to correct the Forms 1041 filed by the trustee before the executor was appointed. The amended Forms 1041 must be filed under the name and TIN of the electing trust and must reflect the items of income, deduction, and credit of the related estate and the electing trust. The name and TIN of the related estate must be provided on the amended Forms 1041 as required in the instructions to that Form. The amended return for the taxable year ending immediately before the executor was appointed must indicate that this Form 1041 is a final return. If the period of limitations for making assessments has expired with respect to the electing trust for any of the Forms 1041 filed by the trustee, the executor must file Forms 1041 for any items of income, deduction, and credit of the related estate that cannot be properly included on amended forms for the electing trust. The personal exemption under section 642(b) is not permitted to be taken on these Forms 1041 filed by the executor.

(ii) *Returns filed after the appointment of the executor.* All returns filed by the combined electing trust and related estate after the appoint-

Reg. § 1.645-1(g)(1)

ment of the executor are to be filed under the name and TIN of the related estate in accordance with paragraph (e)(2) of this section. Regardless of the change in the name and TIN under which the Forms 1041 for the combined electing trust and related estate are filed, the combined electing trust and related estate will be treated as the same entity before and after the executor is appointed.

(3) *Termination of the election period.* If the election period terminates under paragraph (g)(1) of this section, the executor must file Forms 1041 under the name and TIN of the estate for all taxable years of the related estate ending after the death of the decedent. The trustee of the electing trust is not required to amend any returns filed for the electing trust during the election period. Following termination of the election period, the trustee of the electing trust must obtain a new TIN. See § 301.6109-1(a)(4) of this chapter.

(h) *Treatment of an electing trust and related estate following termination of the election*—(1) *The share (or shares) comprising the electing trust is deemed to be distributed upon termination of the election period.* On the close of the last day of the election period, the combined electing trust and related estate, if there is an executor, or the electing trust, if there is no executor, is deemed to distribute the share (or shares, as determined under section 663(c)) comprising the electing trust to a new trust in a distribution to which sections 661 and 662 apply. All items of income, including net capital gains, that are attributable to the share (or shares) comprising the electing trust are included in the calculation of the distributable net income of the electing trust and treated as distributed by the combined electing trust and related estate, if there is an executor, or by the electing trust, if there is no executor, to the new trust. The combined electing trust and related estate, if there is an executor, or the electing trust, if there is no executor, is entitled to a distribution deduction to the extent permitted under section 661 in the taxable year in which the election period terminates as a result of the deemed distribution. The new trust shall include the amount of the deemed distribution in gross income to the extent required under section 662.

(2) *Filing of the Form 1041 upon the termination of the section 645 election*—(i) *If there is an executor*—(A) *Filing the Form 1041 for the year of termination.* If there is an executor, the Form 1041 filed under the name and TIN of the related estate for the taxable year in which the election terminates includes—

(*1*) The items of income, deduction, and credit of the electing trust attributable to the period beginning with the first day of the taxable year of the combined electing trust and related estate and ending with the last day of the election period;

(*2*) The items of income, deduction, and credit, if any, of the related estate for the entire taxable year; and

(*3*) A deduction for the deemed distribution of the share (or shares) comprising the electing trust to the new trust as provided for under paragraph (h)(1) of this section.

(B) *Requirement to file a final Form 1041 under the name and TIN of the electing trust.* If the electing trust terminates during the election period, the trustee of the electing trust must file a Form 1041 under the name and TIN of the electing trust and indicate that the return is a final return to notify the IRS that the electing trust is no longer in existence. The items of income, deduction, and credit of the trust are not reported on this final Form 1041 but on the appropriate Form 1041 filed for the combined electing trust and related estate.

(ii) *If there is no executor.* If there is no executor, the taxable year of the electing trust closes on the last day of the election period. A Form 1041 is filed in the manner prescribed under paragraph (e)(3)(ii) of this section reporting the items of income, deduction, and credit of the electing trust for the short period ending with the last day of the election period. The Form 1041 filed under this paragraph includes a distribution deduction for the deemed distribution provided for under paragraph (h)(1) of this section. The Form 1041 must indicate that it is a final return.

(3) *Use of TINs following termination of the election*—(i) *If there is an executor.* Upon termination of the section 645 election, a former electing trust may need to obtain a new TIN. See § 301.6109-1(a)(4) of this chapter. If the related estate continues after the termination of the election period, the related estate must continue to use the TIN assigned to the estate during the election period.

(ii) *If there is no executor.* If there is no executor, the former electing trust must obtain a new TIN if the trust will continue after the termination of the election period. See § 301.6109-1(a)(4) of this chapter.

(4) *Taxable year of estate and trust upon termination of the election*—(i) *Estate*—Upon termination of the section 645 election period, the taxable year of the estate is the same taxable year used during the election period.

(ii) *Trust.* Upon termination of the section 645 election, the taxable year of the new trust is the calendar year. See section 644.

(i) *Reserved.*

(j) *Effective date.* Paragraphs (a), (b), (c), (d), (f), and (g) of this section apply to trusts and estates of decedents dying on or after December 24, 2002. Paragraphs (e) and (h) of this section apply to taxable years ending on or after December 24, 2002. [Reg. § 1.645-1.]

☐ [T.D. 9032, 12-23-2002.]

[Reg. § 1.651(a)-1]

§ 1.651(a)-1. **Simple trusts; deduction for distributions; in general.**—Section 651 is applicable only to a trust the governing instrument of which:

(a) Requires that the trust distribute all of its income currently for the taxable year, and

(b) Does not provide that any amounts may be paid, permanently set aside, or used in the taxable year for the charitable, etc., purposes specified in section 642(c),

and does not make any distribution other than of current income. A trust to which section 651 applies is referred to in this part as a "simple" trust. Trusts subject to section 661 are referred to as "complex" trusts. A trust may be a simple trust for one year and a complex trust for another year. It should be noted that under section 651 a trust qualifies as a simple trust in a taxable year in which it is required to distribute all its income currently and makes no other distributions, whether or not distributions of current income are in fact made. On the other hand a trust is not a complex trust by reason of distributions of amounts other than income unless such distributions are in fact made during the taxable year, whether or not they are required in that year. [Reg. § 1.651(a)-1.]

☐ [T.D. 6217, 12-19-56.]

[Reg. § 1.651(a)-2]

§ 1.651(a)-2. **Income required to be distributed currently.**—(a) The determination of whether trust income is required to be distributed currently depends upon the terms of the trust instrument and the applicable local law. For this purpose, if the trust instrument provides that the trustee in determining the distributable income shall first retain a reserve for depreciation or otherwise make due allowance for keeping the trust corpus intact by retaining a reasonable amount of the current income for that purpose, the retention of current income for that purpose will not disqualify the trust from being a "simple" trust. The fiduciary must be under a duty to distribute the income currently even if, as a matter of practical necessity, the income is not distributed until after the close of the trust's taxable year. For example: Under the terms of the trust instrument, all of the income is currently distributable to A. The trust reports on the calendar year basis and as a matter of practical necessity makes distribution to A of each quarter's income on the fifteenth day of the month following the close of the quarter. The distribution made by the trust on January 15, 1955, of the income for the fourth quarter of 1954 does not disqualify the trust for treatment in 1955 under section 651, since the income is required to be distributed currently. However, if the terms of a trust require that none of the income be distributed until after the year of its receipt by the trust, the income of the trust is not required to be distributed currently and the trust is not a simple trust. For definition of the term "income" see section 643(b) and § 1.643(b)-1.

(b) It is immaterial, for purposes of determining whether all the income is required to be distributed currently, that the amount of income allocated to a particular beneficiary is not specified in the instrument. For example, if the fiduciary is required to distribute all the income currently, but has discretion to "sprinkle" the income among a class of beneficiaries, or among named beneficiaries in such amount as he may see fit, all the income is required to be distributed currently, even though the amount distributable to a particular beneficiary is unknown until the fiduciary has exercised his discretion.

(c) If in one taxable year of a trust its income for that year is required or permitted to be accumulated, and in another taxable year its income for the year is required to be distributed currently (and no other amounts are distributed), the trust is a simple trust for the latter year. For example, a trust under which income may be accumulated until a beneficiary is 21 years old, and thereafter must be distributed currently, is a simple trust for taxable years beginning after the beneficiary reaches the age of 21 years in which no other amounts are distributed. [Reg. § 1.651(a)-2.]

☐ [T.D. 6217, 12-19-56.]

[Reg. § 1.651(a)-3]

§ 1.651(a)-3. **Distribution of amounts other than income.**—(a) A trust does not qualify for treatment under section 651 for any taxable year in which it actually distributes corpus. For example, a trust which is required to distribute all of its income currently would not qualify as a simple trust under section 651 in the year of its termination since in that year actual distributions of corpus would be made.

Reg. § 1.651(a)-1(a)

(b) A trust, otherwise qualifying under section 651, which may make a distribution of corpus in the discretion of the trustee, or which is required under the terms of its governing instrument to make a distribution of corpus upon the happening of a specified event, will be disqualified for treatment under section 651 only for the taxable year in which an actual distribution of corpus is made. For example: Under the terms of a trust, which is required to distribute all of its income currently, half of the corpus is to be distributed to beneficiary A when he becomes 30 years of age. The trust reports on the calendar year basis. On December 28, 1954, A becomes 30 years of age and the trustee distributes half of the corpus of the trust to him on January 3, 1955. The trust will be disqualified for treatment under section 651 only for the taxable year 1955, the year in which an actual distribution of corpus is made.

(c) See section 661 and the regulations thereunder for the treatment of trusts which distribute corpus or claim the charitable contributions deduction provided by section 642(c). [Reg. § 1.651(a)-3.]

☐ [*T.D. 6217*, 12-19-56.]

[Reg. § 1.651(a)-4]

§ 1.651(a)-4. **Charitable purposes.**—A trust is not considered to be a trust which may pay, permanently set aside, or use any amount for charitable, etc., purposes for any taxable year for which it is not allowed a charitable, etc., deduction under section 642(c). Therefore, a trust with a remainder to a charitable organization is not disqualified for treatment as a simple trust if either (a) the remainder is subject to a contingency, so that no deduction would be allowed for capital gains or other amounts added to corpus as amounts permanently set aside for a charitable, etc., purpose under section 642(c), or (b) the trust receives no capital gains or other income added to corpus for the taxable year for which such a deduction would be allowed. [Reg. § 1.651(a)-4.]

☐ [*T.D. 6217*, 12-19-56.]

[Reg. § 1.651(a)-5]

§ 1.651(a)-5. **Estates.**—Subpart B has no application to an estate. [Reg. § 1.651(a)-5.]

☐ [*T.D. 6217*, 12-19-56.]

[Reg. § 1.651(b)-1]

§ 1.651(b)-1. **Deduction for distributions to beneficiaries.**—In computing its taxable income, a simple trust is allowed a deduction for the amount of income which is required under the terms of the trust instrument to be distributed currently to beneficiaries. If the amount of income [which] is required to be distributed currently exceeds the distributable net income, the deduction allowable to the trust is limited to the amount of the distributable net income. For this purpose the amount of income required to be distributed currently, or distributable net income, whichever is applicable, does not include items of trust income (adjusted for deductions allocable thereto) which are not included in the gross income of the trust. For determination of the character of the income required to be distributed currently, see § 1.652(b)-2. Accordingly, for the purposes of determining the deduction allowable to the trust under section 651, distributable net income is computed without the modifications specified in paragraphs (5), (6), and (7) of section 643(a), relating to tax-exempt interest, foreign income, and excluded dividends. For example: Assume that the distributable net income of a trust as computed under section 643(a) amounts to $99,000 but includes nontaxable income of $9,000. Then distributable net income for the purpose of determining the deduction allowable under section 651 is $90,000 ($99,000 less $9,000 nontaxable income). [Reg. § 1.651(b)-1.]

☐ [*T.D. 6217*, 12-19-56.]

[Reg. § 1.652(a)-1]

§ 1.652(a)-1. **Simple trusts; inclusion of amounts in income of beneficiaries.**—Subject to the rules in §§ 1.652(a)-2 and 1.652(b)-1, a beneficiary of a simple trust includes in his gross income for the taxable year the amounts of income required to be distributed to him for such year, whether or not distributed. Thus, the income of a simple trust is includible in the beneficiary's gross income for the taxable year in which the income is required to be distributed currently even though, as a matter of practical necessity, the income is not distributed until after the close of the taxable year of the trust. See § 1.642(a)(3)-2 with respect to time of receipt of dividends. See § 1.652(c)-1 for treatment of amounts required to be distributed where a beneficiary and the trust have different taxable years. The term "income required to be distributed currently" includes income required to be distributed currently which is in fact used to discharge or satisfy any person's legal obligation as that term is used in § 1.662(a)-4. [Reg. § 1.652(a)-1.]

☐ [*T.D. 6217*, 12-19-56.]

[Reg. § 1.652(a)-2]

§ 1.652(a)-2. **Distributions in excess of distributable net income.**—If the amount of income required to be distributed currently to beneficiaries exceeds the distributable net income of the trust (as defined in section 643(a)), each beneficiary includes in his gross income an amount

Reg. § 1.652(a)-2

equivalent to his proportionate share of such distributable net income. Thus, if beneficiary A is to receive two-thirds of the trust income and B is to receive one-third, and the income required to be distributed currently is $99,000, A will receive $66,000 and B, $33,000. However, if the distributable net income, as determined under section 643(a) is only $90,000, A will include two-thirds ($60,000) of that sum in his gross income, and B will include one-third ($30,000) in his gross income. See §§ 1.652(b)-1 and 1.652(b)-2, however, for amounts which are not includible in the gross income of a beneficiary because of their tax-exempt character. [Reg. § 1.652(a)-2.]

☐ [T.D. 6217, 12-19-56.]

[Reg. § 1.652(b)-1]

§ 1.652(b)-1. **Character of amounts.**—In determining the gross income of a beneficiary, the amounts includible under § 1.652(a)-1 have the same character in the hands of the beneficiary as in the hands of the trust. For example, to the extent that the amounts specified in § 1.652(a)-1 consist of income exempt from tax under section 103, such amounts are not included in the beneficiary's gross income. Similarly, dividends distributed to a beneficiary retain their original character in the beneficiary's hands for purposes of determining the availability to the beneficiary of the dividends received credit under section 34 (for dividends received on or before December 31, 1964) and the dividend exclusion under section 116. Also, to the extent that the amounts specified in § 1.652(a)-1 consist of "earned income" in the hands of the trust under the provisions of section 1348 such amount shall be treated under section 1348 as "earned income" in the hands of the beneficiary. Similarly, to the extent such amounts consist of an amount received as a part of a lump sum distribution from a qualified plan and to which the provisions of section 72(n) would apply in the hands of the trust, such amount shall be treated as subject to such section in the hands of the beneficiary except where such amount is deemed under section 666(a) to have been distributed in a preceding taxable year of the trust and the partial tax described in section 668(a)(2) is determined under section 668(b)(1)(B). The tax treatment of amounts determined under § 1.652(a)-1 depends upon the beneficiary's status with respect to them not upon the status of the trust. Thus, if a beneficiary is deemed to have received foreign income of a foreign trust, the includibility of such income in his gross income depends upon his taxable status with respect to that income. [Reg. § 1.652(b)-1.]

☐ [T.D. 6217, 12-19-56. Amended by T.D. 6777, 12-15-64, and by T.D. 7204, 8-24-72.]

[Reg. § 1.652(b)-2]

§ 1.652(b)-2. **Allocation of income items.**—(a) The amounts specified in § 1.652(a)-1 which are required to be included in the gross income of a beneficiary are treated as consisting of the same proportion of each class of items entering into distributable net income of the trust (as defined in section 643(a)) as the total of each class bears to such distributable net income, unless the terms of the trust specifically allocate different classes of income to different beneficiaries, or unless local law requires such an allocation. For example: Assume that under the terms of the governing instrument, beneficiary A is to receive currently one-half of the trust income and beneficiaries B and C are each to receive currently one-quarter, and the distributable net income of the trust (after allocation of expenses) consists of dividends of $10,000, taxable interest of $10,000, and tax-exempt interest of $4,000. A will be deemed to have received $5,000 of dividends, $5,000 of taxable interest, and $2,000 of tax-exempt interest; B and C will each be deemed to have received $2,500 of dividends, $2,500 of taxable interest, and $1,000 of tax-exempt interest. However, if the terms of the trust specifically allocate different classes of income to different beneficiaries, entirely or in part, or if local law requires such an allocation, each beneficiary will be deemed to have received those items of income specifically allocated to him.

(b) The terms of the trust are considered specifically to allocate different classes of income to different beneficiaries only to the extent that the allocation is required in the trust instrument, and only to the extent that it has an economic effect independent of the income tax consequences of the allocation. For example:

(1) Allocation pursuant to a provision in a trust instrument granting the trustee discretion to allocate different classes of income to different beneficiaries is not a specific allocation by the terms of the trust.

(2) Allocation pursuant to a provision directing the trustee to pay all of one income to A, or $10,000 out of the income to A, and the balance of the income to B, but directing the trustee first to allocate a specific class of income to A's share (to the extent there is income of that class and to the extent it does not exceed A's share) is not a specific allocation by the terms of the trust.

(3) Allocation pursuant to a provision directing the trustee to pay half the class of income (whatever it may be) to A, and the balance of the income to B, is a specific allocation by the terms of the trust. [Reg. § 1.652(b)-2.]

☐ [T.D. 6217, 12-19-56.]

Estates, Trusts, and Beneficiaries

See p. 20,601 for regulations not amended to reflect law changes

[Reg. § 1.652(b)-3]

§ 1.652(b)-3. Allocation of deductions.— Items of deduction of a trust that enter into the computation of distributable net income are to be allocated among the items of income in accordance with the following principles:

(a) All deductible items directly attributable to one class of income (except dividends excluded under section 116) are allocated thereto. For example, repairs to, taxes on, and other expenses directly attributable to the maintenance of rental property or the collection of rental income are allocated to rental income. See § 1.642(e)-1 for treatment of depreciation of rental property. Similarly, all expenditures directly attributable to a business carried on by a trust are allocated to the income from such business. If the deductions directly attributable to a particular class of income exceed that income, the excess is applied against other classes of income in the manner provided in paragraph (d) of this section.

(b) The deductions which are not directly attributable to a specific class of income may be allocated to any item of income (including capital gains) included in computing distributable net income, but a portion must be allocated to nontaxable income (except dividends excluded under section 116) pursuant to section 265 and the regulations thereunder. For example, if the income of a trust is $30,000 (after direct expenses), consisting equally of $10,000 of dividends, tax-exempt interest, and rents, and income commissions amount to $3,000, one-third ($1,000) of such commissions should be allocated to tax-exempt interest, but the balance of $2,000 may be allocated to the rents or dividends in such proportions as the trustee may elect. The fact that the governing instrument or applicable local law treats certain items of deduction as attributable to corpus or to income not included in distributable net income does not affect allocation under this paragraph. For instance, if in the example set forth in this paragraph the trust also had capital gains which are allocable to corpus under the terms of the trust instrument, no part of the deductions would be allocable thereto since the capital gains are excluded from the computation of distributable net income under section 643(a)(3).

(c) Examples of expenses which are considered as not directly attributable to a specific class of income are trustee's commissions, the rental of safe deposit boxes, and State income and personal property taxes.

(d) To the extent that any items of deduction which are directly attributable to a class of income exceed that class of income, they may be allocated to any other class of income (including capital gains) included in distributable net income in the manner provided in paragraph (b) of this section, except that any excess deductions attributable to tax-exempt income (other than dividends excluded under section 116) may not be offset against any other class of income. See section 265 and the regulations thereunder. Thus, if the trust has rents, taxable interest, dividends, and tax-exempt interest, and the deductions directly attributable to the rents exceed the rental income, the excess may be allocated to the taxable interest or dividends in such proportions as the fiduciary may elect. However, if the excess deductions are attributable to the tax-exempt interest, they may not be allocated to either the rents, taxable interest, or dividends. [Reg. § 1.652(b)-3.]

☐ [T.D. 6217, 12-19-56.]

[Reg. § 1.652(c)-1]

§ 1.652(c)-1. Different taxable years.— If a beneficiary has a different taxable year (as defined in section 441 or 442) from the taxable year of the trust, the amount he is required to include in gross income in accordance with section 652(a) and (b) is based on the income of the trust for any taxable year or years ending with or within his taxable year. This rule applies to taxable years of normal duration as well as to so-called short taxable years. Income of the trust for its taxable year or years is determined in accordance with its method of accounting and without regard to that of the beneficiary. [Reg. § 1.652(c)-1.]

☐ [T.D. 6217, 12-19-56.]

[Reg. § 1.652(c)-2]

§ 1.652(c)-2. Death of individual beneficiaries.— If income is required to be distributed currently to a beneficiary, by a trust for a taxable year which does not end with or within the last taxable year of a beneficiary (because of the beneficiary's death), the extent to which the income is included in the gross income of the beneficiary for his last taxable year or in the gross income of his estate is determined by the computations under section 652 for the taxable year of the trust in which his last taxable year ends. Thus, the distributable net income of the taxable year of the trust determines the extent to which the income required to be distributed currently to the beneficiary is included in his gross income for his last taxable year or in the gross income of his estate. (Section 652(c) does not apply to such amounts.) The gross income for the last taxable year of a beneficiary on the cash basis includes only income actually distributed to the beneficiary before his death. Income required to be distributed, but in fact distributed to his estate, is included in the

Reg. § 1.652(c)-2

gross income of the estate as income in respect of a decedent under section 691. See paragraph (e) of § 1.663(c)-3 with respect to separate share treatment for the periods before and after the decedent's death. If the trust does not qualify as a simple trust for the taxable year of the trust in which the last taxable year of the beneficiary ends, see section 662(c) and § 1.662(c)-2. [Reg. § 1.652(c)-2.]

☐ [T.D. 6217, 12-19-56.]

[Reg. § 1.652(c)-3]

§ 1.652(c)-3. Termination of existence of other beneficiaries.—If the existence of a beneficiary which is not an individual terminates, the amount to be included under section 652(a) in its gross income for its last taxable year is computed with reference to §§ 1.652(c)-1 and 1.652(c)-2 as if the beneficiary were a deceased individual, except that income required to be distributed prior to the termination but actually distributed to the beneficiary's successor in interest is included in the beneficiary's income for its last taxable year. [Reg. § 1.652(c)-3.]

☐ [T.D. 6217, 12-19-56.]

[Reg. § 1.652(c)-4]

§ 1.652(c)-4. Illustration of the provisions of sections 651 and 652.—The rules applicable to a trust required to distribute all of its income currently and to its beneficiaries may be illustrated by the following example:

Example. (a) Under the terms of a simple trust all of the income is to be distributed equally to beneficiaries A and B and capital gains are to be allocated to corpus. The trust and both beneficiaries file returns on the calendar year basis. No provision is made in the governing instrument with respect to depreciation. During the taxable year 1955, the trust had the following items of income and expense:

Rents	$25,000
Dividends of domestic corporations	50,000
Tax-exempt interest on municipal bonds	25,000
Long-term capital gains	15,000
Taxes and expenses directly attributable to rents	5,000
Trustee's commissions allocable to income account	2,600
Trustee's commissions allocable to principal account	1,300
Depreciation	5,000

(b) The income of the trust for fiduciary accounting purposes is $92,400, computed as follows:

Rents		$ 25,000
Dividends		50,000
Tax-exempt interest		25,000
Total		100,000
Deductions: Expenses directly attributable to rental income	$5,000	
Trustee's commissions allocable to income account	2,600	7,600
Income computed under section 643(b)		92,400

One-half ($46,200) of the income of $92,400 is currently distributable to each beneficiary.

(c) The distributable net income of the trust computed under section 643(a) is $91,100, determined as follows (cents are disregarded in the computation):

Rents			$25,000
Dividends			50,000
Tax-exempt interest		$25,000	
Less: Expenses allocable thereto (25,000/100,000 × $3,900)		975	24,025
Total			99,025
Deductions:			
Expenses directly attributable to rental income		$ 5,000	
Trustee's commissions ($3,900 less $975 allocable to tax-exempt interest)		2,925	$ 7,925
Distributable net income			91,100

In computing the distributable net income of $91,100, the taxable income of the trust was computed with the following modifications: No deductions were allowed for distributions to the beneficiaries and for personal exemption of the trust (section 643(a)(1) and (2)); capital gains were excluded and no deduction under section 1202 (relating to the 50 percent deduction for long-term capital gains) was taken into account (section 643(a)(3)); the tax-exempt interest (as adjusted for expenses) and the dividend exclusion of $50 were included (section 643(a)(5) and (7)). Since all of the income of the trust is required to be currently distributed, no deduction is allowable

Estates, Trusts, and Beneficiaries

See p. 20,601 for regulations not amended to reflect law changes

for depreciation in the absence of specific provisions in the governing instrument providing for the keeping of the trust corpus intact. See section 167(h) and the regulations thereunder.

Distributable net income computed under section 643(a) (see paragraph (c))		$91,100
Less:		
Tax-exempt interest as adjusted	$24,025	
Dividend exclusion	50	24,075
Distributable net income as determined under section 651(b)		67,025

Since the amount of the income ($92,400) required to be distributed currently by the trust exceeds the distributable net income ($67,025) as computed under section 651(b), the deduction allowable under section 651(a) is limited to the distributable net income of $67,025.

(d) The deduction allowable to the trust under section 651(a) for distributions to the beneficiaries is $67,025, computed as follows:

(e) The taxable income of the trust is $7,200 computed as follows:

Rents		$25,000
Dividends ($50,000 less $50 exclusion)		49,950
Long-term capital gains		15,000
Gross income		89,950
Deductions:		
Rental expenses	$ 5,000	
Trustee's commissions	2,925	
Capital gain deduction	7,500	
Distributions to beneficiaries	67,025	
Personal exemption	300	82,750
Taxable income		7,200

The trust is not allowed a deduction for the portion ($975) of the trustee's commissions allocable to tax-exempt interest in computing its taxable income.

(f) In determining the character of the amounts includible in the gross income of A and B, it is assumed that the trustee elects to allocate to rents the expenses not directly attributable to a specific item of income other than the portion ($975) of such expenses allocated to tax-exempt interest. The allocation of expenses among the items of income is shown below:

	Rents	Dividends	Tax-exempt interest	Total
Income for trust accounting purposes	$25,000	$50,000	$25,000	$100,000
Less:				
Rental expenses	5,000			5,000
Trustee's commissions	2,925		975	3,900
Total deductions	7,925	0	975	8,900
Character of amounts in the hands of the beneficiaries	17,075	50,000	24,025	[1]91,100

[1] Distributable net income.

Inasmuch as the income of the trust is to be distributed equally to A and B, each is deemed to have received one-half of each item of income; that is, rents of $8,537.50, dividends of $25,000, and tax-exempt interest of $12,012.50. The dividends of $25,000 allocated to each beneficiary are to be aggregated with his other dividends (if any) for purposes of the dividend exclusion provided by section 116 and the dividend received credit allowed under section 34. Also, each beneficiary is allowed a deduction of $2,500 for depreciation of rental property attributable to the portion (one-half) of the income of the trust distributed to him. [Reg. § 1.652(c)-4.]

☐ [T.D. 6217, 12-19-56. Amended by T.D. 6712, 3-23-64.]

[Reg. § 1.661(a)-1]

§ 1.661(a)-1. Estates and trusts accumulating income or distributing corpus; general.—Subpart C, part I, subchapter J, chapter 1 of the Code, is applicable to all decedents' estates and their beneficiaries, and to trusts and their beneficiaries other than trusts subject to the provisions of subpart B of such part I (relating to trusts

Reg. § 1.661(a)-1

which distribute current income only, or "simple" trusts). A trust which is required to distribute amounts other than income during the taxable year may be subject to subpart B, and not subpart C, in the absence of an actual distribution of amounts other than income during the taxable year. See §§ 1.651(a)-1 and 1.651(a)-3. A trust to which subpart C is applicable is referred to as a "complex" trust in this part. Section 661 has no application to amounts excluded under section 663(a). [Reg. § 1.661(a)-1.]

☐ [T.D. 6217, 12-19-56.]

[Reg. § 1.661(a)-2]

§ 1.661(a)-2. **Deduction for distributions to beneficiaries.**—(a) In computing the taxable income of an estate or trust there is allowed under section 661(a) as a deduction for distributions to beneficiaries the sum of:

(1) The amount of income for the taxable year which is required to be distributed currently, and

(2) Any other amounts properly paid or credited or required to be distributed for such taxable year.

However, the total amount deductible under section 661(a) cannot exceed the distributable net income as computed under section 643(a) and as modified by section 661(c). See § 1.661(c)-1.

(b) The term "income required to be distributed currently" includes any amount required to be distributed which may be paid out of income or corpus (such as an annuity), to the extent it is paid out of income for the taxable year. See § 1.651(a)-2 which sets forth additional rules which are applicable in determining whether income of an estate or trust is required to be distributed currently.

(c) The term "any other amounts properly paid or credited or required to be distributed" includes all amounts properly paid, credited, or required to be distributed by an estate or trust during the taxable year other than income required to be distributed currently. Thus, the term includes the payment of an annuity to the extent it is not paid out of income for the taxable year, and a distribution of property in kind (see paragraph (f) of this section). However, see section 663(a) and regulations thereunder for distributions which are not included. Where the income of an estate or trust may be accumulated or distributed in the discretion of the fiduciary, or where the fiduciary has a power to distribute corpus to a beneficiary, any such discretionary distribution would qualify under section 661(a)(2). The term also includes an amount applied or distributed for the support of a dependent of a grantor or of a trustee or cotrustee under the circumstances described in section 677(b) or section 678(c) out of corpus or out of other than income for the taxable year.

(d) The terms "income required to be distributed currently" and "any other amounts properly paid or credited or required to be distributed" also include any amount used to discharge or satisfy any person's legal obligation as that term is used in § 1.662(a)-4.

(e) The terms "income required to be distributed currently" and "any other amounts properly paid or credited or required to be distributed" include amounts paid, or required to be paid, during the taxable year pursuant to a court order or decree or under local law, by a decedent's estate as an allowance or award for the support of the decedent's widow or other dependent for a limited period during the administration of the estate. The term "any other amounts properly paid or credited or required to be distributed" does not include the value of any interest in real estate owned by a decedent, title to which under local law passes directly from the decedent to his heirs or devisees.

(f) If property is paid, credited, or required to be distributed in kind:

(1) No gain or loss is realized by the trust or estate (or the other beneficiaries) by reason of the distribution, unless the distribution is in satisfaction of a right to receive a distribution in a specific dollar amount or in specific property other than that distributed.

(2) In determining the amount deductible by the trust or estate and includible in the gross income of the beneficiary the property distributed in kind is taken into account at its fair market value at the time it was distributed, credited, or required to be distributed.

(3) The basis of the property in the hands of the beneficiary is its fair market value at the time it was paid, credited, or required to be distributed, to the extent such value is included in the gross income of the beneficiary. To the extent that the value of property distributed in kind is not included in the gross income of the beneficiary, its basis in the hands of the beneficiary is governed by the rules in sections 1014 and 1015 and the regulations thereunder. For this purpose, if the total value of cash and property distributed, credited, or required to be distributed in kind to a beneficiary in any taxable year exceeds the amount includible in his gross income for that year, the value of the property other than cash is normally considered as includible in his gross income only to the extent that the amount includible exceeds the cash paid, credited, or required to be distributed to the beneficiary in that year.

Further, to the extent that the value of different items of property other than cash is includible in the gross income of a beneficiary in accordance with the preceding sentence, a pro rata portion of the total value of each item of property distributed, credited, or required to be distributed is normally considered as includible in the beneficiary's gross income. [Reg. § 1.661(a)-2.]

☐ [*T.D. 6217, 12-19-56. Amended by T.D. 7287, 9-26-73.*]

[Reg. § 1.661(b)-1]

§ 1.661(b)-1. Character of amounts distributed; in general.—In the absence of specific provisions in the governing instrument for the allocation of different classes of income, or unless local law requires such an allocation, the amount deductible for distributions to beneficiaries under section 661(a) is treated as consisting of the same proportion of each class of items entering into the computation of distributable net income as the total of each class bears to the total distributable net income. For example, if a trust has distributable net income of $20,000, consisting of $10,000 each of taxable interest and royalties and distributes $10,000 to beneficiary A, the deduction of $10,000 allowable under section 661(a) is deemed to consist of $5,000 each of taxable interest and royalties, unless the trust instrument specifically provides for the distribution or accumulation of different classes of income or unless local law requires such an allocation. See also § 1.661(c)-1. [Reg. § 1.661(b)-1.]

☐ [*T.D. 6217, 12-19-56.*]

[Reg. § 1.661(b)-2]

§ 1.661(b)-2. Character of amounts distributed when charitable contributions are made.—In the application of the rule stated in § 1.661(b)-1, the items of deduction which enter into the computation of distributable net income are allocated among the items of income which enter into the computation of distributable net income in accordance with the rules set forth in § 1.652(b)-3, except that, in the absence of specific provisions in the governing instrument, or unless local law requires a different apportionment, amounts paid, permanently set aside, or to be used for the charitable, etc., purposes specified in section 642(c) are first ratably apportioned among each class of items of income entering into the computation of the distributable net income of the estate or trust, in accordance with the rules set out in paragraph (b) of § 1.643(a)-5. [Reg. § 1.661(b)-2.]

☐ [*T.D. 6217, 12-19-56.*]

[Reg. § 1.661(c)-1]

§ 1.661(c)-1. Limitation on deduction.—An estate or trust is not allowed a deduction under section 661(a) for any amount which is treated under section 661(b) as consisting of any item of distributable net income which is not included in the gross income of the estate or trust. For example, if in 1962, a trust, which reports on the calendar year basis, has distributable net income of $20,000, which is deemed to consist of $10,000 of dividends and $10,000 of tax-exempt interest, and distributes $10,000 to beneficiary A, the deduction allowable under section 661(a) (computed without regard to section 661(c)) would amount to $10,000 consisting of $5,000 of dividends and $5,000 of tax-exempt interest. The deduction actually allowable under section 661(a) as limited by section 661(c) is $4,975, since no deduction is allowable for the $5,000 of tax-exempt interest and the $25 deemed distributed out of the $50 of dividends excluded under section 116, items of distributable net income which are not included in the gross income of the estate or trust. [Reg. § 1.661(c)-1.]

☐ [*T.D. 6217, 12-19-56. Amended by T.D. 6777, 12-15-64.*]

[Reg. § 1.661(c)-2]

§ 1.661(c)-2. Illustration of the provisions of section 661.—The provisions of section 661 may be illustrated by the following example:

Example. (a) Under the terms of a trust, which reports on the calendar year basis, $10,000 a year is required to be paid out of income to a designated charity. The balance of the income may, in the trustee's discretion, be accumulated or distributed to beneficiary A. Expenses are allocable against income and the trust instrument requires a reserve for depreciation. During the taxable year 1955 the trustee contributes $10,000 to charity and in his discretion distributes $15,000 of income to A. The trust has the following items of income and expense for the taxable year 1955:

Dividends	$10,000
Partially tax-exempt interest	10,000
Fully tax-exempt interest	10,000
Rents	20,000
Rental expenses	2,000
Depreciation of rental property	3,000
Trustee's commissions	5,000

Reg. § 1.661(c)-2

43,292   Estates, Trusts, and Beneficiaries
See p. 20,601 for regulations not amended to reflect law changes

(b) The income of the trust for fiduciary accounting purposes is $40,000, computed as follows:

Dividends		$10,000
Partially tax-exempt interest		10,000
Fully tax-exempt interest		10,000
Rents		20,000
Total		50,000
Less: Rental expenses	$2,000	
Depreciation	3,000	
Trustee's commissions	5,000	$10,000
Income as computed under section 643(b)		40,000

(c) The distributable net income of the trust as computed under section 643(a) is $30,000, determined as follows:

Rents			$20,000
Dividends			10,000
Partially tax-exempt interest			10,000
Fully tax-exempt interest		$10,000	
Less: Expenses allocable thereto (10,000/50,000 × $5,000)	$1,000		
Charitable contributions allocable thereto (10,000/50,000 × $10,000)	2,000	3,000	7,000
Total			47,000
Deductions:			
Rental expenses		$2,000	
Depreciation of rental property		3,000	
Trustee's commissions ($5,000 less $1,000 allocated to tax-exempt interest)		4,000	
Charitable contributions ($10,000 less $2,000 allocated to tax-exempt interest)		8,000	$17,000
Distributable net income (section 643(a))			30,000

(d) The character of the amounts distributed under section 661(a), determined in accordance with the rules prescribed in §§ 1.661(b)-1 and 1.661(b)-2 is shown by the following table (for the purpose of this allocation, it is assumed that the trustee elected to allocate the trustee's commissions to rental income except for the amount required to be allocated to tax-exempt interest):

	Rental income	Taxable Dividends	Excluded Dividends	Partially tax-exempt interest	Tax-exempt interest	Total
Trust income	$20,000	$9,950	$50	$10,000	$10,000	$50,000
Less:						
Charitable contributions	4,000	2,000	....	2,000	2,000	10,000
Rental expenses	2,000	......	...	......	......	2,000
Depreciation	3,000	......	...	......	......	3,000
Trustee's commissions	4,000	......	...	......	1,000	5,000
Total deductions	13,000	2,000	0	2,000	3,000	20,000
Distributable net income	7,000	7,950	50	8,000	7,000	30,000
Amounts deemed distributed under section 661(a) before applying the limitation of section 661(c)	3,500	3,975	25	4,000	3,500	15,000

In the absence of specific provisions in the trust instrument for the allocation of different classes of income, the charitable contribution is deemed to consist of a pro rata portion of the gross amount of each item of income of the trust (except dividends excluded under section 116) and the trust is deemed to have distributed to A a pro rata portion (one-half) of each item of income included in distributable net income.

Reg. § 1.661(c)-2

(e) The taxable income of the trust is $11,375 computed as follows:

Rental income		$20,000
Dividends ($10,000 less $50 exclusion)		9,950
Partially tax-exempt interest		10,000
Gross income		$39,950
Deductions:		
Rental expenses	$ 2,000	
Depreciation of rental property	3,000	
Trustee's commissions	4,000	
Charitable contributions	8,000	
Distributions to A	11,475	
Personal exemption	100	28,575

In computing the taxable income of the trust no deduction is allowable for the portions of the charitable contributions deduction ($2,000) and trustee's commissions ($1,000) which are treated under section 661(b) as attributable to the tax-exempt interest excludable from gross income. Also, of the dividends of $4,000 deemed to have been distributed to A under section 661(a), $25 (25/50ths of $50) is deemed to have been distributed from the excluded dividends and is not an allowable deduction to the trust. Accordingly, the deduction allowable under section 661 is deemed to be composed of $3,500 rental income, $3,975 of dividends, and $4,000 partially tax-exempt interest. No deduction is allowable for the portion of tax-exempt interest or for the portion of the excluded dividends deemed to have been distributed to the beneficiary.

(f) The trust is entitled to the credit allowed by section 34 with respect to dividends of $5,975 ($9,950 less $3,975 distributed to A) included in gross income. Also, the trust is allowed the credit provided by section 35 with respect to partially tax-exempt interest of $6,000 ($10,000 less $4,000 deemed distributed to A) included in gross income.

(g) Dividends of $4,000 allocable to A are to be aggregated with his other dividends (if any) for purposes of the dividend exclusion under section 116 and the dividend received credit under section 34. [Reg. § 1.661(c)-2.]

☐ [T.D. 6217, 12-19-56.]

[Reg. § 1.662(a)-1]

§ 1.662(a)-1. **Inclusion of amounts in gross income of beneficiaries of estates and complex trusts; general.**—There is included in the gross income of a beneficiary of an estate or complex trust the sum of:

(1) Amounts of income required to be distributed currently to him, and

(2) All other amounts properly paid, credited, or required to be distributed to him by the estate or trust.

The preceding sentence is subject to the rules contained in § 1.662(a)-2 (relating to currently distributable income), § 1.662(a)-3 (relating to other amounts distributed), and §§ 1.662(b)-1 and 1.662(b)-2 (relating to character of amounts). Section 662 has no application to amounts excluded under section 663(a). [Reg. § 1.662(a)-1.]

☐ [T.D. 6217, 12-19-56.]

[Reg. § 1.662(a)-2]

§ 1.662(a)-2. **Currently distributable income.**—(a) There is first included in the gross income of each beneficiary under section 662(a)(1) the amount of income for the taxable year of the estate or trust required to be distributed currently to him, subject to the provisions of paragraph (b) of this section. Such amount is included in the beneficiary's gross income whether or not it is actually distributed.

(b) If the amount of income required to be distributed currently to all beneficiaries exceeds the distributable net income (as defined in section 643(a) but computed without taking into account the payment, crediting, or setting aside of an amount for which a charitable contributions deduction is allowable under section 642(c)) of the estate or trust, then there is included in the gross income of each beneficiary an amount which bears the same ratio to distributable net income (as so computed) as the amount of income required to be distributed currently to the beneficiary bears to the amount required to be distributed currently to all beneficiaries.

(c) The phrase "the amount of income for the taxable year required to be distributed currently" includes any amount required to be paid out of income or corpus to the extent the amount is satisfied out of income for the taxable year. Thus, an annuity required to be paid in all events (either out of income or corpus) would qualify as income required to be distributed currently to the extent there is income (as defined in section 643(b)) not paid, credited, or required to be distributed to other beneficiaries for the taxable

Reg. § 1.662(a)-2(c)

year. If an annuity or a portion of an annuity is deemed under this paragraph to be income required to be distributed currently, it is treated in all respects in the same manner as an amount of income actually required to be distributed currently. The phrase "the amount of income for the taxable year required to be distributed currently" also includes any amount required to be paid during the taxable year in all events (either out of income or corpus) pursuant to a court order or decree or under local law, by a decedent's estate as an allowance or award for the support of the decedent's widow or other dependent for a limited period during the administration of the estate to the extent there is income (as defined in section 643(b)) of the estate for the taxable year not paid, credited, or required to be distributed to other beneficiaries.

(d) If an annuity is paid, credited, or required to be distributed tax free, that is, under a provision whereby the executor or trustee will pay the income tax of the annuitant resulting from the receipt of the annuity, the payment of or for the tax by the executor or trustee will be treated as income paid, credited, or required to be distributed currently to the extent it is made out of income.

(e) The application of the rules stated in this section may be illustrated by the following examples:

Example (1). (1) Assume that under the terms of the trust instrument $5,000 is to be paid to X charity out of income each year; that $20,000 of income is currently distributable to A; and that an annuity of $12,000 is to be paid to B out of income or corpus. All expenses are charges against income and capital gains are allocable to corpus. During the taxable year the trust had income of $30,000 (after the payment of expenses) derived from taxable interest and made the payments to X charity and distributions to A and B as required by the governing instrument.

(2) The amounts treated as distributed currently under section 662(a)(1) total $25,000 ($20,000 to A and $5,000 to B). Since the charitable contribution is out of income, the amount of income available for B's annuity is only $5,000. The distributable net income of the trust computed under section 643(a) without taking into consideration the charitable contributions deduction of $5,000 as provided by section 661(a)(1), is $30,000. Since the amounts treated as distributed currently of $25,000 do not exceed the distributable net income (as modified) of $30,000, A is required to include $20,000 in his gross income and B is required to include $5,000 in his gross income under section 662(a)(1).

Example (2). Assume the same facts as in paragraph (1) of example (1), except that the trust has, in addition, $10,000 of administration expenses, commissions, etc., chargeable to corpus. The amounts treated as distributed currently under section 662(a)(1) total $25,000 ($20,000 to A and $5,000 to B), since trust income under section 643(b) remains the same as in example (1). Distributable net income of the trust computed under section 643(a) but without taking into account the charitable contributions deduction of $5,000 as provided by section 662(a)(1) is only $20,000. Since the amounts treated as distributed currently of $25,000 exceed the distributable net income (as so computed) of $20,000, A is required to include $16,000 (20,000/25,000 of $20,000) in his gross income and B is required to include $4,000 (5,000/25,000 of $20,000) in his gross income under section 662(a)(1). Because A and B are beneficiaries of amounts of income required to be distributed currently, they do not benefit from the reduction of distributable net income by the charitable contributions deduction. [Reg. § 1.662(a)-2.]

☐ [T.D. 6217, 12-19-56. Amended by T.D. 7287, 9-26-73.]

[Reg. § 1.662(a)-3]

§ 1.662(a)-3. Other amounts distributed.— (a) There is included in the gross income of a beneficiary under section 662(a)(2) any amount properly paid, credited, or required to be distributed to the beneficiary for the taxable year, other than (1) income required to be distributed currently, as determined under § 1.662(a)-2, (2) amounts excluded under section 663(a) and the regulations thereunder, and (3) amounts in excess of distributable net income (see paragraph (c) below of this section). An amount which is credited or required to be distributed is included in the gross income of a beneficiary whether or not it is actually distributed.

(b) Some of the payments to be included under paragraph (a) of this section are: (1) A distribution made to a beneficiary in the discretion of the fiduciary; (2) a distribution required by the terms of the governing instrument upon the happening of a specified event; (3) an annuity which is required to be paid in all events but which is payable only out of corpus; (4) a distribution of property in kind (see paragraph (f) of § 1.661(a)-2); and (5) an amount applied or distributed for the support of a dependent of a grantor or a trustee or cotrustee under the circumstances specified in section 677(b) or section 678(c) out of corpus or out of other than income for the taxable year; and (6) an amount required to be paid during the taxable year pursuant to a court order or decree or under local law, by a decedent's estate as an allowance or award for the support of the decedent's widow or other dependent for a limited period during the administration of the estate which is payable only out of corpus of the estate under the order or decree or local law.

(c) If the sum of the amounts of income required to be distributed currently (as determined under § 1.662(a)-2) and other amounts properly paid, credited, or required to be distributed (as determined under paragraph (a) of this section) exceeds distributable net income (as defined in section 643(a)), then such other amounts properly paid, credited, or required to be distributed are included in gross income of the beneficiary but only to the extent of the excess of such distributable net income over the amounts of income required to be distributed currently. If the other amounts are paid, credited, or required to be distributed to more than one beneficiary, each beneficiary includes in gross income his proportionate share of the amount includible in gross income pursuant to the preceding sentence. The proportionate share is an amount which bears the same ratio to distributable net income (reduced by amounts of income required to be distributed currently) as the other amounts (as determined under paragraphs (a) and (d) of this section) distributed to the beneficiary bear to the other amounts distributed to all beneficiaries. For treatment of excess distributions by trusts, see sections 665 to 668, inclusive, and the regulations thereunder.

(d) The application of the rules stated in this section may be illustrated by the following example:

Example. The terms of a trust require the distribution annually of $10,000 of income to A. If any income remains, it may be accumulated or distributed to B, C, and D in amounts in the trustee's discretion. He may also invade corpus for the benefit of A, B, C, or D. In the taxable year, the trust has $20,000 of income after the deduction of all expenses. Distributable net income is $20,000. The trustee distributes $10,000 of income to A. Of the remaining $10,000 of income, he distributes $3,000 each to B, C, and D, and also distributes an additional $5,000 to A. A includes $10,000 in income under section 662(a)(1). The "other amounts distributed" amount to $14,000, includible in the income of the recipients to the extent of $10,000, distributable net income less the income currently distributable to A. A will include an additional $3,571 (5,000/14,000 × $10,000) in income under this section, and B, C, and D will each include $2,143 (3,000/14,000 × $10,000). [Reg. § 1.662(a)-3.]

☐ [*T.D.* 6217, 12-19-56. *Amended by T.D.* 7287, 9-26-73.]

[Reg. § 1.662(a)-4]

§ 1.662(a)-4. **Amounts used in discharge of a legal obligation.**—Any amount which, pursuant to the terms of a will or trust instrument, is used in full or partial discharge or satisfaction of a legal obligation of any person is included in the gross income of such person under section 662(a)(1) or (2), whichever is applicable, as though directly distributed to him as a beneficiary, except in cases to which section 71 (relating to alimony payments) or section 682 (relating to income of a trust in case of divorce, etc.) applies. The term "legal obligation" includes a legal obligation to support another person if, and only if, the obligation is not affected by the adequacy of the dependent's own resources. For example, a parent has a "legal obligation" within the meaning of the preceding sentence to support his minor child if under local law property or income from property owned by the child cannot be used for his support so long as his parent is able to support him. On the other hand, if under local law a mother may use the resources of a child for the child's support in lieu of supporting him herself, no obligation of support exists within the meaning of this paragraph, whether or not income is actually used for support. Similarly, since under local law a child ordinarily is obligated to support his parent only if the parent's earnings and resources are insufficient for the purpose, no obligation exists whether or not the parent's earnings and resources are sufficient. In any event, the amount of trust income which is included in the gross income of a person obligated to support a dependent is limited by the extent of his legal obligation under local law. In the case of a parent's obligation to support his child, to the extent that the parent's legal obligation of support, including education, is determined under local law by the family's station in life and by the means of the parent, it is to be determined without consideration of the trust income in question. [Reg. § 1.662(a)-4.]

☐ [*T.D.* 6217, 12-19-56.]

[Reg. § 1.662(b)-1]

§ 1.662(b)-1. **Character of amounts; when no charitable contributions are made.**—In determining the amount includible in the gross income of a beneficiary, the amounts which are determined under section 662(a) and §§ 1.662(a)-1 through 1.662(a)-4 shall have the same character in the hands of the beneficiary as in the hands of

Reg. § 1.662(b)-1

the estate or trust. The amounts are treated as consisting of the same proportion of each class of items entering into the computation of distributable net income as the total of each class bears to the total distributable net income of the estate or trust unless the terms of the governing instruments specifically allocate different classes of income to different beneficiaries, or unless local law requires such an allocation. For this purpose, the principles contained in § 1.652(b)-1 shall apply. [Reg. § 1.662(b)-1.]

☐ [*T.D.* 6217, 12-19-56.]

[Reg. § 1.662(b)-2]

§ 1.662(b)-2. **Character of amounts; when charitable contributions are made.**—When a charitable contribution is made, the principles contained in §§ 1.652(b)-1 and 1.662(b)-1 generally apply. However, before the allocation of other deductions among the items of distributable net income, the charitable contributions deduction allowed under section 642(c) is (in the absence of specific allocation under the terms of the governing instrument or the requirement under local law of a different allocation) allocated among the classes of income entering into the computation of estate or trust income in accordance with the rules set forth in paragraph (b) of § 1.643(a)-5. In the application of the preceding sentence, for the purpose of allocating items of income and deductions to beneficiaries to whom income is required to be distributed currently, the amount of the charitable contributions deduction is disregarded to the extent that it exceeds the income of the trust for the taxable year reduced by amounts for the taxable year required to be distributed currently. The application of this section may be illustrated by the following examples (of which example (1) is illustrative of the preceding sentence):

Example (1). (a) A trust instrument provides that $30,000 of its income must be distributed currently to A, and the balance may either be distributed to B, distributed to a designated charity, or accumulated. Accumulated income may be distributed to B and to the charity. The trust for its taxable year has $40,000 of taxable interest and $10,000 of tax-exempt income, with no expenses. The trustee distributed $30,000 to A, $50,000 to charity X, and $10,000 to B.

(b) Distributable net income for the purpose of determining the character of the distribution to A is $30,000 (the charitable contributions deduction, for this purpose, being taken into account only to the extent of $20,000, the difference between the income of the trust for the taxable year, $50,000, and the amount required to be distributed currently, $30,000).

(c) The charitable contributions deduction taken into account, $20,000, is allocated proportionately to the items of income of the trust, $16,000 to taxable interest and $4,000 to tax-exempt income.

(d) Under section 662(a)(1), the amount of income required to be distributed currently to A is $30,000, which consists of the balance of these items, $24,000 of taxable interest and $6,000 of tax-exempt income.

(e) In determining the amount to be included in the gross income of B under section 662 for the taxable year, however, the entire charitable contributions deduction is taken into account, with the result that there is no distributable net income and therefore no amount to be included in gross income.

(f) See subpart D (sections 665 and following), part I, subchapter J, chapter 1 of the Code for application of the throwback provisions to the distribution made to B.

Example (2). The net income of a trust is payable to A for life, with the remainder to a charitable organization. Under the terms of the trust instrument and local law capital gains are added to corpus. During the taxable year the trust receives dividends of $10,000 and realized a long-term capital gain of $10,000, for which a long-term capital gains deduction of $5,000 is allowed under section 1202. Since under the trust instrument and local law the capital gains are allocated to the charitable organization, and since the capital gain deduction is directly attributable to the capital gain, the charitable contributions deduction and the capital gain deduction are both allocable to the capital gain, and dividends in the amount of $10,000 are allocable to A. [Reg. § 1.662(b)-2.]

☐ [*T.D.* 6217, 12-19-56.]

[Reg. § 1.662(c)-1]

§ 1.662(c)-1. **Different taxable years.**—If a beneficiary has a different taxable year (as defined in section 441 or 442) from the taxable year of an estate or trust, the amount he is required to include in gross income in accordance with section 662(a) and (b) is based upon the distributable net income of the estate or trust and the amounts properly paid, credited, or required to be distributed to the beneficiary for any taxable year or years of the estate or trust ending with or within his taxable year. This rule applies as to so-called short taxable years as well as taxable years of normal duration. Income of an estate or trust for its taxable year or years is determined in accordance with its method of accounting and without

Reg. § 1.662(b)-2

regard to that of the beneficiary. [Reg. § 1.662(c)-1.]

☐ [T.D. 6217, 12-19-56.]

[Reg. § 1.662(c)-2]

§ 1.662(c)-2. Death of individual beneficiary.—If an amount specified in section 662(a)(1) or (2) is paid, credited, or required to be distributed by an estate or trust for a taxable year which does not end with or within the last taxable year of a beneficiary (because of the beneficiary's death), the extent to which the amount is included in the gross income of the beneficiary for his last taxable year or in the gross income of his estate is determined by the computations under section 662 for the taxable year of the estate or trust in which his last taxable year ends. Thus, the distributable net income and the amounts paid, credited, or required to be distributed for the taxable year of the estate or trust, determine the extent to which the amounts paid, credited, or required to be distributed to the beneficiary are included in his gross income for his last taxable year or in the gross income of his estate. (Section 662(c) does not apply to such amounts.) The gross income for the last taxable year of a beneficiary on the cash basis includes only income actually distributed to the beneficiary before his death. Income required to be distributed, but in fact distributed to his estate, is included in the gross income of the estate as income in respect of a decedent under section 691. See paragraph (e) of § 1.663(c)-3 with respect to separate share treatment for the periods before and after the death of a trust's beneficiary. [Reg. § 1.662(c)-2.]

☐ [T.D. 6217, 12-19-56.]

[Reg. § 1.662(c)-3]

§ 1.662(c)-3. Termination of existence of other beneficiaries.—If the existence of a beneficiary which is not an individual terminates, the amount to be included under section 662(a) in its gross income for the last taxable year is computed with reference to §§ 1.662(c)-1 and 1.662(c)-2 as if the beneficiary were a deceased individual, except that income required to be distributed prior to the termination but actually distributed to the beneficiary's successor in interest is included in the beneficiary's income for its last taxable year. [Reg. § 1.662(c)-3.]

☐ [T.D. 6217, 12-19-56.]

[Reg. § 1.662(c)-4]

§ 1.662(c)-4. Illustration of the provisions of sections 661 and 662.—The provisions of sections 661 and 662 may be illustrated in general by the following example:

Example. (a) Under the terms of a testamentary trust one-half of the trust income is to be distributed currently to W, the decedent's wife, for her life. The remaining trust income may, in the trustee's discretion, either be paid to D, the grantor's daughter, paid to designated charities, or accumulated. The trust is to terminate at the death of W and the principal will then be payable to D. No provision is made in the trust instrument with respect to depreciation of rental property. Capital gains are allocable to the principal account under the applicable local law. The trust and both beneficiaries file returns on the calendar year basis. The records of the fiduciary show the following items of income and deduction for the taxable year 1955:

Rents	$50,000
Dividends of domestic corporations	50,000
Tax-exempt interest	20,000
Partially tax-exempt interest	10,000
Capital gains (long term)	20,000
Depreciation of rental property	10,000
Expenses attributable to rental income	15,400
Trustee's commissions allocable to income account	2,800
Trustee's commissions allocable to principal account	1,100

(b) The income for trust accounting purposes is $111,800, and the trustee distributes one-half ($55,900) to W and in his discretion makes a contribution of one-quarter ($27,950) to charity X and distributes the remaining one-quarter ($27,950) to D. The total of the distributions to beneficiaries is $83,850, consisting of (1) income required to be distributed currently to W of $55,900 and (2) other amounts properly paid or credited to D of $27,950. The income for trust accounting purposes of $111,800 is determined as follows:

Rents		$ 50,000
Dividends		50,000
Tax-exempt interest		20,000
Partially tax-exempt interest		10,000
Total		130,000
Less: Rental expenses	$15,400	
Trustee's commissions allocable to income account	2,800	18,200
Income as computed under section 643(b)		111,800

Reg. § 1.662(c)-4

(c) The distributable net income of the trust as computed under section 643(a) is $82,750, determined as follows:

Rents			$ 50,000
Dividends			50,000
Partially tax-exempt interest			10,000
Tax-exempt interest		$20,000	
Less: Trustee's commissions allocable thereto (20,000/130,000 of $3,900)	$ 600		
Charitable contributions allocable thereto (20,000/130,000 of $27,950)	4,300	4,900	15,100
Total			$125,100
Deductions:			
Rental expenses		$15,400	
Trustee's commissions ($3,900 less $600 allocated to tax-exempt interest)		3,300	
Charitable deduction ($27,950 less $4,300 attributable to tax-exempt interest)		23,650	42,350
Distributable net income			$ 82,750

In computing the distributable net income of $82,750, the taxable income of the trust was computed with the following modifications: No deductions were allowed for distributions to beneficiaries and for personal exemption of the trust (section 643(a)(1) and (2)); capital gains were excluded and no deduction under section 1202 (relating to the 50 percent deduction for long-term capital gains) was taken into account (section 643(a)(3)); and the tax-exempt interest (as adjusted for expenses and charitable contributions) and the dividend exclusion of $50 were included (section 643(a)(5) and (7)).

(d) Inasmuch as the distributable net income of $82,750 as determined under section 643(a) is less than the sum of the amounts distributed to W and D of $83,850, the deduction allowable to the trust under section 661(a) is such distributable net income as modified under section 661(c) to exclude therefrom the items of income not included in the gross income of the trust, as follows:

Distributable net income		$82,750
Less: Tax-exempt interest (as adjusted for expenses and the charitable contributions)	$15,100	
Dividend exclusion allowable under section 116	50	15,150
Deduction allowable under section 661(a)		$67,600

(e) For the purpose of determining the character of the amounts deductible under section 642(c) and section 661(a), the trustee elected to offset the trustee's commissions (other than the portion required to be allocated to tax-exempt interest) against the rental income. The following table shows the determination of the character of the amounts deemed distributed to beneficiaries and contributed to charity:

	Rents	Taxable dividends	Excluded dividends	Tax-exempt interest	Partially tax-exempt interest	Total
Trust income	$50,000	$49,950	$50	$20,000	$10,000	$130,000
Less:						
Charitable contribution	10,750	10,750	...	4,300	2,150	27,950
Rental expenses	15,400	......	...	......	......	15,400
Trustee's commissions	3,300	......	...	600	......	3,900
Total deductions	29,450	10,750	0	4,900	2,150	47,250
Amounts distributable to beneficiaries	20,550	39,200	50	15,100	7,850	82,750

The character of the charitable contribution is determined by multiplying the total charitable contribution ($27,950) by a fraction consisting of each item of trust income, respectively, over the total trust income, except that no part of the dividends excluded from gross income are deemed included in the charitable contribution. For example, the charitable contribution is deemed to consist of rents of $10,750 (50,000/130,000 × $27,950).

(f) The taxable income of the trust is $9,900 determined as follows:

Reg. § 1.662(c)-4

Estates, Trusts, and Beneficiaries

See p. 20,601 for regulations not amended to reflect law changes

Rental income		$ 50,000
Dividends ($50,000 less $50 exclusion)		49,950
Partially tax-exempt interest		10,000
Capital gains		20,000
Gross income		129,950
Deductions:		
Rental expenses	$15,400	
Trustee's commissions	3,300	
Charitable contributions	23,650	
Capital gain deduction	10,000	
Distributions to beneficiaries	67,600	
Personal exemption	100	120,050
Taxable income		9,900

(g) In computing the amount includible in W's gross income under section 662(a)(1), the $55,900 distribution to her is deemed to be composed of the following proportions of the items of income deemed to have been distributed to the beneficiaries by the trust (see paragraph (e) of this example):

Rents (20,550/82,750 × $55,900)	$13,882
Dividends (39,250/82,750 × $55,900)	26,515
Partially tax-exempt interest (7,850/82,750 × $55,900)	5,303
Tax-exempt interest (15,100/82,750 × $55,900)	10,200
Total	55,900

Accordingly, W will exclude $10,200 of tax-exempt interest from gross income and will receive the credits and exclusion for dividends received and for partially tax-exempt interest provided in sections 34, 116, and 35, respectively, with respect to the dividends and partially tax-exempt interest deemed to have been distributed to her, her share of the dividends being aggregated with other dividends received by her for purposes of the dividend credit and exclusion. In addition, she may deduct a share of the depreciation deduction proportionate to the trust income allocable to her; that is, one-half of the total depreciation deduction, or $5,000.

(h) Inasmuch as the sum of the amount of income required to be distributed currently to W ($55,900) and the other amounts properly paid, credited, or required to be distributed to D ($27,950) exceeds the distributable net income ($82,750) of the trust as determined under section 643(a), D is deemed to have received $26,850 ($82,750 less $55,900) for income tax purposes. The character of the amounts deemed distributed to her is determined as follows:

Rents (20,550/82,750 × $26,850)	$ 6,668
Dividends (39,250/82,750 × $26,850)	12,735
Partially tax-exempt interest (7,850/82,750 × $26,850)	2,547
Tax-exempt interest (15,100/82,750 × $26,850)	4,900
Total	26,850

Accordingly, D will exclude $4,900 of tax-exempt interest from gross income and will receive the credits and exclusion for dividends received and for partially tax-exempt interest provided in sections 34, 116, and 35, respectively, with respect to the dividends and partially tax-exempt interest deemed to have been distributed to her, her share of the dividends being aggregated with other dividends received by her for purposes of the dividend credit and exclusion. In addition, she may deduct a share of the depreciation deduction proportionate to the trust income allocable to her; that is, one-fourth of the total depreciation deduction, or $2,500.

(i) [Reserved]

(j) The remaining $2,500 of the depreciation deduction is allocated to the amount distributed to charity X and is hence nondeductible by the trust, W, or D. (See § 1.642(e)-1.) [Reg. § 1.662(c)-4.]

☐ [T.D. 6217, 12-19-56.]

[Reg. § 1.663(a)-1]

§ 1.663(a)-1. Special rules applicable to sections 661 and 662; exclusions; gifts, bequests, etc.—(a) *In general.* A gift or bequest of a specific sum of money or of specific property, which is required by the specific terms of the will or trust instrument and is properly paid or credited to a beneficiary, is not allowed as a deduction to an estate or trust under section 661 and is not in-

Reg. § 1.663(a)-1(a)

cluded in the gross income of a beneficiary under section 662, unless under the terms of the will or trust instrument the gift or bequest is to be paid or credited to the recipient in more than three installments. Thus, in order for a gift or bequest to be excludable from the gross income of the recipient, (1) it must qualify as a gift or bequest of a specific sum of money or of specific property (see paragraph (b) of this section), and (2) the terms of the governing instrument must not provide for its payment in more than three installments (see paragraph (c) of this section). The date when the estate came into existence or the date when the trust was created is immaterial.

(b) *Definition of a gift or bequest of a specific sum of money or of specific property*—(1) In order to qualify as a gift or bequest of a specific sum of money or of specific property under section 663(a), the amount of money or the identity of the specific property must be ascertainable under the terms of a testator's will as of the date of his death, or under the terms of an inter vivos trust instrument as of the date of the inception of the trust. For example, bequests to a decedent's son of the decedent's interest in a partnership and to his daughter of a sum of money equal to the value of the partnership interest are bequests of specific property and of a specific sum of money, respectively. On the other hand, a bequest to the decedent's spouse of money or property, to be selected by the decedent's executor, equal in value to a fraction of the decedent's "adjusted gross estate" is neither a bequest of a specific sum of money or of specific property. The identity of the property and the amount of money specified in the preceding sentence are dependent both on the exercise of the executor's discretion and on the payment of administration expenses and other charges, neither of which are facts existing on the date of the decedent's death. It is immaterial that the value of the bequest is determinable after the decedent's death before the bequest is satisfied (so that gain or loss may be realized by the estate in the transfer of property in satisfaction of it).

(2) The following amounts are not considered as gifts or bequests of a sum of money or of specific property within the meaning of this paragraph:

(i) An amount which can be paid or credited only from the income of an estate or trust, whether from the income for the year of payment or crediting, or from the income accumulated from a prior year;

(ii) An annuity, or periodic gifts of specific property in lieu of or having the effect of an annuity;

(iii) A residuary estate or the corpus of a trust; or

(iv) A gift or bequest paid in a lump sum or in not more than three installments, if the gift or bequest is required to be paid in more than three installments under the terms of the governing instrument.

(3) The provisions of subparagraphs (1) and (2) of this paragraph may be illustrated by the following examples, in which it is assumed that the gift or bequest is not required to be made in more than three installments (see paragraph (c)):

Example 1. Under the terms of a will, a legacy of $5,000 was left to A, 1,000 shares of X company stock was left to W, and the balance of the estate was to be divided equally between W and B. No provision was made in the will for the disposition of income of the estate during the period of administration. The estate had income of $25,000 during the taxable year 1954, which was accumulated and added to corpus for estate accounting purposes. During the taxable year, the executor paid the legacy of $5,000 in a lump sum to A, transferred the X company stock to W, and made no other distributions to beneficiaries. The distributions to A and W qualify for the exclusion under section 663(a)(1).

Example 2. Under the terms of a will, the testator's estate was to be distributed to A. No provision was made in the will for the distribution of the estate's income during the period of administration. The estate had income of $50,000 for the taxable year. The estate distributed to A stock with a basis of $40,000 and with a fair market value of $40,000 on the date of distribution. No other distributions were made during the year. The distribution does not qualify for the exclusion under section 663(a)(1), because it is not a specific gift to A required by the terms of the will. Accordingly, the fair market value of the property ($40,000) represents a distribution within the meaning of sections 661(a) and 662(a) (see § 1.661(a)-2(c)).

Example 3. Under the terms of a trust instrument, trust income is to be accumulated for a period of 10 years. During the eleventh year, the trustee is to distribute $10,000 to B, payable from income or corpus, and $10,000 to C, payable out of accumulated income. The trustee is to distribute the balance of the accumulated income to A. Thereafter, A is to receive all the current income until the trust terminates. Only the distribution to B would qualify for the exclusion under section 663(a)(1).

(4) A gift or bequest of a specific sum of money or of specific property is not disqualified under this paragraph solely because its payment

Reg. § 1.663(a)-1(b)(1)

is subject to a condition. For example, provision for a payment by a trust to beneficiary A of $10,000 when he reaches age 25, and $10,000 when he reaches age 30, with payment over to B of any amount not paid to A because of his death, is a gift to A of a specific sum of money payable in two installments, within the meaning of this paragraph, even though the exact amount payable to A cannot be ascertained with certainty under the terms of the trust instrument.

(c) *Installment payments*—(1) In determining whether a gift or bequest of a specific sum of money or of specific property, as defined in paragraph (b) of this section, is required to be paid or credited to a particular beneficiary in more than three installments—

(i) Gifts or bequests of articles for personal use (such as personal and household effects, automobiles, and the like) are disregarded.

(ii) Specifically devised real property, the title to which passes directly from the decedent to the devisee under local law, is not taken into account, since it would not constitute an amount paid, credited, or required to be distributed under section 661 (see paragraph (e) of § 1.661(a)-2).

(iii) All gifts and bequests under a decedent's will (which are not disregarded pursuant to subdivisions (i) and (ii) of this subparagraph) for which no time of payment or crediting is specified, and which are to be paid or credited in the ordinary course of administration of the decedent's estate, are considered as required to be paid or credited in a single installment.

(iv) All gifts and bequests (which are not disregarded pursuant to subdivisions (i) and (ii) of this subparagraph) payable at any one specified time under the terms of the governing instrument are taken into account as a single installment.

For purposes of determining the number of installments paid or credited to a particular beneficiary, a decedent's estate and a testamentary trust shall each be treated as a separate entity.

(2) The application of the rules stated in subparagraph (1) of this paragraph may be illustrated by the following examples:

Example (1). (i) Under the terms of a decedent's will, $10,000 in cash, household furniture, a watch, an automobile, 100 shares of X company stock, 1,000 bushels of grain, 500 head of cattle, and a farm (title to which passed directly to A under local law) are bequeathed or devised outright to A. The will also provides for the creation of a trust for the benefit of A, under the terms of which there are required to be distributed to A, $10,000 in cash and 100 shares of Y company stock when he reaches 25 years of age, $25,000 in cash and 200 shares of Y company stock when he reaches 30 years of age, and $50,000 in cash and 300 shares of Y company stock when he reaches 35 years of age.

(ii) The furniture, watch, automobile, and the farm are excluded in determining whether any gift or bequest is required to be paid or credited to A in more than three installments. These items qualify for the exclusion under section 663(a)(1) regardless of the treatment of the other items of property bequeathed to A.

(iii) The $10,000 in cash, the shares of X company stock, the grain, the cattle and the assets required to create the trust, to be paid or credited by the estate to A and the trust are considered as required to be paid or credited in a single installment to each, regardless of the manner of payment or distribution by the executor, since no time of payment or crediting is specified in the will. The $10,000 in cash and shares of Y company stock required to be distributed by the trust to A when he is 25 years old are considered as required to be paid or distributed as one installment under the trust. Likewise, the distributions to be made by the trust to A when he is 30 and 35 years old are each considered as one installment under the trust. Since the total number of installments to be made by the estate does not exceed three, all of the items of money and property distributed by the estate qualify for the exclusion under section 663(a)(1). Similarly, the three distributions by the trust qualify.

Example (2). Assume the same facts as in example (1), except that another distribution of a specified sum of money is required to be made by the trust to A when he becomes 40 years old. This distribution would also qualify as an installment, thus making four installments in all under the trust. None of the gifts to A under the trust would qualify for the exclusion under section 663(a)(1). The situation as to the estate, however, would not be changed.

Example (3). A trust instrument provides that A and B are each to receive $75,000 in installments of $25,000, to be paid in alternate years. The trustee distributes $25,000 to A in 1954, 1956, and 1958, and to B in 1955, 1957, and 1959. The gifts to A and B qualify for exclusion under section 663(a)(1), although a total of six payments is made. The gifts of $75,000 to each beneficiary are to be separately treated. [Reg. § 1.663(a)-1.]

☐ [*T.D. 6217, 12-19-56. Amended by T.D. 8849, 12-27-99.*]

Reg. § 1.663(a)-1(c)(2)

Estates, Trusts, and Beneficiaries

See p. 20,601 for regulations not amended to reflect law changes

[Reg. § 1.663(a)-2]

§ 1.663(a)-2. Charitable, etc., distributions.—Any amount paid, permanently set aside, or to be used for the charitable, etc., purposes specified in section 642(c) and which is allowable as a deduction under that section is not allowed as a deduction to an estate or trust under section 661 or treated as an amount distributed for purposes of determining the amounts includible in gross income of beneficiaries under section 662. Amounts paid, permanently set aside, or to be used for charitable, etc., purposes are deductible by estates or trusts only as provided in section 642(c). For purposes of this section, the deduction provided in section 642(c) is computed without regard to the provisions of section 508(d), section 681, or section 4948(c)(4) (concerning unrelated business income and private foundations). [Reg. § 1.663(a)-2.]

☐ [T.D. 6217, 12-19-56. Amended by T.D. 7428, 8-13-76.]

[Reg. § 1.663(a)-3]

§ 1.663(a)-3. Denial of double deduction.—No amount deemed to have been distributed to a beneficiary in a preceding year under section 651 or 661 is included in amounts falling within section 661(a) or 662(a). For example, assume that all of the income of a trust is required to be distributed currently to beneficiary A and both the trust and A report on the calendar year basis. For administrative convenience, the trustee distributes in January and February 1956 a portion of the income of the trust required to be distributed in 1955. The portion of the income for 1955 which was distributed by the trust in 1956 may not be claimed as a deduction by the trust for 1956 since it is deductible by the trust and includible in A's gross income for the taxable year 1955. [Reg. § 1.663(a)-3.]

☐ [T.D. 6217, 12-19-56.]

[Reg. § 1.663(b)-1]

§ 1.663(b)-1. Distributions in first 65 days of taxable year; scope.—(a) *Taxable years beginning after December 31, 1968*—(1) *General rule.* With respect to taxable years beginning after December 31, 1968, the fiduciary of a trust may elect under section 663(b) to treat any amount or portion thereof that is properly paid or credited to a beneficiary within the first 65 days following the close of the taxable year as an amount that was properly paid or credited on the last day of such taxable year.

(2) *Effect of election.* (i) An election is effective only with respect to the taxable year for which the election is made. In the case of distributions made after May 8, 1972, the amount to which the election applies shall not exceed—

(a) The amount of income of the trust (as defined in § 1.643(b)-1) for the taxable year for which the election is made, or

(b) The amount of distributable net income of the trust (as defined in §§ 1.643(a)-1 through 1.643(a)-7) for such taxable year, if greater, reduced by any amounts paid, credited, or required to be distributed in such taxable year other than those amounts considered paid or credited in a preceding taxable year by reason of section 663(b) and this section. An election shall be made for each taxable year for which the treatment is desired. The application of this paragraph may be illustrated by the following example:

Example. X Trust, a calendar year trust, has $1,000 of income (as defined in § 1.643(b)-1) and $800 of distributable net income (as defined in §§ 1.643(a)-1 through 1.643(a)-7) in 1972. The trust properly pays $550 to A, a beneficiary, on January 15, 1972, which the trustee elects to treat under section 663(b) as paid on December 31, 1971. The trust also properly pays to A $600 on July 19, 1972, and $450 on January 17, 1973. For 1972, the maximum amount that may be elected under this subdivision to be treated as properly paid or credited on the last day of 1972 is $400 ($1,000 − $600). The $550 paid on January 15, 1972, does not reduce the maximum amount to which the election may apply, because that amount is treated as properly paid on December 31, 1971.

(ii) If an election is made with respect to a taxable year of a trust, this section shall apply only to those amounts which are properly paid or credited within the first 65 days following such year and which are so designated by the fiduciary in his election. Any amount considered under section 663(b) as having been distributed in the preceding taxable year shall be so treated for all purposes. For example, in determining the beneficiary's tax liability, such amount shall be considered as having been received by the beneficiary in his taxable year in which or with which the last day of the preceding taxable year of the trust ends.

(b) *Taxable years beginning before January 1, 1969.* With respect to taxable years of a trust beginning before January 1, 1969, the fiduciary of the trust may elect under section 663(b) to treat distributions wihtin the first 65 days following such taxable year as amounts which were paid or credited on the last day of such taxable year, if:

(1) The trust was in existence prior to January 1, 1954;

Reg. § 1.663(a)-2

(2) An amount in excess of the income of the immediately preceding taxable year may not (under the terms of the governing instrument) be distributed in any taxable year; and

(3) The fiduciary elects (as provided in § 1.663(b)-2) to have section 663(b) apply. [Reg. § 1.663(b)-1.]

☐ [T.D. 6217, 12-19-56. Amended by T.D. 7204, 8-24-72.]

[Reg. § 1.663(b)-2]

§ 1.663(b)-2. Election.—(a) *Manner and time of election; irrevocability*—(1) *When return is required to be filed.* If a trust return is required to be filed for the taxable year of the trust for which the election is made, the election shall be made in the appropriate place on such return. The election under this subparagraph shall be made not later than the time prescribed by law for filing such return (including extensions thereof). Such election shall become irrevocable after the last day prescribed for making it.

(2) *When no return is required to be filed.* If no return is required to be filed for the taxable year of the trust for which the election is made, the election shall be made in a statement filed with the internal revenue office with which a return by such trust would be filed if such trust were required to file a return for such taxable year. See section 6091 and the regulations thereunder for place for filing return. The election under this subparagraph shall be made not later than the time prescribed by law for filing a return if such trust were required to file a return for such taxable year. Such election shall become irrevocable after the last day prescribed for making it.

(b) *Elections under prior law.* Elections made pursuant to section 663(b) prior to its amendment by section 331(b) of the Tax Reform Act of 1969 (83 Stat. 598), which, under prior law, were irrevocable for the taxable year for which the election was made and all subsequent years, are not effective for taxable years beginning after December 31, 1968. In the case of a trust for which an election was made under prior law, the fiduciary shall make the election for each taxable year beginning after December 31, 1968, for which the treatment provided by section 663(b) is desired. [Reg. § 1.663(b)-2.]

☐ [T.D. 6217, 12-19-56. Amended by T.D. 7204, 8-24-72.]

[Reg. § 1.663(c)-1]

§ 1.663(c)-1. Separate shares treated as separate trusts or as separate estates; in general.—(a) If a single trust (or estate) has more than one beneficiary, and if different beneficiaries have substantially separate and independent shares, their shares are treated as separate trusts (or estates) for the sole purpose of determining the amount of distributable net income allocable to the respective beneficiaries under sections 661 and 662. Application of this rule will be significant in, for example, situations in which income is accumulated for beneficiary A but a distribution is made to beneficiary B of both income and corpus in an amount exceeding the share of income that would be distributable to B had there been separate trusts (or estates). In the absence of a separate share rule B would be taxed on income which is accumulated for A. The division of distributable net income into separate shares will limit the tax liability of B. Section 663(c) does not affect the principles of applicable law in situations in which a single trust instrument creates not one but several separate trusts, as opposed to separate shares in the same trust within the meaning of this section.

(b) The separate share rule does not permit the treatment of separate shares as separate trusts (or estates) for any purpose other than the application of distributable net income. It does not, for instance, permit the treatment of separate shares as separate trusts (or estates) for purposes of:

(1) The filing of returns and payment of tax,

(2) The deduction of personal exemption under section 642(b), and

(3) The allowance to beneficiaries succeeding to the trust (or estate) property of excess deductions and unused net operating loss and capital loss carryovers on termination of the trust (or estate) under section 642(h).

(c) The separate share rule may be applicable even though separate and independent accounts are not maintained and are not required to be maintained for each share on the books of account of the trust (or estate), and even though no physical segregation of assets is made or required.

(d) Separate share treatment is not elective. Thus, if a trust (or estate) is properly treated as having separate and independent shares, such treatment must prevail in all taxable years of the trust (or estate) unless an event occurs as a result of which the terms of the trust (or estate) instrument and the requirements of proper administration require different treatment. [Reg. § 1.663(c)-1.]

☐ [T.D. 6217, 12-19-56. Amended by T.D. 8849, 12-27-99.]

[Reg. § 1.663(c)-2]

§ 1.663(c)-2. Rules of administration.—(a) *When separate shares come into existence.* A separate share comes into existence upon the earliest

Reg. § 1.663(c)-2(a)

moment that a fiduciary may reasonably determine, based upon the known facts, that a separate economic interest exists.

(b) *Computation of distributable net income for each separate share*—(1) *General rule.* The amount of distributable net income for any share under section 663(c) is computed as if each share constituted a separate trust or estate. Accordingly, each separate share shall calculate its distributable net income based upon its portion of gross income that is includible in distributable net income and its portion of any applicable deductions or losses.

(2) *Section 643(b) income.* This paragraph (b)(2) governs the allocation of the portion of gross income includible in distributable net income that is income within the meaning of section 643(b). Such gross income is allocated among the separate shares in accordance with the amount of income that each share is entitled to under the terms of the governing instrument or applicable local law.

(3) *Income in respect of a decedent.* This paragraph (b)(3) governs the allocation of the portion of gross income includible in distributable net income that is income in respect of a decedent within the meaning of section 691(a) and is not income within the meaning of section 643(b). Such gross income is allocated among the separate shares that could potentially be funded with these amounts irrespective of whether the share is entitled to receive any income under the terms of the governing instrument or applicable local law. The amount of such gross income allocated to each share is based on the relative value of each share that could potentially be funded with such amounts.

(4) *Gross income not attributable to cash.* This paragraph (b)(4) governs the allocation of the portion of gross income includible in distributable net income that is not attributable to cash received by the estate or trust (for example, original issue discount, a distributive share of partnership tax items, and the pro rata share of an S corporation's tax items). Such gross income is allocated among the separate shares in the same proportion as section 643(b) income from the same source would be allocated under the terms of the governing instrument or applicable local law.

(5) *Deductions and losses.* Any deduction or any loss which is applicable solely to one separate share of the trust or estate is not available to any other share of the same trust or estate.

(c) *Computations and valuations.* For purposes of calculating distributable net income for each separate share, the fiduciary must use a reasonable and equitable method to make the allocations, calculations, and valuations required by paragraph (b) of this section. [Reg. § 1.663(c)-2.]

☐ [T.D. 6217, 12-19-56. Amended by T.D. 8849, 12-27-99.]

[Reg. § 1.663(c)-3]

§ 1.663(c)-3. **Applicability of separate share rule to certain trusts.**—(a) The applicability of the separate share rule provided by section 663(c) to trusts other than qualified revocable trusts within the meaning of section 645(b)(1) will generally depend upon whether distributions of the trust are to be made in substantially the same manner as if separate trusts had been created. Thus, if an instrument directs a trustee to divide the testator's residuary estate into separate shares (which under applicable law do not constitute separate trusts) for each of the testator's children and the trustee is given discretion, with respect to each share, to distribute or accumulate income or to distribute principal or accumulated income, or to do both, separate shares will exist under section 663(c). In determining whether separate shares exist, it is immaterial whether the principal and any accumulated income of each share is ultimately distributable to the beneficiary of such share, to his descendants, to his appointees under a general or special power of appointment, or to any other beneficiaries (including a charitable organization) designated to receive his share of the trust and accumulated income upon termination of the beneficiary's interest in the share. Thus, a separate share may exist if the instrument provides that upon the death of the beneficiary of the share, the share will be added to the shares of the other beneficiaries of the trust.

(b) Separate share treatment will not be applied to a trust or portion of a trust subject to a power to:

(1) Distribute, apportion, or accumulate income, or

(2) Distribute corpus

to or for one or more beneficiaries within a group or class of beneficiaries, unless payment of income, accumulated income, or corpus of a share of one beneficiary cannot affect the proportionate share of income, accumulated income, or corpus of any shares of the other beneficiaries, or unless substantially proper adjustment must thereafter be made (under the governing instrument) so that substantially separate and independent shares exist.

(c) A share may be considered as separate even though more than one beneficiary has an interest in it. For example, two beneficiaries may have equal, disproportionate, or indeterminate interests in one share which is separate and indepen-

Reg. § 1.663(c)-3(a)

dent from another share in which one or more beneficiaries have an interest. Likewise, the same person may be a beneficiary of more than one separate share.

(d) Separate share treatment may be given to a trust or portion of a trust otherwise qualifying under this section if the trust or portion of a trust is subject to a power to pay out to a beneficiary of a share (of such trust or portion) an amount of corpus in excess of his proportionate share of the corpus of the trust if the possibility of exercise of the power is remote. For example, if the trust is subject to a power to invade the entire corpus for the health, education, support, or maintenance of A, separate share treatment is applied if exercise of the power requires consideration of A's other income which is so substantial as to make the possibility of exercise of the power remote. If instead it appears that A and B have separate shares in a trust subject to a power to invade the entire corpus for the comfort, pleasure, desire, or happiness of A, separate share treatment shall not be applied.

(e) For taxable years ending before January 1, 1979, the separate share rule may also be applicable to successive interests in point of time, as for instance in the case of a trust providing for a life estate to A and a second life estate or outright remainder to B. In such a case, in the taxable year of a trust in which a beneficiary dies items of income and deduction properly allocable under trust accounting principles to the period before a beneficiary's death are attributed to one share, and those allocable to the period after the beneficiary's death are attributed to the other share. Separate share treatment is not available to a succeeding interest, however, with respect to distributions which would otherwise be deemed distributed in a taxable year of the earlier interest under the throwback provisions of subpart D (section 665 and following), Part I, subchapter J, chapter 1 of the Code. The application of this paragraph may be illustrated by the following example:

Example. A trust instrument directs that the income of a trust is to be paid to A for her life. After her death income may be distributed to B or accumulated. A dies on June 1, 1956. The trust keeps its books on the basis of the calendar year. The trust instrument permits invasions of corpus for the benefit of A and B, and an invasion of corpus was in fact made for A's benefit in 1956. In determining the distributable net income of the trust for the purpose of determining the amounts includible in A's income, income and deductions properly allocable to the period before A's death are treated as income and deductions of a separate share, and for that purpose no account is taken of income and deductions allocable to the period after A's death.

[Reg. § 1.663(c)-3.]

☐ [T.D. 6217, 12-19-56. Amended by T.D. 7633, 7-17-79 and T.D. 8849, 12-27-99.]

[Reg. § 1.663(c)-4]

§ 1.663(c)-4. Applicability of separate share rule to estates and qualified revocable trusts.—(a) *General rule.* The applicability of the separate share rule provided by section 663(c) to estates and qualified revocable trusts within the meaning of section 645(b)(1) will generally depend upon whether the governing instrument and applicable local law create separate economic interests in one beneficiary or class of beneficiaries of such estate or trust. Ordinarily, a separate share exists if the economic interests of the beneficiary or class of beneficiaries neither affect nor are affected by the economic interests accruing to another beneficiary or class of beneficiaries. Separate shares include, for example, the income on bequeathed property if the recipient of the specific bequest is entitled to such income and a surviving spouse's elective share that under local law is entitled to income and appreciation or depreciation. Furthermore, a qualified revocable trust for which an election is made under section 645 is always a separate share of the estate and may itself contain two or more separate shares. Conversely, a gift or bequest of a specific sum of money or of property as defined in section 663(a)(1) is not a separate share.

(b) *Special rule for certain types of beneficial interests.* Notwithstanding the provisions of paragraph (a) of this section, a surviving spouse's elective share that under local law is determined as of the date of the decedent's death and is not entitled to income or any appreciation or depreciation is a separate share. Similarly, notwithstanding the provisions of paragraph (a) of this section, a pecuniary formula bequest that, under the terms of the governing instrument or applicable local law, is not entitled to income or to share in appreciation or depreciation constitutes a separate share if the governing instrument does not provide that it is to be paid or credited in more than three installments.

(c) *Shares with multiple beneficiaries and beneficiaries of multiple shares.* A share may be considered as separate even though more than one beneficiary has an interest in it. For example, two beneficiaries may have equal, disproportionate, or indeterminate interests in one share which is economically separate and independent from another share in which one or more beneficiaries have an interest. Moreover, the same person may be a beneficiary of more than one separate share. [Reg. § 1.663(c)-4.]

☐ [T.D. 8849, 12-27-99.]

[Reg. § 1.663(c)-5]

§ 1.663(c)-5. **Examples.**—Section 663(c) may be illustrated by the following examples:

Example 1. (i) A single trust was created in 1940 for the benefit of A, B, and C, who were aged 6, 4, and 2, respectively. Under the terms of the instrument, the trust income is required to be divided into three equal shares. Each beneficiary's share of the income is to be accumulated until he becomes 21 years of age. When a beneficiary reaches the age of 21, his share of the income may thereafter be either accumulated or distributed to him in the discretion of the trustee. The trustee also has discretion to invade corpus for the benefit of any beneficiary to the extent of his share of the trust estate, and the trust instrument requires that the beneficiary's right to future income and corpus will be proportionately reduced. When each beneficiary reaches 35 years of age, his share of the trust estate shall be paid over to him. The interest in the trust estate of any beneficiary dying without issue and before he has attained the age of 35 is to be equally divided between the other beneficiaries of the trust. All expenses of the trust are allocable to income under the terms of the trust instrument.

(ii) No distributions of income or corpus were made by the trustee prior to 1955, although A became 21 years of age on June 30, 1954. During the taxable year 1955, the trust has income from royalties of $20,000 and expenses of $5,000. The trustee in his discretion distributes $12,000 to A. Both A and the trust report on the calendar year basis.

(iii) The trust qualifies for the separate share treatment under section 663(c) and the distributable net income must be divided into three parts for the purpose of determining the amount deductible by the trust under section 661 and the amount includible in A's gross income under section 662.

(iv) The distributable net income of each share of the trust is $5,000 ($6,667 less $1,667). Since the amount $12,000 distributed to A during 1955 exceeds the distributable net income of $5,000 allocated to his share, the trust is deemed to have distributed to him $5,000 of 1955 income and $7,000 of amounts other than 1955 income. Accordingly, the trust is allowed a deduction of $5,000 under section 661. The taxable income of the trust for 1955 is $9,900, computed as follows:

Royalties		$20,000
Deductions:		
Expenses	$5,000	
Distribution to A	5,000	
Personal exemption	100	10,100
Taxable income		9,900

(v) In accordance with section 662, A must include in his gross income for 1955 an amount equal to the portion ($5,000) of the distributable net income of the trust allocated to his share. Also, the excess distribution of $7,000 made by the trust is subject to the throwback provisions of subpart D (section 665 and following), part I, subchapter J, chapter 1 of the Code, and the regulations thereunder.

Example 2. (i) *Facts.* Testator, who dies in 2000, is survived by a spouse and two children. Testator's will contains a fractional formula bequest dividing the residuary estate between the surviving spouse and a trust for the benefit of the children. Under the fractional formula, the marital bequest constitutes 60% of the estate and the children's trust constitutes 40% of the estate. During the year, the executor makes a partial proportionate distribution of $1,000,0000, ($600,000 to the surviving spouse and $400,000 to the children's trust) and makes no other distributions. The estate receives dividend income of $20,000, and pays expenses of $8,000 that are deductible on the estate's federal income tax return.

(ii) *Conclusion.* The fractional formula bequests to the surviving spouse and to the children's trust are separate shares. Because Testator's will provides for fractional formula residuary bequests, the income and any appreciation in the value of the estate assets are proportionately allocated between the marital share and the trust's share. Therefore, in determining the distributable net income of each share, the income and expenses must be allocated 60% to the marital share and 40% to the trust's share. The distributable net income is $7,200 (60% of income less 60% of expenses) for the marital share and $4,800 (40% of income less 40% of expenses) for the trust's share. Because the amount distributed in partial satisfaction of each bequest exceeds the distributable net income of each share, the estate's distribution deduction under section 661 is limited to the sum of the distributable net income for both shares. The estate is allowed a distribution deduction of $12,000 ($7,200 for the marital share and $4,800 for the trust's share). As a result, the estate has zero taxable income ($20,000 income less $8,000 expenses and $12,000 distribution deduction). Under section 662, the surviving spouse and the trust must include in gross income $7,200 and $4,800, respectively.

Example 3. The facts are the same as in *Example 2,* except that in 2000 the executor makes the payment to partially fund the children's trust but makes no payment to the surviving spouse. The fiduciary must use a reasonable and equitable method to allocate income and expenses to the trust's share. Therefore, depending on when the distribution is made to the trust, it may no longer be reasonable or equitable to determine the distributable net income for the trust's share by allocating to it 40% of the estate's income and expenses for the year. The computation of the distributable net income for the trust's share should take into consideration that after the partial distribution the relative size of the trust's separate share is reduced and the relative size of the spouse's separate share is increased.

Example 4. (i) *Facts.* Testator, who dies in 2000, is survived by a spouse and one child. Testator's will provides for a pecuniary formula bequest to be paid in not more than three installments to a trust for the benefit of the child of the largest amount that can pass free of Federal estate tax and a bequest of the residuary to the surviving spouse. The will provides that the bequest to the child's trust is not entitled to any of the estate's income and does not participate in appreciation or depreciation in estate assets. During the 2000 taxable year, the estate receives dividend income of $200,000 and pays expenses of $15,000 that are deductible on the estate's federal income tax return. The executor partially funds the child's trust by distributing to it securities that have an adjusted basis to the estate of $350,000 and a fair market value of $380,000 on the date of distribution. As a result of this distribution, the estate realizes long-term capital gain of $30,000.

(ii) *Conclusion.* The estate has two separate shares consisting of a formula pecuniary bequest to the child's trust and a residuary bequest to the surviving spouse. Because, under the terms of the will, no estate income is allocated to the bequest to the child's trust, the distributable net income for that trust's share is zero. Therefore, with respect to the $380,000 distribution to the child's trust, the estate is allowed no deduction under section 661, and no amount is included in the trust's gross income under section 662. Because no distributions were made to the spouse, there is no need to compute the distributable net income allocable to the marital share. The taxable income of the estate for the 2000 taxable year is $214,400 ($200,000 (dividend income) plus $30,000 (capital gain) minus $15,000 (expenses) and minus $600 (personal exemption)).

Example 5. The facts are the same as in *Example 4,* except that during 2000 the estate reports on its federal income tax return a pro rata share of an S corporation's tax items and a distributive share of a partnership's tax items allocated on Form K-1s to the estate by the S corporation and by the partnership, respectively. Because, under the terms of the will, no estate income from the S corporation or the partnership would be allocated to the pecuniary bequest to child's trust, none of the tax items attributable to the S corporation stock or the partnership interest is allocated to the trust's separate share. Therefore, with respect to the $380,000 distribution to the trust, the estate is allowed no deduction under section 661, and no amount is included in the trust's gross income under section 662.

Example 6. The facts are the same as in *Example 4,* except that during 2000 the estate receives a distribution of $900,000 from the decedent's individual retirement account that is included in the estate's gross income as income in respect of a decedent under section 691(a). The entire $900,000 is allocated to corpus under applicable local law. Both the separate share for the child's trust and the separate share for the surviving spouse may potentially be funded with the proceeds from the individual retirement account. Therefore, a portion of the $900,000 gross income must be allocated to the trust's separate share. The amount allocated to the trust's share must be based upon the relative values of the two separate shares using a reasonable and equitable method. The estate is entitled to a deduction under section 661 for the portion of the $900,000 properly allocated to the trust's separate share, and the trust must include this amount in income under section 662.

Example 7. (i) *Facts.* Testator, who dies in 2000, is survived by a spouse and three adult children. Testator's will divides the residue of the estate equally among the three children. The surviving spouse files an election under the applicable state's elective share statute. Under this statute, a surviving spouse is entitled to one-third of the decedent's estate after the payment of debts and expenses. The statute also provides that the surviving spouse is not entitled to any of the estate's income and does not participate in appreciation or depreciation of the estate's assets. However, under the statute, the surviving spouse is entitled to interest on the elective share from the date of the court order directing the payment until the executor actually makes payment. During the estate's 2001 taxable year, the estate distributes to the surviving spouse $5,000,000 in partial satisfaction of the elective share and pays $200,000 of interest on the delayed payment of

Reg. § 1.663(c)-5

the elective share. During that year, the estate receives dividend income of $3,000,000 and pays expenses of $60,000 that are deductible on the estate's federal income tax return.

(ii) *Conclusion.* The estate has four separate shares consisting of the surviving spouse's elective share and each of the three children's residuary bequests. Because the surviving spouse is not entitled to any estate income under state law, none of the estate's gross income is allocated to the spouse's separate share for purposes of determining that share's distributable net income. Therefore, with respect to the $5,000,000 distribution, the estate is allowed no deduction under section 661, and no amount is included in the spouse's gross income under section 662. The $200,000 of interest paid to the spouse must be included in the spouse's gross income under section 61. Because no distributions were made to any other beneficiaries during the year, there is no need to compute the distributable net income of the other three separate shares. Thus, the taxable income of the estate for the 2000 taxable year is $2,939,400 ($3,000,000 (dividend income) minus $60,000 (expenses) and $600 (personal exemption)). The estate's $200,000 interest payment is a nondeductible personal interest expense described in section 163(h).

Example 8. The will of Testator, who dies in 2000, directs the executor to distribute the X stock and all dividends therefrom to child A and the residue of the estate to child B. The estate has two separate shares consisting of the income on the X stock bequeathed to A and the residue of the estate bequeathed to B. The bequest of the X stock meets the definition of section 663(a)(1) and therefore is not a separate share. If any distributions, other than shares of the X stock, are made during the year to either A or B, then for purposes of determining the distributable net income for the separate shares, gross income attributable to dividends on the X stock must be allocated to A's separate share and any other income must be allocated to B's separate share.

Example 9. The will of Testator, who dies in 2000, directs the executor to divide the residue of the estate equally between Testator's two children, A and B. The will directs the executor to fund A's share first with the proceeds of Testator's individual retirement account. The date of death value of the estate after the payment of debts, expenses, and estate taxes is $9,000,000. During 2000, the $900,000 balance in Testator's individual retirement account is distributed to the estate. The entire $900,000 is allocated to corpus under applicable local law. This amount is income in respect of a decedent within the meaning of section 691(a). The estate has two separate shares, one for the benefit of A and one for the benefit of B. If any distributions are made to either A or B during the year, then, for purposes of determining the distributable net income for each separate share, the $900,000 of income in respect of a decedent must be allocated to A's share.

Example 10. The facts are the same as in *Example 9*, except that the will directs the executor to fund A's share first with X stock valued at $3,000,000, rather than with the proceeds of the individual retirement account. The estate has two separate shares, one for the benefit of A and one for the benefit of B. If any distributions are made to either A or B during the year, then, for purposes of determining the distributable net income for each separate share, the $900,000 of gross income attributable to the proceeds from the individual retirement account must be allocated between the two shares to the extent that they could potentially be funded with those proceeds. The maximum amount of A's share that could potentially be funded with the income in respect of decedent is $1,500,000 ($4,500,000 value of share less $3,000,000 to be funded with stock) and the maximum amount of B's share that could potentially be funded with income in respect of decedent is $4,500,000. Based upon the relative values of these amounts, the gross income attributable to the proceeds of the individual retirement account is allocated $225,000 (or one-fourth) to A's share and $675,000 (or three-fourths) to B's share.

Example 11. The will of Testator, who dies in 2000, provides that after the payment of specific bequests of money, the residue of the estate is to be divided equally among the Testator's three children, A, B, and C. The will also provides that during the period of administration one-half of the income from the residue is to be paid to a designated charitable organization. After the specific bequests of money are paid, the estate initially has three equal separate shares. One share is for the benefit of the charitable organization and A, another share is for the benefit of the charitable organization and B, and the last share is for the benefit of the charitable organization and C. During the period of administration, payments of income to the charitable organization are deductible by the estate to the extent provided in section 642(c) and are not subject to the distribution provisions of sections 661 and 662.

[Reg. § 1.663(c)-5.]

☐ [T.D. 6217, 12-19-56. *Redesignated and amended by T.D. 8849, 12-27-99 (corrected 3-27-2000).*]

Reg. § 1.663(c)-5

[Reg. § 1.663(c)-6]

§ 1.663(c)-6. Effective dates.—Sections 1.663(c)-1 through 1.663(c)-5 are applicable for estates and qualified revocable trusts within the meaning of section 645(b)(1) with respect to decedents who die on or after December 28, 1999. However, for estates and qualified revocable trusts with respect to decedents who died after the date that section 1307 of the Tax Reform Act of 1997 became effective but before December 28, 1999, the IRS will accept any reasonable interpretation of the separate share provisions, including those provisions provided in 1999-11 I.R.B. 41 (see § 601.601(d)(2)(ii)(b) of this chapter). For trusts other than qualified revocable trusts, § 1.663(c)-2 is applicable for taxable years of such trusts beginning after December 28, 1999. [Reg. § 1.663(c)-6.]

☐ [T.D. 8849, 12-27-99 (corrected 3-27-2000).]

[Reg. § 1.664-1]

§ 1.664-1. Charitable remainder trusts.—(a) *In general.*—(1) *Introduction.* (i) *General description of a charitable remainder trust.* Generally, a charitable remainder trust is a trust which provides for a specified distribution, at least annually, to one or more beneficiaries, at least one of which is not a charity, for life or for a term of years, with an irrevocable remainder interest to be held for the benefit of, or paid over to, charity. The specified distribution to be paid at least annually must be a sum certain which is not less than 5 percent of the initial net fair market value of all property placed in trust (in the case of a charitable remainder annuity trust) or a fixed percentage which is not less than 5 percent of the net fair market value of the trust assets, valued annually (in the case of a charitable remainder unitrust). A trust created after July 31, 1969, which is a charitable remainder trust is exempt from all of the taxes imposed by subtitle A of the Code for any taxable year of the trust except a taxable year in which it has unrelated business taxable income.

(ii) *Scope.* This section provides definitions, general rules governing the creation and administration of a charitable remainder trust, and rules governing the taxation of the trust and its beneficiaries. For the application of certain foundation rules to charitable remainder trusts, see paragraph (b) of this section. If the trust has unrelated business taxable income, see paragraph (c) of this section. For the treatment of distributions to recipients, see paragraph (d) of this section. For the treatment of distributions to charity, see paragraph (e) of this section. For the time limitations for amendment of governing instruments, see paragraph (f) of this section. For transitional rules under which particular requirements are inapplicable to certain trusts, see paragraph (g) of this section. Section 1.664-2 provides rules relating solely to a charitable remainder annuity trust. Section 1.664-3 provides rules relating solely to a charitable remainder unitrust. Section 1.664-4 provides rules governing the calculation of the fair market value of the remainder interest in a charitable remainder unitrust. For rules relating to the filing of returns for a charitable remainder trust, see paragraph (a)(6) of § 1.6012-3 and section 6034 and the regulations thereunder.

(iii) *Definitions.* As used in this section and §§ 1.664-2, 1.664-3, and 1.664-4:

(a) *Charitable remainder trust.* The term "charitable remainder trust" means a trust with respect to which a deduction is allowable under section 170, 2055, 2106, or 2522 and which meets the description of a charitable remainder annuity trust (as described in § 1.664-2) or a charitable remainder unitrust (as described in § 1.664-3).

(b) *Annuity amount.* The term "annuity amount" means the amount described in paragraph (a)(1) of § 1.664-2 which is payable, at least annually, to the beneficiary of a charitable remainder annuity trust.

(c) *Unitrust amount.* The term "unitrust amount" means the amount described in paragraph (a)(1) of § 1.664-3 which is payable, at least annually, to the beneficiary of a charitable remainder unitrust.

(d) *Recipient.* The term "recipient" means the beneficiary who receives the possession or beneficial enjoyment of the annuity amount or unitrust amount.

(e) *Governing instrument.* The term "governing instrument" has the same meaning as in section 508(e) and the regulations thereunder.

(2) *Requirement that the trust must be either a charitable remainder annuity trust or a charitable remainder unitrust.* A trust is a charitable remainder trust only if it is either a charitable remainder annuity trust in every respect or a charitable remainder unitrust in every respect. For example, a trust which provides for the payment each year to a noncharitable beneficiary of the greater of a sum certain or a fixed percentage of the annual value of the trust assets is not a charitable remainder trust inasmuch as the trust is neither a charitable remainder annuity trust (for the reason that the payment for the year may be a fixed percentage of the annual value of the trust assets which is not a "sum certain") nor a charitable remainder unitrust (for the reason that the payment for the year may be a sum certain

which is not a "fixed percentage" of the annual value of the trust assets).

(3) *Restrictions on investments.* A trust is not a charitable remainder trust if the provisions of the trust include a provision which restricts the trustee from investing the trust assets in a manner which could result in the annual realization of a reasonable amount of income or gain from the sale or disposition of trust assets. In the case of transactions with, or for the benefit of, a disqualified person, see section 4941(d) and the regulations thereunder for rules relating to the definition of self-dealing.

(4) *Requirement that trust must meet definition of and function exclusively as a charitable remainder trust from its creation.* In order for a trust to be a charitable remainder trust, it must meet the definition of and function exclusively as a charitable remainder trust from the creation of the trust. Solely for the purposes of section 664 and the regulations thereunder, the trust will be deemed to be created at the earliest time that neither the grantor nor any other person is treated as the owner of the entire trust under subpart E, part 1, subchapter J, chapter 1, subtitle A of the Code (relating to grantors and others treated as substantial owners), but in no event prior to the time property is first transferred to the trust. For purposes of the preceding sentence, neither the grantor nor his spouse shall be treated as the owner of the trust under such subpart E merely because the grantor or his spouse is named as a recipient. See examples 1 through 3 of subparagraph (6) of this paragraph for illustrations of the foregoing rule.

(5) *Rules applicable to testamentary transfers*—(i) *Deferral of annuity or unitrust amount.* Notwithstanding subparagraph (4) of this paragraph and §§ 1.664-2 and 1.664-3, for purposes of sections 2055 and 2106 a charitable remainder trust shall be deemed created at the date of death of the decedent (even though the trust is not funded until the end of a reasonable period of administration or settlement) if the obligation to pay the annuity or unitrust amount with respect to the property passing in trust at the death of the decedent begins as of the date of death of the decedent, even though the requirement to pay such amount is deferred in accordance with the rules provided in this subparagraph. If permitted by applicable local law or authorized by the provisions of the governing instrument, the requirement to pay such amount may be deferred until the end of the taxable year of the trust in which occurs the complete funding of the trust. Within a reasonable period after such time, the trust must pay (in the case of an underpayment) or must receive from the recipient (in the case of an overpayment) the difference between—

(*a*) Any annuity or unitrust amounts actually paid, plus interest on such amounts computed at the rate of interest specified in paragraph (a)(5)(iv) of this section, compounded annually, and

(*b*) The annuity or unitrust amounts payable, plus interest on such amounts computed at the rate of interest specified in paragraph (a)(5)(iv) of this section, compounded annually.

The amounts payable shall be retroactively determined by using the taxable year, valuation method, and valuation dates which are ultimately adopted by the charitable remainder trust. See subdivision (ii) of this subparagraph for rules relating to retroactive determination of the amount payable under a charitable remainder unitrust. See paragraph (d)(4) of this section for rules relating to the year of inclusion in the case of an underpayment to a recipient and the allowance of a deduction in the case of an overpayment to a recipient.

(ii) For purposes of retroactively determining the amount under subdivision (i)(*b*) of this subparagraph, the governing instrument of a charitable remainder unitrust may provide that the amount described in subdivision (i)(*b*) of this subparagraph with respect to property passing in trust at the death of the decedent for the period which begins on the date of death of the decedent and ends on the earlier of the date of death of the last recipient or the end of the taxable year of the trust in which occurs the complete funding of the trust shall be computed by multiplying—

(*a*) The sum of (*1*) the value, on the earlier of the date of death of the last recipient or the last day in such taxable year, of the property held in trust which is attributable to property passing to the trust at the death of the decedent, (*2*) any distributions in respect of unitrust amounts made by the trust or estate before such date, and (*3*) interest on such distributions computed at the rate of interest specified in paragraph (a)(5)(iv) of this section, compounded annually, from the date of distribution to such date by—

(*b*)(*1*) In the case of transfers made after November 30, 1983, for which the valuation date is before May 1, 1989, a factor equal to 1.000000 less the factor under the appropriate adjusted payout rate in Table D in § 1.664-4(e)(6) opposite the number of years in column 1 between the date of death of the decedent and the date of the earlier of the death of the last recipient or the last day of such taxable year.

Reg. § 1.664-1(a)(3)

(2) In the case of transfers for which the valuation date is after April 30, 1989, a factor equal to 1.000000 less the factor under the appropriate adjusted payout rate in Table D in § 1.664-4(e)(6) opposite the number of years in column 1 between the date of death of the decedent and the date of the earlier of the death of the last recipient or the last day of such taxable year. The appropriate adjusted payout rate is determined by using the appropriate Table F contained in § 1.664-4(e)(6) for the section 7520 rate for the month of the valuation date.

(3) If the number of years between the date of death and the date of the earlier of the death of the last recipient or the last day of such taxable year is between periods for which factors are provided, a linear interpolation must be made.

(iii) *Treatment of distributions.* The treatment of a distribution to a charitable remainder trust, or to a recipient in respect of an annuity or unitrust amount, paid, credited, or required to be distributed by an estate, or by a trust which is not a charitable remainder trust, shall be governed by the rules of subchapter J of chapter 1 of subtitle A of the Code other than section 664. In the case of a charitable remainder trust which is partially or fully funded during the period of administration of an estate or settlement of a trust (which is not a charitable remainder trust), the treatment of any amounts paid, credited, or required to be distributed by the charitable remainder trust shall be governed by the rules of section 664.

(iv) *Rate of interest.* The following rates of interest shall apply for purposes of paragraphs (a)(5)(i) through (ii) of this section:

(*a*) The section 7520 rate for the month in which the valuation date with respect to the transfer is (or one of the prior two months if elected under § 1.7520-2(b)) after April 30, 1989;

(*b*) 10 percent for instruments executed or amended (other than in the case of a reformation under section 2055(e)(3)) on or after August 9, 1984, and before May 1, 1989, and not subsequently amended;

(*c*) 6 percent or 10 percent for instruments executed or amended (other than in the case of a reformation under section 2055(e)(3)) after October 24, 1983, and before August 9, 1984; and

(*d*) 6 percent for instruments executed before October 25, 1983, and not subsequently amended (other than in the case of a reformation under section 2055(e)(3)).

(6) *Examples.* The application of the rules in paragraphs (a)(4) and (a)(5) of this section require the use of actuarial factors contained in §§ 1.664-4(e) and 1.664-4A(d) and (e) and may be illustrated by use of the following examples:

Example (1). On September 19, 1971, H transfers property to a trust over which he retains an inter vivos power of revocation. The trust is to pay W 5 percent of the value of the trust assets, valued annually, for her life, remainder to charity. The trust would satisfy all of the requirements of section 664 if it were irrevocable. For purposes of section 664, the trust is not deemed created in 1971 because H is treated as the owner of the entire trust under subpart E. On May 26, 1975, H predeceases W at which time the trust becomes irrevocable. For purposes of section 664, the trust is deemed created on May 26, 1975, because that is the earliest date on which H is not treated as the owner of the entire trust under subpart E. The trust becomes a charitable remainder trust on May 26, 1975, because it meets the definition of a charitable remainder trust from its creation.

Example (2). The facts are the same as in example (1), except that H retains the inter vivos power to revoke only one-half of the trust. For purposes of section 664, the trust is deemed created on September 19, 1971, because on that date the grantor is not treated as the owner of the entire trust under subpart E. Consequently, a charitable deduction is not allowable either at the creation of the trust or at H's death because the trust does not meet the definition of a charitable remainder trust from the date of its creation. The trust does not meet the definition of a charitable remainder trust from the date of its creation because the trust is subject to a partial power to revoke on such date.

Example (3). The facts are the same as in example (1), except that the residue of H's estate is to be paid to the trust and the trust is required to pay H's debts. The trust is not a charitable remainder trust at H's death because it does not function exclusively as a charitable remainder trust from the date of its creation which, in this case, is the date it becomes irrevocable.

Example (4). (i) In 1971, H transfers property to Trust A over which he retains an inter vivos power of revocation. Trust A, which is not a charitable remainder trust, is to provide income or corpus to W until the death of H. Upon H's death the trust is required by its governing instrument to pay the debts and administration expenses of H's estate, and then to terminate and distribute all of the remaining assets to a separate Trust B which meets the definition of a charitable remainder annuity trust.

(ii) Trust B will be charitable remainder trust from the date of its funding because it will

Reg. § 1.664-1(a)(6)

function exclusively as a charitable remainder trust from its creation. For purposes of section 2055, Trust B will be deemed created at H's death if the obligation to pay the annuity amount begins on the date of H's death. For purposes of section 664, Trust B becomes a charitable remainder trust as soon as it is partially or completely funded. Consequently, unless Trust B has unrelated business taxable income, the income of the trust is exempt from all taxes imposed by subtitle A of the Code, and any distributions by the trust, even before it is completely funded, are governed by the rules of section 664. Any distributions made by Trust A, including distributions to a recipient in respect of annuity amounts, are governed by the rules of subchapter J, chapter 1, subtitle A of the Code other than section 664.

Example (5). In 1973, H dies testate leaving the net residue of his estate (after payment by the estate of all debts and administration expenses) to a trust which meets the definition of a charitable remainder unitrust. For purposes of section 2055, the trust is deemed created at H's death if the requirement to pay the unitrust amount begins on H's death and is a charitable remainder trust even though the estate is obligated to pay debts and administration expenses. For purposes of section 664, the trust becomes a charitable remainder trust as soon as it is partially or completely funded. Consequently, unless the trust has unrelated business taxable income, the income of the trust is exempt from all taxes imposed by subtitle A of the Code, and any distributions by the trust, even before it is completely funded, are governed by the rules of section 664. Any distributions made by H's estate, including distributions to a recipient in respect of unitrust amounts, are governed by the rules of subchapter J, chapter 1, subtitle A of the Code other than section 664.

Example (6). (i) On January 1, 1974, H dies testate leaving the residue of his estate to a charitable remainder unitrust. The governing instrument provides that, beginning at H's death, the trustee is to make annual payments to W, on December 31 of each year of 5 percent of the net fair market value of the trust assets, valued as of December 31 of each year, for W's life and to pay the remainder to charity at the death of W. The governing instrument also provides that the actual payment of the unitrust amount need not be made until the end of the taxable year of the trust in which occurs the complete funding of the trust. The governing instrument also provides that the amount payable with respect to the period between the date of death and the end of such taxable year shall be computed under the special method provided in subparagraph (5)(ii) of this paragraph. The governing instrument provides that, within a reasonable period after the end of the taxable year of the trust in which occurs the complete funding of the trust, the trustee shall pay (in the case of an underpayment) or shall receive from the recipient (in the case of an overpayment) the difference between the unitrust amounts paid (plus interest at 6 percentage compounded annually) and the amount computed under the special method. The trust is completely funded on September 20, 1976. No amounts were paid before June 30, 1977. The trust adopts a fiscal year of July 1 to June 30. The net fair market value of the trust assets on June 30, 1977, is $100,000.

(ii) Because no amounts were paid prior to the end of the taxable year in which the trust was completely funded, the amount payable at the end of such taxable year is equal to the net fair market value of the trust assets on the last day of such taxable year (June 30, 1977) multiplied by a factor equal to 1.0 minus the factor in Table D corresponding to the number of years in the period between the date of death and the end of such taxable year. The adjusted payout rate (determined under § 1.664-4A(c)) is 5 percent. Because the last day of the taxable year in which the trust is completely funded is June 30, 1977, there are 3-181/365 years in such period. Because there is no factor given in Table D for such period, a linear interpolation must be made:

1.0 minus .814506 (factor at 5 percent for 4 years).............................	.185494
1.0 minus .857375 (factor at 5 percent for 3 years).............................	.142625
Difference...............	.042869

$$\frac{181}{365} = \frac{X}{.042869}$$
$$X = .021258$$

1.0 minus .857375 (factor at 5 percent for 3 years).............................	.142625
Plus: X................................	.021258
Interpolated factor.........	.163883

Thus, the amount payable for the period from January 1, 1974, to June 30, 1977, is $16,388.30 ($100,000 × .163883). Thereafter, the trust assets must be valued on December 31 of each year and 5 percent of such value paid annually to W for her life.

(7) *Valuation of unmarketable assets*—(i) *In general.* If unmarketable assets are transferred to or held by a trust, the trust will not be a trust with respect to which a deduction is available under section 170, 2055, 2106, or 2522, or will be treated as failing to function exclusively as a

Reg. § 1.664-1(a)(7)

charitable remainder trust unless, whenever the trust is required to value such assets, the valuation is—

(a) Performed exclusively by an independent trustee; or

(b) Determined by a *current qualified appraisal*, as defined in § 1.170A-13(c)(3), from a *qualified appraiser*, as defined in § 1.170A-13(c)(5).

(ii) *Unmarketable assets.* Unmarketable assets are assets that are not cash, cash equivalents, or other assets that can be readily sold or exchanged for cash or cash equivalents. For example, unmarketable assets include real property, closely-held stock, and an unregistered security for which there is no available exemption permitting public sale.

(iii) *Independent trustee.* An independent trustee is a person who is not the grantor of the trust, a noncharitable beneficiary, or a related or subordinate party to the grantor, the grantor's spouse, or a noncharitable beneficiary (within the meaning of section 672(c) and the applicable regulations).

(b) *Application of certain foundation rules to charitable remainder trusts.* See section 4947(a)(2) and section 4947(b)(3)(B) and the regulations thereunder for the application to charitable remainder trusts of certain provisions relating to private foundations. See section 508(e) for rules relating to required provisions in governing instruments prohibiting certain activities specified in section 4947(a)(2).

(c) *Taxation of nonexempt charitable remainder trusts.* If the charitable remainder trust has any unrelated business taxable income (within the meaning of section 512 and the regulations thereunder, determined as if part III, subchapter F, chapter 1, subtitle A of the Code applied to such trust) for any taxable year, the trust is subject to all of the taxes imposed by subtitle A of the Code for such taxable year. For taxable years beginning after December 31, 1969, unrelated business taxable income includes debt-financed income. The taxes imposed by subtitle A of the Code upon a nonexempt charitable remainder trust shall be computed under the rules prescribed by subparts A and C, part 1, subchapter J, chapter 1, subtitle A of the Code for trusts which may accumulate income or which distribute corpus. The provisions of subpart E, part 1 of such subchapter J are not applicable with respect to a nonexempt charitable remainder trust. The application of the above rules may be illustrated by the following example:

Example. In 1975, a charitable remainder trust which has a calendar year as its taxable year has $1,000 of ordinary income, including $100 of unrelated business taxable income, and no deductions other than under sections 642(b) and 661(a). The trust is required to pay out $700 for 1975 to a noncharitable recipient. Because the trust has some unrelated business taxable income in 1975, it is not exempt for such year. Consequently, the trust is taxable on all of its income as a complex trust. Under section 661(a) of the Code, the trust is allowed a deduction of $700. Under section 642(b) of the Code, the trust is allowed a deduction of $100. Consequently, the taxable income of the trust for 1975 is $200 ($1,000 − $700 − $100).

(d) *Treatment of annual distributions to recipients*—(1) *Character of distributions*—(i) *Order of distributions.* Annuity and unitrust amounts shall be treated as having the following characteristics in the hands of the recipients (whether or not the trust is exempt) without credit for any taxes which are imposed by subtitle A of the Code on the trust:

(a) *Ordinary income.* First, as ordinary income to the extent of the sum of the trust's ordinary income for the taxable year of the trust and its undistributed ordinary income for prior years. An ordinary loss for the current year shall be used to reduce undistributed ordinary income for prior years and any excess shall be carried forward indefinitely to reduce ordinary income for future years. For purposes of this section, the amount of current and prior years' income shall be computed without regard to the deduction for net operating losses provided by sections 172 or 642(d).

(b) *Capital gain.* Second, as capital gain to the extent of the trust's undistributed capital gains. Undistributed capital gains of the trust are determined on a cumulative net basis under the rules of this subdivision without regard to the provisions of section 1212.

(*1*) *Long and short-term capital gains.* If, in any taxable year of the trust, the trust has both undistributed short-term capital gain and undistributed long-term capital gain, then the short-term capital gain shall be deemed distributed prior to any long-term capital gain.

(*2*) *Capital losses in excess of capital gains.* If the trust has for any taxable year capital losses in excess of capital gains, any excess of the net short-term capital loss over the net long-term capital gain for such year shall be a short-term capital loss in the succeeding taxable year and any excess of the net long-term capital loss over the net short-term capital gain for such year shall be a long-term capital loss in the succeeding taxable year.

Reg. § 1.664-1(d)(1)

(3) *Capital gains in excess of capital losses.* If the trust has for any taxable year capital gains in excess of capital losses, any excess of the net short-term capital gain over the net long-term capital loss for such year shall be, to the extent not deemed distributed, a short-term capital gain in the succeeding taxable year and any excess of the net long-term capital gain over the net short-term capital loss for such year shall be, to the extent not deemed distributed, a long-term capital gain in the succeeding taxable year.

The application of the rules in this subdivision (*b*) may be illustrated by the following example:

Example: (i) The X Trust is a charitable remainder trust created on January 1, 1975, and has the calendar year as its taxable year. During the years indicated, it has the following capital transactions:

1975:	Long-term capital loss	$10
	Short-term capital gain	$ 5
1976:	Short-term capital gain	$20
	Short-term capital loss	$ 5
1977:	Long-term capital gain	$15

Distributions for 1975 and 1976 were not in excess of current and accumulated ordinary income for those years. In 1977, distributions exceeded current and accumulated ordinary income by $5.

(ii) The treatment of the 1975 and 1976 transactions is as follows:

1975:	Long-term capital loss recognized	$(10)
	Short-term capital gain recognized	5
	Net long-term capital loss carried forward to 1976	$(5)
1976:	Short-term capital gain recognized	$ 20
	Short-term capital loss recognized	(5)
	Long-term capital loss carried forward from 1975	(5)
	Net short-term capital gain carried forward to 1977	$ 10
1977:	Long-term capital gain recognized	$ 15
	Net short-term capital gain carried forward from 1976	$ 10

(iii) In 1977, the trust has long-term capital gain of $15 and short-term capital gain of $10. If the trust has both short-term capital gain and long-term capital gain for the same taxable year, the short-term capital gain is deemed distributed prior to the long-term capital gain. Therefore, the distribution of $5 in 1977 is deemed to be short-term capital gain. The undistributed net short-term capital gain of $5 is a short-term capital gain carried forward to 1978. The undistributed net long-term capital gain of $15 is a long-term capital gain carried forward to 1978.

(c) *Other income.* Third, as other income (including income excluded under part III, subchapter B, chapter 1, subtitle A of the Code) to the extent of the sum of the trust's other income for the taxable year and its undistributed other income for prior years. A loss in this category for the current year shall be used to reduce undistributed income in such category for prior years and any excess shall be carried forward indefinitely to reduce such income for future years.

(d) *Corpus.* Finally, as a distribution of trust corpus. For purposes of this section, the term "corpus" means the net fair market value of the trust assets less the total undistributed income (but not loss) in each of the above categories.

(ii) *Rules relating to character of distributions.* The determination of the character of amounts distributed shall be made as of the end of the taxable year of the trust. Amounts treated as paid from one of the categories of income described in (*a*), (*b*) or (*c*) of subdivision (i) of this subparagraph shall be treated as consisting of the same proportion of each class of items included in such category as the total of the current and accumulated income of each class of items bears to the total of the current and accumulated income for that category. A loss in one of such categories may not be used to reduce a gain in any other category. The provisions of subparts D and E, part 1, subchapter J, chapter 1, subtitle A of the Code are not applicable with respect to a charitable remainder trust (regardless of whether the trust is exempt).

(iii) *Application of section 643(a)(7).* For application of the anti-abuse rule of section 643(a)(7) to distributions from charitable remainder trusts, see § 1.643(a)-8.

(iv) *Example.* The following example illustrates the application of this paragraph (d)(1):

Example. (i) X is a charitable remainder unitrust described in section 664(d)(2) and (3). The annual unitrust amount is the lesser of the amount of trust income, as defined in § 1.664-3(a)(1)(i)(*b*), or six percent of the net fair market value of the trust assets valued annually. The net fair market value of the trust assets on the valuation date in 1996 is $150,000. During 1996, X has $7,500 of income after allocating all expenses. All of X's income for 1996 is tax-exempt income. At the end of 1996, X's ordinary income for the current taxable year and undistributed ordinary income for prior years are both zero; X's capital gain for the current taxable year is zero and undistributed capital gain for prior years is $30,000; and X's tax-exempt income for the cur-

Reg. § 1.664-1(d)(1)

rent year is $7,500 and undistributed tax-exempt income for prior years is $2,500.

(ii) Because the trust income of $7,500 is less than the fixed percentage amount of $9,000, the unitrust amount for 1996 is $7,500. The character of that amount in the hands of the recipient of the unitrust amount is determined under section 664(b). Because the unitrust amount is less than X's undistributed capital gain income, the recipient of the unitrust amount treats the distribution of $7,500 as capital gain. At the beginning of 1997, X's undistributed capital gain for prior years is reduced to $22,500, and X's undistributed tax-exempt income is increased to $10,000.

(2) *Allocation of deductions.* Items of deduction of the trust for a taxable year of the trust which are deductible in determining taxable income (other than the deductions permitted by sections 642(b), 642(c), 661, and 1202) which are directly attributable to one or more classes of items within a category of income or to corpus (determined under subparagraph (1)(i) of this paragraph) shall be allocated to such classes of items or to corpus. All other allowable deductions for such taxable year which are not directly attributable to one or more classes of items within a category of income or to corpus (other than the deductions permitted by sections 642(b), 642(c), 661, and 1202) shall be allocated among the classes of items within the category (excluding classes of items with net losses) on the basis of the gross income of such classes for such taxable year reduced by the deductions allocated thereto under the first sentence of this subparagraph, but in no event shall the amount of expenses allocated to any class of items exceed such income of such class for the taxable year. Items of deduction which are not allocable under the above two sentences (other than the deductions permitted by sections 642(b), 642(c), 661, and 1202) may be allocated in any manner. All taxes imposed by subtitle A of the Code for which the trust is liable because it has unrelated business taxable income and all taxes imposed by chapter 42 of the Code shall be allocated to corpus. Any expense which is not deductible in determining taxable income and which is not allocable to any class of items described in subparagraph (1)(i)(c) of this paragraph shall be allocated to corpus. The deductions allowable to a trust under sections 642(b), 642(c), 661, and 1202 are not allowed in determining the amount or character of any class of items within a category of income or to corpus in the categories described in subparagraph (1) of this paragraph.

(3) *Allocation of income among recipients.* If there are two or more recipients, each will be treated as receiving his pro rata portion of the categories of income and corpus. The application of this rule may be illustrated by the following example:

Example. X transfers $40,000 to a charitable remainder annuity trust which is to pay $3,000 per year to X and $2,000 per year to Y for a term of 5 years. During the first taxable year the trust has $3,000 of ordinary income, $500 of capital gain, and $500 of tax exempt income after allocation of all expenses. X is treated as receiving ordinary income of $1,800 ($3,000/$5,000 × $3,000), capital gain of $300 ($3,000/$5,000 × $500), tax exempt income of $300 ($3,000/$5,000 × $500), and corpus of $600 ($3,000/$5,000 × [$5,000 − $4,000]). Y is treated as receiving ordinary income of $1,200 ($2,000/$5,000 × $3,000), capital gain of $200 ($2,000/$5,000 × $500), tax exempt income of $200 ($2,000/$5,000 × $500), and corpus of $400 ($2,000/$5,000 × [$5,000 − $4,000]).

(4) *Year of inclusion*—(i) *General rule.* To the extent required by this paragraph, the annuity or unitrust amount is includible in the recipient's gross income for the taxable year in which the annuity or unitrust amount is required to be distributed even though the annuity or unitrust amount is not distributed until after the close of the taxable year of the trust. If a recipient has a different taxable year (as defined in section 441 or 442) from the taxable year of the trust, the amount he is required to include in gross income to the extent required by this paragraph shall be included in his taxable year in which or with which ends the taxable year of the trust in which such amount is required to be distributed.

(ii) *Payments resulting from incorrect valuations.* Notwithstanding subdivision (i) of this subparagraph, any payments which are made or required to be distributed by a charitable remainder trust pursuant to paragraph (a)(5) of this section, under paragraph (f)(3) of this section because of an amendment to the governing instrument, or under paragraphs (a)(1) of §§ 1.664-2 and 1.664-3 because of an incorrect valuation, shall, to the extent required by this paragraph, be included in the gross income of the recipient in his taxable year in which or with which ends the taxable year of the trust in which the amount is paid, credited, or required to be distributed. For rules relating to required adjustments of underpayments and overpayments of the annuity or unitrust amounts in respect to payments made prior to the amendment of a governing instrument, see paragraph (f)(3) of this section. There is allowable to a recipient a deduction from gross income for any amounts repaid to the trust because of an overpayment during the reasonable

Reg. § 1.664-1(d)(4)

period of administration or settlement or until the trust is fully funded, because of an amendment, or because of an incorrect valuation, to the extent such amounts were included in his gross income. See section 1341 and the regulations thereunder for rules relating to the computation of tax where a taxpayer restores substantial amounts held under a claim of right.

(iii) *Rules applicable to year of recipient's death.* If the taxable year of the trust does not end with or within the last taxable year of the recipient because of the recipient's death, the extent to which the annuity or unitrust amount required to be distributed to him is included in the gross income of the recipient for his last taxable year, or in the gross income of his estate, is determined by making the computations required under this paragraph for the taxable year of the trust in which his last taxable year ends. (The last sentence of subdivision (i) of this subparagraph does not apply to such amounts.) The gross income for the last taxable year of a recipient on the cash basis includes (to the extent required by this paragraph) amounts actually distributed to the recipient before his death. Amounts required to be distributed which are distributed to his estate are included (to the extent required by this paragraph) in the gross income of the estate as income in respect of a decedent under section 691.

(5) *Distributions in kind.* The annuity or unitrust amount may be paid in cash or in other property. In the case of a distribution made in other property, the amount paid, credited, or required to be distributed shall be considered as an amount realized by the trust from the sale or other disposition of property. The basis of the property in the hands of the recipient is its fair market value at the time it was paid, credited, or required to be distributed. The application of these rules may be illustrated by the following example:

Example. On January 1, 1971, X creates a charitable remainder annuity trust, whose taxable year is the calendar year, under which X is to receive $5,000 per year. During 1971, the trust receives $500 ordinary income. On December 31, 1971, the trust distributed cash of $500 and a capital asset of the trust having a fair market value of $4,500 and a basis of $2,200. The trust is deemed to have realized a capital gain of $2,300. X treats the distribution of $5,000 as being ordinary income of $500, capital gain of $2,300 and trust corpus of $2,200. The basis of the distributed property is $4,500 in the hands of X.

(e) *Other distributions*—(1) *Character of distributions.* An amount distributed by the trust to an organization described in section 170(c) other than the annuity or unitrust amount shall be considered as a distribution of corpus and of those categories of income specified in paragraph (d)(1) of this section in an order inverse to that prescribed in such paragraph. The character of such amounts shall be determined as of the end of the taxable year of the trust in which the distribution is made after the character of the annuity or unitrust amount has been determined.

(2) *Distributions in kind.* In the case of a distribution of an amount to which subparagraph (1) of this paragraph applies, no gain or loss is realized by the trust by reason of a distribution in kind unless such distribution is in satisfaction of a right to receive a distribution of a specific dollar amount or in specific property other than that distributed.

(f) *Effective date*—(1) *General rule.* The provisions of this section are effective with respect to transfers in trust made after July 31, 1969. Any trust created (within the meaning of applicable local law) prior to August 1, 1969, is not a charitable remainder trust even if it otherwise satisfies the definition of a charitable remainder trust.

(2) *Transfers to pre-1970 trusts.* Property transferred to a trust created (within the meaning of applicable local law) before August 1, 1969, whose governing instrument provides that an organization described in section 170(c) receives an irrevocable remainder interest in such trust, shall, for purposes of subparagraphs (1) and (3) of this paragraph, be deemed transferred to a trust created on the date of such transfer provided that the transfer occurs after July 31, 1969, and prior to October 18, 1971, and the transferred property and any undistributed income therefrom is severed and placed in a separate trust before December 31, 1972, or if later, on or before the 30th day after the date on which any judicial proceedings begun before December 31, 1972, which are required to sever such property, become final.

(3) *Amendment of post-1969 trusts.* A trust created (within the meaning of applicable local law) subsequent to July 31, 1969, and prior to December 31, 1972, which is not a charitable remainder trust at the date of its creation, may be treated as a charitable remainder trust from the date it would be deemed created under § 1.664-1(a)(4) and (5)(i) for all purposes provided that all the following requirements are met:

(i) At the time of the creation of the trust, the governing instrument provides that an organization described in section 170(c) receives an irrevocable remainder interest in such trust.

(ii) The governing instrument of the trust is amended so that the trust will meet the definition of a charitable remainder trust and, if appli-

Reg. § 1.664-1(d)(5)

cable, will meet the requirement of paragraph (a)(5)(i) of this section that obligation to make payment of the annuity or unitrust amount with respect to property passing at death begin as of the date of death, before December 31, 1972, or if later, on or before the 30th day after the date on which any judicial proceedings which are begun before December 31, 1972, and which are required to amend its governing instrument, become final. In the case of a trust created (within the meaning of applicable local law) subsequent to July 31, 1969, and prior to December 31, 1972, the provisions of section 508(d)(2)(A) shall not apply if the governing instrument of the trust is amended so as to comply with the requirements of section 508(e) before December 31, 1972, or if later, on or before the 30th day after the date on which any judicial proceedings which are begun before December 31, 1972, and which are required to amend its governing instrument, become final. Notwithstanding the provisions of paragraphs (a)(3) and (a)(4) of §§ 1.664-2 and 1.664-3, the governing instrument may grant to the trustee a power to amend the governing instrument for the sole purpose of complying with the requirements of this section and § 1.664-2 or § 1.664-3 provided that at the creation of the trust, the governing instrument (a) provides for the payment of a unitrust amount described in § 1.664-3(a)(1)(i) or an annuity which meets the requirements of paragraph (a)(2) of §§ 1.664-2 or 1.664-3, (b) designates the recipients of the trust and the period for which the amount described in (a) of this subdivision (ii) is to be paid, and (c) provides that an organization described in section 170(c) receives an irrevocable remainder interest in such trust. The mere granting of such a power is not sufficient to meet the requirements of this subparagraph that the governing instrument be amended in the manner and within the time limitations of this subparagraph.

(iii)(a) Where the amount of the distributions which would have been made by the trust to a recipient if the amended provisions of such trust had been in effect from the time of creation of such trust exceeds the amount of the distributions made by the trust prior to its amendment, the trust pays an amount equal to such excess to the recipient.

(b) Where the amount of distributions made to the recipient prior to the amendment of the trust exceeds the amount of the distributions which would have been made by such trust if the amended provisions of such trust had been in effect from the time of creation of such trust, such excess is repaid to the trust by the recipient.

See paragraph (d)(4) of this section for rules relating to the year of inclusion in the case of an underpayment to a recipient and the allowance of a deduction in the case of an overpayment to a recipient. A deduction for a transfer to a charitable remainder trust shall not be allowed until the requirements of this paragraph are met and then only if the deduction is claimed on a timely-filed return (including extensions) or on a claim for refund filed within the period of limitations prescribed by section 6511(a).

(4) *Valuation of unmarketable assets.* The rules contained in paragraph (a)(7) of this section are applicable for trusts created on or after December 10, 1998. A trust in existence as of December 10, 1998, whose governing instrument requires that an independent trustee value the trust's unmarketable assets may be amended or reformed to permit a valuation method that satisfies the requirements of paragraph (a)(7) of this section for taxable years beginning on or after December 10, 1998.

(g) *Transitional effective date.* Notwithstanding any other provision of this section, § 1.664-2, or § 1.664-3, the requirement of paragraph (a)(5)(i) of this section that interest accrue on overpayments and underpayments, the requirement of paragraph (a)(5)(ii) of this section that the unitrust amount accruing under the formula provided therein cease with the death of the last recipient, and the requirement that the governing instrument of the trust contain the provisions specified in paragraph (a)(1)(iv) of § 1.664-2 (relating to computation of the annuity amount in certain circumstances), paragraph (a)(1)(v) of § 1.664-3 (relating to computation of the unitrust amount in certain circumstances), paragraphs (b) of §§ 1.664-2 and 1.664-3 (relating to additional contributions), and paragraph (a)(1)(iii) of § 1.664-3 (relating to incorrect valuations), paragraphs (a)(6)(iv) of §§ 1.664-2 and 1.664-3 (relating to alternative remaindermen) shall not apply to:

(1) A will executed on or before December 31, 1972, if:

(i) The testator dies before December 31, 1975, without having republished the will after December 31, 1972 by codicil or otherwise,

(ii) The testator at no time after December 31, 1972, had the right to change the provisions of the will which pertain to the trust, or

(iii) The will is not republished by codicil or otherwise before December 31, 1975, and the testator is on such date and at all times thereafter under a mental disability to republish the will by codicil or otherwise, or

Reg. § 1.664-1(g)(1)

(2) A trust executed on or before December 31, 1972, if:

(i) The grantor dies before December 31, 1975, without having amended the trust after December 31, 1972,

(ii) The trust is irrevocable on December 31, 1972, or

(iii) The trust is not amended before December 31, 1975, and the grantor is on such date and at all times thereafter under a mental disability to change the terms of the trust. [Reg. § 1.664-1.]

☐ [T.D. 7202, 8-22-72. Amended by T.D. 7955, 5-10-84; T.D. 8540, 6-9-94; T.D. 8791, 12-9-98; T.D. 8819, 4-29-99; T.D. 8886, 6-9-2000 and T.D. 8926, 1-4-2001.]

[Reg. § 8.1]

§ 8.1. Charitable remainder trusts.—(a) *Certain wills and trusts in existence on September 21, 1974.* In the case of a will executed before September 21, 1974, or a trust created (within the meaning of applicable local law) after July 31, 1969, and before September 21, 1974, which is amended pursuant to section 2055(e)(3) and § 24.1 of this chapter (Temporary Estate Tax Regulations), a charitable remainder trust resulting from such amendment will be treated as a charitable remainder trust from the date it would be deemed created under § 1.664-1(a)(4) and (5) of this chapter (Income Tax Regulations), whether or not such date is after September 20, 1974.

(b) *Certain transfers to trusts created before August 1, 1969.* Property transferred to a trust created (within the meaning of applicable local law) before August 1, 1969, whose governing instrument provides that an organization described in section 170(c) receives an irrevocable remainder interest in such trust shall be deemed transferred to a trust created on the date of such transfer, provided that the transfer occurs after July 31, 1969 and prior to October 18, 1971, and pursuant to an amendment provided in § 24.1 of this chapter (Temporary Estate Tax Regulations), the transferred property and any undistributed income therefrom is severed and placed in a separate trust as of the date of the amendment. [Temporary Reg. § 8.1.]

☐ [T.D. 7393, 12-16-75.]

[Reg. § 1.664-2]

§ 1.664-2. Charitable remainder annuity trust.—(a) *Description.* A charitable remainder annuity trust is a trust which complies with the applicable provisions of § 1.664-1 and meets all of the following requirements:

(1) *Required payment of annuity amount*—(i) *Payment of sum certain at least annually.* The governing instrument provides that the trust will pay a sum certain not less often than annually to a person or persons described in paragraph (a)(3) of this section for each taxable year of the period specified in paragraph (a)(5) of this section.

(a) *General rule applicable to all trusts.* A trust will not be deemed to have engaged in an act of self-dealing (within the meaning of section 4941), to have unrelated debt-financed income (within the meaning of section 514), to have received an additional contribution (within the meaning of paragraph (b) of this section), or to have failed to function exclusively as a charitable remainder trust (within the meaning of § 1.664-1(a)(4)) merely because the annuity amount is paid after the close of the taxable year if such payment is made within a reasonable time after the close of such taxable year and the entire annuity amount in the hands of the recipient is characterized only as income from the categories described in section 664(b)(1), (2), or (3), except to the extent it is characterized as corpus described in section 664(b)(4) because—

(*1*) The trust pays the annuity amount by distributing property (other than cash) that it owned at the close of the taxable year to pay the annuity amount, and the trustee elects to treat any income generated by the distribution as occurring on the last day of the taxable year in which the annuity amount is due;

(*2*) The trust pays the annuity amount by distributing cash that was contributed to the trust (with respect to which a deduction was allowable under section 170, 2055, 2106, or 2522); or

(*3*) The trust pays the annuity amount by distributing cash received as a return of basis in any asset that was contributed to the trust (with respect to which a deduction was allowable under section 170, 2055, 2106, or 2522), and that is sold by the trust during the year for which the annuity amount is due.

(b) *Special rule for trusts created before December 10, 1998.* In addition, to the circumstances described in paragraph (a)(1)(i)(a) of this section, a trust created before December 10, 1998, will not be deemed to have engaged in an act of self-dealing (within the meaning of section 4941), to have unrelated debt-financed income (within the meaning of section 514), to have received an additional contribution (within the meaning of paragraph (b) of this section), or to have failed to function exclusively as a charitable remainder trust (within the meaning of § 1.664-1(a)(4)) merely because the annuity amount is paid after the close of the taxable year if such payment is made within a reasonable time after the close of such taxable year and the sum certain to be paid each year as the annuity amount is 15 percent or less of the initial net fair market value of the property irrevocably passing in trust as determined for federal tax purposes.

(c) *Reasonable time.* For this paragraph (a)(1)(i), a reasonable time will not ordinarily extend beyond the date by which the trustee is required to file Form 5227, "Split-Interest Trust Information Return," (including extensions) for the taxable year.

(d) *Example.* The following example illustrates the rules in paragraph (a)(1)(i)(a) of this section:

Example. X is a charitable remainder annuity trust described in section 664(d)(1) that was created after December 10, 1998. The prorated annuity amount payable from X for Year 1 is $100. The trustee does not pay the annuity amount to the recipient by the close of Year 1. At the end of Year 1, X has only $95 in the ordinary income category under section 664(b)(1) and no income in the capital gain or tax-exempt income categories under section 664(b)(2) or (3), respectively. By April 15 of Year 2, in addition to $95 in cash, the trustee distributes to the recipient of the annuity a capital asset with a $5 fair market value and a $2 adjusted basis to pay the $100 annuity amount due for Year 1. The trust owned the asset at the end of Year 1. Under § 1.664-1(d)(5), the distribution is treated as a sale by X, resulting in X recognizing a $3 capital gain. The trustee elects to treat the capital gain as occurring on the last day of Year 1. Under § 1.664-1(d)(1), the character of the annuity amount for Year 1 in the recipient's hands is $95 of ordinary income, $3 of capital gain income, and $2 of trust corpus. For Year 1, X satisfied paragraph (a)(1)(i)(a) of this section.

(e) *Effective date.* This paragraph (a)(1)(i) is applicable for taxable years ending after April 18, 1997. However, paragraphs (a)(1)(i)(a)(2) and (3) of this section apply only to distributions made on or after January 5, 2001.

(ii) *Definition of sum certain.* A sum certain is a stated dollar amount which is the same either as to each recipient or as to the total amount payable for each year of such period. For example, a provision for an amount which is the same every year to A until his death and concurrently an amount which is the same every year to B until his death, with the amount to each recipient to terminate at his death, would satisfy the above rule. Similarly, provision for an amount to A and B for their joint lives and then to the survivor would satisfy the above rule. In the case of a distribution to an organization described in section 170(c) at the death of a recipient or the expiration of a term of years, the governing instrument may provide for a reduction of the stated amount payable after such a distribution provided that:

(a) The reduced amount payable is the same either as to each recipient or as to the total amount payable for each year of the balance of such period, and

(b) The requirements of subparagraph (2)(ii) of this paragraph are met.

(iii) *Sum certain stated as a fraction or percentage.* The stated dollar amount may be expressed as a fraction or a percentage of the initial net fair market value of the property irrevocably passing in trust as finally determined for Federal tax purposes. If the stated dollar amount is so expressed and such market value is incorrectly determined by the fiduciary, the requirement of this subparagraph will be satisfied if the governing instrument provides that in such event the trust shall pay to the recipient (in the case of an undervaluation) or be repaid by the recipient (in the case of an overvaluation) an amount equal to the difference between the amount which the trust should have paid the recipient if the correct value were used and the amount which the trust actually paid the recipient. Such payments or repayments must be made within a reasonable period after the final determination of such value. Any payment due to a recipient by reason of such incorrect valuation shall be considered to be a payment required to be distributed at the time of such final determination for purposes of paragraph (d)(4)(ii) of § 1.664-1. See paragraph (d)(4) of § 1.664-1 for rules relating to the year of inclusion of such payments and the allowance of a deduction for such repayments. See paragraph (b) of this section for rules relating to future contributions. For rules relating to required adjustments for underpayments or overpayments of the amount described in this paragraph in respect of payments made during a reasonable period of administration, see paragraph (a)(5) of § 1.664-1. The application of the rule permitting the stated dollar amount to be expressed as a fraction or a percentage of the initial net fair market value of the property irrevocably passing in trust as finally determined for Federal tax purposes may be illustrated by the following example:

Example. The will of X provides for the transfer of one-half of his residuary estate to a charitable remainder annuity trust which is required to pay to W for life an annuity equal to 5 percent of the initial net fair market value of the interest passing in trust as finally determined for Federal tax purposes. The annuity is to be paid on December 31 of each year computed from the date of X's death. The will also provides that if such initial net fair market value is incorrectly determined, the trust shall pay to W, in the case of an undervaluation, or be repaid by W, in the case of an overvaluation, an amount equal to the difference between the amount which the trust should have paid if the correct value were used and the amount which the trust actually paid. X dies on March 1, 1971. The executor files an estate tax return showing the value of the residuary estate as $250,000 before reduction for taxes and expenses of $50,000. The executor paid to W $4,192 ([$250,000 − $50,000] × ½ × 5% × 306/365) on December 31, 1971. On January 1, 1972, the executor transfers one-half of the residue of the estate to the trust. The trust adopts the calendar year as its taxable year. The value of the residuary estate is finally determined for Federal tax purposes to be $240,000 ($290,000 − $50,000). Accordingly, the amount which the executor should have paid to W is $5,030 ([$290,000 − $50,000] × ½ × 5% × 306/365). Consequently, an additional amount of $838 ($5,030 − $4,192) must be paid to W within a reasonable period after the final determination of value for Federal tax purposes.

(iv) *Computation of annuity amount in certain circumstances*—(a) *Short taxable years.* The governing instrument provides that, in the case of a taxable year which is for a period of less than 12 months other than the taxable year in which occurs the end of the period specified in subparagraph (5) of this paragraph, the annuity amount determined under subdivision (i) of this subparagraph shall be the amount otherwise determined under that subdivision multiplied by a fraction the numerator of which is the number of days in the taxable year of the trust and the denominator of which is 365 (366 if February 29 is a day included in the numerator).

(b) *Last taxable year of period.* The governing instrument provides that, in the case of the taxable year in which occurs the end of the period specified in subparagraph (5) of this paragraph, the annuity amount which must be distributed under subdivision (i) of this subparagraph shall be the amount otherwise determined under that subdivision multiplied by a fraction the numerator of which is the number of days in the period beginning on the first day of such taxable year and ending on the last day of the period specified in subparagraph (5) of this paragraph and the denominator of which is 365 (366 if February 29 is a day included in the numerator). See subparagraph (5) of this paragraph for a special rule allowing termination of payment of the annuity amount with the regular payment next preceding the termination of the period specified therein.

(2) *Minimum annuity amount*—(i) *General rule.* The total amount payable under subparagraph (1) of this paragraph is not less than 5 percent of the initial net fair market value of the property placed in trust as finally determined for Federal tax purposes.

(ii) *Reduction of annuity amount in certain cases.* A trust will not fail to meet the requirements of this subparagraph by reason of the fact that it provides for a reduction of the stated amount payable upon the death of a recipient or the expiration of a term of years provided that:

(a) A distribution is made to an organization described in section 170(c) at the death of such recipient or the expiration of such term of years, and

(b) The total amounts payable each year under subparagraph (1) of this paragraph after such distribution are not less than a stated dollar amount which bears the same ratio to 5 percent of the initial net fair market value of the trust assets as the net fair market value of the trust assets immediately after such distribution bears to the net fair market value of the trust assets immediately before such distribution.

(iii) *Rule applicable to inter vivos trust which does not provide for payment of minimum annuity amount.* In the case where the grantor of an inter vivos trust underestimates in good faith the initial net fair market value of the property placed in trust as finally determined for Federal tax purposes and specifies a fixed dollar amount for the annuity which is less than 5 percent of the initial net fair market value of the property placed in trust as finally determined for Federal tax purposes, the trust will be deemed to have met the 5 percent requirement if the grantor or his representative consents, by appropriate agreement with the District Director, to accept an amount equal to 20 times the annuity as the fair market value of the property placed in trust for purposes of determining the appropriate charitable contributions deduction.

(3) *Permissible recipients*—(i) *General rule.* The amount described in subparagraph (1) of this paragraph is payable to or for the use of a named person or persons, at least one of which is not an organization described in section 170(c). If the amount described in subparagraph (1) of this paragraph is to be paid to an individual or individuals, all such individuals must be living at the time of the creation of the trust. A named person or persons may include members of a named class

Reg. § 1.664-2(a)(2)

provided that, in the case of a class which includes any individual, all such individuals must be alive and ascertainable at the time of the creation of the trust unless the period for which the annuity amount is to be paid to such class consists solely of a term of years. For example, in the case of a testamentary trust, the testator's will may provide that an amount shall be paid to his children living at his death.

(ii) *Power to alter amount paid to recipients.* A trust is not a charitable remainder annuity trust if any person has the power to alter the amount to be paid to any named person other than an organization described in section 170(c) if such power would cause any person to be treated as the owner of the trust, or any portion thereof, if subpart E, Part 1, subchapter J, chapter 1, subtitle A of the Code were applicable to such trust. See paragraph (a)(4) of this section for a rule permitting the retention by a grantor of a testamentary power to revoke or terminate the interest of any recipient other than an organization described in section 170(c). For example, the governing instrument may not grant the trustee the power to allocate the annuity among members of a class unless such power falls within one of the exceptions to section 674(a).

(4) *Other payments.* No amount other than the amount described in subparagraph (1) of this paragraph may be paid to or for the use of any person other than an organization described in section 170(c). An amount is not paid to or for the use of any person other than an organization described in section 170(c) if the amount is transferred for full and adequate consideration. The trust may not be subject to a power to invade, alter, amend, or revoke for the beneficial use of a person other than an organization described in section 170(c). Notwithstanding the preceding sentence, the grantor may retain the power exercisable only by will to revoke or terminate the interest of any recipient other than an organization described in section 170(c). The governing instrument may provide that any amount other than the amount described in subparagraph (1) of this paragraph shall be paid (or may be paid in the discretion of the trustee) to an organization described in section 170(c) provided that, in the case of distributions in kind, the adjusted basis of the property distributed is fairly representative of the adjusted basis of the property available for payment on the date of payment. For example, the governing instrument may provide that a portion of the trust assets may be distributed currently, or upon the death of one or more recipients, to an organization described in section 170(c).

(5) *Period of payment of annuity amount —* (i) *General rules.* The period for which an amount described in subparagraph (1) of this paragraph is payable begins with the first year of the charitable remainder trust and continues either for the life or lives of a named individual or individuals or for a term of years not to exceed 20 years. Only an individual or an organization described in section 170(c) may receive an amount for the life of an individual. If an individual receives an amount for his life, it must be solely for his life. Payment of the amount described in subparagraph (1) of this paragraph may terminate with the regular payment next preceding the termination of the period described in this subparagraph. The fact that the recipient may not receive such last payment shall not be taken into account for purposes of determining the present value of the remainder interest. In the case of an amount payable for a term of years, the length of the term of years shall be ascertainable with certainty at the time of the creation of the trust, except that the term may be terminated by the death of the recipient or by the grantor's exercise by will of a retained power to revoke or terminate the interest of any recipient other than an organization described in section 170(c). In any event, the period may not extend beyond either the life or lives of a named individual or individuals or a term of years not to exceed 20 years. For example, the governing instrument may not provide for the payment of an annuity amount to A for his life and then to B for a term of years because it is possible for the period to last longer than either the lives of recipients in being at the creation of the trust or a term of years not to exceed 20 years. On the other hand, the governing instrument may provide for the payment of an annuity amount to A for his life and then to B for his life or a term of years (not to exceed 20 years), whichever is shorter (but not longer), if both A and B are in being at the creation of the trust because it is not possible for the period to last longer than the lives of recipients in being at the creation of the trust.

(ii) *Relationship to 5 percent requirement.* The 5 percent requirement provided in subparagraph (2) of this paragraph must be met until the termination of all of the payments described in subparagraph (1) of this paragraph. For example, the following provisions would satisfy the above rules:

(*a*) An amount equal to at least 5 percent of the initial net fair market value of the property placed in trust to A and B for their joint lives and then to the survivor for his life;

(*b*) An amount equal to at least 5 percent of the initial net fair market value of the

Reg. § 1.664-2(a)(5)

property placed in trust to A for life or for a term of years not longer than 20 years, whichever is longer (or shorter);

(c) An amount equal to at least 5 percent of the initial net fair market value of the property placed in trust to A for a term of years not longer than 20 years and then to B for life (provided B was living at the date of creation of the trust);

(d) An amount to A for his life and concurrently an amount to B for his life (the amount to each recipient to terminate at his death) if the amount given to each individual is not less than 5 percent of the initial net fair market value of the property placed in trust; or

(e) An amount to A for his life and concurrently an equal amount to B for his life, and at the death of the first to die, the trust to distribute one-half of the then value of its assets to an organization described in section 170(c), if the total of the amounts given to A and B is not less than 5 percent of the initial net fair market value of the property placed in trust.

(6) *Permissible Remaindermen*—(i) *General rule.* At the end of the period specified in subparagraph (5) of this paragraph the entire corpus of the trust is required to be irrevocably transferred, in whole or in part, to or for the use of one or more organizations described in section 170(c) or retained, in whole or in part, for such use.

(ii) *Treatment of Trust.* If all of the trust corpus is to be retained for such use, the taxable year of the trust shall terminate at the end of the period specified in subparagraph (5) of this paragraph and the trust shall cease to be treated as a charitable remainder trust for all purposes. If all or any portion of the trust corpus is to be transferred to or for the use of such organization or organizations, the trustee shall have a reasonable time after the period specified in subparagraph (5) of this paragraph to complete the settlement of the trust. During such time, the trust shall continue to be treated as a charitable remainder trust for all purposes, such as sections 664, 4947(a)(2), and 4947(b)(3)(B). Upon the expiration of such period, the taxable year of the trust shall terminate and the trust shall cease to be treated as a charitable remainder trust for all purposes. If the trust continues in existence, it will be subject to the provisions of section 4947(a)(1) unless the trust is exempt from taxation under section 501(a). For purposes of determining whether the trust is exempt under section 501(a) as an organization described in section 501(c)(3), the trust shall be deemed to have been created at the time it ceases to be treated as a charitable remainder trust.

(iii) *Concurrent or successive remaindermen.* Where interests in the corpus of the trust are given to more than one organization described in section 170(c) such interests may be enjoyed by them either concurrently or successively.

(iv) *Alternative remaindermen.* The governing instrument shall provide that if an organization to or for the use of which the trust corpus is to be transferred or for the use of which the trust corpus is to be retained is not an organization described in section 170(c) at the time any amount is to be irrevocably transferred to or for the use of such organization, such amount shall be transferred to or for the use of one or more alternative organizations which are described in section 170(c) at such time or retained for such use. Such alternative organization or organizations may be selected in any manner provided by the terms of the governing instrument.

(b) *Additional contributions.* A trust is not a charitable remainder annuity trust unless its governing instrument provides that no additional contributions may be made to the charitable remainder annuity trust after the initial contribution. For purposes of this section, all property passing to a charitable remainder annuity trust by reason of death of the grantor shall be considered one contribution.

(c) *Calculation of the fair market value of the remainder interest of a charitable remainder annuity trust.* For purposes of sections 170, 2055, 2106, and 2522, the fair market value of the remainder interest of a charitable remainder annuity trust (as described in this section) is the net fair market value (as of the appropriate valuation date) of the property placed in trust less the present value of the annuity. For purposes of this section, *valuation date* means, in general, the date on which the property is transferred to the trust by the donor regardless of when the trust is created. In the case of transfers to a charitable remainder annuity trust for which the valuation date is after April 30, 1989, if an election is made under section 7520 and § 1.7520-2(b) to compute the present value of the charitable interest by use of the interest rate component for either of the 2 months preceding the month in which the transfer is made, the month so elected is the valuation date for purposes of determining the interest rate and mortality tables. For purposes of section 2055 and 2106, the valuation date is the date of death unless the alternate valuation date is elected in accordance with section 2032, in which event, and within the limitations set forth in section 2032 and the regulations thereunder, the valuation date is the alternate valuation date. If the decedent's estate elects the alternate valuation date

Reg. § 1.664-2(a)(6)

under section 2032 and also elects, under section 7520 and § 1.7520-2(b), to use the interest rate component for one of the 2 months preceding the alternate valuation date, the month so elected is the valuation date for purposes of determining the interest rate and mortality tables. The present value of an annuity is computed under § 20.2031-7(d) of this chapter (Estate Tax Regulations) for transfers for which the valuation date is after April 30, 1999, or under § 20.2031-7A(a) through (e) of this chapter, whichever is applicable, for transfers for which the valuation date is before May 1, 1999. See, however, § 1.7520-3(b) (relating to exceptions to the use of prescribed tables under certain circumstances).

(d) *Deduction for transfers to a charitable remainder annuity trust.* For rules relating to a deduction for transfers to a charitable remainder annuity trust, see sections 170, 2055, 2106 or 2522 and the regulations thereunder. Any claim for deduction on any return for the value of a remainder interest in a charitable remainder annuity trust must be supported by a full statement attached to the return showing the computation of the present value of such interest. The deduction allowed by section 170 is limited to the fair market value of the remainder interest of a charitable remainder annuity trust regardless of whether an organization described in section 170(c) also receives a portion of the annuity. For a special rule relating to the reduction of the amount of a charitable contribution deduction with respect to a contribution of certain ordinary income property or capital gain property, see sections 170(e)(1)(A) or 170(e)(1)(B)(i) and the regulations thereunder. For rules for postponing the time for deduction of a charitable contribution of a future interest in tangible personal property, see section 170(a)(3) and the regulations thereunder. [Reg. § 1.664-2.]

☐ [T.D. 7202, 8-22-72. Amended by T.D. 7955, 5-10-84; T.D. 8540, 6-9-94; T.D. 8791, 12-9-98; T.D. 8819, 4-29-99 (corrected 3-8-2000) and T.D. 8926, 1-4-2001.]

[Reg. § 1.664-3]

§ 1.664-3. **Charitable remainder unitrust.**— (a) *Description.* A charitable remainder unitrust is a trust which complies with the applicable provisions of § 1.664-1 and meets all of the following requirements:

(1) *Required payment of unitrust amount*— (i) *Payment of fixed percentage at least annually*—(a) *General rule.* The governing instrument provides that the trust will pay not less often than annually a fixed percentage of the net fair market value of the trust assets determined annually to a person or persons described in paragraph (a)(3) of this section for each taxable year of the period specified in paragraph (a)(5) of this section. This paragraph (a)(1)(i)(a) is applicable for taxable years ending after April 18, 1997.

(b) *Income exception.* Instead of the amount described in (a) of this subdivision (i), the governing instrument may provide that the trust shall pay for any year either the amount described in (1) or the total of the amounts described in (1) and (2) of this subdivision (b).

(1) The amount of trust income for a taxable year to the extent that such amount is not more than the amount required to be distributed under paragraph (a)(1)(i)(a) of this section.

(2) An amount of trust income for a taxable year that is in excess of the amount required to be distributed under paragraph (a)(1)(i)(a) of this section for such year to the extent that (by reason of paragraph (a)(1)(i)(b)(1) of this section) the aggregate of the amounts paid in prior years was less than the aggregate of such required amounts.

(3) For this paragraph (a)(1)(i)(b), trust income means income as defined under section 643(b) and the applicable regulations.

(4) For this paragraph (a)(1)(i)(b), proceeds from the sale or exchange of any assets contributed to the trust by the donor must be allocated to principal and not to trust income at least to the extent of the fair market value of those assets on the date of contribution.

(5) The rules in paragraphs (a)(1)(i)(b)(1), (2), and (3) of this section are applicable for taxable years ending after April 18, 1997, and the rule in paragraph (a)(1)(i)(b)(4) of this section is applicable for sales or exchanges that occur after April 18, 1997.

(c) *Combination of methods.* Instead of the amount described in paragraph (a)(1)(i)(a) or (b) of this section, the governing instrument may provide that the trust will pay not less often than annually the amount described in paragraph (a)(1)(i)(b) of this section for an initial period and then pay the amount described in paragraph (a)(1)(i)(a) of this section (calculated using the same fixed percentage) for the remaining years of the trust only if the governing instrument provides that—

(1) The change from the method prescribed in paragraph (a)(1)(i)(b) of this section to the method prescribed in paragraph (a)(1)(i)(a) of this section is triggered on a specific date or by a single event whose occurrence is not discretionary with, or within the control of, the trustees or any other persons;

Reg. § 1.664-3(a)(1)

(2) The change from the method prescribed in paragraph (a)(1)(i)(b) of this section to the method prescribed in paragraph (a)(1)(i)(a) of this section occurs at the beginning of the taxable year that immediately follows the taxable year during which the date or event specified under paragraph (a)(1)(i)(c)(1) of this section occurs; and

(3) Following the trust's conversion to the method described in paragraph (a)(1)(i)(a) of this section, the trust will pay at least annually to the permissible recipients the amount described only in paragraph (a)(1)(i)(a) of this section and not any amount described in paragraph (a)(1)(i)(b) of this section.

(d) *Triggering event.* For purposes of paragraph (a)(1)(i)(c)(1) of this section, a triggering event based on the sale of unmarketable assets as defined in § 1.664-1(a)(7)(ii), or the marriage, divorce, death, or birth of a child with respect to any individual will not be considered discretionary with, or within the control of, the trustees or any other persons.

(e) *Examples.* The following examples illustrate the rules in paragraph (a)(1)(i)(c) of this section. For each example, assume that the governing instrument of charitable remainder unitrust Y provides that Y will initially pay not less often than annually the amount described in paragraph (a)(1)(i)(b) of this section and then pay the amount described in paragraph (a)(1)(i)(a) of this section (calculated using the same fixed percentage) for the remaining years of the trust and that the requirements of paragraphs (a)(1)(i)(c)(2) and (3) of this section are satisfied. The examples are as follows:

Example 1. Y is funded with the donor's former personal residence. The governing instrument of Y provides for the change in method for computing the annual unitrust amount as of the first day of the year following the year in which the trust sells the residence. Y provides for a combination of methods that satisfies paragraph (a)(1)(i)(c) of this section.

Example 2. Y is funded with cash and an unregistered security for which there is no available exemption permitting public sale under the Securities and Exchange Commission rules. The governing instrument of Y provides that the change in method for computing the annual unitrust amount is triggered on the earlier of the date when the stock is sold or at the time the restrictions on its public sale lapse or are otherwise lifted. Y provides for a combination of methods that satisfies paragraph (a)(1)(i)(c) of this section.

Example 3. Y is funded with cash and with a security that may be publicly traded under the Securities and Exchange Commission rules. The governing instrument of Y provides that the change in method for computing the annual unitrust amount is triggered when the stock is sold. Y does not provide for a combination of methods that satisfies the requirements of paragraph (a)(1)(i)(c) of this section because the sale of the publicly-traded stock is within the discretion of the trustee.

Example 4. S establishes Y for her granddaughter, G, when G is 10 years old. The governing instrument of Y provides for the change in method for computing the annual unitrust amount as of the first day of the year following the year in which G turns 18 years old. Y provides for a combination of methods that satisfies paragraph (a)(1)(i)(c) of this section.

Example 5. The governing instrument of Y provides for the change in method for computing the annual unitrust amount as of the first day of the year following the year in which the donor is married. Y provides for a combination of methods that satisfies paragraph (a)(1)(i)(c) of this section.

Example 6. The governing instrument of Y provides that if the donor divorces, the change in method for computing the annual unitrust amount will occur as of the first day of the year following the year of the divorce. Y provides for a combination of methods that satisfies paragraph (a)(1)(i)(c) of this section.

Example 7. The governing instrument of Y provides for the change in method for computing the annual unitrust amount as of the first day of the year following the year in which the noncharitable beneficiary's first child is born. Y provides for a combination of methods that satisfies paragraph (a)(1)(i)(c) of this section.

Example 8. The governing instrument of Y provides for the change in method for computing the annual unitrust amount as of the first day of the year following the year in which the noncharitable beneficiary's father dies. Y provides for a combination of methods that satisfies paragraph (a)(1)(i)(c) of this section.

Example 9. The governing instrument of Y provides for the change in method for computing the annual unitrust amount as of the first day of the year following the year in which the noncharitable beneficiary's financial advisor determines that the beneficiary should begin receiving payments under the second prescribed payment method. Because the change in methods for paying the unitrust amount is triggered by an event that is within a person's control, Y does not provide for a combination of methods that satisfies paragraph (a)(1)(i)(c) of this section.

Reg. § 1.664-3(a)(1)

Example 10. The governing instrument of Y provides for the change in method for computing the annual unitrust amount as of the first day of the year following the year in which the noncharitable beneficiary submits a request to the trustee that the trust convert to the second prescribed payment method. Because the change in methods for paying the unitrust amount is triggered by an event that is within a person's control, Y does not provide for a combination of methods that satisfies paragraph (a)(1)(i)(c) of this section.

(*f*) *Effective date*—(*1*) *General rule.* Paragraphs (a)(1)(i)(c), (d), and (e) of this section are applicable for charitable remainder trusts created on or after December 10, 1998.

(*2*) *General rule regarding reformations of combination of method unitrusts.* If a trust is created on or after December 10, 1998, and contains a provision allowing a change in calculating the unitrust amount that does not comply with the provisions of paragraph (a)(1)(i)(c) of this section, the trust will qualify as a charitable remainder unitrust only if it is amended or reformed to use the initial method for computing the unitrust amount throughout the term of the trust, or is reformed in accordance with paragraph (a)(1)(i)(f)(3) of this section. If a trust was created before December 10, 1998, and contains a provision allowing a change in calculating the unitrust amount that does not comply with the provisions of paragraph (a)(1)(i)(c) of this section, the trust may be reformed to use the initial method for computing the unitrust amount throughout the term of the trust without causing the trust to fail to function exclusively as a charitable remainder unitrust under § 1.664-1(a)(4), or may be reformed in accordance with paragraph (a)(1)(i)(f)(3) of this section. Except as provided in paragraph (a)(1)(i)(f)(3) of this section, a qualified charitable remainder unitrust will not continue to qualify as a charitable remainder unitrust if it is amended or reformed to add a provision allowing a change in the method for calculating the unitrust amount.

(*3*) *Special rule for reformations of trusts that begin by June 8, 1999.* Notwithstanding paragraph (a)(1)(i)(f)(2) of this section, if a trust either provides for payment of the unitrust amount under a combination of methods that is not permitted under paragraph (a)(1)(i)(c) of this section, or provides for payment of the unitrust amount under only the method prescribed in paragraph (a)(1)(i)(b) of this section, then the trust may be reformed to allow for a combination of methods permitted under paragraph (a)(1)(i)(c) of this section without causing the trust to fail to function exclusively as a charitable remainder unitrust under § 1.664-1(a)(4) or to engage in an act of self-dealing under section 4941 if the trustee begins legal proceedings to reform by June 8, 1999. The triggering event under the reformed governing instrument may not occur in a year prior to the year in which the court issues the order reforming the trust, except for situations in which the governing instrument prior to reformation already provided for payment of the unitrust amount under a combination of methods that is not permitted under paragraph (a)(1)(i)(c) of this section and the triggering event occurred prior to the reformation.

(*g*) *Payment under general rule for fixed percentage trusts.* When the unitrust amount is computed under paragraph (a)(1)(i)(a) of this section, a trust will not be deemed to have engaged in an act of self-dealing (within the meaning of section 4941), to have unrelated debt-financed income (within the meaning of section 514), to have received an additional contribution (within the meaning of paragraph (b) of this section), or to have failed to function exclusively as a charitable remainder trust (within the meaning of § 1.664-1(a)(4)) merely because the unitrust amount is paid after the close of the taxable year if such payment is made within a reasonable time after the close of such taxable year and the entire unitrust amount in the hands of the recipient is characterized only as income from the categories described in section 664(b)(1), (2), or (3), except to the extent it is characterized as corpus described in section 664(b)(4) because—

(*1*) The trust pays the unitrust amount by distributing property (other than cash) that it owned at the close of the taxable year, and the trustee elects to treat any income generated by the distribution as occurring on the last day of the taxable year in which the unitrust amount is due;

(*2*) The trust pays the unitrust amount by distributing cash that was contributed to the trust (with respect to which a deduction was allowable under section 170, 2055, 2106, or 2522); or

(*3*) The trust pays the unitrust amount by distributing cash received as a return of basis in any asset that was contributed to the trust (with respect to which a deduction was allowable under section 170, 2055, 2106, or 2522), and that is sold by the trust during the year for which the unitrust amount is due.

(*h*) *Special rule for fixed percentage trusts created before December 10, 1998.* When the unitrust amount is computed under paragraph (a)(1)(i)(a) of this section, a trust created

Reg. § 1.664-3(a)(1)

before December 10, 1998, will not be deemed to have engaged in an act of self-dealing (within the meaning of section 4941), to have unrelated debt-financed income (within the meaning of section 514), to have received an additional contribution (within the meaning of paragraph (b) of this section), or to have failed to function exclusively as a charitable remainder trust (within the meaning of § 1.664-1(a)(4)) merely because the unitrust amount is paid after the close of the taxable year if such payment is made within a reasonable time after the close of such taxable year and the fixed percentage to be paid each year as the unitrust amount is 15 percent or less of the net fair market value of the trust assets as determined under paragraph (a)(1)(iv) of this section.

(*i*) *Example.* The following example illustrates the rules in paragraph (a)(1)(i)(*g*) of this section:

Example. X is a charitable remainder unitrust that calculates the unitrust amount under paragraph (a)(1)(i)(*a*) of this section. X was created after December 10, 1998. The prorated unitrust amount payable from X for Year 1 is $100. The trustee does not pay the unitrust amount to the recipient by the end of the Year 1. At the end of Year 1, X has only $95 in the ordinary income category under section 664(b)(1) and no income in the capital gain or tax-exempt income categories under section 664(b)(2) or (3), respectively. By April 15 of Year 2, in addition to $95 in cash, the trustee distributes to the unitrust recipient a capital asset with a $5 fair market value and a $2 adjusted basis to pay the $100 unitrust amount due for Year 1. The trust owned the asset at the end of Year 1. Under § 1.664-1(d)(5), the distribution is treated as a sale by X, resulting in X recognizing a $3 capital gain. The trustee elects to treat the capital gain as occurring on the last day of Year 1. Under § 1.664-1(d)(1), the character of the unitrust amount for Year 1 in the recipient's hands is $95 of ordinary income, $3 of capital gain income, and $2 of trust corpus. For Year 1, X satisfied paragraph (a)(1)(i)(*g*) of this section.

(*j*) *Payment under income exception.* When the unitrust amount is computed under paragraph (a)(1)(i)(*b*) of this section, a trust will not be deemed to have engaged in an act of self-dealing (within the meaning of section 4941), to have unrelated debt-financed income (within the meaning of section 514), to have received an additional contribution (within the meaning of paragraph (b) of this section), or to have failed to function exclusively as a charitable remainder trust (within the meaning of § 1.664-1(a)(4)) merely because payment of the unitrust amount is made after the close of the taxable year if such payment is made within a reasonable time after the close of such taxable year.

(*k*) *Reasonable time.* For paragraphs (a)(1)(i)(*g*), (*h*), and (*j*) of this section, a reasonable time will not ordinarily extend beyond the date by which the trustee is required to file Form 5227, "Split-Interest Trust Information Return," (including extensions) for the taxable year.

(*l*) *Effective date.* Paragraphs (a)(1)(i)(*g*), (*h*), (*i*), (*j*), and (*k*) of this section are applicable for taxable years ending after April 18, 1997. Paragraphs (a)(1)(i)(*g*)(*2*) and (*3*) of this section apply only to distributions made on or after January 5, 2001.

(ii) *Definition of fixed percentage.* The fixed percentage may be expressed either as a fraction or as a percentage and must be payable each year in the period specified in subparagraph (5) of this paragraph. A percentage is fixed if the percentage is the same either as to each recipient or as to the total percentage payable each year of such period. For example, provision for a fixed percentage which is the same every year to A until his death and concurrently a fixed percentage which is the same every year to B until his death, the fixed percentage to each recipient to terminate at his death, would satisfy the rule. Similarly, provision for a fixed percentage to A and B for their joint lives and then to the survivor would satisfy the rule. In the case of a distribution to an organization described in section 170(c) at the death of a recipient or the expiration of a term of years, the governing instrument may provide for a reduction of the fixed percentage payable after such distribution provided that:

(*a*) The reduced fixed percentage is the same either as to each recipient or as to the total amount payable for each year of the balance of such period, and

(*b*) The requirements of subparagraph (2)(ii) of this paragraph are met.

(iii) *Rules applicable to incorrect valuations.* The governing instrument provides that in the case where the net fair market value of the trust assets is incorrectly determined by the fiduciary, the trust shall pay to the recipient (in the case of an undervaluation) or be repaid by the recipient (in the case of an overvaluation) an amount equal to the difference between the amount which the trust should have paid the recipient if the correct value were used and the amount which the trust actually paid the recipient. Such payments or repayments must be made within a reasonable period after the final determination of such value. Any payment due to a recipient by reason of such incorrect valuation shall be considered to be a payment required to be distributed at the time of such final determination for purposes of paragraph (d)(4)(ii) of § 1.664-1. See paragraph (d)(4) of § 1.664-1 for rules relating to the year of inclusion of such payments and the allowance of a deduction for such repayments. See paragraph (b) of this section for rules relating to additional contributions.

(iv) *Rules applicable to valuation.* In computing the net fair market value of the trust assets there shall be taken into account all assets and liabilities without regard to whether particular items are taken into account in determining the income of the trust. The net fair market value of the trust assets may be determined on any one date during the taxable year of the trust, or by taking the average of valuations made on more than one date during the taxable year of the trust, so long as the same valuation date or dates and valuation methods are used each year. If the governing instrument does not specify the valuation date or dates, the trustee must select such date or dates and indicate the selection on the first return on Form 5227, "Split-Interest Trust Information Return," that the trust must file. The amount described in subdivision (i)(a) of this subparagraph which must be paid each year must be based upon the valuation for such year.

(v) *Computation of unitrust amount in certain circumstances*—(a) Short taxable years. The governing instrument provides that, in the case of a taxable year which is for a period of less than 12 months other than the taxable year in which occurs the end of the period specified in subparagraph (5) of this paragraph:

(*1*) The amount determined under subdivision (i)(a) of this subparagraph shall be the amount otherwise determined under that subdivision multiplied by a fraction the numerator of which is the number of days in the taxable year of the trust and the denominator of which is 365 (366 if February 29 is a day included in the numerator),

(*2*) The amount determined under subdivison (i)(b) of this subparagraph shall be computed by using the amount determined under subdivision (a)(*1*) of this subdivision (v), and

(*3*) If no valuation date occurs before the end of the taxable year of the trust, the trust assets shall be valued as of the last day of the taxable year of the trust.

(b) *Last taxable year of period.* (*1*) The governing instrument provides that, in the case of the taxable year in which occurs the end of the period specified in subparagraph (5) of this paragraph:

(*i*) The unitrust amount which must be distributed under subdivision (i)(a) of this subparagraph shall be the amount otherwise determined under that subdivision multiplied by a fraction the numerator of which is the number of days in the period beginning on the first day of such taxable year and ending on the last day of the period specified in subparagraph (5) of this paragraph and the denominator of which is 365 (366 if February 29 is a day included in the numerator),

(*ii*) The amount determined under subdivision (i)(b) of this subparagraph shall be computed by using the amount determined under subdivision (b)(*1*)(*i*) of this subdivision (v), and

(*iii*) If no valuation date occurs before the end of such period, the trust assets shall be valued as of the last day of such period.

(*2*) See subparagraph (5) of this paragraph for a special rule allowing termination of payment of the unitrust amount with the regular payment next preceding the termination of the period specified therein.

(2) *Minimum unitrust amount*—(i) *General rule.* The fixed percentage described in subparagraph (1)(i) of this paragraph with respect to all beneficiaries taken together is not less than 5 percent.

(ii) *Reduction of unitrust amount in certain cases.* A trust will not fail to meet the requirements of this subparagraph by reason of the fact that it provides for a reduction of the fixed percentage payable upon the death of a recipient or the expiration of a term of years provided that:

(a) A distribution is made to an organization described in section 170(c) at the death of such recipient or the expiration of such term of years, and

(b) The total of the percentage payable under subparagraph (1) of this paragraph after such distribution is not less than 5 percent.

(3) *Permissible recipients*—(i) *General rule.* The amount described in subparagraph (1) of this paragraph is payable to or for the use of a named person or persons, at least one of which is not an organization described in section 170(c). If the amount described in subparagraph (1) of this paragraph is to be paid to an individual or individuals, all such individuals must be living at the time of creation of the trust. A named person or persons may include members of a named class except in the case of a class which includes any individual, all such individuals must be alive and ascertainable at the time of the creation of the trust unless the period for which the unitrust amount is to be paid to such class consists solely of

Reg. § 1.664-3(a)(3)

a term of years. For example, in the case of a testamentary trust, the testator's will may provide that the required amount shall be paid to his children living at this death.

(ii) *Power to alter amount paid to recipients.* A trust is not a charitable remainder unitrust if any person has the power to alter the amount to be paid to any named person other than an organization described in section 170(c) if such power would cause any person to be treated as the owner of the trust, or any portion thereof, if subpart E, part 1, subchapter J, chapter 1, subtitle A of the Code were applicable to such trust. See paragraph (a)(4) of this section for a rule permitting the retention by a grantor of a testamentary power to revoke or terminate the interest of any recipient other than an organization described in section 170(c). For example, the governing instrument may not grant the trustee the power to allocate the fixed percentage among members of a class unless such power falls within one of the exceptions to section 674(a).

(4) *Other payments.* No amount other than the amount described in subparagraph (1) of this paragraph may be paid to or for the use of any person other than an organization described in section 170(c). An amount is not paid to or for the use of any person other than an organization described in section 170(c) if the amount is transferred for full and adequate consideration. The trust may not be subject to a power to invade, alter, amend, or revoke for the beneficial use of a person other than an organization described in section 170(c). Notwithstanding the preceding sentence, the grantor may retain the power exercisable only by will to revoke or terminate the interest of any recipient other than an organization described in section 170(c). The governing instrument may provide that any amount other than the amount described in subparagraph (1) of this paragraph shall be paid (or may be paid in the discretion of the trustee) to an organization described in section 170(c) provided that, in the case of distributions in kind, the adjusted basis of the property distributed is fairly representative of the adjusted basis of the property available for payment on the date of payment. For example, the governing instrument may provide that a portion of the trust assets may be distributed currently, or upon the death of one or more recipients, to an organization described in section 170(c).

(5) *Period of payment of unitrust amount* — (i) *General rules.* The period for which an amount described in subparagraph (1) of this paragraph is payable begins with the first year of the charitable remainder trust and continues either for the life or lives of a named individual or individuals or for a term of years not to exceed 20 years. Only an individual or an organization described in section 170(c) may receive an amount for the life of an individual. If an individual receives an amount for life, it must be solely for his life. Payment of the amount described in subparagrah (1) of this paragraph may terminate with the regular payment next preceding the termination of the period described in this subparagraph. The fact that the recipient may not receive such last payment shall not be taken into account for purposes of determining the present value of the remainder interest. In the case of an amount payable for a term of years, the length of the term of years shall be ascertainable with certainty at the time of the creation of the trust, except that the term may be terminated by the death of the recipient or by the grantor's exercise by will of a retained power to revoke or terminate the interest of any recipient other than an organization described in section 170(c). In any event, the period may not extend beyond either the life or lives of a named individual or individuals or a term of years not to exceed 20 years. For example, the governing instrument may not provide for the payment of a unitrust amount to A for his life and then to B for a term of years because it is possible for the period to last longer than either the lives of recipients in being at the creation of the trust or a term of years not to exceed 20 years. On the other hand, the governing instrument may provide for the payment of an unitrust amount to A for his life and then to B for his life or a term of years (not to exceed 20 years), whichever is shorter (but not longer), if both A and B are in being at the creation of the trust because it is not possible for the period to last longer than the lives of recipients in being at the creation of the trust.

(ii) *Relationship to 5 percent requirement.* The 5 percent requirement provided in subparagraph (2) of this paragraph must be met until the termination of all the payments described in subparagraph (1) of this paragraph. For example, the following provisions would satisfy the above rules:

(*a*) A fixed percentage of at least 5 percent to A and B for their joint lives and then to the survivor for his life;

(*b*) A fixed percentage of at least 5 percent to A for life or for a term of years not longer than 20 years, whichever is longer (or shorter);

(*c*) A fixed percentage of at least 5 percent to A for a term of years not longer than 20 years and then to B for life (provided B was living at the creation of the trust);

(*d*) A fixed percentage to A for his life and concurrently a fixed percentage to B for his life (the percentage to each recipient to terminate at his death) if the percentage given to each individual is not less than 5 percent;

(e) A fixed percentage to A for his life and concurrently an equal percentage to B for his life, and at the death of the first to die, the trust to distribute one-half of the then value of its assets to an organization described in section 170(c) if the total of the percentages is not less than 5 percent for the entire period described in this subparagraph.

(6) *Permissible Remaindermen*—(i) *General Rule.* At the end of the period specified in subparagraph (5) of this paragraph, the entire corpus of the trust is required to be irrevocably transferred, in whole or in part, to or for the use of one or more organizations described in section 170(c) or retained, in whole or in part, for such use.

(ii) *Treatment of Trust.* If all of the trust corpus is to be retained for such use, the taxable year of the trust shall terminate at the end of the period specified in subparagraph (5) of this paragraph and the trust shall cease to be treated as a charitable remainder trust for all purposes. If all or any portion of the trust corpus is to be transferred to or for the use of such organization or organizations, the trustee shall have a reasonable time after the period specified in subparagraph (5) of this paragraph to complete the settlement of the trust. During such time, the trust shall continue to be treated as a charitable remainder trust for all purposes, such as sections 664, 4947(a)(2), and 4947(b)(3)(B). Upon the expiration of such period, the taxable year of the trust shall terminate and the trust shall cease to be treated as a charitable remainder trust for all purposes. If the trust continues in existence, it will be subject to the provisions of section 4947(a)(1) unless the trust is exempt from taxation under section 501(a). For purposes of determining whether the trust is exempt under section 501(a) as an organization described in section 501(c)(3), the trust shall be deemed to have been created at the time it ceases to be treated as a charitable remainder trust.

(iii) *Concurrent or successive remaindermen.* Where interests in the corpus of the trust are given to more than one organization described in section 170(c) such interests may be enjoyed by them either concurrently or successively.

(iv) *Alternative remaindermen.* The governing instrument shall provide that if an organization to or for the use of which the trust corpus is to be transferred or for the use of which the trust corpus is to be retained is not an organization described in section 170(c) at the time any amount is to be irrevocably transferred to or for the use of such organization, such amount shall be transferred to or for the use of or retained for the use of one or more alternative organizations which are described in section 170(c) at such time. Such alternative organization or organizations may be selected in any manner provided by the terms of the governing instrument.

(b) *Additional contributions.* A trust is not a charitable remainder unitrust unless its governing instrument either prohibits additional contributions to the trust after the initial contribution or provides that for the taxable year of the trust in which the additional contribution is made:

(1) Where no valuation date occurs after the time of the contribution and during the taxable year in which the contribution is made, the additional property shall be valued as of the time of contribution; and

(2) The amount described in paragraph (a)(1)(i)(a) of this section shall be computed by multiplying the fixed percentage by the sum of (i) the net fair market value of the trust assets (excluding the value of the additional property and any earned income from and any appreciation on such property after its contribution), and (ii) that proportion of the value of the additional property (that was excluded under subdivision (i) of this paragraph), which the number of days in the period which begins with the date of contribution and ends with the earlier of the last day of such taxable year or the last day of the period described in paragraph (a)(5) of this section bears to the number of days in the period which begins with the first day of such taxable year and ends with the earlier of the last day of such taxable year or the last day of the period described in paragraph (a)(5) of this section.

For purposes of this section, all property passing to a charitable remainder unitrust by reason of death of the grantor shall be considered one contribution. The application of the preceding rules may be illustrated by the following examples:

Example (1). On March 2, 1971, X makes an additional contribution of property to a charitable remainder unitrust. The taxable year of the trust is the calendar year and the regular valuation date is January 1 of each year. For purposes of computing the required payout with respect to the additional contribution for the year of contribution, the additional contribution is valued on March 2, 1971, the time of contribution. The property had a value on that date of $5,000. Income from such property in the amount of $250 was received on December 31, 1971. The required payout with respect to the additional contribution for the year of contribution is $208 (5 percent × $5,000 × 305/365). The income earned after the

Reg. § 1.664-3(b)(2)

date of the contribution and after the regular valuation date does not enter into the computation.

Example (2). On July 1, 1971, X makes an additional contribution of $10,000 to a charitable remainder unitrust. The taxable year of the trust is the calendar year and the regular valuation date is December 31 of each year. The fixed percentage is 5 percent. Between July 1, 1971, and December 31, 1971, the additional property appreciates in value to $12,500 and earns $500 of income. Because the regular valuation date for the year of contribution occurs after the date of the additional contribution, the additional contribution including income earned by it is valued on the regular valuation date. Thus, the required payout with respect to the additional contribution is $325.87 (5 percent × [$12,500 + $500] × 183/365).

(c) *Calculation of the fair market value of the remainder interest of a charitable remainder unitrust.* See § 1.664-4 for rules relating to the calculation of the fair market value of the remainder interest of a charitable remainder unitrust.

(d) *Deduction for transfers to a charitable remainder unitrust.* For rules relating to a deduction for transfers to a charitable remainder unitrust, see sections 170, 2055, 2106 or 2522 and the regulations thereunder. The deduction allowed by section 170 for transfers to charity is limited to the fair market value of the remainder interest of a charitable remainder unitrust regardless of whether an organization described in section 170(c) also receives a portion of the amount described in § 1.664-3(a)(1). For a special rule relating to the reduction of the amount of a charitable contribution deduction with respect to a contribution of certain ordinary income property or capital gain property, see section 170(e)(1)(A) or (B)(i) and the regulations thereunder. For rules for postponing the time for deduction of a charitable contribution of a future interest in tangible personal property, see section 170(a)(3) and the regulations thereunder. [Reg. § 1.664-3.]

☐ [T.D. 7202, 8-22-72. Amended by T.D. 8791, 12-9-98 and T.D. 8926, 1-4-2001.]

[Reg. § 1.664-4]

§ 1.664-4. Calculation of the fair market value of the remainder interest in a charitable remainder unitrust.—(a) *Rules for determining present value.* For purposes of sections 170, 2055, 2106, and 2522, the fair market value of a remainder interest in a charitable remainder unitrust (as described in § 1.664-3) is its present value determined under paragraph (d) of this section. The present value determined under this section shall be computed on the basis of—

(1) Life contingencies determined as to each life involved, from the values of lx set forth in Table 90CM contained in § 20.2031-7(d)(7) of this chapter in the case of transfers for which the valuation date is after April 30, 1999; or from Table 80CNSMT contained § 20.2031-7A(e)(4) of this chapter in the case of transfer for which the valuation date is after April 30, 1989, and before May 1, 1999. See § 20.2031-7A(a) through (d) of this chapter, whichever is applicable, for transfers for which the valuation date is before May 1, 1989;

(2) Interest at the section 7520 rate in the case of transfers for which the valuation date is after April 30, 1989, or 10 percent in the case of transfers to charitable remainder unitrusts made after November 30, 1983, for which the valuation date is before May 1, 1989. See § 20.2031-7A(a) through (c) of this chapter, whichever is applicable, for transfers for which the valuation date is before December 1, 1983; and

(3) The assumption that the amount described in § 1.664-3(a)(1)(*i*)(*a*) is distributed in accordance with the payout sequence described in the governing instrument. If the governing instrument does not prescribe when the distribution is made during the period for which the payment is made, for purposes of this section, the distribution is considered payable on the first day of the period for which the payment is made.

(b) *Actuarial Computations by the Internal Revenue Service.* The regulations in this and in related sections provide tables of actuarial factors and examples that illustrate the use of the tables in determining the value of remainder interests in property. Section 1.7520-1(c)(2) refers to government publications that provide additional tables of factors and examples of computations for more complex situations. If the computation requires the use of a factor that is not provided in this section, the Commissioner may supply the factor upon a request for a ruling. A request for a ruling must be accompanied by a recitation of the facts including the date of birth of each measuring life, and copies of the relevant documents. A request for a ruling must comply with the instructions for requesting a ruling published periodically in the Internal Revenue Bulletin (See § 601.601(d)(2)(ii)(*b*) of this chapter) and include payment of the required user fee. If the Commissioner furnishes the factor, a copy of the letter supplying the factor should be attached to the tax return in which the deduction is claimed. If the Commissioner does not furnish the factor, the taxpayer must furnish a factor computed in accordance with the principles set forth in this section.

(c) *Statement supporting deduction required.* Any claim for a deduction on any return for the value of a remainder interest in a charitable remainder unitrust must be supported by a full statement attached to the return showing the computation of the present value of such interest.

(d) *Valuation.* The fair market value of a remainder interest in a charitable remainder unitrust (as described in § 1.664-3) for transfers for which the valuation date is after April 30, 1999, is its present value determined under paragraph (e) of this section. The fair market value of a remainder interest in a charitable remainder unitrust (as described in § 1.664-3) for transfers for which the valuation date is before May 1, 1999, is its present value determined under the following sections:

Valuation Dates		Applicable
After	Before	Regulations
	01-01-52	1.664-4A(a)
12-31-51	01-01-71	1.664-4A(b)
12-31-70	12-01-83	1.664-4A(c)
11-30-83	05-01-89	1.664-4A(d)
04-30-89	05-01-99	1.664-4A(e)

(e) *Valuation of charitable remainder unitrusts having certain payout sequences for transfers for which the valuation date is after April 30, 1999*—(1) *In general.* Except as otherwise provided in paragraph (e)(2) of this section, in the case of transfers for which the valuation date is after April 30, 1999, the present value of a remainder interest is determined under paragraphs (e)(3) through (e)(7) of this section, provided that the amount of the payout as of any payout date during any taxable year of the trust is not larger than the amount that the trust could distribute on such date under § 1.664-3(a)(1)(v) if the taxable year of the trust were to end on such date. See, however, § 1.7520-3(b) (relating to exceptions to the use of the prescribed tables under certain circumstances).

(2) *Transitional rules for valuation of charitable remainder unitrusts*—(i) For purposes of sections 2055, 2106, or 2624, if on May 1, 1999, the decedent was mentally incompetent so that the disposition of the property could not be changed, and the decedent died after April 30, 1999, without having regained competency to dispose of the decedent's property, or the decedent died within 90 days of the date that the decedent first regained competency after April 30, 1999, the present value of a remainder interest under this section is determined as if the valuation date with respect to the decedent's gross estate is either before May 1, 1999, or after April 30, 1999, at the option of the decedent's executor.

(ii) For purposes of sections 170, 2055, 2106, 2522, or 2624, in the case of transfers to a charitable remainder unitrust for which the valuation date is after April 30, 1999, and before July 1, 1999, the present value of a remainder interest based on one or more measuring lives is determined under this section by use of the section 7520 interest rate for the month in which the valuation date occurs (see §§ 1.7520-1(b) and 1.7520-2(a)(2)) and the appropriate actuarial tables under either paragraph (e)(7) of this section or § 1.664-4A(e)(6), at the option of the donor or the decedent's executor, as the case may be.

(iii) For purposes of paragraphs (e)(2)(i) and (ii) of this section, where the donor or decedent's executor is given the option to use the appropriate actuarial tables under either paragraph (e)(7) of this section or § 1.664-4A(e)(6), the donor or decedent's executor must use the same actuarial table with respect to each individual transaction and with respect to all transfers occurring on the valuation date (for example, gift and income tax charitable deductions with respect to the same transfer must be determined based on the same tables, and all assets includible in the gross estate and/or estate tax deductions claimed must be valued based on the same tables).

(3) *Adjusted payout rate.* For transfers for which the valuation date is after April 30, 1989, the adjusted payout rate is determined by using the appropriate Table F in paragraph (e)(6) of this section, for the section 7520 interest rate applicable to the transfer. If the interest rate is between 4.2 and 14 percent, see paragraph (e)(6) of this section. If the interest rate is below 4.2 percent or greater than 14 percent, see paragraph (b) of this section. The adjusted payout rate is determined by multiplying the fixed percentage described in § 1.664-3(a)(1)(i)(*a*) by the factor describing the payout sequence of the trust and the number of months by which the valuation date for the first full taxable year of the trust precedes the first payout date for such taxable year. If the governing instrument does not prescribe when the distribution or distributions shall be made during the taxable year of the trust, see paragraph (a) of this section. In the case of a trust having a payout sequence for which no figures have been provided by the appropriate table, and in the case of a trust that determines the fair market value of the trust assets by taking the average of valuations on more than one date during the taxable year, see paragraph (b) of this section.

Reg. § 1.664-4(e)(3)

(4) *Period is a term of years.* If the period described in § 1.664-3(a)(5) is a term of years, the factor that is used in determining the present value of the remainder interest for transfers for which the valuation date is after November 30, 1983, is the factor under the appropriate adjusted payout rate in Table D of paragraph (e)(6) of this section corresponding to the number of years in the term. If the adjusted payout rate is an amount that is between adjusted payout rates for which factors are provided in Table D, a linear interpolation must be made. The present value of the remainder interest is determined by multiplying the net fair market value (as of the appropriate valuation date) of the property placed in trust by the factor determined under this paragraph. For purposes of this section, the valuation date is, in the case of an inter vivos transfer, the date on which the property is transferred to the trust by the donor. However, if an election is made under section 7520 and § 1.7520-2(b) to compute the present value of the charitable interest by use of the interest rate component for either of the 2 months preceding the month in which the date of transfer falls, the month so elected is the valuation date for purposes of determining the interest rate and mortality tables. In the case of a testamentary transfer under section 2055, 2106, or 2624, the valuation date is the date of death, unless the alternate valuation date is elected under section 2032, in which event, and within the limitations set forth in section 2032 and the regulations thereunder, the valuation date is the alternate valuation date. If the decedent's estate elects the alternate valuation date under section 2032 and also elects, under section 7520 and § 1.7520-2(b), to use the interest rate component for one of the 2 months preceding the alternate valuation date, the month so elected is the valuation date for purposes of determining the interest rate and mortality tables. The application of this paragraph (e)(4) may be illustrated by the following example:

Example. D transfers $100,000 to a charitable remainder unitrust on January 1. The trust instrument requires that the trust pay 8 percent of the fair market value of the trust assets as of January 1st for a term of 12 years to D in quarterly payments (March 31, June 30, September 30, and December 31). The section 7520 rate for January (the month that the transfer occurred) is 9.6 percent. Under Table F(9.6) in paragraph(e)(6) of this section, the appropriate adjustment factor is .944628 for quarterly payments payable at the end of each quarter. The adjusted payout rate is 7.557 (8% × .944628). Based on the remainder factors in Table D in paragraph(e)(6) of this section, the present value of the remainder interest is $38,950.30, computed as follows:

Factor at 7.4 percent for 12 years 397495
Factor at 7.6 percent for 12 years 387314
Difference 010181

Interpolation adjustment:

$$\frac{7.557\% - 7.4\%}{0.2\%} = \frac{x}{.010181}$$

$$x = .007992$$

Factor at 7.4 percent for 12 years 397495
Less: Interpolation adjustment 007992
Interpolated factor 389503

Present value of remainder interest:
($100,000 × .389503) $38,950.30

(5) *Period is the life of one individual.* If the period described in § 1.664-3(a)(5) is the life of one individual, the factor that is used in determining the present value of the remainder interest for transfers for which the valuation date is after April 30, 1999, is the factor in Table U(1) in paragraph (e)(7) of this section under the appropriate adjusted payout. For purposes of the computations described in this paragraph, the age of an individual is the age of that individual at the individual's nearest birthday. If the adjusted payout rate is an amount that is between adjusted payout rates for which factors are provided in the appropriate table, a linear interpolation must be made. The present value of the remainder interest is determined by multiplying the net fair market value (as of the valuation date as determined in paragraph (e)(4) of this section) of the property placed in trust by the factor determined under this paragraph (e)(5). If the adjusted payout rate is between 4.2 and 14 percent, see paragraph (e)(7) of this section. If the adjusted payout rate is below 4.2 percent or greater than 14 percent, see paragraph (b) of this section. The application of this paragraph (e)(5) may be illustrated by the following example:

Example. A, who is 44 years and 11 months old, transfers $100,000 to a charitable remainder unitrust on January 1st. The trust instrument requires that the trust pay to A semiannually (on June 30 and December 31) 9 percent of the fair market value of the trust assets as of January 1st during A's life. The section 7520 rate for January is 9.6 percent. Under Table F(9.6) in paragraph (e)(6) of this section, the appropriate adjustment factor is .933805 for semiannual payments payable at the end of the semiannual period. The adjusted payout rate is 8.404 (9% × .933805). Based on the remainder factors in Table U(1) in paragraph (e)(7) of this section, the present value

Reg. § 1.664-4(e)(4)

of the remainder interest is $10,109.00, computed as follows:

Factor at 8.4 percent at age 45	.10117
Factor at 8.6 percent at age 45	.09715
Difference	.00402

Interpolation adjustment:

$$\frac{8.404\% - 8.4\%}{0.2\%} = \frac{x}{.00402}$$

$$x = .00008$$

Factor at 8.4 percent at age 45	.10117
Less: Interpolation adjustment	.00008
Interpolated Factor	.10109

Present value of remainder interest:
($100,000 × .10109) $10,109.00

(6) *Actuarial Table D and F (4.2 through 14.0) for transfers for which the valuation date is after April 30, 1989.* For transfers for which the valuation date is after April 30, 1989, the present value of a charitable remainder unitrust interest that is dependent upon a term of years is determined by using the section 7520 rate and the tables in this paragraph (e)(6). For transfers for which the valuation date is after April 30, 1999, where the present value of a charitable remainder unitrust interest is dependent on the termination of a life interest, see paragraph (e)(5) of this section. See, however, § 1.7520-3(b) (relating to exceptions to the use of prescribed tables under certain circumstances). Many actuarial factors not contained in the following tables are contained in Internal Revenue Service Publication 1458, "Actuarial Values, Book Beth," (1999). A copy of this publication is available for purchase from the Superintendent of Documents, United States Government Printing Office, Washington, DC 20402.

43,334 **Estates, Trusts, and Beneficiaries**

See p. 20,601 for regulations not amended to reflect law changes

TABLE D
SHOWING THE PRESENT WORTH OF A REMAINDER INTEREST
POSTPONED FOR A TERM CERTAIN IN A CHARITABLE
REMAINDER UNITRUST
APPLICABLE AFTER APRIL 30, 1989

ADJUSTED PAYOUT RATE

YEARS	4.2%	4.4%	4.6%	4.8%	5.0%	5.2%	5.4%	5.6%	5.8%	6.0%
1	.958000	.956000	.954000	.952000	.950000	.948000	.946000	.944000	.942000	.940000
2	.917764	.913936	.910116	.906304	.902500	.898704	.894916	.891136	.887364	.883600
3	.879218	.873723	.868251	.862801	.857375	.851971	.846591	.841232	.835897	.830584
4	.842291	.835279	.828311	.821387	.814506	.807669	.800875	.794123	.787415	.780749
5	.806915	.798527	.790209	.781960	.773781	.765670	.757627	.749652	.741745	.733904
6	.773024	.763392	.753859	.744426	.735092	.725855	.716716	.707672	.698724	.689870
7	.740557	.729802	.719182	.708694	.698337	.688111	.678013	.668042	.658198	.648478
8	.709454	.697691	.686099	.674677	.663420	.652329	.641400	.630632	.620022	.609569
9	.679657	.666993	.654539	.642292	.630249	.618408	.606765	.595317	.584061	.572995
10	.651111	.637645	.624430	.611462	.598737	.586251	.573999	.561979	.550185	.538615
11	.623764	.609589	.595706	.582112	.568800	.555766	.543003	.530508	.518275	.506298
12	.597566	.582767	.568304	.554170	.540360	.526866	.513681	.500800	.488215	.475920
13	.572469	.557125	.542162	.527570	.513342	.499469	.485942	.472755	.459898	.447365
14	.548425	.532611	.517222	.502247	.487675	.473496	.459701	.446281	.433224	.420523
15	.525391	.509177	.493430	.478139	.463291	.448875	.434878	.421289	.408097	.395292
16	.503325	.486773	.470732	.455188	.440127	.425533	.411394	.397697	.384427	.371574
17	.482185	.465355	.449079	.433339	.418120	.403405	.389179	.375426	.362131	.349280
18	.461933	.444879	.428421	.412539	.397214	.382428	.368163	.354402	.341127	.328323
19	.442532	.425304	.408714	.392737	.377354	.362542	.348282	.334555	.321342	.308624
20	.423946	.406591	.389913	.373886	.358486	.343690	.329475	.315820	.302704	.290106

TABLE D
SHOWING THE PRESENT WORTH OF A REMAINDER INTEREST
POSTPONED FOR A TERM CERTAIN IN A CHARITABLE
REMAINDER UNITRUST
APPLICABLE AFTER APRIL 30, 1989

ADJUSTED PAYOUT RATE

YEARS	6.2%	6.4%	6.6%	6.8%	7.0%	7.2%	7.4%	7.6%	7.8%	8.0%
1	.938000	.936000	.934000	.932000	.930000	.928000	.926000	.924000	.922000	.920000
2	.879844	.876096	.872356	.868624	.864900	.861184	.857476	.853776	.850084	.846400
3	.825294	.820026	.814781	.809558	.804357	.799179	.794023	.788889	.783777	.778688
4	.774125	.767544	.761005	.754508	.748052	.741638	.735265	.728933	.722643	.716393
5	.726130	.718421	.710779	.703201	.695688	.688240	.680855	.673535	.666277	.659082
6	.681110	.672442	.663867	.655383	.646990	.638687	.630472	.622346	.614307	.606355
7	.638881	.629406	.620052	.610817	.601701	.592701	.583817	.575048	.566391	.557847
8	.599270	.589124	.579129	.569282	.559582	.550027	.540615	.531344	.522213	.513219
9	.562115	.551420	.540906	.530571	.520411	.510425	.500609	.490962	.481480	.472161
10	.527264	.516129	.505206	.494492	.483982	.473674	.463564	.453649	.443925	.434388
11	.494574	.483097	.471863	.460866	.450104	.439570	.429260	.419171	.409298	.399637
12	.463910	.452179	.440720	.429527	.418596	.407921	.397495	.387314	.377373	.367666
13	.435148	.423239	.411632	.400320	.389295	.378550	.368081	.357879	.347938	.338253
14	.408169	.396152	.384465	.373098	.362044	.351295	.340843	.330680	.320799	.311193
15	.382862	.370798	.359090	.347727	.336701	.326002	.315620	.305548	.295777	.286297
16	.359125	.347067	.335390	.324082	.313132	.302529	.292264	.282326	.272706	.263394
17	.336859	.324855	.313254	.302044	.291213	.280747	.270637	.260870	.251435	.242322
18	.315974	.304064	.292579	.281505	.270828	.260533	.250610	.241044	.231823	.222936
19	.296383	.284604	.273269	.262363	.251870	.241775	.232065	.222724	.213741	.205101
20	.278008	.266389	.255233	.244522	.234239	.224367	.214892	.205797	.197069	.188693

Reg. § 1.664-4(e)(6)

TABLE D
SHOWING THE PRESENT WORTH OF A REMAINDER INTEREST POSTPONED FOR A TERM CERTAIN IN A CHARITABLE REMAINDER UNITRUST APPLICABLE AFTER APRIL 30, 1989

ADJUSTED PAYOUT RATE

YEARS	8.2%	8.4%	8.6%	8.8%	9.0%	9.2%	9.4%	9.6%	9.8%	10.0%
1	.918000	.916000	.914000	.912000	.910000	.908000	.906000	.904000	.902000	.900000
2	.842724	.839056	.835396	.831744	.828100	.824464	.820836	.817216	.813604	.810000
3	.773621	.768575	.763552	.758551	.753571	.748613	.743677	.738763	.733871	.729000
4	.710184	.704015	.697886	.691798	.685750	.679741	.673772	.667842	.661951	.656100
5	.651949	.644878	.637868	.630920	.624032	.617205	.610437	.603729	.597080	.590490
6	.598489	.590708	.583012	.575399	.567869	.560422	.553056	.545771	.538566	.531441
7	.549413	.541089	.532873	.524764	.516761	.508863	.501069	.493377	.485787	.478297
8	.504361	.495637	.487046	.478585	.470253	.462048	.453968	.446013	.438180	.430467
9	.463003	.454004	.445160	.436469	.427930	.419539	.411295	.403196	.395238	.387420
10	.425037	.415867	.406876	.398060	.389416	.380942	.372634	.364489	.356505	.348678
11	.390184	.380934	.371885	.363031	.354369	.345895	.337606	.329498	.321567	.313811
12	.358189	.348936	.339902	.331084	.322475	.314073	.305871	.297866	.290054	.282430
13	.328817	.319625	.310671	.301949	.293453	.285178	.277119	.269271	.261628	.254187
14	.301854	.292777	.283953	.275377	.267042	.258942	.251070	.243421	.235989	.228768
15	.277102	.268184	.259533	.251144	.243008	.235119	.227469	.220053	.212862	.205891
16	.254380	.245656	.237213	.229043	.221137	.213488	.206087	.198928	.192001	.185302
17	.233521	.225021	.216813	.208887	.201235	.193847	.186715	.179830	.173185	.166772
18	.214372	.206119	.198167	.190505	.183124	.176013	.169164	.162567	.156213	.150095
19	.196794	.188805	.181125	.173741	.166643	.159820	.153262	.146960	.140904	.135085
20	.180657	.172946	.165548	.158452	.151645	.145117	.138856	.132852	.127096	.121577

TABLE D
SHOWING THE PRESENT WORTH OF A REMAINDER INTEREST POSTPONED FOR A TERM CERTAIN IN A CHARITABLE REMAINDER UNITRUST APPLICABLE AFTER APRIL 30, 1989

ADJUSTED PAYOUT RATE

YEARS	10.2%	10.4%	10.6%	10.8%	11.0%	11.2%	11.4%	11.6%	11.8%	12.0%
1	.898000	.896000	.894000	.892000	.890000	.888000	.886000	.884000	.882000	.880000
2	.806404	.802816	.799236	.795664	.792100	.788544	.784996	.781456	.777924	.774400
3	.724151	.719323	.714517	.709732	.704969	.700227	.695506	.690807	.686129	.681472
4	.650287	.644514	.638778	.633081	.627422	.621802	.616219	.610673	.605166	.599695
5	.583958	.577484	.571068	.564708	.558406	.552160	.545970	.539835	.533756	.527732
6	.524394	.517426	.510535	.503720	.496981	.490318	.483729	.477214	.470773	.464404
7	.470906	.463613	.456418	.449318	.442313	.435402	.428584	.421858	.415222	.408676
8	.422874	.415398	.408038	.400792	.393659	.386637	.379726	.372922	.366226	.359635
9	.379741	.372196	.364786	.357506	.350356	.343334	.336437	.329663	.323011	.316478
10	.341007	.333488	.326118	.318896	.311817	.304881	.298083	.291422	.284896	.278501
11	.306224	.298805	.291550	.284455	.277517	.270734	.264102	.257617	.251278	.245081
12	.274989	.267729	.260645	.253734	.246990	.240412	.233994	.227734	.221627	.215671
13	.246941	.239886	.233017	.226331	.219821	.213486	.207319	.201317	.195475	.189791
14	.221753	.214937	.208317	.201887	.195641	.189575	.183684	.177964	.172409	.167016
15	.199134	.192584	.186236	.180083	.174121	.168343	.162744	.157320	.152065	.146974
16	.178822	.172555	.166495	.160634	.154967	.149488	.144191	.139071	.134121	.129337
17	.160582	.154609	.148846	.143286	.137921	.132746	.127754	.122939	.118295	.113817
18	.144203	.138530	.133069	.127811	.122750	.117878	.113190	.108678	.104336	.100159
19	.129494	.124123	.118963	.114007	.109247	.104676	.100286	.096071	.092024	.088140
20	.116286	.111214	.106353	.101694	.097230	.092952	.088853	.084927	.081166	.077563

Reg. § 1.664-4(e)(6)

43,336 Estates, Trusts, and Beneficiaries

See p. 20,601 for regulations not amended to reflect law changes

TABLE D
SHOWING THE PRESENT WORTH OF A REMAINDER INTEREST POSTPONED FOR A TERM CERTAIN IN A CHARITABLE REMAINDER UNITRUST APPLICABLE AFTER APRIL 30, 1989

ADJUSTED PAYOUT RATE

YEARS	12.2%	12.4%	12.6%	12.8%	13.0%	13.2%	13.4%	13.6%	13.8%	14.0%
1	.878000	.876000	.874000	.872000	.870000	.868000	.866000	.864000	.862000	.860000
2	.770884	.767376	.763876	.760384	.756900	.753424	.749956	.746496	.743044	.739600
3	.676836	.672221	.667628	.663055	.658503	.653972	.649462	.644973	.640504	.636056
4	.594262	.588866	.583507	.578184	.572898	.567648	.562434	.557256	.552114	.547008
5	.521762	.515847	.509985	.504176	.498421	.492718	.487068	.481469	.475923	.470427
6	.458107	.451882	.445724	.439642	.433626	.427679	.421801	.415990	.410245	.404567
7	.402218	.395848	.389565	.383368	.377255	.371226	.365279	.359415	.353631	.347928
8	.353147	.346763	.340480	.334297	.328212	.322224	.316332	.310535	.304830	.299218
9	.310063	.303764	.297579	.291507	.285544	.279690	.273944	.268302	.262764	.257327
10	.272236	.266098	.260084	.254194	.248423	.242771	.237235	.231813	.226502	.221302
11	.239023	.233102	.227314	.221657	.216128	.210725	.205446	.200286	.195245	.190319
12	.209862	.204197	.198672	.193285	.188032	.182910	.177916	.173047	.168301	.163675
13	.184259	.178877	.173640	.168544	.163588	.158766	.154075	.149513	.145076	.140760
14	.161779	.156696	.151761	.146971	.142321	.137809	.133429	.129179	.125055	.121054
15	.142042	.137266	.132639	.128158	.123819	.119618	.115550	.111611	.107798	.104106
16	.124713	.120245	.115927	.111754	.107723	.103828	.100066	.096432	.092922	.089531
17	.109498	.105334	.101320	.097450	.093719	.090123	.086657	.083317	.080098	.076997
18	.096139	.092273	.088554	.084976	.081535	.078227	.075045	.071986	.069045	.066217
19	.084410	.080831	.077396	.074099	.070936	.067901	.064989	.062196	.059517	.056947
20	.074112	.070808	.067644	.064614	.061714	.058938	.056280	.053737	.051303	.048974

TABLE F(4.2), WITH INTEREST AT 4.2 PERCENT, SHOWING FACTORS FOR COMPUTATION OF THE ADJUSTED PAYOUT RATE FOR CERTAIN VALUATIONS APPLICABLE AFTER APRIL 30, 1989

1 NUMBER OF MONTHS BY WHICH THE VALUATION DATE FOR THE FIRST FULL TAXABLE YEAR OF THE TRUST PRECEDES THE FIRST PAYOUT		2 FACTORS FOR PAYOUT AT THE END OF EACH PERIOD			
AT LEAST	BUT LESS THAN	ANNUAL PERIOD	SEMIANNUAL PERIOD	QUARTERLY PERIOD	MONTHLY PERIOD
....	1	1.000000	.989820	.984755	.981389
1	2	.996577	.986432	.981385	.978030
2	3	.993166	.983056	.978026	
3	4	.989767	.979691	.974679	
4	5	.986380	.976338		
5	6	.983004	.972996		
6	7	.979639	.969666		
7	8	.976286			
8	9	.972945			
9	10	.969615			
10	11	.966296			
11	12	.962989			
12	....	.959693			

Reg. § 1.664-4(e)(6)

Estates, Trusts, and Beneficiaries

See p. 20,601 for regulations not amended to reflect law changes

43,337

TABLE F(4.4), WITH INTEREST AT 4.4 PERCENT, SHOWING FACTORS FOR COMPUTATION OF THE ADJUSTED PAYOUT RATE FOR CERTAIN VALUATIONS APPLICABLE AFTER APRIL 30, 1989

1		2			
NUMBER OF MONTHS BY WHICH THE VALUATION DATE FOR THE FIRST FULL TAXABLE YEAR OF THE TRUST PRECEDES THE FIRST PAYOUT		FACTORS FOR PAYOUT AT THE END OF EACH PERIOD			
AT LEAST	BUT LESS THAN	ANNUAL PERIOD	SEMIANNUAL PERIOD	QUARTERLY PERIOD	MONTHLY PERIOD
....	1	1.000000	.989350	.984054	.980533
1	2	.996418	.985806	.980529	.977021
2	3	.992849	.982275	.977017	
3	4	.989293	.978757	.973517	
4	5	.985749	.975251		
5	6	.982219	.971758		
6	7	.978700	.968277		
7	8	.975195			
8	9	.971702			
9	10	.968221			
10	11	.964753			
11	12	.961298			
12	....	.957854			

TABLE F(4.6), WITH INTEREST AT 4.6 PERCENT, SHOWING FACTORS FOR COMPUTATION OF THE ADJUSTED PAYOUT RATE FOR CERTAIN VALUATIONS APPLICABLE AFTER APRIL 30, 1989

1		2			
NUMBER OF MONTHS BY WHICH THE VALUATION DATE FOR THE FIRST FULL TAXABLE YEAR OF THE TRUST PRECEDES THE FIRST PAYOUT		FACTORS FOR PAYOUT AT THE END OF EACH PERIOD			
AT LEAST	BUT LESS THAN	ANNUAL PERIOD	SEMIANNUAL PERIOD	QUARTERLY PERIOD	MONTHLY PERIOD
....	1	1.000000	.988882	.983354	.979680
1	2	.996259	.985183	.979676	.976015
2	3	.992532	.981498	.976011	
3	4	.988820	.977826	.972360	
4	5	.985121	.974168		
5	6	.981436	.970524		
6	7	.977764	.966894		
7	8	.974107			
8	9	.970463			
9	10	.966832			
10	11	.963216			
11	12	.959613			
12	....	.956023			

Reg. § 1.664-4(e)(6)

43,338   Estates, Trusts, and Beneficiaries

See p. 20,601 for regulations not amended to reflect law changes

TABLE F(4.8), WITH INTEREST AT 4.8 PERCENT, SHOWING FACTORS FOR COMPUTATION OF THE ADJUSTED PAYOUT RATE FOR CERTAIN VALUATIONS APPLICABLE AFTER APRIL 30, 1989

1		2			
NUMBER OF MONTHS BY WHICH THE VALUATION DATE FOR THE FIRST FULL TAXABLE YEAR OF THE TRUST PRECEDES THE FIRST PAYOUT		FACTORS FOR PAYOUT AT THE END OF EACH PERIOD			
AT LEAST	BUT LESS THAN	ANNUAL PERIOD	SEMIANNUAL PERIOD	QUARTERLY PERIOD	MONTHLY PERIOD
....	1	1.000000	.988415	.982657	.978830
1	2	.996101	.984561	.978825	.975013
2	3	.992217	.980722	.975008	
3	4	.988348	.976898	.971206	
4	5	.984494	.973089		
5	6	.980655	.969294		
6	7	.976831	.965515		
7	8	.973022			
8	9	.969228			
9	10	.965448			
10	11	.961684			
11	12	.957934			
12	....	.954198			

TABLE F(5.0), WITH INTEREST AT 5.0 PERCENT, SHOWING FACTORS FOR COMPUTATION OF THE ADJUSTED PAYOUT RATE FOR CERTAIN VALUATIONS APPLICABLE AFTER APRIL 30, 1989

1		2			
NUMBER OF MONTHS BY WHICH THE VALUATION DATE FOR THE FIRST FULL TAXABLE YEAR OF THE TRUST PRECEDES THE FIRST PAYOUT		FACTORS FOR PAYOUT AT THE END OF EACH PERIOD			
AT LEAST	BUT LESS THAN	ANNUAL PERIOD	SEMIANNUAL PERIOD	QUARTERLY PERIOD	MONTHLY PERIOD
....	1	1.000000	.987950	.981961	.977982
1	2	.995942	.983941	.977977	.974014
2	3	.991901	.979949	.974009	
3	4	.987877	.975973	.970057	
4	5	.983868	.972013		
5	6	.979876	.968069		
6	7	.975900	.964141		
7	8	.971940			
8	9	.967997			
9	10	.964069			
10	11	.960157			
11	12	.956261			
12	....	.952381			

Reg. § 1.664-4(e)(6)

TABLE F(5.2), WITH INTEREST AT 5.2 PERCENT, SHOWING FACTORS FOR COMPUTATION OF THE ADJUSTED PAYOUT RATE FOR CERTAIN VALUATIONS APPLICABLE AFTER APRIL 30, 1989

1
NUMBER OF MONTHS BY WHICH THE VALUATION DATE FOR THE FIRST FULL TAXABLE YEAR OF THE TRUST PRECEDES THE FIRST PAYOUT

2
FACTORS FOR PAYOUT AT THE END OF EACH PERIOD

AT LEAST	BUT LESS THAN	ANNUAL PERIOD	SEMIANNUAL PERIOD	QUARTERLY PERIOD	MONTHLY PERIOD
....	1	1.000000	.987486	.981268	.977137
1	2	.995784	.983323	.977132	.973018
2	3	.991587	.979178	.973012	
3	4	.987407	.975050	.968911	
4	5	.983244	.970940		
5	6	.979099	.966847		
6	7	.974972	.962771		
7	8	.970862			
8	9	.966769			
9	10	.962694			
10	11	.958636			
11	12	.954594			
12	....	.950570			

TABLE F(5.4), WITH INTEREST AT 5.4 PERCENT, SHOWING FACTORS FOR COMPUTATION OF THE ADJUSTED PAYOUT RATE FOR CERTAIN VALUATIONS APPLICABLE AFTER APRIL 30, 1989

1
NUMBER OF MONTHS BY WHICH THE VALUATION DATE FOR THE FIRST FULL TAXABLE YEAR OF THE TRUST PRECEDES THE FIRST PAYOUT

2
FACTORS FOR PAYOUT AT THE END OF EACH PERIOD

AT LEAST	BUT LESS THAN	ANNUAL PERIOD	SEMIANNUAL PERIOD	QUARTERLY PERIOD	MONTHLY PERIOD
..	1	1.000000	.987023	.980577	.976295
1	2	.995627	.982707	.976289	.972026
2	3	.991273	.978409	.972019	
3	4	.986938	.974131	.967769	
4	5	.982622	.969871		
5	6	.978325	.965629		
6	7	.974047	.961407		
7	8	.969787			
8	9	.965546			
9	10	.961323			
10	11	.957119			
11	12	.952934			
12	..	.948767			

Reg. § 1.664-4(e)(6)

43,340 Estates, Trusts, and Beneficiaries

See p. 20,601 for regulations not amended to reflect law changes

TABLE F(5.6), WITH INTEREST AT 5.6 PERCENT, SHOWING FACTORS FOR COMPUTATION OF THE ADJUSTED PAYOUT RATE FOR CERTAIN VALUATIONS APPLICABLE AFTER APRIL 30, 1989

1		2			
NUMBER OF MONTHS BY WHICH THE VALUATION DATE FOR THE FIRST FULL TAXABLE YEAR OF THE TRUST PRECEDES THE FIRST PAYOUT		FACTORS FOR PAYOUT AT THE END OF EACH PERIOD			
AT LEAST	BUT LESS THAN	ANNUAL PERIOD	SEMIANNUAL PERIOD	QUARTERLY PERIOD	MONTHLY PERIOD
..	1	1.000000	.986562	.979888	.975455
1	2	.995470	.982092	.975449	.971036
2	3	.990960	.977643	.971029	
3	4	.986470	.973214	.966630	
4	5	.982001	.968805		
5	6	.977552	.964416		
6	7	.973124	.960047		
7	8	.968715			
8	9	.964326			
9	10	.959958			
10	11	.955609			
11	12	.951279			
12	..	.946970			

TABLE F(5.8), WITH INTEREST AT 5.8 PERCENT, SHOWING FACTORS FOR COMPUTATION OF THE ADJUSTED PAYOUT RATE FOR CERTAIN VALUATIONS APPLICABLE AFTER APRIL 30, 1989

1		2			
NUMBER OF MONTHS BY WHICH THE VALUATION DATE FOR THE FIRST FULL TAXABLE YEAR OF THE TRUST PRECEDES THE FIRST PAYOUT		FACTORS FOR PAYOUT AT THE END OF EACH PERIOD			
AT LEAST	BUT LESS THAN	ANNUAL PERIOD	SEMIANNUAL PERIOD	QUARTERLY PERIOD	MONTHLY PERIOD
..	1	1.000000	.986102	.979201	.974618
1	2	.995313	.981480	.974611	.970050
2	3	.990647	.976879	.970043	
3	4	.986004	.972300	.965496	
4	5	.981382	.967743		
5	6	.976782	.963206		
6	7	.972203	.958692		
7	8	.967646			
8	9	.963111			
9	10	.958596			
10	11	.954103			
11	12	.949631			
12	..	.945180			

Reg. § 1.664-4(e)(6)

TABLE F(6.0), WITH INTEREST AT 6.0 PERCENT, SHOWING FACTORS FOR COMPUTATION OF THE ADJUSTED PAYOUT RATE FOR CERTAIN VALUATIONS APPLICABLE AFTER APRIL 30, 1989

1
NUMBER OF MONTHS BY WHICH THE VALUATION DATE FOR THE FIRST FULL TAXABLE YEAR OF THE TRUST PRECEDES THE FIRST PAYOUT

2
FACTORS FOR PAYOUT AT THE END OF EACH PERIOD

AT LEAST	BUT LESS THAN	ANNUAL PERIOD	SEMIANNUAL PERIOD	QUARTERLY PERIOD	MONTHLY PERIOD
..	1	1.000000	.985643	.978516	.973784
1	2	.995156	.980869	.973776	.969067
2	3	.990336	.976117	.969059	
3	4	.985538	.971389	.964365	
4	5	.980764	.966684		
5	6	.976014	.962001		
6	7	.971286	.957341		
7	8	.966581			
8	9	.961899			
9	10	.957239			
10	11	.952603			
11	12	.947988			
12	..	.943396			

TABLE F(6.2), WITH INTEREST AT 6.2 PERCENT, SHOWING FACTORS FOR COMPUTATION OF THE ADJUSTED PAYOUT RATE FOR CERTAIN VALUATIONS APPLICABLE AFTER APRIL 30, 1989

1
NUMBER OF MONTHS BY WHICH THE VALUATION DATE FOR THE FIRST FULL TAXABLE YEAR OF THE TRUST PRECEDES THE FIRST PAYOUT

2
FACTORS FOR PAYOUT AT THE END OF EACH PERIOD

AT LEAST	BUT LESS THAN	ANNUAL PERIOD	SEMIANNUAL PERIOD	QUARTERLY PERIOD	MONTHLY PERIOD
..	1	1.000000	.985185	.977833	.972952
1	2	.995000	.980259	.972944	.968087
2	3	.990024	.975358	.968079	
3	4	.985074	.970481	.963238	
4	5	.980148	.965628		
5	6	.975247	.960799		
6	7	.970371	.955995		
7	8	.965519			
8	9	.960691			
9	10	.955887			
10	11	.951107			
11	12	.946352			
12	..	.941620			

Reg. § 1.664-4(e)(6)

43,342 Estates, Trusts, and Beneficiaries

See p. 20,601 for regulations not amended to reflect law changes

TABLE F(6.4), WITH INTEREST AT 6.4 PERCENT, SHOWING FACTORS FOR COMPUTATION OF THE ADJUSTED PAYOUT RATE FOR CERTAIN VALUATIONS APPLICABLE AFTER APRIL 30, 1989

1		2			
NUMBER OF MONTHS BY WHICH THE VALUATION DATE FOR THE FIRST FULL TAXABLE YEAR OF THE TRUST PRECEDES THE FIRST PAYOUT		FACTORS FOR PAYOUT AT THE END OF EACH PERIOD			
AT LEAST	BUT LESS THAN	ANNUAL PERIOD	SEMIANNUAL PERIOD	QUARTERLY PERIOD	MONTHLY PERIOD
..	1	1.000000	.984729	.977152	.972122
1	2	.994844	.979652	.972114	.967110
2	3	.989714	.974600	.967101	
3	4	.984611	.969575	.962115	
4	5	.979534	.964576		
5	6	.974483	.959602		
6	7	.969458	.954654		
7	8	.964460			
8	9	.959487			
9	10	.954539			
10	11	.949617			
11	12	.944721			
12	..	.939850			

TABLE F(6.6), WITH INTEREST AT 6.6 PERCENT, SHOWING FACTORS FOR COMPUTATION OF THE ADJUSTED PAYOUT RATE FOR CERTAIN VALUATIONS APPLICABLE AFTER APRIL 30, 1989

1		2			
NUMBER OF MONTHS BY WHICH THE VALUATION DATE FOR THE FIRST FULL TAXABLE YEAR OF THE TRUST PRECEDES THE FIRST PAYOUT		FACTORS FOR PAYOUT AT THE END OF EACH PERIOD			
AT LEAST	BUT LESS THAN	ANNUAL PERIOD	SEMIANNUAL PERIOD	QUARTERLY PERIOD	MONTHLY PERIOD
..	1	1.000000	.984274	.976473	.971295
1	2	.994688	.979046	.971286	.966136
2	3	.989404	.973845	.966127	
3	4	.984149	.968672	.960995	
4	5	.978921	.963527		
5	6	.973721	.958408		
6	7	.968549	.953317		
7	8	.963404			
8	9	.958286			
9	10	.953196			
10	11	.948132			
11	12	.943096			
12	..	.938086			

Reg. § 1.664-4(e)(6)

Estates, Trusts, and Beneficiaries

TABLE F(6.8), WITH INTEREST AT 6.8 PERCENT, SHOWING FACTORS FOR COMPUTATION OF THE ADJUSTED PAYOUT RATE FOR CERTAIN VALUATIONS APPLICABLE AFTER APRIL 30, 1989

1		2			
NUMBER OF MONTHS BY WHICH THE VALUATION DATE FOR THE FIRST FULL TAXABLE YEAR OF THE TRUST PRECEDES THE FIRST PAYOUT		FACTORS FOR PAYOUT AT THE END OF EACH PERIOD			
AT LEAST	BUT LESS THAN	ANNUAL PERIOD	SEMIANNUAL PERIOD	QUARTERLY PERIOD	MONTHLY PERIOD
..	1	1.000000	.983821	.975796	.970471
1	2	.994533	.978442	.970461	.965165
2	3	.989095	.973092	.965156	
3	4	.983688	.967772	.959879	
4	5	.978309	.962481		
5	6	.972961	.957219		
6	7	.967641	.951985		
7	8	.962351			
8	9	.957089			
9	10	.951857			
10	11	.946653			
11	12	.941477			
12	..	.936330			

TABLE F(7.0), WITH INTEREST AT 7.0 PERCENT, SHOWING FACTORS FOR COMPUTATION OF THE ADJUSTED PAYOUT RATE FOR CERTAIN VALUATIONS APPLICABLE AFTER APRIL 30, 1989

1		2			
NUMBER OF MONTHS BY WHICH THE VALUATION DATE FOR THE FIRST FULL TAXABLE YEAR OF THE TRUST PRECEDES THE FIRST PAYOUT		FACTORS FOR PAYOUT AT THE END OF EACH PERIOD			
AT LEAST	BUT LESS THAN	ANNUAL PERIOD	SEMIANNUAL PERIOD	QUARTERLY PERIOD	MONTHLY PERIOD
....	1	1.000000	.983368	.975122	.969649
1	2	.994378	.977839	.969639	.964198
2	3	.988787	.972342	.964187	
3	4	.983228	.966875	.958766	
4	5	.977700	.961439		
5	6	.972203	.956033		
6	7	.966736	.950658		
7	8	.961301			
8	9	.955896			
9	10	.950522			
10	11	.945178			
11	12	.939864			
12	....	.934579			

Reg. § 1.664-4(e)(6)

43,344   Estates, Trusts, and Beneficiaries
See p. 20,601 for regulations not amended to reflect law changes

TABLE F(7.2), WITH INTEREST AT 7.2 PERCENT, SHOWING FACTORS FOR COMPUTATION OF THE ADJUSTED PAYOUT RATE FOR CERTAIN VALUATIONS APPLICABLE AFTER APRIL 30, 1989

1		2			
NUMBER OF MONTHS BY WHICH THE VALUATION DATE FOR THE FIRST FULL TAXABLE YEAR OF THE TRUST PRECEDES THE FIRST PAYOUT		FACTORS FOR PAYOUT AT THE END OF EACH PERIOD			
AT LEAST	BUT LESS THAN	ANNUAL PERIOD	SEMIANNUAL PERIOD	QUARTERLY PERIOD	MONTHLY PERIOD
....	1	1.000000	.982917	.974449	.968830
1	2	.994223	.977239	.968819	.963233
2	3	.988479	.971593	.963222	
3	4	.982769	.965980	.957658	
4	5	.977091	.960400		
5	6	.971446	.954851		
6	7	.965834	.949335		
7	8	.960255			
8	9	.954707			
9	10	.949192			
10	11	.943708			
11	12	.938256			
12	....	.932836			

TABLE F(7.4), WITH INTEREST AT 7.4 PERCENT, SHOWING FACTORS FOR COMPUTATION OF THE ADJUSTED PAYOUT RATE FOR CERTAIN VALUATIONS APPLICABLE AFTER APRIL 30, 1989

1		2			
NUMBER OF MONTHS BY WHICH THE VALUATION DATE FOR THE FIRST FULL TAXABLE YEAR OF THE TRUST PRECEDES THE FIRST PAYOUT		FACTORS FOR PAYOUT AT THE END OF EACH PERIOD			
AT LEAST	BUT LESS THAN	ANNUAL PERIOD	SEMIANNUAL PERIOD	QUARTERLY PERIOD	MONTHLY PERIOD
....	1	1.000000	.982467	.973778	.968013
1	2	.994068	.976640	.968002	.962271
2	3	.988172	.970847	.962260	
3	4	.982311	.965088	.956552	
4	5	.976484	.959364		
5	6	.970692	.953673		
6	7	.964935	.948017		
7	8	.959211			
8	9	.953521			
9	10	.947866			
10	11	.942243			
11	12	.936654			
12	....	.931099			

Reg. § 1.664-4(e)(6)

Estates, Trusts, and Beneficiaries 43,345
See p. 20,601 for regulations not amended to reflect law changes

TABLE F(7.6), WITH INTEREST AT 7.6 PERCENT, SHOWING FACTORS FOR COMPUTATION OF THE ADJUSTED PAYOUT RATE FOR CERTAIN VALUATIONS APPLICABLE AFTER APRIL 30, 1989

1			2		
NUMBER OF MONTHS BY WHICH THE VALUATION DATE FOR THE FIRST FULL TAXABLE YEAR OF THE TRUST PRECEDES THE FIRST PAYOUT			FACTORS FOR PAYOUT AT THE END OF EACH PERIOD		
AT LEAST	BUT LESS THAN	ANNUAL PERIOD	SEMIANNUAL PERIOD	QUARTERLY PERIOD	MONTHLY PERIOD
....	1	1.000000	.982019	.973109	.967199
1	2	.993914	.976042	.967187	.961313
2	3	.987866	.970103	.961301	
3	4	.981854	.964199	.955451	
4	5	.975879	.958331		
5	6	.969940	.952499		
6	7	.964037	.946703		
7	8	.958171			
8	9	.952340			
9	10	.946544			
10	11	.940784			
11	12	.935058			
12	....	.929368			

TABLE F(7.8), WITH INTEREST AT 7.8 PERCENT, SHOWING FACTORS FOR COMPUTATION OF THE ADJUSTED PAYOUT RATE FOR CERTAIN VALUATIONS APPLICABLE AFTER APRIL 30, 1989

1			2		
NUMBER OF MONTHS BY WHICH THE VALUATION DATE FOR THE FIRST FULL TAXABLE YEAR OF THE TRUST PRECEDES THE FIRST PAYOUT			FACTORS FOR PAYOUT AT THE END OF EACH PERIOD		
AT LEAST	BUT LESS THAN	ANNUAL PERIOD	SEMIANNUAL PERIOD	QUARTERLY PERIOD	MONTHLY PERIOD
....	1	1.000000	.981571	.972442	.966387
1	2	.993761	.975447	.966374	.960357
2	3	.987560	.969361	.960345	
3	4	.981398	.963312	.954353	
4	5	.975275	.957302		
5	6	.969190	.951329		
6	7	.963143	.945393		
7	8	.957133			
8	9	.951161			
9	10	.945227			
10	11	.939329			
11	12	.933468			
12	....	.927644			

Reg. § 1.664-4(e)(6)

Estates, Trusts, and Beneficiaries

See p. 20,601 for regulations not amended to reflect law changes

TABLE F(8.0), WITH INTEREST AT 8.0 PERCENT, SHOWING FACTORS FOR COMPUTATION OF THE ADJUSTED PAYOUT RATE FOR CERTAIN VALUATIONS APPLICABLE AFTER APRIL 30, 1989

1 NUMBER OF MONTHS BY WHICH THE VALUATION DATE FOR THE FIRST FULL TAXABLE YEAR OF THE TRUST PRECEDES THE FIRST PAYOUT		2 FACTORS FOR PAYOUT AT THE END OF EACH PERIOD			
AT LEAST	BUT LESS THAN	ANNUAL PERIOD	SEMIANNUAL PERIOD	QUARTERLY PERIOD	MONTHLY PERIOD
....	1	1.000000	.981125	.971777	.965578
1	2	.993607	.974853	.965564	.959405
2	3	.987255	.968621	.959392	
3	4	.980944	.962429	.953258	
4	5	.974673	.956276		
5	6	.968442	.950162		
6	7	.962250	.944088		
7	8	.956099			
8	9	.949987			
9	10	.943913			
10	11	.937879			
11	12	.931883			
12	....	.925926			

TABLE F(8.2), WITH INTEREST AT 8.2 PERCENT, SHOWING FACTORS FOR COMPUTATION OF THE ADJUSTED PAYOUT RATE FOR CERTAIN VALUATIONS APPLICABLE AFTER APRIL 30, 1989

1 NUMBER OF MONTHS BY WHICH THE VALUATION DATE FOR THE FIRST FULL TAXABLE YEAR OF THE TRUST PRECEDES THE FIRST PAYOUT		2 FACTORS FOR PAYOUT AT THE END OF EACH PERIOD			
AT LEAST	BUT LESS THAN	ANNUAL PERIOD	SEMIANNUAL PERIOD	QUARTERLY PERIOD	MONTHLY PERIOD
....	1	1.000000	.980680	.971114	.964771
1	2	.993454	.974261	.964757	.958455
2	3	.986951	.967883	.958441	
3	4	.980490	.961547	.952167	
4	5	.974072	.955253		
5	6	.967695	.949000		
6	7	.961361	.942788		
7	8	.955068			
8	9	.948816			
9	10	.942605			
10	11	.936434			
11	12	.930304			
12	....	.924214			

Reg. § 1.664-4(e)(6)

Estates, Trusts, and Beneficiaries

TABLE F(8.4), WITH INTEREST AT 8.4 PERCENT, SHOWING FACTORS FOR COMPUTATION OF THE ADJUSTED PAYOUT RATE FOR CERTAIN VALUATIONS APPLICABLE AFTER APRIL 30, 1989

1		2			
NUMBER OF MONTHS BY WHICH THE VALUATION DATE FOR THE FIRST FULL TAXABLE YEAR OF THE TRUST PRECEDES THE FIRST PAYOUT		FACTORS FOR PAYOUT AT THE END OF EACH PERIOD			
AT LEAST	BUT LESS THAN	ANNUAL PERIOD	SEMIANNUAL PERIOD	QUARTERLY PERIOD	MONTHLY PERIOD
....	1	1.000000	.980237	.970453	.963966
1	2	.993301	.973670	.963952	.957509
2	3	.986647	.967148	.957494	
3	4	.980037	.960669	.951080	
4	5	.973472	.954233		
5	6	.966951	.947841		
6	7	.960473	.941491		
7	8	.954039			
8	9	.947648			
9	10	.941300			
10	11	.934994			
11	12	.928731			
12	....	.922509			

TABLE F(8.6), WITH INTEREST AT 8.6 PERCENT, SHOWING FACTORS FOR COMPUTATION OF THE ADJUSTED PAYOUT RATE FOR CERTAIN VALUATIONS APPLICABLE AFTER APRIL 30, 1989

1		2			
NUMBER OF MONTHS BY WHICH THE VALUATION DATE FOR THE FIRST FULL TAXABLE YEAR OF THE TRUST PRECEDES THE FIRST PAYOUT		FACTORS FOR PAYOUT AT THE END OF EACH PERIOD			
AT LEAST	BUT LESS THAN	ANNUAL PERIOD	SEMIANNUAL PERIOD	QUARTERLY PERIOD	MONTHLY PERIOD
....	1	1.000000	.979794	.969794	.963164
1	2	.993148	.973081	.963149	.956565
2	3	.986344	.966414	.956550	
3	4	.979586	.959793	.949996	
4	5	.972874	.953217		
5	6	.966209	.946686		
6	7	.959589	.940199		
7	8	.953014			
8	9	.946484			
9	10	.940000			
10	11	.933559			
11	12	.927163			
12	....	.920810			

Reg. § 1.664-4(e)(6)

TABLE F(8.8), WITH INTEREST AT 8.8 PERCENT, SHOWING FACTORS FOR COMPUTATION OF THE ADJUSTED PAYOUT RATE FOR CERTAIN VALUATIONS APPLICABLE AFTER APRIL 30, 1989

1		2			
NUMBER OF MONTHS BY WHICH THE VALUATION DATE FOR THE FIRST FULL TAXABLE YEAR OF THE TRUST PRECEDES THE FIRST PAYOUT		FACTORS FOR PAYOUT AT THE END OF EACH PERIOD			
AT LEAST	BUT LESS THAN	ANNUAL PERIOD	SEMIANNUAL PERIOD	QUARTERLY PERIOD	MONTHLY PERIOD
....	1	1.000000	.979353	.969136	.962364
1	2	.992996	.972494	.962349	.955624
2	3	.986041	.965683	.955609	
3	4	.979135	.958919	.948916	
4	5	.972278	.952203		
5	6	.965468	.945534		
6	7	.958706	.938912		
7	8	.951992			
8	9	.945324			
9	10	.938703			
10	11	.932129			
11	12	.925600			
12	....	.919118			

TABLE F(9.0), WITH INTEREST AT 9.0 PERCENT, SHOWING FACTORS FOR COMPUTATION OF THE ADJUSTED PAYOUT RATE FOR CERTAIN VALUATIONS APPLICABLE AFTER APRIL 30, 1989

1		2			
NUMBER OF MONTHS BY WHICH THE VALUATION DATE FOR THE FIRST FULL TAXABLE YEAR OF THE TRUST PRECEDES THE FIRST PAYOUT		FACTORS FOR PAYOUT AT THE END OF EACH PERIOD			
AT LEAST	BUT LESS THAN	ANNUAL PERIOD	SEMIANNUAL PERIOD	QUARTERLY PERIOD	MONTHLY PERIOD
....	1	1.000000	.978913	.968481	.961567
1	2	.992844	.971908	.961551	.954686
2	3	.985740	.964954	.954670	
3	4	.978686	.958049	.947839	
4	5	.971683	.951193		
5	6	.964730	.944387		
6	7	.957826	.937629		
7	8	.950972			
8	9	.944167			
9	10	.937411			
10	11	.930703			
11	12	.924043			
12	....	.917431			

Reg. § 1.664-4(e)(6)

Estates, Trusts, and Beneficiaries

See p. 20,601 for regulations not amended to reflect law changes

TABLE F(9.2), WITH INTEREST AT 9.2 PERCENT, SHOWING FACTORS FOR COMPUTATION OF THE ADJUSTED PAYOUT RATE FOR CERTAIN VALUATIONS APPLICABLE AFTER APRIL 30, 1989

1			2		
NUMBER OF MONTHS BY WHICH THE VALUATION DATE FOR THE FIRST FULL TAXABLE YEAR OF THE TRUST PRECEDES THE FIRST PAYOUT			FACTORS FOR PAYOUT AT THE END OF EACH PERIOD		
AT LEAST	BUT LESS THAN	ANNUAL PERIOD	SEMIANNUAL PERIOD	QUARTERLY PERIOD	MONTHLY PERIOD
....	1	1.000000	.978474	.967827	.960772
1	2	.992693	.971324	.960755	.953752
2	3	.985439	.964226	.953734	
3	4	.978238	.957180	.946765	
4	5	.971089	.950186		
5	6	.963993	.943242		
6	7	.956949	.936350		
7	8	.949956			
8	9	.943014			
9	10	.936123			
10	11	.929283			
11	12	.922492			
12	....	.915751			

TABLE F(9.4), WITH INTEREST AT 9.4 PERCENT, SHOWING FACTORS FOR COMPUTATION OF THE ADJUSTED PAYOUT RATE FOR CERTAIN VALUATIONS APPLICABLE AFTER APRIL 30, 1989

1			2		
NUMBER OF MONTHS BY WHICH THE VALUATION DATE FOR THE FIRST FULL TAXABLE YEAR OF THE TRUST PRECEDES THE FIRST PAYOUT			FACTORS FOR PAYOUT AT THE END OF EACH PERIOD		
AT LEAST	BUT LESS THAN	ANNUAL PERIOD	SEMIANNUAL PERIOD	QUARTERLY PERIOD	MONTHLY PERIOD
....	1	1.000000	.978037	.967176	.959980
1	2	.992541	.970742	.959962	.952820
2	3	.985138	.963501	.952802	
3	4	.977790	.956315	.945695	
4	5	.970497	.949182		
5	6	.963258	.942102		
6	7	.956074	.935075		
7	8	.948942			
8	9	.941865			
9	10	.934839			
10	11	.927867			
11	12	.920946			
12	....	.914077			

Reg. § 1.664-4(e)(6)

43,350   **Estates, Trusts, and Beneficiaries**
See p. 20,601 for regulations not amended to reflect law changes

TABLE F(9.6), WITH INTEREST AT 9.6 PERCENT, SHOWING FACTORS FOR COMPUTATION OF THE ADJUSTED PAYOUT RATE FOR CERTAIN VALUATIONS APPLICABLE AFTER APRIL 30, 1989

1			2		
NUMBER OF MONTHS BY WHICH THE VALUATION DATE FOR THE FIRST FULL TAXABLE YEAR OF THE TRUST PRECEDES THE FIRST PAYOUT			FACTORS FOR PAYOUT AT THE END OF EACH PERIOD		
AT LEAST	BUT LESS THAN	ANNUAL PERIOD	SEMIANNUAL PERIOD	QUARTERLY PERIOD	MONTHLY PERIOD
....	1	1.000000	.977600	.966526	.959190
1	2	.992390	.970161	.959171	.951890
2	3	.984838	.962778	.951872	
3	4	.977344	.955452	.944628	
4	5	.969906	.948181		
5	6	.962526	.940965		
6	7	.955201	.933805		
7	8	.947932			
8	9	.940718			
9	10	.933560			
10	11	.926455			
11	12	.919405			
12	....	.912409			

TABLE F(9.8), WITH INTEREST AT 9.8 PERCENT, SHOWING FACTORS FOR COMPUTATION OF THE ADJUSTED PAYOUT RATE FOR CERTAIN VALUATIONS APPLICABLE AFTER APRIL 30, 1989

1			2		
NUMBER OF MONTHS BY WHICH THE VALUATION DATE FOR THE FIRST FULL TAXABLE YEAR OF THE TRUST PRECEDES THE FIRST PAYOUT			FACTORS FOR PAYOUT AT THE END OF EACH PERIOD		
AT LEAST	BUT LESS THAN	ANNUAL PERIOD	SEMIANNUAL PERIOD	QUARTERLY PERIOD	MONTHLY PERIOD
....	1	1.000000	.977165	.965878	.958402
1	2	.992239	.969582	.958382	.950964
2	3	.984539	.962057	.950945	
3	4	.976898	.954591	.943565	
4	5	.969317	.947183		
5	6	.961795	.939832		
6	7	.954331	.932539		
7	8	.946924			
8	9	.939576			
9	10	.932284			
10	11	.925049			
11	12	.917870			
12	....	.910747			

Reg. § 1.664-4(e)(6)

TABLE F(10.0), WITH INTEREST AT 10.0 PERCENT, SHOWING FACTORS FOR COMPUTATION OF THE ADJUSTED PAYOUT RATE FOR CERTAIN VALUATIONS APPLICABLE AFTER APRIL 30, 1989

1		2			
NUMBER OF MONTHS BY WHICH THE VALUATION DATE FOR THE FIRST FULL TAXABLE YEAR OF THE TRUST PRECEDES THE FIRST PAYOUT		FACTORS FOR PAYOUT AT THE END OF EACH PERIOD			
AT LEAST	BUT LESS THAN	ANNUAL PERIOD	SEMIANNUAL PERIOD	QUARTERLY PERIOD	MONTHLY PERIOD
....	1	1.000000	.976731	.965232	.957616
1	2	.992089	.969004	.957596	.950041
2	3	.984240	.961338	.950021	
3	4	.976454	.953733	.942505	
4	5	.968729	.946188		
5	6	.961066	.938703		
6	7	.953463	.931277		
7	8	.945920			
8	9	.938436			
9	10	.931012			
10	11	.923647			
11	12	.916340			
12	....	.909091			

TABLE F(10.2), WITH INTEREST AT 10.2 PERCENT, SHOWING FACTORS FOR COMPUTATION OF THE ADJUSTED PAYOUT RATE FOR CERTAIN VALUATIONS APPLICABLE AFTER APRIL 30, 1989

1		2			
NUMBER OF MONTHS BY WHICH THE VALUATION DATE FOR THE FIRST FULL TAXABLE YEAR OF THE TRUST PRECEDES THE FIRST PAYOUT		FACTORS FOR PAYOUT AT THE END OF EACH PERIOD			
AT LEAST	BUT LESS THAN	ANNUAL PERIOD	SEMIANNUAL PERIOD	QUARTERLY PERIOD	MONTHLY PERIOD
....	1	1.000000	.976298	.964588	.956833
1	2	.991939	.968428	.956812	.949120
2	3	.983943	.960622	.949099	
3	4	.976011	.952878	.941448	
4	5	.968143	.945196		
5	6	.960338	.937577		
6	7	.952597	.930019		
7	8	.944918			
8	9	.937301			
9	10	.929745			
10	11	.922250			
11	12	.914816			
12	....	.907441			

Reg. § 1.664-4(e)(6)

43,352 Estates, Trusts, and Beneficiaries

See p. 20,601 for regulations not amended to reflect law changes

TABLE F(10.4), WITH INTEREST AT 10.4 PERCENT, SHOWING FACTORS FOR COMPUTATION OF THE ADJUSTED PAYOUT RATE FOR CERTAIN VALUATIONS APPLICABLE AFTER APRIL 30, 1989

1		2			
NUMBER OF MONTHS BY WHICH THE VALUATION DATE FOR THE FIRST FULL TAXABLE YEAR OF THE TRUST PRECEDES THE FIRST PAYOUT		FACTORS FOR PAYOUT AT THE END OF EACH PERIOD			
AT LEAST	BUT LESS THAN	ANNUAL PERIOD	SEMIANNUAL PERIOD	QUARTERLY PERIOD	MONTHLY PERIOD
....	1	1.000000	.975867	.963946	.956052
1	2	.991789	.967854	.956031	.948202
2	3	.983645	.959907	.948181	
3	4	.975568	.952025	.940395	
4	5	.967558	.944208		
5	6	.959613	.936455		
6	7	.951734	.928765		
7	8	.943919			
8	9	.936168			
9	10	.928481			
10	11	.920858			
11	12	.913296			
12	....	.905797			

TABLE F(10.6), WITH INTEREST AT 10.6 PERCENT, SHOWING FACTORS FOR COMPUTATION OF THE ADJUSTED PAYOUT RATE FOR CERTAIN VALUATIONS APPLICABLE AFTER APRIL 30, 1989

1		2			
NUMBER OF MONTHS BY WHICH THE VALUATION DATE FOR THE FIRST FULL TAXABLE YEAR OF THE TRUST PRECEDES THE FIRST PAYOUT		FACTORS FOR PAYOUT AT THE END OF EACH PERIOD			
AT LEAST	BUT LESS THAN	ANNUAL PERIOD	SEMIANNUAL PERIOD	QUARTERLY PERIOD	MONTHLY PERIOD
....	1	1.000000	.975436	.963305	.955274
1	2	.991639	.967281	.955252	.947287
2	3	.983349	.959194	.947265	
3	4	.975127	.951174	.939345	
4	5	.966974	.943222		
5	6	.958890	.935336		
6	7	.950873	.927516		
7	8	.942923			
8	9	.935039			
9	10	.927222			
10	11	.919470			
11	12	.911782			
12	....	.904159			

Reg. § 1.664-4(e)(6)

Estates, Trusts, and Beneficiaries

See p. 20,601 for regulations not amended to reflect law changes

43,353

TABLE F(10.8), WITH INTEREST AT 10.8 PERCENT, SHOWING FACTORS FOR
COMPUTATION OF THE ADJUSTED PAYOUT RATE FOR CERTAIN VALUATIONS
APPLICABLE AFTER APRIL 30, 1989

1		2			
NUMBER OF MONTHS BY WHICH THE VALUATION DATE FOR THE FIRST FULL TAXABLE YEAR OF THE TRUST PRECEDES THE FIRST PAYOUT		FACTORS FOR PAYOUT AT THE END OF EACH PERIOD			
AT LEAST	BUT LESS THAN	ANNUAL PERIOD	SEMIANNUAL PERIOD	QUARTERLY PERIOD	MONTHLY PERIOD
....	1	1.000000	.975007	.962667	.954498
1	2	.991490	.966710	.954475	.946375
2	3	.983052	.958483	.946352	
3	4	.974687	.950327	.938299	
4	5	.966392	.942239		
5	6	.958168	.934221		
6	7	.950014	.926271		
7	8	.941930			
8	9	.933914			
9	10	.925966			
10	11	.918086			
11	12	.910273			
12	....	.902527			

TABLE F(11.0), WITH INTEREST AT 11.0 PERCENT, SHOWING FACTORS FOR
COMPUTATION OF THE ADJUSTED PAYOUT RATE FOR CERTAIN VALUATIONS
APPLICABLE AFTER APRIL 30, 1989

1		2			
NUMBER OF MONTHS BY WHICH THE VALUATION DATE FOR THE FIRST FULL TAXABLE YEAR OF THE TRUST PRECEDES THE FIRST PAYOUT		FACTORS FOR PAYOUT AT THE END OF EACH PERIOD			
AT LEAST	BUT LESS THAN	ANNUAL PERIOD	SEMIANNUAL PERIOD	QUARTERLY PERIOD	MONTHLY PERIOD
....	1	1.000000	.974579	.962030	.953724
1	2	.991341	.966140	.953700	.945466
2	3	.982757	.957774	.945442	
3	4	.974247	.949481	.937255	
4	5	.965811	.941260		
5	6	.957449	.933109		
6	7	.949158	.925029		
7	8	.940939			
8	9	.932792			
9	10	.924715			
10	11	.916708			
11	12	.908770			
12	....	.900901			

Reg. § 1.664-4(e)(6)

Estates, Trusts, and Beneficiaries

See p. 20,601 for regulations not amended to reflect law changes

TABLE F(11.2), WITH INTEREST AT 11.2 PERCENT, SHOWING FACTORS FOR COMPUTATION OF THE ADJUSTED PAYOUT RATE FOR CERTAIN VALUATIONS APPLICABLE AFTER APRIL 30, 1989

1
NUMBER OF MONTHS BY WHICH THE VALUATION DATE FOR THE FIRST FULL TAXABLE YEAR OF THE TRUST PRECEDES THE FIRST PAYOUT

2
FACTORS FOR PAYOUT AT THE END OF EACH PERIOD

AT LEAST	BUT LESS THAN	ANNUAL PERIOD	SEMIANNUAL PERIOD	QUARTERLY PERIOD	MONTHLY PERIOD
....	1	1.000000	.974152	.961395	.952952
1	2	.991192	.965572	.952927	.944559
2	3	.982462	.957068	.944534	
3	4	.973809	.948638	.936215	
4	5	.965232	.940283		
5	6	.956731	.932001		
6	7	.948304	.923792		
7	8	.939952			
8	9	.931673			
9	10	.923467			
10	11	.915333			
11	12	.907272			
12	....	.899281			

TABLE F(11.4), WITH INTEREST AT 11.4 PERCENT, SHOWING FACTORS FOR COMPUTATION OF THE ADJUSTED PAYOUT RATE FOR CERTAIN VALUATIONS APPLICABLE AFTER APRIL 30, 1989

1
NUMBER OF MONTHS BY WHICH THE VALUATION DATE FOR THE FIRST FULL TAXABLE YEAR OF THE TRUST PRECEDES THE FIRST PAYOUT

2
FACTORS FOR PAYOUT AT THE END OF EACH PERIOD

AT LEAST	BUT LESS THAN	ANNUAL PERIOD	SEMIANNUAL PERIOD	QUARTERLY PERIOD	MONTHLY PERIOD
....	1	1.000000	.973726	.960762	.952183
1	2	.991044	.965005	.952157	.943655
2	3	.982168	.956363	.943630	
3	4	.973372	.947798	.935178	
4	5	.964654	.939309		
5	6	.956015	.930896		
6	7	.947452	.922559		
7	8	.938967			
8	9	.930557			
9	10	.922223			
10	11	.913964			
11	12	.905778			
12	....	.897666			

Reg. § 1.664-4(e)(6)

Estates, Trusts, and Beneficiaries

TABLE F(11.6), WITH INTEREST AT 11.6 PERCENT, SHOWING FACTORS FOR COMPUTATION OF THE ADJUSTED PAYOUT RATE FOR CERTAIN VALUATIONS APPLICABLE AFTER APRIL 30, 1989

1		2			
NUMBER OF MONTHS BY WHICH THE VALUATION DATE FOR THE FIRST FULL TAXABLE YEAR OF THE TRUST PRECEDES THE FIRST PAYOUT		FACTORS FOR PAYOUT AT THE END OF EACH PERIOD			
AT LEAST	BUT LESS THAN	ANNUAL PERIOD	SEMIANNUAL PERIOD	QUARTERLY PERIOD	MONTHLY PERIOD
....	1	1.000000	.973302	.960130	.951416
1	2	.990896	.964440	.951389	.942754
2	3	.981874	.955660	.942728	
3	4	.972935	.946959	.934145	
4	5	.964077	.938338		
5	6	.955300	.929795		
6	7	.946603	.921330		
7	8	.937985			
8	9	.929445			
9	10	.920984			
10	11	.912599			
11	12	.904290			
12	....	.896057			

TABLE F(11.8), WITH INTEREST AT 11.8 PERCENT, SHOWING FACTORS FOR COMPUTATION OF THE ADJUSTED PAYOUT RATE FOR CERTAIN VALUATIONS APPLICABLE AFTER APRIL 30, 1989

1		2			
NUMBER OF MONTHS BY WHICH THE VALUATION DATE FOR THE FIRST FULL TAXABLE YEAR OF THE TRUST PRECEDES THE FIRST PAYOUT		FACTORS FOR PAYOUT AT THE END OF EACH PERIOD			
AT LEAST	BUT LESS THAN	ANNUAL PERIOD	SEMIANNUAL PERIOD	QUARTERLY PERIOD	MONTHLY PERIOD
....	1	1.000000	.972878	.959501	.950651
1	2	.990748	.963877	.950624	.941855
2	3	.981582	.954959	.941828	
3	4	.972500	.946124	.933114	
4	5	.963502	.937370		
5	6	.954588	.928698		
6	7	.945756	.920105		
7	8	.937006			
8	9	.928337			
9	10	.919748			
10	11	.911238			
11	12	.902807			
12	....	.894454			

Reg. § 1.664-4(e)(6)

43,356   Estates, Trusts, and Beneficiaries

See p. 20,601 for regulations not amended to reflect law changes

TABLE F(12.0), WITH INTEREST AT 12.0 PERCENT, SHOWING FACTORS FOR COMPUTATION OF THE ADJUSTED PAYOUT RATE FOR CERTAIN VALUATIONS APPLICABLE AFTER APRIL 30, 1989

1		2			
NUMBER OF MONTHS BY WHICH THE VALUATION DATE FOR THE FIRST FULL TAXABLE YEAR OF THE TRUST PRECEDES THE FIRST PAYOUT		**FACTORS FOR PAYOUT AT THE END OF EACH PERIOD**			
AT LEAST	BUT LESS THAN	ANNUAL PERIOD	SEMIANNUAL PERIOD	QUARTERLY PERIOD	MONTHLY PERIOD
....	1	1.000000	.972456	.958873	.949888
1	2	.990600	.963315	.949860	.940960
2	3	.981289	.954260	.940932	
3	4	.972065	.945290	.932087	
4	5	.962928	.936405		
5	6	.953877	.927603		
6	7	.944911	.918884		
7	8	.936029			
8	9	.927231			
9	10	.918515			
10	11	.909882			
11	12	.901329			
12	....	.892857			

TABLE F(12.2), WITH INTEREST AT 12.2 PERCENT, SHOWING FACTORS FOR COMPUTATION OF THE ADJUSTED PAYOUT RATE FOR CERTAIN VALUATIONS APPLICABLE AFTER APRIL 30, 1989

1		2			
NUMBER OF MONTHS BY WHICH THE VALUATION DATE FOR THE FIRST FULL TAXABLE YEAR OF THE TRUST PRECEDES THE FIRST PAYOUT		**FACTORS FOR PAYOUT AT THE END OF EACH PERIOD**			
AT LEAST	BUT LESS THAN	ANNUAL PERIOD	SEMIANNUAL PERIOD	QUARTERLY PERIOD	MONTHLY PERIOD
....	1	1.000000	.972034	.958247	.949128
1	2	.990453	.962754	.949099	.940067
2	3	.980997	.953563	.940038	
3	4	.971632	.944460	.931063	
4	5	.962356	.935443		
5	6	.953168	.926512		
6	7	.944069	.917667		
7	8	.935056			
8	9	.926129			
9	10	.917287			
10	11	.908530			
11	12	.899856			
12	....	.891266			

Reg. § 1.664-4(e)(6)

Estates, Trusts, and Beneficiaries

TABLE F(12.4), WITH INTEREST AT 12.4 PERCENT, SHOWING FACTORS FOR COMPUTATION OF THE ADJUSTED PAYOUT RATE FOR CERTAIN VALUATIONS APPLICABLE AFTER APRIL 30, 1989

1		2			
NUMBER OF MONTHS BY WHICH THE VALUATION DATE FOR THE FIRST FULL TAXABLE YEAR OF THE TRUST PRECEDES THE FIRST PAYOUT		FACTORS FOR PAYOUT AT THE END OF EACH PERIOD			
AT LEAST	BUT LESS THAN	ANNUAL PERIOD	SEMIANNUAL PERIOD	QUARTERLY PERIOD	MONTHLY PERIOD
....	1	1.000000	.971614	.957623	.948370
1	2	.990306	.962195	.948340	.939176
2	3	.980706	.952868	.939147	
3	4	.971199	.943631	.930043	
4	5	.961785	.934484		
5	6	.952461	.925425		
6	7	.943228	.916454		
7	8	.934085			
8	9	.925030			
9	10	.916063			
10	11	.907183			
11	12	.898389			
12	....	.889680			

TABLE F(12.6), WITH INTEREST AT 12.6 PERCENT, SHOWING FACTORS FOR COMPUTATION OF THE ADJUSTED PAYOUT RATE FOR CERTAIN VALUATIONS APPLICABLE AFTER APRIL 30, 1989

1		2			
NUMBER OF MONTHS BY WHICH THE VALUATION DATE FOR THE FIRST FULL TAXABLE YEAR OF THE TRUST PRECEDES THE FIRST PAYOUT		FACTORS FOR PAYOUT AT THE END OF EACH PERIOD			
AT LEAST	BUT LESS THAN	ANNUAL PERIOD	SEMIANNUAL PERIOD	QUARTERLY PERIOD	MONTHLY PERIOD
....	1	1.000000	.971195	.957000	.947614
1	2	.990159	.961638	.947583	.938289
2	3	.980416	.952175	.938258	
3	4	.970768	.942805	.929025	
4	5	.961215	.933527		
5	6	.951756	.924341		
6	7	.942390	.915245		
7	8	.933117			
8	9	.923934			
9	10	.914842			
10	11	.905840			
11	12	.896926			
12	....	.888099			

Reg. § 1.664-4(e)(6)

43,358 Estates, Trusts, and Beneficiaries

See p. 20,601 for regulations not amended to reflect law changes

TABLE F(12.8), WITH INTEREST AT 12.8 PERCENT, SHOWING FACTORS FOR COMPUTATION OF THE ADJUSTED PAYOUT RATE FOR CERTAIN VALUATIONS APPLICABLE AFTER APRIL 30, 1989

\[1\] NUMBER OF MONTHS BY WHICH THE VALUATION DATE FOR THE FIRST FULL TAXABLE YEAR OF THE TRUST PRECEDES THE FIRST PAYOUT			\[2\] FACTORS FOR PAYOUT AT THE END OF EACH PERIOD			
AT LEAST	BUT LESS THAN	ANNUAL PERIOD	SEMIANNUAL PERIOD	QUARTERLY PERIOD	MONTHLY PERIOD
....	1	1.000000	.970777	.956379	.946860
1	2	.990013	.961082	.946828	.937403
2	3	.980126	.951484	.937372	
3	4	.970337	.941981	.928011	
4	5	.960647	.932574		
5	6	.951053	.923260		
6	7	.941554	.914040		
7	8	.932151			
8	9	.922842			
9	10	.913625			
10	11	.904501			
11	12	.895468			
12	....	.886525			

TABLE F(13.0), WITH INTEREST AT 13.0 PERCENT, SHOWING FACTORS FOR COMPUTATION OF THE ADJUSTED PAYOUT RATE FOR CERTAIN VALUATIONS APPLICABLE AFTER APRIL 30, 1989

\[1\] NUMBER OF MONTHS BY WHICH THE VALUATION DATE FOR THE FIRST FULL TAXABLE YEAR OF THE TRUST PRECEDES THE FIRST PAYOUT			\[2\] FACTORS FOR PAYOUT AT THE END OF EACH PERIOD			
AT LEAST	BUT LESS THAN	ANNUAL PERIOD	SEMIANNUAL PERIOD	QUARTERLY PERIOD	MONTHLY PERIOD
....	1	1.000000	.970360	.955760	.946108
1	2	.989867	.960528	.946075	.936521
2	3	.979836	.950795	.936489	
3	4	.969908	.941160	.926999	
4	5	.960079	.931623		
5	6	.950351	.922183		
6	7	.940721	.912838		
7	8	.931188			
8	9	.921753			
9	10	.912412			
10	11	.903167			
11	12	.894015			
12	....	.884956			

Reg. § 1.664-4(e)(6)

Estates, Trusts, and Beneficiaries

TABLE F(13.2), WITH INTEREST AT 13.2 PERCENT, SHOWING FACTORS FOR COMPUTATION OF THE ADJUSTED PAYOUT RATE FOR CERTAIN VALUATIONS APPLICABLE AFTER APRIL 30, 1989

\multicolumn{2}{c	}{1 — NUMBER OF MONTHS BY WHICH THE VALUATION DATE FOR THE FIRST FULL TAXABLE YEAR OF THE TRUST PRECEDES THE FIRST PAYOUT}	\multicolumn{4}{c}{2 — FACTORS FOR PAYOUT AT THE END OF EACH PERIOD}
AT LEAST	BUT LESS THAN	ANNUAL PERIOD	SEMIANNUAL PERIOD	QUARTERLY PERIOD	MONTHLY PERIOD
....	1	1.000000	.969945	.955143	.945359
1	2	.989721	.959975	.945325	.935641
2	3	.979548	.950107	.935608	
3	4	.969479	.940341	.925991	
4	5	.959514	.930675		
5	6	.949651	.921109		
6	7	.939889	.911641		
7	8	.930228			
8	9	.920667			
9	10	.911203			
10	11	.901837			
11	12	.892567			
12	....	.883392			

TABLE F(13.4), WITH INTEREST AT 13.4 PERCENT, SHOWING FACTORS FOR COMPUTATION OF THE ADJUSTED PAYOUT RATE FOR CERTAIN VALUATIONS APPLICABLE AFTER APRIL 30, 1989

\multicolumn{2}{c	}{1 — NUMBER OF MONTHS BY WHICH THE VALUATION DATE FOR THE FIRST FULL TAXABLE YEAR OF THE TRUST PRECEDES THE FIRST PAYOUT}	\multicolumn{4}{c}{2 — FACTORS FOR PAYOUT AT THE END OF EACH PERIOD}
AT LEAST	BUT LESS THAN	ANNUAL PERIOD	SEMIANNUAL PERIOD	QUARTERLY PERIOD	MONTHLY PERIOD
....	1	1.000000	.969530	.954527	.944611
1	2	.989575	.959423	.944577	.934764
2	3	.979260	.949422	.934730	
3	4	.969051	.939524	.924986	
4	5	.958949	.929730		
5	6	.948953	.920038		
6	7	.939060	.910447		
7	8	.929271			
8	9	.919584			
9	10	.909998			
10	11	.900511			
11	12	.891124			
12	....	.881834			

Reg. § 1.664-4(e)(6)

43,360   **Estates, Trusts, and Beneficiaries**
See p. 20,601 for regulations not amended to reflect law changes

TABLE F(13.6), WITH INTEREST AT 13.6 PERCENT, SHOWING FACTORS FOR
COMPUTATION OF THE ADJUSTED PAYOUT RATE FOR CERTAIN VALUATIONS
APPLICABLE AFTER APRIL 30, 1989

1		2			
NUMBER OF MONTHS BY WHICH THE VALUATION DATE FOR THE FIRST FULL TAXABLE YEAR OF THE TRUST PRECEDES THE FIRST PAYOUT		FACTORS FOR PAYOUT AT THE END OF EACH PERIOD			
AT LEAST	BUT LESS THAN	ANNUAL PERIOD	SEMIANNUAL PERIOD	QUARTERLY PERIOD	MONTHLY PERIOD
....	1	1.000000	.969117	.953913	.943866
1	2	.989430	.958873	.943831	.933890
2	3	.978972	.948738	.933854	
3	4	.968624	.938710	.923984	
4	5	.958386	.928788		
5	6	.948256	.918971		
6	7	.938233	.909257		
7	8	.928316			
8	9	.918504			
9	10	.908796			
10	11	.899190			
11	12	.889686			
12	....	.880282			

TABLE F(13.8), WITH INTEREST AT 13.8 PERCENT, SHOWING FACTORS FOR
COMPUTATION OF THE ADJUSTED PAYOUT RATE FOR CERTAIN VALUATIONS
APPLICABLE AFTER APRIL 30, 1989

1		2			
NUMBER OF MONTHS BY WHICH THE VALUATION DATE FOR THE FIRST FULL TAXABLE YEAR OF THE TRUST PRECEDES THE FIRST PAYOUT		FACTORS FOR PAYOUT AT THE END OF EACH PERIOD			
AT LEAST	BUT LESS THAN	ANNUAL PERIOD	SEMIANNUAL PERIOD	QUARTERLY PERIOD	MONTHLY PERIOD
....	1	1.000000	.968704	.953301	.943123
1	2	.989285	.958325	.943087	.933018
2	3	.978685	.948056	.932982	
3	4	.968199	.937898	.922985	
4	5	.957824	.927849		
5	6	.947561	.917907		
6	7	.937408	.908072		
7	8	.927364			
8	9	.917428			
9	10	.907598			
10	11	.897873			
11	12	.888252			
12	....	.878735			

Reg. § 1.664-4(e)(6)

Estates, Trusts, and Beneficiaries 43,361

See p. 20,601 for regulations not amended to reflect law changes

TABLE F(14.0), WITH INTEREST AT 14.0 PERCENT, SHOWING FACTORS FOR
COMPUTATION OF THE ADJUSTED PAYOUT RATE FOR CERTAIN VALUATIONS
APPLICABLE AFTER APRIL 30, 1989

1		2			
NUMBER OF MONTHS BY WHICH THE VALUATION DATE FOR THE FIRST FULL TAXABLE YEAR OF THE TRUST PRECEDES THE FIRST PAYOUT		FACTORS FOR PAYOUT AT THE END OF EACH PERIOD			
AT LEAST	BUT LESS THAN	ANNUAL PERIOD	SEMIANNUAL PERIOD	QUARTERLY PERIOD	MONTHLY PERIOD
....	1	1.000000	.968293	.952691	.942382
1	2	.989140	.957778	.942345	.932148
2	3	.978399	.947377	.932111	
3	4	.967774	.937088	.921989	
4	5	.957264	.926912		
5	6	.946868	.916846		
6	7	.936586	.906889		
7	8	.926415			
8	9	.916354			
9	10	.906403			
10	11	.896560			
11	12	.886824			
12	....	.877193			

(7) *Actuarial Table U(1) for transfers for which the valuation date is after April 30, 1999.* For transfers for which the valuation date is after April 30, 1999, the present value of a charitable remainder unitrust interest that is dependent on the termination of a life interest is determined by using the section 7520 rate, Table U(1) in this paragraph (e)(7), and Table F(4.2) through (14.0) in paragraph (e)(6) of this section. See, however, § 1.7520-3(b) (relating to exceptions to the use of prescribed tables under certain circumstances). Many actuarial factors not contained in the following tables are contained in Internal Revenue Service Publication 1458, "Actuarial Values, Book Beth," (7-1999). A copy of this publication is available for purchase from the Superintendent of Documents, United States Government Printing Office, Washington, DC 20402.

TABLE U(1)
BASED ON LIFE TABLE 90CM
UNITRUST SINGLE LIFE REMAINDER FACTORS
APPLICABLE FOR TRANSFERS AFTER APRIL 30, 1999

ADJUSTED PAYOUT RATE

AGE	4.2%	4.4%	4.6%	4.8%	5.0%	5.2%	5.4%	5.6%	5.8%	6.0%
0	.06177	.05580	.05061	.04609	.04215	.03871	.03570	.03307	.03075	.02872
1	.05543	.04925	.04388	.03919	.03509	.03151	.02838	.02563	.02321	.02109
2	.05716	.05081	.04528	.04045	.03622	.03252	.02927	.02642	.02391	.02170
3	.05920	.05268	.04699	.04201	.03765	.03382	.03046	.02750	.02490	.02260
4	.06143	.05475	.04889	.04376	.03926	.03530	.03182	.02876	.02605	.02366
5	.06384	.05697	.05095	.04567	.04103	.03694	.03334	.03016	.02735	.02487
6	.06637	.05933	.05315	.04771	.04292	.03870	.03497	.03168	.02876	.02618
7	.06905	.06183	.05547	.04987	.04494	.04058	.03673	.03332	.03029	.02761
8	.07186	.06445	.05792	.05216	.04708	.04258	.03859	.03506	.03192	.02914
9	.07482	.06722	.06052	.05460	.04936	.04471	.04060	.03694	.03369	.03079
10	.07793	.07015	.06327	.05718	.05179	.04700	.04274	.03896	.03559	.03259
11	.08120	.07323	.06617	.05991	.05435	.04942	.04502	.04111	.03762	.03450
12	.08461	.07645	.06920	.06277	.05706	.05197	.04744	.04339	.03978	.03655
13	.08812	.07976	.07234	.06574	.05985	.05461	.04993	.04576	.04202	.03867
14	.09168	.08313	.07552	.06874	.06269	.05729	.05247	.04815	.04428	.04081
15	.09527	.08652	.07872	.07176	.06554	.05999	.05501	.05055	.04655	.04296
16	.09886	.08991	.08192	.07478	.06839	.06267	.05754	.05294	.04880	.04508
17	.10249	.09334	.08515	.07782	.07126	.06537	.06008	.05533	.05105	.04720

Reg. § 1.664-4(e)(7)

TABLE U(1)
BASED ON LIFE TABLE 90CM
UNITRUST SINGLE LIFE REMAINDER FACTORS
APPLICABLE FOR TRANSFERS AFTER APRIL 30, 1999

ADJUSTED PAYOUT RATE

AGE	4.2%	4.4%	4.6%	4.8%	5.0%	5.2%	5.4%	5.6%	5.8%	6.0%
18	.10616	.09680	.08842	.08090	.07415	.06809	.06264	.05774	.05332	.04933
19	.10994	.10037	.09178	.08407	.07714	.07091	.06529	.06023	.05566	.05153
20	.11384	.10406	.09527	.08737	.08025	.07383	.06805	.06283	.05811	.05384
21	.11790	.10790	.09891	.09080	.08349	.07690	.07094	.06555	.06068	.05626
22	.12208	.11188	.10267	.09436	.08686	.08008	.07395	.06839	.06336	.05879
23	.12643	.11601	.10659	.09808	.09038	.08342	.07710	.07138	.06618	.06146
24	.13095	.12031	.11069	.10197	.09408	.08692	.08042	.07452	.06915	.06427
25	.13567	.12481	.11497	.10605	.09795	.09060	.08392	.07784	.07230	.06726
26	.14058	.12950	.11945	.11032	.10202	.09447	.08760	.08134	.07563	.07042
27	.14571	.13442	.12415	.11481	.10631	.09856	.09149	.08505	.07916	.07379
28	.15104	.13953	.12904	.11949	.11078	.10284	.09558	.08895	.08288	.07733
29	.15656	.14484	.13414	.12438	.11546	.10731	.09986	.09304	.08679	.08106
30	.16229	.15034	.13943	.12946	.12034	.11198	.10433	.09732	.09089	.08498
31	.16821	.15605	.14493	.13474	.12541	.11685	.10900	.10179	.09517	.08909
32	.17433	.16196	.15063	.14023	.13069	.12193	.11387	.10647	.09966	.09339
33	.18068	.16810	.15655	.14595	.13620	.12723	.11897	.11137	.10437	.09791
34	.18724	.17446	.16270	.15189	.14193	.13275	.12430	.11650	.10930	.10265
35	.19405	.18107	.16910	.15808	.14791	.13853	.12987	.12187	.11448	.10764
36	.20109	.18791	.17574	.16451	.15414	.14456	.13569	.12749	.11990	.11287
37	.20838	.19500	.18263	.17120	.16062	.15083	.14177	.13337	.12558	.11835
38	.21593	.20236	.18979	.17816	.16739	.15739	.14813	.13953	.13154	.12412
39	.22374	.20998	.19723	.18540	.17443	.16423	.15477	.14597	.13779	.13017
40	.23183	.21789	.20496	.19294	.18177	.17138	.16172	.15272	.14434	.13653
41	.24021	.22611	.21299	.20079	.18943	.17885	.16899	.15980	.15123	.14322
42	.24889	.23463	.22134	.20896	.19741	.18665	.17660	.16721	.15845	.15025
43	.25786	.24344	.23000	.21744	.20572	.19477	.18453	.17496	.16601	.15762
44	.26712	.25257	.23896	.22625	.21435	.20322	.19281	.18305	.17391	.16534
45	.27665	.26196	.24821	.23534	.22328	.21198	.20139	.19145	.18213	.17338
46	.28644	.27163	.25774	.24472	.23251	.22105	.21028	.20018	.19068	.18174
47	.29647	.28155	.26754	.25438	.24201	.23040	.21947	.20919	.19952	.19041
48	.30676	.29173	.27760	.26431	.25181	.24004	.22896	.21852	.20868	.19941
49	.31729	.30217	.28794	.27453	.26190	.24999	.23876	.22817	.21817	.20873
50	.32808	.31289	.29856	.28505	.27229	.26026	.24889	.23814	.22799	.21839
51	.33912	.32387	.30946	.29585	.28299	.27083	.25933	.24845	.23815	.22840
52	.35038	.33507	.32060	.30691	.29395	.28168	.27005	.25904	.24861	.23872
53	.36185	.34651	.33198	.31821	.30517	.29280	.28106	.26993	.25937	.24934
54	.37352	.35815	.34358	.32976	.31664	.30418	.29234	.28110	.27042	.26026
55	.38539	.37002	.35542	.34155	.32836	.31583	.30390	.29256	.28177	.27149
56	.39746	.38209	.36748	.35358	.34034	.32774	.31574	.30431	.29342	.28303
57	.40971	.39437	.37976	.36584	.35257	.33992	.32785	.31634	.30536	.29488
58	.42212	.40682	.39222	.37829	.36500	.35231	.34019	.32862	.31756	.30699
59	.43464	.41939	.40482	.39090	.37759	.36488	.35272	.34109	.32996	.31932
60	.44726	.43207	.41754	.40364	.39034	.37761	.36542	.35375	.34257	.33186
61	.45999	.44488	.43041	.41655	.40326	.39053	.37833	.36662	.35540	.34463
62	.47286	.45785	.44345	.42964	.41639	.40367	.39146	.37974	.36848	.35767
63	.48589	.47098	.45667	.44293	.42972	.41703	.40484	.39311	.38184	.37100
64	.49903	.48426	.47005	.45638	.44324	.43060	.41843	.40671	.39544	.38458
65	.51229	.49766	.48357	.47001	.45694	.44435	.43223	.42054	.40927	.39841
66	.52568	.51121	.49726	.48381	.47084	.45833	.44626	.43461	.42337	.41252
67	.53924	.52495	.51115	.49784	.48498	.47256	.46056	.44898	.43778	.42696
68	.55293	.53883	.52521	.51205	.49932	.48701	.47511	.46360	.45246	.44169
69	.56671	.55283	.53940	.52640	.51382	.50165	.48985	.47844	.46738	.45666
70	.58052	.56687	.55365	.54084	.52843	.51639	.50473	.49342	.48245	.47181
71	.59431	.58091	.56791	.55529	.54306	.53118	.51966	.50847	.49761	.48707
72	.60804	.59490	.58213	.56973	.55768	.54598	.53461	.52357	.51283	.50239
73	.62168	.60881	.59629	.58411	.57227	.56076	.54955	.53866	.52806	.51774
74	.63528	.62268	.61042	.59848	.58686	.57555	.56453	.55380	.54335	.53316
75	.64887	.63657	.62458	.61290	.60151	.59041	.57959	.56904	.55875	.54872
76	.66249	.65049	.63880	.62739	.61625	.60538	.59478	.58443	.57432	.56446

Reg. § 1.664-4(e)(7)

Estates, Trusts, and Beneficiaries

See p. 20,601 for regulations not amended to reflect law changes

TABLE U(1)
BASED ON LIFE TABLE 90CM
UNITRUST SINGLE LIFE REMAINDER FACTORS
APPLICABLE FOR TRANSFERS AFTER APRIL 30, 1999

ADJUSTED PAYOUT RATE

AGE	4.2%	4.4%	4.6%	4.8%	5.0%	5.2%	5.4%	5.6%	5.8%	6.0%
77	.67612	.66446	.65307	.64194	.63108	.62046	.61009	.59995	.59005	.58037
78	.68975	.67843	.66736	.65654	.64596	.63561	.62548	.61558	.60590	.59643
79	.70330	.69233	.68160	.67109	.66081	.65074	.64088	.63123	.62178	.61253
80	.71666	.70605	.69566	.68548	.67550	.66573	.65615	.64676	.63755	.62853
81	.72975	.71950	.70946	.69961	.68995	.68047	.67117	.66205	.65310	.64433
82	.74250	.73263	.72293	.71342	.70407	.69490	.68589	.67705	.66837	.65984
83	.75493	.74542	.73608	.72690	.71788	.70902	.70031	.69175	.68333	.67506
84	.76712	.75798	.74900	.74016	.73147	.72292	.71451	.70624	.69810	.69010
85	.77913	.77037	.76175	.75326	.74491	.73668	.72859	.72061	.71276	.70503
86	.79086	.78248	.77423	.76610	.75808	.75019	.74241	.73474	.72719	.71974
87	.80218	.79418	.78628	.77850	.77083	.76326	.75580	.74844	.74118	.73402
88	.81307	.80544	.79790	.79047	.78313	.77589	.76874	.76169	.75473	.74786
89	.82355	.81628	.80909	.80200	.79500	.78808	.78125	.77450	.76783	.76125
90	.83360	.82668	.81985	.81309	.80642	.79982	.79330	.78685	.78048	.77418
91	.84308	.83650	.83000	.82357	.81721	.81092	.80470	.79855	.79246	.78645
92	.85182	.84556	.83937	.83325	.82718	.82119	.81525	.80937	.80356	.79780
93	.85985	.85390	.84800	.84215	.83637	.83064	.82497	.81936	.81379	.80829
94	.86732	.86164	.85601	.85044	.84491	.83944	.83402	.82865	.82333	.81806
95	.87437	.86895	.86359	.85827	.85300	.84778	.84260	.83746	.83237	.82733
96	.88097	.87582	.87070	.86563	.86060	.85561	.85066	.84575	.84088	.83605
97	.88708	.88216	.87727	.87243	.86762	.86285	.85811	.85341	.84875	.84413
98	.89280	.88810	.88343	.87880	.87420	.86964	.86511	.86061	.85614	.85171
99	.89836	.89388	.88943	.88501	.88062	.87626	.87193	.86763	.86336	.85911
100	.90375	.89948	.89525	.89103	.88685	.88269	.87856	.87445	.87037	.86632
101	.90905	.90500	.90097	.89696	.89298	.88902	.88509	.88118	.87729	.87342
102	.91424	.91040	.90658	.90278	.89900	.89524	.89150	.88778	.88408	.88040
103	.91939	.91575	.91214	.90854	.90496	.90139	.89785	.89432	.89081	.88732
104	.92485	.92144	.91805	.91467	.91131	.90796	.90463	.90131	.89800	.89471
105	.93020	.92701	.92383	.92067	.91751	.91437	.91125	.90813	.90502	.90193
106	.93701	.93411	.93122	.92834	.92546	.92260	.91974	.91689	.91405	.91122
107	.94522	.94268	.94013	.93760	.93507	.93254	.93002	.92750	.92499	.92249
108	.95782	.95583	.95385	.95187	.94989	.94791	.94593	.94396	.94199	.94002
109	.97900	.97800	.97700	.97600	.97500	.97400	.97300	.97200	.97100	.97000

TABLE U(1)
BASED ON LIFE TABLE 90CM
UNITRUST SINGLE LIFE REMAINDER FACTORS
APPLICABLE FOR TRANSFERS AFTER APRIL 30, 1999

ADJUSTED PAYOUT RATE

AGE	6.2%	6.4%	6.6%	6.8%	7.0%	7.2%	7.4%	7.6%	7.8%	8.0%
0	.02693	.02534	.02395	.02271	.02161	.02063	.01976	.01898	.01828	.01765
1	.01922	.01756	.01610	.01480	.01365	.01263	.01171	.01090	.01017	.00951
2	.01975	.01802	.01650	.01514	.01393	.01286	.01190	.01104	.01028	.00959
3	.02056	.01876	.01717	.01575	.01449	.01336	.01235	.01145	.01064	.00992
4	.02155	.01967	.01800	.01652	.01520	.01401	.01296	.01201	.01116	.01039
5	.02266	.02071	.01896	.01741	.01603	.01479	.01368	.01269	.01179	.01098
6	.02389	.02184	.02003	.01841	.01696	.01566	.01450	.01345	.01251	.01166
7	.02522	.02309	.02120	.01950	.01799	.01663	.01540	.01431	.01332	.01242
8	.02665	.02444	.02246	.02069	.01910	.01768	.01640	.01524	.01420	.01326
9	.02821	.02590	.02384	.02199	.02033	.01884	.01750	.01629	.01520	.01421
10	.02990	.02750	.02535	.02342	.02169	.02013	.01872	.01745	.01631	.01526
11	.03172	.02922	.02698	.02497	.02316	.02153	.02006	.01872	.01752	.01643
12	.03365	.03106	.02872	.02663	.02474	.02303	.02149	.02010	.01884	.01769
13	.03566	.03297	.03054	.02835	.02638	.02460	.02299	.02154	.02021	.01901
14	.03770	.03490	.03237	.03010	.02804	.02619	.02450	.02298	.02159	.02033
15	.03973	.03682	.03419	.03182	.02968	.02775	.02599	.02439	.02294	.02162
16	.04173	.03871	.03598	.03352	.03129	.02926	.02743	.02576	.02424	.02286

Reg. § 1.664-4(e)(7)

TABLE U(1)
BASED ON LIFE TABLE 90CM
UNITRUST SINGLE LIFE REMAINDER FACTORS
APPLICABLE FOR TRANSFERS AFTER APRIL 30, 1999
ADJUSTED PAYOUT RATE

AGE	6.2%	6.4%	6.6%	6.8%	7.0%	7.2%	7.4%	7.6%	7.8%	8.0%
17	.04372	.04059	.03775	.03519	.03287	.03076	.02884	.02710	.02551	.02406
18	.04573	.04248	.03953	.03686	.03444	.03224	.03024	.02842	.02676	.02524
19	.04780	.04443	.04137	.03859	.03607	.03378	.03169	.02978	.02804	.02646
20	.04997	.04647	.04329	.04040	.03778	.03539	.03321	.03122	.02940	.02773
21	.05226	.04862	.04532	.04232	.03958	.03709	.03481	.03274	.03083	.02909
22	.05465	.05088	.04745	.04432	.04148	.03888	.03650	.03433	.03234	.03052
23	.05716	.05325	.04969	.04645	.04348	.04077	.03830	.03603	.03394	.03203
24	.05983	.05578	.05208	.04871	.04562	.04280	.04021	.03784	.03566	.03367
25	.06266	.05846	.05463	.05112	.04791	.04497	.04227	.03980	.03752	.03543
26	.06566	.06131	.05734	.05369	.05035	.04729	.04448	.04189	.03951	.03732
27	.06887	.06436	.06024	.05646	.05298	.04979	.04686	.04416	.04168	.03939
28	.07225	.06758	.06331	.05938	.05577	.05245	.04940	.04658	.04398	.04159
29	.07581	.07099	.06656	.06248	.05873	.05528	.05210	.04916	.04645	.04394
30	.07956	.07457	.06998	.06575	.06186	.05827	.05495	.05189	.04906	.04644
31	.08348	.07833	.07358	.06920	.06515	.06142	.05797	.05478	.05182	.04908
32	.08761	.08228	.07736	.07282	.06863	.06475	.06116	.05783	.05475	.05189
33	.09195	.08645	.08136	.07666	.07231	.06828	.06454	.06108	.05786	.05488
34	.09651	.09082	.08557	.08070	.07619	.07200	.06812	.06452	.06117	.05805
35	.10131	.09545	.09002	.08498	.08030	.07596	.07193	.06818	.06469	.06144
36	.10635	.10031	.09470	.08949	.08465	.08015	.07596	.07206	.06842	.06503
37	.11165	.10542	.09963	.09424	.08923	.08457	.08022	.07617	.07238	.06885
38	.11722	.11081	.10484	.09927	.09409	.08926	.08475	.08054	.07661	.07293
39	.12308	.11648	.11032	.10458	.09922	.09422	.08955	.08518	.08109	.07726
40	.12925	.12246	.11612	.11020	.10466	.09949	.09465	.09011	.08587	.08189
41	.13575	.12877	.12225	.11614	.11043	.10508	.10007	.09537	.09097	.08683
42	.14259	.13542	.12871	.12243	.11654	.11101	.10583	.10097	.09640	.09210
43	.14977	.14242	.13552	.12905	.12298	.11729	.11193	.10690	.10217	.09771
44	.15731	.14976	.14269	.13604	.12979	.12391	.11838	.11318	.10828	.10367
45	.16516	.15743	.15017	.14334	.13691	.13086	.12516	.11979	.11472	.10994
46	.17334	.16544	.15800	.15099	.14438	.13816	.13228	.12674	.12150	.11656
47	.18184	.17375	.16613	.15895	.15217	.14576	.13972	.13400	.12860	.12349
48	.19066	.18240	.17461	.16724	.16029	.15371	.14749	.14161	.13604	.13077
49	.19981	.19138	.18342	.17588	.16875	.16201	.15562	.14956	.14383	.13839
50	.20931	.20072	.19259	.18489	.17759	.17067	.16412	.15790	.15199	.14639
51	.21917	.21042	.20212	.19426	.18679	.17971	.17299	.16660	.16054	.15477
52	.22933	.22043	.21198	.20395	.19633	.18909	.18220	.17566	.16943	.16350
53	.23981	.23076	.22216	.21399	.20621	.19881	.19176	.18506	.17867	.17258
54	.25060	.24141	.23267	.22434	.21642	.20886	.20166	.19480	.18826	.18201
55	.26171	.25239	.24351	.23504	.22697	.21927	.21192	.20491	.19821	.19182
56	.27313	.26369	.25468	.24608	.23787	.23003	.22254	.21538	.20854	.20199
57	.28487	.27531	.26618	.25746	.24912	.24114	.23351	.22621	.21923	.21254
58	.29688	.28722	.27798	.26914	.26067	.25257	.24481	.23738	.23025	.22343
59	.30913	.29937	.29002	.28107	.27249	.26427	.25639	.24882	.24157	.23461
60	.32159	.31175	.30231	.29325	.28457	.27623	.26823	.26055	.25317	.24608
61	.33429	.32437	.31485	.30571	.29692	.28848	.28037	.27257	.26507	.25786
62	.34728	.33730	.32770	.31847	.30960	.30106	.29285	.28495	.27734	.27001
63	.36057	.35053	.34087	.33157	.32262	.31400	.30569	.29769	.28998	.28255
64	.37412	.36404	.35433	.34498	.33596	.32726	.31887	.31078	.30298	.29545
65	.38794	.37783	.36809	.35868	.34961	.34085	.33239	.32422	.31633	.30871
66	.40205	.39193	.38216	.37272	.36361	.35479	.34628	.33804	.33008	.32238
67	.41650	.40639	.39661	.38715	.37800	.36915	.36059	.35230	.34428	.33651
68	.43126	.42117	.41139	.40193	.39277	.38390	.37530	.36697	.35890	.35108
69	.44628	.43622	.42648	.41703	.40787	.39898	.39037	.38201	.37391	.36604
70	.46150	.45149	.44178	.43236	.42321	.41433	.40571	.39735	.38922	.38132
71	.47683	.46689	.45723	.44785	.43873	.42987	.42126	.41290	.40476	.39685
72	.49225	.48238	.47279	.46346	.45439	.44556	.43697	.42862	.42048	.41257
73	.50770	.49793	.48841	.47915	.47013	.46135	.45280	.44447	.43635	.42844
74	.52324	.51358	.50416	.49498	.48603	.47731	.46880	.46051	.45242	.44454
75	.53894	.52939	.52008	.51100	.50214	.49349	.48505	.47681	.46877	.46092

Reg. § 1.664-4(e)(7)

Estates, Trusts, and Beneficiaries 43,365

TABLE U(1)
BASED ON LIFE TABLE 90CM
UNITRUST SINGLE LIFE REMAINDER FACTORS
APPLICABLE FOR TRANSFERS AFTER APRIL 30, 1999
ADJUSTED PAYOUT RATE

AGE	6.2%	6.4%	6.6%	6.8%	7.0%	7.2%	7.4%	7.6%	7.8%	8.0%
76	.55483	.54543	.53624	.52728	.51852	.50996	.50160	.49344	.48546	.47766
77	.57091	.56167	.55263	.54380	.53516	.52671	.51845	.51038	.50247	.49475
78	.58716	.57809	.56922	.56053	.55203	.54372	.53557	.52760	.51980	.51216
79	.60346	.59459	.58590	.57738	.56904	.56086	.55286	.54501	.53732	.52978
80	.61969	.61102	.60252	.59419	.58601	.57800	.57014	.56243	.55487	.54745
81	.63571	.62726	.61897	.61082	.60283	.59499	.58729	.57974	.57232	.56503
82	.65146	.64324	.63515	.62722	.61942	.61176	.60423	.59683	.58957	.58242
83	.66693	.65893	.65108	.64335	.63575	.62828	.62093	.61371	.60660	.59962
84	.68222	.67447	.66684	.65934	.65195	.64468	.63753	.63049	.62356	.61674
85	.69742	.68993	.68255	.67528	.66812	.66106	.65411	.64727	.64053	.63389
86	.71241	.70517	.69805	.69102	.68410	.67727	.67054	.66390	.65736	.65091
87	.72696	.72000	.71313	.70635	.69967	.69307	.68656	.68014	.67381	.66756
88	.74108	.73438	.72777	.72125	.71480	.70845	.70217	.69597	.68985	.68380
89	.75475	.74832	.74198	.73571	.72951	.72339	.71734	.71137	.70547	.69963
90	.76796	.76180	.75572	.74971	.74376	.73788	.73207	.72633	.72065	.71503
91	.78049	.77460	.76878	.76302	.75732	.75168	.74610	.74058	.73512	.72972
92	.79211	.78647	.78089	.77537	.76990	.76449	.75913	.75383	.74858	.74338
93	.80283	.79743	.79208	.78679	.78154	.77634	.77119	.76610	.76105	.75604
94	.81283	.80765	.80253	.79744	.79240	.78741	.78247	.77756	.77270	.76789
95	.82233	.81737	.81245	.80757	.80274	.79795	.79320	.78849	.78382	.77918
96	.83126	.82651	.82180	.81712	.81248	.80788	.80332	.79880	.79431	.78985
97	.83953	.83498	.83046	.82597	.82152	.81710	.81271	.80836	.80404	.79976
98	.84731	.84294	.83860	.83429	.83002	.82577	.82155	.81737	.81321	.80908
99	.85490	.85071	.84656	.84243	.83832	.83425	.83020	.82618	.82219	.81822
100	.86229	.85828	.85431	.85035	.84642	.84252	.83864	.83478	.83095	.82714
101	.86958	.86575	.86195	.85818	.85442	.85069	.84698	.84329	.83962	.83597
102	.87674	.87310	.86947	.86587	.86229	.85873	.85518	.85166	.84815	.84466
103	.88384	.88038	.87694	.87351	.87010	.86671	.86334	.85998	.85663	.85331
104	.89143	.88817	.88492	.88169	.87847	.87526	.87207	.86889	.86573	.86258
105	.89885	.89578	.89272	.88967	.88664	.88361	.88060	.87760	.87461	.87163
106	.90840	.90559	.90278	.89999	.89720	.89442	.89165	.88888	.88613	.88338
107	.91999	.91750	.91501	.91253	.91005	.90758	.90511	.90265	.90019	.89774
108	.93805	.93609	.93412	.93216	.93020	.92824	.92629	.92434	.92239	.92044
109	.96900	.96800	.96700	.96600	.96500	.96400	.96300	.96200	.96100	.96000

TABLE U(1)
BASED ON LIFE TABLE 90CM
UNITRUST SINGLE LIFE REMAINDER FACTORS
APPLICABLE FOR TRANSFERS AFTER APRIL 30, 1999
ADJUSTED PAYOUT RATE

AGE	8.2%	8.4%	8.6%	8.8%	9.0%	9.2%	9.4%	9.6%	9.8%	10.0%
0	.01709	.01658	.01612	.01570	.01532	.01497	.01466	.01437	.01410	.01386
1	.00892	.00839	.00791	.00747	.00708	.00672	.00639	.00609	.00582	.00557
2	.00896	.00840	.00790	.00744	.00702	.00664	.00629	.00598	.00569	.00542
3	.00926	.00867	.00814	.00765	.00721	.00681	.00644	.00611	.00580	.00552
4	.00970	.00908	.00851	.00800	.00753	.00711	.00672	.00636	.00604	.00574
5	.01026	.00960	.00900	.00846	.00796	.00751	.00710	.00672	.00637	.00606
6	.01089	.01019	.00956	.00899	.00846	.00799	.00755	.00715	.00678	.00644
7	.01161	.01088	.01021	.00960	.00905	.00854	.00808	.00765	.00726	.00690
8	.01241	.01163	.01093	.01029	.00970	.00917	.00867	.00822	.00781	.00743
9	.01331	.01249	.01175	.01107	.01045	.00988	.00936	.00889	.00845	.00804
10	.01432	.01346	.01268	.01196	.01131	.01071	.01016	.00965	.00918	.00875
11	.01543	.01453	.01370	.01295	.01226	.01162	.01104	.01051	.01001	.00956
12	.01664	.01569	.01482	.01403	.01330	.01263	.01202	.01145	.01093	.01045
13	.01791	.01691	.01600	.01516	.01440	.01369	.01304	.01245	.01190	.01139
14	.01918	.01813	.01717	.01629	.01548	.01474	.01406	.01343	.01285	.01231
15	.02041	.01931	.01831	.01738	.01653	.01576	.01504	.01437	.01376	.01320

Reg. § 1.664-4(e)(7)

TABLE U(1)
BASED ON LIFE TABLE 90CM
UNITRUST SINGLE LIFE REMAINDER FACTORS
APPLICABLE FOR TRANSFERS AFTER APRIL 30, 1999

ADJUSTED PAYOUT RATE

AGE	8.2%	8.4%	8.6%	8.8%	9.0%	9.2%	9.4%	9.6%	9.8%	10.0%
16	.02160	.02044	.01938	.01841	.01752	.01670	.01595	.01525	.01460	.01401
17	.02274	.02152	.02041	.01940	.01846	.01760	.01680	.01607	.01539	.01476
18	.02386	.02258	.02142	.02035	.01936	.01846	.01762	.01685	.01613	.01547
19	.02500	.02367	.02245	.02132	.02029	.01933	.01845	.01764	.01689	.01619
20	.02621	.02481	.02353	.02235	.02126	.02025	.01933	.01847	.01768	.01694
21	.02749	.02603	.02468	.02344	.02229	.02124	.02026	.01936	.01852	.01774
22	.02884	.02730	.02589	.02458	.02338	.02227	.02124	.02029	.01940	.01859
23	.03028	.02867	.02718	.02581	.02454	.02337	.02229	.02128	.02035	.01949
24	.03183	.03013	.02857	.02713	.02580	.02456	.02342	.02236	.02138	.02047
25	.03350	.03172	.03008	.02857	.02717	.02587	.02467	.02355	.02251	.02155
26	.03530	.03344	.03172	.03013	.02865	.02729	.02602	.02484	.02375	.02273
27	.03727	.03532	.03351	.03183	.03028	.02885	.02751	.02627	.02511	.02404
28	.03937	.03732	.03543	.03367	.03204	.03052	.02911	.02780	.02658	.02545
29	.04162	.03947	.03748	.03564	.03392	.03233	.03084	.02946	.02818	.02698
30	.04401	.04176	.03967	.03773	.03593	.03425	.03269	.03124	.02988	.02861
31	.04654	.04419	.04200	.03996	.03807	.03630	.03466	.03312	.03169	.03035
32	.04923	.04676	.04447	.04233	.04034	.03849	.03676	.03514	.03363	.03221
33	.05210	.04952	.04711	.04487	.04278	.04083	.03901	.03731	.03571	.03422
34	.05515	.05245	.04993	.04758	.04538	.04333	.04142	.03962	.03794	.03637
35	.05841	.05558	.05295	.05048	.04818	.04603	.04401	.04212	.04035	.03869
36	.06187	.05892	.05616	.05358	.05116	.04890	.04678	.04480	.04293	.04118
37	.06555	.06247	.05958	.05688	.05435	.05198	.04975	.04766	.04570	.04385
38	.06949	.06627	.06325	.06043	.05777	.05528	.05295	.05075	.04868	.04674
39	.07368	.07032	.06717	.06421	.06143	.05882	.05637	.05406	.05189	.04984
40	.07816	.07465	.07137	.06827	.06537	.06263	.06006	.05764	.05535	.05320
41	.08295	.07930	.07587	.07264	.06960	.06674	.06405	.06150	.05910	.05683
42	.08807	.08427	.08069	.07733	.07415	.07116	.06833	.06567	.06315	.06077
43	.09352	.08957	.08585	.08233	.07902	.07589	.07294	.07014	.06750	.06500
44	.09932	.09521	.09134	.08768	.08423	.08096	.07787	.07495	.07218	.06956
45	.10543	.10117	.09715	.09334	.08974	.08634	.08311	.08005	.07716	.07441
46	.11189	.10747	.10329	.09933	.09559	.09204	.08867	.08548	.08245	.07958
47	.11866	.11408	.10974	.10564	.10174	.09805	.09454	.09121	.08805	.08504
48	.12577	.12103	.11654	.11228	.10823	.10439	.10074	.09727	.09397	.09083
49	.13323	.12833	.12368	.11926	.11506	.11107	.10728	.10366	.10022	.09695
50	.14107	.13601	.13120	.12663	.12228	.11813	.11419	.11043	.10685	.10344
51	.14928	.14407	.13910	.13437	.12987	.12558	.12149	.11758	.11386	.11031
52	.15785	.15248	.14735	.14247	.13781	.13337	.12913	.12508	.12122	.11752
53	.16678	.16124	.15597	.15093	.14612	.14153	.13714	.13294	.12893	.12509
54	.17606	.17037	.16493	.15974	.15478	.15004	.14550	.14116	.13700	.13302
55	.18570	.17986	.17428	.16893	.16382	.15893	.15424	.14976	.14546	.14134
56	.19573	.18974	.18400	.17851	.17325	.16821	.16338	.15875	.15430	.15004
57	.20613	.20000	.19412	.18848	.18307	.17789	.17291	.16814	.16355	.15914
58	.21688	.21060	.20458	.19880	.19325	.18792	.18280	.17788	.17316	.16861
59	.22793	.22151	.21535	.20943	.20374	.19827	.19301	.18795	.18309	.17840
60	.23927	.23272	.22642	.22036	.21454	.20893	.20354	.19834	.19334	.18851
61	.25092	.24425	.23782	.23163	.22567	.21993	.21440	.20907	.20393	.19898
62	.26295	.25616	.24961	.24329	.23721	.23134	.22568	.22021	.21494	.20985
63	.27538	.26847	.26180	.25537	.24916	.24316	.23738	.23179	.22639	.22117
64	.28817	.28116	.27438	.26783	.26150	.25539	.24949	.24377	.23825	.23291
65	.30134	.29423	.28735	.28069	.27426	.26803	.26201	.25618	.25054	.24508
66	.31493	.30772	.30075	.29399	.28746	.28113	.27500	.26906	.26331	.25774
67	.32899	.32170	.31464	.30780	.30118	.29475	.28852	.28248	.27663	.27095
68	.34349	.33614	.32901	.32209	.31538	.30887	.30256	.29643	.29047	.28469
69	.35841	.35100	.34381	.33683	.33005	.32346	.31707	.31085	.30481	.29894
70	.37366	.36620	.35896	.35193	.34509	.33844	.33197	.32568	.31957	.31362
71	.38916	.38167	.37440	.36732	.36043	.35372	.34720	.34084	.33466	.32864
72	.40486	.39736	.39006	.38295	.37602	.36927	.36270	.35629	.35005	.34396
73	.42074	.41323	.40591	.39878	.39182	.38504	.37843	.37198	.36568	.35955
74	.43685	.42934	.42202	.41488	.40791	.40110	.39446	.38798	.38165	.37547

Reg. § 1.664-4(e)(7)

Estates, Trusts, and Beneficiaries

43,367

See p. 20,601 for regulations not amended to reflect law changes

TABLE U(1)
BASED ON LIFE TABLE 90CM
UNITRUST SINGLE LIFE REMAINDER FACTORS
APPLICABLE FOR TRANSFERS AFTER APRIL 30, 1999

ADJUSTED PAYOUT RATE

AGE	8.2%	8.4%	8.6%	8.8%	9.0%	9.2%	9.4%	9.6%	9.8%	10.0%
75	.45326	.44577	.43846	.43132	.42435	.41754	.41088	.40438	.39802	.39181
76	.47004	.46259	.45530	.44818	.44122	.43442	.42776	.42125	.41488	.40865
77	.48718	.47979	.47255	.46547	.45853	.45175	.44511	.43861	.43225	.42601
78	.50467	.49735	.49017	.48314	.47626	.46951	.46290	.45643	.45008	.44386
79	.52239	.51515	.50806	.50110	.49427	.48758	.48102	.47459	.46828	.46209
80	.54018	.53304	.52603	.51916	.51242	.50580	.49930	.49292	.48666	.48052
81	.55788	.55085	.54396	.53718	.53053	.52399	.51757	.51126	.50507	.49898
82	.57540	.56851	.56173	.55506	.54851	.54207	.53574	.52951	.52339	.51737
83	.59274	.58598	.57933	.57279	.56635	.56001	.55378	.54765	.54161	.53567
84	.61002	.60341	.59690	.59049	.58418	.57796	.57184	.56582	.55988	.55403
85	.62734	.62090	.61454	.60828	.60211	.59603	.59004	.58414	.57832	.57258
86	.64455	.63828	.63210	.62600	.61999	.61406	.60821	.60244	.59675	.59113
87	.66139	.65531	.64930	.64337	.63752	.63175	.62605	.62043	.61488	.60939
88	.67783	.67194	.66612	.66037	.65469	.64908	.64354	.63807	.63267	.62733
89	.69387	.68817	.68254	.67698	.67148	.66605	.66068	.65537	.65012	.64493
90	.70947	.70398	.69855	.69318	.68786	.68261	.67742	.67228	.66719	.66217
91	.72437	.71908	.71385	.70867	.70354	.69847	.69345	.68848	.68357	.67870
92	.73823	.73314	.72810	.72310	.71816	.71326	.70841	.70361	.69886	.69415
93	.75109	.74618	.74132	.73650	.73173	.72700	.72232	.71768	.71308	.70852
94	.76312	.75839	.75370	.74905	.74445	.73988	.73536	.73087	.72643	.72202
95	.77459	.77004	.76552	.76104	.75660	.75220	.74783	.74350	.73920	.73494
96	.78543	.78105	.77670	.77238	.76810	.76386	.75964	.75546	.75131	.74720
97	.79550	.79128	.78709	.78293	.77880	.77470	.77063	.76659	.76258	.75860
98	.80498	.80091	.79687	.79286	.78888	.78492	.78099	.77709	.77322	.76937
99	.81428	.81036	.80647	.80261	.79877	.79496	.79117	.78741	.78367	.77995
100	.82336	.81959	.81586	.81214	.80845	.80478	.80113	.79751	.79390	.79032
101	.83234	.82873	.82515	.82158	.81804	.81451	.81101	.80753	.80406	.80062
102	.84119	.83774	.83431	.83089	.82750	.82412	.82076	.81742	.81409	.81078
103	.84999	.84670	.84342	.84016	.83691	.83368	.83046	.82726	.82408	.82091
104	.85944	.85632	.85321	.85011	.84703	.84396	.84090	.83786	.83483	.83182
105	.86866	.86570	.86276	.85982	.85690	.85399	.85109	.84820	.84532	.84245
106	.88065	.87792	.87520	.87248	.86978	.86708	.86440	.86172	.85905	.85638
107	.89530	.89286	.89042	.88799	.88557	.88315	.88073	.87833	.87592	.87352
108	.91849	.91654	.91460	.91266	.91072	.90879	.90685	.90492	.90299	.90106
109	.95900	.95800	.95700	.95600	.95500	.95400	.95300	.95200	.95100	.95000

TABLE U(1)
BASED ON LIFE TABLE 90CM
UNITRUST SINGLE LIFE REMAINDER FACTORS
APPLICABLE FOR TRANSFERS AFTER APRIL 30, 1999

ADJUSTED PAYOUT RATE

AGE	10.2%	10.4%	10.6%	10.8%	11.0%	11.2%	11.4%	11.6%	11.8%	12.0%
0	.01363	.01342	.01323	.01305	.01288	.01272	.01258	.01244	.01231	.01219
1	.00534	.00512	.00493	.00474	.00458	.00442	.00427	.00414	.00401	.00389
2	.00518	.00495	.00474	.00455	.00437	.00421	.00405	.00391	.00377	.00365
3	.00526	.00502	.00480	.00459	.00440	.00422	.00406	.00391	.00376	.00363
4	.00546	.00521	.00497	.00475	.00455	.00436	.00419	.00402	.00387	.00373
5	.00576	.00549	.00524	.00501	.00479	.00459	.00440	.00423	.00406	.00391
6	.00613	.00584	.00557	.00532	.00509	.00488	.00468	.00449	.00432	.00415
7	.00657	.00626	.00598	.00571	.00547	.00524	.00502	.00482	.00464	.00446
8	.00707	.00675	.00644	.00616	.00590	.00565	.00542	.00521	.00501	.00482
9	.00766	.00732	.00699	.00669	.00641	.00615	.00591	.00568	.00547	.00527
10	.00835	.00798	.00764	.00732	.00702	.00675	.00649	.00624	.00602	.00580
11	.00913	.00874	.00838	.00804	.00772	.00743	.00715	.00689	.00665	.00642
12	.01000	.00959	.00920	.00884	.00851	.00819	.00790	.00762	.00737	.00712
13	.01091	.01048	.01007	.00969	.00933	.00900	.00869	.00840	.00813	.00787
14	.01181	.01135	.01092	.01052	.01014	.00979	.00947	.00916	.00887	.00860

Reg. § 1.664-4(e)(7)

43,368 Estates, Trusts, and Beneficiaries

See p. 20,601 for regulations not amended to reflect law changes

TABLE U(1)
BASED ON LIFE TABLE 90CM
UNITRUST SINGLE LIFE REMAINDER FACTORS
APPLICABLE FOR TRANSFERS AFTER APRIL 30, 1999

ADJUSTED PAYOUT RATE

AGE	10.2%	10.4%	10.6%	10.8%	11.0%	11.2%	11.4%	11.6%	11.8%	12.0%
15	.01267	.01218	.01173	.01130	.01091	.01054	.01019	.00987	.00956	.00928
16	.01345	.01294	.01246	.01201	.01160	.01121	.01084	.01050	.01018	.00988
17	.01418	.01364	.01313	.01266	.01222	.01181	.01143	.01107	.01073	.01041
18	.01486	.01429	.01375	.01326	.01279	.01236	.01196	.01158	.01122	.01088
19	.01554	.01494	.01438	.01385	.01336	.01291	.01248	.01208	.01170	.01135
20	.01626	.01562	.01503	.01448	.01396	.01348	.01303	.01260	.01220	.01183
21	.01702	.01635	.01573	.01514	.01460	.01409	.01361	.01316	.01274	.01235
22	.01782	.01711	.01645	.01584	.01526	.01472	.01422	.01374	.01330	.01288
23	.01868	.01793	.01724	.01658	.01597	.01540	.01487	.01437	.01390	.01345
24	.01962	.01883	.01809	.01740	.01675	.01615	.01558	.01505	.01455	.01408
25	.02065	.01981	.01903	.01830	.01762	.01698	.01638	.01581	.01528	.01478
26	.02178	.02089	.02006	.01929	.01856	.01789	.01725	.01665	.01609	.01556
27	.02303	.02209	.02122	.02040	.01963	.01891	.01824	.01760	.01700	.01644
28	.02439	.02339	.02247	.02160	.02079	.02002	.01931	.01863	.01800	.01740
29	.02585	.02480	.02382	.02290	.02204	.02123	.02047	.01976	.01908	.01845
30	.02742	.02631	.02527	.02430	.02339	.02253	.02172	.02096	.02025	.01957
31	.02910	.02793	.02683	.02579	.02482	.02391	.02306	.02225	.02149	.02077
32	.03089	.02965	.02849	.02739	.02636	.02540	.02449	.02363	.02282	.02206
33	.03282	.03151	.03028	.02912	.02803	.02701	.02604	.02513	.02427	.02346
34	.03489	.03350	.03220	.03097	.02982	.02873	.02771	.02674	.02583	.02497
35	.03713	.03567	.03429	.03299	.03177	.03061	.02953	.02850	.02753	.02661
36	.03953	.03798	.03653	.03515	.03386	.03263	.03148	.03039	.02936	.02838
37	.04211	.04048	.03894	.03748	.03611	.03481	.03359	.03243	.03134	.03030
38	.04490	.04318	.04155	.04001	.03856	.03719	.03589	.03466	.03350	.03239
39	.04791	.04609	.04437	.04274	.04120	.03975	.03837	.03707	.03583	.03466
40	.05116	.04924	.04742	.04571	.04408	.04254	.04108	.03970	.03839	.03714
41	.05469	.05267	.05075	.04894	.04722	.04559	.04405	.04258	.04119	.03987
42	.05851	.05638	.05436	.05245	.05063	.04891	.04728	.04573	.04425	.04285
43	.06263	.06039	.05827	.05625	.05433	.05252	.05079	.04915	.04759	.04610
44	.06707	.06472	.06248	.06035	.05834	.05642	.05459	.05286	.05121	.04963
45	.07180	.06933	.06698	.06474	.06262	.06059	.05867	.05684	.05509	.05342
46	.07685	.07425	.07178	.06943	.06720	.06507	.06304	.06110	.05926	.05750
47	.08218	.07946	.07687	.07440	.07205	.06981	.06768	.06564	.06369	.06183
48	.08784	.08499	.08228	.07969	.07722	.07487	.07262	.07047	.06842	.06646
49	.09382	.09085	.08801	.08530	.08271	.08024	.07788	.07562	.07346	.07140
50	.10018	.09707	.09410	.09127	.08856	.08597	.08349	.08112	.07885	.07667
51	.10691	.10367	.10057	.09761	.09477	.09206	.08946	.08697	.08459	.08231
52	.11399	.11061	.10738	.10429	.10132	.09849	.09577	.09316	.09066	.08826
53	.12142	.11791	.11454	.11132	.10823	.10526	.10242	.09969	.09707	.09456
54	.12921	.12556	.12206	.11870	.11548	.11239	.10942	.10657	.10383	.10120
55	.13738	.13359	.12995	.12646	.12311	.11989	.11679	.11382	.11096	.10820
56	.14595	.14202	.13824	.13462	.13113	.12778	.12456	.12146	.11847	.11560
57	.15491	.15084	.14693	.14317	.13955	.13607	.13272	.12949	.12638	.12338
58	.16424	.16004	.15599	.15209	.14834	.14473	.14125	.13789	.13465	.13153
59	.17390	.16955	.16537	.16134	.15746	.15371	.15010	.14662	.14325	.14001
60	.18387	.17939	.17507	.17091	.16689	.16302	.15927	.15566	.15217	.14880
61	.19420	.18958	.18513	.18084	.17669	.17268	.16881	.16506	.16145	.15795
62	.20494	.20020	.19561	.19119	.18691	.18277	.17877	.17490	.17115	.16753
63	.21613	.21126	.20654	.20199	.19758	.19331	.18918	.18518	.18131	.17757
64	.22774	.22274	.21791	.21322	.20869	.20429	.20004	.19592	.19192	.18805
65	.23979	.23467	.22971	.22490	.22025	.21573	.21135	.20710	.20299	.19899
66	.25233	.24709	.24202	.23709	.23231	.22767	.22318	.21881	.21457	.21045
67	.26543	.26009	.25489	.24985	.24496	.24021	.23560	.23111	.22676	.22252
68	.27908	.27363	.26833	.26319	.25819	.25332	.24860	.24400	.23954	.23519
69	.29324	.28769	.28230	.27705	.27195	.26699	.26216	.25746	.25288	.24843
70	.30783	.30219	.29671	.29137	.28618	.28112	.27619	.27139	.26672	.26216
71	.32277	.31706	.31150	.30608	.30079	.29564	.29063	.28573	.28096	.27631
72	.33803	.33225	.32661	.32112	.31575	.31052	.30542	.30044	.29559	.29084
73	.35356	.34772	.34201	.33645	.33101	.32571	.32053	.31547	.31053	.30571

Reg. § 1.664-4(e)(7)

Estates, Trusts, and Beneficiaries

43,369

See p. 20,601 for regulations not amended to reflect law changes

TABLE U(1)
BASED ON LIFE TABLE 90CM
UNITRUST SINGLE LIFE REMAINDER FACTORS
APPLICABLE FOR TRANSFERS AFTER APRIL 30, 1999

ADJUSTED PAYOUT RATE

AGE	10.2%	10.4%	10.6%	10.8%	11.0%	11.2%	11.4%	11.6%	11.8%	12.0%
74	.36943	.36354	.35778	.35215	.34666	.34129	.33604	.33091	.32590	.32100
75	.38574	.37980	.37400	.36833	.36278	.35735	.35205	.34686	.34178	.33681
76	.40256	.39660	.39076	.38505	.37947	.37400	.36864	.36340	.35827	.35324
77	.41991	.41394	.40808	.40235	.39674	.39124	.38585	.38056	.37539	.37032
78	.43777	.43180	.42594	.42020	.41457	.40906	.40365	.39834	.39314	.38803
79	.45602	.45007	.44422	.43849	.43287	.42735	.42193	.41661	.41139	.40627
80	.47449	.46856	.46275	.45704	.45143	.44592	.44051	.43519	.42997	.42484
81	.49300	.48712	.48134	.47566	.47008	.46460	.45921	.45391	.44870	.44357
82	.51145	.50563	.49990	.49427	.48873	.48328	.47792	.47265	.46746	.46235
83	.52983	.52407	.51841	.51284	.50735	.50195	.49663	.49139	.48624	.48116
84	.54828	.54261	.53702	.53151	.52609	.52075	.51549	.51030	.50519	.50015
85	.56693	.56135	.55586	.55044	.54510	.53983	.53464	.52952	.52447	.51949
86	.58560	.58013	.57474	.56943	.56418	.55901	.55390	.54886	.54389	.53898
87	.60398	.59864	.59337	.58817	.58303	.57795	.57294	.56799	.56310	.55828
88	.62206	.61685	.61170	.60662	.60159	.59663	.59173	.58688	.58209	.57736
89	.63980	.63474	.62972	.62477	.61987	.61503	.61024	.60551	.60083	.59620
90	.65719	.65227	.64741	.64259	.63783	.63312	.62846	.62385	.61928	.61477
91	.67388	.66912	.66440	.65973	.65511	.65053	.64600	.64152	.63708	.63269
92	.68949	.68487	.68030	.67577	.67129	.66685	.66245	.65809	.65378	.64950
93	.70401	.69954	.69511	.69072	.68637	.68205	.67778	.67355	.66935	.66519
94	.71765	.71332	.70902	.70477	.70055	.69636	.69222	.68810	.68403	.67998
95	.73072	.72653	.72237	.71825	.71416	.71010	.70608	.70209	.69813	.69421
96	.74311	.73906	.73504	.73105	.72709	.72316	.71926	.71539	.71155	.70774
97	.75465	.75073	.74684	.74297	.73914	.73533	.73155	.72780	.72407	.72037
98	.76555	.76175	.75798	.75424	.75052	.74683	.74317	.73953	.73591	.73232
99	.77626	.77260	.76895	.76534	.76174	.75817	.75462	.75109	.74759	.74411
100	.78676	.78323	.77971	.77622	.77274	.76929	.76586	.76245	.75906	.75569
101	.79719	.79379	.79040	.78703	.78368	.78035	.77704	.77375	.77048	.76722
102	.80749	.80422	.80096	.79772	.79450	.79130	.78811	.78494	.78178	.77864
103	.81775	.81461	.81149	.80838	.80529	.80221	.79914	.79609	.79306	.79003
104	.82881	.82582	.82284	.81988	.81693	.81399	.81106	.80815	.80525	.80236
105	.83959	.83674	.83391	.83108	.82826	.82546	.82267	.81988	.81711	.81435
106	.85373	.85108	.84844	.84581	.84319	.84058	.83797	.83537	.83278	.83020
107	.87113	.86875	.86636	.86399	.86161	.85925	.85689	.85453	.85218	.84984
108	.89913	.89721	.89529	.89337	.89145	.88953	.88762	.88571	.88380	.88189
109	.94900	.94800	.94700	.94600	.94500	.94400	.94300	.94200	.94100	.94000

TABLE U(1)
BASED ON LIFE TABLE 90CM
UNITRUST SINGLE LIFE REMAINDER FACTORS
APPLICABLE FOR TRANSFERS AFTER APRIL 30, 1999

ADJUSTED PAYOUT RATE

AGE	12.2%	12.4%	12.6%	12.8%	13.0%	13.2%	13.4%	13.6%	13.8%	14.0%
0	.01208	.01197	.01187	.01177	.01168	.01159	.01151	.01143	.01135	.01128
1	.00378	.00367	.00358	.00348	.00340	.00331	.00323	.00316	.00309	.00302
2	.00353	.00342	.00331	.00322	.00312	.00304	.00295	.00288	.00280	.00273
3	.00350	.00339	.00327	.00317	.00307	.00298	.00289	.00281	.00273	.00265
4	.00359	.00347	.00335	.00324	.00313	.00303	.00294	.00285	.00276	.00268
5	.00377	.00363	.00351	.00339	.00327	.00317	.00306	.00297	.00288	.00279
6	.00400	.00386	.00372	.00359	.00347	.00335	.00325	.00314	.00305	.00295
7	.00430	.00414	.00400	.00386	.00373	.00360	.00349	.00338	.00327	.00317
8	.00465	.00448	.00432	.00417	.00403	.00390	.00378	.00366	.00354	.00344
9	.00508	.00490	.00473	.00457	.00442	.00428	.00414	.00402	.00389	.00378
10	.00560	.00541	.00523	.00506	.00490	.00475	.00460	.00446	.00433	.00421
11	.00620	.00600	.00581	.00563	.00546	.00529	.00514	.00499	.00485	.00472
12	.00689	.00668	.00647	.00628	.00610	.00593	.00576	.00560	.00545	.00531
13	.00763	.00740	.00718	.00698	.00678	.00660	.00642	.00626	.00610	.00595

Reg. § 1.664-4(e)(7)

TABLE U(1)
BASED ON LIFE TABLE 90CM
UNITRUST SINGLE LIFE REMAINDER FACTORS
APPLICABLE FOR TRANSFERS AFTER APRIL 30, 1999

ADJUSTED PAYOUT RATE

AGE	12.2%	12.4%	12.6%	12.8%	13.0%	13.2%	13.4%	13.6%	13.8%	14.0%
14	.00834	.00810	.00787	.00766	.00745	.00726	.00707	.00689	.00673	.00657
15	.00901	.00875	.00851	.00828	.00807	.00786	.00767	.00748	.00730	.00714
16	.00959	.00932	.00907	.00883	.00860	.00839	.00818	.00799	.00780	.00762
17	.01011	.00983	.00956	.00930	.00907	.00884	.00862	.00842	.00822	.00804
18	.01057	.01027	.00999	.00972	.00947	.00923	.00900	.00879	.00858	.00839
19	.01101	.01070	.01040	.01012	.00985	.00960	.00936	.00914	.00892	.00871
20	.01148	.01115	.01083	.01054	.01026	.00999	.00974	.00950	.00927	.00905
21	.01197	.01162	.01129	.01098	.01068	.01040	.01014	.00988	.00964	.00941
22	.01249	.01211	.01176	.01143	.01112	.01082	.01054	.01027	.01002	.00978
23	.01304	.01264	.01227	.01192	.01159	.01127	.01098	.01069	.01042	.01017
24	.01364	.01322	.01283	.01246	.01210	.01177	.01145	.01115	.01087	.01060
25	.01431	.01387	.01345	.01306	.01268	.01233	.01199	.01168	.01137	.01109
26	.01506	.01459	.01415	.01373	.01333	.01295	.01260	.01226	.01194	.01163
27	.01591	.01541	.01494	.01449	.01407	.01367	.01329	.01293	.01259	.01226
28	.01684	.01631	.01580	.01533	.01488	.01445	.01405	.01367	.01330	.01296
29	.01785	.01728	.01675	.01624	.01577	.01531	.01488	.01447	.01408	.01372
30	.01893	.01833	.01776	.01723	.01672	.01623	.01578	.01534	.01493	.01453
31	.02010	.01946	.01885	.01828	.01773	.01722	.01673	.01627	.01582	.01540
32	.02134	.02066	.02002	.01940	.01883	.01828	.01776	.01726	.01679	.01634
33	.02270	.02197	.02128	.02063	.02002	.01943	.01887	.01835	.01784	.01736
34	.02415	.02338	.02265	.02195	.02130	.02067	.02008	.01951	.01897	.01846
35	.02574	.02492	.02414	.02340	.02270	.02203	.02140	.02080	.02022	.01967
36	.02746	.02658	.02575	.02496	.02422	.02350	.02283	.02218	.02157	.02098
37	.02932	.02838	.02750	.02666	.02586	.02510	.02438	.02369	.02303	.02241
38	.03135	.03035	.02941	.02851	.02766	.02685	.02608	.02534	.02464	.02397
39	.03355	.03249	.03149	.03053	.02962	.02876	.02793	.02715	.02640	.02568
40	.03596	.03484	.03377	.03275	.03178	.03086	.02998	.02914	.02833	.02757
41	.03861	.03742	.03628	.03520	.03416	.03318	.03224	.03134	.03048	.02966
42	.04152	.04025	.03903	.03788	.03678	.03573	.03473	.03377	.03285	.03198
43	.04468	.04333	.04205	.04082	.03965	.03853	.03746	.03644	.03546	.03453
44	.04813	.04670	.04533	.04403	.04278	.04159	.04045	.03936	.03832	.03732
45	.05183	.05032	.04887	.04748	.04616	.04489	.04368	.04252	.04141	.04034
46	.05582	.05421	.05267	.05121	.04980	.04846	.04717	.04593	.04475	.04362
47	.06006	.05836	.05673	.05518	.05369	.05226	.05089	.04958	.04832	.04711
48	.06459	.06279	.06107	.05943	.05785	.05634	.05488	.05349	.05216	.05087
49	.06942	.06752	.06571	.06397	.06230	.06070	.05916	.05768	.05626	.05490
50	.07459	.07259	.07068	.06884	.06708	.06538	.06376	.06219	.06069	.05924
51	.08012	.07801	.07599	.07406	.07220	.07041	.06869	.06703	.06544	.06391
52	.08596	.08375	.08163	.07959	.07763	.07574	.07392	.07218	.07049	.06887
53	.09214	.08982	.08759	.08544	.08338	.08139	.07948	.07763	.07586	.07415
54	.09867	.09623	.09389	.09164	.08946	.08737	.08536	.08342	.08154	.07974
55	.10556	.10301	.10055	.09819	.09591	.09371	.09159	.08955	.08757	.08567
56	.11283	.11016	.10759	.10511	.10272	.10042	.09819	.09605	.09397	.09197
57	.12050	.11771	.11502	.11243	.10993	.10751	.10518	.10293	.10075	.09864
58	.12852	.12562	.12281	.12011	.11749	.11496	.11252	.11016	.10787	.10567
59	.13687	.13385	.13092	.12810	.12537	.12273	.12017	.11770	.11531	.11299
60	.14554	.14240	.13935	.13641	.13356	.13080	.12813	.12555	.12305	.12063
61	.15457	.15130	.14813	.14507	.14210	.13923	.13644	.13375	.13113	.12860
62	.16402	.16063	.15734	.15415	.15107	.14808	.14518	.14237	.13964	.13699
63	.17393	.17042	.16700	.16370	.16049	.15738	.15437	.15144	.14860	.14584
64	.18429	.18065	.17712	.17369	.17036	.16714	.16400	.16096	.15800	.15513
65	.19511	.19135	.18769	.18415	.18070	.17735	.17410	.17094	.16787	.16488
66	.20645	.20257	.19880	.19513	.19157	.18810	.18473	.18146	.17827	.17517
67	.21841	.21441	.21052	.20673	.20305	.19947	.19599	.19259	.18929	.18608
68	.23096	.22685	.22284	.21895	.21515	.21146	.20786	.20436	.20094	.19762
69	.24409	.23987	.23575	.23175	.22784	.22404	.22033	.21672	.21320	.20976
70	.25772	.25339	.24918	.24507	.24106	.23715	.23333	.22961	.22598	.22244
71	.27178	.26735	.26304	.25882	.25471	.25070	.24679	.24296	.23923	.23559
72	.28622	.28170	.27729	.27298	.26877	.26467	.26065	.25673	.25290	.24915

Reg. § 1.664-4(e)(7)

Estates, Trusts, and Beneficiaries

See p. 20,601 for regulations not amended to reflect law changes

TABLE U(1)
BASED ON LIFE TABLE 90CM
UNITRUST SINGLE LIFE REMAINDER FACTORS
APPLICABLE FOR TRANSFERS AFTER APRIL 30, 1999

ADJUSTED PAYOUT RATE

AGE	12.2%	12.4%	12.6%	12.8%	13.0%	13.2%	13.4%	13.6%	13.8%	14.0%
73	.30100	.29639	.29189	.28749	.28320	.27899	.27489	.27087	.26694	.26310
74	.31621	.31152	.30694	.30246	.29807	.29378	.28959	.28548	.28146	.27753
75	.33195	.32719	.32253	.31797	.31351	.30914	.30486	.30067	.29657	.29255
76	.34832	.34350	.33877	.33415	.32961	.32517	.32082	.31656	.31238	.30828
77	.36535	.36047	.35570	.35101	.34642	.34192	.33750	.33317	.32892	.32475
78	.38302	.37811	.37329	.36856	.36392	.35937	.35490	.35051	.34621	.34198
79	.40124	.39630	.39145	.38669	.38201	.37742	.37291	.36848	.36413	.35985
80	.41980	.41485	.40998	.40520	.40050	.39588	.39134	.38688	.38249	.37818
81	.43854	.43358	.42871	.42392	.41921	.41457	.41001	.40553	.40112	.39678
82	.45733	.45238	.44752	.44273	.43802	.43338	.42881	.42431	.41989	.41553
83	.47616	.47123	.46638	.46161	.45690	.45227	.44770	.44320	.43877	.43441
84	.49519	.49030	.48548	.48073	.47604	.47143	.46688	.46239	.45797	.45361
85	.51458	.50974	.50496	.50025	.49560	.49102	.48650	.48204	.47763	.47329
86	.53413	.52935	.52463	.51998	.51538	.51084	.50636	.50194	.49758	.49327
87	.55351	.54881	.54416	.53957	.53503	.53055	.52613	.52176	.51744	.51317
88	.57268	.56806	.56349	.55898	.55451	.55010	.54574	.54144	.53718	.53296
89	.59162	.58710	.58262	.57819	.57382	.56949	.56520	.56097	.55678	.55263
90	.61030	.60588	.60151	.59718	.59290	.58866	.58447	.58032	.57621	.57214
91	.62834	.62403	.61977	.61554	.61136	.60722	.60312	.59907	.59505	.59107
92	.64527	.64107	.63692	.63280	.62872	.62468	.62068	.61672	.61279	.60890
93	.66107	.65699	.65294	.64893	.64495	.64101	.63711	.63323	.62940	.62559
94	.67597	.67200	.66806	.66415	.66027	.65643	.65262	.64884	.64509	.64138
95	.69031	.68645	.68262	.67881	.67504	.67130	.66759	.66390	.66025	.65662
96	.70396	.70021	.69648	.69279	.68912	.68548	.68186	.67828	.67471	.67118
97	.71670	.71305	.70943	.70584	.70227	.69872	.69520	.69171	.68824	.68480
98	.72875	.72521	.72169	.71819	.71472	.71127	.70784	.70444	.70106	.69770
99	.74065	.73721	.73379	.73040	.72703	.72368	.72035	.71704	.71375	.71048
100	.75234	.74901	.74570	.74241	.73914	.73589	.73265	.72944	.72625	.72307
101	.76399	.76077	.75757	.75438	.75122	.74807	.74494	.74183	.73873	.73565
102	.77552	.77241	.76932	.76625	.76319	.76015	.75712	.75411	.75111	.74813
103	.78703	.78404	.78106	.77809	.77514	.77221	.76929	.76638	.76348	.76060
104	.79948	.79662	.79377	.79093	.78810	.78528	.78248	.77969	.77691	.77414
105	.81159	.80885	.80612	.80340	.80069	.79799	.79530	.79262	.78995	.78729
106	.82763	.82506	.82250	.81995	.81741	.81488	.81235	.80983	.80732	.80482
107	.84749	.84516	.84283	.84051	.83819	.83587	.83356	.83126	.82896	.82666
108	.87999	.87808	.87618	.87428	.87238	.87049	.86859	.86670	.86481	.86293
109	.93900	.93800	.93700	.93600	.93500	.93400	.93300	.93200	.93100	.93000

(f) *Effective dates.* This section applies after April 30, 1999. [Reg. § 1.664-4.]

☐ [T.D. 7202, 8-22-72. Amended by T.D. 7955, 5-10-84; T.D. 8540, 6-9-94; T.D. 8819, 4-29-99 and T.D. 8886, 6-9-2000.]

[Reg. § 1.664-4A]

§ 1.664-4A. **Valuation of charitable remainder interests for which the valuation date is before May 1, 1999.**—(a) *Valuation of charitable remainder interests for which the valuation date is before January 1, 1952.* There was no provision for the qualification of a charitable remainder unitrust under section 664 until 1969. See § 20.2031-7A(a) of this chapter (Estate Tax Regulations) for the determination of the present value of a charitable interest for which the valuation date is before January 1, 1952.

(b) *Valuation of charitable remainder interests for which the valuation date is after December 31, 1951, and before January 1, 1971.* No charitable deduction is allowable for a transfer to a unitrust for which the valuation date is after the effective dates of the Tax Reform Act of 1969 unless the unitrust meets the requirements of section 664. See § 20.2031-7A(b) of this chapter (Estate Tax Regulations) for the determination of the present value of a charitable remainder interest for which the valuation date is after December 31, 1951, and before January 1, 1971.

(c) *Valuation of charitable remainder unitrusts having certain payout sequences for transfers for which the valuation date is after December 31, 1970, and before December 1, 1983.* For the determination of the present value of a charitable remainder unitrust for which the valuation date is

Reg. § 1.664-4A(c)

after December 31, 1970, and before December 1, 1983, see § 20.2031-7A(c) of this chapter (Estate Tax Regulations) and former § 1.664-4(d) (as contained in the 26 CFR Part 1 edition revised as of April 1, 1994).

(d) *Valuation of charitable remainder unitrusts having certain payout sequences for transfers for which the valuation date is after November 30, 1983, and before May 1, 1989*—(1) *In general.* Except as otherwise provided in paragraph (d)(2) of this section, in the case of transfers made after November 30, 1983, for which the valuation date is before May 1, 1989, the present value of a remainder interest that is dependent on a term of years or the termination of the life of one individual is determined under paragraphs (d)(3) through (d)(6) of this section, provided that the amount of the payout as of any payout date during any taxable year of the trust is not larger than the amount that the trust could distribute on such date under § 1.664-3(a)(1)(v) if the taxable year of the trust were to end on such date. The present value of the remainder interest in the trust is determined by computing the adjusted payout rate (as defined in paragraph (d)(3) of this section) and following the procedure outlined in paragraph (d)(4) or (d)(5) of this section, whichever is applicable. The present value of a remainder interest that is dependent on a term of years is computed under paragraph (d)(4) of this section. The present value of a remainder interest that is dependent on the termination of the life of one individual is computed under paragraph (d)(5) of this section. See paragraph (d)(2) of this section for testamentary transfers for which the valuation date is after November 30, 1983, and before August 9, 1984.

(2) *Rules for determining the present value for testamentary transfers where the decedent dies after November 30, 1983, and before August 9, 1984.* For purposes of section 2055 or 2106, if—

(i) The decedent dies after November 30, 1983, and before August 9, 1984; or

(ii) On December 1, 1983, the decedent was mentally incompetent so that the disposition of the property could not be changed, and the decedent died after November 30, 1983, without regaining competency to dispose of the decedent's property, or died within 90 days of the date on which the decedent first regained competency, the present value determined under this section of a remainder interest is determined in accordance with paragraph (d)(1) and paragraphs (d)(3) through (d)(6) of this section, or § 1.664-4A(c), at the option of the taxpayer.

(3) *Adjusted payout rate.* The adjusted payout rate is determined by multiplying the fixed percentage described in paragraph (a)(1)(i)(a) of § 1.664-3 by the figure in column (2) of Table F(1) which describes the payout sequence of the trust opposite the number in column (1) of Table F(1) which corresponds to the number of months by which the valuation date for the first full taxable year of the trust precedes the first payout date for such taxable year. If the governing instrument does not prescribe when the distribution shall be made during the taxable year of the trust, see § 1.664-4(a). In the case of a trust having a payout sequence for which no figures have been provided by Table F(1) and in the case of a trust which determines the fair market value of the trust assets by taking the average of valuations on more than one date during the taxable year, see § 1.664-4(b).

(4) *Period is a term of years.* If the period described in § 1.664-3(a)(5) is a term of years, the factor which is used in determining the present value of the remainder interest is the factor under the appropriate adjusted payout rate in Table D in § 1.664-4(e)(6) that corresponds to the number of years in the term. If the adjusted payout rate is an amount which is between adjusted payout rates for which factors are provided in Table D, a linear interpolation must be made. The present value of the remainder interest is determined by multiplying the net fair market value (as of the appropriate valuation date) of the property placed in trust by the factor determined under this paragraph (d)(4). For purposes of this section, the term "appropriate valuation date" means the date on which the property is transferred to the trust by the donor except that, for purposes of section 2055 or 2106, it means the date of death unless the alternate valuation date is elected in accordance with section 2032 and the regulations thereunder in which event it means the alternate valuation date. If the adjusted payout rate is greater than 14 percent, see § 1.664-4(b) of this section. The application of this paragraph (d)(4) may be illustrated by the following example:

Example. D transfers $100,000 to a charitable remainder unitrust on January 1, 1985. The trust instrument requires that the trust pay to D semi-annually (on June 30 and December 31) 10 percent of the fair market value of the trust assets as of June 30th for a term of 15 years. The adjusted payout rate is 9.767 percent (10% × 0.976731). The present value of the remainder interest is $21,404.90, computed as follows:

Reg. § 1.664-4A(d)(2)

Estates, Trusts, and Beneficiaries

See p. 20,601 for regulations not amended to reflect law changes

Factor at 9.6 percent for 15 years	0.220053
Factor at 9.8 percent for 15 years	.212862
Difference	.007191

$$\frac{9.767\% - 9.6\%}{0.2\%} = \frac{X}{.007191}$$
$$X = .006004$$

Factor at 9.6 percent for 15 years	0.220053
Less: X	.006004
Interpolated factor	.214049

Present value of remainder interest = $100,000 × 0.214049 = $21,404.90

(5) *Period is the life of one individual.* If the period described in paragraph (a)(5) of § 1.664-3 is the life of one individual, the factor that is used in determining the present value of the remainder interest is the factor under the appropriate adjusted payout rate in column (2) of Table E in paragraph (d)(6) of this section opposite the number in column (1) that corresponds to the age of the individual whose life measures the period. For purposes of the computations described in this paragraph (b)(5), the age of an individual is to be taken as the age of that individual at the individual's nearest birthday. If the adjusted payout rate is an amount which is between adjusted payout rates for which factors are provided for in Table E, a linear interpolation must be made. The present value of the remainder interest is determined by multiplying the net fair market value (as of the appropriate valuation date) of the property placed in trust by the factor determined under this paragraph (b)(5). If the adjusted payout rate is greater than 14 percent, see § 1.664-4(b). The application of this paragraph may be illustrated by the following example:

Example. A, who will be 50 years old on April 15, 1985, transfers $100,000 to a charitable remainder unitrust on January 1, 1985. The trust instrument requires that the trust pay to A at the end of each taxable year of the trust 10 percent of the fair market value of the trust assets as of the beginning of each taxable year of the trust. The adjusted payout rate is 9.091 percent (10 percent × .909091). The present value of the remainder interest is $15,259.00 computed as follows:

Factor at 9 percent at age 50	0.15472
Factor at 9.2 percent at age 50	.15003
Difference	.00469

$$9.091\% - 9\% \div 0.2\% = X \div 0.00469$$
$$x = 0.00213$$

Factor at 9 percent at age 50	.15472
Less: X	.00213
Interpolated factor	.15259

Present value of remainder interest = $100,000 × 0.15259 = $15,259.00

(6) *Actuarial tables for transfers for which the valuation date is after November 30, 1983, and before May 1, 1989.* Table D in § 1.664-4(e)(6) and the following tables shall be used in the application of the provisions of this section:

Reg. § 1.664-4A(d)(6)

Table E—Single Life, Unisex—Table Showing the Present Worth of the Remainder Interest in Property Transferred to a Unitrust Having the Adjusted Payout Rate Shown—Applicable for Transfers After November 30, 1983, and Before May 1, 1989

(1) Age	2.2%	2.4%	2.6%	2.8%	3.0%	3.2%	3.4%	3.6%	3.8%	4.0%
0	.23253	.20635	.18364	.16394	.14683	.13196	.11901	.10774	.09791	.08933
1	.22196	.19506	.17170	.15139	.13372	.11834	.10493	.09324	.08303	.07410
2	.22597	.19884	.17523	.15468	.13676	.12113	.10749	.09557	.08514	.07601
3	.23039	.20304	.17920	.15840	.14024	.12437	.11050	.09835	.08770	.07837
4	.23053	.20747	.18340	.16237	.14397	.12787	.11376	.10138	.09052	.08098
5	.23988	.21211	.18783	.16656	.14793	.13159	.11725	.10465	.09357	.08382
6	.24489	.21693	.19243	.17094	.15207	.13549	.12092	.10810	.09680	.08684
7	.25004	.22189	.19718	.17546	.15637	.13956	.12476	.11171	.10019	.09002
8	.25534	.22701	.20209	.18016	.16084	.14380	.12877	.11549	.10376	.09337
9	.26080	.23230	.20718	.18503	.16549	.14822	.13296	.11946	.10751	.09691
10	.26640	.23774	.21243	.19008	.17031	.15282	.13734	.12361	.11144	.10063
11	.27217	.24335	.21786	.19530	.17532	.15761	.14190	.12795	.11556	.10454
12	.27807	.24911	.22344	.20068	.18049	.16257	.14663	.13247	.11986	.10863
13	.28407	.25497	.22913	.20618	.18579	.16764	.15149	.13711	.12428	.11283
14	.29013	.26089	.23489	.21175	.19115	.17279	.15643	.14182	.12878	.11712
15	.29621	.26684	.24067	.21735	.19655	.17798	.16140	.14657	.13331	.12143
16	.30229	.27279	.24647	.22296	.20196	.18318	.16638	.15133	.13785	.12576
17	.30838	.27876	.25228	.22859	.20739	.18840	.17138	.15611	.14241	.13010
18	.31451	.28477	.25813	.23427	.21287	.19367	.17643	.16094	.14702	.13449
19	.32070	.29085	.26407	.24003	.21844	.19903	.18157	.16586	.15172	.13897
20	.32699	.29704	.27012	.24591	.22413	.20452	.18685	.17092	.15655	.14358
21	.33339	.30335	.27629	.25192	.22996	.21014	.19226	.17612	.16153	.14833
22	.33991	.30977	.28259	.25807	.23592	.21591	.19783	.18146	.16665	.15324
23	.34655	.31634	.28904	.26437	.24205	.22185	.20356	.18698	.17195	.15832
24	.35334	.32306	.29566	.27085	.24836	.22798	.20949	.19270	.17746	.16361
25	.36031	.32998	.30248	.27754	.25490	.23434	.21565	.19866	.18321	.16914
26	.36746	.33710	.30952	.28446	.26167	.24094	.22207	.20489	.18922	.17494
27	.37481	.34443	.31678	.29161	.26869	.24780	.22875	.21138	.19551	.18102
28	.38236	.35197	.32427	.29901	.27596	.25492	.23570	.21814	.20208	.18739
29	.39006	.35968	.33194	.30660	.28344	.26226	.24288	.22514	.20889	.19400
30	.39793	.36757	.33980	.31439	.29113	.26982	.25029	.23239	.21596	.20088
31	.40594	.37561	.34783	.32237	.29902	.27759	.25792	.23985	.22324	.20798
32	.41410	.38383	.35605	.33054	.30711	.28557	.26577	.24755	.23078	.21533
33	.42240	.39220	.36444	.33890	.31541	.29377	.27385	.25548	.23855	.22293
34	.43084	.40072	.37299	.34744	.32389	.30217	.28214	.26364	.24656	.23077
35	.43942	.40941	.38172	.35617	.33258	.31079	.29065	.27203	.25481	.23887
36	.44813	.41824	.39061	.36508	.34146	.31961	.29939	.28065	.26330	.24721
37	.45696	.42720	.39966	.37416	.35053	.32863	.30833	.28950	.27202	.25579
38	.46591	.43630	.40885	.38339	.35977	.33784	.31747	.29855	.28096	.26460
39	.47496	.44552	.41818	.39278	.36917	.34722	.32680	.30780	.29011	.27363
40	.48412	.45486	.42765	.40232	.37875	.35679	.33633	.31727	.29948	.28290
41	.49338	.46432	.43725	.41201	.38849	.36654	.34606	.32693	.30908	.29239
42	.50275	.47391	.44700	.42187	.39840	.37648	.35599	.33683	.31890	.30213
43	.51221	.48360	.45686	.43186	.40847	.38659	.36610	.34691	.32894	.31209
44	.52175	.49340	.46685	.44199	.41870	.39687	.37640	.35720	.33918	.32227
45	.53136	.50327	.47693	.45223	.42905	.40728	.38685	.36765	.34961	.33265
46	.54104	.51323	.48712	.46259	.43953	.41785	.39746	.37828	.36023	.34323
47	.55077	.52327	.49739	.47305	.45013	.42856	.40823	.38908	.37103	.35400
48	.56058	.53339	.50777	.48363	.46087	.43941	.41917	.40006	.38202	.36499
49	.57043	.54358	.51823	.49432	.47173	.45040	.43025	.41121	.39320	.37617
50	.58035	.55384	.52879	.50510	.48271	.46153	.44149	.42252	.40457	.38756
51	.59029	.56415	.53940	.51597	.49379	.47277	.45286	.43398	.41609	.39911
52	.60027	.57450	.55008	.52692	.50496	.48412	.46435	.44558	.42776	.41084
53	.61026	.58488	.56080	.53793	.51620	.49556	.47595	.45731	.43958	.42272
54	.62025	.59528	.57154	.54897	.52750	.50707	.48763	.46913	.45151	.43473
55	.63022	.60567	.58230	.56004	.53884	.51864	.49939	.48104	.46354	.44685
56	.64018	.61606	.59306	.57113	.55021	.53026	.51121	.49303	.47567	.45908
57	.65012	.62644	.60384	.58225	.56163	.54192	.52310	.50510	.48789	.47143
58	.66004	.63681	.61461	.59337	.57306	.55363	.53503	.51723	.50019	.48387
59	.66993	.64717	.62538	.60452	.58453	.56538	.54703	.52945	.51258	.49642
60	.67979	.65751	.63615	.61567	.59602	.57717	.55909	.54173	.52506	.50906
61	.68963	.66784	.64692	.62683	.60754	.58901	.57120	.55408	.53763	.52181
62	.69944	.67815	.65769	.63801	.61908	.60087	.58336	.56650	.55028	.53466

Reg. § 1.664-4A(d)(6)

Estates, Trusts, and Beneficiaries 43,375
See p. 20,601 for regulations not amended to reflect law changes

Table E—Continued. Single Life, Unisex—Table Showing the Present Worth of the Remainder Interest in Property Transferred to a Unitrust Having the Adjusted Payout Rate Shown—Applicable for Transfers After November 30, 1983, and Before May 1, 1989

(1) Age	2.2%	2.4%	2.6%	2.8%	3.0%	3.2%	3.4%	3.6%	3.8%	4.0%
63	.70922	.68844	.66843	.64918	.63063	.61277	.59556	.57898	.56300	.54760
64	.71893	.69868	.67915	.66032	.64217	.62467	.60778	.59149	.57577	.56060
65	.72859	.70886	.68982	.67144	.65369	.63655	.62000	.60402	.58857	.57365
66	.73817	.71897	.70043	.68250	.66517	.64842	.63221	.61654	.60139	.58672
67	.74766	.72901	.71096	.69350	.67660	.66023	.64439	.62905	.61420	.59980
68	.75706	.73896	.72142	.70443	.68796	.67200	.65653	.64154	.62699	.61289
69	.76637	.74882	.73181	.71530	.69928	.68373	.66865	.65400	.63978	.62598
70	.77559	.75861	.74212	.72610	.71053	.69541	.68072	.66645	.65257	.63908
71	.78475	.76833	.75237	.73685	.72176	.70708	.69279	.67890	.66538	.65222
72	.79383	.77799	.76257	.74756	.73294	.71870	.70484	.69134	.67819	.66538
73	.80279	.78753	.77266	.75816	.74403	.73025	.71682	.70372	.69095	.67850
74	.81158	.79689	.78256	.76858	.75494	.74163	.72863	.71595	.70356	.69147
75	.82013	.80602	.79223	.77876	.76561	.75275	.74019	.72792	.71593	.70421
76	.82844	.81488	.80163	.78867	.77599	.76360	.75147	.73962	.72802	.71667
77	.83648	.82347	.81075	.79829	.78609	.77415	.76246	.75102	.73981	.72883
78	.84428	.83182	.81961	.80764	.79592	.78443	.77318	.76214	.75133	.74073
79	.85187	.83994	.82824	.81677	.80552	.79448	.78365	.77303	.76261	.75238
80	.85927	.84787	.83668	.82569	.81491	.80432	.79392	.78371	.77369	.76384
81	.86645	.85556	.84487	.83437	.82404	.81390	.80393	.79413	.78450	.77504
82	.87336	.86299	.85278	.84275	.83288	.82317	.81362	.80423	.79499	.78590
83	.88003	.87014	.86042	.85084	.84142	.83214	.82301	.81402	.80517	.79645
84	.88648	.87708	.86782	.85870	.84971	.84086	.83214	.82355	.81508	.80674
85	.89273	.88381	.87501	.86633	.85778	.84935	.84104	.83284	.82476	.81679
86	.89868	.89021	.88185	.87360	.86547	.85745	.84953	.84172	.83401	.82640
87	.90417	.89613	.88818	.88034	.87260	.86496	.85741	.84996	.84260	.83533
88	.90923	.90158	.89402	.88655	.87917	.87189	.86468	.85757	.85054	.84359
89	.91396	.90668	.89948	.89237	.88533	.87838	.87150	.86471	.85799	.85135
90	.91849	.91156	.90471	.89794	.89124	.88461	.87806	.87157	.86516	.85881
91	.92278	.91620	.90968	.90324	.89686	.89055	.88430	.87812	.87200	.86594
92	.92673	.92046	.91426	.90812	.90204	.89602	.89006	.88416	.87831	.87252
93	.93027	.92429	.91837	.91251	.90670	.90094	.89524	.88959	.88400	.87846
94	.93341	.92768	.92201	.91639	.91082	.90530	.89983	.89441	.88904	.88372
95	.93612	.93062	.92516	.91976	.91440	.90908	.90381	.89859	.89341	.88828
96	.93841	.93309	.92782	.92259	.91740	.91226	.90716	.90211	.89709	.89212
97	.94044	.93529	.93018	.92512	.92009	.91510	.91015	.90525	.90038	.89555
98	.94223	.93723	.93226	.92733	.92244	.91759	.91277	.90800	.90326	.89855
99	.94392	.93905	.93421	.92942	.92466	.91993	.91524	.91058	.90596	.90137
100	.94559	.94086	.93615	.93149	.92685	.92225	.91768	.91315	.90865	.90417
101	.94709	.94248	.93790	.93334	.92882	.92433	.91987	.91544	.91104	.90667
102	.94873	.94424	.93979	.93536	.93096	.92659	.92225	.91793	.91364	.90938
103	.95077	.94645	.94216	.93789	.93365	.92943	.92524	.92107	.91692	.91280
104	.95278	.94862	.94449	.94037	.93628	.93221	.92816	.92413	.92012	.91614
105	.95570	.95178	.94787	.94399	.94012	.93627	.93244	.92863	.92483	.92105
106	.96017	.95662	.95309	.94957	.94607	.94257	.93909	.93562	.93217	.92872
107	.96616	.96313	.96010	.95709	.95408	.95107	.94808	.94509	.94211	.93914
108	.97515	.97291	.97067	.96843	.96620	.96396	.96173	.95950	.95728	.95505
109	.98900	.98800	.98700	.98600	.98500	.98400	.98300	.98200	.98100	.98000

Reg. § 1.664-4A(d)(6)

43,376 Estates, Trusts, and Beneficiaries

See p. 20,601 for regulations not amended to reflect law changes

Table E—Continued. Single Life, Unisex—Table Showing the Present Worth of the Remainder Interest in Property Transferred to a Unitrust Having the Adjusted Payout Rate Shown—Applicable for Transfers After November 30, 1983, and Before May 1, 1989

(1) Age	(2) Adjusted Payout Rate									
	4.2%	4.4%	4.6%	4.8%	5.0%	5.2%	5.4%	5.6%	5.8%	6.0%
0	.08183	.07527	.06952	.06448	.06005	.05615	.05272	.04969	.04701	.04464
1	.06629	.05945	.05344	.04817	.04354	.03945	.03585	.03268	.02986	.02737
2	.06801	.06098	.05481	.04939	.04460	.04039	.03667	.03337	.03046	.02787
3	.07017	.06297	.05663	.05104	.04611	.04176	.03791	.03450	.03147	.02879
4	.07259	.06520	.05868	.05294	.04786	.04336	.03938	.03585	.03272	.02993
5	.07523	.06765	.06096	.05505	.04982	.04518	.04107	.03741	.03416	.03127
6	.07805	.07029	.06342	.05734	.05195	.04717	.04292	.03914	.03577	.03276
7	.08103	.07307	.06603	.05978	.05423	.04929	.04490	.04099	.03750	.03438
8	.08418	.07603	.06880	.06238	.05666	.05158	.04704	.04300	.03938	.03615
9	.08752	.07917	.07175	.06516	.05928	.05404	.04936	.04518	.04143	.03808
10	.09103	.08249	.07488	.06811	.06206	.05666	.05183	.04751	.04364	.04016
11	.09473	.08600	.07820	.07125	.06503	.05947	.05449	.05003	.04602	.04242
12	.09861	.08968	.08169	.07456	.06817	.06245	.05731	.05271	.04856	.04484
13	.10261	.09348	.08530	.07799	.07142	.06554	.06025	.05549	.05121	.04735
14	.10669	.09735	.08899	.08148	.07474	.06869	.06324	.05834	.05391	.04992
15	.11080	.10126	.09269	.08500	.07808	.07186	.06625	.06119	.05662	.05250
16	.11491	.10516	.09640	.08852	.08142	.07502	.06924	.05403	.05931	.05504
17	.11903	.10908	.10012	.09204	.08475	.07817	.07223	.06685	.06199	.05757
18	.12321	.11304	.10387	.09560	.08812	.08136	.07524	.06970	.06468	.06012
19	.12747	.11709	.10771	.09923	.09156	.08462	.07832	.07261	.06743	.06272
20	.13186	.12126	.11168	.10300	.09513	.08800	.08152	.07564	.07029	.06542
21	.13639	.12558	.11578	.10690	.09883	.09151	.08485	.07879	.07327	.06824
22	.14108	.13005	.12004	.11094	.10268	.09516	.08831	.08207	.07638	.07119
23	.14594	.13469	.12446	.11516	.10669	.09897	.09193	.08551	.07964	.07428
24	.15101	.13954	.12910	.11958	.11091	.10299	.09576	.08915	.08310	.07756
25	.15632	.14464	.13398	.12426	.11537	.10725	.09982	.09302	.08679	.08108
26	.16191	.15001	.13914	.12920	.12011	.11179	.10416	.09717	.09075	.08486
27	.16778	.15567	.14459	.13444	.12514	.11661	.10878	.10160	.09500	.08892
28	.17394	.16162	.15032	.13997	.13046	.12173	.11370	.10632	.09953	.09328
29	.18035	.16782	.15632	.14575	.13604	.12710	.11888	.11130	.10432	.09788
30	.18702	.17429	.16259	.15181	.14189	.13276	.12433	.11656	.10938	.10276
31	.19393	.18100	.16909	.15811	.14799	.13865	.13002	.12205	.11469	.10787
32	.20109	.18797	.17586	.16468	.15436	.14482	.13599	.12783	.12026	.11326
33	.20851	.19520	.18290	.17152	.16100	.15126	.14223	.13387	.12612	.11892
34	.21618	.20268	.19018	.17861	.16789	.15796	.14874	.14018	.13223	.12485
35	.22411	.21043	.19775	.18599	.17508	.16494	.15553	.14678	.13864	.13107
36	.23228	.21844	.20558	.19363	.18253	.17221	.16260	.15366	.14533	.13757
37	.24071	.22670	.21367	.20154	.19026	.17975	.16996	.16082	.15231	.14435
38	.24938	.23521	.22201	.20971	.19825	.18756	.17758	.16826	.15955	.15142
39	.25827	.24396	.23060	.21814	.20650	.19563	.18547	.17597	.16708	.15875
40	.26741	.25295	.23945	.22682	.21502	.20397	.19364	.18395	.17488	.16638
41	.27679	.26220	.24855	.23577	.22381	.21259	.20209	.19223	.18298	.17430
42	.28642	.27172	.25793	.24501	.23289	.22152	.21084	.20082	.19140	.18254
43	.29629	.28147	.26756	.25450	.24224	.23071	.21988	.20969	.20010	.19107
44	.30639	.29147	.27745	.26426	.25186	.24019	.22920	.21885	.20910	.19991
45	.31669	.30169	.28756	.27426	.26173	.24992	.23878	.22828	.21837	.20902
46	.32722	.31213	.29791	.28450	.27185	.25991	.24864	.23799	.22793	.21842
47	.33795	.32280	.30849	.29498	.28222	.27016	.25876	.24798	.23777	.22812
48	.34890	.33370	.31932	.30573	.29287	.28070	.26918	.25826	.24792	.23812
49	.36007	.34482	.33039	.31672	.30377	.29150	.27987	.26883	.25837	.24843
50	.37144	.35617	.34170	.32797	.31494	.30258	.29084	.27970	.26911	.25905
51	.38301	.36773	.35322	.33944	.32635	.31391	.30208	.29084	.28014	.26996
52	.39476	.37948	.36495	.35113	.33799	.32548	.31358	.30224	.29144	.28115
53	.40668	.39141	.37688	.36304	.34986	.33729	.32532	.31390	.30302	.29263
54	.41874	.40350	.38897	.37512	.36191	.34931	.33728	.32579	.31482	.30434
55	.43093	.41574	.40123	.38739	.37416	.36152	.34945	.33790	.32686	.31631
56	.44324	.42811	.41364	.39980	.38657	.37392	.36181	.35022	.33912	.32850
57	.45568	.44062	.42620	.41240	.39918	.38652	.37438	.36276	.35162	.34093
58	.48623	.45325	.43890	.42514	.41194	.39929	.38715	.37550	.36432	.35359
59	.48091	.46603	.45175	.43805	.42489	.41226	.40013	.38847	.37727	.36650
60	.49370	.47893	.46475	.45112	.43802	.42542	.41331	.40165	.39044	.37965
61	.50661	.49198	.47790	.46436	.45133	.43878	.42670	.41506	.40386	.39306
62	.51963	.50515	.49120	.47776	.46481	.45233	.44029	.42869	.41750	.40671
63	.53275	.51844	.50463	.49131	.47846	.46606	.45409	.44253	.43138	.42060
64	.54596	.53182	.51817	.50498	.49225	.47994	.46805	.45656	.44545	.43471

Reg. § 1.664-4A(d)(6)

Estates, Trusts, and Beneficiaries

Table E—Continued. Single Life, Unisex—Table Showing the Present Worth of the Remainder Interest in Property Transferred to a Unitrust Having the Adjusted Payout Rate Shown—Applicable for Transfers After November 30, 1983, and Before May 1, 1989

(1) Age	4.2%	4.4%	4.6%	4.8%	5.0%	5.2%	5.4%	5.6%	5.8%	6.0%
65	.55922	.54528	.53180	.51877	.50616	.49397	.48217	.47076	.45971	.44902
66	.57253	.55880	.54551	.53264	.52018	.50811	.49642	.48510	.47413	.46350
67	.58586	.57235	.55926	.54657	.53427	.52235	.51079	.49957	.48869	.47814
68	.59921	.58594	.57306	.56057	.54845	.53668	.52525	.51416	.50339	.49293
69	.61258	.59956	.58692	.57463	.56270	.55110	.53983	.52888	.51823	.50788
70	.62597	.61322	.60082	.58877	.57704	.56563	.55453	.54373	.53322	.52299
71	.63941	.62695	.61481	.60300	.59149	.58029	.56938	.55875	.54839	.53830
72	.65289	.64073	.62887	.61731	.60605	.59507	.58436	.57392	.56374	.55380
73	.66635	.65449	.64293	.63165	.62064	.60990	.59941	.58917	.57918	.56942
74	.67976	.66814	.65688	.64588	.63514	.62465	.61439	.60437	.59458	.58502
75	.69275	.68156	.67061	.65990	.64944	.63920	.62919	.61940	.60983	.60046
76	.70557	.69470	.68407	.67366	.66348	.65351	.64375	.63419	.62484	.61568
77	.71809	.70756	.69724	.68714	.67724	.66755	.65804	.64873	.63961	.63066
78	.73033	.72014	.71015	.70036	.69075	.68133	.67209	.66303	.65414	.64542
79	.74235	.73251	.72284	.71336	.70405	.69492	.68595	.67714	.66850	.66001
80	.75417	.74468	.73535	.72619	.71718	.70834	.69965	.69111	.68272	.67448
81	.76573	.75659	.74759	.73875	.73006	.72151	.71311	.70484	.69671	.68872
82	.77696	.76816	.75951	.75099	.74261	.73436	.72624	.71825	.71039	.70265
83	.78787	.77942	.77110	.76291	.75484	.74689	.73906	.73135	.72376	.71627
84	.79852	.79042	.78243	.77457	.76681	.75917	.75163	.74421	.73688	.72967
85	.80893	.80118	.79353	.78599	.77856	.77122	.76398	.75685	.74980	.74286
86	.81889	.81148	.80417	.79695	.78983	.78280	.77586	.76901	.76224	.75556
87	.82816	.82107	.81408	.80716	.80034	.79359	.78693	.78036	.77386	.76744
88	.83673	.82994	.82324	.81662	.81007	.80360	.79720	.79088	.78463	.77846
89	.84478	.83828	.83186	.82551	.81923	.81302	.80688	.80081	.79480	.78886
90	.85253	.84632	.84018	.83410	.82808	.82213	.81624	.81041	.80465	.79894
91	.85994	.85401	.84813	.84232	.83656	.83086	.82522	.81963	.81410	.80862
92	.86679	.86111	.85549	.84993	.84441	.83895	.83354	.82818	.82287	.81762
93	.87296	.86752	.86213	.85679	.85150	.84626	.84106	.83591	.83081	.82575
94	.87844	.87321	.86803	.86289	.85780	.85275	.84774	.84278	.83787	.83299
95	.88319	.87815	.87314	.86818	.86327	.85839	.85355	.84876	.84400	.83929
96	.88719	.88230	.87745	.87264	.86787	.86313	.85844	.85378	.84916	.84458
97	.89076	.88601	.88129	.87661	.87197	.86737	.86280	.85826	.85377	.84930
98	.89388	.88925	.88465	.88009	.87556	.87107	.86661	.86218	.85779	.85343
99	.89682	.89230	.88781	.88336	.87894	.87455	.87019	.86586	.86157	.85730
100	.89973	.89533	.89095	.88660	.88228	.87800	.87374	.86951	.86532	.86115
101	.90233	.89802	.89374	.88948	.88526	.88106	.87689	.87275	.86863	.86455
102	.90515	.90094	.89676	.89260	.88848	.88437	.88030	.87625	.87222	.86822
103	.90871	.90464	.90059	.89656	.89256	.88858	.88463	.88070	.87679	.87290
104	.91217	.90823	.90431	.90040	.89652	.89266	.88882	.88500	.88120	.87741
105	.91729	.91354	.90981	.90610	.90240	.89872	.89506	.89141	.88778	.88417
106	.92529	.92187	.91846	.91507	.91169	.90832	.90496	.90161	.89828	.89496
107	.93617	.93322	.93027	.92732	.92439	.92146	.91854	.91562	.91271	.90981
108	.95283	.95062	.94840	.94619	.94398	.94177	.93956	.93736	.93516	.93296
109	.97900	.97800	.97700	.97600	.97500	.97400	.97300	.97200	.97100	.97000

Reg. § 1.664-4A(d)(6)

43,378   Estates, Trusts, and Beneficiaries

See p. 20,601 for regulations not amended to reflect law changes

Table E—Continued. Single Life, Unisex—Table Showing the Present Worth of the Remainder Interest in Property Transferred to a Unitrust Having the Adjusted Payout Rate Shown—Applicable for Transfers After November 30, 1983, and Before May 1, 1989

(1) Age	\(2\) Adjusted Payout Rate									
	6.2%	6.4%	6.6%	6.8%	7.0%	7.2%	7.4%	7.6%	7.8%	8.0%
0	.04253	.04066	.03899	.03751	.03618	.03499	.03392	.03296	.03209	.03130
1	.02516	.02320	.02145	.01989	.01850	.01725	.01613	.01513	.01422	.01340
2	.02557	.02353	.02171	.02008	.01862	.01732	.01615	.01509	.01414	.01329
3	.02640	.02427	.02237	.02067	.01915	.01778	.01656	.01545	.01446	.01356
4	.02744	.02523	.02325	.02147	.01988	.01846	.01717	.01601	.01497	.01402
5	.02868	.02638	.02431	.02246	.02080	.01930	.01796	.01674	.01574	.01465
6	.03008	.02767	.02552	.02359	.02185	.02029	.01888	.01761	.01645	.01541
7	.03159	.02909	.02685	.02483	.02302	.02138	.01991	.01857	.01736	.01627
8	.03325	.03065	.02831	.02621	.02432	.02261	.02106	.01966	.01839	.01724
9	.03507	.03236	.02993	.02774	.02576	.02397	.02236	.02089	.01956	.01835
10	.03704	.03423	.03170	.02941	.02735	.02548	.02379	.02225	.02086	.01959
11	.03918	.03626	.03363	.03125	.02910	.02715	.02538	.02377	.02231	.02098
12	.04148	.03845	.03571	.03323	.03099	.02895	.02710	.02542	.02389	.02240
13	.04387	.04073	.03788	.03531	.03297	.03085	.02892	.02716	.02556	.02410
14	.04632	.04305	.04010	.03742	.03499	.03278	.03076	.02893	.02725	.02572
15	.04876	.04538	.04231	.03953	.03699	.03469	.03259	.03067	.02892	.02732
16	.05118	.04767	.04449	.04159	.03896	.03656	.03437	.03237	.03054	.02286
17	.05357	.04994	.04663	.04362	.04088	.03838	.03610	.03401	.03210	.03035
18	.05598	.05221	.04878	.04565	.04280	.04020	.03782	.03564	.03364	.03181
19	.05843	.05453	.05097	.04772	.04476	.04204	.03956	.03729	.03520	.03328
20	.06099	.05694	.05325	.04988	.04679	.04397	.04138	.03901	.03683	.03483
21	.06365	.05946	.05564	.05213	.04893	.04599	.04329	.04081	.03853	.03644
22	.06644	.06210	.05813	.05449	.05116	.04810	.04529	.04270	.04032	.03813
23	.06937	.06488	.06076	.05699	.05352	.05033	.04740	.04470	.04222	.03992
24	.07249	.06784	.06357	.05965	.05605	.05273	.04968	.04686	.04427	.04187
25	.07584	.07103	.06660	.06254	.05879	.05534	.05216	.04922	.04651	.04400
26	.07945	.07447	.06989	.06567	.06178	.05819	.05488	.05182	.04890	.04636
27	.08334	.07819	.07345	.06907	.06503	.06130	.05785	.05466	.05170	.04896
28	.08751	.08219	.07729	.07275	.06856	.06468	.06109	.05777	.05468	.05182
29	.09194	.08645	.08137	.07667	.07233	.06830	.06457	.06110	.05789	.05490
30	.09663	.09096	.08572	.08086	.07635	.07217	.06829	.06469	.06134	.05822
31	.10156	.09572	.09030	.08527	.08060	.07627	.07224	.06849	.06500	.06174
32	.10677	.10074	.09515	.08995	.08512	.08062	.07644	.07254	.06891	.06552
33	.11224	.10604	.10027	.09490	.08990	.08524	.08090	.07686	.07308	.06955
34	.11798	.11159	.10564	.10010	.09494	.09012	.08562	.08142	.07749	.07382
35	.12401	.11744	.11131	.10560	.10026	.09528	.09062	.08626	.08218	.07836
36	.13033	.12357	.11727	.11137	.10586	.10071	.09589	.09137	.08714	.08317
37	.13693	.12999	.12350	.11743	.11175	.10643	.10144	.09676	.09237	.08825
38	.14380	.13668	.13002	.12377	.11791	.11242	.10727	.10243	.09788	.09361
39	.15096	.14366	.13681	.13038	.12436	.11869	.11337	.10837	.10366	.09923
40	.15841	.15092	.14390	.13729	.13109	.12526	.11977	.11460	.10973	.10514
41	.16615	.15848	.15128	.14450	.13812	.13212	.12646	.12113	.11609	.11135
42	.17421	.16637	.15899	.15204	.14549	.13931	.13349	.12799	.12279	.11789
43	.18257	.17456	.16700	.15988	.15316	.14681	.14082	.13515	.12980	.12473
44	.19124	.18306	.17533	.16804	.16115	.15463	.14847	.14264	.13712	.13189
45	.20018	.19184	.18395	.17649	.16943	.16274	.15642	.15042	.14474	.13935
46	.20943	.20092	.19287	.18524	.17802	.17117	.16468	.15853	.15268	.14713
47	.21897	.21030	.20209	.19431	.18692	.17991	.17326	.16694	.16094	.15523
48	.22883	.22001	.21165	.20371	.19616	.18900	.18219	.17571	.16955	.16368
49	.23900	.23004	.22152	.21343	.20573	.19841	.19145	.18481	.17850	.17248
50	.24948	.24039	.23173	.22349	.21565	.20818	.20106	.19428	.18781	.18163
51	.26027	.25104	.24225	.23387	.22589	.21827	.21101	.20407	.19745	.19113
52	.27135	.26200	.25308	.24457	.23645	.22869	.22129	.21421	.20745	.20098
53	.28271	.27325	.26421	.25558	.24733	.23944	.23190	.22468	.21778	.21117
54	.29433	.28476	.27561	.26686	.25848	.25047	.24280	.23545	.22841	.22167
55	.30621	.29654	.28728	.27842	.26993	.26180	.25400	.24653	.23936	.23249
56	.31832	.30856	.29921	.29025	.28165	.27341	.26550	.25790	.25061	.24361
57	.33068	.32085	.31142	.30236	.29367	.28532	.27729	.26959	.26218	.25505
58	.34329	.33339	.32388	.31474	.30595	.29751	.28938	.28157	.27405	.26681
59	.35615	.34620	.33662	.32741	.31855	.31001	.30180	.29388	.28626	.27892
60	.36927	.35927	.34964	.34037	.33143	.32282	.31452	.30652	.29880	.29136
61	.38265	.37262	.37295	.35362	.34463	.33595	.32758	.31950	.31169	.30416
62	.39630	.38625	.37655	.36718	.35814	.34941	.34097	.33282	.32494	.31733
63	.41020	.40014	.39043	.38104	.37196	.36318	.35469	.34648	.33854	.33085
64	.42432	.41428	.40456	.39516	.38606	.37725	.36872	.36046	.35246	.34472

Reg. § 1.664-4A(d)(6)

Estates, Trusts, and Beneficiaries 43,379
See p. 20,601 for regulations not amended to reflect law changes

Table E—Continued. Single Life, Unisex—Table Showing the Present Worth of the Remainder Interest in Property Transferred to a Unitrust Having the Adjusted Payout Rate Shown—Applicable for Transfers After November 30, 1983, and Before May 1, 1989

(1) Age	6.2%	6.4%	6.6%	6.8%	7.0%	7.2%	7.4%	7.6%	7.8%	8.0%
65	.43866	.42864	.41893	.40953	.40042	.39159	.38304	.37474	.36670	.35891
66	.45320	.44321	.43353	.42414	.41503	.40620	.39763	.38931	.38124	.37340
67	.46790	.45796	.44832	.43896	.42987	.42104	.41247	.40414	.39605	.38819
68	.48277	.47289	.46330	.45398	.44492	.43611	.42755	.41923	.41113	.40326
69	.49781	.48802	.47849	.46923	.46021	.45144	.44290	.43459	.42650	.41863
70	.51303	.50333	.49389	.48470	.47574	.46702	.45852	.45025	.44218	.43432
71	.52847	.51888	.50954	.50044	.49156	.48291	.47447	.46623	.45820	.45037
72	.54412	.53466	.52544	.51644	.50766	.49909	.49072	.48255	.47458	.46679
73	.55990	.55059	.54151	.53263	.52396	.51549	.50721	.49912	.49122	.48349
74	.57566	.56652	.55758	.54885	.54030	.53195	.52377	.51578	.50796	.50031
75	.59129	.58232	.57354	.56496	.55655	.54832	.54027	.53238	.52466	.51710
76	.60671	.59792	.58932	.58089	.57263	.56454	.55661	.54884	.54123	.53377
77	.62189	.61330	.60487	.59661	.58851	.58057	.57278	.56514	.55765	.55030
78	.63687	.62847	.62024	.61215	.60422	.59644	.58879	.58129	.57393	.56670
79	.65168	.64349	.63546	.62756	.61981	.61219	.60471	.59736	.59013	.58304
80	.66637	.65841	.65058	.64289	.63532	.62788	.62057	.61338	.60632	.59936
81	.68085	.67312	.66551	.65802	.65066	.64341	.63628	.62926	.62236	.61556
82	.69503	.68753	.68014	.67287	.66571	.65866	.65172	.64488	.63815	.63151
83	.70890	.70164	.69448	.68743	.68048	.67364	.66689	.66024	.65369	.64723
84	.72255	.71553	.70861	.70179	.69506	.68843	.68189	.67544	.66907	.66279
85	.73600	.72924	.72257	.71598	.70948	.70307	.69674	.69050	.68433	.67825
86	.74897	.7446	.73693	.72969	.72342	.71723	.71112	.70508	.69912	.69323
87	.76109	.75483	.74864	.74252	.73647	.73050	.72460	.71877	.71300	.70731
88	.77235	.76631	.76035	.75445	.74862	.74285	.73715	.73151	.72593	.72042
89	.78298	.77717	.77142	.76573	.76011	.75454	.74903	.74358	.73819	.73286
90	.79329	.78770	.78217	.77669	.77127	.76591	.76060	.75534	.75014	.74499
91	.80320	.79783	.79252	.78725	.78204	.77688	.77176	.76670	.76169	.75672
92	.81241	.80725	.80214	.79708	.79206	.78709	.78217	.77729	.77245	.76766
93	.82074	.81578	.81086	.80598	.80115	.79635	.79160	.78690	.78223	.77761
94	.82816	.82337	.81862	.81391	.80924	.80461	.80002	.79547	.79096	.78648
95	.83461	.82997	.82537	.82081	.81629	.81180	.80735	.80394	.79856	.79421
96	.84003	.83552	.83105	.82661	.82221	.81784	.81351	.80921	.80494	.80071
97	.84487	.84048	.83612	.83179	.82750	.82324	.81901	.81481	.81065	.80651
98	.84910	.84481	.84054	.83631	.83211	.82794	.82380	.81969	.81562	.81157
99	.85307	.84887	.84469	.84055	.83644	.83235	.82830	.82427	.82028	.81631
100	.85701	.85290	.84882	.84476	.84073	.83674	.83276	.82882	.82490	.82101
101	.86049	.85645	.85244	.84846	.84451	.84058	.83668	.83280	.82895	.82512
102	.86424	.86029	.85637	.85247	.84859	.84474	.84091	.83710	.83332	.82956
103	.86904	.86520	.86138	.85758	.85381	.85006	.84633	.84262	.83893	.83526
104	.87365	.86991	.86619	.86249	.85880	.85514	.85150	.84787	.84427	.84068
105	.88058	.87700	.87343	.86988	.86635	.86284	.85934	.85585	.85239	.84893
106	.89165	.88835	.88506	.88179	.87852	.87527	.87204	.86881	.86559	.86239
107	.90692	.90404	.90116	.89829	.89542	.89257	.88972	.88688	.88404	.88121
108	.93077	.92858	.92639	.92420	.92201	.91983	.91765	.91547	.91330	.91113
109	.96900	.96800	.96700	.96600	.96500	.96400	.96300	.96200	.96100	.96000

Reg. § 1.664-4A(d)(6)

43,380   Estates, Trusts, and Beneficiaries

See p. 20,601 for regulations not amended to reflect law changes

Table E—Continued. Single Life, Unisex—Table Showing the Present Worth of the Remainder Interest in Property Transferred to a Unitrust Having the Adjusted Payout Rate Shown—Applicable for Transfers After November 30, 1983, and Before May 1, 1989

(1) Age	\(2\) Adjusted Payout Rate									
	8.2%	8.4%	8.6%	8.8%	9.0%	9.2%	9.4%	9.6%	9.8%	10.0%
0	.03059	.02995	.02936	.02882	.02833	.02788	.02747	.02709	.02673	.02641
1	.01267	.01200	.01139	.01084	.01033	.00987	.00945	.00906	.00871	.00838
2	.01251	.01181	.01117	.01059	.01006	.00957	.00913	.00872	.00835	.00800
3	.01274	.01200	.01133	.01072	.01016	.00965	.00918	.00875	.00836	.00799
4	.01316	.01239	.01168	.01103	.01044	.00991	.00941	.00896	.00854	.00815
5	.01375	.01293	.01218	.01150	.01088	.01031	.00979	.00931	.00887	.00846
6	.01446	.01360	.01281	.01209	.01144	.01084	.01028	.00978	.00931	.00888
7	.01527	.01436	.01353	.01277	.01208	.01144	.01086	.01032	.00983	.00937
8	.01619	.01523	.01436	.01356	.01283	.01216	.01154	.01097	.01044	.00996
9	.01725	.01624	.01532	.01448	.01370	.01299	.01234	.01174	.01118	.01067
10	.01843	.01737	.01640	.01551	.01470	.01395	.01326	.01262	.01204	.01149
11	.01976	.01865	.01763	.01669	.01583	.01504	.01432	.01364	.01302	.01245
12	.02122	.02055	.01898	.01800	.01709	.01626	.01549	.01478	.01413	.01352
13	.02276	.02153	.02041	.01937	.01842	.01755	.01674	.01599	.01530	.01466
14	.02432	.02303	.02185	.02077	.01977	.01885	.01800	.01721	.01648	.01581
15	.02585	.02451	.02327	.02213	.02108	.02011	.01922	.01839	.01762	.01691
16	.02732	.02591	.02462	.02342	.02232	.02130	.02036	.01949	.01869	.01794
17	.02874	.02726	.02590	.02465	.02349	.02243	.02144	.02052	.01967	.01888
18	.03013	.02858	.02715	.02584	.02462	.02350	.02246	.02150	.02061	.01978
19	.03152	.02990	.02841	.02703	.02575	.02457	.02348	.02247	.02153	.02065
20	.03298	.03128	.02971	.02826	.02692	.02569	.02454	.02347	.02248	.02156
21	.03451	.03272	.03108	.02956	.02815	.02685	.02564	.02452	.02347	.02250
22	.03611	.03424	.03251	.03091	.02944	.02806	.02679	.02561	.02451	.02348
23	.03781	.03585	.03404	.03236	.03081	.02936	.02802	.02677	.02561	.02453
24	.03965	.03760	.03570	.03393	.03230	.03078	.02937	.02805	.02683	.02569
25	.04168	.03953	.03753	.03568	.03396	.03236	.03087	.02949	.02820	.02699
26	.04393	.04168	.03958	.03764	.03583	.03415	.03258	.03112	.02975	.02848
27	.04642	.04406	.04186	.03982	.03792	.03615	.03450	.03295	.03151	.03017
28	.04916	.04669	.04439	.04224	.04025	.03838	.03664	.03502	.03350	.03208
29	.05212	.04953	.04712	.04487	.04277	.04081	.03898	.03727	.03567	.03416
30	.05531	.05260	.05008	.04772	.04552	.04346	.04154	.03973	.03804	.03646
31	.05871	.05588	.05324	.05077	.04846	.04630	.04427	.04237	.04059	.03892
32	.06236	.05940	.05663	.05405	.05163	.04936	.04723	.04523	.04335	.04159
33	.06625	.06316	.06027	.05756	.05502	.05264	.05041	.04831	.04633	.04448
34	.07038	.06716	.06414	.06131	.05865	.05615	.05381	.05160	.04952	.04757
35	.07478	.07142	.06827	.06531	.06253	.05992	.05746	.05514	.05296	.05090
36	.07944	.07595	.07266	.06957	.06667	.06393	.06135	.05892	.05663	.05447
37	.08438	.08074	.07732	.07410	.07106	.06820	.06550	.06295	.06055	.05828
38	.08958	.08580	.08223	.07888	.07571	.07272	.06990	.06723	.06471	.06233
39	.09506	.09112	.08742	.08392	.08061	.07749	.07454	.07175	.06912	.06662
40	.10081	.09673	.09288	.08924	.08580	.08254	.07946	.07655	.07379	.07117
41	.10687	.10263	.09863	.09484	.09126	.08787	.08466	.08162	.07873	.07599
42	.11325	.10886	.10471	.10078	.09705	.09352	.09018	.08700	.08399	.08112
43	.11993	.11539	.11109	.10701	.10314	.09947	.09599	.09268	.08953	.08654
44	.12694	.12224	.11779	.11356	.10955	.10573	.10211	.09866	.09539	.09227
45	.13424	.12939	.12478	.12040	.11624	.11229	.10852	.10494	.10152	.09827
46	.14186	.13686	.13210	.12757	.12326	.11916	.11525	.11153	.10798	.10459
47	.14980	.14464	.13973	.13505	.13059	.12634	.12229	.11843	.11474	.11122
48	.15810	.15278	.14772	.14289	.13828	.13388	.12969	.12568	.12186	.11820
49	.16674	.16127	.15605	.15107	.14631	.14177	.13743	.13329	.12932	.12553
50	.17574	.17012	.16475	.15962	.15472	.15003	.14555	.14126	.13716	.13322
51	.18510	.17932	.17381	.16853	.16348	.15865	.15402	.14959	.14534	.14127
52	.19480	.18888	.18322	.17779	.17260	.16763	.16286	.15828	.15390	.14969
53	.20484	.19878	.19298	.18741	.18208	.17696	.17205	.16734	.16281	.15847
54	.21520	.20901	.20306	.19735	.19188	.18662	.18157	.17672	.17206	.16758
55	.22589	.21955	.21347	.20763	.20202	.19662	.19144	.18645	.18165	.17703
56	.23688	.23041	.22420	.21822	.21248	.20695	.20163	.19651	.19157	.18682
57	.24820	.24161	.23527	.22917	.22329	.21763	.21218	.20693	.20186	.19698
58	.25984	.25313	.24667	.24044	.23444	.22865	.22307	.21769	.21250	.20749
59	.27184	.26501	.25843	.25209	.24596	.24005	.23435	.22885	.22353	.21839
60	.28417	.27724	.27055	.26409	.25786	.25183	.24601	.24038	.23494	.22969
61	.29688	.28985	.28306	.27650	.27015	.26401	.25808	.25234	.24678	.24141
62	.30996	.30284	.29596	.28929	.28285	.27661	.27056	.26471	.25905	.25356
63	.32341	.31621	.30924	.30249	.29595	.28961	.28347	.27752	.27175	.26615
64	.33721	.32994	.32289	.31605	.30943	.30300	.29677	.29072	.28486	.27916

Reg. § 1.664-4A(d)(6)

Estates, Trusts, and Beneficiaries

See p. 20,601 for regulations not amended to reflect law changes

Table E—Continued. Single Life, Unisex—Table Showing the Present Worth of the Remainder Interest in Property Transferred to a Unitrust Having the Adjusted Payout Rate Shown—Applicable for Transfers After November 30, 1983, and Before May 1, 1989

(1) Age	\(2\) Adjusted Payout Rate									
	8.2%	8.4%	8.6%	8.8%	9.0%	9.2%	9.4%	9.6%	9.8%	10.0%
65	.35134	.34401	.33689	.32999	.32329	.31678	.31046	.30433	.29837	.29259
66	.36580	.35841	.35124	.34427	.33750	.33093	.32454	.31832	.31228	.30641
67	.38055	.37312	.36590	.35889	.35206	.34542	.33897	.33268	.32657	.32062
68	.39559	.38814	.38089	.37383	.36696	.36027	.35376	.34742	.34124	.33522
69	.41096	.40349	.39622	.38913	.38222	.37550	.36894	.36255	.35632	.35024
70	.42665	.41918	.41190	.40480	.39787	.39111	.38452	.37809	.37182	.36570
71	.44273	.43527	.42799	.42089	.41395	.40719	.40058	.39412	.38782	.38166
72	.45919	.45176	.44450	.43741	.43049	.42372	.41710	.41064	.40432	.39814
73	.47594	.46856	.46134	.45428	.44738	.44062	.43402	.42756	.42124	.41506
74	.49283	.48550	.47834	.47132	.46446	.45774	.45116	.44471	.43840	.43223
75	.50969	.50244	.49534	.48838	.48157	.47489	.46834	.46193	.45565	.44949
76	.52646	.51929	.51226	.50537	.49862	.49199	.48550	.47913	.47288	.46675
77	.54309	.53601	.52907	.52226	.51558	.50902	.50258	.49626	.49006	.48397
78	.55960	.55263	.54579	.53907	.53247	.52598	.51962	.51336	.50721	.50117
79	.57606	.56921	.56248	.55586	.54935	.54295	.53667	.53049	.52441	.51843
80	.59253	.58580	.57919	.57269	.56629	.55999	.55380	.54771	.54171	.53581
81	.60887	.60229	.59581	.58943	.58315	.57697	.57088	.56489	.55899	.55317
82	.62498	.61855	.61221	.60597	.59982	.59375	.58778	.58190	.57610	.57039
83	.64086	.63459	.62840	.62230	.61629	.61036	.60451	.59875	.59306	.58746
84	.65660	.65049	.64447	.63852	.63266	.62687	.62116	.61553	.60997	.60448
85	.67224	.66631	.66046	.65468	.64898	.64335	.63779	.63230	.62688	.62152
86	.68742	.68167	.67600	.67040	.66486	.65939	.65398	.64864	.64337	.63816
87	.70168	.69611	.69061	.68518	.67980	.67449	.66924	.66405	.65892	.65384
88	.71497	.70958	.70425	.69897	.69376	.68860	.68350	.67845	.67346	.66852
89	.72758	.72236	.71720	.71208	.70702	.70202	.69706	.69216	.68731	.68250
90	.73989	.73484	.72985	.72490	.72000	.71515	.71035	.70559	.70088	.69622
91	.75180	.74693	.74210	.73732	.73259	.72790	.72325	.71865	.71409	.70957
92	.76292	.75821	.75355	.74894	.74436	.73982	.73533	.73087	.72646	.72208
93	.77302	.76848	.76397	.75951	.75508	.75069	.74634	.74202	.73774	.73350
94	.78204	.77764	.77328	.76895	.76466	.76040	.75618	.75199	.74784	.74372
95	.78991	.78563	.78139	.77719	.77302	.76888	.76477	.76070	.75666	.75265
96	.79651	.79234	.78821	.78411	.78003	.77599	.77199	.76801	.76406	.76014
97	.80241	.79834	.79430	.79029	.78630	.78235	.77843	.77454	.77067	.76684
98	.80755	.80356	.79960	.79567	.79176	.78789	.78404	.78022	.77642	.77266
99	.81236	.80845	.80456	.80071	.79687	.79307	.78929	.78554	.78181	.77811
100	.81715	.81331	.80949	.80571	.80195	.79821	.79450	.79081	.78715	.78351
101	.82132	.81754	.81379	.81006	.80636	.80268	.79902	.79539	.79178	.78819
102	.82582	.82211	.81842	.81476	.81111	.80749	.80389	.80031	.79676	.79322
103	.83162	.82799	.82439	.82080	.81724	.81370	.81018	.80668	.80319	.79973
104	.83711	.83356	.83003	.82652	.82302	.81955	.81609	.81265	.80923	.80582
105	.84550	.84208	.83867	.83528	.83191	.82855	.82520	.82187	.81856	.81526
106	.85920	.85602	.85285	.84969	.84655	.84341	.84029	.83718	.83408	.83099
107	.87839	.87558	.87277	.86997	.86718	.86439	.86162	.85884	.85608	.85332
108	.90896	.90679	.90463	.90246	.90030	.89815	.89599	.89384	.89169	.88955
109	.95900	.95800	.95700	.95600	.95500	.95400	.95300	.95200	.95100	.95000

Reg. § 1.664-4A(d)(6)

Table E—Continued. Single Life, Unisex—Table Showing the Present Worth of the Remainder Interest in Property Transferred to a Unitrust Having the Adjusted Payout Rate Shown—Applicable for Transfers After November 30, 1983, and Before May 1, 1989

(1) Age	(2) Adjusted Payout Rate									
	10.2%	10.4%	10.6%	10.8%	11.0%	11.2%	11.4%	11.6%	11.8%	12.0%
0	.02610	.02582	.02556	.02531	.02508	.02487	.02466	.02447	.02429	.02412
1	.00807	.00779	.00753	.00729	.00707	.00686	.00666	.00648	.00631	.00615
2	.00769	.00739	.00712	.00686	.00663	.00641	.00620	.00601	.00583	.00566
3	.00766	.00735	.00706	.00679	.00654	.00631	.00609	.00589	.00570	.00552
4	.00780	.00747	.00716	.00688	.00662	.00637	.00614	.00593	.00573	.00554
5	.00808	.00773	.00741	.00711	.00683	.00657	.00633	.00610	.00588	.00568
6	.00848	.00811	.00776	.00744	.00715	.00687	.00661	.00637	.00614	.00593
7	.00894	.00855	.00819	.00785	.00753	.00724	.00696	.00670	.00646	.00623
8	.00951	.00909	.00871	.00835	.00801	.00770	.00740	.00713	.00687	.00633
9	.01019	.00975	.00934	.00896	.00860	.00827	.00795	.00766	.00739	.00713
10	.01099	.01052	.01008	.00967	.00930	.00894	.00861	.00830	.00800	.00773
11	.01191	.01142	.01095	.01052	.01012	.00974	.00939	.00906	.00875	.00846
12	.01295	.01243	.01194	.01148	.01106	.01066	.01029	.00993	.00961	.00929
13	.01406	.01351	.01299	.01251	.01206	.01164	.01124	.01087	.01052	.01019
14	.01518	.01459	.01405	.01354	.01306	.01262	.01220	.01181	.01144	.01109
15	.01625	.01563	.01506	.01452	.01402	.01355	.01311	.01270	.01231	.01194
16	.01724	.01659	.01599	.01542	.01489	.01440	.01394	.01350	.01309	.01271
17	.01815	.01747	.01683	.01624	.01568	.01516	.01467	.01421	.01378	.01337
18	.01901	.01829	.01761	.01699	.01640	.01585	.01534	.01485	.01440	.01397
19	.01984	.01908	.01837	.01771	.01709	.01651	.01597	.01546	.01498	.01453
20	.02070	.01990	.01915	.01846	.01780	.01719	.01662	.01608	.01557	.01510
21	.02160	.02075	.01996	.01923	.01854	.01789	.01728	.01672	.01618	.01568
22	.02253	.02164	.02080	.02003	.01930	.01861	.01797	.01737	.01680	.01627
23	.02352	.02258	.02170	.02088	.02010	.01938	.01870	.01806	.01746	.01689
24	.02462	.02362	.02269	.02182	.02100	.02023	.01951	.01883	.01819	.01759
25	.02586	.02481	.02382	.02289	.02203	.02121	.02045	.01973	.01905	.01841
26	.02729	.02617	.02512	.02414	.02322	.02236	.02155	.02078	.02006	.01938
27	.02891	.02772	.02662	.02558	.02460	.02368	.02282	.02200	.02124	.02051
28	.03074	.02949	.02832	.02722	.02618	.02521	.02429	.02342	.02261	.02183
29	.03276	.03143	.03019	.02902	.02792	.02689	.02591	.02499	.02412	.02330
30	.03497	.03357	.03225	.03102	.02985	.02875	.02772	.02674	.02581	.02494
31	.03735	.03587	.03448	.03317	.03193	.03076	.02966	.02863	.02764	.02671
32	.03993	.03837	.03690	.03551	.03420	.03297	.03180	.03070	.02965	.02866
33	.04273	.04108	.03952	.03806	.03667	.03536	.03412	.03295	.03184	.03079
34	.04572	.04399	.04234	.04079	.03933	.03794	.03663	.03539	.03421	.03309
35	.04896	.04713	.04539	.04376	.04221	.04074	.03935	.03803	.03678	.03559
36	.05243	.05049	.04867	.04694	.04530	.04375	.04228	.04089	.03956	.03830
37	.05613	.05410	.05217	.05035	.04862	.04699	.04543	.04395	.04255	.04122
38	.06007	.05793	.05591	.05399	.05217	.05044	.04879	.04723	.04575	.04433
39	.06425	.06200	.05987	.05785	.05593	.05411	.05238	.05073	.04916	.04766
40	.06869	.06633	.06409	.06197	.05995	.05802	.05620	.05445	.05279	.05121
41	.07339	.07092	.06857	.06634	.06421	.06219	.06026	.05843	.05668	.05500
42	.07840	.07581	.07335	.07101	.06878	.06665	.06462	.06269	.06084	.05908
43	.08370	.08099	.07841	.07595	.07361	.07138	.06924	.06721	.06526	.06341
44	.08930	.08646	.08377	.08119	.07874	.07639	.07415	.07202	.06997	.06801
45	.09517	.09222	.08940	.08670	.08413	.08168	.07933	.07708	.07493	.07287
46	.10136	.09828	.09533	.09252	.08983	.08726	.08480	.08244	.08018	.07802
47	.10786	.10464	.10157	.09864	.09582	.09313	.09056	.08809	.08572	.08345
48	.11470	.11136	.10816	.10510	.10216	.09935	.09666	.09408	.09160	.08922
49	.12189	.11842	.11509	.11190	.10884	.10591	.10309	.10039	.09780	.09531
50	.12946	.12585	.12239	.11907	.11588	.11282	.10989	.10707	.10436	.10176
51	.13737	.13363	.13003	.12659	.12327	.12009	.11703	.11409	.11127	.10855
52	.14565	.14177	.13805	.13447	.13103	.12772	.12454	.12147	.11853	.11569
53	.15429	.15028	.14642	.14271	.13914	.13571	.13340	.12922	.12615	.12319
54	.16327	.15912	.15513	.15129	.14759	.14403	.14060	.13729	.13410	.13102
55	.17259	.16831	.16419	.16022	.15639	.15270	.14914	.14571	.14240	.13920
56	.18225	.17784	.17358	.16948	.16553	.16171	.15802	.15447	.15103	.14771
57	.19227	.18773	.18335	.17912	.17503	.17109	.16728	.16360	.16004	.15660
58	.20265	.19798	.19347	.18911	.18490	.18083	.17690	.17309	.16941	.16585
59	.21343	.20863	.20400	.19951	.19518	.19098	.18692	.18299	.17919	.17551
60	.22460	.21968	.21492	.21032	.20586	.20154	.19736	.19331	.18938	.18558
61	.23620	.23117	.22629	.22156	.21698	.21254	.20824	.20407	.20003	.19610
62	.24824	.24309	.23810	.23325	.22856	.22400	.21958	.21530	.21113	.20709
63	.26073	.25546	.25036	.24540	.24060	.23593	.23139	.22699	.22272	.21856
64	.27364	.26827	.26306	.25800	.25308	.24830	.24366	.23915	.23476	.23050

Reg. § 1.664-4A(d)(6)

Estates, Trusts, and Beneficiaries 43,383
See p. 20,601 for regulations not amended to reflect law changes

Table E—Continued. Single Life, Unisex—Table Showing the Present Worth of the Remainder Interest in Property Transferred to a Unitrust Having the Adjusted Payout Rate Shown—Applicable for Transfers After November 30, 1983, and Before May 1, 1989

(1) Age	\(2\) Adjusted Payout Rate									
	10.2%	10.4%	10.6%	10.8%	11.0%	11.2%	11.4%	11.6%	11.8%	12.0%
65	.28696	.28150	.27619	.27103	.26601	.26113	.25638	.25176	.24727	.24290
66	.30070	.29515	.28974	.28449	.27937	.27439	.26955	.26483	.26023	.25576
67	.31483	.30919	.30371	.29836	.29316	.28808	.28314	.27833	.27364	.26906
68	.32936	.32365	.31808	.31266	.30737	.30221	.29718	.29228	.28750	.28283
69	.34432	.33854	.33290	.32741	.32204	.31681	.31170	.30672	.30185	.29710
70	.35972	.35389	.34820	.34264	.33721	.33190	.32673	.32167	.31672	.31189
71	.37565	.36977	.36403	.35842	.35294	.34758	.34234	.33721	.33220	.32731
72	.39210	.38619	.38042	.37477	.36924	.36384	.35855	.35337	.34831	.34335
73	.40900	.40308	.39728	.39161	.38605	.38061	.37529	.37007	.36496	.35996
74	.42618	.42025	.41444	.40876	.40318	.39772	.39237	.38713	.38199	.37695
75	.44345	.43753	.43173	.42604	.42046	.41499	.40962	.40436	.39920	.39413
76	.46073	.45483	.44904	.44336	.43779	.43232	.42695	.42168	.41650	.41142
77	.47799	.47212	.46635	.46069	.45513	.44967	.44431	.43904	.43386	.42878
78	.49524	.48941	.48368	.47805	.47252	.46708	.46173	.45647	.45130	.44622
79	.51256	.50678	.50110	.49551	.49001	.48460	.47928	.47405	.46890	.46383
80	.53001	.52429	.51867	.51313	.50769	.50232	.49705	.49185	.48673	.48169
81	.54745	.54181	.53626	.53079	.52541	.52010	.51487	.50973	.50465	.49965
82	.56476	.55921	.55375	.54835	.54303	.53779	.53263	.52754	.52252	.51757
83	.58193	.57648	.57110	.56579	.56056	.55540	.55031	.54529	.54033	.53544
84	.59907	.59373	.58845	.58325	.57811	.57304	.56804	.56309	.55822	.55340
85	.61624	.61102	.60586	.60077	.59574	.59077	.58586	.58102	.57623	.57150
86	.63300	.62791	.62289	.61791	.61300	.60815	.60335	.59860	.59392	.58928
87	.64883	.64387	.63896	.63411	.62932	.62458	.61989	.61525	.61066	.60613
88	.66363	.65880	.65402	.64929	.64461	.63998	.63540	.63086	.62638	.62194
89	.67775	.67304	.66838	.66377	.65921	.65469	.65022	.64579	.64141	.63707
90	.69160	.68703	.68250	.67802	.67357	.66918	.66482	.66050	.65623	.65199
91	.70509	.70066	.69626	.69191	.68760	.68332	.67909	.67489	.67073	.66661
92	.71775	.71345	.70919	.70496	.70078	.69662	.69251	.68843	.68439	.68038
93	.72929	.72512	.72099	.71689	.71282	.70879	.70479	.70082	.69689	.69299
94	.73964	.73559	.73157	.72758	.72362	.71970	.71581	.71195	.70812	.70432
95	.74867	.74472	.74081	.73692	.73306	.72924	.72544	.72167	.71793	.71422
96	.75625	.75239	.74856	.74476	.74099	.73724	.73353	.72984	.72618	.72254
97	.76303	.75925	.75550	.75177	.74807	.74440	.74076	.73714	.73354	.72998
98	.76892	.76521	.76152	.75786	.75422	.75061	.74703	.74347	.73994	.73643
99	.77443	.77078	.76715	.76355	.75998	.75642	.75290	.74939	.74591	.74245
100	.77990	.77631	.77275	.76921	.76569	.76219	.75872	.75527	.75184	.74844
101	.78463	.78109	.77757	.77407	.77060	.76715	.76372	.76031	.75692	.75356
102	.78971	.78622	.78275	.77930	.77587	.77246	.76908	.76571	.76236	.75904
103	.79629	.79287	.78947	.78608	.78272	.77937	.77605	.77274	.76945	.76618
104	.80244	.79907	.79572	.79239	.78907	.78577	.78249	.77923	.77598	.77275
105	.81198	.80871	.80546	.80222	.79900	.79579	.79259	.78941	.78625	.78310
106	.82792	.82485	.82180	.81876	.81572	.81270	.80969	.80670	.80371	.80073
107	.85057	.84783	.84509	.84237	.83964	.83693	.83422	.83152	.82883	.82614
108	.88740	.88526	.88312	.88098	.87885	.87672	.87459	.87246	.87034	.86822
109	.94900	.94800	.94700	.94600	.94500	.94400	.94300	.94200	.94100	.94000

Reg. § 1.664-4A(d)(6)

43,384 Estates, Trusts, and Beneficiaries

See p. 20,601 for regulations not amended to reflect law changes

Table E—Continued. Single Life, Unisex—Table Showing the Present Worth of the Remainder Interest in Property Transferred to a Unitrust Having the Adjusted Payout Rate Shown—Applicable for Transfers After November 30, 1983, and Before May 1, 1989

(1) Age	(2) Adjusted Payout Rate									
	12.2%	12.4%	12.6%	12.8%	13.0%	13.2%	13.4%	13.6%	13.8%	14.0%
0	.02396	.02380	.02366	.02352	.02338	.02325	.02313	.02301	.02290	.02279
1	.00600	.00585	.00572	.00559	.00547	.00536	.00525	.00514	.00505	.00495
2	.00550	.00535	.00521	.00508	.00495	.00484	.00472	.00462	.00451	.00442
3	.00536	.00520	.00505	.00491	.00478	.00465	.00453	.00442	.00431	.00421
4	.00536	.00519	.00504	.00489	.00475	.00461	.00449	.00437	.00426	.00415
5	.00549	.00532	.00515	.00499	.00484	.00470	.00457	.00444	.00432	.00421
6	.00572	.00554	.00536	.00519	.00503	.00488	.00474	.00460	.00447	.00435
7	.00602	.00582	.00563	.00545	.00528	.00512	.00496	.00482	.00468	.00455
8	.00640	.00618	.00598	.00579	.00561	.00543	.00527	.00512	.00497	.00483
9	.00688	.00665	.00644	.00623	.00604	.00585	.00568	.00551	.00536	.00521
10	.00747	.00723	.00699	.00678	.00657	.00637	.00619	.00601	.00584	.00568
11	.00818	.00792	.00767	.00744	.00722	.00701	.00681	.00662	.00644	.00627
12	.00900	.00873	.00846	.00822	.00798	.00776	.00755	.00735	.00716	.00697
13	.00988	.00959	.00931	.00905	.00880	.00857	.00834	.00813	.00793	.00773
14	.01077	.01046	.01017	.00989	.00963	.00938	.00914	.00892	.00870	.00850
15	.01160	.01127	.01097	.01067	.01040	.01014	.00989	.00965	.00942	.00921
16	.01234	.01200	.01167	.01137	.01108	.01080	.01054	.01029	.01005	.00983
17	.01299	.01263	.01229	.01197	.01166	.01137	.01109	.01083	.01058	.01035
18	.01357	.01319	.01283	.01249	.01217	.01186	.01157	.01130	.01103	.01078
19	.01410	.01370	.01332	.01297	.01263	.01230	.01200	.01171	.01143	.01117
20	.01465	.01422	.01382	.01345	.01309	.01275	.01243	.01212	.01183	.01155
21	.01520	.01475	.01433	.01393	.01355	.01319	.01285	.01253	.01222	.01193
22	.01576	.01529	.01484	.01442	.01402	.01364	.01328	.01293	.01261	.01230
23	.01636	.01586	.01538	.01493	.01450	.01410	.01372	.01336	.01301	.01268
24	.01703	.01649	.01599	.01551	.01505	.01463	.01422	.01383	.01347	.01312
25	.01781	.01724	.01670	.01619	.01571	.01525	.01482	.01441	.01401	.01364
26	.01874	.01813	.01756	.01701	.01650	.01601	.01555	.01511	.01469	.01430
27	.01983	.01918	.01857	.01799	.01744	.01692	.01643	.01596	.01551	.01509
28	.02111	.02042	.01976	.01915	.01856	.01800	.01748	.01697	.01650	.01604
29	.02253	.02179	.02110	.02044	.01981	.01922	.01865	.01812	.01760	.01712
30	.02411	.02333	.02259	.02188	.02121	.02058	.01998	.01940	.01886	.01833
31	.02583	.02500	.02421	.02345	.02274	.02206	.02142	.02080	.02022	.01966
32	.02772	.02683	.02599	.02519	.02443	.02370	.02301	.02236	.02173	.02113
33	.02979	.02885	.02795	.02709	.02628	.02550	.02477	.02407	.02340	.02276
34	.03203	.03102	.03006	.02915	.02829	.02746	.02667	.02592	.02521	.02452
35	.03447	.03340	.03238	.03141	.03048	.02960	.02876	.02796	.02719	.02646
36	.03710	.03597	.03488	.03385	.03286	.03193	.03103	.03017	.02936	.02858
37	.03995	.03874	.03758	.03649	.03544	.03444	.03348	.03257	.03170	.03087
38	.04299	.04170	.04048	.03931	.03820	.03714	.03612	.03515	.03422	.03333
39	.04623	.04487	.04358	.04234	.04115	.04002	.03894	.03791	.03692	.03597
40	.04970	.04826	.04689	.04558	.04432	.04312	.04197	.04087	.03981	.03880
41	.05341	.05189	.05043	.04904	.04771	.04643	.04521	.04404	.04292	.04185
42	.05739	.05578	.05424	.05277	.05136	.05001	.04871	.04747	.04628	.04514
43	.06163	.05993	.05830	.05674	.05525	.05382	.05245	.05113	.04987	.04865
44	.06614	.06435	.06263	.06099	.05941	.05789	.05644	.05505	.05371	.05242
45	.07090	.06901	.06720	.06547	.06380	.06220	.06067	.05919	.05777	.05641
46	.07595	.07396	.07206	.07023	.06847	.06678	.06516	.06360	.06210	.06065
47	.08128	.07919	.07718	.07525	.07340	.07162	.06991	.06826	.06668	.06515
48	.08693	.08474	.08263	.08061	.07866	.07678	.07498	.07324	.07157	.06996
49	.09291	.09061	.08840	.08627	.08423	.08225	.08035	.07852	.07676	.07506
50	.09925	.09684	.09452	.09229	.09014	.08807	.08607	.08415	.08229	.08050
51	.10593	.10341	.10098	.09864	.09638	.09421	.09211	.09009	.08814	.08625
52	.11296	.11032	.10778	.10534	.10297	.10070	.09850	.09637	.09432	.09234
53	.12034	.11759	.11494	.11238	.10991	.10753	.10523	.10300	.10085	.09877
54	.12805	.12519	.12243	.11976	.11718	.11468	.11227	.10994	.10769	.10551
55	.13611	.13313	.13025	.12747	.12478	.12218	.11966	.11722	.11487	.11258
56	.14451	.14141	.13841	.13551	.13271	.12999	.12737	.12483	.12236	.11998
57	.15327	.15005	.14694	.14393	.14101	.13818	.13545	.13279	.13022	.12773
58	.16240	.15906	.15583	.15270	.14967	.14673	.14388	.14112	.13844	.13584
59	.17194	.16848	.16513	.16189	.15874	.15568	.15272	.14985	.14706	.14435
60	.18189	.17831	.17485	.17148	.16822	.16505	.16198	.15899	.15609	.15327
61	.19230	.18860	.18502	.18154	.17816	.17488	.17169	.16859	.16558	.16265
62	.20317	.19936	.19566	.19207	.18857	.18518	.18187	.17866	.17554	.17251
63	.21453	.21060	.20679	.20308	.19947	.19596	.19255	.18923	.18600	.18285
64	.22635	.22231	.21839	.21457	.21085	.20723	.20371	.20028	.19694	.19368

Reg. § 1.664-4A(d)(6)

Estates, Trusts, and Beneficiaries

Table E—Continued. Single Life, Unisex—Table Showing the Present Worth of the Remainder Interest in Property Transferred to a Unitrust Having the Adjusted Payout Rate Shown—Applicable for Transfers After November 30, 1983, and Before May 1, 1989

(1) Age	\(2\) Adjusted Payout Rate								
	12.2%	12.4%	12.6%	12.8%	13.0%	13.2%	13.4%	13.6%	13.8%	14.0%
65	.23864	.23450	.23046	.22653	.22271	.21898	.21535	.21181	.20836	.20500
66	.25140	.24715	.24301	.23898	.23505	.23121	.22748	.22383	.22028	.21681
67	.26461	.26026	.25602	.25188	.24785	.24392	.24008	.23633	.23267	.22910
68	.27828	.27384	.26950	.26527	.26114	.25711	.25317	.24932	.24556	.24189
69	.29246	.28793	.28350	.27918	.27496	.27083	.26680	.26285	.25900	.25523
70	.30718	.30256	.29805	.29364	.28933	.28512	.28100	.27697	.27302	.26916
71	.32251	.31783	.31324	.30876	.30437	.30007	.29587	.29176	.28773	.28378
72	.33850	.33375	.32910	.32455	.32009	.31572	.31145	.30726	.30315	.29913
73	.35506	.35026	.34555	.34094	.33642	.33199	.32765	.32340	.31923	.31514
74	.37201	.36716	.36241	.35776	.35319	.34871	.34431	.34000	.33577	.33162
75	.38916	.38429	.37950	.37481	.37020	.36568	.36124	.35688	.35260	.34840
76	.40644	.40154	.39673	.39200	.38737	.38281	.37833	.37393	.36961	.36537
77	.42378	.41887	.41404	.40930	.40464	.40006	.39555	.39113	.38677	.38249
78	.44123	.43631	.43148	.42673	.42205	.41745	.41293	.40848	.40410	.39980
79	.45885	.45394	.44911	.44436	.43969	.43508	.43055	.42609	.42170	.41737
80	.47673	.47184	.46703	.46229	.45763	.45303	.44850	.44404	.43964	.43531
81	.49473	.48987	.48509	.48037	.47573	.47115	.46663	.46218	.45779	.45347
82	.51269	.50787	.50313	.49845	.49383	.48928	.48479	.48036	.47599	.47168
83	.53062	.52586	.52116	.51653	.51195	.50744	.50298	.49858	.49424	.48995
84	.54864	.54395	.53931	.53473	.53021	.52575	.52134	.51698	.51268	.50843
85	.56683	.56221	.55765	.55314	.54869	.54429	.53994	.53564	.53139	.52720
86	.58470	.58017	.57570	.57127	.56689	.56257	.55829	.55406	.54988	.54574
87	.60164	.59720	.59281	.58847	.58417	.57993	.57572	.57156	.56745	.56338
88	.61754	.61320	.60889	.60464	.60042	.59625	.59212	.58804	.58399	.57999
89	.63277	.62851	.62430	.62013	.61600	.61191	.60786	.60384	.59987	.59594
90	.64780	.64364	.63953	.63545	.63141	.62741	.62344	.61952	.61562	.61177
91	.66252	.65848	.65446	.65049	.64655	.64264	.63877	.63493	.63113	.62736
92	.67640	.67246	.66856	.66468	.66084	.65703	.65326	.64951	.64580	.64212
93	.68912	.68528	.68148	.67770	.67396	.67024	.66656	.66291	.65928	.65568
94	.70055	.69680	.69308	.68941	.68576	.68213	.67854	.67497	.67142	.66791
95	.71054	.70689	.70326	.69966	.69609	.69255	.68903	.68554	.68207	.67863
96	.71893	.71535	.71180	.70827	.70476	.70128	.69783	.69440	.69100	.68762
97	.72643	.72292	.71943	.71596	.71252	.70910	.70570	.70233	.69899	.69566
98	.73294	.72948	.72604	.72263	.71924	.71587	.71252	.70920	.70590	.70263
99	.73902	.73561	.73222	.72886	.72551	.72219	.71889	.71562	.71236	.70913
100	.74506	.74170	.73836	.73504	.73174	.72847	.72522	.72189	.71877	.71558
101	.75021	.74689	.74359	.74030	.73704	.73380	.73058	.72738	.72420	.72104
102	.75573	.75244	.74918	.74593	.74270	.73949	.73630	.73313	.72998	.72685
103	.76293	.75970	.75649	.75329	.75011	.74695	.74381	.74068	.73758	.73449
104	.76954	.76634	.76316	.76000	.75685	.75372	.75060	.74751	.74442	.74136
105	.77996	.77684	.77373	.77064	.76756	.76449	.76144	.75840	.75538	.75237
106	.79777	.79481	.79187	.78894	.78602	.78311	.78021	.77732	.77444	.77157
107	.82346	.82078	.81812	.81546	.81281	.81016	.80752	.80489	.80227	.79965
108	.86610	.86398	.86187	.85976	.85765	.85554	.85344	.85134	.84924	.84715
109	.93900	.93800	.93700	.93600	.93500	.93400	.93300	.93200	.93100	.93000

Reg. § 1.664-4A(d)(6)

Table F(1)—10 Percent—Table Showing Factors for Computations of the Adjusted Payout Rate for Certain Valuations and Payout Sequences—Applicable for Transfers After November 30, 1983, and Before May 1, 1989

Number of Months by Which the Valuation Date Precedes the First Payout		Factors for Payout at the End of Each.			
At least	But Less than	Annual Period	Semiannual Period	Quarterly Period	Monthly Period
..	1		.976731	.965232	.957616
1	2	.992089	.969004	.957596	.950041
2	3	.984240	.961338	.950021	
3	4	.976454	.953733	.942505	
4	5	.968729	.946188		
5	6	.961066	.938703		
6	7	.953463	.931277		
7	8	.945920			
8	9	.938436			
9	10	.931012			
10	11	.923647			
11	12	.916340			
12	..	.909091			

(e) *Valuation of charitable remainder unitrusts having certain payout sequences for transfers for which the valuation date is after April 30, 1989, and before May 1, 1999*—(1) *In general.* Except as otherwise provided in paragraph (e)(2) of this section, in the case of transfers for which the valuation date is after April 30, 1989, and before May 1, 1999, the present value of a remainder interest is determined under paragraphs (e)(3) through (e)(6) of this section, provided that the amount of the payout as of any payout date during any taxable year of the trust is not larger than the amount that the trust could distribute on such date under § 1.664-3(a)(1)(v) if the taxable year of the trust were to end on such date. See, however, § 1.7520-3(b) (relating to exceptions to the use of the prescribed tables under certain circumstances).

(2) *Transitional rules for valuation of charitable remainder unitrusts.* (i) If the valuation date of a transfer to a charitable remainder unitrust is after April 30, 1989, and before June 10, 1994, a transferor can rely upon Notice 89-24, 1989-1 C.B. 660, or Notice 89-60, 1989-1 C.B. 700, in valuing the transferred interest. (See § 601.601(d)(2)(ii)(*b*) of this chapter.)

(ii) For purposes of sections 2055, 2106, or 2624, if on May 1, 1989, the decedent was mentally incompetent so that the disposition of the property could not be changed, and the decedent died after April 30, 1989, without having regained competency to dispose of the decedent's property, or the decedent died within 90 days of the date that the decedent first regained competency after April 30, 1989, the present value of a remainder interest determined under this section is determined as if the valuation date with respect to the decedent's gross estate is either before May 1, 1989, or after April 30, 1989, at the option of the decedent's executor.

(3) *Adjusted payout rate.* For transfers for which the valuation date is after April 30, 1989, and before May 1, 1999, the adjusted payout rate is determined by using the appropriate Table F, contained in § 1.664-4(e)(6), for the section 7520 interest rate applicable to the transfer. If the interest rate is between 4.2 and 14 percent, see § 1.664-4(e)(6). If the interest rate is below 4.2 percent or greater than 14 percent, see § 1.664-4(b). See § 1.664-4(e) for rules applicable in determining the adjusted payout rate.

(4) *Period is a term of years.* If the period described in § 1.664-3(a)(5) is a term of years, the factor that is used in determining the present value of the remainder interest for transfers for which the valuation date is after April 30, 1989, and before May 1, 1999, is the factor under the appropriate adjusted payout rate in Table D in § 1.664-4(e)(6) corresponding to the number of years in the term. If the adjusted payout rate is an amount that is between adjusted payout rates for which factors are provided in Table D, a linear interpolation must be made. The present value of the remainder interest is determined by multiplying the net fair market value (as of the appropriate valuation date) of the property placed in trust by the factor determined under this paragraph. Generally, for purposes of this section, the valuation date is, in the case of an inter vivos transfer, the date on which the property is transferred to the trust by the donor, and, in the case of a testamentary transfer under sections 2055, 2106, or 2624, the valuation date is the date of death. See § 1.664-4(e)(4) for additional rules regarding the valuation date. See § 1.664-4(e)(4) for an example that illustrates the application of this paragraph (e)(4).

(5) *Period is the life of one individual.* If the period described in § 1.664-3(a)(5) is the life of one individual, the factor that is used in determin-

Reg. § 1.664-4A(e)(2)

ing the present value of the remainder interest for transfers for which the valuation date is after April 30, 1989, and before May 1, 1999, is the factor in Table U(1) in paragraph (e)(6) of this section under the appropriate adjusted payout. For purposes of the computations described in this paragraph (e)(5), the age of an individual is the age of that individual at the individual's nearest birthday. If the adjusted payout rate is an amount that is between adjusted payout rates for which factors are provided in the appropriate table, a linear interpolation must be made. The rules provided in § 1.664-4(e)(5) apply for determining the present value of the remainder interest. See § 1.664-4(e)(5) for an example illustrating the application of this paragraph (e)(5)(using current actuarial tables).

(6) *Actuarial tables for transfers for which the valuation date is after April 30, 1989, and before May 1, 1999.* For transfers for which the valuation date is after April 30, 1989, and before May 1, 1999, the present value of a charitable remainder unitrust interest that is dependent on a term of years or the termination of a life interest is determined by using the section 7520 rate and Table D, Tables F(4.2) through F(14.0) in § 1.664-4(e)(6) and Table U(1) of this paragraph (e)(6), as applicable. See, however, § 1.7520-3(b) (relating to exceptions to the use of prescribed tables under certain circumstances). Many actuarial factors not contained in the following tables are contained in Internal Revenue Service Publication 1458, "Actuarial Values, Beta Volume," (8-89). Publication 1458 is no longer available for purchase from the Superintendent of Documents, United States Government Printing Office, Washington, DC 20402. However, pertinent factors in this publication may be obtained by a written request to: CC:DOM:CORP:R (IRS Publication 1458), room 5226, Internal Revenue Service, POB 7604, Ben Franklin Station, Washington, DC 20044.

Reg. § 1.664-4A(e)(6)

TABLE U(1)
BASED ON LIFE TABLE 80CNSMT
UNITRUST SINGLE LIFE REMAINDER FACTORS
APPLICABLE FOR TRANSFERS AFTER APRIL 30, 1989, AND BEFORE MAY 1, 1999

ADJUSTED PAYOUT RATE

AGE	4.2%	4.4%	4.6%	4.8%	5.0%	5.2%	5.4%	5.6%	5.8%	6.0%
0	.06797	.06181	.05645	.05177	.04768	.04410	.04096	.03820	.03578	.03364
1	.05881	.05243	.04686	.04199	.03773	.03400	.03072	.02784	.02531	.02308
2	.06049	.05394	.04821	.04319	.03880	.03494	.03155	.02856	.02593	.02361
3	.06252	.05579	.04990	.04473	.04020	.03621	.03270	.02961	.02688	.02446
4	.06479	.05788	.05182	.04650	.04183	.03771	.03408	.03087	.02804	.02553
5	.06724	.06016	.05393	.04845	.04363	.03937	.03562	.03230	.02936	.02675
6	.06984	.06257	.05618	.05054	.04557	.04117	.03729	.03385	.03080	.02809
7	.07259	.06513	.05856	.05276	.04764	.04310	.03909	.03552	.03236	.02954
8	.07548	.06784	.06109	.05513	.04985	.04517	.04102	.03733	.03405	.03113
9	.07854	.07071	.06378	.05765	.05221	.04738	.04310	.03928	.03588	.03285
10	.08176	.07374	.06663	.06033	.05473	.04976	.04533	.04138	.03786	.03471
11	.08517	.07695	.06966	.06319	.05743	.05230	.04772	.04364	.04000	.03673
12	.08872	.08031	.07284	.06619	.06026	.05498	.05026	.04604	.04227	.03889
13	.09238	.08378	.07612	.06929	.06320	.05776	.05289	.04853	.04463	.04113
14	.09608	.08728	.07943	.07243	.06616	.06056	.05554	.05104	.04701	.04338
15	.09981	.09081	.08276	.07557	.06914	.06337	.05820	.05356	.04938	.04563
16	.10356	.09435	.08612	.07874	.07213	.06619	.06086	.05607	.05176	.04787
17	.10733	.09792	.08949	.08192	.07513	.06902	.06353	.05858	.05413	.05010
18	.11117	.10155	.09291	.08515	.07817	.07189	.06623	.06113	.05652	.05236
19	.11509	.10526	.09642	.08847	.08130	.07484	.06901	.06375	.05899	.05469
20	.11913	.10908	.10003	.09188	.08452	.07788	.07188	.06645	.06154	.05708
21	.12326	.11300	.10375	.09539	.08784	.08101	.07483	.06923	.06416	.05955
22	.12753	.11705	.10758	.09902	.09127	.08426	.07789	.07212	.06688	.06212
23	.13195	.12125	.11156	.10279	.09484	.08763	.08109	.07514	.06973	.06481
24	.13655	.12563	.11573	.10675	.09860	.09119	.08446	.07833	.07274	.06766
25	.14136	.13022	.12010	.11091	.10255	.09495	.08802	.08171	.07595	.07069
26	.14640	.13504	.12471	.11530	.10674	.09893	.09181	.08531	.07937	.07394
27	.15169	.14011	.12956	.11994	.11117	.10316	.09584	.08915	.08302	.07742
28	.15721	.14542	.13465	.12482	.11583	.10762	.10010	.09322	.08691	.08112
29	.16299	.15097	.13999	.12994	.12075	.11233	.10461	.09753	.09104	.08507
30	.16901	.15678	.14559	.13533	.12592	.11729	.10937	.10210	.09541	.08926
31	.17531	.16287	.15146	.14099	.13137	.12254	.11441	.10694	.10006	.09372
32	.18186	.16921	.15759	.14691	.13709	.12804	.11972	.11205	.10497	.09844
33	.18869	.17584	.16401	.15312	.14309	.13384	.12531	.11744	.11017	.10345
34	.19578	.18273	.17070	.15961	.14937	.13992	.13119	.12312	.11565	.10874
35	.20315	.18990	.17767	.16637	.15593	.14628	.13735	.12908	.12142	.11431
36	.21076	.19732	.18490	.17340	.16276	.15291	.14377	.13531	.12745	.12016
37	.21863	.20501	.19239	.18071	.16987	.15982	.15049	.14182	.13377	.12628
38	.22676	.21296	.20016	.18828	.17725	.16701	.15748	.14862	.14037	.13269
39	.23515	.22118	.20820	.19614	.18492	.17448	.16476	.15571	.14727	.13940
40	.24379	.22967	.21652	.20428	.19288	.18225	.17234	.16310	.15447	.14641
41	.25270	.23842	.22511	.21270	.20112	.19031	.18021	.17078	.16197	.15372
42	.26184	.24742	.23395	.22137	.20962	.19864	.18836	.17875	.16975	.16132
43	.27123	.25666	.24305	.23031	.21840	.20724	.19679	.18700	.17782	.16921
44	.28085	.26616	.25241	.23952	.22745	.21613	.20551	.19554	.18618	.17739
45	.29072	.27591	.26203	.24901	.23678	.22530	.21452	.20438	.19485	.18589
46	.30082	.28591	.27191	.25875	.24639	.23476	.22381	.21352	.20382	.19468
47	.31116	.29616	.28204	.26877	.25626	.24449	.23340	.22295	.21309	.20379
48	.32171	.30663	.29241	.27902	.26640	.25449	.24326	.23265	.22264	.21318
49	.33245	.31730	.30300	.28950	.27676	.26473	.25336	.24262	.23246	.22285
50	.34338	.32816	.31379	.30020	.28735	.27521	.26371	.25283	.24253	.23277
51	.35449	.33923	.32479	.31112	.29818	.28593	.27431	.26331	.25287	.24297
52	.36582	.35053	.33603	.32230	.30927	.29692	.28520	.27408	.26352	.25349
53	.37736	.36205	.34751	.33372	.32063	.30819	.29637	.28514	.27446	.26431
54	.38909	.37376	.35921	.34537	.33221	.31970	.30780	.29647	.28569	.27542
55	.40099	.38568	.37111	.35724	.34404	.33146	.31949	.30807	.29719	.28681
56	.41308	.39779	.38322	.36934	.35610	.34348	.33143	.31994	.30898	.29851
57	.42536	.41011	.39555	.38167	.36841	.35575	.34366	.33210	.32106	.31051

Reg. § 1.664-4A(e)(6)

Estates, Trusts, and Beneficiaries

AGE	4.2%	4.4%	4.6%	4.8%	5.0%	5.2%	5.4%	5.6%	5.8%	6.0%
58	.43781	.42262	.40810	.39422	.38096	.36828	.35615	.34454	.33344	.32281
59	.45043	.43530	.42083	.40698	.39373	.38104	.36888	.35724	.34609	.33540
60	.46318	.44813	.43372	.41992	.40668	.39400	.38183	.37017	.35898	.34824
61	.47602	.46107	.44674	.43299	.41979	.40713	.39497	.38329	.37207	.36129
62	.48893	.47410	.45986	.44617	.43303	.42039	.40825	.39657	.38534	.37454
63	.50190	.48720	.47306	.45946	.44638	.43379	.42168	.41001	.39878	.38796
64	.51494	.50038	.48636	.47286	.45986	.44733	.43526	.42362	.41240	.40158
65	.52808	.51368	.49980	.48641	.47350	.46104	.44903	.43743	.42624	.41544
66	.54134	.52711	.51338	.50013	.48733	.47496	.46302	.45148	.44033	.42956
67	.55471	.54068	.52712	.51401	.50134	.48908	.47723	.46577	.45467	.44394
68	.56820	.55437	.54100	.52805	.51552	.50339	.49165	.48027	.46925	.45858
69	.58172	.56812	.55495	.54219	.52982	.51783	.50620	.49494	.48401	.47341
70	.59526	.58190	.56894	.55637	.54417	.53234	.52086	.50971	.49889	.48838
71	.60874	.59564	.58291	.57055	.55854	.54687	.53554	.52453	.51382	.50342
72	.62218	.60934	.59685	.58471	.57291	.56143	.55026	.53939	.52882	.51854
73	.63557	.62301	.61078	.59887	.58728	.57600	.56501	.55431	.54389	.53373
74	.64896	.63669	.62472	.61307	.60171	.59064	.57985	.56932	.55906	.54906
75	.66237	.65040	.63872	.62733	.61622	.60538	.59480	.58447	.57439	.56455
76	.67581	.66416	.65279	.64168	.63083	.62023	.60988	.59977	.58989	.58023
77	.68925	.67793	.66688	.65606	.64550	.63516	.62506	.61517	.60551	.59605
78	.70263	.69166	.68093	.67044	.66016	.65010	.64026	.63062	.62119	.61195
79	.71585	.70525	.69486	.68468	.67471	.66495	.65538	.64600	.63681	.62780
80	.72885	.71860	.70856	.69872	.68906	.67959	.67031	.66120	.65227	.64350
81	.74150	.73162	.72193	.71242	.70308	.69392	.68492	.67609	.66742	.65890
82	.75376	.74425	.73490	.72572	.71671	.70785	.69915	.69059	.68219	.67393
83	.76559	.75643	.74744	.73859	.72989	.72134	.71293	.70466	.69652	.68852
84	.77700	.76821	.75955	.75104	.74266	.73441	.72629	.71831	.71044	.70270
85	.78805	.77961	.77130	.76311	.75505	.74711	.73929	.73158	.72399	.71652
86	.79866	.79056	.78258	.77472	.76697	.75933	.75180	.74438	.73707	.72985
87	.80870	.80094	.79329	.78574	.77829	.77095	.76370	.75656	.74951	.74255
88	.81825	.81081	.80348	.79623	.78908	.78202	.77506	.76818	.76139	.75469
89	.82746	.82035	.81332	.80638	.79952	.79275	.78606	.77945	.77292	.76647
90	.83643	.82963	.82291	.81627	.80971	.80322	.79681	.79047	.78420	.77801
91	.84503	.83854	.83212	.82578	.81950	.81330	.80716	.80109	.79509	.78915
92	.85308	.84689	.84076	.83470	.82870	.82276	.81689	.81107	.80532	.79963
93	.86052	.85460	.84875	.84295	.83721	.83152	.82590	.82033	.81481	.80935
94	.86729	.86163	.85602	.85046	.84496	.83951	.83412	.82877	.82348	.81823
95	.87338	.86795	.86257	.85723	.85195	.84672	.84153	.83639	.83129	.82624
96	.87877	.87354	.86836	.86323	.85814	.85309	.84809	.84313	.83822	.83334
97	.88365	.87861	.87362	.86867	.86375	.85888	.85405	.84926	.84450	.83979
98	.88805	.88318	.87835	.87356	.86880	.86409	.85941	.85477	.85016	.84559
99	.89210	.88739	.88271	.87807	.87347	.86890	.86436	.85986	.85539	.85095
100	.89588	.89131	.88678	.88227	.87780	.87337	.86896	.86459	.86024	.85593
101	.89949	.89506	.89066	.88629	.88195	.87764	.87336	.86911	.86488	.86069
102	.90325	.89897	.89471	.89047	.88627	.88209	.87794	.87381	.86971	.86564
103	.90724	.90311	.89900	.89491	.89085	.88681	.88279	.87880	.87484	.87089
104	.91167	.90770	.90376	.89983	.89593	.89205	.88819	.88435	.88053	.87673
105	.91708	.91333	.90959	.90587	.90217	.89848	.89481	.89116	.88752	.88391
106	.92470	.92126	.91782	.91440	.91100	.90760	.90422	.90085	.89749	.89414
107	.93545	.93246	.92948	.92650	.92353	.92057	.91762	.91467	.91173	.90880
108	.95239	.95016	.94792	.94569	.94346	.94123	.93900	.93678	.93456	.93234
109	.97900	.97800	.97700	.97600	.97500	.97400	.97300	.97200	.97100	.97000

Reg. § 1.664-4A(e)(6)

43,390 Estates, Trusts, and Beneficiaries

See p. 20,601 for regulations not amended to reflect law changes

TABLE U(1)
BASED ON LIFE TABLE 80CNSMT
UNITRUST SINGLE LIFE REMAINDER FACTORS
APPLICABLE FOR TRANSFERS AFTER APRIL 30, 1989, AND BEFORE MAY 1, 1999

ADJUSTED PAYOUT RATE

AGE	6.2%	6.4%	6.6%	6.8%	7.0%	7.2%	7.4%	7.6%	7.8%	8.0%
0	.03176	.03009	.02861	.02730	.02613	.02509	.02416	.02333	.02258	.02191
1	.02110	.01936	.01781	.01644	.01522	.01413	.01316	.01229	.01150	.01080
2	.02156	.01974	.01812	.01669	.01541	.01427	.01325	.01234	.01152	.01078
3	.02233	.02043	.01875	.01725	.01591	.01471	.01364	.01268	.01182	.01105
4	.02330	.02132	.01956	.01800	.01660	.01535	.01422	.01322	.01231	.01149
5	.02443	.02237	.02054	.01890	.01743	.01612	.01494	.01389	.01293	.01208
6	.02568	.02353	.02162	.01990	.01837	.01700	.01576	.01465	.01365	.01275
7	.02704	.02480	.02280	.02102	.01941	.01798	.01668	.01552	.01446	.01351
8	.02852	.02619	.02411	.02224	.02057	.01906	.01770	.01648	.01537	.01437
9	.03014	.02772	.02554	.02360	.02184	.02027	.01885	.01756	.01640	.01535
10	.03190	.02938	.02711	.02508	.02325	.02160	.02012	.01877	.01755	.01645
11	.03381	.03119	.02883	.02672	.02481	.02308	.02153	.02012	.01884	.01768
12	.03585	.03313	.03068	.02847	.02648	.02468	.02305	.02157	.02023	.01902
13	.03798	.03515	.03260	.03030	.02822	.02635	.02464	.02310	.02170	.02042
14	.04012	.03718	.03453	.03213	.02997	.02801	.02623	.02462	.02315	.02181
15	.04225	.03919	.03644	.03395	.03169	.02965	.02779	.02611	.02457	.02317
16	.04436	.04120	.03833	.03574	.03339	.03126	.02932	.02756	.02595	.02449
17	.04647	.04319	.04021	.03752	.03507	.03285	.03082	.02898	.02730	.02577
18	.04860	.04519	.04210	.03930	.03675	.03443	.03232	.03040	.02864	.02703
19	.05079	.04725	.04404	.04113	.03847	.03606	.03386	.03185	.03001	.02833
20	.05304	.04938	.04604	.04301	.04025	.03773	.03543	.03333	.03141	.02965
21	.05537	.05157	.04811	.04495	.04208	.03945	.03705	.03486	.03285	.03101
22	.05779	.05385	.05025	.04698	.04398	.04125	.03874	.03645	.03435	.03242
23	.06032	.05623	.05250	.04910	.04598	.04313	.04052	.03812	.03592	.03390
24	.06302	.05878	.05491	.05136	.04812	.04515	.04242	.03992	.03762	.03550
25	.06589	.06150	.05748	.05380	.05042	.04733	.04448	.04187	.03946	.03725
26	.06897	.06442	.06025	.05643	.05292	.04969	.04673	.04400	.04148	.03916
27	.07228	.06757	.06325	.05928	.05563	.05227	.04917	.04632	.04369	.04126
28	.07582	.07094	.06646	.06234	.05854	.05504	.05182	.04884	.04609	.04355
29	.07958	.07454	.06990	.06562	.06167	.05804	.05468	.05157	.04870	.04604
30	.08360	.07838	.07357	.06913	.06504	.06125	.05775	.05452	.05152	.04874
31	.08788	.08249	.07751	.07291	.06866	.06472	.06108	.05771	.05457	.05167
32	.09242	.08685	.08170	.07694	.07252	.06844	.06465	.06113	.05786	.05483
33	.09724	.09149	.08617	.08124	.07666	.07242	.06848	.06482	.06141	.05824
34	.10234	.09641	.09091	.08581	.08107	.07667	.07257	.06876	.06521	.06191
35	.10773	.10161	.09594	.09066	.08575	.08119	.07694	.07298	.06928	.06583
36	.11338	.10708	.10122	.09577	.09070	.08597	.08156	.07744	.07360	.07001
37	.11932	.11283	.10680	.10117	.09592	.09102	.08645	.08217	.07818	.07444
38	.12554	.11887	.11265	.10685	.10142	.09636	.09162	.08719	.08304	.07915
39	.13206	.12521	.11880	.11282	.10722	.10198	.09708	.09249	.08818	.08414
40	.13888	.13184	.12526	.11909	.11332	.10791	.10284	.09808	.09361	.08942
41	.14601	.13878	.13201	.12567	.11972	.11414	.10890	.10398	.09935	.09499
42	.15342	.14601	.13906	.13254	.12641	.12066	.11525	.11016	.10537	.10086
43	.16112	.15353	.14640	.13970	.13340	.12747	.12189	.11663	.11168	.10701
44	.16913	.16136	.15406	.14718	.14070	.13460	.12885	.12342	.11830	.11347
45	.17745	.16951	.16202	.15497	.14832	.14204	.13612	.13053	.12525	.12025
46	.18608	.17796	.17030	.16308	.15625	.14981	.14372	.13796	.13251	.12735
47	.19501	.18673	.17890	.17150	.16451	.15790	.15164	.14571	.14010	.13478
48	.20425	.19579	.18780	.18024	.17308	.16630	.15987	.15378	.14800	.14252
49	.21375	.20514	.19698	.18926	.18193	.17499	.16840	.16214	.15620	.15056
50	.22352	.21476	.20644	.19856	.19107	.18396	.17721	.17080	.16470	.15890
51	.23358	.22467	.21620	.20816	.20051	.19325	.18634	.17976	.17350	.16755
52	.24396	.23490	.22628	.21809	.21030	.20288	.19581	.18908	.18267	.17655
53	.25465	.24545	.23670	.22836	.22042	.21285	.20563	.19875	.19218	.18592
54	.26563	.25631	.24742	.23895	.23086	.22315	.21579	.20876	.20204	.19562
55	.27692	.26747	.25846	.24986	.24164	.23379	.22628	.21911	.21225	.20568
56	.28850	.27895	.26982	.26109	.25275	.24476	.23712	.22981	.22281	.21611
57	.30041	.29076	.28152	.27267	.26421	.25610	.24833	.24089	.23376	.22691

Reg. § 1.664-4A(e)(6)

Estates, Trusts, and Beneficiaries

See p. 20,601 for regulations not amended to reflect law changes

AGE	6.2%	6.4%	6.6%	6.8%	7.0%	7.2%	7.4%	7.6%	7.8%	8.0%
58	.31263	.30288	.29355	.28460	.27602	.26780	.25991	.25234	.24508	.23811
59	.32515	.31532	.30590	.29685	.28817	.27984	.27184	.26416	.25677	.24968
60	.33793	.32803	.31853	.30940	.30062	.29219	.28409	.27630	.26880	.26159
61	.35093	.34098	.33141	.32220	.31335	.30483	.29663	.28873	.28113	.27381
62	.36414	.35414	.34451	.33524	.32631	.31771	.30942	.30144	.29374	.28631
63	.37754	.36750	.35783	.34850	.33951	.33084	.32247	.31440	.30661	.29910
64	.39115	.38108	.37137	.36200	.35296	.34422	.33579	.32765	.31978	.31217
65	.40500	.39493	.38519	.37579	.36670	.35792	.34943	.34122	.33328	.32560
66	.41914	.40906	.39932	.38990	.38079	.37197	.36343	.35517	.34717	.33943
67	.43355	.42350	.41376	.40434	.39521	.38636	.37780	.36950	.36145	.35365
68	.44824	.43822	.42851	.41909	.40996	.40111	.39252	.38419	.37611	.36827
69	.46313	.45316	.44348	.43409	.42498	.41613	.40754	.39919	.39109	.38322
70	.47818	.46827	.45864	.44929	.44020	.43137	.42279	.41445	.40634	.39845
71	.49331	.48348	.47391	.46461	.45557	.44677	.43821	.42988	.42177	.41388
72	.50853	.49879	.48930	.48007	.47108	.46233	.45380	.44550	.43741	.42952
73	.52384	.51421	.50482	.49566	.48674	.47805	.46957	.46130	.45324	.44538
74	.53930	.52979	.52050	.51145	.50261	.49399	.48557	.47736	.46934	.46152
75	.55495	.54557	.53641	.52747	.51873	.51020	.50187	.49372	.48577	.47799
76	.57079	.56157	.55256	.54374	.53513	.52670	.51847	.51041	.50253	.49483
77	.58680	.57775	.56890	.56024	.55176	.54346	.53534	.52739	.51960	.51198
78	.60291	.59405	.58537	.57687	.56855	.56040	.55241	.54458	.53691	.52940
79	.61898	.61032	.60184	.59353	.58537	.57738	.56954	.56185	.55431	.54691
80	.63491	.62647	.61819	.61007	.60210	.59428	.58660	.57907	.57167	.56441
81	.65054	.64234	.63427	.62636	.61858	.61094	.60344	.59606	.58882	.58170
82	.66582	.65784	.65000	.64229	.63472	.62727	.61994	.61274	.60566	.59870
83	.68065	.67291	.66530	.65781	.65044	.64319	.63605	.62903	.62212	.61532
84	.69508	.68758	.68020	.67293	.66577	.65872	.65178	.64495	.63821	.63158
85	.70915	.70190	.69475	.68770	.68076	.67392	.66718	.66054	.65399	.64754
86	.72274	.71573	.70882	.70200	.69528	.68865	.68212	.67567	.66931	.66304
87	.73569	.72892	.72224	.71565	.70915	.70273	.69639	.69014	.68397	.67788
88	.74807	.74154	.73509	.72872	.72243	.71622	.71009	.70403	.69805	.69214
89	.76010	.75381	.74759	.74144	.73537	.72937	.72344	.71758	.71179	.70607
90	.77189	.76584	.75985	.75394	.74809	.74230	.73659	.73093	.72534	.71981
91	.78327	.77746	.77171	.76603	.76040	.75484	.74933	.74388	.73850	.73316
92	.79399	.78841	.78289	.77743	.77202	.76667	.76137	.75613	.75093	.74579
93	.80394	.79858	.79328	.78803	.78283	.77768	.77258	.76753	.76252	.75757
94	.81303	.80788	.80278	.79773	.79272	.78776	.78284	.77797	.77315	.76837
95	.82124	.81628	.81136	.80649	.80166	.79687	.79213	.78742	.78276	.77814
96	.82851	.82372	.81897	.81426	.80959	.80496	.80036	.79581	.79129	.78682
97	.83512	.83048	.82588	.82132	.81679	.81230	.80785	.80343	.79905	.79471
98	.84106	.83656	.83210	.82767	.82328	.81892	.81459	.81030	.80604	.80181
99	.84655	.84218	.83785	.83354	.82927	.82503	.82082	.81664	.81249	.80837
100	.85165	.84740	.84318	.83899	.83483	.83070	.82660	.82252	.81848	.81446
101	.85652	.85238	.84827	.84419	.84013	.83611	.83210	.82813	.82418	.82026
102	.86159	.85757	.85358	.84960	.84566	.84174	.83784	.83397	.83012	.82630
103	.86697	.86307	.85920	.85535	.85152	.84771	.84392	.84016	.83642	.83270
104	.87295	.86919	.86544	.86172	.85802	.85434	.85068	.84704	.84341	.83981
105	.88030	.87672	.87315	.86959	.86605	.86253	.85903	.85554	.85207	.84861
106	.89081	.88749	.88418	.88088	.87760	.87433	.87106	.86782	.86458	.86135
107	.90588	.90296	.90005	.89715	.89425	.89137	.88849	.88561	.88275	.87989
108	.93013	.92791	.92570	.92350	.92129	.91909	.91689	.91469	.91250	.91031
109	.96900	.96800	.96700	.96600	.96500	.96400	.96300	.96200	.96100	.96000

Reg. § 1.664-4A(e)(6)

TABLE U(1)
BASED ON LIFE TABLE 80CNSMT
UNITRUST SINGLE LIFE REMAINDER FACTORS
APPLICABLE FOR TRANSFERS AFTER APRIL 30, 1989, AND BEFORE MAY 1, 1999

ADJUSTED PAYOUT RATE

AGE	8.2%	8.4%	8.6%	8.8%	9.0%	9.2%	9.4%	9.6%	9.8%	10.0%
0	.02130	.02075	.02025	.01980	.01939	.01901	.01867	.01835	.01806	.01779
1	.01017	.00960	.00908	.00861	.00819	.00780	.00745	.00712	.00683	.00655
2	.01011	.00951	.00897	.00848	.00803	.00762	.00725	.00690	.00659	.00630
3	.01035	.00971	.00914	.00862	.00815	.00771	.00732	.00696	.00663	.00632
4	.01076	.01009	.00948	.00894	.00843	.00798	.00756	.00718	.00683	.00650
5	.01130	.01059	.00996	.00938	.00885	.00836	.00792	.00752	.00714	.00680
6	.01193	.01119	.01051	.00990	.00934	.00883	.00836	.00793	.00754	.00717
7	.01265	.01187	.01116	.01051	.00992	.00938	.00888	.00842	.00800	.00762
8	.01347	.01264	.01189	.01121	.01058	.01001	.00948	.00900	.00856	.00815
9	.01440	.01353	.01274	.01201	.01135	.01075	.01019	.00968	.00921	.00877
10	.01544	.01453	.01369	.01293	.01223	.01159	.01101	.01046	.00997	.00950
11	.01662	.01566	.01478	.01398	.01324	.01257	.01195	.01137	.01085	.01036
12	.01791	.01690	.01597	.01513	.01435	.01364	.01298	.01238	.01182	.01131
13	.01926	.01820	.01722	.01634	.01552	.01477	.01408	.01344	.01285	.01231
14	.02059	.01948	.01846	.01752	.01667	.01588	.01515	.01448	.01386	.01328
15	.02189	.02072	.01965	.01867	.01777	.01694	.01617	.01547	.01481	.01421
16	.02315	.02192	.02080	.01977	.01882	.01795	.01714	.01640	.01572	.01508
17	.02436	.02308	.02190	.02082	.01982	.01891	.01806	.01728	.01656	.01589
18	.02556	.02422	.02298	.02184	.02080	.01983	.01894	.01812	.01736	.01665
19	.02679	.02537	.02408	.02288	.02178	.02077	.01983	.01897	.01817	.01742
20	.02804	.02656	.02519	.02394	.02278	.02172	.02073	.01982	.01898	.01819
21	.02932	.02776	.02633	.02501	.02380	.02268	.02164	.02068	.01979	.01896
22	.03065	.02902	.02751	.02613	.02485	.02367	.02258	.02157	.02063	.01976
23	.03204	.03033	.02876	.02730	.02595	.02471	.02356	.02249	.02150	.02058
24	.03356	.03176	.03010	.02857	.02716	.02585	.02463	.02351	.02246	.02149
25	.03520	.03332	.03158	.02997	.02848	.02710	.02582	.02463	.02352	.02249
26	.03702	.03504	.03321	.03152	.02995	.02850	.02714	.02589	.02472	.02363
27	.03902	.03695	.03502	.03324	.03159	.03006	.02863	.02730	.02607	.02492
28	.04120	.03902	.03700	.03513	.03339	.03178	.03027	.02887	.02757	.02635
29	.04358	.04129	.03917	.03720	.03537	.03367	.03208	.03061	.02923	.02794
30	.04616	.04376	.04154	.03947	.03754	.03575	.03408	.03251	.03106	.02969
31	.04897	.04646	.04413	.04195	.03993	.03804	.03627	.03463	.03309	.03165
32	.05200	.04938	.04693	.04465	.04252	.04053	.03867	.03693	.03531	.03378
33	.05529	.05254	.04998	.04758	.04534	.04325	.04130	.03946	.03775	.03614
34	.05883	.05595	.05326	.05075	.04840	.04620	.04414	.04221	.04040	.03870
35	.06262	.05961	.05680	.05417	.05170	.04939	.04723	.04520	.04329	.04149
36	.06665	.06351	.06057	.05781	.05523	.05280	.05053	.04839	.04638	.04449
37	.07094	.06766	.06459	.06171	.05900	.05646	.05407	.05182	.04971	.04771
38	.07550	.07208	.06888	.06586	.06303	.06037	.05786	.05550	.05327	.05118
39	.08034	.07678	.07344	.07029	.06733	.06454	.06191	.05943	.05709	.05489
40	.08547	.08177	.07828	.07499	.07190	.06898	.06623	.06363	.06118	.05886
41	.09090	.08704	.08341	.07998	.07675	.07371	.07083	.06811	.06553	.06310
42	.09661	.09260	.08882	.08525	.08188	.07870	.07569	.07284	.07015	.06760
43	.10260	.09844	.09451	.09080	.08729	.08397	.08083	.07785	.07503	.07236
44	.10891	.10459	.10051	.09666	.09300	.08954	.08626	.08316	.08021	.07741
45	.11553	.11106	.10683	.10282	.09902	.09542	.09201	.08876	.08568	.08276
46	.12247	.11784	.11346	.10930	.10536	.10161	.09806	.09468	.09146	.08841
47	.12974	.12496	.12042	.11611	.11202	.10813	.10443	.10091	.09756	.09438
48	.13738	.13238	.12769	.12323	.11899	.11495	.11111	.10745	.10397	.10065
49	.14520	.14011	.13526	.13064	.12625	.12207	.11809	.11429	.11066	.10721
50	.15338	.14812	.14312	.13836	.13381	.12948	.12535	.12141	.11765	.11405
51	.16187	.15646	.15130	.14639	.14169	.13721	.13294	.12885	.12495	.12121
52	.17072	.16516	.15985	.15478	.14993	.14531	.14088	.13665	.13261	.12873
53	.17993	.17422	.16876	.16353	.15854	.15377	.14920	.14482	.14064	.13662
54	.18949	.18362	.17801	.17264	.16750	.16258	.15787	.15335	.14902	.14486
55	.19940	.19339	.18763	.18212	.17683	.17176	.16690	.16224	.15777	.15348
56	.20968	.20353	.19762	.19196	.18654	.18132	.17632	.17152	.16691	.16247
57	.22035	.21406	.20802	.20222	.19665	.19129	.18615	.18121	.17646	.17189

Reg. § 1.664-4A(e)(6)

Estates, Trusts, and Beneficiaries

AGE	8.2%	8.4%	8.6%	8.8%	9.0%	9.2%	9.4%	9.6%	9.8%	10.0%
58	.23142	.22499	.21881	.21287	.20717	.20168	.19640	.19132	.18643	.18172
59	.24286	.23630	.23000	.22393	.21809	.21247	.20705	.20184	.19682	.19198
60	.25465	.24797	.24154	.23534	.22938	.22363	.21808	.21274	.20759	.20262
61	.26676	.25996	.25341	.24710	.24101	.23513	.22946	.22399	.21871	.21361
62	.27916	.27225	.26559	.25916	.25295	.24695	.24117	.23557	.23017	.22495
63	.29184	.28483	.27806	.27152	.26520	.25909	.25319	.24748	.24196	.23661
64	.30483	.29772	.29085	.28421	.27779	.27157	.26555	.25973	.25409	.24863
65	.31817	.31098	.30402	.29729	.29076	.28444	.27832	.27240	.26665	.26108
66	.33192	.32466	.31762	.31079	.30418	.29777	.29155	.28552	.27968	.27400
67	.34609	.33876	.33164	.32474	.31805	.31156	.30525	.29913	.29319	.28742
68	.36066	.35328	.34610	.33914	.33238	.32581	.31943	.31323	.30720	.30134
69	.37558	.36815	.36093	.35391	.34709	.34045	.33400	.32773	.32163	.31569
70	.39078	.38332	.37606	.36900	.36213	.35545	.34894	.34260	.33643	.33042
71	.40620	.39872	.39144	.38435	.37744	.37071	.36415	.35776	.35153	.34547
72	.42184	.41435	.40706	.39994	.39301	.38625	.37965	.37322	.36694	.36082
73	.43771	.43023	.42293	.41581	.40886	.40207	.39545	.38899	.38267	.37651
74	.45387	.44641	.43912	.43201	.42505	.41826	.41163	.40514	.39881	.39261
75	.47039	.46296	.45570	.44861	.44167	.43488	.42824	.42175	.41541	.40920
76	.48729	.47991	.47269	.46563	.45872	.45196	.44534	.43886	.43251	.42630
77	.50452	.49722	.49006	.48305	.47619	.46946	.46287	.45642	.45009	.44389
78	.52203	.51481	.50773	.50079	.49399	.48732	.48078	.47437	.46808	.46191
79	.53966	.53254	.52556	.51870	.51198	.50538	.49891	.49255	.48632	.48019
80	.55728	.55028	.54340	.53665	.53002	.52351	.51712	.51083	.50466	.49860
81	.57471	.56784	.56109	.55445	.54792	.54151	.53521	.52901	.52292	.51692
82	.59186	.58512	.57850	.57199	.56558	.55927	.55307	.54697	.54097	.53506
83	.60863	.60204	.59556	.58918	.58289	.57671	.57062	.56462	.55872	.55290
84	.62505	.61862	.61228	.60604	.59989	.59383	.58786	.58198	.57618	.57047
85	.64118	.63491	.62873	.62263	.61663	.61070	.60486	.59911	.59343	.58783
86	.65685	.65075	.64473	.63879	.63294	.62716	.62145	.61583	.61027	.60479
87	.67187	.66594	.66008	.65430	.64859	.64296	.63739	.63190	.62647	.62112
88	.68631	.68054	.67485	.66923	.66367	.65818	.65276	.64740	.64211	.63688
89	.70042	.69483	.68930	.68384	.67845	.67311	.66784	.66262	.65747	.65237
90	.71434	.70894	.70359	.69830	.69307	.68790	.68278	.67772	.67271	.66775
91	.72789	.72266	.71750	.71239	.70733	.70232	.69736	.69246	.68760	.68280
92	.74070	.73567	.73068	.72574	.72085	.71601	.71121	.70647	.70176	.69711
93	.75266	.74780	.74298	.73821	.73348	.72880	.72417	.71957	.71502	.71051
94	.76363	.75893	.75428	.74967	.74510	.74057	.73608	.73163	.72722	.72285
95	.77356	.76901	.76451	.76005	.75562	.75123	.74688	.74257	.73829	.73405
96	.78237	.77797	.77360	.76927	.76497	.76071	.75648	.75229	.74813	.74401
97	.79039	.78612	.78187	.77766	.77348	.76934	.76523	.76115	.75710	.75308
98	.79762	.79345	.78932	.78522	.78115	.77711	.77310	.76913	.76518	.76126
99	.80429	.80023	.79620	.79220	.78823	.78429	.78038	.77649	.77264	.76881
100	.81047	.80651	.80258	.79867	.79479	.79094	.78712	.78332	.77955	.77580
101	.81636	.81249	.80865	.80483	.80104	.79727	.79352	.78981	.78611	.78244
102	.82250	.81872	.81497	.81124	.80754	.80386	.80020	.79656	.79295	.78936
103	.82900	.82532	.82167	.81804	.81442	.81083	.80726	.80371	.80018	.79667
104	.83622	.83266	.82911	.82558	.82207	.81858	.81510	.81165	.80821	.80479
105	.84517	.84174	.83833	.83494	.83156	.82819	.82485	.82151	.81820	.81489
106	.85814	.85494	.85175	.84857	.84540	.84225	.83911	.83598	.83286	.82975
107	.87704	.87420	.87136	.86853	.86571	.86290	.86009	.85729	.85450	.85171
108	.90812	.90593	.90375	.90156	.89939	.89721	.89504	.89286	.89070	.88853
109	.95900	.95800	.95700	.95600	.95500	.95400	.95300	.95200	.95100	.95000

Reg. § 1.664-4A(e)(6)

Estates, Trusts, and Beneficiaries

See p. 20,601 for regulations not amended to reflect law changes

TABLE U(1)
BASED ON LIFE TABLE 80CNSMT
UNITRUST SINGLE LIFE REMAINDER FACTORS
APPLICABLE FOR TRANSFERS AFTER APRIL 30, 1989,
AND BEFORE MAY 1, 1999

ADJUSTED PAYOUT RATE

AGE	10.2%	10.4%	10.6%	10.8%	11.0%	11.2%	11.4%	11.6%	11.8%	12.0%
0	.01754	.01731	.01710	.01690	.01671	.01654	.01638	.01622	.01608	.01594
1	.00630	.00607	.00585	.00565	.00547	.00530	.00514	.00499	.00485	.00472
2	.00604	.00579	.00557	.00536	.00516	.00498	.00481	.00465	.00451	.00437
3	.00604	.00578	.00554	.00532	.00511	.00492	.00474	.00458	.00442	.00427
4	.00621	.00593	.00568	.00544	.00522	.00502	.00483	.00465	.00448	.00433
5	.00648	.00619	.00592	.00567	.00544	.00522	.00502	.00483	.00465	.00449
6	.00684	.00653	.00624	.00597	.00572	.00549	.00528	.00507	.00489	.00471
7	.00726	.00693	.00663	.00634	.00608	.00583	.00560	.00539	.00518	.00499
8	.00777	.00742	.00709	.00679	.00651	.00624	.00600	.00577	.00555	.00535
9	.00837	.00800	.00765	.00733	.00703	.00675	.00649	.00625	.00602	.00580
10	.00908	.00868	.00832	.00797	.00765	.00736	.00708	.00682	.00657	.00634
11	.00991	.00949	.00910	.00874	.00840	.00808	.00779	.00751	.00725	.00700
12	.01083	.01039	.00997	.00959	.00923	.00890	.00858	.00829	.00801	.00775
13	.01181	.01134	.01090	.01049	.01012	.00976	.00943	.00912	.00883	.00855
14	.01275	.01226	.01180	.01137	.01097	.01060	.01025	.00992	.00961	.00932
15	.01365	.01313	.01264	.01219	.01177	.01138	.01101	.01066	.01034	.01003
16	.01449	.01394	.01343	.01295	.01251	.01209	.01171	.01134	.01100	.01068
17	.01526	.01469	.01415	.01365	.01318	.01274	.01233	.01195	.01159	.01125
18	.01600	.01539	.01482	.01430	.01380	.01334	.01291	.01251	.01213	.01177
19	.01673	.01609	.01550	.01494	.01442	.01393	.01348	.01305	.01265	.01227
20	.01747	.01679	.01616	.01557	.01502	.01451	.01403	.01358	.01316	.01276
21	.01820	.01748	.01682	.01620	.01562	.01508	.01457	.01409	.01365	.01323
22	.01895	.01819	.01749	.01683	.01622	.01565	.01511	.01461	.01414	.01369
23	.01972	.01893	.01818	.01749	.01684	.01624	.01567	.01514	.01464	.01417
24	.02058	.01974	.01895	.01822	.01753	.01689	.01629	.01572	.01519	.01469
25	.02154	.02064	.01981	.01903	.01830	.01762	.01698	.01638	.01582	.01529
26	.02262	.02167	.02079	.01996	.01919	.01847	.01779	.01715	.01655	.01599
27	.02385	.02284	.02191	.02103	.02021	.01944	.01872	.01804	.01740	.01680
28	.02521	.02415	.02316	.02222	.02135	.02053	.01977	.01904	.01836	.01772
29	.02673	.02561	.02455	.02357	.02264	.02177	.02095	.02018	.01946	.01877
30	.02842	.02723	.02611	.02506	.02407	.02315	.02227	.02146	.02068	.01996
31	.03030	.02903	.02784	.02673	.02568	.02470	.02377	.02290	.02207	.02130
32	.03235	.03101	.02976	.02857	.02746	.02641	.02543	.02450	.02362	.02279
33	.03463	.03321	.03188	.03062	.02944	.02833	.02728	.02629	.02535	.02447
34	.03711	.03561	.03419	.03286	.03161	.03043	.02931	.02826	.02726	.02632
35	.03981	.03822	.03672	.03531	.03398	.03273	.03154	.03042	.02936	.02836
36	.04271	.04103	.03945	.03796	.03655	.03522	.03396	.03277	.03164	.03057
37	.04584	.04407	.04239	.04081	.03932	.03791	.03657	.03531	.03411	.03297
38	.04920	.04733	.04556	.04389	.04231	.04082	.03940	.03806	.03679	.03558
39	.05280	.05083	.04897	.04721	.04554	.04396	.04246	.04103	.03968	.03840
40	.05667	.05459	.05263	.05077	.04901	.04733	.04575	.04424	.04280	.04144
41	.06080	.05861	.05655	.05459	.05272	.05096	.04928	.04768	.04617	.04472
42	.06518	.06289	.06071	.05864	.05668	.05482	.05305	.05136	.04975	.04822
43	.06982	.06742	.06513	.06296	.06089	.05893	.05706	.05528	.05358	.05196
44	.07475	.07223	.06983	.06754	.06537	.06330	.06133	.05945	.05766	.05595
45	.07998	.07733	.07481	.07242	.07014	.06796	.06588	.06390	.06202	.06021
46	.08550	.08273	.08010	.07758	.07519	.07290	.07072	.06864	.06665	.06474
47	.09134	.08845	.08569	.08306	.08055	.07815	.07586	.07367	.07157	.06957
48	.09748	.09446	.09158	.08882	.08619	.08368	.08128	.07898	.07678	.07467
49	.10391	.10076	.09775	.09487	.09212	.08949	.08697	.08456	.08225	.08003
50	.11062	.10734	.10420	.10120	.09832	.09557	.09293	.09041	.08798	.08566
51	.11764	.11423	.11096	.10783	.10483	.10195	.09919	.09655	.09401	.09158
52	.12503	.12148	.11807	.11481	.11168	.10868	.10581	.10304	.10039	.09784
53	.13278	.12909	.12556	.12216	.11891	.11578	.11278	.10989	.10712	.10445
54	.14088	.13706	.13339	.12986	.12648	.12322	.12009	.11709	.11419	.11141
55	.14936	.14540	.14159	.13793	.13442	.13103	.12778	.12464	.12163	.11872
56	.15821	.15412	.15018	.14639	.14274	.13923	.13584	.13258	.12944	.12642
57	.16749	.16326	.15918	.15526	.15148	.14784	.14433	.14094	.13768	.13453

Reg. § 1.664-4A(e)(6)

Estates, Trusts, and Beneficiaries

See p. 20,601 for regulations not amended to reflect law changes

AGE	10.2%	10.4%	10.6%	10.8%	11.0%	11.2%	11.4%	11.6%	11.8%	12.0%
58	.17719	.17282	.16862	.16456	.16065	.15688	.15324	.14973	.14634	.14306
59	.18731	.18281	.17847	.17429	.17025	.16634	.16258	.15894	.15543	.15203
60	.19782	.19319	.18872	.18440	.18023	.17621	.17231	.16855	.16491	.16139
61	.20869	.20393	.19934	.19489	.19060	.18644	.18242	.17854	.17477	.17113
62	.21990	.21502	.21029	.20573	.20131	.19703	.19289	.18887	.18499	.18123
63	.23144	.22644	.22159	.21690	.21236	.20796	.20370	.19956	.19556	.19167
64	.24335	.23823	.23326	.22845	.22379	.21927	.21489	.21063	.20651	.20250
65	.25568	.25045	.24537	.24044	.23566	.23103	.22653	.22216	.21791	.21379
66	.26850	.26316	.25797	.25293	.24804	.24329	.23868	.23420	.22984	.22560
67	.28182	.27637	.27108	.26594	.26095	.25609	.25137	.24678	.24231	.23797
68	.29565	.29011	.28472	.27949	.27439	.26943	.26461	.25991	.25534	.25089
69	.30991	.30429	.29882	.29349	.28830	.28325	.27833	.27354	.26887	.26432
70	.32457	.31887	.31332	.30791	.30264	.29750	.29249	.28760	.28284	.27820
71	.33955	.33378	.32816	.32267	.31732	.31210	.30701	.30204	.29719	.29246
72	.35485	.34902	.34333	.33778	.33236	.32707	.32190	.31686	.31193	.30711
73	.37049	.36461	.35887	.35326	.34778	.34242	.33719	.33207	.32707	.32218
74	.38656	.38064	.37485	.36920	.36366	.35825	.35296	.34778	.34272	.33776
75	.40312	.39717	.39136	.38566	.38009	.37464	.36930	.36407	.35895	.35394
76	.42022	.41426	.40842	.40271	.39711	.39163	.38625	.38099	.37583	.37077
77	.43782	.43187	.42603	.42031	.41470	.40920	.40380	.39851	.39332	.38823
78	.45586	.44992	.44410	.43839	.43278	.42728	.42188	.41658	.41138	.40627
79	.47418	.46828	.46248	.45679	.45120	.44572	.44033	.43503	.42983	.42472
80	.49264	.48679	.48103	.47538	.46982	.46436	.45900	.45372	.44853	.44343
81	.51103	.50524	.49954	.49394	.48843	.48301	.47768	.47243	.46727	.46219
82	.52925	.52352	.51789	.51235	.50690	.50153	.49624	.49104	.48591	.48087
83	.54718	.54154	.53598	.53051	.52512	.51981	.51459	.50943	.50436	.49936
84	.56484	.55930	.55383	.54844	.54313	.53789	.53273	.52764	.52262	.51767
85	.58231	.57686	.57149	.56619	.56096	.55581	.55072	.54571	.54076	.53588
86	.59939	.59405	.58878	.58358	.57845	.57339	.56839	.56346	.55858	.55377
87	.61583	.61061	.60545	.60035	.59532	.59035	.58545	.58060	.57581	.57108
88	.63171	.62661	.62156	.61658	.61165	.60678	.60196	.59721	.59251	.58786
89	.64733	.64235	.63742	.63255	.62774	.62298	.61827	.61361	.60900	.60444
90	.66285	.65801	.65321	.64847	.64377	.63913	.63453	.62998	.62548	.62103
91	.67804	.67334	.66868	.66407	.65950	.65498	.65050	.64607	.64169	.63735
92	.69250	.68793	.68341	.67893	.67450	.67011	.66575	.66144	.65718	.65295
93	.70604	.70162	.69723	.69288	.68858	.68431	.68008	.67589	.67174	.66762
94	.71852	.71422	.70997	.70575	.70156	.69742	.69331	.68923	.68519	.68119
95	.72984	.72567	.72154	.71744	.71337	.70934	.70534	.70137	.69744	.69354
96	.73992	.73586	.73183	.72784	.72388	.71995	.71605	.71218	.70835	.70454
97	.74910	.74514	.74122	.73733	.73346	.72963	.72582	.72205	.71830	.71458
98	.75737	.75351	.74967	.74587	.74209	.73835	.73463	.73093	.72727	.72363
99	.76501	.76123	.75748	.75376	.75007	.74640	.74276	.73914	.73555	.73198
100	.77208	.76838	.76471	.76107	.75745	.75385	.75028	.74673	.74321	.73971
101	.77879	.77517	.77157	.76800	.76444	.76092	.75741	.75392	.75046	.74702
102	.78579	.78224	.77871	.77521	.77173	.76827	.76483	.76141	.75801	.75463
103	.79318	.78971	.78626	.78283	.77942	.77604	.77266	.76931	.76598	.76267
104	.80139	.79801	.79464	.79129	.78796	.78465	.78136	.77808	.77482	.77157
105	.81161	.80834	.80508	.80184	.79861	.79540	.79220	.78902	.78585	.78270
106	.82665	.82357	.82049	.81743	.81438	.81134	.80831	.80530	.80229	.79930
107	.84893	.84616	.84340	.84064	.83789	.83515	.83241	.82969	.82696	.82425
108	.88637	.88421	.88205	.87989	.87774	.87559	.87344	.87129	.86915	.86701
109	.94900	.94800	.94700	.94600	.94500	.94400	.94300	.94200	.94100	.94000

Reg. § 1.664-4A(e)(6)

Estates, Trusts, and Beneficiaries

See p. 20,601 for regulations not amended to reflect law changes

TABLE U(1)
BASED ON LIFE TABLE 80CNSMT
UNITRUST SINGLE LIFE REMAINDER FACTORS
APPLICABLE FOR TRANSFERS AFTER APRIL 30, 1989,
AND BEFORE MAY 1, 1999

ADJUSTED PAYOUT RATE

AGE	12.2%	12.4%	12.6%	12.8%	13.0%	13.2%	13.4%	13.6%	13.8%	14.0%
0	.01581	.01569	.01557	.01546	.01536	.01526	.01516	.01507	.01499	.01490
1	.00459	.00448	.00437	.00426	.00417	.00407	.00399	.00390	.00382	.00375
2	.00424	.00412	.00400	.00389	.00379	.00369	.00360	.00352	.00343	.00335
3	.00414	.00401	.00389	.00377	.00366	.00356	.00346	.00337	.00328	.00320
4	.00418	.00404	.00391	.00379	.00368	.00357	.00347	.00337	.00327	.00319
5	.00433	.00418	.00405	.00391	.00379	.00368	.00357	.00346	.00336	.00327
6	.00454	.00439	.00424	.00410	.00397	.00384	.00372	.00361	.00351	.00341
7	.00482	.00465	.00449	.00434	.00420	.00407	.00394	.00382	.00371	.00360
8	.00516	.00498	.00481	.00465	.00450	.00436	.00422	.00410	.00397	.00386
9	.00560	.00541	.00523	.00505	.00489	.00474	.00459	.00446	.00433	.00420
10	.00613	.00592	.00573	.00555	.00537	.00521	.00505	.00491	.00477	.00463
11	.00677	.00655	.00635	.00615	.00597	.00580	.00563	.00547	.00532	.00518
12	.00751	.00728	.00706	.00685	.00666	.00647	.00629	.00613	.00597	.00581
13	.00829	.00805	.00782	.00760	.00739	.00719	.00701	.00683	.00666	.00650
14	.00905	.00879	.00854	.00831	.00809	.00789	.00769	.00750	.00732	.00715
15	.00974	.00947	.00921	.00897	.00874	.00852	.00831	.00811	.00793	.00775
16	.01037	.01009	.00982	.00956	.00932	.00909	.00887	.00866	.00846	.00827
17	.01093	.01063	.01034	.01007	.00982	.00958	.00935	.00913	.00892	.00873
18	.01143	.01112	.01082	.01053	.01027	.01001	.00977	.00954	.00933	.00912
19	.01192	.01159	.01127	.01097	.01069	.01043	.01017	.00993	.00970	.00949
20	.01239	.01204	.01170	.01139	.01109	.01081	.01055	.01029	.01005	.00983
21	.01283	.01246	.01211	.01178	.01147	.01117	.01089	.01063	.01037	.01013
22	.01328	.01288	.01251	.01216	.01183	.01152	.01122	.01094	.01067	.01042
23	.01372	.01331	.01292	.01254	.01219	.01186	.01155	.01125	.01097	.01070
24	.01422	.01378	.01336	.01297	.01260	.01225	.01191	.01160	.01130	.01101
25	.01479	.01432	.01388	.01346	.01306	.01269	.01233	.01200	.01168	.01138
26	.01545	.01495	.01448	.01404	.01362	.01322	.01284	.01248	.01214	.01182
27	.01623	.01570	.01520	.01472	.01427	.01385	.01344	.01306	.01270	.01235
28	.01712	.01655	.01601	.01551	.01503	.01457	.01414	.01373	.01334	.01298
29	.01813	.01752	.01695	.01641	.01589	.01541	.01494	.01451	.01409	.01370
30	.01927	.01862	.01801	.01743	.01688	.01635	.01586	.01539	.01495	.01452
31	.02056	.01987	.01922	.01859	.01801	.01745	.01692	.01642	.01594	.01548
32	.02201	.02127	.02057	.01990	.01927	.01868	.01811	.01757	.01706	.01657
33	.02363	.02284	.02209	.02138	.02071	.02007	.01946	.01888	.01833	.01781
34	.02543	.02458	.02378	.02302	.02230	.02162	.02096	.02034	.01975	.01919
35	.02741	.02651	.02565	.02484	.02407	.02333	.02264	.02197	.02134	.02073
36	.02956	.02859	.02768	.02681	.02599	.02520	.02446	.02374	.02307	.02242
37	.03189	.03087	.02990	.02897	.02809	.02725	.02645	.02569	.02496	.02427
38	.03443	.03334	.03230	.03131	.03037	.02948	.02862	.02781	.02703	.02628
39	.03718	.03602	.03491	.03386	.03285	.03190	.03099	.03011	.02928	.02849
40	.04015	.03891	.03774	.03662	.03555	.03453	.03355	.03262	.03173	.03088
41	.04335	.04204	.04079	.03959	.03846	.03737	.03633	.03534	.03439	.03348
42	.04677	.04538	.04405	.04278	.04157	.04042	.03931	.03825	.03724	.03627
43	.05042	.04894	.04754	.04619	.04491	.04368	.04250	.04138	.04030	.03926
44	.05432	.05276	.05127	.04984	.04848	.04718	.04593	.04473	.04358	.04248
45	.05849	.05684	.05526	.05375	.05231	.05092	.04960	.04832	.04710	.04593
46	.06292	.06118	.05952	.05792	.05639	.05492	.05352	.05217	.05087	.04963
47	.06765	.06581	.06405	.06237	.06075	.05920	.05771	.05628	.05491	.05359
48	.07265	.07071	.06886	.06708	.06537	.06373	.06216	.06064	.05919	.05779
49	.07791	.07587	.07392	.07204	.07024	.06851	.06685	.06525	.06371	.06223
50	.08343	.08129	.07923	.07726	.07536	.07354	.07178	.07009	.06847	.06690
51	.08924	.08699	.08483	.08276	.08076	.07884	.07699	.07520	.07349	.07183
52	.09539	.09303	.09076	.08858	.08648	.08446	.08251	.08064	.07883	.07708
53	.10189	.09942	.09704	.09475	.09255	.09043	.08838	.08640	.08450	.08266
54	.10872	.10614	.10365	.10126	.09894	.09672	.09456	.09249	.09049	.08855
55	.11592	.11322	.11062	.10811	.10569	.10335	.10110	.09892	.09682	.09478
56	.12350	.12068	.11796	.11534	.11281	.11036	.10800	.10571	.10350	.10137
57	.13148	.12855	.12572	.12298	.12033	.11777	.11530	.11291	.11060	.10836

Reg. § 1.664-4A(e)(6)

AGE	12.2%	12.4%	12.6%	12.8%	13.0%	13.2%	13.4%	13.6%	13.8%	14.0%
58	.13990	.13685	.13389	.13104	.12828	.12561	.12303	.12053	.11811	.11576
59	.14875	.14557	.14250	.13953	.13665	.13387	.13118	.12856	.12604	.12359
60	.15799	.15469	.15150	.14841	.14542	.14253	.13972	.13700	.13436	.13180
61	.16761	.16419	.16088	.15768	.15457	.15156	.14864	.14580	.14305	.14039
62	.17758	.17404	.17062	.16729	.16407	.16094	.15791	.15496	.15210	.14932
63	.18791	.18425	.18071	.17726	.17392	.17068	.16753	.16447	.16150	.15861
64	.19862	.19484	.19118	.18762	.18417	.18081	.17754	.17437	.17129	.16829
65	.20979	.20590	.20212	.19845	.19487	.19140	.18802	.18474	.18154	.17843
66	.22149	.21748	.21359	.20980	.20612	.20253	.19904	.19564	.19233	.18911
67	.23374	.22962	.22562	.22172	.21792	.21423	.21062	.20712	.20370	.20037
68	.24656	.24234	.23822	.23422	.23031	.22651	.22280	.21919	.21566	.21222
69	.25988	.25556	.25134	.24724	.24323	.23932	.23551	.23179	.22816	.22461
70	.27367	.26925	.26493	.26073	.25662	.25261	.24870	.24488	.24115	.23750
71	.28784	.28333	.27892	.27462	.27042	.26631	.26230	.25839	.25456	.25082
72	.30241	.29781	.29332	.28893	.28464	.28044	.27634	.27233	.26841	.26457
73	.31740	.31272	.30815	.30368	.29930	.29502	.29084	.28674	.28273	.27880
74	.33291	.32817	.32352	.31897	.31452	.31016	.30589	.30171	.29762	.29361
75	.34903	.34422	.33951	.33490	.33038	.32595	.32161	.31735	.31318	.30909
76	.36581	.36095	.35619	.35152	.34694	.34245	.33805	.33373	.32949	.32533
77	.38324	.37835	.37354	.36883	.36420	.35966	.35520	.35083	.34654	.34232
78	.40126	.39634	.39150	.38676	.38210	.37752	.37302	.36861	.36427	.36001
79	.41970	.41476	.40992	.40515	.40047	.39587	.39135	.38690	.38253	.37823
80	.43842	.43348	.42864	.42387	.41918	.41456	.41002	.40556	.40117	.39685
81	.45719	.45228	.44744	.44267	.43799	.43337	.42883	.42436	.41996	.41562
82	.47590	.47101	.46619	.46145	.45677	.45217	.44764	.44317	.43877	.43443
83	.49443	.48957	.48478	.48007	.47542	.47084	.46632	.46187	.45748	.45315
84	.51279	.50798	.50324	.49856	.49394	.48939	.48490	.48048	.47611	.47180
85	.53106	.52630	.52161	.51698	.51241	.50790	.50345	.49906	.49473	.49045
86	.54902	.54434	.53971	.53514	.53062	.52616	.52176	.51741	.51312	.50888
87	.56640	.56178	.55722	.55271	.54826	.54386	.53951	.53521	.53097	.52677
88	.58326	.57872	.57423	.56979	.56541	.56107	.55678	.55254	.54834	.54420
89	.59994	.59548	.59107	.58671	.58240	.57813	.57391	.56973	.56560	.56152
90	.61662	.61226	.60794	.60367	.59944	.59526	.59112	.58702	.58296	.57894
91	.63305	.62879	.62457	.62040	.61627	.61217	.60812	.60411	.60013	.59619
92	.64876	.64461	.64050	.63643	.63239	.62839	.62443	.62051	.61662	.61277
93	.66355	.65950	.65550	.65153	.64759	.64369	.63983	.63600	.63220	.62843
94	.67722	.67328	.66938	.66551	.66167	.65786	.65409	.65035	.64664	.64296
95	.68967	.68583	.68203	.67825	.67451	.67079	.66711	.66345	.65983	.65623
96	.70076	.69701	.69330	.68961	.68595	.68231	.67871	.67513	.67158	.66806
97	.71089	.70722	.70359	.69998	.69640	.69284	.68931	.68581	.68234	.67888
98	.72001	.71642	.71286	.70933	.70582	.70233	.69887	.69544	.69203	.68864
99	.72844	.72492	.72143	.71796	.71452	.71110	.70770	.70433	.70098	.69765
100	.73623	.73278	.72935	.72594	.72256	.71920	.71586	.71254	.70924	.70597
101	.74361	.74021	.73684	.73349	.73016	.72685	.72356	.72029	.71704	.71382
102	.75128	.74794	.74463	.74133	.73806	.73480	.73157	.72835	.72515	.72198
103	.75938	.75610	.75284	.74961	.74639	.74319	.74000	.73684	.73369	.73056
104	.76835	.76514	.76194	.75877	.75561	.75246	.74934	.74623	.74313	.74005
105	.77956	.77643	.77332	.77023	.76714	.76408	.76102	.75798	.75496	.75195
106	.79632	.79334	.79038	.78743	.78449	.78157	.77865	.77575	.77285	.76997
107	.82154	.81884	.81615	.81346	.81079	.80811	.80545	.80279	.80014	.79750
108	.86487	.86274	.86061	.85848	.85635	.85423	.85210	.84998	.84787	.84575
109	.93900	.93800	.93700	.93600	.93500	.93400	.93300	.93200	.93100	.93000

[Reg. § 1.664-4A.]

☐ [T.D. 8540, 6-9-94. Amended by T.D. 8819, 4-29-99 and T.D. 8886, 6-9-2000.]

[Reg. § 1.665(a)-0A]

§ 1.665(a)-0A. Excess distributions by trusts; scope of subpart D.—(a) *In general.* (1) Subpart D (section 665 and following), part I, subchapter J, chapter 1 of the Code, as amended by the Tax Reform Act of 1969, is designed to tax the beneficiary of a trust that accumulates, rather than distributes, all or part of its income currently (i.e., an accumulation trust), in most cases, as if the income had been currently distributed to the beneficiary instead of accumulated by the trust. Accordingly, subpart D provides special rules for the treatment of amounts paid, credited, or required to be distributed by a complex trust (one that is subject to subpart C (section 661 and following) of such part I) in any year in excess of "distributable net income" (as defined in section 643(a)) for that year. Such an excess distribution

Reg. § 1.665(a)-0A(a)

is an "accumulation distribution" (as defined in section 665(b)). The special rules of subpart D are generally inapplicable to amounts paid, credited, or required to be distributed by a trust in a taxable year in which it qualifies as a simple trust (one that is subject to subpart B (section 651 and following) of such part I). However, see § 1.665(e)-1A(b) for rules relating to the treatment of a simple trust as a complex trust.

(2) An accumulation distribution is deemed to consist of, first, "undistributed net income" (as defined in section 665(a)) of the trust from preceding taxable years, and, after all the undistributed net income for all preceding taxable years has been deemed distributed, "undistributed capital gain" (as defined in section 665(f)) of the trust for all preceding taxable years commencing with the first year such amounts were accumulated. An accumulation distribution of undistributed capital gain is a "capital gain distribution" (as defined in section 665(g)). To the extent an accumulation distribution exceeds the "undistributed net income" and "undistributed capital gain" so determined, it is deemed to consist of corpus.

(3) The accumulation distribution is "thrown back" to the earliest "preceding taxable year" of the trust, which, in the case of distributions made for a taxable year beginning after December 31, 1973, from a trust (other than a foreign trust created by a United States person), is any taxable year beginning after December 31, 1968. Special transitional rules apply for distributions made in taxable years beginning before January 1, 1974. In the case of a foreign trust created by a United States person, a "preceding taxable year" is any year of the trust to which the Code applies.

(4) A distribution of undistributed net income (included in an accumulation distribution) and a capital gain distribution will be included in the income of the beneficiary in the year they are actually paid, credited, or required to be distributed to him. The tax on the distribution will be approximately the amount of tax the beneficiary would have paid with respect to the distribution had the income and capital gain been distributed to the beneficiary in the year earned by the trust. An additional amount equal to the "taxes imposed on the trust" for the preceding year is also deemed distributed. To prevent double taxation, however, the beneficiary receives a credit for such taxes.

(b) *Effective dates.* All regulations sections under subpart D (sections 665 through 669) which have an "A" suffix (such as § § 1.665(a)A and 1.666(b)-1A) are applicable to taxable years beginning on or after January 1, 1969, and all references therein to sections 665 through 669 are references to such sections as amended by the Tax Reform Act of 1969. Sections without the "A" suffix (such as § § 1.665(a) and 1.666(b)-1) are applicable only to taxable years beginning before January 1, 1969, and all references therein to sections 665 through 669 are references to such sections before amendment by the Tax Reform Act of 1969.

(c) *Examples.* Where examples contained in the regulations under subpart D refer to tax rates for years after 1968, such tax rates are not necessarily the actual rates for such years, but are only used for example purposes.

(d) *Applicability to estates.* Subpart D does not apply to any estate. [Reg. § 1.665(a)-0A].

☐ [T.D. 7204, 8-24-72.]

[Reg. § 1.665(a)-1A]

§ 1.665(a)-1A. **Undistributed net income.**—(a) *Domestic trusts.* The term "undistributed net income", in the case of a trust (other than a foreign trust created by a U.S. person) means, for any taxable year beginning after December 31, 1968, the distributable net income of the trust for that year (as determined under section 643(a)), less:

(1) The amount of income required to be distributed currently and any other amounts properly paid or credited or required to be distributed to beneficiaries in the taxable year as specified in section 661(a), and

(2) The amount of taxes imposed on the trust allocable to such distributable net income, as defined in § 1.665(d)-1A.

The application of the rule in this paragraph to a taxable year of a trust in which income is accumulated may be illustrated by the following example:

Example. Under the terms of the trust, $10,000 of income is required to be distributed currently to A and the trustee has discretion to make additional distributions to A. During the taxable year 1971 the trust had distributable net income of $30,100 derived from royalties and the trustee made distributions of $20,000 to A. The taxable income of the trust is $10,000 on which a tax of $2,190 is paid. The undistributed net income of the trust for the taxable year 1971 is $7,910, computed as follows:

Distributable net income	$30,100
Less:	
Income currently distributable to A	$10,000
Other amounts distributed to A	10,000

Estates, Trusts, and Beneficiaries

See p. 20,601 for regulations not amended to reflect law changes

Taxes imposed on the trust attributable to the undistributed net income (see § 1.665(d)-1A)	2,190	
		22,190
Undistributed net income		7,910

(b) *Foreign trusts.* The undistributed net income of a foreign trust created by a U.S. person for any taxable year is the distributable net income of such trust (see § 1.643(a)-6 and the examples set forth in paragraph (b) thereof), less:

(1) The amount of income required to be distributed currently and any other amounts properly paid or credited or required to be distributed to beneficiaries in the taxable year as specified in section 661(a), and

(2) The amount of taxes imposed on such trust by chapter 1 of the Internal Revenue Code, which are attributable to items of income which are required to be included in such distributable net income.

For purposes of subparagraph (2) of this paragraph, the amount of taxes imposed on the trust for any taxable year by chapter 1 of the Internal Revenue Code is the amount of taxes imposed pursuant to section 871 (relating to tax on nonresident alien individuals) which is properly allocable to the undistributed portion of the distributable net income. See § 1.665(d)-1A. The amount of taxes imposed pursuant to section 871 is the difference between the total tax imposed pursuant to that section on the foreign trust created by a U.S. person for the year and the amount which would have been imposed on such trust had all the distributable net income, as determined under section 643(a), been distributed. The application of the rule in this paragraph may be illustrated by the following examples:

Example (1). A trust was created in 1952 under the laws of Country X by the transfer to a trustee in Country X of property by U.S. person. The entire trust constitutes a foreign trust created by a U.S. person. The governing instrument of the trust provides that $7,000 of income is required to be distributed currently to a U.S. beneficiary and gives the trustee discretion to make additional distributions to the beneficiary. During the taxable year 1973 the trust had income of $10,000 from dividends of a U.S. corporation (on which Federal income taxes of $3,000 were imposed pursuant to section 871 and withheld under section 1441, resulting in the receipt by the trust of cash in the amount of $7,000), $20,000 in capital gains from the sale of stock of a Country Y corporation and $30,000 from dividends of a Country X corporation, none of the gross income of which was derived from sources within the United States. No income taxes were required to be paid to Country X or Country Y in 1973. The trustee did not file a U.S. income tax return for the taxable year 1973. The distributable net income of the trust before distributions to the beneficiary for 1973 is $60,000 ($57,000 of which is cash). During 1973 the trustee made distributions to the U.S. beneficiary equaling one-half of the trust's distributable net income. Thus, the U.S. beneficiary is treated as having had distributed to him $5,000 (composed of $3,500 as a cash distribution and $1,500 as the tax imposed pursuant to section 871 and withheld under section 1441), representing one-half of the income from U.S. sources; $10,000 in cash, representing one-half of the capital gains from the sale of stock of the Country Y corporation; and $15,000 in cash, representing one-half of the income from Country X sources for a total of $30,000. The undistributed net income of the trust at the close of taxable year 1973 is $28,500 computed as follows:

Distributable net income		$60,000
Less:		
(1) Amounts distributed to the beneficiary		
Income currently distributed to the beneficiary	$7,000	
Other amounts distributed to the beneficiary	21,500	
Taxes under sec. 871 deemed distributed to the beneficiary	1,500	
Total amounts distributed to the beneficiary	30,000	
(2) Amount of taxes imposed on the trust under chapter 1 of the Code attributable to the undistributed net income (See § 1.665(d)-1A) ($3,000 less $1,500)	1,500	
Total		31,500
Undistributed net income		28,500

Example (2). The facts are the same as in example (1) except that property has been transferred to the trust by a person other than a U.S. person, and during 1973 the foreign trust created by a U.S. person was 60 percent of the entire foreign trust. The trustee paid no income taxes to Country X or Country Y in 1973.

(1) The undistributed net income of the portion of the entire trust which is a foreign trust

Reg. § 1.665(a)-1A(b)(2)

created by a U.S. person for 1973 is $17,100, computed as follows:

Distributable net income (60% of each item of gross income of entire trust):
60% of $10,000 U.S. dividends	$ 6,000
60% of $20,000 Country X capital gains	12,000
60% of $30,000 Country X dividends	18,000
Total	36,000

Less:
(i) Amounts distributed to the beneficiary—
Income currently distributed to the beneficiary (60% of $7,000)	$ 4,200	
Other amounts distributed to the beneficiary (60% of $21,500)	12,900	
Taxes under sec. 871 deemed distributed to the beneficiary (60% of $1,500)	900	
Total amounts distributed to the beneficiary	18,000	
(ii) Amount of taxes imposed on the trust under chapter 1 of the Code attributable to the undistributed net income (See § 1.665(d)-1A) (60% of $1,500)	$ 900	
Total		$18,900
Undistributed net income		17,100

(2) The undistributed net income of the portion of the entire trust which is not a foreign trust created by a U.S. person for 1973 is $11,400, computed as follows:

Distributable net income (40% of each item of gross income of entire trust)
40% of $10,000 U.S. dividends	$ 4,000
40% of $30,000 Country X dividends	12,000
Total	24,000

Less:
(i) Amounts distributed to the beneficiary—
Income currently distributed to the beneficiary (40% of $7,000)	$ 2,800	
Other amounts distributed to the beneficiary (40% of $21,500)	8,600	
Taxes under sec. 871 deemed distributed to the beneficiary (40% of $1,500)	600	
Total amounts distributed to the beneficiary	12,000	
(ii) Amount of taxes imposed on the trust under chapter 1 of the Code attributable to the undistributed net income (See § 1.665(d)-1A) (40% of $1,500)	$ 600	
Total		$12,600
Undistributed net income		11,400

(c) *Effect of prior distributions.* The undistributed net income for any year to which an accumulation distribution for a later year may be thrown back will be reduced by accumulation distributions in intervening years that are required to be thrown back to such year. For example, if a trust has undistributed net income for 1975, and an accumulation distribution is made in 1980, there must be taken into account the effect on undistributed net income for 1975 of any accumulation distribution made in 1976, 1977, 1978, or 1979. However, undistributed net income for any year will not be reduced by any distributions in intervening years that are excluded under section 663(a)(1), relating to gifts, bequests, etc. See paragraph (d) of § 1.666(a)-1A for an illustration of the reduction of undistributed net income for any year by a subsequent accumulation distribution.

(d) *Distributions made in taxable years beginning before January 1, 1974.* For special rules relating to accumulation distributions of undistributed net income made in taxable years of the trust beginning before January 1, 1974, see § 1.665(b)-2A. [Reg. § 1.665(a)-1A.]

☐ [T.D. 7204, 8-24-72.]

[Reg. § 1.665(b)-1A]

§ 1.665(b)-1A. **Accumulation distributions.**—(a) *In general.*—(1) For any taxable year of a trust the term "accumulation distribution" means an amount by which the amounts properly paid, credited, or required to be distributed within

Reg. § 1.665(b)-1A(a)(1)

the meaning of section 661(a)(2) (*i.e.*, all amounts properly paid, credited, or required to be distributed to the beneficiary other than income required to be distributed currently within the meaning of section 661(a)(1)) for that year exceed the distributable net income (determined under section 643(a)) of the trust, reduced (but not below zero) by the amount of income required to be distributed currently. To the extent provided in section 663(b) and the regulations thereunder, distributions made within the first 65 days following a taxable year may be treated as having been distributed on the last day of such taxable year.

(2) An accumulation distribution also includes, for a taxable year of the trust, any amount to which section 661(a)(2) and the preceding paragraph are inapplicable and which is paid, credited, or required to be distributed during the taxable year of the trust by reason of the exercise of a power to appoint, distribute, consume, or withdraw corpus of the trust or income of the trust accumulated in a preceding taxable year. No accumulation distribution is deemed to be made solely because the grantor or any other person is treated as owner of a portion of the trust by reason of an unexercised power to appoint, distribute, consume, or withdraw corpus or accumulated income of the trust. Nor will an accumulation distribution be deemed to have been made by reason of the exercise of a power that may affect only taxable income previously attributed to the holders of such power under subpart E (section 671 and following). See example 4 of paragraph (d) of this section for an example of an accumulation distribution occurring as a result of the exercise of a power of withdrawal.

(3) Although amounts properly paid or credited under section 661(a) do not exceed the income of the trust during the taxable year, an accumulation distribution may result if the amounts properly paid or credited under section 661(a)(2) exceed distributable net income reduced (but not below zero) by the amount required to be distributed currently under section 661(a)(1). This may occur, for example, when expenses, interest, taxes, or other items allocable to corpus are taken into account in determining taxable income and hence causing distributable net income to be less than the trust's income.

(b) *Payments that are accumulation distributions.* The following are some instances in which an accumulation distribution may arise:

(1) *One trust to another.* A distribution from one trust to another trust is generally an accumulation distribution. See § 1.643(c)-1. This general rule will apply regardless of whether the distribution is to an existing trust or to a newly created trust and regardless of whether the trust to which the distribution is made was created by the same person who created the trust from which the distribution is made or a different person. However, a distribution made from one trust to a second trust will be deemed an accumulation distribution by the first trust to an ultimate beneficiary of the second trust if the primary purpose of the distribution to the second trust is to avoid the capital gain distribution provisions (see section 669 and the regulations thereunder). An amount passing from one separate share of a trust to another separate share of the same trust is not an accumulation distribution. See § 1.665(g)-2A. For rules relating to the computation of the beneficiary's tax under section 668 by reason of an accumulation distribution from the second trust, see paragraphs (b)(1) and (c)(1)(i) of § 1.668(b)-1A and paragraphs (b)(1) and (c)(1)(i) of § 1.669(b)-1A.

(2) *Income accumulated during minority.* A distribution of income accumulated during the minority of the beneficiary is generally an accumulation distribution. For example, if a trust accumulates income until the beneficiary's 21st birthday, and then distributes the income to the beneficiary, such a distribution is an accumulation distribution. However, see § 1.665(b)-2A for rules governing income accumulated in taxable years beginning before January 1, 1969.

(3) *Amounts paid for support.* To the extent that amounts forming all or part of an accumulation distribution are applied or distributed for the support of a dependent under the circumstances specified in section 677(b) or section 678(c) or are used to discharge or satisfy any person's legal obligation as that term is used in § 1.662(a)-4, such amounts will be considered as having been distributed directly to the person whose obligation is being satisfied.

(c) *Payments which are not accumulation distributions*—(1) *Gifts, bequests, etc., described in section 663(a)(1).* A gift or bequest of a specific sum of money or of specific property described in section 663(a)(1) is not an accumulation distribution.

(2) *Charitable payments.* Any amount paid, permanently set aside, or used for the purposes specified in section 642(c) is not an accumulation distribution, even though no charitable deduction is allowed under such section with respect to such payment.

(3) *Income required to be distributed currently.* No accumulation distribution will arise by reason of a payment of income required to be distributed currently even though such income exceeds the distributable net income of the trust

because the payment is an amount specified in section 661(a)(1).

(d) *Examples.* The provisions of this section may be illustrated by the following examples:

Example (1). A trustee properly makes a distribution to a beneficiary of $20,000 during the taxable year 1976, of which $10,000 is income required to be distributed currently to the beneficiary. The distributable net income of the trust is $15,000. There is an accumulation distribution of $5,000 computed as follows.

Total distribution		$20,000
Less: Income required to be distributed currently (section 661(a)(1))		10,000
Other amounts distributed (section 661(a)(2))		10,000
Distributable net income	$15,000	
Less: Income required to be distributed currently	10,000	
Balance of distributable net income		5,000
Accumulation distribution		5,000

Example (2). Under the terms of the trust instrument, an annuity of $15,000 is required to be paid to A out of income each year and the trustee may in his discretion make distributions out of income or corpus to B. During the taxable year the trust had income of $18,000, as defined in section 643(b), and expenses allocable to corpus of $5,000. Distributable net income amounted to $13,000. The trustee distributed $15,000 of income to A and, in the exercise of his discretion, paid $5,000 to B. There is an accumulation distribution of $5,000 computed as follows:

Total distribution		$20,000
Less: Income required to be distributed currently to A (section 661(a)(1))		15,000
Other amounts distributed (section 661(a)(2))		5,000
Distributable net income	$13,000	
Less: Income required to be distributed currently to A	15,000	
Balance of distributable net income		$ 0
Accumulation distribution to B		5,000

Example (3). Under the terms of a trust instrument, the trustee may either accumulate the trust income or make distributions to A and B. The trustee may also invade corpus for the benefit of A and B. During the taxable year, the trust had income as defined in section 643(b) of $22,000 and expenses of $5,000 allocable to corpus. Distributable net income amounts to $17,000. The trustee distributed $10,000 each to A and B during the taxable year. There is an accumulation distribution of $3,000 computed as follows:

Total distribution		$20,000
Less: Income required to be distributed currently		0
Other amounts distributed (section 661(a)(2))		20,000
Distributable net income	$17,000	
Less: Income required to be distributed currently	0	
Balance of distributable net income		17,000
Accumulation distribution		3,000

Example (4). A dies in 1974 and bequeaths one-half the residue of his estate in trust. His widow, W, is given a power, exercisable solely by her, to require the trustee to pay her each year of the trust $5,000 from corpus. W's right to exercise such power was exercisable at any time during the year but was not cumulative, so that, upon her failure to exercise it before the end of any taxable year of the trust, her right as to that year lapsed. The trust's taxable year is the calendar year. During the calendar years 1975 and 1976, W did not exercise her right and it lapsed as to those years. In the calendar years 1977 and 1978, in which years the trust had no distributable net income, she exercised her right and withdrew $4,000 in 1977 and $5,000 in 1978. No accumulation distribution was made by the trust in the calendar years 1975 and 1976. An accumulation distribution of $4,000 was made in 1977 and an accumulation distribution of $5,000 was made in

Reg. § 1.665(b)-1A(d)

1978. The accumulation distribution for the years 1977 and 1978 is not reduced by any amount of income of the trust attributable to her under section 678 by reason of her power of withdrawal. [Reg. § 1.665(b)-1A.]

☐ [T.D. 7204, 8-24-72.]

[Reg. § 1.665(b)-2A]

§ 1.665(b)-2A. **Special rules for accumulation distributions made in taxable years beginning before January 1, 1974.**—(a) *General rule.* Section 331(d)(2)(A) of the Tax Reform Act of 1969 excludes certain accumulated income from the tax imposed by section 668(a)(2) by providing certain exceptions from the definition of an "accumulation distribution". Any amount paid, credited, or required to be distributed by a trust (other than a foreign trust created by a U.S. person) during a taxable year of the trust beginning after December 31, 1968, and before January 1, 1974, shall not be subject to the tax imposed by section 668(a)(2) to the extent of the portion of such amount that (1) would be allocated under section 666(a) to a preceding taxable year of the trust beginning before January 1, 1969, and (2) would not have been deemed an accumulation distribution because of the provisions of paragraphs (1), (2), (3), or (4) of section 665(b) as in effect on December 31, 1968, had the trust distributed such amounts on the last day of its last taxable year beginning before January 1, 1969. However, the $2,000 *de minimis* exception formerly in section 665(b) does not apply in the case of any distribution made in a taxable year of a trust beginning after December 31, 1968. Amounts to which this exclusion applies shall reduce the undistributed net income of the trust for the preceding taxable year or years to which such amounts would be allocated under section 666(a). However, since section 668(a)(2) does not apply to such amounts, no amount of taxes imposed on the trust allocable to such undistributed net income is deemed distributed under section 666(b) and (c).

(b) *Application of general rule.* The rule expressed in paragraph (a) of this section is applied to the exceptions formerly in section 665(b) as follows:

(1) *Distributions from amounts accumulated while beneficiary is under 21.* (i) Paragraph (1) of section 665(b) as in effect on December 31, 1968, provided that amounts paid, credited, or required to be distributed to a beneficiary as income accumulated before the birth of such beneficiary or before such beneficiary attains the age of 21 were not to be considered to be accumulation distributions. If an accumulation distribution is made in a taxable year of the trust beginning after December 31, 1968, and before January 1, 1974, and under section 666(a) such accumulation distribution would be allocated to a preceding taxable year beginning before January 1, 1969, no tax shall be imposed under section 668(a)(2) to the extent the income earned by the trust for such preceding taxable year would be deemed under § 1.665(b)-2(b)(1) to have been accumulated before the beneficiary's birth or before his 21st birthday. The provisions of this subparagraph may be illustrated by the following example:

Example. A trust on the calendar year basis was established on January 1, 1965, to accumulate the income during the minority of B, and to pay the accumulated income over to B upon his attaining the age of 21. B's 21st birthday is January 1, 1973. On January 2, 1973, the trustee pays over to B all the accumulated income of the trust. The distribution is an accumulation distribution that may be allocated under section 666(a) to 1968, 1969, 1970, 1971, and 1972 (the five preceding taxable years as defined in § 1.665(e)-1A). To the extent the distribution is allocated to 1968, no tax is imposed under section 668(a)(2).

(ii) As indicated in paragraph (a), a distribution of an amount excepted from the tax otherwise imposed under section 668(a)(2) will reduce undistributed net income for the purpose of determining the effect of a future distribution. Thus, under the facts of the example in subdivision (i) of this paragraph, the undistributed net income for the trust's taxable year 1968 would be reduced by the amount of the distribution allocated to that year under section 666(a).

(2) *Emergency distributions.* Paragraph (2) of section 665(b) as in effect on December 31, 1968, provided an exclusion from the definition of an accumulation distribution for amounts properly paid or credited to a beneficiary to meet his emergency needs. Therefore, if an accumulation distribution is made from a trust in a taxable year beginning before January 1, 1974, and under section 666(a) such accumulation distribution would be allocated to a preceding taxable year of the trust beginning before January 1, 1969, no tax shall be imposed under section 668(a)(2) if such distribution would have been considered an emergency distribution under § 1.665(b)-2(b)(2) had it been made in a taxable year of the trust beginning before January 1, 1969. For example, assume a trust on a calendar year basis in 1972 makes an accumulation distribution which under § 1.665(b)-2(b)(2) would be considered an emergency distribution and under section 666(a) the distribution would be allocated to the years 1967, 1968, and 1969. To the extent such amount is allocated to 1967 and 1968, no tax would be imposed under section 668(a)(2).

(3) *Certain distributions at specified ages.* Paragraph (3) of section 665(b) as in effect on December 31, 1968, provided an exclusion (in the case of certain trusts created before January 1, 1954) from the definition of an accumulation distribution for amounts properly paid or credited to a beneficiary upon his attaining a specified age or ages, subject to certain restrictions (see § 1.665(b)-2(b)(3)). Therefore, a distribution from a trust in a taxable year beginning after December 31, 1968, will not be subject to the tax imposed under section 668(a)(2) to the extent such distribution would be allocated to a preceding taxable year of the trust beginning before January 1, 1969, if such distribution would have qualified under the provisions of § 1.665(b)-2(b)(3) had it been made in a taxable year of the trust to which such section was applicable.

(4) *Certain final distributions.* Paragraph (4) of section 665(b) as in effect on December 31, 1968, provided an exclusion from the definition of an accumulation distribution for amounts properly paid or credited to a beneficiary as a final distribution of the trust if such final distribution was made more than 9 years after the date of the last transfer to such trust. Therefore, amounts properly paid or credited to a beneficiary as a final distribution of a trust in a taxable year of the trust beginning after December 31, 1968, and before January 1, 1974, will not be subject to the tax imposed under section 668(a)(2) to the extent such distribution would be allocated to a preceding taxable year of the trust beginning before January 1, 1969, if such final distribution was made more than 9 years after the date of the last transfer to such trust. The provisions of this subparagraph may be illustrated by the following example:

Example. A trust on a calendar year basis was established on January 1, 1958, and no additional transfers were made to it. On January 1, 1973, the trustee terminates the trust and on the same day he makes a final distribution to the beneficiary, B. The distribution is an accumulation distribution that may be allocated under section 666(a) to 1968, 1969, 1970, 1971, and 1972 (the 5 preceding taxable years as defined in § 1.665(e)-1A). Because more than 9 years elapsed between the date of the last transfer to the trust and the date of final distribution, the distribution is not taxed under section 668(a)(2) to the extent it would be allocated to 1968 under section 666(a). [Reg. § 1.665(b)-2A.]

☐ [*T.D.* 7204, 8-24-72.]

Reg. § 1.665(c)-1A(a)

[Reg. § 1.665(c)-1A]

§ 1.665(c)-1A. **Special rule applicable to distributions by certain foreign trusts.**—(a) *In general.* Except as provided in paragraph (b) of this section, for purposes of section 665 any amount paid to a U.S. person which is from a payor who is not a U.S. person and which is derived directly or indirectly from a foreign trust created by a U.S. person shall be deemed in the year of payment to the U.S. person to have been directly paid to the U.S. person by the trust. For example, if a nonresident alien receives a distribution from a foreign trust created by a U.S. person and then pays the amount of the distribution over to a U.S. person, the payment of such amount to the U.S. person represents an accumulation distribution to the U.S. person from the trust to the extent that the amount received would have been an accumulation distribution had the trust paid the amount directly to the U.S. person in the year in which the payment was received by the U.S. person. This section also applies in a case where a nonresident alien receives indirectly an accumulation distribution from a foreign trust created by a U.S. person and then pays it over to a U.S. person. An example of such a transaction is one where the foreign trust created by a U.S. person makes the distribution to an intervening foreign trust created by either a U.S. person or a person other than a U.S. person and the intervening trust distributes the amount received to a nonresident alien who in turn pays it over to a U.S. person. Under these circumstances, it is deemed that the payment received by the U.S. person was received directly from a foreign trust created by a U.S. person.

(b) *Limitation.* In the case of a distribution to a beneficiary who is a U.S. person, paragraph (a) of this section does not apply if the distribution is received by such beneficiary under circumstances indicating lack of intent on the part of the parties to circumvent the purposes for which section 7 of the Revenue Act of 1962 (76 Stat. 985) was enacted. [Reg. § 1.665(c)-1A.]

☐ [*T.D.* 7204, 8-24-72.]

[Reg. § 1.665(d)-1A]

§ 1.665(d)-1A. **Taxes imposed on the trust.**—(a) *In general.* (1) For the purpose of subpart D, the term "taxes imposed on the trust" means the amount of Federal income taxes properly imposed for any taxable year on the trust that are attributable to the undistributed portions of distributable net income and gains in excess of losses from the sales or exchanges of capital assets. Except as provided in paragraph (c)(2) of this section, the minimum tax for tax preferences imposed by section 56 is not a tax attributable to the undistributed portions of distributable net income and gains in excess of losses from the sales or exchanges of capital assets. See section 56 and the regulations thereunder.

(2) In the case of a trust that has received an accumulation distribution from another trust, the term "taxes imposed on the trust" also includes the amount of taxes deemed distributed under §§ 1.666(b)-1A, 1.666(c)-1A, 1.669(d)-1A, and 1.669(e)-1A (whichever are applicable) as a result of such accumulation distribution, to the extent that they were taken into account under paragraphs (b)(2) or (c)(1)(vi) of § 1.668(b)-1A and (b)(2) or (c)(1)(vi) of § 1.669(b)-1A in computing the partial tax on such accumulation distribution. For example, assume that trust A, a calendar year trust, makes an accumulation distribution in 1975 to trust B, also on the calendar year basis, in connection with which $500 of taxes are deemed under § 1.666(b)-1A to be distributed to trust B. The partial tax on the accumulation distribution is computed under paragraph (b) of § 1.668(b)-1A (the exact method) to be $600 and all of the $500 is used under paragraph (b)(2) of § 1.668(b)-1A to reduce the partial tax to $100. The taxes imposed on trust B for 1975 will, in addition to the $100 partial tax, also include the $500 used to reduce the partial tax.

(b) *Taxes imposed on the trust attributable to undistributed net income.* (1) For the purpose of subpart D, the term "taxes imposed on the trust attributable to the undistributed net income" means the amount of Federal income taxes for the taxable year properly allocable to the undistributed portion of the distributable net income for such taxable year. This amount is (i) an amount that bears the same relationship to the total taxes of the trust for the year (other than the minimum tax for tax preferences imposed by section 56), computed after the allowance of credits under section 642(a), as (*a*) the taxable income of the trust, other than the capital gains not included in distributable net income less their share of section 1202 deduction, bears to (*b*) the total taxable income of the trust for such year or, (ii) if the alternative tax computation under section 1201(b) is used and there are no net short-term gains, an amount equal to such total taxes less the amount of the alternative tax imposed on the trust and attributable to the capital gain. Thus, for the purposes of subpart D, in determining the amount of taxes imposed on the trust attributable to the undistributed net income, that portion of the taxes paid by the trust attributable to capital gain allocable to corpus is excluded. The rule stated in this subparagraph may be illustrated by the following example, which assumes that the alternative tax computation is not used:

Example. (1) Under the terms of a trust, which reports on the calendar year basis, the income may be accumulated or distributed to A in the discretion of the trustee and capital gains are allocable to corpus. During the taxable year 1974, the trust had income of $20,000 from royalties, long-term capital gains of $10,000, and expenses of $2,000. The trustee in his discretion made a distribution of $10,000 to A. The taxes imposed on the trust for such year attributable to the undistributed net income are $2,319, determined as shown below.

(2) The distributable net income of the trust computed under section 643(a) is $18,000 (royalties of $20,000 less expenses of $2,000). The total taxes paid by the trust are $3,787, computed as follows:

Royalties	$20,000
Capital gain allocable to corpus	10,000
Gross income	30,000
Deductions:	
Expenses	$ 2,000
Distributions to A	10,000
Capital gain deduction	5,000
Personal exemption	100
	17,100
Taxable income	$12,900
Total income taxes	3,787

(3) Taxable income other than capital gains less the section 1202 deduction is $7,900 ($12,900 − ($10,000 − $5,000)). Therefore, the amount of taxes imposed on the trust attributable to the undistributed net income is $2,319, computed as follows:

$3,787 (total taxes) × $7,900 (taxable income other than capital gains not included in d.n.i. less the 1202 deduction) divided by $12,900 (taxable income) $2,319

(2) If in any taxable year an accumulation distribution of undistributed net income is made by the trust which results in a throwback to a prior year, the taxes of the prior year imposed on

Reg. § 1.665(d)-1A(b)(2)

the trust attributable to any remaining undistributed net income of such prior year are the taxes prescribed in subparagraph (1) of this paragraph reduced by the taxes of the prior year deemed distributed under section 666(b) or (c). The provisions of this subparagraph may be illustrated by the following example:

Example. Assume the same facts as in the example in subparagraph (1) of this paragraph. In 1975 the trust makes an accumulation distribution, of which an amount of undistributed net income is deemed distributed in 1974. Taxes imposed on the trust (in the amount of $1,000) attributable to the undistributed net income are therefore deemed distributed in such year. Consequently, the taxes imposed on the trust subsequent to the 1975 distribution attributable to the remaining undistributed net income are $1,319 ($2,319 less $1,000).

(c) *Taxes imposed on the trust attributable to undistributed capital gain*—(1) *Regular tax.* For the purpose of subpart D, the term "taxes imposed on the trust attributable to undistributed capital gain" means the amount of Federal income taxes for the taxable year properly attributable to that portion of the excess of capital gains over capital losses of the trust which is allocable to corpus for such taxable year. Such amount is the total of—

(i) the amount computed under subparagraph (2) of this paragraph (the minimum tax), plus

(ii) the amount which bears the same relationship to the total taxes of the trust for the year, (other than the minimum tax), computed after the allowance of credits under section 642(a), as (*a*) the excess of capital gains over capital losses for such year that are not included in distributable net income, computed after its share of the deduction under section 1202 (relating to the deduction for capital gains) has been taken into account, bears to the greater of (*b*) the total taxable income of the trust for such year, or (*c*) the amount of capital gains computed under (*a*) of this subdivision. However, if the alternative tax computation under section 1201(b) is used and there are no net short-term gains, the amount is the amount of the alternative tax imposed on the trust and attributable to the capital gain. The application of this subparagraph may be illustrated by the following example, which assumes that the alternative tax computation is not used:

Example. Assume the facts as in the example in paragraph (b)(1). The capital gains not included in d.n.i. are $10,000, and the deduction under section 1202 is $5,000. The amount of taxes imposed on the trust attributable to undistributed capital gain is $1,468, computed as follows:

$3,787 (total taxes) × $5,000 (capital gains not included in d.n.i. less sec. 1202 deductions) divided by $12,900 (taxable income).................. $1,468

(2) *Minimum tax.* The term "taxes imposed on the trust attributable to the undistributed capital gain" also includes the minimum tax for tax preferences imposed on the trust by section 56 with respect to the undistributed capital gain. The amount of such minimum tax so included bears the same relation to the total amount of minimum tax imposed on the trust by section 56 for the taxable year as one-half the net capital gain (net section 1201 gain for taxable years beginning before January 1, 1977) (as defined in section 1222(11)) from such taxable year bears to the sum of the items of tax preference of the trust for such taxable year which are apportioned to the trust in accordance with § 1.58-3(a)(1).

(3) *Reduction for prior distribution.* If in any taxable year a capital gain distribution is made by the trust which results in a throwback to a prior year, the taxes of the prior year imposed on the trust attributable to any remaining undistributed capital gain of the prior year are the taxes prescribed in subparagraph (1) of this paragraph reduced by the taxes of the prior year deemed distributed under section 669(d) or (e). The provisions of this subparagraph may be illustrated by the following example:

Example. Assume the same facts as in the example in subparagraph (1) of this paragraph. In 1976, the trust makes a capital gain distribution, of which an amount of undistributed capital gain is deemed distributed in 1974. Taxes imposed on the trust (in the amount of $500) attributable to the undistributed capital gain are therefore deemed distributed in such year. Consequently, the taxes imposed on the trust attributable to the remaining undistributed capital gain are $968 ($1,468 less $500). [Reg. § 1.665(d)-1A.]

☐ [T.D. 7204, 8-24-72. Amended by T.D. 7728, 10-31-80.]

[Reg. § 1.665(e)-1A]

§ 1.665(e)-1A. **Preceding taxable year.**—(a) *Definition*—(1) *Domestic trusts*—(i) *In general.* For purposes of subpart D, in the case of a trust other than a foreign trust created by a U.S. person, the term "preceding taxable year" serves to identify and limit the taxable years of a trust to which an accumulation distribution consisting of undistributed net income or undistributed capital gain may be allocated (or "thrown back") under sections 666(a) and 669(a). An accumulation distribution consisting of undistributed net income or undistributed capital gain may not be allocated or "thrown back" to a taxable year of a trust if such year is not a "preceding taxable year."

(ii) *Accumulation distributions.* In the case of an accumulation distribution consisting of undistributed net income made in a taxable year beginning before January 1, 1974, any taxable year of the trust that precedes by more than five years the taxable year of the trust in which such accumulation distribution was made is not a "preceding taxable year." Thus, for a domestic trust on a calendar year basis, calendar year 1967 is not a "preceding taxable year" with respect to an accumulation distribution made in calendar year 1973, whereas calendar year 1968 is a "preceding taxable year." In the case of an accumulation distribution made during a taxable year beginning after December 31, 1973, any taxable year of the trust that begins before January 1, 1969, is not a "preceding taxable year." Thus, for a domestic trust on a calendar year basis, calendar year 1968 is not a "preceding taxable year" with respect to an accumulation distribution made in calendar year 1975, whereas calendar year 1969 is a "preceding taxable year."

(iii) *Capital gain distributions.* In the case of an accumulation distribution that is a capital gain distribution, any taxable year of the trust that (*a*) begins before January 1, 1969, or (*b*) is prior to the first year in which income is accumulated, whichever occurs later, is not a "preceding taxable year." Thus, for the purpose of capital gain distributions and section 669, only taxable years beginning after December 31, 1968, can be "preceding taxable years." See § 1.668(a)-1A(c).

(2) *Foreign trusts created by United States persons.* For purposes of subpart D, in the case of a foreign trust created by a U.S. person, the term "preceding taxable year" does not include any taxable year to which part I of subchapter J does not apply. See section 683 and regulations thereunder. Accordingly, the provisions of subpart D may not, in the case of a foreign trust created by a U.S. person, be applied to any taxable year which begins before 1954 or ends before August 17, 1954. For example, if a foreign trust created by a U.S. person (reporting on the calendar year basis) makes a distribution during the calendar year 1970 of income accumulated during prior years, the earliest year of the trust to which the accumulation distribution may be allocated under such subpart D is 1954, but it may not be allocated to 1953 and prior years, since the Internal Revenue Code of 1939 applies to those years.

(b) *Simple trusts.* A taxable year of a trust during which the trust was a simple trust (that is, was subject to subpart B) for the entire year shall not be considered a "preceding taxable year" unless during such year the trust received "outside income" or unless the trustee did not distribute all of the income of the trust that was required to be distributed currently for such year. In such event, undistributed net income for such year shall not exceed the greater of the "outside income" or income not distributed during such year. For purposes of this paragraph, the term "outside income" means amounts that are included in distributable net income of the trust for the year but that are not "income" of the trust as that term is defined in § 1.643(b)-1. Some examples of "outside income" are:

(1) Income taxable to the trust under section 691;

(2) Unrealized accounts receivable that were assigned to the trusts; and

(3) Distributions from another trust that include distributable net income or undistributed net income of such other trust.

The term "outside income", however, does not include amounts received as distributions from an estate, other than income specified in (1) and (2), for which the estate was allowed a deduction under section 661(a). The application of this paragraph may be illustrated by the following examples:

Example (1). By his will D creates a trust for his widow W. The terms of the trust require that the income be distributed currently (*i.e.*, it is a simple trust), and authorize the trustee to make discretionary payments of corpus to W. Upon W's death the trust corpus is to be distributed to D's then living issue. The executor of D's will makes a $10,000 distribution of corpus to the trust that carries out estate income consisting of dividends and interest to the trust under section 662(a)(2). The trust reports this income as its only income on its income tax return for its taxable year in which ends the taxable year of the estate in which the $10,000 distribution was made, and pays a tax thereon of $2,106. Thus, the trust has undistributed net income of $7,894 ($10,000 − $2,106). Several years later the trustee makes a discretionary corpus payment of $15,000 to W. This payment is an accumulation distribution under section 665(b). However, since the trust had no "outside income" in the year of the estate distribution, such year is not a preceding taxable year. Thus, W is not treated as receiving undistributed net income of $7,894 and taxes thereon of $2,106 for the purpose of including the same in her gross income under section 668. The result would be the same if the invasion power were not exercised and the accumulation distribution oc-

Reg. § 1.665(e)-1A(b)(3)

curred as a result of the distribution of the corpus to D's issue upon the death of W.

Example (2). Trust A, a simple trust on the calendar year basis, received in 1972 extraordinary dividends or taxable stock dividends that the trustee in good faith allocated to corpus, but that are determined in 1974 to have been currently distributable to the beneficiary. See section 643(a)(4) and § 1.643(a)-4. Trust A would qualify for treatment under subpart C for 1974, the year of distribution of the extraordinary dividends or taxable stock dividends, because the distribution is not out of income of the current taxable year and is treated as an other amount properly paid or credited or required to be distributed for such taxable year within the meaning of section 661(a)(2). Also, the distribution in 1974 qualifies as an accumulation distribution for the purposes of subpart D. For purposes only of such subpart D, trust A would be treated as subject to the provisions of such subpart C for 1972, the preceding taxable year in which the extraordinary or taxable stock dividends were received, and, in computing undistributed net income for 1972, the extraordinary or taxable stock dividends would be included in distributable net income under section 643(a). The rule stated in the preceding sentence would also apply if the distribution in 1974 was made out of corpus without regard to a determination that the extraordinary dividends or taxable stock dividends in question were currently distributable to the beneficiary. [Reg. § 1.665(e)-1A.]

☐ [T.D. 7204, 8-24-72.]

[Reg. § 1.665(f)-1A]

§ 1.665(f)-1A. Undistributed capital gain.— (a) *Domestic trusts.* (1) The term "undistributed capital gain" means (in the case of a trust other than a foreign trust created by a U.S. person), for any taxable year of the trust beginning after December 31, 1968, the gains in excess of losses for that year from the sale or exchange of capital assets of the trust less:

(i) The amount of such gains that are included in distributable net income under section 643(a)(3) and § 1.643(a)-3,

(ii) The amount of taxes imposed on the trust for such year attributable to such gains, as defined in § 1.665(d)-1A, and

(iii) In the case of a trust that does not use the alternative method for computing taxes on capital gains of the taxable year, the excess of deductions (other than deductions allowed under section 642(b) relating to personal exemption or section 642(c) relating to charitable contributions) over distributable net income for such year to the extent such excess deductions are properly allowable in determining taxable income for such year. For purposes of computing the amount of capital gain under this paragraph, no deduction under section 1202, relating to deduction for excess of capital gains over capital losses, shall be taken into account. The application of this subparagraph may be illustrated by the following example:

Example. Under the terms of the trust, the trustee must distribute all income currently and has discretion to distribute capital gain to A or to allocate it to corpus. During the taxable year 1971 the trust recognized capital gain in the amount of $15,000, and capital losses of $5,000, and had interest income (after expenses) of $6,000. The trustee distributed $8,000 to A, consisting of $6,000 of interest and $2,000 of capital gain. The $2,000 of gain distributed to A is included in the computation of distributable net income under § 1.643(a)-3. The balance of the capital gain is not included in distributable net income since it is allocated to corpus and not paid, credited, or required to be distributed to any beneficiary. The trust paid taxes of $671, all of which are attributable under § 1.665(d)-1A to the undistributed capital gain. The amount of undistributed capital gain of the trust for 1971 is therefore $7,329, computed as follows:

Total capital gains		$15,000
Less: Capital losses		5,000
Gains in excess of losses		$10,000
Less: Amount of capital gain included in distributable net income	2,000	
Taxes imposed on the trust attributable to the undistributed capital gain (see § 1.665(d)-1A)	671	
		2,671
Undistributed capital gain		7,329

(2) For purposes of subparagraph (1) of this paragraph, the term "losses for that year" includes losses of the trust from the sale or exchange of capital assets in preceding taxable years not included in the computation of distributable net income of any year, reduced by such losses taken into account in a subsequent preceding taxable year in computing undistributed capital gain but

Estates, Trusts, and Beneficiaries

See p. 20,601 for regulations not amended to reflect law changes

not reduced by such losses taken into account in determining the deduction under section 1211. See section 1212(b)(2) and the regulations thereunder. For example, assume that a trust had a net long-term capital loss in 1970 of $5,000. During the years 1971 through 1975, the trust had no capital gains or capital losses. In 1976, it has a long-term capital gain of $8,000, which it allocates to corpus and does not distribute to a beneficiary, but has no taxes attributable to such gain. The undistributed capital gain for 1976 is $8,000 − $5,000, or $3,000, even though all or a part of the $5,000 loss was claimed under section 1211 as a deduction in years 1970 through 1975.

(b) *Foreign trusts.* Distributable net income for a taxable year of a foreign trust created by a U.S. person includes capital gains in excess of capital losses for such year (see § 1.643(a)-6(a)(3)). Thus, a foreign trust created by a U.S. person can never have any undistributed capital gain. [Reg. § 1.665(f)-1A.]

☐ [*T.D. 7204, 8-24-72.*]

[Reg. § 1.665(g)-1A]

§ 1.665(g)-1A. Capital gain distribution.—For any taxable year of a trust, the term "capital gain distribution" means, to the extent of the undistributed capital gain of the trust, that portion of an accumulation distribution which exceeds the amount of such accumulation distribution deemed under section 666(a) to be undistributed net income of the trust for all preceding taxable years. See § 1.665(b)-1A for the definition of "accumulation distribution." For any such taxable year the undistributed capital gain includes the total undistributed capital gain for all years of the trust beginning with the first taxable year beginning after December 31, 1968, in which income (as determined under section 643(b)) is accumulated, and ending before such taxable year. See § 1.665(g)-2A for application of the separate share rule. The application of this section may be illustrated by the following example:

Example. A trust on the calendar year basis made the following accumulations. For purposes of this example, the undistributed net income is the same as income under applicable local law. No income was accumulated prior to 1970.

Year	Undistributed net income	Undistributed capital gain
1969	none	$10,000
1970	$1,000	3,000
1971	none	4,000

The trust has distributable net income in 1972 of $2,000, and recognizes capital gains of $4,500 that are allocable to corpus. On December 31, 1972, the trustee makes a distribution of $20,000 to the beneficiary. There is an accumulation distribution of $18,000 ($20,000 distribution less $2,000 d.n.i.) that consists of undistributed net income of $1,000 (see § 1.666(a)-1A) and a capital gain distribution of $7,000. The capital gain distribution is computed as follows:

Accumulation distribution	$18,000
Less: Undistributed net income	1,000
Balance	17,000
Capital gain distribution (Undistributed capital gain of the trust for 1972 ($3,000 from 1970 and $4,000 from 1971))	$ 7,000
Balance (corpus)	10,000

No undistributed capital gain is deemed distributed from 1969 because 1969 is a year prior to the first year in which income is accumulated (1970). The accumulation distribution is not deemed to consist of any part of the capital gain recognized in 1972. [Reg. § 1.665(g)-1A.]

☐ [*T.D. 7204, 8-24-72.*]

[Reg. § 1.665(g)-2A]

§ 1.665(g)-2A. Application of separate share rule.—(a) *In general.* If the separate share rule of section 663(c) is applicable for any taxable year of a trust, subpart D is applied as if each share were a separate trust except as provided in paragraph (c) of this section and in § 1.668(a)-1A(c). Thus, the amounts of an "accumulation distribution", "undistributed net income", "undistributed capital gain", and "capital gain distribution" are computed separately for each share.

(b) *Allocation of taxes—undistributed net income.* The "taxes imposed on the trust attributable to the undistributed net income" are allocated as follows:

(1) There is first allocated to each separate share that portion of the "taxes imposed on the trust attributable to the undistributed net income" (as defined in § 1.665(d)-1A(b)), computed before the allowance of any credits under section 642(a), that bears the same relation to the total of such taxes that the distributable net income of the separate share bears to the distributable net income of the trust, adjusted for this purpose as follows:

Reg. § 1.665(g)-2A(b)(1)

(i) There is excluded from distributable net income of the trust and of each separate share any tax-exempt interest, foreign income of a foreign trust, and excluded dividends, to the extent such amounts are included in distributable net income pursuant to section 643(a)(5), (6), and (7); and

(ii) The distributable net income of the trust is reduced by any deductions allowable under section 661 for amounts paid, credited, or required to be distributed during the taxable year, and the distributable net income of each separate share is reduced by any such deduction allocable to that share.

(2) The taxes so determined for each separate share are then reduced by that portion of the credits against tax allowable to the trust under section 642(a) in computing the "taxes imposed on the trust" that bears the same relation to the total of such credits that the items of distributable net income allocable to the separate share with respect to which the credit is allowed bear to the total of such items of the trust.

(c) *Allocation of taxes—undistributed capital gain.* The "taxes imposed on the trust attributable to undistributed capital gain" are allocated as follows:

(1) There is first allocated to each separate share that portion of the "taxes imposed on the trust attributable to undistributed capital gain" (as defined in § 1.665(d)-1A(c)), computed before the allowance of any credits under section 642(a), that bears the same relation to the total of such taxes that the undistributed capital gain (prior to the deduction of taxes under section 665(c)(2)) of the separate share bears to the total such undistributed capital gain of the trust.

(2) The taxes so determined for each separate share are then reduced by that portion of the credits against tax allowable to the trust under section 642(a) in computing the "taxes imposed on the trust" that bears the same relation to the total of such credits that the capital gain allocable to the separate share with respect to which the credit is allowed bear to the total of such capital gain of the trust.

(d) *Termination of a separate share.* (1) If upon termination of a separate share, an amount is properly paid, credited, or required to be distributed by the trust under section 661(a)(2) to a beneficiary from such share, an accumulation distribution will be deemed to have been made to the extent of such amount. In determining the distributable net income of such share, only those items of income and deduction for the taxable year of the trust in which such share terminates, properly allocable to such share, shall be taken into consideration.

(2) No accumulation distribution will be deemed to have been made upon the termination of a separate share to the extent that the property constituting such share, or a portion thereof, continues to be held as a part of the same trust. The undistributed net income, undistributed capital gain, and the taxes imposed on the trust attributable to such items, if any, for all preceding taxable years (reduced by any amounts deemed distributed under sections 666(a) and 669(a) by reason of any accumulation distribution of undistributed net income or undistributed capital gain in prior years or the current taxable year), which were allocable to the terminating share, shall be treated as being applicable to the trust itself. However, no adjustment will be made to the amounts deemed distributed under sections 666 and 669 by reason of an accumulation distribution of undistributed net income or undistributed capital gain from the surviving share or shares made in years prior to the year in which the terminating share was added to such surviving share or shares.

(3) The provisions of this paragraph may be illustrated by the following example:

Example. A trust was established under the will of X for the benefit of his wife and upon her death the property was to continue in the same trust for his two sons, Y and Z. The separate share rule is applicable to this trust. The trustee had discretion to pay or accumulate the income to the wife, and after her death was to pay each son's share to him after he attained the age of 25. When the wife died, Y was 23 and Z was 28.

(1) Upon the death of X's widow, there is no accumulation distribution. The entire trust is split into two equal shares, and therefore the undistributed net income and the undistributed capital gain of the trust are split into two shares.

(2) The distribution to Z of his share after his mother's death is an accumulation distribution of his separate share of one-half of the undistributed net income and undistributed capital gain. [Reg. § 1.665(g)-2A.]

☐ [T.D. 7204, 8-24-72.]

[Reg. § 1.666(a)-1A]

§ 1.666(a)-1A. **Amount allocated.**—(a) *In general.* In the case of a trust that is subject to subpart C of part I of subchapter J of chapter 1 of the Code (relating to estates and trusts which may accumulate income or which distribute corpus), section 666(a) prescribes rules for determining the taxable years from which an accumulation distribution will be deemed to have been made and the extent to which the accumulation distribution is considered to consist of undistributed net income. In general, an accumulation distribution made in taxable years beginning after December 31, 1969, is deemed to have been made first from the earliest preceding taxable year of the trust for which there is undistributed net income. An accumulation distribution made in a taxable year beginning before January 1, 1970, is deemed to have been made first from the most recent preceding taxable year of the trust for which there is undistributed net income. See § 1.665(e)-1A for the definition of "preceding taxable year."

(b) *Distributions by domestic trusts*—(1) *Taxable years beginning after December 31, 1973.* An accumulation distribution made by a trust (other than a foreign trust created by a U.S. person) in any taxable year beginning after December 31, 1973, is allocated to the preceding taxable years of the trust (defined in § 1.665(e)-1A(a)(1)(ii) as those beginning after December 31, 1968) according to the amount of undistributed net income of the trust for such years. For this purpose, an accumulation distribution is first allocated to the earliest such preceding taxable year in which there is undistributed net income and shall then be allocated in turn, beginning with the next earliest, to any remaining preceding taxable years of the trust. The portion of the accumulation distribution allocated to the earliest preceding taxable year is the amount of the undistributed net income for that preceding taxable year. The portion of the accumulation distribution allocated to any preceding taxable year subsequent to the earliest such preceding taxable year is the excess of the accumulation distribution over the aggregate of the undistributed net income for all earlier preceding taxable years. See paragraph (d) of this section for adjustments to undistributed net income for prior distributions. The provisions of this subparagraph may be illustrated by the following example:

Example. In 1977, a domestic trust reporting on the calendar year basis makes an accumulation distribution of $33,000. Therefore, years before 1969 are ignored. In 1969, the trust had $6,000 of undistributed net income; in 1970, $4,000; in 1971, none; in 1972, $7,000; in 1973, $5,000; in 1974, $8,000; in 1975, $6,000; and $4,000 in 1976. The accumulation distribution is deemed distributed $6,000 in 1969, $4,000 in 1970, none in 1971, $7,000 in 1972, $5,000 in 1973, $8,000 in 1974, and $3,000 in 1975.

(2) *Taxable years beginning after December 31, 1969, and before January 1, 1974.* If a trust (other than a foreign trust created by a U.S. person) makes an accumulation distribution in a taxable year beginning after December 31, 1969, and before January 1, 1974, the distribution will be deemed distributed in the same manner as accumulation distributions qualifying under subparagraph (1) of this paragraph, except that the first year to which the distribution may be thrown back cannot be earlier than the fifth taxable year of the trust preceding the year in which the accumulation distribution is made. Thus, for example, in the case of an accumulation distribution made in the taxable year of a domestic trust which begins on January 1, 1972, the taxable year of the trust beginning on January 1, 1967, would be the first year in which the distribution was deemed made, assuming that there was undistributed net income for 1967. See also § 1.665(e)-1A(a)(1). The provisions of this subparagraph may be illustrated by the following example:

Example. In 1973, a domestic trust, reporting on the calendar year basis, makes an accumulation distribution of $25,000. In 1968, the fifth year preceding 1973, the trust had $7,000 of undistributed net income; in 1969, none; in 1970, $12,000; in 1971, $4,000; in 1972, $4,000. The accumulation distribution is deemed distributed in the amounts of $7,000 in 1968, none in 1969, $12,000 in 1970, $4,000 in 1971, and $2,000 in 1972.

(3) *Taxable years beginning after December 31, 1968, and before January 1, 1970.* Accumulation distributions made in taxable years of the trust beginning after December 31, 1968, and before January 1, 1970, are allocated to prior years according to § 1.666(a)-1.

(c) *Distributions by foreign trusts*—(1) *Foreign trusts created solely by U.S. persons*—(i) *Taxable years beginning after December 31, 1969.* If a foreign trust created by a U.S. person makes an accumulation distribution in any taxable year beginning after December 31, 1969, the distribution is allocated to the trust's preceding taxable years (defined in § 1.665(e)-1A(a)(2) as those beginning after December 31, 1953, and ending after August 16, 1954) according to the amount of undistributed net income of the trust for such years. For this purpose, an accumulation distribution is first allocated to the earliest such preceding taxable year in which there is undistributed net income and shall then be allocated in turn, beginning with the next earliest, to any remaining preceding taxable years of the trust. The portion of the accumulation distribution allocated to the earliest preceding taxable year is the amount of the undistributed net income for that preceding taxable year. The portion of the accumulation distribution allocated to any preceding taxable year subsequent to the earliest such preceding taxable year

Reg. § 1.666(a)-1A(c)(1)

is the excess of the accumulation distribution over the aggregate of the undistributed net income for all earlier preceding taxable years. See paragraph (d) of this section for adjustments to undistributed net income for prior distributions. The provisions of this subdivision may be illustrated by the following example:

Example. In 1971, a foreign trust created by a U.S. person, reporting on the calendar year basis, makes an accumulation distribution of $50,000. In 1961, the trust had $12,000 of undistributed net income; in 1962, none; in 1963, $10,000; in 1964, $8,000; in 1965, $5,000; in 1966, $14,000; in 1967, none; in 1968, $3,000; in 1969, $2,000; and in 1970, $1,000. The accumulation distribution is deemed distributed in the amounts of $12,000 in 1961, none in 1962, $10,000 in 1963, $8,000 in 1964, $5,000 in 1965, $14,000 in 1966, none in 1967, and $1,000 in 1968.

(ii) *Taxable years beginning after December 31, 1968, and before January 1, 1970.* Accumulation distributions made in taxable years of the trust beginning after December 31, 1968, and before January 1, 1970, are allocated to prior years according to § 1.666(a)-1.

(2) *Foreign trusts created partly by U.S. persons*—(i) *Taxable years beginning after December 31, 1969.* If a trust that is in part a foreign trust created by a U.S. person and in part a foreign trust created by a person other than a U.S. person makes an accumulation distribution in any year after December 31, 1969, the distribution is deemed made from the undistributed net income of the foreign trust created by a U.S. person in the proportion that the total undistributed net income for all preceding years of the foreign trust created by the U.S. person bears to the total undistributed net income for all years of the entire foreign trust. In addition, such distribution is deemed made from the undistributed net income of the foreign trust created by a person other than a U.S. person in the proportion that the total undistributed net income for all preceding years of the foreign trust created by a person other than a U.S. person bears to the total undistributed net income for all years of the entire foreign trust. Accordingly, an accumulation distribution of such a trust is composed of two portions with one portion relating to the undistributed net income of the foreign trust created by the U.S. person and the other portion relating to the undistributed net income of the foreign trust created by the person other than a U.S. person. For these purposes, each portion of an accumulation distribution made in any taxable year is first allocated to each of such preceding taxable years in turn, beginning with the earliest preceding taxable year, as defined in § 1.665(e)-1A(a), of the applicable foreign trusts, to the extent of the undistributed net income for the such [sic] trust for each of those years. Thus, each portion of an accumulation distribution is deemed to have been made from the earliest accumulated income of the applicable trust. If the foreign trust created by a U.S. person makes an accumulation distribution in any year beginning after December 31, 1969, the distribution is included in the beneficiary's income for that year to the extent of the undistributed net income of the trust for the trust's preceding taxable years which began after December 31, 1953, and ended after August 16, 1954. The provisions of this subdivision may be illustrated by the following example:

Example. A trust is created in 1962 under the laws of Country X by the transfer to a trustee in Country X of property by both a United States person and a person other than a United States person. Both the trust and the only beneficiary of the trust (who is a U.S. person) report their taxable income on a calendar year basis. On March 31, 1974, the trust makes an accumulation distribution of $150,000 to the beneficiary. The distributable net income of both the portion of the trust which is a foreign trust created by a U.S. person and the portion of the trust which is a foreign trust created by a person other than a U.S. person for each year is computed in accordance with the provisions of paragraph (b)(3) of § 1.643(d)-1 and the undistributed net income for each portion of the trust for each year is computed as described in paragraph (b) of § 1.665(a)-1A. For taxable years 1962 through 1973, the portion of the trust which is a foreign trust created by a United States person and the portion of the trust which is a foreign trust created by a person other than a U.S. person had the following amounts of undistributed net income:

Year	Undistributed net income-portion of the trust created by a U.S. person	Undistributed net income-portion of the trust created by a person other than a U.S. person
1962	$ 7,000	$ 4,000
1963	12,000	7,000
1964	None	None
1965	11,000	5,000
1966	8,000	3,000
1967	None	None
1968	4,000	2,000
1969	17,000	8,000

Reg. § 1.666(a)-1A(c)(2)

Estates, Trusts, and Beneficiaries

Year		
1970	16,000	9,000
1971	None	None
1972	25,000	12,000
1973	20,000	10,000
Totals	120,000	60,000

The accumulation distribution in the amount of $150,000 is deemed to have been distributed in the amount of $100,000 (120,000/180,000 × $150,000) from the portion of the trust which is a foreign trust created by a U.S. person and in the amount of $39,000, which is less than $50,000 (60,000/180,000 × $150,000), from the portion of the trust which is a foreign trust created by a person other than a U.S. person computed as follows:

Year	Throwback to preceding years of foreign trust created by a U.S. person	Throwback to preceding years of portion of the entire foreign trust which is not a foreign trust created by a U.S. person
1962	$ 7,000	None
1963	12,000	None
1964	None	None
1965	11,000	None
1966	8,000	None
1967	None	None
1968	4,000	None
1969	17,000	$ 8,000
1970	16,000	9,000
1971	None	None
1972	25,000	12,000
1973	None	10,000
Totals	$100,000	$39,000

Pursuant to this paragraph, the accumulation distribution in the amount of $100,000 from the portion of the trust which is a foreign trust created by a U.S. person is included in the beneficiary's income for 1974, as the amount represents undistributed net income of the trust for the trust's preceding taxable years which began after December 31, 1953, and ended after August 16, 1954. The accumulation distribution in the amount of $50,000 from the portion of the trust which is a foreign trust created by a person other than a U.S. person is included in the beneficiary's income for 1974 to the extent of the undistributed net income of the trust for the preceding years beginning after December 31, 1968. Accordingly, with respect to the portion of the trust which is a foreign trust created by a person other than a U.S. person, only the undistributed net income for the years 1969 through 1973, which totals $39,000, is includible in the beneficiary's income for 1974. Thus, of the $150,000 distribution made in 1974, the beneficiary is required to include a total of $139,000 in his income for 1974. The balance of $11,000 is deemed to represent a distribution of corpus.

(ii) *Taxable years beginning after December 31, 1968 and before January 1, 1970.* Accumulation distributions made in taxable years of the trust beginning after December 31, 1968, and before January 1, 1970, are allocated to prior years according to § 1.666(a)-1.

(3) *Foreign trusts created by non-U.S. persons.* To the extent that a foreign trust is a foreign trust created by a person other than a U.S. person, an accumulation distribution is included in the beneficiary's income for the year paid, credited, or required to be distributed to the extent provided under paragraph (b) of this section.

(d) *Reduction of undistributed net income for prior accumulation distributions.* For the purposes of allocating to any preceding taxable year an accumulation distribution of the taxable year, the undistributed net income of such preceding taxable year is reduced by the amount from such year deemed distributed in any accumulation distribution of undistributed net income made in any taxable year intervening between such preceding taxable year and the taxable year. Accordingly, for example, if a trust has undistributed net income for 1974 and makes accumulation distributions during the taxable years 1978 and 1979, in determining that part of the 1979 accumulation distribution that is thrown back to 1974 the undistributed net income for 1974 is first reduced by the amount of the undistributed net income for 1974 deemed distributed in the 1978 accumulation distribution.

(e) *Rule when no undistributed net income.* If, before the application of the provisions of subpart D to an accumulation distribution for the taxable year, there is no undistributed net income for a preceding taxable year, then no portion of the

Reg. § 1.666(a)-1A(e)

accumulation distribution is undistributed net income deemed distributed on the last day of such preceding taxable year. Thus, if an accumulation distribution is made during the taxable year 1975 from a trust whose earliest preceding taxable year is taxable year 1970, and the trust had no undistributed net income for 1970, then no portion of the 1975 accumulation distribution is undistributed net income deemed distributed on the last day of 1970. [Reg. § 1.666(a)-1A.]

☐ [T.D. 7204, 8-24-72.]

[Reg. § 1.666(b)-1A]

§ 1.666(b)-1A. **Total taxes deemed distributed.**—(a) If an accumulation distribution is deemed under § 1.666(a)-1A to be distributed on the last day of a preceding taxable year and the amount is not less than the undistributed net income for such preceding taxable year, then an additional amount equal to the "taxes imposed on the trust attributable to the undistributed net income" (as defined in § 1.665(d)-1A(b)) for such preceding taxable year is also deemed distributed under section 661(a)(2). For example, a trust has undistributed net income of $8,000 for the taxable year 1974. The taxes imposed on the trust attributable to the undistributed net income are $3,032. During the taxable year 1977, an accumulation distribution of $8,000 is made to the beneficiary, which is deemed under § 1.666(a)-1A to have been distributed on the last day of 1974. The 1977 accumulation distribution is not less than the 1974 undistributed net income. Accordingly, the taxes of $3,032 imposed on the trust attributable to the undistributed net income for 1974 are also deemed to have been distributed on the last day of 1974. Thus, a total of $11,032 will be deemed to have been distributed on the last day of 1974.

(b) For the purpose of paragraph (a) of this section, the undistributed net income of any preceding taxable year and the taxes imposed on the trust for such preceding taxable year attributable to such undistributed net income are computed after taking into account any accumulation distributions of taxable years intervening between such preceding taxable year and the taxable year. See paragraph (d) of § 1.666(a)-1A. [Reg. § 1.666(b)-1A.]

☐ [T.D. 7204, 8-24-72.]

[Reg. § 1.666(c)-1A]

§ 1.666(c)-1A. **Pro rata portion of taxes deemed distributed.**—(a) If an accumulation distribution is deemed under § 1.666(a)-1A to be distributed on the last day of a preceding taxable year and the amount is less than the undistributed net income for such preceding taxable year, then an additional amount is also deemed distributed under section 661(a)(2). The additional amount is equal to the "taxes imposed on the trust attributable to the undistributed net income" (as defined in § 1.665(a)-1A(b)) for such preceding taxable year, multiplied by a fraction, the numerator of which is the amount of the accumulation distribution allocated to such preceding taxable year and the denominator of which is the undistributed net income for such preceding taxable year. See paragraph (b) of example (1) and paragraphs (c) and (f) of example (2) in § 1.666(c)-2A for illustrations of this paragraph.

(b) For the purpose of paragraph (a) of this section, the undistributed net income of any preceding taxable year and the taxes imposed on the trust for such preceding taxable year attributable to such undistributed net income are computed after taking into account any accumulation distributions of any taxable years intervening between such preceding taxable year and the taxable year. See paragraph (d) of § 1.666(a)-1A and paragraph (c) of example (1) and paragraphs (e) and (h) of example (2) in § 1.666(c)-2A. [Reg. § 1.666(c)-1A.]

☐ [T.D. 7204, 8-24-72.]

[Reg. § 1.666(c)-2A]

§ 1.666(c)-2A. **Illustration of the provisions of section 666(a), (b), and (c).**—The application of the provisions of §§ 1.666(a)-1A, 1.666(b)-1A, and 1.666(c)-1A may be illustrated by the following examples:

Example (1). (a) A trust created on January 1, 1974, makes accumulation distributions as follows:

1979	$ 7,000
1980	26,000

For 1974 through 1978, the undistributed portion of distributable net income, taxes imposed on the trust attributable to the undistributed net income, and undistributed net income are as follows:

Year	Undistributed portion of distributable net income	Taxes imposed on the trust attributable to the undistributed net income	Undistributed net income
1974	$12,100	$3,400	$8,700
1975	16,100	5,200	10,900
1976	6,100	1,360	4,740
1977	None	None	None
1978	10,100	2,640	7,460

The trust has no undistributed capital gain.

Estates, Trusts, and Beneficiaries 43,415
See p. 20,601 for regulations not amended to reflect law changes

(b) Since the entire amount of the accumulation distribution for 1979 ($7,000) is less than the undistributed net income for 1974 ($8,700), an additional amount of $2,736 (7,000/8,700 × $3,400) is deemed distributed under section 666(c).

(c) In allocating the accumulation distribution for 1980, the amount of undistributed net income for 1974 will reflect the accumulation distribution for 1979. The undistributed net income for 1974 will then be $1,700 and the taxes imposed on the trust for 1974 will be $664, determined as follows:

Undistributed net income as of the close of 1974	$8,700
Less: Accumulation distribution (1979)	7,000
Balance (undistributed net income as of the close of 1979)	$1,700
Taxes imposed on the trust attributable to the undistributed net income as of the close of 1979 (1,700/8,700 × $3,400)	$ 664

(d) The accumulation distribution of $26,000 for 1980 is deemed to have been made on the last day of the preceding taxable years of the trust to the extent of $24,800, the total of the undistributed net income for such years, as shown in the tabulation below. In addition, $9,864, the total taxes imposed on the trust attributable to the undistributed net income for such years is also deemed to have been distributed on the last day of such years, as shown below:

Year	Undistributed net income	Taxes imposed on the trust
1974	$ 1,700	$ 664
1975	10,900	5,200
1976	4,740	1,360
1977	None	None
1978	7,460	2,640
1979	None	None

Example (2). (a) Under the terms of a trust instrument, the trustee has discretion to accumulate or distribute the income to X and to invade corpus for the benefit of X. The entire income of the trust is from royalties. Both X and the trust report on the calendar year basis. All of the income for 1974 was accumulated. The distributable net income of the trust for the taxable year 1974 is $20,100 and the income taxes paid by the trust for 1974 attributable to the undistributed net income are $7,260. All of the income for 1975 and 1976 was distributed and in addition the trustee made accumulation distributions within the meaning of section 665(b) of $5,420 for each year.

(b) The undistributed net income of the trust determined under section 665(a) as of the close of 1974, is $12,840, computed as follows:

Distributable net income	$20,100
Less: Taxes imposed on the trust attributable to the undistributed net income	7,260
Undistributed net income as of the close of 1974	$12,840

(c) The accumulation distribution of $5,420 made during the taxable year 1975 is deemed under section 666(a) to have been made on December 31, 1974. Since this accumulation distribution is less than the 1974 undistributed net income of $12,840, a portion of the taxes imposed on the trust for 1974 is also deemed under section 666(c) to have been distributed on December 31, 1974. The total amount deemed to have been distributed to X on December 31, 1974 is $8,484, computed as follows:

Accumulation distribution	$5,420
Taxes deemed distributed (5,420/12,840 × $7,260)	3,064
Total	$8,484

(d) After the application of the provisions of subpart D to the accumulation distribution of 1975, the undistributed net income of the trust for 1974 is $7,420, computed as follows:

Reg. § 1.666(c)-2A

Undistributed net income as of the close of 1974	$12,840
Less: 1975 accumulation distribution deemed distributed on December 31, 1974 (paragraph (c) of this example)	5,420
Undistributed net income for 1974 as of the close of 1975	$7,420

(e) The taxes imposed on the trust attributable to the undistributed net income for the taxable year 1974, as adjusted to give effect to the 1975 accumulation distribution, amount to $4,196, computed as follows:

Taxes imposed on the trust attributable to undistributed net income as of the close of 1974	$7,260
Less: Taxes deemed distributed in 1974	3,064
Taxes attributable to the undistributed net income determined as of the close of 1975	$4,196

(f) The accumulation distribution of $5,420 made during the taxable year 1976 is, under section 666(a), deemed a distribution to X on December 31, 1974, within the meaning of section 661(a)(2). Since the accumulation distribution is less than the 1974 adjusted undistributed net income of $7,420, the trust is deemed under section 666(c) also to have distributed on December 31, 1974, a portion of the taxes imposed on the trust for 1974. The total amount deemed to be distributed on December 31, 1974, with respect to the accumulation distribution made in 1976, is $8,484, computed as follows:

Accumulation distribution	$5,420
Taxes deemed distributed (5,420/7,420 × $4,196)	3,064
Total	$8,484

(g) After the application of the provisions of subpart D to the accumulation distribution of 1976, the undistributed net income of the trust for 1974 is $2,000, computed as follows:

Undistributed net income for 1974 as of the close of 1975	$7,420
Less: 1976 accumulation distribution deemed distributed on December 31, 1974 (paragraph (f) of this example)	5,420
Undistributed net income for 1974 as of the close of 1976	$2,000

(h) The taxes imposed on the trust attributable to the undistributed net income of the trust for the taxable year 1974, determined as of the close of the taxable year 1976, amount to $1,132 ($4,196 less $3,064). [Reg. § 1.666(c)-2A.]

☐ [T.D. 7204, 8-24-72.]

[Reg. § 1.666(d)-1A]

§ 1.666(d)-1A. **Information required from trusts.**—(a) *Adequate records required.* For all taxable years of a trust, the trustee must retain copies of the trust's income tax return as well as information pertaining to any adjustments in the tax shown as due on the return. The trustee shall also keep the records of the trust required to be retained by section 6001 and the regulations thereunder for each taxable year as to which the period of limitations on assessment of tax under section 6501 has not expired. If the trustee fails to produce such copies and records, and such failure is due to circumstances beyond the reasonable control of the trustee or any predecessor trustee, the trustee may reconstruct the amount of corpus, accumulated income, etc., from competent sources (including, to the extent permissible, Internal Revenue Service records). To the extent that an accurate reconstruction can be made for a taxable year, the requirements of this paragraph shall be deemed satisfied for such year.

(b) *Rule when information is not available*—(1) *Accumulation distributions.* If adequate records (as required by paragraph (a) of this section) are not available to determine the proper application of subpart D to an accumulation distribution made in a taxable year by a trust, such accumulation distribution shall be deemed to consist of undistributed net income earned during the earliest preceding taxable year (as defined in § 1.665(e)-1A) of the trust in which it can be established that the trust was in existence. If adequate records are available for some years, but not for others, the accumulation distribution shall be allocated first to the earliest preceding taxable year of the trust for which there are adequate records and then to each subsequent preceding taxable year for which there are adequate records. To the extent that the distribution is not allocated in such manner to years for which adequate records are available, it will be deemed distributed on the last day of the earliest preceding taxable year of the trust in which it is established that the trust was in existence and for which the trust has no records. The provisions of this subparagraph may be illustrated by the following example:

Example. A trust makes a distribution in 1975 of $100,000. The trustee has adequate records for 1973, 1974, and 1975. The records show that the trust is on the calendar year basis, had distributable net income in 1975 of $20,000, and undistributed net income in 1974 of $15,000, and in 1973 of $16,000. The trustee has no other records of the trust except for a copy of the trust instrument showing that the trust was established on January 1, 1965. He establishes that the loss of the records was due to circumstances beyond his control. Since the distribution is made in 1975, the earliest "preceding taxable year," as defined in § 1.665(e)-1A, is 1969. Since $80,000 of the distribution is an accumulation distribution and $31,000 thereof is allocated to 1974 and 1973, $49,000 is deemed to have been distributed on the last day of 1969.

(2) *Taxes.* (i) If an amount is deemed under this paragraph to be undistributed net income allocated to a preceding taxable year for which adequate records are not available, there shall be deemed to be "taxes imposed on the trust" for such preceding taxable year an amount equal to the taxes that the trust would have paid if the deemed undistributed net income were the amount remaining when the taxes were subtracted from taxable income of the trust for such year. For example, assume that an accumulation distribution in 1975 of $100,000 is deemed to be undistributed net income from 1971, and that the taxable income required to produce $100,000 after taxes in 1971 would be $284,966. Therefore the amount deemed to be "taxes imposed on the trust" for such preceding taxable year is $184,966.

(ii) The credit allowed by section 667(b) shall not be allowed for any amount deemed under this subparagraph to be "taxes imposed on the trust". [Reg. § 1.666(d)-1A.]

☐ [*T.D.* 7204, 8-24-72.]

[Reg. § 1.667(a)-1A]

§ 1.667(a)-1A. **Denial of refund to trusts.**—If an amount is deemed under section 666 or 669 to be an amount paid, credited, or required to be distributed on the last day of a preceding taxable year, the trust is not allowed a refund or credit of the amount of "taxes imposed on the trust", as defined in § 1.665(d)-1A. However, such taxes imposed on the trust are allowed as a credit under section 667(b) against the tax of certain beneficiaries who are treated as having received the distributions in the preceding taxable year. [Reg. § 1.667(a)-1A.]

☐ [*T.D.* 7204, 8-24-72.]

[Reg. § 1.667(b)-1A]

§ 1.667(b)-1A. **Authorization of credit to beneficiary for taxes imposed on the trust.**—(a) *Determination of credit*—(1) *In general.* Section 667(b) allows under certain circumstances a credit (without interest) against the tax imposed by subtitle A of the Code on the beneficiary for the taxable year in which the accumulation distribution is required to be included in income under section 668(a). In the case of an accumulation distribution consisting only of undistributed net income, the amount of such credit is the total of the taxes deemed distributed to such beneficiary under section 666(b) and (c) as a result of such accumulation distribution for preceding taxable years of the trust on the last day of which such beneficiary was in being, less the amount of such taxes for such preceding taxable years taken into account in reducing the amount of partial tax determined under § 1.668(b)-1A. In the case of an accumulation distribution consisting only of undistributed capital gain, the amount of such credit is the total of the taxes deemed distributed as a result of the accumulation distribution to such beneficiary under section 669(d) and (e) for preceding taxable years of the trust on the last day of which such beneficiary was in being, less the amount of such taxes for such preceding taxable years taken into account in reducing the amount of partial tax determined under § 1.669(b)-1A. In the case of an accumulation distribution consisting of both undistributed net income and undistributed capital gain, a credit will not be available unless the total taxes deemed distributed to the beneficiary for all preceding taxable years as a result of the accumulation distribution exceeds the beneficiary's partial tax determined under §§ 1.668(b)-1A and 1.669(b)-1A without reference to the taxes deemed distributed. A credit is not allowed for any taxes deemed distributed as a result of an accumulation distribution to a beneficiary by reason of sections 666(b) and (c) or sections 669(d) and (e) for a preceding taxable year of the trust before the beneficiary was born or created. However, if as a result of an accumulation distribution the total taxes deemed distributed under section 668(a)(2) and 668(a)(3) in preceding taxable years before the beneficiary was born or created exceed the partial taxes attributable to amounts deemed distributed in such years, such excess may be used to offset any liability for partial taxes attributable to amounts deemed distributed as a result of the same accumulation distribution in preceding taxable years after the beneficiary was born or created.

(2) *Exact method.* In the case of the tax computed under the exact method provided in §§ 1.668(b)-1A(b) and 1.669(b)-1A(b), the credit allowed by this section is computed as follows:

(i) Compute the total taxes deemed distributed under §§ 1.666(b)-1A and 1.666(c)-1A or §§ 1.669(d)-1A and 1.669(e)-1A, whichever are appropriate for the preceding taxable years of the trust on the last day of which the beneficiary was in being.

(ii) Compute the total of the amounts of tax determined under § 1.668(b)-1A(b)(1) or § 1.669(b)-1A(b)(1), whichever is appropriate, for the prior taxable years of the beneficiary in which he was in being.

If the amount determined under subdivision (i) does not exceed the amount determined under subdivision (ii), no credit is allowable. If the amount determined under subdivision (i) exceeds the amount determined under subdivision (ii), the credit allowable is the lesser of the amount of such excess or the amount of taxes deemed distributed to the beneficiary for all preceding taxable years to the extent that such taxes are not used in § 1.668(b)-1A(b)(2) or § 1.669(b)-1A(b)(2) in determining the beneficiary's partial tax under section 668(a)(2) or 668(a)(3). The application of this subparagraph may be illustrated by the following example:

Example. An accumulation distribution made in 1975 is deemed distributed in 1973 and 1974, years in which the beneficiary was in being. The taxes deemed distributed in such years are $4,000 and $2,000, respectively, totaling $6,000. The amounts of tax computed under § 1.668(b)-1A(b)(1) attributable to the amounts thrown back are $3,000 and $2,000, respectively, totaling $5,000. The credit allowable under this subparagraph is therefore $1,000 ($6,000 less $5,000).

(3) *Short-cut method.* In the case of the tax computed under the short-cut method provided in § 1.668(b)-1A(c) or 1.669(b)-1A(c), the credit allowed by this section is computed as follows:

(i) Compute the total taxes deemed distributed in all preceding taxable years of the trust under §§ 1.666(b)-1A and 1.666(c)-1A or §§ 1.669(d)-1A and 1.669(e)-1A, whichever are appropriate.

(ii) Compute the beneficiary's partial tax determined under either § 1.668(b)-1A(c)(1)(v) or § 1.669(b)-1A(c)(1)(v), whichever is appropriate.

If the amount determined under subdivision (i) does not exceed the amount determined under subdivision (ii), no credit is allowable. If the amount determined under subdivision (i) exceeds the amount determined under subdivision (ii),

(iii) Compute the total taxes deemed distributed under §§ 1.666(b)-1A and 1.666(c)-1A or §§ 1.669(d)-1A and 1.669(e)-1A, which are appropriate, for the preceding taxable years of the trust on the last day of which the beneficiary was in being.

(iv) Multiply the amount by which subdivision (i) exceeds subdivision (ii) by a fraction, the numerator of which is the amount determined under subdivision (iii) of this subparagraph and the denominator of which is the amount determined under subdivision (i) of this subparagraph.

The result is the allowable credit. The application of this subparagraph may be illustrated by the following example:

Example. An accumulation distribution that consists only of undistributed net income is made in 1975. The taxes deemed distributed in the preceding years under §§ 1.666(b)-1A and 1.666(c)-1A are $15,000. The amount determined under § 1.668(b)-1A(c)(1)(v) is $12,000. The beneficiary was in being on the last day of all but one preceding taxable year in which the accumulation distribution was deemed made, and the taxes deemed distributed in those years was $10,000. Therefore, the excess of the subdivision (i) amount over the subdivision (ii) amount is $3,000, and is multiplied by 10,000/15,000, resulting in an answer of $2,000, which is the credit allowable when computed under the short-cut method.

(b) *Year of credit.* The credit to which a beneficiary is entitled under this section is allowed for the taxable year in which the accumulation distribution (to which the credit relates) is required to be included in the income of the beneficiary under section 668(a). Any excess over the total tax liability of the beneficiary for such year is treated as an overpayment of tax by the beneficiary. See section 6401(b) and the regulations thereunder. [Reg. § 1.667(b)-1A.]

☐ [*T.D. 7204*, 8-24-72.]

Reg. § 1.667(b)-1A(a)(2)

[Reg. § 1.671-1]

§ 1.671-1. Grantors and others treated as substantial owners; scope.—(a) Subpart E (section 671 and following), part I, subchapter J, chapter 1 of the Code, contains provisions taxing income of a trust to the grantor or another person under certain circumstances even though he is not treated as a beneficiary under subparts A through D (section 641 and following) of such part I. Section 671 and 672 contain general provisions relating to the entire subpart. Sections 673 through 677 define the circumstances under which income of a trust is taxed to a grantor. These circumstances are in general as follows:

(1) If the grantor has retained a reversionary interest in the trust, within specified time limits (section 673);

(2) If the grantor or a nonadverse party has certain powers over the beneficial interests under the trust (section 674);

(3) If certain administrative powers over the trust exist under which the grantor can or does benefit (section 675);

(4) If the grantor or a nonadverse party has a power to revoke the trust or return the corpus to the grantor (section 676); or

(5) If the grantor or a nonadverse party has the power to distribute income to or for the benefit of the grantor or the grantor's spouse (section 677).

Under section 678, income of a trust is taxed to a person other than the grantor to the extent that he has the sole power to vest corpus or income in himself.

(b) Sections 671 and 677 do not apply if the income of a trust is taxable to a grantor's spouse under section 71 or 682 (relating respectively to alimony and separate maintenance payments, and the income of an estate or trust in the case of divorce, etc.).

(c) Except as provided in such subpart E, income of a trust is not included in computing the taxable income and credits of a grantor or another person solely on the grounds of his dominion and control over the trust. However, the provisions of subpart E do not apply in situations involving an assignment of future income, whether or not the assignment is to a trust. Thus, for example, a person who assigns his right to future income under an employment contract may be taxed on that income even though the assignment is to a trust over which the assignor has retained none of the controls specified in sections 671 through 677. Similarly, a bondholder who assigns his right to interest may be taxed on interest payments even though the assignment is to an uncontrolled trust. Nor are the rules as to family partnerships affected by the provisions of subpart E even though a partnership interest is held in trust. Likewise, these sections have no application in determining the right of a grantor to deductions for payments to a trust under a transfer and leaseback arrangement. In addition, the limitation of the last sentence of section 671 does not prevent any person from being taxed on the income of a trust when it is used to discharge his legal obligation. See § 1.662(a)-4. He is then treated as a beneficiary under subparts A through D or treated as an owner under section 677 because the income is distributed for his benefit, and not because of his dominion or control over the trust.

(d) The provisions of subpart E are not applicable with respect to a pooled income fund as defined in paragraph (5) of section 642(c) and the regulations thereunder, a charitable remainder annuity trust as defined in paragraph (1) of section 664(d) and the regulations thereunder, or a charitable remainder unitrust as defined in paragraph (2) of section 664(d) and the regulations thereunder.

(e) For the effective date of subpart E see section 683 and the regulations thereunder.

(f) For rules relating to the treatment of liabilities resulting on the sale or other disposition of encumbered trust property due to a renunciation of powers by the grantor or other owner, see § 1.1001-2. [Reg. § 1.671-1.]

☐ [T.D. 6217, 12-19-56. Amended by T.D. 7148, 10-28-71, and by T.D. 7741, 12-11-80.]

[Reg. § 1.671-2]

§ 1.671-2. Applicable principles.—(a) Under section 671 a grantor or another person includes in computing his taxable income and credits those items of income, deduction, and credit against tax which are attributable to or included in any portion of a trust of which he is treated as the owner. Sections 673 through 678 set forth the rules for determining when the grantor or another person is treated as the owner of any portion of a trust. The rules for determining the items of income, deduction, and credit against tax that are attributable to or included in a portion of the trust are set forth in § 1.671-3.

(b) Since the principle underlying subpart E (section 671 and following), part I, subchapter J, chapter 1 of the Code, is in general that income of a trust over which the grantor or another person has retained substantial dominion or control should be taxed to the grantor or other person rather than to the trust which receives the income or to the beneficiary to whom the income may be distributed it is ordinarily immaterial whether the income involved constitutes income or corpus for trust accounting purposes. Accordingly, when it is stated in the regulations under subpart E that "income" is attributed to the grantor or another person, the reference, unless specifically limited, is to income determined for tax purposes and not to income for trust accounting purposes. When it is intended to emphasize that income for trust accounting purposes (determined in accordance with the provisions set forth in § 1.643(b)-1), is meant, the phrase "ordinary income" is used.

(c) An item of income, deduction, or credit included in computing the taxable income and credits of a grantor or another person under section 671 is treated as if it had been received or paid directly by the grantor or other person (whether or not an individual). For example, a charitable contribution made by a trust which is attributed to the grantor (an individual) under sections 671 through 677 will be aggregated with his other charitable contributions to determine their deductibility under the limitations of section 170(b)(1). Likewise, dividends received by a trust from sources in a particular foreign country which are attributed to a grantor or another person under subpart E will be aggregated with his other income from sources within that country to determine whether the taxpayer is subject to the limitations of section 904 with respect to credit for the tax paid to that country.

(d) Items of income, deduction, and credit not attributed to or included in any portion of a trust of which the grantor or another person is treated as the owner under subpart E are subject to the provisions of subparts A through D (section 641 and following), of such part I.

(e)(1) For purposes of part I of subchapter J, chapter 1 of the Internal Revenue Code, a grantor includes any person to the extent such person either creates a trust, or directly or indirectly makes a gratuitous transfer (within the meaning of paragraph (e)(2) of this section) of property to a trust. For purposes of this section, the term *property* includes cash. If a person creates or funds a trust on behalf of another person, both persons are treated as grantors of the trust. (See section 6048 for reporting requirements that apply to grantors of foreign trusts.) However, a person who creates a trust but makes no gratuitous transfers to the trust is not treated as an owner of any portion of the trust under sections 671 through 677 or 679. Also, a person who funds a trust with an amount that is directly reimbursed to such person within a reasonable period of time and who makes no other transfers to the trust that constitute gratuitous transfers is not treated as an owner of any portion of the trust under sections 671 through 677 or 679. See also § 1.672(f)-5(a).

(2)(i) A gratuitous transfer is any transfer other than a transfer for fair market value. A transfer of property to a trust may be considered a gratuitous transfer without regard to whether the transfer is treated as a gift for gift tax purposes.

(ii) For purposes of this paragraph (e), a transfer is for fair market value only to the extent of the value of property received from the trust, services rendered by the trust, or the right to use property of the trust. For example, rents, royalties, interest, and compensation paid to a trust are transfers for fair market value only to the extent that the payments reflect an arm's length price for the use of the property of, or for the services rendered by, the trust. For purposes of this determination, an interest in the trust is not property received from the trust. In addition, a person will not be treated as making a transfer for fair market value merely because the transferor recognizes gain on the transaction. See, for example, section 684 regarding the recognition of gain on certain transfers to foreign trusts.

(iii) For purposes of this paragraph (e), a gratuitous transfer does not include a distribution to a trust with respect to an interest held by such trust in either a trust described in paragraph (e)(3) of this section or an entity other than a trust. For example, a distribution to a trust by a corporation with respect to its stock described in section 301 is not a gratuitous transfer.

(3) A grantor includes any person who acquires an interest in a trust from a grantor of the trust if the interest acquired is an interest in certain investment trusts described in § 301.7701-4(c) of this chapter, liquidating trusts described in § 301.7701-4(d) of this chapter, or environmental remediation trusts described in § 301.7701-4(e) of this chapter.

(4) If a gratuitous transfer is made by a partnership or corporation to a trust and is for a business purpose of the partnership or corporation, the partnership or corporation will generally be treated as the grantor of the trust. For example, if a partnership makes a gratuitous transfer to a trust in order to secure a legal obligation of the partnership to a third party unrelated to the partnership, the partnership will be treated as the grantor of the trust. However, if a partnership or a corporation makes a gratuitous transfer to a trust that is not for a business purpose of the partnership or corporation but is for the personal purposes of one or more of the partners or shareholders, the gratuitous transfer will be treated as a constructive distribution to such partners or

Reg. § 1.671-2(c)

shareholders under federal tax principles and the partners or the shareholders will be treated as the grantors of the trust. For example, if a partnership makes a gratuitous transfer to a trust that is for the benefit of a child of a partner, the gratuitous transfer will be treated as a distribution to the partner under section 731 and a subsequent gratuitous transfer by the partner to the trust.

(5) If a trust makes a gratuitous transfer of property to another trust, the grantor of the transferor trust generally will be treated as the grantor of the transferee trust. However, if a person with a general power of appointment over the transferor trust exercises that power in favor of another trust, then such person will be treated as the grantor of the transferee trust, even if the grantor of the transferor trust is treated as the owner of the transferor trust under subpart E of part I, subchapter J, chapter 1 of the Internal Revenue Code.

(6) The following examples illustrate the rules of this paragraph (e). Unless otherwise indicated, all trusts are domestic trusts, and all other persons are United States persons. The examples are as follows:

Example 1. A creates and funds a trust, T, for the benefit of her children. B subsequently makes a gratuitous transfer to T. Under paragraph (e)(1) of this section, both A and B are grantors of T.

Example 2. A makes an investment in a fixed investment trust, T, that is classified as a trust under § 301.7701-4(c)(1) of this chapter. A is a grantor of T. B subsequently acquires A's entire interest in T. Under paragraph (e)(3) of this section, B is a grantor of T with respect to such interest.

Example 3. A, an attorney, creates a foreign trust, FT, on behalf of A's client, B, and transfers $100 to FT out of A's funds. A is reimbursed by B for the $100 transferred to FT. The trust instrument states that the trustee has discretion to distribute the income or corpus of FT to B and B's children. Both A and B are treated as grantors of FT under paragraph (e)(1) of this section. In addition, B is treated as the owner of the entire trust under section 677. Because A is reimbursed for the $100 transferred to FT on behalf of B, A is not treated as transferring any property to FT. Therefore, A is not an owner of any portion of FT under sections 671 through 677 regardless of whether A retained any power over or interest in FT described in sections 673 through 677. Furthermore, A is not treated as an owner of any portion of FT under section 679. Both A and B are responsible parties for purposes of the requirements in section 6048.

Example 4. A creates and funds a trust, T. A does not retain any power or interest in T that would cause A to be treated as an owner of any portion of the trust under sections 671 through 677. B holds an unrestricted power, exercisable solely by B, to withdraw certain amounts contributed to the trust before the end of the calendar year and to vest those amounts in B. B is treated as an owner of the portion of T that is subject to the withdrawal power under section 678(a)(1). However, B is not a grantor of T under paragraph (e)(1) of this section because B neither created T nor made a gratuitous transfer to T.

Example 5. A transfers cash to a trust, T, through a broker, in exchange for units in T. The units in T are not property for purposes of determining whether A has received fair market value under paragraph (e)(2)(ii) of this section. Therefore, A has made a gratuitous transfer to T, and, under paragraph (e)(1) of this section, A is a grantor of T.

Example 6. A borrows cash from T, a trust. A has not made any gratuitous transfers to T. Arm's length interest payments by A to T will not be treated as gratuitous transfers under paragraph (e)(2)(ii) of this section. Therefore, under paragraph (e)(1) of this section, A is not a grantor of T with respect to the interest payments.

Example 7. A, B's brother, creates a trust, T, for B's benefit and transfers $50,000 to T. The trustee invests the $50,000 in stock of Company X. C, B's uncle, purportedly sells property with a fair market value of $1,000,000 to T in exchange for the stock when it has appreciated to a fair market value of $100,000. Under paragraph (e)(2)(ii) of this section, the $900,000 excess value is a gratuitous transfer by C. Therefore, under paragraph (e)(1) of this section, A is a grantor with respect to the portion of the trust valued at $100,000, and C is a grantor of T with respect to the portion of the trust valued at $900,000. In addition, A or C or both will be treated as the owners of the respective portions of the trust of which each person is a grantor if A or C or both retain powers over or interests in such portions under sections 673 through 677.

Example 8. G creates and funds a trust, T1, for the benefit of G's children and grandchildren. After G's death, under authority granted to the trustees in the trust instrument, the trustees of T1 transfer a portion of the assets of T1 to another trust, T2, and retain a power to revoke T2 and revest the assets of T2 in T1. Under paragraphs (e)(1) and (5) of this section, G is the grantor of T1 and T2. In addition, because the trustees of T1 have retained a power to revest the

Reg. § 1.671-2(e)(6)

assets of T2 in T1, T1 is treated as the owner of T2 under section 678(a).

Example 9. G creates and funds a trust, T1, for the benefit of B. G retains a power to revest the assets of T1 in G within the meaning of section 676. Under the trust agreement, B is given a general power of appointment over the assets of T1. B exercises the general power of appointment with respect to one-half of the corpus of T1 in favor of a trust, T2, that is for the benefit of C, B's child. Under paragraph (e)(1) of this section, G is the grantor of T1, and under paragraphs (e)(1) and (5) of this section, B is the grantor of T2.

(7) The rules of this section are applicable to any transfer to a trust, or transfer of an interest in a trust, on or after August 10, 1999. [Reg. § 1.671-2.]

☐ [*T.D.* 6217, 12-19-56. Amended by *T.D.* 8831, 8-5-99 and *T.D.* 8890, 7-3-2000.]

[Reg. § 1.671-3]

§ 1.671-3. Attribution or inclusion of income, deductions, and credits against tax.—(a) When a grantor or another person is treated under subpart E (section 671 and following) as the owner of any portion of a trust, there are included in computing his tax liability those items of income, deduction, and credit against tax attributable to or included in that portion. For example—

(1) If a grantor or another person is treated as the owner of an entire trust (corpus as well as ordinary income), he takes into account in computing his income tax liability all items of income, deduction, and credit (including capital gains and losses) to which he would have been entitled had the trust not been in existence during the period he is treated as owner.

(2) If the portion treated as owned consists of specific trust property and its income, all items directly related to that property are attributable to the portion. Items directly related to trust property not included in the portion treated as owned by the grantor or other person are governed by the provisions of subparts A through D (section 641 and following), part I, subchapter J, chapter 1 of the Code. Items that relate both to the portion treated as owned by the grantor and to the balance of the trust must be apportioned in a manner that is reasonable in the light of all the circumstances of each case, including the terms of the governing instrument, local law, and the practice of the trustee if it is reasonable and consistent.

(3) If the portion of a trust treated as owned by a grantor or another person consists of an undivided fractional interest in the trust, or of an interest represented by a dollar amount, a pro rata share of each item of income, deduction, and credit is normally allocated to the portion. Thus, where the portion owned consists of an interest in or a right to an amount of corpus only, a fraction of each item (including items allocated to corpus, such as capital gains) is attributed to the portion. The numerator of this fraction is the amount which is subject to the control of the grantor or other person and the denominator is normally the fair market value of the trust corpus at the beginning of the taxable year in question. The share not treated as owned by the grantor or other person is governed by the provisions of subparts A through D. See the last three sentences of paragraph (c) of this section for the principles applicable if the portion treated as owned consists of an interest in part of the ordinary income in contrast to an interest in corpus alone.

(b) If a grantor or another person is treated as the owner of a portion of a trust, that portion may or may not include both ordinary income and other income allocable to corpus. For example—

(1) Only ordinary income is included by reason of an interest in or a power over ordinary income alone. Thus, if a grantor is treated under section 673 as an owner by reason of a reversionary interest in ordinary income only, items of income allocable to corpus will not be included in the portion he is treated as owning. Similarly, if a grantor or another person is treated under sections 674-678 as an owner of a portion by reason of a power over ordinary income only, items of income allocable to corpus are not included in that portion. (See paragraph (c) of this section to determine the treatment of deductions and credits when only ordinary income is included in the portion.)

(2) Only income allocable to corpus is included by reason of an interest in or a power over corpus alone, if satisfaction of the interest or an exercise of the power will not result in an interest in or the exercise of a power over ordinary income which would itself cause that income to be included. For example, if a grantor has a reversionary interest in a trust which is not such as to require that he be treated as an owner under section 673, he may nevertheless be treated as an owner under section 677(a)(2) since any income allocable to corpus is accumulated for future distribution to him, but items of income included in determining ordinary income are not included in the portion he is treated as owning. Similarly, he may have a power over corpus which is such that he is treated as an owner under section 674 or 676(a), but ordinary income will not be included in the portion he owns, if his power can only affect income received after a period of time such that

Reg. § 1.671-3(a)(1)

he would not be treated as an owner of the income if the power were a reversionary interest. (See paragraph (c) of this section to determine the treatment of deductions and credits when only income allocated to corpus is included in the portion.)

(3) Both ordinary income and other income allocable to corpus are included by reason of an interest in or a power over both ordinary income and corpus, or an interest in or a power over corpus alone which does not come within the provisions of subparagraph (2) of this paragraph. For example, if a grantor is treated under section 673 as the owner of a portion of a trust by reason of a reversionary interest in corpus, both ordinary income and other income allocable to corpus are included in the portion. Further, a grantor includes both ordinary income and other income allocable to corpus in the portion he is treated as owning if he is treated under section 674 or 676 as an owner because of a power over corpus which can affect income received within a period such that he would be treated as an owner under section 673 if the power were a reversionary interest. Similarly, a grantor or another person includes both ordinary income and other income allocable to corpus in the portion he is treated as owning if he is treated as an owner under section 675 or 678 because of a power over corpus.

(c) If only income allocable to corpus is included in computing a grantor's tax liability, he will take into account in that computation only those items of income, deduction, and credit which would not be included under subparts A through D in the computation of the tax liability of the current income beneficiaries if all distributable net income had actually been distributed to those beneficiaries. On the other hand, if the grantor or another person is treated as an owner solely because of his interest in or power over ordinary income alone, he will take into account in computing his tax liability those items which would be included in computing the tax liability of a current income beneficiary, including expenses allocable to corpus which enter into the computation of distributable net income. If the grantor or other person is treated as an owner because of his power over or right to a dollar amount of ordinary income, he will first take into account a portion of those items of income and expense entering into the computation of ordinary income under the trust instrument or local law sufficient to produce income of the dollar amount required. There will then be attributable to him a pro rata portion of other items entering into the computation of distributable net income under subparts A through D, such as expenses allocable to corpus, and a pro rata portion of credits of the trust. For examples of computations under this paragraph, see paragraph (g) of § 1.677(a)-1. [Reg. § 1.671-3.]

☐ [T.D. 6217, 12-19-56. Amended by T.D. 6989, 1-16-69.]

[Reg. § 1.671-4]

§ 1.671-4. Method of reporting.—(a) *Portion of trust treated as owned by the grantor or another person.* Except as otherwise provided in paragraph (b) of this section, items of income, deduction, and credit attributable to any portion of a trust which, under the provisions of subpart E (section 671 and following), part I, subchapter J, chapter 1 of the Internal Revenue Code, is treated as owned by the grantor or another person are not reported by the trust on Form 1041, but are shown on a separate statement to be attached to that form. Section 301.7701-4(e)(2) of this chapter provides guidance on how these reporting rules apply to an environmental remediation trust.

(b) *A trust all of which is treated as owned by one or more grantors or other persons*—(1) *In general.* In the case of a trust all of which is treated as owned by one or more grantors or other persons, and which is not described in paragraph (b)(6) or (7) of this section, the trustee may, but is not required to, report by one of the methods described in this paragraph (b) rather than by the method described in paragraph (a) of this section. A trustee may not report, however, pursuant to paragraph (b)(2)(i)(A) of this section unless the grantor or other person treated as the owner of the trust provides to the trustee a complete Form W-9 or acceptable substitute Form W-9 signed under penalties of perjury. See section 3406 and the regulations thereunder for the information to include on, and the manner of executing, the Form W-9, depending upon the type of reportable payments made.

(2) *A trust all of which is treated as owned by one grantor or by one other person*—(i) *In general.* In the case of a trust all of which is treated as owned by one grantor or one other person, the trustee reporting under this paragraph (b) must either—

(A) Furnish the name and taxpayer identification number (TIN) of the grantor or other person treated as the owner of the trust, and the address of the trust, to all payors during the taxable year, and comply with the additional requirements described in paragraph (b)(2)(ii) of this section; or

(B) Furnish the name, TIN, and address of the trust to all payors during the taxable year, and comply with the additional requirements described in paragraph (b)(2)(iii) of this section.

Reg. § 1.671-4(b)(2)

(ii) *Additional obligations of the trustee when name and TIN of the grantor or other person treated as the owner of the trust and the address of the trust are furnished to payors.* (A) Unless the grantor or other person treated as the owner of the trust is the trustee or a co-trustee of the trust, the trustee must furnish the grantor or other person treated as the owner of the trust with a statement that—

(*1*) Shows all items of income, deduction, and credit of the trust for the taxable year;

(*2*) Identifies the payor of each item of income;

(*3*) Provides the grantor or other person treated as the owner of the trust with the information necessary to take the items into account in computing the grantor's or other person's taxable income; and

(*4*) Informs the grantor or other person treated as the owner of the trust that the items of income, deduction and credit and other information shown on the statement must be included in computing the taxable income and credits of the grantor or other person on the income tax return of the grantor or other person.

(B) The trustee is not required to file any type of return with the Internal Revenue Service.

(iii) *Additional obligations of the trustee when name, TIN, and address of the trust are furnished to payors*—(A) *Obligation to file Forms 1099.* The trustee must file with the Internal Revenue Service the appropriate Forms 1099, reporting the income or gross proceeds paid to the trust during the taxable year, and showing the trust as the payor and the grantor or other person treated as the owner of the trust as the payee. The trustee has the same obligations for filing the appropriate Forms 1099 as would a payor making reportable payments, except that the trustee must report each type of income in the aggregate, and each item of gross proceeds separately. See paragraph (b)(5) of this section regarding the amounts required to be included on any Forms 1099 filed by the trustee.

(B) *Obligation to furnish statement.* (*1*) Unless the grantor or other person treated as the owner of the trust is the trustee or a co-trustee of the trust, the trustee must also furnish to the grantor or other person treated as the owner of the trust a statement that—

(*i*) Shows all items of income, deduction, and credit of the trust for the taxable year;

(*ii*) Provides the grantor or other person treated as the owner of the trust with the information necessary to take the items into account in computing the grantor's or other person's taxable income; and

(*iii*) Informs the grantor or other person treated as the owner of the trust that the items of income, deduction and credit and other information shown on the statement must be included in computing the taxable income and credits of the grantor or other person on the income tax return of the grantor or other person.

(*2*) By furnishing the statement, the trustee satisfies the obligation to furnish statements to recipients with respect to the Forms 1099 filed by the trustee.

(iv) *Examples.* The following examples illustrate the provisions of this paragraph (b)(2):

Example 1. G, a United States citizen, creates an irrevocable trust which provides that the ordinary income is to be payable to him for life and that on his death the corpus shall be distributed to B, an unrelated person. Except for the right to receive income, G retains no right or power which would cause him to be treated as an owner under sections 671 through 679. Under the applicable local law, capital gains must be added to corpus. Since G has a right to receive income, he is treated as an owner of a portion of the trust under section 677. The tax consequences of any items of capital gain of the trust are governed by the provisions of subparts A, B, C, and D (section 641 and following), part I, subchapter J, chapter 1 of the Internal Revenue Code. Because not all of the trust is treated as owned by the grantor or another person, the trustee may not report by the methods described in paragraph (b)(2) of this section.

Example 2. (i)(A) On January 2, 1996, G, a United States citizen, creates a trust all of which is treated as owned by G. The trustee of the trust is T. During the 1996 taxable year the trust has the following items of income and gross proceeds:

Interest $2,500
Dividends 3,205
Proceeds from sale of B stock 2,000

(B) The trust has no items of deduction or credit.

(ii)(A) The payors of the interest paid to the trust are X ($2,000), Y ($300), and Z ($200). The payors of the dividends paid to the trust are A ($3,200), and D ($5). The payor of the gross proceeds paid to the trust is D, a brokerage firm, which held the B stock as the nominee for the trust. The B stock was purchased by T for $1,500 on January 3, 1996, and sold by T on November 29, 1996. T chooses to report pursuant to para-

Reg. § 1.671-4(b)(2)

graph (b)(2)(i)(B) of this section, and therefore furnishes the name, TIN, and address of the trust to X, Y, Z, A, and D. X, Y, and Z each furnish T with a Form 1099-INT showing the trust as the payee. A furnishes T with a Form 1099-DIV showing the trust as the payee. D does not furnish T with a Form 1099-DIV because D paid a dividend of less than $10 to T. D furnishes T with a Form 1099-B showing the trust as the payee.

(B) On or before February 28, 1997, T files a Form 1099-INT with the Internal Revenue Service on which T reports interest attributable to G, as the owner of the trust, of $2,500; a Form 1099-DIV on which T reports dividends attributable to G, as the owner of the trust, of $3,205; and a Form 1099-B on which T reports gross proceeds from the sale of B stock attributable to G, as the owner of the trust, of $2,000. On or before April 15, 1997, T furnishes a statement to G which lists the following items of income and information necessary for G to take the items into account in computing G's taxable income:

Interest	$2,500
Dividends	3,205
Gain from sale of B stock	500
Information regarding sale of B stock:	
Proceeds	$2,000
Basis	1,500
Date acquired	1/03/96
Date sold	11/29/96

(C) T informs G that any items of income, deduction and credit and other information shown on the statement must be included in computing the taxable income and credits of the grantor or other person on the income tax return of the grantor or other person.

(D) T has complied with T's obligations under this section.

(iii)(A) Same facts as paragraphs (i) and (ii) of this *Example 2*, except that G contributed the B stock to the trust on January 2, 1996. On or before April 15, 1997, T furnishes a statement to G which lists the following items of income and information necessary for G to take the items into account in computing G's taxable income:

Interest	$2,500
Dividends	3,205
Information regarding sale of B stock:	
Proceeds	$2,000
Date sold	11/29/96

(B) T informs G that any items of income, deduction and credit and other information shown on the statement must be included in computing the taxable income and credits of the grantor or other person on the income tax return of the grantor or other person.

(C) T has complied with T's obligations under this section.

Example 3. On January 2, 1996, G, a United States citizen, creates a trust all of which is treated as owned by G. The trustee of the trust is T. The only asset of the trust is an interest in C, a common trust fund under section 584(a). T chooses to report pursuant to paragraph (b)(2)(i)(B) of this section and therefore furnishes the name, TIN, and address of the trust to C. C files a Form 1065 and a Schedule K-1 (Partner's Share of Income, Credits, Deductions, etc.) showing the name, TIN, and address of the trust with the Internal Revenue Service and furnishes a copy to T. Because the trust did not receive any amounts described in paragraph (b)(5) of this section, T does not file any type of return with the Internal Revenue Service. On or before April 15, 1997, T furnishes G with a statement that shows all items of income, deduction, and credit of the trust for the 1996 taxable year. In addition, T informs G that any items of income, deduction and credit and other information shown on the statement must be included in computing the taxable income and credits of the grantor or other person on the income tax return of the grantor or other person. T has complied with T's obligations under this section.

(3) *A trust all of which is treated as owned by two or more grantors or other persons*—(i) *In general.* In the case of a trust all of which is treated as owned by two or more grantors or other persons, the trustee must furnish the name, TIN, and address of the trust to all payors for the taxable year, and comply with the additional requirements described in paragraph (b)(3)(ii) of this section.

(ii) *Additional obligations of trustee*—(A) *Obligation to file Forms 1099.* The trustee must file with the Internal Revenue Service the appropriate Forms 1099, reporting the items of income paid to the trust by all payors during the taxable year attributable to the portion of the trust treated as owned by each grantor or other person, and showing the trust as the payor and each grantor or other person treated as an owner of the trust as the payee. The trustee has the same obligations for filing the appropriate Forms 1099 as would a payor making reportable payments, except that the trustee must report each type of income in the aggregate, and each item of gross proceeds separately. See paragraph (b)(5) of this section regarding the amounts required to be included on any Forms 1099 filed by the trustee.

Reg. § 1.671-4(b)(3)

(B) *Obligation to furnish statement.* (*1*) The trustee must also furnish to each grantor or other person treated as an owner of the trust a statement that—

(*i*) Shows all items of income, deduction, and credit of the trust for the taxable year attributable to the portion of the trust treated as owned by the grantor or other person;

(*ii*) Provides the grantor or other person treated as an owner of the trust with the information necessary to take the items into account in computing the grantor's or other person's taxable income; and

(*iii*) Informs the grantor or other person treated as the owner of the trust that the items of income, deduction and credit and other information shown on the statement must be included in computing the taxable income and credits of the grantor or other person on the income tax return of the grantor or other person.

(*2*) Except for the requirements pursuant to section 3406 and the regulations thereunder, by furnishing the statement, the trustee satisfies the obligation to furnish statements to recipients with respect to the Forms 1099 filed by the trustee.

(4) *Persons treated as payors*—(i) *In general.* For purposes of this section, the term payor means any person who is required by any provision of the Internal Revenue Code and the regulations thereunder to make any type of information return (including Form 1099 or Schedule K-1) with respect to the trust for the taxable year, including persons who make payments to the trust or who collect (or otherwise act as middlemen with respect to) payments on behalf of the trust.

(ii) *Application to brokers and customers.* For purposes of this section, a broker, within the meaning of section 6045, is considered a payor. A customer, within the meaning of section 6045, is considered a payee.

(5) *Amounts required to be included on Forms 1099 filed by the trustee*—(i) *In general.* The amounts that must be included on any Forms 1099 required to be filed by the trustee pursuant to this section do not include any amounts that are reportable by the payor on an information return other than Form 1099. For example, in the case of a trust which owns an interest in a partnership, the trust's distributive share of the income and gain of the partnership is not includible on any Forms 1099 filed by the trustee pursuant to this section because the distributive share is reportable by the partnership on Schedule K-1.

(ii) *Example.* The following example illustrates the provisions of this paragraph (b)(5):

Example. (i)(A) On January 2, 1996, G, a United States citizen, creates a trust all of which is treated as owned by G. The trustee of the trust is T. The assets of the trust during the 1996 taxable year are shares of stock in X, an S corporation, a limited partnership interest in P, shares of stock in M, and shares of stock in N. T chooses to report pursuant to paragraph (b)(2)(i)(B) of this section and therefore furnishes the name, TIN, and address of the trust to X, P, M, and N. M furnishes T with a Form 1099-DIV showing the trust as the payee. N does not furnish T with a Form 1099-DIV because N paid a dividend of less than $10 to T. X and P furnish T with Schedule K-1 (Shareholder's Share of Income, Credits, Deductions, etc.) and Schedule K-1 (Partner's Share of Income, Credits, Deductions, etc.), respectively, showing the trust's name, TIN, and address.

(B) For the 1996 taxable year the trust has the following items of income and deduction:

Dividends paid by M $12

Dividends paid by N 6

Administrative expense $20

Items reported by X on Schedule K-1 attributable to trust's shares of stock in X:

Interest $20

Dividends 35

Items reported by P on Schedule K-1 attributable to trust's limited partnership interest in P:

Ordinary income $300

(ii)(A) On or before February 28, 1997, T files with the Internal Revenue Service a Form 1099-DIV on which T reports dividends attributable to G as the owner of the trust in the amount of $18. T does not file any other returns.

(B) T has complied with T's obligation under paragraph (b)(2)(iii)(A) of this section to file the appropriate Forms 1099.

(6) *Trusts that cannot report under this paragraph (b).* The following trusts cannot use the methods of reporting described in this paragraph (b)—

(i) A common trust fund as defined in section 584(a);

(ii) A trust that has its situs or any of its assets located outside the United States;

(iii) A trust that is a qualified subchapter S trust as defined in section 1361(d)(3);

Reg. § 1.671-4(b)(4)

(iv) A trust all of which is treated as owned by one grantor or one other person whose taxable year is a fiscal year;

(v) A trust all of which is treated as owned by one grantor or one other person who is not a United States person; or

(vi) A trust all of which is treated as owned by two or more grantors or other persons, one of whom is not a United States person.

(7) *Grantors or other persons who are treated as owners of the trust and are exempt recipients for information reporting purposes*—(i) *Trust treated as owned by one grantor or one other person.* The trustee of a trust all of which is treated as owned by one grantor or one other person may not report pursuant to this paragraph (b) if the grantor or other person is an exempt recipient for information reporting purposes.

(ii) *Trust treated as owned by two or more grantors or other persons.* The trustee of a trust, all of which is treated as owned by two or more grantors or other persons, may not report pursuant to this paragraph (b) if one or more grantors or other persons treated as owners are exempt recipients for information reporting purposes unless—

(A) At least one grantor or one other person who is treated as an owner of the trust is a person who is not an exempt recipient for information reporting purposes; and

(B) The trustee reports without regard to whether any of the grantors or other persons treated as owners of the trust are exempt recipients for information reporting purposes.

(8) *Husband and wife who make a single return jointly.* A trust all of which is treated as owned by a husband and wife who make a single return jointly of income taxes for the taxable year under section 6013 is considered to be owned by one grantor for purposes of this paragraph (b).

(c) *Due date for Forms 1099 required to be filed by trustee.* The due date for any Forms 1099 required to be filed with the Internal Revenue Service by a trustee pursuant to this section is the due date otherwise in effect for filing Forms 1099.

(d) *Due date and other requirements with respect to statement required to be furnished by trustee*—(1) *In general.* The due date for the statement required to be furnished by a trustee to the grantor or other person treated as an owner of the trust pursuant to this section is the date specified by section 6034A(a). The trustee must maintain in its records a copy of the statement furnished to the grantor or other person treated as an owner of the trust for a period of three years from the due date for furnishing such statement specified in this paragraph (d).

(2) *Statement for the taxable year ending with the death of the grantor or other person treated as the owner of the trust.* If a trust ceases to be treated as owned by the grantor, or other person, by reason of the death of that grantor or other person (decedent), the due date for the statement required to be furnished for the taxable year ending with the death of the decedent shall be the date specified by section 6034A(a) as though the decedent had lived throughout the decedent's last taxable year. See paragraph (h) of this section for special reporting rules for a trust or portion of the trust that ceases to be treated as owned by the grantor or other person by reason of the death of the grantor or other person.

(e) *Backup withholding requirements*—(1) *Trustee reporting under paragraph (b)(2)(i)(A) of this section.* In order for the trustee to be able to report pursuant to paragraph (b)(2)(i)(A) of this section and to furnish to all payors the name and TIN of the grantor or other person treated as the owner of the trust, the grantor or other person must provide a complete Form W-9 to the trustee in the manner provided in paragraph (b)(1) of this section, and the trustee must give the name and TIN shown on that Form W-9 to all payors. In addition, if the Form W-9 indicates that the grantor or other person is subject to backup withholding, the trustee must notify all payors of reportable interest and dividend payments of the requirement to backup withhold. If the Form W-9 indicates that the grantor or other person is not subject to backup withholding, the trustee does not have to notify the payors that backup withholding is not required. The trustee should not give the Form W-9, or a copy thereof, to a payor because the Form W-9 contains the address of the grantor or other person and paragraph (b)(2)(i)(A) of this section requires the trustee to furnish the address of the trust to all payors and not the address of the grantor or other person. The trustee acts as the agent of the grantor or other person for purposes of furnishing to the payors the information required by this paragraph (e)(1). Thus, a payor may rely on the name and TIN provided to the payor by the trustee, and, if given, on the trustee's statement that the grantor is subject to backup withholding.

(2) *Other backup withholding requirements.* Whether a trustee is treated as a payor for purposes of backup withholding is determined pursuant to section 3406 and the regulations thereunder.

(f) *Penalties for failure to file a correct Form 1099 or furnish a correct statement.* A trustee who

Reg. § 1.671-4(f)

fails to file a correct Form 1099 or to furnish a correct statement to a grantor or other person treated as an owner of the trust as required by paragraph (b) of this section is subject to the penalties provided by sections 6721 and 6722 and the regulations thereunder.

(g) *Changing reporting methods*—(1) *Changing from reporting by filing Form 1041 to a method described in paragraph (b) of this section.* If the trustee has filed a Form 1041 for any taxable year ending before January 1, 1996 (and has not filed a final Form 1041 pursuant to § 1.6714(b)(3) (as contained in the 26 CFR part 1 edition revised as of April 1, 1995)), or files a Form 1041 for any taxable year thereafter, the trustee must file a final Form 1041 for the taxable year which ends after January 1, 1995, and which immediately precedes the first taxable year for which the trustee reports pursuant to paragraph (b) of this section, on the front of which form the trustee must write: "Pursuant to § 1.671-4(g), this is the final Form 1041 for this grantor trust.".

(2) *Changing from reporting by a method described in paragraph (b) of this section to the filing of a Form 1041.* The trustee of a trust who reported pursuant to paragraph (b) of this section for a taxable year may report pursuant to paragraph (a) of this section for subsequent taxable years. If the trustee reported pursuant to paragraph (b)(2)(i)(A) of this section, and therefore furnished the name and TIN of the grantor to all payors, the trustee must furnish the name, TIN, and address of the trust to all payors for such subsequent taxable years. If the trustee reported pursuant to paragraph (b)(2)(i)(B) or (b)(3)(i) of this section, and therefore furnished the name and TIN of the trust to all payors, the trustee must indicate on each Form 1096 (Annual Summary and Transmittal of U.S. Information Returns) that it files (or appropriately on magnetic media) for the final taxable year for which the trustee so reports that it is the final return of the trust.

(3) *Changing between methods described in paragraph (b) of this section*—(i) *Changing from furnishing the TIN of the grantor to furnishing the TIN of the trust.* The trustee of a trust who reported pursuant to paragraph (b)(2)(i)(A) of this section for a taxable year, and therefore furnished the name and TIN of the grantor to all payors, may report pursuant to paragraph (b)(2)(i)(B) of this section, and furnish the name and TIN of the trust to all payors, for subsequent taxable years.

(ii) *Changing from furnishing the TIN of the trust to furnishing the TIN of the grantor.* The trustee of a trust who reported pursuant to paragraph (b)(2)(i)(B) of this section for a taxable year, and therefore furnished the name and TIN of the trust to all payors, may report pursuant to paragraph (b)(2)(i)(A) of this section, and furnish the name and TIN of the grantor to all payors, for subsequent taxable years. The trustee, however, must indicate on each Form 1096 (Annual Summary and Transmittal of U.S. Information Returns) that it files (or appropriately on magnetic media) for the final taxable year for which the trustee reports pursuant to paragraph (b)(2)(i)(B) of this section that it is the final return of the trust.

(4) *Example.* The following example illustrates the provisions of paragraph (g) of this section:

Example. (i) On January 3, 1994, G, a United States citizen, creates a trust all of which is treated as owned by G. The trustee of the trust is T. On or before April 17, 1995, T files with the Internal Revenue Service a Form 1041 with an attached statement for the 1994 taxable year showing the items of income, deduction, and credit of the trust. On or before April 15, 1996, T files with the Internal Revenue Service a Form 1041 with an attached statement for the 1995 taxable year showing the items of income, deduction, and credit of the trust. On the Form 1041, T states that "pursuant to § 1.671-4(g), this is the final Form 1041 for this grantor trust." T may report pursuant to paragraph (b) of this section for the 1996 taxable year.

(ii) T reports pursuant to paragraph (b)(2)(i)(B) of this section, and therefore furnishes the name, TIN, and address of the trust to all payors, for the 1996 and 1997 taxable years. T chooses to report pursuant to paragraph (a) of this section for the 1998 taxable year. On each Form 1096 (Annual Summary and Transmittal of U.S. Information Returns) which T files for the 1997 taxable year (or appropriately on magnetic media), T indicates that it is the trust's final return. On or before April 15, 1999, T files with the Internal Revenue Service a Form 1041 with an attached statement showing the items of income, deduction, and credit of the trust. On the Form 1041, T uses the same TIN which T used on the Forms 1041 and Forms 1099 it filed for previous taxable years. T has complied with T's obligations under paragraph (g)(2) of this section.

(h) *Reporting rules for a trust, or portion of a trust, that ceases to be treated as owned by a grantor or other person by reason of the death of the grantor or other person*—(1) *Definition of decedent.* For purposes of this paragraph (h), the *decedent* is the grantor or other person treated as the owner of the trust, or portion of the trust, under subpart E, part I, subchapter J, chapter 1

Reg. § 1.671-4(g)(1)

of the Internal Revenue Code on the date of death of that person.

(2) *In general.* The provisions of this section apply to a trust, or portion of a trust, treated as owned by a decedent for the taxable year that ends with the decedent's death. Following the death of the decedent, the trust or portion of a trust that ceases to be treated as owned by the decedent, by reason of the death of the decedent, may no longer report under this section. A trust, all of which was treated as owned by the decedent, must obtain a new TIN upon the death of the decedent, if the trust will continue after the death of the decedent. See § 301.6109-1(a)(3)(i) of this chapter for rules regarding obtaining a TIN upon the death of the decedent.

(3) *Special rules*—(i) *Trusts reporting pursuant to paragraph (a) of this section for the taxable year ending with the decedent's death.* The due date for the filing of a return pursuant to paragraph (a) of this section for the taxable year ending with the decedent's death shall be the due date provided for under § 1.6072-1(a)(2). The return filed under this paragraph for a trust all of which was treated as owned by the decedent must indicate that it is a final return.

(ii) *Trust reporting pursuant to paragraph (b)(2)(B) of this section for the taxable year of the decedent's death.* A trust that reports pursuant to paragraph (b)(2)(B) of this section for the taxable year ending with the decedent's death must indicate on each Form 1096 "Annual Summary and Transmittal of the U.S. Information Returns" that it files (or appropriately on magnetic media) for the taxable year ending with the death of the decedent that it is the final return of the trust.

(iii) *Trust reporting under paragraph (b)(3) of this section.* If a trust has been reporting under paragraph (b)(3) of this section, the trustee may not report under that paragraph if any portion of the trust has a short taxable year by reason of the death of the decedent and the portion treated as owned by the decedent does not terminate on the death of the decedent.

(i) *Effective date and transition rule*—(1) *Effective date.* The trustee of a trust any portion of which is treated as owned by one or more grantors or other persons must report pursuant to paragraphs (a), (b), (c), (d)(1), (e), (f), and (g) of this section for taxable years beginning on or after January 1, 1996.

(2) *Transition rule.* For taxable years beginning prior to January 1, 1996, the Internal Revenue Service will not challenge the manner of reporting of—

(i) A trustee of a trust all of which is treated as owned by one or more grantors or other persons who did not report in accordance with § 1.671-4(a) (as contained in the 26 CFR part 1 edition revised as of April 1, 1995) as in effect for taxable years beginning prior to January 1, 1996, but did report in a manner substantially similar to one of the reporting methods described in paragraph (b) of this section; or

(ii) A trustee of two or more trusts all of which are treated as owned by one or more grantors or other persons who filed a single Form 1041 for all of the trusts, rather than a separate Form 1041 for each trust, provided that the items of income, deduction, and credit of each trust were shown on a statement attached to the single Form 1041.

(3) *Effective date for paragraphs (d)(2) and (h) of this section.* Paragraphs (d)(2) and (h) of this section apply for taxable years ending on or after December 24, 2002.

(j) *Cross-reference.* For rules relating to employer identification numbers, and to the obligation of a payor of income or proceeds to the trust to furnish to the payee a statement to recipient, see § 301.6109-1(a)(2) of this chapter. [Reg. § 1.671-4.]

☐ [*T.D.* 6217, 12-19-56. *Amended by T.D.* 7796, 11-23-81; *T.D.* 8633, 12-20-95; *T.D.* 8668, 4-30-96 *and T.D.* 9032, 12-23-2002.]

[Reg. § 1.672(a)-1]

§ 1.672(a)-1. Definition of adverse party.—(a) Under section 672(a) an adverse party is defined as any person having a substantial beneficial interest in a trust which would be adversely affected by the exercise or nonexercise of a power which he possesses respecting the trust. A trustee is not an adverse party merely because of his interest as trustee. A person having a general power of appointment over the trust property is deemed to have a beneficial interest in the trust. An interest is a substantial interest if its value in relation to the total value of the property subject to the power is not insignificant.

(b) Ordinarily, a beneficiary will be an adverse party, but if his right to share in the income or corpus of a trust is limited to only a part, he may be an adverse party only as to that part. Thus, if A, B, C, and D are equal income beneficiaries of a trust and the grantor can revoke with A's consent, the grantor is treated as the owner of a portion which represents three-fourths of the trust; and items of income, deduction, and credit attributable to that portion are included in determining the tax of the grantor.

(c) The interest of an ordinary income beneficiary of a trust may or may not be adverse with respect to the exercise of a power over corpus.

Reg. § 1.672(a)-1(c)

Thus, if the income of a trust is payable to A for life, with a power (which is not a general power of appointment) in A to appoint the corpus to the grantor either during his life or by will, A's interest is adverse to the return of the corpus to the grantor during A's life, but is not adverse to a return of the corpus after A's death. In other words, A's interest is adverse as to ordinary income but is not adverse as to income allocable to corpus. Therefore, assuming no other relevant facts exist, the grantor would not be taxable on the ordinary income of the trust under sections 674, 676, or 677, but would be taxable under section 677 on income allocable to corpus (such as capital gains), since it may in the discretion of a nonadverse party be accumulated for future distribution to the grantor. Similarly, the interest of a contingent income beneficiary is adverse to a return of corpus to the grantor before the termination of his interest but not to a return of corpus after the termination of his interest.

(d) The interest of a remainderman is adverse to the exercise of any power over the corpus of a trust, but not to the exercise of a power over any income interest preceding his remainder. For example, if the grantor creates a trust which provides for income to be distributed to A for 10 years and then for the corpus to go to X if he is then living, a power exercisable by X to revest corpus in the grantor is a power exercisable by an adverse party; however, a power exercisable by X to distribute part or all of the ordinary income to the grantor may be a power exercisable by a nonadverse party (which would cause the ordinary income to be taxed to the grantor). [Reg. § 1.672(a)-1.]

☐ [T.D. 6217, 12-19-56.]

[Reg. § 1.672(b)-1]

§ 1.672(b)-1. **Nonadverse party.**—A "nonadverse party" is any person who is not an adverse party. [Reg. § 1.672(b)-1.]

☐ [T.D. 6217, 12-19-56.]

[Reg. § 1.672(c)-1]

§ 1.672(c)-1. **Related or subordinate party.**—Section 672(c) defines the term "related or subordinate party". The term, as used in sections 674(c) and 675(3), means any nonadverse party who is the grantor's spouse if living with the grantor; the grantor's father, mother, issue, brother or sister; an employee of the grantor; a corporation or any employee of a corporation in which the stock holdings of the grantor and the trust are significant from the viewpoint of voting control; or a subordinate employee of a corporation in which the grantor is an executive. For purposes of sections 674(c) and 675(3), these persons are presumed to be subservient to the grantor in respect of the exercise or nonexercise of the powers conferred on them unless shown not to be subservient by a preponderance of the evidence. [Reg. § 1.672(c)-1.]

☐ [T.D. 6217, 12-19-56.]

[Reg. § 1.672(d)-1]

§ 1.672(d)-1. **Power subject to condition precedent.**—Section 672(d) provides that a person is considered to have a power described in subpart E (section 671 and following), part I, subchapter J, chapter 1 of the Code, even though the exercise of the power is subject to a precedent giving of notice or takes effect only after the expiration of a certain period of time. However, although a person may be considered to have such a power, the grantor will nevertheless not be treated as an owner by reason of the power if its exercise can only affect beneficial enjoyment of income received after the expiration of a period of time such that, if the power were a reversionary interest, he would not be treated as an owner under section 673. See sections 674(b)(2), 676(b), and the last sentence of section 677(a). Thus, for example, if a grantor creates a trust for the benefit of his son and retains a power to revoke which takes effect only after the expiration of 2 years from the date of exercise, he is treated as an owner from the inception of the trust. However, if the grantor retains a power to revoke, exercisable at any time, which can only affect the beneficial enjoyment of the ordinary income of a trust received after the expiration of 10 years commencing with the date of the transfer in trust, or after the death of the income beneficiary, the power does not cause him to be treated as an owner with respect to ordinary income during the first 10 years of the trust or during the income beneficiary's life, as the case may be. See section 676(b). [Reg. § 1.672(d)-1.]

☐ [T.D. 6217, 12-19-56.]

[Reg. § 1.672(f)-1]

§ 1.672(f)-1. **Foreign persons not treated as owners.**—(a) *General rule*—(1) *Application of the general rule.* Section 672(f)(1) provides that subpart E of part I, subchapter J, chapter 1 of the Internal Revenue Code (the grantor trust rules) shall apply only to the extent such application results in an amount (if any) being currently taken into account (directly or through one or more entities) in computing the income of a citizen or resident of the United States or a domestic corporation. Accordingly, the grantor trust rules apply to the extent that any portion of the trust, upon application of the grantor trust rules without regard to section 672(f), is treated as owned by a United States citizen or resident or domestic corporation. The grantor trust rules do not apply to any portion of the trust to the extent that, upon application of the grantor trust rules without regard to section 672(f), that portion is treated as owned by a person other than a United States citizen or resident or domestic corporation, unless the person is described in § 1.672(f)-2(a) (relating to certain foreign corporations treated as domestic corporations), or one of the exceptions set forth in § 1.672(f)-3 is met, (relating to: trusts where the grantor can revest trust assets; trusts where the only amounts distributable are to the grantor or the grantor's spouse; and compensatory trusts). Section 672(f) applies to domestic and foreign trusts. Any portion of the trust that is not treated as owned by a grantor or another person is subject to the rules of subparts A through D (section 641 and following), part I, subchapter J, chapter 1 of the Internal Revenue Code.

(2) *Determination of portion based on application of the grantor trust rules.* The determination of the portion of a trust treated as owned by the grantor or other person is to be made based on the terms of the trust and the application of the grantor trust rules and section 671 and the regulations thereunder.

(b) *Example.* The following example illustrates the rules of this section:

Example. (i) A, a nonresident alien, funds an irrevocable domestic trust, DT, for the benefit of his son, B, who is a United States citizen, with stock of Corporation X. A's brother, C, who also is a United States citizen, contributes stock of Corporation Y to the trust for the benefit of B. A has a reversionary interest within the meaning of section 673 in the X stock that would cause A to be treated as the owner of the X stock upon application of the grantor trust rules without regard to section 672(f). C has a reversionary interest within the meaning of section 673 in the Y stock that would cause C to be treated as the owner of the Y stock upon application of the grantor trust rules without regard to section 672(f). The trustee has discretion to accumulate or currently distribute income of DT to B.

(ii) Because A is a nonresident alien, application of the grantor trust rules without regard to section 672(f) would not result in the portion of the trust consisting of the X stock being treated as owned by a United States citizen or resident. None of the exceptions in § 1.672(f)-3 applies because A cannot revest the X stock in A, amounts may be distributed during A's lifetime to B, who is neither a grantor nor a spouse of a grantor, and the trust is not a compensatory trust. Therefore, pursuant to paragraph (a)(1) of this section, A is not treated as an owner under subpart E of part I, subchapter J, chapter 1 of the Internal Revenue Code, of the portion of the trust consisting of the X stock. Any distributions from such portion of the trust are subject to the rules of subparts A through D (641 and following), part I, subchapter J, chapter 1 of the Internal Revenue Code.

(iii) Because C is a United States citizen, paragraph (a)(1) of this section does not prevent C from being treated under section 673 as the owner of the portion of the trust consisting of the Y stock.

(c) *Effective date.* The rules of this section are applicable to taxable years of a trust beginning after August 10, 1999. [Reg. § 1.672(f)-1.]

☐ [*T.D.* 8831, 8-5-99.]

[Reg. § 1.672(f)-2]

§ 1.672(f)-2. **Certain foreign corporations.**—(a) *Application of general rule.* Subject to the provisions of paragraph (b) of this section, if the owner of any portion of a trust upon application of the grantor trust rules without regard to section 672(f) is a controlled foreign corporation (as defined in section 957), a passive foreign investment company (as defined in section 1297), or a foreign personal holding company (as defined in section 552), the corporation will be treated as a domestic corporation for purposes of applying the rules of § 1.672(f)-1.

(b) *Gratuitous transfers to United States persons*—(1) *Transfer from trust to which corporation made a gratuitous transfer.* If a trust for (or portion of a trust) to which a controlled foreign corporation, passive foreign investment company, or foreign personal holding company has made a gratuitous transfer (within the meaning of § 1.671-2(e)(2)), makes a gratuitous transfer to a United States person, the controlled foreign corporation, passive foreign investment company, or foreign personal holding company, as the case may be, is treated as a foreign corporation for purposes of § 1.672(f)-4(c), relating to gratuitous transfers from trusts (or portions of trusts) to which a partnership or foreign corporation has made a gratuitous transfer.

(2) *Transfer from trust over which corporation has a section 678 power.* If a trust (or portion of a trust) that a controlled foreign corporation, passive foreign investment company, or foreign personal holding company is treated as owning under section 678 makes a gratuitous transfer to a United States person, the controlled foreign corporation, passive foreign investment company, or foreign personal holding company, as the case may be, is treated as a foreign corporation that had made a gratuitous transfer to the trust (or

portion of a trust) and the rules of § 1.672(f)-4(c) apply.

(c) *Special rules for passive foreign investment companies*—(1) *Application of section 1297.* For purposes of determining whether a foreign corporation is a passive foreign investment company as defined in section 1297, the grantor trust rules apply as if section 672(f) had not come into effect.

(2) *References to renumbered Internal Revenue Code section.* For taxable years of shareholders beginning on or before December 31, 1997, and taxable years of passive foreign investment companies ending with or within such taxable years of the shareholders, all references in this § 1.672(f)-2 to section 1297 are deemed to be references to section 1296.

(d) *Examples.* The following examples illustrate the rules of this section. In each example, FT is an irrevocable foreign trust, and CFC is a controlled foreign corporation. The examples are as follows:

Example 1. Application of general rule. CFC creates and funds FT. CFC is the grantor of FT within the meaning of § 1.671-2(e). CFC has a reversionary interest in FT within the meaning of section 673 that would cause CFC to be treated as the owner of FT upon application of the grantor trust rules without regard to section 672(f). Under paragraph (a) of this section, CFC is treated as a domestic corporation for purposes of applying the general rule of § 1.672(f)-1. Thus, § 1.672(f)-1 does not prevent CFC from being treated as the owner of FT under section 673.

Example 2. Distribution from trust to which CFC made gratuitous transfer. A, a nonresident alien, owns 40 percent of the stock of CFC. A's brother B, a resident alien, owns the other 60 percent of the stock of CFC. CFC makes a gratuitous transfer to FT. FT makes a gratuitous transfer to A's daughter, C, who is a resident alien. Under paragraph (b)(1) of this section, CFC will be treated as a foreign corporation for purposes of § 1.672(f)-4(c). For further guidance, see § 1.672(f)-4(g) *Example 2* through *Example 4.*

(e) *Effective date.* The rules of this section are generally applicable to taxable years of shareholders of controlled foreign corporations, passive foreign investment companies, and foreign personal holding companies beginning after August 10, 1999, and taxable years of controlled foreign corporations, passive foreign investment companies, and foreign personal holding companies ending with or within such taxable years of the shareholders. [Reg. § 1.672(f)-2.]

☐ [T.D. 8831, 8-5-99. Amended by T.D. 8890, 7-3-2000.]

[Reg. § 1.672(f)-3]

§ 1.672(f)-3. Exceptions to general rule.—(a) *Certain revocable trusts*—(1) *In general.* Subject to the provisions of paragraph (a)(2) of this section, the general rule of § 1.672(f)-1 does not apply to any portion of a trust for a taxable year of the trust if the power to revest absolutely in the grantor title to such portion is exercisable solely by the grantor (or, in the event of the grantor's incapacity, by a guardian or other person who has unrestricted authority to exercise such power on the grantor's behalf) without the approval or consent of any other person. If the grantor can exercise such power only with the approval of a related or subordinate party who is subservient to the grantor, such power is treated as exercisable solely by the grantor. For the definition of *grantor,* see § 1.671-2(e). For the definition of *related or subordinate party,* see § 1.672(c)-1. For purposes of this paragraph (a), a related or subordinate party is subservient to the grantor unless the presumption in the last sentence of § 1.672(c)-1 is rebutted by a preponderance of the evidence. A trust (or portion of a trust) that fails to qualify for the exception provided by this paragraph (a) for a particular taxable year of the trust will be subject to the general rule of § 1.672(f)-1 for that taxable year and all subsequent taxable years of the trust.

(2) *183-day rule.* For purposes of paragraph (a)(1) of this section, the grantor is treated as having a power to revest for a taxable year of the trust only if the grantor has such power for a total of 183 or more days during the taxable year of the trust. If the first or last taxable year of the trust (including the year of the grantor's death) is less than 183 days, the grantor is treated as having a power to revest for purposes of paragraph (a)(1) of this section if the grantor has such power for each day of the first or last taxable year, as the case may be.

(3) *Grandfather rule for certain revocable trusts in existence on September 19, 1995.* Subject to the rules of paragraph (d) of this section (relating to separate accounting for gratuitous transfers to the trust after September 19, 1995), the general rule of § 1.672(f)-1 does not apply to any portion of a trust that was treated as owned by the grantor under section 676 on September 19, 1995, as long as the trust would continue to be so treated thereafter. However, the preceding sentence does not apply to any portion of the trust attributable to gratuitous transfers to the trust after September 19, 1995.

(4) *Examples.* The following examples illustrate the rules of this paragraph (a):

Estates, Trusts, and Beneficiaries

Example 1. Grantor is owner. FP1, a foreign person, creates and funds a revocable trust, T, for the benefit of FP1's children, who are resident aliens. The trustee is a foreign bank, FB, that is owned and controlled by FP1 and FP2, who is FP1's brother. The power to revoke T and revest absolutely in FP1 title to the trust property is exercisable by FP1, but only with the approval or consent of FB. The trust instrument contains no standard that FB must apply in determining whether to approve or consent to the revocation of T. There are no facts that would suggest that FB is not subservient to FP1. Therefore, the exception in paragraph (a)(1) of this section is applicable.

Example 2. Death of grantor. Assume the same facts as in *Example 1*, except that FP1 dies. After FP1's death, FP2 has the power to withdraw the assets of T, but only with the approval of FB. There are no facts that would suggest that FB is not subservient to FP2. However, the exception in paragraph (a)(1) of this section is no longer applicable, because FP2 is not a grantor of T within the meaning of § 1.671-2(e).

Example 3. Trustee is not related or subordinate party. Assume the same facts as in *Example 1*, except that neither FP1 nor any member of FP1's family has any substantial ownership interest or other connection with FB. FP1 can remove and replace FB at any time for any reason. Although FP1 can replace FB with a related or subordinate party if FB refuses to approve or consent to FP1's decision to revest the trust property in himself, FB is not a related or subordinate party. Therefore, the exception in paragraph (a)(1) of this section is not applicable.

Example 4. Unrelated trustee will consent to revocation. FP, a foreign person, creates and funds an irrevocable trust, T. The trustee is a foreign bank, FB, that is not a related or subordinate party within the meaning of § 1.672(c)-1. FB has the discretion to distribute trust income or corpus to beneficiaries of T, including FP. Even if FB would in fact distribute all the trust property to FP if requested to do so by FP, the exception in paragraph (a)(1) of this section is not applicable, because FP does not have the power to revoke T.

(b) *Certain trusts that can distribute only to the grantor or the spouse of the grantor*—(1) *In general.* The general rule of § 1.672(f)-1 does not apply to any trust (or portion of a trust) if at all times during the lifetime of the grantor the only amounts distributable (whether income or corpus) from such trust (or portion thereof) are amounts distributable to the grantor or the spouse of the grantor. For purposes of this paragraph (b), payments of amounts that are not gratuitous transfers (within the meaning of § 1.671-2(e)(2)) are not amounts distributable. For the definition of *grantor*, see § 1.671-2(e).

(2) *Amounts distributable in discharge of legal obligations*—(i) *In general.* A trust (or portion of a trust) does not fail to satisfy paragraph (b)(1) of this section solely because amounts are distributable from the trust (or portion thereof) in discharge of a legal obligation of the grantor or the spouse of the grantor. Subject to the provisions of paragraph (b)(2)(ii) of this section, an obligation is considered a legal obligation for purposes of this paragraph (b)(2)(i) if it is enforceable under the local law of the jurisdiction in which the grantor (or the spouse of the grantor) resides.

(ii) *Related parties*—(A) *In general.* Except as provided in paragraph (b)(2)(ii)(B) of this section, an obligation to a person who is a related person for purposes of § 1.643(h)-1(e) (other than an individual who is legally separated from the grantor under a decree of divorce or of separate maintenance) is not a legal obligation for purposes of paragraph (b)(2)(i) of this section unless it was contracted bona fide and for adequate and full consideration in money or money's worth (see § 20.2043-1 of this chapter).

(B) *Exceptions*—(*1*) *Amounts distributable in support of certain individuals.* Paragraph (b)(2)(ii)(A) of this section does not apply with respect to amounts that are distributable from the trust (or portion thereof) to support an individual who—

(*i*) Would be treated as a dependent of the grantor or the spouse of the grantor under section 152(a)(1) through (9), without regard to the requirement that over half of the individual's support be received from the grantor or the spouse of the grantor; and

(*ii*) Is either permanently and totally disabled (within the meaning of section 22(e)(3)), or less than 19 years old.

(*2*) *Certain potential support obligations.* The fact that amounts might become distributable from a trust (or portion of a trust) in discharge of a potential obligation under local law to support an individual other than an individual described in paragraph (b)(2)(ii)(B)(*1*) of this section is disregarded if such potential obligation is not reasonably expected to arise under the facts and circumstances.

(*3*) *Reinsurance trusts.* [Reserved]

(3) *Grandfather rule for certain section 677 trusts in existence on September 19, 1995.* Subject to the rules of paragraph (d) of this section (relating to separate accounting for gratuitous transfers

Reg. § 1.672(f)-3(b)(3)

to the trust after September 19, 1995), the general rule of § 1.672(f)-1 does not apply to any portion of a trust that was treated as owned by the grantor under section 677 (other than section 677(a)(3)) on September 19, 1995, as long as the trust would continue to be so treated thereafter. However, the preceding sentence does not apply to any portion of the trust attributable to gratuitous transfers to the trust after September 19, 1995.

(4) *Examples.* The following examples illustrate the rules of this paragraph (b):

Example 1. Amounts distributable only to grantor or grantor's spouse. H and his wife, W, are both nonresident aliens. H is 70 years old, and W is 65. H and W have a 30-year-old child, C, a resident alien. There is no reasonable expectation that H or W will ever have an obligation under local law to support C or any other individual. H creates and funds an irrevocable trust, FT, using only his separate property. H is the grantor of FT within the meaning of § 1.671-2(e). Under the terms of FT, the only amounts distributable (whether income or corpus) from FT as long as either H or W is alive are amounts distributable to H or W. Upon the death of both H and W, C may receive distributions from FT. During H's lifetime, the exception in paragraph (b)(1) of this section is applicable.

Example 2. Effect of grantor's death. Assume the same facts as in *Example 1.* H predeceases W. Assume that W would be treated as owning FT under section 678 if the grantor trust rules were applied without regard to section 672(f). The exception in paragraph (b)(1) of this section is no longer applicable, because W is not a grantor of FT within the meaning of § 1.671-2(e).

Example 3. Amounts temporarily distributable to person other than grantor or grantor's spouse. Assume the same facts as in *Example 1,* except that C (age 30) is a law student at the time FT is created and the trust instrument provides that, as long as C is in law school, amounts may be distributed from FT to pay C's expenses. Thereafter, the only amounts distributable from FT as long as either H or W is alive will be amounts distributable to H or W. Even assuming there is an enforceable obligation under local law for H and W to support C while he is in school, distributions from FT in payment of C's expenses cannot qualify as distributions in discharge of a legal obligation under paragraph (b)(2) of this section, because C is neither permanently and totally disabled nor less than 19 years old. The exception in paragraph (b)(1) of this section is not applicable. After C graduates from law school, the exception in paragraph (b)(1) still will not be applicable, because amounts were distributable to C during the lifetime of H.

Example 4. Fixed investment trust. FC, a foreign corporation, invests in a domestic fixed investment trust, DT, that is classified as a trust under § 301.7701-4(c)(1) of this chapter. Under the terms of DT, the only amounts that are distributable from FC's portion of DT are amounts distributable to FC. The exception in paragraph (b)(1) of this section is applicable to FC's portion of DT.

Example 5. Reinsurance trust. A domestic insurance company, DI, reinsures a portion of its business with an unrelated foreign insurance company, FI. To satisfy state regulatory requirements, FI places the premiums in an irrevocable domestic trust, DT. The trust funds are held by a United States bank and may be used only to pay claims arising out of the reinsurance policies, which are legally enforceable under the local law of the jurisdiction in which FT resides. On the termination of DT, any assets remaining will revert to FI. Because the only amounts that are distributable from DT are distributable either to FI or in discharge of FI's legal obligations within the meaning of paragraph (b)(2)(i) of this section, the exception in paragraph (b)(1) of this section is applicable.

Example 6. Trust that provides security for loan. FC, a foreign corporation, borrows money from B, an unrelated bank, to finance the purchase of an airplane. FC creates a foreign trust, FT, to hold the airplane as security for the loan from B. The only amounts that are distributable from FT while the loan is outstanding are amounts distributable to B in the event that FC defaults on its loan from B. When FC repays the loan, the trust assets will revert to FC. The loan is a legal obligation of FC within the meaning of paragraph (b)(2)(i) of this section, because it is enforceable under the local law of the country in which FC is incorporated. Paragraph (b)(2)(ii) of this section is not applicable, because B is not a related person for purposes of § 1.643(h)-1(e). The exception in paragraph (b)(1) of this section is applicable.

(c) *Compensatory trusts*—(1) *In general.* The general rule of § 1.672(f)-1 does not apply to any portion of—

(i) A nonexempt employees' trust described in section 402(b), including a trust created on behalf of a self-employed individual;

(ii) A trust, including a trust created on behalf of a self-employed individual, that would be a nonexempt employees' trust described in section 402(b) but for the fact that the trust's assets are not set aside from the claims of credi-

Reg. § 1.672(f)-3(b)(4)

tors of the actual or deemed transferor within the meaning of § 1.83-3(e); and

(iii) Any additional category of trust that the Commissioner may designate in revenue procedures, notices, or other guidance published in the Internal Revenue Bulletin (see § 601.601(d)(2) of this chapter).

(2) *Exceptions.* The Commissioner may, in revenue rulings, notices, or other guidance published in the Internal Revenue Bulletin (see § 601.601(d)(2) of this chapter), designate categories of compensatory trusts to which the general rule of paragraph (c)(1) of this section does not apply.

(d) *Separate accounting for gratuitous transfers to grandfathered trusts after September 19, 1995.* If a trust that was treated as owned by the grantor under section 676 or 677 (other than section 677(a)(3)) on September 19, 1995, contains both amounts held in the trust on September 19, 1995, and amounts that were gratuitously transferred to the trust after September 19, 1995, paragraphs (a)(3) and (b)(3) of this section apply only if the amounts that were gratuitously transferred to the trust after September 19, 1995, are treated as a separate portion of the trust that is accounted for under the rules of § 1.671-3(a)(2). If the amounts that were gratuitously transferred to the trust after September 19, 1995 are not so accounted for, the general rule of § 1.672(f)-1 applies to the entire trust. If such amounts are so accounted for, and without regard to whether there is physical separation of the assets, the general rule of § 1.672(f)-1 does not apply to the portion of the trust that is attributable to amounts that were held in the trust on September 19, 1995.

(e) *Effective date.* The rules of this section are generally applicable to taxable years of a trust beginning after August 10, 1999. The initial separate accounting required by paragraph (d) of this section must be prepared by the due date (including extensions) for the tax return of the trust for the first taxable year of the trust beginning after August 10, 1999. [Reg. § 1.672(f)-3.]

☐ [*T.D. 8831, 8-5-99. Amended by T.D. 8890, 7-3-2000.*]

[Reg. § 1.672(f)-4]

§ 1.672(f)-4. **Recharacterization of purported gifts.**—(a) *In general*—(1) *Purported gifts from partnerships.* Except as provided in paragraphs (b), (e), and (f) of this section, and without regard to the existence of any trust, if a United States person (United States donee) directly or indirectly receives a purported gift or bequest (as defined in paragraph (d) of this section) from a partnership, the purported gift or bequest must be included in the United States donee's gross income as ordinary income.

(2) *Purported gifts from foreign corporations.* Except as provided in paragraphs (b), (e), and (f) of this section, and without regard to the existence of any trust, if a United States donee directly or indirectly receives a purported gift or bequest (as defined in paragraph (d) of this section) from any foreign corporation, the purported gift or bequest must be included in the United States donee's gross income as if it were a distribution from the foreign corporation. If the foreign corporation is a passive foreign investment company (within the meaning of section 1297), the rules of section 1291 apply. For purposes of section 1012, the United States donee is not treated as having basis in the stock of the foreign corporation. However, for purposes of section 1223, the United States donee is treated as having a holding period in the stock of the foreign corporation on the date of the deemed distribution equal to the weighted average of the holding periods of the actual interest holders (other than any interest holders who treat the portion of the purported gift attributable to their interest in the foreign corporation in the manner described in paragraph (b)(1) of this section). For purposes of section 902, a United States donee that is a domestic corporation is not treated as owning any voting stock of the foreign corporation.

(b) *Exceptions*—(1) *Partner or shareholder treats transfer as distribution and gift.* Paragraph (a) of this section does not apply to the extent the United States donee can demonstrate to the satisfaction of the Commissioner that either—

(i) A United States citizen or resident alien individual who directly or indirectly holds an interest in the partnership or foreign corporation treated and reported the purported gift or bequest for United States tax purposes as a distribution to such individual and a subsequent gift or bequest to the United States donee; or

(ii) A nonresident alien individual who directly or indirectly holds an interest in the partnership or foreign corporation treated and reported the purported gift or bequest for purposes of the tax laws of the nonresident alien individual's country of residence as a distribution to such individual and a subsequent gift or bequest to the United States donee, and the United States donee timely complied with the reporting requirements of section 6039F, if applicable.

(2) *All beneficial owners of domestic partnership are United States citizens or residents or domestic corporations.* Paragraph (a)(1) of this section does not apply to a purported gift or

bequest from a domestic partnership if the United States donee can demonstrate to the satisfaction of the Commissioner that all beneficial owners (within the meaning of § 1.1441-1(c)(6)) of the partnership are United States citizens or residents or domestic corporations.

(3) *Contribution to capital of corporate United States donee.* Paragraph (a) of this section does not apply to the extent a United States donee that is a corporation can establish that the purported gift or bequest was treated for United States tax purposes as a contribution to the capital of the United States donee to which section 118 applies.

(4) *Charitable transfers.* Paragraph (a) of this section does not apply if either—

(i) The United States donee is described in section 170(c); or

(ii) The transferor has received a ruling or determination letter, which has been neither revoked nor modified, from the Internal Revenue Service recognizing its exempt status under section 501(c)(3), and the transferor made the transfer pursuant to an exempt purpose for which the transferor was created or organized. For purposes of the preceding sentence, a ruling or determination letter recognizing exemption may not be relied upon if there is a material change, inconsistent with exemption, in the character, the purpose, or the method of operation of the organization.

(c) *Certain transfers from trusts to which a partnership or foreign corporation has made a gratuitous transfer*—(1) *Generally treated as distribution from partnership or foreign corporation.* Except as provided in paragraphs (c)(2) and (3) of this section, if a United States donee receives a gratuitous transfer (within the meaning of § 1.671-2(e)(2)) from a trust (or portion of a trust) to which a partnership or foreign corporation has made a gratuitous transfer, the United States donee must treat the transfer as a purported gift or bequest from the partnership or foreign corporation that is subject to the rules of paragraph (a) of this section (including the exceptions in paragraphs (b) and (f) of this section). This paragraph (c) applies without regard to who is treated as the grantor of the trust (or portion thereof) under § 1.671-2(e)(4).

(2) *Alternative rule.* Except as provided in paragraph (c)(3) of this section, if the United States tax computed under the rules of paragraphs (a) and (c)(1) of this section does not exceed the United States tax that would be due if the United States donee treated the transfer as a distribution from the trust (or portion thereof), paragraph (c)(1) of this section does not apply and the United States donee must treat the transfer as a distribution from the trust (or portion thereof) that is subject to the rules of subparts A through D (section 641 and following), part I, subchapter J, chapter 1 of the Internal Revenue Code. For purposes of paragraph (f) of this section, the transfer is treated as a purported gift or bequest from the partnership or foreign corporation that made the gratuitous transfer to the trust (or portion thereof).

(3) *Exception.* Neither paragraph (c)(1) of this section nor paragraph (c)(2) of this section applies to the extent the United States donee can demonstrate to the satisfaction of the Commissioner that the transfer represents an amount that is, or has been, taken into account for United States tax purposes by a United States citizen or resident or a domestic corporation. A transfer will be deemed to be made first out of amounts that have not been taken into account for United States tax purposes by a United States citizen or resident or a domestic corporation, unless the United States donee can demonstrate to the satisfaction of the Commissioner that another ordering rule is more appropriate.

(d) *Definition of purported gift or bequest*—(1) *In general.* Subject to the provisions of paragraphs (d)(2) and (3) of this section, a *purported gift or bequest* for purposes of this section is any transfer of property by a partnership or foreign corporation other than a transfer for fair market value (within the meaning of § 1.671-2(e)(2)(ii)) to a person who is not a partner in the partnership or a shareholder of the foreign corporation (or to a person who is a partner in the partnership or a shareholder of a foreign corporation, if the amount transferred is inconsistent with the partner's interest in the partnership or the shareholder's interest in the corporation, as the case may be). For purposes of this section, the term *property* includes cash.

(2) *Transfers for less than fair market value*—(i) *Excess treated as purported gift or bequest.* Except as provided in paragraph (d)(2)(ii) of this section, if a transfer described in paragraph (d)(1) of this section is for less than fair market value, the excess of the fair market value of the property transferred over the value of the property received, services rendered, or the right to use property is treated as a purported gift or bequest.

(ii) *Exception for transfers to unrelated parties.* No portion of a transfer described in paragraph (d)(1) of this section will be treated as a purported gift or bequest for purposes of this section if the United States donee can demonstrate to the satisfaction of the Commissioner that

Reg. § 1.672(f)-4(b)(3)

the United States donee is not related to a partner or shareholder of the transferor within the meaning of § 1.643(h)-1(e) or does not have another relationship with a partner or shareholder of the transferor that establishes a reasonable basis for concluding that the transferor would make a gratuitous transfer to the United States donee.

(e) *Prohibition against affirmative use of recharacterization by taxpayers.* A taxpayer may not use the rules of this section if a principal purpose for using such rules is the avoidance of any tax imposed by the Internal Revenue Code. Thus, with respect to such taxpayer, the Commissioner may depart from the rules of this section and recharacterize (for all purposes of the Internal Revenue Code) the transfer in accordance with its form or its economic substance.

(f) *Transfers not in excess of $10,000.* This section does not apply if, during the taxable year of the United States donee, the aggregate amount of purported gifts or bequests that is transferred to such United States donee directly or indirectly from all partnerships or foreign corporations that are related (within the meaning of section 643(i)) does not exceed $10,000. The aggregate amount must include gifts or bequests from persons that the United States donee knows or has reason to know are related to the partnership or foreign corporation (within the meaning of section 643(i)).

(g) *Examples.* The following examples illustrate the rules of this section. In each example, the amount that is transferred exceeds $10,000. The examples are as follows:

Example 1. Distribution from foreign corporation. FC is a foreign corporation that is wholly owned by A, a nonresident alien who is resident in Country C. FC makes a gratuitous transfer of property directly to A's daughter, B, who is a resident alien. Under paragraph (a)(2) of this section, B generally must treat the transfer as a dividend from FC to the extent of FC's earnings and profits and as an amount received in excess of basis thereafter. If FC is a passive foreign investment company, B must treat the amount received as a distribution under section 1291. B will be treated as having the same holding period as A. However, under paragraph (b)(1)(ii) of this section, if B can establish to the satisfaction of the Commissioner that, for purposes of the tax laws of Country C, A treated (and reported, if applicable) the transfer as a distribution to himself and a subsequent gift to B, B may treat the transfer as a gift (provided B timely complied with the reporting requirements of section 6039F, if applicable).

Example 2. Distribution of corpus from trust to which foreign corporation made gratuitous transfer. FC is a foreign corporation that is wholly owned by A, a nonresident alien who is resident in Country C. FC makes a gratuitous transfer to a foreign trust, FT, that has no other assets. FT immediately makes a gratuitous transfer in the same amount to A's daughter, B, who is a resident alien. Under paragraph (c)(1) of this section, B must treat the transfer as a transfer from FC that is subject to the rules of paragraph (a)(2) of this section. Under paragraph (a)(2) of this section, B must treat the transfer as a dividend from FC unless she can establish to the satisfaction of the Commissioner that, for purposes of the tax laws of Country C, A treated (and reported, if applicable) the transfer as a distribution to himself and a subsequent gift to B and that B timely complied with the reporting requirements of section 6039F, if applicable. The alternative rule in paragraph (c)(2) of this section would not apply as long as the United States tax computed under the rules of paragraph (a)(2) of this section is equal to or greater than the United States tax that would be due if the transfer were treated as a distribution from FT.

Example 3. Accumulation distribution from trust to which foreign corporation made gratuitous transfer. FC is a foreign corporation that is wholly owned by A, a nonresident alien. FC is not a passive foreign investment company (as defined in section 1297). FC makes a gratuitous transfer of 100X to a foreign trust, FT, on January 1, 2001. FT has no other assets on January 1, 2001. Several years later, FT makes a gratuitous transfer of 1000X to A's daughter, B, who is a United States resident. Assume that the section 668 interest charge on accumulation distributions will apply if the transfer is treated as a distribution from FT. Under the alternative rule of paragraph (c)(2) of this section, B must treat the transfer as an accumulation distribution from FT, because the resulting United States tax liability is greater than the United States tax that would be due if the transfer were treated as a transfer from FC that is subject to the rules of paragraph (a) of this section.

Example 4. Transfer from trust that is treated as owned by United States citizen. Assume the same facts as in *Example 3*, except that A is a United States citizen. Assume that A treats and reports the transfer to FT as a constructive distribution to himself, followed by a gratuitous transfer to FT, and that A is properly treated as the grantor of FT within the meaning of § 1.671-2(e). A is treated as the owner of FT under section 679 and, as required by section 671 and the regulations thereunder, A includes all of FT's items of income, deductions, and credit in computing his taxable income and credits. Neither paragraph

Reg. § 1.672(f)-4(g)

(c)(1) nor paragraph (c)(2) of this section is applicable, because the exception in paragraph (c)(3) of this section applies.

Example 5. Transfer for less than fair market value. FC is a foreign corporation that is wholly owned by A, a nonresident alien. On January 15, 2001, FC transfers property directly to A's daughter, B, a resident alien, in exchange for 90X. The Commissioner later determines that the fair market value of the property at the time of the transfer was 100X. Under paragraph (d)(2)(i) of this section, 10X will be treated as a purported gift to B on January 15, 2001.

(h) *Effective date.* The rules of this section are generally applicable to any transfer after August 10, 1999, by a partnership or foreign corporation, or by a trust to which a partnership or foreign corporation makes a gratuitous transfer after August 10, 1999. [Reg. § 1.672(f)-4.]

☐ [T.D. 8831, 8-5-99. Amended by T.D. 8890, 7-3-2000.]

[Reg. § 1.672(f)-5]

§ 1.672(f)-5. **Special rules.**—(a) *Transfers by certain beneficiaries to foreign grantor*—(1) *In general.* If, but for section 672(f)(5), a foreign person would be treated as the owner of any portion of a trust, any United States beneficiary of the trust is treated as the grantor of a portion of the trust to the extent the United States beneficiary directly or indirectly made transfers of property to such foreign person (without regard to whether the United States beneficiary was a United States beneficiary at the time of any transfer) in excess of transfers to the United States beneficiary from the foreign person. The rule of this paragraph (a) does not apply to the extent the United States beneficiary can demonstrate to the satisfaction of the Commissioner that the transfer by the United States beneficiary to the foreign person was wholly unrelated to any transaction involving the trust. For purposes of this paragraph (a), the term property includes cash, and a transfer of property does not include a transfer that is not a gratuitous transfer (within the meaning of § 1.671-2(e)(2)). In addition, a gift is not taken into account to the extent such gift would not be characterized as a taxable gift under section 2503(b). For a definition of United States beneficiary, see section 679.

(2) *Examples.* The following examples illustrate the rules of this section:

Example 1. A, a nonresident alien, contributes property to FC, a foreign corporation that is wholly owned by A. FC creates a foreign trust, FT, for the benefit of A and A's children. FT is revocable by FC without the approval or consent of any other person. FC funds FT with the property received from A. A and A's family move to the United States. Under paragraph (a)(1) of this section, A is treated as a grantor of FT. (A may also be treated as an owner of FT under section 679(a)(4).)

Example 2. B, a United States citizen, makes a gratuitous transfer of $1 million to B's uncle, C, a nonresident alien. C creates a foreign trust, FT, for the benefit of B and B's children. FT is revocable by C without the approval or consent of any other person. C funds FT with the property received from B. Under paragraph (a)(1) of this section, B is treated as a grantor of FT. (B also would be treated as an owner of FT as a result of section 679.)

(b) *Entity characterization.* Entities generally are characterized under United States tax principles for purposes of §§ 1.672(f)-1 through 1.672(f)-5. See §§ 301.7701-1 through 301.7701-4 of this chapter. However, solely for purposes of § 1.672(f)-4, a transferor that is a wholly owned business entity is treated as a corporation, separate from its single owner.

(c) *Effective date.* The rules in paragraph (a) of this section are applicable to transfers to trusts on or after August 10, 1999. The rules in paragraph (b) of this section are applicable August 10, 1999. [Reg. § 1.672(f)-5.]

☐ [T.D. 8831, 8-5-99. Amended by T.D. 8890, 7-3-2000.]

[Reg. § 1.673(a)-1]

§ 1.673(a)-1. **Reversionary interests; income payable to beneficiaries other than certain charitable organizations; general rule.**—(a) Under section 673(a), a grantor, in general, is treated as the owner of any portion of a trust in which he has a reversionary interest in either the corpus or income if, as of the inception of that portion of the trust, the grantor's interest will or may reasonably be expected to take effect in possession or enjoyment within 10 years commencing with the date of transfer of that portion of the trust. However, the following types of reversionary interests are excepted from the general rule of the preceding sentence:

(1) A reversionary interest after the death of the income beneficiary of a trust (see paragraph (b) of this section); and

(2) Except in the case of transfers in trust made after April 22, 1969, a reversionary interest in a charitable trust meeting the requirements of section 673(b) (see § 1.673(b)-1).

Even though the duration of the trust may be such that the grantor is not treated as its owner under section 673, and therefore is not taxed on the ordinary income, he may nevertheless be treated as an owner under section 677(a)(2) if he has a reversionary interest in the corpus. In the latter case, items of income, deduction, and credit allocable to corpus, such as capital gains and losses, will be included in the portion he owns. See § 1.671-3 and the regulations under section 677. See § 1.673(d)-1 with respect to a postponement of the date specified for reacquisition of a reversionary interest.

(b) Section 673(c) provides that a grantor is not treated as the owner of any portion of a trust by reason of section 673 if his reversionary interest in the portion is not to take effect in possession or enjoyment until the death of the person or persons to whom the income of the portion is payable, regardless of the life expectancies of the income beneficiaries. If his reversionary interest is to take effect on or after the death of an income beneficiary or upon the expiration of a specific term of years, whichever is earlier, the grantor is treated as the owner if the specific term of years is less than 10 years (but not if the term is 10 years or longer).

(c) Where the grantor's reversionary interest in a portion of a trust is to take effect in possession or enjoyment by reason of some event other than the expiration of a specific term of years or the death of the income beneficiary, the grantor is treated as the owner of the portion if the event may reasonably be expected to occur within 10 years from the date of transfer of that portion, but he is not treated as the owner under section 673 if the event may not reasonably be expected to occur within 10 years from that date. For example, if the reversionary interest in any portion of a trust is to take effect on or after the death of the grantor (or any person other than the person to whom the income is payable) the grantor is treated under section 673 as the owner of the portion if the life expectancy of the grantor (or other person) is less than 10 years on the date of transfer of the portion, but not if the life expectancy is 10 years or longer. If the reversionary interest in any portion is to take effect on or after the death of the grantor (or any person other than the person to whom the income is payable) or upon the expiration of a specific term of years, whichever is earlier, the grantor is treated as the owner of the portion if on the date of transfer of the portion either the life expectancy of the grantor (or other person) or the specific term is less than 10 years; however, if both the life expectancy and the specific term are 10 years or longer the grantor is not treated as the owner of the portion under section 673. Similarly, if the grantor has a reversionary interest in any portion which will take effect at the death of the income beneficiary or the grantor, whichever is earlier, the grantor is not treated as an owner of the portion unless his life expectancy is less than 10 years.

(d) It is immaterial that a reversionary interest in corpus or income is subject to a contingency if the reversionary interest may, taking the contingency into consideration, reasonably be expected to take effect in possession or enjoyment within 10 years. For example, the grantor is taxable where the trust income is to be paid to the grantor's son for 3 years, and the corpus is then to be returned to the grantor if he survives that period, or to be paid to the grantor's son if he is already deceased.

(e) See section 671 and §§ 1.671-2 and 1.671-3 for rules for treatment of items of income, deduction, and credit when a person is treated as the owner of all or only a portion of a trust. [Reg. § 1.673(a)-1.]

☐ [T.D. 6217, 12-19-56. Amended by T.D. 7357, 5-30-75.]

[Reg. § 1.673(b)-1]

§ 1.673(b)-1. Income payable to charitable beneficiaries (before amendment by Tax Reform Act of 1969).—(a) Pursuant to section 673(b) a grantor is not treated as an owner of any portion of a trust under section 673, even though he has a reversionary interest which will take effect within 10 years, to the extent that, under the terms of the trust, the income of the portion is irrevocably payable for a period of at least 2 years (commencing with the date of the transfer) to a designated beneficiary of the type described in section 170(b)(1)(A).

(b) Income must be irrevocably payable to a designated beneficiary for at least 2 years commencing with the date of the transfer before the benefit of section 673(b) will apply. Thus, section 673(b) will not apply if income of a trust is irrevocably payable to University A for 1 year and then to University B for the next year; or if income of a trust may be allocated among two or more charitable beneficiaries in the discretion of the trustee or any other person. On the other hand, section 673(b) will apply if half the income of a trust is irrevocably payable to University A and the other half is irrevocably payable to University B for two years.

(c) Section 673(b) applies to the period of 2 years or longer during which income is paid to a designated beneficiary of the type described in section 170(b)(1)(A)(i), (ii), or (iii), even though the trust term is to extend beyond that period. However, the other provisions of section 673 apply to the part of the trust term, if any, that extends beyond that period. This paragraph may be illustrated by the following example:

Example. G transfers property in trust with the ordinary income payable to University C (which qualifies under section 170(b)(1)(A)(ii)) for 3 years, and then to his son, B, for 5 years. At the expiration of the term the trust reverts to G. G is not taxed under section 673 on the trust income payable to University C for the first 3 years because of the application of section 673(b). However, he is taxed on income for the next 5 years because he has a reversionary interest which will take effect within 10 years commencing with the date of the transfer. On the other hand, if the income were payable to University C for 3 years and then to B for 7 years so that the trust corpus would not be returned to G within 10 years, G would not be taxable under section 673 on income payable to University C and to B during any part of the term.

(d) This section does not apply to transfers in trust made after April 22, 1969. [Reg. § 1.673(b)-1.]

☐ [T.D. 6217, 12-19-56. *Amended by* T.D. 6605, 8-14-62, *and by* T.D. 7357, 5-30-75.]

[Reg. § 1.673(c)-1]

§ 1.673(c)-1. **Reversionary interest after income beneficiary's death.**—The subject matter of section 673(c) is covered in paragraph (b) of § 1.673(a)-1. [Reg. § 1.673(c)-1.]

☐ [T.D. 6217, 12-19-56.]

[Reg. § 1.673(d)-1]

§ 1.673(d)-1. **Postponement of date specified for reacquisition.**—Any postponement of the date specified for the reacquisition of possession or enjoyment of any reversionary interest is considered a new transfer in trust commencing with the date on which the postponement is effected and terminating with the date prescribed by the postponement. However, the grantor will not be treated as the owner of any portion of a trust for any taxable year by reason of the foregoing sentence if he would not be so treated in the absence of any postponement. The rules contained in this section may be illustrated by the following example:

Example. G places property in trust for the benefit of his son B. Upon the expiration of 12 years or the earlier death of B the property is to be paid over to G or his estate. After the expiration of 9 years G extends the term of the trust for an additional 2 years. G is considered to have made a new transfer in trust for a term of 5 years (the remaining 3 years of the original transfer plus the 2-year extension). However, he is not treated as the owner of the trust under section 673 for the first 3 years of the new term because he would not be so treated if the term of the trust had not been extended. G is treated as the owner of the trust, however, for the remaining 2 years. [Reg. § 1.673(d)-1.]

☐ [T.D. 6217, 12-19-56.]

[Reg. § 1.674(a)-1]

§ 1.674(a)-1. **Power to control beneficial enjoyment; scope of section 674.**—(a) Under section 674, the grantor is treated as the owner of a portion of trust if the grantor or a nonadverse party has a power, beyond specified limits, to dispose of the beneficial enjoyment of the income or corpus, whether the power is a fiduciary power, a power of appointment, or any other power. Section 674(a) states in general terms that the grantor is treated as the owner in every case in which he or a nonadverse party can affect the beneficial enjoyment of a portion of a trust, the limitations being set forth as exceptions in subsections (b), (c), and (d) of section 674. These exceptions are discussed in detail in §§ 1.674(b)-1 through 1.674(d)-1. Certain limitations applicable to sections 674(b), (c), and (d) are set forth in § 1.674(d)-2. Section 674(b) describes powers which are excepted regardless of who holds them. Section 674(c) describes additional powers of trustees which are excepted if at least half the trustees are independent, and if the grantor is not a trustee. Section 674(d) describes a further power which is excepted if it is held by trustees other than the grantor or his spouse (if living with the grantor).

(b) In general terms the grantor is treated as the owner of a portion of a trust if he or a nonadverse party or both has a power to dispose of the beneficial enjoyment of the corpus or income unless the power is one of the following:

(1) *Miscellaneous powers over either ordinary income or corpus.* (i) A power that can only affect the beneficial enjoyment of income (including capital gains) received after a period of time such that the grantor would not be treated as an owner under section 673 if the power were a reversionary interest (section 674(b)(2));

(ii) A testamentary power held by anyone (other than a testamentary power held by the grantor over accumulated income) (section 674(b)(3));

(iii) A power to choose between charitable beneficiaries or to affect the manner of their enjoyment of a beneficial interest (section 674(b)(4));

(iv) A power to allocate receipts and disbursements between income and corpus (section 674(b)(8)).

(2) *Powers of distribution primarily affecting only one beneficiary.* (i) *A power to distribute corpus* to or for a current income beneficiary, if the distribution must be charged against the share of corpus from which the beneficiary may receive income (section 674(b)(5)(B));

(ii) *A power to distribute income* to or for a current income beneficiary or to accumulate it either (*a*) if accumulated income must either be payable to the beneficiary from whom it was withheld or as described in paragraph (b)(6) of § 1.674(b)-1 (section 674(b)(6)); (*b*) if the power is to apply income to the support of a dependent of the grantor, and the income is not so applied (section 674(b)(1)); or (*c*) if the beneficiary is under 21 or under a legal disability and accumulated income is added to corpus (section 674(b)(7)).

(3) *Powers of distribution affecting more than one beneficiary.* A power to distribute corpus or income to or among one or more beneficiaries or to accumulate income, either (i) if the power is held by a trustee or trustees other than the grantor, at least half of whom are independent (section 674(c)), or (ii) if the power is limited by a reasonably definite standard in the trust instrument, and in the case of a power over income, if in addition the power is held by a trustee or trustees other than the grantor and the grantor's spouse living with the grantor (sections 674(b)(5)(A) and (d)). (These powers include both powers to "sprinkle" income or corpus among current beneficiaries, and powers to shift income or corpus between current beneficiaries and remaindermen; however, certain of the powers described under subparagraph (2) of this paragraph can have the latter effect incidentally.)

(c) See section 671 and §§ 1.671-2 and 1.671-3 for rules for the treatment of income, deductions, and credits when a person is treated as the owner of all or only a portion of a trust. [Reg. § 1.674(a)-1.]

☐ [*T.D.* 6217, 12-19-56.]

[Reg. § 1.674(b)-1]

§ 1.674(b)-1. Excepted powers exercisable by any person.—(a) Paragraph (b)(1) through (8) of this section sets forth a number of powers which may be exercisable by any person without causing the grantor to be treated as an owner of a trust under section 674(a). Further, with the exception of powers described in paragraph (b)(1) of this section, it is immaterial whether these powers are held in the capacity of trustee. It makes no difference under section 674(b) that the person holding the power is the grantor, or a related or subordinate party (with the qualifications noted in paragraph (b)(1) and (3) of this section).

(b) The exceptions referred to in paragraph (a) of this section are as follows (see, however, the limitations set forth in § 1.674(d)-2):

(1) *Powers to apply income to support of a dependent.* Section 674(b)(1) provides, in effect, that regardless of the general rule of section 674(a), the income of a trust will not be considered as taxable to the grantor merely because in the discretion of any person (other than a grantor who is not acting as a trustee or cotrustee) it may be used for the support of a beneficiary whom the grantor is legally obligated to support, except to the extent that it is in fact used for that purpose. See section 677(b) and the regulations thereunder.

(2) *Powers affecting beneficial enjoyment only after a period.* Section 674(b)(2) provides an exception to section 674(a) if the exercise of a power can only affect the beneficial enjoyment of the income of a trust received after a period of time which is such that a grantor would not be treated as an owner under section 673 if the power were a reversionary interest. See §§ 1.673(a)-1 and 1.673(b)-1. For example, if a trust created on January 1, 1955, provides for the payment of income to the grantor's son, and the grantor reserves the power to substitute other beneficiaries of income or corpus in lieu of his son on or after January 1, 1965, the grantor is not treated under section 674 as the owner of the trust with respect to ordinary income received before January 1, 1965. But the grantor will be treated as an owner on and after that date unless the power is relinquished. If the beginning of the period during which the grantor may substitute beneficiaries is postponed, the rules set forth in § 1.673(d)-1 are applicable in order to determine whether the grantor should be treated as an owner during the period following the postponement.

(3) *Testamentary powers.* Under paragraph (3) of section 674(b) a power in any person to control beneficial enjoyment exercisable only by will does not cause a grantor to be treated as an owner under section 674(a). However, this exception does not apply to income accumulated for testamentary disposition by the grantor or to income which may be accumulated for such distribution in the discretion of the grantor or a nonadverse party, or both, without the approval or consent of any adverse party. For example, if a trust instrument provides that the income is to be accumulated during the grantor's life and that the grantor may appoint the accumulated income by will, the grantor is treated as the owner of the trust. Moreover, if a trust instrument provides that the income is payable to another person for

his life, but the grantor has a testamentary power of appointment over the remainder, and under the trust instrument and local law capital gains are added to corpus, the grantor is treated as the owner of a portion of the trust and capital gains and losses are included in that portion. (See § 1.671-3.)

(4) *Powers to determine beneficial enjoyment of charitable beneficiaries.* Under paragraph (4) of section 674(b) a power in any person to determine the beneficial enjoyment of corpus or income which is irrevocably payable (currently or in the future) for purposes specified in section 170(c) (relating to definition of charitable contributions) will not cause the grantor to be treated as an owner under section 674(a). For example, if a grantor creates a trust, the income of which is irrevocably payable solely to educational or other organizations that qualify under section 170(c), he is not treated as an owner under section 674 although he retains the power to allocate the income among such organizations.

(5) *Powers to distribute corpus.* Paragraph (5) of section 674(b) provides an exception to section 674(a) for powers to distribute corpus, subject to certain limitations, as follows:

(i) If the power is limited by a reasonably definite standard which is set forth in the trust instrument, it may extend to corpus distributions to any beneficiary or beneficiaries or class of beneficiaries (whether income beneficiaries or remaindermen) without causing the grantor to be treated as an owner under section 674. See section 674(b)(5)(A). It is not required that the standard consist of the needs and circumstances of the beneficiary. A clearly measurable standard under which the holder of a power is legally accountable is deemed a reasonably definite standard for this purpose. For instance, a power to distribute corpus for the education, support, maintenance, or health of the beneficiary; for his reasonable support and comfort; or to enable him to maintain his accustomed standard of living; or to meet an emergency, would be limited by a reasonably definite standard. However, a power to distribute corpus for the pleasure, desire, or happiness of a beneficiary is not limited by a reasonably definite standard. The entire context of a provision of a trust instrument granting a power must be considered in determining whether the power is limited by a reasonably definite standard. For example, if a trust instrument provides that the determination of the trustee shall be conclusive with respect to the exercise or nonexercise of a power, the power is not limited by a reasonably definite standard. However, the fact that the governing instrument is phrased in discretionary terms is not in itself an indication that no reasonably definite standard exists.

(ii) If the power is not limited by a reasonably definite standard set forth in the trust instrument, the exception applies only if distributions of corpus may be made solely in favor of current income beneficiaries, and any corpus distribution to the current income beneficiary must be chargeable against the proportionate part of corpus held in trust for payment of income to that beneficiary as if it constituted a separate trust (whether or not physically segregated). See section 674(b)(5)(B).

(iii) This subparagraph may be illustrated by the following examples:

Example (1). A trust instrument provides for payment of the income to the grantor's two brothers for life, and for payment of the corpus to the grantor's nephews in equal shares. The grantor reserves the power to distribute corpus to pay medical expenses that may be incurred by his brothers or nephews. The grantor is not treated as an owner by reason of this power because section 674(b)(5)(A) excepts a power, exercisable by any person, to invade corpus for any beneficiary, including a remainderman, if the power is limited by a reasonably definite standard which is set forth in the trust instrument. However, if the power were also exercisable in favor of a person (for example, a sister) who was not otherwise a beneficiary of the trust, section 674(b)(5)(A) would not be applicable.

Example (2). The facts are the same as in example (1) except that the grantor reserves the power to distribute any part of the corpus to his brothers or to his nephews for their happiness. The grantor is treated as the owner of the trust. Paragraph (5)(A) of section 674(b) is inapplicable because the power is not limited by a reasonably definite standard. Paragraph (5)(B) is inapplicable because the power to distribute corpus permits a distribution of corpus to persons other than current income beneficiaries.

Example (3). A trust instrument provides for payment of the income to the grantor's two adult sons in equal shares for 10 years, after which the corpus is to be distributed to his grandchildren in equal shares. The grantor reserves the power to pay over to each son up to one-half of the corpus during the 10-year period, but any such payment shall proportionately reduce subsequent income and corpus payments made to the son receiving the corpus. Thus, if one-half of the corpus is paid to one son, all the income from the remaining half is thereafter payable to the other son. The grantor is not treated as an owner under section 674(a) by reason of this power because it qualifies under the exception of section 674(b)(5)(B).

(6) *Powers to withhold income temporarily.* (i) Section 674(b)(6) excepts a power which, in general, enables the holder merely to effect a postponement in the time when the ordinary income is enjoyed by a current income beneficiary. Specifically, there is excepted a power to distribute or apply ordinary income to or for a current income beneficiary or to accumulate the income, if the accumulated income must ultimately be payable either:

(*a*) To the beneficiary from whom it was withheld, his estate, or his appointees (or persons designated by name, as a class, or otherwise as alternate takers in default of appointment) under a power of appointment held by the beneficiary which does not exclude from the class of possible appointees any person other than the beneficiary, his estate, his creditors, or the creditors of his estate (section 674(b)(6)(A));

(*b*) To the beneficiary from whom it was withheld, or if he does not survive a date of distribution which could reasonably be expected to occur within his lifetime, to his appointees (or alternate takers in default of appointment) under any power of appointment, general or special, or if he has no power of appointment to one or more designated alternate takers (other than the grantor or the grantor's estate) whose shares have been irrevocably specified in the trust instrument (section 674(b)(6)(A) and the flush material following); or

(*c*) On termination of the trust, or in conjunction with a distribution of corpus which is augmented by the accumulated income, to the current income beneficiaries in shares which have been irrevocably specified in the trust instrument, or if any beneficiary does not survive a date of distribution which would reasonably be expected to occur within his lifetime, to his appointees (or alternate takers in default of appointment) under any power of appointment, general or special, or if he has no power of appointment to one or more designated alternate takers (other than the grantor or the grantor's estate) whose shares have been irrevocably specified in the trust instrument (section 674(b)(6)(B) and the flush material following). (In the application of (*a*) above of this subdivision, if the accumulated income of a trust is ultimately payable to the estate of the current income beneficiary, or is ultimately payable to his appointees, or takers in default of appointment, under a power of the type described in (*a*) of this subdivision, it need not be payable to the beneficiary from whom it was withheld under any circumstances. Furthermore, if a trust otherwise qualifies for the exception in (*a*) of this subdivision the trust income will not be considered to be taxable to the grantor under section 677 by reason of the existence of the power of appointment referred to in (*a*) of this subdivision.) In general, the exception in section 674(b)(6) is not applicable if the power is in substance one to shift ordinary income from one beneficiary to another. Thus, a power will not qualify for this exception if ordinary income may be distributed to beneficiary A, or may be added to corpus which is ultimately payable to beneficiary B, a remainderman who is not a current income beneficiary. However, section 674(b)(6)(B), and (*c*) of this subdivision, permit a limited power to shift ordinary income among current income beneficiaries, as illustrated in example (1) below of this subparagraph.

(ii) The application of section 674(b)(6) may be illustrated by the following examples:

Example (1). A trust instrument provides that the income shall be paid in equal shares to the grantor's two adult daughters but the grantor reserves the power to withhold from either beneficiary any part of that beneficiary's share of income and to add it to the corpus of the trust until the younger daughter reaches the age of 30 years. When the younger daughter reaches the age of 30, the trust is to terminate and the corpus is to be divided equally between the two daughters or their estates. Although exercise of this power may permit the shifting of accumulated income from one beneficiary to the other (since the corpus with the accumulations is to be divided equally) the power is excepted under section 674(b)(6)(B) and subdivision (i)(*c*) above of this subparagraph.

Example (2). The facts are the same as in example (1), except that the grantor of the trust reserves the power to distribute accumulated income to the beneficiaries in such shares as he chooses. The combined powers are not excepted by section 674(b)(6)(B) since income accumulated pursuant to the first power is neither required to be payable only in conjunction with a corpus distribution nor required to be payable in shares specified in the trust instrument. See, however, section 674(c) and § 1.674(c)-1 for the effect of such a power if it is exercisable only by independent trustees.

Example (3). A trust provides for payment of income to the grantor's adult son with the grantor retaining the power to accumulate the income until the grantor's death, when all accumulations are to be paid to the son. If the son predeceases the grantor, all accumulations are, at the death of the grantor, to be paid to his daughter, or if she is not living, to alternate takers (which do not include the grantor's estate) in

Reg. § 1.674(b)-1(b)(6)

specified shares. The power is excepted under section 674(b)(6)(A) since the date of distribution (the date of the grantor's death) may, in the usual case, reasonably be expected to occur during the beneficiary's (the son's) lifetime. It is not necessary that the accumulations be payable to the son's estate or his appointees if he should predecease the grantor for this exception to apply.

(7) *Power to withhold income during disability.* Section 674(b)(7) provides an exception for a power which, in general, will permit ordinary income to be withheld during the legal disability of an income beneficiary or while he is under 21. Specifically, there is excepted a power, exercisable only during the existence of a legal disability of any current income beneficiary or the period during which any income beneficiary is under the age of 21 years, to distribute or apply ordinary income to or for that beneficiary or to accumulate the income and add it to corpus. To qualify under this exception it is not necessary that the income ultimately be payable to the income beneficiary from whom it was withheld, his estate, or his appointees; that is, the accumulated income may be added to corpus and ultimately distributed to others. For example, the grantor is not treated as an owner under section 674 if the income of a trust is payable to his son for life, remainder to his grandchildren, although he reserves the power to accumulate income and add it to corpus while his son is under 21.

(8) *Powers to allocate between corpus and income.* Paragraph (8) of section 674(b) provides that a power to allocate receipts and disbursements between corpus and income, even though expressed in broad language, will not cause the grantor to be treated as an owner under the general rule of section 674(a). [Reg. § 1.674(b)-1.]

☐ [*T.D.* 6217, 12-19-56.]

[Reg. § 1.674(c)-1]

§ 1.674(c)-1. **Excepted powers exercisable only by independent trustees.**—Section 674(c) provides an exception to the general rule of section 674(a) for certain powers that are exercisable by independent trustees. This exception is in addition to those provided for under section 674(b) which may be held by any person including an independent trustee. The powers to which section 674(c) apply are powers (a) to distribute, apportion, or accumulate income to or for a beneficiary or beneficiaries, or to, for, or within a class of beneficiaries, or (b) to pay out corpus to or for a beneficiary or beneficiaries or to or for a class of beneficiaries (whether or not income beneficiaries). In order for such a power to fall within the exception of section 674(c) it must be exercisable solely (without the approval or consent of any other person) by a trustee or trustees none of whom is the grantor and no more than half of whom are related or subordinate parties who are subservient to the wishes of the grantor. (See section 672(c) for definitions of these terms.) An example of the application of section 674(c) is a trust whose income is payable to the grantor's three adult sons with power in an independent trustee to allocate without restriction the amounts of income to be paid to each son each year. Such a power does not cause the grantor to be treated as the owner of the trust. See, however, the limitations set forth in § 1.674(d)-2. [Reg. § 1.674(c)-1.]

☐ [*T.D.* 6217, 12-19-56.]

[Reg. § 1.674(d)-1]

§ 1.674(d)-1. **Excepted powers exercisable by any trustees other than grantor or spouse.**—Section 674(d) provides an additional exception to the general rule of section 674(a) for a power to distribute, apportion, or accumulate income to or for a beneficiary or beneficiaries or to, for, or within a class of beneficiaries, whether or not the conditions of section 674(b)(6) or (7) are satisfied, if the power is solely exercisable (without the approval or consent of any other person) by a trustee or trustees none of whom is the grantor or spouse living with the grantor, and if the power is limited by a reasonably definite external standard set forth in the trust instrument (see paragraph (b)(5) of § 1.674(b)-1 with respect to what constitutes a reasonably definite standard). See, however, the limitations set forth in § 1.674(d)-2. [Reg. § 1.674(d)-1.]

☐ [*T.D.* 6217, 12-19-56.]

[Reg. § 1.674(d)-2]

§ 1.674(d)-2. **Limitations on exceptions in section 674(b), (c), and (d).**—(a) *Power to remove trustee.* A power in the grantor to remove, substitute, or add trustees (other than a power exercisable only upon limited conditions which do not exist during the taxable year, such as the death or resignation of, or breach of fiduciary duty by, an existing trustee) may prevent a trust from qualifying under section 674(c) or (d). For example, if a grantor has an unrestricted power to remove an independent trustee and substitute any person including himself as trustee, the trust will not qualify under section 674(c) or (d). On the other hand if the grantor's power to remove, substitute, or add trustees is limited so that its exercise could not alter the trust in a manner that would disqualify it under section 674(c) or (d), as the case may be, the power itself does not disqualify the trust. Thus, for example, a power in the grantor to remove or discharge an independent trustee on the condition that he substitute another independent trustee will not prevent a trust from qualifying under section 674(c).

(b) *Power to add beneficiaries.* The exceptions described in section 674(b)(5), (6), and (7), (c), and (d) are not applicable if any person has a power to add to the beneficiary or beneficiaries or to a class of beneficiaries designated to receive the income or corpus, except where the action is to provide for after-born or after-adopted children. This limitation does not apply to a power held by a beneficiary to substitute other beneficiaries to succeed to his interest in the trust (so that he would be an adverse party as to the exercise or non-exercise of that power). For example, the limitation does not apply to a power in a beneficiary of a nonspendthrift trust to assign his interest. Nor does the limitation apply to a power held by any person which would qualify as an exception under section 674(b)(3) (relating to testamentary powers). [Reg. § 1.674(d)-2.]

☐ [*T.D.* 6217, 12-19-56.]

[Reg. § 1.675-1]

§ 1.675-1. Administrative powers.—(a) *General rule.* Section 675 provides in effect that the grantor is treated as the owner of any portion of a trust if under the terms of the trust instrument or circumstances attendant on its operation administrative control is exercisable primarily for the benefit of the grantor rather than the beneficiaries of the trust. If a grantor retains a power to amend the administrative provisions of a trust instrument which is broad enough to permit an amendment causing the grantor to be treated as the owner of a portion of the trust under section 675, he will be treated as the owner of the portion from its inception. See section 671 and §§ 1.671-2 and 1.671-3 for rules for treatment of items of income, deduction, and credit when a person is treated as the owner of all or only a portion of a trust.

(b) *Prohibited controls.* The circumstances which cause administrative controls to be considered exercisable primarily for the benefit of the grantor are specifically described in paragraphs (1) through (4) of section 675 as follows:

(1) The existence of a power, exercisable by the grantor or a non-adverse party, or both, without the approval or consent of any adverse party, which enables the grantor or any other person to purchase, exchange, or otherwise deal with or dispose of the corpus or the income of the trust for less than adequate consideration in money or money's worth. Whether the existence of the power itself will constitute the holder an adverse party will depend on the particular circumstances.

(2) The existence of a power exercisable by the grantor or a non-adverse party, or both, which enables the grantor to borrow the corpus or income of the trust, directly or indirectly, without adequate interest or adequate security. However, this paragraph does not apply where a trustee (other than the grantor acting alone) is authorized under a general lending power to make loans to any person without regard to interest or security. A general lending power in the grantor, acting alone as trustee, under which he has power to determine interest rates and the adequacy of security is not in itself an indication that the grantor has power to borrow the corpus or income without adequate interest or security.

(3) The circumstance that the grantor has directly or indirectly borrowed the corpus or income of the trust and has not completely repaid the loan, including any interest, before the beginning of the taxable year. The preceding sentence does not apply to a loan which provides for adequate interest and adequate security, if it is made by a trustee other than the grantor or a related or subordinate trustee subservient to the grantor. See section 672(c) for definition of "a related or subordinate party."

(4) The existence of certain powers of administration exercisable in a nonfiduciary capacity by any nonadverse party without the approval or consent of any person in a fiduciary capacity. The term "powers of administration" means one or more of the following powers:

(i) A power to vote or direct the voting of stock or other securities of a corporation in which the holdings of the grantor and the trust are significant from the viewpoint of voting control;

(ii) A power to control the investment of the trust funds either by directing investments or reinvestments, or by vetoing proposed investments or reinvestments, to the extent that the trust funds consist of stocks or securities of corporations in which the holdings of the grantor and the trust are significant from the viewpoint of voting control; or

(iii) A power to reacquire the trust corpus by substituting other property of an equivalent value.

If a power is exercisable by a person as trustee, it is presumed that the power is exercisable in a fiduciary capacity primarily in the interests of the beneficiaries. This presumption may be rebutted only by clear and convincing proof that the power is not exercisable primarily in the interests of the beneficiaries. If a power is not exercisable by a person as trustee, the determination of whether the power is exercisable in a fiduciary or a nonfiduciary capacity depends on all the terms

Reg. § 1.675-1(b)(4)

of the trust and the circumstances surrounding its creation and administration.

(c) *Authority of trustee.* The mere fact that a power exercisable by a trustee is described in broad language does not indicate that the trustee is authorized to purchase, exchange, or otherwise deal with or dispose of the trust property or income for less than an adequate and full consideration in money or money's worth, or is authorized to lend the trust property or income to the grantor without adequate interest. On the other hand, such authority may be indicated by the actual administration of the trust. [Reg. § 1.675-1.]

☐ [*T.D.* 6217, 12-19-56.]

[Reg. § 1.676(a)-1]

§ 1.676(a)-1. Power to revest title to portion of trust property in grantor; general rule.—If a power to revest in the grantor title to any portion of a trust is exercisable by the grantor or a nonadverse party, or both, without the approval or consent of an adverse party, the grantor is treated as the owner of that portion, except as provided in section 676(b) (relating to powers affecting beneficial enjoyment of income only after the expiration of certain periods of time). If the title to a portion of the trust will revest in the grantor upon the exercise of a power by the grantor or a nonadverse party, or both, the grantor is treated as the owner of that portion regardless of whether the power is a power to revoke, to terminate, to alter or amend, or to appoint. See section 671 and §§ 1.671-2 and 1.671-3 for rules for treatment of items of income, deduction, and credit when a person is treated as the owner of all or only a portion of a trust. [Reg. § 1.676(a)-1.]

☐ [*T.D.* 6217, 12-19-56.]

[Reg. § 1.676(b)-1]

§ 1.676(b)-1. Powers exercisable only after a period of time.—Section 676(b) provides an exception to the general rule of section 676(a) when the exercise of a power can only affect the beneficial enjoyment of the income of a trust received after the expiration of a period of time which is such that a grantor would not be treated as an owner under section 673 if the power were a reversionary interest. See §§ 1.673(a)-1 and 1.673(b)-1. Thus, for example, a grantor is excepted from the general rule of section 676 (a) with respect to ordinary income if exercise of a power to revest corpus in him cannot affect the beneficial enjoyment of the income received within 10 years after the date of transfer of that portion of the trust. It is immaterial for this purpose that the power is vested at the time of the transfer. However, the grantor is subject to the general rule of section 676(a) after the expiration of the period unless the power is relinquished. Thus, in the above example, the grantor may be treated as the owner and be taxed on all income in the eleventh and succeeding years if exercise of the power can affect beneficial enjoyment of income received in those years. If the beginning of the period during which the grantor may revest is postponed, the rules set forth in § 1.673(d)-1 are applicable to determine whether the grantor should be treated as an owner during the period following the postponement. [Reg. § 1.676(b)-1.]

☐ [*T.D.* 6217, 12-19-56.]

[Reg. § 1.677(a)-1]

§ 1.677(a)-1. Income for benefit of grantor; general rule.—(a)(1) *Scope.* Section 677 deals with the treatment of the grantor of a trust as the owner of a portion of the trust because he has retained an interest in the income from that portion. For convenience, "grantor" and "spouse" are generally referred to in the masculine and feminine genders, respectively, but if the grantor is a woman the reference to "grantor" is to her and the reference to "spouse" is to her husband. Section 677 also deals with the treatment of the grantor of a trust as the owner of a portion of the trust because the income from property transferred in trust after October 9, 1969, is, or may be, distributed to his spouse or applied to the payment of premiums on policies of insurance on the life of his spouse. However, section 677 does not apply when the income of a trust is taxable to a grantor's spouse under section 71 (relating to alimony and separate maintenance payments) or section 682 (relating to income of an estate or trust in the case of divorce, etc.). See § 1.671-1(b).

(2) *Cross references.* See section 671 and §§ 1.671-2 and 1.671-3 for rules for treatment of items of income, deduction, and credit when a person is treated as the owner of all or a portion of a trust.

(b) *Income for benefit of grantor or his spouse; general rule*—(1) *Property transferred in trust prior to October 10, 1969.* With respect to property transferred in trust prior to October 10, 1969, the grantor is treated, under section 677, in any taxable year as the owner (whether or not he is treated as an owner under section 674) of a portion of a trust of which the income for the taxable year or for a period not within the exception described in paragraph (e) of this section is, or in the discretion of the grantor or a nonadverse party, or both (without the approval or consent of any adverse party) may be:

(i) Distributed to the grantor;

(ii) Held or accumulated for future distribution to the grantor; or

(iii) Applied to the payment of premiums on policies of insurance on the life of the grantor, except policies of insurance irrevocably payable for a charitable purpose specified in section 170(c).

(2) *Property transferred in trust after October 9, 1969.* With respect to property transferred in trust after October 9, 1969, the grantor is treated, under section 677, in any taxable year as the owner (whether or not he is treated as an owner under section 674) of a portion of a trust of which the income for the taxable year or for a period not within the exception described in paragraph (e) of this section is, or in the discretion of the grantor, or his spouse, or a nonadverse party, or any combination thereof (without the approval or consent of any adverse party other than the grantor's spouse) may be:

(i) Distributed to the grantor or the grantor's spouse;

(ii) Held or accumulated for future distribution to the grantor or the grantor's spouse; or

(iii) Applied to the payment of premiums on policies of insurance on the life of the grantor or the grantor's spouse, except policies of insurance irrevocably payable for a charitable purpose specified in section 170(c).

With respect to the treatment of a grantor as the owner of a portion of a trust solely because its income is, or may be, distributed or held or accumulated for future distribution to a beneficiary who is his spouse or applied to the payment of premiums for insurance on the spouse's life, section 677(a) applies to the income of a trust solely during the period of the marriage of the grantor to a beneficiary. In the case of divorce or separation, see sections 71 and 682 and the regulations thereunder.

(c) *Constructive distribution; cessation of interest.* Under section 677 the grantor is treated as the owner of a portion of a trust if he has retained any interest which might, without the approval or consent of an adverse party, enable him to have the income from that portion distributed to him at some time either actually or constructively (subject to the exception described in paragraph (e) of this section). In the case of a transfer in trust after October 9, 1969, the grantor is also treated as the owner of a portion of a trust if he has granted or retained any interest which might, without the approval or consent of an adverse party (other than the grantor's spouse), enable his spouse to have the income from the portion at some time, whether or not within the grantor's life time, distributed to the spouse either actually or constructively. See paragraph (b)(2) of this section for additional rules relating to the income of a trust prior to the grantor's marriage to a beneficiary. Constructive distribution to the grantor or to his spouse includes payment on behalf of the grantor or his spouse to another in obedience to his or her direction and payment of premiums upon policies of insurance on the grantor's, or his spouse's, life (other than policies of insurance irrevocably payable for charitable purposes specified in section 170(c)). If the grantor (in the case of property transferred prior to October 10, 1969) or the grantor and his spouse (in the case of property transferred after October 9, 1969) are divested permanently and completely of every interest described in this paragraph, the grantor is not treated as an owner under section 677 after that divesting. The word "interest" as used in this paragraph does not include the possibility that the grantor or his spouse might receive back from a beneficiary an interest in a trust by inheritance. Further, with respect to transfers in trust prior to October 10, 1969, the word "interest" does not include the possibility that the grantor might receive back from a beneficiary an interest in a trust as a surviving spouse under a statutory right of election or a similar right.

(d) *Discharge of legal obligation of grantor or his spouse.* Under section 677 a grantor is, in general, treated as the owner of a portion of a trust whose income is, or in the discretion of the grantor or a nonadverse party, or both, may be applied in discharge of a legal obligation of the grantor (or his spouse in the case of property transferred in trust by the grantor after October 9, 1969). However, see § 1.677(b)-1 for special rules for trusts whose income may not be applied for the discharge of any legal obligation of the grantor or the grantor's spouse other than the support or maintenance of a beneficiary (other than the grantor's spouse) whom the grantor or grantor's spouse is legally obligated to support. See § 301.7701-4(e) of this chapter for rules on the classification of and application of section 677 to an environmental remediation trust.

(e) *Exception for certain discretionary rights affecting income.* The last sentence of section 677(a) provides that a grantor shall not be treated as the owner when a discretionary right can only affect the beneficial enjoyment of the income of a trust received after a period of time during which a grantor would not be treated as an owner under section 673 if the power were a reversionary interest. See §§ 1.673(a)-1 and 1.673(b)-1. For example, if the ordinary income of a trust is payable to B for 10 years and then in the grantor's discretion income or corpus may be paid to B or to the grantor (or his spouse in the case of property transferred in trust by the grantor after October 9, 1969), the grantor is not treated as an owner

Reg. § 1.677(a)-1(e)

with respect to the ordinary income under section 677 during the first 10 years. He will be treated as an owner under section 677 after the expiration of the 10-year period unless the power is relinquished. If the beginning of the period during which the grantor may substitute beneficiaries is postponed, the rules set forth in § 1.673(d)-1 are applicable in determining whether the grantor should be treated as an owner during the period following the postponement.

(f) *Accumulation of income.* If income is accumulated in any taxable year for future distribution to the grantor (or his spouse in the case of property transferred in trust by the grantor after October 9, 1969), section 677(a)(2) treats the grantor as an owner for that taxable year. The exception set forth in the last sentence of section 677(a) does not apply merely because the grantor (or his spouse in the case of property transferred in trust by the grantor after October 9, 1969) must await the expiration of a period of time before he or she can receive or exercise discretion over previously accumulated income of the trust, even though the period is such that the grantor would not be treated as an owner under section 673 if a reversionary interest were involved. Thus, if income (including capital gains) of a trust is to be accumulated for 10 years and then will be, or at the discretion of the grantor, or his spouse in the case of property transferred in trust after October 9, 1969, or a nonadverse party, may be, distributed to the grantor (or his spouse in the case of property transferred in trust after October 9, 1969), the grantor is treated as the owner of the trust from its inception. If income attributable to transfers after October 9, 1969 is accumulated in any taxable year during the grantor's lifetime for future distribution to his spouse, section 677(a)(2) treats the grantor as an owner for that taxable year even though his spouse may not receive or exercise discretion over such income prior to the grantor's death.

(g) *Examples.* The application of section 677(a) may be illustrated by the following examples:

Example (1). G creates an irrevocable trust which provides that the ordinary income is to be payable to him for life and that on his death the corpus shall be distributed to B, an unrelated person. Except for the right to receive income, G retains no right or power which would cause him to be treated as an owner under sections 671 through 677. Under the applicable local law capital gains must be applied to corpus. During the taxable year 1970 the trust has the following items of gross income and deductions:

Dividends	$5,000
Capital gain	1,000
Expenses allocable to income	200
Expenses allocable to corpus	100

Since G has a right to receive income he is treated as an owner of a portion of the trust under section 677. Accordingly, he should include the $5,000 of dividends, $200 income expense, and $100 corpus expense in the computation of his taxable income for 1970. He should not include the $1,000 capital gain since that is not attributable to the portion of the trust that he owns. See § 1.671-3(b). The tax consequences of the capital gain are governed by the provisions of subparts A, B, C, and D (section 641 and following), part I, subchapter J, chapter 1 of the Code. Had the trust sustained a capital loss in any amount the loss would likewise not be included in the computation of G's taxable income, but would also be governed by the provisions of such subparts.

Example (2). G creates a trust which provides that the ordinary income is payable to his adult son. Ten years and one day from the date of transfer or on the death of his son, whichever is earlier, corpus is to revert to G. In addition, G retains a discretionary right to receive $5,000 of ordinary income each year. (Absent the exercise of this right all the ordinary income is to be distributed to his son.) G retained no other right or power which would cause him to be treated as an owner under subpart E (section 671 and following). Under the terms of the trust instrument and applicable local law capital gains must be applied to corpus. During the taxable year 1970 the trust had the following items of income and deductions:

Dividends	$10,000
Capital gain	2,000
Expenses allocable to income	400
Expenses allocable to corpus	200

Since the capital gain is held or accumulated for future distributions to G, he is treated under section 677(a)(2) as an owner of a portion of the trust to which the gain is attributable. See § 1.671-3(b).

Therefore, he must include the capital gain in the computation of his taxable income. (Had the trust sustained a capital loss in any amount, G would likewise include that loss in the computation of his taxable income.) In addition, because of G's discretionary right (whether exercised or not) he is treated as the owner of a portion of the trust which will permit a distribution of income to him of $5,000. Accordingly, G includes dividends of $5,208.33 and income expenses of $208.33 in computing his taxable income, determined in the following manner:

Reg. § 1.677(a)-1(f)

Total dividends	$10,000.00
Less: Expenses allocable to income	400.00
Distributable income of the trust	9,600.00
Portion of dividends attributable to G (5,000/9,600 × $10,000)	5,208.33
Portion of income expenses attributable to G (5,000/9,600 × $400)	208.33
Amount of income subject to discretionary right	5,000.00

In accordance with § 1.671-3(c), G also takes into account $104.17 (5,000/9,600×$200) of corpus expenses in computing his tax liability. The portion of the dividends and expenses of the trust not attributable to G are governed by the provisions of subparts A through D. [Reg. § 1.677(a)-1.]

☐ [T.D. 6217, 12-19-56. *Amended by* T.D. 7148, 10-28-71 *and* T.D. 8668, 4-30-96.]

[Reg. § 1.677(b)-1]

§ 1.677(b)-1. Trusts for support.—(a) Section 677(b) provides that a grantor is not treated as the owner of a trust merely because its income may in the discretion of any person other than the grantor (except when he is acting as trustee or cotrustee) be applied or distributed for the support or maintenance of a beneficiary (other than the grantor's spouse in the case of income from property transferred in trust after October 9, 1969), such as the child of the grantor, whom the grantor or his spouse is legally obligated to support. If income of the current year of the trust is actually so applied or distributed the grantor may be treated as the owner of any portion of the trust under section 677 to that extent, even though it might have been applied or distributed for other purposes. In the case of property transferred to a trust before October 10, 1969, for the benefit of the grantor's spouse, the grantor may be treated as the owner to the extent income of the current year is actually applied for the support or maintenance of his spouse.

(b) If any amount applied or distributed for the support of a beneficiary, including the grantor's spouse in the case of property transferred in trust before October 10, 1969, whom the grantor is legally obligated to support is paid out of corpus or out of income other than income of the current year, the grantor is treated as a beneficiary of the trust, and the amount applied or distributed is considered to be an amount paid within the meaning of section 661(a)(2), taxable to the grantor under section 662. Thus, he is subject to the other relevant portions of subparts A through D (section 641 and following), part I, subchapter J, chapter 1 of the Code. Accordingly, the grantor may be taxed on an accumulation distribution or a capital gain distribution under subpart D (section 665 and following) of such part I. Those provisions are applied on the basis that the grantor is the beneficiary.

(c) For the purpose of determining the items of income, deduction, and credit of a trust to be included under this section in computing the grantor's tax liability, the income of the trust for the taxable year of distribution will be deemed to have been first distributed. For example, in the case of a trust reporting on the calendar year basis, a distribution made on January 1, 1956, will be deemed to have been made out of ordinary income of the trust for the calendar year 1956 to the extent of the income for that year even though the trust had received no income as of January 1, 1956. Thus, if a distribution of $10,000 is made on January 1, 1956, for the support of the grantor's dependent, the grantor will be treated as the owner of the trust for 1956 to that extent. If the trust received dividends of $5,000 and incurred expenses of $1,000 during that year but subsequent to January 1, he will take into account dividends of $5,000 and expenses of $1,000 in computing his tax liability for 1956. In addition, the grantor will be treated as a beneficiary of the trust with respect to the $6,000 ($10,000 less distributable income of $4,000 (dividends of $5,000 less expenses of $1,000)) paid out of corpus or out of other than income of the current year. See paragraph (b) of this section.

(d) The exception provided in section 677(b) relates solely to the satisfaction of the grantor's legal obligation to support or maintain a beneficiary. Consequently, the general rule of section 677(a) is applicable when in the discretion of the grantor or nonadverse parties income of a trust may be applied in discharge of a grantor's obligations other than his obligation of support or maintenance falling within section 677(b). Thus, if the grantor creates a trust the income of which may in the discretion of a nonadverse party be applied in the payment of the grantor's debts, such as the payment of his rent or other household expenses, he is treated as an owner of the trust regardless of whether the income is actually so applied.

(e) The general rule of section 677(a), and not section 677(b), is applicable if discretion to apply or distribute income of a trust rests solely in the grantor, or in the grantor in conjunction with other persons, unless in either case the grantor has such discretion as trustee or cotrustee.

(f) The general rule of section 677(a), and not section 677(b), is applicable to the extent that income is required, without any discretionary determination, to be applied to the support of a beneficiary whom the grantor is legally obligated to support. [Reg. § 1.677(b)-1.]

☐ [*T.D. 6217*, 12-19-56. *Amended by T.D. 7148*, 10-28-71.]

[Reg. § 1.678(a)-1]

§ 1.678(a)-1. Person other than grantor treated as substantial owner; general rule.—(a) Where a person other than the grantor of a trust has a power exercisable solely by himself to vest the corpus or the income of any portion of a testamentary or inter vivos trust in himself, he is treated under section 678(a) as the owner of that portion, except as provided in section 678(b) (involving taxation of the grantor) and section 678(c) (involving an obligation of support). The holder of such a power also is treated as an owner of the trust even though he has partially released or otherwise modified the power so that he can no longer vest the corpus or income in himself, if he has retained such control of the trust as would, if retained by a grantor, subject the grantor to treatment as the owner under sections 671 to 677, inclusive. See section 671 and §§ 1.671-2 and 1.671-3 for rules for treatment of items of income, deduction, and credit where a person is treated as the owner of all or only a portion of a trust.

(b) Section 678(a) treats a person as an owner of a trust if he has a power exercisable solely by himself to apply the income or corpus for the satisfaction of his legal obligations, other than an obligation to support a dependent (see § 1.678(c)-1) subject to the limitation of section 678(b). Section 678 does not apply if the power is not exercisable solely by himself. However, see § 1.662(a)-4 for principles applicable to income of a trust which, pursuant to the terms of the trust instrument, is used to satisfy the obligations of a person other than the grantor. [Reg. § 1.678(a)-1.]

☐ [*T.D. 6217*, 12-19-56.]

[Reg. § 1.678(b)-1]

§ 1.678(b)-1. If grantor is treated as the owner.—Section 678(a) does not apply with respect to a power over income, as originally granted or thereafter modified, if the grantor of the trust is treated as the owner under sections 671 to 677, inclusive. [Reg. § 1.678(b)-1.]

☐ [*T.D. 6217*, 12-19-56.]

[Reg. § 1.678(c)-1]

§ 1.678(c)-1. Trusts for support.—(a) Section 678(a) does not apply to a power which enables the holder, in the capacity of trustee or cotrustee, to apply the income of the trust to the support or maintenance of a person whom the holder is obligated to support, except to the extent the income is so applied. See paragraph (a), (b), and (c) of § 1.677(b)-1 for applicable principles where any amount is applied for the support or maintenance of a person whom the holder is obligated to support.

(b) The general rule in section 678(a) (and not the exception in section 678(c)) is applicable in any case in which the holder of a power exercisable solely by himself is able, in any capacity other than that of trustee or cotrustee, to apply the income in discharge of his obligation of support or maintenance.

(c) Section 678(c) is concerned with the taxability of income subject to a power described in section 678(a). It has no application to the taxability of income which is either required to be applied pursuant to the terms of the trust instrument or is applied pursuant to a power which is not described in section 678(a), the taxability of such income being governed by other provisions of the Code. See § 1.662(a)-4. [Reg. § 1.678(c)-1.]

☐ [*T.D. 6217*, 12-19-56.]

[Reg. § 1.678(d)-1]

§ 1.678(d)-1. Renunciation of power.—Section 678(a) does not apply to a power which has been renounced or disclaimed within a reasonable time after the holder of the power first became aware of its existence. [Reg. § 1.678(d)-1.]

☐ [*T.D. 6217*, 12-19-56.]

[Reg. § 1.679-0]

§ 1.679-0. Outline of major topics.—This section lists the major paragraphs contained in §§ 1.679-1 through 1.679-7 as follows:

§ 1.679-1 U.S. transferor treated as owner of foreign trust.

(a) In general.
(b) Interaction with sections 673 through 678.
(c) Definitions.
   (1) U.S. transferor.
   (2) U.S. person.
   (3) Foreign trust.
   (4) Property.
   (5) Related person.
   (6) Obligation.
(d) Examples.

Reg. § 1.678(a)-1(a)

Estates, Trusts, and Beneficiaries

§ 1.679-2 Trusts treated as having a U.S. beneficiary.

(a) Existence of U.S. beneficiary.
  (1) In general.
  (2) Benefit to a U.S. person
    (i) In general.
    (ii) Certain unexpected beneficiaries.
    (iii) Examples.
  (3) Changes in beneficiary's status.
    (i) In general.
    (ii) Examples.
  (4) General rules.
    (i) Records and documents.
    (ii) Additional factors.
    (iii) Examples.
(b) Indirect U.S. beneficiaries.
  (1) Certain foreign entities.
  (2) Other indirect beneficiaries.
  (3) Examples.
(c) Treatment of U.S. transferor upon foreign trust's acquisition or loss of U.S. beneficiary.
  (1) Trusts acquiring a U.S. beneficiary.
  (2) Trusts ceasing to have a U.S. beneficiary.
  (3) Examples.

§ 1.679-3 Transfers.

(a) In general.
(b) Transfers by certain trusts.
  (1) In general.
  (2) Example.
(c) Indirect transfers.
  (1) Principal purpose of tax avoidance.
  (2) Principal purpose of tax avoidance deemed to exist.
  (3) Effect of disregarding intermediary.
    (i) In general.
    (ii) Special rule.
    (iii) Effect on intermediary.
  (4) Related parties.
  (5) Examples.
(d) Constructive transfers.
  (1) In general.
  (2) Examples.
(e) Guarantee of trust obligations.
  (1) In general.
  (2) Amount transferred.
  (3) Principal repayments.
  (4) Guarantee.
  (5) Examples.

(f) Transfers to entities owned by a foreign trust.
  (1) General rule.
  (2) Examples.

§ 1.679-4 Exceptions to general rule.

(a) In general.
(b) Transfers for fair market value.
  (1) In general.
  (2) Special rule.
    (i) Transfers for partial consideration.
    (ii) Example.
(c) Certain obligations not taken into account.
(d) Qualified obligations.
  (1) In general.
  (2) Additional loans.
  (3) Obligations that cease to be qualified.
  (4) Transfers resulting from failed qualified obligations.
  (5) Renegotiated loans.
  (6) Principal repayments.
  (7) Examples.

§ 1.679-5 Pre-immigration trusts.

(a) In general.
(b) Special rules.
  (1) Change in grantor trust status.
  (2) Treatment of undistributed income.
(c) Examples.

§ 1.679-6 Outbound migrations of domestic trusts.

(a) In general.
(b) Amount deemed transferred.
(c) Example.

§ 1.679-7 Effective dates.

(a) In general.
(b) Special rules.

[Reg. § 1.679-0.]

☐ [T.D. 8955, 7-19-2001.]

[Reg. § 1.679-1]

§ 1.679-1. U.S. transferor treated as owner of foreign trust.—(a) *In general.* A U.S. transferor who transfers property to a foreign trust is treated as the owner of the portion of the trust attributable to the property transferred if there is a U.S. beneficiary of any portion of the trust, unless an exception in § 1.679-4 applies to the transfer.

(b) *Interaction with sections 673 through 678.* The rules of this section apply without regard to whether the U.S. transferor retains any power or interest described in sections 673 through 677. If

Reg. § 1.679-1(b)

a U.S. transferor would be treated as the owner of a portion of a foreign trust pursuant to the rules of this section and another person would be treated as the owner of the same portion of the trust pursuant to section 678, then the U.S. transferor is treated as the owner and the other person is not treated as the owner.

(c) *Definitions.* The following definitions apply for purposes of this section and §§ 1.679-2 through 1.679-7:

(1) *U.S. transferor.* The term *U.S. transferor* means any U.S. person who makes a transfer (as defined in § 1.679-3) of property to a foreign trust.

(2) *U.S. person.* The term *U.S. person* means a United States person as defined in section 7701(a)(30), a nonresident alien individual who elects under section 6013(g) to be treated as resident of the United States, and an individual who is a dual resident taxpayer within the meaning of § 301.7701(b)-7(a) of this chapter.

(3) *Foreign trust.* Section 7701(a)(31)(B) defines the term *foreign trust.* See also § 301.7701-7 of this chapter.

(4) *Property.* The term *property* means any property including cash.

(5) *Related person.* A person is a *related person* if, without regard to the transfer at issue, the person is—

(i) A grantor of any portion of the trust (within the meaning of § 1.671-2(e)(1));

(ii) An owner of any portion of the trust under sections 671 through 679;

(iii) A beneficiary of the trust; or

(iv) A person who is related (within the meaning of section 643(i)(2)(B)) to any grantor, owner or beneficiary of the trust.

(6) *Obligation.* The term *obligation* means any bond, note, debenture, certificate, bill receivable, account receivable, note receivable, open account, or other evidence of indebtedness, and, to the extent not previously described, any annuity contract.

(d) *Examples.* The following examples illustrate the rules of paragraph (a) of this section. In these examples, *A* is a resident alien, *B* is *A*'s son, who is a resident alien, *C* is *A*'s father, who is a resident alien, *D* is *A*'s uncle, who is a nonresident alien, and *FT* is a foreign trust. The examples are as follows:

Example 1. Interaction with section 678. *A* creates and funds *FT*. *FT* may provide for the education of *B* by paying for books, tuition, room and board. In addition, *C* has the power to vest the trust corpus or income in himself within the meaning of section 678(a)(1). Under paragraph (b) of this section, *A* is treated as the owner of the portion of *FT* attributable to the property transferred to *FT* by *A* and *C* is not treated as the owner thereof.

Example 2. U.S. person treated as owner of a portion of FT. *D* creates and funds *FT* for the benefit of *B*. *D* retains a power described in section 676 and § 1.672(f)-3(a)(1). *A* transfers property to *FT*. Under sections 676 and 672(f), *D* is treated as the owner of the portion of *FT* attributable to the property transferred by *D*. Under paragraph (a) of this section, *A* is treated as the owner of the portion of *FT* attributable to the property transferred by *A*.

[Reg. § 1.679-1.]

☐ [*T.D.* 8955, 7-19-2001.]

[Reg. § 1.679-2]

§ 1.679-2. Trusts treated as having a U.S. beneficiary.—(a) *Existence of U.S. beneficiary*—(1) *In general.* The determination of whether a foreign trust has a U.S. beneficiary is made on an annual basis. A foreign trust is treated as having a U.S. beneficiary unless during the taxable year of the U.S. transferor—

(i) No part of the income or corpus of the trust may be paid or accumulated to or for the benefit of, directly or indirectly, a U.S. person; and

(ii) If the trust is terminated at any time during the taxable year, no part of the income or corpus of the trust could be paid to or for the benefit of, directly or indirectly, a U.S. person.

(2) *Benefit to a U.S. person*—(i) *In general.* For purposes of paragraph (a)(1) of this section, income or corpus may be paid or accumulated to or for the benefit of a U.S. person during a taxable year of the U.S. transferor if during that year, directly or indirectly, income may be distributed to, or accumulated for the benefit of, a U.S. person, or corpus may be distributed to, or held for the future benefit of, a U.S. person. This determination is made without regard to whether income or corpus is actually distributed to a U.S. person during that year, and without regard to whether a U.S. person's interest in the trust income or corpus is contingent on a future event.

(ii) *Certain unexpected beneficiaries.* Notwithstanding paragraph (a)(2)(i) of this section, for purposes of paragraph (a)(1) of this section, a person who is not named as a beneficiary and is not a member of a class of beneficiaries as defined under the trust instrument is not taken into consideration if the U.S. transferor demonstrates to the satisfaction of the Commissioner that the person's contingent interest in the trust is so remote as to be negligible. The preceding sentence does not apply with respect to persons to whom distributions could be made pursuant to a grant of discretion to the trustee or any other person. A class of beneficiaries generally does not include heirs who will benefit from the trust under the laws of intestate succession in the event that the named beneficiaries (or members of the named class) have all deceased (whether or not stated as a named class in the trust instrument).

(iii) *Examples.* The following examples illustrate the rules of paragraphs (a)(1) and (2) of this section. In these examples, *A* is a resident alien, *B* is *A*'s son, who is a resident alien, *C* is *A*'s daughter, who is a nonresident alien, and *FT* is a foreign trust. The examples are as follows:

Example 1. Distribution of income to U.S. person. A transfers property to *FT*. The trust instrument provides that all trust income is to be distributed currently to *B*. Under paragraph (a)(1) of this section, *FT* is treated as having a U.S. beneficiary.

Example 2. Income accumulation for the benefit of a U.S. person. In 2001, *A* transfers property to *FT*. The trust instrument provides that from 2001 through 2010, the trustee of *FT* may distribute trust income to *C* or may accumulate the trust income. The trust instrument further provides that in 2011, the trust will terminate and the trustee may distribute the trust assets to either or both of *B* and *C*, in the trustee's discretion. If the trust terminates unexpectedly prior to 2011, all trust assets must be distributed to *C*. Because it is possible that income may be accumulated in each year, and that the accumulated income ultimately may be distributed to *B*, a U.S. person, under paragraph (a)(1) of this section *FT* is treated as having a U.S. beneficiary during each of *A*'s tax years from 2001 through 2011. This result applies even though no U.S. person may receive distributions from the trust during the tax years 2001 through 2010.

Example 3. Corpus held for the benefit of a U.S. person. The facts are the same as in *Example 2*, except that from 2001 through 2011, all trust income must be distributed to *C*. In 2011, the trust will terminate and the trustee may distribute the trust corpus to either or both of *B* and *C*, in the trustee's discretion. If the trust terminates unexpectedly prior to 2011, all trust corpus must be distributed to *C*. Because during each of *A*'s tax years from 2001 through 2011 trust corpus is held for possible future distribution to *B*, a U.S. person, under paragraph (a)(1) of this section *FT* is treated as having a U.S. beneficiary during each of those years. This result applies even though no U.S. person may receive distributions from the trust during the tax years 2001 through 2010.

Example 4. Distribution upon U.S. transferor's death. A transfers property to *FT*. The trust instrument provides that all trust income must be distributed currently to *C* and, upon *A*'s death, the trust will terminate and the trustee may distribute the trust corpus to either or both of *B* and *C*. Because *B* may receive a distribution of corpus upon the termination of *FT*, and *FT* could terminate in any year, *FT* is treated as having a U.S. beneficiary in the year of the transfer and in subsequent years.

Example 5. Distribution after U.S. transferor's death. The facts are the same as in *Example 4*, except the trust instrument provides that the trust will not terminate until the year following *A*'s death. Upon termination, the trustee may distribute the trust assets to either or both of *B* and *C*, in the trustee's discretion. All trust assets are invested in the stock of *X*, a foreign corporation, and *X* makes no distributions to *FT*. Although no U.S. person may receive a distribution until the year after *A*'s death, and *FT* has no realized income during any year of its existence, during each year in which *A* is living corpus may be held for future distribution to *B*, a U.S. person. Thus, under paragraph (a)(1) of this section *FT* is treated as having a U.S. beneficiary during each of *A*'s tax years from 2001 through the year of *A*'s death.

Example 6. Constructive benefit to U.S. person. A transfers property to *FT*. The trust instrument provides that no income or corpus may be paid directly to a U.S. person. However, the trust instrument provides that trust corpus may be used to satisfy *B*'s legal obligations to a third party by making a payment directly to the third party. Under paragraphs (a)(1) and (2) of this section, *FT* is treated as having a U.S. beneficiary.

Example 7. U.S. person with negligible contingent interest. A transfers property to *FT*. The trust instrument provides that all income is to be distributed currently to *C*, and upon *C*'s death, all corpus is to be distributed to whomever of *C*'s three children is then living. All of *C*'s children are nonresident aliens. Under the laws of intestate succession that would apply to *FT*, if all of *C*'s children are deceased at the time of *C*'s death, the corpus would be distributed to *A*'s heirs. *A*'s living relatives at the time of the transfer consist solely of two brothers and two nieces, all of whom are nonresident aliens, and two first cousins, one of whom, *E*, is a U.S. citizen. Although it is possible under certain circumstances that E could receive a corpus distribution under the applicable laws of intestate succession, for each year the trust is in existence A is able to demonstrate to the satisfaction of the Commissioner under paragraph (a)(2)(ii) of this section that E's contingent interest in FT is so remote as to be negligible. Provided that paragraph (a)(4) of this section does not require a different result, FT is not treated as having a U.S. beneficiary.

Example 8. U.S. person with non-negligible contingent interest. A transfers property to FT. The trust instrument provides that all income is to be distributed currently to D, A's uncle, who is a nonresident alien, and upon A's death, the corpus is to be distributed to D if he is then living. Under the laws of intestate succession that would apply to FT, B and C would share equally in the trust corpus if D is not living at the time of A's death. A is unable to demonstrate to the satisfaction of the Commissioner that B's contingent interest in the trust is so remote as to be negligible. Under paragraph (a)(2)(ii) of this section, FT is treated as having a U.S. beneficiary as of the year of the transfer.

Example 9. U.S. person as member of class of beneficiaries. A transfers property to FT. The trust instrument provides that all income is to be distributed currently to D, A's uncle, who is a nonresident alien, and upon A's death, the corpus is to be distributed to D if he is then living. If D is not then living, the corpus is to be distributed to D's descendants. D's grandson, E, is a resident alien. Under paragraph (a)(2)(ii) of this section, FT is treated as having a U.S. beneficiary as of the year of the transfer.

Example 10. Trustee's discretion in choosing beneficiaries. A transfers property to FT. The trust instrument provides that the trustee may distribute income and corpus to, or accumulate income for the benefit of, any person who is pursuing the academic study of ancient Greek, in the trustee's discretion. Because it is possible that a U.S. person will receive distributions of income or corpus, or will have income accumulated for his benefit, FT is treated as having a U.S. beneficiary. This result applies even if, during a tax year, no distributions or accumulations are actually made to or for the benefit of a U.S. person. A may not invoke paragraph (a)(2)(ii) of this section because a U.S. person could benefit pursuant to a grant of discretion in the trust instrument.

Example 11. Appointment of remainder beneficiary. A transfers property to FT. The trust instrument provides that the trustee may distribute current income to C, or may accumulate income, and, upon termination of the trust, trust assets are to be distributed to C. However, the trust instrument further provides that D, A's uncle, may appoint a different remainder beneficiary. Because it is possible that a U.S. person could be named as the remainder beneficiary, and because corpus could be held in each year for the future benefit of that U.S. person, FT is treated as having a U.S. beneficiary for each year.

Example 12. Trust not treated as having a U.S. beneficiary. A transfers property to FT. The trust instrument provides that the trustee may distribute income and corpus to, or accumulate income for the benefit of C. Upon termination of the trust, all income and corpus must be distributed to C. Assume that paragraph (a)(4) of this section is not applicable under the facts and circumstances and that A establishes to the satisfaction of the Commissioner under paragraph (a)(2)(ii) of this section that no U.S. persons are reasonably expected to benefit from the trust. Because no part of the income or corpus of the trust may be paid or accumulated to or for the benefit of, either directly or indirectly, a U.S. person, and if the trust is terminated no part of the income or corpus of the trust could be paid to or for the benefit of, either directly or indirectly, a U.S. person, FT is not treated as having a U.S. beneficiary.

Example 13. U.S. beneficiary becomes non-U.S. person. In 2001, A transfers property to FT. The trust instrument provides that, as long as B remains a U.S. resident, no distributions of income or corpus may be made from the trust to B. The trust instrument further provides that if B becomes a nonresident alien, distributions of income (including previously accumulated income) and corpus may be made to him. If B remains a U.S. resident at the time of FT's termination, all accumulated income and corpus is to be distributed to C. In 2007, B becomes a nonresident alien and remains so thereafter. Because income may be accumulated during the years 2001 through 2007 for the benefit of a person who is a U.S. person during those years, FT is treated as having a U.S. beneficiary under paragraph (a)(1) of this section during each of those years. This result applies even though B cannot receive distributions from FT during the years he is a resident alien and even though B might remain a resident alien who is not entitled to any distribution from FT. Provided that paragraph (a)(4) of this section does not require a different result, and that A establishes to the satisfaction of the Commissioner under paragraph (a)(2)(ii) of this section that no other U.S. persons are reasonably expected to benefit from the trust, FT is not treated as having a U.S. beneficiary under paragraph (a)(1) of this section during tax years after 2007.

Reg. § 1.679-2(a)(2)

Estates, Trusts, and Beneficiaries 43,455
See p. 20,601 for regulations not amended to reflect law changes

(3) *Changes in beneficiary's status*—(i) *In general.* For purposes of paragraph (a)(1) of this section, the possibility that a person that is not a U.S. person could become a U.S. person will not cause that person to be treated as a U.S. person for purposes of paragraph (a)(1) of this section until the tax year of the U.S. transferor in which that individual actually becomes a U.S. person. However, if a person who is not a U.S. person becomes a U.S. person for the first time more than 5 years after the date of a transfer to the foreign trust by a U.S. transferor, that person is not treated as a U.S. person for purposes of applying paragraph (a)(1) of this section with respect to that transfer.

(ii) *Examples.* The following examples illustrate the rules of paragraph (a)(3) of this section. In these examples, A is a resident alien, B is A's son, who is a resident alien, C is A's daughter, who is a nonresident alien, and FT is a foreign trust. The examples are as follows:

Example 1. Non-U.S. beneficiary becomes U.S. person. In 2001, A transfers property to FT. The trust instrument provides that all income is to be distributed currently to C and that, upon the termination of FT, all corpus is to be distributed to C. Assume that paragraph (a)(4) of this section is not applicable under the facts and circumstances and that A establishes to the satisfaction of the Commissioner under paragraph (a)(2)(ii) of this section that no U.S. persons are reasonably expected to benefit from the trust. Under paragraph (a)(3)(i) of this section, FT is not treated as having a U.S. beneficiary during the tax years of A in which C remains a nonresident alien. If C first becomes a resident alien in 2004, FT is treated as having a U.S. beneficiary commencing in that year under paragraph (a)(3) of this section. See paragraph (c) of this section regarding the treatment of A upon FT's acquisition of a U.S. beneficiary.

Example 2. Non-U.S. beneficiary becomes U.S. person more than 5 years after transfer. The facts are the same as in *Example 1*, except C first becomes a resident alien in 2007. FT is treated as not having a U.S. beneficiary under paragraph (a)(3)(i) of this section with respect to the property transfer by A. However, if C had previously been a U.S. person during any prior period, the 5-year exception in paragraph (a)(3)(i) of this section would not apply in 2007 because it would not have been the first time C became a U.S. person.

(4) *General rules*—(i) *Records and documents.* Even if, based on the terms of the trust instrument, a foreign trust is not treated as having a U.S. beneficiary within the meaning of paragraph (a)(1) of this section, the trust may nevertheless be treated as having a U.S. beneficiary pursuant to paragraph (a)(1) of this section based on the following—

(A) All written and oral agreements and understandings relating to the trust;

(B) Memoranda or letters of wishes;

(C) All records that relate to the actual distribution of income and corpus; and

(D) All other documents that relate to the trust, whether or not of any purported legal effect.

(ii) *Additional factors.* For purposes of determining whether a foreign trust is treated as having a U.S. beneficiary within the meaning of paragraph (a)(1) of this section, the following additional factors are taken into account—

(A) If the terms of the trust instrument allow the trust to be amended to benefit a U.S. person, all potential benefits that could be provided to a U.S. person pursuant to an amendment must be taken into account;

(B) If the terms of the trust instrument do not allow the trust to be amended to benefit a U.S. person, but the law applicable to a foreign trust may require payments or accumulations of income or corpus to or for the benefit of a U.S. person (by judicial reformation or otherwise), all potential benefits that could be provided to a U.S. person pursuant to the law must be taken into account, unless the U.S. transferor demonstrates to the satisfaction of the Commissioner that the law is not reasonably expected to be applied or invoked under the facts and circumstances; and

(C) If the parties to the trust ignore the terms of the trust instrument, or if it is reasonably expected that they will do so, all benefits that have been, or are reasonably expected to be, provided to a U.S. person must be taken into account.

(iii) *Examples.* The following examples illustrate the rules of paragraph (a)(4) of this section. In these examples, A is a resident alien, B is A's son, who is a resident alien, C is A's daughter, who is a nonresident alien, and FT is a foreign trust. The examples are as follows:

Example 1. Amendment pursuant to local law. A creates and funds FT for the benefit of C. The terms of FT (which, according to the trust instrument, cannot be amended) provide that no part of the income or corpus of FT may be paid or accumulated during the taxable year to or for the benefit of any U.S. person, either during the existence of FT or at the time of its termination. However, pursuant to the applicable foreign law, FT can be amended to provide for additional beneficiaries, and there is an oral understanding

Reg. § 1.679-2(a)(4)

between A and the trustee that B can be added as a beneficiary. Under paragraphs (a)(1) and (a)(4)(ii)(B) of this section, FT is treated as having a U.S. beneficiary.

Example 2. Actions in violation of the terms of the trust. A transfers property to FT. The trust instrument provides that no U.S. person can receive income or corpus from FT during the term of the trust or at the termination of FT. Notwithstanding the terms of the trust instrument, a letter of wishes directs the trustee of FT to provide for the educational needs of B, who is about to begin college. The letter of wishes contains a disclaimer to the effect that its contents are only suggestions and recommendations and that the trustee is at all times bound by the terms of the trust as set forth in the trust instrument. Under paragraphs (a)(1) and (a)(4)(ii)(C) of this section, FT is treated as having a U.S. beneficiary.

(b) *Indirect U.S. beneficiaries*—(1) *Certain foreign entities.* For purposes of paragraph (a)(1) of this section, an amount is treated as paid or accumulated to or for the benefit of a U.S. person if the amount is paid to or accumulated for the benefit of—

(i) A controlled foreign corporation, as defined in section 957(a);

(ii) A foreign partnership, if a U.S. person is a partner of such partnership; or

(iii) A foreign trust or estate, if such trust or estate has a U.S. beneficiary (within the meaning of paragraph (a)(1) of this section).

(2) *Other indirect beneficiaries.* For purposes of paragraph (a)(1) of this section, an amount is treated as paid or accumulated to or for the benefit of a U.S. person if the amount is paid to or accumulated for the benefit of a U.S. person through an intermediary, such as an agent or nominee, or by any other means where a U.S. person may obtain an actual or constructive benefit.

(3) *Examples.* The following examples illustrate the rules of this paragraph (b). Unless otherwise noted, A is a resident alien. B is A's son and is a resident alien. FT is a foreign trust. The examples are as follows:

Example 1. Trust benefitting foreign corporation. A transfers property to FT. The beneficiary of FT is FC, a foreign corporation. FC has outstanding solely 100 shares of common stock. B owns 49 shares of the FC stock and FC2, also a foreign corporation, owns the remaining 51 shares. FC2 has outstanding solely 100 shares of common stock. B owns 49 shares of FC2 and nonresident alien individuals own the remaining 51 FC2 shares. FC is a controlled foreign corporation (as defined in section 957(a), after the application of section 958(a)(2)). Under paragraphs (a)(1) and (b)(1)(i) of this section, FT is treated as having a U.S. beneficiary.

Example 2. Trust benefitting another trust. A transfers property to FT. The terms of FT permit current distributions of income to B. A transfers property to another foreign trust, FT2. The terms of FT2 provide that no U.S. person can benefit either as to income or corpus, but permit current distributions of income to FT. Under paragraph (a)(1) of this section, FT is treated as having a U.S. beneficiary and, under paragraphs (a)(1) and (b)(1)(iii) of this section, FT2 is treated as having a U.S. beneficiary.

Example 3. Trust benefitting another trust after transferor's death. A transfers property to FT. The terms of FT require that all income from FT be accumulate during A's lifetime. In the year following A's death, a share of FT is to be distributed to FT2, another foreign trust, for the benefit of B. Under paragraphs (a)(1) and (b)(1)(iii) of this section, FT is treated as having a U.S. beneficiary beginning with the year of A's transfer of property to FT.

Example 4. Indirect benefit through use of debit card. A transfers property to FT. The trust instrument provides that no U.S. person can benefit either as to income or corpus. However, FT maintains an account with FB, a foreign bank, and FB issues a debit card to B against the account maintained by FT and B is allowed to make withdrawals. Under paragraphs (a)(1) and (b)(2) of this section, FT is treated as having a U.S. beneficiary.

Example 5. Other indirect benefit. A transfers property to FT. FT is administered by FTC, a foreign trust company. FTC forms IBC, an international business corporation formed under the laws of a foreign jurisdiction. IBC is the beneficiary of FT. IBC maintains an account with FB, a foreign bank. FB issues a debit card to B against the account maintained by IBC and B is allowed to make withdrawals. Under paragraphs (a)(1) and (b)(2) of this section, FT is treated as having a U.S. beneficiary.

(c) *Treatment of U.S. transferor upon foreign trust's acquisition or loss of U.S. beneficiary*—(1) *Trusts acquiring a U.S. beneficiary.* If a foreign trust to which a U.S. transferor has transferred property is not treated as having a U.S. beneficiary (within the meaning of paragraph (a) of this section) for any taxable year of the U.S. transferor, but the trust is treated as having a U.S. beneficiary (within the meaning of paragraph (a) of this section) in any subsequent taxable year,

Reg. § 1.679-2(b)(1)

the U.S. transferor is treated as having additional income in the first such taxable year of the U.S. transferor in which the trust is treated as having a U.S. beneficiary. The amount of the additional income is equal to the trust's undistributed net income, as defined in section 665(a), at the end of the U.S. transferor's immediately preceding taxable year and is subject to the rules of section 668, providing for an interest charge on accumulation distributions from foreign trusts.

(2) *Trusts ceasing to have a U.S. beneficiary.* If, for any taxable year of a U.S. transferor, a foreign trust that has received a transfer of property from the U.S. transferor ceases to be treated as having a U.S. beneficiary, the U.S. transferor ceases to be treated as the owner of the portion of the trust attributable to the transfer beginning in the first taxable year following the last taxable year of the U.S. transferor during which the trust was treated as having a U.S. beneficiary (unless the U.S. transferor is treated as an owner thereof pursuant to sections 673 through 677). The U.S. transferor is treated as making a transfer of property to the foreign trust on the first day of the first taxable year following the last taxable year of the U.S. transferor during which the trust was treated as having a U.S. beneficiary. The amount of the property deemed to be transferred to the trust is the portion of the trust attributable to the prior transfer to which paragraph (a)(1) of this section applied. For rules regarding the recognition of gain on transfers to foreign trusts, see section 684.

(3) *Examples.* The rules of this paragraph (c) are illustrated by the following examples. *A* is a resident alien, *B* is *A*'s son, and *FT* is a foreign trust. The examples are as follows:

Example 1. Trust acquiring U.S. beneficiary. (i) In 2001, *A* transfers stock with a fair market value of $100,000 to *FT*. The stock has an adjusted basis of $50,000 at the time of the transfer. The trust instrument provides that income may be paid currently to, or accumulated for the benefit of, *B* and that, upon the termination of the trust, all income and corpus is to be distributed to *B*. At the time of the transfer, *B* is a nonresident alien. *A* is not treated as the owner of any portion of *FT* under sections 673 through 677. *FT* accumulates a total of $30,000 of income during the taxable years 2001 through 2003. In 2004, *B* moves to the United States and becomes a resident alien. Assume paragraph (a)(4) of this section is not applicable under the facts and circumstances.

(ii) Under paragraph (c) (1) of this section, *A* is treated as receiving an accumulation distribution in the amount of $30,000 in 2004 and immediately transferring that amount back to the trust. The accumulation distribution is subject to the rules of section 668, providing for an interest charge on accumulation distributions.

(iii) Under paragraphs (a)(1) and (3) of this section, beginning in 2005, *A* is treated as the owner of the portion of *FT* attributable to the stock transferred by *A* to *FT* in 2001 (which includes the portion attributable to the accumulated income deemed to be retransferred in 2004).

Example 2. Trust ceasing to have U.S. beneficiary. (i) The facts are the same as in *Example 1*. In 2008, *B* becomes a nonresident alien. On the date *B* becomes a nonresident alien, the stock transferred by *A* to *FT* in 2001 has a fair market value of $125,000 and an adjusted basis of $50,000.

(ii) Under paragraph (c)(2) of this section, beginning in 2009, *FT* is not treated as having a U.S. beneficiary, and *A* is not treated as the owner of the portion of the trust attributable to the prior transfer of stock. For rules regarding the recognition of gain on the termination of ownership status, see section 684.
[Reg. § 1.679-2.]

☐ [*T.D.* 8955, 7-19-2001.]

[Reg. § 1.679-3]

§ 1.679-3. **Transfers.**—(a) *In general.* A transfer means a direct, indirect, or constructive transfer.

(b) *Transfers by certain trusts*—(1) *In general.* If any portion of a trust is treated as owned by a U.S. person, a transfer of property from that portion of the trust to a foreign trust is treated as a transfer from the owner of that portion to the foreign trust.

(2) *Example.* The following example illustrates this paragraph (b):

Example. In 2001, *A*, a U.S. citizen, creates and funds *DT*, a domestic trust. *A* has the power to revest absolutely in himself the title to the property in *DT* and is treated as the owner of *DT* pursuant to section 676. In 2004, *DT* transfers property to *FT*, a foreign trust. *A* is treated as having transferred the property to *FT* in 2004 for purposes of this section.

(c) *Indirect transfers*—(1) *Principal purpose of tax avoidance.* A transfer to a foreign trust by any person (intermediary) to whom a U.S. person transfers property is treated as an indirect transfer by a U.S. person to the foreign trust if such transfer is made pursuant to a plan one of the principal purposes of which is the avoidance of United States tax.

Reg. § 1.679-3(c)(1)

(2) *Principal purpose of tax avoidance deemed to exist.* For purposes of paragraph (c)(1) of this section, a transfer is deemed to have been made pursuant to a plan one of the principal purposes of which was the avoidance of United States tax if—

(i) The U.S. person is related (within the meaning of paragraph (c)(4) of this section) to a beneficiary of the foreign trust, or has another relationship with a beneficiary of the foreign trust that establishes a reasonable basis for concluding that the U.S. transferor would make a transfer to the foreign trust; and

(ii) The U.S. person cannot demonstrate to the satisfaction of the Commissioner that—

(A) The intermediary has a relationship with a beneficiary of the foreign trust that establishes a reasonable basis for concluding that the intermediary would make a transfer to the foreign trust;

(B) The intermediary acted independently of the U.S. person;

(C) The intermediary is not an agent of the U.S. person under generally applicable United States agency principles; and

(D) The intermediary timely complied with the reporting requirements of section 6048, if applicable.

(3) *Effect of disregarding intermediary*—(i) *In general.* Except as provided in paragraph (c)(3)(ii) of this section, if a transfer is treated as an indirect transfer pursuant to paragraph (c)(1) of this section, then the intermediary is treated as an agent of the U.S. person, and the property is treated as transferred to the foreign trust by the U.S. person in the year the property is transferred, or made available, by the intermediary to the foreign trust. The fair market value of the property transferred is determined as of the date of the transfer by the intermediary to the foreign trust.

(ii) *Special rule.* If the Commissioner determines, or if the taxpayer can demonstrate to the satisfaction of the Commissioner, that the intermediary is an agent of the foreign trust under generally applicable United states agency principles, the property will be treated as transferred to the foreign trust in the year the U.S. person transfers the property to the intermediary. The fair market value of the property transferred will be determined as of the date of the transfer by the U.S. person to the intermediary.

(iii) *Effect on intermediary.* If a transfer of property is treated as an indirect transfer under paragraph (c)(1) of this section, the intermediary is not treated as having transferred the property to the foreign trust.

(4) *Related parties.* For purposes of this paragraph (c), a U.S. transferor is treated as related to a U.S. beneficiary of a foreign trust if the U.S. transferor and the beneficiary are related for purposes of section 643(i)(2)(B), with the following modifications—

(i) For purposes of applying section 267 (other than section 267(f)) and section 707(b)(1), "at least 10 percent" is used instead of "more than 50 percent" each place it appears; and

(ii) The principles of section 267(b)(10), using "at least 10 percent" instead of "more than 50 percent," apply to determine whether two corporations are related.

(5) *Examples.* The rules of this paragraph (c) are illustrated by the following examples:

Example 1. Principal purpose of tax avoidance. A, a U.S. citizen, creates and funds FT, a foreign trust, for the benefit of A's children, who are U.S. citizens. In 2004, A decides to transfer an additional 1000X to the foreign trust. Pursuant to a plan with a principal purpose of avoiding the application of section 679, A transfers 1000X to I, a foreign person. I subsequently transfers 1000X to FT. Under paragraph (c)(1) of this section, A is treated as having made a transfer of 1000X to FT.

Example 2. U.S. person unable to demonstrate that intermediary acted independently. A, a U.S. citizen, creates and funds FT, a foreign trust, for the benefit of A's children, who are U.S. citizens. On July 1, 2004, A transfers XYZ stock to D, A's uncle, who is a nonresident alien. D immediately sells the XYZ stock and uses the proceeds to purchase ABC stock. On January 1, 2007, D transfers the ABC stock to FT. A is unable to demonstrate to the satisfaction of the Commissioner, pursuant to paragraph (c)(2) of this section, that D acted independently of A in making the transfer to FT. Under paragraph (c)(1) of this section, A is treated as having transferred the ABC stock to FT. Under paragraph (c)(3) of this section, D is treated as an agent of A, and the transfer is deemed to have been made on January 1, 2007.

Example 3. Indirect loan to foreign trust. A, a U.S. citizen, previously created and funded FT, a foreign trust, for the benefit of A's children, who are U.S. citizens. On July 1, 2004, A deposits 500X with FB, a foreign bank. On January 1, 2005, FB loans 450X to FT. A is unable to demonstrate to the satisfaction of the Commissioner, pursuant to paragraph (c)(2) of this section, that FB has a relationship with FT that establishes a reasonable basis for concluding that FB would make a loan to *FT* or that *FB* acted independently of *A* in making the loan. Under paragraph (c)(1) of this section, *A* is deemed to have transferred 450X directly to *FT* on January 1, 2005. Under paragraph (c)(3) of this section, *FB* is treated as an agent of *A*. For possible exceptions with respect to qualified obligations of the trust, and the treatment of principal repayments with respect to obligations of the trust that are not qualified obligations, see § 1.679-4.

Example 4. Loan to foreign trust prior to deposit of funds in foreign bank. The facts are the same as in *Example 3*, except that *A* makes the 500X deposit with *FB* on January 2, 2005, the day after *FB* makes the loan to *FT*. The result is the same as in *Example 3*.

(d) *Constructive transfers*—(1) *In general.* For purposes of paragraph (a) of this section, a constructive transfer includes any assumption or satisfaction of a foreign trust's obligation to a third party.

(2) *Examples.* The rules of this paragraph (d) are illustrated by the following examples. In each example, *A* is a U.S. citizen and *FT* is a foreign trust. The examples are as follows:

Example 1. Payment of debt of foreign trust. *FT* owes 1000X to *Y*, an unrelated foreign corporation, for the performance of services by *Y* for *FT*. In satisfaction of *FT*'s liability to *Y*, *A* transfers to *Y* property with a fair market value of 1000X. Under paragraph (d)(1) of this section, *A* is treated as having made a constructive transfer of the property to *FT*.

Example 2. Assumption of liability of foreign trust. *FT* owes 1000X to *Y*, an unrelated foreign corporation, for the performance of services by *Y* for *FT*. *A* assumes *FT*'s liability to pay *Y*. Under paragraph (d)(1) of this section, *A* is treated as having made a constructive transfer of property with a fair market value of 1000X to *FT*.

(e) *Guarantee of trust obligations*—(1) *In general.* If a foreign trust borrows money or other property from any person who is not a related person (within the meaning of § 1.679-1(c)(5)) with respect to the trust (lender) and a U.S. person (U.S. guarantor) that is a related person with respect to the trust guarantees (within the meaning of paragraph (e)(4) of this section) the foreign trust's obligation, the U.S. guarantor is treated for purposes of this section as a U.S. transferor that has made a transfer to the trust on the date of the guarantee in an amount determined under paragraph (e)(2) of this section. To the extent this paragraph causes the U.S. guarantor to be treated as having made a transfer to the trust, a lender that is a U.S. person shall not be treated as having transferred that amount to the foreign trust.

(2) *Amount transferred.* The amount deemed transferred by a U.S. guarantor described in paragraph (e)(1) of this section is the guaranteed portion of the adjusted issue price of the obligation (within the meaning of § 1.1275-1(b)) plus any accrued but unpaid qualified stated interest (within the meaning of § 1.1273-1(c)).

(3) *Principal repayments.* If a U.S. person is treated under this paragraph (e) having made a transfer by reason of the guarantee of an obligation, payments of principal to the lender by the foreign trust with respect to the obligation are taken into account on and after the date of the payment in determining the portion of the trust attributable to the property deemed transferred by the U.S. guarantor.

(4) *Guarantee.* For purposes of this section, the term guarantee—

(i) Includes any arrangement under which a person, directly or indirectly, assures, on a conditional or unconditional basis, the payment of another's obligation;

(ii) Encompasses any form of credit support, and includes a commitment to make a capital contribution to the debtor or otherwise maintain its financial viability; and

(iii) Includes an arrangement reflected in a comfort letter, regardless of whether the arrangement gives rise to a legally enforceable obligation. If an arrangement is contingent upon the occurrence of an event, in determining whether the arrangement is a guarantee, it is assumed that the event has occurred.

(5) *Examples.* The rules of this paragraph (e) are illustrated by the following examples. In all of the examples, *A* is a U.S. resident and *FT* is a foreign trust. The examples are as follows:

Example 1. Foreign lender. *X*, a foreign corporation, loans 1000X of cash to *FT* in exchange for *FT*'s obligation to repay the loan. *A* guarantees the repayment of 600X of *FT*'s obligation. Under paragraph (e)(2) of this section, *A* is treated as having transferred 600X to *FT*.

Example 2. Unrelated U.S. lender. The facts are the same as in *Example 1*, except *X* is a U.S. person that is not a related person within the meaning of § 1.679-1(c)(5). The result is the same as in *Example 1*.

(f) *Transfers to entities owned by a foreign trust*—(1) *General rule.* If a U.S. person is a related person (as defined in § 1.679-1(c)(5)) with respect to a foreign trust, any transfer of property by the U.S. person to an entity in which the foreign trust holds an ownership interest is

Reg. § 1.679-3(f)(1)

treated as a transfer of such property by the U.S. person to the foreign trust followed by a transfer of the property from the foreign trust to the entity owned by the foreign trust, unless the U.S. person demonstrates to the satisfaction of the Commissioner that the transfer to the entity is properly attributable to the U.S. person's ownership interest in the entity.

(2) *Examples*. The rules of this paragraph (f) are illustrated by the following examples. In all of the examples, *A* is a U.S. citizen, *FT* is a foreign trust, and *FC* is a foreign corporation. The examples are as follows:

Example 1. Transfer treated as transfer to trust. A creates and funds *FT*, which is treated as having a U.S. beneficiary under § 1.679-2. *FT* owns all of the outstanding stock of *FC*. *A* transfers property directly to *FC*. Because *FT* is the sole shareholder of *FC*, *A* is unable to demonstrate to the satisfaction of the Commissioner that the transfer is properly attributable to *A*'s ownership interest in *FC*. Accordingly, under this paragraph (f), *A* is treated as having transferred the property to *FT*, followed by a transfer of such property by *FT* to *FC*. Under § 1.679-1(a), *A* is treated as the owner of the portion of *FT* attributable to the property treated as transferred directly to *FT*. Under § 1.367(a)-1T(c)(4)(ii), the transfer of property by *FT* to *FC* is treated as a transfer of the property by *A* to *FC*.

Example 2. Transfer treated as transfer to trust. The facts are the same as in *Example 1*, except that *FT* is not treated as having a U.S. beneficiary under § 1.679-2. Under this paragraph (f), *A* is treated as having transferred the property to *FT*, followed by a transfer of such property by *FT* to *FC*. *A* is not treated as the owner of *FT* for purposes of § 1.679-1(a). For rules regarding the recognition of gain on the transfer, see section 684.

Example 3. Transfer not treated as transfer to trust. A creates and funds *FT*. *FC* has outstanding solely 100 shares of common stock. *FT* owns 50 shares of *FC* stock, and *A* owns the remaining 50 shares. On July 1, 2001, *FT* and *A* each transfer 1000X to *FC*. *A* is able to demonstrate to the satisfaction of the Commissioner that *A*'s transfer to *FC* is properly attributable to *A*'s ownership interest in *FC*. Accordingly, under this paragraph (f), *A*'s transfer to *FC* is not treated as a transfer to *FT*.

[Reg. § 1.679-3.]

☐ [*T.D.* 8955, 7-19-2001.]

[Reg. § 1.679-4]

§ 1.679-4. Exceptions to general rule.—(a) *In general*. Section 1.679-1 does not apply to—

(1) Any transfer of property to a foreign trust by reason of the death of the transferor;

(2) Any transfer of property to a foreign trust described in sections 402(b), 404(a)(4), or 404A;

(3) Any transfer of property to a foreign trust described in section 501(c)(3) (without regard to the requirements of section 508(a)); and

(4) Any transfer of property to a foreign trust to the extent the transfer is for fair market value.

(b) *Transfers for fair market value*—(1) *In general*. For purposes of this section, a transfer is for fair market value only to the extent of the value of property received from the trust, services rendered by the trust, or the right to use property of the trust. For example, rents, royalties, interest, and compensation paid to a trust are transfers for fair market value only to the extent that the payments reflect an arm's length price for the use of the property of, or for the services rendered by, the trust. For purposes of this determination, an interest in the trust is not property received from the trust. For purposes of this section, a distribution to a trust with respect to an interest held by such trust in an entity other than a trust or an interest in certain investment trusts described in § 301.7701-4(c) of this chapter, liquidating trusts described in § 301.7701-4(d) of this chapter, or environmental remediation trusts described in § 301.7701-4(e) of this chapter is considered to be a transfer for fair market value.

(2) *Special rule*—(i) *Transfers for partial consideration*. For purposes of this section, if a person transfers property to a foreign trust in exchange for property having a fair market value that is less than the fair market value of the property transferred, the exception in paragraph (a)(4) of this section applies only to the extent of the fair market value of the property received.

(ii) *Example*. This paragraph (b) is illustrated by the following example:

Example. *A*, a U.S. citizen, transfers property that has a fair market value of 1000X to *FT*, a foreign trust, in exchange for 600X of cash. Under this paragraph (b), § 1.679-1 applies with respect to the transfer of 400X (1000X less 600X) to *FT*.

(c) *Certain obligations not taken into account*. Solely for purposes of this section, in determining whether a transfer by a U.S. transferor that is a related person (as defined in § 1.679-1(c)(5)) with respect to the foreign trust is for fair market value, any obligation (as defined in § 1.679-1(c)(6)) of the trust or a related person (as defined in § 1.679-1(c)(5)) that is not a qualified obligation within the meaning of paragraph (d)(1) of this section shall not be taken into account.

(d) *Qualified obligations*—(1) *In general.* For purposes of this section, an obligation is treated as a qualified obligation only if—

(i) The obligation is reduced to writing by an express written agreement;

(ii) The term of the obligation does not exceed five years (for purposes of determining the term of an obligation, the obligation's maturity date is the last possible date that the obligation can be outstanding under the terms of the obligation);

(iii) All payments on the obligation are denominated in U.S. dollars;

(iv) The yield to maturity is not less than 100 percent of the applicable Federal rate and not greater that 130 percent of the applicable Federal rate (the applicable Federal rate for an obligation is the applicable Federal rate in effect under section 1274(d) for the day on which the obligation is issued, as published in the Internal Revenue Bulletin (see § 601.601(d)(2) of this chapter));

(v) The U.S. transferor extends the period for assessment of any income or transfer tax attributable to the transfer and any consequential income tax changes for each year that the obligation is outstanding, to a date not earlier than three years after the maturity date of the obligation (this extension is not necessary if the maturity date of the obligation does not extend beyond the end of the U.S. transferor's taxable year for the year of the transfer and is paid within such period); when properly executed and filed, such an agreement is deemed to be consented to for purposes of § 301.6501(c)-1(d) of this chapter; and

(vi) The U.S. transferor reports the status of the loan, including principal and interest payments, on Form 3520 for every year that the loan is outstanding.

(2) *Additional loans.* If, while the original obligation is outstanding, the U.S. transferor or a person related to the trust (within the meaning of § 1.679-1(c)(5)) directly or indirectly obtains another obligation issued by the trust, or if the U.S. transferor directly or indirectly obtains another obligation issued by a person related to the trust, the original obligation is deemed to have the maturity date of any such subsequent obligation in determining whether the term of the original obligation exceeds the specified 5-year term. In addition, a series of obligations issued and repaid by the trust (or a person related to the trust) is treated as a single obligation if the transactions giving rise to the obligations are structured with a principal purpose to avoid the application of this provision.

(3) *Obligations that cease to be qualified.* If an obligation treated as a qualified obligation subsequently fails to be a qualified obligation (e.g., renegotiation of the terms of the obligation causes the term of the obligation to exceed five years), the U.S. transferor is treated as making a transfer to the trust in an amount equal to the original obligation's adjusted issue price (within the meaning of § 1.1275-1(b)) plus any accrued but unpaid qualified stated interest (within the meaning of § 1.1273-1(c)) as of the date of the subsequent event that causes the obligation to no longer be a qualified obligation. If the maturity date is extended beyond five years by reason of the issuance of a subsequent obligation by the trust (or person related to the trust), the amount of the transfer will not exceed the issue price of the subsequent obligation. The subsequent obligation is separately tested to determine if it is a qualified obligation.

(4) *Transfers resulting from failed qualified obligations.* In general, a transfer resulting from a failed qualified obligation is deemed to occur on the date of the subsequent event that causes the obligation to no longer be a qualified obligation. However, based on all of the facts and circumstances, the Commissioner may deem a transfer to have occurred on any date on or after the issue date of the original obligation. For example, if at the time the original obligation was issued, the transferor knew or had reason to know that the obligation would not be repaid, the Commissioner could deem the transfer to have occurred on the issue date of the original obligation.

(5) *Renegotiated loans.* Any loan that is renegotiated, extended, or revised is treated as a new loan, and any transfer of funds to a foreign trust after such renegotiation, extension, or revision under a pre-existing loan agreement is treated as a transfer subject to this section.

(6) *Principal repayments.* The payment of principal with respect to any obligation that is not treated as a qualified obligation under this paragraph is taken into account on and after the date of the payment in determining the portion of the trust attributable to the property transferred.

(7) *Examples.* The rules of this paragraph (d) are illustrated by the following examples. In the examples, *A* and *B* are U.S. residents and *FT* is a foreign trust. The examples are as follows:

Example 1. Demand loan. A transfers 500X to *FT* in exchange for a demand note that permits *A* to require repayment by *FT* at any time. *A* is a related person (as defined in § 1.679-1(c)(5)) with respect to *FT*. Because *FT*'s obligation to *A* could remain outstanding for more than five years, the obligation is not a qualified obligation within the meaning of paragraph (d) of this section and, pursuant to paragraph (c) of this section, it is not taken into account for purposes of determining whether *A*'s transfer is eligible for the fair market value exception of paragraph (a)(4) of this section. Accordingly, § 1.679-1 applies with respect to the full 500X transfer to *FT*.

Example 2. Private annuity. *A* transfers 4000X to *FT* in exchange for an annuity from the foreign trust that will pay *A* 100X per year for the rest of *A*'s life. *A* is a related person (as defined in § 1.679-1(c)(5)) with respect to *FT*. Because *FT*'s obligation to *A* could remain outstanding for more than five years, the obligation is not a qualified obligation within the meaning of paragraph (d)(1) of this section and, pursuant to paragraph (c) of this section, it is not taken into account for purposes of determining whether *A*'s transfer is eligible for the fair market value exception of paragraph (a)(4) of this section. Accordingly, § 1.679-1 applies with respect to the full 4000X transfer to *FT*.

Example 3. Loan to unrelated foreign trust. *B* transfers 1000X to *FT* in exchange for an obligation of the trust. The term of the obligation is fifteen years. *B* is not a related person (as defined in § 1.679-1(c)(5)) with respect to *FT*. Because *B* is not a related person, the fair market value of the obligation received by *B* is taken into account for purposes of determining whether *B*'s transfer is eligible for the fair market value exception of paragraph (a)(4) of this section, even though the obligation is not a qualified obligation within the meaning of paragraph (d)(1) of this section.

Example 4. Transfer for an obligation with term in excess of 5 years. *A* transfers property that has a fair market value of 5000X to *FT* in exchange for an obligation of the trust. The term of the obligation is ten years. *A* is a related person (as defined in § 1.679-1(c)(5)) with respect to *FT*. Because the term of the obligation is greater than five years, the obligation is not a qualified obligation within the meaning of paragraph (d)(1) of this section and, pursuant to paragraph (c) of this section, it is not taken into account for purposes of determining whether *A*'s transfer is eligible for the fair market value exception of paragraph (a)(4) of this section. Accordingly, § 1.679-1 applies with respect to the full 5000X transfer to *FT*.

Example 5. Transfer for a qualified obligation. The facts are the same as in *Example 4*, except that the term of the obligation is 3 years. Assuming the other requirements of paragraph (d)(1) of this section are satisfied, the obligation is a qualified obligation and its adjusted issue price is taken into account for purposes of determining whether *A*'s transfer is eligible for the fair market value exception of paragraph (a)(4) of this section.

Example 6. Effect of subsequent obligation on original obligation. *A* transfers property that has a fair market value of 1000X to *FT* in exchange for an obligation that satisfies the requirements of paragraph (d)(1) of this section. *A* is a related person (as defined in § 1. 679-1(c)(5)) with respect to *FT*. Two years later, *A* transfers an additional 2000X to *FT* and receives another obligation from *FT* that has a maturity date four years from the date that the second obligation was issued. Under paragraph (d)(2) of this section, the original obligation is deemed to have the maturity date of the second obligation. Under paragraph (a) of this section, *A* is treated as having made a transfer in an amount equal to the original obligation's adjusted issue price (within the meaning of § 1.1275-1(b)) plus any accrued but unpaid qualified stated interest (within the meaning of § 1.1273-1(c)) as of the date of issuance of the second obligation. The second obligation is tested separately to determine whether it is a qualified obligation for purposes of applying paragraph (a) of this section to the second transfer.

[Reg. § 1.679-4.]

☐ [T.D. 8955, 7-19-2001.]

[Reg. § 1.679-5]

§ 1.679-5. Pre-immigration trusts.—(a) *In general.* If a nonresident alien individual becomes a U.S. person and the individual has a residency starting date (as determined under section 7701(b)(2)(A)) within 5 years after directly or indirectly transferring property to a foreign trust (the original transfer), the individual is treated as having transferred to the trust on the residency starting date an amount equal to the portion of the trust attributable to the property transferred by the individual in the original transfer.

(b) *Special rules*—(1) *Change in grantor trust status.* For purposes of paragraph (a) of this section, if a nonresident alien individual who is treated as owning any portion of a trust under the provisions of subpart E of part I of subchapter J, chapter 1 of the Internal Revenue Code, subsequently ceases to be so treated, the individual is treated as having made the original transfer to the foreign trust immediately before the trust ceases to be treated as owned by the individual.

(2) *Treatment of undistributed income.* For purposes of paragraph (a) of this section, the

property deemed transferred to the foreign trust on the residency starting date includes undistributed net income, as defined in section 665(a), attributable to the property deemed transferred. Undistributed net income for periods before the individual's residency starting date is taken into account only for purposes of determining the amount of the property deemed transferred.

(c) *Examples.* The rules of this section are illustrated by the following examples:

Example 1. Nonresident alien becomes resident alien. On January 1, 2002, *A*, a nonresident alien individual, transfers property to a foreign trust, *FT*. On January 1, 2006, *A* becomes a resident of the United States within the meaning of section 7701(b)(1)(A) and has a residency starting date of January 1, 2006, within the meaning of section 7701(b)(2)(A). Under paragraph (a) of this section, *A* is treated as a U.S. transferor and is deemed to transfer the property to *FT* on January 1, 2006. Under paragraph (b)(2) of this section, the property deemed transferred to *FT* on January 1, 2006, includes the undistributed net income of the trust, as defined in section 665(a), attributable to the property originally transferred.

Example 2. Nonresident alien loses power to revest property. On January 1, 2002, *A*, a nonresident alien individual, transfers property to a foreign trust, *FT*. *A* has the power to revest absolutely in himself the title to such property transferred and is treated as the owner of the trust pursuant to sections 676 and 672(f). On January 1, 2008, the terms of *FT* are amended to remove *A*'s power to revest in himself title to the property transferred, and *A* ceases to be treated as the owner of *FT*. On January 1, 2010, *A* becomes a resident of the United States. Under paragraph (b)(1) of this section, for purposes of paragraph (a) of this section *A* is treated as having originally transferred the property to *FT* on January 1, 2008. Because this date is within five years of *A*'s residency starting date, *A* is deemed to have made a transfer to the foreign trust on January 1, 2010, his residency starting date. Under paragraph (b)(2) of this section, the property deemed transferred to the foreign trust on January 1, 2010, includes the undistributed net income of the trust, as defined in section 665(a), attributable to the property deemed transferred.

[Reg. § 1.679-5.]

☐ [*T.D.* 8955, 7-19-2001.]

[Reg. § 1.679-6]

§ 1.679-6. **Outbound migrations of domestic trusts.**—(a) *In general.* Subject to the provisions of paragraph (b) of this section, if an individual who is a U.S. person transfers property to a trust that is not a foreign trust, and such trust becomes a foreign trust while the U.S. person is alive, the U.S. individual is treated as a U.S. transferor and is deemed to transfer the property to a foreign trust on the date the domestic trust becomes a foreign trust.

(b) *Amount deemed transferred.* For purposes of paragraph (a) of this section, the property deemed transferred to the trust when it becomes a foreign trust includes undistributed net income, as defined in section 665(a), attributable to the property previously transferred. Undistributed net income for periods prior to the migration is taken into account only for purposes of determining the portion of the trust that is attributable to the property transferred by the U.S. person.

(c) *Example.* The following example illustrates the rules of this section. For purposes of the example, *A* is a resident alien, *B* is *A*'s son, who is a resident alien, and *DT* is a domestic trust. The example is as follows:

Example. Outbound migration of domestic trust. On January 1, 2002, *A* transfers property to *DT*, for the benefit of *B*. On January 1, 2003, *DT* acquires a foreign trustee who has the power to determine whether and when distributions will be made to *B*. Under section 7701(a)(30)(E) and § 301.7701-7(d)(ii)(A) of this chapter, *DT* becomes a foreign trust on January 1, 2003. Under paragraph (a) of this section, *A* is treated as transferring property to a foreign trust on January 1, 2003. Under paragraph (b) of this section, the property deemed transferred to the trust when it becomes a foreign trust includes undistributed net income, as defined in section 665(a), attributable to the property deemed transferred.

[Reg. § 1.679-6.]

☐ [*T.D.* 8955, 7-19-2001.]

[Reg. § 1.679-7]

§ 1.679-7. **Effective dates.**—(a) *In general.* Except as provided in paragraph (b) of this section, the rules of §§ 1.679-1, 1.679-2, 1.679-3, and 1.679-4 apply with respect to transfers after August 7, 2000.

(b) *Special rules.* (1) The rules of § 1.679-4(c) and (d) apply to an obligation issued after February 6, 1995, whether or not in accordance with a pre-existing arrangement or understanding. For purposes of the rules of § 1.679-4(c) and (d), if an obligation issued on or before February 6, 1995, is modified after that date, and the modification is a significant modification within the meaning of § 1.1001-3, the obligation is treated as if it were issued on the date of the modification. However, the penalty provided in section 6677 applies only to a failure to report transfers in exchange for obligations issued after August 20, 1996.

(2) The rules of § 1.679-5 apply to persons whose residency starting date is after August 7, 2000.

(3) The rules of § 1.679-6 apply to trusts that become foreign trusts after August 7, 2000. [Reg. § 1.679-7.]

☐ [T.D. 8955, 7-19-2001.]

[Reg. § 1.681(a)-1]

§ 1.681(a)-1. Limitation on charitable contributions deductions of trusts; scope of section 681.—Under section 681, the unlimited charitable contributions deduction otherwise allowable to a trust under section 642(c) is, in general, subject to percentage limitations, corresponding to those applicable to contributions by an individual under section 170(b)(1)(A) and (B), under the following circumstances:

(a) To the extent that the deduction is allocable to "unrelated business income";

(b) For taxable years beginning before January 1, 1970, if the trust has engaged in a prohibited transaction;

(c) For taxable years beginning before January 1, 1970, if income is accumulated for a charitable purpose and the accumulation is (1) unreasonable, (2) substantially diverted to a noncharitable purpose, or (3) invested against the interests of the charitable beneficiaries.

Further, if the circumstance set forth in paragraph (a) or (c) of this section is applicable, the deduction is limited to income actually paid out for charitable purposes, and is not allowed for income only set aside or to be used for those purposes. If the circumstance set forth in paragraph (b) of this section is applicable, deductions for contributions to the trust may be disallowed. The provisions of section 681 are discussed in detail in §§ 1.681(a)-2 through 1.681(c)-1. For definition of the term "income," see section 643(b) and § 1.643(b)-1. [Reg. § 1.681(a)-1.]

☐ [T.D. 6269, 11-15-57. Amended by T.D. 7428, 8-13-76.]

[Reg. § 1.681(a)-2]

§ 1.681(a)-2. Limitation on charitable contributions deduction of trusts with trade or business income.—(a) *In general.* No charitable contributions deduction is allowable to a trust under section 642(c) for any taxable year for amounts allocable to the trust's unrelated business income for the taxable year. For the purpose of section 681(a) the term "unrelated business income" of a trust means an amount which would be computed as the trust's unrelated business taxable income under section 512 and the regulations thereunder, if the trust were an organization exempt from tax under section 501(a) by reason of section 501(c)(3). For the purpose of the computation under section 512, the term "unrelated trade or business" includes a trade or business carried on by a partnership of which a trust is a member, as well as one carried on by the trust itself. While the charitable contributions deduction under section 642(c) is entirely disallowed by section 681(a) for amounts allocable to "unrelated business income," a partial deduction is nevertheless allowed for such amounts by the operation of section 512(b)(11), as illustrated in paragraphs (b) and (c) of this section. This partial deduction is subject to the percentage limitations applicable to contributions by an individual under section 170(b)(1)(A) and (B), and is not allowed for amounts set aside or to be used for charitable purposes but not actually paid out during the taxable year. Charitable contributions deductions otherwise allowable under section 170, 545(b)(2), or 642(c) for contributions to a trust are not disallowed solely because the trust has unrelated business income.

(b) *Determination of amounts allocable to unrelated business income.* In determining the amount for which a charitable contributions deduction would otherwise be allowable under section 642(c) which are allocable to unrelated business income, and therefore not allowable as a deduction, the following steps are taken:

(1) There is first determined the amount which would be computed as the trust's unrelated business taxable income under section 512 and the regulations thereunder if the trust were an organization exempt from tax under section 501(a) by reason of section 501(c)(3), but without taking the charitable contributions deduction allowed under section 512(b)(11).

(2) The amount for which a charitable contributions deduction would otherwise be allowable under section 642(c) is then allocated between the amount determined in subparagraph (1) of this paragraph and any other income of the trust. Unless the facts clearly indicate to the contrary, the allocation to the amount determined in subparagraph (1) of this paragraph is made on the basis of the ratio (but not in excess of 100 percent) of the amount determined in subparagraph (1) of this paragraph to the taxable income of the trust, determined without the deduction for personal exemption under section 642(b), the charitable contributions deduction under section 642(c), or the deduction for distributions to beneficiaries under section 661(a).

Reg. § 1.681(a)-1(a)

(3) The amount for which a charitable contributions deduction would otherwise be allowable under section 642(c) which is allocable to unrelated business income as determined in subparagraph (2) of this paragraph, and therefore not allowable as a deduction, is the amount determined in subparagraph (2) of this paragraph reduced by the charitable contributions deduction which would be allowed under section 512(b)(11) if the trust were an organization exempt from tax under section 501(a) by reason of section 501(c)(3).

(c) *Examples.* (1) The application of this section may be illustrated by the following examples, in which it is assumed that the Y charity is not a charitable organization qualifying under section 170(b)(1)(A) (see subparagraph (2) of this paragraph):

Example (1). The X trust has income of $50,000. There is included in this amount a net profit of $31,000 from the operation of a trade or business. The trustee is required to pay half of the trust income to A, an individual, and the balance of the trust income to the Y charity, an organization described in section 170(c)(2). The trustee pays each beneficiary $25,000. Under these facts, the unrelated business income of the trust (computed before the charitable contributions deduction which would be allowed under section 512(b)(11) is $30,000 ($31,000 less the deduction of $1,000 allowed by section 512(b)(12)). The deduction otherwise allowable under section 642(c) is $25,000, the amount paid to the Y charity. The portion allocable to the unrelated business income (computed as prescribed in paragraph (b)(2) of this section) is $15,000, that is, an amount which bears the same ratio to $25,000 as $30,000 bears to $50,000. The portion allocable to the unrelated business income, and therefore disallowed as a deduction, is $15,000 reduced by $6,000 (20 percent of $30,000, the charitable contributions deduction which would be allowable under section 512(b)(11)), or $9,000.

Example (2). Assume the same facts as in example (1), except that the trustee has discretion as to the portion of the trust income to be paid to each beneficiary, and the trustee pays $40,000 to A and $10,000 to the Y charity. The deduction otherwise allowable under section 642(c) is $10,000. The portion allocable to the unrelated business income computed as prescribed in paragraph (b)(2) of this section is $6,000, that is, an amount which bears the same ratio to $10,000 as $30,000 bears to $50,000. Since this amount does not exceed the charitable contributions deduction which would be allowable under section 512(b)(11) ($6,000, determined as in example (1)), no portion of it is disallowed as a deduction.

Example (3). Assume the same facts as in example (1), except that the terms of the trust instrument require the trustee to pay to the Y charity the trust income, if any, derived from the trade or business, and to pay to A all the trust income derived from other sources. The trustee pays $31,000 to the Y charity and $19,000 to A. The deduction otherwise allowable under section 642(c) is $31,000. Since the entire income from the trade or business is paid to Y charity, the amount allocable to the unrelated business income computed before the charitable contributions deduction under section 512(b)(11) is $30,000 ($31,000 less the deduction of $1,000 allowed by section 512(b)(12)). The amount allocable to the unrelated business income and therefore disallowed as a deduction is $24,000 ($30,000 less $6,000).

Example (4). (i) Under the terms of the trust, the trustee is required to pay half of the trust income to A, an individual, for his life, and the balance of the trust income to the Y charity, an organization described in section 170(c)(2). Capital gains are allocable to corpus and upon A's death the trust is to terminate and the corpus is to be distributed to the Y charity. The trust has taxable income of $50,000 computed without any deduction for personal exemption, charitable contributions, or distributions. The amount of $50,000 includes $10,000 capital gains, $30,000 ($31,000 less the $1,000 deduction allowed under section 512(b)(12)) unrelated business income (computed before the charitable contributions deduction which would be allowed under section 512(b)(11)) and other income of $9,000. The trustee pays each beneficiary $20,000.

(ii) The deduction otherwise allowable under section 642(c) is $30,000 ($20,000 paid to Y charity and $10,000 capital gains allocated to corpus and permanent set aside for charitable purposes). The portion allocable to the unrelated business income is $15,000, that is, an amount which bears the same ratio to $20,000 (the amount paid to Y charity) as $30,000 bears to $40,000 ($50,000 less $10,000 capital gains allocable to corpus). The portion allocable to the unrelated business income, and therefore disallowed as a deduction, is $15,000 reduced by $6,000 (the charitable contributions deduction which would be allowable under section 512(b)(11)), or $9,000.

(2) If, in the examples in subparagraph (1) of this paragraph, the Y charity were a charitable organization qualifying under section 170(b)(1)(A), then the deduction allowable under

Reg. § 1.681(a)-2(c)(2)

section 512(b)(11) would be computed at a rate of 30 percent. [Reg. § 1.681(a)-2.]

☐ [*T.D. 6269, 11-15-57. Amended by T.D. 6605, 8-14-62.*]

[Reg. § 1.681(b)-1]

§ 1.681(b)-1. **Cross reference.**—For disallowance of certain charitable, etc., deductions otherwise allowable under section 642(c), see sections 508(d) and 4948(c)(4). See also 26 CFR §§ 1.681(b)-1 and 1.681(c)-1 (rev. as of Apr. 1, 1974) for provisions applying before January 1, 1970. [Reg. § 1.681(b)-1.]

☐ [*T.D. 7428, 8-13-76.*]

[Reg. § 1.682(a)-1]

§ 1.682(a)-1. **Income of trust in case of divorce, etc.**—(a) *In general.* (1) Section 682(a) provides rules in certain cases for determining the taxability of income of trusts as between spouses who are divorced, or who are separated under a decree of separate maintenance or a written separation agreement. In such cases, the spouse actually entitled to receive payments from the trust is considered the beneficiary rather than the spouse in discharge of whose obligations the payments are made, except to the extent that the payments are specified to be for the support of the obligor spouse's minor children in the divorce or separate maintenance decree, the separation agreement or the governing trust instrument. For convenience, the beneficiary spouse will hereafter in this section and in § 1.682(b)-1 be referred to as the "wife" and the obligor spouse from whom she is divorced or legally separated as the "husband". (See section 7701(a)(17).) Thus, under section 682(a) income of a trust—

(i) Which is paid, credited, or required to be distributed to the wife in a taxable year of the wife, and

(ii) Which, except for the provisions of section 682, would be includible in the gross income of her husband,

is includible in her gross income and is not includible in his gross income.

(2) Section 682(a) does not apply in any case to which section 71 applies. Although section 682(a) and section 71 seemingly cover some of the same situations, there are important differences between them. Thus, section 682(a) applies, for example, to a trust created before the divorce or separation and not in contemplation of it, while section 71 applies only if the creation of the trust or payments by a previously created trust are in discharge of an obligation imposed upon or assumed by the husband (or made specific) under the court order or decree divorcing or legally separating the husband and wife, or a written instrument incident to the divorce status or legal separation status, or a written separation agreement. If section 71 applies, it requires inclusion in the wife's income of the full amount of periodic payments received attributable to property in trust (whether or not out of trust income), while, if section 71 does not apply, section 682(a) requires amounts paid, credited, or required to be distributed to her to be included only to the extent they are includible in the taxable income of a trust beneficiary under subparts A through D (section 641 and following), part I, subchapter J, chapter 1 of the Code.

(3) Section 682(a) is designed to produce uniformity as between cases in which, without section 682(a), the income of a so-called alimony trust would be taxable to the husband because of his continuing obligation to support his wife or former wife, and other cases in which the income of a so-called alimony trust is taxable to the wife or former wife because of the termination of the husband's obligation. Furthermore, section 682(a) taxes trust income to the wife in all cases in which the husband would otherwise be taxed not only because of the discharge of his alimony obligation but also because of his retention of control over the trust income or corpus. Section 682(a) applies whether the wife is the beneficiary under the terms of the trust instrument or is an assignee of a beneficiary.

(4) The application of section 682(a) may be illustrated by the following examples, in which it is assumed that both the husband and wife make their income tax returns on a calendar year basis:

Example (1). Upon the marriage of H and W, H irrevocably transfers property in trust to pay the income to W for her life for support, maintenance, and all other expenses. Some years later, W obtains a legal separation from H under an order of court. W, relying upon the income from the trust payable to her, does not ask for any provision for her support and the decree recites that since W is adequately provided for by the trust, no further provision is being made for her. Under these facts, section 682(a), rather than section 71, is applicable. Under the provisions of section 682(a), the income of the trust which becomes payable to W after the order of separation is includible in her income and is deductible by the trust. No part of the income is includible in H's income or deductible by him.

Example (2). H transfers property in trust for the benefit of W, retaining the power to revoke the trust at any time. H, however, promises that if he revokes the trust he will transfer to W property in the value of $100,000. The transfer in trust and the agreement were not incident to divorce, but some years later W divorces H. The court decree is silent as to alimony and the trust. After the divorce, income of the trust which becomes payable to W is taxable to her, and is not taxable to H or deductible by him. If H later terminates the trust and transfers $100,000 of property to W, the $100,000 is not income to W nor deductible by H.

(b) *Alimony trust income designated for support of minor children.* Section 682(a) does not require the inclusion in the wife's income of trust income which the terms of the divorce or separate maintenance decree, separation agreement, or trust instrument fix in terms of an amount of money or a portion of the income as a sum which is payable for the support of minor children of the husband. The portion of the income which is payable for the support of the minor children is includible in the husband's income. If in such a case trust income fixed in terms of an amount of money is to be paid but a lesser amount becomes payable, the trust income is considered to be payable for the support of the husband's minor children to the extent of the sum which would be payable for their support out of the originally specified amount of trust income. This rule is similar to that provided in the case of periodic payments under section 71. See § 1.71-1. [Reg. § 1.682(a)-1.]

☐ [*T.D.* 6269, 12-15-57.]

[Reg. § 1.682(b)-1]

§ 1.682(b)-1. **Application of trust rules to alimony payments.**—(a) For the purpose of the application subparts A through D (section 641 and following), part I, subchapter J, chapter 1 of the Code, the wife described in section 682 or section 71 who is entitled to receive payments attributable to property in trust is considered a beneficiary of the trust, whether or not the payments are made for the benefit of the husband in discharge of his obligations. A wife treated as a beneficiary of a trust under this section is also treated as the beneficiary of such trust for purposes of the tax imposed by section 56 (relating to the minimum tax for tax preferences). For rules relating to the treatment of items of tax preference with respect to a beneficiary of a trust, see § 1.58-3.

(b) A periodic payment includible in the wife's gross income under section 71 attributable to property in trust is included in full in her gross income in her taxable year in which any part is required to be included under section 652 or 662. Assume, for example, in a case in which both the wife and the trust file income tax returns on the calendar year basis, that an annuity of $5,000 is to be paid to the wife by the trustee every December 31 (out of trust income if possible and, if not, out of corpus) pursuant to the terms of a divorce decree. Of the $5,000 distributable on December 31, 1954, $4,000 is payable out of income and $1,000 out of corpus. The actual distribution is made in 1955. Although the periodic payment is received by the wife in 1955, since under section 662 the $4,000 income distributable on December 31, 1954, is to be included in the wife's income for 1954, the $1,000 payment out of corpus is also to be included in her income for 1954. [Reg. § 1.682(b)-1.]

☐ [*T.D.* 6269, 11-15-57. *Amended by T.D.* 7564, 9-11-78.]

[Reg. § 1.682(c)-1]

§ 1.682(c)-1. **Definitions.**—For definitions of the terms "husband" and "wife" as used in section 682, see section 7701(a)(17) and the regulations thereunder. [Reg. § 1.682(c)-1.]

☐ [*T.D.* 6269, 12-15-57.]

[Reg. § 1.683-1]

§ 1.683-1. **Applicability of provisions; general rule.**—Part I (section 641 and following), subchapter J, chapter 1 of the Code, applies to estates and trusts and to beneficiaries only with respect to taxable years which begin after December 31, 1953, and end after August 16, 1954, the date of enactment of the Internal Revenue Code of 1954. In the case of an estate or trust, the date on which a trust is created or amended or on which an estate commences, and the taxable years of beneficiaries, grantors, or decedents concerned are immaterial. This provision applies equally to taxable years of normal and of abbreviated length. [Reg. § 1.683-1.]

☐ [*T.D.* 6269, 12-15-57.]

[Reg. § 1.683-2]

§ 1.683-2. **Exceptions.**—(a) In the case of any beneficiary of an estate or trust, sections 641 through 682 do not apply to any amount paid, credited, or to be distributed by an estate or trust in any taxable year of the estate or trust which begins before January 1, 1954, or which ends before August 17, 1954. Whether an amount so paid, credited, or to be distributed is to be included in the gross income of a beneficiary is determined with reference to the Internal Revenue Code of 1939. Thus, if a trust in its fiscal year ending June 30, 1954, distributed its current income to a beneficiary on June 30, 1954, the extent to which the distribution is includible in the beneficiary's gross income for his taxable year (the calendar year 1954) and the character of such income will be determined under the Internal

Revenue Code of 1939. The Internal Revenue Code of 1954, however, determines the beneficiary's tax liability for a taxable year of the beneficiary to which such Code applies, with respect even to gross income of the beneficiary determined under the Internal Revenue Code of 1939 in accordance with this paragraph. Accordingly, the beneficiary is allowed credits and deductions pursuant to the Internal Revenue Code of 1954 for a taxable year governed by the Internal Revenue Code of 1954. See subparagraph (ii) of example (1) in paragraph (c) of this section.

(b) For purposes of determining the time of receipt of dividends under sections 34 (for purposes of the credit for dividends received on or before December 31, 1964) and 116, the dividends paid, credited, or to be distributed to a beneficiary are deemed to have been received by the beneficiary ratably on the same dates that the dividends were received by the estate or trust.

(c) The application of this section may be illustrated by the following examples:

Example (1). (i) A trust, reporting on the fiscal year basis, receives in its taxable year ending November 30, 1954, dividends on December 3, 1953, and April 3, July 5, and October 4, 1954. It distributes the dividends to A, its sole beneficiary (who reports on the calendar year basis) on November 30, 1954. Since the trust has received dividends in a taxable year ending after July 31, 1954, it will receive a dividend credit under section 34 with respect to dividends received which otherwise qualify under that section, in this case dividends received on October 4, 1954 (i.e., received after July 31, 1954). See section 7851(a)(1)(C). This credit, however, is reduced to the extent the dividends are allocable to the beneficiary as a result of income being paid, credited, or required to be distributed to him. The trust will also be permitted the dividend exclusion under section 116, since it received its dividends in a taxable year ending after July 31, 1954.

(ii) A is entitled to the section 34 credit with respect to the portion of the October 4, 1954, dividends which is distributed to him even though the determination of whether the amount distributed to him is includible in his gross income is made under the Internal Revenue Code of 1939. The credit allowable to the trust is reduced proportionately to the extent A is deemed to have received the October 4 dividends. A is not entitled to a credit with respect to the dividends received by the trust on December 3, 1953, and April 3, and July 5, 1954, because, although he receives after July 31, 1954, the distribution resulting from the trust's receipt of dividends, he is deemed to have received the dividends ratably with the trust on dates prior to July 31, 1954. In determining the exclusion under section 116 to which he is entitled, all the dividends received by the trust in 1954 and distributed to him are aggregated with any other dividends received by him in 1954, since he is deemed to have received such dividends in 1954 and therefore within a taxable year ending after July 31, 1954. He is not, however, entitled to the exclusion for the dividends received by the trust in December 1953.

Example (2). (i) A simple trust reports on the basis of a fiscal year ending July 31. It receives dividends on October 3, 1953, and January 4, April 3, and July 5, 1954. It distributes the dividends to A, its sole beneficiary, on September 1, 1954. The trust, receiving dividends in a taxable year ending prior to August 17, 1954, is entitled neither to the dividend received credit under section 34 nor the dividend exclusion under section 116.

(ii) A (reporting on the calendar year basis) is not entitled to the section 34 credit, because, although he receives after July 31, 1954, the distribution resulting from the trust's receipt of dividends, he is deemed to have received the dividends ratably with the trust, that is, on October 3, 1953, and January 4, April 3, and July 5, 1954. He is, however, entitled to the section 116 exclusion with respect to the dividends received by the trust in 1954 (along with other dividends received by him in 1954) and distributed to him, since he is deemed to have received such dividends on January 4, April 3, and July 5, 1954, each a date in his taxable year ending after July 31, 1954. He is entitled to no exclusion for the dividends received by the trust on October 3, 1953, since he is deemed to receive the resulting distribution on the same date, which falls within a taxable year of his which ends before August 1, 1954, although he is required to include the October 1953 dividends in his 1954 income. See section 164 of the Internal Revenue Code of 1939.

Example (3). A simple trust on a fiscal year ending July 31, 1954 receives dividends August 5 and November 4, 1953. It distributes the dividends to A, its sole beneficiary (who is on a calendar year basis), on September 1, 1954. Neither the trust nor A is entitled to a credit under section 34 or an exclusion under section 116. [Reg. § 1.683-2.]

☐ [*T.D.* 6217, 12-19-56. Amended by *T.D.* 6777, 12-15-64.]

[Reg. § 1.683-3]

§ 1.683-3. **Application of the 65-day rule of the Internal Revenue Code of 1939.**—If an amount is paid, credited, or to be distributed in the first 65 days of the first taxable year of an estate or trust (heretofore subject to the provisions of the Internal Revenue Code of 1939) to which the Internal Revenue Code of 1954 applies and the amount would be treated, if the Internal Revenue Code of 1939 were applicable, as if paid, credited, or to be distributed on the last day of the preceding taxable year, sections 641 through 682 do not apply to the amount. The amount so paid, credited, or to be distributed is taken into account as provided in the Internal Revenue Code of 1939. See 26 CFR (1939) § 39.162-2(c) and (d) (Regulations 118). [Reg. § 1.683-3.]

☐ [T.D. 6217, 12-19-56.]

[Reg. § 1.684-1]

§ 1.684-1. **Recognition of gain on transfers to certain foreign trusts and estates.**—(a) *Immediate recognition of gain*—(1) *In general.* Any U.S. person who transfers property to a foreign trust or foreign estate shall be required to recognize gain at the time of the transfer equal to the excess of the fair market value of the property transferred over the adjusted basis (for purposes of determining gain) of such property in the hands of the U.S. transferor unless an exception applies under the provisions of § 1.684-3. The amount of gain recognized is determined on an asset-by-asset basis.

(2) *No recognition of loss.* Under this section a U.S. person may not recognize loss on the transfer of an asset to a foreign trust or foreign estate. A U.S. person may not offset gain realized on the transfer of an appreciated asset to a foreign trust or foreign estate by a loss realized on the transfer of a depreciated asset to the foreign trust or foreign estate.

(b) *Definitions.* The following definitions apply for purposes of this section:

(1) *U.S. person.* The term *U.S. person* means a United States person as defined in section 7701(a)(30), and includes a nonresident alien individual who elects under section 6013(g) to be treated as a resident of the United States.

(2) *U.S. transferor.* The term *U.S. transferor* means any U.S. person who makes a transfer (as defined in § 1.684-2) of property to a foreign trust or foreign estate.

(3) *Foreign trust.* Section 7701(a)(31)(B) defines foreign trust. See also § 301.7701-7 of this chapter.

(4) *Foreign estate.* Section 7701(a)(31)(A) defines foreign estate.

(c) *Reporting requirements.* A U.S. person who transfers property to a foreign trust or foreign estate must comply with the reporting requirements under section 6048.

(d) *Examples.* The following examples illustrate the rules of this section. In all examples, A is a U.S. person and *FT* is a foreign trust. The examples are as follows:

Example 1. Transfer to foreign trust. A transfers property that has a fair market value of 1000X to *FT*. A's adjusted basis in the property is 400X. *FT* has no U.S. beneficiary within the meaning of § 1.679-2, and no person is treated as owning any portion of *FT*. Under paragraph (a)(1) of this section, A recognizes gain at the time of the transfer equal to 600X.

Example 2. Transfer of multiple properties. A transfers property Q, with a fair market value of 1000X, and property R, with a fair market value of 2000X, to *FT*. At the time of the transfer, A's adjusted basis in property Q is 700X, and A's adjusted basis in property R is 2200X. *FT* has no U.S. beneficiary within the meaning of § 1.679-2, and no person is treated as owning any portion of *FT*. Under paragraph (a)(1) of this section, A recognizes the 300X of gain attributable to property Q. Under paragraph (a)(2) of this section, A does not recognize the 200X of loss attributable to property R, and may not offset that loss against the gain attributable to property Q.

Example 3. Transfer for less than fair market value. A transfers property that has a fair market value of 1000X to *FT* in exchange for 400X of cash. A's adjusted basis in the property is 200X. *FT* has no U.S. beneficiary within the meaning of § 1.679-2, and no person is treated as owning any portion of *FT*. Under paragraph (a)(1) of this section, A recognizes gain at the time of the transfer equal to 800X.

Example 4. Exchange of property for private annuity. A transfers property that has a fair market value of 1000X to *FT* in exchange for *FT*'s obligation to pay A 50X per year for the rest of A's life. A's adjusted basis in the property is 100X. *FT* has no U.S. beneficiary within the meaning of § 1.679-2, and no person is treated as owning any portion of *FT*. A is required to recognize gain equal to 900X immediately upon transfer of the property to the trust. This result applies even though A might otherwise have been allowed to defer recognition of gain under another provision of the Internal Revenue Code.

Example 5. Transfer of property to related foreign trust in exchange for qualified obligation. A transfers property that has a fair market value of 1000X to *FT* in exchange for *FT*'s obligation to make payments to A during the next four years. *FT* is related to A as defined in § 1.679-1(c)(5). The obligation is treated as a qualified obligation

Reg. § 1.684-1(d)

within the meaning of § 1.679-4(d), and no person is treated as owning any portion of FT. A's adjusted basis in the property is 100X. A is required to recognize gain equal to 900X immediately upon transfer of the property to the trust. This result applies even though A might otherwise have been allowed to defer recognition of gain under another provision of the Internal Revenue Code. Section 1.684-3(d) provides rules relating to transfers for fair market value to unrelated foreign trusts.

[Reg. § 1.684-1.]

☐ [T.D. 8956, 7-19-2001.]

[Reg. § 1.684-2]

§ 1.684-2. Transfers.—(a) *In general.* A transfer means a direct, indirect, or constructive transfer.

(b) *Indirect transfers*—(1) *In general.* Section 1.679-3(c) shall apply to determine if a transfer to a foreign trust or foreign estate, by any person, is treated as an indirect transfer by a U.S. person to the foreign trust or foreign estate.

(2) *Examples.* The following examples illustrate the rules of this paragraph (b). In all examples, A is a U.S. citizen, FT is a foreign trust, and I is A's uncle, who is a nonresident alien. The examples are as follows:

Example 1. Principal purpose of tax avoidance. A creates and funds FT for the benefit of A's cousin, who is a nonresident alien. FT has no U.S. beneficiary within the meaning of § 1.679-2, and no person is treated as owning any portion of FT. In 2004, A decides to transfer additional property with a fair market value of 1000X and an adjusted basis of 600X to FT. Pursuant to a plan with a principal purpose of avoiding the application of section 684, A transfers the property to I. I subsequently transfers the property to FT. Under paragraph (b) of this section and § 1.679-3(c), A is treated as having transferred the property to FT.

Example 2. U.S. person unable to demonstrate that intermediary acted independently. A creates and funds FT for the benefit of A's cousin, who is a nonresident alien. FT has no U.S. beneficiary within the meaning of § 1.679-2, and no person is treated as owning any portion of FT. On July 1, 2004, A transfers property with a fair market value of 1000X and an adjusted basis of 300X to I, a foreign person. On January 1, 2007, at a time when the fair market value of the property is 1100X, I transfers the property to FT. A is unable to demonstrate to the satisfaction of the Commissioner, under § 1.679-3(c)(2)(ii), that I acted independently of A in making the transfer to FT. Under paragraph (b) of this section and § 1.679-3(c), A is treated as having transferred the property to FT. Under paragraph (b) of this section and § 1.679-3(c)(3), I is treated as an agent of A, and the transfer is deemed to have been made on January 1, 2007. Under § 1.684-1(a), A recognizes gain equal to 800X on that date.

(c) *Constructive transfers.* Section 1.679-3(d) shall apply to determine if a transfer to a foreign trust or foreign estate is treated as a constructive transfer by a U.S. person to the foreign trust or foreign estate.

(d) *Transfers by certain trusts*—(1) *In general.* If any portion of a trust is treated as owned by a U.S. person, a transfer of property from that portion of the trust to a foreign trust is treated as a transfer from the owner of that portion to the foreign trust.

(2) *Examples.* The following examples illustrate the rules of this paragraph (d). In all examples, A is a U.S. person, DT is a domestic trust, and FT is a foreign trust. The examples are as follows:

Example 1. Transfer by a domestic trust. On January 1, 2001, A transfers property which has a fair market value of 1000X and an adjusted basis of 200X to DT. A retains the power to revoke DT. On January 1, 2003, DT transfers property which has a fair market value of 500X and an adjusted basis of 100X to FT. At the time of the transfer, FT has no U.S. beneficiary as defined in § 1.679-2 and no person is treated as owning any portion of FT. A is treated as having transferred the property to FT and is required to recognize gain of 400X, under § 1.684-1, at the time of the transfer by DT to FT.

Example 2. Transfer by a foreign trust. On January 1, 2001, A transfers property which has a fair market value of 1000X and an adjusted basis of 200X to FT1. At the time of the transfer, FT1 has a U.S. beneficiary as defined in § 1.679-2 and A is treated as the owner of FT1 under section 679. On January 1, 2003, FT1 transfers property which has a fair market value of 500X and an adjusted basis of 100X to FT2. At the time of the transfer, FT2 has no U.S. beneficiary as defined in § 1.679-2 and no person is treated as owning any portion of FT2. A is treated as having transferred the property to FT2 and is required to recognize gain of 400X, under § 1.684-1, at the time of the transfer by FT1 to FT2.

(e) *Deemed transfers when foreign trust no longer treated as owned by a U.S. person*—(1) *In general.* If any portion of a foreign trust is treated as owned by a U.S. person under subpart E of part I of subchapter J, chapter 1 of the Internal Revenue Code, and such portion ceases to be treated as owned by that person under such subpart (other than by reason of an actual transfer of property from the trust to which § 1.684-2(d) applies), the U.S. person shall be treated as having transferred, immediately before (but on the same date that) the trust is no longer treated as owned by that U.S. person, the assets of such portion to a foreign trust.

(2) *Examples.* The following examples illustrate the rules of this paragraph (e). In all examples, *A* is a U.S. citizen and *FT* is a foreign trust. The examples are as follows:

Example 1. Loss of U.S. beneficiary. (i) On January 1, 2001, *A* transfers property, which has a fair market value of 1000X and an adjusted basis of 400X, to *FT*. At the time of the transfer, *FT* has a U.S. beneficiary within the meaning of § 1.679-2, and *A* is treated as owning *FT* under section 679. Under § 1.684-3(a), § 1.684-1 does not cause *A* to recognize gain at the time of the transfer.

(ii) On July 1, 2003, *FT* ceases to have a U.S. beneficiary as defined in § 1.679-2(c) and as of that date neither *A* nor any other person is treated as owning any portion of *FT*. Pursuant to § 1.679-2(c)(2), if *FT* ceases to be treated as having a U.S. beneficiary, *A* will cease to be treated as owner of *FT* beginning on the first day of the first taxable year following the last taxable year in which there was a U.S. beneficiary. Thus, on January 1, 2004, *A* ceases to be treated as owner of *FT*. On that date, the fair market value of the property is 1200X and the adjusted basis is 350X. Under paragraph (e)(1) of this section, *A* is treated as having transferred the property to *FT* on January 1, 2004, and must recognize 850X of gain at that time under § 1.684-1.

Example 2. Death of grantor. (i) The initial facts are the same as in paragraph (i) of *Example 1*.

(ii) On July 1, 2003, *A* dies, and as of that date no other person is treated as the owner of *FT*. On that date, the fair market value of the property is 1200X, and its adjusted basis equals 350X. Under paragraph (e)(1) of this section, *A* is treated as having transferred the property to *FT* immediately before his death, and generally is required to recognize 850X of gain at that time under § 1.684-1. However, an exception may apply under § 1.684-3(c).

Example 3. Release of a power. (i) On January 1, 2001, *A* transfers property that has a fair market value of 500X and an adjusted basis of 200X to *FT*. At the time of the transfer, *FT* does not have a U.S. beneficiary within the meaning of § 1.679-2. However, *A* retains the power to revoke the trust. *A* is treated as the owner of the trust under section 676 and, therefore, under § 1.684-3(a), *A* is not required to recognize gain under § 1.684-1 at the time of the transfer.

(ii) On January 1, 2007, *A* releases the power to revoke the trust and, as of that date, neither *A* nor any other person is treated as owning any portion of *FT*. On that date, the fair market value of the property is 900X, and its adjusted basis is 200X. Under paragraph (e)(1) of this section, *A* is treated as having transferred the property to *FT* on January 1, 2007, and must recognize 700X of gain at that time.

(f) *Transfers to entities owned by a foreign trust.* Section 1.679-3(f) provides rules that apply with respect to transfers of property by a U.S. person to an entity in which a foreign trust holds an ownership interest. [Reg. § 1.684-2.]

☐ [T.D. 8956, 7-19-2001.]

[Reg. § 1.684-3]

§ 1.684-3. **Exceptions to general rule of gain recognition.**—(a) *Transfers to grantor trusts.* The general rule of gain recognition under § 1.684-1 shall not apply to any transfer of property by a U.S. person to a foreign trust to the extent that any person is treated as the owner of the trust under section 671. Section 1.684-2(e) provides rules regarding a subsequent change in the status of the trust.

(b) *Transfers to charitable trusts.* The general rule of gain recognition under § 1.684-1 shall not apply to any transfer of property to a foreign trust that is described in section 501(c)(3) (without regard to the requirements of section 508(a)).

(c) *Certain transfers at death.* The general rule of gain recognition under § 1.684-1 shall not apply to any transfer of property by reason of death of the U.S. transferor if the basis of the property in the hands of the foreign trust is determined under section 1014(a).

(d) *Transfers for fair market value to unrelated trusts.* The general rule of gain recognition under § 1.684-1 shall not apply to any transfer of property for fair market value to a foreign trust that is not a related foreign trust as defined in § 1.679-1(c)(5). Section 1.671-2(e)(2)(ii) defines fair market value.

(e) *Transfers to which section 1032 applies.* The general rule of gain recognition under § 1.684-1 shall not apply to any transfer of stock (including treasury stock) by a domestic corporation to a foreign trust if the domestic corporation is not required to recognize gain on the transfer under section 1032.

(f) *Certain distributions to trusts.* For purposes of this section, a transfer does not include a distribution to a trust with respect to an interest held by such trust in an entity other than a trust or an

Reg. § 1.684-3(f)

interest in certain investment trusts described in § 301.7701-4(c) of this chapter, liquidating trusts described in § 301.7701-4(d) of this chapter, or environmental remediation trusts described in § 301.7701-4(e) of this chapter.

(g) *Examples.* The following examples illustrate the rules of this section. In all examples, *A* is a U.S. citizen and *FT* is a foreign trust. The examples are as follows:

Example 1. Transfer to owner trust. In 2001, *A* transfers property which has a fair market value of 1000X and an adjusted basis equal to 400X to *FT*. At the time of the transfer, *FT* has a U.S. beneficiary within the meaning of § 1.679-2, and *A* is treated as owning *FT* under section 679. Under paragraph (a) of this section, § 1.684-1 does not cause *A* to recognize gain at the time of the transfer. See § 1.684-2(e) for rules that may require *A* to recognize gain if the trust is no longer owned by *A*.

Example 2. Transfer of property at death: Basis determined under section 1014(a). (i) The initial facts are the same as *Example 1*.

(ii) *A* dies on July 1, 2004. The fair market value at *A*'s death of all property transferred to *FT* by *A* is 1500X. The basis in the property is 400X. *A* retained the power to revoke *FT*, thus, the value of all property owned by *FT* at *A*'s death is includible in *A*'s gross estate for U.S. estate tax purposes. Pursuant to paragraph (c) of this section, *A* is not required to recognize gain under § 1.684-1 because the basis of the property in the hands of the foreign trust is determined under section 1014(a).

Example 3. Transfer of property at death: Basis not determined under section 1014(a). (i) The initial facts are the same as *Example 1*.

(ii) *A* dies on July 1, 2004. The fair market value at *A*'s death of all property transferred to *FT* by *A* is 1500X. The basis in the property is 400X. *A* retains no power over *FT*, and *FT*'s basis in the property transferred is not determined under section 1014(a). Under § 1.684-2(e)(1), *A* is treated as having transferred the property to *FT* immediately before his death, and must recognize 1100X of gain at that time under § 1.684-1.

Example 4. Transfer of property for fair market value to an unrelated foreign trust. *A* sells a house with a fair market value of 1000X to *FT* in exchange for a 30-year note issued by *FT*. *A* is not related to *FT* as defined in § 1.679-1(c)(5). *FT* is not treated as owned by any person. Pursuant to paragraph (d) of this section, *A* is not required to recognize gain under § 1.684-1.

[Reg. § 1.684-3.]

☐ [*T.D. 8956, 7-19-2001.*]

[Reg. § 1.684-4]

§ 1.684-4. **Outbound migrations of domestic trusts.**—(a) *In general.* If a U.S. person transfers property to a domestic trust, and such trust becomes a foreign trust, and neither trust is treated as owned by any person under subpart E of part I of subchapter J, chapter 1 of the Internal Revenue Code, the trust shall be treated for purposes of this section as having transferred all of its assets to a foreign trust and the trust is required to recognize gain on the transfer under § 1.684-1(a). The trust must also comply with the rules of section 6048.

(b) *Date of transfer.* The transfer described in this section shall be deemed to occur immediately before, but on the same date that, the trust meets the definition of a foreign trust set forth in section 7701(a)(31)(B).

(c) *Inadvertent migrations.* In the event of an inadvertent migration, as defined in § 301.7701-7(d)(2) of this chapter, a trust may avoid the application of this section by complying with the procedures set forth in § 301.7701-7(d)(2) of this chapter.

(d) *Examples.* The following examples illustrate the rules of this section. In all examples, *A* is a U.S. citizen, *B* is a U.S. citizen, *C* is a nonresident alien, and *T* is a trust. The examples are as follows:

Example 1. Migration of domestic trust with U.S. beneficiaries. *A* transfers property which has a fair market value of 1000X and an adjusted basis equal to 400X to *T*, a domestic trust, for the benefit of *A*'s children who are also U.S. citizens. *B* is the trustee of *T*. On January 1, 2001, while *A* is still alive, *B* resigns as trustee and *C* becomes successor trustee under the terms of the trust. Pursuant to § 301.7701-7(d) of this chapter, *T* becomes a foreign trust. *T* has U.S. beneficiaries within the meaning of § 1.679-2 and *A* is, therefore, treated as owning *FT* under section 679. Pursuant to § 1.684-3(a), neither *A* nor *T* is required to recognize gain at the time of the migration. Section 1.684-2(e) provides rules that may require *A* to recognize gain upon a subsequent change in the status of the trust.

Example 2. Migration of domestic trust with no U.S. beneficiaries. *A* transfers property which has a fair market value of 1000X and an adjusted basis equal to 400X to *T*, a domestic trust for the benefit of *A*'s mother who is not a citizen or resident of the United States. *T* is not treated as owned by another person. *B* is the trustee of *T*. On January 1, 2001, while *A* is still alive, B resigns as trustee and *C* becomes successor trustee under the terms of the trust. Pursuant to § 301.7701-7(d) of this chapter, *T* becomes a foreign trust, *FT*. *FT*

Income in Respect of Decedents

has no U.S. beneficiaries within the meaning of § 1.679-2 and no person is treated as owning any portion of *FT. T* is required to recognize gain of 600X on January 1, 2001. Paragraph (c) of this section provides rules with respect to an inadvertent migration of a domestic trust. [Reg. § 1.684-4.]

☐ [*T.D.* 8956, 7-19-2001.]

[Reg. § 1.684-5]

§ 1.684-5. **Effective date.**—Sections 1.684-1 through 1.684-4 apply to transfers of property to foreign trusts and foreign estates after August 7, 2000. [Reg. § 1.684-5.]

☐ [*T.D.* 8956, 7-19-2001.]

Income in Respect of Decedents

[Reg. § 1.691(a)-1]

§ 1.691(a)-1. **Income in respect of a decedent.**—(a) *Scope of section 691.* In general, the regulations under section 691 cover: (1) The provisions requiring that amounts which are not includible in gross income for the decedent's last taxable year or for a prior taxable year be included in the gross income of the estate or persons receiving such income to the extent that such amounts constitute "income in respect of a decedent"; (2) the taxable effect of a transfer of the right to such income; (3) the treatment of certain deductions and credit in respect of a decedent which are not allowable to the decedent for the taxable period ending with his death or for a prior taxable year; (4) the allowance to a recipient of income in respect of a decedent of a deduction for estate taxes attributable to the inclusion of the value of the right to such income in the decedent's estate; (5) special provisions with respect to installment obligations acquired from a decedent and with respect to the allowance of a deduction for estate taxes to a surviving annuitant under a joint and survivor annuity contract; and (6) special provisions relating to installment obligations transmitted at death when prior law applied to the transmission.

(b) *General definition.* In general, the term "income in respect of a decedent" refers to those amounts to which a decedent was entitled as gross income but which were not properly includible in computing his taxable income for the taxable year ending with the date of his death or for a previous taxable year under the method of accounting employed by the decedent. See the regulations under section 451. Thus, the term includes—

(1) All accrued income of a decedent who reported his income by use of the cash receipts and disbursements method;

(2) Income accrued solely by reason of the decedent's death in case of a decedent who reports his income by use of an accrual method of accounting; and

(3) Income to which the decedent had a contingent claim at the time of his death.

See sections 736 and 753 and the regulations thereunder for "income in respect of a decedent" in the case of a deceased partner.

(c) *Prior decedent.* The term "income in respect of a decedent" also includes the amount of all items of gross income in respect of a prior decedent, if (1) the right to receive such amount was acquired by the decedent by reason of the death of the prior decedent or by bequest, devise, or inheritance from the prior decedent and if (2) the amount of gross income in respect of the prior decedent was not properly includible in computing the decedent's taxable income for the taxable year ending with the date of his death or for a previous taxable year. See example (2) of paragraph (b) of § 1.691(a)-2.

(d) *Items excluded from gross income.* Section 691 applies only to the amount of items of gross income in respect of a decedent, and items which are excluded from gross income under subtitle A of the Code are not within the provisions of section 691.

(e) *Cross reference.* For items deemed to be income in respect of a decedent for purposes of the deduction for estate taxes provided by section 691(c), see paragraph (c) of § 1.691(c)-1. [Reg. § 1.691(a)-1.]

☐ [*T.D.* 6257, 10-7-57. *Amended by T.D.* 6808, 3-15-65.]

[Reg. § 1.691(a)-2]

§ 1.691(a)-2. **Inclusion in gross income by recipients.**—(a) Under section 691(a)(1), income in respect of a decedent shall be included in the gross income, for the taxable year when received, of—

(1) The estate of the decedent, if the right to receive the amount is acquired by the decedent's estate from the decedent;

(2) The person who, by reason of the death of the decedent, acquires the right to receive the amount, if the right to receive the amount is not acquired by the decedent's estate from the decedent; or

(3) The person who acquires from the decedent the right to receive the amount by bequest,

devise, or inheritance, if the amount is received after a distribution by the decedent's estate of such right.

These amounts are included in the income of the estate or of such persons when received by them whether or not they report income by use of the cash receipts and disbursements method.

(b) The application of paragraph (a) of this section may be illustrated by the following examples, in each of which it is assumed that the decedent kept his books by use of the cash receipts and disbursements method:

Example (1). The decedent was entitled at the date of his death to a large salary payment to be made in equal annual installments over five years. His estate, after collecting two installments, distributed the right to the remaining installment payments to the residuary legatee of the estate. The estate must include in its gross income the two installments received by it, and the legatee must include in his gross income each of the three installments received by him.

Example (2). A widow acquired, by bequest from her husband, the right to receive renewal commissions on life insurance sold by him in his lifetime, which commissions were payable over a period of years. The widow died before having received all of such commissions, and her son inherited the right to receive the rest of the commissions. The commissions received by the widow were includible in her gross income. The commissions received by the son were not includible in the widow's gross income but must be included in the gross income of the son.

Example (3). The decedent owned a Series E United States savings bond, with his wife as co-owner or beneficiary, but died before the payment of such bond. The entire amount of interest accruing on the bond and not includible in income by the decedent, nor just the amount accruing after the death of the decedent, would be treated as income to his wife when the bond is paid.

Example (4). A, prior to his death, acquired 10,000 shares of the capital stock of the X Corporation at a cost of $100 per share. During his lifetime, A had entered into an agreement with X Corporation whereby X Corporation agreed to purchase and the decedent agreed that his executor would sell the 10,000 shares of X Corporation stock owned by him at the book value of the stock at the date of A's death. Upon A's death, the shares are sold by A's executor for $500 a share pursuant to the agreement. Since the sale of stock is consummated after A's death, there is no income in respect of a decedent with respect to the appreciation in value of A's stock to the date of his death. If, in this example, A had in fact sold the stock during his lifetime but payment had not been received before his death, any gain on the sale would constitute income in respect of a decedent when the proceeds were received.

Example (5). (1) A owned and operated an apple orchard. During his lifetime, A sold and delivered 1,000 bushels of apples to X, a canning factory, but did not receive payment before his death. A also entered into negotiations to sell 3,000 bushels of apples to Y, a canning factory, but did not complete the sale before his death. After A's death, the executor received payment from X. He also completed the sale to Y and transferred to Y 1,200 bushels of apples on hand at A's death and harvested and transferred an additional 1,800 bushels. The gain from the sale of apples by A to X constitutes income in respect of a decedent when received. On the other hand, the gain from the sale of apples by the executor to Y does not.

(2) Assume that, instead of the transaction entered into with Y, A had disposed of the 1,200 bushels of harvested apples by delivering them to Z, a cooperative association, for processing and sale. Each year the association commingles the fruit received from all of its members into a pool and assigns to each member a percentage interest in the pool based on the fruit delivered by him. After the fruit is processed and the products are sold, the association distributes the net proceeds from the pool to its members in proportion to their interests in the pool. After A's death, the association made distributions to the executor with respect to A's share of the proceeds from the pool in which A had an interest. Under such circumstances, the proceeds from the disposition of the 1,200 bushels of apples constitute income in respect of a decedent. [Reg. § 1.691(a)-2.]

☐ [T.D. 6257, 10-7-57.]

[Reg. § 1.691(a)-3]

§ 1.691(a)-3. **Character of gross income.**—(a) The right to receive an amount of income in respect of a decedent shall be treated in the hands of the estate, or by the person entitled to receive such amount by bequest, devise, or inheritance from the decedent or by reason of his death, as if it had been acquired in the transaction by which the decedent (or a prior decedent) acquired such right, and shall be considered as having the same character it would have had if the decedent (or a prior decedent) had lived and received such amount. The provisions of section 1014(a), relating to the basis of property acquired from a decedent, do not apply to these amounts in the hands of the estate and such persons. See section 1014(c).

Reg. § 1.691(a)-3(a)

Income in Respect of Decedents

See p. 20,601 for regulations not amended to reflect law changes

(b) The application of paragraph (a) of this section may be illustrated by the following:

(1) If the income would have been capital gain to the decedent, if he had lived and had received it, from the sale of property held for more than 1 year (6 months for taxable years beginning before 1977; 9 months for taxable years beginning in 1977), the income, when received, shall be treated in the hands of the estate or of such person as capital gain from the sale of the property, held for more than 1 year (6 months for taxable years beginning before 1977; 9 months for taxable years beginning in 1977), in the same manner as if such person had held the property for the period the decedent held it, and had made the sale.

(2) If the income is interest on United States obligations which were owned by the decedent, such income shall be treated as interest on United States obligations in the hands of the person receiving it, for the purpose of determining the credit provided by section 35, as if such person had owned the obligations with respect to which such interest is paid.

(3) If the amounts received would be subject to special treatment under part I (section 1301 and following), subchapter Q, chapter 1 of the Code, relating to income attributable to several taxable years, as in effect for taxable years beginning before January 1, 1964, if the decedent had lived and included such amounts in his gross income, such sections apply with respect to the recipient of the income.

(4) The provisions of sections 632 and 1347, relating to the tax attributable to the sale of certain oil or gas property and to certain claims against the United States, apply to any amount included in gross income, the right to which was obtained by the decedent by a sale or claim within the provisions of those sections. [Reg. § 1.691(a)-3.]

☐ [T.D. 6257, 10-7-57. Amended by T.D. 6885, 6-1-66 and by T.D. 7728, 10-31-80.]

[Reg. § 1.691(a)-4]

§ 1.691(a)-4. Transfer of right to income in respect of a decedent.—(a) Section 691(a)(2) provides the rules governing the treatment of income in respect of a decedent (or a prior decedent) in the event a right to receive such income is transferred by the estate or person entitled thereto by bequest, devise, or inheritance, or by reason of the death of the decedent. In general, the transferor must include in his gross income for the taxable period in which the transfer occurs the amount of the consideration, if any, received for the right or the fair market value of the right at the time of the transfer, whichever is greater. Thus, upon a sale of such right by the estate or person entitled to receive it, the fair market value of the right or the amount received upon the sale, whichever is greater, is included in the gross income of the vendor. Similarly, if such right is disposed of by gift, the fair market value of the right at the time of the gift must be included in the gross income of the donor. In the case of a satisfaction of an installment obligation at other than face value, which is likewise considered a transfer under section 691(a)(2), see § 1.691(a)-5.

(b) If the estate of a decedent or any person transmits the right to income in respect of a decedent to another who would be required by section 691(a)(1) to include such income when received in his gross income, only the transferee will include such income when received in his gross income. In this situation, a transfer within the meaning of section 691(a)(2) has not occurred. This paragraph may be illustrated by the following:

(1) If a person entitled to income in respect of a decedent dies before receiving such income, only his estate or other person entitled to such income by bequest, devise, or inheritance from the latter decedent, or by reason of the death of the latter decedent, must include such amount in gross income when received.

(2) If a right to income in respect of a decedent is transferred by an estate to a specific or residuary legatee, only the specific or residuary legatee must include such income in gross income when received.

(3) If a trust to which is bequeathed a right of a decedent to certain payments of income terminates and transfers the right to a beneficiary, only the beneficiary must include such income in gross income when received. If the transferee described in subparagraphs (1), (2), and (3) of this paragraph transfers his right to receive the amounts in the manner described in paragraph (a) of this section, the principles contained in paragraph (a) are applied to such transfer. On the other hand, if the transferee transmits his right in the manner described in this paragraph, the principles of this paragraph are again applied to such transfer. [Reg. § 1.691(a)-4.]

☐ [T.D. 6257, 10-7-57.]

[Reg. § 1.691(a)-5]

§ 1.691(a)-5. Installment obligations acquired from decedent.—(a) Section 691(a)(4) has reference to an installment obligation which remains uncollected by a decedent (or a prior decedent) and which was originally acquired in a transaction the income from which was properly

Reg. § 1.691(a)-5(a)

reportable by the decedent on the installment method under section 453. Under the provisions of section 691(a)(4), an amount equal to the excess of the face value of the obligation over its basis in the hands of the decedent (determined under section 453(d)(2) and the regulations thereunder) shall be considered an amount of income in respect of a decedent and shall be treated as such. The decedent's estate (or the person entitled to receive such income by bequest or inheritance from the decedent or by reason of the decedent's death) shall include in its gross income when received the same proportion of any payment in satisfaction of such obligations as would be returnable as income by the decedent if he had lived and received such payment. No gain on account of the transmission of such obligations by the decedent's death is required to be reported as income in the return of the decedent for the year of his death. See § 1.691(e)-1 for special provisions relating to the filing of an election to have the provisions of section 691(a)(4) apply in the case of installment obligations in respect of which section 44(d) of the Internal Revenue Code of 1939 (or corresponding provisions of prior law) would have applied but for the filing of a bond referred to therein.

(b) If an installment obligation described in paragraph (a) of this section is transferred within the meaning of section 691(a)(2) and paragraph (a) of § 1.691(a)-4, the entire installment obligation transferred shall be considered a right to income in respect of a decedent but the amount includible in the gross income of the transferor shall be reduced by an amount equal to the basis of the obligation in the hands of the decedent (determined under section 453(d)(2) and the regulations thereunder) adjusted, however, to take into account the receipt of any installment payments after the decedent's death and before such transfer. Thus, the amount includible in the gross income of the transferor shall be the fair market value of such obligation at the time of the transfer or the consideration received for the transfer of the installment obligation, whichever is greater, reduced by the basis of the obligation as described in the preceding sentence. For purposes of this paragraph, the term "transfer" in section 691(a)(2) and paragraph (a) of § 1.691(a)-4, includes the satisfaction of an installment obligation at other than face value.

(c) The application of this section may be illustrated by the following example:

Example. An heir of a decedent is entitled to collect an installment obligation with a face value of $100, a fair market value of $80, and a basis in the hands of the decedent of $60. If the heir collects the obligation at face value, the excess of the amount collected over the basis is considered income in respect of a decedent and includible in the gross income of the heir under section 691(a)(1). In this case, the amount includible would be $40 ($100 less $60). If the heir collects the obligation at $90, an amount other than face value, the entire obligation is considered a right to receive income in respect of a decedent but the amount ordinarily required to be included in the heir's gross income under section 691(a)(2) (namely, the consideration received in satisfaction of the installment obligation or its fair market value, whichever is greater) shall be reduced by the amount of the basis of the obligation in the hands of the decedent. In this case, the amount includible would be $30 ($90 less $60). [Reg. § 1.691(a)-5.]

☐ [T.D. 6257, 10-7-57. Amended by T.D. 6808, 3-15-65.]

[Reg. § 1.691(b)-1]

§ 1.691(b)-1. **Allowance of deductions and credit in respect of decedents.**—(a) Under section 691(b), the expenses, interest, and taxes described in sections 162, 163, 164, and 212 for which the decedent (or a prior decedent) was liable, which were not properly allowable as a deduction in his last taxable year or any prior taxable year, are allowed when paid—

(1) As a deduction by the estate; or

(2) If the estate was not liable to pay such obligation, as a deduction by the person who by bequest, devise, or inheritance from the decedent or by reason of the death of the decedent acquires, subject to such obligation, an interest in property of the decedent (or the prior decedent).

Similar treatment is given to the foreign tax credit provided by section 33. For the purposes of subparagraph (2) of this paragraph, the right to receive an amount of gross income in respect of a decedent is considered property of the decedent; on the other hand, it is not necessary for a person, otherwise within the provisions of subparagraph (2) of this paragraph, to receive the right to any income in respect of a decedent. Thus, an heir who receives a right to income in respect of a decedent (by reason of the death of the decedent) subject to an income tax imposed by a foreign country during the decedent's life, which tax must be satisfied out of such income, is entitled to the credit provided by section 33 when he pays the tax. If a decedent who reported income by use of the cash receipts and disbursements method owned real property on which accrued taxes had become a lien, and if such property passed directly to the heir of the decedent in a jurisdiction in which real property does not become a part of a decedent's estate, the heir, upon paying such taxes, may take the same deduction under section 164 that would be allowed to the decedent if, while alive, he had made such payment.

(b) The deduction for percentage depletion is allowable only to the person (described in section 691(a)(1)) who receives the income in respect of the decedent to which the deduction relates, whether or not such person receives the property from which such income is derived. Thus, an heir who (by reason of the decedent's death) receives income derived from sales of units of mineral by the decedent (who reported income by use of the cash receipts and disbursements method) shall be allowed the deduction for percentage depletion, computed on the gross income from such number of units as if the heir had the same economic interest in the property as the decedent. Such heir need not also receive any interest in the mineral property other than such income. If the decedent did not compute his deduction for depletion on the basis of percentage depletion, any deduction for depletion to which the decedent was entitled at the date of his death would be allowable in computing his taxable income for his last taxable year, and there can be no deduction in respect of the decedent by any other person for such depletion. [Reg. § 1.691(b)-1.]

☐ [T.D. 6257, 10-7-57.]

[Reg. § 1.691(c)-1]

§ 1.691(c)-1. Deduction for estate tax attributable to income in respect of a decedent.—(a) *In general.* A person who is required to include in gross income for any taxable year an amount of income in respect of a decedent may deduct for the same taxable year that portion of the estate tax imposed upon the decedent's estate which is attributable to the inclusion in the decedent's estate of the right to receive such amount. The deduction is determined as follows:

(1) Ascertain the net value in the decedent's estate of the items which are included under section 691 in computing gross income. This is the excess of the value included in the gross estate on account of the items of gross income in respect of the decedent (see § 1.691(a)-1 and paragraph (c) of this section) over the deductions from the gross estate for claims which represent the deductions and credit in respect of the decedent (see § 1.691(b)-1). But see section 691(d) and paragraph (b) of § 1.691(d)-1 for computation of the special value of a survivor's annuity to be used in computing the net value for estate tax purposes in cases involving joint and survivor annuities.

(2) Ascertain the portion of the estate tax attributable to the inclusion in the gross estate of such net value. This is the excess of the estate tax over the estate tax computed without including such net value in the gross estate. In computing the estate tax without including such net value in the gross estate, any estate tax deduction (such as the marital deduction) which may be based upon the gross estate shall be recomputed so as to take into account the exclusion of such net value from the gross estate. See example (2), paragraph (e) of § 1.691(d)-1.

For purposes of this section, the term "estate tax" means the tax imposed under section 2001 or 2101 (or the corresponding provisions of the Internal Revenue Code of 1939), reduced by the credits against such tax. Each person including in gross income an amount of income in respect of a decedent may deduct as his share of the portion of the estate tax (computed under subparagraph (2) of this paragraph) an amount which bears the same ratio to such portion as the value in the gross estate of the right to the income included by such person in gross income (or the amount included in gross income if lower) bears to the value in the gross estate of all the items of gross income in respect of the decedent.

(b) *Prior decedent.* If a person is required to include in gross income an amount of income in respect of a prior decedent, such person may deduct for the same taxable year that portion of the estate tax imposed upon the prior decedent's estate which is attributable to the inclusion in the prior decedent's estate of the value of the right to receive such amount. This deduction is computed in the same manner as provided in paragraph (a) of this section and is in addition to the deduction for estate tax imposed upon the decedent's estate which is attributable to the inclusion in the decedent's estate of the right to receive such amount.

(c) *Amounts deemed to be income in respect of a decedent.* For purposes of allowing the deduction under section 691(c), the following items are also considered to be income in respect of a decedent under section 691(a):

(1) The value for estate tax purposes of stock options in respect of which amounts are includible in gross income under section 421(b) (prior to amendment by section 221(a) of the Revenue Act of 1964), in the case of taxable years ending before January 1, 1964, or under section 422(c)(1), 423(c), or 424(c)(1), whichever is applicable, in the case of taxable years ending after December 31, 1963. See section 421(d)(6) (prior to amendment by section 221(a) of the Revenue Act of 1964), in the case of taxable years ending before January 1, 1964, and section 421(c)(2), in

the case of taxable years ending after December 31, 1963.

(2) Amounts received by a surviving annuitant during his life expectancy period as an annuity under a joint and survivor annuity contract to the extent included in gross income under section 72. See section 691(d).

(d) *Examples.* Paragraphs (a) and (b) of this section may be illustrated by the following examples:

Example (1). X, an attorney who kept his books by use of the cash receipts and disbursements method, was entitled at the date of his death to a fee for services rendered in a case not completed at the time of his death, which fee was valued in his estate at $1,000, and to accrued bond interest, which was valued in his estate at $500. In all, $1,500 was included in his gross estate in respect of income described in section 691(a)(1). There were deducted as claims against his estate $150 for business expenses for which his estate was liable and $50 for taxes accrued on certain property which he owned. In all, $200 was deducted for claims which represent amounts described in section 691(b) which are allowable as deductions to his estate or to the beneficiaries of his estate. His gross estate was $185,000 and, considering deductions of $15,000 and an exemption of $60,000, his taxable estate amounted to $110,000. The estate tax on this amount is $23,700 from which is subtracted a $75 credit for State death taxes leaving an estate tax liability of $23,625. In the year following the closing of X's estate, the fee in the amount of $1,200 was collected by X's son, who was the sole beneficiary of the estate. This amount was included under section 691(a)(1)(C) in the son's gross income. The son may deduct, in computing his taxable income for such year, $260 on account of the estate tax attributable to such income, computed as follows:

(1)	(i) Value of income described in section 691(a)(1) included in computing gross estate	$ 1,500
	(ii) Deductions in computing gross estate for claims representing deductions described in section 691(b)	200
	(iii) Net value of items described in section 691(a)(1)	1,300
(2)	(i) Estate tax	23,625
	(ii) Less: Estate tax computed without including $1,300 (item (1)(iii)) in gross estate	23,235
	(iii) Portion of estate tax attributable to net value of items described in section 691(a)(1)	390
(3)	(i) Value in gross estate of items described in section 691(a)(1) received in taxable year (fee)	1,000
	(ii) Value in gross estate of all income items described in section 691(a)(1) (item (1)(i))	1,500
	(iii) Part of estate tax deductible on account of receipt of $1,200 fee (1,000/1,500 of $390)	260

Although $1,200 was later collected as the fee, only the $1,000 actually included in the gross estate is used in the above computations. However, to avoid distortion, section 691(c) provides that if the value included in the gross estate is greater than the amount finally collected, only the amount collected shall be used in the above computations. Thus, if the amount collected as the fee were only $500, the estate tax deductible on the receipt of such amount would be 500/1,500 of $390, or $130. With respect to taxable years ending before January 1, 1964, see paragraph (d)(3) of § 1.421-5 for a similar example involving a restricted stock option. With respect to taxable years ending after December 31, 1963, see paragraph (c)(3) of § 1.421-8 for a similar example involving a stock option subject to the provisions of part II of subchapter D.

Example (2). Assume that in example (1) the fee valued at $1,000 had been earned by prior decedent Y and had been inherited by X who died before collecting it. With regard to the son, the fee would be considered income in respect of a prior decedent. Assume further that the fee was valued at $1,000 in Y's estate, that the net value in Y's estate of items described in section 691(a)(1) was $5,000 and that the estate tax imposed on Y's estate attributable to such net value was $550. In such case, the portion of such estate tax attributable to the fee would be 1,000/5,000 of $550, or $110. When the son collects the $1,200 fee, he will receive for the same taxable year a deduction of $110 with respect to the estate tax imposed on the estate of prior decedent Y as well as the deduction of $260 (as computed in example (1)) with respect to the estate tax imposed on the estate of decedent X. [Reg. § 1.691(c)-1.]

☐ [T.D. 6257, 10-7-57. Amended by T.D. 6887, 6-23-66.]

[Reg. § 1.691(c)-2]

§ 1.691(c)-2. **Estates and trusts.**—(a) In the case of an estate or trust, the deduction prescribed in section 691(c) is determined in the same manner as described in § 1.691(c)-1, with the following exceptions:

(1) If any amount properly paid, credited, or required to be distributed by an estate or trust to a beneficiary consists of income in respect of a

Income in Respect of Decedents

decedent received by the estate or trust during the taxable year—

(i) Such income shall be excluded in determining the income in respect of the decedent with respect to which the estate or trust is entitled to a deduction under section 691(c), and

(ii) Such income shall be considered income in respect of a decedent to such beneficiary for purposes of allowing the deduction under section 691(c) to such beneficiary.

(2) For determination of the amount of income in respect of a decedent received by the beneficiary, see sections 652 and 662, and §§ 1.652(b)-2 and 1.662(b)-2. However, for this purpose, distributable net income as defined in section 643(a) and the regulations thereunder shall be computed without taking into account the estate tax deduction provided in section 691(c) and this section. Distributable net income as modified under the preceding sentence shall be applied for other relevant purposes of subchapter J, chapter 1 of the Code, such as the deduction provided by section 651 or 661, or subpart D, part I of subchapter J, relating to excess distributions by trusts.

(3) The rule stated in subparagraph (1) of this paragraph does not apply to income in respect of a decedent which is properly allocable to corpus by the fiduciary during the taxable year but which is distributed to a beneficiary in a subsequent year. The deduction provided by section 691(c) in such a case is allowable only to the estate or trust. If any amount properly paid, credited, or required to be distributed by a trust qualifies as a distribution under section 666, the fact that a portion thereof constitutes income in respect of a decedent shall be disregarded for the purposes of determining the deduction of the trust and of the beneficiaries under section 691(c) since the deduction for estate taxes was taken into consideration in computing the undistributed net income of the trust for the preceding taxable year.

(b) This section shall apply only to amounts properly paid, credited, or required to be distributed in taxable years of an estate or trust beginning after December 31, 1953, and ending after August 16, 1954, except as otherwise provided in paragraph (c) of this section.

(c) In the case of an estate or trust heretofore taxable under the provisions of the Internal Revenue Code of 1939, amounts paid, credited, or to be distributed during its first taxable year subject to the Internal Revenue Code of 1954 which would have been treated as paid, credited, or to be distributed on the last day of the preceding taxable year if the Internal Revenue Code of 1939 were still applicable shall not be subject to the provisions of section 691(c)(1)(B) or this section. See section 683 and the regulations thereunder.

(d) The provisions of this section may be illustrated by the following example, in which it is assumed that the estate and the beneficiary make their returns on the calendar year basis:

Example. (1) The fiduciary of an estate receives taxable interest of $5,500 and income in respect of a decedent of $4,500 during the taxable year. Neither the will of the decedent nor local law requires the allocation to corpus of income in respect of a decedent. The estate tax attributable to the income in respect of a decedent is $1,500. In his discretion, the fiduciary distributes $2,000 (falling within sections 661(a) and 662(a)) to a beneficiary during that year. On these facts the fiduciary and beneficiary are respectively entitled to estate tax deductions of $1,200 and $300, computed as follows:

(2) Distributable net income computed under section 643(a) without regard to the estate tax deduction under section 691(c) is $10,000, computed as follows:

Taxable interest	$5,500
Income in respect of a decedent	4,500
Total	$10,000

(3) Inasmuch as the distributable net income of $10,000 exceeds the amount of $2,000 distributed to the beneficiary, the deduction allowable to the estate under section 661(a), and the amount taxable to the beneficiary under section 662(a), is $2,000.

(4) The character of the amounts distributed to the beneficiary under section 662(b) is shown in the following table:

	Taxable interest	Income in respect of a decedent	Total
Distributable net income	$5,500	$4,500	$10,000
Amount deemed distributed under section 662(b)	1,100	900	2,000

Reg. § 1.691(c)-2(d)

(5) Accordingly, the beneficiary will be entitled to an estate tax deduction of $300 (900/4,500 × $1,500) and the estate will be entitled to an estate tax deduction of $1,200 (3,600/4,500 × $1,500).

(6) The taxable income of the estate is $6,200, computed as follows:

Gross income		$10,000
Less:		
Distributions to the beneficiary	$2,000	
Estate tax deduction under section 691(c)	1,200	
Personal exemption	600	3,800
Taxable income		$6,200

[Reg. § 1.691(c)-2.]

☐ [T.D. 6257, 10-7-57.]

[Reg. § 1.691(d)-1]

§ 1.691(d)-1. Amounts received by surviving annuitant under joint and survivor annuity contract.—(a) *In general.* Under section 691(d), annuity payments received by a surviving annuitant under a joint and survivor annuity contract (to the extent indicated in paragraph (b) of this section) are treated as income in respect of a decedent under section 691(a) for the purpose of allowing the deduction for estate tax provided for in section 691(c)(1)(A). This section applies only if the deceased annuitant died after December 31, 1953, and after the annuity starting date as defined in section 72(c)(4).

(b) *Special value for surviving annuitant's payments.* Section 691(d) provides a special value for the surviving annuitant's payments to determine the amount of the estate tax deduction provided for in section 691(c)(1)(A). This special value is determined by multiplying—

(1) The excess of the value of the annuity at the date of death of the deceased annuitant over the total amount excludable from the gross income of the surviving annuitant under section 72 during his life expectancy period (see paragraph (d)(1)(i) of this section) by

(2) A fraction consisting of the value of the annuity for estate tax purposes over the value of the annuity at the date of death of the deceased annuitant.

This special value is used for the purpose of determining the net value for estate tax purposes (see section 691(c)(2)(B) and paragraph (a)(1) of § 1.691(c)-1) and for the purpose of determining the portion of estate tax attributable to the survivor's annuity (see paragraph (a) of § 1.691(c)-1).

(c) *Amount of deduction.* The portion of estate tax attributable to the survivor's annuity (see paragraph (a) of § 1.691(c)-1) is allowable as a deduction to the surviving annuitant over his life expectancy period. If the surviving annuitant continues to receive annuity payments beyond this period, there is no further deduction under section 691(d). If the surviving annuitant dies before expiration of such period, there is no compensating adjustment for the unused deduction.

(d) *Definitions.* (1) For purposes of section 691(d) and this section—

(i) The term "life expectancy period" means the period beginning with the first day of the first period for which an amount is received by the surviving annuitant under the contract and ending with the close of the taxable year with or in which falls the termination of the life expectancy of the surviving annuitant.

(ii) The life expectancy of the surviving annuitant shall be determined as of the date of the deceased annuitant, with reference to actuarial Table I set forth in § 1.72-9 (but without making any adjustment under paragraph (a)(2) of § 1.72-5).

(iii) The value of the annuity at the date of death of the deceased annuitant shall be the entire value of the survivor's annuity determined by reference to the principles set forth in section 2031 and the regulations thereunder, relating to the valuation of annuities for estate tax purposes.

(iv) The value of the annuity for estate tax purposes shall be that portion of the value determined under subdivision (iii) of this subparagraph which was includible in the deceased annuitant's gross estate.

(2) The determination of the "life expectancy period" of the survivor for purposes of section 691(d) may be illustrated by the following example:

Example. H and W file their income tax returns on the calendar year basis. H dies on July 15, 1955, on which date W is 70 years of age. On August 1, 1955, W receives a monthly payment under a joint and survivor annuity contract. W's life expectancy determined as of the date of H's death is 15 years as determined from Table I in

§ 1.72-9; thus her life expectancy ends on July 14, 1970. Under the provisions of section 691(d), her life expectancy period begins as of July 1, 1955, and ends as of December 31, 1970, thus giving her a life expectancy period of 15½ years.

(e) *Examples.* The application of section 691(d) and this section may be illustrated by the following examples:

Example (1). (1) H and W, husband and wife, purchased a joint and survivor annuity contract for $203,800 providing for monthly payments of $1,000 starting January 28, 1954, and continuing for their joint lives and for the remaining life of the survivor. H contributed $152,850 and W contributed $50,950 to the cost of the annuity. As of the annuity starting date, January 1, 1954, H's age at his nearest birthday was 70 and W's age at her nearest birthday was 67. H dies on January 1, 1957, and beginning on January 28, 1957, W receives her monthly payments of $1,000. The value of the annuity at the date of H's death is $159,000 (see paragraph (d)(1)(iii) of this section), and the value of the annuity for estate tax purposes (see paragraph (d)(1)(iv) of this section) is $119,250 (152,850/203,800 of $159,000). As of the date of H's death, W's age is 70 and her life expectancy period is 15 years (see paragraph (d) of this section for method of computation). Both H and W reported income by use of the cash receipts and disbursements method and filed income tax returns on the calendar year basis.

(2) The following computations illustrate the application of section 72 in determining the excludable portions of the annuity payments to W during her life expectancy period:

Amount of annuity payments per year (12 × $1,000)	$ 12,000
Life expectancy of H and W as of the annuity starting date (see section 72(c)(3)(A) and Table II of § 1.72-9 (male, age 70; female, age 67))	19.7
Expected return as of the annuity starting date, January 1, 1954 ($12,000 × 19.7 as determined under section 72(c)(3)(A) and paragraph (b) of § 1.72-5)	$236,400
Investment in the contract as of the annuity starting date, Jan. 1, 1954 (see section 72(c)(1) and paragraph (a) of § 1.72-6)	$203,800
Exclusion ratio (203,800/236,400 as determined under section 72(b) and § 1.72-4) (percent)	86.2
Exclusion per year under section 72 ($12,000 × 86.2 percent)	$ 10,344
Excludable during W's life expectancy period ($10,344 × 15)	$155,160

(3) For the purpose of computing the deduction for estate tax under section 691(c), the value for estate tax purposes of the amounts includible in W's gross income and considered income in respect of a decedent by virtue of section 691(d)(1) is $2,880. This amount is arrived at in accordance with the formula contained in section 691(d)(2), as follows:

Value of annuity at date of H's death	$159,000
Total amount excludable from W's gross income under section 72 during W's life expectancy period (see subparagraph (2) of this example)	$155,160
Excess	$ 3,840
Ratio which value of annuity for estate tax purposes bears to value of annuity at date of H's death (119,250/159,000) (percent)	75
Value for estate tax purposes (75 percent of $3,840)	$ 2,880

This amount ($2,880) is included in the items of income under section 691(a)(1) for the purpose of determining the estate tax attributable to each item under section 691(c)(1)(A). The estate tax determined to be attributable to the item of $2,880 is then allowed as a deduction to W over her 15-year life expectancy period (see example (2) of this paragraph).

Example (2). Assume, in addition to the facts contained in example (1) of this paragraph, that H was an attorney and was entitled at the date of his death to a fee for services rendered in a case not completed at the time of his death, which fee was valued at $1,000, and to accrued bond interest, which was valued at $500. Taking into consideration the annuity payments of example (1), valued at $2,880, a total of $4,380 was included in his gross estate in respect of income described in section 691(a)(1). There was deducted as claims against his estate $280 for business expenses for which his estate was liable and $100 for taxes accrued on certain property which he owned. In all, $380 was deducted for claims which represent amounts described in section 691(b) which are allowable as deductions to his estate or to the beneficiaries of his estate. His gross estate was $404,250 and considering deductions of $15,000, a marital deduction of $119,250 (assuming the annuity to be the only qualifying gift) and an exemption of $60,000, his taxable estate amounted to $210,000. The estate tax on this amount is $53,700 from which is subtracted a $175 credit for State death taxes, leaving an estate tax liability of $53,525. W may deduct, in computing her taxable income during each year of her 15-year life expectancy period, $14.73 on account of the estate tax attributable to the value for estate tax purposes of that portion of the annuity payments considered income in respect of a decedent, computed as follows:

Reg. § 1.691(d)-1(e)

(1)	(i) Value of income described in section 691(a)(1) included in computing gross estate ...	$ 4,380.00
	(ii) Deductions in computing gross estate for claims representing deductions described in section 691(b)	380.00
	(iii) Net value of items described in section 691(a)(1)	4,000.00
(2)	(i) Estate tax	53,525.00
	(ii) Less: Estate tax computed without including $4,000 (item (1)(iii)) in gross estate and by reducing marital deduction by $2,880 (portion of item (1)(iii) allowed as a marital deduction)..	53,189.00
	(iii) Portion of estate tax attributable to net value of income items	336.00
(3)	(i) Value in gross estate of income attributable to annuity payments	2,880.00
	(ii) Value in gross estate of all income items described in section 691(a)(1) (item (1)(i)) .	4,380.00
	(iii) Part of estate tax attributable to annuity income (2,880/4,380 of $336)	220.93
	(iv) Deduction each year on account of estate tax attributable to annuity income ($220.93 ÷ 15 (life expectancy period))	14.73

[Reg. § 1.691(d)-1.]

☐ [T.D. 6257, 10-7-57.]

[Reg. § 1.691(e)-1]

§ 1.691(e)-1. **Installment obligations transmitted at death when prior law applied.**—(a) *In general*—(1) *Application of prior law.* Under section 44(d) of the Internal Revenue Code of 1939 and corresponding provisions of prior law, gains and losses on account of the transmission of installment obligations at the death of a holder of such obligations were required to be reported in the return of the decedent for the year of his death. However, an exception to this rule was provided if there was filed with the Commissioner a bond assuring the return as income of any payment in satisfaction of these obligations in the same proportion as would have been returnable as income by the decedent had he lived and received such payments. Obligations in respect of which such bond was filed are referred to in this section as "obligations assured by bond".

(2) *Application of present law.* Section 691(a)(4) of the Internal Revenue Code of 1954 (effective for taxable years beginning after December 31, 1953, and ending after August 16, 1954) in effect makes the exception which under prior law applied to obligations assured by bond the general rule for obligations transmitted at death, but contains no requirement for a bond. Section 691(e)(1) provides that if the holder of the installment obligation makes a proper election, the provisions of section 691(a)(4) shall apply in the case of obligations assured by bond. Section 691(e)(1) further provides that the estate tax deduction provided by section 691(c)(1) is not allowable for any amount included in gross income by reason of filing such an election.

(b) *Manner and scope of election*—(1) *In general.* The election to have obligations assured by bond treated as obligations to which section 691(a)(4) applies shall be made by the filing of a statement with respect to each bond to be released, containing the following information:

(i) The name and address of the decedent from whom the obligations assured by bond were transmitted, the date of his death, the internal revenue district in which the last income tax return of the decedent was filed.

(ii) A schedule of all obligations assured by the bond on which is listed—

(*a*) The name and address of the obligors, face amount, date of maturity, and manner of payment of each obligation,

(*b*) The name, identifying number (provided under section 6109 and the regulations thereunder), and address of each person holding the obligations, and

(*c*) The name, identifying number, and address, of each person who at the time of the election possesses an interest in each obligation, and a description of such interest.

(iii) The total amount of income in respect of the obligations which would have been reportable as income by the decedent if he had lived and received such payment.

(iv) The amount of income referred to in subdivision (iii) of this subparagraph which has previously been included in gross income.

(v) An unqualified statement, signed by all persons holding the obligations, that they elect to have the provisions of section 691(a)(4) apply to such obligations and that such election shall be binding upon them, all current beneficiaries, and any person to whom the obligations may be transmitted by gift, bequest, or inheritance.

(vi) A declaration that the election is made under the penalties of perjury.

(2) *Filing of statement.* The statement with respect to each bond to be released shall be filed in duplicate with the district director of internal revenue for the district in which the bond is maintained. The statement shall be filed not later than the time prescribed for filing the return for the first taxable year (including any extension of time for such filing) to which the election applies.

Reg. § 1.691(e)-1(a)(1)

(3) *Effect of election.* The election referred to in subparagraph (1) of this paragraph shall be irrevocable. Once an election is made with respect to an obligation assured by bond, it shall apply to all payments made in satisfaction of such obligation which were received during the first taxable year to which the election applies and to all such payments received during each taxable year thereafter, whether the recipient is the person who made the election, a current beneficiary, or a person to whom the obligation may be transmitted by gift, bequest, or inheritance. Therefore, all payments received to which the election applies shall be treated as payments made on installment obligations to which section 691(a)(4) applies. However, the estate tax deduction provided by section 691(c) is not allowable for any such payment. The application of this subparagraph may be illustrated by the following example:

Example. A, the holder of an installment obligation, died in 1952. The installment obligation was transmitted at A's death to B who filed a bond on Form 1132 pursuant to paragraph (c) of § 39.44-5 of Regulations 118 (26 CFR Part 39, 1939 ed.) for the necessary amount. On January 1, 1965, B, a calendar year taxpayer, filed an election under section 691(e) to treat the obligation assured by bond as an obligation to which section 691(a)(4) applies, and B's bond was released by 1964 and subsequent taxable years. B died on June 1, 1965, and the obligation was bequeathed to C. On January 1, 1966, C received an installment payment on the obligation which had been assured by the bond. Because B filed an election with respect to the obligation assured by bond, C is required to treat the proper proportion of the January 1, 1966, payment and all subsequent payments made in satisfaction of this obligation as income in respect of a decedent. However, no estate tax deduction is allowable to C under section 691(c)(1) for any estate tax attributable to the inclusion of the value of such obligation in the estate of either A or B.

(c) *Release of bond.* If an election according to the provisions of paragraph (b) of this section is filed, the liability under any bond filed under section 44(d) of the 1939 Code (or the corresponding provisions of prior law) shall be released with respect to each taxable year to which such election applies. However, the liability under any such bond for an earlier taxable year to which the election does not apply shall not be released until the district director of internal revenue for the district in which the bond is maintained is assured that the proper portion of each installment payment received in such taxable year has been reported and the tax thereon paid. [Reg. § 1.691(e)-1.]

☐ [*T.D.* 6808, 3-15-65.]

[Reg. § 1.691(f)-1]

§ **1.691(f)-1. Cross reference.**—See section 753 and the regulations thereunder for application of section 691 to income in respect of a deceased partner. [Reg. § 1.691(f)-1.]

☐ [*T.D.* 6257, 10-7-57. *Amended by T.D.* 6808, 3-15-65.]

[Reg. § 1.692-1]

§ **1.692-1. Abatement of income taxes of certain members of the Armed Forces of the United States upon death.**—(a)(1) This section applies if—

(i) An individual dies while in active service as a member of the Armed Forces of the United States, and

(ii) His death occurs while he is serving in a combat zone (as determined under section 112), or at any place as a result of wounds, disease, or injury incurred while he was serving in a combat zone.

(2) If an individual dies as described in paragraph (a)(1), the following liabilities for tax, under subtitle A of the Internal Revenue Code of 1954 or under chapter 1 of the Internal Revenue Code of 1939, are canceled:

(i) The liability of the deceased individual, for his last taxable year, ending on the date of his death, and for any prior taxable year ending on or after the first day he served in a combat zone in active service as a member of the U.S. Armed Forces after June 24, 1950, and

(ii) The liability of any other person to the extent the liability is attributable to an amount received after the individual's death (including income in respect of a decedent under section 691) which would have been includible in the individual's gross income for his taxable year in which the date of his death falls (determined as if he had survived).

If the tax (including interest, additions to the tax, and additional amounts) is assessed, the assessment will be abated. If the amount of the tax is collected (regardless of the date of collection), the amount so collected will be credited or refunded as an overpayment.

(3) If an individual dies as described in paragraph (a)(1), there will not be assessed any amount of tax of the individual for taxable years preceding the years specified in paragraph (a)(2), under subtitle A of the Internal Revenue Code of 1954, chapter 1 of the Internal Revenue Code of 1939, or corresponding provisions of prior revenue laws, remaining unpaid as of the date of death. If any such unpaid tax (including interest, additions

to the tax, and additional amounts) has been assessed, the assessments will be abated. If the amount of any such unpaid tax is collected after the date of death, the amount so collected will be credited or refunded as an overpayment.

(4) As to what constitutes active service as a member of the Armed Forces, service in a combat zone, and wounds, disease, or injury incurred while serving in a combat zone, see section 112. As to who are members of the Armed Forces, see section 7701(a)(15). As to the period of time within which any claim for refund must be filed, see sections 6511(a) and 7508(a)(1)(E).

(b) If such an individual and his spouse have for any such year filed a joint return, the tax abated, credited, or refunded pursuant to the provisions of section 692 for such year shall be an amount equal to that portion of the joint tax liability which is the same percentage of such joint tax liability as a tax computed upon the separate income of such individual is of the sum of the taxes computed upon the separate income of such individual and his spouse, but with respect to taxable years ending before June 24, 1950, and with respect to taxable years ending before the first day such individual served in a combat zone, as determined under section 112, the amount so abated, credited or refunded shall not exceed the amount unpaid at the date of death. For such purpose, the separate tax of each spouse—

(1) For taxable years beginning after December 31, 1953, and ending after August 16, 1954, shall be the tax computed under subtitle A of the Internal Revenue Code of 1954 before the application of sections 31, 32 6401(b), and 6402, but after the application of section 33, as if such spouse were required to make a separate income tax return; and

(2) For taxable years beginning before January 1, 1954, and for taxable years beginning after December 31, 1953, and ending before August 17, 1954, shall be the tax computed under chapter 1 of the Internal Revenue Code of 1939 before the application of sections 32, 35, and 322(a) but after the application of section 31, as if such spouse were required to make a separate income tax return.

(c) If such an individual and his spouse filed a joint declaration of estimated tax for the taxable year ending with the date of his death, the estimated tax paid pursuant to such declaration may be treated as the estimated tax of either such individual or his spouse, may be divided between them, in such manner as his legal representative and such spouse may agree. Should they agree to treat such estimated tax, or any portion thereof, as the estimated tax of such individual, the estimated tax so paid shall be credited or refunded as an overpayment for the taxable year ending with the date of his death.

(d) For the purpose of determining the tax which is unpaid at the date of death, amounts deducted and withheld under chapter 24, subtitle C of the Internal Revenue Code of 1954, or under subchapter D, chapter 9 of the Internal Revenue Code of 1939 (relating to income tax withheld at source on wages), constitute payment of tax imposed under subtitle A of the Internal Revenue Code of 1954 or under chapter 1 of the Internal Revenue Code of 1939, as the case may be.

(e) This section shall have no application whatsoever with respect to the liability of an individual as a transferee of property of a taxpayer where such liability relates to the tax imposed upon the taxpayer by subtitle A of the Internal Revenue Code of 1954 or by chapter 1 of the Internal Revenue Code of 1939. [Reg. § 1.692-1.]

☐ [*T.D. 6257, 10-7-57. Amended by T.D. 7543, 5-4-78.*]

PARTNERS AND PARTNERSHIPS

Determination of Tax Liability

[Reg. § 1.701-1]

§ 1.701-1. **Partners, not partnership, subject to tax.**—Partners are liable for income tax only in their separate capacities. Partnerships as such are not subject to the income tax imposed by subtitle A but are required to make returns of income under the provisions of section 6031 and the regulations thereunder. For definition of the terms "partner" and "partnership", see sections 761 and 7701(a)(2), and the regulations thereunder. For provisions relating to the election of certain partnerships to be taxed as domestic corporations, see section 1361 and the regulations thereunder. [Reg. § 1.701-1.]

☐ [*T.D. 6175, 5-23-56.*]

[Reg. § 1.701-2]

§ 1.701-2. **Anti-abuse rule.**—(a) *Intent of subchapter K.* Subchapter K is intended to permit taxpayers to conduct joint business (including investment) activities through a flexible economic arrangement without incurring an entity-level tax. Implicit in the intent of subchapter K are the following requirements—

Determination of Tax Liability

See p. 20,601 for regulations not amended to reflect law changes

(1) The partnership must be bona fide and each partnership transaction or series of related transactions (individually or collectively, the transaction) must be entered into for a substantial business purpose.

(2) The form of each partnership transaction must be respected under substance over form principles.

(3) Except as otherwise provided in this paragraph (a)(3), the tax consequences under subchapter K to each partner of partnership operations and of transactions between the partner and the partnership must accurately reflect the partners' economic agreement and clearly reflect the partner's income (collectively, *proper reflection of income*). However, certain provisions of subchapter K and the regulations thereunder were adopted to promote administrative convenience and other policy objectives, with the recognition that the application of those provisions to a transaction could, in some circumstances, produce tax results that do not properly reflect income. Thus, the proper reflection of income requirement of this paragraph (a)(3) is treated as satisfied with respect to a transaction that satisfies paragraphs (a)(1) and (2) of this section to the extent that the application of such a provision to the transaction and the ultimate tax results, taking into account all the relevant facts and circumstances, are clearly contemplated by that provision. See, for example, paragraph (d) *Example 6* of this section (relating to the value-equals-basis rule in § 1.704-1(b)(2)(iii)(*c*)), paragraph (d) *Example 9* of this section (relating to the election under section 754 to adjust basis in partnership property), and paragraph (d) *Examples 10 and 11* of this section (relating to the basis in property distributed by a partnership under section 732). See also, for example, §§ 1.704-3(e)(1) and 1.752-2(e)(4) (providing certain de minimis exceptions).

(b) *Application of subchapter K rules.* The provisions of subchapter K and the regulations thereunder must be applied in a manner that is consistent with the intent of subchapter K as set forth in paragraph (a) of this section (*intent of subchapter K*). Accordingly, if a partnership is formed or availed of in connection with a transaction a principal purpose of which is to reduce substantially the present value of the partners' aggregate federal tax liability in a manner that is inconsistent with the intent of subchapter K, the Commissioner can recast the transaction for federal tax purposes, as appropriate to achieve tax results that are consistent with the intent of subchapter K, in light of the applicable statutory and regulatory provisions and the pertinent facts and circumstances. Thus, even though the transaction may fall within the literal words of a particular statutory or regulatory provision, the Commissioner can determine, based on the particular facts and circumstances, that to achieve tax results that are consistent with the intent of subchapter K—

(1) The purported partnership should be disregarded in whole or in part, and the partnership's assets and activities should be considered, in whole or in part, to be owned and conducted, respectively, by one or more of its purported partners;

(2) One or more of the purported partners of the partnership should not be treated as a partner;

(3) The methods of accounting used by the partnership or a partner should be adjusted to reflect clearly the partnership's or the partner's income;

(4) The partnership's items of income, gain, loss, deduction, or credit should be reallocated; or

(5) The claimed tax treatment should otherwise be adjusted or modified.

(c) *Facts and circumstances analysis; factors.* Whether a partnership was formed or availed of with a principal purpose to reduce substantially the present value of the partners' aggregate federal tax liability in a manner inconsistent with the intent of subchapter K is determined based on all of the facts and circumstances, including a comparison of the purported business purpose for a transaction and the claimed tax benefits resulting from the transaction. The factors set forth below may be indicative, but do not necessarily establish, that a partnership was used in such a manner. These factors are illustrative only, and therefore may not be the only factors taken into account in making the determination under this section. Moreover, the weight given to any factor (whether specified in this paragraph or otherwise) depends on all the facts and circumstances. The presence or absence of any factor described in this paragraph does not create a presumption that a partnership was (or was not) used in such a manner. Factors include:

(1) The present value of the partners' aggregate federal tax liability is substantially less than had the partners owned the partnership's assets and conducted the partnership's activities directly;

(2) The present value of the partners' aggregate federal tax liability is substantially less than would be the case if purportedly separate transactions that are designed to achieve a particular end result are integrated and treated as steps in a

Reg. § 1.701-2(c)(2)

single transaction. For example, this analysis may indicate that it was contemplated that a partner who was necessary to achieve the intended tax results and whose interest in the partnership was liquidated or disposed of (in whole or in part) would be a partner only temporarily in order to provide the claimed tax benefits to the remaining partners;

(3) One or more partners who are necessary to achieve the claimed tax results either have a nominal interest in the partnership, are substantially protected from any risk of loss from the partnership's activities (through distribution preferences, indemnity or loss guaranty agreements, or other arrangements), or have little or no participation in the profits from the partnership's activities other than a preferred return that is in the nature of a payment for the use of capital;

(4) Substantially all of the partners (measured by number or interests in the partnership) are related (directly or indirectly) to one another;

(5) Partnership items are allocated in compliance with the literal language of §§ 1.704-1 and 1.704-2 but with results that are inconsistent with the purpose of section 704(b) and those regulations. In this regard, particular scrutiny will be paid to partnerships in which income or gain is specially allocated to one or more partners that may be legally or effectively exempt from federal taxation (for example, a foreign person, an exempt organization, an insolvent taxpayer, or a taxpayer with unused federal tax attributes such as net operating losses, capital losses, or foreign tax credits);

(6) The benefits and burdens of ownership of property nominally contributed to the partnership are in substantial part retained (directly or indirectly) by the contributing partner (or a related party); or

(7) The benefits and burdens of ownership of partnership property are in substantial part shifted (directly or indirectly) to the distributee partner before or after the property is actually distributed to the distributee partner (or a related party).

(d) *Examples.* The following examples illustrate the principles of paragraphs (a), (b), and (c) of this section. The examples set forth below do not delineate the boundaries of either permissible or impermissible types of transactions. Further, the addition of any facts or circumstances that are not specifically set forth in an example (or the deletion of any facts or circumstances) may alter the outcome of the transaction described in the example. Unless otherwise indicated, parties to the transactions are not related to one another.

Example 1. Choice of entity; avoidance of entity-level tax; use of partnership consistent with the intent of subchapter K. (i) A and B form limited partnership PRS to conduct a bona fide business. A, the corporate general partner, has a 1% partnership interest. B, the individual limited partner, has a 99% interest. PRS is properly classified as a partnership under §§ 301.7701-2 and 301.7701-3. A and B chose limited partnership form as a means to provide B with limited liability without subjecting the income from the business operations to an entity-level tax.

(ii) Subchapter K is intended to permit taxpayers to conduct joint business activity through a flexible economic arrangement without incurring an entity-level tax. See paragraph (a) of this section. Although B has retained, indirectly, substantially all of the benefits and burdens of ownership of the money or property B contributed to PRS (see paragraph (c)(6) of this section), the decision to organize and conduct business through PRS under these circumstances is consistent with this intent. In addition, on these facts, the requirements of paragraphs (a)(1), (2), and (3) of this section have been satisfied. The Commissioner therefore cannot invoke paragraph (b) of this section to recast the transaction.

Example 2. Choice of entity; avoidance of subchapter S shareholder requirements; use of partnership consistent with the intent of subchapter K. (i) A and B form partnership PRS to conduct a bona fide business. A is a corporation that has elected to be treated as an S corporation under subchapter S. B is a nonresident alien. PRS is properly classified as a partnership under §§ 301.7701-2 and 301.7701-3. Because section 1361(b) prohibits B from being a shareholder in A, A and B chose partnership form, rather than admit B as a shareholder in A, as a means to retain the benefits of subchapter S treatment for A and its shareholders.

(ii) Subchapter K is intended to permit taxpayers to conduct joint business activity through a flexible economic arrangement without incurring an entity-level tax. See paragraph (a) of this section. The decision to organize and conduct business through PRS is consistent with this intent. In addition, on these facts, the requirements of paragraphs (a)(1), (2), and (3) of this section have been satisfied. Although it may be argued that the form of the partnership transaction should not be respected because it does not reflect its substance (inasmuch as application of the substance over form doctrine arguably could result in B being treated as a shareholder of A, thereby invalidating A's subchapter S election), the facts indicate otherwise. The shareholders of A are subject to tax

Reg. § 1.701-2(c)(3)

Determination of Tax Liability

on their pro rata shares of A's income (see section 1361 et. seq.), and B is subject to tax on B's distributive share of partnership income (see sections 871 and 875). Thus, the form in which this arrangement is cast accurately reflects its substance as a separate partnership and S corporation. The Commissioner therefore cannot invoke paragraph (b) of this section to recast the transaction.

Example 3. Choice of entity; avoidance of more restrictive foreign tax credit limitation; use of partnership consistent with the intent of subchapter K. (i) X, a domestic corporation, and Y, a foreign corporation, form partnership PRS under the laws of foreign Country A to conduct a bona fide joint business. X and Y each owns a 50% interest in PRS. PRS is properly classified as a partnership under §§ 301.7701-2 and 301.7701-3. PRS pays income taxes to Country A. X and Y chose partnership form to enable X to qualify for a direct foreign tax credit under section 901, with look-through treatment under § 1.904-5(h)(1). Conversely, if PRS were a foreign corporation for U.S. tax purposes, X would be entitled only to indirect foreign tax credits under section 902 with respect to dividend distributions from PRS. The look-through rules, however, would not apply, and pursuant to section 904(d)(1)(E) and § 1.904-4(g), the dividends and associated taxes would be subject to a separate foreign tax credit limitation for dividends from PRS, a noncontrolled section 902 corporation.

(ii) Subchapter K is intended to permit taxpayers to conduct joint business activity through a flexible economic arrangement without incurring an entity-level tax. See paragraph (a) of this section. The decision to organize and conduct business through PRS in order to take advantage of the look-through rules for foreign tax credit purposes, thereby maximizing X's use of its proper share of foreign taxes paid by PRS, is consistent with this intent. In addition, on these facts, the requirements of paragraphs (a)(1), (2), and (3) of this section have been satisfied. The Commissioner therefore cannot invoke paragraph (b) of this section to recast the transaction.

Example 4. Choice of entity; avoidance of gain recognition under sections 351(e) and 357(c); use of partnership consistent with the intent of subchapter K. (i) X, ABC, and DEF form limited partnership PRS to conduct a bona fide real estate management business. PRS is properly classified as a partnership under §§ 301.7701-2 and 301.7701-3. X, the general partner, is a newly formed corporation that elects to be treated as a real estate investment trust as defined in section 856. X offers its stock to the public and contributes substantially all of the proceeds from the public offering to PRS. ABC and DEF, the limited partners, are existing partnerships with substantial real estate holdings. ABC and DEF contribute all of their real property assets to PRS, subject to liabilities that exceed their respective aggregate bases in the real property contributed, and terminate under section 708(b)(1)(A). In addition, some of the former partners of ABC and DEF each have the right, beginning two years after the formation of PRS, to require the redemption of their limited partnership interests in PRS in exchange for cash or X stock (at X's option) equal to the fair market value of their respective interests in PRS at the time of the redemption. These partners are not compelled, as a legal or practical matter, to exercise their exchange rights at any time. X, ABC, and DEF chose to form a partnership rather than have ABC and DEF invest directly in X to allow ABC and DEF to avoid recognition of gain under sections 351(e) and 357(c). Because PRS would not be treated as an investment company within the meaning of section 351(e) if PRS were incorporated (so long as it did not elect under section 856), section 721(a) applies to the contribution of the real property to PRS. See section 721(b).

(ii) Subchapter K is intended to permit taxpayers to conduct joint business activity through a flexible economic arrangement without incurring an entity-level tax. See paragraph (a) of this section. The decision to organize and conduct business through PRS, thereby avoiding the tax consequences that would have resulted from contributing the existing partnerships' real estate assets to X (by applying the rules of sections 721, 731, and 752 in lieu of the rules of sections 351(e) and 357(c)), is consistent with this intent. In addition, on these facts, the requirements of paragraphs (a)(1), (2), and (3) of this section have been satisfied. Although it may be argued that the form of the transaction should not be respected because it does not reflect its substance (inasmuch as the present value of the partners' aggregate federal tax liability is substantially less than would be the case if the transaction were integrated and treated as a contribution of the encumbered assets by ABC and DEF directly to X, see paragraph (c)(2) of this section), the facts indicate otherwise. For example, the right of some of the former ABC and DEF partners after two years to exchange their PRS interests for cash or X stock (at X's option) equal to the fair market value of their PRS interest at that time would not require that right to be considered as exercised prior to its actual exercise. Moreover, X may make other real estate investments and other business decisions, including the decision to raise ad-

Reg. § 1.701-2(d)

ditional capital for those purposes. Thus, although it may be likely that some or all of the partners with the right to do so will, at some point, exercise their exchange rights, and thereby receive either cash or X stock, the form of the transaction as a separate partnership and real estate investment trust is respected under substance over form principles (see paragraph (a)(2) of this section). The Commissioner therefore cannot invoke paragraph (b) of this section to recast the transaction.

Example 5. Special allocations; dividends received deductions; use of partnership consistent with the intent of subchapter K. (i) Corporations X and Y contribute equal amounts to PRS, a bona fide partnership formed to make joint investments. PRS pays $100x for a share of common stock of Z, an unrelated corporation, which has historically paid an annual dividend of $6x. PRS specially allocates the dividend income on the Z stock to X to the extent of the London Inter-Bank Offered Rate (LIBOR) on the record date, applied to X's contribution of $50x, and allocates the remainder of the dividend income to Y. All other items of partnership income and loss are allocated equally between X and Y. The allocations under the partnership agreement have substantial economic effect within the meaning of § 1.704-1(b)(2). In addition to avoiding an entity-level tax, a principal purpose for the formation of the partnership was to invest in the Z common stock and to allocate the dividend income from the stock to provide X with a floating-rate return based on LIBOR, while permitting X and Y to claim the dividends received deduction under section 243 on the dividends allocated to each of them.

(ii) Subchapter K is intended to permit taxpayers to conduct joint business activity through a flexible economic arrangement without incurring an entity-level tax. See paragraph (a) of this section. The decision to organize and conduct business through PRS is consistent with this intent. In addition, on these facts, the requirements of paragraphs (a)(1), (2), and (3) of this section have been satisfied. Section 704(b) and § 1.704-1(b)(2) permit income realized by the partnership to be allocated validly to the partners separate from the partners' respective ownership of the capital to which the allocations relate, provided that the allocations satisfy both the literal requirements of the statute and regulations and the purpose of those provisions (see paragraph (c)(5) of this section). Section 704(e)(2) is not applicable to the facts of this example (otherwise, the allocations would be required to be proportionate to the partners' ownership of contributed capital). The Commissioner therefore cannot invoke paragraph (b) of this section to recast the transaction.

Example 6. Special allocations; nonrecourse financing; low-income housing credit; use of partnership consistent with the intent of subchapter K. (i) A and B, high-bracket taxpayers, and X, a corporation with net operating loss carryforwards, form general partnership PRS to own and operate a building that qualifies for the low-income housing credit provided by section 42. The project is financed with both cash contributions from the partners and nonrecourse indebtedness. The partnership agreement provides for special allocations of income and deductions, including the allocation of all depreciation deductions attributable to the building to A and B equally in a manner that is reasonably consistent with allocations that have substantial economic effect of some other significant partnership item attributable to the building. The section 42 credits are allocated to A and B in accordance with the allocation of depreciation deductions. PRS's allocations comply with all applicable regulations, including the requirements of §§ 1.704-1(b)(2)(ii) (pertaining to economic effect) and 1.704-2(e) (requirements for allocations of nonrecourse deductions). The nonrecourse indebtedness is validly allocated to the partners under the rules of § 1.752-3, thereby increasing the basis of the partners' respective partnership interests. The basis increase created by the nonrecourse indebtedness enables A and B to deduct their distributive share of losses from the partnership (subject to all other applicable limitations under the Internal Revenue Code) against their nonpartnership income and to apply the credits against their tax liability.

(ii) At a time when the depreciation deductions attributable to the building are not treated as nonrecourse deductions under § 1.704-2(c) (because there is no net increase in partnership minimum gain during the year), the special allocation of depreciation deductions to A and B has substantial economic effect because of the value-equals-basis safe harbor contained in § 1.704-1(b)(2)(iii)(*c*) and the fact that A and B would bear the economic burden of any decline in the value of the building (to the extent of the partnership's investment in the building), notwithstanding that A and B believe it is unlikely that the building will decline in value (and, accordingly, they anticipate significant timing benefits through the special allocation). Moreover, in later years, when the depreciation deductions attributable to the building are treated as nonrecourse deductions under § 1.704-2(c), the special allocation of depreciation deductions to A and B is considered to be consistent with the partners' interests in the partnership under § 1.704-2(e).

(iii) Subchapter K is intended to permit taxpayers to conduct joint business activity through a flexible economic arrangement without incurring an entity-level tax. See paragraph (a) of this section. The decision to organize and conduct business through PRS is consistent with this intent. In addition, on these facts, the requirements of paragraphs (a)(1), (2), and (3) of this section have been satisfied. Section 704(b), § 1.704-1(b)(2), and § 1.704-2(e) allow partnership items of income, gain, loss, deduction, and credit to be allocated validly to the partners separate from the partners' respective ownership of the capital to which the allocations relate, provided that the allocations satisfy both the literal requirements of the statute and regulations and the purpose of those provisions (see paragraph (c)(5) of this section). Moreover, the application of the value-equals-basis safe harbor and the provisions of § 1.704-2(e) with respect to the allocations to A and B, and the tax results of the application of those provisions, taking into account all the facts and circumstances, are clearly contemplated. Accordingly, even if the allocations would not otherwise be considered to satisfy the proper reflection of income standard in paragraph (a)(3) of this section, that requirement will be treated as satisfied under these facts. Thus, even though the partners' aggregate federal tax liability may be substantially less than had the partners owned the partnership's assets directly (due to X's inability to use its allocable share of the partnership's losses and credits) (see paragraph (c)(1) of this section), the transaction is not inconsistent with the intent of subchapter K. The Commissioner therefore cannot invoke paragraph (b) of this section to recast the transaction.

Example 7. Partner with nominal interest; temporary partner; use of partnership not consistent with the intent of subchapter K. (i) Pursuant to a plan a principal purpose of which is to generate artificial losses and thereby shelter from federal taxation a substantial amount of income, X (a foreign corporation), Y (a domestic corporation), and Z (a promoter) form partnership PRS by contributing $9,000x, $990x, and $10x, respectively, for proportionate interests (90.0%, 9.9%, and 0.1%, respectively) in the capital and profits of PRS. PRS purchases offshore equipment for $10,000x and validly leases the equipment offshore for a term representing most of its projected useful life. Shortly thereafter, PRS sells its rights to receive income under the lease to a third party for $9,000x, and allocates the resulting $9,000x of income $8,100x to X, $891x to Y, and $9x to Z. PRS thereafter makes a distribution of $9,000x to X in complete liquidation of its interest. Under § 1.704-1(b)(2)(iv)(f), PRS restates the partners' capital accounts immediately before making the liquidating distribution to X to reflect its assets consisting of the offshore equipment worth $1,000x and $9,000x in cash. Thus, because the capital accounts immediately before the distribution reflect assets of $19,000x (that is, the initial capital contributions of $10,000x plus the $9,000x of income realized from the sale of the lease), PRS allocates a $9,000x book loss among the partners (for capital account purposes only), resulting in restated capital accounts for X, Y, and Z of $9,000x, $990x, and $10x, respectively. Thereafter, PRS purchases real property by borrowing the $8,000x purchase price on a recourse basis, which increases Y's and Z's bases in their respective partnership interests from $1,881x and $19x, to $9,801x and $99x, respectively (reflecting Y's and Z's adjusted interests in the partnership of 99% and 1%, respectively). PRS subsequently sells the offshore equipment, subject to the lease, for $1,000x and allocates the $9,000x tax loss $8,910x to Y and $90x to Z. Y's and Z's bases in their partnership interests are therefore reduced to $891x and $9x, respectively.

(ii) On these facts, any purported business purpose for the transaction is insignificant in comparison to the tax benefits that would result if the transaction were respected for federal tax purposes (see paragraph (c) of this section). Accordingly, the transaction lacks a substantial business purpose (see paragraph (a)(1) of this section). In addition, factors (1), (2), (3), and (5) of paragraph (c) of this section indicate that PRS was used with a principal purpose to reduce substantially the partners' tax liability in a manner inconsistent with the intent of subchapter K. On these facts, PRS is not bona fide (see paragraph (a)(1) of this section), and the transaction is not respected under applicable substance over form principles (see paragraph (a)(2) of this section) and does not properly reflect the income of Y (see paragraph (a)(3) of this section). Thus, PRS has been formed and availed of with a principal purpose of reducing substantially the present value of the partners' aggregate federal tax liability in a manner inconsistent with the intent of subchapter K. Therefore (in addition to possibly challenging the transaction under judicial principles or the validity of the allocations under § 1.704-1(b)(2) (see paragraph (h) of this section)), the Commissioner can recast the transaction as appropriate under paragraph (b) of this section.

Example 8. Plan to duplicate losses through absence of section 754 election; use of partnership not consistent with the intent of subchapter K. (i) A owns land with a basis of $100x and a fair market value of $60x. A would like to sell the land to B. A and B devise a plan a principal purpose of which is to permit the duplication, for a substantial period of time, of the tax benefit of A's built-

Reg. § 1.701-2(d)

in loss in the land. To effect this plan, A, C (A's brother), and W (C's wife) form partnership PRS, to which A contributes the land, and C and W each contribute $30x. All partnership items are shared in proportion to the partners' respective contributions to PRS. PRS invests the cash in an investment asset (that is not a marketable security within the meaning of section 731(c)). PRS also leases the land to B under a three-year lease pursuant to which B has the option to purchase the land from PRS upon the expiration of the lease for an amount equal to its fair market value at that time. All lease proceeds received are immediately distributed to the partners. In year 3, at a time when the values of the partnership's assets have not materially changed, PRS agrees with A to liquidate A's interest in exchange for the investment asset held by PRS. Under section 732(b), A's basis in the asset distributed equals $100x, A's basis in A's partnership interest immediately before the distribution. Shortly thereafter, A sells the investment asset to X, an unrelated party, recognizing a $40x loss.

(ii) PRS does not make an election under section 754. Accordingly, PRS's basis in the land contributed by A remains $100x. At the end of year 3, pursuant to the lease option, PRS sells the land to B for $60x (its fair market value). Thus, PRS recognizes a $40x loss on the sale, which is allocated equally between C and W. C's and W's bases in their partnership interests are reduced to $10x each pursuant to section 705. Their respective interests are worth $30x each. Thus, upon liquidation of PRS (or their interests therein), each of C and W will recognize $20x of gain. However, PRS's continued existence defers recognition of that gain indefinitely. Thus, if this arrangement is respected, C and W duplicate for their benefit A's built-in loss in the land prior to its contribution to PRS.

(iii) On these facts, any purported business purpose for the transaction is insignificant in comparison to the tax benefits that would result if the transaction were respected for federal tax purposes (see paragraph (c) of this section). Accordingly, the transaction lacks a substantial business purpose (see paragraph (a)(1) of this section). In addition, factors (1), (2), and (4) of paragraph (c) of this section indicate that PRS was used with a principal purpose to reduce substantially the partners' tax liability in a manner inconsistent with the intent of subchapter K. On these facts, PRS is not bona fide (see paragraph (a)(1) of this section), and the transaction is not respected under applicable substance over form principles (see paragraph (a)(2) of this section). Further, the tax consequences to the partners do not properly reflect the partners' income; and Congress did not contemplate application of section 754 to partnerships such as PRS, which was formed for a principal purpose of producing a double tax benefit from a single economic loss (see paragraph (a)(3) of this section). Thus, PRS has been formed and availed of with a principal purpose of reducing substantially the present value of the partners' aggregate federal tax liability in a manner inconsistent with the intent of subchapter K. Therefore (in addition to possibly challenging the transaction under judicial principles or other statutory authorities, such as the substance over form doctrine or the disguised sale rules under section 707 (see paragraph (h) of this section)), the Commissioner can recast the transaction as appropriate under paragraph (b) of this section.

Example 9. Absence of section 754 election; use of partnership consistent with the intent of subchapter K. (i) PRS is a bona fide partnership formed to engage in investment activities with contributions of cash from each partner. Several years after joining PRS, A, a partner with a capital account balance and basis in its partnership interest of $100x, wishes to withdraw from PRS. The partnership agreement entitles A to receive the balance of A's capital account in cash or securities owned by PRS at the time of withdrawal, as mutually agreed to by A and the managing general partner, P. P and A agree to distribute to A $100x worth of non-marketable securities (see section 731(c)) in which PRS has an aggregate basis of $20x. Upon distribution, A's aggregate basis in the securities is $100x under section 732(b). PRS does not make an election to adjust the basis in its remaining assets under section 754. Thus, PRS's basis in its remaining assets is unaffected by the distribution. In contrast, if a section 754 election had been in effect for the year of the distribution, under these facts section 734(b) would have required PRS to adjust the basis in its remaining assets downward by the amount of the untaxed appreciation in the distributed property, thus reflecting that gain in PRS's retained assets. In selecting the assets to be distributed, A and P had a principal purpose to take advantage of the facts that (i) A's basis in the securities will be determined by reference to A's basis in its partnership interest under section 732(b), and (ii) because PRS will not make an election under section 754, the remaining partners of PRS will likely enjoy a federal tax timing advantage (i.e., from the $80x of additional basis in its assets that would have been eliminated if the section 754 election had been made) that is inconsistent with proper reflection of income under paragraph (a)(3) of this section.

(ii) Subchapter K is intended to permit taxpayers to conduct joint business activity through a

Reg. § 1.701-2(d)

flexible economic arrangement without incurring an entity-level tax. See paragraph (a) of this section. The decision to organize and conduct business through PRS is consistent with this intent. In addition, on these facts, the requirements of paragraphs (a)(1) and (2) of this section have been satisfied. The validity of the tax treatment of this transaction is therefore dependent upon whether the transaction satisfies (or is treated as satisfying) the proper reflection of income standard under paragraph (a)(3) of this section. A's basis in the distributed securities is properly determined under section 732(b). The benefit to the remaining partners is a result of PRS not having made an election under section 754. Subchapter K is generally intended to produce tax consequences that achieve proper reflection of income. However, paragraph (a)(3) of this section provides that if the application of a provision of subchapter K produces tax results that do not properly reflect income, but application of that provision to the transaction and the ultimate tax results, taking into account all the relevant facts and circumstances, are clearly contemplated by that provision (and the transaction satisfies the requirements of paragraphs (a)(1) and (2) of this section), then the application of that provision to the transaction will be treated as satisfying the proper reflection of income standard.

(iii) In general, the adjustments that would be made if an election under section 754 were in effect are necessary to minimize distortions between the partners' bases in their partnership interests and the partnership's basis in its assets following, for example, a distribution to a partner. The electivity of section 754 is intended to provide administrative convenience for bona fide partnerships that are engaged in transactions for a substantial business purpose, by providing those partnerships the option of not adjusting their bases in their remaining assets following a distribution to a partner. Congress clearly recognized that if the section 754 election were not made, basis distortions may result. Taking into account all the facts and circumstances of the transaction, the electivity of section 754 in the context of the distribution from PRS to A, and the ultimate tax consequences that follow from the failure to make the election with respect to the transaction, are clearly contemplated by section 754. Thus, the tax consequences of this transaction will be treated as satisfying the proper reflection of income standard under paragraph (a)(3) of this section. The Commissioner therefore cannot invoke paragraph (b) of this section to recast the transaction.

Example 10. Basis adjustments under section 732; use of partnership consistent with the intent of subchapter K. (i) A, B, and C are partners in partnership PRS, which has for several years been engaged in substantial bona fide business activities. For valid business reasons, the partners agree that A's interest in PRS, which has a value and basis of $100x$, will be liquidated with the following assets of PRS: a nondepreciable asset with a value of $60x$ and a basis to PRS of $40x$, and related equipment with two years of cost recovery remaining and a value and basis to PRS of $40x$. Neither asset is described in section 751 and the transaction is not described in section 732(d). Under section 732(b) and (c), A's $100x$ basis in A's partnership interest will be allocated between the nondepreciable asset and the equipment received in the liquidating distribution in proportion to PRS's bases in those assets, or $50x$ to the nondepreciable asset and $50x$ to the equipment. Thus, A will have a $10x$ built-in gain in the nondepreciable asset ($60x$ value less $50x$ basis) and a $10x$ built-in loss in the equipment ($50x$ basis less $40x$ value), which it expects to recover rapidly through cost recovery deductions. In selecting the assets to be distributed to A, the partners had a principal purpose to take advantage of the fact that A's basis in the assets will be determined by reference to A's basis in A's partnership interest, thus, in effect, shifting a portion of A's basis from the nondepreciable asset to the equipment, which in turn would allow A to recover that portion of its basis more rapidly. This shift provides a federal tax timing advantage to A, with no offsetting detriment to B or C.

(ii) Subchapter K is intended to permit taxpayers to conduct joint business activity through a flexible economic arrangement without incurring an entity-level tax. See paragraph (a) of this section. The decision to organize and conduct business through PRS is consistent with this intent. In addition, on these facts, the requirements of paragraphs (a)(1) and (2) of this section have been satisfied. The validity of the tax treatment of this transaction is therefore dependent upon whether the transaction satisfies (or is treated as satisfying) the proper reflection of income standard under paragraph (a)(3) of this section. Subchapter K is generally intended to produce tax consequences that achieve proper reflection of income. However, paragraph (a)(3) of this section provides that if the application of a provision of subchapter K produces tax results that do not properly reflect income, but the application of that provision to the transaction and the ultimate tax results, taking into account all the relevant facts and circumstances, are clearly contemplated by that provision (and the transaction satisfies the requirements of paragraphs (a)(1) and (2) of this section), then the application of that provision to the transaction will be treated as satisfying the proper reflection of income standard.

(iii) A's basis in the assets distributed to it was determined under section 732(b) and (c). The transaction does not properly reflect A's income due to the basis distortions caused by the distribution and the shifting of basis from a nondepreciable to a depreciable asset. However, the basis rules under section 732, which in some situations can produce tax results that are inconsistent with the proper reflection of income standard (see paragraph (a)(3) of this section), are intended to provide simplifying administrative rules for bona fide partnerships that are engaged in transactions with a substantial business purpose. Taking into account all the facts and circumstances of the transaction, the application of the basis rules under section 732 to the distribution from PRS to A, and the ultimate tax consequences of the application of that provision of subchapter K, are clearly contemplated. Thus, the application of section 732 to this transaction will be treated as satisfying the proper reflection of income standard under paragraph (a)(3) of this section. The Commissioner therefore cannot invoke paragraph (b) of this section to recast the transaction.

Example 11. Basis adjustments under section 732; plan or arrangement to distort basis allocations artificially; use of partnership not consistent with the intent of subchapter K. (i) Partnership PRS has for several years been engaged in the development and management of commercial real estate projects. X, an unrelated party, desires to acquire undeveloped land owned by PRS, which has a value of $95x$ and a basis of $5x$. X expects to hold the land indefinitely after its acquisition. Pursuant to a plan a principal purpose of which is to permit X to acquire and hold the land but nevertheless to recover for tax purposes a substantial portion of the purchase price for the land, X contributes $100x$ to PRS for an interest therein. Subsequently (at a time when the value of the partnership's assets have not materially changed), PRS distributes to X in liquidation of its interest in PRS the land and another asset with a value and basis to PRS of $5x$. The second asset is an insignificant part of the economic transaction but is important to achieve the desired tax results. Under section 732(b) and (c), X's $100x$ basis in its partnership interest is allocated between the assets distributed to it in proportion to their bases to PRS, or $50x$ each. Thereafter, X plans to sell the second asset for its value of $5x$, recognizing a loss of $45x$. In this manner, X will, in effect, recover a substantial portion of the purchase price of the land almost immediately. In selecting the assets to be distributed to X, the partners had a principal purpose to take advantage of the fact that X's basis in the assets will be determined under section 732(b) and (c), thus, in effect, shifting a portion of X's basis economically allocable to the land that X intends to retain to an inconsequential asset that X intends to dispose of quickly. This shift provides a federal tax timing advantage to X, with no offsetting detriment to any of PRS's other partners.

(ii) Although section 732 recognizes that basis distortions can occur in certain situations, which may produce tax results that do not satisfy the proper reflection of income standard of paragraph (a)(3) of this section, the provision is intended only to provide ancillary, simplifying tax results for bona fide partnership transactions that are engaged in for substantial business purposes. Section 732 is not intended to serve as the basis for plans or arrangements in which inconsequential or immaterial assets are included in the distribution with a principal purpose of obtaining substantially favorable tax results by virtue of the statute's simplifying rules. The transaction does not properly reflect X's income due to the basis distortions caused by the distribution that result in shifting a significant portion of X's basis to this inconsequential asset. Moreover, the proper reflection of income standard contained in paragraph (a)(3) of this section is not treated as satisfied, because, taking into account all the facts and circumstances, the application of section 732 to this arrangement, and the ultimate tax consequences that would thereby result, were not clearly contemplated by that provision of subchapter K. In addition, by using a partnership (if respected), the partners' aggregate federal tax liability would be substantially less than had they owned the partnership's assets directly (see paragraph (c)(1) of this section). On these facts, PRS has been formed and availed of with a principal purpose to reduce the taxpayers' aggregate federal tax liability in a manner that is inconsistent with the intent of subchapter K. Therefore (in addition to possibly challenging the transaction under applicable judicial principles and statutory authorities, such as the disguised sale rules under section 707, see paragraph (h) of this section), the Commissioner can recast the transaction as appropriate under paragraph (b) of this section.

(e) *Abuse of entity treatment.*

(1) *General rule.* The Commissioner can treat a partnership as an aggregate of its partners in whole or in part as appropriate to carry out the purpose of any provision of the Internal Revenue Code or the regulations promulgated thereunder.

(2) *Clearly contemplated entity treatment.* Paragraph (e)(1) of this section does not apply to the extent that—

(i) A provision of the Internal Revenue Code or the regulations promulgated thereunder prescribes the treatment of a partnership as an entity, in whole or in part, and

(ii) That treatment and the ultimate tax results, taking into account all the relevant facts and circumstances, are clearly contemplated by that provision.

(f) *Examples.* The following examples illustrate the principles of paragraph (e) of this section. The examples set forth below do not delineate the boundaries of either permissible or impermissible types of transactions. Further, the addition of any facts or circumstances that are not specifically set forth in an example (or the deletion of any facts or circumstances) may alter the outcome of the transaction described in the example. Unless otherwise indicated, parties to the transactions are not related to one another.

Example 1. Aggregate treatment of partnership appropriate to carry out purpose of section 163(e)(5). (i) Corporations X and Y are partners in partnership PRS, which for several years has engaged in substantial bona fide business activities. As part of these business activities, PRS issues certain high yield discount obligations to an unrelated third party. Section 163(e)(5) defers (and in certain circumstances disallows) the interest deductions on this type of obligation if issued by a corporation. PRS, X, and Y take the position that, because PRS is a partnership and not a corporation, section 163(e)(5) is not applicable.

(ii) Section 163(e)(5) does not prescribe the treatment of a partnership as an entity for purposes of that section. The purpose of section 163(e)(5) is to limit corporate-level interest deductions on certain obligations. The treatment of PRS as an entity could result in a partnership with corporate partners issuing those obligations and thereby circumventing the purpose of section 163(e)(5), because the corporate partner would deduct its distributive share of the interest on obligations that would have been deferred until paid or disallowed had the corporation issued its share of the obligation directly. Thus, under paragraph (e)(1) of this section, PRS is properly treated as an aggregate of its partners for purposes of applying section 163(e)(5) (regardless of whether any party had a tax avoidance purpose in having PRS issue the obligation). Each partner of PRS will therefore be treated as issuing its share of the obligations for purposes of determining the deductibility of its distributive share of any interest on the obligations. See also section 163(i)(5)(B).

Example 2. Aggregate treatment of partnership appropriate to carry out purpose of section 1059.

(i) Corporations X and Y are partners in partnership PRS, which for several years has engaged in substantial bona fide business activities. As part of these business activities, PRS purchases 50 shares of Corporation Z common stock. Six months later, Corporation Z announces an extraordinary dividend (within the meaning of section 1059). Section 1059(a) generally provides that if any corporation receives an extraordinary dividend with respect to any share of stock and the corporation has not held the stock for more than two years before the dividend announcement date, the basis in the stock held by the corporation is reduced by the nontaxed portion of the dividend. PRS, X, and Y take the position that section 1059(a) is not applicable because PRS is a partnership and not a corporation.

(ii) Section 1059(a) does not prescribe the treatment of a partnership as an entity for purposes of that section. The purpose of section 1059(a) is to limit the benefits of the dividends received deduction with respect to extraordinary dividends. The treatment of PRS as an entity could result in corporate partners in the partnership receiving dividends through partnerships in circumvention of the intent of section 1059. Thus, under paragraph (e)(1) of this section, PRS is properly treated as an aggregate of its partners for purposes of applying section 1059 (regardless of whether any party had a tax avoidance purpose in acquiring the Z stock through PRS). Each partner of PRS will therefore be treated as owning its share of the stock. Accordingly, PRS must make appropriate adjustments to the basis of the Corporation Z stock, and the partners must also make adjustments to the basis in their respective interests in PRS under section 705(a)(2)(B). See also section 1059(g)(1).

Example 3. Prescribed entity treatment of partnership; determination of CFC status clearly contemplated. (i) X, a domestic corporation, and Y, a foreign corporation, intend to conduct a joint venture in foreign Country A. They form PRS, a bona fide domestic general partnership in which X owns a 40% interest and Y owns a 60% interest. PRS is properly classified as a partnership under §§ 301.7701-2 and 301.7701-3. PRS holds 100% of the voting stock of Z, a Country A entity that is classified as an association taxable as a corporation for federal tax purposes under § 301.7701-2. Z conducts its business operations in Country A. By investing in Z through a domestic partnership, X seeks to obtain the benefit of the look-through rules of section 904(d)(3) and, as a result, maximize its ability to claim credits for its proper share of Country A taxes expected to be incurred by Z.

Reg. § 1.701-2(f)

(ii) Pursuant to sections 957(c) and 7701(a)(30), PRS is a United States person. Therefore, because it owns 10% or more of the voting stock of Z, PRS satisfies the definition of a U.S. shareholder under section 951(b). Under section 957(a), Z is a controlled foreign corporation (CFC) because more than 50% of the voting power or value of its stock is owned by PRS. Consequently, under section 904(d)(3), X qualifies for look-through treatment in computing its credit for foreign taxes paid or accrued by Z. In contrast, if X and Y owned their interests in Z directly, Z would not be a CFC because only 40% of its stock would be owned by U.S. shareholders. X's credit for foreign taxes paid or accrued by Z in that case would be subject to a separate foreign tax credit limitation for dividends from Z, a noncontrolled section 902 corporation. See section 904(d)(1)(E) and § 1.904-4(g).

(iii) Sections 957(c) and 7701(a)(30) prescribe the treatment of a domestic partnership as an entity for purposes of defining a U.S. shareholder, and thus, for purposes of determining whether a foreign corporation is a CFC. The CFC rules prevent the deferral by U.S. shareholders of U.S. taxation of certain earnings of the CFC and reduce disparities that otherwise might occur between the amount of income subject to a particular foreign tax credit limitation when a taxpayer earns income abroad directly rather than indirectly through a CFC. The application of the look-through rules for foreign tax credit purposes is appropriately tied to CFC status. See sections 904(d)(2)(E) and 904(d)(3). This analysis confirms that Congress clearly contemplated that taxpayers could use a bona fide domestic partnership to subject themselves to the CFC regime, and the resulting application of the look-through rules of section 904(d)(3). Accordingly, under paragraph (e) of this section, the Commissioner cannot treat PRS as an aggregate of its partners for purposes of determining X's foreign tax credit limitation.

(g) *Effective date.* Paragraphs (a), (b), (c), and (d) of this section are effective for all transactions involving a partnership that occur on or after May 12, 1994. Paragraphs (e) and (f) of this section are effective for all transactions involving a partnership that occur on or after December 29, 1994.

(h) *Scope and application.* This section applies solely with respect to taxes under subtitle A of the Internal Revenue Code, and for purposes of this section, any reference to a federal tax is limited to any tax imposed under subtitle A of the Internal Revenue Code.

(i) *Application of nonstatutory principles and other statutory authorities.* The Commissioner can continue to assert and to rely upon applicable nonstatutory principles and other statutory and regulatory authorities to challenge transactions. This section does not limit the applicability of those principles and authorities. [Reg. § 1.701-2.]

☐ [*T.D.* 8588, 12-29-94. Amended by *T.D.* 8592, 4-12-95.]

[Reg. § 1.702-1]

§ 1.702-1. **Income and credits of partner.**—(a) *General rule.* Each partner is required to take into account separately in his return his distributive share, whether or not distributed, of each class or item of partnership income, gain, loss, deduction, or credit described in subparagraphs (1) through (9) of this paragraph. (For the taxable year in which a partner includes his distributive share of partnership taxable income, see section 706(a) and § 1.706-1(a). Such distributive share shall be determined as provided in section 704 and § 1.704-1.) Accordingly, in determining his income tax:

(1) Each partner shall take into account, as part of his gains and losses from sales or exchanges of capital assets held for not more than 1 year (6 months for taxable years beginning before 1977; 9 months for taxable years beginning in 1977), his distributive share of the combined net amount of such gains and losses of the partnership.

(2) Each partner shall take into account, as part of his gains and losses from sales or exchanges of capital assets held for more than 1 year (6 months for taxable years beginning before 1977; 9 months for taxable years beginning in 1977), his distributive share of the combined net amount of such gains and losses of the partnership.

(3) Each partner shall take into account, as part of his gains and losses from sales or exchanges of property described in section 1231 (relating to property used in the trade or business and involuntary conversions), his distributive share of the combined net amount of such gains and losses of the partnership. The partnership shall not combine such items with items set forth in subparagraph (1) or (2) of this paragraph.

(4) Each partner shall take into account, as part of the charitable contributions paid by him, his distributive share of each class of charitable contributions paid by the partnership within the partnership's taxable year. Section 170 determines the extent to which such amount may be allowed as a deduction to the partner. For the

definition of the term "charitable contribution", see section 170(c).

(5) Each partner shall take into account, as part of the dividends received by him from domestic corporations, his distributive share of dividends received by the partnership, with respect to which the partner is entitled to a credit under section 34 (for dividends received on or before December 31, 1964), an exclusion under section 116, or a deduction under part VIII, subchapter B, chapter 1 of the Code.

(6) Each partner shall take into account, as part of his taxes described in section 901 which have been paid or accrued to foreign countries or to possessions of the United States, his distributive share of such taxes which have been paid or accrued by the partnership, according to its method of treating such taxes. A partner may elect to treat his total amount of such taxes, including his distributive share of such taxes of the partnership, as a deduction under section 164 or as a credit under section 901, the subject to the provisions of sections 901 through 905.

(7) Each partner shall take into account, as part of the partially tax-exempt interest received by him on obligations of the United States or on obligations of instrumentalities of the United States, as described in section 35 or section 242, his distributive share of such partially tax-exempt interest received by the partnership. However, if the partnership elects to amortize premiums on bonds as provided in section 171, the amount received on such obligations by the partnership shall be reduced by the amortizable bond premium applicable to such obligations as provided in section 171(a)(3).

(8)(i) Each partner shall take into account separately, as part of any class of income, gain, loss, deduction, or credit, his distributive share of the following items: recoveries of bad debts, prior taxes, and delinquency amounts (section 111); gains and losses from wagering transactions (section 165(d)); soil and water conservation expenditures (section 175); nonbusiness expenses as described in section 212; medical, dental, etc., expenses (section 213); expenses for care of certain dependents (section 214); alimony, etc., payments (section 215); amounts representing taxes and interest paid to cooperative housing corporations (section 216); intangible drilling and developments costs (section 263(c)); pre-1970 exploration expenditures (section 615); certain mining exploration expenditures (section 617); income, gain, or loss to the partnership under section 751(b); and any items of income, gain, loss, deduction, or credit subject to a special allocation under the partnership agreement which differs from the allocation of partnership taxable income or loss generally.

(ii) Each partner must also take into account separately the partner's distributive share of any partnership item which, if separately taken into account by any partner, would result in an income tax liability for that partner, or for any other person, different from that which would result if that partner did not take the item into account separately. Thus, if any partner is a controlled foreign corporation, as defined in section 957, items of income that would be gross subpart F income if separately taken into account by the controlled foreign corporation must be separately stated for all partners. Under section 911(a), if any partner is a bona fide resident of a foreign country who may exclude from gross income the part of the partner's distributive share which qualifies as earned income, as defined in section 911(b), the earned income of the partnership for all partners must be separately stated. Similarly, all relevant items of income or deduction of the partnership must be separately stated for all partners in determining the applicability of section 183 (relating to activities not engaged in for profit) and the recomputation of tax thereunder for any partner. This paragraph (a)(8)(ii) applies to taxable years beginning on or after July 23, 2002.

(iii) Each partner shall aggregate the amount of his separate deductions or exclusions and his distributive share of partnership deductions or exclusions separately stated in determining the amount allowable to him of any deduction or exclusion under subtitle A of the Code as to which a limitation is imposed. For example, partner A has individual domestic exploration expenditures of $300,000. He is also a member of the AB partnership which in 1971, in its first year of operation has foreign exploration expenditures of $400,000. A's distributable share of this item is $200,000. However, the total amount of his distributable share that A can deduct as exploration expenditures under section 617(a) is limited to $100,000 in view of the limitation provided in section 617(h). Therefore, the excess of $100,000 ($200,000 minus $100,000) is not deductible by A.

(9) Each partner shall also take into account separately his distributive share of the taxable income or loss of the partnership, exclusive of items requiring separate computations under subparagraphs (1) through (8) of this paragraph. For limitation on allowance of a partner's distributive share of partnership losses, see section 704(d) and paragraph (d) of § 1.704-1.

(b) *Character of items constituting distributive share.* The character in the hands of a partner of

Reg. § 1.702-1(b)

any item of income, gain, loss, deduction, or credit described in section 702(a)(1) through (8) shall be determined as if such item were realized directly from the source from which realized by the partnership or incurred in the same manner as incurred by the partnership. For example, a partner's distributive share of gain from the sale of depreciable property used in the trade or business of the partnership shall be considered as gain from the sale of such depreciable property in the hands of the partner. Similarly, a partner's distributive share of partnership "hobby losses" (section 270) or his distributive share of partnership charitable contributions to organizations qualifying under section 170(b)(1)(A) retains such character in the hands of the partner.

(c) *Gross income of a partner.* (1) Where it is necessary to determine the amount or character of the gross income of a partner, his gross income shall include the partner's distributive share of the gross income of the partnership, that is, the amount of gross income of the partnership from which was derived the partner's distributive share of partnership taxable income or loss (including items described in section 702(a)(1) through (8)). For example, a partner is required to include his distributive share of partnership gross income:

(i) In computing his gross income for the purpose of determining the necessity of filing a return (section 6012(a));

(ii) In determining the application of the provisions permitting the spreading of income for services rendered over a 36-month period (section 1301, as in effect for taxable years beginning before January 1, 1964);

(iii) In computing the amount of gross income received from sources within possessions of the United States (section 931);

(iv) In determining a partner's "gross income from farming" (sections 175 and 6073); and

(v) In determining whether the de minimis or full inclusion rules of section 954(b)(3) apply.

(2) In determining the applicability of the 6-year period of limitation on assessment and collection provided in section 6501(e) (relating to omission of more than 25 percent of gross income), a partner's gross income includes his distributive share of partnership gross income (as described in section 6501(e)(1)(A)(i)). In this respect, the amount of partnership gross income from which was derived the partner's distributive share of any item of partnership income, gain, loss, deduction, or credit (as included or disclosed in the partner's return) is considered as an amount of gross income stated in the partner's return for the purposes of section 6501(e). For example, A, who is entitled to one-fourth of the profits of the ABCD partnership, which has $10,000 gross income and $2,000 taxable income, reports only $300 as his distributive share of partnership profits. A should have shown $500 as his distributive share of profits, which amount was derived from $2,500 of partnership gross income. However, since A included only $300 on his return without explaining in the return the difference of $200, he is regarded as having stated in his return only $1,500 ($300/$500 of $2,500) as gross income from the partnership.

(d) *Partners in community property States.* If separate returns are made by a husband and wife domiciled in a community property State, and only one spouse is a member of the partnership, the part of his or her distributive share of any item or items listed in paragraph (a)(1) through (9) of this section which is community property, or which is derived from community property, should be reported by the husband and wife in equal proportions.

(e) *Special rules on requirement to separately state meal, travel, and entertainment expenses.* Each partner shall take into account separately his or her distributive share of meal, travel, and entertainment expenses paid or incurred after December 31, 1986, by partnerships that have taxable years beginning before January 1, 1987, and ending with or within partners' taxable years beginning on or after January 1, 1987. In addition, with respect to skybox rentals under section 274(l)(2), each partner shall take into account separately his or her distributive share of rents paid or incurred after December 31, 1986, by partnerships that have taxable years beginning before January 1, 1989, and ending with or within partners' taxable years beginning on or after January 1, 1987.

(f) *Cross references.* For special rules in accordance with the principles of section 702 applicable solely for the purpose of the tax imposed by section 56 (relating to the minimum tax for tax preferences) see § 1.58-2(a). In the case of a disposition of an oil or gas property by the partnership, see the rules contained in section 613A(c)(7)(D) and § 1.613A-3(e). [Reg. § 1.702-1.]

☐ [T.D. 6175, 5-23-56. Amended by T.D. 6605, 8-14-62; T.D. 6777, 12-15-64; T.D. 6885, 6-1-66; T.D. 7192, 6-29-72; T.D. 7564, 9-11-78; T.D. 7728, 10-31-80; T.D. 8247, 4-5-89; T.D. 8348, 5-10-91 *and* T.D. 9008, 7-22-2002.]

[Reg. § 1.702-2]

§ 1.702-2. **Net operating loss deduction of partner.**—For the purpose of determining a net operating loss deduction under section 172, a partner shall take into account his distributive share of items of income, gain, loss, deduction, or credit of the partnership. The character of any such item shall be determined as if such item were realized directly from the source from which realized by the partnership, or incurred in the same manner as incurred by the partnership. See section 702(b) and paragraph (b) of § 1.702-1. To the extent necessary to determine the allowance under section 172(d)(4) of the nonbusiness deductions of a partner (arising from both partnership and nonpartnership sources), the partner shall separately take into account his distributive share of the deductions of the partnership which are not attributable to a trade or business and combine such amount with his nonbusiness deductions from nonpartnership sources. Such partner shall also separately take into account his distributive share of the gross income of the partnership not derived from a trade or business and combine such amount with his nonbusiness income from nonpartnership sources. See section 172 and the regulations thereunder. [Reg. § 1.702-2.]

☐ [T.D. 6175, 5-23-56.]

[Reg. § 1.702-3T]

§ 1.702-3T. 4-year spread (temporary).—(a) *Applicability.* This section applies to a partner in a partnership if—

(1) The partnership is required by section 806 of the Tax Reform Act of 1986 (the 1986 Act), Pub. L. No. 99-514, 100 Stat. 2362, to change its taxable year for the first taxable year beginning after December 31, 1986 (partnership's year of change); and

(2) As a result of such change in taxable year, items from more than one taxable year of the partnership would, but for the provisions of this section, be included in the taxable year of the partner with or within which the partnership's year of change ends.

(b) *Partner's treatment of items from the partnership's year of change*—(1) *In general.* Except as provided in paragraph (c) of this section, if a partner's share of "income items" exceeds the partner's share of "expense items," the partner's share of each and every income and expense item shall be taken into account ratably (and retain its character) over the partner's first 4 taxable years beginning with the partner's taxable year with or within which the partnership's year of change ends.

(2) *Definitions*—(i) *Income items.* For purposes of this section, the term "income items" means the sum of—

(A) The partner's distributive share of taxable income (exclusive of separately stated items) from the partnership's year of change,

(B) The partner's distributive share of all separately stated income or gain items from the partnership's year of change, and

(C) Any amount includible in the partner's income under section 707(c) on account of payments during the partnership's year of change.

(ii) *Expense items.* For purposes of this section, the term "expense items" means the sum of—

(A) The partner's distributive share of taxable loss (exclusive of separately stated items) from the partnership's year of change, and

(B) The partner's distributive share of all separately stated items of loss or deduction from the partnership's year of change.

(c) *Electing out of 4-year spread.* A partner may elect out of the rules of paragraph (b) of this section by meeting the requirements of § 301.9100-7T of this chapter (temporary regulations relating to elections under the Tax Reform Act of 1986).

(d) *Special rules for a partner that is a partnership or S corporation*—(1) *In general.* Except as provided in paragraph (d)(2) of this section, a partner that is a partnership or S corporation may, if otherwise eligible, use the 4-year spread (with respect to partnership interests owned by the partner) described in this section.

(2) *Certain partners prohibited from using 4-year spread*—(i) *In general.* Except as provided in paragraph (d)(2)(ii) of this section, a partner that is a partnership or S corporation may not use the 4-year spread (with respect to partnership interests owned by the partner) if such partner is also changing its taxable year pursuant to section 806 of the 1986 Act.

(ii) *Exception.* If a partner's year of change does not include any income or expense items with respect to the partnership's year of change, such partner may, if otherwise eligible, use the 4-year spread (with respect to such partnership interest) described in this section even though the partner is a partnership or S corporation. See examples (13) and (14) in paragraph (h) of this section.

(e) *Basis of partner's interest.* The basis of a partner's interest in a partnership shall be determined as if the partner elected not to spread the partnership items over 4 years, regardless of whether such election was in fact made. Thus, for example, if a partner is eligible for the 4-year spread and does not elect out of the 4-year spread pursuant to paragraph (c) of this section, the partner's basis in the partnership interest will be increased in the first year of the 4-year spread period by an amount equal to the excess of the income items over the expense items. However, the partner's basis will not be increased again, with respect to the unamortized income and expense items, as they are amortized over the 4-year spread period.

(f) *Effect on other provisions of the Code.* Except as provided in paragraph (e) of this section, determinations with respect to a partner, for purposes of other provisions of the Code, must be made with regard to the manner in which partnership items are taken into account under the rules of this section. Thus, for example, a partner who does not elect out of the 4-year spread must take into account, for purposes of determining net earnings from self-employment under section 1402(a) for a taxable year, only the ratable portion of partnership items for that taxable year.

(g) *Treatment of dispositions*—(1) *In general.* If a partnership interest is disposed of before the last taxable year in the 4-year spread period, unamortized income and expense items that are attributable to the interest disposed of and that would be taken into account by the partner for subsequent taxable years in the 4-year spread period shall be taken into account by the partner as determined under paragraph (g)(2) of this section. For purposes of this section, the term "disposed of" means any transfer, including (but not limited to) transfers by sale, exchange, gift, and by reason of death.

(2) *Year unamortized items taken into account.* (i) *In general.* If, at the end of a partner's taxable year, the fraction determined under paragraph (g)(2)(ii) of this section is—

(A) Greater than $2/3$, the partner must continue to take the unamortized income and expense items into account ratably over the 4-year spread period;

(B) Greater than $1/3$ but less than or equal to $2/3$, the partner must, in addition to its ratable amortization, take into account in such year 50 percent of the income and expense items that would otherwise be unamortized at the end of such year (however, this paragraph (g)(2)(i)(B) is only applied once with respect to a partner's interest in a particular partnership); or

(C) Less than or equal to $1/3$, the partner must take into account the entire balance of unamortized income and expense items in such year.

(ii) *Determination of fraction.* For purposes of paragraph (g)(2)(i) of this section, the numerator of the fraction is the partner's proportionate interest in the partnership at the end of the partner's taxable year and the denominator is the partner's proportionate interest in the partnership as of the last day of the partnership's year of change.

(h) *Examples.* The provisions of this section may be illustrated by the following examples.

Example (1). Assume that P1, a partnership with a taxable year ending September 30, is required by the 1986 Act to change its taxable year to a calendar year. All of the partners of P1 are individual taxpayers reporting on a calendar year. P1 is required to change to a calendar year for its taxable year beginning October 1, 1987, and to file a return for the short taxable year ending December 31, 1987. Based on the above facts, the partners of P1 are required to include the items from more than one taxable year of P1 in income for their 1987 taxable year. Thus, under paragraph (b) of this section, if a partner's share of income items exceeds the partner's share of expense items, the partner's share of each and every income and expense item shall be taken into account ratably by such partner in each of the partner's first four taxable years beginning with the partner's 1987 taxable year, unless such partner elects under paragraph (c) of this section to include all such amounts in his 1987 taxable year.

Example (2). Assume the same facts as in example (1), except P1 is a personal service corporation with all of its employee-owners reporting on a calendar year. Although P1 is required to change to a calendar year for its taxable year beginning October 1, 1987, neither P1 nor its employee-owners obtain the benefits of a 4-year spread. Pursuant to section 806 (e)(2)(C) of the 1986 Act, the 4-year spread provision is only applicable to short taxable years of partnerships and S corporations required to change their taxable year under the 1986 Act.

Example (3). Assume the same facts as example (1) and that I is one of the individual partners of P1. Further assume that I's distributive share of P1's taxable income for the short taxable year ended December 31, 1987 (*i.e.*, P1's year of change), is $10,000. In addition, I has $8,000 of separately stated expense from P1's year of change. Since I's income items (*i.e.*, $10,000 of taxable income) exceed I's expense items (*i.e.*, $8,000 of separately stated expense) attributable to P1's year of change, I is eligible for the 4-year spread provided by this section. If I does not elect out of the 4-year spread, I will recognize $2,500 of taxable income and $2,000 of separately stated expense in his 1987 calendar year return. Assuming I does not dispose of his partnership interest in P1 by December 31, 1989, the remaining $7,500 of taxable income and $6,000 of separately stated expense will be amortized (and retain its

Reg. § 1.702-3T(f)

character) over I's next three taxable years (*i.e.*, 1988, 1989 and 1990).

Example (4). Assume the same facts as example (3), except that I disposes of his entire interest in P1 during 1988. Pursuant to paragraph (g) of this section, I would recognize $7,500 of taxable income and $6,000 of separately stated expense in his 1988 calendar year return.

Example (5). Assume the same facts as in example (3), except that I disposes of 50 percent of his interest in P1 during 1989. Pursuant to paragraph (g) of this section, I would recognize $3,750 of taxable income in his 1989 calendar year return ($2,500 ratable portion for 1989 plus 50 percent of the $2,500 of income items that would otherwise be unamortized at the end of 1989). I would also recognize $3,000 of separately stated expense items in 1989 ($2,000 ratable portion for 1989 plus 50 percent of the $2,000 of separately stated expense items that would otherwise be unamortized at the end of 1989).

Example (6). Assume the same facts as in example (1), except that X, a personal service corporation as defined in section 441(i), is a partner of P1. X is a calendar year taxpayer, and thus is not required to change its taxable year under the 1986 Act. The same result occurs as in example 1 (*i.e.*, unless X elects to the contrary, X is required to include one fourth of its share of income and expense items from P1's year of change in the first four taxable years of X beginning with the 1987 taxable year).

Example (7). Assume the same facts as in example (6), except that X is a fiscal year personal service corporation with a taxable year ending September 30. X is required under the 1986 Act to change to a calendar year for its taxable year beginning October 1, 1987, and to file a return for its short year ending December 31, 1987. Based on the above facts, X is not required to include the items from more than one taxable year of P1 in any one taxable year of X. Thus, the provisions of this section do not apply to X, and X is required to include the full amount of income and expense items from P1's year of change in X's taxable income for X's short year ending December 31. Under section 443 of the Code, X is required to annualize the taxable income for its short year ending December 31, 1987.

Example (8). Assume that P2 is a partnership with a taxable year ending September 30. Under the 1986 Act, P2 would have been required to change its taxable year to a calendar year, effective for the taxable year beginning October 1, 1987. However, P2 properly changed its taxable year to a calendar year for the year beginning October 1, 1986, and filed a return for the short period ending December 31, 1986. The provisions of the 1986 Act do not apply to P2 because the short year ending December 31, 1986, was not required by the amendments made by section 806 of the 1986 Act. Thus, the partners of P2 are required to take all items of income and expense for the short taxable year with or within which such short year ends.

Example (9). Assume that P3 is a partnership with a taxable year ending March 31 and I, a calendar year individual, is a partner in P3. Under the 1986 Act, P3 would have been required to change its taxable year to a calendar year. However, under Rev. Proc. 87-32, P3 establishes and changes to a natural business year beginning with the taxable year ending June 30, 1987. Thus, P3 is required to change its taxable year under section 806 of the 1986 Act, and I is required to include items from more than one taxable year of P3 in one of her taxable years. Furthermore, I's share of P3's income items exceeds her share of P3's expense items for the short period April 1, 1987 through June 30, 1987. Accordingly, under this section, unless I elects to the contrary, I is required to take one fourth of her share of items of income and expense from P3's short taxable year ending June 30, 1987 into account for her taxable year ending December 31, 1987.

Example (10). Assume that P4 is a partnership with a taxable year ending March 31. Y, a C corporation, owns a 51 percent interest in the profits and capital of P4. Y reports its income on the basis of a taxable year ending March 31. P4 establishes and changes to a natural business year beginning with the taxable year ending June 30, 1987, under Rev. Proc. 87-32. Under the above facts, P4 is not required to change its taxable year because its March 31 taxable year was the taxable year of Y, the partner owning a majority of the partnership's profits and capital. Therefore, the remaining partners of P4 owning 49 percent of the profits and capital are not permitted the 4-year spread of the items of income and expense with respect to the short year, even though they may be required to include their distributive share of P4's items from more than one taxable year in one of their years.

Example (11). Assume that X and Y are C corporations with taxable years ending June 30. Each owns a 50-percent interest in the profits and capital of partnership P5. P5 has a taxable year ending March 31. Assume that P5 cannot establish a business purpose in order to retain a taxable year ending March 31, and thus P5 must change to a June 30 taxable year, the taxable year of its partners. Furthermore, assume that X's share of P5's income items exceeds its share of P5's ex-

Reg. § 1.702-3T(h)

pense items for P5's short taxable year ending June 30, 1987. Unless X elects out of the 4-year spread, the taxable year ending June 30, 1987, is the first of the four taxable years in which X must take into account its share of the items of income and expense resulting from P5's short taxable year ending June 30, 1987.

Example (12). Assume that I, an individual who reports income on the basis of the calendar year, is a partner in two partnerships, P6 and P7. Both partnerships have a taxable year ending September 30. Neither partnership can establish a business purpose for retaining its taxable year. Consequently, each partnership will change its taxable year to December 31, for the taxable year beginning October 1, 1987. The election to avoid a 4-year spread is made at the partner level; in addition, a partner may make such elections on a partnership-by-partnership basis. Thus, assuming I is eligible to obtain the 4-year spread with respect to income and expense items from partnerships P6 and P7, I may use the 4-year spread with respect to items from P6, while not using the 4-year spread with respect to items from P7.

Example (13). I, an individual taxpayer using a calendar year, owns an interest in P8, a partnership using a taxable year ending June 30. Furthermore, P8 owns an interest in P9, a partnership with a taxable year ending March 31. Under section 806 of the 1986 Act, P8 will be required to change to a taxable year ending December 31, while P9 will be required to change to a taxable year ending June 30. As a result, P8's year of change will be July 1 through December 31, 1987, while P9's year of change will be from April 1 through June 30, 1987. Since P9's year of change does not end with or within P8's year of change, paragraph (d)(2) of this section does not prevent P8 from obtaining a 4-year spread with respect to its interest in P9.

Example (14). The facts are the same as in example (13), except that P9 has a taxable year ending September 30, and under the 1986 Act P9 is required to change to a taxable year ending December 31. Therefore, P9's year of change will be from October 1, 1987 through December 31, 1987. Although P8's year of change from July 1, 1987 through December 31, 1987 includes two taxable years of P9 (*i.e.,* October 1, 1986 through September 30, 1987 and October 1, 1987 through December 31, 1987), paragraph (d)(2) of this section prohibits P8 from using the 4-year spread with respect to its interest in P9, because P9's year of change ends with or within P8's year of change. [Temporary Reg. § 1.702-3T.]

☐ [*T.D. 8167, 12-18-87. Amended by T.D. 8435, 9-18-92.*]

[Reg. § 1.703-1]

§ 1.703-1. Partnership computations.—(a) *Income and deductions.* (1) The taxable income of a partnership shall be computed in the same manner as the taxable income of an individual, except as otherwise provided in this section. A partnership is required to state separately in its return the items described in section 702(a)(1) through (7) and, in addition, to attach to its return a statement setting forth separately those items described in section 702(a)(8) which the partner is required to take into account separately in determining his income tax. See paragraph (a)(8) of § 1.702-1. The partnership is further required to compute and to state separately in its return:

(i) As taxable income under section 702(a)(9), the total of all other items of gross income (not separately stated) over the total of all other allowable deductions (not separately stated), or

(ii) As loss under section 702(a)(9), the total of all other allowable deductions (not separately stated) over the total of all other items of gross income (not separately stated).

The taxable income or loss so computed shall be accounted for by the partners in accordance with their partnership agreement.

(2) The partnership is not allowed the following deductions:

(i) The standard deduction provided in section 141.

(ii) The deduction for personal exemptions provided in section 151.

(iii) The deduction provided in section 164(a) for taxes, described in section 901, paid or accrued to foreign countries or possessions of the United States. Each partner's distributive share of such taxes shall be accounted for separately by him as provided in section 702(a)(6).

(iv) The deduction for charitable contributions provided in section 170. Each partner is considered as having paid within his taxable year his distributive share of any contribution or gift, payment of which was actually made by the partnership within its taxable year ending within or with the partner's taxable year. This item shall be accounted for separately by the partners as provided in section 702(a)(4). See also paragraph (b) of § 1.702-1.

(v) The net operating loss deduction provided in section 172. See § 1.702-2.

(vi) The additional itemized deductions for individuals provided in Part VII of Subchapter B, Chapter 1 of the Code, as follows: expenses for production of income (section 212); medical, dental, etc., expenses (section 213); Expenses for care

Determination of Tax Liability 43,501

See p. 20,601 for regulations not amended to reflect law changes

of certain dependents (section 214); alimony, etc., payments (section 215); and amounts representing taxes and interest paid to cooperative housing corporation (section 216). However, see paragraph (a)(8) of § 1.702-1.

(vii) The deduction for depletion under section 611 with respect to domestic oil or gas which is produced after December 31, 1974, and to which gross income from the property is attributable after such year.

(viii) The deduction for capital gains provided by section 1202 and the deduction for capital loss carryover provided by section 1212.

(b) *Elections of the partnership*—(1) *General rule.* Any elections (other than those described in subparagraph (2) of this paragraph) affecting the computation of income derived from a partnership shall be made by the partnership. For example, elections of methods of accounting, of computing depreciation, of treating soil and water conservation expenditures, and the option to deduct as expenses intangible drilling and development costs, shall be made by the partnership and not by the partners separately. All partnership elections are applicable to all partners equally, but any election made by a partnership shall not apply to any partner's nonpartnership interests.

(2) *Exceptions:* (i) Each partner shall add his distributive share of taxes described in section 901 paid or accrued by the partnership to foreign countries or possessions of the United States (according to its method of treating such taxes) to any such taxes paid or accrued by him (according to his method of treating such taxes), and may elect to use the total amount either as a credit against tax or as a deduction from income.

(ii) Each partner shall add his distributive share of expenses described in section 615 or section 617 paid or accrued by the partnership to any such expenses paid or accrued by him and shall treat the total amount according to his method of treating such expenses, notwithstanding the treatment of the expenses by the partnership.

(iii) Each partner who is a nonresident alien individual or a foreign corporation shall add his distributive share of income derived by the partnership from real property located in the United States, as described in section 871(d)(1) or 882(d)(1), to any such income derived by him and may elect under § 1.871-10 to treat all such income as income which is effectively connected for the taxable year with the conduct of a trade or business in the United States. [Reg. § 1.703-1.]

☐ [*T.D. 6175, 5-23-56. Amended by T.D. 7192, 6-29-72, T.D. 7332, 12-20-74 and T.D. 8348, 5-10-91.*]

[Reg. § 1.704-1]

§ 1.704-1. **Partner's distributive share.**—(a) *Effect of partnership agreement.* A partner's distributive share of any item or class of items of income, gain, loss, deduction, or credit of the partnership shall be determined by the partnership agreement, unless otherwise provided by section 704 and paragraphs (b) through (e) of this section. For definition of partnership agreement see section 761(c).

(b) *Determination of partner's distributive share*—(0) *Cross-references.*

Heading	Section
Cross-references	1.704-1(b)(0)
In general	1.704-1(b)(1)
Basic principles	1.704-1(b)(1)(i)
Effective dates	1.704-1(b)(1)(ii)
Effect of other sections	1.704-1(b)(1)(iii)
Other possible tax consequences	1.704-1(b)(1)(iv)
Purported allocations	1.704-1(b)(1)(v)
Section 704(c) determinations	1.704-1(b)(1)(vi)
Bottom line allocations	1.704-1(b)(1)(vii)
Substantial economic effect	1.704-1(b)(2)
Two-part analysis	1.704-1(b)(2)(i)
Economic effect	1.704-1(b)(2)(ii)
Fundamental principles	1.704-1(b)(2)(ii)(*a*)
Three requirements	1.704-1(b)(2)(ii)(*b*)
Obligation to restore deficit	1.704-1(b)(2)(ii)(*c*)
Alternate test for economic effect	1.704-1(b)(2)(ii)(*d*)
Partial economic effect	1.704-1(b)(2)(ii)(*e*)
Reduction of obligation to restore	1.704-1(b)(2)(ii)(*f*)
Liquidation defined	1.704-1(b)(2)(ii)(*g*)
Partnership agreement defined	1.704-1(b)(2)(ii)(*h*)
Economic effect equivalence	1.704-1(b)(2)(ii)(*i*)
Substantiality	1.704-1(b)(2)(iii)
General rules	1.704-1(b)(2)(iii)(*a*)
Shifting tax consequences	1.704-1(b)(2)(iii)(*b*)
Transitory allocations	1.704-1(b)(2)(iii)(*c*)
Maintenance of capital accounts	1.704-1(b)(2)(iv)
In general	1.704-1(b)(2)(iv)(*a*)
Basic rules	1.704-1(b)(2)(iv)(*b*)
Treatment of liabilities	1.704-1(b)(2)(iv)(*c*)
Contributed property	1.704-1(b)(2)(iv)(*d*)
In general	1.704-1(b)(2)(iv)(*d*)(*1*)
Contribution of promissory notes	1.704-1(b)(2)(iv)(*d*)(*2*)
Section 704(c) considerations	1.704-1(b)(2)(iv)(*d*)(*3*)
Distributed property	1.704-1(b)(2)(iv)(*e*)
In general	1.704-1(b)(2)(iv)(*e*)(*1*)
Distribution of promissory notes	1.704-1(b)(2)(iv)(*e*)(*2*)
Revaluations of property	1.704-1(b)(2)(iv)(*f*)
Adjustments to reflect book value	1.704-1(b)(2)(iv)(*g*)
In general	1.704-1(b)(2)(iv)(*g*)(*1*)
Payables and receivables	1.704-1(b)(2)(iv)(*g*)(*2*)

Reg. § 1.704-1(b)(0)

Determining amount of book items ....
.... 1.704-1(b)(2)(iv)(g)(3)
Determinations of fair market value ....
.... 1.704-1(b)(2)(iv)(h)
Section 705(a)(2)(B) expenditures ....
.... 1.704-1(b)(2)(iv)(i)
In general .... 1.704-1(b)(2)(iv)(i)(1)
Expenses described in section 709 ....
.... 1.704-1(b)(2)(iv)(i)(2)
Disallowed losses ...... 1.704-1(b)(2)(iv)(i)(3)
Basis adjustments to section 38 property ......
.... 1.704-1(b)(2)(iv)(j)
Depletion of oil and gas properties ....
.... 1.704-1(b)(2)(iv)(k)
In general .... 1.704-1(b)(2)(iv)(k)(1)
Simulated depletion ... 1.704-1(b)(2)(iv)(k)(2)
Actual depletion ...... 1.704-1(b)(2)(iv)(k)(3)
Effect of book values .. 1.704-1(b)(2)(iv)(k)(4)
Transfers of partnership interests ....
.... 1.704-1(b)(2)(iv)(l)
Section 754 elections ...... 1.704-1(b)(2)(iv)(m)
In general .... 1.704-1(b)(2)(iv)(m)(1)
Section 743 adjustments....................
.... 1.704-1(b)(2)(iv)(m)(2)
Section 732 adjustments....................
.... 1.704-1(b)(2)(iv)(m)(3)
Section 734 adjustments....................
.... 1.704-1(b)(2)(iv)(m)(4)
Limitations on adjustments ....
.... 1.704-1(b)(2)(iv)(m)(5)
Partnership level characterization ....
.... 1.704-1(b)(2)(iv)(n)
Guaranteed payments ...... 1.704-1(b)(2)(iv)(o)
Minor discrepancies .... 1.704-1(b)(2)(iv)(p)
Adjustments where guidance is lacking ....
.... 1.704-1(b)(2)(iv)(q)
Restatement of capital accounts ....
.... 1.704-1(b)(2)(iv)(r)
Partner's interest in the partnership .. 1.704-1(b)(3)
In general .... 1.704-1(b)(3)(i)
Factors considered .... 1.704-1(b)(3)(ii)
Certain determinations .... 1.704-1(b)(3)(iii)
Special rules .... 1.704-1(b)(4)
Allocations to reflect revaluations 1.704-1(b)(4)(i)
Credits .... 1.704-1(b)(4)(ii)
Excess percentage depletion ... 1.704-1(b)(4)(iii)
Allocations attributable to nonrecourse liabilities .
.... 1.704-1(b)(4)(iv)
Allocations under section 613A(c)(7)(D) ....
.... 1.704-1(b)(4)(v)
Amendments to partnership agreement ....
.... 1.704-1(b)(4)(vi)
Recapture................... 1.704-1(b)(4)(vii)
Examples .... 1.704-1(b)(5)

(1) *In general*—(i) *Basic principles.* Under section 704(b) if a partnership agreement does not provide for the allocation of income, gain, loss, deduction, or credit (or item thereof) to a partner, or if the partnership agreement provides for the allocation of income, gain, loss, deduction, or credit (or item thereof) to a partner but such allocation does not have substantial economic effect, then the partner's distributive share of such income, gain, loss, deduction, or credit (or item thereof) shall be determined in accordance with such partner's interest in the partnership (taking into account all facts and circumstances). If the partnership agreement provides for the allocation of income, gain, loss, deduction, or credit (or item thereof) to a partner, there are three ways in which such allocation will be respected under section 704(b) and this paragraph. First, the allocation can have substantial economic effect in accordance with paragraph (b)(2) of this section. Second, taking into account all facts and circumstances, the allocation can be in accordance with the partner's interest in the partnership. See paragraph (b)(3) of this section. Third, the allocation can be deemed to be in accordance with the partner's interest in the partnership pursuant to one of the special rules contained in paragraph (b)(4) of this section and § 1.704-2. To the extent an allocation under the partnership agreement of income, gain, loss, deduction, or credit (or item thereof) to a partner does not have substantial economic effect, is not in accordance with the partner's interest in the partnership, and is not deemed to be in accordance with the partner's interest in the partnership, such income, gain, loss, deduction, or credit (or item thereof) will be reallocated in accordance with the partner's interest in the partnership (determined under paragraph (b)(3) of this section).

(ii) *Effective dates.* The provisions of this paragraph are effective for partnership taxable years beginning after December 31, 1975. However, for partnership taxable years beginning after December 31, 1975, but before May 1, 1986 (January 1, 1987, in the case of allocations of nonrecourse deductions as defined in paragraph (b)(4)(iv)(a) of this section), an allocation of income, gain, loss, deduction, or credit (or item thereof) to a partner that is not respected under this paragraph nevertheless will be respected under section 704(b) if such allocation has substantial economic effect or is in accordance with the partners' interests in the partnership as those terms have been interpreted under the relevant case law, the legislative history of section 210(d) of the Tax Reform Act of 1976, and the provisions of this paragraph in effect for partnership taxable years beginning before May 1, 1986.

(iii) *Effect of other sections.* The determination of a partner's distributive share of income, gain, loss, deduction, or credit (or item thereof) under section 704(b) and this paragraph is not conclusive as to the tax treatment of a partner with respect to such distributive share. For example, an allocation of loss or deduction to a partner that is respected under section 704(b) and this paragraph may not be deductible by such partner if the partner lacks the requisite motive for economic gain (see, *e.g., Goldstein v. Commissioner,* 364 F.2d 734 (2d Cir. 1966)), or may be disal-

Reg. § 1.704-1(b)(1)

lowed for that taxable year (and held in suspense) if the limitations of section 465 or section 704(d) are applicable. Similarly, an allocation that is respected under section 704(b) and this paragraph nevertheless may be reallocated under other provisions, such as section 482, section 704(e)(2), section 706(d) (and related assignment of income principles), and paragraph (b)(2)(ii) of § 1.751-1. If a partnership has a section 754 election in effect, a partner's distributive share of partnership income, gain, loss, or deduction may be affected as provided in § 1.743-1 (see paragraph (b)(2)(iv)(*m*)(*2*) of this section). A deduction that appears to be a nonrecourse deduction deemed to be in accordance with the partners' interests in the partnership may not be such because purported nonrecourse liabilities of the partnership in fact constitute equity rather than debt. The examples in paragraph (b)(5) of this section concern the validity of allocations under section 704(b) and this paragraph and, except as noted, do not address the effect of other sections or limitations on such allocations.

(iv) *Other possible tax consequences.* Allocations that are respected under section 704(b) and this paragraph may give rise to other tax consequences, such as those resulting from the application of section 61, section 83, section 751, section 2501, paragraph (f) of § 1.46-3, § 1.47-6, paragraph (b)(1) of § 1.721-1 (and related principles), and paragraph (e) of § 1.752-1. The examples in paragraph (b)(5) of this section concern the validity of allocations under section 704(b) and this paragraph and, except as noted, do not address other tax consequences that may result from such allocations.

(v) *Purported allocations.* Section 704(b) and this paragraph do not apply to a purported allocation if it is made to a person who is not a partner of the partnership (see section 7701(a)(2) and paragraph (d) of § 301.7701-3) or to a person who is not receiving the purported allocation in his capacity as a partner (see section 707(a) and paragraph (a) of § 1.707-1).

(vi) *Section 704(c) determinations.* Section 704(c) and § 1.704-3 generally require that if property is contributed by a partner to a partnership, the partners' distributive shares of income, gain, loss, and deduction, as computed for tax purposes, with respect to the property are determined so as to take account of the variation between the adjusted tax basis and fair market value of the property. Although section 704(b) does not directly determine the partners' distributive shares of tax items governed by section 704(c), the partners' distributive shares of tax items may be determined under section 704(c) and § 1.704-3 (depending on the allocation method chosen by the partnership under § 1.704-3) with reference to the partners' distributive shares of the corresponding book items, as determined under section 704(b) and this paragraph. (See paragraphs (b)(2)(iv)(*d*) and (b)(4)(i) of this section.) See § 1.704-3 for methods of making allocations under section 704(c), and § 1.704-3(d)(2) for a special rule in determining the amount of book items if the remedial allocation method is chosen by the partnership. See also paragraph (b)(5) *Example (13)* (i) of this section.

(vii) *Bottom line allocations.* Section 704(b) and this paragraph are applicable to allocations of income, gain, loss, deduction, and credit, allocations of specific items of income, gain, loss, deduction, and credit, and allocations of partnerhip net or "bottom line" taxable income and loss. An allocation to a partner of a share of partnership net or "bottom line" taxable income or loss shall be treated as an allocation to such partner of the same share of each item of income, gain, loss, and deduction that is taken into account in computing such net or "bottom line" taxable income or loss. See example (15)(i) of paragraph (b)(5) of this section.

(2) *Substantial economic effect*—(i) *Two-part analysis.* The determination of whether an allocation of income, gain, loss, or deduction (or item thereof) to a partner has substantial economic effect involves a two-part analysis that is made as of the end of the partnership taxable year to which the allocation relates. First, the allocation must have economic effect (within the meaning of paragraph (b)(2)(ii) of this section). Second, the economic efect of the allocation must be substantial (within the meaning of paragraph (b)(2)(iii) of this section).

(ii) *Economic effect*—(*a*) *Fundamental principles.* In order for an allocation to have economic effect, it must be consistent with the underlying economic arrangement of the partners. This means that in the event there is an economic benefit or economic burden that corresponds to an allocation, the partner to whom the allocation is made must receive such economic benefit or bear such economic burden.

(*b*) *Three requirements.* Based on the principles contained in paragraph (b)(2)(ii)(*a*) of this section, and except as otherwise provided in this paragraph, an allocation of income, gain, loss, or deduction (or item thereof) to a partner will have economic effect if, and only if, throughout the full term of the partnership, the partnership agreement provides—

(*1*) For the determination and maintenance of the partners' capital accounts in accor-

Reg. § 1.704-1(b)(2)

dance with the rules of paragraph (b)(2)(iv) of this section,

(2) Upon liquidation of the partnership (or any partner's interest in the partnership), liquidating distributions are required in all cases to be made in accordance with the positive capital account balances of the partners, as determined after taking into account all capital account adjustments for the partnership taxable year during which such liquidation occurs (other than those made pursuant to this requirement (2) and requirement (3) of this paragraph (b)(2)(ii)(b)), by the end of such taxable year (or, if later, within 90 days after the date of such liquidation), and

(3) If such partner has a deficit balance in his capital account following the liquidation of his interest in the partnership, as determined after taking into account all capital account adjustments for the partnership taxable year during which such liquidation occurs (other than those made pursuant to this requirement (3)), he is unconditionally obligated to restore the amount of such deficit balance to the partnership by the end of such taxable year (or, if later, within 90 days after the date of such liquidation), which amount shall, upon liquidation of the partnership, be paid to creditors of the partnership or distributed to other partners in accordance with their positive capital account balances (in accordance with requirement (2) of this paragraph (b)(2)(ii)(b)).

Requirements (2) and (3) of this paragraph (b)(2)(ii)(b) are not violated if all or part of the partnership interest of one or more partners is purchased (other than in connection with the liquidation of the partnership) by the partnership or by one or more partners (or one or more persons related, within the meaning of section 267(b) (without modification by section 267(e)(1)) or section 707(b)(1), to a partner) pursuant to an agreement negotiated at arm's length by persons who at the time such agreement is entered into have materially adverse interests and if a principal purpose of such purchase and sale is not to avoid the principles of the second sentence of paragraph (b)(2)(ii)(a) of this section. In addition, requirement (2) of this paragraph (b)(2)(ii)(b) is not violated if, upon the liquidation of the partnership, the capital accounts of the partners are increased or decreased pursuant to paragraph (b)(2)(iv)(f) of this section as of the date of such liquidation and the partnership makes liquidating distributions within the time set out in that requirement (2) in the ratios of the partners' positive capital accounts, except that it does not distribute (A) reserves reasonably required to provide for liabilities (contingent or otherwise) of the partnership and (B) installment obligations owed to the partnership, so long as such withheld amounts are distributed as soon as practicable and in the ratios of the partners' positive capital account balances. For purposes of the preceding sentence, a partnership taxable year shall be determined without regard to section 706 (c)(2)(A). See examples (1)(i) and (ii), (4)(i), (8)(i), and (16)(i) of paragraph (b)(5) of this section.

(c) *Obligation to restore deficit.* If a partner is not expressly obligated to restore the deficit balance in his capital account, such partner nevertheless will be treated as obligated to restore the deficit balance in his capital account (in accordance with requirement (3) of paragraph (b)(2)(ii)(b) of this section) to the extent of—

(1) The outstanding principal balance of any promissory note (of which such partner is the maker) contributed to the partnership by such partner (other than a promissory note that is readily tradable on an established securities market), and

(2) The amount of any unconditional obligation of such partner (whether imposed by the partnership agreement or by State or local law) to make subsequent contributions to the partnership (other than pursuant to a promissory note of which such partner is the maker),

provided that such note or obligation is required to be satisfied at a time no later than the end of the partnership taxable year in which such partner's interest is liquidated (or, if later, within 90 days after the date of such liquidation). If a promissory note referred to in the previous sentence is negotiable, a partner will be considered required to satisfy such note within the time period specified in such sentence if the partnership agreement provides that, in lieu of actual satisfaction, the partnership will retain such note and such partner will contribute to the partnership the excess, if any, of the outstanding principal balance of such note over its fair market value at the time of liquidation. See paragraph (b)(2)(iv)(d)(2) of this section. See examples (1)(ix) and (x) of paragraph (b)(5) of this section. A partner in no event will be considered obligated to restore the deficit balance in his capital account to the partnership (in accordance with requirement (3) of paragraph (b)(2)(ii)(b) of this section) to the extent such partner's obligation is not legally enforceable, or the facts and circumstances otherwise indicate a plan to avoid or circumvent such obligation. See paragraphs (b)(2)(ii)(f), (b)(2)(ii)(h), and (b)(4)(vi) of this section for other rules regarding such obligation. For purposes of this paragraph (b)(2), if a partner

Reg. § 1.704-1(b)(2)

contributes a promissory note to the partnership during a partnership taxable year beginning after December 29, 1988, and the maker of such note is a person related to such partner (within the meaning of § 1.752-1T(h), but without regard to subdivision (4) of that section), then such promissory note shall be treated as a promissory note of which such partner is the maker.

(d) *Alternate test for economic effect.* If—

(1) Requirements (1) and (2) of paragraph (b)(2)(ii)(b) of this section are satisfied, and

(2) The partner to whom an allocation is made is not obligated to restore the deficit balance in his capital account to the partnership (in accordance with requirement (3) of paragraph (b)(2)(ii)(b) of this section), or is obligated to restore only a limited dollar amount of such deficit balance, and

(3) The partnership agreement contains a "qualified income offset,"

such allocation will be considered to have economic effect under this paragraph (b)(2)(ii)(d) to the extent such allocation does not cause or increase a deficit balance in such partner's capital account (in excess of any limited dollar amount of such deficit balance that such partner is obligated to restore) as of the end of the partnership taxable year to which such allocation relates. In determining the extent to which the previous sentence is satisfied, such partner's capital account also shall be reduced for—

(4) Adjustments that, as of the end of such year, reasonably are expected to be made to such partner's capital account under paragraph (b)(2)(iv)(k) of this section for depletion allowances with respect to oil and gas properties of the partnership, and

(5) Allocations of loss and deduction that, as of the end of such year, reasonably are expected to be made to such partner pursuant to section 704(e)(2), section 706(d), and paragraph (b)(2)(ii) of § 1.751-1, and

(6) Distributions that, as of the end of such year, reasonably are expected to be made to such partner to the extent they exceed offsetting increases to such partner's capital account that reasonably are expected to occur during (or prior to) the partnership taxable years in which such distributions reasonably are expected to be made (other than increases pursuant to a minimum gain chargeback under paragraph (b)(4)(iv)(e) of this section or under § 1.704-2(f); however, increases to a partner's capital account pursuant to a minimum gain chargeback requirement are taken into account as an offset to distributions of nonrecourse liability proceeds that are reasonably expected to be made and that are allocable to an increase in partnership minimum gain).

For purposes of determining the amount of expected distributions and expected capital account increases described in (6) above, the rule set out in paragraph (b)(2)(iii)(c) of this section concerning the presumed value of partnership property shall apply. The partnership agreement contains a "qualified income offset" if, and only if, it provides that a partner who unexpectedly receives an adjustment, allocation, or distribution described in (4), (5), or (6) above, will be allocated items of income and gain (consisting of a pro rata portion of each item of partnership income, including gross income, and gain for such year) in an amount and manner sufficient to eliminate such deficit balance as quickly as possible. Allocations of items of income and gain made pursuant to the immediately preceding sentence shall be deemed to be made in accordance with the partners' interests in the partnership if requirements (1) and (2) of paragraph (b)(2)(ii)(b) of this section are satisfied. See examples (1)(iii), (iv), (v), (vi), (viii), (ix), and (x), (15), and (16)(ii) of paragraph (b)(5) of this section.

(e) *Partial economic effect.* If only a portion of an allocation made to a partner with respect to a partnership taxable year has economic effect, both the portion that has economic effect and the portion that is reallocated shall consist of a proportionate share of all items that made up the allocation to such partner for such year. See examples (15)(ii) and (iii) of paragraph (b)(5) of this section.

(f) *Reduction of obligation to restore.* If requirements (1) and (2) of paragraph (b)(2)(ii)(b) of this section are satisfied, a partner's obligation to restore the deficit balance in his capital account (or any limited dollar amount thereof) to the partnership may be eliminated or reduced as of the end of a partnership taxable year without affecting the validity of prior allocations (see paragraph (b)(4)(vi) of this section) to the extent the deficit balance (if any) in such partner's capital account, after reduction for the items described in (4), (5), and (6) of paragraph (b)(2)(ii)(d) of this section, will not exceed the partner's remaining obligation (if any) to restore the deficit balance in his capital account. See example (l)(viii) of paragraph (b)(5) of this section.

(g) *Liquidation defined.* For purposes of this paragraph, a liquidation of a partner's interest in the partnership occurs upon the earlier of (1) the date upon which there is a liquidation of the partnership, or (2) the date upon which there

Reg. § 1.704-1(b)(2)

is a liquidation of the partner's interest in the partnership under paragraph (d) of § 1.761-1. For purposes of this paragraph, the liquidation of a partnership occurs upon the earlier of (3) the date upon which the partnership is terminated under section 708(b)(1), or (4) the date upon which the partnership ceases to be a going concern (even though it may continue in existence for the purpose of winding up its affairs, paying its debts, and distributing any remaining balance to its partners). Requirements (2) and (3) of paragraph (b)(2)(ii)(b) of this section will be considered unsatisfied if the liquidation of a partner's interest in the partnership is delayed after its primary business activities have been terminated (for example, by continuing to engage in a relatively minor amount of business activity, if such actions themselves do not cause the partnership to terminate pursuant to section 708(b)(1)) for a principal purpose of deferring any distribution pursuant to requirement (2) of paragraph (b)(2)(ii)(b) of this section or deferring any partner's obligation under requirement (3) of paragraph (b)(2)(ii)(b) of this section.

(h) *Partnership agreement defined.* For purposes of this paragraph, the partnership agreement includes all agreements among the partners, or between one or more partners and the partnership, concerning affairs of the partnership and responsibilities of partners, whether oral or written, and whether or not embodied in a document referred to by the partners as the partnership agreement. Thus, in determining whether distributions are required in all cases to be made in accordance with the partners' positive capital account balances (requirement (2) of paragraph (b)(2)(ii)(b) of this section), and in determining the extent to which a partner is obligated to restore a deficit balance in his capital account (requirement (3) of paragraph (b)(2)(ii)(b) of this section), all arrangements among partners, or between one or more partners and the partnership relating to the partnership, direct and indirect, including puts, options, and other buy-sell agreements, and any other "stop-loss" arrangement, are considered to be part of the partnership agreement. (Thus, for example, if one partner who assumes a liability of the partnership is indemnified by another partner for a portion of such liability, the indemnifying partner (depending upon the particular facts) may be viewed as in effect having a partial deficit makeup obligation as a result of such indemnity agreement.) In addition, the partnership agreement includes provisions of Federal, State, or local law that govern the affairs of the partnership or are considered under such law to be a part of the partnership agreement (see the last sentence of paragraph (c) of § 1.761-1). For purposes of this paragraph (b)(2)(ii)(h), an agreement with a partner or a partnership shall include an agreement with a person related, within the meaning of section 267(b) (without modification by section 267(e)(1)) or section 707(b)(1), to such partner or partnership. For purposes of the preceding sentence, sections 267(b) and 707(b)(1) shall be applied for partnership taxable years beginning after December 29, 1988, by (1) substituting "80 percent or more" for "more than 50 percent" each place it appears in such sections, (2) excluding brothers and sisters from the members of a person's family, and (3) disregarding section 267(f)(1)(A).

(i) *Economic effect equivalence.* Allocations made to a partner that do not otherwise have economic effect under this paragraph (b)(2)(ii) shall nevertheless be deemed to have economic effect, provided that as of the end of each partnership taxable year a liquidation of the partnership at the end of such year or at the end of any future year would produce the same economic results to the partners as would occur if requirements (1), (2), and (3) of paragraph (b)(2)(ii)(b) of this section had been satisfied, regardless of the economic performance of the partnership. See examples (4)(ii) and (iii) of paragraph (b)(5) of this section.

(iii) *Substantiality*—(a) *General rules.* Except as otherwise provided in this paragraph (b)(2)(iii), the economic effect of an allocation (or allocations) is substantial if there is a reasonable possibility that the allocation (or allocations) will affect substantially the dollar amounts to be received by the partners from the partnership, independent of tax consequences. Notwithstanding the preceding sentence, the economic effect of an allocation (or allocations) is not substantial if, at the time the allocation becomes part of the partnership agreement, (1) the after-tax economic consequences of at least one partner may, in present value terms, be enhanced compared to such consequences if the allocation (or allocations) were not contained in the partnership agreement, and (2) there is a strong likelihood that the after-tax economic consequences of no partner will, in present value terms, be substantially diminished compared to such consequences if the allocation (or allocations) were not contained in the partnership agreement. In determining the after-tax economic benefit or detriment to a partner, tax consequences that result from the interaction of the allocation with such partner's tax attributes that are unrelated to the partnership will be taken into account. See examples (5) and (9) of paragraph (b)(5) of this section. The economic effect of an allocation is not substantial in the two situations described in paragraphs (b)(2)(iii)(b) and (c) of

Reg. § 1.704-1(b)(2)

this section. However, even if an allocation is not described therein, its economic effect may be insubstantial under the general rules stated in this paragraph (b)(2)(iii)(a). References in this paragraph (b)(2)(iii) to allocations includes capital account adjustments made pursuant to paragraph (b)(2)(iv)(k) of this section.

(b) *Shifting tax consequences.* The economic effect of an allocation (or allocations) in a partnership taxable year is not substantial if, at the time the allocation (or allocations) becomes part of the partnership agreement, there is a strong likelihood that—

(*1*) The net increases and decreases that will be recorded in the partners' respective capital accounts for such taxable year will not differ substantially from the net increases and decreases that would be recorded in such partners' respective capital accounts for such year if the allocations were not contained in the partnership agreement, and

(*2*) The total tax liability of the partners (for their respective taxable years in which the allocations will be taken into account) will be less than if the allocations were not contained in the partnership agreement (taking into account tax consequences that result from the interaction of the allocation (or allocations) with partner tax attributes that are unrelated to the partnership).

If, at the end of a partnership taxable year to which an allocation (or allocations) relates, the net increases and decreases that are recorded in the partners' respective capital accounts do not differ substantially from the net increases and decreases that would have been recorded in such partners' respective capital accounts had the allocation (or allocations) not been contained in the partnership agreement, and the total tax liability of the partners is (as described in (*2*) above) less than it would have been had the allocation (or allocations) not been contained in the partnership agreement, it will be presumed that, at the time the allocation (or allocations) became part of such partnership agreement, there was a strong likelihood that these results would occur. This presumption may be overcome by a showing of facts and circumstances that prove otherwise. See examples (6), (7)(ii) and (iii), and (10)(ii) of paragraph (b)(5) of this section.

(c) *Transitory allocations.* If a partnership agreement provides for the possibility that one or more allocations (the "original allocation(s)") will be largely offset by one or more other allocations (the "offsetting allocations(s)"), and, at the time the allocations become part of the partnership agreement, there is a strong likelihood that—

(*1*) The net increases and decreases that will be recorded in the partners' respective capital accounts for the taxable years to which the allocations relate will not differ substantially from the net increases and decreases that would be recorded in such partners' respective capital accounts for such years if the original allocation(s) and offsetting allocation(s) were not contained in the partnership agreement, and

(*2*) The total tax liability of the partners (for their respective taxable years in which the allocations will be taken into account) will be less than if the allocations were not contained in the partnership agreement (taking into account tax consequences that result from the interaction of the allocation (or allocations) with partner tax attributes that are unrelated to the partnership)

the economic effect of the original allocation(s) and offsetting allocation(s) will not be substantial. If, at the end of a partnership taxable year to which an offsetting allocation(s) relates, the net increases and decreases recorded in the partners' respective capital accounts do not differ substantially from the net increases and decreases that would have been recorded in such partners' respective capital accounts had the original allocation(s) and the offsetting allocation(s) not been contained in the partnership agreement, and the total tax liability of the partners is (as described in (*2*) above) less than it would have been had such allocations not been contained in the partnership agreement, it will be presumed that, at the time the allocations became part of the partnership agreement, there was a strong likelihood that these results would occur. This presumption may be overcome by a showing of facts and circumstances that prove otherwise. See examples (1)(xi), (2), (3), (7), (8)(ii), and (17) of paragraph (b)(5) of this section. Notwithstanding the foregoing, the original allocation(s) and the offsetting allocation(s) will not be insubstantial (under this paragraph (b)(2)(iii)(c)) and, for purposes of paragraph (b)(2)(iii)(a), it will be presumed that there is a reasonable possibility that the allocations will affect substantially the dollar amounts to be received by the partners from the partnership if, at the time the allocations become part of the partnership agreement, there is a strong likelihood that the offsetting allocation(s) will not, in large part, be made within five years after the original allocation(s) is made (determined on a first-in, first-out basis). See example (2) of paragraph (b)(5) of this section. For purposes of applying the provisions of this paragraph (b)(2)(iii) (and paragraphs (b)(2)(ii)(d)(6) and (b)(3)(iii) of this section), the adjusted tax basis of partnership property (or, if partnership property is properly reflected on the books of the partnership at a book

Reg. § 1.704-1(b)(2)

value that differs from its adjusted tax basis, the book value of such property) will be presumed to be the fair market value of such property, and adjustments to the adjusted tax basis (or book value) of such property will be presumed to be matched by corresponding changes in such property's fair market value. Thus, there cannot be a strong likelihood that the economic effect of an allocation (or allocations) will be largely offset by an allocation (or allocations) of gain or loss from the disposition of partnership property. See examples (1)(vi) and (xi) of paragraph (b)(5) of this section.

(iv) *Maintenance of capital accounts*—(*a*) *In general*. The economic effect test described in paragraph (b)(2)(ii) of this section requires an examination of the capital accounts of the partners of a partnership, as maintained under the partnership agreement. Except as otherwise provided in paragraph (b)(2)(ii)(*i*) of this section, an allocation of income, gain, loss, or deduction will not have economic effect under paragraph (b)(2)(ii) of this section, and will not be deemed to be in accordance with a partner's interest in the partnership under paragraph (b)(4) of this section, unless the capital accounts of the partners are determined and maintained throughout the full term of the partnership in accordance with the capital accounting rules of this paragraph (b)(2)(iv).

(*b*) *Basic rules*. Except as otherwise provided in this paragraph (b)(2)(iv), the partners' capital accounts will be considered to be determined and maintained in accordance with the rules of this paragraph (b)(2)(iv) if, and only if, each partner's capital account is increased by (*1*) the amount of money contributed by him to the partnership, (*2*) the fair market value of property contributed by him to the partnership (net of liabilities secured by such contributed property that the partnership is considered to assume or take subject to under section 752), and (*3*) allocations to him of partnership income and gain (or items thereof), including income and gain exempt from tax and income and gain described in paragraph (b)(2)(iv)(*g*) of this section, but excluding income and gain described in paragraph (b)(4)(i) of this section; and is decreased by (*4*) the amount of money distributed to him by the partnership, (*5*) the fair market value of property distributed to him by the partnership (net of liabilities secured by such distributed property that such partner is considered to assume or take subject to under section 752), (*6*) allocations to him of expenditures of the partnership described in section 705(a)(2)(B), and (*7*) allocations of partnership loss and deduction (or item thereof), including loss and deduction described in paragraph (b)(2)(iv)(*g*) of this section, but excluding items described in (*6*) above and loss or deduction described in paragraphs (b)(4)(i) or (b)(4)(iii) of this section; and is otherwise adjusted in accordance with the additional rules set forth in this paragraph (b)(2)(iv). For purposes of this paragraph, a partner who has more than one interest in a partnership shall have a single capital account that reflects all such interests, regardless of the class of interests owned by such partner (*e.g.*, general or limited) and regardless of the time or manner in which such interests were acquired.

(*c*) *Treatment of liabilities*. For purposes of this paragraph (b)(2)(iv), (*1*) money contributed by a partner to a partnership includes the amount of any partnership liabilities that are assumed by such partner (other than liabilities described in paragraph (b)(2)(iv)(*b*)(*5*) of this section that are assumed by a distributee partner) but does not include increases in such partner's share of partnership liabilities (see section 752(a)), and (*2*) money distributed to a partner by a partnership includes the amount of such partner's individual liabilities that are assumed by the partnership (other than liabilities described in paragraph (b)(2)(iv)(*b*)(*2*) of this section that are assumed by the partnership) but does not include decreases in such partner's share of partnership liabilities (see section 752(b)). For purposes of this paragraph (b)(2)(iv)(*c*), liabilities are considered assumed only to the extent the assuming party is thereby subjected to personal liability with respect to such obligation, the obligee is aware of the assumption and can directly enforce the assuming party's obligation, and, as between the assuming party and the party from whom the liability is assumed, the assuming party is ultimately liable.

(*d*) *Contributed property*—(*1*) *In general*. The basic capital accounting rules contained in paragraph (b)(2)(iv)(*b*) of this section require that a partner's capital account be increased by the fair market value of property contributed to the partnership by such partner on the date of contribution. See *Example 13*(i) of paragraph (b)(5) of this section. Consistent with section 752(c), section 7701(g) does not apply in determining such fair market value.

(*2*) *Contribution of promissory notes*. Notwithstanding the general rule of paragraph (b)(2)(iv)(*b*)(*2*) of this section, except as provided in this paragraph (b)(2)(iv)(*d*)(*2*), if a promissory note is contributed to a partnership by a partner who is the maker of such note, such partner's capital account will be increased with respect to such note only when there is a taxable disposition of such note by the partnership or when the partner makes principal payments on such note. See example (1)(ix) of paragraph (b)(5) of this section. The first sentence of this paragraph (b)(2)(iv)(d)(2) shall not apply if the note referred to therein is readily tradable on an established securities market. See also paragraph (b)(2)(ii)(c) of this section. Furthermore, a partner whose interest is liquidated will be considered as satisfying his obligation to restore the deficit balance in his capital account to the extent of (i) the fair market value, at the time of contribution, of any negotiable promissory note (of which such partner is the maker) that such partner contributes to the partnership on or after the date his interest is liquidated and within the time specified in paragraph (b)(2)(ii)(b)(3) of this section, and (ii) the fair market value, at the time of liquidation, of the unsatisfied portion of any negotiable promissory note (of which such partner is the maker) that such partner previously contributed to the partnership. For purposes of the preceding sentence, the fair market value of a note will be no less than the outstanding principal balance of such note, provided that such note bears interest at a rate no less than the applicable federal rate at the time of valuation.

(3) *Section 704(c) considerations.* Section 704(c) and § 1.704-3 govern the determination of the partners' distributive shares of income, gain, loss, and deduction, as computed for tax purposes, with respect to property contributed to a partnership (see paragraph (b)(1)(vi) of this section). In cases where section 704(c) and § 1.704-3 apply to partnership property, the capital accounts of the partners will not be considered to be determined and maintained in accordance with the rules of this paragraph (b)(2)(iv) unless the partnership agreement requires that the partners' capital accounts be adjusted in accordance with paragraph (b)(2)(iv)(g) of this section for allocations to them of income, gain, loss, and deduction (including depreciation, depletion, amortization, or other cost recovery) as computed for book purposes, with respect to the property. See, however, § 1.704-3(d)(2) for a special rule in determining the amount of book items if the partnership chooses the remedial allocation method. See also *Example (13)* (i) of paragraph (b)(5) of this section. Capital accounts are not adjusted to reflect allocations under section 704(c) and § 1.704-3 (e.g., tax allocations of precontribution gain or loss).

(e) *Distributed property*—(1) *In general.* The basic capital accounting rules contained in paragraph (b)(2)(iv)(b) of this section require that a partner's capital account be decreased by the fair market value of property distributed by the partnership (without regard to section 7701(g)) to such partner (whether in connection with a liquidation or otherwise). To satisfy this requirement, the capital accounts of the partners first must be adjusted to reflect the manner in which the unrealized income, gain, loss, and deduction inherent in such property (that has not been reflected in the capital accounts previously) would be allocated among the partners if there were a taxable disposition of such property for the fair market value of such property (taking section 7701(g) into account) on the date of distribution. See example (14)(v) of paragraph (b)(5) of this section.

(2) *Distribution of promissory notes.* Notwithstanding the general rule of paragraph (b)(2)(iv)(b)(5), except as provided in this paragraph (b)(2)(iv)(e)(2), if a promissory note is distributed to a partner by a partnership that is the maker of such note, such partner's capital account will be decreased with respect to such note only when there is a taxable disposition of such note by the partner or when the partnership makes principal payments on the note. The previous sentence shall not apply if a note distributed to a partner by a partnership who is the maker of such note is readily tradable on an established securities market. Furthermore, the capital account of a partner whose interest in a partnership is liquidated will be reduced to the extent of (i) the fair market value, at the time of distribution, of any negotiable promissory note (of which such partnership is the maker) that such partnership distributes to the partner on or after the date such partner's interest is liquidated and within the time specified in paragraph (b)(2)(ii)(b)(2) of this section, and (ii) the fair market value, at the time of liquidation, of the unsatisfied portion of any negotiable promissory note (of which such partnership is the maker) that such partnership previously distributed to the partner. For purposes of the preceding sentence, the fair market value of a note will be no less than the outstanding principal balance of such note, provided that such note bears interest at a rate no less than the applicable federal rate at the time of valuation.

(f) *Revaluations of property.* A partnership agreement may, upon the occurrence of certain events, increase or decrease the capital accounts of the partners to reflect a revaluation of partnership property (including intangible assets such as goodwill) on the partnership's books. Capital accounts so adjusted will not be considered to be determined and maintained in accordance with the rules of this paragraph (b)(2)(iv) unless—

(1) The adjustments are based on the fair market value of partnership property (taking

Reg. § 1.704-1(b)(2)

section 7701(g) into account) on the date of adjustment, and

(2) The adjustments reflect the manner in which the unrealized income, gain, loss, or deduction inherent in such property (that has not been reflected in the capital accounts previously) would be allocated among the partners if there were a taxable disposition of such property for such fair market value on that date, and

(3) The partnership agreement requires that the partners' capital accounts be adjusted in accordance with paragraph (b)(2)(iv)(g) of this section for allocations to them of depreciation, depletion, amortization, and gain or loss, as computed for book purposes, with respect to such property, and

(4) The partnership agreement requires that the partners' distributive shares of depreciation, depletion, amortization, and gain or loss, as computed for tax purposes, with respect to such property be determined so as to take account of the variation between the adjusted tax basis and book value of such property in the same manner as under section 704(c) (see paragraph (b)(4)(i) of this section), and

(5) The adjustments are made principally for a substantial non-tax business purpose—

(i) In connection with a contribution of money or other property (other than a *de minimis* amount) to the partnership by a new or existing partner as consideration for an interest in the partnership, or

(ii) In connection with the liquidation of the partnership or a distribution of money or other property (other than a *de minimis* amount) by the partnership to a retiring or continuing partner as consideration for an interest in the partnership, or

(iii) Under generally accepted industry accounting practices, provided substantially all of the partnership's property (excluding money) consists of stock, securities, commodities, options, warrants, futures, or similar instruments that are readily tradable on an established securities market.

See examples (14) and (18) of paragraph (b)(5) of this section. If the capital accounts of the partners are not adjusted to reflect the fair market value of partnership property when an interest in the partnership is acquired from or relinquished to the partnership, paragraphs (b)(1)(iii) and (b)(1)(iv) of this section should be consulted regarding the potential tax consequences that may arise if the principles of section 704(c) are not applied to determine the partners' distributive shares of depreciation, depletion, amortization,

and gain or loss, as computed for tax purposes, with respect to such property.

(g) *Adjustments to reflect book value*— (1) *In general.* Under paragraphs (b)(2)(iv)(d) and (b)(2)(iv)(f) of this section, property may be properly reflected on the books of the partnership at a book value that differs from the adjusted tax basis of such property. In these circumstances, paragraphs (b)(2)(iv)(d)(3) and (b)(2)(iv)(f)(3) of this section provide that the capital accounts of the partners will not be considered to be determined and maintained in accordance with the rules of this paragraph (b)(2)(iv) unless the partnership agreement requires the partners' capital accounts to be adjusted in accordance with this paragraph (b)(2)(iv)(g) for allocations to them of depreciation, depletion, amortization, and gain or loss, as computed for book purposes, with respect to such property. In determining whether the economic effect of an allocation of book items is substantial, consideration will be given to the effect of such allocation on the determination of the partners' distributive shares of corresponding tax items under section 704(c) and paragraph (b)(4)(i) of this section. See example (17) of paragraph (b)(5) of this section. If an allocation of book items under the partnership agreement does not have substantial economic effect (as determined under paragraphs (b)(2)(ii) and (b)(2)(iii) of this section), or is not otherwise respected under this paragraph, such items will be reallocated in accordance with the partners' interests in the partnership, and such reallocation will be the basis upon which the partners' distributive shares of the corresponding tax items are determined under section 704(c) and paragraph (b)(4)(i) of this section. See examples (13), (14), and (18) of paragraph (b)(5) of this section.

(2) *Payables and receivables.* References in this paragraph (b)(2)(iv) and paragraph (b)(4)(i) of this section to book and tax depreciation, depletion, amortization, and gain or loss with respect to property that has an adjusted tax basis that differs from book value include, under analogous rules and principles, the unrealized income or deduction with respect to accounts receivable, accounts payable, and other accrued but unpaid items.

(3) *Determining amount of book items.* The partners' capital accounts will not be considered adjusted in accordance with this paragraph (b)(2)(iv)(g) unless the amount of book depreciation, depletion, or amortization for a period with respect to an item of partnership property is the amount that bears the same relationship to the book value of such property as the depreciation (or cost recovery deduction), depletion, or

Reg. § 1.704-1(b)(2)

amortization computed for tax purposes with respect to such property for such period bears to the adjusted tax basis of such property. If such property has a zero adjusted tax basis, the book depreciation, depletion, or amortization may be determined under any reasonable method selected by the partnership.

(h) *Determinations of fair market value.* For purposes of this paragraph (b)(2)(iv), the fair market value assigned to property contributed to a partnership, property distributed by a partnership, or property otherwise revalued by a partnership, will be regarded as correct, provided that (1) such value is reasonably agreed to among the partners in arm's-length negotiations, and (2) the partners have sufficiently adverse interests. If, however, these conditions are not satisfied and the value assigned to such property is overstated or understated (by more than an insignificant amount), the capital accounts of the partners will not be considered to be determined and maintained in accordance with the rules of this paragraph (b)(2)(iv). Valuation of property contributed to the partnership, distributed by the partnership, or otherwise revalued by the partnership shall be on a property-by-property basis, except to the extent the regulations under section 704(c) permit otherwise.

(i) *Section 705(a)(2)(B) expenditures*—(1) *In general.* The basic capital accounting rules contained in paragraph (b)(2)(iv)(b) of this section require that a partner's capital account be decreased by allocations made to such partner of expenditures described in section 705(a)(2)(B). See example (11) of paragraph (b)(5) of this section. If an allocation of these expenditures under the partnership agreement does not have substantial economic effect (as determined under paragraphs (b)(2)(ii) and (b)(2)(iii) of this section), or is not otherwise respected under this paragraph, such expenditures will be reallocated in accordance with the partners' interest in the partnership.

(2) *Expenses described in section 709.* Except for amounts with respect to which an election is properly made under section 709(b), amounts paid or incurred to organize a partnership or to promote the sale of (or to sell) an interest in such a partnership shall, solely for purposes of this paragraph, be treated as section 705(a)(2)(B) expenditures, and upon liquidation of the partnership no further capital account adjustments will be made in respect thereof.

(3) *Disallowed losses.* If a deduction for a loss incurred in connection with the sale or exchange of partnership property is disallowed to the partnership under section 267(a)(1) or section 707(b), that deduction shall, solely for purposes of this paragraph, be treated as a section 705(a)(2)(B) expenditure.

(j) *Basis adjustments to section 38 property.* The capital accounts of the partners will not be considered to be determined and maintained in accordance with the rules of this paragraph (b)(2)(iv) unless such capital accounts are adjusted by the partners' shares of any upward or downward basis adjustments allocated to them under this paragraph (b)(2)(iv)(j). When there is a reduction in the adjusted tax basis of partnership section 38 property under section 48(q)(1) or section 48(q)(3), section 48(q)(6) provides for an equivalent downward adjustment to the aggregate basis of partnership interests (and no additional adjustment is made under section 705(a)(2)(B)). These downward basis adjustments shall be shared among the partners in the same proportion as the adjusted tax basis or cost of (or the qualified investment in) such section 38 property is allocated among the partners under paragraph (f) of § 1.46-3 (or paragraph (a)(4)(iv) of § 1.48-8). Conversely, when there is an increase in the adjusted tax basis of partnership section 38 property under section 48(q)(2), section 48(q)(6) provides for an equivalent upward adjustment to the aggregate basis or partnership interests. These upward adjustments shall be allocated among the partners in the same proportion as the investment tax credit from such property is recaptured by the partners under § 1.47-6.

(k) *Depletion of oil and gas properties*—(1) *In general.* The capital accounts of the partners will not be considered to be determined and maintained in accordance with the rules of this paragraph (b)(2)(iv) unless such capital accounts are adjusted for depletion and gain or loss with respect to the oil or gas properties of the partnership in accordance with this paragraph (b)(2)(iv)(k).

(2) *Simulated depletion.* Except as provided in paragraph (b)(2)(iv)(k)(3) of this section, a partnership shall, solely for purposes of maintaining capital accounts under this paragraph, compute simulated depletion allowances with respect to its oil and gas properties at the partnership level. These allowances shall be computed on each depletable oil or gas property of the partnership by using either the cost depletion method or the percentage depletion method (computed in accordance with section 613 at the rates specified in section 613A(c)(5) without regard to the limitations of section 613A, which theoretically could apply to any partner) for each partnership taxable year that the property is owned by the partnership and subject to depletion. The

Reg. § 1.704-1(b)(2)

choice between the simulated cost depletion method and the simulated percentage depletion method shall be made on a property-by-property basis in the first partnership taxable year beginning after April 30, 1986, for which it is relevant for the property, and shall be binding for all partnership taxable years during which the oil or gas property is held by the partnership. The partnership shall make downward adjustments to the capital accounts of the partners for the simulated depletion allowance with respect to each oil or gas property of the partnership, in the same proportion as such partners (or their predecessors in interest) were properly allocated the adjusted tax basis of each such property. The aggregate capital account adjustments for simulated percentage depletion allowances with respect to an oil or gas property of the partnership shall not exceed the aggregate adjusted tax basis allocated to the partners with respect to such property. Upon the taxable disposition of an oil or gas property by a partnership, such partnership's simulated gain or loss shall be determined by subtracting its simulated adjusted basis in such property from the amount realized upon such disposition. (The partnership's simulated adjusted basis in an oil or gas property is determined in the same manner as adjusted tax basis except that simulated depletion allowances are taken into account instead of actual depletion allowances.) The capital accounts of the partners shall be adjusted upward by the amount of any simulated gain in proportion to such partners' allocable shares of the portion of the total amount realized from the disposition of such property that exceeds the partnership's simulated adjusted basis in such property. The capital accounts of such partners shall be adjusted downward by the amount of any simulated loss in proportion to such partners' allocable shares of the total amount realized from the disposition of such property that represents recovery of the partnership's simulated adjusted basis in such property. See section 613A(c)(7)(D) and the regulations thereunder and paragraph (b)(4)(v) of this section. See example (19)(iv) of paragraph (b)(5) of this section.

(*3*) *Actual depletion.* Pursuant to section 613A(c)(7)(D) and the regulations thereunder, the depletion allowance under section 611 with respect to the oil and gas properties of a partnership is computed separately by the partners. Accordingly, in lieu of adjusting the partners' capital accounts as provided in paragraph (b)(2)(iv)(*k*)(*2*) of this section, the partnership may make downward adjustments to the capital account of each partner equal to such partner's depletion allowance with respect to each oil or gas property of the partnership (for the partner's taxable year that ends with or within the partnership's taxable year). The aggregate adjustments to the capital account of a partner for depletion allowances with respect to an oil or gas property of the partnership shall not exceed the adjusted tax basis allocated to such partner with respect to such property. Upon the taxable disposition of an oil or gas property by a partnership, the capital account of each partner shall be adjusted upward by the amount of any excess of such partner's allocable share of the total amount realized from the disposition of such property over such partner's remaining adjusted tax basis in such property. If there is no such excess, the capital account of such partner shall be adjusted downward by the amount of any excess of such partner's remaining adjusted tax basis in such property over such partner's allocable share of the total amount realized from the disposition thereof. See section 613A(c)(7)(4)(D) and the regulations thereunder and paragraph (b)(4)(v) of this section.

(*4*) *Effect of book values.* If an oil or gas property of the partnership is, under paragraphs (b)(2)(iv)(*d*) or (b)(2)(iv)(*f*) of this section, properly reflected on the books of the partnership at a book value that differs from the adjusted tax basis of such property, the rules contained in this paragraph (b)(2)(iv)(*k*) and paragraph (b)(4)(v) of this section shall be applied with reference to such book value. A revaluation of a partnership oil or gas property under paragraph (b)(2)(iv)(*f*) of this section may give rise to a reallocation of the adjusted tax basis of such property, or a change in the partners' relative shares of simulated depletion from such property, only to the extent permitted by section 613A(c)(7)(D) and the regulations thereunder.

(*l*) *Transfers of partnership interests.* The capital accounts of the partners will not be considered to be determined and maintained in accordance with the rules of this paragraph (b)(2)(iv) unless, upon the transfer of all or a part of an interest in the partnership, the capital account of the transferor that is attributable to the transferred interest carries over to the transferee partner. (See paragraph (b)(2)(iv)(*m*) of this section for rules concerning the effect of a section 754 election on the capital accounts of the partners.) If the transfer of an interest in a partnership causes a termination of the partnership under section 708(b)(1)(B), the capital account of the transferee partner and the capital accounts of the other partners of the terminated partnership carry over to the new partnership that is formed as a result of the termination of the partnership under § 1.708-1(b)(1)(iv). Moreover, the deemed contribution of assets and liabilities by the terminated partnership to a new partnership and the

Reg. § 1.704-1(b)(2)

deemed liquidation of the terminated partnership that occur under § 1.708-1(b)(1)(iv) are disregarded for purposes of paragraph (b)(2)(iv) of this section. See Example 13 of paragraph (b)(5) of this section and the example in § 1.708-1(b)(1)(iv). The previous three sentences apply to terminations of partnerships under section 708(b)(1)(B) occurring on or after May 9, 1997; however, the sentences may be applied to terminations occurring on or after May 9, 1996, provided that the partnership and its partners apply the sentences to the termination in a consistent manner.

(*m*) *Section 754 elections*—(*1*) *In general.* The capital accounts of the partners will not be considered to be determined and maintained in accordance with the rules of this paragraph (b)(2)(iv) unless, upon adjustment to the adjusted tax basis of partnership property under section 732, 734, or 743, the capital accounts of the partners are adjusted as provided in this paragraph (b)(2)(iv)(*m*).

(*2*) *Section 743 adjustments.* In the case of a transfer of all or a part of an interest in a partnership that has a section 754 election in effect for the partnership taxable year in which such transfer occurs, adjustments to the adjusted tax basis of partnership property under section 743 shall not be reflected in the capital account of the transferee partner or on the books of the partnership, and subsequent capital account adjustments for distributions (see paragraph (b)(2)(iv)(*e*)(1) of this section) and for depreciation, depletion, amortization, and gain or loss with respect to such property will disregard the effect of such basis adjustment. The preceding sentence shall not apply to the extent such basis adjustment is allocated to the common basis of partnership property under paragraph (b)(1) of § 1.734-2; in these cases, such basis adjustment shall, except as provided in paragraph (b)(2)(iv)(*m*)(*5*) of this section, give rise to adjustments to the capital accounts of the partners in accordance with their interests in the partnership under paragraph (b)(3) of this section. See examples (13)(iii) and (iv) of paragraph (b)(5) of this section.

(*3*) *Section 732 adjustments.* In the case of a transfer of all or a part of an interest in a partnership that does not have a section 754 election in effect for the partnership taxable year in which such transfer occurs, adjustments to the adjusted tax basis of partnership property under section 732(d) will be treated in the capital accounts of the partners in the same manner as section 743 basis adjustments are treated under paragraph (b)(2)(iv)(*m*)(*2*) of this section.

(*4*) *Section 734 adjustments.* Except as provided in paragraph (b)(2)(iv)(*m*)(.5) of this section, in the case of a distribution of property in liquidation of a partner's interest in the partnership by a partnership that has a section 754 election in effect for the partnership taxable year in which the distribution occurs, the partner who receives the distribution that gives rise to the adjustment to the adjusted tax basis of partnership property under section 734 shall have a corresponding adjustment made to his capital account. If such distribution is made other than in liquidation of a partner's interest in the partnership, however, except as provided in paragraph (b)(2)(iv)(*m*)(.5) of this section, the capital accounts of the partners shall be adjusted by the amount of the adjustment to the adjusted tax basis of partnership property under section 734, and such capital account adjustment shall be shared among the partners in the manner in which the unrealized income and gain that is displaced by such adjustment would have been shared if the property whose basis is adjusted were sold immediately prior to such adjustment for its recomputed adjusted tax basis.

(*5*) *Limitations on adjustments.* Adjustments may be made to the capital account of a partner (or his successor in interest) in respect of basis adjustments to partnership property under sections 732, 734, and 743 only to the extent that such basis adjustments (i) are permitted to be made to one or more items of partnership property under section 755, and (ii) result in an increase or a decrease in the amount at which such property is carried on the partnership's balance sheet, as computed for book purposes. For example, if the book value of partnership property exceeds the adjusted tax basis of such property, a basis adjustment to such property may be reflected in a partner's capital account only to the extent such adjustment exceeds the difference between the book value of such property and the adjusted tax basis of such property prior to such adjustment.

(*n*) *Partnership level characterization.* Except as otherwise provided in paragraph (b)(2)(iv)(*k*) of this section, the capital accounts of the partners will not be considered to be determined and maintained in accordance with the rules of this paragraph (b)(2)(iv) unless adjustments to such capital accounts in respect of partnership income, gain, loss, deduction, and section 705(a)(2)(B) expenditures (or item thereof) are made with reference to the Federal tax treatment of such items (and in the case of book items, with reference to the Federal tax treatment of the corresponding tax items) at the partnership level, without regard to any requisite or elective tax

Reg. § 1.704-1(b)(2)

treatment of such items at the partner level (for example, under section 58(i)). However, a partnership that incurs mining exploration expenditures will determine the Federal tax treatment of income, gain, loss, and deduction with respect to the property to which such expenditures relate at the partnership level only after first taking into account the elections made by its partners under section 617 and section 703(b)(4).

(o) *Guaranteed payments.* Guaranteed payments to a partner under section 707(c) cause the capital account of the recipient partner to be adjusted only to the extent of such partner's distributive share of any partnership deduction, loss, or other downward capital account adjustment resulting from such payment.

(p) *Minor discrepancies.* Discrepancies between the balances in the respective capital accounts of the partners and the balances that would be in such respective capital accounts if they had been determined and maintained in accordance with this paragraph (b)(2)(iv) will not adversely affect the validity of an allocation, provided that such discrepancies are minor and are attributable to good faith error by the partnership.

(q) *Adjustments where guidance is lacking.* If the rules of this paragraph (b)(2)(iv) fail to provide guidance on how adjustments to the capital accounts of the partners should be made to reflect particular adjustments to partnership capital on the books of the partnership, such capital accounts will not be considered to be determined and maintained in accordance with those rules unless such capital account adjustments are made in a manner that (*1*) maintains equality between the aggregate governing capital accounts of the partners and the amount of partnership capital reflected on the partnership's balance sheet, as computed for book purposes, (*2*) is consistent with the underlying economic arrangement of the partners, and (*3*) is based, wherever practicable, on Federal tax accounting principles.

(r) *Restatement of capital accounts.* With respect to partnerships that began operating in a taxable year beginning before May 1, 1986, the capital accounts of the partners of which have not been determined and maintained in accordance with the rules of this paragraph (b)(2)(iv) since inception, such capital accounts shall not be considered to be determined and maintained in accordance with the rules of this paragraph (b)(2)(iv) for taxable years beginning after April 30, 1986, unless either—

(*1*) such capital accounts are adjusted, effective for the first partnership taxable year beginning after April 30, 1986, to reflect the fair market value of partnership property as of the first day of such taxable year, and in connection with such adjustment, the rules contained in paragraph (b)(2)(iv)(*f*)(*2*), (*3*), and (*4*) of this section are satisfied, or

(*2*) the differences between the balance in each partner's capital account and the balance that would be in such partner's capital account if capital accounts had been determined and maintained in accordance with this paragraph (b)(2)(iv) throughout the full term of the partnership are not significant (for example, such differences are solely attributable to a failure to provide for treatment of section 709 expenses in accordance with the rules of paragraph (b)(2)(iv)(*i*)(*2*) of this section or to a failure to follow the rules in paragraph (b)(2)(iv)(*m*) of this section), and capital accounts are adjusted to bring them into conformity with the rules of this paragraph (b)(2)(iv) no later than the end of the first partnership taxable year beginning after April 30, 1986.

With respect to a partnership that began operating in a taxable year beginning before May 1, 1986, modifications to the partnership agreement adopted on or before November 1, 1988, to make the capital account adjustments required to comply with this paragraph, and otherwise to satisfy the requirements of this paragraph, will be treated as if such modifications were included in the partnership agreement before the end of the first partnership taxable year beginning after April 30, 1986. However, compliance with the previous sentences will have no bearing on the validity of allocations that relate to partnership taxable years beginning before May 1, 1986.

(3) *Partner's interest in the partnership*—(i) *In general.* References in section 704(b) and this paragraph to a partner's interest in the partnership, or to the partners' interests in the partnership, signify the manner in which the partners have agreed to share the economic benefit or burden (if any) corresponding to the income, gain, loss, deduction, or credit (or item thereof) that is allocated.

Except with respect to partnership items that cannot have economic effect (such as nonrecourse deductions of the partnership), this sharing arrangement may or may not correspond to the overall economic arrangement of the partners. (For example, in the case of an unexpected downward adjustment to the capital account of a partner who does not have a deficit makeup obligation that causes such partner to have a negative capital account, it may be necessary to allocate a disproportionate amount of gross income of the partnership to such partner for such year so as to

Reg. § 1.704-1(b)(3)

bring that partner's capital account back up to zero.) Thus, a partner who has a 50 percent overall interest in the partnership may have a 90 percent interest in a particular item of income or deduction. The determination of a partner's interest in a partnership shall be made by taking into account all facts and circumstances relating to the economic arrangement of the partners. All partners' interests in the partnership are presumed to be equal (determined on a per capita basis). However, this presumption may be rebutted by the taxpayer or the Internal Revenue Service by establishing facts and circumstances that show that the partners' interests in the partnership are otherwise.

(ii) *Factors considered.* In determining a partner's interest in the partnership, the following factors are among those that will be considered:

(*a*) The partners' relative contributions to the partnership,

(*b*) The interests of the partners in economic profits and losses (if different than that in taxable income or loss),

(*c*) The interests of the partners in cash flow and other non-liquidating distributions, and

(*d*) The rights of the partners to distributions of capital upon liquidation.

The provisions of this subparagraph (b)(3) are illustrated by examples (1)(i) and (ii), (4)(i), (5)(i) and (ii), (6), (7)(i), (ii), and (iv), (8), (10)(ii), (16)(i), and (19)(iii) of paragraph (b)(5) of this section. See paragraph (b)(4)(i) of this section concerning rules for determining the partners' interests in the partnership with respect to certain tax items.

(iii) *Certain determinations.* If—

(*a*) Requirements (*1*) and (*2*) of paragraph (b)(2)(ii)(*b*) of this section are satisfied, and

(*b*) All or a portion of an allocation of income, gain, loss, or deduction made to a partner for a partnership taxable year does not have economic effect under paragraph (b)(2)(ii) of this section,

the partners' interests in the partnership with respect to the portion of the allocation that lacks economic effect will be determined by comparing the manner in which distributions (and contributions) would be made if all partnership property were sold at book value and the partnership were liquidated immediately following the end of the taxable year to which the allocation relates with the manner in which distributions (and contributions) would be made if all partnership property were sold at book value and the partnership were liquidated immediately following the end of the prior taxable year, and adjusting the result for the items described in (*4*), (*5*), and (*6*) of paragraph (b)(2)(ii)(*d*) of this section. A determination made under this paragraph (b)(3)(iii) will have no force if the economic effect of valid allocations made in the same manner is insubstantial under paragraph (b)(2)(iii) of this section. See examples (1)(iv), (v), and (vi), and (15)(ii) and (iii) of paragraph (b)(5) of this section.

(4) *Special rules*—(i) *Allocations to reflect revaluations.* If partnership property is, under paragraphs (b)(2)(iv)(*d*) or (b)(2)(iv)(*f*) of this section, properly reflected in the capital accounts of the partners and on the books of the partnership at a book value that differs from the adjusted tax basis of such property, then depreciation, depletion, amortization, and gain or loss, as computed for book purposes, with respect to such property will be greater or less than the depreciation, depletion, amortization, and gain or loss, as computed for tax purposes, with respect to such property. In these cases the capital accounts of the partners are required to be adjusted solely for allocations of the book items to such partners (see paragraph (b)(2)(iv)(*g*) of this section), and the partners' shares of the corresponding tax items are not independently reflected by further adjustments to the partners' capital accounts. Thus, separate allocations of these tax items cannot have economic effect under paragraph (b)(2)(ii)(*b*)(*1*) of this section, and the partners' distributive shares of such tax items must (unless governed by section 704(c)) be determined in accordance with the partners' interests in the partnership. These tax items must be shared among the partners in a manner that takes account of the variation between the adjusted tax basis of such property and its book value in the same manner as variations between the adjusted tax basis and fair market value of property contributed to the partnership are taken into account in determining the partners' shares of tax items under section 704(c). See examples (14) and (18) of paragraph (b)(5) of this section.

(ii) *Credits.* Allocations of tax credits and tax credit recapture are not reflected by adjustments to the partners' capital accounts (except to the extent that adjustments to the adjusted tax basis of partnership section 38 property in respect of tax credits and tax credit recapture give rise to capital account adjustments under paragraph (b)(2)(iv)(*j*) of this section). Thus, such allocations cannot have economic effect under paragraph (b)(2)(ii)(*b*)(*1*) of this section, and the tax credits and tax credit recapture must be allocated in accordance with the partners' interests in the partnership as of the time the tax credit or credit recapture arises. With respect to the investment tax credit provided by section 38, allocations of

Reg. § 1.704-1(b)(4)

cost or qualified investment made in accordance with paragraph (f) of § 1.46-3 and paragraph (a)(4)(iv) of § 1.48-8 shall be deemed to be made in accordance with the partners' interests in the partnership. With respect to other tax credits, if a partnership expenditure (whether or not deductible) that gives rise to a tax credit in a partnership taxable year also gives rise to valid allocations of partnership loss or deduction (or other downward capital account adjustments) for such year, then the partners' interests in the partnership with respect to such credit (or the cost giving rise thereto) shall be in the same proportion as such partners' respective distributive shares of such loss or deduction (and adjustments). See example (11) of paragraph (b)(5) of this section. Identical principles shall apply in determining the partners' interests in the partnership with respect to tax credits that arise from receipts of the partnership (whether or not taxable).

(iii) *Excess percentage depletion.* To the extent the percentage depletion in respect of an item of depletable property of the partnership exceeds the adjusted tax basis of such property, allocations of such excess percentage depletion are not reflected by adjustments to the partners' capital accounts. Thus, such allocations cannot have economic effect under paragraph (b)(2)(ii)(*b*)(*1*) of this section, and such excess percentage depletion must be allocated in accordance with the partners' interests in the partnership. The partners' interests in the partnership for a partnership taxable year with respect to such excess percentage depletion shall be in the same proportion as such partners' respective distributive shares of gross income from the depletable property (as determined under section 613(c)) for such year. See example (12) of paragraph (b)(5) of this section. See paragraphs (b)(2)(iv)(*k*) and (b)(4)(v) of this section for special rules concerning oil and gas properties of the partnership.

(iv) *Allocations attributable to nonrecourse liabilities.* The rules for allocations attributable to nonrecourse liabilities are contained in § 1.704-2.

(v) *Allocations under section 613A(c)(7)(D).* Allocations of the adjusted tax basis of a partnership oil or gas property are controlled by section 613A(c)(7)(D) and the regulations thereunder. However, if the partnership agreement provides for an allocation of the adjusted tax basis of an oil or gas property among the partners, and such allocation is not otherwise governed under section 704(c) (or related principles under paragraph (b)(4)(i) of this section), that allocation will be recognized as being in accordance with the partners' interests in partnership capital under section 613A(c)(7)(D), provided (*a*) such allocation does not give rise to capital account adjustments under paragraph (b)(2)(iv)(*k*) of this section the economic effect of which is insubstantial (as determined under paragraph (b)(2)(iii) of this section), and (*b*) all other material allocations and capital account adjustments under the partnership agreement are recognized under this paragraph (b). Otherwise, such adjusted tax basis must be allocated among the partners pursuant to section 613A(c)(7)(D) in accordance with the partners' actual interests in partnership capital or income. For purposes of section 613A(c)(7)(D) the partners' allocable shares of the amount realized upon the partnership's taxable disposition of an oil or gas property will, except to the extent governed by section 704(c) (or related principles under paragraph (b)(4)(i) of this section), be determined under this paragraph (b)(4)(v). If, pursuant to paragraph (b)(2)(iv)(*k*)(*2*) of this section, the partners' capital accounts are adjusted to reflect the simulated depletion of an oil or gas property of the partnership, the portion of the total amount realized by the partnership upon the taxable disposition of such property that represents recovery of its simulated adjusted tax basis therein will be allocated to the partners in the same proportion as the aggregate adjusted tax basis of such property was allocated to such partners (or their predecessors in interest). If, pursuant to paragraph (b)(2)(iv)(*k*)(*3*) of this section, the partners' capital accounts are adjusted to reflect the actual depletion of an oil or gas property of the partnership, the portion of the total amount realized by the partnership upon the taxable disposition of such property that equals the partners' aggregate remaining adjusted basis therein will be allocated to the partners in proportion to their respective remaining adjusted tax bases in such property. An allocation provided by the partnership agreement of the portion of the total amount realized by the partnership on its taxable disposition of an oil or gas property that exceeds the portion of the total amount realized allocated under either of the previous two sentences (whichever is applicable) shall be deemed to be made in accordance with the partners' allocable shares of such amount realized, provided (*c*) such allocation does not give rise to capital account adjustments under paragraph (b)(2)(iv)(*k*) of this section the economic effect of which is insubstantial (as determined under paragraph (b)(2)(ii) of this section), and (*d*) all other allocations and capital account adjustments under the partnership agreement are recognized under this paragraph. Otherwise, the partners' allocable shares of the total amount realized by the partnership on its taxable disposition of an oil or gas

Reg. § 1.704-1(b)(4)

property shall be determined in accordance with the partners' interests in the partnership under paragraph (b)(3) of this section. See example (19) of paragraph (b)(5) of this section. (See paragraph (b)(2)(iv)(*k*) of this section for the determination of appropriate adjustments to the partners' capital accounts relating to section 613A(c)(7)(D).)

(vi) *Amendments to partnership agreement.* If an allocation has substantial economic effect under paragraph (b)(2) of this section or is deemed to be made in accordance with the partners' interests in the partnership under paragraph (b)(4) of this section under the partnership agreement that is effective for the taxable year to which such allocation relates, and such partnership agreement thereafter is modified, both the tax consequences of the modification and the facts and circumstances surrounding the modification will be closely scrutinized to determine whether the purported modification was part of the original agreement. If it is determined that the purported modification was part of the original agreement, prior allocations may be reallocated in a manner consistent with the modified terms of the agreement, and subsequent allocations may be reallocated to take account of such modified terms. For example, if a partner is obligated by the partnership agreement to restore the deficit balance in his capital account (or any limited dollar amount thereof) in accordance with requirement (*3*) of paragraph (b)(2)(ii)(*b*) of this section and, thereafter, such obligation is eliminated or reduced (other than as provided in paragraph (b)(2)(ii)(*f*) of this section), or is not complied with in a timely manner, such elimination, reduction, or noncompliance may be treated as if it always were part of the partnership agreement for purposes of making any reallocations and determining the appropriate limitations period.

(vii) *Recapture.* For special rules applicable to the allocation of recapture income or credit, see paragraph (e) of § 1.1245-1, paragraph (f) of § 1.1250-1, paragraph (c) of § 1.1254-1, and paragraph (a) of § 1.47-6.

(5) *Examples.* The operation of the rules in this paragraph is illustrated by the following examples:

Example (1). (i) A and B form a general partnership with cash contributions of $40,000 each, which cash is used to purchase depreciable personal property at a cost of $80,000. The partnership elects under section 48(q)(4) to reduce the amount of investment tax credit in lieu of adjusting the tax basis of such property. The partnership agreement provides that A and B will have equal shares of taxable income and loss (computed without regard to cost recovery deductions) and cash flow and that all cost recovery deductions on the property will be allocated to A. The agreement further provides that the partners' capital accounts will be determined and maintained in accordance with paragraph (b)(2)(iv) of this section, but that upon liquidation of the partnership, distributions will be made equally between the partners (regardless of capital account balances) and no partner will be required to restore the deficit balance in his capital account for distribution to partners with positive capital accounts balances. In the partnership's first taxable year, it recognizes operating income equal to its operating expenses and has an additional $20,000 cost recovery deduction, which is allocated entirely to A. That A and B will be entitled to equal distributions on liquidation, even though A is allocated the entire $20,000 cost recovery deduction, indicates A will not bear the full risk of the economic loss corresponding to such deduction if such loss occurs. Under paragraph (b)(2)(ii) of this section, the allocation lacks economic effect and will be disregarded. The partners made equal contributions to the partnership, share equally in other taxable income and loss and in cash flow, and will share equally in liquidation proceeds, indicating that their actual economic arrangement is to bear the risk imposed by the potential decrease in the value of the property equally. Thus, under paragraph (b)(3) of this section the partners' interests in the partnership are equal, and the cost recovery deduction will be reallocated equally between A and B.

(ii) Assume the same facts as in (i) except that the partnership agreement provides that liquidation proceeds will be distributed in accordance with capital account balances if the partnership is liquidated during the first five years of its existence but that liquidation proceeds will be distributed equally if the partnership is liquidated thereafter. Since the partnership agreement does not provide for the requirement contained in paragraph (b)(2)(ii)(*b*)(*2*) of this section to be satisfied throughout the term of the partnership, the partnership allocations do not have economic effect. Even if the partnership agreement provided for the requirement contained in paragraph (b)(2)(ii)(*b*)(*2*) to be satisfied throughout the term of the partnership, such allocations would not have economic effect unless the requirement contained in paragraph (b)(2)(ii)(*b*)(*3*) of this section or the alternate economic effect test contained in paragraph (b)(2)(ii)(*d*) of this section were satisfied.

(iii) Assume the same facts as in (i) except that distributions in liquidation of the partnership (or any partner's interest) are to be made in

Reg. § 1.704-1(b)(5)

accordance with the partners' positive capital account balances throughout the term of the partnership (as set forth in paragraph (b)(2)(ii)(b)(2) of this section). Assume further that the partnership agreement contains a qualified income offset (as defined in paragraph (b)(2)(ii)(d) of this section) and that, as of the end of each partnership taxable year, the items described in paragraphs (b)(2)(ii)(d)(4), (5), and (6) of this section are not reasonably expected to cause or increase a deficit balance in A's capital account.

	A	B
Capital account upon formation	$40,000	$40,000
Less: year 1 cost recovery deduction	(20,000)	0
Capital account at end of year 1	$20,000	$40,000

Under the alternate economic effect test contained in paragraph (b)(2)(ii)(d) of this section, the allocation of the $20,000 cost recovery deduction to A has economic effect.

(iv) Assume the same facts as in (iii) and that in the partnership's second taxable year it recognizes operating income equal to its operating expenses and has a $25,000 cost recovery deduction which, under the partnership agreement, is allocated entirely to A.

	A	B
Capital account at beginning of year 2	$20,000	$40,000
Less: year 2 cost recovery deduction	(25,000)	0
Capital account at end of year 2	$(5,000)	$40,000

The allocation of the $25,000 cost recovery deduction to A satisfies the alternate economic effect test contained in paragraph (b)(2)(ii)(d) of this section only to the extent of $20,000. Therefore, only $20,000 of such allocation has economic effect, and the remaining $5,000 must be reallocated in accordance with the partners' interests in the partnership. Under the partnership agreement, if the property were sold immediately following the end of the partnership's second taxable year for $35,000 (its adjusted tax basis), the $35,000 would be distributed to B. Thus, B, and not A, bears the economic burden corresponding to $5,000 of the $25,000 cost recovery deduction allocated to A. Under paragraph (b)(3)(iii) of this section, $5,000 of such cost recovery deduction will be reallocated to B.

(v) Assume the same facts as in (iv) except that the cost recovery deduction for the partnership's second taxable year is $20,000 instead of $25,000. The allocation of such cost recovery deduction to A has economic effect under the alternate economic effect test contained in paragraph (b)(2)(ii)(d) of this section. Assume further that the property is sold for $35,000 immediately following the end of the partnership's second taxable year, resulting in a $5,000 taxable loss ($40,000 adjusted tax basis less $35,000 sales price), and the partnership is liquidated.

	A	B
Capital account at beginning of year 2	$20,000	$40,000
Less: year 2 cost recovery deduction	(20,000)	0
Capital account at end of year 2	0	$40,000
Less: loss on sale	(2,500)	(2,500)
Capital account before liquidation	$(2,500)	$37,500

Under the partnership agreement the $35,000 sales proceeds are distributed to B. Since B bears the entire economic burden corresponding to the $5,000 taxable loss from the sale of the property, the allocation of $2,500 of such loss to A does not have economic effect and must be reallocated in accordance with the partners' interests in the partnership. Under paragraph (b)(3)(iii) of this section, such $2,500 loss will be reallocated to B.

(vi) Assume the same facts as in (iv) except that the cost recovery deduction for the partnership's second taxable year is $20,000 instead of $25,000, and that as of the end of the partnership's second taxable year it is reasonably expected that during its third taxable year the partnership will (1) have operating income equal to its operating expenses (but will have no cost recovery deductions), (2) borrow $10,000 (recourse) and distribute such amount $5,000 to A and $5,000 to B, and (3) thereafter sell the partnership property, repay the $10,000 liability, and liquidate. In determining the extent to which the alternate economic effect test contained in paragraph (b)(2)(ii)(d) of this section is satisfied as of the end of the partnership's second taxable year, the fair market value of partnership property is presumed to be equal to its adjusted tax basis (in accordance with paragraph (b)(2)(iii)(c) of this

Reg. § 1.704-1(b)(5)

section). Thus, it is presumed that the selling price of such property during the partnership's third taxable year will be its $40,000 adjusted tax basis. Accordingly, there can be no reasonable expectation that there will be increases to A's capital account in the partnership's third taxable year that will offset the expected $5,000 distribution to A. Therefore, the distribution of the loan proceeds must be taken into account in determining to what extent the alternate economic effect test contained in paragraph (b)(2)(ii)(d) is satisfied.

	A	B
Capital account at beginning of year 2	$20,000	$40,000
Less: expected future distribution	(5,000)	(5,000)
Less: year 2 cost recovery deduction	(20,000)	(0)
Hypothetical capital account at end of year 2	$(5,000)	$35,000

Upon sale of the partnership property, the $40,000 presumed sales proceeds would be used to repay the $10,000 liability, and the remaining $30,000 would be distributed to B. Under these circumstances the allocation of the $20,000 cost recovery deduction to A in the partnership's second taxable year satisfies the alternate economic effect test contained in paragraph (b)(2)(ii)(d) of this section only to the extent of $15,000. Under paragraph (b)(3)(iii) of this section, the remaining $5,000 of such deduction will be reallocated to B. The results in this example would be the same even if the partnership agreement also provided that any gain (whether ordinary income or capital gain) upon the sale of the property would be allocated to A to the extent of the prior allocations of cost recovery deductions to him, and, at end of the partnership's second taxable year, the partners were confident that the gain on the sale of the property in the partnership's third taxable year would be sufficient to offset the expected $5,000 distribution to A.

(vii) Assume the same facts as in (iv) except that the partnership agreement also provides that any partner with a deficit balance in his capital account following the liquidation of his interest must restore that deficit to the partnership (as set forth in paragraph (b)(2)(ii)(b)(3) of this section). Thus, if the property were sold for $35,000 immediately after the end of the partnership's second taxable year, the $35,000 would be distributed to B, A would contribute $5,000 (the deficit balance in his capital account) to the partnership, and that $5,000 would be distributed to B. The allocation of the entire $25,000 cost recovery deduction to A in the partnership's second taxable year has economic effect.

(viii) Assume the same facts as in (vii) except that A's obligation to restore the deficit balance in his capital account is limited to a maximum of $5,000. The allocation of the $25,000 cost recovery deduction to A in the partnership's second taxable year has economic effect under the alternate economic effect test contained in paragraph (b)(2)(ii)(d) of this section. At the end of such year, A makes an additional $5,000 contribution to the partnership (thereby eliminating the $5,000 deficit balance in his capital account). Under paragraph (b)(2)(ii)(f) of this section, A's obligation to restore up to $5,000 of the deficit balance in his capital account may be eliminated after he contributes the additional $5,000 without affecting the validity of prior allocations.

(ix) Assume the same facts as in (iv) except that upon formation of the partnership A also contributes to the partnership his negotiable promissory note with a $5,000 principal balance. The note unconditionally obligates A to pay an additional $5,000 to the partnership at the earlier of (a) the beginning of the partnership's fourth taxable year, or (b) the end of the partnership taxable year in which A's interest is liquidated. Under paragraph (b)(2)(ii)(c) of this section, A is considered obligated to restore up to $5,000 of the deficit balance in his capital account to the partnership. Accordingly, under the alternate economic effect test contained in paragraph (b)(2)(ii)(d) of this section, the allocation of the $25,000 cost recovery deduction to A in the partnership's second taxable year has economic effect. The results in this example would be the same if (1) the note A contributed to the partnership were payable only at the end of the partnership's fourth taxable year (so that A would not be required to satisfy the note upon liquidation of his interest in the partnership), and (2) the partnership agreement provided that upon liquidation of A's interest, the partnership would retain A's note, and A would contribute to the partnership the excess of the outstanding principal balance of the note over its then fair market value.

(x) Assume the same facts as in (ix) except that A's obligation to contribute an additional $5,000 to the partnership is not evidenced by a promissory note. Instead, the partnership agreement imposes upon A the obligation to make an additional $5,000 contribution to the partnership at the earlier of (a) the beginning of the partnership's fourth taxable year, or (b) the end of the partnership taxable year in which A's interest is liquidated. Under paragraph (b)(2)(ii)(c) of this section, as a result of A's deferred contribution

Reg. § 1.704-1(b)(5)

requirement, A is considered obligated to restore up to $5,000 of the deficit balance in his capital account to the partnership. Accordingly, under the alternate economic effect test contained in paragraph (b)(2)(ii)(d) of this section, the allocation of the $25,000 cost recovery deduction to A in the partnership's second taxable year has economic effect.

(xi) Assume the same facts as in (vii) except that the partnership agreement also provides that any gain (whether ordinary income or capital gain) upon the sale of the property will be allocated to A to the extent of the prior allocations to A of cost recovery deductions from such property, and additional gain will be allocated equally between A and B. At the time the allocations of cost recovery deductions were made to A, the partners believed there would be gain on the sale of the property in an amount sufficient to offset the allocations of cost recovery deductions to A. Nevertheless, the existence of the gain chargeback provision will not cause the economic effect of the allocations to be insubstantial under paragraph (b)(2)(iii)(c) of this section, since in testing whether the economic effect of such allocations is substantial, the recovery property is presumed to decrease in value by the amount of such deductions.

Example (2). C and D form a general partnership solely to acquire and lease machinery that is 5-year recovery property under section 168. Each contributes $100,000, and the partnership obtains an $800,000 recourse loan to purchase the machinery. The partnership elects under section 48(q)(4) to reduce the amount of investment tax credit in lieu of adjusting the tax basis of such machinery. The partnership, C, and D have calendar taxable years. The partnership agreement provides that the partners' capital accounts will be determined and maintained in accordance with paragraph (b)(2)(iv) of this section, distributions in liquidation of the partnership (or any partner's interest) will be made in accordance with the partners' positive capital account balances, and any partner with a deficit balance in his capital account following the liquidation of his interest must restore that deficit to the partnership (as set forth in paragraphs (b)(2)(ii)(b)(2) and (3) of this section). The partnership agreement further provides that (a) partnership net taxable loss will be allocated 90 percent to C and 10 percent to D until such time as there is partnership net taxable income, and thereafter C will be allocated 90 percent of such taxable income until he has been allocated partnership net taxable income equal to the partnership net taxable loss previously allocated to him, (b) all further partnership net taxable income or loss will be allocated equally between C and D, and (c) distributions of operating cash flow will be made equally between C and D. The partnership enters into a 12-year lease with a financially secure corporation under which the partnership expects to have a net taxable loss in each of its first 5 partnership taxable years due to cost recovery deductions with respect to the machinery and net taxable income in each of its following 7 partnership taxable years, in part due to the absence of such cost recovery deductions. There is a strong likelihood that the partnership's net taxable loss in partnership taxable years 1 through 5 will be $100,000, $90,000, $80,000, $70,000, and $60,000, respectively, and the partnership's net taxable income in partnership taxable years 6 through 12 will be $40,000, $50,000, $60,000, $70,000, $80,000, $90,000, and $100,000, respectively. Even though there is a strong likelihood that the allocations of net taxable loss in years 1 through 5 will be largely offset by other allocations in partnership taxable years 6 through 12, and even if it is assumed that the total tax liability of the partners in years 1 through 12 will be less than if the allocations had not been provided in the partnership agreement, the economic effect of the allocations will not be insubstantial under paragraph (b)(2)(iii)(c) of this section. This is because at the time such allocations became part of the partnership agreement, there was a strong likelihood that the allocations of net taxable loss in years 1 through 5 would not be largely offset by allocations of income within 5 years (determined on a first-in, first-out basis). The year 1 allocation will not be offset until years 6, 7, and 8, the year 2 allocation will not be offset until years 8 and 9, the year 3 allocation will not be offset until years 9 and 10, the year 4 allocation will not be offset until years 10 and 11, and the year 5 allocation will not be offset until years 11 and 12.

Example (3). E and F enter into a partnership agreement to develop and market experimental electronic devices. E contributes $2,500 cash and agrees to devote his full-time services to the partnership. F contributes $100,000 cash and agrees to obtain a loan for the partnership for any additional capital needs. The partnership agreement provides that all deductions for research and experimental expenditures and interest on partnership loans are to be allocated to F. In addition, F will be allocated 90 percent, and E 10 percent, of partnership taxable income or loss, computed net of the deductions for such research and experimental expenditures and interest, until F has received allocations of such taxable income equal to the sum of such research and experimental expenditures, such interest expense, and his share of such taxable loss. Thereafter, E and F will share all taxable income and loss equally. Operating cash flow will be distributed equally between E and F. The partnership agreement also provides that E's and F's capital accounts will be determined and maintained in accordance with paragraph (b)(2)(iv) of this section, distributions in liquidation of the partnership (or any partner's interest) will be made in accordance with the partners' positive capital account balances, and any partner with a deficit balance in his capital account following the liquidation of his interest must restore that deficit to the partnership (as set forth in paragraphs (b)(2)(ii)(b)(2) and (3) of this section). These allocations have economic effect. In addition, in view of the nature of the partnership's activities, there is not a strong likelihood at the time the allocations become part of the partnership agreement that the economic effect of the allocations to F of deductions for research and experimental expenditures and interest on partnership loans will be largely offset by allocations to F of partnership net taxable income. The economic effect of the allocations is substantial.

Example (4). (i) G and H contribute $75,000 and $25,000, respectively, in forming a general partnership. The partnership agreement provides that all income, gain, loss, and deduction will be allocated equally between the partners, that the partners' capital accounts will be determined and maintained in accordance with paragraph (b)(2)(iv) of this section, but that all partnership distributions will, regardless of capital account balances, be made 75 percent to G and 25 percent to H. Following the liquidation of the partnership, neither partner is required to restore the deficit balance in his capital account to the partnership for distribution to partners with positive capital account balances. The allocations in the partnership agreement do not have economic effect. Since contributions were made in a 75/25 ratio and the partnership agreement indicates that all economic profits and losses of the partnership are to be shared in a 75/25 ratio, under paragraph (b)(3) of this section, partnership income, gain, loss, and deduction will be reallocated 75 percent to G and 25 percent to H.

(ii) Assume the same facts as in (i) except that the partnership maintains no capital accounts and the partnership agreement provides that all income, gain, loss, deduction, and credit will be allocated 75 percent to G and 25 percent to H. G and H are ultimately liable (under a State law right of contribution) for 75 percent and 25 percent, respectively, of any debts of the partnership. Although the allocations do not satisfy the requirements of paragraph (b)(2)(ii)(b) of this section, the allocations have economic effect under the economic effect equivalence test of paragraph (b)(2)(ii)(i) of this section.

(iii) Assume the same facts as in (i) except that the partnership agreement provides that any partner with a deficit balance in his capital account must restore that deficit to the partnership (as set forth in paragraph (b)(2)(ii)(b)(2) of this section). Although the allocations do not satisfy the requirements of paragraph (b)(2)(ii)(b) of this section, the allocations have economic effect under the economic effect equivalence test of paragraph (b)(2)(ii)(i) of this section.

Example (5). (i) Individuals I and J are the only partners of an investment partnership. The partnership owns corporate stocks, corporate debt instruments, and tax-exempt debt instruments. Over the next several years, I expects to be in the 50 percent marginal tax bracket, and J expects to be in the 15 percent marginal tax bracket. There is a strong likelihood that in each of the next several years the partnership will realize between $450 and $550 of tax-exempt interest and between $450 and $550 of a combination of taxable interest and dividends from its investments. I and J made equal capital contributions to the partnership, and they have agreed to share equally in gains and losses from the sale of the partnership's investment securities. I and J agree, however, that rather than share interest and dividends of the partnership equally, they will allocate the partnership's tax-exempt interest 80 percent to I and 20 percent to J and will distribute cash derived from interest received on the tax-exempt bonds in the same percentages. In addition, they agree to allocate 100 percent of the partnership's taxable interest and dividends to J and to distribute cash derived from interest and dividends received on the corporate stocks and debt instruments 100 percent to J. The partnership agreement further provides that the partners' capital accounts will be determined and maintained in accordance with paragraph (b)(2)(iv) of this section, distributions in liquidation of the partnership (or any partner's interest) will be made in accordance with the partner's positive capital account balances, and any partner with a deficit balance in his capital account following the liquidation of his interest must restore that deficit to the partnership (as set forth in paragraphs (b)(2)(ii)(b)(2) and (3) of this section). The allocation of taxable interest and dividends and tax-exempt interest has economic effect, but that economic effect is not substantial under the general rules set forth in paragraph (b)(2)(iii) of this section. Without the allocation I would be allocated between $225 and $275 of tax-exempt interest and between $225 and $275 of a combination of taxable interest and dividends, which (net of Fed-

Reg. § 1.704-1(b)(5)

eral income taxes he would owe on such income) would give I between $337.50 and $412.50 after tax. With the allocation, however, I will be allocated between $360 and $440 of tax-exempt interest and no taxable interest and dividends, which (net of Federal income taxes) will give I between $360 and $440 after tax. Thus, at the time the allocations became part of the partnership agreement, I is expected to enhance his after-tax economic consequences as a result of the allocations. On the other hand, there is a strong likelihood that neither I nor J will substantially diminish his after-tax economic consequences as a result of the allocations. Under the combination of likely investment outcomes least favorable for J, the partnership would realize $550 of tax-exempt interest and $450 of taxable interest and dividends, giving J $492.50 after tax (which is more than the $466.25 after tax J would have received if each of such amounts had been allocated equally between the partners). Under the combination of likely investment outcomes least favorable for I, the partnership would realize $450 of tax-exempt interest and $550 of taxable interest and dividends, giving I $360 after tax (which is not substantially less than the $362.50 he would have received if each of such amounts had been allocated equally between the partners). Accordingly, the allocations in the partnership agreement must be reallocated in accordance with the partners' interests in the partnership under paragraph (b)(3) of this section.

(ii) Assume the same facts as in (i). In addition, assume that in the first partnership taxable year in which the allocation arrangement described in (i) applies, the partnership realizes $450 of tax-exempt interest and $550 of taxable interest and dividends, so that, pursuant to the partnership agreement, I's capital account is credited with $360 (80 percent of the tax-exempt interest), and J's capital account is credited with $640 (20 percent of the tax-exempt interest and 100 percent of the taxable interest and dividends). The allocations of tax-exempt interest and taxable interest and dividends (which do not have substantial economic effect for the reasons stated in (i)) will be disregarded and will be reallocated. Since under the partnership agreement I will receive 36 percent (360/1,000) and J will receive 64 percent (640/1,000) of the partnership's total investment income in such year, under paragraph (b)(3) of this section the partnership's tax-exempt interest and taxable interest and dividends each will be reallocated 36 percent to I and 64 percent to J.

Example (6). K and L are equal partners in a general partnership formed to acquire and operate property described in section 1231(b). The partnership, K, and L have calendar taxable years. The partnership agreement provides that the partners' capital accounts will be determined and maintained in accordance with paragraph (b)(2)(iv) of this section, that distributions in liquidation of the partnership (or any partner's interest) will be made in accordance with the partners' positive capital account balances, and that any partner with a deficit balance in his capital account following the liquidation of his interest must restore that deficit to the partnership (as set forth in paragraphs (b)(2)(ii)(*b*) and (*3*) of this section). For a taxable year in which the partnership expects to incur a loss on the sale of a portion of such property, the partnership agreement is amended (at the beginning of the taxable year) to allocate such loss to K, who expects to have no gains from the sale of depreciable property described in section 1231(b) in that taxable year, and to allocate an equivalent amount of partnership loss and deduction for that year of a different character to L, who expects to have such gains. Any partnership loss and deduction in excess of these allocations will be allocated equally between K and L. The amendment is effective only for that taxable year. At the time the partnership agreement is amended, there is a strong likelihood that the partnership will incur deduction or loss in the taxable year other than loss from the sale of property described in section 1231(b) in an amount that will substantially equal or exceed the expected amount of the section 1231(b) loss. The allocations in such taxable year have economic effect. However, the economic effect of the allocations is insubstantial under the test described in paragraph (b)(2)(iii)(*b*) of this section because there is a stong likelihood, at the time the allocations become part of the partnership agreement, that the net increases and decreases to K's and L's capital accounts will be the same at the end of the taxable year to which they apply with such allocations in effect as they would have been in the absence of such allocations, and that the total taxes of K and L for such year will be reduced as a result of such allocations. If in fact the partnership incurs deduction or loss, other than loss from the sale of property described in section 1231(b), in an amount at least equal to the section 1231(b) loss, the loss and deduction in such taxable year will be reallocated equally between K and L under paragraph (b)(3) of this section. If not, the loss from the sale of property described in section 1231(b) and the items of deduction and other loss realized in such year will be reallocated between K and L in proportion to the net decreases in their capital accounts due to the allocation of such items under the partnership agreement.

Reg. § 1.704-1(b)(5)

Example (7). (i) M and N are partners in the MN general partnership, which is engaged in an active business. Income, gain, loss, and deduction from MN's business is allocated equally between M and N. The partnership, M, and N have calendar taxable years. Under the partnership agreement the partners' capital accounts will be determined and maintained in accordance with paragraph (b)(2)(iv) of this section, distributions in liquidation of the partnership (or any partner's interest) will be made in accordance with the partners' positive capital account balances, and any partner with a deficit balance in his capital account following the liquidation of his interest must restore that deficit to the partnership (as set forth in paragraphs (b)(2)(ii)(*b*)(*2*) and (*3*) of this section). In order to enhance the credit standing of the partnership, the partners contribute surplus funds to the partnership, which the partners agree to invest in equal dollar amounts of tax-exempt bonds and corporate stock for the partnership's first 3 taxable years. M is expected to be in a higher marginal tax bracket than N during those 3 years. At the time the decision to make these investments is made, it is agreed that, during the 3-year period of the investment, M will be allocated 90 percent and N 10 percent of the interest income from the tax-exempt bonds as well as any gain or loss from the sale thereof, and that M will be allocated 10 percent and N 90 percent of the dividend income from the corporate stock as well as any gain or loss from the sale thereof. At the time the allocations concerning the investments become part of the partnership agreement, there is not a strong likelihood that the gain or loss from the sale of the stock will be substantially equal to the gain or loss from the sale of the tax-exempt bonds, but there is a strong likelihood that the tax-exempt interest and the taxable dividends realized from these investments during the 3-year period will not differ substantially. These allocations have economic effect, and the economic effect of the allocations of the gain or loss on the sale of the tax-exempt bonds and corporate stock is substantial. The economic effect of the allocations of the tax-exempt interest and the taxable dividends, however, is not substantial under the test described in paragraph (b)(2)(iii)(c) of this section because there is a strong likelihood, at the time the allocations become part of the partnership agreement, that at the end of the 3-year period to which such allocations relate, the net increases and decreases to M's and N's capital accounts will be the same with such allocations as they would have been in the absence of such allocations, and that the total taxes of M and N for the taxable years to which such allocations relate will be reduced as a result of such allocations. If in fact the amounts of tax-exempt interest and taxable dividends earned by the partnership during the 3-year period are equal, the tax-exempt interest and taxable dividends will be reallocated to the partners in equal shares under paragraph (b)(3) of this section. If not, the tax-exempt interest and taxable dividends will be reallocated between M and N in proportion to the net increases in their capital accounts during such 3-year period due to the allocation of such items under the partnership agreement.

(ii) Assume the same facts as in (i) except that gain or loss from the sale of the tax-exempt bonds and corporate stock will be allocated equally between M and N and the partnership agreement provides that the 90/10 allocation arrangement with respect to the investment income applies only to the first $10,000 of interest income from the tax-exempt bonds and the first $10,000 of dividend income from the corporate stock, and only to the first taxable year of the partnership. There is a strong likelihood at the time the 90/10 allocation of the investment income became part of the partnership agreement that in the first taxable year of the partnership, the partnership will earn more than $10,000 of tax-exempt interest and more than $10,000 of taxable dividends. The allocations of tax-exempt interest and taxable dividends provided in the partnership agreement have economic effect, but under the test contained in paragraph (b)(2)(iii)(*b*) of this section, such economic effect is not substantial for the same reasons stated in (i) (but applied to the 1 taxable year, rather than to a 3-year period). If in fact the partnership realizes at least $10,000 of tax-exempt interest and at least $10,000 of taxable dividends in such year, the allocations of such interest income and dividend income will be reallocated equally between M and N under paragraph (b)(3) of this section. If not, the tax-exempt interest and taxable dividends will be reallocated between M and N in proportion to the net increases in their capital accounts due to the allocations of such items under the partnership agreement.

(iii) Assume the same facts as in (ii) except that at the time the 90/10 allocation of investment income becomes part of the partnership agreement, there is not a strong likelihood that (1) the partnership will earn $10,000 or more of tax-exempt interest and $10,000 or more of taxable dividends in the partnership's first taxable year, and (2) the amount of tax-exempt interest and taxable dividends earned during such year will be substantially the same. Under these facts the economic effect of the allocations generally will be substantial. (Additional facts may exist in certain cases, however, so that the allocation is insubstan-

Reg. § 1.704-1(b)(5)

tial under the second sentence of paragraph (b)(2)(iii). See example (5) above.)

Example (8). (i) O and P are equal partners in the OP general partnership. The partnership, O, and P have calendar taxable years. Partner O has a net operating loss carryover from another venture that is due to expire at the end of the partnership's second taxable year. Otherwise, both partners expect to be in the 50 percent marginal tax bracket in the next several taxable years. The partnership agreement provides that the partners' capital accounts will be determined and maintained in accordance with paragraph (b)(2)(iv) of this section, distributions in liquidation of the partnership (or any partner's interest) will be made in accordance with the partners' positive capital account balances, and any partner with a deficit balance in his capital account following the liquidation of his interest must restore that deficit to the partnership (as set forth in paragraphs (b)(2)(ii)(*b*)(*2*) and (*3*) of this section). The partnership agreement is amended (at the beginning of the partnership's second taxable year) to allocate all the partnership net taxable income for that year to O. Future partnership net taxable loss is to be allocated to O, and future partnership net taxable income to P, until the allocation of income to O in the partnership's second taxable year is offset. It is further agreed orally that in the event the partnership is liquidated prior to completion of such offset, O's capital account will be adjusted downward to the extent of one-half of the allocations of income to O in the partnership's second taxable year that have not been offset by other allocations, P's capital account will be adjusted upward by a like amount, and liquidation proceeds will be distributed in accordance with the partners' adjusted capital account balances. As a result of this oral amendment, all allocations of partnership net taxable income and net taxable loss made pursuant to the amendment executed at the beginning of the partnership's second taxable year lack economic effect and will be disregarded. Under the partnership agreement other allocations are made equally to O and P, and O and P will share equally in liquidation proceeds, indicating that the partners' interests in the partnership are equal. Thus, the disregarded allocations will be reallocated equally between the partners under paragraph (b)(3) of this section.

(ii) Assume the same facts as in (i) except that there is no agreement that O's and P's capital accounts will be adjusted downward and upward, respectively, to the extent of one-half of the partnership net taxable income allocated to O in the partnership's second taxable year that is not offset subsequently by other allocations. The income of the partnership is generated primarily by fixed interest payments received with respect to highly rated corporate bonds, which are expected to produce sufficient net taxable income prior to the end of the partnership's seventh taxable year to offset in large part the net taxable income to be allocated to O in the partnership's second taxable year. Thus, at the time the allocations are made part of the partnership agreement, there is a strong likelihood that the allocation of net taxable income to be made to O in the second taxable year will be offset in large part within 5 taxable years thereafter. These allocations have economic effect. However, the economic effect of the allocation of partnership net taxable income to O in the partnership's second taxable year, as well as the offsetting allocations to P, is not substantial under the test contained in paragraph (b)(2)(iii)(*c*) of this section because there is a strong likelihood that the net increases or decreases in O's and P's capital accounts will be the same at the end of the partnership's seventh taxable year with such allocations as they would have been in the absence of such allocations, and the total taxes of O and P for the taxable years to which such allocations relate will be reduced as a result of such allocations. If in fact the partnership, in its taxable years 3 through 7, realizes sufficient net taxable income to offset the amount allocated to O in the second taxable year, the allocations provided in the partnership agreement will be reallocated equally between the partners under paragraph (b)(3) of this section.

Example (9). Q and R form a limited partnership with contributions of $20,000 and $180,000, respectively. Q, the limited partner, is a corporation that has $2,000,000 of net operating loss carryforwards that will not expire for 8 years. Q does not expect to have sufficient income (apart from the income of the partnership) to absorb any of such net operating loss carryforwards. R, the general partner, is a corporation that expects to be in the 46 percent marginal tax bracket for several years. The partnership agreement provides that the partners' capital accounts will be determined and maintained in accordance with paragraph (b)(2)(iv) of this section, distributions in liquidation of the partnership (or any partner's interest) will be made in accordance with the partners' positive capital account balances, and any partner with a deficit balance in his capital account following the liquidation of his interest must restore that deficit to the partnership (as set forth in paragraph (b)(2)(ii)(*b*)(*2*) and (*3*) of this section). The partnership's cash, together with the proceeds of an $800,000 loan, are invested in assets that are expected to produce taxable income and cash flow (before debt service) of ap-

Reg. § 1.704-1(b)(5)

proximately $150,000 a year for the first 8 years of the partnership's operations. In addition, it is expected that the partnership's total taxable income in its first 8 taxable years will not exceed $2,000,000. The partnership's $150,000 of cash flow in each of its first 8 years will be used to retire the $800,000 loan. The partnership agreement provides that partnership net taxable income will be allocated 90 percent to Q and 10 percent to R in the first through eighth partnership taxable years, and 90 percent to R and 10 percent to Q in all subsequent partnership taxable years. Net taxable loss will be allocated 90 percent to R and 10 percent to Q in all partnership taxable years. All distributions of cash from the partnership to partners (other than the priority distributions to Q described below) will be made 90 percent to R and 10 percent to Q. At the end of the partnership's eighth taxable year, the amount of Q's capital account in excess of one-ninth of R's capital account on such date will be designated as Q's "excess capital account." Beginning in the ninth taxable year of the partnership, the undistributed portion of Q's excess capital account will begin to bear interest (which will be paid and deducted under section 707(c)) at a rate of interest below the rate that the partnership can borrow from commercial lenders, and over the next several years (following the eighth year) the partnership will make priority cash distributions to Q in prearranged percentages of Q's excess capital account designed to amortize Q's excess capital account and the interest thereon over a prearranged period. In addition, the partnership's agreement prevents Q from causing his interest in the partnership from being liquidated (and thereby receiving the balance in his capital account) without R's consent until Q's excess capital account has been eliminated. The below-market rate of interest and the period over which the amortization will take place are prescribed such that, as of the end of the partnership's eighth taxable year, the present value of Q's right to receive such priority distributions is approximately 46 percent of the amount of Q's excess capital account as of such date. However, because the partnership's income for its first 8 taxable years will be realized approximately ratably over that period, the present value of Q's right to receive the priority distributions with respect to its excess capital account is, as of the date the partnership agreement is entered into, less than the present value of the additional Federal income taxes for which R would be liable if, during the partnership's first 8 taxable years, all partnership income were to be allocated 90 percent to R and 10 to Q. The allocations of partnership taxable income to Q and R in the first through eighth partnership taxable years have economic effect. However, such economic effect is not substantial under the general rules set forth in paragraph (b)(2)(iii) of this section. This is true because R may enhance his after-tax economic consequences, on a present value basis, as a result of the allocations to Q of 90 percent of partnership's income during taxable years 1 through 8, and there is a strong likelihood that neither R nor Q will substantially diminish its after-tax economic consequences, on a present value basis, as a result of such allocation. Accordingly, partnership taxable income for partnership taxable years 1 through 8 will be reallocated in accordance with the partners' interests in the partnership under paragraph (b)(3) of this section.

Example (10). (i) S and T form a general partnership to operate a travel agency. The partnership agreement provides that the partners' capital accounts will be determined and maintained in accordance with paragraph (b)(2)(iv) of this section, distributions in liquidation of the partnership (or any partner's interest) will be made in accordance with the partners' positive capital account balances, and any partner with a deficit balance in his capital account following the liquidation of his interest must restore that deficit to the partnership (as set forth in paragraphs (b)(2)(ii)(*b*)(*2*) and (*3*) of this section). The partnership agreement provides that T, a resident of a foreign country, will be allocated 90 percent, and S 10 percent, of the income, gain, loss, and deduction derived from operations conducted by T within his country, and all remaining income, gain, loss, and deduction will be allocated equally. The amount of such income, gain, loss, or deduction cannot be predicted with any reasonable certainty. The allocations provided by the partnership agreement have substantial economic effect.

(ii) Assume the same facts as in (i) except that the partnership agreement provides that all income, gain, loss, and deduction of the partnership will be shared equally, but that T will be allocated all income, gain, loss, and deduction derived from operations conducted by him within his country as a part of his equal share of partnership income, gain, loss, and deduction, up to the amount of such share. Assume the total tax liability of S and T for each year to which these allocations relate will be reduced as a result of such allocation. These allocations have economic effect. However, such economic effect is not substantial under the test stated in paragraph (b)(2)(iii)(*b*) of this section because, at the time the allocations became part of the partnership agreement, there is a strong likelihood that the net increases and decreases to S's and T's capital

Reg. § 1.704-1(b)(5)

accounts will be the same at the end of each partnership taxable year with such allocations as they would have been in the absence of such allocations, and that the total tax liability of S and T for each year to which such allocations relate will be reduced as a result of such allocations. Thus, all items of partnership income, gain, loss, and income, gain, loss, and deduction will be reallocated equally between S and T under paragraph (b)(3) of this section.

Example (11). (i) U and V share equally all income, gain, loss, and deduction of the UV general partnership, as well as all non-liquidating distributions made by the partnership. The partnership agreement provides that the partners' capital accounts will be determined and maintained in accordance with paragraph (b)(2)(iv) of this section, distributions in liquidation of the partnership (or any partner's interest) will be made in accordance with the partners' positive capital account balances, and any partner with a deficit balance in his capital account following the liquidation of his interest must restore such deficit to the partnership (as set forth in paragraphs (b)(2)(ii)(*b*)(*2*) and (*3*) of this section). The agreement further provides that the partners will be allocated equal shares of any section 705(a)(2)(B) expenditures of the partnership. In the partnership's first taxable year, it pays qualified first-year wages of $6,000 and is entitled to a $3,000 targeted jobs tax credit under sections 44B and 51 of the Code. Under section 280C the partnership must reduce its deduction for wages paid by the $3,000 credit claimed (which amount constitutes a section 705(a)(2)(B) expenditure). The partnership agreement allocates the credit to U. Although the allocations of wage deductions and section 705 (a)(2)(B) expenditures have substantial economic effect, the allocation of tax credit cannot have economic effect since it cannot properly be reflected in the partners' capital accounts. Furthermore, the allocation is not in accordance with the special partners' interests in the partnership rule contained in paragraph (b)(4)(ii) of this section. Under that rule, since the expenses that gave rise to the credit are shared equally by the partners, the credit will be shared equally between U and V.

(ii) Assume the same facts as in (i) and that at the beginning of the partnership's second taxable year, the partnership agreement is amended to allocate to U all wage expenses incurred in that year (including wage expenses that constitute section 705(a)(2)(B) expenditures) whether or not such wages qualify for the credit. The partnership agreement contains no offsetting allocations. That taxable year the partnership pays $8,000 in total wages to its employees. Assume that the partnership has operating income equal to its operating expenses (exclusive of expenses for wages). Assume further that $6,000 of the $8,000 wage expense constitutes qualified first-year wages. U is allocated the $3,000 deduction and the $3,000 section 705(a)(2)(B) expenditure attributable to the $6,000 of qualified first-year wages, as well as the deduction for the other $2,000 in wage expenses. The allocations of wage deductions and section 705(a)(2)(B) expenditures have substantial economic effect. Furthermore, since the wage credit is allocated in the same proportion as the expenses that gave rise to the credit, and the allocation of those expenses has substantial economic effect, the allocation of such credit to U is in accordance with the special partners' interests in the partnership rule contained in paragraph (b)(4)(ii) of this section and is recognized thereunder.

Example (12). (i) W and X form a general partnership for the purpose of mining iron ore. W makes an initial contribution of $75,000, and X makes an initial contribution of $25,000. The partnership agreement provides that non-liquidating distributions will be made 75 percent to W and 25 percent to X, and that all items of income, gain, loss, and deduction will be allocated 75 percent to W and 25 percent to X, except that all percentage depletion deductions will be allocated to W. The agreement further provides that the partners' capital accounts will be determined and maintained in accordance with paragraph (b)(2)(iv) of this section, distributions in liquidation of the partnership (or any partner's interest) will be made in accordance with the partners' positive capital account balances, and any partner with a deficit balance in his capital account following the liquidation of his interest must restore such deficit to the partnership (as set forth in paragraphs (b)(2)(ii)(*b*)(*2*) and (*3*) of this section). Assume that the adjusted tax basis of the partnership's only depletable iron ore property is $1,000 and that the percentage depletion deduction for the taxable year with respect to such property is $1,500. The allocation of partnership income, gain, loss, and deduction (excluding the percentage depletion deduction) as well as the allocation of $1,000 of the percentage depletion deduction have substantial economic effect. The allocation to W of the remaining $500 of the percentage depletion deduction, representing the excess of percentage depletion over adjusted tax basis of the iron ore property, cannot have economic effect since such amount cannot properly be reflected in the partners' capital accounts. Furthermore, the allocation to W of that $500 excess percentage depletion deduction is not in accordance with the special partners' interests in the partnership rule contained in paragraph (b)(4)(iii) of this section, under which such $500

Reg. § 1.704-1(b)(5)

excess depletion deduction (and all further percentage depletion deductions from the mine) will be reallocated 75 percent to W and 25 percent to X.

(ii) Assume the same facts as in (i) except that the partnership agreement provides that all percentage depletion deductions of the partnership will be allocated 75 percent to W and 25 percent to X. Once again, the allocation of partnership income, gain, loss, and deduction (excluding the percentage depletion deduction) as well as the allocation of $1,000 of the percentage depletion deduction have substantial economic effect. Furthermore, since the $500 portion of the percentage depletion deduction that exceeds the adjusted basis of such iron ore property is allocated in the same manner as valid allocations of the gross income from such property during the taxable year (i.e., 75 percent to W and 25 percent to X), the allocation of the $500 excess percentage depletion contained in the partnership agreement is in accordance with the special partners' interests in the partnership rule contained in paragraph (b)(4)(iii) of this section.

Example (13). (i) Y and Z form a brokerage general partnership for the purpose of investing and trading in marketable securities. Y contributes cash of $10,000, and Z contributes securities of P corporation, which have an adjusted basis of $3,000 and a fair market value of $10,000. The partnership would not be an investment company under section 351(e) if it were incorporated. The partnership agreement provides that the partners' capital accounts will be determined and maintained in accordance with paragraph (b)(2)(iv) of this section, distributions in liquidation of the partnership (or any partner's interest) will be made in accordance with the partners' positive capital account balances, and any partner with a deficit balance in his capital account following the liquidation of his interest must restore that deficit to the partnership (as set forth in paragraphs (b)(2)(ii)(*b*)(*2*) and (*3*) of this section). The partnership uses the interim closing of the books method for purposes of section 706. The initial capital accounts of Y and Z are fixed at $10,000 each. The agreement further provides that all partnership distributions, income, gain, loss, deduction, and credit will be shared equally between Y and Z, except that the taxable gain attributable to the precontribution appreciation in the value of the securities of P corporation will be allocated to Z in accordance with section 704(c). During the partnership's first taxable year, it sells the securities of P corporation for $12,000, resulting in a $2,000 book gain ($12,000 less $10,000 book value) and a $9,000 taxable gain ($12,000 less $3,000 adjusted tax basis). The partnership has no other income, gain, loss, or deductions for the taxable year. The gain from the sale of the securities is allocated as follows:

	Y Tax	Y Book	Z Tax	Z Book
Capital account upon formation	$10,000	$10,000	$3,000	$10,000
Plus: gain	1,000	1,000	8,000	1,000
Capital account at end of year 1	$11,000	$11,000	$11,000	$11,000

The allocation of the $2,000 book gain, $1,000 each to Y and Z, has substantial economic effect. Furthermore, under section 704(c) the partners' distributive shares of the $9,000 taxable gain are $1,000 to Y and $8,000 to Z.

(ii) Assume the same facts as in (i) and that at the beginning of the partnership's second taxable year, it invests its $22,000 of cash in securities of G Corp. The G Corp. securities increase in value to $40,000, at which time Y sells 50 percent of his partnership interest (i.e., a 25 percent interest in the partnership) to LK for $10,000. The partnership does not have a section 754 election in effect for the partnership taxable year during which such sale occurs. In accordance with paragraph (b)(2)(iv)(*1*) of this section, the partnership agreement provides that LK inherits 50 percent of Y's $11,000 capital account balance. Thus, following the sale, LK and Y each have a capital account of $5,500, and Z's capital account remains at $11,000. Prior to the end of the partnership's second taxable year, the securities are sold for their $40,000 fair market value, resulting in an $18,000 taxable gain ($40,000 less $22,000 adjusted tax basis). The partnership has no other income, gain, loss, or deduction in such taxable year. Under the partnership agreement the $18,000 taxable gain is allocated as follows:

	Y	Z	LK
Capital account before sale of securities	$5,500	$11,000	$5,500
Plus: gain	4,500	9,000	4,500
Capital account at end of year 2	$10,000	$20,000	$10,000

Reg. § 1.704-1(b)(5)

The allocation of the $18,000 taxable gain has substantial economic effect.

(iii) Assume the same facts as in (ii) except that the partnership has a section 754 election in effect for the partnership taxable year during which Y sells 50 percent of his interest to LK. Accordingly, under § 1.743-1 there is a $4,500 basis increase to the G Corp. securities with respect to LK. Notwithstanding this basis adjustment, as a result of the sale of the G Corp. securities, LK's capital account is, as in (ii), increased by $4,500. The fact that LK recognizes no taxable gain from such sale (due to his $4,500 section 743 basis adjustment) is irrelevant for capital accounting purposes since, in accordance with paragraph (b)(2)(iv)(m)(2) of this section, that basis adjustment is disregarded in the maintenance and computation of the partners' capital accounts.

(iv) Assume the same facts as in (iii) except that immediately following Y's sale of 50 percent of this interest to LK, the G Corp. securities decrease in value to $32,000 and are sold. The $10,000 taxable gain ($32,000 less $22,000 adjusted tax basis) is allocated as follows:

	Y	Z	LK
Capital account before sale of securities	$5,500	$11,000	$5,500
Plus: gain	2,500	5,000	2,500
Capital account at end of the year 2	$8,000	$16,000	$8,000

The fact that LK recognizes a $2,000 taxable loss from the sale of the G Corp. securities (due to his $4,500 section 743 basis adjustment) is irrelevant for capital accounting purposes since, in accordance with paragraph (b)(2)(iv)(m)(2) of this section, that basis adjustment is disregarded in the maintenance and computation of the partners' capital accounts.

(v) Assume the same facts as in (ii) except that Y sells 100 percent of his partnership interest (i.e., a 50 percent interest in the partnership) to LK for $20,000. Under section 708(b)(1)(B) the partnership terminates. Under paragraph (b)(1)(iv) of § 1.708-1, there is a constructive liquidation of the partnership. Immediately preceding the constructive liquidation, the capital accounts of Z and LK equal $11,000 each (LK having inherited Y's $11,000 capital account) and the book value of the G Corp. securities is $22,000 (original purchase price of securities). Under paragraph (b)(2)(iv)(l) of this section, the deemed contribution of assets and liabilities by the terminated partnership to the new partnership and the deemed liquidation of the terminated partnership that occur under § 1.708-1(b)(1)(iv) in connection with the constructive liquidation of the terminated partnership are disregarded in the maintenance and computation of the partners' capital accounts. As a result, the capital accounts of Z and LK in the new partnership equal $11,000 each (their capital accounts in the terminated partnership immediately prior to the termination), and the book value of the G Corp. securities remains $22,000 (its book value immediately prior to the termination). This *Example 13*(v) applies to terminations of partnerships under section 708(b)(1)(B) occurring on or after May 9, 1997; however, this *Example 13*(v) may be applied to terminations occurring on or after May 9, 1996, provided that the partnership and its partners apply this *Example 13*(v) to the termination in a consistent manner.

Example (14). (i) MC and RW form a general partnership to which each contributes $10,000. The $20,000 is invested in securities of Ventureco (which are not readily tradable on an established securities market). In each of the partnership's taxable years, it recognizes operating income equal to its operating deductions (excluding gain or loss from the sale of securities). The partnership agreement provides that the partners' capital accounts will be determined and maintained in accordance with paragraph (b)(2)(iv) of this section, distributions in liquidation of the partnership (or any partner's interest) will be made in accordance with the partners' positive capital account balances, and any partner with a deficit balance in his capital account following the liquidation of his interest must restore that deficit to the partnership (as set forth in paragraphs (b)(2)(ii)(b)(2) and (3) of this section). The partnership uses the interim closing of the books method for purposes of section 706. Assume that the Ventureco securities subsequently appreciate in value to $50,000. At that time SK makes a $25,000 cash contribution to the partnership (thereby acquiring a one-third interest in the partnership), and the $25,000 is placed in a bank account. Upon SK's admission to the partnership, the capital accounts of MC and RW (which were $10,000 each prior to SK's admission) are, in accordance with paragraph (b)(2)(iv)(f) of this

Reg. § 1.704-1(b)(5)

Determination of Tax Liability

section, adjusted upward (to $25,000 each) to reflect their shares of the unrealized appreciation in the Ventureco securities that occurred before SK was admitted to the partnership. Immediately after SK's admission to the partnership, the securities are sold for their $50,000 fair market value, resulting in taxable gain of $30,000 ($50,000 less $20,000 adjusted tax basis) and no book gain or loss. An allocation of the $30,000 taxable gain cannot have economic effect since it cannot properly be reflected in the partners' book capital accounts. Under paragraph (b)(2)(iv)(f) of this section and the special partners' interests in the partnership rule contained in paragraph (b)(4)(i) of this section, unless the partnership agreement provides that the $30,000 taxable gain will, in accordance with section 704(c) principles, be shared $15,000 to MC and $15,000 to RW, the partners' capital accounts will not be considered maintained in accordance with paragraph (b)(2)(iv) of this section.

	MC		RW		SK	
	Tax	Book	Tax	Book	Tax	Book
Capital account following SK's admission	$10,000	$25,000	$10,000	$25,000	$25,000	$25,000
Plus: gain	15,000	0	15,000	0	0	0
Capital account following sale	$25,000	$25,000	$25,000	$25,000	$25,000	$25,000

(ii) Assume the same facts as (i), except that after SK's admission to the partnership, the Ventureco securities appreciate in value to $74,000 and are sold, resulting in taxable gain of $54,000 ($74,000 less $20,000 adjusted tax basis) and book gain of $24,000 ($74,000 less $50,000 book value). Under the partnership agreement the $24,000 book gain (the appreciation in value occurring after SK became a partner) is allocated equally among MC, RW, and SK, and such allocations have substantial economic effect. An allocation of the $54,000 taxable gain cannot have economic effect since it cannot properly be reflected in the partners' book capital accounts. Under paragraph (b)(2)(iv)(f) of this section and the special partners' interests in the partnership rule contained in paragraph (b)(4)(i) of this section, unless the partnership agreement provides that the taxable gain will, in accordance with section 704(c) principles, be shared $23,000 to MC, $23,000 to RW, and $8,000 to SK, the partners' capital accounts will not be considered maintained in accordance with paragraph (b)(2)(iv) of this section.

	MC		RW		SK	
	Tax	Book	Tax	Book	Tax	Book
Capital account following SK's admission	$10,000	$25,000	$10,000	$25,000	$25,000	$25,000
Plus: gain	23,000	8,000	23,000	8,000	8,000	8,000
Capital account following sale	$33,000	$33,000	$33,000	$33,000	$33,000	$33,000

(iii) Assume the same facts as (i) except that after SK's admission to the partnership, the Ventureco securities depreciate in value to $44,000 and are sold, resulting in taxable gain of $24,000 ($44,000 less $20,000 adjusted tax basis) and a book loss of $6,000 ($50,000 book value less $44,000). Under the partnership agreement the $6,000 book loss is allocated equally among MC, RW, and SK, and such allocations have substantial economic effect. An allocation of the $24,000 taxable gain cannot have economic effect since it cannot properly be reflected in the partners' book capital accounts. Under paragraph (b)(2)(iv)(f) of this section and the special partners' interests in the partnership rule contained in paragraph (b)(4)(i) of this section, unless the partnership agreement provides that the $24,000 taxable gain will, in accordance with section 704(c) principles, be shared equally between MC and RW, the partners' capital accounts will not be considered maintained in accordance with paragraph (b)(2)(iv) of this section.

	MC		RW		SK	
	Tax	Book	Tax	Book	Tax	Book
Capital account following SK's admission	$10,000	$25,000	$10,000	$25,000	$25,000	$25,000
Plus: gain	12,000	0	12,000	0	0	0
Less: loss	0	(2,000)	0	(2,000)	0	(2,000)
Capital account following sale	$22,000	$23,000	$22,000	$23,000	$25,000	$23,000

That SK bears an economic loss of $2,000 without a corresponding taxable loss is attributable entirely to the "ceiling rule." See paragraph (c)(2) of § 1.704-1.

Reg. § 1.704-1(b)(5)

(iv) Assume the same facts as in (ii) except that upon the admission of SK the capital accounts of MC and RW are not each adjusted upward from $10,000 to $25,000 to reflect the appreciation in the partnership's securities that occurred before SK was admitted to the partnership. Rather, upon SK's admission to the partnership, the partnership agreement is amended to provide that the first $30,000 of taxable gain upon the sale of such securities will be allocated equally between MC and RW, and that all other income, gain, loss, and deduction will be allocated equally between MC, RW, and SK. When the securities are sold for $74,000, the $54,000 of taxable gain is so allocated. These allocations of taxable gain have substantial economic effect. (If the agreement instead provides for all taxable gain (including the $30,000 taxable gain attributable to the appreciation in the securities prior to SK's admission to the partnership) to be allocated equally between MC, RW, and SK, the partners should consider whether, and to what extent, the provisions of paragraphs (b)(1)(iii) and (iv) of this section are applicable.)

(v) Assume the same facts as in (iv) except that instead of selling the securities, the partnership makes a distribution of the securities (which have a fair market value of $74,000). Assume the distribution does not give rise to a transaction described in section 707(a)(2)(B). In accordance with paragraph (b)(2)(iv)(e) of this section, the partners' capital accounts are adjusted immediately prior to the distribution to reflect how taxable gain ($54,000) would have been allocated had the securities been sold for their $74,000 fair market value, and capital account adjustments in respect of the distribution of the securities are made with reference to the $74,000 "booked-up" fair market value.

	MC	RW	SK
Capital account before adjustment	$10,000	$10,000	$25,000
Deemed sale adjustment	23,000	23,000	8,000
Less: distribution	(24,667)	(24,667)	(24,667)
Capital account after distribution	$ 8,333	$ 8,333	$ 8,333

(vi) Assume the same facts as in (i) except that the partnership does not sell the Ventureco securities. During the next 3 years the fair market value of the Ventureco securities remains at $50,000, and the partnership engages in no other investment activities. Thus, at the end of that period the balance sheet of the partnership and the partners' capital accounts are the same as they were at the beginning of such period. At the end of the 3 years, MC's interest in the partnership is liquidated for the $25,000 cash held by the partnership. Assume the distribution does not give rise to a transaction described in section 707(a)(2)(B). Assume further that the partnership has a section 754 election in effect for the taxable year during which such liquidation occurs. Under sections 734(b) and 755 the partnership increases the basis of the Ventureco securities by the $15,000 basis adjustment (the excess of $25,000 over the $10,000 adjusted tax basis of MC's partnership interest).

	MC		RW		SK	
	Tax	Book	Tax	Book	Tax	Book
Capital account before distribution	$10,000	$25,000	$10,000	$25,000	$25,000	$25,000
Plus: basis adjustment	15,000	0	0	0	0	0
Less: distribution	(25,000)	(25,000)	0	0	0	0
Capital account, account after liquidation	0	0	$10,000	$25,000	$25,000	$25,000

(vii) Assume the same facts as in (vi) except that the partnership has no section 754 election in effect for the taxable year during which such liquidation occurs.

	MC		RW		SK	
	Tax	Book	Tax	Book	Tax	Book
Capital account before distribution	$10,000	$25,000	$10,000	$25,000	$25,000	$25,000
Less: distribution	25,000	(25,000)	0	0	0	0
Capital account after liquidation	($15,000)	0	$10,000	$25,000	$25,000	$25,000

Following the liquidation of MC's interest in the partnership, the Ventureco securities are sold for their $50,000 fair market value, resulting in no book gain or loss but a $30,000 taxable gain. An allocation of this $30,000 taxable gain cannot have economic effect since it cannot properly be reflected in the partners' book capital accounts. Under paragraph (b)(2)(iv)(f) of this section and the special partners' interests in the partnership rule contained in paragraph (b)(4)(i) of this section, unless the partnership agreement provides that $15,000 of such taxable gain will, in accordance with section 704(c) principles, be included in RW's distributive share, the partners' capital

Reg. § 1.704-1(b)(5)

accounts will not be considered maintained in accordance with paragraph (b)(2)(iv) of this section. The remaining $15,000 of such gain will, under paragraph (b)(3) of this section, be shared equally between RW and SK.

Example (15). (i) JB and DK form a limited partnership for the purpose of purchasing residential real estate to lease. JB, the limited partner, contributes $13,500, and DK, the general partner, contributes $1,500. The partnership, which uses the cash receipts and disbursements method of accounting, purchases a building for $100,000 (on leased land), incurring a recourse mortgage of $85,000 that requires the payment of interest only for a period of 3 years. The partnership agreement provides that partnership net taxable income and loss will be allocated 90 percent to JB and 10 percent to DK, the partners' capital accounts will be determined and maintained in accordance with paragraph (b)(2)(iv) of this section, distributions in liquidation of the partnership (or any partner's interest) will be made in accordance with the partners' positive capital account balances (as set forth in paragraph (b)(2)(ii)(b)(2) of this section), and JB is not required to restore any deficit balance in his capital account, but DK is so required. The partnership agreement contains a qualified income offset (as defined in paragraph (b)(2)(ii)(d) of this section). As of the end of each of the partnership's first 3 taxable years, the items described in paragraphs (b)(2)(ii)(d)(4), (5), and (6) of this section are not reasonably expected to cause or increase a deficit balance in JB's capital account. In the partnership's first taxable year, it has rental income of $10,000, operating expenses of $2,000, interest expense of $8,000, and cost recovery deductions of $12,000. Under the partnership agreement JB and DK are allocated $10,800 and $1,200, respectively, of the $12,000 net taxable loss incurred in the partnership's first taxable year.

	JB	DK
Capital account upon formation	$13,500	$1,500
Less: year 1 net loss	(10,800)	(1,200)
Capital account at end of year 1	$ 2,700	$ 300

The alternate economic effect test contained in paragraph (b)(2)(ii)(d) of this section is satisfied as of the end of the partnership's first taxable year. Thus, the allocation made in the partnership's first taxable year has economic effect.

(ii) Assume the same facts as in (i) and that in the partnership's second taxable year it again has rental income of $10,000, operating expenses of $2,000, interest expense of $8,000, and cost recovery deductions of $12,000. Under the partnership agreement JB and DK are allocated $10,800 and $1,200, respectively, of the $12,000 net taxable loss incurred in the partnership's second taxable year.

	JB	DK
Capital account at beginning of year 1	$ 2,700	$ 300
Less: year 2 net loss	(10,800)	(1,200)
Capital account at end of year 2	$(8,100)	$ (900)

Only $2,700 of the $10,800 net taxable loss allocated to JB satisfies the alternate economic effect test contained in paragraph (b)(2)(ii)(d) of this section as of the end of the partnership's second taxable year. The allocation of such $2,700 net taxable loss to JB (consisting of $2,250 of rental income, $450 of operating expenses, $1,800 of interest expense, and $2,700 of cost recovery deductions) has economic effect. The remaining $8,100 of net taxable loss allocated by the partnership agreement to JB must be reallocated in accordance with the partners' interests in the partnership. Under paragraph (b)(3)(iii) of this section, the determination of the partners' interests in the remaining $8,100 net taxable loss is made by comparing how distributions (and contributions) would be made if the partnership sold its property at its adjusted tax basis and liquidated immediately following the end of the partnership's first taxable year with the results of such a sale and liquidation immediately following the end of the partnership's second taxable year. If the partnership's real property were sold for its $88,000 adjusted tax basis and the partnership were liquidated immediately following the end of the partnership's first taxable year, the $88,000 sales proceeds would be used to repay the $85,000 note, and there would be $3,000 remaining in the partnership, which would be used to make liquidating distributions to DK and JB of $300 and $2,700, respectively. If such property were sold for its $76,000 adjusted tax basis and the partnership were liquidated immediately following the end of the partnership's second taxable year, DK would be required to contribute $9,000 to the partnership in order for the partnership to repay the $85,000 note, and there would be no assets remaining in the partnership to distribute. A comparison of these outcomes indicates that JB bore $2,700 and DK $9,300 of the economic burden that corresponds to the $12,000 net taxable loss. Thus, in addition to the $1,200 net taxable loss

Reg. § 1.704-1(b)(5)

allocated to DK under the partnership agreement, $8,100 of net taxable loss will be reallocated to DK under paragraph (b)(3)(iii) of this section. Similarly, for subsequent taxable years, absent an increase in JB's capital account, all net taxable loss allocated to JB under the partnership agreement will be reallocated to DK.

(iii) Assume the same facts as in (ii) and that in the partnership's third taxable year there is rental income of $35,000, operating expenses of $2,000, interest expense of $8,000, the cost recovery deductions of $10,000. The capital accounts of the partners maintained on the books of the partnership do not take into account the reallocation to DK of the $8,100 net taxable loss in the partnership's second taxable year. Thus, an allocation of the $15,000 net taxable income $13,500 to JB and $1,500 to DK (as dictated by the partnership agreement and as reflected in the capital accounts of the partners) does not have economic effect. The partners' interests in the partnership with respect to such $15,000 taxable gain again is made in the manner described in paragraph (b)(3)(iii) of this section. If the partnership's real property were sold for its $76,000 adjusted tax basis and the partnership were liquidated immediately following the end of the partnership's second taxable year, DK would be required to contribute $9,000 to the partnership in order for the partnership to repay the $85,000 note, and there would be no assets remaining to distribute. If such property were sold for its $66,000 adjusted tax basis and the partnership were liquidated immediately following the end of the partnership's third taxable year, the $91,000 ($66,000 sales proceeds plus $25,000 cash on hand) would be used to repay the $85,000 note and there would be $6,000 remaining in the partnership, which would be used to make liquidating distributions to DK and JB of $600 and $5,400, respectively. Accordingly, under paragraph (b)(3)(iii) of this section the $15,000 net taxable income in the partnership's third taxable year will be reallocated $9,600 to DK (minus $9,000 at end of the second taxable year to positive $600 at end of the third taxable year) and $5,400 to JB (zero at end of the second taxable year to positive $5,400 at end of the third taxable year).

Example (16). (i) KG and WN form a limited partnership for the purpose of investing in improved real estate. KG, the general partner, contributes $10,000 to the partnership, and WN, the limited partner, contributes $990,000 to the partnership. The $1,000,000 is used to purchase an apartment building on leased land. The partnership agreement provides that (1) the partners' capital accounts will be determined and maintained in accordance with paragraph (b)(2)(iv) of this section; (2) cash will be distributed first to WN until such time as he has received the amount of his original capital contribution ($990,000), next to KG until such time as he has received the amount of his original capital contribution ($10,000), and thereafter equally between WN and KG; (3) partnership net taxable income will be allocated 99 percent to WN and 1 percent to KG until the cumulative net taxable income allocated for all taxable years is equal to the cumulative net taxable loss previously allocated to the partners, and thereafter equally between WN and KG; (4) partnership net taxable loss will be allocated 99 percent to WN and 1 percent to KG, unless net taxable income has previously been allocated equally between WN and KG, in which case such net taxable loss first will be allocated equally until the cumulative net taxable loss allocated for all taxable years is equal to the cumulative net taxable income previously allocated to the partners; and (5) upon liquidation, WN is not required to restore any deficit balance in his capital account, but KG is so required. Since distributions in liquidation are not required to be made in accordance with the partners' positive capital account balances, and since WN is not required, upon the liquidation of his interest, to restore the deficit balance in his capital account to the partnership, the allocations provided by the partnership agreement do not have economic effect and will be reallocated in accordance with the partners' interests in the partnership under paragraph (b)(3) of this section.

(ii) Assume the same facts as in (i) except that the partnership agreement further provides that distributions in liquidation of the partnership (or any partner's interest) are to be made in accordance with the partners' positive capital account balances (as set forth in paragraph (b)(2)(ii)(*b*)(*2*) of this section). Assume further that the partnership agreement contains a qualified income offset (as defined in paragraph (b)(2)(ii)(*d*) of this section) and that, as of the end of each partnership taxable year, the items described in paragraphs (b)(2)(iii)(*d*)(*4*), (*5*), and (*6*) of this section are not reasonably expected to cause or increase a deficit balance in WN's capital account. The allocations provided by the partnership agreement have economic effect.

Example (17). FG and RP form a partnership with FG contributing cash of $100 and RP contributing property, with 2 years of cost recovery deductions remaining, that has an adjusted tax basis of $80 and a fair market value of $100. The partnership, FG, and RP have calendar taxable years. The partnership agreement provides that the partners' capital accounts will be determined and maintained in accordance with paragraph (b)(2)(iv) of this section, liquidation proceeds will be made in accordance with capital account balances, and each partner is liable to restore the deficit balance in his capital account to the partnership upon liquidation of his interest (as set forth in paragraphs (b)(2)(ii)(b)(2) and (3) of this section). FG expects to be in a substantially higher tax bracket than RP in the partnership's first taxable year. In the partnership's second taxable year, and in subsequent taxable years, it is expected that both will be in approximately equivalent tax brackets. The partnership agreement allocates all items equally except that all $50 of book depreciation is allocated to FG in the partnership's first taxable year and all $50 of book depreciation is allocated to RP in the partnership's second taxable year. If the allocation to FG of all book depreciation in the partnership's first taxable year is respected, FG would be entitled under section 704(c) to the entire cost recovery deduction ($40) for such year. Likewise, if the allocation to RP of all the book depreciation in the partnership's second taxable year is respected, RP would be entitled under section 704(c) to the entire cost recovery deduction ($40) for such year. The allocation of book depreciation to FG and RP in the partnership's first 2 taxable years has economic effect within the meaning of paragraph (b)(2)(ii) of this section. However, the economic effect of these allocations is not substantial under the test described in paragraph (b)(2)(iii)(c) of this section since there is a strong likelihood at the time such allocations became part of the partnership agreement that at the end of the 2-year period to which such allocations relate, the net increases and decreases to FG's and RP's capital accounts will be the same with such allocations as they would have been in the absence of such allocation, and the total tax liability of FG and RP for the taxable years to which the section 704(c) determinations relate would be reduced as a result of the allocations of book depreciation. As a result the allocations of book depreciation in the partnership agreement will be disregarded. FG and RP will be allocated such book depreciation in accordance with the partners' interests in the partnership under paragraph (b)(3) of this section. Under these facts the book depreciation deductions will be reallocated equally between the partners, and section 704(c) will be applied with reference to such reallocation of book depreciation.

Example (18). (i) WM and JL form a general partnership by each contributing $300,000 thereto. The partnership uses the $600,000 to purchase an item of tangible personal property, which it leases out. The partnership elects under section 48(q)(4) to reduce the amount of investment tax credit in lieu of adjusting the tax basis of such property. The partnership agreement provides that (1) the partners' capital account will be determined and maintained in accordance with paragraph (b)(2)(iv) of this section, (2) distributions in liquidation of the partnership (or any partner's interest) will be made in accordance with the partners' positive capital account balances (as set forth in paragraph (b)(2)(ii)(b)(2) of this section), (3) any partner with a deficit balance in his capital account following the liquidation of his interest must restore that deficit to the partnership (as set forth in paragraph (b)(2)(ii)(b)(3) of this section), (4) all income, gain, loss, and deduction of the partnership will be allocated equally between the partners, and (5) all non-liquidating distributions of the partnership will be made equally between the partners. Assume that in each of the partnership's taxable years, it recognizes operating income equal to its operating deductions (excluding cost recovery and depreciation deductions and gain or loss on the sale of its property). During its first 2 taxable years, the partnership has an additional $200,000 cost recovery deduction in each year. Pursuant to the partnership agreement these items are allocated equally between WM and JL.

	WM	JL
Capital account upon formation	$300,000	$300,000
Less: net loss for years 1 and 2	(200,000)	(200,000)
Capital account at end of year 2	$100,000	$100,000

The allocations made in the partnership's first 2 taxable years have substantial economic effect.

(ii) Assume the same facts as in (i) and that MK is admitted to the partnership at the beginning of the partnership's third taxable year. At the time of his admission, the fair market value of the partnership property is $600,000. MK contributes $300,000 to the partnership in exchange for an equal one-third interest in the partnership, and, as permitted under paragraph (b)(2)(iv)(g), the capital accounts of WM and JL are adjusted upward to $300,000 each to reflect the fair market value of partnership property. In addition, the partnership agreement is modified to provide that depreciation and gain or loss, as computed for tax purposes, with respect to the partnership property that appreciated prior to MK's admission will be shared among the partners in a manner that takes account of the variation between such property's $200,000 adjusted tax basis and its $600,000 book value in accordance with paragraph (b)(2)(iv)(f) and the special rule contained in paragraph (b)(4)(i) of this section. Depreciation and gain or loss, as computed for book purposes, with respect to such property

Reg. § 1.704-1(b)(5)

will be allocated equally among the partners and, in accordance with paragraph (b)(2)(iv)(g) of this section, will be reflected in the partners' capital accounts, as will all other partnership income, gain, loss, and deduction. Since the requirements of (b)(2)(iv)(g) of this section are satisfied, the capital accounts of the partners (as adjusted) continue to be maintained in accordance with paragraph (b)(2)(iv) of this section.

(iii) Assume the same facts as in (ii) and that immediately after MK's admission to the partnership, the partnership property is sold for $600,000, resulting in a taxable gain of $400,000 ($600,000 less $200,000 adjusted tax basis) and no book gain or loss, and the partnership is liquidated. An allocation of the $400,000 taxable gain cannot have economic effect because such gain cannot properly be reflected in the partners' book capital accounts. Consistent with the special partners' interests in the partnership rule contained in paragraph (b)(4)(i) of this section, the partnership agreement provides that the $400,000 taxable gain will, in accordance with section 704(c) principles, be shared equally between WM and JL.

	WM		JL		MK	
	Tax	Book	Tax	Book	Tax	Book
Capital account at beginning of year 3	$100,000	$300,000	$100,000	$300,000	$300,000	$300,000
Plus: gain	200,000	0	200,000	0	0	0
Capital account before liquidation	$300,000	$300,000	$300,000	$300,000	$300,000	$300,000

The $900,000 of partnership cash ($600,000 sales proceeds plus $300,000 contributed by MK) is distributed equally among WM, JL, and MK in accordance with their adjusted positive capital account balances, each of which is $300,000.

(iv) Assume the same facts as in (iii) except that prior to liquidation the property appreciates and is sold for $900,000, resulting in a taxable gain of $700,000 ($900,000 less $200,000 adjusted tax basis) and a book gain of $300,000 ($900,000 less $600,000 book value). Under the partnership agreement the $300,000 of book gain is allocated equally among the partners, and such allocation has substantial economic effect.

	WM		JL		MK	
	Tax	Book	Tax	Book	Tax	Book
Capital account at beginning of year 3	$100,000	$300,000	$100,000	$300,000	$300,000	$300,000
Plus: gain	300,000	100,000	300,000	100,000	100,000	100,000
Capital account before liquidation	$400,000	$400,000	$400,000	$400,000	$400,000	$400,000

Consistent with the special partners' interests in the partnership rule contained in paragraph (b)(4)(i) of this section, the partnership agreement provides that the $700,000 taxable gain is, in accordance with section 704(c) principles, shared $300,000 to JL, $300,000 to WM, and $100,000 to MK. This ensures that (1) WM and JL share equally the $400,000 taxable gain that is attributable to appreciation in the property that occurred prior to MK's admission to the partnership in the same manner as it was reflected in their capital accounts upon MK's admission, and (2) WM, JL, and MK share equally the additional $300,000 taxable gain in the same manner as they shared the $300,000 book gain.

(v) Assume the same facts as in (ii) except that shortly after MK's admission the property depreciates and is sold for $450,000, resulting in a taxable gain of $250,000 ($450,000 less $200,000 adjusted tax basis) and a book loss of $150,000 (450,000 less $600,000 book value). Under the partnership agreement these items are allocated as follows:

	WM		JL		MK	
	Tax	Book	Tax	Book	Tax	Book
Capital account at beginning of year 3	$100,000	$300,000	$100,000	$300,000	$300,000	$300,000
Plus: gain	125,000	0	125,000	0	0	0
Less: loss	0	(50,000)	0	(50,000)	0	(50,000)
Capital account before liquidation	$225,000	$250,000	$225,000	$250,000	$300,000	$250,000

Reg. § 1.704-1(b)(5)

The $150,000 book loss is allocated equally among the partners, and such allocation has substantial economic effect. Consistent with the special partners' interests in the partnership rule contained in paragraph (b)(4)(i) of this section, the partnership agreement provides that the $250,000 taxable gain is, in accordance with section 704(c) principles, shared equally between WM and JL. The fact that MK bears an economic loss of $50,000 without a corresponding taxable loss is attributable entirely to the "ceiling rule." See paragraph (c)(2) of § 1.704-1.

$170,000, resulting in a $30,000 taxable loss ($200,000 adjusted tax basis less $170,000) and a book loss of $430,000 ($600,000 book value less $170,000). The book loss of $430,000 is allocated equally among the partners ($143,333 each) and has substantial economic effect. Consistent with the special partners' interests in the partnership rule contained in paragraph (b)(4)(i) of this section, the partnership agreement provides that the entire $30,000 taxable loss is, in accordance with section 704(c) principles, included in MK's distributive share.

(vi) Assume the same facts as in (ii) except that the property depreciates and is sold for

	WM Tax	WM Book	JL Tax	JL Book	MK Tax	MK Book
Capital account at beginning of year 3	$100,000	$300,000	$100,000	$300,000	$300,000	$300,000
Less: loss	0	(143,333)	0	(143,333)	(30,000)	(143,333)
Capital account before liquidation	$100,000	$156,667	$100,000	$156,667	$270,000	$156,667

(vii) Assume the same facts as in (ii) and that during the partnership's third taxable year, the partnership has an additional $100,000 cost recovery deduction and $300,000 book depreciation deduction attributable to the property purchased by the partnership in its first taxable year. The $300,000 book depreciation deduction is allocated equally among the partners, and that allocation has substantial economic effect. Consistent with the special partners' interests in the partnership rule contained in paragraph (b)(4)(i) of this section, the partnership agreement provides that the $100,000 cost recovery deduction for the partnership's third taxable year is, in accordance with section 704(c) principles, included in MK's distributive share. This is because under these facts those principles require MK to include the cost recovery deduction for such property in his distributive share up to the amount of the book depreciation deduction for such property properly allocated to him.

	WM Tax	WM Book	JL Tax	JL Book	MK Tax	MK Book
Capital account at beginning of year 3	$100,000	$300,000	$100,000	$300,000	$300,000	$300,000
Less: recovery/depreciation deduction for year 3	0	(100,000)	0	(100,000)	(100,000)	(100,000)
Capital account at the end of year 3	$100,000	$200,000	$100,000	$200,000	$200,000	$200,000

(viii) Assume the same facts as in (vii) except that upon MK's admission the partnership property has an adjusted tax basis of $220,000 (instead of $200,000), and thus the cost recovery deduction for the partnership's third taxable year is $110,000. Assume further that upon MK's admission WM and JL have adjusted capital account balances of $110,000 and $100,000, respectively. Consistent with the special partners' interests in the partnership rule contained in paragraph (b)(4)(i) of this section, the partnership agreement provides that the excess $10,000 cost recovery deduction ($110,000 less $100,000 included in MK's distributive share) is, in accordance with section 704(c) principles, shared equally between WM and JL and is so included in their respective distributive shares for the partnership's third taxable year.

(ix) Assume the same facts as in (vii) except that upon MK's admission the partnership agreement is amended to allocate the first $400,000 of book depreciation and loss on partnership property equally between WM and JL and the last $200,000 of such book depreciation and loss to MK. Assume such allocations have substantial economic effect. Pursuant to this amend-

Reg. § 1.704-1(b)(5)

Determination of Tax Liability

See p. 20,601 for regulations not amended to reflect law changes

ment the $300,000 book depreciation deduction in the partnership's third taxable year is allocated equally between WM and JL. Consistent with the special partners' interests in the partnership rule contained in paragraph (b)(4)(i) of this section, the partnership agreement provides that the $100,000 cost recovery deduction is, in accordance with section 704(c) principles, shared equally between WM and JL. In the partnership's fourth taxable year, it has a $60,000 cost recovery deduction and a $180,000 book depreciation deduction. Under the amendment described above, the $180,000 book depreciation deduction is allocated $50,000 to WM, $50,000 to JL, and $80,000 to MK. Consistent with the special partners' interests in the partnership rule contained in paragraph (b)(4)(i) of this section, the partnership agreement provides that the $60,000 cost recovery deduction is, in accordance with section 704(c) principles, included entirely in MK's distributive share.

	WM		JL		MK	
	Tax	Book	Tax	Book	Tax	Book
Capital account at beginning of year 3	$100,000	$300,000	$100,000	$300,000	$300,000	$300,000
Less: (a) recovery/depreciation deduction for year 3	(50,000)	(150,000)	(50,000)	(150,000)	0	0
(b) recovery/depreciation deduction for year 4	0	(50,000)	0	(50,000)	(60,000)	(80,000)
Capital account at end of year 4	$50,000	$100,000	$50,000	$100,000	$240,000	$220,000

(x) Assume the same facts as in (vii) and that at the beginning of the partnership's third taxable year, the partnership purchases a second item of tangible personal property for $300,000 and elects under section 48(q)(4) to reduce the amount of investment tax credit in lieu of adjusting the tax basis of such property. The partnership agreement is amended to allocate the first $150,000 of cost recovery deductions and loss from such property to WM and the next $150,000 of cost recovery deductions and loss from such property equally between JL and MK. Thus, in the partnership's third taxable year it has, in addition to the items specified in (vii), a cost recovery and book depreciation deduction of $100,000 attributable to the newly acquired property, which is allocated entirely to WM. As in (vii), the allocation of the $300,000 book depreciation attributable to the property purchased in the partnership's first taxable year equally among the partners has substantial economic effect, and consistent with the special partners' interests in the partnership rule contained in paragraph (b)(4)(i) of this section, the partnership agreement properly provides for the entire $100,000 cost recovery deduction attributable to such property to be included in MK's distributive share. Furthermore, the allocation to WM of the $100,000 cost recovery deduction attributable to the property purchased in the partnership's third taxable year has substantial economic effect.

	WM		JL		MK	
	Tax	Book	Tax	Book	Tax	Book
Capital account at beginning of year 3	$100,000	$300,000	$100,000	$300,000	$300,000	$300,000
Less: (a) recovery/depreciation deduction for property bought in year 1	0	(100,000)	0	(100,000)	(100,000)	(100,000)
(b) recovery/depreciation deduction for property bought in year 3	(100,000)	(100,000)	0	0	0	0
Capital account at end of year 3	0	$100,000	$100,000	$200,000	$200,000	$200,000

(xi) Assume the same facts as in (x) and that at the beginning of the partnership's fourth taxable year, the properties purchased in the partnership's first and third taxable years are disposed of for $90,000 and $180,000, respectively, and the partnership is liquidated. With respect to the property purchased in the first taxable year, there is a book loss of $210,000 ($300,000 book value less $90,000) and a taxable loss of $10,000 ($100,000 adjusted tax basis less $90,000). The book loss is allocated equally among the partners, and such allocation has substantial economic effect. Consistent with the special partners' interests in the partnership rule contained in paragraph (b)(4)(i) of this section, the partnership agreement provides that the taxable loss of $10,000 will, in accordance with section 704(c) principles, be included entirely in MK's distributive share. With respect to the property purchased in the partnership's third taxable year,

Reg. § 1.704-1(b)(5)

Determination of Tax Liability 43,537

See p. 20,601 for regulations not amended to reflect law changes

there is a book and taxable loss of $20,000. Pursuant to the partnership agreement this loss is allocated entirely to WM, and such allocation has substantial economic effect.

	WM		JL		MK	
	Tax	Book	Tax	Book	Tax	Book
Capital account at beginning of year 4	0	$100,000	$100,000	$200,000	$200,000	$200,000
Less: (a) loss on property bought in year 1	0	(70,000)	0	(70,000)	(10,000)	(70,000)
(b) loss on property bought in year 3	(20,000)	(20,000)	0	0	0	0
Capital account before liquidation	($20,000)	$10,000	$100,000	$130,000	$190,000	$130,000

Partnership liquidation proceeds ($270,000) are properly distributed in accordance with the partners' adjusted positive book capital account balances ($10,000 to WM, $130,000 to JL and $130,000 to MK).

(xii) Assume the same facts as in (x) and that in the partnership's fourth taxable year it has a cost recovery deduction of $60,000 and book depreciation deduction of $180,000 attributable to the property purchased in the partnership's first taxable year, and a cost recovery and book depreciation deduction of $100,000 attributable to the property purchased in the partnership's third taxable year. The $180,000 book depreciation deduction attributable to the property purchased in the partnership's first taxable year is allocated equally among the partners, and such allocation has substantial economic effect. Consistent with the special partners' interests in the partnership rule contained in paragraph (b)(4)(i) of this section, the partnership agreement provides that the $60,000 cost recovery deduction attributable to the property purchased in the first taxable year is, in accordance with section 704(c) principles, included entirely in MK's distributive share. Furthermore, the $100,000 cost recovery deduction attributable to the property purchased in the third taxable year is allocated $50,000 to WM, $25,000 to JL, and $25,000 to MK, and such allocation has substantial economic effect.

	WM		JL		MK	
	Tax	Book	Tax	Book	Tax	Book
Capital account at beginning of year 4	—0—	$100,000	$100,000	$200,000	$200,000	$200,000
Less: (a) recovery/depreciation deduction for property bought in year 1	—0—	(60,000)	—0—	(60,000)	(60,000)	(60,000)
(b) recovery/depreciation deduction for property bought in year 3	(50,000)	(50,000)	(25,000)	(25,000)	(25,000)	(25,000)
Capital account at end of year 4	($50,000)	($10,000)	$75,000	$115,000	$115,000	$115,000

At the end of the partnership's fourth taxable year the adjusted tax bases of the partnership properties acquired in its first and third taxable years are $40,000 and $100,000, respectively. If the properties are disposed of at the beginning of the partnership's fifth taxable year for their adjusted tax bases, there would be no taxable gain or loss, a book loss of $80,000 on the property purchased in the partnership's first taxable year ($120,000 book value less $40,000), and cash available for distribution of $140,000.

	WM		JL		MK	
	Tax	Book	Tax	Book	Tax	Book
Capital account at beginning of year 5	($50,000)	($10,000)	$75,000	$115,000	$115,000	$115,000
Less: loss	—0—	(26,667)	—0—	(26,667)	—0—	(26,667)
Capital account before liquidation	($50,000)	($36,667)	$75,000	$88,333	$115,000	$88,333

If the partnership is then liquidated, the $140,000 of cash on hand plus the $36,667 balance that WM would be required to contribute to the partnership (the deficit balance in his book capital account) would be distributed equally between JL

Reg. § 1.704-1(b)(5)

and MK in accordance with their adjusted positive book capital account balances.

(xiii) Assume the same facts as in (i). Any tax preferences under section 57(a)(12) attributable to the partnership's cost recovery deductions in the first 2 taxable years will be taken into account equally by WM and JL. If the partnership agreement instead provides that the partnership's cost recovery deductions in its first 2 taxable years are allocated 25 percent to WM and 75 percent to JL (and such allocations have substantial economic effect), the tax preferences attributable to such cost recovery deductions would be taken into account 25 percent by WM and 75 percent by JL. The conclusion in the previous sentence is unchanged even if the partnership's operating expenses (exclusive of cost recovery and depreciation deductions) exceed its operating income in each of the partnership's first 2 taxable years, the resulting net loss is allocated entirely to WM, and the cost recovery deductions are allocated 25 percent to WM and 75 percent to JL (provided such allocations have substantial economic effect). If the partnership agreement instead provides that all income, gain, loss, and deduction (including cost recovery and depreciation deductions) are allocated equally between JL and WM, the tax preferences attributable to the cost recovery deductions would be taken into account equally by JL and WM. In this case, if the partnership has a $100,000 cost recovery deduction in its first taxable year and an additional net loss of $100,000 in its first taxable year (*i.e.*, its operating expenses exceed its operating income by $100,000) and purports to categorize JL's $100,000 distributive share of partnership loss as being attributable to the cost recovery deduction and WM's $100,000 distributive share of partnership loss as being attributable to the net loss, the economic effect of such allocations is not substantial, and each partner will be allocated one-half of all partnership income, gain, loss, and deduction and will take into account one-half of the tax preferences attributable to the cost recovery deductions.

Example (19). (i) DG and JC form a general partnership for the purpose of drilling oil wells. DG contributes an oil lease, which has a fair market value and adjusted tax basis of $100,000. JC contributes $100,000 in cash, which is used to finance the drilling operations. The partnership agreement provides that DG is credited with a capital account of $100,000, and JC is credited with a capital account of $100,000. The agreement further provides that the partners' capital accounts will be determined and maintained in accordance with paragraph (b)(2)(iv) of this section, distributions in liquidation of the partnership (or any partner's interest) will be made in accordance with the partners' positive capital account balances, and any partner with a deficit balance in his capital account following the liquidation of his interest must restore such deficit to the partnership (as set forth in paragraphs (b)(2)(ii)(b)(*2*) and (*3*) of this section). The partnership chooses to adjust capital accounts on a simulated cost depletion basis and elects under section 48(q)(4) to reduce the amount of investment tax credit in lieu of adjusting the basis of its section 38 property. The agreement further provides that (1) all additional cash requirements of the partnership will be borne equally by DG and JC, (2) the deductions attributable to the property (including money) contributed by each partner will be allocated to such partner, (3) all other income, gain, loss, and deductions (and item thereof) will be allocated equally between DG and JC, and (4) all cash from operations will be distributed equally between DG and JC. In the partnership's first taxable year $80,000 of partnership intangible drilling cost deductions and $20,000 of cost recovery deductions on partnership equipment are allocated to JC, and the $100,000 basis of the lease is, for purposes of the depletion allowance under sections 611 and 613A(c)(7)(D), allocated to DG. The allocations of income, gain, loss, and deduction provided in the partnership agreement have substantial economic effect. Furthermore, since the allocation of the entire basis of the lease to DG will not result in capital account adjustments (under paragraph (b)(2)(*iv*)(*k*) of this section) the economic effect of which is insubstantial, and since all other partnership allocations are recognized under this paragraph, the allocation of the $100,000 adjusted basis of the lease to DG is, under paragraph (b)(4)(v) of this section, recognized as being in accordance with the partners' interests in partnership capital for purposes of section 613A(c)(7)(D).

(ii) Assume the same facts as in (i) except that the partnership agreement provides that (1) all additional cash requirements of the partnership for additional expenses will be funded by additional contributions from JC, (2) all cash from operations will first be distributed to JC until the excess of such cash distributions over the amount of such additional expenses equals his initial $100,000 contribution, (3) all deductions attributable to such additional operating expenses will be allocated to JC, and (4) all income will be allocated to JC until the aggregate amount of income allocated to him equals the amount of partnership operating expenses funded by his initial $100,000 contribution plus the amount of additional operating expenses paid from contributions made solely by him. The allocations of income, gain, loss, and deduction provided in the partnership agreement have economic effect. In addition, the economic effect of the allocations provided in the agreement is substantial. Because the partnership's drilling activities are sufficiently speculative, there is not a strong likelihood at the time the disproportionate allocations of loss and deduction to JC are provided for by the partnership agreement that the economic effect of such allocations will be largely offset by allocations of income. In addition, since the allocation of the entire basis of the lease to DG will not result in capital account adjustments (under paragraph (b)(2)(iv)(k) of this section), the economic effect of which is insubstantial, and since all other partnership allocations are recognized under this paragraph, the allocation of the adjusted basis of the lease to DG is, under paragraph (b)(4)(v) of this section, recognized as being in accordance with the partners' interests in partnership capital under section 613A(c)(7)(D).

(iii) Assume the same facts as in (i) except that all distributions, including those made upon liquidation of the partnership, will be made equally between DG and JC, and no partner is obligated to restore the deficit balance in his capital account to the partnership following the liquidation of his interest for distribution to partners with positive capital account balances. Since liquidation proceeds will be distributed equally between DG and JC irrespective of their capital account balances, and since no partner is required to restore the deficit balance in his capital account to the partnership upon liquidation (in accordance with paragraph (b)(2)(ii)(b)(3) of this section), the allocations of income, gain, loss, and deduction provided in the partnership agreement do not have economic effect and must be reallocated in accordance with the partners' interests in the partnership under paragraph (b)(3) of this section. Under these facts all partnership income, gain, loss, and deduction (and item thereof) will be reallocated equally between JC and DG. Furthermore, the allocation of the $100,000 adjusted tax basis of the lease to DG is not, under paragraph (b)(4)(v) of this section, deemed to be in accordance with the partners' interests in partnership capital under section 613A(c)(7)(D), and such basis must be reallocated in accordance with the partners' interests in partnership capital or income as determined under section 613A(c)(7)(D). The results in this example would be the same if JC's initial cash contribution were $1,000,000 (instead of $100,000), but in such case the partners should consider whether, and to what extent, the provisions of paragraph (b)(1) of § 1.721-1, and principles related thereto, may be applicable.

(iv) Assume the same facts as in (i) and that for the partnership's first taxable year the simulated depletion deduction with respect to the lease is $10,000. Since DG properly was allocated the entire depletable basis of the lease (such allocation having been recognized as being in accordance with DG's interest in partnership capital with respect to such lease), under paragraph (b)(2)(iv)(k)(1) of this section the partnership's $10,000 simulated depletion deduction is allocated to DG and will reduce his capital account accordingly. If (prior to any additional simulated depletion deductions) the lease is sold for $100,000, paragraph (b)(4)(v) of this section requires that the first $90,000 (i.e., the partnership's simulated adjusted basis in the lease) out of the $100,000 amount realized on such sale be allocated to DG (but does not directly affect his capital account). The partnersip agreement allocates the remaining $10,000 amount realized equally between JC and DG (but such allocation does not directly affect their capital accounts). This allocation of the $10,000 portion of amount realized that exceeds the partnership's simulated adjusted basis in the lease will be treated as being in accordance with the partners' allocable shares of such amount realized under section 613A(c)(7)(D) because such allocation will not result in capital account adjustments (under paragraph (b)(2)(iv)(k) of this section) the economic effect of which is insubstantial, and all other partnership allocations are recognized under this paragraph. Under paragraph (b)(2)(iv)(k) of this section, the partners' capital accounts are adjusted upward by the partnership's simulated gain of $10,000 ($100,000 sales price less $90,000 simulated adjusted basis) in proportion to such partners' allocable shares of the $10,000 portion of the total amount realized that exceeds the partnership's $90,000 simulated adjusted basis ($5,000 to JC and $5,000 to DG). If the lease is sold for $50,000, under paragraph (b)(4)(v) of this section the entire $50,000 amount realized on the sale of the lease will be allocated to DG (but will not directly affect his capital account). Under paragraph (b)(2)(iv)(k) of this section the partners' capital accounts will be adjusted downward by the partnership's $40,000 simulated loss ($50,000 sales price less $90,000 simulated adjusted basis) in proportion to the partners' allocable shares of the total amount realized from the property that represents recovery of the partnership's simulated adjusted basis therein. Accordingly, DG's capital account will be reduced by such $40,000.

(c) *Contributed property; cross-reference.* See § 1.704-3 for methods of making allocations that take into account precontribution appreciation or

Reg. § 1.704-1(c)

(d) *Limitation on allowance of losses.*

(1) A partner's distributive share of partnership loss will be allowed only to the extent of the adjusted basis (before reduction by current year's losses) of such partner's interest in the partnership at the end of the partnership taxable year in which such loss occurred. A partner's share of loss in excess of his adjusted basis at the end of the partnership taxable year will not be allowed for that year. However, any loss so disallowed shall be allowed as a deduction at the end of the first succeeding partnership taxable year, and subsequent partnership taxable years, to the extent that the partner's adjusted basis for his partnership interest at the end of any such year exceeds zero (before reduction by such loss for such year).

(2) In computing the adjusted basis of a partner's interest for the purpose of ascertaining the extent to which a partner's distributive share of partnership loss shall be allowed as a deduction for the taxable year, the basis shall first be increased under section 705(a)(1) and decreased under section 705(a)(2), except for losses of the taxable year and losses previously disallowed. If the partner's distributive share of the aggregate of items of loss specified in section 702(a)(1), (2), (3), (8), and (9) exceeds the basis of the partner's interest computed under the preceding sentence, the limitation on losses under section 704(d) must be allocated to his distributive share of each such loss. This allocation shall be determined by taking the proportion that each loss bears to the total of all such losses. For purposes of the preceding sentence, the total losses for the taxable year shall be the sum of his distributive share of losses for the current year and his losses disallowed and carried forward from prior years.

(3) For the treatment of certain liabilities of the partner or partnership, see section 752 and § 1.752-1.

(4) The provisions of this paragraph may be illustrated by the following examples:

Example (1). At the end of the partnership taxable year 1955, partnership AB has a loss of $20,000. Partner A's distributive share of this loss is $10,000. At the end [of] such year, A's adjusted basis for his interest in the partnership (not taking into account his distributive share of the loss) is $6,000. Under section 704(d), A's distributive share of partnership loss is allowed to him (in his *taxable year within or with which the partnership taxable year ends*) only to the extent of his adjusted basis of $6,000. The $6,000 loss allowed for 1955 decreases the adjusted basis of A's interest to zero. Assume that, at the end of partnership taxable year 1956, A's share of partnership income has increased the adjusted basis of A's interest in the partnership to $3,000 (not taking into account the $4,000 loss disallowed in 1955). Of the $4,000 loss disallowed for the partnership taxable year 1955, $3,000 is allowed A for the partnership taxable year 1956, thus again decreasing the adjusted basis of his interest to zero. If, at the end of partnership taxable year 1957, A has an adjusted basis of his interest of at least $1,000 (not taking into account the disallowed loss of $1,000), he will be allowed the $1,000 loss previously disallowed.

Example (2). At the end of partnership taxable year 1955, partnership CD has a loss of $20,000. Partner C's distributive share of this loss is $10,000. The adjusted basis of his interest in the partnership (not taking into account his distributive share of such loss) is $6,000. Therefore, $4,000 of the loss is disallowed. At the end of partnership taxable year 1956, the partnership has no taxable income or loss, but owes $8,000 to a bank for money borrowed. Since C's share of this liability is $4,000, the basis of his partnership interest is increased from zero to $4,000. (See sections 752 and 722, and §§ 1.752-1 and 1.722-1.) C is allowed the $4,000 loss, disallowed for the preceding year under section 704(d), for his taxable year within or with which partnership taxable year 1956 ends.

Example (3). At the end of partnership taxable year 1955, partner C has the following distributive share of partnership items described in section 702(a); long-term capital loss, $4,000; short-term capital loss, $2,000; income as described in section 702(a)(9), $4,000. Partner C's adjusted basis for his partnership interest at the end of 1955, before adjustment for any of the above items, is $1,000. As adjusted under section 705(a)(1)(A), C's basis is increased from $1,000 to $5,000 at the end of the year. C's total distributive share of partnership loss is $6,000. Since without regard to losses, C has a basis of only $5,000, C is allowed only $5,000/$6,000 of each loss, that is, $3,333 of his long-term capital loss, and $1,667 of his short-term capital loss. C must carry forward to succeeding taxable years $667 as a long-term capital loss and $333 as a short-term capital loss.

(e) *Family partnerships*—(1) *In general*—(i) *Introduction.* The production of income by a partnership is attributable to the capital or services, or both, contributed by the partners. The provisions of subchapter K, chapter 1 of the Code, are to be read in the light of their relationship to section 61, which requires, inter alia, that income be taxed to the person who earns it through his

Determination of Tax Liability 43,541
See p. 20,601 for regulations not amended to reflect law changes

own labor and skill and the utilization of his own capital.

(ii) *Recognition of donee as partner.* With respect to partnerships in which capital is a material income-producing factor, section 704(e)(1) provides that a person shall be recognized as a partner for income tax purposes if he owns a capital interest in such a partnership whether or not such interest is derived by purchase or gift from any other person. If a capital interest in a partnership in which capital is a material income-producing factor is created by gift, section 704(e)(2) provides that the distributive share of the donee under the partnership agreement shall be includible in his gross income, except to the extent that such distributive share is determined without allowance of reasonable compensation for services rendered to the partnership by the donor, and except to the extent that the portion of such distributive share attributable to donated capital is proportionately greater than the share of the donor attributable to the donor's capital. For rules of allocation in such cases, see subparagraph (3) of this paragraph.

(iii) *Requirement of complete transfer to donee.* A donee or purchaser of a capital interest in a partnership is not recognized as a partner under the principles of section 704(e)(1) unless such interest is acquired in a bona fide transaction, not a mere sham for tax avoidance or evasion purposes, and the donee or purchaser is the real owner of such interest. To be recognized, a transfer must vest dominion and control of the partnership interest in the transferee. The existence of such dominion and control in the donee is to be determined from all the facts and circumstances. A transfer is not recognized if the transferor retains such incidents of ownership that the transferee has not acquired full and complete ownership of the partnership interest. Transactions between members of a family will be closely scrutinized, and the circumstances, not only at the time of the purported transfer but also during the periods preceding and following it, will be taken into consideration in determining the bona fides or lack of bona fides of the purported gift or sale. A partnership may be recognized for income purposes as to some partners but not as to others.

(iv) *Capital as a material income-producing factor.* For purposes of section 704(e)(1), the determination as to whether capital is a material income-producing factor must be made by reference to all the facts of each case. Capital is a material income-producing factor if a substantial portion of the gross income of the business is attributable to the employment of capital in the business conducted by the partnership. In general, capital is not a material income-producing factor where the income of the business consists principally of fees, commissions, or other compensation for personal services performed by members or employees of the partnership. On the other hand, capital is ordinarily a material income-producing factor if the operation of the business requires substantial inventories or a substantial investment in plant, machinery, or other equipment.

(v) *Capital interest in a partnership.* For purposes of section 704(e), a capital interest in a partnership means an interest in the assets of the partnership, which is distributable to the owner of the capital interest upon his withdrawal from the partnership or upon liquidation of the partnership. The mere right to participate in the earnings and profits of a partnership is not a capital interest in the partnership.

(2) *Basic tests as to ownership*—(i) *In general.* Whether an alleged partner who is a donee of a capital interest in a partnership is the real owner of such capital interest, and whether the donee has dominion and control over such interest, must be ascertained from all the facts and circumstances of the particular case. Isolated facts are not determinative; the reality of the donee's ownership is to be determined in the light of the transaction as a whole. The execution of legally sufficient and irrevocable deeds or other instruments of gift under State law is a factor to be taken into account but is not determinative of ownership by the donee for the purposes of section 704(e). The reality of the transfer and of the donee's ownership of the property attributed to him are to be ascertained from the conduct of the parties with respect to the alleged gift and not by any mechanical or formal test. Some of the more important factors to be considered in determining whether the donee has acquired ownership of the capital interest in a partnership are indicated in subdivisions (ii) to (x), inclusive, of this subparagraph.

(ii) *Retained controls.* The donor may have retained such controls of the interest which he has purported to transfer to the donee that the donor should be treated as remaining the substantial owner of the interest. Controls of particular significance include, for example, the following:

(a) Retention of control of the distribution of amounts of income or restrictions on the distributions of amounts of income (other than amounts retained in the partnership annually with the consent of the partners, including the donee partner, for the reasonable needs of the business). If there is a partnership agreement providing for a managing partner or partners,

Reg. § 1.704-1(e)(2)

then amounts of income may be retained in the partnership without the acquiescence of all the partners if such amounts are retained for the reasonable needs of the business.

(*b*) Limitation of the right of the donee to liquidate or sell his interest in the partnership at his discretion without financial detriment.

(*c*) Retention of control of assets essential to the business (for example, through retention of assets leased to the alleged partnership).

(*d*) Retention of management powers inconsistent with normal relationships among partners. Retention by the donor of control of business management or of voting control, such as is common in ordinary business relationships, is not by itself to be considered as inconsistent with normal relationships among partners, provided the donee is free to liquidate his interest at his discretion without financial detriment. The donee shall not be considered free to liquidate his interest unless, considering all the facts, it is evident that the donee is independent of the donor and has such maturity and understanding of his rights as to be capable of deciding to exercise, and capable of exercising, his right to withdraw his capital interest from the partnership. The existence of some of the indicated controls, though amounting to less than substantial ownership retained by the donor, may be considered along with other facts and circumstances as tending to show the lack of reality of the partnership interest of the donee.

(iii) *Indirect controls.* Controls inconsistent with ownership by the donee may be exercised indirectly as well as directly, for example, through a separate business organization, estate, trust, individual, or other partnership. Where such indirect controls exist, the reality of the donee's interest will be determined as if such controls were exercisable directly.

(iv) *Participation in management.* Substantial participation by the donee in the control and management of the business (including participation in the major policy decisions affecting the business) is strong evidence of a donee partner's exercise of dominion and control over his interest. Such participation presupposes sufficient maturity and experience on the part of the donee to deal with the business problems of the partnership.

(v) *Income distributions.* The actual distribution to a donee partner of the entire amount or a major portion of his distributive share of the business income for the sole benefit and use of the donee is substantial evidence of the reality of the donee's interest, provided the donor has not retained controls inconsistent with real ownership by the donee. Amounts distributed are not considered to be used for the donee's sole benefit if, for example, they are deposited, loaned, or invested in such manner that the donor controls or can control the use or enjoyment of such funds.

(vi) *Conduct of partnership business.* In determining the reality of the donee's ownership of a capital interest in a partnership, consideration shall be given to whether the donee is actually treated as a partner in the operation of the business. Whether or not the donee has been held out publicly as a partner in the conduct of the business, in relations with customers, or with creditors or other sources of financing, is of primary significance. Other factors of significance in this connection include:

(*a*) Compliance with local partnership, fictitious names, and business registration statutes.

(*b*) Control of business bank accounts.

(*c*) Recognition of the donee's rights in distributions of partnership property and profits.

(*d*) Recognition of the donee's interest in insurance policies, leases, and other business contracts and in litigation affecting business.

(*e*) The existence of written agreements, records, or memoranda, contemporaneous with the taxable year or years concerned, establishing the nature of the partnership agreement and the rights and liabilities of the respective partners.

(*f*) Filing of partnership tax returns as required by law.

However, despite formal compliance with the above factors, other circumstances may indicate that the donor has retained substantial ownership of the interest purportedly transferred to the donee.

(vii) *Trustees as partners.* A trustee may be recognized as a partner for income tax purposes under the principles relating to family partnerships generally as applied to the particular facts of the trust-partnership arrangement. A trustee who is unrelated to and independent of the grantor, and who participates as a partner and receives distribution of the income distributable to the trust, will ordinarily be recognized as the legal owner of the partnership interest which he holds in trust unless the grantor has retained controls inconsistent with such ownership. However, if the grantor is the trustee, or if the trustee is amenable to the will of the grantor, the provisions of the trust instrument (particularly as to whether the trustee is subject to the responsibilities of a fiduciary), the provisions of the partnership agreement, and the conduct of the parties must all be taken into account in determining whether the trustee in a fiduciary capacity has

Reg. § 1.704-1(e)(2)

become the real owner of the partnership interest. Where the grantor (or person amenable to his will) is the trustee, the trust may be recognized as a partner only if the grantor (or such other person) in his participation in the affairs of the partnership actively represents and protects the interests of the beneficiaries in accordance with the obligations of a fiduciary and does not subordinate such interests to the interests of the grantor. Furthermore, if the grantor (or person amenable to his will) is the trustee, the following factors will be given particular consideration:

(a) Whether the trust is recognized as a partner in business dealings with customers and creditors, and

(b) Whether, if any amount of the partnership income is not properly retained for the reasonable needs of the business, the trust's share of such amount is distributed to the trust annually and paid to the beneficiaries or reinvested with regard solely to the interests of the beneficiaries.

(viii) *Interests (not held in trust) of minor children.* Except where a minor child is shown to be competent to manage his own property and participate in the partnership activities in accordance with his interest in the property, a minor child generally will not be recognized as a member of a partnership unless control of the property is exercised by another person as fiduciary for the sole benefit of the child, and unless there is such judicial supervision of the conduct of the fiduciary as is required by law. The use of the child's property or income for support for which a parent is legally responsible will be considered a use for the parent's benefit. "Judicial supervision of the conduct of the fiduciary" includes filing of such accountings and reports as are required by law of the fiduciary who participates in the affairs of the partnership on behalf of the minor. A minor child will be considered as competent to manage his own property if he actually has sufficient maturity and experience to be treated by disinterested persons as competent to enter business dealings and otherwise to conduct his affairs on a basis of equality with adult persons, notwithstanding legal disabilities of the minor under State law.

(ix) *Donees as limited partners.* The recognition of a donee's interest in a limited partnership will depend, as in the case of other donated interests, on whether the transfer of property is real and on whether the donee has acquired dominion and control over the interest purportedly transferred to him. To be recognized for Federal income tax purposes, a limited partnership must be organized and conducted in accordance with the requirements of the applicable State limited- partnership law. The absence of services and participation in management by a donee in a limited partnership is immaterial if the limited partnership meets all the other requirements prescribed in this paragraph. If the limited partner's right to transfer or liquidate his interest is subject to substantial restrictions (for example, where the interest of the limited partner is not assignable in a real sense or where such interest may be required to be left in the business for a long term of years), or if the general partner retains any other control which substantially limits any of the rights which would ordinarily be exercisable by unrelated limited partners in normal business relationships, such restrictions on the right to transfer or liquidate, or retention of other control, will be considered strong evidence as to the lack of reality of ownership by the donee.

(x) *Motive.* If the reality of the transfer of interest is satisfactorily established, the motives for the transaction are generally immaterial. However, the presence or absence of a tax-avoidance motive is one of many factors to be considered in determining the reality of the ownership of a capital interest acquired by gift.

(3) *Allocation of family partnership income*—(i) *In general.* (a) Where a capital interest in a partnership in which capital is a material income-producing factor is created by gift, the donee's distributive share shall be includible in his gross income, except to the extent that such share is determined without allowance of reasonable compensation for services rendered to the partnership by the donor, and except to the extent that the portion of such distributive share attributable to donated capital is proportionately greater than the distributive share attributable to the donor's capital. For the purpose of section 704, a capital interest in a partnership purchased by one member of a family from another shall be considered to be created by gift from the seller, and the fair market value of the purchased interest shall be considered to be donated capital. The "family" of any individual, for the purpose of the preceding sentence, shall include only his spouse, ancestors, and lineal descendants, and any trust for the primary benefit of such persons.

(b) To the extent that the partnership agreement does not allocate the partnership income in accordance with subdivision (a) of this subdivision, the distributive shares of the partnership income of the donor and donee shall be reallocated by making a reasonable allowance for the services of the donor and by attributing the balance of such income (other than a reasonable allowance for the services, if any, rendered by the donee) to the partnership capital of the donor and

Reg. § 1.704-1(e)(3)

donee. The portion of income, if any, thus attributable to partnership capital for the taxable year shall be allocated between the donor and donee in accordance with their respective interests in partnership capital.

(c) In determining a reasonable allowance for services rendered by the partners, consideration shall be given to all the facts and circumstances of the business, including the fact that some of the partners may have greater managerial responsibility than others. There shall also be considered the amount that would ordinarily be paid in order to obtain comparable services from a person not having an interest in the partnership.

(d) The distributive share of partnership income, as determined under subdivision (b) of this subdivision, of a partner who rendered services to the partnership before entering the Armed Forces of the United States shall not be diminished because of absence due to military service. Such distributive share shall be adjusted to reflect increases or decreases in the capital interest of the absent partner. However, the partners may by agreement allocate a smaller share to the absent partner due to his absence.

(ii) *Special rules.* (a) The provisions of subdivision (i) of this subparagraph, relating to allocation of family partnership income, are applicable where the interest in the partnership is created by gift, indirectly or directly. Where the partnership interest is created indirectly, the term "donor" may include persons other than the nominal transferor. This rule may be illustrated by the following examples:

Example (1). A father gives property to his son who shortly thereafter conveys the property to a partnership consisting of the father and the son. The partnership interest of the son may be considered created by gift and the father may be considered the donor of the son's partnership interest.

Example (2). A father, the owner of a business conducted as a sole proprietorship, transfers the business to a partnership consisting of his wife and himself. The wife subsequently conveys her interest to their son. In such case, the father, as well as the mother, may be considered the donor of the son's partnership interest.

Example (3). A father makes a gift to his son of stock in the family corporation. The corporation is subsequently liquidated. The son later contributes the property received in the liquidation of the corporation to a partnership consisting of his father and himself. In such case, for purposes of section 704, the son's partnership interest may be considered created by gift and the father may be considered the donor of his son's partnership interest.

(b) The allocation rules set forth in section 704(e) and subdivision (i) of this subparagraph apply in any case in which the transfer or creation of the partnership interest has any of the substantial characteristics of a gift. Thus, allocation may be required where transfer of a partnership interest is made between members of a family (including collaterals) under a purported purchase agreement, if the characteristics of a gift are ascertained from the terms of the purchase agreement, the terms of any loan or credit arrangements made to finance the purchase, or from other relevant data.

(c) In the case of a limited partnership, for the purpose of the allocation provisions of subdivision (i) of this subparagraph, consideration shall be given to the fact that a general partner, unlike a limited partner, risks his credit in the partnership business.

(4) *Purchased interest*—(i) *In general.* If a purported purchase of a capital interest in a partnership does not meet the requirements of subdivision (ii) of this subparagraph, the ownership by the transferee of such capital interest will be recognized only if it qualifies under the requirements applicable to a transfer of a partnership interest by gifts. In a case not qualifying under subdivision (ii) of this subparagraph, if payment of any part of the purchase price is made out of partnership earnings, the transaction may be regarded in the same light as a purported gift subject to deferred enjoyment of income. Such a transaction may be lacking in reality either as a gift or as a bona fide purchase.

(ii) *Tests as to reality of purchased interests.* A purchase of a capital interest in a partnership, either directly or by means of a loan or credit extended by a member of the family, will be recognized as bona fide if:

(a) It can be shown that the purchase has the usual characteristics of an arm's-length transaction, considering all relevant factors, including the terms of the purchase agreement (as to price, due date of payment, rate of interest, and security, if any) and the terms of any loan or credit arrangement collateral to the purchase agreement; the credit standing of the purchaser (apart from relationship to the seller) and the capacity of the purchaser to incur a legally binding obligation; or

(b) It can be shown, in the absence of characteristics of an arm's-length transaction, that the purchase was genuinely intended to promote the success of the business by securing par-

Reg. § 1.704-1(e)(4)

ticipation of the purchaser in the business or by adding his credit to that of the other participants.

However, if the alleged purchase price or loan has not been paid or the obligation otherwise discharged, the factors indicated in (a) and (b) of this subdivision shall be taken into account only as an aid in determining whether a bona fide purchase or loan obligation existed. [Reg. § 1.704-1.]

☐ [T.D. 6175, 5-23-56. Amended by T.D. 6771, 11-19-64; T.D. 8065, 12-24-85; T.D. 8099, 9-8-86; T.D. 8237, 12-29-88; T.D. 8385, 12-26-91; T.D. 8500, 12-21-93; T.D. 8585, 12-27-94 and T.D. 8717, 5-8-97.]

[Reg. § 7.704-1]

§ 7.704-1. **Partner's distributive share (Temporary).**—

(a) [Reserved]

(b) [Reserved]

(c) [Reserved]

(d) *Limitation on allowance of losses.*

(1) [Reserved]

(2) [Reserved]

(3)(i) Section 213(e) of the Tax Reform Act of 1976 amended section 704(d) of the Internal Revenue Code relating to the deductions by partners of losses incurred by a partnership. A partner is entitled to deduct the share of partnership loss to the extent of the adjusted basis of the partner's interest in the partnership. As amended, section 704(d) provides, in general, that the adjusted basis of a partner's interest in the partnership for the purpose of deducting partnership losses shall not include any portion of a partnership liability for which the partner has no personal liability. This restriction, however, does not apply to any activity to the extent that section 465 of the Code applies nor to any partnership whose principal activity is investing in real property, other than mineral property. Section 465 does not apply to corporations other than a subchapter S corporation or a personal holding company.

(ii) The restrictions in the amendment to section 704(d) will not apply to any corporate partner with respect to liabilities incurred in an activity described in section 465(c)(1). In all other respects the restrictions in the amendment will apply to all corporate partners unless the partnership's principal activity is investment in real property, other than mineral property. [Temporary Reg. § 7.704-1.]

☐ [T.D. 7445, 12-17-76.]

[Reg. § 1.704-2]

§ 1.704-2. **Allocations attributable to nonrecourse liabilities.**—(a) *Table of contents.* This paragraph contains a listing of the major headings of this § 1.704-2.

§ *1.704-2. Allocations attributable to nonrecourse liabilities.*

(a) Table of contents.

(b) General principles and definitions.

(1) Definition of and allocations of nonrecourse deductions.

(2) Definition of and allocations pursuant to a minimum gain chargeback.

(3) Definition of nonrecourse liability.

(4) Definition of partner nonrecourse debt.

(c) Amount of nonrecourse deductions.

(d) Partnership minimum gain.

(1) Amount of partnership minimum gain.

(2) Property subject to more than one liability.

(i) In general.

(ii) Allocating liabilities.

(3) Partnership minimum gain if there is a book/tax disparity.

(4) Special rule for year of revaluation.

(e) Requirements to be satisfied.

(f) Minimum gain chargeback requirement.

(1) In general.

(2) Exception for certain conversions and refinancings.

(3) Exception for certain capital contributions.

(4) Waiver for certain income allocations that fail to meet minimum gain chargeback requirement if minimum gain chargeback distorts economic arrangement.

(5) Additional exceptions.

(6) Partnership items subject to the minimum gain chargeback requirement.

(7) Examples.

(g) Shares of partnership minimum gain.

(1) Partner's share of partnership minimum gain.

(2) Partner's share of the net decrease in partnership minimum gain.

(3) Conversions of recourse or partner nonrecourse debt into nonrecourse debt.

(h) Distribution of nonrecourse liability proceeds allocable to an increase in partnership minimum gain.

(1) In general.

(2) Distribution allocable to nonrecourse liability proceeds.

(3) Option when there is an obligation to restore.

(4) Carryover to immediately succeeding taxable year.

(i) Partnership nonrecourse liabilities where a partner bears the economic risk of loss.

(1) In general.

(2) Definition of and determination of partner nonrecourse deductions.

(3) Determination of partner nonrecourse debt minimum gain.

(4) Chargeback of partner nonrecourse debt minimum gain.

(5) Partner's share of partner nonrecourse debt minimum gain.

(6) Distribution of partner nonrecourse debt proceeds allocable to an increase in partner nonrecourse debt minimum gain.

(j) Ordering rules.

(1) Treatment of partnership losses and deductions.

(i) Partner nonrecourse deductions.

(ii) Partnership nonrecourse deductions.

(iii) Carryover to succeeding taxable year.

(2) Treatment of partnership income and gains.

(i) Minimum gain chargeback.

(ii) Chargeback attributable to decrease in partner nonrecourse debt minimum gain.

(iii) Carryover to succeeding taxable year.

(k) Tiered partnerships.

(1) Increase in upper-tier partnership's minimum gain.

(2) Decrease in upper-tier partnership's minimum gain.

(3) Nonrecourse debt proceeds distributed from the lower-tier partnership to the upper-tier partnership.

(4) Nonrecourse deductions of lower-tier partnership treated as depreciation by upper-tier partnership.

(5) Coordination with partner nonrecourse debt rules.

(l) Effective dates.

(1) In general.

(i) Prospective application.

(ii) Partnerships subject to temporary regulations.

(iii) Partnerships subject to former regulations.

(2) Special rule applicable to pre-January 30, 1989, related party nonrecourse debt.

(3) Transition rule for pre-March 1, 1984, partner nonrecourse debt.

(4) Election.

(m) Examples.

(b) *General principles and definitions*—(1) *Definition of and allocations of nonrecourse deductions.* Allocations of losses, deductions, or section 705(a)(2)(B) expenditures attributable to partnership nonrecourse liabilities ("nonrecourse deductions") cannot have economic effect because the creditor alone bears any economic burden that corresponds to those allocations. Thus, nonrecourse deductions must be allocated in accordance with the partners' interests in the partnership. Paragraph (e) of this section provides a test that deems allocations of nonrecourse deductions to be in accordance with the partners' interests in the partnership. If that test is not satisfied, the partners' distributive shares of nonrecourse deductions are determined under § 1.704-1(b)(3), according to the partners' overall economic interests in the partnership. See also paragraph (i) of this section for special rules regarding the allocation of deductions attributable to nonrecourse liabilities for which a partner bears the economic risk of loss (as described in paragraph (b)(4) of this section).

(2) *Definition of and allocations pursuant to a minimum gain chargeback.* To the extent a nonrecourse liability exceeds the adjusted tax basis of the partnership property it encumbers, a disposition of that property will generate gain that at least equals that excess ("partnership minimum gain"). An increase in partnership minimum gain is created by a decrease in the adjusted tax basis of property encumbered by a nonrecourse liability below the amount of that liability and by a partnership nonrecourse borrowing that exceeds the adjusted tax basis of the property encumbered by the borrowing. Partnership minimum gain decreases as reductions occur in the amount by which the nonrecourse liability exceeds the adjusted tax basis of the property encumbered by the liability. Allocations of gain attributable to a decrease in partnership minimum gain (a "minimum gain chargeback," as required under paragraph (f) of this section) cannot have economic effect because the gain merely offsets nonrecourse deductions previously claimed by the partnership. Thus, to avoid impairing the economic effect of other allocations, allocations pursuant to a minimum gain chargeback must be made to the partners that either were allocated nonrecourse deductions or received distributions of proceeds attributable to a nonrecourse borrowing. Paragraph (e) of this section provides a test that, if

Reg. § 1.704-2(b)(1)

met, deems allocations of partnership income pursuant to a minimum gain chargeback to be in accordance with the partners' interests in the partnership. If property encumbered by a nonrecourse liability is reflected on the partnership's books at a value that differs from its adjusted tax basis, paragraph (d)(3) of this section provides that minimum gain is determined with reference to the property's book basis. See also paragraph (i)(4) of this section for special rules regarding the minimum gain chargeback requirement for partner nonrecourse debt.

(3) *Definition of nonrecourse liability.* "Nonrecourse liability" means a nonrecourse liability as defined in § 1.752-1(a)(2).

(4) *Definition of partner nonrecourse debt.* "Partner nonrecourse debt" or "partner nonrecourse liability" means any partnership liability to the extent the liability is nonrecourse for purposes of § 1.1001-2, and a partner or related person (within the meaning of § 1.752-4(b)) bears the economic risk of loss under § 1.752-2 because, for example, the partner or related person is the creditor or a guarantor.

(c) *Amount of nonrecourse deductions.* The amount of nonrecourse deductions for a partnership taxable year equals the net increase in partnership minimum gain during the year (determined under paragraph (d) of this section), reduced (but not below zero) by the aggregate distributions made during the year of proceeds of a nonrecourse liability that are allocable to an increase in partnership minimum gain (determined under paragraph (h) of this section). See paragraph (m), *Examples* (1)(i) and (vi), (2), and (3) of this section. However, increases in partnership minimum gain resulting from conversions, refinancings, or other changes to a debt instrument (as described in paragraph (g)(3)) do not generate nonrecourse deductions. Generally, nonrecourse deductions consist first of certain depreciation or cost recovery deductions and then, if necessary, a pro rata portion of other partnership losses, deductions, and section 705(a)(2)(B) expenditures for that year, excess nonrecourse deductions are carried over. See paragraphs (j)(1)(ii) and (iii) of this section for more specific ordering rules. See also paragraph (m), *Example* (1)(vi) of this section.

(d) *Partnership minimum gain*—(1) *Amount of partnership minimum gain.* The amount of partnership minimum gain is determined by first computing for each partnership nonrecourse liability any gain the partnership would realize if it disposed of the property subject to that liability for no consideration other than full satisfaction of the liability, and then aggregating the separately computed gains. The amount of partnership minimum gain includes minimum gain arising from a conversion, refinancing, or other change to a debt instrument, as described in paragraph (g)(3) of this section, only to the extent a partner is allocated a share of that minimum gain. For any partnership taxable year, the net increase or decrease in partnership minimum gain is determined by comparing the partnership minimum gain on the last day of the immediately preceding taxable year with the partnership minimum gain on the last day of the current taxable year. See paragraph (m), *Examples* (l)(i) and (iv), (2), and (3) of this section.

(2) *Property subject to more than one liability.* (i) *In general.* If property is subject to more than one liability, only the portion of the property's adjusted tax basis that is allocated to a nonrecourse liability under paragraph (d)(2)(ii) of this section is used to compute minimum gain with respect to that liability.

(ii) *Allocating liabilities.* If property is subject to two or more liabilities of equal priority, the property's adjusted tax basis is allocated among the liabilities in proportion to their outstanding balances. If property is subject to two or more liabilities of unequal priority, the adjusted tax basis is allocated first to the liability of the highest priority to the extent of its outstanding balance and then to each liability in descending order of priority to the extent of its outstanding balance, until fully allocated. See paragraph (m), *Example* (1)(v) and (vii) of this section.

(3) *Partnership minimum gain if there is a book/tax disparity.* If partnership property subject to one or more nonrecourse liabilities is, under § 1.704-1(b)(2)(iv)(*d*), (*f*), or (*r*), reflected on the partnership's books at a value that differs from its adjusted tax basis, the determinations under this section are made with reference to the property's book value. See section 704(c) and § 1.704-1(b)(4)(i) for principles that govern the treatment of a partner's share of minimum gain that is eliminated by the revaluation. See also paragraph (m), *Example* (3) of this section.

(4) *Special rule for year of revaluation.* If the partners' capital accounts are increased pursuant to § 1.704-1(b)(2)(iv)(*d*), (*f*), or (*r*) to reflect a revaluation of partnership property subject to a nonrecourse liability, the net increase or decrease in partnership minimum gain for the partnership taxable year of the revaluation is determined by:

(i) First calculating the net decrease or increase in partnership minimum gain using the current year's book values and the prior year's partnership minimum gain amount; and

Reg. § 1.704-2(d)(4)

(ii) Then adding back any decrease in minimum gain arising solely from the revaluation. See paragraph (m), *Example* (3)(iii) of this section. If the partners' capital accounts are decreased to reflect a revaluation, the net increases or decreases in partnership minimum gain are determined in the same manner as in the year before the revaluation, but by using book values rather than adjusted tax bases. See section 7701(g) and § 1.704-1(b)(2)(iv)(*f*)(*1*) (property being revalued cannot be booked down below the amount of any nonrecourse liability to which the property is subject).

(e) *Requirements to be satisfied.* Allocations of nonrecourse deductions are deemed to be in accordance with the partners' interests in the partnership only if—

(1) Throughout the full term of the partnership requirements (*1*) and (*2*) of § 1.704-1(b)(2)(ii)(*b*) are satisfied (*i.e.*, capital accounts are maintained in accordance with § 1.704-1(b)(2)(iv) and liquidating distributions are required to be made in accordance with positive capital account balances), and requirement (*3*) of either § 1.704-1(b)(2)(ii)(*b*) or § 1.704-1(b)(2)(ii)(*d*) is satisfied (*i.e.*, partners with deficit capital accounts have an unconditional deficit restoration obligation or agree to a qualified income offset);

(2) Beginning in the first taxable year of the partnership in which there are nonrecourse deductions and thereafter throughout the full term of the partnership, the partnership agreement provides for allocations of nonrecourse deductions in a manner that is reasonably consistent with allocations that have substantial economic effect of some other significant partnership item attributable to the property securing the nonrecourse liabilities;

(3) Beginning in the first taxable year of the partnership that it has nonrecourse deductions or makes a distribution of proceeds of a nonrecourse liability that are allocable to an increase in partnership minimum gain, and thereafter throughout the full term of the partnership, the partnership agreement contains a provision that complies with the minimum gain chargeback requirement of paragraph (f) of this section; and

(4) All other material allocations and capital account adjustments under the partnership agreement are recognized under § 1.704-1(b) (without regard to whether allocations of adjusted tax basis and amount realized under section 613A(c)(7)(D) are recognized under § 1.704-1(b)(4)(v)).

(f) *Minimum gain chargeback requirement*—(1) *In general.* If there is a net decrease in partnership minimum gain for a partnership taxable year, the minimum gain chargeback requirement applies and each partner must be allocated items of partnership income and gain for that year equal to that partner's share of the net decrease in partnership minimum gain (within the meaning of paragraph (g)(2)).

(2) *Exception for certain conversions and refinancings.* A partner is not subject to the minimum gain chargeback requirement to the extent the partner's share of the net decrease in partnership minimum gain is caused by a guarantee, refinancing, or other change in the debt instrument causing it to become partially or wholly recourse debt or partner nonrecourse debt, and the partner bears the economic risk of loss (within the meaning of § 1.752-2) for the newly guaranteed, refinanced, or otherwise changed liability.

(3) *Exception for certain capital contributions.* A partner is not subject to the minimum gain chargeback requirement to the extent the partner contributes capital to the partnership that is used to repay the nonrecourse liability or is used to increase the basis of the property subject to nonrecourse liability, and the partner's share of the net decrease in partnership minimum gain results from the repayment or the increase to the property's basis. See paragraph (m), *Example* (1)(iv) of this section.

(4) *Waiver for certain income allocations that fail to meet minimum gain chargeback requirement if minimum gain chargeback distorts economic arrangement.* In any taxable year that a partnership has a net decrease in partnership minimum gain, if the minimum gain chargeback requirement would cause a distortion in the economic arrangement among the partners and it is not expected that the partnership will have sufficient other income to correct that distortion, the Commissioner has the discretion, if requested by the partnership, to waive the minimum gain chargeback requirement. The following facts must be demonstrated in order for a request for a waiver to be considered:

(i) The partners have made capital contributions or received net income allocations that have restored the previous nonrecourse deductions and the distributions attributable to proceeds of a nonrecourse liability; and

(ii) The minimum gain chargeback requirement would distort the partners' economic arrangement as reflected in the partnership agreement and as evidenced over the term of the partnership by the partnership's allocations and distributions and the partners' contributions.

(5) *Additional exceptions.* The Commissioner may, by revenue ruling, provide additional excep-

tions to the minimum gain chargeback requirement.

(6) *Partnership items subject to the minimum gain chargeback requirement.* Any minimum gain chargeback required for a partnership taxable year consists first of certain gains recognized from the disposition of partnership property subject to one or more partnership nonrecourse liabilities and then if necessary consists of a pro rata portion of the partnership's other items of income and gain for that year. If the amount of the minimum gain chargeback requirement exceeds the partnership's income and gains for the taxable year, the excess carries over. See paragraphs (j)(2)(i) and (iii) of this section for more specific ordering rules.

(7) *Examples.* The following examples illustrate the provisions in § 1.704-2(f).

Example 1. Partnership AB consists of two partners, limited partner A and general partner B. Partner A contributes $90 and partner B contributes $10 to the partnership. The partnership agreement has a minimum gain chargeback provision and provides that, except as otherwise required by section 704(c), all losses will be allocated 90 percent to A and 10 percent to B; and that all income will be allocated first to restore previous losses and thereafter 50 percent to A and 50 percent to B. Distributions are made first to return initial capital to the partners and then 50 percent to A and 50 percent to B. Final distributions are made in accordance with capital account balances. The partnership borrows $200 on a nonrecourse basis from an unrelated third party and purchases an asset for $300. The partnership's only tax item for each of the first three years is $100 of depreciation on the asset. A's and B's shares of minimum gain (under paragraph (g) of this section) and deficit capital account balances are $180 and $20 respectively at the end of the third year. In the fourth year, the partnership earns $400 of net operating income and allocates the first $300 to restore the previous losses (*i.e.*, $270 to A and $30 to B); the last $100 is allocated $50 each. The partnership distributes $200 of the available cash that same year; the first $100 is distributed $90 to A and $10 to B to return their capital contributions; the last $100 is distributed $50 each to reflect their ratio for sharing profits.

	A	B
Capital account on formation	$90	$10
Less: net loss in years 1-3	($270)	($30)
Capital account at end of year 3	($180)	($20)
Allocation of operating income to restore nonrecourse deductions	$180	$20
Allocation of operating income to restore capital contributions	$90	$10
Allocation of operating income to reflect profits	$50	$50
Capital accounts after allocation of operating income	$140	$60
Distribution reflecting capital contribution	($90)	($10)
Distribution in profit-sharing ratio	($50)	($50)
Capital accounts following distribution	($0)	($0)

In the fifth year, the partnership sells the property for $300 and realizes $300 of gain. $200 of the proceeds are used to pay the nonrecourse lender. The partnership has $300 to distribute, and the partners expect to share that equally. Absent a waiver under paragraph (f)(4) of this section, the minimum gain chargeback would require the partnership to allocate the first $200 of the gain $180 to A and $20 to B, which would distort their economic arrangement. This allocation, together with the allocation of the $100 profit $50 to each partner, would result in A having a positive capital account balance of $230 and B having a positive capital account balance of $70. The allocation of income in year 4 in effect anticipated the minimum gain chargeback that did not occur until year 5. Assuming the partnership would not have sufficient other income to correct the distortion that would otherwise result, the partnership may request that the Commissioner exercise his or her discretion to waive the minimum gain chargeback requirement and recognize allocations that would allow A and B to share equally the gain on the sale of the property. These allocations would bring the partners' capital accounts to $150 each, allowing them to share the last $300 equally. The Commissioner may, in his or her discretion, permit this allocation pursuant to paragraph (f)(4) of this section because the minimum gain chargeback would distort the partners' economic arrangement over the term of the partnership as reflected in the partnership agreement and as evidenced by the partners' contributions and the partnership's allocations and distributions.

Example 2. A and B form a partnership, contribute $25 each to the partnership's capital, and agree to share all losses and profits 50 percent each. Neither partner has an unconditional deficit restoration obligation and all the requirements in paragraph (e) of this section are met. The partnership obtains a nonrecourse loan from an unre-

Reg. § 1.704-2(f)(7)

lated third party of $100 and purchases two assets, stock for $50 and depreciable property for $100. The nonrecourse loan is secured by the partnership's depreciable property. The partnership generates $20 of depreciation in each of the first five years as its only tax item. These deductions are properly treated as nonrecourse deductions and the allocation of these deductions 50 percent to A and 50 percent to B is deemed to be in accordance with the partners' interests in the partnership. At the end of year five, A and B each have a $25 deficit capital account and a $50 share of partnership minimum gain. In the beginning of year six, (at the lender's request), A guarantees the entire nonrecourse liability. Pursuant to paragraph (d)(1) of this section, the partnership has a net decrease in minimum gain of $100 and under paragraph (g)(2) of this section, A's and B's shares of that net decrease are $50 each. Under paragraph (f)(1) of this section (the minimum gain chargeback requirement), B is subject to a $50 minimum gain chargeback. Because the partnership has no gross income in year six, the entire $50 carries over as a minimum gain chargeback requirement to succeeding taxable years until there is enough income to cover the minimum gain chargeback requirement. Under the exception to the minimum gain chargeback in paragraph (f)(2) of this section, A is not subject to a minimum gain chargeback for A's $50 share of the net decrease because A bears the economic risk of loss for the liability. Instead, A's share of partner nonrecourse debt minimum gain is $50 pursuant to paragraph (i)(3) of this section. In year seven, the partnership earns $100 of net operating income and uses the money to repay the entire $100 nonrecourse debt (that A has guaranteed). Under paragraph (i)(3) of this section, the partnership has a net decrease in partner nonrecourse debt minimum gain of $50. B must be allocated $50 of the operating income pursuant to the carried over minimum gain chargeback requirement; pursuant to paragraph (i)(4) of this section, the other $50 of operating income must be allocated to A as a partner nonrecourse debt minimum gain chargeback.

(g) *Shares of partnership minimum gain*—(1) *Partner's share of partnership minimum gain.* Except as increased in paragraph (g)(3) of this section, a partner's share of partnership minimum gain at the end of any partnership taxable year equals:

(i) the sum of nonrecourse deductions allocated to that partner (and to that partner's predecessors in interest) up to that time and the distributions made to that partner (and to that partner's predecessors' in interest) up to that time of proceeds of a nonrecourse liability allocable to an increase in partnership minimum gain (see paragraph (h)(1) of this section); minus

(ii) the sum of that partner's (and that partner's predecessors' in interest) aggregate share of the net decreases in partnership minimum gain plus their aggregate share of decreases resulting from revaluations of partnership property subject to one or more partnership nonrecourse liabilities.

For purposes of § 1.704-1(b)(2)(ii)(*d*) a partner's share of partnership minimum gain is added to the limited dollar amount, if any, of the deficit balance in the partner's capital account that the partner is obligated to restore. See paragraph (m), *Examples* (1)(i) and (3)(i) of this section.

(2) *Partner's share of the net decrease in partnership minimum gain.* A partner's share of the net decrease in partnership minimum gain is the amount of the total net decrease multiplied by the partner's percentage share of the partnership's minimum gain at the end of the immediately preceding taxable year. A partner's share of any decrease in partnership minimum gain resulting from a revaluation of partnership property equals the increase in the partner's capital account attributable to the revaluation to the extent the reduction in minimum gain is caused by the revaluation. See paragraph (m), *Example* (3)(ii) of this section.

(3) *Conversions of recourse or partner nonrecourse debt into nonrecourse debt.* A partner's share of partnership minimum gain is increased to the extent provided in this paragraph (g)(3) if a refinancing, the lapse of a guarantee, or other change to a debt instrument causes a recourse or partner nonrecourse liability to become partially or wholly nonrecourse. If a recourse liability becomes a nonrecourse liability, a partner has a share of the partnership's minimum gain that results from the conversion equal to the partner's deficit capital account (determined under § 1.704-1(b)(2)(iv)) to the extent the partner no longer bears the economic burden for the entire deficit capital account as a result of the conversion. For purposes of the preceding sentence, the determination of the extent to which a partner bears the economic burden for a deficit capital account is made by determining the consequences to the partner in the case of a complete liquidation of the partnership immediately after the conversion applying the rules described in § 1.704-1(b)(2)(iii)(*c*) that deem the value of partnership property to equal its basis, taking into account section 7701(g) in the case of property that secures nonrecourse indebtedness. If a partner nonrecourse debt becomes a nonrecourse liability, the partner's share of partnership

Reg. § 1.704-2(g)(1)

minimum gain is increased to the extent the partner is not subject to the minimum gain chargeback requirement under paragraph (i)(4) of this section.

(h) *Distribution of nonrecourse liability proceeds allocable to an increase in partnership minimum gain*—(1) *In general.* If during its taxable year a partnership makes a distribution to the partners allocable to the proceeds of a nonrecourse liability, the distribution is allocable to an increase in partnership minimum gain to the extent the increase results from encumbering partnership property with aggregate nonrecourse liabilities that exceed the property's adjusted tax basis. See paragraph (m), *Example* (1)(vi) of this section. If the net increase in partnership minimum gain for a partnership taxable year is allocable to more than one nonrecourse liability, the net increase is allocated among the liabilities in proportion to the amount each liability contributed to the increase in minimum gain.

(2) *Distribution allocable to nonrecourse liability proceeds.* A partnership nay use any reasonable method to determine whether a distribution by the partnership to one or more partners is allocable to proceeds of a nonrecourse liability. The rules prescribed under § 1.163-8T for allocating debt proceeds among expenditures (applying those rules to the partnership as if it were an individual) constitute a reasonable method for determining whether the nonrecourse liability proceeds are distributed to the partners and the partners to whom the proceeds are distributed.

(3) *Option when there is an obligation to restore.* A partnership may treat any distribution to a partner of the proceeds of a nonrecourse liability (that would otherwise be allocable to an increase in partnership minimum gain) as a distribution that is not allocable to an increase in partnership minimum gain to the extent the distribution does not cause or increase a deficit balance in the partner's capital account that exceeds the amount the partner is otherwise obligated to restore (within the meaning of § 1.704-1(b)(2)(ii)(*c*)) as of the end of the partnership taxable year in which the distribution occurs.

(4) *Carryover to immediately succeeding taxable year.* The carryover rule of this paragraph applies if the net increase in partnership minimum gain for a partnership taxable year that is allocable to a nonrecourse liability under paragraph (h)(2) of this section exceeds the distributions allocable to the proceeds of the liability ("excess allocable amount"), and all or part of the net increase in partnership minimum gain for the year is carried over as an increase in partnership minimum gain for the immediately succeeding taxable year (pursuant to paragraph (j)(1)(iii) of this section). If the carryover rule of this paragraph applies, the excess allocable amount (or the amount carried over under paragraph (j)(1)(iii) of this section, if less) is treated in the succeeding taxable year as an increase in partnership minimum gain that arose in that year as a result of incurring the nonrecourse liability to which the excess allocable amount is attributable. See paragraph (m), *Example* (1)(vi) of this section. If for a partnership taxable year there is an excess allocable amount with respect to more than one partnership nonrecourse liability, the excess allocable amount is allocated to each liability in proportion to the amount each liability contributed to the increase in minimum gain.

(i) *Partnership nonrecourse liabilities where a partner bears the economic risk of loss*—(1) *In general.* Partnership losses, deductions, or section 705(a)(2)(B) expenditures that are attributable to a particular partner nonrecourse liability ("partner nonrecourse deductions," as defined in paragraph (i)(2) of this section) must be allocated to the partner that bears the economic risk of loss for the liability. If more than one partner bears the economic risk of loss for a partner nonrecourse liability, any partner nonrecourse deductions attributable to that liability must be allocated among the partners according to the ratio in which they bear the economic risk of loss. If partners bear the economic risk of loss for different portions of a liability, each portion is treated as a separate partner nonrecourse liability.

(2) *Definition of and determination of partner nonrecourse deductions.* For any partnership taxable year, the amount of partner nonrecourse deductions with respect to a partner nonrecourse debt equals the net increase during the year in minimum gain attributable to the partner nonrecourse debt ("partner nonrecourse debt minimum gain"), reduced (but not below zero) by proceeds of the liability distributed during the year to the partner bearing the economic risk of loss for the liability that are both attributable to the liability and allocable to an increase in the partner nonrecourse debt minimum gain. See paragraph (m), *Example* (1)(viii) and (ix) of this section. The determination of which partnership items constitute the partner nonrecourse deductions with respect to a partner nonrecourse debt must be made in a manner consistent with the provisions of paragraphs (c) and (j)(1)(i) and (iii) of this section.

(3) *Determination of partner nonrecourse debt minimum gain.* For any partnership taxable year, the determination of partner nonrecourse debt minimum gain and the net increase or de-

Reg. § 1.704-2(i)(3)

crease in partner nonrecourse debt minimum gain must be made in a manner consistent with the provisions of paragraphs (d) and (g)(3) of this section.

(4) *Chargeback of partner nonrecourse debt minimum gain.* If during a partnership taxable year there is a net decrease in partner nonrecourse debt minimum gain, any partner with a share of that partner nonrecourse debt minimum gain (determined under paragraph (i)(5) of this section) as of the beginning of the year must be allocated items of income and gain for the year (and, if necessary, for succeeding years) equal to that partner's share of the net decrease in the partner nonrecourse debt minimum gain. A partner's share of the net decrease in partner nonrecourse debt minimum gain is determined in a manner consistent with the provisions of paragraph (g)(2) of this section. A partner is not subject to this minimum gain chargeback, however, to the extent the net decrease in partner nonrecourse debt minimum gain arises because the liability ceases to be partner nonrecourse debt due to a conversion, refinancing, or other change in the debt instrument that causes it to become partially or wholly a nonrecourse liability. The amount that would otherwise be subject to the partner nonrecourse debt minimum gain chargeback is added to the partner's share of partnership minimum gain under paragraph (g)(3) of this section. In addition, rules consistent with the provisions of paragraphs (f)(2), (3), (4), and (5) of this section apply with respect to partner nonrecourse debt in appropriate circumstances. The determination of which items of partnership income and gain must be allocated pursuant to this paragraph (i)(4) is made in a manner that is consistent with the provisions of paragraph (f)(6) of this section. See paragraph (j)(2)(ii) and (iii) of this section for more specific rules.

(5) *Partner's share of partner nonrecourse debt minimum gain.* A partner's share of partner nonrecourse debt minimum gain at the end of any partnership taxable year is determined in a manner consistent with the provisions of paragraphs (g)(1) and (g)(3) of this section with respect to each particular partner nonrecourse debt for which the partner bears the economic risk of loss. For purposes of § 1.704-1(b)(2)(ii)(*d*), a partner's share of partner nonrecourse debt minimum gain is added to the limited dollar amount, if any, of the deficit balance in the partner's capital account that the partner is obligated to restore, and the partner is not otherwise considered to have a deficit restoration obligation as a result of bearing the economic risk of loss for any partner nonrecourse debt. See paragraph (m), *Example* (1)(viii) of this section.

(6) *Distribution of partner nonrecourse debt proceeds allocable to an increase in partner nonrecourse debt minimum gain.* Rules consistent with the provisions of paragraph (h) of this section apply to distributions of the proceeds of partner nonrecourse debt.

(j) *Ordering Rules.* For purposes of this section, the following ordering rules apply to partnership items. Notwithstanding any other provision in this section and § 1.704-1, allocations of partner nonrecourse deductions, nonrecourse deductions, and minimum gain chargebacks are made before any other allocations.

(1) *Treatment of partnership losses and deductions.* (i) *Partner nonrecourse deductions.* Partnership losses, deductions, and section 705(a)(2)(B) expenditures are treated as partner nonrecourse deductions in the amount determined under paragraph (i)(2) of this section (determining partner nonrecourse deductions) in the following order:

(A) First, depreciation or cost recovery deductions with respect to property that is subject to partner nonrecourse debt;

(B) Then, if necessary, a pro rata portion of the partnership's other deductions, losses, and section 705(a)(2)(B) items.

Depreciation or cost recovery deductions with respect to property that is subject to a partnership nonrecourse liability is first treated as a partnership nonrecourse deduction and any excess is treated as a partner nonrecourse deduction under this paragraph (j)(1)(i).

(ii) *Partnership nonrecourse deductions.* Partnership losses, deductions, and section 705(a)(2)(B) expenditures are treated as partnership nonrecourse deductions in the amount determined under paragraph (c) of this section (determining nonrecourse deductions) in the following order:

(A) First, depreciation or cost recovery deductions with respect to property that is subject to partnership nonrecourse liabilities;

(B) Then, if necessary, a pro rata portion of the partnership's other deductions, losses, and section 705(a)(2)(B) items.

Depreciation or cost recovery deductions with respect to property that is subject to partner nonrecourse debt is first treated as a partner nonrecourse deduction and any excess is treated as a partnership nonrecourse deduction under this paragraph (j)(1)(ii). Any other item that is treated as a partner nonrecourse deduction will in

Reg. § 1.704-2(i)(4)

no event be treated as a partnership nonrecourse deduction.

(iii) *Carryover to succeeding taxable year.* If the amount of partner nonrecourse deductions or nonrecourse deductions exceeds the partnership's losses, deductions, and section 705(a)(2)(B) expenditures for the taxable year (determined under paragraphs (j)(1)(i) and (ii) of this section), the excess is treated as an increase in partner nonrecourse debt minimum gain or partnership minimum gain in the immediately succeeding partnership taxable year. See paragraph (m), *Example* (1)(vi) of this section.

(2) *Treatment of partnership income and gains.* (i) *Minimum gain chargeback.* Items of partnership income and gain equal to the minimum gain chargeback requirement (determined under paragraph (f) of this section) are allocated as a minimum gain chargeback in the following order:

(A) First, gain from the disposition of property subject to partnership nonrecourse liabilities;

(B) Then, if necessary, a pro rata portion of the partnership's other items of income and gain for that year. Gain from the disposition of property subject to partner nonrecourse debt is allocated to satisfy a minimum gain chargeback requirement for partnership nonrecourse debt only to the extent not allocated under paragraph (j)(2)(ii) of this section.

(ii) *Chargeback attributable to decrease in partner nonrecourse debt minimum gain.* Items of partnership income and gain equal to the partner nonrecourse debt minimum gain chargeback (determined under paragraph (i)(4) of this section) are allocated to satisfy a partner nonrecourse debt minimum gain chargeback in the following order:

(A) First, gain from the disposition of property subject to partner nonrecourse debt;

(B) Then, if necessary, a pro rata portion of the partnership's other items of income and gain for that year. Gain from the disposition of property subject to a partnership nonrecourse liability is allocated to satisfy a partner nonrecourse debt minimum gain chargeback only to the extent not allocated under paragraph (j)(2)(i) of this section. An item of partnership income and gain that is allocated to satisfy a minimum gain chargeback under paragraph (f) of this section is not allocated to satisfy a minimum gain chargeback under paragraph (i)(4).

(iii) *Carryover to succeeding taxable year.* If a minimum gain chargeback requirement (determined under paragraphs (f) and (i)(4) of this section) exceeds the partnership's income and gains for the taxable year, the excess is treated as a minimum gain chargeback requirement in the immediately succeeding partnership taxable years until fully charged back.

(k) *Tiered partnerships.* For purposes of this section, the following rules determine the effect on partnership minimum gain when a partnership ("upper-tier partnership") is a partner in another partnership ("lower-tier partnership").

(1) *Increase in upper-tier partnership's minimum gain.* The sum of the nonrecourse deductions that the lower-tier partnership allocates to the upper-tier partnership for any taxable year of the upper-tier partnership, and the distributions made during that taxable year from the lower-tier partnership to the upper-tier partnership of proceeds of nonrecourse debt that are allocable to an increase in the lower-tier partnership's minimum gain, is treated as an increase in the upper-tier partnership's minimum gain.

(2) *Decrease in upper-tier partnership's minimum gain.* The upper-tier partnership's share for its taxable year of the lower-tier partnership's net decrease in its minimum gain is treated as a decrease in the upper-tier partnership's minimum gain for that taxable year.

(3) *Nonrecourse debt proceeds distributed from the lower-tier partnership to the upper-tier partnership.* All distributions from the lower-tier partnership to the upper-tier partnership during the upper-tier partnership's taxable year of proceeds of a nonrecourse liability allocable to an increase in the lower-tier partnership's minimum gain are treated as proceeds of a nonrecourse liability of the upper-tier partnership. The increase in the upper-tier partnership's minimum gain (under paragraph (k)(1) of this section) attributable to the receipt of those distributions is, for purposes of paragraph (h) of this section, treated as an increase in the upper-tier partnership's minimum gain arising from encumbering property of the upper-tier partnership with a nonrecourse liability of the upper-tier partnership.

(4) *Nonrecourse deductions of lower-tier partnership treated as depreciation by upper-tier partnership.* For purposes of paragraph (c) of this section, all nonrecourse deductions allocated by the lower-tier partnership to the upper-tier partnership for the upper-tier partnership's taxable year are treated as depreciation or cost recovery deductions with respect to property owned by the upper-tier partnership and subject to a nonrecourse liability of the upper-tier partnership with respect to which minimum gain increased during the year by the amount of the nonrecourse deductions.

Reg. § 1.704-2(k)(4)

(5) *Coordination with partner nonrecourse debt rules.* The lower-tier partnership's liabilities that are treated as the upper-tier partnership's liabilities under § 1.752-4(a) are treated as the upper-tier partnership's liabilities for purposes of applying paragraph (i) of this section. Rules consistent with the provisions of paragraphs (k)(1) through (k)(4) of this section apply to determine the allocations that the upper-tier partnership must make with respect to any liability that constitutes a nonrecourse debt for which one or more partners of the upper-tier partnership bear the economic risk of loss.

(l) *Effective dates*—(1) *In general.* (i) *Prospective application.* Except as otherwise provided in this paragraph (l), this section applies for partnership taxable years beginning on or after December 28, 1991. For the rules applicable to taxable years beginning after December 29, 1988, and before December 28, 1991, see former § 1.704-1T (b)(4)(iv). For the rules applicable to taxable years beginning on or before December 29, 1988, see former § 1.704-1(b)(4)(iv).

(ii) *Partnerships subject to temporary regulations.* If a partnership agreement entered into after December 29, 1988, and before December 28, 1991, or a partnership agreement entered into on or before December 29, 1988, that elected to apply former § 1.704-1T(b)(4)(iv) (as contained in CFR edition revised as of April 1, 1992), complied—

(A) The provisions of former § 1.704-1T (b)(4)(iv) continue to apply to the partnership for any taxable year beginning on or after December 28, 1991, (unless the partnership makes an election under paragraph (l)(4) of this section) and ending before any subsequent material modification to the partnership agreement; and

(B) The provisions of this section do not apply to the partnership for any of those taxable years.

(iii) *Partnerships subject to former regulations.* If a partnership agreement entered into on or before December 29, 1988, complied with the provisions of former § 1.704-1(b) (4)(iv)(d) on or before that date—

(A) The provisions of former § 1.704-1(b)(4)(iv)(a) through (f) continue to apply to the partnership for any taxable year beginning after that date (unless the partnership made an election under § 1.704-1T(b)(4)(iv)(m)(4) in a *partnership taxable year ending before December 28, 1991,* or makes an election under paragraph (l)(4) of this section) and ending before any subsequent material modification to the partnership agreement; and

(B) The provisions of this section do not apply to the partnership for any of those taxable years.

(2) *Special rule applicable to pre-January 30, 1989, related party nonrecourse debt.* For purposes of this section and former § 1.704-1T(b)(4)(iv), if—

(i) A partnership liability would, but for this paragraph (l)(2) of this section, constitute a partner nonrecourse debt; and

(ii) Sections 1.752-1 through -3 or former §§ 1.752-1T through -3T (whichever is applicable) do not apply to the liability;

the liability is, notwithstanding paragraphs (i) and (b)(4) of this section, treated as a nonrecourse liability of the partnership, and not as a partner nonrecourse debt, to the extent the liability would be so treated under this section (or § 1.704-1T(b)(4)(iv)) if the determination of the extent to which one or more partners bears the economic risk of loss for the liability under § 1.752-1 or former § 1.752-1T were made without regard to the economic risk of loss that any partner would otherwise be considered to bear for the liability by reason of any obligation undertaken or interest as a creditor acquired prior to January 30, 1989, by a person related to the partner (within the meaning of § 1.752-4(b) or former § 1.752-1T(h)). For purposes of the preceding sentence, if a related person undertakes an obligation or acquires an interest as a creditor on or after January 30, 1989, pursuant to a written binding contract in effect prior to January 30, 1989, and at all times thereafter, the obligation or interest as a creditor is treated as if it were undertaken or acquired prior to January 30, 1989. However, for partnership taxable years beginning on or after December 29, 1988, a pre-January 30, 1989, liability, other than a liability subject to paragraph (l)(3) of this section or former § 1.704-1T(b)(4)(iv)(m)(3) (whichever is applicable), that is treated as grandfathered under former §§ 1.752-1T through -3T (whichever is applicable) will be treated as a nonrecourse liability for purposes of this section provided that all partners in the partnership consistently treat the liability as nonrecourse for partnership taxable years beginning on or after December 29, 1988.

(3) *Transition rule for pre-March 1, 1984, partner nonrecourse debt.* If a partnership liability would, but for this paragraph (l)(3) or former § 1.704-1T(b)(4)(iv), constitute a partner nonrecourse debt and the liability constitutes grandfathered partner nonrecourse debt that is appropriately treated as a nonrecourse liability of the partnership under § 1.752-1 (as in effect prior to December 29, 1988)—

Reg. § 1.704-2(k)(5)

(i) The liability is, notwithstanding paragraphs (i) and (b)(4) of this section, former § 1.704-1T(b)(4)(iv), and former § 1.704-1(b)(4)(iv), treated as a nonrecourse liability of the partnership for purposes of this section and for purposes of former § 1.704-1T(b)(4)(iv) and former § 1.704-1(b)(4)(iv) to the extent of the amount, if any, by which the smallest outstanding balance of the liability during the period beginning at the end of the first partnership taxable year ending on or after December 31, 1986, and ending at the time of any determination under this paragraph (l)(3)(i) or former § 1.704-1T(b)(4)(iv)(*m*)(*3*)(*i*) exceeds the aggregate amount of the adjusted basis (or book value) of partnership property allocable to the liability (determined in accordance with former § 1.704-1(b)(4)(iv)(*c*)(*1*) and (*2*) at the end of the first partnership taxable year ending on or after December 31, 1986); and

(ii) In applying this section to the liability, former § 1.704-1(b)(4)(iv)(*c*)(*1*) and (*2*) is applied as if all of the adjusted basis of partnership property allocable to the liability is allocable to the portion of the liability that is treated as a partner nonrecourse debt and as if none of the adjusted basis of partnership property that is allocable to the liability is allocable to the portion of the liability that is treated as a nonrecourse liability under this paragraph (l)(3) and former § 1.704-1T(b)(4)(iv)(*m*)(*3*)(*i*).

For purposes of the preceding sentence, a grandfathered partner debt is any partnership liability that was not subject to former §§ 1.752-1T and -3T but that would have been subject to those sections under § 1.752-4T(b) if the liability had arisen (other than pursuant to a written binding contract) on or after March 1, 1984. A partnership liability is not considered to have been subject to §§ 1.752-2T and -3T solely because a portion of the liability was treated as a liability to which those sections apply under § 1.752-4T(e).

(4) *Election.* A partnership may elect to apply the provisions of this section to the first taxable year of the partnership ending on or after December 28, 1991. An election under this paragraph (l)(4) is made by attaching a written statement to the partnership return for the first taxable year of the partnership ending on or after December 28, 1991. The written statement must include the name, address, and taxpayer identification number of the partnership making the statement and must declare that an election is made under this paragraph (l)(4).

(m) *Examples.* The principles of this section are illustrated by the following examples:

Example 1. Nonrecourse deductions and partnership minimum gain. For *Example* 1, unless otherwise provided, the following facts are assumed. LP, the limited partner, and GP, the general partner, form a limited partnership to acquire and operate a commercial office building. LP contributes $180,000, and GP contributes $20,000. The partnership obtains an $800,000 nonrecourse loan and purchases the building (on leased land) for $1,000,000. The nonrecourse loan is secured only by the building, and no principal payments are due for 5 years. The partnership agreement provides that GP will be required to restore any deficit balance in GP's capital account following the liquidation of GP's interest (as set forth in § 1.704-1(b)(2)(ii)(*b*)(*3*)), and LP will not be required to restore any deficit balance in LP's capital account following the liquidation of LP's interest. The partnership agreement contains the following provisions required by paragraph (e) of this section: a qualified income offset (as defined in § 1.704-1(b)(2)(ii)(*d*)); a minimum gain chargeback (in accordance with paragraph (f) of this section); a provision that the partners' capital accounts will be determined and maintained in accordance with § 1.704-1(b)(2)(ii)(*b*)(*1*); and a provision that distributions will be made in accordance with partners' positive capital account balances (as set forth in § 1.704-1(b)(2)(ii)(*b*)(*2*)). In addition, as of the end of each partnership taxable year discussed herein, the items described in § 1.704-1(b)(2)(ii)(*d*)(*4*), (*5*), and (*6*) are not reasonably expected to cause or increase a deficit balance in LP's capital account. The partnership agreement provides that, except as otherwise required by its qualified income offset and minimum gain chargeback provisions, all partnership items will be allocated 90 percent to LP and 10 percent to GP until the first time when the partnership has recognized items of income and gain that exceed the items of loss and deduction it has recognized over its life, and all further partnership items will be allocated equally between LP and GP. Finally, the partnership agreement provides that all distributions, other than distributions in liquidation of the partnership or of a partner's interest in the partnership, will be made 90 percent to LP and 10 percent to GP until a total of $200,000 has been distributed, and thereafter all the distributions will be made equally to LP and GP. In each of the partnership's first 2 taxable years, it generates rental income of $95,000, operating expenses (including land lease payments) of $10,000, interest expense of $80,000, and a depreciation deduction of $90,000, resulting in a net taxable loss of $85,000 in each of those years. The allocations of these losses 90

Reg. § 1.704-2(m)

Determination of Tax Liability

See p. 20,601 for regulations not amended to reflect law changes

percent to LP and 10 percent to GP have substantial economic effect.

	LP	GP
Capital account on formation	$180,000	$20,000
Less: net loss in years 1 and 2	(153,000)	(17,000)
Capital account at end of year 2	$27,000	$3,000

In the partnership's third taxable year, it again generates rental income of $95,000, operating expenses of $10,000, interest expense of $80,000, and a depreciation deduction of $90,000, resulting in a net taxable loss of $85,000. The partnership makes no distributions.

(i) *Calculation of nonrecourse deductions and partnership minimum gain.* If the partnership were to dispose of the building in full satisfaction of the nonrecourse liability at the end of the third year, it would realize $70,000 of gain ($800,000 amount realized less $730,000 adjusted tax basis). Because the amount of partnership minimum gain at the end of the third year (and the net increase in partnership minimum gain during the year) is $70,000, there are partnership nonrecourse deductions for that year of $70,000, consisting of depreciation deductions allowable with respect to the building of $70,000. Pursuant to the partnership agreement, all partnership items comprising the net taxable loss of $85,000, including the $70,000 nonrecourse deduction, are allocated 90 percent to LP and 10 percent to GP. The allocation of these items, other than the nonrecourse deductions, has substantial economic effect.

	LP	GP
Capital account at end of year 2	$27,000	$3,000
Less: net loss in year 3 (without nonrecourse deductions)	(13,500)	(1,500)
Less: nonrecourse deductions in year 3	(63,000)	(7,000)
Capital account at end of year 3	($49,500)	($5,500)

The allocation of the $70,000 nonrecourse deduction satisfies requirement (2) of paragraph (e) of this section because it is consistent with allocations having substantial economic effect of other significant partnership items attributable to the building. Because the remaining requirements of paragraph (e) of this section are satisfied, the allocation of nonrecourse deductions is deemed to be in accordance with the partners' interests in the partnership. At the end of the partnership's third taxable year, LP's and GP's shares of partnership minimum gain are $63,000 and $7,000, respectively. Therefore, pursuant to paragraph (g)(1) of this section, LP is treated as obligated to restore a deficit capital account balance of $63,000, so that in the succeeding year LP could be allocated up to an additional $13,500 of partnership deductions, losses, and section 705(a)(2)(B) items that are not nonrecourse deductions. Even though this allocation would increase a deficit capital account balance, it would be considered to have economic effect under the alternate economic effect test contained in § 1.704-1(b)(2)(ii)(*d*). If the partnership were to dispose of the building in full satisfaction of the nonrecourse liability at the beginning of the partnership's fourth taxable year (and had no other economic activity in that year), the partnership minimum gain would be decreased from $70,000 to zero, and the minimum gain chargeback would require that LP and GP be allocated $63,000 and $7,000, respectively, of the gain from that disposition.

(ii) *Illustration of reasonable consistency requirement.* Assume instead that the partnership agreement provides that all nonrecourse deductions of the partnership will be allocated equally between LP and GP. Furthermore, at the time the partnership agreement is entered into, there is a reasonable likelihood that over the partnership's life it will realize amounts of income and gain significantly in excess of amounts of loss and deduction (other than nonrecourse deductions). The equal allocation of excess income and gain has substantial economic effect.

	LP	GP
Capital account on formation	$180,000	$20,000
Less: net loss years 1 and 2	(153,000)	(17,000)
Less: net loss in year 3 (without nonrecourse deductions)	(13,500)	(1,500)
Less: nonrecourse deductions in year 3	(35,000)	(35,000)
Capital account at end of year 3	($21,500)	($33,500)

The allocation of the $70,000 nonrecourse deduction equally between LP and GP satisfies requirement (2) of paragraph (e) of this section because the allocation is consistent with allocations, which will have substantial economic effect, of other significant partnership items attributable to the

Reg. § 1.704-2(m)

building. Because the remaining requirements of paragraph (e) of this section are satisfied, the allocation of nonrecourse deductions is deemed to be in accordance with the partners' interests in the partnership. The allocation of the nonrecourse deductions 75 percent to LP and 25 percent to GP (or in any other ratio between 90 percent to LP/10 percent to GP and 50 percent to LP/50 percent to GP) also would satisfy requirement (2) of paragraph (e) of this section.

(iii) *Allocation of nonrecourse deductions that fails reasonable consistency requirement.* Assume instead that the partnership agreement provides that LP will be allocated 99 percent, and GP 1 percent, of all nonrecourse deductions of the partnership. Allocating nonrecourse deductions this way does not satisfy requirement (2) of paragraph (e) of this section because the allocations are not reasonably consistent with allocations, having substantial economic effect, of any other significant partnership item attributable to the building. Therefore, the allocation of nonrecourse deductions will be disregarded, and the nonrecourse deductions of the partnership will be reallocated according to the partners' overall economic interests in the partnership, determined under § 1.704-1(b)(3)(ii).

(iv) *Capital contribution to pay down nonrecourse debt.* At the beginning of the partnership's fourth taxable year, LP contributes $144,000 and GP contributes $16,000 of additional capital to the partnership, which the partnership immediately uses to reduce the amount of its nonrecourse liability from $800,000 to $640,000. In addition, in the partnership's fourth taxable year, it generates rental income of $95,000, operating expenses of $10,000, interest expense of $64,000 (consistent with the debt reduction), and a depreciation deduction of $90,000, resulting in a net taxable loss of $69,000. If the partnership were to dispose of the building in full satisfaction of the nonrecourse liability at the end of that year, it would realize no gain ($640,000 amount realized less $640,000 adjusted tax basis). Therefore, the amount of partnership minimum gain at the end of the year is zero, which represents a net decrease in partnership minimum gain of $70,000 during the year. LP's and GP's shares of this net decrease are $63,000 and $7,000 respectively, so that at the end of the partnership's fourth taxable year, LP's and GP's shares of partnership minimum gain are zero. Although there has been a net decrease in partnership minimum gain, pursuant to paragraph (f)(3) of this section LP and GP are not subject to a minimum gain chargeback.

	LP	GP
Capital account at end of year 3	($49,500)	($5,500)
Plus: contribution	144,000	16,000
Less: net loss in year 4	(62,100)	(6,900)
Capital account at end of year 4	$32,400	$3,600
Minimum gain chargeback carryforward	$ 0	$ 0

(v) *Loans of unequal priority.* Assume instead that the building acquired by the partnership is secured by a $700,000 nonrecourse loan and a $100,000 recourse loan, subordinate in priority to the nonrecourse loan. Under paragraph (d)(2) of this section, $700,000 of the adjusted basis of the building at the end of the partnership's third taxable year is allocated to the nonrecourse liability (with the remaining $30,000 allocated to the recourse liability) so that if the partnership disposed of the building in full satisfaction of the nonrecourse liability at the end of that year, it would realize no gain ($700,000 amount realized less $700,000 adjusted tax basis). Therefore, there is no minimum gain (or increase in minimum gain) at the end of the partnership's third taxable year. If, however, the $700,000 nonrecourse loan were subordinate in priority to the $100,000 recourse loan, under paragraph (d)(2) of this section, the first $100,000 of adjusted tax basis in the building would be allocated to the recourse liability leaving only $630,000 of the adjusted basis of the building to be allocated to the $700,000 nonrecourse loan. In that case, the balance of the $700,000 nonrecourse liability would exceed the adjusted tax basis of the building by $70,000, so that there would be $70,000 of minimum gain (and a $70,000 increase in partnership minimum gain) in the partnership's third taxable year.

(vi) *Nonrecourse borrowing; distribution of proceeds in subsequent year.* The partnership obtains an additional nonrecourse loan of $200,000 at the end of its fourth taxable year, secured by a second mortgage on the building, and distributes $180,000 of this cash to its partners at the beginning of its fifth taxable year. In addition, in its fourth and fifth taxable years, the partnership again generates rental income of $95,000, operating expenses of $10,000, interest expense of $80,000 ($100,000 in the fifth taxable year reflecting the interest paid on both liabilities), and a depreciation deduction of $90,000, resulting in a net taxable loss of $85,000 ($105,000 in the fifth taxable year reflecting the interest paid on both

Reg. § 1.704-2(m)

Determination of Tax Liability

liabilities). The partnership has distributed its $5,000 of operating cash flow in each year ($95,000 of rental income less $10,000 of operating expense and $80,000 of interest expense) to LP and GP at the end of each year. If the partnership were to dispose of the building in full satisfaction of both nonrecourse liabilities at the end of its fourth taxable year, the partnership would realize $360,000 of gain ($1,000,000 amount realized less $640,000 adjusted tax basis). Thus, the net increase in partnership minimum gain during the partnership's fourth taxable year is $290,000 ($360,000 of minimum gain at the end of the fourth year less $70,000 of minimum gain at the end of the third year). Because the partnership did not distribute any of the proceeds of the loan it obtained in its fourth year during that year, the potential amount of partnership nonrecourse deductions for that year is $290,000. Under paragraph (c) of this section, if the partnership had distributed the proceeds of that loan to its partners at the end of its fourth year, the partnership's nonrecourse deductions for that year would have been reduced by the amount of that distribution because the proceeds of that loan are allocable to an increase in partnership minimum gain under paragraph (h)(1) of this section. Because the nonrecourse deductions of $290,000 for the partnership's fourth taxable year exceed its total deductions for that year, all $180,000 of the partnership's deductions for that year are treated as nonrecourse deductions, and the $110,000 excess nonrecourse deductions are treated as an increase in partnership minimum gain in the partnership's fifth taxable year under paragraph (c) of this section.

	LP	GP
Capital account at end of year 3 (including cash flow distributions)	($63,000)	($7,000)
Plus: rental income in year 4	85,500	9,500
Less: nonrecourse deductions in year 4	(162,000)	(18,000)
Less: cash flow distributions in year 4	(4,500)	(500)
Capital account at end of year 4	($144,000)	($16,000)

At the end of the partnership's fourth taxable year, LP's and GP's shares of partnership minimum gain are $225,000 and $25,000, respectively (because the $110,000 excess of nonrecourse deductions is carried forward to the next year). If the partnership were to dispose of the building in full satisfaction of the nonrecourse liabilities at the end of its fifth taxable year, the partnership would realize $450,000 of gain ($1,000,000 amount realized less $550,000 adjusted tax basis). Therefore, the net increase in partnership minimum gain during the partnership's fifth taxable year is $200,000 ($110,000 deemed increase plus the $90,000 by which minimum gain at the end of the fifth year exceeds minimum gain at the end of the fourth year ($450,000 less $360,000)). At the beginning of its fifth year, the partnership distributes $180,000 of the loan proceeds (retaining $20,000 to pay the additional interest expense). Under paragraph (h) of this section, the first $110,000 of this distribution (an amount equal to the deemed increase in partnership minimum gain for the year) is considered allocable to an increase in partnership minimum gain for the year. As a result, the amount of nonrecourse deductions for the partnership's fifth taxable year is $90,000 ($200,000 net increase in minimum gain less $110,000 distribution of nonrecourse liability proceeds allocable to an increase in partnership minimum gain), and the nonrecourse deductions consist solely of the $90,000 depreciation deduction allowable with respect to the building. As a result of the distributions during the partnership's fifth taxable year, the total distributions to the partners over the partnership's life equal $205,000. Therefore, the last $5,000 distributed to the partners during the fifth year will be divided equally between them under the partnership agreement. Thus, out of the $185,000 total distribution during the partnership's fifth taxable year, the first $180,000 is distributed 90 percent to LP and 10 percent to GP, and the last $5,000 is divided equally between them.

	LP	GP
Capital account at end of year 4	($144,000)	($16,000)
Less: net loss in year 5 (without nonrecourse deductions)	(13,500)	(1,500)
Less: nonrecourse deductions in year 5	(81,000)	(9,000)
Less: distribution of loan proceeds	(162,000)	(18,000)
Less: cash flow distribution in year 5	(2,500)	(2,500)
Capital account at end of year 5	($403,000)	($47,000)

At the end of the partnership's fifth taxable year, LP's share of partnership minimum gain is $405,000 ($225,000 share of minimum gain at the end of the fourth year plus $81,000 of nonrecourse deductions for the fifth year and a $99,000 distribution of nonrecourse liability proceeds that are allocable to an increase in minimum gain) and GP's share of partnership minimum gain is

Reg. § 1.704-2(m)

$45,000 ($25,000 share of minimum gain at the end of the fourth year plus $9,000 of nonrecourse deductions for the fifth year and an $11,000 distribution of nonrecourse liability proceeds that are allocable to an increase in minimum gain).

(vii) *Partner guarantee of nonrecourse debt.* LP and GP personally guarantee the "first" $100,000 of the $800,000 nonrecourse loan (i.e., only if the building is worth less than $100,000 will they be called upon to make up any deficiency). Under paragraph (d)(2) of this section, only $630,000 of the adjusted tax basis of the building is allocated to the $700,000 nonrecourse portion of the loan because the collateral will be applied first to satisfy the $100,000 guaranteed portion, making it superior in priority to the remainder of the loan. On the other hand, if LP and GP were to guarantee the "last" $100,000 (*i.e.*, if the building is worth less than $800,000, they will be called upon to make up the deficiency up to $100,000), $700,000 of the adjusted tax basis of the building would be allocated to the $700,000 nonrecourse portion of the loan because the guaranteed portion would be inferior in priority to it.

(viii) *Partner nonrecourse debt.* Assume instead that the $800,000 loan is made by LP, the limited partner. Under paragraph (b)(4) of this section, the $800,000 obligation does not constitute a nonrecourse liability of the partnership for purposes of this section because LP, a partner, bears the economic risk of loss for that loan within the meaning of § 1.752-2. Instead, the $800,000 loan constitutes a partner nonrecourse debt under paragraph (b)(4) of this section. In the partnership's third taxable year, partnership minimum gain would have increased by $70,000 if the debt were a nonrecourse liability of the partnership. Thus, under paragraph (i)(3) of this section, there is a net increase of $70,000 in the minimum gain attributable to the $800,000 partner nonrecourse debt for the partnership's third taxable year, and $70,000 of the $90,000 depreciation deduction from the building for the partnership's third taxable year constitutes a partner nonrecourse deduction with respect to the debt. See paragraph (i)(4) of this section. Under paragraph (i)(2) of this section, this partner nonrecourse deduction must be allocated to LP, the partner that bears the economic risk of loss for that liability.

(ix) *Nonrecourse debt and partner nonrecourse debt of differing priorities.* As in Example 1 (viii) of this paragraph (m), the $800,000 loan is made to the partnership by LP, the limited partner, but the loan is a purchase money loan that "wraps around" a $700,000 underlying nonrecourse note (also secured by the building) issued by LP to an unrelated person in connection with LP's acquisition of the building. Under these circumstances, LP bears the economic risk of loss with respect to only $100,000 of the liability within the meaning of § 1.752-2. See § 1.752-2(f) (*Example 6*). Therefore, for purposes of paragraph (d) of this section, the $800,000 liability is treated as a $700,000 nonrecourse liability of the partnership and a $100,000 partner nonrecourse debt (inferior in priority to the $700,000 liability) of the partnership for which LP bears the economic risk of loss. Under paragraph (i)(2) of this section, $70,000 of the $90,000 depreciation deduction realized in the partnership's third taxable year constitutes a partner nonrecourse deduction that must be allocated to LP.

Example 2. Netting of increases and decreases in partnership minimum gain. For *Example 2* unless otherwise provided, the following facts are assumed. X and Y form a general partnership to acquire and operate residential real properties. Each partner contributes $150,000 to the partnership. The partnership obtains a $1,500,000 nonrecourse loan and purchases 3 apartment buildings (on leased land) for $720,000 ("Property A"), $540,000 ("Property B"), and $540,000 ("Property C"). The nonrecourse loan is secured only by the 3 buildings, and no principal payments are due for 5 years. In each of the partnership's first 3 taxable years, it generates rental income of $225,000, operating expenses (including land lease payments) of $50,000, interest expense of $175,000, and depreciation deductions on the 3 properties of $150,000 ($60,000 on Property A and $45,000 on each of Property B and Property C), resulting in a net taxable loss of $150,000 in each of those years. The partnership makes no distributions to X or Y.

(i) *Calculation of net increases and decreases in partnership minimum gain.* If the partnership were to dispose of the 3 apartment buildings in full satisfaction of its nonrecourse liability at the end of its third taxable year, it would realize $150,000 of gain ($1,500,000 amount realized less $1,350,000 adjusted tax basis). Because the amount of partnership minimum gain at the end of that year (and the net increase in partnership minimum gain during that year) is $150,000, the amount of partnership nonrecourse deductions for that year is $150,000, consisting of depreciation deductions allowable with respect to the 3 apartment buildings of $150,000. The result would be the same if the partnership obtained 3 separate nonrecourse loans that were "cross-collateralized" (*i.e.*, if each separate loan were secured by all 3 of the apartment buildings).

(ii) *Netting of increases and decreases in partnership minimum gain when there is a disposition.*

Reg. § 1.704-2(m)

At the beginning of the partnership's fourth taxable year, the partnership (with the permission of the nonrecourse lender) disposes of Property A for $835,000 and uses a portion of the proceeds to repay $600,000 of the nonrecourse liability (the principal amount attributable to Property A), reducing the balance to $900,000. As a result of the disposition, the partnership realizes gain of $295,000 ($835,000 amount realized less $540,000 adjusted tax basis). If the disposition is viewed in isolation, the partnership has generated minimum gain of $60,000 on the sale of Property A ($600,000 of debt reduction less $540,000 adjusted tax basis). However, during the partnership's fourth taxable year it also generates rental income of $135,000, operating expenses of $30,000, interest expense of $105,000, and depreciation deductions of $90,000 ($45,000 on each remaining building). If the partnership were to dispose of the remaining two buildings in full satisfaction of its nonrecourse liability at the end of the partnership's fourth taxable year, it would realize gain of $180,000 ($900,000 amount realized less $720,000 aggregate adjusted tax basis), which is the amount of partnership minimum gain at the end of the year. Because the partnership minimum gain increased from $150,000 to $180,000 during the partnership's fourth taxable year, the amount of partnership nonrecourse deductions for that year is $30,000, consisting of a ratable portion of depreciation deductions allowable with respect to the two remaining apartment buildings. No minimum gain chargeback is required for the taxable year, even though the partnership disposed of one of the properties subject to the nonrecourse liability during the year, because there is no net decrease in partnership minimum gain for the year. See paragraph (f)(1) of this section.

Example 3. Nonrecourse deductions and partnership minimum gain before third partner is admitted. For purposes of *Example* 3, unless otherwise provided, the following facts are assumed. Additional facts are given in each of *Examples* 3 (ii), (iii), and (iv). A and B form a limited partnership to acquire and lease machinery that is 5-year recovery property. A, the limited partner, and B, the general partner, contribute $100,000 each to the partnership, which obtains an $800,000 nonrecourse loan and purchases the machinery for $1,000,000. The nonrecourse loan is secured only by the machinery. The principal amount of the loan is to be repaid $50,000 per year during each of the partnership's first 5 taxable years, with the remaining $550,000 of unpaid principal due on the first day of the partnership's sixth taxable year. The partnership agreement contains all of the provisions required by paragraph (e) of this section, and, as of the end of each partnership taxable year discussed herein, the items described in § 1.704-1(b)(2)(ii)(d)(4), (5), and (6) are not reasonably expected to cause or increase a deficit balance in A's or B's capital account. The partnership agreement provides that, except as otherwise required by its qualified income offset and minimum gain chargeback provisions, all partnership items will be allocated equally between A and B. Finally, the partnership agreement provides that all distributions, other than distributions in liquidation of the partnership or of a partner's interest in the partnership, will be made equally between A and B. In the partnership's first taxable year it generates rental income of $130,000, interest expense of $80,000, and a depreciation deduction of $150,000, resulting in a net taxable loss of $100,000. In addition, the partnership repays $50,000 of the nonrecourse liability, reducing that liability to $750,000. Allocations of these losses equally between A and B have substantial economic effect.

	A	B
Capital account on formation	$100,000	$100,000
Less: net loss in year 1	(50,000)	(50,000)
Capital account at end of year 1	$50,000	$ 50,000

In the partnership's second taxable year, it generates rental income of $130,000, interest expense of $75,000, and a depreciation deduction of $220,000, resulting in a net taxable loss of $165,000. In addition, the partnership repays $50,000 of the nonrecourse liability, reducing that liability to $700,000, and distributes $2,500 of cash to each partner. If the partnership were to dispose of the machinery in full satisfaction of the nonrecourse liability at the end of that year, it would realize $70,000 of gain ($700,000 amount realized less $630,000 adjusted tax basis). Therefore, the amount of partnership minimum gain at the end of that year (and the net increase in partnership minimum gain during the year) is $70,000, and the amount of partnership nonrecourse deductions for the year is $70,000. The partnership nonrecourse deductions for its second taxable year consist of $70,000 of the depreciation deductions allowable with respect to the machinery. Pursuant to the partnership agreement, all partnership items comprising the net taxable loss of $165,000, including the $70,000 nonrecourse deduction, are allocated equally between A and B.

Reg. § 1.704-2(m)

The allocation of these items, other than the nonrecourse deductions, has substantial economic effect.

	A	B
Capital account at end of year 1	$ 50,000	$ 50,000
Less: net loss in year 2 (without nonrecourse deductions)	(47,500)	(47,500)
Less: nonrecourse deductions in year 2	(35,000)	(35,000)
Less: distribution	(2,500)	(2,500)
Capital account at end of year 2	($35,000)	($35,000)

(i) *Calculation of nonrecourse deductions and partnership minimum gain.* Because all of the requirements of paragraph (e) of this section are satisfied, the allocation of nonrecourse deductions is deemed to be made in accordance with the partners' interests in the partnership. At the end of the partnership's second taxable year, A's and B's shares of partnership minimum gain are $35,000 each. Therefore, pursuant to paragraph (g)(1) of this section, A and B are treated as obligated to restore deficit balances in their capital accounts of $35,000 each. If the partnership were to dispose of the machinery in full satisfaction of the nonrecourse liability at the beginning of the partnership's third taxable year (and had no other economic activity in that year), the partnership minimum gain would be decreased from $70,000 to zero. A's and B's shares of that net decrease would be $35,000 each. Upon that disposition, the minimum gain chargeback would require that A and B each be allocated $35,000 of that gain before any other allocation is made under section 704(b) with respect to partnership items for the partnership's third taxable year.

(ii) *Nonrecourse deductions and restatement of capital accounts.* (a) *Additional facts.* C is admitted to the partnership at the beginning of the partnership's third taxable year. At the time of C's admission, the fair market value of the machinery is $900,000. C contributes $100,000 to the partnership (the partnership invests $95,000 of this in undeveloped land and holds the other $5,000 in cash) in exchange for an interest in the partnership. In connection with C's admission to the partnership, the partnership's machinery is revalued on the partnership's books to reflect its fair market value of $900,000. Pursuant to § 1.704-1(b)(2)(iv)(f), the capital accounts of A and B are adjusted upwards to $100,000 each to reflect the revaluation of the partnership's machinery. This adjustment reflects the manner in which the partnership gain of $270,000 ($900,000 fair market value minus $630,000 adjusted tax basis) would be shared if the machinery were sold for its fair market value immediately prior to C's admission to the partnership.

	A	B
Capital account before C's admission	($ 35,000)	($ 35,000)
Deemed sale adjustment	135,000	135,000
Capital account adjusted for C's admission	$100,000	$100,000

The partnership agreement is modified to provide that, except as otherwise required by its qualified income offset and minimum gain chargeback provisions, partnership income, gain, loss, and deduction, as computed for book purposes, are allocated equally among the partners, and those allocations are reflected in the partners' capital accounts. The partnership agreement also is modified to provide that depreciation and gain or loss, as computed for tax purposes, with respect to the machinery will be shared among the partners in a manner that takes account of the variation between the property's $630,000 adjusted tax basis and its $900,000 book value, in accordance with § 1.704-1(b)(2)(iv)(f) and the special rule contained in § 1.704-1(b)(4)(i).

(b) *Effect of revaluation.* Because the requirements of § 1.704-1(b)(2)(iv)(g) are satisfied, the capital accounts of the partners (as adjusted) continue to be maintained in accordance with § 1.704-1(b)(2)(iv). If the partnership were to dispose of the machinery in full satisfaction of the nonrecourse liability immediately following the revaluation of the machinery, it would realize no book gain ($700,000 amount realized less $900,000 book value). As a result of the revaluation of the machinery upward by $270,000, under part (i) of paragraph (d)(4) of this section, the partnership minimum gain is reduced from $70,000 immediately prior to the revaluation to zero; but under part (ii) of paragraph (d)(4) of this section, the partnership minimum gain is increased by the $70,000 decrease arising solely from the revaluation. Accordingly, there is no net increase or decrease solely on account of the revaluation, and so no minimum gain chargeback is triggered. All future nonrecourse deductions that occur will be the nonrecourse deductions as calculated for book purposes, and will be charged to all 3 partners in accordance with the partnership

Reg. § 1.704-2(m)

Determination of Tax Liability

agreement. For purposes of determining the partners' shares of minimum gain under paragraph (g) of this section, A's and B's shares of the decrease resulting from the revaluation are $35,000 each. However, as illustrated below, under section 704(c) principles, the tax capital accounts of A and B will eventually be charged $35,000 each, reflecting their 50 percent shares of the decrease in partnership minimum gain that resulted from the revaluation.

(iii) *Allocation of nonrecourse deductions following restatement of capital accounts.* (a) *Additional facts.* During the partnership's third taxable year, the partnership generates rental income of $130,000, interest expense of $70,000, a tax depreciation deduction of $210,000, and a book depreciation deduction (attributable to the machinery) of $300,000. As a result, the partnership has a net taxable loss of $150,000 and a net book loss of $240,000. In addition, the partnership repays $50,000 of the nonrecourse liability (after the date of C's admission), reducing the liability to $650,000, and distributes $5,000 of cash to each partner.

(b) *Allocations.* If the partnership were to dispose of the machinery in full satisfaction of the nonrecourse liability at the end of the year, $50,000 of book gain would result ($650,000 amount realized less $600,000 book basis). Therefore, the amount of partnership minimum gain at the end of the year is $50,000, which represents a net decrease in partnership minimum gain of $20,000 during the year. (This is so even though there would be an increase in partnership minimum gain in the partnership's third taxable year if minimum gain were computed with reference to the adjusted tax basis of the machinery.) Nevertheless, pursuant to paragraph (d)(4) of this section, the amount of nonrecourse deductions of the partnership for its third taxable year is $50,000 (the net increase in partnership minimum gain during the year determined by adding back the $70,000 decrease in partnership minimum gain attributable to the revaluation of the machinery to the $20,000 net decrease in partnership minimum gain during the year). The $50,000 of partnership nonrecourse deductions for the year consist of book depreciation deductions allowable with respect to the machinery of $50,000. Pursuant to the partnership agreement, all partnership items comprising the net book loss of $240,000, including the $50,000 nonrecourse deduction, are allocated equally among the partners. The allocation of these items, other than the nonrecourse deductions, has substantial economic effect. Consistent with the special partners' interests in the partnership rule contained in § 1.704-1(b)(4)(i), the partnership agreement provides that the depreciation deduction for tax purposes of $210,000 for the partnership's third taxable year is, in accordance with section 704(c) principles, shared $55,000 to A, $55,000 to B, and $100,000 to C.

	A Tax	A Book	B Tax	B Book	C Tax	C Book
Capital account at beginning of year 3	($35,000)	$100,000	($35,000)	$100,000	$100,000	$100,000
Less: nonrecourse deductions	(9,166)	(16,666)	(9,166)	(16,666)	(16,666)	(16,666)
Less: items other than nonrecourse deductions in year 3	(25,834)	(63,334)	(25,834)	(63,334)	(63,334)	(63,334)
Less: distribution	(5,000)	(5,000)	(5,000)	(5,000)	(5,000)	(5,000)
Capital account at end of year 3	($75,000)	$15,000	($75,000)	$15,000	$15,000	$15,000

Because the requirements of paragraph (e) of this section are satisfied, the allocation of the nonrecourse deduction is deemed to be made in accordance with the partners' interests in the partnership. At the end of the partnership's third taxable year, A's, B's, and C's shares of partnership minimum gain are $16,666 each.

(iv) *Subsequent allocation of nonrecourse deductions following restatement of capital accounts.* (a) *Additional facts.* The partners' capital accounts at the end of the second and third taxable years of the partnership are as stated in Example 3 (iii) of this paragraph (m). In addition, during the partnership's fourth taxable year the partnership generates rental income of $130,000,

interest expense of $65,000, a tax depreciation deduction of $210,000, and a book depreciation deduction (attributable to the machinery) of $300,000. As a result, the partnership has a net taxable loss of $145,000 and a net book loss of $235,000. In addition, the partnership repays $50,000 of the nonrecourse liability, reducing that liability to $600,000, and distributes $5,000 of cash to each partner.

(b) *Allocations.* If the partnership were to dispose of the machinery in full satisfaction of the nonrecourse liability at the end of the fourth year, $300,000 of book gain would result ($600,000 amount realized less $300,000 book value). Therefore, the amount of partnership minimum gain as

Reg. § 1.704-2(m)

of the end of the year is $300,000, which represents a net increase in partnership minimum gain during the year of $250,000. Thus, the amount of partnership nonrecourse deductions for that year equals $250,000, consisting of book depreciation deductions of $250,000. Pursuant to the partnership agreement, all partnership items comprising the net book loss of $235,000, including the $250,000 nonrecourse deduction, are allocated equally among the partners. That allocation of all items, other than the nonrecourse deductions, has substantial economic effect. Consistent with the special partners' interests in the partnership rule contained in § 1.704-1(b)(4)(i), the partnership agreement provides that the depreciation deduction for tax purposes of $210,000 in the partnership's fourth taxable year is, in accordance with section 704(c) principles, allocated $55,000 to A, $55,000 to B, and $100,000 to C.

	A Tax	A Book	B Tax	B Book	C Tax	C Book
Capital account at end of year 3	($ 75,000)	$15,000	($ 75,000)	$15,000	$15,000	$15,000
Less: nonrecourse deduction	(45,833)	(83,333)	(45,833)	(83,333)	(83,333)	(83,333)
Plus: items other than nonrecourse deduction in year 4	12,499	5,000	12,499	5,000	5,000	5,000
Less: distribution	(5,000)	(5,000)	(5,000)	(5,000)	(5,000)	(5,000)
Capital account at end of year 4	($113,334)	($68,333)	($113,333)	($68,333)	($68,333)	($68,333)

The allocation of the $250,000 nonrecourse deduction equally among A, B, and C satisfies requirement (2) of paragraph (e) of this section. Because all of the requirements of paragraph (e) of this section are satisfied, the allocation is deemed to be in accordance with the partners' interests in the partnership. At the end of the partnership's fourth taxable year, A's, B's, and C's shares of partnership minimum gain are $100,000 each.

(v) *Disposition of partnership property following restatement of capital accounts.* (a) *Additional facts.* The partners' capital accounts at the end of the fourth taxable year of the partnership are as stated above in (iv). In addition, at the beginning of the partnership's fifth taxable year it sells the machinery for $650,000 (using $600,000 of the proceeds to repay the nonrecourse liability), resulting in a taxable gain of $440,000 ($650,000 amount realized less $210,000 adjusted tax basis) and a book gain of $350,000 ($650,000 amount realized less $300,000 book basis). The partnership has no other items of income, gain, loss, or deduction for the year.

(b) *Effect of disposition.* As a result of the sale, partnership minimum gain is reduced from $300,000 to zero, reducing A's, B's, and C's shares of partnership minimum gain to zero from $100,000 each. The minimum gain chargeback requires that A, B, and C each be allocated $100,000 of that gain (an amount equal to each partner's share of the net decrease in partnership minimum gain resulting from the sale) before any allocation is made to them under section 704(b) with respect to partnership items for the partnership's fifth taxable year. Thus, the allocation of the first $300,000 of book gain $100,000 to each of the partners is deemed to be in accordance with the partners' interests in the partnership under paragraph (e) of this section. The allocation of the remaining $50,000 of book gain equally among the partners has substantial economic effect. Consistent with the special partners' interests in the partnership rule contained in § 1.704-1(b)(4)(i), the partnership agreement provides that the $440,000 taxable gain is, in accordance with section 704(c) principles, allocated $161,667 to A, $161,667 to B, and $116,666 to C.

	A Tax	A Book	B Tax	B Book	C Tax	C Book
Capital account at end of year 4	($113,334)	($ 68,333)	($113,334)	($ 68,333)	($ 68,333)	($ 68,333)
Plus: minimum gain chargeback	138,573	100,000	138,573	100,000	100,000	100,000
Plus: additional gain	23,094	16,666	23,094	16,666	16,666	16,666
Capital account before liquidation	$ 48,333	$ 48,333	$ 48,333	$ 48,333	$ 48,333	$ 48,333

Example 4. Allocations of increase in partnership minimum gain among partnership properties. For *Example* 4, unless otherwise provided, the following facts are assumed. A partnership owns 4 properties, each of which is subject to a nonrecourse liability of the partnership. During a taxable year of the partnership, the following events take place. First, the partnership generates a depreciation deduction (for both book and tax purposes) with respect to Property W of $10,000

Reg. § 1.704-2(m)

and repays $5,000 of the nonrecourse liability secured only by that property, resulting in an increase in minimum gain with respect to that liability of $5,000. Second, the partnership generates a depreciation deduction (for both book and tax purposes) with respect to Property X of $10,000 and repays none of the nonrecourse liability secured by that property, resulting in an increase in minimum gain with respect to that liability of $10,000. Third, the partnership generates a depreciation deduction (for both book and tax purposes) of $2,000 with respect to Property Y and repays $11,000 of the nonrecourse liability secured only by that property, resulting in a decrease in minimum gain with respect to that liability of $9,000 (although at the end of that year, there remains minimum gain with respect to that liability). Finally, the partnership borrows $5,000 on a nonrecourse basis, giving as the only security for that liability Property Z, a parcel of undeveloped land with an adjusted tax basis (and book value) of $2,000, resulting in a net increase in minimum gain with respect to that liability of $3,000.

(i) *Allocation of increase in partnership minimum gain.* The net increase in partnership minimum gain during that partnership taxable year is $9,000, so that the amount of nonrecourse deductions of the partnership for that taxable year is $9,000. Those nonrecourse deductions consist of $3,000 of depreciation deductions with respect to Property W and $6,000 of depreciation deductions with respect to Property X. See paragraph (c) of this section. The amount of nonrecourse deductions consisting of depreciation deductions is determined as follows. With respect to the nonrecourse liability secured by Property Z, for which there is no depreciation deduction, the amount of depreciation deductions that constitutes nonrecourse deductions is zero. Similarly, with respect to the nonrecourse liability secured by Property Y, for which there is no increase in minimum gain, the amount of depreciation deductions that constitutes nonrecourse deductions is zero. With respect to each of the nonrecourse liabilities secured by Properties W and X, which are secured by property for which there are depreciation deductions and for which there is an increase in minimum gain, the amount of depreciation deductions that constitutes nonrecourse deductions is determined by the following formula:

$$\text{net increase in partnership minimum gain} \times \frac{\text{total depreciation deductions for that taxable year on the specific property securing the nonrecourse liability to the extent gain increased on that liability}}{\text{total depreciation deductions for that taxable year on all properties securing nonrecourse liabilities to the extent of the aggregate increase in minimum gain on all those liabilities}}$$

Thus, for the liability secured by Property W, the amount is $9,000 times $5,000/$15,000, or $3,000. For the liability secured by Property X, the amount is $9,000 times $10,000/$15,000, or $6,000. (If one depreciable property secured two partnership nonrecourse liabilities, the amount of depreciation or book depreciation with respect to that property would be allocated among those liabilities in accordance with the method by which adjusted basis is allocated under paragraph (d)(2) of this section).

(ii) *Alternative allocation of increase in partnership minimum gain among partnership properties.* Assume instead that the loan secured by Property Z is $15,000 (rather than $5,000), resulting in a net increase in minimum gain with respect to that liability of $13,000. Thus, the net increase in partnership minimum gain is $19,000, and the amount of nonrecourse deductions of the partnership for that taxable year is $19,000. Those nonrecourse deductions consist of $5,000 of depreciation deductions with respect to Property W, $10,000 of depreciation deductions with respect to Property X, and a pro rata portion of the partnership's other items of deduction, loss, and section 705(a)(2)(B) expenditure for that year. The method for computing the amounts of depreciation deductions that constitute nonrecourse deductions is the same as in (i) of this *Example* 4 for the liabilities secured by Properties Y and Z. With respect to each of the nonrecourse liabilities secured by Properties W and X, the amount of depreciation deductions that constitutes nonrecourse deductions equals the total depreciation deductions with respect to the partnership property securing that particular liability to the extent of the increase in minimum gain with respect to that liability. [Reg. § 1.704-2.]

☐ [T.D. 8385, 12-26-91.]

[Reg. § 1.704-3]

§ 1.704-3. Contributed property.—(a) *In general*—(1) *General principles.* The purpose of section 704(c) is to prevent the shifting of tax consequences among partners with respect to precontribution gain or loss. Under section 704(c), a partnership must allocate income, gain, loss, and deduction with respect to property contributed by

Reg. § 1.704-3(a)(1)

a partner to the partnership so as to take into account any variation between the adjusted tax basis of the property and its fair market value at the time of contribution. Notwithstanding any other provision of this section, the allocations must be made using a reasonable method that is consistent with the purpose of section 704(c). For this purpose, an allocation method includes the application of all of the rules of this section (e.g., aggregation rules). An allocation method is not necessarily unreasonable merely because another allocation method would result in a higher aggregate tax liability. Paragraphs (b), (c), and (d) of this section describe allocation methods that are generally reasonable. Other methods may be reasonable in appropriate circumstances. Nevertheless, in the absence of specific published guidance, it is not reasonable to use an allocation method in which the basis of property contributed to the partnership is increased (or decreased) to reflect built-in gain (or loss), or a method under which the partnership creates tax allocations of income, gain, loss, or deduction independent of allocations affecting book capital accounts. See § 1.704-3(d). Paragraph (e) of this section contains special rules and exceptions.

(2) *Operating rules.* Except as provided in paragraphs (e)(2) and (e)(3) of this section, section 704(c) and this section apply on a property-by-property basis. Therefore, in determining whether there is a disparity between adjusted tax basis and fair market value, the built-in gains and built-in losses on items of contributed property cannot be aggregated. A partnership may use different methods with respect to different items of contributed property, provided that the partnership and the partners consistently apply a single reasonable method for each item of contributed property and that the overall method or combination of methods are reasonable based on the facts and circumstances and consistent with the purpose of section 704(c). It may be unreasonable to use one method for appreciated property and another method for depreciated property. Similarly, it may be unreasonable to use the traditional method for built-in gain property contributed by a partner with a high marginal tax rate while using curative allocations for built-in gain property contributed by a partner with a low marginal tax rate. A new partnership formed as the result of the termination of a partnership under section 708(b)(1)(B) is not required to use the same method as the terminated partnership with respect to section 704(c) property deemed contributed to the new partnership by the terminated partnership under § 1.7081(b)(1)(iv). The previous sentence applies to terminations of partnerships under section 708(b)(1)(B) occurring on or after May 9, 1997; however, the sentence may be applied to terminations occurring on or after May 9, 1996, provided that the partnership and its partners apply the sentence to the termination in a consistent manner.

(3) *Definitions*—(i) *Section 704(c) property.* Property contributed to a partnership is section 704(c) property if at the time of contribution its book value differs from the contributing partner's adjusted tax basis. For purposes of this section, book value is determined as contemplated by § 1.704-1(b). Therefore, book value is equal to fair market value at the time of contribution and is subsequently adjusted for cost recovery and other events that affect the basis of the property. For a partnership that maintains capital accounts in accordance with § 1.704-1(b)(2)(iv), the book value of property is initially the value used in determining the contributing partner's capital account under § 1.704-1(b)(2)(iv)(*d*), and is appropriately adjusted thereafter (e.g., for book cost recovery under § § 1.704-1(b)(2)(iv)(*g*)(*3*) and 1.704-3(d)(2) and other events that affect the basis of the property). A partnership that does not maintain capital accounts under § 1.704-1(b)(2)(iv) must comply with this section using a book capital account based on the same principles (i.e., a book capital account that reflects the fair market value of property at the time of contribution and that is subsequently adjusted for cost recovery and other events that affect the basis of the property). Property deemed contributed to a new partnership as the result of the termination of a partnership under section 708(b)(1)(B) is treated as section 704(c) property in the hands of the new partnership only to the extent that the property was section 704(c) property in the hands of the terminated partnership immediately prior to the termination. See § 1.708-1(b)(1)(iv) for an example of the application of this rule. The previous two sentences apply to terminations of partnerships under section 708(b)(1)(B) occurring on or after May 9, 1997; however, the sentences may be applied to terminations occurring on or after May 9, 1996, provided that the partnership and its partners apply the sentences to the termination in a consistent manner.

(ii) *Built-in gain and built-in loss.* The built-in gain on section 704(c) property is the excess of the property's book value over the contributing partner's adjusted tax basis upon contribution. The built-in gain is thereafter reduced by decreases in the difference between the property's book value and adjusted tax basis. The built-in loss on section 704(c) property is the excess of the contributing partner's adjusted tax basis over the property's book value upon contribution. The

Reg. § 1.704-3(a)(3)

built-in loss is thereafter reduced by decreases in the difference between the property's adjusted tax basis and book value.

(4) *Accounts payable and other accrued but unpaid items.* Accounts payable and other accrued but unpaid items contributed by a partner using the cash receipts and disbursements method of accounting are treated as section 704(c) property for purposes of applying the rules of this section.

(5) *Other provisions of the Internal Revenue Code.* Section 704(c) and this section apply to a contribution of property to the partnership only if the contribution is governed by section 721, taking into account other provisions of the Internal Revenue Code. For example, to the extent that a transfer of property to a partnership is a sale under section 707, the transfer is not a contribution of property to which section 704(c) applies.

(6) *Other applications of section 704(c) principles*—(i) *Revaluations under section 704(b).* The principles of this section apply to allocations with respect to property for which differences between book value and adjusted tax basis are created when a partnership revalues partnership property pursuant to § 1.704-1(b)(2)(iv)(*f*) (reverse section 704(c) allocations). Partnerships are not required to use the same allocation method for reverse section 704(c) allocations as for contributed property, even if at the time of revaluation the property is already subject to section 704(c) and paragraph (a) of this section. In addition, partnerships are not required to use the same allocation method for reverse section 704(c) allocations each time the partnership revalues its property. A partnership that makes allocations with respect to revalued property must use a reasonable method that is consistent with the purposes of section 704(b) and (c).

(ii) *Basis adjustments.* A partnership making adjustments under § 1.743-1(b) or 1.751-1(a)(2) must account for built-in gain or loss under section 704(c) in accordance with the principles of this section.

(7) *Transfers of a partnership interest.* If a contributing partner transfers a partnership interest, built-in gain or loss must be allocated to the transferee partner as it would have been allocated to the transferor partner. If the contributing partner transfers a portion of the partnership interest, the share of built-in gain or loss proportionate to the interest transferred must be allocated to the transferee partner.

(8) *Disposition of property in nonrecognition transaction.* If a partnership disposes of section 704(c) property in a nonrecognition transaction in which no gain or loss is recognized, the substituted basis property (within the meaning of section 7701(a)(42)) is treated as section 704(c) property with the same amount of built-in gain or loss as the section 704(c) property disposed of by the partnership. If gain or loss is recognized in such a transaction, appropriate adjustments must be made. The allocation method for the substituted basis property must be consistent with the allocation method chosen for the original property. If a partnership transfers an item of section 704(c) property together with other property to a corporation under section 351, in order to preserve that item's built-in gain or loss, the basis in the stock received in exchange for the section 704(c) property is determined as if each item of section 704(c) property had been the only property transferred to the corporation by the partnership.

(9) *Tiered partnerships.* If a partnership contributes section 704(c) property to a second partnership (the lower-tier partnership), or if a partner that has contributed section 704(c) property to a partnership contributes that partnership interest to a second partnership (the upper-tier partnership), the upper-tier partnership must allocate its distributive share of lower-tier partnership items with respect to that section 704(c) property in a manner that takes into account the contributing partner's remaining built-in gain or loss. Allocations made under this paragraph will be considered to be made in a manner that meets the requirements of § 1.704-1(b)(2)(iv)(*q*) (relating to capital account adjustments where guidance is lacking).

(10) *Anti-abuse rule.* An allocation method (or combination of methods) is not reasonable if the contribution of property (or event that results in reverse section 704(c) allocations) and the corresponding allocation of tax items with respect to the property are made with a view to shifting the tax consequences of built-in gain or loss among the partners in a manner that substantially reduces the present value of the partners' aggregate tax liability.

(11) *Contributing and noncontributing partners' recapture shares.* For special rules applicable to the allocation of depreciation recapture with respect to property contributed by a partner to a partnership, see §§ 1.1245-1(e)(2) and 1.1250-1(f).

(b) *Traditional method*—(1) *In general.* This paragraph (b) describes the traditional method of making section 704(c) allocations. In general, the traditional method requires that when the partnership has income, gain, loss, or deduction attributable to section 704(c) property, it must make appropriate allocations to the partners to avoid shifting the tax consequences of the built-in gain or loss. Under this rule, if the partnership sells section 704(c) property and recognizes gain or loss, built-in gain or loss on the property is allocated to the contributing partner. If the partnership sells a portion of, or an interest in, section 704(c) property, a proportionate part of the built-in gain or loss is allocated to the contributing partner. For section 704(c) property subject to amortization, depletion, depreciation, or other cost recovery, the allocation of deductions attributable to these items takes into account built-in gain or loss on the property. For example, tax allocations to the noncontributing partners of cost recovery deductions with respect to section 704(c) property generally must, to the extent possible, equal book allocations to those partners. However, the total income, gain, loss, or deduction allocated to the partners for a taxable year with respect to a property cannot exceed the total partnership income, gain, loss, or deduction with respect to that property for the taxable year (the ceiling rule). If a partnership has no property the allocations from which are limited by the ceiling rule, the traditional method is reasonable when used for all contributed property.

(2) *Examples.* The following examples illustrate the principles of the traditional method.

Example 1. Operation of the traditional method—(i) *Calculation of built-in gain on contribution.* A and B form partnership AB and agree that each will be allocated a 50 percent share of all partnership items and that AB will make allocations under section 704(c) using the traditional method under paragraph (b) of this section. A contributes depreciable property with an adjusted tax basis of $4,000 and a book value of $10,000, and B contributes $10,000 cash. Under paragraph (a)(3) of this section, A has built-in gain of $6,000, the excess of the partnership's book value for the property ($10,000) over A's adjusted tax basis in the property at the time of contribution ($4,000).

(ii) *Allocation of tax depreciation.* The property is depreciated using the straight-line method over a 10-year recovery period. Because the property depreciates at an annual rate of 10 percent, B would have been entitled to a depreciation deduction of $500 per year for both book and tax purposes if the adjusted tax basis of the property equalled its fair market value at the time of contribution. Although each partner is allocated $500 of book depreciation per year, the partnership is allowed a tax depreciation deduction of only $400 per year (10 percent of $4,000). The partnership can allocate only $400 of tax depreciation under the ceiling rule of paragraph (b)(1) of this section, and it must be allocated entirely to B.

In AB's first year, the proceeds generated by the equipment exactly equal AB's operating expense. At the end of that year, the book value of the property is $9,000 ($10,000 less the $1,000 book depreciation deduction), and the adjusted tax basis is $3,600 ($4,000 less the $400 tax depreciation deduction). A's built-in gain with respect to the property decreases to $5,400 ($9,000 book value less $3,600 adjusted tax basis). Also, at the end of AB's first year, A has a $9,500 book capital account and a $4,000 tax basis in A's partnership interest. B has a $9,500 book capital account and a $9600 adjusted tax basis in B's partnership interest.

(iii) *Sale of the property.* If AB sells the property at the beginning of AB's second year for $9,000, AB realizes tax gain of $5,400 ($9,000, the amount realized, less the adjusted tax basis of $3,600). Under paragraph (b)(1) of this section, the entire $5,400 gain must be allocated to A because the property A contributed has that much built-in gain remaining. If AB sells the property at the beginning of AB's second year for $10,000, AB realizes tax gain of $6,400 ($10,000, the amount realized, less the adjusted tax basis of $3,600). Under paragraph (b)(1) of this section, only $5,400 of gain must be allocated to A to account for A's built-in gain. The remaining $1,000 of gain is allocated equally between A and B in accordance with the partnership agreement. If AB sells the property for less than the $9,000 book value, AB realizes tax gain of less than $5,400, and the entire gain must be allocated to A.

(iv) *Termination and liquidation of partnership.* If AB sells the property at the beginning of AB's second year for $9,000, and AB engages in no other transactions that year, A will recognize a gain of $5,400, and B will recognize no income or loss. A's adjusted tax basis for A's interest in AB will then be $9,400 ($4,000, A's original tax basis, increased by the gain of $5,400). B's adjusted tax basis for B's interest in AB will be $9,600 ($10,000, B's original tax basis, less the $400 depreciation deduction in he first partnership year). If the partnership then terminates and distributes its assets ($19,000 in cash) to A and B in proportion to their capital account balances, A will recognize a capital gain of $100 ($9,500, the amount distributed to A, less $9,400, the adjusted tax basis of A's interest). B will recognize a capital loss of $100 (the excess of B's adjusted tax basis, $9,600, over the amount received, $9,500).

Example 2. Unreasonable use of the traditional method—(i) *Facts.* C and D form partnership CD and agree that each will be allocated a 50 percent share of all partnership items and that

Reg. § 1.704-3(b)(2)

CD will make allocations under section 704(c) using the traditional method under paragraph (b) of this section. C contributes equipment with an adjusted tax basis of $1,000 and a book value of $10,000, with a view to taking advantage of the fact that the equipment has only one year remaining on its cost recovery schedule although its remaining economic life is significantly longer. At the time of contribution, C has a built-in gain of $9,000 and the equipment is section 704(c) property. D contributes $10,000 of cash, which CD uses to buy securities. D has substantial net operating loss carryforwards that D anticipates will otherwise expire unused. Under § 1.704-1(b)(2)(iv)(*g*)(*3*), the partnership must allocate the $10,000 of book depreciation to the partners in the first year of the partnership. Thus, there is $10,000 of book depreciation and $1,000 of tax depreciation in the partnership's first year. CD sells the equipment during the second year for $10,000 and recognizes a $10,000 gain ($10,000, the amount realized, less the adjusted tax basis of $0).

(ii) *Unreasonable use of method*—(A) At the beginning of the second year, both the book value and adjusted tax basis of the equipment are $0. Therefore, there is no remaining built-in gain. The $10,000 gain on the sale of the equipment in the second year is allocated $5,000 each to C and D. The interaction of the partnership's one-year write-off of the entire book value of the equipment and the use of the traditional method results in a shift of $4,000 of the precontribution gain in the equipment from C to D (D's $5,000 share of CD's $10,000 gain, less the $1,000 tax depreciation deduction previously allocated to D).

(B) The traditional method is not reasonable under paragraph (a)(10) of this section because the contribution of property is made, and the traditional method is used, with a view to shifting a significant amount of taxable income to a partner with a low marginal tax rate and away from a partner with a high marginal tax rate.

(C) Under these facts, if the partnership agreement in effect for the year of contribution had provided that tax gain from the sale of the property (if any) would always be allocated first to C to offset the effect of the ceiling rule limitation, the allocation method would not violate the anti-abuse rule of paragraph (a)(10) of this section. See paragraph (c)(3) of this section. Under other facts, (for example, if the partnership holds multiple section 704(c) properties and either uses multiple allocation methods or uses a single allocation method where one or more of the properties are subject to the ceiling rule) the allocation to C may not be reasonable.

(c) *Traditional method with curative allocations*—(1) *In general.* To correct distortions created by the ceiling rule, a partnership using the traditional method under paragraph (b) of this section may make reasonable curative allocations to reduce or eliminate disparities between book and tax items of noncontributing partners. A curative allocation is an allocation of income, gain, loss, or deduction for tax purposes that differs from the partnership's allocation of the corresponding book item. For example, if a noncontributing partner is allocated less tax depreciation than book depreciation with respect to an item of section 704(c) property, the partnership may make a curative allocation to that partner of tax depreciation from another item of partnership property to make up the difference, notwithstanding that the corresponding book depreciation is allocated to the contributing partner. A partnership may limit its curative allocations to allocations of one or more particular tax items (e.g., only depreciation from a specific property or properties) even if the allocation of those available items does not offset fully the effect of the ceiling rule.

(2) *Consistency.* A partnership must be consistent in its application of curative allocations with respect to each item of section 704(c) property from year to year.

(3) *Reasonable curative allocations*—(i) *Amount.* A curative allocation is not reasonable to the extent it exceeds the amount necessary to offset the effect of the ceiling rule for the current taxable year or, in the case of a curative allocation upon disposition of the property, for prior taxable years.

(ii) *Timing.* The period of time over which the curative allocations are made is a factor in determining whether the allocations are reasonable. Notwithstanding paragraph (c)(3)(i) of this section, a partnership may make curative allocations in a taxable year to offset the effect of the ceiling rule for a prior taxable year if those allocations are made over a reasonable period of time, such as over the property's economic life, and are provided for under the partnership agreement in effect for the year of contribution. See paragraph (c)(4) *Example 3* (ii)(C) of this section.

(iii) *Type*—(A) *In general.* To be reasonable, a curative allocation of income, gain, loss, or deduction must be expected to have substantially the same effect on each partner's tax liability as the tax item limited by the ceiling rule. The expectation must exist at the time the section 704(c) property is obligated to be (or is) contributed to the partnership and the allocation with respect to that property becomes part of the part-

Reg. § 1.704-3(c)(1)

nership agreement. However, the expectation is tested at the time the allocation with respect to that property is actually made if the partnership agreement is not sufficiently specific as to the precise manner in which allocations are to be made with respect to that property. Under this paragraph (c), if the item limited by the ceiling rule is loss from the sale of property, a curative allocation of gain must be expected to have substantially the same effect as would an allocation to that partner of gain with respect to the sale of the property. If the item limited by the ceiling rule is depreciation or other cost recovery, a curative allocation of income to the contributing partner must be expected to have substantially the same effect as would an allocation to that partner of partnership income with respect to the contributed property. For example, if depreciation deductions with respect to leased equipment contributed by a tax-exempt partner are limited by the ceiling rule, a curative allocation of dividend or interest income to that partner generally is not reasonable, although a curative allocation of depreciation deductions from other leased equipment to the noncontributing partner is reasonable. Similarly, under this rule, if depreciation deductions apportioned to foreign source income in a particular statutory grouping under section 904(d) are limited by the ceiling rule, a curative allocation of income from another statutory grouping to the contributing partner generally is not reasonable, although a curative allocation of income from the same statutory grouping and of the same character is reasonable.

(B) *Exception for allocation from disposition of contributed property.* If cost recovery has been limited by the ceiling rule, the general limitation on character does not apply to income from the disposition of contributed property subject to the ceiling rule, but only if properly provided for in the partnership agreement in effect for the year of contribution or revaluation. For example,

if allocations of depreciation deductions to a noncontributing partner have been limited by the ceiling rule, a curative allocation to the contributing partner of gain from the sale of that property, if properly provided for in the partnership agreement, is reasonable for purposes of paragraph (c)(3)(iii)(A) of this section even if not of the same character.

(4) *Examples.* The following examples illustrate the principles of this paragraph (c).

Example 1. Reasonable and unreasonable curative allocations—(i) *Facts.* E and F form partnership EF and agree that each will be allocated a 50 percent share of all partnership items and that EF will make allocations under section 704(c) using the traditional method with curative allocations under paragraph (c) of this section. E contributes equipment with an adjusted tax basis of $4,000 and a book value of $10,000. The equipment has 10 years remaining on its cost recovery schedule and is depreciable using the straight-line method. At the time of contribution, E has a built-in gain of $6,000, and therefore, the equipment is section 704(c) property. F contributes $10,000 of cash, which EF uses to buy inventory for resale. In EF's first year, the revenue generated by the equipment equals EF's operating expenses. The equipment generates $1,000 of book depreciation and $400 of tax depreciation for each of 10 years. At the end of the first year EF sells all the inventory for $10,700, recognizing $700 of income. The partners anticipate that the inventory income will have substantially the same effect on their tax liabilities as income from E's contributed equipment. Under the traditional method of paragraph (b) of this section, E and F would each be allocated $350 of income from the sale of inventory for book and tax purposes and $500 of depreciation for book purposes. The $400 of tax depreciation would all be allocated to F. Thus, at the end of the first year, E and F's book and tax capital accounts would be as follows:

	E		F		
	Book	Tax	Book	Tax	
	$10,000	$4,000	$10,000	$10,000	Initial contribution
	<500>	<0>	<500>	<400>	Depreciation
	350	350	350	350	Sales income
	$ 9,850	$4,350	$ 9,850	$ 9,950	

(ii) *Reasonable curative allocation.* Because the ceiling rule would cause a disparity of $100 between F's book and tax capital accounts, EF may properly allocate to E under paragraph (c) of this section an additional $100 of income from the sale of inventory for tax purposes. This allocation results in capital accounts at the end of EF's first year as follows:

Reg. § 1.704-3(c)(4)

	E		F		
Book	Tax	Book	Tax		
$10,000	$4,000	$10,000	$10,000	Initial contribution
<500>	<0>	<500>	<400>	Depreciation
350	450	350	250	Sales income
$ 9,850	$4,450	$ 9,850	$ 9,850	

(iii) *Unreasonable curative allocation.* (A) The facts are the same as in paragraphs (i) and (ii) of this *Example 1*, except that E and F choose to allocate all the income from the sale of the inventory to E for tax purposes, although they share it equally for book purposes. This allocation results in capital accounts at the end of EF's first year as follows:

	E		F		
Book	Tax	Book	Tax		
$10,000	$4,000	$10,000	$10,000	Initial contribution
<500>	<0>	<500>	<400>	Depreciation
350	700	350	0	Sales income
$ 9,850	$4,700	$ 9,850	$ 9,600	

(B) This curative allocation is not reasonable under paragraph (c)(3)(i) of this section because the allocation exceeds the amount necessary to offset the disparity caused by the ceiling rule.

Example 2. Curative allocations limited to depreciation—(i) *Facts.* G and H form partnership GH and agree that each will be allocated a 50 percent share of all partnership items and that GH will make allocations under section 704(c) using the traditional method with curative allocations under paragraph (c) of this section, but only to the extent that the partnership has sufficient tax depreciation deductions. G contributes property G1, with an adjusted tax basis of $3,000 and a fair market value of $10,000, and H contributes property H1, with an adjusted tax basis of $6,000 and a fair market value of $10,000. Both properties have 5 years remaining on their cost recovery schedules and are depreciable using the straight-line method. At the time of contribution, G1 has a built-in gain of $7,000 and H1 has a built-in gain of $4,000, and therefore, both properties are section 704(c) property. G1 generates $600 of tax depreciation and $2,000 of book depreciation for each of five years. H1 generates $1,200 of tax depreciation and $2,000 of book depreciation for each of 5 years. In addition, the properties each generate $500 of operating income annually. G and H are each allocated $1,000 of book depreciation for each property. Under the traditional method of paragraph (b) of this section, G would be allocated $0 of tax depreciation for G1 and $1,000 for H1, and H would be allocated $600 of tax depreciation for G1 and $200 for H1. Thus, at the end of the first year, G and H's book and tax capital accounts would be as follows:

	G		H		
Book	Tax	Book	Tax		
$10,000	$ 3,000	$10,000	$6,000	Initial contribution
<1,000>	<0>	<1,000>	<600>	G1 depreciation
<1,000>	<1,000>	<1,000>	<200>	H1 depreciation
500	500	500	500	Operating income
$ 8,500	$ 2,500	$ 8,500	$5,700	

(ii) *Curative allocations.* Under the traditional method, G is allocated more depreciation deductions than H, even though H contributed property with a smaller disparity reflected on GH's book and tax capital accounts. GH makes curative allocations to H of an additional $400 of tax depreciation each year, which reduces the disparities between G and H's book and tax capital accounts ratably each year. These allocations are reasonable provided the allocations meet the other requirements of this section. As a result of their agreement, at the end of the first year, G and H's capital accounts are as follows:

	G		H		
Book	Tax	Book	Tax		
$10,000	$3,000	$10,000	$6,000	Initial contribution
<1,000>	<0>	<1,000>	<600>	G1 depreciation
<1,000>	<600>	<1,000>	<600>	H1 depreciation
500	500	500	500	Operating income
$ 8,500	$2,900	$ 8,500	$5,300	

Reg. § 1.704-3(c)(4)

Determination of Tax Liability 43,571
See p. 20,601 for regulations not amended to reflect law changes

Example 3. Unreasonable use of curative allocations—(i) *Facts.* J and K form partnership JK and agree that each will receive a 50 percent share of all partnership items and that JK will make allocations under section 704(c) using the traditional method with curative allocations under paragraph (c) of this section. J contributes equipment with an adjusted tax basis of $1,000 and a book value of $10,000, with a view to taking advantage of the fact that the equipment has only one year remaining on its cost recovery schedule although it has an estimated remaining economic life of 10 years. J has substantial net operating loss carryforwards that J anticipates will otherwise expire unused. At the time of contribution, J has a built-in gain of $9,000, and therefore, the equipment is section 704(c) property. K contributes $10,000 of cash, which JK uses to buy inventory for resale. In JK's first year, the revenues generated by the equipment exactly equal JK's operating expenses. Under § 1.704-1(b)(2)(iv)(g)(3), the partnership must allocate the $10,000 of book depreciation to the partners in the first year of the partnership. Thus, there is $10,000 of book depreciation and $1,000 of tax depreciation in the partnership's first year. In addition, at the end of the first year JK sells all of the inventory for $18,000, recognizing $8,000 of income. The partners anticipate that the inventory income will have substantially the same effect on their tax liabilities as income from J's contributed equipment. Under the traditional method of paragraph (b) of this section, J and K's book and tax capital accounts at the end of the first year would be as follows:

	J			K		
	Book	Tax	Book	Tax		
	$10,000	$1,000	$10,000	$10,000		Initial contribution
	<5,000>	<0>	<5,000>	<1,000>		Depreciation
	4,000	4,000	4,000	4,000		Sales income
	$ 9,000	$5,000	$ 9,000	$13,000		

(ii) *Unreasonable use of method.* (A) The use of curative allocations under these facts to offset immediately the full effect of the ceiling rule would result in the following book and tax capital accounts at the end of JK's first year:

	J			K		
	Book	Tax	Book	Tax		
	$10,000	$1,000	$10,000	$10,000		Initial contribution
	<5,000>	<0>	<5,000>	<1,000>		Depreciation
	4,000	8,000	4,000	0		Sales income
	$ 9,000	$9,000	$ 9,000	$ 9,000		

(B) This curative allocation is not reasonable under paragraph (a)(10) of this section because the contribution of property is made and the curative allocation method is used with a view to shifting a significant amount of partnership taxable income to a partner with a low marginal tax rate and away from a partner with a high marginal tax rate, within a period of time significantly shorter than the economic life of the property.

(C) The property has only one year remaining on its cost recovery schedule even though its economic life is considerably longer. Under these facts, if the partnership agreement had provided for curative allocations over a reasonable period of time, such as over the property's economic life, rather than over its remaining cost recovery period, the allocations would have been reasonable. See paragraph (c)(3)(ii) of this section. Thus, in this example, JK would make a curative allocation of $400 of sales income to J in the partnership's first year (10 percent of $4,000). J and K's book and tax capital accounts at the end of the first year would be as follows:

	J			K		
	Book	Tax	Book	Tax		
	$10,000	$1,000	$10,000	$10,000		Initial contribution
	<5,000>	<0>	<5,000>	<1,000>		Depreciation
	4,000	4,400	4,000	3,600		Sales income
	$ 9,000	$5,400	$ 9,000	$12,600		

(d) *Remedial allocation method*—(1) *In general.* A partnership may adopt the remedial allocation method described in this paragraph to eliminate distortions caused by the ceiling rule. A partnership adopting the remedial allocation method eliminates those distortions by creating remedial items and allocating those items to its partners. Under the remedial allocation method, the partnership first determines the amount of book items under paragraph (d)(2) of this section

Reg. § 1.704-3(d)(1)

and the partners' distributive shares of these items under section 704(b). The partnership then allocates the corresponding tax items recognized by the partnership, if any, using the traditional method described in paragraph (b)(1) of this section. If the ceiling rule (as defined in paragraph (b)(1) of this section) causes the book allocation of an item to a noncontributing partner to differ from the tax allocation of the same item to the noncontributing partner, the partnership creates a remedial item of income, gain, loss, or deduction equal to the full amount of the difference and allocates it to the noncontributing partner. The partnership simultaneously creates an offsetting remedial item in an identical amount and allocates it to the contributing partner.

(2) *Determining the amount of book items.* Under the remedial allocation method, a partnership determines the amount of book items attributable to contributed property in the following manner rather than under the rules of § 1.704-1(b)(2)(iv)(g)(3). The portion of the partnership's book basis in the property equal to the adjusted tax basis in the property at the time of contribution is recovered in the same manner as the adjusted tax basis in the property is recovered (generally, over the property's remaining recovery period under section 168(i)(7) or other applicable Internal Revenue Code section). The remainder of the partnership's book basis in the property (the amount by which book basis exceeds adjusted tax basis) is recovered using any recovery period and depreciation (or other cost recovery) method (including first-year conventions) available to the partnership for newly purchased property (of the same type as the contributed property) that is placed in service at the time of contribution.

(3) *Type.* Remedial allocations of income, gain, loss, or deduction to the noncontributing partner have the same tax attributes as the tax item limited by the ceiling rule. The tax attributes of offsetting remedial allocations of income, gain, loss, or deduction to the contributing partner are determined by reference to the item limited by the ceiling rule. Thus, for example, if the ceiling rule limited item is loss from the sale of contributed property, the offsetting remedial allocation to the contributing partner must be gain from the sale of that property. Conversely, if the ceiling rule limited item is gain from the sale of contributed property, the offsetting remedial allocation to the contributing partner must be loss from the sale of that property. If the ceiling rule limited item is depreciation or other cost recovery from the contributed property, the offsetting remedial allocation to the contributing partner must be income of the type produced (directly or indirectly) by that property. Any partner level tax attributes are determined at the partner level. For example, if the ceiling rule limited item is depreciation from property used in a rental activity, the remedial allocation to the noncontributing partner is depreciation from property used in a rental activity and the offsetting remedial allocation to the contributing partner is ordinary income from that rental activity. Each partner then applies section 469 to the allocations as appropriate.

(4) *Effect of remedial items*—(i) *Effect on partnership.* Remedial items do not affect the partnership's computation of its taxable income under section 703 and do not affect the partnership's adjusted tax basis in partnership property.

(ii) *Effect on partners.* Remedial items are notional tax items created by the partnership solely for tax purposes and do not affect the partners' book capital accounts. Remedial items have the same effect as actual tax items on a partner's tax liability and on the partner's adjusted tax basis in the partnership interest.

(5) *Limitations on use of methods involving remedial allocations*—(i) *Limitation on taxpayers.* In the absence of published guidance, the remedial allocation method described in this paragraph (d) is the only reasonable section 704(c) method permitting the creation of notional tax items.

(ii) *Limitation on Internal Revenue Service.* In exercising its authority under paragraph (a)(10) of this section to make adjustments if a partnership's allocation method is not reasonable, the Internal Revenue Service will not require a partnership to use the remedial allocation method described in this paragraph (d) or any other method involving the creation of notional tax items.

(6) *Adjustments to application of method.* The Commissioner may, by published guidance, prescribe adjustments to the remedial allocation method under this paragraph (d) as necessary or appropriate. This guidance may, for example, prescribe adjustments to the remedial allocation method to prevent the duplication or omission of items of income or deduction or to reflect more clearly the partners' income or the income of a transferee of a partner.

(7) *Examples.* The following examples illustrate the principles of this paragraph (d).

Example 1. Remedial allocation method—(i) *Facts.* On January 1, L and M form partnership LM and agree that each will be allocated a 50 percent share of all partnership items. The partnership agreement provides that LM will make allocations under section 704(c) using the remedial allocation method under this paragraph (d) and that the straight-line method will be used to

Reg. § 1.704-3(d)(2)

recover excess book basis. L contributes depreciable property with an adjusted tax basis of $4,000 and a fair market value of $10,000. The property is depreciated using the straight-line method with a 10-year recovery period and has 4 years remaining on its recovery period. M contributes $10,000, which the partnership uses to purchase land. Except for the depreciation deductions, LM's expenses equal its income in each year of the 10 years commencing with the year the partnership is formed.

(ii) *Years 1 through 4.* Under the remedial allocation method of this paragraph (d), LM has book depreciation for each of its first 4 years of $1,600 [$1,000 ($4,000 adjusted tax basis divided by the 4-year remaining recovery period) plus $600 ($6,000 excess of book value over tax basis, divided by the *new* 10-year recovery period)]. (For the purpose of simplifying the example, the partnership's book depreciation is determined without regard to any first-year depreciation conventions.) Under the partnership agreement, L and M are each allocated 50 percent ($800) of the book depreciation. M is allocated $800 of tax depreciation and L is allocated the remaining $200 of tax depreciation ($1,000 − $800). See paragraph (d)(1) of this section. No remedial allocations are made because the ceiling rule does not result in a book allocation of depreciation to M different from the tax allocation. The allocations result in capital accounts at the end of LM's first 4 years as follows:

	L		M	
Book	Tax	Book	Tax	
$10,000	$4,000	$10,000	$10,000	Initial contribution
<3,200>	<800>	<3,200>	<3,200>	Depreciation
$ 6,800	$3,200	$ 6,800	$ 6,800	

(iii) *Subsequent years.* (A) For each of years 5 through 10, LM has $600 of book depreciation ($6,000 excess of initial book value over adjusted tax basis divided by the 10-year recovery period that commenced in year 1), but no tax depreciation. Under the partnership agreement, the $600 of book depreciation is allocated equally to L and M. Because of the application of the ceiling rule in year 5, M would be allocated $300 of book depreciation, but no tax depreciation. Thus, at the end of LM's fifth year L's and M's book and tax capital accounts would be as follows:

	L		M	
Book	Tax	Book	Tax	
$ 6,800	$3,200	$ 6,800	$ 6,800	End of year 4
<300>		<300>		Depreciation
$ 6,500	$3,200	$ 6,500	$ 6,800	

(B) Because the ceiling rule would cause an annual disparity of $300 between M's allocations of book and tax depreciation, LM must make remedial allocations of $300 of tax depreciation deductions to M under the remedial allocation method for each of years 5 through 10. LM must also make an offsetting remedial allocation to L of $300 of taxable income, which must be of the same type as income produced by the property. At the end of year 5, LM's capital accounts are as follows:

	L		M	
Book	Tax	Book	Tax	
$ 6,800	$3,200	$ 6,800	$ 6,800	End of year 4
<300>		<300>		Depreciation
	300		<300>	Remedial allocations
$ 6,500	$3,500	$ 6,500	$ 6,500	

(C) At the end of year 10, LM's capital accounts are as follows:

	L		M	
Book	Tax	Book	Tax	
$ 6,500	$3,500	$ 6,500	$ 6,500	End of year 5
<1,500>		<1,500>		Depreciation
	1,500		<1,500>	Remedial allocations
$ 5,000	$5,000	$ 5,000	$ 5,000	

Example 2. Remedial allocations on sale—(i) *Facts.* N and P form partnership NP and agree that each will be allocated a 50 percent share of all partnership items. The partnership agreement provides that NP will make allocations under section 704(c) using the remedial allocation method under this paragraph (d). N contributes Blackacre (land) with an adjusted tax basis of $4,000 and a fair market value of $10,000. Because N has a built-in gain of $6,000, Blackacre is section 704(c) property. P contributes Whiteacre (land) with an adjusted tax basis and fair market

Reg. § 1.704-3(d)(7)

value of $10,000. At the end of NP's first year, NP sells Blackacre to Q for $9,000 and recognizes a capital gain of $5,000 ($9,000 amount realized less $4,000 adjusted tax basis) and a book loss of $1,000 ($9,000 amount realized less $10,000 book basis). NP has no other items of income, gain, loss, or deduction. If the ceiling rule were applied, N would be allocated the entire $5,000 of tax gain and N and P would each be allocated $500 of book loss. Thus, at the end of NP's first year N's and P's book and tax capital accounts would be as follows:

N		P		
Book	Tax	Book	Tax	
$10,000	$4,000	$10,000	$10,000	Initial contribution
<500>	5,000	<500>		Sale of Blackacre
$ 9,500	$9,000	$ 9,500	$10,000	

(ii) *Remedial allocation.* Because the ceiling rule would cause a disparity of $500 between P's allocation of book and tax loss, NP must make a remedial allocation of $500 of capital loss to P and an offsetting remedial allocation to N of an additional $500 of capital gain. These allocations result in capital accounts at the end of NP's first year as follows:

N		P		
Book	Tax	Book	Tax	
$10,000	$4,000	$10,000	$10,000	Initial contribution
<500>	5,000	<500>		Sale of Blackacre
	500		<500>	Remedial allocations
$ 9,500	$9,500	$ 9,500	$ 9,500	

Example 3. Remedial allocation where built-in gain property sold for book and tax loss—(i) *Facts.* The facts are the same as in Example 2, except that at the end of NP's first year, NP sells Blackacre to Q for $3,000 and recognizes a capital loss of $1,000 ($3,000 amount realized less $4,000 adjusted tax basis) and a book loss of $7,000 ($3,000 amount realized less $10,000 book basis). If the ceiling rule were applied, P would be allocated the entire $1,000 of tax loss and N and P would each be allocated $3,500 of book loss. Thus, at the end of NP's first year, N's and P's book and tax capital accounts would be as follows:

N		P		
Book	Tax	Book	Tax	
$10,000	$4,000	$10,000	$10,000	Initial contribution
<3,500>	0	<3,500>	<1,000>	Sale of Blackacre
$ 6,500	$4,000	$ 6,500	$ 9,000	

(ii) *Remedial allocation.* Because the ceiling rule would cause a disparity of $2,500 between P's allocation of book and tax loss on the sale of Blackacre, NP must make a remedial allocation of $2,500 of capital loss to P and an offsetting remedial allocation to N of $2,500 of capital gain. These allocations result in capital accounts at the end of NP's first year as follows:

N		P		
Book	Tax	Book	Tax	
$10,000	$4,000	$10,000	$10,000	Initial contribution
<3,500>	0	<3,500>	<1,000>	Sale of Blackacre
	<2,500>		<2,500>	Remedial allocations
$ 6,500	$6,500	$ 6,500	$ 6,500	

(e) *Exceptions and special rules*—(1) *Small disparities*—(i) *General rule.* If a partner contributes one or more items of property to a partnership within a single taxable year of the partnership, and the disparity between the book value of the property and the contributing partner's adjusted tax basis in the property is a small disparity, the partnership may—

(A) Use a reasonable section 704(c) method;

(B) Disregard the application of section 704(c) to the property; or

(C) Defer the application of section 704(c) to the property until the disposition of the property.

(ii) *Definition of small disparity.* A disparity between book value and adjusted tax basis is a small disparity if the book value of all properties contributed by one partner during the partnership taxable year does not differ from the adjusted tax basis by more than 15 percent of the adjusted tax

Reg. § 1.704-3(e)(1)

basis, and the total gross disparity does not exceed $20,000.

(2) *Aggregation.* Each of the following types of property may be aggregated for purposes of making allocations under section 704(c) and this section if contributed by one partner during the partnership taxable year.

(i) *Depreciable property.* All property, other than real property, that is included in the same general asset account of the contributing partner and the partnership under section 168.

(ii) *Zero-basis property.* All property with a basis equal to zero, other than real property.

(iii) *Inventory.* For partnerships that do not use a specific identification method of accounting, each item of inventory, other than qualified financial assets (as defined in paragraph (e)(3)(ii) of this section).

(3) *Special aggregation rule for securities partnerships*—(i) *General rule.* For purposes of making reverse section 704(c) allocations, a securities partnership may aggregate gains and losses from qualified financial assets using any reasonable approach that is consistent with the purpose of section 704(c). Notwithstanding paragraphs (a)(2) and (a)(6)(i) of this section, once a partnership adopts an aggregate approach, that partnership must apply the same aggregate approach to all of its qualified financial assets for all taxable years in which the partnership qualifies as a securities partnership. Paragraphs (e)(3)(iv) and (e)(3)(v) of this section describe approaches for aggregating reverse section 704(c) gains and losses that are generally reasonable. Other approaches may be reasonable in appropriate circumstances. See, however, paragraph (a)(10) of this section, which describes the circumstances under which section 704(c) methods, including the aggregate approaches described in this paragraph (e)(3), are not reasonable. A partnership using an aggregate approach must separately account for any built-in gain or loss from contributed property.

(ii) *Qualified financial assets*—(A) *In general.* A qualified financial asset is any personal property (including stock) that is actively traded. Actively traded means actively traded as defined in § 1.1092(d)-1 (defining actively traded property for purposes of the straddle rules).

(B) *Management companies.* For a management company, qualified financial assets also include the following, even if not actively traded: shares of stock in a corporation; notes, bonds, debentures, or other evidences of indebtedness; interest rate, currency, or equity notional principal contracts; evidences of an interest in, or derivative financial instruments in, any security, currency, or commodity, including any option, forward or futures contract, or short position; or any similar financial instrument.

(C) *Partnership interests.* An interest in a partnership is not a qualified financial asset for purposes of this paragraph (e)(3)(ii). However, for purposes of this paragraph (e)(3), a partnership (upper-tier partnership) that holds an interest in a securities partnership (lower-tier partnership) must take into account the lower-tier partnership's assets and qualified financial assets as follows:

(*1*) In determining whether the upper-tier partnership qualifies as an investment partnership, the upper-tier partnership must treat its proportionate share of the lower-tier securities partnership's assets as assets of the upper-tier partnership; and

(*2*) If the upper-tier partnership adopts an aggregate approach under this paragraph (e)(3), the upper-tier partnership must aggregate the gains and losses from its directly held qualified financial assets with its distributive share of the gains and losses from the qualified financial assets of the lower-tier securities partnership.

(iii) *Securities partnership*—(A) *In general.* A partnership is a securities partnership if the partnership is either a management company or an investment partnership, and the partnership makes all of its book allocations in proportion to the partners' relative book capital accounts (except for reasonable special allocations to a partner that provides management services or investment advisory services to the partnership).

(B) *Definitions*—(*1*) *Management company.* A partnership is a management company if it is registered with the Securities and Exchange Commission as a management company under the Investment Company Act of 1940, as amended (15 U.S.C. 80a).

(*2*) *Investment partnership.* A partnership is an investment partnership if:

(*i*) On the date of each capital account restatement, the partnership holds qualified financial assets that constitute at least 90 percent of the fair market value of the partnership's non-cash assets; and

(*ii*) The partnership reasonably expects, as of the end of the first taxable year in which the partnership adopts an aggregate approach under this paragraph (e)(3) to make revaluations at least annually.

(iv) *Partial netting approach.* This paragraph (e)(3)(iv) describes the partial netting approach of making reverse section 704(c) allocations. See Example 1 of paragraph (e)(3)(ix) of this section for an illustration of the partial netting approach. To use the partial netting approach, the partnership must establish appropriate accounts for each partner for the purpose of taking into account each partner's share of the book gains and losses and determining each partner's share of the tax gains and losses. Under the partial netting approach, on the date of each capital account restatement, the partnership:

(A) Nets its book gains and book losses from qualified financial assets since the last capital account restatement and allocates the net amount to its partners;

(B) Separately aggregates all tax gains and all tax losses from qualified financial assets since the last capital account restatement; and

(C) Separately allocates the aggregate tax gain and aggregate tax loss to the partners in a manner that reduces the disparity between the book capital account balances and the tax capital account balances (book-tax disparities) of the individual partners.

(v) *Full netting approach.* This paragraph (e)(3)(v) describes the full netting approach of making reverse section 704(c) allocations on an aggregate basis. See Example 2 of paragraph (e)(3)(ix) of this section for an illustration of the full netting approach. To use the full netting approach, the partnership must establish appropriate accounts for each partner for the purpose of taking into account each partner's share of the book gains and losses and determining each partner's share of the tax gains and losses. Under the full netting approach, on the date of each capital account restatement, the partnership:

(A) Nets its book gains and book losses from qualified financial assets since the last capital account restatement and allocates the net amount to its partners;

(B) Nets tax gains and tax losses from qualified financial assets since the last capital account restatement; and

(C) Allocates the net tax gain (or net tax loss) to the partners in a manner that reduces the book-tax disparities of the individual partners.

(vi) *Type of tax gain or loss.* The character and other tax attributes of gain or loss allocated to the partners under this paragraph (e)(3) must:

(A) Preserve the tax attributes of each item of gain or loss realized by the partnership;

(B) Be determined under an approach that is consistently applied; and

(C) Not be determined with a view to reducing substantially the present value of the partners' aggregate tax liability.

(vii) *Disqualified securities partnerships.* A securities partnership that adopts an aggregate approach under this paragraph (e)(3) and subsequently fails to qualify as a securities partnership must make reverse section 704(c) allocations on an asset-by-asset basis after the date of disqualification. The partnership, however, is not required to disaggregate the book gain or book loss from qualified asset revaluations before the date of disqualification when making reverse section 704(c) allocations on or after the date of disqualification.

(viii) *Transitional rule for qualified financial assets revalued after effective date.* A securities partnership revaluing its qualified financial assets pursuant to § 1.704-1(b)(2)(iv)(f) on or after the effective date of this section may use any reasonable approach to coordinate with revaluations that occurred prior to the effective date of this section.

(ix) *Examples.* The following examples illustrate the principles of this paragraph (e)(3).

Example 1. Operation of the partial netting approach—(i) Facts. Two regulated investment companies, X and Y, each contribute $150,000 in cash to form PRS, a partnership that registers as a management company. The partnership agreement provides that book items will be allocated in accordance with the partners' relative book capital accounts, that book capital accounts will be adjusted to reflect daily revaluations of property pursuant to § 1.704-1(b)(2)(iv)(f)(5)(iii), and that reverse section 704(c) allocations will be made using the partial netting approach described in paragraph (e)(3)(iv) of this section. X and Y each have an initial book capital account of $150,000. In addition, the partnership establishes for each of X and Y a revaluation account with a beginning balance of $0. On Day 1, PRS buys Stock 1, Stock 2, and Stock 3 for $100,000 each. On Day 2, Stock 1 increases in value from $100,000 to $102,000, Stock 2 increases in value from $100,000 to $105,000, and Stock 3 declines in value from $100,000 to $98,000. At the end of Day 2, Z, a regulated investment company, joins PRS by contributing $152,500 in cash for a one-third interest in the partnership [$152,500 divided by $300,000 (initial values of stock) + $5,000 (net gain at end of Day 2) + $152,500]. PRS uses this cash to purchase Stock 4. PRS establishes a revaluation account for Z with a $0 beginning balance. As of the close of Day 3, Stock 1 increases in value from $102,000 to $105,000, and Stocks 2, 3, and 4 decrease in value from $105,000 to $102,000, from $98,000 to $96,000, and from $152,500 to $151,500, respectively. At the end of Day 3, PRS sells Stocks 2 and 3.

Reg. § 1.704-3(e)(3)

(ii) *Book allocations—Day 2.* At the end of Day 2, PRS revalues the partnership's qualified financial assets and increases X's and Y's book capital accounts by each partner's 50 percent share of the $5,000 ($2,000 + $5,000 − $2,000) net increase in the value of the partnership's assets during Day 2. PRS increases X's and Y's respective revaluation account balances by $2,500 each to reflect the amount by which each partner's book capital account increased on Day 2. Z's capital account is not affected because Z did not join PRS until the end of Day 2. At the beginning of Day 3, the partnership's accounts are as follows:

Stock 1	Stock 2	Stock 3	Stock 4	
$100,000	$100,000	$100,000	—	Opening Balance
2,000	5,000	(2,000)	—	Day 2 Adjustment
$102,000	$105,000	$ 98,000	$152,500	Total

X

Book	Tax	Revaluation Account	
$150,000	$150,000	$ 0	Opening Balance
2,500	0	2,500	Day 2 Adjustment
$152,500	$150,000	$2,500	Closing Balance

Y

Book	Tax	Revaluation Account	
$150,000	$150,000	$ 0	Opening Balance
2,500	0	2,500	Day 2 Adjustment
$152,500	$150,000	$2,500	Closing Balance

Z

Book	Tax	Revaluation Account	
—	—	—	Opening Balance
—	—	—	Day 2 Adjustment
$152,500	$152,500	$ 0	Closing Balance

(iii) *Book and tax allocations—Day 3.* At the end of Day 3, PRS decreases the book capital accounts of X, Y, and Z by $1,000 to reflect each partner's share of the $3,000 ($3,000 − $3,000 − $2,000 − $1,000) net decrease in the value of the partnership's qualified financial assets. PRS also reduces each partner's revaluation account balance by $1,000. Accordingly, X's and Y's revaluation account balances are reduced to $1,500 each and Z's revaluation account balance is ($1,000). PRS then separately allocates the tax gain from the sale of Stock 2 and the tax loss from the sale of Stock 3. The $2,000 of tax gain recognized on the sale of Stock 2 ($102,000 − $100,000) is allocated among the partners with positive revaluation account balances in accordance with the relative balances of those revaluation accounts. X's and Y's revaluation accounts have equal positive balances; thus, PRS allocates $1,000 of the gain from the sale of Stock 2 to X and $1,000 of that gain to Y. PRS allocates none of the gain from the sale to Z because Z's revaluation account balance is negative. The $4,000 of tax loss recognized from the sale of Stock 3 ($96,000 − $100,000) is allocated first to the partners with negative revaluation account balances to the extent of those balances. Because Z is the only partner with a negative revaluation account balance, the tax loss is allocated first to Z to the extent of Z's ($1,000) balance. The remaining $3,000 of tax loss is allocated among the partners in accordance with their distributive shares of the loss. Accordingly, PRS allocates $1,000 of tax loss from the sale of Stock 3 to each of X and Y. PRS also allocates an additional $1,000 of the tax loss to Z, so that Z's total share of the tax loss from the sale of Stock 3 is $2,000. PRS then reduces each partner's revaluation account balance by the amount of any tax gain allocated to that partner and increases each partner's revaluation account balance by the amount of any tax loss allocated to that partner. At the beginning of Day 4, the partnership's accounts are as follows:

Stock 1	Stock 2	Stock 3	Stock 4	
$100,000	$100,000	$100,000	$152,500	Opening Balance
2,000	5,000	(2,000)	—	Day 2 Adjustment
3,000	(3,000)	(2,000)	(1,000)	Day 3 Adjustment
$105,000	$102,000	$ 96,000	$151,500	Total

Reg. § 1.704-3(e)(3)

Determination of Tax Liability

See p. 20,601 for regulations not amended to reflect law changes

X and Y

Book	Tax	Revaluation Account	
$150,000	$150,000	$ 0	Opening Balance
2,500	0	2,500	Day 2 Adjustment
(1,000)	0	(1,000)	Day 3 Adjustment
$151,500	$150,000	$1,500	Total
0	1,000	(1,000)	Gain from Stock 2
0	(1,000)	1,000	Loss from Stock 3
$151,500	$150,000	$1,500	Closing Balance

Z

Book	Tax	Revaluation Account	
$152,500	$152,500	$ 0	Opening Balance
(1,000)	0	(1,000)	Day 3 Adjustment
$151,500	$152,500	($1,000)	Total
0	0	0	Gain from Stock 2
0	(2,000)	2,000	Loss from Stock 3
$151,500	$150,500	$ 1,000	Closing Balance

Example 2. Operation of the full netting approach—(i) *Facts.* The facts are the same as in Example 1, except that the partnership agreement provides that PRS will make reverse section 704(c) allocations using the full netting approach described in paragraph (e)(3)(v) of this section.

(ii) *Book allocations—Days 2 and 3.* PRS allocates its book gains and losses in the manner described in paragraphs (ii) and (iii) of Example 1 (the partial netting approach). Thus, at the end of Day 2, PRS increases the book capital accounts of X and Y by $2,500 to reflect the appreciation in the partnership's assets from the close of Day 1 to the close of Day 2 and records that increase in the revaluation account created for each partner. At the end of Day 3, PRS decreases the book capital accounts of X, Y, and Z by $1,000 to reflect each partner's share of the decline in value of the partnership's assets from Day 2 to Day 3 and reduces each partner's revaluation account by a corresponding amount.

(iii) *Tax allocations—Day 3.* After making the book adjustments described in the previous paragraph, PRS allocates its net tax gain (or net tax loss) from its sales of qualified financial assets during Day 3. To do so, PRS first determines its net tax gain (or net tax loss) recognized from its sales of qualified financial assets for the day. There is a $2,000 net tax loss ($2,000 gain from the sale of Stock 2 less $4,000 loss from the sale of Stock 3) on the sale of PRS's qualified financial assets. Because Z is the only partner with a negative revaluation account balance, the partnership's net tax loss is allocated first to Z to the extent of Z's ($1,000) revaluation account balance. The remaining net tax loss is allocated among the partners in accordance with their distributive shares of loss. Thus, PRS allocates $333.33 of the $2,000 net tax loss to each of X and Y. PRS also allocates an additional $333.33 of the net tax loss to Z, so that the total net tax loss allocation to Z is $1,333.33. PRS then increases each partner's revaluation account balance by the amount of net tax loss allocated to that partner. At the beginning of Day 4, the partnership's accounts are as follows:

Stock 1	Stock 2	Stock 3	Stock 4	
$100,000	$100,000	$100,000	$152,500	Opening Balance
2,000	5,000	(2,000)	—	Day 2 Adjustment
3,000	(3,000)	(2,000)	(1,000)	Day 3 Adjustment
$105,000	$102,000	$ 96,000	$151,500	Total

X and Y

Book	Tax	Revaluation Account	
$150,000	$150,000	$ 0	Opening Balance
2,500	0	2,500	Day 2 Adjustment
(1,000)	0	(1,000)	Day 3 Adjustment
$151,500	$150,000	$1,500	Total
0	(333)	(333)	Net Tax Loss-Stocks 2 & 3
$151,500	$149,667	$1,833	Closing Balance

Reg. § 1.704-3(e)(3)

Z

Book	Tax	Revaluation Account	
$152,500	$152,500	$ 0	Opening Balance
(1,000)	0	(1,000)	Day 3 Adjustment
$151,500	$152,500	($1,000)	Total
0	(1,333)	1,333	Net Tax Loss-Stocks 2 & 3
$151,500	$151,167	$ 333	Closing Balance

(4) *Aggregation as permitted by the Commissioner.* The Commissioner may, by published guidance or by letter ruling, permit:

(i) Aggregation of properties other than those described in paragraphs (e)(2) and (e)(3) of this section;

(ii) Partnerships and partners not described in paragraph (e)(3) of this section to aggregate gain and loss from qualified financial assets; and

(iii) Aggregation of qualified financial assets for purposes of making section 704(c) allocations in the same manner as that described in paragraph (e)(3) of this section.

(f) *Effective date.* With the exception of paragraph (a)(11) of this section, this section applies to properties contributed to a partnership and to restatements pursuant to § 1.704-1(b)(2)(iv)(*f*) on or after December 21, 1993. Paragraph (a)(11) of this section applies to properties contributed by a partner to a partnership on or after August 20, 1997. However, partnerships may rely on paragraph (a)(11) of this section for properties contributed before August 20, 1997, and disposed of on or after August 20, 1997. [Reg. § 1.704-3.]

☐ [*T.D. 8500, 12-21-93. Amended by T.D. 8585, 12-27-94; T.D. 8717, 5-8-97 and T.D. 8730, 8-19-97.*]

[Reg. § 1.704-4]

§ 1.704-4. Distribution of contributed property.—(a) *Determination of gain and loss*—(1) *In general.* A partner that contributes section 704(c) property to a partnership must recognize gain or loss under section 704(c)(1)(B) and this section on the distribution of such property to another partner within five years of its contribution to the partnership in an amount equal to the gain or loss that would have been allocated to such partner under section 704(c)(1)(A) and § 1.704-3 if the distributed property had been sold by the partnership to the distributee partner for its fair market value at the time of the distribution. See § 1.704-3(a)(3)(i) for a definition of section 704(c) property.

(2) *Transactions to which section 704(c)(1)(B) applies.* Section 704(c)(1)(B) and this section apply only to the extent that a distribution by a partnership is a distribution to a partner acting in the capacity of a partner within the meaning of section 731.

(3) *Fair market value of property.* The fair market value of the distributed section 704(c) property is the price at which the property would change hands between a willing buyer and a willing seller at the time of the distribution, neither being under any compulsion to buy or sell and both having reasonable knowledge of the relevant facts. The fair market value that a partnership assigns to distributed section 704(c) property will be regarded as correct, provided that the value is reasonably agreed to among the partners in an arm's-length negotiation and the partners have sufficiently adverse interests.

(4) *Determination of five-year period*—(i) *General rule.* The five-year period specified in paragraph (a)(1) of this section begins on and includes the date of contribution.

(ii) *Section 708(b)(1)(B) terminations.* A termination of the partnership under section 708(b)(1)(B) does not begin a new five-year period for each partner with respect to the built-in gain and built-in loss property that the terminated partnership is deemed to contribute to the new partnership under § 1.7081(b)(1)(iv). See § 1.704-3(a)(3)(ii) for the definitions of built-in gain and built-in loss on section 704(c) property. This paragraph (a)(4)(ii) applies to terminations of partnerships under section 708(b)(1)(B) occurring on or after May 9, 1997; however, this paragraph (a)(4)(ii) may be applied to terminations occurring on or after May 9, 1996, provided that the partnership and its partners apply this paragraph (a)(4)(ii) to the termination in a consistent manner.

(5) *Examples.* The following examples illustrate the rules of this paragraph (a). Unless otherwise specified, partnership income equals partnership expenses (other than depreciation deductions for contributed property) for each year of the partnership, the fair market value of partner-

ship property does not change, all distributions by the partnership are subject to section 704(c)(1)(B), and all partners are unrelated.

Example 1. Recognition of gain. (i) On January 1, 1995, A, B, and C form partnership ABC as equal partners. A contributes $10,000 cash and Property A, nondepreciable real property with a fair market value of $10,000 and an adjusted tax basis of $4,000. Thus, there is a built-in gain of $6,000 on Property A at the time of contribution. B contributes $10,000 cash and Property B, nondepreciable real property with a fair market value and adjusted tax basis of $10,000. C contributes $20,000 cash.

(ii) On December 31, 1998, Property A and Property B are distributed to C in complete liquidation of C's interest in the partnership.

(iii) A would have recognized $6,000 of gain under section 704(c)(1)(A) and § 1.704-3 on the sale of Property A at the time of the distribution ($10,000 fair market value less $4,000 adjusted tax basis). As a result, A must recognize $6,000 of gain on the distribution of Property A to C. B would not have recognized any gain or loss under section 704(c)(1)(A) and § 1.704-3 on the sale of Property B at the time of distribution because Property B was not section 704(c) property. As a result, B does not recognize any gain or loss on the distribution of Property B.

Example 2. Effect of post-contribution depreciation deductions. (i) On January 1, 1995, A, B, and C form partnership ABC as equal partners. A contributes Property A, depreciable property with a fair market value of $30,000 and an adjusted tax basis of $20,000. Therefore, there is a built-in gain of $10,000 on Property A. B and C each contribute $30,000 cash. ABC uses the traditional method of making section 704(c) allocations described in § 1.704-3(b) with respect to Property A.

(ii) Property A is depreciated using the straight-line method over its remaining 10-year recovery period. The partnership has book depreciation of $3,000 per year (10 percent of the $30,000 book basis), and each partner is allocated $1,000 of book depreciation per year (one-third of the total annual book depreciation of $3,000). The partnership has a tax depreciation deduction of $2,000 per year (10 percent of the $20,000 tax basis in Property A). This $2,000 tax depreciation deduction is allocated equally between B and C, the noncontributing partners with respect to Property A.

(iii) At the end of the third year, the book value of Property A is $21,000 ($30,000 initial book value less $9,000 aggregate book depreciation) and the adjusted tax basis is $14,000 ($20,000 initial tax basis less $6,000 aggregate tax depreciation). A's remaining section 704(c)(1)(A) built-in gain with respect to Property A is $7,000 ($21,000 book value less $14,000 adjusted tax basis).

(iv) On December 31, 1997, Property A is distributed to B in complete liquidation of B's interest in the partnership. If Property A had been sold for its fair market value at the time of the distribution, A would have recognized $7,000 of gain under section 704(c)(1)(A) and § 1.704-3(b). Therefore, A recognizes $7,000 of gain on the distribution of Property A to B.

Example 3. Effect of remedial method. (i) On January 1, 1995, A, B, and C form partnership ABC as equal partners. A contributes Property A1, nondepreciable real property with a fair market value of $10,000 and an adjusted tax basis of $5,000, and Property A2, nondepreciable real property with a fair market value and adjusted tax basis of $10,000. B and C each contribute $20,000 cash. ABC uses the remedial method of making section 704(c) allocations described in § 1.704-3(d) with respect to Property A1.

(ii) On December 31, 1998, when the fair market value of Property A1 has decreased to $7,000, Property A1 is distributed to C in a current distribution. If Property A1 had been sold by the partnership at the time of the distribution, ABC would have recognized the $2,000 of remaining built-in gain under section 704(c)(1)(A) on the sale (fair market value of $7,000 less $5,000 adjusted tax basis). All of this gain would have been allocated to A. ABC would also have recognized a book loss of $3,000 ($10,000 original book value less $7,000 current fair market value of the property). Book loss in the amount of $2,000 would have been allocated equally between B and C. Under the remedial method, $2,000 of tax loss would also have been allocated equally to B and C to match their share of the book loss. As a result, $2,000 of gain would also have been allocated to A as an offsetting remedial allocation. A would have recognized $4,000 of total gain under section 704(c)(1)(A) on the sale of Property A1 ($2,000 of section 704(c) recognized gain plus $2,000 remedial gain). Therefore, A recognizes $4,000 of gain on the distribution of Property A1 to C under this section.

(b) *Character of gain or loss*—(1) *General rule.* Gain or loss recognized by the contributing partner under section 704(c)(1)(B) and this section has the same character as the gain or loss that would have resulted if the distributed property had been sold by the partnership to the distributee partner at the time of the distribution.

(2) *Example.* The following example illustrates the rule of this paragraph (b). Unless other-

Reg. § 1.704-4(b)(1)

wise specified, partnership income equals partnership expenses (other than depreciation deductions for contributed property) for each year of the partnership, the fair market value of partnership property does not change, all distributions by the partnership are subject to section 704(c)(1)(B), and all partners are unrelated.

Example. Character of gain. (i) On January 1, 1995, A and B form partnership AB. A contributes $10,000 and Property A, nondepreciable real property with a fair market value of $10,000 and an adjusted tax basis of $4,000, in exchange for a 25 percent interest in partnership capital and profits. B contributes $60,000 cash for a 75 percent interest in partnership capital and profits.

(ii) On December 31, 1998, Property A is distributed to B in a current distribution. Property A is used in a trade or business of B.

(iii) A would have recognized $6,000 of gain under section 704(c)(1)(A) on a sale of Property A at the time of the distribution (the difference between the fair market value ($10,000) and the adjusted tax basis ($4,000) of the property at that time). Because Property A is not a capital asset in the hands of Partner B and B holds more than 50 percent of partnership capital and profits, the character of the gain on a sale of Property A to B would have been ordinary income under section 707(b)(2). Therefore, the character of the gain to A on the distribution of Property A to B is ordinary income.

(c) *Exceptions*—(1) *Property contributed on or before October 3, 1989.* Section 704(c)(1)(B) and this section do not apply to property contributed to the partnership on or before October 3, 1989.

(2) *Certain liquidations.* Section 704(c)(1)(B) and this section do not apply to a distribution of an interest in section 704(c) property to a partner other than the contributing partner in a liquidation of the partnership if—

(i) The contributing partner receives an interest in the section 704(c) property contributed by that partner (and no other property); and

(ii) The built-in gain or loss in the interest distributed to the contributing partner, determined immediately after the distribution, is equal to or greater than the built-in gain or loss on the property that would have been allocated to the contributing partner under section 704(c)(1)(A) and § 1.704-3 on a sale of the contributed property to an unrelated party immediately before the distribution.

(3) *Section 708(b)(1)(B) terminations.* Section 704(c)(1)(B) and this section do not apply to the deemed distribution of interests in a new partnership caused by the termination of a partnership under section 708(b)(1)(B). A subsequent distribution of section 704(c) property by the new partnership to a partner of the new partnership is subject to section 704(c)(1)(B) to the same extent that a distribution by the terminated partnership would have been subject to section 704(c)(1)(B). See also § 1.737-2(a) for a similar rule in the context of section 737. This paragraph (c)(3) applies to terminations of partnerships under section 708(b)(1)(B) occurring on or after May 9, 1997; however, this paragraph (c)(3) may be applied to terminations occurring on or after May 9, 1996, provided that the partnership and its partners apply this paragraph (c)(3) to the termination in a consistent manner.

(4) *Complete transfer to another partnership.* Section 704(c)(1)(B) and this section do not apply to a transfer by a partnership (transferor partnership) of all of its assets and liabilities to a second partnership (transferee partnership) in an exchange described in section 721, followed by a distribution of the interest in the transferee partnership in liquidation of the transferor partnership as part of the same plan or arrangement. A subsequent distribution of section 704(c) property by the transferee partnership to a partner of the transferee partnership is subject to section 704(c)(1)(B) to the same extent that a distribution by the transferor partnership would have been subject to section 704(c)(1)(B). See § 1.737-2(b) for a similar rule in the context of section 737.

(5) *Incorporation of a partnership.* Section 704(c)(1)(B) and this section do not apply to an incorporation of a partnership by any method of incorporation (other than a method involving an actual distribution of partnership property to the partners followed by a contribution of that property to a corporation), provided that the partnership is liquidated as part of the incorporation transaction. See § 1.737-2(c) for a similar rule in the context of section 737.

(6) *Undivided interests.* Section 704(c)(1)(B) and this section do not apply to a distribution of an undivided interest in property to the extent that the undivided interest does not exceed the undivided interest, if any, contributed by the distributee partner in the same property. See § 1.737-2(d)(4) for the application of section 737 in a similar context. The portion of the undivided interest in property retained by the partnership after the distribution, if any, that is treated as contributed by the distributee partner, is reduced to the extent of the undivided interest distributed to the distributee partner.

(7) *Example.* The following example illustrates the rule of paragraph (c)(2) of this section.

Reg. § 1.704-4(c)(7)

Unless otherwise specified, partnership income equals partnership expenses (other than depreciation deductions for contributed property) for each year of the partnership, the fair market value of partnership property does not change, all distributions by the partnership are subject to section 704(c)(1)(B), and all partners are unrelated.

Example. (i) On January 1, 1995, A and B form partnership AB, as equal partners. A contributes Property A, nondepreciable real property with a fair market value and adjusted tax basis of $20,000. B contributes Property B, nondepreciable real property with a fair market value of $20,000 and an adjusted tax basis of $10,000. Property B therefore has a built-in gain of $10,000 at the time of contribution.

(ii) On December 31, 1998, the partnership liquidates when the fair market value of Property A has not changed, but the fair market value of Property B has increased to $40,000.

(iii) In the liquidation, A receives Property A and a 25 percent interest in Property B. This interest in Property B has a fair market value of $10,000 to A, reflecting the fact that A was entitled to 50 percent of the $20,000 post-contribution appreciation in Property B. The partnership distributes to B a 75 percent interest in Property B with a fair market value of $30,000. B's basis in this portion of Property B is $10,000 under section 732(b). As a result, B has a built-in gain of $20,000 in this portion of Property B immediately after the distribution ($30,000 fair market value less $10,000 adjusted tax basis). This built-in gain is greater than the $10,000 of built-in gain in Property B at the time of contribution to the partnership. B therefore does not recognize any gain on the distribution of a portion of Property B to A under this section.

(d) *Special rules*—(1) *Nonrecognition transactions.* Property received by the partnership in exchange for section 704(c) property in a nonrecognition transaction is treated as the section 704(c) property for purposes of section 704(c)(1)(B) and this section to the extent that the property received is treated as section 704(c) property under § 1.704-3(a)(8). See § 1.7372(d)(3) for a similar rule in the context of section 737.

(2) *Transfers of a partnership interest.* The transferee of all or a portion of the partnership interest of a contributing partner is treated as the contributing partner for purposes of section 704(c)(1)(B) and this section to the extent of the share of built-in gain or loss allocated to the transferee partner. See § 1.704-3(a)(7).

(3) *Distributions of like-kind property.* If section 704(c) property is distributed to a partner other than the contributing partner and like-kind property (within the meaning of section 1031) is distributed to the contributing partner no later than the earlier of (i) 180 days following the date of the distribution to the non-contributing partner, or (ii) the due date (determined with regard to extensions) of the contributing partner's income tax return for the taxable year of the distribution to the noncontributing partner, the amount of gain or loss, if any, that the contributing partner would otherwise have recognized under section 704(c)(1)(B) and this section is reduced by the amount of built-in gain or loss in the distributed like-kind property in the hands of the contributing partner immediately after the distribution. The contributing partner's basis in the distributed like-kind property is determined as if the like-kind property were distributed in an unrelated distribution prior to the distribution of any other property distributed as part of the same distribution and is determined without regard to the increase in the contributing partner's adjusted tax basis in the partnership interest under section 704(c)(1)(B) and this section. See § 1.707-3 for provisions treating the distribution of the like-kind property to the contributing partner as a disguised sale in certain situations.

(4) *Example.* The following example illustrates the rules of this paragraph (d). Unless otherwise specified, partnership income equals partnership expenses (other than depreciation deductions for contributed property) for each year of the partnership, the fair market value of partnership property does not change, all distributions by the partnership are subject to section 704(c)(1)(B), and all partners are unrelated.

Example. Distribution of like-kind property. (i) On January 1, 1995, A, B, and C form partnership ABC as equal partners. A contributes Property A, nondepreciable real property with a fair market value of $20,000 and an adjusted tax basis of $10,000. B and C each contribute $20,000 cash. The partnership subsequently buys Property X, nondepreciable real property of a like-kind to Property A with a fair market value and adjusted tax basis of $8,000. The fair market value of Property X subsequently increases to $10,000.

(ii) On December 31, 1998, Property A is distributed to B in a current distribution. At the same time, Property X is distributed to A in a current distribution. The distribution of Property X does not result in the contribution of Property A being properly characterized as a disguised sale to the partnership under § 1.707-3. A's basis in Property X is $8,000 under section 732(a)(1). A therefore has $2,000 of built-in gain in Property X ($10,000 fair market value less $8,000 adjusted tax basis).

Reg. § 1.704-4(d)(1)

(iii) A would generally recognize $10,000 of gain under section 704(c)(1)(B) on the distribution of Property A, the difference between the fair market value ($20,000) of the property and its adjusted tax basis ($10,000). This gain is reduced, however, by the amount of the built-in gain of Property X in the hands of A. As a result, A recognizes only $8,000 of gain on the distribution of Property A to B under section 704(c)(1)(B) and this section.

(e) *Basis adjustments*—(1) *Contributing partner's basis in the partnership interest.* The basis of the contributing partner's interest in the partnership is increased by the amount of the gain, or decreased by the amount of the loss, recognized by the partner under section 704(c)(1)(B) and this section. This increase or decrease is taken into account in determining (i) the contributing partner's adjusted tax basis under section 732 for any property distributed to the partner in a distribution that is part of the same distribution as the distribution of the contributed property, other than like-kind property described in paragraph (d)(3) of this section (pertaining to the special rule for distributions of like-kind property), and (ii) the amount of the gain recognized by the contributing partner under section 731 or section 737, if any, on a distribution of money or property to the contributing partner that is part of the same distribution as the distribution of the contributed property. For a determination of basis in a distribution subject to section 737, see § 1.737-3(a).

(2) *Partnership's basis in partnership property.* The partnership's adjusted tax basis in the distributed section 704(c) property is increased or decreased immediately before the distribution by the amount of gain or loss recognized by the contributing partner under section 704(c)(1)(B) and this section. Any increase or decrease in basis is therefore taken into account in determining the distributee partner's adjusted tax basis in the distributed property under section 732. For a determination of basis in a distribution subject to section 737, see § 1.7373(b).

(3) *Section 754 adjustments.* The basis adjustments to partnership property made pursuant to paragraph (e)(2) of this section are not elective and must be made regardless of whether the partnership has an election in effect under section 754. Any adjustments to the bases of partnership property (including the distributed section 704(c) property) under section 734(b) pursuant to a section 754 election must be made after (and must take into account) the adjustments to basis made under paragraph (e)(2) of this section. See § 1.737-3(c)(4) for a similar rule in the context of section 737.

(4) *Example.* The following example illustrates the rules of this paragraph (e). Unless otherwise specified, partnership income equals partnership expenses (other than depreciation deductions for contributed property) for each year of the partnership, the fair market value of partnership property does not change, all distributions by the partnership are subject to section 704(c)(1)(B), and all partners are unrelated.

Example. Basis adjustment. (i) On January 1, 1995, A, B, and C form partnership ABC as equal partners. A contributes $10,000 cash and Property A, nondepreciable real property with a fair market value of $10,000 and an adjusted tax basis of $4,000. B and C each contribute $20,000 cash.

(ii) On December 31, 1998, Property A is distributed to B in a current distribution.

(iii) Under paragraph (a) of this section, A recognizes $6,000 of gain on the distribution of Property A because that is the amount of gain that would have been allocated to A under section 704(c)(1)(A) and § 1.704-3 on a sale of Property A for its fair market value at the time of the distribution (fair market value of Property A ($10,000) less its adjusted tax basis at the time of distribution ($4,000)). The adjusted tax basis of A's partnership interest is increased from $14,000 to $20,000 to reflect this gain. The partnership's adjusted tax basis in Property A is increased from $4,000 to $10,000 immediately prior to its distribution to B. B's adjusted tax basis in Property A is therefore $10,000 under section 732(a)(1).

(f) *Anti-abuse rule*—(1) *In general.* The rules of section 704(c)(1)(B) and this section must be applied in a manner consistent with the purpose of section 704(c)(1)(B). Accordingly, if a principal purpose of a transaction is to achieve a tax result that is inconsistent with the purpose of section 704(c)(1)(B), the Commissioner can recast the transaction for federal tax purposes as appropriate to achieve tax results that are consistent with the purpose of section 704(c)(1)(B) and this section. Whether a tax result is inconsistent with the purpose of section 704(c)(1)(B) and this section must be determined based on all the facts and circumstances. See § 1.7374 for an anti-abuse rule and examples in the context of section 737.

(2) *Examples.* The following examples illustrate the anti-abuse rule of this paragraph (f). The examples set forth below do not delineate the boundaries of either permissible or impermissible types of transactions. Further, the addition of any facts or circumstances that are not specifically set forth in an example (or the deletion of any facts or

Reg. § 1.704-4(f)(2)

circumstances) may alter the outcome of the transaction described in the example. Unless otherwise specified, partnership income equals partnership expenses (other than depreciation deductions for contributed property) for each year of the partnership, the fair market value of partnership property does not change, all distributions by the partnership are subject to section 704(c)(1)(B), and all partners are unrelated.

Example 1. Distribution in substance made within five-year period; results inconsistent with the purpose of section 704(c)(1)(B). (i) On January 1, 1995, A, B, and C form partnership ABC as equal partners. A contributes Property A, nondepreciable real property with a fair market value of $10,000 and an adjusted tax basis of $1,000. B and C each contributes $10,000 cash.

(ii) On December 31, 1998, the partners desire to distribute Property A to B in complete liquidation of B's interest in the partnership. If Property A were distributed at that time, however, A would recognize $9,000 of gain under section 704(c)(1)(B), the difference between the $10,000 fair market value and the $1,000 adjusted tax basis of Property A, because Property A was contributed to the partnership less than five years before December 31, 1998. On becoming aware of this potential gain recognition, and with a principal purpose of avoiding such gain, the partners amend the partnership agreement on December 31, 1998, and take any other steps necessary to provide that substantially all of the economic risks and benefits of Property A are borne by B as of December 31, 1998, and that substantially all of the economic risks and benefits of all other partnership property are borne by A and C. The partnership holds Property A until January 5, 2000, at which time it is distributed to B in complete liquidation of B's interest in the partnership.

(iii) The actual distribution of Property A occurred more than five years after the contribution of the property to the partnership. The steps taken by the partnership on December 31, 1998, however, are the functional equivalent of an actual distribution of Property A to B in complete liquidation of B's interest in the partnership as of that date. Section 704(c)(1)(B) requires recognition of gain when contributed section 704(c) property is in substance distributed to another partner within five years of its contribution to the partnership. Allowing a contributing partner to avoid section 704(c)(1)(B) through arrangements such as those in this *Example 1* that have the effect of a distribution of property within five years of the date of its contribution to the partnership would effectively undermine the purpose of section 704(c)(1)(B) and this section. As a result, the steps taken by the partnership on December 31, 1998, are treated as causing a distribution of Property A to B for purposes of section 704(c)(1)(B) on that date, and A recognizes gain of $9,000 under section 704(c)(1)(B) and this section at that time.

(iv) Alternatively, if on becoming aware of the potential gain recognition to A on a distribution of Property A on December 31, 1998, the partners had instead agreed that B would continue as a partner with no changes to the partnership agreement or to B's economic interest in partnership operations, the distribution of Property A to B on January 5, 2000, would not have been inconsistent with the purpose of section 704(c)(1)(B) and this section. In that situation, Property A would not have been distributed until after the expiration of the five-year period specified in section 704(c)(1)(B) and this section. Deferring the distribution of Property A until the end of the five-year period for a principal purpose of avoiding the recognition of gain under section 704(c)(1)(B) and this section is not inconsistent with the purpose of section 704(c)(1)(B). Therefore, A would not have recognized gain on the distribution of Property A in that case.

Example 2. Suspension of five-year period in manner consistent with the purpose of section 704(c)(1)(B). (i) A, B, and C form partnership ABC on January 1, 1995, to conduct bona fide business activities. A contributes Property A, nondepreciable real property with a fair market value of $10,000 and an adjusted tax basis of $1,000, in exchange for a 49.5 percent interest in partnership capital and profits. B contributes $10,000 in cash for a 49.5 percent interest in partnership capital and profits. C contributes cash for a 1 percent interest in partnership capital and profits. A and B are wholly owned subsidiaries of the same affiliated group and continue to control the management of Property A by virtue of their controlling interests in the partnership. The partnership is formed pursuant to a plan a principal purpose of which is to minimize the period of time that A would have to remain a partner with a potential acquiror of Property A.

(ii) On December 31, 1997, D is admitted as a partner to the partnership in exchange for $10,000 cash.

(iii) On January 5, 2000, Property A is distributed to D in complete liquidation of D's interest in the partnership.

(iv) The distribution of Property A to D occurred more than five years after the contribution of the property to the partnership. On these facts, however, a principal purpose of the transaction was to minimize the period of time that A would have to remain partners with a potential acquiror of Property A, and treating the five-year period of section 704(c)(1)(B) as running during a time when Property A was still effectively owned through the partnership by members of the contributing affiliated group of which A is a member is inconsistent with the purpose of section 704(c)(1)(B). Prior to the admission of D as a partner, the pooling of assets between A and B, on the one hand, and C, on the other hand, although sufficient to constitute ABC as a valid partnership for federal income tax purposes, is not a sufficient pooling of assets for purposes of running the five-year period with respect to the distribution of Property A to D. Allowing a contributing partner to avoid section 704(c)(1)(B) through arrangements such as those in this *Example 2* would have the effect of substantially nullifying the five-year requirement of section 704(c)(1)(B) and this section and elevating the form of the transaction over its substance. As a result, with respect to the distribution of Property A to D, the five-year period of section 704(c)(1)(B) is tolled until the admission of D as a partner on December 31, 1997. Therefore, the distribution of Property A occurred before the end of the five-year period of section 704(c)(1)(B), and A recognizes gain of $9,000 under section 704(c)(1)(B) on the distribution.

(g) *Effective date.* This section applies to distributions by a partnership to a partner on or after January 9, 1995. [Reg. § 1.704-4.]

☐ [T.D. 8642, 12-22-95. Amended by T.D. 8717, 5-8-97.]

[Reg. § 1.705-1]

§ 1.705-1. **Determination of basis of partner's interest.**—(a) *General rule*—(1) Section 705 and this section provide rules for determining the adjusted basis of a partner's interest in a partnership. A partner is required to determine the adjusted basis of his interest in a partnership only when necessary for the determination of his tax liability or that of any other person. The determination of the adjusted basis of a partnership interest is ordinarily made as of the end of a partnership taxable year. Thus, for example, such year-end determination is necessary in ascertaining the extent to which a partner's distributive share of partnership losses may be allowed. See section 704(d). However, where there has been a sale or exchange of all or a part of a partnership interest or a liquidation of a partner's entire interest in a partnership, the adjusted basis of the partner's interest should be determined as of the date of sale or exchange or liquidation. The adjusted basis of a partner's interest in a partnership is determined without regard to any amount shown in the partnership books as the partner's "capital," "equity," or similar account. For example, A contributes property with an adjusted basis to him of $400 (and a value of $1,000) to a partnership. B contributes $1,000 cash. While under their agreement each may have a "capital account" in the partnership of $1,000, the adjusted basis of A's interest is only $400 and B's interest $1,000.

(2) The original basis of a partner's interest in a partnership shall be determined under section 722 (relating to contributions to a partnership) or section 742 (relating to transfers of partnership interests). Such basis shall be increased under section 722 by any further contributions to the partnership and by the sum of the partner's distributive share for the taxable year and prior taxable years of—

(i) Taxable income of the partnership as determined under section 703(a),

(ii) Tax-exempt receipts of the partnership, and

(iii) The excess of the deductions for depletion over the basis of the depletable property, unless the property is an oil or gas property the basis of which has been allocated to partners under section 613A(c)(7)(D).

(3) The basis shall be decreased (but not below zero) by distributions from the partnership as provided in section 733 and by the sum of the partner's distributive share for the taxable year and prior taxable years of—

(i) Partnership losses (including capital losses), and

(ii) Partnership expenditures which are not deductible in computing partnership taxable income or loss and which are not capital expenditures.

(4) The basis shall be decreased (but not below zero) by the amount of the partner's deduction for depletion allowable under section 611 for any partnership oil and gas property to the extent the deduction does not exceed the proportionate share of the adjusted basis of the property allocated to the partner under section 613A(c)(7)(D).

(5) The basis shall be adjusted (but not below zero) to reflect any gain or loss to the partner resulting from a disposition by the partnership of a domestic oil or gas property after December 31, 1974.

(6) For the effect of liabilities in determining the amount of contributions made by a partner to a partnership or the amount of distributions made by a partnership to a partner, see section 752 and § 1.752-1, relating to the treatment of certain liabilities. In determining the basis of a partnership interest on the effective date of subchapter K, chapter 1 of the Code, or any of the sections

Reg. § 1.705-1(a)(6)

thereof, the partner's share of partnership liabilities on that date shall be included.

(7) For basis adjustments necessary to coordinate sections 705 and 1032 in certain situations in which a partnership disposes of stock or any position in stock to which section 1032 applies of a corporation that holds a direct or indirect interest in the partnership, see § 1.705-2.

(b) *Alternative rule.* In certain cases, the adjusted basis of a partner's interest in a partnership may be determined by reference to the partner's share of the adjusted basis of partnership property which would be distributable upon termination of the partnership. The alternative rule may be used to determine the adjusted basis of a partner's interest where circumstances are such that the partner cannot practicably apply the general rule set forth in section 705(a) and paragraph (a) of this section, or where, from a consideration of all the facts, it is, in the opinion of the Commissioner, reasonable to conclude that the result produced will not vary substantially from the result obtainable under the general rule. Where the alternative rule is used, adjustments may be necessary in determining the adjusted basis of a partner's interest in a partnership. Adjustments would be required, for example, in order to reflect in a partner's share of the adjusted basis of partnership property any significant discrepancies arising as a result of contributed property, transfers of partnership interest, or distributions of property to the partners. The operation of the alternative rules may be illustrated by the following examples:

Example (1). The ABC partnership, in which A, B, and C are equal partners, owns various properties with a total adjusted basis of $1,500 and has earned and retained an additional $1,500. The total adjusted basis of partnership property is thus $3,000. Each partner's share in the adjusted basis of partnership property is one-third of this amount, or $1,000. Under the alternative rule, this amount represents each partner's adjusted basis for his partnership interest.

Example (2). Assume that partner A in example (1) of this paragraph sells his partnership interest to D for $1,250 at a time when the partnership property with an adjusted basis of $1,500 had appreciated in value to $3,000, and when the partnership also had $750 in cash. The total adjusted basis of all partnership property is $2,250 and the value of such property is $3,750. D's basis for his partnership interest is his cost, $1,250. However, his one-third share of the adjusted basis of partnership property is only $750. Therefore, for the purposes of the alternative rule, D has an adjustment of $500 in determining the basis of his interest. This amount represents the difference between the cost of his partnership interest and his share of partnership basis at the time of his purchase. If the partnership subsequently earns and retains an additional $1,500, its property will have an adjusted basis of $3,750. D's adjusted basis for his interest under the alternative rule is $1,750, determined by adding $500, his basis adjustment, to $1,250 (his one-third share of the $3,750 adjusted basis of partnership property). If the partnership distributes $250 to each partner in a current distribution, D's adjusted basis for his interest will be $1,500 ($1,000, his one-third share of the remaining basis of partnership property, $3,000, plus his basis adjustment of $500).

Example (3). Assume the BCD partnership in example (2) of this paragraph continues to operate. In 1960, D proposes to sell his partnership interest and wishes to evaluate the tax consequences of such sale. It is necessary, therefore, to determine the adjusted basis of his interest in the partnership. Assume further that D cannot determine the adjusted basis of his interest under the general rule. The balance sheet of the BCD partnership is as follows:

Assets	Adjusted Basis per Books	Market Value
Cash	$ 3,000	$ 3,000
Receivables	4,000	4,000
Depreciable Property	5,000	5,000
Land held for investment	18,000	30,000
Total	$30,000	$42,000

Liabilities and Capital	Per Books
Liabilities	$ 6,000
Capital Accounts: B	4,500
C	4,500
D	15,000
Total	$30,000

Reg. § 1.705-1(a)(7)

Determination of Tax Liability

The $15,000 representing the amount of D's capital account does not reflect the $500 basis adjustment arising from D's purchase of his interest. See example (2) of this paragraph. The adjusted basis of D's partnership interest determined under the alternative rule is as follows:

D's share of the adjusted basis of partnership property (reduced by the amount of liabilities) at time of proposed sale	$15,000
D's share of partnership liabilities (under the partnership agreement liabilities are shared equally)	2,000
D's basis adjustment from example (2)	500
Adjusted basis of D's interest at the time of proposed sale, as determined under alternative rule	$17,500

[Reg. § 1.705-1.]

☐ [T.D. 6175, 5-23-56. *Amended by* T.D. 8437, 9-22-92; T.D. 8986, 3-28-2002 and T.D. 9049, 3-17-2003.]

[Reg. § 1.705-2]

§ 1.705-2. Basis adjustments coordinating sections 705 and 1032.—(a) *Purpose.* This section coordinates the application of sections 705 and 1032 and is intended to prevent inappropriate increases or decreases in the adjusted basis of a corporate partner's interest in a partnership resulting from the partnership's disposition of the corporate partner's stock. The rules under section 705 generally are intended to preserve equality between the adjusted basis of a partner's interest in a partnership (outside basis) and such partner's share of the adjusted basis in partnership assets (inside basis). However, in situations where a section 754 election was not in effect for the year in which a partner acquired its interest, the partner's inside basis and outside basis may not be equal. Similarly, in situations where a section 754 election was not in effect for the year in which a partnership distributes money or other property to another partner and that partner recognizes gain or loss on the distribution or the basis of the property distributed to that partner is adjusted, the remaining partners' inside basis and outside basis may not be equal. In these situations, gain or loss allocated to the partner upon disposition of the partnership assets that is attributable to the difference between the adjusted basis of the partnership assets absent the section 754 election and the adjusted basis of the partnership assets had a section 754 election been in effect generally will result in an adjustment to the basis of the partner's interest in the partnership under section 705(a). Such gain (or loss) therefore generally will be offset by a corresponding decrease in the gain or increase in the loss (or increase in the gain or decrease in the loss) upon the subsequent disposition by the partner of its interest in the partnership. Where such a difference exists with respect to stock of a corporate partner that is held by the partnership, gain or loss from the disposition of corporate partner stock attributable to the difference is not recognized by the corporate partner under section 1032. To adjust the basis of the corporate partner's interest in the partnership for this unrecognized gain or loss would not be appropriate because it would create an opportunity for the recognition of taxable gain or loss on a subsequent disposition of the partnership interest where no economic gain or loss has been incurred by the corporate partner and no corresponding taxable gain or loss had previously been allocated to the corporate partner by the partnership.

(b) *Single partnership*—(1) *Required adjustments relating to acquisitions of partnership interest*—(i) This paragraph (b)(1) applies in situations where a corporation acquires an interest in a partnership that holds stock in that corporation (or the partnership subsequently acquires stock in that corporation in an exchanged basis transaction), the partnership does not have an election under section 754 in effect for the year in which the corporation acquires the interest, and the partnership later sells or exchanges the stock. In these situations, the increase (or decrease) in the corporation's adjusted basis in its partnership interest resulting from the sale or exchange of the stock equals the amount of gain (or loss) that the corporate partner would have recognized (absent the application of section 1032) if, for the year in which the corporation acquired the interest, a section 754 election had been in effect.

(ii) The provisions of this paragraph (b)(1) are illustrated by the following example:

Example. (i) A, B, and C form equal partnership PRS. Each partner contributes $30,000 in exchange for its partnership interest. PRS has no liabilities. PRS purchases stock in corporation X for $30,000, which appreciates in value to $120,000. PRS also purchases inventory for $60,000, which appreciates in value to $150,000. A sells its interest in PRS to corporation X for $90,000 in a year for which an election under section 754 is not in effect. PRS later sells the X stock for $150,000. PRS realizes a gain of $120,000 on the sale of the X stock. X's share of the gain is $40,000. Under section 1032, X does not recognize its share of the gain.

(ii) Normally, X would be entitled to a $40,000 increase in the basis of its PRS interest for its allocable share of PRS's gain from the sale of the X stock, but a special rule applies in this situation. If a section 754 election had been in effect for the year in which X acquired its interest in PRS, X would have been entitled to a basis adjustment under section 743(b) of $60,000 (the excess of X's basis for the transferred partnership interest over X's share of the adjusted basis to PRS of PRS's property). See § 1.743-1(b). Under § 1.755-1(b), the basis adjustment under section 743(b) would have been allocated $30,000 to the X stock (the amount of the gain that would have been allocated to X from the hypothetical sale of the stock), and $30,000 to the inventory (the amount of the gain that would have been allocated to X from the hypothetical sale of the inventory).

(iii) If a section 754 election had been in effect for the year in which X acquired its interest in PRS, the amount of gain that X would have recognized upon PRS's disposition of X stock (absent the application of section 1032) would be $10,000 (X's share of PRS's gain from the stock sale, $40,000, minus the amount of X's basis adjustment under section 743(b), $30,000). See § 1.743-1(j). Accordingly, the increase in the basis of X's interest in PRS is $10,000.

(2) *Required adjustments relating to distributions*—(i) This paragraph (b)(2) applies in situations where a corporation owns a direct or indirect interest in a partnership that owns stock in that corporation, the partnership distributes money or other property to another partner and that partner recognizes gain or loss on the distribution or the basis of the property distributed to that partner is adjusted during a year in which the partnership does not have an election under section 754 in effect, and the partnership subsequently sells or exchanges the stock. In these situations, the increase (or decrease) in the corporation's adjusted basis in its partnership interest resulting from the sale or exchange of the stock equals the amount of gain (or loss) that the corporate partner would have recognized (absent the application of section 1032) if, for the year in which the partnership made the distribution, a section 754 election had been in effect.

(ii) The provisions of this paragraph (b)(2) are illustrated by the following example:

Example. (i) A, B, and corporation C form partnership PRS. A and B each contribute $10,000 and C contributes $20,000 in exchange for a partnership interest. PRS has no liabilities. PRS purchases stock in corporation C for $10,000, which appreciates in value to $70,000. PRS distributes $25,000 to A in complete liquidation of A's interest in PRS in a year for which an election under section 754 is not in effect. PRS later sells the C stock for $70,000. PRS realizes a gain of $60,000 on the sale of the C stock. C's share of the gain is $40,000. Under section 1032, C does not recognize its share of the gain.

(ii) Normally, C would be entitled to a $40,000 increase in the basis of its PRS interest for its allocable share of PRS's gain from the sale of the C stock, but a special rule applies in this situation. If a section 754 election had been in effect for the year in which PRS made the distribution to A, PRS would have been entitled to adjust the basis of partnership property under section 734(b)(1)(A) by $15,000 (the amount of gain recognized by A with respect to the distribution to A under section 731(a)(1)). See § 1.734-1(b). Under § 1.755-1(c)(1)(ii), the basis adjustment under section 734(b) would have been allocated to the C stock, increasing its basis to $25,000 (where there is a distribution resulting in an adjustment under section 734(b)(1)(A) to the basis of undistributed partnership property, the adjustment is allocated only to capital gain property).

(iii) If a section 754 election had been in effect for the year in which PRS made the distribution to A, the amount of gain that PRS would have recognized upon PRS's disposition of C stock would be $45,000 ($70,000 minus $25,000 basis in the C stock), and the amount of gain C would have recognized upon PRS's disposition of the C stock (absent the application of section 1032) would be $30,000 (C's share of PRS's gain of $45,000 from the stock sale). Accordingly, upon PRS's sale of the C stock, the increase in the basis of C's interest in PRS is $30,000.

(c) *Tiered partnerships and other arrangements*—(1) *Required adjustments.* The purpose of these regulations as set forth in paragraph (a) of this section cannot be avoided through the use of tiered partnerships or other arrangements. For example, if a corporation acquires an indirect interest in its own stock through a chain of two or more partnerships (either where the corporation acquires a direct interest in a partnership or where one of the partnerships in the chain acquires an interest in another partnership), and gain or loss from the sale or exchange of the stock is subsequently allocated to the corporation, then the bases of the interests in the partnerships included in the chain shall be adjusted in a manner that is consistent with the purpose of this section. Similarly, if a corporation owns an indirect interest in its own stock through a chain of two or more partnerships, and a partnership in the chain distributes money or other property to another partner and that partner recognizes gain or loss on the distribution or the basis of the property distributed to that partner is adjusted during a year in which the partnership does not have an election under section 754 in effect, then upon any subsequent sale or exchange of the stock, the bases of the interests in the partnerships included in the chain shall be adjusted in a manner that is consistent with the purpose of this section.

(2) *Examples.* The provisions of this paragraph (c) are illustrated by the following examples:

Example 1. Acquisition of upper-tier partnership interest by corporation. (i) A, B, and C form a partnership (UTP), with each partner contributing $25,000. UTP and D form a partnership (LTP). UTP contributes $75,000 in exchange for its interest in LTP, and D contributes $25,000 in exchange for D's interest in LTP. Neither UTP nor LTP has any liabilities. LTP purchases stock in corporation E for $100,000, which appreciates in value to $1,000,000. C sells its interest in UTP to corporation E for $250,000 in a year for which an election under section 754 is not in effect for UTP or LTP. LTP later sells the E stock for $2,000,000. LTP realizes a $1,900,000 gain on the sale of the E stock. UTP's share of the gain is $1,425,000, and E's share of the gain is $475,000. Under section 1032, E does not recognize its share of the gain.

(ii) With respect to the basis of UTP's interest in LTP, if all of the gain from the sale of the E stock (including E's share) were to increase the basis of UTP's interest in LTP, UTP's basis in such interest would be $1,500,000 ($75,000 + $1,425,000). The fair market value of UTP's interest in LTP is $1,500,000. Because UTP did not have a section 754 election in effect for the taxable year in which E acquired its interest in UTP, UTP's basis in the LTP interest does not reflect the purchase price paid by E for its interest. Increasing the basis of UTP's interest in LTP by the full amount of the gain that would be recognized (in the absence of section 1032) on the sale of the E stock preserves the conformity between UTP's inside basis and outside basis with respect to LTP (i.e., UTP's share of LTP's cash is equal to $1,500,000, and UTP's basis in the LTP interest is $1,500,000) and appropriately would cause UTP to recognize no gain or loss on the sale of UTP's interest in LTP immediately after the sale of the E stock. Accordingly, increasing the basis of UTP's interest in LTP by the entire amount of gain allocated to UTP (including E's share) from LTP's sale of the E stock is consistent with the purpose of this section. The $1,425,000 of gain allocated by LTP to UTP will increase the adjusted basis of UTP's interest in LTP under section 705(a)(1). The basis of UTP's interest in LTP immediately after the sale of the E stock is $1,500,000.

(iii) With respect to the basis of E's interest in UTP, if E's share of the gain allocated to UTP and then to E were to increase the basis of E's interest in UTP, E's basis in such interest would be $725,000 ($250,000 + $475,000) and the fair market value of such interest would be $500,000, so that E would recognize a loss of $225,000 if E sold its interest in UTP immediately after LTP's disposition of the E stock. It would be inappropriate for E to recognize a taxable loss of $225,000 upon a disposition of its interest in UTP because E would not incur an economic loss in the transaction, and E did not recognize a taxable gain upon LTP's disposition of the E stock that appropriately would be offset by a taxable loss on the disposition of its interest in UTP. Accordingly, increasing E's basis in its UTP interest by the entire amount of gain allocated to E from the sale of the E stock is not consistent with the purpose of this section. (Conversely, because A and B were allocated taxable gain on the disposition of the E stock, it would be appropriate to increase A's and B's bases in their respective interests in UTP by the full amount of the gain allocated to them.)

(iv) The appropriate basis adjustment for E's interest in UTP upon the disposition of the E stock by LTP can be determined as the amount of gain that E would have recognized (in the absence of section 1032) upon the sale by LTP of the E stock if both UTP and LTP had made section 754 elections for the taxable year in which E acquired the interest in UTP. If section 754 elections had been in effect for UTP and LTP for the year in which E acquired E's interest in UTP, the following would occur. E would be entitled to a $225,000 positive basis adjustment under section 743(b) with respect to the property of UTP. The entire basis adjustment would be allocated to UTP's only asset, its interest in LTP. In addition,

Reg. § 1.705-2(c)(2)

the sale of C's interest in UTP would be treated as a deemed sale of E's share of UTP's interest in LTP for purposes of sections 754 and 743. The deemed selling price of E's share of UTP's interest in LTP would be $250,000 (E's share of UTP's adjusted basis in LTP, $25,000, plus E's basis adjustment under section 743(b) with respect to the assets of UTP, $225,000). The deemed sale of E's share of UTP's interest in LTP would trigger a basis adjustment under section 743(b) of $225,000 with respect to the assets of LTP (the excess of E's share of UTP's adjusted basis in LTP, including E's basis adjustment ($225,000), $250,000, over E's share of the adjusted basis of LTP's property, $25,000). This $225,000 adjustment by LTP would be allocated to LTP's only asset, the E stock, and would be segregated and allocated solely to E. The amount of LTP's gain from the sale of the E stock (before considering section 743(b)) would be $1,900,000. E's share of this gain, $475,000, would be offset in part by the $225,000 basis adjustment under section 743(b), so that E would recognize gain equal to $250,000 in the absence of section 1032.

(v) If the basis of E's interest in UTP were increased by $250,000, the total basis of E's interest would equal $500,000. This would conform to E's share of UTP's basis in the LTP interest ($1,500,000 × 1/3 = $500,000) as well as E's indirect share of the cash held by LTP ((1/3 × 3/4) × $2,000,000 = $500,000). Such a basis adjustment does not create the opportunity for the recognition of an inappropriate loss by E on a subsequent disposition of E's interest in UTP and is consistent with the purpose of this section. Accordingly, under this paragraph (c), of the $475,000 gain allocated to E, only $250,000 will apply to increase the adjusted basis of E in UTP under section 705(a)(1). E's adjusted basis in its UTP interest following the sale of the E stock is $500,000.

Example 2. Acquisition of lower-tier partnership interest by upper-tier partnership. (i) A, corporation B, and C form an equal partnership (UTP), with each partner contributing $100,000. D, E, and F also form an equal partnership (LTP), with each partner contributing $30,000. LTP purchases stock in corporation B for $90,000, which appreciates in value to $900,000. LTP has no liabilities. UTP purchases D's interest in LTP for $300,000. LTP does not have an election under section 754 in effect for the taxable year of UTP's purchase. LTP later sells the B stock for $900,000. UTP's share of the gain is $270,000, and B's share of that gain is $90,000. Under section 1032, B does not recognize its share of the gain.

(ii) With respect to the basis of UTP's interest in LTP, if all of the gain from the sale of the B stock (including B's share) were to increase the basis of UTP's interest in LTP, UTP's basis in the LTP interest would be $570,000 ($300,000 + $270,000), and the fair market value of such interest would be $300,000, so that B would be allocated a loss of $90,000 (($570,000 − $300,000) × 1/3) if UTP sold its interest in LTP immediately after LTP's disposition of the B stock. It would be inappropriate for B to recognize a taxable loss of $90,000 upon a disposition of UTP's interest in LTP. B would not incur an economic loss in the transaction, and B was not allocated a taxable gain upon LTP's disposition of the B stock that appropriately would be offset by a taxable loss on the disposition of UTP's interest in LTP. Accordingly, increasing UTP's basis in its LTP interest by the gain allocated to B from the sale of the B stock is not consistent with the purpose of this section. (Conversely, because E and F were allocated taxable gain on the disposition of the B stock, it would be appropriate to increase E's and F's bases in their respective interests in LTP by the full amount of such gain.)

(iii) The appropriate basis adjustment for UTP's interest in LTP upon the disposition of the B stock by LTP can be determined as the amount of gain that UTP would have recognized (in the absence of section 1032) upon the sale by LTP of the B stock if the portion of the gain allocated to UTP that subsequently is allocated to B were determined as if LTP had made an election under section 754 for the taxable year in which UTP acquired its interest in LTP. If a section 754 election had been in effect for LTP for the year in which UTP acquired its interest in LTP, then with respect to B, the following would occur. UTP would be entitled to a $90,000 positive basis adjustment under section 743(b), allocable to B, in the property of LTP. The entire basis adjustment would be allocated to LTP's only asset, its B stock. The amount of LTP's gain from the sale of the B stock (before considering section 743(b)) would be $810,000. UTP's share of this gain, $270,000, would be offset, in part, by the basis adjustment under section 743(b), so that UTP would recognize gain equal to $180,000.

(iv) If the basis of UTP's interest in LTP were increased by $180,000, the total basis of UTP's partnership interest would equal $480,000. This would conform to the sum of UTP's share of the cash held by LTP (1/3 × $900,000 = $300,000) and the taxable gain recognized by A and C on the disposition of the B stock that appropriately may be offset on the disposition of their interests in UTP ($90,000 + $90,000 = $180,000). Such a basis adjustment does not inap-

Reg. § 1.705-2(c)(2)

propriately create the opportunity for the allocation of a loss to B on a subsequent disposition of UTP's interest in LTP and is consistent with the purpose of this section. Accordingly, of the $270,000 gain allocated to UTP, only $180,000 will apply to increase the adjusted basis of UTP in LTP under section 705(a)(1). Such $180,000 basis increase must be segregated and allocated $90,000 each to solely A and C. UTP's adjusted basis in its LTP interest following the sale of the B stock is $480,000.

(v) With respect to B's interest in UTP, if B's share of the gain allocated to UTP and then to B were to increase the basis of B's interest in UTP, B would have a UTP partnership interest with an adjusted basis of $190,000 ($100,000 + $90,000) and a value of $100,000, so that B would recognize a loss of $90,000 if B sold its interest in UTP immediately after LTP's disposition of the B stock. It would be inappropriate for B to recognize a taxable loss of $90,000 upon a disposition of its interest in UTP because B would not incur an economic loss in the transaction, and B did not recognize a taxable gain upon LTP's disposition of the B stock that appropriately would be offset by a taxable loss on the disposition of its interest in UTP. Accordingly, increasing B's basis in its UTP interest by the gain allocated to B from the sale of the B stock is not consistent with the purpose of this section. (Conversely, because A and C were allocated taxable gain on the disposition of the B stock that is a result of LTP not having a section 754 election in effect, it would be appropriate for A and C to recognize an offsetting taxable loss on the disposition of A's and C's interests in UTP. Accordingly, it would be appropriate to increase A's and C's bases in their respective interests in UTP by the amount of gain recognized by A and C.)

(vi) The appropriate basis adjustment for B's interest in UTP upon the disposition of the B stock by LTP can be determined as the amount of gain that B would have recognized (in the absence of section 1032) upon the sale by LTP of the B stock if the portion of the gain allocated to UTP that is subsequently allocated to B were determined as if LTP had made an election under section 754 for the taxable year in which UTP acquired its interest in LTP. If a section 754 election had been in effect for LTP for the year in which UTP acquired its interest in LTP, then with respect to B, the following would occur. UTP would be entitled to a basis adjustment under section 743(b) in the property of LTP of $90,000 with respect to B. The entire basis adjustment would be allocated to LTP's only asset, its B stock. The amount of LTP's gain from the sale of the B stock (before considering section 743(b)) would be $810,000. UTP's share of this gain, $270,000, would be offset, in part, by the $90,000 basis adjustment under section 743(b), so that UTP would recognize gain equal to $180,000. The $90,000 basis adjustment would completely offset the gain that otherwise would be allocated to B.

(vii) If no gain were allocated to B so that the basis of B's interest in UTP was not increased, the total basis of B's interest would equal $100,000. This would conform to B's share of UTP's basis in the LTP interest (($480,000 − $180,000 (i.e., A's and C's share of the basis that should offset taxable gain recognized as a result of LTP's failure to have a section 754 election)) × 1/3 = $100,000) as well as B's indirect share of the cash held by LTP ((1/3 × 1/3) × $900,000 = $100,000). Such a basis adjustment does not create the opportunity for the recognition of an inappropriate loss by B on a subsequent disposition of B's interest in UTP and is consistent with the purpose of this section. Accordingly, under this paragraph (c), of the $90,000 gain allocated to B, none will apply to increase the adjusted basis of B in UTP under section 705(a)(1). B's adjusted basis in its UTP interest following the sale of the B stock is $100,000.

(viii) Immediately after LTP's disposition of the B stock, UTP sells its interest in LTP for $300,000. UTP's adjusted basis in its LTP interest is $480,000, $180,000 of which must be allocated $90,000 each to A and C. Accordingly, upon UTP's sale of its interest in LTP, UTP realizes $180,000 of loss, and A and C in turn each realize $90,000 of loss.

(d) *Positions in Stock.* For purposes of this section, stock includes any position in stock to which section 1032 applies.

(e) *Effective date.* This section applies to gain or loss allocated with respect to sales or exchanges of stock occurring after December 6, 1999, except that paragraph (d) of this section is applicable with respect to sales or exchanges of stock occurring on or after March 29, 2002, and the fourth sentence of paragraph (a), paragraph (b)(2), and the third sentence of paragraph (c)(1) of this section are applicable with respect to sales or exchanges of stock occurring on or after March 18, 2003. [Reg. § 1.705-2.]

☐ [T.D. 8986, 3-28-2002. *Amended by T.D.* 9049, 3-17-2003.]

[Reg. § 1.706-1]

§ 1.706-1. **Taxable years of partner and partnership.**—(a) *Year in which partnership income is includible.* (1) In computing taxable income for a taxable year, a partner is required to include the partner's distributive share of partnership items set forth in section 702 and the regulations thereunder for any partnership taxable year ending within or with the partner's taxable year. A partner must also include in taxable income for a taxable year guaranteed payments under section 707(c) that are deductible by the partnership under its method of accounting in the partnership taxable year ending within or with the partner's taxable year.

(2) The rules of this paragraph (a)(1) may be illustrated by the following example:

Example. Partner A reports income using a calendar year, while the partnership of which A is a member reports its income using a fiscal year ending May 31. The partnership reports its income and deductions under the cash method of accounting. During the partnership taxable year ending May 31, 2002, the partnership makes guaranteed payments of $120,000 to A for services and for the use of capital. Of this amount, $70,000 was paid to A between June 1 and December 31, 2001, and the remaining $50,000 was paid to A between January 1 and May 31, 2002. The entire $120,000 paid to A is includible in A's taxable income for the calendar year 2002 (together with A's distributive share of partnership items set forth in section 702 for the partnership taxable year ending May 31, 2002).

(3) If a partner receives distributions under section 731 or sells or exchanges all or part of a partnership interest, any gain or loss arising therefrom does not constitute partnership income.

(b) *Taxable year*—(1) *Partnership treated as a taxpayer.* The taxable year of a partnership must be determined as though the partnership were a taxpayer.

(2) *Partnership's taxable year*—(i) *Required taxable year.* Except as provided in paragraph (b)(2)(ii) of this section, the taxable year of a partnership must be—

(A) The majority interest taxable year, as defined in section 706(b)(4);

(B) If there is no majority interest taxable year, the taxable year of all of the principal partners of the partnership, as defined in 706(b)(3) (the principal partners' taxable year); or

(C) If there is no majority interest taxable year or principal partners' taxable year, the taxable year that produces the least aggregate deferral of income as determined under paragraph (b)(3) of this section.

(ii) *Exceptions.* A partnership may have a taxable year other than its required taxable year if it makes an election under section 444, elects to use a 52-53-week taxable year that ends with reference to its required taxable year or a taxable year elected under section 444, or establishes a business purpose for such taxable year and obtains approval of the Commissioner under section 442.

(3) *Least aggregate deferral*—(i) *Taxable year that results in the least aggregate deferral of income.* The taxable year that results in the least aggregate deferral of income will be the taxable year of one or more of the partners in the partnership which will result in the least aggregate deferral of income to the partners. The aggregate deferral for a particular year is equal to the sum of the products determined by multiplying the month(s) of deferral for each partner that would be generated by that year and each partner's interest in partnership profits for that year. The partner's taxable year that produces the lowest sum when compared to the other partner's taxable years is the taxable year that results in the least aggregate deferral of income to the partners. If the calculation results in more than one taxable year qualifying as the taxable year with the least aggregate deferral, the partnership may select any one of those taxable years as its taxable year. However, if one of the qualifying taxable years is also the partnership's existing taxable year, the partnership must maintain its existing taxable year. The determination of the taxable year that results in the least aggregate deferral of income generally must be made as of the beginning of the partnership's current taxable year. The director, however, may determine that the first day of the current taxable year is not the appropriate testing day and require the use of some other day or period that will more accurately reflect the ownership of the partnership and thereby the actual aggregate deferral to the partners where the partners engage in a transaction that has as its principal purpose the avoidance of the principles of this section. Thus, for example the preceding sentence would apply where there is a transfer of an interest in the partnership that results in a temporary transfer of that interest principally for purposes of qualifying for a specific taxable year under the principles of this section. For purposes of this section, deferral to each partner is measured in terms of months from the end of the partnership's taxable year forward to the end of the partner's taxable year.

(ii) *Determination of the taxable year of a partner or partnership that uses a 52-53-week taxable year.* For purposes of the calculation described in paragraph (b)(3)(i) of this section, the taxable year of a partner or partnership that uses a 52-53-week taxable year must be the same year determined under the rules of section 441(f) and

Determination of Tax Liability

the regulations thereunder with respect to the inclusion of income by the partner or partnership.

(iii) *Special de minimis rule.* If the taxable year that results in the least aggregate deferral produces an aggregate deferral that is less than .5 when compared to the aggregate deferral of the current taxable year, the partnership's current taxable year will be treated as the taxable year with the least aggregate deferral. Thus, the partnership will not be permitted to change its taxable year.

(iv) *Examples.* The principles of this section may be illustrated by the following examples:

Example 1. Partnership P is on a fiscal year ending June 30. Partner A reports income on the fiscal year ending June 30 and Partner B reports income on the fiscal year ending July 31. A and B each have a 50 percent interest in partnership profits. For its taxable year beginning July 1, 1987, the partnership will be required to retain its taxable year since the fiscal year ending June 30 results in the least aggregate deferral of income to the partners. This determination is made as follows:

Test 6/30	Year End	Interest in Partnership Profits	Months of Deferral for 6/30 Year End	Interest × Deferral
Partner A	6/30	.5	0	0
Partner B	7/31	.5	1	.5
Aggregate deferral				.5

Test 7/31	Year End	Interest in Partnership Profits	Months of Deferral for 7/31 Year End	Interest × Deferral
Partner A	6/30	.5	11	5.5
Partner B	7/31	.5	0	0
Aggregate deferral				5.5

Example 2. The facts are the same as in *Example 1* except that A reports income on the calendar year and B reports on the fiscal year ending November 30. For the partnership's taxable year beginning July 1, 1987, the partnership is required to change its taxable year to a fiscal year ending November 30 because such year results in the least aggregate deferral of income to the partners. This determination is made as follows:

Test 12/31	Year End	Interest in Partnership Profits	Months of Deferral for 12/31 Year End	Interest × Deferral
Partner A	12/31	.5	0	0
Partner B	11/30	.5	11	5.5
Aggregate deferral				5.5

Test 11/30	Year End	Interest in Partnership Profits	Months of Deferral for 11/30 Year End	Interest × Deferral
Partner A	12/31	.5	1	.5
Partner B	11/30	.5	0	0
Aggregate deferral				.5

Example 3. The facts are the same as in *Example 2* except that B reports income on the fiscal year ending June 30. For the partnership's taxable year beginning July 1, 1987, each partner's taxable year will result in identical aggregate deferral of income. If the partnership's current taxable year was neither a fiscal year ending June 30 nor the calendar year, the partnership would select either the fiscal year ending June 30 or the calendar year as its taxable year. However, since the partnership's current taxable year ends June 30, it must retain its current taxable year. The determination is made as follows:

Reg. § 1.706-1(b)(3)

Determination of Tax Liability

See p. 20,601 for regulations not amended to reflect law changes

Test 12/31	Year End	Interest in Partnership Profits	Months of Deferral for 12/31 Year End	Interest × Deferral
Partner A	12/31	.5	0	0
Partner B	6/30	.5	6	3.0
Aggregate deferral				3.0

Test 6/30	Year End	Interest in Partnership Profits	Months of Deferral for 6/30 Year End	Interest × Deferral
Partner A	12/31	.5	6	3.0
Partner B	6/30	.5	0	0
Aggregate deferral				3.0

Example 4. The facts are the same as in *Example 1* except that on December 31, 1987, partner A sells a 4 percent interest in the partnership to Partner C, who reports income on the fiscal year ending June 30, and a 40 percent interest in the partnership to Partner D, who also reports income on the fiscal year ending June 30. The taxable year beginning July 1, 1987, is unaffected by the sale. However, for the taxable year beginning July 31, 1988, the partnership must determine the taxable year resulting in the least aggregate deferral as of July 1, 1988. In this case, the partnership will be required to retain its taxable year since the fiscal year ending June 30 continues to be the taxable year that results in the least aggregate deferral of income to the partners.

Example 5. The facts are the same as in *Example 4* except that Partner D reports income on the fiscal year ending April 30. As in *Example 4*, the taxable year during which the sale took place is unaffected by the shifts in interests. However, for its taxable year beginning July 1, 1988, the partnership will be required to change its taxable year to the fiscal year ending April 30. This determination is made as follows:

Test 7/31	Year End	Interest in Partnership Profits	Months of Deferral for 7/31 Year End	Interest × Deferral
Partner A	6/30	.06	11	.66
Partner B	7/31	.5	0	0
Partner C	6/30	.04	11	.44
Partner D	4/30	.4	9	3.60
Aggregate deferral				4.70

Test 6/30	Year End	Interest in Partnership Profits	Months of Deferral for 6/30 Year End	Interest × Deferral
Partner A	6/30	.06	0	0
Partner B	7/31	.5	1	.5
Partner C	6/30	.04	0	0
Partner D	4/30	.4	10	4.0
Aggregate deferral				4.5

Test 4/30	Year End	Interest in Partnership Profits	Months of Deferral for 4/30 Year End	Interest × Deferral
Partner A	6/30	.06	2	.12
Partner B	7/31	.5	3	1.50
Partner C	6/30	.04	2	.08
Partner D	4/30	.4	0	0
Aggregate deferral				1.70

Reg. § 1.706-1(b)(3)

Determination of Tax Liability

§ 1.706-1(b)(3) Test:

Current taxable year (June 30)	4.5
Less: Taxable year producing the least aggregate deferral (April 30)	1.7
Additional aggregate deferral (greater than .5)	2.8

Example 6. (i) Partnership P has two partners, A who reports income on the fiscal year ending March 31, and B who reports income on the fiscal year ending July 31. A and B share profits equally. P has determined its taxable year under paragraph (b)(3) of this section to be the fiscal year ending March 31 as follows:

Test 3/31	Year End	Interest in Partnership Profits	Deferral for 3/31 Year End	Interest × Deferral
Partner A	3/31	.5	0	0
Partner B	7/31	.5	4	2
Aggregate deferral				2

Test 7/31	Year End	Interest in Partnership Profits	Deferral for 7/31 Year End	Interest × Deferral
Partner A	3/31	.5	8	4
Partner B	7/31	.5	0	0
Aggregate deferral				4

(ii) In May 1988, Partner A sells a 45 percent interest in the partnership to C, who reports income on the fiscal year ending April 30. For the taxable period beginning April 1, 1989, the fiscal year ending April 30 is the taxable year that produces the least aggregate deferral of income to the partners. However, under paragraph (b)(3)(iii) of this section the partnership is required to retain its fiscal year ending March 31. This determination is made as follows:

Test 3/31	Year End	Interest in Partnership Profits	Deferral for 3/31 Year End	Interest × Deferral
Partner A	3/31	.05	0	0
Partner B	7/31	.5	4	2.0
Partner C	4/30	.45	1	.45
Aggregate deferral				2.45

Test 7/31	Year End	Interest in Partnership Profits	Deferral for 7/31 Year End	Interest × Deferral
Partner A	3/31	.05	8	.40
Partner B	7/31	.5	0	0
Partner C	4/30	.45	9	4.05
Aggregate deferral				4.45

Test 4/30	Year End	Interest in Partnership Profits	Deferral for 4/30 Year End	Interest × Deferral
Partner A	3/31	.05	11	.55
Partner B	7/31	.5	3	1.50
Partner C	4/30	.45	0	0
Aggregate deferral				2.05

§ 1.706-1(b)(3) Test:

Current taxable year (3/31)	2.45
Less: Taxable year producing the least aggregate deferral (4/30)	2.05
Additional aggregate deferral (less than .5)	.40

(4) *Measurement of partner's profits and capital interest*—(i) *In general.* The rules of this paragraph (b)(4) apply in determining the majority interest taxable year, the principal partners'

Reg. § 1.706-1(b)(4)

taxable year, and the least aggregate deferral taxable year.

(ii) *Profits interest*—(A) *In general.* For purposes of section 706(b), a partner's interest in partnership profits is generally the partner's percentage share of partnership profits for the current partnership taxable year. If the partnership does not expect to have net income for the current partnership taxable year, then a partner's interest in partnership profits instead must be the partner's percentage share of partnership net income for the first taxable year in which the partnership expects to have net income.

(B) *Percentage share of partnership net income.* The partner's percentage share of partnership net income for a partnership taxable year is the ratio of: the partner's distributive share of partnership net income for the taxable year, to the partnership's net income for the year. If a partner's percentage share of partnership net income for the taxable year depends on the amount or nature of partnership income for that year (due to, for example, preferred returns or special allocations of specific partnership items), then the partnership must make a reasonable estimate of the amount and nature of its income for the taxable year. This estimate must be based on all facts and circumstances known to the partnership as of the first day of the current partnership taxable year. The partnership must then use this estimate in determining the partners' interests in partnership profits for the taxable year.

(C) *Distributive share.* For purposes of this paragraph (b)(4)(ii), a partner's distributive share of partnership net income is determined by taking into account all rules and regulations affecting that determination, including, without limitation, sections 704(b), (c), and (e), 736, and 743.

(iii) *Capital interest.* Generally, a partner's interest in partnership capital is determined by reference to the assets of the partnership that the partner would be entitled to upon withdrawal from the partnership or upon liquidation of the partnership. If the partnership maintains capital accounts in accordance with § 1.704-1(b)(2)(iv), then for purposes of section 706(b), the partnership may assume that a partner's interest in partnership capital is the ratio of the partner's capital account to all partners' capital accounts as of the first day of the partnership taxable year.

(5) *Taxable year of a partnership with tax-exempt partners*—(i) *Certain tax-exempt partners disregarded.* In determining the taxable year (the current year) of a partnership under section 706(b) and the regulations thereunder, a partner that is tax-exempt under section 501(a) shall be disregarded if such partner was not subject to tax, under chapter 1 of the Internal Revenue Code, on any income attributable to its investment in the partnership during the partnership's taxable year immediately preceding the current year. However, if a partner that is tax-exempt under section 501(a) was not a partner during the partnership's immediately preceding taxable year, such partner will be disregarded for the current year if the partnership reasonably believes that the partner will not be subject to tax, under chapter 1 of the Internal Revenue Code, on any income attributable to such partner's investment in the partnership during the current year.

(ii) *Example.* The provisions of paragraph (b)(5)(i) of this section may be illustrated by the following example:

Example. Assume that partnership A has historically used the calendar year as its taxable year. In addition, assume that A is owned by 5 partners, 4 calendar year individuals (each owning 10 percent of A's profits and capital) and a tax-exempt organization (owning 60 percent of A's profits and capital). The tax-exempt organization has never had unrelated business taxable income with respect to A and has historically used a June 30 fiscal year. Finally, assume that A desires to retain the calendar year for its taxable year beginning January 1, 2003. Under these facts and but for the special rule in paragraph (b)(5)(i) of this section, A would be required under section 706(b)(1)(B)(i) to change to a year ending June 30, for its taxable year beginning January 1, 2003. However, under the special rule provided in paragraph (b)(5)(i) of this section the partner that is tax-exempt is disregarded, and A must retain the calendar year, under section 706(b)(1)(B)(i), for its taxable year beginning January 1.

(iii) *Effective date.* The provisions of this paragraph (b)(5) are applicable for taxable years beginning on or after July 23, 2002. For taxable years beginning before July 23, 2002, see § 1.706-3T as contained in 26 CFR part 1 revised April 1, 2002.

(6) *Certain foreign partners disregarded*—(i) *Interests of disregarded foreign partners not taken into account.* In determining the taxable year (the current taxable year) of a partnership under section 706(b) and the regulations thereunder, any interest held by a disregarded foreign partner is not taken into account. A foreign partner is a disregarded foreign partner unless such partner is allocated any gross income of the partnership that was effectively connected (or treated as effectively connected) with the conduct of a trade or business within the United States during the partnership's taxable year immediately pre-

ceding the current taxable year (or, if such partner was not a partner during the partnership's immediately preceding taxable year, the partnership reasonably believes that the partner will be allocated any such income during the current taxable year) and taxation of that income is not otherwise precluded under any U.S. income tax treaty.

(ii) *Definition of foreign partner.* For purposes of this paragraph (b)(6), a foreign partner is any partner that is not a U.S. person (as defined in section 7701(a)(30)), except that a partner that is a controlled foreign corporation (as defined in section 957(a)) or a foreign personal holding company (as defined in section 552) shall not be treated as a foreign partner.

(iii) *Minority interest rule.* If each partner that is not a disregarded foreign partner under paragraph (b)(6)(i) of this section (regarded partner) holds less than a 10-percent interest, and the regarded partners, in the aggregate, hold less than a 20-percent interest in the capital or profits of the partnership, then paragraph (b)(6)(i) of this section does not apply. In determining ownership in a partnership for purposes of this paragraph (b)(6)(iii), each regarded partner is treated as owning any interest in the partnership owned by a related partner. For this purpose, partners are treated as related if they are related within the meaning of sections 267(b) or 707(b) (using the language "10 percent" instead of "50 percent" each place it appears). However, for purposes of determining if partners hold less than a 20-percent interest in the aggregate, the same interests will not be considered as being owned by more than one regarded partner.

(iv) *Example.* The provisions of paragraph (b)(6) of this section may be illustrated by the following example:

Example. Partnership B is owned by two partners, F, a foreign corporation that owns a 95-percent interest in the capital and profits of partnership B, and D, a domestic corporation that owns the remaining 5-percent interest in the capital and profits of partnership B. Partnership B is not engaged in the conduct of a trade or business within the United States, and, accordingly, partnership B does not earn any income that is effectively connected with a U.S. trade or business. F uses a March 31 fiscal year, and causes partnership B to maintain its books and records on a March 31 fiscal year as well. D is a calendar year taxpayer. Under paragraph (b)(6)(i) of this section, F would be disregarded and partnership B's taxable year would be determined by reference to D. However, because D owns less than a 10-percent interest in the capital and profits of partnership B, the minority interest rule of paragraph (b)(6)(iii) of this section applies, and partnership B must adopt the March 31 fiscal year for Federal tax purposes.

(v) *Effective date*—(A) *Generally.* The provisions of this paragraph (b)(6) are applicable for the first taxable year of a partnership other than an existing partnership that begins on or after July 23, 2002. For this purpose, an existing partnership is a partnership that was formed prior to September 23, 2002.

(B) *Voluntary change in taxable year.* An existing partnership may change its taxable year to a year determined in accordance with this section. An existing partnership that makes such a change will cease to be exempted from the requirements of paragraph (b)(6) of this section.

(C) *Subsequent sale or exchange of interests.* If an existing partnership terminates under section 708(b)(1)(B), the resulting partnership is not an existing partnership for purposes of paragraph (b)(6)(v)(A) of this section.

(D) *Transition rule.* If, in the first taxable year beginning on or after July 23, 2002, an existing partnership voluntarily changes its taxable year to a year determined in accordance with this paragraph (b)(6), then the partners of that partnership may apply the provisions of § 1.702-3T to take into account all items of income, gain, loss, deduction, and credit attributable to the partnership year of change ratably over a four-year period.

(7) *Adoption of taxable year.* A newly-formed partnership may adopt, in accordance with § 1.441-1(c), its required taxable year, a taxable year elected under section 444, or a 52-53-week taxable year ending with reference to its required taxable year or a taxable year elected under section 444 without securing the approval of the Commissioner. If a newly-formed partnership wants to adopt any other taxable year, it must establish a business purpose and secure the approval of the Commissioner under section 442.

(8) *Change in taxable year*—(i) *Partnerships-*(A) *Approval required.* An existing partnership may change its taxable year only by securing the approval of the Commissioner under section 442 or making an election under section 444. However, a partnership may obtain automatic approval for certain changes, including a change to its required taxable year, pursuant to administrative procedures published by the Commissioner.

(B) *Short period tax return.* A partnership that changes its taxable year must make its return for a short period in accordance with section 443, but must not annualize the partnership taxable income.

Reg. § 1.706-1(b)(8)

(C) *Change in required taxable year.* If a partnership is required to change to its majority interest taxable year, then no further change in the partnership's required taxable year is required for either of the two years following the year of the change. This limitation against a second change within a three-year period applies only if the first change was to the majority interest taxable year and does not apply following a change in the partnership's taxable year to the principal partners' taxable year or the least aggregate deferral taxable year.

(ii) *Partners.* Except as otherwise provided in the Internal Revenue Code or the regulations thereunder (e.g., section 859 regarding real estate investment trusts or § 1.442-2(c) regarding a subsidiary changing to its consolidated parent's taxable year), a partner may not change its taxable year without securing the approval of the Commissioner under section 442. However, certain partners may be eligible to obtain automatic approval to change their taxable years pursuant to the regulations or administrative procedures published by the Commissioner. A partner that changes its taxable year must make its return for a short period in accordance with section 443.

(9) *Retention of taxable year.* In certain cases, a partnership will be required to change its taxable year unless it obtains the approval of the Commissioner under section 442, or makes an election under section 444, to retain its current taxable year. For example, a partnership using a taxable year that corresponds to its required taxable year must obtain the approval of the Commissioner to retain such taxable year if its required taxable year changes as a result of a change in ownership, unless the partnership previously obtained approval for its current taxable year or, if appropriate, makes an election under section 444.

(10) *Procedures for obtaining approval or making a section 444 election.* See § 1.442-1(b) for procedures to obtain the approval of the Commissioner (automatically or otherwise) to adopt, change, or retain a taxable year. See §§ 1.444-1T and 1.444-2T for qualifications, and § 1.444-3T for procedures, for making an election under section 444.

(11) *Effect of partner elections under section 444*—(i) *Election taken into account.* For purposes of section 706(b)(1)(B), any section 444 election by a partner in a partnership shall be taken into account in determining the taxable year of the partnership. See § 1.7519-1T(d), *Example (4).*

(ii) *Effective date.* The provisions of this paragraph (b)(11) are applicable for taxable years beginning on or after July 23, 2002. For taxable years beginning before July 23, 2002, see § 1.706-3T as contained in 26 CFR part 1 revised April 1, 2002.

(c) *Closing of partnership year*—(1) *General rule.* Section 706(c) and this paragraph provide rules governing the closing of partnership years. The closing of a partnership taxable year or a termination of a partnership for Federal income tax purposes is not necessarily governed by the "dissolution", "liquidation", etc., of a partnership under State or local law. The taxable year of a partnership shall not close as the result of the death of a partner, the entry of a new partner, the liquidation of a partner's entire interest in the partnership (as defined in section 761(d)), or the sale or exchange of a partner's interest in the partnership, except in the case of a termination of a partnership and except as provided in subparagraph (2) of this paragraph. In the case of termination, the partnership taxable year closes for all partners as of the date of termination. See section 708(b) and paragraph (b) of § 1.708-1.

(2) *Partner who retires or sells interest in partnership*—(i) *Disposition of entire interest.* A partnership taxable year shall close with respect to a partner who sells or exchanges his entire interest in a partnership, and with respect to a partner whose entire interest is liquidated. However, a partnership taxable year with respect to a partner who dies shall not close prior to the end of such partnership taxable year, or the time when such partner's interest (held by his estate or other successor) is liquidated or sold or exchanged, whichever is earlier. See subparagraph (3) of this paragraph.

(ii) *Inclusions in taxable income.* In the case of a sale, exchange, or liquidation of a partner's entire interest in a partnership, the partner shall include in his taxable income for his taxable year within or with which his membership in the partnership ends, his distributive share of items described in section 702(a), and any guaranteed payments under section 707(c), for his partnership taxable year ending with the date of such sale, exchange, or liquidation. In order to avoid an interim closing of the partnership books, such partner's distributive share of items described in section 702(a) may, by agreement among the partners, be estimated by taking his pro rata part of the amount of such items he would have included in his taxable income had he remained a partner until the end of the partnership taxable year. The proration may be based on the portion of the taxable year that has elapsed prior to the sale, exchange, or liquidation, or may be determined under any other method that is reasonable. Any partner who is the transferee of such partner's interest shall include in his taxable income, as his distributive share of items described in section 702(a) with respect to the acquired interest, the pro rata part (determined by the method used by the transferor partner) of the amount of such items he would have included had he been a partner from the beginning of the taxable year of the partnership. The application of this subdivision may be illustrated by the following example:

Example. Assume that a partner selling his partnership interest on June 30, 1955, has an adjusted basis for his interest of $5,000 on that date; that his pro rata share of partnership income up to June 30 is $15,000; and that he sells his interest for $20,000. Under the provisions of section 706(c)(2), the partnership year with respect to him closes at the time of the sale. The $15,000 is includible in his income as his distributive share and, under section 705, it increases the basis of his partnership interest to $20,000, which is also the selling price of his interest. Therefore, no gain is realized on the sale of his partnership interest. The purchaser of this partnership interest shall include in his income as his distributive share his pro rata part of partnership income for the remainder of the partnership taxable year.

(3) *Partner who dies.* (i) When a partner dies, the partnership taxable year shall not close with respect to such partner prior to the end of the partnership taxable year. The partnership taxable year shall continue both for the remaining partners and the decedent partner. Where the death of a partner results in the termination of the partnership, the partnership taxable year shall close for all partners on the date of such temination under section 708(b)(1)(A). See also paragraph (b)(1)(i)(*b*) of § 1.708-1 for the continuation of a 2-member partnership under certain circumstances after the death of a partner. However, if the decedent partner's estate or other successor sells or exchanges its entire interest in the partnership, or if its entire interest is liquidated, the partnership taxable year with respect to the estate or other successor in interest shall close on the date of such sale or exchange, or the date of completion of the liquidation.

(ii) The last return of a decedent partner shall include only his share of partnership taxable income for any partnership taxable year or years ending within or with the last taxable year for such decedent partner (i.e., the year ending with the date of his death). The distributive share of partnership taxable income for a partnership taxable year ending after the decedent's last taxable year is includible in the return of his estate or other successor in interest. If the estate or other successor in interest of a partner continues to share in the profits or losses of the partnership business, the distributive share thereof is includible in the taxable year of the estate or other successor in interest within or with which the taxable year of the partnership ends. See also paragraph (a)(1)(ii) of § 1.736-1. Where the estate or other successor in interest receives distributions, any gain or loss on such distributions is includible in its gross income for its taxable year in which the distribution is made.

(iii) If a partner (or a retiring partner), in accordance with the terms of the partnership agreement, designates a person to succeed to his interest in the partnership after his death, such designated person shall be regarded as a successor in interest of the deceased for purposes of this chapter. Thus, where a partner designates his widow as the successor in interest, her distributive share of income for the taxable year of the partnership ending within or with her taxable year may be included in a joint return in accordance with the provisions of sections 2 and 6013(a)(2) and (3).

(iv) If, under the terms of an agreement existing at the date of death of a partner, a sale or exchange of the decedent partner's interest in the partnership occurs upon that date, then the taxable year of the partnership with respect to such decedent partner shall close upon the date of death. See section 706(c)(2)(A)(i). The sale or exchange of a partnership interest does not, for the purpose of this rule, include any transfer of a partnership interest which occurs at death as a result of inheritance or any testamentary disposition.

(v) To the extent that any part of a distributive share of partnership income of the estate or other successor in interest of a deceased partner is attributable to the decedent for the period ending with the date of his death, such part of the distributive share is income in respect of the decedent under section 691. See section 691 and the regulations thereunder.

(vi) The provisions of this subparagraph may be illustrated by the following examples:

Example (1). B has a taxable year ending December 31 and is a member of partnership ABC, the taxable year of which ends on June 30. B dies on October 31, 1955. His estate (which as a new taxpayer may, under section 441 and the regulations thereunder, adopt any taxable year) adopts a taxable year ending October 31. The return of the decedent for the period January 1 to October 31, 1955, will include only his distributive share of taxable income of the partnership for its taxable year ending June 30, 1955. The distributive share of taxable income of the partnership for its taxable year ending June 30, 1956, arising

Reg. § 1.706-1(c)(3)

from the interest of the decedent, will be includible in the return of the estate for its taxable year ending October 31, 1956. That part of the distributive share attributable to the decedent for the period ending with the date of his death (July 1 through October 31, 1955) is income in respect of a decedent under section 691.

Example (2). Assume the same facts as in example (1) of this subdivision, except that, prior to B's death, B and D had agreed that, upon B's death, D would purchase B's interest for $10,000. When B dies on October 31, 1955, the partnership taxable year beginning July 1, 1955, closes with respect to him. Therefore, the return for B's last taxable year (January 1 to October 31, 1955) will include his distributive share of taxable income of the partnership for its taxable year ending June 30, 1955, plus his distributive share of partnership taxable income for the period July 1 to October 31, 1955. See subdivision (iv) of this subparagraph.

Example (3). H is a member of a partnership having a taxable year ending December 31. Both H and his wife W are on a calendar year and file joint returns. H dies on March 31, 1955. Administration of the estate is completed and the estate, including the partnership interest, is distributed to W as legatee on November 30, 1955. Such distribution by the estate is not a sale or exchange of H's partnership interest. No part of the taxable income of the partnership for the taxable year ending December 31, 1955, which is allocable to H, will be included in H's taxable income for his last taxable year (January 1 through March 31, 1955) or in the taxable income of H's estate for the taxable year April 1 through November 30, 1955. The distributive share of partnership taxable income for the full calendar year that is allocable to H will be includible in the taxable income of W for her taxable year ending December 31, 1955, and she may file a joint return under sections 2 and 6013(a)(3). That part of the distributive share attributable to the decedent for the period ending with the date of his death (January 1 through March 31, 1955) is income in respect of the decedent under section 691.

Example (4). M is a member of partnership JKM which operates on a calendar year. M and his wife S file joint returns for calendar years. In accordance with the partnership agreement, M designated S to succeed to his interest in the partnership upon his death. M, who had withdrawn $10,000 from the partnership before his death, dies on October 20, 1955. S's distributive share of income for the taxable year 1955 is $15,000 ($10,000 of which represents the amount withdrawn by M). S shall include $15,000 in her income, even though M received $10,000 of this amount before his death. S may file a joint return with M for the year 1955 under sections 2 and 6013(a). That part of the $15,000 distributive share attributable to the decedent for the period ending with the date of his death (January 1 through October 20, 1955) is income in respect of a decedent under section 691.

(4) *Disposition of less than entire interest.* If a partner sells or exchanges a part of his interest in a partnership, or if the interest of a partner is reduced, the partnership taxable year shall continue to its normal end. In such case, the partner's distributive share of items which he is required to include in his taxable income under the provisions of section 702(a) shall be determined by taking into account his varying interests in the partnership during the partnership taxable year in which such sale, exchange, or reduction of interest occurred.

(5) *Transfer of interest by gift.* The transfer of a partnership interest by gift does not close the partnership taxable year with respect to the donor. However, the income up to the date of gift attributable to the donor's interest shall be allocated to him under section 704(e)(2).

(d) *Effective date.* The rules of this section are applicable for taxable years ending on or after May 17, 2002, except for paragraph (c), which applies for taxable years beginning after December 31, 1953. [Reg. § 1.706-1.]

☐ [T.D. 6175, 5-23-56. Amended by T.D. 7286, 9-26-73; T.D. 8123, 2-4-87; T.D. 8996, 5-16-2002 and T.D. 9009, 7-22-2002.]

[Reg. § 1.706-2T]

§ 1.706-2T. **Temporary regulations; question and answer under the Tax Reform Act of 1984 (Temporary).**—*Question 1:* For purposes of section 706(d), how is an otherwise deductible amount that is deferred under section 267(a)(2) treated?

Answer 1: In the year the deduction is allowed, the deduction will constitute an allocable cash basis item under section 706(d)(2)(B)(iv). [Temporary Reg. § 1.706-2T.]

☐ [T.D. 7991; 11-29-84.]

[Reg. § 1.707-0]

§ 1.707-0. **Table of contents.**—This section lists the captions that appear in §§ 1.707-1 through 1.707-9.

§ 1.707-1. *Transactions between partner and partnership.*

(a) Partner not acting in capacity as partner.

Determination of Tax Liability

See p. 20,601 for regulations not amended to reflect law changes

(b) Certain sales or exchanges of property with respect to controlled partnerships.
    (1) Losses disallowed.
    (2) Gains treated as ordinary income.
    (3) Ownership of a capital or profits interest.
(c) Guaranteed payments.

§ 1.707-2. *Disguised payments for services.* [Reserved]

§ 1.707-3. *Disguised sales of property to partnership; general rules.*
  (a) Treatment of transfers as a sale.
    (1) In general.
    (2) Definition and timing of sale.
    (3) Application of disguised sale rules.
    (4) Deemed terminations under section 708.
  (b) Transfers treated as a sale.
    (1) In general.
    (2) Facts and circumstances.
  (c) Transfers made within two years presumed to be a sale.
    (1) In general.
    (2) Disclosure of transfers made within two years.
  (d) Transfers made more than two years apart presumed not to be a sale.
  (e) Scope.
  (f) Examples.

§ 1.707-4. *Disguised sales of property to partnership; special rules applicable to guaranteed payments, preferred returns, operating cash flow distributions, and reimbursements of preformation expenditures.*
  (a) Guaranteed payments and preferred returns.
    (1) Guaranteed payment not treated as part of a sale.
      (i) In general.
      (ii) Reasonable guaranteed payments.
      (iii) Unreasonable guaranteed payments.
    (2) Presumption regarding reasonable preferred returns.
    (3) Definition of reasonable preferred returns and guaranteed payments.
      (i) In general.
      (ii) Reasonable amount.
    (4) Examples.
  (b) Presumption regarding operating cash flow distributions.
    (1) In general.
    (2) Operating cash flow distributions.
      (i) In general.
      (ii) Operating cash flow safe harbor.
      (iii) Tiered partnerships.
  (c) Accumulation of guaranteed payments, preferred returns, and operating cash flow distributions.
  (d) Exception for reimbursements of preformation expenditures.
  (e) Other exceptions.

§ 1.707-5. *Disguised sales of property to partnership; special rules relating to liabilities.*
  (a) Liability assumed or taken subject to by partnership.
    (1) In general.
    (2) Partner's share of liability.
      (i) Recourse liability.
      (ii) Nonrecourse liability.
    (3) Reduction of partner's share of liability.
    (4) Special rule applicable to transfers of encumbered property to a partnership by more than one partner pursuant to a plan.
    (5) Special rule applicable to qualified liabilities.
    (6) Qualified liability of a partner defined.
    (7) Liability incurred within two years of transfer presumed to be in anticipation of the transfer.
      (i) In general.
      (ii) Disclosure of transfers of property subject to liabilities incurred within two years of the transfer.
  (b) Treatment of debt-financed transfers of consideration by partnerships.
    (1) In general.
    (2) Partner's allocable share of liability.
      (i) In general.
      (ii) Debt-financed transfers made pursuant to a plan.
        (A) In general.
        (B) Special rule.
      (iii) Reduction of partner's share of liability.
  (c) Refinancings.
  (d) Share of liability where assumption accompanied by transfer of money.
  (e) Tiered partnerships and other related persons.
  (f) Examples.

§ 1.707-6. *Disguised sales of property by partnership to partner; general rules.*
  (a) In general.
  (b) Special rules relating to liabilities.

Reg. § 1.707-0

(1) In general.

(2) Qualified liabilities.

(c) Disclosure rules.

(d) Examples.

§ 1.707-7. Disguised sales of partnership interests. [Reserved]

§ 1.707-8. Disclosure of certain information.

(a) In general.

(b) Method of providing disclosure.

(c) Disclosure by certain partnerships.

§ 1.707-9. Effective dates and transitional rules.

(a) Sections 1.707-3 through 1.707-6.

(1) In general.

(2) Transfers occurring on or before April 24, 1991.

(3) Effective date of section 73 of the Tax Reform Act of 1984.

(b) Section 1.707-8 disclosure of certain information. [Reg. § 1.707-0.]

☐ [T.D. 8439, 9-25-92.]

[Reg. § 1.707-1]

§ 1.707-1. Transactions between partner and partnership—(a) *Partner not acting in capacity as partner.* A partner who engages in a transaction with a partnership other than in his capacity as a partner shall be treated as if he were not a member of the partnership with respect to such transaction. Such transactions include, for example, loans of money or property by the partnership to the partner or by the partner to the partnership, the sale of property by the partner to the partnership, the purchase of property by the partner from the partnership, and the rendering of services by the partnership to the partner or by the partner to the partnership. Where a partner retains the ownership of property but allows the partnership to use such separately owned property for partnership purposes (for example, to obtain credit or to secure firm creditors by guaranty, pledge, or other agreement) the transaction is treated as one between a partnership and a partner not acting in his capacity as a partner. However, transfers of money or property by a partner to a partnership as contributions, or transfers of money or property by a partnership to a partner as distributions, are not transactions included within the provisions of this section. In all cases, the substance of the transaction will govern rather than its form. See paragraph (c)(3) of § 1.731-1.

(b) *Certain sales or exchanges of property with respect to controlled partnerships*—(1) *Losses disallowed.* (i) No deduction shall be allowed for a loss on a sale or exchange of property (other than an interest in the partnership), directly or indirectly, between a partnership and a partner who owns, directly or indirectly, more than 50 percent of the capital interest or profits interest in such partnership. A loss on a sale or exchange of property, directly or indirectly, between two partnerships in which the same persons own, directly or indirectly, more than 50 percent of the capital interest or profits interests in each partnership shall not be allowed.

(ii) If a gain is realized upon the subsequent sale or exchange by transferee of property with respect to which a loss was disallowed under the provisions of subdivision (i) of this subparagraph, section 267(d) (relating to amount of gain where loss previously disallowed) shall apply as though the loss were disallowed under section 267(a)(1).

(2) *Gains treated as ordinary income.* Any gain recognized upon the sale or exchange, directly or indirectly, of property which, in the hands of the transferee immediately after the transfer, is property other than a capital asset, as defined in section 1221, shall be ordinary income if the transaction is between a partnership and a partner who owns, directly or indirectly, more than 80 percent of the capital interest or profits interest in the partnership. This rule also applies where such a transaction is between partnerships in which the same persons own, directly or indirectly, more than 80 percent of the capital interests or profits interests in each partnership. The term "property other than a capital asset" includes (but is not limited to) trade accounts receivable, inventory, stock in trade, and depreciable or real property used in the trade or business.

(3) *Ownership of a capital or profits interest.* In determining the extent of the ownership by a partner, as defined in section 761(b), of his capital interest or profits interest in a partnership, the rules for constructive ownership of stock provided in section 267(c)(1), (2), (4), and (5) shall be applied for the purpose of section 707(b) and this paragraph. Under these rules, ownership of a capital or profits interest in a partnership may be attributed to a person who is not a partner as defined in section 761(b) in order that another partner may be considered the constructive owner of such interest under section 267(c). However, section 707(b)(1)(A) does not apply to a constructive owner of a partnership interest since he is not a partner as defined in section 761(b). For example, where trust T is a partner in the partnership ABT, and AW, A's wife, is the sole beneficiary of the trust, the ownership of a capital and profits interest in the partnership by T will be attributed

to AW only for the purpose of further attributing the ownership of such interest to A. See section 267(c)(1) and (5). If A, B, and T are equal partners, then A will be considered as owning more than 50 percent of the capital and profits interest in the partnership, and losses on transactions between him and the partnership will be disallowed by section 707(b)(1)(A). However, a loss sustained by AW on a sale or exchange of property with the partnership would not be disallowed by section 707, but will be disallowed to the extent provided in paragraph (b) of § 1.267(b)-1. See section 267(a) and (b), and the regulations thereunder.

(c) *Guaranteed payments.* Payments made by a partnership to a partner for services or for the use of capital are considered as made to a person who is not a partner, to the extent such payments are determined without regard to the income of the partnership. However, a partner must include such payments as ordinary income for his taxable year within or with which ends the partnership taxable year in which the partnership deducted such payments as paid or accrued under its method of accounting. See section 706(a) and paragraph (a) of § 1.706-1. Guaranteed payments are considered as made to one who is not a member of the partnership, only for the purposes of section 61(a) (relating to gross income) and section 162(a) (relating to trade or business expenses). For a guaranteed payment to be a partnership deduction, it must meet the same tests under section 162(a) as it would if the payment had been made to a person who is not a member of the partnership, and the rules of section 263 (relating to capital expenditures) must be taken into account. This rule does not affect the deductibility to the partnership of a payment described in section 736(a)(2) to a retiring partner or to a deceased partner's successor in interest. Guaranteed payments do not constitute an interest in partnership profits for purposes of sections 706(b)(3), 707(b), and 708(b). For the purposes of other provisions of the internal revenue laws, guaranteed payments are regarded as a partner's distributive share of ordinary income. Thus, a partner who receives guaranteed payments for a period during which he is absent from work because of personal injuries or sickness is not entitled to exclude such payments from his gross income under section 105(d). Similarly, a partner who receives guaranteed payments is not regarded as an employee of the partnership for the purposes of withholding of tax at source, deferred compensation plans, etc. The provisions of this paragraph may be illustrated by the following examples:

Example (1). Under the ABC partnership agreement, partner A is entitled to a fixed annual payment of $10,000 for services, without regard to the income of the partnership. His distributive share is 10 percent. After deducting the guaranteed payment, the partnership has $50,000 ordinary income. A must include $15,000 as ordinary income for his taxable year within or with which the partnership taxable year ends ($10,000 guaranteed payment plus $5,000 distributive share).

Example (2). Partner C in the CD partnership is to receive 30 percent of partnership income as determined before taking into account any guaranteed payments, but not less than $10,000. The income of the partnership is $60,000, and C is entitled to $18,000 (30 percent of $60,000) as his distributive share. No part of this amount is a guaranteed payment. However, if the partnership had income of $20,000 instead of $60,000, $6,000 (30 percent of $20,000) would be partner C's distributive share, and the remaining $4,000 payable to C would be a guaranteed payment.

Example (3). Partner X in the XY partnership is to receive a payment of $10,000 for services, plus 30 percent of the taxable income or loss of the partnership. After deducting the payment of $10,000 to partner X, the XY partnership has a loss of $9,000. Of this amount, $2,700 (30 percent of the loss) is X's distributive share of partnership loss and, subject to section 704(d), is to be taken into account by him in his return. In addition, he must report as ordinary income the guaranteed payment of $10,000 made to him by the partnership.

Example (4). Assume the same facts as in example (3) of this paragraph except that, instead of a $9,000 loss, the partnership has $30,000 in capital gains and no other items of income or deduction except the $10,000 paid X as a guaranteed payment. Since the items of partnership income or loss must be segregated under section 702(a), the partnership has a $10,000 ordinary loss and $30,000 in capital gains. X's 30 percent distributive shares of these amounts are $3,000 ordinary loss and $9,000 capital gain. In addition, X has received a $10,000 guaranteed payment which is ordinary income to him. [Reg. § 1.707-1.]

☐ [T.D. 6175, 5-23-56. *Amended by* T.D. 6312, 9-10-58 *and* T.D. 7891, 5-3-83.]

[Reg. § 1.707-2]

§ 1.707-2. Disguised payments for services.—[Reserved]

☐ [T.D. 8439, 9-25-92.]

[Reg. § 1.707-3]

§ 1.707-3. **Disguised sales of property to partnership; general rules.**—(a) *Treatment of transfers as a sale*—(1) *In general.* Except as otherwise provided in this section, if a transfer of property by a partner to a partnership and one or more transfers of money or other consideration by the partnership to that partner are described in paragraph (b)(1) of this section, the transfers are treated as a sale of property, in whole or in part, to the partnership.

(2) *Definition and timing of sale.* For purposes of §§ 1.707-3 through 1.707-5, the use of the term *sale* (or any variation of that word) to refer to a transfer of property by a partner to a partnership and a transfer of consideration by a partnership to a partner means a sale or exchange of that property, in whole or in part, to the partnership by the partner acting in a capacity other than as a member of the partnership, rather than a contribution and distribution to which sections 721 and 731, respectively, apply. A transfer that is treated as a sale under paragraph (a)(1) of this section is treated as a sale for all purposes of the Internal Revenue Code (*e.g.,* sections 453, 483, 1001, 1012, 1031 and 1274). The sale is considered to take place on the date that, under general principles of Federal tax law, the partnership is considered the owner of the property. If the transfer of money or other consideration from the partnership to the partner occurs after the transfer of property to the partnership, the partner and the partnership are treated as if, on the date of the sale, the partnership transferred to the partner an obligation to transfer to the partner money or other consideration.

(3) *Application of disguised sale rules.* If a person purports to transfer property to a partnership in a capacity as a partner, the rules of this section apply for purposes of determining whether the property was transferred in a disguised sale, even if it is determined after the application of the rules of this section that such person is not a partner. If after the application of the rules of this section to a purported transfer of property to a partnership, it is determined that no partnership exists because the property was actually sold, or it is otherwise determined that the contributed property is not owned by the partnership for tax purposes, the transferor of the property is treated as having sold the property to the person (or persons) that acquired ownership of the property for tax purposes.

(4) *Deemed terminations under section 708.* In applying the rules of this section, transfers resulting from a termination of a partnership under section 708(b)(1)(B) are disregarded.

(b) *Transfers treated as a sale*—(1) *In general.* A transfer of property (excluding money or an obligation to contribute money) by a partner to a partnership and a transfer of money or other consideration (including the assumption of or the taking subject to a liability) by the partnership to the partner constitute a sale of property, in whole or in part, by the partner to the partnership only if based on all the facts and circumstances—

(i) The transfer of money or other consideration would not have been made but for the transfer of property; and

(ii) In cases in which the transfers are not made simultaneously, the subsequent transfer is not dependent on the entrepreneurial risks of partnership operations.

(2) *Facts and circumstances.* The determination of whether a transfer of property by a partner to the partnership and a transfer of money or other consideration by the partnership to the partner constitute a sale, in whole or in part, under paragraph (b)(1) of this section is made based on all the facts and circumstances in each case. The weight to be given each of the facts and circumstances will depend on the particular case. Generally, the facts and circumstances existing on the date of the earliest of such transfers are the ones considered in determining whether a sale exists under paragraph (b)(1) of this section. Among the facts and circumstances that may tend to prove the existence of a sale under paragraph (b)(1) of this section are the following:

(i) That the timing and amount of a subsequent transfer are determinable with reasonable certainty at the time of an earlier transfer;

(ii) That the transferor has a legally enforceable right to the subsequent transfer;

(iii) That the partner's right to receive the transfer of money or other consideration is secured in any manner, taking into account the period during which it is secured;

(iv) That any person has made or is legally obligated to make contributions to the partnership in order to permit the partnership to make the transfer of money or other consideration;

(v) That any person has loaned or has agreed to loan the partnership the money or other consideration required to enable the partnership to make the transfer, taking into account whether any such lending obligation is subject to contingencies related to the results of partnership operations;

(vi) That the partnership has incurred or is obligated to incur debt to acquire the money or other consideration necessary to permit it to make the transfer, taking into account the likelihood that the partnership will be able to incur that debt (considering such factors as whether any person has agreed to guarantee or otherwise assume personal liability for that debt);

Reg. § 1.707-3(a)(2)

(vii) That the partnership holds money or other liquid assets, beyond the reasonable needs of the business, that are expected to be available to make the transfer (taking into account the income that will be earned from those assets);

(viii) That partnership distributions, allocations or control of partnership operations is designed to effect an exchange of the burdens and benefits of ownership of property;

(ix) That the transfer of money or other consideration by the partnership to the partner is disproportionately large in relationship to the partner's general and continuing interest in partnership profits; and

(x) That the partner has no obligation to return or repay the money or other consideration to the partnership, or has such an obligation but it is likely to become due at such a distant point in the future that the present value of that obligation is small in relation to the amount of money or other consideration transferred by the partnership to the partner.

(c) *Transfers made within two years presumed to be a sale*—(1) *In general.* For purposes of this section, if within a two-year period a partner transfers property to a partnership and the partnership transfers money or other consideration to the partner (without regard to the order of the transfers), the transfers are presumed to be a sale of the property to the partnership unless the facts and circumstances clearly establish that the transfers do not constitute a sale.

(2) *Disclosure of transfers made within two years.* Disclosure to the Internal Revenue Service in accordance with § 1.707-8 is required if—

(i) A partner transfers property to a partnership and the partnership transfers money or other consideration to the partner within a two-year period (without regard to the order of the transfers);

(ii) The partner treats the transfers other than as a sale for tax purposes; and

(iii) The transfer of money or other consideration to the partner is not presumed to be a guaranteed payment for capital under § 1.707-4(a)(1)(ii), is not a reasonable preferred return within the meaning of § 1.707-4(a)(3), and is not an operating cash flow distribution within the meaning of § 1.707-4(b)(2).

(d) *Transfers made more than two years apart presumed not to be a sale.* For purposes of this section, if a transfer of money or other consideration to a partner by a partnership and the transfer of property to the partnership by that partner are more than two years apart, the transfers are presumed not to be a sale of the property to the partnership unless the facts and circumstances clearly establish that the transfers constitute a sale.

(e) *Scope.* This section and §§ 1.707-4 through 1.707-9 apply to contributions and distributions of property described in section 707(a)(2)(A) and transfers described in section 707(a)(2)(B) of the Internal Revenue Code.

(f) *Examples.* The following examples illustrate the application of this section.

Example 1. Treatment of simultaneous transfers as a sale. A transfers property X to partnership AB on April 9, 1992, in exchange for an interest in the partnership. At the time of the transfer, property X has a fair market value of $4,000,000 and an adjusted tax basis of $1,200,000. Immediately after the transfer, the partnership transfers $3,000,000 in cash to A. Assume that, under this section, the partnership's transfer of cash to A is treated as part of a sale of property X to the partnership. Because the amount of cash A receives on April 9, 1992, does not equal the fair market value of the property, A is considered to have sold a portion of property X with a value of $3,000,000 to the partnership in exchange for the cash. Accordingly, A must recognize $2,100,000 of gain ($3,000,000 amount realized less $900,000 adjusted tax basis ($1,200,000 multiplied by $3,000,000/$4,000,000)). Assuming A receives no other transfers that are treated as consideration for the sale of the property under this section, A is considered to have contributed to the partnership, in A's capacity as a partner, $1,000,000 of the fair market value of the property with an adjusted tax basis of $300,000.

Example 2. Treatment of transfers at different times as a sale. (i) The facts are the same as in *Example 1*, except that the $3,000,000 is transferred to A one year after A's transfer of property X to the partnership. Assume that under this section the partnership's transfer of cash to A is treated as part of a sale of property X to the partnership. Assume also that the applicable Federal short-term rate for April, 1992, is 10 percent, compounded semiannually.

(ii) Under paragraph (a)(2) of this section, A and the partnership are treated as if, on April 9, 1992, A sold a portion of property X to the partnership in exchange for an obligation to transfer $3,000,000 to A one year later. Section 1274 applies to this obligation because it does not bear interest and is payable more than six months after the date of the sale. As a result, A's amount realized from the receipt of the partnership's obligation will be the imputed principal amount of the partnership's obligation to transfer $3,000,000 to A, which equals $2,721,088 (the present value

Reg. § 1.707-3(f)

on April 9, 1992, of a $3,000,000 payment due one year later, determined using a discount rate of 10 percent, compounded semiannually). Therefore, A's amount realized from the receipt of the partnership's obligation is $2,721,088 (without regard to whether the sale is reported under the installment method). A is therefore considered to have sold only $2,721,088 of the fair market value of property X. The remainder of the $3,000,000 payment ($278,912) is characterized in accordance with the provisions of section 1272. Accordingly, A must recognize $1,904,761 of gain ($2,721,088 amount realized less $816,327 adjusted tax basis ($1,200,000 multiplied by $2,721,088/$4,000,000)) on the sale of property X to the partnership. The gain is reportable under the installment method of section 453 if the sale is otherwise eligible. Assuming A receives no other transfers that are treated as consideration for the sale of property under this section, A is considered to have contributed to the partnership, in A's capacity as a partner, $1,278,912 of the fair market value of property X with an adjusted tax basis of $383,673.

Example 3. Operation of presumption for transfers within two years. (i) C transfers undeveloped land to the CD partnership in exchange for an interest in the partnership. The partnership intends to construct a building on the land. At the time the land is transferred to the partnership, it is unencumbered and has an adjusted tax basis of $500,000 and a fair market value of $1,000,000. The partnership agreement provides that upon completing construction of the building the partnership will distribute $900,000 to C.

(ii) If, within two years of C's transfer of land to the partnership, a transfer is made to C pursuant to the provision requiring a distribution upon completion of the building, the transfer is presumed to be, under paragraph (c) of this section, part of a sale of the land to the partnership. C may rebut the presumption that the transfer is part of a sale if the facts and circumstances clearly establish that—

(A) The transfer to C would have been made without regard to C's transfer of land to the partnership; or

(B) The partnership's obligation or ability to make this transfer to C depends, at the time of the transfer to the partnership, on the entrepreneurial risks of partnership operations.

(iii) For example, if the partnership will be able to fund the transfer of cash to C only to the extent that permanent loan proceeds exceed the cost of constructing the building, the fact that excess permanent loan proceeds will be available only if the cost to complete the building is significantly less than the amount projected by a reasonable budget would be evidence that the transfer to C is not part of a sale. Similarly, a condition that limits the amount of the permanent loan to the cost of constructing the building (and thereby limits the partnership's ability to make a transfer to C) unless all or a substantial portion of the building is leased would be evidence that the transfer to C is not part of a sale, if a significant risk exists that the partnership may not be able to lease the building to that extent. Another factor that may prove that the transfer of cash to C is not part of a sale would be that, at the time the land is transferred to the partnership, no lender has committed to make a permanent loan to fund the transfer of cash to C.

(iv) Facts indicating that the transfer of cash to C is not part of a sale, however, may be offset by other factors. An offsetting factor to restrictions on the permanent loan proceeds may be that the permanent loan is to be a recourse loan and certain conditions to the loan are likely to be waived by the lender because of the creditworthiness of the partners or the value of the partnership's other assets. Similarly, the factor that no lender has committed to fund the transfer of cash to C may be offset by facts establishing that the partnership is obligated to attempt to obtain such a loan and that its ability to obtain such a loan is not significantly dependent on the value that will be added by successful completion of the building, or that the partnership reasonably anticipates that it will have (and will utilize) an alternative source to fund the transfer of cash to C if the permanent loan proceeds are inadequate.

Example 4. Operation of presumption for transfers within two years. E is a partner in the equal EF partnership. The partnership owns two parcels of unimproved real property (*parcels 1 and 2*). Parcels 1 and 2 are unencumbered. Parcel 1 has a fair market value of $500,000, and parcel 2 has a fair market value of $1,500,000. E transfers additional unencumbered, unimproved real property (*parcel 3*) with a fair market value of $1,000,000 to the partnership in exchange for an increased interest in partnership profits of 66 2/3 percent. Immediately after this transfer, the partnership sells parcel 1 for $500,000 in a transaction not in the ordinary course of business. The partnership transfers the proceeds of the sale $333,333 to E and $166,667 to F in accordance with their respective partnership interests. The transfer of $333,333 to E is presumed to be, in accordance with paragraph (c) of this section, a sale, in part, of parcel 3 to the partnership. However, the facts of this example clearly establish that $250,000 of the transfer to E is not part of a sale of parcel 3 to the partnership because E would have been dis-

Reg. § 1.707-3(f)

tributed $250,000 from the sale of parcel 1 whether or not E had transferred parcel 3 to the partnership. The transfer to E exceeds by $83,333 ($333,333 minus $250,000) the amount of the distribution that would have been made to E if E had not transferred parcel 3 to the partnership. Therefore, $83,333 of the transfer is presumed to be part of a sale of a portion of parcel 3 to the partnership by E.

Example 5. Operation of presumption for transfers more than two years apart. (i) G transfers undeveloped land to the GH partnership in exchange for an interest in the partnership. At the time the land is transferred to the partnership, it is unencumbered and has an adjusted tax basis of $500,000 and a fair market value of $1,000,000. H contributes $1,000,000 in cash in exchange for an interest in the partnership. Under the partnership agreement, the partnership is obligated to construct a building on the land. The projected construction cost is $5,000,000, which the partnership plans to fund with its $1,000,000 in cash and the proceeds of a construction loan secured by the land and improvements.

(ii) Shortly before G's transfer of the land to the partnership, the partnership secures commitments from lending institutions for construction and permanent financing. To obtain the construction loan, H guarantees completion of the building for a cost of $5,000,000. The partnership is not obligated to reimburse or indemnify H if H must make payment on the completion guarantee. The permanent loan will be funded upon completion of the building, which is expected to occur two years after G's transfer of the land. The amount of the permanent loan is to equal the lesser of $5,000,000 or 80 percent of the appraised value of the improved property at the time the permanent loan is closed. Under the partnership agreement, the partnership is obligated to apply the proceeds of the permanent loan to retire the construction loan and to hold any excess proceeds for transfer to G 25 months after G's transfer of the land to the partnership. The appraised value of the improved property at the time the permanent loan is closed is expected to exceed $5,000,000 only if the partnership is able to lease a substantial portion of the improvements by that time, and there is a significant risk that the partnership will not be able to achieve a satisfactory occupancy level. The partnership completes construction of the building for the projected cost of $5,000,000 approximately two years after G's transfer of the land. Shortly thereafter, the permanent loan is funded in the amount of $5,000,000. At the time of funding the land and building have an appraised value of $7,000,000. The partnership transfers the $1,000,000 excess permanent loan proceeds to G 25 months after G's transfer of the land to the partnership.

(iii) G's transfer of the land to the partnership and the partnership's transfer of $1,000,000 to G occurred more than two years apart. In accordance with paragraph (d) of this section, those transfers are presumed not to be a sale unless the facts and circumstances clearly establish that the transfers constitute a sale of the property, in whole or part, to the partnership. The transfer of $1,000,000 to G would not have been made but for G's transfer of the land to the partnership. In addition, at the time G transferred the land to the partnership, G had a legally enforceable right to receive a transfer from the partnership at a specified time an amount that equals the excess of the permanent loan proceeds over $4,000,000. In this case, however, there was a significant risk that the appraised value of the property would be insufficient to support a permanent loan in excess of $4,000,000 because of the risk that the partnership would not be able to achieve a sufficient occupancy level. Therefore, the facts of this example indicate that at the time G transferred the land to the partnership the subsequent transfer of $1,000,000 to G depended on the entrepreneurial risks of partnership operations. Accordingly, G's transfer of the land to the partnership is not treated as part of a sale.

Example 6. Rebuttal of presumption for transfers more than two years apart. The facts are the same as in *Example 5*, except that the partnership is able to secure a commitment for a permanent loan in the amount of $5,000,000 without regard to the appraised value of the improved property at the time the permanent loan is funded. Under these facts, at the time that G transferred the land to the partnership the subsequent transfer of $1,000,000 to G was not dependent on the entrepreneurial risks of partnership operations, because during the period before the permanent loan is funded, the permanent lender's obligation to make a loan in the amount necessary to fund the transfer is not subject to contingencies related to the risks of partnership operations, and after the permanent loan is funded, the partnership holds liquid assets sufficient to make the transfer. Therefore, the facts and circumstances clearly establish that G's transfer of the land to the partnership is part of a sale.

Example 7. Operation of presumption for transfers more than two years apart. The facts are the same as in *Example 6*, except that H does not guarantee either that the improvements will be completed or that the cost to the partnership of completing the improvements will not exceed $5,000,000. Under these facts, if there is a signifi-

Reg. § 1.707-3(f)

cant risk that the improvements will not be completed, G's transfer of the land to the partnership will not be treated as part of a sale because the lender is not required to make the permanent loan if the improvements are not completed. Similarly, the transfers will not be treated as a sale to the extent that there is a significant risk that the cost of constructing the improvements will exceed $5,000,000, because, in the absence of a guarantee of the cost of the improvements by H, the $5,000,000 proceeds of the permanent loan might not be sufficient to retire the construction loan and fund the transfer to G. In either case, the transfer of cash to G would be dependent on the entrepreneurial risks of partnership operations.

Example 8. Rebuttal of presumption for transfers more than two years apart. (i) On February 1, 1992, I, J, and K form partnership IJK. On formation of the partnership, I transfers an unencumbered office building with a fair market value of $50,000,000 and an adjusted tax basis of $20,000,000 to the partnership, and J and K each transfer United States government securities with a fair market value and an adjusted tax basis of $25,000,000 to the partnership. Substantially all of the rentable space in the office building is leased on a long-term basis. The partnership agreement provides that all items of income, gain, loss, and deduction from the office building are to be allocated 45 percent to J, 45 percent to K, and 10 percent to I. The partnership agreement also provides that all items of income, gain, loss, and deduction from the government securities are to be allocated 90 percent to I, 5 percent to J, and 5 percent to K. The partnership agreement requires that cash flow from the office building and government securities be allocated between partners in the same manner as the items of income, gain, loss, and deduction from those properties are allocated between them. The partnership agreement complies with the requirements of § 1.704-1(b)(2)(ii)(*b*) It is not expected that the partnership will need to resort to the government securities or the cash flow therefrom to operate the office building. At the time the partnership is formed, I, J, and K contemplated that I's interest in the partnership would be liquidated sometime after January 31, 1994, in exchange for a transfer of the government securities and cash (if necessary). On March 1, 1995, the partnership transfers cash and the government securities to I in liquidation of I's interest in the partnership. The cash transferred to I represents the excess of I's share of the appreciation in the office building since the formation of the partnership over J's and K's share of the appreciation in the government securities since they were acquired by the partnership.

(ii) I's transfer of the office building to the partnership and the partnership's transfer of the government securities and cash to I occurred more than two years apart. Therefore, those transfers are presumed not to be a sale unless the facts and circumstances clearly establish that the transfers constitute a sale. Absent I's transfer of the office building to the partnership, I would not have received the government securities from the partnership. The facts (including the amount and nature of partnership assets) indicate that, at the time that I transferred the office building to the partnership, the timing of the transfer of the government securities to I was anticipated and was not dependent on the entrepreneurial risks of partnership operations. Moreover, the facts indicate that the partnership allocations were designed to effect an exchange of the burdens and benefits of ownership of the government securities in anticipation of the transfer of those securities to I and those burdens and benefits were effectively shifted to I on formation of the partnership. Accordingly, the facts and circumstances clearly establish that I sold the office building to the partnership on February 1, 1992, in exchange for the partnership's obligation to transfer the government securities to I and to make certain other cash transfers to I. [Reg. § 1.707-3.]

☐ [*T.D.* 8439, 9-25-92.]

[Reg. § 1.707-4]

§ 1.707-4. Disguised sales of property to partnership; special rules applicable to guaranteed payments, preferred returns, operating cash flow distributions, and reimbursements of preformation expenditures.—(a) *Guaranteed payments and preferred returns*—(1) *Guaranteed payment not treated as part of a sale*—(i) *In general.* A guaranteed payment for capital made to a partner is not treated as part of a sale of property under § 1.707-3(a) (relating to treatment of transfers as a sale). A party's characterization of a payment as a guaranteed payment for capital will not control in determining whether a payment is, in fact, a guaranteed payment for capital. The term *guaranteed payment for capital* means any payment to a partner by a partnership that is determined without regard to partnership income and is for the use of that partner's capital. See section 707(c). For this purpose, one or more payments are not made for the use of a partner's capital if the payments are designed to liquidate all or part of the partner's interest in property contributed to the partnership rather than to provide the partner with a return on an investment in the partnership.

(ii) *Reasonable guaranteed payments.* Notwithstanding the presumption set forth in

§ 1.707-3(c) (relating) to transfers made within two years of each other), for purposes of section 707(a)(2) and the regulations thereunder a transfer of money to a partner that is characterized by the parties as a guaranteed payment for capital, is determined without regard to the income of the partnership and is reasonable (within the meaning of paragraph (a)(3) of this section) is presumed to be a guaranteed payment for capital unless the facts and circumstances clearly establish that the transfer is not a guaranteed payment for capital and is part of a sale.

(iii) *Unreasonable guaranteed payments.* A transfer of money to a partner that is characterized by the parties as a guaranteed payment for capital but that is not reasonable (within the meaning of paragraph (a)(3) of this section) is presumed not to be a guaranteed payment for capital unless the facts and circumstances clearly establish that the transfer is a guaranteed payment for capital. A transfer that is not a guaranteed payment for capital is subject to the rules of § 1.707-3.

(2) *Presumption regarding reasonable preferred returns.* Notwithstanding the presumption set forth in § 1.707-3(c) (relating to transfers made within two years of each other), a transfer of money to a partner that is characterized by the parties as a preferred return and that is reasonable (within the meaning of paragraph (a)(3) of this section) is presumed not to be part of a sale of property to the partnership unless the facts and circumstances (including the likelihood and expected timing of the subsequent allocation of income or gain to support the preferred return) clearly establish that the transfer is part of a sale. The term *preferred return* means a preferential distribution of partnership cash flow to a partner with respect to capital contributed to the partnership by the partner that will be matched, to the extent available, by an allocation of income or gain.

(3) *Definition of reasonable preferred returns and guaranteed payments*—(i) *In general.* A transfer of money to a partner that is characterized as a preferred return or guaranteed payment for capital is reasonable only to the extent that the transfer is made to the partner pursuant to a written provision of a partnership agreement that provides for payment for the use of capital in a reasonable amount, and only to the extent that the payment is made for the use of capital after the date on which that provision is added to the partnership agreement.

(ii) *Reasonable amount.* A transfer of money that is made to a partner during any partnership taxable year and is characterized as a preferred return or guaranteed payment for capital is reasonable in amount if the sum of any preferred return and any guaranteed payment for capital that is payable for that year does not exceed the amount determined by multiplying either the partner's unreturned capital at the beginning of the year or, at the partner's option, the partner's weighted average capital balance for the year (with either amount appropriately adjusted, taking into account the relevant compounding periods, to reflect any unpaid preferred return or guaranteed payment for capital that is payable to the partner) by the safe harbor interest rate for that year. The safe harbor interest rate for a partnership's taxable year equals 150 percent of the highest applicable Federal rate, at the appropriate compounding period or periods, in effect at any time from the time that the right to the preferred return or guaranteed payment for capital is first established pursuant to a binding, written agreement among the partners through the end of the taxable year. A partner's unreturned capital equals the excess of the aggregate amount of money and the fair market value of other consideration (net of liabilities) contributed by the partner to the partnership over the aggregate amount of money and the fair market value of other consideration (net of liabilities) distributed by the partnership to the partner other than transfers of money that are presumed to be guaranteed payments for capital under paragraph (a)(1)(ii) of this section, transfers of money that are reasonable preferred returns within the meaning of this paragraph (a)(3), and operating cash flow distributions within the meaning of paragraph (b)(2) of this section.

(4) *Examples.* The following examples illustrate the application of paragraph (a) of this section:

Example 1. Transfer presumed to be a guaranteed payment. (i) A transfers property with a fair market value of $100,000 to partnership AB. At the time of A's transfer, the partnership agreement is amended to provide that A is to receive a guaranteed payment for the use of A's capital of 10 percent (compounded annually) of the fair market value of the transferred property in each of the three years following the transfer. The partnership agreement provides that partnership net taxable income and loss will be allocated equally between partners A and B, and that partnership cash flow will be distributed in accordance with the allocation of partnership net taxable income and loss. The partnership would be allowed a deduction in the year paid if the transfers made to A are treated as guaranteed payments under section 707(c). Under the partnership agreement, that deduction would be allocated in

Reg. § 1.707-4

the same manner as any other item of partnership deduction. The partnership agreement complies with the requirements of § 1.704-1(b)(2)(ii)(b). The partnership agreement does not provide for the payment of a preferred return and, other than the guaranteed payment to be paid to A, no transfer is expected to be made during the three year period following A's transfer that is not an operating cash flow distribution (within the meaning of paragraph (b)(2) of this section). Assume that the highest applicable Federal rate in effect at the time of A's transfer is eight percent compounded annually.

(ii) The transfer of money to be made to A under the partnership agreement is characterized by the parties as a guaranteed payment for capital and is determined without regard to the income of the partnership. The transfer is also reasonable within the meaning of § 1.707-4(a)(3). The transfer, therefore, is presumed to be a guaranteed payment for capital. The presumption set forth in § 1.707-3(c) (relating to transfers made within two years of each other) thus does not apply to this transfer. The transfer will not be treated as part of a sale of property to the partnership unless the facts and circumstances clearly establish that the transfer is not a guaranteed payment for capital but is part of a sale.

(iii) The presumption that the transfer is a guaranteed payment for capital is not rebutted, because there are no facts indicating that the transfer is not a guaranteed payment for the use of capital.

Example 2. Transfers characterized as guaranteed payments treated as part of a sale. (i) C and D form partnership CD. C transfers property with a fair market value of $100,000 and an adjusted tax basis of $20,000 in exchange for a partnership interest. D is responsible for managing the day-to-day operations of the partnership and makes no capital contribution to the partnership upon its formation. The partnership agreement provides that C is to receive payments characterized as guaranteed payments and determined without regard to partnership income of $8,333 per year for the first four years of partnership operations for the use of C's capital. In addition, the partnership agreement provides that—

(A) Partnership net taxable income and loss will be allocated 75 percent to C and 25 percent to D; and

(B) All partnership cash flow (determined prior to consideration of the guaranteed payment) will be distributed 75 percent to C and 25 percent to D except that guaranteed payments that the partnership is obligated to make to C are payable solely out of D's share of the partnership's cash flow.

(ii) If D's share of the partnership's cash flow is not sufficient to make the guaranteed payment to C, then D is obligated to contribute any shortfall to the partnership, even in the event the partnership is liquidated. Thus, the effect of the guaranteed payment arrangement is that the guaranteed payment to C is funded entirely by D. The partnership agreement complies with the requirements of § 1.704-1(b)(2)(ii)(b). Assume that, at the time the partnership is formed, the partnership or D could borrow $25,000 pursuant to a loan requiring equal payments of principal and interest over a four-year term at the current market interest rate of approximately 12 percent (compounded annually). Assume that the highest applicable Federal rate in effect at the time the partnership is formed is 10 percent compounded annually.

(iii) The transfer of money to be made to C under the partnership agreement is characterized by the parties as a guaranteed payment for capital and is determined without regard to the income of the partnership. The transfer is also reasonable within the meaning of § 1.707-4(a)(3). The transfer, therefore, is presumed to be a guaranteed payment for capital. The presumption set forth in § 1.707-3(c) (relating to transfers made within two years of each other) thus does not apply to this transfer. The transfer will not be treated as part of a sale of property to the partnership unless the facts and circumstances clearly establish that the transfer is not a guaranteed payment for capital and is part of a sale.

(iv) For the first four years of partnership operations, the total guaranteed payments made to C under the partnership agreement will equal $33,332. If the characterization of those payments as guaranteed payments for capital within the meaning of section 707(c) were respected, C would be allocated $24,999 of the deductions that would be claimed by the partnership for those payments, thereby leaving the balance in C's capital account approximately $25,000 less than it would have been if the guaranteed payments had not been made. The guaranteed payments thus have the effect of offsetting approximately $25,000 of the credit made to C's capital account for the property transferred to the partnership by C. C's resulting capital account is approximately equivalent to the capital account C would have had if C had only contributed 75 percent of the property to the partnership. Furthermore, the effect of D's funding the guaranteed payment to C (either through reduced distributions of cash flow to D or additional contributions) is that D's capi-

Reg. § 1.707-4

tal account is approximately equivalent to the capital account D would have had if D had contributed 25 percent of the property (or contributed cash so that the partnership could purchase the 25 percent). Moreover, a $25,000 loan requiring equal payments of principal and interest over a four-year term at the current market interest rate of 12 percent (compounded annually), would have resulted in annual payments of principal and interest of $8,230.86. Consequently, the guaranteed payments effectively place the partners in the same economic position that they would have been in had D purchased a one-quarter interest in the property from C financed at the current market rate of interest, and then C and D each contributed their share of the property to the partnership. In view of the burden the guaranteed payments place on D's right to transfers of partnership cash flow and D's legal obligation to make contributions to the partnership to the extent necessary to fund the guaranteed payments, D has effectively purchased through the partnership a one-quarter interest in the property from C.

(v) Under these facts, the presumption that the transfers to C are guaranteed payments for capital is rebutted, because the facts and circumstances clearly establish that the transfers are part of a sale and not guaranteed payments for capital. Under § 1.707-3(a), C and the partnership are treated as if C sold a one-quarter interest in the property to the partnership in exchange for a promissory note evidencing the partnership's obligation to make the guaranteed payments.

(b) *Presumption regarding operating cash flow distributions*—(1) *In general.* Notwithstanding the presumption set forth in § 1.707-3(c) (relating to transfers made within two years of each other), an operating cash flow distribution is presumed not to be part of a sale of property to the partnership unless the facts and circumstances clearly establish that the transfer is part of a sale.

(2) *Operating cash flow distributions*—(i) *In general.* One or more transfers of money by the partnership to a partner during a taxable year of the partnership are operating cash flow distributions for purposes of paragraph (b)(1) of this section to the extent that those transfers are not presumed to be guaranteed payments for capital under paragraph (a)(1)(ii) of this section, are not reasonable preferred returns within the meaning of paragraph (a)(3) of this section, are not characterized by the parties as distributions to the partner acting in a capacity other than as a partner, and to the extent they do not exceed the product of the net cash flow of the partnership from operations for the year multiplied by the lesser of the partner's percentage interest in overall partnership profits for that year or the partner's percentage interest in overall partnership profits for the life of the partnership. For purposes of the preceding sentence, the net cash flow of the partnership from operations for a taxable year is an amount equal to the taxable income or loss of the partnership arising in the ordinary course of the partnership's business and investment activities, increased by tax exempt interest, depreciation, amortization, cost recovery allowances and other noncash charges deducted in determining such taxable income and decreased by—

(A) Principal payments made on any partnership indebtedness;

(B) Property replacement or contingency reserves actually established by the partnership;

(C) Capital expenditures when made other than from reserves or from borrowings the proceeds of which are not included in operating cash flow; and

(D) Any other cash expenditures (including preferred returns) not deducted in determining such taxable income or loss.

(ii) *Operating cash flow safe harbor.* For any taxable year, in determining a partner's operating cash flow distributions for the year, the partner may use the partner's smallest percentage interest under the terms of the partnership agreement in any material item of partnership income or gain that may be realized by the partnership in the three-year period beginning with such taxable year. This provision is merely intended to provide taxpayers with a safe harbor and is not intended to preclude a taxpayer from using a different percentage under the rules of paragraph (b)(2)(i) of this section.

(iii) *Tiered partnerships.* In the case of tiered partnerships, the upper-tier partnership must take into account its share of the net cash flow from operations of the lower-tier partnership applying principles similar to those described in paragraph (b)(2)(i) of this section, so that the amount of the upper-tier partnership's operating cash flow distributions is neither overstated nor understated.

(c) *Accumulation of guaranteed payments, preferred returns, and operating cash flow distributions.* Guaranteed payments for capital, preferred returns, and operating cash flow distributions presumed not to be part of a sale under the rules of paragraphs (a) and (b) of this section do not lose the benefit of the presumption by reason of being retained for distribution in a later year.

(d) *Exception for reimbursements of preformation expenditures.* A transfer of money or other

Reg. § 1.707-4(d)

consideration by the partnership to a partner is not treated as part of a sale of property by the partner to the partnership under § 1.707-3(a) (relating to treatment of transfers as a sale) to the extent that the transfer to the partner by the partnership is made to reimburse the partner for, and does not exceed the amount of, capital expenditures that—

(1) Are incurred during the two-year period preceding the transfer by the partner to the partnership; and

(2) Are incurred by the partner with respect to—

(i) Partnership organization and syndication costs described in section 709; or

(ii) Property contributed to the partnership by the partner, but only to the extent the reimbursed capital expenditures do not exceed 20 percent of the fair market value of such property at the time of the contribution. However, the 20 percent of fair market value limitation of this paragraph (d)(2)(ii) does not apply if the fair market value of the contributed property does not exceed 120 percent of the partner's adjusted basis in the contributed property at the time of contribution.

(e) *Other exceptions.* The Commissioner may provide by guidance published in the Internal Revenue Bulletin that other payments or transfers to a partner are not treated as part of a sale for purposes of section 707(a)(2) and the regulations thereunder. [Reg. § 1.707-4.]

☐ [*T.D. 8439, 9-25-92.*]

[Reg. § 1.707-5]

§ 1.707-5. Disguised sales of property to partnership; special rules relating to liabilities.—(a) *Liability assumed or taken subject to by partnership*—(1) *In general.* For purposes of this section and §§ 1.707-3 and 1.707-4, if a partnership assumes or takes property subject to a qualified liability (as defined in paragraph (a)(6) of this section) of a partner, the partnership is treated as transferring consideration to the partner only to the extent provided in paragraph (a)(5) of this section. By contrast, if the partnership assumes or takes property subject to a liability of the partner other than a qualified liability, the partnership is treated as transferring consideration to the partner to the extent that the amount of the liability exceeds the partner's share of that liability immediately after the partnership assumes or takes subject to the liability as provided in paragraphs (a)(2), (3) and (4) of this section.

(2) *Partner's share of liability.* A partner's share of any liability of the partnership is determined under the following rules:

(i) *Recourse liability.* A partner's share of a recourse liability of the partnership equals the partner's share of the liability under the rules of section 752 and the regulations thereunder. A partnership liability is a recourse liability to the extent that the obligation is a recourse liability under § 1.752-1(a)(1) or would be treated as a recourse liability under that section if it were treated as a partnership liability for purposes of that section.

(ii) *Nonrecourse liability.* A partner's share of a nonrecourse liability of the partnership is determined by applying the same percentage used to determine the partner's share of the excess nonrecourse liability under § 1.752-3(a)(3). A partnership liability is a nonrecourse liability of the partnership to the extent that the obligation is a nonrecourse liability under § 1.752-1(a)(2) or would be a nonrecourse liability of the partnership under § 1.752-1(a)(2) if it were treated as a partnership liability for purposes of that section.

(3) *Reduction of partner's share of liability.* For purposes of this section, a partner's share of a liability, immediately after a partnership assumes or takes subject to the liability, is determined by taking into account a subsequent reduction in the partner's share if—

(i) At the time that the partnership assumes or takes subject to a liability, it is anticipated that the transferring partner's share of the liability will be subsequently reduced; and

(ii) The reduction of the partner's share of the liability is part of a plan that has as one of its principal purposes minimizing the extent to which the assumption of or taking subject to the liability is treated as part of a sale under § 1.707-3.

(4) *Special rule applicable to transfers of encumbered property to a partnership by more than one partner pursuant to a plan.* For purposes of paragraph (a)(1) of this section, if the partnership assumes or takes property or properties subject to the liabilities of more than one partner pursuant to a plan, a partner's share of the liabilities assumed or taken subject to by the partnership pursuant to that plan immediately after the transfers equals the sum of that partner's shares of the liabilities (other than that partner's qualified liabilities, as defined in paragraph (a)(6) of this section) assumed or taken subject to by the partnership pursuant to the plan. This paragraph (a)(4) does not apply to any liability assumed or taken subject to by the partnership with a principal purpose of reducing the extent to which any other liability assumed or taken subject to by the

Reg. § 1.707-5(a)(1)

partnership is treated as a transfer of consideration under paragraph (a)(1) of this section.

(5) *Special rule applicable to qualified liabilities.* (i) If a transfer of property by a partner to a partnership is not otherwise treated as part of a sale, the partnership's assumption of or taking subject to a qualified liability in connection with a transfer of property is not treated as part of a sale. If a transfer of property by a partner to the partnership is treated as part of a sale without regard to the partnership's assumption of or taking subject to a qualified liability (as defined in paragraph (a)(6) of this section) in connection with the transfer of property, the partnership's assumption of or taking subject to that liability is treated as a transfer of consideration made pursuant to a sale of such property to the partnership only to the extent of the lesser of—

(A) The amount of consideration that the partnership would be treated as transferring to the partner under paragraph (a)(1) of this section if the liability were not a qualified liability; or

(B) The amount obtained by multiplying the amount of the qualified liability by the partner's net equity percentage with respect to that property.

(ii) A partner's net equity percentage with respect to an item of property equals the percentage determined by dividing—

(A) The aggregate transfers of money or other consideration to the partner by the partnership (other than any transfer described in this paragraph (a)(5)) that are treated as proceeds realized from the sale of the transferred property; by

(B) The excess of the fair market value of the property at the time it is transferred to the partnership over any qualified liability encumbering the property or, in the case of any qualified liability described in paragraph (a)(6)(i)(C) or (D) of this section, that is properly allocable to the property.

(6) *Qualified liability of a partner defined.* A liability assumed or taken subject to by a partnership in connection with a transfer of property to the partnership by a partner is a qualified liability of the partner only to the extent—

(i) The liability is—

(A) A liability that was incurred by the partner more than two years prior to the earlier of the date the partner agrees in writing to transfer the property or the date the partner transfers the property to the partnership and that has encumbered the transferred property throughout that two-year period;

(B) A liability that was not incurred in anticipation of the transfer of the property to a partnership, but that was incurred by the partner within the two-year period prior to the earlier of the date the partner agrees in writing to transfer the property or the date the partner transfers the property to the partnership and that has encumbered the transferred property since it was incurred (see paragraph (a)(7) of this section for further rules regarding a liability incurred within two years of a property transfer or of a written agreement to transfer);

(C) A liability that is allocable under the rules of § 1.163-8T to capital expenditures with respect to the property; or

(D) A liability that was incurred in the ordinary course of the trade or business in which property transferred to the partnership was used or held but only if all the assets related to that trade or business are transferred other than assets that are not material to a continuation of the trade or business; and

(ii) If the liability is a recourse liability, the amount of the liability does not exceed the fair market value of the transferred property (less the amount of any other liabilities that are senior in priority and that either encumber such property or are liabilities described in paragraph (a)(6)(i)(C) or (D) of this section) at the time of the transfer.

(7) *Liability incurred within two years of transfer presumed to be in anticipation of the transfer*—(i) *In general.* For purposes of this section, if within a two-year period a partner incurs a liability (other than a liability described in paragraph (a)(6)(i)(C) or (D) of this section) and transfers property to a partnership or agrees in writing to transfer the property, and in connection with the transfer the partnership assumes or takes the property subject to the liability, the liability is presumed to be incurred in anticipation of the transfer unless the facts and circumstances clearly establish that the liability was not incurred in anticipation of the transfer.

(ii) *Disclosure of transfers of property subject to liabilities incurred within two years of the transfer.* If a partner treats a liability assumed or taken subject to by a partnership as a qualified liability under paragraph (a)(6)(i)(B) of this section, such treatment is to be disclosed to the Internal Revenue Service in accordance with § 1.707-8.

(b) *Treatment of debt-financed transfers of consideration by partnerships*—(1) *In general.* For purposes of § 1.707-3, if a partner transfers property to a partnership, and the partnership incurs a liability and all or a portion of the proceeds of that liability are allocable under § 1.163-8T to a transfer of money or other consideration to the partner made within 90 days of incurring the liability, the transfer of money or other consideration to the partner is taken into account only to the extent that the amount of money or the fair market value of the other consideration transferred exceeds that partner's allocable share of the partnership liability.

(2) *Partner's allocable share of liability*—(i) *In general.* A partner's allocable share of a partnership liability for purposes of paragraph (b)(1) of this section equals the amount obtained by multiplying the partner's share of the liability as described in paragraph (a)(2) of this section by the fraction determined by dividing—

(A) The portion of the liability that is allocable under § 1.163-8T to the money or other property transferred to the partner; by

(B) The total amount of the liability.

(ii) *Debt-financed transfers made pursuant to a plan.*

(A) *In general.* Except as provided in paragraph (b)(2)(iii) of this section, if a partnership transfers to more than one partner pursuant to a plan all or a portion of the proceeds of one or more partnership liabilities, paragraph (b)(1) of this section is applied by treating all of the liabilities incurred pursuant to the plan as one liability, and each partner's allocable share of those liabilities equals the amount obtained by multiplying the sum of the partner's shares of each of the respective liabilities (as defined in paragraph (a)(2) of this section) by the fraction obtained by dividing—

(*1*) The portion of those liabilities that is allocable under § 1.163-8T to the money or other consideration transferred to the partners pursuant to the plan; by

(*2*) The total amount of those liabilities.

(B) *Special rule.* Paragraph (b)(2)(ii)(A) of this section does not apply to any transfer of money or other property to a partner that is made with a principal purpose of reducing the extent to which any transfer is taken into account under paragraph (b)(1) of this section.

(iii) *Reduction of partner's share of liability.* For purposes of paragraph (b)(2) of this section, a partner's share of a liability, immediately after the partnership assumes or takes subject to the liability, is determined by taking into account a subsequent reduction in the partner's share if—

(A) It is anticipated that the partner's share of the liability that is allocable to a transfer of money or other consideration to the partner will be reduced subsequent to the transfer; and

(B) The reduction of the partner's share of the liability is part of a plan that has as one of its principal purposes minimizing the extent to which the partnership's distribution of the proceeds of the borrowing is treated as part of a sale.

(c) *Refinancings.* To the extent that the proceeds of a partner or partnership liability (the *refinancing debt*) are allocable under the rules of § 1.163-8T to payments discharging all or part of any other liability of that partner or of the partnership, as the case may be, the refinancing debt is treated as the other liability for purposes of applying the rules of this section.

(d) *Share of liability where assumption accompanied by transfer of money.* For purposes of §§ 1.707-3 through 1.707-5, if pursuant to a plan a partner pays or contributes money to the partnership and the partnership assumes or takes subject to one or more liabilities (other than qualified liabilities) of the partner, the amount of those liabilities that the partnership is treated as assuming or taking subject to is reduced (but not below zero) by the money transferred.

(e) *Tiered partnerships and other related persons.* If a lower-tier partnership succeeds to a liability of an upper-tier partnership, the liability in the lower-tier partnership retains the characterization as qualified or nonqualified that it had under these rules in the upper-tier partnership. A similar rule applies to other related party transactions involving liabilities to the extent provided by guidance published in the Internal Revenue Bulletin.

(f) *Examples.* The following examples illustrate the application of this section.

Example 1. Partnership's assumption of nonrecourse liability encumbering transferred property. (i) A and B form partnership AB, which will engage in renting office space. A transfers $500,000 in cash to the partnership, and B transfers an office building to the partnership. At the time it is transferred to the partnership, the office building has a fair market value of $1,000,000, an adjusted basis of $400,000, and is encumbered by a $500,000 liability, which B incurred 12 months earlier to finance the acquisition of other property. No facts rebut the presumption that the liability was incurred in anticipation of the transfer of the property to the partnership. Assume that this liability is a nonrecourse liability of the partnership within the meaning of section 752 and the regulations thereunder. The partnership agreement provides that partnership items will be allocated equally between A and B, including excess nonrecourse deductions under § 1.752-3(a)(3).

Reg. § 1.707-5(b)(2)

The partnership agreement complies with the requirements of § 1.704-1(b)(2)(ii)(*b*).

(ii) The nonrecourse liability secured by the office building is not a qualified liability within the meaning of paragraph (a)(6) of this section. B would be allocated 50 percent of the excess nonrecourse liability under the partnership agreement. Accordingly, immediately after the partnership's assumption of that liability, B's share of the liability equals $250,000, which is equal to B's 50 percent share of the excess nonrecourse liability of the partnership as determined in accordance with B's share of partnership profits under § 1.752-3(a)(3).

(iii) The partnership's taking subject to the liability encumbering the office building is treated as a transfer of $250,000 of consideration to B (the amount by which the liability ($500,000) exceeds B's share of that liability immediately after taking subject to ($250,000)). B is treated as having sold $250,000 of the fair market value of the office building to the partnership in exchange for the partnership's taking subject to a $250,000 liability. This results in a gain of $150,000 ($250,000 minus ($250,000/$1,000,000 multiplied by $400,000)).

Example 2. Partnership's assumption of recourse liability encumbering transferred property. (i) C transfers property Y to a partnership. At the time of its transfer to the partnership, property Y has a fair market value of $10,000,000 and is subject to an $8,000,000 liability that C incurred, immediately before transferring property Y to the partnership, in order to finance other expenditures. Upon the transfer of property Y to the partnership, the partnership assumed the liability encumbering that property. The partnership assumed this liability solely to acquire property Y. Under section 752 and the regulations thereunder, immediately after the partnership's assumption of the liability encumbering property Y, the liability is a recourse liability of the partnership and C's share of that liability is $7,000,000.

(ii) Under the facts of this example, the liability encumbering property Y is not a qualified liability. Accordingly, the partnership's assumption of the liability results in a transfer of consideration to C in connection with C's transfer of property Y to the partnership in the amount of $1,000,000 (the excess of the liability assumed by the partnership ($8,000,000) over C's share of the liability immediately after the assumption ($7,000,000)). See paragraphs (a)(1) and (2) of this section.

Example 3. Subsequent reduction of transferring partner's share of liability. (i) The facts are the same as in *Example 2*. In addition, property Y is a fully leased office building, the rental income from property Y is sufficient to meet debt service, and the remaining term of the liability is ten years. It is anticipated that, three years after the partnership's assumption of the liability, C's share of the liability under section 752 will be reduced to zero because of a shift in the allocation of partnership losses pursuant to the terms of the partnership agreement. Under the partnership agreement, this shift in the allocation of partnership losses is dependent solely on the passage of time.

(ii) Under paragraph (a)(3) of this section, if the reduction in C's share of the liability was anticipated at the time of C's transfer, and the reduction was part of a plan that has as one of its principal purposes minimizing the extent of sale treatment under § 1.707-3 (*i.e.*, a principal purpose of allocating a large percentage of losses to C in the first three years when losses were not likely to be realized was to minimize the extent to which C's transfer would be treated as part of a sale), C's share of the liability immediately after the assumption is treated as equal to C's reduced share.

Example 4. Trade payables as qualified liabilities. (i) D and E form partnership DE which will engage in a consulting business that requires no overhead and minimal cash on hand for daily operating expenses. Previously, D and E, as individual sole proprietors, operated separate consulting businesses. D and E each transfer to the partnership sufficient cash to cover daily operating expenses together with the goodwill and trade payables related to each sole proprietorship. Due to uncertainty over the collection rate on the trade receivables related to their sole proprietorships, D and E agree that none of the trade receivables will be transferred to the partnership.

(ii) Under the facts of this example, all the assets related to the consulting business (other than the trade receivables) together with the trade payables were transferred to partnership DE. The trade receivables retained by D and E are not material to a continuation of the trade or business by the partnership because D and E contributed sufficient cash to cover daily operating expenses. Accordingly, the trade payables transferred to the partnership constitute qualified liabilities under paragraph (a)(6) of this section.

Example 5. Partnership's assumption of a qualified liability as sole consideration. (i) F transfers property Z to a partnership. At the time of its transfer to the partnership, property Z has a fair market value of $165,000 and an adjusted tax basis of $75,000. Also, at the time of the transfer, property Z is subject to a $75,000 liability that F

Reg. § 1.707-5(f)

incurred more than two years before transferring property Z to the partnership. The liability has been secured by property Z since it was incurred by F. Upon the transfer of property Z to the partnership, the partnership assumed the liability encumbering that property. The partnership made no other transfers to F in consideration for the transfer of property Z to the partnership. Assume that, under section 752 and the regulations thereunder, immediately after the partnership's assumption of the liability encumbering property Z, the liability is a recourse liability of the partnership and F's share of that liability is $25,000.

(ii) The $75,000 liability secured by property Z is a qualified liability of F because F incurred the liability more than two years prior to the assumption of the liability by the partnership and the liability has encumbered property Z for more than two years prior to that assumption. See paragraph (a)(6) of this section. Therefore, since no other transfer to F was made as consideration for the transfer of property Z, under paragraph (a)(5) of this section, the partnership's assumption of the qualified liability of F encumbering property Z is not treated as part of a sale.

Example 6. Partnership's assumption of a qualified liability in addition to other consideration. (i) The facts are the same as in Example 5, except that the partnership makes a transfer to D of $30,000 in money that is consideration for F's transfer of property Z to the partnership under § 1.707-3.

(ii) As in Example 5, the $75,000 liability secured by property Z is a qualified liability of F. Since the partnership transferred $30,000 to F in addition to assuming the qualified liability under paragraph (a)(5) of this section, the partnership's assumption of this qualified liability is treated as a transfer of additional consideration to F to the extent of the lesser of—

(A) The amount that the partnership would be treated as transferring to F if the liability were not a qualified liability ($50,000 (i.e., the excess of the $75,000 qualified liability over F's $25,000 share of that liability)); or

(B) The amount obtained by multiplying the qualified liability ($75,000) by F's net equity percentage with respect to property Z (one-third).

(iii) F's net equity percentage with respect to property Z equals the fraction determined by dividing—

(A) The aggregate amount of money or other consideration (other than the qualified liability) transferred to F and treated as part of a sale of property Z under § 1.707-3(a) ($30,000 transfer of money); by

(B) F's net equity in property Z ($90,000 (i.e., the excess of the $165,000 fair market value over the $75,000 qualified liability)).

(iv) Accordingly, the partnership's assumption of the qualified liability of F encumbering property Z is treated as a transfer of $25,000 (one-third of $75,000) of consideration to F pursuant to a sale. Therefore, F is treated as having sold $55,000 of the fair market value of property Z to the partnership in exchange for $30,000 in money and the partnership's assumption of $25,000 of the qualified liability. Accordingly, F must recognize $30,000 of gain on the sale (the excess of the $55,000 amount realized over $25,000 of F's adjusted basis for property Z (i.e., one-third of F's adjusted basis for the property, because F is treated as having sold one-third of the property to the partnership)).

Example 7. Partnership's assumptions of liabilities encumbering properties transferred pursuant to a plan. (i) Pursuant to a plan, G and H transfer property 1 and property 2, respectively, to an existing partnership in exchange for interests in the partnership. At the time the properties are transferred to the partnership, property 1 has a fair market value of $10,000 and an adjusted tax basis of $6,000, and property 2 has a fair market value of $10,000 and an adjusted tax basis of $4,000. At the time properties 1 and 2 are transferred to the partnership, a $6,000 nonrecourse liability (liability 1) is secured by property 1 and a $7,000 recourse liability of F (liability 2) is secured by property 2. Properties 1 and 2 are transferred to the partnership, and the partnership takes subject to liability 1 and assumes liability 2. G and H incurred liabilities 1 and 2 immediately prior to transferring properties 1 and 2 to the partnership and used the proceeds for personal expenditures. The liabilities are not qualified liabilities. Assume that G and H are each allocated $2,000 of liability 1 in accordance with § 1.707-5(a)(2)(ii) (which determines a partner's share of a nonrecourse liability). Assume further that G's share of liability 2 is $3,500 and H's share is $0 in accordance with § 1.707-5(a)(2)(i) (which determines a partner's share of a recourse liability).

(ii) G and H transferred properties 1 and 2 to the partnership pursuant to a plan. Accordingly, the partnership's taking subject to liability 1 is treated as a transfer of only $500 of consideration to G (the amount by which liability 1 ($6,000) exceeds G's share of liabilities 1 and 2 ($5,500)), and the partnership's assumption of liability 2 is treated as a transfer of only $5,000 of consideration to H (the amount by which liability 2 ($7,000) exceeds H's share of liabilities 1 and 2

Reg. § 1.707-5(f)

($2,000)). G is treated under the rule in § 1.707-3 as having sold $500 of the fair market value of property 1 in exchange for the partnership's taking subject to liability 1 and H is treated as having sold $5,000 of the fair market value of property 2 in exchange for the assumption of liability 2.

Example 8. Partnership's assumption of liability pursuant to a plan to avoid sale treatment of partnership assumption of another liability. (i) The facts are the same as in *Example 7,* except that—

(A) H transferred the proceeds of liability 2 to the partnership; and

(B) H incurred liability 2 in an attempt to reduce the extent to which the partnership's taking subject to liability 1 would be treated as a transfer of consideration to G (and thereby reduce the portion of G's transfer of property 1 to the partnership that would be treated as part of a sale).

(ii) Because the partnership assumed liability 2 with a principal purpose of reducing the extent to which the partnership's taking subject to liability 1 would be treated as a transfer of consideration to G, liability 2 is ignored in applying paragraph (a)(3) of this section. Accordingly, the partnership's taking subject to liability 1 is treated as a transfer of $4,000 of consideration to G (the amount by which liability 1 ($6,000) exceeds G's share of liability 1 ($2,000)). On the other hand, the partnership's assumption of liability 2 is not treated as a transfer of any consideration to H because H's share of that liability equals $7,000 as a result of H's transfer of $7,000 in money to the partnership.

Example 9. Partnership's assumptions of qualified liabilities encumbering properties transferred pursuant to a plan in addition to other consideration. (i) Pursuant to a plan, I transfers property 1 and J transfers property 2 plus $10,000 in cash to partnership IJ in exchange for equal interests in the partnership. At the time the properties are transferred to the partnership, property 1 has a fair market value of $100,000, an adjusted tax basis of $5,000, and is encumbered by a qualified liability of $50,000 (*liability 1*). Property 2 has a fair market value of $100,000, an adjusted tax basis of $5,000, and is encumbered by a qualified liability of $70,000 (*liability 2*). Pursuant to the plan, the partnership transferred to I $10,000 in cash. That amount is consideration for I's transfer of property 1 to the partnership under § 1.707-3. In accordance with § 1.707-5(a)(2), I and J are each allocated $25,000 of liability 1 and $35,000 of liability 2.

(ii) Because the partnership transferred $10,000 to I as consideration for the transfer of property, under § 1.707-5(a)(5), the partnership's assumption of liability 1 is treated as a transfer of additional consideration to I, even though liability 1 is a qualified liability, to the extent of the lesser of—

(A) The amount that the partnership would be treated as transferring to I if the liability were not a qualified liability; or

(B) The amount obtained by multiplying the qualified liability by I's net equity percentage with respect to property 1.

(iii) Because I and J transferred properties 1 and 2 to the partnership pursuant to a plan, treating I's qualified liability as a nonqualified liability under § 1.707-5(a)(5)(i)(A) enables I to apply the special rule applicable to transfers of encumbered property to a partnership by more than one partner pursuant to a plan under § 1.707-5(a)(4). Under this alternative test, the partnership's assumption of liability 1 encumbering property 1 is treated as a transfer of zero ($0) additional consideration to I pursuant to a sale. This is because the amount of liability 1 ($50,000) does not exceed the sum of I's share of liability 1 treated as a nonqualified liability ($25,000) and I's share of liability 2 ($35,000)).

(iv) The alternative under § 1.707-5(a)(5)(i)(B) is the amount obtained by multiplying the qualified liability ($50,000) by I's net equity percentage with respect to property 1. I's net equity percentage with respect to property 1 equals one-fifth, the fraction determined by dividing—

(A) The aggregate amount of money or other consideration (other than the qualified liability) transferred to I and treated as part of a sale of property 1 under § 1.707-3(a) (the $10,000 transfer of money); by

(B) I's net equity in property 1 ($50,000, *i.e.,* the excess of the $100,000 fair market value over the $50,000 qualified liability).

(v) Under this alternative test, the partnership's assumption of the qualified liability encumbering property 1 is treated as a transfer of $10,000 (one-fifth of the $50,000 qualified liability) of additional consideration to I pursuant to a sale.

(vi) Applying § 1.707-5(a)(5) to these facts, the partnership's assumption of liability 1 is treated as a transfer of additional consideration to I to the extent of the lesser of—

(A) zero; or

(B) $10,000.

(vii) Therefore, the partnership's assumption of I's qualified liability encumbering property 1 is

Reg. § 1.707-5(f)

not treated as a transfer of any additional consideration to I pursuant to a sale, and I is treated as having only received $10,000 of the fair market value of property 1 to the partnership in exchange for $10,000 in cash. Accordingly, I must recognize $9,500 of gain on the sale, that is, the excess of the $10,000 amount realized over $500 of I's adjusted tax basis for property 1 (one-tenth of I's adjusted tax basis for the property, because I is treated as having sold one-tenth of the property to the partnership). Since no other transfer to J was made as consideration for the transfer of property 2, the partnership's assumption of the qualified liability of J encumbering property 2 is not treated as part of a sale.

Example 10. Treatment of debt-financed transfers of consideration by partnership. (i) K transfers property Z to partnership KL in exchange for an interest therein on April 9, 1992. On September 13, 1992, the partnership incurs a liability of $20,000. On November 17, 1992, the partnership transfers $20,000 to K, and $10,000 of this transfer is allocable under the rules of § 1.163-8T to proceeds of the partnership liability incurred on September 13, 1992. The remaining $10,000 is paid from other partnership funds. Assume that, under section 752 and the corresponding regulations, the $20,000 liability incurred on September 13, 1992, is a recourse liability of the partnership and K's share of that liability is $10,000 on November 17, 1992.

(ii) Because a portion of the transfer made to K on November 17, 1992, is allocable under § 1.163-8T to proceeds of a partnership liability that was incurred by the partnership within 90 days of that transfer, K is required to take the transfer into account in applying the rules of this section and § 1.707-3 only to the extent that the amount of the transfer exceeds K's allocable share of the liability used to fund the transfer. K's allocable share of the $20,000 liability used to fund $10,000 of the transfer to K is $5,000 (K's share of the liability ($10,000) multiplied by the fraction obtained by dividing—

(A) The amount of the liability that is allocable to the distribution to K ($10,000); by

(B) The total amount of such liability ($20,000)).

(iii) Therefore, K is required to take into account only $15,000 of the $20,000 partnership transfer to K for purposes of this section and § 1.707-3. Under these facts, assuming the within-two-year presumption is not rebutted, this $15,000 transfer will be treated under the rule in § 1.707-3 as part of a sale by K of property Z to the partnership.

Example 11. Borrowing against pool of receivables. (i) M generates receivables which have an adjusted basis of zero in the ordinary course of its business. For M to use receivables as security for a loan, a commercial lender requires M to transfer the receivables to a partnership in which M has a 90 percent interest. In January, 1992, M transfers to the partnership receivables with a face value of $100,000. N (who is not related to M) transfers $10,000 cash to the partnership in exchange for a 10 percent interest. The partnership borrows $80,000, secured by the receivables, and makes a distribution of $72,000 of the proceeds to M and $8,000 of the proceeds to N within 90 days of incurring the liability. M's share of the liability under § 1.707-5(a)(2) is $72,000 (90 percent × $80,000).

(ii) Because the transfer of the loan proceeds to M is allocable under § 1.163-8T to proceeds of a partnership loan that was incurred by the partnership within 90 days of that transfer, M is required to take the transfer into account in applying the rules of this section and § 1.707-3 only to the extent that the amount of the transfer ($72,000) exceeds M's allocable share of the liability used to fund the transfer. Because the distribution was a debt-financed transfer pursuant to a plan, M's allocable share of the liability is $72,000 ($72,000 × $80,000/80,000) under § 1.707-5(b)(2)(ii). Therefore, M is not required to take into account any of the loan proceeds for purposes of this section and § 1.707-3.

(iii) When the receivables are collected, M must be allocated the gain on the contributed receivables under section 704(c). However, the lender permits the partnership to distribute cash to the partners only to the extent of the value of new receivables contributed to the partnership. In 1993, M contributes additional receivables and receives a distribution of cash. The taxable income recognized by the partnership on the receivables is taxable income of the partnership arising in the ordinary course of the partnership's activities. To the extent the distribution does not exceed 90 percent (M's percentage interest in overall partnership profits) of the partnership's operating cash flow under § 1.707-4(b), the distribution to M is presumed not to be a part of a sale of receivables by M to the partnership, and the presumption is not rebutted under these facts. [Reg. § 1.707-5.]

☐ [*T.D.* 8439, 9-25-92.]

[Reg. § 1.707-6]

§ 1.707-6. Disguised sales of property by partnership to partner; general rules.—(a) *In general.* Rules similar to those provided in § 1.707-3 apply in determining whether a transfer of property by a partnership to a partner and one or more transfers of money or other consideration by that partner to the partnership are treated as a sale of property, in whole or in part, to the partner.

(b) *Special rules relating to liabilities*—(1) *In general.* Rules similar to those provided in § 1.707-5 apply to determine the extent to which an assumption of or taking subject to a liability by a partner, in connection with a transfer of property by a partnership, is considered part of a sale. Accordingly, if a partner assumes or takes property subject to a qualified liability (as defined in paragraph (b)(2) of this section) of a partnership, the partner is treated as transferring consideration to the partnership only to the extent provided in this paragraph (b). If the partner assumes or takes subject to a liability that is not a qualified liability, the amount treated as consideration transferred to the partnership is the amount that the liability assumed or taken subject to by the partner exceeds the partner's share of that liability (determined under the rules of § 1.707-5(a)(2)) immediately before the transfer. Similar to the rules provided in § 1.707-5(a)(4), if more than one partner assumes or takes subject to a liability pursuant to a plan, the amount that is treated as a transfer of consideration by each partner is the amount by which all of the liabilities (other than qualified liabilities) assumed or taken subject to by the partner pursuant to the plan exceed the partner's share of all of those liabilities immediately before the assumption or taking subject to. This paragraph (b)(1) does not apply to any liability assumed or taken subject to by a partner with a principal purpose of reducing the extent to which any other liability assumed or taken subject to by a partner is treated as a transfer of consideration under this paragraph (b).

(2) *Qualified liabilities.* (i) If a transfer of property by a partnership to a partner is not otherwise treated as part of a sale, the partner's assumption of or taking subject to a qualified liability is not treated as part of a sale. If a transfer of property by a partnership to the partner is treated as part of a sale without regard to the partner's assumption of or taking subject to a qualified liability, the partner's assumption of or taking subject to that liability is treated as a transfer of consideration made pursuant to a sale of such property to the partner only to the extent of the lesser of—

(A) The amount of consideration that the partner would be treated as transferring to the partnership under paragraph (b) of this section if the liability were not a qualified liability; or

(B) The amount obtained by multiplying the amount of the liability at the time of its assumption or taking subject to by the partnership's net equity percentage with respect to that property.

(ii) A partnership's net equity percentage with respect to an item of property encumbered by a qualified liability equals the percentage determined by dividing—

(A) The aggregate transfers to the partnership from the partner (other than any transfer described in this paragraph (b)(2)) that are treated as the proceeds realized from the sale of the transferred property to the partner; by

(B) The excess of the fair market value of the property at the time it is transferred to the partner over any qualified liabilities of the partnership that are assumed or taken subject to by the partner at that time.

(iii) For purposes of this section, the definition of a qualified liability is that provided in § 1.707-5(a)(6) with the following exceptions—

(A) In applying the definition, the qualified liability is one that is originally an obligation of the partnership and is assumed or taken subject to by the partner in connection with a transfer of property to the partner; and

(B) If the liability was incurred by the partnership more than two years prior to the earlier of the date the partnership agrees in writing to transfer the property or the date the partnership transfers the property to the partner, that liability is a qualified liability whether or not it has encumbered the transferred property throughout the two-year period.

(c) *Disclosure rules.* Similar to the rules provided in §§ 1.707-3(c)(2) and 1.707-5(a)(7)(ii), a partnership is to disclose to the Internal Revenue Service, in accordance with § 1.707-8, the facts in the following circumstances:

(1) When a partnership transfers property to a partner and the partner transfers money or other consideration to the partnership within a two-year period (without regard to the order of the transfers) and the partnership treats the transfers as other than a sale for tax purposes; and

(2) When a partner assumes or takes subject to a liability of a partnership in connection with a transfer of property by the partnership to the partner, and the partnership incurred the liability within the two-year period prior to the earlier of the date the partnership agrees in writing to the transfer of property or the date the partnership transfers the property, and the partnership treats

Reg. § 1.707-6(c)

the liability as a qualified liability under rules similar to § 1.707-5(a)(6)(i)(B).

(d) *Examples.* The following examples illustrate the rules of this section.

Example 1. Sale of property by partnership to partner. (i) A is a member of a partnership. The partnership transfers property X to A. At the time of the transfer, property X has a fair market value of $1,000,000. One year after the transfer, A transfers $1,100,000 to the partnership. Assume that under the rules of section 1274 the imputed principal amount of an obligation to transfer $1,100,000 one year after the transfer of property X is $1,000,000 on the date of the transfer.

(ii) Since the transfer of $1,100,000 to the partnership by A is made within two years of the transfer of property X to A, under rules similar to those provided in § 1.707-3(c), the transfers are presumed to be a sale unless the facts and circumstances clearly establish otherwise. If no facts exist that would rebut this presumption, on the date that the partnership transfers property X to A, the partnership is treated as having sold property X to A in exchange for A's obligation to transfer $1,100,000 to the partnership one year later.

Example 2. Assumption of liability by partner. (i) B is a member of an existing partnership. The partnership transfers property Y to B. On the date of the transfer, property Y has a fair market value of $1,000,000 and is encumbered by a nonrecourse liability of $600,000. B takes the property subject to the liability. The partnership incurred the nonrecourse liability six months prior to the transfer of property Y to B and used the proceeds to purchase an unrelated asset. Assume that, under rule of § 1.707-5(a)(2)(ii) (which determines a partner's share of a nonrecourse liability), B's share of the nonrecourse liability immediately before the transfer of property Y was $100,000.

(ii) The liability is not allocable under the rules of § 1.163-8T to capital expenditures with respect to the property transferred to B and was not incurred in the ordinary course of the trade or business in which the property transferred to the partner was used or held. Since the partnership incurred the nonrecourse liability within two years of the transfer to B, under rules similar to those provided in § 1.707-5(a)(5), the liability is presumed to be incurred in anticipation of the transfer unless the facts and circumstances clearly establish the contrary. Assuming no facts exist to rebut this presumption, the liability taken subject to by B is not a qualified liability. The partnership is treated as having received, on the date of the transfer of property Y to B, $500,000 ($600,000 liability assumed by B less B's share of the $100,000 liability immediately prior to the transfer) as consideration for the sale of one-half ($500,000/$1,000,000) of property Y to B. The partnership is also treated as having distributed to B, in B's capacity as a partner, the other one-half of property Y. [Reg. § 1.707-6.]

☐ [*T.D.* 8439, 9-25-92.]

[Reg. § 1.707-7]

§ 1.707-7. Disguised sales of partnership interests.—[Reserved]

☐ [*T.D.* 8439, 9-25-92.]

[Reg. § 1.707-8]

§ 1.707-8. Disclosure of certain information.—(a) *In general.* The disclosure referred to in § 1.707-3(c)(2) (regarding certain transfers made within two years of each other), § 1.707-5(a)(7)(ii) (regarding a liability incurred within two years prior to a transfer of property), and § 1.707-6(c) (relating to transfers of property from a partnership to a partner in situations analogous to those listed above) is to be made in accordance with paragraph (b) of this section.

(b) *Method of providing disclosure.* Disclosure is to be made on a completed Form 8275 or on a statement attached to the return of the transferor of property for the taxable year of the transfer that includes the following:

(1) A caption identifying the statement as disclosure under section 707;

(2) An identification of the item (or group of items) with respect to which disclosure is made;

(3) The amount of each item; and

(4) The facts affecting the potential tax treatment of the item (or items) under section 707.

(c) *Disclosure by certain partnerships.* If more than one partner transfers property to a partnership pursuant to a plan, the disclosure required by this section may be made by the partnership on behalf of all the transferors rather than by each transferor separately. [Reg. § 1.707-8.]

☐ [*T.D.* 8439, 9-25-92.]

[Reg. § 1.707-9]

§ 1.707-9. Effective dates and transitional rules.—(a) *Sections 1.707-3 through 1.707-6*—(1) *In general.* Except as provided in paragraph (a)(3) of this section, §§ 1.707-3 through 1.707-6 apply to any transaction with respect to which all transfers that are part of a sale of an item of property occur after April 24, 1991.

(2) *Transfers occurring on or before April 24, 1991.* Except as otherwise provided in paragraph

Determination of Tax Liability

(a)(3) of this section, in the case of any transaction with respect to which one or more of the transfers occurs on or before April 24, 1991, the determination of whether the transaction is a disguised sale of property (including a partnership interest) under section 707(a)(2) is to be made on the basis of the statute and the guidance provided regarding that provision in the legislative history of section 73 of the Tax Reform Act of 1984 (Pub. L. 98-369, 98 Stat. 494). See H.R. Rep. No. 861, 98th Cong., 2d Sess. 859-62 (1984); S. Prt. No. 169 (Vol. I), 98th Cong., 2d Sess. 223-32 (1984); H.R. Rep. No. 432 (Pt. 2), 98th Cong., 2d Sess. 1216-21 (1984).

(3) *Effective date of section 73 of the Tax Reform Act of 1984.* Sections 1.707-3 through 1.707-6 do not apply to any transfer of money or other consideration to which section 73(a) of the Tax Reform Act of 1984 (Pub. L. 98-369, 98 Stat. 494) does not apply pursuant to section 73(b) of that Act.

(b) *Section 1.707-8 disclosure of certain information.* The disclosure provisions described in § 1.707-8 apply to transactions with respect to which all transfers that are part of a sale of property occur after September 30, 1992. [Reg. § 1.707-9.]

☐ [T.D. 8439, 9-25-92.]

[Reg. § 1.708-1]

§ 1.708-1. Continuation of partnership.—(a) *General rule.* For purposes of subchapter K, chapter 1 of the Code, an existing partnership shall be considered as continuing if it is not terminated.

(b) *Termination*—(1) *General rule.* A partnership shall terminate when the operations of the partnership are discontinued and no part of any business, financial operation, or venture of the partnership continues to be carried on by any of its partners in a partnership. For example, on November 20, 1956, A and B, each of whom is a 20-percent partner in partnership ABC, sell their interests to C, who is a 60-percent partner. Since the business is no longer carried on by any of its partners in a partnership, the ABC partnership is terminated as of November 20, 1956. However, where partners DEF agree on April 30, 1957, to dissolve their partnership, but carry on the business through a winding up period ending September 30, 1957, when all remaining assets, consisting only of cash, are distributed to the partners, the partnership does not terminate because of cessation of business until September 30, 1957.

(i) Upon the death of one partner in a 2-member partnership, the partnership shall not be considered as terminated if the estate or other successor in interest of the deceased partner continues to share in the profits or losses of the partnership business.

(ii) For the continuation of a partnership where payments are being made under section 736 (relating to payments to a retiring partner or a deceased partner's successor in interest), see paragraph (a)(6) of § 1.736-1.

(2) A partnership shall terminate when 50 percent or more of the total interest in partnership capital and profits is sold or exchanged within a period of 12 consecutive months. Such sale or exchange includes a sale or exchange to another member of the partnership. However, a disposition of a partnership interest by gift (including assignment to a successor in interest), bequest, or inheritance, or the liquidation of a partnership interest, is not a sale or exchange for purposes of this subparagraph. Moreover, if the sale or exchange of an interest in a partnership (upper-tier partnership) that holds an interest in another partnership (lower-tier partnership) results in a termination of the upper-tier partnership, the upper-tier partnership is treated as exchanging its entire interest in the capital and profits of the lower-tier partnership. If the sale or exchange of an interest in an upper-tier partnership does not terminate the upper-tier partnership, the sale or exchange of an interest in the upper-tier partnership is not treated as a sale or exchange of a proportionate share of the upper-tier partnership's interest in the capital and profits of the lower-tier partnership. The previous two sentences apply to terminations of partnerships under section 708(b)(1)(B) occurring on or after May 9, 1997; however, the sentences may be applied to terminations occurring on or after May 9, 1996, provided that the partnership and its partners apply the sentences to the termination in a consistent manner. Furthermore, the contribution of property to a partnership does not constitute such a sale or exchange. See, however, paragraph (c)(3) of § 1.731-1. Fifty percent or more of the total interest in partnership capital and profits means 50 percent or more of the total interest in partnership capital plus 50 percent or more of the total interest in partnership profits. Thus, the sale of a 30-percent interest in partnership capital and a 60-percent interest in partnership profits is not the sale or exchange of 50 percent or more of the total interest in partnership capital and profits. If one or more partners sell or exchange interests aggregating 50 percent or more of the total interest in partnership capital and 50 percent or more of the total interest in partnership profits within a period of 12 consecutive months, such sale or exchange is considered as being within the provisions of this subparagraph. When interests are sold or exchanged on

Reg. § 1.708-1(b)(2)

different dates, the percentages to be added are determined as of the date of each sale. For example, with respect to the ABC partnership, the sale by A on May 12, 1956, of a 30-percent interest in capital and profits to D, and the sale by B on March 27, 1957, of a 30-percent interest in capital and profits to E, is a sale of a 50-percent or more interest. Accordingly, the partnership is terminated as of March 27, 1957. However, if, on March 27, 1957, D, instead of B, sold his 30-percent interest in capital and profits to E, there would be no termination since only one 30-percent interest would have been sold or exchanged within a 12-month period.

(3) For purposes of subchapter K, chapter 1 of the Code, a partnership taxable year closes with respect to all partners on the date on which the partnership terminates. See section 706(c)(1) and paragraph (c)(1) of § 1.706-1. The date of termination is:

(i) For purposes of section 708(b)(1)(A), the date on which the winding up of the partnership affairs is completed.

(ii) For purposes of section 708(b)(1)(B), the date of the sale or exchange of a partnership interest which, of itself or together with sales or exchanges in the preceding 12 months, transfers an interest of 50 percent or more in both partnership capital and profits.

(4) If a partnership is terminated by a sale or exchange of an interest, the following is deemed to occur: The partnership contributes all of its assets and liabilities to a new partnership in exchange for an interest in the new partnership; and, immediately thereafter, the terminated partnership distributes interests in the new partnership to the purchasing partner and the other remaining partners in proportion to their respective interests in the terminated partnership in liquidation of the terminated partnership, either for the continuation of the business by the new partnership or for its dissolution and winding up. In the latter case, the new partnership terminates in accordance with (b)(1) of this section. This paragraph (b)(4) applies to terminations of partnerships under section 708(b)(1)(B) occurring on or after May 9, 1997; however, this paragraph (b)(4) may be applied to terminations occurring on or after May 9, 1996, provided that the partnership and its partners apply this paragraph (b)(4) to the termination in a consistent manner. The provisions of this paragraph (b)(4) are illustrated by the following example:

Example. (i) A and B each contribute $10,000 cash to form AB, a general partnership, as equal partners. AB purchases depreciable Property X for $20,000. Property X increases in value to $30,000, at which time A sells its entire 50 percent interest to C for $15,000 in a transfer that terminates the partnership under section 708(b)(1)(B). At the time of the sale, Property X had an adjusted tax basis of $16,000 and a book value of $16,000 (original $20,000 tax basis and book value reduced by $4,000 of depreciation). In addition, A and B each had a capital account balance of $8,000 (original $10,000 capital account reduced by $2,000 of depreciation allocations with respect to Property X).

(ii) Following the deemed contribution of assets and liabilities by the terminated AB partnership to a new partnership (new AB) and the liquidation of the terminated AB partnership, the adjusted tax basis of Property X in the hands of new AB is $16,000. See Section 723. The book value of Property X in the hands of new partnership AB is also $16,000 (the book value of Property X immediately before the termination) and B and C each have a capital account of $8,000 in new AB (the balance of their capital accounts in AB prior to the termination). See § 1.7041(b)(2)(iv)(l) (providing that the deemed contribution and liquidation with regard to the terminated partnership are disregarded in determining the capital accounts of the partners and the books of the new partnership). Additionally, under § 301.6109-1(d)(2)(iii) of this chapter, new AB retains the taxpayer identification number of the terminated AB partnership.

(iii) Property X was not section 704(c) property in the hands of terminated AB and is therefore not treated as section 704(c) property in the hands of new AB, even though Property X is deemed contributed to new AB at a time when the fair market value of Property X ($30,000) was different from its adjusted tax basis ($16,000). See § 1.704-3(a)(3)(i) (providing that property contributed to a new partnership under § 1.708-1(b)(4) is treated as section 704(c) property only to the extent that the property was section 704(c) property in the hands of the terminated partnership immediately prior to the termination).

(5) If a partnership is terminated by a sale or exchange of an interest in the partnership, a section 754 election (including a section 754 election made by the terminated partnership on its final return) that is in effect for the taxable year of the terminated partnership in which the sale occurs, applies with respect to the incoming partner. Therefore, the bases of partnership assets are adjusted pursuant to sections 743 and 755 prior to their deemed contribution to the new partnership. This paragraph (b)(5) applies to terminations of partnerships under section 708(b)(1)(B) occurring

Reg. § 1.708-1(b)(3)

on or after May 9, 1997; however, this paragraph (b)(5) may be applied to terminations occurring on or after May 9, 1996, provided that the partnership and its partners apply this paragraph (b)(5) to the termination in a consistent manner.

(c) *Merger or consolidation*—(1) *General rule.* If two or more partnerships merge or consolidate into one partnership, the resulting partnership shall be considered a continuation of the merging or consolidating partnership the members of which own an interest of more than 50 percent in the capital and profits of the resulting partnership. If the resulting partnership can, under the preceding sentence, be considered a continuation of more than one of the merging or consolidating partnerships, it shall, unless the Commissioner permits otherwise, be considered the continuation solely of that partnership which is credited with the contribution of assets having the greatest fair market value (net of liabilities) to the resulting partnership. Any other merging or consolidating partnerships shall be considered as terminated. If the members of none of the merging or consolidating partnerships have an interest of more than 50 percent in the capital and profits of the resulting partnership, all of the merged or consolidated partnerships are terminated, and a new partnership results.

(2) *Tax returns.* The taxable years of any merging or consolidating partnerships which are considered terminated shall be closed in accordance with the provisions of section 706(c) and the regulations thereunder, and such partnerships shall file their returns for a taxable year ending upon the date of termination, i.e., the date of merger or consolidation. The resulting partnership shall file a return for the taxable year of the merging or consolidating partnership that is considered as continuing. The return shall state that the resulting partnership is a continuation of such merging or consolidating partnership, shall retain the employer identification number (EIN) of the partnership that is continuing, and shall include the names, addresses, and EINs of the other merged or consolidated partnerships. The respective distributive shares of the partners for the periods prior to and including the date of the merger or consolidation and subsequent to the date of merger or consolidation shall be shown as a part of the return.

(3) *Form of a merger or consolidation*—(i) *Assets-over form.* When two or more partnerships merge or consolidate into one partnership under the applicable jurisdictional law without undertaking a form for the merger or consolidation, or undertake a form for the merger or consolidation that is not described in paragraph (c)(3)(ii) of this section, any merged or consolidated partnership that is considered terminated under paragraph (c)(1) of this section is treated as undertaking the assets-over form for Federal income tax purposes. Under the assets-over form, the merged or consolidated partnership that is considered terminated under paragraph (c)(1) of this section contributes all of its assets and liabilities to the resulting partnership in exchange for an interest in the resulting partnership, and immediately thereafter, the terminated partnership distributes interests in the resulting partnership to its partners in liquidation of the terminated partnership.

(ii) *Assets-up form.* Despite the partners' transitory ownership of the terminated partnership's assets, the form of a partnership merger or consolidation will be respected for Federal income tax purposes if the merged or consolidated partnership that is considered terminated under paragraph (c)(1) of this section distributes all of its assets to its partners (in a manner that causes the partners to be treated, under the laws of the applicable jurisdiction, as the owners of such assets) in liquidation of the partners' interests in the terminated partnership, and immediately thereafter, the partners in the terminated partnership contribute the distributed assets to the resulting partnership in exchange for interests in the resulting partnership.

(4) *Sale of an interest in the merging or consolidating partnership.* In a transaction characterized under the assets-over form, a sale of all or part of a partner's interest in the terminated partnership to the resulting partnership that occurs as part of a merger or consolidation under section 708(b)(2)(A), as described in paragraph (c)(3)(i) of this section, will be respected as a sale of a partnership interest if the merger agreement (or another document) specifies that the resulting partnership is purchasing interests from a particular partner in the merging or consolidating partnership and the consideration that is transferred for each interest sold, and if the selling partner in the terminated partnership, either prior to or contemporaneous with the transaction, consents to treat the transaction as a sale of the partnership interest. See section 741 and § 1.741-1 for determining the selling partner's gain or loss on the sale or exchange of the partnership interest.

(5) *Examples.* The following examples illustrate the rules in paragraphs (c)(1) through (4) of this section:

Example 1. Partnership AB, in whose capital and profits A and B each own a 50-percent interest, and partnership CD, in whose capital and profits C and D each own a 50-percent interest, merge on September 30, 1999, and form partner-

Reg. § 1.708-1(c)(5)

ship ABCD. Partners A, B, C, and D are on a calendar year, and partnership AB and partnership CD also are on a calendar year. After the merger, the partners have capital and profits interests as follows: A, 30 percent; B, 30 percent; C, 20 percent; and D, 20 percent. Since A and B together own an interest of more than 50 percent in the capital and profits of partnership ABCD, such partnership shall be considered a continuation of partnership AB and shall continue to file returns on a calendar year basis. Since C and D own an interest of less than 50 percent in the capital and profits of partnership ABCD, the taxable year of partnership CD closes as of September 30, 1999, the date of the merger, and partnership CD is terminated as of that date. Partnership ABCD is required to file a return for the taxable year January 1 to December 31, 1999, indicating thereon that, until September 30, 1999, it was partnership AB. Partnership CD is required to file a return for its final taxable year, January 1 through September 30, 1999.

Example 2. (i) Partnership X, in whose capital and profits A owns a 40-percent interest and B owns a 60-percent interest, and partnership Y, in whose capital and profits B owns a 60-percent interest and C owns a 40-percent interest, merge on September 30, 1999. The fair market value of the partnership X assets (net of liabilities) is $100X, and the fair market value of the partnership Y assets (net of liabilities) is $200X. The merger is accomplished under state law by partnership Y contributing its assets and liabilities to partnership X in exchange for interests in partnership X, with partnership Y then liquidating, distributing interests in partnership X to B and C.

(ii) B, a partner in both partnerships prior to the merger, owns a greater than 50-percent interest in the resulting partnership following the merger. Accordingly, because the fair market value of partnership Y's assets (net of liabilities) was greater than that of partnership X's, under paragraph (c)(1) of this section, partnership X will be considered to terminate in the merger. As a result, even though, for state law purposes, the transaction was undertaken with partnership Y contributing its assets and liabilities to partnership X and distributing interests in partnership X to its partners, pursuant to paragraph (c)(3)(i) of this section, for Federal income tax purposes, the transaction will be treated as if partnership X contributed its assets to partnership Y in exchange for interests in partnership Y and then liquidated, distributing interests in partnership Y to A and B.

Example 3. (i) The facts are the same as in *Example 2*, except that partnership X is engaged in a trade or business and has, as one of its assets, goodwill. In addition, the merger is accomplished under state law by having partnership X convey an undivided 40-percent interest in each of its assets to A and an undivided 60-percent interest in each of its assets to B, with A and B then contributing their interests in such assets to partnership Y. Partnership Y also assumes all of the liabilities of partnership X.

(ii) Under paragraph (c)(3)(ii) of this section, the form of the partnership merger will be respected so that partnership X will be treated as following the assets-up form for Federal income tax purposes.

Example 4. (i) Partnership X and partnership Y merge when the partners of partnership X transfer their partnership X interests to partnership Y in exchange for partnership Y interests. Immediately thereafter, partnership X liquidates into partnership Y. The resulting partnership is considered a continuation of partnership Y, and partnership X is considered terminated.

(ii) The partnerships are treated as undertaking the assets-over form described in paragraph (c)(3)(i) of this section because the partnerships undertook a form that is not the assets-up form described in paragraph (c)(3)(ii) of this section. Accordingly, for Federal income tax purposes, partnership X is deemed to contribute its assets and liabilities to partnership Y in exchange for interests in partnership Y, and, immediately thereafter, partnership X is deemed to have distributed the interests in partnership Y to its partners in liquidation of their interests in partnership X.

Example 5. (i) A, B, and C are partners in partnership X. D, E, and F are partners in Partnership Y. Partnership X and partnership Y merge, and the resulting partnership is considered a continuation of partnership Y. Partnership X is considered terminated. Under state law, partnerships X and Y undertake the assets-over form of paragraph (c)(3)(i) of this section to accomplish the partnership merger. C does not want to become a partner in partnership Y, and partnership X does not have the resources to buy C's interest before the merger. C, partnership X, and partnership Y enter into an agreement specifying that partnership Y will purchase C's interest in partnership X for $150 before the merger, and as part of the agreement, C consents to treat the transaction in a manner that is consistent with the agreement. As part of the merger, partnership X receives from partnership Y $150 that will be distributed to C immediately before the merger, and interests in partnership Y in exchange for partnership X's assets and liabilities.

Reg. § 1.708-1(c)(5)

Determination of Tax Liability

See p. 20,601 for regulations not amended to reflect law changes

(ii) Because the merger agreement satisfies the requirements of paragraph (c)(4) of this section and C provides the necessary consent, C will be treated as selling its interest in partnership X to partnership Y for $150 before the merger. See section 741 and § 1.741-1 to determine the amount and character of C's gain or loss on the sale or exchange of its interest in partnership X.

(iii) Because the merger agreement satisfies the requirements of paragraph (c)(4) of this section, partnership Y is considered to have purchased C's interest in partnership X for $150 immediately before the merger. See § 1.704-1(b)(2)(iv)(*l*) for determining partnership Y's capital account in partnership X. Partnership Y's adjusted basis of its interest in partnership X is determined under section 742 and § 1.742-1. To the extent any built-in gain or loss on section 704(c) property in partnership X would have been allocated to C (including any allocations with respect to property revaluations under section 704(b) (reverse section 704(c) allocations)), see section 704 and § 1.704-3(a)(7) for determining the built-in gain or loss or reverse section 704(c) allocations apportionable to partnership Y. Similarly, after the merger is completed, the built-in gain or loss and reverse section 704(c) allocations attributable to C's interest are apportioned to D, E, and F under section 704(c) and § 1.704-3(a)(7).

(iv) Under paragraph (c)(3)(i) of this section, partnership X contributes its assets and liabilities attributable to the interests of A and B to partnership Y in exchange for interests in partnership Y; and, immediately thereafter, partnership X distributes the interests in partnership Y to A and B in liquidation of their interests in partnership X. At the same time, partnership X distributes assets to partnership Y in liquidation of partnership Y's interest in partnership X. Partnership Y's bases in the distributed assets are determined under section 732(b).

(6) *Prescribed form not followed in certain circumstances*—(i) If any transactions described in paragraph (c)(3) or (4) of this section are part of a larger series of transactions, and the substance of the larger series of transactions is inconsistent with following the form prescribed in such paragraph, the Commissioner may disregard such form, and may recast the larger series of transactions in accordance with their substance.

(ii) *Example.* The following example illustrates the rules in paragraph (c)(6) of this section:

Example. A, B, and C are equal partners in partnership ABC. ABC holds no section 704(c) property. D and E are equal partners in partnership DE. B and C want to exchange their interests in ABC for all of the interests in DE. However, rather than exchanging partnership interests, DE merges with ABC by undertaking the assets-up form described in paragraph (c)(3)(ii) of this section, with D and E receiving title to the DE assets and then contributing the assets to ABC in exchange for interests in ABC. As part of a prearranged transaction, the assets acquired from DE are contributed to a new partnership, and the interests in the new partnership are distributed to B and C in complete liquidation of their interests in ABC. The merger and division in this example represent a series of transactions that in substance are an exchange of interests in ABC for interests in DE. Even though paragraph (c)(3)(ii) of this section provides that the form of a merger will be respected for Federal income tax purposes if the steps prescribed under the assets-up form are followed, and paragraph (d)(3)(i) of this section provides a form that will be followed for Federal income tax purposes in the case of partnership divisions, these forms will not be respected for Federal income tax purposes under these facts, and the transactions will be recast in accordance with their substance as a taxable exchange of interests in ABC for interests in DE.

(7) *Effective date.* This paragraph (c) is applicable to partnership mergers occurring on or after January 4, 2001. However, a partnership may apply paragraph (c) of this section to partnership mergers occurring on or after January 11, 2000.

(d) *Division of a partnership*—(1) *General rule.* Upon the division of a partnership into two or more partnerships, any resulting partnership (as defined in paragraph (d)(4)(iv) of this section) or resulting partnerships shall be considered a continuation of the prior partnership (as defined in paragraph (d)(4)(ii) of this section) if the members of the resulting partnership or partnerships had an interest of more than 50 percent in the capital and profits of the prior partnership. Any other resulting partnership will not be considered a continuation of the prior partnership but will be considered a new partnership. If the members of none of the resulting partnerships owned an interest of more than 50 percent in the capital and profits of the prior partnership, none of the resulting partnerships will be considered a continuation of the prior partnership, and the prior partnership will be considered to have terminated. Where members of a partnership which has been divided into two or more partnerships do not become members of a resulting partnership which is considered a continuation of the prior partnership, such members' interests shall be considered liquidated as of the date of the division.

Reg. § 1.708-1(d)(1)

(2) *Tax consequences*—(i) *Tax returns.* The resulting partnership that is treated as the divided partnership (as defined in paragraph (d)(4)(i) of this section) shall file a return for the taxable year of the partnership that has been divided and retain the employer identification number (EIN) of the prior partnership. The return shall include the names, addresses, and EINs of all resulting partnerships that are regarded as continuing. The return shall also state that the partnership is a continuation of the prior partnership and shall set forth separately the respective distributive shares of the partners for the periods prior to and including the date of the division and subsequent to the date of division. All other resulting partnerships that are regarded as continuing and new partnerships shall file separate returns for the taxable year beginning on the day after the date of the division with new EINs for each partnership. The return for a resulting partnership that is regarded as continuing and that is not the divided partnership shall include the name, address, and EIN of the prior partnership.

(ii) *Elections.* All resulting partnerships that are regarded as continuing are subject to preexisting elections that were made by the prior partnership. A subsequent election that is made by a resulting partnership does not affect the other resulting partnerships.

(3) *Form of a division*—(i) *Assets-over form.* When a partnership divides into two or more partnerships under applicable jurisdictional law without undertaking a form for the division, or undertakes a form that is not described in paragraph (d)(3)(ii) of this section, the transaction will be characterized under the assets-over form for Federal income tax purposes.

(A) *Assets-over form where at least one resulting partnership is a continuation of the prior partnership.* In a division under the assets-over form where at least one resulting partnership is a continuation of the prior partnership, the divided partnership (as defined in paragraph (d)(4)(i) of this section) contributes certain assets and liabilities to a recipient partnership (as defined in paragraph (d)(4)(iii) of this section) or recipient partnerships in exchange for interests in such recipient partnership or partnerships; and, immediately thereafter, the divided partnership distributes the interests in such recipient partnership or partnerships to some or all of its partners in partial or complete liquidation of the partners' interests in the divided partnership.

(B) *Assets-over form where none of the resulting partnerships is a continuation of the prior partnership.* In a division under the assets-over form where none of the resulting partnerships is a continuation of the prior partnership, the prior partnership will be treated as contributing all of its assets and liabilities to new resulting partnerships in exchange for interests in the resulting partnerships; and, immediately thereafter, the prior partnership will be treated as liquidating by distributing the interests in the new resulting partnerships to the prior partnership's partners.

(ii) *Assets-up form*—(A) *Assets-up form where the partnership distributing assets is a continuation of the prior partnership.* Despite the partners' transitory ownership of some of the prior partnership's assets, the form of a partnership division will be respected for Federal income tax purposes if the divided partnership (which, pursuant to § 1.708-1(d)(4)(i), must be a continuing partnership) distributes certain assets (in a manner that causes the partners to be treated, under the laws of the applicable jurisdiction, as the owners of such assets) to some or all of its partners in partial or complete liquidation of the partners' interests in the divided partnership, and immediately thereafter, such partners contribute the distributed assets to a recipient partnership or partnerships in exchange for interests in such recipient partnership or partnerships. In order for such form to be respected for transfers to a particular recipient partnership, all assets held by the prior partnership that are transferred to the recipient partnership must be distributed to, and then contributed by, the partners of the recipient partnership.

(B) *Assets-up form where none of the resulting partnerships are a continuation of the prior partnership.* If none of the resulting partnerships are a continuation of the prior partnership, then despite the partners' transitory ownership of some or all of the prior partnership's assets, the form of a partnership division will be respected for Federal income tax purposes if the prior partnership distributes certain assets (in a manner that causes the partners to be treated, under the laws of the applicable jurisdiction, as the owners of such assets) to some or all of its partners in partial or complete liquidation of the partners' interests in the prior partnership, and immediately thereafter, such partners contribute the distributed assets to a resulting partnership or partnerships in exchange for interests in such resulting partnership or partnerships. In order for such form to be respected for transfers to a particular resulting partnership, all assets held by the prior partnership that are transferred to the resulting partnership must be distributed to, and then contributed by, the partners of the resulting partnership. If the prior partnership does not liquidate under the applicable jurisdictional law, then with respect to the assets and liabilities that, in form, are not transferred to a new resulting partnership, the prior partnership will be treated as transferring these assets and liabilities to a new resulting partnership under the assets-over form described in paragraph (d)(3)(i)(B) of this section.

(4) *Definitions*—(i) *Divided partnership.* For purposes of paragraph (d) of this section, the divided partnership is the continuing partnership which is treated, for Federal income tax purposes, as transferring the assets and liabilities to the recipient partnership or partnerships, either directly (under the assets-over form) or indirectly (under the assets-up form). If the resulting partnership that, in form, transferred the assets and liabilities in connection with the division is a continuation of the prior partnership, then such resulting partnership will be treated as the divided partnership. If a partnership divides into two or more partnerships and only one of the resulting partnerships is a continuation of the prior partnership, then the resulting partnership that is a continuation of the prior partnership will be treated as the divided partnership. If a partnership divides into two or more partnerships without undertaking a form for the division that is recognized under paragraph (d)(3) of this section, or if the resulting partnership that had, in form, transferred assets and liabilities is not considered a continuation of the prior partnership, and more than one resulting partnership is considered a continuation of the prior partnership, the continuing resulting partnership with the assets having the greatest fair market value (net of liabilities) will be treated as the divided partnership.

(ii) *Prior partnership.* For purposes of paragraph (d) of this section, the prior partnership is the partnership subject to division that exists under applicable jurisdictional law before the division.

(iii) *Recipient partnership.* For purposes of paragraph (d) of this section, a recipient partnership is a partnership that is treated as receiving, for Federal income tax purposes, assets and liabilities from a divided partnership, either directly (under the assets-over form) or indirectly (under the assets-up form).

(iv) *Resulting partnership.* For purposes of paragraph (d) of this section, a resulting partnership is a partnership resulting from the division that exists under applicable jurisdictional law after the division and that has at least two partners who were partners in the prior partnership. For example, where a prior partnership divides into two partnerships, both partnerships existing after the division are resulting partnerships.

(5) *Examples.* The following examples illustrate the rules in paragraphs (d)(1), (2), (3), and (4) of this section:

Example 1. Partnership ABCD is in the real estate and insurance businesses. A owns a 40-percent interest, and B, C, and D each owns a 20-percent interest, in the capital and profits of the partnership. The partnership and the partners report their income on a calendar year. On November 1, 1999, they separate the real estate and insurance businesses and form two partnerships. Partnership AB takes over the real estate business, and partnership CD takes over the insurance business. Because members of resulting partnership AB owned more than a 50-percent interest in the capital and profits of partnership ABCD (A, 40 percent, and B, 20 percent), partnership AB shall be considered a continuation of partnership ABCD. Partnership AB is required to file a return for the taxable year January 1 to December 31, 1999, indicating thereon that until November 1, 1999, it was partnership ABCD. Partnership CD is considered a new partnership formed at the beginning of the day on November 2, 1999, and is required to file a return for the taxable year it adopts pursuant to section 706(b) and the applicable regulations.

Example 2. (i) Partnership ABCD owns properties W, X, Y, and Z, and divides into partnership AB and partnership CD. Under paragraph (d)(1) of this section, partnership AB is considered a continuation of partnership ABCD and partnership CD is considered a new partnership. Partnership ABCD distributes property Y to C and titles property Y in C's name. Partnership ABCD distributes property Z to D and titles property Z in D's name. C and D then contribute properties Y and Z, respectively, to partnership CD in exchange for interests in partnership CD. Properties W and X remain in partnership AB.

(ii) Under paragraph (d)(3)(ii) of this section, partnership ABCD will be treated as following the assets-up form for Federal income tax purposes.

Example 3. (i) The facts are the same as in *Example 2,* except partnership ABCD distributes property Y to C and titles property Y in C's name. C then contributes property Y to partnership CD. Simultaneously, partnership ABCD contributes property Z to partnership CD in exchange for an interest in partnership CD. Immediately thereafter, partnership ABCD distributes the interest in partnership CD to D in liquidation of D's interest in partnership ABCD.

(ii) Under paragraph (d)(3)(i) of this section, because partnership ABCD did not undertake the assets-up form with respect to all of the assets transferred to partnership CD, partnership ABCD will be treated as undertaking the assets-over form in transferring the assets to partnership CD. Accordingly, for Federal income tax purposes, partnership ABCD is deemed to contribute property Y and property Z to partnership CD in exchange for interests in partnership CD, and immediately thereafter, partnership ABCD is deemed to distribute the interests in partnership CD to partner C and partner D in liquidation of their interests in partnership ABCD.

Example 4. (i) Partnership ABCD owns three parcels of property: property X, with a value of $500; property Y, with a value of $300; and property Z, with a value of $200. A and B each own a 40-percent interest in the capital and profits of partnership ABCD, and C and D each own a 10 percent interest in the capital and profits of partnership ABCD. On November 1, 1999, partnership ABCD divides into three partnerships (AB1, AB2, and CD) by contributing property X to a newly formed partnership (AB1) and distributing all interests in such partnership to A and B as equal partners, and by contributing property Z to a newly formed partnership (CD) and distributing all interests in such partnership to C and D as equal partners in exchange for all of their interests in partnership ABCD. While partnership ABCD does not transfer property Y, C and D cease to be partners in the partnership. Accordingly, after the division, the partnership holding property Y is referred to as partnership AB2.

(ii) Partnerships AB1 and AB2 both are considered a continuation of partnership ABCD, while partnership CD is considered a new partnership formed at the beginning of the day on November 2, 1999. Under paragraph (d)(3)(i)(A) of this section, partnership ABCD will be treated as following the assets-over form, with partnership ABCD contributing property X to partnership AB1 and property Z to partnership CD, and distributing the interests in such partnerships to the designated partners.

Example 5. (i) The facts are the same as in *Example 4*, except that partnership ABCD divides into three partnerships by operation of state law, without undertaking a form.

(ii) Under the last sentence of paragraph (d)(4)(i) of this section, partnership AB1 will be treated as the resulting partnership that is the divided partnership. Under paragraph (d)(3)(i)(A) of this section, partnership ABCD will be treated as following the assets-over form, with partnership ABCD contributing property Y to partnership AB2 and property Z to partnership CD, and distributing the interests in such partnerships to the designated partners.

Example 6. (i) The facts are the same as in *Example 4*, except that partnership ABCD divides into three partnerships by contributing property X to newly-formed partnership AB1 and property Y to newly-formed partnership AB2 and distributing all interests in each partnership to A and B in exchange for all of their interests in partnership ABCD.

(ii) Because resulting partnership CD is not a continuation of the prior partnership (partnership ABCD), partnership CD cannot be treated, for Federal income tax purposes, as the partnership that transferred assets (i.e., the divided partnership), but instead must be treated as a recipient partnership. Under the last sentence of paragraph (d)(4)(i) of this section, partnership AB1 will be treated as the resulting partnership that is the divided partnership. Under paragraph (d)(3)(i)(A) of this section, partnership ABCD will be treated as following the assets-over form, with partnership ABCD contributing property Y to partnership AB2 and property Z to partnership CD, and distributing the interests in such partnerships to the designated partners.

Example 7. (i) Partnership ABCDE owns Blackacre, Whiteacre, and Redacre, and divides into partnership AB, partnership CD, and partnership DE. Under paragraph (d)(1) of this section, partnership ABCDE is considered terminated (and, hence, none of the resulting partnerships are a continuation of the prior partnership) because none of the members of the new partnerships (partnership AB, partnership CD, and partnership DE) owned an interest of more than 50 percent in the capital and profits of partnership ABCDE.

(ii) Partnership ABCDE distributes Blackacre to A and B and titles Blackacre in the names of A and B. A and B then contribute Blackacre to partnership AB in exchange for interests in partnership AB. Partnership ABCDE will be treated as following the assets-up form described in paragraph (d)(3)(ii)(B) of this section for Federal income tax purposes.

(iii) Partnership ABCDE distributes Whiteacre to C and D and titles Whiteacre in the names of C and D. C and D then contribute Whiteacre to partnership CD in exchange for interests in partnership CD. Partnership ABCDE will be treated as following the assets-up form described in paragraph (d)(3)(ii)(B) of this section for Federal income tax purposes.

(iv) Partnership ABCDE does not liquidate under state law so that, in form, the assets in new partnership DE are not considered to have been transferred under state law. Partnership ABCDE will be treated as undertaking the assets-over form described in paragraph (d)(3)(i)(B) of this section for Federal income tax purposes with respect to the assets of partnership DE. Thus, partnership ABCDE will be treated as contributing Redacre to partnership DE in exchange for interests in partnership DE; and, immediately thereafter, partnership ABCDE will be treated as distributing interests in partnership DE to D and E in liquidation of their interests in partnership ABCDE. Partnership ABCDE then terminates.

(6) *Prescribed form not followed in certain circumstances.* If any transactions described in paragraph (d)(3) of this section are part of a larger series of transactions, and the substance of the larger series of transactions is inconsistent with following the form prescribed in such paragraph, the Commissioner may disregard such form, and may recast the larger series of transactions in accordance with their substance.

(7) *Effective date.* This paragraph (d) is applicable to partnership divisions occurring on or after January 4, 2001. However, a partnership may apply paragraph (d) of this section to partnership divisions occurring on or after January 11, 2000. [Reg. § 1.708-1.]

☐ [T.D. 6175, 5-23-56. Amended by T.D. 8717, 5-8-97 and T.D. 8925, 1-3-2001 (corrected 9-9-2002).]

[Reg. § 1.709-1]

§ 1.709-1. **Treatment of organization and syndication costs.**—(a) *General rule.* Except as provided in paragraph (b) of this section, no deduction shall be allowed under chapter 1 of the Code to a partnership or to any partner for any amounts paid or incurred, directly or indirectly, in partnership taxable years beginning after December 31, 1975, to organize a partnership, or to promote the sale of, or to sell, an interest in the partnership.

(b) *Amortization of organization expenses.* (1) Under section 709(b) of the Code, a partnership may elect to treat its organizational expenses (as defined in section 709(b)(2) and in § 1.709-2(a)) paid or incurred in partnership taxable years beginning after December 31, 1976, as deferred expenses. If a partnership elects to amortize organizational expenses, it must select a period of not less than 60 months, over which the partnership will amortize all such expenses on a straight line basis. This period must begin with the month in which the partnership begins business (as determined under § 1.709-2(c)). However, in the case of a partnership on the cash receipts and disbursements method of accounting, no deduction shall be allowed for a taxable year with respect to any such expenses that have not been paid by the end of that taxable year. Portions of such expenses which would have been deductible under section 709(b) in a prior taxable year if the expenses had been paid are deductible in the year of payment. The election is irrevocable and the period selected by the partnership in making its election may not be subsequently changed.

(2) If there is a winding up and complete liquidation of the partnership prior to the end of the amortization period, the unamortized amount of organizational expenses is a partnership deduction in its final taxable year to the extent provided under section 165 (relating to losses). However, there is no partnership deduction with respect to its capitalized syndication expenses.

(c) *Time and manner of making election.* The election to amortize organizational expenses provided by section 709(b) shall be made by attaching a statement to the partnership's return of income for the taxable year in which the partnership begins business. The statement shall set forth a description of each organizational expense incurred (whether or not paid) with the amount of the expense, the date each expense was incurred, the month in which the partnership began business, and the number of months (not less than 60) over which the expenses are to be amortized. A taxpayer on the cash receipts and disbursements method of accounting shall also indicate the amount paid before the end of the taxable year with respect to each such expense. Expenses less than $10 need not be separately listed, provided the total amount of these expenses is listed with the dates on which the first and last of such expenses were incurred, and, in the case of a taxpayer on the cash receipts and disbursements method of accounting, the aggregate amount of such expenses that was paid by the end of the taxable year is stated. In the case of a partnership which begins business in a taxable year that ends after March 31, 1983, the original return and statement must be filed (and the election made) not later than the date prescribed by law for filing the return (including any extensions of time) for that taxable year. Once an election has been made, an amended return (or returns) and statement (or statements) may be filed to include any organizational expenses not included in the partnership's original return and statement. [Reg. § 1.709-1.]

☐ [T.D. 7891, 5-3-83.]

[Reg. § 1.709-2]

§ 1.709-2. **Definitions.**—(a) *Organizational expenses.* Section 709(b)(2) of the Internal Revenue Code defines organizational expenses as expenses which:

Reg. § 1.709-2(a)

(1) Are incident to the creation of the partnership;

(2) Are chargeable to capital account; and

(3) Are of a character which, if expended incident to the creation of a partnership having an ascertainable life, would (but for section 709(a)) be amortized over such life.

An expenditure which fails to meet one or more of these three tests does not qualify as an organizational expense for purposes of section 709(b) and this section. To satisfy the statutory requirement described in paragraph (a)(1) of this section, the expense must be incurred during the period beginning at a point which is a reasonable time before the partnership begins business and ending with the date prescribed by law for filing the partnership return (determined without regard to any extensions of time) for the taxable year the partnership begins business. In addition, the expenses must be for creation of the partnership and not for operation or starting operation of the partnership trade or business. To satisfy the statutory requirement described in paragraph (a)(3) of this section, the expense must be for an item of a nature normally expected to benefit the partnership throughout the entire life of the partnership. The following are examples of organizational expenses within the meaning of section 709 and this section: Legal fees for services incident to the organization of the partnership, such as negotiation and preparation of a partnership agreement; accounting fees for services incident to the organization of the partnership; and filing fees. The following are examples of expenses that are not organizational expenses within the meaning of section 709 and this section (regardless of how the partnership characterizes them): Expenses connected with acquiring assets for the partnership or transferring assets to the partnership; expenses connected with the admission or removal of partners other than at the time the partnership is first organized; expenses connected with a contract relating to the operation of the partnership trade or business (even where the contract is between the partnership and one of its members); and syndication expenses.

(b) *Syndication expenses.* Syndication expenses are expenses connected with the issuing and marketing of interests in the partnership. Examples of syndication expenses are brokerage fees; registration fees; legal fees of the underwriter or placement agent and the issuer (the general partner or the partnership) for securities advice and for advice pertaining to the adequacy of tax disclosures in the prospectus or placement memorandum for securities law purposes; accounting fees for preparation of representations to be included in the offering materials; and printing costs of the prospectus, placement memorandum, and other selling and promotional material. These expenses are not subject to the election under section 709(b) and must be capitalized.

(c) *Beginning business.* The determination of the date a partnership begins business for purposes of section 709 presents a question of fact that must be determined in each case in light of all the circumstances of the particular case. Ordinarily, a partnership begins business when it starts the business operation for which it was organized. The mere signing of a partnership agreement is not alone sufficient to show the beginning of business. If the activities of the partnership have advanced to the extent necessary to establish the nature of its business operations, it will be deemed to have begun business. Accordingly, the acquisition of operating assets which are necessary to the type of business contemplated may constitute beginning business for these purposes. The term "operating assets", as used herein, means assets that are in a state of readiness to be placed in service within a reasonable period following their acquisition. [Reg. § 1.709-2.]

☐ [T.D. 7891, 5-3-83.]

Contributions, Distributions and Transfers
[Reg. § 1.721-1]

§ 1.721-1. Nonrecognition of gain or loss on contribution.—(a) No gain or loss shall be recognized either to the partnership or to any of its partners upon a contribution of property, including installment obligations, to the partnership in exchange for a partnership interest. This rule applies whether the contribution is made to a partnership in the process of formation or to a partnership which is already formed and operating. Section 721 shall not apply to a transaction between a partnership and a partner not acting in his capacity as a partner since such a transaction is governed by section 707. Rather than contributing property to a partnership, a partner may sell property to the partnership or may retain the ownership of property and allow the partnership to use it. In all cases, the substance of the transaction will govern, rather than its form. See paragraph (c)(3) of § 1.731-1. Thus, if the transfer of property by the partner to the partnership results in the receipt by the partner of money or other consideration, including a promissory obligation fixed in amount and time for payment, the transaction will be treated as a sale or exchange under section 707 rather than as a contribution under section 721. For the rules governing the treatment of liabilities to which contributed property is subject, see section 752 and § 1.752-1.

(b)(1) Normally, under local law, each partner is entitled to be repaid his contributions of money or other property to the partnership (at the value placed upon such property by the partnership at the time of the contribution) whether made at the formation of the partnership or subsequent thereto. To the extent that any of the partners gives up any part of his right to be repaid his contributions (as distinguished from a share in partnership profits) in favor of another partner as compensation for services (or in satisfaction of an obligation), section 721 does not apply. The value of an interest in such partnership capital so transferred to a partner as compensation for services constitutes income to the partner under section 61. The amount of such income is the fair market value of the interest in capital so transferred, either at the time the transfer is made for past services, or at the time the services have been rendered where the transfer is conditioned on the completion of the transferee's future services. The time when such income is realized depends on all the facts and circumstances, including any substantial restrictions or conditions on the compensated partner's right to withdraw or otherwise dispose of such interest. To the extent that an interest in capital representing compensation for services rendered by the decedent prior to his death is transferred after his death to the decedent's successor in interest, the fair market value of such interest is income in respect of a decedent under section 691.

(2) To the extent that the value of such interest is: (i) compensation for services rendered to the partnership, it is a guaranteed payment for services under section 707(c); (ii) compensation for services rendered to a partner, it is not deductible by the partnership, but is deductible only by such partner to the extent allowable under this chapter.

(c) *Underwritings of partnership interests*—(1) *In general.* For the purpose of section 721, if a person acquires a partnership interest from an underwriter in exchange for cash in a qualified underwriting transaction, the person who acquires the partnership interest is treated as transferring cash directly to the partnership in exchange for the partnership interest and the underwriter is disregarded. A qualified underwriting transaction is a transaction in which a partnership issues partnership interests for cash in an underwriting in which either the underwriter is an agent of the partnership or the underwriter's ownership of the partnership interests is transitory.

(2) *Effective date.* This paragraph (c) is effective for qualified underwriting transactions occurring on or after May 1, 1996. [Reg. § 1.721-1.]

☐ [*T.D. 6175, 5-23-56. Amended by T.D. 8665, 4-30-96.*]

[Reg. § 1.722-1]

§ 1.722-1. **Basis of contributing partner's interest.**—The basis to a partner of a partnership interest acquired by a contribution of property, including money, to the partnership shall be the amount of money contributed plus the adjusted basis at the time of contribution of any property contributed. If the acquisition of an interest in partnership capital results in taxable income to a partner, such income shall constitute an addition to the basis of the partner's interest. See paragraph (b) of § 1.721-1. If the contributed property is subject to indebtedness or if liabilities of the partner are assumed by the partnership, the basis of the contributing partner's interest shall be reduced by the portion of the indebtedness assumed by the other partners, since the partnership's assumption of his indebtedness is treated as a distribution of money to the partner. Conversely, the assumption by the other partners of a portion of the contributor's indebtedness is treated as a contribution of money by them. See section 752 and § 1.752-1. The provisions of this section may be illustrated by the following examples:

Example (1). A acquired a 20-percent interest in a partnership by contributing property. At the time of A's contribution, the property had a fair market value of $10,000, an adjusted basis to A of $4,000, and was subject to a mortgage of $2,000. Payment of the mortgage was assumed by the partnership. The basis of A's interest in the partnership is $2,400, computed as follows:

Adjusted basis to A of property contributed	$4,000
Less portion of mortgage assumed by other partners which must be treated as a distribution (80 percent of $2,000)	1,600
Basis of A's interest	2,400

Example (2). If, in example (1) of this section, the property contributed by A was subject to a mortgage of $6,000, the basis of A's interest would be zero, computed as follows:

Reg. § 1.722-1

Adjusted basis to A of property contributed	$4,000
Less portion of mortgage assumed by other partners which must be treated as a distribution (80 percent of $6,000)	4,800
	(800)

Since A's basis cannot be less than zero, the $800 in excess of basis, which is considered as a distribution of money under section 752(b), is treated as capital gain from the sale or exchange of a partnership interest. See section 731(a). [Reg. § 1.722-1.]

☐ [T.D. 6175, 5-23-56.]

[Reg. § 1.723-1]

§ 1.723-1. **Basis of property contributed to partnership.**—The basis to the partnership of property contributed to it by a partner is the adjusted basis of such property to the contributing partner at the time of the contribution. Since such property has the same basis in the hands of the partnership as it had in the hands of the contributing partner, the holding period of such property for the partnership includes the period during which it was held by the partner. See section 1223(2). For elective adjustments to the basis of partnership property arising from distributions or transfers of partnership interests, see sections 732(d), 734(b), and 743(b). [Reg. § 1.723-1.]

☐ [T.D. 6175, 5-23-56.]

[Reg. § 1.731-1]

§ 1.731-1. **Extent of recognition of gain or loss on distribution**—(a) *Recognition of gain or loss to partner*—(1) *Recognition of gain.*(i) Where money is distributed by a partnership to a partner, no gain shall be recognized to the partner except to the extent that the amount of money distributed exceeds the adjusted basis of the partner's interest in the partnership immediately before the distribution. This rule is applicable both to current distributions (i. e., distributions other than in liquidation of an entire interest) and to distributions in liquidation of a partner's entire interest in a partnership. Thus, if a partner with a basis for his interest of $10,000 receives a distribution of cash of $8,000 and property with a fair market value of $3,000, no gain is recognized to him. If $11,000 cash were distributed, gain would be recognized to the extent of $1,000. No gain shall be recognized to a distributee partner with respect to a distribution of property (other than money) until he sells or otherwise disposes of such property, except to the extent otherwise provided by section 736 (relating to payments to a retiring partner or a deceased partner's successor in interest) and section 751 (relating to unrealized receivables and inventory items). See section 731(c) and paragraph (c) of this section.

(ii) For the purposes of sections 731 and 705, advances or drawings of money or property against a partner's distributive share of income shall be treated as current distributions made on the last day of the partnership taxable year with respect to such partner.

(2) *Recognition of loss.* Loss is recognized to a partner only upon liquidation of his entire interest in the partnership, and only if the property distributed to him consists solely of money, unrealized receivables (as defined in section 751(c)), and inventory items (as defined in section 751(d)(2)). The term "liquidation of a partner's interest", as defined in section 761(d), is the termination of the partner's entire interest in the partnership by means of a distribution or a series of distributions. Loss is recognized to the distributee partner in such cases to the extent of the excess of the adjusted basis of such partner's interest in the partnership at the time of the distribution over the sum of—

(i) Any money distributed to him, and

(ii) The basis to the distributee, as determined under section 732, of any unrealized receivables and inventory items that are distributed to him. If the partner whose interest is liquidated receives any property other than money, unrealized receivables, or inventory items, then no loss will be recognized. Application of the provisions of this subparagraph may be illustrated by the following examples:

Example (1). Partner A has a partnership interest in partnership ABC with an adjusted basis to him of $10,000. He retires from the partnership and receives, as a distribution in liquidation of his entire interest, his share of partnership property. This share is $5,000 cash and inventory with a basis to him (under section 732) of $3,000. Partner A realizes a capital loss of $2,000, which is recognized under section 731(a)(2).

Example (2). Partner B has a partnership interest in partnership BCD with an adjusted basis to him of $10,000. He retires from the partnership and receives, as a distribution in liquidation of his entire interest, his share of partnership property. This share is $4,000 cash, real property (used in the trade or business) with an adjusted basis to the partnership of $2,000, and unrealized receivables having a basis to him (under section 732) of $3,000. No loss will be recognized to B on the transaction because he received property other than money, unrealized receivables, and inventory items. As determined under section 732, the basis to B for the real property received is $3,000.

(3) *Character of gain or loss.* Gain or loss recognized under section 731(a) on a distribution is considered gain or loss from the sale or exchange of the partnership interest of the distributee partner, that is, capital gain or loss.

(b) *Gain or loss recognized by partnership.* A distribution of property (including money) by a partnership to a partner does not result in recognized gain or loss to the partnership under section 731. However, recognized gain or loss may result to the partnership from certain distributions which, under section 751(b), must be treated as a sale or exchange of property between the distributee partner and the partnership.

(c) *Exceptions.* (1) Section 731 does not apply to the extent otherwise provided by—

(i) Section 736 (relating to payments to a retiring partner or to a deceased partner's successor in interest), and

(ii) Section 751 (relating to unrealized receivables and inventory items). For example, payments under section 736(a), which are considered as a distributive share or guaranteed payment, are taxable as such under that section.

(2) The receipt by a partner from the partnership of money or property under an obligation to repay the amount of such money or to return such property does not constitute a distribution subject to section 731 but is a loan governed by section 707(a). To the extent that such an obligation is canceled, the obligor partner will be considered to have received a distribution of money or property at the time of cancellation.

(3) If there is a contribution of property to a partnership and within a short period:

(i) Before or after such contribution other property is distributed to the contributing partner and the contributed property is retained by the partnership, or

(ii) After such contribution the contributed property is distributed to another partner,

such distribution may not fall within the scope of section 731. Section 731 does not apply to a distribution of property, if, in fact, the distribution was made in order to effect an exchange of property between two or more of the partners or between the partnership and a partner. Such a transaction shall be treated as an exchange of property. [Reg. § 1.731-1.]

☐ [*T.D. 6175, 5-23-56.*]

[Reg. § 1.731-2]

§ 1.731-2. **Partnership distributions of marketable securities.**—(a) *Marketable securities treated as money.* Except as otherwise provided in section 731(c) and this section, for purposes of sections 731(a)(1) and 737, the term *money* includes marketable securities and such securities are taken into account at their fair market value as of the date of the distribution.

(b) *Reduction of amount treated as money*—(1) *Aggregation of securities.* For purposes of section 731(c)(3)(B) and this paragraph (b), all marketable securities held by a partnership are treated as marketable securities of the same class and issuer as the distributed security.

(2) *Amount of reduction.* The amount of the distribution of marketable securities that is treated as a distribution of money under section 731(c) and paragraph (a) of this section is reduced (but not below zero) by the excess, if any, of—

(i) The distributee partner's distributive share of the net gain, if any, which would be recognized if all the marketable securities held by the partnership were sold (immediately before the transaction to which the distribution relates) by the partnership for fair market value; over

(ii) The distributee partner's distributive share of the net gain, if any, which is attributable to the marketable securities held by the partnership immediately after the transaction, determined by using the same fair market value as used under paragraph (b)(2)(i) of this section.

(3) *Distributee partner's share of net gain.* For purposes of section 731(c)(3)(B) and paragraph (b)(2) of this section, a partner's distributive share of net gain is determined—

(i) By taking into account any basis adjustments under section 743(b) with respect to that partner;

(ii) Without taking into account any special allocations adopted with a principal purpose of avoiding the effect of section 731(c) and this section; and

(iii) Without taking into account any gain or loss attributable to a distributed security to which paragraph (d)(1) of this section applies.

(c) *Marketable securities*—(1) *In general.* For purposes of section 731(c) and this section, the term *marketable securities* is defined in section 731(c)(2).

(2) *Actively traded.* For purposes of section 731(c) and this section, a financial instrument is actively traded (and thus is a marketable security) if it is of a type that is, as of the date of distribution, actively traded within the meaning of section 1092(d)(1). Thus, for example, if *XYZ*

common stock is listed on a national securities exchange, particular shares of XYZ common stock that are distributed by a partnership are marketable securities even if those particular shares cannot be resold by the distributee partner for a designated period of time.

(3) *Interests in an entity*—(i) *Substantially all.* For purposes of section 731(c)(2)(B)(v) and this section, substantially all of the assets of an entity consist (directly or indirectly) of marketable securities, money, or both only if 90 percent or more of the assets of the entity (by value) at the time of the distribution of an interest in the entity consist (directly or indirectly) of marketable securities, money, or both.

(ii) *Less than substantially all.* For purposes of section 731(c)(2)(B)(vi) and this section, an interest in an entity is a marketable security to the extent that the value of the interest is attributable (directly or indirectly) to marketable securities, money, or both, if less than 90 percent but 20 percent or more of the assets of the entity (by value) at the time of the distribution of an interest in the entity consist (directly or indirectly) of marketable securities, money, or both.

(4) *Value of assets.* For purposes of section 731(c) and this section, the value of the assets of an entity is determined without regard to any debt that may encumber or otherwise be allocable to those assets, other than debt that is incurred to acquire an asset with a principal purpose of avoiding or reducing the effect of section 731(c) and this section.

(d) *Exceptions*—(1) *In general.* Except as otherwise provided in paragraph (d)(2) of this section, section 731(c) and this section do not apply to the distribution of a marketable security if—

(i) The security was contributed to the partnership by the distributee partner;

(ii) The security was acquired by the partnership in a nonrecognition transaction, and the following conditions are satisfied—

(A) The value of any marketable securities and money exchanged by the partnership in the nonrecognition transaction is less than 20 percent of the value of all the assets exchanged by the partnership in the nonrecognition transaction; and

(B) The partnership distributed the security within five years of either the date the security was acquired by the partnership or, if later, the date the security became marketable; or

(iii) The security was not a marketable security on the date acquired by the partnership, and the following conditions are satisfied—

(A) The entity that issued the security had no outstanding marketable securities at the time the security was acquired by the partnership;

(B) The security was held by the partnership for at least six months before the date the security became marketable; and

(C) The partnership distributed the security within five years of the date the security became marketable.

(2) *Anti-stuffing rule.* Paragraph (d)(1) of this section does not apply to the extent that 20 percent or more of the value of the distributed security is attributable to marketable securities or money contributed (directly or indirectly) by the partnership to the entity to which the distributed security relates after the security was acquired by the partnership (other than marketable securities contributed by the partnership that were originally contributed to the partnership by the distributee partner). For purposes of this paragraph (d)(2), money contributed by the distributing partnership does not include any money deemed contributed by the partnership as a result of section 752.

(3) *Successor security.* Section 731(c) and this section apply to the distribution of a marketable security acquired by the partnership in a nonrecognition transaction in exchange for a security the distribution of which immediately prior to the exchange would have been excepted under this paragraph (d) only to the extent that section 731(c) and this section otherwise would have applied to the exchanged security.

(e) *Investment partnerships*—(1) *In general.* Section 731(c) and this section do not apply to the distribution of marketable securities by an investment partnership (as defined in section 731(c)(3)(C)(i)) to an eligible partner (as defined in section 731(c)(3)(C)(iii)).

(2) *Eligible partner*—(i) *Contributed services.* For purposes of section 731(c)(3)(C)(iii) and this section, a partner is not treated as a partner other than an eligible partner solely because the partner contributed services to the partnership.

(ii) *Contributed partnership interests.* For purposes of determining whether a partner is an eligible partner under section 731(c)(3)(C), if the partner has contributed to the investment partnership an interest in another partnership that meets the requirements of paragraph (e)(4)(i) of this section after the contribution, the contributed interest is treated as property specified in section 731(c)(3)(C)(i).

(3) *Trade or business activities.* For purposes of section 731(c)(3)(C) and this section, a partner-

Reg. § 1.731-2(c)(3)

ship is not treated as engaged in a trade or business by reason of—

(i) Any activity undertaken as an investor, trader, or dealer in any asset described in section 731(c)(3)(C)(i), including the receipt of commitment fees, break-up fees, guarantee fees, director's fees, or similar fees that are customary in and incidental to any activities of the partnership as an investor, trader, or dealer in such assets;

(ii) Reasonable and customary management services (including the receipt of reasonable and customary fees in exchange for such management services) provided to an investment partnership (within the meaning of section 731(c)(3)(C)(i)) in which the partnership holds a partnership interest; or

(iii) Reasonable and customary services provided by the partnership in assisting the formation, capitalization, expansion, or offering of interests in a corporation (or other entity) in which the partnership holds or acquires a significant equity interest (including the provision of advice or consulting services, bridge loans, guarantees of obligations, or service on a company's board of directors), provided that the anticipated receipt of compensation for the services, if any, does not represent a significant purpose for the partnership's investment in the entity and is incidental to the investment in the entity.

(4) *Partnership tiers.* For purposes of section 731(c)(3)(C)(iv) and this section, a partnership (upper-tier partnership) is not treated as engaged in a trade or business engaged in by, or as holding (instead of a partnership interest) a proportionate share of the assets of, a partnership (lower-tier partnership) in which the partnership holds a partnership interest if—

(i) The upper-tier partnership does not actively and substantially participate in the management of the lower-tier partnership; and

(ii) The interest held by the upper-tier partnership is less than 20 percent of the total profits and capital interests in the lower-tier partnership.

(f) *Basis rules*—(1) *Partner's basis*—(i) *Partner's basis in distributed securities.* The distributee partner's basis in distributed marketable securities with respect to which gain is recognized by reason of section 731(c) and this section is the basis of the security determined under section 732, increased by the amount of such gain. Any increase in the basis of the marketable securities attributable to gain recognized by reason of section 731(c) and this section is allocated to marketable securities in proportion to their respective amounts of unrealized appreciation in the hands of the partner before such increase.

(ii) *Partner's basis in partnership interest.* The basis of the distributee partner's interest in the partnership is determined under section 733 as if no gain were recognized by the partner on the distribution by reason of section 731(c) and this section.

(2) *Basis of partnership property.* No adjustment is made to the basis of partnership property under section 734 as a result of any gain recognized by a partner, or any step-up in the basis in the distributed marketable securities in the hands of the distributee partner, by reason of section 731(c) and this section.

(g) *Coordination with other sections*—(1) *Sections 704(c)(1)(B) and 737*—(i) *In general.* If a distribution results in the application of sections 731(c) and one or both of sections 704(c)(1)(B) and 737, the effect of the distribution is determined by applying section 704(c)(1)(B) first, section 731(c) second, and finally section 737.

(ii) *Section 704(c)(1)(B).* The basis of the distributee partner's interest in the partnership for purposes of determining the amount of gain, if any, recognized by reason of section 731(c) (and for determining the basis of the marketable securities in the hands of the distributee partner) includes the increase or decrease, if any, in the partner's basis that occurs under section 704(c)(1)(B)(iii) as a result of a distribution to another partner of property contributed by the distributee partner in a distribution that is part of the same distribution as the marketable securities.

(iii) *Section 737*—(A) *Marketable securities as other property.* A distribution of marketable securities is treated as a distribution of property other than money for purposes of section 737 to the extent that the marketable securities are not treated as money under section 731(c). In addition, marketable securities contributed to the partnership are treated as property other than money in determining the contributing partner's net precontribution gain under section 737(b).

(B) *Basis increase under section 737.* The basis of the distributee partner's interest in the partnership for purposes of determining the amount of gain, if any, recognized by reason of section 731(c) (and for determining the basis of the marketable securities in the hands of the distributee partner) does not include the increase, if any, in the partner's basis that occurs under section 737(c)(1) as a result of a distribution of property to the distributee partner in a distribution that is part of the same distribution as the marketable securities.

(2) *Section 708(b)(1)(B).* If a partnership termination occurs under section 708(b)(1)(B), the

Reg. § 1.731-2(g)(2)

successor partnership will be treated as if there had been no termination for purposes of section 731(c) and this section. Accordingly, a section 708(b)(1)(B) termination will not affect whether a partnership qualifies for any of the exceptions in paragraphs (d) and (e) of this section. In addition, a deemed distribution that may occur as a result of a section 708(b)(1)(B) termination will not be subject to section 731(c) and this section.

(h) *Anti-abuse rule.* The provisions of section 731(c) and this section must be applied in a manner consistent with the purpose of section 731(c) and the substance of the transaction. Accordingly, if a principal purpose of a transaction is to achieve a tax result that is inconsistent with the purpose of section 731(c) and this section, the Commissioner can recast the transaction for Federal tax purposes as appropriate to achieve tax results that are consistent with the purpose of section 731(c) and this section. Whether a tax result is inconsistent with the purpose of section 731(c) and this section must be determined based on all the facts and circumstances. For example, under the provisions of this paragraph (h)—

(1) A change in partnership allocations or distribution rights with respect to marketable securities may be treated as a distribution of the marketable securities subject to section 731(c) if the change in allocations or distribution rights is, in substance, a distribution of the securities;

(2) A distribution of substantially all of the assets of the partnership other than marketable securities and money to some partners may also be treated as a distribution of marketable securities to the remaining partners if the distribution of the other property and the withdrawal of the other partners is, in substance, equivalent to a distribution of the securities to the remaining partners; and

(3) The distribution of multiple properties to one or more partners at different times may also be treated as part of a single distribution if the distributions are part of a single plan of distribution.

(i) [Reserved]

(j) *Examples.* The following examples illustrate the rules of this section. Unless otherwise specified, all securities held by a partnership are marketable securities within the meaning of section 731(c); the partnership holds no marketable securities other than the securities described in the example; all distributions by the partnership are subject to section 731(a) and are not subject to sections 704(c)(1)(B), 707(a)(2)(B), 751(b), or 737; and no securities are eligible for an exception to section 731(c). The examples read as follows:

Example 1. Recognition of gain. (i) A and B form partnership AB as equal partners. A contributes property with a fair market value of $1,000 and an adjusted tax basis of $250. B contributes $1,000 cash. AB subsequently purchases Security X for $500 and immediately distributes the security to A in a current distribution. The basis in A's interest in the partnership at the time of distribution is $250.

(ii) The distribution of Security X is treated as a distribution of money in an amount equal to the fair market value of Security X on the date of distribution ($500). (The amount of the distribution that is treated as money is not reduced under section 731(c)(3)(B) and paragraph (b) of this section because, if Security X had been sold immediately before the distribution, there would have been no gain recognized by AB and A's distributive share of the gain would therefore have been zero.) As a result, A recognizes $250 of gain under section 731(a)(1) on the distribution ($500 distribution of money less $250 adjusted tax basis in A's partnership interest).

Example 2. Reduction in amount treated as money—in general. (i) A and B form partnership AB as equal partners. AB subsequently distributes Security X to A in a current distribution. Immediately before the distribution, AB held securities with the following fair market values, adjusted tax bases, and unrecognized gain or loss:

	Value	Basis	Gain (Loss)
Security X	100	70	30
Security Y	100	80	20
Security Z	100	110	(10)

(ii) If AB had sold the securities for fair market value immediately before the distribution to A, the partnership would have recognized $40 of net gain ($30 gain on Security X plus $20 gain on Security Y minus $10 loss on Security Z). A's distributive share of this gain would have been $20 (one-half of $40 net gain). If AB had sold the remaining securities immediately after the distribution of Security X to A, the partnership would have $10 of net gain ($20 of gain on Security Y minus $10 loss on Security Z). A's distributive share of this gain would have been $5 (one-half of $10 net gain). As a result, the distribution resulted in a decrease of $15 in A's distributive share of the net gain in AB's securities ($20 net gain before distribution minus $5 net gain after distribution).

Reg. § 1.731-2(h)(1)

(iii) Under paragraph (b) of this section, the amount of the distribution of Security X that is treated as a distribution of money is reduced by $15. The distribution of Security X is therefore treated as a distribution of $85 of money to A ($100 fair market value of Security X minus $15 reduction).

Example 3. Reduction in amount treated as money—carried interest. (i) A and B form partnership AB. A contributes $1,000 and provides substantial services to the partnership in exchange for a 60 percent interest in partnership profits. B contributes $1,000 in exchange for a 40 percent interest in partnership profits. AB subsequently distributes Security X to A in a current distribution. Immediately before the distribution, AB held securities with the following fair market values, adjusted tax bases, and unrecognized gain:

	Value	Basis	Gain
Security X	100	80	20
Security Y	100	90	10

(ii) If AB had sold the securities for fair market value immediately before the distribution to A, the partnership would have recognized $30 of net gain ($20 gain on Security X plus $10 gain on Security Y). A's distributive share of this gain would have been $18 (60 percent of $30 net gain). If AB had sold the remaining securities immediately after the distribution of Security X to A, the partnership would have $10 of net gain ($10 gain on Security Y). A's distributive share of this gain would have been $6 (60 percent of $10 net gain). As a result, the distribution resulted in a decrease of $12 in A's distributive share of the net gain in AB's securities ($18 net gain before distribution minus $6 net gain after distribution).

(iii) Under paragraph (b) of this section, the amount of the distribution of Security X that is treated as a distribution of money is reduced by $12. The distribution of Security X is therefore treated as a distribution of $88 of money to A ($100 fair market value of Security X minus $12 reduction).

Example 4. Reduction in amount treated as money—change in partnership allocations. (i) A is admitted to partnership ABC as a partner with a 1 percent interest in partnership profits. At the time of A's admission, ABC held no securities. ABC subsequently acquires Security X. A's interest in partnership profits is subsequently increased to 2 percent for securities acquired after the increase. A retains a 1 percent interest in all securities acquired before the increase. ABC then acquires Securities Y and Z and later distributes Security X to A in a current distribution. Immediately before the distribution, the securities held by ABC had the following fair market values, adjusted tax bases, and unrecognized gain or loss:

	Value	Basis	Gain (Loss)
Security X	1,000	500	500
Security Y	1,000	800	200
Security Z	1,000	1,100	(100)

(ii) If ABC had sold the securities for fair market value immediately before the distribution to A, the partnership would have recognized $600 of net gain ($500 gain on Security X plus $200 gain on Security Y minus $100 loss on Security Z). A's distributive share of this gain would have been $7 (1 percent of $500 gain on Security X plus 2 percent of $200 gain on Security Y minus 2 percent of $100 loss on Security Z).

(iii) If ABC had sold the remaining securities immediately after the distribution of Security X to A, the partnership would have $100 of net gain ($200 gain on Security Y minus $100 loss on Security Z). A's distributive share of this gain would have been $2 (2 percent of $200 gain on Security Y minus 2 percent of $100 loss on Security Z). As a result, the distribution resulted in a decrease of $5 in A's distributive share of the net gain in ABC's securities ($7 net gain before distribution minus $2 net gain after distribution).

(iv) Under paragraph (b) of this section, the amount of the distribution of Security X that is treated as a distribution of money is reduced by $5. The distribution of Security X is therefore treated as a distribution of $995 of money to A ($1000 fair market value of Security X minus $5 reduction).

Example 5. Basis consequences—distribution of marketable security. (i) A and B form partnership AB as equal partners. A contributes nondepreciable real property with a fair market value and adjusted tax basis of $100.

(ii) AB subsequently distributes Security X with a fair market value of $120 and an adjusted tax basis of $90 to A in a current distribution. At the time of distribution, the basis in A's interest in the partnership is $100. The amount of the distribution that is treated as money is reduced under section 731(c)(3)(B) and paragraph (b)(2) of this section by $15 (one-half of $30 net gain in Security X). As a result, A recognizes $5 of gain under section 731(a) on the distribution (excess of $105 distribution of money over $100 adjusted tax basis in A's partnership interest).

Reg. § 1.731-2(j)

(iii) *A*'s adjusted tax basis in Security *X* is $95 ($90 adjusted basis of Security *X* determined under section 732(a)(1) plus $5 of gain recognized by *A* by reason of section 731(c)). The basis in *A*'s interest in the partnership is $10 as determined under section 733 ($100 pre-distribution basis minus $90 basis allocated to Security *X* under section 732).

Example 6. Basis consequences—distribution of marketable security and other property. (i) *A* and *B* form partnership *AB* as equal partners. *A* contributes nondepreciable real property, with a fair market value of $100 and an adjusted tax basis of $10.

(ii) *AB* subsequently distributes Security *X* with a fair market value and adjusted tax basis of $40 to *A* in a current distribution and, as part of the same distribution, *AB* distributes Property *Z* to *A* with an adjusted tax basis and fair market value of $40. At the time of distribution, the basis in *A*'s interest in the partnership is $10. *A* recognizes $30 of gain under section 731(a) on the distribution (excess of $40 distribution of money over $10 adjusted tax basis in *A*'s partnership interest).

(iii) *A*'s adjusted tax basis in Security *X* is $35 ($5 adjusted basis determined under section 732(a)(2) plus $30 of gain recognized by *A* by reason of section 731(c)). *A*'s basis in Property *Z* is $5, as determined under section 732(a)(2). The basis in *A*'s interest in the partnership is $0 as determined under section 733 ($10 pre-distribution basis minus $10 basis allocated between Security *X* and Property *Z* under section 732).

(iv) *AB*'s adjusted tax basis in the remaining partnership assets is unchanged unless the partnership has a section 754 election in effect. If *AB* made such an election, the aggregate basis of *AB*'s assets would be increased by $70 (the difference between the $80 combined basis of Security *X* and Property *Z* in the hands of the partnership before the distribution and the $10 combined basis of the distributed property in the hands of *A* under section 732 after the distribution). Under section 731(c)(5), no adjustment is made to partnership property under section 734 as a result of any gain recognized by *A* by reason of section 731(c) or as a result of any step-up in basis in the distributed marketable securities in the hands of *A* by reason of section 731(c).

Example 7. Coordination with section 737. (i) *A* and *B* form partnership *AB*. *A* contributes Property *A*, nondepreciable real property with a fair market value of $200 and an adjusted basis of $100 in exchange for a 25 percent interest in partnership capital and profits. *AB* owns marketable Security *X*.

(ii) Within five years of the contribution of Property *A*, *AB* subsequently distributes Security *X*, with a fair market value of $120 and an adjusted tax basis of $100, to *A* in a current distribution that is subject to section 737. As part of the same distribution, *AB* distributes Property *Y* to *A* with a fair market value of $20 and an adjusted tax basis of $0. At the time of distribution, there has been no change in the fair market value of Property *A* or the adjusted tax basis in *A*'s interest in the partnership.

(iii) If *AB* had sold Security *X* for fair market value immediately before the distribution to *A*, the partnership would have recognized $20 of gain. *A*'s distributive share of this gain would have been $5 (25 percent of $20 gain). Because *AB* has no other marketable securities, *A*'s distributive share of gain in partnership securities after the distribution would have been $0. As a result, the distribution resulted in a decrease of $5 in *A*'s share of the net gain in *AB*'s securities ($5 net gain before distribution minus $0 net gain after distribution). Under paragraph (b)(2) of this section, the amount of the distribution of Security *X* that is treated as a distribution of money is reduced by $5. The distribution of Security *X* is therefore treated as a distribution of $115 of money to *A* ($120 fair market value of Security *X* minus $5 reduction). The portion of the distribution of the marketable security that is not treated as a distribution of money ($5) is treated as other property for purposes of section 737.

(iv) *A* recognizes total gain of $40 on the distribution. *A* recognizes $15 of gain under section 731(a)(1) on the distribution of the portion of Security *X* treated as money ($115 distribution of money less $100 adjusted tax basis in *A*'s partnership interest). *A* recognizes $25 of gain under section 737 on the distribution of Property *Y* and the portion of Security *X* that is not treated as money. *A*'s section 737 gain is equal to the lesser of (i) *A*'s precontribution gain ($100) or (ii) the excess of the fair market value of property received ($20 fair market value of Property *Y* plus $5 portion of Security *X* not treated as money) over the adjusted basis in *A*'s interest in the partnership immediately before the distribution ($100) reduced (but not below zero) by the amount of money received in the distribution ($115).

(v) *A*'s adjusted tax basis in Security *X* is $115 ($100 basis of Security *X* determined under section 732(a) plus $15 of gain recognized by reason of section 731(c)). *A*'s adjusted tax basis in Property *Y* is $0 under section 732(a). The basis in *A*'s interest in the partnership is $25 ($100 basis before distribution minus $100 basis allocated to

Reg. § 1.731-2(j)

Security X under section 732(a) plus $25 gain recognized under section 737).

(k) *Effective date.* This section applies to distributions made on or after December 26, 1996. However, taxpayers may apply the rules of this section to distributions made after December 8, 1994, and before December 26, 1996. [Reg. § 1.731-2.]

☐ [*T.D.* 8707, 12-24-96.]

[Reg. § 1.732-1]

§ 1.732-1. Basis of distributed property other than money—(a) *Distributions other than in liquidation of a partner's interest.* The basis of property (other than money) received by a partner in a distribution from a partnership, other than in liquidation of his entire interest, shall be its adjusted basis to the partnership immediately before such distribution. However, the basis of the property to the partner shall not exceed the adjusted basis of the partner's interest in the partnership, reduced by the amount of any money distributed to him in the same transaction. The provisions of this paragraph may be illustrated by the following examples:

Example (1). Partner A, with an adjusted basis of $15,000 for his partnership interest, receives in a current distribution property having an adjusted basis of $10,000 to the partnership immediately before distribution, and $2,000 cash. The basis of the property in A's hands will be $10,000. Under sections 733 and 705, the basis of A's partnership interest will be reduced by the distribution to $3,000 ($15,000, less $2,000 cash, less $10,000, the basis of the distributed property to A).

Example (2). Partner R has an adjusted basis of $10,000 for his partnership interest. He receives a current distribution of $4,000 cash and property with an adjusted basis to the partnership of $8,000. The basis of the distributed property to partner R is limited to $6,000 ($10,000, the adjusted basis of his interest, reduced by $4,000, the cash distributed).

(b) *Distribution in liquidation.* Where a partnership distributes property (other than money) in liquidation of a partner's entire interest in the partnership, the basis of such property to the partner shall be an amount equal to the adjusted basis of his interest in the partnership reduced by the amount of any money distributed to him in the same transaction. Application of this rule may be illustrated by the following example:

Example. Partner B, with a partnership interest having an adjusted basis to him of $12,000, retires from the partnership and receives cash of $2,000, and real property with an adjusted basis to the partnership of $6,000 and a fair market value of $14,000. The basis of the real property to B is $10,000 (B's basis for his partnership interest, $12,000, reduced by $2,000, the cash distributed).

(c) *Allocation of basis among properties distributed to a partner*—(1) *General rule*—(i) *Unrealized receivables and inventory items.* The basis to be allocated to properties distributed to a partner under section 732(a)(2) or (b) is allocated first to any unrealized receivables (as defined in section 751(c)) and inventory items (as defined in section 751(d)(2)) in an amount equal to the adjusted basis of each such property to the partnership immediately before the distribution. If the basis to be allocated is less than the sum of the adjusted bases to the partnership of the distributed unrealized receivables and inventory items, the adjusted basis of the distributed property must be decreased in the manner provided in paragraph (c)(2)(i) of this section.

(ii) *Other distributed property.* Any basis not allocated to unrealized receivables or inventory items under paragraph (c)(1)(i) of this section is allocated to any other property distributed to the partner in the same transaction by assigning to each distributed property an amount equal to the adjusted basis of the property to the partnership immediately before the distribution. However, if the sum of the adjusted bases to the partnership of such other distributed property does not equal the basis to be allocated among the distributed property, any increase or decrease required to make the amounts equal is allocated among the distributed property as provided in paragraph (c)(2) of this section.

(2) *Adjustment to basis allocation*—(i) *Decrease in basis.* Any decrease to the basis of distributed property required under paragraph (c)(1) of this section is allocated first to distributed property with unrealized depreciation in proportion to each property's respective amount of unrealized depreciation before any decrease (but only to the extent of each property's unrealized depreciation). If the required decrease exceeds the amount of unrealized depreciation in the distributed property, the excess is allocated to the distributed property in proportion to the adjusted bases of the distributed property, as adjusted pursuant to the immediately preceding sentence.

(ii) *Increase in basis.* Any increase to the basis of distributed property required under paragraph (c)(1)(ii) of this section is allocated first to distributed property (other than unrealized receivables and inventory items) with unrealized appreciation in proportion to each property's respective amount of unrealized appreciation before any increase (but only to the extent of each property's unrealized appreciation). If the required increase exceeds the amount of unrealized appreciation in the distributed property, the excess is allocated to the distributed property (other than unrealized receivables or inventory items) in proportion to the fair market value of the distributed property.

(3) *Unrealized receivables and inventory items.* If the basis to be allocated upon a distribution in liquidation of the partner's entire interest in the partnership is greater than the adjusted basis to the partnership of the unrealized receivables and inventory items distributed to the partner, and if there is no other property distributed to which the excess can be allocated, the distributee partner sustains a capital loss under section 731(a)(2) to the extent of the unallocated basis of the partnership interest.

(4) *Examples.* The provisions of this paragraph (c) are illustrated by the following examples:

Example 1. A is a one-fourth partner in partnership PRS and has an adjusted basis in its partnership interest of $650. PRS distributes inventory items and Assets X and Y to A in liquidation of A's entire partnership interest. The distributed inventory items have a basis to the partnership of $100 and a fair market value of $200. Asset X has an adjusted basis to the partnership of $50 and a fair market value of $400. Asset Y has an adjusted basis to the partnership and a fair market value of $100. Neither Asset X nor Asset Y consists of inventory items or unrealized receivables. Under this paragraph (c), A's basis in its partnership interest is allocated first to the inventory items in an amount equal to their adjusted basis to the partnership. A, therefore, has an adjusted basis in the inventory items of $100. The remaining basis, $550, is allocated to the distributed property first in an amount equal to the property's adjusted basis to the partnership. Thus, Asset X is allocated $50 and Asset Y is allocated $100. Asset X is then allocated $350, the amount of unrealized appreciation in Asset X. Finally, the remaining basis, $50, is allocated to Assets X and Y in proportion to their fair market values: $40 to Asset X (400/500 × $50), and $10 to Asset Y (100/500 × $50). Therefore, after the distribution, A has an adjusted basis of $440 in Asset X and $110 in Asset Y.

Example 2. B is a one-fourth partner in partnership PRS and has an adjusted basis in its partnership interest of $200. PRS distributes Asset X and Asset Y to B in liquidation of its entire partnership interest. Asset X has an adjusted basis to the partnership and fair market value of $150. Asset Y has an adjusted basis to the partnership of $150 and a fair market value of $50. Neither of the assets consists of inventory items or unrealized receivables. Under this paragraph (c), B's basis is first assigned to the distributed property to the extent of the partnership's basis in each distributed property. Thus, Asset X and Asset Y are each assigned $150. Because the aggregate adjusted basis of the distributed property, $300, exceeds the basis to be allocated, $200, a decrease of $100 in the basis of the distributed property is required. Assets X and Y have unrealized depreciation of zero and $100, respectively. Thus, the entire decrease is allocated to Asset Y. After the distribution, B has an adjusted basis of $150 in Asset X and $50 in Asset Y.

Example 3. C, a partner in partnership PRS, receives a distribution in liquidation of its entire partnership interest of $6,000 cash, inventory items having an adjusted basis to the partnership of $6,000, and real property having an adjusted basis to the partnership of $4,000. C's basis in its partnership interest is $9,000. The cash distribution reduces C's basis to $3,000, which is allocated entirely to the inventory items. The real property has a zero basis in C's hands. The partnership bases not carried over to C for the distributed properties are lost unless an election under section 754 is in effect requiring the partnership to adjust the bases of remaining partnership properties under section 734(b).

Example 4. Assume the same facts as in *Example 3* of this paragraph except C receives a distribution in liquidation of its entire partnership interest of $1,000 cash and inventory items having a basis to the partnership of $6,000. The cash distribution reduces C's basis to $8,000, which can be allocated only to the extent of $6,000 to the inventory items. The remaining $2,000 basis, not allocable to the distributed property, constitutes a capital loss to partner C under section 731(a)(2). If the election under section 754 is in effect, see section 734(b) for adjustment of the basis of undistributed partnership property.

(5) *Effective date.* This paragraph (c) applies to distributions of property from a partnership that occur on or after December 15, 1999.

(d) *Special partnership basis to transferee under section 732(d).*—(1)(i) A transfer of a partnership interest occurs upon a sale or exchange of an interest or upon the death of a partner. Section 732(d) provides a special rule for the determination of the basis of property distributed to a transferee partner who acquired any part of his partnership interest in a transfer with respect to which the election under section 754 (relating to the optional adjustment to basis of partnership property) was not in effect.

Reg. § 1.732-1(c)(3)

(ii) Where an election under section 754 is in effect, see section 743(b) and §§ 1.743-1 and 1.732-2.

(iii) If a transferee partner receives a distribution of property (other than money) from the partnership within 2 years after he acquired his interest or part thereof in the partnership by a transfer with respect to which the election under section 754 was not in effect, he may elect to treat as the adjusted partnership basis of such property the adjusted basis such property would have if the adjustment provided in section 743(b) were in effect.

(iv) If an election under section 732(d) is made upon a distribution of property to a transferee partner, the amount of the adjustment with respect to the transferee partner is not diminished by any depletion or depreciation on that portion of the basis of partnership property which arises from the special basis adjustment under section 732(d), since depletion or depreciation on such portion for the period prior to distribution is allowed or allowable only if the optional adjustment under section 743(b) is in effect.

(v) If property is distributed to a transferee partner who elects under section 732(d), and if such property is not the same property which would have had a special basis adjustment, then such special basis adjustment shall apply to any like property received in the distribution, provided that the transferee, in exchange for the property distributed, has relinquished his interest in the property with respect to which he would have had a special basis adjustment. This rule applies whether the property in which the transferee has relinquished his interest is retained or disposed of by the partnership. (For a shift of transferee's basis adjustment under section 743(b) to like property, see § 1.743-1(g).)

(vi) The provisions of this paragraph (d)(1) may be illustrated by the following example:

Example. (i) Transferee partner, T, purchased a one-fourth interest in partnership PRS for $17,000. At the time T purchased the partnership interest, the election under section 754 was not in effect and the partnership inventory had a basis to the partnership of $14,000 and a fair market value of $16,000. T's purchase price reflected $500 of this difference. Thus, $4,000 of the $17,000 paid by T for the partnership interest was attributable to T's share of partnership inventory with a basis of $3,500. Within 2 years after T acquired the partnership interest, T retired from the partnership and received in liquidation of its entire partnership interest the following property:

	Assets Adjusted Basis to PRS	Fair Market Value
Cash	$1,500	$1,500
Inventory	$3,500	$4,000
Asset X	$2,000	$4,000
Asset Y	$4,000	$5,000

(ii) The fair market value of the inventory received by T was one-fourth of the fair market value of all partnership inventory and was T's share of such property. It is immaterial whether the inventory T received was on hand when T acquired the interest. In accordance with T's election under section 732(d), the amount of T's share of partnership basis that is attributable to partnership inventory is increased by $500 (one-fourth of the $2,000 difference between the fair market value of the property, $16,000, and its $14,000 basis to the partnership at the time T purchased its interest). This adjustment under section 732(d) applies only for purposes of distributions to T, and not for purposes of partnership depreciation, depletion, or gain or loss on disposition. Thus, the amount to be allocated among the properties received by T in the liquidating distribution is $15,500 ($17,000, T's basis for the partnership interest, reduced by the amount of cash received, $1,500). This amount is allocated as follows: The basis of the inventory items received is $4,000, consisting of the $3,500 common partnership basis, plus the basis adjustment of $500 which T would have had under section 743(b). The remaining basis of $11,500 ($15,500 minus $4,000) is allocated among the remaining property distributed to T by assigning to each property the adjusted basis to the partnership of such property and adjusting that basis by any required increase or decrease. Thus, the adjusted basis to T of Asset X is $5,111 ($2,000, the adjusted basis of Asset X to the partnership, plus $2,000, the amount of unrealized appreciation in Asset X, plus $1,111 ($4,000/$9,000 multiplied by $2,500)). Similarly, the adjusted basis of Asset Y to T is $6,389 ($4,000, the adjusted basis of Asset Y to the partnership, plus $1,000, the amount of unrealized appreciation in Asset Y, plus, $1,389 ($5,000/$9,000 multiplied by $2,500)).

(2) A transferee partner who wishes to elect under section 732(d) shall make the election with his tax return—

(i) For the year of the distribution, if the distribution includes any property subject to the allowance for depreciation, depletion, or amortization, or

(ii) For any taxable year no later than the first taxable year in which the basis of any of the distributed property is pertinent in determining his income tax, if the distribution does not include any such property subject to the allowance for depreciation, depletion or amortization.

(3) A taxpayer making an election under section 732(d) shall submit with the return in which the election is made a schedule setting forth the following:

(i) That under section 732(d) he elects to adjust the basis of property received in a distribution; and

(ii) The computation of the special basis adjustment for the property distributed and the properties to which the adjustment has been allocated. For rules of allocation, see section 755.

(4) A partner who acquired any part of his partnership interest in a transfer to which the election provided in section 754 was not in effect, is required to apply the special basis rule contained in section 732(d) to a distribution to him, whether or not made within 2 years after the transfer, if at the time of his acquisition of the transferred interest—

(i) The fair market value of all partnership property (other than money) exceeded 110 percent of its adjusted basis to the partnership,

(ii) An allocation of basis under section 732(c) upon a liquidation of his interest immediately after the transfer of the interest would have resulted in a shift of basis from property not subject to an allowance for depreciation, depletion, or amortization, to property subject to such an allowance, and

(iii) A basis adjustment under section 743(b) would change the basis to the transferee partner of the property actually distributed.

(5) *Required statements*. If a transferee partner notifies a partnership that it plans to make the election under section 732(d) under paragraph (d)(3) of this section, or if a partnership makes a distribution to which paragraph (d)(4) of this section applies, the partnership must provide the transferee with such information as is necessary for the transferee properly to compute the transferee's basis adjustments under section 732(d).

(e) *Exception*. When a partnership distributes unrealized receivables (as defined in section 751(c)) or substantially appreciated inventory items (as defined in section 751(d)) in exchange for any part of a partner's interest in other partnership property (including money), or, conversely, partnership property (including money) other than unrealized receivables or substantially appreciated inventory items in exchange for any part of a partner's interest in the partnership's unrealized receivables or substantially appreciated inventory items, the distribution will be treated as a sale or exchange of property under the provisions of section 751(b). In such case, section 732 (including subsection (d) thereof) applies in determining the partner's basis of the property which he is treated as having sold to or exchanged with the partnership (as constituted after the distribution). The partner is considered as having received such property in a current distribution and, immediately thereafter, as having sold or exchanged it. See section 751(b) and paragraph (b) of § 1.751-1. However, section 732 does not apply in determining the basis of that part of property actually distributed to a partner which is treated as received by him in a sale or exchange under section 751(b). Consequently, the basis of such property shall be its cost to the partner. [Reg. § 1.732-1.]

☐ [T.D. 6175, 5-23-56. Amended by T.D. 8847, 12-14-99.]

[Reg. § 1.732-2]

§ 1.732-2. **Special partnership basis of distributed property**—(a) *Adjustments under section 734(b)*. In the case of a distribution of property to a partner, the partnership bases of the distributed properties shall reflect any increases or decreases to the basis of partnership property which have been made previously under section 734(b) (relating to the optional adjustment to basis of undistributed partnership property) in connection with previous distributions.

(b) *Adjustments under section 743(b)*. In the case of a distribution of property to a partner who acquired any part of his interest in a transfer as to which an election under section 754 was in effect, then, for the purposes of section 732 (other than subsection (d) thereof), the adjusted partnership bases of the distributed property shall take into account, in addition to any adjustments under section 734(b), the transferee's special basis adjustment for the distributed property under section 743(b). The application of this paragraph may be illustrated by the following example:

Example. Partner D acquired his interest in partnership ABD from a a previous partner. Since the partnership had made an election under section 754, a special basis adjustment with respect to D is applicable to the basis of partnership property in accordance with section 743(b). One of the assets of the partnership at the time D acquired his interest was property X, which is later distributed to D in a current distribution. Property X has an adjusted basis to the partnership of $1,000 and with respect to D it has a special basis adjustment of $500. Therefore, for purposes of section 732(a)(1), the adjusted basis of such property to the partnership with respect to D immediately before its distribution is $1,500. However, if property X is distributed to partner

A, a nontransferee partner, its adjusted basis to the partnership for purposes of section 732(a)(1) is only $1,000. In such case, D's $500 special basis adjustment may shift over to other property. See § 1.743-1(g).

(c) *Adjustments to basis of distributed inventory and unrealized receivables.* Under section 732, the basis to be allocated to distributed properties shall be allocated first to any unrealized receivables and inventory items. If the distributee partner is a transferee of a partnership interest and has a special basis adjustment for unrealized receivables or inventory items under either section 743(b) or section 732(d), then the partnership adjusted basis immediately prior to distribution of any unrealized receivables or inventory items distributed to such partner shall be determined as follows: If the distributee partner receives his entire share of the fair market value of the inventory items or unrealized receivables of the partnership, the adjusted basis of such distributed property to the partnership, for the purposes of section 732, shall take into account the entire amount of any special basis adjustment which the distributee partner may have for such assets. If the distributee partner receives less than his entire share of the fair market value of partnership inventory items or unrealized receivables, then, for purposes of section 732, the adjusted basis of such distributed property to the partnership shall take into account the same proportion of the distributee's special basis adjustment for unrealized receivables or inventory items as the value of such items distributed to him bears to his entire share of the total value of all such items of the partnership. The provisions of this paragraph may be illustrated by the following example:

Example. Partner C acquired his 40-percent interest in partnership AC from a previous partner. Since the partnership had made an election under section 754, C has a special basis adjustment to partnership property under section 743(b). C retires from the partnership when the adjusted basis of his partnership interest is $3,000. He receives from the partnership in liquidation of his entire interest, $1,000 cash, certain capital assets, depreciable property, and certain inventory items and unrealized receivables. C has a special basis adjustment of $800 with respect to partnership inventory items and of $200 with respect to unrealized receivables. The common partnership basis for the inventory items distributed to him is $500 and for the unrealized receivables is zero. If the value of inventory items and the unrealized receivables distributed to C in [is] his 40-percent share of the total value of all partnership inventory items and unrealized receivables, then, for purposes of section 732, the adjusted basis of such property in C's hands will be $1,300 for the inventory items ($500 plus $800) and $200 for the unrealized receivables (zero plus $200). The remaining basis of $500, which constitutes the basis of the capital assets and depreciable property distributed to C, is determined as follows: $3,000 (total basis) less $1,000 cash, or $2,000 (the amount to be allocated to the basis of all distributed property), less $1,500 ($800 and $200 special basis adjustments, plus $500 common partnership basis, the amount allocated to inventory items and unrealized receivables). However, if the value of the inventory items and unrealized receivables distributed to C consisted of only 20 percent of the total fair market value of such property (i.e., only one-half of C's 40-percent share), then only one-half of C's special basis adjustment of $800 for partnership inventory items and $200 for unrealized receivables would be taken into account. In that case, the basis of the inventory items in C's hands would be $650 ($250, the common partnership basis for inventory items distributed to him, plus $400, one-half of C's special basis adjustment for inventory items). The basis of the unrealized receivables in C's hands would be $100 (zero plus $100, one-half of C's special basis adjustment for unrealized receivables). [Reg. § 1.732-2.]

☐ [*T.D.* 6175, 5-23-56. *Amended by T.D.* 8847, 12-14-99.]

[Reg. § 1.732-3]

§ 1.732-3. Corresponding adjustment to basis of assets of a distributed corporation controlled by a corporate partner.—The determination of whether a corporate partner has control of a distributed corporation for purposes of section 732(f) shall be made by applying the special aggregate stock ownership rules of § 1.1502-34. [Reg. § 1.732-3.]

☐ [*T.D.* 8949, 6-18-2001.]

[Reg. § 1.733-1]

§ 1.733-1. Basis of distributee partner's interest.—In the case of a distribution by a partnership to a partner other than in liquidation of a partner's entire interest, the adjusted basis to such partner of his interest in the partnership shall be reduced (but not below zero) by the amount of any money distributed to such partner and by the amount of the basis to him of distributed property other than money as determined under section 732 and §§ 1.732-1 and 1.732-2. [Reg. § 1.733-1.]

☐ [*T.D.* 6175, 5-23-56.]

Contributions, Distributions and Transfers
See p. 20,601 for regulations not amended to reflect law changes

[Reg. § 1.734-1]

§ 1.734-1. Optional adjustment to basis of undistributed partnership property.—(a) *General rule.* A partnership shall not adjust the basis of partnership property as the result of a distribution of property to a partner, unless the election provided in section 754 (relating to optional adjustment to basis of partnership property) is in effect.

(b) *Method of adjustment* —(1) *Increase in basis.* Where an election under section 754 is in effect and a distribution of partnership property is made whether or not in liquidation of the partner's entire interest in the partnership, the adjusted basis of the remaining partnership assets shall be increased by—

(i) The amount of any gain recognized under section 731(a)(1) to the distributee partner, or [and]*

(ii) The excess of the adjusted basis to the partnership immediately before the distribution of any property distributed (including adjustments under section 743(b) or section 732(d) when applied) over the basis under section 732 (including such special basis adjustments) of such property to the distributee partner.

The provisions of this subparagraph may be illustrated by the following examples:

Example (1). Partner A has a basis of $10,000 for his one-third interest in partnership ABC. The partnership has no liabilities and has assets consisting of cash of $11,000 and property with a partnership basis of $19,000 and a value of $22,000. A receives $11,000 in cash in liquidation of his entire interest in the partnership. He has a gain of $1,000 under section 731(a)(1). If the election under section 754 is in effect, the partnership basis for the property becomes $20,000 ($19,000 plus $1,000).

Example (2). Partner D has a basis of $10,000 for his one-third interest in partnership DEF. The partnership balance sheet before the distribution shows the following:

Assets	Adjusted Basis	Value
Cash	$ 4,000	$ 4,000
Property X	11,000	11,000
Property Y	15,000	18,000
Totals	30,000	33,000

Liabilities and Capital		
Liabilities	$ 0	$ 0
Capital: D	10,000	11,000
E	10,000	11,000
F	10,000	11,000
Totals	30,000	33,000

In liquidation of his entire interest in the partnership, D received property X with a partnership basis of $11,000. D's basis for property X is $10,000 under section 732(b). Where the election under section 754 is in effect, the excess of $1,000 (the partnership basis before the distribution less D's basis for property X after distribution) is added to the basis of property Y. The basis of property Y becomes $16,000 ($15,000 plus $1,000). If the distribution is made to a transferee partner who elects under section 732(d), see § 1.734-2.

(2) *Decrease in basis.* Where the election provided in section 754 is in effect and a distribution is made in liquidation of a partner's entire interest, the partnership shall decrease the adjusted basis of the remaining partnership property by—

(i) The amount of loss, if any, recognized under section 731(a)(2) to the distributee partner, or [and]**

(ii) The excess of the basis of the distributed property to the distributee, as determined under section 732 (including adjustments under section 743(b) or section 732(d) when applied) over the adjusted basis of such property to the partnership (including such special basis adjustments) immediately before such distribution.

The provisions of this subparagraph may be illustrated by the following examples:

Example (1). Partner G has a basis of $11,000 for his one-third interest in partnership GHI. Partnership assets consist of cash of $10,000 and property with a basis of $23,000 and a value of $20,000. There are no partnership liabilities. In liquidation of his entire interest in the partnership, G receives $10,000 in cash. He has a loss of $1,000 under section 731(a)(2). If the election under section 754 is in effect, the partnership basis for the property becomes $22,000 ($23,000 less $1,000).

Example (2). Partner J has a basis of $11,000 for his one-third interest in partnership JKL. The partnership balance sheet before the distribution shows the following:

Assets	Adjusted Basis	Value
Cash	$ 5,000	$ 5,000
Property X	10,000	10,000
Property Y	18,000	15,000
Total	33,000	30,000

Liabilities and Capital		
Liabilities	$ 0	$ 0
Capital: J	11,000	10,000
K	11,000	10,000
L	11,000	10,000
Total	33,000	30,000

---

* As it appears in Code Sec. 734(b)(1)(A).

** As it appears in Code Sec. 734(b)(2)(A).

Reg. § 1.734-1(a)

In liquidation of his entire interest in the partnership, J receives property X with a partnership basis of $10,000. J's basis for property X under section 732(b) is $11,000. Where the election under section 754 is in effect, the excess of $1,000 ($11,000 basis of property X to J, the distributee, less its $10,000 adjusted basis to the partnership immediately before the distribution) decreases the basis of property Y in the partnership. Thus, the basis of property Y becomes $17,000 ($18,000 less $1,000). If the distribution is made to a transferee partner who elects under section 732(d), see § 1.734-2.

(c) *Allocation of basis.* For allocation among the partnership properties of basis adjustments under section 734(b) and paragraph (b) of this section, see section 755 and § 1.755-1.

(d) *Returns.* A partnership which must adjust the bases of partnership properties under section 734 shall attach a statement to the partnership return for the year of the distribution setting forth the computation of the adjustment and the partnership properties to which the adjustment has been allocated.

(e) *Recovery of adjustments to basis of partnership property*—(1) *Increases in basis.* For purposes of section 168, if the basis of a partnership's recovery property is increased as a result of the distribution of property to a partner, then the increased portion of the basis must be taken into account as if it were newly-purchased recovery property placed in service when the distribution occurs. Consequently, any applicable recovery period and method may be used to determine the recovery allowance with respect to the increased portion of the basis. However, no change is made for purposes of determining the recovery allowance under section 168 for the portion of the basis for which there is no increase.

(2) *Decreases in basis.* For purposes of section 168, if the basis of a partnership's recovery property is decreased as a result of the distribution of property to a partner, then the decrease in basis must be accounted for over the remaining recovery period of the property beginning with the recovery period in which the basis is decreased.

(3) *Effective date.* This paragraph (e) applies to distributions of property from a partnership that occur on or after December 15, 1999. [Reg. § 1.734-1.]

☐ [*T.D.* 6175, 5-23-56. Amended by T.D. 8847, 12-14-99.]

[Reg. § 1.734-2]

§ 1.734-2. **Adjustment after distribution to transferee partner.**—(a) In the case of a distribution of property by the partnership to a partner who has obtained all or part of his partnership interest by transfer, the adjustments to basis provided in section 743(b) and section 732(d) shall be taken into account in applying the rules under section 734(b). For determining the adjusted basis of distributed property to the partnership immediately before the distribution where there has been a prior transfer of a partnership interest with respect to which the election provided in section 754 or section 732(d) is in effect, see §§ 1.732-1 and 1.732-2.

(b)(1) If a transferee partner, in liquidation of his entire partnership interest, receives a distribution of property (including money) with respect to which he has no special basis adjustment, in exchange for his interest in property with respect to which he has a special basis adjustment, and does not utilize his entire special basis adjustment in determining the basis of the distributed property to him under section 732, the unused special basis adjustment of the distributee shall be applied as an adjustment to the partnership basis of the property retained by the partnership and as to which the distributee did not use his special basis adjustment. The provisions of this subparagraph may be illustrated by the following example:

Example. Upon the death of his father, partner S acquires by inheritance a half-interest in partnership ACS. Partners A and C each have a one-quarter interest. The assets of the partnership consist of $10,000 cash and land used in farming worth $10,000 with a basis of $1,000 to the partnership. Since the partnership had made the election under section 754 at the time of the transfer, partner S has a special basis adjustment of $4,500 under section 743(b) with respect to his undivided half-interest in the real estate. The basis of S's partnership interest, in accordance with section 742, is $10,000. S retires from the partnership and receives $10,000 in cash in exchange for his entire interest. Since S has received no part of the real estate, his special basis adjustment of $4,500 will be allocated to the real estate, the remaining partnership property, and will increase its basis to the partnership to $5,500.

(2) The provisions of this paragraph do not apply to the extent that certain distributions are treated as sales or exchanges under section 751(b) (relating to unrealized receivables and substantially appreciated inventory items). See section 751(b) and paragraph (b) of § 1.751-1. [Reg. § 1.734-2.]

☐ [*T.D.* 6175, 5-23-56.]

Reg. § 1.734-2(b)

[Reg. § 1.735-1]

§ 1.735-1. Character of gain or loss on disposition of distributed property.—(a) *Sale or exchange of distributed property*—(1) *Unrealized receivables.* Any gain realized or loss sustained by a partner on a sale or exchange or other disposition of unrealized receivables (as defined in paragraph (c)(1) of § 1.751-1) received by him in a distribution from a partnership shall be considered gain or loss from the sale or exchange of property other than a capital asset.

(2) *Inventory items.* Any gain realized or loss sustained by a partner on a sale or exchange of inventory items (as defined in section 751(d)(2)) received in a distribution from a partnership shall be considered gain or loss from the sale or exchange of property other than a capital asset if such inventory items are sold or exchanged within 5 years from the date of the distribution by the partnership. The character of any gain or loss from a sale or exchange by the distributee partner of such inventory items after 5 years from the date of distribution shall be determined as of the date of such sale or exchange by reference to the character of the assets in his hands at that date (inventory items, capital assets, property used in a trade or business, etc.).

(b) *Holding period for distributed property.* A partner's holding period for property distributed to him by a partnership shall include the period such property was held by the partnership. The provisions of this paragraph do not apply for the purpose of determining the 5-year period described in section 735(a)(2) and paragraph (a)(2) of this section. If the property has been contributed to the partnership by a partner, then the period that the property was held by such partner shall also be included. See section 1223(2). For a partnership's holding period for contributed property, see § 1.723-1.

(c) *Effective date.* Section 735(a) applies to any property distributed by a partnership to a partner after March 9, 1954. See section 771(b)(2) and paragraph (b)(2) of § 1.771-1. However, see section 771(c). [Reg. § 1.735-1.]

☐ [*T.D.* 6175, 5-23-56. *Amended by T.D.* 6832, 7-6-65.]

[Reg. § 1.736-1]

§ 1.736-1. Payments to a retiring partner or a deceased partner's successor in interest.—(a) *Payments considered as distributive share or guaranteed payment.*—(1)(i) Section 736 and this section apply only to payments made to a retiring partner or to a deceased partner's successor in interest in liquidation of such partner's entire interest in the partnership. See section 761(d). Section 736 and this section do not apply if the estate or other successor in interest of a deceased partner continues as a partner in its own right under local law. Section 736 and this section apply only to payments made by the partnership and not to transactions between the partners. Thus, a sale by partner A to partner B of his entire one-fourth interest in partnership ABCD would not come within the scope of section 736.

(ii) A partner retires when he ceases to be a partner under local law. However, for the purposes of subchapter K, chapter 1 of the Code, a retired partner or a deceased partner's successor will be treated as a partner until his interest in the partnership has been completely liquidated.

(2) When payments (including assumption of liabilities treated as a distribution of money under section 752) are made to a withdrawing partner, that is, a retiring partner or the estate or other successor in interest of a deceased partner, the amounts paid may represent several items. In part, they may represent the fair market value at the time of his death or retirement of the withdrawing partner's interest in all the assets of the partnership (including inventory) unreduced by partnership liabilities. Also, part of such payments may be attributable to his interest in unrealized receivables and part to an arrangement among the partners in the nature of mutual insurance. When a partnership makes such payments, whether or not related to partnership income, to retire the withdrawing partner's entire interest in the partnership, the payments must be allocated between (i) payments for the value of his interest in assets, except unrealized receivables and, under some circumstances, good will (section 736(b)), and (ii) other payments (section 736(a)). The amounts paid for his interest in assets are treated in the same manner as a distribution in complete liquidation under sections 731, 732, and where applicable, 751. See paragraph (b)(4)(ii) of § 1.751-1. The remaining partners are allowed no deduction for these payments since they represent either a distribution or a purchase of the withdrawing partner's capital interest by the partnership (composed of the remaining partners).

(3) Under section 736(a), the portion of the payments made to a withdrawing partner for his share of unrealized receivables, good will (in the absence of an agreement to the contrary), or otherwise not in exchange for his interest in assets under the rules contained in paragraph (b) of this section will be considered either—

(i) A distributive share of partnership income, if the amount of payment is determined with regard to income of the partnership; or

Reg. § 1.735-1(a)(1)

(ii) A guaranteed payment under section 707(c), if the amount of the payment is determined without regard to income of the partnership.

(4) Payments, to the extent considered as a distributive share of partnership income under section 736(a)(1), are taken into account under section 702 in the income of the withdrawing partner and thus reduce the amount of the distributive shares of the remaining partners. Payments, to the extent considered as guaranteed payments under section 736(a)(2), are deductible by the partnership under section 162(a) and are taxable as ordinary income to the recipient under section 61(a). See section 707(c).

(5) The amount of any payments under section 736(a) shall be included in the income of the recipient for his taxable year with or within which ends the partnership taxable year for which the payment is a distributive share, or in which the partnership is entitled to deduct such amount as a guaranteed payment. On the other hand, payments under section 736(b) shall be taken into account by the recipient for his taxable year in which such payments are made. See paragraph (b)(4) of this section.

(6) A retiring partner or a deceased partner's successor in interest receiving payments under section 736 is regarded as a partner until the entire interest of the retiring or deceased partner is liquidated. Therefore, if one of the members of a 2-man partnership retires under a plan whereby he is to receive payments under section 736, the partnership will not be considered terminated, nor will the partnership year close with respect to either partner, until the retiring partner's entire interest is liquidated, since the retiring partner continues to hold a partnership interest in the partnership until that time. Similarly, if a partner in a 2-man partnership dies, and his estate or other successor in interest receives payments under section 736, the partnership shall not be considered to have terminated upon the death of the partner but shall terminate as to both partners only when the entire interest of the decedent is liquidated. See section 708(b).

(b) *Payments for interest in partnership.* (1) Payments made in liquidation of the entire interest of a retiring partner or deceased partner shall, to the extent made in exchange for such partner's interest in partnership property (except for unrealized receivables and good will as provided in subparagraphs (2) and (3) of this paragraph), be considered as a distribution by the partnership (and not as a distributive share or guaranteed payment under section 736(a)). Generally, the valuation placed by the partners upon a partner's interest in partnership property in an arm's length agreement will be regarded as correct. If such valuation reflects only the partner's net interest in the property (i.e., total assets less liabilities), it must be adjusted so that both the value of the partner's interest in property and the basis for his interest take into account the partner's share of partnership liabilities. Gain or loss with respect to distributions under section 736(b) and this paragraph will be recognized to the distributee to the extent provided in section 731 and, where applicable, section 751.

(2) Payments made to a retiring partner or to the successor in interest of a deceased partner for his interest in unrealized receivables of the partnership in excess of their partnership basis, including any special basis adjustment for them to which such partner is entitled, shall not be considered as made in exchange for such partner's interest in partnership property. Such payments shall be treated as payments under section 736(a) and paragraph (a) of this section. For definition of unrealized receivables, see section 751(c).

(3) For the purposes of section 736(b) and this paragraph, payments made to a retiring partner or to a successor in interest of a deceased partner in exchange for the interest of such partner in partnership property shall not include any amount paid for the partner's share of good will of the partnership in excess of its partnership basis, including any special basis adjustments for it to which such partner is entitled, except to the extent that the partnership agreement provides for a reasonable payment with respect to such good will. Such payments shall be considered as payments under section 736(a). To the extent that the partnership agreement provides for a reasonable payment with respect to good will, such payments shall be treated under section 736(b) and this paragraph. Generally, the valuation placed upon good will be an arm's length agreement of the partners, whether specific in amount or determined by a formula, shall be regarded as correct.

(4) Payments made to a retiring partner or to a successor in interest of a deceased partner for his interest in inventory shall be considered as made in exchange for such partner's interest in partnership property for the purposes of section 736(b) and this paragraph. However, payments for an interest in substantially appreciated inventory items, as defined in section 751(d), are subject to the rules provided in section 751(b) and paragraph (b) of § 1.751-1. The partnership basis in inventory items as to a deceased partner's successor in interest does not change because of the death of the partner unless the partnership has elected the optional basis adjustment under

Reg. § 1.736-1(b)(4)

section 754. But see paragraph (b)(3)(iii) of § 1.751-1.

(5) Where payments made under section 736 are received during the taxable year, the recipient must segregate that portion of each such payment which is determined to be in exchange for the partner's interest in partnership property and treated as a distribution under section 736(b) from that portion treated as a distributive share or guaranteed payment under section 736(a). Such allocation shall be made as follows—

(i) If a fixed amount (whether or not supplemented by any additional amounts) is to be received over a fixed number of years, the portion of each payment to be treated as a distribution under section 736(b) for the taxable year shall bear the same ratio to the total fixed agreed payments for such year (as distinguished from the amount actually received) as the total fixed agreed payments under section 736(b) bear to the total fixed agreed payments under sections 736(a) and (b). The balance, if any, of such amount received in the same taxable year shall be treated as a distributive share or a guaranteed payment under section 736(a)(1) or (2). However, if the total amount received in any one year is less than the amount considered as a distribution under section 736(b) for that year, then any unapplied portion shall be added to the portion of the payments for the following year or years which are to be treated as a distribution under section 736(b). For example, retiring partner W who is entitled to an annual payment of $6,000 for 10 years for his interest in partnership property, receives only $3,500 in 1955. In 1956, he receives $10,000. Of this amount, $8,500 ($6,000 plus $2,500 from 1955) is treated as a distribution under section 736(b) for 1956; $1,500, as a payment under section 736(a).

(ii) If the retiring partner or deceased partner's successor in interest receives payments which are not fixed in amount, such payments shall first be treated as payments in exchange for his interest in partnership property under section 736(b) to the extent of the value of that interest and, thereafter, as payments under section 736(a).

(iii) In lieu of the rules provided in subdivisions (i) and (ii) of this subparagraph, the allocation of each annual payment between section 736(a) and (b) may be made in any manner to which all the remaining partners and the withdrawing partner or his successor in interest agree, provided that the total amount allocated to property under section 736(b) does not exceed the fair market value of such property at the date of death or retirement.

(6) Except to the extent section 751(b) applies, the amount of any gain or loss with respect to payments under section 736(b) for a retiring or deceased partner's interest in property for each year of payment shall be determined under section 731. However, where the total of section 736(b) payments is a fixed sum, a retiring partner or a deceased partner's successor in interest may elect (in his tax return for the first taxable year for which he receives such payments), to report and to measure the amount of any gain or loss by the difference between—

(i) The amount treated as a distribution under section 736(b) in that year, and

(ii) The portion of the adjusted basis of the partner for his partnership interest attributable to such distribution (i.e., the amount which bears the same proportion to the partner's total adjusted basis for his partnership interest as the amount distributed under section 736(b) in that year bears to the total amount to be distributed under section 736(b)).

A recipient who elects under this subparagraph shall attach a statement to his tax return for the first taxable year for which he receives such payments, indicating his election and showing the computation of the gain included in gross income.

(7) The provisions of this paragraph may be illustrated by the following examples:

Example (1). Partnership ABC is a personal service partnership and its balance sheet is as follows:

Assets	Adjusted basis per books	Market value
Cash	$13,000	$13,000
Unrealized receivables	0	30,000
Capital and sec. 1231 assets	20,000	23,000
Total	$33,000	$66,000

Liabilities and Capital	Per books	Value
Liabilities	$ 3,000	$ 3,000
Capital:		
A	10,000	21,000
B	10,000	21,000
C	10,000	21,000
Total	$33,000	$66,000

Partner A retires from the partnership in accordance with an agreement whereby his share of liabilities ($1,000) is assumed. In addition he is to receive $9,000 in the year of retirement plus $10,000 in each of the two succeeding years. Thus, the total that A receives for his partnership interest is $30,000 ($29,000 in cash and $1,000 in liabilities assumed). Under the agreement termi-

Reg. § 1.736-1(b)(5)

nating A's interest, the value of A's interest in section 736(b) partnership property is $12,000 (one-third of $36,000, the sum of $13,000 cash and $23,000, the fair market value of capital and section 1231 assets). A's share in unrealized receivables is not included in his interest in partnership property described in section 736(b). Since the basis of A's interest is $11,000 ($10,000 plus $1,000, his share of partnership liabilities), he will realize a capital gain of $1,000 ($12,000 minus $11,000) from the disposition of his interest in partnership property. The remaining $18,000 ($30,000 minus $12,000) will constitute payments under section 736(a)(2) which are taxable to A as guaranteed payments under section 707(c). The payment for the first year is $10,000, consisting of $9,000 in cash, plus $1,000 in liability assumed (section 752(b)). Thus, unless the partners agree otherwise under subparagraph (5)(iii) of this paragraph, each annual payment of $10,000 will be allocated as follows: $6,000 (18,000/30,000 of $10,000) is a section 736(a)(2) payment and $4,000 (12,000/30,000 of $10,000) is a payment for an interest in section 736(b) partnership property. (The Partnership may deduct the $6,000 guaranteed payment made to A in each of the 3 years.) The gain on the payments for partnership property will be determined under section 731, as provided in subparagraph (6) of this paragraph. A will treat only $4,000 of each payment as a distribution in a series in liquidation of his entire interest and, under section 731, will have a capital gain of $1,000 when the last payment is made. However, if A so elects, as provided in subparagraph (6) of this paragraph, he may treat such gain as follows: Of each $4,000 payment attributable to A's interest in partnership property, $333 is capital gain (one-third of the total capital gain of $1,000), and $3,667 is a return of capital.

Example (2). Assume the same facts as in example (1) of this subparagraph except that the agreement between the partners provides for payments to A for 3 years of a percentage of annual income instead of a fixed amount. Unless the partners agree otherwise under subparagraph (5)(iii) of this paragraph, all payments received by A up to $12,000 shall be treated under section 736(b) as payments for A's interest in partnership property. His gain of $1,000 will be taxed only after he has received his full basis under section 731. Since the payments are not fixed in amount, the election provided in subparagraph (6) of this paragraph is not available. Any payments in excess of $12,000 shall be treated as a distributive share of partnership income to A under section 736(a)(1).

Example (3). Assume the same facts as in example (1) of this subparagraph except that the partnership agreement provides that the payment for A's interest in partnership property shall include payment for his interest in the good will of the partnership. At the time of A's retirement, the partners determine the value of partnership good will to be $9,000. The value of A's interest in partnership property described in section 736(b) is thus $15,000 (one-third of $45,000, the sum of $13,000 cash, plus $23,000, the value of capital and section 1231 assets, plus $9,000 good will). From the disposition of his interest in partnership property, A will realize a capital gain of $4,000 ($15,000, minus $11,000, the basis of his interest). The remaining $15,000 ($30,000 minus $15,000) will constitute payments under section 736(a)(2) which are taxable to A as guaranteed payments under section 707(c).

Example (4). Assume the same facts as in example (1) of this subparagraph except that the capital and section 1231 assets consist of an item of section 1245 property (as defined in section 1245(a)(3)). Assume further that under paragraph (c)(4) of § 1.751-1 the section 1245 property is an unrealized receivable to the extent of $2,000. Therefore, the value of A's interest in section 736(b) partnership property is only $11,333 (one-third of $34,000, the sum of $13,000 cash and $21,000, the fair market value of section 1245 property to the extent not an unrealized receivable). From the disposition of his interest in partnership property, A will realize a capital gain of $333 ($11,333 minus $11,000, the basis of his interest). The remaining $18,667 ($30,000 minus $11,333) will constitute payments under section 736(a)(2) which are taxable to A as guaranteed payments under section 707(c).

(c) *Cross reference.* See section 753 for treatment of payments under section 736(a) as income in respect of a decedent under section 691. [Reg. § 1.736-1.]

☐ [*T.D. 6175, 5-23-56. Amended by T.D. 6832, 7-6-65.*]

[§ 1.737-1]

§ **1.737-1. Recognition of precontribution gain.**—(a) *Determination of gain*—(1) *In general.* A partner that receives a distribution of property (other than money) must recognize gain under section 737 and this section in an amount equal to the lesser of the excess distribution (as defined in paragraph (b) of this section) or the partner's net precontribution gain (as defined in paragraph (c) of this section). Gain recognized under section 737 and this section is in addition to any gain recognized under section 731.

(2) *Transactions to which section 737 applies.* Section 737 and this section apply only to

Reg. § 1.737-1(a)(2)

the extent that a distribution by a partnership is a distribution to a partner acting in the capacity of a partner within the meaning of section 731, except that section 737 and this section do not apply to the extent that section 751(b) applies to the distribution.

(b) *Excess distribution*—(1) *Definition.* The excess distribution is the amount (if any) by which the fair market value of the distributed property (other than money) exceeds the distributee partner's adjusted tax basis in the partner's partnership interest.

(2) *Fair market value of property.* The fair market value of the distributed property is the price at which the property would change hands between a willing buyer and a willing seller at the time of the distribution, neither being under any compulsion to buy or sell and both having reasonable knowledge of the relevant facts. The fair market value that a partnership assigns to distributed property will be regarded as correct, provided that the value is reasonably agreed to among the partners in an arm's-length negotiation and the partners have sufficiently adverse interests.

(3) *Distributee partner's adjusted tax basis*—(i) *General rule.* In determining the amount of the excess distribution, the distributee partner's adjusted tax basis in the partnership interest includes any basis adjustment resulting from the distribution that is subject to section 737 (for example, adjustments required under section 752) and from any other distribution or transaction that is part of the same distribution, except for—

(A) The increase required under section 737(c)(1) for the gain recognized by the partner under section 737; and

(B) The decrease required under section 733(2) for any property distributed to the partner other than property previously contributed to the partnership by the distributee partner. See § 1.704-4(e)(1) for a rule in the context of section 704(c)(1)(B). See also § 1.737-3(b)(2) for a special rule for determining a partner's adjusted tax basis in distributed property previously contributed by the partner to the partnership.

(ii) *Advances or drawings.* The distributee partner's adjusted tax basis in the partnership interest is determined as of the last day of the partnership's taxable year if the distribution to which section 737 applies is properly characterized as an advance or drawing against the partner's distributive share of income. See § 1.731-1(a)(1)(ii).

(c) *Net precontribution gain*—(1) *General rule.* The distributee partner's net precontribution gain is the net gain (if any) that would have been recognized by the distributee partner under section 704(c)(1)(B) and § 1.704-4 if all property that had been contributed to the partnership by the distributee partner within five years of the distribution and is held by the partnership immediately before the distribution had been distributed by the partnership to another partner other than a partner who owns, directly or indirectly, more than 50 percent of the capital or profits interest in the partnership. See § 1.704-4 for provisions determining a contributing partner's gain or loss under section 704(c)(1)(B) on an actual distribution of contributed section 704(c) property to another partner.

(2) *Special rules*—(i) *Property contributed on or before October 3, 1989.* Property contributed to the partnership on or before October 3, 1989, is not taken into account in determining a partner's net precontribution gain. See § 1.704-4(c)(1) for a similar rule in the context of section 704(c)(1)(B).

(ii) *Section 734(b)(1)(A) adjustments.* For distributions to a distributee partner of money by a partnership with a section 754 election in effect that are part of the same distribution as the distribution of property subject to section 737, for purposes of paragraph (a) and (c)(1) of this section the distributee partner's net precontribution gain is reduced by the basis adjustments (if any) made to section 704(c) property contributed by the distributee partner under section 734(b)(1)(A). See § 1.737-3(c)(4) for rules regarding basis adjustments for partnerships with a section 754 election in effect.

(iii) *Transfers of a partnership interest.* The transferee of all or a portion of a contributing partner's partnership interest succeeds to the transferor's net precontribution gain, if any, in an amount proportionate to the interest transferred. See § 1.704-3(a)(7) and § 1.704-4(d)(2) for similar provisions in the context of section 704(c)(1)(A) and section 704(c)(1)(B).

(iv) *Section 704(c)(1)(B) gain recognized in related distribution.* A distributee partner's net precontribution gain is determined after taking into account any gain or loss recognized by the partner under section 704(c)(1)(B) and § 1.704-4 (or that would have been recognized by the partner except for the like-kind exception in section 704(c)(2) and § 1.704-4(d)(3)) on an actual distribution to another partner of section 704(c) property contributed by the distributee partner that is part of the same distribution as the distribution to the distributee partner.

(v) *Section 704(c)(2) disregarded.* A distributee partner's net precontribution gain is determined without regard to the provisions of

Reg. § 1.737-1(b)(1)

section 704(c)(2) and § 1.704-4(d)(3) in situations in which the property contributed by the distributee partner is not actually distributed to another partner in a distribution related to the section 737 distribution.

(d) *Character of gain.* The character of the gain recognized by the distributee partner under section 737 and this section is determined by, and is proportionate to, the character of the partner's net precontribution gain. For this purpose, all gains and losses on section 704(c) property taken into account in determining the partner's net precontribution gain are netted according to their character. Character is determined at the partnership level for this purpose, and any character with a net negative amount is disregarded. The character of the partner's gain under section 737 is the same as, and in proportion to, any character with a net positive amount. Character for this purpose is determined as if the section 704(c) property had been sold by the partnership to an unrelated third party at the time of the distribution and includes any item that would have been taken into account separately by the contributing partner under section 702(a) and § 1.702-1(a).

(e) *Examples.* The following examples illustrate the provisions of this section. Unless otherwise specified, partnership income equals partnership expenses (other than depreciation deductions for contributed property) for each year of the partnership, the fair market value of partnership property does not change, all distributions by the partnership are subject to section 737, and all partners are unrelated.

Example 1. Calculation of excess distribution and net precontribution gain. (i) On January 1, 1995, A, B, and C form partnership ABC as equal partners. A contributes Property A, a depreciable real property with a fair market value of $30,000 and an adjusted tax basis of $20,000. B contributes Property B, nondepreciable real property with a fair market value and adjusted tax basis of $30,000. C contributes $30,000 cash.

(ii) Property A has 10 years remaining on its cost recovery schedule and is depreciated using the straight-line method. The partnership uses the traditional method for allocating items under section 704(c) described in § 1.704-3(b)(1) for Property A. The partnership has book depreciation of $3,000 per year (10 percent of the $30,000 book basis in Property A) and each partner is allocated $1,000 of book depreciation per year (one-third of the total annual book depreciation of $3,000). The partnership also has tax depreciation of $2,000 per year (10 percent of the $20,000 adjusted tax basis in Property A). This $2,000 tax depreciation is allocated equally between B and C, the noncontributing partners with respect to Property A.

(iii) At the end of 1997, the book value of Property A is $21,000 ($30,000 initial book value less $9,000 aggregate book depreciation) and its adjusted tax basis is $14,000 ($20,000 initial tax basis less $6,000 aggregate tax depreciation).

(iv) On December 31, 1997, Property B is distributed to A in complete liquidation of A's partnership interest. The adjusted tax basis of A's partnership interest at that time is $20,000. The amount of the excess distribution is $10,000, the difference between the fair market value of the distributed Property B ($30,000) and A's adjusted tax basis in A's partnership interest ($20,000). A's net precontribution gain is $7,000, the difference between the book value of Property A ($21,000) and its adjusted tax basis at the time of the distribution ($14,000). A recognizes gain of $7,000 on the distribution, the lesser of the excess distribution and the net precontribution gain.

Example 2. Determination of distributee partner's basis. (i) On January 1, 1995, A, B, and C form general partnership ABC as equal partners. A contributes Property A, nondepreciable real property with a fair market value of $10,000 and an adjusted tax basis of $4,000. B and C each contributes $10,000 cash.

(ii) The partnership purchases Property B, nondepreciable real property with a fair market value of $9,000, subject to a $9,000 nonrecourse liability. This nonrecourse liability is allocated equally among the partners under section 752, increasing A's adjusted tax basis in A's partnership interest from $4,000 to $7,000.

(iii) On December 31, 1998, A receives $2,000 cash and Property B, subject to the $9,000 liability, in a current distribution.

(iv) In determining the amount of the excess distribution, the adjusted tax basis of A's partnership interest is adjusted to take into account the distribution of money and the shift in liabilities. A's adjusted tax basis is therefore increased to $11,000 for this purpose ($7,000 initial adjusted tax basis, less $2,000 distribution of money, less $3,000 (decrease in A's share of the $9,000 partnership liability), plus $9,000 (increase in A's individual liabilities)). As a result of this basis adjustment, the adjusted tax basis of A's partnership interest ($11,000) is greater than the fair market value of the distributed property ($9,000) and therefore, there is no excess distribution. A recognizes no gain under section 737.

Example 3. Net precontribution gain reduced for gain recognized under section 704(c)(1)(B). (i) On January 1, 1995, A, B, and C form partnership ABC as equal partners. A contributes Properties

Reg. § 1.737-1(e)

A1 and A2, nondepreciable real properties located in the United States each with a fair market value of $10,000 and an adjusted tax basis of $6,000. B contributes Property B, nondepreciable real property located outside the United States, with a fair market value and adjusted tax basis of $20,000. C contributes $20,000 cash.

(ii) On December 31, 1998, Property B is distributed to A in complete liquidation of A's interest and, as part of the same distribution, Property A1 is distributed to B in a current distribution.

(iii) A's net precontribution gain before the distribution is $8,000 ($20,000 fair market value of Properties A1 and A2 less $12,000 adjusted tax basis of such properties). A recognizes $4,000 of gain under section 704(c)(1)(B) and § 1.704-4 on the distribution of Property A1 to B ($10,000 fair market value of Property A1 less $6,000 adjusted tax basis of Property A1). This gain is taken into account in determining A's excess distribution and net precontribution gain. As a result, A's net precontribution gain is reduced from $8,000 to $4,000, and the adjusted tax basis in A's partnership interest is increased by $4,000 to $16,000.

(iv) A recognizes gain of $4,000 on the receipt of Property B under section 737, an amount equal to the lesser of the excess distribution of $4,000 ($20,000 fair market value of Property B less $16,000 adjusted tax basis of A's interest in the partnership) and A's remaining net precontribution gain of $4,000.

Example 4. Character of gain. (i) On January 1, 1995, A, B, and C form partnership ABC as equal partners. A contributes the following nondepreciable property to the partnership:

	Fair Market Value	Adjusted Tax Basis
Property A1	$30,000	$20,000
Property A2	30,000	38,000
Property A3	10,000	9,000

(ii) The character of gain or loss on Property A1 and Property A2 is long-term, U.S.-source capital gain or loss. The character of gain on Property A3 is long-term, foreign-source capital gain. B contributes Property B, nondepreciable real property with a fair market value and adjusted tax basis of $70,000. C contributes $70,000 cash.

(iii) On December 31, 1998, Property B is distributed to A in complete liquidation of A's interest in the partnership. A recognizes $3,000 of gain under section 737, an amount equal to the excess distribution of $3,000 ($70,000 fair market value of Property B less $67,000 adjusted tax basis in A's partnership interest) and A's net precontribution gain of $3,000 ($70,000 aggregate fair market value of properties contributed by A less $67,000 aggregate adjusted tax basis of such properties).

(iv) In determining the character of A's gain, all gains and losses on property taken into account in determining A's net precontribution gain are netted according to their character and allocated to A's recognized gain under section 737 based on the relative proportions of the net positive amounts. U.S.-source and foreign-source gains must be netted separately because A would have been required to take such gains into account separately under section 702. As a result, A's net precontribution gain of $3,000 consists of $2,000 of net long-term, U.S.-source capital gain ($10,000 gain on Property A1 and $8,000 loss on Property A2) and $1,000 of net long-term, foreign-source capital gain ($1,000 gain on Property A3).

(v) The character of A's gain under paragraph (d) of this section is therefore $2,000 long-term, U.S.-source capital gain ($3,000 gain recognized under section 737 x $2,000 net long-term, U.S.-source capital gain/$3,000 total net precontribution gain) and $1,000 long-term, foreign-source capital gain ($3,000 gain recognized under section 737 x $1,000 net long-term, foreign-source capital gain/$3,000 total net precontribution gain). [Reg. § 1.737-1.]

☐ [T.D. 8642, 12-22-95.]

[Reg. § 1.737-2]

§ 1.737-2. Exceptions and special rules.—(a) *Section 708(b)(1)(B) terminations.* Section 737 and this section do not apply to the deemed distribution of interests in a new partnership caused by the termination of a partnership under section 708(b)(1)(B). A subsequent distribution of property by the new partnership to a partner of the new partnership that was formerly a partner of the terminated partnership is subject to section 737 to the same extent that a distribution from the terminated partnership would have been subject to section 737. See also § 1.704-4(c)(3) for a similar rule in the context of section 704(c)(1)(B). This paragraph (a) applies to terminations of partnerships under section 708(b)(1)(B) occurring on or after May 9, 1997; however, this paragraph (a) may be applied to terminations occurring on or after May 9, 1996, provided that the partnership and its partners apply this paragraph (a) to the termination in a consistent manner.

(b) *Transfers to another partnership*—(1) *Complete transfer.* Section 737 and this section do not apply to a transfer by a partnership (transferor partnership) of all of its assets and liabilities to a second partnership (transferee partnership) in an exchange described in section 721, followed by a distribution of the interest in the transferee partnership in liquidation of the transferor partnership as part of the same plan or arrangement. See § 1.704-4(c)(4) for a similar rule in the context of section 704(c)(1)(B).

(2) *Certain divisive transactions.* Section 737 and this section do not apply to a transfer by a partnership (transferor partnership) of all of the section 704(c) property contributed by a partner to a second partnership (transferee partnership) in an exchange described in section 721, followed by a distribution as part of the same plan or arrangement of an interest in the transferee partnership (and no other property) in complete liquidation of the interest of the partner that originally contributed the section 704(c) property to the transferor partnership.

(3) *Subsequent distributions.* A subsequent distribution of property by the transferee partnership to a partner of the transferee partnership that was formerly a partner of the transferor partnership is subject to section 737 to the same extent that a distribution from the transferor partnership would have been subject to section 737.

(c) *Incorporation of a partnership.* Section 737 and this section do not apply to an incorporation of a partnership by any method of incorporation (other than a method involving an actual distribution of partnership property to the partners followed by a contribution of that property to a corporation), provided that the partnership is liquidated as part of the incorporation transaction. See § 1.704-4(c)(5) for a similar rule in the context of section 704(c)(1)(B).

(d) *Distribution of previously contributed property*—(1) *General rule.* Any portion of the distributed property that consists of property previously contributed by the distributee partner (previously contributed property) is not taken into account in determining the amount of the excess distribution or the partner's net precontribution gain. The previous sentence applies on or after May 9, 1997. See § 1.737-3(b)(2) for a special rule for determining the basis of previously contributed property in the hands of a distributee partner who contributed the property to the partnership.

(2) *Limitation for distribution of previously contributed interest in an entity.* An interest in an entity previously contributed to the partnership is not treated as previously contributed property to the extent that the value of the interest is attributable to property contributed to the entity after the interest was contributed to the partnership. The preceding sentence does not apply to the extent that the property contributed to the entity was contributed to the partnership by the partner that also contributed the interest in the entity to the partnership.

(3) *Nonrecognition transactions.* Property received by the partnership in exchange for contributed section 704(c) property in a nonrecognition transaction is treated as the contributed property with regard to the contributing partner for purposes of section 737 to the extent that the property received is treated as section 704(c) property under § 1.704-3(a)(8). See § 1.7044(d)(1) for a similar rule in the context of section 704(c)(1)(B).

(4) *Undivided interests.* The distribution of an undivided interest in property is treated as the distribution of previously contributed property to the extent that the undivided interest does not exceed the undivided interest, if any, contributed by the distributee partner in the same property. See § 1.704-4(c)(6) for the application of section 704(c)(1)(B) in a similar context. The portion of the undivided interest in property retained by the partnership after the distribution, if any, that is treated as contributed by the distributee partner, is reduced to the extent of the undivided interest distributed to the distributee partner.

(e) *Examples.* The following examples illustrate the rules of this section. Unless otherwise specified, partnership income equals partnership expenses (other than depreciation deductions for contributed property) for each year of the partnership, the fair market value of partnership property does not change, all distributions by the partnership are subject to section 737, and all partners are unrelated.

Example 1. Distribution of previously contributed property. (i) On January 1, 1995, A, B, and C form partnership ABC as equal partners. A contributes the following nondepreciable real property to the partnership:

	Fair Market Value	Adjusted Tax Basis
Property A1	$20,000	$10,000
Property A2	10,000	6,000

(ii) A's total net precontribution gain on the contributed property is $14,000 ($10,000 on Property A1 plus $4,000 on Property A2). B contributes $10,000 cash and Property B, nondepreciable real property with a fair market value and adjusted tax basis of $20,000. C contributes $30,000 cash.

(iii) On December 31, 1998, Property A2 and Property B are distributed to A in complete liquidation of A's interest in the partnership. Property

Reg. § 1.737-2(e)

A2 was previously contributed by A and is therefore not taken into account in determining the amount of the excess distribution or A's net precontribution gain. The adjusted tax basis of Property A2 in the hands of A is also determined under section 732 as if that property were the only property distributed to A.

(iv) As a result of excluding Property A2 from these determinations, the amount of the excess distribution is $10,000 ($20,000 fair market value of distributed Property B less $10,000 adjusted tax basis in A's partnership interest). A's net precontribution gain is also $10,000 ($14,000 total net precontribution gain less $4,000 gain with respect to previously contributed Property A2). A therefore recognizes $10,000 of gain on the distribution, the lesser of the excess distribution and the net precontribution gain.

Example 2. Distribution of a previously contributed interest in an entity. (i) On January 1, 1995, A, B, and C form partnership ABC as equal partners. A contributes Property A, nondepreciable real property with a fair market value of $10,000 and an adjusted tax basis of $5,000, and all of the stock of Corporation X with a fair market value and adjusted tax basis of $500. B contributes $500 cash and Property B, nondepreciable real property with a fair market value and adjusted tax basis of $10,000. Partner C contributes $10,500 cash. On December 31, 1996, ABC contributes Property B to Corporation X in a nonrecognition transaction under section 351.

(ii) On December 31, 1998, all of the stock of Corporation X is distributed to A in complete liquidation of A's interest in the partnership. The stock is treated as previously contributed property with respect to A only to the extent of the $500 fair market value of the Corporation X stock contributed by A. The fair market value of the distributed stock for purposes of determining the amount of the excess distribution is therefore $10,000 ($10,500 total fair market value of Corporation X stock less $500 portion treated as previously contributed property). The $500 fair market value and adjusted tax basis of the Corporation X stock is also not taken into account in determining the amount of the excess distribution and the net precontribution gain.

(iii) A recognizes $5,000 of gain under section 737, the amount of the excess distribution ($10,000 fair market value of distributed property less $5,000 adjusted tax basis in A's partnership interest) and A's net precontribution gain ($10,000 fair market value of Property A less $5,000 adjusted tax basis in Property A).

Example 3. Distribution of undivided interest in property. (i) On January 1, 1995, A and B form partnership AB as equal partners. A contributes $500 cash and an undivided one-half interest in Property X. B contributes $500 cash and an undivided one-half interest in Property X.

(ii) On December 31, 1998, an undivided one-half interest in Property X is distributed to A in a current distribution. The distribution of the undivided one-half interest in Property X is treated as a distribution of previously contributed property because A contributed an undivided one-half interest in Property X. As a result, A does not recognize any gain under section 737 on the distribution. [Reg. § 1.737-2.]

☐ [T.D. 8642, 12-22-95. Amended by T.D. 8717, 5-8-97.]

[Reg. § 1.737-3]

§ 1.737-3. **Basis adjustments; Recovery rules.**—(a) *Distributee partner's adjusted tax basis in the partnership interest.* The distributee partner's adjusted tax basis in the partnership interest is increased by the amount of gain recognized by the distributee partner under section 737 and this section. This increase is not taken into account in determining the amount of gain recognized by the partner under section 737(a)(1) and this section or in determining the amount of gain recognized by the partner under section 731(a) on the distribution of money in the same distribution or any related distribution. See § 1.704-4(e)(1) for a determination of the distributee partner's adjusted tax basis in a distribution subject to section 704(c)(1)(B).

(b) *Distributee partner's adjusted tax basis in distributed property*—(1) *In general.* The distributee partner's adjusted tax basis in the distributed property is determined under section 732(a) or (b) as applicable. The increase in the distributee partner's adjusted tax basis in the partnership interest under paragraph (a) of this section is taken into account in determining the distributee partner's adjusted tax basis in the distributed property other than property previously contributed by the partner. See § 1.704-4(e)(2) for a determination of basis in a distribution subject to section 704(c)(1)(B).

(2) *Previously contributed property.* The distributee partner's adjusted tax basis in distributed property that the partner previously contributed to the partnership is determined as if it were distributed in a separate and independent distribution prior to the distribution that is subject to section 737 and § 1.737-1.

(c) *Partnership's adjusted tax basis in partnership property*—(1) *Increase in basis.* The partnership's adjusted tax basis in eligible property is increased by the amount of gain recognized by the distributee partner under section 737.

(2) *Eligible property.* Eligible property is property that—

(i) Entered into the calculation of the distributee partner's net precontribution gain;

(ii) Has an adjusted tax basis to the partnership less than the property's fair market value at the time of the distribution;

(iii) Would have the same character of gain on a sale by the partnership to an unrelated party as the character of any of the gain recognized by the distributee partner under section 737; and

(iv) Was not distributed to another partner in a distribution subject to section 704(c)(1)(B) and § 1.704-4 that was part of the same distribution as the distribution subject to section 737.

(3) *Method of adjustment.* For the purpose of allocating the basis increase under paragraph (c)(2) of this section among the eligible property, all eligible property of the same character is treated as a single group. Character for this purpose is determined in the same manner as the character of the recognized gain is determined under § 1.737-1(d). The basis increase is allocated among the separate groups of eligible property in proportion to the character of the gain recognized under section 737. The basis increase is then allocated among property within each group in the order in which the property was contributed to the partnership by the partner, starting with the property contributed first, in an amount equal to the difference between the property's fair market value and its adjusted tax basis to the partnership at the time of the distribution. For property that has the same character and was contributed in the same (or a related) transaction, the basis increase is allocated based on the respective amounts of unrealized appreciation in such properties at the time of the distribution.

(4) *Section 754 adjustments.* The basis adjustments to partnership property made pursuant to paragraph (c)(1) of this section are not elective and must be made regardless of whether the partnership has an election in effect under section 754. Any adjustments to the bases of partnership property (including eligible property as defined in paragraph (c)(2) of this section) under section 734(b) pursuant to a section 754 election (other than basis adjustments under section 734(b)(1)(A) described in the following sentence) must be made after (and must take into account) the adjustments to basis made under paragraph (a) and paragraph (c)(1) of this section. Basis adjustments under section 734(b)(1)(A) that are attributable to distributions of money to the distributee partner that are part of the same distribution as the distribution of property subject to section 737 are made before the adjustments to basis under paragraph (a) and paragraph (c)(1) of this section. See § 1.737-1(c)(2)(ii) for the effect, if any, of basis adjustments under section 734(b)(1)(A) on a partner's net precontribution gain. See also § 1.704-4(e)(3) for a similar rule regarding basis adjustments pursuant to a section 754 election in the context of section 704(c)(1)(B).

(d) *Recovery of increase to adjusted tax basis.* Any increase to the adjusted tax basis of partnership property under paragraph (c)(1) of this section is recovered using any applicable recovery period and depreciation (or other cost recovery) method (including first-year conventions) available to the partnership for newly purchased property (of the type adjusted) placed in service at the time of the distribution.

(e) *Examples.* The following examples illustrate the rules of this section. Unless otherwise specified, partnership income equals partnership expenses (other than depreciation deductions for contributed property) for each year of the partnership, the fair market value of partnership property does not change, all distributions by the partnership are subject to section 737, and all partners are unrelated.

Example 1. Partner's basis in distributed property. (i) On January 1, 1995, A, B, and C form partnership ABC as equal partners. A contributes Property A, nondepreciable real property with a fair market value of $10,000 and an adjusted tax basis of $5,000. B contributes Property B, nondepreciable real property with a fair market value and adjusted tax basis of $10,000. C contributes $10,000 cash.

(ii) On December 31, 1998, Property B is distributed to A in complete liquidation of A's interest in the partnership. A recognizes $5,000 of gain under section 737, an amount equal to the excess distribution of $5,000 ($10,000 fair market value of Property B less $5,000 adjusted tax basis in A's partnership interest) and A's net precontribution gain of $5,000 ($10,000 fair market value of Property A less $5,000 adjusted tax basis of such property).

(iii) A's adjusted tax basis in A's partnership interest is increased by the $5,000 of gain recognized under section 737. This increase is taken into account in determining A's basis in the distributed property. Therefore, A's adjusted tax basis in distributed Property B is $10,000 under section 732(b).

Example 2. Partner's basis in distributed property in connection with gain recognized under

Reg. § 1.737-3(e)

43,656 **Contributions, Distributions and Transfers**

See p. 20,601 for regulations not amended to reflect law changes

section 704(c)(1)(B). (i) On January 1, 1995, A, B, and C form partnership ABC as equal partners. A contributes the following nondepreciable real property located in the United States to the partnership:

	Fair Market Value	Adjusted Tax Basis
Property A1	$10,000	$5,000
Property A2	10,000	2,000

(ii) B contributes $10,000 cash and Property B, nondepreciable real property located outside the United States, with a fair market value and adjusted tax basis of $10,000. C contributes $20,000 cash.

(iii) On December 31, 1998, Property B is distributed to A in a current distribution and Property A1 is distributed to B in a current distribution. A recognizes $5,000 of gain under section 704(c)(1)(B) and § 1.704-4 on the distribution of Property A1 to B, the difference between the fair market value of such property ($10,000) and the adjusted tax basis in distributed Property A1 ($5,000). The adjusted tax basis of A's partnership interest is increased by this $5,000 of gain under section 704(c)(1)(B) and § 1.704-4(e)(1).

(iv) The increase in the adjusted tax basis of A's partnership interest is taken into account in determining the amount of the excess distribution. As a result, there is no excess distribution because the fair market value of Property B ($10,000) is less than the adjusted tax basis of A's interest in the partnership at the time of distribution ($12,000). A therefore recognizes no gain under section 737 on the receipt of Property B. A's adjusted tax basis in Property B is $10,000 under section 732(a)(1). The adjusted tax basis of A's partnership interest is reduced from $12,000 to $2,000 under section 733. See *Example 3* of § 1.737-1(e).

Example 3. Partnership's basis in partnership property after a distribution with section 737 gain. (i) On January 31, 1995, A, B, and C form partnership ABC as equal partners. A contributes the following nondepreciable property to the partnership:

	Fair Market Value	Adjusted Tax Basis
Property A1	$1,000	$ 500
Property A2	4,000	1,500
Property A3	4,000	6,000
Property A4	6,000	4,000

(ii) The character of gain or loss on Properties A1, A2, and A3 is long-term, U.S.-source capital gain or loss. The character of gain on Property A4 is long-term, foreign-source capital gain. B contributes Property B, nondepreciable real property with a fair market value and adjusted tax basis of $15,000. C contributes $15,000 cash.

(iii) On December 31, 1998, Property B is distributed to A in complete liquidation of A's interest in the partnership. A recognizes gain of $3,000 under section 737, an amount equal to the excess distribution of $3,000 ($15,000 fair market value of Property B less $12,000 adjusted tax basis in A's partnership interest) and A's net precontribution gain of $3,000 ($15,000 aggregate fair market value of the property contributed by A less $12,000 aggregate adjusted tax basis of such property).

(iv) $2,000 of A's gain is long-term, foreign-source capital gain ($3,000 total gain under section 737 x $2,000 net long-term, foreign-source capital gain/$3,000 total net precontribution gain). $1,000 of A's gain is long-term, U.S.-source capital gain ($3,000 total gain under section 737 x $1,000 net long-term, U.S.-source capital gain/$3,000 total net precontribution gain).

(v) The partnership must increase the adjusted tax basis of the property contributed by A by $3,000. All property contributed by A is eligible property. Properties A1, A2, and A3 have the same character and are grouped into a single group for purposes of allocating this basis increase. Property A4 is in a separate character group.

(vi) $2,000 of the basis increase must be allocated to long-term, foreign-source capital assets because $2,000 of the gain recognized by A was long-term, foreign-source capital gain. The adjusted tax basis of Property A4 is therefore increased from $4,000 to $6,000. $1,000 of the increase must be allocated to Properties A1 and A2 because $1,000 of the gain recognized by A is long-term, U.S.-source capital gain. No basis increase is allocated to Property A3 because its fair market value is less than its adjusted tax basis. The $1,000 basis increase is allocated between Properties A1 and A2 based on the unrealized appreciation in each asset before such basis adjustment. As a result, the adjusted tax basis of Property A1 is increased by $167 ($1,000 x $500/$3,000) and the adjusted tax basis of Property A2 is increased by $833 ($1,000 x $2,500/3,000). [Reg. § 1.737-3.]

☐ [T.D. 8642, 12-22-95.]

Reg. § 1.737-3(e)

[Reg. § 1.737-4]

§ 1.737-4. Anti-abuse rule.—(a) *In general.* The rules of section 737 and §§ 1.737-1, 1.737-2, and 1.737-3 must be applied in a manner consistent with the purpose of section 737. Accordingly, if a principal purpose of a transaction is to achieve a tax result that is inconsistent with the purpose of section 737, the Commissioner can recast the transaction for federal tax purposes as appropriate to achieve tax results that are consistent with the purpose of section 737. Whether a tax result is inconsistent with the purpose of section 737 must be determined based on all the facts and circumstances. See § 1.704-4(f) for an anti-abuse rule and examples in the context of section 704(c)(1)(B). The anti-abuse rule and examples under section 704(c)(1)(B) and § 1.704-4(f) are relevant to section 737 and §§ 1.737-1, 1.737-2, and 1.737-3 to the extent that the net precontribution gain for purposes of section 737 is determined by reference to section 704(c)(1)(B).

(b) *Examples.* The following examples illustrate the rules of this section. The examples set forth below do not delineate the boundaries of either permissible or impermissible types of transactions. Further, the addition of any facts or circumstances that are not specifically set forth in an example (or the deletion of any facts or circumstances) may alter the outcome of the transaction described in the example. Unless otherwise specified, partnership income equals partnership expenses (other than depreciation deductions for contributed property) for each year of the partnership, the fair market value of partnership property does not change, all distributions by the partnership are subject to section 737, and all partners are unrelated.

Example 1. Increase in distributee partner's basis by temporary contribution; results inconsistent with the purpose of section 737. (i) On January 1, 1995, A, B, and C form partnership ABC as equal partners. A contributes Property A1, nondepreciable real property with a fair market value of $10,000 and an adjusted tax basis of $1,000. B contributes Property B, nondepreciable real property with a fair market value of $10,000 and an adjusted tax basis of $10,000. C contributes $10,000 cash.

(ii) On January 1, 1999, pursuant to a plan a principal purpose of which is to avoid gain under section 737, A transfers to the partnership Property A2, nondepreciable real property with a fair market value and adjusted tax basis of $9,000. A treats the transfer as a contribution to the partnership pursuant to section 721 and increases the adjusted tax basis of A's partnership interest from $1,000 to $10,000. On January 1, 1999, the partnership agreement is amended and all other necessary steps are taken so that substantially all of the economic risks and benefits of Property A2 are retained by A. On February 1, 1999, Property B is distributed to A in a current distribution. If the contribution of Property A2 is treated as a contribution to the partnership for purposes of section 737, there is no excess distribution because the fair market value of distributed Property B ($10,000) does not exceed the adjusted tax basis of A's interest in the partnership ($10,000), and therefore section 737 does not apply. A's adjusted tax basis in distributed Property B is $10,000 under section 732(a)(1) and the adjusted tax basis of A's partnership interest is reduced to zero under section 733.

(iii) On March 1, 2000, A receives Property A2 from the partnership in complete liquidation of A's interest in the partnership. A recognizes no gain on the distribution of Property A2 because the property was previously contributed property. See § 1.737-2(d).

(iv) Although A has treated the transfer of Property A2 as a contribution to the partnership that increased the adjusted tax basis of A's interest in the partnership, it would be inconsistent with the purpose of section 737 to recognize the transfer as a contribution to the partnership. Section 737 requires recognition of gain when the value of distributed property exceeds the distributee partner's adjusted tax basis in the partnership interest. Section 737 assumes that any contribution or other transaction that affects a partner's adjusted tax basis in the partnership interest is a contribution or transaction in substance and is not engaged in with a principal purpose of avoiding recognition of gain under section 737. Because the transfer of Property A2 to the partnership was not a contribution in substance and was made with a principal purpose of avoiding recognition of gain under section 737, the Commissioner can disregard the contribution of Property A2 for this purpose. As a result, A recognizes gain of $9,000 under section 737 on the receipt of Property B, an amount equal to the lesser of the excess distribution of $9,000 ($10,000 fair market value of distributed Property B less the $1,000 adjusted tax basis of A's partnership interest, determined without regard to the transitory contribution of Property A2) or A's net precontribution gain of $9,000 on Property A1.

Example 2. Increase in distributee partner's basis; section 752 liability shift; results consistent with the purpose of section 737. (i) On January 1, 1995, A and B form general partnership AB as equal partners. A contributes Property A, nondepreciable real property with a fair market value of $10,000 and an adjusted tax basis of $1,000. B contributes Property B, nondepreciable real property with a fair market value and adjusted tax basis of $10,000. The partnership also borrows

$10,000 on a recourse basis and purchases Property C. The $10,000 liability is allocated equally between A and B under section 752, thereby increasing the adjusted tax basis in A's partnership interest to $6,000.

(ii) On December 31, 1998, the partners agree that A is to receive Property B in a current distribution. If A were to receive Property B at that time, A would recognize $4,000 of gain under section 737, an amount equal to the lesser of the excess distribution of $4,000 ($10,000 fair market value of Property B less $6,000 adjusted tax basis in A's partnership interest) or A's net precontribution gain of $9,000 ($10,000 fair market value of Property A less $1,000 adjusted tax basis of Property A).

(iii) With a principal purpose of avoiding such gain, A and B agree that A will be solely liable for the repayment of the $10,000 partnership liability and take the steps necessary so that the entire amount of the liability is allocated to A under section 752. The adjusted tax basis in A's partnership interest is thereby increased from $6,000 to $11,000 to reflect A's share of the $5,000 of liability previously allocated to B. As a result of this increase in A's adjusted tax basis, there is no excess distribution because the fair market value of distributed Property B ($10,000) is less than the adjusted tax basis of A's partnership interest. Recognizing A's increased adjusted tax basis as a result of the shift in liabilities is consistent with the purpose of section 737 and this section. Section 737 requires recognition of gain only when the value of the distributed property exceeds the distributee partner's adjusted tax basis in the partnership interest. The $10,000 recourse liability is a bona fide liability of the partnership that was undertaken for a substantial business purpose and A's and B's agreement that A will assume responsibility for repayment of that debt has substance. Therefore, the increase in A's adjusted tax basis in A's interest in the partnership due to the shift in partnership liabilities under section 752 is respected, and A recognizes no gain under section 737. [Reg. § 1.737-4.]

☐ [T.D. 8642, 12-22-95.]

[Reg. § 1.737-5]

§ 1.737-5. Effective date.—Sections 1.737-1, 1.737-2, 1.737-3, and 1.737-4 apply to distributions by a partnership to a partner on or after January 9, 1995. [Reg. § 1.737-5.]

☐ [T.D. 8642, 12-22-95.]

[Reg. § 1.741-1]

§ 1.741-1. Recognition and character of gain or loss on sale or exchange.—(a) The sale or exchange of an interest in a partnership shall, except to the extent section 751(a) applies, be treated as the sale or exchange of a capital asset, resulting in capital gain or loss measured by the difference between the amount realized and the adjusted basis of the partnership interest, as determined under section 705. For treatment of selling partner's distributive share up to date of sale, see section 706(c)(2). Where the provisions of section 751 require the recognition of ordinary income or loss with respect to a portion of the amount realized from such sale or exchange, the amount realized shall be reduced by the amount attributable under section 751 to unrealized receivables and substantially appreciated inventory items, and the adjusted basis of the transferor partner's interest in the partnership shall be reduced by the portion of such basis attributable to such unrealized receivables and substantially appreciated inventory items. See section 751 and § 1.751-1.

(b) Section 741 shall apply whether the partnership interest is sold to one or more members of the partnership or to one or more persons who are not members of the partnership. Section 741 shall also apply even though the sale of the partnership interest results in a termination of the partnership under section 708(b). Thus, the provisions of section 741 shall be applicable (1) to the transferor partner in a 2-man partnership when he sells his interest to the other partner, and (2) to all the members of a partnership when they sell their interest to one or more persons outside the partnership.

(c) See section 351 for nonrecognition of gain or loss upon transfer of a partnership interest to a corporation controlled by the transferor.

(d) For rules relating to the treatment of liabilities on the sale or exchange of interests in a partnership see §§ 1.752-1 and 1.1001-2.

(e) For rules relating to the capital gain or loss recognized when a partner sells or exchanges an interest in a partnership that holds appreciated collectibles or section 1250 property with section 1250 capital gain, see § 1.1(h)-1. This paragraph (e) applies to transfers of interests in partnerships that occur on or after September 21, 2000.

(f) For rules relating to dividing the holding period of an interest in a partnership, see § 1.1223-3. This paragraph (f) applies to transfers of partnership interests and distributions of property from a partnership that occur on or after September 21, 2000. [Reg. § 1.741-1.]

☐ [T.D. 6175, 5-23-56. Amended by T.D. 7741, 12-11-80 and T.D. 8902, 9-20-2000.]

Contributions, Distributions and Transfers

See p. 20,601 for regulations not amended to reflect law changes

[Reg. § 1.742-1]

§ 1.742-1. Basis of transferee partner's interest.—The basis to a transferee partner of an interest in a partnership shall be determined under the general basis rules for property provided by part II (section 1011 and following), subchapter O, chapter 1 of the Code. Thus, the basis of a purchased interest will be its cost. The basis of a partnership interest acquired from a decedent is the fair market value of the interest at the date of his death or at the alternate valuation date, increased by his estate's or other successor's share of partnership liabilities, if any, on that date, and reduced to the extent that such value is attributable to items constituting income in respect of a decedent (see section 753 and paragraph (c)(3)(v) of § 1.706-1 and paragraph (b) of § 1.753-1) under section 691. See section 1014(c). For basis of contributing partner's interest, see section 722. The basis so determined is then subject to the adjustments provided in section 705. [Reg. § 1.742-1.]

☐ [T.D. 6175, 5-23-56.]

[Reg. § 1.743-1]

§ 1.743-1. Optional adjustment to basis of partnership property.—(a) *Generally.* The basis of partnership property is adjusted as a result of the transfer of an interest in a partnership by sale or exchange or on the death of a partner only if the election provided by section 754 (relating to optional adjustments to the basis of partnership property) is in effect with respect to the partnership. Whether or not the election provided in section 754 is in effect, the basis of partnership property is not adjusted as the result of a contribution of property, including money, to the partnership.

(b) *Determination of adjustment.* In the case of the transfer of an interest in a partnership, either by sale or exchange or as a result of the death of a partner, a partnership that has an election under section 754 in effect—

(1) Increases the adjusted basis of partnership property by the excess of the transferee's basis for the transferred partnership interest over the transferee's share of the adjusted basis to the partnership of the partnership's property; or

(2) Decreases the adjusted basis of partnership property by the excess of the transferee's share of the adjusted basis to the partnership of the partnership's property over the transferee's basis for the transferred partnership interest.

(c) *Determination of transferee's basis in the transferred partnership interest.* In the case of the transfer of a partnership interest by sale or exchange or as a result of the death of a partner, the transferee's basis in the transferred partnership interest is determined under section 742 and § 1.742-1. See also section 752 and §§ 1.752-1 through 1.752-5.

(d) *Determination of transferee's share of the adjusted basis to the partnership of the partnership's property*—(1) *Generally.* A transferee's share of the adjusted basis to the partnership of partnership property is equal to the sum of the transferee's interest as a partner in the partnership's previously taxed capital, plus the transferee's share of partnership liabilities. Generally, a transferee's interest as a partner in the partnership's previously taxed capital is equal to—

(i) The amount of cash that the transferee would receive on a liquidation of the partnership following the hypothetical transaction, as defined in paragraph (d)(2) of this section (to the extent attributable to the acquired partnership interest); increased by

(ii) The amount of tax loss (including any remedial allocations under § 1.704-3(d)), that would be allocated to the transferee from the hypothetical transaction (to the extent attributable to the acquired partnership interest); and decreased by

(iii) The amount of tax gain (including any remedial allocations under § 1.704-3(d)), that would be allocated to the transferee from the hypothetical transaction (to the extent attributable to the acquired partnership interest).

(2) *Hypothetical transaction defined.* For purposes of paragraph (d)(1) of this section, the hypothetical transaction means the disposition by the partnership of all of the partnership's assets, immediately after the transfer of the partnership interest, in a fully taxable transaction for cash equal to the fair market value of the assets.

(3) *Examples.* The provisions of this paragraph (d) are illustrated by the following examples:

Example 1. (i) A is a member of partnership PRS in which the partners have equal interests in capital and profits. The partnership has made an election under section 754, relating to the optional adjustment to the basis of partnership property. A sells its interest to T for $22,000. The balance sheet of the partnership at the date of sale shows the following:

Assets

	Adjusted Basis	Fair Market Value
Cash	$ 5,000	$ 5,000
Accounts receivable	10,000	10,000
Inventory	20,000	21,000
Depreciable assets	20,000	40,000
Total	$55,000	$76,000

Reg. § 1.743-1(d)(3)

43,660   Contributions, Distributions and Transfers

See p. 20,601 for regulations not amended to reflect law changes

Liabilities and Capital

	Adjusted Per Books	Fair Market Value
Liabilities	$10,000	$10,000
Capital:		
A	15,000	22,000
B	15,000	22,000
C	15,000	22,000
Total	$55,000	$76,000

(ii) The amount of the basis adjustment under section 743(b) is the difference between the basis of T's interest in the partnership and T's share of the adjusted basis to the partnership of the partnership's property. Under section 742, the basis of T's interest is $25,333 (the cash paid for A's interest, $22,000, plus $3,333, T's share of partnership liabilities). T's interest in the partnership's previously taxed capital is $15,000 ($22,000, the amount of cash T would receive if PRS liquidated immediately after the hypothetical transaction, decreased by $7,000, the amount of tax gain allocated to T from the hypothetical transaction). T's share of the adjusted basis to the partnership of the partnership's property is $18,333 ($15,000 share of previously taxed capital, plus $3,333 share of the partnership's liabilities). The amount of the basis adjustment under section 743(b) to partnership property therefore, is $7,000, the difference between $25,333 and $18,333.

Example 2. A, B, and C form partnership PRS, to which A contributes land (Asset 1) with a fair market value of $1,000 and an adjusted basis to A of $400, and B and C each contribute $1,000 cash. Each partner has $1,000 credited to it on the books of the partnership as its capital contribution. The partners share in profits equally. During the partnership's first taxable year, Asset 1 appreciates in value to $1,300. A sells its one-third interest in the partnership to T for $1,100, when an election under section 754 is in effect. The amount of tax gain that would be allocated to T from the hypothetical transaction is $700 ($600 section 704(c) built-in gain, plus one-third of the additional gain). Thus, T's interest in the partnership's previously taxed capital is $400 ($1,100, the amount of cash T would receive if PRS liquidated immediately after the hypothetical transaction, decreased by $700, T's share of gain from the hypothetical transaction). The amount of T's basis adjustment under section 743(b) to partnership property is $700 (the excess of $1,100, T's cost basis for its interest, over $400, T's share of the adjusted basis to the partnership of partnership property).

(e) *Allocation of basis adjustment.* For the allocation of the basis adjustment under this section among the individual items of partnership property, see section 755 and the regulations thereunder.

(f) *Subsequent transfers.* Where there has been more than one transfer of a partnership interest, a transferee's basis adjustment is determined without regard to any prior transferee's basis adjustment. In the case of a gift of an interest in a partnership, the donor is treated as transferring, and the donee as receiving, that portion of the basis adjustment attributable to the gifted partnership interest. The provisions of this paragraph (f) are illustrated by the following example:

Example. (i) A, B, and C form partnership PRS. A and B each contribute $1,000 cash, and C contributes land with a basis and fair market value of $1,000. When the land has appreciated in value to $1,300, A sells its interest to T1 for $1,100 (one-third of $3,300, the fair market value of the partnership property). An election under section 754 is in effect; therefore, T1 has a basis adjustment under section 743(b) of $100.

(ii) After the land has further appreciated in value to $1,600, T1 sells its interest to T2 for $1,200 (one-third of $3,600, the fair market value of the partnership property). T2 has a basis adjustment under section 743(b) of $200. This amount is determined without regard to any basis adjustment under section 743(b) that T1 may have had in the partnership assets.

(iii) During the following year, T2 makes a gift to T3 of fifty percent of T2's interest in PRS. At the time of the transfer, T2 has a $200 basis adjustment under section 743(b). T2 is treated as transferring $100 of the basis adjustment to T3 with the gift of the partnership interest.

(g) *Distributions*—(1) *Distribution of adjusted property to the transferee*—(i) *Coordination with section 732.* If a partnership distributes property to a transferee and the transferee has a basis adjustment for the property, the basis adjustment is taken into account under section 732. See § 1.732-2(b).

(ii) *Coordination with section 734.* For certain adjustments to the common basis of remaining partnership property after the distribution of adjusted property to a transferee, see § 1.734-2(b).

(2) *Distribution of adjusted property to another partner*—(i) *Coordination with section 732.* If a partner receives a distribution of property with respect to which another partner has a basis

Reg. § 1.743-1(e)

adjustment, the distributee does not take the basis adjustment into account under section 732.

(ii) *Reallocation of basis.* A transferee with a basis adjustment in property that is distributed to another partner reallocates the basis adjustment among the remaining items of partnership property under § 1.755-1(c).

(3) *Distributions in complete liquidation of a partner's interest.* If a transferee receives a distribution of property (whether or not the transferee has a basis adjustment in such property) in liquidation of its interest in the partnership, the adjusted basis to the partnership of the distributed property immediately before the distribution includes the transferee's basis adjustment for the property in which the transferee relinquished an interest (either because it remained in the partnership or was distributed to another partner). Any basis adjustment for property in which the transferee is deemed to relinquish its interest is reallocated among the properties distributed to the transferee under § 1.755-1(c).

(4) *Coordination with other provisions.* The rules of sections 704(c)(1)(B), 731, 737, and 751 apply before the rules of this paragraph (g).

(5) *Example.* The provisions of this paragraph (g) are illustrated by the following example:

Example. (i) A, B, and C are equal partners in partnership PRS. Each partner originally contributed $10,000 in cash, and PRS used the contributions to purchase five nondepreciable capital assets. PRS has no liabilities. After five years, PRS's balance sheet appears as follows:

Assets

	Adjusted Basis	Fair Market Value
Asset 1	$10,000	$10,000
Asset 2	4,000	6,000
Asset 3	6,000	6,000
Asset 4	7,000	4,000
Asset 5	3,000	13,000
Total	$30,000	$39,000

Capital

	Adjusted Per Books	Fair Market Value
Partner A	$10,000	$13,000
Partner B	10,000	13,000
Partner C	10,000	13,000
Total	$30,000	$39,000

(ii) A sells its interest to T for $13,000 when PRS has an election in effect under section 754. T receives a basis adjustment under section 743(b) in the partnership property that is equal to $3,000 (the excess of T's basis in the partnership interest, $13,000, over T's share of the adjusted basis to the partnership of partnership property, $10,000). The basis adjustment is allocated under section 755, and the partnership's balance sheet appears as follows:

Assets

	Adjusted Basis	Fair Market Value	Basis Adjustment
Asset 1	$10,000	$10,000	$ 0.00
Asset 2	4,000	6,000	666.67
Asset 3	6,000	6,000	0.00
Asset 4	7,000	4,000	(1,000.00)
Asset 5	3,000	13,000	3,333.33
Total	$30,000	$39,000	$ 3,000.00

Capital

	Adjusted Per Books	Fair Market Value	Special Basis
Partner T	$10,000	$13,000	$3,000
Partner B	10,000	13,000	0
Partner C	10,000	13,000	0
Total	$30,000	$39,000	$3,000

(iii) Assume that PRS distributes Asset 2 to T in partial liquidation of T's interest in the partnership. T has a basis adjustment under section 743(b) of $666.67 in Asset 2. Under paragraph (g)(1)(i) of this section, T takes the basis adjustment into account under section 732. Therefore, T will have a basis in Asset 2 of $4,666.67 following the distribution.

(iv) Assume instead that PRS distributes Asset 5 to C in complete liquidation of C's interest in PRS. T has a basis adjustment under section 743(b) of $3,333.33 in Asset 5. Under paragraph (g)(2)(i) of this section, C does not take T's basis adjustment into account under section 732. Therefore, the partnership's basis for purposes of sections 732 and 734 is $3,000. Under paragraph (g)(2)(ii) of this section, T's $3,333.33 basis adjustment is reallocated among the remaining partnership assets under $1.755-1(c).

(v) Assume instead that PRS distributes Asset 5 to T in complete liquidation of its interest in PRS. Under paragraph (g)(3) of this section, immediately prior to the distribution of Asset 5 to T, PRS must adjust the basis of Asset 5. Therefore, immediately prior to the distribution, PRS's basis in Asset 5 is equal to $6,000, which is the sum of (A) $3,000, PRS's common basis in Asset 5, plus (B) $3,333.33, T's basis adjustment to Asset 5, plus (C) ($333.33), the sum of T's basis adjustments in Assets 2 and 4. For purposes of sections 732 and 734, therefore, PRS will be treated as having a basis in Asset 5 equal to $6,000.

(h) *Contributions of adjusted property*—(1) *Section 721(a) transactions.* If, in a transaction described in section 721(a), a partnership (the upper tier) contributes to another partnership (the lower tier) property with respect to which a basis adjustment has been made, the basis adjustment is treated as contributed to the lower-tier partnership, regardless of whether the lower-tier partnership makes a section 754 election. The lower tier's basis in the contributed assets and the upper tier's basis in the partnership interest received in the transaction are determined with reference to the basis adjustment. However, that portion of the basis of the upper tier's interest in the lower tier attributable to the basis adjustment must be segregated and allocated solely to the transferee partner for whom the basis adjustment was made. Similarly, that portion of the lower tier's basis in its assets attributable to the basis adjustment must be segregated and allocated solely to the upper tier and the transferee. A partner with a basis adjustment in property held by a partnership that terminates under section 708(b)(1)(B) will continue to have the same basis adjustment with respect to property deemed contributed by the terminated partnership to the new partnership under §1.708-1(b)(1)(iv), regardless of whether the new partnership makes a section 754 election.

(2) *Section 351 transactions*—(i) *Basis in transferred property.* A corporation's adjusted tax basis in property transferred to the corporation by a partnership in a transaction described in section 351 is determined with reference to any basis adjustments to the property under section 743(b) (other than any basis adjustment that reduces a partner's gain under paragraph (h)(2)(ii) of this section).

(ii) *Partnership gain.* The amount of gain, if any, recognized by the partnership on a transfer of property by the partnership to a corporation in a transfer described in section 351 is determined without reference to any basis adjustment to the transferred property under section 743(b). The amount of gain, if any, recognized by the partnership on the transfer that is allocated to a partner with a basis adjustment in the transferred property is adjusted to reflect the partner's basis adjustment in the transferred property.

(iii) *Basis in stock.* The partnership's adjusted tax basis in stock received from a corporation in a transfer described in section 351 is determined without reference to the basis adjustment in property transferred to the corporation in the section 351 exchange. A partner with a basis adjustment in property transferred to the corporation, however, has a basis adjustment in the stock received by the partnership in the section 351 exchange in an amount equal to the partner's basis adjustment in the transferred property, reduced by any basis adjustment that reduced the partner's gain under paragraph (h)(2)(ii) of this section.

(iv) *Example.* The following example illustrates the principles of this paragraph (h)(2):

Example. (i) A, B, and C are equal partners in partnership PRS. The partnership's only asset, Asset 1, has an adjusted tax basis of $60 and a fair market value of $120. Asset 1 is a nondepreciable capital asset and is not section 704(c) property. A has a basis in its partnership interest of $40, and a positive section 743(b) adjustment of $20 in Asset 1. In a transaction to which section 351 applies, PRS contributes Asset 1 to X, a corporation, in exchange for $15 in cash and X stock with a fair market value of $105.

(ii) Under paragraph (h)(2)(ii) of this section, PRS realizes $60 of gain on the transfer of Asset 1 to X ($120, its amount realized, minus $60, its adjusted basis), but recognizes only $15 of that gain under section 351(b)(1). Of this amount, $5 is allocated to each partner. A must use $5 of its basis adjustment in Asset 1 to offset A's share of PRS's gain. Under paragraph (h)(2)(iii) of this section, PRS's basis in the stock received from X is $60. However, A has a basis adjustment in the stock received by PRS equal to $15 (its basis adjustment in Asset 1, $20, reduced by the portion of the adjustment which reduced A's gain, $5). Under paragraph (h)(2)(i) of this section, X's basis in Asset 1 equals $90 (PRS's common basis in the asset, $60, plus the gain recognized by PRS under section 351(b)(1), $15, plus A's basis adjustment under section 743(b), $20, less the portion of the adjustment which reduced A's gain, $5).

(i) [Reserved].

(j) *Effect of basis adjustment*—(1) *In general.* The basis adjustment constitutes an adjustment to the basis of partnership property with respect to the transferee only. No adjustment is made to the common basis of partnership property. Thus, for purposes of calculating income, deduction, gain, and loss, the transferee will have a special basis for those partnership properties the bases of which are adjusted under section 743(b) and this section. The adjustment to the basis of partnership property under section 743(b) has no effect on the partnership's computation of any item under section 703.

(2) *Computation of partner's distributive share of partnership items.* The partnership first computes its items of income, deduction, gain, or loss at the partnership level under section 703. The partnership then allocates the partnership items among the partners, including the transferee, in accordance with section 704, and adjusts

the partners' capital accounts accordingly. The partnership then adjusts the transferee's distributive share of the items of partnership income, deduction, gain, or loss, in accordance with paragraphs (j)(3) and (4) of this section, to reflect the effects of the transferee's basis adjustment under section 743(b). These adjustments to the transferee's distributive shares must be reflected on Schedules K and K-1 of the partnership's return (Form 1065). These adjustments to the transferee's distributive shares do not affect the transferee's capital account.

(3) *Effect of basis adjustment in determining items of income, gain, or loss*—(i) *In general.* The amount of a transferee's income, gain, or loss from the sale or exchange of a partnership asset in which the transferee has a basis adjustment is equal to the transferee's share of the partnership's gain or loss from the sale of the asset (including any remedial allocations under $1.704-3(d)), minus the amount of the transferee's positive basis adjustment for the partnership asset (determined by taking into account the recovery of the basis adjustment under paragraph (j)(4)(i)(B) of this section) or plus the amount of the transferee's negative basis adjustment for the partnership asset (determined by taking into the account the recovery of the basis adjustment under paragraph (j)(4)(ii)(B) of this section).

(ii) *Examples.* The following examples illustrate the principles of this paragraph (j)(3):

Example 1. A and B form equal partnership PRS. A contributes nondepreciable property with a fair market value of $50 and an adjusted tax basis of $100. PRS will use the traditional allocation method under § 1.704-3(b). B contributes $50 cash. A sells its interest to T for $50. PRS has an election in effect to adjust the basis of partnership property under section 754. T receives a negative $50 basis adjustment under section 743(b) that, under section 755, is allocated to the nondepreciable property. PRS then sells the property for $60. PRS recognizes a book gain of $10 (allocated equally between T and B) and a tax loss of $40. T will receive an allocation of $40 of tax loss under the principles of section 704(c). However, because T has a negative $50 basis adjustment in the nondepreciable property, T recognizes a $10 gain from the partnership's sale of the property.

Example 2. A and B form equal partnership PRS. A contributes nondepreciable property with a fair market value of $100 and an adjusted tax basis of $50. B contributes $100 cash. PRS will use the traditional allocation method under $1.704-3(b). A sells its interest to T for $100. PRS has an election in effect to adjust the basis of partnership property under section 754. Therefore, T receives a $50 basis adjustment under section 743(b) that, under section 755, is allocated to the nondepreciable property. PRS then sells the nondepreciable property for $90. PRS recognizes a book loss of $10 (allocated equally between T and B) and a tax gain of $40. T will receive an allocation of the entire $40 of tax gain under the principles of section 704(c). However, because T has a $50 basis adjustment in the property, T recognizes a $10 loss from the partnership's sale of the property.

Example 3. A and B form equal partnership PRS. PRS will make allocations under section 704(c) using the remedial allocation method described in $1.704-3(d). A contributes nondepreciable property with a fair market value of $100 and an adjusted tax basis of $150. B contributes $100 cash. A sells its partnership interest to T for $100. PRS has an election in effect to adjust the basis of partnership property under section 754. T receives a negative $50 basis adjustment under section 743(b) that, under section 755, is allocated to the property. The partnership then sells the property for $120. The partnership recognizes a $20 book gain and a $30 tax loss. The book gain will be allocated equally between the partners. The entire $30 tax loss will be allocated to T under the principles of section 704(c). To match its $10 share of book gain, B will be allocated $10 of remedial gain, and T will be allocated an offsetting $10 of remedial loss. T was allocated a total of $40 of tax loss with respect to the property. However, because T has a negative $50 basis adjustment to the property, T recognizes a $10 gain from the partnership's sale of the property.

(4) *Effect of basis adjustment in determining items of deduction*—(i) *Increases*—(A) *Additional deduction.* The amount of any positive basis adjustment that is recovered by the transferee in any year is added to the transferee's distributive share of the partnership's depreciation or amortization deductions for the year. The basis adjustment is adjusted under section 1016(a)(2) to reflect the recovery of the basis adjustment.

(B) *Recovery period*—(1) *In general.* Except as provided in paragraph (j)(4)(i)(B)(2) of this section, for purposes of section 168, if the basis of a partnership's recovery property is increased as a result of the transfer of a partnership interest, then the increased portion of the basis is taken into account as if it were newly-purchased recovery property placed in service when the transfer occurs. Consequently, any applicable recovery period and method may be used to determine the recovery allowance with respect to the increased portion of the basis. However, no change

Reg. § 1.743-1(j)(4)

is made for purposes of determining the recovery allowance under section 168 for the portion of the basis for which there is no increase.

(2) *Remedial allocation method.* If a partnership elects to use the remedial allocation method described in §1.704-3(d) with respect to an item of the partnership's recovery property, then the portion of any increase in the basis of the item of the partnership's recovery property under section 743(b) that is attributable to section 704(c) built-in gain is recovered over the remaining recovery period for the partnership's excess book basis in the property as determined in the final sentence of §1.704-3(d)(2). Any remaining portion of the basis increase is recovered under paragraph (j)(4)(i)(B)(*1*) of this section.

(C) *Examples.* The provisions of this paragraph (j)(4)(i) are illustrated by the following examples:

Example 1. (i) A, B, and C are equal partners in partnership PRS, which owns Asset 1, an item of depreciable property that has a fair market value in excess of its adjusted tax basis. C sells its interest in PRS to T while PRS has an election in effect under section 754. PRS, therefore, increases the basis of Asset 1 with respect to T.

(ii) Assume that in the year following the transfer of the partnership interest to T, T's distributive share of the partnership's common basis depreciation deductions from Asset 1 is $1,000. Also assume that, under paragraph (j)(4)(i)(B) of this section, the amount of the basis adjustment under section 743(b) that T recovers during the year is $500. The total amount of depreciation deductions from Asset 1 reported by T is equal to $1,500.

Example 2. (i) A and B form equal partnership PRS. A contributes property with an adjusted basis of $100,000 and a fair market value of $500,000. B contributes $500,000 cash. When PRS is formed, the property has five years remaining in its recovery period. The partnership's adjusted basis of $100,000 will, therefore, be recovered over the five years remaining in the property's recovery period. PRS elects to use the remedial allocation method under §1.704-3(d) with respect to the property. If PRS had purchased the property at the time of the partnership's formation, the basis of the property would have been recovered over a 10-year period. The $400,000 of section 704(c) built-in gain will, therefore, be amortized under §1.704-3(d) over a 10-year period beginning at the time of the partnership's formation.

(ii)(A) Except for the depreciation deductions, PRS's expenses equal its income in each year of the first two years commencing with the year the partnership is formed. After two years, A's share of the adjusted basis of partnership property is $120,000, while B's is $440,000:

Capital Accounts

	A Book	A Tax	B Book	B Tax
Initial Contribution	$500,000	$100,000	$500,000	$500,000
Depreciation Year 1	(30,000)		(30,000)	(20,000)
Remedial		10,000		(10,000)
	470,000	110,000	470,000	470,000
Depreciation Year 2	(30,000)		(30,000)	(20,000)
Remedial		10,000		(10,000)
	$440,000	$120,000	$440,000	$440,000

(B) A sells its interest in PRS to T for its fair market value of $440,000. A valid election under section 754 is in effect with respect to the sale of the partnership interest. Accordingly, PRS makes an adjustment, pursuant to section 743(b), to increase the basis of partnership property. Under section 743(b), the amount of the basis adjustment is equal to $320,000. Under section 755, the entire basis adjustment is allocated to the property.

(iii) At the time of the transfer, $320,000 of section 704(c) built-in gain from the property was still reflected on the partnership's books, and all of the basis adjustment is attributable to section 704(c) built-in gain. Therefore, the basis adjustment will be recovered over the remaining recovery period for the section 704(c) built-in gain under §1.704-3(d).

(ii) *Decreases*—(A) *Reduced deduction.* The amount of any negative basis adjustment allocated to an item of depreciable or amortizable property that is recovered in any year first decreases the transferee's distributive share of the partnership's depreciation or amortization deduc-

Reg. § 1.743-1(j)(4)

tions from that item of property for the year. If the amount of the basis adjustment recovered in any year exceeds the transferee's distributive share of the partnership's depreciation or amortization deductions from the item of property, then the transferee's distributive share of the partnership's depreciation or amortization deductions from other items of partnership property is decreased. The transferee then recognizes ordinary income to the extent of the excess, if any, of the amount of the basis adjustment recovered in any year over the transferee's distributive share of the partnership's depreciation or amortization deductions from all items of property.

(B) *Recovery period.* For purposes of section 168, if the basis of an item of a partnership's recovery property is decreased as the result of the transfer of an interest in the partnership, then the decrease is recovered over the remaining useful life of the item of the partnership's recovery property. The portion of the decrease that is recovered in any year during the recovery period is equal to the product of—

(*1*) The amount of the decrease to the item's adjusted basis (determined as of the date of the transfer); multiplied by

(*2*) A fraction, the numerator of which is the portion of the adjusted basis of the item recovered by the partnership in that year, and the denominator of which is the adjusted basis of the item on the date of the transfer (determined prior to any basis adjustments).

(C) *Examples.* The provisions of this paragraph (j)(4)(ii) are illustrated by the following examples:

Example 1. (i) A, B, and C are equal partners in partnership PRS, which owns Asset 2, an item of depreciable property that has a fair market value that is less than its adjusted tax basis. C sells its interest in PRS to T while PRS has an election in effect under section 754. PRS, therefore, decreases the basis of Asset 2 with respect to T.

(ii) Assume that in the year following the transfer of the partnership interest to T, T's distributive share of the partnership's common basis depreciation deductions from Asset 2 is $1,000. Also assume that, under paragraph (j)(4)(ii)(B) of this section, the amount of the basis adjustment under section 743(b) that T recovers during the year is $500. The total amount of depreciation deductions from Asset 2 reported by T is equal to $500.

Example 2. (i) A and B form equal partnership PRS. A contributes property with an adjusted basis of $100,000 and a fair market value of $50,000. B contributes $50,000 cash. When PRS is formed, the property has five years remaining in its recovery period. The partnership's adjusted basis of $100,000 will, therefore, be recovered over the five years remaining in the property's recovery period. PRS uses the traditional allocation method under § 1.704-3(b) with respect to the property. As a result, B will receive $5,000 of depreciation deductions from the property in each of years 1-5, and A, as the contributing partner, will receive $15,000 of depreciation deductions in each of these years.

(ii) Except for the depreciation deductions, PRS's expenses equal its income in each of the first two years commencing with the year the partnership is formed. After two years, A's share of the adjusted basis of partnership property is $70,000, while B's is $40,000. A sells its interest in PRS to T for its fair market value of $40,000. A valid election under section 754 is in effect with respect to the sale of the partnership interest. Accordingly, PRS makes an adjustment, pursuant to section 743(b), to decrease the basis of partnership property. Under section 743(b), the amount of the adjustment is equal to ($30,000). Under section 755, the entire adjustment is allocated to the property.

(iii) The basis of the property at the time of the transfer of the partnership interest was $60,000. In each of years 3 through 5, the partnership will realize depreciation deductions of $20,000 from the property. Thus, one third of the negative basis adjustment ($10,000) will be recovered in each of years 3 through 5. Consequently, T will be allocated, for tax purposes, depreciation of $15,000 each year from the partnership and will recover $10,000 of its negative basis adjustment. Thus, T's net depreciation deduction from the partnership in each year is $5,000.

Example 3. (i) A, B, and C are equal partners in partnership PRS, which owns Asset 2, an item of depreciable property that has a fair market value that is less than its adjusted tax basis. C sells its interest in PRS to T while PRS has an election in effect under section 754. PRS, therefore, decreases the basis of Asset 2 with respect to T.

(ii) Assume that in the year following the transfer of the partnership interest to T, T's distributive share of the partnership's common basis depreciation deductions from Asset 2 is $500. PRS allocates no other depreciation to T. Also assume that, under paragraph (j)(4)(ii)(B) of this section, the amount of the negative basis adjustment that T recovers during the year is $1,000. T will report $500 of ordinary income because the amount of the negative basis adjustment recovered during the year exceeds T's dis-

Reg. § 1.743-1(j)(4)

tributive share of the partnership's common basis depreciation deductions from Asset 2.

(5) *Depletion.* Where an adjustment is made under section 743(b) to the basis of partnership property subject to depletion, any depletion allowance is determined separately for each partner, including the transferee partner, based on the partner's interest in such property. See § 1.702-1(a)(8). For partnerships that hold oil and gas properties that are depleted at the partner level under section 613A(c)(7)(D), the transferee partner (and not the partnership) must make the basis adjustments, if any, required under section 743(b) with respect to such properties. See § 1.613A-3(e)(6)(iv).

(6) *Example.* The provisions of paragraph (j)(5) of this section are illustrated by the following example:

Example. A, B, and C each contributes $5,000 cash to form partnership PRS, which purchases a coal property for $15,000. A, B, and C have equal interests in capital and profits. C subsequently sells its partnership interest to T for $100,000 when the election under section 754 is in effect. T has a basis adjustment under section 743(b) for the coal property of $95,000 (the difference between T's basis, $100,000, and its share of the basis of partnership property, $5,000). Assume that the depletion allowance computed under the percentage method would be $21,000 for the taxable year so that each partner would be entitled to $7,000 as its share of the deduction for depletion. However, under the cost depletion method, at an assumed rate of 10 percent, the allowance with respect to T's one-third interest which has a basis to him of $100,000 ($5,000, plus its basis adjustment of $95,000) is $10,000, although the cost depletion allowance with respect to the one-third interest of A and B in the coal property, each of which has a basis of $5,000, is only $500. For partners A and B, the percentage depletion is greater than cost depletion and each will deduct $7,000 based on the percentage depletion method. However, as to T, the transferee partner, the cost depletion method results in a greater allowance and T will, therefore, deduct $10,000 based on cost depletion. See section 613(a).

(k) *Returns*—(1) *Statement of adjustments*—(i) *In general.* A partnership that must adjust the bases of partnership properties under section 743(b) must attach a statement to the partnership return for the year of the transfer setting forth the name and taxpayer identification number of the transferee as well as the computation of the adjustment and the partnership properties to which the adjustment has been allocated.

(ii) *Special rule.* Where an interest is transferred in a partnership which holds oil and gas properties that are depleted at the partner level under section 613A(c)(7)(D), the transferee must attach a statement to the transferee's return for the year of the transfer, setting forth the computation of the basis adjustment under section 743(b) which is allocable to such properties and the specific properties to which the adjustment has been allocated.

(iii) *Example.* The provisions of paragraph (k)(1)(ii) of this section are illustrated by the following example:

Example. (i) Partnership XYZ owns a single section 613A(c)(7)(D) domestic oil and gas property (Property) and other non-depletable assets. A, a partner in XYZ with an adjusted tax basis in Property of $100 (excluding any prior adjustments under section 743(b)), sells its partnership interest to B for $800 cash. Under § 1.613A-3(e)(6)(iv), A's adjusted basis of $100 in Property carries over to B.

(ii) Under section 755, XYZ determines that Property accounts for 50% of the fair market value of all partnership assets. The remaining 50% of B's purchase price ($400) is attributable to non-depletable property. XYZ must provide a statement to B containing the portion of B's adjusted basis attributable to non-depletable property ($400). Under this paragraph (k)(1), XYZ must report basis adjustments under section 743(b) to non-depletable property. B must report basis adjustments under section 743(b) to Property.

(2) *Requirement that transferee notify partnership*—(i) *Sale or exchange.* A transferee that acquires, by sale or exchange, an interest in a partnership with an election under section 754 in effect for the taxable year of the transfer, must notify the partnership, in writing, within 30 days of the sale or exchange. The written notice to the partnership must be signed under penalties of perjury and must include the names and addresses of the transferee and (if ascertainable) of the transferor, the taxpayer identification numbers of the transferee and (if ascertainable) of the transferor, the relationship (if any) between the transferee and the transferor, the date of the transfer, the amount of any liabilities assumed or taken subject to by the transferee, and the amount of any money, the fair market value of any other property delivered or to be delivered for the transferred interest in the partnership, and any other information necessary for the partnership to compute the transferee's basis.

(ii) *Transfer on death.* A transferee that acquires, on the death of a partner, an interest in a partnership with an election under section 754 in effect for the taxable year of the transfer, must notify the partnership, in writing, within one year of the death of the deceased partner. The written notice to the partnership must be signed under penalties of perjury and must include the names and addresses of the deceased partner and the transferee, the taxpayer identification numbers of the deceased partner and the transferee, the relationship (if any) between the transferee and the transferor, the deceased partner's date of death, the date on which the transferee became the owner of the partnership interest, the fair market value of the partnership interest on the applicable date of valuation set forth in section 1014, and the manner in which the fair market value of the partnership interest was determined.

(iii) *Nominee reporting.* If a partnership interest is transferred to a nominee which is required to furnish the statement under section 6031(c)(1) to the partnership, the nominee may satisfy the notice requirement contained in this paragraph (k)(2) by providing the statement required under § 1.6031(c)-1T, provided that the statement satisfies all requirements of § 1.6031(c)-1T and this paragraph (k)(2).

(3) *Reliance.* In making the adjustments under section 743(b) and any statement or return relating to such adjustments under this section, a partnership may rely on the written notice provided by a transferee pursuant to paragraph (k)(2) of this section to determine the transferee's basis in a partnership interest. The previous sentence shall not apply if any partner who has responsibility for federal income tax reporting by the partnership has knowledge of facts indicating that the statement is clearly erroneous.

(4) *Partnership not required to make or report adjustments under section 743(b) until it has notice of the transfer.* A partnership is not required to make the adjustments under section 743(b) (or any statement or return relating to those adjustments) with respect to any transfer until it has been notified of the transfer. For purposes of this section, a partnership is notified of a transfer when either—

(i) The partnership receives the written notice from the transferee required under paragraph (k)(2) of this section; or

(ii) Any partner who has responsibility for federal income tax reporting by the partnership has knowledge that there has been a transfer of a partnership interest.

(5) *Effect on partnership of the failure of the transferee to comply.* If the transferee fails to provide the partnership with the written notice required by paragraph (k)(2) of this section, the partnership must attach a statement to its return in the year that the partnership is otherwise notified of the transfer. This statement must set forth the name and taxpayer identification number (if ascertainable) of the transferee. In addition, the following statement must be prominently displayed in capital letters on the first page of the partnership's return for such year, and on the first page of any schedule or information statement relating to such transferee's share of income, credits, deductions, etc.: "RETURN FILED PURSUANT TO § 1.743-1(k)(5)." The partnership will then be entitled to report the transferee's share of partnership items without adjustment to reflect the transferee's basis adjustment in partnership property. If, following the filing of a return pursuant to this paragraph (k)(5), the transferee provides the applicable written notice to the partnership, the partnership must make such adjustments as are necessary to adjust the basis of partnership property (as of the date of the transfer) in any amended return otherwise to be filed by the partnership or in the next annual partnership return of income to be regularly filed by the partnership. At such time, the partnership must also provide the transferee with such information as is necessary for the transferee to amend its prior returns to properly reflect the adjustment under section 743(b).

(l) *Effective date.* This section applies to transfers of partnership interests that occur on or after December 15, 1999. [Reg. § 1.743-1.]

☐ [*T.D.* 6175, 5-23-56. Amended by *T.D.* 8717, 5-8-97 and *T.D.* 8847, 12-14-99 (*corrected 2-23-2000*).]

[Reg. § 1.751-1]

§ 1.751-1. **Unrealized receivables and inventory items**—(a) *Sale or exchange of interest in a partnership*—(1) *Character of amount realized.* To the extent that money or property received by a partner in exchange for all or part of his partnership interest is attributable to his share of the value of partnership unrealized receivables or substantially appreciated inventory items, the money or fair market value of the property received shall be considered as an amount realized from the sale or exchange of property other than a capital asset. The remainder of the total amount realized on the sale or exchange of the partnership interest is realized from the sale or exchange of a capital asset under section 741. For definition of "unrealized receivables" and "inventory items which have appreciated substantially in value", see section 751(c) and (d). Unrealized receivables and substantially appreciated inventory items are hereafter in this section referred to as "section 751 property". See paragraph (e) of this section.

Reg. § 1.751-1(a)(1)

(2) *Determination of gain or loss.* The income or loss realized by a partner upon the sale or exchange of its interest in section 751 property is the amount of income or loss from section 751 property (including any remedial allocations under § 1.704-3(d)) that would have been allocated to the partner (to the extent attributable to the partnership interest sold or exchanged) if the partnership had sold all of its property in a fully taxable transaction for cash in an amount equal to the fair market value of such property (taking into account section 7701(g)) immediately prior to the partner's transfer of the interest in the partnership. Any gain or loss recognized that is attributable to section 751 property will be ordinary gain or loss. The difference between the amount of capital gain or loss that the partner would realize in the absence of section 751 and the amount of ordinary income or loss determined under this paragraph (a)(2) is the transferor's capital gain or loss on the sale of its partnership interest.

(3) *Statement required.* A partner selling or exchanging any part of an interest in a partnership that has any section 751 property at the time of sale or exchange must submit with its income tax return for the taxable year in which the sale or exchange occurs a statement setting forth separately the following information—

(i) The date of the sale or exchange;

(ii) The amount of any gain or loss attributable to the section 751 property; and

(iii) The amount of any gain or loss attributable to capital gain or loss on the sale of the partnership interest.

(b) *Certain distributions treated as sales or exchanges*—(1) *In general.* (i) Certain distributions to which section 751(b) applies are treated in part as sales or exchanges of property between the partnership and the distributee partner, and not as distributions to which sections 731 through 736 apply. A distribution treated as a sale or exchange under section 751(b) is not subject to the provisions of section 707(b). Section 751(b) applies whether or not the distribution is in liquidation of the distributee partner's entire interest in the partnership. However, section 751(b) applies only to the extent that a partner either receives section 751 property in exchange for his relinquishing any part of his interest in other property, or receives other property in exchange for his relinquishing any part of his interest in section 751 property.

(ii) Section 751(b) does not apply to a distribution to a partner which is not in exchange for his interest in other partnership property. Thus, section 751(b) does not apply to the extent that a distribution consists of the distributee partner's share of section 751 property or his share of other property. Similarly, section 751(b) does not apply to current drawings or to advances against the partner's distributive share, or to a distribution which is, in fact, a gift or payment for services or for the use of capital. In determining whether a partner has received only his share of either section 751 property or of other property, his interest in such property remaining in the partnership immediately after a distribution must be taken into account. For example, the section 751 property in partnership ABC has a fair market value of $100,000 in which partner A has an interest of 30 percent, or $30,000. If A receives $20,000 of section 751 property in a distribution, and continues to have a 30-percent interest in the $80,000 of section 751 property remaining in the partnership after the distribution, only $6,000 ($30,000 minus $24,000 (30 percent of $80,000)) of the section 751 property received by him will be considered to be his share of such property. The remaining $14,000 ($20,000 minus $6,000) received is in excess of his share.

(iii) If a distribution is, in part, a distribution of the distributee partner's share of section 751 property, or of other property (including money) and, in part, a distribution in exchange of such properties, the distribution shall be divided for the purpose of applying section 751(b). The rules of section 751(b) shall first apply to the part of the distribution treated as a sale or exchange of such properties, and then the rules of sections 731 through 736 shall apply to the part of the distribution not treated as a sale or exchange. See paragraph (b)(4)(ii) of this section for treatment of payments under section 736(a).

(2) *Distribution of section 751 property (unrealized receivables or substantially appreciated inventory items).* (i) To the extent that a partner receives section 751 property in a distribution in exchange for any part of his interest in partnership property (including money) other than section 751 property, the transaction shall be treated as a sale or exchange of such properties between the distributee partner and the partnership (as constituted after the distribution).

(ii) At the time of the distribution, the partnership (as constituted after the distribution) realizes ordinary income or loss on the sale or exchange of the section 751 property. The amount of the income or loss to the partnership will be measured by the difference between the adjusted basis to the partnership of the section 751 property considered as sold to or exchanged with the partner, and the fair market value of the distributee partner's interest in other partnership property which he relinquished in the exchange. In

Reg. § 1.751-1(a)(2)

computing the partners' distributive shares of such ordinary income or loss, the income or loss shall be allocated only to partners other than the distributee and separately taken into account under section 702(a)(8).

(iii) At the time of the distribution, the distributee partner realizes gain or loss measured by the difference between his adjusted basis for the property relinquished in the exchange (including any special basis adjustment which he may have) and the fair market value of the section 751 property received by him in exchange for his interest in other property which he has relinquished. The distributee's adjusted basis for the property relinquished is the basis such property would have had under section 732 (including subsection (d) thereof) if the distributee partner had received such property in a current distribution immediately before the actual distribution which is treated wholly or partly as a sale or exchange under section 751(b). The character of the gain or loss to the distributee partner shall be determined by the character of the property in which he relinquished his interest.

(3) *Distribution of partnership property other than section 751 property.* (i) To the extent that a partner receives a distribution of partnership property (including money) other than section 751 property in exchange for any part of his interest in section 751 property of the partnership, the distribution shall be treated as a sale or exchange of such properties between the distributee partner and the partnership (as constituted after the distribution).

(ii) At the time of the distribution, the partnership (as constituted after the distribution) realizes gain or loss on the sale or exchange of the property other than section 751 property. The amount of the gain to the partnership will be measured by the difference between the adjusted basis to the partnership of the distributed property considered as sold to or exchanged with the partner, and the fair market value of the distributee partner's interest in section 751 property which he relinquished in the exchange. The character of the gain or loss to the partnership is determined by the character of the distributed property treated as sold or exchanged by the partnership. In computing the partners' distributive shares of such gain or loss, the gain or loss shall be allocated only to partners other than the distributee and separately taken into account under section 702(a)(8).

(iii) At the time of the distribution, the distributee partner realizes ordinary income or loss on the sale or exchange of the section 751 property. The amount of the distributee partner's income or loss shall be measured by the difference between his adjusted basis for the section 751 property relinquished in the exchange (including any special basis adjustment which he may have), and the fair market value of other property (including money) received by him in exchange for his interest in the section 751 property which he has relinquished. The distributee partner's adjusted basis for the section 751 property relinquished is the basis such property would have had under section 732 (including subsection (d) thereof) if the distributee partner had received such property in a current distribution immediately before the actual distribution which is treated wholly or partly as a sale or exchange under section 751(b).

(4) *Exceptions.* (i) Section 751(b) does not apply to the distribution to a partner of property which the distributee partner contributed to the partnership. The distribution of such property is governed by the rules set forth in sections 731 through 736, relating to distributions by a partnership.

(ii) Section 751(b) does not apply to payments made to a retiring partner or to a deceased partner's successor in interest to the extent that, under section 736(a), such payments constitute a distributive share of partnership income or guaranteed payments. Payments to a retiring partner or to a deceased partner's successor in interest for his interest in unrealized receivables of the partnership in excess of their partnership basis, including any special basis adjustment for them to which such partner is entitled, constitute payments under section 736(a) and, therefore, are not subject to section 751(b). However, payments under section 736(b) which are considered as made in exchange for an interest in partnership property are subject to section 751(b) to the extent that they involve an exchange of substantially appreciated inventory items for other property. Thus, payments to a retiring partner or to a deceased partner's successor in interest under section 736 must first be divided between payments under section 736(a) and section 736(b).

The section 736(b) payments must then be divided, if there is an exchange of substantially appreciated inventory items for other property, between the payments treated as a sale or exchange under section 751(b) and payments treated as a distribution under sections 731 through 736. See subparagraph (1)(iii) of this paragraph, and section 736 and § 1.736-1.

(5) *Statement required.* A partnership which distributes section 751 property to a partner in exchange for his interest in other partnership property, or which distributes other property in

Reg. § 1.751-1(b)(5)

exchange for any part of the partner's interest in section 751 property, shall submit with its return for the year of the distribution a statement showing the computation of any income, gain, or loss to the partnership under the provisions of section 751(b) and this paragraph. The distributee partner shall submit with his return a statement showing the computation of any income, gain, or loss to him. Such statement shall contain information similar to that required under paragraph (a)(3) of this section.

(c) *Unrealized receivables.* (1) The term "unrealized receivables", as used in subchapter K, chapter 1 of the Code, means any rights (contractual or otherwise) to payment for—

(i) Goods delivered or to be delivered (to the extent that such payment would be treated as received for property other than a capital asset), or

(ii) Services rendered or to be rendered, to the extent that income arising from such rights to payment was not previously includible in income under the method of accounting employed by the partnership. Such rights must have arisen under contracts or agreements in existence at the time of sale or distribution, although the partnership may not be able to enforce payment until a later time. For example, the term includes trade accounts receivable of a cash method taxpayer, and rights to payment for work or goods begun but incomplete at the time of the sale or distribution.

(2) The basis for such unrealized receivables shall include all costs or expenses attributable thereto paid or accrued but not previously taken into account under the partnership method of accounting.

(3) In determining the amount of the sale price attributable to such unrealized receivables, or their value in a distribution treated as a sale or exchange, full account shall be taken not only of the estimated cost of completing performance of the contract or agreement, but also of the time between the sale or distribution and the time of payment.

(4)(i) With respect to any taxable year of a partnership ending after September 12, 1966 (but only in respect of expenditures paid or incurred after that date), the term *unrealized receivables*, for purposes of this section and sections 731, 736, 741, and 751, also includes potential gain from mining property defined in section 617(f)(2). With respect to each item of partnership mining property so defined, the potential gain is the amount that would be treated as gain to which section 617(d)(1) would apply if (at the time of the transaction described in section 731, 736, 741,

or 751, as the case may be) the item were sold by the partnership at its fair market value.

(ii) With respect to sales, exchanges, or other dispositions after December 31, 1975, in any taxable year of a partnership ending after that date, the term *unrealized receivables*, for purposes of this section and sections 731, 736, 741, and 751, also includes potential gain from stock in a DISC as described in section 992(a). With respect to stock in such a DISC, the potential gain is the amount that would be treated as gain to which section 995(c) would apply if (at the time of the transaction described in section 731, 736, 741, or 751, as the case may be) the stock were sold by the partnership at its fair market value.

(iii) With respect to any taxable year of a partnership beginning after December 31, 1962, the term *unrealized receivables*, for purposes of this section and sections 731, 736, 741, and 751, also includes potential gain from section 1245 property. With respect to each item of partnership section 1245 property (as defined in section 1245(a)(3)), potential gain from section 1245 property is the amount that would be treated as gain to which section 1245(a)(1) would apply if (at the time of the transaction described in section 731, 736, 741, or 751, as the case may be) the item of section 1245 property were sold by the partnership at its fair market value. See § 1.1245-1(e)(1). For example, if a partnership would recognize under section 1245(a)(1) gain of $600 upon a sale of one item of section 1245 property and gain of $300 upon a sale of its only other item of such property, the potential section 1245 income of the partnership would be $900.

(iv) With respect to transfers after October 9, 1975, and to sales, exchanges, and distributions taking place after that date, the term *unrealized receivables*, for purposes of this section and sections 731, 736, 741, and 751, also includes potential gain from stock in certain foreign corporations as described in section 1248. With respect to stock in such a foreign corporation, the potential gain is the amount that would be treated as gain to which section 1248(a) would apply if (at the time of the transaction described in section 731, 736, 741, or 751, as the case may be) the stock were sold by the partnership at its fair market value.

(v) With respect to any taxable year of a partnership ending after December 31, 1963, the term *unrealized receivables*, for purposes of this section and sections 731, 736, 741, and 751, also includes potential gain from section 1250 property. With respect to each item of partnership section 1250 property (as defined in section 1250(c)), potential gain from section 1250 prop-

Reg. § 1.751-1(c)(2)

erty is the amount that would be treated as gain to which section 1250(a) would apply if (at the time of the transaction described in section 731, 736, 741, or 751, as the case may be) the item of section 1250 property were sold by the partnership at its fair market value. See § 1.1250-1(f)(1).

(vi) With respect to any taxable year of a partnership beginning after December 31, 1969, the term *unrealized receivables*, for purposes of this section and sections 731, 736, 741, and 751, also includes potential gain from farm recapture property as defined in section 1251(e)(1) (as in effect before enactment of the Tax Reform Act of 1984). With respect to each item of partnership farm recapture property so defined, the potential gain is the amount which would be treated as gain to which section 1251(c) (as in effect before enactment of the Tax Reform Act of 1984) would apply if (at the time of the transaction described in section 731, 736, 741, or 751, as the case may be) the item were sold by the partnership at its fair market value.

(vii) With respect to any taxable year of a partnership beginning after December 31, 1969, the term *unrealized receivables*, for purposes of this section and sections 731, 736, 741, and 751, also includes potential gain from farm land as defined in section 1252(a)(2). With respect to each item of partnership farm land so defined, the potential gain is the amount that would be treated as gain to which section 1252(a)(1) would apply if (at the time of the transaction described in section 731, 736, 741, or 751, as the case may be) the item were sold by the partnership at its fair market value.

(viii) With respect to transactions which occur after December 31, 1976, in any taxable year of a partnership ending after that date, the term *unrealized receivables*, for purposes of this section and sections 731, 736, 741, and 751, also includes potential gain from franchises, trademarks, or trade names referred to in section 1253(a). With respect to each such item so referred to in section 1253(a), the potential gain is the amount that would be treated as gain to which section 1253(a) would apply if (at the time of the transaction described in section 731, 736, 741, or 751, as the case may be) the items were sold by the partnership at its fair market value.

(ix) With respect to any taxable year of a partnership ending after December 31, 1975, the term *unrealized receivables*, for purposes of this section and sections 731, 736, 741, and 751, also includes potential gain under section 1254(a) from natural resource recapture property as defined in § 1.1254-1(b)(2). With respect to each separate partnership natural resource recapture property so described, the potential gain is the amount that would be treated as gain to which section 1254(a) would apply if (at the time of the transaction described in section 731, 736, 741, or 751, as the case may be) the property were sold by the partnership at its fair market value.

(5) For purposes of subtitle A of the Internal Revenue Code, the basis of any potential gain described in paragraph (c)(4) of this section is zero.

(6)(i) If (at the time of any transaction referred to in paragraph (c)(4) of this section) a partnership holds property described in paragraph (c)(4) of this section and if—

(A) A partner had a special basis adjustment under section 743(b) in respect of the property;

(B) The basis under section 732 of the property if distributed to the partner would reflect a special basis adjustment under section 732(d); or

(C) On the date a partner acquired a partnership interest by way of a sale or exchange (or upon the death of another partner) the partnership owned the property and an election under section 754 was in effect with respect to the partnership, the partner's share of any potential gain described in paragraph (c)(4) of this section is determined under paragraph (c)(6)(ii) of this section.

(ii) The partner's share of the potential gain described in paragraph (c)(4) of this section in respect of the property to which this paragraph (c)(6)(ii) applies is that amount of gain that the partner would recognize under section 617(d)(1), 995(c), 1245(a), 1248(a), 1250(a), 1251(c) (as in effect before the Tax Reform Act of 1984), 1252(a), 1253(a), or 1254(a) (as the case may be) upon a sale of the property by the partnership, except that, for purposes of this paragraph (c)(6) the partner's share of such gain is determined in a manner that is consistent with the manner in which the partner's share of partnership property is determined; and the amount of a potential special basis adjustment under section 732(d) is treated as if it were the amount of a special basis adjustment under section 743(b). For example, in determining, for purposes of this paragraph (c)(6), the amount of gain that a partner would recognize under section 1245 upon a sale of partnership property, the items allocated under § 1.1245-1(e)(3)(ii) are allocated to the partner in the same manner as the partner's share of partnership property is determined. See § 1.1250-1(f) for rules similar to those contained in § 1.1245-1(e)(3)(ii).

Reg. § 1.751-1(c)(6)

(d) *Inventory items which have substantially appreciated in value*—(1) *Substantial appreciation.* Partnership inventory items shall be considered to have appreciated substantially in value if, at the time of the sale or distribution, the total fair market value of all the inventory items of the partnership exceeds 120 percent of the aggregate adjusted basis for such property in the hands of the partnership (without regard to any special basis adjustment of any partner) and, in addition, exceeds 10 percent of the fair market value of all partnership property other than money. The terms "inventory items which have appreciated substantially in value" or "substantially appreciated inventory items" refer to the aggregate of all partnership inventory items. These terms do not refer to specific partnership inventory items or to specific groups of such items. For example, any distribution of inventory items by a partnership the inventory items of which as a whole are substantially appreciated in value shall be a distribution of substantially appreciated inventory items for the purposes of section 751(b), even though the specific inventory items distributed may not be appreciated in value. Similarly, if the aggregate of partnership inventory items are not substantially appreciated in value, a distribution of specific inventory items, the value of which is more than 120 percent of their adjusted basis, will not constitute a distribution of substantially appreciated inventory items. For the purpose of this paragraph, the "fair market value" of inventory items has the same meaning as "market" value in the regulations under section 471, relating to general rule for inventories.

(2) *Inventory items.* The term "inventory items" as used in subchapter K, chapter 1 of the Code, includes the following types of property:

(i) Stock in trade of the partnership, or other property of a kind which would properly be included in the inventory of the partnership if on hand at the close of the taxable year, or property held by the partnership primarily for sale to customers in the ordinary course of its trade or business. See section 1221(1).

(ii) Any other property of the partnership which, on sale or exchange by the partnership, would be considered property other than a capital asset and other than property described in section 1231. Thus, accounts receivable acquired in the ordinary course of business for services or from the sale of stock in trade constitute inventory items (see section 1221(4)), as do any unrealized receivables.

(iii) Any other property retained by the partnership which, if held by the partner selling his partnership interest or receiving a distribution described in section 751(b), would be considered property described in subdivisions (i) or (ii) of this subparagraph. Property actually distributed to the partner does not come within the provisions of section 751(d)(2)(C) and this subdivision.

(e) *Section 751 property and other property.* For the purposes of this section, "section 751 property" means unrealized receivables or substantially appreciated inventory items, and "other property" means all property (including money) except section 751 property.

(f) *Effective date.* Section 751 applies to gain or loss to a seller, distributee, or partnership in the case of a sale, exchange, or distribution occurring after March 9, 1954. For the purpose of applying this paragraph in the case of a taxable year beginning before January 1, 1955, a partnership or a partner may elect to treat as applicable any other section of subchapter K, chapter 1 of the Code. Any such election shall be made by a statement submitted not later than the time prescribed by law for the filing of the return for such taxable year, or submitted within 90 days after the promulgation of the regulations under this section, whichever date is later (but not later than 6 months after the time prescribed by law for the filing of the return for such year). See section 771(b)(3) and paragraph (b)(3) of § 1.771-1. See also section 771(c) and paragraph (c) of § 1.771-1. The rules contained in paragraphs (a)(2) and (a)(3) of this section apply to transfers of partnership interests that occur on or after December 15, 1999.

(g) *Examples.* Application of the provisions of section 751 may be illustrated by the following examples:

Example 1. (i)(A) A and B are equal partners in personal service partnership PRS. B transfers its interest in PRS to T for $15,000 when PRS's balance sheet (reflecting a cash receipts and disbursements method of accounting) is as follows:

Assets

	Adjusted Basis	Fair Market Value
Cash	$ 3,000	$ 3,000
Loans Receivable	10,000	10,000
Capital Assets	7,000	5,000
Unrealized Receivables	0	14,000
Total	20,000	32,000

Liabilities and Capital

	Adjusted Per Books	Fair Market Value
Liabilities	$ 2,000	$ 2,000
Capital:		
A	9,000	15,000
B	9,000	15,000
Total	20,000	32,000

Reg. § 1.751-1(d)(1)

Contributions, Distributions and Transfers 43,673

(B) None of the assets owned by PRS is section 704(c) property, and the capital assets are nondepreciable. The total amount realized by B is $16,000, consisting of the cash received, $15,000, plus $1,000, B's share of the partnership liabilities assumed by T. See section 752. B's undivided half-interest in the partnership property includes a half-interest in the partnership's unrealized receivables items. B's basis for its partnership interest is $10,000 ($9,000, plus $1,000, B's share of partnership liabilities). If section 751(a) did not apply to the sale, B would recognize $6,000 of capital gain from the sale of the interest in PRS. However, section 751(a) does apply to the sale.

(ii) If PRS sold all of its section 751 property in a fully taxable transaction immediately prior to the transfer of B's partnership interest to T, B would have been allocated $7,000 of ordinary income from the sale of PRS's unrealized receivables. Therefore, B will recognize $7,000 of ordinary income with respect to the unrealized receivables. The difference between the amount of capital gain or loss that the partner would realize in the absence of section 751 ($6,000) and the amount of ordinary income or loss determined under paragraph (a)(2) of this section ($7,000) is the transferor's capital gain or loss on the sale of its partnership interest. In this case, B will recognize a $1,000 capital loss.

Example (2). (a) *Facts*. Partnership ABC makes a distribution to partner C in liquidation of his entire one-third interest in the partnership. At the time of the distribution, the balance sheet of the partnership, which uses the accrual method of accounting, is as follows:

Assets

	Adjusted basis per books	Market value
Cash	$15,000	$15,000
Accounts receivable	9,000	9,000
Inventory	21,000	30,000
Depreciable property	42,000	48,000
Land	9,000	9,000
Total	96,000	111,000

Liabilities and Capital

	Per books	Value
Current liabilities	$15,000	$15,000
Mortgage payable	21,000	21,000
Capital:		
A	20,000	25,000
B	20,000	25,000
C	20,000	25,000
Total	96,000	111,000

The distribution received by C consists of $10,000 cash and depreciable property with a fair market value of $15,000 and an adjusted basis to the partnership of $15,000.

(b) *Presence of section 751 property*. The partnership has no unrealized receivables, but the dual test provided in section 751(d)(1) must be applied to determine whether the inventory items of the partnership, in the aggregate, have appreciated substantially in value. The fair market value of all partnership inventory items, $39,000 (inventory $30,000, and accounts receivable $9,000), exceeds 120 percent of the $30,000 adjusted basis of such items to the partnership. The fair market value of the inventory items, $39,000, also exceeds 10 percent of the fair market value of all partnership property other than money (10 percent of $96,000 or $9,600). Therefore, the partnership inventory items have substantially appreciated in value.

(c) *The properties exchanged*. Since C's entire partnership interest is to be liquidated, the provisions of section 736 are applicable. No part of the payment, however, is considered as a distributive share or as a guaranteed payment under section 736(a) because the entire payment is made for C's interest in partnership property. Therefore, the entire payment is for an interest in partnership property under section 736(b), and, to the extent applicable, subject to the rules of section 751. In the distribution, C received his share of cash ($5,000) and $15,000 in depreciable property ($1,000 less than his $16,000 share). In addition, he received other partnership property ($5,000 cash and $12,000 liabilities assumed, treated as money distributed under section 752(b)) in exchange for his interest in accounts receivable ($3,000), inventory ($10,000), land ($3,000), and the balance of his interest in depreciable property ($1,000). Section 751(b) applies only to the extent of the exchange of other property for section 751 property (i.e., inventory items, which include trade accounts receivable). The section 751 property exchanged has a fair market value of $13,000 ($3,000 in accounts receivable and $10,000 in inventory). Thus, $13,000 of the total amount C received is considered as received for the sale of section 751 property.

(d) *Distributee partner's tax consequences*. C's tax consequences on the distribution are as follows:

(1) *The section 751(b) sale or exchange*. C's share of the inventory items is treated as if he received them in a current distribution, and his basis for such items is $10,000 ($7,000 for inventory and $3,000 for accounts receivable) as determined under paragraph (b)(3)(iii) of this section. Then C is considered as having sold his share of inventory items to the partnership for $13,000. Thus, on the sale of his share of inventory items, C realizes $3,000 of ordinary income.

(2) *The part of the distribution not under section 751(b)*. Section 751(b) does not apply to the balance of the distribution. Before the distribution, C's basis for his partnership interest was

Reg. § 1.751-1(g)

$32,000 ($20,000 plus $12,000, his share of partnership liabilities). See section 752(a). This basis is reduced by $10,000, the basis attributed to the section 751 property treated as distributed to C and sold by him to the partnership. Thus, C has a basis of $22,000 for the remainder of his partnership interest. The total distribution to C was $37,000 ($22,000 in cash and liabilities assumed, and $15,000 in depreciable property). Since C received no more than his share of the depreciable property, none of the depreciable property constitutes proceeds of the sale under section 751(b). C did receive more than his share of money. Therefore, the sale proceeds, treated separately in subparagraph (1) of this paragraph of this example, must consist of money and therefore must be deducted from the money distribution. Consequently, in liquidation of the balance of C's interest, he receives depreciable property and $9,000 in money ($22,000 less $13,000). Therefore, no gain or loss is recognized to C on the distribution. Under section 732(b), C's basis for the depreciable property is $13,000 (the remaining basis of this partnership interest, $22,000, reduced by $9,000, the money received in the distribution).

(e) *Partnership's tax consequences.* The tax consequences to the partnership on the distribution are as follows:

(1) *The section 751(b) sale or exchange.* The partnership consisting of the remaining members has no ordinary income on the distribution since it did not give up any section 751 property in the exchange. Of the $22,000 money distributed (in cash and the assumption of C's share of liabilities), $13,000 was paid to acquire C's interest in inventory ($10,000 fair market value) and in accounts receivable ($3,000). Since under section 751(b) the partnership is treated as buying these properties, it has a new cost basis for the inventory and accounts receivable acquired from C. Its basis for C's share of inventory and accounts receivable is $13,000, the amount which the partnership is considered as having paid C in the exchange. Since the partnership is treated as having distributed C's share of inventory and accounts receivable to him, the partnership must decrease its basis for inventory and accounts receivable ($30,000) by $10,000, the basis of C's share treated as distributed to him, and then increase the basis for inventory and accounts receivable by $13,000 to reflect the purchase prices of the items acquired. Thus, the basis of the partnership inventory is increased from $21,000 to $24,000 in the transaction. (Note that the basis of property acquired in a section 751(b) exchange is determined under section 1012 without regard to any elections of the partnership. See § 1.732-1(e).) Further, the partnership realizes no capital gain or loss on the portion of the distribution treated as a sale under section 751(b) since, to acquire C's interest in the inventory and accounts receivable, it gave up money and assumed C's share of liabilities.

(2) *The part of the distribution not under section 751(b).* In the remainder of the distribution to C which was not in exchange for C's interest in section 751 property, C received only other property as follows: $15,000 in depreciable property (with a basis to the partnership of $15,000) and $9,000 in money ($22,000 less $13,000 treated under subparagraph (1) of this paragraph of this example). Since this part of the distribution is not an exchange of section 751 property for other property, section 751(b) does not apply. Instead, the provisions which apply are sections 731 through 736, relating to distributions by a partnership. No gain or loss is recognized to the partnership on the distribution. (See section 731(b).) Further, the partnership makes no adjustment to the basis of remaining depreciable property unless an election under section 754 is in effect. (See section 734(a).) Thus, the basis of the depreciable property before the distribution, $42,000, is reduced by the basis of the depreciable property distributed, $15,000, leaving a basis for the depreciable property in the partnership of $27,000. However, if an election under section 754 is in effect, the partnership must make the adjustment required under section 734(b) as follows: Since the adjusted basis of the distributed property to the partnership had been $15,000, and is only $13,000 in C's hands (see paragraph (d)(2) of this example), the partnership will increase the basis of the depreciable property remaining in the partnership by $2,000 (the excess of the adjusted basis to the partnership of the distributed depreciable property immediately before the distribution over its basis to the distributee). Whether or not an election under section 754 is in effect, the basis for each of the remaining partner's partnership interests will be $38,000 ($20,000 original contribution, plus $12,000, each partner's original share of the liabilities, plus $6,000, the share of C's liabilities each assumed).

(f) *Partnership trial balance.* A trial balance of the AB partnership after the distribution in liquidation of C's entire interest would reflect the results set forth in the schedule below. Column I shows the amounts to be reflected in the records if

Reg. § 1.751-1(g)

Contributions, Distributions and Transfers

See p. 20,601 for regulations not amended to reflect law changes

an election is in effect under section 754 with respect to an optional adjustment under section 734(b) to the basis of undistributed partnership property. Column II shows the amounts to be reflected in the records where an election under section 754 is not in effect. Note that in column II, the total bases for the partnership assets do not equal the total of the bases for the partnership interests.

	I Sec. 754, Election in effect		II Sec. 754, Election not in effect	
	Basis	Fair market value	Basis	Fair market value
Cash	$ 5,000	$ 5,000	$ 5,000	$ 5,000
Accounts receivable	9,000	9,000	9,000	9,000
Inventory	24,000	30,000	24,000	30,000
Depreciable property	29,000	33,000	27,000	33,000
Land	9,000	9,000	9,000	9,000
	76,000	86,000	74,000	86,000
Current liabilities	15,000	15,000	15,000	15,000
Mortgage	21,000	21,000	21,000	21,000
Capital: A	20,000	25,000	20,000	25,000
B	20,000	25,000	20,000	25,000
	76,000	86,000	76,000	86,000

Example (3). (a) *Facts.* Assume that the distribution to partner C in example (2) of this paragraph in liquidation of his entire interest in partnership ABC consists of $5,000 in cash and $20,000 worth of partnership inventory with a basis of $14,000.

(b) *Presence of section 751 property.* For the same reason as stated in paragraph (b) of that example, the partnership inventory items have substantially appreciated in value.

(c) *The properties exchanged.* In the distribution, C received his share of cash ($5,000) and his share of appreciated inventory items ($13,000). In addition, he received appreciated inventory with a fair market value of $7,000 (and with an adjusted basis to the partnership of $4,900) and $12,000 in money (liabilities assumed). C has relinquished his interest in $16,000 of depreciable property and $3,000 of land. Although C relinquished his interest in $3,000 of accounts receivable, such accounts receivable are inventory items and, therefore, that exchange was not an exchange of section 751 property for other property. Section 751(b) applies only to the extent of the exchange of other property for section 751 property (i.e., depreciable property or land for inventory items). Assume that the partners agree that the $7,000 of inventory in excess of C's share was received by him in exchange for $7,000 of depreciable property.

(d) *Distributee partner's tax consequences.* C's tax consequence on the distributions are as follows:

(1) *The section 751(b) sale or exchange.* C is treated as if he had received his 7/16ths share of the depreciable property in a current distribution. His basis for that share is $6,125 (42,000/48,000 of $7,000), as determined under paragraph (b)(2)(iii) of this section. Then C is considered as having sold his 7/16ths share of depreciable property to the partnership for $7,000, realizing a gain of $875.

(2) *The part of the distribution not under section 751(b).* Section 751(b) does not apply to the balance of the distribution. Before the distribution, C's basis for his partnership interest was $32,000 ($20,000, plus $12,000, his share of partnership liabilities). See section 752(a). This basis is reduced by $6,125, the basis of property treated as distributed to C and sold by him to the partnership. Thus, C will have a basis of $25,875 for the remainder of his partnership interest. Of the $37,000 total distribution to C, $30,000 ($17,000 in money, including liabilities assumed, and $13,000 in inventory) is not within section 751(b). Under section 732(b), C's basis for the inventory with a fair market value of $13,000 (which had an adjusted basis to the partnership of $9,100) is limited to $8,875, the amount of the remaining basis for his partnership interest, $25,875, reduced by $17,000, the money received. Thus, C's total aggregate basis for the inventory received is $15,875 ($7,000 plus $8,875), and not its $14,000 basis in the hands of the partnership.

(e) *Partnership's tax consequences.* The tax consequences to the partnership on the distribution are as follows:

(1) *The section 751(b) sale or exchange.* The partnership consisting of the remaining members has $2,100 of ordinary income on the sale of the $7,000 of inventory which had a basis to the partnership of $4,900 (21,000/30,000 of $7,000). This $7,000 of inventory was paid to acquire 7/16ths of C's interest in the depreciable prop-

Reg. § 1.751-1(g)

erty. Since, under section 751(b), the partnership is treated as buying this property from C, it has a new cost basis for such property. Its basis for the depreciable property is $42,875 ($42,000 less $6,125, the basis of the 7/16ths share considered as distributed to C, plus $7,000, the partnership purchase price for this share).

(2) *The part of the distribution not under section 751(b).* In the remainder of the distribution to C which was not a sale or exchange of section 751 property for other property, the partnership realizes no gain or loss. See section 731(b). Further, under section 734(a), the partnership makes no adjustment to the basis of the accounts receivable or the 9/16ths interest in depreciable property which C relinquished. However, if an election under section 754 is in effect, the partnership must make the adjustment required under section 734(b) since the adjusted basis to the partnership of the inventory distributed had been $9,100, and C's basis for such inventory after distribution is only $8,875. The basis of the inventory remaining in the partnership must be increased by $225. Whether or not an election under section 754 is in effect, the basis for each of the remaining partnership interests will be $39,050 ($20,000 original contribution, plus $12,000, each partner's original share of the liabilities, plus $6,000, the share of C's liabilities now assumed, plus $1,050, each partner's share of ordinary income realized by the partnership upon that part of the distribution treated as a sale or exchange).

Example (4). (a) *Facts.* Assume the same facts as in example (3) of this paragraph, except that the partners did not identify the property which C relinquished in exchange for the $7,000 of inventory which he received in excess of his share.

(b) *Presence of section 751 property.* For the same reasons stated in paragraph (b) of example (2) of this paragraph, the partnership inventory items have substantially appreciated in value.

(c) *The properties exchanged.* The analysis stated in paragraph (c) of example (3) of this paragraph is the same in this example, except that, in the absence of a specific agreement among the partners as to the properties exchanged, C will be presumed to have sold to the partnership a proportionate amount of each property in which he relinquished an interest. Thus, in the absence of an agreement, C has received $7,000 of inventory in exchange for his release of 7/19ths of the depreciable property and 7/19ths of the land. ($7,000, fair market value of property released, over $19,000, the sum of the fair market values of C's interest in the land and C's interest in the depreciable property.)

(d) *Distributee partner's tax consequences.* C's tax consequences on the distribution are as follows:

(1) *The section 751(b) sale or exchange.* C is treated as if he had received his 7/19ths shares of the depreciable property and land in a current distribution. His basis for those shares is $6,263 (51,000/57,000 of $7,000, their fair market value), as determined under paragraph (b)(2)(iii) of this section. Then C is considered as having sold his 7/19ths shares of depreciable property and land to the partnership for $7,000, realizing a gain of $737.

(2) *The part of the distribution not under section 751(b).* Section 751(b) does not apply to the balance of the distribution. Before the distribution C's basis for his partnership interest was $32,000 ($20,000 plus $12,000, his share of partnership liabilities). See section 752(a). This basis is reduced by $6,263, the bases of C's shares of depreciable property and land treated as distributed to him and sold by him to the partnership. Thus, C will have a basis of $25,737 for the remainder of his partnership interest. Of the total $37,000 distributed to C, $30,000 ($17,000 in money, including liabilities assumed, and $13,000 in inventory) is not within section 751(b). Under section 732(b), C's basis for the inventory (with a fair market value of $13,000 and an adjusted basis to the partnership of $9,100) is limited to $8,737, the amount of the remaining basis for his partnership interest ($25,737 less $17,000, money received). Thus, C's total aggregate basis for the inventory he received is $15,737 ($7,000 plus $8,737), and not the $14,000 basis it had in the hands of the partnership.

(e) *Partnership's tax consequences.* The tax consequences to the partnership on the distribution are as follows:

(1) *The section 751(b) sale or exchange.* The partnership consisting of the remaining members has $2,100 of ordinary income on the sale of $7,000 of inventory which had a basis to the partnership of $4,900 (21,000/30,000 of $7,000). This $7,000 of inventory was paid to acquire 7/19ths of C's interest in the depreciable property and land. Since, under section 751(b), the partnership is treated as buying this property from C, it has a new cost basis for such property. The bases of the depreciable property and land would be $42,737 and $9,000, respectively. The basis for the depreciable property is computed as follows: The common partnership basis of $42,000 is reduced by the $5,158 basis (42,000/48,000 of $5,895) for C's 7/19ths interest constructively distributed, and increased by $5,895 (16,000/19,000 of $7,000), the part of the

Reg. § 1.751-1(g)

Contributions, Distributions and Transfers 43,677
See p. 20,601 for regulations not amended to reflect law changes

purchase price allocated to the depreciable property. The basis of the land would be computed in the same way. The $9,000 original partnership basis is reduced by $1,105 basis (9,000/9,000 of $1,105) of the land constructively distributed to C, and increased by $1,105 (3,000/19,000 of $7,000), the portion of the purchase price allocated to the land.

(2) *The part of the distribution not under section 751(b).* In the remainder of the distribution to C which was not a sale or exchange of section 751 property for other property, the partnership realizes no gain or loss. See section 731(b). Further, under section 734(a), the partnership makes no adjustment to the basis of the accounts receivable or the 12/19ths interests in depreciable property and land which C relinquished. However, if an election under section 754 is in effect, the partnership must make the adjustment required under section 734(b) since the adjusted basis to the partnership of the inventory distributed had been $9,100 and C's basis for such inventory after the distribution is only $8,737. The basis of the inventory remaining in the partnership must be increased by the difference of $363. Whether or not an election under section 754 is in effect, the basis for each of the remaining partnership interests will be $39,050 ($20,000 original contribution plus $12,000, each partner's original share of the liabilities, plus $6,000, the share of C's liabilities assumed, plus $1,050, each partner's share of ordinary income realized by the partnership upon the part of the distribution treated as a sale or exchange).

Example (5). (a) *Facts.* Assume that partner C in example (2) of this paragraph agrees to reduce his interest in capital and profits from 1/3 to 1/5 for a current distribution consisting of $5,000 in cash, and $7,500 of accounts receivable with a basis to the partnership of $7,500. At the same time, the total liabilities of the partnership are not reduced. Therefore, after the distribution, C's share of the partnership liabilities has been reduced by $4,800 from $12,000 (1/3 of $36,000) to $7,200 (1/5 of $36,000).

(b) *Presence of section 751 property.* For the same reasons as stated in paragraph (b) of example (2) of this paragraph, the partnership inventory items have substantially appreciated in value.

(c) *The properties exchanged.* C's interest in the fair market value of the partnership properties before and after the distribution can be illustrated by the following table:

	C's interest Fair Market Value		C received		
Item	One-third before	One-fifth after	Distribution of share	In excess of share	C relinquished
Cash	$ 5,000	$ 2,000	$3,000	$ 2,000	......
Liabilities assumed	(12,000)	(7,200)	.....	$ 4,800	......
Inventory items:					
Accounts receivable	$ 3,000	$ 300	$2,700	$ 4,800	......
Inventory	10,000	6,000	.....	.....	$ 4,000
Depreciable property	16,000	9,600	.....	.....	6,400
Land	3,000	1,800	.....	.....	1,200
Total	$25,000	$12,500	$5,700	$11,600	$11,600

Although C relinquished his interest in $4,000 of inventory and received $4,800 of accounts receivable, both items constitute section 751 property and C has received only $800 of accounts receivable for $800 worth of depreciable property or for an $800 undivided interest in land. In the absence of an agreement identifying the properties exchanged, it is presumed C received $800 for proportionate shares of his interests in both depreciable property and land. To the extent that inventory was exchanged for accounts receivable, or to the extent cash was distributed for the release of C's interest in the balance of the depreciable property and land, the transaction does not fall within section 751(b) and is a current distribution under section 732(a). Thus, the remaining $6,700 of accounts receivable are received in a current distribution.

(d) *Distributee partner's tax consequences.* C's tax consequences on the distribution are as follows:

(1) *The Section 751(b) sale or exchange.* Assuming that the partners paid $800 worth of accounts receivable for $800 worth of depreciable property, C is treated as if he received the depreciable property in a current distribution, and his basis for the $800 worth of depreciable property is $700 (42,000/48,000 of $800, its fair market value), as determined under paragraph (b)(2)(iii) of this section. Then C is considered as having sold his $800 share of depreciable property to the partnership for $800. On the sale of the depreciable property, C realizes a gain of $100. If, on the other hand, the partners had agreed that C exchanged an $800 interest in the land for $800

Reg. § 1.751-1(g)

worth of accounts receivable, C would realize no gain or loss, because under paragraph (b)(2)(iii) of this section his basis for the land sold would be $800. In the absence of an agreement, the basis for the depreciable property and land (which C is considered as having received in a current distribution and then sold back to the partnership) would be $716 (51,000/57,000 of $800). In that case, on the sale of the balance of the $800 share of depreciable property and land, C would realize $84 of gain ($800 less $716).

(2) *The part of the distribution not under section 751(b).* Section 751(b) does not apply to the balance of the distribution. Under section 731, C does not realize either gain or loss on the balance of the distribution. The adjustments to the basis of C's interest are illustrated in the following table:

	If accounts receivable received for depreciable property	If accounts receivable received for land	If there is no agreement
Original basis for C's interest	$32,000	$32,000	$32,000
Less basis of property distributed prior to sec. 751(b) sale or exchange	− 700	− 800	− 716
	31,300	31,200	31,284
Less money received in distribution	−9,800	−9,800	−9,800
	21,500	21,400	21,484
Less basis of property received in a current distribution under sec. 732	−6,700	−6,700	−6,700
Resulting basis for C's interest	14,800	14,700	14,784

C's basis for the $7,500 worth of accounts receivable which he received in the distribution will be $7,500, composed of $800 for the portion purchased in the section 751(b) exchange, plus $6,700, the basis carried over under section 732(a) for the portion received in the current distribution.

(e) *Partnership's tax consequences.* The tax consequences to the partnership on the distribution are as follows:

(1) *The section 751(b) sale or exchange.* The partnership realizes no gain or loss in the section 751 sale or exchange because it had a basis of $800 for the accounts receivable for which it received $800 worth of other property. If the partnership agreed to purchase $800 worth of depreciable property, the partnership basis of depreciable property becomes $42,100 ($42,000 less $700 basis of property constructively distributed to C, plus $800, price of property purchased). If the partnership purchased land with the accounts receivable, there would be no change in the basis of the land to the partnership because the basis of land distributed was equal to its purchase price. If there were no agreement, the basis of the depreciable property and land would be $51,084 (depreciable property, $42,084 and land, $9,000). The basis for the depreciable property is computed as follows: The common partnership basis of $42,000 is reduced by the $590 basis (42,000/48,000 of $674) for C's $674 interest constructively distributed, and increased by $674 (6,400/7,600 of $800, the part of the purchase price allocated to the depreciable property. The basis of the land would be computed in the same way. The $9,000 original partnership basis is reduced by $126 basis (9,000/9,000 of $126) of the land constructively distributed to C, and increased by $126 (1,200/7,600 of $800), the portion of the purchase price allocated to the land.

(2) *The part of the distribution not under section 751(b).* The partnership will realize no gain or loss in the balance of the distribution under section 731. Since the property in C's hands after the distribution will have the same basis it had in the partnership, the basis of partnership property remaining in the partnership after the distribution will not be adjusted (whether or not an election under 754 is in effect).

Example (6). (a) *Facts.* Partnership ABC distributes to partner C, in liquidation of his entire one-third interest in the partnership, a machine which is section 1245 property with a recomputed basis (as defined in section 1245(a)(2)) of $18,000. At the time of the distribution, the balance sheet of the partnership is as follows:

Assets	Adjusted basis per books	Market value
Cash	$ 3,000	$ 3,000
Machine (section 1245 property)	9,000	15,000
Land	18,000	27,000
Total	$30,000	$45,000

Liabilities and Capital	Per books	Value
Liabilities	$ 0	$ 0
Capital:		
A	10,000	15,000
B	10,000	15,000
C	10,000	15,000
Total	$30,000	$45,000

Reg. § 1.751-1(g)

Contributions, Distributions and Transfers

See p. 20,601 for regulations not amended to reflect law changes

(b) *Presence of section 751 property.* The section 1245 property is an unrealized receivable of the partnership to the extent of the potential section 1245 income in respect of the property. Since the fair market value of the property ($15,000) is lower than its recomputed basis ($18,000), the excess of the fair market value over its adjusted basis ($9,000), or $6,000, is the potential section 1245 income of the partnership in respect of the property. The partnership has no other section 751 property.

(c) *The properties exchanged.* In the distribution C received his share of section 751 property (potential section 1245 income of $2,000, i.e., 1/3 of $6,000) and his share of section 1245 property (other than potential section 1245 income) with a fair market value of $3,000, i.e., 1/3 of ($15,000 minus $6,000), and an adjusted basis of $3,000, i.e., 1/3 of $9,000. In addition he received $4,000 of section 751 property (consisting of $4,000 ($6,000 minus $2,000) of potential section 1245 income) and section 1245 property (other than potential section 1245 income) with a fair market value of $6,000 ($9,000 minus $3,000) and an adjusted basis of $6,000 ($9,000 minus $3,000). C relinquished his interest in $1,000 of cash and $9,000 of land. Assume that the partners agree that the $4,000 of section 751 property in excess of C's share was received by him in exchange for $4,000 of land.

(d) *Distributee partner's tax consequences.* C's tax consequences on the distributions are as follows:

(1) *The section 751(b) sale or exchange.* C is treated as if he received in a current distribution 4/9ths of his share of the land with a basis of $2,667 (18,000/27,000 × $4,000). Then C is considered as having sold his 4/9ths share of the land to the partnership for $4,000, realizing a gain of $1,333. C's basis for the remainder of his partnership interest after the current distribution is $7,333, i.e., the basis of his partnership interest before the current distribution ($10,000) minus the basis of the land treated as distributed to him ($2,667).

(2) *The part of the distribution not under section 751(b).* Of the $15,000 total distribution to C, $11,000 ($2,000 of potential section 1245 income and $9,000 section 1245 property other than potential section 1245 income) is not within section 751(b). Under section 732(b) and (c), C's basis for his share of potential section 1245 income is zero (see paragraph (c)(5) of this section) and his basis for $9,000 of section 1245 property (other than potential section 1245 income) is $7,333, i.e., the amount of the remaining basis for his partnership interest ($7,333) reduced by the basis for his share of potential section 1245 income (zero). Thus C's total aggregate basis for the section 1245 property (fair market value of $15,000) distributed to him is $11,333 ($4,000 plus $7,333). For an illustration of the computation of his recomputed basis for the section 1245 property immediately after the distribution, see example (2) of paragraph (f)(3) of § 1.1245-4.

(e) *Partnership's tax consequences.* The tax consequences to the partnership on the distribution are as follows:

(1) *The section 751(b) sale or exchange.* Upon the sale of $4,000 potential section 1245 income, with a basis of zero, for 4/9ths of C's interest in the land, the partnership consisting of the remaining members has $4,000 ordinary income under sections 751(b) and 1245(a)(1). See section 1245(b)(3) and (6)(A). The partnership's new basis for the land is $19,333, i.e., $18,000, less the basis of the 4/9ths share considered as distributed to C ($2,667), plus the partnership purchase price for this share ($4,000).

(2) *The part of the distribution not under section 751(b).* The analysis under this subparagraph should be made in accordance with the principles illustrated in paragraph (e)(2) of examples (3), (4), and (5) of this paragraph.

[Reg. § 1.751-1.]

☐ [T.D. 6175, 5-23-56. Amended by T.D. 6832, 7-6-65; T.D. 7084, 1-7-71; T.D. 8586, 1-9-95 and T.D. 8847, 12-14-99.]

[Reg. § 1.752-0]

§ 1.752-0. **Table of contents.**—This section lists the captions that appear in §§ 1.752-1 through 1.752-5.

§ 1.752-1. *Treatment of partnership liabilities.*

(a) Definitions.

(1) Recourse liability defined.

(2) Nonrecourse liability defined.

(3) Related person.

(b) Increase in partner's share of liabilities.

(c) Decrease in partner's share of liabilities.

(d) Assumption of liability.

(e) Property subject to a liability.

(f) Netting of increases and decreases in liabilities resulting from same transaction.

(g) Example.

(h) Sale or exchange of partnership interest.

(i) Bifurcation of partnership liabilities.

§ 1.752-2. *Partner's share of recourse liabilities.*

(a) In general.

(b) Obligation to make a payment.

Reg. § 1.752-0

(1) In general.
(2) Treatment upon deemed disposition.
(3) Obligations recognized.
(4) Contingent obligations.
(5) Reimbursement rights.
(6) Deemed satisfaction of obligation.
(c) Partner or related person as lender.
(1) In general.
(2) Wrapped debt.
(d) De minimis exceptions.
(1) Partner as lender.
(2) Partner as guarantor.
(e) Special rule for nonrecourse liability with interest guaranteed by a partner.
(1) In general.
(2) Computation of present value.
(3) Safe harbor.
(4) De minimis exception.
(f) Examples.
(g) Time-value-of-money considerations.
(1) In general.
(2) Valuation of an obligation.
(3) Satisfaction of obligation with partner's promissory note.
(4) Example.
(h) Partner providing property as security for partnership liability.
(1) Direct pledge.
(2) Indirect pledge.
(3) Valuation.
(4) Partner's promissory note.
(i) Treatment of recourse liabilities in tiered partnerships.
(j) Anti-abuse rules.
(1) In general.
(2) Arrangements tantamount to a guarantee.
(3) Plan to circumvent or avoid the regulations.
(4) Example.
§ 1.752-3. Partner's share of nonrecourse liabilities.
(a) In general.
(b) Examples.
§ 1.752-4. Special rules.
(a) Tiered partnerships.
(b) Related person definition.
(1) In general.
(2) Person related to more than one partner.

(i) In general.
(ii) Natural persons.
(iii) Related partner exception.
(iv) Special rule where entity structured to avoid related person status.
(A) In general.
(B) Ownership interest.
(C) Example.
(c) Limitation.
(d) Time of determination.
§ 1.752-5. Effective dates and transition rules.
(a) In general.
(b) Election.
(1) In general.
(2) Time and manner of election.
(c) Effect of section 708(b)(1)(B) termination on determining date liabilities are incurred or assumed. [Reg. § 1.752-0.]
☐ [T.D. 8380, 12-20-91.]

[Reg. § 1.752-1]

§ 1.752-1. Treatment of partnership liabilities.—(a) *Definitions.* For purposes of section 752, the following definitions apply:

(1) *Recourse liability defined.* A partnership liability is a recourse liability to the extent that any partner or related person bears the economic risk of loss for that liability under § 1.752-2.

(2) *Nonrecourse liability defined.* A partnership liability is a nonrecourse liability to the extent that no partner or related person bears the economic risk of loss for that liability under § 1.752-2.

(3) *Related person.* Related person means a person having a relationship to a partner that is described in § 1.752-4(b).

(b) *Increase in partner's share of liabilities.* Any increase in a partner's share of partnership liabilities, or any increase in a partner's individual liabilities by reason of the partner's assumption of partnership liabilities, is treated as a contribution of money by that partner to the partnership.

(c) *Decrease in partner's share of liabilities.* Any decrease in a partner's share of partnership liabilities, or any decrease in a partner's individual liabilities by reason of the partnership's assumption of the individual liabilities of the partner, is treated as a distribution of money by the partnership to that partner.

(d) *Assumption of liability.* Except as otherwise provided in paragraph (e) of this section, a person is considered to assume a liability only to the extent that:

(1) The assuming person is personally obligated to pay the liability; and

(2) If a partner or related person assumes a partnership liability, the person to whom the liability is owed knows of the assumption and can directly enforce the partner's or related person's obligation for the liability, and no other partner or person that is a related person to another partner would bear the economic risk of loss for the liability immediately after the assumption.

(e) *Property subject to a liability.* If property is contributed by a partner to the partnership or distributed by the partnership to a partner and the property is subject to a liability of the transferor, the transferee is treated as having assumed the liability, to the extent that the amount of the liability does not exceed the fair market value of the property at the time of the contribution or distribution.

(f) *Netting of increases and decreases in liabilities resulting from same transaction.* If, as a result of a single transaction, a partner incurs both an increase in the partner's share of the partnership liabilities (or the partner's individual liabilities) and a decrease in the partner's share of the partnership liabilities (or the partner's individual liabilities), only the net decrease is treated as a distribution from the partnership and only the net increase is treated as a contribution of money to the partnership. Generally, the contribution to or distribution from a partnership of property subject to a liability or the termination of the partnership under section 708(b) will require that increases and decreases in liabilities associated with the transaction be netted to determine if a partner will be deemed to have made a contribution or received a distribution as a result of the transaction. When two or more partnerships merge or consolidate under section 708(b)(2)(A), as described in § 1.708-1(c)(3)(i), increases and decreases in partnership liabilities associated with the merger or consolidation are netted by the partners in the terminating partnership and the resulting partnership to determine the effect of the merger under section 752.

(g) *Example.* The following example illustrates the principles of paragraphs (b), (c), (e), and (f) of this section.

Example 1. Property contributed subject to a liability; netting of increase and decrease in partner's share of liability. B contributes property with an adjusted basis of $1,000 to a general partnership in exchange for a one-third interest in the partnership. At the time of the contribution, the partnership does not have any liabilities outstanding and the property is subject to a recourse debt of $150 and has a fair market value in excess of $150. After the contribution, B remains personally liable to the creditor and none of the other partners bears any of the economic risk of loss for the liability under state law or otherwise. Under paragraph (e) of this section, the partnership is treated as having assumed the $150 liability. As a result, B's individual liabilities decrease by $150. At the same time, however, B's share of liabilities of the partnership increases by $150. Only the net increase or decrease in B's share of the liabilities of the partnership and B's individual liabilities is taken into account in applying section 752. Because there is no net change, B is not treated as having contributed money to the partnership or as having received a distribution of money from the partnership under paragraph (b) or (c) of this section. Therefore B's basis for B's partnership interest is $1,000 (B's basis for the contributed property).

Example 2. Merger or consolidation of partnerships holding property encumbered by liabilities. (i) B owns a 70 percent interest in partnership T. Partnership T's sole asset is property X, which is encumbered by a $900 liability. Partnership T's adjusted basis in property X is $600, and the value of property X is $1,000. B's adjusted basis in its partnership T interest is $420. B also owns a 20 percent interest in partnership S. Partnership S's sole asset is property Y, which is encumbered by a $100 liability. Partnership S's adjusted basis in property Y is $200, the value of property Y is $1,000, and B's adjusted basis in its partnership S interest is $40.

(ii) Partnership T and partnership S merge under section 708(b)(2)(A). Under section 708(b)(2)(A) and § 1.708-1(c)(1), partnership T is considered terminated and the resulting partnership is considered a continuation of partnership S. Partnerships T and S undertake the form described in § 1.708-1(c)(3)(i) for the partnership merger. Under § 1.708-1(c)(3)(i), partnership T contributes property X and its $900 liability to partnership S in exchange for an interest in partnership S. Immediately thereafter, partnership T distributes the interests in partnership S to its partners in liquidation of their interests in partnership T. B owns a 25 percent interest in partnership S after partnership T distributes the interests in partnership S to B.

(iii) Under paragraph (f) of this section, B nets the increases and decreases in its share of partnership liabilities associated with the merger of partnership T and partnership S. Before the merger, B's share of partnership liabilities was $650 (B had a $630 share of partnership liabilities in partnership T and a $20 share of partnership liabilities in partnership S immediately before the

Reg. § 1.752-1(g)

merger). B's share of S's partnership liabilities after the merger is $250 (25 percent of S's total partnership liabilities of $1,000). Accordingly, B has a $400 net decrease in its share of S's partnership liabilities. Thus, B is treated as receiving a $400 distribution from partnership S under section 752(b). Because B's adjusted basis in its partnership S interest before the deemed distribution under section 752(b) is $460 ($420 + $40), B will not recognize gain under section 731. After the merger, B's adjusted basis in its partnership S interest is $60.

(h) *Sale or exchange of a partnership interest.* If a partnership interest is sold or exchanged, the reduction in the transferor partner's share of partnership liabilities is treated as an amount realized under section 1001 and the regulations thereunder. For example, if a partner sells an interest in a partnership for $750 cash and transfers to the purchaser the partner's share of partnership liabilities in the amount of $250, the seller realizes $1,000 on the transaction.

(i) *Bifurcation of partnership liabilities.* If one or more partners bears the economic risk of loss as to part, but not all, of a partnership liability represented by a single contractual obligation, that liability is treated as two or more separate liabilities for purposes of section 752. The portion of the liability as to which one or more partners bear the economic risk of loss is a recourse liability and the remainder of the liability, if any, is a nonrecourse liability. [Reg. § 1.752-1.]

☐ [T.D. 8380, 12-20-91. Amended by T.D. 8925, 1-3-2001.]

[Reg. § 1.752-2]

§ 1.752-2. **Partner's share of recourse liabilities.**—(a) *In general.* A partner's share of a recourse partnership liability equals the portion of that liability, if any, for which the partner or related person bears the economic risk of loss. The determination of the extent to which a partner bears the economic risk of loss for a partnership liability is made under the rules in paragraphs (b) through (j) of this section.

(b) *Obligation to make a payment.*

(1) *In general.* Except as otherwise provided in this section, a partner bears the economic risk of loss for a partnership liability to the extent that, if the partnership constructively liquidated, the partner or related person would be obligated to make a payment to any person (or a contribution to the partnership) because that liability becomes due and payable and the partner or related person would not be entitled to reimbursement from another partner or person that is a related person to another partner. Upon a constructive liquidation, all of the following events are deemed to occur simultaneously:

(i) All of the partnership's liabilities become payable in full;

(ii) With the exception of property contributed to secure a partnership liability (see § 1.752-2(h)(2)), all of the partnership's assets, including cash, have a value of zero;

(iii) The partnership disposes of all of its property in a fully taxable transaction for no consideration (except relief from liabilities for which the creditor's right to repayment is limited solely to one or more assets of the partnership);

(iv) All items of income, gain, loss, or deduction are allocated among the partners; and

(v) The partnership liquidates.

(2) *Treatment upon deemed disposition.* For purposes of paragraph (b)(1) of this section, gain or loss on the deemed disposition of the partnership's assets is computed in accordance with the following:

(i) If the creditor's right to repayment of a partnership liability is limited solely to one or more assets of the partnership, gain or loss is recognized in an amount equal to the difference between the amount of the liability that is extinguished by the deemed disposition and the tax basis (or book value to the extent section 704(c) or § 1.704-1(b)(4)(i) applies) in those assets.

(ii) A loss is recognized equal to the remaining tax basis (or book value to the extent section 704(c) or § 1.704-1(b)(4)(i) applies) of all of the partnership's assets not taken into account in paragraph (b)(2)(i) of this section.

(3) *Obligations recognized.* The determination of the extent to which a partner or related person has an obligation to make a payment under paragraph (b)(1) of this section is based on the facts and circumstances at the time of the determination. All statutory and contractual obligations relating to the partnership liability are taken into account for purposes of applying this section, including:

(i) Contractual obligations outside the partnership agreement such as guarantees, indemnifications, reimbursement agreements, and other obligations running directly to creditors or to other partners, or to the partnership;

(ii) Obligations to the partnership that are imposed by the partnership agreement, including the obligation to make a capital contribution and to restore a deficit capital account upon liquidation of the partnership; and

(iii) Payment obligations (whether in the form of direct remittances to another partner or a contribution to the partnership) imposed by state

Reg. § 1.752-2(a)

law, including the governing state partnership statute.

To the extent that the obligation of a partner to make a payment with respect to a partnership liability is not recognized under this paragraph (b)(3), paragraph (b) of this section is applied as if the obligation did not exist.

(4) *Contingent obligations.* A payment obligation is disregarded if, taking into account all the facts and circumstances, the obligation is subject to contingencies that make it unlikely that the obligation will ever be discharged. If a payment obligation would arise at a future time after the occurrence of an event that is not determinable with reasonable certainty, the obligation is ignored until the event occurs.

(5) *Reimbursement rights.* A partner's or related person's obligation to make a payment with respect to a partnership liability is reduced to the extent that the partner or related person is entitled to reimbursement from another partner or a person who is a related person to another partner.

(6) *Deemed satisfaction of obligation.* For purposes of determining the extent to which a partner or related person has a payment obligation and the economic risk of loss, it is assumed that all partners and related persons who have obligations to make payments actually perform those obligations, irrespective of their actual net worth, unless the facts and circumstances indicate a plan to circumvent or avoid the obligation. See § 1.752-2(j).

(c) *Partner or related person as lender*—(1) *In general.* A partner bears the economic risk of loss for a partnership liability to the extent that the partner or a related person makes (or acquires an interest in) a nonrecourse loan to the partnership and the economic risk of loss for the liability is not borne by another partner.

(2) *Wrapped debt.* If a partnership liability is owed to a partner or related person and that liability includes (*i.e.*, is "wrapped" around) a nonrecourse obligation encumbering partnership property that is owed to another person, the partnership liability will be treated as two separate liabilities. The portion of the partnership liability corresponding to the wrapped debt is treated as a liability owed to another person.

(d) *De minimis exceptions*—(1) *Partner as lender.* The general rule contained in paragraph (c)(1) of this section does not apply if a partner or related person whose interest (directly or indirectly through one or more partnerships including the interest of any related person) in each item of partnership income, gain, loss, deduction, or credit for every taxable year that the partner is a partner in the partnership is 10 percent or less, makes a loan to the partnership which constitutes qualified nonrecourse financing within the meaning of section 465(b)(6) (determined without regard to the type of activity financed).

(2) *Partner as guarantor.* The general rule contained in paragraph (b)(1) of this section does not apply if a partner or related person whose interest (directly or indirectly through one or more partnerships including the interest of any related person) in each item of partnership income, gain, loss, deduction, or credit for every taxable year that the partner is a partner in the partnership is 10 percent or less, guarantees a loan that would otherwise be a nonrecourse loan of the partnership and which would constitute qualified nonrecourse financing within the meaning of section 465(b)(6) (without regard to the type of activity financed) if the guarantor had made the loan to the partnership.

(e) *Special rule for nonrecourse liability with interest guaranteed by a partner*—(1) *In general.* For purposes of this section, if one or more partners or related persons have guaranteed the payment of more than 25 percent of the total interest that will accrue on a partnership nonrecourse liability over its remaining term, and it is reasonable to expect that the guarantor will be required to pay substantially all of the guaranteed future interest if the partnership fails to do so, then the liability is treated as two separate partnership liabilities. If this rule applies, the partner or related person that has guaranteed the payment of interest is treated as bearing the economic risk of loss for the partnership liability to the extent of the present value of the guaranteed future interest payments. The remainder of the stated principal amount of the partnership liability constitutes a nonrecourse liability. Generally, in applying this rule, it is reasonable to expect that the guarantor will be required to pay substantially all of the guaranteed future interest if, upon a default in payment by the partnership, the lender can enforce the interest guaranty without foreclosing on the property and thereby extinguishing the underlying debt. The guarantee of interest rule continues to apply even after the point at which the amount of guaranteed interest that will accrue is less than 25 percent of the total interest that will accrue on the liability.

(2) *Computation of present value.* The present value of the guaranteed future interest payments is computed using a discount rate equal to either the interest rate stated in the loan documents, or if interest is imputed under either section 483 or section 1274, the applicable federal rate, compounded semi-annually. The computation takes into account any payment of interest

Reg. § 1.752-2(e)(2)

that the partner or related person may be required to make only to the extent that the interest will accrue economically (determined in accordance with section 446 and the regulations thereunder) after the date of the interest guarantee. If the loan document contains a variable rate of interest that is an interest rate based on current values of an objective interest index, the present value is computed on the assumption that the interest determined under the objective interest index on the date of the computation will remain constant over the term of the loan. The term "objective interest index" has the meaning given to it in section 1275 and the regulations thereunder (relating to variable rate debt instruments). Examples of an objective interest index include the prime rate of a designated financial institution, LIBOR (London Interbank Offered Rate), and the applicable federal rate under section 1274(d).

(3) *Safe harbor.* The general rule contained in paragraph (e)(1) of this section does not apply to a partnership nonrecourse liability if the guarantee of interest by the partner or related person is for a period not in excess of the lesser five years or one-third of the term of the liability.

(4) *De minimis exception.* The general rule contained in paragraph (e)(1) of this section does not apply if a partner or related person whose interest (directly or indirectly through one or more partnerships including the interest of any related person) in each item of partnership income, gain, loss, deduction, or credit for every taxable year that the partner is a partner in the partnership is 10 percent or less, guarantees the interest on a loan to that partnership which constitutes qualified nonrecourse financing within the meaning of section 465(b)(6) (determined without regard to the type of activity financed). An allocation of interest to the extent paid by the guarantor is not treated as a partnership item of deduction or loss subject to the 10 percent or less rule.

(f) *Examples.* The following examples illustrate the principles of paragraphs (a) through (e) of this section.

Example 1. Determining when a partner bears the economic risk of loss. A and B form a general partnership with each contributing $100 in cash. The partnership purchases an office building on leased land for $1,000 from an unrelated seller, paying $200 in cash and executing a note to the seller for the balance of $800. The note is a general obligation of the partnership, *i.e.*, no partner has been relieved from personal liability. The partnership agreement provides that all items are allocated equally except that tax losses are specially allocated 90% to A and 10% to B and that capital accounts will be maintained in accordance with the regulations under section 704(b), including a deficit capital account restoration obligation on liquidation. In a constructive liquidation, the $800 liability becomes due and payable. All of the partnership's assets, including the building, are deemed to be worthless. The building is deemed sold for a value of zero. Capital accounts are adjusted to reflect the loss on the hypothetical disposition, as follows:

	A	B
Initial contribution	$100	$100
Loss on hypothetical sale	(900)	(100)
	($800)	$–0–

Other than the partners' obligation to fund negative capital accounts on liquidation, there are no other contractual or statutory payment obligations existing between the partners, the partnership and the lender. Therefore, $800 of the partnership liability is classified as a recourse liability because one or more partners bears the economic risk of loss for non-payment. B has no share of the $800 liability since the constructive liquidation produces no payment obligation for B. A's share of the partnership liability is $800 because A would have an obligation in that amount to make a contribution to the partnership.

Example 2. Recourse liability; deficit restoration obligation. C and D each contribute $500 in cash to the capital of a new general partnership, CD. CD purchases property from an unrelated seller for $1,000 in cash and a $9,000 mortgage note. The note is a general obligation of the partnership, *i.e.*, no partner has been relieved from personal liability. The partnership agreement provides that profits and losses are to be divided 40% to C and 60% to D. C and D are required to make up any deficit in their capital accounts. In a constructive liquidation, all partnership assets are deemed to become worthless and all partnership liabilities become due and payable in full. The partnership is deemed to dispose of all its assets in a fully taxable transaction for no consideration. Capital accounts are adjusted to reflect the loss on the hypothetical disposition, as follows:

Reg. § 1.752-2(e)(3)

Contributions, Distributions and Transfers

See p. 20,601 for regulations not amended to reflect law changes

	C	D
Initial contribution	$ 500	$ 500
Loss on hypothetical sale	(4,000)	(6,000)
	($3,500)	($5,500)

C's capital account reflects a deficit that C would have to make up of $3,500 and D's capital account reflects a deficit that D would have to make up of $5,500. Therefore, the $9,000 mortgage note is a recourse liability because one or more partners bears the economic risk of loss for the liability. C's share of the recourse liability is $3,500 and D's share is $5,500.

Example 3. Guarantee by limited partner; partner deemed to satisfy obligation. E and F form a limited partnership. E, the general partner, contributes $2,000 and F, the limited partner, contributes $8,000 in cash to the partnership. The partnership agreement allocates losses 20% to E and 80% to F until F's capital account is reduced to zero, after which all losses are allocated to E. The partnership purchases depreciable property for $25,000 using its $10,000 cash and a $15,000 recourse loan from a bank. F guarantees payment of the $15,000 loan to the extent the loan remains unpaid after the bank has exhausted its remedies against the partnership. In a constructive liquidation, the $15,000 liability becomes due and payable. All of the partnership's assets, including the depreciable property, are deemed to be worthless. The depreciable property is deemed sold for a value of zero. Capital accounts are adjusted to reflect the loss on the hypothetical disposition, as follows:

	E	F
Initial contribution	$ 2,000	$ 8,000
Loss on hypothetical sale	(17,000)	(8,000)
	($15,000)	–0–

E, as a general partner, would be obligated by operation of law to make a net contribution to the partnership of $15,000. Because E is assumed to satisfy that obligation, it is also assumed that F would not have to satisfy F's guarantee. The $15,000 mortgage is treated as a recourse liability because one or more partners bear the economic risk of loss. E's share of the liability is $15,000, and F's share is zero. This would be so even if E's net worth at the time of the determination is less than $15,000, unless the facts and circumstances indicate a plan to circumvent or avoid E's obligation to contribute to the partnership.

Example 4. Partner guarantee with right of subrogation. G, a limited partner in the GH partnership, guarantees a portion of a partnership liability. The liability is a general obligation of the partnership, *i.e.,* no partner has been relieved from personal liability. If under state law G is subrogated to the rights of the lender, G would have the right to recover the amount G paid to the recourse lender from the general partner. Therefore, G does not bear the economic risk of loss for the partnership liability.

Example 5. Bifurcation of partnership liability; guarantee of part of nonrecourse liability. A partnership borrows $10,000, secured by a mortgage on real property. The mortgage note contains an exoneration clause which provides that in the event of default, the holder's only remedy is to foreclose on the property. The holder may not look to any other partnership asset or to any partner to pay the liability. However, to induce the lender to make the loan, a partner guarantees payment of $200 of the loan principal. The exoneration clause does not apply to the partner's guarantee. If the partner paid pursuant to the guarantee, the partner would be subrogated to the rights of the lender with respect to $200 of the mortgage debt, but the partner is not otherwise entitled to reimbursement from the partnership or any partner. For purposes of section 752, $200 of the $10,000 mortgage liability is treated as a recourse liability of the partnership and $9,800 is treated as a nonrecourse liability of the partnership. The partner's share of the recourse liability of the partnership is $200.

Example 6. Wrapped debt. I, an individual, purchases real estate from an unrelated seller for $10,000, paying $1,000 in cash and giving a $9,000 purchase mortgage note on which I has no personal liability and as to which the seller can look only to the property for satisfaction. At a time when the property is worth $15,000, I sells the property to a partnership in which I is a general partner. The partnership pays for the property with a partnership purchase money mortgage note of $15,000 on which neither the partnership nor any partner (or person related to a partner) has personal liability. The $15,000 mortgage note is a wrapped debt that includes the $9,000 obligation to the original seller. The liability is a recourse liability to the extent of $6,000 because I is the creditor with respect to the loan and I bears the economic risk of loss for $6,000. I's share of the recourse liability is $6,000. The remaining $9,000 is treated as a partnership nonre-

Reg. § 1.752-2(f)

course liability that is owed to the unrelated seller.

Example 7. Guarantee of interest by partner treated as part recourse and part nonrecourse. On January 1, 1992, a partnership obtains a $4,000,000 loan secured by a shopping center owned by the partnership. Neither the partnership nor any partner has any personal liability under the loan documents for repayment of the stated principal amount. Interest accrues at a 15 percent annual rate and is payable on December 31 of each year. The principal is payable in a lump sum on December 31, 2006. A partner guarantees payment of 50 percent of each interest payment required by the loan. The guarantee can be enforced without first foreclosing on the property. When the partnership obtains the loan, the present value (discounted at 15 percent, compounded annually) of the future interest payments is $3,508,422, and of the future principal payment is $491,578. If tested on that date, the loan would be treated as a partnership liability of $1,754,211 ($3,508,422 × .5) for which the guaranteeing partner bears the economic risk of loss and a partnership nonrecourse liability of $2,245,789 ($1,754,211 + $491,578).

Example 8. Contingent obligation not recognized. J and K form a general partnership with cash contributions of $2,500 each. J and K share partnership profits and losses equally. The partnership purchases an apartment building for its $5,000 of cash and a $20,000 nonrecourse loan from a commercial bank. The nonrecourse loan is secured by a mortgage on the building. The loan documents provide that the partnership will be liable for the outstanding balance of the loan on a recourse basis to the extent of any decrease in the value of the apartment building resulting from the partnership's failure properly to maintain the property. There are no facts that establish with reasonable certainty the existence of any liability on the part of the partnership (and its partners) for damages resulting from the partnership's failure properly to maintain the building. Therefore, no partner bears the economic risk of loss, and the liability constitutes a nonrecourse liability. Under § 1.752-3, J and K share this nonrecourse liability equally because they share all profits and losses equally.

(g) *Time-value-of-money considerations*—(1) *In general.* The extent to which a partner or related person bears the economic risk of loss is determined by taking into account any delay in the time when a payment or contribution obligation with respect to a partnership liability is to be satisfied. If a payment obligation with respect to a partnership liability is not required to be satisfied within a reasonable time after the liability becomes due and payable, or if the obligation to make a contribution to the partnership is not required to be satisfied before the later of—

(i) The end of the year in which the partner's interest is liquidated, or

(ii) 90 days after the liquidation,

the obligation is recognized only to the extent of the value of the obligation.

(2) *Valuation of an obligation.* The value of a payment or contribution obligation that is not required to be satisfied within the time period specified in paragraph (g)(1) of this section equals the entire principal balance of the obligation only if the obligation bears interest equal to or greater than the applicable federal rate under section 1274(d) at the time of valuation, commencing on—

(i) In the case of a payment obligation, the date that the partnership liability to a creditor or other person to whom the obligation relates becomes due and payable, or

(ii) In the case of a contribution obligation, the date of the liquidation of the partner's interest in the partnership.

If the obligation does not bear interest at a rate at least equal to the applicable federal rate at the time of valuation, the value of the obligation is discounted to the present value of all payments due from the partner or related person (*i.e.*, the imputed principal amount computed under section 1274(b)). For purposes of making this present value determination, the partnership is deemed to have constructively liquidated as of the date on which the payment obligation is valued and the payment obligation is assumed to be a debt instrument subject to the rules of section 1274 (*i.e.*, the debt instrument is treated as if it were issued for property at the time of the valuation).

(3) *Satisfaction of obligation with partner's promissory note.* An obligation is not satisfied by the transfer to the obligee of a promissory note by a partner or related person unless the note is readily tradeable on an established securities market.

(4) *Example.* The following example illustrates the principle of paragraph (g) of this section.

Example. Value of obligation not required to be satisfied within specified time period. A, the general partner, and B, the limited partner, each contributes $10,000 to partnership AB. AB purchases property from an unrelated seller for $20,000 in cash and a $70,000 recourse purchase money note. The partnership agreement provides that profits and losses are to be divided equally. A

Reg. § 1.752-2(g)(1)

and B are required to make up any deficit in their capital accounts. While A is required to restore any deficit balance in A's capital account within 90 days after the date of liquidation of the partnership, B is not required to restore any deficit for two years following the date of liquidation. The deficit in B's capital account will not bear interest during that two-year period. In a constructive liquidation, all partnership assets are deemed to become worthless and all partnership liabilities become due and payable in full. The partnership is deemed to dispose of all its assets in a fully taxable transaction for no consideration. Capital accounts are adjusted to reflect the loss on the hypothetical disposition, as follows:

	A	B
Initial contribution	$10,000	$10,000
Loss on hypothetical sale	(45,000)	(45,000)
	($35,000)	($35,000)

A's and B's capital accounts each reflect deficits of $35,000. B's obligation to make a contribution pursuant to B's deficit restoration obligation is recognized only to the extent of the fair market value of that obligation at the time of the constructive liquidation because B is not required to satisfy that obligation by the later of the end of the partnership taxable year in which B's interest is liquidated or within 90 days after the date of the liquidation. Because B's obligation does not bear interest, the fair market value is deemed to equal the imputed principal amount under section 1274(b). Under section 1274(b), the imputed principal amount of a debt instrument equals the present value of all payments due under the debt instrument. Assume the applicable federal rate with respect to B's obligation is 10 percent compounded semiannually. Using this discount rate, the present value of the $35,000 payment that B would be required to make two years after the constructive liquidation to restore the deficit balance in B's capital account equals $28,795. To the extent that B's deficit restoration obligation is not recognized, it is assumed that B's obligation does not exist. Therefore, A, as the sole general partner, would be obligated by operation of law to contribute an additional $6,205 of capital to the partnership. Accordingly, under paragraph (g) of this section, B bears the economic risk of loss for $28,795 and A bears the economic risk of loss for $41,205 ($35,000 + $6,205).

(h) *Partner providing property as security for partnership liability*—(1) *Direct pledge.* A partner is considered to bear the economic risk of loss for a partnership liability to the extent of the value of any of the partner's or related person's separate property (other than a direct or indirect interest in the partnership) that is pledged as security for the partnership liability.

(2) *Indirect pledge.* A partner is considered to bear the economic risk of loss for a partnership liability to the extent of the value of any property that the partner contributes to the partnership solely for the purpose of securing a partnership liability. Contributed property is not treated as contributed solely for the purpose of securing a partnership liability unless substantially all of the items of income, gain, loss, and deduction attributable to the contributed property are allocated to the contributing partner, and this allocation is generally greater than the partner's share of other significant items of partnership income, gain, loss, or deduction.

(3) *Valuation.* The extent to which a partner bears the economic risk of loss as a result of a direct pledge described in paragraph (h)(1) of this section or an indirect pledge described in paragraph (h)(2) of this section is limited to the fair market value of the property at the time of the pledge or contribution.

(4) *Partner's promissory note.* For purposes of paragraph (h)(2) of this section, a promissory note of the partner or related person that is contributed to the partnership shall not be taken into account unless the note is readily tradeable on an established securities market.

(i) *Treatment of recourse liabilities in tiered partnerships.* If a partnership (the "upper-tier partnership") owns (directly or indirectly through one or more partnerships) an interest in another partnership (the "lower-tier partnership"), the liabilities of the lower-tier partnership are allocated to the upper-tier partnership in an amount equal to the sum of the following—

(1) The amount of the economic risk of loss that the upper-tier partnership bears with respect to the liabilities; and

(2) Any other amount of the liabilities with respect to which partners of the upper-tier partnership bear the economic risk of loss.

(j) *Anti-abuse rules*—(1) *In general.* An obligation of a partner or related person to make a payment may be disregarded or treated as an obligation of another person for purposes of this section if facts and circumstances indicate that a principal purpose of the arrangement between the parties is to eliminate the partner's economic risk of loss with respect to that obligation or create the appearance of the partner or related person bear-

Reg. § 1.752-2(j)(1)

ing the economic risk of loss when, in fact, the substance of the arrangement is otherwise. Circumstances with respect to which a payment obligation may be disregarded include, but are not limited to, the situations described in paragraphs (j)(2) and (j)(3) of this section.

(2) *Arrangements tantamount to a guarantee.* Irrespective of the form of a contractual obligation, a partner is considered to bear the economic risk of loss with respect to a partnership liability, or a portion thereof, to the extent that:

(i) The partner or related person undertakes one or more contractual obligations so that the partnership may obtain a loan;

(ii) The contractual obligations of the partner or related person eliminate substantially all the risk to the lender that the partnership will not satisfy its obligations under the loan; and

(iii) One of the principal purposes of using the contractual obligations is to attempt to permit partners (other than those who are directly or indirectly liable for the obligation) to include a portion of the loan in the basis of their partnership interests.

The partners are considered to bear the economic risk of loss for the liability in accordance with their relative economic burdens for the liability pursuant to the contractual obligations. For example, a lease between a partner and a partnership which is not on commercially reasonable terms may be tantamount to a guarantee by the partner of a partnership liability.

(3) *Plan to circumvent or avoid the obligation.* An obligation of a partner to make a payment is not recognized if the facts and circumstances evidence a plan to circumvent or avoid the obligation.

(4) *Example.* The following example illustrates the principle of paragraph (j)(3) of this section.

Example. Plan to circumvent or avoid obligation. A and B form a general partnership. A, a corporation, contributes $20,000 and B contributes $80,000 to the partnership. A is obligated to restore any deficit in its partnership capital account. The partnership agreement allocates losses 20% to A and 80% to B until B's capital account is reduced to zero, after which all losses are allocated to A. The partnership purchases depreciable property for $250,000 using its $100,000 cash and a $150,000 recourse loan from a bank. B guarantees payment of the $150,000 loan to the extent the loan remains unpaid after the bank has exhausted its remedies against the partnership. A is a subsidiary, formed by a parent of a consolidated group, with capital limited to $20,000 to allow the consolidated group to enjoy the tax losses generated by the property while at the same time limiting its monetary exposure for such losses. These facts, when considered together with B's guarantee, indicate a plan to circumvent or avoid A's obligation to contribute to the partnership. The rules of section 752 must be applied as if A's obligation to contribute did not exist. Accordingly, the $150,000 liability is a recourse liability that is allocated entirely to B. [Reg. § 1.752-2.]

☐ [T.D. 8380, 12-20-91.]

[Reg. § 1.752-3]

§ 1.752-3. **Partner's share of nonrecourse liabilities.**—(a) *In general.* A partner's share of the nonrecourse liabilities of a partnership equals the sum of paragraphs (a)(1) through (a)(3) of this section as follows—

(1) The partner's share of partnership minimum gain determined in accordance with the rules of section 704(b) and the regulations thereunder;

(2) The amount of any taxable gain that would be allocated to the partner under section 704(c) (or in the same manner as section 704(c) in connection with a revaluation of partnership property) if the partnership disposed of (in a taxable transaction) all partnership property subject to one or more nonrecourse liabilities of the partnership in full satisfaction of the liabilities and for no other consideration; and

(3) The partner's share of the excess nonrecourse liabilities (those not allocated under paragraphs (a)(1) and (a)(2) of this section) of the partnership as determined in accordance with the partner's share of partnership profits. The partner's interest in partnership profits is determined by taking into account all facts and circumstances relating to the economic arrangement of the partners. The partnership agreement may specify the partners' interests in partnership profits for purposes of allocating excess nonrecourse liabilities provided the interests so specified are reasonably consistent with allocations (that have substantial economic effect under the section 704(b) regulations) of some other significant item of partnership income or gain. Alternatively, excess nonrecourse liabilities may be allocated among the partners in accordance with the manner in which it is reasonably expected that the deductions attributable to those nonrecourse liabilities will be allocated. Additionally, the partnership may first allocate an excess nonrecourse liability to a partner up to the amount of built-in gain that is allocable to the partner on section 704(c) property (as defined under § 1.704-3(a)(3)(ii)) or property for which reverse section 704(c) allocations

Reg. § 1.752-3(a)(1)

are applicable (as described in § 1.704-3(a)(6)(i)) where such property is subject to the nonrecourse liability to the extent that such built-in gain exceeds the gain described in paragraph (a)(2) of this section with respect to such property. This additional method does not apply for purposes of § 1.707-5(a)(2)(ii). To the extent that a partnership uses this additional method and the entire amount of the excess nonrecourse liability is not allocated to the contributing partner, the partnership must allocate the remaining amount of the excess nonrecourse liability under one of the other methods in this paragraph (a)(3). Excess nonrecourse liabilities are not required to be allocated under the same method each year.

(b) *Allocation of a single nonrecourse liability among multiple properties*—(1) *In general.* For purposes of determining the amount of taxable gain under paragraph (a)(2) of this section, if a partnership holds multiple properties subject to a single nonrecourse liability, the partnership may allocate the liability among the multiple properties under any reasonable method. A method is not reasonable if it allocates to any item of property an amount of the liability that, when combined with any other liabilities allocated to the property, is in excess of the fair market value of the property at the time the liability is incurred. The portion of the nonrecourse liability allocated to each item of partnership property is then treated as a separate loan under paragraph (a)(2) of this section. In general, a partnership may not change the method of allocating a single nonrecourse liability under this paragraph (b) while any portion of the liability is outstanding. However, if one or more of the multiple properties subject to the liability is no longer subject to the liability, the portion of the liability allocated to that property must be reallocated among the properties still subject to the liability so that the amount of the liability allocated to any property does not exceed the fair market value of such property at the time of reallocation.

(2) *Reductions in principal.* For purposes of this paragraph (b), when the outstanding principal of a partnership liability is reduced, the reduction of outstanding principal is allocated among the multiple properties in the same proportion that the partnership liability originally was allocated to the properties under paragraph (b)(1) of this section.

(c) *Examples.* The following examples illustrate the principles of this section:

Example 1. Partner's share of nonrecourse liabilities. The AB partnership purchases depreciable property for a $1,000 purchase money note that is a nonrecourse liability under the rules of this section. Assume that this is the only nonrecourse liability of the partnership, and that no principal payments are due on the purchase money note for a year. The partnership agreement provides that all items of income, gain, loss, and deduction are allocated equally. Immediately after purchasing the depreciable property, the partners share the nonrecourse liability equally because they have equal interests in partnership profits. A and B are each treated as if they contributed $500 to the partnership to reflect each partner's increase in his or her share of partnership liabilities (from $0 to $500). The minimum gain with respect to an item of partnership property subject to a nonrecourse liability equals the amount of gain that would be recognized if the partnership disposed of the property in full satisfaction of the nonrecourse liability and for no other consideration. Therefore, if the partnership claims a depreciation deduction of $200 for the depreciable property for the year it acquires that property, partnership minimum gain for the year will increase by $200 (the excess of the $1,000 nonrecourse liability over the $800 adjusted tax basis of the property). See section 704(b) and the regulations thereunder. A and B each have a $100 share of partnership minimum gain at the end of that year because the depreciation deduction is treated as a nonrecourse deduction. See section 704(b) and the regulations thereunder. Accordingly, at the end of that year, A and B are allocated $100 each of the nonrecourse liability to match their shares of partnership minimum gain. The remaining $800 of the nonrecourse liability will be allocated equally between A and B ($400 each).

Example 2. Excess nonrecourse liabilities allocated consistently with reasonably expected deductions. The facts are the same as in *Example 1* except that the partnership agreement provides that depreciation deductions will be allocated to A. The partners agree to allocate excess nonrecourse liabilities in accordance with the manner in which it is reasonably expected that the deductions attributable to those nonrecourse liabilities will be allocated. Assuming that the allocation of all of the depreciation deductions to A is valid under section 704(b), immediately after purchasing the depreciable property, A's share of the nonrecourse liability is $1,000. Accordingly, A is treated as if A contributed $1,000 to the partnership.

Example 3. Allocation of liability among multiple properties. (i) A and B are equal partners in a partnership (PRS). A contributes $70 of cash in exchange for a 50-percent interest in PRS. B contributes two items of property, X and Y, in exchange for a 50-percent interest in PRS. Property

Reg. § 1.752-3(c)

X has a fair market value (and book value) of $70 and an adjusted basis of $40, and is subject to a nonrecourse liability of $50. Property Y has a fair market value (and book value) of $120, an adjusted basis of $40, and is subject to a nonrecourse liability of $70. Immediately after the initial contributions, PRS refinances the two separate liabilities with a single $120 nonrecourse liability. All of the built-in gain attributable to Property X ($30) and Property Y ($80) is section 704(c) gain allocable to B.

(ii) The amount of the nonrecourse liability ($120) is less than the total book value of all of the properties that are subject to such liability ($70+$120=$190), so there is no partnership minimum gain. § 1.704-2(d). Accordingly, no portion of the liability is allocated pursuant to paragraph (a)(1) of this section.

(iii) Pursuant to paragraph (b)(1) of this section, PRS decides to allocate the nonrecourse liability evenly between the Properties X and Y. Accordingly, each of Properties X and Y are treated as being subject to a separate $60 nonrecourse liability for purposes of applying paragraph (a)(2) of this section. Under paragraph (a)(2) of this section, B will be allocated $20 of the liability for each of Properties X and Y (in each case, $60 liability minus $40 adjusted basis). As a result, a portion of the liability is allocated pursuant to paragraph (a)(2) of this section as follows:

Partner	Property	Tier 1	Tier 2
A	X	$0	$ 0
	Y	$0	$ 0
B	X	$0	$20
	Y	$0	$20

(iv) PRS has $80 of excess nonrecourse liability that it may allocate in any manner consistent with paragraph (a)(3) of this section. PRS determines to allocate the $80 of excess nonrecourse liabilities to the partners up to their share of the remaining section 704(c) gain on the properties, with any remaining amount of liabilities being allocated equally to A and B consistent with their equal interests in partnership profits. B has $70 of remaining section 704(c) gain ($10 on Property X and $60 on Property Y), and thus will be allocated $70 of the liability in accordance with this gain. The remaining $10 is divided equally between A and B. Accordingly, the overall allocation of the $120 nonrecourse liability is as follows:

Partner	Tier 1	Tier 2	Tier 3	Total
A	$0	$ 0	$ 5	$ 5
B	$0	$40	$75	$115

[Reg. § 1.752-3.]

☐ [T.D. 8380, 12-20-91. Amended by T.D. 8906, 10-30-2000.]

[Reg. § 1.752-4]

§ 1.752-4. Special rules.—(a) *Tiered partnerships.* An upper-tier partnership's share of the liabilities of a lower-tier partnership (other than any liability of the lower-tier partnership that is owed to the upper-tier partnership) is treated as a liability of the upper-tier partnership for purposes of applying section 752 and the regulations thereunder to the partners of the upper-tier partnership.

(b) *Related person definition.*—(1) *In general.* A person is related to a partner if the person and the partner bear a relationship to each other that is specified in sections 267(b) or 707(b)(1), subject to the following modifications:

(i) Substitute "80 percent or more" for "more than 50 percent" each place it appears in those sections;

(ii) A person's family is determined by excluding brothers and sisters; and

(iii) Disregard sections 267(e)(1) and 267(f)(1)(A).

(2) *Person related to more than one partner*—(i) *In general.* If, in applying the related person rules in paragraph (b)(1) of this section, a person is related to more than one partner, paragraph (b)(1) of this section is applied by treating the person as related only to the partner with whom there is the highest percentage of related ownership. If two or more partners have the same percentage of related ownership and no other partner has a greater percentage, the liability is allocated equally among the partners having the equal percentages of related ownership.

(ii) *Natural persons.* For purposes of determining the percentage of related ownership between a person and a partner, natural persons who are related by virtue of being members of the same family are treated as having a percentage relationship of 100 percent with respect to each other.

(iii) *Related partner exception.* Notwithstanding paragraph (b)(1) of this section (which defines related person), persons owning interests directly or indirectly in the same partnership are not treated as related persons for purposes of determining the economic risk of loss borne by each of them for the liabilities of the partnership. This paragraph (iii) does not apply when determining a partner's interest under the de minimis rules in § 1.752-2(d) and (e).

(iv) *Special rule where entity structured to avoid related person status*—(A) *In general.* If—

(*1*) A partnership liability is owed to or guaranteed by another entity that is a partnership, an S corporation, a C corporation, or a trust;

(2) A partner or related person owns (directly or indirectly) a 20 percent or more ownership interest in the other entity; and

(3) A principal purpose of having the other entity act as a lender or guarantor of the liability was to avoid the determination that the partner that owns the interest bears the economic risk of loss for federal income tax purposes for all or part of the liability;

then the partner is treated as holding the other entity's interest as a creditor or guarantor to the extent of the partner's or related person's ownership interest in the entity.

(B) *Ownership interest.* For purposes of paragraph (b)(2)(iv)(A) of this section, a person's ownership interest in:

(1) A partnership equals the partner's highest percentage interest in any item of partnership loss or deduction for any taxable year;

(2) An S corporation equals the percentage of the outstanding stock in the S corporation owned by the shareholder;

(3) A C corporation equals the percentage of the fair market value of the issued and outstanding stock owned by the shareholder; and

(4) A trust equals the percentage of the actuarial interests owned by the beneficial owner of the trust.

(C) *Example. Entity structured to avoid related person status.* A, B, and C form a general partnership, ABC. A, B, and C are equal partners, each contributing $1,000 to the partnership. A and B want to loan money to ABC and have the loan treated as nonrecourse for purposes of section 752. A and B form partnership AB to which each contributes $50,000. A and B share losses equally in partnership AB. Partnership AB loans partnership ABC $100,000 on a nonrecourse basis secured by the property ABC buys with the loan. Under these facts and circumstances, A and B bear the economic risk of loss with respect to the partnership liability equally based on their percentage interest in losses of partnership AB.

(c) *Limitation.* The amount of an indebtedness is taken into account only once, even though a partner (in addition to the partner's liability for the indebtedness as a partner) may be separately liable therefor in a capacity other than as a partner.

(d) *Time of determination.* A partner's share of partnership liabilities must be determined whenever the determination is necessary in order to determine the tax liability of the partner or any other person. See § 1.705-1(a) for rules regarding when the adjusted basis of a partner's interest in the partnership must be determined. [Reg. § 1.752-4.]

☐ [*T.D.* 8380, 12-20-91.]

[Reg. § 1.752-5]

§ 1.752-5. **Effective dates and transitional rules.**—(a) *In general.* Unless a partnership makes an election under paragraph (b)(1) of this section to apply the provisions of §§ 1.752-1 through 1.752-4 earlier, §§ 1.752-1 through 1.752-4 apply to any liability incurred or assumed by a partnership on or after December 28, 1991, other than a liability incurred or assumed by the partnership pursuant to a written binding contract in effect prior to December 28, 1991 and at all times thereafter. However, § 1.752-3(a)(3) fifth, sixth, and seventh sentences, (b), and (c) *Example 3,* do not apply to any liability incurred or assumed by a partnership prior to October 31, 2000. Nevertheless, § 1.752-3(a)(3) fifth, sixth, and seventh sentences, (b), and (c) *Example 3,* may be relied upon for any liability incurred or assumed by a partnership prior to October 31, 2000 for taxable years ending on or after October 31, 2000. In addition, § 1.752-1(f) last sentence and (g) *Example 2,* do not apply to any liability incurred or assumed by a partnership prior to January 4, 2001. Nevertheless, § 1.752-1(f) last sentence and (g) *Example 2,* may be relied on for any liability incurred or assumed by a partnership prior to January 4, 2001 and, unless the partnership makes an election under paragraph (b)(1) of this section, on or after December 28, 1991, other than a liability incurred or assumed by the partnership pursuant to a written binding contract in effect prior to December 28, 1991 and at all times thereafter. For liabilities incurred or assumed by a partnership prior to December 28, 1991 (or pursuant to a written binding contract in effect prior to December 28, 1991 and at all times thereafter), unless an election to apply these regulations has been made, see §§ 1.752-0T to 1.752-4T, set forth in 26 CFR 1.752-0T through 1.752-4T as contained in 26 CFR edition revised April 1, 1991, (TD 8237, TD 8274, and TD 8355) and § 1.752-1, set forth in 26 CFR 1.752-1 as contained in 26 CFR edition revised April 1, 1988 (TD 6175 and TD 6500).

(b) *Election*—(1) *In general.* A partnership may elect to apply the provisions of §§ 1.752-1 through 1.752-4 to all of its liabilities to which the provisions of those sections do not otherwise apply as of the beginning of the first taxable year of the partnership ending on or after December 28, 1991.

(2) *Time and manner of election.* An election under this paragraph (b) is made by attaching a written statement to the partnership return for

the first taxable year of the partnership ending on or after December 28, 1991. The written statement must include the name, address, and taxpayer identification number of the partnership making the statement and contain a declaration that an election is being made under this paragraph (b).

(c) *Effect of section 708(b)(1)(B) termination on determining date liabilities are incurred or assumed.* For purposes of applying this section, a termination of the partnership under section 708(b)(1)(B) will not cause partnership liabilities incurred or assumed prior to the termination to be treated as incurred or assumed on the date of the termination. [Reg. § 1.752-5.]

☐ [T.D. 8380, 12-20-91. Amended by T.D. 8906, 10-30-2000 and T.D. 8925, 1-3-2001.]

[Reg. § 1.752-6T]

§ 1.752-6T. **Partnership assumption of partner's section 358(h)(3) liability after October 18, 1999, and before June 24, 2003 (temporary).**—(a) *In general.* If, in a transaction described in section 721(a), a partnership assumes a liability (defined in section 358(h)(3)) of a partner (other than a liability to which section 752(a) and (b) apply), then, after application of section 752(a) and (b), the partner's basis in the partnership is reduced (but not below the adjusted value of such interest) by the amount (determined as of the date of the exchange) of the liability. For purposes of this section, the adjusted value of a partner's interest in a partnership is the fair market value of that interest increased by the partner's share of partnership liabilities under §§ 1.752-1 through 1.752-5.

(b) *Exceptions*—(1) *In general.* Except as provided in paragraph (b)(2) of this section, the exceptions contained in section 358(h)(2)(A) and (B) apply to this section.

(2) *Transactions described in Notice 2000-44.* The exception contained in section 358(h)(2)(B) does not apply to an assumption of a liability (defined in section 358(h)(3)) by a partnership as part of a transaction described in, or a transaction that is substantially similar to the transactions described in, Notice 2000-44 (2000-2 C.B. 255). See § 601.601(d)(2) of this chapter.

(c) *Example.* The following example illustrates the principles of paragraph (a) of this section:

Example. In 1999, A and B form partnership PRS. A contributes property with a value and basis of $200, subject to a nonrecourse debt obligation of $50 and a fixed or contingent obligation of $100 that is not a liability to which section 752(a) and (b) applies, in exchange for a 50% interest in PRS. Assume that, after the contribution, A's share of partnership liabilities under §§ 1.752-1 through 1.752-5 is $25. Also assume that the $100 liability is not associated with a trade or business contributed by A to PRS or with assets contributed by A to PRS. After the contribution, A's basis in PRS is $175 (A's basis in the contributed land ($200) reduced by the nonrecourse debt assumed by PRS ($50), increased by A's share of partnership liabilities under §§ 1.752-1 through 1.752-5 ($25)). Because A's basis in the PRS interest is greater than the adjusted value of A's interest, $75 (the fair market value of A's interest ($50) increased by A's share of partnership liabilities ($25)), paragraph (a) of this section operates to reduce A's basis in the PRS interest (but not below the adjusted value of that interest) by the amount of liabilities described in section 358(h)(3) (other than liabilities to which section 752(a) and (b) apply) assumed by PRS. Therefore, A's basis in PRS is reduced to $75.

(d) *Effective dates*—(1) *In general.* This section applies to assumptions of liabilities occurring after October 18, 1999 and before June 24, 2003.

(2) *Election to apply § 1.752-7.* The partnership may elect, under provisions of REG-106736-00 in 2003-28 I.R.B. (see § 601.601(d)(2) of this chapter) to apply those provisions and related Income Tax Regulations to all assumptions of liabilities by the partnership occurring after October 18, 1999, and before June 24, 2003. Provisions of REG-106736-00 in 2003-28 I.R.B. (see § 601.601(d)(2) of this chapter) describe the manner in which the election is made. [Temporary Reg. § 1.752-6T.]

☐ [T.D. 9062, 6-23-2003.]

[Reg. § 1.753-1]

§ 1.753-1. **Partner receiving income in respect of decedent.**—(a) *Income in respect of a decedent under section 736(a).* All payments coming within the provisions of section 736(a) made by a partnership to the estate or other successor in interest of a deceased partner are considered income in respect of the decedent under section 691. The estate or other successor in interest of a deceased partner shall be considered to have received income in respect of a decedent to the extent that amounts are paid by a third person in exchange for rights to future payments from the partnership under section 736(a). When a partner who is receiving payments under section 736(a) dies, section 753 applies to any remaining payments under section 736(a) made to his estate or other successor in interest.

(b) *Other income in respect of a decedent.* When a partner dies, the entire portion of the distributive share which is attributable to the period ending with the date of his death and which is taxable to his estate or other successor constitutes income in respect of a decedent under section 691. This rule applies even though that part of the distributive share for the period before death which the decedent withdrew is not included in the value of the decedent's partnership interest for estate tax purposes. See paragraph (c)(3) of § 1.706-1.

(c) *Example.* The provisions of this section may be illustrated by the following example:

Example. A and the decedent B were equal partners in a business having assets (other than money) worth $40,000 with an adjusted basis of $10,000. Certain partnership business was well advanced towards completion before B's death and, after B's death but before the end of the partnership year, payment of $10,000 was made to the partnership for such work. The partnership agreement provided that, upon the death of one of the partners, all partnership property, including unfinished work, would pass to the surviving partner, and that the surviving partner would pay the estate of the decedent the undrawn balance of his share of partnership earnings at the date of death, plus $10,000 in each of the three years after death. B's share of earnings to the date of his death was $4,000, of which he had withdrawn $3,000. B's distributive share of partnership income of $4,000 to the date of his death is income in respect of a decedent (although only the $1,000 undrawn at B's death will be reflected in the value of B's partnership interest on B's estate tax return). Assume that the value of B's interest in partnership property at date of his death was $22,000, composed of the following items: B's one-half share of the assets of $40,000, plus $2,000, B's interest in partnership cash. It should be noted that B's $1,000 undrawn share of earnings to the date of his death is not a separate item but will be paid from partnership assets. Under the partnership agreement, A is to pay B's estate a total of $31,000. The difference of $9,000 between the amount to be paid by A ($31,000) and the value of B's interest in partnership property ($22,000) comes within section 736(a) and, thus, also constitutes income in respect of a decedent. (However, the $17,000 difference between the $5,000 basis for B's share of the partnership property and its $22,000 value at the date of his death does not constitute income in respect of a decedent.) If, before the close of the partnership taxable year, A pays B's estate $11,000, of which they agree to allocate $3,000 as the payment under section 736(a), B's estate will include $7,000 in its gross income (B's $4,000 distributive share plus $3,000 payment under section 736(a)). In computing the deduction under section 691(c), this $7,000 will be considered as the value for estate tax purposes of such income in respect of a decedent, even though only $4,000 ($1,000 of distributive share not withdrawn, plus $3,000, payment under section 736(a)) of this amount can be identified on the estate tax return as part of the partnership interest.

(d) *Effective date.* The provisions of section 753 apply only in the case of payments made with respect to decedents whose death occurred after December 31, 1954. See Section 771(b)(4) and paragraph (b)(4) of § 1.771. [Reg. § 1.753-1.]

☐ [*T.D.* 6175, 5-23-56.]

[Reg. § 1.754-1]

§ 1.754-1. **Time and manner of making election to adjust basis of partnership property.—** (a) *In general.* A partnership may adjust the basis of partnership property under sections 734(b) and 743(b) if it files an election in accordance with the rules set forth in paragraph (b) of this section. An election may not be filed to make the adjustments provided in either section 734(b) or section 743(b) alone, but such an election must apply to both sections. An election made under the provisions of this section shall apply to all property distributions and transfers of partnership interests taking place in the partnership taxable year for which the election is made and in all subsequent partnership taxable years unless the election is revoked pursuant to paragraph (c) of this section.

(b) *Time and method of making election*—(1) An election under section 754 and this section to adjust the basis of partnership property under sections 734(b) and 743(b), with respect to a distribution of property to a partner or a transfer of an interest in a partnership, shall be made in a written statement filed with the partnership return for the taxable year during which the distribution or transfer occurs. For the election to be valid, the return must be filed not later than the time prescribed by paragraph (e) of § 1.6031-1 (including extensions thereof) for filing the return for such taxable year (or before August 23, 1956, whichever is later). Notwithstanding the preceding two sentences, if a valid election has been made under section 754 and this section for a preceding taxable year and not revoked pursuant to paragraph (c) of this section, a new election is not required to be made. The statement required by this subparagraph shall (i) set forth the name and address of the partnership making the election, (ii) be signed by any one of the partners, and (iii) contain a declaration that the partnership elects under section 754 to apply the provisions of section 734(b) and section 743(b). For rules regarding extensions of time for filing elections, see § 1.9100-1.

(2) The principles of this paragraph may be illustrated by the following example:

Example. A, a U.S. citizen, is a member of partnership ABC, which has not previously made an election under section 754 to adjust the basis of partnership property. The partnership and the partners use the calendar year as the taxable year. A sells his interest in the partnership to D on January 1, 1971. The partnership may elect under section 754 and this section to adjust the basis of partnership property under sections 734(b) and 743(b). Unless an extension of time to make the election is obtained under the provisions of § 1.9100-1, the election must be made in a written statement filed with the partnership return for 1971 and must contain the information specified in subparagraph (1) of this paragraph. Such return must be filed by April 17, 1972 (unless an extension of time for filing the return is obtained). The election will apply to all distributions of property to a partner and transfers of an interest in the partnership occurring in 1971 and subsequent years, unless revoked pursuant to paragraph (c) of this section.

(c) *Revocation of election*—(1) *In general.* A partnership having an election in effect under this section may revoke such election with the approval of the district director for the internal revenue district in which the partnership return is required to be filed. A partnership which wishes to revoke such an election shall file with the district director for the internal revenue district in which the partnership return is required to be filed an application setting forth the grounds on which the revocation is desired. The application shall be filed not later than 30 days after the close of the partnership taxable year with respect to which revocation is intended to take effect and shall be signed by any one of the partners. Examples of situations which may be considered sufficient reason for approving an application for revocation include a change in the nature of the partnership business, a substantial increase in the assets of the partnership, a change in the character of partnership assets, or an increased frequency of retirements or shifts of partnership interests, so that an increased administrative burden would result to the partnership from the election. However, no application for revocation of an election shall be approved when the purpose of the revocation is primarily to avoid stepping down the basis of partnership assets upon a transfer or distribution.

(2) *Revocations effective on December 15, 1999.* Notwithstanding paragraph (c)(1) of this section, any partnership having an election in effect under this section for its taxable year that includes December 15, 1999, may revoke such election effective for transfers or distributions occurring on or after December 15, 1999, by attaching a statement to the partnership's return for such year. For the revocation to be valid, the statement must be filed not later than the time prescribed by § 1.6031(a)-1(e) (including extensions thereof) for filing the return for such taxable year, and must set forth the name and address of the partnership revoking the election, be signed by any one of the partners who is authorized to sign the partnership's federal income tax return, and contain a declaration that the partnership revokes its election under section 754 to apply the provisions of section 734(b) and 743(b). In addition, the following statement must be prominently displayed in capital letters on the first page of the partnership's return for such year: "RETURN FILED PURSUANT TO § 1.754-1(c)(2)." [Reg. § 1.754-1.]

☐ [*T.D.* 6175, 5-23-56. Amended by *T.D.* 7208, 10-2-72 and *T.D.* 8847, 12-14-99 (corrected 2-23-2000).]

[Reg. § 1.755-1]

§ 1.755-1. **Rules for allocation of basis.**—(a) *In general*—(1) *Scope.* This section provides rules for allocating basis adjustments under sections 743(b) and 734(b) among partnership property. If there is a basis adjustment to which this section applies, the basis adjustment is allocated among the partnership's assets as follows. First, the partnership must determine the value of each of its assets under paragraphs (a)(2) through (5) of this section. Second, the basis adjustment is allocated between the two classes of property described in section 755(b). These classes of property consist of capital assets and section 1231(b) property (capital gain property), and any other property of the partnership (ordinary income property). For purposes of this section, properties and potential gain treated as unrealized receivables under section 751(c) and the regulations thereunder shall be treated as separate assets that are ordinary income property. Third, the portion of the basis adjustment allocated to each class is allocated among the items within the class. Basis adjustments under section 743(b) are allocated among partnership assets under paragraph (b) of this section. Basis adjustments under section 734(b) are allocated among partnership assets under paragraph (c) of this section.

(2) *Coordination of sections 755 and 1060.* If there is a basis adjustment to which this section applies, and the assets of the partnership constitute a trade or business (as described in § 1.1060-1(b)(2)), then the partnership is required to use the residual method to assign values to the partnership's section 197 intangibles. To do so,

the partnership must, first, determine the value of partnership assets other than section 197 intangibles under paragraph (a)(3) of this section. The partnership then must determine partnership gross value under paragraph (a)(4) of this section. Last, the partnership must assign values to the partnership's section 197 intangibles under paragraph (a)(5) of this section. For purposes of this section, the term *section 197 intangibles* includes all section 197 intangibles (as defined in section 197), as well as any goodwill or going concern value that would not qualify as a section 197 intangible under section 197.

(3) *Values of properties other than section 197 intangibles.* For purposes of this section, the fair market value of each item of partnership property other than section 197 intangibles shall be determined on the basis of all the facts and circumstances, taking into account section 7701(g).

(4) *Partnership gross value*—(i) *Basis adjustments under section 743(b)*—(A) *In general.* Except as provided in paragraph (a)(4)(ii) of this section, in the case of a basis adjustment under section 743(b), partnership gross value generally is equal to the amount that, if assigned to all partnership property, would result in a liquidating distribution to the partner equal to the transferee's basis in the transferred partnership interest immediately following the relevant transfer (reduced by the amount, if any, of such basis that is attributable to partnership liabilities).

(B) *Special situations.* In certain circumstances, such as where income or loss with respect to particular section 197 intangibles are allocated differently among partners, partnership gross value may vary depending on the values of particular section 197 intangibles held by the partnership. In these special situations, the partnership must assign value, first, among section 197 intangibles (other than goodwill and going concern value) in a reasonable manner that is consistent with the ordering rule in paragraph (a)(5) of this section and would cause the appropriate liquidating distribution under paragraph (a)(4)(i)(A) of this section. If the actual fair market values, determined on the basis of all the facts and circumstances, of all section 197 intangibles (other than goodwill and going concern value) is not sufficient to cause the appropriate liquidating distribution, then the fair market value of goodwill and going concern value shall be presumed to equal an amount that if assigned to goodwill and going concern value would cause the appropriate liquidating distribution.

(C) *Income in respect of a decedent.* Solely for the purpose of determining partnership gross value under this paragraph (a)(4)(i), where a partnership interest is transferred as a result of the death of a partner, the transferee's basis in its partnership interest is determined without regard to section 1014(c), and is deemed to be adjusted for that portion of the interest, if any, that is attributable to items representing income in respect of a decedent under section 691.

(ii) *Basis adjustments under section 743(b) resulting from substituted basis transactions.* This paragraph (a)(4)(ii) applies to basis adjustments under section 743(b) that result from exchanges in which the transferee's basis in the partnership interest is determined in whole or in part by reference to the transferor's basis in the interest or to the basis of other property held at any time by the transferee (substituted basis transactions). In the case of a substituted basis transaction, partnership gross value equals the value of the entire partnership as a going concern, increased by the amount of partnership liabilities at the time of the exchange giving rise to the basis adjustment.

(iii) *Basis adjustments under section 734(b).* In the case of a basis adjustment under section 734(b), partnership gross value equals the value of the entire partnership as a going concern immediately following the distribution causing the adjustment, increased by the amount of partnership liabilities immediately following the distribution.

(5) *Determining the values of section 197 intangibles*—(i) *Two classes.* If the aggregate value of partnership property other than section 197 intangibles (as determined in paragraph (a)(3) of this section) is equal to or greater than partnership gross value (as determined in paragraph (a)(4) of this section), then all section 197 intangibles are deemed to have a value of zero for purposes of this section. In all other cases, the aggregate value of the partnership's section 197 intangibles (the residual section 197 intangibles value) is deemed to equal the excess of partnership gross value over the aggregate value of partnership property other than section 197 intangibles. The residual section 197 intangibles value must be allocated between two asset classes in the following order—

(A) Among section 197 intangibles other than goodwill and going concern value; and

(B) To goodwill and going concern value.

(ii) *Values assigned to section 197 intangibles other than goodwill and going concern value.* The fair market value assigned to a section 197 intangible (other than goodwill and going concern value) shall not exceed the actual fair market value (determined on the basis of all the

Reg. § 1.755-1(a)(5)

facts and circumstances) of that asset on the date of the relevant transfer. If the residual section 197 intangibles value is less than the sum of the actual fair market values (determined on the basis of all the facts and circumstances) of all section 197 intangibles (other than goodwill and going concern value) held by the partnership, then the residual section 197 intangibles value must be allocated among the individual section 197 intangibles (other than goodwill and going concern value) as follows. The residual section 197 intangibles value is assigned first to any section 197 intangibles (other than goodwill and going concern value) having potential gain that would be treated as unrealized receivables under the flush language of section 751(c) (flush language receivables) to the extent of the basis of those section 197 intangibles and the amount of income arising from the flush language receivables that the partnership would recognize if the section 197 intangibles were sold for their actual fair market values (determined based on all the facts and circumstances) (collectively, the flush language receivables value). If the value assigned to section 197 intangibles (other than goodwill and going concern value) is less than the flush language receivables value, then the assigned value is allocated among the properties giving rise to the flush language receivables in proportion to the flush language receivables value in those properties. Any remaining residual section 197 intangibles value is allocated among the remaining portions of the section 197 intangibles (other than goodwill and going concern value) in proportion to the actual fair market values of such portions (determined based on all the facts and circumstances).

(iii) *Value assigned to goodwill and going concern value.* The fair market value of goodwill and going concern value is the amount, if any, by which the residual section 197 intangibles value exceeds the aggregate value of the partnership's section 197 intangibles (other than goodwill and going concern value).

(6) *Examples.* The provisions of paragraphs (a)(2) through (5) are illustrated by the following examples, which assume that the partnerships have an election in effect under section 754 at the time of the transfer and that the assets of each partnership constitute a trade or business (as described in § 1.1060-1(b)(2)). Except as provided, no partnership asset (other than inventory) is property described in section 751(a), and partnership liabilities are secured by all partnership assets. The examples are as follows:

Example 1. (i) A is the sole general partner in PRS, a limited partnership having three equal partners. PRS has goodwill and going concern value, two section 197 intangibles other than goodwill and going concern value (Intangible 1 and Intangible 2), and two other assets with fair market values (determined using all the facts and circumstances) as follows: inventory worth $1,000,000 and a building (a capital asset) worth $2,000,000. The fair market value of each of Intangible 1 and Intangible 2 is $50,000. PRS has one liability of $1,000,000, for which A bears the entire risk of loss under section 752 and the regulations thereunder. D purchases A's partnership interest for $650,000, resulting in a basis adjustment under section 743(b). After the purchase, D bears the entire risk of loss for PRS's liability under section 752 and the regulations thereunder. Therefore, D's basis in its interest in PRS is $1,650,000.

(ii) D's basis in the transferred partnership interest (reduced by the amount of such basis that is attributable to partnership liabilities) is $650,000 ($1,650,000 − $1,000,000). Under paragraph (a)(4)(i) of this section, partnership gross value is $2,950,000 (the amount that, if assigned to all partnership property, would result in a liquidating distribution to D equal to $650,000).

(iii) Under paragraph (a)(3) of this section, the inventory has a fair market value of $1,000,000, and the building has a fair market value of $2,000,000. Thus, the aggregate value of partnership property other than section 197 intangibles, $3,000,000, is equal to or greater than partnership gross value, $2,950,000, Accordingly, under paragraphs (a)(3) and (5) of this section, the value assigned to each of the partnership's assets is as follows: inventory, $1,000,000; building, $2,000,000; Intangibles 1 and 2, $0; and goodwill and going concern value, $0. D's section 743(b) adjustment must be allocated under paragraph (b) of this section using these assigned fair market values.

Example 2. (i) Assume the same facts as in *Example 1,* except that the fair market values of Intangible 1 and Intangible 2 are each $300,000, and that D purchases A's interest in PRS for $1,000,000. After the purchase, D's basis in its interest in PRS is $2,000,000.

(ii) D's basis in the transferred partnership interest (reduced by the amount of such basis that is attributable to partnership liabilities) is $1,000,000 ($2,000,000 − $1,000,000). Under paragraph (a)(4)(i) of this section, partnership gross value is $4,000,000 (the amount that, if assigned to all partnership property, would result in a liquidating distribution to D equal to $1,000,000).

(iii) Under paragraph (a)(5) of this section, the residual section 197 intangibles value is

Reg. § 1.755-1(a)(6)

$1,000,000 (the excess of partnership gross value, $4,000,000, over the aggregate value of assets other than section 197 intangibles, $3,000,000 (the sum of the value of the inventory, $1,000,000, and the value of the building, $2,000,000)). The partnership must determine the values of section 197 assets by allocating the residual section 197 intangibles value among the partnership's assets. The residual section 197 intangibles value is assigned first to section 197 intangibles other than goodwill and going concern value, and then to goodwill and going concern value. Thus, $300,000 is assigned to each of Intangible 1 and Intangible 2, and $400,000 is assigned to goodwill and going concern value (the amount by which the residual section 197 intangibles value, $1,000,000, exceeds the fair market value of section 197 intangibles other than goodwill and going concern value, $600,000). D's section 743(b) adjustment must be allocated under paragraph (b) of this section using these assigned fair market values.

Example 3. (i) Assume the same facts as in Example 1, except that the fair market values of Intangible 1 and Intangible 2 are each $300,000, and that D purchases A's interest in PRS for $750,000. After the purchase, D's basis in its interest in PRS is $1,750,000. Also assume that Intangible 1 was originally purchased for $300,000, and that its adjusted basis has been decreased to $50,000 as a result of amortization. Assume that, if PRS were to sell Intangible 1 for $300,000, it would recognize $250,000 of gain that would be treated as an unrealized receivable under the flush language in section 751(c).

(ii) D's basis in the transferred partnership interest (reduced by the amount of such basis that is attributable to partnership liabilities) is $750,000 ($1,750,000 − $1,000,000). Under paragraph (a)(4)(i) of this section, partnership gross value is $3,250,000 (the amount that, if assigned to all partnership property, would result in a liquidating distribution to D equal to $750,000).

(iii) Under paragraph (a)(5) of this section, the residual section 197 intangibles value is $250,000 (the amount by which partnership gross value, $3,250,000, exceeds the aggregate value of partnership property other than section 197 intangibles, $3,000,000). Intangible 1 has potential gain that would be treated as unrealized receivables under the flush language of section 751(c). The flush language receivables value in Intangible 1 is $300,000 (the sum of PRS's basis in Intangible 1, $50,000, and the amount of ordinary income, $250,000, that the partnership would recognize if Intangible 1 were sold for its actual fair market value). Because the residual section 197 intangibles value, $250,000, is less than the flush language receivables value of Intangible 1, Intangible 1 is assigned a value of $250,000, and Intangible 2 and goodwill and going concern value are assigned a value of zero. D's section 743(b) adjustment must be allocated under paragraph (b) of this section using these assigned fair market values.

Example 4. Assume the same facts as in Example 1, except that the fair market values of Intangible 1 and Intangible 2 are each $300,000, and that A does not sell its interest in PRS. Instead, A contributes its interest in PRS to E, a newly formed corporation wholly-owned by A, in a transaction described in section 351. Assume that the contribution results in a basis adjustment under section 743(b) (other than zero). PRS determines that its value as a going concern immediately following the contribution is $3,000,000. Under paragraph (a)(4)(ii) of this section, partnership gross value is $4,000,000 (the value of PRS as a going concern, $3,000,000, increased by the partnership's liability, $1,000,000, immediately after the contribution). Under paragraph (a)(5) of this section, the residual section 197 intangibles value is $1,000,000 (the amount by which partnership gross value, $4,000,000, exceeds the aggregate value of partnership property other than section 197 intangibles, $3,000,000). Of the residual section 197 intangibles value, $300,000 is assigned to each of Intangible 1 and Intangible 2, and $400,000 is assigned to goodwill and going concern value (the amount by which the residual section 197 intangibles value, $1,000,000, exceeds the fair market value of section 197 intangibles other than goodwill and going concern value, $600,000). E's section 743(b) adjustment must be allocated under paragraph (b)(5) of this section using these assigned fair market values.

Example 5. G is the sole general partner in PRS, a limited partnership having three equal partners (G, H, and I). PRS has goodwill and going concern value, two section 197 intangibles other than goodwill and going concern value (Intangible 1 and Intangible 2), and two capital assets with fair market values (determined using all the facts and circumstances) as follows: vacant land worth $1,000,000, and a building worth $2,000,000. The fair market value of each of Intangible 1 and Intangible 2 is $300,000. PRS has one liability of $1,000,000, for which G bears the entire risk of loss under section 752 and the regulations thereunder. PRS distributes the land to H in liquidation of H's interest in PRS. Immediately prior to the distribution, PRS's basis in the land is $800,000, and H's basis in its interest in PRS is $750,000. The distribution causes the partnership to increase the basis of its remaining property by $50,000 under section 734(b)(1)(B). PRS determines that its value as a going concern immediately following the distribution is $2,000,000. Under paragraph (a)(4)(iii) of this section, partnership gross value is $3,000,000 (the value of PRS as a going concern, $2,000,000, increased by the partnership's liability, $1,000,000, immediately after the distribution). Under paragraph (a)(5) of this section, the residual section 197 intangibles value of PRS's section 197 intangibles is $1,000,000 (the amount by which partnership gross value, $3,000,000, exceeds the aggregate value of partnership property other than section 197 intangibles, $2,000,000). Of the residual section 197 intangibles value, $300,000 is assigned to each of Intangible 1 and Intangible 2, and $400,000 is assigned to goodwill and going concern value (the amount by which the residual section 197 intangibles value, $1,000,000, exceeds the fair market value of section 197 intangibles other than goodwill and going concern value, $600,000). PRS's section 734(b) adjustment must be allocated under paragraph (c) of this section using these assigned fair market values.

(b) *Adjustments under section 743(b)*—(1) *Generally*—(i) *Application.* For basis adjustments under section 743(b) resulting from substituted basis transactions, paragraph (b)(5) of this section shall apply. For basis adjustments under section 743(b) resulting from all other transfers, paragraphs (b)(2) through (4) of this section shall apply. Except as provided in paragraph (b)(5) of this section, the portion of the basis adjustment allocated to one class of property may be an increase while the portion allocated to the other class is a decrease. This would be the case even though the total amount of the basis adjustment is zero. Except as provided in paragraph (b)(5) of this section, the portion of the basis adjustment allocated to one item of property within a class may be an increase while the portion allocated to another is a decrease. This would be the case even though the basis adjustment allocated to the class is zero.

(ii) *Hypothetical transaction.* For purposes of paragraphs (b)(2) through (b)(4) of this section, the allocation of the basis adjustment under section 743(b) between the classes of property and among the items of property within each class are made based on the allocations of income, gain, or loss (including remedial allocations under § 1.704-3(d)) that the transferee partner would receive (to the extent attributable to the acquired partnership interest) if, immediately after the transfer of the partnership interest, all of the partnership's property were disposed of in a fully taxable transaction for cash in an amount equal to the fair market value of such property (the hypothetical transaction).

(2) *Allocations between classes of property*—(i) *In general.* The amount of the basis adjustment allocated to the class of ordinary income property is equal to the total amount of income, gain, or loss (including any remedial allocations under § 1.704-3(d)) that would be allocated to the transferee (to the extent attributable to the acquired partnership interest) from the sale of all ordinary income property in the hypothetical transaction. The amount of the basis adjustment to capital gain property is equal to—

(A) The total amount of the basis adjustment under section 743(b); less

(B) The amount of the basis adjustment allocated to ordinary income property under the preceding sentence; provided, however, that in no event may the amount of any decrease in basis allocated to capital gain property exceed the partnership's basis (or in the case of property subject to the remedial allocation method, the transferee's share of any remedial loss under § 1.704-3(d) from the hypothetical transaction) in capital gain property. In the event that a decrease in basis allocated to capital gain property would otherwise exceed the partnership's basis in capital gain property, the excess must be applied to reduce the basis of ordinary income property.

(ii) *Examples.* The provisions of this paragraph (b)(2) are illustrated by the following examples:

Example 1. (i) A and B form equal partnership PRS. A contributes $50,000 and Asset 1, a nondepreciable capital asset with a fair market value of $50,000 and an adjusted tax basis of $25,000. B contributes $100,000. PRS uses the cash to purchase Assets 2, 3, and 4. After a year, A sells its interest in PRS to T for $120,000. At the time of the transfer, A's share of the partnership's basis in partnership assets is $75,000. Therefore, T receives a $45,000 basis adjustment.

(ii) Immediately after the transfer of the partnership interest to T, the adjusted basis and fair market value of PRS's assets are as follows:

Assets

	Adjusted Basis	Fair Market Value
Capital Gain Property:		
Asset 1	$ 25,000	$ 75,000
Asset 2	100,000	117,500
Ordinary Income Property:		
Asset 3	$ 40,000	$ 45,000
Asset 4	10,000	2,500
Total	$175,000	$240,000

Reg. § 1.755-1(b)(1)

(iii) If PRS sold all of its assets in a fully taxable transaction at fair market value immediately after the transfer of the partnership interest to T, the total amount of capital gain that would be allocated to T is equal to $46,250 ($25,000 section 704(c) built-in gain from Asset 1, plus fifty percent of the $42,500 appreciation in capital gain property). T would also be allocated a $1,250 ordinary loss from the sale of the ordinary income property.

(iv) The amount of the basis adjustment that is allocated to ordinary income property is equal to ($1,250) (the amount of the loss allocated to T from the hypothetical sale of the ordinary income property).

(v) The amount of the basis adjustment that is allocated to capital gain property is equal to $46,250 (the amount of the basis adjustment, $45,000, less ($1,250), the amount of loss allocated to T from the hypothetical sale of the ordinary income property).

Example 2. (i) A and B form equal partnership PRS. A and B each contribute $1,000 cash which the partnership uses to purchase Assets 1, 2, 3, and 4. After a year, A sells its partnership interest to T for $1,000. T's basis adjustment under section 743(b) is zero.

(ii) Immediately after the transfer of the partnership interest to T, the adjusted basis and fair market value of PRS's assets are as follows:

Assets

	Adjusted Basis	Fair Market Value
Capital Gain Property:		
Asset 1	$ 500	$ 750
Asset 2	500	500
Ordinary Income Property:		
Asset 3	$ 500	$ 250
Asset 4	500	500
Total	$2,000	$2,000

(iii) If, immediately after the transfer of the partnership interest to T, PRS sold all of its assets in a fully taxable transaction at fair market value, T would be allocated a loss of $125 from the sale of the ordinary income property. Thus, the amount of the basis adjustment to ordinary income property is ($125). The amount of the basis adjustment to capital gain property is $125 (zero, the amount of the basis adjustment under section 743(b), less ($125), the amount of the basis adjustment allocated to ordinary income property).

(3) *Allocation within the class*—(i) *Ordinary income property.* The amount of the basis adjustment to each item of property within the class of ordinary income property is equal to—

(A) The amount of income, gain, or loss (including any remedial allocations under § 1.704-3(d)) that would be allocated to the transferee (to the extent attributable to the acquired partnership interest) from the hypothetical sale of the item; reduced by

(B) The product of—

(*1*) Any decrease to the amount of the basis adjustment to ordinary income property required pursuant to the last sentence of paragraph (b)(2)(i) of this section; multiplied by

(*2*) A fraction, the numerator of which is the fair market value of the item of property to the partnership and the denominator of which is the total fair market value of all of the partnership's items of ordinary income property.

(ii) *Capital gain property.* The amount of the basis adjustment to each item of property within the class of capital gain property is equal to—

(A) The amount of income, gain, or loss (including any remedial allocations under § 1.704-3(d)) that would be allocated to the transferee (to the extent attributable to the acquired partnership interest) from the hypothetical sale of the item; minus

(B) The product of—

(*1*) The total amount of gain or loss (including any remedial allocations under § 1.704-3(d)) that would be allocated to the transferee (to the extent attributable to the acquired partnership interest) from the hypothetical sale of all items of capital gain property, minus the amount of the positive basis adjustment to all items of capital gain property or plus the amount of the negative basis adjustment to capital gain property; multiplied by

(*2*) A fraction, the numerator of which is the fair market value of the item of property to the partnership, and the denominator of which is the fair market value of all of the partnership's items of capital gain property.

(iii) *Special rules*—(A) *Assets in which partner has no interest.* An asset with respect to which the transferee partner has no interest in income, gain, losses, or deductions shall not be taken into account in applying paragraph (b)(3)(ii)(B) of this section.

(B) *Limitation in decrease of basis.* In no event may the amount of any decrease in basis allocated to an item of capital gain property under paragraph (b)(3)(ii)(B) of this section exceed the partnership's adjusted basis in that item (or in the case of property subject to the remedial allocation method, the transferee's share of any remedial loss under § 1.704-3(d) from the hypo-

Reg. § 1.755-1(b)(3)

thetical transaction). In the event that a decrease in basis allocated under paragraph (b)(3)(ii)(B) of this section to an item of capital gain property would otherwise exceed the partnership's adjusted basis in that item, the excess must be applied to reduce the remaining basis, if any, of other capital gain assets pro rata in proportion to the bases of such assets (as adjusted under this paragraph (b)(3)).

(iv) *Examples.* The provisions of this paragraph (b)(3) are illustrated by the following examples:

Example 1. (i) Assume the same facts as Example 1 in paragraph (b)(2)(ii) of this section. Of the $45,000 basis adjustment, $46,250 was allocated to capital gain property. The amount allocated to ordinary income property was ($1,250).

(ii) Asset 1 is a capital gain asset, and T would be allocated $37,500 from the sale of Asset 1 in the hypothetical transaction. Therefore, the amount of the adjustment to Asset 1 is $37,500.

(iii) Asset 2 is a capital gain asset, and T would be allocated $8,750 from the sale of Asset 2 in the hypothetical transaction. Therefore, the amount of the adjustment to Asset 2 is $8,750.

(iv) Asset 3 is ordinary income property, and T would be allocated $2,500 from the sale of Asset 3 in the hypothetical transaction. Therefore, the amount of the adjustment to Asset 3 is $2,500.

(v) Asset 4 is ordinary income property, and T would be allocated ($3,750) from the sale of Asset 4 in the hypothetical transaction. Therefore, the amount of the adjustment to Asset 4 is ($3,750).

Example 2. (i) Assume the same facts as Example 1 in paragraph (b)(2)(ii) of this section, except that A sold its interest in PRS to T for $110,000 rather than $120,000. T, therefore, receives a basis adjustment under section 743(b) of $35,000. Of the $35,000 basis adjustment, ($1,250) is allocated to ordinary income property, and $36,250 is allocated to capital gain property.

(ii) Asset 3 is ordinary income property, and T would be allocated $2,500 from the sale of Asset 3 in the hypothetical transaction. Therefore, the amount of the adjustment to Asset 3 is $2,500.

(iii) Asset 4 is ordinary income property, and T would be allocated ($3,750) from the sale of Asset 4 in the hypothetical transaction. Therefore, the amount of the adjustment to Asset 4 is ($3,750).

(iv) Asset 1 is a capital gain asset, and T would be allocated $37,500 from the sale of Asset 1 in the hypothetical transaction. Asset 2 is a capital gain asset, and T would be allocated $8,750 from the sale of Asset 2 in the hypothetical transaction. The total amount of gain that would be allocated to T from the sale of the capital gain assets in the hypothetical transaction is $46,250, which exceeds the amount of the basis adjustment allocated to capital gain property by $10,000. The amount of the adjustment to Asset 1 is $33,604 ($37,500 minus $3,896 ($10,000 × $75,000/192,500)). The amount of the basis adjustment to Asset 2 is $2,646 ($8,750 minus $6,104 ($10,000 × $117,500/192,500)).

(4) *Income in respect of a decedent*—(i) *In general.* Where a partnership interest is transferred as a result of the death of a partner, under section 1014(c) the transferee's basis in its partnership interest is not adjusted for that portion of the interest, if any, which is attributable to items representing income in respect of a decedent under section 691. See § 1.742-1. Accordingly, if a partnership interest is transferred as a result of the death of a partner, and the partnership holds assets representing income in respect of a decedent, no part of the basis adjustment under section 743(b) is allocated to these assets. See § 1.743-1(b).

(ii) The provisions of this paragraph (b)(4) are illustrated by the following example:

Example. (i) A and B are equal partners in personal service partnership PRS. In 2004, as a result of B's death, B's partnership interest is transferred to T when PRS's balance sheet (reflecting a cash receipts and disbursements method of accounting) is as follows (based on all the facts and circumstances):

Assets

	Adjusted Basis	Fair Market Value
Section 197 Intangible	$ 2,000	$ 5,000
Unrealized Receivables	0	15,000
Total	$ 2,000	$20,000

Liabilities and Capital

	Adjusted Per Books	Fair Market Value
Capital:		
A	$ 1,000	$10,000
B	1,000	10,000
Total	$ 2,000	$20,000

(ii) None of the assets owned by PRS is section 704(c) property, and the section 197 intangible is not amortizable. The fair market value of T's partnership interest on the applicable date of valuation set forth in section 1014 is $10,000. Of this amount, $2,500 is attributable to T's 50% share of the partnership's section 197 intangible,

Reg. § 1.755-1(b)(4)

and $7,500 is attributable to T's 50% share of the partnership's unrealized receivables. The partnership's unrealized receivables represent income in respect of a decedent. Accordingly, under section 1014(c), T's basis in its partnership interest is not adjusted for that portion of the interest which is attributable to the unrealized receivables. Therefore, T's basis in its partnership interest is $2,500.

(iii) Under paragraph (a)(4)(i)(C) of this section, solely for purposes of determining partnership gross value, T's basis in its partnership interest is deemed to be $10,000. Under paragraph (a)(4)(i) of this section, partnership gross value is $20,000 (the amount that, if assigned to all partnership property, would result in a liquidating distribution to T equal to $10,000).

(iv) Under paragraph (a)(5) of this section, the residual section 197 intangibles value is $5,000 (the excess of partnership gross value, $20,000, over the aggregate value of assets other than section 197 intangibles, $15,000). The residual section 197 intangibles value is assigned first to section 197 intangibles other than goodwill and going concern value, and then to goodwill and going concern value. Thus, $5,000 is assigned to the section 197 intangible, and $0 is assigned to goodwill and going concern value. T's section 743(b) adjustment must be allocated using these assigned fair market values.

(v) At the time of the transfer, B's share of the partnership's basis in partnership assets is $1,000. Accordingly, T receives a $1,500 basis adjustment under section 743(b). Under this paragraph (b)(4), the entire basis adjustment is allocated to the partnership's section 197 intangible.

(5) *Substituted basis transactions*—(i) *In general.* This paragraph (b)(5) applies to basis adjustments under section 743(b) that result from exchanges in which the transferee's basis in the partnership interest is determined in whole or in part by reference to the transferor's basis in that interest. For exchanges on or after June 9, 2003, this paragraph (b)(5) also applies to basis adjustments under section 743(b) that result from exchanges in which the transferee's basis in the partnership interest is determined by reference to other property held at any time by the transferee. For example, this paragraph (b)(5) applies if a partnership interest is contributed to a corporation in a transaction to which section 351 applies, if a partnership interest is contributed to a partnership in a transaction to which section 721(a) applies, or if a partnership interest is distributed by a partnership in a transaction to which section 731(a) applies.

(ii) *Allocations between classes of property.* If the total amount of the basis adjustment under section 743(b) is zero, then no adjustment to the basis of partnership property will be made under this paragraph (b)(5). If there is an increase in basis to be allocated to partnership assets, such increase must be allocated to capital gain property or ordinary income property, respectively, only if the total amount of gain or loss (including any remedial allocations under § 1.704-3(d)) that would be allocated to the transferee (to the extent attributable to the acquired partnership interest) from the hypothetical sale of all such property would result in a net gain or net income, as the case may be, to the transferee. Where, under the preceding sentence, an increase in basis may be allocated to both capital gain assets and ordinary income assets, the increase shall be allocated to each class in proportion to the net gain or net income, respectively, which would be allocated to the transferee from the sale of all assets in each class. If there is a decrease in basis to be allocated to partnership assets, such decrease must be allocated to capital gain property or ordinary income property, respectively, only if the total amount of gain or loss (including any remedial allocations under § 1.704-3(d)) that would be allocated to the transferee (to the extent attributable to the acquired partnership interest) from the hypothetical sale of all such property would result in a net loss to the transferee. Where, under the preceding sentence, a decrease in basis may be allocated to both capital gain assets and ordinary income assets, the decrease shall be allocated to each class in proportion to the net loss which would be allocated to the transferee from the sale of all assets in each class.

(iii) *Allocations within the classes*—(A) *Increases.* If there is an increase in basis to be allocated within a class, the increase must be allocated first to properties with unrealized appreciation in proportion to the transferee's share of the respective amounts of unrealized appreciation before such increase (but only to the extent of the transferee's share of each property's unrealized appreciation). Any remaining increase must be allocated among the properties within the class in proportion to the transferee's share of the amount that would be realized by the partnership upon the hypothetical sale of each asset in the class.

(B) *Decreases.* If there is a decrease in basis to be allocated within a class, the decrease must be allocated first to properties with unrealized depreciation in proportion to the transferee's shares of the respective amounts of unrealized depreciation before such decrease (but only to the extent of the transferee's share of each property's unrealized depreciation). Any remaining decrease must be allocated among the properties within the class in proportion to the transferee's shares of their adjusted bases (as adjusted under the preceding sentence).

(C) *Limitation in decrease of basis.* Where, as the result of a transaction to which this paragraph (b)(5) applies, a decrease in basis must be allocated to capital gain assets, ordinary income assets, or both, and the amount of the decrease otherwise allocable to a particular class exceeds the transferee's share of the adjusted basis to the partnership of all depreciated assets in that class, the transferee's negative basis adjustment is limited to the transferee's share of the partnership's adjusted basis in all depreciated assets in that class.

(D) *Carryover adjustment.* Where a transferee's negative basis adjustment under section 743(b) cannot be allocated to any asset, because the adjustment exceeds the transferee's share of the adjusted basis to the partnership of all depreciated assets in a particular class, the adjustment is made when the partnership subsequently acquires property of a like character to which an adjustment can be made.

(iv) *Examples.* The provisions of this paragraph (b)(5) are illustrated by the following examples:

Example 1. A is a member of partnership LTP, which has made an election under section 754. The three partners in LTP have equal interests in capital and profits. Solely in exchange for a partnership interest in UTP, A contributes its interest in LTP to UTP in a transaction described in section 721. At the time of the transfer, A's basis in its partnership interest ($5,000) equals its share of inside basis (also $5,000). Under section 723, UTP's basis in its interest in LTP is $5,000. LTP's only two assets on the date of contribution are inventory with a basis of $5,000 and a fair market value of $7,500, and a nondepreciable capital asset with a basis of $10,000 and a fair market value of $7,500. The amount of the basis adjustment under section 743(b) to partnership property is $0 ($5,000, UTP's basis in its interest in LTP, minus $5,000, UTP's share of LTP's basis in partnership assets). Because UTP acquired its interest in LTP in a substituted basis transaction, and the total amount of the basis adjustment under section 743(b) is zero, UTP receives no special basis adjustments under section 743(b) with respect to the partnership property of LTP.

Example 2. (i) A purchases a partnership interest in LTP at a time when an election under section 754 is not in effect. The three partners in LTP have equal interests in capital and profits. During a later year for which LTP has an election under section 754 in effect, and in a transaction that is unrelated to A's purchase of the LTP interest, A contributes its interest in LTP to UTP in a transaction described in section 721 (solely in exchange for a partnership interest in UTP). At the time of the transfer, A's adjusted basis in its interest in LTP is $20,433. Under section 721, A recognizes no gain or loss as a result of the contribution of its partnership interest to UTP. Under section 723, UTP's basis in its partnership interest in LTP is $20,433. The balance sheet of LTP on the date of the contribution shows the following:

Assets

	Adjusted Basis	Fair Market Value
Cash	$ 5,000	$ 5,000
Accounts receivable	10,000	10,000
Inventory	20,000	21,000
Nondepreciable capital asset	20,000	40,000
Total	$55,000	$76,000

Liabilities and Capital

	Adjusted Per Books	Fair Market Value
Liabilities	$10,000	$10,000
Capital:		
A	15,000	22,000
B	15,000	22,000
C	15,000	22,000
Total	$55,000	$76,000

(ii) The amount of the basis adjustment under section 743(b) is the difference between the basis of UTP's interest in LTP and UTP's share of the adjusted basis to LTP of partnership property. UTP's interest in the previously taxed capital of LTP is $15,000 ($22,000, the amount of cash UTP would receive if LTP liquidated immediately after the hypothetical transaction, decreased by $7,000, the amount of tax gain allocated to UTP from the hypothetical transaction). UTP's share of the adjusted basis to LTP of partnership property is $18,333 ($15,000 share of previously taxed capital, plus $3,333 share of LTP's liabilities). The amount of the basis adjustment under section 743(b) to partnership property therefore, is $2,100 ($20,433 minus $18,333).

(iii) The total amount of gain that would be allocated to UTP from the hypothetical sale of capital gain property is $6,666.67 (one-third of the excess of the fair market value of LTP's nondepreciable capital asset, $40,000, over its basis, $20,000). The total amount of gain that would be allocated to UTP from the hypothetical sale of ordinary income property is $333.33 (one-third of the excess of the fair market value of LTP's in-

Reg. § 1.755-1(b)(5)

Contributions, Distributions and Transfers

See p. 20,601 for regulations not amended to reflect law changes

ventory, $21,000, over its basis, $20,000). Under this paragraph (b)(5), LTP must allocate $2,000 ($6,666.67 divided by $7,000 times $2,100) of UTP's basis adjustment to the nondepreciable capital asset. LTP must allocate $100 ($333.33 divided by $7,000 times $2,100) of UTP's basis adjustment to the inventory.

(c) *Adjustments under section 734(b)*—(1) *Allocations between classes of property*—(i) *General rule.* Where there is a distribution of partnership property resulting in an adjustment to the basis of undistributed partnership property under section 734(b)(1)(B) or (b)(2)(B), the adjustment must be allocated to remaining partnership property of a character similar to that of the distributed property with respect to which the adjustment arose. Thus, when the partnership's adjusted basis of distributed capital gain property immediately prior to distribution exceeds the basis of the property to the distributee partner (as determined under section 732), the basis of the undistributed capital gain property remaining in the partnership is increased by an amount equal to the excess. Conversely, when the basis to the distributee partner (as determined under section 732) of distributed capital gain property exceeds the partnership's adjusted basis of such property immediately prior to the distribution, the basis of the undistributed capital gain property remaining in the partnership is decreased by an amount equal to such excess. Similarly, where there is a distribution of ordinary income property, and the basis of the property to the distributee partner (as determined under section 732) is not the same as the partnership's adjusted basis of the property immediately prior to distribution, the adjustment is made only to undistributed property of the same class remaining in the partnership.

(ii) *Special rule.* Where there is a distribution resulting in an adjustment under section 734(b)(1)(A) or (b)(2)(A) to the basis of undistributed partnership property, the adjustment is allocated only to capital gain property.

(2) *Allocations within the classes*—(i) *Increases.* If there is an increase in basis to be allocated within a class, the increase must be allocated first to properties with unrealized appreciation in proportion to their respective amounts of unrealized appreciation before such increase (but only to the extent of each property's unrealized appreciation). Any remaining increase must be allocated among the properties within the class in proportion to their fair market values.

(ii) *Decreases.* If there is a decrease in basis to be allocated within a class, the decrease must be allocated first to properties with unrealized depreciation in proportion to their respective

amounts of unrealized depreciation before such decrease (but only to the extent of each property's unrealized depreciation). Any remaining decrease must be allocated among the properties within the class in proportion to their adjusted bases (as adjusted under the preceding sentence).

(3) *Limitation in decrease of basis.* Where a decrease in the basis of partnership assets is required under section 734(b)(2) and the amount of the decrease exceeds the adjusted basis to the partnership of property of the required character, the basis of such property is reduced to zero (but not below zero).

(4) *Carryover adjustment.* Where, in the case of a distribution, an increase or a decrease in the basis of undistributed property cannot be made because the partnership owns no property of the character required to be adjusted, or because the basis of all the property of a like character has been reduced to zero, the adjustment is made when the partnership subsequently acquires property of a like character to which an adjustment can be made.

(5) *Example.* The following example illustrates this paragraph (c):

Example. (i) A, B, and C form equal partnership PRS. A contributes $50,000 and Asset 1, nondepreciable capital gain property with a fair market value of $50,000 and an adjusted tax basis of $25,000. B and C each contributes $100,000. PRS uses the cash to purchase Assets 2, 3, 4, 5, and 6. Assets 2 and 3 are nondepreciable capital assets, and Assets 4, 5, and 6 are inventory that has not appreciated substantially in value within the meaning of section 751(b)(3). Assets 4, 5, and 6 are the only assets held by the partnership that are subject to section 751. The partnership has an election in effect under section 754. After seven years, the adjusted basis and fair market value of PRS's assets are as follows:

Assets

	Adjusted Basis	Fair Market Value
Capital Gain Property:		
Asset 1	$ 25,000	$ 75,000
Asset 2	100,000	117,500
Asset 3	50,000	60,000
Ordinary Income Property:		
Asset 4	$ 40,000	$ 45,000
Asset 5	50,000	60,000
Asset 6	10,000	2,500
Total	$275,000	$360,000

(ii) *Allocation between classes.* Assume that PRS distributes Assets 3 and 5 to A in complete liquidation of A's interest in the partnership. A's

Reg. § 1.755-1(c)(5)

43,704

Definitions

See p. 20,601 for regulations not amended to reflect law changes

basis in the partnership interest was $75,000. The partnership's basis in Assets 3 and 5 was $50,000 each. A's $75,000 basis in its partnership interest is allocated between Assets 3 and 5 under sections 732(b) and (c). A will, therefore, have a basis of $25,000 in Asset 3 (capital gain property), and a basis of $50,000 in Asset 5 (section 751 property). The distribution results in a $25,000 increase in the basis of capital gain property. There is no change in the basis of ordinary income property.

(iii) *Allocation within class.* The amount of the basis increase to capital gain property is $25,000 and must be allocated among the remaining capital gain assets in proportion to the difference between the fair market value and basis of each. The fair market value of Asset 1 exceeds its basis by $50,000. The fair market value of Asset 2 exceeds its basis by $17,500. Therefore, the basis of Asset 1 will be increased by $18,519 ($25,000, multiplied by $50,000, divided by $67,500), and the basis of Asset 2 will be increased by $6,481 ($25,000 multiplied by $17,500, divided by $67,500).

(d) *Required statements.* See § 1.743-1(k)(2) for provisions requiring the transferee of a partnership interest to provide information to the partnership relating to the transfer of an interest in the partnership. See § 1.743-1(k)(1) for a provision requiring the partnership to attach a statement to the partnership return showing the computation of a basis adjustment under section 743(b) and the partnership properties to which the adjustment is allocated under section 755. See § 1.732-1(d)(3) for a provision requiring a transferee partner to attach a statement to its return showing the computation of a basis adjustment under section 732(d) and the partnership properties to which the adjustment is allocated under section 755. See § 1.732-1(d)(5) for a provision requiring the partnership to provide information to a transferee partner reporting a basis adjustment under section 732(d).

(e) *Effective date*—(1) *Generally.* Except as provided in paragraphs (b)(5) and (e)(2) of this section, this section applies to transfers of partnership interests and distributions of property from a partnership that occur on or after December 15, 1999.

(2) *Special rules.* Paragraphs (a) and (b)(3)(iii) of this section apply to transfers of partnership interests and distributions of property from a partnership that occur on or after June 9, 2003. [Reg. § 1.755-1.]

☐ [T.D. 6175, 5-23-56. Amended by T.D. 8847, 12-14-99 (corrected 2-23-2000) and T.D. 9059, 6-6-2003.]

Definitions

[Reg. § 1.761-1]

§ 1.761-1. **Terms defined.**—(a) *Partnership.* The term *partnership* means a partnership as determined under §§ 301.7701-1, 301.7701-2, and 301.7701-3 of this chapter.

(b) *Partner.* The term "partner" means a member of a partnership.

(c) *Partnership agreement.* For the purposes of subchapter K, a partnership agreement includes the original agreement and any modifications thereof agreed to by all the partners or adopted in any other manner provided by the partnership agreement. Such agreement or modifications can be oral or written. A partnership agreement may be modified with respect to a particular taxable year subsequent to the close of such taxable year, but not later than the date (not including any extension of time) prescribed by law for the filing of the partnership return. As to any matter on which the partnership agreement, or any modification thereof, is silent, the provisions of local law shall be considered to constitute a part of the agreement.

(d) *Liquidation of partner's interest.* The term "liquidation of a partner's interest" means the termination of a partner's entire interest in a partnership by means of a distribution, or a series of distributions, to the partner by the partnership. A series of distributions will come within the meaning of this term whether they are made in one year or in more than one year. Where a partner's interest is to be liquidated by a series of distributions, the interest will not be considered as liquidated until the final distribution has been made. For the basis of property distributed in one liquidating distribution, or in a series of distributions in liquidation, see section 732(b). A distribution which is not in liquidation of a partner's entire interest, as defined in this paragraph, is a current distribution. Current distributions, therefore, include distributions in partial liquidation of a partner's interest, and distributions of the partner's distributive share. See paragraph (a)(1)(ii) of § 1.731-1.

(e) *Distribution of partnership interest.* For purposes of section 708(b)(1)(B) and § 1.708-1(b)(1)(iv), the deemed distribution of an interest in a new partnership by a partnership that terminates under section 708(b)(1)(B) is not a sale or exchange of an interest in the new partnership. However, the deemed distribution of an interest in a new partnership by a partnership that terminates under section 708(b)(1)(B) is

Reg. § 1.761-1(a)

treated as an exchange of the interest in the new partnership for purposes of section 743. This paragraph (e) applies to terminations of partnerships under section 708(b)(1)(B) occurring on or after May 9, 1997; however, this paragraph (e) may be applied to terminations occurring on or after May 9, 1996, provided that the partnership and its partners apply this paragraph (e) to the termination in a consistent manner. [Reg. § 1.761-1.]

☐ [T.D. 6175, 5-23-56. Amended by T.D. 6198, 8-15-56; T.D. 7012, 5-14-69; T.D. 7208, 10-2-72; T.D. 8697, 12-17-96 and T.D. 8717, 5-8-97.]

[Reg. § 1.761-2]

§ 1.761-2. **Exclusion of certain unincorporated organizations from the application of all or part of subchapter K of chapter 1 of the Internal Revenue Code.**—(a) *Exclusion of eligible unincorporated organizations*—(1) *In general.* Under conditions set forth in this section, an unincorporated organization described in subparagraph (2) or (3) of this paragraph may be excluded from the application of all or a part of the provisions of subchapter K of chapter 1 of the Code. Such organization must be availed of (i) for investment purposes only and not for the active conduct of a business, or (ii) for the joint production, extraction or use of property, but not for the purpose of selling services or property produced or extracted. The members of such organization must be able to compute their income without the necessity of computing partnership taxable income. Any syndicate, group, pool, or joint venture which is classifiable as an association, or any group operating under an agreement which creates an organization classifiable as an association, does not fall within these provisions.

(2) *Investing partnership.* Where the participants in the joint purchase, retention, sale, or exchange of investment property—

(i) Own the property as coowners,

(ii) Reserve the right separately to take or dispose of their shares of any property acquired or retained, and

(iii) Do not actively conduct business or irrevocably authorize some person or persons acting in a representative capacity to purchase, sell, or exchange such investment property, although each separate participant may delegate authority to purchase, sell, or exchange his share of any such investment property for the time being for his account, but not for a period of more than a year, then

such group may be excluded from the application of the provisions of subchapter K under the rules set forth in paragraph (b) of this section.

(3) *Operating agreements.* Where the participants in the joint production, extraction, or use of property—

(i) Own the property as coowners, either in fee or under lease or other form of contract granting exclusive operating rights, and

(ii) Reserve the right separately to take in kind or dispose of their shares of any property produced, extracted, or used, and

(iii) Do not jointly sell services or the property produced or extracted, although each separate participant may delegate authority to sell his share of the property produced or extracted for the time being for his account, but not for a period of time in excess of the minimum needs of the industry, and in no event for more than one year, then

such group may be excluded from the application of the provisions of subchapter K under the rules set forth in paragraph (b) of this section. However, the preceding sentence does not apply to any unincorporated organization one of whose principal purposes is cycling, manufacturing, or processing for persons who are not members of the organization. In addition, except as provided in paragraph (d)(2)(i) of this section, this paragraph (a)(3) does not apply to any unincorporated organization that produces natural gas under a joint operating agreement, unless all members of the unincorporated organization comply with paragraph (d) of this section.

(b) *Complete exclusion from subchapter K* — (1) *Time for making election for exclusion.* Any unincorporated organization described in subparagraphs (1) and either (2) or (3) of paragraph (a) of this section which wishes to be excluded from all of subchapter K must make the election provided in section 761(a) not later than the time prescribed by paragraph (e) of § 1.6031-1 (including extensions thereof) for filing the partnership return for the first taxable year for which exclusion from subchapter K is desired. Notwithstanding the prior sentence such organization may be deemed to have made the election in the manner prescribed in subparagraph (2)(ii) of this paragraph.

(2) *Method of making election.*—(i) Except as provided in subdivision (ii) of this subparagraph, any unincorporated organization described in subparagraphs (1) and either (2) or (3) of paragraph (a) of this section which wishes to be excluded from all of subchapter K must make the election provided in section 761(a) in a statement attached to, or incorporated in, a properly executed partnership return, Form 1065, which shall contain the information required in this subdivision. Such return shall be filed with the internal

Reg. § 1.761-2(b)(2)

revenue officer with whom a partnership return, Form 1065, would be required to be filed if no election were made. Where, for the purpose of determining such officer, it is necessary to determine the internal revenue district (or service center serving such district) in which the electing organization has its principal office or place of business, the principal office or place of business of the person filing the return shall be considered the principal office or place of business of the organization. The partnership return must be filed not later than the time prescribed by paragraph (e) of § 1.6031-1 (including extensions thereof) for filing the partnership return with respect to the first taxable year for which exclusion from subchapter K is desired. Such partnership return shall contain, in lieu of the information required by Form 1065 and by the instructions relating thereto, only the name or other identification and the address of the organization together with information on the return, or in the statement attached to the return, showing the names, addresses, and identification numbers of all the members of the organization; a statement that the organization qualifies under subparagraphs (1) and either (2) or (3) of paragraph (a) of this section; a statement that all of the members of the organization elect that it be excluded from all of subchapter K; and a statement indicating where a copy of the agreement under which the organization operates is available (or if the agreement is oral, from whom the provisions of the agreement may be obtained).

(ii) If an unincorporated organization described in subparagraphs (1) and either (2) or (3) of paragraph (a) of this section does not make the election provided in section 761(a) in the manner prescribed by subdivision (i) of this subparagraph, it shall nevertheless be deemed to have made the election if it can be shown from all the surrounding facts and circumstances that it was the intention of the members of such organization at the time of its formation to secure exclusion from all of subchapter K beginning with the first taxable year of the organization. Although the following facts are not exclusive, either one of such facts may indicate the requisite intent:

(a) at the time of the formation of the organization there is an agreement among the members that the organization be excluded from subchapter K beginning with the first taxable year of the organization, or

(b) the members of the organization owning substantially all of the capital interest report their respective shares of the items of income, deductions, and credits of the organization on their respective returns (making such elections as to individual items as may be appropriate) in a manner consistent with the exclusion of the organization from subchapter K beginning with the first taxable year of the organization.

(3) *Effect of election*—(i) *In general.* An election under this section to be excluded will be effective unless within 90 days after the formation of the organization (or by October 15, 1956, whichever is later) any member of the organization notifies the Commissioner that the member desires subchapter K to apply to such organization, and also advises the Commissioner that he has so notified all other members of the organization by registered or certified mail. Such election is irrevocable as long as the organization remains qualified under subparagraphs (1) and either (2) or (3) of paragraph (a) of this section, or unless approval of revocation of the election is secured from the Commissioner. Application for permission to revoke the election must be submitted to the Commissioner of Internal Revenue, Attention: T:I, Washington, D.C. 20224, no later than 30 days after the beginning of the first taxable year to which the revocation is to apply.

(ii) *Special rule.* Notwithstanding subdivision (i) of this subparagraph, an election deemed made pursuant to subparagraph (2)(ii) of this paragraph will not be effective in the case of an organization which had a taxable year ending on or before [the last day of the first calendar month which begins after the date of the publication of the Treasury decision in the Federal Register] if any member of the organization notifies the Commissioner that the member desires subchapter K to apply to such organization, and also advises the Commissioner that he has so notified all other members of the organization by registered or certified mail. Such notification to the Commissioner must be made on or before [the 90th day after the date of the publication of the Treasury decision in the Federal Register] and must include the names and addresses of all of the members of the organization.

(c) *Partial exclusion from subchapter K.* An unincorporated organization which wishes to be excluded from only certain sections of subchapter K must submit to the Commissioner, no later than 90 days after the beginning of the first taxable year for which partial exclusion is desired, a request for permission to be excluded from certain provisions of subchapter K. The request shall set forth the sections of subchapter K from which exclusion is sought and shall state that such organization qualifies under subparagraphs (1) and either (2) or (3) of paragraph (a) of this section, and that the members of the organization elect to be excluded to the extent indicated. Such exclu-

(d) *Rules for gas producers that produce natural gas under joint operating agreements*—(1) *Joint operating agreements and gas balancing.* Co-owners of a property producing natural gas enter into a joint operating agreement (JOA) to define the rights and obligations of each co-producer of the gas in place. The JOA determines, among other things, each co-producer's proportionate share of the natural gas as it is produced from the reservoir, together with the associated production expenses. A gas imbalance arises when a co-producer does not take its proportionate share of current gas production under the JOA (underproducer) and another co-producer takes more than its proportionate share of current production (overproducer). The co-producers often enter into a gas balancing agreement (GBA) as an addendum to their JOA to establish their rights and obligations when a gas imbalance arises. A GBA typically allows the overproducer to take the amount of the gas imbalance (overproduced gas) and entitles the underproducer to recoup the overproduced gas either from the volume of the gas remaining in the reservoir or by a cash balancing payment.

(2) *Permissible gas balancing methods*—(i) *General requirement.* All co-producers of natural gas operating under the same JOA must use the cumulative gas balancing method, as described in paragraph (d)(3) of this section, unless they use the annual gas balancing method described in paragraph (d)(4) of this section. A co-producer's failure to comply with the provisions of this paragraph (d)(2)(i) generally constitutes the use of an impermissible method of accounting, requiring a change to a permissible method under § 1.446-1(e)(3) with any terms and conditions as may be imposed by the Commissioner. The co-producers' election to be excluded from all or part of subchapter K will not be revoked, unless the Commissioner determines that there was willful failure to comply with the requirements of this paragraph (d)(2)(i).

(ii) *Change in method of accounting; adoption of method of accounting*—(A) *In general.* The annual gas balancing method and the cumulative gas balancing method are methods of accounting. Accordingly, a change to or from either of these methods is a change in method of accounting that requires the consent of the Commissioner. See section 446(e) and § 1.446-1(e). For purposes of this section, each JOA is treated as a separate trade or business. Paragraph (d)(2)(ii)(B) of this section provides rules for adopting either permissible method of accounting. Paragraph (d)(2)(ii)(C) of this section provides rules on the timing of required changes to either permissible method during the transitional period, and paragraph (d)(5) of this section contains the procedural provisions for making a change in method of accounting required in paragraph (d)(2)(ii)(C) of this section.

(B) *Adoption of method of accounting.* A co-producer must adopt a permissible method for each JOA entered into on or after the start of the co-producer's first taxable year beginning after December 31, 1994 (or, in the case of the use of the annual gas balancing method by co-producers not having the same taxable year, the start of the first taxable year beginning after December 31, 1994, of the co-producer whose taxable year begins latest in the calendar year). If a co-producer is adopting the cumulative method, the co-producer may adopt the method by using the method on its timely filed return for the taxable year of adoption. A co-producer may adopt the annual gas balancing method with the permission of the Commissioner under guidelines set forth in paragraph (d)(4)(ii) of this section.

(C) *Required change in method of accounting for certain joint operating agreements.* This paragraph (d)(2)(ii)(C) applies to certain JOAs entered into prior to 1996. Except in the case of a part-year change in method of accounting or in the case of the cessation of a JOA (both of which are described in this paragraph (d)(2)(ii)(C)), for each JOA entered into prior to a co-producer's first taxable year beginning after December 31, 1994, and in effect as of the beginning of that year, the co-producer must change its method of accounting for sales of gas and its treatment of certain related deductions and credits to a permissible method as of the start of its first taxable year beginning after December 31, 1994. In the case of a JOA of co-producers that do not all have the same taxable year and that choose the annual gas balancing method, if the JOA is entered into prior to the first taxable year beginning after December 31, 1994 of the co-producer whose taxable year begins latest in the calendar year and the JOA is in effect as of January 1, 1996, a change to the annual gas balancing method by each co-producer under that JOA is made as of January 1, 1996 (part-year change in method of accounting). If the co-producers would have made a part-year change to the annual gas balancing method but for the fact that their JOA ceased to be in effect before January 1, 1996 (cessation of a JOA), the co-producers do not change their method of accounting with respect to the JOA. Rather, for their taxable years in which the JOA ceases to be in effect, the co-producers

Reg. § 1.761-2(d)(2)

use their current method of accounting with respect to that JOA.

(3) *Cumulative gas balancing method*—(i) *In general*. The cumulative gas balancing method (cumulative method), solely for purposes of reporting income from gas sales and certain related deductions and credits, treats each co-producer under the same JOA as the sole owner of its percentage share of the total gas in the reservoir and disregards the ownership arrangement described in the JOA for gas as it is produced from the reservoir. Each co-producer is considered to be taking only its share of the total gas in the reservoir as long as the gas remaining in the reservoir is sufficient to satisfy the ownership rights of the co-producers in their percentage shares of the total gas in the reservoir. After a co-producer has taken its entire share of the total gas in the reservoir, any additional gas taken by that co-producer (taking co-producer) is treated as having been taken from its other co-producers' shares of the total gas in the reservoir. The effect of being treated as a taking co-producer under the cumulative method is that the taking co-producer generally may not claim an allowance for depletion and a production credit on its sales of its other co-producers' percentage shares of the total gas in the reservoir.

(ii) *Requirements*—(A) *Reporting of income from sales of gas*. Under the cumulative method, each co-producer must include in gross income under its overall method of accounting the amount of its sales from all gas produced from the reservoir, including sales of gas taken from another co-producer's share of the gas in the reservoir.

(B) *Reporting of deduction of taking co-producer*. A taking co-producer deducts the amount of a payment (in cash or property, other than gas produced under the JOA) made to another co-producer for sales of that co-producer's gas, but only for the taxable year in which the payment is made. Thus, an accrual method taking co-producer is not permitted a deduction for any obligation it has to pay another co-producer for sales of that co-producer's gas until a payment is made. See paragraph (d)(3)(iii)(B) of this section for a rule requiring a reduction of the amount of the deduction described in this paragraph (d)(3)(ii)(B) if the taking co-producer had mistakenly claimed a depletion deduction relating to those sales.

(C) *Reporting of income by other co-producers*. Any co-producer that is entitled to receive a payment from a taking co-producer must include the amount of the payment in gross income as proceeds from the sale of its gas only for the taxable year that the payment is actually received, regardless of its overall method of accounting.

(D) *Reporting of production expenses*. Each co-producer deducts its proportionate share of production expenses, as provided in the JOA, under its regular method of accounting for the expenses.

(iii) *Special rules for production credits and depletion deductions under the cumulative method*—(A) *In general*. Under the cumulative method, a co-producer's depletion allowance and production credit for a taxable year are based on its income from gas sales and production of gas from its percentage share of the total gas in the reservoir, and are not based on its current proportionate share of income and production as determined under the JOA. Thus, in general, a taking co-producer is not allowed a production credit or an allowance for depletion on its sales of gas in excess of its percentage share of the total gas in the reservoir. However, the Service will not disallow depletion deductions or production credits claimed by a taking co-producer on the gas of other co-producers if the taking co-producer had a reasonable but mistaken belief that the deductions or credits were claimed with respect to the taking co-producer's percentage share of total gas in the reservoir and the taking co-producer makes the appropriate reductions and additions to tax required in paragraphs (d)(3)(iii)(B) and (d)(3)(iii)(C) of this section. The reasonableness of the mistaken belief is determined at the time of filing the return claiming the deductions or credits. A co-producer receiving a payment for sales of its gas from a taking co-producer claims a production credit and an allowance for depletion relating to those sales only for the taxable year in which the amount of the payment is included in its gross income.

(B) *Reduction of taking co-producer's payment deduction for depletion claimed on another co-producer's gas*. If a taking co-producer claims an allowance for depletion on another co-producer's gas, the taking co-producer must reduce its deduction claimed in a later year for making a payment to the other co-producer for sales of that co-producer's gas by the amount of any percentage depletion deduction allowed on the gas sales to which the payment relates. If the percentage limitation of section 613A(d)(1) applied to disallow a depletion deduction for a previous year, the taking co-producer must reduce the amount of any carried over depletion deduction allowable in the year of the payment or in a future year by the portion of the carried over

Reg. § 1.761-2(d)(3)

depletion deduction, if any, that relates to another co-producer's gas.

(C) *Addition to tax of taking co-producer for production credit claimed on another co-producer's gas.* If a taking co-producer claims a production credit on another co-producer's gas, the taking co-producer must add to its tax for the taxable year that it makes a payment to the other co-producer for sales of that co-producer's gas any production credit allowed in an earlier taxable year on the gas sales to which the payment relates, but only to the extent the credit allowed actually reduced the taking co-producer's tax in any earlier year. The taking co-producer also must reduce the amount of its minimum tax credit allowable by reason of section 53(d)(1)(B)(iii) in the year of the payment or in a future year by the portion of the credit, if any, that relates to another co-producer's gas.

(iv) *Anti-abuse rule.* If the Commissioner determines that co-producers using the cumulative method have arranged or altered their taking of production for a taxable year with a principal purpose of shifting the income, deductions, or credits relating to that production to avoid tax, the co-producers' election to be excluded from all or part of subchapter K will be revoked for that year and for subsequent years. In determining that a principal purpose was to avoid tax, the Commissioner will examine all the facts and circumstances surrounding the use of the cumulative method by the co-producers. See *Examples 3* and *4* of paragraph (d)(6) of this section.

(4) *Annual gas balancing method*—(i) *In general.* The annual gas balancing method (annual method) takes into account each co-producer's ownership rights and obligations, as described in the JOA, with respect to the co-producer's current proportionate share of gas as it is produced from the reservoir. Under the annual method, gas imbalances relating to a JOA must be eliminated annually through a balancing payment, which may be in the form of cash, gas produced under the same JOA, or other property. If all the co-producers under a JOA have the same taxable year, any gas imbalance remaining at the end of a taxable year must be eliminated by a balancing payment from the overproducer to the underproducer by the due date of the overproducer's tax return for that taxable year (including extensions). If all the co-producers under a JOA do not have the same taxable year, any gas imbalance remaining at the end of a calendar year must be eliminated by a balancing payment from the overproducer to the underproducer by September 15 of the following calendar year. The annual method may be used only if the Commissioner's permission is obtained. Paragraph (d)(4)(ii) of this section provides guidelines for applying for this permission. The annual method is not available for a JOA with respect to which any co-producer made an election under paragraph (d)(5)(i)(B)(*3*) of this section (to take an aggregate section 481(a) adjustment for all JOAs of a co-producer into account in the year of change).

(ii) *Obtaining the Commissioner's permission to use the annual method.* A request for the Commissioner's permission to adopt the annual method for a new JOA must be in writing and must set forth the names of all the co-producers under the JOA and the respective taxable year of adoption. See paragraphs (d)(2)(ii) and (d)(5)(ii) of this section for the rules for a change in method of accounting to the annual method. In addition, the request must contain an explanation of how the co-producers will report income from gas sales, the making or receiving of a balancing payment, production expenses, depletion deductions, and production credits. Permission will be granted under appropriate conditions, including, but not limited to, an agreement in writing by all co-producers to use the annual method and to eliminate any gas imbalances annually in accordance with paragraph (d)(4)(i) of this section.

(5) *Transitional rules for making a change in method of accounting required in paragraph (d)(2)(ii)(C) of this section*—(i) *Change in method of accounting to the cumulative method*—(A) *Automatic consent to change in method of accounting to the cumulative method.* A co-producer changing to the cumulative method for any JOA entered into prior to its first taxable year beginning after December 31, 1994, and in effect as of the beginning of that year is granted the consent of the Commissioner to change its method of accounting with respect to each JOA to the cumulative method, provided the co-producer—

(*1*) Makes the change on its timely filed return for its first taxable year beginning after December 31, 1994;

(*2*) Attaches a completed and signed Form 3115 to the co-producer's tax return for the year of change, stating that, pursuant to § 1.761-2(d)(2)(ii) of the regulations, the co-producer is changing its method of accounting for sales of gas and its treatment of certain related deductions and credits under each JOA to the cumulative method;

(*3*) In the case of a co-producer making an election under paragraph (d)(5)(i)(B)(*3*) of this section to take the aggregate section 481(a) adjustment into account in the year of change,

Reg. § 1.761-2(d)(5)

attaches the statement described in paragraph (d)(5)(i)(B)(*3*)(*ii*) of this section; and

(*4*) In the case of a co-producer not making an election under paragraph (d)(5)(i)(B)(*3*) of this section, attaches a list of each JOA with respect to which there is a section 481(a) adjustment computed in accordance with paragraph (d)(5)(i)(B)(*2*)(*i*) of this section.

(B) *Section 481(a) adjustment*—(*1*) *Application of section 481(a).* A change in method of accounting to the cumulative method under the automatic consent procedure in paragraph (d)(5)(i)(A) of this section is a change in method of accounting to which the provisions of section 481(a) apply. Thus, a section 481(a) adjustment must be taken into account in the manner provided by this paragraph (d)(5)(i)(B) to prevent the omission or duplication of income. Paragraph (d)(5)(i)(B)(*2*) of this section provides the general rules for computing the amount of the section 481(a) adjustment of a co-producer relating to a particular JOA and for taking the section 481(a) adjustment into account. Paragraph (d)(5)(i)(B)(*3*) of this section provides rules for electing to take a co-producer's section 481(a) adjustment computed on an aggregate basis for all JOAs into account in the year of change. Paragraph (d)(5)(i)(C) of this section provides rules to coordinate the taking of a depletion deduction or a production credit with the inclusion of a section 481(a) adjustment arising from a change in method of accounting to the cumulative method under this paragraph (d)(5)(i).

(*2*) *Computation of the section 481(a) adjustment relating to a joint operating agreement*—(*i*) *In general.* The section 481(a) adjustment of a co-producer relating to a JOA is computed as of the first day of the co-producer's year of change and is equal to the difference between the amount of income reported under the co-producer's former method of accounting for all taxable years prior to the year of change and the amount of income that would have been reported if the co-producer's new method had been used in all those taxable years.

(*ii*) *Section 481(a) adjustment period.* Except to the extent that paragraph (d)(5)(i)(B)(*3*) of this section applies, a co-producer's section 481(a) adjustment relating to a JOA, whether positive or negative, is taken into account in computing taxable income ratably over the 6-taxable-year period beginning with the year of change (the section 481(a) adjustment period). If the co-producer has been in existence less than 6 taxable years, the adjustment is taken into account over the number of years the co-producer has been in existence. If the co-producer ceases to engage in the trade or business that gave rise to the section 481(a) adjustment at any time during the section 481(a) adjustment period, the entire remaining balance of the section 481(a) adjustment relating to that trade or business must be taken into account in the year of the cessation. For purposes of this paragraph (d)(5)(i)(B)(*2*)(*ii*), production under each JOA is treated as a separate trade or business. The determination as to whether the co-producer ceases to engage in its trade or business is to be made under the principles of § 1.446-1(e)(3)(ii) and its underlying administrative procedures. For example, the permanent cessation of production under a co-producer's JOA constitutes the cessation of a trade or business of the co-producer. Accordingly, for the year that production under a JOA permanently ceases, the remaining balance of the section 481(a) adjustment relating to the JOA must be taken into account.

(*3*) *Election to take aggregate section 481(a) adjustment for all joint operating agreements into account in the year of change*—(*i*) *In general.* A co-producer may elect to take into account its section 481(a) adjustment, computed on an aggregate basis for all of its JOAs, whether negative or positive, in the year of change, provided the co-producer uses the cumulative method for all of its JOAs entered into prior to its first taxable year beginning after December 31, 1994, and in effect as of the beginning of that year. The aggregate section 481(a) adjustment of a co-producer is equal to the difference between the amount of income reported under the co-producer's former method of accounting for all taxable years prior to the year of change and the amount of income that would have been reported if the co-producer's new method had been used in all of those taxable years for all JOAs for which the co-producer changes its method of accounting. An election made under this paragraph (d)(5)(i)(B)(*3*) is irrevocable. If any person who, together with another person, would be treated as a single taxpayer under section 41(f)(1)(A) or (B) makes an election under this paragraph (d)(5)(i)(B)(*3*), all persons within that single taxpayer group will be treated as if they had made an election under this paragraph (d)(5)(i)(B)(*3*) and, as such, will be irrevocably bound by that election. If a co-producer does not make an election under this paragraph, each JOA entered into prior to the start of its first taxable year beginning after December 31, 1994, and in effect as of the beginning of that year must be accounted for separately in computing the section 481(a) adjustment and taxable income of the co-producer for any year to which this paragraph (d) applies.

Reg. § 1.761-2(d)(5)

(ii) *Time and manner for making the election.* An election under this paragraph (d)(5)(i)(B)(*3*) is made by attaching a statement to the co-producer's timely filed return for its year of change indicating that the co-producer is electing under § 1.761-2(d)(5)(i)(B)(*3*) to take its aggregate section 481(a) adjustment into account in the year of change.

(C) *Treatment of section 481(a) adjustment as a sale for purposes of computing a production credit and as gross income from the property for purposes of depletion deductions.* Any positive section 481(a) adjustment arising as a result of a change in method of accounting for gas imbalances under this paragraph (d)(5)(i) and taken into account in computing taxable income under paragraph (d)(5)(i)(B) of this section is considered a sale by the taxpayer for purposes of computing any production credit in the year that the adjustment is taken into account. Similarly, the positive section 481(a) adjustment is considered *gross income from the property* and *taxable income from the property* for purposes of computing depletion deductions in the year the adjustment is taken into account. Sales amounts used in computing any production credit in any year in which a negative section 481(a) adjustment is taken into account in computing taxable income under paragraph (d)(5)(i)(B) of this section must be reduced by the amount of the negative section 481(a) adjustment taken into account in that year. Similarly, gross income from the property and taxable income from the property used in computing any depletion deduction in any year in which the negative section 481(a) adjustment is taken into account must be reduced by the amount of the negative adjustment. For these purposes, any taxpayer that makes an aggregate section 481(a) adjustment election under paragraph (d)(5)(i)(B)(*3*) of this section must allocate the adjustment among its properties in any reasonable manner that prevents a duplication or omission of depletion deductions.

(ii) *Change in method of accounting to the annual method*—(A) *In general.* A co-producer changing to the annual method in accordance with paragraph (d)(2)(ii) of this section must request a change under § 1.446-1(e)(3) and will be subject to any terms and conditions as may be imposed by the Commissioner.

(B) *Section 481(a) adjustment.* A change in method of accounting to the annual method is a change in method of accounting to which the provisions of section 481(a) apply. Thus, a section 481(a) adjustment must be taken into account to prevent the omission or duplication of income. If all the co-producers under a JOA have the same taxable year, the section 481(a) adjustment involved in a change to the annual method by a co-producer relating to the JOA is computed as of the first day of the co-producer's year of change. If the co-producers under a JOA do not all have the same taxable year (that is, in the case of a part-year change described in paragraph (d)(2)(ii)(C) of this section), the change in method of accounting occurs on January 1, 1996, and the section 481(a) adjustment is computed on that date.

(iii) *Untimely change in method of accounting to comply with this section.* Unless a co-producer required by this section to change its method of accounting complies with the provisions of this paragraph (d)(5) for its first applicable taxable year within the time prescribed by this paragraph (d)(5), the co-producer must take the section 481(a) adjustment into account under the provisions of any applicable administrative procedure that is prescribed by the Commissioner specifically for purposes of complying with this section. Absent such an administrative procedure, a co-producer must request a change under § 1.446-1(e)(3) and will be subject to any terms and conditions as may be imposed by the Commissioner.

(6) *Examples.* The following examples illustrate the application of the cumulative method described in paragraph (d)(3) of this section.

Example 1. Operation of the cumulative method. (i) L, a corporation using the cash receipts and disbursements method of accounting, and M, a corporation using an accrual method, file returns on a calendar year basis. On January 1, 1995, L and M enter into a JOA to produce natural gas as an unincorporated organization from a reservoir located in State Y. The JOA allocates reservoir production 60 percent to L and 40 percent to M. L and M enter into a GBA as an addendum to the JOA. L and M agree to use the cumulative method to account for gas sales from the reservoir and elect under section 761(a) and this section to exclude the organization from the application of subchapter K. Production from the reservoir is eligible for the section 29 credit for producing fuel from a nonconventional source. L and M produce and sell the following amounts of natural gas (in mmcf) until 2000 during which year production from the reservoir ceases:

	1995	1996	1997	1998	1999	2000
L	720	480	600	-0-	-0-	-0-
M	240	60	120	160	80	40

Reg. § 1.761-2(d)(6)

43,712   Definitions

See p. 20,601 for regulations not amended to reflect law changes

(ii) By the end of 1996, neither L nor M has fully produced its percentage share of the total gas in the reservoir. In 1997, L produces a total of 600 mmcf of gas at the rate of 50 mmcf per month. Prior to filing its return for 1997, L determines that it fully produced its percentage share of gas in the reservoir as of June 30, 1997. Pursuant to the GBA executed by L and M, L pays M at the end of 2000 for the 300 mmcf of M's gas (as determined under the cumulative method) that L sold in the last half of 1997.

(iii) For 1995, L and M must include in their gross income the amounts relating to gas sales of 720 mmcf and 240 mmcf, respectively. For 1996, L and M must include the amounts relating to gas sales of 480 mmcf and 60 mmcf, respectively. For both 1995 and 1996, L and M compute an allowance for depletion and a section 29 credit based upon gas taken and sold by each from the reservoir for each taxable year.

(iv) For 1997, L and M must include in gross income the amounts relating to their gas sales of 600 mmcf and 120 mmcf, respectively. Under paragraph (d)(3)(iii)(A) of this section, L computes an allowance for depletion and the section 29 credit based only on production from L's proportionate share of gas in the reservoir (that is, based on L's production through June 30, 1997). Accordingly, for 1997, L claims depletion and the section 29 credit only with respect to 300 mmcf of gas (50 mmcf per month x 6 months). For 1997, because M has not fully produced from its percentage share of the total gas in the reservoir as of the end of 1997, M claims depletion and the section 29 credit on the 120 mmcf that M produced in 1997.

(v) In 1998 and 1999, M must include in gross income the amounts relating to M's sales of gas, that is, 160 mmcf for 1998 and 80 mmcf for 1999. For 2000, M must include in gross income the amount relating to sales of 340 mmcf of gas,

	1995
L	720
M	240

(ii) In addition, L does not realize until December 31, 1999, that L fully produced its percentage share of the total gas in the reservoir as of June 30, 1997. At the time of filing its returns for 1997 and 1998, L reasonably believes that during 1997 and 1998, respectively, it did not fully produce its percentage share of the total gas in the reservoir. Thus, L claims depletion and the section 29 credit for its total sales of 600 mmcf in 1997 and 60 mmcf in 1998. Pursuant to the GBA executed by L and M, L pays M at the end of 2000 for the 420 mmcf of M's gas (as determined under the cumulative method) that L sold (300

which consists of its own sales of 40 mmcf plus the payment for 300 mmcf of gas that L made to M for having sold from M's share of the total gas in the reservoir during the last half of 1997. Because M produced from its percentage share of the total gas in the reservoir during 1998, 1999, and 2000, M claims a depletion deduction and a section 29 credit on its income and production for those years, that is, 160 mmcf for 1998, 80 mmcf for 1999, and 40 mmcf for 2000. Additionally, for 2000, M claims depletion and the section 29 credit relating to the payment that M received from L for the 300 mmcf of M's gas that L sold in the last half of 1997. Under paragraph (d)(3)(ii)(B) of this section, L's deduction for its payment to M for the 300 mmcf of M's gas that L sold in 1997 is allowable only for 2000.

Example 2. Adjustments under the cumulative method for depletion deductions and production credits that were claimed for sales in excess of a co-producer's percentage share of total gas in the reservoir. (i) L, a corporation using the cash receipts and disbursements method of accounting, and M, a corporation using an accrual method, file returns on a calendar year basis. On January 1, 1995, L and M enter into a JOA to produce natural gas as an unincorporated organization from a reservoir located in State Y. The JOA allocates reservoir production 60 percent to L and 40 percent to M. L and M enter into a GBA as an addendum to the JOA. L and M agree to use the cumulative method to account for gas sales from the reservoir and elect under section 761(a) and this section to exclude the organization from the application of subchapter K. Production from the reservoir is eligible for the section 29 credit for producing fuel from a nonconventional source. L and M produce and sell the following amounts of natural gas (in mmcf) until 2000 during which year production from the reservoir ceases:

1996	1997	1998	1999	2000
480	600	60	60	-0-
60	120	60	60	40

mmcf in the last half of 1997 (assuming that production was at a rate of 50 mmcf per month), 60 mmcf in 1998, and 60 mmcf in 1999).

(iii) In 1997 and 1998, L and M include in gross income the amounts relating to their respective sales of gas, that is, for L 600 mmcf for 1997 and 60 mmcf for 1998, and for M 120 mmcf for 1997 and 60 mmcf for 1998.

(iv) For 1999, L must include in gross income the amount of its sales of 60 mmcf, but may not claim depletion or the section 29 credit on those sales. For 1999, M must include in gross income the amount of its sales of 60 mmcf and claims

Reg. § 1.761-2(d)(6)

Definitions

See p. 20,601 for regulations not amended to reflect law changes

depletion and the section 29 credit with respect to those 60 mmcf.

(v) For 2000, M must include in gross income the amount relating to gas sales of 460 mmcf, that is, the amount of M's own gas sales of 40 mmcf and the amount of the payment received from L for the 420 mmcf of M's gas that L sold (consisting of 300 mmcf in 1997, 60 mmcf in 1998, and 60 mmcf in 1999). Under paragraph (d)(3)(iii)(A) of this section, M computes a depletion deduction and a production credit relating to the amount of M's actual gas sales for 2000 and the payment received from L, that is, relating to a total of 460 mmcf of gas (M's sales of 40 mmcf for 2000, plus L's payment for 420 mmcf of gas). Under paragraph (d)(3)(ii)(B) of this section, L's deduction for making its payment to M for 420 mmcf of gas is allowable only for 2000. Under paragraph (d)(3)(iii)(B) of this section, L must reduce its deduction by the amount of any percentage depletion deductions allowed on its sales of M's gas, that is, relating to 360 mmcf of gas (300 mmcf for 1997 and 60 mmcf for 1998). In addition, under paragraph (d)(3)(iii)(C) of this section, L must increase its tax for 2000 by the amount of any section 29 credit L claimed on its sales of M's gas, but only to the extent that the credit claimed actually reduced L's tax in any earlier year.

Example 3. Non-abusive altering of the taking of production for a taxable year. (i) C and D enter into a JOA and a GBA on December 1, 1994, for gas production from a reservoir. The JOA allocates production at 50 percent to C and 50 percent to D. C and D agree in writing to use the cumulative method to account for gas sales. Additionally, C and D elect under section 761(a) and this section to exclude their organization from the application of subchapter K. C and D arrange to sell all their production under annually renewable contracts. In 1995, C and D each sell 480 mmcf of gas from the reservoir.

(ii) In November 1995, D is notified that its contract with its purchaser will not be renewed for 1996. D is unable to find a new purchaser for its gas for 1996. In December 1995, D notifies C that it will not be taking production from the reservoir in 1996. Pursuant to the GBA, C then contracts with its current gas purchaser to sell an additional 20 mmcf per month in 1996. Accordingly, C sells 720 mmcf in 1996 (60 mmcf per month x 12 months). Under the facts described in this example, a principal purpose of altering the taking of production is not to avoid tax. Accordingly, the co-producers' election under section 761(a) will not be revoked by reason of altering the taking of production.

Example 4. Abusive altering of the taking of production for a taxable year. The facts are the same as in *Example 3* (i). For 1996, C anticipates that C's regular tax (reduced by the credits allowable under sections 27 and 28) will not exceed C's tentative minimum tax. Accordingly, under section 29(b)(6), C's credit allowed under section 29(a) for sales of its gas will be zero. For 1997, C anticipates that its credit allowed under section 29(a) will not be limited by section 29(b)(6). On the other hand, D anticipates that any credit it may claim under section 29(a) for 1996, even including a credit based on sales of C's share of current production under the JOA, will not be limited by section 29(b)(6). However, for 1997, D anticipates that its credit under section 29(a) will be limited by section 29(b)(6). On January 1, 1996, C and D agree that D will contract with its purchaser to sell the entire 960 mmcf produced from the reservoir in 1996 and that C will contract with its purchaser to sell the entire 960 mmcf produced from the reservoir in 1997. Under these facts, a principal purpose of altering the taking of production is to avoid tax. Accordingly, the co-producers' election under section 761(a) will be revoked for 1996 and for subsequent years.

(7) *Effective date.* Except in the case of a part-year change to the annual method or the cessation of a JOA, both of which are described in paragraph (d)(2)(ii)(C) of this section, the provisions of this paragraph (d) apply to all taxable years beginning after December 31, 1994, of any producer that is a member of an unincorporated organization that produces natural gas under a JOA in effect on or after the start of the producer's first taxable year beginning after December 31, 1994. In the case of a part-year change, the provisions of this paragraph (d) apply on and after January 1, 1996. In the case of the cessation of a JOA, the co-producers use their current method of accounting with respect to that JOA until the JOA ceases to be in effect.

(e) *Cross reference.* For requirements with respect to the filing of a return on Form 1065 by a partnership, see § 1.6031-1. [Reg. § 1.761-2.]

☐ [T.D. 7208, 10-2-72. Amended by T.D. 8578, 12-22-94.]

[The next page is 45,701.]

Reg. § 1.761-2(e)

INSURANCE COMPANIES

Life Insurance Companies

→ *Caution: New Code Secs. 801–818 replaced former Code Secs. 801–820 (pre-1984 years), which were repealed. The following Regulations were issued under new Code Secs. 801–818.* ←

[Reg. § 1.807-1]

§ 1.807-1. Mortality and morbidity tables.

(a) *Tables to be used.* If there are no commissioners' standard tables applicable to an insurance contract when the contract is issued, then the mortality and morbidity tables set forth in this subsection are used to compute reserves under section 807(d)(2) for the contract.

	Type of Contract	Table
1.	Group term life insurance (active life reserves)	1960 Commissioners' Standard Group Mortality Table
2.	Group life insurance (active life reserves); accidental death benefits	1959 Accidental Death Benefits Table
3.	Permanent and paid-up group life insurance (active life reserves)	Same tables as are applicable to males for ordinary life insurance
4a.	Group life insurance disability income benefits (active life reserves)	The tables of period 2 disablement rates and the 1930 to 1950 termination rates of the 1952 Disability Study of the Society of Actuaries
4b.	Group life insurance disability income benefits (disabled life reserves)	The 1930 to 1950 termination rates of the 1952 Disability Study of the Society of Actuaries
5.	Group life insurance; survivor income benefits insurance	Same tables as are applicable to group annuities
6.	Group life insurance; extended death benefits for disabled lives	1970 Intercompany Group Life Disability Valuation Table
7.	Credit life insurance	1958 Commissioners' Extended Term Table
8.	Supplementary contracts involving life contingencies	Same tables as are applicable to individual immediate annuities
9.	Noncancellable accident and health insurance (active life reserves); benefits issued before 1984	Tables used for NAIC annual statement reserves as of December 31, 1983
10a.	Noncancellable accident and health insurance (active life reserves); group disability benefits issued after 1983 and individual disability benefits issued after 1983 and before 1989	1964 Commissioners' Disability Tables
10b.	Noncancellable accident and health insurance (active life reserves); individual disability benefits issued after 1988	1985 Commissioners' Individual Disability Table A or Commissioners' Individual Disability Table B
11.	Noncancellable accident and health insurance (active life reserves); accidental death benefits issued after 1983	1959 Accidental Death Benefits Tables
12.	Noncancellable accident and health insurance (active life reserves); all benefits issued after 1983 other than disability and accidental death	Tables used for NAIC annual statement reserves
13a.	Noncancellable accident and health insurance (claim reserves); group disability benefits for all years of issue and individual disability benefits for years before 1989	1964 Commissioners' Disability Tables

Reg. § 1.807-1(a)

45,702 Life Insurance Companies

See p. 20,601 for regulations not amended to reflect law changes

→ *Caution: New Code Secs. 801–818 replaced former Code Secs. 801–820 (pre-1984 years), which were repealed. The following Regulations were issued under new Code Secs. 801–818.*←

	Type of Contract	Table
13b.	Noncancellable accident and health insurance (claim reserves); individual disability benefits for years after 1988	1985 Commissioners' Individual Disability Table A or Commissioners' Individual Disability Table B
14.	Noncancellable accident and health insurance (claim reserves); all benefits other than disability for all years of issue	Tables used for annual statement reserves

(b) *Adjustments.* An appropriate adjustment may be made to the tables in paragraph (a) of this section to reflect risks (such as substandard risks) incurred under the contract which are not otherwise taken into account.

(c) *Special rule where more than 1 table or option applicable.* If, with respect to any category of risks, there are 2 or more tables (or options under 1 or more tables) in paragraph (a) of this section, the table (and option thereunder) which generally yields the lowest reserves shall be used to compute reserves under section 807(b)(2) for the contract.

(d) *Effective date.* This section is effective for taxable years beginning after December 31, 1983, except that the 1985 Commissioners' Individual Disability Tables A and B shall be treated (for purposes of section 807(d)(5)(B) and for purposes of determining the issue dates of contracts for which they shall be used) as if the tables were new prevailing commissioners' standard tables adopted by the twenty-sixth State on December 26, 1989. [Reg. § 1.807-1.]

☐ [*T.D.* 8278, 12-22-89.]

[Reg. § 1.807-2]

§ 1.807-2. **Cross-reference.**—For special rules regarding the treatment of modified guaranteed contracts (as defined in section 817A and § 1.817A-1(a)(1)), see § 1.817A-1. [Reg. § 1.807-2.]

☐ [*T.D.* 9058, 5-6-2003.]

[Reg. § 1.809-9]

§ 1.809-9. **Computation of the differential earnings rate and the recomputed differential earnings rate.**—(a) *In general.* Neither the differential earnings rate under section 809(c) nor the recomputed differential earnings rate that is used in computing the recomputed differential earnings amount under section 809(f)(3) may be less than zero.

(b) *Definitions*—(1) *Recomputed differential earnings amount.* The recomputed differential earnings amount, with respect to any taxable year, is the amount equal to the product of—

(i) The life insurance company's average equity base for the taxable year; multiplied by

(ii) The recomputed differential earnings rate for that taxable year.

(2) *Recomputed differential earnings rate.* The recomputed differential earnings rate for any taxable year equals the excess of—

(i) The imputed earnings rate for the taxable year; over

(ii) The average mutual earning[s] rate for the calendar year in which the taxable year begins.

(c) *Effective date.* The regulations are effective for all taxable years beginning after December 31, 1986. [Reg. § 1.809-9.]

☐ [*T.D.* 8499, 12-7-93.]

[Reg. § 1.809-10]

§ 1.809-10. **Computation of equity base.**—(a) *In general.* For purposes of section 809, the equity base of a life insurance company includes the amount of any asset valuation reserve and the amount of any interest maintenance reserve.

(b) *Effective date.* This section is effective for taxable years ending after December 31, 1991. [Reg. § 1.809-10.]

☐ [*T.D.* 8564, 9-28-94.]

[Reg. § 1.811-3]

§ 1.811-3. **Cross-reference.**—For special rules regarding the treatment of modified guaranteed contracts (as defined in section 817A and § 1.817A-1(a)(1)), see § 1.817A-1. [Reg. § 1.811-3.]

☐ [*T.D.* 9058, 5-6-2003.]

[Reg. § 1.812-9]

§ 1.812-9. **Cross-reference.**—For special rules regarding the treatment of modified guaranteed contracts (as defined in section 817A and § 1.817A-1(a)(1)), see § 1.817A-1. [Reg. § 1.812-9.]

☐ [*T.D.* 9058, 5-6-2003.]

Life Insurance Companies

See p. 20,601 for regulations not amended to reflect law changes

→ **Caution:** *New Code Secs. 801–818 replaced former Code Secs. 801–820 (pre-1984 years), which were repealed. The following Regulations were issued under new Code Secs. 801–818.*←

[Reg. § 1.817-5]

§ 1.817-5. **Diversification requirements for variable annuity, endowment, and life insurance contracts.**—(a) *Consequences of nondiversification*—(1) *In general.* Except as provided in paragraph (a)(2) of this section, for purposes of subchapter L, section 72, and section 7702(a), a variable contract (as defined in section 817(d)), other than a pension plan contract (as defined in section 818(a)), which is based on one or more segregated asset accounts shall not be treated as an annuity, endowment, or life insurance contract for any calendar quarter period for which the investments of any such account are not adequately diversified. For this purpose, a variable contract shall be treated as based on a segregated asset account for a calendar quarter period if amounts received under the contract (or earnings thereon) are allocated to the segregated asset account at any time during the period. In addition, a variable contract that is not treated as an annuity, endowment, or life insurance contract for any period by reason of this paragraph (a)(1) shall not be treated as an annuity, endowment, or life insurance contract for any subsequent period even if the investments are adequately diversified for such subsequent period. If a variable contract which is a life insurance or endowment contract under other applicable (e.g., State or foreign) law is not treated as a life insurance or endowment contract under section 7702(a), the income on the contract for any taxable year of the policyholder is treated as ordinary income received or accrued by the policyholder during such year in accordance with section 7702(g) and (h). Likewise, if a variable contract is not treated as an annuity contract under section 72, the income on the contract for any taxable year of the policyholder shall be treated as ordinary income received or accrued by the policyholder during such year in the same manner as a life insurance or endowment contract under section 7702(g) and (h).

(2) *Inadvertent failure to diversify.* The investments of a segregated asset account shall be treated as satisfying the requirements of paragraph (b) of this section for one or more periods, provided the following conditions are satisfied—

(i) The issuer or holder must show the Commissioner that the failure of the investments to satisfy the requirements of paragraph (b) of this section for such period or periods was inadvertent;

(ii) The investments of the account must satisfy the requirements of paragraph (b) of this section within a reasonable time after the discovery of such failure, and

(iii) The issuer or holder of the variable contract must agree to make such adjustments or pay such amounts as may be required by the Commissioner with respect to the period or periods during which the investments of the account did not satisfy the requirements of paragraph (b) of this section. The amount required by the Commissioner to be paid shall be an amount based upon the tax that would have been owed by the policyholders if they were treated as receiving the income on the contract (as defined in section 7702(g)(1)(B), without regard to section 7702(g)(1)(C)) for such period or periods.

(b) *Diversification of investments*—(1) *In general.* (i) Except as otherwise provided in this paragraph and paragraph (c) of this section, the investments of a segregated asset account shall be considered adequately diversified for purposes of this section and section 817(h) only if—

(A) No more than 55% of the value of the total assets of the account is represented by any one investment;

(B) No more than 70% of the value of the total assets of the account is represented by any two investments;

(C) No more than 80% of the value of the total assets of the account is represented by any three investments; and

(D) No more than 90% of the value of the total assets of the account is represented by any four investments.

(ii) For purposes of this section—

(A) All securities of the same issuer, all interests in the same real property project, and all interests in the same commodity are each treated as a single investment; and

(B) In the case of government securities, each government agency or instrumentality shall be treated as a separate issuer.

(iii) See paragraph (f) of this section for circumstances in which a segregated asset account is treated as the owner of assets held indirectly through certain pass-through entities and corporations taxed under subchapter M, chapter 1 of the Code.

(2) *Safe harbor.* A segregated asset account will be considered adequately diversified for purposes of this section and section 817(h) if—

Reg. § 1.817-5(b)(2)

→ *Caution: New Code Secs. 801–818 replaced former Code Secs. 801–820 (pre-1984 years), which were repealed. The following Regulations were issued under new Code Secs. 801–818.*←

(i) The account meets the requirements of section 851(b)(4) and the regulations thereunder; and

(ii) No more than 55% of the value of the total assets of the account is attributable to cash, cash items (including receivables), government securities, and securities of other regulated investment companies.

(3) *Alternative diversification requirements for variable life insurance contracts.* (i) A segregated asset account with respect to variable life insurance contracts will be considered adequately diversified for purposes of this section and section 817(h) if the requirements of paragraph (b)(1) or (b)(2) of this section are satisfied or if the assets of such account, other than Treasury securities, satisfy the percentage limitations prescribed in paragraph (b)(1) of this section increased by the product of (A) .5 and (B) the percentage of the value of the total assets of the account that is represented by Treasury securities. In determining whether the assets of an account, other than Treasury securities, satisfy the increased percentage limitations, such limitations are applied as if the Treasury securities were not included in the account (*i.e.*, the increased percentage limitations are not applied to Treasury securities and the value of the total assets of the account is reduced by the value of the Treasury securities).

(ii) The provisions of this paragraph (b)(3) may be illustrated by the following examples:

Example (1). On the last day of a quarter of a calendar year, a segregated asset account with respect to variable life insurance contracts holds assets having a total value of $100,000. The assets of the account are represented by Treasury securities having a total value of $90,000 and securities of Corporation A having a total value of $10,000. The 55% limit described in paragraph (b)(1)(i) of this section would be increased by 45% (0.5 × 90%) to 100%, and would then be applied to the assets of the account other than Treasury securities. Because no more than 100% of the value of the assets other than Treasury securities is represented by securities of Corporation A, the investments of the account will be considered adequately diversified.

Example (2). On the last day of a quarter of a calendar year, a segregated asset account with respect to variable life insurance contracts holds assets having a total value of $100,000. The assets of the account are represented by Treasury securities having a total value of $60,000, securities of Corporation A having a total value of $30,000, and securities of Corporation B having a total value of $10,000. The 55% and 70% limits described in paragraph (b)(1)(i) of this section would be increased by 30% (0.5 × 60%) to 85% and 100%, respectively, and would then be applied to the assets of the account other than Treasury securities. Securities of Corporation A represent 75%, and securities of Corporation B represent 25%, of the value of the assets of the account other than Treasury securities. Because no more than 85% of the value of the assets other than Treasury securities is represented by securities of Corporation A or B and no more than 100% of the value of the assets other than Treasury securities is represented by securities of Corporations A and B, the investments of the account will be considered adequately diversified.

(c) *Periods for which an account is adequately diversified*—(1) *In general.* A segregated asset account that satisfies the requirements of paragraph (b) of this section on the last day of a quarter of a calendar year (*i.e.*, March 31, June 30, September 30, and December 31) or within 30 days after such last day shall be considered adequately diversified for such quarter.

(2) *Start-up period.* (i) Except as provided in paragraph (c)(2)(iv) of this section, a segregated asset account that is not a real property account on its first anniversary shall be considered adequately diversified until such first anniversary.

(ii) Except as provided in paragraph (c)(2)(iv) of this section, a segregated asset account that is a real property account on its first anniversary shall be considered adequately diversified until the earlier of its fifth anniversary or the anniversary on which the account ceases to be a real property account.

(iii) For purposes of paragraph (c)(2)(i) and (ii) of this section, the anniversary of a segregated asset account is the anniversary of the date on which any amount received under a life insurance or annuity contract, other than a pension plan contract (as defined in section 818(a)), is first allocated to the account.

(iv) If more than 30 percent of the amount allocated to a segregated asset account as of the last day of a calendar quarter is attributable to contracts entered into more than one year before such date, paragraph (c)(2)(i) of this section shall not apply to the segregated asset account for any period after such date. Similarly, if more than 30 percent of the amount allocated to a segregated

Reg. § 1.817-5(b)(3)

Life Insurance Companies 45,705

See p. 20,601 for regulations not amended to reflect law changes

→ *Caution: New Code Secs. 801–818 replaced former Code Secs. 801–820 (pre-1984 years), which were repealed. The following Regulations were issued under new Code Secs. 801–818.*←

asset account as of the last day of a calendar quarter is attributable to contracts entered into more than 5 years before such date, paragraph (c)(2)(ii) of this section shall not apply to the segregated asset account for any period after such date. For purposes of this paragraph (c)(2), amounts transferred to the account from a diversified account (determined without regard to this paragraph (c)(2)) or as a result of an exchange pursuant to section 1035 in which the issuer of the contract received in the exchange is not related in a manner specified in section 267(b) to the issuer of the contract transferred in the exchange are not treated as—

    (A) Amounts attributable to contracts entered into more than one year before such date, in the case of accounts subject to paragraph (c)(2)(i) of this section, or

    (B) Amounts attributable to contracts entered into more than five years before such date, in the case of accounts subject to paragraph (c)(2)(ii) of this section.

  (3) *Liquidation period.* A segregated asset account that satisfies the requirements of paragraph (b) of this section on the date a plan of liquidation is adopted shall be considered adequately diversified for—

    (i) The one-year period beginning on the date the plan of liquidation is adopted if the account is not a real property account on such date; or

    (ii) The two-year period beginning on the date the plan of liquidation is adopted if the account is a real property account on such date.

 (d) *Market fluctuations.* A segregated asset account that satisfies the requirements of paragraph (b) of this section at the end of any calendar quarter (or within 30 days after the end of such calendar quarter) shall not be considered nondiversified in a subsequent quarter because of a discrepancy between the value of its assets and the diversification requirements unless such discrepancy exists immediately after the acquisition of any asset and such discrepancy is wholly or partly the result of such acquisition.

 (e) *Segregated asset account.* For purposes of section 817(h) and this section, a segregated asset account shall consist of all assets the investment return and market value of each of which must be allocated in an identical manner to any variable contract invested in any of such assets. See paragraph (g) for examples illustrating the application of this paragraph (e).

 (f) *Look-through rule for assets held through certain investment companies, partnerships, or trusts*—(1) *In general.* If this paragraph (f) applies, a beneficial interest in a regulated investment company, a real estate investment trust, a partnership, or a trust that is treated under sections 671 through 679 as owned by the grantor or another person ("investment company, partnership, or trust") shall not be treated as a single investment of a segregated asset account. Instead, a pro rata portion of each asset of the investment company, partnership, or trust shall be treated, for purposes of this section, as an asset of the segregated asset account. For purposes of this section, the ratable interest of a partner in a partnership's assets shall be determined in accordance with the partner's capital interest in the partnership.

  (2) *Applicability*—(i) *Certain investment companies, partnerships, and trusts.* This paragraph (f) shall apply to an investment company, partnership, or trust if—

    (A) All the beneficial interests in the investment company, partnership, or trust (other than those described in paragraph (f)(3) of this section) are held by one or more segregated asset accounts of one or more insurance companies; and

    (B) Public access to such investment company, partnership, or trust is available exclusively (except as otherwise permitted in paragraph (f)(3) of this section) through the purchase of a variable contract. Solely for this purpose, the status of a contract as a variable contract will be determined without regard to section 817(h) and this section.

    (ii) *Nonregistered partnerships.* This paragraph (f) shall also apply to a partnership interest if the partnership interest is not registered under a Federal or State law regulating the offering or sale of securities.

    (iii) *Trusts holding Treasury securities.* This paragraph (f) shall also apply to a trust that is treated under section 671 through 679 as owned by the grantor or another person if substantially all of the assets of the trust are represented by Treasury securities.

  (3) *Interests not held by segregated asset accounts.* Satisfaction of the requirements of paragraph (f)(2)(i) of this section shall not be prevented by reason of beneficial interests in the investment company, partnership, or trust that are—

Reg. § 1.817-5(f)(3)

45,706 **Life Insurance Companies**

See p. 20,601 for regulations not amended to reflect law changes

→ *Caution: New Code Secs. 801–818 replaced former Code Secs. 801–820 (pre-1984 years), which were repealed. The following Regulations were issued under new Code Secs. 801–818.*←

(i) Held by the general account of a life insurance company or a corporation related in a manner specified in section 267(b) to a life insurance company, but only if the return on such interests is computed in the same manner as the return on an interest held by a segregated asset account is computed (determined without regard to expenses attributable to variable contracts), there is no intent to sell such interests to the public, and a segregated asset account of such life insurance company also holds or will hold a beneficial interest in the investment company, partnership, or trust;

(ii) Held by the manager, or a corporation related in a manner specified in section 267(b) to the manager, of the investment company, partnership, or trust, but only if the holding of the interests is in connection with the creation or management of the investment company, partnership, or trust, the return on such interest is computed in the same manner as the return on an interest held by a segregated asset account is computed (determined without regard to expenses attributable to variable contracts), and there is no intent to sell such interests to the public;

(iii) Held by the trustee of a qualified pension or retirement plan; or

(iv) Held by the public, or treated as owned by policyholders pursuant to Rev. Rul. 81-225, 1981-2 C.B. 12, but only if (A) the investment company, partnership, or trust was closed to the public in accordance with Rev. Rul. 82-55, 1982-1 C.B. 12, or (B) all the assets of the segregated asset account are attributable to premium payments made by policyholders prior to September 26, 1981, to premium payments made in connection with a qualified pension or retirement plan, or to any combination of such premium payments.

(g) *Examples.* The provisions of paragraphs (e) and (f) of this section may be illustrated by the following examples.

Example (1). (i) The assets underlying variable contracts issued by a life insurance company consist of two groups of assets: (a) a diversified portfolio of debt securities and (b) interests in P, a partnership that is publicly registered. All of the beneficial interests in P are held by one or more segregated asset accounts of one or more insurance companies and public access to P is available exclusively through the purchase of a variable contract. The variable contracts provide that policyholders may specify which portion of each premium is to be invested in the debt securities and which portion is to be invested in P interests. The portfolio of debt securities and the assets of P, considered separately, each satisfy the diversification requirements of paragraph (b) of this section.

(ii) As a result of the ability of policyholders to allocate premiums among the two groups of assets, the investment return and market value of the interests in P and the debt securities may be allocated to different variable contracts in a nonidentical manner. Accordingly, under paragraph (e) of this section, the interests in P are treated as part of a single segregated asset account ("Account 1") and the debt securities are treated as part of a different segregated asset account ("Account 2").

(iii) Since P is described in paragraph (f)(2)(i) of this section, interests in P will not be treated as a single investment of Account 1. Rather, Account 1 is treated as owning a pro rata portion of the assets of P.

(iv) Since Account 1 and Account 2 each satisfy the requirements of paragraph (b) of this section, variable contracts that are based on either or both accounts are treated as annuity, endowment, or life insurance contracts.

Example (2). The facts are the same as in example (1) except that some of the beneficial interests in P are held by persons not described in paragraph (f)(3) of this section. Since P is not described in paragraph (f)(2) of this section, interests in P will be treated as a single investment of Account 1. As a result, Account 1 does not satisfy the requirements of paragraph (b) of this section. Variable contracts based in whole or in part on Account 1 are not treated as annuity, endowment, or life insurance contracts. Variable contracts that are not based on Account 1 at any time during the period in which such account fails to satisfy the requirements of paragraph (b) of this section (*i.e.,* contracts based entirely on Account 2), are treated as annuity, endowment, or life insurance contracts. See paragraph (a)(1).

Example (3). The facts are the same as in example (2) except that P is not publicly registered. Since P is described in paragraph (e)(2)(ii) of this section, the result is the same as in example (1).

Example (4). The facts are the same as in example (2) except that the variable contracts do not permit policyholders to allocate premiums between or among the debt securities and interests in P. Thus, the investment return and market

Reg. § 1.817-5(g)

Life Insurance Companies

See p. 20,601 for regulations not amended to reflect law changes

→ *Caution: New Code Secs. 801–818 replaced former Code Secs. 801–820 (pre-1984 years), which were repealed. The following Regulations were issued under new Code Secs. 801–818.* ←

value of the interests in P and the debt securities must be allocated to the same variable contracts and in an identical manner. Under paragraph (e) of this section, the interests in P and the debt securities are treated as part of a single segregated asset account. If the interests in P and the debt securities, considered together, satisfy the requirements of paragraph (b) of this section, contracts based on this segregated asset account will be treated as annuity, endowment, or life insurance contracts.

(h) *Definitions.* The terms defined below shall, for purposes of this section, have the meanings set forth in such definitions:

(1) *Government security*—(i) *General rule.* The term "government security" shall mean any security issued or guaranteed or insured by the United States or an instrumentality of the United States; or any certificate of deposit for any of the foregoing. Any security or certificate of deposit insured or guaranteed only in part by the United States or an instrumentality thereof is treated as issued by the United States or its instrumentality only to the extent so insured or guaranteed, and as issued by the direct obligor to the extent not so insured or guaranteed. For purposes of this paragraph (h)(1), an instrumentality of the United States shall mean any person that is treated for purposes of 15 U.S.C. 80a-2(16), as amended, as a person controlled or supervised by and acting an an instrumentality of the Government of the United States pursuant to authority granted by the Congress of the United States.

(ii) *Example.* A segregated asset account purchases a certificate of deposit in the amount of $150,000 from bank A. Deposits in bank A are insured by the Federal Deposit Insurance Corporation, an instrumentality of the United States, to the extent of $100,000 per depositor. The certificate of deposit is treated as a government security to the extent of the $100,000 insured amount and is treated as a security issued by bank A to the extent of the $50,000 excess of the value of the certificate of deposit over the insured amount.

(2) *Treasury security*—(i) *General rule.* For purposes of paragraph (b)(3) of this section and section 817(h)(3), the term "Treasury security" shall mean a security the direct obligor of which is the United States Treasury.

(ii) *Example.* A segregated asset account purchases put and call options on U.S. Treasury securities issued by the Options Clearing Corporation. The options are not Treasury securities for purposes of paragraph (b)(3) and section 817(h)(3) because the direct obligor of the options is not the United States Treasury.

(3) *Real property.* The term "real property" shall mean any property that is treated as real property under Reg. § 1.856-3(d) except that it shall not include interests in real property.

(4) *Real property account.* A segregated asset account is a real property account on an anniversary of the account (within the meaning of paragraph (c)(2)(iii) of this section) or on the date a plan of liquidation is adopted if not less than the applicable percentage of the total assets of the account is represented by real property or interests in real property on such anniversary or date. For this purpose, the applicable percentage is 40% for the period ending on the first anniversary of the date on which premium income is first received, 50% for the year ending on the second anniversary, 60% for the year ending on the third anniversary, 70% for the year ending on the fourth anniversary, and 80% thereafter. A segregated asset account will also be treated as a real property account on its first anniversary if on or before such first anniversary the issuer has stated in the contract or prospectus or in a submission to a regulatory agency, an intention that the assets of the account will be primarily invested in real property or interests in real property, provided that at least 40% of the total assets of the account are so invested within six months after such first anniversary.

(5) *Commodity.* The term "commodity" shall mean any type of personal property other than a security.

(6) *Security.* The term "security" shall include a cash item and any partnership interest registered under a Federal or State law regulating the offering or sale of securities. The term shall not include any other partnership interest, any interest in real property, or any interest in a commodity.

(7) *Interest in real property.* The term "interest in real property" shall include the ownership and co-ownership of land or improvements thereon and leaseholds of land or improvements thereon. Such term shall not, however, include mineral, oil, or gas royalty interests, such as a retained economic interest in coal or iron ore with respect to which the special provisions of section 631(c) apply. The term "interest in real property" also shall include options to acquire land or im-

Reg. § 1.817-5(h)(7)

45,708   **Life Insurance Companies**

See p. 20,601 for regulations not amended to reflect law changes

→ *Caution: New Code Secs. 801–818 replaced former Code Secs. 801–820 (pre-1984 years), which were repealed. The following Regulations were issued under new Code Secs. 801–818.* ←

provements thereon, and options to acquire leaseholds of land or improvements thereon.

(8) *Interest in a commodity.* The term "interest in a commodity" shall include the ownership and co-ownership of any type of personal property other than a security, and any leaseholds thereof. Such term shall include mineral, oil, and gas royalty interests, including any fractional undivided interest therein. Such term also shall include any put, call, straddle, option, or privilege on any type of personal property other than a security.

(9) *Value.* The term "value" shall mean, with respect to investments for which market quotations are readily available, the market value of such investments; and with respect to other investments, fair value as determined in good faith by the managers of the segregated asset account.

(10) *Terms used in section 851.* To the extent not inconsistent with this paragraph (h) all terms used in this section shall have the same meaning as when used in section 851.

(i) *Effective date*—(1) *In general.* This section is effective for taxable years beginning after December 31, 1983.

(2) *Exceptions.* (i) If, at all times after December 31, 1983, an insurance company would be considered the owner of the assets of a segregated asset account under the principles of Rev. Rul. 81-225, 1981-2 C.B. 12, this section will not apply to such account until December 15, 1986.

(ii) This section will not apply to any variable contract to which Rev. Rul. 77-85, 1977-1 C.B. 12, or Rev. Rul. 81-225, 1981-2 C.B. 12, did not apply by reason of the limited retroactive effect of such rulings.

(iii) In determining whether a segregated asset account is adequately diversified for any calendar quarter ending before July 1, 1988, debt instruments that are issued, guaranteed, or insured by the United States or an instrumentality of the United States shall not be treated as government securities if such debt instruments are secured by a mortgage on real property (other than real property owned by the United States or an instrumentality of the United States) or represent an interest in a pool of debt instruments secured by such mortgages.

(iv) This section shall not apply until January 1, 1989, with respect to a variable contract (as defined in section 817(d)) that (1) provides for the payment of an immediate annuity (as defined in section 72(u)(4)); (2) was outstanding on September 12, 1986; and (3) the segregated asset account on which it was based was, on September 12, 1986, wholly invested in deposits insured by the Federal Deposit Insurance Corporation or the Federal Savings and Loan Insurance Corporation. [Reg. § 1.817-5.]

☐ [T.D. 8242, 3-1-89.]

[Reg. § 1.817A-0]

§ 1.817A-0. Table of contents.—This section lists the captions that appear in section § 1.817A-1:

§ 1.817A-1. Certain modified guaranteed contracts.

(a) Definitions.

(1) Modified guaranteed contract.

(2) Temporary guarantee period.

(3) Equity-indexed modified guaranteed contract.

(4) Non-equity-indexed modified guaranteed contract.

(5) Current market rate for non-equity-indexed modified guaranteed contract.

(6) Current market rate for equity-indexed modified guaranteed contract. [Reserved.]

(b) Applicable interest rates for non-equity-indexed modified guaranteed contracts.

(1) Tax reserves during temporary guarantee period.

(2) Required interest during temporary guarantee period.

(3) Application of section 811(d).

(4) Periods after the end of the temporary guarantee period.

(5) Examples.

(c) Applicable interest rates for equity-indexed modified guaranteed contracts. [Reserved.]

(d) Effective date.

[Reg. § 1.817A-0.]

☐ [T.D. 9058, 5-6-2003.]

[Reg. § 1.817A-1]

§ 1.817A-1. Certain modified guaranteed contracts.—(a) *Definitions*—(1) *Modified guaranteed contract.* The term *modified guaranteed contract* (MGC) is defined in section 817A(d) as an annuity, life insurance, or pension plan contract (other than a variable contract described in section 817) under which all or parts of the amounts received under the contract are allocated to a segregated account. Assets and reserves in

Reg. § 1.817A-0

Life Insurance Companies

See p. 20,601 for regulations not amended to reflect law changes

→ *Caution: New Code Secs. 801–818 replaced former Code Secs. 801–820 (pre-1984 years), which were repealed. The following Regulations were issued under new Code Secs. 801–818.*←

this segregated account must be valued from time to time with reference to market values for annual statement purposes. Further, an MGC must provide either for a net surrender value or for a policyholder's fund (as defined in section 807(e)(1)). If only a portion of a contract is not described in section 817, such portion is treated as a separate contract for purposes of applying section 817A.

(2) *Temporary guarantee period.* An MGC may temporarily guarantee a return other than the permanently guaranteed crediting rate for a period specified in the contract (the *temporary guarantee period*). During the temporary guarantee period, the amount paid to the policyholder upon surrender is usually increased or decreased by a market value adjustment, which is determined by a formula set forth under the terms of the MGC.

(3) *Equity-indexed modified guaranteed contract.* An equity-indexed MGC is an MGC, as defined in paragraph (a)(1) of this section, that provides a return during or at the end of the temporary guarantee period based on the performance of stocks, other equity instruments, or equity-based derivatives.

(4) *Non-equity-indexed modified guaranteed contract.* A non-equity-indexed MGC is an MGC, as defined in paragraph (a)(1) of this section, that provides a return during or at the end of the temporary guarantee period not based on the performance of stocks, other equity instruments, or equity-based derivatives.

(5) *Current market rate for non-equity-indexed modified guaranteed contracts.* The current market rate for a non-equity-indexed MGC issued by an insurer (whether issued in that tax year or a previous one) is the appropriate Treasury constant maturity interest rate published by the Board of Governors of the Federal Reserve System for the month containing the last day of the insurer's taxable year. The appropriate rate is that rate published for Treasury securities with the shortest published maturity that is greater than (or equal to) the remaining duration of the current temporary guarantee period under the MGC.

(6) *Current market rate for equity-indexed modified guaranteed contracts.* [Reserved.]

(b) *Applicable interest rates for non-equity-indexed modified guaranteed contracts*—(1) *Tax reserves during temporary guarantee period.* An insurance company is required to determine the tax reserves for an MGC under sections 807(c)(3) or (d)(2). During a non-equity-indexed MGC's temporary guarantee period, the applicable interest rate to be used under sections 807(c)(3) and (d)(2)(B) is the current market rate, as defined in paragraph (a)(5) of this section.

(2) *Required interest during temporary guarantee period.* During the temporary guarantee period of a non-equity-indexed MGC, the applicable interest rate to be used to determine required interest under section 812(b)(2)(A) is the same current market rate, defined in paragraph (a)(5) of this section, that applies for that period for purposes of sections 807(c)(3) or (d)(2)(B).

(3) *Application of section 811(d).* An additional reserve computation rule applies under section 811(d) for contracts that guarantee certain interest payments beyond the end of the taxable year. Section 811(d) is waived for non-equity-indexed MGCs.

(4) *Periods after the end of the temporary guarantee period.* For periods after the end of the temporary guarantee period, sections 807(c)(3), 807(d)(2)(B), 811(d) and 812(b)(2)(A) are not modified when applied to non-equity-indexed MGCs. None of these sections are affected by the definition of current market rate contained in paragraph (a)(5) of this section once the temporary guarantee period has expired.

(5) *Examples.* The following examples illustrate this paragraph (b):

Example 1. (i) *IC*, a life insurance company as defined in section 816, issues a MGC (the Contract) on August 1 of 1996. The Contract is an annuity contract that gives rise to life insurance reserves, as defined in section 816(b). *IC* is a calendar year taxpayer. The Contract guarantees that interest will be credited at 8 percent per year for the first 8 contract years and 4 percent per year thereafter. During the 8-year temporary guarantee period, the Contract provides for a market value adjustment based on changes in a published bond index and not on the performance of stocks, other equity instruments or equity based derivatives. *IC* has chosen to avail itself of the provisions of these regulations for 1996 and taxable years thereafter. The 10-year Treasury constant maturity interest rate published for December of 1996 was 6.30 percent. The next shortest maturity published for Treasury constant maturity interest rates is 7 years. As of the end of 1996, the remaining duration of the temporary

Reg. § 1.817A-1(b)(5)

45,710 **Life Insurance Companies**

See p. 20,601 for regulations not amended to reflect law changes

→ *Caution: New Code Secs. 801–818 replaced former Code Secs. 801–820 (pre-1984 years), which were repealed. The following Regulations were issued under new Code Secs. 801–818.*←

guarantee period for the Contract was 7 years and 7 months.

(ii) To determine under section 807(d)(2) the end of 1996 reserves for the Contract, *IC* must use a discount interest rate of 6.30 percent for the temporary guarantee period. The interest rate to be used in computing required interest under section 812(b)(2)(A) for 1996 reserves is also 6.30 percent.

(iii) The discount rate applicable to periods outside the 8-year temporary guarantee period is determined under sections 807(c)(3), 807(d)(2)(B), 811(d) and 812(b)(2)(A) without regard to the current market rate.

Example 2. Assume the same facts as in *Example 1* except that it is now the last day of 1998. The remaining duration of the temporary guarantee period under the Contract is now 5 years and 7 months. The 7-year Treasury constant maturity interest rate published for December of 1998 was 4.65 percent. The next shortest duration published for Treasury constant maturity interest rates is 5 years. A discount rate of 4.65 percent is used for the remaining duration of the temporary guarantee period for the purpose of determining a reserve under section 807(d) and for the purpose of determining required interest under section 812(b)(2)(A).

Example 3. Assume the same facts as in *Example 1* except that it is now the last day of 2001. The remaining duration of the temporary guarantee period under the Contract is now 2 years and 7 months. The 3-year Treasury constant maturity interest rate published for December of 2001 was 3.62 percent. The next shortest duration published for Treasury constant maturity interest rates is 2 years. A discount rate of 3.62 percent is used for the remaining duration of the temporary guarantee period for the purpose of determining a reserve under section 807(d) and for the purpose of determining required interest under section 812(b)(2)(A).

(c) *Applicable interest rates for equity-indexed modified guaranteed contracts.* [Reserved.]

(d) *Effective date.* Paragraphs (a), (b) and (d) of this section are effective on May 7, 2003. However, pursuant to section 7805(b)(7), taxpayers may elect to apply those paragraphs retroactively for all taxable years beginning after December 31, 1995, the effective date of section 817A. [Reg. § 1.817A-1.]

☐ [*T.D.* 9058, 5-6-2003.]

→ *Caution: Former Code Secs. 801-820 for pre-1984 years were repealed and replaced by new Code Secs. 801-818. The following Regulations were issued under old Code Secs. 801-820.*←

[Reg. § 1.801-2]

§ 1.801-2. Taxable years affected.—Section 1.801-1 is applicable only to taxable years beginning after December 31, 1953, and before January 1, 1955, and all references to sections of part I, subchapter L, chapter 1 of the Code are to the Internal Revenue Code of 1954, before amendments. Section 1.801-3 through 1.801-7 are applicable only to taxable years beginning after December 31, 1957, and all references to sections of part I, subchapter L, chapter 1 of the Code are to the Internal Revenue Code of 1954, as amended by the Life Insurance Company Income Tax Act of 1959 (73 Stat. 112). Section 1.801-8 is applicable only to taxable years beginning after December 31, 1961, and all references to sections of part I, subchapter L, chapter 1 of the Code are to the Internal Revenue Code of 1954, as amended by the Life Insurance Company Income Tax Act of 1959 (73 Stat. 112) and section 3 of the Act of October 23, 1962 (76 Stat. 1134). [Reg. § 1.801-2.]

☐ [*T.D.* 6513, 12-9-60. Amended by *T.D.* 6886, 6-22-66.]

[Reg. § 1.801-3]

§ 1.801-3. Definitions.—For purposes of part I, subchapter L, chapter 1 of the Code, this section defines the following terms, which are to be used in determining if a taxpayer is a life insurance company (as defined in section 801(a) and paragraph (b) of this section):

(a) *Insurance company.* (1) The term "insurance company" means a company whose primary and predominant business activity during the taxable year is the issuing of insurance or annuity contracts or the reinsuring of risks underwritten by insurance companies. Thus, though its name, charter powers, and subjection to State insurance laws are significant in determining the business which a company is authorized and intends to

Reg. § 1.801-2

Life Insurance Companies

See p. 20,601 for regulations not amended to reflect law changes

→ *Caution: Former Code Secs. 801-820 for pre-1984 years were repealed and replaced by new Code Secs. 801-818. The following Regulations were issued under old Code Secs. 801-820.* ←

carry on, it is the character of the business actually done in the taxable year which determines whether a company is taxable as an insurance company under the Internal Revenue Code.

(2) Insurance companies include both stock and mutual companies, as well as mutual benefit insurance companies. For taxable years beginning before January 1, 1970, a voluntary unincorporated association of employees, including an association fulfilling the requirements of section 801(b)(2)(B) (as in effect for such years) formed for the purpose of relieving sick and aged members, and the dependents of deceased members, is an insurance company, whether the fund for such purpose is created wholly by membership dues or partly by contributions from the employer. A corporation which merely sets aside a fund for the insurance of its employees is not an insurance company, and the income from such fund shall be included in the return of the corporation.

(b) *Life insurance company.* (1) The term "life insurance company", as used in subtitle A of the Code, is defined in section 801(a). For the purpose of determining whether a company is a "life insurance company" within the meaning of that term as used in section 801(a), it must first be determined whether the company is taxable as an insurance company (as defined in paragraph (a) of this section). An insurance company shall be taxed as a life insurance company if it is engaged in the business of issuing life insurance and annuity contracts (either separately or combined with health and accident insurance), or noncancellable contracts of health and accident insurance, and its life insurance reserves (as defined in section 801(b) and § 1.801-4), plus unearned premiums, and unpaid losses (whether or not ascertained), on noncancellable life, health, or accident policies not included in life insurance reserves, comprise more than 50 percent of its total reserves (as defined in section 801(c) and § 1.801-5). For purposes of determining whether it satisfies the percentage requirements of the preceding sentence, a company shall first make any adjustments to life insurance reserves and total reserves required by section 806(a) (relating to adjustments for certain changes in reserves and assets) and then as required by section 801(d) (relating to adjustments in reserves for policy loans). For examples of the adjustments required under section 806(a), see paragraph (b)(4) of § 1.806-3. For an example of the adjustments required under section 801(d), see paragraph (c) of § 1.801-6. Furthermore, if an insurance company which computes its life insurance reserves on a preliminary term basis elects to revalue such reserves on a net level premium basis under section 818(c), such revalued basis shall be disregarded for purposes of section 801.

(2) An insurance company writing only noncancellable life, health, or accident policies and having no "life insurance reserves" may qualify as a life insurance company if its unearned premiums, and unpaid losses (whether or not ascertained), on such policies comprise more than 50 percent of its total reserves.

(3) Section 801(f) provides that a burial or funeral benefit insurance company engaged directly in the manufacture of funeral supplies or the performance of funeral services shall not be taxable under section 802 but shall be taxable under section 821 or section 831 as an insurance company other than life.

(c) *Noncancellable life, health, or accident insurance policy.* The term "noncancellable life, health, or accident insurance policy" means a health and accident contract, or a health and accident contract combined with a life insurance or annuity contract, which the insurance company is under an obligation to renew or continue at a specified premium and with respect to which a reserve in addition to the unearned premiums (as defined in paragraph (e) of this section) must be carried to cover the obligation. Such a health and accident contract shall be considered noncancellable even though it states a termination date at a stipulated age, if, with respect to the health and accident contract, such age termination date is 60 or over. Such a contract, however, shall not be considered to be noncancellable after the age of termination date stipulated in the contract has passed. However, if the age termination date stipulated in the contract occurs during the period covered by a premium received by the life insurance company prior to such date, and the company cannot cancel or modify the contract during such period, the age termination date shall be deemed to occur at the expiration of the period for which the premium has been received.

(d) *Guaranteed renewable life, health, and accident insurance policy.* The term "guaranteed renewable life, health, and accident insurance policy" means a health and accident contract, or a health and accident contract combined with a life insurance or annuity contract, which is not cancellable by the company but under which the company reserves the right to adjust premium rates by classes in accordance with its experience under the type of policy involved, and with re-

Reg. § 1.801-3(d)

45,712 Life Insurance Companies

See p. 20,601 for regulations not amended to reflect law changes

→ *Caution: Former Code Secs. 801-820 for pre-1984 years were repealed and replaced by new Code Secs. 801-818. The following Regulations were issued under old Code Secs. 801-820.*←

spect to which a reserve in addition to the unearned premiums (as defined in paragraph (e) of this section) must be carried to cover that obligation. Section 801(e) provides that such policies shall be treated in the same manner as noncancellable life, health, and accident insurance policies. For example, the age termination date requirements applicable to noncancellable health and accident insurance policies shall also apply to guaranteed renewable life, health, and accident insurance policies. See paragraph (c) of this section.

(e) *Unearned premiums.* The term "unearned premiums" means those amounts which shall cover the cost of carrying the insurance risk for the period for which the premiums have been paid in advance. Such term includes all unearned premiums, whether or not required by law.

(f) *Life insurance reserves.* For the definition of the term "life insurance reserves", see section 801(b) and § 1.801-4.

(g) *Unpaid losses (whether or not ascertained).* The term "unpaid losses (whether or not ascertained)" means a reasonable estimate of the amount of the losses (based upon the facts in each case and the company's experience with similar cases)—

(1) Reported and ascertained by the end of the taxable year but where the amount of the loss has not been paid by the end of the taxable year,

(2) Reported by the end of the taxable year but where the amount thereof has not been either ascertained or paid by the end of the taxable year, or

(3) Which have occurred by the end of the taxable year but which have not been reported or paid by the end of the taxable year.

(h) *Total reserves.* For the definition of the term "total reserves", see section 801(c) and § 1.801-5.

(i) *Amount of reserves.* For purposes of subsections (a), (b), and (c) of section 801 and this section, section 801(b)(5) provides that the amount of any reserve (or portion thereof) for any taxable year shall be the mean of such reserve (or portion thereof) at the beginning and end of the taxable year. [Reg. § 1.801-3.]

☐ [T.D. 6513, 12-9-60. Amended by T.D. 7172, 3-16-72.]

[Reg. § 1.801-4]

§ 1.801-4. **Life insurance reserves.**—(a) *Life insurance reserves defined.* For purposes of part I, subchapter L, chapter 1 of the Code, the term "life insurance reserves" (as defined in section 801(b)) means those amounts—

(1) Which are computed or estimated on the basis of recognized mortality or morbidity tables and assumed rates of interest;

(2) Which are set aside to mature or liquidate, either by payment or reinsurance, future unaccrued claims arising from life insurance, annuity, and noncancellable health and accident insurance contracts (including life insurance or annuity contracts combined with noncancellable health and accident insurance) involving, at the time with respect to which the reserve is computed, life, health, or accident contingencies; and

(3) Which, except as otherwise provided by section 801(b)(2) and paragraphs (b) and (c) of this section, are required by law. For the meaning of the term "reserves required by law", see paragraph (b) of § 1.801-5.

For purposes of determining life insurance reserves, only those amounts shall be taken into account which must be reserved either by express statutory provisions or by rules and regulations of the insurance department of a State, Territory, or the District of Columbia when promulgated in the exercise of a power conferred by statute. Moreover, such amounts must actually be held by the company during the taxable year for which the reserve is claimed. However, reserves held by the company with respect to the net value of risks reinsured in other solvent companies (whether or not authorized) shall be deducted from the company's life insurance reserves. For example, if an ordinary life policy with a reserve of $100 is reinsured in another solvent company on a yearly renewable term basis, and the reserve on such yearly renewable term policy is $10, the reinsured company shall include $90 ($100 minus $10) in determining its life insurance reserves. Generally, life insurance reserves, as in the case of level premium life insurance, are held to supplement the future premium receipts when the latter, alone, are insufficient to cover the increased risk in the later years. For examples of reserves which qualify as life insurance reserves, see paragraph (d) of this section. For examples of reserves which do not qualify as life insurance reserves, see paragraph (e) of this section.

(b) *Certain reserves which need not be required by law.* Section 801(b)(2) sets forth certain reserves which, though not required by law, may still qualify as life insurance reserves, provided,

Reg. § 1.801-4(a)(1)

Life Insurance Companies

See p. 20,601 for regulations not amended to reflect law changes

→ *Caution: Former Code Secs. 801-820 for pre-1984 years were repealed and replaced by new Code Secs. 801-818. The following Regulations were issued under old Code Secs. 801-820.*←

however, that they first satisfy the requirements of section 801(b)(1)(A) and (B) and paragraph (a)(1) and (2) of this section. Thus, reserves need not be required by law—

(1) In the case of policies covering life, health, and accident insurance combined in one policy issued on the weekly premium payment plan, continuing for life and not subject to cancellation, and

(2) For taxable years beginning before January 1, 1970, in the case of policies issued by an organization which met the requirements of section 501(c)(9) (as it existed prior to amendment by the Tax Reform Act of 1969) other than the requirement of subparagraph (B) thereof.

(c) *Assessment companies.* Section 801(b)(3) provides that in the case of an assessment life insurance company or association, the term "life insurance reserves" includes—

(1) Sums actually deposited by such company or association with officers of a State or Territory pursuant to law as guaranty or reserve funds, and

(2) Any funds maintained, under the charter or articles of incorporation or association of such company or association (or bylaws approved by the State insurance commissioner) of such company or association, exclusively for the payment of claims arising under certificates of membership or policies issued upon the assessment plan and not subject to any other use.

For purposes of part I, subchapter L, chapter 1 of the Code, the reserves described in this paragraph shall be included as life insurance reserves even though such reserves do not meet the requirements of section 801(b) and paragraph (a) of this section. However, for such reserves to be included as life insurance reserves, they must be deposited or maintained to liquidate future unaccrued claims arising from life insurance, annuity, or noncancellable health and accident insurance contracts (including life insurance or annuity contracts combined with noncancellable health and accident insurance) involving, at the time with respect to which the reserve is deposited or maintained, life, health, or accident contingencies. The rate of interest assumed in calculating the reserves described in this paragraph shall be 3 percent, regardless of the rate of interest (if any) specified in the contract in respect of such reserves.

(d) *Reserves which qualify as life insurance reserves.* The following reserves, provided they meet the requirements of section 801(b) and paragraph (a) of this section, are illustrative of reserves which shall be included as life insurance reserves:

(1) Reserves held under life insurance contracts.

(2) Reserves held under annuity contracts (including reserves held under variable annuity contracts as described in section 801(g)(1)).

(3) Reserves held under noncancellable health and accident insurance contracts (as defined in paragraph (c) of § 1.801-3) and reserves held under guaranteed renewable health, and accident insurance contracts (as defined in paragraph (d) of § 1.801-3).

(4) Reserves held either separately or combined under contracts described in subparagraphs (1), (2), or (3) of this paragraph.

(5) Reserves held under deposit administration contracts. Generally, the reserves held by a life insurance company on both the active and retired lives under deposit administration contracts will meet the requirements of section 801(b) and paragraph (a) of this section. However, reserves held by the company with respect to the net value of risks reinsured in other solvent companies (whether or not authorized) shall be deducted from the company's life insurance reserves. See paragraph (a) of this section.

(e) *Reserves and liabilities which do not qualify as life insurance reserves.* The following are illustrative of reserves and liabilities which do not meet the requirements of section 801(b) and paragraph (a) of this section and, accordingly, shall not be included as life insurance reserves:

(1) Liability for supplementary contracts not involving at the time with respect to which the liability is computed, life, health, or accident contingencies.

(2) In the case of cancellable health and accident policies and similar cancellable contracts, the unearned premiums and unpaid losses (whether or not ascertained).

(3) The unearned premiums, and unpaid losses (whether or not ascertained), on noncancellable life, health, or accident policies (and guaranteed renewable life, or accident policies) not included in life insurance reserves. (However, such amounts shall be taken into account under section 801(a)(2) for purposes of determining whether an insurance company is a life insurance company.)

Reg. § 1.801-4(e)(3)

Life Insurance Companies

See p. 20,601 for regulations not amended to reflect law changes

→ *Caution: Former Code Secs. 801-820 for pre-1984 years were repealed and replaced by new Code Secs. 801-818. The following Regulations were issued under old Code Secs. 801-820.* ←

(4) The deficiency reserve (as defined in section 801(b)(4)) for each individual contract, that is, that portion of the reserve for such contract equal to the amount (if any) by which—

(i) The present value of the future net premiums required for such contracts, exceeds

(ii) The present value of the future actual premiums and consideration charged for such contract.

(5) Reserves required to be maintained to provide for the ordinary operating expenses of a business which must be currently paid by every company from its income if its business is to continue, such as taxes, salaries, and unpaid brokerage.

(6) Liability for premiums received in advance.

(7) Liability for premium deposit funds.

(8) Liability for annual and deferred dividends declared or apportioned.

(9) Liability for dividends left on deposit at interest.

(10) Liability for accrued but unsettled policy claims whether known or unreported.

(11) A mandatory securities valuation reserve.

(f) *Adjustments to life insurance reserves.* In the event it is determined on the basis of the facts of a particular case that premiums deferred and uncollected and premiums due and unpaid are not properly accruable for the taxable year under section 809 and, accordingly, are not properly includible unders assets (as defined in section 805(b)(4)) for the taxable year, appropriate reduction shall be made in the life insurance reserves. This reduction shall be made when the insurance company has calculated life insurance reserves on the assumption that the premiums on all policies are paid annually or that all premiums due on or prior to the date of the annual statement have been paid. [Reg. § 1.801-4.]

☐ [T.D. 6513, 12-9-60. Amended by T.D. 7172, 3-16-72.]

[Reg. § 1.801-5]

§ 1.801-5. **Total reserves.**—(a) *Total reserves defined.* For purposes of section 801(a) and § 1.801-3, the term "total reserves" is defined in section 801(c) as the sum of—

(1) Life insurance reserves (as defined in section 801(b) and § 1.801-4),

(2) Unearned premiums (as defined in paragraph (e) of § 1.801-3), and unpaid losses (whether or not ascertained) (as defined in paragraph (g) of § 1.801-3), not included in life insurance reserves, and

(3) All other insurance reserves required by law.

The term "total reserves" does not, however, include deficiency reserves (within the meaning of section 801(b)(4) and paragraph (e)(4) of § 1.801-4), even though such deficiency reserves are required by State law. In determining total reserves, a company is permitted to make use of the highest aggregate reserve required by any State or Territory or the District of Columbia in which it transacts business, but the reserve must have been actually held during the taxable year for which the reserve is claimed. For example, during the taxable year 1958 a life insurance company sells life insurance and annuity contracts in States A and B. State A requires reserves of 10 against the life and 5 against the annuity business. State B requires reserves of 9 against the life and 7 against the annuity business. Assuming the company actually holds these reserves during the taxable year 1958, its highest aggregate reserve for such taxable year is the 16 required by State B. Thus, the company is not permitted to compute its highest aggregate reserve by taking State A's requirement of 10 against its life insurance business and adding it to State B's requirement of 7 against its annuity business.

(b) *Reserves required by law defined.* For purposes of part I, subchapter L, chapter 1 of the Code, the term "reserves required by law" means reserves which are required either by express statutory provisions or by rules and regulations of the insurance department of a State, Territory, or the District of Columbia when promulgated in the exercise of a power conferred by statute, and which are reported in the annual statement of the company and accepted by state regulatory authorities as held for the fulfillment of the claims of policyholders or beneficiaries.

(c) *Information to be filed.* In any case where reserves are claimed, sufficient information must be filed with the return to enable the district director to determine the validity of the claim. See section 6012 and paragraph (c) of § 1.6012-2. If the basis (for Federal income tax purposes) for determining the amount of any of the life insurance reserves as of the close of the taxable year differs from the basis for such determination as of the beginning of the taxable year then the follow-

Life Insurance Companies

See p. 20,601 for regulations not amended to reflect law changes

→ *Caution: Former Code Secs. 801-820 for pre-1984 years were repealed and replaced by new Code Secs. 801-818. The following Regulations were issued under old Code Secs. 801-820.* ←

ing information must be filed with respect to all such changes in basis:

(1) The nature of the life insurance reserve (i.e., life, annuity, etc.);

(2) The mortality or morbidity table, assumed rate of interest, method used in computing or estimating such reserve on the old basis, and the amount of such reserve at the beginning and close of the taxable year computed on the old basis;

(3) The mortality or morbidity table, assumed rate of interest, method used in computing or estimating such reserve on the new basis, and the amount of such reserve at the close of the taxable year computed on the new basis;

(4) The deviation, if any, from recognized mortality or morbidity tables, or recognized methods of computation;

(5) The reasons for the change in basis of such reserve; and

(6) Whether such change in the reserve has been approved or accepted by the regulatory authorities of the State of domicile, and if so, a copy of the letter, certificate, or other evidence of such approval or acceptance.

(d) *Illustration of principles.* The provisions of section 801 relating to the percentage requirements for qualification as a life insurance company may be illustrated by the following example:

Example. The books of Y, an insurance company, selling life insurance, noncancellable health and accident insurance, and cancellable accident and health insurance, reflect (after adjustment under sections 806(a) and 801(d)) the following facts for the taxable year 1958:

	Jan. 1	Dec. 31	Mean of Year
1. Life insurance reserves	$3,000	$5,000	$4,000
2. Unearned premiums, and unpaid losses (whether or not ascertained), on noncancellable accident and health insurance not included in life insurance reserves	400	600	500
3. Unearned premiums, and unpaid losses (whether or not ascertained), on cancellable accident and health insurance	1,800	2,200	2,000
4. All other insurance reserves required by law	900	1,100	1,000
5. Total reserves			$7,500

The rules provided by section 801 require that the sum of the mean of the year figures in items 1 and 2 comprise more than 50 percent of the mean of the year figure in item 5 for an insurance company to qualify as a life insurance company. Thus, Y would qualify as a life insurance company for the taxable year 1958 as the sum of the mean of the year figures in items 1 and 2 ($4,500) comprise 60 percent of the mean of the year figure in item 5 ($7,500). [Reg. § 1.801-5.]

☐ [T.D. 6513, 12-9-60.]

[Reg. § 1.801-6]

§ 1.801-6. **Adjustments in reserves for policy loans.**—(a) *In general.* Section 801(d) provides that for purposes only of determining whether or not an insurance company is a life insurance company (as defined in section 801(a) and paragraph (b) of § 1.801-3), the life insurance reserves (as defined in section 801(b) and § 1.801-4), and the total reserves (as defined in section 801(c) and paragraph (a) of § 1.801-5], shall each be reduced by an amount equal to the mean of the aggregates, at the beginning and end of the taxable year, of the policy loans outstanding with respect to contracts for which life insurance reserves are maintained. Such reduction shall be made after any adjustments required under section 806(a) and § 1.806-3 have been made.

(b) *Policy loans defined.* The term "policy loans" includes loans made by the insurance company, by whatever name called, for which the reserve on a contract is the collateral.

(c) *Illustration of principles.* The provisions of section 801(d) and this section may be illustrated by the following example:

Example. The books of T, an insurance company, selling only life insurance and cancellable accident and health insurance, reflect (after adjustment under section 806(a)) the following facts for the taxable year 1958:

Reg. § 1.801-6(c)

Life Insurance Companies

See p. 20,601 for regulations not amended to reflect law changes

→ *Caution: Former Code Secs. 801-820 for pre-1984 years were repealed and replaced by new Code Secs. 801-818. The following Regulations were issued under old Code Secs. 801-820.* ←

	Jan.1	Dec..31	Mean of Year
1. Life insurance reserves	$1,000	$2,000	$1,500
2. Policy loans	50	850	450
3. Life insurance reserves less policy loans			$1,050
4. Unearned premiums, and unpaid losses (whether or not ascertained), on cancellable accident and health insurance	$900	$1,600	$1,250
5. Total reserves adjusted for policy loans (item 3 plus item 4)			$2,300

As the rules provided by section 801(a) and (d) require that the figure in item 3 ($1,050) be more than 50 percent of the mean of the year figure in item 5 ($2,300) for an insurance company to qualify as a life insurance company, T would not qualify as a life insurance company for the taxable year 1958. [Reg. § 1.801-6.]

☐ [*T.D.* 6513, 12-9-60.]

[Reg. § 1.801-7]

§ 1.801-7. Variable annuities.—(a) *In general.*—(1) Section 801(g)(1) provides that for purposes of part I, subchapter L, chapter 1 of the Code, an annuity contract includes a contract which provides for the payment of a variable annuity computed on the basis of recognized mortality tables and the investment experience of the company issuing such a contract. A variable annuity differs from the ordinary or fixed dollar annuity in that the annuity benefits payable under a variable annuity contract vary with the insurance company's investment experience with respect to such contracts while the annuity benefits paid under a fixed dollar annuity contract are guaranteed irrespective of the company's actual investment earnings.

(2) The reserves held with respect to the annuity contracts described in section 801(g)(1) and subparagraph (1) of this paragraph shall qualify as life insurance reserves within the meaning of section 801(b)(1) and paragraph (a) of § 1.801-4 provided such reserves are required by law (as defined in paragraph (b) of § 1.801-5) and are set aside to mature or liquidate, either by payment or reinsurance, future unaccrued claims arising from such contracts involving, at the time with respect to which the reserve is computed, life, health, or accident contingencies. Accordingly, a company issuing variable annuity contracts shall qualify as a life insurance company for Federal income tax purposes if it satisfies the requirements of section 801(a) (relating to the definition of a life insurance company) and paragraph (b) of § 1.801-3.

(b) *Special rules for variable annuities*—(1) *Adjusted reserves rate; assumed rate.* The adjusted reserves rate for any taxable year with respect to the annuity contracts described in section 801(g)(1) and paragraph (a)(1) of this section, and the rate of interest assumed by the taxpayer for any taxable year in calculating the reserve on any such contract, shall be a rate equal to the current earnings rate determined under section 801(g)(3) and subparagraph (2) of this paragraph. However, any change in the rate of interest assumed by the taxpayer in calculating the reserve on a variable annuity contract for any taxable year which is attributable to an increase or decrease in the current earnings rate, shall not be treated as a change of basis in computing reserves for purposes of section 806(b) (relating to certain changes in reserves) or section 810(d)(1) (relating to adjustment for change in computing reserves).

(2) *Current earnings rate.* (i) The current earnings rate for any taxable year with respect to the annuity contracts described in section 801(g)(1) and paragraph (a)(1) of this section shall be the current earnings rate determined under section 805(b)(2) and paragraph (a)(2) of § 1.805-5 with respect to such contracts, reduced by the percentage obtained by dividing (*a*) the amount of the actuarial margin charge on all such variable annuity contracts issued by the taxpayer, by (*b*) the mean of the reserves for such contracts.

(ii) For purposes of section 801(g)(3) and subdivision (i) of this subparagraph, the term "actuarial margin charge" means any amount retained by the company from gross investment income pursuant to the terms of the variable annuity contract in excess of any portion of the investment expenses which is attributable to such contract and which is deductible under section 804(c) and paragraph (b) of § 1.804-4.

(3) *Increases and decreases in reserves.* (i) Section 801(g)(4) provides that for purposes of section 810(a) and (b) (relating to adjustments for increases or decreases in certain reserves), the sum of the items described in section 810(c) and paragraph (b) of § 1.810-2 taken into account as of the close of the taxable year shall be adjusted—

Reg. § 1.801-7(a)(1)

Life Insurance Companies

See p. 20,601 for regulations not amended to reflect law changes

→ *Caution: Former Code Secs. 801-820 for pre-1984 years were repealed and replaced by new Code Secs. 801-818. The following Regulations were issued under old Code Secs. 801-820.*←

(*a*) By subtracting therefrom the sum of any amounts added from time to time (for the taxable year) to the reserves for variable annuity contracts described in section 801(g)(1) and paragraph (a)(1) of this section by reason of realized or unrealized appreciation in the value of the assets held in relation thereto, and

(*b*) By adding thereto the sum of any amounts subtracted from time to time (for the taxable year) from such reserves by reason of realized or unrealized depreciation in the value of such assets.

(ii) The application of section 801(g)(4) and subdivision (i) of this subparagraph may be illustrated by the following example:

Example. Company M, a life insurance company issuing only variable annuity contracts of the type described in section 801(g)(1) and paragraph (a)(1) of this section, increased its life insurance reserves held with respect to such contracts during the taxable year 1959 by $275,000. Of the total increase in the reserves, $100,000 was attributable to premium receipts, $50,000 to dividends and interest, $100,000 to unrealized appreciation in the value of the assets held in relation to such reserves, and $25,000 to realized capital gains on the sale of such assets. As of the close of the taxable year 1959, the reserves held by Company M with respect to all variable annuity contracts amounted to $1,275,000. However, under section 801(g)(4) and subdivision (i) of this subparagraph, this amount must be reduced by the $100,000 unrealized asset value appreciation and the $25,000 of realized capital gains. Accordingly, for purposes of section 810(a) and (b), the amount of these reserves which is to be taken into account as of the close of the taxable year 1959 under section 810(c) is $1,150,000 ($1,275,000 less $125,000).

(c) *Companies issuing variable annuities and other contracts.* (1) In the case of a life insurance company which issues both annuity contracts described in section 801(g)(1) and paragraph (a)(1) of this section and other contracts, the policy and other contract liability requirements (as defined in section 805(a) and paragraph (b) of § 1.805-4) of such a company for any taxable year shall be considered to be the sum of—

(i) The policy and other contract liability requirements computed with respect to the items which relate to such variable annuity contracts, and

(ii) The policy and other contract liability requirements computed by excluding the items taken into account under subdivision (i) of this subparagraph.

(2) [Reserved for regulations to be issued under section 801(g)(5)(B).]

(d) *Termination.* Paragraphs (1), (2), (3), (4), and (5) of section 801(g) and paragraphs (a), (b), and (c) of § 1.801-7 shall not apply with respect to any taxable year beginning after December 31, 1962. [Reg. § 1.801-7.]

☐ [*T.D.* 6610, 8-30-62.]

[Reg. § 1.801-8]

§ 1.801-8. **Contracts with reserves based on segregated asset accounts.**—(a) *Definitions*—(1) *Annuity contracts include variable annuity contracts.* Section 801(g)(1)(A) provides that for purposes of part I, subchapter L, chapter 1 of the Code, an annuity contract includes a contract which provides for the payment of a variable annuity computed on the basis of recognized mortality tables and the investment experience of the company issuing such a contract. A variable annuity differs from the ordinary or fixed dollar annuity in that the annuity benefits payable under a variable annuity contract vary with the insurance company's investment experience with respect to such contracts while the annuity benefits paid under a fixed dollar annuity contract are guaranteed irrespective of the company's actual investment earnings.

(2) *Contracts with reserves based on a segregated asset account.* (i) For purposes of part I, section 801(g)(1)(B) defines the term "contract with reserves based on a segregated asset account" as a contract (individual or group)—

(*a*) Which provides for the allocation of all or part of the amounts received under the contract to an account which, pursuant to State law or regulation, is segregated from the general asset accounts of the company,

(*b*) Which provides for the payment of annuities, and

(*c*) Under which the amounts paid in, or the amount paid as annuities, reflect the investment return and the market value of the segregated asset account.

(ii) The term "contract with reserves based on a segregated asset account" includes a contract such as a variable annuity contract, which reflects the investment return and the market value of the segregated asset account, even

→ **Caution:** *Former Code Secs. 801-820 for pre-1984 years were repealed and replaced by new Code Secs. 801-818. The following Regulations were issued under old Code Secs. 801-820.* ←

though such contract provides for the payment of an annuity computed on the basis of recognized mortality tables, but the term includes such contract only for the period during which it satisfies the requirements of section 801(g)(1)(B) and the subdivision (i) of this subparagraph. However, such term does not include a pension contract written on the basis of the so-called new-money concept. Thus, for example, such term does not include a pension contract whereby reserves are credited on the basis of the company's new high yield investments. Furthermore, such term does not include a contract which during the taxable year contains a right to participate in the divisible surplus of the company where such right merely reflects the company's investment return. Nevertheless, the term does include a contract which meets the requirements of section 801(g)(1)(B) and of this subparagraph even if part of the amounts received are, for example, allocated to reserves under provisions of the contract which are written on the basis of the new-money concept. However, such reserves do not qualify as a segregated asset account referred to in section 801(g) and this section.

(iii) If at any time during the taxable year a contract otherwise satisfying the requirements of section 801(g)(1)(B) and subdivision (i) of this subparagraph ceases to reflect current investment return and current market value, such contract shall not be considered as meeting the requirements of section 801(g)(1)(B)(iii) and subdivision (i)(c) of this subparagraph after such cessation. Thus, a contract with reserves based on a segregated asset account includes a contract under which the reflection of investment return and market value terminates at the beginning of the annuity payments, but only for the period prior to such termination. For example, if the purchaser of a variable annuity contract which meets such requirements elects an option which provides for the payment of a fixed dollar annuity, then such contract shall be considered as satisfying such requirements only for the period prior to the time such contract ceases to reflect current investment return and current market value. Furthermore, a group annuity contract which satisfies the requirements of section 801(g)(1)(B) and subdivision (i) of this subparagraph shall be considered as continuing to meet such requirements even though a certificate holder under the group contract elects an option which provides for the payment of a fixed dollar annuity. However, the annuity attributable to such certificate holder shall not be considered as satisfying such requirements as of the time such annuity ceases to reflect current investment return and current market value. On the other hand, a group annuity contract which does not reflect current market value shall not be considered as satisfying such requirements even though a certificate holder under the group contract elects an option which provides for the payment of a variable annuity. However, the variable annuity attributable to such certificate holder shall be considered as satisfying such requirements as of the time such variable annuity commences to reflect current investment return and current market value.

(b) *Life insurance reserves.* Section 801(g)(2) provides that for purposes of section 801(b)(1)(A), the reflection of the investment return and the market value of the segregated asset account shall be considered an assumed rate of interest. Thus, the reserves held with respect to contracts described in section 801(g)(1) and paragraph (a) of this section shall qualify as life insurance reserves within the meaning of section 801(b)(1) and paragraph (a) of § 1.801-4 provided such reserves are required by law (as defined in paragraph (b) of § 1.801-5) and are set aside to mature or liquidate, either by payment or reinsurance, future unaccrued claims arising from such contracts with reserves based on segregated asset accounts involving, at the time with respect to which the reserve is computed, life, health, or accident contingencies. Accordingly, a company issuing contracts with reserves based on segregated asset accounts shall qualify as a life insurance company for Federal income tax purposes if it satisfies the requirements of section 801(a) (relating to the definition of a life insurance company) and paragraph (b) of § 1.801-3.

(c) *Separate accounting.* (1) For purposes of part I, section 801(g)(3) provides that a life insurance company (as defined in section 801(a) and paragraph (b) of § 1.801-3) which issues contracts with reserves based on segregated asset accounts (as defined in section 801(g)(1)(B) and paragraph (a)(2) of this section) shall separately account for each and every income, exclusion, deduction, asset, reserve, and other liability item which is properly attributable to such segregated asset accounts. In those cases where such items are not directly accounted for, separate accounting shall be made—

(i) According to the method regularly employed by the company, if such method is reasonable, and

Reg. § 1.801-8(b)

Life Insurance Companies

→ Caution: Former Code Secs. 801-820 for pre-1984 years were repealed and replaced by new Code Secs. 801-818. The following Regulations were issued under old Code Secs. 801-820. ←

(ii) In all other cases in a manner which, in the opinion of the district director, is reasonable.

A method of separate accounting for such items as are not accounted for directly will be deemed "regularly employed" by a life insurance company if the method was consistently followed in prior taxable years, or if, in the case of a company which has never before issued contracts with reserves based on segregated asset accounts, the company initiates in the first taxable year for which it issues such contracts a reasonable method of separate accounting for such items and consistently follows such method thereafter. Ordinarily, a company regularly employs a method of accounting in accordance with the statute of the State, Territory, or the District of Columbia, in which it operates.

(2) Every life insurance company issuing contracts with reserves based on segregated asset accounts shall keep such permanent records and other data relating to such contracts as is necessary to enable the district director to determine the correctness of the application of the rules prescribed in section 801(g) and this section and to ascertain the accuracy of the computations involved.

(d) *Investment yield.* (1) For purposes of part I, section 801(g)(4)(A) provides that the policy and other contract liability requirements (as determined under section 805), and the life insurance company's share of investment yield (as determined under section 804(a) or 809(b)), shall be separately computed—

(i) With respect to the items separately accounted for in accordance with section 801(g)(3) and paragraph (c) of this section, and

(ii) Excluding the items taken into account under subdivision (i) of this subparagraph.

Thus, for purposes of determining both taxable investment income and gain or loss from operations, a life insurance company shall separately compute the life insurance company's share of the investment yield on the assets in its segregated asset account without regard to the policy and other contract liability requirements of, and the investment income attributable to, contracts with reserves that are not based on the segregated asset account. Such separate computations shall be made after any allocation required under section 801(g)(4)(B) and subparagraph (2) of this paragraph.

(2)(i) Section 801(g)(4)(B) provides that if the net short-term capital gain (as defined in section 1222(5)) exceeds the net long-term capital loss (as defined in section 1222(8)), determined without regard to any separate computations under section 801(g)(4)(A) and subparagraph (1) of this paragraph, then such excess shall be allocated between section 801(g)(4)(A)(i) and (ii) and subparagraph (1)(i) and (ii) of this paragraph. Such allocation shall be in proportion to the respective contributions to such excess of the items taken into account under each such section and subparagraph. The allocation under this subparagraph shall be made before the separate computations prescribed by section 801(g)(4)(A) and subparagraph (1) of this paragraph.

(ii) The operation of the allocation required under section 801(g)(4)(B) and subdivision (i) of this subparagraph may be illustrated by the following examples:

Example (1). For the taxable year 1962, T, a life insurance company which issues regular life insurance and annuity contracts and contracts with reserves based on segregated asset accounts, had (without regard to section 801(g)(4)(A)) realized short-term capital gains of $10,000 and short-term capital losses of $10,000 attributable to its general asset accounts and realized short-term capital gains of $12,000 attributable to its segregated asset accounts. For the taxable year 1962, the excess of the net short-term capital gain ($10,000 plus $12,000 minus $10,000, or $12,000) over the net long-term capital loss (0) was $12,000. Of the excess of $12,000, 100 percent was contributed by the segregated asset accounts. Applying the provisions of section 801(g)(4)(B), T would allocate the entire $12,000 to its segregated asset accounts for such taxable year.

Example (2). The facts are the same as in example (1), except that for the taxable year 1962, T had (without regard to section 801(g)(4)(A)) realized short-term capital losses of $8,000 attributable to its general asset accounts and realized long-term capital gains of $1,000 and long-term capital losses of $5,000 attributable to its segregated asset accounts. For the taxable year 1962, the excess of the net short-term capital gain ($10,000 plus $12,000 minus $8,000, or $14,000) over the net long-term capital loss ($5,000 minus $1,000, or $4,000) was $10,000. Of the excess of $10,000, the general asset accounts contributed 20 percent ($2,000 ($10,000 minus $8,000) ÷ $10,000) and the segregated asset accounts contributed 80 percent ($8,000 ($12,000 minus $4,000) ÷ $10,000). Applying the provisions of section 801(g)(4)(B), T would allocate $2,000

Reg. § 1.801-8(d)(2)

45,720 Life Insurance Companies

See p. 20,601 for regulations not amended to reflect law changes

→ *Caution: Former Code Secs. 801-820 for pre-1984 years were repealed and replaced by new Code Secs. 801-818. The following Regulations were issued under old Code Secs. 801-820.*←

($10,000 multiplied by 20 percent) to its general asset accounts and $8,000 ($10,000 multiplied by 80 percent) to its segregated asset accounts for such taxable year.

Example (3). W is a life insurance company which issues regular life insurance and annuity contracts and contracts with reserves based on either of two segregated asset accounts, Separate Account C or Separate Account D. For the taxable year 1962, W had (without regard to section 801(g)(4)(A)) realized short-term capital gains of $16,000 and long-term capital losses of $15,000 attributable to its general asset accounts, long-term capital gains of $12,000 and short-term capital losses of $6,000 attributable to Separate Account C and long-term capital gains of $7,000 and short-term capital losses of $5,000 attributable to Separate Account D. For the taxable year 1962, the excess of the net short-term capital gain ($16,000—$6,000—$5,000) over the net long-term capital loss (0) was $5,000. Of the $5,000 excess, 20 percent ($16,000 − $15,000 ÷ $5,000) was contributed by the general asset accounts, leaving 80 percent as the amount contributed by the segregated asset accounts. Applying the provisions of section 801(g)(4)(B), W would allocate $1,000 (20% of $5,000) to the general asset accounts, leaving $4,000 (80% of $5,000) to be allocated among the segregated asset accounts, Separate Account C and Separate Account D. W would allocate $3,000 of the $4,000 to Separate Account C computed as follows:

$$\$3{,}000 = \frac{(\$4{,}000) \times (\$12{,}000 - \$6{,}000)}{(\$12{,}000 - \$6{,}000) + (\$7{,}000 - \$5{,}000)}$$

W would allocate $1,000 of the $4,000 to Separate Account D computed as follows:

$$\$1{,}000 = \frac{(\$4{,}000) \times (\$7{,}000 - \$5{,}000)}{(\$12{,}000 - \$6{,}000) + (\$7{,}000 - \$5{,}000)}$$

(e) *Policy and other contract liability requirements.*—(1) For purposes of part I, section 8001(g)(5)(A) provides that with respect to life insurance reserves based on segregated asset accounts (as defined in section 801(g)(1)(B) and paragraph (a)(2) of this section), the adjusted reserves rate and the current earnings rate for purposes of section 805(b), and the rate of interest assumed by the taxpayer for purposes of sections 805(c) and 809(a)(2), shall be a rate equal to the current earnings rate determined under section 805(b)(2) and paragraph (a)(2) of § 1.805-5 with respect to the items separately accounted for in accordance with section 801(g)(3), reduced by the percentage obtained by dividing—

(i) Any amount retained with respect to all of the reserves based on a segregated asset account by the life insurance company from gross investment income (as defined in section 804(b) and paragraph (a) of § 1.804-3) on segregated assets, to the extent such retained amount exceeds the deductions allowable under section 804(c) which are attributable to such reserves, by

(ii) The means of such reserves.

(2) For purposes of part I, section 801(g)(5)(B) provides that with respect to reserves based on segregated asset accounts other than life insurance reserves, there shall be included as interest paid within the meaning of section 805(e)(1) and paragraph (b)(1) of § 1.805-8 an amount equal to the product of the means of such reserves multiplied by the rate of interest assumed as defined in section 801(g)(5)(A) and subparagraph (1) of this paragraph.

(3) For purposes of this paragraph, any change in the rate of interest assumed by the taxpayer in calculating the reserve on a contract with reserves based on a segregated asset account for any taxable year beginning after December 31, 1961, which is attributable to an increase or decrease in the current earnings rate, shall not be treated as a change of basis in computing reserves for purposes of section 806(b) (relating to certain changes in reserves) or section 810(d)(1) (relating to adjustment for change in computing reserves).

(4) The provisions of section 801(g)(3) through (5) may be illustrated by the following example. For purposes of this example, it is assumed that all computations have been carried out to a sufficient number of decimal places to insure substantial accuracy and to eliminate any significant error in the resulting tax liability.

Example. The books of R, a life insurance company, discloses the following facts with respect to items of investment yield, deductions, assets, and reserves for the taxable year 1962:

(a) *Excerpts from Company Financial Statements.*

Reg. § 1.801-8(e)(1)

Life Insurance Companies

See p. 20,601 for regulations not amended to reflect law changes

→ *Caution: Former Code Secs. 801-820 for pre-1984 years were repealed and replaced by new Code Secs. 801-818. The following Regulations were issued under old Code Secs. 801-820.*←

	Company Regular Account	Separate Account A	Separate Account B
(1) Investment yield:			
Interest wholly tax-exempt	$100,000	$3,000	$1,000
Interest—other	10,000,000	8,000	15,000
Dividends received	200,000	25,000	27,000
Other items of investment yield	100,000	2,000	1,000
Gross investment income	10,400,000	38,000	44,000
Less deductions (sec. 804(c))	1,000,000	4,000	4,400
Investment yield	9,400,000	34,000	39,600
(2) Assets and reserves:			
(i) Assets:			
January 1, 1962	190,000,000		
December 31, 1962	210,000,000	1,600,000	1,800,000
Mean	200,000,000	800,000	900,000
(ii) Life insurance reserves:			
January 1, 1962	152,000,000		
December 31, 1962	168,000,000	1,600,000	1,640,000
Mean	160,000,000	800,000	820,000
(iii) Reserves based on segregated asset accounts other than life insurance reserves:			
January 1, 1962			
December 31, 1962			120,000
Mean	160,000,000	800,000	820,000

(b) *Additional facts.* In addition to the facts assumed in (a) above, assume the following: The company retained with respect to reserves based upon segregated asset accounts a total of $4,720 from gross investment income on Separate Account A and $5,720 from gross investment income on Separate Account B. With respect to the Company Regular Account computed without regard to the items in either of the separate accounts, the policy and other contract liability requirement is $6,580,000 and the required interest is $5,640,000. There are no items of interest paid with respect to the separate accounts other than those computed under section 801(g)(5)(B). Based on these facts, the current earnings rate (sec. 805(b)); adjusted reserves rate (sec. 805(b)); and rate of interest assumed (secs. 805(c) and 809(a)(2)); and the policy and other contract liability requirements are determined for each of the Separate Accounts A and B (and the policy and other contract liability requirements for the Company Regular Account) as set forth in items (c) through (l) below.

(c) *Separate Account A.* The current earnings rate determined under section 805(b)(2) with respect to the items separately accounted for under Separate Account A, prior to the reduction provided for under section 801(g)(5)(A), is 4.25 percent (the investment yield, $34,000, divided by the mean of the assets, $800,000). The company retained with respect to such reserves from gross investment income on Separate Account A a total of $4,720. The company had deductions allowable under section 804(c) with respect to such account of $4,000. Accordingly, for purposes of section 801(g)(5)(A)(i), the amount retained by the company was $720 (the total amount retained of $4,720 less the deductions allowable under section 804(c) of $4,000). The reduction percentage for purposes of section 801(g)(5)(A) is 0.09 percent (the amount retained of $720 divided by the mean of the life insurance reserves of $800,000). Therefore, the adjusted reserves rate and the current earnings rate for purposes of section 805(b), and the rate of interest assumed for purposes of sections 805(c) and 809(a)(2) is equal to 4.16% (the current earnings rate of 4.25% less the reduction percentage of 0.09 percent).

The policy and other contract liability requirements with respect to Separate Account A is determined as follows: For purposes of section 805(a)(1) and (2), the amount is $33,280 (the mean of the life insurance reserves, $800,000, multiplied by the current earnings rate, as determined under section 801(g)(5)(A), 4.16 percent). Thus, the policy and other contract liability requirement for Separate Account A is $33,280.

(d) *Separate Account B.* The current earnings rate determined under section 805(b)(2) with respect to the items separately accounted for under Separate Account B, prior to the reduction provided for under section 801(g)(5)(A), is 4.40 percent (the investment yield, $39,600 divided by the mean of the assets, $900,000). The company retained with respect to such reserves from gross investment income on Separate Account B a total

Reg. § 1.801-8(e)(4)

→ *Caution: Former Code Secs. 801-820 for pre-1984 years were repealed and replaced by new Code Secs. 801-818. The following Regulations were issued under old Code Secs. 801-820.*←

of $5,720. The company had deductions allowable under section 804(c) with respect to such account of $4,400. Accordingly, for purposes of section 801(g)(5)(A)(i) the amount retained by the company was $1,320 (the total amount retained of $5,720 less the deductions allowable under section 804(c) of $4,400). The reduction percentage for purposes of section 801(g)(5)(A) is 0.15 percent (the amount retained of $1,320 divided by the mean of the reserves based on Separate Account B of $880,000 ($820,000 plus $60,000)). Therefore, the adjusted reserves rate and the current earnings rate for purposes of section 805(b), and the rate of interest assumed for purposes of section 805(c) and 809(a)(2) is equal to 4.25 percent (the current earnings rate of 4.40 percent less the reduction percentage of 0.15 percent).

With respect to reserves based on segregated asset accounts other than life insurance reserves, Separate Account B had such reserves at December 31, 1962, of $120,000. The mean of such reserves was $60,000. The rate of interest assumed with respect to such reserves is 4.25 percent, as computed above. Accordingly, there shall be included as interest paid within the meaning of section 805(e)(1) the amount of $2,550 (the mean of such reserves, $60,000 multiplied by the rate of interest assumed of 4.25 percent).

The policy and other contract liability requirements with respect to Separate Account B is determined as follows:

(1) For purposes of section 805(a)(1) and (2), the amount is $34,850 (the mean of the life insurance reserves, $820,000, multiplied by the current earnings rate, as determined under section 801(g)(5)(A), 4.25 percent).

(2) For purposes of section 805(a)(3), the amount is $2,550 (the mean of the reserves based on Separate Account B other than life insurance reserves $60,000, multiplied by the rate of interest assumed, as determined under section 801(g)(5)(A), 4.25 percent). It has been assumed that there was no other interest paid on Separate Account B within the meaning of section 805(e).

If there was other interest paid with respect to Separate Account B that met the requirements of section 805(e), however, then such interest would be included under section 805(a)(3). Thus, the policy and other contract liability requirement for Separate Account B is $37,400 ($34,850 plus $2,550).

(e) *Company Regular Account.* The policy and other contract liability requirement with respect to the Company Regular Account is $6,580,000 (this amount is determined by the company in the manner provided by section 805 (and the regulations thereunder) without regard to either Separate Account A or Separate Account B).

(f) *Policyholders' share and company's share of investment yield—section 804.* The policyholders' and company's share of investment yield and taxable investment income are computed as follows:

(1) Company Regular Account:
Policyholders' share of investment yield .. 70% ($6,580,000 divided by $9,400,000)
Company's share of investment yield (100% less 70%) ... 30%

(2) Separate Account A:
Policyholders' share of investment yield .. 97.8824% ($33,280 divided by $34,000)
Company's share of investment yield (100% less 97.8824%) 2.1176%

(3) Separate Account B:
Policyholders' share of investment yield .. 94.444% ($37,400 divided by $39,600)
Company's share of investment yield (100% less 94.444%) 5.556%

(g) The company's share of investment yield under section 804 is determined as follows:

Investment Yield (from item (a)(1))	Company Regular Acct. (30 percent × each amount in item (a)(1))	Separate Acct. A (2.1176 percent × each amount in item (a)(1))	Separate Acct. B (5.556 percent × each amount in item (a)(1))
Interest wholly tax exempt	$ 30,000	$ 63.53	$ 55.56
Interest—other	3,000,000	169.41	833.40

Reg. § 1.801-8(e)(4)

Life Insurance Companies

See p. 20,601 for regulations not amended to reflect law changes

→ *Caution: Former Code Secs. 801-820 for pre-1984 years were repealed and replaced by new Code Secs. 801-818. The following Regulations were issued under old Code Secs. 801-820.* ←

Dividends received	60,000	529.40	1,500.12
Other items of gross investment income	30,000	42.35	55.56
	3,120,000	804.69	2,444.64
Less deductions	300,000	84.70	244.46
Investment yield	$2,820,000	$719.99	$2,200.18

(h) *Taxable investment income.* The company's taxable investment income (without regard to any excess of net long-term capital gain over net short-term capital loss) is determined as follows:

Life insurance company's share of investment yield ($2,820,000 plus $719.99 plus $2,200.18)	$2,822,920.17
Less:	
Company's share of interest wholly tax-exempt ($30,000 plus $63.53 plus $55.56)	$30,119.09
85% of company's share of dividends received (but not to exceed 85% of taxable investment income computed without regard to this deduction) (85% × $62,029.52) ($60,000 plus $529.40 plus $1,500.12)	52,725.09
Small business deduction (10% of investment yield, $9,473,600, not to exceed $25,000)	25,000.00
	$ 107,844.18
Taxable Investment Income	$2,715,075.99

(i) *Required interest—section 809(a)(2)*—

(1) *Separate Account A.* The rate of interest assumed by the company with respect to Separate Account A is 4.16% (see (c) above). The required interest for purposes of section 809(a)(2) is determined as follows:

Life insurance reserves: 4.16% (rate assumed) times $800,000 (mean of life insurance reserves)	$33,280.00

(2) *Separate Account B.* The rate of interest assumed by the company with respect to Separate Account B is 4.25% (see (d) above). The required interest for purposes of section 809(a)(2) is determined as follows:

(i) Life insurance reserves: 4.25% (rate assumed) times $820,000 (mean of life insurance reserves)	$34,850.00
(ii) Other section 810(c) reserves: 4.25% (rate assumed) times $60,000 (mean of reserves other than life insurance reserves)	2,550.00
	$37,400.00

(3) *Company Regular Account.* The required interest with respect to the Company Regular Account is $5,640,000 (this amount is assumed for purposes of this example but it would be determined by the company in the manner provided by section 809 without regard to either Separate Account A or Separate Account B).

(j) *Policyholders' share and company's share of investment yield—section 809.* The policyholders' share and the company's share of investment yield for purposes of section 809 is determined as follows:

(1) *Company Regular Account:*		
Policyholders' share of investment yield	60%	($5,640,000 divided by $9,400,000)
Company's share of investment yield (100% minus 60%)	40%	
(2) *Separate Account A:*		
Policyholders' share of investment yield	97.8824%	($33,280 divided by $34,000)
Company's share of investment yield (100% minus 97.8824%)	2.1176%	
(3) *Separate Account B:*		
Policyholders' share of investment yield	94.444%	($37,400 divided by $39,600)
Company's share of investment yield (100% minus 94.444%)	5.556%	

Reg. § 1.801-8(e)(4)

Life Insurance Companies

See p. 20,601 for regulations not amended to reflect law changes

→ *Caution: Former Code Secs. 801-820 for pre-1984 years were repealed and replaced by new Code Secs. 801-818. The following Regulations were issued under old Code Secs. 801-820.*←

(k) The company's share of investment yield under section 809 is determined as follows:

	Investment Yield (from item (a)(1))	Company Regular Acct. (40% × each amount in item (a)(1))	Separate Acct. A (2.1176% × each amount in item (a)(1))	Separate Acct. B (5.556% × each amount in item (a)(1))
Interest wholly tax-exempt		$ 40,000	$ 63.53	$ 55.56
Interest—other		4,000,000	169.41	833.40
Dividends received		80,000	529.40	1,500.12
Other items of gross investment income		40,000	42.35	55.56
		4,160,000	804.69	2,444.64
Less deductions		400,000	84.70	244.46
Investment yield		3,760,000	719.99	2,200.18

(l) *Deductions under section 809(d)(8).* For purposes of section 809(d)(8), the life insurance company's share of each of such items is determined as follows:

(1) Wholly tax-exempt interest ($40,000 plus $63.53 plus $55.56) . . $40,119.09
(2) Dividends received 85% × $82,029.52 ($80,000 plus $529.40 plus $1,500.12) (it is assumed for purposes of this example that this amount does not exceed 85% of the gain from operations as computed under sec. 809(d)(8)(B)) 69,725.09

(f) *Increases and decreases in reserves.* (1) Section 801(g)(6) provides that for purposes of section 810(a) and (b) (relating to adjustments for increases or decreases in certain reserves), the sum of the items described in section 810(c) and paragraph (b) of § 1.810-2 taken into account as of the close of the taxable year shall be adjusted—

(i) By subtracting therefrom the sum of any amounts added from time to time (for the taxable year) to the reserves separately accounted for in accordance with section 801(g)(3) and paragraph (c) of this section by reason of realized or unrealized appreciation in value of the assets held in relation thereto, and

(ii) By adding thereto the sum of any amounts subtracted from time to time (for the taxable year) from such reserves by reason of realized or unrealized depreciation in the value of such assets.

(2) The provisions of subparagraph (1) of this paragraph may be illustrated by the following example:

Example: Company M, a life insurance company issuing only contracts with reserves based on segregated asset accounts as defined in section 801(g)(1)(B) and paragraph (a)(2) of this section (other than contracts described in section 805(d)(1)(A), (B), (C), (D), or (E), increased its life insurance reserves held with respect to such contracts during the taxable year 1962 by $275,000. Of the total increase in the reserves, $100,000 was attributable to premium receipts, $50,000 to dividends and interest, $100,000 to unrealized appreciation in the value of the assets held in relation to such reserves, and $25,000 to realized capital gains on the sale of such assets. As of the close of the taxable year 1962, the reserves held by company M with respect to all such contracts amounted to $1,275,000. However, under section 801(g)(6) and this subparagraph, this amount must be reduced by the $100,000 unrealized asset value appreciation and the $25,000 of realized capital gains. Accordingly, for purposes of section 810(a) and (b), the amount of these reserves which is to be taken into account as of the close of the taxable year 1962 under section 810(c) is $1,150,000 ($1,275,000 less $125,000). However, for purposes of section 810(a) and (b), the amount of these reserves which is to be taken into account as of the beginning of the taxable year 1963 under section 810(c) is $1,275,000 (the amount as of the close of the taxable year 1962 before reduction of $125,000 for unrealized appreciation and realized capital gains).

(3)(i) Under section 801(g)(6), the deduction allowable for items described in section 809(d)(1) and (7) (relating to death benefits and assumption reinsurance, respectively) with respect to segregated asset accounts shall be reduced to the extent that the amount of such items is increased for the taxable year by appreciation (or shall be increased to the extent that the amount of such items is decreased for the taxable year by depreci-

Reg. § 1.801-8(f)(2)

Life Insurance Companies

See p. 20,601 for regulations not amended to reflect law changes

→ *Caution: Former Code Secs. 801-820 for pre-1984 years were repealed and replaced by new Code Secs. 801-818. The following Regulations were issued under old Code Secs. 801-820.*←

ation) not reflected in adjustments required to be made under subparagraph (1) of this paragraph.

(ii) The provisions of this subparagraph may be illustrated by the following example:

Example: On June 30, 1962, X, a life insurance company, reinsured a portion of its insurance contracts with reserves based on segregated asset accounts with Y, a life insurance company, under an agreement whereby Y agreed to assume and become solely liable under the contracts reinsured. The reserves on the contracts reinsured by X were $90,000, of which $10,000 was attributable to unrealized appreciation in the value of the assets held in relation to such reserves. However, no amounts had been added to the reserves by reason of the unrealized appreciation of $10,000 and consequently, the $10,000 was not reflected in adjustments to reserves under section 809(g)(6) or subparagraph (1) of this paragraph. Under the reinsurance agreement, X made a payment of $90,000 in cash to Y for assuming such contracts. Applying the provisions of section 809 (d)(7), and assuming no other such reinsurance transactions by X during the taxable year, X would have an allowable deduction of $90,000 as a result of this payment on June 30, 1962. However, applying the provisions of section 801(g)(6) and this subparagraph, the actual deduction allowed would be $80,000 ($90,000 less $10,000). See section 806(a) and § 1.806-3 for the adjustments in reserves and assets to be made by X and Y as a result of this transaction. For the treatment by Y of this $90,000 payment, see section 809(c)(1) and paragraph (a)(1)(i) of § 1.809-4.

(g) *Basis of assets held for certain pension plan contracts.* Section 801(g)(7) provides that in the case of contracts described in section 805(d)(1)(A), (B), (C), (D), or (E) (relating to the definition of pension plan reserves), the basis of each asset in a segregated asset account shall (in addition to all other adjustments to basis) be (i) increased by the amount of any appreciation in value, and (ii) decreased by the amount of any depreciation in value; but only to the extent that such appreciation and depreciation are reflected in the increases and decreases in reserves, or other items described in section 801(g)(6), with respect to such contracts. Thus, there shall be no capital gains tax payable by a life insurance company on appreciation realized on assets in a segregated asset account to the extent such appreciation has been reflected in reserves, or other items, described in section 801(g)(6), for contracts described in section 805(d)(1)(A), (B), (C), or (D), based on segregated asset accounts.

(h) *Additional separate computation*—(1) *Assets and total insurance liabilities.* A life insurance company which issues contracts with reserves based on segregated asset accounts (as defined in section 801(g)(1)(B) and paragraph (a)(2) of this section) shall separately compute and report with its return the assets and total insurance liabilities which are properly attributable to all of such segregated asset accounts. Each foreign corporation carrying on a life insurance business which issues such contracts shall separately compute and report with its return assets held in the United States and total insurance liabilities on United States business which are properly attributable to all of such segregated asset accounts.

(2) *Foreign life insurance companies.* For adjustment under section 819 in the case of a foreign life insurance company which issues contracts based on segregated asset accounts under section 801(g), see § 1.819-2(b)(4). [Reg. § 1.801-8.]

☐ [*T.D. 6886, 6-22-66. Amended by T.D. 6970, 8-23-68 and T.D. 7501, 8-22-77.*]

[Reg. § 1.802-2]

§ 1.802-2. **Taxable years affected.**—Section 1.802(b)-1 is applicable only to taxable years beginning after December 31, 1953, and before January 1, 1955, and all references to sections of part I, subchapter L, chapter 1 of the Code are to the Internal Revenue Code of 1954, before amendments. Sections 1.802-3 through 1.802-5 (other than paragraph (f)(2) of § 1.802-3), except as otherwise provided therein, are applicable only to taxable years beginning after December 31, 1957, and all references to sections of part I, subchapter L, chapter 1 of the Code are to the Internal Revenue Code of 1954, as amended by the Life Insurance Company Income Tax Act of 1959 (73 Stat. 112) and section 235(c)(1) of the Revenue Act of 1964 (78 Stat. 126). Paragraph (f)(2) of § 1.802-3 is applicable only to taxable years beginning after December 31, 1961, and all references to sections of part I, subchapter L, chapter 1 of the Code are to the Internal Revenue Code of 1954, as amended by the Life Insurance Company Income Tax Act of 1959 (73 Stat. 112), section 3 of the Act of October 23, 1962 (76 Stat. 1134) and section 235(c)(1) of the Revenue Act of 1964 (78 Stat. 126). [Reg. § 1.802-2.]

☐ [*T.D. 6513, 12-9-60. Amended by T.D. 6845, 8-4-65 and T.D. 6886, 6-22-66.*]

Reg. § 1.802-2

→ **Caution:** *Former Code Secs. 801-820 for pre-1984 years were repealed and replaced by new Code Secs. 801-818. The following Regulations were issued under old Code Secs. 801-820.* ←

[Reg. § 1.802-3]

§ 1.802-3. Tax imposed on life insurance companies.—(a) *In general.* For taxable years beginning after December 31, 1957, section 802(a)(1) imposes a tax on the life insurance company taxable income (as defined in section 802(b) and paragraph (a) of § 1.802-4) of every life insurance company (including a foreign life insurance company carrying on a life insurance business within the United States if with respect to its United States business it would qualify as a life insurance company under section 801(a)). The tax imposed by section 802(a)(1) is payable upon the basis of returns rendered by the life insurance companies liable thereto. See subchapter A, chapter 61 (section 6001 and following) of the Code.

(b) *Tax imposed.* The tax imposed by section 802(a)(1) consists of a normal tax and a surtax computed as provided in section 11 as though the life insurance company taxable income (as defined in section 802(b)) were the taxable income referred to in section 11.

(c) *Normal tax.* The normal tax is computed by applying to the life insurance company taxable income the regular corporate normal tax rate (as in effect for the taxable year) provided by section 11(b).

(d) *Surtax.* The surtax is computed by applying the regular corporate surtax rate (as in effect for the taxable year) provided by section 11(c) to the amount by which the life insurance company taxable income exceeds the surtax exemption for the taxable year as determined under section 11(d). See sections 269 and 1551 and the regulations thereunder, for certain circumstances in which the surtax exemption may be disallowed in whole or in part.

(e) *Special rule for 1959 and 1960.* See section 802(a)(3) and paragraph (a) of § 1.802-5 for a transitional rule applicable in certain cases in determining tax liability for the taxable years 1959 and 1960 by reason of the operation of section 802(b)(3).

(f) *Tax imposed in case of certain capital gains*—(1) *Taxable years beginning after December 31, 1958, and before January 1, 1962.* For taxable years beginning after December 31, 1958, and before January 1, 1962, if the net long-term capital gain (as defined in section 1222(7)) of any life insurance company exceeds its net short-term capital loss (as defined in section 1222(6)), section 802(a)(2) imposes a separate tax equal to 25 percent of such excess. This separate 25 percent tax rate applies whether or not there is life insurance company taxable income, taxable investment income, or a gain or loss from operations for the taxable year. For taxable years beginning after December 31, 1958, and before January 1, 1962, only the excess (if any) of net short-term capital gain (as defined in section 1222(5)) over net long-term capital loss (as defined in section 1222 (8)) shall be taken into account in computing taxable investment income and gain or loss from operations. See sections 804(b) and 809(b). Except as modified by section 817 (rules relating to certain gains and losses), the general rules of the Code relating to gains and losses (such as the rules for determining the amount, characterization, and treatment thereof) shall apply with respect to life insurance companies.

(2) *Alternative tax in case of capital gains for taxable years beginning after December 31, 1961.* For taxable years beginning after December 31, 1961, if the net long-term capital gain (as defined in section 1222(7)) of any life insurance company exceeds its net short-term capital loss (as defined in section 1222(6)), section 802(a)(2) imposes an alternative tax in lieu of the tax imposed by section 802(a)(1), if and only if such alternative tax is less than the tax imposed by section 802(a)(1). The alternative tax is the sum of—

(i) A partial tax, computed as provided by section 802(a)(1), on the life insurance company taxable income determined by reducing the taxable investment income, and the gain from operations, by the amount of the excess of its net long-term capital gain over its net short-term capital loss, and

(ii)(a) In the case of a taxable year beginning before January 1, 1970, an amount equal to 25 percent of such excess, or

(b) In the case of a taxable year beginning after December 31, 1969, an amount determined as provided in section 1201(a) and paragraph (a)(3) of § 1.1201-1 on such excess.

In the computation of the partial tax, the deductions provided by sections 170 (as modified by section 809(e)(3)), 243, 244, 245 (as modified by sections 804(a)(5) and 809(d)(8)(B)), and the limitation provided by section 809(f), shall not be recomputed as a result of the reduction of taxable investment income, and gain from operations, by the amount of such excess. Except as modified by section 817 (rules relating to certain gains and losses), the general rules of the Code relating to gains and losses (such as the rules for determining

Reg. § 1.802-3(a)

Life Insurance Companies

See p. 20,601 for regulations not amended to reflect law changes

→ *Caution: Former Code Secs. 801-820 for pre-1984 years were repealed and replaced by new Code Secs. 801-818. The following Regulations were issued under old Code Secs. 801-820.* ←

the amount, characterization and treatment thereof) shall apply with respect to life insurance companies.

(g) *Foreign life insurance companies.* Foreign life insurance companies not carrying on an insurance business within the United States are not taxable under section 802, but are taxable as other foreign corporations. See section 881.

(h) *Assessment and collection of tax imposed.* All provisions of the Internal Revenue Code and of the regulations in this part not inconsistent with the specific provisions of sections 801 to 820, inclusive, are applicable to the assessment and collection of the tax imposed by section 802(a), and life insurance companies are subject to the same penalties as are provided in the case of returns and payment of income tax by other corporations. The return shall be on Form 1120L.

(i) *Illustration of principles.* The provisions of section 802(a), other than paragraph (3) thereof, and this section may be illustrated by the following example:

Example. For the taxable year 1959, T, a life insurance company, has life insurance company taxable income of $300,000 (including $25,000 of net short-term capital gain) and $80,000 of net long-term capital gain. The tax of T under section 802(a) for 1959 is $170,500 ($90,000 normal tax, $60,500 surtax, and $20,000 capital gains tax) computed as follows:

Computation of Normal Tax

Life insurance company taxable income	$300,000
Normal tax (30% of $300,000)	90,000

Computation of Surtax

Life insurance company taxable income	$300,000
Less: Exemption from surtax	25,000
Excess of life insurance company taxable income subject to surtax	$275,000
Surtax (22% of $275,000)	60,500

Computation of Capital Gains Tax

Excess of net long-term capital gain over net short-term capital loss	$ 80,000
Capital gains tax (25% of $80,000)	20,000

(j) *Cross reference.* In the case of a taxable year of a life insurance company ending after December 31, 1963, for which an election under section 1562(a)(1) by a controlled group of corporations is effective, the additional tax imposed by section 1562 may apply. See section 1562 and the regulations thereunder. [Reg. § 1.802-3.]

☐ [*T.D.* 6513, 12-9-60. *Amended by T.D.* 6845, 8-4-65, *T.D.* 6886, 6-22-66, *and T.D.* 7337, 12-26-74.]

[Reg. § 1.802-4]

§ 1.802-4. **Life insurance company taxable income.**—(a) *Life insurance company taxable income defined.* Section 802(b) defines the term "life insurance company taxable income", for purposes of part I, subchapter L, chapter 1 of the Code, as the sum of—

(1) The taxable investment income (as defined in section 804), or, if smaller, the gain from operations (as defined in section 809),

(2) If the gain from operations exceeds the taxable investment income, an amount equal to 50 percent of such excess, plus

(3) The amount subtracted from the policyholders surplus account for the taxable year, as determined under section 815.

If for any taxable year there is a loss from operations (as defined in section 809(b)(2)), the amount taken into account under paragraphs (1) and (2) of section 802(b) and subparagraphs (1) and (2) of this paragraph shall be zero. However, even in such a case, there may still be an amount includible in life insurance company taxable income (and hence an amount subject to tax) by reason of an amount includible under section 802(b)(3) and subparagraph (3) of this paragraph.

(b) *Illustration of principles.* The provisions of section 802(b) and this section may be illustrated by the following examples:

Example (1). For the taxable year 1959, Y, a life insurance company, has taxable investment income of $250,000, and a gain from operations of $175,000. Y made no subtractions from the policyholders surplus account during such taxable year. For the taxable year 1959, Y has life insurance company taxable income of $175,000.

Example (2). The facts are the same as in example (1) except that for the taxable year 1959, Y has a gain from operations of $400,000. For the taxable year 1959, Y has life insurance company taxable income of $325,000, computed by adding taxable investment income ($250,000) and 50 percent ($75,000) of the amount ($150,000) by which the gain from operations ($400,000) exceeds the taxable investment income ($250,000).

Example (3). For the taxable year 1959, W, a life insurance company, has taxable investment income of zero (0) and a gain from operations of $90,000. W made no subtractions from the policy-

Reg. § 1.802-4(b)

Life Insurance Companies

See p. 20,601 for regulations not amended to reflect law changes

→ *Caution: Former Code Secs. 801-820 for pre-1984 years were repealed and replaced by new Code Secs. 801-818. The following Regulations were issued under old Code Secs. 801-820.* ←

holders surplus account during such taxable year. For the taxable year 1959, W has life insurance company taxable income of $45,000, computed by adding taxable investment income (0) and 50 percent ($45,000) of the amount ($90,000) by which the gain from operations ($90,000) exceeds the taxable investment income (0).

Example (4). For the taxable year 1961, Z, a life insurance company, has taxable investment income of $100,000, a policyholders surplus account of $50,000 as of the beginning of such taxable year, a loss from operations (as defined in section 809(b)(2)) of $25,000, and subtractions from the policyholders surplus account in the amount of $20,000. For the taxable year 1961, Z has life insurance company taxable income of $20,000, as only the amount ($20,000) subtracted from the policyholders surplus account is taken into account. [Reg. § 1.802-4.]

☐ [T.D. 6315, 12-9-60.]

[Reg. § 1.804-1]

§ 1.804-1. Taxable years affected.—Sections 1.804-2 through 1.804-4 (other than paragraph (d)(1)(ii) of § 1.804-2) are applicable only to taxable years beginning after December 31, 1957, and all references to sections of part I, subchapter L, chapter 1 of the Code are to the Internal Revenue Code of 1954, as amended by the Life Insurance Company Income Tax Act of 1959 (73 Stat. 112). Paragraph (d)(1)(ii) of § 1.804-2 is applicable only to taxable years beginning after December 31, 1961, and all references to sections of part I, subchapter L, chapter 1 of the Code are to the Internal Revenue Code of 1954, as amended by the Life Insurance Company Income Tax Act of 1959 (73 Stat. 112), section 3 of the Act of October 23, 1962 (Public Law 87-858, 76 Stat. 1134), and section 214(b)(3) of the Revenue Act of 1964 (78 Stat. 55). [Reg. § 1.804-1.]

☐ [T.D. 6513, 12-9-60. Amended by T.D. 6886, 6-22-66 and T.D. 6992, 1-17-69.]

[Reg. § 1.804-2]

§ 1.804-2. Taxable investment income.—(a) *In general.* Section 804 provides the rules for determining the taxable investment income of a life insurance company, which amount is necessary to determine life insurance company taxable income. In order to determine taxable investment income, a life insurance company must first determine its gross investment income (as defined in section 804(b) and § 1.804-3). After making such determination, the next step is to determine its investment yield (as defined in section 804(c) and § 1.804-4). After determining its investment yield, a company shall then determine the policyholders' share of each and every item of its investment yield (as computed under section 804(a)(1) and paragraph (b) of this section), as this share is excluded from taxable investment income (as defined in section 804(a)(2) and paragraph (d) of this section). Thus, only the life insurance company's share of the items comprising investment yield (less certain reductions) shall be taken into account in computing taxable investment income.

(b) *Exclusion of policyholder's share of investment yield.* Section 804(a)(1) provides that the policyholders' share of each and every item of investment yield (including tax-exempt interest, partially tax-exempt interest, and dividends received) of any life insurance company shall not be included in taxable investment income. For this purpose, the percentage used in determining the policyholders' share of each of these items comprising the investment yield shall be determined by dividing the policy and other contract liability requirements (as defined in section 805(a) and paragraph (b) of § 1.805-4) by the investment yield. The percentage thus obtained is then applied to each and every item of the investment yield so that the policyholders' share of each and every item of investment yield shall be excluded from taxable investment income. However, if in any case the policy and other contract liability requirements exceed the investment yield, then the policyholders' share of any item shall be 100 percent.

(c) *Computation of life insurance company's share of investment yield.* Section 804(a)(2) provides that the percentage used in determining the life insurance company's share of each and every item of investment yield (including tax-exempt interest, partially tax-exempt interest, and dividends received) shall be the percentage obtained by subtracting the percentage obtained under paragraph (b) of this section from 100 percent. Only the life insurance company's share of the items comprising investment yield (less certain reductions specified in section 804(a)(2) and paragraph (d)(1) of this section) shall be taken into account in computing taxable investment income. For example, if the policyholders' percentage (as determined under section 804(a)(1) and paragraph (b) of this section) is 80 percent, then the life insurance company's share is 20 percent (100 percent minus 80 percent). In such a case, if the amount of a particular item is $1,000, then the

Life Insurance Companies

See p. 20,601 for regulations not amended to reflect law changes

→ *Caution: Former Code Secs. 801-820 for pre-1984 years were repealed and replaced by new Code Secs. 801-818. The following Regulations were issued under old Code Secs. 801-820.* ←

life insurance company's share of such item included in determining taxable investment income is $200 ($1,000 multiplied by 20 percent) and the policyholders' share of such item (which is excluded from taxable investment income) is $800 ($1,000 multiplied by 80 percent).

(d) *Taxable investment income of a life insurance company.*—(1) *Definition.* Section 804(a)(2) defines the term "taxable investment income," for purposes of part I, as an amount (not less than zero) equal to the amount (if any) by which the net long-term capital gain exceeds the net short-term capital loss, plus the sum of the life insurance company's share (as determined under paragraph (c) of this section) of each and every item of investment yield (including tax-exempt interest, partially tax-exempt interest, and dividends received), reduced by the sum of—

(i) The life insurance company's share of interest which under section 103 is excluded from gross income,

(ii) The deduction for partially tax-exempt interest provided by section 242 (as modified by section 804(a)(3) and subparagraph (2)(i) of this paragraph) computed with respect to the life insurance company's share of such interest,

(iii) The deduction for dividends received provided by sections 243, 244, and 245 (as modified by section 804(a)(5) and subparagraph (2)(ii) of this paragraph) computed with respect to the life insurance company's share of the dividends received, and

(iv) The small business deduction provided by section 804(a)(4). For purposes of part I, such small business deduction shall be an amount equal to 10 percent of the investment yield for the taxable year, except that such amount shall not exceed $25,000, or, in the case of a component member of a controlled group of corporations (as defined in section 1563), the amount allowable under section 1561 (for taxable years beginning after December 31, 1974) or section 1564(a) (for taxable years beginning before January 1, 1975).

(2) *Modifications*—(i) *Partially tax-exempt interest.* For purposes of part I, the deduction allowed by section 242 (relating to partially tax-exempt interest) shall be determined by applying to the life insurance company's share of such interest the ratio which the normal tax rate (as prescribed by section 11) for the taxable year bears to the sum of the normal tax rate and the surtax rate (as prescribed by section 11) for the taxable year. For example, if for the taxable year 1959 the life insurance company's share of partially tax-exempt interest is $104, the deduction provided by section 804(a)(2)(A)(ii) (as modified by this subdivision) is $60 (thirty fifty-seconds of such partially tax-exempt interest).

(ii) *Application of section 246(b).* The sum of the deductions allowed by sections 243(a)(1) (relating to dividends received by corporations), 244(a) (relating to dividends received on certain preferred stock), and 245 (relating to dividends received from certain foreign corporations) shall be limited to 85 percent of the taxable investment income (as defined in subparagraph (1) of this paragraph). The taxable investment income of the company for this purpose shall be computed without regard to the deductions provided in sections 243(a)(1), 244(a), and 245.

(e) *Illustration of principles.* The provisions of section 804(a) (1) through (5) and paragraphs (a) through (d) of this section may be illustrated by the following example:

Example. For the taxable year 1958, R, a life insurance company, had investment yield of $1,000,000, including $200,000 of dividends received from domestic corporations subject to taxation under chapter 1 of the Code, $16,800 of wholly tax-exempt interest, and $83,200 of partially tax-exempt interest. For such taxable year, the policyholders' share of each and every item of investment yield was 75 percent and the company's share of each and every item of investment yield was 25 percent. Based upon these figures, R had taxable investment income of $166,300 for the taxable year 1958, computed as follows:

	Col. 1 Total	Col. 2 (75% × Col. 1) Policyholders' share	Col. 3 (25% × Col. 1) Company's share
Interest wholly tax-exempt	$ 16,800	$ 12,600	$ 4,200
Interest partially tax-exempt	83,200	62,400	20,800
Dividends received	200,000	150,000	50,000
Other items of investment yield	700,000	525,000	175,000
Investment yield	1,000,000	750,000	250,000

Reg. § 1.804-2(e)

→ **Caution:** *Former Code Secs. 801-820 for pre-1984 years were repealed and replaced by new Code Secs. 801-818. The following Regulations were issued under old Code Secs. 801-820.* ←

	Col. 1 Total	Col. 2 (75% × Col. 1) Policyholders' share	Col. 3 (25% × Col. 1) Company's share
Less: Company's share of interest wholly tax-exempt . . . . $	4,200		
30/52 of company's share of interest partially tax-exempt (30/52 × $20,800)	12,000		
85% of company's share of dividends received (but not to exceed 85% of taxable investment income computed without regard to this deduction)(85% × $50,000)	42,500		
Small business deduction (10% of investment yield, not to exceed $25,000) . . . . $	25,000		83,700
Taxable investment income			$166,300

(f) *Exception.* (1) In accordance with section 804(a)(6), if it is established in any case to the satisfaction of the Commissioner, or by a determination of the Tax Court of the United States, or of any other court of competent jurisdiction, which has become final, that the application of the definition of taxable investment income contained in section 804(a)(2) results in the imposition of tax on—

(i) Any interest which under section 103 is excluded from gross income,

(ii) Any amount of interest which under section 242 (as modified by section 804(a)(3)) is allowable as a deduction, or

(iii) Any amount of dividends received which under sections 243, 244, and 245 (as modified by section 804(a)(5)) is allowable as a deduction,

adjustment shall be made to the extent necessary to prevent such imposition.

(2) For the date upon which a decision by the Tax Court becomes final, see section 7481. For the date upon which a judgment of any other court becomes final, see paragraph (c) of § 1.1313(a)-1. [Reg. § 1.804-2.]

☐ [T.D. 6513, 12-9-60. Amended by T.D. 6886, 6-22-66, T.D. 6992, 1-17-69, T.D. 7181, 4-25-72 and T.D. 7528, 12-27-77.]

[Reg. § 1.804-3]

§ 1.804-3. **Gross investment income of a life insurance company.**—(a) *Gross investment income defined.* For purposes of part I, subchapter L, chapter 1 of the Code, section 804(b) defines the term "gross investment income" of a life insurance company as the sum of the following:

(1) The gross amount of income from—

(i) Interest (including tax-exempt interest and partially tax-exempt interest), as described in § 1.61-7. Interest shall be adjusted for amortization of premium and accrual of discount in accordance with the rules prescribed in section 818(b) and the regulations thereunder.

(ii) Dividends, as described in § 1.61-9.

(iii) Rents and royalties, as described in § 1.61-8.

(iv) The entering into of any lease, mortgage, or other instrument or agreement from which the life insurance company may derive interest, rents, or royalties.

(v) The alteration or termination of any instrument or agreement described in subdivision (iv) of this subparagraph.

For example, gross investment income includes amounts received as commitment fees, as a bonus for the entering into of a lease, or as a penalty for the early payment of a mortgage.

(2) In the case of a taxable year beginning after December 31, 1958, the amount (if any) by which the net short-term capital gain (as defined in section 1222(5)) exceeds the net long-term capital loss (as defined in section 1222(8)), and

(3) The gross income from any trade or business (other than an insurance business) carried on by the life insurance company, or by a partnership of which the life insurance company is a partner.

(b) *No double inclusion of income.* In computing the gross income from any trade or business (other than an insurance business) carried on by the life insurance company, or by a partnership of which the life insurance company is a partner, any item described in section 804(b)(1) and paragraph (a)(1) of this section shall not be considered as gross income arising from the conduct of such trade or business or partnership, but shall be taken into account under section 804(b)(1) and paragraph (a)(1) of this section.

→ *Caution: Former Code Secs. 801-820 for pre-1984 years were repealed and replaced by new Code Secs. 801-818. The following Regulations were issued under old Code Secs. 801-820.*←

(c) *Exclusion of net long-term capital gains.* Any net long-term capital gains from the sale or exchange of a capital asset (or any gain considered to be from the sale or exchange of a capital asset under applicable law) shall be excluded from the gross investment income of a life insurance company. However, section 804(b)(2) and paragraph (a)(2) of this section provide that the amount (if any) by which the net short-term capital gain exceeds the net long-term capital loss shall be included in the gross investment income of a life insurance company. [Reg. § 1.804-3.]

☐ [T.D. 6513, 12-9-60.]

[Reg. § 1.804-4]

§ 1.804-4. **Investment yield of a life insurance company.**—(a) *Investment yield defined.* Section 804(c) defines the term "investment yield" of a life insurance company for purposes of part I, subchapter L, chapter 1 of the Code. Investment yield means gross investment income (as defined in section 804(b) and paragraph (a) of § 1.804-3), less the deductions provided in section 804(c) and paragraph (b) of this section for investment expenses, real estate expenses, depreciation, depletion, and trade or business (other than an insurance business) expenses. However, such expenses are deductible only to the extent that they relate to investment income and the deduction of such expenses is not disallowed by any other provision of subtitle A of the Code. For example, investment expenses are not allowable unless they are ordinary and necessary expenses within the meaning of section 162, and under section 265, no deduction is allowable for interest on indebtedness incurred or continued to purchase or carry obligations the interest on which is wholly exempt from taxation under chapter 1 of the Code. A deduction shall not be permitted with respect to the same item more than once.

(b) *Deductions from gross investment income*— (1) *Investment expenses.* (i) Section 804(c)(1) provides for the deduction of investment expenses by a life insurance company in determining investment yield. "Investment expenses" are those expenses of the taxable year which are fairly chargeable against gross investment income. For example, investment expenses include salaries and expenses paid exclusively for work in looking after investments, and amounts expended for printing, stationery, postage, and stenographic work incident to the collection of interest. An itemized schedule of such expenses shall be attached to the return.

(ii) Any assignment of general expenses to the investment department of a life insurance company for which a deduction is claimed under section 804(c)(1) subjects the entire deduction for investment expenses to the limitation provided in that section and subdivision (iii) of this subparagraph. As used in section 804(c)(1), the term "general expenses" means any expense paid or incurred for the benefit of more than one department of the company rather than for the benefit of a particular department thereof. For example, if real estate taxes, depreciation, or other expenses attributable to office space owned by the company and utilized by it in connection with its investment function are assigned to investment expenses, such items shall be deductible as general expenses assigned to or included in investment expenses and as such shall be subject to the limitation of section 804(c)(1) and subdivision (iii) of this subparagraph. Similarly, if an expense, such as a salary, is attributable to more than one department, including the investment department, such expense may be properly allocated among these departments. If such expenses are allocated, the amount properly allocable to the investment department shall be deductible as general expenses assigned to or included in investment expenses and as such shall be subject to the limitation of section 804(c)(1) and subdivision (iii) of this subparagraph. If general expenses are in part assigned to or included in investment expenses, the maximum allowance (as determined under section 804(c)(1)) shall not be granted unless it is shown to the satisfaction of the district director that such allowance is justified by a reasonable assignment of actual expenses. The accounting procedure employed is not conclusive as to whether any assignment has in fact been made. Investment expenses do not include Federal income and excess profits taxes, if any. In cases where the investment expenses allowable as deductions under section 804(c)(1) exceed the limitation contained therein, see section 809(d)(9).

(iii) If any general expenses are in part assigned to or included in investment expenses, the total deduction under section 804(c)(1) shall not exceed the sum of—

(*a*) One-fourth of one percent of the mean of the assets (as defined in section 805(b)(4) and paragraph (a)(4) of § 1.805-5) held at the beginning and end of the taxable year,

Reg. § 1.804-4(b)(1)

45,732   Life Insurance Companies

See p. 20,601 for regulations not amended to reflect law changes

→ *Caution: Former Code Secs. 801-820 for pre-1984 years were repealed and replaced by new Code Secs. 801-818. The following Regulations were issued under old Code Secs. 801-820.* ←

(b) The amount of the mortgage service fees for the taxable year, plus

(c) Whichever of the following is the greater:

(1) One-fourth of the amount by which the investment yield (computed without any deduction for investment expenses allowed by section 804(c)(1)) exceeds 3¾ percent of the mean of the assets (as defined in section 805(b)(4)) held at the beginning and end of the taxable year, reduced by the amount of the mortgage service fees for the taxable year, or

(2) One-fourth of one percent of the mean of the value of mortgages held at the beginning and end of the taxable year for which there are no mortgage service fees for the taxable year. For purposes of the preceding sentence, the term "mortgages held" refers to mortgages, and other similar liens, on real property which are held by the company as security for "mortgage loans".

For purposes of section 804(c)(1)(B) and (C)(i) and (b) and (c)(1) of this subdivision, the term "mortgage service fees" includes mortgage origination fees. Such mortgage origination fees shall be amortized in accordance with the rules prescribed in section 818(b) and the regulations thereunder.

(iv) The operation of the limitation contained in section 804(c)(1) and subdivision (iii) of this subparagraph may be illustrated by the following example:

Example. The books of S, a life insurance company, reflect the following items for the taxable year 1958:

Investment expenses (including general expenses assigned to or included in investment expenses)	$ 125,000
Mean of the assets held at the beginning and end of the taxable year	20,000,000
Mortgage service fees	25,000
Investment yield computed without regard to investment expenses	1,200,000
Mean of the value of mortgages held at the beginning and end of the taxable year for which there are no mortgage service fees	6,000,000

In order to determine the limitation on investment expenses, S would make up the following schedule:

1. Mean of the assets held at the beginning and end of the taxable year		$20,000,000
2. One-fourth of 1 percent of item 1 (¼ of 1% of $20,000,000)		$ 50,000
3. Mortgage service fees		25,000
4. The greater of (a) or (b):		
(a) (i) Investment yield computed without regard to investment expenses	$1,200,000	
(ii) Three and three-fourths percent of item 1 (3¾% × $20,000,000)	750,000	
(iii) Excess of (i) over (ii) ($1,200,000 minus $750,000)	450,000	
(iv) One-fourth of (iii) (¼ × $450,000)	112,500	
(v) Less: Mortgage service fees (item 3)	25,000	
(vi) Excess of (iv) over (v) ($112,500 minus $25,000)	87,500	
(b) One-fourth of 1 percent of the mean of the value of mortgages held at the beginning and end of the taxable year for which there are no mortgage service fees (¼ of 1% × $6,000,000)	15,000	
5. The greater of item 4(a) or (b)		$ 87,500
6. Limitation on investment expenses (items 2, 3, and 4(a))		$ 162,500

As the investment expenses (including general expenses assigned to or included in investment expenses) of S for the taxable year 1958 ($125,000) do not exceed the limitation on such expenses ($162,500), S would be entitled to deduct the entire $125,000 under section 804(c)(1).

(2) *Real estate expenses and taxes.* The deduction for expenses and taxes under section 804(c)(2) includes taxes (as defined in section 164), and other expenses for the taxable year exclusively on or with respect to real estate owned by the company. For example, no deduction shall be allowed under section 804(c)(2) for amounts allowed as a deduction under section 164(e) (relating to taxes of shareholders paid by a corporation). No deduction shall be allowed under section 804(c)(2) for any amount paid out for new buildings, or for permanent improvements or better-

Reg. § 1.804-4(b)(2)

Life Insurance Companies

See p. 20,601 for regulations not amended to reflect law changes

→ *Caution: Former Code Secs. 801-820 for pre-1984 years were repealed and replaced by new Code Secs. 801-818. The following Regulations were issued under old Code Secs. 801-820.*←

ments made to increase the value of any property. An itemized schedule of such taxes and expenses shall be attached to the return. See subparagraph (4) of this paragraph for a limitation of such deduction.

(3) *Depreciation.* The deduction allowed for depreciation is, except as provided in section 804(c)(3) and subparagraph (4) of this paragraph, identical to that allowed other corporations by section 167. Such amount allowed as a deduction from gross investment income in determining investment yield is limited to depreciation sustained on the property used, and to the extent used, for the purpose of producing the income specified in section 804(b). An election with respect to any of the methods of depreciation provided in section 167 shall not be affected in any way by the enactment of the Life Insurance Company Income Tax Act of 1959 (73 Stat. 112). However, in appropriate cases, the method of depreciation may be changed with the consent of the Commissioner. See section 167(e) and § 1.167(e)-1. See subparagraph (4) of this paragraph for limitation of such deduction. See section 809(d)(12) and the regulations thereunder for the treatment of depreciable property used in the operation of a life insurance business.

(4) *Limitation on deductions allowable under section 804(c)(2) and (c)(3).* Section 804(c)(3) provides that the amount allowable as a deduction for taxes, expenses, and depreciation on or with respect to any real estate owned and occupied for insurance purposes in whole or in part by a life insurance company shall be limited to an amount which bears the same ratio to such deduction (computed without regard to this limitation) as the rental value of the space not so occupied bears to the rental value of the entire property. For example, T, a life insurance company, owns a twenty-story downtown home office building. The rental value of each floor of the building is identical. T rents nine floors to various tenants, one floor is utilized by it in operating its investment department, and the remaining ten floors are occupied by it in carrying on its insurance business. Since floor space equivalent to eleven-twentieths, or 55 percent, of the rental value of the entire property is owned and occupied for insurance purposes by the company, the deductions allowable under section 804(c)(2) and (3) for taxes, depreciation, and other real estate expenses shall be limited to nine-twentieths, or 45 percent, of the taxes, depreciation, and other real estate expenses on account of the entire property. However, the portion of such allowable deductions attributable to the operation of the investment department (one-twentieth, or 5 percent) may be deductible as general expenses assigned to or included in investment expenses and as such shall be subject to the limitations of section 804(c)(1). Where a deduction is claimed as provided in this section, the parts of the property occupied and the parts not occupied by the company in carrying on its insurance business, together with the respective rental values thereof, must be shown in a schedule accompanying the return.

(5) *Depletion.* The deduction for depletion (and depreciation) provided in section 804(c)(4) is identical to that allowed other corporations by section 611. The amount allowed by section 611 in the case of a life insurance company is limited to depletion (and depreciation) sustained on the property used, and to the extent used, for the purpose of producing the income specified in section 804(b). See section 611 and § 1.611-5 for special rules relating to the depreciation of improvements in the case of mines, oil and gas wells, other natural deposits, and timber.

(6) *Trade or business deductions.* (i) Under section 804(c)(5), the deductions allowed by subtitle A of the Code (without regard to this part) which are attributable to any trade or business (other than an insurance business) carried on by the life insurance company, or by a partnership of which the life insurance company is a partner are, subject to the limitations in subdivisions (ii), (iii), and (iv) of this subparagraph, allowable as deductions from the gross investment income of a life insurance company in determining its investment yield. Such deductions are allowable, however, only to the extent that they are attributable to the production of income which is included in the life insurance company's gross investment income by reason of section 804(b)(3). However, since any interest, dividends, rents, and royalties received by any trade or business (other than an insurance business) carried on by the life insurance company, or by a partnership of which the life insurance company is a partner, is included in the life insurance company's gross investment income by reason of section 804(b)(1) and paragraph (b) of § 1.804-3, any expenses fairly chargeable against the production of such income may be deductible under section 804(c)(1), (2), (3), or (4). The allowable deductions may exceed the gross income from such business.

(ii) In computing the deductions under section 804(c)(5), there shall be excluded losses—

Reg. § 1.804-4(b)(6)

→ **Caution:** *Former Code Secs. 801-820 for pre-1984 years were repealed and replaced by new Code Secs. 801-818. The following Regulations were issued under old Code Secs. 801-820.* ←

(a) From (or considered as from) sales or exchanges of capital assets,

(b) From sales or exchanges of property used in the trade or business (as defined in section 1231(b)), and

(c) From the compulsory or involuntary conversion (as a result of destruction, in whole or in part, theft or seizure, or an exercise of the power of requisition or condemnation or the threat or imminence thereof) of property used in the trade or business (as so defined).

(iii) Any item, to the extent attributable to the carrying on of the insurance business, shall not be taken into account. For example, if a life insurance company operates a radio station primarily to advertise its own insurance services, a portion of the expenses of the radio station shall not be allowed as a deduction. The portion disallowed shall be an amount which bears the same ratio to the total expenses of the station as the value of advertising furnished to the insurance company bears to the total value of services rendered by the station.

(iv) The deduction for net operating losses provided in section 172, and the special deductions for corporations provided in part VIII, subchapter B, chapter 1 of the Code, shall not be allowed. [Reg. § 1.804-4.]

☐ [*T.D.* 6513, 12-9-60.]

[Reg. § 1.805-7]

§ 1.805-7. Pension plan reserves.—(a) *In general.* One of the elements to be taken into account in computing the amount of the policy and other contract liability requirements (as defined in section 805(a) and paragraph (b) of § 1.805-4) of a life insurance company is the investment income attributable to pension plan reserves (as defined in section 805(d)(1) and paragraph (b) of this section). The amount of this element to be included in the policy and other contract liability requirements shall be determined by multiplying the mean of such pension plan reserves at the beginning and end of the taxable year by the current earnings rate (as defined in section 805(b)(2)) of the company. However, the amount of such reserves taken into account must be adjusted first as required by section 818(c) (relating to an election with respect to life insurance reserves computed on a preliminary term basis) and then as required by section 806(a) (relating to adjustments for certain changes in reserves and assets) before applying the current earnings rate thereto. Reserves held by a life insurance company under deposit administration contracts shall be included in pension plan reserves if they qualify as life insurance reserves (as defined in section 801(b) and paragraph (a) of § 1.801-4) and otherwise meet the definition of pension plan reserves.

(b) *Pension plan reserves defined.* For purposes of part I, subchapter L, chapter 1 of the Code, section 805(d)(1) defines the term "pension plan reserves" as that portion of the life insurance reserves (as defined in section 801(b)) which is allocable to contracts—

(1) Purchased under contracts entered into with trusts which (as of the time the contracts were entered into) were deemed to be trusts described in section 401(a) and exempt from tax under section 501(a) of the Internal Revenue Code of 1954, or trusts exempt from tax under section 165 of the Internal Revenue Code of 1939 (prior to, or after, the 1942 amendments) or the corresponding provisions of prior revenue laws;

(2) Purchased under contracts entered into under plans which (as of the time the contracts were entered into) were deemed to be plans—

(i) Meeting the requirements of section 165(a)(3), (4), (5) and (6) of the Internal Revenue Code of 1939, for taxable years beginning before January 1, 1954, and ending before August 17, 1954, or

(ii) Described in section 403(a) of the Internal Revenue Code of 1954;

(3) Provided for employees of the life insurance company under a plan which for the taxable year meet the requirements of section 401(a)(3), (4), (5), (6), (7), (8), (11), (12), (13), (14), (15), (16), and (19) for the taxable year to which such paragraphs apply. For purposes of this subparagraph, the term "employees" includes full-time life insurance salesmen treated as employees under section 7701(a)(20);

(4) Purchased to provide retirement annuities—

(i) For its employees by an organization which (as of the time the contracts were purchased) was an organization described in section 501(c)(3) which was exempt from tax under section 501(a) or was an organization exempt from tax under section 101(6) of the Internal Revenue Code of 1939 or the corresponding provisions of prior revenue laws, or

(ii) For taxable years beginning after December 31, 1963, for employees described in section 403(b)(1)(A)(ii) by an employer which is a State, a political subdivision of a State, or an

→ **Caution:** *Former Code Secs. 801-820 for pre-1984 years were repealed and replaced by new Code Secs. 801-818. The following Regulations were issued under old Code Secs. 801-820.* ←

agency or instrumentality of any one or more of the foregoing.

The definition of pension plan reserves described in paragraph (b)(4)(i) of this section includes only life insurance reserves held under contracts purchased by those organizations described in section 501(c)(3) and exempt from tax under section 501(a), and does not include life insurance reserves under contracts purchased by organizations described under any other provision of section 501(c). Accordingly, the reserves held under contracts purchased by such other exempt organizations, or by entities not subject to Federal income tax (such as a State, municipality, etc.), shall not be treated as pension plan reserves unless they qualify as such under section 805(d)(1), (2), (3), or (5) or paragraph (b)(4)(ii) of this section.

(5) Purchased under contracts entered into with trusts which (at the time the contracts were entered into) were individual retirement accounts described in section 408(a) or under contracts entered into with individual retirement annuities described in section 408(b). [Reg. § 1.805-7.]

☐ [*T.D.* 6513, 12-9-60. Amended by *T.D.* 6886, 6-22-66, *T.D.* 7326, 9-30-74, *T.D.* 7501, 8-22-77, and *T.D.* 7531, 1-5-78.]

[Reg. § 1.806-2]

§ 1.806-2. Taxable years affected.—Section 1.806-1 is applicable only to taxable years beginning after December 31, 1953, and before January 1, 1955, and all references to sections of part I, subchapter L, chapter 1 of the Code are to the Internal Revenue Code of 1954, before amendments. Sections 1.806-3 and 1.806-4 are applicable only to taxable years beginning after December 31, 1957, and all references to sections of part I, subchapter L, chapter 1 of the Code are to the Internal Revenue Code of 1954, as amended by the Life Insurance Company Income Tax Act of 1959 (73 Stat. 112). [Reg. § 1.806-2.]

☐ [*T.D.* 6513, 12-9-60.]

[Reg. § 1.806-3]

§ 1.806-3. Certain changes in reserves and assets.—(a) *In general.* For purposes of part I, subchapter L, chapter 1 of the Code, section 806(a) provides that if there is a change in life insurance reserves (as defined in section 801(b)), during the taxable year, which is attributable to the transfer between the taxpayer and another person of liabilities under contracts taken into account in computing such life insurance reserves, then the means of such reserves, and the mean of the assets, shall be appropriately adjusted to reflect the amounts involved in such transfer. For example, the adjustments required under section 806(a) are applicable to transfers in which one life insurance company purchases or acquires a part or all of the business of another life insurance company under an arrangement whereby the purchaser or transferee becomes solely liable on the contracts transferred. This provision shall apply in the case of assumption reinsurance but not in the case of indemnity reinsurance or reinsurance ceded. Thus, no adjustments shall be required under section 806(a) when, in the ordinary course of business, an indemnity reinsurance contract is entered into with another company (on a yearly renewable term basis, on a coinsurance basis, or otherwise) whereby there is a sharing of risks under one or more individual contracts. It will be necessary for each life insurance company participating in a transfer described in section 806(a) to make the adjustments required by such section. Such adjustments shall be made without regard to whether or not the transferor of the liabilities was the original insurer.

(b) *Manner in which adjustments shall be made*—(1) *Daily basis.* The means of the life insurance reserves, and the mean of the assets, shall be appropriately adjusted, on a daily basis, to reflect the amounts involved in a transfer described in section 806(a) and paragraph (a) of this section. The transferor and the transferee shall be treated as having held such life insurance reserves and assets for a fraction of the year in which the transfer occurs.

(2) *Determination of period held.* In determining the fraction which represents the fractional year that such reserves and assets were held, the numerator shall be the number of days during the taxable year which such reserves and assets were actually held, and the denominator shall be the number of days in the calendar year of the transfer. In computing the period held for purposes of the numerator, the day on which such reserves and assets are transferred is included by the transferor and excluded by the transferee.

(3) *Adjustments to the means of life insurance reserves and assets not transferred.* All life insurance reserves and assets transferred during the taxable year, within the meaning of section 806(a), shall be excluded from the beginning and end of the taxable year balances of the transferor and transferee, respectively. The amount of assets to be excluded from the beginning of the taxable

45,736 Life Insurance Companies

See p. 20,601 for regulations not amended to reflect law changes

→ *Caution: Former Code Secs. 801-820 for pre-1984 years were repealed and replaced by new Code Secs. 801-818. The following Regulations were issued under old Code Secs. 801-820.*←

year balance of the transferor shall be an amount equal to the value of such reserves at the beginning of the taxable year. The amount of assets to be excluded from the end of the taxable year balance of the transferee shall be an amount equal to the value of such reserves at the end of the taxable year. The means of the life insurance reserves and assets not so transferred shall be determined in the ordinary manner, that is, the arithmetic means. There shall be added to these means an amount to appropriately adjust them, on a daily basis, for the life insurance reserves and assets that were transferred during the taxable year. This adjustment shall be determined by multiplying (i) the mean of the transferred life insurance reserves (or assets, as the case may be) at the beginning of the taxable year (or, if acquired later, at the beginning of the period held as defined in subparagraph (2) of this paragraph) and the end of the period held, as defined in subparagraph (2) of this paragraph (or at the end of the taxable year, if held at such time) by (ii) the fraction determined under subparagraph (2) of this paragraph.

(4) *Examples.* The application of this paragraph may be illustrated by the following examples:

Example (1). On March 14, 1958, the M Company, a life insurance company, transferred to the N Company, a life insurance company, pursuant to an assumption reinsurance agreement, all of its life insurance reserves, and related assets, on one block of policies. The reserves (and assets) for this block were held by the M Company on January 1, 1958, and totaled $60,000; on March 14, the reserves (and assets) totaled $64,000. The M Company had life insurance reserves of $1,000,000 at the beginning of 1958 (including those subsequently transferred) and $1,040,000 at the end of 1958. The M Company had assets of $1,300,000 at the beginning of 1958 (including those subsequently transferred) and $1,380,000 at the end of 1958. The mean of M's life insurance reserves for the taxable year 1958 is computed as follows:

```
Reserves at 1-1-58 ............................................$1,000,000
    Exclude reserves (at beginning of year) on contracts
    transferred to N ..........................................    60,000
                                                                 ----------
        Recomputed amount at 1-1-58...........................               $  940,000
Reserves at 12-31-58 .........................................                 1,040,000
                                                                              ----------
        Sum ...................................................               $1,980,000
        Mean ..................................................               $  990,000
Adjustment for reserves transferred on 3-14-58:
    Reserves at 1-1-58 on contracts transferred to N .......  $ 60,000
    Reserves at 3-14-58 on such contracts ..................    64,000
                                                              ---------
        Sum..................................................   $124,000
        Mean.................................................   $ 62,000
Fraction taken into account .................................     73/365
        Adjustment (73/365 × $62,000) .........................               $   12,400
                                                                              ----------
Mean of M's life insurance reserves after section 806(a) adjustment ........  $1,002,400
```

Example (2). Assuming the facts to be the same as in example (1), the mean of M's assets for the taxable year 1958 is computed as follows:

```
Assets at 1-1-58 .............................................$1,300,000
    Exclude assets (at beginning of year) on contracts
    transferred to N ..........................................    60,000
                                                                 ----------
        Recomputed amount at 1-1-58...........................               $1,240,000
Assets at 12-31-58 ...........................................                 1,380,000
                                                                              ----------
        Sum ...................................................               $2,620,000
```

Reg. § 1.806-3(b)(4)

Life Insurance Companies 45,737

See p. 20,601 for regulations not amended to reflect law changes

→ *Caution: Former Code Secs. 801-820 for pre-1984 years were repealed and replaced by new Code Secs. 801-818. The following Regulations were issued under old Code Secs. 801-820.*←

Mean		$1,310,000
Adjustments for assets transferred on 3-14-58:		
Assets at 1-1-58 on contracts transferred to N	$ 60,000	
Assets at 3-14-58 on such contracts	64,000	
Sum	$ 124,000	
Mean	$ 62,000	
Fraction taken into account	73/365	
Adjustment (73/365 × $62,000)		$ 12,400
Mean of M's assets after section 806(a) adjustment		$1,322,400

Example (3). Assume the facts are the same as in example (1). At the end of 1958, N Company had life insurance reserves (and assets) of $80,000 on the contracts transferred on March 14, 1958. The N Company had life insurance reserves of $6,000,000 at the beginning of 1958 and $6,400,000 at the end of 1958 (including those transferred). The N Company had assets of $6,800,000 at the beginning of 1958 and $7,300,000 at the end of 1958 (including those on the contracts transferred). The mean of N's life insurance reserves for the taxable year 1958 is computed as follows:

Reserves at 1-1-58		$6,000,000
Reserves at 12-31-58	$6,400,000	
Exclude reserves (at end of year) on contracts transferred from M	80,000	
Recomputed amount at 12-31-58		6,320,000
Sum		$2,320,000
Mean		$6,160,000
Adjustment for reserves transferred on 3-14-58:		
Reserves at 3-14-58 on contracts transferred from M	$ 64,000	
Reserves at 12-31-58 on such contracts	80,000	
Sum	$ 144,000	
Mean	$ 72,000	
Fraction taken into account	292/365	
Adjustment (292/365 × $72,000)		$ 57,600
Mean of N's life insurance reserves after section 806(a) adjustment		$6,217,600

Example (4). Assuming the facts to be the same as in example (3), the mean of N's assets for the taxable year 1958 is computed as follows:

Assets at 1-1-58		$6,800,000
Assets at 12-31-58	$7,300,000	
Exclude assets (at end of year) on contracts transferred from M	80,000	
Recomputed amount at 12-31-58		7,220,000
Sum		$4,020,000
Mean		$7,010,000
Adjustments for assets transferred on 3-14-58:		
Assets at 3-14-58 on contracts transferred from M	$ 64,000	
Assets at 12-31-58 on such contracts	80,000	
Sum	$ 144,000	
Mean	$ 72,000	

Reg. § 1.806-3(b)(4)

45,738   **Life Insurance Companies**

See p. 20,601 for regulations not amended to reflect law changes

→ *Caution: Former Code Secs. 801-820 for pre-1984 years were repealed and replaced by new Code Secs. 801-818. The following Regulations were issued under old Code Secs. 801-820.*←

Fraction taken into account	292/365
Adjustment (292/365 × $72,000)	$ 57,600
Mean of N's assets after section 806(a) adjustment	$7,067,600

Example (5). The facts are the same as in example (1), except that on October 19, 1958, company N transfers to company P, a life insurance company, all of the life insurance reserves, and related assets, on the block of policies it had received from company M on March 14, 1958. The reserves (and assets) for this block totaled $76,000 on October 19, 1958. The means of company M's life insurance reserves and assets, as computed in examples (1) and (2), respectively, would be unchanged by the transfer of October 19, 1958. Since company N did not own this block of policies at either the beginning or end of the taxable year, it would not have to recompute its beginning or end of the taxable year reserves or assets. Company N will, however, have to adjust (or increase) the mean of its life insurance reserves and assets on account of the policies it received from company M. This adjustment will be $42,000, which is determined by multiplying the means of the life insurance reserves (or assets) on these policies as of March 15, 1958, and October 19, 1958, $70,000 ($64,000 + $76,000 = $140,000 ÷ 2) by the fraction 219/365 (the numerator of 219 is determined by excluding the day of the transfer to N, March 14, 1958, and including the day of the transfer from N to P, October 19, 1958). Company P will have to recompute its end of the year life insurance reserves and assets (in the same manner as illustrated in examples (3) and (4)). Assuming the end of the year reserves (and assets) on this block of policies is $80,000, company P will have an adjustment under section 806(a) of $15,600, which is determined by multiplying the means of the reserves on these policies as of October 20, 1958, and December 31, 1958, $78,000 ($76,000 + $80,000 = $156,000 ÷ 2) by the fraction 73/365. [Reg. § 1.806-3].

☐ [T.D. 6513, 12-9-60.]

[Reg. § 1.806-4]

§ 1.806-4. **Change of basis in computing reserves.**—(a) *In general.* For purposes of subpart B, part I, subchapter L, chapter 1 of the Code, section 806(b) provides that if the basis for determining the amount of any item referred to in section 810(c) (relating to items taken into account) as of the close of the taxable year differs from the basis for such determination as of the beginning of the taxable year, then in determining taxable investment income the amount of the item as of the close of the taxable year shall be the amount computed on the old basis, and the amount of the item as of the beginning of the next taxable year shall be the amount computed on the new basis. For purposes of the preceding sentence, an election under section 818(c) shall not be treated as a change in basis for determining the amount of an item referred to in section 810(c). A change of basis in computing any of the items referred to in section 810(c) is not a change of accounting method requiring the consent of the Secretary or his delegate under section 446(e).

(b) *Illustration of change of basis in computing reserves.* The application of section 806(b) and paragraph (a) of this section may be illustrated by the following examples:

Example (1). Assume that the life insurance reserves of Y, a life insurance company, at the beginning of the taxable year 1959 are $100 and that during such taxable year a portion of the reserves is strengthened (by reason of a change in mortality or interest assumptions, or otherwise), so that at the end of the taxable year 1959 the reserves (computed on the new basis) are $130 but computed on the old basis would be $120. Assume further that at the close of the next taxable year, 1960, the reserves (computed on the new basis) are $142. Under the provisions of section 806(b) and paragraph (a) of this section, the mean of such reserves for the taxable year of the reserve strengthening, namely 1959, is $110 (the mean of $100, the balance at the beginning of the taxable year 1959, and $120, the balance at the end of the taxable year 1959 computed on the old basis). The mean of such reserves for the next taxable year, 1960, is $136 (the mean of $130, the balance at the beginning of the taxable year 1960 computed on the new basis, and $142, the balance at the end of the taxable year 1960 computed on the new basis).

Example (2). The life insurance reserves of S, a life insurance company, computed with respect to contracts for which such reserves are determined on a recognized preliminary term basis amount to $50 on January 1, 1959, and $80 on December 31, 1959. For the taxable year 1959, S elects to revalue such reserves on a net level premium basis under section 818(c). Such reserves computed under section 818(c) amount to $60 on January 1, 1959, and $96 on December 31, 1959. Under the

Reg. § 1.806-4(a)

Life Insurance Companies

See p. 20,601 for regulations not amended to reflect law changes

→ **Caution: Former Code Secs. 801-820 for pre-1984 years were repealed and replaced by new Code Secs. 801-818. The following Regulations were issued under old Code Secs. 801-820.** ←

provisions of paragraph (a) of this section, the mean of such reserves for the taxable year 1959 is $78 (the mean of $60, the balance at the beginning of the taxable year 1959 computed under section 818(c), and $96, the balance at the end of the taxable year 1959 computed under section 818(c)). [Reg. § 1.806-4.]

☐ [*T.D.* 6513, 12-9-60.]

[Reg. § 1.809-1]

§ 1.809-1. Taxable years affected.—Sections 1.809 through 1.809-8, except as otherwise provided therein, are applicable only to taxable years beginning after December 31, 1957, and all references to sections of part I, subchapter L, chapter 1 of the Code are to the Internal Revenue Code of 1954, as amended by the Life Insurance Company Income Tax Act of 1959 (73 Stat. 112), the Act of June 27, 1961 (75 Stat. 120), the Act of October 10, 1962 (76 Stat. 808); the Act of October 23, 1962 (76 Stat. 1134), and section 214(b)(4) of the Revenue Act of 1964 (78 Stat. 55). [Reg. § 1.809-1.]

☐ [*T.D.* 6535, 1-19-61. *Amended by T.D.* 6886, 6-22-66 *and T.D.* 6992, 1-17-69.]

[Reg. § 1.809-2]

§ 1.809-2. Exclusion of share of investment yield set aside for policyholders.—(a) *In general.* Section 809 provides the rules for determining the gain or loss from operations of a life insurance company, which amount is necessary to determine life insurance company taxable income. In order to determine gain or loss from operations, a life insurance company must first determine the share of each and every item of its investment yield (as defined in section 804(c) and paragraph (a) of § 1.804-4) set aside for policyholders (as computed under section 809(a)(1) and paragraph (b) of this section), as this share is excluded from gain or loss from operations (as defined in section 809(b)(1) and (2) and paragraphs (a) and (b) of § 1.809-3 respectively). The life insurance company shall then add its share of each and every item of its investment yield to the sum of the items comprising gross amount (as described in section 809(c) and paragraph (a) of § 1.809-4). In addition, the life insurance company shall, for taxable years beginning after December 31, 1961, add the amount (if any) by which its net long-term capital gain exceeds its net short-term loss. From the sum so computed (which includes the capital gains item only for taxable years beginning after December 31, 1961) there shall then be subtracted the deductions provided in section 809(d) and paragraph (a) of § 1.809-5 of this chapter. The amount thus obtained is the gain or loss from operations for the taxable year.

(b) *Computation of share of investment yield set aside for policyholders.* Section 809(a)(1) provides that the share of each and every item of investment yield (including tax-exempt interest, partially tax-exempt interest, and dividends received) of any life insurance company set aside for policyholders shall not be included in gain or loss from operations. For this purpose, the percentage used in determining the share of each of these items comprising the investment yield set aside for policyholders shall be determined by dividing the required interest (as defined in section 809(a)(2) and paragraph (d) of this section) by the investment yield (as defined in section 804(c) and paragraph (a) of § 1.804-4). The percentage thus obtained is then applied to each and every item of the investment yield so that the share of each and every item of investment yield set aside for policyholders shall be excluded from gain or loss from operations. However, if in any case the required interest exceeds the investment yield, then the share of any item set aside for policyholders shall be 100 percent.

(c) *Computation of life insurance company's share of investment yield.* For purposes of subpart C, part I, subchapter L, chapter 1 of the Code, section 809(b)(3) provides that the percentage used in determining the life insurance company's share of each and every item of investment yield (including tax-exempt interest, partially tax-exempt interest, and dividends received) shall be obtained by subtracting the percentage obtained under paragraph (b) of this section from 100 percent. For example, if the policyholders' percentage (as determined under section 809(a)(1) and paragraph (b) of this section) is 72.38 percent, then the life insurance company's share is 27.62 percent (100 percent minus 72.38 percent). In such a case, if the amount of a particular item is $200, then the life insurance company's share of such item included in determining gain or loss from operations is $55.24 ($200 multiplied by 27.62 percent) and the share of such item set aside for policyholders (which is excluded from gain or loss from operations) is $144.76 ($200 multiplied by 72.38 percent). For purposes of determining gain or loss from operations, the life insurance commpany's share of each and every item of investment yield (including tax-exempt interest, partially tax-exempt interest, and dividends re-

Reg. § 1.809-2(c)

45,740 **Life Insurance Companies**
See p. 20,601 for regulations not amended to reflect law changes

→ *Caution: Former Code Secs. 801-820 for pre-1984 years were repealed and replaced by new Code Secs. 801-818. The following Regulations were issued under old Code Secs. 801-820.*←

ceived) shall be added to the sum of the items comprising gross amount (as described in section 809(c) and paragraph (a) of § 1.809-4).

(d) *Required interest defined.* (1) For purposes of part I, section 809(a)(2) defines the term "required interest" for any taxable year as the sum of the products obtained by multiplying (i) each rate of interest required, or assumed by the taxpayer, in calculating the reserves described in section 810(c), by (ii) the means of the amount of such reserves computed at that rate at the beginning and end of the taxable year. In the case of the reserves described in section 810(c)(1), such rate of interest shall be the same as that used by the taxpayer for purposes of paragraph (b) of § 1.801-5 (relating to the definition of reserves required by law) with respect to such reserves. In the case of the reserves described in section 810(c)(2) through (5), such rate of interest shall be the same as that actually paid, credited, or accrued by the taxpayer with respect to such reserves. Thus, the required interest for any taxable year includes the elements of interest paid (as defined in section 805(e)) with respect to the reserves described in section 810(c).

(2) For purposes of computing required interest under section 809(a)(2) and subparagraph (1) of this paragraph, the amount of life insurance reserves taken into account shall be adjusted first as required by section 818(c) (relating to an election with respect to life insurance reserves computed on a preliminary term basis) and then as required by section 806(a) (relating to adjustments for certain changes in reserves and assets) before applying the rate of interest required, or assumed by the taxpayer, thereto. However, in the case of the adjustments required by section 810(d) as a result of a change in the basis of computing reserves, the adjustments to any of the reserves described in section 810(c) shall be taken into account in accordance with the rules prescribed in section 810(d) and § 1.810-3. [Reg. § 1.809-2.]

☐ [T.D. 6535, 1-19-61. Amended by T.D. 6886, 6-22-66.]

[Reg. § 1.809-4]

§ 1.809-4. **Gross amount.**—(a) *Items taken into account.* For purposes of determining gain or loss from operations under section 809(b)(1) and (2), respectively, section 809(c) specifies three categories of items which shall be taken into account. Such items are in addition to the life insurance company's share of the investment yield (as determined under section 809(a)(1) and paragraph (c) of § 1.809-2), and the amount (if any) by which the net long-term capital gain exceeds the net short-term capital loss (such capital gains item is included in determining gain or loss from operations only for taxable years beginning after December 31, 1961). The additional three categories of items taken into account are:

(1) *Premiums.* (i) The gross amount of all premiums and other consideration on insurance and annuity contracts (including contracts supplementary thereto); less return premiums and premiums and other consideration arising out of reinsurance ceded. The term "gross amount of all premiums" means the premiums and other consideration provided in the insurance or annuity contract. Thus, the amount to be taken into account shall be the total of the premiums and other consideration provided in the insurance or annuity contract without any deduction for commissions, return premiums, reinsurance, dividends to policyholders, dividends left on deposit with the company, discounts on premiums paid in advance, interest applied in reduction of premiums (whether or not required to be credited in reduction of premiums under the terms of the contract), or any other item of similar nature. Such term includes advance premiums, premiums deferred and uncollected and premiums due and unpaid, deposits, fees, assessments, and consideration in respect of assuming liabilities under contracts not issued by the taxpayer (such as a payment or transfer of property in an assumption reinsurance transaction as defined in paragraph (a)(7)(ii) of § 1.809-5). The term also includes amounts a life insurance company charges itself representing premiums with respect to liability for insurance and annuity benefits for its employees (including full-time life insurance salesmen within the meaning of section 7701(a)(20)).

(ii) The term "return premiums" means amounts returned or credited which are fixed by contract and do not depend on the experience of the company or the discretion of the management. Thus, such term includes amounts refunded due to policy cancellations or erroneously computed premiums. Furthermore, amounts of premiums or other consideration returned to another life insurance company in respect of reinsurance ceded shall be included in return premiums. For the treatment of amounts which do not meet the requirements of return premiums, see section 811 (relating to dividends to policyholders).

Reg. § 1.809-4(a)(1)

Life Insurance Companies

See p. 20,601 for regulations not amended to reflect law changes

→ *Caution: Former Code Secs. 801-820 for pre-1984 years were repealed and replaced by new Code Secs. 801-818. The following Regulations were issued under old Code Secs. 801-820.* ←

(iii) For purposes of section 809(c)(1) and this subparagraph, the term "reinsurance ceded" means an arrangement whereby the taxpayer (the reinsured) remains solely liable to the policyholder, whether all or only a portion of the risk has been transferred to the reinsurer. Such term includes indemnity reinsurance transactions but does not include assumption reinsurance transactions. See paragraph (a)(7)(ii) of § 1.809-5 for the definition of assumption reinsurance.

(2) *Decreases in certain reserves*. Each net decrease in reserves which is required by section 810(a) and (d)(1) or 811(b)(2) to be taken into account for the taxable year as a net decrease for purposes of section 809(c)(2).

(3) *Other amounts*. All amounts, not included in computing investment yield and not otherwise taken into account under section 809(c)(1) or (2), shall be taken into account under section 809(c)(3) to the extent that such amounts are includible in gross income under subtitle A of the Code. See section 61 (relating to gross income defined) and the regulations thereunder.

(b) *Treatment of net long-term capital gains*. For taxable years beginning before January 1, 1962, any net long-term capital gains (as defined in section 1222(7)) from the sale or exchange of a capital asset (or any gain considered to be from the sale or exchange of a capital asset under applicable law) shall be excluded from the determination of gain or loss from operations of a life insurance company. On the other hand, with respect to taxable years beginning after December 31, 1961, the amount (if any) by which the net long-term capital gain exceeds the net short-term capital loss (as defined in section 1222(6)) shall be taken into account in determining gain or loss from operations under section 809. However, for any taxable year beginning after December 31, 1958, the excess of net short-term capital gain (as defined in section 1222(5)) over net long-term capital loss (as defined in section 1222(8)) is included in computing investment yield (as defined in section 804(c)) and, to that extent, is taken into account in determining gain or loss from operations under section 809. [Reg. § 1.809-4.]

☐ [T.D. 6535, 1-19-61. Amended by T.D. 6610, 8-30-62 and T.D. 6886, 6-22-66.]

[Reg. § 1.809-5]

§ 1.809-5. Deductions.—(a) *Deductions allowed*. Section 809(d) provides the following deductions for purposes of determining gain or loss from operations under section 809(b)(1) and (2), respectively:

(1) *Death benefits, etc*. All claims and benefits accrued (less reinsurance recoverable), and all losses incurred (whether or not ascertained), during the taxable year on insurance and annuity contracts (including contracts supplementary thereto). The term "all claims and benefits accrued" includes, for example, matured endowments and amounts allowed on surrender. The term "losses incurred (whether or not ascertained)" includes a reasonable estimate of the amount of the losses (based upon the facts in each case and the company's experience with similar cases) incurred but not reported by the end of the taxable year as well as losses reported but where the amount thereof cannot be ascertained by the end of the taxable year.

(2) *Increases in certain reserves*. The net increase in reserves which is required by section 810(b) and (d)(1) to be taken into account for the taxable year as a net increase for purposes of section 809(d)(2).

(3) *Dividends to policyholders*. The deduction for dividends to policyholders as determined under section 811(b) and § 1.811-2. Except as provided in section 809(d)(3) and this subparagraph, no amount shall be allowed as a deduction in respect of dividends to policyholders under section 809(d). See section 809(f) and § 1.809-7 for limitation of such deduction.

(4) *Operations loss deduction*. The operations loss deduction as determined under section 812.

(5) *Certain nonparticipating contracts*. (i) An amount equal to the greater of:

(*a*) 10 percent of the increase for the taxable year in certain life insurance reserves for nonparticipating contracts (other than group contracts); or

(*b*) 3 percent of the premiums for the taxable year attributable to nonparticipating contracts (other than group contracts) which are issued or renewed for periods of 5 years or more.

(ii) For purposes of section 809(d)(5) and this subparagraph, the term "nonparticipating contracts" means those contracts which during the taxable year contain no right to participate in the divisible surplus of the company. For example, if at any time during the taxable year for which the deduction allowed under section 809(d)(5) and this subparagraph is claimed such contracts have rights to dividends or similar distributions (as defined in section 811(a) and paragraph (a) of

Reg. § 1.809-5(a)(5)

45,742   Life Insurance Companies

See p. 20,601 for regulations not amended to reflect law changes

→ *Caution: Former Code Secs. 801-820 for pre-1984 years were repealed and replaced by new Code Secs. 801-818. The following Regulations were issued under old Code Secs. 801-820.*←

§ 1.811-2), such contracts shall no longer be deemed nonparticipating contracts and, therefore, no deduction shall be allowed. Thus, if a class of contracts having no right to participate in the divisible surplus of the company is in force for nine years and on March 10, 1958, it is announced that such contracts shall be accorded dividend rights as of August 1, 1958, no deduction shall be allowed under section 809(d)(5) and this subparagraph for the taxable year 1958 or any succeeding taxable year, whether or not dividends are actually paid on such contracts. However, if the announcement of March 10, 1958, states that such contracts shall be accorded dividend rights as of January 1, 1959, a deduction under section 809(d)(5) and this subparagraph shall be allowed for the taxable year 1958 but not for any succeeding taxable year.

(iii) For purposes of section 809(d)(5) and this subparagraph, the term "reserves for nonparticipating contracts" means such part of the life insurance reserves (as defined in section 801(b) and § 1.801-4), other than that portion of such reserves which is allocable to annuity features, as relates to nonparticipating contracts (as defined in subdivision (ii) of this subparagraph). The amount of life insurance reserves taken into account shall be adjusted first as required by section 818(c) (relating to an election with respect to life insurance reserves computed on a preliminary term basis) and then as required by section 806(a) (relating to adjustments for certain changes in reserves and assets). In the case of the adjustments required by section 810(d) (relating to adjustment for change in computing reserves), the increase in life insurance reserves attributable to reserve strengthening shall be taken into account in accordance with the rules prescribed in section 810(d) and § 1.810-3.

(iv) For purposes of section 809(d)(5) and this subparagraph, the term "premiums" means the net amount of the premiums and other consideration attributable to nonparticipating contracts (as defined in subdivision (ii) of this subparagraph) which are taken into account under section 809(c)(1). For this purpose, premiums include only such amounts attributable to such contracts which are issued or renewed for periods of 5 years or more, but does not include that portion of the premiums which is allocable to annuity features. No portion of a premium shall be deemed allocable to annuity features solely because a contract, such as an endowment contract, provides that at maturity the insured shall have an option to take an annuity. The determination of whether a contract meets the 5-year requirement shall be made as of the date the contract is issued, or as of the date it is renewed, whichever is applicable. Thus, a 20-year nonparticipating endowment policy shall qualify for the deduction under section 809(d)(5), even though the insured subsequently dies at the end of the second year, since the policy is issued for a period of 5 years or more. However, a 1-year renewable term contract shall not qualify, since as of the date it is issued (or of any renewal date) it is not issued (or renewed) for a period of 5 years or more. In like manner, a policy originally issued for a 3-year period and subsequently renewed for an additional 3-year period shall not qualify. However, if this policy is renewed for a period of 5 years or more, the policy shall qualify for the deduction under section 809(d)(5) from the date it is renewed.

(v) The provisions of section 809(d)(5) and this subparagraph may be illustrated by the following example:

Example. Assume the following facts with respect to X, a life insurance company, for the taxable year 1958:

Life insurance reserves on nonparticipating contracts without annuity features (other than group contracts) at 1-1-58	$150,000
Life insurance reserves on nonparticipating contracts without annuity features (other than group contracts) at 12-31-58	225,000
Annuity reserves on nonparticipating contracts (other than group contracts) at 1-1-58	48,000
Annuity reserves on nonparticipating contracts (other than group contracts) at 12-31-58	57,000
Premiums on nonparticipating contracts without annuity features (other than group contracts) issued or renewed for 5 years or more	85,000
Premiums on nonparticipating contracts allocable to annuity features (other than group contracts) issued or renewed for 5 years or more	14,000
Return premiums on nonparticipating contracts without annuity features (other than group contracts)	5,000

Reg. § 1.809-5(a)(5)

Life Insurance Companies

45,743

See p. 20,601 for regulations not amended to reflect law changes

→ **Caution:** *Former Code Secs. 801-820 for pre-1984 years were repealed and replaced by new Code Secs. 801-818. The following Regulations were issued under old Code Secs. 801-820.* ←

In order to determine the deduction under section 809(d)(5) (without regard to the limitation of section 809(f)), X would make up the following schedule:

(1) Life insurance reserves on nonparticipating contracts without annuity features (other than group contracts) at 12-31-58	$225,000	
(2) Life insurance reserves on nonparticipating contracts without annuity features (other than group contracts) at 1-1-58	$150,000	
(3) Excess of item (1) over item (2) ($225,000 minus $150,000)	$ 75,000	
(4) 10 percent of item (3) (10% × $75,000)		$7,500
(5) Net premiums on nonparticipating contracts without annuity features issued or renewed for 5 years or more (other than group contracts) (gross premiums on such contracts ($85,000) minus return premiums ($5,000) on such contracts)	$ 80,000	
(6) 3 percent of item (5) (3% × $80,000)		$2,400
(7) The greater of item (4) or item (6)		7,500
(8) Tentative deduction under sec. 809(d)(5) (computed without regard to the limitation of sec. 809(f))		$7,500

(vi) See section 809(f) and § 1.809-7 for limitation of the deduction provided by this subparagraph.

(6) *Certain accident and health insurance and group life insurance.* (i) For taxable years beginning before January 1, 1963, an amount equal to two percent of the premiums for the taxable year attributable to group life insurance contracts, group accident and health insurance contracts, or group accident and health insurance contracts with a life feature. For taxable years beginning after December 31, 1962, the deduction shall be an amount equal to two percent of the premiums for the taxable year attributable to group life insurance contracts, accident and health insurance contracts (other than those to which section 809(d)(5) applies), or accident and health insurance contracts with a life feature (other than those to which section 809(d)(5) applies). For purposes of section 809(d)(6) and this subparagraph, the term "premiums" means the net amount of the premiums and other consideration attributable to such contracts taken into account under section 809(c)(1). The deduction allowed by section 809(d)(6) and this subparagraph for the taxable year and all preceding taxable years shall not exceed 50 percent of the net amount of the premiums attributable to such contracts for the taxable year. For example, assume that premiums attributable to group life insurance and group accident and health insurance contracts are $103,000 for the taxable year 1962. Assume further that there are $3,000 of return premiums attributable to such contracts for the taxable year. Under the provisions of section 809(d)(6) and this subparagraph, a deduction (determined without regard to section 809(f)) of $2,000 (2 percent of $100,000 ($103,000 − $3,000)) is allowed. Assuming that the company continues to receive net premiums of $100,000 attributable to such contracts for 15 years, the cumulative amount of these deductions is $30,000 ($2,000 for 15 years). If, in the sixteenth year, net premiums attributable to such contracts amount to $60,000, no deduction shall be allowed under section 809(d)(6) and this subparagraph since the cumulative amount of these deductions ($30,000) equals 50 percent of the current year's premiums ($60,000) from such contracts.

(ii) In computing the deduction under section 809(d)(6), the determination as to when the 50 percent limitation on such deduction has been reached shall be based upon the amount allowed as a deduction for the taxable year and all preceding taxable years after the application of the limitation provided in section 809(f) and § 1.809-7. Thus, if in the example set forth in paragraph (c) of § 1.809-7 the application of the limitation provided by section 809(f) limited the deduction allowed for the taxable year under section 809(d)(6) to $3,250,000, then for purposes of determining the 50 percent limitation on such deduction, only $3,250,000 (the amount allowed) shall be taken into account.

(iii) For purposes of determining whether the 50 percent limitation applies to any taxable year, the deduction provided by section 809(d)(6) for all preceding taxable years shall be taken into account, irrespective of whether or not the life insurance company claimed a deduction for these amounts for such preceding taxable years.

(iv) See section 809(f) and § 1.809-7 for limitation of the deduction provided by this subparagraph.

Reg. § 1.809-5(a)(6)

Life Insurance Companies

See p. 20,601 for regulations not amended to reflect law changes

→ **Caution: Former Code Secs. 801-820 for pre-1984 years were repealed and replaced by new Code Secs. 801-818. The following Regulations were issued under old Code Secs. 801-820.** ←

(7) *Assumption by another person of liabilities under insurance, etc., contracts.* (i) The consideration (other than consideration arising out of reinsurance ceded as defined in paragraph (a)(1)(iii) of § 1.809-4) in respect of the assumption by another person of liabilities under insurance and annuity contracts (including contracts supplementary thereto) of the taxpayer.

(ii) For purposes of section 809(d)(7) and this subparagraph, the term "assumption reinsurance" means an arrangement whereby another person (the reinsurer) becomes solely liable to the policyholders on the contracts transferred by the taxpayer. Such term does not include indemnity reinsurance or reinsurance ceded (as defined in paragraph (a)(1)(iii) of § 1.809-4).

(iii) The provisions of section 809(d)(7) and this subparagraph may be illustrated by the following example:

Example. During the taxable year 1958, T, a life insurance company, transferred a block of insurance policies and made a payment of $50,000 to R, a life insurance company, under an arrangement whereby R became solely liable to the policyholders on the policies transferred by T. Under the provisions of section 809(d)(7) and this subparagraph, T is allowed a deduction of $50,000 for the taxable year 1958. For the treatment by R of this $50,000 payment, see section 809(c)(1) and paragraph (a)(1)(i) of § 1.809-4. See section 806(a) and § 1.806-3 for the adjustments in reserves and assets to be made by T and R as a result of this transaction.

(8) *Tax-exempt interest, dividends, etc.* (i) Each of the following items:

(*a*) The life insurance company's share of interest which under section 103 is excluded from gross income;

(*b*) The deduction for partially tax-exempt interest provided by section 242 (as modified by section 804(a)(3) and paragraph (d)(2)(i) of § 1.804-2) computed with respect to the life insurance company's share of such interest; and

(*c*) The deductions for dividends received provided by sections 243, 244, and 245 (as modified by section 809(d)(8)(B) and subdivision (ii) of this subparagraph) computed with respect to the life insurance company's share of the dividends received.

(ii) The modification contained in section 809(d)(8)(B) provides the method for applying section 246(b) (relating to limitation on aggregate amount of deductions for dividends received) for purposes of section 809(d)(8)(A)(iii) and subdivision (i)(*c*) of this subparagraph. Under this method, the sum of the deductions allowed by sections 243(a)(1) (relating to dividends received by corporations), 244(a) (relating to dividends received on certain preferred stock), and 245 (relating to dividends received from certain foreign corporations) shall be limited to 85 percent of the gain from operations computed without regard to:

(*a*) The deductions provided by section 809(d)(3), (5), and (6);

(*b*) The operations loss deductions provided by section 812; and

(*c*) The deductions allowed by sections 243(a)(1), 244(a), and 245.

If a life insurance company has a loss from operations (as determined under section 812) for the taxable year, the limitation provided in section 809(d)(8)(B) and this subdivision shall not be applicable for such taxable year. In that event, the deductions provided by sections 243(a)(1), 244(a), and 245 shall be allowable for all tax purposes to the life insurance company for such taxable year without regard to such limitation. If the life insurance company does not have a loss from operations for the taxable year, however, the limitation shall be applicable for all tax purposes for such taxable year. In determining whether a life insurance company has a loss from operations for the taxable year under section 812, the deductions allowed by sections 243(a)(1), 244(a), and 245 shall be computed without regard to the limitation provided in section 809(d)(8)(B) and this subdivision.

(9) *Investment expenses, etc.* (i) The amount of investment expenses to the extent not allowed as a deduction under section 804(c)(1) in computing investment yield. For example, if a deduction in the amount of $100,000 is claimed for investment expenses, which amount includes general expenses assigned to or included in investment expenses, and due to the operation of the limitation provided by section 804(c)(1) only $85,000 is allowed, then the excess ($15,000) shall be allowed as a deduction under section 809(d)(9) and this subparagraph.

(ii) The amount (if any) by which the sum of the deductions allowable under section 804(c) exceeds the gross investment income. For example, if gross investment income under section 840(b) equals $400,000, and the sum of the deductions allowable under section 804(c) equals $425,000, then the excess ($25,000) shall be al-

Reg. § 1.809-5(a)(7)

Life Insurance Companies

See p. 20,601 for regulations not amended to reflect law changes

→ *Caution: Former Code Secs. 801-820 for pre-1984 years were repealed and replaced by new Code Secs. 801-818. The following Regulations were issued under old Code Secs. 801-820.* ←

lowed as a deduction under section 809(d)(9) and this subparagraph.

(iii) In determining the amount of the deductions allowed under subdivisions (i) and (ii) of this subparagraph, a life insurance company shall first take such deductions to the full extent allowable under section 804(c)(1), and any amount which is allowed as a deduction under section 804(c) shall not again be allowed as a deduction under section 809(d)(9).

(10) *Small business deduction.* The small business deduction as determined under section 804(a)(4).

(11) *Certain mutualization distributions.* The amount of distributions to shareholders actually made by the life insurance company in 1958, 1959, 1960, and 1961 in acquisition of stock pursuant to a plan of mutualization adopted by the company before January 1, 1958. If such deduction is claimed, there must be attached to the return of the company claiming such deduction a certified copy of the plan of mutualization and proof that such plan was adopted prior to January 1, 1958. See section 809(g) and § 1.809-8 for limitation of such deduction.

(12) *Other deductions.* Except as modified by section 809(e) and § 1.809-6, all other deductions allowed under subtitle A of the Code for purposes of computing taxable income to the extent not allowed as a deduction in computing investment yield. For example, a life insurance company shall be allowed a deduction under section 809(d)(12) and this subparagraph for amounts representing premiums charged itself with respect to liability for insurance and annuity benefits for its employees (including full-time life insurance salesmen within the meaning of section 7701(a)(20)) in accordance with the rules prescribed in sections 162 and 404 and the regulations thereunder, to the extent that a deduction for such amounts is not allowed under section 804(c)(1) and paragraph (b)(1) of § 1.804-4 or section 809(d)(9) and subparagraph (9) of this paragraph.

(b) *Denial of double deduction.* Nothing in section 809(d) shall permit the same item to be deducted more than once in determining gain or loss from operations. For example, if an item is allowed as a deduction for the taxable year by reason of its being a loss incurred within such taxable year (whether or not ascertained) under section 809(d)(1), such item, or any portion thereof, shall not also be allowed as a deduction

for such taxable year under section 809(d)(2). [Reg. § 1.809-5.]

☐ [T.D. 6535, 1-19-61. Amended by T.D. 6610, 8-30-62, T.D. 6886, 6-22-66, and T.D. 6992, 1-17-69.]

[Reg. § 1.809-6]

§ 1.809-6. **Modifications.**—Under section 809(e), the deductions allowed under section 809(d)(12) and paragraph (a)(12) of § 1.809-5 (relating to other deductions) are subject to the following modifications—

(a) *Interest.* No deduction shall be allowed under section 163 for interest in respect of items described in section 810(c) since such interest is taken into account in the determination of required interest under section 809.

(b) *Bad debts.* No deduction shall be allowed for an addition to reserves for bad debts under section 166(c). However, a deduction for specific bad debts shall be allowed to the extent that such deduction is allowed under section 166 and the regulations thereunder. In the case of a loss incurred on the sale of mortgaged or pledged property, see § 1.166-6.

(c) *Charitable, etc., contributions and gifts.* (1) The deduction by a life insurance company in any taxable year for a charitable contribution (as defined in section 170(c)) shall be limited to 5 percent of the gain from operations (as determined under section 809(b)(1)), computed without regard to any deductions for:

(i) Charitable contributions under section 170;

(ii) Dividends to policyholders under section 811(b);

(iii) Certain nonparticipating contracts under section 809(d)(5);

(iv) Group life insurance contracts and group accident and health insurance contracts under section 809(d)(6);

(v) Tax-exempt interest, dividends, etc., under section 809(d)(8); and

(vi) Any operations loss carryback to the taxable year under section 812.

(2) In applying the first sentence of section 170(b)(2) as contained in § 1.170 or, in the case of taxable years beginning after December 31, 1969, section 170(d)(2)(B) as contained in § 1.170A, any excess of the charitable contributions made by a life insurance company in a taxable year over the amount deductible in such year under the limita-

Reg. § 1.809-6(c)(2)

→ *Caution: Former Code Secs. 801-820 for pre-1984 years were repealed and replaced by new Code Secs. 801-818. The following Regulations were issued under old Code Secs. 801-820.* ←

tion contained in subparagraph (1) of this paragraph, shall be reduced to the extent that such excess:

(i) Reduces life insurance company taxable income (computed without regard to section 802(b)(3)) for the purpose of determining the offsets referred to in section 812(b)(2); and

(ii) Increases an operations loss carryover under section 812 for a succeeding taxable year.

(3) The application of the rules provided in section 809(e)(3) and this paragraph may be illustrated by the following example:

Example. Assume that life insurance company P is organized on January 1, 1958, and has a loss from operations for that year in the amount of $100,000 which is an operations loss carryover to 1959. In 1959, company P has a gain from operations and tax base (computed without regard to section 802(b)(3)) of $100,000 before the allowance of a deduction for a $5,000 charitable contribution made in 1959 and before the application of the operations loss carryover from 1958. Under section 170(b)(2), the operations loss carryover from 1958 is first applied to eliminate the $100,000 gain from operations and tax base in 1959 and the $5,000 charitable contributions carryover would (except for the limitation contained in this paragraph) become a charitable contribution carryover to 1960. However, for the purpose of computing the offsets referred to in section 812(b)(2), the $5,000 charitable contribution is applied to reduce the gain from operations and tax base for 1959 to $95,000 before the application of the operations carryover from 1958. Since only $95,000 of the $100,000 loss from operations in 1958 is an offset for 1959, the remaining $5,000 becomes an operations loss carryover to 1960. Accordingly, under the limitation contained in this paragraph, the charitable contributions carryover provided under the second sentence of section 170(b)(2) is eliminated.

(d) *Amortizable bond premium.* No deduction shall be allowed under section 171 for the amortization of bond premiums since a special deduction for such premiums is specifically taken into account under section 818(b).

(e) *Net operating loss deduction.* No deduction shall be allowed under section 172 since section 812 allows an "operations loss deduction."

(f) *Partially tax-exempt interest.* No deduction shall be allowed under section 242 for partially tax-exempt interest since section 809(d)(8) allows a deduction for such interest.

(g) *Dividends received.* No deduction shall be allowed under sections 243, 244, and 245 for dividends received since section 809(d)(8) allows a deduction for such dividends. [Reg. § 1.809-6.]

☐ [T.D. 6535, 1-19-61. Amended by T.D. 7207, 10-3-72.]

[Reg. § 1.809-7]

§ 1.809-7. **Limitation on certain deductions.**—(a) *In general.* Section 809(f)(1) limits the deductions under section 809(d)(3), (5), and (6), relating to deductions for dividends to policyholders, certain nonparticipating contracts, and group life, accident, and health insurance contracts, respectively. This limitation provides that the amount of such deductions shall not exceed the sum of (1) the amount (if any) by which the gain from operations for the taxable year (determined without regard to such deductions) exceeds the taxpayer's taxable investment income for such year, plus (2) $250,000.

(b) *Application of limitation.* Section 809(f)(2) provides a priority system for applying the limitation contained in section 809(f)(1) and paragraph (a) of this section. Under this priority system, the limitation shall be applied in the following order—

(1) For taxable years beginning before January 1, 1962:

(i) First to the amount of the deduction under section 809(d)(6) (relating to group life, accident, and health insurance);

(ii) Then to the amount of the deduction under section 809(d)(5) (relating to certain nonparticipating contracts); and

(iii) Finally to the amount of the deduction under section 809(d)(3) (relating to dividends to policyholders).

(2) For taxable years beginning after December 31, 1961, the limitation shall be applied in the following order:

(i) First to the amount of the deduction under section 809(d)(3);

(ii) Then to the amount of the deduction under section 809(d)(6); and

(iii) Finally to the amount of the deduction under section 809(d)(5).

Thus, for taxable years beginning after December 31, 1961, the limitation and priority system would operate first to disallow a deduction under section 809(d)(5), then a deduction under section 809(d)(6), and finally a deduction under section

Life Insurance Companies

45,747

See p. 20,601 for regulations not amended to reflect law changes

→ *Caution: Former Code Secs. 801-820 for pre-1984 years were repealed and replaced by new Code Secs. 801-818. The following Regulations were issued under old Code Secs. 801-820.* ←

809(d)(3). For purposes of applying the 50 percent limitation contained in section 809(d)(6) with respect to a taxable year beginning after December 31, 1961, the amount of the deductions for taxable years beginning before January 1, 1962, shall be determined by applying the priority system contained in subparagraph (1) of this paragraph.

(c) *Illustration of principles.* The operation of the limitation and priority system provided by section 809(f) and this section may be illustrated by the following examples:

Example (1). Assume the following facts with respect to M, a life insurance company, for the taxable year 1958:

Gain from operations computed without regard to the deductions under sec. 809(d)(3), (5), and (6)	$100,000,000
Taxable investment income	83,000,000
Tentative deduction for group life, accident, and health insurance under sec. 809(d)(6)	4,000,000
Tentative deduction for certain nonparticipating contracts under sec. 809(d)(5)	6,000,000
Tentative deduction for dividends to policyholders under sec. 809(d)(3)	10,000,000

In order to determine the limitation on the deductions under section 809(d)(3), (5), and (6), M would make up the following schedule:

(1) Statutory amount provided under sec. 809(f)(1)		$ 250,000
(2) Gain from operations computed without regard to the deductions under sec. 809(d)(3), (5), and (6)	$100,000,000	
(3) Taxable investment income	83,000,000	
(4) Excess of item (2) over item (3)		17,000,000
(5) Limitation on deductions under sec. 809(d)(3), (5), and (6) (item (1) plus item (4))		17,250,000

Since the total tentative deductions under section 809(d)(3), (5), and (6) ($20,000,000) exceeds the limitation on such deductions ($17,250,000), M would make up the following schedule to determine the application of the priority system:

(6) Maximum possible deduction under sec. 809(d)(3), (5), and (6) (item (5))	$17,250,000
(7) Deduction for group life, accident, and health insurance under sec. 809(d)(6) (not in excess of item (6))	4,000,000
(8) Maximum possible deduction under sec. 809(d)(5) (item (6) less item (7))	13,250,000
(9) Deduction for certain nonparticipating contracts under sec. 809(d)(5) (not in excess of item (8))	6,000,000
(10) Maximum possible deduction under sec. 809(d)(3) (item (8) less item (9))	$ 7,250,000
(11) Deduction for dividends to policyholders under sec. 809(d)(3) (not in excess of item (10))	7,250,000

Thus, as a result of the application of the limitation and priority system for the taxable year 1958, M shall be allowed a deduction of $4,000,000 under section 809(d)(6), $6,000,000 under section 809(d)(5), and only $7,250,000 of the $10,000,000 tentative deduction under section 809(d)(3).

Example (2). The facts are the same as in example (1), except that the taxable year is 1962. Since the total tentative deductions under section 809(d)(3), (5), and (6) ($20,000,000) exceeds the limitation on such deductions ($17,250,000), M would make up the following schedule to determine the application of the priority system:

(1) Maximum possible deductions under sec. 809(d)(3), (5), and (6) (item (5) in example (1))	$17,250,000
(2) Deduction for dividends to policyholders under sec. 809(d)(3) (not in excess of item (1))	10,000,000
(3) Maximum possible deduction under sec. 809(d)(6) (item (1) less item (2))	$ 7,250,000
(4) Deduction for certain accident, health, and group life insurance under sec. 809(d)(6) (not in excess of item (3))	$ 4,000,000
(5) Maximum possible deduction under sec. 809(d)(5) (item (4) less item (5))	$ 3,250,000

Reg. § 1.809-7(c)

Life Insurance Companies

See p. 20,601 for regulations not amended to reflect law changes

→ *Caution: Former Code Secs. 801-820 for pre-1984 years were repealed and replaced by new Code Secs. 801-818. The following Regulations were issued under old Code Secs. 801-820.*←

(6) Deduction for certain nonparticipating contracts under sec. 809(d)(5) (not in excess of item (5)) 3,250,000

Thus, as a result of the application of the limitation and priority system for the taxable year 1962, M shall be allowed a deduction of $10,000,000 under section 809(d)(3), $4,000,000 under section 809(d)(6), and only $3,250,000 of the $6,000,000 tentative deduction under section 809(d)(5). [Reg. § 1.809-7.]

☐ [*T.D.* 6535, 1-19-61. Amended by *T.D.* 6886, 6-22-66.]

[Reg. § 1.810-1]

§ 1.810-1. Taxable years affected.—Sections 1.810-2 through 1.810-4 are applicable only to taxable years beginning after December 31, 1957, and all references to sections of part I, subchapter L, chapter 1 of the Code are to the Internal Revenue Code of 1954, as amended by the Life Insurance Company Income Tax Act of 1959 (73 Stat. 112). [Reg. § 1.810-1.]

☐ [*T.D.* 6535, 1-19-61.]

[Reg. § 1.810-2]

§ 1.810-2. Rules for certain reserves.—(a) *Adjustment for decrease or increase in certain reserve items*—(1) *Adjustment for decrease.* Section 810(a) provides that if the sum of the items described in section 810(c) and paragraph (b) of this section at the beginning of the taxable year exceeds the sum of such items at the end of the taxable year (reduced by the amount of investment yield not included in gain or loss from operations for the taxable year by reason of section 809(a)(1)), the amount of such excess shall be taken into account as a net decrease referred to in section 809(c)(2) and paragraph (a)(2) of § 1.809-4 in determining gain or loss from operations.

(2) *Adjustment for increase.* Section 810(b) provides that if the sum of the items described in section 810(c) and paragraph (b) of this section at the end of the taxable year (reduced by the amount of investment yield not included in gain or loss from operations for the taxable year by reason of section 809(a)(1)) exceeds the sum of such items at the beginning of the taxable year, the amount of such excess shall be taken into account as a net increase referred to in section 809(d)(2) and paragraph (a)(2) of § 1.809-5 in determining gain or loss from operations.

(b) *Items taken into account.* The items described in section 810(c) and referred to in section 810(a) and (b) and paragraph (a) of this section are:

(1) The life insurance reserves (as defined in section 801(b) and § 1.801-4);

(2) The unearned premiums and unpaid losses included in total reserves under section 801(c)(2) and § 1.801-5;

(3) The amounts (discounted at the rates of interest assumed by the company) necessary to satisfy the obligations under insurance or annuity contracts (including contracts supplementary thereto), but only if such obligations do not involve (at the time with respect to which the computation is made under this subparagraph) life, health, or accident contingencies;

(4) Dividend accumulations, and other amounts, held at interest in connection with insurance or annuity contracts (including contracts supplementary thereto);

(5) Premiums received in advance, and liabilities for premium deposit funds; and

(6) Special contingency reserves under contracts of group term life insurance or group health and accident insurance which are established and maintained for the provision of insurance on retired lives, for premium stabilization, or for a combination thereof.

For purposes of this paragraph, the same item shall be counted only once and deficiency reserves (as defined in section 801(b)(4) and paragraph (e)(4) of § 1.801-4) shall not be taken into account.

(c) *Special rules.* For purposes of section 810(a) and (b) and paragraph (a) of this section, in determining whether there is a net increase or decrease in the sum of the items described in section 810(c) and paragraph (b) of this section for the taxable year, the following rules shall apply.

(1) *Computation of net increase or decrease in reserves.* The sum of the items described in section 810(c) and paragraph (b) of this section at the beginning of the taxable year shall be the aggregate of the sums of each of such items at the beginning of the taxable year. The sum of the items described in section 810(c) and paragraph (b) of this section at the end of the taxable year shall be the aggregate of the sums of each of such items at the end of the taxable year. However, in order to determine whether there is a net increase or decrease in such items for the taxable year, the

Reg. § 1.810-1

Life Insurance Companies

→ *Caution: Former Code Secs. 801-820 for pre-1984 years were repealed and replaced by new Code Secs. 801-818. The following Regulations were issued under old Code Secs. 801-820.* ←

aggregate of the sums of the items at the end of the taxable year must first be reduced by the amount of investment yield not included in gain or loss from operations for the taxable year by reason of section 809(a)(1).

(2) *Effect of change in basis in computing reserves.* Any increase or decrease in the sum of the items described in section 810(c) and paragraph (b) of this section for the taxable year which is attributable to a change in the basis used in computing such items during the taxable year shall not be taken into account under section 810(a) and (b) and paragraph (a) of this section but shall be taken into account in the manner prescribed in section 810(d) and paragraph (a) of § 1.810-3.

(3) *Effect of section 818(c) election.* If a company which computes its life insurance reserves on a preliminary term basis elects to revalue such reserves on a net level premium basis under section 818(c), the sum of such reserves at the beginning and end of all taxable years (including the first taxable year) for which the election applies shall be the sum of such reserves computed on such net level premium basis.

(4) *Cross references.* For taxable years beginning before January 1, 1970, see section 810(e) (as in effect for such years) and § 1.810-4 for special rules for determining the net increase or decrease in the sum of the items described in section 810(c) and paragraph (b) of this section in the case of certain voluntary employees' beneficiary associations. For similar special rules in the case of life insurance companies issuing variable annuity contracts, see section 801(g)(4) and the regulations thereunder.

(d) *Illustration of principles.* The provisions of section 810(a) and (b) and this section may be illustrated by the following examples:

Example (1). Assume the following facts with respect to R, a life insurance company:

Sum of items described in section 810(c)(1) through (6) at beginning of taxable year	$ 940
Sum of items described in section 810(c)(1) through (6) at end of taxable year	1,060
Required interest (as defined in section 809(a)(2))	70
Investment yield (as defined in section 804(c))	100
Amount of investment yield not included in gain or loss from operations for the taxable year by reason of section 809(a)(1)	70

In order to determine the adjustment for decrease or increase in the sum of the items described in section 810(c) for the taxable year, R must first reduce the sum of such items at the end of the taxable year ($1,060) by the amount of investment yield ($70) not included in gain or loss from operations for the taxable year by reason of section 809(a)(1). Since the adjusted sum of such items at the end of the taxable year, $990 ($1,060 minus $70), exceeds the sum of such items at the beginning of the taxable year, $940, the excess of $50 ($990 minus $940) shall be taken into account as a net increase under section 809(d)(2) and paragraph (a)(2) of § 1.809-5 in determining gain or loss from operations.

Example (2). Assume the facts are the same as in example (1), except that the sum of the items described in section 810(c) at the beginning of the taxable year is $1,000. Since the sum of the items described in section 810(c) at the beginning of the taxable year, $1,000, exceeds the sum of such items at the end of the taxable year after adjustment for the amount of investment yield not included in gain or loss from operations for the taxable year by reason of section 809(a)(1), $990 ($1,060 minus $70), the excess of $10 ($1,000 minus $990) shall be taken into account as a net decrease under section 809(c)(2) and paragraph (a)(2) of § 1.809-4 in determining gain or loss from operations.

Example (3). Assume the following facts with respect to S, a life insurance company:

Sum of items described in section 810(c)(1) through (6) at beginning of taxable year	$1,970
Sum of items described in section 810(c)(1) through (6) at end of taxable year	2,040
Required interest (as defined in section 809(a)(2))	60
Investment yield (as defined in section 804(c))	$ 40
Amount of investment yield not included in gain or loss from operations by reason of section 809(a)(1)	40

Under the provisions of section 809(a)(1), since the required interest ($60) exceeds the investment yield ($40), the share of each and every item of investment yield set aside for policyholders and not included in gain or loss from operations for the

Reg. § 1.810-2(d)

→ **Caution:** *Former Code Secs. 801-820 for pre-1984 years were repealed and replaced by new Code Secs. 801-818. The following Regulations were issued under old Code Secs. 801-820.* ←

taxable year shall be 100 percent. Thus, applying the provisions of section 810(a) and (b), the sum of the items described in section 810(c) at the end of the taxable year ($2,040) must first be reduced by the entire amount of the investment yield ($40) in order to determine the net increase or decrease in the sum of such items for the taxable year. Since the adjusted sum of such items at the end of the taxable year, $2,000 ($2,040 minus $40), is greater than the sum of such items at the beginning of the taxable year, $1,970, the excess of $30 ($2,000 minus $1,970) shall be taken into account as a net increase under section 809(d)(2) and paragraph (a)(2) of § 1.809-5 in determining gain or loss from operations. No additional deduction is allowed under section 809(d) for the amount ($20) by which the required interest exceeds the investment yield for the taxable year.

Example (4). Assume the facts are the same as in example (1), except that as a result of a change in the basis used in computing an item described in section 810(c) during the taxable year, the sum of such items at the end of the taxable year is $1,200. Under the provisions of paragraph (c)(2) of this section, any increase or decrease in the sum of the section 810(c) items for the taxable year which is attributable to a change in the basis used in computing such items during the taxable year shall not be taken into account under section 810(a) and (b). Thus, for purposes of section 810(a) and (b), the sum of the items described in section 810(c) at the end of the taxable year shall be $1,060 (the amount computed without regard to the change in basis) and S shall treat the $50 computed in the manner described in example (1) as a net increase under section 809(d)(2) and paragraph (a)(2) of § 1.809-5 in determining its gain or loss from operations for the taxable year. The amount of the increase in the section 810(c) items which is attributable to the change in basis during the taxable year, $140 ($1,200 minus $1,060), shall be taken into account in the manner prescribed in section 810(d) and paragraph (a) of § 1.810-3.

Example (5). The life insurance reserves of M, a life insurance company, computed with respect to contracts for which such reserves are determined on a recognized preliminary term basis amount to $100 on January 1, 1960, and $110 on December 31, 1960. For the taxable year 1960, M elects to revalue such reserves on a net level premium basis under section 818(c). Such reserves computed under section 818(c) amount to $115 on January 1, 1960, and $127 on December 31, 1960. Under the provisions of paragraph (c)(3) of this section, a company which makes the section 818(c) election must use the net level premium basis in computing the sum of its life insurance reserves at the beginning and end of all taxable years for which the election applies. Thus, for purposes of section 810(a) and (b), in determining whether there is a net increase or decrease in the sum of the section 810(c) items for the taxable year 1960, M shall include $115 as its reserves with respect to such contracts under section 810(c)(1) at the beginning of the taxable year and $127 as its reserves with respect to such contracts under section 810(c)(1) at the end of the taxable year. [Reg. § 1.810-2.]

☐ [*T.D.* 6535, 1-19-61. *Amended by T.D.* 7163, 2-28-72 *and T.D.* 7172, 3-16-72.]

[Reg. § 1.810-3]

§ 1.810-3. **Adjustment for change in computing reserves.**—(a) *Reserve strengthening or weakening.* Section 810(d)(1) provides that if the basis for determining any item referred to in section 810(c) and paragraph (b) of § 1.810-2 at the end of any taxable year differs from the basis for such determination at the end of the preceding taxable year, then so much of the difference between—

(1) The amount of the item at the end of the taxable year, computed on the new basis, and

(2) The amount of the item at the end of the taxable year, computed on the old basis,

as is attributable to contracts issued before the taxable year shall be taken into account as follows:

(i) If the amount of the item at the end of the taxable year computed on the new basis exceeds the amount of the item at the end of the taxable year computed on the old basis, 1/10 of such excess shall be taken into account, for each of the succeeding 10 taxable years, as a net increase to which section 809(d)(2) and paragraph (a)(2) of § 1.809-5 applies; or

(ii) If the amount of the item at the end of the taxable year computed on the old basis exceeds the amount of the item at the end of the taxable year computed on the new basis, 1/10 of such excess shall be taken into account, for each of the 10 succeeding taxable years, as a net decrease to which section 809(c)(2) and paragraph (a)(2) of § 1.809-4 applies.

Reg. § 1.810-3(a)(1)

Life Insurance Companies

See p. 20,601 for regulations not amended to reflect law changes

→ *Caution: Former Code Secs. 801-820 for pre-1984 years were repealed and replaced by new Code Secs. 801-818. The following Regulations were issued under old Code Secs. 801-820.* ←

(b) *Illustration of principles.* The provisions of section 810(d)(1) and paragraph (a) of this section may be illustrated by the following examples:

Example (1). Assume that the amount of an item described in section 810(c) of L, a life insurance company, at the beginning of the taxable year 1959 is $100. Assume that at the end of the taxable year 1959, as a result of a change in the basis used in computing such item during the taxable year, the amount of the item (computed on the new basis) is $200 but computed on the old basis would have been $150. Since the amount of the item at the end of the taxable year computed on the new basis, $200, exceeds the amount of the item at the end of the taxable year computed on the old basis, $150, by $50, 1/10 of the amount of such excess, or $5, shall be taken into account as a net increase referred to in section 809(d)(2) and paragraph (a)(2) of § 1.809-5 in determining gain or loss from operations for each of the 10 taxable years immediately following the taxable year 1959. Any increase (or decrease) in the sum of the section 810(c) items computed on the old basis at the end of the taxable year 1959 ($150) after adjustment for investment yield not included in gain or loss from operations for the taxable year by reason of section 809(a)(1), over the sum of such items computed on the old basis at the beginning of the taxable year 1959 ($100), shall be taken into account in the manner prescribed in section 810(a) or (b) and § 1.810-2 for purposes of determining L's gain or loss from operations for 1959.

Example (2). Assume the facts are the same as in example (1), and that the sum of the items described in section 810(c) (computed on the new basis) is $200 on January 1, 1960, and $260 on December 31, 1960. Under the provisions of section 810(d)(1), as a result of the reserve strengthening attributable to the change in basis which occurred in 1959, L would include $5 (computed in the manner described in example (1)) as a net increase under section 809(d)(2) and paragraph (a)(2) of § 1.809-5 in determining its gain or loss from operations for 1960. In addition to this amount, any increase (or decrease) in the sum of the items described in section 810(c) at the end of the taxable year 1960 ($260) after adjustment for investment yield not included in gain or loss from operations for the taxable year by reason of section 809(a)(1), over the sum of such items at the beginning of the taxable year 1960 ($200), shall be taken into account in the manner prescribed in section 810(a) or (b) and § 1.810-2 for purposes of determining L's gain or loss from operations for 1960.

(c) *Termination as life insurance company.* Section 810(d)(2) provides, subject to the provisions of section 381(c)(22) and the regulations thereunder (relating to carryovers in certain corporate readjustments), that if for any taxable year a company which previously was a life insurance company no longer meets the requirements of section 801(a) and paragraph (b) of § 1.801-3 (relating to the definition of a life insurance company), the balance of any adjustments remaining to be made under section 810(d)(1) and paragraph (a) of this section shall be taken into account for the preceding taxable year.

(d) *Illustration of principles.* The provisions of section 810(d)(2) and paragraph (c) of this section may be illustrated by the following example:

Example. Assume the facts are the same as in example (1) of paragraph (b) of this section, except that for the taxable year 1962, L no longer meets the requirements of section 801(a) (relating to the definition of a life insurance company) and that the provisions of section 381(c)(22) are not applicable. Under the provisions of section 810(d)(2), the entire balance of the adjustment remaining to be made with respect to the change in basis which occurred in 1959, 8/10 of $50, or $40, shall be taken into account for the taxable year 1961, the last year L was a life insurance company. Thus, for the taxable year 1961, the total amount to be taken into account by L as a net increase referred to in section 809(d)(2) and paragraph (a)(2) of § 1.809-5 in determining its gain or loss from operations shall be $45. Of this amount, $5 (1/10 of $50) represents the amount determined under the provisions of section 810(d)(1), and $40 represents the amount determined under the provisions of section 810(d)(2).

(e) *Effect of preliminary term election.* (1) Section 810(d)(3) provides that if a company which computes its life insurance reserves on a preliminary term basis elects to revalue such reserves on a net level premium basis under section 818(c), such election shall not be treated as a change in basis within the meaning of section 810(d)(1) and paragraph (a) of this section. Thus, any increase or decrease in reserves attributable to such election shall not be taken into account under section 810(d)(1) and paragraph (a) of this section but shall be taken into account in the manner prescribed in section 810(a) and (b) and paragraph (a) of § 1.810-2. See paragraph (c)(3) of § 1.810-2.

Reg. § 1.810-3(e)

Life Insurance Companies

See p. 20,601 for regulations not amended to reflect law changes

→ **Caution: Former Code Secs. 801-820 for pre-1984 years were repealed and replaced by new Code Secs. 801-818. The following Regulations were issued under old Code Secs. 801-820.** ←

(2) Section 810(d)(3) further provides that where an election under section 818(c) would apply to an item referred to in section 810(c) but for the fact that the basis used in computing such item has actually been changed, any increase or decrease in such item attributable to such actual change in basis shall be subject to the adjustment required under section 810(d)(1) and paragraph (a) of this section. In such a case, however, for purposes of section 810(d)(1)(B) and paragraph (a)(2) of this section, the amount of such item at the end of the taxable year computed on the old basis shall be the amount of such item at the end of the taxable year computed as if the election under section 818(c) applied in respect of such item for the taxable year.

(f) *Illustration of principles.* The provisions of section 810(d)(3) and paragraph (e) of this section may be illustrated by the following examples:

Example (1). Assume that S, a life insurance company which computes its life insurance reserves on a 3-percent assumed rate and the Commissioner's reserve valuation method (one of the recognized preliminary term reserve methods), elects to revalue such reserves on a net level premium method under section 818(c) and that the significant facts are as follows:

	Jan. 1, 1958	Dec. 31, 1958
Book reserves at 3-percent assumed rate, Commissioner's reserve valuation method	100	118
Reserves at 3-percent assumed rate, after restatement under section 818(c)	110	131

Under the provisions of section 810(d)(3), an election under section 818(c) is not treated as a change in basis for purposes of section 810(d)(1). Accordingly, the increase of $21, ($131 minus $110) attributable to such election shall not be subject to the adjustment provided by section 810(d)(1) but shall be taken into account in the manner prescribed in section 810(b). For purposes of determining the amount to be taken into account under section 810(b), the reserves with respect to the contracts subject to the section 818(c) election shall be $110 at the beginning of the taxable year 1958 and $131 at the end of the taxable year 1958. However, as a result of making the election under section 818(c), the difference ($10) between the reserves computed on the preliminary term basis on January 1, 1958 ($100) and the reserves restated on the net level premium basis on January 1, 1958 ($110) shall not be taken into account under section 809(d) for the year 1958, or for any subsequent taxable year.

Example (2). Assume the facts are the same as in example (1), except that during the taxable year 1959, S actually changed from the preliminary term basis to a net level premium basis which was identical with the net level premium basis used under the section 818(c) election and that the significant facts are as follows:

	Jan. 1, 1958	Dec. 31, 1958
Book reserves at 3-percent assumed rate, Commissioner's reserve valuation method	118	127
Reserves at 3-percent assumed rate, after restatement under section 818(c)	131	142
Strengthened reserves at 3-percent assumed rate and net level premium method	...	142

Under the provisions of section 810(d)(3), if a company which has made an election under section 818(c) which has not been revoked actually changes the basis used by it in computing the reserves subject to such election, any increase or decrease in reserves attributable to such change in basis shall be taken into account in the manner prescribed in section 810(d)(1). Since S actually changed to the same basis which it used in computing its reserves under section 818(c), the reserves at the end of the taxable year computed on the new basis ($142) are the same as the reserves at the end of the taxable year computed on the old basis ($142), i.e., the basis which would have applied under section 818(c) if the election applied for 1959. Accordingly, no adjustment under section 810(d)(1) is required.

Example (3). Assume the facts are the same as in example (1), except that during the taxable year 1960, S actually changed the basis used by it in computing its reserves on a certain block of contracts subject to the election under section 818(c) and that the significant facts with respect to this block of contracts are as follows:

	Jan. 1, 1958	Dec. 31, 1958
Book reserves at 3-percent assumed rate, Commissioner's reserve valuation method	50	63

Reg. § 1.810-3(e)(2)

Life Insurance Companies

See p. 20,601 for regulations not amended to reflect law changes

→ *Caution: Former Code Secs. 801-820 for pre-1984 years were repealed and replaced by new Code Secs. 801-818. The following Regulations were issued under old Code Secs. 801-820.* ←

Reserves at 3-percent assumed rate, after restatement under section 818(c)	60	75
Strengthened reserves at 2-percent assumed rate and net level premium method	...	95

Under the provisions of section 810(d)(3), the amount of the reserves subject to the section 818(c) election at the end of the taxable year computed on the old basis shall be the amount of such reserves at the end of the taxable year determined under section 818(c) ($75). Since the reserves at the end of the taxable year computed on the new basis, $95, exceeds the reserves at the end of the taxable year computed on the old basis, $75, by $20, 1/10 of the excess of $20, or $2, shall be taken into account as a net increase referred to in section 809(d)(2) and paragraph (a)(2) of § 1.809-5 in determining gain or loss from operations for each of the 10 taxable years immediately following the taxable year 1960. For purposes of determining whether there is a net increase or decresae in the sum of the items described in section 810(c) for the taxable year 1960 under section 810(a) or (b), the sum of the reserves with respect to such block of contracts shall be $60 at the beginning of the taxable year and $75 at the end of the taxable year (the amount of such reserves computed under section 818(c) at the beginning and end of the taxable year). The difference ($10) between the reserves computed on the preliminary term basis on January 1, 1960 ($50) and the reserves restated on the net level premium basis on January 1, 1960 ($60) shall not be taken into account under section 809(d) for the year 1960, or for any subsequent taxable year. [Reg. § 1.810-3.]

☐ [*T.D. 6535, 1-19-61.*]

[Reg. § 1.810-4]

§ 1.810-4. Certain decreases in reserves of voluntary employees' beneficiary associations.—(a) *Decreases due to voluntary lapses of policies issued before January 1, 1958.*—(1) Section 810(e) provides that if for any taxble year a life insurance company which meets the requirements of section 501(c)(9), other than the requirement of subparagraph (B) thereof, makes an election in the manner provided in section 810(e)(3) and paragraph (b) of this section, only 11½ percent of any decrease in life insurance reserves (as defined in section 801(b) and § 1.801-4) attributable to the voluntary lapse on or after January 1, 1958, of any policy issued prior to that date shall be taken into account under section 810(a) or (b) and paragraph (a) of § 1.810-2 in determining the net increase or decrease in the sum of the items described in section 810(c) during the taxable year. In applying the preceding sentence, the decrease in the reserve for any policy shall be determined by reference to the amount of such reserve at the beginning of the taxable year, reduced by any amount allowable as a deduction under section 809(d)(1) and paragraph (a)(1) of § 1.809-5 in respect of such policy by reason of such lapse. The election under section 810(e) shall be adhered to in computing the company's gain or loss from operation for the taxable year for which the election is made and for all subsequent taxable years, unless consent to revoke such election is obtained from the Commissioner.

(2) The application of the election provided under section 810(e) and subparagraph (1) of this paragraph may be illustrated by the following example:

Example. For the taxable year 1960, M, a life insurance company which meets the requirements of section 501(c)(9), other than the requirement of subparagraph (B) thereof, makes the election under section 810(e). Assume the following facts with respect to a policy issued in 1955 which voluntarily lapsed during the taxable year:

(1) Life insurance reserve on January 1, 1960 . $600
(2) Amount allowable as a deduction under sec. 809(d)(1) 200
(3) Decrease in life insurance reserves for sec. 810(e) purposes (item (1) minus item (2)) 400
(4) Amount taken into account under sec. 810(a) and (b) by reason of sec. 810(e) election (11½% × $400)   46

Under the provisions of section 810(e) and subparagraph (1) of this paragraph, M would include $46 as its life insurance reserve with respect to such policy under section 810(c)(1) at the beginning of the taxable year 1960 for purposes of determining the net increase or decrease in the sum of the items described in section 810(c) for the taxable year under section 810(a) or (b).

(b) *Time and manner of making election.* The election provided by section 810(e)(3) shall be made in a statement attached to the life insurance company's income tax return for the first taxable year for which the company desires the election to apply. The return and statement must be filed not later than the date prescribed by law (including extensions thereof) for filing the return

Life Insurance Companies

See p. 20,601 for regulations not amended to reflect law changes

→ *Caution: Former Code Secs. 801-820 for pre-1984 years were repealed and replaced by new Code Secs. 801-818. The following Regulations were issued under old Code Secs. 801-820.* ←

for such taxable year. However, if the last day prescribed by law (including extensions thereof) for filing a return for the first taxable year for which the company desires the election to apply falls before January 20, 1961, the election provided by section 810(e)(3) may be made for such year by filing the statement and an amended return for such taxable year (and all subsequent taxable years for which returns have been filed) before April 21, 1961. The statement shall indicate that the company meets the requirements of section 501(c)(9), other than the requirement of subparagraph (B) thereof, and has made the election provided under section 810(e) and paragraph (a) of this section. The statement shall set forth the following information with respect to each policy described in paragraph (a) of this section which has voluntarily lapsed during such year:

(1) Type of policy.

(2) Date issued.

(3) Date lapsed.

(4) Reason for lapse.

(5) Policy reserve as of beginning of taxable year.

(6) Deduction allowable under section 809(d)(1) and paragraph (a)(1) of § 1.809-5 during taxable year by reason of lapse.

(7) Decrease in policy reserve for section 810(e) purposes (excess of (5) over (6)).

In addition, the statement shall set forth the total of the amounts referred to in subparagraph (7) of this paragraph with respect to all policies described in paragraph (a) of this section which have voluntarily lapsed during the taxable year.

(c) *Scope of election.* An election made under section 810(e)(3) and paragraph (a) of this section shall be effective for the taxable year for which made and for all succeeding taxable years, unless consent to revoke the election is obtained from the Commissioner. However, for taxable years beginning prior to January 20, 1961, a company may revoke the election provided by section 810(e)(3) without obtaining consent from the Commissioner by filing, before April 21, 1961, a statement that the company desires to revoke such election. An amended return reflecting such revocation must accompany the statement for all taxable years for which returns have been filed with respect to such election.

(d) *Disallowance of carryovers from pre-1958 losses from operations.* For any taxable year for which the election provided under section 810(e)(3) and paragraph (b) of this section is effective, the provisions of section 812(b)(1) and § 1.812-4 shall not apply with respect to any loss from operations for any taxable year beginning before January 1, 1958.

(e) *Effective date; cross reference.* The provisions of section 810(e) (as in effect for such years) and this section apply only with respect to taxable years beginning before January 1, 1970. For provisions relating to certain funded pension trusts applicable to taxable years beginning after December 31, 1969, see section 501(c)(18) and the regulations thereunder. [Reg. § 1.810-4.]

☐ [*T.D.* 6535, 1-19-61. Amended by T.D. 7172, 3-16-72.]

[Reg. § 1.811-1]

§ 1.811-1. **Taxable years affected.**—Section 1.811-2, except as otherwise provided therein, is applicable only to taxable years beginning after December 31, 1957, and all references to sections of part I, subchapter L, chapter 1 of the Code are to the Internal Revenue Code of 1954, as amended by the Life Insurance Company Income Tax Act of 1959 (73 Stat. 112). [Reg. § 1.811-1.]

☐ [*T.D.* 6535, 1-19-61.]

[Reg. § 1.811-2]

§ 1.811-2. **Dividends to policyholders.**—(a) *Dividends to policyholders defined.* Section 811(a) defines the term "dividends to policyholders", for purposes of part I, subchapter L, chapter 1 of the Code, to mean dividends and similar distributions to policyholders in their capacity as such. The term includes amounts returned to policyholders where the amount is not fixed in the contract but depends on the experience of the company or the discretion of the management. In general, any payment not fixed in the contract which is made with respect to a participating contract (that is, a contract which during the taxable year contains a right to participate in the divisible surplus of the company) shall be treated as a dividend to policyholders. Similarly, any amount refunded or allowed as a rate credit with respect to either a participating or nonparticipating contract shall be treated as a dividend to policyholders if such amount depends on the experience of the company. However, the term does not include interest paid (as defined in section 805(e) and paragraph (b) of § 1.805-8) or return premiums (as defined in section 809(c) and paragraph (a)(1)(ii) of § 1.809-4). Thus, so-called excess-interest dividends and amounts returned by one life insurance

Reg. § 1.811-1

Life Insurance Companies

See p. 20,601 for regulations not amended to reflect law changes

→ **Caution: Former Code Secs. 801-820 for pre-1984 years were repealed and replaced by new Code Secs. 801-818. The following Regulations were issued under old Code Secs. 801-820.** ←

company to another in respect of reinsurance ceded shall not be treated as dividends to policyholders even though such amounts are not fixed in the contract but depend upon the experience of the company or the discretion of the management.

(b) *Amount of deduction*—(1) *In general.* Section 811(b)(1) provides, subject to the limitation of section 809(f), that the deduction for dividends to policyholders paid during the taxable year—

(i) Increased by the excess of the amounts held as reserves for dividends to policyholders at the end of the taxable year for payment during the year following the taxable year, over the amounts held as reserves for dividends to policyholders at the end of the preceding taxable year for payment during the taxable year, or

(ii) Decreased by the excess of the amounts held as reserves for dividends to policyholders at the end of the preceding taxable year for payment during the taxable year, over the amounts held as reserves for dividends to policyholders at the end of the taxable year for payment during the year following the taxable year.

For the rule as to when dividends are considered paid, see section 561 and the regulations thereunder. For the determination of the amounts held as reserves for dividends to policyholders, see paragraph (c) of this section. For special provisions relating to the treatment of dividends to policyholders paid with respect to policies reinsured under modified coinsurance contracts, see section 820(c)(5) and the regulation thereunder.

(2) *Certain amounts to be treated as net decreases.* Section 811(b)(2) provides that if the amount determined under subparagraph (1)(ii) of this paragraph exceeds the dividends to policyholders paid during the taxable year, the amount of such excess shall be a net decrease referred to in section 809(c)(2).

(c) *Reserves for dividends to policyholders defined*—(1) *In general.* The term "reserves for dividends to policyholders", as used in section 811(b)(1) (A) and (B) and paragraph (b)(1) of this section, means only those amounts—

(i) Actually held, or set aside as provided in subparagraph (2) of this paragraph and thus treated as actually held, by the company at the end of the taxable year, and

(ii) With respect to which, at the end of the taxable year or, if set aside, within the period prescribed in subparagraph (2) of this paragraph, the company is under an obligation, which is either fixed or determined according to a formula which is fixed and not subject to change by the company, to pay such amounts as dividends to policyholders (as defined in section 811(a) and paragraph (a) of this section) during the year following the taxable year.

(2) *Amounts set aside.* (i) In the case of a life insurance company (as defined in section 801(a) and paragraph (b) of § 1.801-3), all amounts set aside before the 16th day of the 3rd month of the year following the taxable year for payment as dividends to policyholders (as defined in section 811(a) and paragraph (a) of this section) during the year following such taxable year shall be treated as amounts actually held at the end of the taxable year.

(ii) In the case of a mutual savings bank subject to the tax imposed by section 594, all amounts set aside before the 16th day of the 4th month of the year following the taxable year for payment as dividends to policyholders (as defined in section 811(a) and paragraph (a) of this section) during the year following such taxable year shall be treated as amounts actually held at the end of the taxable year.

(3) *1958 reserve for dividends to policyholders.* For purposes of section 811(b) and paragraph (b) of this section, the amounts held at the end of 1957 as reserves for dividends to policyholders payable during 1958 shall be determined as if part I, subchapter L, chapter 1 of the Code (as in effect for 1958) applied for 1957. Any adjustment in the reserves for dividends to policyholders at the beginning of 1957 required as a result of an understatement or overstatement of such reserves by the company shall be made to the balance of such reserves as of the beginning of 1957. For example, if at the beginning of 1957 the reserves for dividends to policyholders are stated to be $100 and it is subsequently determined that such reserves should have been $90, the reserves at the beginning of 1957 shall be reduced by $10. Under no circumstances shall an adjustment required with regard to the beginning 1957 reserves be made to the reserves at the end of 1957.

(4) *Information to be filed.* Every company claiming a deduction for dividends to policyholders shall keep such permanent records as are necessary to establish the amount of dividends actually paid during the taxable year. Such company shall also keep a copy of the dividend resolution and any necessary supporting data relating to the amounts of dividends declared and to the amounts held or set aside as reserves for dividends to policyholders during the taxable year. The com-

Reg. § 1.811-2(c)(4)

45,756   **Life Insurance Companies**
See p. 20,601 for regulations not amended to reflect law changes

→ *Caution: Former Code Secs. 801-820 for pre-1984 years were repealed and replaced by new Code Secs. 801-818. The following Regulations were issued under old Code Secs. 801-820.* ←

pany shall file with its return a concise statement of the pertinent facts relating to its dividend policy for the year, the amount of dividends actually paid during the taxable year, and the amounts held or set aside as reserves for dividends to policyholders during the taxable year.

(d) *Illustration of principles.* The provisions of section 811(b) and this section may be illustrated by the following examples:

Example (1). On December 31, 1959, M, a life insurance company, held $200 as reserves for dividends to policyholders due and payable in 1960.

On March 10, 1960, M set aside an additional $50 as reserves for dividends to policyholders due and payable in 1960. During the taxable year 1960, M paid $240 as dividends to its policyholders and at the end of the taxable year 1960, held $175 as reserves for dividends to policyholders due and payable in 1961. No additional amount was set aside before March 16, 1961, as reserves for dividends to policyholders due and payable in 1961. For the taxable year 1960, subject to the limitation of section 809(f), M's deduction for dividends to policyholders is $165, computed as follows:

(1) Dividends paid to policyholders during the taxable year 1960		$240
(2) Decreased by the excess of item (a) over item (b):		
(a) Reserves for dividends to policyholders as of 12-31-59 (including amounts set aside as provided in paragraph (c)(2) of this section)...	$250	
(b) Reserves for dividends to policyholders as of 12-31-60	$175	$ 75
(3) Deduction for dividends to policyholders under sec. 811(b) (computed without regard to the limitation of sec. 809(f))		$165

Example (2). On December 31, 1960, S, a life insurance company, held $100 as reserves for dividends to policyholders due and payable in 1961. During the taxable year 1961, S paid $125 as dividends to its policyholders and at the end of the taxable year 1961, held $110 as reserves for dividends to policyholders due and payable in 1962. No additional amount was set aside for dividends to policyholders as provided in paragraph (c)(2).

(1) Dividends paid to policyholders during the taxable year 1961		$125
(2) Increased by the excess of item (a) over item (b):		
(a) Reserves for dividends to policyholders as of 12-31-61	$110	
(b) Reserves for dividends to policyholders as of 12-31-60	$100	$ 10
(3) Deduction for dividends to policyholders under sec. 811(b) (computed without regard to the limitation of sec. 809(f))		$135

Example (3). Assume the facts are the same as in example (2), except that on December 31, 1960, the amount held as reserves for dividends to policyholders due and payable in 1961 is $250. For the taxable year 1961, S's deduction for dividends to policyholders is zero, computed as follows:

(1) Dividends paid to policyholders during the taxable year 1961		$125
(2) Decreased by the excess of item (a) over item (b):		
(a) Reserves for dividends to policyholders as of 12-31-60	$250	
(b) Reserves for dividends to policyholders as of 12-31-61	$110	$140
(3) Deduction for dividends to policyholders under sec. 811(b) (computed without regard to the limitation of sec. 809(f))		$ 0

Under the provisions of section 811(b)(2) and paragraph (b)(2) of this section, since the decrease in the reserves for dividends to policyholders during the taxable year, $140 ($250 minus $110), exceeds the dividends to policyholders paid during the taxable year 1961, $125, S shall include $15 (the amount of such excess) as a net decrease under section 809(c)(2) and paragraph (a)(2) of § 1.809-4 in determining its gain or loss from operations for 1961. [Reg. § 1.811-2.]

☐ [T.D. 6535, 1-19-61.]

[Reg. § 1.812-1]

§ 1.812-1. Taxable years affected.—Sections 1.812-2 through 1.812-8, except as otherwise provided therein, are applicable only to taxable years beginning after December 31, 1957, and all references to sections of part I, subchapter L, chapter 1 of the Code are to the Internal Revenue Code of 1954, as amended by the Life Insurance Company

Reg. § 1.812-1

Life Insurance Companies

→ **Caution:** *Former Code Secs. 801-820 for pre-1984 years were repealed and replaced by new Code Secs. 801-818. The following Regulations were issued under old Code Secs. 801-820.* ←

Income Tax Act of 1959 (73 Stat. 112) and the Act of October 23, 1962 (76 Stat. 1134). [Reg. § 1.812-1.]

☐ [*T.D.* 6535, 1-19-61. *Amended by T.D.* 6886, 6-22-66.]

[Reg. § 1.812-2]

§ 1.812-2. Operations loss deduction.—(a) *Allowance of deduction.* Section 812 provides that a life insurance company shall be allowed a deduction in computing gain or loss from operations for any taxable year beginning after December 31, 1957, in an amount equal to the aggregate of the operations loss carryovers and operations loss carrybacks to such taxable year. This deduction is referred to as the operations loss deduction. The loss from operations (computed under section 809), is the basis for the computation of the operations loss carryovers and operations loss carrybacks and ultimately for the operations loss deduction itself. Section 809(e)(5) provides that the net operating loss deduction provided in section 172 shall not be allowed a life insurance company since the operations loss deduction provided in section 812 and this paragraph shall be allowed in lieu thereof.

(b) *Steps in computation of operations loss deduction.* The three steps to be taken in the ascertainment of the operations loss deduction for any taxable year beginning after December 31, 1957, are as follows:

(1) Compute the loss from operations for any preceding or succeeding taxable year from which a loss from operations may be carried over or carried back to such taxable year.

(2) Compute the operations loss carryovers to such taxable year from such preceding taxable years and the operations loss carrybacks to such taxable year from such succeeding taxable years.

(3) Add such operations loss carryovers and carrybacks in order to determine the operations loss deduction for such taxable year.

(c) *Statement with tax return.* Every life insurance company claiming an operations loss deduction for any taxable year shall file with its return for such year a concise statement setting forth the amount of the operations loss deduction claimed and all material and pertinent facts relative thereto, including a detailed schedule showing the computation of the operations loss deduction.

(d) *Ascertainment of deduction dependent upon operations loss carryback.* If a life insurance company is entitled in computing its operations loss deduction to a carryback which it is not able to ascertain at the time its return is due, it shall compute the operations loss deduction on its return without regard to such operations loss carryback. When the life insurance company ascertains the operations loss carryback, it may within the applicable period of limitations file a claim for credit or refund of the overpayment, if any, resulting from the failure to compute the operations loss deduction for the taxable year with the inclusion of such carryback; or it may file an application under the provisions of section 6411 for a tentative carryback adjustment.

(e) *Law applicable to computations.* The following rules shall apply to all taxable years beginning after December 31, 1957—

(1) In determining the amount of any operations loss carryback or carryover to any taxable year, the necessary computations involving any other taxable year shall be made under the law applicable to such other taxable year.

(2) The loss from operations for any taxable year shall be determined under the law applicable to that year without regard to the year to which it is to be carried and in which, in effect, it is to be deducted as part of the operations loss deduction.

(3) The amount of the operations loss deduction which shall be allowed for any taxable year shall be determined under the law applicable for that year.

(f) *Special rules.* For purposes of taxable years beginning after December 31, 1954, and before January 1, 1958—

(1) The amount of any:

(i) Loss from operations;

(ii) Operations loss carryback; and

(iii) Operations loss carryover

shall be computed as if part I, subchapter L, chapter 1 of the Code (as in effect for 1958) and section 381(c)(22) applied to such taxable years.

(2) A loss from operations (determined in accordance with the provisions of section 812(b)(1)(C) and this paragraph) for such taxable years shall in no way affect the tax liability of any life insurance company for such taxable years. However, such loss may, to the extent allowed as an operations loss carryover under section 812, affect the tax liability of a life insurance company for a taxable year beginning after December 31, 1957. For example, for the taxable year 1956, X, a life insurance company, has a loss from operations (determined in accordance with the provisions of

Reg. § 1.812-2(f)(2)

Life Insurance Companies

See p. 20,601 for regulations not amended to reflect law changes

→ **Caution:** *Former Code Secs. 801-820 for pre-1984 years were repealed and replaced by new Code Secs. 801-818. The following Regulations were issued under old Code Secs. 801-820.* ←

section 812(b)(1)(C) and this paragraph). Such loss shall in no way affect X's tax liability for the taxable years 1956 (the year of the loss), 1955 (a year to which such loss shall be carried back), or 1957 (a year to which such loss shall be carried forward). However, to the extent allowed under section 812, any amount of the loss for 1956 remaining after such carryback and carryforward shall be taken into account in determining X's tax liability for taxable years beginning after December 31, 1957. [Reg. § 1.812-2.]

☐ [*T.D.* 6535, 1-19-61.]

[Reg. § 1.812-3]

§ 1.812-3. Computation of loss from operations.—(a) *Modification of deductions.* A loss from operations is sustained by a life insurance company in any taxable year, if and to the extent that, for such year, there is an excess of the sum of the deductions provided by section 809(d) over the sum of (1) the life insurance company's share of each and every item of investment yield (including tax-exempt interest, partially tax-exempt interest, and dividends received) as determined under section 809(b)(3), and (2) the sum of the items of gross amount taken into account under section 809(c). In determining the loss from operations for purposes of section 812—

(i) No deduction shall be allowed under section 812 for the operations loss deduction.

(ii) The 85 percent limitation on dividends received provided by section 246(b) as modified by section 809(d)(8)(B) shall not apply to the deductions otherwise allowed under—

(*a*) Section 243(a) in respect to dividends received by corporations,

(*b*) Section 244 in respect of dividends received on certain preferred stock of public utilities, and

(*c*) Section 245 in respect of dividends received from certain foreign corporations.

(b) *Illustration of principles.* The application of paragraph (a) of this section may be illustrated by the following example:

Example. For the taxable year 1960, X, a life insurance company, has items taken into account under section 809(c) amount to $150,000, its share of the investment yield amounts to $250,000, and total deductions allowed by section 809(d) of $375,000, exclusive of any operations loss deduction and exclusive of any deduction for dividends received. In 1960, X received as its share of dividends entitled to the benefits of section 243(a) the amount of $100,000. These dividends are included in X's share of the investment yield. X has no other deductions to which section 812(c) applies. On the basis of these facts, X has a loss from operations for the taxable year 1960 of $60,000, computed as follows:

Deductions for 1960	$375,000
Plus: Deduction for dividends received computed without regard to the limitation provided by sec. 246(b), as modified by sec. 809(d)(8)(B) (85% of $100,000)	85,000
Total deductions as modified by sec. 812(c)	460,000
Less: Sum of sec. 809(c) items and X's share of investment yield (including $100,000 of dividends)	400,000
Loss from operations for 1960	($60,000)

[Reg. § 1.812-3.]

☐ [*T.D.* 6535, 1-19-61.]

[Reg. § 1.812-4]

§ 1.812-4. Operations loss carrybacks and operations loss carryovers.—(a) *In general*—(1) *Years to which loss may be carried.* In order to compute the operations loss deduction of a life insurance company the company must first determine the part of any losses from operations for any preceding or succeeding taxable years which are carryovers or carrybacks to the taxable year in issue. Except as otherwise provided by this paragraph, a loss from operations for taxable years beginning after December 31, 1954, shall be carried back to each of the 3 taxable years preceding the loss year and shall be carried forward to each of the 5 taxable years succeeding the loss year. Except as limited by section 812(e)(2) and paragraph (b) of § 1.812-6, if the life insurance company is a new company (as defined in section 812(e)(1)) for the loss year, the loss from operations shall be carried back to each of the 3 taxable years preceding the loss year and shall be carried forward to each of the 8 taxable years succeeding the loss year. In determining the span of years for which a loss from operations may be carried, taxable years in which a company does not qualify as a life insurance company (as defined in section 801(a)), or is not treated as a new company, shall be taken into account.

(2) *Special transitional rules.* (i) A loss from operations for any taxable year beginning before January 1, 1958, shall not be carried back to any taxable year beginning before January 1, 1955. Furthermore, a loss from operations for any taxa-

Reg. § 1.812-3(a)

Life Insurance Companies

See p. 20,601 for regulations not amended to reflect law changes

→ *Caution: Former Code Secs. 801-820 for pre-1984 years were repealed and replaced by new Code Secs. 801-818. The following Regulations were issued under old Code Secs. 801-820.*←

ble year beginning after December 31, 1957, shall not be carried back to any taxable year beginning before January 1, 1958.

(ii) If for any taxable year a life insurance company has made an election under section 810(e) (relating to certain decreases in reserves for voluntary employees' beneficiary associations) which is effective for such taxable year, the provisions of section 812(b)(1) and subparagraph (1) of this paragraph shall not apply with respect to any loss from operations for any taxable year beginning before January 1, 1958.

(3) *Illustration of principles.* The provisions of section 812(b)(1) and of this paragraph may be illustrated by the following examples:

Example (1). P, a life insurance company, organized in 1940, has a loss from operations of $1,000 in 1958. This loss cannot be carried back, but shall be carried forward to each of the 5 taxable years following 1958.

Example (2). Q, a life insurance company, organized in 1940, has a loss from operations of $1,200 in 1959. This loss shall be carried back to the taxable year 1958 and then shall be carried forward to each of the 5 taxable years following 1959.

Example (3). R, a life insurance company organized in 1940, has a loss from operations of $1,300 for the taxable year 1956. This loss shall first be carried back to the taxable year 1955 and then shall be carried forward to each of the 5 taxable years following 1956. The loss for 1956, carryback to 1955, and carryover to 1957 shall each be computed as if part I, subchapter L, chapter 1 of the Code (as in effect for 1958) applied to such taxable years.

Example (4). S, a life insurance company, organized in 1958 and meeting the provisions of section 812(e) (rules relating to new companies), has a loss from operations of $1,400 for the taxable year 1958. This loss cannot be carried back, but shall be carried forward to each of the 8 taxable years following 1958, provided, however, S is not a nonqualified corporation at any time during the loss year (1958) or any taxable year thereafter.

Example (5). T, a life insurance company, organized in 1954 and meeting the provisions of section 812(e) (rules relating to new companies), has a loss from operations of $1,500 for the taxable year 1956. This loss shall first be carried back to the taxable year 1955 and then carried forward to each of the 8 taxable years following 1956, provided, however, T is not a nonqualified corporation at any time during the loss year (1956) or any taxable year thereafter. The loss for 1956, carryback to 1955, and carryover to 1957 shall each be computed as if part I of subchapter L (as in effect for 1958) applied to such taxable years.

(4) *Periods of less than 12 months.* A fractional part of a year which is a taxable year under sections 441(b) and 7701(a)(23) is a preceding or a succeeding taxable year for the purpose of determining under section 812 the first, second, etc., preceding or succeeding taxable year. For the determination of the loss from operations for periods of less than 12 months, see section 818(d) and the regulations thereunder.

(5) *Amount of loss to be carried.* The amount which is carried back or carried over to any taxable year is the loss from operations to the extent it was not absorbed in the computation of gain from operations for other taxable years, preceding such taxable year, to which it may be carried back or carried over. For the purpose of determining the gain from operations for any such preceding taxable year, the various operations loss carryovers and carrybacks to such taxable year are considered to be applied in reduction of the gain from operations in the order of the taxable years from which such losses are carried over or carried back, beginning with the loss for the earliest taxable year.

(6) *Corporate acquisitions.* For the computation of the operations loss carryovers in the case of certain acquisitions of the assets of a life insurance company by another life insurance company, see section 381(c)(22) and the regulations thereunder.

(b) *Portion of loss from operations which is a carryback or a carryover to the taxable year in issue*—(1) *Manner of computation.* (i) A loss from operations shall first be carried back to the earliest taxable year permissible under section 812(b) and paragraph (a) of this section for which such loss is allowable as a carryback or a carryover. The entire amount of the loss from operations shall be carried back to such earliest year.

(ii) Section 812(b)(2) provides that the portion of the loss from operations which shall be carried to each of the taxable years subsequent to the earliest taxable year shall be the excess (if any) of the amount of the loss from operations over the sum of the offsets (as defined in section 812(d) and paragraph (a) of § 1.812-5) for all

Reg. § 1.812-4(b)

45,760 Life Insurance Companies

See p. 20,601 for regulations not amended to reflect law changes

→ **Caution: Former Code Secs. 801-820 for pre-1984 years were repealed and replaced by new Code Secs. 801-818. The following Regulations were issued under old Code Secs. 801-820.** ←

prior taxable years to which the loss from operations may be carried.

(2) *Illustration of principles.* The application of this paragraph may be illustrated by the following example:

Example. T, a life insurance company (which is not a new company as defined in section 812(e)(1)), has a loss from operations for 1960. The entire amount of the loss from operations for 1960 shall first be carried back to 1958. The amount of the carryback to 1959 is the excess (if any) of the 1960 loss over the offset for 1958. The amount of the carryover to 1961 is the excess (if any) of the 1960 loss over the sum of the offsets for 1958 and 1959. The amount of the 1960 loss remaining (if any) to be carried over to 1962, 1963, or 1964 shall be computed in a like manner. [Reg. § 1.812-4.]

☐ [*T.D.* 6535, 1-19-61.]

[Reg. § 1.812-5]

§ 1.812-5. **Offset.**—(a) *Offset defined.* Section 812(d) defines the term "offset" for purposes of section 812(b)(2) and paragraph (b)(1)(ii) of § 1.812-4. For any taxable year the offset is only that portion of the increase in the operations loss deduction for the taxable year which is necessary to reduce the life insurance company taxable income (computed without regard to section 802(b)(3)) for such year to zero. For purposes of the preceding sentence, the offset shall be determined with the modifications prescribed in paragraph (b) of this section. Such modifications shall be made independently of, and without reference to, the modifications required by paragraph (a) of § 1.812-3 for purposes of computing the loss from operations itself.

(b) *Modifications*—(1) *Operations loss deduction*—(i) *In general.* Section 812(d)(2) provides that for purposes of section 812(d)(1) (relating to the definition of offset), the operations loss deduction for any taxable year shall be computed by taking into account only such losses from operations otherwise allowable as carryovers or as carrybacks to such taxable year as were sustained in taxable years preceding the taxable year in which the life insurance company sustained the loss from operations from which the offset is to be deducted. Thus, for such purposes the loss from operations for the loss year or for any taxable year thereafter shall not be taken into account.

(ii) *Illustration of principles.* The provisions of this subparagraph may be illustrated by the following example:

Example. In computing the operations loss deduction for 1960, Y, a life insurance company, has a carryover from 1958 of $9,000, a carryover from 1959 of $6,000, a carryback from 1961 of $18,000, and a carryback from 1962 of $10,000, or an aggregate of $43,000 in carryovers and carrybacks. Thus, the operations loss deduction for 1960, for purposes of determining the tax liability for 1960, is $43,000. However, in computing the offset for 1960 which is subtracted from the loss from operations for 1961 for the purpose of determining the portion of such loss which may be carried over to subsequent taxable years, the operations loss deduction for 1960 is $15,000, that is, the aggregate of the $9,000 carryover from 1958 and the $6,000 carryover from 1959. In computing the operations loss deduction for such purpose, the $18,000 carryback from 1961 and the $10,000 carryback from 1962 are disregarded. In computing the offset for 1960, however, which is subtracted from the loss from operations for 1962 for the purpose of determining the portion of such 1962 loss which may be carried over for subsequent taxable years, the operations loss deduction for 1960 is $33,000, that is, the aggregate of the $9,000 carryover from 1958, the $6,000 carryover from 1959, and the $18,000 carryback from 1961. In computing the operations loss deduction for such purpose, the $10,000 carryback from 1962 is disregarded.

(2) *Recomputation of deductions limited by section 809(f)*—(i) *In general.* If in any taxable year a life insurance company has deductions under section 809(d)(3), (5), and (6), as limited by section 809(f), and sustains a loss from operations in a succeeding taxable year which may be carried back as an operations loss deduction, such limitation and deductions shall be recomputed. This recomputation is required since the carryback must be taken into account for purposes of determining such limitation and deductions.

(ii) *Illustration of principles.* The provisions of this subparagraph may be illustrated by the following example:

(*a*) *Facts.* The books of P, a life insurance company, reveal the following facts:

Reg. § 1.812-5(a)

Life Insurance Companies

→ **Caution:** *Former Code Secs. 801-820 for pre-1984 years were repealed and replaced by new Code Secs. 801-818. The following Regulations were issued under old Code Secs. 801-820.*←

Taxable year	Taxable investment income	Gain from operations	Loss from operations
1959	$9,000,000	$10,000,000	....
1960	....	....	($9,800,000)

The gain from operations thus shown is computed without regard to any operations loss deduction or deductions under section 809(d)(3), (5), and (6), as limited by section 809(f). Assume that for the taxable year 1959, P has (without regard to the limitation of section 809(f) or the operations loss deduction for 1959), a deduction under section 809(d)(3) of $2,500,000 for dividends to policyholders and no deductions under section 809(d)(5) or (6).

(*b*) *Determination of section 809(f) limitation and deduction for dividends to policyholders without regard to the operations loss deduction for 1959.* In order to determine gain or loss from operations for 1959, P must determine the deduction for dividends to policyholders for such year. Under the provisions of section 809(f), the amount of such deduction shall not exceed the sum of (*1*) the amount (if any) by which the gain from operations for such year (determined without regard to such deduction) exceeds P's taxable investment income for such year, plus (*2*) $250,000. Since the gain from operations as thus determined ($10,000,000) exceeds the taxable investment income ($9,000,000) by $1,000,000, the limitation on such deduction is $1,250,000 ($1,000,000 plus $250,000). Accordingly, only $1,250,000 of the $2,500,000 deduction for dividends to policyholders shall be allowed. The gain from operations for such year is $8,750,000 ($10,000,000 minus $1,250,000).

(*c*) *Recomputation of section 809(f) limitation and deduction for dividends to policyholders after application of the operations loss deduction for 1959.* Since P has sustained a loss from operations for 1960 which shall be carried back to 1959 as an operations loss deduction, it must recompute the section 809(f) limitation and deduction for dividends to policyholders. Taking into account the $9,800,000 operations loss deduction for 1959 reduces gain from operations for such year to $200,000 ($10,000,000 minus $9,800,000). Since the gain from operations as thus determined ($200,000) is less than the taxable investment income ($9,000,000), the limitation on the deduction for dividends to policyholders is $250,000. Thus, only $250,000 of the $2,500,000 deduction for dividends to policyholders shall be allowed. The gain from operations for such year as thus determined is $9,750,000 ($10,000,000 minus $250,000) since for purposes of this determination the operations loss deduction for 1959 is not taken into account (see section 812(c)(1)). Accordingly, the offset for 1959 is $9,750,000 (the increase in the operations loss deduction for 1959, computed without regard to the carryback for 1960, which reduces life insurance company taxable income for 1959 to zero); thus, the portion of the 1960 loss from operations which shall be carried forward to 1961 is $50,000 (the excess of the 1960 loss ($9,800,000) over the offset for 1959 ($9,750,000)).

(*3*) *Minimum limitation.* The life insurance company taxable income, as modified under this paragraph, shall in no case be considered less than zero. [Reg. § 1.812-5.]

☐ [*T.D.* 6535, 1-19-61.]

[Reg. § 1.812-6]

§ 1.812-6. New company defined.—Section 812(e) provides that for purposes of part I, subchapter L, chapter 1 of the Code, a life insurance company is a "new company" for any taxable year only if such taxable year begins not more than 5 years after the first day on which it (or any predecessor if section 381(c)(22) applies or would have applied if in effect) was authorized to do business as an insurance company. [Reg. § 1.812-6.]

☐ [*T.D.* 6535, 1-19-61. *Amended by T.D.* 6886, 6-22-66 *and T.D.* 7326, 9-30-79.]

[Reg. § 1.812-7]

§ 1.812-7. Application of subtitle A and subtitle F.—Section 812(f) provides that except as modified by section 809(e) (relating to modifications of deduction items otherwise allowable under subtitle A of the Code) subtitles A and F of the Code shall apply to operations loss carrybacks and carryovers, and to the operations loss deduction, in the same manner and to the same extent that such subtitles apply in respect of net operation loss carrybacks, net operation loss carryovers, and the net operating loss deduction of corporations generally. For the computation of the operations loss carrybacks and carryovers, and of the operations loss deduction in the case of certain acquisitions of the assets of a life insurance company by another life insurance company, see section 381(c)(22) and the regulations thereunder. [Reg. § 1.812-7.]

☐ [*T.D.* 6535, 1-19-61.]

→ **Caution:** *Former Code Secs. 801-820 for pre-1984 years were repealed and replaced by new Code Secs. 801-818. The following Regulations were issued under old Code Secs. 801-820.* ←

[Reg. § 1.812-8]

§ **1.812-8. Illustration of operations loss carrybacks and carryovers.**—The application of § 1.812-4 may be illustrated by the following example:

(a) *Facts.* The books of M, a life insurance company, organized in 1940, reveal the following facts:

Taxable year	Taxable investment income	Gain from operations	Loss from operations
1958	$11,000	$15,000	....
1959	23,000	30,000	....
1960	......	......	($ 75,000)
1961	25,000	20,000	....
1962	......	......	(150,000)
1963	22,000	30,000	....
1964	40,000	35,000	....
1965	62,000	75,000	....
1966	25,000	17,000	....
1967	39,000	53,000	....

The gain from operations thus shown is computed without regard to any operations loss deduction. The assumption is also made that none of the other modifications prescribed in paragraph (b) of § 1.812-5 apply. There are no losses from operations for 1955, 1956, 1957, 1968, 1969, 1970.

(b) *Loss sustained in 1960.* The portions of the $75,000 loss from operations for 1960 which shall be used as carrybacks to 1958 and 1959 and as carryovers to 1961, 1962, 1963, 1964, and 1965 are computed as follows:

(1) *Carryback to 1958.* The carryback to this year is $75,000, that is, the amount of the loss from operations.

(2) *Carryback to 1959.* The carryback to this year is $60,000 (the excess of the loss for 1960 over the offset for 1958), computed as follows:

Loss from operations		$ 75,000
Less: Offset for 1958 (the $15,000 gain from operations for such year computed without the deduction of the carryback from 1960)		15,000
Carryback		$ 60,000

(3) *Carryover to 1961.* The carryover to this year is $30,000 (the excess, if any, of the loss for 1960 over the sum of the offsets for 1958 and 1959), computed as follows:

Loss from operations		$ 75,000
Less: Offset for 1958 (the $15,000 gain from operations for such year computed without the deduction of the carryback from 1960)	$15,000	
Offset for 1959 (the $30,000 gain from operations for such year computed without the deduction of the carryback from 1960 or the carryback from 1962)	30,000	
Sum of offsets		$ 45,000
Carryover		$ 30,000

(4) *Carryover to 1962.* The carryover to this year is $10,000 (the excess, if any, of the loss for 1960 over the sum of the offsets for 1958, 1959, and 1961), computed as follows:

Loss from operations		$ 75,000
Less: Offset for 1958 (the $15,000 gain from operations for such year computed without the deduction of the carryback from 1960)	$15,000	
Offset for 1959 (the $30,000 gain from operations for such year computed without the deduction of the carryback from 1960 or the carryback from 1962)	30,000	

Life Insurance Companies   45,763
See p. 20,601 for regulations not amended to reflect law changes

→ *Caution: Former Code Secs. 801-820 for pre-1984 years were repealed and replaced by new Code Secs. 801-818. The following Regulations were issued under old Code Secs. 801-820.*←

Offset for 1961 (the $20,000 gain from operations for such year computed without the deduction of the carryover from 1960 or the carryback from 1962)	20,000	
Sum of offsets		$ 65,000
Carryover		$ 10,000

(5) *Carryover to 1963.* The carryover to this year is $10,000 (the excess, if any, of the loss for 1960 over the sum of the offsets for 1958, 1959, 1961, and 1962), computed as follows:

Loss from operations		$ 75,000
Less:		
Offset for 1958 (the $15,000 gain from operations for such year computed without the deduction of the carryback from 1960)	$15,000	
Offset for 1959 (the $30,000 gain from operations for such year computed without the deduction of the carryback from 1960 or the carryback from 1962)	30,000	
Offset for 1961 (the $20,000 gain from operations for such year computed without the deduction of the carryover from 1960 or the carryback from 1962)	20,000	
Offset for 1962 (a year in which a loss from operations was sustained)	0	
Sum of offsets		$ 65,000
Carryover		$ 10,000

(6) *Carryover to 1964.* The carryover to this year is $0 (the excess, if any, of the loss from 1960 over the sum of the offsets for 1958, 1959, 1961, 1962, and 1963), computed as follows:

Loss from operations		$ 75,000
Less:		
Offset for 1958 (the $15,000 gain from operations for such year computed without the deduction of the carryback from 1960)	$15,000	
Offset for 1959 (the $30,000 gain from operations for such year computed without the deduction of the carryback from 1960 or the carryback from 1962)	30,000	
Offset for 1961 (the $20,000 gain from operations for such year computed without the deduction of the carryover from 1960 or the carryback from 1962)	20,000	
Offset for 1962 (a year in which a loss from operations was sustained)	0	
Offset for 1963 (the $30,000 gain from operations for such year computed without the deduction of the carryover from 1960 or the carryover from 1962)	30,000	
Sum of offsets		$ 95,000
Carryover		$ 0

(7) *Carryover to 1965.* The carryover to this year is $0 (the excess, if any, of the loss from 1960 over the sum of the offsets for 1958, 1959, 1961, 1962, 1963, and 1964), computed as follows:

Loss from operations		$ 75,000
Less:		
Offset for 1958 (the $15,000 gain from operations for such year computed without the deduction of the carryback from 1960)	$15,000	
Offset for 1959 (the $30,000 gain from operations for such year computed without the deduction for the carryback from 1960 or the carryback from 1962)	30,000	
Offset for 1961 (the $20,000 gain from operations for such year computed without the deduction for the carryover from 1960 or the carryback from 1962)	20,000	
Offset for 1962 (a year in which a loss from operations was sustained)	0	
Offset for 1963 (the $30,000 gain from operations for such year computed without the deduction for the carryover from 1960 or the carryover from 1962)	30,000	

Reg. § 1.812-8(b)(7)

Life Insurance Companies

See p. 20,601 for regulations not amended to reflect law changes

→ *Caution: Former Code Secs. 801-820 for pre-1984 years were repealed and replaced by new Code Secs. 801-818. The following Regulations were issued under old Code Secs. 801-820.*←

Offset for 1964 (the $35,000 gain from operations for such year computed without the deduction of the carryover from 1960 or the carryover from 1962)	30,000
Sum of offsets...	$130,000
Carryover	$ 0

(c) *Loss sustained in 1962.* The portions of the $150,000 loss from operations for 1962 which shall be used as carrybacks to 1959, 1960, and 1961 and as carryovers to 1963, 1964, 1965, 1966, and 1967 are computed as follows:

(1) *Carryback to 1959.* The carryback to this year is $150,000, that is, the amount of the loss from operations.

(2) *Carryback to 1960.* The carryback to this year is $150,000, the excess, if any, of the loss from 1962 over the offset for 1959), computed as follows:

Loss from operations	$150,000
Less:	
Offset for 1959 (the $30,000 gain from operations for such year reduced by the carryback to such year of $60,000 from 1960, the carryback from 1962 to 1959 not being taken into account)...............	0
Carryback	$150,000

(3) *Carryback to 1961.* The carryback to this year is $150,000 (the excess, if any, of the loss from 1962 over the sum of the offsets for 1959 and 1960), computed as follows:

Loss from operations	$150,000
Less:	
Offset for 1959 (the $30,000 gain from operations for such year reduced by the carryback to such year of $60,000 from 1960, the carryback from 1962 to 1959 not being taken into account)	0
Offset for 1960 (a year in which a loss from operations was sustained)...	0
Sum of offsets...	0
Carryback	$150,000

(4) *Carryover to 1963.* The carryover to this year is $150,000 (the excess, if any, of the loss from 1962 over the sum of the offsets for 1959, 1960, and 1961), computed as follows:

Loss from operations	$150,000
Less:	
Offset for 1959 (the $30,000 gain from operations for such year reduced by the carryback to such year of $60,000 from 1960, the carryback from 1962 to 1959 not being taken into account)	0
Offset for 1960 (a year in which a loss from operations was sustained)...	0
Offset for 1961 (the $20,000 gain from operations for such year reduced by the carryover to such year of $30,000 from 1960, the carryback from 1962 to 1961 not being taken into account)	0
Sum of offsets...	0
Carryover	$150,000

(5) *Carryover to 1964.* The carryover to this year is $130,000 (the excess, if any, of the loss from 1962 over the sum of the offsets for 1959, 1960, 1961, and 1963), computed as follows:

Loss from operations	$150,000
Less:	
Offset for 1959 (the $30,000 gain from operations for such year reduced by the carryback to such year of $60,000 from 1960, the carryback from 1962 to 1959 not being taken into account)	0
Offset for 1960 (a year in which a loss from operations was sustained)	0

Reg. § 1.812-8(c)(1)

Life Insurance Companies

See p. 20,601 for regulations not amended to reflect law changes

→ **Caution: Former Code Secs. 801-820 for pre-1984 years were repealed and replaced by new Code Secs. 801-818. The following Regulations were issued under old Code Secs. 801-820.** ←

Offset for 1961 (the $20,000 gain from operations for such year reduced by the carryover to such year of $30,000 from 1960, the carryback from 1962 to 1961 not being taken into account)	0	
Offset for 1963 (the $30,000 gain from operations for such year reduced by the carryover to such year of $10,000 from 1960, the carryover from 1962 to 1963 not being taken into account)	$ 20,000	
Sum of offsets...		$ 20,000
Carryover...		$130,000

(6) *Carryover to 1965.* The carryover to this year is $95,000 (the excess, if any, of the loss from 1962 over the sum of the assets for 1959, 1960, 1961, 1963, and 1964), computed as follows:

Loss from operations...		$150,000
Less:		
Offset for 1959 (the $30,000 gain from operations for such year reduced by the carryback to such year of $60,000 from 1960, the carryback from 1962 to 1959 not being taken into account .	0	
Offset for 1960 (a year in which a loss from operations was sustained)	0	
Offset for 1961 (the $20,000 gain from operations for such year reduced by the carryover to such year of $30,000 from 1960, the carryback from 1962 to 1961 not being taken into account)	0	
Offset for 1963 (the $30,000 gain from operations for such year reduced by the carryover to such year of $10,000 from 1960, the carryover from 1962 to 1963 not being taken into account)	$ 20,000	
Offset for 1964 (the $35,000 gain from operations for such year reduced by the carryover to such year of $0 from 1960, the carryover from 1962 to 1964 not being taken into account)....	35,000	
Sum of offsets...		$ 55,000
Carryover...		$ 95,000

(7) *Carryover to 1966.* The carryover to this year is $20,000 (the excess, if any, of the loss from 1962 over the sum of the offsets for 1959, 1960, 1961, 1963, 1964, and 1965), computed as follows:

Loss from operations...		$150,000
Less:		
Offset for 1959 (the $30,000 gain from operations for such year reduced by the carryback to such year of $60,000 from 1960, the carryback from 1962 to 1959 not being taken into account)	0	
Offset for 1960 (a year in which a loss from operations was sustained)	0	
Offset for 1961 (the $20,000 gain from operations for such year reduced by the carryover to such year of $30,000 from 1960, the carryback from 1962 to 1961 not being taken into account)	0	
Offset for 1963 (the $30,000 gain from operations for such year reduced by the carryover for such year of $10,000 from 1960, the carryover from 1962 to 1963 not being taken into account)	$ 20,000	
Offset for 1964 (the $35,000 gain from operations for such year reduced by the carryover to such year of $0 from 1960, the carryover from 1962 to 1964 not being taken into account)....	35,000	
Offset for 1965 (the $75,000 gain from operations for such year reduced by the carryover to such year of $0 from 1960, the carryover from 1962 to 1965 not being taken into account)....	75,000	
Sum of offsets...		130,000
Carryover...		$ 20,000

(8) *Carryover to 1967.* The carryover to this year is $3,000 (the excess, if any, of the loss from 1962 over the sum of the offsets for 1959, 1960, 1961, 1963, 1964, 1965, and 1966), computed as follows:

Reg. § 1.812-8(c)(8)

45,766 Life Insurance Companies

See p. 20,601 for regulations not amended to reflect law changes

→ **Caution:** *Former Code Secs. 801-820 for pre-1984 years were repealed and replaced by new Code Secs. 801-818. The following Regulations were issued under old Code Secs. 801-820.* ←

Loss from operations	$150,000
Less:	
Offset for 1959 (the $30,000 gain from operations for such year reduced by the carryback to such year of $60,000 from 1960, the carryback from 1962 to 1959 not being taken into account)	0
Offset for 1960 (a year in which a loss from operations was sustained)	0
Offset for 1961 (the $20,000 gain from operations for such year reduced by the carryover to such year of $30,000 from 1960, the carryback from 1962 to 1961 not being taken into account)	0
Offset for 1963 (the $30,000 gain from operations for such year reduced by the carryover to such year of $10,000 from 1960, the carryover from 1962 to 1963 not being taken into account)	$ 20,000
Offset for 1964 (the $35,000 gain from operations for such year reduced by the carryover to such year of $0 from 1960, the carryover from 1962 to 1964 not being taken into account)	35,000
Offset for 1965 (the $75,000 gain from operations for such year reduced by the carryover to such year of $0 from 1960, the carryover from 1962 to 1965 not being taken into account)	75,000
Offset for 1966 (the $17,000 gain from operations for such year computed without the deduction of the carryover from 1962)	17,000
Sum of offsets	$147,000
Carryover	$ 3,000

(d) *Determination of operations loss deduction for each year.* The carryovers and carrybacks computed under paragraphs (b) and (c) of this section are used as a basis for the computation of the operations loss deduction in the following manner:

Taxable year	Carryover From 1960	Carryover From 1962	Carryback From 1960	Carryback From 1962	Operations loss deductions
1958			$75,000		$ 75,000
1959			60,000	$150,000	210,000
1961	$30,000			150,000	180,000
1963	10,000	$150,000			160,000
1964		130,000			130,000
1965		95,000			95,000
1966		20,000			20,000
1967		3,000			3,000

[Reg. § 1.812-8.]

☐ [*T.D. 6535, 1-19-61.*]

[Reg. § 1.815-1]

§ 1.815-1. Taxable years affected.—Sections 1.815-2 through 1.815-6, except as otherwise provided therein, are applicable only to taxable years beginning after December 31, 1957, and all reference to sections of part I, subchapter L, chapter 1 of the Code are to the Internal Revenue Code of 1954, as amended by the Life Insurance Company Income Tax Act of 1959 (73 Stat. 112), the Act of October 10, 1962 (76 Stat. 808), and the Act of October 23, 1962 (76 Stat. 1134). [Reg. § 1.815-1.]

☐ [*T.D. 6535, 1-19-61. Amended by T.D. 6886, 6-22-66.*]

[Reg. § 1.815-2]

§ 1.815-2. Distributions to shareholders.—(a) *In general.* Section 815 provides that every stock life insurance company subject to the tax imposed by section 802 shall establish and maintain two special surplus accounts for Federal income tax purposes. These special accounts are the shareholders surplus account (as defined in section 815(b) and § 1.815-3) and the policyholders surplus account (as defined in section 815(c) and § 1.815-4). To the extent that a distribution to shareholders (as defined in paragraph (c) of this section) is treated as being made out of the shareholders surplus account, no tax is imposed on the company with respect to such distribution. However, to the extent that a distribution to shareholders is treated as being made out of the policyholders surplus account, the amount subtracted from the policyholders surplus account by reason of such distribution shall be taken into

Reg. § 1.815-1

Life Insurance Companies

See p. 20,601 for regulations not amended to reflect law changes

→ *Caution: Former Code Secs. 801-820 for pre-1984 years were repealed and replaced by new Code Secs. 801-818. The following Regulations were issued under old Code Secs. 801-820.*←

account in determining life insurance company taxable income under section 802(b).

(b) *Priority system for distributions to shareholders.* (1) For purposes of section 815 (other than subsection (e) thereof relating to certain mutualizations) and section 802(b)(3) (relating to the determination of life insurance company taxable income), any distribution made to shareholders after December 31, 1958, shall be treated in the following manner:

(i) Distributions shall be treated as first being made out of the shareholders surplus account (as defined in section 815(b) and § 1.815-3);

(ii) Once the shareholders surplus account has been reduced to zero, distributions shall then be treated as being made out of the policyholders surplus account (as defined in section 815(c) and § 1.815-4) until that account has been reduced to zero; and

(iii) Finally, any distributions in excess of the amounts in the shareholders surplus account and the policyholders surplus account shall be treated as being made out of other accounts (as defined in § 1.815-5).

(2) For purposes of subparagraph (1) of this paragraph, in order to determine whether a distribution (or any portion thereof) shall be treated as being made out of the shareholders surplus account, policyholders surplus account, or other accounts, the amount in such accounts at the end of any taxable year shall be the cumulative balance in such accounts at the end of the taxable year, computed without diminution by reason of a distribution (or any portion thereof) during the taxable year which is treated as being made out of such accounts. For example, on January 1, 1960, S, a stock life insurance company, had $1,000 in its shareholders surplus account and $3,000 in its policyholders surplus account. On November 1, 1960, S distributed $4,000 to its shareholders. Under the provisions of section 815(b)(2) and paragraph (b) of § 1.815-3, S added $5,000 to its shareholders surplus account for the taxable year 1960. Since the distributions to shareholders during the taxable year 1960, $4,000, does not exceed the cumulative balance in the shareholders surplus account at the end of the taxable year, computed without diminution by reason of distributions treated as made out of such account during the taxable year, $6,000 ($1,000 plus $5,000), the entire distribution is treated as being made out of the shareholders surplus account.

(3) Except in the case of a distribution in cash and as otherwise provided herein, the amount to be charged to the special surplus accounts referred to in subparagraph (1) of this paragraph with respect to any distributions to shareholders (as defined in section 815(a) and paragraph (c) of this section) shall be the fair market value of the property distributed, determined as of the date of distribution. However, for the amount of the adjustment to earnings and profits reflecting such distributions, see section 312 and the regulations thereunder. For a special rule relating to the determination of the amount to be charged to such special surplus accounts in the case of a distribution by a foreign life insurance company carrying on a life insurance business within the United States, see section 819(c)(1) and the regulations thereunder.

(c) *Distributions to shareholders defined.* (1) Except as otherwise provided in section 815(f) and subparagraph (2) of this paragraph, the term "distribution", as used in section 815(a) and paragraph (b) of this section, means any distribution of property made by a life insurance company to its shareholders. For purposes of the preceding sentence, the term "property" means any property (including money, securities, and indebtedness to the company) other than stock, or rights to acquire stock, in the company making the distribution. Thus, for example, the term includes a distribution which is considered a dividend under section 316, but is not limited to the extent that such distribution must be made out of the accumulated or current earnings and profits of the company making the distribution. For example, except as otherwise provided in section 815(f) and subparagraph (2) of this paragraph, there is a distribution within the meaning of this paragraph in any case in which a corporation acquires the stock of a shareholder in exchange for property in a redemption treated as a distribution in exchange for stock under section 302(a) or treated as a distribution of property under section 302(d). For special rules relating to distributions to shareholders in acquisition of stock pursuant to a plan of mutualization, see section 815(e) and paragraph (e) of § 1.815-6.

(2) The term "distribution", as used in section 815(a) and paragraph (b) of this section, does not (except for purposes of section 815(a) and (e)(2)(B)) include any distribution in redemption of stock issued prior to January 1, 1958, where such stock was at all times on and after the date of its issuance and on and before the date of its

Reg. § 1.815-2(c)(2)

Life Insurance Companies

See p. 20,601 for regulations not amended to reflect law changes

→ *Caution: Former Code Secs. 801-820 for pre-1984 years were repealed and replaced by new Code Secs. 801-818. The following Regulations were issued under old Code Secs. 801-820.* ←

redemption limited as to the amount of dividends payable and was callable, at the option of the issuer, at a price not in excess of 105 percent of the sum of its issue price plus the amount of contribution to surplus (if any) made by the original purchaser at the time of his purchase. [Reg. § 1.815-2.]

☐ [*T.D.* 6535, 1-19-61. *Amended by T.D.* 7189, 6-28-72.]

[Reg. § 1.815-3]

§ 1.815-3. Shareholders surplus account.—(a) *In general.* Every stock life insurance company subject to the tax imposed by section 802 shall establish and maintain a shareholders surplus account. This account shall be established as of January 1, 1958, and the beginning or opening balance of the shareholders surplus account on that date shall be zero.

(b) *Additions to shareholders surplus account.*—(1) The amount added to the shareholders surplus account for any taxable year beginning after December 31, 1957, shall be the amount by which the sum of—

(i) The life insurance company taxable income (computed without regard to section 802(b)(3)),

(ii) In the case of a taxable year beginning after December 31, 1958, the amount (if any) by which the net long-term capital gain exceeds the net short-term capital loss, reduced (in the case of a taxable year beginning after December 31, 1961) by the amount referred to subdivision (i) of this paragraph,

(iii) The deduction for partially tax-exempt interest provided by section 242 (as modified by section 804(a)(3)), the deductions for dividends received provided by sections 243, 244, and 245 (as modified by section 809(d)(8)(B)), and the amount of interest excluded from gross income under section 103, and

(iv) The small business deduction provided by section 809(d)(10),

exceeds the taxes imposed for the taxable year by section 802(a), computed without regard to section 802(b)(3).

(2) For amounts which are to be added to the shareholders surplus account at the beginning of the succeeding taxable year, see section 815(d)(1) and (4) and paragraphs (a) and (d) of § 1.815-6.

(c) *Subtractions from shareholders surplus account.*—(1) *In general.* There shall be subtracted from the cumulative balance in the shareholders surplus account at the end of any taxable year, computed without diminution by reason of distributions made during the taxable year, the amount which is treated as being distributed out of such account under section 815(a) and paragraph (b) of § 1.815-2.

(2) *Special rule; distributions in 1958.* There shall be subtracted from the shareholders surplus account (to the extent thereof) for any taxable year beginning in 1958 the amount of the distributions to shareholders made by the company during 1958. For example, assume S, a stock life insurance company, had additions to its shareholders surplus account (as determined under section 815(b)(2) and paragraph (b) of this section) for the taxable year 1958 of $10,000, and actually distributed as dividends to its shareholders $8,000 during the year 1958. The balance in S's shareholders surplus account as of January 1, 1959, shall be $2,000. If S had distributed $12,000 as dividends in 1958, the balance in its shareholders surplus account as of January 1, 1959, would be zero and the other accounts referred to in section 815(a)(3) and paragraph (b)(1)(iii) of § 1.815-2 would be reduced by $2,000.

(d) *Illustration of principles.* The application of section 815(b) and this section may be illustrated by the following example:

Example. The books of S, a stock life insurance company, reflect the following items for the taxable year 1960:

Balance in shareholders surplus account as of 1-1-60	$5,000
Life insurance company taxable income computed without regard to sec. 802(b)(3)	4,000
Excess of net long-term capital gain over net short-term capital loss	1,700
Tax-exempt interest included in gross investment income under sec. 804(b)	100
Small business deduction (determined under sec. 809(d)(10))	200
Tax liability under sec. 802(a)(1) and (2) computed without regard to sec. 802(b)(3)	1,625
Amount distributed to shareholders	9,000

For purposes of determining the amount to be subtracted from its shareholders surplus account for the taxable year, S would first make up the following schedule in order to determine the cu-

Reg. § 1.815-3(a)

Life Insurance Companies   45,769

See p. 20,601 for regulations not amended to reflect law changes

→ *Caution: Former Code Secs. 801-820 for pre-1984 years were repealed and replaced by new Code Secs. 801-818. The following Regulations were issued under old Code Secs. 801-820.* ←

mulative balance in the shareholders surplus account at the end of the taxable year, computed without diminution by reason of distributions made during the taxable year:

(1) Balance in shareholders surplus account as of 1-1-60			$5,000
(2) Additions to account:			
(a) Life insurance company taxable income computed without regard to sec. 802(b)(3)	$4,000		
(b) Excess of net long-term capital gain over net short-term capital loss	1,700		
(c) Tax-exempt interest included in gross investment income under sec. 804(b)	100		
(d) Small business deduction (determined under sec. 809(d)(10)) .	200		
Total		$6,000	
Less: Tax liability under sec. 802(a)(1) and (2) computed without regard to sec. 802(b)(3)		1,625	$4,375
(3) Cumulative balance in shareholders surplus account as of 12-31-60 (item (1) plus item (2))			$9,375

Since the amount distributed to shareholders during the taxable year, $9,000, does not exceed the cumulative balance in the shareholders surplus account at the end of the taxable year, computed without diminution by reason of distributions made during the taxable year, $9,375, under the provisions of section 815(a), the entire distribution shall be treated as being made out of the shareholders surplus account. Thus, $9,000 shall be subtracted from the shareholders surplus account (leaving a balance of $375 in such account at the end of the taxable year) and S shall incur no additional tax liability by reason of the distribution to its shareholders during the taxable year 1960. [Reg. § 1.815-3.]

☐ [T.D. 6535, 1-19-61. Amended by T.D. 7189, 6-28-72.]

[Reg. § 1.815-4]

§ 1.815-4. **Policyholders surplus account.**—(a) *In general.* Every stock life insurance company subject to the tax imposed by section 802 shall establish and maintain a policyholders surplus account. This account shall be established as of January 1, 1959, and the beginning or opening balance of the policyholders surplus account on that date shall be zero.

(b) *Additions to policyholders surplus account.* The amount added to the policyholders surplus account for any taxable year beginning after December 31, 1958, shall be the sum of—

(1) An amount equal to 50 percent of the amount by which the gain from operations for the taxable year exceeds the taxable investment income,

(2) The deduction allowed or allowable under section 809(d)(5) (as limited by section 809(f)) for certain nonparticipating contracts, and

(3) The deduction allowed or allowable under section 809(d)(6) (as limited by section 809(f)) for taxable years beginning before January 1, 1963, for group life and group accident and health insurance contracts, and for taxable years beginning after December 31, 1962, for accident and health insurance and group life insurance contracts.

(c) *Subtractions from policyholders surplus account*—(1) *In general.* There shall be subtracted from the cumulative balance in the policyholders surplus account at the end of any taxable year, computed without diminution by reason of distributions made during the taxable year, an amount equal to the sum of—

(i) The amount which (without regard to subdivision (ii) of this subparagraph) is treated under section 815(a) as distributed out of the policyholders surplus account for the taxable year, plus

(ii) The amount (determined without regard to section 802(a)(3)) by which the tax imposed for taxable years beginning before January 1, 1962, by section 802(a)(1), and for taxable years beginning after December 31, 1961, by section 802(a), is increased by reason of section 802(b)(3).

In addition, there shall be subtracted from the policyholders surplus account for the taxable year those amounts which, at the close of the taxable year, are subtracted or treated as subtracted from the policyholders surplus account under section 815(d)(1) and (4) and paragraphs (a) and (d) of § 1.815-6. For purposes of this paragraph, the

Reg. § 1.815-4(c)(1)

Life Insurance Companies

See p. 20,601 for regulations not amended to reflect law changes

→ **Caution:** *Former Code Secs. 801-820 for pre-1984 years were repealed and replaced by new Code Secs. 801-818. The following Regulations were issued under old Code Secs. 801-820.*←

subtractions from the policyholders surplus account shall be treated as made in the following order:

(a) First the amount determined under section 815(c)(3) by reason of distributions to shareholders during the taxable year which are treated as being made out of the policyholders surplus account;

(b) Next the amount elected to be subtracted from the policyholders surplus account for the taxable year under section 815(d)(1);

(c) Then the amount which is treated as a subtraction from the policyholders surplus account for the taxable year by reason of the limitation provided in section 815(d)(4); and

(d) Finally the amount taken into account upon termination as a life insurance company as provided in section 815(d)(2).

(2) *Method of computing amount subtracted from policyholders surplus account*—(i) *Where life insurance company taxable income, computed without regard to section 802(b)(3), exceeds $25,000.* If the life insurance company taxable income for any taxable year computed under section 802(b), computed without regard to section 802(b)(3), exceeds $25,000, the amount subtracted from the policyholders surplus account shall be determined by multiplying the amount treated as distributed out of such account by a ratio, the numerator of which is 100 percent and the denominator of which is 100 percent minus the sum of the normal tax rate and the surtax rate for the taxable year.

(ii) *Where life insurance company taxable income does not exceed $25,000.* If the life insurance company taxable income for any taxable year, computed under section 802(b), does not exceed $25,000, the amount subtracted from the policyholders surplus account shall be determined by multiplying the amount treated as distributed out of such account by a ratio, the numerator of which is 100 percent and the denominator of which is 100 percent minus the normal tax rate for the taxable year.

(iii) *Where life insurance company taxable income, computed without regard to section 802(b)(3) does not exceed $25,000, but computed with regard to section 802(b)(3) does exceed $25,000.* If the life insurance company taxable income for any taxable year, computed without regard to section 802(b)(3) does not exceed $25,000, but computed with regard to section 802(b)(3) does exceed $25,000, the amount subtracted from the policyholders surplus account shall be determined in the following manner:

(a) First, determine the amount by which $25,000 exceeds the amount determined under section 802(b)(1) and (2);

(b) Then, multiply the amount determined under (a) by a ratio, the numerator of which is 100 percent minus the normal tax rate and the denominator of which is 100 percent;

(c) Next, determine the amount by which the amount treated as distributed out of the policyholders surplus account exceeds the amount determined under (b) and multiply such excess by a ratio, the numerator of which is 100 percent and the denominator of which is 100 percent minus the sum of the normal tax rate and the surtax rate; and

(d) Finally, add the amounts determined under (a) and (c).

(3) *Illustration of principles.* The application of section 815(c)(3) and subparagraph (2) of this paragraph may be illustrated by the following examples:

Example (1). The life insurance company taxable income of S, a stock life insurance company, computed without regard to section 802(b)(3), exceeds $25,000 for the taxable year 1959. Assume that of the amount distributed by S to its shareholders during the taxable year, $9,600 (as determined under section 815(a) and without regard to section 815(c)(3)(B)) is treated as distributed out of the policyholders surplus account. Since the sum of the normal tax rate (30%) and the surtax rate (22%) in effect for 1959 is 52 percent, S shall subtract $20,000 from its policyholders surplus account for the taxable year 1959, computed as follows:

$$\$9,600 \times \frac{100}{(100-52)} = \$9,600 \times \frac{100}{48} = \$20,000$$

Of this amount, $9,600 is due to the application of section 815(c)(3)(A) and $10,400 to the application of section 815(c)(3)(B).

Example (2). Assume that for the taxable year 1960, S, a stock life insurance company, has taxable investment income of $1,000 and a gain from operations of $2,000. Assume further that of

Reg. § 1.815-4(c)(2)

Life Insurance Companies

See p. 20,601 for regulations not amended to reflect law changes

→ *Caution: Former Code Secs. 801-820 for pre-1984 years were repealed and replaced by new Code Secs. 801-818. The following Regulations were issued under old Code Secs. 801-820.* ←

the amount distributed by S to its shareholders during the taxable year, $3,500 (as determined under section 815(a) and without regard to section 815(c)(3)(B)) is treated as distributed out of the policyholders surplus account. Since S's life insurance company taxable income does not exceed $25,000 for the taxable year and the normal tax rate in effect for 1960 is 30 percent, S shall subtract $5,000 from its policyholders surplus account for the taxable year 1960, computed as follows:

$$\$3,500 \times \frac{100}{(100-30)} = \$3,500 \times \frac{100}{70} = \$5,000$$

Of this amount, $3,500 is due to the application of section 815(c)(3)(A), and $1,500 to the application of section 815(c)(3)(B).

Example (3). For the taxable year 1960, the life insurance company taxable income of S, a stock life insurance company, computed without regard to section 802(b)(3), is $10,000. Assume that of the amount distributed by S to its shareholders during the taxable year, $12,000 (as determined under section 815(a) and without regard to section 815(c)(3)(B)) is treated as distributed out of the policyholders surplus account. Since the life insurance company taxable income of S, computed with regard to section 802(b)(3), exceeds $25,000, in order to determine the amount to be subtracted from its policyholders surplus account, S would make up the following schedule:

(1) $25,000 minus life insurance company taxable income, computed without regard to sec. 802(b)(3) ($25,000 minus $10,000) $15,000
(2) Item (1) multiplied by 100 percent minus the normal tax rate as in effect for 1960, over 100 percent

$$(15,000 \times \frac{(100-30)}{100})\ \dots\dots\dots\dots\dots\dots\dots\dots\dots\dots\dots\dots\ 10,500$$

(3) Amount by which the amount treated as distributed out of policyholders surplus account ($12,000) exceeds item (2) ($10,500), multiplied by 100 percent over 100 percent minus the sum of the normal tax rate and the surtax rate as in effect for 1960

$$(\$1,500 \times \frac{100}{(100-52)})\ \dots\dots\dots\dots\dots\dots\dots\dots\dots\dots\dots\dots\dots\ 3,125$$

(4) Item (1) plus item (3) ($15,000 plus $3,125)............................. 18,125

For the taxable year 1960, S shall subtract $18,125 from its policyholders surplus account. Of this amount, $10,500 represents the distribution from the policyholders surplus account which is taxed at a 30 percent tax rate and $1,500 the distribution from the policyholders surplus account which is taxed at a 52 percent tax rate. Thus, of the amount subtracted from the policyholders surplus account for the taxable year 1960, $12,000 is due to the application of section 815(c)(3)(A), and $6,125 to the application of section 815(c)(3)(B).

(d) *Illustration of principles.* The application of section 815(c) and this section may be illustrated by the following example:

Example. The books of S, a stock life insurance company, reflect the following items for the taxable year 1960:

Taxable investment income	$25,000
Gain from operations	30,000
Tax base (sec. 802(b)(1) and (2))	27,500
Deduction for certain nonparticipating policies provided by sec. 809(d)(5) (as limited by sec. 809(f))	600
Deduction for group policies provided by sec. 809(d)(6) (as limited by sec. 809(f))	400
Amount distributed to shareholders	60,000
Cumulative balance in shareholders surplus account as of 12-31-60	36,000
Balance in policyholders surplus account as of 1-1-60	48,000

For purposes of determining the amount to be subtracted from its policyholders surplus account for the taxable year, S would first make up the following schedule in order to determine the cumulative balance in the policyholders surplus account at the end of the taxable year, computed without diminution by reason of distributions made during the taxable year:

Reg. § 1.815-4(d)

45,772 Life Insurance Companies

See p. 20,601 for regulations not amended to reflect law changes

→ *Caution: Former Code Secs. 801-820 for pre-1984 years were repealed and replaced by new Code Secs. 801-818. The following Regulations were issued under old Code Secs. 801-820.*←

(1)	Balance in policyholders surplus account as of 1-1-60		$48,000
(2)	Additions to account:		
(a)	50 percent of the amount by which the gain from operations ($30,000) exceeds the taxable investment income ($25,000) (½ × $5,000)	$2,500	
(b)	The deduction for certain nonparticipating contracts provided by sec. 809(d)(5) (as limited by sec. 809(f))	600	
(c)	The deduction for group contracts provided by sec. 809(d)(6) as limited by sec. 809(f))	400	3,500
(3)	Cumulative balance in policyholders account as of 12-31-60 (item (1) plus item (2))		$51,500

Under the provisions of section 815(a), since the amount distributed to shareholders during the taxable year, $60,000, exceeds the cumulative balance in the shareholders surplus at the end of the taxable year, computed without diminution by reason of distribution during the taxable year, $36,000, the shareholders surplus account shall first be reduced to zero. The remaining $24,000 ($60,000 minus $36,000) of the distribution shall then be treated as made out of the policyholders surplus account. Thus, since the tax base under section 802(b)(1) and (2) is in excess of $25,000, the total amount to be subtracted from the policyholders surplus account at the end of the taxable year would be $50,000 ($24,000 × $\frac{100}{(100-52)}$). Of this amount $26,000 ($50,000 minus $24,000) represents the tax on the portion of the distribution to shareholders which is treated as being out of the policyholders surplus account.

(e) *Special rule for 1959 and 1960.* For a special transitional rule applicable to any increase in tax liability under section 802(b)(3) for the taxable years 1959 and 1960 which is due solely to the operation of section 815(c)(3) and this section, see section 802(a)(3) and § 1.802-5. [Reg. § 1.815-4.]

☐ [*T.D. 6535, 1-19-61. Amended by T.D. 6886, 6-22-66.*]

[Reg. § 1.815-5]

§ 1.815-5. **Other accounts defined.**—The term "other accounts," as used in section 815(a)(3) and paragraph (b) of § 1.815-2, means all amounts which are not specifically included in the shareholders surplus account under section 815(b) and paragraph (b) of § 1.815-3, or in the policyholders surplus account under section 815(c) and paragraph (b) of § 1.815-4. Thus, for example, other accounts include amounts representing the increase in tax due to the operation of section 802(b)(3) which is not taken into account for the taxable years 1959 and 1960 because of the special transitional rule provided in section 802(a)(3) and § 1.802-5, earnings and profits accumulated prior to January 1, 1958, paid-in surplus, capital, etc. To the extent that a distribution (or any portion thereof) is treated as being made out of other accounts, no tax is imposed on the company with respect to such distribution. [Reg. § 1.815-5.]

☐ [*T.D. 6535, 1-19-61.*]

[Reg. § 1.815-6]

§ 1.815-6. **Special rules.**—(a) *Election to transfer amounts from policyholders surplus account to shareholders surplus account*—(1) *In general.* Section 815(d)(1) permits a life insurance company to elect, after the close of any taxable year for which it is a life insurance company, to subtract any amount (or any portion thereof) in its policyholders surplus account as of the close of the taxable year. The effect of such election is to subject the company to tax on the amounts elected to be subtracted for the taxable year for which the election applies. The amount so subtracted, less the amount of tax imposed with respect to such amount by reason of section 802(b)(3), shall be added to the shareholders surplus account as of the beginning of the taxable year following the taxable year for which the election applies and no further tax shall be imposed upon the company if the amount elected to be transferred to the shareholders surplus account is subsequently distributed to shareholders.

(2) *Manner and effect of election.* (i) The election provided by section 815(d)(1) and this section shall be made in a statement attached to the life insurance company's income tax return for any taxable year for which the company desires the election to apply. The statement shall include the name and address of the taxpayer, shall be signed by the taxpayer (or his duly authorized representative), and shall be filed not later than the date prescribed by law (including extensions thereof) for filing the return for such taxable year. In addition, the statement shall indicate that the company has made the election

Reg. § 1.815-5

Life Insurance Companies

See p. 20,601 for regulations not amended to reflect law changes

→ *Caution: Former Code Secs. 801-820 for pre-1984 years were repealed and replaced by new Code Secs. 801-818. The following Regulations were issued under old Code Secs. 801-820.*←

provided under section 815(d)(1) for the taxable year and the amount elected to be subtracted from the policyholders surplus account.

(ii) An election made under section 815(d)(1)(B) and subdivision (i) of this subparagraph shall be effective only with respect to the taxable year for which the election is made. Thus, the company must make a new election for each taxable year for which it desires the election to apply. Once such an election has been made for any taxable year it may not be revoked.

(3) The application of subparagraph (1) of this paragraph may be illustrated by the following example:

Example. For the taxable year 1960, the life insurance company taxable income of S, a stock life insurance company, computed without regard to section 802(b)(3), exceeds $25,000. Assume that S elects to subtract $20,000 from its policyholders surplus account under section 815(d)(1) for the taxable year. Since S is subject to a 52 percent tax rate, the tax on the amount elected to be subtracted from the policyholders surplus account (as of the close of the taxable year 1960) is $10,400 ($20,000 × 52 percent). Thus, the amount to be added to the shareholders surplus account as of January 1, 1961, is $9,600 (the amount subtracted from the policyholders surplus account by virtue of the section 815(d)(1) election, less the tax imposed upon such amount by reason of section 802(b)(3), or $20,000 minus $10,400).

(b) *Termination as life insurance company*—(1) *Effect of termination.* Except as provided in section 381(c)(22) (relating to carryovers in certain corporate readjustments), section 815(d)(2)(A) provides that if for any taxable year the taxpayer is not an insurance company (as defined in paragraph (a) of § 1.801-3), or if for any two successive taxable years the taxpayer is not a life insurance company (as defined in section 801(a) and paragraph (b) of § 1.801-3), the amount taken into account under section 802(b)(3) for the last preceding year for which the company was a life insurance company shall be increased (after the application of section 815(d)(2)(B)) by the entire balance in the policyholders surplus account at the close of such last preceding taxable year.

(2) *Effect of certain distributions.* If for any taxable year the taxpayer is an insurance company (as defined in paragraph (a) of § 1.801-3) but is not a life insurance company (as defined in section 801(a) and paragraph (b) of § 1.801-3),

section 815(d)(2)(B) provides that any distribution to shareholders during such taxable year shall be treated as having been made on the last day of the last preceding taxable year for which the company was a life insurance company.

(3) *Examples.* The application of section 815(d)(2) and this paragraph may be illustrated by the following examples:

Example (1). At the end of the taxable year 1959, the balance in the policyholders surplus account of S, a life insurance company within the meaning of section 801(a) and paragraph (b) of § 1.801-3, is $12,000. If S fails to qualify as an insurance company (as defined in paragraph (a) of § 1.801-3) for the taxable year 1960, and section 381(c)(22) does not apply, under the provisions of section 815(d)(2)(A), the entire balance of $12,000 in the policyholders surplus account at the end of 1959, the last year S was a life insurance company, shall be taken into account under section 802(b)(3) for purposes of determining S's tax liability for the taxable year 1959.

Example (2). Assume the facts are the same as in example (1), except that for the taxable years 1960 and 1961, S qualifies as an insurance company (as defined in paragraph (a) of § 1.801-3) but does not qualify as a life insurance company within the meaning of section 801(a) and paragraph (b) of § 1.801-3. Assume further that as a result of a distribution by S to its shareholders in 1960, $4,800 (as determined under section 815(a) and without regard to section 815(c)(3)(B)) is treated as distributed out of the policyholders surplus account. Under the provisions of section 815(d)(2)(B), if section 381(c)(22) does not apply, any distribution to shareholders during the taxable years 1960 and 1961 shall be treated as having been made on December 31, 1959 (the last day of the last preceding taxable year for which S was a life insurance company). Thus, assuming S is subject to a 52 percent tax rate on additions to life insurance company taxable income, $10,000 ($4,800 plus $5,200, the tax on the portion of the distribution treated as made out of the policyholders surplus account) shall be treated as being subtracted from the policyholders surplus account at the end of 1959 and shall be taken into account under section 802(b)(3) for purposes of determining S's tax liability for the taxable year 1959. Under the provisions of section 815(d)(2)(A), the entire balance of $2,000 ($12,000 minus $10,000) in the policyholders surplus account at the end of 1959 (after the application of section 815(d)(2)(B)), shall also be taken

Reg. § 1.815-6(b)(3)

Life Insurance Companies

See p. 20,601 for regulations not amended to reflect law changes

→ *Caution: Former Code Secs. 801-820 for pre-1984 years were repealed and replaced by new Code Secs. 801-818. The following Regulations were issued under old Code Secs. 801-820.*←

into account under section 802(b)(3) for purposes of determining S's tax liability for the taxable year 1959.

(c) *Treatment of certain indebtedness.* Section 815(d)(3) provides that if a taxpayer makes any payment in discharge of its indebtedness and such indebtedness is attributable to a distribution by the taxpayer to its shareholders after February 9, 1959, the amount of such payment shall be treated as a distribution in cash to the shareholders both for purposes of section 802(b)(3) and section 815. However, this paragraph shall only apply to the extent that the distribution of such indebtedness to shareholders was treated as being out of accounts other than the shareholders and policyholders surplus accounts at the time of distribution.

(d) *Limitation on amount in policyholders surplus account.*—(1) *In general.* Section 815(d)(4) provides a limitation on the amount that any life insurance company may accumulate in its policyholders surplus account. If the policyholders surplus account at the end of any taxable year (computed without regard to this paragraph) exceeds whichever of the following is the greatest—

(i) 15 percent of life insurance reserves (as defined in section 801(b) and paragraph (a) of § 1.801-4) at the end of the taxable year,

(ii) 25 percent of the amount by which the life insurance reserves at the end of the taxable year exceed the life insurance reserves at the end of 1958, or

(iii) 50 percent of the net amount of the premiums and other consideration taken into account for the taxable year under section 809(c)(1), then such excess shall be treated as a subtraction from the policyholders surplus account as of the end of such taxable year. The amount so treated as subtracted, less the amount of tax imposed with respect to such amount by reason of section 802(b)(3), shall be added to the shareholders surplus account at the beginning of the succeeding year.

(2) *Example.* The application of the limitation contained in subparagraph (1) of this paragraph may be illustrated by the following example:

Example. The books of S, a stock life insurance company, reflect the following items for the taxable year 1960:

Balance in policyholders surplus account, computed without regard to sec. 815(d)(4), as of 12-31-60	$ 175
Life insurance reserves (as defined in sec. 801(b)) as of 12-31-60	4,500
Life insurance reserves (as defined in sec. 801(b)) as of 12-31-58	3,900
Premiums and other consideration taken into account for the taxable year under sec. 809(c)(1)	310

In order to determine the limitations on the amount that it may accumulate in its policyholders surplus account at the end of the taxable year under section 815(d)(4), S would make up the following schedule:

(1) 15 percent of life insurance reserves at the end of the taxable year (15% × $4,500)	$675
(2) 25 percent of amount by which life insurance reserves at the end of the taxable year ($4,500) exceed life insurance reserves as of 12-31-58 ($3,900) (25% × $600)	150
(3) 50 percent of premiums and other consideration taken into account under sec. 809(c)(1) for the taxable year (50% × $310)	155
(4) Limitation on policyholders surplus account (the greatest of items (1), (2), or (3))	675

Since the balance in the policyholders surplus account at the end of the taxable year 1960, $175, does not exceed the limitation provided by section 815(d)(4), $675, S is not required to make any further adjustment to its policyholders surplus account at the end of the taxable year.

(e) *Special rule for certain mutualizations*—(1) *In general.* Section 815(e) provides a rule for determining priorities which shall operate in place of section 815(a) and paragraph (b) of § 1.815-2 where a life insurance company makes any distribution to its shareholders after December 31, 1958, in acquisition of stock pursuant to a plan of mutualization. Section 815(e)(1) provides that such a distribution shall first be treated as being made out of paid-in capital and paid-in surplus, and, to the extent thereof, no tax shall be imposed on the company with respect to such distribution. Thereafter, distributions made pursuant to such plan of mutualization shall be treated as made in two allocable parts. One part shall be treated as being made out of other accounts (as defined in § 1.815-5) and the company shall incur no tax with respect to such portion of the distribution. The other part shall be treated as a distribution to which section 815(a) and paragraph (b) of § 1.815-2 applies. Thus, such portion of the distribution shall be treated as first being made out of

Reg. § 1.815-6(c)

Life Insurance Companies

See p. 20,601 for regulations not amended to reflect law changes

→ *Caution: Former Code Secs. 801-820 for pre-1984 years were repealed and replaced by new Code Secs. 801-818. The following Regulations were issued under old Code Secs. 801-820.* ←

the shareholders surplus account (as defined in section 815(b) and § 1.815-3), to the extent thereof, and then out of the policyholders surplus account (as defined in section 815(c) and § 1.815-4), to the extent thereof. See paragraph (a) of § 1.815-2. For purposes of this paragraph, a distribution shall be considered as being made pursuant to a plan of mutualization only if the requirements of applicable State law for the adoption of such plan (as, for example, approval by the requisite majority of the board of directors, shareholders, and policyholders) have been fulfilled.

(2) *Allocation ratio.* Section 815(e)(2)(A) provides an allocation ratio which when applied to the amount distributed under a plan of mutualization in excess of the balance in the paid-in capital and paid-in surplus accounts determines the portion of such excess to be treated as distributed out of the shareholders surplus account, policyholders surplus account, or other accounts. The numerator of this ratio is the excess of the assets of the company (as defined in section 805(b)(4) and paragraph (a)(4) of § 1.805-5) over the total liabilities (including reserves), both determined as of December 31, 1958, and adjusted in the manner provided in subparagraph (3) of this paragraph. The denominator of this ratio is the amount included in the numerator plus the amounts in the shareholders surplus account and policyholders surplus account, all determined as of the beginning of the year of the distribution.

(3) *Adjustment for certain distributions.* Section 815(e)(2)(B) provides that if between 1958 and the year of distribution the taxpayer has been treated as having made a distribution (under a plan of mutualization or otherwise) which is treated as a return of paid-in capital and paid-in surplus or as out of other accounts (as defined in § 1.815-5), the aggregate amount of any such prior distributions must be subtracted from the numerator and denominator in all cases where the allocation ratio provided by subparagraph (2) of this paragraph applies.

(f) *Recomputation required as a result of a subsequent loss from operations under section 812*—(1) *In general.* Any amounts added to or subtracted from the special surplus accounts referred to in section 815(a) and paragraph (b) of § 1.815-2 for any taxable year shall be adjusted to the extent necessary to properly reflect a subsequent loss from operations which under section 812 is carried back to the taxable year for which such additions or subtractions were made.

(2) *Example.* The application of subparagraph (1) of this paragraph may be illustrated by the following example.

Example. Assume that for the taxable years 1959 through 1961, the books of S, a stock life insurance company subject to a 30 percent tax rate for all taxable years involved, reflect the following items:

	1959	1960	1961
Taxable investment income	$40.00	$40.00	$40.00
Gain from operations	60.00	60.00	60.00
Tax base (sec. 802(b)(1) and (2))	50.00	50.00	50.00
Tax (sec. 802(b)(1) and (2) base)	15.00	15.00	15.00
Shareholders surplus account—			
At beginning of year	0	35.00	37.00
Added at beginning of year by reason of election under sec. 815(d)(1)	0	7.00	0
Added for year (without regard to election under sec. 815(d)(1))	35.00	35.00	35.00
Subtracted (distributions)	0	40.00	40.00
Policyholders surplus account—			
At beginning of year	0	0	10.00
Added for year	10.00	10.00	10.00
Subtracted (distributions)	0	0	0
Subtracted (by reason of election under sec. 815(d)(1))	10.00	0	0
Tax base (sec. 802(b)(3))	10.00	0	0
Tax (sec. 802(b)(3) base)	3.00	0	0

Assume further that S has a loss from operations for the taxable year 1962 of $25. Under provisions of section 812, the $25 loss from operations would be carried back to the taxable year 1959 and would reduce the 1959 tax base under section 802(b)(1) and (2) to $35 ($60 minus $25). After adjustments reflecting the 1962 loss from operations, the results for the taxable years 1959 through the beginning of 1962 would be as follows:

Reg. § 1.815-6(f)(2)

45,776   Life Insurance Companies

See p. 20,601 for regulations not amended to reflect law changes

→ *Caution: Former Code Secs. 801-820 for pre-1984 years were repealed and replaced by new Code Secs. 801-818. The following Regulations were issued under old Code Secs. 801-820.*←

	1959	1960	1961	1962
Taxable investment income	$40.00	$40.00	$40.00	.....
Gain from operations	35.00	60.00	60.00	.....
Tax base (sec. 802(b)(1) and (2))	35.00	50.00	50.00	.....
Tax (sec. 802(b)(1) and (2) base)	10.50	15.00	15.00	.....
Shareholders surplus account—				
At beginning of year	0	24.50	19.50	$14.50
Added for year (without regard to election under sec. 815(d)(1)	24.50	35.00	35.00	.....
Added by reason of election under sec. 815(d)(1)	0	0	0	.....
Subtracted (distributions)	0	40.00	40.00	.....
Policyholders surplus account—				
At beginning of year	0	0	10.00	20.00
Added for year	0	10.00	10.00	.....
Subtracted (distributions)	0	0	0	.....
Subtracted (by reason of election under sec. 815(d)(1))	0	0	0	.....
Tax base (sec. 802(b)(3))	0	0	0	.....
Tax (sec. 802(b)(3) base)	0	0	0	.....

As a result of the loss from operations for 1962, the election under section 815(d)(1) for the taxable year 1959 has become inapplicable in its entirety since the balance in the policyholders surplus account at the end of 1959, as recomputed, is zero. Thus, S would be entitled to a total refund of $7.50 for the taxable year 1959. Of this amount, $4.50 is due to the recomputation of the section 802(b)(1) and (2) tax base and $3 to the amount of tax paid by reason of the election under section 815(d)(1). [Reg. § 1.815-6.]

☐ [*T.D. 6535, 1-19-61.*]

[Reg. § 1.817-1]

§ 1.817-1. Taxable years affected.—Except as otherwise provided therein, §§ 1.817-2 through 1.817-4 are applicable only to taxable years beginning after December 31, 1957, and all references to sections of part I, subchapter L, chapter 1 of the Code are to the Internal Revenue Code of 1954, as amended by the Life Insurance Company Income Tax Act of 1959 (73 Stat. 112) and section 3 of the Act of October 23, 1962 (76 Stat. 1134). [Reg. § 1.817-1.]

☐ [*T.D. 6558, 4-3-61. Amended by T.D. 6886, 6-22-66.*]

[Reg. § 1.817-2]

§ 1.817-2. Treatment of capital gains and losses.—(a) *In general.* For taxable years beginning after December 31, 1958, and before January 1, 1962, if the net long-term capital gain (as defined in section 1222 (7)) of any life insurance company exceeds its net short-term capital loss (as defined in section 1222(6)), section 802(a)(2) prior to its amendment by section 3 of the Act of October 23, 1962 (76 Stat. 1134), imposes a separate tax equal to 25 percent of such excess. For taxable years beginning after December 31, 1961, if the net long-term capital gain of any life insurance company exceeds its net short-term capital loss, section 802(a)(2) imposes an alternative tax in lieu of the tax imposed by section 802(a)(1), if and only if such alternative tax is less than the tax imposed by section 802(a)(1). Except as modified by section 817 (rules relating to certain gains and losses), the general rules of the Code relating to gains and losses, such as subchapter O (relating to gain or loss on disposition of property), subchapter P (relating to capital gains and losses), etc., shall apply with respect to life insurance companies.

(b) *Modification of sections 1221 and 1231.* (1) In the case of a life insurance company, section 817(a)(1) provides that for purposes of applying section 1231(a) (relating to property used in the trade or business and involuntary conversions), the term "property used in the trade or business" shall be treated as including only—

(i) Property used in carrying on an insurance business, of a character subject to the allowance for depreciation under section 167 (even though fully depreciated), held for more than 1 year (6 months for taxable years beginning before 1977; 9 months for taxable years beginning in 1977), and real property used in carrying on an insurance business, held for more than 1 year (6 months for taxable years beginning before 1977; 9 months for taxable years beginning in 1977), and which is not—

(*a*) Property of a kind which would properly be includible in the inventory of the taxpayer if on hand at the close of the taxable year;

(*b*) Property held by the taxpayer primarily for sale to customers in the ordinary course of business; or

(*c*) A copyright, a literary, musical, or artistic composition, a letter or memorandum, or

Reg. § 1.817-1

→ **Caution:** *Former Code Secs. 801-820 for pre-1984 years were repealed and replaced by new Code Secs. 801-818. The following Regulations were issued under old Code Secs. 801-820.* ←

similar property held by a taxpayer described in section 1221(3). In the case of a letter, memorandum, or property similar to a letter or memorandum, this subdivision (c) applies only to sales and other dispositions occurring after July 25, 1969.

(ii) The cutting or disposal of timber, or the disposal of coal or iron ore, to the extent considered arising from a sale or exchange by reason of the provisions of section 631 and the regulations thereunder.

(2) In the case of a life insurance company, section 817(a)(2) provides that for purposes of applying section 1221(2) (relating to the exclusion of certain property from the term capital asset), the reference to property used in trade or business shall be treated as including only property used in carrying on an insurance business.

(3) Section 1231(a), as modified by section 817(a)(1) and subparagraph (1) of this paragraph, shall apply to recognized gains and losses from the following:

(i) The sale, exchange, or involuntary conversion of the following property, if held for more than 1 year (6 months for taxable years beginning before 1977; 9 months for taxable years beginning in 1977)—

(*a*) The home office and branch office buildings (including land) owned and occupied by the life insurance company;

(*b*) Furniture and equipment owned by the life insurance company and used in the home office and branch office buildings occupied by the life insurance company; and

(*c*) Automobiles and other depreciable personal property used in connection with the operations conducted in the home office and branch office buildings occupied by the life insurance company.

(ii) The involuntary conversion of capital assets held for more than 1 year (6 months for taxable years beginning before 1977; 9 months for taxable years beginning in 1977).

(iii) The cutting or disposal of timber, or the disposal of coal or iron ore, to the extent considered arising from a sale or exchange by reason of the provisions of section 631 and the regulations thereunder.

(4) Section 1221(2), as modified by section 817(a)(2) and subparagraph (2) of this paragraph, shall include only the following property:

(i) The home office and branch office buildings (including land) owned and occupied by the life insurance company;

(ii) Furniture and equipment owned by the life insurance company and used in the home office and branch office buildings occupied by the life insurance company; and

(iii) Automobiles and other depreciable personal property used in connection with the operations conducted in the home office and branch office buildings occupied by the life insurance company.

(5) If an asset described in subparagraph (3)(i)(*a*), (*b*), or (*c*) or subparagraph (4) of this paragraph, or any portion thereof, is also an "investment asset" (an asset from which gross investment income, as defined in section 804(b), is derived), such asset, or portion thereof, shall not be treated as an asset used in carrying on an insurance business. Accordingly, the gains or losses from the sale or exchange (or considered as from the sale or exchange) of depreciable assets attributable to any trade or business, other than the insurance trade or business, carried on by the life insurance company, such as operating a radio station, housing development, or a farm, or renting various pieces of real estate shall be treated as gains or losses from the sale or exchange of a capital asset unless such asset is involuntarily converted (within the meaning of paragraph (e) of § 1.1231-1).

(c) *Illustration of principles.* The provisions of section 817(a) and this section may be illustrated by the following examples:

Example (1). L, a life insurance company, has recognized gains and losses for the taxable year 1959 from the sale or involuntary conversion of the following items:

	Gains	Losses
Stocks, held for more than 6 months	$100,000	
Bonds, held for more than 6 months		$ 5,000
Housing development, held for more than 6 months		400,000
Branch office building owned and occupied by L, held for more than 6 months		115,000
Furniture and equipment used in the investment department, held for more than 6 months	30,000	
Radio station, held for more than 6 months	200,000	

Reg. § 1.817-2(c)

→ **Caution:** *Former Code Secs. 801-820 for pre-1984 years were repealed and replaced by new Code Secs. 801-818. The following Regulations were issued under old Code Secs. 801-820.* ←

Involuntary conversion of apartment building, held for more than 6 months .... 7,000 ....

The recognized gains and losses from the sale of the stocks, bonds, housing development, and radio station shall be treated as gains and losses from the sale of capital assets since such items are capital assets within the meaning of section 1221 (as modified by section 817(a)(2)). Accordingly, the provisions of section 1231 shall not apply to the sale of such capital assets. However, the provisions of section 1231 (as modified by section 817(a)(1)) shall apply to the sale of the branch office building and the furniture and equipment, and the apartment building involuntarily converted. Since the aggregate of the recognized losses ($115,000) exceeds the aggregate of the recognized gains ($37,000), the gains and losses are treated as ordinary gains and losses.

Example (2). Y, a life insurance company, owns a twenty-story home office building, having an adjusted basis of $15,000,000, ten floors of which it rents to various tenants, one floor of which is utilized by it in operating its investment department, and the remaining nine floors of which are occupied by it in carrying on its insurance business. If in 1960, Y sells the building for $10,000,000, Y must first apportion its basis between that portion of the building (one-half) used in carrying on an insurance business, and that portion of the building (one-half) classified as an "investment asset," before it can determine the character of the loss attributable to each portion of the building. For such purpose, the one floor utilized by Y in operating its investment department is treated as used in carrying on an insurance business. Assuming that each portion of the building bears an equal (one-half) relation to the basis of the entire building, Y (without regard to section 817(b)) would have a $2,500,000 ordinary loss on that portion used in carrying on an insurance business (assuming that Y had no gains subject to section 1231), and a $2,500,000 capital loss on that portion of the building classified as an investment asset. [Reg. § 1.817-2.]

☐ [T.D. 6558, 4-3-61. Amended by T.D. 6886, 6-22-66, by T.D. 7369, 7-15-75, and by T.D. 7728, 10-31-80.]

[Reg. § 1.817-3]

§ 1.817-3. Gain on property held on December 31, 1958, and certain substituted property acquired after 1958.—(a) *Limitation of gain recognized on property held on December 31, 1958.* (1) Section 817(b)(1) limits the amount of gain that shall be recognized on the sale or other disposition of property other than insurance and annuity contracts (and contracts supplementary thereto) and property described in section 1221(1) (relating to stock in trade or inventory-type property) if:

(i) The property was held (or treated as held within the meaning of paragraph (c)(1) of this section) by a life insurance company on December 31, 1958;

(ii) The taxpayer has been a life insurance company at all times on and after December 31, 1958, including the date of the sale or other disposition of the property; and

(iii) The fair market value of the property on December 31, 1958, exceeds the adjusted basis for determining gain as of such date.

The gain on the sale or other disposition of such property shall be limited to an amount (but not less than zero) equal to the amount by which the gain (determined without regard to section 817(b)(1)) exceeds the difference between the fair market value of such property on December 31, 1958, and the adjusted basis for determining gain as of such date. Accordingly, the tax imposed under section 802(a) shall apply with respect to the amount of gain so limited. In addition, in the case of a stock life insurance company, the amount of such gain shall be taken into account under section 815(b)(2)(A)(ii) for purposes of determining the amount to be added to the shareholders surplus account (as defined in section 815(b) and § 1.815-3) for the taxable year. Furthermore, the amount of the gain (determined without regard to section 817(b)(1) and this paragraph) which is not taken into account under section 802(a) and under paragraph (f) of § 1.802-3 by reason of the application of section 817(b)(1) shall be included in other accounts (as defined in § 1.815-5) by such a company for the taxable year.

(2) Section 817(b)(1) and subparagraph (1) of this paragraph shall not apply for purposes of determining loss with respect to property held on December 31, 1958.

(b) *Illustration of principles.* The application of section 817(b)(1) and paragraph (a) of this section may be illustrated by the following examples:

Example (1). On December 31, 1958, J, a stock life insurance company, owned stock of Z Corporation and on such date the stock had an adjusted

Life Insurance Companies

See p. 20,601 for regulations not amended to reflect law changes

→ *Caution: Former Code Secs. 801-820 for pre-1984 years were repealed and replaced by new Code Secs. 801-818. The following Regulations were issued under old Code Secs. 801-820.* ←

basis for determining gain of $5,000 and a fair market value of $6,000. On August 1, 1959, the company sells such stock for $8,000. Assuming J qualifies as a life insurance company for the taxable year 1959, and applying the provisions of section 817(b)(1) and paragraph (a) of this section, the gain recognized (assuming no adjustment to basis for the period since December 31, 1958) on the sale shall be limited to $2,000 (the amount by which the gain realized, $3,000, exceeds the difference, $1,000, between the fair market value, $6,000, and the adjusted basis, $5,000, for determining gain on December 31, 1958). Thus, J shall take into account $2,000 under section 815(b)(2)(A)(ii) for purposes of determining the amount to be added to its shareholders' surplus account for the taxable year and shall include $1,000 in other accounts for the taxable year.

Example (2). The facts are the same as in example (1), except that the selling price is $5,800. In such case, no gain shall be recognized even though there is a realized gain of $800 since such realized gain does not exceed the difference ($1,000) between the fair market value ($6,000) and the adjusted basis ($5,000) for determining gain on December 31, 1958. Furthermore, no loss shall be realized or recognized as a result of this transaction. Thus, J shall include $800 in other accounts for the taxable year and shall not take into account any amount under section 815(b)(2)(A)(ii).

Example (3). The facts are the same as in example (1), except that the adjusted basis for determining loss is $5,000 and the selling price is $4,500. In such case, since J has sustained a loss, section 817(b)(1) does not apply.

(c) *Certain substituted property acquired after December 31, 1958.* Section 817(b)(2) provides that if a life insurance company acquires property after December 31, 1958, in exchange for property actually held by the company on December 31, 1958, and the property acquired has a substituted basis within the meaning of section 1016(b) and § 1.1016-10, the following rules shall apply:

(1) For purposes of section 817(b)(1), such acquired property shall be deemed as having been held continuously by the taxpayer since the beginning of the holding period thereof as determined under section 1223;

(2) The fair market value and adjusted basis referred to in section 817(b)(1) shall be that of that property for which the holding period taken into account includes December 31, 1958;

(3) Section 817(b)(1) shall apply only if the property or properties, the holding periods of which are taken into account, were held only by life insurance companies after December 31, 1958, during the holding periods so taken into account;

(4) The difference between the fair market value and adjusted basis referred to in section 817(b)(1) shall be reduced (but not below zero) by the excess of (i) the gain that would have been recognized but for section 817(b) on all prior sales or other dispositions after December 31, 1958, of properties referred to in section 817(b)(2)(C) over (ii) the gain that was recognized on such sales or other dispositions; and

(5) The basis of such acquired property shall be determined as if the gain which would have been recognized but for section 817(b) were recognized gain.

For purposes of section 817(b)(2) and this paragraph, the term "property" does not include insurance and annuity contracts (and contracts supplementary thereto) and property described in section 1221(1) (relating to stock in trade or inventory-type property). Furthermore, the provisions of section 817(b)(1) and paragraph (a)(1) of this section shall not apply for purposes of determining loss with respect to property described in section 817(b)(2) and this paragraph.

(d) *Illustration of principles.* The application of section 817(b)(2) and paragraph (c) of this section may be illustrated by the following example:

Example. Assume that W, a life insurance company, owns property B on December 31, 1958, at which time its adjusted basis was $1,000 and its fair market value was $1,800. On January 31, 1960, in a transaction to which section 1031 (relating to exchange of property held for productive use or investment) applies, W receives property H having a fair market value of $1,700 plus $300 in cash in exchange for property B. The gain realized on the transaction, without regard to section 817(b), is $1,000 (assuming no adjustments to basis for the period since December 31, 1958). Under the provisions of section 817(b)(1) the gain is limited to $200. The entire $200 shall be recognized since such amount is less than the amount of gain ($300) which would be recognized under section 1031. Applying the provisions of section 817(b)(2) and paragraph (c) of this section, the basis of property H shall be determined as if the entire $300 of cash received is recognized gain. Thus, the basis of property H under section 1031

Reg. § 1.817-3(d)

45,780 Life Insurance Companies

See p. 20,601 for regulations not amended to reflect law changes

→ *Caution: Former Code Secs. 801-820 for pre-1984 years were repealed and replaced by new Code Secs. 801-818. The following Regulations were issued under old Code Secs. 801-820.* ←

is $1,000 ($1,000 the basis of property B) minus $300 (the amount of money received) plus $300 (the recognized gain of $200 plus $100 which would have been recognized but for section 817(b)). If W later sells property H for $2,200 cash, and assuming no further adjustments to its basis of $1,000, the gain realized is $1,200, but due to the application of section 817(b)(2) the amount of gain recognized is $500, computed as follows:

Selling price		$ 2,200
Less: Adjusted basis as of date of sale		− 1,000
Gain realized		$ 1,200
Fair market value as of 12-31-58	$1,800	
Adjusted basis as of 12-31-85	1,000	
Excess of fair market value over adjusted basis	800	
Less: Excess of gain which would have been recognized on all prior dispositions but for sec. 817(b) over gain recognized on all prior dispositions ($300 minus $200)	100	700
Gain recognized		$ 500

[Reg. § 1.817-3.]

□ [*T.D. 6558, 4-3-61. Amended by T.D. 6886, 6-22-66.*]

[Reg. § 1.817-4]

§ 1.817-4. Special rules.—(a) *Limitation on capital loss carryovers.* Section 817(c) provides that a net capital loss (as defined in section 1222(10)) for any taxable year beginning before January 1, 1959, shall not be taken into account. For any taxable year beginning after December 31, 1958, the provisions of part II, subchapter P, chapter 1 of the Code (relating to the treatment of capital losses) shall be applicable to life insurance companies for purposes of determining the tax imposed by section 802(a) and § 1.802-3 (relating to the imposition of tax in case of capital gains).

(b) *Gain on transactions occurring prior to January 1, 1959.* For purposes of part I, subchapter L, chapter 1 of the Code, section 817(d) provides that—

(1) There shall be excluded from tax any gain from the sale or exchange of a capital asset, and any gain considered as gain from sale or exchange of a capital asset, which results from sales or other dispositions of property prior to January 1, 1959; and

(2) Any gain after December 31, 1958, resulting from the sale or other disposition of property prior to January 1, 1959, which, but for this subparagraph, would be taken into account under section 1231, shall not be taken into account under section 1231.

For example, if a life insurance company makes an installment sale of a capital asset prior to January 1, 1959, and payments are received after such date, any capital gain attributable to such sale shall not be taken into account for purposes of section 802(a). Furthermore, any gain referred to in subparagraphs (1) and (2) and the preceding sentence shall not be taken into account in determining the excess of the net short-term capital gain over the net long-term capital loss (and for taxable years beginning after December 31, 1961, the excess of the net long-term capital gain over the net short-term capital loss) for purposes of computing taxable investment income under section 804(a)(2) or gain or loss from operations under section 809(b).

(c) *Certain reinsurance transactions in 1958.* For purposes of part I, section 817(e) provides that where a life insurance company reinsures (or sells) all of its insurance contracts of a particular type, such as an entire industrial department, in either a single transaction, or in a series of related transactions, all of which occurred during 1958, and the reinsuring (or purchasing) company or companies assume all liabilities under such contracts, such reinsurance (or sale) shall be treated as the sale of a capital asset. However, such transaction shall be subject to the provisions of section 805(a) and § 1.806-3 (relating to adjustments for certain changes in reserves and assets).

(d) *Certain other reinsurance transactions.* (1) For any taxable year beginning after December 31, 1958, the reinsurance of all or a part of the insurance contracts of a particular type by a life insurance company, in either a single transaction, or in a series of related transactions, occurring in any such taxable year, whereby the reinsuring company or companies assume all liabilities under such contracts, shall not be treated as the sale or exchange of a capital asset but shall be subject to the provisions of sections 806(a) and 809 and the regulations thereunder. However, if in connection

Reg. § 1.817-4(a)

Life Insurance Companies

See p. 20,601 for regulations not amended to reflect law changes

→ *Caution: Former Code Secs. 801-820 for pre-1984 years were repealed and replaced by new Code Secs. 801-818. The following Regulations were issued under old Code Secs. 801-820.* ←

with a transaction described in the preceding sentence the reinsured or reinsurer transfers an asset which is a capital asset within the meaning of section 1221 (as modified by section 817(a)(2)), such transfer shall be treated as the sale or exchange of a capital asset by the transferor.

(2)(i) The consideration paid by the reinsured to the reinsurer in connection with a transaction described in subparagraph (1) of this paragraph shall be treated as an item of deduction under section 809(d)(7). However, any amount received by the reinsured from the reinsurer shall be applied against and reduce (but not below zero) the amount of such consideration, and to the extent that is exceeds such consideration, shall be treated as an item of gross amount under section 809(c)(3).

(ii) In connection with an assumption reinsurance (as defined in paragraph (a)(7)(ii) of § 1.809-5) transaction, a reinsurer shall in any taxable year beginning after December 31, 1957:

(A) Treat the consideration received from the reinsured in any such taxable year as an item of gross amount under section 809(c)(1), and

(B) Treat any amount paid to the reinsured for the purchase of such contracts, to the extent such amount meets the requirements of section 162, as a deferred expense that may be amortized over the reasonably estimated life (as defined in paragraph (d)(2)(iv) of this section) of the contracts reinsured and treat the portion of the expense so amortized in each taxable year as a deduction under section 809(d)(12) irrespective of the taxable year in which such amount was paid to the reinsured.

(iii) For purposes of paragraph (d)(2)(ii) of this section where the reinsured transfers to the reinsurer in connection with the assumption reinsurance transaction a net amount which is less than the increase in the reinsurer's reserves resulting from the transaction, the reinsurer shall be treated as:

(A) Having received from the reinsured consideration in an amount equal to the net amount of the increase in the reinsurer's reserves resulting from the transaction, and

(B) Having paid the reinsured an amount for the purchase of the contracts equal to the excess of the amount of such increase in the reinsurer's reserves over the net amount received from the reinsured.

(iv) For purposes of this subparagraph, the term "reasonably estimated life" means the period during which the contract reinsured remains in force. Such period shall be based on the facts in each case (such as age, health, and sex of the insured, type of contract reinsured, etc.) and the assuming company's experience (such as mortality, lapse rate, etc.) with similar risks.

(3) The provisions of this paragraph may be illustrated by the following examples:

Example (1). On June 30, 1959, X, a life insurance company, reinsured a portion of its insurance contracts with Y, a life insurance company, under an agreement whereby Y agreed to assume and to become solely liable under the contracts reinsured. The reserves on the contracts reinsured by X were $100,000. Under the reinsurance agreement X agreed to pay Y $100,000 for assuming such contracts and Y agreed to pay X $17,000 for the right to receive future premium payments under this block of contracts. Rather than exchange payments of money, X agreed to pay Y a net amount of $83,000 in cash. Assuming that the reasonably estimated life of the contracts reinsured is 17 years, that there are no other insurance transactions by X or Y during the taxable year, and assuming that X and Y compute the reserves on the contracts reinsured on the same basis, X has income of $100,000 under section 809(c)(2) as a result of the net decrease in its reserves. X has a net deduction of $83,000 ($100,000 − $17,000) under section 809(d)(7). For the taxable year 1959, Y has income of $100,000 under section 809(c)(1) as a result of the consideration received from X and a deduction of $100,000 under section 809(d)(2) for the net increase in reserves and $1,000 ($17,000 divided by 17, the reasonably estimated life of the contracts reinsured), under section 809(d)(12). The remaining $16,000 shall be amortized over the next 16 succeeding taxable years (16 × $1,000 = $16,000) under section 809(d)(12) at the rate of $1,000 for each such taxable year.

Example (2). The facts are the same as in example (1), except X agreed to pay Y a consideration of $100,000 in cash for assuming these contracts and Y paid X a bonus of $17,000 in cash and that this bonus meets the requirements of section 162. Assuming that the reasonably estimated life of the contracts reinsured is 17 years, X has income of $100,000 under section 809(c)(2) as a result of this net decrease in its reserves and a deduction of $83,000 under section 809(d)(7) for the amount of the consideration ($100,000) paid to Y for assuming these contracts, reduced by the bonus ($17,000) received from Y. For the taxable

Reg. § 1.817-4(d)(3)

→ **Caution:** *Former Code Secs. 801-820 for pre-1984 years were repealed and replaced by new Code Secs. 801-818. The following Regulations were issued under old Code Secs. 801-820.* ←

year 1959, Y has income of $100,000 under section 809(c)(1) as a result of the consideration received from X and deductions of $100,000 under section 809(d)(2) for the net increase in reserves and $1,000 (the bonus of $17,000 divided by 17, the reasonably estimated life of the contracts reinsured), under section 809(d)(12). The remaining amount of the bonus ($16,000) shall be amortized over the next 16 succeeding taxable years (16 × $1,000 = $16,000) under section 809(d)(12) at the rate of $1,000 for each such taxable year.

Example (3). The facts are the same as in Example (1), except that the reinsurance agreement does not specifically provide that X agreed to pay Y $100,000 for assuming the contracts reinsured and Y agreed to pay X $17,000 for the right to receive future premium payments under such contracts. Instead, X agreed to pay Y a net amount of $83,000 in cash for assuming such contracts. Nevertheless, Y is treated as having received from X consideration equal to $100,000, the amount of the increase in Y's reserves, and as having paid $17,000 ($100,000 less $83,000) for the purchase of such contracts. Therefore, for the taxable year 1959, Y has income of $100,000 under section 809(c)(1). Y also has a deduction of $100,000 under section 809(d)(2) for the net increase in its reserves and an amortization deduction under section 809(d)(12) of $1,000 ($17,000 divided by 17, the reasonably estimated life of the contracts reinsured). The remaining $16,000 shall be amortized by Y over the next 16 succeeding years at the rate of $1,000 for each such year. For 1959, X has income of $100,000 under section 809(c)(2) as a result of the net decrease in its reserves and a deduction of $83,000 under section 809(d)(7) for the net amount of consideration paid to Y for assuming the contracts reinsured.

Example (4). The facts are the same as in example (1), except that X agreed to pay Y a consideration of $130,000 in cash for assuming such contracts. Based upon these facts, X has income of $100,000 under section 809(c)(2) as a result of this net decrease in its reserves and a deduction of $130,000 under section 809(d)(7) for the amount of the consideration paid to Y for assuming these contracts. Y has income of $130,000 under section 809(c)(1) as a result of the consideration received from X and a deduction of $100,000 under section 809(d)(2) for the net increase in its reserves.

Example (5). On August 1, 1960, R, a life insurance company, reinsured all of its insurance policies with S, a life insurance company, under an agreement whereby S agreed to assume and become solely liable under the contracts reinsured. The reserves on the contracts reinsured by R were $3,000,000. Under the reinsurance agreement, R agreed to pay S a consideration of $3,000,000 in stocks and bonds for assuming such contracts. Assuming no other insurance transactions by R or S during the taxable year, that R and S compute the reserves on the contracts reinsured on the same basis, and that R has a recognized gain (after the application of the limitation of section 817(b)(1)) of $20,000 due to appreciation in value of the assets transferred, the results to each company are as follows:

INCOME

Company R (reinsured)
Net decrease in reserves (sec. 809(c)(2))................. $3,000,000

Capital gain (as limited by sec. 817(b)(1)) to be taxed separately under sec. 802(a)(2).......... 20,000

Company S (reinsurer)
Consideration received by S in respect of assuming liabilities under contracts issued by R (sec. 809(c)(1))................... $3,000,000

DEDUCTIONS

Company R (reinsured)
Consideration paid by R to S in respect of S's assuming liabilities under contracts issued by R (sec. 809(d)(7))................. $3,000,000

Company S (reinsurer)
Net increase in reserves (sec. 809(d)(2))................. $3,000,000

[Reg. § 1.817-4.]

☐ [T.D. 6558, 4-3-61. Amended by T.D. 6625, 12-18-62; T.D. 6886, 6-22-66 and T.D. 7401, 2-3-76.]

[Reg. § 1.817-5]

§ 1.817-5. Diversification requirements for variable annuity, endowment, and life insurance contracts.—(a) *Consequences of nondiversification*—(1) *In general.* Except as provided in

Reg. § 1.817-5(a)(1)

Life Insurance Companies

See p. 20,601 for regulations not amended to reflect law changes

→ *Caution: Former Code Secs. 801-820 for pre-1984 years were repealed and replaced by new Code Secs. 801-818. The following Regulations were issued under old Code Secs. 801-820.*←

paragraph (a)(2) of this section, for purposes of subchapter L, section 72, and section 7702(a), a variable contract (as defined in section 817(d)), other than a pension plan contract (as defined in section 818(a)), which is based on one or more segregated asset accounts shall not be treated as an annuity, endowment, or life insurance contract for any calendar quarter period for which the investments of any such account are not adequately diversified. For this purpose, a variable contract shall be treated as based on a segregated asset account for a calendar quarter period if amounts received under the contract (or earnings thereon) are allocated to the segregated asset account at any time during the period. In addition, a variable contract that is not treated as an annuity, endowment, or life insurance contract for any period by reason of this paragraph (a)(1) shall not be treated as an annuity, endowment, or life insurance contract for any subsequent period even if the investments are adequately diversified for such subsequent period. If a variable contract which is a life insurance or endowment contract under other applicable (e.g., State or foreign) law is not treated as a life insurance or endowment contract under section 7702(a), the income on the contract for any taxable year of the policyholder is treated as ordinary income received or accrued by the policyholder during such year in accordance with section 7702(g) and (h). Likewise, if a variable contract is not treated as an annuity contract under section 72, the income on the contract for any taxable year of the policyholder shall be treated as ordinary income received or accrued by the policyholder during such year in the same manner as a life insurance or endowment contract under section 7702(g) and (h).

(2) *Inadvertent failure to diversify.* The investments of a segregated asset account shall be treated as satisfying the requirements of paragraph (b) of this section for one or more periods, provided the following conditions are satisfied—

(i) The issuer or holder must show the Commissioner that the failure of the investments to satisfy the requirements of paragraph (b) of this section for such period or periods was inadvertent;

(ii) The investments of the account must satisfy the requirements of paragraph (b) of this section within a reasonable time after the discovery of such failure; and

(iii) The issuer or holder of the variable contract must agree to make such adjustments or pay such amounts as may be required by the Commissioner with respect to the period or periods during which the investments of the account did not satisfy the requirements of paragraph (b) of this section. The amount required by the Commissioner to be paid shall be an amount based upon the tax that would have been owed by the policyholders if they were treated as receiving the income on the contract (as defined in section 7702(g)(1)(B), without regard to section 7702(g)(1)(C)) for such period or periods.

(b) *Diversification of investments*—(1) *In general.* (i) Except as otherwise provided in this paragraph and paragraph (c) of this section, the investments of a segregated asset account shall be considered adequately diversified for purposes of this section and section 817(h) only if—

(A) No more than 55% of the value of the total assets of the account is represented by any one investment;

(B) No more than 70% of the value of the total assets of the account is represented by any two investments;

(C) No more than 80% of the value of the total assets of the account is represented by any three investments; and

(D) No more than 90% of the value of the total assets of the account is represented by any four investments.

(ii) For purposes of this section—

(A) All securities of the same issuer, all interests in the same real property project, and all interests in the same commodity are each treated as a single investment; and

(B) In the case of government securities, each government agency or instrumentality shall be treated as a separate issuer.

(iii) See paragraph (f) of this section for circumstances in which a segregated asset account is treated as the owner of assets held indirectly through certain pass-through entities and corporations taxed under subchapter M, chapter 1 of the Code.

(2) *Safe harbor.* A segregated asset account will be considered adequately diversified for purposes of this section and section 817(h) if—

(i) The account meets the requirements of section 851(b)(4) and the regulations thereunder; and

(ii) No more than 55% of the value of the total assets of the account is attributable to cash, cash items (including receivables), government se-

Reg. § 1.817-5(b)(2)

→ *Caution: Former Code Secs. 801-820 for pre-1984 years were repealed and replaced by new Code Secs. 801-818. The following Regulations were issued under old Code Secs. 801-820.*←

curities, and securities of other regulated investment companies.

(3) *Alternative diversification requirements for variable life insurance contracts.* (i) A segregated asset account with respect to variable life insurance contracts will be considered adequately diversified for purposes of this section and section 817(h) if the requirements of paragraph (b)(1) or (b)(2) of this section are satisfied or if the assets of such account, other than Treasury securities, satisfy the percentage limitations prescribed in paragraph (b)(1) of this section increased by the product of (A) .5 and (B) the percentage of the value of the total assets of the account that is represented by Treasury securities. In determining whether the assets of an account, other than Treasury securities, satisfy the increased percentage limitations, such limitations are applied as if the Treasury securities were not included in the account (*i.e.*, the increased percentage limitations are not applied to Treasury securities and the value of the total assets of the account is reduced by the value of the Treasury securities).

(ii) The provisions of this paragraph (b)(3) may be illustrated by the following examples:

Example (1). On the last day of a quarter of a calendar year, a segregated asset account with respect to variable life insurance contracts holds assets having a total value of $100,000. The assets of the account are represented by Treasury securities having a total value of $90,000 and securities of Corporation A having a total value of $10,000. The 55% limit described in paragraph (b)(1)(i) of this section would be increased by 45% (0.5 × 90%) to 100%, and would then be applied to the assets of the account other than Treasury securities. Because no more than 100% of the value of the assets other than Treasury securities is represented by securities of Corporation A, the investments of the account will be considered adequately diversified.

Example (2). On the last day of a quarter of a calendar year, a segregated asset account with respect to variable life insurance contracts holds assets having a total value of $100,000. The assets of the account are represented by Treasury securities having a total value of $60,000, securities of Corporation A having a total value of $30,000, and securities of Corporation B having a total value of $10,000. The 55% and 70% limits described in paragraph (b)(1)(i) of this section would be increased by 30% (0.5 × 60%) to 85% and 100%, respectively, and would then be applied to the assets of the account other than Treasury securities. Securities of Corporation A represent 75%, and securities of Corporation B represent 25%, of the value of the assets of the account other than Treasury securities. Because no more than 85% of the value of the assets other than Treasury securities is represented by securities of Corporation A or B and no more than 100% of the value of the assets other than Treasury securities is represented by securities of Corporations A and B, the investments of the account will be considered adequately diversified.

(c) *Periods for which an account is adequately diversified*—(1) *In general.* A segregated asset account that satisfies the requirements of paragraph (b) of this section on the last day of a quarter of a calendar year (*i.e.*, March 31, June 30, September 30, and December 31) or within 30 days after such last day shall be considered adequately diversified for such quarter.

(2) *Start-up period.* (i) Except as provided in paragraph (c)(2)(iv) of this section, a segregated asset account that is not a real property account on its first anniversary shall be considered adequately diversified until such first anniversary.

(ii) Except as provided in paragraph (c)(2)(iv) of this section, a segregated asset account that is a real property account on its first anniversary shall be considered adequately diversified until the earlier of its fifth anniversary or the anniversary on which the account ceases to be a real property account.

(iii) For purposes of paragraph (c)(2)(i) and (ii) of this section, the anniversary of a segregated asset account is the anniversary of the date on which any amount received under a life insurance or annuity contract, other than a pension plan contract (as defined in section 818(a)), is first allocated to the account.

(iv) If more than 30 percent of the amount allocated to a segregated asset account as of the last day of a calendar quarter is attributable to contracts entered into more than one year before such date, paragraph (c)(2)(i) of this section shall not apply to the segregated asset account for any period after such date. Similarly, if more than 30 percent of the amount allocated to a segregated asset account as of the last day of a calendar quarter is attributable to contracts entered into more than 5 years before such date, paragraph (c)(2)(ii) of this section shall not apply to the segregated asset account for any period after such date. For purposes of this paragraph (c)(2), amounts transferred to the account from a diver-

Reg. § 1.817-5(b)(3)

Life Insurance Companies

See p. 20,601 for regulations not amended to reflect law changes

→ *Caution: Former Code Secs. 801-820 for pre-1984 years were repealed and replaced by new Code Secs. 801-818. The following Regulations were issued under old Code Secs. 801-820.*←

sified account (determined without regard to this paragraph (c)(2)) or as a result of an exchange pursuant to section 1035 in which the issuer of the contract received in the exchange is not related in a manner specified in section 267(b) to the issuer of the contract transferred in the exchange are not treated as—

(A) Amounts attributable to contracts entered into more than one year before such date, in the case of accounts subject to paragraph (c)(2)(i) of this section, or

(B) Amounts attributable to contracts entered into more than five years before such date, in the case of accounts subject to paragraph (c)(2)(ii) of this section.

(3) *Liquidation period.* A segregated asset account that satisfies the requirements of paragraph (b) of this section on the date a plan of liquidation is adopted shall be considered adequately diversified for—

(i) The one-year period beginning on the date the plan of liquidation is adopted if the account is not a real property account on such date; or

(ii) The two-year period beginning on the date the plan of liquidation is adopted if the account is a real property account on such date.

(d) *Market fluctuations.* A segregated asset account that satisfies the requirements of paragraph (b) of this section at the end of any calendar quarter (or within 30 days after the end of such calendar quarter) shall not be considered nondiversified in a subsequent quarter because of a discrepancy between the value of its assets and the diversification requirements unless such discrepancy exists immediately after the acquisition of any asset and such discrepancy is wholly or partly the result of such acquisition.

(e) *Segregated asset account.* For purposes of section 817(h) and this section, a segregated asset account shall consist of all assets the investment return and market value of each of which must be allocated in an identical manner to any variable contract invested in any of such assets. See paragraph (g) for examples illustrating the application of this paragraph (e).

(f) *Look-through rule for assets held through certain investment companies, partnerships, or trusts*—(1) *In general.* If this paragraph (f) applies, a beneficial interest in a regulated investment company, a real estate investment trust, a partnership, or a trust that is treated under sections 671 through 679 as owned by the grantor or another person ("investment company, partnership, or trust") shall not be treated as a single investment of a segregated asset account. Instead, a pro rata portion of each asset of the investment company, partnership, or trust shall be treated, for purposes of this section, as an asset of the segregated asset account. For purposes of this section, the ratable interest of a partner in a partnership's assets shall be determined in accordance with the partner's capital interest in the partnership.

(2) *Applicability*—(i) *Certain investment companies, partnerships, and trusts.* This paragraph (f) shall apply to an investment company, partnership, or trust if—

(A) All the beneficial interests in the investment company, partnership, or trust (other than those described in paragraph (f)(3) of this section) are held by one or more segregated asset accounts of one or more insurance companies; and

(B) Public access to such investment company, partnership, or trust is available exclusively (except as otherwise permitted in paragraph (f)(3) of this section) through the purchase of a variable contract. Solely for this purpose, the status of a contract as a variable contract will be determined without regard to section 817(h) and this section.

(ii) *Nonregistered partnerships.* This paragraph (f) shall also apply to a partnership interest if the partnership interest is not registered under a Federal or State law regulating the offering or sale of securities.

(iii) *Trusts holding Treasury securities.* This paragraph (f) shall also apply to a trust that is treated under section 671 through 679 as owned by the grantor or another person if substantially all of the assets of the trust are represented by Treasury securities.

(3) *Interests not held by segregated asset accounts.* Satisfaction of the requirements of paragraph (f)(2)(i) of this section shall not be prevented by reason of beneficial interests in the investment company, partnership, or trust that are—

(i) Held by the general account of a life insurance company or a corporation related in a manner specified in section 267(b) to a life insurance company, but only if the return on such interests is computed in the same manner as the return on an interest held by a segregated asset account is computed (determined without regard to expenses attributable to variable contracts),

Reg. § 1.817-5(f)(3)

Life Insurance Companies

See p. 20,601 for regulations not amended to reflect law changes

→ *Caution: Former Code Secs. 801-820 for pre-1984 years were repealed and replaced by new Code Secs. 801-818. The following Regulations were issued under old Code Secs. 801-820.* ←

there is no intent to sell such interests to the public, and a segregated asset account of such life insurance company also holds or will hold a beneficial interest in the investment company, partnership, or trust;

(ii) Held by the manager, or a corporation related in a manner specified in section 267(b) to the manager, of the investment company, partnership, or trust, but only if the holding of the interests is in connection with the creation or management of the investment company, partnership, or trust, the return on such interest is computed in the same manner as the return on an interest held by a segregated asset account is computed (determined without regard to expenses attributable to variable contracts), and there is no intent to sell such interests to the public;

(iii) Held by the trustee of a qualified pension or retirement plan; or

(iv) Held by the public, or treated as owned by policyholders pursuant to Rev. Rul. 81-225, 1981-2 C.B. 12, but only if (A) the investment company, partnership, or trust was closed to the public in accordance with Rev. Rul. 82-55, 1982-1 C.B. 12, or (B) all the assets of the segregated asset account are attributable to premium payments made by policyholders prior to September 26, 1981, to premium payments made in connection with a qualified pension or retirement plan, or to any combination of such premium payments.

(g) *Examples.* The provisions of paragraphs (e) and (f) of this section may be illustrated by the following examples.

Example (1). (i) The assets underlying variable contracts issued by a life insurance company consist of two groups of assets: (a) a diversified portfolio of debt securities and (b) interests in P, a partnership that is publicly registered. All of the beneficial interests in P are held by one or more segregated asset accounts of one or more insurance companies and public access to P is available exclusively through the purchase of a variable contract. The variable contracts provide that policyholders may specify which portion of each premium is to be invested in the debt securities and which portion is to be invested in P interests. The portfolio of debt securities and the assets of P, considered separately, each satisfy the diversification requirements of paragraph (b) of this section.

(ii) As a result of the ability of policyholders to allocate premiums among the two groups of assets, the investment return and market value of the interests in P and the debt securities may be allocated to different variable contracts in a non-identical manner. Accordingly, under paragraph (e) of this section, the interests in P are treated as part of a single segregated asset account ("Account 1") and the debt securities are treated as part of a different segregated asset account ("Account 2").

(iii) Since P is described in paragraph (f)(2)(i) of this section, interests in P will not be treated as a single investment of Account 1. Rather, Account 1 is treated as owning a pro rata portion of the assets of P.

(iv) Since Account 1 and Account 2 each satisfy the requirements of paragraph (b) of this section, variable contracts that are based on either or both accounts are treated as annuity, endowment, or life insurance contracts.

Example (2). The facts are the same as in example (1) except that some of the beneficial interests in P are held by persons not described in paragraph (f)(3) of this section. Since P is not described in paragraph (f)(2) of this section, interests in P will be treated as a single investment of Account 1. As a result, Account 1 does not satisfy the requirements of paragraph (b) of this section. Variable contracts based in whole or in part on Account 1 are not treated as annuity, endowment, or life insurance contracts. Variable contracts that are not based on Account 1 at any time during the period in which such account fails to satisfy the requirements of paragraph (b) of this section (*i.e.*, contracts based entirely on Account 2), are treated as annuity, endowment, or life insurance contracts. See paragraph (a)(1).

Example (3). The facts are the same as in example (2) except that P is not publicly registered. Since P is described in paragraph (e)(2)(ii) of this section, the result is the same as in example (1).

Example (4). The facts are the same as in example (2) except that the variable contracts do not permit policyholders to allocate premiums between or among the debt securities and interests in P. Thus, the investment return and market value of the interests in P and the debt securities must be allocated to the same variable contracts and in an identical manner. Under paragraph (e) of this section, the interests in P and the debt securities are treated as part of a single segregated asset account. If the interests in P and the debt securities, considered together, satisfy the requirements of paragraph (b) of this section,

Reg. § 1.817-5(g)

Life Insurance Companies

See p. 20,601 for regulations not amended to reflect law changes

→ **Caution:** *Former Code Secs. 801-820 for pre-1984 years were repealed and replaced by new Code Secs. 801-818. The following Regulations were issued under old Code Secs. 801-820.* ←

contracts based on this segregated asset account will be treated as annuity, endowment, or life insurance contracts.

(h) *Definitions.* The terms defined below shall, for purposes of this section, have the meanings set forth in such definitions:

(1) *Government security*—(i) *General rule.* The term "government security" shall mean any security issued or guaranteed or insured by the United States or an instrumentality of the United States; or any certificate of deposit for any of the foregoing. Any security or certificate of deposit insured or guaranteed only in part by the United States or an instrumentality thereof is treated as issued by the United States or its instrumentality only to the extent so insured or guaranteed, and as issued by the direct obligor to the extent not so insured or guaranteed. For purposes of this paragraph (h)(1), an instrumentality of the United States shall mean any person that is treated for purposes of 15 U.S.C. 80a-2(16), as amended, as a person controlled or supervised by and acting an an instrumentality of the Government of the United States pursuant to authority granted by the Congress of the United States.

(ii) *Example.* A segregated asset account purchases a certificate of deposit in the amount of $150,000 from bank A. Deposits in bank A are insured by the Federal Deposit Insurance Corporation, an instrumentality of the United States, to the extent of $100,000 per depositor. The certificate of deposit is treated as a government security to the extent of the $100,000 insured amount and is treated as a security issued by bank A to the extent of the $50,000 excess of the value of the certificate of deposit over the insured amount.

(2) *Treasury security*—(i) *General rule.* For purposes of paragraph (b)(3) of this section and section 817(h)(3), the term "Treasury security" shall mean a security the direct obligor of which is the United States Treasury.

(ii) *Example.* A segregated asset account purchases put and call options on U.S. Treasury securities issued by the Options Clearing Corporation. The options are not Treasury securities for purposes of paragraph (b)(3) and section 817(h)(3) because the direct obligor of the options is not the United States Treasury.

(3) *Real property.* The term "real property" shall mean any property that is treated as real property under Reg. § 1.856-3(d) except that it shall not include interests in real property.

(4) *Real property account.* A segregated asset account is a real property account on an anniversary of the account (within the meaning of paragraph (c)(2)(iii) of this section) or on the date a plan of liquidation is adopted if not less than the applicable percentage of the total assets of the account is represented by real property or interests in real property on such anniversary or date. For this purpose, the applicable percentage is 40% for the period ending on the first anniversary of the date on which premium income is first received, 50% for the year ending on the second anniversary, 60% for the year ending on the third anniversary, 70% for the year ending on the fourth anniversary, and 80% thereafter. A segregated asset account will also be treated as a real property account on its first anniversary if on or before such first anniversary the issuer has stated in the contract or prospectus or in a submission to a regulatory agency, an intention that the assets of the account will be primarily invested in real property or interests in real property, provided that at least 40% of the total assets of the account are so invested within six months after such first anniversary.

(5) *Commodity.* The term "commodity" shall mean any type of personal property other than a security.

(6) *Security.* The term "security" shall include a cash item and any partnership interest registered under a Federal or State law regulating the offering or sale of securities. The term shall not include any other partnership interest, any interest in real property, or any interest in a commodity.

(7) *Interest in real property.* The term "interest in real property" shall include the ownership and co-ownership of land or improvements thereon and leaseholds of land or improvements thereon. Such term shall not, however, include mineral, oil, or gas royalty interests, such as a retained economic interest in coal or iron ore with respect to which the special provisions of section 631(c) apply. The term "interest in real property" also shall include options to acquire land or improvements thereon, and options to acquire leaseholds of land or improvements thereon.

(8) *Interest in a commodity.* The term "interest in a commodity" shall include the ownership and co-ownership of any type of personal property other than a security, and any leaseholds thereof. Such term shall include mineral, oil, and gas royalty interests, including any fractional undivided interest therein. Such term also shall in-

Reg. § 1.817-5(h)(8)

→ **Caution:** *Former Code Secs. 801-820 for pre-1984 years were repealed and replaced by new Code Secs. 801-818. The following Regulations were issued under old Code Secs. 801-820.*←

clude any put, call, straddle, option, or privilege on any type of personal property other than a security.

(9) *Value.* The term "value" shall mean, with respect to investments for which market quotations are readily available, the market value of such investments; and with respect to other investments, fair value as determined in good faith by the managers of the segregated asset account.

(10) *Terms used in section 851.* To the extent not inconsistent with this paragraph (h) all terms used in this section shall have the same meaning as when used in section 851.

(i) *Effective date*—(1) *In general.* This section is effective for taxable years beginning after December 31, 1983.

(2) *Exceptions.*—(i) If, at all times after December 31, 1983, an insurance company would be considered the owner of the assets of a segregated asset account under the principles of Rev. Rul. 81-225, 1981-2 C.B. 12, this section will not apply to such account until December 15, 1986.

(ii) This section will not apply to any variable contract to which Rev. Rul. 77-85, 1977-1 C.B. 12, or Rev. Rul. 81-225, 1981-2 C.B. 12, did not apply by reason of the limited retroactive effect of such rulings.

(iii) In determining whether a segregated asset account is adequately diversified for any calendar quarter ending before July 1, 1988, debt instruments that are issued, guaranteed, or insured by the United States or an instrumentality of the United States shall not be treated as government securities if such debt instruments are secured by a mortgage on real property (other than real property owned by the United States or an instrumentality of the United States) or represent an interest in a pool of debt instruments secured by such mortgages.

(iv) This section shall not apply until January 1, 1989, with respect to a variable contract (as defined in section 817(d)) that (1) provides for the payment of an immediate annuity (as defined in section 72(u)(4)); (2) was outstanding on September 12, 1986; and (3) the segregated asset account on which it was based was, on September 12, 1986, wholly invested in deposits insured by the Federal Deposit Insurance Corporation or the Federal Savings and Loan Insurance Corporation. [Reg. § 1.817-5.]

☐ [*T.D. 8242, 3-1-89.*]

[Reg. § 1.818-1]

§ 1.818-1. **Taxable years affected.**—Sections 1.818-2 through 1.818-8, except as otherwise provided therein, are applicable only to taxable years beginning after December 31, 1957, and all references to sections of part I, subchapter L, chapter 1 of the Code are to the Internal Revenue Code of 1954, as amended by the Life Insurance Company Income Tax Act of 1959 (73 Stat. 112). [Reg. § 1.818-1.]

☐ [*T.D. 6558, 4-3-61. Amended by T.D. 7469, 2-28-77.*]

[Reg. § 1.818-2]

§ 1.818-2. **Accounting provisions.**—(a) *Method of accounting.* (1) Section 818(a)(1) provides the general rule that all computations entering into the determination of taxes imposed by part I, subchapter L, chapter 1 of the Code, shall be made under an accrual method of accounting. Thus, the over-all method of accounting for life insurance companies shall be the accrual method. Except as otherwise provided in part I, the term "accrual method" shall have the same meaning and application in section 818 as it does under section 446 (relating to general rule for methods of accounting) and the regulations thereunder. For general rules relating to the taxable year for inclusion of income and deduction of expenses under an accrual method of accounting, see sections 451 and 461 and the regulations thereunder.

(2) Section 818(a)(2) provides that, to the extent permitted under this section, a life insurance company's method of accounting may be a combination of the accrual method with any other method of accounting permitted by chapter 1 of the Internal Revenue Code of 1954, other than the cash receipts and disbursements method. Thus, section 818(a)(2) specifically prohibits the use by a life insurance company of the cash receipts and disbursements method either separately or in combination with a permissible method of accounting. The term "method of accounting" includes not only the over-all method of accounting of the taxpayer but also the accounting treatment of any item. For purposes of section 818(a)(2), a life insurance company may elect to compute its taxable income under an over-all method of accounting consisting of the accrual method combined with the special methods of accounting for particular items of income and expense provided under other sections of chapter 1 of the Internal Revenue Code of 1954, other than the cash receipts and disbursements method.

Life Insurance Companies

See p. 20,601 for regulations not amended to reflect law changes

→ *Caution: Former Code Secs. 801-820 for pre-1984 years were repealed and replaced by new Code Secs. 801-818. The following Regulations were issued under old Code Secs. 801-820.* ←

These methods of accounting for special items include the accounting treatment provided for depreciation (section 167), research and experimental expenditures (section 174), soil and water conservation expenditures (section 175), organizational expenditures (section 248), etc. In addition, a life insurance company may, where applicable, use the crop method of accounting (as provided in the regulations under sections 61 and 162), and the installment method of accounting for sales of realty and casual sales of personalty (as provided in section 453(b)). To the extent not inconsistent with the provisions of the Internal Revenue Code of 1954 or the regulations thereunder and the method of accounting adopted by the taxpayer pursuant to this section, all computations entering into the determination of taxes imposed by part I shall be made in a manner consistent with the manner required for purposes of the annual statement approved by the National Association of Insurance Commissioners.

(3)(i) An election to use any of the special methods of accounting referred to in subparagraph (2) of this paragraph which was made pursuant to any provisions of the Internal Revenue Code of 1954 or prior revenue laws for purposes of determining a company's tax liabilities for prior years, shall have the same force and effect in determining the items of gross investment income under section 804(b) and the items of deduction under section 804(c) of the Life Insurance Company Income Tax Act of 1959 (73 Stat. 112) as if such Act had not been enacted.

(ii) For purposes of determining gain or loss from operations under section 809(b), in computing the life insurance company's share of investment yield under section 809(b)(1)(A) and (2)(A), an election with respect to any of the special methods of accounting referred to in subparagraph (2) of this paragraph which was made pursuant to any provision of the Internal Revenue Code of 1954 or prior revenue laws, shall not be affected in any way by the enactment of the Life Insurance Company Income Tax Act of 1959 (73 Stat. 112).

(iii) For purposes of determining gain or loss from operations under section 809(b), in computing the items of gross amount under section 809(c) and the deduction items under section 809(d), an election to use any of the special methods of accounting referred to in subparagraph (2) of this paragraph must be made in accordance with the specific statutory provisions of the sections containing such elections and the regulations thereunder. However, where a particular election may be made only with the consent of the Commissioner (either because the time for making the election without the consent of the Commissioner has expired or because the particular section contained no provision for making an election without consent), and the time prescribed by the applicable regulations for submitting a request for permission to make such an election for the taxable year 1958 has expired, a life insurance company may make such an election for the year 1958 at the time of filing its return for that year (including extensions thereof). For example, a life insurance company may elect any of the methods of depreciation prescribed in section 167 (to the extent permitted under that section and the regulations thereunder) with respect to those assets, or any portion thereof, for which no depreciation was allowable under prior revenue laws, for example, furniture and fixtures used in the underwriting department. Similarly, a life insurance company shall be permitted to make an election under section 461(c) (relating to the accrual of real property taxes) with respect to real property for which no deduction was allowable under prior revenue laws. Any such election shall be made in the manner and form prescribed in the applicable regulations.

(iv) For purposes of subdivision (ii) of this subparagraph, the method used under section 1016(a)(3)(C) (relating to adjustments to basis) in determining the amount of exhaustion, wear and tear, obsolescence, and amortization actually sustained shall not preclude a taxpayer from electing any of the methods prescribed in section 167 in accordance with the provisions of that section and the regulations thereunder for determining the amount of such exhaustion, wear and tear, obsolescence, and amortization for the year 1958. For example, if the amount of depreciation actually sustained, under section 1016(a)(3)(C), on a life insurance company's home office building (other than that portion for which depreciation was allowable under prior revenue laws) is determined on the straight line method, the life insurance company may elect for the year 1958 to use any of the methods prescribed in section 167 for determining its depreciation allowance for 1958. However, such election shall be binding for 1958, and for all subsequent taxable years, unless consent to change such election, if required, is obtained from the Commissioner in accordance with the provisions of section 167 and the regulations thereunder.

Reg. § 1.818-2(a)(3)

Life Insurance Companies

See p. 20,601 for regulations not amended to reflect law changes

→ *Caution: Former Code Secs. 801-820 for pre-1984 years were repealed and replaced by new Code Secs. 801-818. The following Regulations were issued under old Code Secs. 801-820.*←

(4)(i) For purposes of section 805(b)(3)(B)(i) (relating to the determination of the current earnings rate for any taxable year beginning before January 1, 1958), the determination for any year of the investment yield and the assets shall be made as though the taxpayer had been on the accrual method prescribed in subparagraph (1) of this paragraph for such year, or the accrual method in combination with the other methods of accounting prescribed in subparagraph (2) of this paragraph, if these other methods of accounting are used by the taxpayer in determining the investment yield and assets for the taxable year 1958. However, where the method used for determining the deduction under section 167 for the year 1958 differs from the method used in prior years, the amount of the deduction actually allowed or allowable for such prior years for purposes of section 1016(a)(2) (relating to adjustments to basis) shall be the amount to be taken into account in determining the current earnings rate under section 805(b)(3)(B)(i).

(ii) For purposes of section 812(b)(1)(C) (relating to operations loss carrybacks and carryovers for years prior to 1958), the determination for those years of the gain or loss from operations shall be made as though the taxpayer had been on the accrual method of accounting prescribed in subparagraph (1) of this paragraph for such year, or the accrual method in combination with the other methods of accounting prescribed in subparagraph (2) of this paragraph, if these other methods of accounting are used by the taxpayer in the determination of gain or loss from operations for the taxable year 1958. However, where any adjustment to basis is required under section 1016(a)(3)(C) on account of exhaustion, wear and tear, obsolescence, amortization, and depletion sustained, the amount actually sustained as determined under section 1016(a)(3)(C) for each of the years involved shall be the amount allowed in the determination of gain or loss from operations for purposes of section 812(b)(1)(C).

(b) *Adjustments required if accrual method of accounting was not used in 1957.* The items of gross amount taken into account under section 809(c) and the items of deductions allowed under section 809(d) for the taxable year 1958 shall be determined as though the taxpayer had been on the accrual method of accounting prescribed in paragraph (a) of this section for all prior years. Thus, life insurance companies not on the accrual method for the year 1957 shall accrue, as of December 31, 1957, those items of gross amount which would have been properly taken into account for the year 1957 if the company had been on the accrual method described in section 818(a). Likewise, life insurance companies not on the accrual method for the year 1957 shall accrue, as of December 31, 1957, those items of deductions which would have been properly allowed for the year 1957 if the company had been on the accrual method described in section 818(a). For example, if certain premium amounts were received during the year 1958 but such amounts would have been properly taken into account for the year 1957 if the taxpayer had been on the accrual method for the year 1957, then the taxpayer will not be required to take such premium amounts into account for the year 1958. If, for example, certain claims, benefits, and losses were paid during the year 1958 but such items would have been properly taken into account for the year 1957 if the taxpayer had been on the accrual method for the year 1957, then the taxpayer will not be permitted to deduct such expense items for the year 1958. For a special transitional rule applicable with respect to changes in method of accounting required by section 818(a) and paragraph (a) of this section, see section 818(e) and § 1.818-6.

(c) *Change of basis in computing reserves.* (1) Section 806(b) provides that if the basis for determining the amount of any item referred to in section 810(c) as of the close of the taxable year differs from the basis for such determination as of the beginning of the taxable year, then for purposes of subpart B, part I, subchapter L, chapter 1 of the Code (relating to the determination of taxable investment income), the amount of such item shall be the amount computed on the old basis as of the close of the taxable year and the amount computed on the new basis as of the beginning of the next taxable year. Similarly, section 810(d)(1) provides rules for determining the amount of the adjustment to be made for purposes of subpart C, part I, subchapter L, chapter 1 of the Code (relating to the determination of gain or loss from operations), if the basis for determining any item referred to in section 810(c) as of the close of any taxable year differs from the basis for such determination as of the close of the preceding taxable year. Under an accrual method of accounting, a change in the basis or method of computing the amount of liability of any item referred to in section 810(c) occurs in the taxable year in which all the events have occurred which determine the change in the basis or method of computing the amount of such liability and, in

Reg. § 1.818-2(a)(4)

Life Insurance Companies

45,791

See p. 20,601 for regulations not amended to reflect law changes

→ **Caution:** *Former Code Secs. 801-820 for pre-1984 years were repealed and replaced by new Code Secs. 801-818. The following Regulations were issued under old Code Secs. 801-820.* ←

which, the amount thereof (whether increased or decreased) can be determined with reasonable accuracy.

(2) The application of subparagraph (1) of this paragraph may be illustrated by the following examples:

Example (1). Assume that during the taxable year 1960, M, a life insurance company, determines that the amount of its life insurance reserves held with respect to a particular block of contracts is understated on the present basis being used in valuing such liability and that such liability can be more accurately reflected by changing from the present basis to a particular new basis. Assume that M uses such new basis in computing its reserves under such contracts at the end of the taxable year 1960. Under the provisions of section 818(a) and subparagraph (1) of this paragraph, the change in basis for purposes of sections 806(b) and 810(d) occurs during the taxable year 1960, the year in which all the events have occurred which determine the change in basis and the amount of any increase (or decrease) attributable to such change can be determined with reasonable accuracy. Such change shall be treated as having occurred during the taxable year 1960 whether M determines that its liability under such contracts was understated for the first time during 1960, or that its liability under such contracts has, in fact, been understated for a number of prior years.

Example (2). Assume the facts are the same as in example (1), except that during the taxable year 1960 the insurance department of State X issues a ruling, pursuant to authority conferred by statute, requiring M to use the particular new basis which more accurately reflects its liability with respect to such contracts and that as a result of such ruling, M uses the new basis in computing its reserves under such contracts for the taxable years 1958, 1959, and 1960. Under the provisions of section 818(a) and subparagraph (1) of this paragraph, the change in basis for purposes of sections 806(b) and 810(d) occurs during the taxable year 1960, the year in which all the events have occurred which determine that a change in basis should be made and the amount of any increase (or decrease) attributable to such change can be determined with reasonable accuracy. [Reg. § 1.818-2.]

☐ [*T.D.* 6558, 4-3-61.]

[Reg. § 1.818-3]

§ 1.818-3. Amortization of premium and accrual of discount.—(a) *In general.* Section 818(b) provides that the appropriate items of income, deductions, and adjustments under part I, subchapter L, chapter 1 of the Code, shall be adjusted to reflect the appropriate amortization of premium and the appropriate accrual of discount on bonds, notes, debentures, or other evidences of indebtedness held by a life insurance company. Such adjustments are limited to the amount of appropriate amortization or accrual attributable to the taxable year with respect to such securities which are not in default as to principal or interest and which are amply secured. The question of ample security will be resolved according to the rules laid down from time to time by the National Association of Insurance Commissioners. The adjustment for amortization of premium decreases the gross investment income, the exclusion and reduction for wholly tax-exempt interest, the exclusion and deduction for partially tax-exempt interest, and the basis or adjusted basis of such securities. The adjustment for accrual of discount increases the gross investment income, the exclusion and reduction for wholly tax-exempt interest, the exclusion and deduction for partially tax-exempt interest, and the basis or adjusted basis of such securities. However, for taxable years beginning after May 31, 1960, only the accrual of discount relating to issue discount will increase the exclusion and reduction for wholly tax-exempt interest. See section 103.

(b) *Acquisitions before January 1, 1958.* (1) In the case of any such security acquired before January 1, 1958, the premium is the excess of its acquisition value over its maturity value and the discount is the excess of its maturity value over its acquisition value. The acquisition value of any such security is its cost (including buying commissions or brokerages but excluding any amounts paid for accrued interest) if purchased for cash, or if not purchased for cash, its then fair market value. The maturity value of any such security is the amount payable thereunder either at the maturity date or an earlier call date. The earlier call date of any such security may be the earliest interest payment date if it is callable or payable at such date, the earliest date at which it is callable at par, or such other call or payment date, prior to maturity, specified in the security as may be selected by the life insurance company. A life insurance company which adjusts amortization of premium or accrual of discount with refer-

Reg. § 1.818-3(b)

45,792   **Life Insurance Companies**
See p. 20,601 for regulations not amended to reflect law changes

→ *Caution: Former Code Secs. 801-820 for pre-1984 years were repealed and replaced by new Code Secs. 801-818. The following Regulations were issued under old Code Secs. 801-820.* ←

ence to a particular call or payment date must make the adjustments with reference to the value on such date and may not, after selecting such date, use a different call or payment date, or value, in the calculation of such amortization or discount with respect to such security unless the security was not in fact called or paid on such selected date.

(2) The adjustments for amortization of premium and accrual of discount will be determined—

(i) According to the method regularly employed by the company, if such method is reasonable, or

(ii) According to the method prescribed by this section.

A method of amortization of premium or accrual of discount will be deemed "regularly employed" by a life insurance company if the method was consistently followed in prior taxable years, or if, in the case of a company which has never before made such adjustments, the company initiates in the first taxable year for which the adjustments are made a reasonable method of amortization of premium or accrual of discount and consistently follows such method thereafter. Ordinarily, a company regularly employs a method in accordance with the statute of some State, Territory, or the District of Columbia, in which it operates.

(3) The method of amortization and accrual prescribed by this section is as follows:

(i) The premium (or discount) shall be determined in accordance with this section; and

(ii) The appropriate amortization of premium (or accrual of discount) attributable to the taxable year shall be an amount which bears the same ratio to the premium (or discount) as the number of months in the taxable year during which the security was owned by the life insurance company bears to the number of months between the date of acquisition of the security and its maturity or earlier call date determined in accordance with this section. For purposes of this section, a fractional part of a month shall be disregarded unless it amounts to more than half a month, in which case it shall be considered a month.

(c) *Acquisitions after December 31, 1957.* (1) In the case of—

(i) Any bond, as defined in section 171(d), acquired after December 31, 1957, the amount of the premium and the amortizable premium for the taxable year, shall be determined under section 171(b) and the regulations thereunder, as if the election set forth in section 171(c) had been made, and

(ii) Any bond, note, debenture, or other evidence of indebtedness not described in subdivision (i) of this subparagraph and acquired after December 31, 1957, the amount of the premium and the amortizable premium for the taxable year, shall be determined under paragraph (b) of this section.

(2) In the case of any bond, note, debenture, or other evidence of indebtedness acquired after December 31, 1957, the amount of the discount and the accrual of discount attributable to the taxable year shall be determined under paragraph (b) of this section.

(d) *Convertible evidences of indebtedness.* Section 818(b)(2)(B) provides that in no case shall the amount of premium on a convertible evidence of indebtedness (including any bond, note, or debenture) include any amount attributable to the conversion features of the evidence of indebtedness. This provision is the same as the one contained in section 171(b), and the rules prescribed in paragraph (c) of § 1.171-2 shall be applicable for purposes of section 818(b)(2)(B). This provision is to be applied without regard to the date upon which the evidence of indebtedness was acquired. Thus, where a convertible evidence of indebtedness was acquired before January 1, 1958, and a portion or all of the premium attributable to the conversion features of the evidence of indebtedness has been amortized for taxable years beginning before January 1, 1958, no adjustment for such amortization will be required by reason of section 818(b)(2)(B). Such amortization will, however, require an adjustment to the basis of the evidence of indebtedness under section 1016(a)(17). For taxable years beginning after December 31, 1957, no further amortization of the premium attributable to the conversion features of such an evidence of indebtedness will be taken into account.

(e) *Adjustments to basis.* Section 1016(a)(17) (relating to adjustments to basis) provides that in the case of any evidence of indebtedness referred to in section 818(b) and this section, the basis shall be adjusted to the extent of the adjustments required under section 818(b) (or the corresponding provisions of prior income tax laws) for the taxable year and all prior taxable years. The basis of any evidence of indebtedness shall be reduced by the amount of the adjustment required under section 818(b) (or the corresponding provision of

Reg. § 1.818-3(b)(2)

→ **Caution:** *Former Code Secs. 801-820 for pre-1984 years were repealed and replaced by new Code Secs. 801-818. The following Regulations were issued under old Code Secs. 801-820.*←

prior income tax laws) on account of amortizable premium and shall be increased by the amount of the adjustment required under section 818(b) on account of accruable discounts.

(f) *Denial of double inclusion.* Any amount which is includible in gross investment income by reason of section 818(b) and paragraph (a) of this section shall not be includible in gross income under section 1232(a) (relating to the taxation of bonds and other evidences of indebtedness). See section 1232(a)(2)(c) and the regulations thereunder. [Reg. § 1.818-3.]

☐ [*T.D. 6558, 4-3-61.*]

[Reg. § 1.818-4]

§ 1.818-4. Election with respect to life insurance reserves computed on preliminary term basis.—(a) *In general.* Section 818(c) permits a life insurance company issuing contracts with respect to which the life insurance reserves are computed on one of the recognized preliminary term bases to elect to revalue such reserves on a net level premium basis for the purpose of determining the amount which may be taken into account as life insurance reserves for purposes of part I, subchapter L, chapter 1 of the Code, other than section 801 (relating to the definition of a life insurance company). If such an election is made, the method to be used in making this revaluation of reserves shall be either the exact revaluation method (as described in section 818(c)(1) and paragraph (b)(1) of this section) or the approximate revaluation method (as described in section 818(c)(2) and paragraph (b)(2) of this section).

(b) *Revaluation of reserves computed on preliminary term basis.* If a life insurance company makes an election under section 818(c) in the manner provided in paragraph (e) of this section, the amount to be taken into account as life insurance reserves with respect to contracts for which such reserves are computed on a preliminary term basis may be determined on either of the following bases:

(1) *Exact revaluation method.* As if the reserves for all such contracts had been computed on a net level premium basis (using the same mortality or morbidity assumptions and interest rates for both the preliminary term basis and the net level premium basis).

(2) *Approximate revaluation method.* The amount computed without regard to section 818(c)—

(i) Increased by $21 per $1,000 of insurance in force (other than term insurance) under such contracts, less 2.1 percent of reserves under such contracts, and

(ii) Increased by $5 per $1,000 of term insurance in force under such contracts which at the time of issuance cover a period of more than 15 years, less 0.5 percent of reserves under such contracts.

(c) *Exception.* If a life insurance company which makes an election under section 818(c)(2) and paragraph (b)(2) of this section has life insurance reserves with respect to both life insurance and noncancellable accident and health contracts for which such reserves are computed on a preliminary term basis, it shall use the approximate revaluation method for all its life insurance reserves other than that portion of such reserves held with respect to its noncancellable accident and health contracts, and shall use the exact revaluation method for all its life insurance reserves held with respect to such noncancellable accident and health contracts.

(d) *Reserves subject to recomputation.* (1) For the first taxable year for which the election under section 818(c) and paragraph (b) of this section applies, a company making such election must revalue all its life insurance reserves held with respect to contracts for which such reserves are computed on a preliminary term basis at the end of such taxable year on the basis elected under section 818(c) and paragraph (b) of this section. However, for purposes of the preceding sentence, an election under section 818(c) shall not apply with respect to such reserves which would not be treated as being computed on the preliminary term basis at the end of such taxable year except for the provisions of section 810(a) or (b). See paragraph (c)(2) of § 1.810-2. For example, if S, a life insurance company which computes its life insurance reserves on a recognized preliminary term basis at the beginning of the taxable year 1958, strengthens a portion of such reserves during the taxable year by actually changing to a net level premium basis in computing such reserves, and then makes the election under section 818(c) and paragraph (b) of this section for 1958, such election shall not apply with respect to the strengthened contracts.

(2) For any taxable year other than the first taxable year for which the election under section 818(c) and paragraph (b) of this section applies, a company making such election must revalue all its life insurance reserves held with respect to

Reg. § 1.818-4(d)(2)

→ **Caution:** *Former Code Secs. 801-820 for pre-1984 years were repealed and replaced by new Code Secs. 801-818. The following Regulations were issued under old Code Secs. 801-820.* ←

contracts for which such reserves are computed on a preliminary term basis at the beginning or end of the taxable year on the basis elected under section 818(c) and paragraph (b) of this section. For example, if M, a life insurance company which made a valid outstanding election under section 818(c) in the manner provided in paragraph (e) of this section for the taxable year 1959, sells a block of contracts subject to such election on September 1, 1960, M would value such contracts on the basis elected under section 818(c) and paragraph (b) of this section on January 1, 1960, for purposes of determining the net decrease or increase in the sum of the items described in section 810(c) for the taxable year under section 810(a) or (b).

(3) For the effect of an election under section 818(c) and paragraph (b) of this section in determining gain or loss from operations for the taxable year, see paragraph (c)(3) of § 1.810-2 and paragraph (e) of § 1.810-3.

(e) *Time and manner of making election.* The election provided by section 818(c) shall be made in a statement attached to the life insurance company's income tax return of the first taxable year for which the company desires the election to apply. The return and statement must be filed not later than the date prescribed by law (including extensions thereof) for filing the return for such taxable year. However, if the last day prescribed by law (including extensions thereof) for filing a return for the first taxable year for which the company desires the election to apply falls before April 4, 1961, the election provided by section 818(c) may be made for such year by filing the statement and an amended return for such taxable year (and all subsequent taxable years for which returns have been filed) before July 4, 1961. The statement shall indicate whether the exact or the approximate method of revaluation has been adopted. The statement shall also set forth sufficient information as to mortality and morbidity assumptions; interest rates; the valuation method used; the amount of the reserves and the amount and type of insurance in force under all contracts for which reserves are computed on a preliminary term basis; and such other pertinent data as will enable the Commissioner to determine the correctness of the application of the revaluation method adopted and the accuracy of the computations involved in revaluing the reserves. The election to use either the exact revaluation method or the approximate revaluation method shall, except for the purposes of section 801, be adhered to in making the computations under part I for the taxable year for which such election is made and for all subsequent taxable years.

(f) *Scope of election.* An election made under section 818(c) and paragraph (b) of this section to use either the exact or the approximate method of revaluing the company life insurance reserves shall be binding for the taxable year for which made, and, except as provided in paragraph (g) of this section, shall be binding for all succeeding taxable years, unless consent to revoke the election is obtained from the Commissioner. However, for taxable years beginning prior to April 4, 1961, a company may revoke the election provided by section 818(c) without obtaining consent from the Commissioner by filing before July 4, 1961, a statement that the company desires to revoke such election. An amended return reflecting such revocation must accompany the statement for all taxable years for which the returns have been filed with respect to such election.

(g) *Special rule for 1958.* If an election is made for a taxable year beginning in 1958 to use the approximate revaluation method described in section 818(c)(2) and paragraph (b)(2) of this section, the company may, for its first taxable year beginning after 1958, elect to change to the exact revaluation method described in section 818(c)(1) and paragraph (b)(1) of this section without obtaining the consent of the Commissioner. In such case, the election to change shall be made in a statement attached to the company's income tax return for such taxable year and filed not later than the date prescribed by law (including extensions thereof) for filing the return for such year. The statement shall indicate that the company has elected to change from the approximate to the exact revaluation method for such taxable year and shall include such information and data referred to in paragraph (e) of this section as will enable the Commissioner to determine the correctness and accuracy of the computations involved. [Reg. § 1.818-4.]

☐ [T.D. 6558, 4-3-61.]

[Reg. § 1.818-5]

§ 1.818-5. Short taxable years.—(a) *In general.* Section 818(d) provides that if any return of a corporation made under part I, subchapter L, chapter 1 of the Code is for a period of less than the entire calendar year, then section 443 (relating to returns for a period of less than 12 months) shall not apply. This section further provides certain rules to be used in determining the life insur-

Life Insurance Companies

See p. 20,601 for regulations not amended to reflect law changes

→ **Caution:** *Former Code Secs. 801-820 for pre-1984 years were repealed and replaced by new Code Secs. 801-818. The following Regulations were issued under old Code Secs. 801-820.* ←

ance company taxable income for a period of less than the entire calendar year.

(b) *Returns for periods of less than the entire calendar year.* A return for a short period, that is, for a taxable year consisting of a period of less than the entire calendar year, shall be made only under the following circumstances:

(1) If a company which qualifies as a life insurance company is not in existence for the entire taxable year, a return is required for the short period during which the taxpayer was in existence. For example, a life insurance company organized on August 1, is required to file a return for the short period from August 1 to December 31, and returns for each calendar year thereafter. Similarly, if a company which qualifies as a life insurance company completely dissolves during the taxable year it is required to file a return for the short period from January 1 to the date it goes out of existence. All items entering into the computation of taxable investment income and gain or loss from operations for the short period shall be determined on a consistent basis and in the manner provided in paragraph (c) of this section.

(2) A return must be filed for a short period resulting from the termination by the district director of a taxpayer's taxable year for jeopardy. See section 6851 and the regulations thereunder.

A company which was an insurance company for the preceding taxable year (but not a life insurance company as defined in section 801(a) and paragraph (b) of § 1.801-3) and which for the current taxable year qualifies as a life insurance company shall not file a return for the short period from the time during the taxable year that it first qualifies as a life insurance company to the end of the taxable year. Similarly, an insurance company which was a life insurance company for the preceding taxable year but which for the current taxable year does not qualify as a life insurance company shall not file a return for the short period from the beginning of the taxable year to the time during the taxable year that it no longer qualifies as a life insurance company.

(c) *Computation of life insurance company taxable income for short period.* (1) If a return is made for a short period, section 818(d)(1) provides that the taxable investment income and the gain or loss from operations shall be determined on an annual basis by a ratable daily projection of the appropriate figures for the short period. The appropriate figures for the short period shall be determined on an annual basis by multiplying such figures by a fraction, the numerator of which is the number of days in the calendar year in which the short period occurs and the denominator of which is the number of days in the short period.

(2)(i) In computing taxable investment income for a short period, the investment yield, the policy and other contract liability requirements, the policyholders' share of each and every item of investment yield, and the company's share of any item of investment yield shall be determined on an annual basis.

(ii) For purposes of determining the investment yield on an annual basis, each item of gross investment income under section 804(b) and each item of deduction under section 804(c) shall be annualized in the manner provided in subparagraph (1) of this paragraph. In any case in which a limitation is placed on the amount of a deduction provided under section 804(c), the limitation shall apply to the item of deduction computed on an annual basis.

(iii) The policy and other contract liability requirements shall be determined on an annual basis in the following manner:

(a) The interest paid (as defined in section 805(e) and § 1.805-8) for the short period shall be annualized in the manner prescribed in subparagraph (1) of this paragraph.

(b) The current earnings rate for the taxable year in which the short period occurs shall be determined by dividing the taxpayer's investment yield, as determined on an annual basis under subdivision (ii) of this subparagraph, by the mean of the taxpayer's assets at the beginning and end of the short period. For purposes of section 805, any reference to the current earnings rate for the taxable year in which the short period occurs means the current earnings rate as determined under this subdivision.

(c) The adjusted life insurance reserves shall be determined as provided in section 805(c), and the pension plan reserves shall be determined as provided in section 805(d).

(iv) The policyholders' share of each and every item of investment yield (as defined in section 804(a)) shall be that percentage obtained by dividing the policy and other contract liability requirements, determined under subdivision (iii) of this subparagraph, by the investment yield, determined under subdivision (ii) of this subparagraph.

Reg. § 1.818-5(c)(2)

Life Insurance Companies

See p. 20,601 for regulations not amended to reflect law changes

→ **Caution:** *Former Code Secs. 801-820 for pre-1984 years were repealed and replaced by new Code Secs. 801-818. The following Regulations were issued under old Code Secs. 801-820.* ←

(v) The taxable investment income for the short period shall be an amount (not less than zero) equal to the life insurance company's share of each and every item of investment yield, as determined under subdivision (ii) of this subparagraph, reduced by the items described in section 804(a)(2)(A) and (B). In determining these reductions under section 804(a)(2)(A) the amount of the respective items shall be the amount that is determined on an annual basis under subdivision (ii) of this subparagraph. The small business deduction, under section 804(a)(2)(B) shall be an amount (not to exceed $25,000) equal to 10 percent of the investment yield, determined under subdivision (ii) of this subparagraph, for the short period.

(vi) Except as provided in this paragraph, the determination of taxable investment income under subpart B, part I, subchapter L, chapter 1 of the Code, shall be made in accordance with all the provisions of that subpart.

(3)(i) In computing gain or loss from operations for a short period, the share of each and every item of investment yield set aside for policyholders, the life insurance company's share of each and every item of investment yield, the items of gross amount, and the items of deduction shall, except as modified by this subparagraph, be determined on an annual basis in the manner provided in subparagraph (1) of this paragraph. In any case in which a limitation is placed on the amount of a deduction provided under section 809, the limitation shall apply to the item of deduction computed on an annualized basis.

(ii) For purposes of section 809 and 810, the investment yield shall be determined in the manner provided in subparagraph (2)(ii) of this paragraph. The share of any item of investment yield set aside for policyholders shall be that percentage obtained by dividing the required interest as determined under section 809(a)(2), by the investment yield, as determined in this subparagraph, except that if the required interest exceeds the investment yield, then the share of any item of investment yield set aside for policyholders shall be 100 percent.

(iii) The items of gross amount and the items of deduction, other than the operations loss deduction under section 809(d)(4), shall be determined on an annual basis. See subdivision (iv) of this subparagraph for the manner in which the net decrease or net increase in reserves under section 810 shall be annualized.

(iv) For purposes of determining either a net decrease in reserves under section 810(a) or a net increase in reserves under section 810(b), the sum of the items described in section 810(c) as of the end of the short period shall be reduced by the amount of the investment yield not included in gain or loss from operations for the short period by reason of section 809(a)(1). The amount of investment yield excluded under section 809(a)(1) has been determined upon an annualized basis while the sum of the items described in section 810(c) at the end of the short period has been determined on an actual basis. In order to place these on the same basis, the amount of investment yield not included in gain or loss from operation by reason of section 809(a)(1), determined under subdivision (ii), shall, for purposes of section 810(a) and section 810(b), be reduced to an amount which bears the same ratio to the full amount as the number of days in the short period bears to the number of days in the entire calendar year. The net decrease or the net increase of the items referred to in section 810(c) for the short period shall then be determined, as provided in section 810(a) and section 810(b), respectively, and the result annualized.

(4) The portion of the life insurance company taxable income described in section 802(b)(1) and (2) (relating to taxable investment income and gain or loss from operations) shall be determined on an annual basis by treating the amounts ascertained under subparagraph (2) of this paragraph as the taxable investment income, and the amount ascertained under subparagraph (3) of this paragraph as the gain or loss from operations, for the taxable year.

(5) The portion of the life insurance company taxable income described in section 802(b)(1) and (2) for the short period shall be the amount which bears the same ratio to the amount ascertained under section 818(d)(2) and subparagraph (4) of this paragraph as the number of days in the short period bears to the number of days in the entire year.

(d) *Special rules.* (1) For purposes of determining the average earnings rate (as defined in section 805(b)(3)) for subsequent taxable years, the current earnings rate for the taxable year in which the short period occurs shall be the rate determined under paragraph (c)(2) of this section.

(2) For purposes of determining an operations loss deduction under section 812, the loss from operations for the short period shall be the

Reg. § 1.818-5(c)(3)

→ **Caution: Former Code Secs. 801-820 for pre-1984 years were repealed and replaced by new Code Secs. 801-818. The following Regulations were issued under old Code Secs. 801-820.** ←

loss from operations determined under paragraph (c)(5) of this section. [Reg. § 1.818-5.]

☐ [*T.D.* 6558, 4-3-61.]

[Reg. § 1.818-6]

§ 1.818-6. Transition rule for change in method of accounting.—(a) *In general.* Section 818(e) prescribes the rules to be followed in recomputing the taxes of a life insurance company for the taxable year 1957 in cases where the method of accounting required to be used in computing the company's taxes for 1958 under section 818(a) and paragraph (a) of § 1.818-2 is different from the method used in 1957.

(b) *Recomputation of 1957 taxes.* (1) For purposes of recomputing its taxes for 1957, a life insurance company must ascertain the net amount of those adjustments which are determined (as of the close of 1957) to be necessary solely by reason of the change to the method of accounting required by section 818(a) and paragraph (a) of § 1.818-2 in order to prevent amounts from being duplicated or omitted. Thus, for example, life insurance companies not on the accrual method of accounting for the year 1957 shall accrue, as of December 31, 1957, those items of gross investment income under section 803(b) and those items of deduction under section 803(c), as in effect for 1957, which would have been properly accruable for the year 1957 if the company had been on the accrual method of accounting.

(2) In the case of a change in the over-all method of accounting, the term "net amount of those adjustments" means the consolidation of adjustments (whether the amounts thereof represent increases or decreases in items of income or deductions) arising with respect to balances in the various accounts on December 31, 1957. In the case of a change in the treatment of a single material item, the amount of the adjustment shall be determined with reference only to the net dollar balances in that particular account.

(3)(i) The amount of the taxpayer's tax for 1957 shall be recomputed (under the law applicable to 1957, modified as provided in section 818(e)(4) and paragraph (e) of this section) by taking into account an amount equal to one-tenth of the net amount of the adjustments determined under subparagraph (1) of this paragraph. The increase or decrease in tax attributable to the adjustments for such year is the difference between the tax for such year computed with the allocation of one-tenth of the net amount of the adjustments to such taxable year over the tax computed without the allocation of any part of the adjustments to such year.

(ii) The amount of increase or decrease (as the case may be) referred to in section 818(e)(2) or (3) and paragraph (c) or (d) of this section, shall be the amount of the increase or decrease in tax ascertained in the manner described in subdivision (i) of this subparagraph, multiplied by 10.

(c) *Treatment of decrease.* Section 818(e)(2) provides that for purposes of subtitle F of the Code, if the recomputation under paragraph (b)(3)(ii) of this section results in a decrease, the amount of such decrease shall be treated as a decrease in the tax imposed for 1957; except that for purposes of computing the period of limitation on the making of refunds or allowance of credits with respect to such overpayments, the amount of such decrease shall be treated as an overpayment of tax for 1959. No interest shall be paid, for any period before March 16, 1960, on any overpayment of the tax imposed for 1957 which is attributable to such decrease.

(d) *Treatment of increase*—(1) *In general.* Section 818(e)(3)(A) provides that for purposes of subtitle F of the Code, other than section 6016 (relating to declarations of estimated income tax by corporations) and section 6655 (relating to failure by corporations to pay estimated income tax), if the recomputation under paragraph (b)(3)(ii) of this section results in an increase, the amount of such increases shall be treated as a tax imposed for 1959. Such tax shall be payable in 10 equal annual installments, beginning with March 15, 1960.

(2) *Special rules.* Section 818(e)(3)(B) provides that for purposes of section 818(e)(3)(A) and subparagraph (1) of this paragraph—

(i) No interest shall be paid on any installment described in section 818(e)(3)(A) and subparagraph (1) of this paragraph before the time prescribed therein for the payment of such installment.

(ii) Section 6152(c) (relating to proration of deficiencies to installments) and the regulations thereunder shall apply. However, section 6152(a) (relating to the election to make installment payments) and the regulations thereunder shall not apply.

(iii) In applying section 6502(a)(1) (relating to collection after assessment) and the regulations thereunder, the assessment of any installment described in section 818(e)(3)(A) and subparagraph (1) of this paragraph shall be

Reg. § 1.818-6(d)(2)

Life Insurance Companies

See p. 20,601 for regulations not amended to reflect law changes

→ **Caution:** *Former Code Secs. 801-820 for pre-1984 years were repealed and replaced by new Code Secs. 801-818. The following Regulations were issued under old Code Secs. 801-820.* ←

treated as made at the time prescribed therein for the payment of such installment.

(iv) If for any taxable year the taxpayer is not a life insurance company, the amount of the increase in tax (as determined under paragraph (b)(3)(ii) of this section), to the extent not taken into account for prior taxable years, shall be payable on the date the return for such taxable year is due (determined without regard to any extensions of time for filing such return), unless such amount is required to be taken into account by the acquiring corporation under section 381(c)(22) and the regulations thereunder.

(e) *Modifications of 1957 tax computation.* Section 818(e)(4) provides that in recomputing the taxpayer's tax for 1957 for purposes of section 818(e)(1) and paragraph (b) of this section—

(1) Section 804(b), as in effect for 1957 (relating to the maximum reserve and other policy liability deduction), shall not apply with respect to any amount required to be taken into account by reason of section 818(e)(1) and paragraph (b) of this section; and

(2) The amount of the deduction allowed by section 805, as in effect for 1957 (relating to the special interest deduction), shall not be reduced by reason of any amount required to be taken into account under section 818(e)(1) and paragraph (b) of this section.

(f) *Illustration of principles.* The application of section 818(e) and this section may be illustrated by the following examples:

Example (1). For the taxable year 1957, the life insurance taxable income of M, a life insurance company, is $200,000 computed on the cash receipts and disbursements method of accounting. The net amount of the adjustments required under section 818(e)(1) by reason of the change to the accrual method of accounting for 1958, increases M's life insurance taxable income for 1957 by $50,000. The increase in tax attributable to the change in method of accounting required by section 818(a) is $26,000, computed as follows:

(1) Life insurance taxable income
before adjustments $200,000
(2) Adjustments required by sec.
818(e)(1) (¹⁄₁₀ × $50,000) ... 5,000
(3) Life insurance taxable income
after adjustments (item (1)
plus item (2)) 205,000
(4) Tax liability after adjustments
(52% × $205,000, minus
$5,500) 101,100
(5) Tax liability before adjustments
(52% × $200,000, minus
$5,500) 98,500
(6) Excess of item (4) over item (5)... 2,600
(7) Increase in tax for purposes of sec.
818(e)(3) (item (6) multiplied
by 10) 26,000

Under the provisions of section 818(e)(3), one-tenth of the increase in tax for 1957 attributable to the change in method of accounting required by section 818(a), $2,600 (¹⁄₁₀ × $26,000), was due and payable on March 15, 1960, and the balance, $23,400 (⁹⁄₁₀ × $26,000), is due and payable in equal installments on March 15th of the nine succeeding taxable years. However, if for the taxable year 1965, M is no longer a life insurance company, and section 381(c)(22) does not apply, the balance of the installments not paid in prior taxable years, $10,400 (⁴⁄₁₀ × $26,000), shall be due and payable on March 15, 1966.

Example (2). Assume the facts are the same as in example (1), except that the net amount of the adjustments required by section 818(e)(1) decreases M's life insurance taxable income for 1957 by $25,000. The decrease in tax attributable to the change in method of accounting required by section 818(a) is $13,000, computed as follows:

(1) Life insurance taxable income
before adjustments $200,000
(2) Adjustments required by sec.
818(e)(1) (¹⁄₁₀ × $25,000) ... 2,500
(3) Life insurance taxable income
after adjustments (item (1)
minus item (2)) 197,500
(4) Tax liability after adjustments
(52% × $197,500, minus
$5,500) 97,200
(5) Tax liability before adjustments
(52% × $200,000, minus
$5,500) 98,500
(6) Excess of item (5) over item (4)... 1,300
(7) Decrease in tax for purposes of
sec. 818(e)(2) (item (6)
multiplied by 10) 13,000

Under the provisions of section 818(e)(2), the entire $13,000 decrease in tax for 1957 attributable to the change in method of accounting required by section 818(a) shall be treated as an overpayment of tax for the taxable year 1959. [Reg. § 1.818-6.]

☐ [T.D. 6558, 4-3-61.]

[Reg. § 1.818-7]

§ 1.818-7. **Denial of double deductions.**—Section 818(f) provides that the same item may not be deducted more than once under subpart B, part I, subchapter L, chapter 1 of the Code (relating to the determination of taxable investment income),

Reg. § 1.818-7

Life Insurance Companies

See p. 20,601 for regulations not amended to reflect law changes

→ *Caution: Former Code Secs. 801-820 for pre-1984 years were repealed and replaced by new Code Secs. 801-818. The following Regulations were issued under old Code Secs. 801-820.* ←

and more than once under subpart C, part I, subchapter L, chapter 1 of the Code (relating to the determination of gain or loss from operations). [Reg. § 1.818-7.]

☐ [T.D. 6558, 4-3-61.]

[Reg. § 1.818-8]

§ 1.818-8. Special rules relating to consolidated returns and certain capital losses.—Section 818(g) provides that, in the case of a life insurance company filing or required to file a consolidated return under section 1501 for a taxable year, the computations of the policyholders' share of investment yield under subparts B and C, part I, subchapter L, chapter 1 of the Code (including all determinations and computations incident thereto) shall be made as if such company were not filing a consolidated return. Thus, for example, if X and Y are life insurance companies which are entitled to file a consolidated return for 1975 and X has paid dividends to Y during such taxable year, Y must include such dividends in the computation of gross investment income under section 804(b). For other rules relating to the filing of consolidated returns, see sections 1501 through 1504 and the regulations thereunder. [Reg. § 1.818-8.]

☐ [T.D. 7469, 2-28-77.]

[Reg. § 1.819-1]

§ 1.819-1. Taxable years affected.—Section 1.819-2 is applicable only to taxable years beginning after December 31, 1957, and all references to sections of part I, subchapter L, chapter 1 of the Code, are to the Internal Revenue Code of 1954, as amended by the Life Insurance Company Income Tax Act of 1959 (73 Stat. 112). [Reg. § 1.819-1.]

☐ [T.D. 6558, 4-3-61.]

[Reg. § 1.819-2]

§ 1.819-2. Foreign life insurance companies.—(a) *Carrying on United States insurance business.* Section 819(a) provides that a foreign life insurance company carrying on a life insurance business within the United States, if with respect to its United States business it would qualify as a life insurance company under section 801, shall be taxable on its United States business under section 802 in the same manner as a domestic life insurance company. Thus, the life insurance company taxable income of such a foreign life insurance company shall not be determined in the manner provided by part I, subchapter N, chapter 1 of the Code (relating to determination of sources of income), but shall be determined in the manner provided by part I, subchapter L, chapter 1 of the Code (relating to life insurance companies). See section 842. Accordingly, in determining its life insurance company taxable income from its United States business, such a foreign life insurance company shall take into account the appropriate items of income irrespective of whether such items of income are from sources within or without the United States. A foreign life insurance company shall take into account the appropriate items of expenses, losses, and other deductions properly allocable to such items of income from its United States business. To the extent not inconsistent with the provisions of this paragraph, section 818(a), and section 819(b), all computations entering into the determination of taxes imposed by part I shall be made in a manner consistent with the manner required for purposes of the annual statement approved by the National Association of Insurance Commissioners.

(b) *Adjustment where surplus held in the United States is less than specified minimum*—(1) *In general.* Section 819(b)(1) provides that if the minimum figure for the taxable year determined under section 819(b)(2) and subparagraph (2)(i) of this paragraph exceeds the surplus held in the United States as of the end of the taxable year (as defined in section 819(b)(2)(B) and subparagraph (2)(ii) of this paragraph) by a foreign life insurance company carrying on a life insurance business within the United States and taxable under section 802, then—

(i) The amount of the policy and other contract liability requirements (determined under section 805 and § 1.805-4 without regard to this subparagraph), and

(ii) The amount of the required interest (determined under section 809(a)(2) and paragraph (d) of § 1.809-2 without regard to this subparagraph),

shall each be reduced by an amount determined by multiplying such excess by the current earnings rate (as defined in section 805(b)(2) and paragraph (a)(2) of § 1.805-5) of such company. Such current earnings rate shall be determined by reference to the assets held by the company in the United States.

(2) *Definitions.* For purposes of section 819(b)(1) and subparagraph (1) of this paragraph—

Reg. § 1.819-2(b)(2)

45,800 Life Insurance Companies

See p. 20,601 for regulations not amended to reflect law changes

→ *Caution: Former Code Secs. 801-820 for pre-1984 years were repealed and replaced by new Code Secs. 801-818. The following Regulations were issued under old Code Secs. 801-820.*←

(i) The term "minimum figure", in the case of a taxable year beginning after December 31, 1957, but before January 1, 1959, means the amount obtained by multiplying the company's total insurance liabilities on United States business by 9 percent. In the case of any taxable year beginning after December 31, 1958, such term means the amount obtained by multiplying the company's total insurance liabilities on United States business by the percentage determined and proclaimed by the Secretary as being applicable for such year;

(ii) The term "surplus held in the United States" means the excess of the assets held in the United States (as of the end of the taxable year) over the total insurance liabilities on United States business (as of the end of the taxable year);

(iii) The term "total insurance liabilities" means the sum of the total reserves (as defined in section 801(c) and paragraph (a) of § 1.801-5) as of the end of the taxable year plus (to the extent not included in total reserves) the items referred to in section 810(c)(3), (4), and (5) and paragraph (b)(3), (4), and (5) of § 1.810-2 as of the end of the taxable year; and

(iv) The term "assets" shall have the same meaning as that contained in section 805(b)(4) and paragraph (a)(4) of § 1.805-5.

(3) *Illustration of principles.* The provisions of section 819(b) and this paragraph may be illustrated by the following example:

Example. For the taxable year 1958, P, a foreign life insurance company carrying on a life insurance business within the United States and taxable under section 802, has total insurance liabilities on United States business (as of the end of the taxable year) of $940,000, assets held in the United States of $1,000,000 (as of the end of the taxable year), policy and other contract liability requirements in the amount of $30,000, required interest in the amount of $20,000, and a current earnings rate of 4 percent. In order to determine whether section 819(b) applies for the taxable year 1958, P must first compute its minimum figure, for if the minimum figure is less than the surplus held in the United States (as of the end of the taxable year), no section 819(b) adjustments need by made. Since the minimum figure, $84,600 ($940,000, the total insurance liabilities on United States business multiplied by 9 percent, the percentage applicable for 1958), exceeds the surplus held in the United States, $60,000 (the excess of the assets held in the United States, $1,000,000, over the total insurance liabilities on United States business, $940,000), by $24,600, section 819(b) applies for the taxable year 1958. Thus, the amount of the policy and other contract liability requirements, $30,000, and the amount of the required interest, $20,000, shall each be reduced by $984 ($24,600, the amount of such excess, multiplied by 4 percent, the current earnings rate).

(4) *Segregated asset accounts.* For taxable years beginning after December 31, 1967, pursuant to the provisions of section 801(g)—

(i) A foreign corporation carrying on a life insurance business which issues contracts based on segregated asset accounts shall separately compute in a manner consistent with the subparagraph the adjustment (if any) under section 819 to the amount of policy and other contract liability requirements and the amount of required interest properly attributable to each of such segregated asset accounts. The "minimum figure" used in section 819 in making the adjustment with respect to each of the segregated asset accounts shall be computed as provided in subdivision (ii) of this subparagraph in lieu of the manner provided in subparagraphs (1), (2) and (3) of this paragraph.

(ii) The minimum figure applicable to a segregated asset account referred to in subdivision (i) of this subparagraph is the amount determined by multiplying the total insurance liabilities on U.S. business attributable to such a segregated asset account, by 1 percent.

(iii) The minimum figure as computed under subdivision (ii) of this subparagraph shall be compared only with the surplus held in the United States attributable to each segregated asset account referred to in subdivision (i) of this subparagraph. Such surplus is the excess of assets held in the United States properly attributable to such segregated asset account over the total insurance liabilities on U.S. business properly attributable to such account.

(iv) If the minimum figure applicable to accounts other than segregated asset accounts exceeds the surplus held in the United States attributable to such other accounts, for purposes of section 819 and this paragraph, the amount of such excess shall not exceed the company's overall excess as defined in this subdivision. No adjustment under section 819 or this paragraph shall be made with respect to any account if there is no such overall excess. For purposes of this subdivi-

Reg. § 1.819-2(b)(3)

Life Insurance Companies

See p. 20,601 for regulations not amended to reflect law changes

→ **Caution:** *Former Code Secs. 801-820 for pre-1984 years were repealed and replaced by new Code Secs. 801-818. The following Regulations were issued under old Code Secs. 801-820.* ←

sion and of subdivision (v) of this subparagraph, the term "overall excess" means the amount, if any, by which the aggregate minimum figures applicable to segregated asset accounts plus the minimum figure applicable to accounts other than segregated asset accounts exceeds the surplus held in the United States with respect to the company's entire U.S. life insurance business, including segregated asset accounts as well as other accounts.

(v) In the case of a company which issues contracts based on one or more than one segregated asset account, if the minimum figure applicable to a segregated asset account exceeds the surplus held in the United States attributable to such account, then for purposes of section 819 and this paragraph, the amount of such excess shall not exceed the account limitation figure, as defined in this subdivision. Therefore, no adjustment under section 819 or under this subparagraph shall be made with respect to any segregated asset account if the aggregate of the account limitation figures is zero, but nothing in this subdivision shall preclude an adjustment under section 819 with respect to accounts other than segregated asset accounts. For purposes of this subdivision, the term "account limitation figure" is a segregated asset account's proportionate share of the aggregate of the account limitation figures. Such aggregate of the account limitation figures is equal to the lesser of either the company's overall excess as defined in subdivision (iv) of this subparagraph, or the amount, if any, by which the aggregate of the minimum figures applicable to segregated asset accounts exceeds the surplus held in the United States with respect to all such segregated asset accounts. For purposes of this subdivision, a segregated asset account's proportionate share of the aggregate of the account limitation figures is determined by multiplying the amount of such aggregate of account limitation figures by a percentage, the numerator of which is the amount by which the minimum figure applicable to such account exceeds the surplus held in the United States attributable to such account, and the denominator of which is the aggregate of the amounts by which the minimum figure applicable to each segregated asset account exceeds the surplus held in the United States attributable to such account.

(vi) Subdivisions (i), (ii), (iii), (iv) and (v) of this subparagraph may be illustrated by the following examples:

Example (1). (a) For the taxable year 1968, T, a foreign life insurance company carrying on a life insurance business within the United States and taxable under section 802, has the following assets and total insurance liabilities with respect to such U.S. business:

	Regular Account	Separate Account A	Separate Account B
Assets	$9,300,000	$1,810,000	$515,000
Total insurance liabilities	$8,000,000	$1,800,000	$500,000

It is further assumed that the percentage determined and proclaimed by the Secretary under section 819(a)(2)(A) for the taxable year 1968 is 15 percent.

(b) In order to determine whether any adjustment under section 819 must be made, T must compute the minimum figure applicable to its Regular Account as well as each of its Separate Accounts. The minimum figure for the Regular Account is $1,200,000 (15 percent of $8,000,000). The minimum figure applicable to Separate Account A is $18,000 (1 percent of $1,800,000). The minimum figure applicable to Separate Account B is $5,000 (1 percent of $500,000). The aggregate of the minimum figures is $1,223,000 ($1,200,000 + $18,000 + $5,000). The surplus held in the United States with respect to the Regular Account is $1,300,000 ($9,300,000 − $8,000,000), with respect to Separate Account A is $10,000 ($1,810,000 − $1,800,000) and with respect to Separate Account B is $15,000 ($515,000 − $500,000). The surplus held in the United States with respect to T's entire U.S. life insurance business is $1,325,000 ($1,300,000 + $10,000 + $15,000).

(c) Since the aggregate of the minimum figures ($1,223,000) does not exceed the surplus held in the United States attributable to T's entire U.S. life insurance business ($1,325,000), under subdivision (iv) of this subparagraph no adjustment under section 819 shall be made with respect to the Regular Account or either of the Separate Accounts.

Example (2). (a) The facts are the same as in example (1) except that the assets held in the United States with respect to the Regular Account is $8,300,000 instead of $9,300,000. Thus, the surplus held in the United States with respect

Reg. § 1.819-2(b)(4)

45,802   **Life Insurance Companies**
See p. 20,601 for regulations not amended to reflect law changes

→ *Caution: Former Code Secs. 801-820 for pre-1984 years were repealed and replaced by new Code Secs. 801-818. The following Regulations were issued under old Code Secs. 801-820.* ←

to the Regular Account is $300,000 ($8,300,000 − $8,000,000), and the surplus held in the United States with respect to T's entire U.S. life insurance business is $325,000 ($300,000 + $10,000 + $15,000).

(b) Since the aggregate of the minimum figures with respect to the Separate Accounts, $23,000 ($18,000 + $5,000), does not exceed the surplus held in the United States with respect to both of such Separate Accounts, $25,000 ($10,000 + $15,000), under subdivision (v) of this subparagraph, no adjustment under section 819 must be made with respect to either of the Separate Accounts.

(c) The excess of the minimum figure for the Regular Account ($1,200,000) over the surplus held in the United States with respect to the Regular Account ($300,000) is equal to $900,000 ($1,200,000 − $300,000). However, the company's overall excess as defined in subdivision (iv) of this subparagraph, is $898,000 ($1,223,000 − $325,000). Under subdivision (iv) of this subparagraph the excess with respect to the Regular Account ($900,000) is limited to the amount of overall excess ($898,000). Thus, the amount of policy and other contract liability requirements with respect to T's Regular Account and the amount of required interest with respect to T's Regular Account (both computed without regard to section 819) shall each be reduced by an amount equal to the product of $898,000 and the current earnings rate computed only with respect to T's Regular Account.

(c) *Distributions to shareholders*—(1) *In general.* In the case of a foreign life insurance company carrying on a life insurance business within the United States and taxable under section 802, section 819(c)(1) provides alternative methods for determining the amount of distributions to shareholders for purposes of section 815 (relating to distributions to shareholders) and section 802(b)(3) (relating to life insurance company taxable income). Such a foreign life insurance company may elect (in the manner provided by subparagraph (4) of this paragraph) for each taxable year, whichever of the alternative methods provided by section 819(c)(1) and this subparagraph it desires, and the method elected for any one taxable year shall be effective only with respect to the taxable year for which the election is made. Such alternative methods are:

(i) The amount of the distributions to shareholders shall be the amount determined by multiplying the total amount of distributions to shareholders by the percentage which the minimum figure for the taxable year is of the excess of the assets of the company over the total insurance liabilities; or

(ii) The amount of the distributions for shareholders shall be the amount determined by multiplying the total amount of distributions for shareholders by the percentage which the total insurance liabilities on United States business for the taxable year is of the total insurance liabilities of the company.

(2) *Definitions.* For purposes of section 819(c)(1) and subparagraph (1) of this paragraph:

(i) The term "total amount of the distributions to shareholders" means all distributions (within the meaning of section 815 and § 1.815-2) by a foreign life insurance company to all of its shareholders whether or not in the United States;

(ii) The term "minimum figure for the taxable year" means the amount determined under section 819(b)(2)(A) and paragraph (b)(2) of this section;

(iii) The term "assets of the company" means all of the assets (as defined in section 805(b)(4) and paragraph (e) of § 1.805-2) of the foreign life insurance company whether or not in the United States (as of the end of the taxable year); and

(iv) The term "total insurance liabilities of the company" means the total insurance liabilities (as defined in section 819(b)(2) and paragraph (b)(2) of this section) on all of its business whether or not in the United States (as of the end of the taxable year).

(3) *Illustration of principles.* The provisions of section 819(c)(1) and subparagraphs (1) and (2) of this paragraph may be illustrated by the following examples:

Example (1). For the taxable year 1958, T, a foreign life insurance company carrying on a life insurance business within the United States and taxable under section 802, has a minimum figure of $40,000, total amount of distributions to all shareholders (within the meaning of section 815) of $5,000, assets (as of the end of the year) of $500,000, total insurance liabilities (as of the end of the year) of $450,000, and total insurance liabilities on United States business (as of the end of the year) of $180,000. Based upon these facts, if T elects the method provided in section 819(c)(1)(A) and subparagraph (1)(i) of this paragraph, the amount of T's distributions to shareholders for the taxable year 1958 is $4,000, that is, $5,000 (the

Reg. § 1.819-2(c)(1)

Life Insurance Companies

See p. 20,601 for regulations not amended to reflect law changes

→ *Caution: Former Code Secs. 801-820 for pre-1984 years were repealed and replaced by new Code Secs. 801-818. The following Regulations were issued under old Code Secs. 801-820.* ←

total amount of distributions to shareholders) multiplied by 80 percent (the percentage which the minimum figure for the taxable year, $40,000, is of $50,000, the excess of the assets of the company ($500,000) over the total insurance liabilities ($450,000)).

Example (2). The facts are the same as in example (1), except that for the taxable year 1958, T elects the method provided in section 819(c)(1)(B) and subparagraph (1)(ii) of this paragraph. Based upon these facts, the amount of T's distributions to shareholders for the taxable year 1958 is $2,000, that is, $5,000 (the total amount of distributions to shareholders) multiplied by 40 percent (the percentage which the total insurance liabilities on United States business ($180,000) is of the total insurance liabilities of the company ($450,000)).

(4) *Manner and effect of election.* (i) The election provided by section 819(c)(1) shall be made in a statement attached to the foreign life insurance company's income tax return for any taxable year for which the company desires the election to apply. The return and statement must be filed not later than the date prescribed by law (including extensions thereof) for filing the return for such taxable year. The statement shall indicate the method elected, the name and address of the taxpayer, and shall be signed by the taxpayer (or his duly authorized representative).

(ii) An election made under section 819(c)(1) and this paragraph shall be effective only with respect to the taxable year for which the election is made. Thus, the company must make a new election for each taxable year for which it desires the election to apply. Once such election has been made for any taxable year it may not be revoked. However, for taxable years beginning prior to April 4, 1961, a company may revoke the election provided by section 819(c)(1) without obtaining consent from the Commissioner by filing, before July 4, 1961, a statement that the company desires to revoke such election. An amended return reflecting such revocation and the selection of the other percentage must accompany the statement for all taxable years for which returns have been filed with respect to such election.

(5) *Application of section 815.* Once the amount of distributions to shareholders is determined under the provisions of section 819(c)(1) and this paragraph, the rules of section 815 (relating to distributions to shareholders) shall apply to the shareholders surplus account and the policyholders surplus account of a foreign stock life insurance company in the same manner as they would apply to a domestic stock life insurance company.

(d) *Distributions pursuant to certain mutualizations.* Section 819(c)(2) provides that for purposes of applying section 815(e) and paragraph (e) of § 1.815-6 (relating to a special rule for certain mutualizations) in the case of a foreign life insurance company subject to tax under section 802—

(1) The paid-in capital and paid-in surplus referred to in section 815(e)(1)(A) of a foreign life insurance company is the portion of such capital and surplus determined by multiplying such amounts by the percentage selected for the taxable year under section 819(c)(1) and paragraph (c)(1) of this section; and

(2) The excess referred to in section 815(e)(2)(A)(i) (without the adjustment provided by section 815(e)(2)(B)), is whichever of the following is the greater:

(i) The minimum figure for 1958 determined under section 819(b)(2)(A); or

(ii) The surplus held in the United States (as defined in section 819(b)(2)(B)) determined as of December 31, 1958.

(e) *No United States insurance business.* Foreign life insurance companies not carrying on an insurance business within the United States shall not be taxable under part I, subchapter L, chapter 1 of the Code, but shall be taxable as other foreign corporations. See section 811 and the regulations thereunder. [Reg. § 1.819-2.]

☐ [T.D. 6558, 4-3-61. Amended by T.D. 6970, 8-23-68.]

[Reg. § 1.821-4]

§ 1.821-4. **Tax on mutual insurance companies other than life insurance companies and other than fire, flood, or marine insurance companies subject to tax imposed by section 831.**—(a) *In general*—(1) *Tax imposed.* (i) For taxable years beginning after December 31, 1962, all mutual insurance companies, including foreign insurance companies carrying on an insurance business within the United States, not taxable under section 802 or 831, and not specifically exempt under the provisions of section 501(c)(15), are subject either to the tax imposed by section 821(a) on mutual insurance company taxable income or, in the case of certain small companies, to the tax imposed by section 821(c) on taxable investment income. The determination of whether a

Reg. § 1.821-4

mutual insurance company is taxable under section 821(a) or (c) for the taxable year is dependent upon the gross amount received by the company during such taxable year from the items described in section 822(b) (other than paragraph (1)(D) thereof) and premiums (including deposits and assessments). If such gross amount received exceeds $150,000, but does not exceed $500,000 for the taxable year, the company is subject to the tax imposed by section 821(c) on taxable investment income, unless (a) the company elects under section 821(d) in the manner provided in paragraph (f) of this section to be subject to the tax imposed by section 821(a), or (b) there is a balance in its protection against loss account at the beginning of the taxable year. A company having a gross amount received in excess of $500,000 is subject to the tax imposed by section 821(a). For exemption from income tax of companies having a gross amount received not in excess of $150,000, see section 501(c)(15). For the alternative tax, in lieu of the tax imposed by section 821(a) or (c), where the net long-term capital gain for any taxable year exceeds the net short-term capital loss, see section 1201(a) and the regulations thereunder. For the definition of an insurance company, see § 1.801-3(a).

(ii) The term "premiums" as used in section 821 and this section has the same meaning as in section 501(c)(15) and § 1.501(c)(15)-1, and means the total amount of the premiums and other consideration provided in the insurance contract without any deduction for commissions, return premiums, reinsurance, dividends to policyholders, dividends left on deposit with the company, discounts on premiums paid in advance, interest applied in reduction of premiums (whether or not required to be credited in reduction of premiums under the terms of the contract), or any other item of similar nature. Such term includes advance premiums, premiums deferred and uncollected and premiums due and unpaid, deposits, fees, assessments, and consideration in respect of assuming liabilities under contracts not issued by the taxpayer (such as a payment or transfer of property in an assumption reinsurance transaction), but does not include amounts received from other insurance companies for losses paid under reinsurance contracts.

(2) *Tax base.* The taxable income of mutual insurance companies taxable under section 821 differs from the taxable income of other corporations. See sections 821(b) and 822. Mutual insurance companies have special items of income and special deductions not provided for other corporations. See, for example, sections 821(b)(1)(C), 822(d), 823(b), 824(a), and 825(a). Thus, the computation of mutual insurance company taxable income for a company taxable under section 821(a), and the computation of taxable investment income for a company taxable under section 821(c), must be made in strict accordance with the provisions of part II of subchapter L of the Code.

(3) *Applicability of other provisions.* All provisions of the Code and of the regulations in this part not inconsistent with the specific provisions of part II of subchapter L of the Code are applicable to the assessment and collection of the tax imposed by section 821(a) or (c), and mutual insurance companies subject to the tax imposed by section 821 are subject to the same penalties as are provided in the case of returns and payment of income tax by other corporations. The return shall be on Form 1120M.

(4) *Certain foreign companies.* Foreign mutual insurance companies (other than a life insurance company and other than a fire, flood, or marine insurance company subject to the tax imposed by section 831) not carrying on an insurance business within the United States are not taxable under section 821(a) or (c), but are taxable as other foreign corporations. See section 881.

(b) *Rates of tax imposed by section 821(a)* — (1) *Normal tax.* For taxable years beginning before January 1, 1964, the normal tax imposed under section 821(a) is the lesser of 30 percent of mutual insurance company taxable income, or 60 percent of the amount by which mutual insurance company taxable income exceeds $6,000. In the case of taxable years beginning after December 31, 1963, the normal tax is imposed at the rate of 22 percent of mutual insurance company taxable income, or 44 percent of the amount by which mutual insurance company taxable income exceeds $6,000, whichever is the lesser. For example, a company subject to tax under section 821(a) will file a return but will pay no normal tax if mutual insurance company taxable income does not exceed $6,000. When mutual insurance company taxable income exceeds $6,000 but does not exceed $12,000, the company will pay a normal tax equal to 44 percent (60 percent in the case of taxable years beginning before January 1, 1964), of the amount by which mutual insurance company taxable income exceeds $6,000. When mutual insurance company taxable income exceeds $12,000, the company will pay normal tax at the rate of 22 percent (30 percent in the case of taxable years beginning before January 1, 1964) of such income.

(2) *Surtax*—(i) *Taxable years beginning before January 1, 1964.* For taxable years beginning before January 1, 1964, companies taxable under section 821(a) are subject to a surtax equal to 22 percent of so much of their mutual insur-

ance company taxable income (computed without regard to the deduction provided in section 242 for partially tax-exempt interest) as exceeds $25,000. In the case of an interinsurer or reciprocal underwriter electing to be subject to the limitation provided in section 826(b), the surtax applies to any increase in mutual insurance company taxable income attributable to such election, without regard to the $25,000 surtax exemption otherwise provided by this subparagraph, and without regard to whether the company is liable for any normal tax under subparagraph (1) of this paragraph. See section 826(f) and § 1.826-2.

(ii) *Taxable years beginning after December 31, 1963.* For taxable years beginning after December 31, 1963, companies taxable under section 821(a) are subject to a surtax at the rates and with the exemptions provided in section 11(c) on their mutual insurance company taxable income. In the case of an interinsurer or reciprocal underwriter electing to be subject to the limitation provided in section 826(b), the surtax applies to any increase in mutual insurance company taxable income attributable to such election, without regard to the surtax exemption otherwise provided by section 11(d), and without regard to whether the company is liable for any normal tax under section 821(a)(1) and subparagraph (1) of this paragraph. See section 826(f) and § 1.826-2.

(c) *Mutual insurance company taxable income defined.* The tax imposed by section 821(a) with respect to any taxable year is computed upon mutual insurance company taxable income for the taxable year. Section 821(b) provides that in the case of a mutual insurance company subject to the tax imposed by section 821(a), mutual insurance company taxable income means the amount by which—

(1) The sum of—

(i) The taxable investment income (as defined in section 822(a)(1) and paragraph (a)(1) of § 1.822-8),

(ii) The statutory underwriting income (as defined in section 823(a)(1) and paragraph (b)(1) of § 1.823-6), and

(iii) The amounts required by section 824(d) and paragraph (b)(3) of § 1.824-1 to be subtracted from the protection against loss account, exceeds

(2) The sum of—

(i) The investment loss (as defined in section 822(a)(2) and paragraph (a)(2) of § 1.822-8),

(ii) The statutory underwriting loss (as defined in section 823(a)(2) and paragraph (b)(2) of § 1.823-6), and

(iii) The unused loss deduction provided by section 825(a) and paragraph (a) of § 1.825-1.

If for any taxable year the amount determined under subparagraph (2) of this paragraph equals or exceeds the amount determined under subparagraph (1) of this paragraph, the mutual insurance company taxable income for such year shall be zero.

(d) *Examples.* The application of the tax imposed by section 821(a) may be illustrated by the following examples:

Example (1). (a) M, a mutual casualty insurance company, for the calendar year 1963 has gross receipts from the items described in section 822(b) (other than paragraph (1)(D) thereof) and premiums (including deposits and assessments) in excess of $500,000, and therefore is subject to the tax imposed by section 821(a). M's taxable investment income, computed under section 822, is $30,000 and its statutory underwriting income, computed under section 823, is $15,000. M subtracts $3,000 from its protection against loss account in accordance with the computation made under section 824(d). M has no unused loss deduction. M received no partially tax exempt interest. If M is not subject to section 826, its mutual insurance company taxable income for the taxable year 1963 is $48,000, computed as follows:

(1)	Taxable investment income	$30,000
(2)	Statutory underwriting income	15,000
(3)	Subtractions from protection against loss account	3,000
(4)	Total income items	$48,000
(5)	Investment loss	0
(6)	Statutory underwriting loss	0
(7)	Unused loss deduction	0
(8)	Total loss items	0
(9)	Mutual insurance company taxable income (item (4) minus item (8))	$48,000

(b) Since M's mutual insurance company taxable income is in excess of $12,000, M will pay normal tax on its mutual insurance company taxable income at a rate of 30 percent. In addition, since M's mutual insurance company taxable income exceeds $25,000, M will pay surtax on such excess at a rate of 22 percent. M's total tax liability for the taxable year 1963 is $19,460, computed as follows:

(1)	Mutual insurance company taxable income as computed in item (a)(9)	$48,000
(2)	Normal tax; 30 percent of mutual insurance company taxable income	14,400
(3)	Surtax exemption	25,000
(4)	Mutual insurance company taxable income subject to the surtax (item (1) minus item (3))	23,000

Reg. § 1.821-4(d)

(5) Surtax: 22 percent of mutual insurance company taxable income subject to the surtax 5,060
(6) Total tax (item (2) plus item (5)) 19,460

Example (2). If in example (1), M's mutual insurance company taxable income for 1963 had been in excess of $6,000 but not in excess of $12,000, M would pay normal tax in an amount equal to 60 percent of the amount by which such income exceeded $6,000. Thus, if M had mutual insurance company taxable income of $11,000, M's total tax liability for the taxable year 1963 would be $3,000, computed as follows:

(1) Mutual insurance company taxable income $11,000
(2) Mutual insurance company taxable income in excess of $6,000 ($11,000 minus $6,000).................. 5,000
(3) 30 percent of item (1) 3,300
(4) 60 percent of item (2) 3,000
(5) Normal tax (lesser of items (3) or (4)). 3,000
(6) Surtax exemption 25,000

Since the surtax exemption exceeds the mutual insurance company taxable income for purposes of the surtax, there is no surtax liability. Since the normal tax under section 821(a) is the lesser of 30 percent of mutual insurance company taxable income or 60 percent of the amount by which such income exceeds $6,000, M's normal tax (and total income tax liability) is $3,000. If M's mutual insurance company taxable income was not in excess of $6,000, M would be required to file a return, but would not be liable for any normal tax, since, in such a case, 60 percent of M's mutual insurance company taxable income in excess of $6,000 would be zero.

Example (3). Assume the same income as in example (1) in the 1965 calendar year and that M is not a corporation to which section 1561 (with respect to certain controlled corporations) applies. Since M's mutual insurance company taxable income is in excess of $12,000, M will pay normal tax on its mutual insurance company taxable income at a rate of 22 percent. In addition, since M's mutual insurance company taxable income exceeds the surtax exemption provided in section 11(d) of $25,000, M will pay a surtax on such excess at the rate provided in section 11(c), 26 percent. M's total liability for the taxable year 1964 is $16,540, computed as follows:

(1) Mutual insurance company taxable income as computed in example (1) $48,000
(2) Normal tax: 22 percent of mutual insurance company taxable income for normal tax purposes 10,560
(3) Surtax exemption provided by section 11(d) 25,000

(4) Mutual insurance company taxable income subject to the surtax (item (1) minus item (3)) 23,000
(5) Surtax: at rates provided in section 11(c): 26 percent of mutual insurance company taxable income subject to the surtax............ 5,980
(6) Total tax (item (2) plus item (5)) 16,540

(e) *Alternative tax for certain small mutual insurance companies*—(1) *In general.* (i) Section 821(c) provides an alternative tax for certain small mutual insurance companies. This alternative tax, which is in lieu of the tax imposed by section 821(a), is imposed on taxable investment income (as defined in section 822(a)(1) and paragraph (a)(1) of § 1.822-8) and consists of a normal tax and a surtax. The tax provided by section 821(c) is imposed on every mutual insurance company (other than a life insurance company and other than a fire, flood, or marine insurance company subject to the tax imposed by section 831) which received during the taxable year from the items described in section 822(b) (other than paragraph (1)(D) thereof) and premiums (including deposits and assessments) a gross amount in excess of $150,000 but not in excess of $500,000, except a company which has properly elected under section 821(d) and paragraph (f) of this section to be subject to the tax imposed by section 821(a), or a company which has a balance in its protection against loss account at the beginning of the taxable year.

(ii) Any company which would be taxable under section 821(c) but for the presence of an amount in its protection against loss account at the beginning of the taxable year may elect to subtract the balance from such account. See section 824(d)(5) and § 1.824-3. If such an election is made in such a case, the company shall not be subject to the tax imposed by section 812(a), but shall be subject to the tax imposed by section 821(c).

(2) *Rates of tax imposed by section 821(c)* — (i) *Normal tax.* The normal tax for taxable years beginning before January 1, 1964, is the lesser of 30 percent of taxable investment income or 60 percent of the amount by which taxable investment income exceeds $3,000. For taxable years beginning after December 31, 1963, the normal tax is imposed at the rate of 22 percent of taxable investment income, or 44 percent of the amount by which taxable investment income exceeds $3,000, whichever is the lesser. Thus, a company subject to tax under section 821(c) will file a return but will pay no tax if for the taxable year its taxable investment income does not exceed $3,000; or will pay a normal tax equal to 44 percent (60 percent in the case of taxable years beginning before January 1, 1964), of taxable in-

vestment income in excess of $3,000 when such income exceeds $3,000 but does not exceed $6,000. When taxable investment income exceeds $6,000, the normal tax is imposed at the rate of 22 percent (30 percent in the case of taxable years beginning before January 1, 1964) of such income.

(ii) *Surtax.* For taxable years beginning before January 1, 1964, a surtax is imposed at the rate of 22 percent of taxable investment income (computed without regard to the deduction provided in section 242 for partially tax-exempt interest) in excess of $25,000. For taxable years beginning after December 31, 1963, a surtax is imposed at the rate provided in section 11(c) on taxable investment income in excess of the surtax exemption provided in section 11(d).

(f) *Election to be taxed under section 821(a) —* (1) *In general.* Section 821(d) provides that any mutual insurance company taxable under section 821(c) may elect, in the manner provided by subparagraph (3) of this paragraph, to be taxed under section 821(a).

(2) *Scope of election.* Except as otherwise provided herein, an election made under section 821(d) and this paragraph to be taxable under section 821(a) shall be binding for the taxable year for which made and for all succeeding taxable years unless the Commissioner consents to a revocation of such election. If for any taxable year the gross amount received from the items described in section 822(b) (other than paragraph (1)(D) thereof) and premiums (including deposits and assessments) does not exceed $150,000, a company's prior election made under section 821(d) to be taxable under section 821(a) will automatically terminate and any balance in the protection against loss account will be taken into account for the preceding taxable year. (See section 824(d)(4) and § 1.824-2 for automatic termination of protection against loss account if company is not subject to the tax imposed by section 821(a).) If for any taxable year thereafter the gross amount received exceeds $150,000 but does not exceed $500,000, the company shall be taxable under section 821(c) unless it makes a new election to be taxable under section 821(a). If a company subject to tax under section 821(c) for a taxable year elects under section 821(d) and this section to be taxed under section 821(a) and, in a subsequent taxable year, the gross receipts of such company exceed $500,000, the election made for such earlier taxable year shall be considered as continuing in effect. Thus, such a company will continue to be taxable under section 821(a) notwithstanding that its gross receipts subsequently fall below $500,000 (so long as they do not fall below $150,000) unless the Commissioner consents to a revocation of the prior election. Whether revocation is permissible in any case will depend on the facts and circumstances of the particular case, but in no case will revocation be granted in the absence of a showing that the election creates an undue burden or material hardship on the company due to a substantial change in the character of its operations.

(3) *Time and manner of making election.* The election provided by section 821(d) shall be made in a statement attached to the company's income tax return for the first taxable year for which the election is to apply. The statement shall include the name and address of the taxpayer, shall be signed by the taxpayer (or its duly authorized representative), and shall be filed not later than the date prescribed by law (including extensions thereof) for filing the return for such taxable year.

(g) *Examples.* The application of the tax imposed by section 821(c) may be illustrated by the following examples:

Example (1). M, a mutual casualty insurance company, for the calendar year 1963 has a gross amount received from the items described in section 822(b) (other than paragraph (1)(D) thereof) and premiums (including deposits and assessments) of $400,000. Since M's gross amount received exceeds $150,000, but does not exceed $500,000, M is subject to the tax imposed by section 821(c) on taxable investment income unless it elects to be subject to the tax imposed on mutual insurance company taxable income by section 821(a). M computes its taxable investment income under section 822 to be $35,000. In computing taxable investment income, M deducted $2,000 of partially tax-exempt interest under section 242. If M does not make an election to be taxed under section 821(a), its total tax liability for the taxable year 1963 is $13,140 computed as follows:

(1)	Taxable investment income as computed under section 822	$35,000
(2)	30 percent of taxable investment income	10,500
(3)	60 percent of taxable investment income in excess of $3,000	19,200
(4)	Normal tax (lesser of items (2) or (3))	10,500
(5)	Partially tax-exempt interest deducted in computing taxable investment income	2,000
(6)	Taxable investment income for purposes of the surtax (item (1) plus item (5))	37,000
(7)	Surtax exemption	25,000
(8)	Taxable investment income subject to surtax (item (6) minus item (7))	12,000
(9)	Surtax (22 percent of item (8))	2,640
(10)	Total tax liability (item (4) plus item (9))	13,140

Reg. § 1.821-4(g)

Example (2). N, a mutual casualty insurance company, for the taxable year 1963 has a gross amount received from the items described in section 822(b) (other than paragraph (1)(D) thereof) and premiums (including deposits and assessments) of $210,000. Since N's gross amount received exceeds $150,000 but does not exceed $500,000, N is subject to the tax imposed by section 821(c) on taxable investment income unless it elects to be subject to the tax imposed by section 821(a). Furthermore, since the gross amount received by N does not exceed $250,000, N is entitled to the special tax reduction provided by section 821(c)(2). N computes its taxable investment income under section 822 to be $24,000. In computing taxable investment income, N deducted $2,000 of partially tax-exempt interest under section 242. If N does not make an election to be taxed under section 821(a), its total tax liability for the taxable year 1963 is $4,452 computed as follows:

(1)	Taxable investment income as computed under section 822	$24,000
(2)	30 percent of taxable investment income	7,200
(3)	60 percent of taxable investment income in excess of $3,000	12,600
(4)	Normal tax (lesser of items (2) or (3))	7,200
(5)	Partially tax-exempt interest deducted in computing taxable investment income	2,000
(6)	Taxable investment income for purposes of the surtax (item (1) plus item (5))	26,000
(7)	Surtax exemption	25,000
(8)	Taxable investment income subject to surtax (item (6) minus item (7))	1,000
(9)	Surtax (22 percent of item (8))	220
(10)	Tax liability computed without regard to special reduction (item (4) plus item (9))	7,420
(11)	Amount by which gross receipts exceed $150,000 ($210,000 gross receipts minus $150,000)	60,000
(12)	Percentage which item (11) bears to $100,000 ($60,000 over $100,000)	60 percent
(13)	Tax as adjusted (percentage determined in item (12) applied to item (10))	4,452

If N's taxable investment income for purposes of the surtax did not exceed $3,000, N would file a return but would pay no tax. Had N elected (under section 821(d)) to be subject to tax under section 821(a), N would not be entitled to the special reduction afforded by section 821(c)(2), since that provision applies only to companies taxable under section 821(c). [Reg. § 1.821-4.]

☐ [T.D. 6681, 10-16-63. Amended by T.D. 7100, 3-19-71.]

[Reg. § 1.821-5]

§ 1.821-5. **Special transitional underwriting loss.**—(a) *In general.* Section 821(f) provides a special reduction in the statutory underwriting income (as defined by section 823(a)(1) and paragraph (b)(1) of § 1.823-6) of any company taxable under section 821(a) which was taxable under section 821 for the five taxable years immediately preceding January 1, 1962, and which incurred an underwriting loss (as defined in section 821(f)(3) and paragraph (c) of this section) for each of such five taxable years.

(b) *Amount of reduction.* In the case of a company described in section 821(f)(1) and paragraph (a) of this section the statutory underwriting income for the taxable year (determined without regard to this paragraph) shall be reduced by an amount equal to the amount by which—

(1) The sum of the underwriting losses of such company for the five taxable years immediately preceding January 1, 1962, exceeds

(2) The total amount by which the company's statutory underwriting income was reduced by reason of section 821(f) and this section for prior taxable years.

(c) *Underwriting loss defined.* For purposes of computing the amount of the reduction available under section 821(f) and paragraph (a) of this section, the term underwriting loss means statutory underwriting loss (as defined by section 823(a)(2) and paragraph (b)(2) of § 1.823-6) computed without any deduction under section 824(a) and paragraph (a) of § 1.824-1 (relating to deduction to provide protection against losses) and without any deduction under section 832(c)(11) (relating to dividends and similar distributions paid or declared to policyholders). For rules relating to the definition of dividends and similar distributions paid or declared to policyholders, see paragraph (a) of § 1.832-5.

(d) *Years of applicability.* Section 821(f)(4) provides that the special reduction of statutory underwriting income allowed by section 821(f)(2) and paragraph (b) of this section shall apply to any taxable year beginning after December 31, 1962, and before January 1, 1968, for which the taxpayer is subject to the tax imposed by section 821(a). [Reg. § 1.821-5.]

☐ [T.D. 6681, 10-16-63.]

Reg. § 1.821-5(a)

Life Insurance Companies

See p. 20,601 for regulations not amended to reflect law changes

→ *Caution: Reg. §§ 1.822-4–1.822-12, below, were issued under former Code Sec. 822, which was redesignated as Code Sec. 834.* ←

[Reg. § 1.822-4]

§ 1.822-4. **Taxable years affected.**—Sections 1.822-1 through 1.822-3 are applicable only to taxable years beginning after December 31, 1953, but before January 1, 1955, and ending after August 16, 1954, and all references to sections of Part II, subchapter L, chapter 1 of the Code are to the Internal Revenue Code of 1954, before amendments. Sections 1.822-5 through 1.822-7 [reproduced at 674 CCH ¶ 4042B-4042D] are applicable only to taxable years beginning after December 31, 1954, but before January 1, 1963, and all references to sections of part II, subchapter L, chapter 1 of the Code are to the Internal Revenue Code of 1954, as amended by the Life Insurance Company Tax Act for 1955 (70 Stat. 36). Sections 1.822-8 through 1.822-12 are applicable only to taxable years beginning after December 31, 1962, and all references to sections of parts II and III, subchapter L, chapter 1 of the Code are to the Internal Revenue Code of 1954 as amended by section 8 of the Revenue Act of 1962 (76 Stat. 989). [Reg. § 1.822-4.]

☐ [*T.D.* 6610, 8-30-62. Amended by *T.D.* 6681, 10-16-63.]

[Reg. § 1.822-8]

§ 1.822-8. **Determination of taxable investment income.**—(a) *In general*—(1) *Taxable investment income defined.* Section 822(a)(1) defines the term "taxable investment income" for purposes of part II, subchapter L, chapter 1 of the Code as the gross investment income (as defined in section 822(b) and paragraph (b) of this section), less the deductions provided in section 822(c) and paragraph (c) of this section for wholly tax-exempt interest, investment expenses, real estate expenses, depreciation, interest paid or accrued, capital losses, special deductions, trade or business (other than an insurance business) expenses, and depletion. However, such expenses are deductible only to the extent that they relate to investment income and the deduction of such expenses is not disallowed by any other provision of subtitle A of the Code. For example, investment expenses are not allowable unless they are ordinary and necessary expenses within the meaning of section 162. In addition to the limitations on deductions relating to real estate owned and occupied by a mutual insurance company subject to the tax imposed by section 821 provided in section 822(d)(1), the adjustment for amortization of premium and accrual of discount provided in section 822(d)(2), and the limitation on the deduction for investment expenses where general expenses are allocated to investment income provided in section 822(c)(2), mutual insurance companies subject to the tax imposed by section 821(a) or (c) are subject to the limitation on deductions relating to wholly tax-exempt income provided in section 265. Such companies are not entitled to the net operating loss deduction provided in section 172. See, however, section 825 and paragraph (a) of § 1.825-1 for unused loss deduction allowed companies taxable under section 821(a). A deduction shall not be permitted with respect to the same item more than once.

(2) *Investment loss defined.* The term "investment loss" is defined by section 822(a)(2) as the amount by which the deductions allowable under section 822(c) and paragraph (c) of this section exceed the gross investment income (as defined in section 822(b) and paragraph (b) of this section).

(b) *Gross investment income defined.* For purposes of part II, subchapter L, chapter 1 of the Code, section 822(b) defines the term "gross investment income" of a mutual insurance company subject to the tax imposed by section 821(a) or (c) as the sum of the following:

(1) The gross amount of income during the taxable year from—

(i) Interest (including tax-exempt interest and partially tax-exempt interest), as described in § 1.61-7. Interest shall be adjusted for amortization of premium and accrual of discount in accordance with the rules prescribed in section 822(d)(2) and § 1.822-10;

(ii) Dividends, as described in § 1.61-9;

(iii) Rents and royalties, as described in § 1.61-8;

(iv) The entering into of any lease, mortgage or other instrument or agreement from which the company may derive interest, rents, or royalties;

(v) The alteration or termination of any instrument or agreement described in subdivision (iv) of this subparagraph;

(vi) Gains from sales or exchanges of capital assets to the extent provided in subchapter P (section 1201 and following, relating to capital gains and losses), chapter 1 of the Code.

(2) The gross income from any trade or business (other than an insurance business) carried on by a mutual insurance company subject to the tax imposed by section 821(a) or (c), or by a partnership of which the insurance company is a partner. For example, gross investment income includes amounts received as commitment fees, or as a

Reg. § 1.822-8(b)(2)

Life Insurance Companies

See p. 20,601 for regulations not amended to reflect law changes

→ *Caution: Reg. §§ 1.822-4–1.822-12, below, were issued under former Code Sec. 822, which was redesignated as Code Sec. 834.* ←

bonus for the entering into of a lease, or as a penalty for the early payment of a mortgage. In computing the gross income from any trade or business (other than an insurance business) carried on by the insurance company, or by a partnership of which the insurance company is a partner, any item described in section 822(b)(1) and paragraph (b)(1) of this section shall not be considered as gross income arising from the conduct of such trade or business, but shall be taken into account under section 822(b)(1) and paragraph (b)(1) of this section.

(c) *Deductions from gross investment income*—(1) *Wholly tax-exempt interest.* Interest which in the case of other taxpayers is excluded from gross income by section 103 but included in the gross investment income by section 822(b) is allowed as a deduction from gross investment income by section 822(c)(1).

(2) *Investment expenses.* (i) The deduction for investment expenses under section 822(c)(2) includes only those expenses of the taxable year which are fairly chargeable against gross investment income. For example, investment expenses include salaries and expenses paid exclusively for work in looking after investments, and amounts expended for printing, stationery, postage, and stenographic work incident to the collection of interest. An itemized schedule of such expenses shall be attached to the return.

(ii) Any assignment of general expenses to the investment department of a mutual insurance company subject to the tax imposed by section 821(a) or (c) subjects the entire deduction for investment expenses to the limitation provided in section 822(c)(2) and subdivision (iii) of this subparagraph. As used in section 822(c)(2), the term "general expenses" means any expense paid or incurred for the benefit of more than one department of the company rather than for the benefit of a particular department thereof. For example, if an expense, such as a salary, is attributable to more than one department, including the investment department, such expense may be properly allocated among these departments. If such expense is allocated, the amount properly allocable to the investment department shall be deductible as general expenses assigned to or included in investment expenses and as such shall be subject to the limitation of section 822(c)(2) and subdivision (iii) of this subparagraph. However, a company subject to the tax imposed by section 821(a) or (c) shall not deduct under section 822(c)(2) its real estate taxes, depreciation, or other expenses with respect to any portion of the real estate which it owns, irrespective of whether such items are properly allocable to its investment department. For the rules relating to the deductibility of these items, see section 822(c)(3) and (4) and subparagraphs (3) and (4) of this paragraph. If general expenses are in part assigned to or included in investment expenses, the maximum allowance (as determined under section 822(c)(2)) shall not be granted unless it is shown to the satisfaction of the district director that such allowance is justified by a reasonable assignment of actual expenses. The accounting procedure employed is not conclusive as to whether any assignment has in fact been made. Investment expenses do not include Federal income and excess profits taxes, if any.

(iii) If any general expenses are in part assigned to or included in investment expenses, the total deduction under section 822(c)(2) shall not exceed the sum of—

(*a*) One-fourth of 1 percent of the mean of the book value of the invested assets held at the beginning and end of the taxable year, plus

(*b*) One-fourth of the amount by which taxable investment income (computed without any deduction for investment expenses, tax-free interest, partially tax-exempt interest, or dividends received) exceeds $3\frac{3}{4}$ percent of the book value of the mean of the invested assets held at the beginning and end of the taxable year.

For purposes of section 822(c)(2) and this paragraph, the term "invested assets" means only those assets which are owned and used, and to the extent used, for the purpose of producing the income specified in section 822(b). See paragraph (b) of this section. The term does not include real estate owned and occupied, and to the extent owned and occupied, by the company.

(3) *Real estate expenses and taxes.* The deduction for real estate expenses and taxes under section 822(c)(3) includes taxes (as defined in section 164) and other expenses for the taxable year exclusively on or with respect to real estate owned by the company. For example, no deduction shall be allowed under section 822(c)(3) for amounts allowed as a deduction under section 164(e) (relating to taxes of shareholders paid by a corporation). No deduction shall be allowed under section 822(c)(3) for any amount paid out for new buildings, or for permanent improvements or betterments made to increase the value of any property. An itemized schedule of such taxes and expenses shall be attached to the return. See § 1.822-9 for limitation of such deduction.

Reg. § 1.822-8(c)(1)

Life Insurance Companies

See p. 20,601 for regulations not amended to reflect law changes

→ *Caution: Reg. §§ 1.822-4–1.822-12, below, were issued under former Code Sec. 822, which was redesignated as Code Sec. 834.* ←

(4) *Depreciation.* The deduction allowed by section 822(c)(4) for depreciation is, except as provided in section 822(d)(1) and § 1.822-9, identical to that allowed other corporations by section 167. Such amount allowed as a deduction from gross investment income in determining taxable investment income is limited to depreciation sustained on the property used, and to the extent used, for the purpose of producing the income specified in section 822(b).

(5) *Interest paid or accrued.* The deduction allowed by section 822(c)(5) for interest on indebtedness is the same as that allowed other corporations by section 163. See § 1.163-1.

(6) *Capital losses.* (i) The deduction for capital losses under section 822(c)(6) includes not only capital losses to the extent provided in subchapter P, chapter 1 of the Code but in addition thereto losses from capital assets sold or exchanged to provide funds to meet abnormal insurance losses and to provide for the payment of dividends and similar distributions to policyholders. Losses in the latter case may be deducted from ordinary income while the deduction for losses under subchapter P is limited to the gains. See section 1211.

(ii) Capital assets are considered as sold or exchanged to provide for the funds or payments specified in section 822(c)(6), to the extent that the gross receipts from the sale or exchange of such assets are not greater than the excess, if any, for the taxable year of the sum of dividends and similar distributions paid to policyholders, and losses and expenses paid over the sum of the items described in section 822(b) (other than paragraph (1)(D) thereof) and net premiums received. If, by reason of a particular sale or exchange of a capital asset, gross receipts are greater than such excess, the gross receipts and the resulting loss should be apportioned and the excess included in capital losses subject to the provisions of subchapter P. Capital losses actually used to reduce net income in any taxable year may not again be used in a succeeding taxable year as an offset against capital gains in that year and for that purpose a special rule is set forth for the application of section 1212.

(iii) The application of section 822(c)(6) may be illustrated by the following examples:

Example (1). The X Company, a mutual fire insurance company subject to tax under section 821, in the taxable year 1963 sells capital assets in order to obtain funds to meet abnormal insurance losses and to provide for the payment of dividends and similar distributions to policyholders. The gross receipts from the sale are $60,000, resulting in losses of $20,000. It pays dividends to policyholders of $150,000. It sustains losses of $25,000, and pays expenses of $25,000. It receives interest of $50,000, dividends of $5,000, royalties of $4,000, and net premiums of $66,000. The excess of the sum of dividends, losses, and expenses paid ($200,000) over the sum of the items described in section 822(b) (other than paragraph (1)(D) thereof) and net premiums received ($125,000) is $75,000. Since the gross receipts from the sale of capital assets ($60,000) do not exceed such excess ($75,000), the losses of $20,000 are allowable as a deduction from gross investment income in computing taxable investment income under section 822.

Example (2). If in example (1) the gross receipts were $76,000 and the last capital asset sold, for the purpose therein specified, resulted in gross receipts of $2,000 and a loss of $500, the losses allowable as a deduction from gross investment income would be $19,750. The last sale made the gross receipts of $76,000 exceed by $1,000 the excess ($75,000) of the sum of dividends, losses, and expenses paid ($200,000) over the sum of the items described in section 822(b) (other than paragraph (1)(D) thereof) and net premiums received ($125,000). The gross receipts and the resulting loss from the last sale are apportioned on the basis of the ratio of the excess of $1,000 to the gross receipts of $2,000, or 50 percent. Fifty percent of the loss of $500 is deducted from the total loss of $20,000. The remaining gross receipts of $1,000 and the proportionate loss of $250 should be reported as capital losses under subchapter P.

Example (3). If in example (1) the X Company had taxable investment income for purposes of the surtax of $9,750 and, under the provisions of subchapter P, chapter 1 of the Code, had capital losses of $18,000 and capital gains of $10,000, the net capital loss for the taxable year 1963, in applying section 1212 for the purposes of section 822(c)(6), would be $8,000. This is determined by subtracting from total losses of $38,000 ($18,000 capital losses under subchapter P plus $20,000 other capital losses under section 822(c)(6)) the sum of capital gains of $10,000 and losses from the sale or exchange of capital assets sold or exchanged to obtain funds to meet abnormal insurance losses and to provide for the payment of dividends and similar distributions to policyholders of $20,000. Such losses of $20,000 are added to capital gains of $10,000, since they are less than taxable investment income for purposes of the surtax, computed without regard to gains or losses

Reg. § 1.822-8(c)(6)

45,812 **Life Insurance Companies**

See p. 20,601 for regulations not amended to reflect law changes

→ *Caution: Reg. §§ 1.822-4–1.822-12, below, were issued under former Code Sec. 822, which was redesignated as Code Sec. 834.*←

from sales or exchanges of capital assets, of $29,750 ($9,750 taxable investment income for purposes of the surtax plus $20,000 other capital losses under section 822(c)(6) plus the portion of capital losses allowable under subchapter P of $10,000 minus capital gains under subchapter P of $10,000).

(7) *Special deductions.* Section 822(c)(7) allows a mutual insurance company the special deductions provided by part VIII (section 241 and following), except section 248, subchapter B, chapter 1 of the Code, relating to partially tax-exempt interest and to dividends received. In applying section 246(b) (relating to limitation on aggregate amount of deductions for dividends received) for purposes of this subparagraph, the reference in such section to "taxable income" shall be treated as a reference to "taxable investment income".

(8) *Trade or business deductions.* (i) Under section 822(c)(8), the deductions allowed by subtitle A of the Code (without regard to this part) which are attributable to any trade or business (other than an insurance business) carried on by the insurance company, or by a partnership of which the company is a partner are, subject to the limitations in subdivision (ii) of this subparagraph, allowable as deductions from gross investment income in computing taxable investment income. Such deductions are allowable, however, only to the extent that they relate to income which is included in the company's gross investment income by reason of section 822(b)(2). Thus, a deduction shall not be allowed under section 822(c)(8) with respect to any item described in section 822(b)(1). The allowable deductions may exceed the gross income from such business.

(ii) In computing the deductions under section 822(c)(8)—

(a) Any item, to the extent attributable to the carrying on of the insurance business, shall not be taken into account. For example, if the company operates a radio station primarily to advertise its own insurance services, a portion of the expenses of the radio station shall not be allowed as a deduction. The portion disallowed shall be an amount which bears the same ratio to the total expenses of the station as the value of advertising furnished to the insurance company bears to the total value of services rendered by the station.

(b) The deduction for net operating losses provided in section 172 shall not be allowed.

(9) *Depletion.* The deduction allowed by Section 822(c)(9) for depletion is the same as that allowed life insurance companies under section 804(c)(4). See paragraph (b)(5) of § 1.804-4. [Reg. § 1.822-8.]

☐ [T.D. 6681, 10-16-63.]

[Reg. § 1.822-9]

§ 1.822-9. Real estate owned and occupied.—Section 822(d)(1) provides that the amount allowable as a deduction for taxes, expenses, and depreciation on or with respect to any real estate owned and occupied in whole or in part by a mutual insurance company subject to the tax imposed by section 821(a) or (c) shall be limited to an amount which bears the same ratio to such deduction (computed without regard to this limitation) as the rental value of the space not so occupied bears to the rental value of the entire property. For example, if the rental value of the space not occupied by the company is equal to one-half of the rental value of the entire property, the deduction for taxes, expenses, and depreciation is one-half of the taxes, expenses, and depreciation on account of the entire property. Where a deduction is claimed as provided in this section, the parts of the property occupied and the parts not occupied by the company, together with the respective rental values thereof, must be shown in a statement accompanying the return. [Reg. § 1.822-9.]

☐ [T.D. 6681, 10-16-63.]

[Reg. § 1.822-10]

§ 1.822-10. Amortization of premium and accrual of discount.—(a) *In general.* In computing taxable investment income for the taxable year, the gross amount of income from interest, the deduction under section 822(c)(1) for wholly tax-exempt interest, and the deduction under section 242 for partially tax-exempt interest, are, under the provisions of section 822(d)(2), each to be decreased by the appropriate amortization of premium and increased by the appropriate accrual of discount attributable to the taxable year on bonds, notes, debentures, or other evidences of indebtedness held by a mutual insurance company subject to the tax imposed by section 821(a) or (c). However, only the accrual of discount relating to issue discount will increase the deduction for wholly tax-exempt interest. See section 103. Such amortization and accrual is the same as that provided for life insurance companies by section 818(b)(1), as amended by the Life Insurance Company Income Tax Act of 1959 (73 Stat. 133), and shall be determined in accordance with

Reg. § 1.822-9

→ **Caution:** Reg. §§ 1.822-4–1.822-12, below, were issued under former Code Sec. 822, which was redesignated as Code Sec. 834. ←

paragraphs (a) and (b) of § 1.818-3, except as provided by paragraph (b) of this section.

(b) *Modifications.* (1) Paragraph (b) of § 1.818-3 shall apply to mutual casualty insurance companies subject to the tax imposed by section 821(a) or (c) without regard to the date of acquisition of the particular securities to which the amortization of premium or accrual of discount is attributable.

(2) In computing the amount of premium or discount for purposes of section 822(d)(2) with respect to securities held by a company taxable under section 821, the basis provided by section 1012 shall be used in lieu of the acquisition value provided by paragraph (b) of § 1.818-3. In the case of a company subject to the tax imposed by section 821(c), adjustments to basis to reflect the accrual of discount and the amortization of premium shall be made in the manner provided by paragraphs (a) and (b) of § 1.818-3. However, for purposes of determining statutory underwriting income or loss for the taxable year under section 823, a company subject to the tax imposed by section 821(a) is not required to accrue discount or to amortize premium in computing its income under section 832 as if it were subject to the tax imposed by section 831. Thus, the accrual of discount and amortization of premium required in the computation of taxable investment income by a company subject to the tax imposed by section 821(a) neither increases nor decreases the mutual insurance company taxable income of such a company and, except to the extent such a company actually accrues discount or amortizes premium for purposes of making the section 832 computation, no adjustment shall be made to the basis of obligations held by it to reflect accrual of discount or amortization of premium. [Reg. § 1.822-10.]

☐ [*T.D.* 6681, 10-16-63.]

[Reg. § 1.822-11]

§ 1.822-11. Net premiums.—The term "net premiums", defined in section 822(f)(1), includes deposits and assessments, but excludes amounts returned to policyholders which are treated as dividends under section 822(f)(2). Net premiums are used in sections 822(c)(6) and 832(c)(5) in determining the limitation on certain capital losses and in the application of section 1212. [Reg. § 1.822-11.]

☐ [*T.D.* 6681, 10-16-63.]

[Reg. § 1.822-12]

§ 1.822-12. Dividends to policyholders.—(a) Dividends to policyholders are used in determining the "underwriting loss" for purposes of the special transitional underwriting loss deduction provided by section 821(f), and the limitation on capital losses under section 822(c)(6); in computing statutory underwriting income or loss under section 823, and the subtractions from the protection against loss account under section 824(d). The term "dividends to policyholders" is defined in section 822(f)(2) as dividends and similar distributions paid or declared to policyholders. It includes amounts returned to policyholders where the amount is not fixed in the insurance contract but depends upon the experience of the company or the discretion of the management. Such amounts are not to be treated as return premiums under section 822(f)(1). Savings credited to the individual accounts of the subscribers of a reciprocal underwriter or interinsurer under section 823(b)(2) are not dividends paid or declared within the meaning of this paragraph. However, distributions in respect of such credits shall be considered as dividends paid. See section 823(b)(2) and paragraph (c)(2) of § 1.823-6. The term "paid or declared" is to be construed according to the method of accounting regularly employed in keeping the books of the insurance company, and such method shall be consistently followed with respect to all deductions (including dividends and similar distributions to policyholders) and all items of income.

(b) If the method of accounting so employed is the cash receipts and disbursements method, the deduction is limited to the dividends and similar distributions actually paid to policyholders in the taxable year. If, on the other hand, the method of accounting so employed is the accrual method, the deduction, or a reasonably accurate estimate thereof, for dividends and similar distributions declared to policyholders for any taxable year will, in general, be computed by adding the amount of dividends and similar distributions declared but unpaid at the end of the taxable year to dividends and similar distributions paid during the taxable year and deducting dividends and similar distributions declared but unpaid at the beginning of the taxable year. If an insurance company using the accrual method does not compute the deduction for dividends and similar distributions declared to policyholders in the manner stated, it must submit with its return a full and complete explanation of the manner in which the deduction is computed. For the rule as to when dividends are considered paid, see the regulations under section 561. [Reg. § 1.822-12.]

☐ [*T.D.* 6681, 10-16-63.]

[Reg. § 1.823-6]

§ 1.823-6. Determination of statutory underwriting income or loss.—(a) *In general.* Section 823(a) and this section provide that for purposes of determining statutory underwriting income or loss for the taxable year, a mutual insurance company subject to the tax imposed by section 821(a) must first take into account the same gross income and deduction items (except as modified by section 823(b) and paragraph (c) of this section) as a taxpayer subject to tax under section 831 would take into account for purposes of determining its taxable income under section 832. These items are then reduced to the extent that they include amounts which are included in determining taxable investment income or loss under section 822(a) and § 1.822-8. In addition, in computing its statutory underwriting income or loss for the taxable year, a company taxable under section 821(a) is allowed to deduct the amount determined under section 824(a) (relating to deduction to provide protection against losses) and, if its gross amount received is less than $1,000,000, is allowed to deduct the amount determined under section 823(c) and paragraph (d) of this section (relating to special deduction for certain small companies), subject to the limitations provided therein.

(b) *Definitions*—(1) *Statutory underwriting income defined.* Section 823(a)(1) defines the term "statutory underwriting income" for purposes of part II of subchapter L of the Code. Subject to the modifications provided by section 823(b) and paragraph (c) of this section, statutory underwriting income is defined as the amount by which—

(i) The gross income which would be taken into account in computing taxable income under section 832 if the taxpayer were subject to the tax imposed by section 831, reduced by the gross investment income (as determined under section 822(b)), exceeds

(ii) The sum of—

(*a*) The deductions which would be taken into account in computing taxable income if the taxpayer were subject to the tax imposed by section 831, reduced by the deductions provided in section 822(c) (relating to deductions allowed in computing taxable investment income), plus

(*b*) The deductions provided in section 823(c) (relating to special deduction for small company having gross amount of less than $1,100,000) and section 824(a) (relating to deduction to provide protection against losses).

For purposes of subdivision (ii)(*a*), the limitations on the amounts deductible under paragraphs (9) (relating to charitable, etc., contributions) and (12) (relating to partially tax-exempt interest and to dividends received) of section 832(c) shall be computed by reference to taxable income as defined by section 832(a), and as modified by section 823(b) and paragraph (c) of this section.

(2) *Statutory underwriting loss defined.* "Statutory underwriting loss" is defined in section 823(a)(2) as the amount by which the amount determined under section 823(a)(1)(B) and subparagraph (1)(ii) of this paragraph exceeds the amount determined under section 823(a)(1)(A) and subparagraph (1)(i) of this paragraph.

(c) *Modifications*—(1) *Net operating losses.* In applying section 832 for purposes of determining statutory underwriting income or loss under section 823(a) and paragraph (b) of this section, the deduction for net operating losses provided by section 172 is not allowed. However, see section 825(a) and § 1.825-1 for unused loss deduction allowed companies taxable under section 821(a) in computing mutual insurance company taxable income under section 821(b).

(2) *Interinsurers and reciprocal underwriters*—(i) *In general.* Section 823(b)(2) provides that in computing the statutory underwriting income or loss of a mutual insurance company which is an interinsurer or reciprocal underwriter, there shall be allowed as a deduction the increase for the taxable year in savings credited to subscriber accounts, or there shall be included as an item of gross income the decrease for the taxable year in savings credited to subscriber accounts. For purposes of this subparagraph, the term "savings credited to subscriber accounts" means such portion of the surplus for the taxable year as is credited to the individual accounts of subscribers before the 16th day of the third month following the close of the taxable year, but only if the company would be obligated to pay such amount promptly to such subscriber if he terminated his contract at the close of the company's taxable year, and only if the company mails notification to such subscriber of the amount credited to his individual account in the manner provided by subdivision (v) of this subparagraph.

(ii) *Limitations.* Amounts representing return premiums (as defined in paragraph (a)(1)(ii) of § 1.809-4) which the company would be obligated to pay to any subscriber terminating his contract at the close of the company's taxable year are not savings credited to subscriber accounts within the meaning of section 823(b)(2) and subdivision (i) of this subparagraph. The deduction for savings credited to individual subscriber accounts is allowed only in the case of reciprocal underwriters or interinsurers where the

Reg. § 1.823-6(a)

subscriber or policyholder has not only a legally enforceable right to receive the amount so credited if he withdraws from the exchange, but where the amounts credited, as a matter of actual practice, are paid to subscribers or policyholders who terminate their contracts. Thus, no deduction shall be allowed for savings credited to subscriber accounts if such savings are not in fact promptly returned to subscribers when they terminate their contracts.

(iii) *Computation of increase or decrease in savings credited to subscriber accounts.* For purposes of determining the increase or decrease for the taxable year in savings credited to subscriber accounts, every reciprocal underwriter or interinsurer claiming a deduction under section 823(b)(2) and this section shall establish and maintain an account for savings credited to subscriber accounts. The opening balance in such account for the first taxable year for which a deduction is claimed under section 823(b)(2) and this section shall be zero. In each taxable year there shall be added to such account the total amount of savings credited to subscriber accounts for the taxable year, and there shall be subtracted from such account the total amount of savings subtracted from subscriber accounts for the taxable year. However, in no case may the amount added to the account exceed the total amount of savings to subscribers for the taxable year, irrespective of the amount of savings credited to subscriber accounts for the taxable year. Credits made to subscriber accounts after the close of the taxable year and before the 16th day of the third month following the close of the taxable year will be taken into account as if such amounts had been credited on the last day of the taxable year to the extent such amounts would have become fixed and determinable legal obligations due subscribers if such subscribers had terminated their contracts on the last day of the company's taxable year unless, at the time the amounts are credited, the company specifically designates such amounts as being from surplus for the taxable year in which the amounts were actually credited. Such a designation, once made, shall be irrevocable. However, if a company credited savings to subscriber accounts after December 31, 1962, and before March 16, 1963, and failed to designate such credits as being from surplus for the taxable year 1963, such company may designate such credits as being from surplus for the taxable year 1963 for purposes of determining the total amount of credits to subscriber accounts for such year. In determining the total amount of savings subtracted from subscriber accounts for the taxable year, only amounts subtracted from savings credited for taxable years beginning with the first taxable year for which a deduction was claimed under section 823(b)(2) and this subparagraph will be taken into account. The method of accounting regularly employed by the taxpayer in keeping its books of account will be used for purposes of determining whether the amounts subtracted from the subscriber accounts are from savings for taxable years beginning before the first taxable year for which a deduction is claimed under section 823(b)(2) and this subparagraph, or from savings for taxable years beginning with such first taxable year. Where the method of accounting regularly employed by the taxpayer in keeping its books of account does not clearly indicate whether an amount was subtracted from savings credited to subscriber accounts for taxable years beginning before the first taxable year for which a deduction is claimed under section 823(b)(2) and this subparagraph, or from savings credited for such first taxable year and subsequent taxable years, the amount subtracted will be deemed to have come from savings credited to subscriber accounts for all taxable years, on a pro rata basis. Where an amount is subtracted from a subscriber's account for record purposes, but such subtraction does not reflect the discharge of the company's legal obligation to pay the amount subtracted promptly to the subscriber if he terminates his contract, then such subtraction shall not be taken into account for purposes of section 823(b)(2) and this subparagraph. On the other hand, where the company ceases to be under a legal obligation to pay promptly to any subscriber the amount credited to his individual account, then such amount shall be considered as having been subtracted from such subscriber's account at the time such obligation ceased to exist. For purposes of section 823(b)(2) and this subparagraph, the increase (if any) for the taxable year in savings credited to subscriber accounts shall be the amount by which the balance in the account for savings credited to subscriber accounts as of the close of the taxable year exceeds the balance in such account as of the close of the preceding taxable year; and the decrease (if any) for the taxable year in savings credited to subscriber accounts shall be the amount by which the balance in the account for savings credited to subscriber accounts as of the close of the preceding taxable year exceeds the balance in such account as of the close of the taxable year.

(iv) *Legal obligation.* For purposes of this subparagraph, the existence of a legal obligation on the part of the company to pay to the subscriber the savings credited to him will be determined under the insurance contract pursuant to which the credits are made. Where it appears that the company is otherwise legally obligated to pay

Reg. § 1.823-6(c)(2)

amounts credited to its subscribers, the requisite legal obligation will not be considered absent merely because a subscriber's credits remain subject to absorption by future losses incurred if left on deposit with the company.

(v) *Notification to subscribers.* Every reciprocal underwriter or interinsurer claiming a deduction under section 823(b)(2) and this subparagraph for amounts credited to the individual accounts of its subscribers must mail to each such subscriber written notification of the amount credited to the subscriber's account for the taxable year, the date on which such amount was credited, and the date on which the subscriber's right to such amount first would have become fixed if such subscriber had terminated his contract at the close of the company's taxable year. As an alternative to providing each subscriber with specific information relating to the amount of savings credited to his individual account, the notification required by this subdivision may be provided in the form of a table or formula mailed to the subscribers. However, a table or formula may not be used in lieu of the specific notification required by this subdivision unless such table or formula has been approved by the Commissioner. Generally, a table or formula will be approved if it enables the subscriber to simply and readily ascertain the amount of savings credited to his individual account for the taxable year, the date on which such amount was credited, and the date on which his right to such amount first would have become fixed if he had terminated his contract at the close of the company's taxable year. A reciprocal underwriter or interinsurer which desires to use such a table or formula should direct a written request for approval of such table or formula to the Commissioner of Internal Revenue, Attention: T:R, Washington, D.C., 20224. Such request must set forth a copy of the table or formula proposed to be used, together with sufficient information to permit the Commissioner to determine the basis upon which such table or formula was prepared and the manner in which the subscribers will use such table or formula in determining the amounts credited to their individual accounts. Once a table or formula has been approved, the use of such table or formula with respect to savings credited for subsequent taxable years will not require further approval unless the basis upon which such table or formula was prepared, or the manner in which such table or formula is to be applied, is substantially changed. The table or formula method of notification may be used with respect to all or less than all of the company's subscribers. For example, the company might provide the notification required by this subdivision to one class of subscribers in the form of a table or formula mailed to the individual subscribers, while providing another class of subscribers with specific statements of the amounts credited to their individual accounts. The notification required by this subdivision must be mailed before the 16th day of the third month following the close of the reciprocal's taxable year for which the account was credited. Where for any taxable year a reciprocal underwriter or interinsurer claims a deduction under section 823(b) and this subparagraph and fails to give notice as required by this subdivision, such deduction shall not be allowed unless the reciprocal establishes to the satisfaction of the district director that the failure to mail such notice within the prescribed period was due to reasonable cause.

(d) *Special deduction for small company having gross amount of less than $1,100,000*—(1) *In general.* In the case of a taxpayer subject to the tax imposed by section 821(a), section 823(c) provides that if the gross amount received during the taxable year from the items described in section 822(b) (other than paragraph (1)(D) thereof) and premiums (including deposits and assessments) is less than $1,100,000, then, subject to the limitation provided in section 823(c)(2) and subparagraph (2) of this paragraph, there shall be allowed an additional deduction for purposes of determining statutory underwriting income or loss under section 823(a) for the taxable year. The amount of the additional deduction is $6,000; except that if the gross amount received for the taxable year exceeds $500,000, the additional deduction is limited to an amount equal to 1 percent of the amount by which $1,100,000 exceeds such gross amount.

(2) *Limitation.* The amount of the deduction provided by section 823(c)(1) may not exceed the statutory underwriting income for the taxable year, computed without regard to the deduction allowed under section 823(c)(1) and subparagraph (1) of this paragraph, and the deduction allowed under section 824(a) (relating to deduction for protection against losses).

(3) *Example.* The application of section 823(c) and this paragraph may be illustrated by the following example:

M, a mutual insurance company subject to the tax imposed by section 821(a), has the following items for the taxable year 1963:

Gross amount for purposes of section 823(c)(1)	$800,000
Gross investment income (including capital gains)	150,000
Capital gains	100,000
Gross income under section 832	900,000
Deductions under section 822(c)	22,000

Reg. § 1.823-6(d)(1)

Deductions under section 832 (as modified
by section 823(b)(2)) 746,000

Under the provisions of section 823(c), M's special small company deduction for the taxable year 1963 would be $3,000, computed as follows:

(1) Gross amount for purposes of section
  823(c)(1) $800,000
(2) Amount by which $1,100,000 exceeds
  item (1) ($1,100,000 minus
  $800,000)...................... 300,000
(3) 1 percent of item (2) (not to exceed
  $6,000) 3,000
(4) Gross income under section 832,
  reduced by gross investment income
  ($900,000 minus $150,000)........ 750,000
(5) Deductions under section 832 (as
  modified by section 823(b)), reduced
  by deductions under section 822(c)
  ($746,000 minus $22,000)......... 724,000
(6) Limitation on deduction under section
  823(c)(1) (excess, if any, of item (4)
  over item (5)) 26,000
(7) Deduction under section 823(c)(1)
  (item (3) or item (6), whichever is
  the lesser) 3,000

[Reg. § 1.823-6.]

☐ [*T.D.* 6681, 10-16-63.]

[Reg. § 1.823-7]

§ 1.823-7. Subscribers of reciprocal underwriters and interinsurers.—A subscriber or policyholder of a reciprocal underwriter or interinsurer entitled to the deduction allowed by section 823(b)(2) and paragraph (c)(2) of § 1.823-6 shall treat amounts representing savings credited to his individual account for the taxable year as a dividend paid or declared for purposes of computing his taxable income. If a reciprocal credits savings to subscriber accounts after the close of its taxable year, but before the 16th day of the third month following the close of the taxable year, and the reciprocal takes such credits into account as if they had been made on the last day of its taxable year, the subscribers of such reciprocal must take such savings into account as if they had in fact been credited on the last day of the company's taxable year. The subscriber shall take savings credited to his account into account without regard to whether the amounts credited are actually distributed to him in cash. To the extent the insurance premium constituted a deductible expense when paid or accrued, the subscriber's taxable income for the taxable year will be increased and any loss for the taxable year will be decreased, by the amount credited to his account. Amounts credited to a subscriber's account which are taken into income by him and which subsequently are used to absorb losses of the reciprocal shall be treated by the subscriber as an additional insurance expense for the taxable year in which the amounts are absorbed. Such amounts may be deducted in computing taxable income to the extent insurance constitutes an otherwise properly deductible expense for such taxable year. [Reg. § 1.823-7.]

☐ [*T.D.* 6681, 10-16-63.]

[Reg. § 1.825-1]

§ 1.825-1. Unused loss deduction; in general.—(a) *Amount of deduction.* Section 825(a) provides that the unused loss deduction of a mutual insurance company subject to the tax imposed by section 821(a) shall be an amount equal to the sum of the unused loss carryovers and carrybacks to the taxable year. The amount so determined is used in the computation of mutual insurance company taxable income for the taxable year. See section 821(b) and § 1.821-4.

(b) *Unused loss defined.* Section 825(b) defines the term "unused loss" as the amount (if any) by which—

(1) The sum of the statutory underwriting loss (as defined in section 823(a)(2)) and the investment loss (as defined in section 822(a)(2)) exceeds

(2) The sum of—

  (i) The taxable investment income (as defined in section 822(a)(1)),

  (ii) The statutory underwriting income (as defined in section 823(a)(1)), and

  (iii) The amounts required to be subtracted from the protection against loss account under section 824(d).

(c) *Steps in computation of unused loss deduction.* The three steps to be taken in the ascertainment of the unused loss deduction for any taxable year are as follows:

(1) Compute the unused loss for any preceding or succeeding taxable year from which an unused loss may be carried over or carried back to the taxable year.

(2) Compute the unused loss carryovers to the taxable year from such preceding taxable years and the unused loss carrybacks to the taxable year from such succeeding taxable years.

(3) Add such unused loss carryovers and carrybacks in order to determine the unused loss deduction for the taxable year.

(d) *Statement with tax return.* Every mutual insurance company taxable under section 821(a) claiming an unused loss deduction for any taxable year shall file with its return for such year a concise statement setting forth the amount of the unused loss deduction claimed and all material and pertinent facts relative thereto, including a detailed schedule showing the computation of the unused loss deduction.

Reg. § 1.825-1(d)

(e) *Ascertainment of deduction dependent upon unused loss carryback.* If a mutual insurance company taxable under section 821(a) is entitled in computing its unused loss deduction to a carryback which it is not able to ascertain at the time its return is due, it shall compute the unused loss deduction on its return without regard to such unused loss carryback. When the company ascertains the unused loss carryback, it may within the applicable period of limitations file a claim for credit or refund of the overpayment, if any, resulting from the failure to compute the unused loss deduction for the taxable year with the inclusion of such carryback; or it may file an application under the provisions of section 6411 for a tentative carryback adjustment.

(f) *Law applicable to computations.* The following rules shall apply to taxable years for which the taxpayer is subject to the tax imposed by section 821(a)—

(1) In determining the amount of any unused loss carryback or carryover to any taxable year, the necessary computations involving any other taxable year shall be made under the law applicable to such other taxable year.

(2) The unused loss for any taxable year shall be determined under the law applicable to that year without regard to the year to which it is to be carried and in which, in effect, it is to be deducted as part of the unused loss deduction.

(3) The amount of the unused loss deduction which shall be allowed for any taxable year shall be determined under the law applicable for that year. [Reg. § 1.825-1.]

☐ [T.D. 6681, 10-16-63.]

[Reg. § 1.825-2]

§ 1.825-2. **Unused loss carryovers and carrybacks.**—(a) *Years to which loss may be carried*—(1) *In general.* In order to determine its unused loss deduction for any taxable year, a mutual insurance company taxable under section 821(a) must first determine the part of any unused losses for any preceding or succeeding taxable years which are carryovers or carrybacks to the taxable year in issue. An unused loss is to be an unused loss carryback to each of the 3 taxable years preceding the loss year, and an unused loss carryover to each of the 5 taxable years following the loss year, subject to the limitations provided in section 825(g) and subparagraph (2) of this paragraph.

(2) *Limitations.* An unused loss may not be carried—

(i) To or from any taxable year beginning before January 1, 1963,

(ii) To or from any taxable year for which the taxpayer is not subject to the tax imposed by section 821(a), nor

(iii) To any taxable year if, between the loss year and such taxable year, there is an intervening taxable year for which the taxpayer was not subject to the tax imposed by section 821(a).

(3) *Periods of less than 12 months.* A fractional part of a year which is a taxable year under sections 441(b) and 7701(a)(23) is a preceding or a succeeding taxable year for the purpose of determining under section 825 the first, second, etc., preceding or succeeding taxable year.

(b) *Loss year defined.* The term "loss year" as used in this section means any taxable year for which a company subject to the tax imposed by section 821(a) has an unused loss in excess of zero.

(c) *Amount of carrybacks and carryovers.* Section 825(e) provides that in the case of a loss year for a company taxable under section 821(a), the entire amount of the unused loss shall be carried to the earliest taxable year to which such loss may be carried under section 825(d) (subject to the limitations of section 825(g)). The amount of the unused loss carried to each of the other taxable years to which such loss may be carried under section 825(d) following such earliest taxable year shall be the excess (if any) of such loss over the sum of the offsets for each taxable year preceding the taxable year to which the unused loss is carried.

(d) *Offset defined*—(1) *In general.* Section 825(f) defines the term "offset" and provides that the taxable year to which an unused loss is carried shall be referred to as the "offset year". The definition of the term offset in the case of an unused loss carryback to an offset year, differs from the definition of such term in the case of an unused loss carryover to an offset year.

(2) *Offset in case of carryback.* In the case of an unused loss carryback from the loss year to the offset year, the offset is the mutual insurance company taxable income for the offset year, computed without regard to any unused loss carryback from the loss year or any taxable year thereafter.

(3) *Offset in case of carryover.* In the case of an unused loss carryover from the loss year to the offset year, the offset is equal to the sum of—

(i) The amount required to be subtracted from the protection against loss account under section 824(d)(1)(C) (relating to amounts equal to the unused loss carryovers to the offset year), plus

(ii) The mutual insurance company taxable income for the taxable year, computed without regard to any unused loss carryback or carryover from the loss year or any taxable year thereafter. [Reg. § 1.825-2.]

☐ [T.D. 6681, 10-16-63.]

[Reg. § 1.825-3]

§ 1.825-3. Examples.—The application of section 825 may be illustrated by the following examples:

Example (1). For the taxable year 1967, F, a mutual insurance company subject to the tax imposed by section 821(a), has the following items:

Taxable investment income	1
Underwriting loss	59
Addition to protection against loss account	8
Statutory underwriting loss	67

The subtractions from the protection against loss account are as follows:

Amount subtracted from amounts in account with respect to taxable years 1963 through 1966	18
Amount subtracted from amounts in account with respect to taxable year 1967	8
Total subtractions from protection against loss account under section 824(d)	26

The application of section 825 in this case may be illustrated by the facts and results shown in the following table and explained below:

	\multicolumn{6}{c}{Taxable year}
	1963	1964	1965	1966	1967	1968
Protection against loss account:						
Addition to account during taxable year	6	2	3	7	8	7
Subtraction from account during taxable year	0	0	0	0	8	7
Protection against loss account (at end of year)	6	2	3	7	0	0
Protection against loss account (at end of taxable year 1968)	0	0	0	0	0	0
Unused loss	0	0	0	0	40	0
Unused loss carryback	0	40	35	25	0	0
Unused loss carryover	0	0	0	0	0	18
Unused loss deduction	0	40	35	25	0	18
Mutual insurance company taxable income (computed without regard to unused loss)	13	5	10	7	0	2
Mutual insurance company taxable income (computed with regard to unused loss)	13	0	0	0	0	0
Offset for year	0	5	10	7	0	9
Offset total	0	5	15	22	22	31

1967: Under the provisions of section 825(b), F's unused loss for 1967 is 40, the amount by which the sum of the statutory underwriting loss and the investment loss, 67 (67 plus 0), exceeds the sum of the taxable investment income, the statutory underwriting income, and the amounts required to be subtracted from the protection against loss account under section 824(d) for the taxable year, 27 (the sum of 1, 0, and 26, respectively).

1967 carryback to 1964: Under the provisions of section 825(e), the entire unused loss for 1967 of 40 is carried back to 1964, the earliest year to which the loss may be carried under section 825(d). Since there are no other amounts carried to 1964, the unused loss deduction for 1964 is 40. Thus, after taking the unused loss deduction into account, the mutual insurance company taxable income for 1964 is zero, and the offset for 1964 is 5 (the mutual insurance company taxable income for 1964 determined without regard to the unused loss carryback from 1967 or any year thereafter).

1967 carryback to 1965: The portion of the unused loss for 1967 which is carried back to 1965 is 35 (40 minus 5, the offset for 1964). After taking the unused loss deduction into account, the mutual insurance company taxable income for 1965 is zero. The offset for 1965 is 10, the mutual insurance company taxable income for 1965 determined without regard to any unused loss carryback from 1967 or any year thereafter.

1967 carryback to 1966: The portion of the unused loss for 1967 which is carried back to 1966 is 25. This amount is the excess of the unused loss for 1967 of 40 over the sum of the offset for 1964 (5) and the offset for 1965 (10). As a result of the unused loss deduction the mutual insurance company taxable income for 1966 is reduced to zero. The offset for 1966 is 7.

1967 carryover to 1968: Under the provisions of section 825(d), the portion of the unused loss for 1967 which is carried forward to 1968 is 18 (40 minus the sum of 5, 10, and 7, the offsets for 1964, 1965, and 1966, respectively). Under section 825(f)(2), this amount is first applied against any amounts in the protection against loss account at the end of 1968, and is then applied against the mutual insurance company taxable income for 1968 (computed without regard to any unused loss carryovers or carrybacks from 1967 or any taxable year thereafter). Thus, assuming that there are no other subtractions from its protection

Reg. § 1.825-3

against loss account under section 824(d) for 1968, F's protection against loss account of 7 is reduced to zero by reason of the subtraction under section 824(d)(1)(C). The remaining portion of the unused loss for 1967 which is carried to 1968, 11 (18 minus 7, the amount of the unused loss carryover to 1968 which is subtracted from the protection against loss account under section 824(d)(1)(C)), is then applied against the mutual insurance company taxable income for 1968 computed without regard to any unused carryback or carryover from the loss year (1967) or any taxable year thereafter. After the application of the unused loss deduction for 1968, the mutual insurance company taxable income for 1968 is zero. The offset for 1968 is 9, the sum of the amount required to be subtracted from the protection against loss account under section 824(d)(1)(C) for 1968 (7), plus the mutual insurance company taxable income for 1968, determined without regard to any unused loss carryover or carryback from 1967 or any year thereafter (2). The remaining 9 of the unused loss for 1967 (40 minus the sum of 5, 10, 7, and 9, the offsets for 1964, 1965, 1966, and 1968, respectively), is carried forward to 1969, and to the extent not used in that year or any year thereafter, may be carried forward to 1970, 1971, and 1972, in that order.

Example (2). If in example (1) F had an unused loss in 1966 of 22, then, with respect to F's 1967 unused loss of 40, the offset for 1964 would be zero; the offset for 1965 would be 6—the 1965 mutual insurance company taxable income of 10 less an unused loss carryback of 4 from 1966 (the 1966 unused loss of 22 minus the 1963 offset of 13 and the 1964 offset of 5); the offset for the loss year 1966 would be zero, and 34 (the 1967 unused loss of 40 minus the offset for 1965 of 6) would remain as an unused loss carryover to 1968, 1969, 1970, 1971, 1972, in that order. Thus, the unused loss carrybacks or carryovers to an offset year are applied against the mutual insurance company taxable income for such year in the order in which the losses occurred, with the earliest loss being offset first.

Example (3). For the taxable year 1963, M, a mutual insurance company subject to tax imposed by section 821(a), has an unused loss (as defined in section 825(b)) of $65,000. Under section 825(g), the loss may not be carried back to any taxable year beginning before 1963. However, the loss may be carried forward to each of the 5 taxable years following 1963 provided that for each of such succeeding taxable years M is subject to the tax imposed by section 821(a).

Example (4). Assume the facts are the same as in example (3), except that for the taxable year 1964, the gross amount received by M from the items described in section 822(b) (other than paragraph (1)(D) thereof) and premiums (including deposits and assessments) exceeds $150,000 but does not exceed $500,000. If M does not make the election under section 821(d) (relating to election to be taxed under section 821(a)) for 1964, M's 1963 unused loss of $65,000 will not be allowed as an unused loss carryover or carryback since, by reason of section 825(g)(3), the unused loss may not be carried to any taxable year if, between the loss year and such taxable year, there is an intervening taxable year for which the insurance company was not subject to the tax imposed by section 821(a), and by reason by section 825(g)(1), the unused loss may not be carried to any taxable year beginning before 1963. [Reg. § 1.825-3.]

☐ [T.D. 6681, 10-16-63.]

→ *Caution: Reg. §§ 1.826-1–1.826-7 were issued under former Code Sec. 826, which was redesignated as Code Sec. 835.* ←

[Reg. § 1.826-1]

§ 1.826-1. Election by reciprocal underwriters and interinsurers.—(a) *In general.* Except as otherwise provided in section 826(c), any mutual insurance company which is an interinsurer or reciprocal underwriter taxable under section 821(a) may elect under section 826(a) to limit its deductions for amounts paid or incurred to its attorney-in-fact to the deductions of its attorney-in-fact which are allocable to income received by the attorney-in-fact from the reciprocal during the taxable year. See § 1.826-4 for rules relating to allocation of expenses. In no case may such an election increase the amount deductible by the reciprocal for amounts paid or due its attorney-in-fact for the taxable year. The election allowed by section 826(a) and this section in effect increases the income of the reciprocal by the net income of the attorney-in-fact attributable to its business with the reciprocal. A reciprocal making the election is allowed a credit for the amount of tax paid by the attorney-in-fact for the taxable year which is attributable to income received by the attorney-in-fact from the reciprocal. See section 826(e) and § 1.826-5.

(b) *Companies eligible to elect under section 826(a).* Any mutual insurance company which is a reciprocal underwriter or interinsurer subject to the tax imposed by section 821(a) may elect (in the manner prescribed by paragraph (c) of this section) to be subject to the limitation provided by section 826(b) and paragraph (a) of this sec-

Reg. § 1.826-1(a)

Life Insurance Companies

See p. 20,601 for regulations not amended to reflect law changes

→ *Caution: Reg. §§ 1.826-1–1.826-7 were issued under former Code Sec. 826, which was redesignated as Code Sec. 835.* ←

tion provided the attorney-in-fact of the electing reciprocal—

(1) Is subject to the taxes imposed by section 11(b) and (c) and the regulations thereunder;

(2) Consents (in the manner provided by paragraph (a) of § 1.826-3) to provide the information required under paragraph (b) of § 1.826-3 during the period in which the election made under section 826(a) and this section is in effect;

(3) Reports the income received from the reciprocal and the deductions allocable thereto under the same method of accounting used by the reciprocal in reporting its deductions for amounts paid or due its attorney-in-fact; and

(4) Files its income tax return on a calendar year basis.

(c) *Manner of making election.* The election provided by section 826(a) and this section shall be made in a statement attached to the taxpayer's income tax return for the first taxable year for which such election is to apply. The statement shall include the name and address of the taxpayer, shall be signed by the taxpayer (or [its] duly authorized representative), and shall be filed not later than the time prescribed by law for filing the income tax return (including extensions thereof) for the first taxable year for which such election is to apply. For information required of an electing reciprocal, see paragraph (e) of this section.

(d) *Scope of election.* The election allowed by section 826(a) is binding for the taxable year for which made and all succeeding taxable years unless the Commissioner consents to a revocation of such election. Whether revocation will be permitted will depend upon the facts and circumstances of each particular case.

(e) *Information required of an electing company.* Every reciprocal underwriter or interinsurer making the election provided by section 826(a) and this section shall, in the manner provided by paragraph (f) of this section, furnish the following information for each taxable year during which such election is in effect:

(1) The name and address of the attorney-in-fact with respect to which the election allowed by section 826(a) and this section is in effect; the district in which such attorney-in-fact filed its return for the taxable year; and a copy of the consent required by section 826 and § 1.826-3 and the date and district in which such consent was filed;

(2) The deductible amount paid or due to such attorney-in-fact from the reciprocal computed without regard to the limitation provided by section 826(b);

(3) The total amount claimed as a deduction by the reciprocal for amounts paid to its attorney-in-fact after giving effect to the limitation provided by section 826(b);

(4) The amount of the increase (if any) in underwriting gain (as defined in section 824(a)) attributable to the election allowed by section 826(a);

(5) The amount of the increase (if any) in the deduction allowed by section 824(a) (relating to deduction to provide protection against losses) attributable to the election allowed by section 826(a);

(6) The amount of any increase or decrease in the statutory underwriting income or loss for the taxable year (as computed under section 823) attributable to the election allowed by section 826(a);

(7) The amount of any increase or decrease in the mutual insurance company taxable income or unused loss for the taxable year attributable to the election allowed by section 826(a);

(8) The amount of the increase (if any) in the tax liability of the reciprocal for the taxable year attributable to the election allowed by section 826(a) before taking into account the credit provided by section 826(e);

(9) The amount of tax attributable to income received by the attorney-in-fact from the reciprocal during the taxable year (as determined under § 1.826-5) claimed (under section 826(e) and paragraph (a) of this section) by the reciprocal as a credit for the taxable year; and

(10) The information which the attorney-in-fact is required to submit to the reciprocal under paragraphs (b) and (c) of § 1.826-3.

(f) *Manner in which information is to be provided.* The information required by paragraph (e) of this section shall be set forth in a statement attached to the taxpayer's income tax return for each taxable year for which such information is required. Such statement shall include the name and address of the taxpayer; and shall be filed not later than the date prescribed by law (including extensions thereof) for filing the income tax return for the taxable year with respect to which such information is being provided. [Reg. § 1.826-1.]

☐ [*T.D.* 6681, 10-16-63.]

[Reg. § 1.826-2]

§ 1.826-2. **Special rules applicable to electing reciprocals.**—(a) *Protection against loss account.*

Life Insurance Companies

See p. 20,601 for regulations not amended to reflect law changes

→ *Caution: Reg. §§ 1.826-1–1.826-7 were issued under former Code Sec. 826, which was redesignated as Code Sec. 835.* ←

Section 826(d) provides that for purposes of determining the amount to be subtracted from the protection against loss account under section 824(d)(1)(D) and the regulations thereunder (relating to amounts added to the account for the fifth preceding taxable year) for any taxable year, any amount which was added to such account by reason of the election under section 826(a) and paragraph (a) of § 1.826-1 shall be treated as having been added by reason of section 824(a)(1)(A) and the regulations thereunder (relating to amounts equal to 1 percent of losses incurred during the taxable year). Thus, no amount added to the protection against loss account by reason of an election made under section 826(a) may remain in such account beyond the end of the fifth taxable year following the taxable year with respect to which such amount was added. See section 824(d)(1)(D) and paragraph (b)(3) of § 1.824-1. The amount added to the protection against loss account by reason of an election under section 826(a) is that amount which is equal to 25 percent (plus, in the case of a reciprocal which qualifies as a concentrated risk company under section 824(a), so much of the concentrated wind-storm, etc., premium percentage as exceeds 40 percent) of the amount by which—

(1) The underwriting gain (as defined by section 824(a)(1)) computed after taking into account the limitation provided by section 826(b) and § 1.826-1, exceeds

(2) The underwriting gain computed without regard to the limitation provided by section 826(b) and § 1.826-1.

(b) *Denial of surtax exemption.* Section 826(f) provides that the tax imposed upon any increase in the mutual insurance company taxable income of a reciprocal which is attributable to the limitation provided by section 826(b) shall be computed without regard to the surtax exemption provided by section 821(a)(2) and the regulations thereunder. Thus, a company making the election provided under section 826(a) will be subject to surtax, as well as normal tax, on the increase in its mutual insurance company taxable income for the taxable year which is attributable to such election. Similarly, any amount which was added to the protection against loss account by reason of an election under section 826(a) and § 1.826-1, and which is subtracted from such account in accordance with section 826(d) and paragraph (a) of this section, will be subject to surtax, as well as normal tax, to the extent such amount increases mutual insurance company taxable income in the year in which the subtraction is made. Furthermore, the company will be subject to surtax on such increases notwithstanding the fact that it may have no normal tax liability for the taxable year, because its mutual insurance company taxable income (after giving effect to the election provided by section 826(a)) does not exceed $6,000.

(c) *Adjustment for refunds.* Section 826(g) provides that if for any taxable year an attorney-in-fact is allowed a credit or refund for taxes paid with respect to which credit or refund to the reciprocal resulted under section 826(e), the taxes of such reciprocal for such taxable year shall be properly adjusted. The reciprocal shall make the adjustment required by section 826(g) by increasing its income tax liability for its taxable year in which the credit or refund is allowed to the attorney-in-fact by the amount of such credit or refund which is attributable to taxes paid by the attorney-in-fact on income received from the reciprocal, as determined under § 1.826-6, but only to the extent that the payment of such amount by the attorney-in-fact resulted in a credit or refund to the reciprocal. However, if the refund or credit to the attorney-in-fact is the result of an error in determining its items of income or deduction for the taxable year with respect to which the refund or credit is allowed, and such error affects the amount of deductions allocable to its reciprocal for such taxable year, then, if the reciprocal's period for filing an amended return has not otherwise expired, the preceding sentence shall not apply and the reciprocal shall make the adjustment required by section 826(g) by filing an amended return for such taxable year and all subsequent taxable years for which an adjustment is required. The reciprocal's amended return or returns shall give effect to the change in the deductions of the attorney-in-fact allocable to income received from the reciprocal and the tax paid by the attorney-in-fact attributable to such income. The amount of any adjustment required by section 826(g) and this section and the computation thereof shall be set forth in a statement attached to and filed with the taxpayer's income tax return for the taxable year for which the adjustment is made. Such statement shall include the name and address of the taxpayer, and a copy of the notification received by the attorney-in-fact indicating that it has been allowed the credit or refund requiring adjustment of the reciprocal's taxes. [Reg. § 1.826-2.]

☐ [*T.D. 6681, 10-16-63. Amended by T.D. 7100, 3-19-71.*]

Reg. § 1.826-2(a)(1)

Life Insurance Companies

→ **Caution: Reg. §§ 1.826-1–1.826-7 were issued under former Code Sec. 826, which was redesignated as Code Sec. 835.** ←

[Reg. § 1.826-3]

§ 1.826-3. Attorney-in-fact of electing reciprocals.—(a) *Manner of making consent.* Section 826(c)(2) provides that a reciprocal may not elect to be subject to the limitation provided by section 826(b) unless its attorney-in-fact consents to make certain information available. See paragraph (b) of this section. The attorney-in-fact of a reciprocal making the election provided by section 826(a) shall signify the consent required by section 826(c) in a statement attached to its income tax return for the first taxable year for which the reciprocal's election is to apply. Such statement shall include the name and address of the consenting taxpayer [and] the name and address of the reciprocal with respect to which such consent is to apply; shall be signed by the taxpayer (or its duly authorized representative); and shall be filed not later than the date prescribed by law (including extensions thereof) for filing the income tax return for the first taxable year for which such consent is to apply. In addition, such statement shall specify that the taxpayer is subject to the taxes imposed by section 11(b) and (c); the method of accounting used in reporting income received from its reciprocal and the deductions allocable thereto; and that its return is filed on the calendar year basis. Consent, once given, shall be irrevocable for the period during which the election provided for the reciprocal by section 826(a) is in effect. See paragraph (e) of § 1.826-1.

(b) *Information required of consenting attorney-in-fact.* Every attorney-in-fact making the consent provided by section 826(c)(2) and paragraph (a) of this section shall, in the manner prescribed by paragraph (c) of this section, furnish the following information for each taxable year during which the consent provided by section 826(c)(2) and paragraph (a) of this section is in effect:

(1) The name and address of the reciprocal with respect to which the consent required by section 826(c)(2) and paragraph (a) of this section is to apply;

(2) Gross income in total and by sources, adjusted for returns and allowances;

(3) Deductions (itemized to the same extent as on taxpayer's income tax return and accompanying schedules) allocable to each source of gross income and in total (see § 1.826-4);

(4) Method of allocation used in subparagraph (3) of this paragraph;

(5) Taxable income (if any) in total and by sources, as in subparagraph (2) of this paragraph (income by sources from subparagraph (2) of this paragraph minus expenses allocable thereto under subparagraph (3) of this paragraph);

(6) Total income tax liability (if any) for the taxable year;

(7) Taxes paid attributable (under § 1.826-5) to income earned by the taxpayer in dealing with the reciprocal;

(8) Such other information as may be required by the district director.

(c) *Manner in which information is to be provided.* (1) The information required by paragraph (b) of this section shall be set forth in a statement attached to the taxpayer's income tax return for each taxable year for which the consent provided by section 826(c)(2) and paragraph (a) of this section is in effect. Such statement shall include the name and address of the taxpayer, and shall be filed not later than the date prescribed by law (including extensions thereof) for filing the income tax return for each taxable year for which such information is required.

(2) A copy of the statement containing the information required by paragraph (b) of this section shall be submitted to the board of advisors (or other comparable body) of the reciprocal on whose behalf the consent provided under section 826(c)(2) is given. The copy shall be executed in the same manner as the original and shall be delivered to such board not later than 10 days before the last date prescribed by law (including extensions thereof) for filing the reciprocal's income tax return for the taxable year for which the information is required unless the attorney-in-fact establishes to the satisfaction of the district director that the failure to furnish such copy or the failure to furnish such copy within the prescribed 10 day period was due to circumstances beyond its control. In addition, there shall be attached to and made a part of such copy, a copy of the income tax return of the attorney-in-fact (including accompanying schedules) for each taxable year for which such statement is required. [Reg. § 1.826-3.]

☐ [T.D. 6681, 10-16-63.]

[Reg. § 1.826-4]

§ 1.826-4. Allocation of expenses.—An attorney-in-fact allocating expenses as required by section 826(b) and paragraph (b) of § 1.826-3 shall allocate each expense itemized in its income tax return (and accompanying schedules) for the taxable year to each source of gross income (as set forth pursuant to paragraph (b)(2) of § 1.826-3).

Reg. § 1.826-4

Life Insurance Companies

See p. 20,601 for regulations not amended to reflect law changes

→ *Caution: Reg. §§ 1.826-1–1.826-7 were issued under former Code Sec. 826, which was redesignated as Code Sec. 835.* ←

However, no portion of the net operating loss deduction allowed by section 172 shall be allocated to income received or due from the reciprocal, and no expenses, other than those directly related thereto, shall be allocated to capital gains. Where the method of allocation used by the taxpayer does not reasonably reflect the expenses of the taxpayer allocable to income received or due from the reciprocal, the district director may require the taxpayer to use such other method of allocation as is reasonable under the circumstances. [Reg. § 1.826-4.]

☐ [T.D. 6681, 10-16-63.]

[Reg. § 1.826-5]

§ 1.826-5. Attribution of tax.—(a) *In general.* Section 826(e) provides that a reciprocal making the election allowed by section 826(a) shall be credited with so much of the tax paid by the attorney-in-fact as is attributable to the income received by the attorney-in-fact from the reciprocal in such taxable year.

(b) *Computation.* For purposes of section 826(e) and paragraph (a) of this section, the amount of tax attributable to income received by the attorney-in-fact from the reciprocal in the taxable year shall be computed in the following manner:

(1) First, compute the taxable income (if any) from each source of gross income set forth in paragraph (b)(2) of § 1.826-3 by deducting from each such amount the expenses allocable thereto under § 1.826-4;

(2) Second, compute the normal tax on each amount of taxable income computed in subparagraph (1) of this paragraph at the rate provided by section 11(b) of the Code;

(3) Third, deduct from each amount determined in subparagraph (1) of this paragraph an amount which bears the same proportion to the surtax exemption provided by section 11(c) of the Code as each amount computed under subparagraph (1) of this paragraph bears to the total of the amounts computed under subparagraph (1) of this paragraph;

(4) Fourth, compute the surtax on each remainder computed in subparagraph (3) of this paragraph at the rate provided by section 11(c) of the Code;

(5) Fifth, add the normal tax computed under subparagraph (2) of this paragraph to the surtax computed under subparagraph (4) of this paragraph for each amount computed under subparagraph (1) of this paragraph;

(6) Sixth, deduct from each amount of tax computed under subparagraph (5) of this paragraph any tax credits (other than those arising from payments made with respect to the tax liability for the taxable year or other taxable years) allocable (in the same manner as provided for expenses under § 1.826-4) to such amount;

(7) Seventh, compute that amount which bears the same proportion to the tax actually paid with respect to the taxable year as each individual amount computed under subparagraph (6) of this paragraph bears to the total of the amounts computed under subparagraph (6) of this paragraph. The amount so determined with respect to each amount computed under subparagraph (6) of this paragraph is the tax paid which is attributable to the amount computed under subparagraph (1) of this paragraph.

To the extent the amounts determined under subparagraph (1) of this paragraph are attributable to amounts received from the reciprocal for the taxable year, the tax attributable to such amounts (as determined under subparagraph (7) of this paragraph) shall be the amount of tax attributable to income received by the attorney-in-fact from the reciprocal during the taxable year.

(c) *Taxes of attorney-in-fact unaffected.* Nothing in section 826 or the regulations thereunder shall increase or decrease the taxes imposed on the income of the attorney-in-fact. [Reg. § 1.826-5.]

☐ [T.D. 6681, 10-16-63.]

[Reg. § 1.826-6]

§ 1.826-6. Credit or refund.—(a) *Notification required.* In any case where a taxpayer applies for a credit or refund of taxes paid by it in respect of a taxable year for which the taxpayer was the consenting attorney-in-fact of a reciprocal making the election provided by section 826(a), such taxpayer shall give written notice to its reciprocal for such taxable year, first, upon applying for the credit or refund; and again, within 10 days from the date on which a final determination is made that such credit or refund has been allowed or denied.

(b) *Notice form.* The notices required by this section shall include the name and address of the taxpayer and shall be signed by the taxpayer or its duly authorized representative. In addition, there shall be attached to and made a part of each first notice a concise statement of the claim upon which the application for refund or credit is based; and there shall be attached to and made a part of each second notice:

Reg. § 1.826-5(a)

Life Insurance Companies

See p. 20,601 for regulations not amended to reflect law changes

→ *Caution: Reg. §§ 1.826-1–1.826-7 were issued under former Code Sec. 826, which was redesignated as Code Sec. 835.* ←

(1) A copy of the notification (if any) received by the taxpayer indicating that the credit or refund has been allowed; and

(2) A statement setting forth the amount of such credit or refund attributable to taxes paid by the taxpayer on income received from the reciprocal, and the computation by which such amount was determined.

(c) *Manner of apportioning refund or credit.* The taxpayer shall determine the amount of the refund or credit attributable to taxes paid on income received from its reciprocal by reallocating its income and expense items for the taxable year, with respect to which the refund or credit is allowed, in the manner provided by §§ 1.826-3 and 1.826-4 so as to reflect the adjustments (if any) in such items which resulted in the credit or refund of tax for the taxable year. The taxpayer shall then recompute the tax attributable to income received from its reciprocal for such taxable year in the manner provided by § 1.826-5. The district director may require such additional information as may be necessary in the circumstances to verify the computations required by this paragraph. [Reg. § 1.826-6.]

☐ [T.D. 6681, 10-16-63.]

[Reg. § 1.826-7]

§ 1.826-7. Examples.—The application of section 826 may be illustrated by the following examples:

Example (1). For the taxable year 1963, R, a reciprocal underwriter subject to the taxes imposed by section 821(a), has the following items (determined before applying any election under section 826):

Gross income under sec. 832	578
Gross investment income	50
Deductions under sec. 832 (as modified by sec. 823(b)):	
Deduction for amounts paid by R to attorney-in-fact A	100
All other deductions	500
Total deductions under sec. 832	600
Deductions under sec. 822(c)	40
Incurred losses	400
Protection against loss deduction	4
Underwriting gain	0
Mutual insurance company taxable income	0
Unused loss	22
Credit or refund for taxes paid	0

Assume that the deductions of attorney-in-fact A allocable to the income received by A from R are 60 and the tax paid by A allocable to the income received from R is 16. If R elects to be subject to the limitation provided in section 826(b), the results for 1963 would be as follows:

Gross income under sec. 832	578
Gross investment income	50
Deductions under sec. 832 (as modified by sec. 823(b)):	
Deduction for amounts paid by R to attorney-in-fact A	60
All other deductions	500
Total deduction under sec. 832	560
Deductions under sec. 822(c)	40
Incurred losses	400
Underwriting gain	8
Protection against loss deduction	6
Mutual insurance company taxable income	12
Unused loss	0
Credit or refund for taxes paid	16

Under the provisions of section 826(b), R's deduction for amounts paid or incurred to the attorney-in-fact in the taxable year 1963 would be limited to the deductions of A allocable to the income received by A from R. Thus, R's deductions under section 832 (as modified by section 823(b)) for 1963 would be 60 (the deductions of A which are allocable to the income received by A from R). As a result of making the election under section 826(a) for the taxable year 1963, R's underwriting gain would be 8, and its statutory underwriting income would be 2 (the underwriting gain of 8 minus the protection against loss deduction of 6—of which 4 represents the amount determined under section 824(a)(1)(A)—and 2 represents the amount determined under section 824(a)(1)(B)—or 8 minus 6). R's mutual insurance company taxable income for 1963 would be 12, consisting of taxable investment income of 10 (gross investment income minus deductions under section 822(c), or 50 minus 40) plus statutory underwriting income of 2. Since all of R's mutual insurance company taxable income of 12 is attributable to the limitation under section 826(b), the entire amount is subject to the surtax under section 821(a)(2) without regard to the $25,000 surtax exemption. The credit of 16, representing that part of the tax paid by A which is allocable to the income received by A from R, may be applied by R against its taxes with respect to its mutual insurance company taxable income of 12 for 1963, and R would be entitled to a refund of any excess of the amount of such credit over its tax liability for 1963.

Under the provisions of section 826(d), no portion of the amount added to the protection against loss account in 1963 by reason of the election under section 826(a), (25 percent of the amount by which the consolidated underwriting gain ex-

Reg. § 1.826-7

45,826 Life Insurance Companies

See p. 20,601 for regulations not amended to reflect law changes

→ **Caution:** *Reg. §§ 1.826-1–1.826-7 were issued under former Code Sec. 826, which was redesignated as Code Sec. 835.* ←

ceeds 25 percent of the underwriting gain determined without regard to the election under section 826(a), or the amount by which 25 percent of 8 exceeds 25 percent of 0), may remain in such account beyond the taxable year 1968.

Example (2). For the taxable year 1963, F is a corporate attorney-in-fact subject to the taxes imposed by section 11(b) and (c) of the Code. F files its return on the calendar year basis and reports income received from its reciprocal and the deductions allocable thereto under the same method of accounting used by its reciprocal in reporting its deductions for amounts paid to F. F properly consents to provide the information required by paragraph (b) of § 1.826-3. In addition to its attorney-in-fact business, F owns real estate for investment purposes, and operates a real estate management service. For the taxable year 1963, F has gross income from these various sources as follows:

Attorney-in-fact fees	$85,000
Real estate management fees	18,000
Rental income	25,000

F allocates its expenses for the taxable year on the basis of their direct relation to each source of income. During 1963, F acquired property for use in its attorney-in-fact operations which entitled F to an investment credit of $800 under section 38. For 1963, F determines that the tax paid by it which is attributable to its reciprocal is $21,863, computed as follows:

	Attorney-in-Fact Fees	Real Estate Management	Rental Income	Total
Gross income	$85,000	$18,000	$25,000	$128,000
Allocable expenses	25,000	3,000	35,000	63,000
Taxable income (loss)	60,000	15,000	(10,000)	65,000
Normal tax (30 percent)	18,000	4,500	0	25,000
Surtax exemption	20,000	5,000	0	25,000
Income subject to surtax	40,000	10,000	0	40,000
Surtax (22 percent)	8,800	2,200	0	8,800
Total tax	26,800	6,700	0	28,300
Investment credit	800	0	0	800
1963 tax liability	26,000	6,700	0	27,500
1963 tax paid	......	......	......	27,500
Allocation of tax paid	21,863	5,637	0	27,500

Under paragraph (b)(1) of § 1.826-5, F computes its taxable income from its attorney-in-fact fees to be $60,000 ($85,000 minus $25,000), and its taxable income from its real estate management to be $15,000 ($18,000 minus $3,000). Since F's rental operations resulted in a $10,000 loss for the taxable year ($25,000 minus $35,000), F's taxable income from its rental operations is zero. Using the 30 percent rate provided by section 11(b), F computes its normal tax to be $18,000 on its attorney-in-fact fees and $4,500 on its real estate management operations. F's normal tax on total income is $19,500. The $3,000 difference between the normal tax on F's total income and the normal taxes on F's profitable operations results from the loss on F's rental operations. Under paragraph (b)(3) of § 1.826-5, F allocates its surtax exemption as follows: $20,000 ($60,000/$75,000 × $25,000) to its attorney-in-fact fees; and $5,000 ($15,000/$75,000 × $25,000) to its real estate management operations. F computes its surtax on its profitable operations at the 22 percent rate provided by section 11(c) as follows: $8,800 (22 percent of $40,000) on attorney-in-fact fees; and $2,200 (22 percent of $10,000) on real estate management income. F adds its normal tax and surtax on its profitable operations and determines its total tax to be $26,800 on its attorney-in-fact operations; $6,700 on its real estate management operations; and $28,300 on its total income. F must allocate its investment credit on the same basis as it used to allocate its expenses. Thus, F's entire investment credit must be allocated to its attorney-in-fact operations. Accordingly, F's 1963 tax liability is $26,000 on its attorney-in-fact fees; $6,700 on its real estate management operations; $0 on its rental operations; and $27,500 on its total income. Under paragraph (b)(7) of § 1.826-5, F allocates $21,863 ($26,000/$32,700 × $27,500) of its 1963 tax paid to its attorney-in-fact fees; and $5,637 ($6,700/$32,700 × $27,500) of its 1963 tax paid to its real estate management business. F's reciprocal will be allowed a credit or refund of $21,863 for taxes paid by F which are attributable to F's income received from its reciprocal.

Example (3). Assume the same facts as in example (2), and assume further that in 1966 F sustains a net operating loss on its overall operations of $5,000. In carrying the loss back to 1963 as a net operating loss deduction under section 172, F must allocate the deduction under the same method it used in allocating its 1963 deduc-

Reg. § 1.826-7

Other Insurance Companies

See p. 20,601 for regulations not amended to reflect law changes

→ *Caution: Reg. §§ 1.826-1–1.826-7 were issued under former Code Sec. 826, which was redesignated as Code Sec. 835.* ←

tions. Thus, if the loss was entirely attributable to F's rental operations for the taxable year 1966, F would reduce its taxable income attributable to those operations by the entire amount of the loss and would recompute the tax attributable to those operations under paragraph (b) of § 1.826-5. As recomputed in the table below, F's 1963 tax liability from attorney-in-fact fees would be $19,800 and F's total tax liability would be $24,900.

	Attorney-in-Fact Fees	Real Estate Management	Rental Income	Total
Gross income	$85,000	$18,000	$25,000	$128,000
Allocable expenses	25,000	3,000	35,000	63,000
Net operating loss deduction	0	0	5,000	5,000
Taxable income (loss)	60,000	15,000	(15,000)	60,000
Normal tax (30 percent)	18,000	4,500	0	18,000
Surtax exemption	20,000	5,000	0	25,000
Income subject to surtax	40,000	10,000	0	35,000
Surtax (22 percent)	8,800	2,200	0	7,700
Total tax	26,800	6,700	0	25,700
Investment credit	800	0	0	800
1963 tax liability	26,000	6,700	0	24,900
1963 tax paid				24,900
Allocation of tax paid	19,800	5,100	0	24,900

As a result of its 1966 net operating loss, F would be entitled to a refund of $2,600 (1963 taxes paid of $27,500 minus recomputed 1963 taxes of $24,900). Under paragraph (a) of § 1.826-6, F would be required to notify its reciprocal of its claim for refund and of the amount of the refund or credit attributable to taxes paid on income received from the reciprocal. Since the 1963 tax paid by F attributable to its reciprocal (as recomputed) is less than the amount claimed in 1963 by F's reciprocal as a credit, F's reciprocal would be required, under section 826(g), to add the difference—$2,063 ($21,863 minus $19,800), to its tax liability for 1966. Thus, F's reciprocal would first compute its tax liability for 1966 without regard to section 826(g) and then would increase such liability by $2,063. [Reg. § 1.826-7.]

☐ [T.D. 6681, 10-16-63.]

Other Insurance Companies

[Reg. § 1.831-2]

§ 1.831-2. Taxable years affected.—Section 1.831-1 [reproduced at ¶ 4055 of the CCH 1974 STANDARD FEDERAL TAX REPORTS] is applicable only to taxable years beginning after December 31, 1953, but before January 1, 1963, and ending after August 16, 1954, and all references therein to sections of the Code and regulations are to sections of the Internal Revenue Code of 1954 and the regulations thereunder before amendments. Section 1.831-3 is applicable only to taxable years beginning after December 31, 1962, and all references therein to sections of the Code and regulations are to sections of the Internal Revenue Code of 1954 as amended. Section 1.831-4 is applicable only with respect to the companies described therein, and only with respect to taxable years beginning after December 31, 1961. [Reg. § 1.831-2.]

☐ [T.D. 6681, 10-16-63.]

[Reg. § 1.831-3]

§ 1.831-3. Tax on insurance companies (other than life or mutual), mutual marine insurance companies, mutual fire insurance companies issuing perpetual policies, and mutual fire or flood insurance companies operating on the basis of premium deposits; taxable years beginning after December 31, 1962.—(a) All insurance companies, other than life or mutual or foreign insurance companies not carrying on an insurance business within the United States, and all mutual marine insurance companies and mutual fire or flood insurance companies exclusively issuing perpetual policies or whose principal business is the issuance of policies for which the premium deposits are the same regardless of the length of the term for which the policies are written, are subject to the tax imposed by section 831 if the unabsorbed portion of such premium deposits not required for losses, expenses or reserves is returned or credited to the policyholder on cancellation or expiration of the policy. For purposes of section 831 and this section, in the case of a mutual flood insurance company, the premium deposits will be considered to be the same if the payment of a premium increases the total insurance under the policy in an amount equal to the amount of such premium and the omission of any

Reg. § 1.831-3

annual premium does not result in the reduction or suspension of coverage under the policy. As used in this section and section 832 and the regulations thereunder, the term "insurance companies" means only those companies which qualify as insurance companies under the definition provided by paragraph (b) of § 1.801-1 and which are subject to the tax imposed by section 831.

(b) All provisions of the Code and of the regulations in this part not inconsistent with the specific provisions of section 831 are applicable to the assessment and collection of the tax imposed by section 831(a), and insurance companies are subject to the same penalties as are provided in the case of returns and payment of income tax by other corporations.

(c) Since section 832 provides that the underwriting and investment exhibit of the annual statement approved by the National Convention of Insurance Commissioners shall be the basis for computing gross income and since the annual statement is rendered on the calendar year basis, the returns under section 831 shall be made on the basis of the calendar year and shall be on Form 1120. Insurance companies are entitled, in computing insurance company taxable income, to the deductions provided in part VIII (section 241 and following), subchapter B, chapter 1 of the Code.

(d) Foreign insurance companies not carrying on an insurance business within the United States are not taxable under section 831 but are taxable as other foreign corporations. See section 881.

(e) Insurance companies are subject to both normal tax and surtax. The normal tax shall be computed as provided in section 11(b) and the surtax shall be computed as provided in section 11(c). For the circumstances under which the $25,000 exemption from surtax for certain taxable years may be disallowed in whole or in part, see section 1551. For alternative tax where the net long-term capital gain for any taxable year exceeds the net short-term capital loss, see section 1201(a) and the regulations thereunder. [Reg. § 1.831-3.]

☐ [T.D. 6681, 10-16-63.]

[Reg. § 1.831-4]

§ 1.831-4. **Election of multiple line companies to be taxed on total income.**—(a) *In general.* Section 831(c) provides that any mutual insurance company engaged in writing marine, fire, and casualty insurance which, for any 5-year period beginning after December 31, 1941, and ending before January 1, 1962, was subject to the tax imposed by section 831 (or the tax imposed by corresponding provisions of prior law) may elect, in the manner provided by paragraph (b) of this section, to be subject to the tax imposed by section 831, whether or not marine insurance is its predominant source of premium income. A company making an election under section 831(c) and this section will be subject to the tax imposed by section 831 for taxable years beginning after December 31, 1961, rather than subject to the tax imposed by section 821.

(b) *Time and manner of making election.* The election provided by section 831(c) and paragraph (a) of this section shall be made in a statement attached to the taxpayer's return for the taxable year 1962. The statement shall indicate that the taxpayer has made the election provided by section 831(c) and this section; shall include the name and address of the taxpayer, and shall be signed by the taxpayer or his duly authorized representative. In addition, the statement shall list the 5 consecutive taxable years prior to 1962 for which the taxpayer was subject to tax under section 831 (or the corresponding provisions of prior law); the types of insurance written by the company; and the percentage of marine insurance to total insurance written. The return and statement must be filed not later than the date prescribed by law (including extensions thereof) for filing the return for the taxable year 1962. However, if the last date prescribed by law (including extensions thereof) for filing the income tax return for the taxable year 1962 falls before October 17, 1963, the election provided by section 831(c) and this section may be made for such year by filing the statement and an amended return for such taxable year (and all subsequent taxable years for which returns have been filed) before January 16, 1964.

(c) *Scope of election.* An election made under section 831(c) and paragraph (b) of this section shall be binding for all taxable years beginning after December 31, 1961, unless consent to revoke the election is obtained from the Commissioner. However, if a taxpayer made the election provided by section 831(c) and this section for taxable years beginning prior to October 17, 1963, the taxpayer may revoke such election without obtaining consent from the Commissioner by filing, before January 16, 1964, a statement that the taxpayer desires to revoke such election. Such statement shall be signed by the taxpayer or its duly authorized representative. An amended return reflecting such revocation must accompany the statement for all taxable years for which returns have been filed with respect to such election.

(d) *Limitation on certain net operating loss carryovers and carrybacks.* In the case of a taxpayer making the election allowed under section

831(c) and this section, a net operating loss shall not be carried—

(1) To or from any taxable year for which the insurance company is not subject to the tax imposed by section 831(a) (or predecessor sections); or

(2) To any taxable year if, between the loss year and such taxable year, there is an intervening taxable year for which the insurance company was not subject to the tax imposed by section 831(a) (or predecessor sections). [Reg. § 1.831-4.]

☐ [*T.D.* 6681, 10-16-63.]

[Reg. § 1.832-3]

§ 1.832-3. Taxable years affected.—Sections 1.832-1 and 1.832-2 [reproduced at ¶ 4058-4058A of the CCH 1974 STANDARD FEDERAL TAX REPORTS] are applicable only to taxable years beginning after December 31, 1953, and before January 1, 1963, and ending after August 16, 1954, and all references therein to sections of the Code and regulations are to sections of the Internal Revenue Code of 1954 and the regulations thereunder before amendments. Sections 1.832-4, 1.832-5, and 1.832-6 are applicable only to taxable years beginning after December 31, 1962, and all references therein to sections of the Code and regulations are to sections of the Internal Revenue Code of 1954 as amended. [Reg. § 1.832-3.]

☐ [*T.D.* 6681, 10-16-63.]

[Reg. § 1.832-4]

§ 1.832-4. Gross income.—(a) (1) Gross income as defined in section 832(b)(1) means the gross amount of income earned during the taxable year from interest, dividends, rents, and premium income, computed on the basis of the underwriting and investment exhibit of the annual statement approved by the National Convention of Insurance Commissioners, as well as the gain derived from the sale or other disposition of property, and all other items constituting gross income under section 61, except that in the case of a mutual fire insurance company described in section 831(a)(3)(A) the amount of single deposit premiums received, but not assessments, shall be excluded from gross income. Section 832(b)(1)(D) provides that in the case of a mutual fire or flood insurance company described in section 831(a)(3)(B), there shall be included in gross income an amount equal to 2 percent of the premiums earned during the taxable year on contracts described in section 831(a)(3)(B) after deduction of premium deposits returned or credited during such taxable year with respect to such contracts. Gross income does not include increase in liabilities during the year on account of reinsurance treaties, remittances from the home office of a foreign insurance company to the United States branch, borrowed money, or gross increase due to adjustments in book value of capital assets.

(2) The underwriting and investment exhibit is presumed to reflect the true net income of the company, and insofar as it is not inconsistent with the provisions of the Code will be recognized and used as a basis for that purpose. All items of the exhibit, however, do not reflect an insurance company's income as defined in the Code. By reason of the definition of investment income, miscellaneous items which are intended to reflect surplus but do not properly enter into the computation of income, such as dividends declared to shareholders in their capacity as such, home office remittances and receipts, and special deposits, are ignored. Gain or loss from agency balances and bills receivable not admitted as assets on the underwriting and investment exhibit will be ignored, excepting only such agency balances and bills receivable as have been allowed as deductions for worthless debts or, having been previously so allowed, are recovered during the taxable year.

(3) *Premiums earned.* The determination of premiums earned on insurance contracts during the taxable year begins with the insurance company's gross premiums written on insurance contracts during the taxable year, reduced by return premiums and premiums paid for reinsurance. Subject to the exceptions in sections 832(b)(7), 832(b)(8), and 833(a)(3), this amount is increased by 80 percent of the unearned premiums on insurance contracts at the end of the preceding taxable year, and is decreased by 80 percent of the unearned premiums on insurance contracts at the end of the current taxable year.

(4) *Gross premiums written*—(i) *In general.* Gross premiums written are amounts payable for insurance coverage. The label placed on a payment in a contract does not determine whether an amount is a gross premium written. Gross premiums written do not include other items of income described in section 832(b)(1)(C) (for example, charges for providing loss adjustment or claims processing services under administrative services or cost-plus arrangements). Gross premiums written on an insurance contract include all amounts payable for the effective period of the insurance contract. To the extent that amounts paid or payable with respect to an arrangement are not gross premiums written, the insurance company may not treat amounts payable to customers under the applicable portion of such arrangements as losses incurred described in section 832(b)(5).

Reg. § 1.832-4(a)(4)

(ii) *Items included.* Gross premiums written include—

(A) Any additional premiums resulting from increases in risk exposure during the effective' period of an insurance contract;

(B) Amounts subtracted from a premium stabilization reserve to pay for insurance coverage; and

(C) Consideration in respect of assuming insurance liabilities under insurance contracts not issued by the taxpayer (such as a payment or transfer of property in an assumption reinsurance transaction).

(5) *Method of reporting gross premiums written*—(i) *In general.* Except as otherwise provided under this paragraph (a)(5), an insurance company reports gross premiums written for the earlier of the taxable year that includes the effective date of the insurance contract or the year in which the company receives all or a portion of the gross premium for the insurance contract. The effective date of the insurance contract is the date on which the insurance coverage provided by the contract commences. The effective period of an insurance contract is the period over which one or more rates for insurance coverage are guaranteed in the contract. If a new rate for insurance coverage is guaranteed after the effective date of an insurance contract, the making of such a guarantee generally is treated as the issuance of a new insurance contract with an effective period equal to the duration of the new guaranteed rate for insurance coverage.

(ii) *Special rule for additional premiums resulting from an increase in risk exposure.* An insurance company reports additional premiums that result from an increase in risk exposure during the effective period of an insurance contract in gross premiums written for the taxable year in which the change in risk exposure occurs. Unless the increase in risk exposure is of temporary duration (for example, an increase in risk exposure under a workers' compensation policy due to seasonal variations in the policyholder's payroll), the company reports additional premiums resulting from an increase in risk exposure based on the remainder of the effective period of the insurance contract.

(iii) *Exception for certain advance premiums.* If an insurance company receives a portion of the gross premium for an insurance contract prior to the first day of the taxable year that includes the effective date of the contract, the company may report the advance premium (rather than the full amount of the gross premium for the contract) in gross premiums written for the taxable year in which the advance premium is received. An insurance company may adopt this method of reporting advance premiums only if the company's deduction for premium acquisition expenses for the taxable year in which the company receives the advance premium does not exceed the limitation of paragraph (a)(5)(vii) of this section. A company that reports an advance premium in gross premiums written under this paragraph (a)(5)(iii) takes into account the remainder of the gross premium written and premium acquisition expenses for the contract in the taxable year that includes the effective date of the contract. A company that adopts this method of reporting advance premiums must use the method for all contracts with advance premiums.

(iv) *Exception for certain cancellable accident and health insurance contracts with installment premiums.* If an insurance company issues or proportionally reinsures a cancellable accident and health insurance contract (other than a contract with an effective period that exceeds 12 months) for which the gross premium is payable in installments over the effective period of the contract, the company may report the installment premiums (rather than the total gross premium for the contract) in gross premiums written for the earlier of the taxable year in which the installment premiums are due under the terms of the contract or the year in which the installment premiums are received. An insurance company may adopt this method of reporting installment premiums for a cancellable accident and health insurance contract only if the company's deduction for premium acquisition expenses for the first taxable year in which an installment premium is due or received under the contract does not exceed the limitation of paragraph (a)(5)(vii) of this section. A company that adopts this method of reporting installment premiums for a cancellable accident and health contract must use the method for all of its cancellable accident and health insurance contracts with installment premiums.

(v) *Exception for certain multi-year insurance contracts.* If an insurance company issues or proportionally reinsures an insurance contract, other than a contract described in paragraph (a)(5)(vi) of this section, with an effective period that exceeds 12 months, for which the gross premium is payable in installments over the effective period of the contract, the company may treat the insurance coverage provided under the multi-year contract as a series of separate insurance contracts. The first contract in the series is treated as having been written for an effective period of twelve months. Each subsequent contract in the series is treated as having been written for an effective period equal to the lesser of 12 months or the remainder of the period for which the rates for

Reg. § 1.832-4(a)(5)

insurance coverage are guaranteed in the multi-year insurance contract. An insurance company may adopt this method of reporting premiums on a multi-year contract only if the company's deduction for premium acquisition expenses for each year of the multi-year contract does not exceed the limitation of paragraph (a)(5)(vii) of this section. A company that adopts this method of reporting premiums for a multi-year contract must use the method for all multi-year contracts with installment premiums.

(vi) *Exception for insurance contracts described in section 832(b)(7).* If an insurance company issues or reinsures the risks related to a contract described in section 832(b)(7), the company may report gross premiums written for the contract in the manner required by sections 803 and 811(a) for life insurance companies. An insurance company may adopt this method of reporting premiums on contracts described in section 832(b)(7) only if the company also determines the deduction for premium acquisition costs for the contract in accordance with section 811(a), as adjusted by the amount required to be taken into account under section 848 in connection with the net premiums of the contract. A company that adopts this method of reporting premiums for a contract described in section 832(b)(7) must use the method for all of its contracts described in that section.

(vii) *Limitation on deduction of premium acquisition expenses.* An insurance company's deduction for premium acquisition expenses (for example, commissions, state premium taxes, overhead reimbursements to agents or brokers, and other similar amounts) related to an insurance contract is within the limitation of this paragraph (a)(5)(vii) if—

(A) The ratio obtained by dividing the sum of the company's deduction for premium acquisition expenses related to the insurance contract for the taxable year and previous taxable years by the total premium acquisition expenses attributable to the insurance contract; does not exceed

(B) The ratio obtained by dividing the sum of the amounts included in gross premiums written with regard to the insurance contract for the taxable year and previous taxable years by the total gross premium written for the insurance contract.

(viii) *Change in method of reporting gross premiums.* An insurance company that adopts a method of accounting for gross premiums written and premium acquisition expenses described in paragraph (a)(5)(iii), (iv), (v), or (vi) of this section must continue to use the method to report gross premiums written and premium acquisition expenses unless the company obtains the consent of the Commissioner to change to a different method under section 446(e) and § 1.446-1(e).

(6) *Return premiums*—(i) *In general.* An insurance company's liability for return premiums includes amounts previously included in an insurance company's gross premiums written, which are refundable to a policyholder or ceding company, provided that the amounts are fixed by the insurance contract and do not depend on the experience of the insurance company or the discretion of its management.

(ii) *Items included.* Return premiums include amounts—

(A) Which were previously paid and become refundable due to policy cancellations or decreases in risk exposure during the effective period of an insurance contract;

(B) Which reflect the unearned portion of unpaid premiums for an insurance contract that is canceled or for which there is a decrease in risk exposure during its effective period; or

(C) Which are either previously paid and refundable or which reflect the unearned portion of unpaid premiums for an insurance contract, arising from the redetermination of a premium due to correction of posting or other similar errors.

(7) *Method of reporting return premiums.* An insurance company reports the liability for a return premium resulting from the cancellation of an insurance contract for the taxable year in which the contract is canceled. An insurance company reports the liability for a return premium attributable to a reduction in risk exposure under an insurance contract for the taxable year in which the reduction in risk exposure occurs.

(8) *Unearned premiums*—(i) *In general.* The unearned premium for a contract, other than a contract described in section 816(b)(1)(B), generally is the portion of the gross premium written that is attributable to future insurance coverage during the effective period of the insurance contract. However, unearned premiums held by an insurance company with regard to the net value of risks reinsured with other solvent companies (whether or not authorized to conduct business under state law) are subtracted from the company's unearned premiums. Unearned premiums also do not include any additional liability established by the insurance company on its annual statement to cover premium deficiencies. Unearned premiums do not include an insurance company's estimate of its liability for amounts to be paid or credited to a customer with regard to the expired portion of a retrospectively rated con-

Reg. § 1.832-4(a)(8)

tract (retro credits). An insurance company's estimate of additional amounts payable by its customers with regard to the expired portion of a retrospectively rated contract (retro debits) cannot be subtracted from unearned premiums.

(ii) *Special rules for unearned premiums.* For purposes of computing "premiums earned on insurance contracts during the taxable year" under section 832(b)(4), the amount of unearned premiums includes—

(A) Life insurance reserves (as defined in section 816(b), but computed in accordance with section 807(d) and sections 811(c) and (d));

(B) In the case of a mutual flood or fire insurance company described in section 832(b)(1)(D) (with respect to contracts described in that section), the amount of unabsorbed premium deposits that the company would be obligated to return to its policyholders at the close of the taxable year if all its insurance contracts were terminated at that time;

(C) In the case of an interinsurer or reciprocal underwriter that reports unearned premiums on its annual statement net of premium acquisition expenses, the unearned premiums on the company's annual statement increased by the portion of premium acquisition expenses allocable to those unearned premiums; and

(D) In the case of a title insurance company, its discounted unearned premiums (computed in accordance with section 832(b)(8)).

(9) *Method of determining unearned premiums.* If the risk of loss under an insurance contract does not vary significantly over the effective period of the contract, the unearned premium attributable to the unexpired portion of the effective period of the contract is determined on a pro rata basis. If the risk of loss varies significantly over the effective period of the contract, the insurance company may consider the pattern and incidence of the risk in determining the portion of the gross premium that is attributable to the unexpired portion of the effective period of the contract. An insurance company that uses a method of computing unearned premiums other than the pro rata method must maintain sufficient information to demonstrate that its method of computing unearned premiums accurately reflects the pattern and incidence of the risk for the insurance contract.

(10) *Examples.* The provisions of paragraphs (a)(4) through (a)(9) of this section are illustrated by the following examples:

Example 1. (i) IC is a non-life insurance company which, pursuant to section 843, files its returns on a calendar year basis. IC writes a casualty insurance contract that provides insurance coverage for a one-year period beginning on July 1, 2000 and ending on June 30, 2001. IC charges a $500 premium for the insurance contract, which may be paid either in full by the effective date of the contract or in quarterly installments over the contract's one year term. The policyholder selects the installment payment option. As of December 31, 2000, IC collected $250 of installment premiums for the contract.

(ii) The effective period of the insurance contract begins on July 1, 2000 and ends on June 30, 2001. For the taxable year ending December 31, 2000, IC includes the $500 gross premium, based on the effective period of the contract, in gross premiums written under section 832(b)(4)(A). IC's unearned premium with respect to the contract was $250 as of December 31, 2000. Pursuant to section 832(b)(4)(B), to determine its premiums earned, IC deducts $200 ($250 × .8) for the insurance contract at the end of the taxable year.

Example 2. (i) The facts are the same as *Example 1*, except that the insurance contract has a stated term of 5 years. On each contract anniversary date, IC may adjust the rate charged for the insurance coverage for the succeeding 12 month period. The amount of the adjustment in the charge for insurance coverage is not substantially limited under the insurance contract.

(ii) Under paragraph (a)(5)(i) of this section, IC is required to report gross premiums written for the insurance contract based on the effective period for the contract. The effective period of the insurance contract is the period for which a rate for insurance coverage is guaranteed in the contract. Although the insurance contract issued by IC has a stated term of 5 years, a rate for insurance coverage is guaranteed only for a period of 12 months beginning with the contract's effective date and each anniversary date thereafter. Thus, for the taxable year ending December 31, 2000, IC includes the $500 gross premium for the 12 month period beginning with the contract's effective date in gross premiums written. IC's unearned premium with respect to the contract was $250 as of December 31, 2000. Pursuant to section 832(b)(4)(B), to determine its premiums earned, IC deducts $200 ($250 × .8) for the insurance contract at the end of the taxable year.

Example 3. (i) The facts are the same as *Example 1*, except that coverage under the insurance contract begins on January 1, 2001 and ends on December 31, 2001. On December 15, 2000, IC collects the first $125 premium installment on the insurance contract. For the taxable year ended December 31, 2000, IC deducts $20 of premium acquisition expenses related to the insurance con-

Reg. § 1.832-4(a)(9)

tract. IC's total premium acquisition expenses, based on the insurance contract's $500 gross premium, are $80.

(ii) Under paragraph (a)(5)(iii) of this section, IC may elect to report only the $125 advance premium (rather than the contract's $500 gross premium) in gross premiums written for the taxable year ended December 31, 2000, provided that IC's deduction for the premium acquisition expenses related to the insurance contract does not exceed the limitation in paragraph (a)(5)(vii). IC's deduction for premium acquisition expenses is within this limitation only if the ratio of the insurance contract's premium acquisition expenses deducted for the taxable year and any previous taxable year to the insurance contract's total premium acquisition expenses does not exceed the ratio of the amounts included in gross premiums written for the taxable year and any previous taxable year for the contract to the total gross premium written for the contract.

(iii) For the taxable year ended December 31, 2000, IC deducts $20 of premium acquisition expenses related to the insurance contract. This deduction represents 25% of the total premium acquisition expenses for the insurance contract ($20/$80 = 25%). This ratio does not exceed the ratio of the $125 advance premium to the insurance contract's $500 gross premium ($125/$500 = 25%). Therefore, under paragraph (a)(5)(iii) of this section, IC may elect to report only the $125 advance premium (rather than the $500 gross premium) in gross premiums written for the taxable year ending December 31, 2000. IC reports the balance of the gross premium for the insurance contract ($375) and deducts the remaining premium acquisition expenses ($60) for the insurance contract in the taxable year ending December 31, 2001.

Example 4. (i) The facts are the same as *Example 3,* except that for the taxable year ending December 31, 2000, IC deducts $60 of premium acquisition expenses related to the insurance contract.

(ii) For the taxable year ended December 31, 2000, IC deducted 75% of total premium acquisition expenses for the insurance contract ($60/$80 = 75%). This ratio exceeds the ratio of the $125 advance premium to the $500 gross premium ($125/$500 = 25%). Because IC's deduction for premium acquisition expenses allocable to the contract exceeds the limitation in paragraph (a)(5)(vii) of this section, paragraph (a)(5)(i) of this section requires IC to report the $500 gross premium in gross premiums written for the taxable year ending December 31, 2000. IC's unearned premium with respect to the contract was $500 as of December 31, 2000. Pursuant to section 832(b)(4)(B), to determine its premiums earned, IC deducts $400 ($500 × .8) for the insurance contract at the end of the taxable year.

Example 5. (i) IC is a non-life insurance company which, pursuant to section 843, files its returns on a calendar year basis. On August 1, 2000, IC issues a one-year cancellable accident and health insurance policy to X, a corporation with 80 covered employees. The gross premium written for the insurance contract is $320,000. Premiums are payable in monthly installments. As of December 31, 2000, IC has collected $150,000 of installment premiums from X. For the taxable year ended December 31, 2000, IC has paid or incurred $21,000 of premium acquisition expenses related to the insurance contract. IC's total premium acquisition expenses for the insurance contract, based on the $320,000 gross premium, are $48,000.

(ii) Under paragraph (a)(5)(iv) of this section, IC may elect to report only the $150,000 of installment premiums (rather than the $320,000 estimated gross premium) in gross premiums written for the taxable year ended December 31, 2000, provided that its deduction for premium acquisition expenses allocable to the insurance contract does not exceed the limitation in paragraph (a)(5)(vii). For the taxable year ended December 31, 2000, IC deducts $21,000 of premium acquisition expenses related to the insurance contract, or 43.75% of total premium acquisition expenses for the insurance contract ($21,000/$48,000 = 43.75%). This ratio does not exceed the ratio of installment premiums to the gross premium for the contract ($150,000/$320,000 = 46.9%). Therefore, under paragraph (a)(5)(iv) of this section, IC may elect to report only $150,000 of installment premiums for the insurance contract (rather than $320,000 of gross premium) in gross premiums written for the taxable year ending December 31, 2000.

Example 6. (i) IC is a non-life insurance company which, pursuant to section 843, files its returns on a calendar year basis. On July 1, 2000, IC issues a one-year workers' compensation policy to X, an employer. The gross premium for the policy is determined by applying a monthly rate of $25 to each of X's employees. This rate is guaranteed for a period of 12 months, beginning with the effective date of the contract. On July 1, 2000, X has 1,050 employees. Based on the assumption that X's payroll would remain constant during the effective period of the contract, IC determines an estimated gross premium for the contract of $315,000 (1,050 × $25 × 12 = $315,000). The estimated gross premium is payable by X in equal monthly installments. At the end of each calendar quarter, the premiums payable under the contract are adjusted based on an audit of X's actual payroll during the preceding three months of coverage.

(ii) Due to an expansion of X's business in 2000, the actual number of employees covered under the contract during each month of the period between July 1, 2000 and December 31, 2000 is 1,050 (July), 1,050 (August), 1,050 (September), 1,200 (October), 1,200 (November), and 1,200 (December). The increase in the number of employees during the year is not attributable to a temporary or seasonal variation in X's business activities and is expected to continue for the remainder of the effective period of the contract.

(iii) Under paragraph(a)(5)(i) of this section, IC is required to report gross premiums written for the insurance contract based the effective period of the contract. The effective period of X's contract is based on the 12 month period for which IC has guaranteed rates for insurance coverage. Under paragraph (a)(5)(ii), IC must also report the additional premiums resulting from the change in risk exposure under the contract for the taxable year in which the change in such exposure occurs. Unless the change in risk exposure is of temporary duration, the additional gross premiums are included in gross premiums written for the remainder of the effective period of the contract. Thus, for the taxable year ending December 31, 2000, IC reports gross premiums written of $348,750 with respect to the workers' compensation contract issued to X, consisting of the sum of the initial gross premium for the contract ($315,000) plus the additional gross premium attributable to the 150 employees added to X's payroll who will be covered during the last nine months of the contract's effective period (150 × $25 (monthly premium) × 9 = $33,750). IC's unearned premium with respect to the contract was $180,000 as of December 31, 2000, which consists of the sum of the remaining portion of the original gross premium ($315,000 × 6/12 = $157,500), plus the additional premiums resulting from the change in risk exposure ($33,750 × 6/9 = $22,500) that are allocable to the remaining six months of the contract's effective period. Pursuant to section 832(b)(4)(B), to determine its premiums earned, IC deducts $144,000 ($180,000 = .8) for the insurance contract at the end of the taxable year.

Example 7. (i) The facts are the same as Example 6, except that the increase in the number of X's employees for the period ending December 31, 2000 is attributable to a seasonal variation in X's business activity.

(ii) Under paragraph (a)(5)(ii) of this section, for the taxable year ending December 31, 2000, IC reports gross premiums written of $326,500, consisting of the sum of the initial gross premium for the contract ($315,000) plus the additional premium attributable to the temporary increase in risk exposure during the taxable year (150 × $25 × 3 = $11,250). The unearned premium that is allocable to the remaining six months of the effective period of the contract is $157,500. Pursuant to section 832(b)(4)(B), to determine its premiums earned, IC deducts $126,000 ($157,500 × .8) for the insurance contract at the end of the taxable year.

Example 8. (i) IC, a non-life insurance company, issues a noncancellable accident and health insurance contract (other than a qualified long-term care insurance contract, as defined in section 7702B(b)) to A, an individual, on July 1, 2000. The contract has an entry-age annual premium of $2,400, which is payable by A in equal monthly installments of $200 on the first day of each month of coverage. IC incurs agents' commissions, premium taxes, and other premium acquisition expenses equal to 10% of the gross premiums received for the contract. As of December 31, 2000, IC has collected $1,200 of installment premiums for the contract.

(ii) A noncancellable accident and health insurance contract is a contract described in section 832(b)(7). Thus, under paragraph (a)(5)(vi) of this section, IC may report gross premiums written in the manner required for life insurance companies under sections 803 and 811. Accordingly, for the taxable year ending December 31, 2000, IC may report gross premiums written of $1,200, based on the premiums actually received on the contract. Pursuant to section (a)(5)(vi) of this section, IC deducts a total of $28 of premium acquisition costs for the contract, based on the difference between the acquisition costs actually paid or incurred under section 811(a) ($1,200 × .10 = $120) and the amount required to taken into account under section 848 in connection with the net premiums for the contract ($1,200 × .077 = $92).

(iii) Under paragraph (a)(8)(ii)(A) of this section, IC includes the amount of life insurance reserves (as defined in section 816(b), but computed in accordance with section 807(d) and sections 811(c) and (d)) in unearned premiums under section 832(b)(4)(B). Section 807(d)(3)(A)(iii) requires IC to use a two-year preliminary term method to compute the amount of life insurance reserves for a noncancellable accident and health insurance contract (other than a qualified long-term care contract). Under this tax reserve

Reg. § 1.832-4(a)(10)

method, no portion of the $1,200 gross premium received by IC for A's contract is allocable to future insurance coverage. Accordingly, for the taxable year ending December 31, 2000, no life insurance reserves are included in IC's unearned premiums under section 832(b)(4)(B) with respect to the contract.

Example 9. (i) IC, a non-life insurance company, issues an insurance contract with a twelve month effective period for $1,200 on December 1, 2000. Immediately thereafter, IC reinsures 90% of its liability under the insurance contract for $900 with IC-2, an unrelated and solvent insurance company. On December 31, 2000, IC-2 has an $825 unearned premium with respect to the reinsurance contract it issued to IC. In computing its earned premiums, pursuant to section 832(b)(4)(B), IC-2 deducts $660 of unearned premiums ($825 × .8) with respect to the reinsurance contract.

(ii) Under paragraph (a)(8)(i) of this section, unearned premiums held by an insurance company with regard to the net value of the risks reinsured in other solvent companies are deducted from the ceding company's unearned premiums taken into account for purposes of section 832(b)(4)(B). If IC had not reinsured 90% of its risks, IC's unearned premium for the insurance contract would have been $1,100 ($1,200 × 11/12) and IC would have deducted $880 ($1,100 × .8) of unearned premiums with respect to such contract. However, because IC reinsured 90% of its risks under the contract with IC-2, as of December 31, 2000, the net value of the risks retained by IC for the remaining 11 months of the effective period of the contract is $110 ($1,100 − $990). For the taxable year ending December 31, 2000, IC includes the $1,200 gross premium in its gross premiums written and deducts the $900 reinsurance premium paid to IC-2 under section 832(b)(4)(A). Pursuant to section 832(b)(4)(B), to determine its premiums earned, IC deducts $88 ($110 × .8) for the insurance contract at the end of the taxable year.

(11) *Change in method of accounting*—(i) *In general.* A change in the method of determining premiums earned to comply with the provisions of paragraphs (a)(3) through (a)(10) of this section is a change in method of accounting for which the consent of the Commissioner is required under section 446(e) and § 1.446-1(e).

(ii) *Application.* For the first taxable year beginning after December 31, 1999, a taxpayer is granted consent of the Commissioner to change its method of determining premiums earned to comply with the provisions of paragraphs (a)(3) through (a)(10) of this section. A taxpayer changing its method of accounting in accordance with this section must follow the automatic change in accounting provisions of Rev. Proc. 99-49, 1999-52 I.R.B. 725 (see § 601.601(d)(2) of this chapter), except that—

(A) The scope limitations in section 4.02 of Rev. Proc. 99-49 shall not apply;

(B) The timely duplicate filing requirement in section 6.02(2) of Rev. Proc. 99-49 shall not apply; and

(C) If the method of accounting for determining premiums earned is an issue under consideration within the meaning of section 3.09 of Rev. Proc. 99-49 as of January 5, 2000, then section 7.01 of Rev. Proc. 99-49 shall not apply.

(12) *Effective date.* Paragraphs (a)(3) through (a)(11) of this section are applicable with respect to the determination of premiums earned for taxable years beginning after December 31, 1999.

(13) In computing the amount of unabsorbed premium deposits which a mutual fire or flood insurance company described in section 831(a)(3)(B) would be obligated to return to its policyholders at the close of its taxable year, the company must use its own schedule of unabsorbed premium deposit returns then in effect. A copy of the applicable schedule must be filed with the company's income tax return for each taxable year for which a computation based upon such schedule is made. In addition, a taxpayer making such a computation must provide the following information for each taxable year for which the computation is made:

(i) The amount of gross premiums received during the taxable year, and the amount of premiums paid for reinsurance during the taxable year, on the policies described in section 831(a)(3)(B) and on other policies;

(ii) The amount of insurance written during the taxable year under the policies described in section 831(a)(3)(B) and under other policies, and the amount of such insurance written which was reinsured during the taxable year. The information required under this subdivision shall only be submitted upon the specific request of the district director for a statement setting forth such information, and, if required, such statement shall be filed in the manner provided by this subparagraph or in such other manner as is satisfactory to the district director;

(iii) The amount of premiums earned during the taxable year on the policies described in section 831(a)(3)(B) and on other policies and the computations by which such amounts were determined, including sufficient information to support

Reg. § 1.832-4(a)(13)

the taxpayer's determination of the amount of unearned premiums on premium deposit plan and other policies at the beginning and end of the taxable year, and the amount of unabsorbed premium deposits at the beginning and end of the taxable year on policies described in section 831(a)(3)(B).

The information required by this subparagraph shall be set forth in a statement attached to the taxpayer's income tax return for the taxable year for which such information is being provided. Such statement shall include the name and address of the taxpayer, and shall be filed not later than the date prescribed by law (including extensions thereof) for filing the income tax return for the taxable year.

(14) In computing "losses incurred" the determination of unpaid losses at the close of each year must represent actual unpaid losses as nearly as it is possible to ascertain them.

(b) *Losses incurred.* Every insurance company to which this section applies must be prepared to establish to the satisfaction of the district director that the part of the deduction for "losses incurred" which represents unpaid losses at the close of the taxable year comprises only actual unpaid losses. See section 846 for rules relating to the determination of discounted unpaid losses. These losses must be stated in amounts which, based upon the facts in each case and the company's experience with similar cases, represent a fair and reasonable estimate of the amount the company will be required to pay. Amounts included in, or added to, the estimates of unpaid losses which, in the opinion of the district director, are in excess of a fair and reasonable estimate will be disallowed as a deduction. The district director may require any insurance company to submit such detailed information with respect to its actual experience as is deemed necessary to establish the reasonableness of the deduction for "losses incurred."

(c) *Losses incurred are reduced by salvage.* Under section 832(b)(5)(A), losses incurred are computed by taking into account losses paid reduced by salvage and reinsurance recovered, the change in discounted unpaid losses, and the change in estimated salvage and reinsurance recoverable. For purposes of section 832(b)(5)(A)(iii), estimated salvage recoverable includes all anticipated recoveries on account of salvage, whether or not the salvage is treated, or may be treated, as an asset for state statutory accounting purposes. Estimates of salvage recoverable must be based on the facts of each case and the company's experience with similar cases. Except as otherwise provided in guidance published by the Commissioner in the Internal Revenue Bulletin, estimated salvage recoverable must be discounted either—

(1) By using the applicable discount factors published by the Commissioner for estimated salvage recoverable; or

(2) By using the loss payment pattern for a line of business as the salvage recovery pattern for that line of business and by using the applicable interest rate for calculating unpaid losses under section 846(c).

For purposes of section 832(b)(5)(A) and the regulations thereunder, the term "salvage recoverable" includes anticipated recoveries on account of subrogation claims arising with respect to paid or unpaid losses.

(d) *Increase in unpaid losses shown on annual statement in certain circumstances*—(1) *In general.* An insurance company that takes estimated salvage recoverable into account in determining the amount of its unpaid losses shown on its annual statement is allowed to increase its unpaid losses by the amount of estimated salvage recoverable taken into account if the company complies with the disclosure requirement of paragraph (d)(2) of this section. This adjustment shall not be used in determining under section 846(d) the loss payment pattern for a line of business.

(2) *Disclosure requirement*—(i) *In general.* A company described in paragraph (d)(1) of this section is allowed to increase the unpaid losses shown on its annual statement only if the company either—

(A) Discloses on its annual statement, by line of business and accident year, the extent to which estimated salvage recoverable is taken into account in computing the unpaid losses shown on the annual statement filed by the company for the calendar year ending with or within the taxable year of the company; or

(B) Files a statement on or before the due date of its Federal income tax return (determined without regard to extensions) with the appropriate state regulatory authority of each state to which the company is required to submit an annual statement. The statement must be contained in a separate document captioned "DISCLOSURE CONCERNING LOSS RESERVES" and must disclose, by line of business and accident year, the extent to which estimated salvage recoverable is taken into account in computing the unpaid losses shown on the annual statement filed by the company for the calendar year ending with or within the taxable year of the company.

(ii) *Transitional rule.* For a taxable year ending before December 31, 1991, a taxpayer is deemed to satisfy the disclosure requirement of paragraph (d)(2)(i)(B) of this section if the taxpayer files the statement described in paragraph (d)(2)(i)(B) of this section before March 17, 1992.

(3) *Failure to disclose in a subsequent year.* If a company that claims the increase permitted by paragraph (d)(1) of this section fails in a subsequent taxable year to make the disclosure described in paragraph (d)(2) of this section, the company cannot claim an increase under paragraph (d)(1) of this section in any subsequent taxable year without the consent of the Commissioner.

(e) *Treatment of estimated salvage recoverable*—(1) *In general.* An insurance company is required to take estimated salvage recoverable (including that which cannot be treated as an asset for state statutory accounting purposes) into account in computing the deduction for losses incurred. Except as provided in paragraph (e)(2)(iii) of this section, an insurance company must apply this method of accounting to estimated salvage recoverable for all lines of business and for all accident years.

(2) *Change in method of accounting*—(i) If an insurance company did not take estimated salvage recoverable into account as required by paragraph (c) of this section for its last taxable year beginning before January 1, 1990, taking estimated salvage recoverable into account as required by paragraph (c) of this section is a change in method of accounting.

(ii) If a company does not claim the deduction under section 11305(c)(3) of the 1990 Act, the company must take into account 13 percent of the adjustment that would otherwise be required under section 481 for pre-1990 accident years as a result of the change in accounting method. This paragraph (e)(2)(ii) applies only to an insurance company subject to tax under section 831.

(iii) If a company claims the deduction under section 11305(c)(3) of the 1990 Act and paragraph (f) of this section, the company must implement the change in method of accounting for estimated salvage recoverable for post-1989 taxable years pursuant to a "cut-off" method.

(3) *Rule for overestimates.* An insurance company is required under section 11305(c)(4) of the 1990 Act to include in gross income 87 percent of any amount (adjusted for discounting) by which the section 481 adjustment is overestimated. The rule is applied by comparing the amount of the section 481 adjustment (determined without regard to paragraph (e)(2)(ii) of this section and any discounting) to the sum of the actual salvage recoveries and remaining undiscounted estimated salvage recoverable that are attributable to losses incurred in accident years beginning before 1990. For any taxable year beginning after December 31, 1989, any excess of the section 481 adjustment over this sum (reduced by amounts treated as overestimates in prior taxable years pursuant to this paragraph (e)(3)) is an overestimate. To determine the amount to be included in income, it is necessary to discount this excess and multiply the resulting amount by 87 percent.

(f) *Special deduction*—(1) *In general.* Under section 11305(c)(3) of the 1990 Act, an insurance company may deduct an amount equal to 87 percent of the discounted amount of estimated salvage recoverable that the company took into account in determining the deduction for losses incurred under section 832(b)(5) in the last taxable year beginning before January 1, 1990. A company that claims the special deduction must establish to the satisfaction of the district director that the deduction represents only the discounted amount of estimated salvage recoverable that was actually taken into account by the company in computing losses incurred for that taxable year.

(2) *Safe harbor.* The requirements of paragraph (f)(1) of this section are deemed satisfied and the amount that the company reports as bona fide estimated salvage recoverable is not subject to adjustment by the district director, if—

(i) The company files with the insurance regulatory authority of the company's state of domicile, on or before September 16, 1991, a statement disclosing the extent to which losses incurred for each line of business reported on its 1989 annual statement were reduced by estimated salvage recoverable,

(ii) The company attaches a statement to its Federal income tax return filed for the first taxable year beginning after December 31, 1989, agreeing to apply the special rule for overestimates under section 11305(c)(4) of the 1990 Act to the amount of estimated salvage recoverable for which it has taken the special deduction, and

(iii) In the case of a company that is a member of a consolidated group, each insurance company subject to tax under section 831 that is included in the consolidated group complies with paragraph (f)(2)(ii) of this section with respect to its special deduction, if any.

(3) *Limitations on special deduction*—(i) The special deduction under section 11305(c)(3) of the 1990 Act is available only to an insurance company subject to tax under section 831.

(ii) An insurance company that claimed the benefit of the "fresh start" with respect to estimated salvage recoverable under section 1023(e) of the Tax Reform Act of 1986 may not claim the special deduction allowed by section 11305(c)(3) of the 1990 Act to the extent of the estimated salvage recoverable for which a fresh start benefit was previously claimed.

(iii) A company that claims the special deduction is precluded from also claiming the section 481 adjustment provided in paragraph (e)(2)(ii) of this section for pre-1990 accident years.

(g) *Effective date.* Paragraphs (b) through (f) of this section are effective for taxable years beginning after December 31, 1989. [Reg. § 1.832-4.]

☐ [T.D. 8390, 1-27-92. Amended by T.D. 8857, 1-5-2000.]

[Reg. § 1.832-5]

§ 1.832-5. Deductions.—(a) The deductions allowable are specified in section 832(c) and by reason of the provisions of section 832(c)(10) and (12) include in addition certain deductions provided in sections 161, and 241 and following. The deductions, however, are subject to the limitation provided in section 265, relating to expenses and interest in respect of tax-exempt income. The net operating loss deduction is computed under section 172 and the regulations thereunder. For the purposes of section 172, relating to net operating loss deduction, "gross income" shall mean gross income as defined in section 832(b)(1) and the allowable deductions shall be those allowed by section 832(c) with the exceptions and limitations set forth in section 172(d). In addition to the deduction for capital losses provided in subchapter P (section 1201 and following), chapter 1 of the Code, insurance companies are allowed a deduction for losses from capital assets sold or exchanged in order to obtain funds to meet abnormal insurance losses and to provide for the payment of dividends and similar distributions to policyholders. A special rule is provided for the application of the capital loss carryover provisions of section 1212. The deduction is the same as that allowed mutual insurance companies subject to the tax imposed by section 821; see section 822(c)(6) and the regulations thereunder. Insurance companies, other than mutual fire insurance companies described in section 831(a)(3)(A) and the regulations thereunder, are also allowed a deduction for dividends and similar distributions paid or declared to policyholders in their capacity as such. Similar distributions include such payments as the so-called unabsorbed premium deposits returned to policyholders by factory mutual insurance companies. The deduction is otherwise the same as that allowed mutual insurance companies subject to the tax imposed by section 821; see section 822(f)(2) and the regulations thereunder.

(b) Among the items which may not be deducted are income and profits taxes imposed by the United States, income and profits taxes imposed by any foreign country or possession of the United States (in cases where the company chooses to claim to any extent a credit for such taxes), taxes assessed against local benefits, decrease during the year due to adjustments in the book value of capital assets, decrease in liabilities during the year on account of reinsurance treaties, dividends paid to shareholders in their capacity as such, remittances to the home office of a foreign insurance company by the United States branch, and borrowed money repaid.

(c) In computing taxable income of insurance companies, losses sustained during the taxable year from the sale or other disposition of property are deductible subject to the limitation contained in section 1211. Insurance companies are entitled to the alternative taxes provided in section 1201. [Reg. § 1.832-5.]

☐ [T.D. 6681, 10-16-63. Amended by T.D. 6867, 12-6-65.]

[Reg. § 1.832-6]

§ 1.832-6. Policyholders of mutual fire or flood insurance companies operating on the basis of premium deposits.—For purposes of determining his taxable income for any taxable year, a taxpayer insured by a mutual fire or flood insurance company under a policy for which the premium deposit is the same regardless of the length of the term for which the policy is written, and who is entitled to have returned or credited to him on the cancellation or expiration of such policy the unabsorbed portion of the premium deposit not required for losses, expenses, or establishment of reserves, may, if such amount is otherwise deductible under this chapter, deduct so much of his premium deposit as was absorbed by the company during the taxpayer's taxable year. The amount of the premium deposit absorbed during the taxpayer's taxable year shall be determined in accordance with the schedule of unabsorbed premium deposit returns in effect for the company during such taxable year. If the taxpayer is unable to determine the applicable rate of absorption in effect during his taxable year, he shall compute his deduction on the basis of the rate of absorption in effect at the end of the company's taxable year which next preceded the end of the taxpayer's taxable year. In such a case, an appropriate adjustment will be made upon the final determination of the rate of absorption applicable to the taxable year. [Reg. § 1.832-6.]

☐ [T.D. 6681, 10-16-63.]

Provisions of General Application

See p. 20,601 for regulations not amended to reflect law changes

[Reg. § 1.832-7T]

§ 1.832-7T. Treatment of salvage and reinsurance in computing "losses incurred" deduction, taxable years beginning before January 1, 1990 (temporary).—(a) In computing "losses incurred" the determination of unpaid losses at the close of each year must represent actual unpaid losses as nearly as it is possible to ascertain them.

(b) Every insurance company to which this section applies must be prepared to establish to the satisfaction of the district director that the part of the deduction for "losses incurred" which represents unpaid losses at the close of the taxable year comprises only actual unpaid losses stated in amounts which, based upon the facts in each case and the company's experience with similar cases, can be said to represent a fair and reasonable estimate of the amount the company will be required to pay. Amounts included in, or added to, the estimates of such losses which in the opinion of the district director are in excess of the actual liability determined as provided in the preceding sentence will be disallowed as a deduction. The district director may require any such insurance company to submit such detailed information with respect to its actual experience as is deemed necessary to establish the reasonableness of the deduction for "losses incurred".

(c) That part of the deduction for "losses incurred" which represents an adjustment to losses paid for salvage and reinsurance recoverable shall, except as hereinafter provided, include all salvage in course of liquidation, and all reinsurance in process of collection not otherwise taken into account as a reduction of losses paid, outstanding at the end of the taxable year. Salvage in course of liquidation includes all property (other than cash), real or personal, tangible or intangible, except that which may not be included by reason of express statutory provisions (or rules and regulations of an insurance department) of any State or Territory or the District of Columbia in which the company transacts business. Such salvage in course of liquidation shall be taken into account to the extent of the value thereof at the end of the taxable year as determined from a fair and reasonable estimate based upon either the facts in each case or the company's experience with similar cases. Cash received during the taxable year with respect to items of salvage or reinsurance shall be taken into account in computing losses paid during such taxable year.

(d) This section is effective for taxable years beginning before January 1, 1990. [Temporary Reg. § 1.832-7T.]

☐ [T.D. 8266, 9-21-89. Amended by T.D. 8293, 3-13-90.]

→ *Caution: Code Sec. 834 was formerly Code Sec. 822. See Reg. §§ 1.822-4–1.822-12 for rules issued under former Code Sec. 822.* ←

→ *Caution: Code Sec. 835 was formerly Code Sec. 826. See Reg. §§ 1.826-1–1.826-7 for rules issued under former Code Sec. 826.* ←

Provisions of General Application

[Reg. § 1.846-0]

§ 1.846-0. Outline of provisions.

The following is a list of the headings in §§ 1.846-1 through 1.846-4.

§ 1.846-1. Application of discount factors.

(a) In general.

   (1) Rules.

   (2) Examples.

   (3) Increase in discounted unpaid losses shown on the annual statement.

   (4) Increase in unpaid losses which take into account estimated salvage recoverable.

(b) Applicable discount factors.

   (1) In general.

      (i) Discount factors published by the Service.

      (ii) Composite discount factors.

      (iii) Annual statement changes.

   (2) Title insurance company reserves.

   (3) Reinsurance business.

      (i) Proportional reinsurance for accident years after 1987.

      (ii) Non-proportional reinsurance.

         (A) Accident years after 1991.

         (B) Accident years 1988 through 1991.

      (iii) Reinsurance for accident years before 1988.

      (iv) 90 percent exception.

   (4) International business.

   (5) Composite discount factors.

§ 1.846-2. Election by taxpayer to use its own historical loss payment pattern.

Reg. § 1.846-0

Provisions of General Application

See p. 20,601 for regulations not amended to reflect law changes

(a) In general.
(b) Eligible line of business.
   (1) In general.
   (2) Other published guidance.
   (3) Special rule for 1987 determination year.
(c) Anti-abuse rule.

§ 1.846-3. Fresh start and reserve strengthening.
(a) In general.
(b) Applicable discount factors.
   (1) Calculation of beginning balance.
   (2) Example.
(c) Rules for determining the amount of reserve strengthening.
   (1) In general.
   (2) Accident years after 1985.
     (i) In general.
     (ii) Hypothetical unpaid loss reserve.
   (3) Accident years before 1986.
     (i) In general.
     (ii) Exceptions.
     (iii) Certain transactions deemed to be reinsurance assumed (ceded) in 1986.
(d) Section 845.
(e) Treatment of reserve strengthening.
(f) Examples.

§ 1.846-4. Effective date. [Reg. § 1.846-0.]
☐ [T.D. 8433, 9-4-92.]

[Reg. § 1.846-1]

§ 1.846-1. Application of discount factors.— (a) *In general*—(1) *Rules.* A separate series of discount factors are computed for, and applied, to undiscounted unpaid losses attributable to each accident year of each line of business shown on the annual statement (as defined by section 846(f)(3)) filed by that taxpayer for the calendar year ending with or within the taxable year of the taxpayer. See § 1.832-4(b) relating to the determination of unpaid losses. Paragraph (b) of this section provides rules relating to applicable discount factors and § 1.846-3(b) contains guidance relating to discount factors applicable to accident years prior to the 1987 accident year. Once a taxpayer applies a series of discount factors to unpaid losses attributable to an accident year of a line of business, that series of discount factors must be applied to discount the unpaid losses for that accident year for that line of business for all future taxable years. The discount factors cannot be changed to reflect a change in the taxpayer's loss payment pattern during a subsequent year or to reflect a different interest rate assumption. However, discount factors may be changed for taxpayers who elect to use their own historical loss payment pattern, if information upon which the pattern is based is adjusted upon examination by the district director.

(2) *Examples.* The following examples illustrate the principles of paragraph (a)(1) of this section:

Example 1. A taxpayer discounts unpaid losses attributable to all accident years prior to 1992 using discount factors published by the Service. In 1992, the taxpayer elects, under § 1.846-2, to compute discount factors using its own historical loss payment pattern. The taxpayer must continue to discount unpaid losses attributable to pre-1992 accident years using the discount factors published for those accident years by the Service.

Example 2. On its annual statements through 1987, a taxpayer did not allocate unpaid losses attributable to proportional reinsurance to the line of business associated with the risks being reinsured. Beginning with the 1988 annual statement, the taxpayer allocated those losses for all accident years to the line of business being reinsured. The taxpayer must continue to discount the unpaid losses attributable to proportional reinsurance from pre-1988 accident years using the discount factors that were used in determining tax reserves for the 1987 tax year. (See paragraph (b)(3) of this section for rules relating to the application of discount factors to reinsurance unpaid losses.)

(3) *Increase in discounted unpaid losses shown on the annual statement.* If the amount of unpaid losses shown on the annual statement is determined on a discounted basis, and the extent to which the unpaid losses were discounted can be determined on the basis of information disclosed on or with the annual statement, the amount of the unpaid losses to which the discount factors are applied shall be determined without regard to any reduction attributable to the discounting reflected on the annual statement.

(4) *Increase in unpaid losses which take into account estimated salvage recoverable.* If the amount of unpaid losses shown on the annual statement reflects a reduction for estimated salvage recoverable and the extent to which the unpaid losses were reduced by estimated salvage recoverable is appropriately disclosed as required by § 1.832-4(d)(2), the amount of unpaid losses shall be determined without regard to the reduction for salvage recoverable.

(b) *Applicable discount factors*—(1) *In general.* Except as otherwise provided in section 846(f)(6) (relating to certain accident and health lines of business), in § 1.846-2 (relating to a taxpayer's election to use its own historical loss payment pattern), in this paragraph (b), or in other guidance published in the Internal Revenue Bulletin, the following factors must be used—

(i) *Discount factors published by the Service.* If the Service has published discount factors for a line of business, a taxpayer must discount unpaid losses attributable to that line by applying those discount factors; and

(ii) *Composite discount factors.* If the Service has not published discount factors for a line of business, a taxpayer must discount unpaid losses attributable to that line by applying composite discount factors.

(iii) *Annual statement changes.* If the groupings of individual lines of business on the annual statement changes, taxpayers must discount the unpaid losses on the resulting lines of business with the discounting patterns that would have applied to those unpaid losses based on their annual statement classification prior to the change.

(2) *Title insurance company reserves.* A title insurance company may only take into account case reserves (relating to claims which have been reported to the insurance company). Unless the Service publishes other guidance, the reserves must be discounted using the "Miscellaneous Casualty" discount factors published by the Service. Section 832(b)(8) provides rules for determining the discounted unearned premiums of a title insurance company.

(3) *Reinsurance business*—(i) *Proportional reinsurance for accident years after 1987.* For the 1988 accident year and subsequent accident years, unpaid losses for proportional reinsurance must be discounted using discount factors applicable to the line of business to which those unpaid losses are allocated as required on the annual statement.

(ii) *Non-proportional reinsurance*—(A) *Accident years after 1991.* For the 1992 accident year and subsequent accident years, unpaid losses for non-proportional reinsurance must be discounted using the applicable discount factors published by the Service for the appropriate reinsurance line of business.

(B) *Accident years 1988 through 1991.* For the 1988, 1989, 1990, and 1991 accident years unpaid losses for non-proportional reinsurance must be discounted using composite discount factors.

(iii) *Reinsurance for accident years before 1988.* If on its annual statement a taxpayer does not allocate unpaid losses to the applicable line of business for proportional or nonproportional reinsurance attributable to the 1987 accident year or a prior accident year, those losses must be discounted using composite discount factors. If on its annual statement a taxpayer allocates to the underlying line of business reinsurance unpaid losses that are attributable to the 1987 accident year or a prior accident year, those losses must be discounted using discount factors applicable to the underlying line of business.

(iv) *90 percent exception.* For purposes of § 1.846-1(b)(3)(ii) and (iii), if more than 90 percent of all the unallocated losses of a taxpayer for an accident year relate to one underlying line of business, the taxpayer must discount all unallocated reinsurance unpaid losses attributable to that accident year using the discount factors published by the Service for the underlying line of business.

(4) *International business.* For any accident year, unpaid losses which are attributable to international business must be discounted using composite discount factors unless more than 90 percent of all losses for that accident year relate to one underlying line of business. If more than 90 percent of all losses for an accident year relate to one underlying line of business, the taxpayer must discount the losses attributable to that accident year using discount factors published by the Service for the underlying line of business.

(5) *Composite discount factors.* For purposes of the regulations under section 846, "composite discount factors" means the series of discount factors published annually by the Service determined on the basis of the appropriate composite loss payment pattern. [Reg. § 1.846-1.]

☐ [*T.D.* 8433, 9-4-92.]

[Reg. § 1.846-2]

§ 1.846-2. **Election by taxpayer to use its own historical loss payment pattern.**—(a) *In general.* If a taxpayer has one or more eligible lines of business in a determination year, the taxpayer may elect on the taxpayer's timely filed Federal income tax return for the determination year to discount unpaid losses using its own historical loss payment pattern instead of the industry-wide pattern determined by the Secretary. A taxpayer making the election must use its own historical loss payment pattern in discounting unpaid losses for each line of business that is an eligible line of business in that determination year. The election applies to accident years ending with the determination year and to each of the four succeeding accident years. If a taxpayer makes the election for the 1987 determination year, the taxpayer must use its 1987 loss payment pattern (determined by reference to its 1985 annual statement) to discount unpaid losses attributable to all accident years prior to 1988.

(b) *Eligible line of business*—(1) *In general.* A line of business is an eligible line of business in a determination year if, on the most recent annual statement filed by the taxpayer before the beginning of that determination year, the taxpayer reports losses and loss expenses incurred (in Schedule P, part 1, column 24 of the 1990 annual statement or comparable location in an earlier or subsequently revised blank) for at least the number of accident years for which losses and loss expenses incurred for that line of business are required to be separately reported on that annual statement. For example, for the 1987 determination year, the 1985 annual statement is used. The annual statement to be used to determine eligibility in subsequent determination years is the annual statement for each fifth year after 1985 (e.g., 1990, 1995, etc.).

(2) *Other published guidance.* A line of business is also an eligible line of business for purposes of the election if the line is an eligible line under requirements published for this purpose in the Internal Revenue Bulletin.

(3) *Special rule for 1987 determination year.* A line of business is an eligible line of business in the 1987 determination year if it is eligible under paragraph (b)(1) or (2) of this section, or if on the most recent annual statement filed by the taxpayer before the beginning of the 1987 determination year, the taxpayer reports written premiums for the line of business for at least the number of accident years that unpaid losses for that line of business are required to be separately reported on that annual statement.

(c) *Anti-abuse rule.* To prevent avoidance of the requirement that the election to use historical loss payment patterns apply to all eligible lines of business of a taxpayer, the district director may—

(1) Nullify a taxpayer's election to compute discounted unpaid losses based on its historical loss payment pattern;

(2) Adjust a taxpayer's historical loss payment pattern; or

(3) Make other proper adjustments. [Reg. § 1.846-2.]

☐ [*T.D.* 8433, 9-4-92.]

[Reg. § 1.846-3]

§ 1.846-3. **Fresh start and reserve strengthening.**—(a) *In general.* Section 1023(e) of the Tax Reform Act of 1986 ("the 1986 Act") provides rules relating to fresh start and reserve strengthening. For purposes of section 1023(e) of the 1986 Act, a taxpayer must discount its unpaid losses as of the end of the last taxable year beginning before January 1, 1987. The excess of undiscounted unpaid losses over discounted unpaid losses as of that time is not required to be included in income, except (as provided in paragraph (e) of this section) to the extent of any "reserve strengthening" in a taxable year beginning in 1986. The exclusion from income of this excess is known as "fresh start." The amount of fresh start is, however, included in earnings and profits for the first taxable year beginning after December 31, 1986.

(b) *Applicable discount factors*—(1) *Calculation of beginning balance.* For purposes of section 1023(e) of the 1986 Act, a taxpayer discounts unpaid losses as of the end of the last taxable year beginning before January 1, 1987—

(i) By using the same discount factors that are used in the succeeding taxable year to discount unpaid losses attributable to the 1987 accident year and prior accident years (see section 1023(e)(2) of the 1986 Act); and

(ii) By applying those discount factors as if the 1986 accident year were the 1987 accident year.

(2) *Example.* The following example illustrates the principles of this paragraph (b):

Example. X, a calendar year taxpayer, does not make an election in 1987 to use its own historical loss payment pattern. When X computes discounted unpaid losses for its last taxable year beginning before January 1, 1987, the discount factor for AY + 0 published in Rev. Rul. 87-34, 1987-1 C.B. 168, must be applied to unpaid losses attributable to the 1986 accident year; the discount factor for AY + 1 is applied to unpaid losses attributable to the 1985 accident year; etc.

(c) *Rules for determining the amount of reserve strengthening (weakening)*—(1) *In general.* The amount of reserve strengthening (weakening) is the amount that is determined under paragraph (c)(2) or (3) to have been added to (subtracted from) an unpaid loss reserve in a taxable year beginning in 1986. For purposes of section 1023(e)(3)(B) of the 1986 Act, the amount of reserve strengthening (weakening) must be determined separately for each unpaid loss reserve by applying the rules of this paragraph (c). This determination is made without regard to the reasonableness of the amount of the unpaid loss reserve and without regard to the taxpayer's discretion, or lack thereof, in establishing the amount of the unpaid loss reserve. The amount of reserve strengthening for an unpaid loss reserve may not exceed the amount of the reserve, including any undiscounted strengthening amount, as of the end of the last taxable year beginning before January 1, 1987. For purposes of this section, an "unpaid loss reserve" is the aggregate of the unpaid loss estimates for losses (whether or not reported) incurred in an accident year of a line of business.

(2) *Accident years after 1985*—(i) *In general.* The amount of reserve strengthening (weakening) for an unpaid loss reserve for an accident year after 1985 is the amount by which that reserve at the end of the last taxable year beginning in 1986 exceeds (is less than) a hypothetical unpaid loss reserve.

(ii) *Hypothetical unpaid loss reserve.* For purposes of this paragraph (c)(2), the term "hypothetical unpaid loss reserve" means a reserve computed for losses the estimates of which were included, at the end of the last taxable year beginning in 1986, in the unpaid loss reserve for which reserve strengthening (weakening) is being determined. The hypothetical unpaid loss reserve must be computed using the same assumptions, other than the assumed interest rates in the case of reserves determined on a discounted basis for annual statement reporting purposes, that were used to determine the 1985 accident year reserve, if any, for the line of business for which the hypothetical reserve is being computed. If there was no 1985 accident year reserve for that line of business, the hypothetical unpaid loss reserve is the reserve, at the end of the last taxable year beginning in 1986, for which reserve strengthening (weakening) is being determined (and thus there is no reserve strengthening or weakening).

(3) *Accident years before 1986*—(i) *In general.* For each taxable year beginning in 1986, the amount of reserve strengthening (weakening) for an unpaid loss reserve for an accident year before 1986 is the amount by which the reserve at the end of that taxable year exceeds (is less than)—

(A) The reserve at the end of the immediately preceding taxable year; reduced by

(B) Claims paid and loss adjustment expenses paid ("loss payments") in the taxable year beginning in 1986 with respect to losses that are attributable to the reserve. The amount by which a reserve is reduced as a result of reinsurance ceded during a taxable year beginning in 1986 is treated as a loss payment made in that taxable year.

(ii) *Exceptions.* Notwithstanding paragraph (c)(3)(i) of this section, the amount of reserve strengthening (weakening) for an unpaid loss reserve for an accident year before 1986 does not include—

(A) An amount added to the reserve in a taxable year beginning in 1986 as a result of a loss reported to the taxpayer from a mandatory state or federal assigned risk pool if the amount of the loss reported is not discretionary with the taxpayer; or

(B) Payments made with respect to reinsurance assumed during a taxable year beginning in 1986 or amounts added to the reserve to take into account reinsurance assumed for a line of business during a taxable year beginning in 1986, but only to the extent that the amount does not exceed the amount of a hypothetical reserve for the reinsurance assumed. The amount of the hypothetical reserve is determined using the same assumptions (other than the assumed interest rates) that were used to determine a reserve for reinsurance assumed for the line of business in a taxable year beginning in 1985.

(iii) *Certain transactions deemed to be reinsurance assumed (ceded) in 1986.* For purposes of this paragraph (c)(3), reinsurance assumed (ceded) in a taxable year beginning in 1985 is treated as assumed (ceded) during the succeeding taxable year if the appropriate unpaid loss reserve is not adjusted to take into account the reinsurance transaction until that succeeding taxable year.

(d) *Section 845.* Any reinsurance transaction that has as one of its purposes the avoidance of the reserve strengthening limitation is subject to section 845.

(e) *Treatment of reserve strengthening.* The fresh start provision of section 1023(e)(3)(A) of the 1986 Act does not apply to the portion of the taxpayer's unpaid losses attributable to reserve strengthening. Thus, the difference between the undiscounted unpaid losses attributable to reserve strengthening and the discounted unpaid losses attributable to reserve strengthening must be included in income and, therefore, included in earnings and profits for the first taxable year beginning after December 31, 1986. The amount that a taxpayer must include in income for its first taxable year beginning after December 31, 1986, as a result of reserve strengthening is equal to the excess (if any) of—

(1) The sum of each amount of reserve strengthening multiplied by the difference between 100 percent and the discount factor that, under paragraph (b) of this section, is applicable to the unpaid loss reserve which was strengthened; over

(2) The sum of each reserve weakening multiplied by the difference between 100 percent and the discount factor that, under paragraph (b) of this section, is applicable to the unpaid loss reserve which was weakened.

Reg. § 1.846-3(e)(2)

(f) *Examples.* The following examples illustrate the principles of this section. For purposes of these examples, it is assumed that the taxpayers are property and casualty insurance companies that in 1987 did not elect to use their own historical loss payment patterns.

Example 1. (i) As of the end of 1985, X, a calendar year taxpayer, had undiscounted unpaid losses of $1,000,000 in the workers' compensation line of business for the 1984 accident year. The same reserve had undiscounted unpaid losses of $900,000 at the end of 1986. During 1986, X's loss payments for this reserve were $300,000. Accordingly, under paragraph (c)(3)(i) of this section, X has a reserve strengthening of $200,000 ($900,000 − ($1,000,000 − $300,000)).

(ii) This was X's only reserve strengthening or weakening. Thus, under paragraph (e) of this section, for 1987 X must include in income $54,361.40 ($200,000 × (100% − 72.8193%)). The factor of 72.8193% is the AY + 2 factor from the workers' compensation series of discount factors published in Rev. Rul. 87-34, 1987-1 C.B. 168.

Example 2. The facts are the same as in *Example 1*, except that X's 1986 loss payments for the reserve were $1,100,000. If only paragraph (c)(3)(i) of this section were applied, X would have a $1,000,000 reserve strengthening ($900,000 − ($1,000,000 − $1,100,000)). Under paragraph (c)(1) of this section, however, the amount of reserve strengthening for the reserve is limited to the amount of the reserve at the end of 1986. Accordingly, X has a reserve strengthening of $900,000 and for 1987 must include in income $244,626.30 ($900,000 × (100% − 72.1893%)).

Example 3. (i) As of the end of 1985, Y, a calendar year taxpayer, had undiscounted unpaid losses of $1,000,000 in the auto physical damage line of business for the 1985 accident year. The same reserve included undiscounted unpaid losses of $600,000 at the end of 1986. During 1986, Y had loss payments of $300,000 for this line of business. Under paragraph (c)(3)(i) of this section Y has a $100,000 reserve weakening ($600,000 − ($1,000,000 − $300,000)).

(ii) Under paragraph (e) of this section, the only effect of the reserve weakening is to reduce the amount that Y is required to include in income as a result of any strengthening of another reserve.

Example 4. The facts are the same as in *Example 1* except that X also has a $100,000 reserve weakening for the 1985 accident year in its auto physical damage line of business. Under paragraph (b) of this section, the reserve discount factor for the reserve is 93.3400, the AY + 1 factor from the auto physical damage series of discount factors published in Rev. Rul. 87-34. Thus, under paragraph (e) of this section, the amount that X is required to include in income in 1987 is reduced by $6,660 ($100,000 × (100% − 93.3400%)), resulting in an amount of $47,761.40 ($54,361.40 − $6,660).

Example 5. (i) At the end of 1985, Z, a calendar year taxpayer, had undiscounted unpaid losses of $1,000,000 in the workers' compensation line of business for the 1984 accident year. On May 1, 1986, Z ceded $130,000 of the reserve to an unrelated reinsurer. Z added $250,000 to the 1985 year end reserve to take into account workers' compensation risks for the 1984 accident year that Z assumed in a reinsurance transaction on September 1, 1986. Z had $230,000 of 1986 loss payments related to the 1984 accident year of its workers' compensation line, $60,000 of which was attributable to the reinsurance assumed by Z. At the end of 1986, Z's reserve for the workers' compensation line for the 1984 accident year was $1,100,000.

(ii) If only paragraph (c)(3)(i) of this section were applied, Z would have a $460,000 reserve strengthening ($1,100,000 − ($1,000,000 − $230,000 − $130,000)). Under paragraph (c)(3)(ii)(B) of this section, however, reserve strengthening does not include the $250,000 that Z added to the reserve to take into account the reinsurance assumed. Also, none of the $60,000 of loss payments attributable to the reinsurance assumed in 1986 are taken into account. Accordingly, Z has $150,000 of reserve strengthening ($460,000 − $250,000 − $60,000). If this is Z's only reserve strengthening or weakening, then the amount that Z must include in income for 1987 under paragraph (e) of this section is $40,771.05 ($150,000 × (100% − 72.8193%)). The factor of 72.8193% is the AY + 2 factor from the workers' compensation series of discount factors published in Rev. Rul. 87-34.

Example 6. (i) X was a calendar year taxpayer before July 1, 1986, the date on which X became a member of an affiliated group of corporations that files a consolidated return with a June 30 year end. Thus, X had two taxable years beginning in 1986: a short taxable year ending June 30, 1986, and a fiscal taxable year ending June 30, 1987.

(ii) As of the end of 1985, X had undiscounted unpaid losses of $800,000 in the automobile liability line of business for the 1983 accident year. At the end of the short taxable year, X had reserves of $700,000 of undiscounted unpaid losses, and on June 30, 1987, had reserves of $600,000 of undiscounted unpaid losses. During the short taxable year, ending June 30, 1986, X's loss payments for

Reg. § 1.846-3(f)

Provisions of General Application

this reserve were $120,000. During the taxable year ending June 30, 1987, X's loss payments for this reserve were $180,000. Under paragraph (c)(3)(i) of this section, X has a $100,000 reserve strengthening: of which $20,000 ($700,000 − ($800,000 − $120,000)) is attributable to the short taxable year ending June 30, 1986 and $80,000 ($600,000 − ($700,000 − $180,000)) is attributable to the taxable year ending June 30, 1987.

(iii) The amount of reserve strengthening for this line of business is determined pursuant to the principles of paragraph (c)(2) of this section. [Reg. § 1.846-3.]

☐ [T.D. 8433, 9-4-92.]

[Reg. § 1.846-4]

§ 1.846-4. **Effective date.**—Sections 1.846-1 through Sections 1.846-3 apply to taxable years beginning after December 31, 1986. [Reg. § 1.846-4.]

☐ [T.D. 8433, 9-4-92.]

[Reg. § 1.848-0]

§ 1.848-0. **Outline of regulations under section 848.**

This section lists the paragraphs in §§ 1.848-1 through 1.848-3.

§ 1.848-1. *Definitions and special provisions.*

(a) Scope and effective date.

(b) Specified insurance contract.

(1) In general.

(2) Exceptions.

(i) In general.

(ii) Reinsurance of qualified foreign contracts.

(c) Life insurance contract.

(d) Annuity contract.

(e) Noncancellable accident and health insurance contract.

(f) Guaranteed renewable accident and health insurance contract.

(g) Combination contract.

(1) Definition.

(2) Treatment of premiums on a combination contract.

(i) In general.

(ii) De minimis premiums.

(3) Example.

(h) Group life insurance contract.

(1) In general.

(2) Group affiliation requirement.

(i) In general.

(ii) Employee group.

(iii) Debtor group.

(iv) Labor union group.

(v) Association group.

(vi) Credit union group.

(vii) Multiple group.

(viii) Certain discretionary groups.

(ix) Employees treated as members.

(x) Class or classes of a group determined without regard to individual health characteristics.

(A) In general.

(B) Limitation of coverage based on certain work and age requirements permissible.

(3) Premiums determined on a group basis.

(i) In general.

(ii) Exception for substandard premium rates for certain high risk insureds.

(iii) Flexible premium contracts.

(iv) Determination of actual age.

(4) Underwriting practices used by company. [Reserved]

(5) Disqualification of group.

(i) In general.

(ii) Exception for de minimis failures.

(6) Supplemental life insurance coverage.

(7) Special rules relating to the payment of proceeds.

(i) Contracts issued to a welfare benefit fund.

(ii) Credit life insurance contracts.

(iii) "Organization or association" limited to the sponsor of the contract or the group policyholder.

(i) General deductions.

§ 1.848-2. *Determination of net premiums.*

(a) Net premiums.

(1) In general.

(2) Separate determination of net premiums for certain reinsurance agreements.

(b) Gross amount of premiums and other consideration.

(1) General rule.

(2) Items included.

(3) Treatment of premium deposits.

(i) In general.

(ii) Amounts irrevocably committed to the payment of premiums.

(iii) Retired lives reserves.

(4) Deferred and uncollected premiums.

Reg. § 1.848-0

(c) Policy exchanges.
(1) General rule.
(2) External exchanges.
(3) Internal exchanges resulting in fundamentally different contracts.
(i) In general.
(ii) Certain modifications treated as not changing the mortality, morbidity, interest, or expense guarantees.
(iii) Exception for contracts restructured by a court supervised rehabilitation or similar proceeding.
(4) Value of the contract.
(i) In general.
(ii) Special rule for group term life insurance contracts.
(iii) Special rule for certain policy enhancement and update programs.
(A) In general.
(B) Policy enhancement or update program defined.
(5) Example.
(d) Amounts excluded from the gross amount of premiums and other consideration.
(1) In general.
(2) Amounts received or accrued from a guaranty association.
(3) Exclusion not to apply to dividend accumulations.
(e) Return premiums.
(f) Net consideration for a reinsurance agreement.
(1) In general.
(2) Net consideration determined by a ceding company.
(i) In general.
(ii) Net negative and net positive consideration.
(3) Net consideration determined by the reinsurer.
(i) In general.
(ii) Net negative and net positive consideration.
(4) Timing consistency required.
(5) Modified coinsurance and funds-withheld reinsurance agreements.
(i) In general.
(ii) Special rule for certain funds-withheld reinsurance agreements.
(6) Treatment of retrocessions.
(7) Mixed reinsurance agreements.
(8) Treatment of policyholder loans.
(9) Examples.
(g) Reduction in the amount of net negative consideration to ensure consistency of capitalization for reinsurance agreements.
(1) In general.
(2) Application to reinsurance agreements subject to the interim rules.
(3) Amount of reduction.
(4) Capitalization shortfall.
(5) Required capitalization amount.
(i) In general.
(ii) Special rule with respect to net negative consideration.
(6) General deductions allocable to reinsurance agreements.
(7) Allocation of capitalization shortfall among reinsurance agreements.
(8) Election to determine specified policy acquisition expenses for an agreement without regard to general deductions limitation.
(i) In general.
(ii) Manner of making election.
(iii) Election statement.
(iv) Effect of election.
(9) Examples.
(h) Treatment of reinsurance agreements with parties not subject to U.S. taxation.
(1) In general.
(2) Agreements to which this paragraph (h) applies.
(i) In general.
(ii) Parties subject to U.S. taxation.
(A) In general.
(B) Effect of a closing agreement.
(3) Election to separately determine the amounts required to be capitalized for reinsurance agreements with parties not subject to U.S. taxation.
(i) In general.
(ii) Manner of making the election.
(4) Amount taken into account for purposes of determining specified policy acquisition expenses.
(5) Net foreign capitalization amount.
(i) In general.
(ii) Foreign capitalization amounts by category.
(6) Treatment of net negative foreign capitalization amount.

Reg. § 1.848-0

Provisions of General Application

(i) Applied as a reduction to previously capitalized amounts.

(ii) Carryover of remaining net negative foreign capitalization amount.

(7) Reduction of net positive foreign capitalization amount by carryover amounts allowed.

(8) Examples.

(i) Carryover of excess negative capitalization amount.

(1) In general.

(2) Excess negative capitalization amount.

(3) Treatment of excess negative capitalization amount.

(4) Special rule for the treatment of an excess negative capitalization amount of an insolvent company.

(i) When applicable.

(ii) Election to forego carryover of excess negative capitalization amount.

(iii) Amount of reduction to the excess negative capitalization amount and specified policy acquisition expenses.

(iv) Manner of making election.

(v) Presumptions relating to the insolvency of an insurance company undergoing a court supervised rehabilitation or similar state proceeding.

(vi) Example.

(j) Ceding commissions with respect to reinsurance of contracts other than specified insurance contracts.

(k) Effective dates.

(1) In general.

(2) Reduction in the amount of net negative consideration to ensure consistency of capitalization for reinsurance agreements.

(3) Net consideration rules.

(4) Determination of the date on which a reinsurance agreement is entered into.

(5) Special rule for certain reinsurance agreements with parties not subject to U.S. taxation.

(6) Carryover of excess negative capitalization amount.

§ 1.848-3. Interim rules for certain reinsurance agreements.

(a) Scope and effective dates.

(b) Interim rules.

(c) Adjustments and special rules.

(1) Assumption reinsurance.

(2) Reimbursable dividends.

(3) Ceding commissions.

(i) In general.

(ii) Amount of ceding commission.

(4) Termination payments.

(5) Modified coinsurance agreements.

(d) Examples.

[Reg. § 1.848-0.]

☐ [*T.D.* 8456, 12-28-92.]

[Reg. § 1.848-1]

§ 1.848-1. Definitions and special provisions.—(a) *Scope and effective date.* The definitions and special provisions in this section apply solely for purposes of determining specified policy acquisition expenses under section 848 of the Internal Revenue Code, this section, and §§ 1.848-2 and 1.848-3. Unless otherwise specified, the rules of this section are effective for the taxable years of an insurance company beginning after November 14, 1991.

(b) *Specified insurance contract*—(1) *In general.* A "specified insurance contract" is any life insurance contract, annuity contract, noncancellable or guaranteed renewable accident and health insurance contract, or combination contract. A reinsurance agreement that reinsures the risks under a specified insurance contract is treated in the same manner as the reinsured contract.

(2) *Exceptions*—(i) *In general.* A "specified insurance contract" does not include any pension plan contract (as defined in section 818(a)), flight insurance or similar contract, or qualified foreign contract (as defined in section 807(e)(4)).

(ii) *Reinsurance of qualified foreign contracts.* The exception for qualified foreign contracts does not apply to reinsurance agreements that reinsure qualified foreign contracts.

(c) *Life insurance contract.* A "life insurance contract" is any contract—

(1) Issued after December 31, 1984, that qualifies as a life insurance contract under section 7702(a) (including an endowment contract as defined in 7702(h)); or

(2) Issued prior to January 1, 1985, if the premiums on the contract are reported as life insurance premiums on the insurance company's annual statement (or could be reported as life insurance premiums if the company were required to file the annual statement for life and accident and health companies).

(d) *Annuity contract.* An "annuity contract" is any contract (other than a life insurance contract as defined in paragraph (c) of this section) if amounts received under the contract are subject to the rules in section 72(b) or section 72(e) (determined without regard to section 72(u)). The term "annuity contract" also includes a contract that is a qualified funding asset under section 130(d).

(e) *Noncancellable accident and health insurance contract.* The term "noncancellable accident and health insurance contract" has the same meaning for purposes of section 848 as the term has for purposes of section 816(b).

(f) *Guaranteed renewable accident and health insurance contract.* The term "guaranteed renewable accident and health insurance contract" has the same meaning for purposes of section 848 as the term has for purposes of section 816(e).

(g) *Combination contract*—(1) *Definition.* A "combination contract" is a contract (other than a contract described in section 848(e)(3)) that provides two or more types of insurance coverage, at least one of which if offered separately would be a life insurance contract, an annuity contract, or a noncancellable or guaranteed renewable accident and health insurance contract.

(2) *Treatment of premiums on a combination contract*—(i) *In general.* If the premium allocable to each type of insurance coverage is separately stated on the insurance company's annual statement (or could be separately stated if the insurance company were required to file the annual statement for life and accident and health companies), the premium allocable to each type of insurance coverage in a combination contract is subject to the capitalization rate, if any, that would apply if that coverage was provided in a separate contract. If the premium allocable to each type of insurance coverage in a combination contract is not separately stated, the entire premium is subject to the highest capitalization percentage applicable to any of the coverages provided.

(ii) *De minimis premiums.* For purposes of this paragraph (g)(2)—

(A) A de minimis premium is not required to be separately stated;

(B) In determining the highest capitalization percentage applicable to a combination contract, the coverage to which a de minimis premium is allocable is disregarded;

(C) If the separate statement requirement of this paragraph (g)(2) is satisfied, a de minimis premium is treated in accordance with its characterization on the insurance company's annual statement; and

(D) Whether a premium for an insurance coverage is de minimis is determined by comparing that premium with the aggregate of the premiums for the combination contract. A premium that is not more than 2 percent of the premium for the entire contract is considered de minimis. Whether a premium that is more than 2 percent is de minimis is determined based on all the facts and circumstances.

(3) *Example.* The principles of this paragraph (g) are illustrated by the following example.

Example. A life insurance company (L1) issues a contract to an employer (X) which provides cancellable accident and health insurance coverage and group term life insurance coverage to X's employees. L1 charges a premium of $1,000 for the contract, $950 of which is attributable to the cancellable accident and health insurance coverage and $50 of which is attributable to the group term life insurance coverage. On its annual statement, L1 reports the premiums attributable to the accident and health insurance coverage separately from the premiums attributable to the group term life insurance coverage. The contract issued by L1 is a combination contract as defined in paragraph (g)(1) of this section. Pursuant to paragraph (g)(2)(i) of this section, only the premiums attributable to the group term life insurance coverage ($50) are subject to the provisions of section 848. The premiums attributable to the cancellable accident and health insurance coverage ($950) are not subject to the provisions of section 848.

(h) *Group life insurance contract*—(1) *In general.* A life insurance contract (as defined in paragraph (c) of this section) is a group life insurance contract if—

(i) The contract is a group life insurance contract under the applicable law;

(ii) The coverage is provided under a master contract issued to the group policyholder, which may be a trust, trustee, or agent;

(iii) The premiums on the contract are reported either as group life insurance premiums or credit life insurance premiums on the insurance company's annual statement (or could be reported as group life insurance premiums or credit life insurance premiums if the company were required to file the annual statement for life and accident and health companies);

(iv) The group affiliation requirement of paragraph (h)(2) of this section is satisfied;

(v) The premiums on the contract are determined on a group basis within the meaning of paragraph (h)(3) of this section; and

(vi) The proceeds of the contract are not payable to or for the benefit of the insured's employer, an organization or association to which the insured belongs, or other similar person. (See paragraph (h)(7) of this section for special rules that apply in determining if this requirement is satisfied.)

Reg. § 1.848-1(e)

(2) *Group affiliation requirement*—(i) *In general.* The group affiliation requirement of section 848(e)(2)(A) and this paragraph (h)(2) is satisfied only if all of the individuals eligible for coverage under the contract constitute a group described in paragraphs (h)(2)(ii) through (viii) of this section.

(ii) *Employee group.* An employee group consists of all of the employees (including statutory employees within the meaning of section 3121(d)(3) and individuals who are treated as employed by a single employer under section 414(b), (c), or (m)), or any class or classes thereof within the meaning of paragraph (h)(2)(x) of this section, of an employer. For this purpose, the term "employee" includes—

(A) A retired or former employee;

(B) The sole proprietor, if the employer is a sole proprietorship;

(C) A partner of the partnership, if the employer is a partnership;

(D) A director of the corporation, if the employer is a corporation; and

(E) An elected or appointed official of the public body, if the employer is a public body.

(iii) *Debtor group.* A debtor group consists of all of the debtors, or any class or classes thereof within the meaning of paragraph (h)(2)(x) of this section, of a creditor. For this purpose, the term "debtor" includes a borrower of money or purchaser or lessee of goods, services, or property for which payment is arranged through a credit transaction.

(iv) *Labor union group.* A labor union group consists of all of the members, or any class or classes thereof within the meaning of paragraph (h)(2)(x) of this section, of a labor union or similar employee organization.

(v) *Association group.* An association group consists of all of the members, or any class or classes thereof within the meaning of paragraph (h)(2)(x) of this section, of an association that, at the time the master contract is issued—

(A) Is organized and maintained for purposes other than obtaining insurance;

(B) Has been in active existence for at least two years (including, in the case of a merged or successor association, the years of active existence of any predecessor association); and

(C) Has at least 100 members.

(vi) *Credit union group.* A credit union group consists of all of the members or borrowers, or any class or classes thereof within the meaning of paragraph (h)(2)(x) of this section, of a credit union.

(vii) *Multiple group.* A multiple group consists of two or more groups from any single category described in paragraphs (h)(2)(ii) through (vi) of this section. A multiple group may not include two or more groups from different categories described in paragraphs (h)(2)(ii) through (vi) of this section.

(viii) *Certain discretionary groups.* Provided that the contract otherwise satisfies the requirements of paragraph (h)(1) of this section, a contract issued to one of the following discretionary groups is treated as satisfying the group affiliation requirement of this paragraph (h)(2)—

(A) A contract issued to a group consisting of students of one or more universities or other educational institutions;

(B) A contract issued to a group consisting of members or former members of the U.S. Armed Forces;

(C) A contract issued to a group of individuals for the payment of future funeral expenses; and

(D) A contract issued to any other discretionary group as specified by the Commissioner in subsequent guidance published in the Internal Revenue Bulletin. (See § 601.601(d)(2)(ii)(*b*) of this chapter).

(ix) *Employees treated as members.* In determining whether the group affiliation requirement of paragraph (h)(2) of this section is satisfied, the employees of a labor union, credit union, or association may be treated as members of a labor union group, a credit union group, or an association group, respectively.

(x) *Class or classes of a group determined without regard to individual health characteristics*—(A) *In general.* A class or classes of a group described in paragraphs (h)(2)(ii) through (viii) of this section may be determined using any reasonable characteristics (for example, amount of insurance, location, or occupation) other than individual health characteristics. The employees of a single employer covered under a policy issued to a multi-employer trust are considered a class of a group described in paragraph (h)(2)(ii) of this section.

(B) *Limitation of coverage based on certain work and age requirements permissible.* A limitation of coverage under a group contract to persons who are actively at work or of a preretirement age (for example, age 65 or younger) is not treated as based on individual health characteristics.

(3) *Premiums determined on a group basis*—(i) *In general.* Premiums for a contract are determined on a group basis for purposes of section

848(e)(2)(B) and this paragraph (h) only if the premium charged by the insurance company for each member of the group (or any class thereof) is determined on the basis of the same rates for the corresponding amount of coverage (for example, per $1,000 of insurance) or on the basis of rates which differ only because of the gender, smoking habits, or age of the member.

(ii) *Exception for substandard premium rates for certain high risk insureds.* Any difference in premium rates is disregarded for purposes of this paragraph (h)(3) if the difference is charged for an individual who was accepted for coverage at a substandard rate prior to January 1, 1993.

(iii) *Flexible premium contracts.* In the case of a group universal life insurance contract, the identical premium requirement is satisfied if the premium rates used by the insurance company in determining the periodic mortality charges applied to the policy account value of any member insured by the contract differ from those of other members (within the same class) only because of the gender, smoking habits, or age of the member.

(iv) *Determination of actual age.* For purposes of this paragraph (h)(3), determinations of actual age may be made using any reasonable method, provided that this method is applied consistently for all members of the group.

(4) *Underwriting practices used by company.* [Reserved]

(5) *Disqualification of group*—(i) *In general.* Except as otherwise provided in this paragraph (h)(5), if the requirements of paragraphs (h)(1), (2), and (3) of this section are not satisfied with respect to one or more members of the group, or of a class within a group (within the meaning of paragraph (h)(2)(x) of this section), the premiums for the entire group (or class) are treated as individual life insurance premiums.

(ii) *Exception for de minimis failures.* If the requirements of paragraphs (h)(1), (2), or (3) of this section are not satisfied with respect to one or more members of the group (or class), but the sum of the premiums charged by the insurance company for those individuals is no more than 5 percent of the aggregate premiums for the group (or class), only the premiums charged for those individuals are treated as premiums for an individual life insurance contract.

(6) *Supplemental life insurance coverage.* For purposes of determining whether the requirement in paragraph (h)(3)(i) of this section is satisfied, any supplemental life insurance coverage (including optional coverage for members of the group, their spouses, or their dependent children) is (or is treated as) a separate contract. In determining whether the group affiliation requirement of paragraph (h)(2) of this section is satisfied for the supplemental coverage, a member's spouse and dependent children are treated as members of the group if they are eligible for coverage.

(7) *Special rules relating to the payment of proceeds.* The following rules apply for purposes of section 848(e)(2) and paragraph (h)(1)(vi) of this section.

(i) *Contracts issued to a welfare benefit fund.* If a contract issued to a welfare benefit fund (as defined in section 419) provides for payment of proceeds to the welfare benefit fund, the proceeds of the contract are not considered payable to or for the benefit of the insured's employer, an organization or association to which the insured belongs, or other similar person, provided the proceeds are paid as benefits to the employee or the employee's beneficiary.

(ii) *Credit life insurance contracts.* If a credit life insurance contract provides for payment of proceeds to the insured's creditor, the proceeds of the contract are not treated as payable to or for the benefit of the insured's employer, an organization or association to which the insured belongs, or other similar person, provided the proceeds are applied against an outstanding indebtedness of the insured.

(iii) *"Organization or association" limited to the sponsor of the contract or the group policyholder.* The term "organization or association" means the organization or association that is either the sponsor of the contract or the group policyholder.

(i) *General deductions.* The term "general deductions" is defined in section 848(c)(2). An insurance company determines its general deductions for the taxable year without regard to amounts capitalized or amortized under section 848(a). The amount of a company's general deductions is also determined without regard to the rules of § 1.848-2(f), which apply only for purposes of determining net consideration for reinsurance agreements. [Reg. § 1.848-1.]

☐ [*T.D.* 8456, 12-28-92.]

[Reg. § 1.848-2]

§ 1.848-2. **Determination of net premiums.**—(a) *Net premiums*—(1) *In general.* An insurance company must use the accrual method of accounting (as prescribed by section 811(a)(1)) to determine the net premiums with respect to each category of specified insurance contracts. With respect to any category of contracts, net premiums means—

Provisions of General Application

(i) The gross amount of premiums and other consideration (see paragraph (b) of this section); reduced by

(ii) The sum of—

(A) The return premiums (see paragraph (e) of this section); and

(B) The net negative consideration for a reinsurance agreement (other than an agreement described in paragraph (h)(2) of this section). See paragraphs (f) and (g) of this section for rules relating to the determination of net negative consideration.

(2) *Separate determination of net premiums for certain reinsurance agreements.* Net premiums with respect to reinsurance agreements for which an election under paragraph (h)(3) of this section has been made (certain reinsurance agreements with parties not subject to United States taxation) are treated separately and are subject to the rules of paragraph (h) of this section.

(b) *Gross amount of premiums and other consideration*—(1) *General rule.* The term "gross amount of premiums and other consideration" means the sum of—

(i) All premiums and other consideration (other than amounts on reinsurance agreements); and

(ii) The net positive consideration for any reinsurance agreement (other than an agreement for which an election under paragraph (h)(3) of this section has been made).

(2) *Items included.* The gross amount of premiums and other consideration includes—

(i) Advance premiums;

(ii) Amounts in a premium deposit fund or similar account, to the extent provided in paragraph (b)(3) of this section;

(iii) Fees;

(iv) Assessments;

(v) Amounts that the insurance company charges itself representing premiums with respect to benefits for its employees (including full-time life insurance salesmen treated as employees under section 7701(a)(20)); and

(vi) The value of a new contract issued in an exchange described in paragraph (c)(2) or (c)(3) of this section.

(3) *Treatment of premium deposits*—(i) *In general.* An amount in a premium deposit fund or similar account is taken into account in determining the gross amount of premiums and other consideration at the earlier of the time that the amount is applied to, or irrevocably committed to, the payment of a premium on a specified insurance contract. If an amount is irrevocably committed to the payment of a premium on a specified insurance contract, then neither that amount nor any earnings allocable to that amount are included in the gross amount of premiums and other consideration when applied to the payment of a premium on the same contract.

(ii) *Amounts irrevocably committed to the payment of premiums.* Except as provided in paragraph (b)(3)(iii) of this section, an amount in a premium deposit fund or similar account is irrevocably committed to the payment of premiums on a contract only if neither the amount nor any earnings allocable to that amount may be—

(A) Returned to the policyholder or any other person (other than on surrender of the contract); or

(B) Used by the policyholder to fund another contract.

(iii) *Retired lives reserves.* Premiums received by an insurance company under a retired lives reserve arrangement are treated as irrevocably committed to the payment of premiums on a specified insurance contract.

(4) *Deferred and uncollected premiums.* The gross amount of premiums and other consideration does not include deferred and uncollected premiums.

(c) *Policy exchanges*—(1) *General rule.* Except as otherwise provided in this paragraph (c), an exchange of insurance contracts (including a change in the terms of a specified insurance contract) does not result in any amount being included in the gross amount of premiums and other consideration.

(2) *External exchanges.* If a contract is exchanged for a specified insurance contract issued by another insurance company, the company that issues the new contract must include the value of the new contract in the gross amount of premiums and other consideration.

(3) *Internal exchanges resulting in fundamentally different contracts*—(i) *In general.* If a contract is exchanged for a specified insurance contract issued by the same insurance company that issued the original contract, the company must include the value of the new contract in the gross amount of premiums and other consideration if the new contract—

(A) Relates to a different category of specified insurance contract than the original contract;

(B) Does not cover the same insured as the original contract; or

(C) Changes the interest, mortality, morbidity, or expense guarantees with respect to

Reg. § 1.848-2(c)(3)

the nonforfeiture benefits provided in the original contract.

(ii) *Certain modifications treated as not changing the mortality, morbidity, interest, or expense guarantees.* For purposes of paragraph (c)(3)(i)(C) of this section, the following items are not treated as changing the interest, mortality, morbidity, or expense guarantees with respect to the nonforfeiture benefits provided in the contract—

(A) A change in a temporary guarantee with respect to the amounts to be credited as interest to the policyholder's account, or charged as mortality, morbidity, or expense charges, if the new guarantee applies for a period of ten years or less;

(B) The determination of benefits on annuitization using rates which are more favorable to the policyholder than the permanently guaranteed rates; and

(C) Other items as specified by the Commissioner in subsequent guidance published in the Internal Revenue Bulletin.

(iii) *Exception for contracts restructured by a court supervised rehabilitation or similar proceeding.* No amount is included in the gross amount of premiums and other consideration with respect to any change made to the interest, mortality, morbidity, or expense guarantees with respect to the nonforfeiture benefits of contracts of an insurance company that is the subject of a rehabilitation, conservatorship, insolvency, or similar state proceeding. This treatment applies only if the change—

(A) Occurs as part of the rehabilitation, conservatorship, insolvency, or similar state proceeding; and

(B) Is approved by the state court, the state insurance department, or other state official with authority to act in the rehabilitation, conservatorship, insolvency, or similar state proceeding.

(4) *Value of the contract*—(i) *In general.* For purposes of paragraph (c)(2) or (c)(3) of this section, the value of the new contract is established through the most recent sale by the company of a comparable contract. If the value of the new contract is not readily ascertainable, the value may be approximated by using the interpolated terminal reserve of the original contract as of the date of the exchange.

(ii) *Special rule for group term life insurance contracts.* In the case of any exchange involving a group term life insurance contract without cash value, the value of the new contract is deemed to be zero.

(iii) *Special rule for certain policy enhancement and update programs*—(A) *In general.* If the interest, mortality, morbidity, or expense guarantees with respect to the nonforfeiture benefits of a specified insurance contract are changed pursuant to a policy enhancement or update program, the value of the contract included in the gross amount of premiums and other consideration equals 30 percent of the value determined under paragraph (c)(4) of this section.

(B) *Policy enhancement or update program defined.* For purposes of paragraph (c)(4)(iii)(A) of this section, a policy enhancement or update program means any offer or commitment by the insurance company to all of the policyholders holding a particular policy form to change the interest, mortality, morbidity, or expense guarantees used to determine the contract's nonforfeiture benefits.

(5) *Example.* The principles of this paragraph (c) are illustrated by the following example.

Example. (i) An individual (A) owns a life insurance policy issued by a life insurance company (L1). On January 1, 1993, A purchases additional term insurance for $250, which is added as a rider to A's life insurance policy. The purchase of the additional term insurance does not change the interest, mortality, morbidity, or expense guarantees with respect to the nonforfeiture benefits provided by A's life insurance policy.

(ii) A's purchase of the term insurance rider is not considered to result in a fundamentally different contract under paragraph (c)(3) of this section because the addition of the rider did not change the interest, mortality, morbidity, or expense guarantees with respect to the nonforfeiture values of A's original life insurance policy. Therefore, L1 includes only the $250 received from A in the gross amount of premiums and other consideration.

(d) *Amounts excluded from the gross amount of premiums and other consideration*—(1) *In general.* The following items are not included in the gross amount of premiums and other consideration—

(i) Items treated by section 808(e) as policyholder dividends that are paid to the policyholder and immediately returned to the insurance company as a premium on the same contract that generated the dividends, including—

(A) A policyholder dividend applied to pay a premium under the contract that generated the dividend;

(B) Excess interest accumulated within the contract;

Reg. § 1.848-2(c)(4)

(C) A policyholder dividend applied for additional coverage (for example, a paid-up addition, extension of the period for which insurance protection is provided, or reduction of the period for which premiums are paid) on the contract that generated the dividend;

(D) A policyholder dividend applied to reduce premiums otherwise payable on the contract that generated the dividend;

(E) An experience-rated refund applied to pay a premium on the group contract that generated the refund; and

(F) An experience-rated refund applied to a premium stabilization reserve held with respect to the group contract that generated the refund;

(ii) Premiums waived as a result of the disability of an insured or the disability or death of a premium payor;

(iii) Premiums considered to be paid on a contract as the result of a partial surrender or withdrawal from the contract, or as a result of the surrender or withdrawal of a paid-up addition previously issued with respect to the same contract; and

(iv) Amounts treated as premiums upon the selection by a policyholder or by a beneficiary of a settlement option provided in a life insurance contract.

(2) *Amounts received or accrued from a guaranty association.* Amounts received or accrued from a guaranty association relating to an insurance company that is subject to an insolvency, delinquency, conservatorship, rehabilitation, or similar proceeding are not included in the gross amount of premiums and other consideration.

(3) *Exclusion not to apply to dividend accumulations.* For purposes of section 848(d)(3) and paragraph (d)(1) of this section, amounts applied from a dividend accumulation account to pay premiums on a specified insurance contract are not amounts treated as paid to, and immediately returned by, the policyholder.

(e) *Return premiums.* For purposes of section 848(d)(1)(B) and this section, return premiums do not include policyholder dividends (as defined in section 808), claims or benefits payments, or amounts returned to another insurance company under a reinsurance agreement. For the treatment of amounts returned to another insurance company under a reinsurance agreement, see paragraph (f) of this section.

(f) *Net consideration for a reinsurance agreement*—(1) *In general.* For purposes of section 848, the ceding company and the reinsurer must treat amounts arising from the reinsurance of a specified insurance contract consistently in determining their net premiums. See paragraph (g) of this section for restrictions on the amount of the net negative consideration for any reinsurance agreement that may be taken into account. See paragraph (h) of this section for special rules applicable to reinsurance agreements with parties not subject to United States taxation.

(2) *Net consideration determined by a ceding company*—(i) *In general.* The net consideration determined by a ceding company for a reinsurance agreement equals—

(A) The gross amount incurred by the reinsurer with respect to the reinsurance agreement, including any ceding commissions, annual allowances, reimbursements of claims and benefits, modified coinsurance reserve adjustments under paragraph (f)(5) of this section, experience-rated adjustments, and termination payments; less

(B) The gross amount of premiums and other consideration incurred by the ceding company with respect to the reinsurance agreement.

(ii) *Net negative and net positive consideration.* If the net consideration is less than zero, the ceding company has net negative consideration for the reinsurance agreement. If the net consideration is greater than zero, the ceding company has net positive consideration for the reinsurance agreement.

(3) *Net consideration determined by the reinsurer*—(i) *In general.* The net consideration determined by a reinsurer for a reinsurance agreement equals—

(A) The amount described in paragraph (f)(2)(i)(B) of this section; less

(B) The amount described in paragraph (f)(2)(i)(A) of this section.

(ii) *Net negative and net positive consideration.* If the net consideration is less than zero, the reinsurer has net negative consideration for the reinsurance agreement. If the net consideration is greater than zero, the reinsurer has net positive consideration for the reinsurance agreement.

(4) *Timing consistency required.* For purposes of determining the net consideration of a party for a reinsurance agreement, an income or expense item is taken into account for the first taxable year for which the item is required to be taken into account by either party. Thus, the ceding company and the reinsurer must take the item into account for the same taxable year (or for the same period if the parties have different taxable years).

Reg. § 1.848-2(f)(4)

45,854 **Provisions of General Application**
See p. 20,601 for regulations not amended to reflect law changes

(5) *Modified coinsurance and funds-withheld reinsurance agreements*—(i) *In general.* In the case of a modified coinsurance or funds-withheld reinsurance agreement, the net consideration for the agreement includes the amount of any payments or reserve adjustments, as well as any related loan transactions between the ceding company and the reinsurer. The amount of any investment income transferred between the parties as the result of a reserve adjustment or loan transaction is treated as an item of consideration under the reinsurance agreement.

(ii) *Special rule for certain funds-withheld reinsurance agreements.* In the case of a funds-withheld reinsurance agreement that is entered into after November 14, 1991, but before the first day of the first taxable year beginning after December 31, 1991, and is terminated before January 1, 1995, the parties' net consideration in the year of termination must include the amount of the original reserve for any reinsured specified insurance contract that, in applying the provisions of subchapter L, was treated as premiums and other consideration incurred for reinsurance for the taxable year in which the agreement became effective.

(6) *Treatment of retrocessions.* For purposes of this paragraph (f), a retrocession agreement is treated as a separate reinsurance agreement. The party that is relieved of liability under a retrocession agreement is treated as the ceding company.

(7) *Mixed reinsurance agreements.* If a reinsurance agreement includes more than one category of specified insurance contracts (or specified insurance contracts and contracts that are not specified insurance contracts), the portion of the agreement relating to each category of reinsured specified insurance contracts is treated as a separate agreement. The portion of the agreement relating to reinsured contracts that are not specified insurance contracts is similarly treated as a separate agreement.

(8) *Treatment of policyholder loans.* For purposes of determining the net consideration under a reinsurance agreement, the transfer of a policyholder loan receivable is treated as an item of consideration under the agreement. The interest credited with respect to a policyholder loan receivable is treated as investment income earned directly by the party holding the receivable. The amounts taken into account as claims and benefit reimbursements under the agreement must be determined without reduction for the policyholder loan.

(9) *Examples.* The principles of this paragraph (f) are illustrated by the following examples.

Example 1. On July 1, 1992, a life insurance company (L1) transfers a block of individual life insurance contracts to an unrelated life insurance company (L2) under an agreement whereby L2 becomes solely liable to the policyholders under the contracts reinsured. L1 and L2 are calendar year taxpayers. Under the assumption reinsurance agreement, L1 agrees to pay L2 $100,000 for assuming the life insurance contracts, and L2 agrees to pay L1 a $17,000 ceding commission. Under paragraph (f)(2) of this section, L1 has net negative consideration of ($83,000) ($17,000 ceding commission incurred by L2 − $100,000 incurred by L1 for reinsurance). Under paragraph (f)(3) of this section, L2 has net positive consideration of $83,000. Under paragraph (b)(1)(ii) of this section, L2 includes the net positive consideration in its gross amount of premiums and other consideration.

Example 2. (i) On July 1, 1992, a life insurance company (L1) transfers a block of individual life insurance contracts to an unrelated life insurance company (L2) under an agreement whereby L1 remains liable to the policyholders under the reinsured contracts. L1 and L2 are calendar year taxpayers. Under the indemnity reinsurance agreement, L1 agrees to pay L2 $100,000 for reinsuring the life insurance contracts, and L2 agrees to pay L1 a $17,000 ceding commission. L1 agrees to pay L2 an amount equal to the future premiums on the reinsured contracts. L2 agrees to indemnify L1 for claims and benefits and administrative expenses incurred by L1 while the reinsurance agreement is in effect.

(ii) For the period beginning July 1, 1992, and ending December 31, 1992, the following income and expense items are determined with respect to the reinsured contracts:

Item	Income	Expense
Premiums	$25,000	
Death benefits		$10,000
Surrender benefits		8,000
Premium taxes and other expenses		2,000
		$20,000

(iii) Under paragraph (f)(2) of this section, L1's net negative consideration equals ($88,000), which is determined by subtracting the $125,000 ($100,000 + $25,000) incurred by L1 from the $37,000 incurred by L2 under the reinsurance agreement ($17,000 + $10,000 + $8,000 + $2,000). L2's net positive consideration is $88,000. Under paragraph (b)(1)(ii) of this section, L2 includes the $88,000 net positive consideration in its gross amount of premiums and other consideration.

Reg. § 1.848-2(f)(5)

Example 3. (i) Assume that the reinsurance agreement referred to in *Example 2* is terminated on December 31, 1993. During the period from January 1, 1993 through December 31, 1993, the following income and expense items are determined with respect to the reinsured contracts:

Item	Income	Expense
Premiums	$45,000	
Death benefits		$18,000
Surrender benefits		6,000
Premium taxes and other expenses		8,000
		$32,000

(ii) On the termination date of the reinsurance agreement, L1 receives a payment of $70,000 from L2 as consideration for releasing L2 from liability with respect to the reinsured contracts.

(iii) L1's net positive consideration equals $57,000, which is the excess of the $102,000 incurred by L2 for the year ($18,000 + $6,000 + $8,000 + $70,000) over the $45,000 incurred by L1. L2's net negative consideration is ($57,000). L1 includes the net positive consideration in its gross amount of premiums and other consideration.

Example 4. (i) On January 1, 1993, an insurance company (L1) enters into a modified coinsurance agreement with another insurance company (L2), covering a block of individual life insurance contracts. Both L1 and L2 are calendar year taxpayers. Under the agreement, L2 is credited with an initial reinsurance premium equal to L1's reserves on the reinsured contracts at the inception of the agreement, any new premiums received with respect to the reinsured contracts, any decrease in L1's reserves on the reinsured contracts, and an amount of investment income determined by reference to L1's reserves on the reinsured contracts. L2 is charged for all claims and expenses incurred with respect to the reinsured contracts plus an amount reflecting any increase in L1's reserves. The agreement further provides that cash settlements between the parties are made at the inception and termination of the agreement, as well as at the end of each calendar year while the agreement is in effect. The cash settlement is determined by netting the sum of the amounts credited to L2 against the sum of the amounts charged to L2 with respect to the reinsured policies. L1's reserves on the reinsured policies at the inception of the reinsurance agreement are $375,000.

(ii) Under the cash settlement formula, L2 is credited with an initial reinsurance premium equal to L1's reserves on the reinsured policies ($375,000), but is charged an amount reflecting L1's policy reserve requirements ($375,000).

(iii) For the period ending December 31, 1993, L2 is also credited and charged the following amounts with respect to the reinsured contracts.

Item	Income	Expense
Premiums	$100,000	
Investment income	39,000	
Death benefits		$65,000
Increase in reserves		75,000

(iv) Under paragraph (f)(5) of this section, L2's net negative consideration for the 1993 taxable year equals ($1,000) which is determined by subtracting the sum of the amounts charged to L2 ($375,000 + $65,000 + $75,000 = $515,000) from the sum of the amounts credited to L2 ($375,000 + $100,000 + $39,000 = $514,000). L1's net positive consideration for calendar year 1993 equals $1,000. Under paragraph (b)(1)(ii) of this section, L1 includes the $1,000 net positive consideration in its gross amount of premiums and other consideration.

Example 5. (i) On January 1, 1993, an insurance company (L1) enters into a coinsurance agreement with another insurance company (L2) covering a block of individual life insurance contracts. Both L1 and L2 are calendar year taxpayers. Under the agreement, L2 is credited with an initial reinsurance premium equal to L1's reserves on the effective date of the agreement, any new premiums received on the reinsured contracts, but must indemnify L1 for all claims and expenses incurred with respect to the contracts. As part of the agreement, L2 makes a loan to L1 equal to the amount of the reserves on the reinsured contracts. L1's reserves on the reinsured contracts on the effective date of the agreement are $375,000. Thus, on the inception date of the reinsurance agreement, L1 transfers to L2 its note for $375,000 as consideration for reinsurance.

(ii) The reinsurance agreement between L1 and L2 is a funds-withheld reinsurance agreement. Under paragraph (f)(5) of this section, the amount of any loan transaction is taken into account in determining the parties' net consideration. At the inception of the reinsurance agreement, L2 is credited with a reinsurance premium equal to L1's reserves on the reinsured contracts ($375,000). L2's $375,000 loan to L1 is treated as an amount returned to L1 under the agreement.

(iii) For the period ending December 31, 1993, L2 is credited and charged the following amounts with respect to the reinsured contracts and the loan transaction with L1.

Reg. § 1.848-2(f)(9)

Provisions of General Application

See p. 20,601 for regulations not amended to reflect law changes

Item	Income	Expense
Premiums	$100,000	
Accrued interest	39,000	
Death benefits		$65,000
Increase in loan to L1		75,000

(iv) Under paragraph (f)(5) of this section, L2's net negative consideration for the 1993 taxable year equals ($1,000), which is determined by subtracting the sum of amounts incurred by L2 with respect to death benefits and the loan transaction ($375,000 + $65,000 + $75,000 = $515,000) from the sum of the amounts credited to L2 as reinsurance premiums and interest on the loan transaction ($375,000 + $100,000 + $39,000 = $514,000). L1's net positive consideration for calendar year 1993 equals $1,000. Under paragraph (b)(1)(ii) of this section, L1 includes the $1,000 net positive consideration in its gross amount of premiums and other consideration.

Example 6. (i) On December 31, 1993, an insurance company (L1) enters into a reinsurance agreement with another insurance company (L2) covering a block of individual life insurance contracts. Both L1 and L2 are calendar year taxpayers. Under the agreement, L2 is credited with L1's reserves on the reinsured contracts on the effective date of the agreement, plus any new premiums received on the reinsured contracts, but must indemnify L1 for all claims and expenses incurred with respect to the contracts. Under the agreement, L1 transfers cash of $325,000 to L2 plus rights to its policyholder loan receivables on the reinsured contracts ($50,000). L2 reports the reinsurance agreement by including the transferred policyholder loan receivables as an asset on its books.

(ii) For the period beginning January 1, 1994 and ending December 31, 1994, the following income and expense items are incurred with respect to the reinsured contracts.

Item	Income	Expense
Premiums	$100,000	
Death benefits		$25,000
Surrender benefits		5,000
Premium taxes and other expenses		8,000
		$38,000

(iii) These amounts are net of the outstanding policyholder loans held by L2 of $20,000 with respect to death benefits and $15,000 with respect to surrender benefits.

(iv) Under paragraph (f)(8) of this section, the transferred policyholder loan receivables are treated as an item of consideration under the reinsurance agreement. In determining the parties' net consideration for the agreement, the transferred policyholder loan receivables ($50,000) are treated as an item of consideration incurred by L1 under paragraph (f)(2)(i)(B) of this section. Therefore, for the 1993 taxable year, L1 has net negative consideration of ($375,000). L2 has net positive consideration of $375,000. Under paragraph (b)(1)(ii) of this section, L2 includes the $375,000 net positive consideration in its gross amount of premiums and other consideration.

(v) For the 1994 taxable year, L2 has net positive consideration for the reinsurance agreement of $62,000 before adjustment for the transferred policyholder loans. Under paragraph (f)(8) of this section, the amounts taken into account as claim and benefit payments must be adjusted by the amount of any transferred policyholder loan receivables which are netted against the reinsurer's claim and benefit reimbursements. Therefore, L2 takes into account $45,000 ($25,000 + $20,000 = $45,000) as reimbursements for death benefits, and $20,000 ($5,000 + $15,000 = $20,000) as reimbursements for surrender benefits. After adjustment for these items, L2 has net positive consideration of $27,000, which is determined by subtracting the sum of the amounts charged to L2 ($45,000 + $20,000 + $8,000 = $73,000) from the sum of the amounts credited to L2 ($100,000). L1 has net negative consideration of ($27,000) under the agreement. Under paragraph (b)(1)(ii) of this section, L2 includes the $27,000 net positive consideration in its gross amount of premiums and other consideration. The amount of any interest earned on the policyholder loan receivables after their transfer to L2 is treated as investment income earned directly by L2, and is not taken into account as an item of consideration under the agreement.

(g) *Reduction in the amount of net negative consideration to ensure consistency of capitalization for reinsurance agreements*—(1) *In general.* Paragraph (g)(3) of this section provides for a reduction in the amount of net negative consideration that a party to a reinsurance agreement (other than a reinsurance agreement described in paragraph (h)(2) of this section) may take into account in determining net premiums under paragraph (a)(2)(ii) of this section if the party with net positive consideration has a capitalization shortfall (as defined in paragraph (g)(4) of this section). Unless the party with net negative consideration demonstrates that the party with net positive consideration does not have a capitalization shortfall or demonstrates the amount of the other party's capitalization shortfall which is allocable to the reinsurance agreement, the net negative consideration that may be taken into account under paragraph (a)(2)(ii) of this section is zero. However, the reduction of paragraph (g)(3) of this section does not apply to a reinsurance agreement

Reg. § 1.848-2(g)

if the parties make a joint election under paragraph (g)(8) of this section. Under the election, the party with net positive consideration capitalizes specified policy acquisition expenses with respect to the agreement without regard to the general deductions limitation of section 848(c)(1).

(2) *Application to reinsurance agreements subject to the interim rules.* In applying this paragraph (g) to a reinsurance agreement that is subject to the interim rules of § 1.848-3, the term "premiums and other consideration incurred for reinsurance under section 848(d)(1)(B)" is substituted for "net negative consideration," and the term "gross amount of premiums and other consideration under section 848(d)(1)(A)" is substituted for "net positive consideration." If an insurance company has "premiums and other consideration incurred for reinsurance under section 848(d)(1)(B)" and a "gross amount of premiums and other consideration under section 848(d)(1)(A)" for the same agreement, the net of these amounts is taken into account for purposes of this paragraph (g).

(3) *Amount of reduction.* The reduction required by this paragraph (g)(3) equals the amount obtained by dividing—

(i) The portion of the capitalization shortfall (as defined in paragraph (g)(4) of this section) allocated to the reinsurance agreement under paragraph (g)(7) of this section; by

(ii) The applicable percentage set forth in section 848 (c)(1) for the category of specified insurance contracts reinsured by the agreement.

(4) *Capitalization shortfall.* A "capitalization shortfall" equals the excess of—

(i) The sum of the required capitalization amounts (as defined in paragraph (g)(5) of this section) for all reinsurance agreements (other than reinsurance agreements for which an election has been made under paragraph (h)(3) of this section); over

(ii) The general deductions allocated to those reinsurance agreements, as determined under paragraph (g)(6) of this section.

(5) *Required capitalization amount*—(i) *In general.* The "required capitalization amount" for a reinsurance agreement (other than a reinsurance agreement for which an election has been made under paragraph (h)(3) of this section) equals the amount (either positive or negative) obtained by multiplying—

(A) The net positive or negative consideration for an agreement not described in paragraph (h)(2) of this section, and the net positive consideration for an agreement described in paragraph (h)(2) of this section, but for which an election under paragraph (h)(3) of this section has not been made; by

(B) The applicable percentage set forth in section 848(c)(1) for that category of specified insurance contracts.

(ii) *Special rule with respect to net negative consideration.* Solely for purposes of computing a party's required capitalization amount under this paragraph (g)(5)—

(A) If either party to the reinsurance agreement is the direct issuer of the reinsured contracts, the party computing its required capitalization amount takes into account the full amount of any net negative consideration without regard to any potential reduction under paragraph (g)(3) of this section; and

(B) If neither party to the reinsurance agreement is the direct issuer of the reinsured contracts, any net negative consideration is deemed to equal zero in computing a party's required capitalization amount except to the extent that the party with the net negative consideration establishes that the other party to that reinsurance agreement capitalizes the appropriate amount.

(6) *General deductions allocable to reinsurance agreements.* An insurance company's general deductions allocable to its reinsurance agreements equals the excess, if any, of—

(i) The company's general deductions (excluding additional amounts treated as general deductions under paragraph (g)(8) of this section); over

(ii) The amount determined under section 848(c)(1) on specified insurance contracts that the insurance company has issued directly (determined without regard to any reinsurance agreements).

(7) *Allocation of capitalization shortfall among reinsurance agreements.* The capitalization shortfall is allocated to each reinsurance agreement for which the required capitalization amount (as determined in paragraph (g)(5) of this section) is a positive amount. The portion of the capitalization shortfall allocable to each agreement equals the amount which bears the same ratio to the capitalization shortfall as the required capitalization amount for the reinsurance agreement bears to the sum of the positive required capitalization amounts.

(8) *Election to determine specified policy acquisition expenses for an agreement without regard to general deductions limitation*—(i) *In general.* The reduction specified by paragraph (g)(3) of this section does not apply if the parties to a reinsurance agreement make an election

Reg. § 1.848-2(g)(8)

under this paragraph (g)(8). The election requires the party with net positive consideration to capitalize specified policy acquisition expenses with respect to the reinsurance agreement without regard to the general deductions limitation of section 848(c)(1). That party must reduce its deductions under section 805 or section 832(c) by the amount, if any, of the party's capitalization shortfall allocable to the reinsurance agreement. The additional capitalized amounts are treated as specified policy acquisition expenses attributable to premiums and other consideration on the reinsurance agreement, and are deductible in accordance with section 848(a)(2).

(ii) *Manner of making election.* To make an election under paragraph (g)(8) of this section, the ceding company and the reinsurer must include an election statement in the reinsurance agreement, either as part of the original terms of the agreement or by an addendum to the agreement. The parties must each attach a schedule to their federal income tax returns which identifies the reinsurance agreement for which the joint election under this paragraph (g)(8) has been made. The schedule must be attached to each of the parties' federal income tax returns filed for the later of—

(A) The first taxable year ending after the election becomes effective; or

(B) The first taxable year ending on or after December 29, 1992.

(iii) *Election statement.* The election statement in the reinsurance agreement must—

(A) Provide that the party with net positive consideration for the reinsurance agreement for each taxable year will capitalize specified policy acquisition expenses with respect to the reinsurance agreement without regard to the general deductions limitation of section 848(c)(1);

(B) Set forth the agreement of the parties to exchange information pertaining to the amount of net consideration under the reinsurance agreement each year to ensure consistency;

(C) Specify the first taxable year for which the election is effective; and

(D) Be signed by both parties.

(iv) *Effect of election.* An election under this paragraph (g)(8) is effective for the first taxable year specified in the election statement and for all subsequent taxable years for which the reinsurance agreement remains in effect. The election may not be revoked without the consent of the Commissioner.

(9) *Examples.* The principles of this paragraph (g) are illustrated by the following examples.

Example 1. (i) On December 31, 1992, a life insurance company (L1) transfers a block of individual life insurance contracts to an unrelated life insurance company (L2) under an agreement in which L2 becomes solely liable to the policyholders on the reinsured contracts. L1 transfers $105,000 to L2 as consideration for the reinsurance of the contracts.

(ii) L1 and L2 do not make an election under paragraph (g)(8) of this section to capitalize specified policy acquisition expenses with respect to the reinsurance agreement without regard to the general deductions limitation. L2 has no other insurance business, and its general deductions for the taxable year are $3,500.

(iii) Under paragraph (f)(2) of this section, L1's net negative consideration is ($105,000). Under paragraph (f)(3) of this section, L2's net positive consideration is $105,000. Pursuant to paragraph (b)(1)(ii) of this section, L2 includes the net positive consideration in its gross amount of premiums and other consideration.

(iv) The required capitalization amount under paragraph (g)(5) of this section for the reinsurance agreement is $8,085 ($105,000 × .077). L2's general deductions, all of which are allocable to the reinsurance agreement with L1, are $3,500. The $4,585 difference between the required capitalization amount ($8,085) and general deductions allocable to the reinsurance agreement ($3,500) represents L2's capitalization shortfall under paragraph (g)(4) of this section.

(v) Since L2 has a capitalization shortfall allocable to the agreement, the rules of paragraph (g)(1) of this section apply for purposes of determining the amount by which L1 may reduce its net premiums. Under paragraph (g)(3) of this section, L1 must reduce the amount of net negative consideration that it takes into account under paragraph (a)(2)(ii) of this section by $59,545 ($4,585/.077). Thus, of the $105,000 net negative consideration under the reinsurance agreement, L1 may take into account only $45,455 as a reduction of its net premiums.

Example 2. The facts are the same as *Example 1*, except that L1 and L2 make the election under paragraph (g)(8) of this section to capitalize specified policy acquisition expenses with respect to the reinsurance agreement without regard to the general deductions limitation. Pursuant to this election, L2 must capitalize as specified policy acquisition expenses an amount equal to $8,085 ($105,000 × .077). L1 may reduce its net premiums by the $105,000 of net negative consideration.

Example 3. (i) A life insurance company (L1) is both a direct issuer and a reinsurer of life

Reg. § 1.848-2(g)(9)

insurance and annuity contracts. For 1993, L1's net premiums under section 848(d)(1) for directly issued individual life insurance and annuity contracts are as follows:

Category	Net Premiums
Life insurance contracts	$17,000,000
Annuity contracts	8,000,000

(ii) L1's general deductions for 1993 are $1,500,000.

(iii) For 1993, L1 is a reinsurer under four separate indemnity reinsurance agreements with unrelated insurance companies (L2, L3, L4, and L5). The agreements with L2, L3, and L4 cover life insurance contracts issued by those companies. The agreement with L5 covers annuity contracts issued by L5. The parties to the reinsurance agreements have not made the election under paragraph (g)(8) of this section to capitalize specified policy acquisition expenses with respect to these agreements without regard to the general deductions limitation.

(iv) L1's net consideration for 1993 with respect to its reinsurance agreements is as follows:

Agreement	Net consideration
L2	$1,200,000
L3	(350,000)
L4	300,000
L5	600,000

(v) To determine whether a reduction under paragraph (g)(3) of this section applies with respect to these reinsurance agreements, L1 must determine the required capitalization amounts for its reinsurance agreements and the amount of its general deductions allocable to these agreements.

(vi) Pursuant to paragraph (g)(5) of this section, the required capitalization amount for each reinsurance agreement is determined as follows:

L2 $1,200,000 × .077 = $92,400
L3 ($350,000) × .077 = ($26,950)
L4 $300,000 × .077 = $23,100
L5 $600,000 × .0175 = $10,500

(vii) Thus, the sum of L1's required capitalization amounts on its reinsurance agreements equals $99,050.

(viii) Pursuant to paragraph (g)(6) of this section, L1 determines its general deductions allocable to its reinsurance agreements. The amount determined under section 848(c)(1) on its directly issued contracts is:

Category	Required Capitalization Amount
Annuity contracts	$8,000,000 × .0175 = $140,000
Life insurance contracts	$17,000,000 × .077 = 1,309,000
	$1,449,000

(ix) L1's general deductions allocable to its reinsurance agreements are $51,000 ($1,500,000 − $1,449,000).

(x) Pursuant to paragraph (g)(4) of this section, L1's capitalization shortfall equals $48,050, reflecting the excess of L1's required capitalization amounts for its reinsurance agreements ($99,050) over the general deductions allocable to its reinsurance agreements ($51,000).

(xi) Pursuant to paragraph (g)(7) of this section, the capitalization shortfall of $48,050 must be allocated between each of L1's reinsurance agreements with net positive consideration in proportion to their respective required capitalization amounts. The allocation of the shortfall between L1's reinsurance agreements is determined as follows:

L2 = $35,237 ($48,050 × 92,400/126,000)
L4 = $8,809 ($48,050 × 23,100/126,000)
L5 = $4,004 ($48,050 × 10,500/126,000)

(xii) Accordingly, the reduction under paragraph (g)(3) of this section that applies to the amount of net negative consideration that may be taken into account by L2, L4, and L5 under paragraph (a)(1)(ii)(B) of this section is determined as follows:

L2 = $457,623 ($35,237/.077)
L4 = $114,403 ($8,809/.077)
L5 = $228,800 ($4,004/.0175)

Example 4. The facts are the same as *Example 3,* except that L1 and L4 make a joint election under paragraph (g)(8) of this section to capitalize specified policy acquisition expenses with respect to the reinsurance agreement without regard to the general deductions limitation. Pursuant to this election, L1 must reduce its deductions under section 805 by an amount equal to the capitalization shortfall allocable to the reinsurance agreement with L4 ($8,809). L1 treats the additional capitalized amounts as specified policy acquisition expenses allocable to premiums and other consideration under the agreement. L4 may reduce its net premiums by the $300,000 net negative consideration. The election by L1 and L4 does not change the amount of the capitalization shortfall allocable under paragraph (g)(7) of this section to the reinsurance agreements with L2 and L5. Thus, the reduction required by paragraph (g)(3) of this section with respect to the amount of the net negative consideration that L2 and L5 may recognize under paragraph (a)(2)(ii) of this section is $457,623 and $228,800, respectively.

(h) *Treatment of reinsurance agreements with parties not subject to U.S. taxation*—(1) *In general.* Unless an election under paragraph (h)(3) of this section is made, an insurance company may

Reg. § 1.848-2(h)(1)

not reduce its net premiums by the net negative consideration for the taxable year (or, with respect to a reinsurance agreement that is subject to the interim rules of § 1.848-3, by the premiums and other consideration incurred for reinsurance) under a reinsurance agreement to which this paragraph (h) applies.

(2) *Agreements to which this paragraph (h) applies*—(i) *In general.* This paragraph (h) applies to a reinsurance agreement if, with respect to the premiums and other consideration under the agreement, one party to that agreement is subject to United States taxation and the other party is not.

(ii) *Parties subject to U.S. taxation*—(A) *In general.* A party is subject to United States taxation for this purpose if the party is subject to United States taxation either directly under the provisions of subchapter L of chapter 1 of the Internal Revenue Code (subchapter L), or indirectly under the provisions of subpart F of Part III of subchapter N of chapter 1 of the Internal Revenue Code (subpart F).

(B) *Effect of a closing agreement.* If a reinsurer agrees in a closing agreement with the Internal Revenue Service to be subject to tax under rules equivalent to the provisions of subchapter L on its premiums and other consideration from reinsurance agreements with parties subject to United States taxation, the reinsurer is treated as an insurance company subject to tax under subchapter L.

(3) *Election to separately determine the amounts required to be capitalized for reinsurance agreements with parties not subject to U.S. taxation*—(i) *In general.* This paragraph (h)(3) authorizes an insurance company to make an election to separately determine the amounts required to be capitalized for the taxable year with respect to reinsurance agreements with parties that are not subject to United States taxation. If this election is made, an insurance company separately determines a net foreign capitalization amount for the taxable year for all reinsurance agreements to which this paragraph (h) applies.

(ii) *Manner of making the election.* An insurance company makes the election authorized by this paragraph (h)(3) by attaching an election statement to the federal income tax return (including an amended return) for the taxable year for which the election becomes effective. The election applies to that taxable year and all subsequent taxable years unless permission to revoke the election is obtained from the Commissioner.

(4) *Amount taken into account for purposes of determining specified policy acquisition expenses.* If for a taxable year an insurance company has a net positive foreign capitalization amount (as defined in paragraph (h)(5)(i) of this section), any portion of that amount remaining after the reduction described in paragraph (h)(7) of this section is treated as additional specified policy acquisition expenses for the taxable year (determined without regard to amounts taken into account under this paragraph (h)). A net positive capitalization amount is treated as an amount otherwise required to be capitalized for the taxable year for purposes of the reduction under section 848(f)(1)(A).

(5) *Net foreign capitalization amount*—(i) *In general.* An insurance company's net foreign capitalization amount equals the sum of the foreign capitalization amounts (netting positive and negative amounts) determined under paragraph (h)(5)(ii) of this section for each category of specified insurance contracts reinsured by agreements described in paragraph (h)(2) of this section. If the amount is less than zero, the company has a net negative foreign capitalization amount. If the amount is greater than zero, the company has a net positive foreign capitalization amount.

(ii) *Foreign capitalization amounts by category.* The foreign capitalization amount for a category of specified insurance contracts is determined by—

(A) Combining the net positive consideration and the net negative consideration for the taxable year (or, with respect to a reinsurance agreement that is subject to the interim rules of § 1.848-3, by combining the gross amount of premiums and other consideration and the premiums and other consideration incurred for reinsurance) for all agreements described in paragraph (h)(2) of this section which reinsure specified insurance contracts in that category; and

(B) Multiplying the result (either positive or negative) by the percentage for that category specified in section 848(c)(1).

(6) *Treatment of net negative foreign capitalization amount*—(i) *Applied as a reduction to previously capitalized amounts.* If for a taxable year an insurance company has a net negative foreign capitalization amount, the negative amount reduces (but not below zero) the unamortized balances of the amounts previously capitalized (beginning with the amount capitalized for the most recent taxable year) to the extent attributable to prior years' net positive foreign capitalization amounts. The amount by which previously capitalized amounts is reduced is allowed as a deduction for the taxable year.

(ii) *Carryover of remaining net negative foreign capitalization amount.* The net negative foreign capitalization amount, if any, remaining after the reduction described in paragraph (h)(6)(i) of this section is carried over to reduce a future net positive capitalization amount. The remaining net negative foreign capitalization amount may only offset a net positive foreign capitalization amount in a future year, and may not be used to reduce the amounts otherwise required to be capitalized under section 848(a) for the taxable year, or to reduce the unamortized balances of specified policy acquisition expenses from preceding taxable years, with respect to directly written business or reinsurance agreements other than agreements for which the election under paragraph (h)(3) of this section has been made.

(7) *Reduction of net positive foreign capitalization amount by carryover amounts allowed.* If for a taxable year an insurance company has a net positive foreign capitalization amount, that amount is reduced (but not below zero) by any carryover of net negative foreign capitalization amounts from preceding taxable years. Any remaining net positive foreign capitalization amount is taken into account as provided in paragraph (h)(4) of this section.

(8) *Examples.* The principles of this paragraph (h) are illustrated by the following examples.

Example 1. (i) On January 1, 1993, a life insurance company (L1) enters into a reinsurance agreement with a foreign corporation (X) covering a block of annuity contracts issued to residents of the United States. X is not subject to taxation either directly under subchapter L or indirectly under subpart F on the premiums for the reinsurance agreement with L1. L1 makes the election under paragraph (h)(3) of this section to separately determine the amounts required to be capitalized for the taxable year with respect to parties not subject to United States taxation.

(ii) For the taxable year ended December 31, 1993, L1 has net negative consideration of ($25,000) under its reinsurance agreement with X. L1 has no other reinsurance agreements with parties not subject to United States taxation.

(iii) Under paragraph (h)(5) of this section, L1's net negative foreign capitalization amount for the 1993 taxable year equals ($437.50), which is determined by multiplying L1's net negative consideration on the agreement with X ($25,000) by the percentage in section 848(c)(1) for the reinsured specified insurance contracts (1.75%). Under paragraph (h)(6)(ii) of this section, L1 carries over the net negative foreign capitalization amount of ($437.50) to future taxable years. The net negative foreign capitalization amount may not be used to reduce the amounts which L1 is required to capitalize on directly written business or reinsurance agreements other than those agreements described in paragraph (h)(2) of this section.

Example 2. (i) The facts are the same as *Example 1* except that L1 terminates its reinsurance agreement with X and receives $35,000 on December 31, 1994. For the 1994 taxable year, L1 has net positive consideration of $35,000 under its agreement with X. L1 has no other reinsurance agreements with parties not subject to United States taxation.

(ii) Under paragraph (h)(5) of this section, L1's net positive net foreign capitalization amount for the 1984 taxable year equals $612.50, which is determined by multiplying the net positive consideration on the agreement with X ($35,000) by the percentage in section 848(c)(1) for the reinsured specified insurance contracts (1.75%). Under paragraph (h)(4) of this section, L1 reduces the net positive foreign capitalization amount for the taxable year by the net negative foreign capitalization amount carried over from preceding taxable years ($437.50). After this reduction, L1 includes $175 ($612.50 − $437.50) as specified policy acquisition expenses for the 1994 taxable year.

(i) *Carryover of excess negative capitalization amount*—(1) *In general.* This paragraph (i) authorizes a carryover of an excess negative capitalization amount (as defined in paragraph (i)(2) of this section) to reduce amounts otherwise required to be capitalized under section 848. Paragraph (i)(4) provides special rules for the treatment of excess negative capitalization amounts of insolvent insurance companies.

(2) *Excess negative capitalization amount.* The excess negative capitalization amount with respect to a category of specified insurance contracts for a taxable year is equal to the excess of—

(A) The negative capitalization amount with respect to that category; over

(B) The amount that can be utilized under section 848(f)(1).

(3) *Treatment of excess negative capitalization amount.* The excess negative capitalization amount for a taxable year reduces the amounts that are otherwise required to be capitalized by an insurance company under section 848(c)(1) for future years.

(4) *Special rule for the treatment of an excess negative capitalization amount of an insolvent company*—(i) *When applicable.* This paragraph (i)(4) applies only for the taxable year in which an insolvent insurance company has an excess negative capitalization amount and has net negative

Reg. § 1.848-2(i)(4)

consideration under a reinsurance agreement. See paragraph (i)(4)(v) of this section for the definition of "insolvent."

(ii) *Election to forego carryover of excess negative capitalization amount.* At the joint election of the insolvent insurance company and the other party to the reinsurance agreement—

(A) The insolvent insurance company reduces the excess negative capitalization amount which would otherwise be carried over under paragraph (i)(1) of this section by the amount determined under paragraph (i)(4)(iii) of this section; and

(B) The other party reduces the amount of its specified policy acquisition expenses for the taxable year by the amount determined under paragraph (i)(4)(iii) of this section.

(iii) *Amount of reduction to the excess negative capitalization amount and specified policy acquisition expenses.* To determine the reduction to the carryover of an insolvent insurance company's excess negative capitalization amount and the specified policy acquisition expenses of the other party with respect to a reinsurance agreement—

(A) Multiply the net negative consideration for each reinsurance agreement of the insolvent insurer for which there is net negative consideration for the taxable year by the appropriate percentage specified in section 848(c)(1) for the category of specified insurance contracts reinsured by the agreement;

(B) Sum the results for each agreement;

(C) Calculate the ratio between the results in paragraphs (i)(4)(iii)(A) and (B) of this section for each agreement; and

(D) Multiply that result by the increase in the excess negative capitalization amount of the insolvent insurer for the taxable year.

(iv) *Manner of making election.* To make an election under paragraph (i)(4) of this section, each party to the reinsurance agreement must attach an election statement to its federal income tax return (including an amended return) for the taxable year for which the election is effective. The election statement must identify the reinsurance agreement for which the joint election under this paragraph (i)(4) has been made, state the amount of the reduction to the insolvent insurance company's excess negative capitalization amount that is attributable to the agreement, and be signed by both parties. An election under this paragraph (i)(4) is effective for the taxable year specified in the election statement, and may not be revoked without the consent of the Commissioner.

(v) *Presumptions relating to the insolvency of an insurance company undergoing a court supervised rehabilitation or similar state proceeding.* For purposes of this paragraph (i)(4), an insurance company which is undergoing a rehabilitation, conservatorship, or similar state proceeding shall be presumed to be insolvent if the state proceeding results in—

(A) An order of the state court finding that the fair market value of the insurance company's assets is less than its liabilities;

(B) The use of funds, guarantees, or reinsurance from a guaranty association;

(C) A reduction of the policyholders' available account balances; or

(D) A substantial limitation on access to funds (for example, a partial or total moratorium on policyholder withdrawals or surrenders that applies for a period of 5 years).

(vi) *Example.* The principles of this paragraph (i)(4) are illustrated by the following example.

Example. (i) An insurance company (L1) is the subject of a rehabilitation proceeding under the supervision of a state court. The state court has made a finding that the fair market value of L1's assets is less than its liabilities. On December 31, 1993, L1 transfers a block of individual life insurance contracts to an unrelated insurance company (L2) under an assumption reinsurance agreement whereby L2 becomes solely liable to the policyholders under the contracts reinsured. Under the agreement, L1 agrees to pay L2 $2,000,000 for assuming the life insurance contracts. This negative net consideration causes L1 to incur an excess negative capitalization amount of $138,600 for the 1993 taxable year. L1 has no other reinsurance agreements for the taxable year.

(ii) As part of the reinsurance agreement, L1 and L2 agree to make an election under paragraph (i)(4) of this section. Under the election, L1 agrees to forego the carryover of the $138,600 excess negative capitalization amount for future taxable years. L2 must include the $2,000,000 net positive consideration for the reinsurance agreement in its gross amount of premiums and other consideration. L2 reduces its specified policy acquisition expenses for the 1993 taxable year by $138,600.

(j) *Ceding commissions with respect to reinsurance of contracts other than specified insurance contracts.* A ceding commission incurred with respect to the reinsurance of an insurance contract that is not a specified insurance contract is not subject to the provisions of section 848(g).

Reg. § 1.848-2(j)

(k) *Effective dates*—(1) *In general.* Unless otherwise specified in this paragraph, the rules of this section are effective for the taxable years of an insurance company beginning after November 14, 1991.

(2) *Reduction in the amount of net negative consideration to ensure consistency of capitalization for reinsurance agreements.* Section 1.848-2(g) (which provides for an adjustment to ensure consistency) is effective for—

(i) All amounts arising under any reinsurance agreement entered into after November 14, 1991; and

(ii) All amounts arising under any reinsurance agreement for taxable years beginning after December 31, 1991, without regard to the date on which the reinsurance agreement was entered into.

(3) *Net consideration rules.* Section 1.848-2(f) (which provides rules for determining the net consideration for a reinsurance agreement) applies to—

(i) Amounts arising in taxable years beginning after December 31, 1991, under a reinsurance agreement entered into after November 14, 1991; and

(ii) Amounts arising in taxable years beginning after December 31, 1994, under a reinsurance agreement entered into before November 15, 1991.

(4) *Determination of the date on which a reinsurance agreement is entered into.* A reinsurance agreement is considered entered into at the earlier of—

(i) The date of the reinsurance agreement; or

(ii) The date of a binding written agreement to enter into a reinsurance transaction if the written agreement evidences the parties' agreement on substantially all material items relating to the reinsurance transaction.

(5) *Special rule for certain reinsurance agreements with parties not subject to U.S. taxation.* The election and special rules in paragraph (h) of this section relating to the determination of amounts required to be capitalized on reinsurance agreements with parties not subject to United States taxation apply to taxable years ending on or after September 30, 1990.

(6) *Carryover of excess negative capitalization amount.* The provisions of paragraph (i) of this section, including the special rule for the treatment of excess negative capitalization amounts of insolvent insurance companies, are effective with respect to amounts arising in taxable years ending on or after September 30, 1990. [Reg. § 1.848-2.]

☐ [*T.D.* 8456, 12-28-92.]

[Reg. § 1.848-3]

§ 1.848-3. Interim rules for certain reinsurance agreements.—(a) *Scope and effective dates.* The rules of this section apply in determining net premiums for a reinsurance agreement with respect to—

(1) Amounts arising in taxable years beginning before January 1, 1992, under a reinsurance agreement entered into after November 14, 1991; and

(2) Amounts arising in taxable years beginning before January 1, 1995, under a reinsurance agreement entered into before November 15, 1991.

(b) *Interim rules.* In determining a company's gross amount of premiums and other consideration under section 848(d)(1)(A) and premiums and other consideration incurred for reinsurance under section 848(d)(1)(B), the general rules of subchapter L of the Internal Revenue Code apply with the adjustments and special rules set forth in paragraph (c) of this section. Except as provided in paragraph (c)(5) of this section (which applies to modified coinsurance transactions), the gross amount of premiums and other consideration is determined without any reduction for ceding commissions, annual allowances, reimbursements of claims and benefits, or other amounts incurred by a reinsurer with respect to reinsured contracts.

(c) *Adjustments and special rules.* This paragraph sets forth certain adjustments and special rules that apply for reinsurance agreements in determining the gross amount of premiums and other consideration under section 848(d)(1)(A) and premiums and other consideration incurred for reinsurance under section 848(d)(1)(B).

(1) *Assumption reinsurance.* The ceding company must treat the gross amount of consideration incurred with respect to an assumption reinsurance agreement as premiums and other consideration incurred for reinsurance under section 848(d)(1)(B). The reinsurer must include the same amount in the gross amount of premiums and other consideration under section 848(d)(1)(A). For rules relating to the determination and treatment of ceding commissions, see paragraph (c)(3) of this section.

(2) *Reimbursable dividends.* The reinsurer must treat the amount of policyholder dividends reimbursable to the ceding company (other than under a modified coinsurance agreement covered by paragraph (c)(5) of this section) as a return premium under section 848(d)(1)(B). The ceding

company must include the same amount in the gross amount of premiums and other consideration under section 848(d)(1)(A). The amount of any experience-related refund due the ceding company is treated as a policyholder dividend reimbursable to the ceding company.

(3) *Ceding commissions*—(i) *In general.* The reinsurer must treat ceding commissions as a general deduction. The ceding company must treat ceding commissions as non-premium related income under section 803(a)(3). The ceding company may not reduce its general deductions by the amount of the ceding commission.

(ii) *Amount of ceding commission.* For purposes of this section, the amount of a ceding commission equals the excess, if any, of—

(A) The increase in the reinsurer's tax reserves resulting from the reinsurance agreement (computed in accordance with section 807(d)); over

(B) The gross consideration incurred by the ceding company for the reinsurance agreement, less any amount incurred by the reinsurer as part of the reinsurance agreement.

(4) *Termination payments.* The reinsurer must treat the gross amount of premiums and other consideration payable as a termination payment to the ceding company (including the tax reserves on the reinsured contracts) as premiums and other consideration incurred for reinsurance under section 848(d)(1)(B). The ceding company must include the same amount in the gross amount of premiums and other consideration under section 848(d)(1)(A). This paragraph does not apply to modified coinsurance agreements.

(5) *Modified coinsurance agreements.* In the case of a modified coinsurance agreement, the parties must determine their net premiums on a net consideration basis as described in § 1.848-2(f)(5).

(d) *Examples.* The principles of this section are illustrated by the following examples.

Example 1. On July 1, 1991, an insurance company (L1) transfers a block of individual life insurance contracts to an unrelated insurance company (L2) under an arrangement whereby L2 becomes solely liable to the policyholder under the contracts reinsured. The tax reserves on the reinsured contracts are $100,000. Under the assumption reinsurance agreement, L1 pays L2 $83,000 for assuming the life insurance contracts. Under paragraph (c)(3) of this section, since the increase in L2's tax reserves ($100,000) exceeds the net consideration transferred by L1 ($83,000), the reinsurance agreement provides for a ceding commission. The ceding commission equals $17,000 ($100,000 − $83,000). Under paragraph (c)(3) of this section, L1 reduces its gross amount of premiums and other consideration for the 1991 taxable year under section 848(d)(1)(B) by the $100,000 premium incurred for reinsurance, and L2 includes the $100,000 premium for reinsurance in its gross amount of premiums and other consideration under section 848(d)(1)(A). L1 treats the $17,000 ceding commission as non-premium related income under section 803(a)(3).

Example 2. On July 1, 1991, a life insurance company (L1) transfers a block of individual life insurance contracts to an unrelated insurance company (L2) under an arrangement whereby L2 becomes solely liable to the policyholder under the contracts reinsured. The tax reserves on the reinsured contracts are $100,000. Under the assumption reinsurance agreement, L1 pays L2 $100,000 for assuming the contracts, and L2 pays L1 a $17,000 ceding commission. Under paragraph (c)(1) of this section, L1 reduces its gross amount of premiums and other consideration under section 848(d)(1)(B) by $100,000. L2 includes $100,000 in its gross amount of premiums and other consideration under section 848(d)(1)(A). Under paragraph (c)(3) of this section, since the increase in L2's tax reserves ($100,000) exceeds the net consideration transferred by L1, the reinsurance agreement provides for a ceding commission. The ceding commission equals $17,000 ($100,000 increase in L2's tax reserves less $83,000 net consideration transferred by L1). L1 treats the $17,000 ceding commission as non-premium related income under section 803(a)(3).

Example 3. On July 1, 1991, a life insurance company (L1) transfers a block of individual life insurance contracts to an unrelated insurance company (L2) under an arrangement whereby L2 becomes solely liable to the policyholder under the contracts reinsured. Under the assumption reinsurance agreement, L1 transfers assets of $105,000 to L2. The tax reserves on the reinsured contracts are $100,000. Under paragraph (c)(1) of this section, L1 reduces its gross amount of premiums and other consideration under section 848(d)(1)(B) by $105,000, and L2 increases its gross amount of premiums and other consideration under section 848(d)(1)(A) by $105,000. Since the net consideration transferred by L1 exceeds the increase in L2's tax reserves, there is no ceding commission under paragraph (c)(3) of this section.

Example 4. (i) On June 30, 1991, a life insurance company (L1) reinsures 40% of certain individual life insurance contracts to be issued after that date with an unrelated insurance company (L2) under an agreement whereby L1 remains directly liable to the policyholders with respect to the contracts reinsured. The agreement provides that L2 is credited with 40% of any premiums received with respect to the reinsured contracts, but must indemnify L1 for 40% of any claims, expenses, and policyholder dividends. During the period from July 1 through December 31, 1991, L1 has the following income and expense items with respect to the reinsured policies:

Item	Income	Expense
Premiums	$8,000	
Benefits paid		$1,000
Commissions		6,000
Policyholder dividends		500
		$7,500

(ii) Under paragraphs (b) and (c)(2) of this section, L1 includes $8,200 in its gross amount of premiums and other consideration under section 848(d)(1)(A) ($8,000 gross premiums on the reinsured contracts plus $200 of policyholder dividends reimbursed by L2 ($500 × 40%)). L1 reduces its gross amount of premiums and other consideration by $3,200 (40% × $8,000) as premiums and other consideration incurred for reinsurance under section 848(d)(1)(B). The benefits and commissions incurred by L1 with respect to the reinsured contracts do not reduce L1's gross amount of premiums and other consideration under section 848(d)(1)(B). L2 includes $3,200 in its gross amount of premiums and other consideration (40% × $8,000) and is treated as having paid return premiums of $200 (the amount of reimbursable dividends paid to L1). L2 is also treated as having incurred the following expenses with respect to the reinsured contracts: $400 as benefits paid (40% × $1,000) and $2,400 as commissions expense (40% × $6,000). Under paragraph (b) of this section, these expenses do not reduce L2's gross amount of premiums and other consideration under section 848(d)(1)(A).

Example 5. On December 31, 1991, an insurance company (L1) terminates a reinsurance agreement with an unrelated insurance company (L2). The termination applies to a reinsurance agreement under which L1 had ceded 40% of its liability on a block of individual life insurance contracts to L2. Upon termination of the reinsurance agreement, L2 makes a final payment of $116,000 to L1 for assuming full liability under the contracts. The tax reserves attributable to L2's portion of the reinsured contracts are $120,000. Under paragraph (c)(4) of this section, L2 reduces its gross amount of premiums and other consideration under section 848(d)(1)(B) by $120,000. L1 includes $120,000 in its gross amount of premiums and other consideration under section 848(d)(1)(A).

Example 6. (i) On June 30, 1991, an insurance company (L1) reinsures 40% of its existing life insurance contracts with an unrelated life insurance company (L2) under a modified coinsurance agreement. For the period July 1, 1991 through December 31, 1991, L1 reports the following income and expense items with respect to L2's 40% share of the reinsured contracts:

Item	Income	Expense
Premiums	$10,000	
Benefits paid		$4,000
Policyholder dividends		500
Reserve adjustment		1,500
Total		$6,000

(ii) Pursuant to paragraph (c)(5) of this section, L1 reduces its gross amount of premiums and other consideration under section 848(d)(1)(B) by the $4,000 net consideration for the modified coinsurance agreement ($10,000 − $6,000). L2 includes the $4,000 net consideration in its gross amount of premiums and other consideration under section 848(d)(1)(A). [Reg. § 1.848-3.]

☐ [T.D. 8456, 12-28-92.]

REGULATED INVESTMENT COMPANIES AND REAL ESTATE INVESTMENT TRUSTS

Regulated Investment Companies

[Reg. § 1.851-1]

§ 1.851-1. **Definition of regulated investment company.**—(a) *In general.* The term "regulated investment company" is defined to mean any domestic corporation (other than a personal holding company as defined in section 542) which meets (1) the requirements of section 851(a) and paragraph (b) of this section, and (2) the limitations of section 851(b) and § 1.851-2. As to the definition of the term "corporation", see section 7701(a)(3).

(b) *Requirement.* To qualify as a regulated investment company, a corporation must be:

(1) Registered at all times during the taxable year, under the Investment Company Act of 1940, as amended (15 U.S.C. 80 a-1 to 80 b-2), either as a management company or a unit investment trust, or

(2) A common trust fund or similar fund excluded by section 3(c)(3) of the Investment Company Act of 1940 (15 U.S.C. 80a-3(c)) from the definition of "investment company" and not

included in the definition of "common trust fund" by section 584(a). [Reg. § 1.851-1.]

☐ [T.D. 6236, 6-3-57.]

[Reg. § 1.851-2]

§ 1.851-2. Limitations.—(a) *Election to be a regulated investment company.* Under the provisions of section 851(b)(1), a corporation, even though it satisfies the other requirements of part 1, subchapter M, chapter 1 of the Code, for the taxable year, will not be considered a regulated investment company for such year, within the meaning of such part I, unless it elects to be a regulated investment company for such taxable year, or has made such an election for a previous taxable year which began after December 31, 1941. The election shall be made by the taxpayer by computing taxable income as a regulated investment company in its return for the first taxable year for which the election is applicable. No other method of making such election is permitted. An election once made is irrevocable for such taxable year and all succeeding taxable years.

(b) *Gross income requirement.*—(1) *General rule.* Section 851(b)(2) and (3) provides that (i) at least 90 percent of the corporation's gross income for the taxable year must be derived from dividends, interest, and gains from the sale or other disposition of stocks or securities, and (ii) less than 30 percent of its gross income must have been derived from the sale or other disposition of stock or securities held for less than three months. In determining the gross income requirements under section 851(b)(2) and (3), a loss from the sale or other disposition of stock or securities does not enter into the computation. A determination of the period for which stock or securities have been held shall be governed by the provisions of section 1223 insofar as applicable.

(2) *Special rules.* (i) For purposes of section 851(b)(2), there shall be treated as dividends amounts which are included in gross income for the taxable year under section 951(a)(1)(A)(i) to the extent that (*a*) a distribution out of a foreign corporation's earnings and profits of the taxable year is not included in gross income by reason of section 959(a)(1), and (*b*) the earnings and profits are attributable to the amounts which were so included in gross income under section 951(a)(1)(A)(i). For allocation of distributions to earnings and profits of foreign corporations, see § 1.959-3. The provisions of this subparagraph shall apply with respect to taxable years of controlled foreign corporations beginning after December 31, 1975, and to taxable years of United States shareholders (within the meaning of section 951(b)) within which or with which such taxable years of such controlled foreign corporations end.

(ii) For purposes of subdivision (i) of this subparagraph, if by reason of section 959(a)(1) a distribution of a foreign corporation's earnings and profits for a taxable year described in section 959(c)(2) is not included in a shareholder's gross income, then such distribution shall be allocated proportionately between amounts attributable to amounts included under each clause of section 951(a)(1)(A). Thus, for example, M is a United States shareholder in X Corporation, a controlled foreign corporation. M and X each use the calendar year as the taxable year. For 1977, M is required by section 951(a)(1)(A) to include $3,000 in its gross income, $1,000 of which is included under clause (i) thereof. In 1977, M received a distribution described in section 959(c)(2) of $2,700 out of X's earnings and profits for 1977, which is, by reason of section 959(a)(1), excluded from M's gross income. The amount of the distribution attributable to the amount included under section 951(a)(1)(A)(i) is $900, *i.e.*, $2,700 multiplied by ($1,000/$3,000).

(c) *Diversification of investments.* (1) Subparagraph (A) of section 851(b)(4) requires that at the close of each quarter of the taxable year at least 50 percent of the value of the total assets of the taxpayer corporation be represented by one or more of the following:

(i) Cash and cash items, including receivables;

(ii) Government securities;

(iii) Securities of other regulated investment companies; or

(iv) Securities (other than those described in subdivisions (ii) and (iii) of this subparagraph) of any one or more issuers which meet the following limitations: (*a*) The entire amount of the securities of the issuer owned by the taxpayer corporation is not greater in value than 5 percent of the value of the total assets of the taxpayer corporation, and (*b*) the entire amount of the securities of such issuer owned by the taxpayer corporation does not represent more than 10 percent of the outstanding voting securities of such issuer. For the modification of the percentage limitations applicable in the case of certain venture capital investment companies, see section 851(e) and § 1.851-6.

Assuming that at least 50 percent of the value of the total assets of the corporation satisfies the requirements specified in this subparagraph, and that the limiting provisions of subparagraph (B) of section 851(b)(4) and subparagraph (2) of this paragraph are not violated, the corporation will satisfy the requirements of section 851(b)(4), notwithstanding that the remaining assets do not satisfy the diversification requirements of subparagraph (A) of section 851(b)(4). For example, a corporation may own all the stock of another corporation, provided it otherwise meets the requirements of subparagraphs (A) and (B) of section 851(b)(4).

(2) Subparagraph (B) of section 851(b)(4) prohibits the investment at the close of each quarter of the taxable year of more than 25 percent of the value of the total assets of the corporation (including the 50 percent or more mentioned in subparagraph (A) of section 851(b)(4)) in the securities (other than Government securities or the securities of other regulated investment companies) of any one issuer, or of two or more issuers which the taxpayer company controls and which are engaged in the same or similar trades or businesses or related trades or businesses, including such issuers as are merely a part of a unit contributing to the completion and sale of a product or the rendering of a particular service. Two or more issuers are not considered as being in the same or similar trades or businesses merely because they are engaged in the broad field of manufacturing or of any other general classification of industry, but issuers shall be construed to be engaged in the same or similar trades or businesses if they are engaged in a distinct branch of business, trade, or manufacture in which they render the same kind of service or produce or deal in the same kind of product, and such service or products fulfill the same economic need. If two or more issuers produce more than one product or render more than one type of service, then the chief product or service of each shall be the basis for determining whether they are in the same trade or business. [Reg. § 1.851-2.]

☐ [T.D. 6236, 6-3-57. Amended by T.D. 6598, 4-25-62 and T.D. 7555, 7-25-78.]

[Reg. § 1.851-3]

§ 1.851-3. **Rules applicable to section 851(b)(4).**—In determining the value of the taxpayer's investment in the securities of any one issuer, for the purposes of subparagraph (B) of section 851(b)(4), there shall be included its proper proportion of the investment of any other corporation, a member of a controlled group, in the securities of such issuer. See example (4) in § 1.851-5. For purposes of §§ 1.851-2, 1.851-4, 1.851-5, and 1.851-6, the terms "controls", "controlled group", and "value" have the meaning assigned to them by section 851(c). All other terms used in such sections have the same meaning as when used in the Investment Company Act of 1940 (15 U.S.C., ch. 2D) or that act as amended. [Reg. § 1.851-3.]

☐ [T.D. 6236, 6-3-57.]

[Reg. § 1.851-4]

§ 1.851-4. **Determination of status.**—With respect to the effect which certain discrepancies between the value of its various investments and the requirements of section 851(b)(4) and paragraph (c) of § 1.851-2, or the effect that the elimination of such discrepancies will have on the status of a company as a regulated investment company for purposes of part I, subchapter M, chapter 1 of the Code, see section 851(d). A company claiming to be a regulated investment company shall keep sufficient records as to investments so as to be able to show that it has complied with the provisions of section 851 during the taxable year. Such records shall be kept at all times available for inspection by any internal revenue officer or employee and shall be retained so long as the contents thereof may become material in the administration of any internal revenue law. [Reg. § 1.851-4.]

☐ [T.D. 6236, 6-3-57. Amended by T.D. 6598, 4-25-62.]

[Reg. § 1.851-5]

§ 1.851-5. **Examples.**—The provisions of section 851 may be illustrated by the following examples:

Example (1). Investment Company W at the close of its first quarter of the taxable year has its assets invested as follows:

	Percent
Cash	5
Government securities	10
Securities of regulated investment companies	20
Securities of Corporation A	10
Securities of Corporation B	15
Securities of Corporation C	20
Securities of various corporations (not exceeding 5 percent of its assets in any one company)	20
Total	100

Investment Company W owns all of the voting stock of Corporations A and B, 15 percent of the voting stock of Corporation C, and less than 10 percent of the voting stock of the other corporations. None of the corporations is a member of a controlled group. Investment Company W meets the requirements under section 851(b)(4) at the end of its first quarter. It complies with subparagraph (A) of section 851(b)(4) since it has 55 percent of its assets invested as provided in such subparagraph. It complies with subparagraph (B) of section 851(b)(4) since it does not have more than 25 percent of its assets invested in the securities of any one issuer, or of two or more issuers which it controls.

Reg. § 1.851-5

Example (2). Investment Company V at the close of a particular quarter of the taxable year has its assets invested as follows:

	Percent
Cash	10
Government securities	35
Securities of Corporation A	7
Securities of Corporation B	12
Securities of Corporation C	15
Securities of Corporation D	21
Total	100

Investment Company V fails to meet the requirements of subparagraph (A) of section 851(b)(4) since its assets invested in Corporations A, B, C, and D exceed in each case 5 percent of the value of the total assets of the company at the close of the particular quarter.

Example (3). Investment Company X at the close of the particular quarter of the taxable year has its assets invested as follows:

	Percent
Cash and Government securities	20
Securities of Corporation A	5
Securities of Corporation B	10
Securities of Corporation C	25
Securities of various corporations (not exceeding 5 percent of its assets in any one company)	40
Total	100

Investment Company X owns more than 20 percent of the voting power of Corporations B and C and less than 10 percent of the voting power of all of the other corporations. Corporation B manufactures radios and Corporation C acts as its distributor and also distributes radios for other companies. Investment Company X fails to meet the requirements of subparagraph (B) of section 851(b)(4) since it has 35 percent of its assets invested in the securities of two issuers which it controls and which are engaged in related trades or businesses.

Example (4). Investment Company Y at the close of a particular quarter of the taxable year has its assets invested as follows:

	Percent
Cash and Government securities	15
Securities of Corporation K (a regulated investment company)	30
Securities of Corporation A	10
Securities of Corporation B	20
Securities of various corporations (not exceeding 5 percent of its assets in any one company)	25
Total	100

Corporation K has 20 percent of its assets invested in Corporation L and Corporation L has 40 percent of its assets invested in Corporation B. Corporation A also has 30 percent of its assets invested in Corporation B, and owns more than 20 percent of the voting power in Corporation B. Investment Company Y owns more than 20 percent of the voting power of Corporations A and K. Corporation K owns more than 20 percent of the voting power of Corporation L, and Corporation L owns more than 20 percent of the voting power of Corporation B. Investment Company Y is disqualified under subparagraph (B) of section 851(b)(4) since more than 25 percent of its assets are considered invested in Corporation B as shown by the following calculation:

Percentage of assets invested directly in Corporation B	20.0
Percentage invested through the controlled group, Y-K-L-B (40 percent of 20 percent of 30 percent)	2.4
Percentage invested in the controlled group, Y-A-B (30 percent of 10 percent)	3.0
Total percentage of assets of Investment Company Y invested in Corporation B	25.4

Example (5). Investment Company Z, which keeps its books and makes its returns on the basis of the calendar year, at the close of the first quarter of 1955 meets the requirements of section 851(b)(4) and has 20 percent of its assets invested in Corporation A. Later during the taxable year it makes distributions to its shareholders and because of such distributions it finds at the close of the taxable year that it has more than 25 percent of its remaining assets invested in Corporation A. Investment Company Z does not lose its status as a regulated investment company for the taxable year 1955 because of such distributions, nor will it lose its status as a regulated investment company for 1956 or any subsequent year solely as a result of such distributions.

Example (6). Investment Company Q, which keeps its books and makes its returns on the basis of a calendar year, at the close of the first quarter of 1955, meets the requirements of section 851(b)(4) and has 20 percent of its assets invested in Corporation P. At the close of the taxable year 1955 it finds that it has more than 25 percent of its assets invested in Corporation P. This situation results entirely from fluctuations in the market values of the securities in Investment Company Q's portfolio and is not due in whole or in part to the acquisition of any security or other property. Corporation Q does not lose its status as a regulated investment company for the taxable year 1955 because of such fluctuations in the market values of the securities in its portfolio, nor will it lose its status as a regulated investment company for 1956 or any subsequent year solely as a result of such market value fluctuations. [Reg. § 1.851-5.]

☐ [T.D. 6236, 6-3-57.]

Reg. § 1.851-5

Regulated Investment Companies

See p. 20,601 for regulations not amended to reflect law changes

[Reg. § 1.851-6]

§ 1.851-6. **Investment companies furnishing capital to development corporations.**—(a) *Qualifying requirements.*—(1) In the case of a regulated investment company which furnishes capital to development corporations, section 851(e) provides an exception to the rule relating to the diversification of investments, made applicable to regulated investment companies by section 851(b)(4)(A). This exception (as provided in paragraph (b) of this section) is available only to registered management investment companies which the Securities and Exchange Commission determines, in accordance with regulations issued by it, and certifies to the Secretary or his delegate, not earlier than 60 days before the close of the taxable year of such investment company, to be principally engaged in the furnishing of capital to other corporations which are principally engaged in the development or exploitation of inventions, technological improvements, new processes, or products not previously generally available.

(2) For the purpose of the aforementioned determination and certification, unless the Securities and Exchange Commission determines otherwise, a corporation shall be considered to be principally engaged in the development or exploitation of inventions, technological improvements, new processes, or products not previously generally available, for at least 10 years after the date of the first acquisition of any security in such corporation or any predecessor thereof by such investment company if at the date of such acquisition the corporation or its predecessor was principally so engaged, and an investment company shall be considered at any date to be furnishing capital to any company whose securities it holds if within 10 years before such date it had acquired any of such securities, or any securities surrendered in exchange therefor, from such other company or its predecessor.

(b) *Exception to general rule.* (1) The registered management investment company, which for the taxable year meets the requirements of paragraph (a) of this section, may (subject to the limitations of section 851(e)(2) and paragraph (c) of this section) in the computation of 50 percent of the value of its assets under section 851(b)(4)(A) and paragraph (c)(1) of § 1.851-2 for any quarter of such taxable year, include the value of any securities of an issuer (whether or not the investment company owns more than 10 percent of the outstanding voting securities of such issuer) if at the time of the latest acquisition of any securities of such issuer the basis of all such securities in the hands of the investment company does not exceed 5 percent of the value of the total assets of the investment company at that time. The exception provided by section 851(e)(1) and this subparagraph is not applicable to the securities of an issuer if the investment company has continuously held any security of such issuer or of any predecessor company (as defined in paragraph (d) of this section) for 10 or more years preceding such quarter of the taxable year. The rule of section 851(e)(1) with respect to the relationship of the basis of the securities of an issuer to the value of the total assets of the investment company is, in substance, a qualification of the 5-percent limitation in section 851(b)(4)(A)(ii) and paragraph (c)(1)(iv) of § 1.851-2. All other provisions and requirements of section 851 and §§ 1.851-1 through 1.851-6 are applicable in determining whether such registered management investment company qualifies as a regulated investment company.

(2) The application of subparagraph (1) of this paragraph may be illustrated by the following examples:

Example (1). (i) The XYZ Corporation, a regulated investment company, qualified under section 851(e) as an investment company furnishing capital to development corporations. On June 30, 1954, the XYZ Corporation purchased 1,000 shares of the stock of the A Corporation at a cost of $30,000. On June 30, 1954, the value of the total assets of the XYZ Corporation was $1,000,000. Its investment in the stock of the A Corporation ($30,000) comprised 3 percent of the value of its total assets, and it therefore met the requirements prescribed by section 851(b)(4)(A)(ii) as modified by section 851(e)(1).

(ii) On June 30, 1955, the value of the total assets of the XYZ Corporation was $1,500,000 and the 1,000 shares of stock of the A Corporation which the XYZ Corporation owned appreciated in value so that they were then worth $60,000. On that date, the XYZ Investment Company increased its investment in the stock of the A Corporation by the purchase of an additional 500 shares of that stock at a total cost of $30,000. The securities of the A Corporation owned by the XYZ Corporation had a value of $90,000 (6 percent of the value of the total assets of the XYZ Corporation) which exceeded the limit provided by section 851(b)(4)(A)(ii). However, the investment of the XYZ Corporation in the A Corporation on June 30, 1955, qualified under section 851(b)(4)(A) as modified by section 851(e)(1), since the basis of those securities to the investment company did not exceed 5 percent of the value of its total assets as of June 30, 1955, illustrated as follows:

Reg. § 1.851-6(b)(2)

Regulated Investment Companies

See p. 20,601 for regulations not amended to reflect law changes

Basis to the XYZ Corporation of the A Corporation's stock acquired on
June 30, 1954 .... $30,000
Basis of the 500 shares of the A Corporation's stock acquired by the XYZ
Corporation on June 30, 1955 30,000

Basis of all stock of A Corporation 60,000

$$\frac{\text{Basis of stock of A Corporation}}{\text{Value of XYZ Corporation's total assets at June 30, 1955, time of the latest acquisition.}} = \frac{\$60,000}{\$1,500,000} = 4 \text{ percent}$$

Example (2). The same facts existed as in example (1), except that on June 30, 1955, the XYZ Corporation increased its investment in the stock of the A Corporation by the purchase of an additional 1,000 shares of that stock (instead of 500 shares) at a total cost of $60,000. No part of the investment of the XYZ Corporation in the A Corporation qualified under the 5-percent limitation provided by section 851(b)(4)(A) as modified by section 851(e)(1), illustrated as follows:

Basis to the XYZ Corporation of the 1,000 shares of the A Corporation's stock acquired on
June 30, 1954 .... $30,000
Basis of the 1,000 shares of the A Corporation's stock acquired on June 30, 1955 60,000

Total 90,000

$$\frac{\text{Basis of stock of A Corporation}}{\text{Value of XYZ Corporation's total assets at June 30, 1955, time of the latest acquisition.}} = \frac{\$90,000}{\$1,500,000} = 6 \text{ percent}$$

Example (3). The same facts existed as in example (2) and on June 30, 1956, the XYZ Corporation increased its investment in the stock of the A Corporation by the purchase of an additional 100 shares of that stock at a total cost of $6,000. On June 30, 1956, the value of the total assets of the XYZ Corporation was $2,000,000 and on that date the investment in the A Corporation qualified under section 851(b)(4)(A) as modified by section 851(e)(1), illustrated as follows:

Basis to the XYZ Corporation of investments in the A Corporation's stock:
1,000 shares acquired June 30, 1954 .... $30,000
1,000 shares acquired June 30, 1955 60,000
100 shares acquired June 30, 1956 6,000

Total 96,000

$$\frac{\text{Basis of stock of A Corporation}}{\text{Value of XYZ Corporation's total assets at June 30, 1956, time of the latest acquisition.}} = \frac{\$96,000}{\$2,000,000} = 4.8 \text{ percent}$$

(c) *Limitation.* Section 851(e) and this section do not apply in the quarterly computation of 50 percent of the value of the assets of an investment company under subparagraph (A) of section 851(b)(4) and paragraph (c)(1) of § 1.851-2 for any taxable year if at the close of any quarter of such taxable year more than 25 percent of the value of its total assets (including the 50 percent or more mentioned in such subparagraph (A)) is represented by securities (other than Government securities or the securities of other regulated investment companies) of issuers as to each of which such investment company (1) holds more than 10 percent of the outstanding voting securities of such issuer, and (2) has continuously held any security of such issuer (or any security of a predecessor of such issuer) for 10 or more years preceding such quarter, unless the value of its total assets so represented is reduced to 25 percent or less within 30 days after the close of such quarter.

(d) *Definition of predecessor company.* As used in section 851(e) and this section, the term "predecessor company" means any corporation the basis of whose securities in the hands of the investment company was, under the provisions of section 358 or corresponding provisions of prior law, the same in whole or in part as the basis of any of the securities of the issuer and any corporation with respect to whose securities any of the securities of the issuer were received directly or

Reg. § 1.851-6(c)

Regulated Investment Companies

indirectly by the investment company in a transaction or series of transactions involving nonrecognition of gain or loss in whole or in part. The other terms used in this section have the same meaning as when used in section 851(b)(4). See paragraph (c) of § 1.851-2 and § 1.851-3. [Reg. § 1.851-6.]

☐ [*T.D. 6236, 6-3-57. Amended by T.D. 6369, 3-16-59.*]

[Reg. § 1.851-7]

§ 1.851-7. Certain unit investment trusts.— (a) *In general.* For purposes of the Internal Revenue Code, a unit investment trust (as defined in paragraph (d) of this section) shall not be treated as a person (as defined in section 7701(a)(1)) except for years ending before January 1, 1969. A holder of an interest in such a trust will be treated as directly owning the assets of such trust for taxable years of such holder which end with or within any year of the trust to which section 851(f) and this section apply.

(b) *Treatment of unit investment trust.* A unit investment trust shall not be treated as an individual, a trust, estate, partnership, association, company, or corporation for purposes of the Internal Revenue Code. Accordingly, a unit investment trust is not a taxpayer subject to taxation under the Internal Revenue Code. No gain or loss will be recognized by the unit investment trust if such trust distributes a holder's proportionate share of the trust assets in exchange for his interest in the trust. Also, no gain or loss will be recognized by the unit investment trust if such trust sells the holder's proportionate share of the trust assets and distributes the proceeds from such share to the holder in exchange for his interest in the trust.

(c) *Treatment of holder of interest in unit investment trust.* (1) Each holder of an interest in a unit investment trust shall be treated (to the extent of such interest) as owning a proportionate share of the assets of the trust. Accordingly, if the trust distributes to the holder of an interest in such trust his proportionate share, or any portion thereof, of the trust assets in exchange for his interest in the trust, no gain or loss shall be recognized by such holder (or by any other holder of an interest in such trust). For purposes of this paragraph, each purchase of an interest in the trust by the holder will be considered a separate interest in the trust. Items of income, gain, loss, deduction, or credit received by the trust or a custodian thereof shall be taxed to the holders of interests in the trust (and not to the trust) as though they had received their proportionate share of the items directly on the date such items were received by the trust or custodian.

(2) The basis of the assets of such trust which are treated under subparagraph (1) of this paragraph as being owned by the holder of an interest in such trust shall be the same as the basis of his interest in such trust. Accordingly, the amount of the gain or loss recognized by the holder upon the sale by the unit investment trust of the holder's pro rata share of the trust assets shall be determined with reference to the basis of his interest in the trust. Also, the basis of the assets received by the holder, if the trust distributes a holder's pro rata share of the trust assets in exchange for his interest in the trust, will be the same as the basis of his interest in the trust. If the unit investment trust sells less than all of the holder's pro rata share of the trust assets and the holder retains an interest in the trust, the amount of the gain or loss recognized by the holder upon the sale shall be determined with reference to the basis of his interest in the assets sold by the trust, and the basis of his interest in the trust shall be reduced accordingly. If the trust distributes a portion of the holder's pro rata share of the trust assets in exchange for a portion of his interest in the trust, the basis of the assets received by the holder shall be determined with reference to the basis of his interest in the assets distributed by the trust, and the basis of his interest in the trust shall be reduced accordingly. For purposes of this subparagraph, the basis of the holder's interest in assets sold by the trust or distributed to him shall be an amount which bears the same relationship to the basis of his total interest in the trust that the fair market value of the assets so sold or distributed bears to the fair market value of such total interest in the trust, such fair market value to be determined on the date of such sale or distribution.

(3) The period for which the holder of an interest in such trust has held the assets of the trust which are treated under subparagraph (1) of this paragraph as being owned by him is the same as the period for which such holder has held his interest in such trust. Accordingly, the character of the gain, loss, deduction, or credit recognized by the holder upon the sale by the unit investment trust of the holder's proportionate share of the trust assets shall be determined with reference to the period for which he has held his interest in the trust. Also, the holding period of the assets received by the holder if the trust distributes the holder's proportionate share of the trust assets in exchange for his interest in the trust will include the period for which the holder has held his interest in the trust.

(4) The application of the provisions of this paragraph may be illustrated by the following example:

Reg. § 1.851-7(c)(4)

Example. B entered a periodic payment plan of a unit investment trust (as defined in paragraph (d) of this section) with X Bank as custodian and Z as plan sponsor. Under this plan, upon B's demand, X must either redeem B's interest at a price substantially equal to the fair market value of the number of shares in Y, a management company, which are credited to B's account by X in connection with the unit investment trust, or at B's option distribute such shares of Y to B. B's plan provides for quarterly payments of $1,000. On October 1, 1969, B made his initial quarterly payment of $1,000 and X credited B's account with 110 shares of Y. On December 1, 1969, Y declared and paid a dividend of 25 cents per share, 5 cents of which was designated as a capital gain dividend pursuant to section 852(b)(3) and § 1.852-4. X credited B's account with $27.50 but did not distribute the money to B in 1969. On December 31, 1969, X charged B's account with $1 for custodial fees for calendar year 1969. On January 1, 1970, B paid X $1,000 and X credited B's account with 105 shares of Y. On April 1, 1970, B paid X $1,000 and X credited B's account with 100 shares of Y. B must include in his tax return for 1969 a dividend of $22 and a long-term capital gain of $5.50. In addition, B is entitled to deduct the annual custodial fee of $1 under section 212 of the Code.

(a) On April 4, 1970, at B's request, X sells the shares of Y credited to B's account (315 shares) for $10 per share and distributes the proceeds ($3,150) to B together with the remaining balance of $26.50 in B's account. The receipt of the $26.50 does not result in any tax consequences to B. B recognizes a long-term capital gain of $100 and a short-term capital gain of $50, computed as follows:

(1) B is treated as owning 110 shares of Y as of October 1, 1969. The basis of these shares is $1,000, and they were sold for $1,100 (110 shares at $10 per share). Therefore, B recognizes a gain from the sale or exchange of a capital asset held for more than 6 months in the amount of $100.

(2) B is treated as owning 105 shares of Y as of January 1, 1970, and 100 shares as of April 1, 1970. With respect to the shares acquired on April 1, 1970, there is no gain recognized as the shares were sold for $1,000, which is B's basis of the shares. The shares acquired on January 1, 1970, were sold for $1,050 (105 shares at $10 per share), and B's basis of these shares is $1,000. Therefore, B recognizes a gain of $50 from the sale or exchange of a capital asset held for not more than 6 months.

(b) On April 4, 1970, at B's request, X distributes to B the shares of Y credited to his account and $26.50 in cash. The receipt of the $26.50 does not result in any tax consequences to B. B does not recognize gain or loss on the distribution of the shares of Y to him. The bases and holding periods of B's interest in Y are as follows:

No. of shares	Date acquired	Basis
110	10-1-69	$ 9.09
105	1-1-70	9.52
100	4-1-70	10.00

(d) *Definition.* A unit investment trust to which this section refers is a business arrangement (other than a segregated asset account, whether or not it holds assets pursuant to a variable annuity contract, under the insurance laws or regulations of a State) which (except for taxable years ending before Jan. 1, 1969)—

(1) Is a unit investment trust (as defined in the Investment Company Act of 1940);

(2) Is registered under such Act;

(3) Issues periodic payment plan certificates (as defined in such Act) in one or more series;

(4) Possesses, as substantially all of its assets, as to all such series, securities issued by—

(i) Except as otherwise provided by paragraph (e) of this section, a single management company (as defined in such Act), and securities acquired pursuant to subparagraph (5) of this paragraph, or

(ii) A single other corporation; and

(5) Except as otherwise provided by paragraph (e) of this section, has no power to invest in any other securities except securities issued by a single other management company, when permitted by such Act or the rules and regulations of the Securities and Exchange Commission.

(e) *Investment in two single management companies.* (1) A unit investment trust may, when such investment is permitted by the Investment Company Act of 1940 or the rules and regulations of the Securities and Exchange Commission, possess securities issued by two or more single management companies (as defined in such Act) if—

(i) The trust issues a separate series of periodic payment plan certificates (as defined in such Act) with respect to the securities of each single management company which it possesses; and

(ii) None of the periodic payment plan certificates issued by the trust permits joint acquisition of an interest in each series nor the

Reg. § 1.851-7(d)(1)

application of payments in whole or in part first to a series issued by one of the single management companies and then to any other series issued by any other single management company.

(2) If a unit investment trust possesses securities of two or more separate single management companies as described in subparagraph (1) of this paragraph and issues a separate series of periodic payment plan certificates with respect to the securities of each such management company, then the holder of an interest in a series shall be treated as the owner of the securities in the single management company represented by such interest.

(i) A holder of an interest in a series of periodic payment plan certificates of a trust who exchanges his interest in the series for an interest in another series of periodic payment plan certificates of the trust shall recognize gain or loss on the exchange as if the trust had sold the shares credited to his interest in the series at fair market value and distributed the proceeds of the sale to him.

(ii) The basis of the interest in the series so acquired by the holder shall be the fair market value of his interest in the series exchanged by him.

(iii) The period for which the holder has held his interest in the series so acquired shall be measured from the date of his acquisition of his interest in that series.

(f) *Cross references.* (1) For reporting requirements imposed on custodians of unit investment trusts described in this section, see §§ 1.852-4, 1.852-9, 1.853-3, 1.854-2, and 1.6042-2.

(2) For the rules relating to redemptions of certain unit investment trusts not described in this section, see § 1.852-10. [Reg. § 1.851-7.]

☐ [*T.D. 7187, 7-5-72.*]

[Reg. § 1.852-1]

§ 1.852-1. **Taxation of regulated investment companies.**—(a) *Requirements applicable thereto*—(1) *In general.* Section 852(a) denies the application of the provisions of part I, subchapter M, chapter 1 of the Code (other than section 852(c), relating to earnings and profits), to a regulated investment company for a taxable year beginning after February 28, 1958, unless—

(i) The deduction for dividends paid for such taxable year as defined in section 561 (computed without regard to capital gain dividends) is equal to at least 90 percent of its investment company taxable income for such taxable year (determined without regard to the provisions of section 852(b)(2)(D) and paragraph (d) of § 1.852-3); and

(ii) The company complies for such taxable year with the provisions of § 1.852-6 (relating to records required to be maintained by a regulated investment company).

See section 853(b)(1)(B) and paragraph (a) of § 1.853-2 for amounts to be added to the dividends paid deduction, and section 855 and § 1.855-1, relating to dividends paid after the close of the taxable year.

(2) *Special rule for taxable years of regulated investment companies beginning before March 1, 1958.* The provisions of part I of subchapter M (including section 852(c)) are not applicable to a regulated investment company for a taxable year beginning before March 1, 1958, unless such company meets the requirements of section 852(a) and subparagraph (1)(i) and (ii) of this paragraph.

(b) *Failure to qualify.* If a regulated investment company does not meet the requirements of section 852(a) and paragraph (a)(1)(i) and (ii) of this section for the taxable year, it will, even though it may otherwise be classified as a regulated investment company, be taxed in such year as an ordinary corporation and not as a regulated investment company. In such case, none of the provisions of part I of subchapter M (other than section 852(c) in the case of taxable years beginning after February 28, 1958) will be applicable to it. For the rules relating to the applicability of section 852(c), see § 1.852-5. [Reg. § 1.852-1.]

☐ [*T.D. 6236, 6-3-57. Amended by T.D. 6369, 3-16-59 and T.D. 6598, 4-25-62.*]

[Reg. § 1.852-2]

§ 1.852-2. **Method of taxation of regulated investment companies.**—(a) *Imposition of normal tax and surtax.* Section 852(b)(1) imposes a normal tax and surtax, computed at the rates and in the manner prescribed in section 11, on the investment company taxable income, as defined in section 852(b)(2) and § 1.852-3, for each taxable year of a regulated investment company. The tax is imposed as if the investment company taxable income were the taxable income referred to in section 11. In computing the normal tax under section 11, the regulated investment company's taxable income and the dividends paid deduction (computed without regard to the capital gains dividends) shall both be reduced by the deduction for partially tax-exempt interest provided by section 242.

(b) *Taxation of capital gains*—(1) *In general.* Section 852(b)(3)(A) imposes (i) in the case of a taxable year beginning before January 1, 1970, a tax of 25 percent, or (ii) in the case of a taxable year beginning after December 31, 1969, a tax determined as provided in section 1201(a) and paragraph (a)(3) of § 1.1201-1, on the excess, if any, of the net long-term capital gain of a regulated investment company (subject to tax under part I, subchapter M, chapter 1 of the Code) over the sum of its net short-term capital loss and its deduction for dividends paid (as defined in section 561) determined with reference to capital gain dividends only. For the definition of capital gain dividend paid by a regulated investment company, see section 852(b)(3)(C) and paragraph (c) of § 1.852-4. In the case of a taxable year ending after December 31, 1969, and beginning before January 1, 1975, such deduction for dividends paid shall first be made from the amount subject to tax in accordance with section 1201(a)(1)(B), to the extent thereof, and then from the amount subject to tax in accordance with section 1201(a)(1)(A). See § 1.852-10, relating to certain distributions in redemption of interests in unit investment trusts which, for purposes of the deduction for dividends paid with reference to capital gain dividends only, are not considered preferential dividends under section 562(c). See section 855 and § 1.855-1, relating to dividends paid after the close of the taxable year.

(2) *Undistributed capital gains*—(i) *In general.* A regulated investment company (subject to tax under part I of subchapter M) may, for taxable years beginning after December 31, 1956, designate under section 852(b)(3)(D) an amount of undistributed capital gains to each shareholder of the company. For the definition of the term "undistributed capital gains" and for the treatment of such amounts by a shareholder, see paragraph (b)(2) of § 1.852-4. For the rules relating to the method of making such designation, the returns to be filed, and the payment of the tax in such cases, see paragraph (a) of § 1.852-9.

(ii) *Effect on earnings and profits of a regulated investment company.* If a regulated investment company designates an amount as undistributed capital gains for a taxable year, the earnings and profits of such regulated investment company for such taxable year shall be reduced by the total amount of the undistributed capital gains so designated. In such case, its capital account shall be increased—

(a) In the case of a taxable year ending before January 1, 1970, by 75 percent of the total amount designated,

(b) In the case of a taxable year ending after December 31, 1969, and beginning before January 1, 1975, by the total amount designated decreased by the amount of tax imposed by section 852(b)(3)(A) with respect to such amount, or

(c) In the case of a taxable year beginning after December 31, 1974, by 70 percent of the total amount designated.

The earnings and profits of a regulated investment company shall not be reduced by the amount of tax which is imposed by section 852(b)(3)(A) on an amount designated as undistributed capital gains and which is paid by the corporation but deemed paid by the shareholder. [Reg. § 1.852-2.]

☐ [T.D. 6326, 6-3-57. *Amended by T.D.* 6369, 3-16-59; T.D. 6598, 4-25-62; T.D. 6921, 6-19-67 and T.D. 7337, 12-26-74.]

[Reg. § 1.852-3]

§ 1.852-3. *Investment company taxable income.*—Section 852(b)(2) requires certain adjustments to be made to convert taxable income of the investment company to investment company taxable income, as follows:

(a) The excess, if any, of the net long-term capital gain over the net short-term capital loss shall be excluded;

(b) The net operating loss deduction provided in section 172 shall not be allowed;

(c) The special deductions provided in part VIII (section 241 and following, except section 248), subchapter B, chapter 1 of the Code, shall not be allowed. Those not allowed are the deduction for partially tax-exempt interest provided by section 242, the deductions for dividends received provided by sections 243, 244, and 245, and the deduction for certain dividends paid provided by section 247. However, the deduction provided by section 248 (relating to organizational expenditures), otherwise allowable in computing taxable income, shall likewise be allowed in computing the investment company taxable income. See section 852(b)(1) and paragraph (a) of § 1.852-2 for treatment of the deduction for partially tax-exempt interest (provided by section 242) for purposes of computing the normal tax under section 11;

(d) The deduction for dividends paid (as defined in section 561) shall be allowed, but shall be computed without regard to capital gains dividends (as defined in section 852(b)(3)(C) and paragraph (c) of § 1.852-4); and

(e) The taxable income shall be computed without regard to section 443(b). Thus, the taxable income for a period of less than 12 months shall not be placed on an annual basis even though such short taxable year results from a change of accounting period. [Reg. § 1.852-3.]

☐ [T.D. 6236, 6-3-57. *Amended by T.D.* 6369, 3-16-59.]

Reg. § 1.852-3(a)

[Reg. § 1.852-4]

§ 1.852-4. Method of taxation of shareholders of regulated investment companies.—(a) *Ordinary income.* (1) Except as otherwise provided in paragraph (b) of this section (relating to capital gains), a shareholder receiving dividends from a regulated investment company shall include such dividends in gross income for the taxable year in which they are received.

(2) See section 853(b)(2) and (c) and paragraph (b) of § 1.853-2 and § 1.853-3 for the treatment by shareholders of dividends received from a regulated investment company which has made an election under section 853(a) with respect to the foreign tax credit. See section 854 and §§ 1.854-1 through 1.854-3 for limitations applicable to dividends received from regulated investment companies for the purpose of the credit under section 34 (for dividends received on or before December 31, 1964), the exclusion from gross income under section 116, and the deduction under section 243. See section 855(b) and (d) and paragraphs (c) and (f) of § 1.855-1 for treatment by shareholders of dividends paid by a regulated investment company after the close of the taxable year in the case of an election under section 855(a).

(b) *Capital gains*—(1) *In general.* Under section 852(b)(3)(B), shareholders of a regulated investment company who receive capital gain dividends (as defined in paragraph (c) of this section), in respect of the capital gains of an investment company for a taxable year for which it is taxable under part I, subchapter M, chapter 1 of the Code, as a regulated investment company, shall treat such capital gain dividends as gains from the sale or exchange of capital assets held for more than 1 year (6 months for taxable years beginning before 1977; 9 months for taxable years beginning in 1977) and realized in the taxable year of the shareholder in which the dividend was received. In the case of dividends with respect to any taxable year of a regulated investment company ending after December 31, 1969, and beginning before January 1, 1975, the portion of a shareholder's capital gain dividend to which section 1201(d)(1) or (2) applies is the portion so designated by the regulated investment company pursuant to paragraph (c)(2) of this section.

(2) *Undistributed capital gains.* (i) A person who is a shareholder of a regulated investment company at the close of a taxable year of such company for which it is taxable under part I of subchapter M shall include in his gross income as a gain from the sale or exchange of a capital asset held for more than 1 year (6 months for taxable years beginning before 1977; 9 months for taxable years beginning in 1977) any amount of undistributed capital gains. The term "undistributed capital gains" means the amount designated as undistributed capital gains in accordance with paragraph (a) of § 1.852-9, but the amount so designated shall not exceed the shareholder's proportionate part of the amount subject to tax under section 852(b)(3)(A). Such amount shall be included in gross income for the taxable year of the shareholder in which falls the last day of the taxable year of the regulated investment company in respect of which the undistributed capital gains were designated. The amount of such gains designated under paragraph (a) of § 1.852-9 as gain described in section 1201(d)(1) or (2) shall be included in the shareholder's gross income as gain described in section 1201(d)(1) or (2). For certain administrative provisions relating to undistributed capital gains, see § 1.852-9.

(ii) Any shareholder required to include an amount of undistributed capital gains in gross income under section 852(b)(3)(D)(i) and subdivision (i) of this subparagraph shall be deemed to have paid for his taxable year for which such amount is so includible—

(a) In the case of an amount designated with respect to a taxable year of the company ending before January 1, 1970, a tax equal to 25 percent of such amount,

(b) In the case of a taxable year of the company ending after December 31, 1969, and beginning before January 1, 1975, a tax equal to the tax designated under paragraph (a)(1) of § 1.852-9 by the regulated investment company as his proportionate share of the capital gains tax paid with respect to such amount, or

(c) In the case of an amount designated with respect to a taxable year of the company beginning after December 31, 1974, a tax equal to 30 percent of such amount.

Such shareholder is entitled to a credit or refund of the tax so deemed paid in accordance with the rules provided in paragraph (c)(2) of § 1.852-9.

(iii) Any shareholder required to include an amount of undistributed capital gains in gross income under section 852(b)(3)(D)(i) and subdivision (i) of this subparagraph shall increase the adjusted basis of the shares of stock with respect to which such amount is so includible—

(a) In the case of an amount designated with respect to a taxable year of the company ending before January 1, 1970, by 75 percent of such amount,

(b) In the case of an amount designated with respect to a taxable year of the company ending after December 31, 1969, and beginning before January 1, 1975, by the amount designated under paragraph (a)(1)(iv) of §1.852-9 by the regulated investment company, or

(c) In the case of an amount designated with respect to a taxable year of the company beginning after December 31, 1974, by 70 percent of such amount.

(3) *Partners and partnerships.* If the shareholder required to include an amount of undistributed capital gains in gross income under section 852(b)(3)(D) and subparagraph (2) of this paragraph is a partnership, such amount shall be included in the gross income of the partnership for the taxable year of the partnership in which falls the last day of the taxable year or the regulated investment company in respect of which the undistributed capital gains were designated. The amount so includible by the partnership shall be taken into account by the partners as distributive shares of the partnership gains and losses from sales or exchanges of capital assets held for more than 1 year (6 months for taxable years beginning before 1977; 9 months for taxable years beginning in 1977) pursuant to section 702(a)(2) and paragraph (a)(2) of § 1.702-1. The tax with respect to the undistributed capital gains is deemed paid by the partnership (under section 852(b)(3)(D)(ii) and subparagraph (2)(ii) of this paragraph), and the credit or refund of such tax shall be taken into account by the partners in accordance with section 702(a)(8) and paragraph (a)(8)(ii) of § 1.702-1 and paragraph (c)(2) of § 1.852-9. In accordance with section 705(a), the partners shall increase the basis of their partnership interests under section 705(a)(1) by the distributive shares of such gains, and shall decrease the basis of their partnership interests by the distributive shares of the amount of the tax under section 705(a)(2)(B) (relating to certain non-deductible expenditures) and paragraph (a)(3) of § 1.705-1.

(4) *Nonresident alien individuals.* If the shareholder required to include an amount of undistributed capital gains in gross income under section 852(b)(3)(D) and subparagraph (2) of this paragraph is a nonresident alien individual, such shareholder shall be treated, for purposes of section 871 and the regulations thereunder, as having realized a long-term capital gain in such amount on the last day of the taxable year of the regulated investment company in respect of which the undistributed capital gains were designated.

(5) *Effect on earnings and profits of corporate shareholders of a regulated investment company.* If a shareholder required to include an amount of undistributed capital gains in gross income under section 852(b)(3)(D) and subparagraph (2) of this paragraph is a corporation, such corporation, in computing its earnings and profits for the taxable year for which such amount is so includible, shall treat such amount as if it had actually been received and the taxes paid shall include any amount of tax liability satisfied by a credit under section 852(b)(3)(D) and subparagraph (2) of this paragraph.

(c) *Definition of capital gain dividend*—(1) *General rule.* A capital gain dividend, as defined in section 852(b)(3)(C), is any dividend or part thereof which is designated by a regulated investment company as a capital gain dividend in a written notice mailed to its shareholders within the period specified in paragraph (c)(4) of this section. If the aggregate amount so designated with respect to the taxable year (including capital gain dividends paid after the close of the taxable year pursuant to an election under section 855) is greater than the excess of the net long-term capital gain over the net short-term capital loss of the taxable year, the portion of each distribution which shall be a capital gain dividend shall be only that proportion of the amount so designated which such excess of the net long-term capital gain over the net short-term capital loss bears to the aggregate amount so designated. For example, a regulated investment company making its return on the calendar year basis advised its shareholders by written notice mailed December 30, 1955, that of a distribution of $500,000 made December 15, 1955, $200,000 constituted a capital gain dividend, amounting to $2 per share. It was later discovered that an error had been made in determining the excess of the net long-term capital gain over the net short-term capital loss of the taxable year, and that such excess was $100,000 instead of $200,000. In such case each shareholder would have received a capital gain dividend of $1 per share instead of $2 per share.

(2) *Shareholder of record custodian of certain unit investment trusts.* In any case where a notice is mailed pursuant to subparagraph (1) of this paragraph by a regulated investment company with respect to a taxable year of the regulated investment company ending after December 8, 1970, to a shareholder of record who is a nominee acting as a custodian of a unit investment trust described in section 851(f)(1) and paragraph (d) of § 1.851-7, the nominee shall furnish each holder of an interest in such trust with a written notice mailed on or before the 55th day following the close of the regulated investment company's taxable year. The notice shall designate the holder's proportionate share of the capital gain dividend shown on the notice received by the nominee pursuant to subparagraph (1) of this paragraph. The notice shall include the name and address of

Reg. § 1.852-4(b)(3)

the nominee identified as such. This subparagraph shall not apply if the regulated investment company agrees with the nominee to satisfy the notice requirements of subparagraph (1) of this paragraph with respect to each holder of an interest in the unit investment trust whose shares are being held by the nominee as custodian and, not later than 45 days following the close of the company's taxable year, files with the Internal Revenue Service office where the company's income tax return is to be filed for the taxable year, a statement that the holders of the unit investment trust with whom the agreement was made have been directly notified by the regulated investment company. Such statement shall include the name, sponsor, and custodian of each unit investment trust whose holders have been directly notified. The nominee's requirements under this paragraph shall be deemed met if the regulated investment company transmits a copy of such statement to the nominee within such 45-day period; provided, however, if the regulated investment company fails or is unable to satisfy the requirements of this subparagraph with respect to the holders of interest in the unit investment trust, it shall so notify the Internal Revenue Service within 45 days following the close of its taxable year. The custodian shall, upon notice by the Internal Revenue Service that the regulated investment company has failed to comply with the agreement, satisfy the requirements of this subparagraph within 30 days of such notice. If a notice under paragraph (c)(1) of this section is mailed within the 120-day period following the date of a determination pursuant to paragraph (c)(4)(ii) of this section, the 120-day period and the 130-day period following the date of the determination shall be substituted for the 45-day period and the 55-day period following the close of the regulated investment company's taxable year prescribed by this subparagraph (2).

(3) *Subsection (d) gain for certain taxable years.* In the case of capital gain dividends with respect to any taxable year of a regulated investment company ending after December 31, 1969, and beginning before January 1, 1975 (including capital gain dividends paid after the close of the taxable year pursuant to an election under section 855), the company must include in its written notice under paragraph (c)(1) of this section a statement showing the shareholder's proportionate share of the capital gain dividend which is gain described in section 1201(d)(1) and his proportionate share of such dividend which is gain described in section 1201(d)(2). In determining the portion of the capital gain dividend which, in the hands of a shareholder, is gain described in section 1201(d)(1) or (2), the regulated investment company shall consider that capital gain dividends for a taxable year are first made from its long-term capital gains for such year which are not described in section 1201(d)(1) or (2), to the extent thereof, and then from its long-term capital gains for such year which are described in section 1201(d)(1) or (2). A shareholder's proportionate share of gains which are described in section 1201(d)(1) is the amount which bears the same ratio to the amount paid to him as a capital gain dividend in respect of such year as (i) the aggregate amount of the company's gains which are described in section 1201(d)(1) and paid to all shareholders bears to (ii) the aggregate amount of the capital gain dividend paid to all shareholders in respect of such year. A shareholder's proportionate share of gains which are described in section 1201(d)(2) shall be determined in a similar manner. Every regulated investment company shall keep a record of the proportion of each capital gain dividend (to which this paragraph applies) which is gain described in section 1201(d)(1) or (2). If, for his taxable year, a shareholder must include in his gross income a capital gain dividend to which this paragraph applies, he shall attach to his income tax return for such taxable year a statement showing, with respect to the total of such dividends for such taxable year received from each regulated investment company, the name and address of the regulated investment company from which such dividends are received, the amount of such dividends, the portion of such dividends which was designated as gain described in section 1201(d)(1), and the portion of such dividends which was designated as gain described in section 1201(d)(2).

(4) *Mailing of written notice to shareholders.* (i) Except as provided in paragraph (c)(4)(ii) of this section, the written notice designating a dividend or part thereof as a capital gain dividend must be mailed to the shareholders not later than 45 days (30 days for a taxable year ending before February 26, 1964) after the close of the taxable year of the regulated investment company.

(ii) If a determination (as defined in section 860(e)) after November 6, 1978, increases the excess for the taxable year of the net capital gain over the deduction for capital gains dividends paid, then a regulated investment company may designate all or part of any dividend as a capital gain dividend in a written notice mailed to its shareholders at any time during the 120-day period immediately following the date of the determination. The aggregate amount designated during this period may not exceed this increase. A dividend may be designated if it is actually paid during the taxable year, is one paid after the close of the taxable year to which section 855 applies,

Reg. § 1.852-4(c)(4)

or is a deficiency dividend (as defined in section 860(f)), including a deficiency dividend paid by an acquiring corporation to which section 381(c)(25) applies. The date of a determination is established under § 1.860-2(b)(1).

(d) *Special treatment of loss on the sale or exchange of regulated investment company stock held less than 31 days*—(1) *In general.* Under section 852(b)(4), if any person, with respect to a share of regulated investment company stock acquired by such person after December 31, 1957, and held for a period of less than 31 days, is required by section 852(b)(3)(B) or (D) to include in gross income as a gain from the sale or exchange of a capital asset held for more than 1 year (6 months for taxable years beginning before 1977; 9 months for taxable years beginning in 1977)—

    (i) The amount of a capital gain dividend, or

    (ii) An amount of undistributed capital gains,

then such person shall, to the extent of such amount, treat any loss on the sale or exchange of such share of stock as a loss from the sale or exchange of a capital asset held for more than 6 months. Such special treatment with respect to the sale of regulated investment company stock held for a period of less than 31 days is applicable to losses for taxable years ending after December 31, 1957.

(2) *Determination of holding period.* The rules contained in section 246(c)(3) (relating to the determination of holding periods for purposes of the deduction for dividends received) shall be applied in determining whether, for purposes of section 852(b)(4) and this paragraph, a share of regulated investment company stock has been held for a period of less than 31 days. In applying those rules, however, "30 days" shall be substituted for the number of days specified in subparagraph (B) of section 246(c)(3).

(3) *Example.* The application of section 852(b)(4) and this paragraph may be illustrated by the following example:

    Example. On December 15, 1958, A purchased a share of stock in the X regulated investment company for $20. The X regulated investment company declared a capital gain dividend of $2 per share to shareholders of record on December 31, 1958. A, therefore, received a capital gain dividend of $2 which, pursuant to section 852(b)(3)(B), he must treat as a gain from the sale or exchange of a capital asset held for more than 6 months. On January 5, 1959, A sold his share of stock in the X regulated investment company for $17.50, which sale resulted in a loss of $2.50.

Under section 852(b)(4) and this paragraph, A must treat $2 of such loss (an amount equal to the capital gain dividend received with respect to such share of stock) as a loss from the sale or exchange of a capital asset held for more than 6 months. [Reg. § 1.852-4.]

☐ [*T.D. 6236, 6-3-57. Amended by T.D. 6369, 3-16-59, T.D. 6531, 1-18-61, T.D. 6598, 4-25-62, T.D. 6777, 12-15-64, T.D. 6921, 6-19-67, T.D. 7187, 7-5-72, T.D. 7337, 12-26-74, T.D. 7728, 10-31-80, and T.D. 7936, 1-17-84.*]

[Reg. § 1.852-5]

§ 1.852-5. **Earnings and profits of a regulated investment company.**—(a) Any regulated investment company, whether or not such company meets the requirements of section 852(a) and paragraph (a)(1)(i) and (ii) of § 1.852-1, shall apply paragraph (b) of this section in computing its earnings and profits for a taxable year beginning after February 28, 1958. However, for a taxable year of a regulated investment company beginning before March 1, 1958, paragraph (b) of this section shall apply only if the regulated investment company meets the requirements of section 852(a) and paragraph (a)(1)(i) and (ii) of § 1.852-1.

(b) In the determination of the earnings and profits of a regulated investment company, section 852(c) provides that such earnings and profits for any taxable year (but not the accumulated earnings and profits) shall not be reduced by any amount which is not allowable as a deduction in computing its taxable income for the taxable year. Thus, if a corporation would have had earnings and profits of $500,000 for the taxable year except for the fact that it had a net capital loss of $100,000, which amount was not deductible in determining its taxable income, its earnings and profits for that year if it is a regulated investment company would be $500,000. If the regulated investment company had no accumulated earnings and profits at the beginning of the taxable year, in determining its accumulated earnings and profits as of the beginning of the following taxable year, the earnings and profits for the taxable year to be considered in such computation would amount to $400,000 assuming that there had been no distribution from such earnings and profits. If distributions had been made in the taxable year in the amount of the earnings and profits then available for distribution, $500,000, the corporation would have as of the beginning of the following taxable year neither accumulated earnings and profits nor a deficit in accumulated earnings and profits, and would begin such year with its paid-in capital reduced by $100,000, an amount equal to the excess of the $500,000 distributed over the

Reg. § 1.852-5(a)

$400,000 accumulated earnings and profits which would otherwise have been carried into the following taxable year. [Reg. § 1.852-5.]

☐ [*T.D. 6236, 6-3-57. Amended by T.D. 6369, 3-16-59.*]

[Reg. § 1.852-6]

§ 1.852-6. Records to be kept for purpose of determining whether a corporation claiming to be a regulated investment company is a personal holding company.—(a) Every regulated investment company shall maintain in the internal revenue district in which it is required to file its income tax return permanent records showing the information relative to the actual owners of its stock contained in the written statements required by this section to be demanded from the shareholders. The actual owner of stock includes the person who is required to include in gross income in his return the dividends received on the stock. Such records shall be kept at all times available for inspection by any internal revenue officer or employee, and shall be retained so long as the contents thereof may become material in the administration of any internal revenue law.

(b) For the purpose of determining whether a domestic corporation claiming to be a regulated investment company is a personal holding company as defined in section 542, the permanent records of the company shall show the maximum number of shares of the corporation (including the number and face value of securities convertible into stock of the corporation) to be considered as actually or constructively owned by each of the actual owners of any of its stock at any time during the last half of the corporation's taxable year, as provided in section 544.

(c) Statements setting forth the information (required by paragraph (b) of this section) shall be demanded not later than 30 days after the close of the corporation's taxable year as follows:

(1) In the case of a corporation having 2,000 or more record owners of its stock on any dividend record date, from each record holder of 5 percent or more of its stock; or

(2) In the case of a corporation having less than 2,000 and more than 200 record owners of its stock, on any dividend record date, from each record holder of 1 percent or more of its stock; or

(3) In the case of a corporation having 200 or less record owners of its stock, on any dividend record date, from each record holder of one-half of 1 percent or more of its stock.

When making demand for the written statements required of each shareholder by this paragraph, the company shall inform each of the shareholders of his duty to submit as a part of his income tax return the statements which are required by § 1.852-7 if he fails or refuses to comply with such demand. A list of the persons failing or refusing to comply in whole or in part with a company's demand shall be maintained as a part of its record required by this section. A company which fails to keep such records to show the actual ownership of its outstanding stock as are required by this section shall be taxable as an ordinary corporation and not as a regulated investment company. [Reg. § 1.852-6.]

☐ [*T.D. 6236, 6-3-57.*]

[Reg. § 1.852-7]

§ 1.852-7. Additional information required in returns of shareholders.—Any person who fails or refuses to comply with the demand of a regulated investment company for the written statements which § 1.852-6 requires the company to demand from its shareholders shall submit as a part of his income tax return a statement showing, to the best of his knowledge and belief—

(a) The number of shares actually owned by him at any and all times during the period for which the return is filed in any company claiming to be a regulated investment company;

(b) The dates of acquisition of any such stock during such period and the names and addresses of persons from whom it was acquired;

(c) The dates of disposition of any such stock during such period and the names and addresses of the transferees thereof;

(d) The names and addresses of the members of his family (as defined in section 544(a)(2)); the names and addresses of his partners, if any, in any partnership; and the maximum number of shares, if any, actually owned by each in any corporation claiming to be a regulated investment company, at any time during the last half of the taxable year of such company;

(e) The names and addresses of any corporation, partnership, association, or trust in which he had a beneficial interest to the extent of at least 10 percent at any time during the period for which such return is made, and the number of shares of any corporation claiming to be a regulated investment company actually owned by each;

(f) The maximum number of shares (including the number and face value of securities convertible into stock of the corporation) in any domestic corporation claiming to be a regulated investment company to be considered as constructively owned by such individual at any time during the last half of the corporation's taxable year, as provided in section 544 and the regulations thereunder; and

Reg. § 1.852-7

(g) The amount and date of receipt of each dividend received during such period from every corporation claiming to be a regulated investment company. [Reg. § 1.852-7.]

☐ [*T.D.* 6236, 6-3-57.]

[Reg. § 1.852-8]

§ 1.852-8. Information returns.—Nothing in §§ 1.852-6 and 1.852-7 shall be construed to relieve regulated investment companies or their shareholders from the duty of filing information returns required by regulations prescribed under the provisions of subchapter A, chapter 61 of the Code. [Reg. § 1.852-8.]

☐ [*T.D.* 6236, 6-3-57.]

[Reg. § 1.852-9]

§ 1.852-9. Special procedural requirements applicable to designation under section 852(b)(3)(D).—(a) *Regulated investment company*—(1) *Notice to shareholders.* (i) A designation of undistributed capital gains under section 852(b)(3)(D) and paragraph (b)(2)(i) of § 1.852-2 shall be made by notice on Form 2439 mailed by the regulated investment company to each person who is a shareholder of record of the company at the close of the company's taxable year. The notice on Form 2439 shall show the name, address, and employer identification number of the regulated investment company; the taxable year of the company for which the designation is made; the name, address, and identifying number of the shareholder; the amount designated by the company for inclusion by the shareholder in computing his long-term capital gains; and the tax paid with respect thereto by the company which is deemed to have been paid by the shareholder.

(ii) In the case of a designation of undistributed capital gains with respect to a taxable year of the regulated investment company ending after December 31, 1969, and beginning before January 1, 1975, Form 2439 shall also show the shareholder's proportionate share of such gains which is gain described in section 1201(d)(1), his proportionate share of such gains which is gain described in section 1201(d)(2), and the amount (determined pursuant to subdivision (iv) of this subparagraph) by which the shareholder's adjusted basis in his shares shall be increased.

(iii) In determining under subdivision (ii) of this subparagraph the portion of the undistributed capital gains which, in the hands of the shareholder, is gain described in section 1201(d)(1) or (2), the company shall consider that capital gain dividends for a taxable year are made first from its long-term capital gains for such year which are not described in section 1201(d)(1) or (2), to the extent thereof, and then from its long-term capital gains for such year which are described in section 1201(d)(1) or (2). A shareholder's proportionate share of undistributed capital gains for a taxable year which is gain described in section 1201(d)(1) is the amount which bears the same ratio to the amount included in his income as designated undistributed capital gains for such year as *(a)* the aggregate amount of the company's gains for such year which are described in section 1201(d)(1) and designated as undistributed capital gains bears to *(b)* the aggregate amount of the company's gains for such year which are designated as undistributed capital gains. A shareholder's proportionate share of gains which are described in section 1201(d)(2) shall be determined in a similar manner. Every regulated investment company shall keep a record of the proportion of undistributed capital gains (to which this subdivision applies) which is gain described in section 1201(d)(1) or (2).

(iv) In the case of a designation of undistributed capital gains for any taxable year ending after December 31, 1969, and beginning before January 1, 1975, Form 2439 shall also show with respect to the undistributed capital gains of each shareholder the amount by which such shareholder's adjusted basis in his shares shall be increased under section 852(b)(3)(D)(iii). The amount by which each shareholder's adjusted basis in his shares shall be increased is the amount includible in his gross income with respect to such shares under section 852(b)(3)(D)(i) less the tax which the shareholder is deemed to have paid with respect to such shares. The tax which each shareholder is deemed to have paid with respect to such shares is the amount which bears the same ratio to the amount of the tax imposed by section 852(b)(3)(A) for such year with respect to the aggregate amount of the designated undistributed capital gains as the amount of such gains includible in the shareholder's gross income bears to the aggregate amount of such gains so designated.

(v) Form 2439 shall be prepared in triplicate, and copies B and C of the form shall be mailed to the shareholder on or before the 45th day (30th day for a taxable year ending before February 26, 1964) following the close of the company's taxable year. Copy A of each Form 2439 must be associated with the duplicate copy of the undistributed capital gains tax return of the company (Form 2438), as provided in subparagraph (2)(ii) of this paragraph.

(2) *Return of undistributed capital gains tax*—(i) *Form 2438.* Every regulated investment company which designates undistributed capital

gains for any taxable year beginning after December 31, 1956, in accordance with subparagraph (1) of this paragraph, shall file for such taxable year an undistributed capital gains tax return on Form 2438 including on such return the total of its undistributed capital gains so designated and the tax with respect thereto. The return on Form 2438 shall be prepared in duplicate and shall set forth fully and clearly the information required to be included therein. The original of Form 2438 shall be filed on or before the 30th day after the close of the company's taxable year with the internal revenue officer designated in instructions applicable to Form 2438. The duplicate copy of Form 2438 for the taxable year shall be attached to and filed with the income tax return of the company on Form 1120 for such taxable year.

(ii) *Copies A of Form 2439.* For each taxable year which ends on or before December 31, 1965, there shall be submitted with the company's return on Form 2438 all copies A of Form 2439 furnished by the company to its shareholders in accordance with subparagraph (1) of this paragraph. For each taxable year which ends after December 31, 1965, there shall be submitted with the duplicate copy of the company's return on Form 2438, which is attached to and filed with the income tax return of the company on Form 1120 for the taxable year, all copies A of Form 2439 furnished by the company to its shareholders in accordance with subparagraph (1) of this paragraph. The copies A of Form 2439 shall be accompanied by lists (preferably in the form of adding machine tapes) of the amounts of undistributed capital gains and of the tax paid with respect thereto shown on such forms. The totals of the listed amounts of undistributed capital gains and of tax paid with respect thereto must agree with the corresponding entries on Form 2438.

(3) *Payment of tax.* The tax required to be returned on Form 2438 shall be paid by the regulated investment company on or before the 30th day after the close of the company's taxable year to the internal revenue officer with whom the return on Form 2438 is filed.

(b) *Shareholder of record not actual owner*—(1) *Notice to actual owner.* In any case in which a notice on Form 2439 is mailed pursuant to paragraph (a)(1) of this section by a regulated investment company to a shareholder of record who is a nominee of the actual owner or owners of the shares of stock to which the notice relates, the nominee shall furnish to each such actual owner notice of the owner's proportionate share of the amounts of undistributed capital gains and tax with respect thereto, as shown on the Form 2439 received by the nominee from the regulated investment company. The nominee's notice to the actual owner shall be prepared in triplicate on Form 2439 and shall contain the information prescribed in paragraph (a)(1) of this section, except that the name and address of the nominee, identified as such, shall be entered on the form in addition to, and in the space provided for, the name and address of the regulated investment company, and the amounts of undistributed capital gains and tax with respect thereto entered on the form shall be the actual owner's proportionate share of the corresponding items shown on the nominee's notice from the regulated investment company. Copies B and C of the Form 2439 prepared by the nominee shall be mailed to the actual owner—

(i) For taxable years of regulated investment companies ending after February 25, 1964, on or before the 75th day (55th day in the case of a nominee who is acting as a custodian of a unit investment trust described in section 851(f)(1) and paragraph (d) of § 1.851-7 for taxable years of regulated investment companies ending after December 8, 1970, and 135th day if the nominee is a resident of a foreign country) following the close of the regulated investment company's taxable year, or

(ii) For taxable years of regulated investment companies ending before February 26, 1964, on or before the 60th day (120th day if the nominee is a resident of a foreign country) following the close of the regulated investment company's taxable year.

(2) *Transmittal of Form 2439.* The nominee shall enter the word "Nominee" in the upper right hand corner of Copy B of the notice on Form 2439 received by him from the regulated investment company, and on or before the appropriate day specified in subdivision (i) or (ii) of subparagraph (1) of this paragraph shall transmit such copy B, together with all copies A of Form 2439 prepared by him pursuant to subparagraph (1) of this paragraph, to the internal revenue officer with whom his income tax return is required to be filed.

(3) *Custodian of certain unit investment trusts.* The requirements of this paragraph shall not apply to a nominee who is acting as a custodian of the unit investment trust described in section 851(f)(1) and paragraph (d) of § 1.851-7 provided that the regulated investment company agrees with the nominee to satisfy the notice requirements of paragraph (a) of this section with respect to each holder of an interest in the unit investment trust whose shares are being held by such nominee as custodian and on or before the 45th day following the close of the company's taxable year, files with the Internal Revenue Ser-

Reg. § 1.852-9(b)(3)

vice office where the company's income tax return is to be filed for the taxable year, a statement that the holders of the unit investment trust with whom the agreement was made have been directly notified by the regulated investment company. Such statement shall include the name, sponsor, and custodian of each unit investment trust whose holders have been directly notified. The nominee's requirements under this paragraph shall be deemed met if the regulated investment company transmits a copy of such statement to the nominee within such 45-day period; provided however, if the regulated investment company fails or is unable to satisfy the requirements of this paragraph with respect to the holders of interest in the unit investment trust, it shall so notify the Internal Revenue Service within 45 days following the close of its taxable year. The custodian shall, upon notice by the Internal Revenue Service that the regulated investment company has failed to comply with the agreement, satisfy the requirements of this paragraph within 30 days of such notice.

(c) *Shareholders*—(1) *Return and Recordkeeping Requirements*—(i) *Return requirements for taxable years beginning before January 1, 2002.* For taxable years beginning before January 1, 2002, the copy B of Form 2439 furnished to a shareholder by the regulated investment company or by a nominee, as provided in § 1.852-9(a) or (b) shall be attached to the income tax return of the shareholder for the taxable year in which the amount of undistributed capital gains is includible in gross income as provided in § 1.852-4(b)(2).

(ii) *Recordkeeping requirements for taxable years beginning after December 31, 2001.* For taxable years beginning after December 31, 2001, the shareholder shall retain a copy of Form 2439 for as long as its contents may become material in the administration of any internal revenue law.

(2) *Credit or refund*—(i) *In general.* The amount of the tax paid by the regulated investment company with respect to the undistributed capital gains required under section 852(b)(3)(D) and paragraph (b)(2) of § 1.852-4 to be included by a shareholder in his computation of long-term capital gains for any taxable year is deemed paid by such shareholder under section 852(b)(3)(D)(ii) and such payment constitutes for purposes of section 6513(a) (relating to time tax considered paid), an advance payment in like amount of the tax imposed under chapter 1 of the Code for such taxable year. In the case of an overpayment of tax within the meaning of section 6401, see section 6402 and the regulations in Part 301 of this chapter (Regulations on Procedure and Administration) for rules applicable to the treatment of an overpayment of tax and section 6511 and the regulations in Part 301 of this chapter (Regulations on Procedure and Administration) with respect to the limitations applicable to the credit or refund of an overpayment of tax.

(ii) *Form to be used.* Claim for refund or credit of the tax deemed to have been paid by a shareholder with respect to an amount of undistributed capital gains shall be made on the shareholder's income tax return for the taxable year in which such amount of undistributed capital gains is includible in gross income. In the case of a shareholder which is a partnership, claim shall be made by the partners on their income tax returns for refund or credit of their distributive shares of the tax deemed to have been paid by the partnership. In the case of a shareholder which is exempt from tax under section 501(a) and to which section 511 does not apply for the taxable year, claim for refund of the tax deemed to have been paid by such shareholder on an amount of undistributed capital gains for such year shall be made on Form 843 and copy B of Form 2439 furnished to such shareholder shall be attached to its claim. For other rules applicable to the filing of claims for credit or refund of an overpayment of tax, see § 301.6402-2 of this chapter (Regulations on Procedure and Administration), relating to claims for credit or refund, and § 301.6402-32 of such regulations, relating to special rules applicable to income tax.

(3) *Records.* The shareholder is required to keep copy C of the Form 2439 furnished for the regulated investment company's taxable years ending after December 31, 1969, and beginning before January 1, 1975, as part of his records to show increases in the adjusted basis of his shares in such company.

(d) *Penalties.* For criminal penalties for willful failure to file a return, supply information, or pay tax, and for filing a false or fraudulent return, statement, or other document, see sections 7203, 7206, and 7207. [Reg. § 1.852-9.]

☐ [*T.D.* 6369, 3-16-59. *Amended by T.D.* 6531, 1-18-61, *T.D.* 6921, 6-19-67; *T.D.* 7012, 5-14-69, *T.D.* 7187, 7-5-72, *T.D.* 7332, 12-20-74; *T.D.* 7337, 12-26-74; *T.D.* 8989, 4-23-2002 *and T.D.* 9040, 1-30-2003.]

[Reg. § 1.852-10]

§ 1.852-10. **Distributions in redemption of interests in unit investment trusts**—(a) *In general.* In computing that part of the excess of its net long-term capital gain over net short-term capital loss on which it must pay a capital gains tax, a regulated investment company is allowed under section 852 (b) (3) (A) (ii) a deduction for dividends paid (as defined in section 561) determined with reference to capital gains dividends only. Section 561(b) provides that in determining the deduction for dividends paid, the rules provided in section 562 are applicable. Section 562(c) (relating to preferential dividends) provides that the amount of any distribution shall not be considered as a dividend unless such distribution is prorata, with no preference to any share of stock as compared with other shares of the same class except to the extent that the former is entitled to such preference.

(b) *Redemption distributions made by unit investment trust* —(1) *In general.* Where a unit investment trust (as defined in par. (c) of this section) liquidates part of its portfolio represented by shares in a management company in order to make a distribution to a holder of an interest in the trust in redemption of part or all of such interest, and by so doing, the trust realizes net long-term capital gain, that portion of the distribution by the trust which is equal to the amount of the net long-term capital gain realized by the trust on the liquidation of the shares in the management company will not be considered a preferential dividend under section 562(c). For example, where the entire amount of net long-term capital gain realized by the trust on such a liquidation is distributed to the redeeming interest holder, the trust will be allowed the entire amount of net long-term capital gain so realized in determining the deduction under section 852(b)(3)(A)(ii) for dividends paid determined with reference to capital gains dividends only. This paragraph and section 852(d) shall apply only with respect to the capital gain net income (net capital gain for taxable years beginning before January 1, 1977) realized by the trust which is attributable to a redemption by a holder of an interest in such trust. Such dividend may be designated as a capital gain dividend by a written notice to the certificate holder. Such designation should clearly indicate to the holder that the holder's gain or loss on the redemption of the certificate may differ from such designated amount, depending upon the holder's basis for the redeemed certificate, and that the holder's own records are to be used in computing the holder's gain or loss on the redemption of the certificate.

(2) *Example.* The application of the provisions of this paragraph may be illustrated by the following example:

Example. B entered into a periodic payment plan contract with X as custodian and Z as plan sponsor under which he purchased a plan certificate of X. Under this contract, upon B's demand, X must redeem B's certificate at a price substantially equal to the value of the number of shares in Y, a management company, which are credited to B's account by X in connection with the unit investment trust. Except for a small amount of cash which X is holding to satisfy liabilities and to invest for other plan certificate holders, all of the assets held by X in connection with the trust consist of shares in Y. Pursuant to the terms of the periodic payment plan contract, 100 shares of Y are credited to B's account. Both X and Y have elected to be treated as regulated investment companies. On March 1, 1965, B notified X that he wished to have his entire interest in the unit investment trust redeemed. In order to redeem B's interest, X caused Y to redeem 100 shares of Y which X held. At the time of redemption, each share of Y had a value of $15. X then distributed the $1,500 to B. X's basis for each of the Y shares which was redeemed was $10. Therefore, X realized a long-term capital gain of $500.00 ($5 × 100 shares) which is attributable to the redemption by B of his interest in the trust. Under section 852(d), the $500 capital gain distributed to B will not be considered a preferential dividend. Therefore, X is allowed a deduction of $500 under section 852(b)(3)(A)(ii) for dividends paid determined with reference to capital gains dividends only, with the result that X will not pay a capital gains tax with respect to such amount.

(c) *Definition of unit investment trust.* A unit investment trust to which paragraph (a) of this section refers is a business arrangement which—

(1) Is registered under the Investment Company Act of 1940 as a unit investment trust;

(2) Issues periodic payment plan certificates (as defined in such Act);

(3) Possesses, as substantially all of its assets, securities issued by a management company (as defined in such Act);

(4) Qualifies as a regulated investment company under section 851; and

(5) Complies with the requirements provided for by section 852(a). Paragraph (a) of this section does not apply to a unit investment trust described in section 851(f)(1) and paragraph (d) of § 1.851-7. [Reg. § 1.852-10.]

☐ [T.D. 6921, 6-19-67. Amended by T.D. 7187, 7-5-72 and T.D. 7728, 10-31-80.]

[Reg. § 1.852-11]

§ 1.852-11. **Treatment of certain losses attributable to periods after October 31 of a taxable year.**—(a) *Outline of provisions.* This paragraph lists the provisions of this section.

(a) Outline of provisions.

(b) Scope.

(1) In general.

Regulated Investment Companies

See p. 20,601 for regulations not amended to reflect law changes

(2) Limitation on application of section.
(c) Post-October capital loss defined.
   (1) In general.
   (2) Methodology.
   (3) October 31 treated as last day of taxable year for purpose of determining taxable income under certain circumstances.
      (i) In general.
      (ii) Effect on gross income.
(d) Post-October currency loss defined.
   (1) Post-October currency loss.
   (2) Net foreign currency loss.
   (3) Foreign currency gain or loss.
(e) Limitation on capital gain dividends.
   (1) In general.
   (2) Amount taken into account in current year.
      (i) Net capital loss.
      (ii) Net long-term capital loss.
   (3) Amount taken into account in succeeding year.
(f) Regulated investment company may elect to defer certain losses for purposes of determining taxable income.
   (1) In general.
   (2) Effect of election in current year.
   (3) Amount of loss taken into account in current year.
      (i) If entire amount of net capital loss deferred.
      (ii) If part of net capital loss deferred.
         (A) In general.
         (B) Character of capital loss not deferred.
      (iii) If entire amount of net long-term capital loss deferred.
      (iv) If part of net long-term capital loss deferred.
      (v) If entire amount of post-October currency loss deferred.
      (vi) If part of post-October currency loss deferred.
   (4) Amount of loss taken into account in succeeding year and subsequent years.
   (5) Effect on gross income.
(g) Earnings and profits.
   (1) General rule.
   (2) Special Rule—Treatment of losses that are deferred for purposes of determining taxable income.
(h) Examples.

(i) Procedure for making election.
   (1) In general.
   (2) When applicable instructions not available.
(j) Transition rules.
   (1) In general.
   (2) Retroactive election.
      (i) In general.
      (ii) Deadline for making election.
   (3) Amended return required for succeeding year in certain circumstances.
      (i) In general.
      (ii) Time for filing amended return.
   (4) Retroactive dividend.
      (i) In general.
      (ii) Method of making election.
      (iii) Deduction for dividends paid.
         (A) In general.
         (B) Limitation on ordinary dividends.
         (C) Limitation on capital gain dividends.
         (D) Effect on other years.
      (iv) Earnings and profits.
      (v) Receipt by shareholders.
      (vi) Foreign tax election.
      (vii) Example.
   (5) Certain distributions may be designated.
(k) Effective date.

(b) *Scope*—(1) *In general.* This section prescribes the manner in which a regulated investment company must treat a post-October capital loss (as defined in paragraph (c) of this section) or a post-October currency loss (as defined in paragraph (d)(1) of this section) for purposes of determining its taxable income, its earnings and profits, and the amount that it may designate as capital gain dividends for the taxable year in which the loss is incurred and the succeeding taxable year (the "succeeding year").

(2) *Limitation on application of section.* This section shall not apply to any post-October capital loss or post-October currency loss of a regulated investment company attributable to a taxable year for which an election is in effect under section 4982(e)(4) of the Code with respect to the company.

(c) *Post-October capital loss defined*—(1) *In general.* For purposes of this section, the term "post-October capital loss" means—

(i) Any net capital loss attributable to the portion of a regulated investment company's taxable year after October 31; or

Reg. § 1.852-11(b)(1)

(ii) If there is no such net capital loss, any net long-term capital loss attributable to the portion of a regulated investment company's taxable year after October 31.

(2) *Methodology.* The amount of any net capital loss or any net long-term capital loss attributable to the portion of the regulated investment company's taxable year after October 31 shall be determined in accordance with general tax law principles (other than section 1212) by treating the period beginning on November 1 of the taxable year of the regulated investment company and ending on the last day of such taxable year as though it were the taxable year of the regulated investment company. For purposes of this paragraph (c)(2), any item (other than a capital loss carryover) that is required to be taken into account or any rule that must be applied, for purposes of section 4982, on October 31 as if it were the last day of the regulated investment company's taxable year must also be taken into account or applied in the same manner as required under section 4982, both on October 31 and again on the last day of the regulated investment company's taxable year.

(3) *October 31 treated as last day of taxable year for purpose of determining taxable income under certain circumstances*—(i) *In general.* If a regulated investment company has a post-October capital loss for a taxable year, any item that must be marked to market for purposes of section 4982 on October 31 as if it were the last day of the regulated investment company's taxable year must also be marked to market on October 31 and again on the last day of the regulated investment company's taxable year for purposes of determining its taxable income. If the regulated investment company does not have a post-October capital loss for a taxable year, the regulated investment company must treat items that must be marked to market for purposes of section 4982 on October 31 as if it were the last day of the regulated investment company's taxable year as marked to market only on the last day of its taxable year for purposes of determining its taxable income.

(ii) *Effect on gross income.* The marking to market of any item on October 31 of a regulated investment company's taxable year for purposes of determining its taxable income under paragraph (c)(3)(i) of this section shall not affect the amount of the gross income of such company for such taxable year for purposes of section 851(b)(2) or (3).

(d) *Post-October currency loss defined.* For purposes of this section—

(1) *Post-October currency loss.* The term "post-October currency loss" means any net foreign currency loss attributable to the portion of the regulated investment company's taxable year after October 31. For purposes of the preceding sentence, principles similar to those of paragraph (c)(2) and (c)(3) of this section shall apply.

(2) *Net foreign currency loss.* The term "net foreign currency loss" means the excess of foreign currency losses over foreign currency gains.

(3) *Foreign currency gain or loss.* The terms "foreign currency gain" and "foreign currency loss" have the same meaning as provided in section 988(b).

(e) *Limitation on capital gain dividends*—(1) *In general.* For purposes of determining the amount a regulated investment company may designate as capital gain dividends for a taxable year, the amount of net capital gain for the taxable year shall be determined without regard to any post-October capital loss for such year.

(2) *Amount taken into account in current year*—(i) *Net capital loss.* If the post-October capital loss referred to in paragraph (e)(1) of this section is a post-October capital loss as defined in paragraph (c)(1)(i) of this section, the net capital gain of the company for the taxable year in which the loss arose shall be determined without regard to any capital gains or losses (both long-term and short-term) taken into account in computing the post-October capital loss for the taxable year.

(ii) *Net long-term capital loss.* If the post-October capital loss referred to in paragraph (e)(1) of this section is a post-October capital loss as defined in paragraph (c)(2)(ii) of this section, the net capital gain of the company for the taxable year in which the loss arose shall be determined without regard to any long-term capital gain or loss taken into account in computing the post-October capital loss for the taxable year.

(3) *Amount taken into account in succeeding year.* If a regulated investment company has a post-October capital loss (as defined in paragraph (c)(1)(i) or (c)(2)(ii) of this section) for any taxable year, then, for purposes of determining the amount the company may designate as capital gain dividends for the succeeding year, the net capital gain for the succeeding year shall be determined by treating all gains and losses taken into account in computing the post-October capital loss as arising on the first day of the succeeding year.

(f) *Regulated investment company may elect to defer certain losses for purposes of determining taxable income*—(1) *In general.* A regulated investment company may elect, in accordance with the procedures of paragraph (i) of this section, to

Reg. § 1.852-11(f)

compute its taxable income for a taxable year without regard to part or all of any post-October capital loss or post-October currency loss for that year.

(2) *Effect of election in current year.* The taxable income of a regulated investment company for a taxable year to which an election under paragraph (f)(1) of this section applies shall be computed without regard to that part of any post-October capital loss or post-October currency loss to which the election applies.

(3) *Amount of loss taken into account in current year*—(i) *If entire amount of net capital loss deferred.* If a regulated investment company elects, under paragraph (f)(1) of this section, to defer the entire amount of a post-October capital loss as defined in paragraph (c)(1)(i) of this section, the taxable income of the company for the taxable year in which the loss arose shall be determined without regard to any capital gains or losses (both long-term and short-term) taken into account in computing the post-October capital loss for the taxable year.

(ii) *If part of net capital loss deferred*—(A) *In general.* If a regulated investment company elects, under paragraph (f)(1) of this section, to defer less than the entire amount of a post-October capital loss as defined in paragraph (c)(1)(i) of this section, the taxable income of the company for the taxable year in which the loss arose shall be determined by including an amount of capital loss taken into account in computing the post-October capital loss for the taxable year equal to the amount of the post-October capital loss that is not deferred. No amount of capital gain taken into account in computing the post-October capital loss for the taxable year shall be taken into account in the determination.

(B) *Character of capital loss not deferred.* The capital loss includible in the taxable income of the company under this paragraph (f)(3)(ii) for the taxable year in which the loss arose shall consist first of any short-term capital losses to the extent thereof, and then of any long-term capital losses, taken into account in computing the post-October capital loss for the taxable year.

(iii) *If entire amount of net long-term capital loss deferred.* If a regulated investment company elects, under paragraph (f)(1) of this section, to defer the entire amount of a post-October capital loss as defined in paragraph (c)(2)(ii) of this section, the taxable income of the company for the taxable year in which the loss arose shall be determined without regard to any long-term capital gains or losses taken into account in computing the post-October capital loss for the taxable year.

(iv) *If part of net long-term capital loss deferred.* If a regulated investment company elects, under paragraph (f)(1) of this section, to defer less than the entire amount of a post-October capital loss as defined in paragraph (c)(2)(ii) of this section, the taxable income of the company for the taxable year in which the loss arose shall be determined by including an amount of long-term capital loss taken into account in computing the post-October capital loss for the taxable year equal to the amount of the post-October capital loss that is not deferred. No amount of long-term capital gain taken into account in computing the post-October capital loss for the taxable year shall be taken into account in the determination.

(v) *If entire amount of post-October currency loss deferred.* If a regulated investment company elects, under paragraph (f)(1) of this section, to defer the entire amount of a post-October currency loss, the taxable income of the company for the taxable year in which the loss arose shall be determined without regard to any foreign currency gains or losses taken into account in computing the post-October currency loss for the taxable year.

(vi) *If part of post-October currency loss deferred.* If a regulated investment company elects, under paragraph (f)(1) of this section, to defer less than the entire amount of a post-October currency loss, the taxable income of the company for the taxable year in which the loss arose shall be determined by including an amount of foreign currency loss taken into account in computing the post-October currency loss for the taxable year equal to the amount of the post-October currency loss that is not deferred. No amount of foreign currency gain taken into account in computing the post-October currency loss for the taxable year shall be taken into account in the determination.

(4) *Amount of loss taken into account in succeeding year and subsequent years.* If a regulated investment company has a post-October capital loss or a post-October currency loss for any taxable year and an election under paragraph (f)(1) is made for that year, then, for purposes of determining the taxable income of the company for the succeeding year and all subsequent years, all capital gains and losses taken into account in determining the post-October capital loss, and all foreign currency gains and losses taken into account in determining the post-October currency loss, that are not taken into account under the rules of paragraph (f)(3) of this section in determining the taxable income of the regulated investment company for the taxable year in which the

Regulated Investment Companies

loss arose shall be treated as arising on the first day of the succeeding year.

(5) *Effect on gross income.* An election by a regulated investment company to defer any post-October capital loss or any post-October currency loss for a taxable year under paragraph (f)(1) of this section shall not affect the amount of the gross income of such company for such taxable year (or the succeeding year) for purposes of section 851(b)(2) or (3).

(g) *Earnings and profits*—(1) *General rule.* The earnings and profits of a regulated investment company for a taxable year are determined without regard to any post-October capital loss or post-October currency loss for that year. If a regulated investment company distributes with respect to a calendar year amounts in excess of the limitation described in the succeeding sentence, then, with respect to those excess amounts, for the taxable year with respect to which the amounts are distributed, the earnings and profits of the company are computed without regard to the preceding sentence. The limitation described in this sentence is the amount that would be the required distribution for that calendar year under section 4982 if "100 percent" were substituted for each percentage set forth in section 4982(b)(1).

(2) *Special Rule—Treatment of losses that are deferred for purposes of determining taxable income.* If a regulated investment company elects to defer, under paragraph (f)(1) of this section, any part of a post-October capital loss or post-October currency loss arising in a taxable year, then, for both the taxable year in which the loss arose and the succeeding year, both the earnings and profits and the accumulated earnings and profits of the company are determined as if the part of the loss so deferred had arisen on the first day of the succeeding year.

(h) *Examples.* The provisions of paragraphs (e), (f), and (g) of this section may be illustrated by the following examples. For each example, assume that X is a regulated investment company that computes its income on a calendar year basis, and that no election is in effect under section 4982(e)(4).

Example (1). X has a $25 net foreign currency gain, a $50 net short-term capital loss, and a $75 net long-term capital gain for the post-October period of 1988. X has no post-October currency loss and no post-October capital loss for 1988, and this section does not apply.

Example (2). X has the following capital gains and losses for the periods indicated:

	Long-term	Short-term
01/01 – 10/31/88	115 (15) 100	80 (20) 60
11/01 – 12/31/88	75 (150) (75)	150 (50) 100
01/01 – 10/31/89	30 (5) 25	40 (20) 20
11/01 – 12/31/89	35 (0) 35	100 (50) 50

X has a post-October capital loss of $75 for its 1988 taxable year due to a net long-term capital loss for the post-October period of 1988. X does not make an election under paragraph (f)(1) of this section.

(i) *Capital gain dividends.* X may designate up to $100 as a capital gain dividend for 1988 because X must disregard the $75 long-term capital gain and the $150 long-term capital loss for the post-October period of 1988 in computing its net capital gain for this purpose. In computing its net capital gain for 1989 for the purposes of determining the amount it may designate as a capital gain dividend for 1989, X must take into account the $75 long-term capital gain and the $150 long-term capital loss for the post-October period of 1988 in addition to the long-term and short-term capital gains and losses for 1989. Accordingly, X may not designate any amount as a capital gain dividend for 1989.

(ii) *Taxable income.* X must include the $75 long-term capital gain and the $150 long-term capital loss for its post-October period of 1988 in its taxable income for 1988 because it did not make an election under paragraph (f)(1) of this section for 1988. Accordingly, X's taxable income for 1988 will include a net capital gain of $25 and a net short-term capital gain of $160. X's taxable income for 1989 will include a net capital gain of $60 and a net short-term capital gain of $70.

(iii) *Earnings and profits.* X must determine its earnings and profits for 1988 without regard to the $75 long-term capital gain and the $150 long-term capital loss for the post-October period of 1988. X must, however, include the $75 long-term capital gain and $150 long-term capital loss for the post-October period of 1988 in determining its accumulated earnings and profits for 1988. Thus, X includes $260 of capital gain in its earnings and profits for 1988, includes $185 in its

Reg. § 1.852-11(h)

accumulated earnings and profits for 1988, and includes $130 of capital gain in its earnings and profits for 1989.

Example (3). Same facts as example (2), except that X elects to defer the entire $75 post-October capital loss for 1988 under paragraph (f)(1) of this section for purposes of determining its taxable income for 1988.

(i) *Capital gain dividends.* Some result as in example (2).

(ii) *Taxable income.* X must compute its taxable income for 1988 without regard to the $75 long-term capital gain and the $150 long-term capital loss for the post-October period of 1988 because it made an election to defer the entire $75 post-October capital loss for 1988 under paragraph (f)(1) of this section. Accordingly, X's taxable income for 1988 will include a net capital gain of $100 and a net short-term capital gain of $160. X must include the $75 long-term capital gain and the $150 long-term capital loss for the post-October period of 1988 in its taxable income for 1989 in addition to the long-term and short-term capital gains and losses for 1989. Accordingly, X's taxable income for 1989 will include a net long-term capital loss of $15 and a net short-term capital gain of $70.

(iii) *Earnings and profits.* For 1988, X must determine both its earnings and profits and its accumulated earnings and profits without regard to the $75 long-term capital gain and $150 long-term capital loss for the post-October period of 1988. In determining both its earnings and profits and its accumulated earnings and profits for 1989, X must include (in addition to the long-term and short-term capital gains and losses for 1989) the $75 long-term capital gain and $150 long-term capital loss for the post-October period of 1988 as if those deferred gains and losses arose on January 1, 1989. Thus, X will include $260 of capital gain in its earnings and profits for 1988 and $55 of capital gain in its earnings and profits for 1989.

Example (4). Same facts as example (2), except that X elects to defer only $50 of the post-October capital loss for 1988 under paragraph (f)(1) of this section for purposes of determining its taxable income for 1988.

(i) *Capital gain dividends.* Same results as in example (2).

(ii) *Taxable income.* X must compute its taxable income for 1988 without regard to the $75 long-term capital gain and $125 of the $150 long-term capital loss for the post-October period of 1988 because it made an election to defer $50 of the $75 post-October capital loss for 1988 under paragraph (f)(1) of this section. Accordingly, X's taxable income for 1988 will include a net capital gain of $75 and a net short-term capital gain of $160. X must include the $75 long-term capital gain and $125 of the $150 long-term capital loss for the post-October period of 1988 in its taxable income for 1989 in addition to the long-term and short-term capital gains and losses for 1989. Accordingly, X's taxable income for 1989 will include a net capital gain of $10 and a net short-term capital gain of $70.

(iii) *Earnings and profits.* X must determine its earnings and profits for 1988 without regard to the $75 long-term capital gain and the $150 long-term capital loss for the post-October period of 1988. X must include $25 of the $150 long-term capital loss for the post-October period of 1988 in determining its accumulated earnings and profits for 1988. In determining both its earnings and profits and its accumulated earnings and profits for 1989, X must include (in addition to the long-term and short-term capital gains and losses for 1989) the $75 long-term capital gain and $125 of the $150 long-term capital loss for the post-October period of 1988 as if those deferred gains and losses arose on January 1, 1989. Thus, X includes $260 of capital gain in its earnings and profits for 1988, includes $235 in its accumulated earnings and profits for 1988, and includes $80 of capital gain in its earnings and profits for 1989.

Example (5). X has the following capital gains and losses for the periods indicated:

	Long-term	Short-term
01/01 – 10/31/88	115	80
	(15)	(20)
	100	60
11/01 – 12/31/88	150	50
	(75)	(150)
	75	(100)
01/01 – 10/31/89	30	40
	(5)	(20)
	25	20
11/01 – 12/31/89	35	100
	(0)	(50)
	35	50

X has a post-October capital loss of $25 for its 1988 taxable year due to a net capital loss for the post-October period of 1988. X does not make an election under paragraph (f)(1) of this section.

(i) *Capital gain dividends.* X may designate up to $100 as a capital gain dividend for 1988 because X must disregard the $150 long-term capital gain, the $75 long-term capital loss, the $50 short-term capital gain, and the $150

Reg. § 1.852-11(h)

short-term capital loss for the post-October period of 1988 in computing its net capital gain for this purpose. In computing its net capital gain for 1989 for purposes of determining the amount it may designate as a capital gain dividend for 1989, X must take into account the $150 long-term capital gain, the $75 long-term capital loss, the $50 short-term capital gain, and the $150 short-term capital loss for the post-October period of 1988 in addition to the long-term and short-term capital gains and losses for 1989. Accordingly, X may designate up to $105 as a capital gain dividend for 1989.

(ii) *Taxable income.* X must include the $150 long-term capital gain, the $75 long-term capital loss, the $50 short-term capital gain, and the $150 short-term capital loss for the post-October period of 1988 in its taxable income for 1988 because it did not make an election under paragraph (f)(1) of this section for 1988. Accordingly, X's taxable income for 1988 will include a net capital gain of $135 (consisting of a net long-term capital gain of $175 and a net short-term capital loss of $40). X's taxable income for 1989 will include a net capital gain of $60 and a net short-term capital gain of $70.

(iii) *Earnings and profits.* X must determine its earnings and profits for 1988 without regard to the $150 long-term capital gain, the $75 long-term capital loss, the $50 short-term capital gain, and the $150 short-term capital loss for the post-October period of 1988. X must, however, include the $150 long-term capital gain, the $75 long-term capital loss, the $50 short-term capital gain, and the $150 short-term capital loss for the post-October period of 1988 in determining its accumulated earnings and profits for 1988. Thus, X includes $160 of capital gain in its earnings and profits for 1988, includes $135 in its accumulated earnings and profits for 1988, and includes $130 of capital gain in its earnings and profits for 1989.

Example (6). Same facts as example (5), except that X elects to defer the entire $25 post-October capital loss for 1988 under paragraph (f)(1) of this section for purposes of determining its taxable income for 1988.

(i) *Capital gain dividends.* Same result as in example (5).

(ii) *Taxable income.* X must compute its taxable income for 1988 without regard to the $150 long-term capital gain, the $75 long-term capital loss, the $50 short-term capital gain, and the $150 short-term capital loss for the post-October period of 1988 because it made an election to defer the entire $25 post-October capital loss for 1988 under paragraph (f)(1) of this section. Accordingly, X's taxable income for 1988 will include a net capital gain of $100 and a net short-term capital gain of $60. X must include the $150 long-term capital gain, the $75 long-term capital loss, the $50 short-term capital gain, and the $150 short-term capital loss for the post-October period of 1988 in its taxable income for 1989 in addition to the long-term and short-term capital gains and losses for 1989. Accordingly, X's taxable income for 1989 will include a net capital gain of $105 (consisting of a net long-term capital gain of $135 and a net short-term capital loss of $30).

(iii) *Earnings and profits.* For 1988, X must determine both its earnings and profits and its accumulated earnings and profits without regard to the $150 long-term capital gain, the $75 long-term capital loss, the $50 short-term capital gain, and the $150 short-term capital loss for the post-October period of 1988. In determining both its earnings and profits and its accumulated earnings and profits for 1989, X must include (in addition to the long-term and short-term capital gains and losses for 1989) the $150 long-term capital gain, the $75 long-term capital loss, the $50 short-term capital gain, and the $150 short-term capital loss for the post-October period of 1988 as if those deferred gains and losses arose on January 1, 1989. Thus, X will include $160 of capital gain in its earnings and profits for 1988 and $105 of capital gain in its earnings and profits for 1989.

Example (7). Same facts as example (5), except that X elects to defer only $20 of the post-October capital loss for 1988 under paragraph (f)(1) of this section for purposes of determining its taxable income for 1988.

(i) *Capital gain dividends.* Same result as in example (5).

(ii) *Taxable income.* X must compute its taxable income for 1988 by including $5 of the $150 short-term capital loss for the post-October period of 1988, but without regard to the $150 long-term capital gain, the $75 long-term capital loss, the $50 short-term capital gain, and $145 of the $150 short-term capital loss for the post-October period of 1988 because it made an election to defer $20 of the $25 post-October capital loss for 1988 under paragraph (f)(1) of this section. Accordingly, X's taxable income for 1988 will include a net capital gain of $100 and a net short-term capital gain of $55. X must include the $150 long-term capital gain, the $75 long-term capital loss, the $50 short-term capital gain, and $145 of the $150 short-term capital loss for the post-October period of 1988 in its taxable income for 1989 in addition to the long-term and short-term capital gains and losses for 1989. Accordingly, X's taxable income for 1989 will include a net capital gain of $110 (consisting of a long-term capital gain of $135 and a net short-term capital loss of $25).

(iii) *Earnings and profits.* X must determine its earnings and profits for 1988 without regard to the $150 long-term capital gain, the $75 long-term capital loss, the $50 short-term capital gain, and the $150 short-term capital loss for the post-October period of 1988. In determining its accumulated earnings and profits for 1988, X must include $5 of the $150 short-term capital loss for the post-October period of 1988. In determining its accumulated earnings and profits for 1989, X must include (in addition to the long-term and short-term capital gains and losses for 1989) the $150 long-term capital gain, the $75 long-term capital loss, the $50 short-term capital gain, and $145 of the $150 short-term capital loss for the post-October period of 1988 as if those deferred gains and losses arose on January 1, 1989. Thus, X includes $160 of capital gain in its earnings and profits for 1988, includes $155 in its accumulated earnings and profits for 1988, and includes $110 of capital gain in its earnings and profits for 1989.

Example (8). X has the following capital gains and losses for the periods indicated:

	Long-term	Short-term
01/01—10/31/88	115	80
	(15)	(20)
	100	60
11/01—12/31/88	15	25
	(75)	(10)
	(60)	15
01/01—10/31/89	80	50
	(5)	(100)
	75	(50)
11/01—12/31/89	85	40
	(0)	(20)
	85	20

X has a post-October capital loss of $45 for its 1988 taxable year due to a net capital loss for the post-October period of 1988. X does not make an election under paragraph (f)(1) of this section.

(i) *Capital gain dividends.* X may designate up to $100 as a capital gain dividend for 1988 because X must disregard the $15 long-term capital gain, the $75 long-term capital loss, the $25 short-term capital gain, and the $10 short-term capital loss for the post-October period of 1988 in computing its net capital gain for this purpose. In computing its net capital gain for 1989 for purposes of determining the amount it may designate as a capital gain dividend for 1989, X must take into account the $15 long-term capital gain, the $75 long-term capital loss, the $25 short-term capital gain, and the $10 short-term capital loss for the post-October period of 1988 in addition to the long-term and short-term capital gains and losses for 1989. Accordingly, X may designate up to $85 as a capital gain dividend for 1989.

(ii) *Taxable income.* X must include the $15 long-term capital gain, the $75 long-term capital loss, the $25 short-term capital gain, and the $10 short-term capital loss for the post-October period of 1988 in its taxable income for 1988 because it did not make an election under paragraph (f)(1) of this section for 1988. Accordingly, X's taxable income for 1988 will include a net capital gain of $40 and a net short-term capital gain of $75. X's taxable income for 1989 will include a net capital gain of $130 for 1989 (consisting of a net long-term capital gain of $160 and a net short-term capital loss of $30).

(iii) *Earnings and profits.* X must determine its earnings and profits for 1988 without regard to the $15 long-term capital gain, the $75 long-term capital loss, the $25 short-term capital gain, and the $10 short-term capital loss for the post-October period of 1988. X must, however, include the $15 long-term capital gain, the $75 long-term capital loss, the $25 short-term capital gain, and the $10 short-term capital loss for the post-October period of 1988 in determining its accumulated earnings and profits for 1988. Thus, X includes $160 of capital gain in its earnings and profits for 1988, includes $115 in its accumulated earnings and profits for 1988, and includes $130 of capital gain in its earnings and profits for 1989.

Example (9). Same facts as example (8), except that X elects to defer the entire $45 post-October capital loss for 1988 under paragraph (f)(1) of this section for purposes of determining its taxable income for 1988.

(i) *Capital gain dividends.* Same result as in example (8).

(ii) *Taxable income.* X must compute its taxable income for 1988 without regard to the $15 long-term capital gain, the $75 long-term capital loss, the $25 short-term capital gain, and the $10 short-term capital loss for the post-October period of 1988 because it made an election to defer the entire $45 post-October capital loss for 1988 under paragraph (f)(1) of this section. Accordingly, X's taxable income for 1988 will include a net capital gain of $100 and a net short-term capital gain of $60. X must include the $15 long-

Reg. § 1.852-11(h)

term capital gain, the $75 long-term capital loss, the $25 short-term capital gain, and the $10 short-term capital loss for the post-October period of 1988 in its taxable income for 1989 in addition to the long-term and short-term capital gains and losses for 1989. Accordingly, X's taxable income for 1989 will include a net capital gain of $85 (consisting of a net long-term capital gain of $100 and a net short-term capital loss of $15).

(iii) *Earnings and profits.* For 1988, X must determine both its earnings and profits and its accumulated earnings and profits without regard to the $15 long-term capital gain, the $75 long-term capital loss, the $25 short-term capital gain, and the $10 short-term capital loss for the post-October period of 1988. In determining both its earnings and profits and its accumulated earnings and profits for 1989, X must include (in addition to the long-term and short-term capital gains and losses for 1989) the $15 long-term capital gain, the $75 long-term capital loss, the $25 short-term capital gain, and the $10 short-term capital loss for the post-October period of 1988 as if those deferred gains and losses arose on January 1, 1989. Thus, X will include $160 of capital gain in its earnings and profits for 1988 and $85 of capital gain in its earnings and profits for 1989.

Example (10). Same facts as example (8), except that X elects to defer only $30 of the post-October capital loss for 1988 under paragraph (f)(1) of this section for purposes of determining its taxable income for 1988.

(i) *Capital gain dividends.* Same result as in example (8).

(ii) *Taxable income.* X must compute its taxable income for 1988 by including $5 of the $75 long-term capital loss and the $10 short-term capital loss for the post-October period of 1988, but without regard to the $15 long-term capital gain, the $70 of the $75 long-term capital loss, and the $25 short-term capital gain for the post-October period of 1988 because it made an election to defer $30 of the $45 post-October capital loss for 1988 under paragraph (f)(1) of this section. Accordingly, X's taxable income for 1988 will include a net capital gain of $95 and a net short-term capital gain of $50. X must include the $15 long-term capital gain, $70 of the $75 long-term capital loss, and the $25 short-term capital gain for the post-October period of 1988 in its taxable income for 1989 in addition to the long-term and short-term capital gains and losses for 1989. Accordingly, X's taxable income for 1989 will include a net capital gain of $100 (consisting of a net long-term capital gain of $105 and a net short-term capital loss of $5).

(iii) *Earnings and profits.* X must determine its earnings and profits for 1988 without regard to the $15 long-term capital gain, the $75 long-term capital loss, the $25 short-term capital gain, and the $10 short-term capital loss for the post-October period of 1988. In determining its accumulated earnings and profits for 1988, X must include $5 of the $75 long-term capital loss and the $10 short-term capital loss for the post-October period of 1988. In determining both its earnings and profits and its accumulated earnings and profits for 1989, X must include (in addition to the long-term and short-term capital gains and losses for 1989) the $15 long-term capital gain, $70 of the $75 long-term capital loss, and the $25 short-term capital gain for the post-October period of 1988 as if those deferred gains and losses arose on January 1, 1989. Thus, X includes $160 of capital gain in its earnings and profits for 1988, includes $145 in its accumulated earnings and profits for 1989, and includes $100 of capital gain in its earnings and profits for 1989 (consisting of a net long-term capital gain of $105 and a net short-term capital loss of $5).

Example (11). X has the following foreign currency gains and losses attributable to the periods indicated:

01/01—10/31/88	200
11/01—12/31/88	(100)
01/01—10/31/89	110
11/01—12/31/89	40

X has a $100 post-October currency loss for its 1988 taxable year due to a net foreign currency loss for the post-October period of 1988. X does not make an election under paragraph (f)(1) of this section.

(i) *Taxable income.* X must compute its taxable income for 1988 by including the $100 foreign currency loss for the post-October period of 1988 because it did not make an election under paragraph (f)(1) of this section. Accordingly, X's taxable income for 1988 will include a net foreign currency gain of $100. X's taxable income for 1989 will include a net foreign currency gain of $150.

(ii) *Earnings and profits.* X must determine its earnings and profits for 1988 without regard to the foreign currency loss for the post-October period of 1988. X must, however, include the $100 foreign currency loss for the post-October period of 1988 in determining its accumulated earnings and profits for 1988. Thus, X includes $200 of foreign currency gain in its earnings and profits for 1988, includes $100 in its accumulated earnings and profits for 1988, and includes $150 of foreign currency gain in its earnings and profits for 1989.

Reg. § 1.852-11(h)

Example (12). Same facts as example (11), except that X elects to defer the entire $100 post-October currency loss for 1988 under paragraph (f)(1) of this section for purposes of determining its taxable income for 1988.

(i) *Taxable income.* X must compute its taxable income for 1988 without regard to the $100 foreign currency loss for the post-October period of 1988 because it made an election to defer the entire $100 post-October currency loss for 1988 under paragraph (f)(1) of this section. Accordingly, X's taxable income for 1988 will include a net foreign currency gain of $200. X's taxable income for 1989 will include a net foreign currency gain of $50 because X must compute its taxable income for 1989 by including the $100 foreign currency loss for the post-October period of 1988 in addition to the foreign currency gains and losses for 1989.

(ii) *Earnings and profits.* For 1988, X must determine both its earnings and profits and its accumulated earnings and profits without regard to the $100 foreign currency loss for the post-October period of 1988. In determining both its earnings and profits and its accumulated earnings and profits for 1989, X must include (in addition to the foreign currency gains and losses for 1989) the $100 foreign currency loss for the post-October period of 1988 as if that deferred loss arose on January 1, 1989. Thus, X will include $200 of foreign currency gain in its earnings and profits for 1988 and $50 of foreign currency gain in its earnings and profits for 1989.

Example (13). Same facts as example (11), except that X elects to defer only $75 of the post-October currency loss under paragraph (f)(1) of this section for purposes of determining its taxable income for 1988.

(i) *Taxable income.* X must compute its taxable income for 1988 by including $25 of the $100 foreign currency loss for the post-October period of 1988, but without regard to $75 of the $100 foreign currency loss for the post-October period of 1988 because it made an election to defer $75 of the $100 post-October currency loss for 1988 under paragraph (f)(1) of this section. Accordingly, X's taxable income for 1988 will include a net foreign currency gain of $175. X's taxable income will include a net foreign currency gain of $75 for 1989 because X must compute its taxable income for 1989 by including $75 of the $100 foreign currency loss for the post-October period of 1988 in addition to the foreign currency gains and losses for 1989.

(ii) *Earnings and profits.* X must determine its earnings and profits for 1988 without regard to the $100 foreign currency loss for the post-October period of 1988. X must, however, include $25 of the $100 foreign currency loss for the post-October period of 1988 in determining its accumulated earnings and profits for 1988. In determining both its earnings and profits and its accumulated earnings and profits for 1989, X must include (in addition to the foreign currency gains and losses for 1989) the $75 of the $100 foreign currency loss for the post-October period of 1988 as if that loss arose on January 1, 1989. Thus, X includes $200 of foreign currency gain in its earnings and profits for 1988, includes $175 in its accumulated earnings and profits for 1988, and includes $75 of foreign currency gain in its earnings and profits for 1989.

(i) *Procedure for making election*—(1) *In general.* Except as provided in paragraph (i)(2) of this section, a regulated investment company may make an election under paragraph (f)(1) of this section for a taxable year to which this section applies by completing its income tax return (including any necessary schedules) for that taxable year in accordance with the instructions for the form that are applicable to the election.

(2) *When applicable instructions not available.* If the instructions for the income tax returns of regulated investment companies for a taxable year to which this section applies do not reflect the provisions of this section, a regulated investment company may make an election under paragraph (f)(1) of this section for that year by entering the appropriate amounts on its income tax return (including any necessary schedules) for that year, and by attaching a written statement to the return that states—

(i) The taxable year for which the election under this section is made;

(ii) The fact that the regulated investment company elects to defer all or a part of its post-October capital loss or post-October currency loss for that taxable year for purposes of computing its taxable income under the terms of this section,

(iii) The amount of the post-October capital loss or post-October currency loss that the regulated investment company elects to defer for that taxable year; and

(iv) The name, address, and employer identification number of the regulated investment company.

(j) *Transition rules*—(1) *In general.* For a taxable year ending before March 2, 1990 in which a regulated investment company incurred a post-October capital loss or post-October currency loss, the company may use any method that is consistently applied and in accordance with reasonable business practice to determine the amounts taken into account in that taxable year for purposes of

Reg. § 1.852-11(i)(1)

paragraphs (e)(2), (f)(3), and (g) of this section and to determine the amount taken into account in the succeeding year for purposes of paragraphs (e)(3), (f)(4), and (g) of this section. For example, for purposes of paragraph (e), a taxpayer may use a method that treats as incurred in a taxable year all capital gains taken into account in computing the post-October loss for that year and an amount of capital loss for such period equal to the amount of such gains and that treats the remaining amount of capital loss for such period as arising on the first day of the succeeding year. Similarly, for purposes of paragraph (e)(3), a taxpayer may use a method that treats as arising on the first day of the succeeding year only the excess of the capital losses from sales or exchanges after October 31 over the capital gains for such period (that is, the net capital loss or net long-term capital loss for such period).

(2) *Retroactive election*—(i) *In general.* A regulated investment company may make an election (a "retroactive election") under paragraph (f)(1) for a taxable year with respect to which it has filed an income tax return on or before May 1, 1990 (a "retroactive election year") by filing an amended return (including any necessary schedules) for the retroactive election year reflecting the appropriate amounts and by attaching a written statement to the return that complies with the requirements of paragraph (i)(2) of this section.

(ii) *Deadline for making election.* A retroactive election may be made no later than December 31, 1990.

(3) *Amended return required for succeeding year in certain circumstances*—(i) *In general.* If, at the time a regulated investment company makes a retroactive election under this section, it has already filed an income tax return for the succeeding year, the company must file an amended return for such succeeding year reflecting the appropriate amounts.

(ii) *Time for filing amended return.* An amended return required under paragraph (j)(3)(i) of this section must be filed together with the amended return described in paragraph (j)(2)(i).

(4) *Retroactive dividend*—(i) *In general.* A regulated investment company that makes a retroactive election under this section for a retroactive election year may elect to treat any dividend (or portion thereof) declared and paid (or treated as paid under section 852(b)(7)) by the regulated investment company after the retroactive election year and on or before December 31, 1990 as having been paid during the retroactive election year (a "retroactive dividend"). This election shall be irrevocable with respect to the retroactive dividend to which it applies.

(ii) *Method of making election.* The election under this paragraph (j)(4) must be made by the regulated investment company by treating the dividend (or portion thereof) to which the election applies as a dividend paid during the retroactive election year in computing its deduction for dividends paid in its tax returns for all applicable years (including the amended return(s) required to be filed under paragraphs (j)(2) and (3) of this section).

(iii) *Deduction for dividends paid*—(A) *In general.* Subject to the rules of sections 561 and 562, a regulated investment company shall include the amount of any retroactive dividend in computing its deduction for dividends paid for the retroactive election year. No deduction for dividends paid shall be allowed under this paragraph (j)(4)(iii)(A) for any amount not paid (or treated as paid under section 852(b)(7)) on or before December 31, 1990.

(B) *Limitation on ordinary dividends.* The amount of retroactive dividends (other than retroactive dividends qualifying as capital gain dividends) paid for a retroactive election year under this section shall not exceed the increase, if any, in the investment company taxable income of the regulated investment company (determined without regard to the deduction for dividends paid (as defined in section 561)) that is attributable solely to the regulated investment company having made the retroactive election.

(C) *Limitation on capital gain dividends.* The amount of retroactive dividends qualifying as capital gain dividends paid for a retroactive election year under this section shall not exceed the increase, if any, in the amount of the excess described in section 852(b)(3)(A) (relating to the excess of the net capital gain over the deduction for capital gain dividends paid) that is attributable solely to the regulated investment company having made the retroactive election.

(D) *Effect on other years.* A retroactive dividend shall not be includible in computing the deduction for dividends paid for—

(*1*) The taxable year in which such distribution is actually paid (or treated as paid under section 852(b)(7)); or

(*2*) Under section 855(a), the taxable year preceding the retroactive election year.

(iv) *Earnings and profits.* A retroactive dividend shall be considered as paid out of the earnings and profits of the retroactive election year (computed with the application of sections 852(c) and 855, § 1.852-5, § 1.855-1, and this sec-

Reg. § 1.852-11(j)(4)

tion), and not out of the earnings and profits of the taxable year in which the distribution is actually paid (or treated as paid under section 852(b)(7)).

(v) *Receipt by shareholders.* Except as provided in section 852(b)(7), a retroactive dividend shall be included in the gross income of the shareholders of the regulated investment company for the taxable year in which the dividend is received by them.

(vi) *Foreign tax election.* If a regulated investment company to which section 853 (relating to foreign taxes) is applicable for a retroactive election year elects to treat a dividend paid (or treated as paid under section 852(b)(7)) during the taxable year as a retroactive dividend, the shareholders of the regulated investment company shall consider the amounts described in section 853(b)(2) allocable to such distribution as paid or received, as the case may be, in the shareholder's taxable year in which the distribution is made.

(vii) *Example.* The provisions of this paragraph (j)(4) may be illustrated by the following example:

Example. X is a regulated investment company that computes its income on a calendar year basis. No election is in effect under section 4982(e)(4). X has the following income for 1988:

FOREIGN CURRENCY GAINS AND LOSSES:

	Gains and Losses
Jan. 1—Oct. 31	100
Nov. 1—Dec. 31	(75)

CAPITAL GAINS AND LOSSES:

	Short-Term	Long-Term
Jan. 1—Oct. 31	100	100
Nov. 1—Dec. 31	50	(100)

(A) X had investment company taxable income of $175 and no net capital gain for 1988 for taxable income purposes. X distributed $175 of investment company taxable income as an ordinary dividend for 1988.

(B) If X makes a retroactive election under this section to defer the entire $75 post-October currency loss and the entire $50 post-October capital loss for the post-October period of its 1988 taxable year for purposes of computing its taxable income, that deferral increases X's investment company taxable income for 1988 by $25 (due to an increase in foreign currency gain of $75 and a decrease in short-term capital gain of $50) to $200 and increases the excess described in section 852(b)(3)(A) for 1988 by $100 from $0 to $100. The amount that X may treat as a retroactive ordinary dividend is limited to $25, and the amount that X may treat as a retroactive capital gain dividend is limited to $100.

(5) *Certain distributions may be designated retroactively as capital gain dividends.* To the extent that a regulated investment company designated as capital gain dividends for a taxable year less than the maximum amount permitted under paragraph (e) of this section for that taxable year, the regulated investment company may designate an additional amount of dividends paid (or treated as paid under sections 852(b)(7) or 855, or paragraph (j)(4) of this section) for the taxable year as capital gain dividends, notwithstanding that a written notice was not mailed to its shareholders within 60 days after the close of the taxable year in which the distribution was paid (or treated as paid under section 852(b)(7)).

(k) *Effective date.* The provisions of this section shall apply to taxable years ending after October 31, 1987. [Reg. § 1.852-11.]

☐ [*T.D. 8320, 11-29-90.*]

[Reg. § 1.852-12]

§ 1.852-12. **Non-RIC earnings and profits.**—(a) *Applicability of section 852(a)(2)(A)*—(1) *In general.* An investment company does not satisfy section 852(a)(2)(A) unless—

(i) Part I of subchapter M applied to the company for all its taxable years ending on or after November 8, 1983; and

(ii) For each corporation to whose earnings and profits the investment company succeeded by the operation of section 381, part I of subchapter M applied for all the corporation's taxable years ending on or after November 8, 1983.

(2) *Special rule.* See section 1071(a)(5)(D) of the Tax Reform Act of 1984, Pub. L. 98-369 (98 Stat. 1051), for a special rule which treats part I of subchapter M as having applied to an investment company's first taxable year ending after November 8, 1983.

(b) *Applicability of section 852(a)(2)(B)*—(1) *In general.* An investment company does not satisfy section 852(a)(2)(B) unless, as of the close of the taxable year, it has no earnings and profits other than earnings and profits that—

(i) Were earned by a corporation in a year for which part I of subchapter M applied to the corporation and, at all times thereafter, were the earnings and profits of a corporation to which part I of subchapter M applied;

(ii) By the operation of section 381 pursuant to a transaction that occurred before December 22, 1992, became the earnings and profits of a corporation to which part I of subchapter M applied and, at all times thereafter, were the earnings and profits of a corporation to which part I of subchapter M applied;

(iii) Were accumulated in a taxable year ending before January 1, 1984, by a corporation to which part I of subchapter M applied for any taxable year ending before November 8, 1983; or

(iv) Were accumulated in the first taxable year of an investment company that began business in 1983 and that was not a successor corporation.

(2) *Prior law.* For purposes of paragraph (b) of this section, a reference to part I of subchapter M includes a reference to the corresponding provisions of prior law.

(c) *Effective date.* This regulation is effective for taxable years ending on or after December 22, 1992.

(d) For treatment of net built-in gain assets of a C corporation that become assets of a RIC, see § 1.337(d)-5T. [Reg. § 1.852-12.]

☐ [T.D. 8483, 8-17-93. Amended by T.D. 8872, 2-4-2000.]

[Reg. § 1.853-1]

§ 1.853-1. **Foreign tax credit allowed to shareholders.**—(a) *In general.* Under section 853, a regulated investment company, meeting the requirements set forth in section 853(a) and paragraph (b) of this section, may make an election with respect to the income, war-profits, and excess profits taxes described in section 901(b)(1) which it pays to foreign countries or possessions of the United States during the taxable year, including such taxes as are deemed paid by it under the provisions of any income tax convention to which the United States is a party. If an election is made, the shareholders of the regulated investment company shall apply their proportionate share of such foreign taxes paid, or deemed to have been paid by it pursuant to any income tax convention, as either a credit (under section 901) or as a deduction (under section 164(a)) as provided by section 853(b)(2) and paragraph (b) of § 1.853-2. The election is not applicable with respect to taxes deemed to have been paid under section 902 (relating to the credit allowed to corporate stockholders of a foreign corporation for taxes paid by such foreign corporation).

(b) *Requirements.* To qualify for the election provided in section 853(a), a regulated investment company (1) must have more than 50 percent of the value of its total assets, at the close of the taxable year for which the election is made, invested in stocks and securities of foreign corporations, and (2) must also, for that year, comply with the requirements prescribed in section 852(a) and paragraph (a) of § 1.852-1. The term "value", for purposes of the first requirement, is defined in section 851(c)(4). For the definition of foreign corporation, see section 7701(a). [Reg. § 1.853-1.]

☐ [T.D. 6236, 6-3-57.]

[Reg. § 1.853-2]

§ 1.853-2. **Effect of election.**—(a) *Regulated investment company.* A regulated investment company making a valid election with respect to a taxable year under the provisions of section 853(a) is, for such year, denied both the deduction for foreign taxes provided by section 164(a) and the credit for foreign taxes provided by section 901 with respect to all income, war-profits, and excess profits taxes (described in section 901(b)(1)) which it has paid to any foreign country or possession of the United States. See section 853(b)(1)(A). However, under section 853(b)(1)(B), the regulated investment company is permitted to add the amount of such foreign taxes paid to its dividends paid deduction for that taxable year. See paragraph (a) of § 1.852-1.

(b) *Shareholder.* Under section 853(b)(2), a shareholder of an investment company, which has made the election under section 853, is, in effect, placed in the same position as a person directly owning stock in foreign corporations, in that he must include in his gross income (in addition to taxable dividends actually received) his proportionate share of such foreign taxes paid and must treat such amount as foreign taxes paid by him for the purposes of the deduction under section 164(a) and the credit under section 901. For such purposes he must treat as gross income from a foreign country or possession of the United States (1) his proportionate share of the taxes paid by the regulated investment company to such foreign country or possession and (2) the portion of any dividend paid by the investment company which represents income derived from such sources.

(c) *Dividends paid after the close of the taxable year.* For additional rules applicable to certain distributions made after the close of the taxable year which may be designated as income received from sources within and taxes paid to foreign countries or possessions of the United States, see section 855(d) and paragraph (f) of § 1.855-1.

(d) *Example.* This section may be illustrated as follows:

(1) The X Corporation, a regulated investment company, has total assets, at the close of the taxable year, of $10 million invested as follows:

Regulated Investment Companies

See p. 20,601 for regulations not amended to reflect law changes

Domestic corporations		$ 4,000,000
Foreign corporations in:		
Country A	$3,500,000	
Country B	2,500,000	
		6,000,000
Total assets		10,000,000

(2) The dividend income of X Corporation is received from the following sources:

Domestic corporations		$ 300,000
Foreign corporations:		
Country A	$ 250,000	
Country B	250,000	
		500,000
Total dividend income		800,000
Operation and management expenses		80,000
Net dividend income		720,000
Taxes withheld by Country A on dividends of $250,000 at a rate of 10 percent	$ 25,000	
Taxes withheld by Country B on dividends of $250,000 at a rate of 20 percent	50,000	
Total foreign taxes withheld		$ 75,000
Income available for distribution		645,000

(3) X Corporation has 250,000 shares of common stock outstanding and distributes the entire $645,000 as a dividend of $2.58 per share of stock.

(4) The X Corporation meets the 50 percent requirement of section 851(b)(4) and the requirements of section 852(a). It notifies each shareholder by mail, within the time prescribed by section 853(c), that by reason of the election they are to treat as foreign taxes paid $0.30 per share of stock ($75,000 of foreign taxes paid, divided by the 250,000 shares of stock outstanding), of which $0.20 represents taxes paid to Country B and $0.10 taxes paid to Country A. The shareholders must report as income $2.88 per share ($2.58 of dividends actually received plus the $0.30 representing foreign taxes paid). Of the $2.88 per share, $1.80 per share ($450,000 (which represents such part of the net dividend income of $720,000 as the foreign dividend income of $500,000 bears to the total dividend income of $800,000) divided by 250,000 shares) is to be considered as received from foreign sources. Ninety cents is to be considered as received from Country A, and ninety cents from Country B. [Reg. § 1.853-2.]

☐ [T.D. 6236, 6-3-57.]

[Reg. § 1.853-3]

§ 1.853-3. Notice to shareholders.—(a) *General rule.* If a regulated investment company makes an election under section 853(a), in the manner provided in § 1.853-4, the investment company is required, under section 853(c), to furnish its shareholders with a written notice mailed not later than 45 days (30 days for taxable years ending before February 26, 1964) after the close of its taxable year. The notice must designate the shareholder's portion of foreign taxes paid to each such country or possession and the portion of the dividend which represents income derived from sources within each such country or possession. For purposes of section 853(b)(2) and paragraph (b) of § 1.853-2, the amount that a shareholder may treat as his proportionate share of foreign taxes paid and the amount to be included as gross income derived from any foreign country or possession of the United States shall not exceed the amounts so designated by the company in such written notice. If, however, the amount designated by the company in the notice exceeds the shareholder's proper proportionate share of foreign taxes or gross income from sources within any foreign country or possession, the shareholder is limited to the amount correctly ascertained.

(b) *Shareholder of record custodian of certain unit investment trusts.* In any case where a notice is mailed pursuant to paragraph (a) of this section by a regulated investment company with respect to a taxable year of the regulated investment company ending after December 8, 1970, to a shareholder of record who is a nominee acting as a custodian of a unit investment trust described in section 851(f)(1) and paragraph (b) of § 1.851-7, the nominee shall furnish each holder of an interest in such trust with a written notice mailed on or before the 55th day following the close of the regulated investment company's taxable year. The notice shall designate the holder's proportionate share of the amounts of foreign taxes paid to each such country or possession and the holder's proportionate share of the dividend which represents income derived from sources within each country or possession shown on the notice received by the nominee pursuant to paragraph (a) of this section. The notice shall include the name and address of the nominee identified as such. This paragraph shall not apply if the regulated investment company agrees with the nominee to satisfy the notice requirements of paragraph (a) of this section with respect to each holder of an interest in the unit investment trust whose shares are being held by the nominee as custodian and not later than 45 days following the close of the company's taxable year, files with the Internal Revenue Service office where such company's return for the taxable year is to be filed, a statement that the holders of the unit investment trust with whom the agreement was made have been directly notified by the regulated investment company. Such statement shall include the name, sponsor, and custodian of each unit investment trust whose holders have been directly notified. The nominee's requirements under this paragraph shall be deemed met if the regulated investment company transmits a copy of such statement to the nominee within such 45-day period; provided however, if the regulated investment company fails or is unable to satisfy the requirements of this paragraph with respect to the holders of interest in the unit investment trust, it shall so notify the Internal Revenue Service within 45 days following the close of its taxable year. The custodian shall, upon notice by the Internal Revenue Service that the regulated investment company has failed to comply with the agreement, satisfy the requirements of this paragraph within 30 days of such notice. [Reg. § 1.853-3.]

☐ [T.D. 6236, 6-3-57. Amended by T.D. 6369, 3-16-59; T.D. 6921, 6-19-67 and T.D. 7187, 7-5-72.]

[Reg. § 1.853-4]

§ 1.853-4. Manner of making election.—(a) *General rule.* A regulated investment company, to make a valid election under section 853, must—

(1) File with Form 1099 and Form 1096 a statement as part of its return which sets forth the following information:

(i) The total amount of income received from sources within foreign countries and possessions of the United States;

(ii) The total amount of income, war-profits, or excess profits taxes (described in section 901(b)(1)) paid, or deemed to have been paid under the provisions of any treaty to which the United States is a party, to such foreign countries or possessions;

(iii) The date, form, and contents of the notice to its shareholders;

(iv) The proportionate share of such taxes paid during the taxable year and foreign income received during such year attributable to one share of stock of the regulated investment company; and

(2) File as part of its return for the taxable year a Form 1118 modified so that it becomes a statement in support of the election made by a regulated investment company for taxes paid to a foreign country or a possession of the United States.

(b) *Irrevocability of the election.* The election is applicable only with respect to taxable years subject to the Code, shall be made with respect to all such foreign taxes, and must be made not later than the time prescribed for filing the return (including extensions thereof). Such election, if made, shall be irrevocable with respect to the dividend (or portion thereof), and the foreign taxes paid with respect thereto, to which the election applies. [Reg. § 1.853-4.]

☐ [T.D. 6236, 6-3-57.]

[Reg. § 1.854-1]

§ 1.854-1. **Limitations applicable to dividends received from regulated investment company.**—(a) *In general.* Section 854 provides special limitations applicable to dividends received from a regulated investment company for purposes of the exclusion under section 116 for dividends received by individuals, the deduction under section 243 for dividends received by corporations, and, in the case of dividends received by individuals before January 1, 1965, the credit under section 34.

(b) *Capital gain dividend.* Under the provisions of section 854(a) a capital gain dividend as defined in section 852(b)(3) and paragraph (c) of § 1.852-4 shall not be considered a dividend for purposes of the exclusion under section 116, the deduction under section 243, and, in the case of taxable years ending before January 1, 1965, the credit under section 34.

(c) *Rule for dividends other than capital gain dividends.* (1) Section 854(b)(1) limits the amount that may be treated as a dividend (other than a capital gain dividend) by the shareholder of a regulated investment company, for the purposes of the credit, exclusion, and deduction specified in paragraph (b) of this section, where the investment company receives substantial amounts of income (such as interest, etc.) from sources other than dividends from domestic corporations, which dividends qualify for the exclusion under section 116.

(2) Where the "aggregate dividends received" (as defined in section 854(b)(3)(B) and paragraph (b) of § 1.854-3) during the taxable year by a regulated investment company (which meets the requirements of section 852(a) and paragraph (a) of § 1.852-1 for the taxable year during which it paid such dividend) are less than 75 percent of its gross income for such taxable year (as defined in section 854(b)(3)(A) and paragraph (a) of § 1.854-3), only that portion of the dividend paid by the regulated investment company which bears the same ratio to the amount of such dividend paid as the aggregate dividends received by the regulated investment company, during the taxable year, bears to its gross income for such taxable year (computed without regard to gains from the sale or other disposition of stocks or securities) may be treated as a dividend for purposes of such credit, exclusion, and deduction.

(3) Subparagraph (2) of this paragraph may be illustrated by the following example:

Example. The XYZ regulated investment company meets the requirements of section 852(a) for the taxable year and has received income from the following sources:

Capital gains (from the sale of stock or securities)	$100,000
Dividends (from domestic sources other than dividends described in section 116(b))	70,000
Dividends (from foreign corporation)	5,000
Interest	25,000
Total	$200,000
Expenses	20,000
Taxable Income	$180,000

The regulated investment company decides to distribute the entire $180,000. It distributes a capital gain dividend of $100,000 and a dividend of ordinary income of $80,000. The aggregate dividends received by the regulated investment company from domestic corporations ($70,000) is less than 75 percent of its gross income ($100,000) computed without regard to capital gains from sales of securities. Therefore, an apportionment is required. Since $70,000 is 70 percent of $100,000, out of every $1 dividend of ordinary income paid by the regulated investment company only 70 cents would be available for the credit, exclusion, or deduction referred to in section 854(b)(1). The capital gains dividend and the dividend received from foreign corporations are excluded from the computation.

(d) *Dividends received from a regulated investment company during taxable years of shareholders ending after July 31, 1954, and subject to the Internal Revenue Code of 1939.* For the application of section 854 to taxable years of shareholders of a regulated investment company ending after July 31, 1954, and subject to the Internal Revenue Code of 1939, see § 1.34-5 and § 1.116.2. [Reg. § 1.854-1.]

☐ [T.D. 6236, 6-3-57. Amended by T.D. 6369, 3-16-59 and T.D. 6921, 6-19-67.]

[Reg. § 1.854-2]

§ 1.854-2. Notice to shareholders.—(a) *General rule.* Section 854(b)(2) provides that the amount that a shareholder may treat as a dividend for purposes of the exclusion under section 116 for dividends received by individuals, the deduction under section 243 for dividends received by corporations, and, in the case of dividends received by individuals before January 1, 1965, the credit under section 34, shall not exceed the amount so designated by the company in a written notice to its shareholders mailed not later than 45 days (30 days for a taxable year ending before February 26, 1964) after the close of the company's taxable year. If, however, the amount so designated by the company in the notice exceeds the amount which may be treated by the shareholder as a dividend for such purposes, the shareholder is limited to the amount as correctly ascertained under section 854(b)(1) and paragraph (c) of § 1.854-1.

(b) *Shareholder of record custodian of certain unit investment trusts.* In any case where a notice is mailed pursuant to paragraph (a) of this section by a regulated investment company with respect to a taxable year of the regulated investment company ending after [insert date of publication of notice in Federal Register] to a shareholder of record who is a nominee acting as a custodian of a unit investment trust described in section 851(f)(1) and paragraph (d) of § 1.851-7, the nominee shall furnish each holder of an interest in such trust with a written notice mailed on or before the 55th day following the close of the regulated investment company's taxable year. The notice shall designate the holder's proportionate share of the amounts that may be treated as a dividend for purposes of the exclusion under section 116 for dividends received by individuals and the deduction under section 243 for dividends received by corporations shown on the notice received by the nominee pursuant to paragraph (a) of this section. This notice shall include the name and address of the nominee identified as such. This paragraph shall not apply if the regulated investment company agrees with the nominee to satisfy the notice requirements of paragraph (a) of this section with respect to each holder of an interest in the unit investment trust whose shares

Reg. § 1.854-2(a)

are being held by the nominee as custodian and not later than 45 days following the close of the company's taxable year, files with the Internal Revenue Service office where such company's return is to be filed for the taxable year, a statement that the holders of the unit investment trust with whom the agreement was made have been directly notified by the regulated investment company. Such statement shall include the name, sponsor, and custodian of each unit investment trust whose holders have been directly notified. The nominee's requirement under this paragraph shall be deemed met if the regulated investment company transmits a copy of such statement to the nominee within such 45-day period; provided, however, if the regulated investment company fails or is unable to satisfy the requirements of this paragraph with respect to the holders of interest in the unit investment trust, it shall so notify the Internal Revenue Service within 45 days following the close of its taxable year. The custodian shall, upon notice by the Internal Revenue Service that the regulated investment company has failed to comply with the agreement, satisfy the requirements of this paragraph within 30 days of such notice. [Reg. § 1.854-2.]

☐ [T.D. 6236, 6-3-57. Amended by T.D. 6921, 6-19-67 and T.D. 7187, 7-5-72.]

[Reg. § 1.854-3]

§ 1.854-3. Definitions.—(a) For the purpose of computing the limitation prescribed by section 854(b)(1)(B) and paragraph (c) of § 1.854-1, the term "gross income" does not include gain from the sale or other disposition of stock or securities. However, capital gains arising from the sale or other dispostion of capital assets, other than stock or securities, shall not be excluded from gross income for this purpose.

(b) The term "aggregate dividends received" includes only dividends received from domestic corporations other than dividends described in section 116(b) (relating to dividends not eligible for exclusion from gross income). Accordingly, dividends received from foreign corporations will not be included in the computation of "aggregate dividends received". In determining the amount of any dividend for purposes of this section, the rules provided in section 116(c) (relating to certain distributions) shall apply. [Reg. § 1.854-3.]

☐ [T.D. 6236, 6-3-57.]

[Reg. § 1.855-1]

§ 1.855-1. Dividends paid by regulated investment company after close of taxable year.—(a) *General rule.* In—

(1) Determining under section 852(a) in paragraph (a) of § 1.852-1 whether the deduction for dividends paid during the taxable year (without regard to capital gain dividends) by a regulated investment company equals or exceeds 90 percent of its investment company taxable income (determined without regard to the provisions of section 852(b)(2)(D)),

(2) Computing its investment company taxable income (under section 852(b)(2) and § 1.852-3), and

(3) Determining the amount of capital gain dividends, (as defined in section 852(b)(3) and paragraph (c) of § 1.852-4) paid during the taxable year, any dividend (or portion thereof) declared by the investment company either before or after the close of the taxable year but in any event before the time prescribed by law for the filing of its return for the taxable year (including the period of any extension of time granted for filing such return) shall, to the extent the company so elects in such return, be treated as having been paid during such taxable year. This rule is applicable only if the entire amount of such dividend is actually distributed to the shareholders in the 12-month period following the close of such taxable year and not later than the date of the first regular dividend payment made after such declaration.

(b) *Election*—(1) *Method of making election.* The election must be made in the return filed by the company for the taxable year. The election shall be made by the taxpayer (the regulated investment company) by treating the dividend (or portion thereof) to which such election applies as a dividend paid during the taxable year in computing its investment company taxable income, or if the dividend (or portion thereof) to which such election applies is to be designated by the company as a capital gain dividend, in computing the amount of capital gain dividends paid during such taxable year. The election provided in section 855(a) may be made only to the extent that the earnings and profits of the taxable year (computed with the application of section 852(c) and § 1.852-5) exceed the total amount of distributions out of such earnings and profits actually made during the taxable year (not including distributions with respect to which an election has been made for a prior year under section 855(a)). The dividend or portion thereof, with respect to which the regulated investment company has made a valid election under section 855(a), shall be considered as paid out of the earnings and profits of the taxable year for which such election is made, and not out of the earnings and profits of the

Reg. § 1.855-1(b)(1)

taxable year in which the distribution is actually made.

(2) *Irrevocability of the election.* After the expiration of the time for filing the return for the taxable year for which an election is made under section 855(a), such election shall be irrevocable with respect to the dividend or portion thereof to which it applies.

(c) *Receipt by shareholders.* Under section 855(b), the dividend or portion thereof, with respect to which a valid election has been made, will be includible in the gross income of the shareholders of the regulated investment company for the taxable year in which the dividend is received by them.

(d) *Examples.* The application of paragraphs (a), (b), and (c) of this section may be illustrated by the following examples:

Example (1). The X Company, a regulated investment company, had taxable income (and earnings or profits) for the calendar year 1954 of $100,000. During that year the company distributed to shareholders taxable dividends aggregating $88,000. On March 10, 1955, the company declared a dividend of $37,000 payable to shareholders on March 20, 1955. Such dividend consisted of the first regular quarterly dividend for 1955 of $25,000 plus an additional $12,000 representing that part of the taxable income for 1954 which was not distributed in 1954. On March 15, 1955, the X Company filed its Federal income tax return and elected therein to treat $12,000 of the total dividend of $37,000 to be paid to shareholders on March 20, 1955, as having been paid during the taxable year 1954. Assuming that the X Company actually distributed the entire amount of the dividend of $37,000 on March 20, 1955, an amount equal to $12,000 thereof will be treated for the purposes of section 852(a) as having been paid during the taxable year 1954. Such amount ($12,000) will be considered by the X Company as a distribution out of the earnings and profits for the taxable year 1954, and will be treated by the shareholders as a taxable dividend for the taxable year in which such distribution is received by them.

Example (2). The Y Company, a regulated investment company, had taxable income (and earnings or profits) for the calendar year 1954 of $100,000, and for 1955 taxable income (and earnings or profits) of $125,000. On January 1, 1954, the company had a deficit in its earnings and profits accumulated since February 28, 1913, of $115,000. During the year 1954 the company distributed to shareholders taxable dividends aggregating $85,000. On March 5, 1955, the company declared a dividend of $65,000 payable to shareholders on March 31, 1955. On March 15, 1955, the Y Company filed its Federal income tax return in which it included $40,000 of the total dividend of $65,000 payable to shareholders on March 31, 1955, as a dividend paid by it during the taxable year 1954. On March 31, 1955, the Y Company distributed the entire amount of the dividend of $65,000 declared on March 5, 1955. The election under section 855(a) is valid only to the extent of $15,000, the amount of the undistributed earnings and profits for 1954 ($100,000 earnings and profits less $85,000 distributed during 1954). The remainder ($50,000) of the $65,000 dividend paid on March 31, 1955, could not be the subject of an election, and such amount will be regarded as a distribution by the Y Company out of earnings and profits for the taxable year 1955. Assuming that the only other distribution by the Y Company during 1955 was a distribution of $75,000 paid as a dividend on October 31, 1955, the total amount of the distribution of $65,000 paid on March 31, 1955, is to be treated by the shareholders as taxable dividends for the taxable year in which such dividend is received. The Y Company will treat the amount of $15,000 as a distribution of the earnings or profits of the company for the taxable year 1954, and the remaining $50,000 as a distribution of the earnings or profits for the year 1955. The distribution of $75,000 on October 31, 1955, is, of course, a taxable dividend out of the earnings and profits for the year 1955.

(e) *Notice to shareholders.* Section 855(c) provides that in the case of dividends, with respect to which a regulated investment company has made an election under section 855(a), any notice to shareholders required under subchapter M, chapter 1 of the Code, with respect to such amounts, shall be made not later than 45 days (30 days for a taxable year ending before February 26, 1964) after the close of the taxable year in which the distribution is made. Thus, the notice requirements of section 852(b)(3)(C) and paragraph (c) of § 1.852-4 with respect to capital gain dividends, section 853(c) and § 1.853-3 with respect to allowance to shareholder of foreign tax credit, and section 854(b)(2) and § 1.854-2 with respect to the amount of a distribution which may be treated as a dividend, may be satisfied with respect to amounts to which section 855(a) and this section apply if the notice relating to such amounts is mailed to the shareholders not later than 45 days (30 days for a taxable year ending before February 26, 1964) after the close of the taxable year in which the distribution is made. If the notice under section 855(c) relates to an election with respect to any capital gain dividends, such capital gain dividends shall be aggregated by the investment company with the designated capital gain dividends actually paid during the taxable year to which an election applies (not including such dividends with respect to which an election has been made for a prior year under section 855) for the purpose of determining whether the aggregate of the designated capital gain dividends with respect to such taxable year of the company is greater than the excess of the net long-term capital gain over the net short-term capital loss of the company. See section 852(b)(3)(C) and paragraph (c) of § 1.852-4.

(f) *Foreign tax election.* Section 855(d) provides that in the case of an election made under section 853 (relating to foreign taxes), the shareholder of the investment company shall consider the foreign income received, and the foreign tax paid, as received and paid, respectively, in the shareholder's taxable year in which distribution is made. [Reg. § 1.855-1.]

☐ [T.D. 6236, 6-3-57. *Amended by* T.D. 6369, 3-16-59 *and* T.D. 6921, 6-19-67.]

Real Estate Investment Trusts

[Reg. § 1.856-0]

§ 1.856-0. **Revenue Act of 1978 amendments not included.**—The regulations under part II of subchapter M of the Code do not reflect the amendments made by the Revenue Act of 1978, other than the changes made by section 362 of the Act, relating to deficiency dividends. [Reg. § 1.856-0.]

☐ [T.D. 7767, 2-3-81. *Amended by* T.D. 7936, 1-17-84.]

[Reg. § 1.856-1]

§ 1.856-1. **Definition of real estate investment trust.**—(a) *In general.* The term "real estate investment trust" means a corporation, trust, or association which (1) meets the status conditions in section 856(a) and paragraph (b) of this section, and (2) satisfies the gross income and asset diversification requirements under the limitations of section 856(c) and § 1.856-2. (See, however, paragraph (f) of this section, relating to the requirement that, for taxable years beginning before October 5, 1976, a real estate investment trust must be an unincorporated trust or unincorporated association.)

(b) *Qualifying conditions.* To qualify as a "real estate investment trust" an organization must be one—

(1) Which is managed by one or more trustees or directors,

(2) The beneficial ownership of which is evidenced by transferable shares or by transferable certificates of beneficial interest,

(3) Which would be taxable as a domestic corporation but for the provisions of part II, subchapter M, chapter 1 of the Code,

(4) Which, in the case of a taxable year beginning before October 5, 1976, does not hold any property (other than foreclosure property) primarily for sale to customers in the ordinary course of its trade or business,

(5) Which is neither (i) a financial institution to which section 585, 586, or 593 applies, nor (ii) an insurance company to which subchapter L applies,

(6) The beneficial ownership of which is held by 100 or more persons, and

(7) Which would not be a personal holding company (as defined in section 542) if all of its gross income constituted personal holding company income (as defined in section 543).

(c) *Determination of status.* The conditions described in subparagraphs (1) through (5) of paragraph (b) of this section must be met during the entire taxable year and the condition described in subparagraph (6) of paragraph (b) of this section must exist during at least 335 days of a taxable year of 12 months or during a proportionate part of a taxable year of less than 12 months. The days during which the latter condition must exist need not be consecutive. In determining the minimum number of days during which the condition described in paragraph (b)(6) of this section is required to exist in a taxable year of less than 12 months, fractional days shall be disregarded. For example, in a taxable year of 310 days, the actual number of days prescribed would be 284 38/73 days (310/365 of 335). The fractional day is disregarded so that the required condition in such taxable year need exist for only 284 days.

(d) *Rules applicable to status requirements.* For purposes of determining whether an organization meets the conditions and requirements in section 856(a), the following rules shall apply.

(1) *Trustee.* The term "trustee" means a person who holds legal title to the property of the real estate investment trusts, and has such rights and powers as will meet the requirement of "centralization of management" under paragraph (c) of § 301.7701-2 of this chapter. (Regulations on Procedures Administration). Thus, the trustee must have continuing exclusive authority over the management of the trust, the conduct of its affairs, and (except as limited by section 856(d)(3)

Reg. § 1.856-1(d)(1)

and § 1.856-4) the management and disposition of the trust property. For example, such authority will be considered to exist even though the trust instrument grants to the shareholders any or all of the following rights and powers: To elect or remove trustees; to terminate the trust, and to ratify amendments to the trust instrument proposed by the trustee. The existence of a mere fiduciary relationship does not, in itself, make one a trustee for purposes of section 856(a)(1). The trustee will be considered to hold legal title to the property of the trust, for purposes of this subparagraph, whether the title is held in the name of the trust itself, in the name of one or more of the trustees, or in the name of a nominee for the exclusive benefit of the trust.

(2) *Beneficial ownership.* Beneficial ownership shall be evidenced by transferable shares, or by transferable certificates of beneficial interest, and (subject to the provisions of paragraph (c) of this section) must be held by 100 or more persons, determined without reference to any rules of attribution. Provisions in the trust instrument or corporate charter or bylaws which permit the trustee or directors to redeem shares or to refuse to transfer shares in any case where the trustee or directors, in good faith, believe that a failure to redeem shares or that a transfer of shares would result in the loss of status as a real estate investment trust will not render the shares "nontransferable." For purposes of the regulations under part II of subchapter M, the terms "stockholder," "stockholders," "shareholder," and "shareholders" include holders of beneficial interest in a real estate investment trust, the terms "stock," "shares," and "shares of stock" include certificates of beneficial interest, and the term "shares" includes shares of stock.

(3) *Unincorporated organization taxable as a domestic corporation.* The determination of whether an unincorporated organization would be taxable as a domestic corporation, in the absence of the provisions of part II of subchapter M, shall be made in accordance with the provisions of section 7701(a)(3) and (4) and the regulations thereunder and for such purposes an otherwise qualified real estate investment trust is deemed to satisfy the "objective to carry on business" requirement of paragraph (a) of § 301.7701-2 of this chapter (Regulations on Procedure and Administration).

(4) *Property held for sale to customers.* In the case of a taxable year beginning before October 5, 1976, a real estate investment trust may not hold any property (other than foreclosure property) primarily for sale to customers in the ordinary course of its trade or business. Whether property is held for sale to customers in the ordinary course of the trade or business of a real estate investment trust depends upon the facts and circumstances in each case.

(5) *Personal holding company.* A corporation, trust, or association, even though it may otherwise meet the requirements of part II of subchapter M, will not be a real estate investment trust if, by considering all of its gross income as personal holding company income under section 543, it would be a personal holding company as defined in section 542. Thus, if at any time during the last half of the trust's taxable year more than 50 percent in value of its outstanding stock is owned (directly or indirectly under the provisions of section 544) by or for not more than 5 individuals, the stock ownership requirement in section 542(a)(2) will be met and the trust would be a personal holding company. See § 1.857-8, relating to record requirements for purposes of determining whether the trust is a personal holding company.

(e) *Other rules applicable.* To the extent that other provisions of chapter 1 of the Code are not inconsistent with those under part II of subchapter M thereof and the regulations thereunder, such provisions will apply with respect to both the real estate investment trust and its shareholders in the same manner that they would apply to any other organization which would be taxable as a domestic corporation. For example:

(1) Taxable income of a real estate investment trust is computed in the same manner as that of a domestic corporation;

(2) Section 301, relating to distributions of property, applies to distributions by a real estate investment trust in the same manner as it would apply to a domestic corporation;

(3) Sections 302, 303, 304, and 331 are applicable in determining whether distributions by a real estate investment trust are to be treated as in exchange for stock;

(4) Section 305 applies to distributions by a real estate investment trust of its own stock;

(5) Section 311 applies to distributions by a real estate investment trust;

(6) Except as provided in section 857(d), earnings and profits of a real estate investment trust are computed in the same manner as in the case of a domestic corporation;

(7) Section 316, relating to the definition of a dividend, applies to distributions by a real estate investment trust; and

(8) Section 341, relating to collapsible corporations, applies to gain on the sale or exchange of, or a distribution which is in exchange for, stock in

a real estate investment trust in the same manner that it would apply to a domestic corporation.

(f) *Unincorporated status required for certain taxable years.* In the case of a taxable year beginning before October 5, 1976, a real estate investment trust must be an unincorporated trust or unincorporated association. Accordingly, in applying the regulations under part II of subchapter M of the Code with respect to such a taxable year, the term "an unincorporated trust or unincorporated association" is to be substituted for the term "a corporation, trust, or association" each place it appears, and the references to "directors" and "corporate charter or bylaws" are to be disregarded. [Reg. § 1.856-1.]

☐ [*T.D.* 6598, 4-25-62. *Amended by T.D.* 6928, 9-18-67 *and T.D.* 7767, 2-3-81.]

[Reg. § 1.856-2]

§ 1.856-2. Limitations.—(a) *Effective date.* The provisions of part II, subchapter M, chapter 1 of the Code and the regulations thereunder apply only to taxable years of a real estate investment trust beginning after December 31, 1960.

(b) *Election.* Under the provisions of section 856(c)(1), a trust, even though it satisfies the other requirements of part II of subchapter M for the taxable year, will not be considered a "real estate investment trust" for such year, within the meaning of such part II, unless it elects to be a real estate investment trust for such taxable year, or has made such an election for a previous taxable year which has not been terminated or revoked under section 856(g)(1) or (2). The election shall be made by the trust by computing taxable income as a real estate investment trust in its return for the first taxable year for which it desires the election to apply, even though it may have otherwise qualified as a real estate investment trust for a prior year. No other method of making such election is permitted. An election cannot be revoked with respect to a taxable year beginning before October 5, 1976. Thus, the failure of an organization to be a qualified real estate investment trust for a taxable year beginning before October 5, 1976, does not have the effect of revoking a prior election by the organization to be a real estate investment trust, even though the organization is not taxable under part II of subchapter M for such taxable year. See section 856(g) and § 1.856-8 for rules under which an election may be revoked with respect to taxable years beginning after October 4, 1976.

(c) *Gross income requirements.* Section 856(c)(2), (3), and (4) provides that a corporation, trust, or association is not a "real estate investment trust" for a taxable year unless it meets certain requirements with respect to the sources of its gross income for the taxable year. In determining whether the gross income of a real estate investment trust satisfies the percentage requirements of section 856(c)(2), (3), and (4), the following rules shall apply:

(1) *Gross income.* For purposes of both the numerator and denominator in the computation of the specified percentages, the term "gross income" has the same meaning as that term has under section 61 and the regulations thereunder. Thus, in determining the gross income requirements under section 856(c)(2), (3), and (4), a loss from the sale or other disposition of stock, securities, real property, etc. does not enter into the computation.

(2) *Lapse of options.* Under section 856(c)(6)(C), the term "interests in real property" includes options to acquire land or improvements thereon, and options to acquire leaseholds of land and improvements thereon. However, where a corporation, trust, or association writes an option giving the holder the right to acquire land or improvements thereon, or writes an option giving the holder the right to acquire a leasehold of land or improvements thereon, any income that the corporation, trust, or association recognizes because the option expires unexercised is not considered to be gain from the sale or other disposition of real property (including interests in real property) for purposes of section 856(c)(2)(D) and (3)(C). The rule in the preceding sentence also applies for purposes of section 856(c)(4)(C) in determining gain from the sale or other disposition of real property for the 30-percent-of-gross-income limitation.

(3) *Commitment fees.* For purposes of section 856(c)(2)(G) and (3)(G), if consideration is received or accrued for an agreement to make a loan secured by a mortgage covering both real property and other property, or for an agreement to purchase or lease both real property and other property, an apportionment of the consideration is required. The apportionment of consideration received or accrued for an agreement to make a loan secured by a mortgage covering both real property and other property shall be made under the principles of § 1.856-5(c), relating to the apportionment of interest income.

(4) *Holding period of property.* For purposes of the 30-percent limitation of section 856(c)(4), the determination of the period for which property described in such section has been held is governed by the provisions of section 1223 and the regulations thereunder.

Reg. § 1.856-2(c)(4)

(5) *Rents from real property and interest.* See §§ 1.856-4 and 1.856-5 for rules relating to rents from real property and interest.

(d) *Diversification of investment requirements*—(1) *75-percent test.* Section 856(c)(5)(A) requires that at the close of each quarter of the taxable year at least 75 percent of the value of the total assets of the trust be represented by one or more of the following:

(i) Real estate assets;

(ii) Government securities; and

(iii) Cash and cash items (including receivables).

For purposes of this subparagraph the term "receivables" means only those receivables which arise in the ordinary course of the trust's operation and does not include receivables purchased from another person. Subject to the limitations in section 856(c)(5)(B) and subparagraph (2) of this paragraph, the character of the remaining 25 percent (or less) of the value of the total assets is not restricted.

(2) *Limitations on certain securities.* Under section 856(c)(5)(B), not more than 25 percent of the value of the total assets of the trust may be represented by securities other than those described in section 856(c)(5)(A). The ownership of securities under the 25-percent limitation in section 856(c)(5)(B) is further limited in respect of any one issuer to an amount not greater in value than 5 percent of the value of the total assets of the trust and to not more than 10 percent of the outstanding voting securities of such issuer. Thus, if the real estate investment trust meets the 75-percent asset diversification requirement in section 856(c)(5)(A), it will also meet the first test under section 856(c)(5)(B) since it will, of necessity, have not more than 25 percent of its total assets represented by securities other than those described in section 856(c)(5)(A). However, the trust must also meet two additional tests under section 856(c)(5)(B), i.e. it cannot own the securities of any one issuer in an amount (i) greater in value than 5 percent of the value of the trust's total assets, or (ii) representing more than 10 percent of the outstanding voting securities of such issuer.

(3) *Determination of investment status.* The term "total assets" means the gross assets of the trust determined in accordance with generally accepted accounting principles. In order to determine the effect, if any, which an acquisition of any security or other property may have with respect to the status of a trust as a real estate investment trust, section 856(c)(5) requires a revaluation of the trust's assets at the end of the quarter in which such acquisition was made. A revaluation of assets is not required at the end of any quarter during which there has been no acquisition of a security or other property since the mere change in market value of property held by the trust does not, of itself, affect the status of the trust as a real estate investment trust. A change in the nature of "cash items," for example, the prepayment of insurance or taxes, does not constitute the acquisition of "other property" for purposes of this subparagraph. A real estate investment trust shall keep sufficient records as to investments so as to be able to show that it has complied with the provisions of section 856(c)(5) during the taxable year. Such records shall be kept at all times available for inspection by any internal revenue officer or employee and shall be retained so long as the contents thereof may become material in the administration of any internal revenue law.

(4) *Illustrations.* The application of section 856(c)(5) and this paragraph may be illustrated by the following examples:

Example (1). Real Estate Investment Trust M, at the close of the first quarter of its taxable year, has its assets invested as follows:

	Percent
Cash	6
Government securities	7
Real estate assets	63
Securities of various corporations (not exceeding, with respect to any one issuer, 5 percent of the value of the total assets of the trust nor 10 percent of the outstanding voting securities of such issuer)	24
Total	100

Trust M meets the requirements of section 856(c)(5) for that quarter of its taxable year.

Example (2). Real Estate Investment Trust P, at the close of the first quarter of its taxable year, has its assets invested as follows:

	Percent
Cash	6
Government securities	7
Real estate assets	63
Securities of Corporation Z	20
Securities of Corporation X	4
Total	100

Trust P meets the requirement of section 856(c)(5)(A) since at least 75 percent of the value of the total assets is represented by cash, Government securities, and real estate assets. However, Trust P does not meet the diversification requirements of section 856(c)(5)(B) because its investment in the voting securities of Corporation Z exceeds 5 percent of the value of the trust's total assets.

Reg. § 1.856-2(c)(5)

Example (3). Real Estate Investment Trust G, at the close of the first quarter of its taxable year, has its assets invested as follows:

	Percent
Cash	4
Government securities	9
Real estate assets	70
Securities of Corporation S	5
Securities of Corporation L	4
Securities of Corporation U	4
Securities of Corporation M (which equals 25 percent of Corporation M's outstanding voting securities)	4
Total	100

Trust G meets the 75-percent requirement of section 856(c)(5)(A), but does not meet the requirements of section 856(c)(5)(B) because its investment in the voting securities of Corporation M exceeds 10 percent of Corporation M's outstanding voting securities.

Example (4). Real Estate Investment Trust R, at the close of the first quarter of its taxable year (i.e. calendar year), is a qualified real estate investment trust and has its assets invested as follows:

Cash	$ 5,000
Government securities	4,000
Receivables	4,000
Real estate assets	68,000
Securities of Corporation P	4,000
Securities of Corporation O	5,000
Securities of Corporation U	5,000
Securities of Corporation T	5,000
Total assets	$100,000

During the second calendar quarter the stock in Corporation P increases in value to $50,000 while the value of the remaining assets has not changed. If Real Estate Investment Trust R has made no acquisition of stock or other property during such second quarter it will not lose its status as a real estate investment trust merely by reason of the appreciation in the value of P's stock. If, during the third quarter, Trust R acquires stock of Corporation S worth $2,000, such acquisition will necessitate a revaluation of all of the assets of Trust R as follows:

Cash	$ 3,000
Government securities	4,000
Receivables	4,000
Real estate assets	68,000
Securities in Corporation P	50,000
Securities in Corporation O	5,000
Securities in Corporation U	5,000
Securities in Corporation T	5,000
Securities in Corporation S	2,000
Total assets	$146,000

Because of the discrepancy between the value of its various investments and the 25-percent limitation in section 856(c)(5), resulting in part from the acquisition of the stock of Corporation S, Trust R, at the end of the third quarter, loses its status as a real estate investment trust. However, if Trust R, within 30 days after the close of such quarter, eliminates the discrepancy so that it meets the 25-percent limitation, the trust will be considered to have met the requirements of section 856(c)(5) at the close of the third quarter, even though the discrepancy between the value of its investment in Corporation P and the 5-percent limitation in section 856(c)(5) (resulting solely from appreciation) may still exist. If instead of acquiring stock of Corporation S, Trust R had acquired additional stock of Corporation P, then, because of the discrepancy between the value of its investments and both the 5-percent and the 25-percent limitations in section 856(c)(5) resulting in part from this acquisition, Trust R, at the end of the third quarter, would lose its status as a real estate investment trust, unless within 30 days after the close of such quarter both of the discrepancies are eliminated.

Example (5). If, in the previous example, the stock of Corporation P appreciates only to $10,000 during the second quarter and, in the third quarter, Trust R acquires stock of Corporation S worth $1,000, the assets as of the end of the third quarter would be as follows:

Cash	$ 4,000
Government securities	4,000
Receivables	4,000
Real estate assets	68,000
Securities in Corporation P	10,000
Securities in Corporation O	5,000
Securities in Corporation U	5,000
Securities in Corporation T	5,000
Securities in Corporation S	1,000
Total assets	$106,000

Because the discrepancy between the value of its investment in Corporation P and the 5-percent limitation in section 856(c)(5) results solely from appreciation, and because there is no discrepancy between the value of its various investments and the 25-percent limitation, Trust R, at the end of the third quarter, does not lose its status as a real estate investment trust. If, instead of acquiring stock of Corporation S, Trust R had acquired additional stock of Corporation P worth $1,000, then, because of the discrepancy between the value of its investment in Corporation P and the 5-percent limitation resulting in part from this acquisition, Trust R, at the end of the third quarter, would lose its status as a real estate investment trust, unless within 30 days after the close of such quarter this discrepancy is eliminated. [Reg. § 1.856-2.]

☐ [T.D. 6598, 4-25-62. Amended by T.D. 7728, 10-31-80 and T.D. 7767, 2-3-81.]

Reg. § 1.856-2(d)(4)

[Reg. § 1.856-3]

§ 1.856-3. *Definitions.*—For purposes of the regulations under part II, subchapter M, chapter 1 of the Code, the following definitions shall apply.

(a) *Value.* The term "value" means, with respect to securities for which market quotations are readily available, the market value of such securities; and with respect to other securities and assets, fair value as determined in good faith by the trustees of the real estate investment trust. In the case of securities of other qualified real estate investment trusts, fair value shall not exceed market value or asset value, whichever is higher.

(b) *Real estate assets.*—(1) *In general.* The term "real estate assets" means real property, interests in mortgages on real property (including interests in mortgages on leaseholds of land or improvements thereon), and shares in other qualified real estate investment trusts. The term "mortgages on real property" includes deeds of trust on real property.

(2) *Treatment of REMIC interests as real estate assets*—(i) *In general.* If, for any calendar quarter, at least 95 percent of a REMIC's assets (as determined in accordance with § 1.860F-4(e)(1)(ii) or § 1.6049-7(f)(3)) are real estate assets (as defined in paragraph (b)(1) of this section), then, for that calendar quarter, all the regular and residual interests in that REMIC are treated as real estate assets and, except as provided in paragraph (b)(2)(iii) of this section, any amount includible in gross income with respect to those interests is treated as interest on obligations secured by mortgages on real property. If less than 95 percent of a REMIC's assets are real estate assets, then the real estate investment trust is treated as holding directly its proportionate share of the assets and as receiving directly its proportionate share of the income of the REMIC. See §§ 1.860F-4(e)(1)(ii)(B) and 1.6049-7(f)(3) for information required to be provided to regular and residual interest holders if the 95-percent test is not met.

(ii) *Treatment of REMIC assets for section 856 purposes*—(A) *Manufactured housing treated as real estate asset.* For purposes of paragraphs (b)(1) and (2) of this section, the term "real estate asset" includes manufactured housing treated as a single family residence under section 25(e)(10).

(B) *Status of cash flow investments.* For purposes of this paragraph (b)(2), cash flow investments (as defined in section 860G(a)(6) and § 1.860G-2(g)(1)) are real estate assets.

(iii) *Certain contingent interest payment obligations held by a REIT.* If a REIT holds a residual interest in a REMIC for a principal purpose of avoiding the limitation set out in section 856(f) (concerning interest based on mortgagor net profits) or section 856(j) (concerning shared appreciation provisions), then, even if the REMIC satisfies the 95-percent test of paragraph (b)(i) of this section, the REIT is treated as receiving directly the REMIC's items of income for purposes of section 856.

(c) *Interests in real property.* The term "interests in real property" includes fee ownership and co-ownership of land or improvements thereon, leaseholds of land or improvements thereon, options to acquire land or improvements thereon, and options to acquire leaseholds of land or improvements thereon. The term also includes timeshare interests that represent an undivided fractional fee interest, or undivided leasehold interest, in real property, and that entitle the holders of the interests to the use and enjoyment of the property for a specified period of time each year. The term also includes stock held by a person as a tenant-stockholder in a cooperative housing corporation (as those terms are defined in section 216). Such term does not, however, include mineral, oil, or gas royalty interests, such as a retained economic interest in coal or iron ore with respect to which the special provisions of section 631(c) apply.

(d) *Real property.* The term "real property" means land or improvements thereon, such as buildings or other inherently permanent structures thereon (including items which are structural components of such buildings or structures). In addition, the term "real property" includes interests in real property. Local law definitions will not be controlling for purposes of determining the meaning of the term "real property" as used in section 856 and the regulations thereunder. The term includes, for example, the wiring in a building, plumbing systems, central heating or central air-conditioning machinery, pipes or ducts, elevators or escalators installed in the building, or other items which are structural components of a building or other permanent structure. The term does not include assets accessory to the operation of a business, such as machinery, printing press, transportation equipment which is not a structural component of the building, office equipment, refrigerators, individual air-conditioning units, grocery counters, furnishings of a motel, hotel, or office building, etc. even though such items may be termed fixtures under local law.

(e) *Securities.* The term "securities" does not include "interests in real property" or "real estate assets" as those terms are defined in section 856 and this section.

(f) *Qualified real estate investment trusts.* The term "qualified real estate investment trust" means a real estate investment trust within the meaning of part II of subchapter M which is taxable under such part as a real estate investment trust. For purposes of the 75-percent requirement in section 856(c)(5)(A), the trust whose stock has been included by another trust as "real estate assets" must be a "qualified real estate investment trust" for its full taxable year in which falls the close of each quarter of the trust's taxable year for which the computation is made. For example, Real Estate Investment Trust Z for its taxable year ending December 31, 1963, holds as "real estate assets" stock in Real Estate Investment Trust Y, which is also on a calendar year.

If Trust Y is not a qualified real estate investment trust for its full taxable year ending December 31, 1963, Trust Z may not include the stock of Trust Y as "real estate assets" in computing the 75-percent requirement as of the close of any quarter of its taxable year ending December 31, 1963.

(g) *Partnership interest.* In the case of a real estate investment trust which is a partner in a partnership, as defined in section 7701(a)(2) and the regulations thereunder, the trust will be deemed to own its proportionate share of each of the assets of the partnership and will be deemed to be entitled to the income of the partnership attributable to such share. For purposes of section 856, the interest of a partner in the partnership's assets shall be determined in accordance with his capital interest in the partnership. The character of the various assets in the hands of the partnership and items of gross income of the partnership shall retain the same character in the hands of the partners for all purposes of section 856. Thus, for example, if the trust owns a 30-percent capital interest in a partnership which owns a piece of rental property the trust will be treated as owning 30 percent of such property and as being entitled to 30 percent of the rent derived from the property by the partnership. Similarly, if the partnership holds any property primarily for sale to customers in the ordinary course of its trade or business, the trust will be treated as holding its proportionate share of such property primarily for such purpose. Also, for example, where a partnership sells real property or a trust sells its interest in a partnership which owns real property, any gross income realized from such sale, to the extent that it is attributable to the real property, shall be deemed gross income from the sale or disposition of real property held for either the period that the partnership has held the real property or the period that the trust was a member of the partnership, whichever is the shorter.

(h) *Net capital gain.* The term "net capital gain" means the excess of the net long-term capital gain for the taxable year over the net shortterm capital loss for the taxable year. [Reg. § 1.856-3.]

☐ [*T.D.* 6598, 4-25-62. *Amended by T.D.* 6841, 7-26-65; *T.D.* 7767, 2-3-81 *and T.D.* 8458, 12-23-93.]

[Reg. § 1.856-4]

§ 1.856-4. Rents from real property.—(a) *In general.* Subject to the exceptions of section 856(d) and paragraph (b) of this section, the term "rents from real property" means, generally, the gross amounts received for the use of, or the right to use, real property of the real estate investment trust.

(b) *Amounts specifically included or excluded*—(1) *Charges for customary services.* For taxable years beginning after October 4, 1976, the term "rents from real property", for purposes of paragraphs (2) and (3) of section 856(c), includes charges for services customarily furnished or rendered in connection with the rental of real property, whether or not the charges are separately stated. Services furnished to the tenants of a particular building will be considered as customary if, in the geographic market in which the building is located, tenants in buildings which are of a similar class (such as luxury apartment buildings) are customarily provided with the service. The furnishing of water, heat, light, and air-conditioning, the cleaning of windows, public entrances, exits, and lobbies, the performance of general maintenance and of janitorial and cleaning services, the collection of trash, and the furnishing of elevator services, telephone answering services, incidental storage space, laundry equipment, watchman or guard services, parking facilities, and swimming pool facilities are examples of services which are customarily furnished to the tenants of a particular class of buildings in many geographic marketing areas. Where it is customary, in a particular geographic marketing area, to furnish electricity or other utilities to tenants in buildings of a particular class, the submetering of such utilities to tenants in such buildings will be considered a customary service. To qualify as a service customarily furnished, the service must be furnished or rendered to the tenants of the real estate investment trust or, primarily for the convenience or benefit of the tenant, to the guests, customers, or subtenants of the tenant. The service must be furnished through an independent contractor from whom the trust does not derive or receive any income. See paragraph (b)(5) of this

Reg. § 1.856-4(b)(1)

section. For taxable years beginning before October 5, 1976, the rules in paragraph (b)(3) of 26 CFR 1.856-4 (revised as of April 1, 1977), relating to the furnishing of services, shall continue to apply.

(2) *Amounts received with respect to certain personal property.* (i) *In general.* In the case of taxable years beginning after October 4, 1976, rent attributable to personal property that is leased under, or in connection with, the lease of real property is treated under section 856(d)(1)(C) as "rents from real property" (and thus qualified for purposes of the income source requirements) if the rent attributable to the personal property is not more than 15 percent of the total rent received or accrued under the lease for the taxable year. If, however, the rent attributable to personal property is greater than 15 percent of the total rent received or accrued under the lease for the taxable year, then the portion of the rent from the lease that is attributable to personal property will not qualify as "rents from real property".

(ii) *Application.* In general, the 15-percent test in section 856(d)(1)(C) is applied separately to each lease of real property. However, where the real estate investment trust rents all (or a portion of all) the units in a multiple unit project under substantially similar leases (such as the leasing of apartments in an apartment building or complex to individual tenants), the 15-percent test may be applied with respect to the aggregate rent received or accrued for the taxable year under the similar leases of the property, by using the average of the trust's aggregate adjusted bases of all the personal property subject to such leases, and the average of the trust's aggregate adjusted bases of all real and personal property subject to such leases. A lease of a furnished apartment is not considered to be substantially similar to a lease of an unfurnished apartment (including an apartment where the trust provides only personal property, such as major appliances, that is commonly provided by a landlord in connection with the rental of unfurnished living quarters).

(iii) *Taxable years beginning before October 5, 1976.* In the case of taxable years beginning before October 5, 1976, any amount of rent that is attributable to personal property does not qualify as rent from real property.

(3) *Disqualification of rent which depends on income or profits of any person.* Except as provided in paragraph (b)(6)(ii) of this section, no amount received or accrued, directly or indirectly, with respect to any real property (or personal property leased under, or in connection with, real property) qualifies as "rents from real property"

where the determination of the amount depends in whole or in part on the income or profits derived by any person from the property. However, any amount so accrued or received shall not be excluded from the term "rents from real property" solely by reason of being based on a fixed percentage or percentages of receipts or sales (whether or not receipts or sales are adjusted for returned merchandise, or Federal, State, or local sales taxes). Thus, for example, "rents from real property" would include rents where the lease provides for differing percentages of receipts or sales from different departments or from separate floors of a retail store so long as each percentage is fixed at the time of entering into the lease and a change in such percentage is not renegotiated during the term of the lease (including any renewal periods of the lease) in a manner which has the effect of basing the rent on income or profits. See paragraph (b)(6) of this section for rules relating to certain amounts received or accrued by a trust which are considered to be based on the income or profits of a sublessee of the prime tenant. The amount received or accrued as rent for the taxable year which is based on a fixed percentage or percentages of the lessee's receipts or sales reduced by escalation receipts (including those determined under a formula clause) will qualify as "rents from real property". Escalation receipts include amounts received by a prime tenant from subtenants by reason of an agreement that rent shall be increased to reflect all or a portion of an increase in real estate taxes, property insurance, operating costs of the prime tenant, or similar items customarily included in lease escalation clauses. Where in accordance with the terms of an agreement and amount received or accrued as rent for the taxable year includes both a fixed rental and a percentage of all or a portion of the lessee's income or profits, neither the fixed rental nor the additional amount will qualify as "rents from real property". However, where the amount received or accrued for the taxable year under such an agreement includes only the fixed rental, the determination of which does not depend in whole or in part on the income or profits derived by the lessee, such amount may qualify as "rents from real property". An amount received or accrued as rent for the taxable year which consists, in whole or in part, of one or more percentages of the lessee's receipts or sales in excess of determinable dollar amounts may qualify as "rents from real property", but only if two conditions exist. First, the determinable amounts must not depend in whole or in part on the income or profits of the lessee. Second, the percentages and, in the case of leases entered into after July 7, 1978, the determinable amounts, must be fixed at

Reg. § 1.856-4(b)(2)

the time the lease is entered into and a change in percentages and determinable amounts is not re-negotiated during the term of the lease (including any renewal periods of the lease) in a manner which has the effect of basing rent on income or profits. In any event, an amount will not qualify as "rents from real property" if, considering the lease and all the surrounding circumstances, the arrangement does not conform with normal business practice but is in reality used as a means of basing the rent on income or profits. The provisions of this subparagraph may be illustrated by the following example:

Example. A real estate investment trust owns land underlying an office building. On January 1, 1975, the trust leases the land for 50 years to a prime tenant for an annual rental of $100x plus 20% of the prime tenant's annual gross receipts from the office building in excess of a fixed base amount of $5,000x and 10 percent of such gross receipts in excess of $10,000x. For this purpose the lease defines gross receipts as all amounts received by the prime tenant from occupancy tenants pursuant to leases of space in the office building reduced by the amount by which real estate taxes, property insurance, and operating costs related to the office building for a particular year exceed the amount of such items for 1974. The exclusion from gross receipts of increases since 1974 in real estate taxes, property insurance, and other expenses relating to the office building reflects the fact that the prime tenant passes on to occupancy tenants by way of a customary lease escalation provision the risk that such expenses might increase during the term of an occupancy lease. The exclusion from gross receipts of these expense escalation items will not cause the rental received by the real estate investment trust from the prime tenant to fail to qualify as "rents from real property" for purposes of section 856(c).

(4) *Disqualification of amounts received from persons owned in whole or in part by the trust.* "Rents from real property" does not include any amount received or accrued, directly or indirectly, from any person in which the real estate investment trust owns, at any time during the taxable year, the specified percentage or number of shares of stock (or interest in the assets or net profits) of that person. Any amount received from such person will not qualify as "rents from real property" if such person is a corporation and the trust owns 10 percent or more of the total combined voting power of all classes of its stock entitled to vote or 10 percent or more of the total number of shares of all classes of its outstanding stock, or if such person is not a corporation and the trust owns a 10-percent-or-more interest in its assets or net profits. For example, a trust leases an office building to a tenant for which it receives rent of $100,000 for the taxable year 1962. The lessee of the building subleases space to various subtenants for which it receives gross rent of $500,000 for the year 1962. The trust owns 15 percent of the total assets of an unincorporated subtenant. The rent paid by this subtenant for the taxable year is $50,000. Therefore, $10,000 (50,000/500,000 × $100,000) of the rent paid to the trust does not qualify as "rents from real property". Where the real estate investment trust receives, directly or indirectly, any amount of rent from any person in which it owns any proprietary interest, the trust shall submit, at the time it files its return for the taxable year (or before June 1, 1962, whichever is later), a schedule setting forth—

(i) The name and address of such person and the amount received as rent from such person; and

(ii) If such person is a corporation, the highest percentage of the total combined voting power of all classes of its stock entitled to vote, and the highest percentage of the total number of shares of all classes of its outstanding stock, owned by the trust at any time during the trust's taxable year; or

(iii) If such person is not a corporation, the highest percentage of the trust's interest in the assets or net profits of such person, owned by the trust at any time during its taxable year.

(5) *Furnishing of services or management of property must be through an independent contractor*—(i) *In general.* No amount received or accrued, directly or indirectly, with respect to any real property (or any personal property leased under, or in connection with, the real property) qualifies as "rents from real property" if the real estate investment trust furnishes or renders services to the tenants of the property or manages or operates the property, other than through an independent contractor from whom the trust itself does not derive or receive any income. The prohibition against the trust deriving or receiving any income from the independent contractor applies regardless of the source from which the income was derived by the independent contractor. Thus, for example, the trust may not receive any dividends from the independent contractor. The requirement that the trust not receive any income from an independent contractor requires that the relationship between the two be an arm's-length relationship. The independent contractor must be adequately compensated for any services which are performed for the trust. Compensation to an independent contractor determined by reference

Reg. § 1.856-4(b)(5)

to an unadjusted percentage of gross rents will generally be considered to be adequate where the percentage is reasonable taking into account the going rate of compensation for managing similar property in the same locality, the services rendered, and other relevant factors. The independent contractor must not be an employee of the trust (*i.e.*, the manner in which he carries out his duties as independent contractor must not be subject to the control of the trust). Although the cost of services which are customarily rendered or furnished in connection with the rental of real property may be borne by the trust, the services must be furnished or rendered through an independent contractor. Furthermore, the facilities through which the services are furnished must be maintained and operated by an independent contractor. For example, if a heating plant is located in the building, it must be maintained and operated by an independent contractor. To the extent that services (other than those customarily furnished or rendered in connection with the rental of real property) are rendered to the tenants of the property by the independent contractor, the cost of the services must be borne by the independent contractor, a separate charge must be made for the services, the amount of the separate charge must be received and retained by the independent contractor, and the independent contractor must be adequately compensated for the services.

(ii) *Trustee or director functions.* The trustees or directors of the real estate investment trust are not required to delegate or contract out their fiduciary duty to manage the trust itself, as distinguished from rendering or furnishing services to the tenants of its property or managing or operating the property. Thus, the trustees or directors may do all those things necessary, in their fiduciary capacities, to manage and conduct the affairs of the trust itself. For example, the trustees or directors may establish rental terms, choose tenants, enter into and renew leases, and deal with taxes, interest, and insurance, relating to the trust's property. The trustees or directors may also make capital expenditures with respect to the trust's property (as defined in section 263) and may make decisions as to repairs of the trust's property (of the type which would be deductible under section 162), the cost of which may be borne by the trust.

(iii) *Independent contractor defined.* The term "independent contractor" means—

(*a*) A person who does not own, directly or indirectly, at any time during the trust's taxable year more than 35 percent of the shares in the real estate investment trust, or

(*b*) A person—

(1) If a corporation, not more than 35 percent of the total combined voting power of whose stock (or 35 percent of the total shares of all classes of whose stock), or

(2) If not a corporation, not more than 35 percent of the interest in whose assets or net profits

is owned, directly or indirectly, at any time during the trust's taxable year by one or more persons owning at any time during such taxable year 35 percent or more of the shares in the trust.

(iv) *Information required.* The real estate investment trust shall submit with its return for the taxable year (or before June 1, 1962, whichever is later) a statement setting forth the name and address of each independent contractor; and

(*a*) The highest percentage of the outstanding shares in the trust owned at any time during its taxable year by such independent contractor and by any person owning at any time during such taxable year any shares of stock or interest in the independent contractor.

(*b*) If the independent contractor is a corporation such statement shall set forth the highest percentage of the total combined voting power of its stock and the highest percentage of the total number of shares of all classes of its stock owned at any time during its taxable year by any person owning shares in the trust at any time during such taxable year.

(*c*) If the independent contractor is not a corporation such statement shall set forth the highest percentage of any interest in its assets or net profits owned at any time during its taxable year by any person owning shares in the trust at any time during such taxable year.

(6) *Amounts based on income or profits of subtenants.* (i) Except as provided in paragraph (b)(6)(ii) of this section, if a trust leases real property to a tenant under terms other than solely on a fixed sum rental (for example, a percentage of the tenant's gross receipts), and the tenant subleases all or a part of such property under an agreement which provides for a rental based in whole or in part on the income or profits of the sublessee, the entire amount of the rent received by the trust from the prime tenant with respect to such property is disqualified as "rents from real property."

(ii) *Exception.* For taxable years beginning after October 4, 1976, section 856(d)(4) provides an exception to the general rule that amounts received or accrued, directly or indirectly, by a real estate investment trust do not qualify as rents from real property if the determination of the amount depends in whole or in part on the

Reg. § 1.856-4(b)(6)

income or profits derived by any person from the property. This exception applies where the trust rents property to a tenant (the prime tenant) for a rental which is based, in whole or in part, on a fixed percentage or percentages of the receipts or sales of the prime tenant, and the rent which the trust receives or accrues from the prime tenant pursuant to the lease would not qualify as "rents from real property" solely because the prime tenant receives or accrues from subtenants (including concessionaires) rents or other amounts based on the income or profits derived by a person from the property. Under the exception, only a proportionate part of the rent received or accrued by the trust does not qualify as "rents from real property." The proportionate part of the rent received or accrued by the trust which is nonqualified is the lesser of the following two amounts:

(A) The rent received or accrued by the trust from the prime tenant pursuant to the lease, that is based on a fixed percentage or percentages of receipts or sales, or

(B) The product determined by multiplying the total rent which the trust receives or accrues from the prime tenant pursuant to the lease by a fraction, the numerator of which is the rent or other amount received by the prime tenant that is based, in whole or in part, on the income or profits derived by any person from the property, and the denominator of which is the total rent or other amount received by the prime tenant from the property. For example, assume that a real estate investment trust owns land underlying a shopping center. The trust rents the land to the owner of the shopping center for an annual rent of $10.00 plus 2 percent of the gross receipts which the prime tenant receives from subtenants who lease space in the shopping center. Assume further that, for the year in question, the prime tenant derives total rent from the shopping center of $100.00 and, of that amount, $25.00 is received from subtenants whose rent is based, in whole or in part, on the income or profits derived from the property. Accordingly, the trust will receive a total rent of $12.00, of which $2.00 is based on a percentage of the gross receipts of the prime tenant. The portion of the rent which is disqualified is the lesser of $2.00 (the rent received by the trust which is based on a percentage of gross receipts), or $3.00 ($2.00 multiplied by $25.00/$100.00). Accordingly, $10.00 of the rent received by the trust qualifies as "rents from real property" and $2.00 does not qualify.

(7) *Attribution rules.* Paragraphs (2) and (3) of section 856(d) relate to direct or indirect ownership of stock, assets, or net profits by the persons described therein. For purposes of determining such direct or indirect ownership, the rules prescribed by section 318(a) (for determining the ownership of stock) shall apply except that "10 percent" shall be substituted for "50 percent" in section 318(a)(2)(C) and (3)(C). [Reg. § 1.856-4.]

☐ [*T.D.* 6598, 4-25-62. *Amended by T.D.* 6969, 8-22-68 *and by T.D.* 7767, 2-3-81.]

[Reg. § 1.856-5]

§ 1.856-5. Interest.—(a) *In general.* In computing the percentage requirements in section 856(c)(2)(B) and (3)(B), the term "interest" includes only an amount which constitutes compensation for the use or forbearance of money. For example, a fee received or accrued by a lender which is in fact a charge for services performed for a borrower rather than a charge for the use of borrowed money is not includable as interest.

(b) *Where amount depends on income or profits of any person.* Except as provided in paragraph (d) of this section, any amount received or accrued, directly or indirectly, with respect to an obligation is not includable as interest for purposes of section 856(c)(2)(B) and (3)(B) if, under the principles set forth in paragraph (b)(3) and (6)(i) of § 1.856-4, the determination of the amount depends in whole or in part on the income or profits of any person (whether or not derived from property secured by the obligation). Thus, for example, if in accordance with a loan agreement an amount is received or accrued by the trust with respect to an obligation which includes both a fixed amount of interest and a percentage of the borrower's income or profits, neither the fixed interest nor the amount based upon the percentage will qualify as interest for purposes of section 856(c)(2)(B) and (3)(B). This paragraph and paragraph (d) of this section apply only to amounts received or accrued in taxable years beginning after October 4, 1976, pursuant to loans made after May 27, 1976. For purposes of the preceding sentence, a loan is considered to be made before May 28, 1976, if it is made pursuant to a binding commitment entered into before May 28, 1976.

(c) *Apportionment of interest*—(1) *In general.* Where a mortgage covers both real property and other property, an apportionment of the interest income must be made for purposes of the 75-percent requirement of section 856(c)(3). For purposes of the 75-percent requirement, the apportionment shall be made as follows:

(i) If the loan value of the real property is equal to or exceeds the amount of the loan, then the entire interest income shall be apportioned to the real property.

Reg. § 1.856-5(c)(1)

(ii) If the amount of the loan exceeds the loan value of the real property, then the interest income apportioned to the real property is an amount equal to the interest income multiplied by a fraction, the numerator of which is the loan value of the real property, and the denominator of which is the amount of the loan. The interest income apportioned to the other property is an amount equal to the excess of the total interest income over the interest income apportioned to the real property.

(2) *Loan value.* For purposes of this paragraph, the loan value of the real property is the fair market value of the property, determined as of the date on which the commitment by the trust to make the loan becomes binding on the trust. In the case of a loan purchased by the trust, the loan value of the real property is the fair market value of the property, determined as of the date on which the commitment by the trust to purchase the loan becomes binding on the trust. However, in the case of a construction loan or other loan made for purposes of improving or developing real property, the loan value of the real property is the fair market value of the land plus the reasonably estimated cost of the improvements or developments (other than personal property) which will secure the loan and which are to be constructed from the proceeds of the loan. The fair market value of the land and the reasonably estimated cost of improvements or developments shall be determined as of the date on which a commitment to make the loan becomes binding on the trust. If the trust does not make the construction loan but commits itself to provide long-term financing following completion of construction, the loan value of the real property is determined by using the principles for determining the loan value for a construction loan. Moreover, if the mortgage on the real property is given as additional security (or as a substitute for other security) for the loan after the trust's commitment is binding, the real property loan value is its fair market value when it becomes security for the loan (or, if earlier, when the borrower makes a binding commitment to add or substitute the property as security).

(3) *Amount of loan.* For purposes of this paragraph, the amount of the loan means the highest principal amount of the loan outstanding during the taxable year.

(d) *Exception.* Section 856(f)(2) provides an exception to the general rule that amounts received, directly or indirectly, with respect to an obligation do not qualify as "interest" where the determination of the amounts depends in whole or in part on the income or profits of any person. The exception applies where the trust receives or accrues, with respect to the obligation of its debtor, an amount that is based in whole or in part on a fixed percentage or percentages of receipts or sales of the debtor, and the amount would not qualify as interest solely because the debtor has receipts or sale proceeds that are based on the income or profits of any person. Under this exception only a proportionate part of the amount received or accrued by the trust fails to qualify as interest for purposes of the percentage-of-income requirements of section 856(c)(2) and (3). The proportionate part of the amount received or accrued by the trust that is non-qualified is the lesser of the following two amounts:

(1) The amount received or accrued by the trust from the debtor with respect to the obligation that is based on a fixed percentage or percentages of receipts or sales, or

(2) The product determined by multiplying by a fraction the total amount received or accrued by the trust from the debtor with respect to the obligation. The numerator of the fraction is the amount of receipts or sales of the debtor that is based, in whole or in part, on the income or profits of any person and the denominator is the total amount of the receipts or sales of the debtor. For purposes of the preceding sentence, the only receipts or sales to be taken into account are those taken into account in determining the payment to the trust pursuant to the loan agreement. [Reg. § 1.856-5.]

☐ [T.D. 7767, 2-3-81.]

[Reg. § 1.856-6]

§ 1.856-6. *Foreclosure property.*—(a) *In general.* Under section 856(e) a real estate investment trust may make an irrevocable election to treat as "foreclosure property" certain real property (including interests in real property), and any personal property incident to the real property, acquired by the trust after December 31, 1973. This section prescribes rules relating to the election, including rules relating to property eligible for the election. This section also prescribes rules relating to extensions of the general two-year period (hereinafter the "grace period") during which property retains its status as foreclosure property, as well as rules relating to early termination of the grace period under section 856(e)(4). The election to treat property as foreclosure property does not alter the character of the income derived therefrom (other than for purposes of section 856(c)(2)(F) and (c)(3)(F)). For example, if foreclosure property is sold, the determination of whether it is property described in section 1221(1) will not be affected by the fact that it is foreclosure property.

Reg. § 1.856-6(a)

Real Estate Investment Trusts

See p. 20,601 for regulations not amended to reflect law changes

(b) *Property eligible for the election*—(1) *Rules relating to acquisitions.* In general, the trust must acquire the property after December 31, 1973, as the result of having bid in the property at foreclosure, or having otherwise reduced the property to ownership or possession by agreement or process of law, after there was default (or default was imminent) on a lease of the property (where the trust was the lessor) or on an indebtedness owed to the trust which the property secured. Foreclosure property which secured an indebtedness owed to the trust is acquired for purposes of section 856(e) on the date on which the trust acquires ownership of the property for Federal income tax purposes. Foreclosure property which a trust owned and leased to another is acquired for purposes of section 856(e) on the date on which the trust acquires possession of the property from its lessee. A trust will not be considered to have acquired ownership of property for purposes of section 856(e) where it takes control of the property as a mortgagee-in-possession and cannot receive any profit or sustain any loss with respect to the property except as a creditor of the mortgagor. A trust may be considered to have acquired ownership of property for purposes of section 856(e) even though legal title to the property is held by another person. For example, where, upon foreclosure of a mortgage held by the trust, legal title to the property is acquired in the name of a nominee for the exclusive benefit of the trust and the trust is the equitable owner of the property, the trust will be considered to have acquired ownership of the property for purposes of section 856(e). Generally, the fact that under local law the mortgagor has a right of redemption after foreclosure is not relevant in determining whether the trust has acquired ownership of the property for purposes of section 856(e). Property is not ineligible for the election solely because the property, in addition to securing an indebtedness owed to the trust, also secures debts owed to other creditors. Property eligible for the election includes a building or other improvement which has been constructed on land owned by the trust and which is acquired by the trust upon default of a lease of the land.

(2) *Personal property.* Personal property (including personal property not subject to a mortgage or lease of the real property) will be considered incident to a particular item of real property if the personal property is used in a trade or business conducted on the property or the use of the personal property is otherwise an ordinary and necessary corollary of the use to which the real property is put. In the case of a hotel, such items as furniture, appliances, linens, china, food, etc. would be examples of incidental personal property. Personal property incident to the real property is eligible for the election even though it is acquired after the real property is acquired or is placed in the building or other improvement in the course of the completion of construction.

(3) *Property with respect to which default is anticipated.* Property is not eligible for the election to be treated as foreclosure property if the loan or lease with respect to which the default occurs (or is imminent) was made or entered into (or the lease or indebtedness was acquired) by the trust with an intent to evict or foreclose, or when the trust knew or had reason to know that default would occur ("improper knowledge"). For purposes of the preceding sentence, a trust will not be considered to have improper knowledge with respect to a particular lease or loan if the lease or loan was made pursuant to a binding commitment entered into by the trust at a time when it did not have improper knowledge. Moreover, if the trust, in an attempt to avoid default or foreclosure, advances additional amounts to the borrower in excess of amounts contemplated in the original loan commitment or modifies the lease or loan, such advance or modification will be considered not to have been made with an intent to evict or foreclose, or with improper knowledge, unless the original loan or lease was entered into with that intent or knowledge.

(c) *Election*—(1) *In general.* (i) An election to treat property as foreclosure property applies to all of the eligible real property acquired in the same taxable year by the trust upon the default (or as a result of the imminence of default) on a particular lease (where the trust is the lessor) or on a particular indebtedness owed to the trust. For example, if a loan made by a trust is secured by two separate tracts of land located in different cities, and in the same taxable year the trust acquires both tracts on foreclosure upon the default (or imminence of default) of the loan, the trust must include both tracts in the election. For a further example, the trust may choose to make a separate election for only one of the tracts if they are acquired in different taxable years or were not security for the same loan. If real property subject to the same election is acquired at different times in the same taxable year, the grace period for a particular property begins when that property is acquired.

(ii) If the trust acquires separate pieces of real property that secure the same indebtedness (or are under the same lease) in different taxable years because the trust delays acquiring one of them until a later taxable year, and the primary purpose for the delay is to include only one of them in an election, then if the trust makes an

Reg. § 1.856-6(c)(1)

election for one piece it must also make an election for the other piece. A trust will not be considered to have delayed the acquisition of property for this purpose if there is a legitimate business reason for the delay (such as an attempt to avoid foreclosure by further negotiations with the debtor or lessee).

(iii) All of the eligible personal property incident to the real property must also be included in the election.

(2) *Time for making election.* The election to treat property as foreclosure property must be made on or before the due date (including extensions of time) for filing the trust's income tax return for the taxable year in which the trust acquires the property with respect to which the election is being made, or April 3, 1975, whichever is later.

(3) *Manner of making the election.* An election made after February 6, 1981, shall be made by a statement attached to the income tax return for the taxable year in which the trust acquired the property with respect to which the election is being made. The statement shall indicate that the election is made under section 856(e) and shall identify the property to which the election applies. The statement shall also set forth—

(i) The name, address, and taxpayer identification number of the trust,

(ii) The date the property was acquired by the trust, and

(iii) A brief description of how the real property was acquired, including the name of the person or persons from whom the real property was acquired and a description of the lease or indebtedness with respect to which default occurred or was imminent.

An election made on or before February 6, 1981, shall be filed in the manner prescribed in 26 CFR 10.1 (f) (revised as of April 1, 1977) (temporary regulations relating to the election to treat property as foreclosure property) as in effect when the election is made.

(4) *Status of taxpayer.* In general, a taxpayer may make an election with respect to an acquisition of property only if the taxpayer is a qualified real estate investment trust for the taxable year in which the acquisition occurs. If, however, the taxpayer establishes, to the satisfaction of the district director for the internal revenue district in which the taxpayer maintains its principal place of business or principal office or agency, that its failure to be a qualified real estate investment trust for a taxable year was due to reasonable cause and not due to willful neglect, the taxpayer may make the election with respect to property acquired in such taxable year. The principles of §§ 1.856-7(c) and 1.856-8(d) (including the principles relating to expert advice) will apply in determining whether, for purposes of this subparagraph, the failure of the taxpayer to be a qualified real estate investment trust for the taxable year in which the property is acquired was due to reasonable cause and not due to willful neglect. If a taxpayer makes a valid election to treat property as foreclosure property, the property will not lose its status as foreclosure property solely because the taxpayer is not a qualified real estate investment trust for a subsequent taxable year (including a taxable year which encompasses an extension of the grace period). However, the rules relating to the termination of foreclosure property status in section 856(e)(4) (but not the tax on income from foreclosure property imposed by section 857(b)(4)) apply to the year in which the property is acquired and all subsequent years, even though the taxpayer is not a qualified real estate investment trust for such year.

(d) *Termination of 2-year grace period; subsequent leases*—(1) *In general.* Under section 856(e)(4)(A), all real property (and any incidental personal property) for which a particular election has been made (see paragraph (c)(1) of this section) shall cease to be foreclosure property on the first day (occurring on or after the day on which the trust acquired the property) on which the trust either—

(i) Enters into a lease with respect to any of the property which, by its terms, will give rise to income of the trust which is not described in section 856(c)(3) (other than section 856(c)(3)(F)), or

(ii) Receives or accrues, directly or indirectly, any amount which is not described in section 856(c)(3) (other than section 856(c)(3)(F)) pursuant to a lease with respect to any of the real property entered into by the trust on or after the day the trust acquired the property.

For example, assume the trust acquires, in a particular taxable year, a shopping center upon the default of an indebtedness owed to the trust. Also assume that the trust subsequently enters into a lease with respect to one of several stores in the shopping center that requires the lessee to pay rent to the trust which is not income described in section 856(c)(3) (other than section 856(c)(3)(F)). In such case, the entire shopping center will cease to be foreclosure property on the day the trust enters into the lease.

(2) *Extensions or renewals of leases.* Generally, the extension or renewal of a lease of foreclosure property will be treated as the entering into of a new lease only if the trust has a right to

Reg. § 1.856-6(c)(2)

renegotiate the terms of the lease. If, however, by operation of law or by contract, the acquisition of the foreclosure property by the trust terminates a preexisting lease of the property, or gives the trust a right to terminate the lease, then for purposes of section 856(e)(4)(A), a trust, in such circumstances, will not be considered to have entered into a lease with respect to the property solely because the terms of the preexisting lease are continued in effect after foreclosure without substantial modification. The letting of rooms in a hotel or motel does not constitute the entering into a lease for purposes of section 856(e)(4)(A).

(3) *Rent attributable to personal property.* Solely for the purposes of section 856(e)(4)(A), if a trust enters into a lease with respect to real property on or after the day upon which the trust acquires such real property by foreclosure, and a portion of the rent from such lease is attributable to personal property which is foreclosure property incident to such real property, such rent attributable to the incidental personal property will not be considered to terminate the status of such real property (or such incidental personal property) as foreclosure property.

(e) *Termination of 2-year grace period; completion of construction*—(1) *In general.* Under section 856(e)(4)(B), all real property (and any incidental personal property) for which a particular election has been made (see paragraph (c)(1) of this section) shall cease to be foreclosure property on the first day (occurring on or after the day on which the trust acquired the property) on which any construction takes place on the property, other than completion of a building (or completion of any other improvement) where more than 10 percent of the construction of the building (or other improvement) was completed before default became imminent. If more than one default occurred with respect to an indebtedness or lease in respect of which there is an acquisition, the more-than-10-percent test (including the rules prescribed in this paragraph relating to the test) will not be applied at the time a particular default became imminent if it is clear that the acquisition did not occur as the result of such default. For example, if the debtor fails to make four consecutive payments of principal and interest on the due dates, and the trust takes action to acquire the property securing the debt only after the fourth default becomes imminent, the 10-percent test is applied at the time the fourth default became imminent (even though the trust would not have foreclosed on the property had not all four defaults occurred).

(2) *Determination of percentage of completion.* The determination of whether the construction of a building or other improvement was more than 10-percent complete when default became imminent shall be made by comparing the total direct costs of construction incurred with respect to the building or other improvement as of the date default became imminent with the estimated total direct costs of construction as of such date. If the building or other improvement qualifies as more than 10-percent complete under this method, the building or other improvement shall be considered to be more than 10-percent complete. For purposes of this subparagraph, direct costs of construction include the cost of labor and materials which are directly connected with the construction of the building or improvement. Thus, for example, direct costs of construction incurred as of the date default became imminent would include amounts paid, or for which liability has been incurred, for labor which has been performed as of such date that is directly connected with the construction of the building or other improvement and for building materials and supplies used or consumed in connection with the construction as of such date. For purposes of applying the 10-percent test the trust may also take into account the cost of building materials and supplies which have been delivered to the construction site as of the date default became imminent and which are to be used or consumed in connection with the construction. On the other hand, architect's fees, administrative costs of the developer or builder, lawyers' fees, and expenses incurred in connection with obtaining zoning approval or building permits are not considered to be direct costs of construction. Any construction by the trust as mortgagee-in-possession is considered to have taken place after default resulting in acquisition of the property became imminent. Generally, the trust's estimate of the total direct costs of completing construction as of the date the default became imminent will be accepted, provided that the estimate is reasonable, in good faith, and is based on all of the data reasonably available to the trust when the trust undertakes completion of construction of the building or other improvement. Appropriate documentation which shows that construction was more than 10-percent complete when default became imminent must be available at the principal place of business of the trust for inspection in connection with an examination of the income tax return. Construction includes the renovation of a building, such as the remodeling of apartments, or the renovation of an apartment building to convert units to a condominium. The renovation must be more than 10-percent complete (determined by comparing the total direct cost of the physical renovation which has been incurred when default became

imminent with the estimated total direct cost of renovation as of such date) when default became imminent in order for the property not to lose its status as foreclosure property if the trust undertakes the renovation.

(3) *Modification of a building or improvement.* Generally, the terms "building" and "improvement" in section 856(e)(4)(B) mean the building or improvement (including any integral part thereof) as planned by the mortgagor or lessee (or other person in possession of the property, if appropriate) as of the date default became imminent. The trust, however, may estimate the total direct costs of construction and complete the construction of the building or other improvement by modifying the building or other improvement as planned as of the date default became imminent so as to reduce the estimated direct cost of construction of the building or improvement. If the trust does so modify the planned construction of the building or improvement, the 10-percent test is to be applied by comparing the direct costs of construction incurred as of the date default became imminent that are attributable to the building or improvement as modified, with the estimated total direct costs (as of such date) of construction of the building or other improvement as modified. The trust, in order to meet the 10-percent test, may not, however, modify the planned building or improvement by reducing the estimated direct cost of construction to such an extent that the building or improvement is not functional.

Also, the trust may make subsequent modifications which increase the direct cost of construction of the building or improvement if such modifications—

(i) Are required by a Federal, State, or local agency, or

(ii) Are alterations that are either required by a prospective lessee or purchaser as a condition of leasing or buying the property or are necessary for the property to be used for the purpose planned at the time default became imminent.

Subdivision (ii) of the preceding sentence applies, however, only if the building or improvement, as modified was more than 10-percent complete when default became imminent. A building completed by the trust will not cease to be foreclosure property solely because the building is used in a manner other than that planned by the defaulting mortgagor or lessee. Thus, for example, assume a trust acquired on foreclosure a planned apartment building which was 20-percent complete when default became imminent and that the trust completes the building without modifications which increase the direct cost of construction. The property will not cease to be foreclosure property by reason of section 856(e)(4)(B) solely because the trust sells the dwelling units in the building as condominium units, rather than holding them for rent as planned by the defaulting mortgagor. (See, however, section 856(e)(4)(C) and paragraph (f)(2) of this section for rules relating to the requirement that where foreclosure property is used in a trade or business (including a trade or business of selling the foreclosure property), the trade or business must be conducted through an independent contractor after 90 days after the property is acquired.)

(4) *Application on building-by-building basis.* Generally the more-than-10-percent test is to be applied on a building-by-building basis. Thus, for example, if a trust has foreclosed on land held by a developer building a housing subdivision, the trust may complete construction of the houses which were more than 10-percent complete when default became imminent. The trust, however, may not complete construction of houses which were only 10-percent (or less) complete, nor may the trust begin construction of other houses planned for the subdivision on which construction has not begun. The trust, however, may construct an additional building or improvement (whether or not the construction thereof has begun) which is an integral part of another building or other improvement that was more than 10-percent complete when default became imminent if the additional building or improvement and the other building or improvement, taken together as a unit, meet the more-than-10-percent test. For purposes of this paragraph, an additional building or other improvement will be considered to be an integral part of another building or improvement if—

(i) It is ancillary to the other building or improvement and its principal intended use is to furnish services or facilities which either supplement the use of such other building or improvement or are necessary for such other building or improvement to be utilized in the manner or for the purpose for which it is intended, or

(ii) The buildings or improvements are intended to comprise constituent parts of an interdependent group of buildings or other improvements.

However, a building or other improvement will not be considered to be an integral part of another building or improvement unless the buildings or improvements were planned as part of the same overall construction plan or project before default became imminent. An additional building or other improvement (such as, for example, an outdoor swimming pool or a parking garage) may be con-

Reg. § 1.856-6(e)(3)

sidered to be an integral part of another building or improvement, even though the additional building or improvement was also intended to be used to provide facilities or services for use in connection with several other buildings or improvements which will not be completed. If the trust chooses not to undertake the construction of an additional building or other improvement which qualifies as an integral part of another building or improvement, so much of the costs of construction (including both the direct costs of construction incurred before the default became imminent and the estimated costs of completion) as are attributable to that "integral part" shall not be taken into account in determining whether any other building or improvement was more than 10-percent when default became imminent. For example, assume the trust acquires on foreclosure a property on which the defaulting mortgagor had begun construction of a motel. The motel, as planned by the mortgagor, was to consist of a two-story building containing 30 units, and two detached one-story wings, each of which was to contain 20 units. At the time default became imminent, the defaulting mortgagor had completed more than 10 percent of the construction of the two-story structure but the two wings, an access road, a parking lot, and an outdoor swimming pool planned for the motel were each less than 10-percent complete. The trust may construct the two wings of the motel, the access road, the parking lot, and the swimming pool, provided that the motel and the other improvements which the trust undertakes to construct, taken together as a unit, were more than 10-percent complete when default became imminent. If, however, the trust chooses not to undertake construction of the swimming pool, the costs of construction attributable to the swimming pool, whether incurred before default became imminent or estimated as the cost of completion, shall not be taken into account in determining whether the trust can complete construction of the other buildings and improvements. For another example, assume that the trust acquires a planned shopping center on foreclosure. At the time default became imminent several large buildings intended to house shops and stores in the shopping center were more than 10-percent complete. Less than 10 percent of the construction, however, had been completed on a separate structure intended to house a bank. The bank was planned as a component of the shopping center in order to provide, in conjunction with the other shops and stores, a specific range and variety of goods and services with which to attract customers to the shopping center. The trust may complete construction of the bank, provided that the bank and the other buildings and improvements which the trust undertakes to complete, taken together as a unit, were more than 10-percent complete when default became imminent. If the trust chooses not to construct the bank, no actual or estimated construction costs attributable to the bank are to be taken into account in applying the 10-percent test with respect to the other buildings and improvements in the shopping center. For a third example, assume that a defaulting mortgagor had planned to construct two identical apartment buildings, A and B, on the same tract of land, that neither building is to provide substantial facilities or services to be used in connection with the other, and that only building A was more than 10-percent complete when default became imminent. The trust, in this case, may not complete building B. On the other hand, if the facts are the same except that pursuant to the plans of the defaulting mortgagor, one of the buildings is to contain the furnace and central air conditioning machinery for both buildings A and B, the trust may complete both buildings A and B, provided that, taken together as a unit, the two buildings meet the more-than-10-percent test.

(5) *Repair and maintenance.* Under this paragraph (e), "construction" does not include—

(i) The repair or maintenance of a building or other improvement, such as the replacement of worn or obsolete furniture and appliances to offset normal wear and tear or obsolescence and the restoration of property required because of damage from fire, storm, vandalism or other casualty,

(ii) The preparation of leased space for a new tenant which does not substantially extend the useful life of the building or other improvement or significantly increase its value, even though, in the case of commercial space, this preparation includes adapting the property to the conduct of a different business, or

(iii) The performing of repair or maintenance described in paragraph (e)(5)(i) of this section after property is acquired that was deferred by the defaulting party and that does not constitute renovation under paragraph (e)(2) of this section.

(6) *Independent contractor required.* If any construction takes place on the foreclosure property more than 90 days after the day on which such property was acquired by the trust, such construction must be performed by an independent contractor (as defined in section 856(d)(3) and § 1.856-4(b)(5)(iii)) from whom the trust does not derive or receive any income. Otherwise, the property will cease to be foreclosure property.

(7) *Failure to complete construction.* Property will not cease to be foreclosure property solely because a trust which undertakes the com-

pletion of construction of a building or other improvement on the property that was more than 10-percent complete when default became imminent does not complete the construction. Thus, for example, if a trust continues construction of a building that was 20-percent complete when default became imminent, and the trust constructs an additional 40 percent of the building and then sells the property, the property will not lose its status as foreclosure property solely because the trust fails to complete construction of the building.

(f) *Termination of 2-year grace period; use of foreclosure property in a trade or business*—(1) *In general.* Under section 856(e)(4)(C), all real property (and any incidental personal property) for which a particular election has been made (see paragraph (c)(1) of this section) shall cease to be foreclosure property on the first day (occurring more than 90 days after the day on which the trust acquired the property) on which the property is used in a trade or business conducted by the trust, other than a trade or business conducted by the trust through an independent contractor from whom the trust itself does not derive or receive any income. (See section 856(d)(3) for the definition of independent contractor.)

(2) *Property held primarily for sale to customers.* For the purposes of section 856(e)(4)(C), foreclosure property held by the trust primarily for sale to customers in the ordinary course of a trade or business is considered to be property used in a trade or business conducted by the trust. Thus, if a trust holds foreclosure property (whether real property or personal property incident to real property) for sale to customers in the ordinary course of a trade or business more than 90 days after the day on which the trust acquired the real property, the trade or business of selling the property must be conducted by the trust through an independent contractor from whom the trust does not derive or receive any income. Otherwise, after such 90th day the property will cease to be foreclosure property.

(3) *Change in use.* Foreclosure property will not cease to be foreclosure property solely because the use of the property in a trade or business by the trust differs from the use to which the property was put by the person from whom it was acquired. Thus, for example, if a trust acquires a rental apartment building on foreclosure, the property will not cease to be foreclosure property solely because the trust converts the building to a condominium apartment building and, through an independent contractor from whom the trust derives no income, engages in the trade or business of selling the individual condominium units.

(g) *Extension of 2-year grace period*—(1) *In general.* A real estate investment trust may apply to the district director of the internal revenue district in which is located the principal place of business (or principal office or agency) of the trust for an extension of the 2-year grace period. If the trust establishes to the satisfaction of the district director that an extension of the grace period is necessary for the orderly liquidation of the trust's interest in foreclosure property, or for an orderly renegotiation of a lease or leases of the property, the district director may extend the 2-year grace period. See section 856(e)(3) (as in effect with respect to the particular extension) for rules relating to the maximum length of an extension, and the number of extensions which may be granted. An extension of the grace period may be granted by the district director either before or after the date on which the grace period, but for the extension, would expire. The extension shall be effective as of the date on which the grace period, but for the extension, would expire.

(2) *Showing required.* Generally, in order to establish the necessity of an extension, the trust must demonstrate that it has made good faith efforts to renegotiate leases with respect to, or dispose of, the foreclosure property. In certain cases, however, the trust may establish the necessity of an extension even though it has not made such efforts. For example, if the trust demonstrates that, for valid business reasons, construction of the foreclosure property could not be completed before the expiration of the grace period, the necessity of the extension could be established even though the trust had made no effort to sell the property. For another example, if the trust demonstrates that due to a depressed real estate market, it could not sell the foreclosure property before the expiration of the grace period except at a distress price, the necessity of an extension could be established even though the trust had made no effort to sell the property. The fact that property was acquired as foreclosure property prior to January 3, 1975 (the date of enactment of section 856(e)), generally will be considered as a factor (but not a controlling factor) which tends to establish that an extension of the grace period is necessary.

(3) *Time for requesting an extension of the grace period.* A request for an extension of the grace period must be filed with the appropriate district director more than 60 days before the day on which the grace period would otherwise expire. In the case of a grace period which would otherwise expire before August 6, 1976, a request for an extension will be considered to be timely filed if filed on or before June 7, 1976.

Reg. § 1.856-6(f)(1)

(4) *Information required.* The request for an extension of the grace period shall identify the property with respect to which the request is being made and shall also include the following information:

(i) The name, address, and taxpayer identification number of the trust,

(ii) The date the property was acquired as foreclosure property by the trust,

(iii) The taxable year of the trust in which the property was acquired,

(iv) If the trust has been previously granted an extension of the grace period with respect to the property, a statement to that effect (which shall include the date on which the grace period, as extended, expires) and a copy of the information which accompanied the request for the previous extension,

(v) A statement of the reasons why the grace period should be extended,

(vi) A description of any efforts made by the trust after the acquisition of the property to dispose of the property or to renegotiate any lease with respect to the property, and

(vii) A description of any other factors which tend to establish that an extension of the grace period is necessary for the orderly liquidation of the trust's interest in the property, or for an orderly renegotiation of a lease or leases of the property. The trust shall also furnish any additional information requested by the district director after the request for extension is filed.

(5) *Automatic extension.* If a real estate investment trust files a request for an extension with the district director more than 60 days before the expiration of the grace period, the grace period shall be considered to be extended until the end of the 30th day after the date on which the district director notifies the trust by certified mail sent to its last known address that the period of extension requested by the trust is not granted. For further guidance regarding the definition of last known address, see § 301.6212-2 of this chapter. In no event, however, shall the rule in the preceding sentence extend the grace period beyond the expiration of (i) the period of extension requested by the trust, or (ii) the one-year period following the date that the grace period (but for the automatic extension) would expire. The date of the postmark on the sender's receipt is considered to be the date of the certified mail for purposes of this subparagraph. This subparagraph does not apply, however, if the date of the notification by certified mail described in the first sentence is more than 30 days before the date that the grace period (determined without regard to this subparagraph) expires; moreover, this subparagraph shall not operate to allow any period of extension that is prohibited by the last sentence of section 856(e)(3) (as in effect with respect to the particular extension).

(6) *Extension of time for filing.* If a real estate investment trust fails to file the request for an extension of the grace period within the time provided in paragraph (g)(3) of this section, then the district director shall grant a reasonable extension of time for filing such request, provided (i) it is established to the satisfaction of the district director that there was reasonable cause for failure to file the request within the prescribed time and (ii) a request for such extension is filed within such time as the district director considers reasonable under the circumstances.

(7) *Status of taxpayer.* The reference to "real estate investment trust" or "trust" in this paragraph (g) shall be considered to include a taxpayer that is not a qualified real estate investment trust, if the taxpayer establishes to the satisfaction of the district director that its failure to be a qualified real estate investment trust for the taxable year was due to reasonable cause and not due to willful neglect. The principles of § 1.856-7(c) and § 1.856-8(d) (including the principles relating to expert advice) shall apply for determining reasonable cause (and absence of willful neglect) for this purpose. [Reg. § 1.856-6.]

☐ [T.D. 7767, 2-3-81. Amended by T.D. 8939, 1-11-2001.]

[Reg. § 1.856-7]

§ 1.856-7. Certain corporations, etc., that are considered to meet the gross income requirements.—(a) *In general.* A corporation, trust, or association which fails to meet the requirements of paragraph (2) or (3) of section 856(c), or of both such paragraphs, for any taxable year nevertheless is considered to have satisfied these requirements if the corporation, trust, or association meets the requirements of subparagraphs (A), (B), and (C) of section 856(c)(7) (relating to a schedule attached to the return, the absence of fraud, and reasonable cause).

(b) *Contents of the schedule.* The schedule required by subparagraph (A) of section 856(c)(7) must contain a breakdown, or listing, of the total amount of gross income falling under each of the separate subparagraphs of section 856(c)(2) and (3). Thus, for example, the real estate investment trust, for purposes of listing its income from the sources described in section 856(c)(2), would list separately the total amount of dividends, the total amount of interest, the total amount of rents from real property, etc. The listing is not required to be on a lease-by-lease, loan-by-loan, or project-by-project basis, but the real estate investment trust must maintain adequate records on such a basis with which to substantiate each total amount listed in the schedule.

(c) *Reasonable cause*—(1) *In general.* The failure to meet the requirements of paragraph (2) or (3) of section 856(c) (or of both paragraphs) will be considered due to reasonable cause and not due to willful neglect if the real estate investment trust exercised ordinary business care and prudence in attempting to satisfy the requirements. Such care and prudence must be exercised at the time each transaction is entered into by the trust. However, even if the trust exercised ordinary business care and prudence in entering into a transaction, if the trust later determines that the transaction results in the receipt or accrual of nonqualified income and that the amounts of such nonqualified income, in the context of the trust's overall portfolio, reasonably can be expected to cause a source-of-income requirement to be failed, the trust must use ordinary business care and prudence in an effort to renegotiate the terms of the transaction, dispose of property acquired or leased in the transaction, or alter other elements of its portfolio. In any case, failure to meet an income source requirement will be considered due to willful neglect and not due to reasonable cause if the failure is willful and the trust could have avoided such failure by taking actions not inconsistent with ordinary business care and prudence. For example, if the trust enters into a lease knowing that it will produce nonqualified income which reasonably can be expected to cause a source-of-income requirement to be failed, the failure is due to willful neglect even if the trust has a legitimate business purpose for entering into the lease.

(2) *Expert advice*—(i) *In general.* The reasonable reliance on a reasoned, written opinion as to the characterization for purposes of section 856 of gross income to be derived (or being derived) from a transaction generally constitutes "reasonable cause" if income from the transaction causes the trust to fail to meet the requirements of paragraph (2) or (3) of section 856(c) (or of both paragraphs). The absence of such a reasoned, written opinion with respect to a transaction does not, by itself, give rise to any inference that the failure to meet a percentage of income requirement was without reasonable cause. An opinion as to the character of income from a transaction includes an opinion pertaining to the use of a standard form of transaction or standard operating procedure in a case where such standard form or procedure is in fact used or followed.

(ii) If the opinion indicates that a portion of the income from a transaction will be nonqualified income, the trust must still exercise ordinary business care and prudence with respect to the nonqualified income and determine that the amount of that income, in the context of its overall portfolio, reasonably cannot be expected to cause a source-of-income requirement to be failed. Reliance on an opinion is not reasonable if the trust has reason to believe that the opinion is incorrect (for example, because the trust withholds facts from the person rendering the opinion).

(iii) *Reasoned written opinion.* For purposes of this subparagraph (2), a written opinion means an opinion, in writing, rendered by a tax advisor (including house counsel) whose opinion would be relied on by a person exercising ordinary business care and prudence in the circumstances of the particular transaction. A written opinion is considered "reasoned" even if it reaches a conclusion which is subsequently determined to be incorrect, so long as the opinion is based on a full disclosure of the factual situation by the real estate investment trust and is addressed to the facts and law which the person rendering the opinion believes to be applicable. However, an opinion is not considered "reasoned" if it does nothing more than recite the facts and express a conclusion.

(d) *Application of section 856(c)(7) to taxable years beginning before October 5, 1976.* Pursuant to section 1608(b) of the Tax Reform Act of 1976, paragraph (7) of section 856(c) and this section apply to a taxable year of a real estate investment trust which begins before October 5, 1976, only if as the result of a determination occurring after October 4, 1976, the trust does not meet the requirements of paragraph (2) or (3) of section 856(c), or both paragraphs, as in effect for the taxable year. The requirement that the schedule described in subparagraph (A) of section 856(c)(7) be attached to the income tax return of a real estate investment trust in order for section 856(c)(7) to apply is not applicable to taxable years beginning before October 5, 1976. For purposes of section 1608(b) of the Tax Reform Act of 1976 and this paragraph, the rules relating to determinations prescribed in section 860(e) and § 1.860-2(b)(1) (other than the second, third, and last sentences of § 1.860-2(b)(1)(ii)) shall apply. However, a determination consisting of an agreement between the taxpayer and the district director (or other official to whom authority to sign the agreement is delegated) shall set forth the amount of gross income for the taxable year to which the determination applies, the amount of the 90 percent and 75 percent source-of-income require-

Reg. § 1.856-7(c)(1)

ments for the taxable year to which the determination applies, and the amount by which the real estate investment trust failed to meet either or both of the requirements. The agreement shall also set forth the amount of tax for which the trust is liable pursuant to section 857(b)(5). The agreement shall also contain a finding as to whether the failure to meet the requirements of paragraph (2) or (3) of section 856(c) (or of both paragraphs) was due to reasonable cause and not due to willful neglect. [Reg. § 1.856-7.]

☐ [T.D. 7767, 3-2-81. Amended by T.D. 7936, 1-17-84.]

[Reg. § 1.856-8]

§ 1.856-8. Revocation or termination of election.—(a) *Revocation of an election to be a real estate investment trust.* A corporation, trust, or association that has made an election under section 856(c)(1) to be a real estate investment trust may revoke the election for any taxable year after the first taxable year for which the election is effective. (This election terminates whether the failure to be a qualified real estate investment trust is intentional or inadvertent.) The revocation must be made by filing a statement with the district director for the internal revenue district in which the taxpayer maintains its principal place of business or principal office or agency. The statement must be filed on or before the 90th day after the first day of the first taxable year for which the revocation is to be effective. The statement must be signed by an official authorized to sign the income tax return of the taxpayer and must—

(1) Contain the name, address, and taxpayer identification number of the taxpayer,

(2) Specify the taxable year for which the election was made, and

(3) Include a statement that the taxpayer, pursuant to section 856(g)(2), revokes its election under section 856(c)(1) to be a real estate investment trust.

The revocation may be made only with respect to a taxable year beginning after October 4, 1976, and is effective for the taxable year in which made and for all succeeding taxable years. A revocation with respect to a taxable year beginning after October 4, 1976, that is filed before February 6, 1981, in the time and manner prescribed in § 7.856(g)-1 of this chapter (as in effect when the revocation was filed) is considered to meet the requirements of this paragraph.

(b) *Termination of election to be a real estate investment trust.* An election of a corporation, trust, or association under section 856(c)(1) to be a real estate investment trust shall terminate if the corporation, trust, or association is not a qualified real estate investment trust for any taxable year (including the taxable year with respect to which the election is made) beginning after October 4, 1976. The term "taxable year" includes a taxable year of less than 12 months for which a return is made under section 443. The termination of the election is effective for the first taxable year beginning after October 4, 1976, for which the corporation, trust, or association is not a qualified real estate investment trust and for all succeeding taxable years.

(c) *Restrictions on election after termination or revocation.*—(1) *General rule.* Except as provided in paragraph (d) of this section, if a corporation, trust, or association has made an election under section 856(c)(1) to be a real estate investment trust and the election has been terminated or revoked under section 856(g)(1) or (2), the corporation, trust, or association (and any successor corporation, trust, or association) is not eligible to make a new election under section 856(c)(1) for any taxable year prior to the fifth taxable year which begins after the first taxable year for which the termination or revocation is effective.

(2) *Successor corporation.* The term "successor corporation, trust, or association", as used in section 856(g)(3), means a corporation, trust, or association which meets both a continuity of ownership requirement and a continuity of assets requirement with respect to the corporation, trust, or association whose election has been terminated under section 856(g)(1) or revoked under section 856(g)(2). A corporation, trust, or association meets the continuity of ownership requirement only if at any time during the taxable year the persons who own, directly or indirectly, 50 percent or more in value of its outstanding shares owned, at any time during the first taxable year for which the termination or revocation was effective, 50 percent or more in value of the outstanding shares of the corporation, trust, or association whose election has been terminated or revoked. A corporation, trust, or association meets the continuity of assets requirement only if either (i) a substantial portion of its assets were assets of the corporation, trust, or association whose election has been revoked or terminated, or (ii) it acquires a substantial portion of the assets of the corporation, trust, or association whose election has been terminated or revoked.

(3) *Effective date.* Section 856(g)(3) does not apply to the termination of an election that was made by a taxpayer pursuant to section 856(c)(1) on or before October 4, 1976, unless the taxpayer is a qualified real estate investment trust for a taxable year ending after October 4, 1976, for

which the pre-October 5, 1976, election is in effect. For example, assume that Trust X, a calendar year taxpayer, files a timely election under section 856(c)(1) with respect to its taxable year 1974, and is a qualified real estate investment trust for calendar years 1974 and 1975. Assume further that Trust X is not a qualified real estate investment trust for 1976 and 1977 because it willfully fails to meet the asset diversification requirements of section 856(c)(5) for both years. The failure (whether or not willful) to meet these requirements in 1977 terminates the election to be a real estate investment trust made with respect to 1974. (See paragraph (b) of this section.) The termination is effective for 1977 and all succeeding taxable years. However, under section 1608(d)(3) of the Tax Reform Act of 1976, Trust X is not prohibited by section 856(g)(3) from making a new election under section 856(c)(1) with respect to 1978.

(d) *Exception.* Section 856(g)(4) provides an exception to the general rule of section 856(g)(3) that the termination of an election to be a real estate investment trust disqualifies the corporation, trust, or association from making a new election for the four taxable years following the first taxable year for which the termination is effective. This exception applies where the corporation, trust, or association meets the requirements of section 856(g)(4)(A), (B) and (C) (relating to the timely filing of a return, the absence of fraud, and reasonable cause, respectively) for the taxable year with respect to which the termination of election occurs. In order to meet the requirements of section 856(g)(4)(C), the corporation, trust, or association must establish, to the satisfaction of the district director for the internal revenue district in which the corporation, trust, or association maintains its principal place of business or principal office or agency, that its failure to be a qualified real estate investment trust for the taxable year in question was due to reasonable cause and not due to willful neglect. The principles of § 1.856-7(c) (including the principles relating to expert advice) will apply in determining whether, for purposes of section 856(g)(4), the failure of a corporation, trust, or association to be a qualified real estate investment trust for a taxable year was due to reasonable cause and not due to willful neglect. Thus, for example, the corporation, trust, or association must exercise ordinary business care and prudence in attempting to meet the status conditions of section 856(a) and the distribution and record keeping requirements of section 857(a), as well as the gross income requirements of section 856(c). The provisions of section 856(g)(4) do not apply to a taxable year in which the corporation, trust, or association makes a valid revocation, under section 856(g)(2), of an election to be a real estate investment trust. [Reg. § 1.856-8.]

☐ [*T.D. 7767*, 2-3-81.]

[Reg. § 5.856-1]

§ 5.856-1. **Extension of the grace period for foreclosure property by a real estate investment trust (Temporary).**—(a) *In general.* Under section 856(e), a real estate investment trust ("REIT") may elect to treat as foreclosure property certain real property (including interests in real property), and any personal property incident to such real property, that the REIT acquires after December 31, 1973. In general, the REIT must acquire the property as the result of having bid on the property at foreclosure, or having otherwise reduced the property to ownership or possession by agreement or process of law, after there was default (or default was imminent) on a lease of such property (where the REIT was the lessor) or on an indebtedness owed to the REIT which such property secured. Property that a REIT elects to treat as foreclosure property ceases to be foreclosure property with respect to such REIT at the end of a grace period. The grace period ends on the date which is 2 years after the date on which the REIT acquired the property, unless the REIT has been granted an extension or extensions of the grace period. If the grace period is extended, the property ceases to be foreclosure property on the day immediately following the last day of the grace period, as extended.

(b) *Rules for extensions of the grace period.* In general, § 1.856-6(g) prescribes rules regarding extensions of the grace period. However, in order to reflect the amendment of section 856(e)(3) of the Code by section 363(c) of the Revenue Act of 1978, the following rules also apply:

(1) In the case of extensions granted after November 6, 1978, with respect to extension periods beginning after December 31, 1977, the district director may grant one or more extensions of the grace period for the property, subject to the limitation that no extension shall extend the grace period beyond the date which is 6 years after the date the REIT acquired the property. In any other case, an extension shall be for a period of not more than 1 year, and not more than two extensions can be granted with respect to the property.

(2) In the case of an extension period beginning after December 31, 1977, a request for an extension filed on or before March 28, 1980, will be considered to be timely if the limitation on the number and length of extensions in section 856(e)(3), as in effect before the amendment made by section 363(c) of the Revenue Act of

Reg. § 5.856-1(a)

1978, would have barred the extension. [Temporary Reg. § 5.856-1.]

☐ [T.D. 7767, 2-3-81.]

[Reg. § 1.857-1]

§ 1.857-1. Taxation of real estate investment trusts.—(a) *Requirements applicable thereto.* Section 857(a) denies the application of the provisions of part II, subchapter M, chapter 1 of the Code (other than sections 856(g), relating to the revocation or termination of an election, and 857(d), relating to earnings and profits) to a real estate investment trust for a taxable year unless—

(1) The deduction for dividends paid for the taxable year as defined in section 561 (computed without regard to capital gain dividends) equals or exceeds the amount specified in section 857(a)(1) as in effect for the taxable year; and

(2) The trust complies for such taxable year with the provisions of § 1.857-8 (relating to records required to be maintained by a real estate investment trust).

See Section 585 and § 1.858-1, relating to dividends paid after the close of the taxable year.

(b) *Failure to qualify.* If a real estate investment trust does not meet the requirements of section 857(a) and paragraph (a) of this section for the taxable year, it will, even though it may otherwise be classified as a real estate investment trust, be taxed in such year as an ordinary corporation and not as a real estate investment trust. In such case, none of the provisions of part II of subchapter M (other than sections 856(g) and 857(d)) will be applicable to it. For the rules relating to the applicability of section 857(d), see § 1.857-7. [Reg. § 1.857-1.]

☐ [T.D. 6598, 4-25-62. Amended by T.D. 7767, 2-3-81.]

[Reg. § 1.857-2]

§ 1.857-2. Real estate investment trust taxable income and net capital gain.—(a) *Real estate investment trust taxable income.* Section 857(b)(1) imposes a normal tax and surtax, computed at the rates and in the manner prescribed in section 11, on the "real estate investment trust taxable income", as defined in section 857(b)(2). Section 857(b)(2) requires certain adjustments to be made to convert taxable income of the real estate investment trust to "real estate investment trust taxable income". The adjustments are as follows:

(1) *Net capital gain.* In the case of taxable years ending before October 5, 1976, the net capital gain, if any, is excluded.

(2) *Special deductions disallowed.* The special deductions provided in part VIII, subchapter B, chapter 1 of the Code (except the deduction under section 248) are not allowed.

(3) *Deduction for dividends paid*—(i) *General rule.* The deduction for dividends paid (as defined in section 561) is allowed. In the case of taxable years ending before October 5, 1976, the deduction for dividends paid is computed without regard to capital gains dividends.

(ii) *Deduction for dividends paid if there is net income from foreclosure property.* If for any taxable year the trust has net income from foreclosure property (as defined in section 857(b)(4)(B) and § 1.857-3), the deduction for dividends paid is an amount equal to the amount which bears the same proportion to the total dividends paid or considered as paid during the taxable year that otherwise meet the requirements for the deduction for dividends paid (as defined in section 561) as the real estate investment trust taxable income (determined without regard to the deduction for dividends paid) bears to the sum of—

(A) The real estate investment trust taxable income (determined without regard to the deduction for dividends paid), and

(B) The amount by which the net income from foreclosure property exceeds the tax imposed on such income by section 857(b)(4)(A).

For purposes of the preceding sentence, the term "total dividends paid or considered as paid during the taxable year" includes deficiency dividends paid with respect to the taxable year that are not otherwise excluded under this subdivision or section 857(b)(3)(A). The term, however, does not include either deficiency dividends paid during the taxable year with respect to a preceding taxable year or, in the case of taxable years ending before October 5, 1976, capital gains dividends.

(iii) *Deduction for dividends paid for purposes of the alternative tax.* The rules in section 857(b)(3)(A) apply in determining the amount of the deduction for dividends paid that is taken into account in computing the alternative tax. Thus, for example, if a real estate investment trust has net income from foreclosure property for a taxable year ending after October 4, 1976, then for purposes of determining the partial tax described in section 857(b)(3)(A)(i), the amount of the deduction for dividends paid is computed pursuant to paragraph (a)(3)(ii) of this section, except that capital gains dividends are excluded from the dividends paid or considered as paid during the taxable year, and the net capital gain is excluded in computing real estate investment trust taxable income.

Reg. § 1.857-2(a)(3)

Real Estate Investment Trusts

(4) *Section 443(b) disregarded.* The taxable income is computed without regard to section 443(b). Thus, the taxable income for a period of less than 12 months is not placed on an annual basis even though the short taxable year results from a change of accounting period.

(5) *Net operating loss deduction.* In the case of a taxable year ending before October 5, 1976, the net operating loss deduction provided in section 172 is not allowed.

(6) *Net income from foreclosure property.* An amount equal to the net income from foreclosure property (as defined in section 857(b)(4)(B) and paragraph (a) of § 1.857-3), if any, is excluded.

(7) *Tax imposed by section 857(b)(5).* An amount equal to the tax (if any) imposed on the trust by section 857(b)(5) for the taxable year is excluded.

(8) *Net income or loss from prohibited transactions.* An amount equal to the amount of any net income derived from prohibited transactions (as defined in section 857(b)(6)(B)(i)) is excluded. On the other hand, an amount equal to the amount of any net loss derived from prohibited transactions (as defined in section 857(b)(6)(B)(ii)) is included. Because the amount of the net loss derived from prohibited transactions is taken into account in computing taxable income before the adjustments required by section 857(b)(2) and this section are made, the effect of including an amount to the amount of the loss is to disallow a deduction for the loss.

(b) *Net capital gain in taxable years ending before October 5, 1976.* The rules relating to the taxation of capital gains in 26 CFR 1.857-2(b) (revised as of April 1, 1977) apply to taxable years ending before October 5, 1976. [Reg. § 1.857-2.]

☐ [T.D. 6598, 4-25-62. Amended by T.D. 7767, 2-3-81.]

[Reg. § 1.857-3]

§ 1.857-3. **Net income from foreclosure property.**—(a) *In general.* For purposes of section 857(b)(4)(B), net income from foreclosure property means the aggregate of—

(1) All gains and losses from sales or other dispositions of foreclosure property described in section 1221(1), and

(2) The difference (hereinafter called "net gain or loss from operations") between (i) the gross income derived from foreclosure property (as defined in section 856(c)) to the extent such gross income is not described in subparagraph (A), (B), (C), (D), (E), or (G) of section 856(c)(3), and (ii) the deductions allowed by chapter 1 of the Code which are directly connected with the production of such gross income.

Thus, the sum of the gains and losses from sales or other dispositions of foreclosure property described in section 1221(1) is aggregated with the net gain or loss from operations in arriving at net income from foreclosure property. For example, if for a taxable year a real estate investment trust has gain of $100 from the sale of an item of foreclosure property described in section 1221(1), a loss of $50 from the sale of an item of foreclosure property described in section 1221(1), gross income of $25 from the rental of foreclosure property that is not gross income described in subparagraph (A), (B), (C), (D), or (G) of section 856(c)(3), and deductions of $35 allowed by chapter 1 of the Code which are directly connected with the production of the rental income, the net income from foreclosure property for the taxable year is $40 (($100 − $50) + ($25 − $35)).

(b) *Directly connected deductions.* A deduction which is otherwise allowed by chapter 1 of the Code is "directly connected" with the production of gross income from foreclosure property if it has a proximate and primary relationship to the earning of the income. Thus, in the case of gross income from real property that is foreclosure property, "directly connected" deductions would include depreciation on the property, interest paid or accrued on the indebtedness of the trust (whether or not secured by the property) to the extent attributable to the carrying of the property, real estate taxes, and fees paid to an independent contractor hired to manage the property. On the other hand, general overhead and administrative expenses of the trust are not "directly connected" deductions. Thus, salaries of officers and other administrative employees of the trust are not "directly connected" deductions. The net operating loss deduction provided by section 172 is not allowed in computing net income from foreclosure property.

(c) *Net loss from foreclosure property.* The tax imposed by section 857(b)(4) applies only if there is net income from foreclosure property. If there is a net loss from foreclosure property (that is, if the aggregate computed under paragraph (a) of this section results in a negative amount) the loss is taken into account in computing real estate investment trust taxable income under section 857(b)(2).

(d) *Gross income not subject to tax on foreclosure property.* If the gross income derived from foreclosure property consists of two classes, a deduction directly connected with the production of both classes (including interest attributable to the

Reg. § 1.857-3(a)(1)

carrying of the property) must be apportioned between them. The two classes are:

(1) Gross income which is taken into account in computing net income from foreclosure property and

(2) Other income (such as income described in subparagraph (A), (B), (C), (D), or (G) of section 856(c)(3)).

The apportionment may be made on any reasonable basis.

(e) *Allocation and apportionment of interest.* For purposes of determining the amount of interest attributable to the carrying of foreclosure property under paragraph (b) of this section, the following rules apply:

(1) *Deductible interest.* Interest is taken into account under this paragraph (e) only if it is otherwise deductible under chapter 1 of the Code.

(2) *Interest specifically allocated to property.* Interest that is specifically allocated to an item of property is attributable only to the carrying of that property. Interest is specifically allocated to an item of property if (i) the indebtedness on which the interest is paid or accrued is secured only by that property, (ii) such indebtedness was specifically incurred for the purpose of purchasing, constructing, maintaining, or improving that property, and (iii) the proceeds of the borrowing were applied for that purpose.

(3) *Other interest.* Interest which is not specifically allocated to property is apportioned between foreclosure property and other property under the principles of § 1.861-8(e)(2)(v).

(4) *Effective date.* The rules in this paragraph (e) are mandatory for all taxable years ending after February 6, 1981. [Reg. § 1.857-3.]

☐ [T.D. 7767, 2-3-81.]

[Reg. § 1.857-4]

§ 1.857-4. Tax imposed by reason of the failure to meet certain source-of-income requirements.—Section 857(b)(5) imposes a tax on a real estate investment trust that is considered, by reason of section 856(c)(7), as meeting the source-of-income requirements of paragraph (2) or (3) of section 856(c) (or both such paragraphs). The amount of the tax is determined in the manner prescribed in section 857(b)(5). [Reg. § 1.857-4.]

☐ [T.D. 7767, 2-3-81.]

[Reg. § 1.857-5]

§ 1.857-5. Net income and loss from prohibited transactions.—(a) *In general.* Section 857(b)(6) imposes, for each taxable year, a tax equal to 100 percent of the net income derived from prohibited transactions. A prohibited transaction is a sale or other disposition of property described in section 1221(1), that is not foreclosure property. The 100-percent tax is imposed to preclude a real estate investment trust from retaining any profit from ordinary retailing activities such as sales to customers of condominium units or subdivided lots in a development tract. In order to prevent a trust from receiving any tax benefit from such activities, a net loss from prohibited transactions effectively is disallowed in computing real estate investment trust taxable income. See § 1.857-2(a)(8). Such loss, however, does reduce the amount which a trust is required to distribute as dividends. For purposes of applying the provisions of the Code, other than those provisions of part II of subchapter M which relate to prohibited transactions, no inference is to be drawn from the fact that a type of transaction does not constitute a prohibited transaction.

(b) *Special rules.* In determining whether a particular transaction constitutes a prohibited transaction, the activities of a real estate investment trust with respect to foreclosure property and its sales of such property are disregarded. Also, if a real estate investment trust enters into a purchase and leaseback of real property with an option in the seller-lessee to repurchase the property at the end of the lease period, and the seller exercises the option pursuant to its terms, income from the sale generally will not be considered to be income from a prohibited transaction solely because the purchase and leaseback was entered into with an option in the seller to repurchase and because the option was exercised pursuant to its terms. Other facts and circumstances, however, may require a conclusion that the property is held primarily for sale to customers in the ordinary course of a trade or business. Gain from the sale or other disposition of property described in section 1221(1) (other than foreclosure property) that is included in gross income for a taxable year of a qualified real estate investment trust constitutes income from a prohibited transaction, even though the sale or other disposition from which the gain is derived occurred in a prior taxable year. For example, if a corporation that is a qualified real estate investment trust for the current taxable year elected to report the income from the sale of an item of section 1221(1) property (other than foreclosure property) on the installment method of reporting income, the gain from the sale that is taken into income by the real estate investment trust for the current taxable year is income from a prohibited transaction. This result follows even though the sale occurred in a prior taxable year for which the corporation did not qualify as a real estate investment trust. On the other hand, if the gain is taken into income in a

Reg. § 1.857-5(b)

taxable year for which the taxpayer is not a qualified real estate investment trust, the 100-percent tax does not apply.

(c) *Net income or loss from prohibited transactions.* Net income or net loss from prohibited transactions is determined by aggregating all gains from the sale or other disposition of property (other than foreclosure property) described in section 1221(1) with all losses from the sale or other disposition of such property. Thus, for example, if a real estate investment trust sells two items of property described in section 1221(1) (other than foreclosure property) and recognizes a gain of $100 on the sale of one item and a loss of $40 on the sale of the second item, the net income from prohibited transactions will be $60. [Reg. § 1.857-5.]

☐ [T.D. 7767, 2-3-81.]

[Reg. § 1.857-6]

§ 1.857-6. **Method of taxation of shareholders of real estate investment trusts.**—(a) *Ordinary income.* Except as otherwise provided in paragraph (b) of this section (relating to capital gains), a shareholder receiving dividends from a real estate investment trust shall include such dividends in gross income for the taxable year in which they are received. See section 858(b) and paragraph (c) of § 1.858-1 for treatment by shareholders of dividends paid by a real estate investment trust after the close of its taxable year in the case of an election under section 858(a).

(b) *Capital gains.* Under section 857(b)(3)(B), shareholders of a real estate investment trust who receive capital gain dividends (as defined in paragraph (e) of this section), in respect of the capital gains of a corporation, trust or association for a taxable year for which it is taxable under part II of subchapter M as real estate investment trust, shall treat such capital gain dividends as gains from the sale or exchange of capital assets held more than 1 year (6 months for taxable years beginning before 1977; 9 months for taxable years beginning in 1977) and realized in the taxable year of the shareholder in which the dividend was received. In the case of dividends with respect to any taxable year of a real estate investment trust ending after December 31, 1969, and beginning before January 1, 1975, the portion of a shareholder's capital gain dividend which in his hands is gain to which section 1201(d)(1) or (2) applies is the portion so designated by the real estate investment trust pursuant to paragraph (e)(2) of this section.

(c) *Special treatment of loss on the sale or exchange of real estate investment trust stock held less than 31 days*—(1) *In general.* Under section 857(b)(7), if any person with respect to a share of real estate investment trust stock held for a period of less than 31 days, is required by section 857(b)(3)(B) to include in gross income as a gain from the sale or exchange of a capital asset held for more than 1 year (6 months for taxable years beginning before 1977; 9 months for taxable years beginning in 1977) the amount of a capital gains dividend, then such person shall, to the extent of such amount, treat any loss on the sale or exchange of such share as a loss from the sale or exchange of a capital asset held for more than 1 year (6 months for taxable years beginning before 1977; 9 months for taxable years beginning in 1977).

(2) *Determination of holding period.* The rules contained in section 246(c)(3) (relating to the determination of holding periods for purposes of the deduction for dividends received) shall be applied in determining whether, for purposes of section 857(b)(7)(B) and this paragraph, a share of real estate investment trust stock has been held for a period of less than 31 days. In applying those rules, however, "30 days" shall be substituted for the number of days specified in subparagraph (B) of such section.

(3) *Illustration.* The application of section 857(b)(7) and this paragraph may be illustrated by the following example:

Example. On December 15, 1961, A purchased a share of stock in the S Real Estate Investment Trust for $20. The S trust declared a capital gains dividend of $2 per share to shareholders of record on December 31, 1961. A, therefore, received a capital gain dividend of $2 which, pursuant to section 857(b)(3)(B), he must treat as a gain from the sale or exchange of a capital asset held for more than six months. On January 5, 1962, A sold his share of stock in the S trust for $17.50, which sale resulted in a loss of $2.50. Under section 857(b)(4) and this paragraph, A must treat $2 of such loss (an amount equal to the capital gain dividend received with respect to such share of stock) as a loss from the sale or exchange of a capital asset held for more than six months.

(d) *Dividend received credit, exclusion, and deduction not allowed.* Any dividend received from a real estate investment trust which, for the taxable year to which the dividend relates, is a qualified real estate investment trust, shall not be eligible for the dividend received credit (for dividends received on or before December 31, 1964) under section 34(a), the dividend received exclusion under section 116, or the dividend received deduction under section 243.

Reg. § 1.857-6(a)

(e) *Definition of capital gain dividend.* (1)(i) A capital gain dividend, as defined in section 857(b)(3)(C), is any dividend or part thereof which is designated by a real estate investment trust as a capital gain dividend in a written notice mailed to its shareholders within the period specified in section 857(b)(3)(C) and paragraph (f) of this section. If the aggregate amount so designated with respect to the taxable year (including capital gain dividends paid after the close of the taxable year pursuant to an election under section 858) is greater than the net capital gain of the taxable year, the portion of each distribution which shall be a capital gain dividend shall be only that proportion of the amount so designated which such net capital gain bears to the aggregate of the amount so designated. For example, a real estate investment trust making its return on the calendar year basis advised its shareholders by written notice mailed December 30, 1961, that $200,000 of a distribution of $500,000 made December 15, 1961, constituted a capital gain dividend, amounting to $2 per share. It was later discovered that an error had been made in determining the net capital gain of the taxable year and that the net capital gain was $100,000, instead of $200,000. In such case, each shareholder would have received a capital gain dividend of $1 per share instead of $2 per share. For purposes of section 857(b)(3)(C) and this paragraph, the net capital gain for a taxable year ending after October 4, 1976, shall be deemed not to exceed the real estate investment trust taxable income (determined without regard to the deduction for dividends paid) for the taxable year.

(ii) For purposes of section 857(b)(3)(C) and this paragraph, the net capital gain for a taxable year ending after October 4, 1976, is deemed not to exceed the real estate investment trust taxable income determined by taking into account the net operating loss deduction for the taxable year but not the deduction for dividends paid. See example (2) in § 1.172-5(a)(4).

(2) In the case of capital gain dividends designated with respect to any taxable year of a real estate investment trust ending after December 31, 1969, and beginning before January 1, 1975 (including capital gain dividends paid after the close of the taxable year pursuant to an election under section 858), the real estate investment trust must include in its written notice designating the capital gain dividend a statement showing the shareholder's proportionate share of such dividend which is gain described in section 1201(d)(1) and his proportionate share of such dividend which is gain described in section 1201(d)(2). In determining the portion of the capital gain dividend which, in the hands of a shareholder, is gain described in section 1201(d)(1) or (2), the real estate investment trust shall consider that capital gain dividends for a taxable year are first made from its long-term capital gains which are not described in section 1201(d)(1) or (2), to the extent thereof, and then from its long-term capital gains for such year which are described in section 1201(d)(1) or (2). A shareholder's proportionate share of gains which are described in section 1201(d)(1) is the amount which bears the same ratio to the amount paid to him as a capital gain dividend in respect of such year as (i) the aggregate amount of the trust's gains which are described in section 1201(d)(1) and paid to all shareholders bears to (ii) the aggregate amount of the capital gain dividend paid to all shareholders in respect of such year. A shareholder's proportionate share of gains which are described in section 1201(d)(2) shall be determined in a similar manner. Every real estate investment trust shall keep a record of the proportion of each capital gain dividend (to which this subparagraph applies) which is gain described in section 1201(d)(1) or (2).

(f) *Mailing of written notice to shareholders.* (1) *General rule.* Except as provided in paragraph (f)(2) of this section, the written notice designating a dividend or part thereof as a capital gain dividend must be mailed to the shareholders not later than 30 days after the close of the taxable year of the real estate investment trust.

(2) *Net capital gain resulting from a determination.* If, as a result of a determination (as defined in section 860(e)), occurring after October 4, 1976, there is an increase in the amount by which the net capital gain exceeds the deduction for dividends paid (determined with reference to capital gains dividends only) or the taxable year, then a real estate investment trust may designate a dividend (or part thereof) as a capital gain dividend in a written notice mailed to its shareholders at any time during the 120-day period immediately following the date of the determination. The designation may be made with respect to a dividend (or part thereof) paid during the taxable year to which the determination applies (including a dividend considered as paid during the taxable year pursuant to section 858). A deficiency dividend (as defined in section 860(f)), or a part thereof, that is paid with respect to the taxable year also may be designated as a capital gain dividend by the real estate investment trust (or by the acquiring corporation to which section 381(c)(25) applies) before the expiration of the 120 day period immediately following the determination. However, the aggregate amount of the dividends (or parts thereof) that may be designated as capital gain dividends after the date of

Reg. § 1.857-6(f)(2)

the determination shall not exceed the amount of the increase in the excess of the net capital gain over the deduction for dividends paid (determined with reference to capital gains dividends only) that results from the determination. The date of a determination shall be established in accordance with § 1.860-2(b)(1). [Reg. § 1.857-6.]

☐ [T.D. 6598, 4-25-62. Amended by T.D. 6777, 12-15-65; T.D. 7337, 12-26-74; T.D. 7728, 10-31-80; T.D. 7767, 2-3-81; T.D. 7936, 1-17-84 and T.D. 8107, 12-1-86.]

[Reg. § 1.857-7]

§ 1.857-7. **Earnings and profits of a real estate investment trust.**—(a) Any real estate investment trust, whether or not such trust meets the requirements of section 857(a) and paragraph (a) of § 1.857-1 for any taxable requirements of section 857(a) and paragraph (a) of § 1.857-1 for any taxable year beginning after December 31, 1960, shall apply paragraph (b) of this section in computing its earnings and profits for such taxable year.

(b) In the determination of the earnings and profits of a real estate investment trust, section 857(d) provides that such earnings and profits for any taxable year (but not the accumulated earnings and profits) shall not be reduced by any amount which is not allowable as a deduction in computing its taxable income for the taxable year. Thus, if a trust would have had earnings and profits of $500,000 for the taxable year except for the fact that it had a net capital loss of $100,000, which amount was not deductible in determining its taxable income, its earnings and profits for that year if it is a real estate investment trust would be $500,000. If the real estate investment trust had no accumulated earnings and profits at the beginning of the taxable year, in determining its accumulated earnings and profits as of the beginning of the following taxable year, the earnings and profits for the taxable year to be considered in such computation would amount to $400,000 assuming that there had been no distribution from such earnings and profits. If distributions had been made in the taxable year in the amount of the earnings and profits then available for distribution, $500,000, the trust would have as of the beginning of the following taxable year neither accumulated earnings and profits nor a deficit in accumulated earnings and profits, and would begin such year with its paid-in capital reduced by $100,000, an amount equal to the excess of the $500,000 distributed over the $400,000 accumulated earnings and profits which would otherwise have been carried into the following taxable year. For purposes of section 857(d) and this section, if an amount equal to any net loss derived from prohibited transactions is included in real estate investment trust taxable income pursuant to section 857(b)(2)(F), that amount shall be considered to be an amount which is not allowable as a deduction in computing taxable income for the taxable year. The earnings and profits for the taxable year (but not the accumulated earnings and profits) shall not be considered to be less than (i) in the case of a taxable year ending before October 5, 1976 the amount (if any) of the net capital gain for the taxable year, or (ii) in the case of a taxable year ending after December 31, 1973, the amount (if any) of the excess of the net income from foreclosure property for the taxable year over the tax imposed thereon by section 857(b)(4)(A). [Reg. § 1.857-7.]

☐ [T.D. 6598, 4-25-62. Amended by T.D. 7767, 2-3-81.]

[Reg. § 1.857-8]

§ 1.857-8. **Records to be kept by a real estate investment trust.**—(a) *In general.* Under section 857(a)(2) a real estate investment trust is required to keep such records as will disclose the actual ownership of its outstanding stock. Thus, every real estate investment trust shall maintain in the internal revenue district in which it is required to file its income tax return permanent records showing the information relative to the actual owners of its stock contained in the written statements required by this section to be demanded from its shareholders. Such records shall be kept at all times available for inspection by any internal revenue officer or employee, and shall be retained so long as the contents thereof may become material in the administration of any internal revenue law.

(b) *Actual owner of stock.* The actual owner of stock of a real estate investment trust is the person who is required to include in gross income in his return the dividends received on the stock. Generally, such person is the shareholder of record of the real estate investment trust. However, where the shareholder of record is not the actual owner of the stock, the stockholding record of the real estate investment trust may not disclose the actual ownership of such stock. Accordingly, the real estate investment trust shall demand written statements from shareholders of record disclosing the actual owners of stock as required in paragraph (d) of this section.

(c) *Stock ownership for personal holding company determination.* For the purpose of determining under section 856(a)(6) whether a trust, claiming to be a real estate investment trust, is a personal holding company, the permanent records of the trust shall show the maximum number of shares of the trust (including the number and face

Reg. § 1.857-7(a)

Real Estate Investment Trusts

See p. 20,601 for regulations not amended to reflect law changes

value of securities convertible into stock of the trust) to be considered as actually or constructively owned by each of the actual owners of any of its stock at any time during the last half of the trust's taxable year, as provided in section 544.

(d) *Statements to be demanded from shareholders.* The information required by paragraphs (b) and (c) of this section shall be set forth in written statements which shall be demanded from shareholders of record as follows:

(1) In the case of a trust having 2,000 or more shareholders of record of its stock on any dividend record date, from each record holder of 5 percent or more of its stock; or

(2) In the case of a trust having less than 2,000 and more than 200 shareholders of record of its stock on any dividend record date, from each record holder of 1 percent or more of its stock; or

(3) In the case of a trust having 200 or less shareholders of record of its stock on any dividend record date, from each record holder of one-half of 1 percent or more of its stock.

(e) *Demands for statements.* The written statements from shareholders of record shall be demanded by the real estate investment trust in accordance with paragraph (d) of this section within 30 days after the close of the real estate investment trust's taxable year (or before June 1, 1962, whichever is later). When making demand for such written statements, the trust shall inform each such shareholder of his duty to submit at the time he files his income tax return (or before July 1, 1962, whichever is later) the statements which are required by § 1.857-9 if he fails or refuses to comply with such demand. A list of the persons failing or refusing to comply in whole or in part with the trust's demand for statements under this section shall be maintained as a part of the trust's records required by this section. A trust which fails to keep such records to show, to the extent required by this section, the actual ownership of its outstanding stock shall be taxable as an ordinary corporation and not as a real estate investment trust. [Reg. § 1.857-8.]

☐ [*T.D. 6598, 4-25-62. Amended by T.D. 7767, 2-3-81.*]

[Reg. § 1.857-9]

§ 1.857-9. Information required in returns of shareholders.—(a) *In general.* Any person who fails or refuses to submit to a real estate investment trust the written statements required under § 1.857-8 to be demanded by such trust from its shareholders of record shall submit at the time he files his income tax return for his taxable year which ends with, or includes, the last day of the trust's taxable year (or before July 1, 1962, whichever is later) a statement setting forth the information required by this section.

(b) *Information required.*—(1) *Shareholder of record not actual owner.* In the case of any person holding shares of stock in any trust claiming to be a real estate investment trust who is not the actual owner of such stock, the name and address of each actual owner, the number of shares owned by each actual owner at any time during such person's taxable year, and the amount of dividends belonging to each actual owner.

(2) *Actual owner of shares.* In the case of an actual owner of shares of stock in any trust claiming to be a real estate investment trust—

(i) The name and address of each such trust, the number of shares actually owned by him at any and all times during his taxable year, and the amount of dividends from each such trust received during his taxable year;

(ii) If shares of any such trust were acquired or disposed of during such person's taxable year, the name and address of the trust, the number of shares acquired or disposed of, the dates of acquisition or disposition, and the names and addresses of the persons from whom such shares were acquired or to whom they were transferred;

(iii) If any shares of stock (including securities convertible into stock) of any such trust are also owned by any member of such person's family (as defined in section 544(a) (2)), or by any of its partners, the name and address of the trust, the names and addresses of such members of his family and his partners, and the number of shares owned by each such member of his family or partner at any and all times during such person's taxable year; and

(iv) The names and addresses of any corporation, partnership, association, or trust, in which such person had a beneficial interest of 10 percent or more at any time during his taxable year. [Reg. § 1.857-9.]

☐ [*T.D. 6598, 4-25-62. Amended by T.D. 6628, 12-27-62 and T.D. 7767, 2-3-81.*]

[Reg. § 1.857-10]

§ 1.857-10. Information returns.—Nothing in §§ 1.857-8 and 1.857-9 shall be construed to relieve a real estate investment trust or its shareholders from the duty of filing information returns required by regulations prescribed under the provisions of subchapter A, chapter 61 of the Code. [Reg. § 1.857-10.]

☐ [*T.D. 6598, 4-25-62. Amended by T.D. 7767, 2-3-81.*]

Real Estate Investment Trusts

See p. 20,601 for regulations not amended to reflect law changes

[Reg. § 1.857-11]

§ 1.857-11. Non-REIT earnings and profits.—(a) *Applicability of section 857(a)(3)(A).* A real estate investment trust does not satisfy section 857(a)(3)(A) unless—

(1) Part II of subchapter M applied to the trust for all its taxable years beginning after February 28, 1986; and

(2) For each corporation to whose earnings and profits the trust succeeded by the operation of section 381, part II of subchapter M applied for all the corporation's taxable years beginning after February 28, 1986.

(b) *Applicability of section 857(a)(3)(B); in general.* A real estate investment trust does not satisfy section 857(a)(3)(B) unless, as of the close of the taxable year, it has no earnings and profits other than earnings and profits that—

(1) Were earned by a corporation in a year for which part II of subchapter M applied to the corporation and, at all times thereafter, were the earnings and profits of a corporation to which part II of subchapter M applied; or

(2) By the operation of section 381 pursuant to a transaction that occurred before December 22, 1992, became the earnings and profits of a corporation to which part II of subchapter M applied and, at all times thereafter, were the earnings and profits of a corporation to which part II of subchapter M applied.

(c) *Distribution procedures similar to those for regulated investment companies to apply.* Distribution procedures similar to those in section 852(e) for regulated investment companies apply to non-REIT earnings and profits of real estate investment trusts.

(d) *Effective date.* This regulation is effective for taxable years ending on or after December 22, 1992.

(e) For treatment of net built-in gain assets of a C corporation that become assets of a REIT, see § 1.337(d)5T. [Reg. § 1.857-11.]

☐ [T.D. 8483, 8-17-93. Amended by T.D. 8872, 2-4-2000.]

[Reg. § 1.858-1]

§ 1.858-1. Dividends paid by a real estate investment trust after close of taxable year.—(a) *General rule.* Under section 858, a real estate investment trust may elect to treat certain dividends that are distributed within a specified period after the close of a taxable year as having been paid during the taxable year. The dividend is taken into account in determining the deduction for dividends paid for the taxable year in which it is treated as paid. The dividend may be an ordinary dividend or, subject to the requirements of sections 857(b)(3)(C) and 858(c), a capital gain dividend. The trust may make the dividend declaration required by section 858(a)(1) either before or after the close of the taxable year as long as the declaration is made before the time prescribed by law for filing its return for the taxable year (including the period of any extension of time granted for filing the return).

(b) *Election*—(1) *Method of making election.* The election must be made in the return filed by the trust for the taxable year. The election shall be made by treating the dividend (or portion thereof) to which the election applies as a dividend paid during the taxable year of the trust in computing its real estate investment trust taxable income and, if applicable, the alternative tax imposed by section 857(b)(3)(A). (In the case of an election with respect to a taxable year ending before October 5, 1976, if the dividend (or portion thereof) to which election is to apply is a capital gain dividend, the trust shall treat the dividend as paid during such taxable year in computing the amount of capital gains dividends paid during the taxable year.) In the case of an election with respect to a taxable year beginning after October 4, 1976, the trust must also specify in its return (or in a statement attached to its return) the exact dollar amount that is to be treated as having been paid during the taxable year.

(2) *Limitation based on earnings and profits.* The election provided in section 858(a) may be made only to the extent that the earnings and profits of the taxable year (computed with the application of section 857(d) and § 1.857-7) exceed the total amount of distributions out of such earnings and profits actually made during the taxable year. For purposes of the preceding sentence, deficiency dividends and distributions with respect to which an election has been made for a prior year under section 858(a) are disregarded in determining the total amount of distributions out of earnings and profits actually made during the taxable year. The dividend or portion thereof, with respect to which the real estate investment trust has made a valid election under section 858(a), shall be considered as paid out of the earnings and profits of the taxable year for which such election is made, and not out of the earnings and profits of the taxable year in which the distribution is actually made.

(3) *Additional limitation based on amount specified.* The amount treated under section 858(a) as having been paid in a taxable year beginning after October 4, 1976, cannot exceed the lesser of (i) the dollar amount specified by the trust in its return (or a statement attached

Reg. § 1.857-11(a)(1)

thereto) in making the election or (ii) the amount allowable under the limitation prescribed in paragraph (b)(2) of this section.

(4) *Irrevocability of the election.* After the expiration of the time for filing the return for the taxable year for which an election is made under section 858(a), such election shall be irrevocable with respect to the dividend or portion thereof to which it applies.

(c) *Receipt by shareholders.* Under section 858(b), the dividend or portion thereof, with respect to which a valid election has been made, will be includible in the gross income of the shareholders of the real estate investment trust for the taxable year in which the dividend is received by them.

(d) *Illustrations.* The application of paragraphs (a), (b), and (c) of this section may be illustrated by the following examples:

Example (1). The X Trust, a real estate investment trust, had taxable income (and earnings and profits) for the calendar year 1961 of $100,000. During that year the trust distributed to shareholders taxable dividends aggregating $88,000. On March 10, 1962, the trust declared a dividend of $37,000 payable to shareholders on March 20, 1962. Such dividend consisted of the first regular quarterly dividend for 1962 of $25,000 plus an additional $12,000 representing that part of the taxable income for 1961 which was not distributed in 1961. On March 15, 1962, the X Trust filed its Federal income tax return and elected therein to treat $12,000 of the total dividend of $37,000 to be paid to shareholders on March 20, 1962, as having been paid during the taxable year 1961. Assuming that the X Trust actually distributed the entire amount of the dividend of $37,000 on March 20, 1962, an amount equal to $12,000 thereof will be treated for the purposes of section 857(a) as having been paid during the taxable year 1961. Upon distribution of such dividend the trust becomes a qualified real estate investment trust for the taxable year 1961. Such amount ($12,000) will be considered by the X Trust as a distribution out of the earnings and profits for the taxable year 1961, and will be treated by the shareholders as a taxable dividend for the taxable year in which such distribution is received by them. However, assuming that the X Trust is not a qualified real estate investment trust for the calendar year 1962, nevertheless, the $12,000 portion of the dividend (paid on March 20, 1962) which the trust elected to relate to the calendar year 1961, will not qualify as a dividend for purposes of section 34, 116, or 243.

Example (2). The Y Trust, a real estate investment trust, had taxable income (and earnings and profits) for the calendar year 1964 of $100,000, and for 1965 taxable income (and earnings and profits) of $125,000. On January 1, 1964, the trust had a deficit in its earnings and profits accumulated since February 28, 1913, of $115,000. During the year 1964 the trust distributed to shareholders taxable dividends aggregating $85,000. On March 5, 1965, the trust declared a dividend of $65,000 payable to shareholders on March 31, 1965. On March 15, 1965, the Y Trust filed its Federal income tax return in which it included $40,000 of the total dividend of $65,000 payable to shareholders on March 31, 1965, as a dividend paid by it during the taxable year 1964. On March 31, 1965, the Y Trust distributed the entire amount of the dividend of $65,000 declared on March 5, 1965. The election under section 858(a) is valid only to the extent of $15,000, the amount of the undistributed earnings and profits for 1964 ($100,000 earnings and profits less $85,000 distributed during 1964). The remainder ($50,000) of the $65,000 dividend paid on March 31, 1965, could not be the subject of an election, and such amount will be regarded as a distribution by the Y Trust out of earnings and profits for the taxable year 1965. Assuming that the only other distribution by the Y Trust during 1965 was a distribution of $75,000 paid as a dividend on October 31, 1965, the total amount of the distribution of $65,000 paid on March 31, 1965, is to be treated by the shareholders as taxable dividends for the taxable year in which such dividend is received. The Y Trust will treat the amount of $15,000 as a distribution of the earnings or profits of the trust for the taxable year 1964, and the remaining $50,000 as a distribution of the earnings or profits for the year 1965. The distribution of $75,000 on October 31, 1965, is, of course, a taxable dividend out of the earnings and profits for the year 1965.

Example (3). Assume the facts are the same as in example (2), except that the taxable years involved are calendar years 1977 and 1978, and Y Trust specified in its Federal income tax return for 1977 that the dollar amount of $40,000 of the $65,000 distribution payable to shareholders on March 31, 1978, is to be treated as having been paid in 1977. The result will be the same as in example (2), since the amount of the undistributed earnings and profits for 1977 is less than the $40,000 amount specified by Y Trust in making its election. Accordingly, the election is valid only to the extent of $15,000. Y Trust will treat the amount of $15,000 as a distribution, in 1977, of earnings and profits of the trust for the taxable year 1977 and the remaining $50,000 as a distribution, in 1978, of the earnings and profits for 1978.

Reg. § 1.858-1(d)

Provisions Which Apply Both to RICs and REITs

See p. 20,601 for regulations not amended to reflect law changes

(e) *Notice to shareholders.* Section 858(c) provides that, in the case of dividends with respect to which a real estate investment trust has made an election under section 858(a), any notice to shareholders required under part II, subchapter M, chapter 1 of the Code, with respect to such amounts, shall be made not later than 30 days after the close of the taxable year in which the distribution is made. Thus, the notice requirement of section 857(b)(3)(C) and paragraph (f) of § 1.857-6 with respect to capital gains dividends may be satisfied with respect to amounts to which section 858(a) and this section apply if the notice relating to such amounts is mailed to the shareholders not later than 30 days after the close of the taxable year in which the distribution is made. If the notice under section 858(c) relates to an election with respect to any capital gains dividends, such capital gains dividends shall be aggregated by the real estate investment trust with the designated capital gains dividends actually paid during the taxable year to which the election applies (not including deficiency dividends or dividends with respect to which an election has been made for a prior taxable year under section 858) to determine whether the aggregate of the designated capital gains dividends with respect to such taxable year exceeds the net capital gain of the trust. See section 857(b)(3)(C) and paragraph (f) of § 1.857-6. [Reg. § 1.858-1.]

☐ [T.D. 6598, 4-25-62. Amended by T.D. 7767, 2-3-81.]

Provisions Which Apply Both to RICs and REITs

[Reg. § 1.860-1]

§ 1.860-1. **Deficiency dividends.**—Section 860 allows a qualified investment entity to be relieved from the payment of a deficiency in (or to be allowed a credit or refund of) certain taxes. "Qualified investment entity" is defined in section 860(b). The taxes referred to are those imposed by sections 852(b)(1) and (3), 857(b)(1) or (3), the minimum tax on tax preferences imposed by section 56 and, if the entity fails the distribution requirements of section 852(a)(1)(A) or 857(a)(1) (as applicable), the corporate income tax imposed by section 11(a) or 1201(a). The method provided by section 860 is to allow an additional deduction for a dividend distribution (that meets the requirements of section 860 and § 1.860-2) in computing the deduction for dividends paid for the taxable year for which the deficiency is determined. A deficiency dividend may be an ordinary dividend or, subject to the limitations of sections 852(b)(3)(C), 857(b)(3)(C), and 860(f)(2)(B), may be a capital gain dividend. [Reg. § 1.860-1.]

☐ [T.D. 7767, 2-3-81. Amended by T.D. 7936, 1-17-84.]

[Reg. § 1.860-2]

§ 1.860-2. **Requirements for deficiency dividends.**—(a) *In general*—(1) *Determination, etc.* A qualified investment entity is allowed a deduction for a deficiency dividend only if there is a determination (as defined in section 860(e) and paragraph (b)(1) of this section) that results in an adjustment (as defined in section 860(d)(1) or (2)) for the taxable year for which the deficiency dividend is paid. An adjustment does not include an increase in the excess of (i) the taxpayer's interest income excludable from gross income under section 103(a) over (ii) its deductions disallowed under section 265 and 171(a)(2).

(2) *Payment date and claim.* The deficiency dividend must be paid on, or within 90 days after, the date of the determination and before the filing of a claim under section 860(g) and paragraph (b)(2) of this section. This claim must be filed within 120 days after the date of the determination.

(3) *Nature and amount of distribution.* (i) The deficiency dividend must be a distribution of property (including money) that would have been property taken into account in computing the dividends paid deduction under section 561 for the taxable year for which tax liability resulting from the determination exists if the property had been distributed during that year. Thus, if the distribution would have been a dividend under section 316(a) if it had been made during the taxable year for which the determination applies, the distribution may qualify under sections 316(b)(3), 562(a), and 860(f)(1), even though the distributing corporation, trust, or association has no current or accumulated earnings and profits for the taxable year in which the distribution is actually made. The amount of the distribution is determined under section 301 as of the date of the distribution.

The amount of the deduction is subject to the applicable limitations under sections 562 and 860(f)(2). Thus, if the entity distributes to an individual shareholder property (other than money) which on the date of the distribution has a fair market value in excess of its adjusted basis in the hands of the entity, the amount of the deficiency dividend in the individual's hands for purposes of section 316(b)(3) is determined by using the property's fair market value on that date. Nevertheless, the amount of the deficiency dividend the entity may deduct is limited, under § 1.562-1(a), to the adjusted basis of the property

Reg. § 1.860-1

and the amount taxable to the individual as a dividend is determined by reference to the current and accumulated earnings and profits for the year to which the determination applies.

(ii) The qualified investment entity does not have to distribute the full amount of the adjustment in order to pay a deficiency dividend. For example, assume that in 1983 a determination with respect to a calendar year regulated investment company results in an increase of $100 in investment company taxable income (computed without the dividends paid deduction) for 1981 and no other change. The regulated investment company may choose to pay a deficiency dividend of $100 or of any lesser amount and be allowed a dividends paid deduction for 1981 for the amount of that deficiency dividend.

(4) *Status of distributor.* The corporation, trust, or association that pays the deficiency dividend does not have to be a qualified investment entity at the time of payment.

(5) *Certain definitions to apply.* For purposes of sections 860(d) (defining adjustment) and (f)(2) (limitations) the definitions of the terms "investment company taxable income," "real estate investment trust taxable income," and "capital gains dividends" in sections 852(b)(2), 857(b)(2), and 857(b)(3)(C) apply, as appropriate to the particular entity.

(b) *Determination and claim for deduction—* (1) *Determination.* For purposes of applying section 860(e), the following rules apply:

(i) The date of determination by a decision of the United States Tax Court, the date upon which a judgment of a court becomes final, and the date of determination by a closing agreement shall be determined under the rules in § 1.547-2(b)(1)(ii), (iii), and (iv).

(ii) A determination under section 860(e)(3) may be made by an agreement signed by the district director or another official to whom authority to sign the agreement is delegated, and by or on behalf of the taxpayer. The agreement shall set forth the amount, if any, of each adjustment described in subparagraphs (A), (B), and (C) of section 860(d)(1) or (2) (as appropriate) for the taxable year and the amount of the liability for any tax imposed by section 11(a), 56(a), 852(b)(1), 852(b)(3)(A), 857(b)(1), 857(b)(3)(A), or 1201(a) for the taxable year. The agreement shall also set forth the amount of the limitation (determined under section 860(f)(2)) on the amount of deficiency dividends that can qualify as capital gain dividends and ordinary dividends, respectively, for the taxable year. An agreement under this subdivision (ii) which is signed by the district director (or other delegate) shall be sent to the taxpayer at its last known address by either registered or certified mail. For further guidance regarding the definition of last known address, see § 301.6212-2 of this chapter. If registered mail is used, the date of registration is the date of determination. If certified mail is used, the date of the postmark on the sender's receipt is the date of determination. However, if a dividend is paid by the taxpayer before the registration or postmark date, but on or after the date the agreement is signed by the district director (or other delegate), the date of determination is the date of signing.

(2) *Claim for deduction.* A claim for deduction for a deficiency dividend shall be made, with the requisite declaration, on Form 976 and shall contain the following information and have the following attachments:

(i) The name, address, and taxpayer identification number of the corporation, trust, or association;

(ii) The amount of the deficiency and the taxable year or years involved;

(iii) The amount of the unpaid deficiency or, if the deficiency has been paid in whole or in part, the date of payment and the amount thereof;

(iv) A statement as to how the deficiency was established (*i.e.,* by an agreement under section 860(e)(3), by a closing agreement under section 7121, or by a decision of the Tax Court or court judgment);

(v) Any date or other information with respect to the determination that is required by Form 976;

(vi) The amount and date of payment of the dividend with respect to which the claim for the deduction for deficiency dividends is filed;

(vii) The amount claimed as a deduction for deficiency dividends;

(viii) If the amount claimed as a deduction for deficiency dividends includes any amount designated (or to be designated) as capital gain dividends, the amount of capital gain dividends for which a deficiency dividend deduction is claimed;

(ix) Any other information required by the claim form;

(x) A certified copy of the resolution of the trustees, directors, or other authority authorizing the payment of the dividend with respect to which the claim is filed; and

(xi) A copy of any court decision, judgment, agreement, or other document required by Form 976.

(3) *Filing claim.* The claim, together with the accompanying documents, shall be filed with the

Reg. § 1.860-2(b)(3)

district director, or director of the internal revenue service center, with whom the income tax return for the taxable year for which the determination applies was filed. In the event that the determination is an agreement with the district director (or other delegate) described in section 860(e)(3) and paragraph (b)(1)(ii) of this section, the claim may be filed with the district director with whom (or pursuant to whose delegation) the agreement was made. [Reg. § 1.860-2.]

☐ [T.D. 7767, 2-3-81. Amended by T.D. 7936, 1-17-84 and T.D. 8939, 1-11-2001.]

[Reg. § 1.860-3]

§ 1.860-3. Interest and additions to tax.—(a) *In general.* If a qualified investment entity is allowed a deduction for deficiency dividends with respect to a taxable year, under section 860(c)(1) the tax imposed on the entity by chapter 1 of the Code (computed by taking into account the deduction) for that year is deemed to be increased by the amount of the deduction. This deemed increase in tax, however, applies solely for purposes of determining the liability of the entity for interest under subchapter A of chapter 67 of the Code and for additions to tax and additional amounts under chapter 68 of the Code. For purposes of applying subchapter A of chapter 67 and chapter 68, the last date prescribed for payment of the deemed increase in tax is considered to be the last date prescribed for the payment of tax (determined in the manner provided in section 6601(b)) for the taxable year for which the deduction for deficiency dividends is allowed. The deemed increase in tax is considered to be paid as of the date that the claim for the deficiency dividend deduction described in section 860(g) is filed.

(b) *Overpayments of tax.* If a qualified investment entity is entitled to a credit or refund of an overpayment of the tax imposed by chapter 1 of the Code for the taxable year for which the deficiency dividend deduction is allowed, then, for purposes of computing interest, additions to tax, and additional amounts, the payment (or payments) that result in the overpayment and that precede the filing of the claim described in section 860(g) will be applied against and reduce the increase in tax that is deemed to occur under section 860(c)(1).

(c) *Examples.* This section is illustrated by the following examples:

Example (1). Corporation X is a real estate investment trust that files its income tax return on a calendar year basis. X receives an extension of time until June 15, 1978, to file its 1977 income tax return and files the return on May 15, 1978. X does not elect to pay any tax due in installments. For 1977, X reports real estate investment trust taxable income (computed without the dividends paid deduction) of $100, a dividends paid deduction of $100, and no tax liability. Following an examination of X's 1977 return, the district director and X enter into an agreement which is a determination under section 860(e)(3). The determination is dated November 1, 1979, and increases X's real estate investment trust taxable income (computed without the dividends paid deduction) by $20 to $120. Thus, taking into account the $100 of dividends paid in 1977, X has undistributed real estate investment trust taxable income of $20 as a result of the determination. X pays a dividend of $20 on November 10, 1979, files a claim for a deficiency dividend deduction of this $20 pursuant to section 860(g) on November 15, 1979, and is allowed a deficiency dividend deduction of $20 for 1977. After taking into account this deduction, X has no real estate investment trust taxable income and meets the distribution requirements of section 857(a)(1). However, for purposes of section 6601 (relating to interest on underpayment of tax), the tax imposed by chapter 1 of the Code on X for 1977 is deemed increased by this $20, and the last date prescribed for payment of the tax is March 15, 1978 (the due date of the 1977 return determined without any extension of time). The tax of $20 is deemed paid on November 15, 1979, the date the claim for the deficiency dividend deduction is filed. Thus, X is liable for interest on $20, at the rate established under section 6621, for the period from March 15, 1978, to November 15, 1979. Also, for purposes of determining whether X is liable for any addition to tax or additional amount imposed by chapter 68 of the Code (including the penalty prescribed by section 6697), the amount of tax imposed on X by chapter 1 of the Code is deemed to be increased by $20 (the amount of the deficiency dividend deduction allowed), the last date prescribed for payment of such tax is March 15, 1978, and the tax of $20 is deemed to be paid on November 15, 1979. X, however, is not subject to interest and penalties for the amount of any tax for which it would have been liable under section 11(a), 56(a), 1201(a), or 857(b) had it not been allowed the $20 deduction for deficiency dividends.

Example (2). Assume the facts are the same as in example (1) except that the district director, upon examining X's income tax return, asserts an income tax deficiency of $4, based on an asserted increase of $10 in real estate investment trust taxable income, and no agreement is entered into between the parties. X pays the $4 on June 1, 1979, and files suit for refund in the United States District Court. The District Court, in a decision which becomes final on November 1, 1980, holds that X did fail to report $10 of real estate investment trust taxable income and is not entitled to any refund. (No other item of income or deduction is in issue.) X pays a dividend of $10 on November 10, 1980, files a claim for a deficiency dividend deduction of this $10 on November 15, 1980, and is allowed a deficiency dividend deduction of $10 for 1977. Assume further that $4 is refunded to X on December 31, 1980, as the result of the $10 deficiency dividend deduction being allowed. Also assume that any assessable penalties, additional amounts, and additions to tax (including the penalty imposed by section 6697) for which X is liable are paid within 10 days of notice and demand, so that no interest is imposed on such penalties, etc. X's liability for interest for the period March 15, 1978, to June 1, 1979, is determined with respect to $10 (the amount of the deficiency dividend deduction allowed). X's liability for interest for the period June 1, 1979, to November 15, 1980, is determined with respect to $6, i.e., $10 minus the $4 payment. X is entitled to interest on the $4 overpayment for the period described in section 6611(b)(2), beginning on November 15, 1980. [Reg. § 1.860-3.]

☐ [T.D. 7767, 2-3-81. Amended by T.D. 7936, 1-17-84.]

[Reg. § 1.860-4]

§ 1.860-4. Claim for credit or refund.—If the allowance of a deduction for a deficiency dividend results in an overpayment of tax, the taxpayer, in order to secure credit or refund of the overpayment, must file a claim on Form 1120X in addition to the claim for the deficiency dividend deduction required under section 860(g). The credit or refund will be allowed as if on the date of the determination (as defined in section 860(e)) two years remained before the expiration of the period of limitations on the filing of claim for refund for the taxable year to which the overpayment relates. [Reg. § 1.860-4.]

☐ [T.D. 7767, 2-3-81. Amended by T.D. 7936, 1-17-84.]

[Reg. § 1.860-5]

§ 1.860-5. Effective date.—(a) *In general.* Section 860 and §§ 1.860-1 through 1.860-4 apply with respect to determinations after November 6, 1978.

(b) *Prior determination of real estate investments trusts.* Section 859 (as in effect before the enactment of the Revenue Act of 1978) applies to determinations with respect to real estate investment trusts occurring after October 4, 1976, and before November 7, 1978. In the case of such a determination, the rules in §§ 1.860-1 through 1.860-4 apply, a reference in this chapter 1 to section 860 (or to a particular provision of section 860) shall be considered to be a reference to section 859 (or to the corresponding substantive provision of section 859), as in effect before enactment of the Revenue Act of 1978, and "qualified investment entity" in §§ 1.381(c)25-1(a) and 1.860-1 through 1.860-3 means a real estate investment trust. [Reg. § 1.860.5.]

☐ [T.D. 7936, 1-17-84.]

Real Estate Mortgage Investment Conduits

[Reg. § 1.860A-0]

§ 1.860A-0. Outline of REMIC provisions.—This section lists the paragraphs contained in §§ 1.860A-1 through 1.860G-3.

§ 1.860A-1. Effective dates and transition rules.

(a) In general.

(b) Exceptions.

(1) Reporting regulations.

(2) Tax avoidance rules.

(i) Transfers of certain residual interests.

(ii) Transfers to foreign holders.

(iii) Residual interests that lack significant value.

(3) Excise taxes.

(4) Rate based on current interest rate.

(i) In general.

(ii) Rate based on index.

(iii) Transition obligations.

§ 1.860C-1. Taxation of holders of residual interests.

(a) Pass-thru of income or loss.

(b) Adjustments to basis of residual interests.

(1) Increase in basis.

(2) Decrease in basis.

(3) Adjustments made before disposition.

(c) Counting conventions.

§ 1.860C-2. Determination of REMIC taxable income or net loss.

(a) Treatment of gain or loss.

(b) Deductions allowable to a REMIC.

(1) In general.

(2) Deduction allowable under section 163.

(3) Deduction allowable under section 166.

(4) Deduction allowable under section 212.

(5) Expenses and interest relating to tax-exempt income.

Reg. § 1.860A-0

Real Estate Mortgage Investment Conduits

See p. 20,601 for regulations not amended to reflect law changes

§ 1.860D-1. Definition of a REMIC.
  (a) In general.
  (b) Specific requirements.
    (1) Interests in a REMIC.
      (i) In general.
      (ii) De minimis interests.
    (2) Certain rights not treated as interests.
      (i) Payments for services.
      (ii) Stripped interests.
      (iii) Reimbursement rights under credit enhancement contracts.
      (iv) Rights to acquire mortgages.
    (3) Asset test.
      (i) In general.
      (ii) Safe harbor.
    (4) Arrangements test.
    (5) Reasonable arrangements.
      (i) Arrangements to prevent disqualified organizations from holding residual interests.
      (ii) Arrangements to ensure that information will be provided.
    (6) Calendar year requirement.
  (c) Segregated pool of assets.
    (1) Formation of REMIC.
    (2) Identification of assets.
    (3) Qualified entity defined.
  (d) Election to be treated as a real estate mortgage investment conduit.
    (1) In general.
    (2) Information required to be reported in the REMIC's first taxable year.
    (3) Requirement to keep sufficient records.

§ 1.860E-1. Treatment of taxable income of a residual interest holder in excess of daily accruals.
  (a) Excess inclusion cannot be offset by otherwise allowable deductions.
    (1) In general.
    (2) Affiliated groups.
    (3) Special rule for certain financial institutions.
      (i) In general.
      (ii) Ordering rule.
        (A) In general.
        (B) Example.
      (iii) Significant value.
      (iv) Determining anticipated weighted average life.
        (A) Anticipated weighted average life of the REMIC.
        (B) Regular interests that have a specified principal amount.
        (C) Regular interests that have no specified principal amount or that have only a nominal principal amount, and all residual interests.
        (D) Anticipated payments.
  (b) Treatment of a residual interest held by REITs, RICs, common trust funds, and subchapter T cooperatives. [Reserved]
  (c) Transfers of noneconomic residual interests.
    (1) In general.
    (2) Noneconomic residual interest.
    (3) Computations.
    (4) Safe harbor for establishing lack of improper knowledge.
    (5) Asset test.
    (6) Definitions for asset test.
    (7) Formula test.
    (8) Conditions and limitations on formula test.
    (9) Examples.
    (10) Effective dates.
  (d) Transfers to foreign persons.

§ 1.860E-2. Tax on transfers of residual interest to certain organizations.
  (a) Transfers to disqualified organizations.
    (1) Payment of tax.
    (2) Transitory ownership.
    (3) Anticipated excess inclusions.
    (4) Present value computation.
    (5) Obligation of REMIC to furnish information.
    (6) Agent.
    (7) Relief from liability.
      (i) Transferee furnishes information under penalties of perjury.
      (ii) Amount required to be paid.
  (b) Tax on pass-thru entities.
    (1) Tax on excess inclusions.
    (2) Record holder furnishes information under penalties of perjury.
    (3) Deductibility of tax.
    (4) Allocation of tax.

§ 1.860F-1. Qualified liquidations.
§ 1.860F-2. Transfers to a REMIC.
  (a) Formation of a REMIC.
    (1) In general.
    (2) Tiered arrangements.
      (i) Two or more REMICs formed pursuant to a single set of organizational documents.

Reg. § 1.860A-0

(ii) A REMIC and one or more investment trusts formed pursuant to a single set of documents.

(b) Treatment of sponsor.

(1) Sponsor defined.

(2) Nonrecognition of gain or loss.

(3) Basis of contributed assets allocated among interests.

(i) In general.

(ii) Organizational expenses.

(A) Organizational expense defined.

(B) Syndication expenses.

(iii) Pricing date.

(4) Treatment of unrecognized gain or loss.

(i) Unrecognized gain on regular interests.

(ii) Unrecognized loss on regular interests.

(iii) Unrecognized gain on residual interests.

(iv) Unrecognized loss on residual interests.

(5) Additions to or reductions of the sponsor's basis.

(6) Transferred basis property.

(c) REMIC's basis in contributed assets.

§ 1.860F-4. *REMIC reporting requirements and other administrative rules.*

(a) In general.

(b) REMIC tax return.

(1) In general.

(2) Income tax return.

(c) Signing of REMIC return.

(1) In general.

(2) REMIC whose startup day is before November 10, 1988.

(i) In general.

(ii) Startup day.

(iii) Exception.

(d) Designation of tax matters person.

(e) Notice to holders of residual interests.

(1) Information required.

(i) In general.

(ii) Information with respect to REMIC assets.

(A) 95 percent asset test.

(B) Additional information required if the 95 percent test not met.

(C) For calendar quarters in 1987.

(D) For calendar quarters in 1988 and 1989.

(iii) Special provisions.

(2) Quarterly notice required.

(i) In general.

(ii) Special rule for 1987.

(3) Nominee reporting.

(i) In general.

(ii) Time for furnishing statement.

(4) Reports to the Internal Revenue Service.

(f) Information returns for persons engaged in a trade or business.

§ 1.860G-1. *Definition of regular and residual interests.*

(a) Regular interest.

(1) Designation as a regular interest.

(2) Specified portion of the interest payments on qualified mortgages.

(i) In general.

(ii) Specified portion cannot vary.

(iii) Defaulted or delinquent mortgages.

(iv) No minimum specified principal amount is required.

(v) Specified portion includes portion of interest payable on regular interest.

(vi) Examples.

(3) Variable rate.

(i) Rate based on current interest rate.

(ii) Weighted average rate.

(A) In general.

(B) Reduction in underlying rate.

(iii) Additions, subtractions, and multiplications.

(iv) Caps and floors.

(v) Funds-available caps.

(A) In general.

(B) Facts and circumstances test.

(C) Examples.

(vi) Combination of rates.

(4) Fixed terms on the startup day.

(5) Contingencies prohibited.

(b) Special rules for regular interests.

(1) Call premium.

(2) Customary prepayment penalties received with respect to qualified mortgages.

(3) Certain contingencies disregarded.

(i) Prepayments, income, and expenses.

(ii) Credit losses.

(iii) Subordinated interests.

(iv) Deferral of interest.

(v) Prepayment interest shortfalls.

(vi) Remote and incidental contingencies.

Reg. § 1.860A-0

45,938 **Real Estate Mortgage Investment Conduits**
See p. 20,601 for regulations not amended to reflect law changes

(4) Form of regular interest.

(5) Interest disproportionate to principal.

   (i) In general.

   (ii) Exception.

(6) Regular interest treated as a debt instrument for all Federal income tax purposes.

(c) Residual interest.

(d) Issue price of regular and residual interests.

   (1) In general.

   (2) The public.

§ 1.860G-2. Other rules.

(a) Obligations principally secured by an interest in real property.

   (1) Tests for determining whether an obligation is principally secured.

     (i) The 80-percent test.

     (ii) Alternative test.

   (2) Treatment of liens.

   (3) Safe harbor.

     (i) Reasonable belief that an obligation is principally secured.

     (ii) Basis for reasonable belief.

     (iii) Later discovery that an obligation is not principally secured.

   (4) Interests in real property; real property.

   (5) Obligations secured by an interest in real property.

   (6) Obligations secured by other obligations; residual interests.

   (7) Certain instruments that call for contingent payments are obligations.

   (8) Defeasance.

   (9) Stripped bonds and coupons.

(b) Assumptions and modifications.

   (1) Significant modifications are treated as exchanges of obligations.

   (2) Significant modification defined.

   (3) Exceptions.

   (4) Modifications that are not significant modifications.

   (5) Assumption defined.

   (6) Pass-thru certificates.

(c) Treatment of certain credit enhancement contracts.

   (1) In general.

   (2) Credit enhancement contracts.

   (3) Arrangements to make certain advances.

     (i) Advances of delinquent principal and interest.

     (ii) Advances of taxes, insurance payments, and expenses.

     (iii) Advances to ease REMIC administration.

   (4) Deferred payment under a guarantee arrangement.

(d) Treatment of certain purchase agreements with respect to convertible mortgages.

   (1) In general.

   (2) Treatment of amounts received under purchase agreements.

   (3) Purchase agreement.

   (4) Default by the person obligated to purchase a convertible mortgage.

   (5) Convertible mortgage.

(e) Prepayment interest shortfalls.

(f) Defective obligations.

   (1) Defective obligation defined.

   (2) Effect of discovery of defect.

(g) Permitted investments.

   (1) Cash flow investment.

     (i) In general.

     (ii) Payments received on qualified mortgages.

     (iii) Temporary period.

   (2) Qualified reserve funds.

   (3) Qualified reserve asset.

     (i) In general.

     (ii) Reasonably required reserve.

        (A) In general.

        (B) Presumption that a reserve is reasonably required.

        (C) Presumption may be rebutted.

(h) Outside reserve funds.

(i) Contractual rights coupled with regular interests in tiered arrangements.

   (1) In general.

   (2) Example.

(j) Clean-up call.

   (1) In general.

   (2) Interest rate changes.

   (3) Safe harbor.

(k) Startup day.

§ 1.860G-3. *Treatment of foreign persons.*

(a) Transfer of a residual interest with tax avoidance potential.

   (1) In general.

   (2) Tax avoidance potential.

     (i) Defined.

     (ii) Safe harbor.

Reg. § 1.860A-0

(3) Effectively connected income.

(4) Transfer by a foreign holder.

(b) [Reserved]

[Reg. § 1.860A-0.]

☐ [T.D. 8458, 12-23-92. Amended by T.D. 8614, 8-16-95 and T.D. 9004, 7-18-2002.]

[Reg. § 1.860A-1]

§ 1.860A-1. Effective dates and transition rules.—(a) *In general.* Except as otherwise provided in paragraph (b) of this section, the regulations under sections 860A through 860G are effective only for a qualified entity (as defined in § 1.860D-1(c)(3)) whose startup day (as defined in section 860G(a)(9) and § 1.860G-2(k)) is on or after November 12, 1991.

(b) *Exceptions*—(1) *Reporting regulations*—(i) Sections 1.860D-1(c)(1) and (3), and § 1.860D-1(d)(1) through (3) are effective after December 31, 1986.

(ii) Sections 1.860F-4(a) through (e) are effective after December 31, 1986 and are applicable after that date except as follows:

(A) Section 1.860F-4(c)(1) is effective for REMICs with a startup day on or after November 10, 1988.

(B) Sections 1.860F-4(e)(1)(ii)(A) and (B) are effective for calendar quarters and calendar years beginning after December 31, 1988.

(C) Section 1.860F-4(e)(1)(ii)(C) is effective for calendar quarters and calendar years beginning after December 31, 1986 and ending before January 1, 1988.

(D) Section 1.860F-4(e)(1)(ii)(D) is effective for calendar quarters and calendar years beginning after December 31, 1987 and ending before January 1, 1990.

(2) *Tax avoidance rules*—(i) *Transfers of certain residual interests.* Section 1.860E-1(c) (concerning transfers of noneconomic residual interests) and § 1.860G-3 (a)(4) (concerning transfers by a foreign holder to a United States person) are effective for transfers of residual interests on or after September 27, 1991.

(ii) *Transfers to foreign holders.* Generally, § 1.860G-3(a) (concerning transfers of residual interests to foreign holders) is effective for transfers of residual interests after April 20, 1992. However, § 1.860G-3(a) does not apply to a transfer of a residual interest in a REMIC by the REMIC's sponsor (or by another transferor contemporaneously with formation of the REMIC) on or before June 30, 1992, if—

(A) The terms of the regular interests and the prices at which regular interests were offered had been fixed on or before April 20, 1992;

(B) On or before June 30, 1992, a substantial portion of the regular interests in the REMIC were transferred, with the terms and at the prices that were fixed on or before April 20, 1992, to investors who were unrelated to the REMIC's sponsor at the time of the transfer; and

(C) At the time of the transfer of the residual interest, the expected future distributions on the residual interest were equal to at least 30 percent of the anticipated excess inclusions (as defined in § 1.860E-2(a)(3)), and the transferor reasonably expected that the transferee would receive sufficient distributions from the REMIC at or after the time at which the excess inclusions accrue in an amount sufficient to satisfy the taxes on the excess inclusions.

(iii) *Residual interests that lack significant value.* The significant value requirement in § 1.860E-1(a)(1) and (3) (concerning excess inclusions accruing to organizations to which section 593 applies) generally is effective for residual interests acquired on or after September 27, 1991. The significant value requirement in 1.860E-1(a)(1) and (3) does not apply, however, to residual interests acquired by an organization to which section 593 applies as a sponsor at formation of a REMIC in a transaction described in § 1.860F-2(a)(1) if more than 50 percent of the interests in the REMIC (determined by reference to issue price) were sold to unrelated investors before November 12, 1991. The exception from the significant value requirement provided by the preceding sentence applies only so long as the sponsor owns the residual interests.

(3) *Excise taxes.* Section 1.860E-2(a)(1) is effective for transfers of residual interests to disqualified organizations after March 31, 1988. Section 1.860E-2(b)(1) is effective for excess inclusions accruing to pass-thru entities after March 31, 1988.

(4) *Rate based on current interest rate*—(i) *In general.* Section 1.860G-1(a)(3)(i) applies to obligations (other than transition obligations described in paragraph (b)(4)(iii) of this section) intended to qualify as regular interests that are issued on or after April 4, 1994.

(ii) *Rate based on index.* Section 1.860G-1(a)(3)(i) (as contained in 26 CFR part 1 revised as of April 1, 1994) applies to obligations intended to qualify as regular interests that—

(A) Are issued by a qualified entity (as defined in § 1.860D-1(c)(3)) whose startup date (as defined in section 860G(a)(9) and

§ 1.860G-2(k)) is on or after November 12, 1991; and

(B) Are either—

(1) Issued before April 4, 1994; or

(2) Transition obligations described in paragraph (b)(4)(iii) of this section.

(iii) *Transition obligations.* Obligations are described in this paragraph (b)(4)(iii) if—

(A) The terms of the obligations and the prices at which the obligations are offered are fixed before April 4, 1994; and

(B) On or before June 1, 1994, a substantial portion of the obligations are transferred, with the terms and at the prices that are fixed before April 4, 1994, to investors who are unrelated to the REMIC's sponsor at the time of the transfer. [Reg. § 1.860A-1.]

☐ [T.D. 8458, 12-23-92. Amended by T.D. 8614, 8-16-95.]

[Reg. § 1.860C-1]

§ 1.860C-1. **Taxation of holders of residual interests.**—(a) *Pass-thru of income or loss.* Any holder of a residual interest in a REMIC must take into account the holder's daily portion of the taxable income or net loss of the REMIC for each day during the taxable year on which the holder owned the residual interest.

(b) *Adjustments to basis of residual interests*— (1) *Increase in basis.* A holder's basis in a residual interest is increased by—

(i) The daily portions of taxable income taken into account by that holder under section 860C(a) with respect to that interest; and

(ii) The amount of any contribution described in section 860G(d)(2) made by that holder.

(2) *Decrease in basis.* A holder's basis in a residual interest is reduced (but not below zero) by—

(i) First, the amount of any cash or the fair market value of any property distributed to that holder with respect to that interest; and

(ii) Second, the daily portions of net loss of the REMIC taken into account under section 860C(a) by that holder with respect to that interest.

(3) *Adjustments made before disposition.* If any person disposes of a residual interest, the adjustments to basis prescribed in paragraph (b)(1) and (2) of this section are deemed to occur immediately before the disposition.

(c) *Counting conventions.* For purposes of determining the daily portion of REMIC taxable income or net loss under section 860C(a)(2), any reasonable convention may be used. An example of a reasonable convention is "30 days per month/90 days per quarter/360 days per year." [Reg. § 1.860C-1.]

☐ [T.D. 8458, 12-23-92.]

[Reg. § 1.860C-2]

§ 1.860C-2. **Determination of REMIC taxable income or net loss.**—(a) *Treatment of gain or loss.* For purposes of determining the taxable income or net loss of a REMIC under section 860C(b), any gain or loss from the disposition of any asset, including a qualified mortgage (as defined in section 860G(a)(3)) or a permitted investment (as defined in section 860G(a)(5) and § 1.860G-2(g)), is treated as gain or loss from the sale or exchange of property that is not a capital asset.

(b) *Deductions allowable to a REMIC*—(1) *In general.* Except as otherwise provided in section 860C(b) and in paragraph (b)(2) through (5) of this section, the deductions allowable to a REMIC for purposes of determining its taxable income or net loss are those deductions that would be allowable to an individual, determined by taking into account the same limitations that apply to an individual.

(2) *Deduction allowable under section 163.* A REMIC is allowed a deduction, determined without regard to section 163(d), for any interest expense accrued during the taxable year.

(3) *Deduction allowable under section 166.* For purposes of determining a REMIC's bad debt deduction under section 166, debt owed to the REMIC is not treated as nonbusiness debt under section 166(d).

(4) *Deduction allowable under section 212.* A REMIC is not treated as carrying on a trade or business for purposes of section 162. Ordinary and necessary operating expenses paid or incurred by the REMIC during the taxable year are deductible under section 212, without regard to section 67. Any expenses that are incurred in connection with the formation of the REMIC and that relate to the organization of the REMIC and the issuance of regular and residual interests are not treated as expenses of the REMIC for which a deduction is allowable under section 212. See § 1.860F-2(b)(3)(ii) for treatment of those expenses.

(5) *Expenses and interest relating to tax-exempt income.* Pursuant to section 265(a), a REMIC is not allowed a deduction for expenses and interest allocable to tax-exempt income. The portion of a REMIC's interest expense that is allocable to tax-exempt interest is determined in

Reg. § 1.860C-1(a)

the manner prescribed in section 265(b)(2), without regard to section 265(b)(3). [Reg. § 1.860C-2.]

☐ [T.D. 8458, 12-23-92.]

[Reg. § 1.860D-1]

§ 1.860D-1. Definition of a REMIC.—(a) *In general.* A real estate mortgage investment conduit (or REMIC) is a qualified entity, as defined in paragraph (c)(3) of this section, that satisfies the requirements of section 860D(a). See paragraph (d)(1) of this section for the manner of electing REMIC status.

(b) *Specific requirements*—(1) *Interests in a REMIC*—(i) *In general.* A REMIC must have one class, and only one class, of residual interests. Except as provided in paragraph (b)(1)(ii) of this section, every interest in a REMIC must be either a regular interest (as defined in section 860G(a)(1) and § 1.860G-1(a)) or a residual interest (as defined in section 860G(a)(2) and § 1.860G-1(c)).

(ii) *De minimis interests.* If, to facilitate the creation of an entity that elects REMIC status, an interest in the entity is created and, as of the startup day (as defined in section 860G(a)(9) and § 1.860G-2(k)), the fair market value of that interest is less than the lesser of $1,000 or 1/1,000 of one percent of the aggregate fair market value of all the regular and residual interests in the REMIC, then, unless that interest is specifically designated as an interest in the REMIC, the interest is not treated as an interest in the REMIC for purposes of section 860D(a)(2) and (3) and paragraph (b)(1)(i) of this section.

(2) *Certain rights not treated as interests.* Certain rights are not treated as interests in a REMIC. Although not an exclusive list, the following rights are not interests in a REMIC.

(i) *Payments for services.* The right to receive from the REMIC payments that represent reasonable compensation for services provided to the REMIC in the ordinary course of its operation is not an interest in the REMIC. Payments made by the REMIC in exchange for services may be expressed as a specified percentage of interest payments due on qualified mortgages or as a specified percentage of earnings from permitted investments. For example, a mortgage servicer's right to receive reasonable compensation for servicing the mortgages owned by the REMIC is not an interest in the REMIC.

(ii) *Stripped interests.* Stripped bonds or stripped coupons not held by the REMIC are not interests in the REMIC even if, in a transaction preceding or contemporaneous with the formation of the REMIC, they and the REMIC's qualified mortgages were created from the same mortgage obligation. For example, the right of a mortgage servicer to receive a servicing fee in excess of reasonable compensation from payments it receives on mortgages held by a REMIC is not an interest in the REMIC. Further, if an obligation with a fixed principal amount provides for interest at a fixed or variable rate and for certain contingent payment rights (*e.g.*, a shared appreciation provision or a percentage of mortgagor profits provision), and the owner of the obligation contributes the fixed payment rights to a REMIC and retains the contingent payment rights, the retained contingent payment rights are not an interest in the REMIC.

(iii) *Reimbursement rights under credit enhancement contracts.* A credit enhancer's right to be reimbursed for amounts advanced to a REMIC pursuant to the terms of a credit enhancement contract (as defined in § 1.860G-2(c)(2)) is not an interest in the REMIC even if the credit enhancer is entitled to receive interest on the amounts advanced.

(iv) *Rights to acquire mortgages.* The right to acquire or the obligation to purchase mortgages and other assets from a REMIC pursuant to a clean-up call (as defined in § 1.860G-2(j)) or a qualified liquidation (as defined in section 860F(a)(4)), or on conversion of a convertible mortgage (as defined in § 1.860G-2(d)(5)), is not an interest in the REMIC.

(3) *Asset test*—(i) *In general.* For purposes of the asset test of section 860D(a)(4), substantially all of a qualified entity's assets are qualified mortgages and permitted investments if the qualified entity owns no more than a de minimis amount of other assets.

(ii) *Safe harbor.* The amount of assets other than qualified mortgages and permitted investments is de minimis if the aggregate of the adjusted bases of those assets is less than one percent of the aggregate of the adjusted bases of all of the REMIC's assets. Nonetheless, a qualified entity that does not meet this safe harbor may demonstrate that it owns no more than a de minimis amount of other assets.

(4) *Arrangements test.* Generally, a qualified entity must adopt reasonable arrangements designed to ensure that—

(i) Disqualified organizations (as defined in section 860E(e)(5)) do not hold residual interests in the qualified entity; and

(ii) If a residual interest is acquired by a disqualified organization, the qualified entity will provide to the Internal Revenue Service, and to the persons specified in section 860E(e)(3), information needed to compute the tax imposed under section 860E(e) on transfers of residual interests to disqualified organizations.

(5) *Reasonable arrangements*—(i) *Arrangements to prevent disqualified organizations from holding residual interests.* A qualified entity is considered to have adopted reasonable arrangements to ensure that a disqualified organization (as defined in section 860E(e)(5)) will not hold a residual interest if—

(A) The residual interest is in registered form (as defined in § 5f.103-1(c) of this chapter); and

(B) The qualified entity's organizational documents clearly and expressly prohibit a disqualified organization from acquiring beneficial ownership of a residual interest, and notice of the prohibition is provided through a legend on the document that evidences ownership of the residual interest or through a conspicuous statement in a prospectus or private offering document used to offer the residual interest for sale.

(ii) *Arrangements to ensure that information will be provided.* A qualified entity is considered to have made reasonable arrangements to ensure that the Internal Revenue Service and persons specified in section 860E(e)(3) as liable for the tax imposed under section 860E(e) receive the information needed to compute the tax if the qualified entity's organizational documents require that it provide to the Internal Revenue Service and those persons a computation showing the present value of the total anticipated excess inclusions with respect to the residual interest for periods after the transfer. See § 1.860E-2(a)(5) for the obligation to furnish information on request.

(6) *Calendar year requirement.* A REMIC's taxable year is the calendar year. The first taxable year of a REMIC begins on the startup day and ends on December 31 of the same year. If the startup day is other than January 1, the REMIC has a short first taxable year.

(c) *Segregated pool of assets*—(1) *Formation of REMIC.* A REMIC may be formed as a segregated pool of assets rather than as a separate entity. To constitute a REMIC, the assets identified as part of the segregated pool must be treated for all Federal income tax purposes as assets of the REMIC and interests in the REMIC must be based solely on assets of the REMIC.

(2) *Identification of assets.* Formation of the REMIC does not occur until—

(i) The sponsor identifies the assets of the REMIC, such as through execution of an indenture with respect to the assets; and

(ii) The REMIC issues the regular and residual interests in the REMIC.

(3) *Qualified entity defined.* For purposes of this section, the term "qualified entity" includes an entity or a segregated pool of assets within an entity.

(d) *Election to be treated as a real estate mortgage investment conduit*—(1) *In general.* A qualified entity, as defined in paragraph (c)(3) of this section, elects to be treated as a REMIC by timely filing, for the first taxable year of its existence, a Form 1066, U.S. Real Estate Mortgage Investment Conduit Income Tax Return, signed by a person authorized to sign that return under § 1.860F-4(c). See § 1.9100-1 for rules regarding extensions of time for making elections. Once made, this election is irrevocable for that taxable year and all succeeding taxable years.

(2) *Information required to be reported in the REMIC's first taxable year.* For the first taxable year of the REMIC's existence, the qualified entity, as defined in paragraph (c)(3) of this section, must provide either on its return or in a separate statement attached to its return—

(i) The REMIC's employer identification number, which must not be the same as the identification number of any other entity,

(ii) Information concerning the terms and conditions of the regular interests and the residual interest of the REMIC, or a copy of the offering circular or prospectus containing such information,

(iii) A description of the prepayment and reinvestment assumptions that are made pursuant to section 1272(a)(6) and the regulations thereunder, including a statement supporting the selection of the prepayment assumption,

(iv) The form of the electing qualified entity under State law or, if an election is being made with respect to a segregated pool of assets within an entity, the form of the entity that holds the segregated pool of assets, and

(v) Any other information required by the form.

(3) *Requirement to keep sufficient records.* A qualified entity, as defined in paragraph (c)(3) of this section, that elects to be a REMIC must keep sufficient records concerning its investments to show that it has complied with the provisions of sections 860A through 860G and the regulations thereunder during each taxable year. [Reg. § 1.860D-1.]

☐ [T.D. 8366, 9-27-91. Amended by T.D. 8458, 12-23-92.]

Reg. § 1.860D-1(b)(5)

Real Estate Mortgage Investment Conduits

See p. 20,601 for regulations not amended to reflect law changes

[Reg. § 1.860E-1]

§ 1.860E-1. Treatment of taxable income of a residual interest holder in excess of daily accruals.—(a) *Excess inclusion cannot be offset by otherwise allowable deductions*—(1) *In general.* Except as provided in paragraph (a)(3) of this section, the taxable income of any holder of a residual interest for any taxable year is in no event less than the sum of the excess inclusions attributable to that holder's residual interests for that taxable year. In computing the amount of a net operating loss (as defined in section 172(c)) or the amount of any net operating loss carryover (as defined in section 172(b)(2)), the amount of any excess inclusion is not included in gross income or taxable income. Thus, for example, if a residual interest holder has $100 of gross income, $25 of which is an excess inclusion, and $90 of business deductions, the holder has taxable income of $25, the amount of the excess inclusion, and a net operating loss of $15 ($75 of other income − $90 of business deductions).

(2) *Affiliated groups.* If a holder of a REMIC residual interest is a member of an affiliated group filing a consolidated income tax return, the taxable income of the affiliated group cannot be less than the sum of the excess inclusions attributable to all residual interests held by members of the affiliated group.

(3) *Special rule for certain financial institutions*—(i) *In general.* If an organization to which section 593 applies holds a residual interest that has significant value (as defined in paragraph (a)(3)(iii) of this section), section 860E(a)(1) and paragraph (a)(1) of this section do not apply to that organization with respect to that interest. Consequently, an organization to which section 593 applies may use its allowable deductions to offset an excess inclusion attributable to a residual interest that has significant value, but, except as provided in section 860E(a)(4)(A), may not use its allowable deductions to offset an excess inclusion attributable to a residual interest held by any other member of an affiliated group, if any, of which the organization is a member. Further, a net operating loss of any other member of an affiliated group of which the organization is a member may not be used to offset an excess inclusion attributable to a residual interest held by that organization.

(ii) *Ordering rule*—(A) *In general.* In computing taxable income for any year, an organization to which section 593 applies is treated as having applied its allowable deductions for the year first to offset that portion of its gross income that is not an excess inclusion and then to offset that portion of its income that is an excess inclusion.

(B) *Example.* The following example illustrates the provisions of paragraph (a)(3)(ii) of this section:

Example. Corp. X, a corporation to which section 593 applies, is a member of an affiliated group that files a consolidated return. For a particular taxable year, Corp. X has gross income of $1,000, and of this amount, $150 is an excess inclusion attributable to a residual interest that has significant value. Corp. X has $975 of allowable deductions for the taxable year. Corp. X must apply its allowable deductions first to offset the $850 of gross income that is not an excess inclusion, and then to offset the portion of its gross income that is an excess inclusion. Thus, Corp. X has $25 of taxable income ($1,000 − $975), and that $25 is an excess inclusion that may not be offset by losses sustained by other members of the affiliated group.

(iii) *Significant value.* A residual interest has significant value if—

(A) The aggregate of the issue prices of the residual interests in the REMIC is at least 2 percent of the aggregate of the issue prices of all residual and regular interests in the REMIC; and

(B) The anticipated weighted average life of the residual interests is at least 20 percent of the anticipated weighted average life of the REMIC.

(iv) *Determining anticipated weighted average life*—(A) *Anticipated weighted average life of the REMIC.* The anticipated weighted average life of a REMIC is the weighted average of the anticipated weighted average lives of all classes of interests in the REMIC. This weighted average is determined under the formula in paragraph (a)(3)(iv)(B) of this section, applied by treating all payments taken into account in computing the anticipated weighted average lives of regular and residual interests in the REMIC as principal payments on a single regular interest.

(B) *Regular interests that have a specified principal amount.* Generally, the anticipated weighted average life of a regular interest is determined by—

(*1*) Multiplying the amount of each anticipated principal payment to be made on the interest by the number of years (including fractions thereof) from the startup day (as defined in section 860G(a)(9) and § 1.860G-2(k)) to the related principal payment date;

(*2*) Adding the results; and

(*3*) Dividing the sum by the total principal paid on the regular interest.

Reg. § 1.860E-1(a)(3)

(C) *Regular interests that have no specified principal amount or that have only a nominal principal amount, and all residual interests.* If a regular interest has no specified principal amount, or if the interest payments to be made on a regular interest are disproportionately high relative to its specified principal amount (as determined by reference to § 1.860G-1(b)(5)(i)), then, for purposes of computing the anticipated weighted average life of the interest, all anticipated payments on that interest, regardless of their designation as principal or interest, must be taken into account in applying the formula set out in paragraph (a)(3)(iv)(B) of this section. Moreover, for purposes of computing the weighted average life of a residual interest, all anticipated payments on that interest, regardless of their designation as principal or interest, must be taken into account in applying the formula set out in paragraph (a)(3)(iv)(B) of this section.

(D) *Anticipated payments.* The anticipated principal payments to be made on a regular interest subject to paragraph (a)(3)(iv)(B) of this section, and the anticipated payments to be made on a regular interest subject to paragraph (a)(3)(iv)(C) of this section or on a residual interest, must be determined based on—

(*1*) The prepayment and reinvestment assumptions adopted under section 1272(a)(6), or that would have been adopted had the REMIC's regular interests been issued with original issue discount; and

(*2*) Any required or permitted clean up calls or any required qualified liquidation provided for in the REMIC's organizational documents.

(b) *Treatment of residual interests held by REITs, RICs, common trust funds, and subchapter T cooperatives.* [Reserved]

(c) *Transfers of noneconomic residual interests*—(1) *In general.* A transfer of a noneconomic residual interest is disregarded for all Federal tax purposes if a significant purpose of the transfer was to enable the transferor to impede the assessment or collection of tax. A significant purpose to impede the assessment or collection of tax exists if the transferor, at the time of the transfer, either knew or should have known (had "improper knowledge") that the transferee would be unwilling or unable to pay taxes due on its share of the taxable income of the REMIC.

(2) *Noneconomic residual interest.* A residual interest is a noneconomic residual interest unless, at the time of the transfer—

(i) The present value of the expected future distributions on the residual interest at least equals the product of the present value of the anticipated excess inclusions and the highest rate of tax specified in section 11(b)(1) for the year in which the transfer occurs; and

(ii) The transferor reasonably expects that, for each anticipated excess inclusion, the transferee will receive distributions from the REMIC at or after the time at which the taxes accrue on the anticipated excess inclusion in an amount sufficient to satisfy the accrued taxes.

(3) *Computations.* The present value of the expected future distributions and the present value of the anticipated excess inclusions must be computed under the procedure specified in § 1.860E-2(a)(4) for determining the present value of anticipated excess inclusions in connection with the transfer of a residual interest to a disqualified organization.

(4) *Safe harbor for establishing lack of improper knowledge.* A transferor is presumed not to have improper knowledge if—

(i) The transferor conducted, at the time of the transfer, a reasonable investigation of the financial condition of the transferee and, as a result of the investigation, the transferor found that the transferee had historically paid its debts as they came due and found no significant evidence to indicate that the transferee will not continue to pay its debts as they come due in the future;

(ii) The transferee represents to the transferor that it understands that, as the holder of the noneconomic residual interest, the transferee may incur tax liabilities in excess of any cash flows generated by the interest and that the transferee intends to pay taxes associated with holding the residual interest as they become due;

(iii) The transferee represents that it will not cause income from the noneconomic residual interest to be attributable to a foreign permanent establishment or fixed base (within the meaning of an applicable income tax treaty) of the transferee or another U.S. taxpayer; and

(iv) The transfer satisfies either the asset test in paragraph (c)(5) of this section or the formula test in paragraph (c)(7) of this section.

(5) *Asset test.* The transfer satisfies the asset test if it meets the requirements of paragraphs (c)(5)(i), (ii) and (iii) of this section.

(i) At the time of the transfer, and at the close of each of the transferee's two fiscal years preceding the transferee's fiscal year of transfer, the transferee's gross assets for financial reporting purposes exceed $100 million and its net assets for financial reporting purposes exceed $10 million. For purposes of the preceding sentence, the gross assets and net assets of a transferee do not include any obligation of any related person (as defined in paragraph (c)(6)(ii) of this section) or any other asset if a principal purpose for holding or acquiring the other asset is to permit the transferee to satisfy the conditions of this paragraph (c)(5)(i).

(ii) The transferee must be an eligible corporation (defined in paragraph (c)(6)(i) of this section) and must agree in writing that any subsequent transfer of the interest will be to another eligible corporation in a transaction that satisfies paragraphs (c)(4)(i), (ii), and (iii) and this paragraph (c)(5). The direct or indirect transfer of the residual interest to a foreign permanent establishment (within the meaning of an applicable income tax treaty) of a domestic corporation is a transfer that is not a transfer to an eligible corporation. A transfer also fails to meet the requirements of this paragraph (c)(5)(ii) if the transferor knows, or has reason to know, that the transferee will not honor the restrictions on subsequent transfers of the residual interest.

(iii) A reasonable person would not conclude, based on the facts and circumstances known to the transferor on or before the date of the transfer, that the taxes associated with the residual interest will not be paid. The consideration given to the transferee to acquire the noneconomic residual interest in the REMIC is only one factor to be considered, but the transferor will be deemed to know that the transferee cannot or will not pay if the amount of consideration is so low compared to the liabilities assumed that a reasonable person would conclude that the taxes associated with holding the residual interest will not be paid. In determining whether the amount of consideration is too low, the specific terms of the formula test in paragraph (c)(7) of this section need not be used.

(6) *Definitions for asset test.* The following definitions apply for purposes of paragraph (c)(5) of this section:

(i) *Eligible corporation* means any domestic C corporation (as defined in section 1361(a)(2)) other than—

(A) A corporation which is exempt from, or is not subject to, tax under section 11;

(B) An entity described in section 851(a) or 856(a);

(C) A REMIC; or

(D) An organization to which part I of subchapter T of chapter 1 of subtitle A of the Internal Revenue Code applies.

(ii) *Related person* is any person that—

(A) Bears a relationship to the transferee enumerated in section 267(b) or 707(b)(1), using "20 percent" instead of "50 percent" where it appears under the provisions; or

(B) Is under common control (within the meaning of section 52(a) and (b)) with the transferee.

(7) *Formula test.* The transfer satisfies the formula test if the present value of the anticipated tax liabilities associated with holding the residual interest does not exceed the sum of—

(i) The present value of any consideration given to the transferee to acquire the interest;

(ii) The present value of the expected future distributions on the interest; and

(iii) The present value of the anticipated tax savings associated with holding the interest as the REMIC generates losses.

(8) *Conditions and limitations on formula test.* The following rules apply for purposes of the formula test in paragraph (c)(7) of this section.

(i) The transferee is assumed to pay tax at a rate equal to the highest rate of tax specified in section 11(b)(1). If the transferee has been subject to the alternative minimum tax under section 55 in the preceding two years and will compute its taxable income in the current taxable year using the alternative minimum tax rate, then the tax rate specified in section 55(b)(1)(B) may be used in lieu of the highest rate specified in section 11(b)(1).

(ii) The direct or indirect transfer of the residual interest to a foreign permanent establishment or fixed base (within the meaning of an applicable income tax treaty) of a domestic transferee is not eligible for the formula test.

(iii) Present values are computed using a discount rate equal to the Federal short-term rate prescribed by section 1274(d) for the month of the transfer and the compounding period used by the taxpayer.

(9) *Examples.* The following examples illustrate the rules of this section:

Example 1. Transfer to partnership. X transfers a noneconomic residual interest in a REMIC to Partnership *P* in a transaction that does not satisfy the formula test of paragraph (c)(7) of this section. *Y* and *Z* are the partners of *P*. Even if *Y* and *Z* are eligible corporations that satisfy the requirements of paragraph (c)(5)(i) of this section, the transfer fails to satisfy the asset test requirements found in paragraph (c)(5)(ii) of this section because *P* is a partnership rather than an eligible corporation within the meaning of (c)(6)(i) of this section.

Example 2. Transfer to a corporation without capacity to carry additional residual interests. During the first ten months of a year, Bank transfers five residual interests to Corporation U under circumstances meeting the requirements of the asset test in paragraph (c)(5) of this section. Bank is the major creditor of U and consequently has access to U's financial records and has knowledge of U's financial circumstances. During the last month of the year, Bank transfers three additional residual interests to U in a transaction that does not meet the formula test of paragraph (c)(7) of this section. At the time of this transfer, U's financial records indicate it has retained the previously transferred residual interests. U's financial circumstances, including the aggregate tax liabilities it has assumed with respect to REMIC residual interests, would cause a reasonable person to conclude that U will be unable to meet its tax liabilities when due. The transfers in the last month of the year fail to satisfy the investigation requirement in paragraph (c)(4)(i) of this section and the asset test requirement of paragraph (c)(5)(iii) of this section because Bank has reason to know that U will not be able to pay the tax due on those interests.

Example 3. Transfer to a foreign permanent establishment of an eligible corporation. R transfers a noneconomic residual interest in a REMIC to the foreign permanent establishment of Corporation T. Solely because of paragraph (c)(8)(ii) of this section, the transfer does not satisfy the formula test of paragraph (c)(7) of this section. In addition, even if T is an eligible corporation, the transfer does not satisfy the asset test because the transfer fails the requirements of paragraph (c)(5)(ii) of this section.

(10) *Effective dates.* Paragraphs (c)(4) through (c)(9) of this section are applicable to transfers occurring on or after February 4, 2000, except for paragraphs (c)(4)(iii) and (c)(8)(iii) of this section, which are applicable for transfers occurring on or after August 19, 2002. For the dates of applicability of paragraphs (a) through (c)(3) and (d) of this section, see § 1.860A-1.

(d) *Transfers to foreign persons.* Paragraph (c) of this section does not apply to transfers of residual interests to which § 1.860G-3(a)(1), concerning transfers to certain foreign persons, applies. [Reg. § 1.860E-1.]

☐ [T.D. 8458, 12-23-92. Amended by T.D. 9004, 7-18-2002.]

[Reg. § 1.860E-2]

§ 1.860E-2. Tax on transfers of residual interests to certain organizations.—(a) *Transfers to disqualified organizations*—(1) *Payment of tax.* Any excise tax due under section 860E(e)(1) must be paid by the later of March 24, 1993, or April 15th of the year following the calendar year in which the residual interest is transferred to a disqualified organization. The Commissioner may prescribe rules for the manner and method of collecting the tax.

(2) *Transitory ownership.* For purposes of section 860E(e) and this section, a transfer of a residual interest to a disqualified organization in connection with the formation of a REMIC is disregarded if the disqualified organization has a binding contract to sell the interest and the sale occurs within 7 days of the startup day (as defined in section 860G(a)(9) and § 1.860G-2(k)).

(3) *Anticipated excess inclusions.* The anticipated excess inclusions are the excess inclusions that are expected to accrue in each calendar quarter (or portion thereof) following the transfer of the residual interest. The anticipated excess inclusions must be determined as of the date the residual interest is transferred and must be based on—

(i) Events that have occurred up to the time of the transfer;

(ii) The prepayment and reinvestment assumptions adopted under section 1272(a)(6), or that would have been adopted had the REMIC's regular interests been issued with original issue discount; and

(iii) Any required or permitted clean up calls, or required qualified liquidation provided for in the REMIC's organizational documents.

(4) *Present value computation.* The present value of the anticipated excess inclusions is determined by discounting the anticipated excess inclusions from the end of each remaining calendar quarter in which those excess inclusions are expected to accrue to the date the disqualified organization acquires the residual interest. The discount rate to be used for this present value computation is the applicable Federal rate (as specified in section 1274(d)(1)) that would apply to a debt instrument that was issued on the date the disqualified organization acquired the residual interest and whose term ended on the close of the last quarter in which excess inclusions were expected to accrue with respect to the residual interest.

(5) *Obligation of REMIC to furnish information.* A REMIC is not obligated to determine if its residual interests have been transferred to a disqualified organization. However, upon request of a person designated in section 860E(e)(3), the REMIC must furnish information sufficient to compute the present value of the anticipated excess inclusions. The information must be furnished to the requesting party and to the Internal Revenue Service within 60 days of the request. A reasonable fee charged to the requestor is not

income derived from a prohibited transaction within the meaning of section 860F(a).

(6) *Agent.* For purposes of section 860E(e)(3), the term "agent" includes a broker (as defined in section 6045(c) and § 1.6045-1(a)(1)), nominee, or other middleman.

(7) *Relief from liability*—(i) *Transferee furnishes information under penalties of perjury.* For purposes of section 860E(e)(4), a transferee is treated as having furnished an affidavit if the transferee furnishes—

(A) A social security number, and states under penalties of perjury that the social security number is that of the transferee; or

(B) A statement under penalties of perjury that it is not a disqualified organization.

(ii) *Amount required to be paid.* The amount required to be paid under section 860E(e)(7)(B) is equal to the product of the highest rate specified in section 11(b)(1) for the taxable year in which the transfer described in section 860E(e)(1) occurs and the amount of excess inclusions that accrued and were allocable to the residual interest during the period that the disqualified organization held the interest.

(b) *Tax on pass-thru entities*—(1) *Tax on excess inclusions.* Any tax due under section 860E(e)(6) must be paid by the later of March 24, 1993, or by the fifteenth day of the fourth month following the close of the taxable year of the pass-thru entity in which the disqualified person is a record holder. The Commissioner may prescribe rules for the manner and method of collecting the tax.

(2) *Record holder furnishes information under penalties of perjury.* For purposes of section 860E(e)(6)(D), a record holder is treated as having furnished an affidavit if the record holder furnishes—

(i) A social security number and states, under penalties of perjury, that the social security number is that of the record holder; or

(ii) A statement under penalties of perjury that it is not a disqualified organization.

(3) *Deductibility of tax.* Any tax imposed on a pass-thru entity pursuant to section 860E(e)(6)(A) is deductible against the gross amount of ordinary income of the pass-thru entity. For example, in the case of a REIT, the tax is deductible in determining real estate investment trust taxable income under section 857(b)(2).

(4) *Allocation of tax.* Dividends paid by a RIC or by a REIT are not preferential dividends within the meaning of section 562(c) solely because the tax expense incurred by the RIC or REIT under section 860E(e)(6) is allocated solely to the shares held by disqualified organizations. [Reg. § 1.860E-2.]

☐ [T.D. 8458, 12-23-92.]

[Reg. § 1.860F-1]

§ 1.860F-1. Qualified liquidations.—A plan of liquidation need not be in any special form. If a REMIC specifies the first day in the 90-day liquidation period in a statement attached to its final return, then the REMIC will be considered to have adopted a plan of liquidation on the specified date. [Reg. § 1.860F-1.]

☐ [T.D. 8458, 12-23-92.]

[Reg. § 1.860F-2]

§ 1.860F-2. Transfers to a REMIC.—(a) *Formation of a REMIC*—(1) *In general.* For Federal income tax purposes, a REMIC formation is characterized as the contribution of assets by a sponsor (as defined in paragraph (b)(1) of this section) to a REMIC in exchange for REMIC regular and residual interests. If, instead of exchanging its interest in mortgages and related assets for regular and residual interests, the sponsor arranges to have the REMIC issue some or all of the regular and residual interests for cash, after which the sponsor sells its interests in mortgages and related assets to the REMIC, the transaction is, nevertheless, viewed for Federal income tax purposes as the sponsor's exchange of mortgages and related assets for regular and residual interests, followed by a sale of some or all of those interests. The purpose of this rule is to ensure that the tax consequences associated with the formation of a REMIC are not affected by the actual sequence of steps taken by the sponsor.

(2) *Tiered arrangements*—(i) *Two or more REMICs formed pursuant to a single set of organizational documents.* Two or more REMICs can be created pursuant to a single set of organizational documents even if for state law purposes or for Federal securities law purposes those documents create only one organization. The organizational documents must, however, clearly and expressly identify the assets of, and the interests in, each REMIC, and each REMIC must satisfy all of the requirements of section 860D and the related regulations.

(ii) *A REMIC and one or more investment trusts formed pursuant to a single set of documents.* A REMIC (or two or more REMICs) and one or more investment trusts can be created pursuant to a single set of organizational documents and the separate existence of the REMIC(s) and the investment trust(s) will be respected for Federal income tax purposes even if for state law purposes or for Federal securities law

Reg. § 1.860F-2(a)(2)

purposes those documents create only one organization. The organizational documents for the REMIC(s) and the investment trust(s) must, however, require both the REMIC(s) and the investment trust(s) to account for items of income and ownership of assets for Federal tax purposes in a manner that respects the separate existence of the multiple entities. See § 1.860G-2(i) concerning issuance of regular interests coupled with other contractual rights for an illustration of the provisions of this paragraph.

(b) *Treatment of sponsor*—(1) *Sponsor defined.* A sponsor is a person who directly or indirectly exchanges qualified mortgages and related assets for regular and residual interests in a REMIC. A person indirectly exchanges interests in qualified mortgages and related assets for regular and residual interests in a REMIC if the person transfers, other than in a nonrecognition transaction, the mortgages and related assets to another person who acquires a transitory ownership interest in those assets before exchanging them for interests in the REMIC, after which the transitory owner then transfers some or all of the interests in the REMIC to the first person.

(2) *Nonrecognition of gain or loss.* The sponsor does not recognize gain or loss on the direct or indirect transfer of any property to a REMIC in exchange for regular or residual interests in the REMIC. However, the sponsor, upon a subsequent sale of the REMIC regular or residual interests, may recognize gain or loss with respect to those interests.

(3) *Basis of contributed assets allocated among interests*—(i) *In general.* The aggregate of the adjusted bases of the regular and residual interests received by the sponsor in the exchange described in paragraph (a) of this section is equal to the aggregate of the adjusted bases of the property transferred by the sponsor in the exchange, increased by the amount of organizational expenses (as described in paragraph (b)(3)(ii) of this section). That total is allocated among all the interests received in proportion to their fair market values on the pricing date (as defined in paragraph (b)(3)(iii) of this section) if any, or, if none, the startup day (as defined in section 860G(a)(9) and § 1.860G-2(k)).

(ii) *Organizational expenses*—(A) *Organizational expense defined.* An organizational expense is an expense that is incurred by the sponsor or by the REMIC and that is directly related to the creation of the REMIC. Further, the organizational expense must be incurred during a period beginning a reasonable time before the startup day and ending before the date prescribed by law for filing the first REMIC tax return (determined without regard to any extensions of time to file). The following are examples of organizational expenses: legal fees for services related to the formation of the REMIC, such as preparation of a pooling and servicing agreement and trust indenture; accounting fees related to the formation of the REMIC; and other administrative costs related to the formation of the REMIC.

(B) *Syndication expenses.* Syndication expenses are not organizational expenses. Syndication expenses are those expenses incurred by the sponsor or other person to market the interests in a REMIC, and, thus, are applied to reduce the amount realized on the sale of the interests. Examples of syndication expenses are brokerage fees, registration fees, fees of an underwriter or placement agent, and printing costs of the prospectus or placement memorandum and other selling or promotional material.

(iii) *Pricing date.* The term "pricing date" means the date on which the terms of the regular and residual interests are fixed and the prices at which a substantial portion of the regular interests will be sold are fixed.

(4) *Treatment of unrecognized gain or loss*—(i) *Unrecognized gain on regular interests.* For purposes of section 860F(b)(1)(C)(i), the sponsor must include in gross income the excess of the issue price of a regular interest over the sponsor's basis in the interest as if the excess were market discount (as defined in section 1278(a)(2)) on a bond and the sponsor had made an election under section 1278(b) to include this market discount currently in gross income. The sponsor is not, however, by reason of this paragraph (b)(4)(i), deemed to have made an election under section 1278(b) with respect to any other bonds.

(ii) *Unrecognized loss on regular interests.* For purposes of section 860F(b)(1)(D)(i), the sponsor treats the excess of the sponsor's basis in a regular interest over the issue price of the interest as if that excess were amortizable bond premium (as defined in section 171(b)) on a taxable bond and the sponsor had made an election under section 171(c). The sponsor is not, however, by reason of this paragraph (b)(4)(ii), deemed to have made an election under section 171(c) with respect to any other bonds.

(iii) *Unrecognized gain on residual interests.* For purposes of section 860F(b)(1)(C)(ii), the sponsor must include in gross income the excess of the issue price of a residual interest over the sponsor's basis in the interest ratably over the anticipated weighted average life of the REMIC (as defined in § 1.860E-1(a)(3)(iv)).

(iv) *Unrecognized loss on residual interests.* For purposes of section 860F(b)(1)(D)(ii), the sponsor deducts the excess of the sponsor's basis in a residual interest over the issue price of the interest ratably over the anticipated weighted average life of the REMIC.

(5) *Additions to or reductions of the sponsor's basis.* The sponsor's basis in a regular or residual interest is increased by any amount included in the sponsor's gross income under paragraph (b)(4) of this section. The sponsor's basis in a regular or residual interest is decreased by any amount allowed as a deduction and by any amount applied to reduce interest payments to the sponsor under paragraph (b)(4)(ii) of this section.

(6) *Transferred basis property.* For purposes of paragraph (b)(4) of this section, a transferee of a regular or residual interest is treated in the same manner as the sponsor to the extent that the basis of the transferee in the interest is determined in whole or in part by reference to the basis of the interest in the hands of the sponsor.

(c) *REMIC's basis in contributed assets.* For purposes of section 860F(b)(2), the aggregate of the REMIC's bases in the assets contributed by the sponsor to the REMIC in a transaction described in paragraph (a) of this section is equal to the aggregate of the issue prices (determined under section 860G(a)(10) and § 1.860G-1(d)) of all regular and residual interests in the REMIC. [Reg. § 1.860F-2.]

☐ [*T.D.* 8458, 12-23-92.]

[Reg. § 1.860F-4]

§ 1.860F-4. REMIC reporting requirements and other administrative rules.—(a) *In general.* Except as provided in paragraph (c) of this section, for purposes of subtitle F of the Internal Revenue Code, a REMIC is treated as a partnership and any holder of a residual interest in the REMIC is treated as a partner. A REMIC is not subject, however, to the rules of subchapter C of chapter 63 of the Internal Revenue Code, relating to the treatment of partnership items, for a taxable year if there is at no time during the taxable year more than one holder of a residual interest in the REMIC.

(b) *REMIC tax return*—(1) *In general.* To satisfy the requirement under section 6031 to make a return of income for each taxable year, a REMIC must file the return required by paragraph (b)(2) of this section. The due date and any extensions for filing the REMIC's annual return are determined as if the REMIC were a partnership.

(2) *Income tax return.* The REMIC must make a return, as required by section 6011(a), for each taxable year on Form 1066, U.S. Real Estate Mortgage Investment Conduit Income Tax Return. The return must include—

(i) The amount of principal outstanding on each class of regular interests as of the close of the taxable year,

(ii) The amount of the daily accruals determined under section 860E(c), and

(iii) The information specified in § 1.860D-1(d)(2)(i), (iv), and (v).

(c) *Signing of REMIC return*—(1) *In general.* Although a REMIC is generally treated as a partnership for purposes of subtitle F, for purposes of determining who is authorized to sign a REMIC's income tax return for any taxable year, the REMIC is not treated as a partnership and the holders of residual interests in the REMIC are not treated as partners. Rather, the REMIC return must be signed by a person who could sign the return of the entity absent the REMIC election. Thus, the return of a REMIC that is a corporation or trust under applicable State law must be signed by a corporate officer or a trustee, respectively. The return of a REMIC that consists of a segregated pool of assets must be signed by a person who could sign the return of the entity that owns the assets of the REMIC under applicable State law.

(2) *REMIC whose startup day is before November 10, 1988*—(i) *In general.* The income tax return of a REMIC whose startup day is before November 10, 1988, may be signed by any person who held a residual interest during the taxable year to which the return relates, or, as provided in section 6903, by a fiduciary, as defined in section 7701(a)(6), who is acting for the REMIC and who has furnished adequate notice in the manner prescribed in § 301.6903-1(b) of this chapter.

(ii) *Startup day.* For purposes of paragraph (c)(2) of this section, startup day means any day selected by a REMIC that is on or before the first day on which interests in such REMIC are issued.

(iii) *Exception.* A REMIC whose startup day is before November 10, 1988, may elect to have paragraph (c)(1) of this section apply, instead of paragraph (c)(2) of this section, in determining who is authorized to sign the REMIC return. See section 1006(t)(18)(B) of the Technical and Miscellaneous Revenue Act of 1988 (102 Stat. 3426) and § 5h.6(a)(1) of this chapter for the time and manner for making this election.

(d) *Designation of tax matters person.* A REMIC may designate a tax matters person in the same manner in which a partnership may designate a tax matters partner under § 301.6231(a)(7)-1T of this chapter. For purposes of applying that section, all holders of residual interests in the REMIC are treated as general partners.

(e) *Notice to holders of residual interests*—(1) *Information required.* As of the close of each calendar quarter, a REMIC must provide to each person who held a residual interest in the REMIC during that quarter notice on Schedule Q (Form 1066) of information specified in paragraphs (e)(1)(i) and (ii) of this section.

(i) *In general.* Each REMIC must provide to each of its residual interest holders the following information—

(A) That person's share of the taxable income or net loss of the REMIC for the calendar quarter;

(B) The amount of the excess inclusion (as defined in section 860E and the regulations thereunder), if any, with respect to that person's residual interest for the calendar quarter;

(C) If the holder of a residual interest is also a pass-through interest holder (as defined in § 1.67-3T(a)(2)), the allocable investment expenses (as defined in § 1.67-3T(a)(4)) for the calendar quarter, and

(D) Any other information required by Schedule Q (Form 1066).

(ii) *Information with respect to REMIC assets*—(A) *95 percent asset test.* For calendar quarters after 1988, each REMIC must provide to each of its residual interest holders the following information—

(*1*) The percentage of REMIC assets that are qualifying real property loans under section 593,

(*2*) The percentage of REMIC assets that are assets described in section 7701(a)(19), and

(*3*) The percentage of REMIC assets that are real estate assets defined in section 856(c)(6)(B),

computed by reference to the average adjusted basis (as defined in section 1011) of the REMIC assets during the calendar quarter (as described in paragraph (e)(1)(iii) of this section). If the percentage of REMIC assets represented by a category is at least 95 percent, then the REMIC need only specify that the percentage for that category was at least 95 percent.

(B) *Additional information required if the 95 percent test not met.* If, for any calendar quarter after 1988, less than 95 percent of the assets of the REMIC are real estate assets defined in section 856(c)(6)(B), then, for that calendar quarter, the REMIC must also provide to any real estate investment trust (REIT) that holds a residual interest the following information—

(*1*) The percentage of REMIC assets described in section 856(c)(5)(A), computed by reference to the average adjusted basis of the REMIC assets during the calendar quarter (as described in paragraph (e)(1)(iii) of this section),

(*2*) The percentage of REMIC gross income (other than gross income from prohibited transactions defined in section 860F (a)(2)) described in section 856(c)(3)(A) through (E), computed as of the close of the calendar quarter, and

(*3*) The percentage of REMIC gross income (other than gross income from prohibited transactions defined in section 860F(a)(2)) described in section 856(c)(3)(F), computed as of the close of the calendar quarter. For purposes of this paragraph (e)(1)(ii)(B)(*3*), the term "foreclosure property" contained in section 856(c)(3)(F) has the meaning specified in section 860G(a)(8).

In determining whether a REIT satisfies the limitations of section 856(c)(2), all REMIC gross income is deemed to be derived from a source specified in section 856(c)(2).

(C) *For calendar quarters in 1987.* For calendar quarters in 1987, the percentages of assets required in paragraphs (e)(1)(ii)(A) and (B) of this section may be computed by reference to the fair market value of the assets of the REMIC as of the close of the calendar quarter (as described in paragraph (e)(1)(iii) of this section), instead of by reference to the average adjusted basis during the calendar quarter.

(D) *For calendar quarters in 1988 and 1989.* For calendar quarters in 1988 and 1989, the percentages of assets required in paragraphs (e)(1)(ii)(A) and (B) of this section may be computed by reference to the average fair market value of the assets of the REMIC during the calendar quarter (as described in paragraph (e)(1)(iii) of this section), instead of by reference to the average adjusted basis of the assets of the REMIC during the calendar quarter.

(iii) *Special provisions.* For purposes of paragraph (e)(1)(ii) of this section, the percentage of REMIC assets represented by a specified category computed by reference to average adjusted basis (or fair market value) of the assets during a calendar quarter is determined by dividing the average adjusted bases (or for calendar quarters before 1990, fair market value) of the assets in the specified category by the average adjusted basis (or, for calendar quarters before 1990, fair market value) of all the assets of the REMIC as of the close of each month, week, or day during that calendar quarter. The monthly, weekly, or daily computation period must be applied uniformly during the calendar quarter to all categories of assets and may not be changed in succeeding calendar quarters without the consent of the Commissioner.

Reg. § 1.860F-4(e)(1)

(2) *Quarterly notice required*—(i) *In general.* Schedule Q must be mailed (or otherwise delivered) to each holder of a residual interest during a calendar quarter no later than the last day of the month following the close of the calendar quarter.

(ii) *Special rule for 1987.* Notice to any holder of a REMIC residual interest of the information required in paragraph (e)(1) of this section for any of the four calendar quarters of 1987 must be mailed (or otherwise delivered) to each holder no later than March 28, 1988.

(3) *Nominee reporting*—(i) *In general.* If a REMIC is required under paragraphs (e)(1) and (2) of this section to provide notice to an interest holder who is a nominee of another person with respect to an interest in the REMIC, the nominee must furnish that notice to the person for whom it is a nominee.

(ii) *Time for furnishing statement.* The nominee must furnish the notice required under paragraph (e)(3)(i) of this section to the person for whom it is a nominee no later than 30 days after receiving this information.

(4) *Reports to the Internal Revenue Service.* For each person who was a residual interest holder at any time during a REMIC's taxable year, the REMIC must attach a copy of Schedule Q to its income tax return for that year for each quarter in which that person was a residual interest holder. Quarterly notice to the Internal Revenue Service is not required.

(f) *Information returns for persons engaged in a trade or business.* See § 1.6041-1(b)(2) for the treatment of a REMIC under sections 6041 and 6041A. [Reg. § 1.860F-4.]

☐ [T.D. 8366, 9-27-91. *Amended by T.D.* 8458, 12-23-92.]

[Reg. § 1.860G-1]

§ 1.860G-1. **Definition of regular and residual interests.**—(a) *Regular interest*—(1) *Designation as a regular interest.* For purposes of section 860G(a)(1), a REMIC designates an interest as a regular interest by providing to the Internal Revenue Service the information specified in § 1.860D-1(d)(2)(ii) in the time and manner specified in § 1.860D-1(d)(2).

(2) *Specified portion of the interest payments on qualified mortgages*—(i) *In general.* For purposes of section 860G(a)(1)(B)(ii), a specified portion of the interest payments on qualified mortgages means a portion of the interest payable on qualified mortgages, but only if the portion can be expressed as—

(A) A fixed percentage of the interest that is payable at either a fixed rate or at a variable rate described in paragraph (a)(3) of this section on some or all of the qualified mortgages;

(B) A fixed number of basis points of the interest payable on some or all of the qualified mortgages; or

(C) The interest payable at either a fixed rate or at a variable rate described in paragraph (a)(3) of this section on some or all of the qualified mortgages in excess of a fixed number of basis points or in excess of a variable rate described in paragraph (a)(3) of this section.

(ii) *Specified portion cannot vary.* The portion must be established as of the startup day (as defined in section 860G(a)(9) and § 1.860G-2(k)) and, except as provided in paragraph (a)(2)(iii) of this section, it cannot vary over the period that begins on the startup day and ends on the day that the interest holder is no longer entitled to receive payments.

(iii) *Defaulted or delinquent mortgages.* A portion is not treated as varying over time if an interest holder's entitlement to a portion of the interest on some or all of the qualified mortgages is dependent on the absence of defaults or delinquencies on those mortgages.

(iv) *No minimum specified principal amount is required.* If an interest in a REMIC consists of a specified portion of the interest payments on the REMIC's qualified mortgages, no minimum specified principal amount need be assigned to that interest. The specified principal amount can be zero.

(v) *Specified portion includes portion of interest payable on regular interest.* (A) The specified portions that meet the requirements of paragraph (a)(2)(i) of this section include a specified portion that can be expressed as a fixed percentage of the interest that is payable on some or all of the qualified mortgages where—

(*1*) Each of those qualified mortgages is a regular interest issued by another REMIC; and

(*2*) With respect to that REMIC in which it is a regular interest, each of those regular interests bears interest that can be expressed as a specified portion as described in paragraph (a)(2)(i)(A), (B), or (C) of this section.

(B) See § 1.860A-1(a) for the effective date of this paragraph (a)(2)(v).

(vi) *Examples.* The following examples, each of which describes a pass-thru trust that is intended to qualify as a REMIC, illustrate the provisions of this paragraph (a)(2).

Example 1. (i) A sponsor transferred a pool of fixed rate mortgages to a trustee in exchange for two classes of certificates. The Class A certificate holders are entitled to all principal payments on the mortgages and to interest on outstanding principal at a variable rate based on the current value of One-Month LIBOR, subject to a lifetime cap equal to the weighted average rate payable on the mortgages. The Class B certificate holders are entitled to all interest payable on the mortgages in excess of the interest paid on the Class A certificates. The Class B certificates are subordinate to the Class A certificates so that cash flow shortfalls due to defaults or delinquencies on the mortgages will be borne first by the Class B certificate holders.

(ii) The Class B certificate holders are entitled to all interest payable on the pooled mortgages in excess of a variable rate described in paragraph (a)(3)(vi) of this section. Moreover, the portion of the interest payable to the Class B certificate holders is not treated as varying over time solely because payments on the Class B certificates may be reduced as a result of defaults or delinquencies on the pooled mortgages. Thus, the Class B certificates provide for interest payments that consist of a specified portion of the interest payable on the pooled mortgages under paragraph (a)(2)(i)(C) of this section.

Example 2. (i) A sponsor transferred a pool of variable rate mortgages to a trustee in exchange for two classes of certificates. The mortgages call for interest payments at a variable rate based on the current value of the One-Year Constant Maturity Treasury Index (hereinafter "CMTI") plus 200 basis points, subject to a lifetime cap of 12 percent. Class C certificate holders are entitled to all principal payments on the mortgages and interest on the outstanding principal at a variable rate based on the One-Year CMTI plus 100 basis points, subject to a lifetime cap of 12 percent. The interest rate on the Class C certificates is reset at the same time the rate is reset on the pooled mortgages.

(ii) The Class D certificate holders are entitled to all interest payments on the mortgages in excess of the interest paid on the Class C certificates. So long as the One-Year CMTI is at 10 percent or lower, the Class D certificate holders are entitled to 100 basis points of interest on the pooled mortgages. If, however, the index exceeds 10 percent on a reset date, the Class D certificate holders' entitlement shrinks, and it disappears if the index is at 11 percent or higher.

(iii) The Class D certificate holders are entitled to all interest payable on the pooled mortgages in excess of a qualified variable rate described in paragraph (a)(3) of this section. Thus, the Class D certificates provide for interest payments that consist of a specified portion of the interest payable on the qualified mortgages under paragraph (a)(2)(i)(C) of this section.

Example 3. (i) A sponsor transferred a pool of fixed rate mortgages to a trustee in exchange for two classes of certificates. The fixed interest rate payable on the mortgages varies from mortgage to mortgage, but all rates are between 8 and 10 percent. The Class E certificate holders are entitled to receive all principal payments on the mortgages and interest on outstanding principal at 7 percent. The Class F certificate holders are entitled to receive all interest on the mortgages in excess of the interest paid on the Class E certificates.

(ii) The Class F certificates provide for interest payments that consist of a specified portion of the interest payable on the mortgages under paragraph (a)(2)(i) of this section. Although the portion of the interest payable to the Class F certificate holders varies from mortgage to mortgage, the interest payable can be expressed as a fixed percentage of the interest payable on each particular mortgage.

(3) *Variable rate.* A regular interest may bear interest at a variable rate. For purposes of section 860G(a)(1)(B)(i), a variable rate of interest is a rate described in this paragraph (a)(3).

(i) *Rate based on current interest rate.* A qualified floating rate as defined in § 1.1275-5(b)(1) (but without the application of paragraph (b)(2) or (3) of that section) set at a current value, as defined in § 1.1275-5(a)(4), is a variable rate. In addition, a rate equal to the highest, lowest, or average of two or more qualified floating rates is a variable rate. For example, a rate based on the average cost of funds of one or more financial institutions is a variable rate.

(ii) *Weighted average rate*—(A) *In general.* A rate based on a weighted average of the interest rates on some or all of the qualified mortgages held by a REMIC is a variable rate. The qualified mortgages taken into account must, however, bear interest at a fixed rate or at a rate described in this paragraph (a)(3). Generally, a weighted average interest rate is a rate that, if applied to the aggregate outstanding principal balance of a pool of mortgage loans for an accrual period, produces an amount of interest that equals the sum of the interest payable on the pooled loans for that accrual period. Thus, for an accrual period in which a pool of mortgage loans comprises $300,000 of loans bearing a 7 percent interest rate and $700,000 of loans bearing a 9.5 percent interest rate, the weighted average rate for the pool of loans is 8.75 percent.

(B) *Reduction in underlying rate.* For purposes of paragraph (a)(3)(ii)(A) of this section, an interest rate is considered to be based on a weighted average rate even if, in determining that rate, the interest rate on some or all of the qualified mortgages is first subject to a cap or a floor, or is first reduced by a number of basis points or a fixed percentage. A rate determined by taking a weighted average of the interest rates on the qualified mortgage loans net of any servicing spread, credit enhancement fees, or other expenses of the REMIC is a rate based on a weighted average rate for the qualified mortgages. Further, the amount of any rate reduction described above may vary from mortgage to mortgage.

(iii) *Additions, subtractions, and multiplications.* A rate is a variable rate if it is—

(A) Expressed as the product of a rate described in paragraph (a)(3)(i) or (ii) of this section and a fixed multiplier;

(B) Expressed as a constant number of basis points more or less than a rate described in paragraph (a)(3)(i) or (ii) of this section; or

(C) Expressed as the product, plus or minus a constant number of basis points, of a rate described in paragraph (a)(3)(i) or (ii) of this section and a fixed multiplier (which may be either a positive or a negative number).

(iv) *Caps and floors.* A rate is a variable rate if it is a rate that would be described in paragraph (a)(3)(i) through (iii) of this section except that it is—

(A) Limited by a cap or ceiling that establishes either a maximum rate or a maximum number of basis points by which the rate may increase from one accrual or payment period to another or over the term of the interest; or

(B) Limited by a floor that establishes either a minimum rate or a maximum number of basis points by which the rate may decrease from one accrual or payment period to another or over the term of the interest.

(v) *Funds-available caps*—(A) *In general.* A rate is a variable rate if it is a rate that would be described in paragraph (a)(3)(i) through (iv) of this section except that it is subject to a "funds-available" cap. A funds-available cap is a limit on the amount of interest to be paid on an instrument in any accrual or payment period that is based on the total amount available for the distribution, including both principal and interest received by an issuing entity on some or all of its qualified mortgages as well as amounts held in a reserve fund. The term "funds-available cap" does not, however, include any cap or limit on interest payments used as a device to avoid the standards of paragraph (a)(3)(i) through (iv) of this section.

(B) *Facts and circumstances test.* In determining whether a cap or limit on interest payments is a funds-available cap within the meaning of this section and not a device used to avoid the standards of paragraph (a)(3)(i) through (iv) of this section, one must consider all of the facts and circumstances. Facts and circumstances that must be taken into consideration are—

(*1*) Whether the rate of the interest payable to the regular interest holders is below the rate payable on the REMIC's qualified mortgages on the start-up day; and

(*2*) Whether, historically, the rate of interest payable to the regular interest holders has been consistently below that payable on the qualified mortgages.

(C) *Examples.* The following examples, both of which describe a pass-thru trust that is intended to qualify as a REMIC, illustrate the provisions of this paragraph (a)(3)(v).

Example 1. (i) A sponsor transferred a pool of mortgages to a trustee in exchange for two classes of certificates. The pool of mortgages has an aggregate principal balance of $100x. Each mortgage in the pool provides for interest payments based on the eleventh district cost of funds index (hereinafter COFI) plus a margin. The initial weighted average rate for the pool is COFI plus 200 basis points. The trust issued a Class X certificate that has a principal amount of $100x and that provides for interest payments at a rate equal to One-Year LIBOR plus 100 basis points, subject to a cap described below. The Class R certificate, which the sponsor designated as the residual interest, entitles its holder to all funds left in the trust after the Class X certificates have been retired. The Class R certificate holder is not entitled to current distributions.

(ii) At the time the certificates were issued, COFI equalled 4.874 percent and One-Year LIBOR equalled 3.375 percent. Thus, the initial weighted average pool rate was 6.874 percent and the Class X certificate rate was 4.375 percent. Based on historical data, the sponsor does not expect the rate paid on the Class X certificate to exceed the weighted average rate on the pool.

(iii) Initially, under the terms of the trust instrument, the excess of COFI plus 200 over One-Year LIBOR plus 100 (excess interest) will be applied to pay expenses of the trust, to fund any required reserves, and then to reduce the principal balance on the Class X certificate. Consequently, although the aggregate principal balance of the mortgages initially matched the principal balance of the Class X certificate, the principal balance on the Class X certificate will pay down faster than the principal balance on the

Reg. § 1.860G-1(a)(3)

mortgages as long as the weighted average rate on the mortgages is greater than One-Year LIBOR plus 100. If, however, the rate on the Class X certificate (One-Year LIBOR plus 100) ever exceeds the weighted average rate on the mortgages, then the Class X certificate holders will receive One-Year LIBOR plus 100 subject to a cap based on the current funds that are available for distribution.

(iv) The funds available cap here is not a device used to avoid the standards of paragraph (a)(3)(i) through (iv) of this section. First, on the date the Class X certificates were issued, a significant spread existed between the weighted average rate payable on the mortgages and the rate payable on the Class X certificate. Second, historical data suggest that the weighted average rate payable on the mortgages will continue to exceed the rate payable on the Class X certificate. Finally, because the excess interest will be applied to reduce the outstanding principal balance of the Class X certificate more rapidly than the outstanding principal balance on the mortgages is reduced, One-Year LIBOR plus 100 basis points would have to exceed the weighted average rate on the mortgages by an increasingly larger amount before the funds available cap would be triggered. Accordingly, the rate paid on the Class X certificates is a variable rate.

Example 2. (i) The facts are the same as those in *Example 1*, except that the pooled mortgages are commercial mortgages that provide for interest payments based on the gross profits of the mortgagors, and the rate on the Class X certificates is 400 percent of One-Year LIBOR (a variable rate under paragraph (a)(3)(iii) of this section), subject to a cap equal to current funds available to the trustee for distribution.

(ii) Initially, 400 percent of One-Year LIBOR exceeds the weighted average rate payable on the mortgages. Furthermore, historical data suggest that there is a significant possibility that, in the future, 400 percent of One-Year LIBOR will exceed the weighted average rate on the mortgages.

(iii) The facts and circumstances here indicate that the use of 400 percent of One-Year LIBOR with the above-described cap is a device to pass through to the Class X certificate holder contingent interest based on mortgagor profits. Consequently, the rate paid on the Class X certificate here is not a variable rate.

(vi) *Combination of rates.* A rate is a variable rate if it is based on—

(A) One fixed rate during one or more accrual or payment periods and a different fixed rate or rates, or a rate or rates described in paragraph (a)(3)(i) through (v) of this section, during other accrual or payment periods; or

(B) A rate described in paragraph (a)(3)(i) through (v) of this section during one or more accrual or payment periods and a fixed rate or rates, or a different rate or rates described in paragraph (a)(3)(i) through (v) of this section in other periods.

(4) *Fixed terms on the startup day.* For purposes of section 860G(a)(1), a regular interest in a REMIC has fixed terms on the startup day if, on the startup day, the REMIC's organizational documents irrevocably specify—

(i) The principal amount (or other similar amount) of the regular interest;

(ii) The interest rate or rates used to compute any interest payments (or other similar amounts) on the regular interest; and

(iii) The latest possible maturity date of the interest.

(5) *Contingencies prohibited.* Except for the contingencies specified in paragraph (b)(3) of this section, the principal amount (or other similar amount) and the latest possible maturity date of the interest must not be contingent.

(b) *Special rules for regular interests*—(1) *Call premium.* An interest in a REMIC does not qualify as a regular interest if the terms of the interest entitle the holder of that interest to the payment of any premium that is determined with reference to the length of time that the regular interest is outstanding and is not described in paragraph (b)(2) of this section.

(2) *Customary prepayment penalties received with respect to qualified mortgages.* An interest in a REMIC does not fail to qualify as a regular interest solely because the REMIC's organizational documents provide that the REMIC must allocate among and pay to its regular interest holders any customary prepayment penalties that the REMIC receives with respect to its qualified mortgages. Moreover, a REMIC may allocate prepayment penalties among its classes of interests in any manner specified in the REMIC's organizational documents. For example, a REMIC could allocate all or substantially all of a prepayment penalty that it receives to holders of an interest-only class of interests because that class would be most significantly affected by prepayments.

(3) *Certain contingencies disregarded.* An interest in a REMIC does not fail to qualify as a regular interest solely because it is issued subject to some or all of the contingencies described in paragraph (b)(3)(i) through (vi) of this section.

Reg. § 1.860G-1(a)(4)

(i) *Prepayments, income, and expenses.* An interest does not fail to qualify as a regular interest solely because—

(A) The timing of (but not the right to or amount of) principal payments (or other similar amounts) is affected by the extent of prepayments on some or all of the qualified mortgages held by the REMIC or the amount of income from permitted investments (as defined in § 1.860G-2(g)); or

(B) The timing of interest and principal payments is affected by the payment of expenses incurred by the REMIC.

(ii) *Credit losses.* An interest does not fail to qualify as a regular interest solely because the amount or the timing of payments of principal or interest (or other similar amounts) with respect to a regular interest is affected by defaults on qualified mortgages and permitted investments, unanticipated expenses incurred by the REMIC, or lower than expected returns on permitted investments.

(iii) *Subordinated interests.* An interest does not fail to qualify as a regular interest solely because that interest bears all, or a disproportionate share, of the losses stemming from cash flow shortfalls due to defaults or delinquencies on qualified mortgages or permitted investments, unanticipated expenses incurred by the REMIC, lower than expected returns on permitted investments, or prepayment interest shortfalls before other regular interests or the residual interest bear losses occasioned by those shortfalls.

(iv) *Deferral of interest.* An interest does not fail to qualify as a regular interest solely because that interest, by its terms, provides for deferral of interest payments.

(v) *Prepayment interest shortfalls.* An interest does not fail to qualify as a regular interest solely because the amount of interest payments is affected by prepayments of the underlying mortgages.

(vi) *Remote and incidental contingencies.* An interest does not fail to qualify as a regular interest solely because the amount or timing of payments of principal or interest (or other similar amounts) with respect to the interest is subject to a contingency if there is only a remote likelihood that the contingency will occur. For example, an interest could qualify as a regular interest even though full payment of principal and interest on that interest is contingent upon the absence of significant cash flow shortfalls due to the operation of the Soldiers and Sailors Civil Relief Act, 50 U.S.C. app. § 526 (1988).

(4) *Form of regular interest.* A regular interest in a REMIC may be issued in the form of debt, stock, an interest in a partnership or trust, or any other form permitted by state law. If a regular interest in a REMIC is not in the form of debt, it must, except as provided in paragraph (a)(2)(iv) of this section, entitle the holder to a specified amount that would, were the interest issued in debt form, be identified as the principal amount of the debt.

(5) *Interest disproportionate to principal*—(i) *In general.* An interest in a REMIC does not qualify as a regular interest if the amount of interest (or other similar amount) payable to the holder is disproportionately high relative to the principal amount or other specified amount described in paragraph (b)(4) of this section (specified principal amount). Interest payments (or other similar amounts) are considered disproportionately high if the issue price (as determined under paragraph (d) of this section) of the interest in the REMIC exceeds 125 percent of its specified principal amount.

(ii) *Exception.* A regular interest in a REMIC that entitles the holder to interest payments consisting of a specified portion of interest payments on qualified mortgages qualifies as a regular interest even if the amount of interest is disproportionately high relative to the specified principal amount.

(6) *Regular interest treated as a debt instrument for all Federal income tax purposes.* In determining the tax under chapter 1 of the Internal Revenue Code, a REMIC regular interest (as defined in section 860G(a)(1)) is treated as a debt instrument that is an obligation of the REMIC. Thus, sections 1271 through 1288, relating to bonds and other debt instruments, apply to a regular interest. For special rules relating to the accrual of original issue discount on regular interests, see section 1272(a)(6).

(c) *Residual interest.* A residual interest is an interest in a REMIC that is issued on the startup day and that is designated as a residual interest by providing the information specified in § 1.860D-1(d)(2)(ii) at the time and in the manner provided in § 1.860D-1(d)(2). A residual interest need not entitle the holder to any distributions from the REMIC.

(d) *Issue price of regular and residual interests*—(1) *In general.* The issue price of any REMIC regular or residual interest is determined under section 1273(b) as if the interest were a debt instrument and, if issued for property, as if the requirements of section 1273(b)(3) were met. Thus, if a class of interests is publicly offered, then the issue price of an interest in that class is

Reg. § 1.860G-1(d)(1)

the initial offering price to the public at which a substantial amount of the class is sold. If the interest is in a class that is not publicly offered, the issue price is the price paid by the first buyer of that interest regardless of the price paid for the remainder of the class. If the interest is in a class that is retained by the sponsor, the issue price is its fair market value on the pricing date (as defined in § 1.860F-2(b)(3)(iii)), if any, or, if none, the startup day, regardless of whether the property exchanged therefor is publicly traded.

(2) *The public.* The term "the public" for purposes of this section does not include brokers or other middlemen, nor does it include the sponsor who acquires all of the regular and residual interests from the REMIC on the startup day in a transaction described in § 1.860F-2(a). [Reg. § 1.860G-1.]

☐ [T.D. 8458, 12-23-92. Amended by T.D. 8614, 8-16-95.]

[Reg. § 1.860G-2]

§ 1.860G-2. Other rules.—(a) *Obligations principally secured by an interest in real property*— (1) *Tests for determining whether an obligation is principally secured.* For purposes of section 860G(a)(3)(A), an obligation is principally secured by an interest in real property only if it satisfies either the test set out in paragraph (a)(1)(i) or the test set out in paragraph (a)(1)(ii) of this section.

(i) *The 80-percent test.* An obligation is principally secured by an interest in real property if the fair market value of the interest in real property securing the obligation—

(A) Was at least equal to 80 percent of the adjusted issue price of the obligation at the time the obligation was originated (see paragraph (b)(1) of this section concerning the origination date for obligations that have been significantly modified); or

(B) Is at least equal to 80 percent of the adjusted issue price of the obligation at the time the sponsor contributes the obligation to the REMIC.

(ii) *Alternative test.* For purposes of section 860G(a)(3)(A), an obligation is principally secured by an interest in real property if substantially all of the proceeds of the obligation were used to acquire or to improve or protect an interest in real property that, at the origination date, is the only security for the obligation. For purposes of this test, loan guarantees made by the United States or any state (or any political subdivision, agency, or instrumentality of the United States or of any state), or other third party credit enhancement are not viewed as additional security for a loan. An obligation is not considered to be secured by property other than real property solely because the obligor is personally liable on the obligation.

(2) *Treatment of liens.* For purposes of paragraph (a)(1)(i) of this section, the fair market value of the real property interest must be first reduced by the amount of any lien on the real property interest that is senior to the obligation being tested, and must be further reduced by a proportionate amount of any lien that is in parity with the obligation being tested.

(3) *Safe harbor*—(i) *Reasonable belief that an obligation is principally secured.* If, at the time the sponsor contributes an obligation to a REMIC, the sponsor reasonably believes that the obligation is principally secured by an interest in real property within the meaning of paragraph (a)(1) of this section, then the obligation is deemed to be so secured for purposes of section 860G(a)(3). A sponsor cannot avail itself of this safe harbor with respect to an obligation if the sponsor actually knows or has reason to know that the obligation fails both of the tests set out in paragraph (a)(1) of this section.

(ii) *Basis for reasonable belief.* For purposes of paragraph (a)(3)(i) of this section, a sponsor may base a reasonable belief concerning any obligation on—

(A) Representations and warranties made by the originator of the obligation; or

(B) Evidence indicating that the originator of the obligation typically made mortgage loans in accordance with an established set of parameters, and that any mortgage loan originated in accordance with those parameters would satisfy at least one of the tests set out in paragraph (a)(1) of this section.

(iii) *Later discovery that an obligation is not principally secured.* If, despite the sponsor's reasonable belief concerning an obligation at the time it contributed the obligation to the REMIC, the REMIC later discovers that the obligation is not principally secured by an interest in real property, the obligation is a defective obligation and loses its status as a qualified mortgage 90 days after the date of discovery. See paragraph (f) of this section, relating to defective obligations.

(4) *Interests in real property; real property.* The definition of "interests in real property" set out in § 1.856-3(c), and the definition of "real property" set out in § 1.856-3(d), apply to define those terms for purposes of section 860G(a)(3) and paragraph (a) of this section.

(5) *Obligations secured by an interest in real property.* Obligations secured by interests in real

property include the following: mortgages, deeds of trust, and installment land contracts; mortgage pass-thru certificates guaranteed by GNMA, FNMA, FHLMC, or CMHC (Canada Mortgage and Housing Corporation); other investment trust interests that represent undivided beneficial ownership in a pool of obligations principally secured by interests in real property and related assets that would be considered to be permitted investments if the investment trust were a REMIC, and provided the investment trust is classified as a trust under § 301.7701-4(c) of this chapter; and obligations secured by manufactured housing treated as single family residences under section 25(e)(10) (without regard to the treatment of the obligations or the properties under state law).

(6) *Obligations secured by other obligations; residual interests.* Obligations (other than regular interests in a REMIC) that are secured by other obligations that are not principally secured by interests in real property even if the underlying obligations are secured by interests in real property. Thus, for example, a collateralized mortgage obligation issued by an issuer that is not a REMIC is not an obligation principally secured by an interest in real property. A residual interest (as defined in section 860G(a)(2)) is not an obligation principally secured by an interest in real property.

(7) *Certain instruments that call for contingent payments are obligations.* For purposes of section 860G(a)(3) and (4), the term "obligation" includes any instrument that provides for total noncontingent principal payments that at least equal the instrument's issue price even if that instrument also provides for contingent payments. Thus, for example, an instrument that was issued for $100x and that provides for noncontingent principal payments of $100x, interest payments at a fixed rate, and contingent payments based on a percentage of the mortgagor's gross receipts, is an obligation.

(8) *Defeasance.* If a REMIC releases its lien on real property that secures a qualified mortgage, that mortgage ceases to be a qualified mortgage on the date the lien is released unless—

(i) The mortgagor pledges substitute collateral that consists solely of government securities (as defined in section 2(a)(16) of the Investment Company Act of 1940 as amended (15 U.S.C. 80a-1));

(ii) The mortgage documents allow such a substitution;

(iii) The lien is released to facilitate the disposition of the property or any other customary commercial transaction, and not as part of an arrangement to collateralize a REMIC offering with obligations that are not real estate mortgages; and

(iv) The release is not within 2 years of the startup day.

(9) *Stripped bonds and coupons.* The term "qualified mortgage" includes stripped bonds and stripped coupons (as defined in section 1286(e)(2) and (3)) if the bonds (as defined in section 1286(e)(1)) from which such stripped bonds or stripped coupons arose would have been qualified mortgages.

(b) *Assumptions and modifications*—(1) *Significant modifications are treated as exchanges of obligations.* If an obligation is significantly modified in a manner or under circumstances other than those described in paragraph (b)(3) of this section, then the modified obligation is treated as one that was newly issued in exchange for the unmodified obligation that it replaced. Consequently—

(i) If such a significant modification occurs after the obligation has been contributed to the REMIC and the modified obligation is not a qualified replacement mortgage, the modified obligation will not be a qualified mortgage and the deemed disposition of the unmodified obligation will be a prohibited transaction under section 860F(a)(2); and

(ii) If such a significant modification occurs before the obligation is contributed to the REMIC, the modified obligation will be viewed as having been originated on the date the modification occurs for purposes of the tests set out in paragraph (a)(1) of this section.

(2) *Significant modification defined.* For purposes of paragraph (b)(1) of this section, a "significant modification" is any change in the terms of an obligation that would be treated as an exchange of obligations under section 1001 and the related regulations.

(3) *Exceptions.* For purposes of paragraph (b)(1) of this section, the following changes in the terms of an obligation are not significant modifications regardless of whether they would be significant modifications under paragraph (b)(2) of this section—

(i) Changes in the terms of the obligation occasioned by default or a reasonably foreseeable default;

(ii) Assumption of the obligation;

(iii) Waiver of a due-on-sale clause or a due on encumbrance clause; and

(iv) Conversion of an interest rate by a mortgagor pursuant to the terms of a convertible mortgage.

Reg. § 1.860G-2(b)(3)

(4) *Modifications that are not significant modifications.* If an obligation is modified and the modification is not a significant modification for purposes of paragraph (b)(1) of this section, then the modified obligation is not treated as one that was newly originated on the date of modification.

(5) *Assumption defined.* For purposes of paragraph (b)(3) of this section, a mortgage has been assumed if—

(i) The buyer of the mortgaged property acquires the property subject to the mortgage, without assuming any personal liability;

(ii) The buyer becomes liable for the debt but the seller also remains liable; or

(iii) The buyer becomes liable for the debt and the seller is released by the lender.

(6) *Pass-thru certificates.* If a REMIC holds as a qualified mortgage a pass-thru certificate or other investment trust interest of the type described in paragraph (a)(5) of this section, the modification of a mortgage loan that backs the pass-thru certificate or other interest is not a modification of the pass-thru certificate or other interest unless the investment trust structure was created to avoid the prohibited transaction rules of section 860F(a).

(c) *Treatment of certain credit enhancement contracts*—(1) *In general.* A credit enhancement contract (as defined in paragraph (c)(2) and (3) of this section) is not treated as a separate asset of the REMIC for purposes of the asset test set out in section 860D(a)(4) and § 1.860D-1(b)(3), but instead is treated as part of the mortgage or pool of mortgages to which it relates. Furthermore, any collateral supporting a credit enhancement contract is not treated as an asset of the REMIC solely because it supports the guarantee represented by that contract. See paragraph (g)(1)(ii) of this section for the treatment of payments made pursuant to credit enhancement contracts as payments received under a qualified mortgage.

(2) *Credit enhancement contracts.* For purposes of this section, a credit enhancement contract is any arrangement whereby a person agrees to guarantee full or partial payment of the principal or interest payable on a qualified mortgage or on a pool of such mortgages, or full or partial payment on one or more classes of regular interests or on the class of residual interests, in the event of defaults or delinquencies on qualified mortgages, unanticipated losses or expenses incurred by the REMIC, or lower than expected returns on cash flow investments. Types of credit enhancement contracts may include, but are not limited to, pool insurance contracts, certificate guarantee insurance contracts, letters of credit, guarantees, or agreements whereby the REMIC sponsor, a mortgage servicer, or other third party agrees to make advances described in paragraph (c)(3) of this section.

(3) *Arrangements to make certain advances.* The arrangements described in this paragraph (c)(3) are credit enhancement contracts regardless of whether, under the terms of the arrangement, the payor is obligated, or merely permitted, to advance funds to the REMIC.

(i) *Advances of delinquent principal and interest.* An arrangement by a REMIC sponsor, mortgage servicer, or other third party to advance to the REMIC out of its own funds an amount to make up for delinquent payments on qualified mortgages is a credit enhancement contract.

(ii) *Advances of taxes, insurance payments, and expenses.* An arrangement by a REMIC sponsor, mortgage servicer, or other third party to pay taxes and hazard insurance premiums on, or other expenses incurred to protect the REMIC's security interest in, property securing a qualified mortgage in the event that the mortgagor fails to pay such taxes, insurance premiums, or other expenses is a credit enhancement contract.

(iii) *Advances to ease REMIC administration.* An agreement by a REMIC sponsor, mortgage servicer, or other third party to advance temporarily to a REMIC amounts payable on qualified mortgages before such amounts are actually due to level out the stream of cash flows to the REMIC or to provide for orderly administration of the REMIC is a credit enhancement contract. For example, if two mortgages in a pool have payment due dates on the twentieth of the month, and all the other mortgages have payment due dates on the first of each month, an agreement by the mortgage servicer to advance to the REMIC on the fifteenth of each month the payments not yet received on the two mortgages together with the amounts received on the other mortgages is a credit enhancement contract.

(4) *Deferred payment under a guarantee arrangement.* A guarantee arrangement does not fail to qualify as a credit enhancement contract solely because the guarantor, in the event of a default on a qualified mortgage, has the option of immediately paying to the REMIC the full amount of mortgage principal due on acceleration of the defaulted mortgage, or paying principal and interest to the REMIC according to the original payment schedule for the defaulted mortgage, or according to some other deferred payment schedule. Any deferred payments are payments pursuant to a credit enhancement contract even if the mortgage is foreclosed upon and the guarantor, pursuant to subrogation rights set out in the

Reg. § 1.860G-2(b)(4)

guarantee arrangement, is entitled to receive immediately the proceeds of foreclosure.

(d) *Treatment of certain purchase agreements with respect to convertible mortgages*—(1) *In general.* For purposes of sections 860D(a)(4) and 860G(a)(3), a purchase agreement (as described in paragraph (d)(3) of this section) with respect to a convertible mortgage (as described in paragraph (d)(5) of this section) is treated as incidental to the convertible mortgage to which it relates. Consequently, the purchase agreement is part of the mortgage or pool of mortgages and is not a separate asset of the REMIC.

(2) *Treatment of amounts received under purchase agreements.* For purposes of sections 860A through 860G and for purposes of determining the accrual of original issue discount and market discount under sections 1272(a)(6) and 1276, respectively, a payment under a purchase agreement described in paragraph (d)(3) of this section is treated as a prepayment in full of the mortgage to which it relates. Thus, for example, a payment under a purchase agreement with respect to a qualified mortgage is considered a payment received under a qualified mortgage within the meaning of section 860G(a)(6) and the transfer of the mortgage is not a disposition of the mortgage within the meaning of section 860F(a)(2)(A).

(3) *Purchase agreement.* A purchase agreement is a contract between the holder of a convertible mortgage and a third party under which the holder agrees to sell and the third party agrees to buy the mortgage for an amount equal to its current principal balance plus accrued but unpaid interest if and when the mortgagor elects to convert the terms of the mortgage.

(4) *Default by the person obligated to purchase a convertible mortgage.* If the person required to purchase a convertible mortgage defaults on its obligation to purchase the mortgage upon conversion, the REMIC may sell the mortgage in a market transaction and the proceeds of the sale will be treated as amounts paid pursuant to a purchase agreement.

(5) *Convertible mortgage.* A convertible mortgage is a mortgage that gives the obligor the right at one or more times during the term of the mortgage to elect to convert from one interest rate to another. The new rate of interest must be determined pursuant to the terms of the instrument and must be intended to approximate a market rate of interest for newly originated mortgages at the time of the conversion.

(e) *Prepayment interest shortfalls.* An agreement by a mortgage servicer or other third party to make payments to the REMIC to make up prepayment interest shortfalls is not treated as a separate asset of the REMIC and payments made pursuant to such an agreement are treated as payments on the qualified mortgages. With respect to any mortgage that prepays, the prepayment interest shortfall for the accrual period in which the mortgage prepays is an amount equal to the excess of the interest that would have accrued on the mortgage during that accrual period had it not prepaid, over the interest that accrued from the beginning of that accrual period up to the date of the prepayment.

(f) *Defective obligations*—(1) *Defective obligation defined.* For purposes of sections 860G(a)(4)(B)(ii) and 860F(a)(2), a defective obligation is a mortgage subject to any of the following defects.

(i) The mortgage is in default, or a default with respect to the mortgage is reasonably foreseeable.

(ii) The mortgage was fraudulently procured by the mortgagor.

(iii) The mortgage was not in fact principally secured by an interest in real property within the meaning of paragraph (a)(1) of this section.

(iv) The mortgage does not conform to a customary representation or warranty given by the sponsor or prior owner of the mortgage regarding the characteristics of the mortgage, or the characteristics of the pool of mortgages of which the mortgage is a part. A representation that payments on a qualified mortgage will be received at a rate no less than a specified minimum or no greater than a specified maximum is not customary for this purpose.

(2) *Effect of discovery of defect.* If a REMIC discovers that an obligation is a defective obligation, and if the defect is one that, had it been discovered before the startup day, would have prevented the obligation from being a qualified mortgage, then, unless the REMIC either causes the defect to be cured or disposes of the defective obligation within 90 days of discovering the defect, the obligation ceases to be a qualified mortgage at the end of that 90 day period. Even if the defect is not cured, the defective obligation is, nevertheless, a qualified mortgage from the startup day through the end of the 90 day period. Moreover, even if the REMIC holds the defective obligation beyond the 90 day period, the REMIC may, nevertheless, exchange the defective obligation for a qualified replacement mortgage so long as the requirements of section 860G(a)(4)(B) are satisfied. If the defect is one that does not affect the status of an obligation as a qualified mortgage, then the obligation is always a qualified

Reg. § 1.860G-2(f)(2)

mortgage regardless of whether the defect is or can be cured. For example, if a sponsor represented that all mortgages transferred to a REMIC had a 10 percent interest rate, but it was later discovered that one mortgage had a 9 percent interest rate, the 9 percent mortgage is defective, but the defect does not affect the status of that obligation as a qualified mortgage.

(g) *Permitted investments*—(1) *Cash flow investment*—(i) *In general.* For purposes of section 860G(a)(6) and this section, a cash flow investment is an investment of payments received on qualified mortgages for a temporary period between receipt of those payments and the regularly scheduled date for distribution of those payments to REMIC interest holders. Cash flow investments must be passive investments earning a return in the nature of interest.

(ii) *Payments received on qualified mortgages.* For purposes of paragraph (g)(1) of this section, the term "payments received on qualified mortgages" includes—

(A) Payments of interest and principal on qualified mortgages, including prepayments of principal and payments under credit enhancement contracts described in paragraph (c)(2) of this section;

(B) Proceeds from the disposition of qualified mortgages;

(C) Cash flows from foreclosure property and proceeds from the disposition of such property;

(D) A payment by a sponsor or prior owner in lieu of the sponsor's or prior owner's repurchase of a defective obligation, as defined in paragraph (f) of this section, that was transferred to the REMIC in breach of a customary warranty; and

(E) Prepayment penalties required to be paid under the terms of a qualified mortgage when the mortgagor prepays the obligation.

(iii) *Temporary period.* For purposes of section 860G(a)(6) and this paragraph (g)(1), a temporary period generally is that period from the time a REMIC receives payments on qualified mortgages and permitted investments to the time the REMIC distributes the payments to interest holders. A temporary period may not exceed 13 months. Thus, an investment held by a REMIC for more than 13 months is not a cash flow investment. In determining the length of time that a REMIC has held an investment that is part of a commingled fund or account, the REMIC may employ any reasonable method of accounting. For example, if a REMIC holds mortgage cash flows in a commingled account pending distribution, the first-in, first-out method of accounting is a reasonable method for determining whether all or part of the account satisfies the 13 month limitation.

(2) *Qualified reserve funds.* The term qualified reserve fund means any reasonably required reserve to provide for full payment of expenses of the REMIC or amounts due on regular or residual interests in the event of defaults on qualified mortgages, prepayment interest shortfalls (as defined in paragraph (e) of this section), lower than expected returns on cash flow investments, or any other contingency that could be provided for under a credit enhancement contract (as defined in paragraph (c)(2) and (3) of this section).

(3) *Qualified reserve asset*—(i) *In general.* The term "qualified reserve asset" means any intangible property (other than a REMIC residual interest) that is held both for investment and as part of a qualified reserve fund. An asset need not generate any income to be a qualified reserve asset.

(ii) *Reasonably required reserve*—(A) *In general.* In determining whether the amount of a reserve is reasonable, it is appropriate to consider the credit quality of the qualified mortgages, the extent and nature of any guarantees relating to either the qualified mortgages or the regular and residual interests, the expected amount of expenses of the REMIC, and the expected availability of proceeds from qualified mortgages to pay the expenses. To the extent that a reserve exceeds a reasonably required amount, the amount of the reserve must be promptly and appropriately reduced. If at any time, however, the amount of the reserve fund is less than is reasonably required, the amount of the reserve fund may be increased by the addition of payments received on qualified mortgages or by contributions from holders of residual interests.

(B) *Presumption that a reserve is reasonably required.* The amount of a reserve fund is presumed to be reasonable (and an excessive reserve is presumed to have been promptly and appropriately reduced) if it does not exceed—

(*1*) The amount required by a nationally recognized independent rating agency as a condition of providing the rating for REMIC interests desired by the sponsor; or

(*2*) The amount required by a third party insurer or guarantor, who does not own directly or indirectly (within the meaning of section 267(c)) an interest in the REMIC (as defined in § 1.860D-1(b)(1)), as a condition of providing credit enhancement.

(C) *Presumption may be rebutted.* The presumption in paragraph (g)(3)(ii)(B) of this sec-

Reg. § 1.860G-2(g)(1)

tion may be rebutted if the amounts required by the rating agency or by the third party insurer are not commercially reasonable considering the factors described in paragraph (g)(3)(ii)(A) of this section.

(h) *Outside reserve funds.* A reserve fund that is maintained to pay expenses of the REMIC, or to make payments to REMIC interest holders is an outside reserve fund and not an asset of the REMIC only if the REMIC's organizational documents clearly and expressly—

(1) Provide that the reserve fund is an outside reserve fund and not an asset of the REMIC;

(2) Identify the owner(s) of the reserve fund, either by name, or by description of the class (*e.g.*, subordinated regular interest holders) whose membership comprises the owners of the fund; and

(3) Provide that, for all Federal tax purposes, amounts transferred by the REMIC to the fund are treated as amounts distributed by the REMIC to the designated owner(s) or transferees of the designated owner(s).

(i) *Contractual rights coupled with regular interests in tiered arrangements*—(1) *In general.* If a REMIC issues a regular interest to a trustee of an investment trust for the benefit of the trust certificate holders and the trustee also holds for the benefit of those certificate holders certain other contractual rights, those other rights are not treated as assets of the REMIC even if the investment trust and the REMIC were created contemporaneously pursuant to a single set of organizational documents. The organizational documents must, however, require that the trustee account for the contractual rights as property that the trustee holds separate and apart from the regular interest.

(2) *Example.* The following example, which describes a tiered arrangement involving a pass-thru trust that is intended to qualify as a REMIC and a pass-thru trust that is intended to be classified as a trust under § 301.7701-4(c) of this chapter, illustrates the provisions of paragraph (i)(1) of this section.

Example. (i) A sponsor transferred a pool of mortgages to a trustee in exchange for two classes of certificates. The pool of mortgages has an aggregate principal balance of $100x. Each mortgage in the pool provides for interest payments based on the eleventh district cost of funds index (hereinafter COFI) plus a margin. The trust (hereinafter REMIC trust) issued a Class N bond, which the sponsor designates as a regular interest, that has a principal amount of $100x and that provides for interest payments at a rate equal to One-Year LIBOR plus 100 basis points, subject to a cap equal to the weighted average pool rate. The Class R interest, which the sponsor designated as the residual interest, entitles its holder to all funds left in the trust after the Class N bond has been retired. The Class R interest holder is not entitled to current distributions.

(ii) On the same day, and under the same set of documents, the sponsor also created an investment trust. The sponsor contributed to the investment trust the Class N bond together with an interest rate cap contract. Under the interest rate cap contract, the issuer of the cap contract agrees to pay to the trustee for the benefit of the investment trust certificate holders the excess of One-Year LIBOR plus 100 basis points over the weighted average pool rate (COFI plus a margin) times the outstanding principal balance of the Class N bond in the event One-Year LIBOR plus 100 basis points ever exceeds the weighted average pool rate. The trustee (the same institution that serves as REMIC trust trustee), in exchange for the contributed assets, gave the sponsor certificates representing undivided beneficial ownership interests in the Class N bond and the interest rate cap contract. The organizational documents require the trustee to account for the regular interest and the cap contract as discrete property rights.

(iii) The separate existence of the REMIC trust and the investment trust are respected for all Federal income tax purposes. Thus, the interest rate cap contract is an asset beneficially owned by the several certificate holders and is not an asset of the REMIC trust. Consequently, each certificate holder must allocate its purchase price for the certificate between its undivided interest in the Class N bond and its undivided interest in the interest rate cap contract in accordance with the relative fair market values of those two property rights.

(j) *Clean-up call*—(1) *In general.* For purposes of section 860F(a)(5)(B), a clean-up call is the redemption of a class of regular interests when, by reason of prior payments with respect to those interests, the administrative costs associated with servicing that class outweigh the benefits of maintaining the class. Factors to consider in making this determination include—

(i) The number of holders of that class of regular interests;

(ii) The frequency of payments to holders of that class;

(iii) The effect the redemption will have on the yield of that class of regular interests;

(iv) The outstanding principal balance of that class; and

Reg. § 1.860G-2(j)(1)

(v) The percentage of the original principal balance of that class still outstanding.

(2) *Interest rate changes.* The redemption of a class of regular interests undertaken to profit from a change in interest rates is not a clean-up call.

(3) *Safe harbor.* Although the outstanding principal balance is only one factor to consider, the redemption of a class of regular interests with an outstanding principal balance of no more than 10 percent of its original principal balance is always a clean-up call.

(k) *Startup day.* The term "startup day" means the day on which the REMIC issues all of its regular and residual interests. A sponsor may, however, contribute property to a REMIC in exchange for regular and residual interests over any period of 10 consecutive days and the REMIC may designate any one of those 10 days as its startup day. The day so designated is then the startup day, and all interests are treated as issued on that day. [Reg. § 1.860G-2.]

☐ [T.D. 8458, 12-23-92.]

[Reg. § 1.860G-3]

§ 1.860G-3. Treatment of foreign persons.—(a) *Transfer of a residual interest with tax avoidance potential*—(1) *In general.* A transfer of a residual interest that has tax avoidance potential is disregarded for all Federal tax purposes if the transferee is a foreign person. Thus, if a residual interest with tax avoidance potential is transferred to a foreign holder at formation of the REMIC, the sponsor is liable for the tax on any excess inclusion that accrues with respect to that residual interest.

(2) *Tax avoidance potential*—(i) *Defined.* A residual interest has tax avoidance potential for purposes of this section unless, at the time of the transfer, the transferor reasonably expects that, for each excess inclusion, the REMIC will distribute to the transferee residual interest holder an amount that will equal at least 30 percent of the excess inclusion, and that each such amount will be distributed at or after the time at which the excess inclusion accrues and not later than the close of the calendar year following the calendar year of accrual.

(ii) *Safe harbor.* For purposes of paragraph (a)(2)(i) of this section, a transferor has a reasonable expectation if the 30-percent test would be satisfied were the REMIC's qualified mortgages to prepay at each rate within a range of rates from 50 percent to 200 percent of the rate assumed under section 1272(a)(6) with respect to the qualified mortgages (or the rate that would have been assumed had the mortgages been issued with original issue discount).

(3) *Effectively connected income.* Paragraph (a)(1) of this section will not apply if the transferee's income from the residual interest is subject to tax under section 871(b) or section 882.

(4) *Transfer by a foreign holder.* If a foreign person transfers a residual interest to a United States person or a foreign holder in whose hands the income from a residual interest would be effectively connected income, and if the transfer has the effect of allowing the transferor to avoid tax on accrued excess inclusions, then the transfer is disregarded and the transferor continues to be treated as the owner of the residual interest for purposes of section 871(a), 881, 1441, or 1442.

(b) [Reserved] [Reg. § 1.860G-3.]

☐ [T.D. 8458, 12-23-92.]

INCOME FROM SOURCES WITHIN OR WITHOUT THE UNITED STATES

Determination of Sources of Income

[Reg. § 1.861-1]

§ 1.861-1. Income from sources within the United States.—(a) *Categories of income.* Part 1 (section 861 and following), subchapter N, chapter 1 of the Code, and the regulations thereunder determine the sources of income for purposes of the income tax. These sections explicitly allocate certain important sources of income to the United States or to areas outside the United States, as the case may be; and, with respect to the remaining income (particularly that derived partly from sources within and partly from sources without the United States), authorize the Secretary or his delegate to determine the income derived from sources within the United States, either by rules of separate allocation or by processes or formulas of general apportionment. The statute provides for the following three categories of income:

(1) *Within the United States.* The gross income from sources within the United States, consisting of the items of gross income specified in section 861(a) plus the items of gross income allocated or apportioned to such sources in accordance with section 863(a). See §§ 1.861-2 to 1.861-7, inclusive, and § 1.863-1. The taxable income from sources within the United States, in

Determination of Sources of Income

See p. 20,601 for regulations not amended to reflect law changes

the case of such income, shall be determined by deducting therefrom, in accordance with sections 861(b) and 863(a), the expenses, losses, and other deductions properly apportioned or allocated thereto and a ratable part of any other expenses, losses, or deductions which cannot definitely be allocated to some item or class of gross income. See §§ 1.861-8 and 1.863-1.

(2) *Without the United States.* The gross income from sources without the United States, consisting of the items of gross income specified in section 862(a) plus the items of gross income allocated or apportioned to such sources in accordance with section 863(a). See §§ 1.862-1 and 1.863-1. The taxable income from sources without the United States, in the case of such income, shall be determined by deducting therefrom, in accordance with sections 862(b) and 863(a), the expenses, losses, and other deductions properly apportioned or allocated thereto and a ratable part of any other expenses, losses, or deductions which cannot definitely be allocated to some item or class of gross income. See §§ 1.862-1 and 1.863-1.

(3) *Partly within and partly without the United States.* The gross income derived from sources partly within and partly without the United States, consisting of the items specified in section 863(b)(1), (2), and (3). The taxable income allocated or apportioned to sources within the United States, in the case of such income, shall be determined in accordance with section 863(a) or (b). See §§ 1.863-2 to 1.863-5, inclusive.

(4) *Exceptions.* An owner of certain aircraft or vessels first leased on or before December 28, 1980, may elect to treat income in respect of these aircraft or vessels as income from sources within the United States for purposes of sections 861(a) and 862(a). See § 1.861-9. An owner of certain aircraft, vessels, or spacecraft first leased after December 28, 1980, must treat income in respect of these craft as income from sources within the United States for purposes of sections 861(a) and 862(a). See § 1.861-9A.

(b) *Taxable income from sources within the United States.* The taxable income from sources within the United States shall consist of the taxable income described in paragraph (a)(1) of this section plus the taxable income allocated or apportioned to such sources, as indicated in paragraph (a)(3) of this section.

(c) *Computation of income.* If a taxpayer has gross income from sources within or without the United States, together with gross income derived partly from sources within and partly from sources without the United States, the amounts thereof, together with the expenses and investment applicable thereto, shall be segregated; and the taxable income from sources within the United States shall be separately computed therefrom. [Reg. § 1.861-1.]

☐ [*T.D.* 6258, 10-23-57. *Amended by T.D.* 7635, 8-7-79 *and T.D.* 7928, 12-15-83.]

[Reg. § 1.861-2]

§ 1.861-2. Interest.—(a) *In general.*—(1) Gross income consisting of interest from the United States or any agency or instrumentality thereof (other than a possession of the United States or an agency or instrumentality of a possession), a State or any political subdivision thereof, or the District of Columbia, and interest from a resident of the United States on a bond, note, or other interest-bearing obligation issued or assumed or incurred by such person shall be treated as income from sources within the United States. Thus, for example, income from sources within the United States includes interest received on any refund of income tax imposed by the United States, a State or any political subdivision thereof, or the District of Columbia. Interest other than that described in this paragraph is not to be treated as income from sources within the United States. See paragraph (a)(7) of this section for special rules concerning substitute interest paid or accrued pursuant to a securities lending transaction.

(2) The term "resident of the United States", as used in this paragraph, includes (i) an individual who at the time of payment of the interest is a resident of the United States, (ii) a domestic corporation, (iii) a domestic partnership which at any time during its taxable year is engaged in trade or business in the United States, or (iv) a foreign corporation or a foreign partnership, which at any time during its taxable year is engaged in trade or business in the United States.

(3) The method by which, or the place where, payment of the interest is made is immaterial in determining whether interest is derived from sources within the United States.

(4) For purposes of this section, the term "interest" includes all amounts treated as interest under section 483, and the regulations thereunder. It also includes original issue discount, as defined in section 1232(b)(1), whether or not the underlying bond, debenture, note, certificate, or other evidence of indebtedness is a capital asset in the hands of the taxpayer within the meaning of section 1221.

(5) If interest is paid on an obligation of a resident of the United States by a nonresident of the United States acting in the nonresident's capacity as a guarantor of the obligation of the

Reg. § 1.861-2(a)(5)

resident, the interest will be treated as income from sources within the United States.

(6) In the case of interest received by a nonresident alien individual or foreign corporation this paragraph (a) applies whether or not the interest is effectively connected for the taxable year with the conduct of a trade or business in the United States by such individual or corporation.

(7) A substitute interest payment is a payment, made to the transferor of a security in a securities lending transaction or a sale-repurchase transaction, of an amount equivalent to an interest payment which the owner of the transferred security is entitled to receive during the term of the transaction. A securities lending transaction is a transfer of one or more securities that is described in section 1058(a) or a substantially similar transaction. A sale-repurchase transaction is an agreement under which a person transfers a security in exchange for cash and simultaneously agrees to receive substantially identical securities from the transferee in the future in exchange for cash. A substitute interest payment shall be sourced in the same manner as the interest accruing on the transferred security for purposes of this section and § 1.862-1. See also §§ 1.864-5(b)(2)(iii), 1.871-7(b)(2), 1.881-2(b)(2) and for the character of such payments and § 1.894-1(c) for the application tax treaties to these transactions.

(b) *Interest not derived from U.S. sources.* Notwithstanding paragraph (a) of this section, interest shall be treated as income from sources without the United States to the extent provided by subparagraphs (A) through (H), of section 861(a)(1) and by the following subparagraphs of this paragraph.

(1) *Interest on bank deposits and on similar amounts.* (i) Interest paid or credited before January 1, 1977, to a nonresident alien individual or foreign corporation on—

(*a*) Deposits with persons, including citizens of the United States or alien individuals and foreign or domestic partnerships or corporations, carrying on the banking business in the United States,

(*b*) Deposits or withdrawable accounts with savings institutions chartered and supervised as savings and loan or similar associations under Federal or State law, or

(*c*) Amounts held by an insurance company under an agreement to pay interest thereon, shall be treated as income from sources without the United States if such interest is not effectively connected for the taxable year with the conduct of a trade or business in the United States by such nonresident alien individual or foreign corporation. If such interest is effectively connected for the taxable year with the conduct of a trade or business in the United States by such nonresident alien individual or foreign corporation, it shall be treated as income from sources within the United States under paragraph (a) of this section unless it is treated as income from sources without the United States under another subparagraph of this paragraph. For a special rule for determining whether such interest is effectively connected for the taxable year with the conduct of a trade or business in the United States, see paragraph (c)(1)(ii) or § 1.864-4.

(ii) Subdivision (i)(*b*) of this subparagraph applies to interest on deposits or withdrawable accounts described therein only to the extent that the interest paid or credited by the savings institution described therein is deductible under section 591 in determining the taxable income of such institution; and, for this purpose, whether an amount is deductible under section 591 shall be determined without regard to section 265, relating to deductions allocable to tax-exempt income. Thus, for example, such subdivision does not apply to amounts paid by a savings and loan or similar association on or with respect to its nonwithdrawable capital stock or on or with respect to funds held in restricted accounts which represent a proprietary interest in such association. Subdivision (i)(*b*) of this subparagraph also applies to so-called dividends paid or credited on deposits or withdrawable accounts if such dividends are deductible under section 591 without reference to section 265.

(iii) For purposes of subdivision (i)(*c*) of this subparagraph, amounts held by an insurance company under an agreement to pay interest thereon include policyholder dividends left with the company to accumulate, prepaid insurance premiums, proceeds of policies left on deposit with the company, and overcharges of premiums. Such subdivision does not apply to (*a*) the so-called "interest element" in the case of annuity or installment payments under life insurance or endowment contracts or (*b*) interest paid by an insurance company to its creditors on notes, bonds, or similar evidences of indebtedness, if the debtor-creditor relationship does not arise by virtue of a contract of insurance with the insurance company.

(iv) For purposes of subdivision (i) of this subparagraph, interest received by a partnership shall be treated as received by each partner of such partnership to the extent of his distributive share of such item.

Reg. § 1.861-2(a)(6)

(2) *Interest from a resident alien individual or domestic corporation deriving substantial income from sources without the United States.* Interest received from a resident alien individual or a domestic corporation shall be treated as income from sources without the United States when it is shown to the satisfaction of the district director (or, if applicable, the Director of International Operations) that less than 20 percent of the gross income from all sources of such individual or corporation has been derived from sources within the United States, as determined under the provisions of sections 861 to 863, inclusive, and the regulations thereunder, for the 3-year period ending with the close of the taxable year of such individual or corporation preceding its taxable year in which such interest is paid or credited, or for such part of such period as may be applicable. If 20 percent or more of the gross income from all sources of such individual or corporation has been derived from sources within the United States, as so determined, for such 3-year period (or part thereof), the entire amount of the interest from such individual or corporation shall be treated as income from sources within the United States.

(3) *Interest from a foreign corporation not deriving major portion of its income from a U.S. business.* (i) Interest from a foreign corporation which, at any time during the taxable year, is engaged in trade or business in the United States shall be treated as income from sources without the United States when it is shown to the satisfaction of the district director (or, if applicable, the Director of International Operations) that (*a*) less than 50 percent of the gross income from all sources of such foreign corporation for the 3-year period ending with the close of its taxable year preceding its taxable year in which such interest is paid or credited (or for such part of such period as the corporation has been in existence) was effectively connected with the conduct by such corporation of a trade or business in the United States, as determined under section 864(c) and § 1.864-3, or (*b*) such foreign corporation had gross income for such 3-year period (or part thereof) but none was effectively connected with the conduct of a trade or business in the United States.

(ii) If 50 percent or more of the gross income from all sources of such foreign corporation for such 3-year period (or part thereof) was effectively connected with the conduct by such corporation of a trade or business in the United States, see section 861(a)(1)(D) and paragraph (c)(1) of this section for determining the portion of interest from such corporation which is treated as income from sources within the United States.

(iii) For purposes of this subparagraph the gross income which is effectively connected with the conduct of a trade or business in the United States includes the gross income which, pursuant to section 882(d) or (e) and the regulations thereunder, is treated as income which is effectively connected with the conduct of a trade or business in the United States.

(iv) This subparagraph does not apply to interest paid or credited after December 31, 1969, by a branch in the United States of a foreign corporation if, at the time of payment or crediting, such branch is engaged in the commercial banking business in the United States; furthermore, such interest is treated under paragraph (a) of this section as income from sources within the United States unless it is treated as income from sources without the United States under subparagraph (1) or (4) of this paragraph.

(4) *Bankers' acceptances.* Interest derived by a foreign central bank of issue from bankers' acceptances shall be treated as income from sources without the United States. For this purpose, a foreign central bank of issue is a bank which is by law or government sanction the principal authority, other than the government itself, issuing instruments intended to circulate as currency. Such a bank is generally the custodian of the banking reserves of the country under whose law it is organized.

(5) *Foreign banking branch of a domestic corporation or partnership.* Interest paid or credited on deposits with a branch outside the United States (as defined in section 7701(a)(9)) of a domestic corporation or of a domestic partnership shall be treated as income from sources without the United States if, at the time of payment or crediting, such branch is engaged in the commercial banking business. For purposes of applying this subparagraph, it is immaterial (i) whether the domestic corporation or domestic partnership is carrying on a banking business in the United States, (ii) whether the recipient of the interest is a citizen or resident of the United States, a foreign corporation, or a foreign partnership, (iii) whether the interest is effectively connected with the conduct of a trade or business in the United States by the recipient, or (iv) whether the deposits with the branch located outside the United States are payable in the currency of a foreign country. Notwithstanding the provisions of § 1.863-6, interest to which this subparagraph applies shall be treated as income from sources within the foreign country, possession of the United States, or other territory in which the branch is located.

Reg. § 1.861-2(b)(5)

Determination of Sources of Income
See p. 20,601 for regulations not amended to reflect law changes

(6) *Section 4912(c) debt obligations*—(i) *In general.* Under section 861(a)(1)(G), interest on a debt obligation shall not be treated as income from sources within the United States if—

(*a*) The debt obligation was part of an issue of debt obligations with respect to which an election has been made under section 4912(c) (relating to the treatment of such debt obligations as debt obligations of a foreign obligor for purposes of the interest equalization tax),

(*b*) The debt obligation had a maturity not exceeding 15 years (within the meaning of subdivision (ii) of this subparagraph) on the date it is originally issued or on the date it is treated under section 4912(c)(2) as issued by reason of being assumed by a certain domestic corporation,

(*c*) The debt obligation, when originally issued, was purchased by one or more underwriters (within the meaning of subdivision (iii) of this subparagraph) with a view to distribution through resale (within the meaning of subdivision (iv) of this subparagraph), and

(*d*) The interest on the debt obligation is attributable to periods after the effective date of an election under section 4912(c) to treat such debt obligations as debt obligations of a foreign obligor for purposes of the interest equalization tax.

(ii) *Maturity not exceeding 15 years.* The date the debt obligation is issued or treated as issued is not included in the 15 year computation, but the date of maturity of the debt obligation is included in such computation.

(iii) *Purchased by one or more underwriters.* For purposes of this subparagraph, the debt obligation when originally issued will not be treated as purchased by one or more underwriters unless the underwriter purchases the debt obligation for his own account and bears the risk of gain or loss on resale. Thus, for example, a debt obligation, when originally issued, will not be treated as purchased by one or more underwriters if the underwriter acts only in the capacity of an agent of the issuer. Neither will a debt obligation, when originally issued, be treated as purchased by one or more underwriters if the agreement between the underwriter and issuer is merely for a "best efforts" underwriting, for the purchase by the underwriter of all or a portion of the debt obligations remaining unsold at the expiration of a fixed period of time, or for any other arrangement under the terms of which the debt obligations are not purchased by the underwriter with a view to distribution through resale. The fact that an underwriter is related to the issuer will not prevent the underwriter from meeting the requirements of this subparagraph. In determining whether a related underwriter meets the requirement of this subparagraph consideration shall be given to whether the purchase by the underwriter of the debt obligation from the issuer for resale was effected by a transaction subject to conditions similar to those which would have been imposed between independent persons.

(iv) *With a view to distribution through resale.* (*a*) An underwriter who purchased a debt obligation shall be deemed to have purchased it with a view to distribution through resale if the requirements of (*b*) or (*c*) of this subdivision (iv) are met.

(*b*) The requirement of this subdivision (*b*) is that—

(*1*) The debt obligation is registered, approved, or listed for trading on one or more foreign securities exchanges or foreign established securities markets within 4 months after the date on which the underwriter purchases the debt obligation, or by the date of the first interest payment on the debt obligation, whichever is later, or

(*2*) The debt obligation, or any substantial portion of the issue of which the debt obligation is a part, is actually traded on one or more foreign securities markets on or within 15 calendar days after the date on which the underwriter purchases the debt obligation.

For purposes of this subdivison (iv), a foreign established securities market includes any foreign over-the-counter market as reflected by the existence of an inter-dealer quotation system for regularly disseminating to brokers and dealers quotations of obligations by identified brokers or dealers, other than quotations prepared and distributed by a broker or dealer in the regular course of his business and containing only quotations of such broker or dealer.

(*c*) The requirements of this subdivision (*c*) are that, except as provided in (*d*) of this subdivision, the underwriter is under no written or implied restriction imposed by the issuer with respect to whom he may resell the debt obligation and either—

(*1*) Within 30 calendar days after he purchased the debt obligation the underwriter or underwriters either (*i*) sold it or (*ii*) sold at least 95 percent of the face amount of the issue of which the debt obligation is a part, or

(*2*)(*i*) The debt obligation is evidenced by an instrument which, under the laws of the jurisdiction in which it is issued, is either negotiable or transferable by assignment (whether or not it is registered for trading), and (*ii*) it appears from all the relevant facts and circumstances, including any written statements or as-

Reg. § 1.861-2(b)(6)

surances made by the purchasing underwriter or underwriters, that such debt obligation was purchased with a view to distribution through resale.

(d) The requirements of (c) of this subdivision may be met whether or not the underwriter is restricted from reselling the debt obligations—

(1) To a United States person (as defined in section 7701(a)(30)) or

(2) To any particular person or persons pursuant to a restriction imposed by, or required to be met in order to comply with, United States or foreign securities or other law.

(v) *Statement with return.* Any taxpayer who is required to file a tax return and who excludes from gross income interest of the type specified in this subparagraph must comply with the requirements of paragraph (d) of this section.

(vi) *Effect of termination of IET.* If the interest equalization tax expires, the provisions of section 861(a)(1)(G) and this subparagraph shall apply to interest paid on debt obligations only with respect to which a section 4912(c) election was made.

(vii) *Definition of term underwriter.* For purposes of section 861(a)(1)(G) and this subparagraph, the term "underwriter" shall mean any underwriter as defined in section 4919(c)(1).

(c) *Special rules*—(1) *Proration of interest from a foreign corporation deriving major portion of its income from U.S. business.* If, after applying the first sentence of paragraph (b)(3) of this section to interest to which that paragraph applies, it is determined that the interest may not be treated as income from sources without the United States, the amount of the interest from the foreign corporation which at some time during the taxable year is engaged in trade or business in the United States which is to be treated as income from sources within the United States shall be the amount that bears the same ratio to such interest as the gross income of such foreign corporation for the 3-year period ending with the close of its taxable year preceding its taxable year in which such interest is paid or credited (or for such part of such period as the corporation has been in existence) which was effectively connected with the conduct by such corporation of a trade or business in the United States bears to its gross income from all sources for such period.

(2) *Payors having no gross income for period preceding taxable year of payment.* If the resident alien individual, domestic corporation, or foreign corporation, as the case may be, paying interest has no gross income from any source for the 3-year period (or part thereof) specified in subparagraph (2) or (3) of paragraph (b) of this section, or subparagraph (1) of this paragraph, the 20-percent test or the 50-percent test, or the apportionment formula, as the case may be, described in such subparagraph shall be applied solely with respect to the taxable year of the payor in which the interest is paid or credited. This subparagraph applies whether the lack of gross income for the 3-year period (or part thereof) stems from the business inactivity of the payor, from the fact that the payor is a corporation which is newly created or organized, or from any other cause.

(3) *Transitional rule.* For purposes of applying paragraph (b)(3) of this section, and subparagraph (1) of this paragraph, the gross income of the foreign corporation for any period before the first taxable year beginning after December 31, 1966, which is from sources within the United States (determined as provided by sections 861 through 863, and the regulations thereunder, as in effect immediately before amendment by section 102 of the Foreign Investors Tax Act of 1966 (Pub. L. 89-809, 80 Stat. 1541)) shall be treated as gross income for such period which is effectively connected with the conduct of a trade or business in the United States by such foreign corporation.

(4) *Gross income determinations.* In making determinations under subparagraph (2) or (3) of paragraph (b) of this section, or subparagraph (1) or (3) of this paragraph—

(i) The gross income of a domestic corporation or a resident alien individual is to be determined by excluding any items specifically excluded from gross income under chapter 1 of the Code, and

(ii) The gross income of a foreign corporation which is effectively connected with the conduct of a trade or business in the United States is to be determined under section 882(b)(2) and by excluding any items specifically excluded from gross income under chapter 1 of the Code, and

(iii) The gross income from all sources of a foreign corporation is to be determined without regard to section 882(b) and without excluding any items otherwise specifically excluded from gross income under chapter 1 of the Code.

(d) *Statement with return.* Any taxpayer who is required to file a return and applies any provision of this section to exclude an amount of interest from his gross income must file with his return a statement setting forth the amount so excluded, the date of its receipt, the name and address of the obligor of the interest, and, if known, the location of the records which substantiate the amount of the exclusion. A statement from the obligor setting forth such information and indicat-

Reg. § 1.861-2(d)

ing the amount of interest to be treated as income from sources without the United States may be used for this purpose. See §§ 1.6012-1(b)(1)(i) and 1.6012-2(g)(1)(i).

(e) *Effective dates.* Except as otherwise provided, this section applies with respect to taxable years beginning after December 31, 1966. For corresponding rules applicable to taxable years beginning before January 1, 1967, (see 26 CFR part 1 revised April 1, 1971). Paragraph (a)(7) of this section is applicable to payments made after November 13, 1997. [Reg. § 1.861-2.]

☐ [T.D. 6258, 10-23-57. Amended by T.D. 6873, 1-24-66; T.D. 7314, 5-22-74; T.D. 7378, 9-29-75; T.D. 8257, 8-1-89 and T.D. 8735, 10-6-97.]

[Reg. § 1.861-3]

§ 1.861-3. Dividends.—(a) [*In*] *General*—(1) *Dividends included in gross income.* Gross income from sources within the United States includes a dividend described in subparagraph (2), (3), (4), or (5) of this paragraph. For purposes of subparagraphs (2), (3), and (4) of this paragraph, the term "dividend" shall have the same meaning as set forth in section 316 and the regulations thereunder. See subparagraph (5) of this paragraph for special rules with respect to certain dividends from a DISC or former DISC. See also paragraph (a)(6) of this section for special rules concerning substitute dividend payments received pursuant to a securities lending transaction.

(2) *Dividend from a domestic corporation.* A dividend described in this subparagraph is a dividend from a domestic corporation other than a domestic corporation entitled to the benefits of section 931, and other than a domestic corporation less than 20 percent of the gross income of which is shown to the satisfaction of the district director (or, if applicable, the Director of International Operations) to have been derived from sources within the United States, as determined under the provisions of sections 861 to 864, inclusive, and the regulations thereunder, for the 3-year period ending with the close of the taxable year of such corporation preceding the declaration of such dividend, or for such part of such period as the corporation has been in existence. See subparagraph (5) of this paragraph for the treatment of certain dividends from a DISC or former DISC.

(3) *Dividend from a foreign corporation*—(i) *In general.* (a) A dividend described in this subparagraph is a dividend from a foreign corporation (other than a dividend to which subparagraph (4) of this paragraph applies) unless less than 50 percent of the gross income from all sources of such foreign corporation for the 3-year period ending with the close of its taxable year preceding the taxable year in which occurs the declaration of such dividend (or for such part of such period as the corporation has been in existence) was effectively connected with the conduct by such corporation of a trade or business in the United States, as determined under section 864(c) and § 1.864-3. Thus, no portion of a dividend from a foreign corporation shall be treated as income from sources within the United States under section 861(a)(2)(B) if less than 50 percent of the gross income of such foreign corporation from all sources for such 3-year period (or part thereof) was effectively connected with the conduct of a trade or business in the United States or if such foreign corporation had gross income for such 3-year period (or part thereof) but none was effectively connected with the conduct by such corporation of a trade or business in the United States.

(b) If 50 percent or more of the gross income from all sources of such foreign corporation for such 3-year period (or part thereof) was effectively connected with the conduct by such corporation of a trade or business in the United States, the amount of the dividend which is to be treated as income from sources within the United States under section 861(a)(2)(B) shall be the amount that bears the same ratio to such dividend as the gross income of such foreign corporation for such 3-year period (or part thereof) which was effectively connected with the conduct by such corporation of a trade or business in the United States bears to its gross income from all sources for such period.

(c) For purposes of this subdivision (i), the gross income which is effectively connected with the conduct of a trade or business in the United States includes the gross income which, pursuant to section 882(d) or (e), is treated as income which is effectively connected with the conduct of a trade or business in the United States.

(ii) *Rule applicable in applying limitation on amount of foreign tax credit.* For purposes of determining under section 904 the limitation upon the amount of the foreign tax credit—

(a) So much of a dividend from a foreign corporation as exceeds (and only to the extent it so exceeds) the amount which is 100/85ths of the amount of the deduction allowable under section 245(a) in respect of such dividend, plus

(b) An amount which bears the same proportion to any section 78 dividend to which the dividend from the foreign corporation gives rise as the amount of the excess determined under (a) of this subdivision bears to the total amount of the dividend from the foreign corporation,

shall, notwithstanding subdivision (i) of this subparagraph, be treated as income from sources without the United States. This subdivision applies to a dividend for which no dividends-received deduction is allowed under section 245 or for which the 85 percent dividends-received deduction is allowed under section 245(a) but does not apply to a dividend for which a deduction is allowable under section 245(b). All of a dividend for which the 100 percent dividends-received deduction is allowed under section 245(b) shall be treated as income from sources within the United States for purposes of determining under section 904 the limitation upon the amount of the foreign tax credit. If the amount of a distribution of property other than money (constituting a dividend under section 316) is determined by applying section 301(b)(1)(C), such amount must be used as the dividend for purposes of applying (a) of this subdivision even though the amount used for purposes of section 245(a) is determined by applying section 301(b)(1)(D). In making determinations under this subdivision, a dividend (other than a section 78 dividend referred to in (b) of this subdivision) shall be determined without regard to section 78.

(iii) *Illustrations.* The application of this subparagraph may be illustrated by the following examples:

Example (1). D, a domestic corporation, owns 80 percent of the outstanding stock of M, a foreign manufacturing corporation. M, which makes its returns on the basis of the calendar year, has earnings and profits of $200,000 for 1971 and 60 percent of its gross income for that year is effectively connected for 1971 with the conduct of a trade or business in the United States. For an uninterrupted period of 36 months ending on December 31, 1970, M has been engaged in trade or business in the United States and has received gross income effectively connected with the conduct of a trade or business in the United States amounting to 60 percent of its gross income from all sources for such period. The only distribution by M to D for 1971 is a cash dividend of $100,000; of this amount, $60,000 ($100,000 × 60%) is treated under subdivision (i) of this subparagraph as income from sources within the United States, and $40,000 ($100,000 − $60,000) is treated under § 1.862-1(a)(2) as income from sources without the United States. Accordingly, under section 245(a), D is entitled to a dividends-received deduction of $51,000 ($60,000 × 85%), and under subdivision (ii) of this subparagraph $40,000 ($100,000 − [$51,000 × 100/85]) is treated as income from sources without the United States for purposes of determining under section 904(a)(1) or (2) the limitation upon the amount of the foreign tax credit.

Example (2). (a) The facts are the same as in example (1) except that the distribution for 1971 consists of property which has a fair market value of $100,000 and an adjusted basis of $30,000 in M's hands immediately before the distribution. The amount of the dividend under section 316 is $58,000, determined by applying section 301(b)(1)(C) as follows:

Portion of adjusted basis of property attributable to gross income of M effectively connected for 1971 with conduct of trade or business in United States ($30,000 × 60%)	$18,000
Portion of fair market value of property attributable to gross income of M not effectively connected for 1971 with conduct of trade or business in United States ($100,000 × 40%)	40,000
Total dividend	$58,000

(b) Of the total dividend, $34,800 ($58,000 × 60% (percentage applicable to 3-year period)) is treated under subdivision (i) of this subparagraph as income from sources within the United States, and $23,200 ($58,000 × 40%) is treated under § 1.862-1(a)(2) as income from sources without the United States. However, by reason of section 245(c) the adjusted basis of the property ($30,000) is used under section 245(a) in determining the dividends-received deduction. Thus, under section 245(a), D is entitled to a dividends-received deduction of $15,300 ($30,000 × 60% × 85%).

(c) Under subdivision (ii) of this subparagraph, the amount of the dividend for purposes of applying (a) of that subdivision is the amount ($58,000) determined by applying section 301(b)(1)(C) rather than the amount ($30,000) determined by applying section 301(b)(1)(B). Accordingly, under subdivision (ii) of this subparagraph $40,000 ($58,000 − [$15,300 × 100/85]) is treated as income from sources without the United States for purposes of determining under section 904(a) (1) or (2) the limitation upon the amount of the foreign tax credit.

Example (3). (a) D, a domestic corporation which makes its returns on the basis of the calendar year, owns 100 percent of the outstanding stock of N, a foreign corporation which is not a less developed country corporation under section 902(d). N, which makes its returns on the basis of the calendar year, has total gross income for 1971 of $100,000, of which $80,000 (including $60,000

Reg. § 1.861-3(a)(3)

from sources within foreign country X) is effectively connected for that year with the conduct of a trade or business in the United States. For 1971 N is assumed to have paid $27,000 of income taxes to Country X and to have accumulated profits of $81,000 for purposes of section 902(c)(1)(A). N's accumulated profits in excess of foreign income taxes amount to $54,000. For 1971 D receives a cash dividend of $42,000 from N, which is D's only income for that year.

(b) For 1971 D chooses the benefits of the foreign tax credit under section 901, and as a result is required under section 78 to include in gross income an amount equal to the foreign income taxes of $21,000 ($27,000 × $42,000/$54,000) it is deemed to have paid under section 902(a)(1). Thus, assuming no other deductions for the taxable year, D has gross income of $63,000 ($42,000 + $21,000) for 1971 less a dividends-received deduction under section 245(a) of $28,560 ([$42,000 × $80,000/$100,000] × 85%), or taxable income for 1971 of $34,440.

(c) Under subdivision (ii) of this subparagraph, for purposes of determining under section 904(a) (1) or (2) the limitation upon the amount of the foreign tax credit, $12,600 is treated as income from sources without the United States, determined as follows:

Excess of dividend from N over amount which is 100/85ths of amount of sec. 245(a) deduction ($42,000 − [$28,560 × 100/85]) . .	$ 8,400
Proportionate part of sec. 78 dividend ($21,000 × $8,400/$42,000)	4,200
Taxable income from sources without the United States	$12,600

Example (4). A, an individual citizen of the United States who makes his return on the basis of the calendar year, receives in 1971 a cash dividend of $10,000 from M, a foreign corporation, which makes its return on the basis of the calendar year. For the 3-year period ending with 1970 M has been engaged in trade or business in the United States and has received gross income effectively connected with the conduct of a trade or business in the United States amounting to 80 percent of its gross income from all sources for such period. Of the total dividend, $8,000 ($10,000 × 80%) is treated under subdivision (i) of this subparagraph as income from sources within the United States and $2,000 ($10,000 − $8,000) is treated under § 1.862-1(a)(2) as income from sources without the United States. Since under section 245 no dividends-received deduction is allowable to an individual, A is entitled under subdivision (ii) of this subparagraph to treat the entire dividend of $10,000 ($10,000 − [$0 ×

100/85]) as income from sources without the United States for purposes of determining under section 904(a) (1) or (2) the limitation upon the amount of the foreign tax credit.

(4) *Dividend from a foreign corporation succeeding to earnings of a domestic corporation.* A dividend described in this subparagraph is a dividend from a foreign corporation, if such dividend is received by a corporation after December 31, 1959, but only to the extent that such dividend is treated by such recipient corporation under the provisions of § 1.243-3 as a dividend from a domestic corporation subject to taxation under chapter 1 of the Code. To the extent that this subparagraph applies to a dividend received from a foreign corporation, subparagraph (3) of this paragraph shall not apply to such dividend.

(5) *Certain dividends from a DISC or former DISC*—(i) *General rule.* A dividend described in this subparagraph is a dividend from a corporation that is a DISC or former DISC (as defined in section 992(a)) other than a dividend that—

(*a*) Is deemed paid by a DISC, for taxable years beginning before January 1, 1976, under section 995(b)(1)(D) as in effect for taxable years beginning before January 1, 1976, and for taxable years beginning after December 31, 1975, under section 995(b)(1)(D), (E), and (F) to the extent provided in subdivision (iii) of this subparagraph or

(*b*) Reduces under § 1.996-3(b)(3) accumulated DISC income (as defined in subdivision (ii)(*b*) of this subparagraph) to the extent provided in subdivision (iv) of this subparagraph.

Thus, a dividend deemed paid under section 995(b)(1)(A), (B), or (C) (relating to certain deemed distributions in qualified years) will be treated in full as gross income from sources within the United States. To the extent that a dividend from a DISC or former DISC is paid out of other earnings and profits (as defined in § 1.996-3(d)), subparagraph (2) of this paragraph shall apply. To the extent that a dividend from a DISC or former DISC is paid out of previously taxed income (as defined in § 1.996-3(c)), see section 996(a)(3) (relating to the exclusion from gross income of amounts distributed out of previously taxed income). In determining the source of income of certain dividends from a DISC or former DISC, the source of income from any transaction which gives rise to gross receipts (as defined in § 1.993-6), in the hands of the DISC or former DISC, is immaterial.

(ii) *Definitions.* For purposes of this subparagraph, the term—

(*a*) "Dividend from" means any amount actually distributed which is a dividend within

Reg. § 1.861-3(a)(4)

the meaning of section 316 (including distributions to meet qualification requirements under section 992(c)) and any amount treated as a distribution taxable as a dividend pursuant to section 995(b) (relating to deemed distributions in qualified years or upon disqualification) or included in gross income as a dividend pursuant to section 995(c) (relating to gain on certain dispositions of stock in a DISC or former DISC), and

(*b*) "Accumulated DISC income" means the amount of accumulated DISC income as of the close of the taxable year immediately preceding the taxable year in which the dividend was made increased by the amount of DISC income for the taxable year in which the dividend was made (as determined under § 1.996-3(b)(2)).

(*c*) "Nonqualified export taxable income" means the taxable income of a DISC from any transaction which gives rise to gross receipts (as defined in § 1.993-6) which are not qualified export receipts (as defined in § 1.993-1) other than a transaction giving rise to gain described in section 995(b)(1)(B) or (C).

For purposes of subdivisions (i) (*b*) and (iv) of this subparagraph, if by reason of section 995(c), gain is included in the shareholder's gross income as a dividend, accumulated DISC income shall be treated as if it were reduced under § 1.996-3(b)(3).

(iii) *Determination of source of income for deemed distributions, for taxable years beginning before January 1, 1976, under section 995(b)(1)(D) as in effect for taxable years beginning before January 1, 1976, and for taxable years beginning after December 31, 1975, under section 995(b)(1)(D), (E), and (F).*

(*a*) If for its taxable year a DISC does not have any nonqualified export taxable income, then for such year the entire amount treated, for taxable years beginning before January 1, 1976, under section 995(b)(1)(D) as in effect for taxable years beginning before January 1, 1976, and for taxable years beginning after December 31, 1975, under section 995(b)(1)(D), (E), and (F) as a deemed distribution taxable as a dividend will be treated as gross income from sources without the United States.

(*b*) If for its taxable year a DISC has any nonqualified export taxable income, then for such year the portion of the amount treated, for taxable years beginning before January 1, 1976, under section 995(b)(1)(D) as in effect for taxable years beginning before January 1, 1976, and for taxable years beginning after December 31, 1975, under section 995(b)(1)(D), (E), and (F) as a deemed distribution taxable as a dividend that will be treated as income from sources within the United States shall be equal to the amount of such nonqualified export taxable income multiplied by the following fraction. The numerator of the fraction is the sum of the amounts treated, for taxable years beginning before January 1, 1976, under section 995(b)(1)(D) as in effect for taxable years beginning before January 1, 1976, and for taxable years beginning after December 31, 1975, under section 995(b)(1)(D), (E), and (F) as deemed distributions taxable as dividends. The denominator of the fraction is the taxable income of the DISC for the taxable year, reduced by the amounts treated under section 995(b)(1)(A), (B), and (C) as deemed distributions taxable as dividends. However, in no event shall the numerator exceed the denominator. The remainder of such dividend will be treated as gross income from sources without the United States.

(iv) *Determination of source of income for dividends that reduce accumulated DISC income.* (*a*) If no portion of the accumulated DISC income of a DISC or former DISC is attributable to nonqualified export taxable income from any transaction during a year for which it is (or is treated as) a DISC, then the entire amount of any dividend that reduces under § 1.996-3(b)(3) accumulated DISC income will be treated as income from sources without the United States.

(*b*) If any portion of the accumulated DISC income of a DISC or former DISC is attributable to nonqualified export taxable income from any transaction during a year for which it is (or is treated as) a DISC, then the portion of any dividend during its taxable year that reduces under § 1.996-3(b)(3) accumulated DISC income that will be treated as income from sources within the United States shall be equal to the amount of such dividend multiplied by a fraction (determined as of the close of such year) the numerator of which is the amount of accumulated DISC income attributable to nonqualified export taxable income, and the denominator of which is the total amount of accumulated DISC income. The remainder of such dividend will be treated as gross income from sources without the United States.

(v) *Special rules.* For purposes of subdivisions (iii) and (iv) of this subparagraph—

(*a*) Taxable income shall be determined under § 1.992-3(b)(2)(i) (relating to the computation of deficiency distribution), and

(*b*) The portion of any deemed distribution taxable as a dividend, for taxable years beginning before January 1, 1976, under section 995(b)(1)(D) as in effect for taxable years beginning before January 1, 1976, and for taxable years beginning after December 31, 1975, under section 995(b)(1)(D), (E), and (F) or amount under

§ 1.996-3(b)(3)(i) through (iv) that is treated as gross income from sources within the United States during the taxable year shall be considered to reduce the amount of nonqualified export taxable income as of the close of such year.

(vi) *Illustrations.* This subparagraph may be illustrated by the following examples:

Example (1). (a) Y is a corporation which uses the calendar year as its taxable year and which elects to be treated as a DISC beginning with 1972. X is its sole shareholder. In 1973, Y has $18,000 of taxable income from qualified export receipts (none of which are interest and gains described in section 995(b)(1)(A), (B), and (C)) and $1,000 of nonqualified export taxable income. Under these facts, X is deemed to have received a distribution under section 995(b)(1)(D) as in effect for taxable years beginning before January 1, 1976, of $9,500, i.e., $19,000 × 1/2. X is treated under subdivision (iii)(*b*) of this subparagraph as having $500, *i.e.,* $1,000 × $9,500/$19,000, from sources within the United States and $9,000 from sources without the United States.

(b) For 1972, assume that Y did not have any nonqualified export taxable income. Pursuant to subdivision (v)(*b*) of this subparagraph, at the beginning of 1974, $500 of Y's accumulated DISC income is attributable to nonqualified export taxable income, i.e., $1,000 − $500.

Example (2). The facts are the same as in example (1) except that in 1973, in addition to the taxable income described in such example, Y has $450 of taxable income from gross interest from producer's loans described in section 995(b)(1)(A). Under these facts, the deemed distribution of $450 under section 995(b)(1)(A) is treated in full under subdivision (i) of this subparagraph as gross income from sources within the United States. The deemed distribution under section 995(b)(1)(D) as in effect for taxable years beginning before January 1, 1976, of $9,500 will be treated in the same manner as in example (1), *i.e.,* $1,000 × $9,500/($19,450 − $450).

Example (3). (a) The facts are the same as in example (1) except that in 1973, in addition to the distribution described in such example, Y makes a deemed distribution taxable as a dividend of $100 under section 995(b)(1)(G) (relating to foreign investment attributable to producer's loans) and actual distributions of all of its previously taxed income and of $2,000 taxable as a dividend which reduces accumulated DISC income (as defined in subdivision (ii)(*b*) of this subparagraph). Undre § 1.996-3(b)(3), accumulated DISC income is first reduced by the deemed distribution of $100 and then by the actual distribution taxable as a dividend of $2,000. As indicated in example (1), for 1972 Y did not have any nonqualified export taxable income. Assume that Y had accumulated DISC income of $12,000 at the end of 1973, $500 of which under example (1) is attributable to nonqualified export taxable income.

(b) The distribution from previously taxed income is excluded from gross income pursuant to section 996(a)(3).

(c) Of the deemed distribution of $100, X is treated under subdivision (iv)(*b*) as having $4.17, i.e., $100 × 500/12,000, from sources within the United States and $95.83, i.e., $100 − $4.17, from sources without the United States.

(d) Of the actual distribution taxable as a dividend of $2,000, X is treated under subdivision (iv)(*b*) as having $83.33, i.e., $2000 × 500/12,000, from sources within the United States and $1,916.67, i.e., $2,000 − $83.33, from sources without the United States.

(e) The sum of the amounts deemed and actually distributed as dividends for 1973 that are treated as gross income from sources within the United States is as follows:

	Total dividend	Amount of dividend from sources within the United States
Deemed distribution under sec. 995(b)(1)(D) as in effect for taxable years beginning before Jan. 1, 1976	$ 9,500	$500.00
Deemed distribution under sec. 995(b)(1)(G)	100	4.17
Actual distribution that reduces accumulated DISC income	2,000	83.33
Totals	$11,600	$587.50

Thus, pursuant to subdivision (v)(*b*) of this subparagraph, at the beginning of 1974 Y has $412.50, *i.e.,* $1,000 − $587.50, of nonqualified export taxable income.

(f) The result would be the same if Y made an actual distribution taxable as a dividend of $1,500 on March 30, 1973, and another distribution of $500 on December 31, 1973.

Example (4). (a) Z is a corporation which uses the calendar year as its taxable year and which elects to be treated as a DISC beginning with 1972. W is its sole shareholder. At the end of

Determination of Sources of Income 45,973
See p. 20,601 for regulations not amended to reflect law changes

1976 Z has previously taxed income of $12,000 and accumulated DISC income of $4,000, $900 of which is attributable to nonqualified export taxable income. In 1977, Z has $20,050 of taxable income from qualified export receipts, of which $550 is from gross income from producer's loans described in section 995(b)(1)(A); Z has $950 of taxable income giving rise to gross receipts which are not qualified export receipts, of which $450 is gain described in section 995(b)(1)(B). Of its total taxable income of $21,000 (which is equal to its earnings and profits for 1977), $1,000 is attributable to sales of military property. Z has an international boycott factor (determined under section 999) of .10, and made an illegal bribe (within the meaning of section 162(c)) of $1,265. The proportion which the amount of Z's adjusted base period export receipts bears to Z's export gross receipts for 1977 is .40 (see section 995(e)(1)). Z makes a deemed distribution taxable as a dividend of $1,000 under section 995(b)(1)(G) (relating to foreign investment attributable to producer's loans) and actual distributions of $32,000.

(b) The deemed distributions of $550 under section 995(b)(1)(A) and $450 under section 995(b)(1)(B) are treated in full under subdivision (i) of this subparagraph as gross income from sources within the United States.

(c) Under these facts, Z has also made the following deemed distributions taxable as dividends to W under the following subdivisions of section 995(b)(1):

(D)	$ 500, i.e., ½ × $1,000.
(E)	7,800, i.e., 40 × [$21,000 − ($550 + 450 + 500)].
(F) (i)	5,850, i.e., ½ × [$21,000 − ($550 + 450 + 500 + 7,800)].
(F) (ii)	585, i.e., $5,850 × .10.
(F) (iii)	1,265
Total	$16,000

(d) The portion of the total amount of these deemed distributions ($16,000) that is treated under subdivision (iii)(*b*) as gross income from sources within the United States is computed as follows:

(1) The amount of nonqualified export taxable income is $500, i.e., taxable income giving rise to gross receipts which are not qualified export receipts ($950) minus gain described in section 995(b)(1)(B) or (C) ($450).

(2) $500 × {$16,000/$[21,000 − (550 + 450)]} = $400. The remainder of these distributions, $15,600 ($16,000 minus $400), is treated under subdivision (iii)(*b*) of this subparagraph as gross income from sources without the United States.

(e) The earnings and profits accounts of Z at the end of 1977 are computed as follows:

	Total earnings and profits	Previously taxed income	Accumulated DISC income attributable to taxable income from transactions which give rise to gross receipts which are qualified export receipts	Accumulated DISC income attributable to taxable income from transactions which give rise to gross receipts which are not qualified export receipts
(1) Balance—January 1, 1977	$16,000	$12,000	$3,100	$ 900
(2) Earnings and profits for 1977, before actual and section 995(b)(1)(G) distributions	21,000	17,000	3,900	100 [1]
(3) Balance—December 31, 1977	$37,000	$29,000	$7,000	$1,000
(4) Distribution under section 995(b)(1)(G)	....	1,000	(875)	(125) [2]
(5) Balance	$37,000	$30,000	$6,125	$ 875
(6) Actual distribution	(32,000)	(30,000)	(1,750)	(250) [3]
(7) Balance—January 1, 1978	$ 5,000	....	$4,375	$ 625

---

[1] The total of nonqualified export taxable income ($500) minus the portion of such income, under subdivision (iii)(*b*) of this subparagraph, deemed distributed pursuant to section 995(b)(1)(D), (E), and (F) ($400), as computed under (d)(2) of this example.

[2] Under subdivision (iv)(*b*) of this subparagraph,

Reg. § 1.861-3(a)(5)

45,974 Determination of Sources of Income

See p. 20,601 for regulations not amended to reflect law changes

$$\frac{\$1,000}{\$8,000} \times \$1,000.$$

[3] Under subdivision (iv)(*b*) of this subparagraph,

$$\frac{\$1,000}{\$8,000} \times \$2,000 \text{ (amount of actual distribution that reduces accumulated DISC income)}.$$

(6) *Substitute dividend payments.* A substitute dividend payment is a payment, made to the transferor of a security in a securities lending transaction or a sale-repurchase transaction, of an amount equivalent to a dividend distribution which the owner of the transferred security is entitled to receive during the term of the transaction. A securities lending transaction is a transfer of one or more securities that is described in section 1058(a) or a substantially similar transaction. A sale-repurchase transaction is an agreement under which a person transfers a security in exchange for cash and simultaneously agrees to receive substantially identical securities from the transferee in the future in exchange for cash. A substitute dividend payment shall be sourced in the same manner as the distributions with respect to the transferred security for purposes of this section and § 1.862-1. See also § § 1.864-5(b)(2)(iii), 1.871-7(b)(2) and 1.881-2(b)(2) for the character of such payments and § 1.894-1(c) for the application of tax treaties to these transactions.

(b) *Special rules*—(1) *Foreign corporation having no gross income for period preceding declaration of dividend.* If the foreign corporation has no gross income from any source for the 3-year period (or part thereof) specified in paragraph (a)(3)(i) of this section, the 50-percent test, or the apportionment formula, as the case may be, described in such paragraph shall be applied solely with respect to the taxable year of such corporation in which the declaration of the dividend occurs. This subparagraph applies whether the lack of gross income for the 3-year period (or part thereof) stems from the business inactivity of the foreign corporation, from the fact that such corporation is newly created or organized, or from any other cause.

(2) *Transitional rule.* For purposes of applying paragraph (a)(3)(i) of this section, the gross income of the foreign corporation for any period before the first taxable year beginning after December 31, 1966, which is from sources within the United States (determined as provided by sections 861 through 863, and the regulations thereunder, as in effect immediately before amendment by section 102 of the Foreign Investors Tax Act of 1966 (Pub. L. 89-809, 80 Stat. 1541)) shall be treated as gross income for such period which is effectively connected with the conduct of a trade or business within the United States by such foreign corporation.

(3) *Gross income determinations.* In making determinations under subparagraph (2) or (3) of paragraph (a) of this section, or subparagraph (2) of this paragraph—

(i) The gross income of a domestic corporation is to be determined by excluding any items specifically excluded from gross income under chapter 1 of the Code,

(ii) The gross income of a foreign corporation which is effectively connected with the conduct of a trade or business in the United States is to be determined under section 882(b)(2) and by excluding any items specifically excluded from gross income under chapter 1 of the Code, and

(iii) The gross income from all sources of a foreign corporation is to be determined without regard to section 882(b) and without excluding any items otherwise specifically excluded from gross income under chapter 1 of the Code.

(c) *Statement with return.* Any taxpayer who is required to file a return and applies any provision of this section to exclude any dividend from his gross income must file with his return a statement setting forth the amount so excluded, the date of its receipt, the name and address of the corporation paying the dividend, and, if known, the location of the records which substantiate the amount of the exclusion. A statement from the paying corporation setting forth such information and indicating the amount of the dividend to be treated as income from sources within the United States may be used for this purpose. See § § 1.6012-1(b)(1)(i) and 1.6012-2(g)(1)(i).

(d) *Effective date.* Except as otherwise provided in this paragraph this section applies with respect to dividends received or accrued after December 31, 1966. Paragraph (a)(5) of this section applies to certain dividends from a DISC or former DISC in taxable years ending after December 31, 1971. Paragraph (a)(6) of this section is applicable to payments made after November 13, 1997. For purposes of paragraph (a)(5) of this section, any reference to a distribution taxable as a dividend under section 995(b)(1)(F)(ii) and (iii) for taxable years beginning after December 31, 1975, shall also constitute a reference to any distribution taxable as a dividend under section 995(b)(1)(F)(ii) and (iii) for taxable years begin-

Reg. § 1.861-3(a)(6)

ning after November 30, 1975, but before January 1, 1976. For corresponding rules applicable with respect to dividends received or accrued before January 1, 1967, see 26 CFR 1.861-3 (Rev. as of Jan. 1, 1972). [Reg. § 1.861-3.]

☐ [*T.D.* 6258, 10-23-57. *Amended by T.D.* 6830, 6-22-65, *T.D.* 7378, 9-29-75, *T.D.* 7472, 2-28-77, *T.D.* 7591, 1-19-79; *T.D.* 7854, 11-15-82 *and T.D.* 8735, 10-6-97.]

[Reg. § 1.861-4]

§ 1.861-4. **Compensation for labor or personal services.**—(a) *In general.* (1) Gross income from sources within the United States includes compensation for labor or personal services performed in the United States irrespective of the residence of the payer, the place in which the contract for service was made, or the place or time of payment; except that such compensation shall be deemed not to be income from sources within the United States, if—

(i) The labor or services are performed by a nonresident alien individual temporarily present in the United States for a period or periods not exceeding a total of 90 days during his taxable year,

(ii) The compensation for such labor or services does not exceed in the aggregate a gross amount of $3,000, and

(iii) The compensation is for labor or services performed as an employee of, or under any form of contract with—

(*a*) A nonresident alien individual, foreign partnership, or foreign corporation, not engaged in trade or business within the United States, or

(*b*) An individual who is a citizen or resident of the United States, a domestic partnership, or a domestic corporation, if such labor or services are performed for an office or place of business maintained in a foreign country or in a possession of the United States by such individual, partnership, or corporation.

(2) As a general rule, the term "day," as used in subparagraph (1)(i) of this paragraph, means a calendar day during any portion of which the nonresident alien individual is physically present in the United States.

(3) Solely for purposes of applying this paragraph, the nonresident alien individual, foreign partnership, or foreign corporation for which the nonresident alien individual is performing personal services in the United States shall not be considered to be engaged in trade or business in the United States by reason of the performance of such services by such individual.

(4) In determining for purposes of subparagraph (1)(ii) of this paragraph whether compensation received by the nonresident alien individual exceeds in the aggregate a gross amount of $3,000, any amounts received by the individual from an employer as advances or reimbursements for travel expenses incurred on behalf of the employer shall be omitted from the compensation received by the individual, to the extent of expenses incurred, where he was required to account and did account to his employer for such expenses and has met the tests for such accounting provided in § 1.162-17 and paragraph (e)(4) of § 1.274-5. If advances or reimbursements exceed such expenses, the amount of the excess shall be included as compensation for personal services for purposes of such subparagraph. Pensions and retirement pay attributable to labor or personal services performed in the United States are not to be taken into account for purposes of subparagraph (1)(ii) of this paragraph.

(5) For definition of the term "United States," when used in a geographical sense, see sections 638 and 7701(a)(9).

(b) *Amount includible in gross income*—(1) *Taxable years beginning after December 31, 1975.* (i) If a specific amount is paid for labor or personal services performed in the United States, that amount (if income from sources within the United States) shall be included in the gross income. If no accurate allocation or segregation of compensation for labor or personal services performed in the United States can be made, or when such labor or service is performed partly within and partly without the United States, the amount to be included in the gross income shall be determined on the basis that most correctly reflects the proper source of income under the facts and circumstances of the particular case. In many cases the facts and circumstances will be such that an apportionment on the time basis will be acceptable, that is, the amount to be included in gross income will be that amount which bears the same relation to the total compensation as the number of days of performance of the labor or services within the United States bears to the total number of days of performance of labor or services for which the payment is made. In other cases, the facts and circumstances will be such that another method of apportionment will be acceptable.

(ii) The application of this subparagraph may be illustrated by the following examples:

Example (1). B, a nonresident alien individual, was employed by M from March 1, 1976, to June 12, 1976, a total of 104 days, for which he received compensation in the amount of $12,240. During that period B was present in the United

States 59 days. Under his contract B was subject to call at all times by his employer and was in a payment status on a 7-day week basis. There was no specific agreement as to the amount of pay for services performed within the United States; moreover, he received his stipulated salary payments regardless of the number of days per week he actually performed services. Under these circumstances the amount of compensation to be included in gross income as income from sources within the United States will be $6,943.85 ($12,240 × 59/104).

Example (2). C, a citizen of the United States, was a resident of a foreign country during his entire taxable year. He is employed by N, a domestic corporation, and paid a salary of $17,600 per annum. Under his contract C is required to work only on a 5-day week basis, Monday through Friday. During 1976 he was in the United States for 6 weeks, performing services therein for N for 30 work days. During the year he worked 240 days for N for which payment was made, determined by eliminating his vacation period for which no payment was made. Under these circumstances the amount of compensation for personal services performed in the United States is $2,200 ($17,600 × 30/240).

(2) *Taxable years beginning before January 1, 1976.* If a specific amount is paid for labor or personal services performed in the United States, that amount (if income from sources within the United States) shall be included in the gross income. If no accurate allocation or segregation of compensation for labor or personal services performed in the United States can be made, or when such labor or service is performed partly within and partly without the United States, the amount to be included in the gross income shall be determined by an apportionment on the time basis; that is, there shall be included in the gross income an amount which bears the same relation to the total compensation as the number of days of performance of the labor or services within the United States bears to the total number of days of performance of labor or services for which the payment is made.

(c) *Coastwise travel.* Except as to income excluded by paragraph (a) of this section, wages received for services rendered inside the territorial limits of the United States and wages of an alien seaman earned on a coastwise vessel are to be regarded as from sources within the United States.

(d) *Effective date.* This section applies with respect to taxable years beginning after December 31, 1966. For corresponding rules applicable to taxable years beginning before January 1, 1967, see 26 CFR 1.861-4 (Rev. as of Jan. 1, 1972). [Reg. § 1.861-4.]

☐ [T.D. 6258, 10-23-57. *Amended by T.D. 7378, 9-29-75.*]

[Reg. § 1.861-5]

§ 1.861-5. Rentals and royalties.—Gross income from sources within the United States includes rentals or royalties from property located in the United States or from any interest in such property, including rentals or royalties for the use of, or for the privilege of using, in the United States, patents, copyrights, secret processes and formulas, good will, trademarks, trade brands, franchises, and other like property. The income arising from the rental of property, whether tangible or intangible, located within the United States, or from the use of property, whether tangible or intangible, within the United States, is from sources within the United States. For taxable years beginning after December 31, 1966, gains described in section 871(a)(1)(D) and section 881(a)(4) from the sale or exchange after October 4, 1966, of patents, copyrights, and other like property shall be treated, as provided in section 871(e)(2), as rentals or royalties for the use of, or privilege of using, property or an interest in property. See paragraph (e) of § 1.871-11. [Reg. § 1.861-5.]

☐ [T.D. 6258, 10-23-57. *Amended by T.D. 7378, 9-29-75.*]

[Reg. § 1.861-6]

§ 1.861-6. Sale of real property.—Gross income from sources within the United States includes gain, computed under the provisions of section 1001 and the regulations thereunder, derived from the sale or other disposition of real property located in the United States. For the treatment of capital gains and losses, see subchapter P (section 1201 and following) chapter 1 of the Code, and the regulations thereunder. [Reg. § 1.861-6.]

☐ [T.D. 6258, 10-23-57.]

[Reg. § 1.861-7]

§ 1.861-7. Sale of personal property.—(a) *General.* Gains, profits, and income derived from the purchase and sale of personal property shall be treated as derived entirely from the country in which the property is sold. Thus, gross income from sources within the United States includes gains, profits, and income derived from the purchase of personal property without the United States and its sale within the United States.

(b) *Purchase within a possession.* Notwithstanding paragraph (a) of this section, income derived from the purchase of personal property within a possession of the United States and its sale within the United States shall be treated as derived partly from sources within and partly from sources without the United States. See section 863(b)(3) and § 1.863-2.

(c) *Country in which sold.* For the purposes of part I (section 861 and following), subchapter N, chapter 1 of the Code, and the regulations thereunder, a sale of personal property is consummated at the time when, and the place where, the rights, title, and interest of the seller in the property are transferred to the buyer. Where bare legal title is retained by the seller, the sale shall be deemed to have occurred at the time and place of passage to the buyer of beneficial ownership and the risk of loss. However, in any case in which the sales transaction is arranged in a particular manner for the primary purpose of tax avoidance, the foregoing rules will not be applied. In such cases, all factors of the transaction, such as negotiations, the execution of the agreement, the location of the property, and the place of payment, will be considered, and the sale will be treated as having been consummated at the place where the substance of the sale occurred.

(d) *Production and sale.* For provisions respecting the source of income derived from the sale of personal property produced by the taxpayer, see section 863(b)(2) and paragraphs (b) of §§ 1.863-1 and 1.863-2.

(e) *Section 306 stock.* For determining the source of gain on the disposition of section 306 stock, see section 306(f) and the regulations thereunder. [Reg. § 1.861-7.]

☐ [*T.D.* 6258, 10-23-57.]

[Reg. § 1.861-8]

§ 1.861-8. Computation of taxable income from sources within the United States and from other sources and activities.—(a) *In general*—(1) *Scope.* Sections 861(b) and 863(a) state in general terms how to determine taxable income of a taxpayer from sources within the United States after gross income from sources within the United States has been determined. Sections 862(b) and 863(a) state in general terms how to determine taxable income of a taxpayer from sources without the United States after gross income from sources without the United States has been determined. This section provides specific guidance for applying the cited Code sections by prescribing rules for the allocation and apportionment of expenses, losses, and other deductions (referred to collectively in this section as "deductions") of the taxpayer. The rules contained in this section apply in determining taxable income of the taxpayer from specific sources and activities under other sections of the Code, referred to in this section as operative sections. See paragraph (f)(1) of this section for a list and description of operative sections. The operative sections include, among others, sections 871(b) and 882 (relating to taxable income of a nonresident alien individual or a foreign corporation which is effectively connected with the conduct of a trade or business in the United States), section 904(a)(1) (as in effect before enactment of the Tax Reform Act of 1976, relating to taxable income from sources within specific foreign countries), and section 904(a)(2) (as in effect before enactment of the Tax Reform Act of 1976, or section 904(a) after such enactment, relating to taxable income from all sources without the United States).

(2) *Allocation and apportionment of deductions in general.* A taxpayer to which this section applies is required to allocate deductions to a class of gross income and, then, if necessary to make the determination required by the operative section of the Code, to apportion deductions within the class of gross income between the statutory grouping of gross income (or among the statutory groupings) and the residual grouping of gross income. Except for deductions, if any, which are not definitely related to gross income (see paragraphs (c)(2) and (e)(9) of this section) and which, therefore, are ratably apportioned to all gross income, all deductions of the taxpayer (except the deductions for personal exemptions enumerated in paragraph (e)(11) of this section) must be so allocated and apportioned. As further detailed below, allocations and apportionments are made on the basis of the factual relationship of deductions to gross income.

(3) *Class of gross income.* For purposes of this section, the gross income to which a specific deduction is definitely related is referred to as a "class of gross income" and may consist of one or more items (or subdivisions of these items) of gross income enumerated in section 61, namely:

(i) Compensation for services, including fees, commissions, and similar items;

(ii) Gross income derived from business;

(iii) Gains derived from dealings in property;

(iv) Interest;

(v) Rents;

(vi) Royalties;

(vii) Dividends;

(viii) Alimony and separate maintenance payments;

(ix) Annuities;

(x) Income from life insurance and endowment contracts;

(xi) Pensions;

(xii) Income from discharge of indebtedness;

(xiii) Distributive share of partnership gross income;

(xiv) Income in respect of a decedent;

(xv) Income from an interest in an estate or trust.

(4) *Statutory grouping of gross income and residual grouping of gross income.* For purposes of this section, the term "statutory grouping of gross income" or "statutory grouping" means the gross income from a specific source or activity which must first be determined in order to arrive at taxable income" from such specific source or activity under an operative section. (See paragraph (f)(1) of this section.) Gross income from other sources or activities is referred to as the "residual grouping of gross income" or "residual grouping". For example, for purposes of determining taxable income from sources within specific foreign countries and possessions of the United States, in order to apply the per-country limitation to the foreign tax credit (as in effect before enactment of the Tax Reform Act of 1976), the statutory groupings are the separate gross incomes from sources within each country and possession. Moreover, if the taxpayer has income subject to section 904(d) (as in effect after enactment of the Tax Reform Act of 1976), such income constitutes one or more separate statutory groupings. In the case of the per-country limitation, the residual grouping is the aggregate of gross income from sources within the United States. In some instances, where the operative section so requires, the statutory grouping or the residual grouping may include, or consist entirely of, excluded income. See paragraph (d)(2) of this section with respect to the allocation and apportionment of deductions to excluded income.

(5) *Effective date*—(i) *Taxable years beginning after December 31 1976.* The provisions of this section apply to taxable years beginning after December 31, 1976.

(ii) *Taxable years beginning before January 1, 1977.* For taxable years beginning before January 1, 1977, § 1.861-8 applies as in effect on October 23, 1957 (T.D. 6258), as amended on August 22, 1966 (T.D. 6892) and on September 29, 1975 (T.D. 7378). The specific rules for allocation and apportionment of deductions set forth in this section may, at the option of the taxpayer, apply to those taxable years on a deduction-by-deduction basis if the rules are applied consistently to all taxable years with respect to which action by the Internal Revenue Service is not barred by any statute of limitations. Thus, for example, a calendar year taxpayer may choose to have the rules of paragraph (e)(2) of this section apply for the allocation and apportionment of all interest expenses for the two taxable years ending December 31, 1975 and 1976, which are open years under examination, and may justify the allocation and apportionment of all research and development expenses for those years on a basis supportable under § 1.861-8 as in effect for 1975 and 1976 without regard to the rules of paragraph (e)(3) of this section.

(b) *Allocation*—(1) *In general.* For purposes of this section, the gross income to which a specific deduction is definitely related is referred to as a "class of gross income" and may consist of one or more items of gross income. The rules emphasize the factual relationship between the deduction and a class of gross income. See paragraph (d)(1) of this section which provides that in a taxable year there may be no item of gross income in a class or less gross income than deductions allocated to the class, and paragraph (d)(2) of this section which provides that a class of gross income may include excluded income. Allocation is accomplished by determining, with respect to each deduction, the class of gross income to which the deduction is definitely related and then allocating the deduction to such class of gross income (without regard to the taxable year in which such gross income is received or accrued or is expected to be received or accrued). The classes of gross income are not predetermined but must be determined on the basis of the deductions to be allocated. Although most deductions will be definitely related to some class of a taxpayer's total gross income, some deductions are related to all gross income. In addition, some deductions are treated as not definitely related to any gross income and are ratably apportioned to all gross income. (See paragraph (e)(9) of this section.) In allocating deductions it is not necessary to differentiate between deductions related to one item of gross income and deductions related to another item of gross income where both items of gross income are exclusively within the same statutory grouping or exclusively within the residual grouping.

(2) *Relationship to activity or property.* A deduction shall be considered definitely related to a class of gross income and therefore allocable to such class if it is incurred as a result of, or incident to, an activity or in connection with property from which such class of gross income is derived. Where a deduction is incurred as a result of, or incident to, an activity or in connection with property, which activity or property generates, has generated, or could reasonably have been expected to generate gross income, such deduction shall be considered definitely related to such gross

income as a class whether or not there is any item of gross income in such class which is received or accrued during the taxable year and whether or not the amount of deductions exceeds the amount of the gross income in such class. See paragraph (d)(1) of this section and example (17) of paragraph (g) of this section with respect to cases in which there is an excess of deductions. In some cases, it will be found that this subparagraph can most readily be applied by determining, with respect to a deduction, the categories of gross income to which it is not related and concluding that it is definitely related to a class consisting of all other gross income.

(3) *Supportive functions.* [Reserved] For guidance, see § 1.861-8T(b)(3).

(4) *Deductions related to a class of gross income.* See paragraph (e) of this section for rules relating to the allocation and apportionment of certain specific deductions definitely related to a class of gross income. See paragraph (c)(1) of this section for rules relating to the apportionment of deductions.

(5) *Deductions related to all gross income.* If a deduction does not bear a definite relationship to a class of gross income constituting less than all of gross income, it shall ordinarily be treated as definitely related and allocable to all of the taxpayer's gross income except where provided to the contrary under paragraph (e) of this section. Paragraph (e)(9) of this section lists various deductions which generally are not definitely related to any gross income and are ratably apportioned to all gross income.

(c) *Apportionment of deductions*—(1) *Deductions definitely related to a class of gross income.* [Reserved] For guidance, see § 1.861-8T(c)(1).

(2) *Apportionment based on assets.* [Reserved] For guidance, see § 1.861-8T(c)(2).

(3) *Deductions not definitely related to any gross income.* If a deduction is not definitely related to any gross income (see paragraph (e)(9) of this section), the deduction must be apportioned ratably between the statutory grouping (or among the statutory groupings) of gross income and the residual grouping. Thus, the amount apportioned to each statutory grouping shall be equal to the same proportion of the deduction which the amount of gross income in the statutory grouping bears to the total amount of gross income. The amount apportioned to the residual grouping shall be equal to the same proportion of the deduction which the amount of the gross income in the residual grouping bears to the total amount of gross income.

(d) *Excess of deductions and excluded and eliminated income*—(1) *Excess of deductions.* Each deduction which bears a definite relationship to a class of gross income shall be allocated to that class in accordance with paragraph (b)(1) of this section even though, for the taxable year, no gross income in such class is received or accrued or the amount of the deduction exceeds the amount of such class of gross income. In apportioning deductions, it may be that, for the taxable year, there is no gross income in the statutory grouping (or residual grouping), or that deductions exceed the amount of gross income in the statutory grouping (or residual grouping). If there is no gross income in a statutory grouping or the amount of deductions allocated and apportioned to a statutory grouping exceeds the amount of gross income in the statutory grouping, the effects are determined under the operative section. If the taxpayer is a member of a group filing a consolidated return, such excess of deductions allocated or apportioned to a statutory grouping of income of such member is taken into account in determining the consolidated taxable income from such statutory grouping, and such excess of deductions allocated or apportioned to the residual grouping of income is taken into account in determining the consolidated taxable income from the residual grouping. See § 1.1502-4(d)(1) and the last sentence of § 1.1502-12. For an illustration of the principles of this paragraph (d)(1), see example (17) of paragraph (g) of this section.

(2) *Allocation and apportionment to exempt, excluded, or eliminated income.* [Reserved] For guidance, see § 1.861-8T(d)(2).

(e) *Allocation and apportionment of certain deductions*—(1) *In general.* Subparagraphs (2) and (3) of this paragraph contain rules with respect to the allocation and apportionment of interest expense and research and development expenditures, respectively. Subparagraphs (4) through (8) of this paragraph contain rules with respect to the allocation of certain other deductions. Subparagraph (9) of this paragraph lists those deductions which are ordinarily considered as not being definitely related to any class of gross income. Subparagraph (10) of this paragraph lists special deductions of corporations which must be allocated and apportioned. Subparagraph (11) of this paragraph lists personal exemptions which are neither allocated nor apportioned. Examples of allocation and apportionment are contained in paragraph (g) of this section.

(2) *Interest.* [Reserved] For guidance, see § 1.861-8T(e)(2).

(3) *Research and experimental expenditures.* For rules regarding the allocation and apportionment of research and experimental expenditures, see § 1.861-17.

Reg. § 1.861-8(e)(3)

(4) *Stewardship expenses attributable to dividends received.* If a corporation renders services for the benefit of a related corporation and the corporation charges the related corporation for such services (see section 482 and the regulations thereunder which provide for an allocation where the charge is not on an arm's length basis as determined therein), the deductions for expenses of the corporation attributable to the rendering of such services are considered definitely related to the amounts so charged and are to be allocated to such amounts. However, the regulations under section 482 (§ 1.482-2(b)(2)(ii)) recognize a type of activity which is not considered to be for the benifit of a related corporation but is considered to constitute "stewardship" or "overseeing" functions undertaken for the corporation's own benefit as an investor in the related corporation, and therefore, a charge to the related corporation for such stewardship or overseeing functions is not provided for. Services undertaken by a corporation of a stewardship or overseeing character generally represent a duplication of services which the related corporation has independently performed for itself. For example, assume that a related corporation, which has a qualified financial staff, makes an analysis to determine the amount and source of its borrowing needs and submits a report of its findings and a plan of borrowing to the parent corporation, and the parent corporation's financial staff reviews the findings and plans to determine whether to advise the related corporation to reconsider its plan. The services of review performed by the parent corporation for its own benefit are of a stewardship or overseeing character. The deductions resulting from stewardship or overseeing functions are incurred as a result of, or incident to, the ownership of the related corporation and, thus, shall be considered definitely related and allocable to dividends received or to be received from the related corporation. If a corporation has a foreign or international department which exercises stewardship or overseeing functions with respect to related foreign corporations and, in addition, the department has other functions which are attributable to other foreign-source income (such as fees for services rendered outside of the United States for the benefit of foreign related corporations, foreign royalties, and gross income of foreign branches) to which its deductions are also to be allocated, some part of the deductions with respect to that department are considered definitely related to the other foreign-source income. In some instances, the operations of a foreign or international department will also be attributable to United States source income (such as fees for services performed in the United States) to which

its deductions are to be allocated. Methods of apportionment which could possibly be utilized with respect to stewardship expenses include comparisons of time spent by employees weighted to take into account differences in compensation, or comparisons of each related corporation's gross receipts, gross income, or unit sales volume, assuming that stewardship activities are not substantially disproportionate to such factors. See paragraph (f)(5) of this section for the type of verification that may be required in this respect. See examples (17) and (18) of paragraph (g) of this section for the allocation and apportionment of stewardship expenses. See paragraph (b)(3) of this section for the allocation and apportionment of deductions attributable to supportive functions other than stewardship activities.

(5) *Legal and accounting fees and expenses.* Fees and other expenses for legal and accounting services are ordinarily definitely related and allocable to specific classes of gross income or to all the taxpayer's gross income, depending on the nature of the services rendered (and are apportioned as provided in paragraph (c)(1) of this section). For example, accounting fees for the preparation of a study of the costs involved in manufacturing a specific product will ordinarily be definitely related to the class of gross income derived from (or which could reasonably have been expected to be derived from) that specific product. The taxpayer is not relieved from his responsibility to make a proper allocation and apportionment of fees on the grounds that the statement of services rendered does not identify the services performed beyond a generalized designation such as "professional," or does not provide any type of allocation, or does not properly allocate the fees involved.

(6) *Income taxes*—(i) *In general.* The deduction for state, local, and foreign income, war profits and excess profits taxes ("state income taxes") allowed by section 164 shall be considered definitely related and allocable to the gross income with respect to which such state income taxes are imposed. For example, if a domestic corporation is subject to state income taxation and the state income tax is imposed in part on an amount of foreign source income, then that part of the taxpayer's deduction for state income tax that is attributable to foreign source income is definitely related and allocable to foreign source income. In allocating and apportioning the deduction for state income tax for purposes including (but not limited to) the computation of the foreign tax credit limitation under section 904 of the Code and the consolidated foreign tax credit under § 1.1502-4 of the regulations, the income upon which the state income tax is imposed is deter-

Reg. § 1.861-8(e)(4)

mined by reference to the law of the jurisdiction imposing the tax. Thus, if a state attributes taxable income to a corporate taxpayer by applying an apportionment formula that takes into consideration the income and factors of one or more corporations related by ownership to the corporate taxpayer and engaging in activities related to the business of the corporate taxpayer, then the income so attributed is the income upon which the state income tax is imposed. If the income so attributed to the corporate taxpayer includes foreign source income, then, in computing the taxpayer's foreign tax credit limitation under section 904, for example, the taxpayer's deduction for state income tax will be considered definitely related and allocable to a class of gross income that includes the statutory grouping of foreign source income. When the law of the state includes dividends that are treated under section 862(a)(2) as income from sources without the United States in taxable income apportionable to the state, but does not include factors of the corporation paying such dividends in the apportionment formula used to determine state taxable income, an appropriate portion of the deduction for state income tax will be considered definitely related and allocable to a class of gross income consisting solely of foreign source dividend income. A deduction for state income tax will not be considered definitely related to a hypothetical amount of income calculated under federal tax principles when the jurisdiction imposing the tax computes taxable income under different principles. A corporate taxpayer's deduction for a state franchise tax that is computed on the basis of income attributable to business activities conducted within the state must be allocated and apportioned in the same manner as the deduction for state income taxes. In determining, for example, both the foreign tax credit under section 904 of the Code and the consolidated foreign tax credit limitation under § 1.1502-4 of the regulations, the deduction for state income tax may be allocable and apportionable to foreign source income in a statutory grouping described in section 904(d) in a taxable year in which the taxpayer has no foreign source income in such statutory grouping. Alternatively, such an allocation or apportionment may be appropriate if a taxpayer corporation has no foreign source income in a statutory grouping, but its deduction is attributable to foreign source income in such grouping that is attributed to the taxpayer corporation under the law of a state which attributes taxable income to a corporation by applying an apportionment formula that takes into consideration the income and factors of one or more corporations related by ownership to the taxpayer corporation and engaging in activities related to the business of the taxpayer corporation. *Example 30* of paragraph (g) of this section illustrates the application of this last rule.

(ii) *Methods of allocation and apportionment*—(A) *In general.* A taxpayer's deduction for a state income tax is to be allocated (and then apportioned, if necessary, subject to the rules of § 1.861-8(d)) by reference to the taxable income that the law of the taxing jurisdiction attributes to the taxpayer ("state taxable income").

(B) *Effect of subsequent recomputations of state income tax.* [Reserved]

(C) *Illustrations*—(1) *In general.* Examples 25 through 32 of paragraph (g) of § 1.861-8 illustrate, in the given factual situations, the application of this paragraph (e)(6) and the general rule of paragraph (b)(1) of this section that a deduction must be allocated to the class of gross income to which the deduction is factually related. In general, these examples employ a presumption that state income taxes are allocable to a class of gross income that includes the statutory grouping of income from sources without the United States when the total amount of taxable income determined under state law exceeds the amount of taxable income determined under the Code (without taking into account the deduction for state income taxes) in the residual grouping of income from sources within the United States. A taxpayer that allocates and apportions the deduction for state income tax in accordance with the methodology of *Example 25* of paragraph (g) of this section must also apply the modifications illustrated in *Examples 26* and *27* of paragraph (g) of this section, when applicable. The modification illustrated in *Example 26* is applicable when the deduction for state income tax is attributable in part to taxes imposed by a state which factually excludes foreign source income (as determined for federal income tax purposes) from state taxable income. The modification illustrated in *Example 27* is applicable when the taxpayer has income-producing activities in a state which does not impose a corporate income tax. The specific allocation of state income tax illustrated in *Example 28* follows the rule in paragraph (e)(6)(i) of this section, and must be applied whenever a taxpayer's state taxable income includes dividends apportioned to the state under a formula that does not take into account the factors of the corporations paying those dividends, regardless of whether the taxpayer uses the methodology of *Example 25* with respect to the remainder of the deduction for state income taxes.

(2) *Modifications.* Before applying a method of allocation and apportionment illustrated in the examples, the computation of state

Reg. § 1.861-8(e)(6)

taxable income under state law may be modified, subject to the approval of the District Director, to reflect more accurately the income with respect to which the state income tax is imposed. Any modification to the state law computation of state taxable income must yield an allocation and apportionment of the deduction for state income taxes that is consistent with the rules contained in this paragraph (e)(6), and that accurately reflects the factual relationship between the state income tax and the income on which that tax is imposed. For example, a modification to the computation of taxable income under state law might be appropriate to compensate for differences between the state law definition of taxable income and the federal definition of taxable income, due to a difference in the rate of allowable depreciation or the amount of another deduction that is allowable under both systems. This rule is illustrated in *Example 31* of paragraph (g) of this section. However, a modification to the computation of taxable income under state law will not be appropriate, and will not more accurately reflect the factual relationship between the state tax and the income on which the tax is imposed, to the extent such modification reflects the fact that the state does not follow federal tax principles in attributing income to the taxpayer's activities in the state. This rule is illustrated in *Example 32* of paragraph (g) of this section. A taxpayer may not modify the methods illustrated in the examples, or use an alternative method of allocation and apportionment of the deduction for state income taxes, if the modification or alternative method would be inconsistent with the rules of paragraph (e)(6)(i) of this section. A taxpayer that uses a method of allocation and apportionment other than one illustrated in *Example 25* (as modified by *Examples 26* and *27*), or *29* with respect to a factual situation similar to those of the examples, must describe the alternative method on an attachment to its federal income tax return and establish to the satisfaction of the District Director, upon examination, that the result of the alternative method more accurately reflects the factual relationship between the state income tax and the income on which the tax is imposed.

(D) *Elective safe harbor methods.* (*1*) *In general.* In lieu of applying the rules set forth in paragraphs (e)(6)(ii)(A) through (C) of this section, a taxpayer may elect to allocate and apportion the deduction for state income tax in accordance with one of the two safe harbor methods described in paragraph (e)(6)(ii)(D)(*2*) and (*3*) of this section. A taxpayer shall make this election for a taxable year by filing a timely tax return for that year that reflects an allocation and apportionment of the deduction for state income tax under one of the safe harbor methods and attaching to such return a statement that the taxpayer has elected to use the safe harbor method provided in either paragraph (e)(6)(ii)(D)(*2*) or (*3*) of this section, as appropriate. Once made, this election is effective for the taxable year for which made and all subsequent taxable years, and may be revoked only with the consent of the Commissioner. *Example 33* of paragraph (g) of this section illustrates the application of these safe harbor methods.

(*2*) *Method One.* (*i*) *Step One—Specific allocation to foreign source portfolio dividends and other income.* If any portion of the deduction for state income tax is attributable to tax imposed by a state which includes in a corporate taxpayer's taxable income apportionable to the state, portfolio dividends (as defined in paragraph (i) of *Example 28* of paragraph (g) of this section) that are treated under section 862(a)(2) as income from sources without the United States, but does not include factors of the corporations paying the portfolio dividends in the apportionment formula used to determine state taxable income, the taxpayer shall allocate an appropriate portion of the deduction to a class of gross income consisting solely of foreign source portfolio dividends. The portion of the deduction so allocated, and the amount of foreign source portfolio dividends included in such class, shall be determined in accordance with the methodology illustrated in paragraph (ii) of *Example 28* of paragraph (g). If a state income tax is determined based upon formulary apportionment of the total taxable income attributable to the taxpayer's unitary business, the taxpayer must also apply the methodology illustrated in paragraph (ii)(C) through (G) of *Example 29* of paragraph (g) of this section to make specific allocations of appropriate portions of the deduction for state income tax on the basis of income that, under separate accounting, would have been attributed to other members of the unitary group. The taxpayer shall reduce its aggregate state taxable income by the amount of foreign source portfolio dividends and other income to which a specific allocation is made (the reduced amount being referred to hereinafter as "adjusted state taxable income").

(*ii*) *Step Two—Adjustment of U.S. source federal taxable income.* If the taxpayer has significant income producing activities in a state which does not impose a corporate income tax or other state tax measured by income derived from business activities in the state, the taxpayer shall reduce its U.S. source federal taxable income (solely for purposes of this safe harbor method) by the amount of federal taxable income attributable to its activities in such state. This amount shall be determined in accordance with the methodology illustrated in paragraph (ii) of *Example 27* of paragraph (g) of this section, provided that the taxpayer shall be required to use the rules of the Uniform Division of Income for Tax Purposes Act to attribute income to the relevant state. The taxpayer's U.S. source federal taxable income, as so reduced, is referred to hereinafter as "adjusted U.S. source federal taxable income."

(*iii*) *Step Three—Allocation.* The taxpayer shall allocate the remainder of the deduction for state income tax (after reduction by the portion allocated to foreign source portfolio dividends and other income under Step One) in accordance with the methodology illustrated in paragraph (ii) of *Example 25* of paragraph (g) of this section. However, the taxpayer shall substitute for the comparison of aggregate state taxable income to U.S. source federal taxable income, illustrated in paragraph (ii) of *Example 25* of paragraph (g), a comparison of its adjusted state taxable income to an amount equal to 110% of its adjusted U.S. source federal taxable income.

(*iv*) *Step Four—Apportionment.* In the event that apportionment of the remainder of the deduction for state income tax is required, the taxpayer shall apportion that remaining deduction to U.S. source income in accordance with the methodology illustrated in paragraph (iii) of *Example 25* of paragraph (g) of this section, substituting for domestic source income in that paragraph an amount equal to 110% of the taxpayer's adjusted U.S. source federal taxable income. The remaining portion of the deduction shall be apportioned to the statutory groupings of foreign source income described in section 904(d) of the Code in accordance with the proportion of the income in each statutory grouping of foreign source income described in section 904(d) to the taxpayer's total foreign source federal taxable income (after reduction by the amount of foreign source portfolio dividends to which tax has been specifically allocated under Step One, above).

(*3*) *Method Two.* (*i*) *Step One—Specific allocation to foreign source portfolio dividends and other income.* Step One of this method is the same as Step One of Method One (as described in paragraph (e)(6)(ii)(D)(*2*)(*i*) of this section).

(*ii*) *Step Two—Adjustment of U.S. source federal taxable income.* Step Two of this method is the same as Step Two of Method One (as described in paragraph (e)(6)(ii)(D)(*2*)(*ii*) of this section).

(*iii*) *Step Three—Allocation.* The taxpayer shall allocate the remainder of the deduction for state income tax (after reduction by the portion allocated to foreign source portfolio dividends and other income under Step One) in accordance with the methodology illustrated in paragraph (ii) of *Example 25* of paragraph (g) of this section. However, the taxpayer shall substitute for the comparison of aggregate state taxable income to U.S. source federal taxable income, illustrated in paragraph (ii) of *Example 25* of paragraph (g) of this section, a comparison of its adjusted state taxable income to its adjusted U.S. source federal taxable income.

(*iv*) *Step Four—Apportionment.* In the event that apportionment of the deduction is required, the taxpayer shall apportion to U.S. source income that portion of the deduction that is attributable to state income taxes imposed upon an amount of state taxable income equal to adjusted U.S. source federal taxable income. The taxpayer shall apportion the remaining amount of the deduction to U.S. and foreign source income in the same proportions that the taxpayer's adjusted U.S. source federal taxable income and foreign source federal taxable income (after reduction by the amount of foreign source portfolio dividends to which tax has been specifically allocated under Step One, above) bear to its total federal taxable income (taking into account the adjustment of U.S. source federal taxable income under Step Two and after reduction by the amount of foreign source portfolio dividends to which tax has been specifically allocated under Step One). The portion of the deduction apportioned to foreign source income shall be apportioned among the statutory groupings described in section 904(d) of the Code in accordance with the proportions of the taxpayer's total foreign source federal taxable income (after reduction by the amount of foreign source portfolio dividends to which tax has been specifically allocated under Step One, above) in each grouping.

(*iii*) *Effective dates.* The rules of § 1.861-8(e)(6)(i) and the language preceding the examples in § 1.861-8(g) are effective for taxable years beginning after December 31, 1976. The rules of § 1.861-8(e)(6)(ii) (other than § 1.861-8(e)(6)(ii)(D)) and *Examples 25* through *32* of § 1.861-8(g) are effective for taxable years beginning on or after January 1, 1988. The rules of § 1.861-8(e)(6)(ii)(D) and *Example 33* of § 1.861-8(g) are effective for taxable years ending after [date of publication of this regulation in the Federal Register]. At the option of the taxpayer, however, the rules of § 1.861-8(e)(6)(ii) (other than § 1.861-8(e)(6)(ii)(D)) and *Examples 25* through *32* of § 1.861-8(g) may be applied with respect to deductions for state taxes incurred in taxable years beginning before January 1, 1988.

Reg. § 1.861-8(e)(6)

(7) *Losses on the sale, exchange, or other disposition of property*—(i) *Allocation.* The deduction allowed for loss recognized on the sale, exchange, or other disposition of a capital asset or property described in section 1231(b) shall be considered a deduction which is definitely related and allocable to the class of gross income to which such asset or property ordinarily gives rise in the hands of the taxpayer. Where the nature of gross income generated from the asset or property has varied significantly over several taxable years of the taxpayer, such class of gross income shall generally be determined by reference to gross income generated from the asset or property during the taxable year or years immediately preceding the sale, exchange, or other disposition of such asset or property. Thus, for example, where an asset generates primarily sales income from domestic sources in the early years of its operation and then is leased by the taxpayer to a foreign subsidiary in later years, the class of gross income to which the asset gives rise will be considered to be the rental income derived from the lease and will not include sales income from domestic sources.

(ii) *Apportionment of losses.* Where in the unusual circumstances that an apportionment of a deduction for losses on the sale, exchange, or other disposition of a capital asset or property described in section 1231(b) is necessary, the amount of such deduction shall be apportioned between the statutory grouping (or among the statutory groupings) of gross income (within the class of gross income) and the residual grouping (within the class of gross income) in the same proportion that the amount of gross income within such statutory grouping (or statutory groupings) and such residual grouping bear, respectively, to the total amount of gross income within the class of gross income. Apportionment will be necessary where, for example, the class of gross income to which the deduction is allocated consists of gross income (such as royalties) attributable to an intangible asset used both within and without the United States, or gross income (such as from sales or services) attributable to a tangible asset used both within and without the United States.

(iii) *Allocation of loss recognized in taxable years after 1986.* See §§ 1.865-1 and 1.865-2 for rules regarding the allocation of certain loss recognized in taxable years beginning after December 31, 1986.

(8) *Net operating loss deduction.* A net operating loss deduction allowed under section 172 shall be allocated and apportioned in the same manner as the deductions giving rise to the net operating loss deduction.

(9) *Deductions which are not definitely related.* Deductions which shall generally be considered as not definitely related to any gross income, and therefore are ratably apportioned as provided in paragraph (c)(2) of this section, are—

(i) The deduction allowed by section 163 for interest described in subparagraph (2)(iii) of this paragraph (e);

(ii) The deduction allowed by section 164 for real estate taxes on a personal residence or for sales tax on the purchase of items for personal use;

(iii) The deduction for medical expenses allowed by section 213;

(iv) The deduction for charitable contributions allowed by sections 170, 873(b)(2), and 882(c)(1)(B); and

(v) The deduction for alimony payments allowed by section 215.

(10) *Special deductions.* The special deductions allowed in the case of a corporation by section 241 (relating to the deductions for partially tax exempt interest, dividends received, etc.), section 922 (relating to Western Hemisphere trade corporations), and section 941 (relating to China Trade Act corporations) shall be allocated and apportioned consistent with the principles of this section.

(11) *Personal exemptions.* The deductions for the personal exemptions allowed by section 151, 642(b), or 873(b)(3) shall not be taken into account for purposes of allocation and apportionment under this section.

(f) *Miscellaneous matters*—(1) *Operative sections.* The operative sections of the Code which require the determination of taxable income of the taxpayer from specific sources or activities and which give rise to statutory groupings to which this section is applicable include the sections described below.

(i) *Overall limitation to the foreign tax credit.* Under the overall limitation to the foreign tax credit, as provided in section 904(a)(2) (as in effect before enactment of the Tax Reform Act of 1976, or section 904(a) after such enactment) the amount of the foreign tax credit may not exceed the tentative U.S. tax (i.e., the U.S. tax before application of the foreign tax credit) multiplied by a fraction, the numerator of which is the taxable income from sources without the United States and the denominator of which is the entire taxable income. Accordingly, in this case, the statutory grouping is foreign source income (including, for example, interest received from a domestic corporation which meets the tests of section 861(a)(1)(B), dividends received from a domestic corporation which has an election in effect under

Reg. § 1.861-8(e)(7)

Determination of Sources of Income

section 936, and other types of income specified in section 862). Pursuant to sections 862(b) and 863(a) and §§ 1.862-1 and 1.863-1, this section provides rules for identifying the deductions to be taken into account in determining taxable income from sources without the United States. See section 904(d) (as in effect after enactment of the Tax Reform Act of 1976) and the regulations thereunder which require separate treatment of certain types of income. See example (3) of paragraph (g) of this section for one example of the application of this section to the overall limitation.

(ii) [Reserved].

(iii) *DISC and FSC taxable income.* Sections 925 and 994 provide rules for determining the taxable income of a FSC and DISC, respectively, with respect to qualified sales and leases of export property and qualified services. The combined taxable income method available for determining a DISC's taxable income provides, without consideration of export promotion expenses, that the taxable income of the DISC shall be 50 percent of the combined taxable income of the DISC and the related supplier derived from sales and leases of export property and from services. In the FSC context, the taxable income of the FSC equals 23 percent of the combined taxable income of the FSC and the related supplier. Pursuant to regulations under sections 925 and 994, this section provides rules for determining the deductions to be taken into account in determining combined taxable income, except to the extent modified by the marginal costing rules set forth in the regulations under sections 925(b)(2) and 994(b)(2) if used by the taxpayer. See *Examples* (22) and (23) of paragraph (g) of this section. In addition, the computation of combined taxable income is necessary to determine the applicability of the section 925(d) limitation and the "no loss" rules of the regulations under sections 925 and 994.

(iv) *Effectively connected taxable income.* Nonresident alien individuals and foreign corporations engaged in trade or business within the United States are taxed, as provided under sections 871(b)(1) and 882(a)(1), on taxable income which is effectively connected with the conduct of a trade or business within the United States. Such taxable income is determined in most instances by initially determining, under section 864(c), the amount of gross income which is effectively connected with the conduct of a trade or business within the United States. Pursuant to sections 873 and 882(c), this section is applicable for purposes of determining the deductions from such gross income (other than the deduction for interest expense allowed to foreign corporations (see § 1.882-5)) which are to be taken into account in determining taxable income. See example (21) of paragraph (g) of this section.

(v) *Foreign base company income.* Section 954 defines the term "foreign base company income" with respect to controlled foreign corporations. Section 954(b)(5) provides that in determining foreign base company income the gross income shall be reduced by the deductions of the controlled foreign corporation "properly allocable to such income". This section provides rules for identifying which deductions are properly allocable to foreign base company income.

(vi) *Other operative sections.* The rules provided in this section also apply in determining—

(A) The amount of foreign source items of tax preference under section 58(g) determined for purposes of the minimum tax;

(B) The amount of foreign mineral income under section 901(e);

(C) [Reserved];

(D) The amount of foreign oil and gas extraction income and the amount of foreign oil related income under section 907;

(E) The tax base for citizens entitled to the benefits of section 931 and the section 936 tax credit of a domestic corporation which has an election in effect under section 936;

(F) The exclusion for income from Puerto Rico for residents of Puerto Rico under section 933;

(G) The limitation under section 934 on the maximum reduction in income tax liability incurred to the Virgin Islands;

(H) The income derived from Guam by an individual who is subject to section 935;

(I) The special deduction granted to China Trade Act corporations under section 941;

(J) The amount of certain U.S. source income excluded from the subpart F income of a controlled foreign corporation under section 952(b);

(K) The amount of income from the insurance of U.S. risks under section 953(b)(5);

(L) The international boycott factor and the specifically attributable taxes and income under section 999; and

(M) The taxable income attributable to the operation of an agreement vessel under section 607 of the Merchant Marine Act of 1936, as amended, and the Capital Construction Fund Regulations thereunder (26 CFR, pt. 3). See 26 CFR 3.2(b)(3).

Reg. § 1.861-8(f)(1)

(2) *Application to more than one operative section.* (i) Where more than one operative section applies, it may be necessary for the taxpayer to apply this section separately for each applicable operative section. In such a case, the taxpayer is required to use the same method of allocation and the same principles of apportionment for all operative sections.

(ii) When expenses, losses, and other deductions that have been properly allocated and apportioned between combined gross income of a related supplier and a DISC or former DISC and residual gross income, regardless of which of the administrative pricing methods of section 994 has been applied, such deductions are not also allocated and apportioned to gross income consisting of distributions from the DISC or former DISC attributable to income of the DISC or former DISC as determined under the administrative pricing methods with respect to DISC or former DISC taxable years beginning after December 31, 1986. Accordingly, *Example* (22) of paragraph (g) of this section does not apply to distributions from a DISC or former DISC with respect to DISC or former DISC taxable years beginning after December 31, 1986. This rule does not apply to the extent that the taxable income of the DISC or former DISC is determined under the section 994(a)(3) transfer pricing method. In addition, for taxable years beginning after December 31, 1986, in the case of expenses, losses, and other deductions that have been properly allocated and apportioned between combined gross income of a related supplier and a FSC and residual gross income, regardless of which of the administrative pricing methods of section 925 has been applied, such deductions are not also allocated and apportioned to gross income consisting of distributions from the FSC or former FSC which are attributable to the foreign trade income of the FSC or former FSC as determined under the administrative pricing methods. This rule does not apply to the extent that the foreign trade income of the FSC or former FSC is determined under the section 925(a)(3) transfer pricing method. See *Example* (23) of paragraph (g) of this section.

(3) *Special rules of section 863(b)* —(i) *In general.* Special rules under section 863(b) provide for the application of rules of general apportionment provided in §§ 1.863-3 to 1.863-5, to worldwide taxable income in order to attribute part of such worldwide taxable income to U.S. sources and the remainder of such worldwide taxable income to foreign sources. The activities specified in section 863(b) are—

(A) Transportation or other services rendered partly within and partly without the United States,

(B) Sales of personal property produced by the taxpayer within and sold without the United States, or produced by the taxpayer without and sold within the United States, and

(C) Sales within the United States of personal property purchased within a possession of the United States.

In the instances provided in §§ 1.863-3 and 1.863-4 with respect to the activities described in (A), (B), and (C) of this subsection, this section is applicable only in determining worldwide taxable income attributable to these activities.

(ii) *Relationship of sections 861, 862, 863(a), and 863(b).* Sections 861, 862, 863(a), and 863(b) are the four provisions applicable in determining taxable income from specific sources. Each of these four provisions applies independently. Where a deduction has been allocated and apportioned to income under one of these four provisions, the deduction shall not again be allocated and apportioned to gross income under any of the other three provisions. However, two or more of these provisions may have to be applied at the same time to determine the proper allocation and apportionment of a deduction. The special rules under section 863(b) take precedence over the general rules of Code sections 861, 862 and 863(a). For example, where a deduction is allocable in whole or in part to gross income to which section 863(b) applies, such deduction or part thereof shall not otherwise be allocated under section 861, 862, or 863(a). However, where the gross income to which the deduction is allocable includes both gross income to which section 863(b) applies and gross income to which section 861, 862, or 863(a) applies, more than one section must be applied at the same time in order to determine the proper allocation and apportionment of the deduction.

(4) *Adjustments made under other provisions of the Code*—(i) *In general.* If an adjustment which affects the taxpayer is made under section 482 or any other provision of the Code, it may be necessary to recompute the allocations and apportionments required by this section in order to reflect changes resulting from the adjustment. The recomputation made by the District Director shall be made using the same method of allocation and apportionment as was originally used by the taxpayer, provided such method as originally used conformed with paragraph (a)(5) of this section and, in light of the adjustment, such method does not result in a material distortion. In addition to adjustments which would be made aside from this

Reg. § 1.861-8(f)(2)

Determination of Sources of Income

See p. 20,601 for regulations not amended to reflect law changes

section, adjustments to the taxpayer's income and deductions which would not otherwise be made may be required before applying this section in order to prevent a distortion in determining taxable income from a particular source of activity. For example, if an item included as a part of the cost of goods sold has been improperly attributed to specific sales, and, as a result, gross income under one of the operative sections referred to in paragraph (f)(1) of this section is improperly determined, it may be necessary for the District Director to make an adjustment to the cost of goods sold, consistent with the principles of this section, before applying this section. Similarly, if a domestic corporation transfers the stock in its foreign subsidiaries to a domestic subsidiary and the parent continues to incur expenses in connection with the supervision of the foreign subsidiaries (see paragraph (e)(4) of this section), it may be necessary for the District Director to make an allocation under section 482 with respect to such expenses before making allocations and apportionments required by this section, even though the section 482 allocation might not otherwise be made.

(ii) *Example.* X, a domestic corporation, purchases and sells consumer items in the United States and foreign markets. Its sales in foreign markets are made to related foreign subsidiaries. X reported $1,500,000 as sales during the taxable year of which $1,000,000 was domestic sales and $500,000 was foreign sales. X took a deduction for expenses incurred by its marketing department during the taxable year in the amount of $150,000. These expenses were determined to be allocable to both domestic and foreign sales and are apportionable between such sales. Thus, X allocated and apportioned the marketing department deduction as follows:

To gross income from domestic sales:

$$\$150,000 \times \frac{\$1,000,000}{1,500,000} \ldots\ldots\ldots\ldots\ldots\ldots\ldots\ldots\ldots\ldots\ldots\ldots \$100,000$$

To gross income from foreign sales:

$$\$150,000 \times \frac{\$500,000}{1,500,000} \ldots\ldots\ldots\ldots\ldots\ldots\ldots\ldots\ldots\ldots\ldots\ldots 50,000$$

Total 150,000

On audit of X's return for the taxable year, the District Director adjusted, under section 482, X's sales to related foreign subsidiaries by increasing the sales price by a total of $100,000, thereby increasing X's foreign sales and total sales by the same amount. As a result of the section 482 adjustment, the apportionment of the deduction for the marketing department expenses is redetermined as follows:

To gross income from domestic sales:

$$\$150,000 \times \frac{\$1,000,000}{1,600,000} \ldots\ldots\ldots\ldots\ldots\ldots\ldots\ldots\ldots\ldots\ldots\ldots \$\,93,750$$

To gross income from foreign sales:

$$\$150,000 \times \frac{\$600,000}{1,600,000} \ldots\ldots\ldots\ldots\ldots\ldots\ldots\ldots\ldots\ldots\ldots\ldots \$\,56,250$$

Total 150,000

(5) *Verification of allocations and apportionments.* Since, under this section, allocations and apportionments are made on the basis of the factual relationship between deductions and gross income, the taxpayer is required to furnish, at the request of the District Director, information from which such factual relationships can be determined. In reviewing the overall limitation to the foreign tax credit of a domestic corporation, for example, the District Director should consider information which would enable him to determine the extent to which deductions attributable to functions performed in the United States are related to earning foreign source income, United States source income, or income from both sources. In addition to functions with a specific international purpose, consideration should be given to the functions of management, the direction and results of an acquisition program, the functions of operating units and personnel located at the head office, the functions of support units (including but not limited to engineering, legal, budget, accounting, and industrial relations), the functions of selling and advertising units and personnel, the direction and uses of research and development, and the direction and uses of services furnished by independent contractors. Thus, for example when requested by the District Direc-

Reg. § 1.861-8(f)(5)

tor, the taxpayer shall make available any of its organization charts, manuals, and other writings which relate to the manner in which its gross income arises and to the functions of organizational units, employees, and assets of the taxpayer and arrange for the interview of such of its employees as the District Director deems desirable in order to determine the gross income to which deductions relate. See section 7602 and the regulations thereunder which generally provide for the examination of books and witnesses. See also section 905(b) and the regulations thereunder which require proof of foreign tax credits to the satisfaction of the Secretary or his delegate.

(g) *General examples.* The following examples illustrate the principles of this section. In each example, unless otherwise specified, the operative section which is applied and gives rise to the statutory grouping of gross income is the overall limitation to the foreign tax credit under section 904(a). In addition, in each example, where a method of allocation or apportionment is illustrated as an acceptable method, it is assumed that such method is used by the taxpayer on a consistent basis from year to year (except in the case of the optional method for apportioning research and development expense under paragraph (e)(3)(iii) of § 1.861-8). Further, it is assumed that each party named in each example operates on a calendar year accounting basis and, where the party is a U.S. taxpayer, files returns on a calendar year basis.

Example (1)—[Reserved]

Example (2)—[Reserved]

Example (3)—[Reserved]

Example (4)—[Reserved]

Example (5)—[Reserved]

Example (6)—[Reserved]

Example (7)—[Reserved]

Example (8)—[Reserved]

Example (9)—[Reserved]

Example (10)—[Reserved]

Example (11)—[Reserved]

Example (12)—[Reserved]

Example (13)—[Reserved]

Example (14)—[Reserved]

Example (15)—[Reserved]

Example (16)—[Reserved]

Example (17)—*Stewardship Expenses (Consolidation)*—(i) *Facts.* X, a domestic corporation, wholly owns M, N, and O, also domestic corporations. X, M, N, and O file a consolidated income tax return. All the income of X and O is from sources within the United States, all of M's income is from sources within South America, and all of N's income is from sources within Africa. X receives no dividends from M, N, or O. During the taxable year, the consolidated group of corporations earned consolidated gross income of $550,000 and incurred total deductions of $370,000 as follows:

	Gross income	Deductions
Corporations:		
X	$100,000	$50,000
M	250,000	100,000
N	150,000	200,000
O	50,000	20,000
Total	$550,000	$370,000

Of the $50,000 of deductions incurred by X, $15,000 relates to X's ownership of M; $10,000 relates to X's ownership of N; $5,000 relates to X's ownership of O; and the entire $30,000 constitute stewardship expenses. The remainder of X's deductions ($20,000) relates to production of income from its plant in the United States.

(ii) *Allocation.* In accordance with § 1.1502-4, each corporation must first compute its separate taxable income for purposes of computing the limitation on the foreign tax credit. X's deductions of $50,000 are definitely related and thus allocable to the types of gross income to which they give rise, namely $25,000 wholly to income from sources outside the United States ($15,000 for stewardship of M and $10,000 for stewardship of N) and the remainder ($25,000) wholly to gross income from sources within the United States. Expenses incurred by M and N are entirely related and thus wholly allocable to income earned from sources without the United States and expenses incurred by O are entirely related and thus wholly allocable to income earned within the United States. Hence, no apportionment of expenses of X, M, N, or O is necessary. For purposes of applying the overall limitation, the statutory grouping is gross income from sources without the United States and the residual grouping is gross income from sources within the United States. As a result of the allocation of deductions, X, M, and N have separate taxable income (losses) from sources without the United States in the amounts of ($25,000), $150,000 and ($50,000), respectively, computed as follows:

Determination of Sources of Income

	X	M	N
Foreign gross income		$250,000	$150,000
Less: Deductions allocable to foreign gross income	$ 25,000	100,000	200,000
Total, taxable income (loss)	($ 25,000)	$150,000	($ 50,000)

Thus, in the combined computation of the overall limitation, the numerator of the limiting fraction (taxable income from sources outside the United States) is $75,000 ($150,000 or separate taxable income of M less $50,000 of losses of N and less $25,000 of losses of X).

Example (18)—Stewardship and Supportive Expenses—(i) *Facts.* X, a domestic corporation, manufactures and sells pharmaceuticals in the United States. X's domestic subsidiary S, and X's foreign subsidiaries T, U, and V perform similar functions in the United States and foreign countries T, U, and V, respectively. Each corporation derives substantial net income during the taxable year. X's gross income for the taxable year consists of:

Domestic sales income	$32,000,000
Dividends from S (before dividends received deduction)	3,000,000
Dividends from T	2,000,000
Dividends from U	1,000,000
Dividends from V	0
Royalties from T and U	1,000,000
Fees from U for services performed in the United States	1,000,000
Total gross income	$40,000,000

Among other deductions, X incurs the following:

Expenses of supervision department	$ 1,600,000
Charitable contributions	$ 100,000

X's Supervision Department (the Department) is responsible for the supervision of its four subsidiaries and for rendering certain services to the subsidiaries, and this Department provides all the supportive functions necessary for X's foreign activities. The Department performs three principal types of activities. The first type consists of services for the direct benefit of U for which a fee is paid by U to X. The cost of the services for U is $1,000,000. The second type consists of stewardship activities which are in the nature of a management review and generally duplicate functions performed by the subsidiaries' own employees (and are, therefore, of a type described in § 1.482-2(b)(2)(ii) which would not be subject to an allocation under section 482). For example, a team of auditors from X's accounting department periodically audits the subsidiaries' books and prepares internal reports for use by X's management. Similarly, X's treasurer periodically reviews for the board of directors of X the subsidiaries' financial policies. The cost of the duplicative services and related supportive expenses is $540,000. The third type of activity consists of providing services which are ancillary to the license agreements which X maintains with subsidiaries T and U. The cost of the ancillary services is $60,000.

(ii) *Allocation.* The Department's outlay of $1,000,000 is the basis for the charge to U for services rendered, and therefore $1,000,000 is allocated to the fees paid by U. The remaining $600,000 in the Department's deductions are definitely related to the types of gross income to which they give rise, namely dividends from subsidiaries S, T, U and V and royalties from T and U. However, $60,000 of the $600,000 in deductions are found to be attributable to the ancillary services and are definitely related (and therefore allocable) solely to royalties received from T and U, while the remaining $540,000 in deductions are definitely related (and therefore allocable) to dividends received from all the subsidiaries.

(iii) *Apportionment.* For purposes of applying the overall limitation, the statutory grouping is gross income from sources outside the United States and the residual grouping is gross income from sources within the United States. X's deduction of $540,000 for the Supervision Department expenses and related supportive expenses which is allocable to dividends received from the subsidiaries must be apportioned between the statutory and residual groupings before the overall limitation may be applied. In determining an appropriate method for apportioning the $540,000, a basis other than X's gross income must be used since the dividend payment policies of the subsidiaries bear no relationship either to the activities of the Department or to the amount of income earned by each subsidiary. This is evidenced by the fact that V paid no dividends during the year, whereas S, T, and U paid dividends of $1 million or more each. In the absence of facts that would indicate a material distortion resulting from the use of such method, the stewardship expenses ($540,000) may be apportioned on the basis of the gross receipts of each subsidiary.

The gross receipts of the subsidiaries were as follows:

Reg. § 1.861-8(g)

45,990   Determination of Sources of Income

See p. 20,601 for regulations not amended to reflect law changes

S	$4,000,000
T	3,000,000
U	500,000
V	1,500,000
Total	$9,000,000

$$\$540,000 \times \frac{(\$3,000,000 + \$500,000 + \$1,500,000)}{\$9,000,000}$$

Apportionment of supervisory expenses to the residual grouping of gross income:

$$\$540,000 \times \frac{\$4,000,000}{9,000,000} \quad \ldots \ldots \ldots \ldots \ldots \ldots \ldots \ldots \ldots \ldots \quad 240,000$$

Total: Apportioned stewardship expense $540,000

(iv) *Allocation and apportionment of charitable contributions.* Pursuant to paragraph (e)(9) of this section, charitable contributions are generally treated as deductions which are not definitely related to any gross income and are, accordingly, apportioned ratably on the basis of gross income for purposes of the overall limitation as follows:

Apportionment of charitable contributions to the statutory grouping of gross income:

$$\$100,000 \times \frac{(\$2,000,000 + \$1,000,000 + \$1,000,000)}{\$40,000,000} \quad \ldots \ldots \ldots \ldots \ldots \ldots \ldots \quad \$10,000$$

Apportionment of charitable contributions to the residual grouping of gross income:

$$\$100,000 \times \frac{(\$32,000,000 + \$3,000,000 + \$1,000,000)}{\$40,000,000} \quad \ldots \ldots \ldots \ldots \ldots \ldots \ldots \quad 90,000$$

Total apportioned charitable contributions $100,000

Example (19)—Supportive Expense—(i) *Facts.* X, a domestic corporation, purchases and sells products both in the United States and in foreign countries. X has no foreign subsidiary and no international department. During the taxable year, X incurs the following expenses with respect to its worldwide activities:

Personnel department expenses	$ 50,000
Training department expenses	35,000
General and administrative expenses	55,000
President's salary	40,000
Sales manager's salary	20,000
Total	$200,000

X has domestic gross receipts from sales of $750,000 and foreign gross receipts from sales of $500,000 and has gross income from such sales in the same ratio, namely $300,000 from domestic sources and $200,000 from foreign sources.

(ii) *Allocation.* The above expenses are definitely related and allocable to all of X's gross income derived from both domestic and foreign markets.

Thus, the expenses of the Department are apportioned for purposes of the overall limitation as follows:

Apportionment of stewardship expenses to the statutory grouping of gross income:

.... $300,000

(iii) *Apportionment.* For purposes of applying the overall limitation, the statutory grouping is gross income from sources outside the United States and the residual grouping is gross income from sources within the United States. X's deductions for its worldwide sales activities must be apportioned between these groupings. Company X in this example (unlike Company X in example (18)) does not have a separate international division which performs essentially all of the functions required to manage and oversee its foreign activities. The president and sales manager do not maintain time records. The division of their time between domestic and foreign activities varies from day to day and cannot be estimated on an annual basis with any reasonable degree of accuracy. Similarly, there are no facts which would justify a method of apportionment of their salaries or of one of the other listed deductions based on more specific factors than gross receipts or gross income. An acceptable method of apportionment would be on the basis of gross receipts. The apportionment of the $200,000 deduction is as follows:

Apportionment of the $200,000 expense to the statutory grouping of gross income:

Reg. § 1.861-8(g)

Determination of Sources of Income

See p. 20,601 for regulations not amended to reflect law changes

$$200{,}000 \times \frac{\$500{,}000}{(\$500{,}000 + \$750{,}000)} \quad \ldots\ldots\ldots\ldots\ldots\ldots\ldots\ldots\ldots\ldots\ldots\ldots\ldots\ldots\ldots\ldots\ldots \quad \$80{,}000$$

Apportionment of the $200,000 expense to the residual grouping of gross income:

$$200{,}000 \times \frac{\$750{,}000}{(\$500{,}000 + \$750{,}000)} \quad \ldots\ldots\ldots\ldots\ldots\ldots\ldots\ldots\ldots\ldots\ldots\ldots\ldots\ldots \quad 120{,}000$$

Total apportioned supportive expense $200,000

Example (20)—Supportive Expense—(i) *Facts.* Assume the same facts as above except that X's president devotes only 5 percent of his time to the foreign operations and 95 percent of his time to the domestic operations and that X's sales manager devotes approximately 10 percent of his time to foreign sales and 90 percent of his time to domestic sales.

(ii) *Allocation.* The expenses incurred by X with respect to its worldwide activities are definitely related, and therefore allocable to X's gross income from both its foreign and domestic markets.

(iii) *Apportionment.* On the basis of the additional facts it is not acceptable to apportion the salaries of the president and the sales manager on the basis of gross receipts. It is acceptable to apportion such salaries between the statutory grouping (gross income from sources without the United States) and residual grouping (gross income from sources within the United States) on the basis of time devoted to each sales activity. Remaining expenses may still be apportioned on the basis of gross receipts. The apportionment is as follows:

Apportionment of the $200,000 expense to the statutory grouping of gross income:

President's salary: $40,000 × 5%	$2,000
Sales manager's salary: $20,000 × 10%	2,000
Remaining expenses: $140{,}000 \times \dfrac{\$500{,}000}{(\$500{,}000 + \$750{,}000)}$	$56,000
Subtotal: Apportionment of expense to statutory grouping	60,000

Apportionment of the $200,000 expense to the residual grouping of gross income:

President's salary: $40,000 × 95%	38,000
Sales manager's salary: $20,000 × 90%	18,000
Remaining expenses: $140{,}000 \times \dfrac{\$750{,}000}{(\$500{,}000 + \$750{,}000)}$	84,000
Subtotal: Apportionment of expense to residual grouping	$140,000
Total: Apportioned general and administrative expense	$200,000

Example (21)—Supportive Expense—(i) *Facts.* X, a foreign corporation doing business in the United States, is a manufacturer of metal stamping machines. X has no United States subsidiaries and no separate division to manage and oversee its business in the United States. X manufactures and sells these machines in the United States and in foreign countries A and B and has a separate manufacturing facility in each country. Sales of these machines are X's only source of income. In 1977, X incurs general and administrative expenses related to both its U.S. and foreign operations of $100,000. It has machine sales of $500,000, $1,000,000 and $1,000,000 on which it earns gross income of $200,000, $400,000 and $400,000 in the United States, country A, and country B, respectively. The income from the manufacture and sale of the machines in countries A and B is not effectively connected with X's business in the United States.

(ii) *Allocation.* The $100,000 of general and administrative expense is definitely related to the income to which it gives rise, namely a part of the gross income from sales of machines in the United States, in country A, and in country B. The expenses are allocable to this class of income,

Reg. § 1.861-8(g)

even though X's gross income from sources outside the United States is excluded income since it is not effectively connected with a U.S. trade or business.

(iii) *Apportionment.* Since X is a foreign corporation, the statutory grouping is gross income effectively connected with X's trade or business in the United States, namely gross income from sources within the United States, and the residual grouping is gross income not effectively connected with a trade or business in the United States, namely gross income from countries A and B. Since there are no facts which would require a method of apportionment other than on the basis of sales or gross income, the amount may be apportioned between the two groupings on the basis of amounts of gross income as follows:

Apportionment of general and administrative expense to the statutory grouping, gross income from sources within the United States:

$$\$100,000 \times \frac{\$200,000}{(\$200,000 + \$400,000 + \$400,000)} \dots\dots\dots\dots\dots\dots\dots\dots\dots\dots\dots\dots\dots \quad \$\ 20,000$$

Apportionment of general and administrative expense to the residual grouping, gross income from sources within the United States:

$$\$100,000 \times \frac{(\$400,000 + \$400,000)}{(\$200,000 + \$400,000 + \$400,000)} \dots\dots\dots\dots\dots\dots\dots\dots\dots\dots\dots\dots\dots \quad 80,000$$

Total apportioned general and administrative expense $100,000

Example (22)—Domestic International Sales Corporations—(i) *Facts.* X, a domestic corporation, manufactures a line of kitchenware and sells it to retailers in the United States, France, and the United Kingdom. After the Domestic International Sales Corporation (DISC) legislation was passed in 1971, X established, as of January 1, 1972, a DISC and thereafter did all of its foreign marketing through sales by the DISC. In 1977 the DISC has total sales of $7,700,000 for which X's cost of goods sold is $6,000,000. Thus, the gross income attributable to exports through the DISC is $1,700,000 ($7,700,000 − $6,000,000). Moreover, X has U.S. domestic sales of kitchenware of $12,000,000 on which it earned gross income of $900,000, and X receives royalty income from the foreign license of its kitchenware technology in the amount of $800,000. The DISC's expenses attributable to the resale of export property are $400,000 of which $300,000 qualify as export promotion expenses. X also incurs $125,000 of general and administrative expenses in connection with its domestic and foreign sales activities, and its foreign licensing activities. X and the DISC determine transfer prices charged on the basis of a single product grouping and the "50-50" combined taxable income method (without marginal costing) which permits the DISC to have a taxable income equal to 50 percent of the combined taxable income attributable to the production and sales of the export property, plus 10 percent of the DISC's export promotion expenses.

(ii) *Allocation.* For purposes of determining combined taxable income of X and the DISC from export sales, general and administrative expenses of $125,000 must be allocated to and apportioned between gross income resulting from the production and sale of kitchenware for export, and from the production and sale of kitchenware for the domestic market. The deduction of $400,000 for expenses attributable to the resale of export property is allocated solely to gross income from the production and sale of kitchenware in foreign markets.

(iii) *Apportionment.* Apportionment of expense takes place in two stages. In the first stage, for computing combined taxable income from the production and sale of export property, the general and administrative expense should be apportioned between the statutory grouping of gross income from the export of kitchenware and the residual grouping of gross income from domestic sales and foreign licenses. In the second stage, since the limitation on the foreign tax credit requires the use of a separate limitation with respect to dividends from a DISC (section 904(d)), the general and administrative expense should be apportioned between two statutory groupings, DISC dividends and foreign royalty income (for which the overall limitation is used), and the residual grouping of gross income from sales within the United States. In the first stage, in the absence of more specific or contrary information, the general and administrative expense may be apportioned on the basis of gross income in the respective groupings, as follows:

Apportionment of general and administrative expense to the statutory grouping, gross income from exports of kitchenware:

Reg. § 1.861-8(g)

Determination of Sources of Income

$$125{,}000 \times \frac{\$1{,}700{,}000}{(\$1{,}700{,}000 + \$900{,}000 + \$800{,}000)} \quad \ldots\ldots\ldots\ldots\ldots\ldots\ldots\ldots\ldots\ldots \quad \$\ 62{,}500$$

Apportionment of general and administrative expense to the residual grouping, gross income from domestic sales of kitchenware and foreign royalty income from licensing kitchenware technology:

$$125{,}000 \times \frac{(\$900{,}000 + \$800{,}000)}{(\$1{,}700{,}000 + \$900{,}000 + \$800{,}000)} \quad \ldots\ldots\ldots\ldots\ldots\ldots\ldots\ldots\ldots\ldots \quad 62{,}500$$

Total apportionment of general and administrative expense $125,000

On the basis of this apportionment, the combined taxable income, and the DISC portion of taxable income may be calculated as follows:

Gross income from exports $1,700,000

Less:

DISC expense for resale of export property	$400,000	
Apportioned general and administrative expense	62,500	
		462,500

Combined taxable income from production and export of kitchenware $1,237,500

DISC income:

50 pct. of combined taxable income	618,750
10 pct. of export promotion expense of $300,000	30,000
Total DISC income	$ 648,750
DISC income as a percentage of combined taxable income	52.4

In the second stage, in the absence of more specific or contrary information, the general and administrative expense may also be apportioned on the basis of gross income in the respective groupings. Since DISC taxable income is 52.4 percent of combined taxable income, DISC gross income is treated as 52.4 percent of the gross income from exports, $1,700,000. The apportionment follows:

Apportionment of general and administrative expense to the statutory grouping, DISC dividends:

$$125{,}000 \times \frac{(0.524 \times \$1{,}700{,}00)}{(\$1{,}700{,}000 + \$900{,}000 + \$800{,}000)} \quad \ldots\ldots\ldots\ldots\ldots\ldots\ldots\ldots\ldots\ldots \quad \$\ 32{,}750$$

Apportionment of general and administrative expense to the statutory grouping, foreign royalty income:

$$125{,}000 \times \frac{\$800{,}000}{(\$1{,}700{,}000 + \$900{,}000 + \$800{,}000)} \quad \ldots\ldots\ldots\ldots\ldots\ldots\ldots\ldots\ldots\ldots \quad \$\ 29{,}412$$

Apportionment of general and administrative expense to the residual grouping, gross income from sources within the United States:

$$125{,}000 \times \frac{(\$900{,}000 + (0.476 \times \$1{,}700{,}000))}{(\$1{,}700{,}000 + \$900{,}000 + \$800{,}000)} \quad \ldots\ldots\ldots\ldots\ldots\ldots\ldots\ldots\ldots\ldots \quad 62{,}838$$

Total apportioned general and administrative expense $125,000

(iv) This *Example (22)* applies only to DISC taxable years ending before January 1, 1987, and to distributions from a DISC or former DISC with respect to DISC or former DISC taxable years ending before January 1, 1987.

Example (23)—[Reserved]

Example (24)—[Reserved] For guidance, see § 1.861-8T(g) *Example (24).*

Example 25—Income Taxes—(i) *Facts.* X, a domestic corporation, is a manufacturer and distributor of electronic equipment with operations in states A, B, and C. X also has a branch in country Y which manufactures and distributes the same type of electronic equipment. In 1988, X has taxable income from these activities, as determined under the Code (without taking into ac-

Reg. § 1.861-8(g)

count the deduction for state income taxes), of $1,000,000, of which $200,000 is foreign source general limitation income subject to a separate limitation under section 904(d)(1)(1) ("general limitation income") and $800,000 is domestic source income. States A, B, and C each determine X's income subject to tax within their state by making adjustments to X's taxable income as determined under the Code, and then apportioning the adjusted taxable income on the basis of the relative amounts of X's payroll, property, and sales within each state as compared to X's worldwide payroll, property, and sales. The adjustments made by states A, B, and C all involve adding and subtracting enumerated items from taxable income as determined under the Code. However, in making these adjustments to taxable income, none of the states specifically exempts foreign source income as determined under the Code. On this basis, it is determined that X has taxable income of $550,000, $200,000, and $200,000 in states A, B, and C, respectively. The corporate tax rates in states A, B, and C are 10 percent, 5 percent, and 2 percent, respectively, and X has total state income tax liabilities of $69,000 ($55,000 + $10,000 + $4,000), which it deducts as an expense for federal income tax purposes.

(ii) *Allocation.* X's deduction of $69,000 for state income taxes is definitely related and thus allocable to the gross income with respect to which the taxes are imposed. Since the statutes of states A, B, and C do not specifically exempt foreign source income (as determined under the Code) from taxation and since, in the aggregate, states A, B, and C tax $950,000 of X's income while only $800,000 is domestic source income under the Code, it is presumed that state income taxes are imposed on $150,000 of foreign source income. The deduction for state income taxes is therefore related and allocable to both X's foreign source and domestic source income.

(iii) *Apportionment.* For purposes of computing the foreign tax credit limitation, X's income is comprised of one statutory grouping, foreign source general limitation gross income, and one residual grouping, gross income from sources within the United States. The state income tax deduction of $69,000 must be apportioned between these two groupings. Corporation X calculates the apportionment on the basis of the relative amounts of foreign source general limitation taxable income and U.S. source taxable income subject to state taxation. In this case, state income taxes are presumed to be imposed on $800,000 of domestic source income and $150,000 of foreign source general limitation income.

State income tax deduction apportioned to foreign source general limitation income (statutory grouping): $69,000 × ($150,000/$950,000) ...	$10,895
State income tax deduction apportioned to income from sources within the United States (residual grouping): $69,000 × ($800,000/$950,000) ...	$58,105
Total apportioned state income tax deduction	$69,000

Example 26—Income Taxes—(i) *Facts.* Assume the same facts as in *Example 25* except that the language of state A's statute and the statute's operation exempt from taxation all foreign source income, as determined under the Code, so that foreign source income is not included in adjusted taxable income subject to apportionment in state A (and factors relating to X's country Y branch are not taken into account in computing the state A apportionment fraction).

(ii) *Allocation.* X's deduction of $69,000 for state income taxes is definitely related and thus allocable to the gross income with respect to which the taxes are imposed. Since state A exempts all foreign source income by statute, state A is presumed to impose tax on $550,000 of X's $800,000 of domestic source income. X's state A tax of $55,000 is allocable, therefore, solely to domestic source income. Since the statutes of states B and C do not specifically exclude all foreign source income as determined under the Code, and since states B and C impose tax on $400,000 ($200,000 + $200,000) of X's income of which only $250,000 ($800,000 − $550,000) is presumed to be domestic source, the deduction for the $14,000 of income taxes imposed by states B and C is related and allocable to both foreign source and domestic source income.

(iii) *Apportionment.* (A) For purposes of computing the foreign tax credit limitation, X's income is comprised of one statutory grouping, foreign source general limitation gross income, and one residual grouping, gross income from sources within the United States. The deduction of $14,000 for income taxes of states B and C must be apportioned between these two groupings.

(B) Corporation X calculates the apportionment on the basis of the relative amounts of foreign source general limitation income and U.S. source income subject to state taxation.

States B and C income tax deduction apportioned to foreign source general limitation income (statutory grouping): $14,000 × ($150,000/$400,000) ...	$ 5,250

Reg. § 1.861-8(g)

Determination of Sources of Income

States B and C income tax deduction apportioned to income from sources within the United States (residual grouping):
$14,000 × ($250,000/$400,000) ... $ 8,750
Total apportioned state income tax deduction $14,000

(C) Of X's total income taxes of $69,000, the amount allocated and apportioned to foreign source general limitation income equals $5,250. The total amount of state income taxes allocated and apportioned to U.S. source income equals $63,750 ($55,000 + $8,750).

Example 27—Income Tax—(i) *Facts.* Assume the same facts as in *Example 25* except that state A, in which X has significant income-producing activities, does not impose a corporate income tax or other state tax computed on the basis of income derived from business activities conducted in state A. X therefore has a total state income tax liability in 1988 of $14,000 ($10,000 paid to state B plus $4,000 paid to state C), all of which is subject to allocation and apportionment under paragraph (b) of this section.

(ii) *Allocation.* (A) X's deduction of $14,000 for state income taxes is definitely related and allocable to the gross income with respect to which the taxes are imposed. However, in these facts, an adjustment is necessary before the aggregate state taxable incomes can be compared with U.S. source income on the federal income tax return in the manner described in *Examples 25* and *26*. Unlike the facts in *Examples 25* and *26*, state A imposes no income tax and does not define taxable income attributable to activities in state A. The total amount of X's income subject to state taxation is, therefore, $400,000 ($200,000 in state B and $200,000 in state C). This total presumptively does not include any income attributable to activities performed in state A and therefore can not properly be compared to total U.S. source taxable income reported by X for federal income tax purposes, which does include income attributable to state A activities.

(B)(1) Accordingly, before applying the method used in *Examples 25* and *26* to the facts of this example, it is necessary first to estimate the amount of taxable income that state A could reasonably attribute to X's activities in state A, and then to reduce federal taxable income by that amount.

(2) Any reasonable method may be used to attribute taxable income to X's activities in state A. For example, the rules of the Uniform Division of Income for Tax Purposes Act ("UDITPA") attribute income to a state on the basis of the average of three ratios that are based upon the taxpayer's facts—property within the state over total property, payroll within the state over total payroll, and sales within the state over total sales—and, with adjustments, provide a reasonable method for this purpose. When applying the rules of UDITPA to estimate U.S. source income derived from state A activities, the taxpayer's UDITPA factors must be adjusted to eliminate both taxable income and factors attributable to a foreign branch. Therefore, in this example all taxable income as well as UDITPA apportionment factors (property, payroll, and sales) attributable to X's country Y branch must be eliminated.

(C)(1) Since it is presumed that, if state A had had an income tax, state A would not attempt to tax the income derived by X's country Y branch, any reasonable estimate of the income that would be taxed by state A must exclude any foreign source income.

(2) When using the rules of UDITPA to estimate the income that would have been taxable by state A in these facts, foreign source income is excluded by starting with federally defined taxable income (before deduction for state income taxes) and subtracting any income derived by X's country Y branch. The hypothetical state A taxable income is then determined by multiplying the resulting difference by the average of X's state A property, payroll, and sales ratios, determined using the principles of UDITPA (after adjustment by eliminating the country Y branch factors). The resulting product is presumed to be exclusively U.S. source income, and the allocation and apportionment method described in *Example 26* must then be applied.

(3) If, for example, state A taxable income were determined to equal $550,000, then $550,000 of U.S. source income for federal income tax purposes would be presumed to constitute state A taxable income. Under *Example 26*, the remaining $250,000 ($800,000 - $550,000) of U.S. source income for federal income tax purposes would be presumed to be subject to tax in states B and C. Since states B and C impose tax on $400,000, the application of *Example 25* would result in a presumption that $150,000 is foreign source income and $250,000 is domestic source income. The deduction for the $14,000 of income taxes of states B and C would therefore be related and allocable to both foreign source and domestic source income and would be subject to apportionment.

(iii) *Apportionment.* The deduction of $14,000 for income taxes of states B and C is apportioned in the same manner as in *Example 26*. As a result, $5,250 of the $14,000 of state B and state C income taxes is apportioned to foreign source general limitation income ($14,000×

Reg. § 1.861-8(g)

$150,000/$400,000), and $8,750 ($14,000×$250,000/$400,000) of the $14,000 of state B and state C income taxes is apportioned to U.S. source income.

Example 28—Income Tax—(i) *Facts.* (A) Assume the same facts as in *Example 25* (X has $1,000,000 of taxable income for federal income tax purposes, $800,000 of which is U.S. source income and $200,000 of which is foreign source general limitation income), except that $100,000 of X's $200,000 of foreign source general limitation income consists of dividends from first-tier controlled foreign corporations ("CFCs") (as defined in section 957(a) of the Code) which derive exclusively foreign source general limitation income. X owns stock representing 10 to 50 percent of the vote and value in such CFCs.

(B) State A taxable income is computed by first making adjustments to X's federal taxable income. These adjustments result in X having a total of $1,100,000 of apportionable taxable income for state A tax purposes. None of the $100,000 of adjustments made by state A relate to the dividends paid by the CFCs. As in *Example 25*, the amount of apportionable taxable income attributable to business activities conducted in state A is determined by multiplying apportionable taxable income by a fraction (the "state apportionment fraction") that compares the relative amounts of X's payroll, property, and sales within state A with X's worldwide payroll, property and sales. An analysis of state A law indicates that state A law includes in its definition of the taxable business income of X which is apportionable to X's state A activities, dividends paid to X by its subsidiaries that are in the same business as X, but are less than 50 percent owned by X ("portfolio dividends"). The dividends received by X from the 10 to 50 percent owned first-tier CFCs, therefore, are considered to be portfolio dividends includable in apportionable business income for state A tax purposes. However, the factors of these CFCs are not included in the state A apportionment fraction for purposes of apportioning income to X's activities in the state. The comparison of X's state A factors with X's worldwide factors results in a state apportionment fraction of 50 percent. Applying this fraction to apportionable taxable income of $1,100,000, as determined under state law, results in attributing 50 percent of apportionable taxable income to state A, and produces total state A taxable income of $550,000. State A imposes an income tax at a rate of 10 percent on the amount of income that is attributed to state A, which results in $55,000 of tax imposed by state A.

(ii) *Allocation.* (A) States A, B, and C impose income taxes of $69,000 which must be allocated to the classes of gross income upon which the taxes are imposed. A portion of X's federal income tax deduction of $55,000 for state A income tax is definitely related and thus allocable to the class of gross income consisting of foreign source portfolio dividends. A definite relationship exists between a deduction for state income tax and portfolio dividends when a state includes portfolio dividends in state taxable income apportionable to the state, but determines state taxable income by applying an apportionment fraction that excludes the factors of the corporations paying those dividends. By applying a state apportionment fraction that excludes factors of the corporations paying portfolio dividends to apportionable taxable income that includes the $100,000 of foreign source portfolio dividends, $50,000 (50 percent of the $100,000) of the portfolio dividends is attributed to X's activities in state A and subjected to state A income tax. Applying the state A income tax rate of 10 percent to the $50,000 of foreign source portfolio dividends subjected to state A income tax, $5,000 of X's $55,000 total state A income tax liability is definitely related and allocable to a class of gross income consisting of the foreign source portfolio dividends. Since under the look-through rules of section 904(d)(3) the foreign source portfolio dividends from the first-tier CFCs are included within the general limitation described in section 904(d)(1)(I), the $5,000 of state A tax on foreign source portfolio dividends is allocated entirely to foreign source general limitation income and, therefore, is not apportioned. (If the total amount of state A tax imposed on foreign source portfolio dividends were to exceed the actual amount of X's state A income tax liability (for example, due to net operating losses), the actual amount of state A tax would be allocated entirely to those foreign source portfolio dividends.) After allocation of a portion of the state A tax to portfolio dividends, $50,000 ($55,000 - $5,000) of state A tax remains to be allocated.

(B) A total of $64,000 (the aggregate of the $50,000 remaining state A tax, and the $10,000 and $4,000 of taxes imposed by states B and C, respectively) is to be allocated (as provided in *Example 25*) by comparing U.S. source taxable income (as determined under the Code) with the aggregate of the state taxable incomes determined by states A, B, and C (after reducing state apportionable taxable incomes by the amount of any portfolio dividends included in apportionable taxable income to which tax has been specifically allocated). X's state A taxable income, after reduction by the $50,000 of portfolio dividends taxed by state A, equals $500,000. X also has

Reg. § 1.861-8(g)

taxable income of $200,000 and $200,000 in states B and C, respectively. In the aggregate, therefore, states A, B, and C tax $900,000 of X's income, after excluding state taxable income attributable to portfolio dividends. Since X has only $800,000 of U.S. source taxable income for federal income tax purposes, it is presumed that state income taxes are imposed on $100,000 of foreign source income. The remaining deduction of $64,000 for state income taxes is therefore related and allocable to both foreign source and domestic source income and is subject to apportionment.

(iii) *Apportionment.* For purposes of computing the foreign tax credit limitation, X's income is comprised of one statutory grouping, foreign source general limitation income, and one residual grouping, gross income from sources within the United States. The remaining state income tax deduction of $64,000 must be apportioned between these two groupings on the basis of relative amounts of foreign source general limitation taxable income and U.S. source taxable income subject to state taxation. In this case, the $64,000 of state income taxes is considered to be imposed on $800,000 of domestic source income and $100,000 of foreign source general limitation income and is apportioned as follows:

State income tax deduction apportioned to foreign source general limitation income (statutory grouping): $64,000 × ($100,000/$900,000) ...	$ 7,111
State income tax deduction apportioned to income from sources within the United States (residual grouping): $64,000 × ($800,000/$900,000) ...	$56,889
Total apportioned state income tax deduction	$64,000

Of the total state income taxes of $69,000, the amount allocated and apportioned to foreign source general limitation income equals $12,111 ($5,000+$7,111). The total amount of state income taxes allocated and apportioned to U.S. source income equals $56,889.

Example 29—Income Taxes—(i) *Facts.* (A) P, a domestic corporation, is a manufacturer and distributor of electronic equipment with operations in states F, G, and H. P also has a branch in country Y which manufactures and distributes the same type of electronic equipment. In addition, P has three wholly owned subsidiaries, US1, US2, and FS, the latter a controlled foreign corporation ("CFC") as defined in section 957(a) of the Code. P also owns stock representing 10 to 50 percent of the vote and value of various other first-tier CFCs that derive exclusively foreign source general limitation income.

(B) In 1988, P derives $1,000,000 of federal taxable income (without taking into account the deduction for state income taxes), which consists of $250,000 of foreign source general limitation income and $750,000 of U.S. source income. The foreign source general limitation income consists of a $25,000 subpart F inclusion with respect to FS, $150,000 of dividends from the other first-tier CFCs deriving exclusively foreign source general limitation income, in which P owns stock representing 10 to 50 percent of the vote and value, and $75,000 of manufacturing and sales income derived by P's U.S. operations and country Y branch. The $750,000 of U.S. source income consists of manufacturing and sales income derived by P's U.S. operations.

(C) For federal income tax purposes, US1 derives $75,000 of taxable income, before deduction for state income taxes, which consists entirely of U.S. source income. US2, a so-called "80/20" corporation described in section 861(c) (1), derives $250,000 of federal taxable income before deduction for state or foreign income taxes, all of which is derived from foreign operations and consists entirely of foreign source general limitation income. FS is not engaged in a U.S. trade or business and derives $550,000 of foreign source general limitation income before deduction for foreign income taxes.

(D) State F imposes a corporate income tax of 10 percent on P's state F taxable income, which is determined by formulary apportionment of the total taxable income attributable to P's worldwide unitary business. State F determines P's taxable income for state F tax purposes by first making adjustments to the taxable income, as determined for federal income tax purposes, of the members of the unitary business group to determine the total taxable income of the group. State F then computes P's state taxable income by attributing a portion of that unitary business taxable income to activities of P that are conducted in state F. State F does this by multiplying the unitary business taxable income (federal taxable income with state adjustments) by a fraction (the "state apportionment fraction") that compares the relative amounts of the unitary business group's payroll, property, and sales (the "factors") in state F with the payroll, property, and sales of the unitary business group. P is the only member of its unitary business group that has state F factors and that is thereby subject to state F income tax and filing requirements. State F defines the unitary business group to include any corporation more than 50 percent of which is directly or indirectly owned by a state F taxpayer and is engaged in the same unitary business. P's unitary business group, therefore, includes P, US1, US2, and FS, but does

Reg. § 1.861-8(g)

not include the 10 to 50 percent owned CFCs. The income of the unitary business group excludes intercompany dividends between members of the unitary business group and subpart F inclusions with respect to a member of the unitary business group. Dividends paid from nonmembers of the unitary group (the 10 to 50 percent owned CFCs) for state F tax purposes are referred to as "portfolio dividends" and are included in taxable income of the unitary business. None of the factors (in state F or worldwide) of the corporations paying portfolio dividends are included in the state F apportionment fraction for purposes of apportioning total taxable income of the unitary business to P's state F activities.

(E) After state adjustments to the taxable income of the unitary business group, as determined under federal tax principles, the total taxable income of P's unitary business group equals $2,000,000, consisting of $1,050,000 of P's income ($100,000 of foreign source manufacturing and sales income, $150,000 of foreign source portfolio dividends, and $800,000 of U.S. source manufacturing and sales income, but excluding the $25,000 subpart F inclusion attributable to FS since FS is a member of the unitary business group), $100,000 of US1's income (from sales made in the United States), $275,000 of US2's income (from an active business outside the United States), and $575,000 of FS's income. The differences between taxable income under federal tax principles and state F apportionable taxable income for P, US1, US2, and FS represent adjustments to taxable income under federal tax principles that are made pursuant to the tax laws of state F.

(F) The taxable income for each member of the unitary business group under federal tax principles and state law principles is summarized in the following table. (The items of income listed in the "Federal" column of the table refer to taxable income before deduction for state income tax.)

		Federal	State F
P	U.S. source income	$ 750,000	$ 800,000
	Foreign source general limitation income:		
	Portfolio dividends	150,000	150,000
	Subpart F income	25,000	0
	Manufacturing and sales income	75,000	100,000
	Total taxable income	$1,000,000	$1,050,000
US1	U.S. source income	$ 75,000	100,000
US2	Foreign source general limitation income	$ 250,000	275,000
FS	Foreign source general limitation income	$ 550,000	575,000
	Taxable income of the unitary business group		$2,000,000

(G) State F deems P to have state F taxable income of $500,000, which is determined by multiplying the total taxable income of the unitary business group ($2,000,000) by the group's state F apportionment fraction, which is assumed to be 25 percent in these facts. P's state F taxable income is then multiplied by the state F tax rate of 10 percent, resulting in a state F tax liability of $50,000. State G and state H, unlike state F, do not tax portfolio dividends. Although state G and state H apportion taxable income, respectively, on the basis of an apportionment fraction that compares state factors to total factors, state G and state H, unlike state F, do not apply a unitary business theory and consider only P's taxable income and factors in computing P's taxable income. P's taxable income under state G law equals $300,000, which is subject to a 5 percent tax rate resulting in a state G tax liability of $15,000. P's taxable income under state H law is $300,000, which is subject to a tax rate of 2 percent resulting in a state H tax liability of $6,000. P has a total federal income tax deduction for state income taxes of $71,000 ($50,000 + 15,000 + 6,000).

(ii) *Allocation.* (A) P's deduction of $71,000 for state income taxes is definitely related and allocable to the gross income with respect to which the taxes are imposed. Adjustments may be necessary, however, before aggregate state taxable incomes can be compared with U.S. source taxable income on the federal income tax return in the manner described in *Examples 25* and *26*. In allocating P's deduction for state income taxes, it is necessary first to determine the portion, if any, of the deduction that is definitely related and allocable to a particular class of gross income. A definite relationship exists between a deduction for state income tax and dividend income when a state includes portfolio dividends in state taxable income apportionable to the taxpayer's activities in the state, but determines state taxable income by applying an apportionment formula that excludes

Reg. § 1.861-8(g)

the factors of the corporations paying portfolio dividends.

(B) In this case, $150,000 of foreign source portfolio dividends are subject to a state F apportionment fraction of 25 percent, which results in a total of $37,500 of state F taxable income attributable to such dividends. As illustrated in *Example 28*, $3,750 ($150,000 × 25 percent state F apportionment percentage × 10 percent state F tax rate) of P's state F income tax is definitely related and allocable to a class of gross income consisting entirely of the foreign source portfolio dividends. Since under the look-through rules of section 904(d)(3) the foreign source portfolio dividends paid by first-tier CFCs are included within the general limitation described in section 904(d)(1)(I), the $3,750 of state F tax on foreign source portfolio dividends is allocated entirely to foreign source general limitation income and, therefore, is not apportioned.

(C) After reducing state F taxable income of the unitary business group by the taxable income attributable to portfolio dividends, P's remaining state F taxable income equals $462,500 ($500,000 − $37,500), the portion of the taxable income of the unitary business that state F attributes to P's activities in state F. Accordingly, in order to allocate and apportion the remaining $46,250 of state F tax ($50,000 of state F tax minus the $3,750 of state F tax allocated to foreign source portfolio dividends), it is necessary first to determine if state F is taxing only P's non-unitary taxable income (as defined below) or is imposing its tax partly on other unitary business income that is attributed under state F law to P's activities in state F. P's state F non-unitary taxable income is computed by applying the state F apportionment formula, solely on the basis of P's income (excluding portfolio dividends) and state F apportionment factors. If the state F taxable income (after reduction by the portfolio dividends attributed to state F) attributed to P under state F law exceeds P's non-unitary taxable income, a portion of the state F tax must be allocated and apportioned on the basis of the other unitary business income that is attributed to and taxable to P under state F law. If P's non-unitary taxable income equals or exceeds the $462,500 of remaining state F taxable income, it is presumed that state F is only taxing P's non-unitary taxable income, so that the entire amount of the remaining state F tax should be allocated and apportioned in the manner described in *Example 25*.

(D) If P's non-unitary taxable income is less than the $462,500 of remaining state F taxable income (after reduction for the $37,500 of state F taxable income attributable to portfolio dividends), it is presumed that state F is attributing to P, and taxing P upon, other unitary business income. In such a case, it is necessary to determine if state F is attributing to P, and imposing its income tax on, a part of the foreign source income that would be generally presumed under separate accounting to be the income of foreign affiliates and 80/20 companies included in the unitary group, or whether state F is limiting the income it attributes to P, and its taxation of P, to the U.S. source income that would be generally presumed under separate accounting to be the income of domestic members of the unitary group.

(E) Assume for purposes of this example that the non-unitary taxable income attributable to P equals $396,000, computed by multiplying P's state F taxable income of $900,000 (P's state F taxable income (before state F apportionment) of $1,050,000 less the $150,000 of foreign source portfolio dividends) by P's non-unitary state F apportionment fraction, which is assumed to be 44 percent. Because P's non-unitary taxable income of $396,000 is less than the $462,500 of remaining state F taxable income, state F is presumed to be attributing to P and taxing the income that would have been generally attributed under separate accounting to P's affiliates in the unitary group. To determine if state F tax is being imposed on members of the unitary group (other than P) that produce foreign source income, it is necessary to compute a hypothetical state F taxable income for all companies in the unitary group with significant U.S. operations. (For this purpose, the hypothetical group of companies with significant domestic operations is referred to as the "water's edge group.") State F is presumed to be attributing to P and taxing income that would have been generally attributable under separate accounting to foreign corporations and 80/20 companies to the extent that the remaining state F taxable income ($462,500) of P exceeds the hypothetical state F taxable income that would have been attributed under state F law to P if state F had defined the unitary group to be the water's edge group.

(F) The members of the water's edge group would have been P and US1. The unitary business income of this water's edge group is $1,000,000, the sum of $900,000 (P's state F taxable income (before state F apportionment) of $1,050,000 less the $150,000 of foreign source portfolio dividends) and $100,000 (US1's state F taxable income). For purposes of this example, the state F apportionment fraction determined on a unitary basis for this water's edge group is assumed to equal 40 percent, the average of P and US1's state F payroll, property, and sales factor ratios (the water's edge group's state F factors over its worldwide

Reg. § 1.861-8(g)

factors). Applying this apportionment fraction to the $1,000,000 of unitary business income of the water's edge group yields state F water's edge taxable income of $400,000. The excess of the remaining $462,500 of P's state F taxable income over the $400,000 of P's state F water's edge taxable income equals $62,500, and is attributable to the inclusion of US2 and FS in the unitary group. The state F tax attributable to the $62,500 of taxable income attributed to P under state F law, and that would have generally been attributed to US2 and FS under non-unitary accounting, equals $6,250 and is allocated entirely to a class of gross income consisting of foreign source general limitation income, because the income of FS and US2 consists entirely of such income. After the $6,250 of state F tax attributable to US2 and FS is subtracted from the remaining $46,250 of net state F tax, P has $40,000 of state F tax remaining to be allocated and apportioned.

(G) To the extent that the remainder of P's state F taxable income ($400,000) exceeds P's non-unitary state F taxable income ($396,000), it is presumed that state F is attributing to and imposing on P a tax on U.S. source income that would have been attributed under separate accounting to members of the water's edge group other than P. In these facts, the $4,000 difference in P's state F taxable income results from the inclusion of US1 in the unitary group. The $400 of P's state F tax attributable to this $4,000 is allocated entirely to P's U.S. source income. P's remaining $39,600 of state F tax ($40,000 of P's state F tax resulting from the attribution to P of income that would have been attributed under non-unitary accounting to other members of the water's edge group, minus $400 of state F tax attributable to US1 and allocated to P's U.S. source income) is the state F tax attributable to P's non-unitary state F taxable income that is to be allocated and apportioned together with P's state G tax of $15,000 and state H tax of $6,000 as illustrated in *Example 25*.

(H) In allocating the $60,600 of state tax liabilities ($39,600 state F tax attributable to P's non-unitary state F income + $15,000 state G tax + $6,000 state H tax) under *Example 25*, P's state taxable income in state G and state H ($300,000 + $300,000) must be added to P's non-unitary state F taxable income ($396,000). The resulting $996,000 of combined state taxable incomes is compared with $750,000 of U.S. source income on P's federal income tax return. Because P's combined state taxable incomes exceed P's federal U.S. source taxable income, it is presumed that the remaining $60,600 of P's total state income taxes is imposed in part on foreign source income. Accordingly, P's remaining deduction of $60,600

($39,600 + $15,000 + $6,000) for state income taxes is related and allocable to both P's foreign source and domestic source income and is subject to apportionment.

(iii) *Apportionment.* The $60,600 of state taxes (the remaining $39,600 of state F tax + $15,000 of state G tax + $6,000 of state H tax) must be apportioned between foreign source general limitation income and U.S. source income for federal income tax purposes. This apportionment is based upon the relative amounts of foreign source general limitation taxable income and U.S. source taxable income comprising the $996,000 of income subject to tax by the states, after reducing the total amount of income subject to tax by the portfolio dividends and the income attributed to P under state F law that would have been attributed under arm's length principles to other members of P's state F unitary business group. The deduction for the $60,600 of state income taxes is apportioned as follows:

State income tax deduction apportioned to foreign source general limitation income (statutory grouping): $60,600 × ($246,000/$996,000) . . .	$14,967
State income tax deduction apportioned to income from sources within the United States (residual grouping): $60,600 × ($750,000/$996,000) . . .	$45,633
Total apportioned state income tax deduction	$60,600

Of the total state income taxes of $71,000, the amount allocated and apportioned to foreign source general limitation income is $24,967—the sum of $14,967 of state F, state G, and state H taxes apportioned to foreign source general limitation income, $3,750 of state F tax allocated to foreign source apportionable dividend income, and the $6,250 of state F tax allocated to foreign source general limitation income as the result of state F's worldwide unitary business theory of taxation. The total amount of state income taxes allocated and apportioned to U.S. source income equals $46,033—the sum of the $400 of state F tax attributable to the inclusion of US1 in the state F unitary business group and $45,633 of combined state F, G, and H tax apportioned under the method provided in *Example 25*.

Example 30—Income Taxes—(i) *Facts.* (A) As in *Example 17* of § 1.861-8(g), X is a domestic corporation that wholly owns M, N, and O, also domestic corporations. X, M, N, and O file a consolidated income tax return. All the income of X and O is from sources within the United States, all of M's income is from sources within South America, and all of N's income is from sources within Africa. X receives no dividends from M, N,

Reg. § 1.861-8(g)

Determination of Sources of Income

See p. 20,601 for regulations not amended to reflect law changes

or O. During the taxable year, the consolidated group of corporations earned consolidated gross income of $550,000 and incurred total deductions of $370,000. X has gross income of $100,000 and deductions of $50,000, without regard to its deduction for state income tax. Of the $50,000 of deductions incurred by X, $15,000 relates to X's ownership of M; $10,000 relates to X's ownership of N; $5,000 relates to X's ownership of O; and the entire $30,000 constitutes stewardship expenses. The remainder of X's $20,000 of deductions (which is assumed not to include state income tax) relates to production of income from its plant in the United States. M has gross income of $250,000 and deductions of $100,000, which yield foreign source taxable income of $150,000. N has gross income of $150,000 and deductions of $200,000, which yield a foreign source loss of $50,000. O has gross income of $50,000 and deductions of $20,000, which yield U.S. source taxable income of $30,000.

(B) Unlike *Example 17* of § 1.861-8(g), however, X also has a deduction of $1,800 for state A income taxes. X's state A taxable income is computed by first making adjustments to the federal taxable income of X to derive apportionable taxable income for state A tax purposes. An analysis of state A law indicates that state A law also includes in its definition of the taxable business income of X which is apportionable to X's state A activities, the taxable income of M, N, and O, which is related to X's business. As in *Example 25*, the amount of apportionable taxable income attributable to business activities conducted in state A is determined by multiplying apportionable taxable income by a fraction (the "state apportionment fraction") that compares the relative amounts of payroll, property, and sales within state A with worldwide payroll, property and sales. Assuming that X's apportionable taxable income equals $180,000, $100,000 of which is from sources without the United States, and $80,000 is from sources within the United States, and that the state apportionment fraction is equal to 10 percent, X has state A taxable income of $18,000. The state A income tax of $1,800 is then derived by applying the state A income tax rate of 10 percent to the $18,000 of state A taxable income.

(ii) *Allocation and apportionment.* In accordance with § 1.1502-4, each corporation must first compute its separate taxable income for purposes of computing the consolidated limitation on the foreign tax credit. Assume that under *Example 29*, it is determined that X's deduction for state A income tax is definitely related to a class of gross income consisting of income from sources both within and without the United States, and that

the state A tax is apportioned $1,000 to sources without the United States, and $800 to sources within the United States. Under *Example 17*, without regard to the deduction for X's state A income tax, X has a separate loss of ($25,000) from sources without the United States. After taking into account the deduction for state A income tax, X's separate loss from sources without the United States is increased by the $1,000 state A tax apportioned to sources without the United States, and equals a loss of ($26,000), for purposes of computing the numerator of the consolidated foreign tax credit limitation.

Example 31—Income Taxes—(i) *Facts.* Assume that the facts are the same as in *Example 29*, except that state G requires P to adjust its federal taxable income by depreciating an asset at a different rate than is allowed P under the Internal Revenue Code for the same asset. Before using the methodology of *Example 25* to determine whether a portion of its deduction for state income taxes is allocable to a class of gross income that includes foreign source income, P recomputes its taxable income under state G law by using the rate of depreciation that it is entitled to use under the Code, and uses this recomputed amount in applying the methodology of *Example 25*.

(ii) *Allocation.* P's modification of its state G taxable income is permissible. Under the methodology of *Example 25*, this modification of state G taxable income will produce a reasonable determination of the portion (if any) of P's state income taxes that is allocable to a class of gross income that includes foreign source income.

Example 32—Income Taxes—(i) *Facts.* Assume the facts are the same as *Example 29*, except that P's state F taxable income differs from the amount of its U.S. source income under federal income tax principles solely because state F determines P's state taxable income under a worldwide unitary business theory instead of the arm's length principles applied in the Code. Before using the methodology of *Example 25* to determine whether a portion of its deduction for state income taxes is allocable to a class of gross income that includes foreign source income, P recomputes state F taxable income under the arm's length principles applied in the Code. P substitutes that recomputed amount for the amount of taxable income actually determined under state F law in applying the methodology of *Example 25*.

(ii) *Allocation.* P's modification of state F taxable income does not accurately reflect the factual relationship between the deduction for state F income tax and the income on which the tax is imposed, because there is no factual relationship

Reg. § 1.861-8(g)

between the state F income tax and the state F taxable income as recomputed under Code principles. State F does not impose its income tax upon P's income as it might have been defined under the Internal Revenue Code. Consequently, P's modification of state F taxable income is impermissible because it will not produce a reasonable determination of the portion (if any) of P's state income taxes that is allocable to a class of gross income that includes foreign source income.

Example 33—Income Taxes—(i) *Facts.* Assume the same facts as in *Example 29*, except that state G does not impose an income tax on corporations and P's non-unitary state F taxable income equals $462,500. Thus only $56,000 of state income taxes ($50,000 of state F income tax and $6,000 of state H income tax) are deductible and required to be allocated and (if necessary) apportioned. As in *Example 29*, P has $800,000 of aggregate state taxable income ($500,000 of state F taxable income and $300,000 of state H taxable income).

(ii) *Method One.* Assume that P has elected to allocate and apportion its deduction for state income tax under the safe harbor method provided in § 1.861-8(e)(6)(ii)(D)(*2*) ("Method One").

(A) *Step One—Specific allocation to foreign source portfolio dividends.* P applies the methodology of paragraph (ii) of *Example 28* to determine the portion of the deduction that must be allocated to a class of gross income consisting solely of foreign source portfolio dividends. As illustrated in paragraphs (ii) (A) and (B) of *Example 29*, $3,750 of the deduction for state F income tax is attributable to the $37,500 of foreign source portfolio dividends attributed under state F law to P's activities in state F. Thus $3,750 of P's deduction for state income tax must be specifically allocated to a class of gross income consisting solely of $37,500 of foreign source portfolio dividends. No apportionment of the $3,750 is necessary. P's adjusted state taxable income is $762,500 (aggregate state taxable income of $800,000 reduced by $37,500 of foreign source portfolio dividends). Because the remaining amount of state F taxable income ($462,500) equals P's non-unitary state F taxable income, no further specific allocation of state tax is required.

(B) *Step Two—Adjustment of U.S. source federal taxable income.* P applies the methodology illustrated in paragraph (ii) of *Example 27* (including the rules of UDITPA described therein) to determine the amount of its federal taxable income attributable to its activities in state G. Assume that P determines under this methodology that $300,000 of its federal taxable income is attributable to activities in state G. P's adjusted U.S. source federal taxable income equals $450,000 ($750,000 minus the $300,000 attributed to P's activities in state G).

(C) *Step Three—Allocation.* The portion of P's deduction for state income tax remaining to be allocated equals $52,250 ($56,000 minus the $3,750 specifically allocated to foreign source portfolio dividends). P allocates this portion by applying the methodology illustrated in paragraph (ii) of *Example 25*, as modified by paragraph (e)(6)(ii)(D)(*2*)(*iii*) of this section. Thus, P compares its adjusted state taxable income (as determined under Step One in paragraph (A) above) with an amount equal to 110% of its adjusted U.S. source federal taxable income (as determined under Step Two in paragraph (B) above). Because P's adjusted state taxable income ($762,500) exceeds 110% of P's adjusted U.S. source federal taxable income ($495,000, or 110% of $450,000), the remaining portion of P's deduction for state income tax ($52,500) must be allocated to a class of gross income that includes both U.S. and foreign source income.

(D) *Step Four—Apportionment.* P must apportion to U.S. source income the portion of the deduction that is attributable to state income tax imposed upon state taxable income in an amount equal to 110% of P's adjusted U.S. source federal taxable income. The remainder of the deduction must be apportioned to foreign source general limitation income and reduced by the amount of foreign source portfolio dividends to which the tax has been specifically allocated.

Amount of deduction to be apportioned $52,250.00
Less
Portion of deduction to be apportioned to income from sources within the United States (residual grouping):
($52,250 × ($495,000/$762,500))
.... $33,919.67
Equals
Portion of deduction to be apportioned to foreign source general limitation income (statutory grouping): $18,330.33

(iii) *Method Two.* Assume that P has elected to allocate and apportion its deduction for state income tax under the safe harbor method provided in § 1.861-8(e)(6)(ii)(D)(*3*) ("Method Two").

(A) *Step One—Specific allocation.* Step One of Method Two is the same as Step One of Method One. Therefore, as described in paragraph (A) of paragraph (ii) above, $3,750 of P's deduction for state income tax must be specifically allocated to a class of gross income consisting solely of $37,500 of foreign source portfolio dividends. No appor-

Determination of Sources of Income 46,003
See p. 20,601 for regulations not amended to reflect law changes

tionment of the $3,750 is necessary. P's adjusted state taxable income is $762,500 (aggregate state taxable income of $800,000 reduced by $37,500 of foreign source portfolio dividends).

(B) *Step Two—Adjustment of U.S. source federal taxable income.* Step Two of Method Two is the same as Step Two of Method One. Therefore, as described in paragraph (B) of paragraph (ii) above, assume that P determines that $300,000 of its federal taxable income is attributable to activities in state G. P's adjusted U.S. source federal taxable income equals $450,000 ($750,000 minus the $300,000 attributed to P's activities in state G).

(C) *Step Three—Allocation.* The portion of P's deduction for state income tax remaining to be allocated equals $52,250 ($56,000 minus the $3,750 of state F income tax specifically allocated to foreign source portfolio dividends). P allocates this portion by applying the methodology illustrated in paragraph (ii) of *Example 25,* as modified by paragraph (e)(6)(ii)(D)(*3*)(*iii*) of this section. Thus, P compares its adjusted state taxable income (as determined under Step One in paragraph (A) above) with its adjusted U.S. source federal taxable income (as determined under Step Two in paragraph (B) above). Because P's adjusted state taxable income ($762,500) exceeds P's adjusted U.S. source federal taxable income ($450,000), the remaining portion of P's deduction for state income tax ($52,500) must be allocated to a class of gross income that includes both U.S. and foreign source income.

(D) *Step Four—Apportionment.* P must apportion to U.S. source income the portion of the deduction that is attributable to state income tax imposed upon state taxable income in an amount equal to P's adjusted U.S. source federal taxable income.

Amount of deduction to be apportioned....................	$52,250.00
Less	
Portion of deduction initially apportioned to income from sources within the United States (residual grouping): $52,250 × ($450,000/$762,500).	$30,836.07
Remainder requiring further apportionment: $52,250 × ($312,500/$762,500).	$21,413.93

The remainder of $21,413.93 must be further apportioned between foreign source general limitation income and U.S. source federal taxable income in the same proportions that P's adjusted U.S. source federal taxable income and foreign source general limitation income bear to P's total federal taxable income (taking into account the adjustment of U.S. source federal taxable income).

Portion of remainder apportioned to foreign source general limitation income (statutory grouping): $21,413.93 × ($212,500/$662,500)..........	$6,868.62
Remaining state income tax deduction to be apportioned to income from sources within the United States (residual grouping): $21,413.93 × ($450,000/$662,500)..........	$14,545.31

Of P's total deduction of $56,000 for state income tax, the portion allocated and apportioned to foreign source general limitation income equals $10,618.62—the sum of $6,868.62 apportioned under Step Four and the $3,750.00 specifically allocated to foreign source portfolio dividend income under Step One. The portion of the deduction allocated and apportioned to U.S. source income equals $45,381.38—the sum of the $30,836.07 and the $14,545.31 apportioned under Step Four. [Reg. § 1.861-8.]

☐ [T.D. 6258, 10-23-57. Amended by T.D. 6892, 8-22-66; T.D. 7378, 9-29-75; T.D. 7456, 1-3-77; T.D. 7749, 12-30-80; T.D. 7939, 2-2-84; T.D. 8228, 9-9-88; T.D. 8236, 12-7-88; T.D. 8286, 1-29-90; T.D. 8337, 3-11-91; T.D. 8646, 12-21-95; T.D. 8805, 1-8-99 and T.D. 8973, 12-27-2001.]

[Reg. § 1.861-8T]

§ 1.861-8T. **Computation of taxable income from sources within the United States and from other sources and activities (Temporary).**—(a) *In general.*

(1) [Reserved]

(2) *Allocation and apportionment of deductions in general.* If an affiliated group of corporations joins in filing a consolidated return under section 1501, the provisions of this section are to be applied separately to each member in that affiliated group for purposes of determining such member's taxable income, except to the extent that expenses, losses, and other deductions are allocated and apportioned as if all domestic members of an affiliated group were a single corporation under section 864(e) and the regulations thereunder. See § 1.861-9T through § 1.861-11T for rules regarding the affiliated group allocation and apportionment of interest expense, and § 1.861-14T for rules regarding the affiliated group allocation and apportionment of expenses other than interest.

(3) through (5) [Reserved]

(b) *Allocation.*

(1) and (2) [Reserved]

Reg. § 1.861-8T(b)(1)

(3) *Supportive functions.* Deductions which are supportive in nature (such as overhead, general and administrative, and supervisory expenses) may relate to other deductions which can more readily be allocated to gross income. In such instance, such supportive deductions may be allocated and apportioned along with the deductions to which they relate. On the other hand, it would be equally acceptable to attribute supportive deductions on some reasonable basis directly to activities or property which generate, have generated, or could be reasonably expected to generate gross income. This would ordinarily be accomplished by allocating the supportive expenses to all gross income or to another broad class of gross income and apportioning the expenses in accordance with paragraph (c)(1) of this section. For this purpose, reasonable departmental overhead rates may be utilized. For examples of the application of the principles of this paragraph (b)(3) other than to expenses attributable to stewardship activities, see examples (19) through (21) of paragraph (g) of this section. See paragraph (e)(4) of this section for the allocation and apportionment of deductions attributable to stewardship activities. However, supportive deductions that are described in § 1.861-14T(e)(3) shall be allocated and apportioned in accordance with the rules of § 1.861-14T and shall not be allocated and apportioned by reference only to the gross income of a single member of an affiliated group of corporations as defined in § 1.861-14T(d).

(4) and (5) [Reserved]

(c) *Apportionment of deductions*—(1) *Deductions definitely related to a class of gross income.* Where a deduction has been allocated in accordance with paragraph (b) of this section to a class of gross income which is included in one statutory grouping and the residual grouping, the deduction must be apportioned between the statutory grouping and the residual grouping. Where a deduction has been allocated to a class of gross income which is included in more than one statutory grouping, such deduction must be apportioned among the statutory groupings and, where necessary, the residual grouping. Thus, in determining the separate limitations on the foreign tax credit imposed by section 904(d)(1) or by section 907, the income within a separate limitation category constitutes a statutory grouping of income and all other income not within that separate limitation category (whether domestic or within a different separate limitation category) constitutes the residual grouping. In this regard, the same method of *apportionment* must be used in apportioning a deduction to each separate limitation category. Also, see paragraph (f)(1)(iii) of this section with respect to the apportionment of deductions among the statutory groupings designated in section 904(d)(1). If the class of gross income to which a deduction has been allocated consists entirely of a single statutory grouping or the residual grouping, there is no need to apportion that deduction. If a deduction is not definitely related to any gross income, it must be apportioned ratably as provided in paragraph (c)(3) of this section. A deduction is apportioned by attributing the deduction to gross income (within the class to which the deduction has been allocated) which is in one or more statutory groupings and to gross income (within the class) which is in the residual grouping. Such attribution must be accomplished in a manner which reflects to a reasonably close extent the factual relationship between the deduction and the grouping of gross income. In apportioning deductions, it may be that for the taxable year there is no gross income in the statutory grouping or that deductions will exceed the amount of gross income in the statutory grouping. See paragraph (d)(1) of this section with respect to cases in which deductions exceed gross income. In determining the method of apportionment for a specific deduction, examples of bases and factors which should be considered include, but are not limited to—

(i) Comparison of units sold,

(ii) Comparison of the amount of gross sales or receipts,

(iii) Comparison of costs of goods sold,

(iv) Comparison of profit contribution,

(v) Comparison of expenses incurred, assets used, salaries paid, space utilized, and time spent which are attributable to the activities or properties giving rise to the class of gross income, and

(vi) Comparison of the amount of gross income.

Paragraph (e)(2) through (8) of this section provides the applicable rules for allocation and apportionment of deductions for interest, research and development expenses, and certain other deductions. The effects on tax liability of the apportionment of deductions and the burden of maintaining records not otherwise maintained and making computations not otherwise made shall be taken into consideration in determining whether a method of apportionment and its application are sufficiently precise. A method of apportionment described in this paragraph (c)(1) may not be used when it does not reflect, to a reasonably close extent, the factual relationship between the deduction and the groupings of income. Furthermore, certain methods of apportionment described in this paragraph (c)(1) may not be used in connection with any deduction for which an-

Reg. § 1.861-8T(b)(3)

Determination of Sources of Income

See p. 20,601 for regulations not amended to reflect law changes

other method is prescribed. The principles set forth above are applicable in apportioning both deductions definitely related to a class which constitutes less than all of the taxpayer's gross income and to deductions related to all of the taxpayer's gross income. If a deduction is not related to any class of gross income, it must be apportioned ratably as provided in paragraph (c)(3) of this section.

(2) *Apportionment based on assets.* Certain taxpayers are required by paragraph (e)(2) of this section and § 1.861-9T to apportion interest expense on the basis of assets. A taxpayer may apportion other deductions based on the comparative value of assets that generate income within each grouping, provided that such method reflects the factual relationship between the deduction and the groupings of income and is applied in accordance with the rules of § 1.861-9T(g). In general, such apportionments must be made either on the basis of the tax book value of those assets or on their fair market value. However, once the taxpayer uses fair market value, the taxpayer and all related persons must continue to use such method unless expressly authorized by the Commissioner to change methods. For purposes of this paragraph (c)(2) the term "related persons" means two or more persons in a relationship described in section 267(b). In determining whether two or more corporations are members of same controlled group under section 267(b)(3), a person is considered to own stock owned directly by such person, stock owned with the application of section 1563(e)(1), and stock owned by the application of section 267(c). In determining whether a corporation is related to a partnership under section 267(b)(10), a person is considered to own the partnership interest owned directly by such person and the partnership interest owned with the application of section 267(e)(3). In the case of any corporate taxpayer that—

(i) Uses tax book value, and

(ii) Owns directly or indirectly (within the meaning of § 1.861-11T(b)(2)(ii)) 10 percent or more of the total combined voting power of all classes of stock entitled to vote in any other corporation (domestic or foreign) that is not a member of the affiliated group (as defined in section 864(e)(5)), such taxpayer shall adjust its basis in that stock in the manner described in § 1.861-11T(b).

(3) [Reserved]

(d) *Excess of deductions and excluded and eliminated items of income.*

(1) [Reserved]

(2) *Allocation and apportionment to exempt, excluded or eliminated income*—(i) *In general.* In the case of taxable years beginning after December 31, 1986, except to the extent otherwise permitted by § 1.861-13T, the following rules shall apply to take account of income that is exempt or excluded, or assets generating such income, with respect to allocation and apportionment of deductions.

(A) *Allocation of deductions.* In allocating deductions that are definitely related to one or more classes of gross income, exempt income (as defined in paragraph (d)(2)(ii) of this section) shall be taken into account.

(B) *Apportionment of deductions.* In apportioning deductions that are definitely related either to a class of gross income consisting of multiple groupings of income (whether statutory or residual) or to all gross income, exempt income and exempt assets (as defined in paragraph (d)(2)(ii) of this section) shall not be taken into account.

For purposes of apportioning deductions which are not taken into account under § 1.1502-13 in determining gain or loss from intercompany transactions, as defined in § 1.1502-13, income from such transactions shall be taken into account in the year such income is ultimately included in gross income.

(ii) *Exempt income and exempt assets defined*—(A) *In general.* For purposes of this section, the term "exempt income" means any income that is, in whole or in part, exempt, excluded, or eliminated for federal income tax purposes. The term "exempt asset" means any asset the income from which is, in whole or in part, exempt, excluded, or eliminated for federal tax purposes.

(B) *Certain stock and dividends.* The term "exempt income" includes the portion of the dividends that are deductible under—

(*1*) Section 243(a)(1) or (2) (relating to the dividends received deduction),

(*2*) Section 245(a) (relating to the dividends received deduction for dividends from certain foreign corporations).

Thus, for purposes of apportioning deductions using a gross income method, gross income would not include a dividend to the extent that it gives rise to a dividends received deduction under either section 243(a)(1), section 243(a)(2), or section 245(a). In the case of a life insurance company taxable under section 801, the amount of such stock that is treated as tax exempt shall not be reduced because a portion of the dividends received deduction is disallowed as attributable to the policyholder's share of such dividends. See § 1.861-14T(h) for a special rule concerning the

Reg. § 1.861-8T(d)(2)

allocation of reserve expenses of a life insurance company. In addition, for purposes of apportioning deductions using an asset method, assets would not include that portion of stock equal to the portion of dividends paid thereon that would be deductible under either section 243(a)(1), section 243(a)(2), or section 245(a). In the case of stock which generates, has generated, or can reasonably be expected to generate qualifying dividends deductible under section 243(a)(3), such stock shall not constitute a tax exempt asset. Such stock and the dividends thereon will, however, be eliminated from consideration in the apportionment of interest expense under the consolidation rule set forth in § 1.861-10T(c), and in the apportionment of other expenses under the consolidation rules set forth in § 1.861-14T.

(iii) *Income that is not considered tax exempt.* The following items are not considered to be exempt, eliminated, or excluded income and, thus, may have expenses, losses, or other deductions allocated and apportioned to them:

(A) In the case of a foreign taxpayer (including a foreign sales corporation (FSC)) computing its effectively connected income, gross income (whether domestic or foreign source) which is not effectively connected to the conduct of a United States trade or business;

(B) In computing the combined taxable income of a DISC or FSC and its related supplier, the gross income of a DISC or a FSC;

(C) For all purposes under subchapter N of the Code, including the computation of combined taxable income of a possessions corporation and its affiliates under section 936(h), the gross income of a possessions corporation for which a credit is allowed under section 936(a); and

(D) Foreign earned income as defined in section 911 and the regulations thereunder (however, the rules of § 1.911-6 do not require the allocation and apportionment of certain deductions, including home mortgage interest, to foreign earned income for purposes of determining the deductions disallowed under section 911(d)(6)).

(iv) *Prior years.* For expense allocation and apportionment rules applicable to taxable years beginning before January 1, 1987, and for later years to the extent permitted by § 1.861-13T, see § 1.861-8(d)(2) (Revised as of April 1, 1986).

(e) *Allocation and apportionment of certain deductions.*

(1) [Reserved]. For further guidance, see § 1.861-8(e)(1).

(2) *Interest.* The rules concerning the allocation and apportionment of interest expense and certain interest equivalents are set forth in §§ 1.861-9T through 1.861-13T.

(3) through (11) [Reserved]. For further guidance, see § 1.861-8(e)(3) through (e)(11).

(f) *Miscellaneous matters*—(1) *Operative sections.*

(i) [Reserved]

(ii) *Separate limitations to the foreign tax credit.* Section 904(d)(1) requires that the foreign tax credit limitation be determined separately in the case of the types of income specified therein. Accordingly, the income within each separate limitation category constitutes a statutory grouping of income and all other income not within that separate limitation category (whether domestic or within a different separate limitation category) constitutes the residual grouping.

(iii) [Reserved]

(2)-(5) [Reserved]

(g) *General examples.*

Examples (1) through (23). [Reserved]

Example (24)—*Exempt, excluded, or eliminated income*—(i) *Income method*—(A) *Facts.* X, a domestic corporation organized on January 1, 1987, is engaged in a number of businesses worldwide. X owns a 25-percent voting interest in each of five corporations engaged in the business A, two of which are domestic and three of which are foreign. X incurs stewardship expenses in connection with these five stock investments in the amount of $100. X apportions its stewardship expenses using a gross income method. Each of the five companies pays a dividend in the amount of $100. X is entitled to claim the 80-percent dividends received deduction on dividends paid by the two domestic companies. Because tax exempt income is considered in the allocation of deductions, X's $100 stewardship expense is allocated to the class of income consisting of dividends from business A companies. However, because tax exempt income is not considered in the apportionment of deductions within a class of gross income, the gross income of the two domestic companies must be reduced to reflect the availability of the dividends received deduction. Thus, for purposes of apportionment, the gross income paid by the three foreign companies is considered to be $100 each, while the gross income paid by the domestic companies is considered to be $20 each. Accordingly, X has total gross income from business A companies, for purposes of apportionment, of $340. As a result, $29.41 of X's stewardship expense is apportioned to each of the foreign companies and $5.88 of X's stewardship expense is apportioned to each of the domestic companies.

Determination of Sources of Income

(ii) *Asset method*—(A) *Facts.* X, a domestic corporation organized on January 1, 1987, carries on a trade or business in the United States. X has deductible interest expense incurred in 1987 of $60,000. X owns all the stock of Y, a foreign corporation. X also owns 49 percent of the voting stock of Z, a domestic corporation. Neither Y nor Z has retained earnings and profits at the end of 1987. X apportions its interest expense on the basis of the fair market value of its assets. X has assets worth $1,500,000 that generate domestic source income, among which are tax exempt municipal bonds worth $100,000, and the stock of Z, which has a value of $500,000. The Y stock owned by X has a fair market value of $2,000,000 and generates solely foreign source general limitation income.

(B) *Allocation.* No portion of X's interest expense is directly allocable solely to identified property within the meaning of § 1.861-10T. Thus, X's deduction for interest is definitely related to all its gross income as a class.

(C) *Apportionment.* For purposes of apportioning expenses, assets that generate exempt, eliminated, or excluded income are not taken into account. Because X's municipal bonds are tax exempt, they are not taken into account in apportioning interest expense. Since X is entitled to claim under section 243 the 80-percent dividends received deduction with respect to the dividend it received from Z, 80 percent of the value of that stock is not taken into account as an asset for purposes of apportionment under the asset method. X apportions its interest deduction between the statutory grouping of foreign source general limitation income and the residual grouping of domestic source income as follows:

To foreign source general limitation income:

$$\text{Interest expense} \times \frac{\text{General limitation assets that are not tax exempt}}{\text{Worldwide assets that are not tax exempt}}$$

$$\$60,000 \times \frac{\$2,000,000}{(\$100,000 + \$900,000 + \$2,000,000)} = \$40,000$$

$$\underbrace{}_{\text{nonexempt foreign assets}}$$

$$\underbrace{\text{20 percent of Z stock value}}_{} + \underbrace{\text{nonexempt domestic assets}}_{} + \underbrace{\text{nonexempt foreign assets}}_{}$$

To domestic source income:

$$\text{Interest expense} \times \frac{\text{Domestic assets that are not tax exempt}}{\text{Worldwide assets that are not tax exempt}}$$

$$\$60,000 \times \frac{\$100,000 + \$900,000}{(\$100,000 + \$900,000 + \$2,000,000)} = \$20,000$$

$$\underbrace{\text{20 percent of Z stock value}}_{} + \underbrace{\text{nonexempt domestic assets}}_{}$$

$$\underbrace{\text{20 percent of Z stock value}}_{} + \underbrace{\text{nonexempt domestic assets}}_{} + \underbrace{\text{nonexempt foreign assets}}_{}$$

(h) *Effective dates.* In general, the rules of this section, as well as the rules of §§ 1.861-9T, 1.861-10T, 1.861-11T, 1.861-12T, and 1.861-14T shall apply for taxable years beginning after December 31, 1986. In the case of corporate taxpayers, transition rules set forth in § 1.861-13T provide for the gradual phase-in of certain [of] the provisions of this and the foregoing sections. However, the following rules are effective for taxable years commencing after December 31, 1988:

(1) Section 1.861-9T(b)(2) (concerning the treatment of certain foreign currency borrowings),

(2) Section 1.861-9T(d)(2) (concerning the treatment of interest incurred by nonresident aliens),

(3) Section 1.861-10T(b)(3)(ii) (providing an operating costs test for purposes of the nonrecourse indebtedness exception), and

Reg. § 1.861-8T(h)(3)

46,008 Determination of Sources of Income

See p. 20,601 for regulations not amended to reflect law changes

(4) Section 1.861-10T(b)(6) (concerning excess collateralization of nonrecourse borrowings).

In addition, 1.861-10T(e) (concerning the treatment of related controlled foreign corporation indebtedness) is effective for taxable years commencing after December 31, 1987. For rules for taxable years beginning before January 1, 1987, and for later years to the extent permitted by § 1.861-13T, see § 1.861-8 (Revised as of April 1, 1986). [Temporary Reg. § 1.861-8T.]

☐ [T.D. 8228, 9-9-88. Amended by T.D. 8236, 12-7-88; T.D. 8286, 1-29-90; T.D. 8337, 3-11-91; T.D. 8597, 7-12-95; T.D. 8805, 1-8-99 and T.D. 8973, 12-27-2001.]

[Reg. § 1.861-9]

§ 1.861-9. Allocation and apportionment of interest expense.—(a) through (h)(4) [Reserved]. For further guidance, see § 1.861-9T(a) through (h)(4).

(h)(5) *Characterizing stock in related persons*—(i) *General rule.* Stock in a related person held by the taxpayer or by another related person shall be characterized on the basis of the fair market value of the taxpayer's pro rata share of assets held by the related person attributed to each statutory grouping and the residual grouping under the stock characterization rules of § 1.861-12T(c)(3)(ii), except that the portion of the value of intangible assets of the taxpayer and related persons that is apportioned to the related person under § 1.861-9T(h)(2) shall be characterized on the basis of the net income before interest expense of the related person within each statutory grouping or residual grouping (excluding income that is passive under § 1.904-4(b)).

(ii) *Special rule for section 936 corporations regarding alternative minimum tax.* For purposes of characterizing stock in a related section 936 corporation in determining foreign source alternative minimum taxable income within each separate category and the alternative minimum tax foreign tax credit pursuant to section 59(a), the rules of § 1.861-9T(g)(3) shall apply and § 1.861-9(h)(5)(i) shall not apply. Thus, for taxable years beginning after December 31, 1989, and before January 1, 1994, stock in a related section 936 corporation is characterized for alternative minimum tax purposes as a foreign source passive asset because the stock produces foreign source passive dividend income under sections 861(a)(2)(A), 862(a)(2), and 904(d)(2)(A) and the regulations under those sections. For taxable years beginning after December 31, 1993, stock in a related section 936 corporation would be characterized for alternative minimum tax purposes as an asset subject to the separate limitation for section 936 corporation dividends because the stock produces foreign source dividend income that, for alternative minimum tax purposes, is subject to a separate foreign tax credit limitation under section 56(g)(4)(C)(iii)(IV). However, stock in a section 936 corporation is characterized as a U.S. source asset to the extent required by section 904(g). For the definition of the term *section 936 corporation* see § 1.861-11(d)(2)(ii).

(iii) *Effective date.* This paragraph (h)(5) applies to taxable years beginning after December 31, 1989. [Reg. § 1.861-9.]

☐ [T.D. 8916, 12-29-2000.]

[Reg. § 1.861-9T]

§ 1.861-9T. Allocation and apportionment of interest expense (Temporary).—(a) *In general.* Any expense that is deductible under section 163 (including original issue discount) constitutes interest expense for purposes of this section, as well as for purposes of §§ 1.861-10T, 1.861-11T, 1.861-12T, and 1.861-13T. The term interest refers to the gross amount of interest expense incurred by a taxpayer in a given tax year. The method of allocation and apportionment for interest set forth in this section is based on the approach that, in general, money is fungible and that interest expense is attributable to all activities and property regardless of any specific purpose for incurring an obligation on which interest is paid. Exceptions to the fungibility rule are set forth in § 1.861-10T. The fungibility approach recognizes that all activities and property require funds and that management has a great deal of flexibility as to the source and use of funds. When borrowing will generally free other funds for other purposes, and it is reasonable under this approach to attribute part of the cost of borrowing to such other purposes. Consistent with the principles of fungibility, except as otherwise provided, the aggregate of deductions for interest in all cases shall be considered related to all income producing activities and assets of the taxpayer and, thus, allocable to all the gross income which the assets of the taxpayer generate, have generated, or could reasonably have been expected to generate. In the case of the interest expense of members of an affiliated group, interest expense shall be considered to be allocable to all the gross income of the members of the group under § 1.861-11T. That section requires the members of an affiliated group to allocate and apportion the interest expense of each member of the group as if all members of such group were a single corporation. For the method of determining the interest deduction allowed to foreign corporations under section 882(c), see § 1.882-5.

Reg. § 1.861-9(a)

(b) *Interest equivalents*—(1) *Certain expenses and losses.*—(i) *General rule.* Any expense or loss (to the extent deductible) incurred in a transaction or series of integrated or related transactions in which the taxpayer secures the use of funds for a period of time shall be subject to allocation and apportionment under the rules of this section if such expense or loss is substantially incurred in consideration of the time value of money. However, the allocation and apportionment of a loss under this paragraph (b) shall not affect the characterization of such loss as capital or ordinary for other purposes of the Code and the regulations thereunder.

(ii) *Examples.* The rule of this paragraph (b)(1) may be illustrated by the following example.

Example (1). W, a domestic corporation, borrows from X two ounces of gold at a time when the spot price for gold is $500 per ounce. W agrees to return the two ounces of gold in six months. W sells the two ounces of gold to Y for $1000. W then enters into a contract with Z to purchase two ounces of gold six months in the future for $1,050. In exchange for the use of $1,000 in cash, W has sustained a loss of $50 on related transactions. This loss is subject to allocation and apportionment under the rules of this section in the same manner as interest expense.

Example (2). X, a domestic corporation with a dollar functional currency, borrows 100 pounds on January 1, 1987 for a three-year term at an interest rate greater than the applicable federal rate for dollar loans. At this time, the interest rate on the pound was approximately equal to the interest rate on dollar borrowings and the forward price on the pound, vis-a-vis the dollar, was approximately equal to the spot price. On January 1, 1987, X converted 100 pounds into dollars and entered into a currency swap that substantially hedged X's foreign currency exposure on the pound borrowing, both with respect to interest and principal. The borrowing, coupled with the swap, represents a series of related transactions in which the taxpayer secures the use of funds in its functional currency. Any net foreign currency loss on this series of transactions constitutes a loss incurred substantially in consideration of the time value of money and shall be apportioned in the same manner as interest expense. Thus, if the pound depreciates against the dollar, such that when the first payment on the pound borrowing is due the taxpayer has a currency loss on the swap payment hedging its first interest payment, such loss shall, even if the transaction is not integrated under section 988(d), be allocated and apportioned in the same manner as interest expense under the authority of this paragraph (b)(1).

Example (3). On January 1, 1987, X, a domestic corporation with a dollar functional currency, enters into a dollar interest rate swap contract with Y, a domestic counterparty. Under the terms of this agreement, X agrees to pay Y floating rate interest with respect to a notional principal amount of $100 for five years. In return, Y agrees to pay X fixed rate interest at 10 percent with respect to a notional principal amount of $100 for five years. On the same day, Y prepays the fixed leg of the swap by making a lump sum payment of $37 to X. This lump sum payment represents the present value of five $10 swap payments. Because X secures the use of $37 in this transaction, any net swap expense arising from the transaction represents an expense incurred substantially in consideration of the time value of money. Assuming this lump sum payment is not otherwise characterized as a loan from Y to X, and that X must amortize the $37 lump sum payment under the principles of Notice 89-21, any net swap expense incurred by X with respect to this transaction (*i.e.*, the excess, if any, of X's annual swap payment to Y over the annual amortization of the $37 lump sum payment that is taken into income by X) represents an expense equivalent to interest expense. The result would be the same if X sold the fixed leg to a third party for $37. While this example presents the case of a lump sum payment, the rules of paragraph (b)(1) would also apply to any transaction in which the swap payments are not substantially contemporaneous if the pricing of the transaction is materially affected by the time value of money. Thus, expenses and losses will be subject to apportionment under the rules of this section to the extent that such expenses or losses were incurred in consideration of the time value of money.

(2) *Certain foreign currency borrowings*—(i) *Rule.* If a taxpayer borrows in a nonfunctional currency at a rate of interest that is less than the applicable federal rate (or its equivalent in functional currency if the functional currency is not the dollar), any swap, forward, future, option, or similar financial arrangement (or any combination thereof) entered into by the taxpayer or by a related person (as defined in § 1.861-8T(c)(2)) that exists during the term of the borrowing and that substantially diminishes currency risk with respect to the borrowing or interest expense thereon will be presumed to constitute a hedge of such borrowing, unless the taxpayer can demonstrate on the basis of facts and circumstances that the two transactions are in fact unrelated. Under this presumption, the currency loss incurred on the borrowing during taxable years beginning af-

Reg. § 1.861-9T(b)(2)

ter December 31, 1988, in connection with hedged nonfunctional currency borrowings, reduced or increased by the gain or loss on the hedge, will be apportioned in the same manner as interest expense. This presumption can be rebutted by a showing that the financial arrangement was entered into in connection with hedging currency exposure arising in the ordinary course of a trade or business (other than with respect to the borrowing).

(ii) *Examples.* The principles of this paragraph (b)(2) may be illustrated by the following examples.

Example (1). Taxpayer has a dollar functional currency and does not have any qualified business units with a functional currency other than the dollar. On January 1, 1989, when the unit of foreign currency is worth $1, taxpayer borrows 100 units of foreign currency for a three-year period bearing interest at the annual rate of 3 percent and immediately converts the proceeds of the borrowing into dollars for use in its business. In the ordinary course of its business, taxpayer has no foreign currency exposure in this currency. In March 1989, taxpayer enters into a three-year swap agreement that covers most, but not all, of the payment of interest and principal. Because the swap substantially diminishes currency risk with respect to the borrowing, it is presumed to hedge the loan. Since taxpayer cannot demonstrate that it was hedging currency exposure arising in the ordinary course of its business (other than currency exposure with respect to the borrowing), the net currency loss on the borrowing adjusted for any gain or loss on the swap must be apportioned in the same manner as interest expense.

Example (2). Assume the same facts as in Example 1, except that the taxpayer borrows in two separate foreign currencies on terms described in Example 1 and enters into a swap agreement in a single currency that substantially diminishes the taxpayer's aggregate foreign currency risk. The net currency loss on the borrowings adjusted for any gain or loss on the swap must be apportioned in the same manner as interest expense.

(3) *Losses on sale of certain receivables*—(i) *General rule.* Any loss on the sale of a trade receivable (as defined in § 1.954-2(h)) shall be allocated and apportioned, solely for purposes of this section and §§ 1.861-10T, 1.861-11T, 1.861-12T, and 1.861-13T, in the same manner as interest expense, unless at the time of sale of the receivable, it bears interest at a rate which is at least 120 percent of the short term applicable federal rate (as determined under section 1274(d) of the Code), or its equivalent in foreign currency in the case of receivables denominated in foreign currency, determined at the time the receivable arises. This treatment shall not affect the characterization of such expense as interest for other purposes of the Internal Revenue Code.

(ii) *Exceptions.* To the extent that a loss on the sale of a trade receivable exceeds the discount on the receivable that would be computed applying to the amount received on the sale of the receivable 120 percent of the applicable federal rate (or its equivalent in foreign currency in the case of receivables denominated in foreign currency) for the period commencing with the date on which the receivable is sold and ending with the earlier of the date on which the receivable begins to bear interest at such rate or the anticipated payment date of the receivable, such excess shall not be allocated and apportioned in the same manner as interest expense but rather shall be allocated and apportioned to the gross income generated by the receivable. In cases of transfers of receivables to a domestic international sales corporation described in § 1.994-1(c)(6)(v), the rule of this paragraph (b)(3) shall not apply for purposes of computing combined taxable income. In computing the combined taxable income of a foreign sales corporation and its related supplier, loss on the sale of receivables to a third party incurred either by the foreign sales corporation or its related supplier shall offset combined taxable income, notwithstanding the provisions of this paragraph (b)(3). See § 1.924(a)-1T(g)(7).

Example. On October 1, X sells a widget to Y for $100 payable in 30 days, after which the receivable will bear stated interest at 13 percent. On October 4, X sells Y's obligation to Z for $98. Assume that the applicable federal rate for the month of October is 10 percent. Applying 120 percent of the applicable federal rate to the $98 received on the sale of the receivable, the obligation is discounted at a 12 percent rate for a period of 27 days. At this discount rate, the obligation would have sold for $99.22. Thus, 88 cents of the $2 loss on the sale is apportioned in the same manner as interest expense, and $1.22 of the $2 loss on the sale is directly allocated to the income generated on the widget sale.

(4) *Rent in certain leasing transactions.* [Reserved.]

(5) *Treatment of bond premium*—(i) *Treatment by the issuer.* If a bond or other debt obligation is issued at a premium, an amount of interest expense incurred by the issuer on that bond or other debt obligation equal to the amortized portion of that premium that is included in gross income for the year shall be allocated and appor-

tioned solely to the amortized portion of premium derived by the issuer for the year.

(ii) *Treatment by the holder.* If a bond or debt obligation is purchased at a premium, the portion of that premium amortized during the year by the holder under section 171 and the regulations thereunder shall be allocated and apportioned solely to interest income derived from the bond by the holder for the year.

(6) *Financial products that alter effective cost of borrowing*—(i) *In general.* Various derivative financial products can be part of transactions or series of transactions described in paragraph (b)(1) of this section. Such derivative financial products, including interest rate swaps, options, forwards, caps, and collars, potentially alter a taxpayer's effective cost of borrowing with respect to an actual liability of the taxpayer. For example, a taxpayer that is obligated to pay interest at a fixed rate may, in effect, pay interest at a floating rate by entering into an interest rate swap. Similarly, a taxpayer that is obligated to pay interest at a floating rate may, in effect, limit its exposure to rising interest rates by purchasing a cap. Such a taxpayer may have gains or losses associated with such derivative financial products. This paragraph (b)(6) provides rules for the treatment of gains and losses from such derivative financial products ("financial products") that are part of transactions described in paragraph (b)(1) of this section and that are used by the taxpayer to alter its effective cost of borrowing with respect to an actual liability. This paragraph (b)(6) shall only apply where the hedge and the borrowing are in the same currency and shall not apply to the extent otherwise provided in section 988 and the regulations thereunder. The allocation and apportionment of a loss under this paragraph (b) shall not affect the characterization of such loss as capital or ordinary for other purposes of the Code and the regulations thereunder.

(ii) *Definition of gain and loss.* For purposes of this paragraph (b)(6), the term "gain" refers to the excess of the amounts properly taken into income under a financial product that alters the effective cost of borrowing over the amounts properly allowed as a deduction thereunder within a given taxable year. *See, e.g.,* Notice 89-21. The term "loss" refers to the excess of the amounts properly allowed as a deduction under such a financial product over the amounts properly taken into income thereunder within a given taxable year.

(iii) *Treatment of gain or loss on the disposition of a financial product.* [Reserved.]

(iv) *Entities that are not financial services entities.* An entity that does not constitute a financial services entity within the meaning of § 1.904-4(e)(3) shall treat gains and losses on financial products described in paragraph (b)(6)(i) of this section as follows.

(A) *Losses.* Losses on any financial product described in paragraph (b)(6)(i) of this section shall be apportioned in the same manner as interest expense whether or not such financial product is identified by the taxpayer under paragraph (b)(6)(iv)(C) of this section as a liability hedge.

(B) *Gains.* Gains on any financial product described in paragraph (b)(6)(i) of this section shall reduce the taxpayer's total interest expense that is subject to apportionment, but only if such financial product is identified by the taxpayer under paragraph (b)(6)(iv)(C) of this section as a liability hedge. Such reduction is accomplished by directly allocating interest expense to the income derived from such a financial product.

(C) *Identification of financial products.* A taxpayer can identify a financial product described in paragraph (b)(6)(i) of this section as hedging a particular interest-bearing liability (or any group of such liabilities) by clearly identifying on its books and records on the same day that it becomes a party to such arrangement that such arrangement hedges a given liability (or group of liabilities). In the case of a partial hedge, such identification shall apply to only that part of the liability that is hedged. If the taxpayer clearly identifies on its books and records a financial product as a hedge of an interest-bearing asset (or any group of such assets), it will create a rebuttable presumption that such financial product is not described in paragraph (b)(6)(i) of this section. A taxpayer may identify a hedge as relating to an anticipated liability, provided that such liability is in fact incurred within 120 days following the date of such identification. Gains and losses on such an anticipatory arrangement accruing prior to the time at which the liability is incurred shall constitute an adjustment to interest expense.

(v) *Financial services entities.* [Reserved.]

(vi) *Dealers.* The rule of paragraph (b)(6)(iv) of this section shall not apply to a person acting in its capacity as a regular dealer in the financial products described in paragraph (b)(6)(i) of this section. Instead, losses sustained by a regular dealer in connection with such financial products shall be allocated to the class of gross income from such arrangements. Gains of a regular dealer in notional principal contracts are governed by the rules of § 1.863-7T(b). Amounts received or accrued by any person from any financial product that is integrated as specified in Notice 89-90 with an asset shall not be treated as amounts received or accrued by a person acting in

Reg. § 1.861-9T(b)(6)

its capacity as a regular dealer in financial products.

(vii) *Examples*. The principles of this paragraph (b)(6) may be illustrated by the following examples.

Example (1). X is not a financial services entity or regular dealer in the financial products described in paragraph (b)(6)(i) of this section and has a dollar functional currency. In 1990, X incurred a total of $200 of interest expense. On January 1, 1990, X entered into an interest rate swap agreement with Y, in order to hedge its interest rate exposure with respect to a pre-existing floating rate liability. On the same day, X properly identified the agreement as a hedge of such liability. Under the agreement, X is required to pay Y an amount equal to a fixed rate of 10 percent on a notional principal amount of $1,000. Y is required to pay X an amount equal to a floating rate of interest on the same notional principal amount. Under the agreement, X received from Y during 1990 a net payment of $25. Because X identified the swap agreement as a liability hedge under the rules of paragraph (b)(6)(iv)(C), X may effectively reduce its total allocable interest expense for 1990 to $175 by directly allocating $25 of interest expense to the swap income. Had X not properly identified the swap as a liability hedge, this swap payment would have been treated as domestic source income in accordance with the rule of § 1.863-7T(b).

Example (2). Assume the same facts as Example (1), except that X did not properly identify the agreement as a liability hedge on January 1, 1990. In 1990, X made a net payment of $25 to Y under the swap agreement. This swap payment is allocated and apportioned in the same manner as interest expense under the rules of paragraph (b)(6)(iv)(A).

(viii) *Effective dates*—(A) *Losses*. The rules of this paragraph (b)(6) shall apply to losses on any transaction described in paragraph (b)(6)(i) of this section that was entered into after September 14, 1988.

(B) *Gains*. Except as provided in paragraph (b)(6)(viii)(C) of this section, the rules of this paragraph (b)(6) shall apply to any gain that was realized on any transaction described in paragraph (b)(6)(i) of this section that was entered into after August 11, 1989.

(C) *Exception for interim gains*. Taxpayers shall be permitted to apply the rules of this paragraph (b)(6) to any gain that was realized on any transaction described in paragraph (b)(6)(i) of this section that was entered into after September 14, 1988 and on or before August 11, 1989 if the taxpayer can demonstrate to the satisfaction of the Commissioner that substantially all of the arrangements described in paragraph (b)(6)(i) of this section to which the taxpayer became a party during that interim period were identified on the taxpayer's books and records with the liabilities of the taxpayer in a substantially contemporaneous manner and that all losses and expenses that are subject to the rules of this paragraph (b)(6) were treated in the same manner as interest expense. For this purpose, arrangements that were identified in a substantially contemporaneous manner with the taxpayer's assets shall be ignored.

(7) *Foreign currency gain or loss*. In addition to the rules of paragraph (b)(1), (b)(2), and (b)(6) of this section, any foreign currency loss that is treated as an adjustment to interest expense under regulations issued under section 988 shall be allocated and apportioned in the same manner as interest expense. Any foreign currency gain that is treated as an adjustment to interest expense under regulations issued under section 988 shall offset apportionable interest expense.

(c) *Allowable deductions*. In order for an interest expense to be allocated and apportioned, it must first be determined that the interest expense is currently deductible. A number of provisions in the Code disallow or suspend deductions of interest expense or require the capitalization thereof.

(1) *Disallowed deductions*. A taxpayer does not allocate and apportion interest expense under this section that is permanently disallowed as a deduction by operation of section 163(h), section 265, or any other provision or rule that permanently disallows the deduction of interest expense.

(2) *Section 263A*. Section 263A requires the capitalization of interest expense that is allocable to designated types of property. Any interest expense that is capitalized under section 263A does not constitute deductible interest expense for purposes of this section. Furthermore, interest expense capitalized in inventory or depreciable property is not separately allocated and apportioned when the inventory is sold or depreciation is allowed. Capitalized interest expense is effectively allocated and apportioned as part of, and in the same manner as, the cost of goods sold, amortization, or depreciation deduction.

(3) *Section 163(d)*. Section 163(d) suspends the deduction for interest expense to the extent that it exceeds net investment income. In the year that suspended investment interest expense becomes allowable under the rules of section 163(d), that interest expense is apportioned under rules set forth in paragraph (d)(1) of this section as though it were incurred in the taxable year in which the expense is deducted.

Reg. § 1.861-9T(b)(7)

(4) *Section 469*—(i) *General rule.* Section 469 suspends the deduction of passive activity losses to the extent that they exceed passive activity income for the year. Passive activity losses may consist in part of interest expense properly allocable to passive activity. In the year that suspended interest expense becomes allowable as a deduction under the rules of section 469, that interest expense is apportioned under rules set forth in paragraph (d)(1) of this section as though it were incurred in the taxable year in which the expense is deducted.

(ii) *Identification of the interest component of a suspended passive loss.* A suspended passive loss may consist of a variety of items of expense other than interest expense. Suspended interest expense for any taxable year is computed by multiplying the total suspended passive loss for the year by a fraction, the numerator of which is passive interest expense for the year (determined under regulations issued under section 163) and the denominator of which is total passive expenses for the year. The amount of the suspended interest expense that is considered to be deductible in a subsequent taxable year is computed by multiplying the amount of any cumulative suspended interest expense (reduced by suspended interest expense allowed as a deduction in prior taxable years) times a fraction, the numerator of which is the portion of cumulative suspended passive losses that become deductible in the taxable year and the denominator of which is the cumulative suspended passive losses for prior taxable years (reduced by suspended passive losses allowed as deductions in prior taxable years).

(iii) *Example.* The rules of this paragraph (c)(4) may be illustrated by the following example.

Example. On January 1, 1987, A, a United States citizen, invested in a passive activity. In 1987, the passive activity generated no passive income and $100 in passive losses, all of which were suspended by operation of section 469. The suspended loss included $10 of suspended interest expense. In 1988, the passive activity generated $50 in passive income and $150 in passive expenses which included $30 of interest expense. The entire $100 passive loss was suspended in 1988 and included $20 of interest expense ($100 suspended passive loss × $30 passive interest expense / $150 total passive expenses). Thus, at the end of 1988, A had total suspended passive losses of $200, including $30 of suspended interest expense. In 1989, the passive activity generated $100 in passive income and no passive expenses. Thus, $100 of A's cumulative suspended passive loss was therefore allowed in 1989. The $100 of deductible passive loss includes $15 of suspended interest expense ($30 cumulative suspended interest expense × $100 of cumulative suspended passive losses allowable in 1989 / $200 of total cumulative suspended passive losses). The $15 of interest expense is apportioned under the rules of paragraph (d) of this section as though it were incurred in 1989.

(d) *Apportionment rules for individuals, estates, and certain trusts*—(1) *United States individuals.* In the case of taxable years beginning after December 31, 1986, individuals generally shall apportion interest expense under different rules according to the type of interest expense incurred. The interest expense of individuals shall be characterized under the regulations issued under section 163. However, in the case of an individual whose foreign source income (including income that is excluded under section 911) does not exceed a gross amount of $5,000, the apportionment of interest expense under this section is not required. Such an individual's interest expense may be allocated entirely to domestic source income.

(i) *Interest incurred in the conduct of a trade or business.* An individual who incurs business interest described in section 163(h)(2)(A) shall apportion such interest expense using an asset method by reference to the individual's business assets.

(ii) *Investment interest.* An individual who incurs investment interest described in section 163(h)(2)(B) shall apportion that interest expense on the basis of the individual's investment assets.

(iii) *Interest incurred in a passive activity.* An individual who incurs passive activity interest described in section 163(h)(2)(C) shall apportion that interest expense on the basis of the individual's passive activity assets. Individuals who receive a distributive share of interest expense incurred in a partnership are subject to special rules set forth in paragraph (e) of this section.

(iv) *Qualified residence and deductible personal interest.* Individuals who incur qualified residence interest described in section 163(h)(2)(D) shall apportion that interest expense under a gross income method, taking into account all income (including business, passive activity, and investment income) but excluding income that is exempt under section 911. For purposes of this section, any qualified residence that is rented shall be considered to be a business asset for the period in which it is rented, with the result that the interest on such a residence is not apportioned under this subdivision (iv) but instead under subdivisions (i) or (iii) of this paragraph (d)(1). To

Reg. § 1.861-9T(d)(1)

Determination of Sources of Income

See p. 20,601 for regulations not amended to reflect law changes

the extent that personal interest described in section 163(h)(2) remains deductible under transitional rules, individuals shall apportion such interest expense in the same manner as qualified residence interest.

(v) *Example.* The following example illustrates the principles of this section.

Example—(i) *Facts.* A is a resident individual taxpayer engaged in the active conduct of a trade or business, which A operates as a sole proprietor. A's business generates only domestic source income. A's investment portfolio consists of several less than 10 percent stock investments. Certain stocks in which A's adjusted basis is $40,000 generate domestic source income and other stocks in which A's adjusted basis is $60,000 generate foreign source passive income. In addition, A owns his personal residence, which is subject to a mortgage in the amount of $100,000. All interest expense incurred with respect to A's mortgage is qualified residence interest for purposes of section 163(h)(2)(D). A's other indebtedness consists of a bank loan in the amount of $40,000. Under the regulations issued under section 163(h), it is determined that the proceeds of the $40,000 loan were divided equally between A's business and his investment portfolio. In 1987, the gross income of A's business, before the apportionment of interest expense, was $50,000. A's investment portfolio generated $4,000 in domestic source income and $6,000 in foreign source passive income. All of A's debt obligations bear interest at the annual rate of 10 percent.

(ii) *Analysis of business interest.* Under section 163(h) of the Code, $2,000 of A's interest expense is attributable to his business. Under the rules of paragraph (d)(1)(i), such interest must be apportioned on the basis of the business assets. Applying the asset method described in paragraph (g) of this section, it is determined that all of A's business assets generate domestic income and, therefore, constitute domestic assets. Thus, the $2,000 in interest expense on the business loan is allocable to domestic source income.

(iii) *Analysis of investment interest.* Under section 163(h) of the Code, $2,000 of A's interest expense is investment interest. Under the rules of paragraph (d)(1)(ii) of this section, such interest must be apportioned on the basis of investment assets. Applying the asset method, A's investment assets consist of stock generating domestic source income with an adjusted basis of $40,000 and stock generating foreign source passive income with an adjusted basis of $60,000. Thus, 40 percent ($800) of A's investment interest is apportioned to domestic source income and 60 percent ($1,200) of A's investment interest is apportioned to foreign source passive income for purposes of section 904.

(iv) *Analysis of qualified residence interest.* The $10,000 of qualified residence interest expense is apportioned under the rules of paragraph (d)(1)(iv) of this section on the basis of all of A's gross income. A's gross income consists of $60,000, $54,000 of which is domestic source and $6,000 of which is foreign source passive income. Thus, $9,000 of A's qualified residence interest is apportioned to domestic source income and $1,000 of A's qualified residence interest is apportioned to foreign source passive income.

(2) *Nonresident aliens*—(i) *General rule.* For taxable years beginning on or after January 1, 1988, interest expense incurred by a nonresident alien shall be considered to be connected with income effectively connected with a United States trade or business only to the extent that interest expense is incurred with respect to liabilities that—

(A) Are entered on the books and records of the United States trade or business when incurred, or

(B) Are secured by assets that generate such effectively connected income.

(ii) *Limitations*—(A) *Maximum debt capitalization.* Interest expense incurred by a nonresident alien is not considered to be connected with effectively connected income to the extent that it is incurred with respect to liabilities that exceed 80 percent of the gross assets of the United States trade or business.

(B) *Collateralization by other assets.* Interest expense on indebtedness that is secured by specific assets (not including the general credit of the nonresident alien) other than the assets of the United States trade or business shall not be considered to be connected with effectively connected income.

(3) *Estates and trusts.* Estates shall be treated in the same manner as individuals. In the case of a trust that is beneficially owned by individuals and is a complex trust, the trust shall be treated in the same manner as individuals under the rules of paragraph (d) of this section, except that no de minimis amount shall apply. In the case of a trust that is beneficially owned by one or more corporations, the trust shall be treated either as a partnership or as a corporation depending on how the trust is characterized under the rules of section 7701 and the regulations thereunder.

(e) *Partnerships*—(1) *In general*—*aggregate rule.* A partner's distributive share of the interest expense of a partnership that is directly allocable

Reg. § 1.861-9T(d)(2)

under § 1.861-10T to income from specific partnership property shall be treated as directly allocable to the income generated by such partnership property. Subject to the exceptions set forth in paragraph (e)(4), a partner's distributive share of the interest expense of a partnership that is not directly allocable under § 1.861-10T generally is considered related to all income producing activities and assets of the partner and shall be subject to apportionment under the rules described in this paragraph. For purposes of this section, a partner's percentage interest in a partnership shall be determined by reference to the partner's interest in partnership income for the year. Similarly, a partner's pro rata share of partnership assets shall be determined by reference to the partner's interest in partnership income for the year.

(2) *Corporate partners whose interest in the partnership is 10 percent or more.* A corporate partner shall apportion its distributive share of partnership interest expense by reference to the partner's assets, including the partner's pro rata share of partnership assets, under the rules of paragraph (f) of this section if the corporate partner's direct and indirect interest in the partnership (as determined under the attribution rules of section 318) is 10 percent or more. A corporation using the tax book value method of apportionment shall use the partnership's inside basis in its assets, adjusted to the extent required under § 1.861-10T(d)(2). A corporation using the fair market value method of apportionment shall use the fair market value of the partnership's assets, adjusted to the extent required under § 1.861-10T(d)(2).

(3) *Individual partners who are general partners or who are limited partners with an interest in the partnership of 10 percent or more.* An individual partner is subject to the rules of this paragraph (e)(3) if either the individual is a general partner or the individual's direct and indirect interest (as determined under the attribution rules of section 318) in the partnership is 10 percent or more. The individual shall first classify his or her distributive share of partnership interest expense as interest incurred in the active conduct of a trade or business, as passive activity interest, or as investment interest under regulations issued under sections 163 and 469. The individual must then apportion his or her interest expense (including the partner's distributive share of partnership interest expense) under the rules of paragraph (d) of this section. Each such individual partner shall take into account his or her distributive share of partnership gross income or pro rata share of the partnership assets in applying such rules. An individual using the tax book value method of apportionment shall use the partnership's inside basis in its assets, adjusted to the extent required under § 1.861-10T(d)(2). An individual using the fair market value method of apportionment shall use the fair market value of the partnership's assets, adjusted to the extent required under § 1.861-10T(d)(2).

(4) *Less than 10 percent limited partners and less than 10 percent corporate general partners—entity rule—*(i) *Partnership interest expense.* A limited partner (whether individual or corporate) or corporate general partner whose direct and indirect interest (as determined under the attribution rules of section 318) in the partnership is less than 10 percent shall directly allocate its distributive share of partnership interest expense to its distributive share of partnership gross income. Under § 1.904-7(i)(2) of the regulations, such a partner's distributive share of foreign source income of the partnership is treated as passive income (subject to the high taxed income exception of section 904(d)(2)(F)), except in the case of high withholding tax interest or income from a partnership interest held in the ordinary course of the partner's active trade or business, as defined in § 1.904-7(i)(2). A partner's distributive share of partnership interest expense (other than partnership interest expense that is directly allocated to identified property under § 1.861-10T) shall be apportioned in accordance with the partner's relative distributive share of gross foreign source income in each limitation category and of domestic source income from the partnership. To the extent that partnership interest expense is directly allocated under § 1.861-10T, a comparable portion of the income to which such interest expense is allocated shall be disregarded in determining the partner's relative distributive share of gross foreign source income in each limitation category and domestic source income. The partner's distributive share of the interest expense of the partnership that is directly allocable under § 1.861-10T shall be allocated according to the treatment, after application of § 1.904-7(i)(2), of the partner's distributive share of the income to which the expense is allocated.

(ii) *Other interest expense of the partner.* For purposes of apportioning other interest expense of the partner on an asset basis, the partner's interest in the partnership, and not the partner's pro rata share of partnership assets, is considered to be the relevant asset. The value of this asset for apportionment purposes is either the tax book value or fair market value of the partner's partnership interest, depending on the method of apportionment used by the taxpayer. This amount of a partner's interest in the partnership is allocated among various limitation categories in the same manner as partnership interest

Reg. § 1.861-9T(e)(4)

expense (that is not directly allocable under § 1.861-10T) is apportioned in subdivision (i) of this paragraph (e)(4). If the partner uses the tax book value method of apportionment, the partner's interest in the partnership must be reduced, for this purpose, to the extent that the partner's basis consists of liabilities that are taken into account under section 752. Under either the tax book value or fair market value method of apportionment, for purposes of this section only, the value of the partner's interest in the partnership must be reduced by the principal amount of any indebtedness of the partner the interest on which is directly allocated to its partnership interest under § 1.861-10T.

(5) *Tiered partnerships.* If a partnership is a partner in another partnership, the distributive share of interest expense of a lower-tier partnership that is subject to the rules of paragraph (e)(4) shall not be reapportioned in the hands of any higher-tier partner. However, the distributive share of interest expense of lower-tier partnership that is subject to the rules of paragraph (e)(2) or (3) shall be apportioned by the partner of the higher-tier partnership or by any higher-tier partnership to which the rules of paragraph (e)(4) apply, taking into account the partner's indirect pro rata share of the lower-tier partnership's income or assets.

(6) *Example*—(i) *Facts.* A, B, and C are partners in a limited partnership. A is a corporate general partner, owns a 5 percent interest in the partnership, and has an adjusted basis in its partnership interest, determined without regard to section 752 of the Code, of $5. A's investment in the partnership is not held in the ordinary course of the taxpayer's active trade or business, as defined in § 1.904-7(i)(2). B, a corporate limited partner, owns a 70 percent interest in the partnership, and has an adjusted basis in its partnership interest, determined without regard to section 752 of the Code, of $70. C is an individual limited partner, owns a 25 percent interest in the partnership, and has an adjusted basis in the partnership interest, determined without regard to section 752 of the Code, of $25. The partners' interests in the profits and losses of the partnership conform to their respective interests. None of the interest expense incurred directly by any of the partners is directly allocable to their partnership interest under § 1.861-10T. The ABC partnership's sole assets are two apartment buildings, one domestic and the other foreign. The domestic building has an adjusted inside basis of $600 and the foreign building has an adjusted inside basis of $500. Each of the buildings is subject to a nonrecourse liability in the amount of $500. The ABC partnership's total interest expense for the taxable year is $120, both nonrecourse liabilities bearing interest at the rate of 12 percent. The indebtedness on the domestic building qualifies for direct allocation under the rules of § 1.861-10T. The indebtedness on the foreign building does not so qualify. The partnership incurred no foreign taxes. The partnership's gross income for the taxable year is $360, consisting of $100 in foreign source income and $260 in domestic source income. Under § 1.752-1(e), the nonrecourse liabilities of the partnership are allocated among the partners according to their share of the partnership profits. Accordingly, the adjusted basis of A, B, and C in their respective partnership interests (for other than apportionment purposes) is, respectively, $55, $770, and $275.

(ii) *Determination of the amount of partnership interest expense that is subject to allocation and apportionment.* Interest on the nonrecourse loan on the domestic building is, under § 1.861-10T, directly allocable to income from that investment. The interest expense is therefore directly allocable to domestic income. Interest on the nonrecourse loan on the foreign building is not directly allocable. The interest expense is therefore subject to allocation and apportionment. Thus, $60 of interest expense is directly allocable to domestic income and $60 of interest expense is subject to allocation and apportionment.

(iii) *Analysis for Partner A.* A's distributive share of the partnership's gross income is $18, which consists of $5 in foreign source income and $13 in domestic source income. A's distributive share of the ABC interest expense is $6, $3 of which is directly allocable to domestic income and $3 of which is subject to apportionment. After direct allocation of qualifying interest expense, A's distributive share of the partnership's gross income consists of $5 in foreign source income and $10 in domestic source income. Because A is a less than 10 percent corporate partner, A's distributive share of any foreign source partnership income is considered to be passive income. Accordingly, in apportioning the $3 of partnership interest expense that is subject to apportionment on a gross income method, one-third ($1) is apportioned to foreign source passive income and two-thirds ($2) is apportioned to domestic source income. In apportioning its other interest expense, A uses the tax book value method. A's adjusted basis in A's partnership interest ($55) includes A's share of the partnership's liabilities ($50), which are included in basis under section 752. For purposes of apportioning other interest expense, A's adjusted basis in the partnership must be reduced to the extent of such liabilities. Thus, A's adjusted basis in the partnership, for purposes of apportionment, is $5. For the purpose of apportioning

Reg. § 1.861-9T(e)(5)

A's other interest expense, this $5 in basis is characterized one-third as a foreign passive asset and two-thirds as a domestic asset, which is the ratio determined in paragraph (e)(4)(i).

(iv) *Analysis for Partner B.* B's distributive share of the ABC interest expense is $84, $42 of which is directly allocable to domestic income and $42 of which is subject to apportionment. As a corporate limited partner whose interest in the partnership is 10 percent or more, B is subject to the rules of paragraph (e)(2) and paragraph (f) of this section. These rules require that a corporate partner apportion its distributive share of partnership interest expense at the partner level on the asset method described in paragraph (g) of this section by reference to its corporate assets, which include, for this purpose, 70 percent of the partnership's assets, adjusted in the manner described in § 1.861-10T(e) to reflect directly allocable interest expense.

(v) *Analysis for Partner C.* C's distributive share of the ABC interest expense is $30, $15 of which is directly allocable to domestic income and $15 of which is subject to apportionment. As an individual limited partner whose interest in the partnership is 10 percent or more, C is subject to the rules of paragraph (e)(3) of this section. These rules require that an individual's share of partnership interest expense be classified under regulations issued under section 163(h) and then apportioned under the rules applicable to individuals, which are set forth in paragraph (d) of this section.

(7) *Foreign partners.* The distributive share of partnership interest expense of a nonresident alien who is a partner in a partnership shall be considered to be connected with effectively connected income based on the percentage of the assets of the partnership that generate effectively connected income. No interest expense directly incurred by the partner may be allocated and apportioned to effectively connected income derived by the partnership.

(f) *Corporations*—(1) *Domestic corporations.* Domestic corporations shall apportion interest expense using the asset method described in paragraph (g) of this section and the applicable rules of §§ 1.861-10T through 1.861-13T.

(2) *Foreign branches of domestic corporations.* In the application of the asset method described in paragraph (g) of this section, a domestic corporation shall—

(i) Take into account the assets of any foreign branch, translated according to the rules set forth in paragraph (g) of this section, and

(ii) Combine with its own interest expense any deductible interest expense incurred by a branch, translated according to the rules of section 987 and the regulations thereunder.

For purposes of computing currency gain or loss on any remittance from a branch or other qualified business unit (as defined in § 1.989(a)-1T) under section 987, the rules of this paragraph (f) shall not apply. The branch shall compute its currency gain or loss on remittances by taking into account only its separate expenses and its separate income.

Example—(i) *Facts.* X is a domestic corporation which operates B, a branch doing business in a foreign country. In 1988, without regard to branch B, X has gross domestic source income of $1,000 and gross foreign source general limitation income of $500 and incurs $200 of interest expense. Using the tax book value method of apportionment, X, without regard to branch B, determines the value of its assets that generate domestic source income to be $6,000 and the value of its assets that generate foreign source general limitation income to be $1,000. B constitutes a qualified business unit within the meaning of section 989 with a functional currency other than the U.S. dollar and uses the profit and loss method prescribed by section 987. Applying the translation rules of section 987, B earned $500 of gross foreign general limitation income and incurred $100 of interest expense. B incurred no other expenses. For 1988, the average functional currency book value of B's assets that generate foreign general limitation income translated at the year-end rate for 1988 is $3,000.

(ii) *Computation of net income.* The combined assets of X and B for 1988 (averaged under the rules of § 1.861-9T(g)(3)) consist 60 percent of assets generating domestic source income and 40 percent of assets generating foreign source general limitation income. The combined interest expense of both X and B is $300. Thus, $180 of the combined interest expense is apportioned to domestic source income and $120 is apportioned to the foreign source income, yielding net domestic source income of $820 and net foreign source general limitation income of $880.

(iii) *Computation of currency gain or loss.* For purposes of computing currency gain or loss on branch remittances, B takes into account only its gross income and its separate expenses. In 1988, B therefore has a net amount of income in foreign currency units equal in value to $400. Gain or loss on remittances shall be computed by reference to this amount.

(3) *Controlled foreign corporations*—(i) *In general.* For purposes of computing subpart F income and computing earnings and profits for all other federal tax purposes, the interest expense of

a controlled foreign corporation may be apportioned either using the asset method described in paragraph (g) of this section or using the modified gross income method described in paragraph (j) of this section, subject to the rules of subdivisions (ii) and (iii) of this paragraph (f)(2). However, the gross income method described in paragraph (j) of this section is not available to any controlled foreign corporation if a United States shareholder and the members of its affiliated group (as defined in § 1.861-11T(d)) constitute controlling shareholders of such controlled foreign corporation and such affiliated group elects the fair market value method of apportionment under paragraph (g) of this section.

(ii) *Manner of election.* The election to use the asset method described in paragraph (g) of this section or the modified gross income method described in paragraph (j) of this section may be made either by the controlled foreign corporation or by the controlling United States shareholders on behalf of the controlled foreign corporation. The term "controlling United States shareholders" means those United States shareholders (as defined in section 951(b)) who, in aggregate, own (within the meaning of section 958(a)) greater than 50 percent of the total combined voting power of all classes of stock of the foreign corporation entitled to vote. In the case of a controlled foreign corporation in which the United States shareholders own stock representing more than 50 percent of the value of the stock in such corporation, but less than 50 percent of the combined voting power of all classes of stock in such corporation, the term "controlling United States shareholders" means all the United States shareholders (as defined in section 951(b)) who own (within the meaning of section 958(a)) stock of the controlled foreign corporation. All United States shareholders are bound by the election of either the controlled foreign corporation or the controlling United States shareholders. The election shall be made by filing a written statement described in § 1.964-1(c)(3)(ii) at the time and in the manner described therein and providing a written notice described in § 1.964-1(c)(3)(iii), except that no such written statement or notice is required to be filed or sent before March 13, 1989.

(iii) *Consistency requirement.* The same method of apportionment must be employed by all controlled foreign corporations in which a United States taxpayer and the members of its affiliated group (as defined in § 1.861-11T(d)) constitute controlling United States shareholders. A controlled foreign corporation that is required by this paragraph (f)(3)(iii) to utilize a particular method of apportionment must do so with respect to all United States shareholders.

(iv) *Stock characterization.* Pursuant to § 1.861-12T(c)(2), the stock of a controlled foreign corporation shall be characterized in the hands of any United States shareholder using the same method that the controlled foreign corporation uses to apportion its interest expense.

(4) *Other relevant provisions.* Affiliated groups of corporations are subject to special rules set forth in § 1.861-11T. Section 1.861-12T sets forth rules relating to basis adjustments for stock in nonaffiliated 10 percent owned corporations, special rules relating to the consideration and characterization of certain assets in the apportionment of interest expense, and to other special rules pertaining to the apportionment of interest expense. Section 1.861-13T contains transition rules limiting the application of the rules of §§ 1.861-8T through 1.861-12T, which are otherwise applicable to taxable years beginning after 1986. In the case of an affiliated group of corporations as defined in § 1.861-11T(d), any reference in §§ 1.861-8T through 1.861-13T to the "taxpayer" with respect to the allocation and apportionment of interest expense generally denotes the entire affiliated group of corporations and not the separate members thereof, unless the context otherwise requires.

(g) *Asset method*—(1) *In general.* (i) Under the asset method, the taxpayer apportions interest expense to the various statutory groupings based on the average total value of assets within each such grouping for the taxable year, as determined under the asset valuation rules of this paragraph (g)(1) and paragraph (g)(2) of this section and the asset characterization rules of paragraph (g)(3) of this section and § 1.861-12T. Except to the extent otherwise provided (see, e.g., paragraph (d)(1)(iv) of this section), taxpayers must apportion interest expense only on the basis of asset values and may not apportion any interest deduction on the basis of gross income.

(ii) A taxpayer may elect to determine the value of its assets on the basis of either the tax book value or the fair market value of its assets. For rules concerning the application of the fair market value method, see paragraph (h) of this section. In the case of an affiliated group—

(A) The parent of which used the fair market value method prior to 1987, or

(B) A substantial portion of which used the fair market value method prior to 1987, such a taxpayer may use either the fair market value method or the tax book value method for its tax year commencing in 1987 and may use either such method in its tax year commencing in 1988 without regard to which method was used in its tax year commencing in 1987 and without secur-

Reg. § 1.861-9T(f)(4)

ing the Commissioner's consent. The use of the fair market value method in 1988, however, shall operate as a binding election as described in § 1.861-8T(c)(2). For rules requiring consistency in the use of the tax book value or fair market value method, see § 1.861-8T(c)(2).

(iii) A taxpayer electing to apportion its interest expense on the basis of the fair market value of its assets must establish the fair market value to the satisfaction of the Commissioner. If a taxpayer fails to establish the fair market value of an asset to the satisfaction of the Commissioner, the Commissioner may determine the appropriate asset value. If a taxpayer fails to establish the value of a substantial portion of its assets to the satisfaction of the Commissioner, the Commissioner may require the taxpayer to use the tax book value method of apportionment.

(iv) For rules relating to earnings and profits adjustments by taxpayers using the tax book value method for the stock in certain nonaffiliated 10 percent owned corporations, see § 1.861-12T(b).

(v) The provisions of this paragraph (g)(1) may be illustrated by the following examples.

Example (1)—(i) *Facts.* X, a domestic corporation organized on January 1, 1987, has deductible interest expense in 1987 in the amount of $150,000. X apportions its expenses according to the tax book value method. The adjusted basis of X's assets is $3,600,000, $3,000,000 of which generate domestic source income and $600,000 of which generate foreign source general limitation income.

(ii) *Allocation.* No portion of the $150,000 deduction is directly allocable solely to identified property within the meaning of § 1.861-10T. Thus, X's deduction for interest is related to all its activities and assets.

(iii) *Apportionment.* X apportions its interest expense as follows:

To foreign source general limitation income:

$$\$150,000 \times \frac{\$600,000}{\$3,600,000} \ldots\ldots\ldots\ldots \$25,000$$

To domestic source income:

$$\$150,000 \times \frac{\$3,000,000}{\$3,600,000} \ldots\ldots\ldots\ldots \$125,000$$

Example (2)—(i) *Facts.* Assume the same facts as in Example (1), except that X apportions its interest expense on the basis of the fair market value of its assets. X's total assets have a fair market value of $4,000,000, $3,200,000 of which generate domestic source income and $800,000 of which generate foreign source general limitation income.

(ii) *Allocation.* No portion of the $150,000 deduction is directly allocable solely to identified property within the meaning of § 1.861-10T. Thus, X's deduction for interest is related to all its activities and properties.

(iii) *Apportionment.* If it establishes the fair market value of its assets to the satisfaction of the Commissioner, X may apportion its interest expense as follows:

To foreign source general limitation income:

$$\$150,000 \times \frac{\$800,000}{\$4,000,000} \ldots\ldots\ldots\ldots \$30,000$$

To domestic source income:

$$\$150,000 \times \frac{\$3,200,000}{\$4,000,000} \ldots\ldots\ldots\ldots \$120,000$$

(2) *Asset values*—(i) *General rule.* For purposes of determining the value of assets under this section, an average of values (book or market) within each statutory grouping and the residual grouping shall be computed for the year on the basis of values of assets at the beginning and end of the year. For the first taxable year beginning after 1986, a taxpayer may choose to determine asset values solely by reference to the year-end value of its assets, provided that all the members of an affiliated group as defined in § 1.861-11T(d) make the same choice. Thus, no averaging is required for the first taxable year beginning after 1986. Where a substantial distortion of asset values would result from averaging beginning-of-year and year-end values, as might be the case in the event of a major corporate acquisition or disposition, the taxpayer must use a different method of asset valuation that more clearly reflects the average value of assets weighted to reflect the time such assets are held by the taxpayer during the taxable year.

(ii) *Special rule for qualified business units of domestic corporations with functional currency other than the U.S. dollar*—(A) *Tax book value method.* In the case of taxpayers using the tax book value method of apportionment, the following rules shall apply to determine the value of the assets of a qualified business unit (as defined in section 989(a)) of a domestic corporation with a functional currency other than the dollar.

(*1*) *Profit and loss branch.* In the case of a branch for which an election is not effective under § 1.985-2T to use the dollar approximate separate transactions method of computing currency gain or loss, the tax book value shall be determined by applying the rules of paragraph (g)(2)(i) and (3) of this section with respect to beginning-of-year and end-of-year tax book value in units of functional currency that are translated

Reg. § 1.861-9T(g)(2)

into dollars at the end-of-year exchange rate between the functional currency and the U.S. dollar.

Example. At the end of 1987, a profit and loss branch has assets that generate foreign source general limitation income with a tax book value in units of functional currency of 100. At the end of 1987, the unit is worth $1. At the end of 1988, the branch has assets that generate foreign source general limitation income with a tax book value in units of functional currency of 80. At the end of 1988, the unit is worth $2. The average value of foreign source general limitation assets for 1988 is 90 units, which is worth $180.

(2) *Approximate separate transactions method.* In the case of a branch for which an election is effective under § 1.985-2T to use the dollar approximate separate transactions method to compute currency gain or loss, the beginning-of-year dollar amount of the assets shall be determined by reference to the end-of-year balance sheet of the branch for the immediately preceding taxable year, adjusted for United States generally accepted accounting principles and United States tax accounting principles, and translated into U.S. dollars as provided in § 1.985-3T. The year-end dollar amount of the assets of the branch shall be determined in the same manner by reference to the end-of-year balance sheet for the current taxable year. The beginning-of-year and end-of-year dollar tax book value of assets, as so determined, within each grouping must then be averaged as provided in paragraph (g)(2)(i) of this section.

(B) *Fair market value method.* In the case of taxpayers using the fair market value method of apportionment, the beginning-of-year and end-of-year fair market values of branch assets within each grouping shall be computed in dollars and averaged as provided in this paragraph (g)(2).

(iii) *Adjustment for directly allocated interest.* Prior to averaging, the year-end value of any asset to which interest expense is directly allocated during the current taxable year under the rules of § 1.861-10T(b) or (c) shall be reduced (but not below zero) by the percentage of the principal amount of indebtedness outstanding at year-end equal to the percentage of all interest on the debt for the taxable year that is directly allocated.

(iv) *Assets in intercompany transactions.* In the application of the asset method described in this paragraph (g), the tax book value of assets transferred between affiliated corporations in intercompany transactions shall be determined without regard to the gain or loss that is deferred under the regulations issued under section 1502.

(v) *Example.* X is a domestic corporation that uses the fair market value method of apportionment. X is a calendar year taxpayer. X owns 25 percent of the stock of A, a noncontrolled section 902 corporation. At the end of 1987, the fair market value of X's assets by income grouping are as follows:

Domestic	$1,000,000
Foreign general limitation	500,000
Foreign passive	500,000
Noncontrolled section 902 corporation	50,000

For its 1987 tax year, X apportions its interest expense by reference to the 1987 year-end values. In July of 1988, X sells a portion of its investment in A and in an asset acquisition purchases a shipping business, the assets of which generate exclusively foreign shipping income. At the end of 1988, the fair market values of X's assets by income grouping are as follows:

Domestic	$ 800,000
Foreign general limitation	900,000
Foreign passive	300,000
Noncontrolled section 902 corporation	40,000
Foreign shipping	100,000

For its 1988 tax year, X shall apportion its interest expense by reference to the average of the 1988 beginning-of-year values (the 1987 year-end values) and the 1988 year-end values, assuming that the averaging of beginning-of-year and end-of-year values does not cause a substantial distortion of asset values. These averages are as follows:

Domestic	$ 900,000
Foreign general limitation	700,000
Foreign passive	400,000
Foreign shipping	50,000
Noncontrolled section 902 corporation	45,000

(3) *Characterization of assets.* Assets are characterized for purposes of this section according to the source and type of the income that they generate, have generated, or may reasonably be expected to generate. The physical location of assets is not relevant to this determination. Subject to the special rules of paragraph (h) concerning the application of the fair market value method of apportionment, the value of assets within each statutory grouping and the residual grouping at the beginning and end of each year shall be determined by dividing the taxpayer's assets into three types—

(i) *Single category assets.* Assets that generate income that is exclusively within a single statutory grouping or the residual grouping;

(ii) *Multiple category assets.* Assets that generate income within more than one grouping of income (statutory or residual); and

(iii) *Assets without directly identifiable yield.* Assets that produce no directly identifiable

Determination of Sources of Income 46,021
See p. 20,601 for regulations not amended to reflect law changes

income yield or that contribute equally to the generation of all the income of the taxpayer (such as assets used in general and administrative functions).

Single category assets are directly attributable to the relevant statutory or residual grouping of income. In order to attribute multiple category assets to the relevant groupings of income, the income yield of each such asset for the taxable year must be analyzed to determine the proportion of gross income generated by it within each relevant grouping. The value of each asset is then prorated among the relevant groupings of income according to their respective proportions of gross income. The value of each asset without directly identifiable income yield must be identified. However, because prorating the value of such assets cannot alter the ratio of assets within the various groupings of income (as determined by reference to the single and multiple category assets), they are not taken into account in determining that ratio. Special asset characterization rules that are set forth in § 1.861-12T. An example demonstrating the application of the asset method is set forth in § 1.861-12T(d).

(h) *The fair market value method.* An affiliated group (as defined in § 1.861-11T(d)) or other taxpayer (the "taxpayer") that elects to use the fair market value method of apportionment shall value its assets according to the following methodology.

(1) *Determination of values*—(i) *Valuation of group assets.* The taxpayer shall first determine the aggregate value of the assets of the taxpayer on the last day of its taxable year without excluding the value of stock in foreign subsidiaries or any other asset. In the case of a publicly traded corporation, this determination shall be equal to the aggregate trading value of the taxpayer's stock traded on established securities markets at year-end increased by the taxpayer's year-end liabilities to unrelated persons and its pro rata share of year-end liabilities of all related persons owed to unrelated persons. In determining whether persons are related, § 1.861-8T(c)(2) shall apply. In the case of a corporation that is not publicly traded, this determination shall be made by reference to the capitalization of corporate earnings, in accordance with the rules of Rev. Rul. 68-609. In either case, control premium shall not be taken into account.

(ii) *Valuation of tangible assets.* The taxpayer shall determine the value of all assets held by the taxpayer and its pro rata share of assets held by other related persons on the last day of its taxable year, excluding stock or indebtedness in such persons, any intangible property as defined in section 936(h)(3)(B), or goodwill or going concern value intangibles. Such valuations shall be made using generally accepted valuation techniques. For this purpose, assets may be combined into reasonable groupings. Statistical methods of valuation may only be used in connection with fungible property, such as commodities. The value of stock in any corporation that is not a related person shall be determined under the rules of paragraph (h)(1)(i) of this section, except that no liabilities shall be taken into account.

(iii) *Computation of intangible asset value.* The value of the intangible assets of the taxpayer and of intangible assets of all related persons attributable to the taxpayer's ownership in related persons is equal to the amount obtained by subtracting the amount determined under paragraph (h)(1)(ii) of this section from the amount determined under paragraph (h)(1)(i) of this section.

(2) *Apportionment of intangible asset value.* The value of the intangible assets determined under paragraph (h)(1)(iii) of this section is apportioned among the taxpayer and all related persons in proportion to the net income before interest expense of the taxpayer and the taxpayer's pro rata share of the net income before interest expense of each related person held by the taxpayer, excluding income that is passive under § 1.904-4(b). For this purpose, net income is determined before reduction for income taxes. Net income of the taxpayer and of related persons shall be computed without regard to dividends or interest received from any person that is related to the taxpayer.

(3) *Characterization of affiliated group's portion of intangible asset value.* The portion of the value of intangible assets of the taxpayer and related persons that is apportioned to the taxpayer under paragraph (h)(2) of this section is characterized on the basis of net income before interest expense, as determined under paragraph (h)(2) of this section, of the taxpayer within each statutory or residual grouping of income.

(4) *Valuing stock in related persons held by the taxpayer.* The value of stock in a related person held by the taxpayer or by another person related to the taxpayer equals the sum of the following amounts reduced by the taxpayer's pro rata share of liabilities of such related person:

(i) The portion of the value of intangible assets of the taxpayer and related persons that is apportioned to such related person under paragraph (h)(2) of this section;

(ii) The taxpayer's pro rata share of tangible assets held by the related person (as deter-

Reg. § 1.861-9T(h)(4)

mined under paragraph (h)(1)(ii) of this section); and

(iii) The total value of stock in all related person held by the related person as determined under this paragraph (h)(4).

(5) [Reserved]. For further guidance, see § 1.861-9(h)(5).

(6) *Adjustments for apportioning related person expenses.* For purposes of apportioning expenses of a related person, the value of stock in a second related person as otherwise determined under paragraph (h)(4) of this section (which is determined on the basis of the taxpayer's percentage ownership interest in the second related person) shall be increased to reflect the first related person's percentage ownership interest in the second related person to the extent it is larger.

Example. Assume that a taxpayer owns 80 percent of CFC1, which owns 100 percent of CFC2. The value of CFC1 is determined generally under paragraph (h)(4) on the basis of the taxpayer's 80 percent indirect interest in CFC2. For purposes of apportioning expenses of CFC1, 100 percent of the stock of CFC1 must be taken into account. Therefore, the value of CFC2 stock in the hands of CFC1 shall equal the value of CFC2 stock in the hands of CFC1 as determined under paragraph (h)(4) of this section, increased by 25 percent of such amount to reflect the fact that CFC1 owns 100 percent and not 80 percent of CFC2.

(i) [Reserved.]

(j) *Modified gross income method.* Subject to rules set forth in paragraph (f)(3) of this section, the interest expense of a controlled foreign corporation may be allocated according to the following rules.

(1) *Single-tier controlled foreign corporation.* In the case of a controlled foreign corporation that does not hold stock in any lower-tier controlled foreign corporation, the interest expense of the controlled foreign corporation shall be apportioned based on its gross income.

(2) *Multiple vertically owned controlled foreign corporations.* In the case of a controlled foreign corporation that holds stock in any lower-tier controlled foreign corporation, the interest expense of that controlled foreign corporation and each upper-tier controlled foreign corporation shall be apportioned based on the following methodology:

(i) *Step 1.* Commencing with the lowest-tier controlled foreign corporation in the chain, allocate and apportion its interest expense based on its gross income as provided in paragraph (j)(1) of this section, yielding gross income in each grouping net of interest expense.

(ii) *Step 2.* Moving to the next higher-tier controlled foreign corporation, combine the gross income of such corporation within each grouping with its pro rata share of the gross income net of interest expense of all lower-tier controlled foreign corporations held by such higher-tier corporation within the same grouping adjusted as follows:

(A) Exclude from the gross income of the upper-tier corporation any dividends or other payments received from the lower-tier corporation other than interest subject to look-through under section 904(d)(3); and

(B) Exclude from the gross income net of interest expense of any lower-tier corporation any subpart F income (net of interest expense apportioned to such income).

Then apportion the interest expense of the higher-tier controlled foreign corporation based on the adjusted combined gross income amounts. Repeat this step 2 for each next higher-tier controlled foreign corporation in the chain. For purposes of this paragraph (j)(2)(ii), pro rata share shall be determined under principles similar to section 951(a)(2). [Temporary Reg. § 1.861-9T.]

☐ [T.D. 8228, 9-9-88. Amended by T.D. 8257, 8-1-89; T.D. 8597, 7-12-95; T.D. 8658, 3-5-96 and T.D. 8916, 12-29-2000.]

[Reg. § 1.861-10]

§ 1.861-10. **Special allocations of interest expense.**—(a) through (d). [Reserved]

(e) *Treatment of certain related group indebtedness*—(1) *In general.* If, for any taxable year beginning after December 31, 1991, a U.S. shareholder (as defined in paragraph (e)(5)(i) of this section) has both—

(i) Excess related group indebtedness (as determined under Step One in paragraph (e)(2) of this section) and

(ii) Excess U.S. shareholder indebtedness (as determined under Step Two in paragraph (e)(3) of this section),

the U.S. shareholder shall allocate, to its gross income in the various separate limitation categories described in section 904(d)(1), a portion of its interest expense paid or accrued to any obligee who is not a member of the affiliated group (as defined in § 1.861-11T(d)) of the U.S. shareholder ("third party interest expense"), excluding amounts allocated under paragraphs (b) and (c) of § 1.861-10T. The amount of third party interest expense so allocated shall equal the total amount of interest income derived by the U.S. shareholder during the year from related group indebtedness,

Determination of Sources of Income

multiplied by the ratio of the lesser of the foregoing two amounts of excess indebtedness for the year to related group indebtedness for the year. This amount of third party interest expense is allocated as described in Step Three in paragraph (e)(4) of this section.

(2) *Step One: Excess related group indebtedness.*

(i) The excess related group indebtedness of a U.S. shareholder for the year equals the amount by which its related group indebtedness for the year exceeds its allowable related group indebtedness for the year.

(ii) The "related group indebtedness" of the U.S. shareholder is the average of the aggregate amounts at the beginning and end of the year of indebtedness owed to the U.S. shareholder by each controlled foreign corporation which is a related person (as defined in paragraph (e)(5)(ii) of this section) with respect to the U.S. shareholder.

(iii) The "allowable related group indebtedness" of a U.S. shareholder for the year equals—

(A) The average of the aggregate values at the beginning and end of the year of the assets (including stock holdings in and obligations of related persons, other than related controlled foreign corporations) of each related controlled foreign corporation, multiplied by

(B) The foreign base period ratio of the U.S. shareholder for the year.

(iv) The "foreign base period ratio" of the U.S. shareholder for the year is the average of the related group debt-to-asset ratios of the U.S. shareholder for each taxable year comprising the foreign base period for the current year (each a "base year"). For this purpose, however, the related group debt-to-asset ratio of the U.S. shareholder for any base year may not exceed 110 percent of the foreign base period ratio for that base year. This limitation shall not apply with respect to any of the five taxable years chosen as initial base years by the U.S. shareholder under paragraph (e)(2)(v) of this section or with respect to any base year for which the related group debt-to-asset ratio does not exceed 0.10.

(v)(A) The foreign base period for any current taxable year (except as described in paragraphs (e)(2)(v)(B) and (C) of this section) shall consist of the five taxable years immediately preceding the current year.

(B) The U.S. shareholder may choose as foreign base periods for all of its first five taxable years for which this paragraph (e) is effective the following alternative base periods:

(*1*) For the first effective taxable year, the 1982, 1983, 1984, 1985 and 1986 taxable years;

(*2*) For the second effective taxable year, the 1983, 1984, 1985 and 1986 taxable years and the first effective taxable year;

(*3*) For the third effective taxable year, the 1984, 1985 and 1986 taxable years and the first and second effective taxable years;

(*4*) For the fourth effective taxable year, the 1985 and 1986 taxable years and the first, second and third effective taxable years; and

(*5*) For the fifth effective taxable year, the 1986 taxable year and the first, second, third and fourth effective taxable years.

(C) If, however, the U.S. shareholder does not choose, under paragraph (e)(10)(ii) of this section, to apply this paragraph (e) to one or more taxable years beginning before January 1, 1992, the U.S. shareholder may not include within any foreign base period the taxable year immediately preceding the first effective taxable year. Thus, for example, a U.S. shareholder for which the first effective taxable year is the taxable year beginning on October 1, 1992, may not include the taxable year beginning on October 1, 1991, in any foreign base period. Assuming that the U.S. shareholder does not elect the alternative base periods described in paragraph (e)(2)(v)(B) of this section, the initial foreign base period for the U.S. shareholder will consist of the taxable years beginning on October 1 of 1986, 1987, 1988, 1989, and 1990. The foreign base period for the U.S. shareholder for the following taxable year, beginning on October 1, 1993, will consist of the taxable years beginning on October 1 of 1987, 1988, 1989, 1990, and 1992.

(D) If the U.S. shareholder chooses the base periods described in paragraph (e)(2)(v)(B) of this section as foreign base periods, it must make a similar election under paragraph (e)(3)(v)(B) of this section with respect to its U.S. base periods.

(vi) The "related group debt-to-asset ratio" of a U.S. shareholder for a year is the ratio between—

(A) The related group indebtedness of the U.S. shareholder for the year (as determined under paragraph (e)(2)(ii) of this section); and

(B) The average of the aggregate values at the beginning and end of the year of the assets (including stock holdings in and obligations of related persons, other than related controlled foreign corporations) of each related controlled foreign corporation.

Reg. § 1.861-10(e)(2)

(vii) Notwithstanding paragraph (e)(2)(i) of this section, a U.S. shareholder is considered to have no excess related group indebtedness for the year if—

(A) Its related group indebtedness for the year does not exceed its allowable related group indebtedness for the immediately preceding year (as determined under paragraph (e)(2)(iii) of this section); or

(B) Its related group debt-to-asset ratio (as determined under paragraph (e)(2)(vi) of this section) for the year does not exceed 0.10.

(3) *Step Two: Excess U.S. shareholder indebtedness.*

(i) The excess indebtedness of a U.S. shareholder for the year equals the amount by which its unaffiliated indebtedness for the year exceeds its allowable indebtedness for the year.

(ii) The "unaffiliated indebtedness" of the U.S. shareholder is the average of the aggregate amounts at the beginning and end of the year of indebtedness owed by the U.S. shareholder to any obligee, other than a member of the affiliated group (as defined in § 1.861-11T(d)) of the U.S. shareholder.

(iii) The "allowable indebtedness" of a U.S. shareholder for the year equals—

(A) The average of the aggregate values at the beginning and end of the year of the assets of the U.S. shareholder (including stock holdings in and obligations of related controlled foreign corporations, but excluding stock holdings in and obligations of members of the affiliated group (as defined in § 1.861-11T(d)) of the U.S. shareholder), reduced by the amount of the excess related group indebtedness of the U.S. shareholder for the year (as determined under Step One in paragraph (e)(2) of this section), multiplied by

(B) The U.S. base period ratio of the U.S. shareholder for the year.

(iv) The "U.S. base period ratio" of the U.S. shareholder for the year is the average of the debt-to-asset ratios of the U.S. shareholder for each taxable year comprising the U.S. base period for the current year (each a "base year"). For this purpose, however, the debt-to-asset ratio of the U.S. shareholder for any base year may not exceed 110 percent of the U.S. base period ratio for that base year. This limitation shall not apply with respect to any of the five taxable years chosen as initial base years by the U.S. shareholder under paragraph (e)(3)(v) of this section or with respect to any base year for which the debt-to-asset ratio does not exceed 0.10.

(v)(A) The U.S. base period for any current taxable year (except as described in paragraphs (e)(3)(v)(B) and (C) of this section) shall consist of the five taxable years immediately preceding the current year.

(B) The U.S. shareholder may choose as U.S. base periods for all of its first five taxable years for which this paragraph (e) is effective the following alternative base periods:

(*1*) For the first effective taxable year, the 1982, 1983, 1984, 1985 and 1986 taxable years;

(*2*) For the second effective taxable year, the 1983, 1984, 1985 and 1986 taxable years and the first effective taxable year;

(*3*) For the third effective taxable year, the 1984, 1985 and 1986 taxable years and the first and second effective taxable years;

(*4*) For the fourth effective taxable year, the 1985 and 1986 taxable years and the first, second and third effective taxable years; and

(*5*) For the fifth effective taxable year, the 1986 taxable year and the first, second, third and fourth effective taxable years.

(C) If, however, the U.S. shareholder does not choose, under paragraph (e)(10)(ii) of this section, to apply this paragraph (e) to one or more taxable years beginning before January 1, 1992, the U.S. shareholder may not include within any U.S. base period the taxable year immediately preceding the first effective taxable year. Thus, for example, a U.S. shareholder for which the first effective taxable year is the taxable year beginning on October 1, 1992, may not include the taxable year beginning on October 1, 1991, in any U.S. base period. Assuming that the U.S. shareholder does not elect the alternative base periods described in paragraph (e)(3)(v)(B) of this section, the initial U.S. base period for the U.S. shareholder will consist of the taxable years beginning on October 1 of 1986, 1987, 1988, 1989, and 1990. The U.S. base period for the U.S. shareholder for the following taxable year, beginning on October 1, 1993, will consist of the taxable years beginning on October 1, 1987, 1988, 1989, 1990, and 1992.

(D) If the U.S. shareholder chooses the base periods described in paragraph (e)(3)(v)(B) of this section as U.S. base periods, it must make a similar election under paragraph (e)(2)(v)(B) of this section with respect to its foreign base periods.

(vi) The "debt-to-asset ratio" of a U.S. shareholder for a year is the ratio between—

(A) The unaffiliated indebtedness of the U.S. shareholder for the year (as determined under paragraph (e)(3)(ii) of this section); and

(B) The average of the aggregate values at the beginning and end of the year of the assets

Reg. § 1.861-10(e)(3)

of the U.S. shareholder. For this purpose, the assets of the U.S. shareholder include stock holdings in and obligations of related controlled foreign corporations but do not include stock holdings in and obligations of members of the affiliated group (as defined in § 1.861-11T(d)).

(vii) A U.S. shareholder is considered to have no excess indebtedness for the year if its debt-to-asset ratio (as determined under paragraph (e)(3)(vi) of this section) for the year does not exceed 0.10.

(4) *Step Three: Allocation of third party interest expense.* (i) A U.S. shareholder shall allocate to its gross income in the various separate limitation categories described in section 904(d)(1) a portion of its third party interest expense incurred during the year equal in amount to the interest income derived by the U.S. shareholder during the year from allocable related group indebtedness.

(ii) The "allocable related group indebtedness" of a U.S. shareholder for any year is an amount of related group indebtedness equal to the lesser of—

(A) The excess related group indebtedness of the U.S. shareholder for the year (determined under Step One in paragraph (e)(2) of this section); or

(B) The excess U.S. shareholder indebtedness for the year (determined under Step Two in paragraph (e)(3) of this section).

(iii) The amount of interest income derived by a U.S. shareholder from allocable related group indebtedness during the year equals the total amount of interest income derived by the U.S. shareholder during the year with respect to related group indebtedness, multiplied by the ratio of allocable related group indebtedness for the year to the aggregate amount of related group indebtedness for the year.

(iv) The portion of third party interest expense described in paragraph (e)(4)(i) of this section shall be allocated in proportion to the relative average amounts of related group indebtedness held by the U.S. shareholder in each separate limitation category during the year. The remaining portion of third party interest expense of the U.S. shareholder for the year shall be apportioned as provided in §§ 1.861-8T through 1.861-13T, excluding paragraph (e) of § 1.861-10T and this paragraph (e).

(v) The average amount of related group indebtedness held by the U.S. shareholder in each separate limitation category during the year equals the average of the aggregate amounts of such indebtedness in each separate limitation category at the beginning and end of the year. Solely for purposes of this paragraph (e)(4), each debt obligation of a related controlled foreign corporation held by the U.S. shareholder at the beginning or end of the year is attributed to separate limitation categories in the same manner as the stock of the obligor would be attributed under the rules of § 1.861-12T(c)(3), whether or not such stock is held directly by the U.S. shareholder.

(vi) The amount of third party interest expense of a U.S. shareholder allocated pursuant to this paragraph (e)(4) shall not exceed the total amount of the third party interest expense of the U.S. shareholder for the year (excluding any third party interest expense allocated under paragraphs (b) and (c) of § 1.861-10T).

(5) *Definitions.* For purposes of this paragraph (e), the following terms shall have the following meanings.

(i) *U.S. shareholder.* The term "U.S. shareholder" has the same meaning as the term "United States shareholder" when used in section 957, except that, in the case of a United States shareholder that is a member of an affiliated group (as defined in § 1.861-11T(d)), the entire affiliated group is considered to constitute a single U.S. shareholder.

(ii) *Related person.* For the definition of the term "related person", see § 1.861-8T(c)(2). A controlled foreign corporation is considered "related" to a U.S. shareholder if it is a related person with respect to the U.S. shareholder.

(6) *Determination of asset values.* A U.S. shareholder shall determine the values of the assets of each related controlled foreign corporation (for purposes of Step One in paragraph (e)(2) of this section) and the assets of the U.S. shareholder (for purposes of Step Two in paragraph (e)(3) of this section) for any year in accordance with the valuation method (tax book value or fair market value) elected for that year pursuant to § 1.861-9T(g). However, solely for purposes of this paragraph (e), a U.S. shareholder may instead choose to determine the values of the assets of all related controlled foreign corporations by reference to their values as reflected on Forms 5471 (the annual information return with respect to each related controlled foreign corporation), subject to the translation rules of paragraph (e)(8)(i) of this section. This method of valuation may be used only if the taxable years of each of the related controlled foreign corporations begin with, or no more than one month earlier than, the taxable year of the U.S. shareholder. Once chosen for a taxable year, this method of valuation must be used in each subsequent taxable year and may

be changed only with the consent of the Commissioner.

(7) *Adjustments to asset value.* For purposes of apportioning remaining interest expense under § 1.861-9T, a U.S. shareholder shall reduce (but not below zero) the value of its assets for the year (as determined under § 1.861-9T(g)(3) or (h)) by an amount equal to the allocable related group indebtedness of the U.S. shareholder for the year (as determined under Step Three in paragraph (e)(4)(ii) of this section). This reduction is allocated among assets in each separate limitation category in proportion to the average amount of related group indebtedness held by the U.S. shareholder in each separate limitation category during the year (as determined under Step Three in paragraph (e)(4)(v) of this section).

(8) *Special rules*—(i) *Exchange rates.* All indebtedness amounts and asset values (including current year and base year amounts and values) denominated in a foreign currency shall be translated into U.S. dollars at the exchange rate for the current year. The exchange rate for the current year may be determined under any reasonable method (*e.g.*, average of month-end exchange rates for each month in the current year) if it is consistently applied to the current year and all base years. Once chosen for a taxable year, a method for determining an exchange rate must be used in each subsequent taxable year and will be treated as a method of accounting for purposes of section 446. A taxpayer may apply a different translation rule only with the prior consent of the Commissioner. In this regard, the Commissioner will be guided by the extent to which a different rule would reduce the comparability of dollar amounts of indebtedness and dollar asset values for the base years and the current year.

(ii) *Exempt assets.* Solely for purposes of this paragraph (e), any exempt assets otherwise excluded under section 864(e)(3) and § 1.861-8T(d) shall be included as assets of the U.S. shareholder or related controlled foreign corporation.

(iii) *Exclusion of certain directly allocated indebtedness and assets.* Qualified nonrecourse indebtedness (as defined in § 1.861-10T(b)(2)) and indebtedness incurred in connection with an integrated financial transaction (as defined in § 1.861-10T(c)(2)) shall be excluded from U.S. shareholder indebtedness and related group indebtedness. In addition, assets which are the subject of qualified nonrecourse indebtedness or integrated financial transactions shall be excluded from the assets of the U.S. shareholder and each related controlled foreign corporation.

(iv) *Exclusion of certain receivables.* Receivables between related controlled foreign corporations (or between members of the affiliated group constituting the U.S. shareholder) shall be excluded from the assets of the related controlled foreign corporation (or affiliated group member) holding such receivables. See also § 1.861-11T(e)(1).

(v) *Classification of certain loans as related group indebtedness.* If—

(A) A U.S. shareholder owns stock in a related controlled foreign corporation which is a resident of a country that—

(*1*) Does not impose a withholding tax of 5 percent or more upon payments of dividends to a U.S. shareholder; and

(*2*) Does not, for the taxable year of the controlled foreign corporation, subject the income of the controlled foreign corporation to an income tax which is greater than that percentage specified under § 1.954-1T (d)(1)(i) of the maximum rate of tax specified under section 11 of the Code, and

(B) The controlled foreign corporation has outstanding a loan or loans to one or more other related controlled foreign corporations, or the controlled foreign corporation has made a direct or indirect capital contribution to one or more other related controlled foreign corporations which have outstanding a loan or loans to one or more other related controlled foreign corporations,

then, to the extent of the aggregate amount of its capital contributions in taxable years beginning after December 31, 1986, to the related controlled foreign corporation that made such loans or additional contributions, the U.S. shareholder itself shall be treated as having made the loans described in paragraph (e)(8)(v)(B) of this section and, thus, such loan amounts shall be considered related group indebtedness. However, for purposes of paragraph (e)(4) of this section, interest income derived by the U.S. shareholder during the year from related group indebtedness shall not include any income derived with respect to the U.S. shareholder's ownership of stock in the related controlled foreign corporation that made such loans or additional contributions.

(vi) *Classification of certain stock as related person indebtedness.* In determining the amount of its related group indebtedness for any taxable year, a U.S. shareholder must treat as related group indebtedness its holding of stock in a related controlled foreign corporation if, during such taxable year, such related controlled foreign corporation claims a deduction for interest under foreign law for distributions on such stock. However, for purposes of paragraph (e)(4) of this sec-

Reg. § 1.861-10(e)(7)

tion, interest income derived by the U.S. shareholder during the year from related group indebtedness shall not include any income derived with respect to the U.S. shareholder's ownership of stock in the related controlled foreign corporation.

(9) *Corporate events*—(i) *Initial acquisition of a controlled foreign corporation.* If the foreign base period of the U.S. shareholder for any year includes a base year in which the U.S. shareholder did not hold stock in any related controlled foreign corporation, then, in computing the foreign base period ratio, the related group debt-to-asset ratio of the U.S. shareholder for any such base year shall be deemed to be 0.10.

(ii) *Incorporation of U.S. shareholder.*

(A) *Nonapplication.* This paragraph (e) does not apply to the first taxable year of the U.S. shareholder. However, this paragraph (e) does apply to all following years, including years in which later members of the affiliated group may be incorporated.

(B) *Foreign and U.S. base period ratios.* In computing the foreign and U.S. base period ratios, the foreign and U.S. base periods of the U.S. shareholder shall be considered to be only the period prior to the current year that the U.S. shareholder was in existence if this prior period is less than five taxable years.

(iii) *Acquisition of additional corporations.* (A) If a U.S. shareholder acquires (directly or indirectly) stock of a foreign or domestic corporation which, by reason of the acquisition, then becomes a related controlled foreign corporation or a member of the affiliated group, then in determining excess related group indebtedness or excess U.S. shareholder indebtedness, the indebtedness and assets of the acquired corporation shall be taken into account only at the end of the acquisition year and in following years. Thus, amounts of indebtedness and assets and the various debt-to-asset ratios of the U.S. shareholder existing at the beginning of the acquisition year or relating to preceding years are not recalculated to take account of indebtedness and assets of the acquired corporation existing as of dates before the end of the year. If, however, a major acquisition is made within the last three months of the year and a substantial distortion of values for the year would otherwise result, the taxpayer must take into account the average values of the acquired indebtedness and assets weighted to reflect the time such indebtedness is owed and such assets are held by the taxpayer during the year.

(B) In the case of a reverse acquisition subject to this paragraph (e)(9), the rules of § 1.1502-75(d)(3) apply in determining which corporations are the acquiring and acquired corporations. For this purpose, whether corporations are affiliated is determined under § 1.861-11T(d).

(C) If the stock of a U.S. shareholder is acquired by (and, by reason of such acquisition, the U.S. shareholder becomes affiliated with) a corporation described below, then such U.S. shareholder shall be considered to have acquired such corporation for purposes of the application of the rules of this paragraph (e). A corporation to which this paragraph (e)(9)(iii)(C) applies is—

(*1*) A corporation which is not affiliated with any other corporation (other than another similarly described corporation); and

(*2*) Substantially all of the assets of which consist of cash, securities and stock.

(iv) *Election to compute base period ratios by including acquired corporations.* A U.S. shareholder may choose, solely for purposes of paragraph (e)(9)(i) and (iii) of this section, to compute its foreign and U.S. base period ratios for the acquisition year and all subsequent years by taking into account the indebtedness and asset values of the acquired corporation or corporations (including related group indebtedness owed to a former U.S. shareholder) at the beginning of the acquisition year and in each of the five base years preceding the acquisition year. This election, if made for an acquisition, must be made for all other acquisitions occurring during the same taxable year or initiated in that year and concluded in the following year.

(v) *Dispositions.* If a U.S. shareholder disposes of stock of a foreign or domestic corporation which, by reason of the disposition, then ceases to be a related controlled foreign corporation or a member of the affiliated group (unless liquidated or merged into a related corporation), in determining excess related group indebtedness or excess U.S. shareholder indebtedness, the indebtedness and assets of the divested corporation shall be taken into account only at the beginning of the disposition year and for the relevant preceding years. Thus, amounts of indebtedness and assets and the various debt-to-asset ratios of the U.S. shareholder existing at the end of the year or relating to following years are not affected by indebtedness and assets of the divested corporation existing as of dates after the beginning of the year. If, however, a major disposition is made within the first three months of the year and a substantial distortion of values for the year would otherwise result, the taxpayer must take into account the average values of the divested indebtedness and assets weighted to reflect the time such indebtedness is owed and such assets are held by the taxpayer during the year.

Reg. § 1.861-10(e)(9)

Determination of Sources of Income

See p. 20,601 for regulations not amended to reflect law changes

(vi) *Election to compute base period ratios by excluding divested corporations.* A U.S. shareholder may choose, solely for purposes of paragraph (e)(9)(v) and (vii) of this section, to compute its foreign and U.S. base period ratios for the disposition year and all subsequent years without taking into account the indebtedness and asset values of the divested corporation or corporations at the beginning of the disposition year and in each of the five base years preceding the disposition year. This election, if made for a disposition, must be made for all other dispositions occurring during the same taxable year or initiated in that year and concluded in the following year.

(vii) *Section 355 transactions.* A U.S. corporation which becomes a separate U.S. shareholder as a result of a distribution of its stock to which section 355 applies shall be considered—

(A) As disposed of by the U.S. shareholder of the affiliated group of which the distributing corporation is a member, with this disposition subject to the rules of paragraphs (e)(9)(v) and (vi) of this section; and

(B) As having the same related group debt-to-asset ratio and debt-to-asset ratio as the distributing U.S. shareholder in each year preceding the year of distribution for purposes of applying this paragraph (e) to the year of distribution and subsequent years of the distributed corporation.

(10) *Effective date—(i) Taxable years beginning after December 31, 1991.* The provisions of this paragraph (e) apply to all taxable years beginning after December 31, 1991.

(ii) *Taxable years beginning after December 31, 1987 and before January 1, 1992.* The provisions of § 1.861-10T(e) apply to taxable years beginning after December 31, 1987, and before January 1, 1992. The taxpayer may elect to apply the provisions of this paragraph (e) (in lieu of the provisions of § 1.861-10T(e)) for any taxable year beginning after December 31, 1987, but this paragraph (e) must then be applied to all subsequent taxable years.

	1985	1986-88	1989	1990
(A) Related group indebtedness	$ 11,000	24,000	26,000	50,000
(B) Average Value of Assets of Related CFC	$100,000	200,000	200,000	250,000
(C) Related Group Debt-to-Asset Ratio	.11	.12	.13	.20

(*1*) X's "foreign base period ratio" for 1990, an average of its ratios of related group indebtedness to related group assets for 1985 through 1989, is:

(.11 + .12 + .12 + .12 + .13)/5 = .12

(11) The following example illustrates the provisions of this paragraph (e):

Example. (i) *Facts.* X, a domestic corporation, elects to apply this paragraph (e) to its 1990 tax year. X has a calendar taxable year and apportions its interest expense on the basis of the tax book value of its assets. In 1990, X incurred deductible third-party interest expense of $24,960 on an average amount of indebtedness (determined on the basis of beginning-of-year and end-of-year amounts) of $249,600. X manufactures widgets, all of which are sold in the United States. X owns all of the stock of Y, a controlled foreign corporation that also has a calendar taxable year and is also engaged in the manufacture and sale of widgets. Y has no earnings and profits or deficit of earnings and profits attributable to taxable years prior to 1987. X's total assets and their average tax book values (determined on the basis of beginning-of-year and end-of-year tax book values) for 1990 are:

Asset	Average Tax Book Value
Plant and equipment	$315,000
Corporate headquarters	60,000
Y stock	75,000
Y note	50,000
	$500,000

Y had $25,000 of income before the deduction of any interest expense. Of this total, $5,000 is high withholding tax interest income. The remaining $20,000 is derived from widget sales, and constitutes foreign source general limitation income. Assume that Y has no deductions from gross income other than interest expense. During 1990, Y paid $5,000 of interest expense to X on the Y note and $10,000 of interest expense to third parties, giving Y total interest expense of $15,000. X elects pursuant to § 1.861-9T to apportion Y's interest expense under the gross income method prescribed in section 1.861-9T(j).

(ii) *Step 1:* Using a beginning and end of year average, X (the U.S. shareholder) held the following average amounts of indebtedness of Y and Y had the following average asset values:

(*2*) X's "allowable related group indebtedness" for 1990 is:

$250,000 × .12 = $30,000

(*3*) X's "excess related group indebtedness" for 1990 is:

$50,000 − $30,000 = $20,000

Reg. § 1.861-10(e)(10)

Determination of Sources of Income

See p. 20,601 for regulations not amended to reflect law changes

X's related group indebtedness of $50,000 for 1990 is greater than its allowable related group indebtedness of $24,000 for 1989 (assuming a foreign base period ratio in 1989 of .12), and X's related group debt-to-asset ratio for 1990 is .20, which is greater than the ratio of .10 described in paragraph (e)(2)(vii)(B) of this section. Therefore,

	1985	1986	1987	1988	1989	1990
(1)	$231,400	225,000	225,000	225,000	220,800	249,600
(2)	$445,000	450,000	450,000	450,000	460,000	480,000 (a)
(3)	.52	.50	.50	.50	.48	.52

(1) U.S. and foreign indebtedness
(2) Average value of assets of U.S. shareholder
(3) Debt-to-Asset ratio of U.S. shareholder
(a) [500,000 − 20,000 (excess related group indebtedness determined in Step 1)]

X's "U.S. base period ratio" for 1990 is:
(.52 + .50 + .50 + .50 + .48)/5 = .50

X's "allowable indebtedness" for 1990 is:
$480,000 × .50 = $240,000

X's "excess U.S. shareholder indebtedness" for 1990 is:
$249,600 − $240,000 = $9,600

X's debt-to-asset ratio for 1990 is .52, which is greater than the ratio of .10 described in paragraph (e)(3)(vii) of this section. Therefore, X's excess U.S. shareholder indebtedness for 1990 remains at $9,600.

(iv) *Step 3:* (a) Since X's excess U.S. shareholder indebtedness of $9,600 is less than its excess related group indebtedness of $20,000, X's allocable related group indebtedness for 1990 is $9,600. The amount of interest received by X during 1990 on allocable related group indebtedness is:

$$\$5,000 \times \frac{\$9,600}{\$50,000} = \$960$$

Foreign source high withholding tax interest income = $5,000 − [($15,000) multiplied by ($5,000)/($5,000 + $20,000)]
= $2,000

and

Foreign source general limitation income = $20,000 − [($15,000) multiplied by ($20,000)/($5,000 + $20,000)]
= $8,000

(c) Therefore, $192 [($960 × $2,000/($2,000+$8,000)] of X's third party interest expense is allocated to foreign source high withholding tax interest income and $768 [$960 × $8,000/($2,000+$8,000)] is allocated to foreign source general limitation income.

X's excess related group indebtedness for 1990 remains at $20,000.

(iii) *Step 2:* Using a beginning and end of year average, X has the following average amounts of U.S. and foreign indebtedness and average asset values:

(b) Therefore, $960 of X's third party interest expense ($24,960) shall be allocated among various separate limitation categories in proportion to the relative average amounts of Y obligations held by X in each such category. The amount of Y obligations in each limitation category is determined in the same manner as the stock of Y would be attributed under the rules of § 1.861-12T(c)(3). Since Y's interest expense is apportioned under the gross income method prescribed in § 1.861-9T(j), the Y stock must be characterized under the gross income method described in § 1.861-12T(c)(3)(iii). Y's gross income net of interest expense is determined as follows:

(v) As a result of these direct allocations, for purposes of apportioning X's remaining interest expense under § 1.861-9T, the value of X's assets generating foreign source general limitation income is reduced by the principal amount of indebtedness the interest on which is directly allocated to foreign source general limitation in-

Reg. § 1.861-10(e)(11)

46,030   Determination of Sources of Income

See p. 20,601 for regulations not amended to reflect law changes

come ($7,680), and the value of X's assets generating foreign source high withholding tax interest income is reduced by the principal amount of indebtedness the interest on which is directly allocated to foreign source high withholding tax interest income ($1,920), determined as follows:

Reduction of X's assets generating foreign source general limitation income:

$$\text{X's allocable related group indebtedness} \times \frac{\text{Y's Foreign source general limitation income}}{\text{Y's Foreign source income}}$$

$$\$9{,}600 \times \$8{,}000/(\$8{,}000 + \$2{,}000) = \$7{,}680$$

Reduction of X's assets generating foreign source high withholding tax interest income:

$$\text{X's allocable related group indebtedness} \times \frac{\text{Y's Foreign source high withholding tax interest income}}{\text{Y's Foreign source income}}$$

$$\$9{,}600 \times \$2{,}000/(\$8{,}000 + \$2{,}000) = \$1{,}920$$

[Reg. § 1.861-10.]

☐ [T.D. 8410, 4-14-92.]

[Reg. § 1.861-10T]

§ 1.861-10T. Special allocations of interest expense (Temporary).—(a) *In general.* This section applies to all taxpayers and provides three exceptions to the rules of § 1.861-9T that require the allocation and apportionment of interest expense on the basis of all assets of all members of the affiliated group. Paragraph (b) of this section describes the direct allocation of interest expense to the income generated by certain assets that are subject to qualified nonrecourse indebtedness. Paragraph (c) of this section describes the direct allocation of interest expense to income generated by certain assets that are acquired in integrated financial transactions. Paragraph (d) of this section provides special rules that are applicable to all transactions described in paragraphs (b) and (c) of this section. Paragraph (e) of this section requires the direct allocation of third party interest of an affiliated group to such group's investment in related controlled foreign corporations in cases involving excess related person indebtedness (as defined therein). See also § 1.861-9T(b)(5), which requires direct allocation of amortizable bond premium.

(b) *Qualified nonrecourse indebtedness*—(1) *In general.* In the case of qualified nonrecourse indebtedness (as defined in paragraph (b)(2) of this section), the deduction for interest shall be considered directly allocable solely to the gross income which the property acquired, constructed, or improved with the proceeds of the indebtedness generates, has generated, or could reasonably be expected to generate.

(2) *Qualified nonrecourse indebtedness defined.* The term "qualified nonrecourse indebtedness" means any borrowing that is not excluded by paragraph (b)(4) of this section if:

(i) The borrowing is specifically incurred for the purpose of purchasing, constructing, or improving identified property that is either depreciable tangible personal property or real property with a useful life of more than one year or for the purpose of purchasing amortizable intangible personal property with a useful life of more than one year;

(ii) The proceeds are actually applied to purchase, construct, or improve the identified property;

(iii) Except as provided in paragraph (b)(7)(ii) (relating to certain third party guarantees in leveraged lease transactions), the creditor can look only to the identified property (or any lease or other interest therein) as security for payment of the principal and interest on the loan and, thus, cannot look to any other property, the borrower, or any third party with respect to repayment of principal or interest on the loan;

(iv) The cash flow from the property, as defined in paragraph (b)(3) of this section, is reasonably expected to be sufficient in the first year of ownership as well as in each subsequent year of ownership to fulfill the terms and conditions of the loan agreement with respect to the amount and timing of payments of interest and original issue discount and periodic payments of principal in each such year; and

(v) There are restrictions in the loan agreement on the disposal or use of the property consistent with the assumptions described in subdivisions (iii) and (iv) of this paragraph (b)(2).

(3) *Cash flow defined*—(i) *In general.* The term "cash flow from the property" as used in paragraph (b)(2)(iv) of this section means a stream of revenue (as computed under paragraph (b)(3)(ii) of this section) substantially all of which

Reg. § 1.861-10T(a)

derives directly from the property. The phrase "cash flow from the property" does not include revenue if a significant portion thereof is derived from activities such as sales, labor, services, or the use of other property. Thus, revenue derived from the sale or lease of inventory or of similar property does not constitute cash flow from the property, including plant or equipment used in the manufacture and sale or lease, or purchase and sale or lease, of such inventory or similar property. In addition, revenue derived in part from the performance of services that are not ancillary and subsidiary to the use of property does not constitute cash flow from the property.

(ii) *Self-constructed assets.* The activities associated with self-construction of assets shall be considered to constitute labor or services for purposes of paragraph (b)(3)(i) only if the self-constructed asset—

(A) Is constructed for the purposes of resale, or

(B) Without regard to purpose, is sold to an unrelated person within one year from the date that the property is placed in service for purposes of section 167.

(iii) *Computation of cash flow.* Cash flow is computed by subtracting cash disbursements excluding debt service from cash receipts.

(iv) *Analysis of operating costs.* [Reserved]

(v) *Examples.* The principles of this paragraph may be demonstrated by the following examples.

Example (1). In 1987, X borrows $100,000 in order to purchase an apartment building, which X then purchases. The loan is secured only by the building and the leases thereon. Annual debt service on the loan is $12,000. Annual gross rents from the building are $20,000. Annual taxes on the building are $2,000. Other expenses deductible under section 162 are $2,000. Rents are reasonably expected to remain stable or increase in subsequent years, and taxes and expenses are reasonably expected to remain proportional to gross rents in subsequent years. X provides security, maintenance, and utilities to the tenants of the building. Based on facts and circumstances, it is determined that, although services are provided to tenants, these services are ancillary and subsidiary to the occupancy of the apartments. Accordingly, the cash flow of $16,000 is considered to constitute a return from the property. Furthermore, such cash flow is sufficient to fulfill the terms and conditions of the loan agreement as required by paragraph (b)(2)(iii).

Example (2). In 1987, X borrows funds in order to purchase a hotel, which X then purchases and operates. The loan is secured only by the hotel. Based on facts and circumstances, it is determined that the operation of the hotel involves services the value of which is significant in relation to amounts paid to occupy the rooms. Thus, a significant portion of the cash flow is derived from the performance of services incidental to the occupancy of hotel rooms. Accordingly, the cash flow from the hotel is considered not to constitute a return on or from the property.

Example (3). In 1987, X borrows funds in order to build a factory, which X then builds and operates. The loan is secured only by the factory and the equipment therein. Based on the facts and circumstances, it is determined that the operation of the factory involves significant expenditures for labor and raw materials. Thus, a significant portion of the cash flow is derived from labor and the processing of raw materials. Accordingly, the cash flow from the factory is considered not to constitute a return on or from the property.

(4) *Exclusions.* The term "qualified nonrecourse indebtedness" shall not include any transaction that—

(i) Lacks economic significance within the meaning of paragraph (b)(5) of this section;

(ii) Involves cross collateralization within the meaning of paragraph (b)(6) of this section;

(iii) Except in the case of a leveraged lease described in paragraph (b)(7)(ii) of this section, involves credit enhancement within the meaning of paragraph (b)(7) of this section or, with respect to loans made on or after October 14, 1988, does not, under the terms of the loan documents, prohibit the acquisition by the holder of bond insurance or similar forms of credit enhancement;

(iv) Involves the purchase of inventory;

(v) Involves the purchase of any financial asset, including stock in a corporation, an interest in a partnership or a trust, or the debt obligation of any obligor (although interest incurred in order to purchase certain financial instruments may qualify for direct allocation under paragraph (c) of this section);

(vi) Involves interest expense that constitutes qualified residence interest as defined in section 163(h)(3); or

(vii) [Reserved].

(5) *Economic significance.* Indebtedness that otherwise qualifies under paragraph (b)(2) shall nonetheless be subject to apportionment under § 1.861-9T if, taking into account all the facts and circumstances, the transaction (including the security arrangement) lacks economic significance.

Reg. § 1.861-10T(b)(5)

(6) *Cross collateralization.* The term "cross collateralization" refers to the pledge as security for a loan of—

(i) Any asset of the borrower other than the identified property described in paragraph (b)(2) of this section, or

(ii) Any asset belonging to any related person, as defined in § 1.861-8T(c)(2).

(7) *Credit enhancement*—(i) *In general.* Except as provided in paragraph (b)(7)(ii) of this section, the term "credit enhancement" refers to any device, including a contract, letter of credit, or guaranty, that expands the creditor's rights, directly or indirectly, beyond the identified property purchased, constructed, or improved with the funds advanced and, thus, effectively provides as security for a loan the assets of any person other than the borrower. The acquisition of bond insurance or any other contract of suretyship by an initial or subsequent holder of an obligation shall constitute credit enhancement.

(ii) *Special rule for leveraged leases.* For purposes of this paragraph (b), the term "credit enhancement" shall not include any device under which any person that is not a related person within the meaning of § 1.861-8T(c)(2) agrees to guarantee, without recourse to the lessor or any person related to the lessor, a lessor's payment of principal and interest on indebtedness that was incurred in order to purchase or improve an asset that is depreciable tangible personal property or depreciable tangible real property (and the land on which such real property is situated) that is leased to a lessee that is not a related person in a transaction that constitutes a lease for federal income tax purposes.

(iii) *Syndication of credit risk and sale of loan participations.* The term "syndication of credit risk" refers to an arrangement in which one primary lender secures the promise of a secondary lender to bear a portion of the primary lender's credit risk on a loan. The term "sale of loan participations" refers to an arrangement in which one primary lender divides a loan into several portions, sells and assigns all rights with respect to one or more portions to participating secondary lenders, and does not remain at risk in any manner with respect to the portion assigned. For purposes of this paragraph (b), the syndication of credit risk shall constitute credit enhancement because the primary lender can look to secondary lenders for payment of the loan, notwithstanding limitations on the amount of the secondary lender's liability. Conversely, the sale of loan participations does not constitute credit enhancement, because the holder of each portion of the loan can look solely to the asset securing the loan and not to the credit or other assets of any person.

(8) *Other arrangements that do not constitute cross collateralization or credit enhancement.* For purposes of paragraphs (b)(6) and (7) of this section, the following arrangements do not constitute cross collateralization or credit enhancement:

(i) *Integrated projects.* A taxpayer's pledge of multiple assets of an integrated project, provided that the integrated project. An integrated project consists of functionally related and geographically contiguous assets that, as to the taxpayer, are used in the same trade or business.

(ii) *Insurance.* A taxpayer's purchase of third-party casualty and liability insurance on the collateral or, by contract, bearing the risk of loss associated with destruction of the collateral or with respect to the attachment of third party liability claims.

(iii) *After-acquired property.* Extension of a creditor's security interest to improvements made to the collateral, provided that the extension does not constitute excess collateralization under paragraph (b)(6), determined by taking into account the value of improvements at the time the improvements are made and the value of the original property at the time the loan was made.

(iv) *Warranties of completion and maintenance.* A taxpayer's warranty to a creditor that it will complete construction or manufacture of the collateral or that it will maintain the collateral in good condition.

(v) *Substitution of collateral.* A taxpayer's right to substitute collateral under any loan contract. However, after the right is exercised, the loan shall no longer constitute qualified nonrecourse indebtedness.

(9) *Refinancings.* If a taxpayer refinances qualified nonrecourse indebtedness (as defined in paragraph (b)(2) of this section) with new indebtedness, such new indebtedness shall continue to qualify only if—

(i) The principal amount of the new indebtedness does not exceed by more than five percent the remaining principal amount of the original indebtedness,

(ii) The term of the new indebtedness does not exceed by more than six months the remaining term of the original indebtedness, and

(iii) The requirements of this paragraph (other than those of paragraph (b)(2)(i) and (ii) of this section) are satisfied at the time of the refinancing, and the exclusions contained in this paragraph (b)(4) do not apply.

Reg. § 1.861-10T(b)(6)

(10) *Post-construction permanent financing.* Financing that is obtained after the completion of constructed property will be deemed to satisfy the requirements of paragraph (b)(2)(i) and (ii) of this section if—

(i) The financing is obtained within one year after the constructed property or substantially all of a constructed integrated project (as defined in paragraph (b)(9)(i) of this section) is placed in service for purposes of section 167; and

(ii) The financing does not exceed the cost of construction (including construction period interest).

(11) *Assumptions of pre-existing qualified nonrecourse indebtedness.* If a transferee of property that is subject to qualified nonrecourse indebtedness assumes such indebtedness, the indebtedness shall continue to constitute qualified nonrecourse indebtedness, provided that the assumption in no way alters the qualified status of the debt.

(12) *Excess collateralization.* [Reserved]

(c) *Direct allocations in the case of certain integrated financial transactions*—(1) *General rule.* Interest expense incurred on funds borrowed in connection with an integrated financial transaction (as defined in paragraph (c)(2) of this section) shall be directly allocated to the income generated by the investment funded with the borrowed amounts.

(2) *Definition.* The term "integrated financial transaction" refers to any transaction in which—

(i) The taxpayer—

(A) Incurs indebtedness for the purpose of making an identified term investment,

(B) Identifies the indebtedness as incurred for such purpose at the time the indebtedness is incurred, and

(C) Makes the identified term investment within ten business days after incurring the indebtedness;

(ii) The return on the investment is reasonably expected to be sufficient throughout the term of the investment to fulfill the terms and conditions of the loan agreement with respect to the amount and timing of payments of principal and interest or original issue discount;

(iii) The income constitutes interest or original issue discount or would constitute income equivalent to interest if earned by a controlled foreign corporation (as described in § 1.954-2T(h));

(iv) The debt incurred and the investment mature within ten business days of each other;

(v) The investment does not relate in any way to the operation of, and is not made in the normal course of, the trade or business of the taxpayer or any related person, including the financing of the sale of goods or the performance of services by the taxpayer or any related person, or the compensation of the taxpayer's employees (including any contribution or loan to an employee stock ownership plan (as defined in section 4975(e)(7)) or other plan that is qualified under section 401(a)); and

(vi) The borrower does not constitute a financial services entity (as defined in section 904 and the regulations thereunder).

(3) *Roll-overs.* In the event that a taxpayer sells or otherwise liquidates an investment described in paragraph (c)(2) of this section, the interest expense incurred on the borrowing shall, subsequent to that liquidation, no longer qualify for direct allocation under this paragraph (c).

(4) *Examples.* The principles of this paragraph (c) may be demonstrated by the following examples.

Example (1). X is a manufacturer and does not constitute a financial services entity as defined in the regulations under section 904. On January 1, 1988, X borrows $100 for 6 months at an annual interest rate of 10 percent. X identifies on its books and records by the close of that day that the indebtedness is being incurred for the purpose of making an investment that is intended to qualify as an integrated financial transaction. On January 5, 1988, X uses the proceeds to purchase a portfolio of stock that approximates the composition of the Standard & Poor's 500 Index. On that day, X also enters into a forward sale contract that requires X to sell the stock on June 1, 1988 for $110. X identifies on its books and records by the close of January 5, 1988, that the portfolio stock purchases and the forward sale contract constitute part of the integrated financial transaction with respect to which the identified borrowing was incurred. Under § 1.954-2T(h), the income derived from the transaction would constitute income equivalent to interest. Assuming that the return on the investment to be derived on June 1, 1988, will be sufficient to pay the interest due on June 1, 1988, the interest on the borrowing is directly allocated to the gain from the investment.

Example (2). X does not constitute a financial services entity as defined in the regulations under section 904. X is in the business of, among other things, issuing credit cards to consumers and purchasing from merchants who accept the X card the receivables of consumers who make purchases with the X card. X borrows from Y in

Reg. § 1.861-10T(c)(4)

order to purchase X credit card receivables from Z, a merchant. Assuming that the Y borrowing satisfies the other requirements of paragraph (c)(2) of this section, the transaction nonetheless cannot constitute an integrated financial transaction because the purchase relates to the operation of X's trade or business.

Example (3). Assume the same facts as in Example 2, except that X borrows in order to purchase the receivables of A, a merchant who does not accept the X card and is not otherwise engaged directly or indirectly in any business transaction with X. Because the borrowing is not related to the operation of X's trade or business, the borrowing may qualify as an integrated financial transaction if the other requirements of paragraph (c)(2) of this section are satisfied.

(d) *Special rules.* In applying paragraphs (b) and (c) of this section, the following special rules shall apply.

(1) *Related person transactions.* The rules of this section shall not apply to the extent that any transaction—

(i) Involves either indebtedness between related persons (as defined in section § 1.861-8T(c)(2)) or indebtedness incurred from unrelated persons for the purpose of purchasing property from a related person; or

(ii) Involves the purchase of property that is leased to a related person (as defined in section § 1.861-8T(c)(2)) in a transaction described in paragraph (b) of this section. If a taxpayer purchases property and leases such property in whole or in part to a related person, a portion of the interest incurred in connection with such an acquisition, based on the ratio that the value of the property leased to the related person bears to the total value of the property, shall not qualify for direct allocation under this section.

(2) *Consideration of assets or income to which interest is directly allocated in apportioning other interest expense.* In apportioning interest expense under § 1.861-9T, the year-end value of any asset to which interest expense is directly allocated under this section during the current taxable year shall be reduced to the extent provided in § 1.861-9T(g)(2)(iii) to reflect the portion of the principal amount of the indebtedness outstanding at year-end relating to the interest which is directly allocated. A similar adjustment shall be made to the end-of-year value of assets for the prior year for purposes of determining the beginning-of-year value of assets for the current year. These adjustments shall be made prior to averaging beginning-of-year and end-of-year values pursuant to § 1.861-9T(g)(2). In apportioning interest expense under the modified gross income method, gross income shall be reduced by the amount of income to which interest expense is directly allocated under this section.

(e) *Treatment of certain related controlled foreign corporation indebtedness*—(1) *In general.* In taxable years beginning after 1987, if a United States shareholder has incurred substantially disproportionate indebtedness in relation to the indebtedness of its related controlled foreign corporations so that such corporations have excess related person indebtedness (as determined under step 4 in subdivision (iv) of this paragraph (e)(1)), the third party interest expense of the related United States shareholder (excluding amounts allocated under paragraphs (b) and (c)) in an amount equal to the interest income received on such excess related person indebtedness shall be allocated to gross income in the various separate limitation categories described in section 904(d)(1) in the manner prescribed in step 6 in subdivision (vi) of this paragraph (e)(1). This computation shall be performed as follows.

(i) *Step 1: Compute the debt-to-asset ratio of the related United States shareholder.* The debt-to-asset ratio of the related United States shareholder is the ratio between—

(A) The average month-end debt level of the related United States shareholder taking into account debt owing to any obligee who is not a related person as defined in section § 1.861-8T(c)(2), and

(B) The value of assets (tax book or fair market) of the related United States shareholder including stockholdings and obligations of related controlled foreign corporations but excluding stockholdings and obligations of members of the affiliated group (as defined in § 1.861-11T(d)).

(ii) *Step 2: Compute aggregate debt-to-asset ratio of all related controlled foreign corporations.* The aggregate debt-to-asset ratio of all related controlled foreign corporations is the ratio between—

(A) The average aggregate month-end debt level of all related controlled foreign corporations for their taxable years ending during the related United States shareholder's taxable year taking into account only indebtedness owing to persons other than the related United States shareholder or the related United States shareholder's other related controlled foreign corporations ("third party indebtedness"), and

(B) The aggregate value (tax book or fair market) of the assets of all related controlled foreign corporations for their taxable years ending during the related United States shareholder's taxable year excluding stockholdings in and obligations of the related United States shareholder or

Reg. § 1.861-10T(d)(1)

the related United States shareholder's other related controlled foreign corporations.

(iii) *Step 3: Compute aggregate related person debt of all related controlled foreign corporations.* This amount equals the average aggregate month-end debt level of all related controlled foreign corporations for their taxable years ending with or within the related United States shareholder's taxable year, taking into account only debt which is owed to the related United States shareholder ("related person indebtedness").

(iv) *Step 4: Computation of excess related person indebtedness and computation of the income therefrom*— (A) *General rule.* If the ratio computed under step 2 is less than applicable percentage of the ratio computed under step 1, the taxpayer shall add to the aggregate third party indebtedness of all related controlled foreign corporations determined under paragraph (e)(1)(ii)(A) of this section that portion of the related person indebtedness computed under step 3 that, when combined with the aggregate third party indebtedness of all controlled foreign corporations, makes the ratio computed under step 2 equal to applicable percentage of the ratio computed under step 1. The amount of aggregate related person debt that is so added to the aggregate third party debt of related controlled foreign corporations is considered to constitute excess related person indebtedness. For purposes of this paragraph (e)(1)(iv)(A), the term "applicable percentage" means the designated percentages for taxable years beginning during the following calendar years:

Taxable Years Beginning In	Applicable Percentage
1988	50
1989	65
1990 and thereafter	80

(B) *Elective quadratic formula.* In calculating the amount of excess related party indebtedness of related controlled foreign corporations, the United States shareholder's debt-to-asset ratio may be adjusted to reflect the amount by which its debt and assets would be reduced had the related controlled foreign corporations incurred the excess related party indebtedness directly to third parties. In such case, the ratio computed in Step 1 is adjusted to reflect a reduction of both portions of the ratio by the amount of excess related person indebtedness as computed under this paragraph (e)(1)(ii)(A). Excess related person indebtedness may be computed under the following formula, under which excess related person indebtedness equals the smallest positive amount (not exceeding the aggregate amount of related controlled foreign corporation indebtedness) that is a solution to the following formula (with X equalling the amount of excess related person indebtedness):

$$\frac{\text{Aggregate Third Party Debt of Related US Shareholder} - X}{\text{US Shareholder Assets} - X} \times \text{Applicable Percentage For Year} = \frac{\text{Aggregate Third Party Debt of Related CFCs} + X}{\text{Related CFC Assets}}$$

Guidance concerning the solution of this equation is set forth in Example (2) of § 1.861-12(k).

(C) *Computation of interest income received on excess related party indebtedness.* The amount of interest income received on excess related person indebtedness equals the total interest income on related person indebtedness derived by the related United States shareholder during the taxable year multiplied by the ratio of excess related person indebtedness over the aggregate related person indebtedness for the taxable year.

(v) *Step 5: Determine the aggregate amount of related controlled foreign corporation obligations held by the related United States shareholder in each limitation category.* The aggregate amount of related controlled foreign corporation obligations held by the related United States shareholder in each limitation category equals the sum of the value of all such obligations in each limitation category. Solely for purposes of this paragraph (e)(1)(v), each debt obligation in a related controlled foreign corporation held by a related United States shareholder shall be attributed to separate limitation categories in the same manner as the stock of the obligor would be attributed under the rules of § 1.861-12T(c)(3), whether or not such stock is held directly by such related United States shareholder.

(vi) *Step 6: Direct allocation of United States shareholder third party interest expense.* Third party interest expense of the related United States shareholder equal to the amount of interest income received on excess related person indebtedness as determined in step 4 shall be allocated among the various separate limitation categories in proportion to the relative aggregate amount of related controlled foreign corporation obligations held by the related United States shareholder in

Reg. § 1.861-10T(e)(1)

each such category, as determined under step 5. The remaining portion of third party interest expense will be apportioned as provided in §§ 1.861-8T through 1.861-13T, excluding this paragraph.

(2) *Definitions*—(i) *United States shareholder.* For purposes of this paragraph, the term "United States shareholder" has the same meaning as defined by section 957, except that, in the case of a United States shareholder that is a member an affiliated group (as defined in § 1.861-11T(d)), the entire affiliated group shall be considered to constitute a single United States shareholder. The term "related United States shareholder" is the United States shareholder (as defined in this paragraph (e)(2)(i)) with respect to which related controlled foreign corporations (as defined in paragraph (e)(2)(ii) of this section) are related within the meaning of that paragraph.

(ii) *Related controlled foreign corporation.* For purposes of this section, the term "related controlled foreign corporation" means any controlled foreign corporation which is a related person (as defined in § 1.861-8T(c)(2)) to a United States shareholder (as defined paragraph (e)(2)(i) of this section).

(iii) *Value of assets and amount of liabilities.* For purposes of this section, the value of assets is determined under § 1.861-9T(g). Thus, in the case of assets that are denominated in foreign currency, the average of the beginning-of-year and end-of-year values is determined in foreign currency and translated into dollars using exchange rates on the last day of the related United States shareholder's taxable year. In the case of liabilities that are denominated in foreign currency, the average month-end debt level of such liabilities is determined in foreign currency and then translated into dollars using exchange rates on the last day of the related United States shareholder's taxable year.

(3) *Treatment of certain stock.* To the extent that there is insufficient related person indebtedness of all related controlled foreign corporations under step 3 in paragraph (e)(1)(iii) of this section to achieve an equal ratio in step 4 of paragraph (e)(1)(iv) of this section, certain stock held by the related United States shareholder will be treated as related person indebtedness. Such stock includes—

(i) Any stock in the related controlled foreign corporation that is treated in the same manner as debt under the law of any foreign country that grants a deduction for interest or original issue discount relating to such stock, and

(ii) Any stock in a related controlled foreign corporation that has made loans to, or held stock described in this paragraph (e)(3) in, another related controlled foreign corporation. However, such stock shall be treated as related person indebtedness only to the extent of the principal amount of such loans.

For purposes of computing income from excess related person indebtedness in step 4 of paragraph (e)(1)(iv) of this section, stock that is treated under this paragraph as related person indebtedness shall be considered to yield interest in an amount equal to the interest that would be computed on an equal amount of indebtedness under section 1274. Only dividends actually paid thereon shall be included in gross income for other purposes.

(4) *Adjustments to assets in apportioning other interest expense.* In apportioning interest expense under § 1.861-9T, the value of assets in each separate limitation category for the taxable year as determined under § 1.861-9T(g)(3) shall be reduced (but not below zero) by the principal amount of third party indebtedness of the related United States shareholder the interest expense on which is allocated to each such category under paragraph (e)(1) of this section.

(5) *Exceptions*—(i) *Per company rule.* If—

(A) A related controlled foreign corporation with obligations owing to a related United States shareholder has a greater proportion of passive assets than the proportion of passive assets held by the related United States shareholder,

(B) Such passive assets are held in liquid or short term investments, and

(C) There are frequent cash transfers between the related controlled foreign corporation and the related United States shareholder,

the Commissioner, in his discretion, may choose to exclude such a corporation from other related controlled foreign corporations in the application of the rules of this paragraph (e).

(ii) *Aggregate rule.* If it is determined that, in aggregate, the application of the rules of this paragraph (e) increases a taxpayer's foreign tax credit as determined under section 901(a), the Commissioner, in his discretion, may choose not to apply the rules of this paragraph. If the Commissioner exercises discretion under this paragraph (e)(5)(ii), then paragraph (e) shall not apply to any extent to any interest expense of the taxpayer. [Temporary Reg. § 1.861-10T.]

☐ [T.D. 8228, 9-9-88.]

[Reg. § 1.861-11]

§ 1.861-11. **Special rules for allocating and apportioning interest expense of an affiliated group of corporations.**—(a) through (c) [Re-

Determination of Sources of Income

served]. For further guidance, see § 1.861-11T(a) through (c).

(d) *Definition of affiliated group*—(1) *General rule.* For purposes of this section, in general, the term *affiliated group* has the same meaning as is given that term by section 1504, except that section 936 corporations are also included within the affiliated group to the extent provided in paragraph (d)(2) of this section. Section 1504(a) defines an affiliated group as one or more chains of includible corporations connected through 80-percent stock ownership with a common parent corporation which is an includible corporation (as defined in section 1504(b)). In the case of a corporation that either becomes or ceases to be a member of the group during the course of the corporation's taxable year, only the interest expense incurred by the group member during the period of membership shall be allocated and apportioned as if all members of the group were a single corporation. In this regard, assets held during the period of membership shall be taken into account. Other interest expense incurred by the group member during its taxable year but not during the period of membership shall be allocated and apportioned without regard to the other members of the group.

(2) *Inclusion of section 936 corporations*—(i) *Rule*—(A) *In general.* Except as otherwise provided in paragraph (d)(2)(i)(B) of this section, the exclusion of section 936 corporations from the affiliated group under section 1504(b)(4) does not apply for purposes of this section. Thus, a section 936 corporation that meets the ownership requirements of section 1504(a) is a member of the affiliated group.

(B) *Exception for purposes of alternative minimum tax.* The exclusion from the affiliated group of section 936 corporations under section 1504(b)(4) shall be operative for purposes of the application of this section solely in determining the amount of foreign source alternative minimum taxable income within each separate category and the alternative minimum tax foreign tax credit pursuant to section 59(a). Thus, a section 936 corporation that meets the ownership requirements of section 1504(a) is not a member of the affiliated group for purposes of determining the amount of foreign source alternative minimum taxable income within each separate category and the alternative minimum tax foreign tax credit pursuant to section 59(a).

(ii) *Section 936 corporation defined.* For purposes of this section, § 1.861-9, and § 1.861-14, the term *section 936 corporation* means, for any taxable year, a corporation with an election in effect to be eligible for the credit provided under section 936(a)(1) or section 30A for the taxable year.

(iii) *Example.* This example illustrates the provisions of paragraph (d)(2)(i) of this section:

Example—(A) *Facts.* X owns all of the stock of Y. XY constitutes an affiliated group of corporations within the meaning of section 1504(a) and uses the tax book value method of apportionment. In 2000, Y owns all of the stock of Z, a section 936 corporation. Z manufactures widgets in Puerto Rico. Y purchases these widgets and markets them exclusively in the United States. Of the three corporations, only Z has foreign source income, which includes both qualified possessions source investment income and general limitation income. For purposes of section 904, Z's qualified possessions source investment income constitutes foreign source passive income. In computing the section 30A benefit, Y and Z have elected the cost sharing method. Of the three corporations, only X has debt and, thus, only X incurs interest expense.

(B) *Analysis for regular tax.* Assume first that X has no alternative minimum tax liability. Under paragraph (d)(2) of this section, Z is treated as a member of the XY affiliated group for purposes of allocating and apportioning interest expense for regular tax purposes. As provided in § 1.861-11T(b)(2), section 864(e)(1) and (5) do not apply in computing the combined taxable income of Y and Z under section 936, but these rules do apply in computing the foreign source taxable income of the XY affiliated group. The effect of including Z in the affiliated group is that X, the only debtor corporation in the group, must, under the asset method described in § 1.861-9T(g), apportion a part of its interest expense to foreign source passive income and foreign source general limitation income. This is because the assets of Z that generate qualified possessions source investment income and general limitation income are included in computing the group apportionment fractions. The result is that, under section 904(f), X has an overall foreign loss in both the passive and general limitation categories, which currently offsets domestic income and must be recaptured against any subsequent years' foreign passive income and general limitation income, respectively, under the rules of that section.

(C) *Analysis for alternative minimum tax.* Assume, alternatively, that X is liable to pay the alternative minimum tax. Pursuant to section 59(a), X must compute its alternative minimum tax foreign tax credit as if section 904 were applied on the basis of alternative minimum taxable income instead of taxable income. Under paragraph (d)(2)(i)(B) of this section, for purposes of

Reg. § 1.861-11(d)(2)

the apportionment of interest expense in determining alternative minimum taxable income within each limitation category, Z is not considered a member of the XY affiliated group. Thus, the stock (and not the assets) of Z are included in computing the group apportionment fractions. Pursuant to sections 59(g)(4)(C)(iii)(IV), 861(a)(2)(A), and 862(a)(2), dividends paid by a section 936 corporation are foreign source income subject to a separate foreign tax credit limitation for alternative minimum tax purposes. Thus, under § 1.861-9T(g)(3), the stock of Z must be considered attributable solely to the statutory grouping consisting of foreign source dividends from Z. The effect of excluding Z from the affiliated group is that X must apportion a part of its interest expense to the separate category for foreign source dividends from Z in computing alternative minimum taxable income within each separate category. If, as a result, under section 904(f), X has a separate limitation loss or an overall foreign loss in the category for dividends from Z for alternative minimum tax purposes, then that loss must be allocated against X's other income (separate limitation or United States source, as the case may be). The loss must be recaptured in subsequent years under the rules of section 904(f) for purposes of the alternative minimum tax foreign tax credit.

(iv) *Effective date.* This paragraph (d)(2) applies to taxable years beginning after December 31, 1989.

(d)(3) through (6) [Reserved]. For further guidance see § 1.861-11T(d)(3) through (6).

(7) *Special rules for the application of § 1.861-11T(d)(6).* The attribution rules of section 1563(e) and the regulations under that section shall apply in determining indirect ownership under § 1.861-11T(d)(6). The Commissioner shall have the authority to disregard trusts, partnerships, and pass-through entities that break affiliated status. Corporations described in § 1.861-11T(d)(6) shall be considered to constitute members of an affiliated group that does not file a consolidated return and shall therefore be subject to the limitations imposed under § 1.861-11T(g). The affiliated group filing a consolidated return shall be considered to constitute a single corporation for purposes of applying the rules of § 1.861-11T(g). For taxable years beginning after December 31, 1989, § 1.861-11T(d)(6)(i) shall not apply in determining foreign source alternative minimum taxable income within each separate category and the alternative minimum tax foreign tax credit pursuant to section 59(a) to the extent that such application would result in the inclusion of a section 936 corporation within the affiliated group. This paragraph (d)(7) applies to taxable years beginning after December 31, 1986.

(e) through (g) [Reserved]. For further guidance, see § 1.861-11T(e) through (g). [Reg. § 1.861-11.]

☐ [T.D. 8916, 12-29-2000.]

[Reg. § 1.861-11T]

§ 1.861-11T. **Special rules for allocating and apportioning interest expense of an affiliated group of corporations (Temporary regulations.)**—(a) *In general.* Sections 1.861-9T, 1.861-10T, 1.861-12T, and 1.861-13T provide rules that are generally applicable in apportioning interest expense. The rules of this section relate to affiliated groups of corporations and implement section 864(e)(1) and (5), which requires affiliated group allocation and apportionment of interest expense. The rules of this section apply to taxable years beginning after December 31, 1986, except as otherwise provided in § 1.861-13T. Paragraph (b) of this section describes the scope of the application of the rule for the allocation and apportionment of interest expense of affiliated groups of corporations, which is contained in paragraph (c) of this section. Paragraph (d) of this section sets forth the definition of the term "affiliated group" for purposes of this section. Paragraph (e) describes the treatment of loans between members of an affiliated group. Paragraph (f) of this section provides rules concerning the affiliated group allocation and apportionment of interest expense in computing the combined taxable income of a FSC or DISC and its related supplier. Paragraph (g) of this section describes the treatment of losses caused by apportionment of interest expense in the case of an affiliated group that does not file a consolidated return.

(b) *Scope of application*—(1) *Application of section 864(e)(1) and (5) (concerning the definition and treatment of affiliated groups).* Section 864(e)(1) and (5) and the portions of this section implementing section 864(e)(1) and (5) apply to the computation of foreign source taxable income for purposes of section 904 (relating to various limitations on the foreign tax credit). Section 904 imposes separate foreign tax credit limitations on passive income, high withholding interest income, financial services income, shipping income, income consisting of dividends from each noncontrolled section 902 corporation, income consisting of dividends from a DISC or former DISC, taxable income attributable to foreign trade income within the meaning of section 923(b), distributions from an FSC or former FSC, and all other forms of foreign source income not enumerated above ("general limitation income"). Section 864(e)(1) and (5) and the portions of this section implementing section 864(e)(1) and (5) also apply in connection with section 907 to determine reductions in the amount allowed as a foreign tax credit under section 901. Section 864(e)(1) and (5) and the portions of this section implementing section 864(e)(1) and (5) also apply to the computation of the combined taxable income of the related supplier and a foreign sales corporation (FSC) (under sections 921 through 927) as well as the combined taxable income of the related supplier and a domestic international sales corporation (DISC) (under sections 991 through 997).

(2) *Nonapplication of section 864(e)(1) and (5) (concerning the definition and treatment of affiliated groups).* Section 864(e)(1) and (5) and the portions of this section implementing section 864(e)(1) and (5) do not apply to the computation of subpart F income of controlled foreign corporations (under sections 951 through 964), the computation of combined taxable income of a possessions corporation and its affiliates (under section 936), or the computation of effectively connected taxable income of foreign corporations. For the rules with respect to the allocation and apportionment of interest expenses of foreign corporations other than controlled foreign corporations, see §§ 1.882-4 and 1.882-5.

(c) *General rule for affiliated corporations.* Except as otherwise provided in this section, the taxable income of each member of an affiliated group within each statutory grouping shall be determined by allocating and apportioning the interest expense of each member according to apportionment fractions which are computed as if all members of such group were a single corporation. For purposes of determining these apportionment fractions, stock in corporations within the affiliated group (as defined in section 864(e)(5) and the rules of this section) shall not be taken into account. In the case of an affiliated group of corporations that files a consolidated return, consolidated foreign tax credit limitations are computed for the group in accordance with the rules of § 1.1502-4. Except as otherwise provided, all the interest expense of all members of the group will be treated as definitely related and therefore allocable to all the gross income of the members of the group and all the assets of all the members of the group shall be taken into account in apportioning this interest expense. For purposes of this section, the term "taxpayer" refers to the affiliated group (regardless of whether the group files a consolidated return), rather than to the separate members thereof.

(d)(1) and (2) [Reserved]. For further guidance, see § 1.861-11(d)(1) and (2).

(3) *Treatment of life insurance companies subject to taxation under section 801*—(i) *General rule.* A life insurance company that is subject to taxation under section 801 shall be considered to constitute a member of the affiliated group composed of companies not taxable under section 801 only if a parent corporation so elects under section 1504(c)(2)(A) of the Code. If a parent does not so elect, no adjustments shall be required with respect to such an insurance company under paragraph (g) of this section.

(ii) *Treatment of stock.* Stock of a life insurance company that is subject to taxation under section 801 that is not included in an affiliated group shall be disregarded in the allocation and apportionment of the interest expense of such affiliated group.

(4) *Treatment of certain financial corporations*—(i) *In general.* In the case of an affiliated group (as defined in paragraph (d)(1) of this section), any members that constitute financial corporations as defined in paragraph (d)(4)(ii) of this section shall be treated as a separate affiliated group consisting of financial corporations (the "financial group"). The members of the group that do not constitute financial corporations shall be treated as members of a separate affiliated group consisting of nonfinancial corporations ("the nonfinancial group").

(ii) *Financial corporation defined.* The term "financial corporation" means any corporation which meets all of the following conditions:

(A) It is described in section 581 (relating to the definition of a bank) or section 591 (relating to the deduction for dividends paid on deposits by mutual savings banks, cooperative banks, domestic building and loan associations, and other savings institutions chartered and supervised as savings and loan or similar associations);

(B) Its business is predominantly with persons other than related persons (within the meaning of section 864(d)(4) and the regulations thereunder) or their customers; and

(C) It is required by state or Federal law to be operated separately from any other entity which is not such an institution.

(iii) *Treatment of bank holding companies.* The total aggregate interest expense of any member of an affiliated group that constitutes a bank holding company subject to regulation under the Bank Holding Company Act of 1956 shall be prorated between the financial group and the nonfinancial group on the basis of the assets in the financial and nonfinancial groups. For purposes of making this proration, the assets of each member of each group, and not the stock basis in each member, shall be taken into account. Any direct or indirect subsidiary of a bank holding company that is predominantly engaged in the active conduct of a banking, financing, or similar business shall be considered to be a financial corporation for purposes of this paragraph (d)(4). The interest expense of the bank holding company must be further apportioned in accordance with § 1.861-9T(f) to the various section 904(d) categories of income contained in both the financial group and the nonfinancial group on the basis of the assets owned by each group. For purposes of computing the apportionment fractions for each group, the assets owned directly by a bank holding company within each limitation category described in section 904(d)(1) (other than stock in affiliates or assets described in § 1.861-9T(f)) shall be treated as owned pro rata by the nonfinancial group and the financial group based on the relative amounts of investment of the bank holding company in the nonfinancial group and financial group.

(iv) *Consideration of stock of the members of one group held by members of the other group.* In apportioning interest expense, the nonfinancial group shall not take into account the stock of any lower-tier corporation that is treated as a member of the financial group under paragraph (d)(4)(i) of this section. Conversely, in apportioning interest expense, the financial group shall not take into account the stock of any lower-tier corporation that is treated as a member of the nonfinancial group under paragraph (d)(4)(i) of this section. For the treatment of loans between members of the financial group and members of the nonfinancial group, see paragraph (e)(1) of this section.

(5) *Example*—(i) *Facts.* X, a domestic corporation which is not a bank holding company, is the parent of domestic corporations Y and Z. Z owns 100 percent of the stock Z1, which is also a domestic corporation. X, Y, Z, and Z1 were organized after January 1, 1987, and constitute an affiliated group within the meaning of paragraph (d)(1) of this section. Y and Z are financial corporations described in paragraph (d)(4) of this section. X also owns 25 percent of the stock of A, a domestic corporation. Y owns 25 percent of the voting stock of B, a foreign corporation that is not a controlled foreign corporation. Z owns less than 10 percent of the voting stock of C, another foreign corporation. The foreign source income generated by Y's or Z's direct assets is exclusively financial services income. The foreign source income generated by X's or Z1's direct assets is exclusively general limitation income. X and Z1 are not financial corporations described in paragraph (d)(4)(ii) of this section. Y and Z, therefore, constitute a separate affiliated group apart from X and Z1 for purposes of section 864(e). The combined interest expense of Y and Z of $100,000 ($50,000 each) is apportioned separately on the basis of their assets. The combined interest expense of X and Z1 of $50,000 ($25,000 each) is allocated on the basis of the assets of the XZ1 group.

Analysis of the YZ group assets

Adjusted basis of assets of the YZ group that generate foreign source financial services income (excluding stock of foreign subsidiaries not included in the YZ affiliated group)	$ 200,000
Z's basis in the C stock (not adjusted by the allocable amount of C's earnings and profits because Z owns less than 10 percent of the stock) which would be considered to generate passive income in the hands of a nonfinancial services entity but is considered to generate financial services income when in the hands of Z, a financial services entity	$ 100,000
Y's basis in the B stock (adjusted by the allocable amount of B's earnings and profits) which generates dividends subject to a separate limitation for B dividends	$ 100,000
Adjusted basis of assets of the YZ group that generate U.S. source income	$ 600,000
Total assets	$1,000,000

Analysis of the XZ1 group assets

Adjusted basis of assets of the XZ1 group that generate foreign source general limitation income	$ 500,000
Adjusted basis of assets of the XZ1 group other than A stock that generate domestic source income	$1,900,000
X's basis in the A stock adjusted by the allocable amount of A's earnings and profits	$ 100,000
Total domestic assets	$2,000,000
Total assets	$2,500,000

Reg. § 1.861-11T(d)(5)

Determination of Sources of Income

(ii) *Allocation.* No portion of the $50,000 deduction of the YZ group is definitely related solely to specific property within the meaning of § 1.861-10T. Thus, the YZ group's deduction for interest is related to all its activities and properties. Similarly, no portion of the $50,000 deduction of the XZ1 group is definitely related solely to specific property within the meaning of § 1.861-10T. Thus, the XZ1 group's deduction for interest is related to all its activities and properties.

(iii) *Apportionment.* The YZ group would apportion its interest expense as follows:

To gross financial services income from sources outside the United States:

$50,000 × $\dfrac{\$300,000}{\$1,000,000}$ $15,000

To gross income subject to a separate limitation for dividends from B:

$50,000 × $\dfrac{\$100,000}{\$1,000,000}$ .... $ 5,000

To gross income from sources inside the United States:

$50,000 × $\dfrac{\$600,000}{\$1,000,000}$ $30,000

The XZ1 group would apportion its interest expense as follows:

To gross general limitation income from sources outside the United States:

$50,000 × $\dfrac{\$500,000}{\$2,500,000}$ $10,000

To gross income from sources inside the United States:

$50,000 × $\dfrac{\$2,000,000}{\$2,500,000}$ $40,000

(6) *Certain unaffiliated corporations.* Certain corporations that are not described in paragraph (d)(1) of this section will nonetheless be considered to constitute affiliated corporations for purposes of §§ 1.861-9T through 1.861-13T. These corporations include:

(i) Any includible corporation (as defined in section 1504(b) without regard to section 1504(b)(4)) if 80 percent of either the vote or value of all outstanding stock of such corporation is owned directly or indirectly by an includible corporation or by members of an affiliated group, and

(ii) Any foreign corporation if 80 percent of the either the vote or value of all outstanding stock of such corporation is owned directly or indirectly by members of an affiliated group, and if more than 50 percent of the gross income of such corporation for the taxable year is effectively connected with the conduct of a United States trade or business. If 80 percent or more of the gross income of such corporation is effectively connected income, then all the assets of such corporation and all of its interest expense shall be taken into account. If between 50 and 80 percent of the gross income of such corporation is effectively connected income, then only the assets of such corporation that generate effectively connected income and a percentage of its interest expense equal to the percentage of its assets that generate effectively connected income shall be taken into account.

(7) *Special rules for the application of § 1.861-11T(d)(6).* [Reserved]. For special rules for the application of § 1.861-11T(d)(6), see § 1.861-11(d)(7).

(e) *Loans between members of an affiliated group*—(1) *General rule.* In the case of loans (including any receivable) between members of an affiliated group, as defined in paragraph (d) of this section, for purposes of apportioning interest expense, the indebtedness of the member borrower shall not be considered an asset of the member lender. However, in the case of members of separate financial and nonfinancial groups under paragraph (d)(4) of this section, the indebtedness of the member borrower shall be considered an asset of the member lender and such asset shall be characterized by reference to the member lender's income from the asset as determined under paragraph (e)(2)(ii) of this section. For purposes of this paragraph (e), the terms "related person interest income" and "related person interest payment" refer to interest paid and received by members of the same affiliated group as defined in paragraph (d) of this section.

(2) *Treatment of interest expense within the affiliated group*—(i) *General rule.* A member borrower shall deduct related person interest payments in the same manner as unrelated person

Reg. § 1.861-11T(e)(2)

Determination of Sources of Income

See p. 20,601 for regulations not amended to reflect law changes

interest expense using group apportionment fractions computed under § 1.861-9T(f). A member lender shall include related person interest income in the same class of gross income as the class of gross income from which the member borrower deducts the related person interest payment.

(ii) *Special rule for loans between financial and nonfinancial affiliated corporations.* In the case of a loan between two affiliated corporations only one of which constitutes a financial corporation under paragraph (d)(4) of this section, the member borrower shall allocate and apportion related person interest payments in the same manner as unrelated person interest expense using group apportionment fractions computed under § 1.861-9T(f). The source of the related person interest income to the member lender shall be determined under section 861(a)(1).

(iii) *Special rule for high withholding tax interest.* In the case of an affiliated corporation that pays interest that is high withholding tax interest under § 1.904-5(f)(1) to another affiliated corporation, the interest expense of the payor shall be allocated to high withholding tax interest.

(3) *Back-to-back loans.* If a member of the affiliated group makes a loan to a nonmember who makes a loan to a member borrower, the rule of paragraph (e)(1) and (2) of this section shall apply, in the Commissioner's discretion, as if the member lender made the loan directly to the member borrower, provided that the loans constitute a back-to-back loan transaction. Such loans will constitute a back-to-back loan for purposes of this paragraph (e) if the loan by the nonmember would not have been made or maintained on substantially the same terms irrespective of the loan of funds by the lending member to the nonmember or other intermediary party.

(4) *Examples.* The rules of this paragraph (e) may be illustrated by the following examples.

Example (1). X, a domestic corporation, is the parent of Y, a domestic corporation. X and Y were organized after January 1, 1987, and constitute an affiliated group within the meaning of paragraph (d)(1) of this section. Among X's assets is the note of Y for the amount of $100,000. Because X and Y are members of an affiliated group, Y's note does not constitute an asset for purposes of apportionment. The apportionment fractions for the relevant tax year of the XY group are 50 percent domestic, 40 percent foreign general, and 10 percent foreign passive. Y deducts its related person interest payment using those apportionment fractions. Of the $10,000 in related person interest income received by X, $5,000 consists of domestic source income, $4,000 consists of foreign general limitation income, and $1,000 consists of foreign passive income.

Example (2). X is a domestic corporation organized after January 1, 1987. X owns all the stock of Y, a domestic corporation. On June 1, 1987, X loans $100,000 to Z, an unrelated person. On June 2, 1987, Z makes a loan to Y with terms substantially similar to those of the loan from X to Z. Based on the facts and circumstances of the transaction, it is determined that Z would not have made the loan to Y on the same terms if X had not made the loan to Z. Because the transaction constitutes a back-to-back loan, as defined in paragraph (e)(3) of this section, the Commissioner may require, in his discretion, that neither the note of Y nor the note of Z may be considered an asset of X for purposes of this section.

(f) *Computations of combined taxable income.* In the computation of the combined taxable income of any FSC or DISC and its related supplier which is a member of an affiliated group under the pricing rules of sections 925 or 994, the combined taxable income of such FSC or DISC and its related supplier shall be reduced by the portion of the total interest expense of the affiliated group that is incurred in connection with those assets of the group used in connection with export sales involving that FSC or DISC. This amount shall be computed by multiplying the total interest expense of the affiliated group and interest expense of the FSC or DISC by a fraction the numerator of which is the assets of the affiliated group and of the FSC or DISC generating foreign trade income or gross income attributable to qualified export receipts, as the case may be, and the denominator of which is the total assets of the affiliated group and the FSC or DISC. Under this rule, interest of other group members may be attributed to the combined taxable income of a FSC or DISC and its related supplier without affecting the amount of interest otherwise deductible by the FSC or DISC, the related supplier or other member of the affiliated group. The FSC or DISC is entitled to only the statutory portion of the combined taxable income, net of any deemed interest expense, which determines the commission paid to the FSC or DISC or the transfer price of qualifying export property sold to the FSC or DISC.

(g) *Losses created through apportionment*—(1) *General rules.* In the case of an affiliated group that is eligible to file, but does not file, a consolidated return and in the case of any corporation described in paragraph (d)(6) of this section, the foreign tax credits in any separate limitation category are limited to the credits computed under the rules of this paragraph (g). As a consequence of the affiliated group allocation and apportion-

Determination of Sources of Income

ment of interest expense required by section 864(e)(1) and this section, interest expense of a group member may be apportioned for section 904 purposes to a limitation category in which that member has no gross income, resulting in a loss in that limitation category. The same is true in connection with any expense other than interest that is subject to apportionment under the rules of section 864(e)(6) of the Code. Any reference to "interest expense" in this paragraph (g) shall be treated as including such expenses. For purposes of this paragraph, the term "limitation category" includes domestic source income, as well as the types of income described in section 904(d)(1)(A) through (I). A loss of one affiliate in a limitation category will reduce the income of another member in the same limitation category if a consolidated return is filed. (See § 1.1502-4.) If a consolidated return is not filed, this netting does not occur. Accordingly, in such a case, the following adjustments among members are required in order to give effect to the group allocation of interest expense:

(i) Losses created through group apportionment of interest expense in one or more limitation categories within a given member must be eliminated; and

(ii) A corresponding amount of income of other members in the same limitation category must be recharacterized.

Such adjustments shall be accomplished, in accordance with paragraph (g)(2) of this section, without changing the total taxable income of any member and before the application of section 904(f). Section 904(f) (including section 904(f)(5)) does not apply to a loss created through the apportionment of interest expense to the extent that the loss is eliminated pursuant to paragraph (g)(2)(ii) of this section. For purposes of this section, the terms "limitation adjustment" and "recharacterization" mean the recharacterization of income in one limitation category as income in another limitation category.

(2) *Mechanics of computation*—(i) *Step 1: Computation of consolidated taxable income.* The members of an affiliated group must first allocate and apportion all other deductible expenses other than interest. The members must then deduct from their respective gross incomes within each limitation category interest expense apportioned under the rules of § 1.861-9T(f). The taxable income of the entire affiliated group within each limitation category is then totalled.

(ii) *Step 2: Loss offset adjustments.* If, after step 1, a member has losses in a given limitation category or limitation categories created through apportionment of interest expense, any such loss (*i.e.*, the portion of such loss equal to interest expense) shall be eliminated by offsetting that loss against taxable income in other limitation categories of that member to the extent of the taxable income of other members within the same limitation category as the loss. If the member has taxable income in more than one limitation category, then the loss shall offset taxable income in all such limitation categories on a pro rata basis. If there is insufficient domestic income of the member to offset the net losses in all foreign limitation categories caused by the apportionment of interest expense, the losses in each limitation category shall be recharacterized as domestic losses to the extent of the taxable income of other members in the same respective limitation categories. After these adjustments are made, the income of the entire affiliated group within each limitation category is totalled again.

(iii) *Step 3: Determination of amount subject to recharacterization.* In order to determine the amount of income to be recharacterized in step 4, the income totals computed under step 1 in each limitation category shall be subtracted from the income totals computed under step 2 in each limitation category.

(iv) *Step 4: Recharacterization.* Because any differences determined under step 3 represent deviations from the consolidated totals computed under step 1, such differences (in any limitation category) must be eliminated.

(A) *Limitation categories to be reduced.* In the case of any limitation category in which there is a positive change, the income of group members with income in that limitation category must be reduced on a pro rata basis (by reference to net income figures as determined under Step 2) to the extent of such positive change ("limitation reductions"). Each member shall separately compute the sum of the limitation reductions.

(B) *Limitation categories to be increased.* In any case in which only one limitation category has a negative change in Step 3, the sum of the limitation reductions within each member is added to that limitation category. In the case in which multiple limitation categories have negative changes in Step 3, the sum of the limitation reductions within each member is prorated among the negative change limitation categories based on the ratio that the negative change for the entire group in each limitation category bears to the total of all negative changes for the entire group in all limitation categories.

(3) *Examples.* The following examples illustrate the principles of this paragraph.

Example (1)—(i) *Facts.* X, a domestic corporation, is the parent of domestic corporations Y

46,044   Determination of Sources of Income

See p. 20,601 for regulations not amended to reflect law changes

and Z. X, Y, and Z were organized after January 1, 1987, constitute an affiliated group within the meaning of paragraph (d)(1) of this section, but do not file a consolidated return. The XYZ group apportions its interest expense on the basis of the fair market value of its assets. X, Y, and Z have the following assets, interest expense, and taxable income before apportioning interest expense:

Assets	X	Y	Z	Total
Domestic	2,000.00	0	1,000.00	3,000.00
Foreign Passive	0	50.00	50.00	100.00
Foreign General	0	700.00	200.00	900.00
Interest expense	48.00	12.00	80.00	140.00

Taxable Income (pre-interest)				
Domestic	100.00	0	63.00	163.00
Foreign Passive	0	5.00	5.00	10.00
Foreign General	0	60.00	35.00	95.00

(ii) *Step 1: Computation of consolidated taxable income.* Each member of the XYZ group apportions its interest expense according to group apportionment ratios determined under the asset method described in § 1.861-9T(f), yielding the following results:

Apportioned interest expense	X	Y	Z	Total
Domestic	36.00	9.00	60.00	105.00
Foreign Passive	1.20	0.30	2.00	3.50
Foreign General	10.80	2.70	18.00	31.50
Total	48.00	12.00	80.00	140.00

The members of the group then compute taxable income within each category by deducting the apportioned interest expense from the amounts of pre-interest taxable income specified in the facts in paragraph (i), yielding the following results:

Taxable Income	X	Y	Z	Total
Domestic	64.00	−9.00	3.00	58.00
Foreign Passive	−1.20	4.70	3.00	6.50
Foreign General	−10.80	57.30	17.00	63.50
Total	52.00	53.00	23.00	128.00

(iii) *Step 2: Loss offset adjustments.* Because X and Y have losses created through apportionment, these losses must be eliminated by reducing taxable income of the member in other limitation categories. Because X has a total of $12 in apportionment losses and because it has only one limitation category with income (*i.e.*, domestic), domestic income must be reduced by $12, thus eliminating its apportionment losses. Because Y has a total of $9 in apportionment losses and because it has two limitation categories with income (*i.e.*, foreign passive and foreign general limitation), the income in these two limitation categories must be reduced on a pro rata basis in order to eliminate its apportionment losses. In summary, the following adjustments are required:

Loss Offset Adjustments	X	Y	Z	Total
Domestic	−12.00	+9.00	0	−3.00
Foreign Passive	+1.20	−0.68	0	+0.52
Foreign General	+10.80	−8.32	0	+2.48

These adjustments yield the following adjusted taxable income figures:

Adjusted Taxable Income	X	Y	Z	Total
Domestic	52.00	0	3.00	55.00
Foreign Passive	0	4.02	3.00	7.02
Foreign General	0	48.98	17.00	65.98
Total	52.00	53.00	23.00	128.00

(iv) *Step 3: Determination of amount subject to recharacterization.* The adjustments performed under Step 2 led to a change in the group's taxable income within each limitation category. The total loss offset adjustments column shown in paragraph (iii) above shows the net deviations between Steps 1 and 2.

(v) *Step 4: Recharacterization.* The loss offset adjustments yield a positive change in the

Reg. § 1.861-11T(g)(3)

Determination of Sources of Income

foreign passive and the foreign general limitation categories. Y and Z both have income in these limitation categories. Accordingly, the income of Y and Z in each of these limitation categories must be reduced on a pro rata basis (by reference to the adjusted taxable income figures) to the extent of the positive change in each limitation category. The total positive change in the foreign passive limitation category is $0.52. The adjusted taxable income of Y in the foreign passive limitation category is $4.02 and the adjusted taxable income of Z in the foreign passive limitation category is $3. Therefore, $0.30 is drawn from Y and $0.22 is drawn from Z. The total positive change in the foreign general limitation category is $2.48. The adjusted taxable income of Y in the foreign general limitation category is $48.98, and the adjusted taxable income of Z in the foreign general limitation category is $17. Therefore, $1.84 is drawn from Y and $.64 is drawn from Z.

The members must then separately compute the sum of the limitation reductions. Y has limitation reductions of $0.30 in the foreign passive limitation category and $1.84 in the foreign general limitation category, yielding total limitation reduction of $2.14. Under these facts, domestic income is the only limitation category requiring a positive adjustment. Accordingly, Y's domestic income is increased by $2.14. Z has limitation reductions of $0.22 in the foreign passive limitation category and $0.64 in the foreign general limitation category, yielding total limitation reductions of $0.86. Under these facts, domestic income is the only limitation category of Z requiring a positive adjustment. Accordingly, Z's domestic income is increased by $0.86.

Recharacterization Adjustments	X	Y	Z	Total
Domestic	0	+2.14	+0.86	+3.00
Foreign Passive	0	−0.30	−0.22	−0.52
Foreign General	0	−1.84	−0.64	−2.48

These recharacterization adjustments yield the following final taxable income figures:

Final Taxable Income	X	Y	Z	Total
Domestic	52.00	2.14	3.86	58.00
Foreign Passive	0	3.72	2.78	6.50
Foreign General	0	47.14	16.36	63.50
Total	52.00	53.00	23.00	128.00

Example (2)—(i) *Facts.* X, a domestic corporation, is the parent of domestic corporations Y and Z. X, Y, and Z were organized after January 1, 1987, constitute an affiliated group within the meaning of paragraph (d)(1) of this section, but do not file a consolidated return. Moreover, X has served as the sole borrower in the group and, as a result, has sustained an overall loss. The XYZ group apportions its interest expense on the basis of the fair market value of its assets. X, Y, and Z have the following assets, interest expense, and taxable income before interest expense:

Assets	X	Y	Z	Total
Domestic	2,000.00	0	1,000.00	3,000.00
Foreign Passive	0	50.00	50.00	100.00
Foreign General	0	700.00	200.00	900.00
Interest Expense	140.00	0	0	140.00

Taxable Income (pre-interest)	X	Y	Z	Total
Domestic	100.00	0	100.00	200.00
Foreign Passive	0	5.00	5.00	10.00
Foreign General	0	70.00	35.00	105.00

(ii) *Step 1: Computation of consolidated taxable income.* Each member of the XYZ group apportions its interest expense according to group apportionment ratios determined under the asset method described in § 1.861-9T(g), yielding the following results:

Apportioned Interest Expense	X	Y	Z	Total
Domestic	105.00	0	0	105.00
Foreign Passive	3.50	0	0	3.50
Foreign General	31.50	0	0	31.50
Total	140.00	0	0	140.00

Reg. § 1.861-11T(g)(3)

46,046   Determination of Sources of Income
See p. 20,601 for regulations not amended to reflect law changes

The members of the group then compute taxable income within each category by deducting the apportioned interest expense from the amounts of pre-interest taxable income specified in the facts in paragraph (i), yielding the following results:

Taxable Income	X	Y	Z	Total
Domestic	−5.00	0	100.00	95.00
Foreign Passive	−3.50	5.00	5.00	6.50
Foreign General	−31.50	70.00	35.00	73.50
Total	−40.00	75.00	140.00	175.00

(iii) *Step 2: Loss offset adjustment.* Because X has insufficient domestic income to offset the sum of the losses in the foreign limitation categories caused by apportionment, the amount of apportionment losses in each limitation category shall be recharacterized as domestic losses to the extent of taxable income of other members in the same limitation category. This is accomplished by adding to each foreign limitation categories an amount equal to the loss therein and by subtracting the sum of such foreign losses from domestic income, as follows:

Loss Offset Adjustments	X	Y	Z	Total
Domestic	−35.00	0	0	−35.00
Foreign Passive	+3.50	0	0	+3.50
Foreign General	+31.50	0	0	+31.50

These adjustments yield the following adjusted taxable income figures:

Adjusted Taxable Income	X	Y	Z	Total
Domestic	−40.00	0	100.00	60.00
Foreign Passive	0	5.00	5.00	10.00
Foreign General	0	70.00	35.00	105.00
Total	−40.00	75.00	140.00	175.00

(iv) *Step 3: Determination of amount subject to recharacterization.* The adjustments performed under Step 2 led to a change in the group's taxable income within each limitation category. The total loss offset adjustments column shown in paragraph (iii) above shows the net deviations between Steps 1 and 2.

(v) *Step 4: Recharacterization.* The loss offset adjustments yield a positive change in the foreign passive and the foreign general limitation categories. Y and Z both have income in these limitation categories. Accordingly, the income of Y and Z in each of these limitation categories must be reduced on a pro rata basis (by reference to the adjusted taxable income figures) to the extent of the positive change in each limitation category. The total positive change in the foreign passive limitation category is $3.50. The adjusted taxable income of Y in the foreign passive limitation category is $5, and the adjusted taxable income of Z in the foreign passive limitation category is $5. Therefore, $1.75 is drawn from Y and $1.75 is drawn from Z. The total positive change in the foreign general limitation category is $31.50. The adjusted taxable income of Y in the foreign general limitation category is $70, and the adjusted taxable income of Z in the foreign general limitation category is $35. Therefore, $21 is drawn from Y and $10.50 is drawn from Z.

The members must then separately compute the sum of the limitation reductions. Y has limitation reductions of $1.75 in the foreign passive limitation category and $21 in the foreign general limitation category, yielding total limitation reductions of $22.75. Under these facts, domestic income is the only limitation category requiring a positive adjustment. Accordingly, Y's domestic income is increased by $22.75. Z has limitation reductions of $1.75 in the foreign passive limitation category and $10.50 in the foreign general limitation category, yielding total limitation reductions of $12.25. Under these facts, domestic income is the only limitation category requiring a positive adjustment. Accordingly, Z's domestic income is increased by $12.25.

Recharacterization Adjustments	X	Y	Z	Total
Domestic	0	+22.75	+12.25	+35.00
Foreign Passive	0	−1.75	−1.75	−3.50
Foreign General	0	−21.00	−10.50	−31.50

These recharacterization adjustments yield the following final taxable income figures:

Reg. § 1.861-11T(g)(3)

Determination of Sources of Income 46,047

See p. 20,601 for regulations not amended to reflect law changes

Final Taxable Income	X	Y	Z	Total
Domestic	−40.00	22.75	112.25	95.00
Foreign Passive	0	3.25	3.25	6.50
Foreign General	0	49.00	24.50	73.50
Total	−40.00	75.00	140.00	175.00

[Temporary Reg. § 1.861-11T.]

☐ [T.D. 8228, 9-9-88. Amended by T.D. 8916, 12-29-2000.]

[Reg. § 1.861-12T]

§ 1.861-12T. Characterization rules and adjustments for certain assets (Temporary regulations.)—(a) *In general.* These rules are applicable to taxpayers in apportioning expenses under an asset method to income in various separate limitation categories under section 904(d), and supplement other rules provided in §§ 1.861-9T, 1.861-10T, and 1.861-11T. The rules of this section apply to taxable years beginning after December 31, 1986, except as otherwise provided in § 1.861-13T. Paragraph (b) of this section describes the treatment of inventories. Paragraph (c)(1) of this section concerns the treatment of various stock assets. Paragraph (c)(2) of this section describes a basis adjustment for stock in nonaffiliated 10 percent owned corporations. Paragraph (c)(3) of this section sets forth rules for characterizing the stock in controlled foreign corporations. Paragraph (c)(4) of this section describes the treatment of stock of noncontrolled section 902 corporations. Paragraph (d)(1) of this section concerns the treatment of notes. Paragraph (d)(2) of this section concerns the treatment of the notes of controlled foreign corporations. Paragraph (e) of this section describes the treatment of certain portfolio securities that constitute inventory or generate income primarily in the form of gains. Paragraph (f) of this section describes the treatment of assets that are subject to the capitalization rules of section 263A. Paragraph (g) of this section concerns the treatment of FSC stock and of assets of the related supplier generating foreign trade income. Paragraph (h) of this section concerns the treatment of DISC stock and of assets of the related supplier generating qualified export receipts. Paragraph (i) of this section is reserved. Paragraph (j) of this section sets forth an example illustrating the rules of this section, as well as the rules of § 1.861-9T(g).

(b) *Inventories.* Inventory must be characterized by reference to the source and character of sales income, or sales receipts in the case of LIFO inventory, from that inventory during the taxable year. If a taxpayer maintains separate inventories for any federal tax purpose, including the rules for establishing pools of inventory items under sections 472 and 474 of the Code, each separate inventory shall be separately characterized in accordance with the previous sentence.

(c) *Treatment of stock*—(1) *In general.* Subject to the adjustment and special rules of this paragraphs 160 (c) and (e) of this section, stock in a corporation is taken into account in the application of the asset method described in § 1.861-9T(g). However, an affiliated group (as defined in § 1.861-11T(d)) does not take into account the stock of any member in the application of the asset method.

(2) *Basis adjustment for stock in nonaffiliated 10 percent owned corporations*—(i) *Taxpayers using the tax book value method.* For purposes of apportioning expenses on the basis of the tax book value of assets, the adjusted basis of any stock in a 10 percent owned corporation owned directly by the taxpayer shall be—

(A) Increased by the amount of the earnings and profits of such corporation (and of lower-tier 10 percent owned corporations) attributable to such stock and accumulated during the period the taxpayer or other members of its affiliated group held 10 percent or more of such stock, or

(B) Reduced (but not below zero) by any deficit in earnings and profits of such corporation (and of lower-tier 10 percent owned corporations) attributable to such stock for such period.

Solely for purposes of this section, a taxpayer's basis in the stock of a controlled foreign corporation shall not include any amount included in basis under section 961 or 1293(d) of the Code. For purposes of this paragraph (c)(2), earnings and profits and deficits are computed under the rules of section 312 and, in the case of a foreign corporation, section 902 and the regulations thereunder for taxable years of the 10 percent owned corporation ending on or before the close of the taxable year of the taxpayer. The rules of section 1248 and the regulations thereunder shall apply to determine the amount of earnings and profits that is attributable to stock without regard to whether earned and profits (or deficits) were derived (or incurred) during taxable years beginning before or after December 31, 1962. This adjustment is to be made annually and is noncumulative. Thus, the adjusted basis of the stock (determined without prior years' adjustments under this section) is to be adjusted annually by

Reg. § 1.861-12T(c)(2)

the amount of accumulated earnings and profits (or any deficit) attributable to such stock as of the end of each year. Earnings and profits or deficits of a qualified business unit that has a functional currency other than the dollar must be computed under this paragraph (c)(2) in functional currency and translated into dollars using the exchange rate at the end of the taxpayer's current taxable year with respect to which interest is being allocated (and not the exchange rates for the years in which the earnings and profits or deficits were derived or incurred).

(ii) *10 percent owned corporation defined*—(A) *In general.* The term "10 percent owned corporation" means any corporation (domestic or foreign)—

(*1*) Which is not included within the taxpayer's affiliated group as defined in § 1.861-11T(d)(1) or (6),

(*2*) In which the members of the taxpayer's affiliated group own directly or indirectly 10 percent or more of the total combined voting power of all classes of the stock entitled to vote, and

(*3*) Which is taken into account for purposes of apportionment.

(B) *Rule of attribution.* Stock that is owned by a corporation, partnership, or trust shall be treated as being indirectly owned proportionately by its shareholders, partners, or beneficiaries. For this purpose, a partner's interest in stock held by a partnership shall be determined by reference to the partner's distributive share of partnership income.

(iii) *Earnings and profits of lower-tier corporations taken into account.* For purposes of the adjustment to the basis of the stock of the 10 percent owned corporation owned by the taxpayer under paragraph (c)(2)(i) of this section, the earnings and profits of that corporation shall include its pro rata share of the earnings and profits (or any deficit therein) of each succeeding lower-tier 10 percent owned corporation. Thus, a first-tier 10 percent owned corporation shall combine with its own earnings and profits its pro rata share of the earnings and profits of all such lower-tier corporations. The affiliated group shall then adjust its basis in the stock of the first-tier corporation by its pro rata share of the total combined earnings and profits of the first-tier and the lower-tier corporations. In the case of a 10 percent owned corporation whose tax year does not conform to that of the taxpayer, the taxpayer shall include the annual earnings and profits of such 10 percent owned corporation for the tax year ending within the tax year of the taxpayer, whether or not such 10 percent owned corporation is owned directly by the taxpayer.

(iv) *Special rules for foreign corporations in pre-effective date tax years.* Solely for purposes of determining the adjustment required under paragraph (c)(2)(i) of this section, for tax years beginning after 1912 and before 1987, financial earnings (or losses) of a foreign corporation computed using United States generally accepted accounting principles may be substituted for earnings and profits in making the adjustment required by paragraph (c)(2)(i) of this section. A taxpayer is not required to isolate the financial earnings of a foreign corporation derived or incurred during its period of 10 percent ownership or during the post-1912 taxable years and determine earnings and profits (or deficits) attributable under section 1248 principles to the taxpayer's stock in a 10 percent owned corporation. Instead, the taxpayer may include all historic financial earnings for purposes of this adjustment. If the affiliated group elects to use financial earnings with respect to any foreign corporation, financial earnings must be used by that group with respect to all foreign corporations, except that earnings and profits may in any event be used for controlled foreign corporations for taxable years beginning after 1962 and before 1987. However, if the affiliated group elects to use earnings and profits with respect to any single controlled foreign corporation for the 1963 through 1986 period, such election shall apply with respect to all its controlled foreign corporations.

(v) *Taxpayers using the fair market value method.* Because the fair market value of any asset which is stock will reflect retained earnings and profits, taxpayers who use the fair market value method shall not adjust stock basis by the amount of retained earnings and profits, as otherwise required by paragraph (c)(2)(i) of this section.

(vi) *Examples.* Certain of the rules of this paragraph (c)(2) may be illustrated by the following examples.

Example (1). X, an affiliated group that uses the tax book value method of apportionment, owns 20 percent of the stock of Y, which owns 50 percent of the stock of Z. X's basis in the Y stock is $1000. X, Y, and Z have calendar taxable years. The undistributed earnings and profits of Y and Z at year-end attributable to X's period of ownership are $80 and $40, respectively. Because Y owns half of the Z stock, X's pro rata share of Z's earnings and profits attributable to X's Y stock is $4. X's pro rata share of Y's earnings attributable to X's Y stock is $16. For purposes of

Reg. § 1.861-12T(c)(2)

Determination of Sources of Income

apportionment, the tax book value of the Y stock is, therefore, considered to be $1,020.

Example (2). X, an unaffiliated domestic corporation that was organized on January 1, 1987, has owned all the stock of Y, a foreign corporation with a functional currency other than the U.S. dollar, since January 1, 1987. Both X and Y have calendar taxable years. All of Y's assets generate general limitation income. X has a deductible interest expense incurred in 1987 of $160,000. X apportions its interest expense using the tax book value method. The adjusted basis of its assets that generate domestic income is $7,500,000. The adjusted basis of its assets that generate foreign source general limitation income (other than the stock of Y) is $400,000. X's adjusted basis in the Y stock is $2,000,000. Y has undistributed earnings and profits for 1987 of $100,000, translated into dollars from Y's functional currency at the exchange rate on the last day of X's taxable year. Because X is required under paragraph (b)(1) of this § 1.861-10T to increase its basis in the Y stock by the computed amount of earnings and profits, X's adjusted basis in the Y stock is considered to be $2,100,000, and its adjusted basis of assets that generates foreign source general limitation income is, thus, considered to be $2,500,000. X would apportion its interest expense as follows:

To foreign source general limitation income:

$$\text{Interest expense} \times \frac{\text{Adjusted basis of foreign general limitation assets}}{\text{Adjusted basis of foreign general limitation assets} + \text{Adjusted basis of domestic assets}}$$

$$\$160{,}000 \times \frac{\$2{,}500{,}000}{\$2{,}500{,}000 + \$7{,}500{,}000} = \$40{,}000$$

To domestic source income:

$$\text{Interest expense} \times \frac{\text{Adjusted basis of domestic assets}}{\text{Adjusted basis of foreign general limitation assets} + \text{Adjusted basis of domestic assets}}$$

$$\$160{,}000 \times \frac{\$7{,}500{,}000}{\$2{,}500{,}000 + \$7{,}500{,}000} = \$120{,}000$$

(3) *Characterization of stock of controlled foreign corporations*—(i) *In general.* Stock in a controlled foreign corporation (as defined in section 957) shall be characterized as an asset in the various separate limitation categories either on the basis of:

(A) The asset method described in paragraph (c)(3)(ii) of this section, or

(B) The modified gross income method described in paragraph (c)(3)(iii) of this section.

Stock in a controlled foreign corporation whose interest expense is apportioned on the basis of assets shall be characterized in the hands of its United States shareholders under the asset method described in paragraph (c)(3)(ii). Stock in a controlled foreign corporation whose interest expense is apportioned on the basis of gross income shall be characterized in the hands of its United States shareholders under the gross income method described in paragraph (c)(3)(iii).

(ii) *Asset method.* Under the asset method, the taxpayer characterizes the tax book value or fair market value of the stock of a controlled foreign corporation based on an analysis of the assets owned by the controlled foreign corporation during the foreign corporation's taxable year that ends with or within the taxpayer's taxable year. This process is based on the application of § 1.861-9T(g) at the level of the controlled foreign corporation. In the case of a controlled foreign corporation that owns stock in one or more lower-tier controlled foreign corporations in which the United States taxpayer is a United States shareholder, the characterization of the tax book value or the fair market value of the stock of the first-tier controlled foreign corporation to the various separate limitation categories of the affiliated group must take into account the stock in lower-tier corporations. For this purpose, the stock of each such lower-tier corporation shall be characterized by reference to the assets owned during the lower-tier corporation's taxable year that ends during the taxpayer's taxable year. The analysis of assets within a chain of controlled foreign corporations must begin at the lowest-tier controlled foreign corporation and proceed up the chain to the first-tier controlled foreign corporation. For purposes of this paragraph (c), the value of any passive asset to which related person interest is

Reg. § 1.861-12T(c)(3)

allocated under § 1.904-5(c)(2)(ii) must be reduced by the principal amount of indebtedness on which such interest is incurred. Furthermore, the value of any asset to which interest expense is directly allocated under § 1.861-10T must be reduced as provided in § 1.861-9T(g)(2)(iii). See § 1.861-9T(h)(5) for further guidance concerning characterization of stock in a related person under the fair market value method.

(iii) *Modified gross income method.* Under the gross income method, the taxpayer characterizes the tax book value of the stock of the first-tier controlled foreign corporation based on the gross income net of interest expense of the controlled foreign corporation (as computed under § 1.861-9T(j)) within each relevant category for the taxable year of the controlled foreign corporation ending with or within the taxable year of the taxpayer. For this purpose, however, the gross income of the first-tier controlled foreign corporation shall include the total amount of net subpart F income of any lower-tier controlled foreign corporation that was excluded under the rules of § 1.861-9T(j)(2)(ii)(B).

(4) *Stock of noncontrolled section 902 corporations*—(i) *General rule.* Because each noncontrolled section 902 corporation constitutes a separate limitation category, the value of such stock, increased to the extent required under paragraph (c)(2) of this section, is attributable solely to each such category.

(ii) *Special rule for separate limitation losses*—(A) *Election.* If, as a result of the allocation and apportionment of interest expense using the asset method described in § 1.861-9T(g), the taxpayer has a loss in the separate limitation category for a given noncontrolled section 902 corporation, the taxpayer may elect to reallocate interest expense equal to such loss to any other separate limitation category that is in excess credit (without regard to carryovers from other years), to the extent that the reallocation of such interest to such other category does not create a loss in that category. For this purpose, the term "category in excess credit" means any category of income with respect to which the foreign income taxes paid or accrued for the current taxable year exceed the limitation computed under section 904 with respect to such category. The election to reallocate interest expense under this paragraph shall be made in the manner prescribed in § 1.861-9T(f)(3) (relating to the election to use a gross income method for controlled foreign corporations). Furthermore, such election is irrevocable and, thus, cannot be amended by an amended return.

(B) *Example.* X, a domestic corporation organized on January 1, 1987, incurred deductible interest expense in 1987 in the amount of $1,000,000. X uses the tax book value method of apportionment. X owns 25 percent of the stock of A, a noncontrolled section 902 corporation. At the end of 1987, the tax book value of X's assets by income grouping are as follows:

Domestic $3,500,000
Foreign general limitation 1,000,000
Noncontrolling section 902 corporation . 500,000

In 1987, A paid no dividends. X received $100,000 of foreign general limitation income, on which it incurred $50,000 of tax to foreign governments.

The stock of A constitutes ten percent of X's assets. Therefore, ten percent of X's interest expense ($100,000) is allocated and apportioned to the separate limitation category for dividends on the A stock. Since A paid no dividends, this amount would constitute a separate limitation loss under the rules of section 904(f)(5).

Because X incurred more tax to foreign governments on its foreign general limitation income than it can credit against its U.S. tax liability, for the current tax year, and because the reallocation of interest expense allocated and apportioned to dividends from A to foreign general limitation income would not create a loss in that category, X may elect to reallocate such interest expense to the foreign general limitation category to the extent of the loss in the separate limitation category for dividends received from A.

(d) *Treatment of notes*—(1) *General rule.* Subject to the adjustments and special rules of this paragraph (d) and paragraph (e) of this section, all notes held by a taxpayer are taken into account in the application of the asset method described in § 1.861-9T(g). However, the notes of an affiliated corporation are subject to special rules set forth in § 1.861-11T(e). For purposes of this section, the term notes means all interest bearing debt, including debt bearing original issue discount.

(2) *Characterization of related controlled foreign corporation notes.* The debt of a controlled foreign corporation shall be characterized according to the taxpayer's treatment of the interest income derived from that debt obligation after application of the look-through rule of section 904(d)(3)(C). Thus, a United States shareholder includes interest income from a controlled foreign corporation in the same category of income as the category of income from which the controlled foreign corporation deducts the interest expense. See section 954(b)(5) and § 1.904-5(c)(2) for rules concerning the allocation of related person interest

Reg. § 1.861-12T(c)(4)

Determination of Sources of Income

payments to the foreign personal holding company income of a controlled foreign corporation.

(e) *Portfolio securities that constitute inventory or generate primarily gains.* Because gain on the sale of securities is sourced by reference to the residence of the seller, a resident of the United States will generally receive domestic source income (and a foreign resident will generally receive foreign source income) upon sale or disposition of securities that otherwise generate foreign source dividends and interest (or domestic source dividends and interest in the case of a foreign resident). Although under paragraphs (c) and (d) of this section securities are characterized by reference to the source and character of dividends and interest, the source and character of income on gain or disposition must also be taken into account for purposes of characterizing portfolio securities if:

(1) The securities constitute inventory in the hands of the holder, or

(2) 80 percent or more of the gross income generated by a taxpayer's entire portfolio of such securities during a taxable year consists of gains.

For this purpose, a portfolio security is a security in any entity other than a controlled foreign corporation with respect to which the taxpayer is a United States shareholder under section 957, a noncontrolled section 902 corporation with respect to the taxpayer, or a 10 percent owned corporation as defined in § 1.861-12(c)(2)(ii). In taking gains into account, a taxpayer must treat all portfolio securities generating foreign source dividends and interest as a single asset and all portfolio securities generating domestic source dividends as a single asset and shall characterize the total value of that asset based on the source of all income and gain generated by those securities in the taxable year.

(f) *Assets funded by disallowed interest*—(1) *Rule.* In the case of any asset in connection with which interest expense accruing at the end of the taxable year is capitalized, deferred, or disallowed under any provision of the Code, the adjusted basis or fair market value (depending on the taxpayer's choice of apportionment methods) of such an asset shall be reduced by the principal amount of indebtedness the interest on which is so capitalized, deferred, or disallowed.

(2) *Example.* The rules of this paragraph (f) may be illustrated by the following example.

Example. X is a domestic corporation which uses the tax book value method of apportionment. X has $1000 of indebtedness and $100 of interest expense. X constructs an asset with an adjusted basis of $800 before interest capitalization and is required under the rules of section 263A to capitalize $80 in interest expense. Because interest on $800 of debt is capitalized and because the production period is in progress at the end of X's taxable year, $800 of the principal amount of X's debt is allocable to the building. The $800 of debt allocable to the building reduces its adjusted basis for purposes of apportioning the balance of X's interest expense ($20).

(g) *Special rules for FSCs*—(1) *Treatment of FSC stock.* No interest expense shall be allocated or apportioned to stock of a foreign sales corporation ("FSC") to the extent that the FSC stock is attributable to the separate limitation for certain FSC distributions described in section 904(d)(1)(H). FSC stock is considered to be attributable solely to the separate limitation category described in section 904(d)(1)(H) unless the taxpayer can demonstrate that more than 20 percent of the FSC's gross income for the taxable year consists of income other than foreign trading income.

(2) *Treatment of assets that generate foreign trade income.* Assets of the related supplier that generate foreign trade income must be prorated between assets attributable to foreign source general limitation income and assets attributable to domestic source income in proportion to foreign source general limitation income and domestic source income derived from transactions generating foreign trade income.

(i) *Value of assets attributable to foreign source income.* The value of assets attributable to foreign source general limitation income is computed by multiplying the value of assets for the taxable year generating foreign trading gross receipts by a fraction:

(A) The numerator of which is foreign source general limitation income for the taxable year derived from transactions giving rise to foreign trading gross receipts, after the application of the limitation provided in section 927(e)(1), and

(B) The denominator of which is total income for the taxable year derived from the transactions giving rise to foreign trading gross receipts.

(ii) *Value of assets attributable to domestic source income.* The value of assets attributable to domestic source income is computed by subtracting from the total value of assets for the taxable year generating foreign trading gross receipts the value of assets attributable to foreign source general limitation income as computed under paragraph (g)(2)(i) of this section.

(h) *Special rules for DISCs*—(1) *Treatment of DISC stock.* No interest shall be allocated or apportioned to stock in a DISC (or stock in a former

Reg. § 1.861-12T(h)(1)

Determination of Sources of Income

See p. 20,601 for regulations not amended to reflect law changes

DISC to the extent that the stock in the former DISC is attributable to the separate limitation category described in section 904(d)(1)(F)).

(2) *Treatment of assets that generate qualified export receipts.* Assets of the related supplier that generate qualified export receipts must be prorated between assets attributable to foreign source general limitation income and assets attributable to domestic source income in proportion to foreign source general limitation income and domestic source income derived from transactions during the taxable year from transactions generating qualified export receipts.

(i) [Reserved.]

(j) *Examples.* Certain of the rules in this section and §§ 1.861-9T(g) and 1.861-10(e) are illustrated by the following example.

Example (1):

(1) *Facts.* X, a domestic corporation organized on January 1, 1987, has a calendar taxable year and apportions its interest expense on the basis of the tax book value of its assets. In 1987, X incurred a deductible third-party interest expense of $100,000 on an average month-end debt amount of $1 million. The total tax book value of X's assets (adjusted as required under paragraph (b) of this section for retained earnings and profits) is $2 million. X manufactures widgets. One-half of the widgets are sold in the United States and one-half are exported and sold through a foreign branch with title passing outside the United States.

X owns all the stock of Y, a controlled foreign corporation that also has a calendar taxable year and is also engaged in the manufacture and sale of widgets. Y has no earnings and profits or deficits in earnings and profits prior to 1987. For 1987, Y has taxable income and earnings and profits of $50,000 before the deduction for related person interest expense. Half of the $50,000 is foreign source personal holding company income and the other half is derived from widget sales and constitutes foreign source general limitation income. Assume that Y has no deductions from gross income other than interest expense. Y's foreign personal holding company taxable income is included in X's gross income under section 951. Y paid no dividends in 1987. Prior to 1987, Y did not borrow any funds from X. The average month-end level of borrowings by Y from X in 1987 is $100,000, on which Y paid a total of $10,000 in interest. The total tax book value of Y's assets in 1987 is $500,000. Y has no liabilities to third parties. X elects pursuant to § 1.861-9T for Y to apportion Y's interest expense under the gross income method prescribed in § 1.861-9T(g).

In addition to its stock in Y, X owns 20 percent of the stock of Z, a noncontrolled section 902 corporation.

X's total assets and their tax book values are:

Asset	Tax Book Value
Plant & equipment	$1,000,000
Corporate headquarters	500,000
Inventory	200,000
Automobiles	20,000
Patents	50,000
Trademarks	10,000
Y stock (including paragraph (c)(2) adjustment)	80,000
Y note	100,000
Z stock	40,000

(2) *Categorization of Assets*

Single Category Assets

1. Automobiles: X's automobiles are used exclusively by its domestic sales force in the generation of United States source income. Thus, these assets are attributable solely to the grouping of domestic income.

2. Y Note: Under paragraph (d)(2) of this section, the Y note in the hands of X is characterized according to X's treatment of the interest income received on the Y note. In determining the source and character of the interest income on the Y note, the look-through rules of sections 904(d)(3)(C) and 904(g) apply. Under section 954(b)(5) and § 1.904-5(c)(2)(ii), Y's $10,000 interest payment to X is allocated directly to, and thus reduces, Y's foreign personal holding company income of $25,000 (yielding foreign personal holding company taxable income of $15,000). Therefore, the Y note is attributable solely to the statutory grouping of foreign source passive income.

3. Z stock: Because Z is a noncontrolled section 902 corporation, the dividends paid by Z are subject to a separate limitation under section 904(d)(1)(E). Thus, this asset is attributable solely to the statutory grouping consisting of Z dividends.

Multiple Category Assets

1. Plant & equipment, inventory, patents, and trademarks: In 1987, X sold half its widgets in the United States and exported half outside the United States. A portion of the taxable income from export sales will be foreign source income, since the export sales were accomplished through a foreign branch and title passed outside the United States. Thus, these assets are attributable both to the statutory grouping of foreign general limitation and the grouping of domestic income.

2. Y Stock: Since Y's interest expense is apportioned under the gross income method prescribed

Reg. § 1.861-12T(h)(2)

in § 1.861-9T(j), the Y stock must be characterized under the gross income method described in paragraph (c)(3)(iii) of this section.

Assets without Directly Identifiable Yield

1. Corporate headquarters: This asset generates no directly identifiable income yield. The value of the asset is disregarded.

(3) *Analysis of Income Yield for Multiple Category Assets*

1. Plant & equipment, inventory, patents, and trademarks: As noted above, X's 1987 widget sales were half domestic and half foreign. Assume that Example 2 of § 1.863-3(b)(2) applies in sourcing the export income from the export sales. Under Example 2, the income generated by the export sales is sourced half domestic and half foreign. The income generated by the domestic sales is entirely domestic source. Accordingly, three-quarters of the income generated on all sales is domestic source and one-quarter of the income is foreign source. Thus, three-quarters of the fair market value of these assets are attributed to the grouping of domestic source income and one-quarter of the fair market value of these assets is attributed to the statutory grouping of foreign source general limitation income.

2. Y Stock: Under the gross income method described in paragraph (c)(3)(iii) of this section, Y's gross income net of interest expense in each limitation category must be determined— $25,000 foreign source general limitation income and $15,000 of foreign source passive income. Of X's adjusted basis of $80,000 in Y stock, $50,000 is attributable to foreign source general limitation income and $30,000 is attributable to foreign source passive income.

(4) *Application of the Special Allocation Rule of § 1.861-10T(e).* Assume that the taxable year in question is 1990 and that the applicable percentage prescribed by § 1.861-10T(e)(1)(iv)(A) is 80 percent. Assume that X has elected to use the quadratic formula provided in § 1.861-10T(e)(1)(iv)(B).

Step 1. X's average month-end level of debt owing to unrelated persons is $1 million. The tax book value of X's assets is $2 million. Thus, X's debt-to-asset ratio computed under § 1.861-10T(e)(1)(i) is 1 to 2.

Step 2. The tax book value of Y's assets is $500,000. Because Y has no debt to persons other than X, Y's debt-to-asset ratio computed under § 1.861-10T(e)(1)(ii) is $0 to $500,000.

Step 3. Y's average month-end liabilities to X, as computed under § 1.861-10T(e)(1)(iii) for 1987 are $100,000.

Step 4. Adding the $100,000 of Y's liabilities owed to X as computed under Step 3 to Y's third party liabilities ($0) would be insufficient to make Y's debt-to-asset ratio computed in Step 2 ($100,000-to-$500,000, or 1:5) equal to at least 80 percent of X's debt-to-asset ratio computed under Step 1, as adjusted to reflect a reduction in X's debt and assets by the $100,000 of excess related person indebtedness (.80 × $900,000/$1,900,000 or 1:2.6). Therefore, the entire amount of Y's liabilities to X ($100,000) constitute excess related person indebtedness under § 1.861-10T(e)(1)(ii). Thus, the entire $10,000 of interest received by X from Y during 1987 constitutes interest received on excess related person indebtedness.

Step 5. The Y note held by X has a tax book value of $100,000. Solely for purposes of § 1.861-10(e)(1)(v), the Y note is attributed to separate limitation categories in the same manner as the Y stock. Under paragraph (c)(3)(iii) of this section, of the $80,000 of Y stock held by X, $50,000 is attributable to foreign source general limitation income, and $30,000 is attributable to foreign source passive income. Thus, for purposes of § 1.861-10T(e)(1)(v), $62,500 of the $100,000 Y note is considered to be a foreign source general limitation asset and $37,500 of the $100,000 Y note is considered to be a foreign source passive asset.

Step 6. Since $8,000 of the $10,000 in related person interest income received by Y constitutes interest received on excess related person indebtedness, $10,000 of X's third party interest expense is allocated to X's debt investment in Y. Under § 1.861-10T(e)(1)(vi), 62.5 percent of the $10,000 of X's third party interest expense ($6,250) is allocated to foreign source general limitation income and 37.5 percent of the $10,000 of X's third party interest expense ($3,750) is allocated to foreign source passive income. As a result of this direct allocation, the value of X's assets generating foreign source general limitation income shall be reduced by the principal amount of indebtedness the interest on which is directly allocated to foreign source general limitation income ($62,500), and X's assets generating foreign general limitation income shall be reduced by the principal amount of indebtedness the interest on which is directly allocated to foreign passive income ($37,500).

(5) *Totals*

Having allocated $10,000 of its third party interest expense to its debt investment in Y, X would apportion the $90,000 balance of its interest according to the following apportionment fractions:

Reg. § 1.861-12T(j)

Determination of Sources of Income

See p. 20,601 for regulations not amended to reflect law changes

Asset	Domestic Source	Foreign General	Foreign Passive	Noncontrolled Section 902
Plant & equipment	$750,000	$250,000		
Inventory	150,000	50,000		
Automobiles	20,000			
Patents	37,500	12,500		
Trademarks	7,500	2,500		
Y stock		50,000	30,000	
Y note			100,000	
Z stock				$ 40,000
TOTALS:	965,000	365,000	130,000	40,000
Adjustments for directly allocable interest		(62,250)	(37,750)	
ADJUSTED TOTALS:	965,000	302,750	92,250	40,000
Percentage	69%	22%	6%	3%

Example 2: Assume the same facts as in Example 1, except that Y has $100,000 of third party indebtedness. Further, assume for purposes of the application of the special allocation rule of § 1.861-10T(e) that the taxable year is 1990 and that the applicable percentage prescribed by § 1.861-10T(e)(1)(iv)(A) is 80 percent. The application of the § 1.861-10(e) would be modified as follows.

Step 1. X's debt-to-asset ratio computed under § 1.861-10T(e)(1)(i) remains 1 to 2 (or 0.5).

Step 2. The tax book value of Y's assets is $500,000. Y has $100,000 of indebtedness to third parties. Y's debt-to-asset ratio computed under § 1.861-10T(e)(1)(ii) is $100,000 to $500,000 (1:5 or 0.2).

Step 3. Y's average month-end liabilities to X, as computed under § 1.861-10T(e)(1)(iii) remain $100,000.

Step 4. X's debt-to-asset ratio is 0.5 and 80 percent of 0.5 is 0.4. Because Y's debt-to-asset ratio is 0.2, there is excess related person indebtedness, the amount of which can be computed based on the following formula:

$$\frac{\text{Aggregate Third Party Debt of Related US Shareholder} - X}{\text{US Shareholder} - X \text{ Assets}} \times \text{Applicable Percentage For Year (0.8)} = \frac{\text{Aggregate Third Party Debt of Related CFCs} + X}{\text{Related CFC Assets}}$$

Supplying the facts as given, this equation is as follows:

$$\frac{1,000,000 - X}{2,000,000 - X} \times .8 = \frac{100,000 + X}{500,000}$$

Multiply both sides by 500,000 and $(2,000,000 - X)$, yielding:

$$4 \times 10^{11} - 400,000X = 2 \times 10^{11} + 2,000,000X - 100,000X - X^2$$

Since there is an X^2 in this equation, a quadratic formula must be utilized to solve for X. Group the components in this equation, segregating the X and the X^2:

$$X^2 + (-2,300,000)X + (2 \times 10^{11}) = 0$$

Apply the quadratic formula:

$$X = \frac{-b \pm \sqrt{b^2 - 4(a)(c)}}{2(a)}$$

a = 1 (coefficient of X^2)
b = −2,300,000 (coefficient of X)
c = 2 × 10^{11} (remaining element of equation)

Therefore, X equals either 90,519 or (2.21×10^{11}). For purposes of computing excess related person indebtedness, X is the lowest positive amount derived from this equation, which is 90,519.

Reg. § 1.861-12T(j)

Steps 5 and 6 are unchanged from *Example* 1, except that the total amount of interest on excess related party indebtedness is $9,051.
[Temporary Reg. § 1.861-12T.]

☐ [T.D. 8228, 9-9-88.]

[Reg. § 1.861-13T]

§ 1.861-13T. Transition rules for interest expenses (Temporary.)—(a) *In general*—(1) *Optional application.* The rules of this section may be applied at the choice of a corporate taxpayer. In the case of an affiliated group, however, the choice must be made on a consistent basis for all members. Therefore, a corporate taxpayer (or affiliated group) may allocate and apportion its interest expense entirely on the basis of the rules contained in § § 1.861-8T through 1.861-12T and without regard to the rules of this section. The choice is made on an annual basis and, thus, is not binding with respect to subsequent tax years.

(2) *Transition relief.* This section contains transitional rules that limit the application of the rules for allocating and apportioning interest expense of corporate taxpayers contained in § § 1.861-8T through 1.861-12T, which are applicable in allocating and apportioning the interest expense of corporate taxpayers generally for taxable years beginning after 1986. Sections 1.861-9(d) (relating to individuals, estates, and certain trusts) and 1.861-9(e) (relating to partnerships) are effective for taxable years beginning after 1986. Thus, the taxpayers to whom those sections apply do not qualify for transition relief under this section. To the extent that the rules of § § 1.861-8T through 1.861-12T do not apply by reason of these transition rules, interest expense shall be allocated and apportioned under the rules of § 1.861-8 as in effect for taxable years beginning before 1987.

(3) *Indebtedness defined.* For purposes of this section, the term "indebtedness" means any obligation or other evidence of indebtedness that generates an expense that constitutes interest expense within the meaning of § 1.861-9T(a). In the case of an obligation that does not bear interest initially, but becomes interest bearing with the lapse of time or upon the occurrence of an event, such obligation shall only be considered to constitute indebtedness when it first bears interest. Obligations that are outstanding as of November 16, 1985 shall only qualify for transition relief under this section if they bear interest-bearing as of that date. For this purpose, any obligation that has original issue discount within the meaning of section 1273(a)(1) of the Code shall be considered to be interest-bearing.

(4) *Exceptions.* The term "indebtedness" shall not include any obligation existing between affiliated corporations, as defined in § 1.861-11T(d). Moreover, the term "indebtedness" shall not include any obligation the interest on which is directly allocable under § § 1.861-10T(b) and 1.861-10T(c). Under § 1.861-9T(b)(6)(iv)(B), certain interest expense is directly allocated to the gain derived from an appropriately identified financial product. When interest expense on a liability is reduced by such gain, the principal amount of such liability shall be reduced pro rata by the relative amount of interest expense that is directly allocated.

(b) *General phase-in*—(1) *In general.* In the case of each of the first three taxable years of the taxpayer beginning after December 31, 1986, the rules of § § 1.861-8T through 1.861-12T shall not apply to interest expenses paid or accrued by the taxpayer during the taxable year with respect to an aggregate amount of indebtedness which does not exceed the general phase-in amount, as defined in paragraph (b)(2) of this section.

(2) *General phase-in amount defined.* Subject to the limitation imposed by paragraph (b)(3) of this section, the general phase-in amount means the amount which is the applicable percentage (determined under the following table) of the aggregate amount of indebtedness of the taxpayer outstanding on November 16, 1985:

Taxable year beginning after December 31, 1986	Percentage
First	75
Second	50
Third	25

(3) *Reductions in indebtedness.* The general phase-in amount shall not exceed the taxpayer's historic lowest month-end debt level taking into account all months after October 1985. However, for the taxable year in which a taxpayer attains a new historic lowest month-end debt level (but not for subsequent taxable years), the general phase-in amount shall not exceed the average of month-end debt levels within that taxable year (without taking into account any increase in month-end debt levels occurring in such taxable year after the new historic lowest month-end debt level is attained).

Example. X is a calendar year taxpayer that had $100 of indebtedness outstanding on November 16, 1985. X's month-end debt level remained $100 for all subsequent months until July 1987, when X's month-end debt level fell to $50. In computing transition relief for 1987, X's general phase-in amount cannot exceed $75 (900 divided by 12), which is the average of month-end debt levels in 1987. Assuming that X's month-end debt level for any subsequent month does not fall

Reg. § 1.861-13T(b)(3)

below $50, the limitation on its general phase-in amount for all taxable years after 1987 will be $50, its historic lowest month-end debt level after October 1985.

(c) *Nonapplication of the consolidation rule*—(1) *General rule.* In the case of each of the first five taxable years of the taxpayer beginning after December 31, 1986, the consolidation rule contained in § 1.861-11T(c) shall not apply to interest expenses paid or accrued by the taxpayer during the taxable year with respect to an aggregate amount of indebtedness which does not exceed the special phase-in amount, as defined in paragraph (c)(2) of this section.

(2) *Special phase-in amount.* The special phase-in amount is the sum of—

(i) The general phase-in amount,

(ii) The five-year phase-in amount, and

(iii) The four-year phase-in amount.

(3) *Five-year phase-in amount.* The five-year phase-in amount is the lesser of—

(i) The applicable percentage (the "unreduced percentage" in the following table) of the five-year debt amount, or

(ii) The applicable percentage (the "reduced percentage" in the following table) of the five-year debt amount reduced by paydowns (if any):

Transition Year	Unreduced Percentage	Reduced Percentage
Year 1	8 1/3	10
Year 2	16 2/3	25
Year 3	25	50
Year 4	33 1/3	100
Year 5	16 2/3	100

(4) *Four-year phase-in amount.* The four-year phase-in amount is the lesser of—

(i) The applicable percentage (the "unreduced percentage" in the following table) of the four-year debt amount, or

(ii) The applicable percentage (the "reduced percentage" in the following table) of the four-year debt amount reduced by paydowns (if any) to the extent that such paydowns exceed the five-year debt amount:

Transition Year	Unreduced Percentage	Reduced Percentage
Year 1	5	6 1/4
Year 2	10	16 2/3
Year 3	15	37 1/2
Year 4	20	100

(5) *Five-year debt amount.* The "five-year debt amount" means the excess (if any) of—

(i) The amount of the outstanding indebtedness of the taxpayer on May 29, 1985, over

(ii) The amount of the outstanding indebtedness of the taxpayer on December 31, 1983.

The five-year debt amount shall not exceed the aggregate amount of indebtedness of the taxpayer outstanding on November 16, 1985.

(6) *Four-year debt amount.* The "four-year debt amount" means the excess (if any) of—

(i) The amount of the outstanding indebtedness of the taxpayer on December 31, 1983, over

(ii) The amount of the outstanding indebtedness of the taxpayer on December 31, 1982.

The four-year debt amount shall not exceed the aggregate amount of indebtedness of the taxpayer outstanding on November 16, 1985, reduced by the five-year debt amount.

(7) *Paydowns.* The term "paydowns" means the excess (if any) of—

(i) The aggregate amount of indebtedness of the taxpayer outstanding on November 16, 1985, over

(ii) The limitation on the general phase-in amount described in paragraph (b)(3) of this section.

Paydowns are first applied to the five-year debt amount to the extent thereof and then to the four-year debt amount for purposes of computing the five-year and the four-year phase-in amounts.

(d) *Treatment of affiliated group.* For purposes of this section, all members of the same affiliated group of corporations (as defined in § 1.861-11(d)) shall be treated as one taxpayer whether or not such members filed a consolidated return. Interaffiliate debt is not taken into account in computing transition relief. Moreover, any reduction in the amount of interaffiliate debt is not taken into account in determining the amount of paydowns.

(e) *Mechanics of computation*—(1) *Step 1: Determination of the amounts within the various categories of debt.* Each separate member of an

Determination of Sources of Income

affiliated group must determine each of its following amounts:

(i) *November 16, 1985 amount.* The amount of its debt outstanding on November 16, 1985 (after the elimination of interaffiliate indebtedness),

(ii) *Unreduced five-year debt.* The amount of any net increase in the amount of its indebtedness on May 29, 1985 (after elimination of interaffiliate indebtedness) over the amount of its indebtedness on December 31, 1983 (after elimination of interaffiliate indebtedness),

(iii) *Unreduced four-year debt.* The amount of any net increase in the amount of its indebtedness on December 31, 1983 (after elimination of interaffiliate indebtedness) over the amount of its indebtedness on December 31, 1982 (after elimination of interaffiliate indebtedness), and

(iv) *Month-end debt.* The amount of its month-end debt level for all months after October 1985 (after elimination of interaffiliate indebtedness).

(2) *Step 2: Aggregation of the separate company amounts.* Each of the designated amounts for the separate companies identified in Step 1 must be aggregated in order to compute consolidated transition relief. Paragraph (e)(10)(iv) of this section (Step 10) requires the use of the taxpayer's current year average debt level for the purpose of computing the percentages of debt that are subject to the three sets of rules that are identified in Step 10. For use in that computation, the taxpayer should compute the current year average debt level by aggregating separate company month-end debt levels and then by averaging those aggregate amounts.

(3) *Step 3: Calculation of the lowest historic month-end debt level of the taxpayer.* In order to calculate the lowest historic month-end debt level of the taxpayer, determine the month-end debt level of each separate company for each month ending after October 1985 and aggregate these amounts on a month-by-month basis. On such aggregate basis, in any taxable year in which the taxpayer attains an aggregate new lowest historic month-end debt level, add together all the aggregate month-end debt levels within the taxable year (without taking into account any increase in aggregate debt level subsequent to the attainment of such lowest historic month-end debt level) and divide by the number of months in that taxable year, yielding the average of month-end debt levels for such year. Such average shall constitute the taxpayer's lowest historic month-end debt level for that taxable year in which the aggregate new lowest historic month-end debt level was attained. Unless otherwise specified, all subsequent references to any amount refer to the aggregate amount for all members of the same affiliated group of corporations.

(4) *Step 4: Computation of paydowns.* Paydowns equal the amount by which the November 16, 1985 amount exceeds the taxpayer's lowest historic month-end debt level, determined under Step 3.

(5) *Step 5: Computation of limitations on unreduced five-year debt and unreduced four-year debt.* (i) The unreduced five-year debt cannot exceed the November 16, 1985 amount.

(ii) The unreduced four-year debt cannot exceed the November 16, 1985 amount less the unreduced five-year debt.

(6) *Step 6: Computation of reduced five-year and reduced four-year debt*—(i) *Reduced five-year debt.* Compute the amount of reduced five-year debt by subtracting from the unreduced five-year debt (see Step 5) the amount of paydowns (see Step 4).

(ii) *Reduced four-year debt.* To the extent that the amount of paydowns (see step 4) exceeds the amount of unreduced five-year debt (see Step 5), compute the amount of reduced four-year debt by subtracting such excess from the unreduced four-year debt (see Step 1).

(iii) To the extent that paydowns do not offset either the unreduced five-year amount or the unreduced four-year amount, the reduced and the unreduced amounts are the same.

(7) *Step 7: Computation of the general phase-in amount.* The general phase-in amount is the lesser of—

(i) The percentage of the November 16, 1985 amount designated for the relevant transition year in the table below, or

(ii) The lowest group month-end debt level (see Step 3).

General Phase-in Table

Transition Year	Percentage
Year 1	75
Year 2	50
Year 3	25

Reg. § 1.861-13T(e)(7)

46,058 Determination of Sources of Income

See p. 20,601 for regulations not amended to reflect law changes

(8) *Step 8: Computation of Five-year Phase-in Amount.* The five-year phase-in amount is the lesser of—

(i) The percentage of the unreduced five-year debt designated for the relevant transition year in the table below, or

(ii) The percentage of the reduced five-year debt designated for the relevant transition year in the table below.

Five-year Phase-in Table

Transition Year	Unreduced Percentage	Reduced Percentage
Year 1	8 1/3	10
Year 2	16 2/3	25
Year 3	25	50
Year 4	33 1/3	100
Year 5	16 2/3	100

(9) *Step 9: Computation of Four-year Phase-in Amount.* The four-year phase-in amount is the lesser of—

(i) The percentage of the unreduced four-year debt designated for the relevant transition year in the table below, or

(ii) The percentage of the reduced four-year debt designated for the relevant transition year in the table below.

Four-year Phase-in Table

Transition Year	Unreduced Percentage	Reduced Percentage
Year 1	5	6 1/4
Year 2	10	16 2/3
Year 3	15	37 1/2
Year 4	20	100

(10) *Step 10: Determination of group debt ratio and application of transition relief to separate company interest expense.* (i) The general phase-in amount consists of the amount computed under Step 7. Interest expense on this amount is subject to pre-1987 rules of allocation and apportionment.

(ii) The post-1986 separate company amount consists of the sum of the amounts determined under Steps 8 and 9. Interest expense on this amount is subject to post-1986 rules of allocation and apportionment as applied on a separate company basis. Thus, § 1.861-11T(c) does not apply with respect to this amount of indebtedness. Because the consolidation rule does not apply, stock in affiliated corporations shall be taken into account in computing the apportionment fractions for each separate company in the same manner as under pre-1987 rules.

(iii) The post-1986 one-taxpayer amount consists of any indebtedness that does not qualify for transition relief under Steps 7, 8, and 9. Interest expense on this amount is subject to post-1986 rules as applied on a consolidated basis.

(iv) To determine the extent to which the interest expense of each separate company is subject to any of these sets of allocation and apportionment rules, each company shall prorate its own interest expense using two fractions. The general phase-in fraction is the general phase-in amount over the current year average debt level of the affiliated group (see Step 2). The post-1986 separate company fraction is the post-1986 separate company amount over the current year average debt level of the affiliated group. The balance of each separate company's interest expense is subject to post-1986 one-taxpayer rules.

(f) *Example.* XYZ form an affiliated group.

(1) *Step 1:* Determination of the amounts within the various debt categories.

Company X	Historic 3rd party Debt		Increase
November 16, 1985	$100,000		
May 29, 1985	90,000	5-year	$ 10,000
December 31, 1983	80,000	4-year	10,000
December 31, 1982	70,000		
Current Interest Expense	10,000		

Reg. § 1.861-13T(e)(8)

Determination of Sources of Income

See p. 20,601 for regulations not amended to reflect law changes

Company Y		Historic 3rd party Debt		Increase
November 16, 1985		$200,000		
May 29, 1985		170,000	5-year	$120,000
December 31, 1983		50,000	4-year	10,000
December 31, 1982		40,000		
Current Interest Expense		30,000		

Company Z		Historic 3rd party Debt		Increase
November 16, 1985		$300,000		
May 29, 1985		300,000	5-year	$ 50,000
December 31, 1983		250,000	4-year	100,000
December 31, 1982		150,000		
Current Interest Expense		30,000		

(2) *Step 2:* Aggregation of the separate company amounts.

Aggregate November 16, 1985	$600,000
Aggregate 5-year debt	180,000
Aggregate 4-year debt	120,000
Current year average debt level	700,000

(3) *Step 3:* Calculation of lowest historic month-end debt level.

An analysis of historic month-end debt levels indicates that in 1986, XYZ's aggregate month-end debt level fell to $500,000, which represents the lowest sum for all years under consideration. Because this historic low occurred in a prior tax year, there is no averaging of month-end debt levels in the current taxable year.

Aggregate November 16, 1985 amount	$600,000
Aggregate unreduced 5-year debt	180,000
Aggregate unreduced 4-year debt	120,000

Because the November 16, 1985 amount exceeds the unreduced 4- and 5-year debt, the full amount of the 4- and 5-year debt qualify for transition relief. In cases where the November 16, 1985 amount is less than the 4- or 5-year debt (or the sum of both), the latter amounts are limited to the November 16, 1985 amount. See the limitations on the 4-year and 5-year debt amounts in paragraphs (c)(6) and (c)(5), respectively, of this section.

(6) *Step 6:* Computation of reduced five-year and four-year debt.

The paydowns computed under Step 4 are deemed to first offset the aggregate unreduced five-year debt. Accordingly, the reduced amount of five-year debt is $80,000. Since the paydowns are less than the aggregate unreduced five-year debt, there is no paydown in connection with aggregate unreduced four-year debt. Accordingly, the unreduced four-year debt and the reduced four-year debt are both considered to be $120,000.

(7) *Step 7:* Computation of the general phase-in amount.

In transition year 1, the general transition amount is the lesser of:

(4) *Step 4:* Computation of paydowns.

The aggregate November 16, 1985 amount ($600,000), less the lowest historic month-end debt level ($500,000), yields a total paydown in the amount of $100,000.

(5) *Step 5:* Computation of limitations on aggregate unreduced five-year debt and aggregate unreduced four-year debt.

(i) 75 percent of the aggregate November 16, 1985 amount (75% of $600,000 = $450,000); or

(ii) the lowest month-end debt level since November 16, 1985 ($500,000).

Therefore, the general transition amount is $450,000.

(8) *Step 8:* Computation of the five-year phase-in amount.

In transition year 1, the five-year phase-in amount is the lesser of:

(i) 8 1/3 percent of the unreduced five-year amount (8 1/3% of $180,000 = $15,000); or

(ii) 10 percent of the reduced five-year amount (10% of $80,000 = $8,000).

Therefore, the five-year phase-in amount is $8,000.

(9) *Step 9:* Computation of the four-year phase-in amount.

In transition year 1, the four-year phase-in amount is the lesser of:

(i) 5 percent of the unreduced four-year amount (5% of $120,000 = $6,000); or

(ii) 6 1/4 percent of the reduced four-year amount (6 1/4% of $120,000 = $7,500).

Reg. § 1.861-13T(f)(9)

Therefore, the four-year phase-in amount is $6,000.

(10) *Step 10:* Determination of group debt ratio and application of relief to separate company interest expense.

(i) As determined under Step 7, interest expense on a total of $450,000 of the XYZ debt in the first transition year is computed under pre-1987 rules of allocation and apportionment.

(ii) The sum of Steps 8 ($8,000) and 9 ($6,000) is $14,000. Interest expense on a total of $14,000 of XYZ debt is computed under post-1986 rules of allocation and apportionment as applied on a separate company basis.

(iii) The balance of XYZ's current year interest expense is computed under post-1986 rules of allocation and apportionment as applied on a consolidated basis. X, Y, and Z, respectively, have current interest expense of $10,000, $30,000, and $30,000. Thus, 64.3 percent (450,000/700,000) of the interest expense of each separate company is subject to pre-1987 rules. Two percent (14,000/700,000) of the interest expense of each separate company is subject to post-1986 rules applied on a separate company basis. Finally, the balance of each separate company's current year interest expense (33.7 percent) is subject to post-1986 rules applied on a consolidated basis.

(g) *Corporate transfers*—(1) *Effect on transferee*—(i) *General rule.* Except as provided in paragraph (g)(1)(ii) of this section, if a domestic corporation or an affiliated group acquires stock in a domestic corporation that was not a member of the transferee's affiliated group before the acquisition, but becomes a member of the transferee's affiliated group after the acquisition, the transferee group shall take into account the following transition attributes of the acquired corporation in computing its transition relief:

(A) November 16, 1985 amount,

(B) Unreduced five-year amount,

(C) Unreduced four-year amount, and

(D) The amount of any transferor paydowns attributed to the acquired corporation under the rules of paragraph (h)(1) of this section.

(ii) *Special rule for year of acquisition.* To compute the amount of the transition attributes described in paragraph (g)(1)(i) of this section that a transferee takes into account in the transferee's taxable year of the acquisition, such transition attributes shall be multiplied by a fraction, the numerator of which is the number of months within the taxable year that the transferee held the acquired corporation and the denominator of which is the number of months in such taxable year. In order for the transferee to assert ownership of a subsidiary for a given month, the transferee and the acquired corporation must be affiliated corporations as of the last day of the month. In addition, the transferor and the transferee shall take account of the month-end debt level of the transferred corporation only for those months at the end of which the transferred corporation was a member of the transferor's or the transferee's respective affiliated group.

(iii) *Aggregation of transition attributes.* The transition attributes of the acquired corporation shall be aggregated with the respective amounts of the transferee group.

(iv) *Conveyance of transferor paydowns.* The total paydowns of the transferee group shall include the amount of any paydown of the transferor group that was attributed to the acquired corporation under the rules of paragraph (h)(1) of this section.

(v) *Effect of certain elections.* If an election—

(A) Is made under section 338(g) (whether or not an election under 338(h)(10) is made),

(B) Is deemed to be made under section 338(e) (other than (e)(2)), or section 338(f), or,

(C) Is made under section 336(e), no indebtedness of the acquired corporation shall qualify for transition relief for the year such election first becomes effective and for subsequent taxable years, and no other transition attributes of the acquired corporation shall be taken into account by the transferee group.

(2) *Effect on transferor*—(i) *General rule.* Except as provided in paragraph (g)(2)(ii) of this section, in the case of an acquisition of a member of an affiliated group by a nonmember of the group, the transferor shall not take into account the transition attributes of the acquired corporation in computing the transition relief of the transferor group in subsequent taxable years. Thus, the November 16, 1985 amount, the unreduced five-year and four-year debt amounts, and the end-of-month debt levels of the transferor group shall be computed without regard to the acquired corporation's respective amounts for purposes of computing transition relief of the transferor group for years thereafter.

(ii) *Special rule for the year of disposition.* To compute the amount of the transition attributes described in paragraph (g)(2)(i) of this section that a transferor shall take into account in the transferor's taxable year of the disposition, such transition attributes shall be multiplied by a fraction, the numerator of which is the number of months within the taxable year that the transferor held the acquired corporation and the denominator of which is the number of months in such taxable year. In order for the transferor to assert ownership of a subsidiary for a given

Reg. § 1.861-13T(f)(10)

month, the transferor and the acquired corporation must be affiliated corporations as of the last day of the month.

(iii) *Effect of prior paydowns.* Any paydowns of the acquired corporation that are considered to reduce the debt of other members of the transferor group under the rules of paragraph (h)(1) of this section (whether incurred in a prior taxable year or in that portion of a year of disposition that is taken into account by the transferor) shall continue to be taken into account by the transferor group after the disposition.

(3) *Special rule for assumptions of indebtedness.* In connection with the transfer of a corporation, if the indebtedness of an acquired corporation is assumed by any party other than the transferee or another member of the transferee's affiliated group, the transition attributes of the acquired corporation shall not be taken into account in computing the transition relief of the transferee group. See paragraph (g)(2) of this section concerning the treatment of the transferor group. Also in connection with the transfer of a corporation, if the transferee or another member of the transferee's affiliated group assumes the indebtedness of an acquired corporation, such assumed indebtedness shall only qualify for transition relief during the period in which the acquired corporation remains a member of the transferee group. Further, if the transferee group subsequently disposes of the acquired corporation, the indebtedness of the acquired corporation will continue to qualify for transition relief only if the indebtedness is assumed by the new purchaser as of the time such corporation is acquired.

(4) *Effect of asset sales.* If substantially all of the assets of a corporation are sold, the indebtedness of such corporation shall cease to be qualified for transition relief. Thus, the transition attributes of such corporation shall not be taken into account in computing transition relief.

(h) *Rules for attributing paydowns among separate companies*—(1) *General rule.* In the case of a corporate transfer under paragraph (g) of this section, it is necessary to determine the amount of paydowns attributable to the acquired corporation. Under paragraph (c)(7) of this section, paydowns are deemed to reduce first the five-year phase-in amount, then the four-year phase-in amount, and then the general phase-in amount. Thus, for example, a reduction in indebtedness of the group caused by a reduction in the debt of a group member that has no five-year debt will nevertheless be deemed under this ordering rule to reduce the indebtedness of those group members that do have five-year debt. In order to preserve the effect of paydowns caused by a reduction, each member must determine on a separate company basis at the time of any transfer of any member of the affiliated group the impact of paydowns (including those paydowns occurring in the year of transfer prior to the time of the transfer) on the various categories of indebtedness.

(2) *Mechanics of computation.* Separate company accounts of paydowns are determined by prorating any paydown among all group members with five-year debt to the extent thereof on the basis of the relative amounts of five-year debt. Paydowns in excess of five-year debt are prorated on a similar basis among all group members with four-year debt to the extent thereof on the basis of the relative amounts of four-year debt. Paydowns in excess of four-year and five-year debt are prorated among all group members with general phase-in debt to the extent thereof on the basis of the relative amounts of general phase-in debt. After an initial paydown has been prorated among the members of an affiliated group, any further reduction in the amount of aggregate month-end debt level as compared to the November 16, 1985 amount is prorated among all members of the affiliated group based on the remaining net amounts of four-year and five-year debt.

(3) *Examples.* The rules of paragraphs (g) and (h) of this section may be illustrated by the following examples.

Example (1): Computing separate company accounts of reductions—(i) *Facts.* XYZ constitutes an affiliated group of corporations that has a calendar taxable year and the following transition attributes:

Company X	Historic 3rd party Debt		Increase
November 16, 1985	$100,000		
May 29, 1985	80,000	5-year	$ 0
December 31, 1983	80,000	4-year	10,000
December 31, 1982	70,000		

Company Y	Historic 3rd party Debt		Increase
November 16, 1985	$200,000		
May 29, 1985	170,000	5-year	$120,000
December 31, 1983	50,000	4-year	10,000
December 31, 1982	40,000		

Reg. § 1.861-13T(h)(3)

46,062   Determination of Sources of Income

See p. 20,601 for regulations not amended to reflect law changes

Company Z	Historic 3rd party Debt		Increase
November 16, 1985	$300,000		
May 29, 1985	290,000	5-year	$ 40,000
December 31, 1983	250,000	4-year	100,000
December 31, 1982	150,000		

In 1986, the XYZ group attained its lowest historic month-end debt level of $500,000. Because the November 16, 1985 amount is $600,000, the XYZ group therefore has a paydown in the amount of $100,000. This paydown partially offsets the $160,000 of five-year debt in the XYZ group.

(ii) *Analysis.* Applying the rule of paragraph (h)(1) of this section, separate company accounts of paydowns are computed by prorating the $100,000 paydown among those members of the group that have five-year debt. Accordingly, the paydown is prorated between Y and Z as follows:

To Y: $100,000 × $\dfrac{\$120{,}000}{\$160{,}000}$ = $75,000.

To Z: $100,000 × $\dfrac{\$40{,}000}{\$160{,}000}$ = $25,000.

Example (2): Corporate acquisitions—(i) *Facts.* The facts are the same as in example (1). On July 15, 1987, the XYZ group sells all the stock of Y to A. Having held the stock of Y for six months in 1987, the XZ group computes its transition relief for that year taking into account half of the transition attributes of Y. AY constitutes an affiliated group of corporations after the acquisition. Having held the stock of Y for six months in 1987, the AY group computes its transition relief for that year taking into account half of the transition attributes of Y. In 1987, the AY group attained a new lowest month-end debt level that yields an average lowest month-end debt level for 1987 of $150,000.

(ii) *Transferee group.* The following analysis applies in determining transition relief for purposes of apportioning the interest expense of the transferee group for 1987. The AY group has the following transition attributes for 1987:

Company A	Historic 3rd party Debt		Increase
November 16, 1985	$100,000		
May 29, 1985	250,000	5-year	$ 5,000
December 31, 1983	245,000	4-year	10,000
December 31, 1982	235,000		

Company Y (half-year amounts)	Historic 3rd party Debt		Increase
November 16, 1985	$100,000		
May 29, 1985	85,000	5-year	$60,000
December 31, 1983	25,000	4-year	5,000
December 31, 1982	20,000		
Pre-acquisition year paydown by another member of the transferor group that reduced Y's five-year debt	37,500 (one half of $75,000)		

Because the November 16, 1985 amount of the AY group in 1987 is $200,000 and because the 1987 average of historic month-end debt levels was $150,000, the AY group has a paydown in the amount of $50,000. In addition, the 1986 paydown by the XYZ group that was deemed to reduce Y debt is added to the paydown computed above, yielding a total paydown of $87,500. This amount is prorated between members, eliminating the four and five year debt of the AY group. Note that Y is only a member of the AY group for half of the 1987 taxable year. In 1988, Y's entire transition indebtedness and a $75,000 paydown must be taken into account in computing the amount of interest expense eligible for transition relief.

(iii) *Transferor group.* The following analysis applies in determining transition relief for purposes of apportioning the interest expense of the transferor group for 1987. The XZ group has the transition attributes stated below for 1987. In 1987, the XZ group attained a new lowest month-end debt level that yields an average lowest month-end debt level for 1987 of $250,000.

Reg. § 1.861-13T(h)(3)

Determination of Sources of Income 46,063

See p. 20,601 for regulations not amended to reflect law changes

	Historic 3rd party debt	Increase
Company X:		
Nov. 16, 1985	$100,000	......
May 29, 1985 (5-year)	80,000	$ 0
Dec. 31, 1983 (4-year)	80,000	10,000
Dec. 31, 1982	70,000	......
Pre-disposition paydown that reduced X's debt	0	......
Company Y (half-year amounts):		
Nov. 16, 1985	100,000	......
May 29, 1985 (5-year)	85,000	60,000
Dec. 31, 1983 (4-year)	25,000	5,000
Dec. 31, 1982	20,000	......
Pre-disposition paydown that reduced Y's debt	37,500	......
Company Z:		
Nov. 16, 1985	300,000	......
May 29, 1985 (5-year)	290,000	40,000
Dec. 31, 1983 (4-year)	250,000	100,000
Dec. 31, 1982	150,000	......
Pre-disposition paydown that reduced Z's debt	25,000	......

Because the revised November 16, 1985 amount of the XZ group is $500,000 and because the 1987 average of lowest historic month-end debt levels of the XZ group was $250,000, the XZ group has a paydown in the amount of $250,000. This paydown offsets the total five and four year debt of the XZ group. Had the 1987 paydown of the XZ group been an amount less than the five-year amount, the paydown would have been pro-rated based on Y's adjusted 5-year amount of $22,500 and Z's adjusted 5-year amount of $15,000. [Temporary Reg. § 1.861-13T.]

☐ [T.D. 8257, 8-1-89.]

[Reg. § 1.861-14]

§ 1.861-14. Special rules for allocating and apportioning certain expenses (other than interest expense) of an affiliated group of corporations.—(a) through (c) [Reserved]. For further guidance, see § 1.861-14T(a) through (c).

(d) *Definition of affiliated group*—(1) *General rule.* For purposes of this section, the term *affiliated group* has the same meaning as is given that term by section 1504, except that section 936 corporations (as defined in § 1.861-11(d)(2)(ii)) are also included within the affiliated group to the extent provided in paragraph (d)(2) of this section. Section 1504(a) defines an affiliated group as one or more chains of includible corporations connected through 80% stock ownership with a common parent corporation which is an includible corporation (as defined in section 1504(b)). In the case of a corporation that either becomes or ceases to be a member of the group during the course of the corporation's taxable year, only the expenses incurred by the group member during the period of membership shall be allocated and apportioned as if all members of the group were a single corporation. In this regard, the apportionment factor chosen shall relate only to the period of membership. For example, if apportionment on the basis of assets is chosen, the average amount of assets (tax book value or fair market value) for the taxable year shall be multiplied by a fraction, the numerator of which is the number of months of the corporation's taxable year during which the corporation was a member of the affiliated group, and the denominator of which is the number of months within the corporation's taxable year. If apportionment on the basis of gross income is chosen, only gross income generated during the period of membership shall be taken into account. If apportionment on the basis of units sold or sales receipts is chosen, only units sold or sales receipts during the period of membership shall be taken into account. Expenses incurred by the group member during its taxable year, but not during the period of membership, shall be allocated and apportioned without regard to other members of the group. This paragraph (d)(1) applies to taxable years beginning after December 31, 1989.

(2) *Inclusion of section 936 corporations*—(i) *General rule.* Except as otherwise provided in paragraph (d)(2)(ii) of this section, the exclusion from the affiliated group of section 936 corporations under section 1504(b)(4) does not apply for purposes of this section. Thus, a section 936 corporation that meets the ownership requirements of section 1504(a) is a member of the affiliated group.

(ii) *Exception for purposes of alternative minimum tax.* The exclusion from the affiliated group of section 936 corporations under section 1504(b)(4) shall be operative for purposes of the application of this section solely in determining the amount of foreign source alternative minimum taxable income within each separate category and the alternative minimum tax foreign tax credit pursuant to section 59(a). Thus, a section 936 corporation that meets the ownership requirements of section 1504(a) is not a member of the affiliated group for purposes of determining the

Reg. § 1.861-14(d)(2)

amount of foreign source alternative minimum taxable income within each separate category and the alternative minimum tax foreign tax credit pursuant to section 59(a).

(iii) *Effective date.* This paragraph (d)(2) applies to taxable years beginning after December 31, 1989.

(d)(3) through (j) [Reserved]. For further guidance see § 1.861-14T(d)(3) through (j). [Reg. § 1.861-14.]

☐ [T.D. 8916, 12-29-2000.]

[Reg. § 1.861-14T]

§ 1.861-14T. **Special rules for allocating and apportioning certain expenses (other than interest expense) of an affiliated group of corporations (Temporary.)**—(a) *In general.* Section 1.861-11T provides special rules for allocating and apportioning interest expense of an affiliated group of corporations. The rules of this § 1.861-14T also relate to affiliated groups of corporations and implement section 864(e)(6), which requires affiliated group allocation and apportionment of expenses other than interest which are not directly allocable and apportionable to any specific income producing activity or property. In general, the rules of this section apply to taxable years beginning after December 31, 1986. Paragraph (b) of this section describes the scope of the application of the rule for the allocation and apportionment of such expenses of affiliated groups of corporations. Such rule is then set forth in paragraph (c) of this section. Paragraph (d) of this section contains the definition of the term "affiliated group" for purposes of this section. Paragraph (e) of this section describes the expenses subject to allocation and apportionment under the rules of this section. Paragraph (f) of this section provides rules concerning the affiliated group allocation and apportionment of such expenses in computing the combined taxable income of a FSC or DISC and its related supplier. Paragraph (g) of this section describes the treatment of losses caused by apportionment of such expenses in the case of an affiliated group that does not file a consolidated return. Paragraph (h) of this section provides rules concerning the treatment of the reserve expenses of a life insurance company. Paragraph (j) of this section provides examples illustrating the application of this section.

(b) *Scope*—(1) *Application of section 864(e)(6).* Section 864(e)(6) and this section apply to the computation of taxable income for purposes of computing separate limitations on the foreign tax credit under section 904. Section 864(e)(6) and this section also apply in connection with section 907 to determine reductions in the amount allowed as a foreign tax credit under section 901. Section 864(e)(6) and this section also apply to the computation of the combined taxable income of the related supplier and a foreign sales corporation (FSC) (under sections 921 through 927) as well as the combined taxable income of the related supplier and a domestic international sales corporation (DISC) (under sections 991 through 997).

(2) *Nonapplication of section 864(e)(6).* Section 864(e)(6) and this section do not apply to the computation of subpart F income of controlled foreign corporations (under sections 951 through 964) or the computation of effectively connected taxable income of foreign corporations.

(3) *Application of section 864(e)(6) to the computation of combined taxable income of a possessions corporation and its affiliates.* [Reserved.]

(c) *General rule for affiliated corporations*—(1) *General rule.* (i) Except as otherwise provided in paragraph (c)(2) of this section, the taxable income of each member of an affiliated group within each statutory grouping shall be determined by allocating and apportioning the expenses described in paragraph (e) of this section of each member according to apportionment fractions which are computed as if all members of such group were a single corporation. For purposes of determining these apportionment fractions, any interaffiliate transactions or property that are duplicative with respect to the measure of apportionment chosen shall be eliminated. For example, in the application of an asset method of apportionment, stock in affiliated corporations shall not be taken into account, and loans between members of an affiliated group shall be treated in accordance with the rules of § 1.861-11T(e). Similarly, in the application of a gross income method of apportionment, interaffiliate dividends and interest, gross income from sales or services, and other interaffiliate gross income shall be eliminated. Likewise, in the application of a method of apportionment based on units sold or sales receipts, interaffiliate sales shall be eliminated.

(ii) Except as otherwise provided in this section, the rules of § 1.861-8T apply to the allocation and apportionment of the expenses described in paragraph (e) of this section. Thus, allocation under this paragraph (c) is accomplished by determining, with respect to each expense described in paragraph (e), the class of gross income to which the expense is definitely related and then allocating the deduction to such class of gross income. For this purpose, the gross income of all members of the affiliated group must be taken in account. Then, the expense is apportioned by attributing

Determination of Sources of Income 46,065
See p. 20,601 for regulations not amended to reflect law changes

the expense to gross income (within the class to which the expense has been allocated) which is in the statutory grouping and to gross income (within the class) which is in the residual grouping. Section 1.861-8T(c)(1) identifies a number of factors upon which apportionment may be based, such as comparison of units sold, gross sales or receipts, assets used, or gross income. The apportionment method chosen must be applied consistently by each member of the affiliated group in apportioning the expense when more than one member incurred the expense or when members incurred separate portions of the expense. The apportionment fraction must take into account the apportionment factors contributed by all members of the affiliated group. In the case of an affiliated group of corporations that files a consolidated return, consolidated foreign tax credit limitations are computed for the group in accordance with the rules of § 1.1502-4. For purposes of this section the term "taxpayer" refers to the affiliated group (regardless of whether the group files a consolidated return), rather than to the separate members thereof.

(2) *Expenses relating to fewer than all members.* An expense relates to fewer than all members of an affiliated group if the expense is allocable under paragraph (e)(1) of this section to gross income of at least one member other than the member that incurred the expense but fewer than all members of the affiliated group. The taxable income of the member that incurred the expense shall be determined by apportioning that expense under the rules of paragraph (c)(1) of this section as if the members of the affiliated group that derive gross income to which such expense is allocable under paragraph (e)(1) were treated as a single corporation.

(3) *Prior application of section 482.* The rules of this section do not supersede the application of section 482 and the regulations thereunder. Section 482 may be applied effectively to deny a deduction for an expense to one member of an affiliated group and to allow a deduction for that expense to another member of the affiliated group. In cases to which section 482 is applied, expenses shall be reallocated and reapportioned under section 864(e)(6) and this section after taking into account the application of section 482.

(d)(1) and (2) [Reserved]. For further guidance, see § 1.861-14(d)(1) and (2).

(3) *Inclusion of financial corporations.* For purposes of this section, in the case of an affiliated group (as defined in paragraph (d)(1) of this section), any members that constitute financial corporations as defined in § 1.861-11T(d)(4)(ii) shall be treated as members of the affiliated group. The rule of § 1.861-11T(d)(4)(i), which treats such financial corporations as a separate affiliated group, applies only for purposes of allocation and apportionment of interest expense and does not apply to the allocation and apportionment of other expenses under this section.

(4) *Treatment of life insurance companies subject to taxation under section 801.* A life insurance company that is subject to taxation under section 801 shall be considered to constitute a member of the affiliated group composed of companies not taxable under section 801 only if a parent corporation so elects under section 1504(c)(2)(A) of the Code.

(e) *Expenses to be allocated and apportioned under this section*—(1) *Expenses not directly traceable to specific income producing activities or property.* (i) The expenses that are required to be allocated and apportioned under the rules of this section are expenses related to certain supportive functions, research and experimental expenses, stewardship expenses, and legal and accounting expenses, to the extent that such expenses are not directly allocable to specific income producing activities or property solely of the member of the affiliated group that incurred the expense. Interest expense of members of an affiliated group of corporations is allocated and apportioned under § 1.861-11T and not under the rules of this section. Expenses that are included in inventory costs or that are capitalized are not subject to allocation and apportionment under the rules of this section.

(ii) An item of expense is not considered to be directly allocable to specific income producing activities or property solely of the member incurring the expense if, were all members of the affiliated group treated as a single corporation, the expense would not be considered definitely related, within the meaning of § 1.861-8T(b)(2), only to a class of gross income derived solely by the member which actually incurred the expense. Furthermore, the expense is presumed not to be definitely related only to a class of gross income derived solely by the member incurring the expense (and is, therefore, presumed not to be directly allocable to specific income producing activities or property of that member) unless the taxpayer is able affirmatively to establish otherwise. As provided in paragraph (c)(1) of this section, expenses described in this paragraph (e)(1) generally shall be apportioned by the member incurring the expense according to apportionment fractions computed as if all members of the affiliated group were a single corporation. Under paragraph (c)(2) of this section, however, an expense shall be apportioned according to apportionment

Reg. § 1.861-14T(e)(1)

fractions computed as if only some (but fewer than all) members of the affiliated group were a single corporation, if the expense is considered allocable to gross income of at least one member other than the member incurring the expense but fewer than all members of the affiliated group. An item of expense shall be considered to be allocable to gross income of fewer than all members of the group if, were all members of the affiliated group treated as a single corporation, the expense would not be considered definitely related within the meaning of § 1.861-8T(b)(2) to gross income derived by all members of the group. In such case, the expense shall be considered allocable, for purposes of paragraph (c)(2) of this section, to gross income of those members of the group that generated (or could reasonably be expected to generate) the gross income to which the expense would be considered definitely related if the group were treated as a single corporation.

(2) *Research and experimental expenses*—(i) *In general.* The allocation and apportionment of research and experimental expenses is governed by the rules of § 1.861-8T(e)(3). In the case of research and experimental expenses incurred by a member of an affiliated group, the rules of § 1.861-8T(e)(3) shall be applied as if all members of the affiliated group were a single taxpayer. Thus, research and experimental expenses shall be allocated to all income of all members of the affiliated group reasonably connected with the relevant broad product category to which such expenses are definitely related under § 1.861-8T(e)(3)(i). If fewer than all members of the affiliated group derive gross income reasonably connected with that relevant broad product category, then such expenses shall be apportioned under the rules of this paragraph (c)(2) only among those members, as if those members were a single corporation. See *Example* (1) of paragraph (j) of this section. Such expenses shall then be apportioned, if the sales method is used, in accordance with the rules of § 1.861-8T(e)(3)(ii) between the statutory grouping (within the class of gross income) and the residual grouping (within the class of gross income) taking into account the amount of sales of all members of the affiliated group from the product category which resulted in such gross income. Section 1.861-8T(e)(3)(ii)(D), relating to sales of controlled parties, shall be applied as if all members of the affiliated group were the "taxpayer" referred to therein. If either of the optional gross income methods of apportionment is used, gross income of all members of the affiliated group that generate, have generated, or could reasonably have been expected to generate gross income within the relevant class of gross income must be taken into account.

(ii) *Expenses subject to the statutory moratorium.* The rules of this section do not apply to research and experimental expenses allocated under section 126 of P.L. 98-369.

(3) *Expenses related to supportive functions.* Expenses which are supportive in nature (such as overhead, general and administrative, supervisory expenses, advertising, marketing, and other sales expenses) are to be allocated and apportioned in accordance with the rules of § 1.861-8T(b)(3). To the extent that such expenses are not directly allocable under paragraph (e)(1)(ii) of this section to specific income producing activities or property of the member of the affiliated group that incurred the expense, such expenses must be allocated and apportioned as if all members of the affiliated group were a single corporation in accordance with the rules of paragraph (c) of this section. Specifically, such expenses must be allocated to a class of gross income that takes into account gross income that is generated, has been generated, or could reasonably have been expected to have been generated by the members of the affiliated group. If the expenses relate to the gross income of fewer than all members of the affiliated group as determined under paragraph (c)(2) of this section, then those expenses must be apportioned under the rules of paragraph (c)(2) of this section, as if those fewer members were a single corporation. See *Example* (3) of paragraph (j) of this section. Such expenses must be apportioned between statutory and residual groupings of income within the appropriate class of gross income by reference to the apportionment factors contributed by the members of the affiliated group that are treated as a single corporation.

(4) *Stewardship expenses.* Stewardship expenses are to be allocated and apportioned in accordance with the rules of § 1.861-8T(e)(4). In general, stewardship expenses are considered definitely related and allocable to dividends received or to be received from a related corporation. If members of the affiliated group, other than the member that incurred the stewardship expense, receive or may receive dividends from the related corporation, such expense must be allocated and apportioned in accordance with the rules of paragraph (c) of this section as if all such members of the affiliated group that receive or may receive dividends were a single corporation. See *Example* (4) of paragraph (j) of this section. Such expenses must be apportioned between statutory and residual groupings of income within the appropriate class of gross income by reference to the apportionment factors contributed by the members of the affiliated group treated as a single corporation.

Reg. § 1.861-14T(e)(2)

Determination of Sources of Income

(5) *Legal and accounting fees and expenses.* Legal and accounting fees and expenses are to be allocated and apportioned under the rules of § 1.861-8T(e)(5). To the extent that such expenses are not directly allocable under paragraph (e)(1)(ii) of this section to specific income producing activities or property of the member of the affiliated group that incurred the expense, such expenses must be allocated and apportioned as if all members of the affiliated group were a single corporation. Specifically, such expenses must be allocated to a class of gross income that takes into account the gross income which is generated, has been generated, or could reasonably have been expected to have been generated by the other members of the affiliated group. If the expenses relate to the gross income of fewer than all members of the affiliated group as determined under paragraph (c)(2) of this section, then those expenses must be apportioned under the rules of paragraph (c)(2) of this section, as if those fewer members were a single corporation. See *Example* (5) of paragraph (j) of this section. Such expenses must be apportioned taking into account the apportionment factors contributed by the members of the group that are treated as a single corporation.

(f) *Computation of FSC or DISC combined taxable income.* In the computation under the pricing rules of sections 925 and 994 of the combined taxable income of any FSC or DISC and its related supplier which are members of an affiliated group, the combined taxable income of such FSC or DISC and its related supplier shall be reduced by the portion of the expenses of the affiliated group described in paragraph (e) of this section that is incurred in connection with export sales involving that FSC or DISC. In order to determine the portion of the expenses of the affiliated group that is incurred in connection with export sales by or through a FSC or DISC, the portion of the total of the apportionment factor chosen that relates to the generation of that export income must be determined. Thus, if gross income is the apportionment factor chosen, the portion of total gross income of the affiliated group that consists of combined gross income derived from transactions involving the FSC or DISC and related supplier must be determined. Similarly, if units sold or sales receipts is the apportionment factor chosen, the portion of total units sold or sales receipts that generated export income of the FSC or DISC and related supplier must be determined. The amount of the expense shall then be multiplied by a fraction, the numerator of which is the export related apportionment factor as determined above, and the denominator of which is the total apportionment factor. Thus, if gross income is the apportionment factor chosen, apportionment is based on a fraction, the numerator of which is export related combined gross income of the FSC or DISC and related supplier and the denominator of which is the total gross income of the affiliated group. Similarly, if units sold or sales receipts is the apportionment factor chosen, the fraction is the units sold or sales receipts that generated export income of the FSC or DISC and related supplier over the total units sold or sales receipts of the affiliated group. Under this rule, expenses of other group members may be attributed to the combined gross income of a FSC or DISC and its related supplier without affecting the amount of expenses (other than any commission payable by the related supplier to the FSC or DISC) otherwise deductible by the FSC or DISC, the related supplier, or other members of the affiliated group. The FSC or DISC must calculate combined taxable income, taking into account any reduction by expenses attributed from other members of the affiliated group to determine the commission derived by the FSC or DISC or the transfer price of qualifying export property sold to the FSC or DISC.

(g) *Losses created through apportionment.* In the case of an affiliated group that does not file a consolidated return, the taxable income in any separate limitation category must be adjusted under this paragraph (g) for purposes of computing the separate foreign tax credit limitations under section 904(d). As a consequence of the affiliated group allocation and apportionment of expenses required by section 864(e)(6) and this section, expenses of a group member may be apportioned for section 904 purposes to a limitation category with a consequent loss in that limitation category. For purposes of this paragraph, the term "limitation category" includes domestic source income, as well as the types of income described in section 904(d)(1)(A) through (I). A loss of one affiliate in a limitation category will reduce the income of another member in the same limitation category if a consolidated return is filed. (See § 1.1502-4.) If a consolidated return is not filed, this netting does not occur. Accordingly, in such a case, the following adjustments among members are required, in order to give effect to the group allocation of expense:

(1) Losses created through group apportionment of expense in one or more limitation categories within a given member must be eliminated; and

(2) A corresponding amount of income of other members in the same limitation category must be recharacterized.

Reg. § 1.861-14T(g)(2)

Such adjustments shall be accomplished in accordance with the rules of § 1.861-11T(g).

(h) *Special rule for the allocation of reserve expenses of a life insurance company.* An amount of reserve expenses of a life insurance company equal to the dividends received deduction that is disallowed because it is attributable to the policyholders' share of dividends received shall be treated as definitely related to such dividends. The remaining reserve expenses of such company shall be allocated and apportioned under the rules of § 1.861-8 and this section.

(i) [Reserved.]

(j) *Examples.* The rules of this section may be illustrated by the following examples. All of these examples assume that section 482 has not been applied by the Commissioner.

Example (1)—(i) *Facts.* P owns all of the stock of X and all of the stock of Y. P, X and Y are domestic corporations. P is a holding company for the stock of X and Y. Both X and Y manufacture and sell a product which is included in a broad product category listed in § 1.861-8(e)(3)(i). During 1988, X incurred $100,000 on research connected with that product. All of the research was performed in the United States. In 1988, the domestic sales by X of the product totalled $400,000 and the foreign sales of the product totalled $200,000; Y's domestic sales of the product totalled $200,000 and Y's foreign sales of the product totalled $200,000. In 1988, X's gross income is $300,000, of which $200,000 is from domestic sales and $100,000 is from foreign sales; Y's gross income is $200,000 of which $100,000 is from domestic sales and $100,000 is from foreign sales.

(ii) P, X and Y are affiliated corporations within the meaning of section 864(e)(5) and this section. The research expenses incurred by X are allocable to all income connected with the relevant broad category listed in § 1.861-8T(e)(3)(i). Both X and Y have gross income includible within the class of gross income related to that product category. Accordingly, the research and experimental expenses incurred by X are to be allocated and apportioned as if X and Y were a single corporation. The apportionment for 1988 is as follows:

Tentative Apportionment on the Basis of Sales

Research expenses to be apportioned...	$100,000
Exclusive apportionment to United States source gross income	$ 30,000
Research expense to be apportioned on the basis of sales	$ 70,000

Apportionment of research expense to foreign source general limitation income:

$$\$70{,}000 \times \frac{\$200{,}000 + \$200{,}000}{\$600{,}000 + \$400{,}000} \quad \ldots\ldots \quad \$28{,}000$$

Apportionment of research expense to United States source gross income:

$$\$70{,}000 \times \frac{\$400{,}000 + \$200{,}000}{\$600{,}000 + \$400{,}000} \quad \ldots\ldots \quad \$42{,}000$$

Total apportioned deduction for research	$100,000
Of which—	
Apportioned to foreign source gross income	$ 28,000
Apportioned to U.S. source gross income ($30,000 + $42,000)	$ 72,000

Tentative Apportionment on the Basis of Gross Income

Research expense apportioned to foreign source gross income:

$$\$100{,}000 \times \frac{\$100{,}000 + \$100{,}000}{\$300{,}000 + \$200{,}000} \quad \ldots\ldots \quad \$40{,}000$$

Research expense apportioned to United States income:

$$\$100{,}000 \times \frac{\$200{,}000 + \$100{,}000}{\$300{,}000 + \$200{,}000} \quad \ldots\ldots \quad \$60{,}000$$

Example (2)—(i) *Facts.* P owns all of the stock of X, which owns all of the stock of Y. P, X and Y are all domestic corporations. P has incurred general training program expenses of $100,000 in 1987. Employees of P, X and Y participate in the training program. In 1987, P had United States source gross income of $200,000 and foreign source general limitation income of $200,000; X had U.S. source gross income of $100,000 and foreign source general limitation income of $100,000; and Y had U.S. source gross income of $300,000 and foreign source general limitation income of $100,000.

Reg. § 1.861-14T(h)

(ii) *Analysis.* P, X and Y are an affiliated group of corporations within the meaning of section 864(e)(5). The training expenses incurred by P are not definitely related solely to specific income producing activities or property of P. The employees of X and Y also participate in the training program. Thus, this expense relates to gross income generated by P, X and Y. This expense is definitely related and allocable to all of the gross income from foreign and domestic sources of P, X and Y. It is assumed that apportionment on the basis of gross income is reasonable. The apportionment of the expense is as follows:

Apportionment of $100,000 expense to foreign source general limitation income:

$$\$100{,}000 \times \frac{\$200{,}000 + \$100{,}000 + \$100{,}000}{\$400{,}000 + \$200{,}000 + \$400{,}000} \ldots \ \$ \ 40{,}000$$

Apportionment of $100,000 expense to United States source gross income:

$$\$100{,}000 \times \frac{\$200{,}000 + \$100{,}000 + \$300{,}000}{\$400{,}000 + \$200{,}000 + \$400{,}000} \ldots \ \$ \ 60{,}000$$

Total apportioned expense .... $ 100,000

Example (3)—(i) *Facts.* The facts are the same as in *Example (2)* above, except that only employees of P and X participate in the training program.

(ii) *Analysis.* Because only the employees of P and X participate in the training program and they perform no services for Y, the expense relates only to gross income generated by P and X. Accordingly, the $100,000 expense must be allocated and apportioned as if P and X were a single corporation. The apportionment of the $100,000 expense is as follows:

Apportionment of $100,000 expense to foreign source general limitation income:

$$\$100{,}000 \times \frac{\$200{,}000 + \$100{,}000}{\$400{,}000 + \$200{,}000} \ldots \ \$ \ 50{,}000$$

Apportionment of $100,000 expense to United States source gross income:

$$\$100{,}000 \times \frac{\$200{,}000 + \$100{,}000}{\$400{,}000 + \$200{,}000} \ldots \ \$ \ 50{,}000$$

Example (4)—(i) *Facts.* P owns all of the stock of X which owns all of the stock of Y. P and X are domestic corporations; Y is a foreign corporation. In 1987 P incurred $10,000 of stewardship expenses relating to an audit of Y.

(ii) *Analysis.* The stewardship expenses incurred by P are not directly allocable to specific income producing activities or property of P. The expense is definitely related and allocable to dividends received or to be received by X. Accordingly, the expense of P is allocated and apportioned as if P and X were a single corporation. The expense is definitely related to dividends received or to be received by X from Y, a foreign corporation. Such dividends are foreign source general limitation income. Thus, the entire amount of the expense must be allocated to foreign source dividend income.

Example (5)—(i) *Facts.* P owns all of the stock of X which owns all of the stock of Y. P, X and Y are all domestic corporations. In 1987, P incurred $10,000 legal expense relating to the testimony of certain employees of P in connection with litigation to which Y is a party. This expense is not allocable to specific income of Y. In 1987, Y had $100,000 foreign source general limitation income and $300,000 U.S. source gross income.

(ii) *Analysis.* The legal expenses incurred by P are not definitely related solely to specific income producing activities or property of P. The expense is definitely related and allocable to the class of gross income which includes only gross income generated by Y. Accordingly, the expense of P is allocated and apportioned as if Y were the only member of the affiliated group, as follows:

Apportionment of legal expenses to foreign source general limitation income:

$$\$10{,}000 \times \frac{\$100{,}000}{\$400{,}000} \ldots \ \$ \ 2{,}500$$

Apportionment of legal expenses to U.S. source gross income:

Reg. § 1.861-14T(j)

Determination of Sources of Income

See p. 20,601 for regulations not amended to reflect law changes

$$\$10,000 \times \frac{\$300,000}{\$400,000} \ldots\ldots\ldots\ldots \$7,500$$

Example (6)—(i) *Facts.* P owns all of the stock of R, which owns all of the stock of F. P and R are domestic corporations, and F is a foreign sales corporation under section 922 of the Code. R and F have entered into an agreement whereby F is paid a commission with respect to sales of product A. In 1987, P had gross receipts of $1,000,000 from domestic sales of product A, and gross receipts of $1,000,000 from foreign sales of product A. R had gross receipts of $1,000,000 from domestic sales of product A, and $1,000,000 from export sales of product A. R's cost of goods sold attributable to export sales is $500,000. R has deductible expenses of $100,000 directly related to its export sales, and F has such deductible expenses of $100,000. During 1987, P incurred an expense of $100,000 for marketing studies involving the worldwide market for product A.

(ii) *Analysis.* P and R are an affiliated group of corporations within the meaning of section 864(e)(5) and this section. The expense incurred by P for marketing studies regarding the worldwide market for product A is an expense that is not directly related solely to the activities of P, but also to the activities of R. This expense must be allocated and apportioned under the rules of paragraph (c)(1) of this section, as if P and R were a single corporation. The expense is allocable to the class of gross income that includes all gross income generated by sales of product A. Apportionment on the basis of gross receipts is reasonable under these facts. F, a foreign corporation, is not a member of the affiliated group. However, for purposes of determining F's commission on its sales, the combined gross income of F and R must be reduced by the portion of the marketing studies expense of P that is incurred in connection with export sales involving F under the rules of paragraph (f) of this section. The computation of the combined taxable income of R and F is as follows:

Combined Taxable Income of R and F

R's gross receipts from export sales	$1,000,000
R's cost of goods sold	$ 500,000
Combined Gross Income	$ 500,000
Less:	
R's other deductible expenses	$ 100,000
F's other deductible expenses	$ 100,000
Apportionment of P's expense:	
$\$100,000 \times \dfrac{\$1,000,000}{\$2,000,000 + \$2,000,000}$	$ 25,000
Total	$ 225,000
Combined Taxable Income	$ 275,000

[Temporary Reg. § 1.861-14T.]

☐ [T.D. 8228, 9-9-88. Amended by T.D. 8916, 12-29-2000.]

[Reg. § 1.861-15]

§ 1.861-15. Income from certain aircraft or vessels first leased on or before December 28, 1980.—(a) *General rule.* A taxpayer who owns an aircraft or vessel described in paragraph (b) of this section and who leases the aircraft or vessel to a United States person (other than a member of the same controlled group of corporations (as defined in section 1563) as the taxpayer) may elect under paragraph (f) of this section to treat all amounts includible in gross income with respect to the aircraft or vessel as income from sources within the United States for any taxable year ending after the commencement of the lease. This paragraph (a) applies only with respect to taxable years ending after August 15, 1971, and only with respect to leases entered into after that date of aircraft or vessels first leased by the taxpayer on or before December 28, 1980. An election once made applies to the taxable year for which made and to all subsequent taxable years unless it is revoked or terminated in accordance with paragraph (g) of this section. A taxpayer need not be a United States person to be eligible to make the election under this section, unless otherwise required by a provision of law not contained in the Internal Revenue Code of 1954. In addition, the taxpayer need not be a bank or other financial institution to be eligible to make this election. The term "United States person" as used in this section has the meaning assigned to it by section 7701(a)(30).

(b) *Property to which the election applies*—(1) *Section 38 property.* An election made under this

Reg. § 1.861-15(a)

section may be made only if the aircraft or vessel is section 38 property, or property which would be section 38 property but for section 48(a)(5) (relating to property used by governmental units), at the time the election is made and for all taxable years to which the election applies. The aircraft or vessel must be property which qualifies for the investment credit under section 38 unless the property does not qualify because it is described in section 48(a)(5). If an aircraft is used predominantly outside the United States (determined under § 1.48-1(g)(1)), it must qualify under the provisions of section 48(a)(2)(B)(i) and § 1.48-1(g)(2)(i). If a vessel is used predominantly outside the United States, it must qualify under the provisions of section 48(a)(2)(B)(iii) and § 1.48-1(g)(2)(iii). The aircraft or vessel may not be suspension or termination period property described in section 48(h) or section 49(a) (as in effect before the enactment of the Revenue Act of 1978). See paragraphs (g)(3) and (4) of this section for rules which apply if the property ceases to be section 38 property.

(2) *United States manufacture or construction.* An election under this section may be made only if the aircraft or vessel is manufactured or constructed in the United States. The aircraft or vessel will be considered to be manufactured or constructed in the United States if 50 percent or more of the basis of the aircraft or vessel is attributable to value added within the United States.

(3) *Exclusion of certain property used outside the United States.* The term "aircraft or vessel" as used in this paragraph (b) does not include any property which is used predominantly outside the United States and which qualifies as section 38 property under—

(i) Section 48(a)(2)(B)(v), relating to containers used in the transportation of property to and from the United States,

(ii) Section 48(a)(2)(B)(vi), relating to certain property used for the purpose of exploring for, developing, removing, or transporting resources from the Outer Continental Shelf, or

(iii) Section 48(a)(2)(B)(x), relating to certain property used in international or territorial waters.

(c) *Leases or subleases to which the election applies.* At the time the election under this section is made and for all taxable years for which the election applies, the lessee of the aircraft or vessel must be a United States person. In addition, the aircraft or vessel may not be subleased to a person who is not a United States person unless the sublease is a short-term sublease. For purposes of this section, a short-term sublease is a sublease for a period of time (including any period for which the sublease may be renewed or extended) which is less than 30 percent of the asset guideline period of the aircraft or vessel leased (determined under section 167(m)). See paragraph (g)(3) and (4) of this section for rules which apply if the requirements of this paragraph (c) are not met.

(d) *Income to which the election applies.* An election under this section applies to all amounts derived by the taxpayer with respect to the aircraft or vessel which is subject to the election. The election applies to all amounts which are includible in the taxpayer's gross income whether or not includible during or after the period of a lease to which the election applies. Amounts derived by the taxpayer with respect to the aircraft or vessel include any gain from the sale, exchange, or other disposition of the aircraft or vessel. If by reason of the allowance of expenses and other deductions, there is a loss with respect to an aircraft or vessel, the election applies to treat the loss as having a source within the United States. Similarly, if the sale, exchange or other disposition of the aircraft or vessel which is subject to an election results in a loss, it is treated as having a source within the United States. See paragraph (e)(2) of this section for the application of an election under this section to the income of certain transferees or distributees.

(e) *Effect of election*—(1) *In general.* An election under this section applies to the taxable year for which it is made and to all subsequent taxable years for which amounts in respect of the aircraft or vessel to which the election relates are includible in gross income. However, the election may be revoked under paragraph (g)(1) or (2) of this section or terminated under paragraph (g)(3) of this section.

(2) *Certain transfers involving carryover of basis.* (i) If an electing taxpayer transfers or distributes an aircraft or vessel which is subject to the election under this section, the transferee or distributee will be treated as having made an election under this section with respect to the aircraft or vessel if the basis of the aircraft or vessel in the hands of the transferee or distributee is determined by reference to its basis in the hands of the transferor or distributor. This paragraph (e)(2)(i) applies even though the transferor or distributor recognizes an amount of gain which increases basis in the hands of the transferee or distributee and even though the transferee or distributee is a nonresident alien individual or foreign corporation. For example, if a corporation distributes a vessel which is subject to an election under this section to its parent corporation in a complete liquidation described in section 332(b), the parent corporation will be required to treat all

Reg. § 1.861-15(e)(2)

amounts includible in its gross income with respect to the vessel as income from sources within the United States if, unless the election is revoked or terminated under paragraph (g) of this section, the basis of the property in the hands of the parent is determined under section 334(b)(1) (relating to the general rule on carryover of basis). In further illustration, if a corporation distributes a vessel (subject to an election) in a distribution to which section 301(a) applies, the distributee will be treated as having made the election with respect to the vessel if its basis is determined under section 301(d)(2) (relating to basis of corporate distributees) even though the basis is the fair market value of the vessel under section 301(d)(2)(A).

(ii) If a member of an affiliated group which files a consolidated return transfers an aircraft or vessel subject to an election to another member of that group, the transferee will be treated as having made the election with respect to the aircraft or vessel. In addition, if a partnership distributes an aircraft or vessel subject to an election to a partner, the partner will be treated as having made the election with respect to the aircraft or vessel.

(iii) If paragraphs (e)(2)(i) and (ii) of this section do not apply, the election under this section with respect to an aircraft or vessel will not be considered as made by a transferee or distributee.

(f) *Election*—(1) *Time for making the election.* The election under this section must be made before the expiration of the period prescribed by section 6511(a) (or section 6511(c) if the period is extended by agreement) for making a claim for credit or refund of the tax imposed by chapter 1 for the first taxable year for which the election is to apply. The period for that first taxable year is determined without regard to the special periods prescribed by section 6511(d).

(2) *Manner of making the election.* An election under this section must be made by filing with the income tax return (or an amended return) for the first taxable year for which the election is to apply a statement, signed by the taxpayer, to the effect that the election under section 861(e) is being made. The statement must—

(i) Set forth sufficient facts to identify the aircraft or vessel which is the subject of the election,

(ii) State that the aircraft or vessel was manufactured or constructed in the United States,

(iii) State that the aircraft or vessel is section 38 property described in § 1.861-9(b) which was leased to a United States person (as defined in section 7701(a)(30) of the Code) pursuant to a lease entered into after August 15, 1971,

(iv) State that the electing taxpayer is the owner of the aircraft or vessel,

(v) State that the lessee of the aircraft or vessel is not a member of a controlled group of corporations (as defined in section 1563) of which the taxpayer is a member,

(vi) Give the name and taxpayer identification number of the lessee of the aircraft or vessel, and

(vii) State that the aircraft or vessel is not subject to a sublease (other than a short-term sublease) to any person who is not a United States person.

(3) *Election by partnership.* Any election under this section with respect to an aircraft or vessel owned by a partnership shall be made by the partnership. Any partnership election is applicable to each partner's partnership interest in the aircraft or vessel. However, an election made by a partner before August 8, 1979 will be recognized where the partnership made no election and the election can no longer be revoked without the consent of the Commissioner under paragraph (g)(1) of this section.

(g) *Termination of election*—(1) *Revocation without consent.* A taxpayer may revoke an election within the time prescribed in paragraph (f)(1) of this section without the consent of the Commissioner. In such a case, the taxpayer must file an amended income tax return for any taxable year to which the election applied.

(2) *Revocation with consent.* Except as provided in paragraph (g)(1) or (3) of this section, an election made under this section is binding unless consent to revoke is obtained from the Commissioner. A request to revoke the election must be made in writing and addressed to the Assistant Commissioner of Internal Revenue (Technical), Attention: T:C:C:3, Washington, D.C. 20224. The request must include the name and address of the taxpayer and be signed by the taxpayer or his duly authorized representative. It must specify the taxable year or years for which the revocation is to be effective and must be filed at least 90 days prior to the time (not including extensions) prescribed by law for filing the income tax return for the first taxable year for which the revocation of the election is to be effective or by November 6, 1979 whichever is later. The request must specify the grounds which are considered to justify the revocation. The Commissioner may require such additional information as may be necessary in order to determine whether the proposed revocation will be permitted. Consent will generally not

Reg. § 1.861-15(f)(1)

be given to revoke an election where the revocation would result in treating gross income with respect to the aircraft or vessel (including any gain from the sale, exchange, or other disposition of such aircraft or vessel) as income from sources without the United States where, during the period the election was in effect, there were losses from sources within the United States. A copy of the consent of the Commissioner to revoke must be attached to the taxpayer's income tax return (or amended return) for each taxable year affected by the revocation.

(3) *Automatic termination.* If an aircraft or vessel subject to an election under section 861(e) ceases to be section 38 property, ceases to be leased by its owner directly to a United States person, or is subleased (other than a short-term sublease) to a person who is not a United States person, within the period set forth in section 6511(a) (or section 6511(c) if the period is extended by agreement) for making a claim for credit or refund of the tax imposed by chapter 1 for the first taxable year for which the election applied, then the election with respect to such aircraft or vessel will automatically terminate. If the election terminates, the taxpayer who made the election must file an amended tax return or claim for credit or refund, as the case may be, for any taxable year to which the election applied.

(4) *Factors not causing revocation or termination.* The fact that an aircraft or vessel ceases to be section 38 property, ceases to be leased by its owner directly to a United States person, or is leased or subleased for any period of time to a person who is not a United States person, after expiration of the period set forth in section 6511(a) (or section 6511(c) if the period is extended by agreement) for making a claim for credit or refund of the tax imposed by chapter 1 for the first taxable year for which the election applied, will not cause a termination of the election made under this section with respect to the aircraft or vessel. For example, the electing taxpayer is not relieved from any of the consequences of making the election merely because the aircraft or vessel is subleased to a person who is not a United States person for a period in excess of that allowed for short-term subleases under paragraph (c) of this section after expiration of the later of 3 years from the time the return was filed for the first taxable year to which the election applied or 2 years from the time the tax was paid for that year where the period set forth in section 6511(a) has not been extended by agreement.

(5) *Effect of revocation or termination.* If an election is revoked or terminated under this paragraph (g), the taxpayer is required to recompute the tax for the appropriate taxable years without reference to section 861(e)(1).

(6) *Revocation or termination after December 28, 1980.* The rules in paragraph (g)(1) through (g)(5) continue to apply with respect to any election made pursuant to this section even though the revocation or termination may occur after December 28, 1980. [Reg. § 1.861-15.]

☐ [*T.D. 7635, 8-7-79. Amended by T.D. 7928, 12-15-83 and T.D. 8228, 9-9-88.*]

[Reg. § 1.861-16]

§ 1.861-16. **Income from certain craft first leased after December 28, 1980.**—(a) *General rule.* If a taxpayer—

(1) Owns a qualified craft (as defined in paragraph (b) of this section),

(2) Leases such qualified craft after December 28, 1980, to a United States person that is not a member of the same controlled group of corporations as the taxpayer, and

(3) The lease is the taxpayer's first lease of the craft and the taxpayer is not considered to have made an election with respect to the craft under § 1.861-9(e)(2),

then the taxpayer shall treat all amounts includible in gross income with respect to the qualified craft as income from sources within the United States for each taxable year ending after commencement of the lease. If this section applies to income with respect to a craft, it applies to all such amounts that are includible in the taxpayer's gross income, whether or not includible during or after the period of a lease to a United States person. Amounts derived by the taxpayer with respect to the qualified craft include any gain from the sale, exchange, or other disposition of the qualifed craft. If this section applies to income with respect to a craft and there is a loss with respect to that craft (either due to the allowance of expenses and other deductions or due to a sale, exchange, or other disposition of the qualified craft), such loss is treated as allocable or apportionable to sources within the United States. The fact that a craft ceases to be section 38 property, ceases to be leased by the taxpayer to a United States person, or is leased or subleased for any period of time to a person who is not a United States person will not terminate the application of this section.

(b) *Qualified craft* —(1) *In general.* A qualified craft is a vessel, aircraft, or spacecraft that—

(i) Is section 38 property (or would be section 38 property but for section 48(a)(5), relating to use by governmental units), and

(ii) Is manufactured or constructed in the United States.

(2) *Vessel.* The term "vessel" includes every type of watercraft capable of being used as a means of transportation on water, and any items of property that are affixed in a permanent fashion or are integral to the vessel. A vessel that is used predominately outside the United States must be described in section 48(a)(2)(B)(iii) and § 1.48-1(g)(2)(iii), relating to vessels documented for use in the foreign or domestic commerce of the United States, to be a qualified craft.

(3) *Aircraft.* An aircraft used predominantly outside the United States must be described in section 48(a)(2)(B)(i) and § 1.48-1(g)(2)(i), relating to aircraft registered by the Administrator of the Federal Aviation Agency, and operated to and from the United States or operated under contract with the United States, to be a qualified craft.

(4) *Spacecraft.* A spacecraft must be described in section 48(a)(2)(B)(viii) and § 1.48-1(g)(2)(viii), relating to communications satellites, or any interest therein, of a United States person, to be a qualified craft.

(5) *United States manufacture or construction.* A craft will be considered to be manufactured or constructed in the United States if 50 percent or more of the basis of the craft on the date of the lease to a United States person is attributable to value added within the United States.

(c) *United States person.* For purposes of this section, the term "United States person" includes those persons described in section 7701(a)(30) and individuals with respect to whom an election under section 6013(g) or (h) (relating to nonresident alien individuals married to United States citizens or residents) is in effect.

(d) *Controlled group.* For purposes of paragraph (a)(2) of this section, whether a taxpayer and a United States person are members of the same controlled group of corporations is determined under section 1563. Solely for purposes of this section, if at least 80% of the capital interest, or the profits interest, in a partnership is owned, directly or indirectly, by a member or members of a controlled group of corporations, then the partnership shall be considered a member of that controlled group of corporations. In addition, if at least 80% of the capital interest, or the profits interest, in a partnership is owned, directly or indirectly, by a corporation, then the partnership and that corporation shall be considered members of a controlled group of corporations.

(e) *Certain transfers and distributions*—(1) *Transfers and distributions involving carryover of basis.* If—

(i) The income with respect to a craft is subject to this section,

(ii) The taxpayer transfers or distributes such craft, and

(iii) The basis of such craft in the hands of the transferee or distributee is determined by reference to its basis in the hands of the transferor or distributor,

then this section will apply to the income with respect to the craft includible in the gross income of the transferee or distributee. This paragraph (e)(1) applies even though the transferor or distributor recognizes an amount of gain that increases basis in the hands of the transferee or distributee and even though the transferee or distributee is a nonresident alien or foreign corporation. For example, if a corporation distributes a craft the income of which is subject to this section to its parent corporation in a complete liquidation described in section 332(b), the parent corporation will be treated as if it satisfied the requirements of paragraph (a) of this section with respect to such craft if the basis of the property in the hands of the parent corporation is determined under section 334(b) (relating to the general rule on carryover of basis in liquidations). In further illustration, if a corporation distributes a craft the income of which is subject to this section, in a distribution to which section 301(a) applies, the distributee will be treated as if it satisfied the requirements of paragraph (a) of this section with respect to such craft if its basis is determined under section 301(d)(2) (relating to basis of corporate distributees) even though the basis may be the fair market value of the craft under section 301(d)(2)(A).

(2) *Partnerships.* If a partnership satisfies the requirements of paragraph (a)(1), (2), and (3) of this section, each partner shall treat all amounts includible in gross income with respect to the craft as income from sources within the United States for any taxable year of the partnership ending after commencement of the lease. In addition, if a partnership distributes a craft the income of which is subject to this section, to a partner, the partner will be treated as if he or she satisfied the requirements of paragraph (a) of this section with respect to such craft.

(3) *Affiliated groups.* If a member of a controlled group of corporations that files a consolidated return transfers a craft, the income of which is subject to this section, to another member of that same group, the transferee will be treated as if it satisfied the requirements of paragraph (a) of this section with respect to the craft. [Reg. § 1.861-16.]

☐ [T.D. 7928, 12-15-83. Amended by T.D. 8228, 9-9-88.]

Determination of Sources of Income

[Reg. § 1.861-17]

§ 1.861-17. Allocation and apportionment of research and experimental expenditures.—(a) *Allocation*—(1) *In general.* The methods of allocation and apportionment of research and experimental expenditures set forth in this section recognize that research and experimentation is an inherently speculative activity, that findings may contribute unexpected benefits, and that the gross income derived from successful research and experimentation must bear the cost of unsuccessful research and experimentation. Expenditures for research and experimentation that a taxpayer deducts under section 174 ordinarily shall be considered deductions that are definitely related to all income reasonably connected with the relevant broad product category (or categories) of the taxpayer and therefore allocable to all items of gross income as a class (including income from sales, royalties, and dividends) related to such product category (or categories). For purposes of this allocation, the product category (or categories) that a taxpayer may be considered to have shall be determined in accordance with the provisions of paragraph (a)(2) of this section.

(2) *Product categories*—(i) *Allocation based on product categories.* Ordinarily, a taxpayer's research and experimental expenditures may be divided between the relevant product categories. Where research and experimentation is conducted with respect to more than one product category, the taxpayer may aggregate the categories for purposes of allocation and apportionment; however, the taxpayer may not subdivide the categories. Where research and experimentation is not clearly identified with any product category (or categories), it will be considered conducted with respect to all the taxpayer's product categories.

(ii) *Use of three digit standard industrial classification codes.* A taxpayer shall determine the relevant product categories by reference to the three digit classification of the Standard Industrial Classification Manual (SIC code). A copy may be purchased from the Superintendent of Documents, United States Government Printing Office, Washington, DC 20402. The individual products included within each category are enumerated in Executive Office of the President, Office of Management and Budget, Standard Industrial Classification Manual, 1987 (or later edition, as available).

(iii) *Consistency.* Once a taxpayer selects a product category for the first taxable year for which this section is effective with respect to the taxpayer, it must continue to use that product category in following years, unless the taxpayer establishes to the satisfaction of the Commissioner that, due to changes in the relevant facts, a change in the product category is appropriate. For this purpose, a change in the taxpayer's selection of a product category shall include a change from a three digit SIC code category to a two digit SIC code category, a change from a two digit SIC code category to a three digit SIC code category, or any other aggregation, disaggregation or change of a previously selected SIC code category.

(iv) *Wholesale trade category.* The two digit SIC code category "Wholesale trade" is not applicable with respect to sales by the taxpayer of goods and services from any other of the taxpayer's product categories and is not applicable with respect to a domestic international sales corporation (DISC) or foreign sales corporation (FSC) for which the taxpayer is a related supplier of goods and services from any of the taxpayer's product categories.

(v) *Retail trade category.* The two digit SIC code category "Retail trade" is not applicable with respect to sales by the taxpayer of goods and services from any other of the taxpayer's product categories, except wholesale trade, and is not applicable with respect to a DISC or FSC for which the taxpayer is a related supplier of goods and services from any other of the taxpayer's product categories, except wholesale trade.

(3) *Affiliated Groups*—(i) In general. Except as provided in paragraph (a)(3)(ii) of this section, the allocation and apportionment required by this section shall be determined as if all members of the affiliated group (as defined in § 1.861-14T(d)) were a single corporation. See § 1.861-14T.

(ii) *Possessions corporations.* (A) For purposes of the allocation and apportionment required by this section, sales and gross income from products produced in whole or in part in a possession by an electing corporation (within the meaning of section 936(h)(5)(E)), and dividends from an electing corporation, shall not be taken into account, except that this paragraph (a)(3)(ii) shall not apply to sales of (and gross income and dividends attributable to sales of) products with respect to which an election under section 936(h)(5)(F) is not in effect.

(B) The research and experimental expenditures taken into account for purposes of this section shall be reduced by the amount of such expenditures included in computing the cost-sharing amount (determined under section 936(h)(5)(C)(i)).

(4) *Legally mandated research and experimentation.* Where research and experimentation is undertaken solely to meet legal requirements

Reg. § 1.861-17(a)(4)

imposed by a political entity with respect to improvement or marketing of specific products or processes, and the results cannot reasonably be expected to generate amounts of gross income (beyond de minimis amounts) outside a single geographic source, the deduction for such research and experimentation shall be considered definitely related and therefore allocable only to the grouping (or groupings) of gross income within that geographic source as a class (and apportioned, if necessary, between such groupings as set forth in paragraphs (c) and (d) of this section). For example, where a taxpayer performs tests on a product in response to a requirement imposed by the U.S. Food and Drug Administration, and the test results cannot reasonably be expected to generate amounts of gross income (beyond de minimis amounts) outside the United States, the costs of testing shall be allocated solely to gross income from sources within the United States.

(b) *Exclusive apportionment*—(1) *In general.* An exclusive apportionment shall be made under this paragraph (b), where an apportionment based upon geographic sources of income of a deduction for research and experimentation is necessary (after applying the exception in paragraph (a)(4) of this section).

(i) *Exclusive apportionment under the sales method.* If the taxpayer apportions on the sales method under paragraph (c) of this section, an amount equal to fifty percent of such deduction for research and experimentation shall be apportioned exclusively to the statutory grouping of gross income or the residual grouping of gross income, as the case may be, arising from the geographic source where the research and experimental activities which account for more than fifty percent of the amount of such deduction were performed.

(ii) *Exclusive apportionment under the optional gross income methods.* If the taxpayer apportions on the optional gross income methods under paragraph (d) of this section, an amount equal to twenty-five percent of such deduction for research and experimentation shall be apportioned exclusively to the statutory grouping or the residual grouping of gross income, as the case may be, arising from the geographic source where the research and experimental activities which account for more than fifty percent of the amount of such deduction were performed.

(iii) *Exception.* If the applicable fifty percent geographic source test of the preceding paragraph (b)(1)(i) or (ii) is not met, then no part of the deduction shall be apportioned under this paragraph (b)(1).

(2) *Facts and circumstances supporting an increased exclusive apportionment*—(i) *In general.* The exclusive apportionment provided for in paragraph (b)(1) of this section reflects the view that research and experimentation is often most valuable in the country where it is performed, for two reasons. First, research and experimentation often benefits a broad product category, consisting of many individual products, all of which may be sold in the nearest market but only some of which may be sold in foreign markets. Second, research and experimentation often is utilized in the nearest market before it is used in other markets, and in such cases, has a lower value per unit of sales when used in foreign markets. The taxpayer may establish to the satisfaction of the Commissioner that, in its case, one or both of the conditions mentioned in the preceding sentences warrant a significantly greater exclusive allocation percentage than allowed by paragraph (b)(1) of this section because the research and experimentation is reasonably expected to have very limited or long delayed application outside the geographic source where it was performed. Past experience with research and experimentation may be considered in determining reasonable expectations.

(ii) *Not all products sold in foreign markets.* For purposes of establishing that only some products within the product category (or categories) are sold in foreign markets, the taxpayer shall compare the commercial production of individual products in domestic and foreign markets made by itself, by uncontrolled parties (as defined under paragraph (c)(2)(i) of this section) of products involving intangible property which was licensed or sold by the taxpayer, and by those controlled corporations (as defined under paragraph (c)(3)(ii) of this section) that can reasonably be expected to benefit directly or indirectly from any of the taxpayer's research expense connected with the product category (or categories). The individual products compared for this purpose shall be limited, for nonmanufactured categories, solely to those enumerated in Executive Office of the President, Office of Management and Budget Standard Industrial Classification Manual, 1987 (or later edition, as available), and, for manufactured categories, solely to those enumerated at a 7-digit level in the U.S. Bureau of the Census, Census of Manufacturers: 1992, Numerical List of Manufactured Products, 1993, (or later edition, as available). Copies of both of these documents may be purchased from the Superintendent of Documents, United States Government Printing Office, Washington, DC 20402.

(iii) *Delayed application of research findings abroad.* For purposes of establishing the

Reg. § 1.861-17(b)(1)

Determination of Sources of Income

delayed application of research findings abroad, the taxpayer shall compare the commercial introduction of its own particular products and processes (not limited by those listed in the Standard Industrial Classification Manual or the Numerical List of Manufactured Products) in the United States and foreign markets, made by itself, by uncontrolled parties (as defined under paragraph (c)(2)(i) of this section) of products involving intangible property that was licensed or sold by the taxpayer, and by those controlled corporations (as defined under paragraph (c)(3)(i) of this section) that can reasonably be expected to benefit, directly or indirectly, from the taxpayer's research expense. For purposes of evaluating the delay in the application of research findings in foreign markets, the taxpayer shall use a safe haven discount rate of 10 percent per year of delay unless he is able to establish to the satisfaction of the Commissioner, by reference to the cost of money and the number of years during which economic benefit can be directly attributable to the results of the taxpayer's research, that another discount rate is more appropriate.

(c) *Sales method*—(1) *In general.* The amount equal to the remaining portion of such deduction for research and experimentation, not apportioned under paragraph (a)(4) or (b)(1)(i) of this section, shall be apportioned between the statutory grouping (or among the statutory groupings) within the class of gross income and the residual grouping within such class in the same proportions that the amount of sales from the product category (or categories) that resulted in such gross income within the statutory grouping (or statutory groupings) and in the residual grouping bear, respectively, to the total amount of sales from the product category (or categories).

(i) *Apportionment in excess of gross income.* Amounts apportioned under this section may exceed the amount of gross income related to the product category within the statutory grouping. In such case, the excess shall be applied against other gross income within the statutory grouping. See § 1.861-8(d)(1) for instances where the apportionment leads to an excess of deductions over gross income within the statutory grouping.

(ii) *Leased property.* For purposes of this paragraph (c), amounts received from the lease of equipment during a taxable year shall be regarded as sales receipts for such taxable year.

(2) *Sales of uncontrolled parties.* For purposes of the apportionment under paragraph (c)(1) of this section, the sales from the product category (or categories) by each party uncontrolled by the taxpayer, of particular products involving intangible property that was licensed or sold by the taxpayer to such uncontrolled party shall be taken fully into account both for determining the taxpayer's apportionment and for determining the apportionment of any other member of a controlled group of corporations to which the taxpayer belongs if the uncontrolled party can reasonably be expected to benefit directly or indirectly (through any member of the controlled group of corporations to which the taxpayer belongs) from the research expense connected with the product category (or categories) of such other member. An uncontrolled party can reasonably be expected to benefit from the research expense of a member of a controlled group of corporations to which the taxpayer belongs if such member can reasonably be expected to license, sell, or transfer intangible property to that uncontrolled party or transfer secret processes to that uncontrolled party, directly or indirectly through a member of the controlled group of corporations to which the taxpayer belongs. Past experience with research and experimentation shall be considered in determining reasonable expectations.

(i) *Definition of uncontrolled party.* For purposes of this paragraph (c)(2) the term *uncontrolled party* means a party that is not a person with a relationship to the taxpayer specified in section 267(b), or is not a member of a controlled group of corporations to which the taxpayer belongs (within the meaning of section 993(a)(3) or 927(d)(4)).

(ii) *Licensed products.* In the case of licensed products, if the amount of sales of such products is unknown (for example, where the licensed product is a component of a large machine), a reasonable estimate based on the principles of section 482 should be made.

(iii) *Sales of intangible property.* In the case of sales of intangible property, regardless of whether the consideration received in exchange for the intangible is a fixed amount or is contingent on the productivity, use, or disposition of the intangible, if the amount of sales of products utilizing the intangible property is unknown, a reasonable estimate of sales shall be made annually. If necessary, appropriate economic analyses shall be used to estimate sales.

(3) *Sales of controlled parties.* For purposes of the apportionment under paragraph (c)(1) of this section, the sales from the product category (or categories) of the taxpayer shall be taken fully into account and the sales from the product category (or categories) of a corporation controlled by the taxpayer shall be taken into account to the extent provided in this paragraph (c)(3) for deter-

Reg. § 1.861-17(c)(3)

mining the taxpayer's apportionment, if such corporation can reasonably be expected to benefit directly or indirectly (through another member of the controlled group of corporations to which the taxpayer belongs) from the taxpayer's research expense connected with the product category (or categories). A corporation controlled by the taxpayer can reasonably be expected to benefit from the taxpayer's research expense if the taxpayer can be expected to license, sell, or transfer intangible property to that corporation or transfer secret processes to that corporation, either directly or indirectly through a member of the controlled group of corporations to which the taxpayer belongs. Past experience with research and experimentation shall be considered in determining reasonable expectations.

(i) *Definition of a corporation controlled by the taxpayer.* For purposes of this paragraph (c)(3), the term *a corporation controlled by the taxpayer* means any corporation that has a relationship to the taxpayer specified in section 267(b) or is a member of a controlled group of corporations to which the taxpayer belongs (within the meaning of section 993(a)(3) or 927(d)(4)).

(ii) *Sales to be taken into account.* The sales from the product category (or categories) of a corporation controlled by the taxpayer taken into account shall be equal to the amount of sales that bear the same proportion to the total sales of the controlled corporation as the total value of all classes of the stock of such corporation owned directly or indirectly by the taxpayer, within the meaning of section 1563, bears to the total value of all classes of stock of such corporation.

(iii) *Sales not to be taken into account more than once.* Sales from the product category (or categories) between or among such controlled corporations or the taxpayer shall not be taken into account more than once; in such a situation, the amount sold by the selling corporation to the buying corporation shall be subtracted from the sales of the buying corporation.

(iv) *Effect of cost-sharing arrangements.* If the corporation controlled by the taxpayer has entered into a bona fide cost-sharing arrangement, in accordance with the provisions of § 1.482-7, with the taxpayer for the purpose of developing intangible property, then that corporation shall not reasonably be expected to benefit from the taxpayer's share of the research expense.

(d) *Gross income methods*—(1)(i) *In general.* In lieu of applying the sales method of paragraph (c) of this section, the remaining amount of the deduction for research and experimentation, not apportioned under paragraph (a)(4) or (b)(1)(ii) of this section, shall be apportioned as prescribed in paragraphs (d)(2) and (3) of this section, between the statutory grouping (or among the statutory groupings) of gross income and the residual grouping of gross income.

(ii) *Optional methods to be applied to all research and experimental expenditures.* These optional methods must be applied to the taxpayer's entire deduction for research and experimental expense remaining after applying the exception in paragraph (a)(4) of this section, and may not be applied on a product category basis. Thus, after the allocation of the taxpayer's entire deduction for research and experimental expense under paragraph (a)(2) of this section (by attribution to SIC code categories), the taxpayer must then apportion as necessary the entire deduction as allocated by separate amounts to various product categories, using only the sales method under paragraph (c) of this section or only the optional gross income methods under this paragraph (d). The taxpayer may not use the sales method for a portion of the deduction and optional gross income methods for the remainder of the deduction separately allocated.

(2) *Option one.* The taxpayer may apportion its research and experimental expenditures ratably on the basis of gross income between the statutory grouping (or among the statutory groupings) of gross income and the residual grouping of gross income in the same proportions that the amount of gross income in the statutory grouping (or groupings) and the amount of gross income in the residual grouping bear, respectively, to the total amount of gross income, if the conditions described in paragraph (d)(2)(i) and (ii) of this section are both met.

(i) The amount of research and experimental expense ratably apportioned to the statutory grouping (or groupings in the aggregate) is not less than fifty percent of the amount that would have been so apportioned if the taxpayer had used the method described in paragraph (c) of this section; and

(ii) The amount of research and experimental expense ratably apportioned to the residual grouping is not less than fifty percent of the amount that would have been so apportioned if the taxpayer had used the method described in paragraph (c) of this section.

(3) *Option two.* If, when the amount of research and experimental expense is apportioned ratably on the basis of gross income, either of the conditions described in paragraph (d)(2)(i) or (ii) of this section is not met, the taxpayer may either—

Reg. § 1.861-17(d)(1)

Determination of Sources of Income 46,079

See p. 20,601 for regulations not amended to reflect law changes

(i) Where the condition of paragraph (d)(2)(i) of this section is not met, apportion fifty percent of the amount of research and experimental expense that would have been apportioned to the statutory grouping (or groupings in the aggregate) under paragraph (c) of this section to such statutory grouping (or to such statutory groupings in the aggregate and then among such groupings on the basis of gross income within each grouping), and apportion the balance of the amount of research and experimental expenses to the residual grouping; or

(ii) Where the condition of paragraph (d)(2)(ii) of this section is not met, apportion fifty percent of the amount of research and experimental expense that would have been apportioned to the residual grouping under paragraph (c) of this section to such residual grouping, and apportion the balance of the amount of research and experimental expenses to the statutory grouping (or to the statutory groupings in the aggregate and then among such groupings ratably on the basis of gross income within each grouping).

(e) *Binding election*—(1) *In general.* A taxpayer may choose to use either the sales method under paragraph (c) of this section or the optional gross income methods under paragraph (d) of this section for its original return for its first taxable year to which this section applies. The taxpayer's use of either the sales method or the optional gross income methods for its return filed for its first taxable year to which this section applies shall constitute a binding election to use the method chosen for that year and for four taxable years thereafter.

(2) *Change of method.* The taxpayer's election of a method may not be revoked during the period referred to in paragraph (e)(1) of this section without the prior consent of the Commissioner. After the expiration of that period, the taxpayer may change methods without the prior consent of the Commissioner. However, the taxpayer's use of the new method shall constitute a binding election to use the new method for its return filed for the first year for which the taxpayer uses the new method and for four taxable years thereafter. The taxpayer's election of the new method may not be revoked during that period without the prior consent of the Commissioner.

(i) *Short taxable years.* For purposes of this paragraph (e), the term taxable year includes a taxable year of less than twelve months.

(ii) *Affiliated groups.* In the case of an affiliated group, the period referred to in paragraph (e)(1) of this section shall commence as of the latest taxable year in which any member of the group has changed methods.

(f) *Special rules for partnerships*—(1) *Research and experimental expenditures.* For purposes of applying this section, if research and experimental expenditures are incurred by a partnership in which the taxpayer is a partner, the taxpayer's research and experimental expenditures shall include the taxpayer's distributive share of the partnership's research and experimental expenditures.

(2) *Purpose and location of expenditures.* In applying the exception for expenditures undertaken to meet legal requirements under paragraph (a)(4) of this section and the exclusive apportionment for the sales method and the optional gross income methods under paragraph (b) of this section, a partner's distributive share of research and experimental expenditures incurred by a partnership shall be treated as incurred by the partner for the same purpose and in the same location as incurred by the partnership.

(3) *Apportionment under the sales method.* In applying the remaining apportionment for the sales method under paragraph (c) of this section, a taxpayer's sales from a product category shall include the taxpayer's share of any sales from the product category of any partnership in which the taxpayer is a partner. For purposes of the preceding sentence, a taxpayer's share of sales shall be proportionate to the taxpayer's distributive share of the partnership's gross income in the product category.

(g) *Effective date.* This section applies to taxable years beginning after December 31, 1995. However, a taxpayer may at its option, apply this section in its entirety to all taxable years beginning after August 1, 1994.

(h) *Examples.* The following examples illustrate the application of this section:

Example 1—(i) *Facts.* X, a domestic corporation, is a manufacturer and distributor of small gasoline engines for lawn mowers. Gasoline engines are a product within the category, Engines and Turbines (SIC Industry Group 351). Y, a wholly owned foreign subsidiary of X, also manufactures and sells these engines abroad. During 1996, X incurred expenditures of $60,000 on research and experimentation, which it deducts as a current expense, to invent and patent a new and improved gasoline engine. All of the research and experimentation was performed in the United States. In 1996, the domestic sales by X of the new engine total $500,000 and foreign sales by Y total $300,000. X provides technology for the manufacture of engines to Y via a license that requires the payment of an arm's length royalty.

Reg. § 1.861-17(h)

46,080   Determination of Sources of Income
See p. 20,601 for regulations not amended to reflect law changes

In 1996, X's gross income is $160,000, of which $140,000 is U.S. source income from domestic sales of gasoline engines and $10,000 is foreign source royalties from Y, and $10,000 is U.S. source interest income.

(ii) *Allocation.* The research and experimental expenditures were incurred in connection with small gasoline engines and they are definitely related to the items of gross income to which the research gives rise, namely gross income from the sale of small gasoline engines in the United States and royalties received from subsidiary Y, a foreign manufacturer of gasoline engines. Accordingly, the expenses are allocable to this class of gross income. The U.S. source interest income is not within this class of gross income and, therefore, is not taken into account.

(iii) *Apportionment.* (A) For purposes of applying the foreign tax credit limitation, the statutory grouping is general limitation gross income from sources without the United States and the residual grouping is gross income from sources within the United States. Since the related class of gross income derived from the use of engine technology consists of both gross income from sources without the United States (royalties from Y) and gross income from sources within the United States (gross income from engine sales), X's deduction of $60,000 for its research and experimental expenditure must be apportioned between the statutory and residual grouping before the foreign tax credit limitation may be determined. Because more than 50 percent of X's research and experimental activity was performed in the United States, 50 percent of that deduction can be apportioned exclusively to the residual grouping of gross income, gross income from sources within the United States. The remaining 50 percent of the deduction can then be apportioned between the residual and statutory groupings on the basis of sales of small gasoline engines by X and Y. Alternatively, X's deduction for research and experimentation can be apportioned under the optional gross income method. The apportionment for 1996 is as follows:

(*1*) *Tentative Apportionment on the Basis of Sales.*

(*i*) Research and experimental expense to be apportioned between residual and statutory groupings of gross income: $60,000

(*ii*) Less: Exclusive apportionment of research and experimental expense to the residual grouping of gross income ($60,000 × 50 percent): $30,000

(*iii*) Research and experimental expense to be apportioned between residual and statutory groupings of gross income on the basis of sales: $30,000

(*iv*) Apportionment of research and experimental expense to the residual grouping of gross income ($30,000 × $500,000/($500,000 + $300,000)): $18,750

(*v*) Apportionment of research and experimental expense to the statutory grouping of gross income ($30,000 × $300,000/($500,000 + $300,000)): $11,250

(*vi*) Total apportioned deduction for research and experimentation: $60,000

(*vii*) Amount apportioned to the residual grouping ($30,000 + $18,750): $48,750

(*viii*) Amount apportioned to the statutory grouping: $11,250

(*2*) *Tentative Apportionment on the Basis of Gross Income.*

(*i*) Exclusive apportionment of research and experimental expense to the residual grouping of gross income ($60,000 × 25 percent): $15,000

(*ii*) Research and experimental expense apportioned to sources within the United States (residual grouping) ($45,000 × $140,000/($140,000 + $10,000)): $42,000

(*iii*) Research and experimental expense apportioned to sources within country Y (statutory grouping) ($45,000 × $10,000/($140,000 + $10,000)): $3,000

(*iv*) Amount apportioned to the residual grouping: $57,000

(*v*) Amount apportioned to the statutory grouping: $3,000

(B) The total research and experimental expense apportioned to the statutory grouping ($3,000) under the gross income method is approximately 26 percent of the amount apportioned to the statutory grouping under the sales method. Thus, X may use option two of the gross income method (paragraph (d)(3) of this section) and apportion to the statutory grouping fifty percent (50%) of the $11,250 apportioned to that grouping under the sales method. Thus, X apportions $5,625 of research and experimental expense to the statutory grouping. X's use of the optional gross income methods will constitute a binding election to use the optional gross income methods for 1996 and four taxable years thereafter.

Example 2—(i) *Facts.* Assume the same facts as in *Example 1* except that X also spends $30,000 in 1996 for research on steam turbines, all of which is performed in the United States, and X has steam turbine sales in the United States of $400,000. X's foreign subsidiary Y neither manufactures nor sells steam turbines. The steam turbine research is in addition to the $60,000 in research which X does on gasoline engines for lawnmowers. X thus has a deduction of $90,000

Reg. § 1.861-17(h)

for its research activity. X's gross income is $200,000, of which $140,000 is U.S. source income from domestic sales of gasoline engines, $50,000 is U.S. source income from domestic sales of steam turbines, and $10,000 is foreign source royalties from Y.

(ii) *Allocation.* X's research expenses generate income from sales of small gasoline engines and steam turbines. Both of these products are in the same three digit SIC code category, Engines and Turbines (SIC Industry Group 351). Therefore, the deduction is definitely related to this product category and allocable to all items of income attributable to it. These items of X's income are gross income from the sale of small gasoline engines and steam turbines in the United States and royalties from foreign subsidiary Y, a foreign manufacturer and seller of small gasoline engines.

(iii) *Apportionment.* (A) For purposes of applying the foreign tax credit limitation, the statutory grouping is general limitation gross income from sources outside the United States and the residual grouping is gross income from sources within the United States. X's deduction of $90,000 must be apportioned between the statutory and residual groupings. Because more than 50 percent of X's research and experimental activity was performed in the United States, 50 percent of that deduction can be apportioned exclusively to the residual grouping, gross income from sources within the United States. The remaining 50 percent of the deduction can then be apportioned between the residual and statutory groupings on the basis of total sales of small gasoline engines and steam turbines by X and Y. Alternatively, X's deduction for research and experimentation can be apportioned under the optional gross income methods. The apportionment for 1996 is as follows:

(*1*) *Tentative Apportionment on the Basis of Sales.*

(*i*) Research and experimental expense to be apportioned between residual and statutory groupings of gross income: $90,000

(*ii*) Less: Exclusive apportionment of the research and experimental expense to the residual grouping of gross income ($90,000 × 50 percent): $45,000

(*iii*) Research and experimental expense to be apportioned between the residual and statutory groupings of gross income on the basis of sales: $45,000

(*iv*) Apportionment of research and experimental expense to the residual grouping of gross income ($45,000 × ($500,000 + $400,000)/($500,000 + $400,000 + $300,000)): $33,750

(*v*) Apportionment of research and experimental expense to the statutory grouping of gross income ($45,000 × $300,000/($500,000 + $400,000 + $300,000)): $11,250

(*vi*) Total apportioned deduction for research and experimentation: $90,000

(*vii*) Amount apportioned to the residual grouping ($45,000 + $33,750): $78,750

(*viii*) Amount apportioned to the statutory grouping: $11,250

(*2*) *Tentative Apportionment on the Basis of Gross Income.*

(*i*) Exclusive apportionment of research and experimental expense to the residual grouping of gross income ($90,000 × 25 percent): $22,500

(*ii*) Research and experimental expense apportioned to sources within the United States (residual grouping) ($67,500 × $190,000/($140,000 + $50,000 + $10,000)): $64,125

(*iii*) Research and experimental expense apportioned to sources within country Y (statutory grouping) ($67,500 × $10,000/($140,000 + $50,000 + $10,000)): $3,375

(*iv*) Amount apportioned to the residual grouping: $86,625

(*v*) Amount apportioned to the statutory grouping: $3,375

(B) The total research and experimental expense apportioned to the statutory grouping ($3,375) under the gross income method is 30 percent of the amount apportioned to the statutory grouping under the sales method. Thus, X may use option two of the gross income method (paragraph (d)(3) of this section) and apportion to the statutory grouping fifty percent (50%) of the $11,250 apportioned to that grouping under the sales method. Thus, X apportions $5,625 of research and experimental expense to the statutory grouping. X's use of the optional gross income methods will constitute a binding election to use the optional gross income methods for 1996 and four taxable years thereafter.

Example 3—(i) *Facts.* Assume the same facts as in *Example 1* except that in 1997 X continues its sales of the new engines, with sales of $600,000 in the United States and $400,000 abroad by subsidiary Y. X also acquires a 60 percent (by value) ownership interest in foreign corporation Z and a 100 percent ownership interest in foreign corporation C. X transfers its engine technology to Z for a royalty equal to 5 percent of sales, and X enters into an arm's length cost-sharing arrangement with C to share the funding of all of X's research activity. In 1997, corporation Z has sales in country Z equal to $1,000,000. X incurs ex-

Reg. § 1.861-17(h)

pense of $80,000 on research and experimentation in 1997, and in addition, X performs $15,000 of research on gasoline engines which was funded by the cost-sharing arrangement with C. All of Z's sales are from the product category, Engines and Turbines (SIC Industry Group 351). X performs all of its research in the United States and $20,000 of its expenditure of $80,000 is made solely to meet pollution standards mandated by law. X establishes, to the satisfaction of the Commissioner, that the expenditure in response to pollution standards is not expected to generate gross income (beyond *de minimis* amounts) outside the United States.

(ii) *Allocation.* The $20,000 of research expense which X incurred in connection with pollution standards is definitely related and thus allocable to the residual grouping, gross income from sources within the United States. The remaining $60,000 in research and experimental expenditure incurred by X is definitely related to all gasoline engines and is therefore allocable to the class of gross income to which the engines give rise, gross income from sales of gasoline engines in the United States, royalties from country Y, and royalties from country Z. No part of the $60,000 research expense is allocable to dividends from country C, because corporation C has already paid, through its cost-sharing arrangement, for research activity performed by X which may benefit C.

(iii) *Apportionment.* For purposes of applying the foreign tax credit limitation, the statutory grouping is general limitation gross income from sources without the United States, and the residual grouping is gross income from sources within the United States. X's deduction of $60,000 for its research and experimental expenditure must be apportioned between these groupings. Because more than 50 percent of the research and experimentation was performed in the United States, 50 percent of the $60,000 deduction can be apportioned exclusively to the residual grouping. The remaining 50 percent of the deduction can then be apportioned between the residual and the statutory grouping on the basis of sales of gasoline engines by X, Y, and Z. (If X utilized the optional gross income methods in 1996, then its use of such methods constituted a binding election to use the optional gross income methods in 1996 and for four taxable years thereafter. If X utilized the sales method in 1996, then its use of such method constituted a binding election to use the sales method in 1996 and for four taxable years thereafter.) The optional gross income methods are not illustrated in this *Example 3* (see instead *Examples 1* and *2*). Since X has only a 60 percent ownership interest in corpora-

tion Z, only 60 percent of Z's sales (60% of $1,000,000, or $600,000) are included for purposes of apportionment. The allocation and apportionment for 1997 is as follows:

(A) X's total research expense: $80,000

(B) Less: Legally mandated research directly allocated to the residual grouping of gross income: $20,000

(C) Tentative apportionment on the basis of sales.

(*1*) Research and experimental expense to be apportioned between residual and statutory groupings of gross income: $60,000

(*2*) Less: Exclusive apportionment of research and experimental expense to the residual grouping of gross income ($60,000 × 50 percent): $30,000

(*3*) Research and experimental expense to be apportioned between the residual and the statutory groupings on the basis of sales: $30,000

(*4*) Apportionment of research and experimental expense to gross income from sources within the United States (residual grouping) ($30,000 × $600,000 / ($600,000 + $400,000 + $600,000)): $11,250

(*5*) Apportionment of research and experimental expense to general limitation gross income from countries Y and Z (statutory grouping) ($30,000 × $400,000 + $600,000/($600,000 + $400,000 +$600,000)): $18,750

(*6*) Total apportioned deduction for research and experimentation ($30,000 + $30,000): $60,000

(*7*) Amount apportioned to the residual grouping ($30,000 + $11,250): $41,250

(*8*) Amount apportioned to the statutory grouping of gross income from sources within countries Y and Z: $18,750

Example 4—Research and Experimentation— (i) *Facts.* X, a domestic corporation, manufactures and sells forklift trucks and other types of materials handling equipment in the United States. The manufacture and sale of forklift trucks and other materials handling equipment belongs to the product category, Construction, Mining, and Materials Handling Machinery and Equipment (SIC Industry Group 353). X also sells its forklift trucks to a wholesaling subsidiary located in foreign country Y (but title passes in the United States), and X manufactures forklift trucks in foreign country Z. The wholesaling of forklift trucks to country Y also belongs to X's product category Transportation equipment and, therefore, may not belong to the product category, Wholesale trade (SIC Major Group 50 and 51). In 1997, X sold $7,000,000 of forklift trucks to purchasers in the United States, $3,000,000 of forklift trucks to the wholesaling subsidiary in Y, and transferred forklift truck components with an FOB export value of $2,000,000 to its branch in Z. The branch's sales of finished forklift trucks were $5,000,000. In response to legally mandated emission control requirements, X's United States research department has been engaged in a research project to improve the performance and quality of engine exhaust systems used on its products in the United States. It incurs expenses of $100,000 for this purpose in 1997. In the past, X has customarily adapted the product improvements developed originally for the domestic market to its forklift trucks manufactured abroad. During the taxable year 1997, development of an improved engine exhaust system is completed and X begins installing the new system during the latter part of the taxable year in products manufactured and sold in the United States. X continues to manufacture and sell forklift trucks in foreign countries without the improved engine exhaust systems.

(ii) *Allocation.* X's deduction for its research expense is definitely related to the income to which it gives rise, namely income from the manufacture and sale of forklift trucks within the United States and in country Z. Although the research is undertaken in response to a legal mandate, it can reasonably be expected to generate gross income from the manufacture and sale of trucks by the branch in Z. Therefore, the deduction is not allocable solely to income from X's domestic sales of forklift trucks. It is allocable to income from such sales and income from the sales of X's branch in Z.

(iii) *Apportionment.* For the method of apportionment on the basis of either sales or gross income, see *Example 3.* However, in determining the amount of research apportioned to income from foreign and domestic sources, the net sales of the branch in Z are $3,000,000 ($5,000,000 less $2,000,000) and the sales within the United States are $12,000,000 ($7,000,000 plus $3,000,000 plus $2,000,000). See § 1.861-17(c)(3)(iii).

Example 5—(i) *Facts.* X, a domestic corporation, is a drug company that manufactures a wide variety of pharmaceutical products for sale in the United States. Pharmaceutical products belong to the product category, Drugs (SIC Industry Group 283). X exports its pharmaceutical products through a foreign sales corporation (FSC). X's wholly owned foreign subsidiary Y also manufactures pharmaceutical products. In 1997, X has domestic sales of pharmaceutical products of $10,000,000, the FSC has sales of pharmaceutical products of $3,000,000, and Y has sales of pharmaceutical products of $5,000,000. In that same year, 1997, X incurs expense of $200,000 on research to test a product in response to requirements imposed by the United States Food and Drug Administration (FDA). X is able to show that, even though country Y imposes certain testing requirements on pharmaceutical products, the research performed in the United States is not accepted by country Y for purposes of its own licensing requirements, and the research has minimal use abroad. X is further able to show that FSC sells goods to countries that do not accept or do not require research performed in the United States for purposes of their own licensing standards.

(ii) *Allocation.* Since X's research expense of $200,000 is undertaken to meet the requirements of the United States Food and Drug Administration, and since it is reasonable to expect that the expenditure will not generate gross income (beyond *de minimis* amounts) outside the United States, the deduction is definitely related and thus allocable to the residual grouping.

(iii) *Apportionment.* No apportionment is necessary since the entire expense is allocated to the residual grouping, gross income from sales within the United States.

Example 6—(i) *Facts.* X, a domestic corporation, is engaged in continuous research and experimentation to improve the quality of the products that it manufactures and sells, which are floodlights, flashlights, fuse boxes, and solderless connectors. X incurs and deducts $100,000 of expenditure for research and experimentation in 1997 that was performed exclusively in the United States. As a result of this research activity, X acquires patents that it uses in its own manufacturing activity. X licenses its floodlight patent to Y and Z, uncontrolled foreign corporations, for use in their own territories, countries Y and Z, respectively. Corporation Y pays X an arm's length royalty of $3,000 plus $0.20 for each floodlight sold. Sales of floodlights by Y for the taxable year are $135,000 (at $4.50 per unit) or 30,000 units, and the royalty is $9,000 ($3,000 + $0.20 × 30,000). Y has sales of other products of $500,000. Z pays X an arm's length royalty of $3,000 plus $0.30 for each unit sold. Z manufactures 30,000 floodlights in the taxable year, and the royalty is $12,000 ($3,000 + $0.30 × 30,000). The dollar value of Z's floodlight sales is not known and cannot be reasonably estimated because, in this case, the floodlights are not sold separately by Z but are instead used as a component in Z's manufacture of lighting equipment for theaters. The sales of all Z's products, including the lighting equipment for theaters, are $1,000,000. Y and Z each sell the floodlights ex-

Reg. § 1.861-17(h)

clusively within their respective countries. X's sales of floodlights for the taxable year are $500,000 and its sales of its other products, flashlights, fuse boxes, and solderless connectors, are $400,000. X has gross income of $500,000, consisting of gross income from domestic sources from sales of floodlights, flashlights, fuse boxes, and solderless connectors of $479,000, and royalty income of $9,000 and $12,000 from foreign corporations Y and Z respectively. X utilized the optional gross income methods of apportionment for its return filed for its first taxable year to which this section applies.

(ii) *Allocation.* X's research and experimental expenses are definitely related to all of the products that it produces, which are floodlights, flashlights, fuse boxes, and solderless connectors. All of these products are in the same three digit SIC Code category, Electric Lighting and Wiring Equipment (SIC Industry Group 364). Thus, X's research and experimental expenses are allocable to all items of income attributable to this product category, domestic sales income and royalty income from the foreign countries in which corporations Y and Z operate.

(iii) *Apportionment.* (A) The statutory grouping of gross income is general limitation income from sources without the United States. The residual grouping is gross income from sources within the United States. X's deduction of $100,000 for its research expenditures must be apportioned between the groupings. For apportionment on the basis of sales in accordance with paragraph (c) of this section, X is entitled to an exclusive apportionment of 50 percent of its research and experimental expense to the residual grouping, gross income from sources within the United States, since more than 50 percent of the research activity was performed in the United States. The remaining 50 percent of the deduction can then be apportioned between the residual and statutory groupings on the basis of sales. Since Y and Z are unrelated licensees of X, only their sales of the licensed product, floodlights, are included for purposes of apportionment. Floodlight sales of Z are unknown, but are estimated at ten times royalties from Z, or $120,000. All of X's sales from the entire product category are included for purposes of apportionment on the basis of sales. Alternatively, X may apportion its deduction on the basis of gross income, in accordance with paragraph (d) of this section. The apportionment is as follows:

(*1*) Tentative Apportionment on the basis of sales.

(*i*) Research and experimental expense to be apportioned between statutory and residual groupings of gross income: $100,000

(*ii*) Less: Exclusive apportionment of research and experimental expense to the residual groupings of gross income ($100,000 × 50 percent): $50,000

(*iii*) Research and experimental expense to be apportioned between the statutory and residual groupings of gross income on the basis of sales: $50,000

(*iv*) Apportionment of research and experimental expense to the residual groupings of gross income ($50,000 × $900,000/($900,000 + $135,000 + $120,000)): $38,961

(*v*) Apportionment of research and experimental expense to the statutory grouping, royalty income from countries Y and Z ($50,000 × $135,000 + $120,000/($900,000 + $135,000 + $120,000)): $11,039

(*vi*) Total apportioned deduction for research and experimentation: $100,000

(*vii*) Amount apportioned to the residual grouping ($50,000 + $38,961): $88,961

(*viii*) Amount apportioned to the statutory grouping of sources within countries Y and Z: $11,039

(*2*) *Tentative apportionment on gross income basis.*

(*i*) Exclusive apportionment of research and experimental expense to the residual grouping of gross income ($100,000 × 25 percent): $25,000

(*ii*) Apportionment of research and experimental expense to the residual grouping of gross income ($75,000 × $479,000/$500,000): $71,850

(*iii*) Apportionment of research and experimental expense to the statutory grouping of gross income ($75,000 × $9,000 + $12,000/$500,000): $3,150

(*iv*) Amount apportioned to the residual grouping: $96,850

(*v*) Amount apportioned to the statutory grouping of general limitation income from sources without the United States: $3,150

(B) Since X has elected to use the optional gross income methods of apportionment and its apportionment on the basis of gross income to the statutory grouping, $3,150, is less than 50 percent of its apportionment on the basis of sales to the statutory grouping, $11,039, it must use Option two of paragraph (d)(3) of this section and apportion $5,520 (50 percent of $11,039) to the statutory grouping. [Reg. § 1.861-17.]

☐ [T.D. 8646, 12-21-95.]

Determination of Sources of Income

[Reg. § 1.861-18]

§ 1.861-18. Classification of transactions involving computer programs.—(a) *General*—(1) *Scope.* This section provides rules for classifying transactions relating to computer programs for purposes of subchapter N of chapter 1 of the Internal Revenue Code, sections 367, 404A, 482, 551, 679, 1059A, chapter 3, chapter 5, sections 842 and 845 (to the extent involving a foreign person), and transfers to foreign trusts not covered by section 679.

(2) *Categories of transactions.* This section generally requires that such transactions be treated as being solely within one of four categories (described in paragraph (b)(1) of this section) and provides certain rules for categorizing such transactions. In the case of a transfer of a copyright right, this section provides rules for determining whether the transaction should be classified as either a sale or exchange, or a license generating royalty income. In the case of a transfer of a copyrighted article, this section provides rules for determining whether the transaction should be classified as either a sale or exchange, or a lease generating rental income.

(3) *Computer program.* For purposes of this section, a computer program is a set of statements or instructions to be used directly or indirectly in a computer in order to bring about a certain result. For purposes of this paragraph (a)(3), a computer program includes any media, user manuals, documentation, data base or similar item if the media, user manuals, documentation, data base or similar item is incidental to the operation of the computer program.

(b) *Categories of transactions*—(1) *General.* Except as provided in paragraph (b)(2) of this section, a transaction involving the transfer of a computer program, or the provision of services or of know-how with respect to a computer program (collectively, a transfer of a computer program) is treated as being solely one of the following—

(i) A transfer of a copyright right in the computer program;

(ii) A transfer of a copy of the computer program (a copyrighted article);

(iii) The provision of services for the development or modification of the computer program; or

(iv) The provision of know-how relating to computer programming techniques.

(2) *Transactions consisting of more than one category.* Any transaction involving computer programs which consists of more than one of the transactions described in paragraph (b)(1) of this section shall be treated as separate transactions, with the appropriate provisions of this section being applied to each such transaction. However, any transaction that is de minimis, taking into account the overall transaction and the surrounding facts and circumstances, shall not be treated as a separate transaction, but as part of another transaction.

(c) *Transfers involving copyright rights and copyrighted articles*—(1) *Classification*—(i) *Transfers treated as transfers of copyright rights.* A transfer of a computer program is classified as a transfer of a copyright right if, as a result of the transaction, a person acquires any one or more of the rights described in paragraphs (c)(2)(i) through (iv) of this section. Whether the transaction is treated as being solely the transfer of a copyright right or is treated as separate transactions is determined pursuant to paragraph (b)(1) and (b)(2) of this section. For example, if a person receives a disk containing a copy of a computer program which enables it to exercise, in relation to that program, a non-de minimis right described in paragraphs (c)(2)(i) through (iv) of this section (and the transaction does not involve, or involves only a de minimis provision of services as described in paragraph (d) of this section or of know-how as described in paragraph (e) of this section), then, under paragraph (b)(2) of this section, the transfer is classified solely as a transfer of a copyright right.

(ii) *Transfers treated solely as transfers of copyrighted articles.* If a person acquires a copy of a computer program but does not acquire any of the rights described in paragraphs (c)(2)(i) through (iv) of this section (or only acquires a de minimis grant of such rights), and the transaction does not involve, or involves only a de minimis, provision of services as described in paragraph (d) of this section or of know-how as described in paragraph (e) of this section, the transfer of the copy of the computer program is classified solely as a transfer of a copyrighted article.

(2) *Copyright rights.* The copyright rights referred to in paragraph (c)(1) of this section are as follows—

(i) The right to make copies of the computer program for purposes of distribution to the public by sale or other transfer of ownership, or by rental, lease or lending;

(ii) The right to prepare derivative computer programs based upon the copyrighted computer program;

(iii) The right to make a public performance of the computer program; or

(iv) The right to publicly display the computer program.

Reg. § 1.861-18(c)(2)

(3) *Copyrighted article.* A copyrighted article includes a copy of a computer program from which the work can be perceived, reproduced, or otherwise communicated, either directly or with the aid of a machine or device. The copy of the program may be fixed in the magnetic medium of a floppy disk, or in the main memory or hard drive of a computer, or in any other medium.

(d) *Provision of services.* The determination of whether a transaction involving a newly developed or modified computer program is treated as either the provision of services or another transaction described in paragraph (b)(1) of this section is based on all the facts and circumstances of the transaction, including, as appropriate, the intent of the parties (as evidenced by their agreement and conduct) as to which party is to own the copyright rights in the computer program and how the risks of loss are allocated between the parties.

(e) *Provision of know-how.* The provision of information with respect to a computer program will be treated as the provision of know-how for purposes of this section only if the information is—

(1) Information relating to computer programming techniques;

(2) Furnished under conditions preventing unauthorized disclosure, specifically contracted for between the parties; and

(3) Considered property subject to trade secret protection.

(f) *Further classification of transfers involving copyright rights and copyrighted articles*—(1) *Transfers of copyright rights.* The determination of whether a transfer of a copyright right is a sale or exchange of property is made on the basis of whether, taking into account all facts and circumstances, there has been a transfer of all substantial rights in the copyright. A transaction that does not constitute a sale or exchange because not all substantial rights have been transferred will be classified as a license generating royalty income. For this purpose, the principles of sections 1222 and 1235 may be applied. Income derived from the sale or exchange of a copyright right will be sourced under section 865(a), (c), (d), (e), or (h), as appropriate. Income derived from the licensing of a copyright right will be sourced under section 861(a)(4) or 862(a)(4), as appropriate.

(2) *Transfers of copyrighted articles.* The determination of whether a transfer of a copyrighted article is a sale or exchange is made on the basis of whether, taking into account all facts and circumstances, the benefits and burdens of ownership have been transferred. A transaction that does not constitute a sale or exchange because insufficient benefits and burdens of ownership of the copyrighted article have been transferred, such that a person other than the transferee is properly treated as the owner of the copyrighted article, will be classified as a lease generating rental income. Income from transactions that are classified as sales or exchanges of copyrighted articles will be sourced under sections 861(a)(6), 862(a)(6), 863, 865(a), (b), (c), or (e), as appropriate. Income derived from the leasing of a copyrighted article will be sourced under section 861(a)(4) or section 862(a)(4), as appropriate.

(3) *Special circumstances of computer programs.* In connection with determinations under this paragraph (f), consideration must be given as appropriate to the special characteristics of computer programs in transactions that take advantage of these characteristics (such as the ability to make perfect copies at minimal cost). For example, a transaction in which a person acquires a copy of a computer program on disk subject to a requirement that the disk be destroyed after a specified period is generally the equivalent of a transaction subject to a requirement that the disk be returned after such period. Similarly, a transaction in which the program deactivates itself after a specified period is generally the equivalent of returning the copy.

(g) *Rules of operation*—(1) *Term applied to transaction by parties.* Neither the form adopted by the parties to a transaction, nor the classification of the transaction under copyright law, shall be determinative. Therefore, for example, if there is a transfer of a computer program on a single disk for a one-time payment with restrictions on transfer and reverse engineering, which the parties characterize as a license (including, but not limited to, agreements commonly referred to as shrink-wrap licenses), application of the rules of paragraphs (c) and (f) of this section may nevertheless result in the transaction being classified as the sale of a copyrighted article.

(2) *Means of transfer not to be taken into account.* The rules of this section shall be applied irrespective of the physical or electronic or other medium used to effectuate a transfer of a computer program.

(3) *To the public*—(i) *In general.* For purposes of paragraph (c)(2)(i) of this section, a transferee of a computer program shall not be considered to have the right to distribute copies of the program to the public if it is permitted to distribute copies of the software to only either a related person, or to identified persons who may be identified by either name or by legal relationship to the original transferee. For purposes of this subparagraph, a related person is a person

Reg. § 1.861-18(c)(3)

who bears a relationship to the transferee specified in section 267(b)(3), (10), (11), or (12), or section 707(b)(1)(B). In applying section 267(b), 267(f), 707(b)(1)(B), or 1563(a), "10 percent" shall be substituted for "50 percent."

(ii) *Use by individuals.* The number of employees of a transferee of a computer program who are permitted to use the program in connection with their employment is not relevant for purposes of this paragraph (g)(3). In addition, the number of individuals with a contractual agreement to provide services to the transferee of a computer program who are permitted to use the program in connection with the performance of those services is not relevant for purposes of this paragraph (g)(3).

(h) *Examples.* The provisions of this section may be illustrated by the following examples:

Example 1. (i) *Facts.* Corp A, a U.S. corporation, owns the copyright in a computer program, Program X. It copies Program X onto disks. The disks are placed in boxes covered with a wrapper on which is printed what is generally referred to as a shrink-wrap license. The license is stated to be perpetual. Under the license no reverse engineering, decompilation, or disassembly of the computer program is permitted. The transferee receives, first, the right to use the program on two of its own computers (for example, a laptop and a desktop) provided that only one copy is in use at any one time, and, second, the right to make one copy of the program on each machine as an essential step in the utilization of the program. The transferee is permitted by the shrink-wrap license to sell the copy so long as it destroys any other copies it has made and imposes the same terms and conditions of the license on the purchaser of its copy. These disks are made available for sale to the general public in Country Z. In return for valuable consideration, P, a Country Z resident, receives one such disk.

(ii) *Analysis.* (A) Under paragraph (g)(1) of this section, the label license is not determinative. None of the copyright rights described in paragraph (c)(2) of this section have been transferred in this transaction. P has received a copy of the program, however, and, therefore, under paragraph (c)(1)(ii) of this section, P has acquired solely a copyrighted article.

(B) Taking into account all of the facts and circumstances, P is properly treated as the owner of a copyrighted article. Therefore, under paragraph (f)(2) of this section, there has been a sale of a copyrighted article rather than the grant of a lease.

Example 2. (i) *Facts.* The facts are the same as those in *Example 1,* except that instead of selling disks, Corp A, the U.S. corporation, decides to make Program X available, for a fee, on a World Wide Web home page on the Internet. P, the Country Z resident, in return for payment made to Corp A, downloads Program X (via modem) onto the hard drive of his computer. As part of the electronic communication, P signifies his assent to a license agreement with terms identical to those in *Example 1,* except that in this case P may make a back-up copy of the program on to a disk.

(ii) *Analysis.* (A) None of the copyright rights described in paragraph (c)(2) of this section have passed to P. Although P did not buy a physical copy of the disk with the program on it, paragraph (g)(2) of this section provides that the means of transferring the program is irrelevant. Therefore, P has acquired a copyrighted article.

(B) As in *Example 1,* P is properly treated as the owner of a copyrighted article. Therefore, under paragraph (f)(2) of this section, there has been a sale of a copyrighted article rather than the grant of a lease.

Example 3. (i) *Facts.* The facts are the same as those in *Example 1,* except that Corp A only allows P, the Country Z resident, to use Program X for one week. At the end of that week, P must return the disk with Program X on it to Corp A. P must also destroy any copies made of Program X. If P wishes to use Program X for a further period he must enter into a new agreement to use the program for an additional charge.

(ii) *Analysis.* (A) Under paragraph (c)(2) of this section, P has received no copyright rights. Because P has received a copy of the program under paragraph (c)(1)(ii) of this section, he has, therefore, received a copyrighted article.

(B) Taking into account all of the facts and circumstances, P is not properly treated as the owner of a copyrighted article. Therefore, under paragraph (f)(2) of this section, there has been a lease of a copyrighted article rather than a sale. Taking into account the special characteristics of computer programs as provided in paragraph (f)(3) of this section, the result would be the same if P were required to destroy the disk at the end of the one week period instead of returning it since Corp A can make additional copies of the program at minimal cost.

Example 4. (i) *Facts.* The facts are the same as those in *Example 2,* where P, the Country Z resident, receives Program X from Corp A's home page on the Internet, except that P may only use Program X for a period of one week at the end of which an electronic lock is activated and the program can no longer be accessed. Thereafter, if P wishes to use Program X, it must return to the

Reg. § 1.861-18(h)

home page and pay Corp A to send an electronic key to reactivate the program for another week.

(ii) *Analysis.* (A) As in *Example 3*, under paragraph (c)(2) of this section, P has not received any copyright rights. P has received a copy of the program, and under paragraph (g)(2) of this section, the means of transmission is irrelevant. P has, therefore, under paragraph (c)(1)(ii) of this section, received a copyrighted article.

(B) As in *Example 3*, P is not properly treated as the owner of a copyrighted article. Therefore, under paragraph (f)(2) of this section, there has been a lease of a copyrighted article rather than a sale. While P does retain Program X on its computer at the end of the one week period, as a legal matter P no longer has the right to use the program (without further payment) and, indeed, cannot use the program without the electronic key. Functionally, Program X is no longer on the hard drive of P=s computer. Instead, the hard drive contains only a series of numbers which no longer perform the function of Program X. Although in *Example 3*, P was required to physically return the disk, taking into account the special characteristics of computer programs as provided in paragraph (f)(3) of this section, the result in this *Example 4* is the same as in *Example 3*.

Example 5. (i) *Facts.* Corp A, a U.S. corporation, transfers a disk containing Program X to Corp B, a Country Z corporation, and grants Corp B an exclusive license for the remaining term of the copyright to copy and distribute an unlimited number of copies of Program X in the geographic area of Country Z, prepare derivative works based upon Program X, make public performances of Program X, and publicly display Program X. Corp B will pay Corp A a royalty of $y a year for three years, which is the expected period during which Program X will have commercially exploitable value.

(ii) *Analysis.* (A) Although Corp A has transferred a disk with a copy of Program X on it to Corp B, under paragraph (c)(1)(i) of this section because this transfer is accompanied by a copyright right identified in paragraph (c)(2)(i) of this section, this transaction is a transfer solely of copyright rights, not of copyrighted articles. For purposes of paragraph (b)(2) of this section, the disk containing a copy of Program X is a de minimis component of the transaction.

(B) Applying the all substantial rights test under paragraph (f)(1) of this section, Corp A will be treated as having sold copyright rights to Corp B. Corp B has acquired all of the copyright rights in Program X, has received the right to use them exclusively within Country Z, and has received the rights for the remaining life of the copyright in Program X. The fact the payments cease before the copyright term expires is not controlling. Under paragraph (g)(1) of this section, the fact that the agreement is labelled a license is not controlling (nor is the fact that Corp A receives a sum labelled a royalty). (The result in this case would be the same if the copy of Program X to be used for the purposes of reproduction were transmitted electronically to Corp B, as a result of the application of the rule of paragraph (g)(2) of this section.)

Example 6. (i) *Facts.* Corp A, a U.S. corporation, transfers a disk containing Program X to Corp B, a Country Z corporation, and grants Corp B the non exclusive right to reproduce (either directly or by contracting with either Corp A or another person to do so) and distribute for sale to the public an unlimited number of disks at its factory in Country Z in return for a payment related to the number of disks copied and sold. The term of the agreement is two years, which is less than the remaining life of the copyright.

(ii) *Analysis.* (A) As in *Example 5*, the transfer of the disk containing the copy of the program does not constitute the transfer of a copyrighted article under paragraph (c)(1) of this section because Corp B has also acquired a copyright right under paragraph (c)(2)(i) of this section, the right to reproduce and distribute to the public. For purposes of paragraph (b)(2) of this section, the disk containing Program X is a de minimis component of the transaction.

(B) Taking into account all of the facts and circumstances, there has been a license of Program X to Corp B, and the payments made by Corp B are royalties. Under paragraph (f)(1) of this section, there has not been a transfer of all substantial rights in the copyright to Program X because Corp A has the right to enter into other licenses with respect to the copyright of Program X, including licenses in Country Z (or even to sell that copyright, subject to Corp B's interest). Corp B has acquired no right itself to license the copyright rights in Program X. Finally, the term of the license is for less than the remaining life of the copyright in Program X.

Example 7. (i) *Facts.* Corp C, a distributor in Country Z, enters into an agreement with Corp A, a U.S. corporation, to purchase as many copies of Program X on disk as it may from time-to-time request. Corp C will then sell these disks to retailers. The disks are shipped in boxes covered by shrink-wrap licenses (identical to the license described in *Example 1*).

(ii) *Analysis.* (A) Corp C has not acquired any copyright rights under paragraph (c)(2) of this section with respect to Program X. It has ac-

Reg. § 1.861-18(h)

quired individual copies of Program X, which it may sell to others. The use of the term license is not dispositive under paragraph (g)(1) of this section. Under paragraph (c)(1)(ii) of this section, Corp C has acquired copyrighted articles.

(B) Taking into account all of the facts and circumstances, Corp C is properly treated as the owner of copyrighted articles. Therefore, under paragraph (f)(2) of this section, there has been a sale of copyrighted articles.

Example 8. (i) *Facts.* Corp A, a U.S. corporation, transfers a disk containing Program X to Corp D, a foreign corporation engaged in the manufacture and sale of personal computers in Country Z. Corp A grants Corp D the non-exclusive right to copy Program X onto the hard drive of an unlimited number of computers, which Corp D manufactures, and to distribute those copies (on the hard drive) to the public. The term of the agreement is two years, which is less than the remaining life of the copyright in Program X. Corp D pays Corp A an amount based on the number of copies of Program X it loads on to computers.

(ii) *Analysis.* The analysis is the same as in *Example 6.* Under paragraph (c)(2)(i) of this section, Corp D has acquired a copyright right enabling it to exploit Program X by copying it on to the hard drives of the computers that it manufactures and then sells. For purposes of paragraph (b)(2) of this section, the disk containing Program X is a de minimis component of the transaction. Taking into account all of the facts and circumstances, Corp D has not, however, acquired all substantial rights in the copyright to Program X (for example, the term of the agreement is less than the remaining life of the copyright). Under paragraph (f)(1) of this section, this transaction is, therefore, a license of Program X to Corp D rather than a sale and the payments made by Corp D are royalties. (The result would be the same if Corp D included with the computers it sells an archival copy of Program X on a floppy disk.)

Example 9. (i) *Facts.* The facts are the same as in *Example 8,* except that Corp D, the Country Z corporation, receives physical disks. The disks are shipped in boxes covered by shrink-wrap licenses (identical to the licenses described in *Example 1*). The terms of these licenses do not permit Corp D to make additional copies of Program X. Corp D uses each individual disk only once to load a single copy of Program X onto each separate computer. Corp D transfers the disk with the computer when it is sold.

(ii) *Analysis.* (A) As in *Example 7* (unlike *Example 8*) no copyright right identified in paragraph (c)(2) of this section has been transferred. Corp D acquires the disks without the right to reproduce and distribute publicly further copies of Program X. This is therefore the transfer of copyrighted articles under paragraph (c)(1)(ii) of this section.

(B) Taking into account all of the facts and circumstances, Corp D is properly treated as the owner of copyrighted articles. Therefore, under paragraph (f)(2) of this section, the transaction is classified as the sale of a copyrighted article. (The result would be the same if Corp D used a single physical disk to copy Program X onto each computer, and transferred an unopened box containing Program X with each computer, if Corp D were not permitted to copy Program X onto more computers than the number of individual copies purchased.)

Example 10. (i) *Facts.* Corp A, a U.S. corporation, transfers a disk containing Program X to Corp E, a Country Z corporation, and grants Corp E the right to load Program X onto 50 individual workstations for use only by Corp E employees at one location in return for a one-time per-user fee (generally referred to as a site license or enterprise license). If additional workstations are subsequently introduced, Program X may be loaded onto those machines for additional one-time per-user fees. The license which grants the rights to operate Program X on 50 workstations also prohibits Corp E from selling the disk (or any of the 50 copies) or reverse engineering the program. The term of the license is stated to be perpetual.

(ii) *Analysis.* (A) The grant of a right to copy, unaccompanied by the right to distribute those copies to the public, is not the transfer of a copyright right under paragraph (c)(2) of this section. Therefore, under paragraph (c)(1)(ii) of this section, this transaction is a transfer of copyrighted articles (50 copies of Program X).

(B) Taking into account all of the facts and circumstances, P is properly treated as the owner of copyrighted articles. Therefore, under paragraph (f)(2) of this section, there has been a sale of copyrighted articles rather than the grant of a lease. Notwithstanding the restriction on sale, other factors such as, for example, the risk of loss and the right to use the copies in perpetuity outweigh, in this case, the restrictions placed on the right of alienation.

(C) The result would be the same if Corp E were permitted to copy Program X onto an unlimited number of workstations used by employees of either Corp E or corporations that had a relationship to Corp E specified in paragraph (g)(3) of this section.

Reg. § 1.861-18(h)

46,090   Determination of Sources of Income
See p. 20,601 for regulations not amended to reflect law changes

Example 11. (i) *Facts.* The facts are the same as in *Example 10,* except that Corp E, the Country Z corporation, acquires the right to make Program X available to workstation users who are Corp E employees by way of a local area network (LAN). The number of users that can use Program X on the LAN at any one time is limited to 50. Corp E pays a one-time fee for the right to have up to 50 employees use the program at the same time.

(ii) *Analysis.* Under paragraph (g)(2) of this section the mode of utilization is irrelevant. Therefore, as in *Example 10,* under paragraph (c)(2) of this section, no copyright right has been transferred, and, thus, under paragraph (c)(1)(ii) of this section, this transaction will be classified as the transfer of a copyrighted article. Under the benefits and burdens test of paragraph (f)(2) of this section, this transaction is a sale of copyrighted articles. The result would be the same if an unlimited number of Corp E employees were permitted to use Program X on the LAN or if Corp E were permitted to copy Program X onto LANs maintained by corporations that had a relationship to Corp E specified in paragraph (g)(3) of this section.

Example 12. (i) *Facts.* The facts are the same as in *Example 11,* except that Corp E pays a monthly fee to Corp A, the U.S. corporation, calculated with reference to the permitted maximum number of users (which can be changed) and the computing power of Corp E's server. In return for this monthly fee, Corp E receives the right to receive upgrades of Program X when they become available. The agreement may be terminated by either party at the end of any month. When the disk containing the upgrade is received, Corp E must return the disk containing the earlier version of Program X to Corp A. If the contract is terminated, Corp E must delete (or otherwise destroy) all copies made of the current version of Program X. The agreement also requires Corp A to provide technical support to Corp E but the agreement does not allocate the monthly fee between the right to receive upgrades of Program X and the technical support services. The amount of technical support that Corp A will provide to Corp E is not foreseeable at the time the contract is entered into but is expected to be de minimis. The agreement specifically provides that Corp E has not thereby been granted an option to purchase Program X.

(ii) *Analysis.* (A) Corp E has received no copyright rights under paragraph (c)(2) of this section. Corp A has not provided any services described in paragraph (d) of this section. Based on all the facts and circumstances of the transaction, Corp A has provided de minimis technical services to Corp E. Therefore, under paragraph (c)(1)(ii) of this section, the transaction is a transfer of a copyrighted article.

(B) Taking into account all facts and circumstances, under the benefits and burdens test Corp E is not properly treated as the owner of the copyrighted article. Corp E does not receive the right to use Program X in perpetuity, but only for so long as it continues to make payments. Corp E does not have the right to purchase Program X on advantageous (or, indeed, any) terms once a certain amount of money has been paid to Corp A or a certain period of time has elapsed (which might indicate a sale). Once the agreement is terminated, Corp E will no longer possess any copies of Program X, current or superseded. Therefore under paragraph (f)(2) of this section there has been a lease of a copyrighted article.

Example 13. (i) *Facts.* The facts are the same as in *Example 12,* except that, while Corp E must return copies of Program X as new upgrades are received, if the agreement terminates, Corp E may keep the latest version of Program X (although Corp E is still prohibited from selling or otherwise transferring any copy of Program X).

(ii) *Analysis.* For the reasons stated in *Example 10,* paragraph (ii)(B), the transfer of the program will be treated as a sale of a copyrighted article rather than as a lease.

Example 14. (i) *Facts.* Corp G, a Country Z corporation, enters into a contract with Corp A, a U.S. corporation, for Corp A to modify Program X so that it can be used at Corp G's facility in Country Z. Under the contract, Corp G is to acquire one copy of the program on a disk and the right to use the program on 5,000 workstations. The contract requires Corp A to rewrite elements of Program X so that it will conform to Country Z accounting standards and states that Corp A retains all copyright rights in the modified Program X. The agreement between Corp A and Corp G is otherwise identical as to rights and payment terms as the agreement described in *Example 10.*

(ii) *Analysis.* (A) As in *Example 10,* no copyright rights are being transferred under paragraph (c)(2) of this section. In addition, since no copyright rights are being transferred to Corp G, this transaction does not involve the provision of services by Corp A under paragraph (d) of this section. This transaction will be classified, therefore, as a transfer of copyrighted articles under paragraph (c)(1)(ii) of this section.

(B) Taking into account all facts and circumstances, Corp G is properly treated as the owner of copyrighted articles. Therefore, under paragraph (f)(2) of this section, there has been the sale

Reg. § 1.861-18(h)

of a copyrighted article rather than the grant of a lease.

Example 15. (i) *Facts.* Corp H, a Country Z corporation, enters into a license agreement for a new computer program. Program Q is to be written by Corp A, a U.S. corporation. Corp A and Corp H agree that Corp A is writing Program Q for Corp H and that, when Program Q is completed, the copyright in Program Q will belong to Corp H. Corp H gives instructions to Corp A programmers regarding program specifications. Corp H agrees to pay Corp A a fixed monthly sum during development of the program. If Corp H is dissatisfied with the development of the program, it may cancel the contract at the end of any month. In the event of termination, Corp A will retain all payments, while any procedures, techniques or copyrightable interests will be the property of Corp H. All of the payments are labelled royalties. There is no provision in the agreement for any continuing relationship between Corp A and Corp H, such as the furnishing of updates of the program, after completion of the modification work.

(ii) *Analysis.* Taking into account all of the facts and circumstances, Corp A is treated as providing services to Corp H. Under paragraph (d) of this section, Corp A is treated as providing services to Corp H because Corp H bears all of the risks of loss associated with the development of Program Q and is the owner of all copyright rights in Program Q. Under paragraph (g)(1) of this section, the fact that the agreement is labelled a license is not controlling (nor is the fact that Corp A receives a sum labelled a royalty).

Example 16. (i) *Facts.* Corp A, a U.S. corporation, and Corp I, a Country Z corporation, agree that a development engineer employed by Corp A will travel to Country Z to provide know-how relating to certain techniques not generally known to computer programmers, which will enable Corp I to more efficiently create computer programs. These techniques represent the product of experience gained by Corp A from working on many computer programming projects, and are furnished to Corp I under nondisclosure conditions. Such information is property subject to trade secret protection.

(ii) *Analysis.* This transaction contains the elements of know-how specified in paragraph (e) of this section. Therefore, this transaction will be treated as the provision of know-how.

Example 17. (i) *Facts.* Corp A, a U.S. corporation, transfers a disk containing Program Y to Corp E, a Country Z corporation, in exchange for a single fixed payment. Program Y is a computer program development program, which is used to create other computer programs, consisting of several components, including libraries of reusable software components that serve as general building blocks in new software applications. No element of these libraries is a significant component of any overall new program. Because a computer program created with the use of Program Y will not operate unless the libraries are also present, the license agreement between Corp A and Corp E grants Corp E the right to distribute copies of the libraries with any program developed using Program Y. The license agreement is otherwise identical to the license agreement in *Example 1.*

(ii) *Analysis.* (A) No non-de minimis copyright rights described in paragraph (c)(2) of this section have passed to Corp E. For purposes of paragraph (b)(2) of this section, the right to distribute the libraries in conjunction with the programs created using Program Y is a de minimis component of the transaction. Because Corp E has received a copy of the program under paragraph (c)(1)(ii) of this section, it has received a copyrighted article.

(B) Taking into account all the facts and circumstances, Corp E is properly treated as the owner of a copyrighted article. Therefore, under paragraph (f)(2) of this section, there has been the sale of a copyrighted article rather than the grant of a lease.

Example 18. (i) *Facts.* (A) Corp A, a U.S. corporation, transfers a disk containing Program X to Corp E, a country Z Corporation. The disk contains both the object code and the source code to Program X and the license agreement grants Corp E the right to—

(*1*) Modify the source code in order to correct minor errors and make minor adaptations to Program X so it will function on Corp E=s computer; and

(*2*) Recompile the modified source code.

(B) The license does not grant Corp E the right to distribute the modified Program X to the public. The license is otherwise identical to the license agreement in *Example 1.*

(ii) *Analysis.* (A) No non-de minimis copyright rights described in paragraph (c)(2) of this section have passed to Corp E. For purposes of paragraph (b)(2) of this section, the right to modify the source code and recompile the source code in order to create new code to correct minor errors and make minor adaptations is a de minimis component of the transaction. Because Corp E has received a copy of the program under paragraph (c)(1)(ii) of this section, it has received a copyrighted article.

(B) Taking into account all the facts and circumstances, Corp E is properly treated as the

Reg. § 1.861-18(h)

owner of a copyrighted article. Therefore, under paragraph (f)(2) of this section, there has been the sale of a copyrighted article rather than the grant of a lease.

(i) *Effective date*—(1) *General.* This section applies to transactions occurring pursuant to contracts entered into on or after December 1, 1998.

(2) *Elective transition rules*—(i) *Contracts entered into in taxable years ending on or after October 2, 1998.* A taxpayer may elect to apply this section to transactions occurring pursuant to contracts entered into in taxable years ending on or after October 2, 1998. A taxpayer that makes an election under this paragraph (i)(2)(i) must apply this section to all contracts entered into in taxable years ending on or after October 2, 1998.

(ii) *Contracts entered into before October 2, 1998.* A taxpayer may elect to apply this section to transactions occurring in taxable years ending on or after October 2, 1998, pursuant to contracts entered into before October 2, 1998, provided the taxpayer would not be required under this section to change its method of accounting as a result of such election, or the taxpayer would be required to change its method of accounting but the resulting section 481(a) adjustment would be zero. A taxpayer that makes an election under this paragraph (i)(2)(ii) must apply this section to all transactions occurring in taxable years ending on or after October 2, 1998, pursuant to contracts entered into before October 2, 1998.

(3) *Manner of making election.* Taxpayers may elect, under paragraph (i)(2)(i) or (i)(2)(ii) of this section, to apply this section, by treating the transactions in accordance with these regulations on their original tax return.

(4) *Examples.* The following examples illustrate application of the transition rule of paragraph (i)(2)(ii) of this section:

Example 1. Corp A develops computer programs for sale to third parties. Corp A uses an overall accrual method of accounting and files its tax return on a calendar-year basis. In year 1, Corp A enters into a contract to deliver a computer program in that year, and to provide updates for each of the following four years. Under the contract, the computer program and the updates are priced separately, and Corp A is entitled to receive payments for the computer program and each of the updates upon delivery. Assume Corp A properly accounts for the contract as a contract for the provision of services. Corp A properly includes the payments under the contract in gross income in the taxable year the payments are received and the computer program or updates are delivered. Corp A properly deducts the cost of developing the computer program and updates when the costs are incurred. Year 3 includes October 2, 1998. Assume under the rules of this section, the provision of updates would properly be accounted for as the transfer of copyrighted articles. If Corp A made an election under paragraph (i)(2)(ii) of this section, Corp A would not be required to change its method of accounting for income under the contract as a result of the election. Corp A would also not be required to change its method of accounting for the cost of developing the computer program and the updates under the contract as a result of the election. Therefore, under paragraph (i)(2)(ii) of this section, Corp A may elect to apply the provisions of this section to the updates provided in years 3, 4, and 5, because Corp A is not required to change from its method of accounting for the contract as a result of the election.

Example 2. Corp A develops computer programs for sale to third parties. Corp A uses an overall accrual method of accounting and files its tax return on a calendar-year basis. In year 1, Corp A enters into a contract to deliver a computer program and to provide one update the following year. Under the contract, the computer program and the update are priced separately, and Corp A is entitled to receive payment for the computer program and the update upon delivery of the computer program. Assume Corp A properly accounts for the contract as a contract for the provision of services. Corp A properly includes the portion of the payment relating to the computer program in gross income in year 1, the taxable year the payment is received and the program delivered. Corp A properly includes the portion of the payment relating to the update in gross income in year 2, the taxable year the update is provided, under Rev. Proc. 71-21, 1971-2 CB 549 (see § 601.601(d)(2) of this chapter). Corp A properly deducts the cost of developing the computer program and update when the costs are incurred. Year 2 includes October 2, 1998. Assume under the rules of this section, provision of the update would properly be accounted for as the transfer of a copyrighted article. If Corp A made an election under paragraph (i)(2)(ii) of this section, Corp A would be required to change its method of accounting for deferring income under its contract as a result of the election. However, the section 481(a) adjustment would be zero because the portion of the payment relating to the update would be includible in gross income in year 2, the taxable year the update is provided, under both Rev. Proc. 71-21 and § 1.451-5. Corp A would not be required to change its method of accounting for the cost of developing the computer program and the update under the contract as a result of the election. Therefore, under paragraph (i)(2)(ii) of this section, Corp A may elect to apply the provisions of this section to the update in year 2, because the section 481(a) adjustment resulting from the change in method of accounting for deferring advance payments under the contract is zero, and because Corp A is not required to change from its method of accounting for the cost of developing the computer program and updates under the contract as a result of the election.

Example 3. Assume the same facts as in *Example 1* except that Corp A is entitled to receive payments for the computer program and each of the updates 30 days after delivery. Corp A properly includes the amounts due under the contract in gross income in the taxable year the computer program or updates are provided. Assume that Corp A properly uses the nonaccrual-experience method described in section 448(d)(5) and § 1.448-2T to account for income on its contracts. If Corp A made an election under paragraph (i)(2)(ii) of this section, Corp A would be required to change from the nonaccrual-experience method for income as a result of the election, because the method is only available with respect to amounts to be received for the performance of services. Therefore, Corp A may not elect to apply the provisions of this section to the updates provided in years 3, 4, and 5, under paragraph (i)(2)(ii) of this section, because Corp A would be required to change from the nonaccrual-experience method of accounting for income on the contract as a result of the election.

(j) *Change in method of accounting required by this section*—(1) *Consent.* A taxpayer is granted consent to change its method of accounting for contracts involving computer programs, to conform with the classification prescribed in this section. The consent is granted for contracts entered into on or after December 1, 1998, or in the case of a taxpayer making an election under paragraph (i)(2)(i) of this section, the consent is granted for contracts entered into in taxable years ending on or after October 2, 1998. In addition, a taxpayer that makes an election under paragraph (i)(2)(ii) of this section is granted consent to change its method of accounting for any contract with transactions subject to the election, if the taxpayer is required to change its method of accounting as a result of the election.

(2) *Year of change.* The year of change is the taxable year that includes December 1, 1998, or in the case of a taxpayer making an election under paragraph (i)(2)(i) or (i)(2)(ii) of this section, the taxable year that includes October 2, 1998.

(k) *Time and manner of making change in method of accounting*—(1) *General.* A taxpayer changing its method of accounting in accordance with this section must file a Form 3115, Application for Change in Method of Accounting, in duplicate. The taxpayer must type or print the following statement at the top of page 1 of the Form 3115: "FILED UNDER TREASURY REGULATION § 1.861-18." The original Form 3115 must be attached to the taxpayers original return for the year of change. A copy of the Form 3115 must be filed with the National Office no later than when the original Form 3115 is filed for the year of change.

(2) *Copy of Form 3115.* The copy required by this paragraph (k)(l) to be sent to the national office should be sent to the Commissioner of Internal Revenue, Attention: CC:DOM:IT&A, P.O. Box 7604, Benjamin Franklin Station, Washington DC 20044 (or in the case of a designated private delivery service: Commissioner of Internal Revenue, Attention: CC:DOM:IT&A, 1111 Constitution Avenue, NW., Washington, DC 20224).

(3) *Effect of consent and Internal Revenue Service review.* A change in method of accounting granted under this section is subject to review by the district director and the national office and may be modified or revoked in accordance with the provisions of Rev. Proc. 97-37 (1997-33 IRB 18) (or its successors) (see § 601.601(d)(2) of this chapter). [Reg. § 1.861-18.]

☐ [*T.D.* 8785, 9-30-98 (*corrected* 11-24-98).]

[Reg. § 1.862-1]

§ 1.862-1. **Income specifically from sources without the United States.**—(a) *Gross income.* (1) The following items of gross income shall be treated as income from sources without the United States:

(i) Interest other than that specified in section 861(a)(1) and § 1.861-2 as being derived from sources within the United States;

(ii) Dividends other than those derived from sources within the United States as provided in section 861(a)(2) and § 1.861-3;

(iii) Compensation for labor or personal services performed without the United States;

(iv) Rentals or royalties from property located without the United States or from any interest in such property, including rentals or royalties for the use of, or for the privilege of using, without the United States, patents, copyrights, secret processes and formulas, goodwill, trademarks, trade brands, franchises, and other like property;

Reg. § 1.862-1(a)

Determination of Sources of Income

See p. 20,601 for regulations not amended to reflect law changes

(v) Gains, profits, and income from the sale of real property located without the United States; and

(vi) Gains, profits, and income derived from the purchase of personal property within the United States and its sale without the United States.

For rules treating certain interest as income from sources without the United States, see paragraph (b) of § 1.861-2. For the treatment of compensation for labor or personal services performed partly within the United States and partly without the United States, see paragraph (b) of § 1.861-4.

(2) In applying subparagraph (1)(iv) of this paragraph for taxable years beginning after December 31, 1966, gains described in section 871(a)(1)(D) and section 881(a)(4) from the sale or exchange after October 4, 1966, of patents, copyrights, and other like property shall be treated, as provided in section 871(e)(2), as rentals or royalties for the use of, or privilege of using, property or an interest in property. See paragraph (e) of § 1.871-11.

(3) For determining the time and place of sale of personal property for purposes of subparagraph (1)(vi) of this paragraph, see paragraph (c) of § 1.861-7.

(4) Income derived from the purchase of personal property within the United States and its sale within a possession of the United States shall be treated as derived entirely from within that possession.

(5) If interest is paid on an obligation of a nonresident of the United States by a resident of the United States acting in the resident's capacity as a guarantor of the obligation of the nonresident, the interest will be treated as income from sources without the United States.

(6) For rules treating certain interest as income from sources without the United States, see paragraph (b) of § 1.861-2.

(7) For the treatment of compensation for labor or personal services performed partly within the United States and partly without the United States, see paragraph (b) of § 1.861-4.

(b) *Taxable income.* The taxable income from sources without the United States, in the case of the items of gross income specified in paragraph (a) of this section, shall be determined on the same basis as that used in § 1.861-8 for determining the taxable income from sources within the United States.

(c) *Income from certain property.* For provisions permitting a taxpayer to elect to treat amounts of gross income attributable to certain aircraft or vessels first leased on or before December 28, 1980, as income from sources within the United States which would otherwise be treated as income from sources without the United States under paragraph (a) of this section, see § 1.861-9. For provisions requiring amounts of gross income attributable to certain aircraft, vessels, or spacecraft first leased by the taxpayer after December 28, 1980, to be treated as income from sources within the United States which would otherwise be treated as income from sources without the United States under paragraph (a) of this section, see § 1.861-9A. [Reg. § 1.862-1.]

☐ [T.D. 6258, 10-23-57. Amended by T.D. 7378, 9-29-75, T.D. 7635, 8-7-79 and T.D. 7928, 12-15-83.]

[Reg. § 1.863-0]

§ 1.863-0. **Table of contents.**—This section lists captions contained in §§ 1.863-1, 1.863-2, and 1.863-3.

§ 1.863-1. *Allocation of gross income.*

(a) In general.

(b) Natural resources.

(1) In general.

(2) Additional production prior to export terminal.

(3) Definitions.

(i) Production activity.

(ii) Additional production activities.

(iii) Export terminal.

(4) Determination of fair market value.

(5) Determination of gross income.

(6) Tax return disclosure.

(7) Examples.

(c) Determination of taxable income.

(e) Effective dates.

§ 1.863-2. *Allocation and apportionment of taxable income.*

(a) Determination of taxable income.

(b) Determination of source of taxable income.

(c) Effective dates.

§ 1.863-3. *Allocation and apportionment of income from certain sales of inventory.*

(a) In general.

(1) Scope

(2) Special rules

(b) Methods to determine income attributable to production activity and sales activity.

(1) 50/50 method.

(i) Determination of gross income.

(ii) Example.

Reg. § 1.863-0

Determination of Sources of Income 46,095

See p. 20,601 for regulations not amended to reflect law changes

(2) IFP method.
    (i) Establishing an IFP.
    (ii) Applying the IFP method.
    (iii) Determination of gross income.
    (iv) Examples.
(3) Books and records method.

(c) Determination of the source of gross income from production activity and sales activity.

(1) Income attributable to production activity.
    (i) Production only within the United States or only within foreign countries.
        (A) Source of income.
        (B) Definition of production assets.
        (C) Location of production assets.
    (ii) Production both within the United States and within foreign countries.
        (A) Source of income.
        (B) Adjusted basis of production assets.
    (iii) Anti-abuse rule.
    (iv) Examples.
(2) Income attributable to sales activity.

(d) Determination of source of taxable income.

(e) Election and reporting rules.

(1) Elections under paragraph (b) of this section.

(2) Disclosure on tax return.

(f) Income partly from sources within a possession of the United States.

(g) Special rules for partnerships.

(h) Effective dates.

[Reg. § 1.863-0.]

☐ [*T.D.* 8687, 11-27-96.]

[Reg. § 1.863-1]

§ 1.863-1. Allocation of gross income.—(a) *In general.* Items of gross income other than those specified in section 861(a) and section 862(a) will generally be separately allocated to sources within or without the United States. See § 1.863-2 for alternate methods to determine the income from sources within or without the United States in the case of items specified in § 1.863-2(a). See also sections 865(b) and (e)(2). In the case of sales of property involving partners and partnerships, the rules of § 1.863-3(g) apply.

(b) *Natural resources*—(1) *In general.* Notwithstanding any other provision, except to the extent provided in paragraph (b)(2) of this section, gross receipts from the sale outside the United States of products derived from the ownership or operation of any farm, mine, oil or gas well, other natural deposit, or timber within the United States, must be allocated between sources within and without the United States based on the fair market value of the product at the export terminal (as defined in paragraph (b)(3)(iii) of this section). Notwithstanding any other provision, except to the extent provided in paragraph (b)(2) of this section, gross receipts from the sale within the United States of products derived from the ownership or operation of any farm, mine, oil or gas well, other natural deposit, or timber outside the United States must be allocated between sources within and without the United States based on the fair market value of the product at the export terminal. For place of sale, see §§ 1.861-7(c) and 1.863-3(c)(2). The source of gross receipts equal to the fair market value of the product at the export terminal will be from sources where the farm, mine, well, deposit, or uncut timber is located. The source of gross receipts from the sale of the product in excess of its fair market value at the export terminal (excess gross receipts) will be determined as follows—

(i) If the taxpayer engages in additional production activities subsequent to shipment from the export terminal and outside the country of sale, the source of excess gross receipts must be determined under § 1.863-3. For purposes of applying § 1.863-3, only production assets used in additional production activity subsequent to the export terminal are taken into account.

(ii) In all other cases, excess gross receipts will be from sources within the country of sale. This paragraph (b)(1)(ii) applies to a taxpayer that engages in additional production activities in the country of sale, as well as to a taxpayer that does not engage in additional production activities at all.

(2) *Additional production prior to export terminal.* Notwithstanding any other provision of this section, gross receipts from the sale of products derived by a taxpayer who performs additional production activities as defined in paragraph (b) (3) (ii) of this section before the relevant product is shipped from the export terminal are allocated between sources within and without the United States based on the fair market value of the product immediately prior to the additional production activities. The source of gross receipts equal to the fair market value of the product immediately prior to the additional production activities will be from sources where the farm, mine, well, deposit, or uncut timber is located. The source of gross receipts from the sale of the product in excess of the fair market value immediately prior to the additional production activities must be determined under § 1.863-3.

Reg. § 1.863-1(b)(2)

For purposes of applying § 1.863-3, only production assets used in the additional production activities are taken into account.

(3) *Definitions*—(i) *Production activity.* For purposes of this section, production activity means an activity that creates, fabricates, manufactures, extracts, processes, cures, or ages inventory. See § 1.864-1. Except as otherwise provided in §§ 1.1502-13 or 1.863-3(g)(2), only production activities conducted directly by the taxpayer are taken into account.

(ii) *Additional production activities.* For purposes of this section, additional production activities are substantial production activities performed directly by the taxpayer in addition to activities from the ownership or operation of any farm, mine, oil or gas well, other natural deposit, or timber. Whether a taxpayer's activities constitute additional production activities will be determined under the principles of § 1.954-3(a)(4). However, in no case will activities that prepare the natural resource itself for export, including those that are designed to facilitate the transportation of the natural resource to or from the export terminal, be considered additional production activities for purposes of this section.

(iii) *Export terminal.* Where the farm, mine, well, deposit, or uncut timber is located without the United States, the export terminal will be the final point in a foreign from which goods are shipped to the United States. If there no such final point in a foreign country (e.g., the property is extracted and produced on the high seas), the export terminal will be the place of production. Where the farm, mine, well, deposit, or uncut timber is located within the United States, the export terminal will be the final point in the United States from which goods are shipped from the United States to a foreign country. The location of the export terminal is determined without regard to any contractual terms agreed to by the taxpayer and without regard to whether there is an actual sale of the products at the export terminal.

(4) *Determination of fair market value.* For purposes of this section, fair market value depends on all of the facts and circumstances as they exist relative to a party in any particular case. Where the products are sold to a related party in a transaction subject to section 482, the determination of fair market value under this section must be consistent with the arm's length price determined under section 482.

(5) *Determination of gross income.* To determine the amount of a taxpayer's gross income from sources within or without the United States, the taxpayer's gross receipts from sources within or without the United States determined under this paragraph (b) must be reduced by the cost of goods sold properly attributable to gross receipts from sources within or without the United States.

(6) *Tax return disclosure.* A taxpayer that determines the source of its income under this paragraph (b) shall attach a statement to its return explaining the methodology used to determine fair market value under paragraph (b)(4) of this section, and explaining any additional production activities (as defined in paragraph (b)(3)(ii) of this section) performed by the taxpayer. In addition, the taxpayer must provide such other information as is required by § 1.863-3.

(7) *Examples.* The following examples illustrate the rules of this paragraph (b):

Example 1. No additional production. U.S. Mines, a U.S. corporation, operates a copper mine and mill in country X. U.S. Mines extracts copper-bearing rocks from the ground and transports the rocks to the mill where the rocks are ground and processed to produce copper-bearing concentrate. The concentrate is transported to a port where it is dried in preparation for export, stored and then shipped to purchasers in the United States. Because title to the property is passed in the United States and, under the facts and circumstances, none of U.S. Mine's activities constitutes additional production prior to the export terminal within the meaning of paragraph (b)(3)(ii) of this section, under paragraph (b)(1) and (b)(1)(ii) of this section, gross receipts equal to the fair market value of the concentrate at the export terminal will be from sources without the United States, and excess gross receipts will be from sources within the United States.

Example 2. No additional production. US Gas, a U.S. corporation, extracts natural gas within the United States, and transports the natural gas to a U.S. port where it is liquified in preparation for shipment. The liquified natural gas is then transported via freighter and sold without additional production activities in a foreign country. Liquefaction of natural gas is not an additional production activity because liquefaction prepares the natural gas for transportation from the export terminal. Therefore, under paragraph (b)(1) and (b)(1)(ii) of this section, gross receipts equal to the fair market value of the liquefied natural gas at the export terminal will be from sources within the United States, and excess gross receipts will be from sources without the United States.

Example 3. Sale in third country. US Gold, a U.S. corporation, mines gold in country X, produces gold jewelry in the United States, and sells the jewelry in country Y. Assume that the fair

Reg. § 1.863-1(b)(3)

market value of the gold at the export terminal in country X is $40, and that US Gold ultimately sells the gold jewelry in country Y for $100. Under § 1.863-1(b), $40 of US Gold's gross receipts will be allocated to sources without the United States. Under paragraph (b)(1)(i) of this section, the source of the remaining $60 of gross receipts will be determined under § 1.863-3. If US Gold applies the 50/50 method described in § 1.863-3, $20 of cost of goods sold is properly attributable to activities subsequent to the export terminal, and all of US Gold's production assets subsequent to the export terminal are located in the United States, then $20 of gross income will be allocated to sources within the United States and $20 of gross income will be allocated to sources without the United States.

Example 4. Production in country of sale. US Oil, a U.S. corporation, extracts oil in country X, transports the oil via pipeline to the export terminal in country Y, refines the oil in the United States, and sells the refined product in the United States to unrelated persons. Assume that the fair market value of the oil at the export terminal in country Y is $80, and that US Oil ultimately sells the refined product for $100. Under paragraph (b)(1) of this section, $80 of US Oil's gross receipts will be allocated to sources without the United States, and under paragraph (b)(1)(ii) of this section the remaining $20 of gross receipts will be allocated to sources within the United States.

Example 5. Additional production prior to export. The facts are the same as in *Example 1*, except that U.S. Mines also operates a smelter in country X. The concentrate output from the mill is transported to the smelter where it is transformed into smelted copper. The smelted copper is exported to purchasers in the United States. Under the facts and circumstances, all of the processes applied to make copper concentrate are considered mining. Therefore, under paragraph (b)(2) of this section, gross receipts equal to the fair market value of the concentrate at the smelter will be from sources without the United States. Under the facts and circumstances, the conversion of the concentrate into smelted copper is an additional production activity in a foreign country within the meaning of paragraph (b)(3)(ii) of this section. Therefore, the source of U.S. Mine's excess gross receipts will be determined pursuant to paragraph (b)(2) of this section.

(c) *Determination of taxable income.* The taxpayer's taxable income from sources within or without the United States will be determined under the rules of §§ 1.861-8 through 1.861-14T for determining taxable income from sources within the United States.

(d) *Scholarships, fellowship grants, grants, prizes and awards*—(1) *In general.* This paragraph (d) applies to scholarships, fellowship grants, grants, prizes and awards. The provisions of this paragraph (d) do not apply to amounts paid as salary or other compensation for services.

(2) *Source of income.* The source of income from scholarships, fellowship grants, grants, prizes and awards is determined as follows:

(i) *United States source income.* Except as provided in paragraph (d)(2)(iii) of this section, scholarships, fellowship grants, grants, prizes and awards made by a U.S. citizen or resident, a domestic partnership, a domestic corporation, an estate or trust (other than a foreign estate or trust within the meaning of section 7701(a)(31)), the United States (or an instrumentality or agency thereof), a State (or any political subdivision thereof), or the District of Columbia shall be treated as income from sources within the United States.

(ii) *Foreign source income.* Scholarships, fellowship grants, grants, prizes and awards made by a foreign government (or an instrumentality, agency, or any political subdivision thereof), an international organization (as defined in section 7701(a)(18)), or a person other than a U.S. person (as defined in section 7701(a)(30)) shall be treated as income from sources without the United States.

(iii) *Certain activities conducted outside the United States.* Scholarships, fellowship grants, targeted grants, and achievement awards received by a person other than a U.S. person (as defined in section 7701(a)(30)) with respect to activities previously conducted (in the case of achievement awards) or to be conducted (in the case of scholarships, fellowships grants, and targeted grants) outside the United States shall be treated as income from sources without the United States.

(3) *Definitions.* The following definitions apply for purposes of this paragraph (d):

(i) *Scholarships* are defined in section 117 and the regulations thereunder.

(ii) *Fellowship grants* are defined in section 117 and the regulations thereunder.

(iii) *Prizes and awards* are defined in section 74 and the regulations thereunder.

(iv) *Grants* are amounts described in subparagraph (3) of section 4945(g) and the regulations thereunder, and are not amounts otherwise described in paragraphs (d)(3)(i), (ii), or (iii) of this section. For purposes of this paragraph (d), the reference to section 4945(g)(3) is applied without regard to the identity of the payor or recipient

Determination of Sources of Income

See p. 20,601 for regulations not amended to reflect law changes

and without the application of the objective and nondiscriminatory basis test and the requirement of a procedure approved in advance.

(v) *Targeted grants* are grants—

(A) Issued by an organization described in section 501(c)(3), the United States (or an instrumentality or agency thereof), a State (or any political subdivision thereof), or the District of Columbia; and

(B) For an activity undertaken in the public interest and not primarily for the private financial benefit of a specific person or persons or organization.

(vi) *Achievement awards* are awards—

(A) Issued by an organization described in section 501(c)(3), the United States (or an instrumentality or agency thereof), a State (or political subdivision thereof), or the District of Columbia; and

(B) For a past activity undertaken in the public interest and not primarily for the private financial benefit of a specific person or persons or organization.

(4) *Effective dates.* The following are the effective dates concerning this paragraph (d):

(i) *Scholarships and fellowship grants.* This paragraph (d) is effective for scholarship and fellowship grant payments made after December 31, 1986. However, for scholarship and fellowship grant payments made after May 14, 1989, and before June 16, 1993, the residence of the payor rule of paragraph (d)(2)(i) and (ii) of this section may be applied without applying paragraph (d)(2)(iii) of this section.

(ii) *Grants, prizes and awards.* This paragraph (d) is effective for payments made for grants, prizes and awards, targeted grants, and achievement awards after September 25, 1995. However, the taxpayer may elect to apply the provisions of this paragraph (d) to payments made for grants, prizes and awards, targeted grants, and achievement awards after December 31, 1986, and before September 26, 1995.

(e) *Effective dates.* The rules of paragraphs (a), (b) and (c) of this section will apply to taxable years beginning after December 30, 1996. However, taxpayers may apply the rules of this section for taxable years beginning after July 11, 1995, and on or before December 30, 1996. For years beginning before December 30, 1996, see § 1.863-1 (as contained in 26 CFR part 1 revised as of April 1, 1996). [Reg. § 1.863-1.]

☐ [T.D. 6258, 10-23-57. *Amended by* T.D. 6348, 12-21-58; T.D. 8615, 8-24-95 *and* T.D. 8687, 11-27-96.]

Reg. § 1.863-2(a)(1)

[Reg. § 1.863-2]

§ 1.863-2. Allocation and apportionment of taxable income.—(a) *Determination of taxable income.* Section 863(b) provides an alternate method for determining taxable income from sources within the United States in the case of gross income derived from sources partly within and partly without the United States. Under this method, taxable income is determined by deducting from such gross income the expenses, losses, or other deductions properly apportioned or allocated thereto and a ratable part of any other expenses, losses, or deductions that cannot definitely be allocated to some item or class of gross income. The income to which this section applies (and that is treated as derived partly from sources within and partly from sources without the United States) will consist of gains, profits, and income

(1) From certain transportation or other services rendered partly within and partly without the United States to the extent not within the scope of section 863(c) or other specific provisions of this title;

(2) From the sale of inventory property (within the meaning of section 865(i)) produced (in whole or in part) by the taxpayer in the United States and sold outside the United States or produced (in whole or in part) by the taxpayer outside the United States and sold in the United States; or

(3) Derived from the purchase of personal property within a possession of the United States and its sale within the United States, to the extent not excluded from the scope of these regulations under § 1.936-6(a)(5), Q&A 7.

(b) *Determination of source of taxable income.* Income treated as derived from sources partly within and partly without the United States under paragraph (a) of this section may be allocated to sources within and without the United States pursuant to § 1.863-1 or apportioned to such sources in accordance with the methods described in other regulations under section 863. To determine the source of certain types of income described in paragraph (a) (1) of this section, see § 1.863-4. To determine the source of gross income described in paragraph (a)(2) of this section, see § 1.863-1 for natural resources and see § 1.863-3 for other inventory. Taxpayers, at their election, may apply the principles of § 1.863-3(b)(1) and (c) to determine the source of taxable income (rather than gross income) from sales of inventory property (other than natural resources). To determine the source of income partly from sources within a possession of the United States, including

Determination of Sources of Income

income described in paragraph (a)(3) of this section, see § 1.863-3(f).

(c) *Effective dates.* This section will apply to taxable years beginning after December 30, 1996. However, taxpayers may apply the rules of this section for taxable years beginning after July 11, 1995, and on or before December 30, 1996. For years beginning before December 30, 1996, see § 1.863-2 (as contained in 26 CFR part 1 revised as of April 1, 1996). [Reg. § 1.863-2.]

☐ [T.D. 6258, 10-23-57. *Amended by T.D.* 8687, 11-27-96.]

[Reg. § 1.863-3]

§ 1.863-3. Allocation and apportionment of income from certain sales of inventory.—(a) *In general*—(1) *Scope.* Paragraphs (a) through (e) of this section apply to determine the source of income derived from the sale of inventory property (inventory), which a taxpayer produces (in whole or in part) within the United States and sells outside the United States, or which a taxpayer produces (in whole or in part) outside the United States and sells within the United States (Section 863 Sales). A taxpayer must divide gross income from Section 863 Sales between production activity and sales activity using one of the methods described in paragraph (b) of this section. The source of gross income from production activity and from sales activity must then be determined under paragraph (c) of this section. Taxable income from Section 863 Sales is determined under paragraph (d) of this section. Paragraph (e) of this section describes the rules for electing the methods described in paragraph (b) of this section and the information that a taxpayer must disclose on a tax return. Paragraph (f) of this section applies to determine the source of certain income derived from a possession of the United States. Paragraph (g) of this section provides special rules for partnerships for all sales subject to §§ 1.863-1 through 1.863-3. Paragraph (h) of this section provides effective dates for the rules in this section.

(2) *Rules of application for Section 863 Sales.* Once a taxpayer has elected a method described in paragraph (b) of this section, the taxpayer must separately apply that method to Section 863 Sales in the United States and to Section 863 Sales outside the United States. In addition, the taxpayer must apply the rules of paragraphs (c) and (d) of this section by aggregating all Section 863 Sales to which a method described in paragraph (b) of this section applies, after separately applying that method to Section 863 Sales in the United States and to Section 863 Sales outside the United States. See section 865(i)(1) for the definition of inventory property. See also section 865(e)(2). See

§ 1.861-7(c) and paragraph (c)(2) of this section for the time and place of sale.

(b) *Methods to determine income attributable to production activity and sales activity*—(1) *50/50 method*—(i) *Determination of gross income.* Generally, gross income from Section 863 Sales will be apportioned between production activity and sales activity under the 50/50 method as described in this paragraph (b)(1). Under the 50/50 method, one-half of the taxpayer's gross income will be considered income attributable to production activity and the source of that income will be determined under the rules of paragraph (c)(1) of this section. The remaining one-half of such gross income will be considered income attributable to sales activity and the source of that income will be determined under the rules of paragraph (c)(2) of this section. In lieu of the 50/50 method, the taxpayer may elect to determine the source of income from Section 863 Sales under the IFP method described in paragraph (b)(2) of this section or, with the consent of the District Director, the books and records method described in paragraph (b)(3) of this section.

(ii) *Example.* The following example illustrates the rules of this paragraph (b)(1):

Example. 50/50 method. (i) P, a U.S. corporation, produces widgets in the United States. P sells the widgets for $100 to D, an unrelated foreign distributor, in another country. P's cost of goods sold is $40. Thus, P's gross income is $60.

(ii) Pursuant to the 50/50 method, one-half of P's gross income, or $30, is considered income attributable to production activity, and one-half of P's gross income, or $30, is considered income attributable to sales activity.

(2) *IFP method*—(i) *Establishing an IFP.* A taxpayer may elect to allocate gross income earned from production activity and sales activity using the independent factory price (IFP) method described in this paragraph (b)(2) if an IFP is fairly established. An IFP is fairly established based on a sale by the taxpayer only if the taxpayer regularly sells part of its output to wholly independent distributors or other selling concerns in such a way as to reasonably reflect the income earned from production activity. A sale will not be considered to fairly establish an IFP if sales activity by the taxpayer with respect to that sale is significant in relation to all of the activities with respect to that product.

(ii) *Applying the IFP method.* If the taxpayer elects to use the IFP method, the amount of the gross sales price equal to the IFP will be treated as attributable to production activity, and the excess of the gross sales price over the IFP will be treated as attributable to sales activity. If a

Reg. § 1.863-3(b)(2)

taxpayer elects to use the IFP method, the IFP must be applied to all Section 863 Sales of inventory that are substantially similar in physical characteristics and function, and are sold at a similar level of distribution as the inventory sold in the sale fairly establishing an IFP. The IFP will only be applied to sales that are reasonably contemporaneous with the sale fairly establishing the IFP. An IFP cannot be applied to sales in other geographic markets if the markets are substantially different. If the taxpayer elects the IFP method, the rules of this paragraph will also apply to determine the division of gross receipts between production activity and sales activity in a Section 863 Sale that itself fairly establishes an IFP. If the taxpayer elects to apply the IFP method, the IFP method must be applied to all sales for which an IFP may be fairly established and applied for that taxable year and each subsequent taxable year. The taxpayer will apply either the 50/50 method described in paragraph (b)(1) of this section or the books and records method described in paragraph (b)(3) of this section to any other Section 863 Sale for which an IFP cannot be established or applied for each taxable year.

(iii) *Determination of gross income.* The amount of a taxpayer's gross income from production activity is determined by reducing the amount of gross receipts from production activity by the cost of goods sold properly attributable to production activity. The amount of a taxpayer's gross income from sales activity is determined by reducing the amount of gross receipts from sales activity by the cost of goods sold (if any) properly attributable to sales activity. The source of gross income from production activity is determined under the rules of paragraph (c)(1) of this section, and the source of gross income from sales activity will be determined under the rules of paragraph (c)(2) of this section.

(iv) *Examples.* The following examples illustrate the rules of this paragraph (b)(2):

Example 1. IFP method. (i) P, a U.S. producer, purchases cotton and produces cloth in the United States. P sells cloth in country X to D, an unrelated foreign clothing manufacturer, for $100. Cost of goods sold for cloth is $80, entirely attributable to production activity. P does not engage in significant sales activity in relation to its other activities in the sales to D. Under these facts, the sale to D fairly establishes an IFP of $100. Assume that P elects to use the IFP method. Accordingly, $100 of the gross sales price is treated as attributable to production activity, and no amount of income from this sale is attributable to sales activity. After reducing the gross sales price by cost of goods sold, $20 of the gross income is treated as attributable to production activity ($100-$80).

(ii) P also sells cloth in country X to A, a unrelated foreign retail outlet, for $110. Because P elected the IFP method and the cloth is substantially similar to the cloth sold to D, the IFP fairly established in the sales to D must be used to determine the amount attributable to production activity in the sale to A. Accordingly, $100 of the gross sales price is treated as attributable to production activity and $10 ($110-$100) is attributable to sales activity. After reducing the gross sales price by cost of goods sold, $20 of the gross income is treated as attributable to production activity ($100-$80) and $10 is attributable to sales activity.

Example 2. Scope of IFP Method. (i) USCo manufactures three dissimilar products. USCo elects to apply the IFP method. In year 1, an IFP can be established for sales of product X, but not for products Y and Z. In year 2, an IFP cannot be established for any of USCo's products. In year 3, an IFP can be established for products X and Y, but not for product Z.

(ii) In year 1, USCo must apply the IFP method to sales of product X. In year 2, although USCo's IFP election remains in effect, USCo is not required to apply the IFP election to any products. In year 3, USCo is required to apply the IFP method to sales of products X and Y.

(3) *Books and records method.* A taxpayer may elect to determine the amount of its gross income from Section 863 Sales that is attributable to production and sales activities for the taxable year based upon its books of account if it has received in advance the permission of the District Director having audit responsibility over its tax return. The taxpayer must establish to the satisfaction of the District Director that the taxpayer, in good faith and unaffected by considerations of tax liability, will regularly employ in its books of account a detailed allocation of receipts and expenditures which clearly reflects the amount of the taxpayer's income from production and sales activities. If a taxpayer receives permission to apply the books and records method, but does not comply with a material condition set forth by the District Director, the District Director may, in its discretion, revoke permission to use the books and records method. The source of gross income treated as attributable to production activity under this method may be determined under the rules of paragraph (c)(1) of this section, and the source of gross income attributable to sales activity will be determined under the rules of paragraph (c)(2) of this section.

Reg. § 1.863-3(b)(3)

Determination of Sources of Income

See p. 20,601 for regulations not amended to reflect law changes

(c) *Determination of the source of gross income from production activity and sales activity*—(1) *Income attributable to production activity*—(i) *Production only within the United States or only within foreign countries*—(A) *Source of income.* For purposes of this section, production activity means an activity that creates, fabricates, manufactures, extracts, processes, cures, or ages inventory. See § 1.864-1. Subject to the provisions in § 1.1502-13 or paragraph (g)(2)(ii) of this section, the only production activities that are taken into account for purposes of §§ 1.863-1, 1.863-2, and this section are those conducted directly by the taxpayer. Where the taxpayer's production assets are located only within the United States or only outside the United States, the income attributable to production activity is sourced where the taxpayer's production assets are located. For rules regarding the source of income when production assets are located both within the United States and without the United States, see paragraph (c)(1)(ii) of this section.

(B) *Definition of production assets.* Subject to the provisions of § 1.1502-13 and paragraph (g)(2)(ii) of this section, production assets include only tangible and intangible assets owned directly by the taxpayer that are directly used by the taxpayer to produce inventory described in paragraph (a) of this section. Production assets do not include assets that are not directly used to produce inventory described in paragraph (a) of this section. Thus, production assets do not include such assets as accounts receivables, intangibles not related to production of inventory (e.g., marketing intangibles, including trademarks and customer lists), transportation assets, warehouses, the inventory itself, raw materials, or work-in-process. In addition, production assets do not include cash or other liquid assets (including working capital), investment assets, prepaid expenses, or stock of a subsidiary.

(C) *Location of production assets.* For purposes of this section, a tangible production asset will be considered located where the asset is physically located. An intangible production asset will be considered located where the tangible production assets owned by the taxpayer to which it relates are located.

(ii) *Production both within the United States and within foreign countries*—(A) *Source of income.* Where the taxpayer's production assets are located both within and without the United States, income from sources without the United States will be determined by multiplying the income attributable to the taxpayer's production activity by a fraction, the numerator of which is the average adjusted basis of production assets that are located outside the United States and the denominator of which is the average adjusted basis of all production assets within and without the United States. The remaining income is treated as from sources within the United States.

(B) *Adjusted basis of production assets.* For purposes of paragraph (c)(1)(ii)(A) of this section, the adjusted basis of an asset is determined under section 1011. The average adjusted basis is computed by averaging the adjusted basis of the asset at the beginning and end of the taxable year, unless by reason of material changes during the taxable year such average does not fairly represent the average for such year. In this event, the average adjusted basis will be determined upon a more appropriate basis. If production assets are used to produce inventory sold in Section 863 Sales and are also used to produce other property during the taxable year, the portion of its adjusted basis that is included in the fraction described in paragraph (c) (1) (ii) (A) of this section will be determined under any method that reasonably reflects the portion of the assets that produces inventory sold in Section 863 Sales. For example, the portion of such an asset that is included in the formula may be determined by multiplying the asset's average adjusted basis by a fraction, the numerator of which is the gross receipts from sales of inventory from Section 863 Sales produced by the asset, and the denominator of which is the gross receipts from all property produced by that asset.

(iii) *Anti-abuse rule.* The purpose of this paragraph (c)(1) is to attribute the source of the taxpayer's production income to the location of the taxpayer's production activity. Therefore, if the taxpayer has entered into or structured one or more transactions with a principal purpose of reducing its U.S. tax liability by manipulating the formula described in paragraph (c)(1)(ii)(A) of this section in a manner inconsistent with the purpose of this paragraph (c)(1), the District Director may make appropriate adjustments so that the source of the taxpayer's income from production activity more clearly reflects the source of that income.

(iv) *Examples.* The following examples illustrate the rules of this paragraph (c)(1):

Example 1. Source of production income. (i) A, a U.S. corporation, produces widgets that are sold both within the United States and within a foreign country. The initial manufacture of all widgets occurs in the United States. The second stage of production of widgets that are sold within a foreign country is completed within the country of sale. A's U.S. plant and machinery which is involved in the initial manufacture of the widgets

Reg. § 1.863-3(c)(1)

has an average adjusted basis of $200. A also owns warehouses used to store work-in-process. A owns foreign equipment with an average adjusted basis of $25. A's gross receipts from all sales of widgets is $100, and its gross receipts from export sales of widgets is $25. Assume that apportioning average adjusted basis using gross receipts is reasonable. Assume A's cost of goods sold from the sale of widgets in the foreign countries is $13 and thus, its gross income from widgets sold in foreign countries is $12. A uses the 50/50 method to divide its gross income between production activity and sales activity.

(ii) A determines its production gross income from sources without the United States by multiplying one-half of A's $12 of gross income from sales of widgets in foreign countries, or $6, by a fraction, the numerator of which is all relevant foreign production assets, or $25, and the denominator of which is all relevant production assets, or $75 ($25 foreign assets + ($200 U.S. assets X $25 gross receipts from export sales/$100 gross receipts from all sales)). Therefore, A's gross production income from sources without the United States is $2 ($6 X ($25/$75).

Example 2. Location of intangible property. Assume the same facts as *Example 1,* except that A employs a patented process that applies only to the initial production of widgets. In computing the formula used to determine the source of income from production activity, A's patent, if it has an average adjusted basis, would be located in the United States.

Example 3. Anti-abuse rule. (i) Assume the same facts as *Example 1.* A sells its U.S. assets to B, an unrelated U.S. corporation, with a principal purpose of reducing its U.S. tax liability by manipulating the property fraction. A then leases these assets from B. After this transaction, under the general rule of paragraph (c)(1)(ii) of this section, all of A's production income would be considered from sources without the United States, because all of A's relevant production assets are located within a foreign country. Since the leased property is not owned by the taxpayer, it is not included in the fraction.

(ii) Because A has entered into a transaction with a principal purpose of reducing its U.S. tax liability by manipulating the formula described in paragraph (c)(1)(ii)(A) of this section, A's income must be adjusted to more clearly reflect the source of that income. In this case, the District Director may redetermine the source of A's production income by ignoring the sale-leaseback transactions.

(2) *Income attributable to sales activity.* The source of the taxpayer's income that is attributable to sales activity will be determined under the provisions of § 1.861-7(c). However, notwithstanding any other provision, for purposes of section 863, the place of sale will be presumed to be the United States if personal property is wholly produced in the United States and the property is sold for use, consumption, or disposition in the United States. See § 1.864-6(b)(3)(ii) to determine the country of use, consumption, or disposition. Also, in applying this paragraph, property will be treated as wholly produced in the United States if it is subject to no more than packaging, repackaging, labeling, or other minor assembly operations outside the United States, within the meaning of § 1.954-3(a)(4)(iii)(property manufactured or produced by a controlled foreign corporation).

(d) *Determination of source of taxable income.* Once the source of gross income has been determined under paragraph (c) of this section, the taxpayer must properly allocate and apportion separately under §§ 1.861-8 through 1.861-14T the amounts of its expenses, losses, and other deductions to its respective amounts of gross income from Section 863 Sales determined separately under each method described in paragraph (b) of this section. In addition, if the taxpayer deducts expenses for research and development under section 174 that may be attributed to its Section 863 Sales under § 1.861-8(e)(3), the taxpayer must separately allocate or apportion expenses, losses, and other deductions to its respective amounts of gross income from each relevant product category that the taxpayer uses in applying the rules of § 1.861-8(e)(3)(i)(A). In the case of gross income from Section 863 Sales determined under the IFP method or the books and records method, the rules of §§ 1.861-8 through 1.861-14T must apply to properly allocate or apportion amounts of expenses, losses and other deductions allocated and apportioned to such gross income between gross income from sources within and without the United States. In the case of gross income from Section 863 Sales determined under the 50/50 method, the amounts of expenses, losses, and other deductions allocated and apportioned to such gross income must be apportioned between sources within and without the United States pro rata based on the relative amounts of gross income from sources within and without the United States determined under the 50/50 method. Research and experimental expenditures qualifying under § 1.861-17 are allocated under that section, and are not allocated and apportioned pro rata under the 50/50 method.

(e) *Election and reporting rules*—(1) *Elections under paragraph (b) of this section.* If a taxpayer does not elect a method specified in paragraph

Reg. § 1.863-3(c)(2)

Determination of Sources of Income

See p. 20,601 for regulations not amended to reflect law changes

(b)(2) or (3) of this section, the taxpayer must apply the method specified in paragraph (b)(1) of this section. The taxpayer may elect to apply the method specified in paragraph (b)(2) of this section by using the method on a timely filed original return (including extensions). A taxpayer may elect to apply the method specified in paragraph (b)(3) of this section by using the method on a timely filed original return (including extensions), but only if the taxpayer has received permission from the District Director to apply that method. Once a method under paragraph (b) of this section has been used, that method must be used in later taxable years unless the Commissioner consents to a change. However, if a taxpayer elects to change to or from the method specified in paragraph (b)(3) of this section, the taxpayer must obtain permission from the District Director instead of the Commissioner. Permission to change methods from one year to another year will not be withheld unless the change would result in a substantial distortion of the source of the taxpayer's income.

(2) *Disclosure on tax return.* A taxpayer who uses one of the methods described in paragraph (b) of this section must fully explain in a statement attached to the return the methodology used, the circumstances justifying use of that methodology, the extent that sales are aggregated, and the amount of income so allocated.

(f) *Income partly from sources within a possession of the United States*—(1) *In general.* This paragraph (f) relates to gains, profits, and income, which are treated as derived partly from sources within the United States and partly from sources within a possession of the United States (Section 863 Possession Sales). This paragraph (f) applies to determine the source of income derived from the sale of inventory produced (in whole or in part) by the taxpayer within the United States and sold within a possession, or produced (in whole or in part) by a taxpayer in a possession and sold within the United States (Possession Production Sales). It also applies to determine the source of income derived from the purchase of personal property within a possession of the United States and its sale within the United States (Possession Purchase Sales). A taxpayer subject to this paragraph (f) must divide gross income from Section 863 Possession Sales using one of the methods described in either paragraph (f)(2)(i) of this section (in the case of Possession Production Sales) or paragraph (f)(3)(i) of this section (in the case of Possession Purchase Sales). Once a taxpayer has elected a method, the taxpayer must separately apply that method to the applicable category of Section 863 Possession Sales in the United States and to those in a possession. The source of gross income from each type of activity must then be determined under either paragraph (f)(2)(ii) or (3)(ii) of this section, as appropriate. The source of taxable income from Section 863 Possession Sales is determined under paragraph (f)(4) of this section. The taxpayer must apply the rules for computing gross and taxable income by aggregating all Section 863 Possession Sales to which a method in this section applies after separately applying that method to Section 863 Possession Sales in the United States and to Section 863 Possession Sales in a possession. This section does not apply to determine the source of a taxpayer's gross income derived from a sale of inventory purchased from a corporation that has an election in effect under section 936, if the taxpayer's income from sales of that inventory is taken into account to determine benefits under section 936 for the section 936 corporation. For rules to be applied to determine the source of such income, see § 1.936-6(a)(5) Q&A 7a and 1.936-6(b)(1) Q&A 13.

(2) *Allocation or apportionment for Possession Production Sales*—(i) *Methods for determining the source of gross income for Possession Production Sales*—(A) *Possession 50/50 method.* Under the possession 50/50 method, gross income from Possession Production Sales is allocated between production activity and business sales activity as described in this paragraph (f)(2)(i)(A). Under the possession 50/50 method, one-half of the taxpayer's gross income will be considered income attributable to production activity and the source of that income will be determined under the rules of paragraph (f)(2)(ii)(A) of this section. The remaining one-half of such gross income will be considered income attributable to business sales activity and the source of that income will be determined under the rules of paragraph (f)(2)(ii)(B) of this section.

(B) *IFP method.* In lieu of the possession 50/50 method, a taxpayer may elect the independent factory price (IFP) method. Under the IFP method, gross income from Possession Production Sales is allocated to production activity or sales activity using the IFP method, as described in paragraph (b)(2) of this section, if an IFP is fairly established under the rules of paragraph (b)(2) of this section. See paragraphs (f)(2)(ii)(A) and (C) of this section for rules for determining the source of gross income attributable to production activity and sales activity.

(C) *Books and records method.* A taxpayer may elect to allocate gross income using the books and records method described in paragraph (b)(3) of this section, if it has received in advance the permission of the District Director having audit responsibility over its return. See paragraph

Reg. § 1.863-3(f)(2)

46,104   Determination of Sources of Income
See p. 20,601 for regulations not amended to reflect law changes

(f)(2)(ii) of this section for rules for determining the source of gross income.

(ii) *Determination of source of gross income from production, business sales, and sales activity*—(A) *Gross income attributable to production activity.* The source of gross income from production activity is determined under the rules of paragraph (c)(1) of this section, except that the term possession is substituted for foreign country wherever it appears.

(B) *Gross income attributable to business sales activity*—(*1*) *Source of gross income.* Gross income from the taxpayer's business sales activity is sourced in the possession in the same proportion that the amount of the taxpayer's business sales activity for the taxable year within the possession bears to the amount of the taxpayer's business sales activity for the taxable year both within the possession and outside the possession, with respect to Possession Production Sales. The remaining income is sourced in the United States.

(*2*) *Business sales activity.* For purposes of this paragraph (f)(2)(ii)(B), the taxpayer's business sales activity is equal to the sum of—

(*i*) The amounts for the taxable period paid for wages, salaries, and other compensation of employees, and other expenses attributable to Possession Production Sales (other than amounts that are nondeductible under section 263A, interest, and research and development); and

(*ii*) Possession Production Sales for the taxable period.

(*3*) *Location of business sales activity.* For purposes of determining the location of the taxpayer's business activity within a possession, the following rules apply:

(*i*) *Sales.* Receipts from gross sales will be attributed to a possession under the provisions of paragraph (c)(2) of this section.

(*ii*) *Expenses.* Expenses will be attributed to a possession under the rules of §§ 1.861-8 through 1.861-14T.

(C) *Gross income attributable to sales activity.* The source of the taxpayer's income that is attributable to sales activity, as determined under the IFP method or the books and records method, will be determined under the provisions of paragraph (c)(2) of this section.

(3) *Allocation or apportionment for Possession Purchase Sales*—(i) *Methods for determining the source of gross income for Possession Purchase Sales*—(A) *Business activity method.* Gross income from Possession Purchase Sales is allocated in its entirety to the taxpayer's business activity, and is then apportioned between U.S. and possession sources under paragraph (f)(3)(ii) of this section.

(B) *Books and records method.* A taxpayer may elect to allocate gross income using the books and records method described in paragraph (b)(3) of this section, subject to the conditions set forth in paragraph (b)(3) of this section. See paragraph (f)(2)(ii) of this section for rules for determining the source of gross income.

(ii) *Determination of source of gross income from business activity*—(A) *Source of gross income.* Gross income from the taxpayer's business activity is sourced in the possession in the same proportion that the amount of the taxpayer's business activity for the taxable year within the possession bears to the amount of the taxpayer's business activity for the taxable year both within the possession and outside the possession, with respect to Possession Purchase Sales. The remaining income is sourced in the United States.

(B) *Business activity.* For purposes of this paragraph (f)(3)(ii), the taxpayer's business activity is equal to the sum of—

(*1*) The amounts for the taxable period paid for wages, salaries, and other compensation of employees, and other expenses attributable to Possession Purchase Sales (other than amounts that are nondeductible under section 263A, interest, and research and development);

(*2*) Cost of goods sold attributable to Possession Purchase Sales during the taxable period; and

(*3*) Possession Purchase Sales for the taxable period.

(C) *Location of business activity.* For purposes of determining the location of the taxpayer's business activity within a possession, the following rules apply:

(*1*) *Sales.* Receipts from gross sales will be attributed to a possession under the provisions of paragraph (c)(2) of this section.

(*2*) *Cost of goods sold.* Payments for cost of goods sold will be properly attributable to gross receipts from sources within the possession only to the extent that the property purchased was manufactured, produced, grown, or extracted in the possession (within the meaning of section 954(d)(1)(A)).

(*3*) *Expenses.* Expenses will be attributed to a possession under the rules of §§ 1.861-8 through 1.861-14T.

(iii) *Examples.* The following examples illustrate the rules of paragraph (f)(3)(ii) of this

Reg. § 1.863-3(f)(3)

section relating to the determination of source of gross income from business activity:

Example 1. (i) U.S. Co. purchases in a possession product X for $80 from A. A manufactures X in the possession. Without further production, U.S. Co. sells X in the United States for $100. Assume U.S. Co. has sales and administrative expenses in the possession of $10.

(ii) To determine the source of U.S. Co.'s gross income, the $100 gross income from sales of X is allocated entirely to U.S. Co.'s business activity. Forty-seven dollars of U.S. Co.'s gross income is sourced in the possession. [Possession expenses ($10) plus possession purchases (i.e., cost of goods sold) ($80) plus possessions sales ($0), divided by total expenses ($10) plus total purchases ($80) plus total sales ($100).] The remaining $53 is sourced in the United States.

Example 2. (i) Assume the same facts as in Example 1, except that A manufactures X outside the possession.

(ii) To determine the source of U.S. Co.'s gross income, the $100 gross income is allocated entirely to U.S. Co.'s business activity. Five dollars of U.S. Co.'s gross income is sourced in the possession. [Possession expenses ($10) plus possession purchases ($0) plus possession sales ($0), divided by total expenses ($10) plus total purchases ($80) plus total sales ($100).] The $80 purchase is not included in the numerator used to determine U.S. Co.'s business activity in the possession, since product X was not manufactured in the possession. The remaining $95 is sourced in the United States.

(4) *Determination of source of taxable income.* Once the source of gross income has been determined under paragraph (f)(2) or (3) of this section, the taxpayer must properly allocate and apportion separately under §§ 1.861-8 through 1.861-14T the amounts of its expenses, losses, and other deductions to its respective amounts of gross income from Section 863 Possession Sales determined separately under each method described in paragraph (f)(2) or (3) of this section. In addition, if the taxpayer deducts expenses for research and development under section 174 that may be attributed to its Section 863 Possession Sales under § 1.861-17, the taxpayer must separately allocate or apportion expenses, losses, and other deductions to its respective amounts of gross income from each relevant product category that the taxpayer uses in applying the rules of § 1.861-17. Thus, in the case of gross income from Section 863 Possession Sales determined under the IFP method or books and records method, a taxpayer must apply the rules of §§ 1.861-8 through 1.861-14T to properly allocate or apportion amounts of expenses, losses and other deductions, allocated and apportioned to such gross income, between gross income from sources within and without the United States. However, in the case of gross income from Possession Production Sales determined under the possessions 50/50 method or gross income from Possession Purchase Sales computed under the business activity method, the amounts of expenses, losses, and other deductions allocated and apportioned to such gross income must be apportioned between sources within and without the United States pro rata based on the relative amounts of gross income from sources within and without the United States determined under those methods, except that the rules regarding the allocation and apportionment of research and experimental expenditures in § 1.861-17 shall apply to such expenditures of taxpayers using the 50/50 method.

(5) *Special rules for partnerships.* In applying the rules of this paragraph (f) to transactions involving partners and partnerships, the rules of paragraph (g) of this section apply.

(6) *Election and reporting rules*—(i) *Elections under paragraph (f)(2) or (3) of this section.* If a taxpayer does not elect one of the methods specified in paragraph (f)(2) or (3) of this section, the taxpayer must apply the possession 50/50 method in the case of Possession Production Sales or the business activity method in the case of Possession Purchase Sales. The taxpayer may elect to apply a method specified in either paragraph (f)(2) or (3) of this section by using the method on a timely filed original return (including extensions). Once a method has been used, that method must be used in later taxable years unless the Commissioner consents to a change. Permission to change methods from one year to another year will be granted unless the change would result in a substantial distortion of the source of the taxpayer's income.

(ii) *Disclosure on tax return.* A taxpayer who uses one of the methods described in paragraph (f)(2) or (3) of this section must fully explain in a statement attached to the tax return the methodology used, the circumstances justifying use of that methodology, the extent that sales are aggregated, and the amount of income so allocated.

(g) *Special rules for partnerships*—(1) *General rule.* For purposes of § 1.863-1 and this section, a taxpayer's production or sales activity does not include production and sales activities conducted by a partnership of which the taxpayer is a partner either directly or through one or more partnerships, except as otherwise provided in paragraph (g)(2) of this section.

Reg. § 1.863-3(g)(1)

(2) *Exceptions*—(i) *In general.* For purposes of determining the source of the partner's distributive share of partnership income or determining the source of the partner's income from the sale of inventory property which the partnership distributes to the partner in kind, the partner's production or sales activity includes an activity conducted by the partnership. In addition, the production activity of a partnership includes the production activity of a taxpayer that is a partner either directly or through one or more partnerships, to the extent that the partner's production activity is related to inventory that the partner contributes to the partnership in a transaction described under section 721.

(ii) *Attribution of production assets to or from a partnership.* A partner will be treated as owning its proportionate share of the partnership's production assets only to the extent that, under paragraph (g)(2)(i) of this section, the partner's activity includes production activity conducted through a partnership. A partner's share of partnership assets will be determined by reference to the partner's distributive share of partnership income for the year attributable to such production assets. Similarly, to the extent a partnership's activities include the production activities of a partner, the partnership will be treated as owning the partner's production assets related to the inventory that is contributed in kind to the partnership. See paragraph (c)(1)(ii)(B) of this section for rules apportioning the basis of assets to Section 863 Sales.

(iii) *Basis.* For purposes of this section, in those cases where the partner is treated as owning its proportionate share of the partnership's production assets, the partner's basis in production assets held through a partnership shall be determined by reference to the partnership's adjusted basis in its assets (including a partner's special basis adjustment, if any, under section 743). Similarly, a partnership's basis in a partner's production assets is determined with reference to the partner's adjusted basis in its assets.

(iv) *Separate application of methods.* If, under paragraph (g)(2) of this section, a partner is treated as conducting the activity of a partnership, and is treated as owning its proportionate share of a partnership's production assets, a partner must apply the method it has elected under paragraph (b) of this section separately to Section 863 Sales described in this paragraph (g) and all other Section 863 Sales.

(3) *Examples.* The following examples illustrate the rules of this paragraph (g):

Example 1. Distributive share of partnership income. A, a U.S. corporation, forms a partnership in the United States with B, a country X corporation. A and B each have a 50 percent interest in the income, gains, losses, deductions and credits of the partnership. The partnership is engaged in the manufacture and sale of widgets. The widgets are manufactured in the partnership's plant located in the United States and are sold by the partnership outside the United States. The partnership owns the manufacturing facility and all other production assets used to produce the widgets. A's distributive share of partnership income includes 50 percent of the sales income from these sales. In applying the rules of section 863 to determine the source of its distributive share of partnership income from the export sales of widgets, A is treated as carrying on the activity of the partnership related to production of these widgets and as owning a proportionate share of the partnership's assets related to production of the widgets, based upon its distributive share of partnership income.

Example 2. Distribution in kind. Assume the same facts as in *Example 1* except that the partnership, instead of selling the widgets, distributes the widgets to A and B. A then further processes the widgets and then sells them outside the United States. In determining the source of the income earned by A on the sales outside the United States, A is treated as conducting the activities of the partnership related to production of the distributed widgets. Thus, the source of gross income on the sale of the widgets is determined under section 863 and these regulations. A applies the 50/50 method described in paragraph (b)(1) of this section to determine the source of income from the sales. In applying paragraph (c)(1) of this section, A is treated as owning its proportionate share of the partnership's production assets based upon its distributive share of partnership income.

(h) *Effective dates.* The rules of this section apply to taxable years beginning after December 30, 1996. However, taxpayers may apply these regulations for taxable years beginning after July 11, 1995, and on or before December 30, 1996. For years beginning before December 30, 1996, see §§ 1.863-3A and 1.863-3AT. However, the rules of paragraph (f) of this section apply to taxable years beginning on or after November 13, 1998. [Reg. § 1.863-3.]

☐ *[T.D. 8687, 11-27-96. Amended by T.D. 8786, 10-13-98.]*

Determination of Sources of Income

See p. 20,601 for regulations not amended to reflect law changes

→ Caution: Reg. § 1.863-3 was redesignated as Reg. § 1.863-3A, below, by T.D. 8687 and applies to tax years beginning before December 30, 1996. ←

[Reg. § 1.863-3A]

§ 1.863-3A. **Income from the sale of personal property derived partly from within and partly from without the United States.**—(a) *General*—(1) *Classes of income.* Income from the sale of property to which paragraph (b)(2) and (3) of § 1.863-2 applies is divided into two classes for purposes of this section, namely, income which is treated as derived partly from sources within the United States and partly from sources within a foreign country, and income which is treated as derived partly from sources within the United States and partly from sources within a possession of the United States.

(2) *Definition.* For purposes of this section, the word "produced" includes created, fabricated, manufactured, extracted, processed, cured, or aged. For determining the time and place of sale of personal property for purposes of this section, see paragraph (c) of § 1.861-7.

(b) *Income partly from sources within a foreign country*—(1) *General.* This paragraph relates to gains, profits, and income derived from the sale of personal property produced (in whole or in part) by the taxpayer within the United States and sold within a foreign country, or produced (in whole or in part) by the taxpayer within a foreign country and sold within the United States. Pursuant to section 863(b) such items shall be treated as derived partly from sources within the United States and partly from sources within a foreign country.

(2) *Allocation or apportionment.* The taxable income from sources within the United States, in the case of the items to which this paragraph applies, shall be determined according to the examples set forth in this subparagraph. For such purposes, the deductions for the personal exemptions shall not be taken into account, but the special deductions described in paragraph (c) of § 1.861-8 shall be taken into account.

Example (1). Where the manufacturer or producer regularly sells part of his output to wholly independent distributors or other selling concerns in such a way as to establish fairly an independent factory or production price—or shows to the satisfaction of the district director (or, if applicable, the Director of International Operations) that such an independent factory or production price has been otherwise established—unaffected by considerations of tax liability, and the selling or distributing branch or department of the business is located in a different country from that in which the factory is located or the production carried on, the taxable income attributable to sources within the United States shall be computed by an accounting which treats the products as sold by the factory or productive department of the business to the distributing or selling department at the independent factory price so established. In all such cases the basis of the accounting shall be fully explained in a statement attached to the return for the taxable year.

Example (2). (i) and (ii) [Reserved] For guidance, see § 1.863-3T(b)(2) *Example* (2)(i) and (ii).

(iii) The term "gross sales", as used in this example, refers only to the sales of personal property produced (in whole or in part) by the taxpayer within the United States and sold within a foreign country or produced (in whole or in part) by the taxpayer within a foreign country and sold within the United States.

(iv) The term "property", as used in this example, includes only the property held or used to produce income which is derived from such sales. Such property should be taken at its actual value, which in the case of property valued or appraised for purposes of inventory, depreciation, depletion, or other purposes of taxation shall be the highest amount at which so valued or appraised, and which in other cases shall be deemed to be its book value in the absence of affirmative evidence showing such value to be greater or less than the actual value. The average value during the taxable year or period shall be employed. The average value of property as above prescribed at the beginning and end of the taxable year or period ordinarily may be used, unless by reason of material changes during the taxable year or period such average does not fairly represent the average for such year or period, in which event the average shall be determined upon a monthly or daily basis.

(v) Bills and accounts receivable shall (unless satisfactory reason for a different treatment is shown) be assigned or allocated to the United States when the debtor resides in the United States, unless the taxpayer has no office, branch, or agent in the United States.

Example (3). Application for permission to base the return upon the taxpayer's books of account will be considered by the district director (or, if applicable, the Director of International Operations) in the case of any taxpayer who, in good faith and unaffected by considerations of tax liability, regularly employs in his books of account a detailed allocation of receipts and expenditures which reflects more clearly than the processes or formula herein prescribed the taxable income derived from sources within the United States.

Reg. § 1.863-3A(b)(2)

Determination of Sources of Income

See p. 20,601 for regulations not amended to reflect law changes

→ *Caution: Reg. § 1.863-3 was redesignated as Reg. § 1.863-3A, below, by T.D. 8687 and applies to tax years beginning before December 30, 1996.* ←

(c) *Income partly from sources within a possession of the United States*—(1) *General.* This paragraph relates to gains, profits, and income which, pursuant to section 863(b), are treated as derived partly from sources within the United States and partly from sources within a possession of the United States. The items so treated are described in subparagraphs (3) and (4) of this paragraph.

(2) *Allocation or apportionment.* The taxable income from sources within the United States, in the case of the items to which this paragraph applies, shall be determined according to the examples set forth in subparagraphs (3) and (4) of this paragraph. For such purposes, the deductions for the personal exemptions shall not be taken into account, but the special deductions described in paragraph (c) of § 1.861-8 shall be taken into account.

(3) *Personal property produced and sold.* This subparagraph relates to gross income derived from the sale of personal property produced (in whole or in part) by the taxpayer within the United States and sold within a possession of the United States, or produced (in whole or in part) by the taxpayer within a possession of the United States and sold within the United States.

Example (1). Same as example (1) under paragraph (b)(2) of this section.

Example (2). (i) Where an independent factory or production price has not been established as provided under example (1), the taxable income shall first be computed by deducting from the gross income derived from the sale of personal property produced (in whole or in part) by the taxpayer within the United States and sold within a possession of the United States, or produced (in whole or in part) by the taxpayer within a possession of the United States and sold within the United States, the expenses, losses, or other deductions properly allocated and apportioned thereto in accordance with the rules set forth in § 1.861-8.

(ii) Of the amount of taxable income so determined, one-half shall be apportioned in accordance with the value of the taxpayer's property within the United States and within the possession of the United States, the portion attributable to sources within the United States being determined by multiplying such one-half by a fraction the numerator of which consists of the value of the taxpayer's property within the United States, and the denominator of which consists of the value of the taxpayer's property both within the United States and within the possession of the United States. The remaining one-half of such taxable income shall be apportioned in accordance with the total business of the taxpayer within the United States and within the possession of the United States, the portion attributable to sources within the United States being determined by multiplying such one-half by a fraction the numerator of which consists of the amount of the taxpayer's business for the taxable year or period within the United States, and the denominator of which consists of the amount of the taxpayer's business for the taxable year or period both within the United States and within the possession of the United States.

(iii) The "business of the taxpayer", as used in this example, shall be measured by the amounts which the taxpayer paid out during the taxable year or period for wages, salaries, and other compensation of employees and for the purchase of goods, materials, and supplies consumed in the regular course of business, plus the amounts received during the taxable year or period from gross sales, such expenses, purchases, and gross sales being limited to those attributable to the production (in whole or in part) of personal property within the United States and its sale within a possession of the United States or to the production (in whole or in part) of personal property within a possession of the United States and its sale within the United States. The term "property", as used in this example, includes only the property held or used to produce income which is derived from such sales.

Example (3). Same as example (3) under paragraph (b)(2) of this section.

(4) *Personal property purchased and sold.* This subparagraph relates to gross income derived from the purchase of personal property within a possession of the United States and its sale within the United States.

Example (1). (i) The taxable income shall first be computed by deducting from such gross income the expenses, losses, or other deductions properly allocated or apportioned thereto in accordance with the rules set forth in § 1.861-8.

(ii) The amount of taxable income so determined shall be apportioned in accordance with the total business of the taxpayer within the United States and within the possession of the United States, the portion attributable to sources within the United States being that percentage of such taxable income which the amount of the taxpayer's business for the taxable year or period within the United States bears to the amount of the taxpayer's business for the taxable year or

Reg. § 1.863-3A(c)(1)

Determination of Sources of Income

See p. 20,601 for regulations not amended to reflect law changes

→ *Caution: Reg. § 1.863-3 was redesignated as Reg. § 1.863-3A, below, by T.D. 8687 and applies to tax years beginning before December 30, 1996.*←

period both within the United States and within the possession of the United States.

(iii) The "business of the taxpayer", as that term is used in this example, shall be measured by the amounts which the taxpayer paid out during the taxable year or period for wages, salaries, and other compensation of employees and for the purchase of goods, materials, and supplies sold or consumed in the regular course of business, plus the amount received during the taxable year or period from gross sales, such expenses, purchases, and gross sales being limited to those attributable to the purchase of personal property within a possession of the United States and its sale within the United States.

Example (2). Same as example (3) under paragraph (b)(2) of this section. [Reg. § 1.863-3A.]

☐ [*T.D.* 6258, 10-23-57. Amended by *T.D.* 7456, 1-3-77 *and T.D.* 8228, 9-9-88. Redesignated by *T.D.* 8687, 11-27-96.]

→ *Caution: Temporary Reg. § 1.863-3T was redesignated as Temporary Reg. § 1.863-3AT, below, by T.D. 8687 and applies to tax years beginning before December 30, 1996.*←

[Reg. § 1.863-3AT]

§ 1.863-3AT. **Income from the sale of personal property derived partly from within and partly from without the United States (Temporary regulations).**—(a) and (b)(1) [Reserved]

(b) *Income partly from sources within a foreign country.*

* * *

(2) *Allocation or apportionment.*

Example (1) [Reserved]

Example (2). (i) Where an independent factory or production price has not been established as provided under *Example* (1), the gross income derived from the sale of personal property produced (in whole or in part) by the taxpayer within the United States and sold within a foreign country or produced (in whole or in part) by the taxpayer within a foreign country and sold within the United States shall be computed.

(ii) Of this gross amount, one-half shall be apportioned in accordance with the value of the taxpayer's property within the United States and within the foreign country, the portion attributable to sources within the United States being determined by multiplying such one-half by a fraction, the numerator of which consists of the value of the taxpayer's property within the United States and the denominator of which consists of the value of the taxpayer's property both within the United States and within the foreign country. The remaining one-half of such gross income shall be apportioned in accordance with the gross sales of the taxpayer within the United States and within the foreign country, the portion attributable to sources within the United States being determined by multiplying such one-half by a fraction the numerator of which consists of the taxpayer's gross sales for the taxable year or period within the United States, and the denominator of which consists of the taxpayer's gross sales for the taxable year or period both within the United States and within the foreign country. Deductions from gross income that are allocable and apportionable to gross income described in paragraph (i) of this *Example* (2) shall be apportioned between the United States and foreign source portions of such income, as determined under this paragraph (ii), on a pro rata basis, without regard to whether the deduction relates primarily or exclusively to the production of property or to the sale of property.

(b)(2) *Example* (2)(iii) through (c)(4) [Reserved] [Temporary Reg. § 1.863-3AT.]

☐ [*T.D.* 8228, 9-9-88. Redesignated by *T.D.* 8687, 11-27-96.]

[Reg. § 1.863-4]

§ 1.863-4. **Certain transportation services.**—(a) *General.* A taxpayer carrying on the business of transportation service (other than an activity giving rise to transportation income described in section 863(c) or to income subject to other specific provisions of this title) between points in the United States and points outside the United States derives income partly from sources within and partly from sources without the United States.

(b) *Gross income.* The gross income from sources within the United States derived from such services shall be determined by taking such a portion of the total gross revenues therefrom as (1) the sum of the costs or expenses of such transportation business carried on by the taxpayer within the United States and a reasonable return upon the property used in its transportation business while within the United States bears to (2) the sum of the total costs or expenses of such

Reg. § 1.863-4(b)

transportation business carried on by the taxpayer and a reasonable return upon the total property used in such transportation business. Revenues from operations incidental to transportation services, such as the sale of money orders, shall be apportioned on the same basis as direct revenues from transportation services.

(c) *Allocation of costs or expenses.* In allocating the total costs or expenses incurred in such transportation business, costs or expenses incurred in connection with that part of the services which was wholly rendered in the United States shall be assigned to the cost of transportation business within the United States. For example, expenses of loading and unloading in the United States, rentals, office expenses, salaries, and wages wholly incurred for services rendered to the taxpayer in the United States belong to this class. Costs and expenses incurred in connection with services rendered partly within and partly without the United States may be prorated on a reasonable basis between such services. For example, ship wages, charter money, insurance, and supplies chargeable to voyage expenses shall ordinarily be prorated for each voyage on the basis of the proportion which the number of days the ship was within the territorial limits of the United States bears to the total number of days on the voyage; and fuel consumed on each voyage may be prorated on the basis of the proportion which the number of miles sailed within the territorial limits of the United States bears to the total number of miles sailed on the voyage. For other expenses entering into the cost of services, only such expenses as are allowable deductions under the internal revenue laws shall be taken into account.

(d) *Items not included as costs or expenses*—(1) *Taxes and interest.* Income, war profits, and excess profits taxes shall not be regarded as costs or expenses for the purpose of determining the proportion of gross income from sources within the United States; and, for such purpose, interest and other expenses for the use of borrowed capital shall not be taken into the cost of services rendered, for the reason that the return upon the property used measures the extent to which such borrowed capital is the source of the income. See paragraph (f)(2) of this section.

(2) *Other business activity and general expenses.* If a taxpayer subject to this section is also engaged in a business other than that of providing transportation service between points in the United States and points outside the United States, the costs and expenses, including taxes, properly apportioned or allocated to such other business shall be excluded both from the deductions and from the apportionment process prescribed in paragraph (c) of this section; but, for the purpose of determining taxable income, a ratable part of any general expenses, losses, or deductions, which cannot definitely be allocated to some item or class of gross income, may be deducted from the gross income from sources within the United States after the amount of such gross income has been determined. Such ratable part shall ordinarily be based upon the ratio of gross income from sources within the United States to the total gross income. See paragraph (f)(3) of this section.

(3) *Personal exemptions and special deductions.* The deductions for the personal exemptions, and the special deductions described in paragraph (c) of § 1.861-8, shall not be taken into account for purposes of paragraph (c) of this section.

(e) *Property used while within the United States*—(1) *General.* The value of the property used shall be determined upon the basis of cost less depreciation. Eight percent may ordinarily be taken as a reasonable rate of return to apply to such property. The property taken shall be the average property employed in the transportation service between points in the United States and points outside the United States during the taxable year.

(2) *Average property.* For ships, the average shall be determined upon a daily basis for each ship, and the amount to be apportioned for each ship as assets employed within the United States shall be computed upon the proportion which the number of days the ship was within the territorial limits of the United States bears to the total number of days the ship was in service during the taxable period. For other assets employed in the transportation business, the average of the assets at the beginning and end of the taxable period ordinarily may be taken, but if the average so obtained does not, by reason of material changes during the taxable year, fairly represent the average for such year either for the assets employed in the transportation business in the United States or in total, the average must be determined upon a monthly or daily basis.

(3) *Current assets.* Current assets shall be decreased by current liabilities and allocated to services between the United States and foreign countries and to other services. The part allocated to services between the United States and foreign countries shall be based on the proportion which the gross receipts from such services bear to the gross receipts from all services. The amount so allocated to services between the United States and foreign countries shall be further allocated to services rendered within the United States and to services rendered without the United States. The

Reg. § 1.863-4(c)

portion allocable to services rendered within the United States shall be based on the proportion which the expenses incurred within the territorial limits of the United States bear to the total expenses incurred in services between the United States and foreign countries.

(f) *Taxable income*—(1) *General.* In computing taxable income from sources within the United States there shall be allowed as deductions from the gross income from such sources, determined in accordance with paragraph (b) of this section, (i) the expenses of the transportation business carried on within the United States (as determined under paragraphs (c) and (d) of this section) and (ii) the expenses and deductions determined in accordance with this paragraph.

(2) *Interest and taxes.* Interest and income, war-profits, and excess profits taxes shall be excluded from the apportionment process, as indicated in paragraph (d) of this section; but, for the purpose of computing taxable income, there may be deducted from the gross income from sources within the United States, after the amount of such gross income has been determined, a ratable part of all interest deductible under section 163 and of all income, war-profits, and excess profits taxes deductible under section 164, paid or accrued in respect of the business of transportation service between points in the United States and points outside the United States. The ratable part shall ordinarily be based upon the ratio of gross income from sources within the United States to the total gross income, from such transportation service.

(3) *General expenses.* General expenses, losses, or deductions shall be deducted under this paragraph to the extent indicated in paragraph (d)(2) of this section.

(4) *Personal exemptions.* The deductions for the personal exemptions shall be allowed under this paragraph to the same extent as provided by paragraph (b) of § 1.861-8.

(5) *Special deductions.* The special deductions allowed in the case of a corporation by sections 241, 922, and 941 shall be allowed under this paragraph to the same extent as provided by paragraph (c) of § 1.861-8.

(g) *Allocation based on books of account.* Application for permission to base the return upon the taxpayer's books of account will be considered by the district director (or, if applicable, the Director of International Operations) in the case of any taxpayer subject to this section, who, in good faith and unaffected by considerations of tax liability, regularly employs in his books of account a detailed allocation of receipts and expenditures which more clearly reflects the income derived from sources within the United States than does the process prescribed by paragraphs (b) to (f), inclusive, of this section. [Reg. § 1.863-4.]

☐ [T.D. 6258, 10-23-57. Amended by T.D. 8687, 11-27-96.]

[Reg. § 1.863-6]

§ 1.863-6. Income from sources within a foreign country or possession of the United States.—The principles applied in §§ 1.861-1 to 1.863-5, inclusive, for determining the gross and the taxable income from sources within and without the United States shall generally be applied, for purposes of the income tax, in determining the gross and the taxable income from sources within and without a foreign country, or within and without a possession of the United States. This section shall not apply, however, to the extent it is determined by applying § 1.863-3 that a portion of the taxable income is from sources within the United States and the balance of the taxable income is from sources within a foreign country or possession of the United States. In the application of this section the name of the particular foreign country or possession of the United States shall be substituted for the term "United States," and the term "domestic" shall be construed to mean created or organized in such foreign country or possession. In applying section 861 and the regulations thereunder for purposes of this section, references to sections 243, 245, and 931 shall be excluded, and the exception in section 861(a)(3) shall not apply. In the case of any item of income, the income from sources wtihin a foreign country or possession of the United States shall not exceed the amount which, by applying any provision of §§ 1.861-1 to 1.863-5, inclusive, without reference to this section, is treated as income from sources without the United States. [Reg. § 1.863-6.]

☐ [T.D. 6258, 10-23-57. Amended by T.D. 7378, 9-29-75.]

[Reg. § 1.863-7]

§ 1.863-7. Allocation of income attributable to certain notional principal contracts under section 863(a).—(a) *Scope*—(1) *Introduction.* This section provides rules relating to the source and, in certain cases, the character of notional principal contract income. However, this section does not apply to income from a section 988 transaction within the meaning of section 988 and the regulations thereunder, relating to the treatment of certain nonfunctional currency transactions. Notional principal contract income is income attributable to a notional principal contract. A notional principal contract is a financial instrument that provides for the payment of amounts by one party to another at specified intervals calculated by reference to a specified index upon a notional principal amount in exchange for specified consideration or a promise to pay similar amounts. An agreement between a taxpayer and a qualified business unit (as defined in section 989(a)) of the taxpayer, or among qualified business units of the same taxpayer, is not a notional principal contract, because a taxpayer cannot enter into a contract with itself.

(2) *Effective date.* This section applies to notional principal contract income includible in income on or after February 13, 1991. However, any taxpayer desiring to apply paragraph (b)(2)(iv) of this section to notional principal contract income includible in income prior to February 13, 1991 in lieu of temporary Income Tax Regulations § 1.863-7T(b)(2)(iv) may (on a consistent basis) so choose. See paragraph (c) of this section for an election to apply the rules of this section to notional principal contract income includible in income before December 24, 1986.

(b) *Source of notional principal contract income*—(1) *General rule.* Unless paragraph (b)(2) or (3) of this section applies, the source of notional principal contract income shall be determined by reference to the residence of the taxpayer as determined under section 988(a)(3)(B)(i).

(2) *Qualified business unit exception.* The source of notional principal contract income shall be determined by reference to the residence of a qualified business unit of a taxpayer if—

(i) The taxpayer's residence, determined under section 988(a)(3)(B)(i), is the United States;

(ii) The qualified business unit's residence, determined under section 988(a)(3)(B)(ii), is outside the United States;

(iii) The qualified business unit is engaged in the conduct of a trade or business where it is a resident as determined under section 988(a)(3)(B)(ii); and

(iv) The notional principal contract is properly reflected on the books of the qualified business unit. Whether a notional principal contract is properly reflected on the books of such qualified business unit is a question of fact. The degree of participation in the negotiation and acquisition of a notional principal contract shall be considered in this determination. Participation in connection with the negotiation or acquisition of a notional principal contract may be disregarded if the district director determines that a purpose for such participation was to affect the source of notional principal contract income.

(3) *Effectively connected notional principal contract income.* Notional principal contract income that under principles similar to those set forth in § 1.864-4(c) arises from the conduct of a United States trade or business shall be sourced in the United States and such income shall be treated as effectively connected to the conduct of a United States trade or business for purposes of sections 871(b) and 882(a)(1).

(c) *Election*—(1) *Eligibility and effect.* A taxpayer described in paragraph (b)(2)(i) of this section may make an election to apply the rules of this section to all, but not part, of the taxpayer's income attributable to notional principal contracts for all taxable years (or portion thereof) beginning before December 24, 1986, for which the period of limitations for filing a claim for refund under section 6511(a) has not expired. A taxpayer not described in paragraph (b)(2)(i) of this section that is engaged in trade or business within the United States may make an election to apply the rules of this section to all, but not part, of the taxpayer's income described in paragraph (b)(3) of this section for all taxable years (or portion thereof) beginning before December 24, 1986, for which the period of limitations for filing a claim for refund under section 6511(a) has not expired. If a taxpayer makes an election pursuant to this paragraph (c)(1) in the time and manner provided in paragraph (c)(2) and (3) of this section, then, with respect to such taxable years (or portion thereof), no tax shall be deducted or withheld under sections 1441 and 1442 with respect to payments made by the taxpayer pursuant to a notional principal contract the income attributable to which is subject to such election. The election may be revoked only with the consent of the Commissioner.

(2) *Time for making election.* The election specified in paragraph (c)(1) of this section shall be made by May 15, 1991.

(3) *Manner of making election.* The election described in paragraph (c)(1) of this section shall be made by attaching a statement to the tax return or an amended tax return for each taxable year beginning before December 24, 1986, in which the taxpayer accrued or received notional principal contract income. The statement shall—

(i) Contain the name, address, and taxpayer identifying number of the electing taxpayer;

(ii) Identify the election as a "Notional Principal Contract Election under § 1.863-7"; and

(iii) Specify each taxable year described in paragraph (c)(1) of this section in which payments were made.

Reg. § 1.863-7(a)(2)

Determination of Sources of Income

See p. 20,601 for regulations not amended to reflect law changes

(d) *Example.* The operation of this section is illustrated by the following example:

(1) On January 1, 1990, X, a calendar year domestic corporation, entered into an interest rate swap contract with FZ, an unrelated foreign corporation. X does not have a qualified business unit outside the United States. Under the contract, X is required to pay FZ fixed rate dollar amounts, and FZ is required to pay X floating rate dollar amounts, each determined solely by reference to a notional dollar denominated principal amount specified under the contract. The contract is a notional principal contract under § 1.863-7(a) because the contract provides for the payment of amounts at specified intervals calculated by reference to a specified index upon a notional principal amount in exchange for a promise to pay similar amounts.

(2) Assume that during 1990 X had notional principal contract income of $100 in connection with the notional principal contract described in (1) above. Also assume that the contract provides that payments more than 30 days late give rise to a $5 fee, and that X receives such a fee in 1990. Under paragraph (b)(1) of this section, the source of X's $100 of income attributable to the swap agreement is domestic. The $5 fee is not notional principal contract income.

(e) *Cross References.* See § 1.861-9T(b) for the allocation of expense to certain notional principal contracts. For rules relating to the source of income from nonfunctional currency notional principal contracts, see § 1.988-4T. For rules relating to the taxable amount of notional principal contract income allocable under this section to sources inside or outside the United States, see § 1.863-1(c). [Reg. § 1.863-7.]

☐ [*T.D.* 8330, 1-11-91.]

[Reg. § 1.864-1]

§ 1.864-1. **Meaning of sale, etc.**—For purposes of §§ 1.861 through 1.864-7, the word "sale" includes "exchange"; the word "sold" includes "exchanged"; and the word "produced" includes "created", "fabricated", "manufactured", "extracted", "processed", "cured", and "aged". [Reg. § 1.864-1.]

☐ [*T.D.* 6948, 3-27-68.]

[Reg. § 1.864-2]

§ 1.864-2. **Trade or business within the United States.**—(a) *In general.* As used in part I (section 861 and following) and part II (section 871 and following), subchapter N, chapter 1 of the Code, and chapter 3 (section 1441 and following) of the Code, and the regulations thereunder, the term "engaged in trade or business within the United States" does not include the activities described in paragraphs (c) and (d) of this section, but includes the performance of personal services within the United States at any time within the taxable year except to the extent otherwise provided in this section.

(b) *Performance of personal services for foreign employer*—(1) *Excepted services.* For purposes of paragraph (a) of this section, the term "engaged in trade or business within the United States" does not include the performance of personal services—

(i) For a nonresident alien individual, foreign partnership, or foreign corporation, not engaged in trade or business within the United States at any time during the taxable year, or

(ii) For an office or place of business maintained in a foreign country or in a possession of the United States by an individual who is a citizen or resident of the United States or by a domestic partnership or a domestic corporation,

by a nonresident alien individual who is temporarily present in the United States for a period or periods not exceeding a total of 90 days during the taxable year and whose compensation for such services does not exceed in the aggregate a gross amount of $3,000.

(2) *Rules of application.* (i) As a general rule, the term "day", as used in subparagraph (1) of this paragraph, means a calendar day during any portion of which the nonresident alien individual is physically present in the United States.

(ii) Solely for purposes of applying this paragraph, the nonresident alien individual, foreign partnership, or foreign corporation for which the nonresident alien individual is performing personal services in the United States shall not be considered to be engaged in trade or business in the United States by reason of the performance of such services by such individual.

(iii) In applying subparagraph (1) of this paragraph it is immaterial whether the services performed by the nonresident alien individual are performed as an employee for his employer or under any form of contract with the person for whom the services are performed.

(iv) In determining for purposes of subparagraph (1) of this paragraph whether compensation received by the nonresident alien individual exceeds in the aggregate a gross amount of $3,000, any amounts received by the individual from an employer as advances or reimbursements for travel expenses incurred on behalf of the employer shall be omitted from the compensation received by the individual, to the extent of expenses incurred, where he was required to account and did

Reg. § 1.864-2(b)(2)

account to his employer for such expenses and has met the tests for such accounting provided in § 1.162-17 and paragraph (e)(4) of § 1.274-5. If advances or reimbursements exceed such expenses, the amount of the excess shall be included as compensation for personal services for purposes of such subparagraph. Pensions and retirement pay attributable to personal services performed in the United States are not to be taken into account for purposes of subparagraph (1) of this paragraph.

(v) See section 7701(a)(5) and § 301.7701-5 of this chapter (Procedure and Administration Regulations) for the meaning of "foreign" when applied to a corporation or partnership.

(vi) As to the source of compensation for personal services, see §§ 1.861-4 and 1.862-1.

(3) *Illustrations.* The application of this paragraph may be illustrated by the following examples:

Example (1). During 1967, A, a nonresident alien individual, is employed by the London office of a domestic partnership. A, who uses the calendar year as his taxable year, is temporarily present in the United States during 1967 for 60 days performing personal service in the United States for the London office of the partnership and is paid by that office a total gross salary of $2,600 for such services. During 1967, A is not engaged in trade or business in the United States solely by reason of his performing such personal services for the London office of the domestic partnership.

Example (2). The facts are the same as in example (1), except that A's total gross salary for the services performed in the United States during 1967 amounts to $3,500, of which $2,625 is received in 1967 and $875 is received in 1968. During 1967, A is engaged in trade or business in the United States by reason of his performance of personal services in the United States.

(c) *Trading in stocks or securities.* For purposes of paragraph (a) of this section—

(1) *In general.* The term "engaged in trade or business within the United States" does not include the effecting of transactions in the United States in stocks or securities through a resident broker, commission agent, custodian, or other independent agent. This subparagraph shall apply to any taxpayer, including a broker or dealer in stocks or securities, except that it shall not apply if at any time during the taxable year the taxpayer has an office or other fixed place of business in the United States through which, or by the direction of which, the transactions in stocks or securities are effected. The volume of stock or security transactions effected during the taxable year shall not be taken into account in determining under this subparagraph whether the taxpayer is engaged in trade or business within the United States.

(2) *Trading for taxpayer's own account.*—(i) *In general.* The term "engaged in trade or business within the United States" does not include the effecting of transactions in the United States in stocks or securities for the taxpayer's own account, irrespective of whether such transactions are effected by or through—

(a) The taxpayer himself while present in the United States,

(b) Employees of the taxpayer, whether or not such employees are present in the United States while effecting the transactions, or

(c) A broker, commission agent, custodian, or other agent of the taxpayer, whether or not such agent while effecting the transactions is (1) dependent or independent, or (2) resident, nonresident, or present, in the United States,

and irrespective of whether any such employee or agent has discretionary authority to make decisions in effecting such transactions. For purposes of this paragraph, the term "securities" means any note, bond, debenture, or other evidence of indebtedness, or any evidence of an interest in or right to subscribe to or purchase any of the foregoing; and the effecting of transactions in stocks or securities includes buying, selling (whether or not by entering into short sales), or trading in stocks, securities, or contracts or options to buy or sell stocks or securities, on margin or otherwise, for the account and risk of the taxpayer, and any other activity closely related thereto (such as obtaining credit for the purpose of effectuating such buying, selling, or trading). The volume of stock or security transactions effected during the taxable year shall not be taken into account in determining under this subparagraph whether the taxpayer is engaged in trade or business within the United States. The application of this subdivision may be illustrated by the following example:

Example. A, a nonresident alien individual who is not a dealer in stocks or securities, authorizes B, an individual resident of the United States, as his agent to effect transactions in the United States in stocks and securities for the account of A. B is empowered with complete authority to trade in stocks and securities for the account of A and to use his own discretion as to when to buy or sell for A's account. This grant of discretionary authority from A to B is also communicated in writing by A to various domestic brokerage firms through which A ordinarily effects transactions in the United States in stocks or securities. Under the agency arrangement B has

Reg. § 1.864-2(b)(3)

the authority to place orders with the brokers, and all confirmations are to be made by the brokers to B, subject to his approval. The brokers are authorized by A to make payments to B and to charge such payments to the account of A. In addition, B is authorized to obtain and advance the necessary funds, if any, to maintain credits with the brokerage firms. Pursuant to his authority B carries on extensive trading transactions in the United States during the taxable year through the various brokerage firms for the account of A. During the taxable year A makes several visits to the United States in order to discuss with B various aspects of his trading activities and to make necessary changes in his trading policy. A is not engaged in trade or business within the United States during the taxable year solely because of the effecting by B of transactions in the United States in stocks or securities during such year for the account of A.

(ii) *Partnerships.* A nonresident alien individual, foreign partnership, foreign estate, foreign trust, or foreign corporation shall not be considered to be engaged in trade or business within the United States solely because such person is a member of a partnership (whether domestic or foreign) which, pursuant to discretionary authority granted to such partnership by such person, effects transactions in the United States in stock or securities for the partnership's own account or solely because an employee of such partnership, or a broker, commission agent, custodian, or other agent, pursuant to discretionary authority granted by such partnership, effects transactions in the United States in stocks or securities for the account of such partnership. This subdivision shall not apply, however, to any member of *(a)* a partnership which is a dealer in stocks or securities or *(b)* a partnership (other than a partnership in which, at any time during the last half of its taxable year, more than 50 percent of either the capital interest or the profits interest is owned, directly or indirectly, by five or fewer partners who are individuals) the principal business of which is trading in stocks or securities for its own account, if the principal office of such partnership is in the United States at any time during the taxable year. The principles of subdivision (iii) of this subparagraph for determining whether a foreign corporation has its principal office in the United States shall apply in determining under this subdivision whether a partnership has its principal office in the United States. See section 707(b)(3) and paragraph (b)(3) of § 1.707-1 for rules for determining the extent of the ownership by a partner of a capital interest or profits interest in a partnership. The application of this subdivision may be illustrated by the following examples:

Example (1). B, a nonresident alien individual, is a member of partnership X, the members of which are U.S. citizens, nonresident alien individuals, and foreign corporations. The principal business of partnership X is trading in stocks or securities for its own account. Pursuant to discretionary authority granted by B, partnership X effects transactions in the United States in stock or securities for its own account. Partnership X is not a dealer in stocks or securities, and more than 50 percent of either the capital interest or the profits interest in partnership X is owned throughout its taxable year by five or fewer partners who are individuals. B is not engaged in trade or business within the United States solely by reason of such effecting of transactions in the United States in stocks or securities by partnership X for its own account.

Example (2). The facts are the same as in example (1), except that not more than 50 percent of either the capital interest or the profits interest in partnership X is owned throughout the taxable year by five or fewer partners who are individuals. However, partnership X does not maintain its principal office in the United States at any time during the taxable year. B is not engaged in trade or business within the United States solely by reason of the trading in stocks or securities by partnership X for its own account.

Example (3). The facts are the same as in example (1), except that, pursuant to discretionary authority granted by partnership X, domestic broker D effects transactions in the United States in stocks or securities for the account of partnership X. B is not engaged in trade or business in the United States solely by reason of such trading in stocks or securities for the account of partnership X.

(iii) *Dealers in stocks or securities and certain foreign corporations.* This subparagraph shall not apply to the effecting of transactions in the United States for the account of *(a)* a dealer in stocks or securities or *(b)* a foreign corporation (other than a corporation which is, or but for section 542(c)(7) or 543(b)(1)(C) would be, a personal holding company) the principal business of which is trading in stocks or securities for its own account, if the principal office of such corporation is in the United States at any time during the taxable year. Whether a foreign corporation's principal office is in the United States for this purpose is to be determined by comparing the activities (other than trading in stocks or securities) which the corporation conducts from its office or other fixed place of business located in the

Reg. § 1.864-2(c)(2)

United States with the activities it conducts from its offices or other fixed places of business located outside the United States. For purposes of this subdivision, a foreign corporation is considered to have only one principal office, and an office of such corporation will not be considered to be its principal office merely because it is a statutory office of such corporation. For example, a foreign corporation which carries on most or all of its investment activities in the United States but maintains a general business office or offices outside the United States in which its management is located will not be considered as having its principal office in the United States if all or a substantial portion of the following functions is carried on at or from an office or offices located outside the United States:

(1) Communicating with its shareholders (including the furnishing of financial reports),

(2) Communicating with the general public,

(3) Soliciting sales of its own stock,

(4) Accepting the subscriptions of new stockholders,

(5) Maintaining its principal corporate records and books of account,

(6) Auditing its books of account,

(7) Disbursing payments of dividends, legal fees, accounting fees, and officers' and directors' salaries,

(8) Publishing or furnishing the offering and redemption price of the shares of stock issued by it,

(9) Conducting meetings of its shareholders and board of directors, and

(10) Making redemptions of its own stock.

The application of this subdivision may be illustrated by the following examples:

Example (1). (a) Foreign corporation X (not a corporation which is, or but for section 542(c)(7) or 543(b)(1)(C) would be, a personal holding company) was organized to sell its shares to nonresident alien individuals and foreign corporations and to invest the proceeds from the sale of such shares in stocks or securities in the United States. Foreign corporation X is engaged primarily in the business of investing, reinvesting, and trading in stocks or securities for its own account.

(b) For a period of three years, foreign corporation X irrevocably authorizes domestic corporation Y to exercise its discretion in effecting transactions in the United States in stocks or securities for the account and risk of foreign corporation X. Foreign corporation X issues a prospectus in which it is stated that its funds will be invested pursuant to an investment advisory contract with domestic corporation Y and otherwise advertises its services. Shares of foreign corporation X are sold to nonresident aliens and foreign corporations who are customers of United States brokerage firms unrelated to domestic corporation Y or foreign corporation X. The principal functions performed for foreign corporation X by domestic corporation Y are the rendering of investment advice and the effecting of transactions in the United States in stocks or securities for the account of foreign corporation X. Moreover, domestic corporation Y occasionally communicates with prospective foreign investors in foreign corporation X (through speaking engagements abroad by management of domestic corporation Y, and otherwise) for the purpose of explaining the investment techniques and policies used by domestic corporation Y in investing the funds of foreign corporation X. However, domestic corporation Y does not participate in the day-to-day conduct of other business activities of foreign corporation X.

(c) Foreign corporation X maintains a general business office or offices outside the United States in which its management is permanently located and from which it carries on, except to the extent noted heretofore, the functions enumerated in (b)(1) through (10) of this subdivision. The management of foreign corporation X at all times retains the independent power to cancel the investment advisory contract with domestic corporation Y subject to the contractual limitations contained therein and is in all other respects independent of the management of domestic corporation Y. The managing personnel of foreign corporation X communicate on a regular basis with domestic corporation Y, and periodically visit the offices of domestic corporation Y, in connection with the business activities of foreign corporation X.

(d) The principal office of foreign corporation X will not be considered to be in the United States; and, therefore, foreign corporation X is not engaged in trade or business within the United States solely by reason of its relationship with domestic corporation Y.

Example (2). The facts are the same as in example (1) except that, in lieu of having the investment advisory contract with domestic corporation Y, foreign corporation X has an office in the United States in which its employees perform the same functions as are performed by domestic corporation Y in example (1). Foreign corporation X is not engaged in trade or business within the United States during the taxable year solely be-

Reg. § 1.864-2(c)(2)

Determination of Sources of Income

cause the employees located in its United States office effect transactions in the United States in stocks or securities for the account of that corporation.

(iv) *Definition of dealer in stocks or securities*—*(a) In general.* For purposes of this subparagraph, a dealer in stocks or securities is a merchant of stocks or securities, with an established place of business, regularly engaged as a merchant in purchasing stocks or securities and selling them to customers with a view to the gains and profits that may be derived therefrom. Persons who buy and sell, or hold, stocks or securities for investment or speculation, irrespective of whether such buying or selling constitutes the carrying on of a trade or business, and officers of corporations, members of partnerships, or fiduciaries, who in their individual capacities buy and sell, or hold, stocks or securities for investment or speculation are not dealers in stocks or securities within the meaning of this subparagraph solely by reason of that activity. In determining under this subdivision whether a person is a dealer in stocks or securities such person's transactions in stocks or securities effected both in and outside the United States shall be taken into account.

(b) Underwriting syndicates and dealers trading for others. A foreign person who otherwise may be considered a dealer in stocks or securities under *(a)* of this subdivision shall not be considered a dealer in stocks or securities for purposes of this subparagraph—

(1) Solely because he acts as an underwriter, or as a selling group member, for the purpose of making a distribution of stocks or securities of a domestic issuer to foreign purchasers of such stocks or securities, irrespective of whether other members of the selling group distribute the stocks or securities of the domestic issuer to domestic purchasers, or

(2) Solely because of transactions effected in the United States in stocks or securities pursuant to his grant of discretionary authority to make decisions in effecting those transactions, if he can demonstrate to the satisfaction of the Commissioner that the broker, commission agent, custodian, or other agent through whom the transactions were effected acted pursuant to his written representation that the funds in respect of which such discretion was granted were the funds of a customer who is neither a dealer in stocks or securities, a partnership described in subdivision (ii)*(b)* of this subparagraph, or a foreign corporation described in subdivision (iii)*(b)* of this subparagraph.

For purposes of this *(b)*, a foreign person includes a nonresident alien individual, a foreign corporation, or a partnership any member of which is a nonresident alien individual or a foreign corporation. This *(b)* shall apply only if the foreign person at no time during the taxable year has an office or other fixed place of business in the United States through which, or by the direction of which, the transaction in stocks or securities are effected.

(c) Illustrations. The application of this subdivision may be illustrated by the following examples:

Example (1). Foreign corporation X is a member of an underwriting syndicate organized to distribute stock issued by domestic corporation Y. Foreign corporation X distributes the stock of domestic corporation Y to foreign purchasers only. Domestic corporation M is syndicate manager of the underwriting syndicate and, pursuant to the terms of the underwriting agreement, reserves the right to sell certain quantities of the underwritten stock on behalf of all the members of the syndicate so as to engage in stabilizing transactions and to take certain other actions which may result in the realization of profit by all members of the underwriting syndicate. Foreign corporation X is not engaged in trade or business within the United States solely by reason of its participation as a member of such underwriting syndicate for the purpose of distributing the stock of domestic corporation Y to foreign purchasers or by reason of the exercise by M corporation of its discretionary authority as manager of such syndicate.

Example (2). Foreign corporation Y, a calendar year taxpayer, is a bank which trades in stocks or securities both for its own account and for the account of others. During 1967 foreign corporation Y authorizes domestic corporation M, a broker, to exercise its discretion in effecting transactions in the United States in stocks or securities for the account of B, a nonresident alien individual who has a trading account with foreign corporation Y. Foreign corporation Y furnishes a written representation to domestic corporation M to the effect that the funds in respect of which foreign corporation Y has authorized domestic corporation M to use its discretion in trading in the United States in stocks or securities are not funds in respect of which foreign corporation Y is trading for its own account but are the funds of one of its customers who is neither a dealer in stocks or securities, a partnership described in subdivision (ii)*(b)* of this subparagraph, or a foreign corporation described in subdivision (iii)*(b)* of this subparagraph. Pursuant to the discretionary authority so granted, domestic corporation M effects transactions in the United States during 1967 in stocks or securities for the account of the customer of foreign corporation Y. At no time

Reg. § 1.864-2(c)(2)

during 1967 does foreign corporation Y have an office or other fixed place of business in the United States through which, or by the direction of which, such transactions in stocks or securities are effected by domestic corportion M. During 1967 foreign corporation Y is not engaged in trade or business within the United States solely by reason of such trading in stocks or securities during such year by domestic corporation M for the account of the customer of foreign corporation Y. Copies of the written representations furnished to domestic corporation M should be retained by foreign corporation Y for inspection by the Commissioner, if inspection is requested.

(d) *Trading in commodities.* For purposes of paragraph (a) of this section—

(1) *In general.* The term "engaged in trade or business within the United States" does not include the effecting of transactions in the United States in commodities (including hedging transactions) through a resident broker, commission agent, custodian, or other independent agent if (i) the commodities are of a kind customarily dealt in on an organized commodity exchange, such as a grain futures or a cotton futures market, (ii) the transaction is of a kind customarily consummated at such place, and (iii) the taxpayer at no time during the taxable year has an office or other fixed place of business in the United States through which, or by the direction of which, the transactions in commodities are effected. The volume of commodity transactions effected during the taxable year shall not be taken into account in determining under this subparagraph whether the taxpayer is engaged in trade or business within the United States.

(2) *Trading for taxpayer's own account* —(i) *In general.* The term "engaged in trade or business within the United States" does not include the effecting of transactions in the United States in commodities (including hedging transactions) for the taxpayer's own account if the commodities are of a kind customarily dealt in on an organized commodity exchange and if the transaction is of a kind customarily consummated at such place. This rule shall apply irrespective of whether such transactions are effected by or through—

(*a*) The taxpayer himself while present in the United States,

(*b*) Employees of the taxpayer, whether or not such employees are present in the United States while effecting the transactions, or

(*c*) A broker, commission agent, custodian, or other agent of the taxpayer, whether or not such agent while effecting the transactions is (*1*) dependent or independent, or (*2*) resident, nonresident, or present, in the United States,

and irrespective of whether any such employee or agent has discretionary authority to make decisions in effecting such transactions. The volume of commodity transactions effected during the taxable year shall not be taken into account in determining under this subparagraph whether the taxpayer is engaged in trade or business within the United States. This subparagraph shall not apply to the effecting of transactions in the United States for the account of a dealer in commodities.

(ii) *Partnerships.* A nonresident alien individual, foreign partnership, foreign estate, foreign trust, or foreign corporation shall not be considered to be engaged in trade or business within the United States solely because such person is a member of a partnership (whether domestic or foreign) which, pursuant to discretionary authority granted to such partnership by such person, effects transactions in the United States in commodities for the partnership's account or solely because an employee of such partnership, or a broker, commission agent, custodian, or other agent, pursuant to discretionary authority granted by such partnership, effects transactions in the United States in commodities for the account of such partnership. This subdivision shall not apply to any member of a partnership which is a dealer in commodities.

(iii) *Illustration.* The application of this subparagraph may be illustrated by the following example:

Example. Foreign corporation X, a calendar year taxpayer, is engaged as a merchant in the business of purchasing grain in South America and selling such cash grain outside the United States under long-term contracts for delivery in foreign countries. Foreign corporation X consummates a sale of 100,000 bushels of cash grain in February 1967 for July delivery to Sweden. Because foreign corporation X does not actually own such grain at the time of the sales transaction, such corporation buys as a hedge a July "futures contract" for delivery of 100,000 bushels of grain, in order to protect itself from loss by reason of a possible rise in the price of grain between February and July. The "futures contract" is ordered through domestic corporation Y, a futures commission merchant registered under the Commodity Exchange Act. Foreign corporation X is not engaged in trade or business within the United States during 1967 solely by reason of its effecting of such futures contract for its own account through domestic corporation Y.

(3) *Definition of commodity.* For purposes of section 864(b)(2)(B) and this paragraph the term

Reg. § 1.864-2(d)(1)

Determination of Sources of Income 46,119
See p. 20,601 for regulations not amended to reflect law changes

"commodities" does not include goods or merchandise in the ordinary channels of commerce.

(e) *Other rules.* The fact that a person is not determined by reason of this section to be not engaged in trade or business with the United States is not to be considered a determination that such person is engaged in trade or business within the United States. Whether or not such person is engaged in trade or business within the United States shall be determined on the basis of the facts and circumstances in each case. For other rules relating to the determination of whether a taxpayer is engaged in trade or business in the United States see section 875 and the regulations thereunder.

(f) *Effective date.* The provisions of this section shall apply only in the case of taxable years beginning after December 31, 1966. [Reg. § 1.864-2.]

☐ [T.D. 6948, 3-27-68. Amended by T.D. 7378, 9-29-75.]

[Reg. § 1.864-3]

§ 1.864-3. Rules for determining income effectively connected with U.S. business of nonresident aliens or foreign corporations.—(a) *In general.* For purposes of the Income Revenue Code, in the case of a nonresident alien individual or a foreign corporation that is engaged in a trade or business in the United States at any time during the taxable year, the rules set forth in §§ 1.864-4 through 1.864-7 and this section shall apply in determining whether income, gain, or loss shall be treated as effectively connected for a taxable year beginning after December 31, 1966, with the conduct of a trade or business in the United States. Except as provided in sections 871(c) and (d) and 882(d) and (e), and the regulations thereunder, in the case of a nonresident alien individual or a foreign corporation that is at no time during the taxable year engaged in a trade or business in the United States, no income, gain, or loss shall be treated as effectively connected for the taxable year with the conduct of a trade or business in the United States. The general rule prescribed by the preceding sentence shall apply even though the income, gain, or loss would have been treated as effectively connected with the conduct of a trade or business in the United States if such income or gain had been received or accrued, or such loss had been sustained, in an earlier taxable year when the taxpayer was engaged in a trade or business in the United States. In applying §§ 1.864-4 through 1.864-7 and this section, the determination whether an item of income, gain, or loss is effectively connected with the conduct of a trade or business in the United States shall not be controlled by any administrative, judicial, or other interpretation made under the laws of any foreign country.

(b) *Illustrations.* The application of this section may be illustrated by the following examples:

Example (1). During 1967 foreign corporation N, which uses the calendar year as the taxable year, is engaged in the business of purchasing and selling household equipment on the installment plan. During 1967 N is engaged in business in the United States by reason of the sales activities it carries on in the United States for the purpose of selling therein some of the equipment which it has purchased. During 1967 N receives installment payments of $800,000 on sales it makes that year in the United States, and the income from sources within the United States for 1967 attributable to such payments is $200,000. By reason of section 864(c)(3) and paragraph (b) of § 1.864-4 this income of $200,000 is effectively connected for 1967 with the conduct of a trade or business in the United States by N. In December of 1967, N discontinues its efforts to make any further sales of household equipment in the United States, and at no time during 1968 is N engaged in a trade or business in the United States. During 1968 N receives installment payments of $500,000 on the sales it made in the United States during 1967, and the income from sources within the United States for 1968 attributable to such payments is $125,000. By reason of section 864(c)(1)(B) and this section, this income of $125,000 is not effectively connected for 1968 with the conduct of a trade or business in the United States by N, even though such amount, if it had been received by N during 1967, would have been effectively connected for 1967 with the conduct of a trade or business in the United States by that corporation.

Example (2). R, a foreign holding company, owns all of the voting stock in five corporations, two of which are domestic corporations. All of the subsidiary corporations are engaged in the active conduct of a trade or business. R has an office in the United States where its chief executive officer, who is also the chief executive officer of one of the domestic corporations, spends a substantial portion of the taxable year supervising R's investment in its operating subsidiaries and performing his function as chief executive officer of the domestic operating subsidiary. R is not considered to be engaged in a trade or business in the United States during the taxable year by reason of the activities carried on in the United States by its chief executive officer in the supervision of its investment in its operating subsidiary corporations. Accordingly, the dividends from sources within the United States received by R during the taxable year from its domestic subsidiary corpora-

Reg. § 1.864-3(b)

tions are not effectively connected for that year with the conduct of a trade or business in the United States by R.

Example (3). During the months of June through December 1971, B, a nonresident alien individual who uses the calendar year as the taxable year and the cash receipts and disbursements method of accounting, is employed in the United States by domestic corporation M for a salary of $2,000 per month, payable semimonthly. During 1971, B receives from M salary payments totaling $13,000, all of which income by reason of section 864(c)(2) and paragraph (c)(6)(ii) of § 1.864-4, is effectively connected for 1971 with the conduct of a trade or business in the United States by B. On December 31, 1971, B terminates his employment with M and departs from the United States. At no time during 1972 is B engaged in a trade or business in the United States. In January of 1972, B receives from M salary of $1,000 for the last half of December 1971, and a bonus of $1,000 in consideration of the services B performed in the United States during 1971 for that corporation. By reason of section 864(c)(1)(B) and this section, the $2,000 received by B during 1972 from sources within the United States is not effectively connected for that year with the conduct of a trade or business in the United States, even though such amount, if it had been received by B during 1971, would have been effectively connected for 1971 with the conduct of a trade or business in the United States by B. [Reg. § 1.864-3.]

☐ [T.D. 7216, 11-2-72.]

[Reg. § 1.864-4]

§ 1.864-4. **U.S. source income effectively connected with U.S. business.**—(a) *In general.* This section applies only to a nonresident alien individual or a foreign corporation that is engaged in a trade or business in the United States at some time during a taxable year beginning after December 31, 1966, and to the income, gain, or loss of such person from sources within the United States. If the income, gain, or loss of such person for the taxable year from sources within the United States consists of (1) gain or loss from the sale or exchange of capital assets or (2) fixed or determinable annual or periodical gains, profits, and income or certain other gains described in section 871(a)(1) or 881(a), certain factors must be taken into account, as prescribed by section 864(c)(2) and paragraph (c) of this section, in order to determine whether the income, gain, or loss is effectively connected for the taxable year with the conduct of a trade or business in the United States by that person. All other income, gain, or loss of such person for the taxable year from sources within the United States shall be treated as effectively connected for the taxable year with the conduct of a trade or business in the United States by that person, as prescribed by section 864(c)(3) and paragraph (b) of this section.

(b) *Income other than fixed or determinable income and capital gains.* All income, gain, or loss for the taxable year derived by a nonresident alien individual or foreign corporation engaged in a trade or business in the United States from sources within the United States which does not consist of income, gain, or loss described in section 871(a)(1) or 881(a), or of gain or loss from the sale or exchange of capital assets, shall, for purposes of paragraph (a) of this section, be treated as effectively connected for the taxable year with the conduct of a trade or business in the United States. This income, gain, or loss shall be treated as effectively connected for the taxable year with the conduct of a trade or business in the United States, whether or not the income, gain, or loss is derived from the trade or business being carried on in the United States during the taxable year. The application of this paragraph may be illustrated by the following examples:

Example (1). M, a foreign corporation which uses the calendar year as the taxable year, is engaged in the business of manufacturing machine tools in a foreign country. It establishes a branch office in the United States during 1968 which solicits orders from customers in the United States for the machine tools manufactured by that corporation. All negotiations with respect to such sales are carried on in the United States. By reason of its activity in the United States M is engaged in business in the United States during 1968. The income or loss from sources within the United States from such sales during 1968 is treated as effectively connected for that year with the conduct of a business in the United States by M. Occasionally, during 1968 the customers in the United States write directly to the home office of M, and the home office makes sales directly to such customers without routing the transactions through its branch office in the United States. The income or loss from sources within the United States for 1968 from these occasional direct sales by the home office is also treated as effectively connected for that year with the conduct of a business in the United States by M.

Example (2). The facts are the same as in example (1) except that during 1967 M was also engaged in the business of purchasing and selling office machines and that it used the installment method of accounting for the sales made in this separate business. During 1967 M was engaged in

Reg. § 1.864-4(a)

Determination of Sources of Income 46,121
See p. 20,601 for regulations not amended to reflect law changes

business in the United States by reason of the sales activities it carried on in the United States for the purpose of selling therein a number of the office machines which it had purchased. Although M discontinued this business activity in the United States in December of 1967, it received in 1968 some installment payments on the sales which it had made in the United States during 1967. The income of M for 1968 from sources within the United States which is attributable to such installment payments is effectively connected for 1968 with the conduct of a business in the United States, even though such income is not connected with the business carried on in the United States during 1968 through its sales office located in the United States for the solicitation of orders for the machine tools it manufactures.

Example (3). Foreign corporation S, which uses the calendar year as the taxable year, is engaged in the business of purchasing and selling electronic equipment. The home office of such corporation is also engaged in the business of purchasing and selling vintage wines. During 1968, S establishes a branch office in the United States to sell electronic equipment to customers, some of whom are located in the United States and the balance, in foreign countries. This branch office is not equipped to sell, and does not participate in sale of, wine purchased by the home office. Negotiations for the sales of the electronic equipment take place in the United States. By reason of the activity of its branch office in the United States, S is engaged in business in the United States during 1968. As a result of advertisements which the home office of S places in periodicals sold in the United States, customers in the United States frequently place orders for the purchase of wines with the home office in the foreign country, and the home office makes sales of wine in 1968 directly to such customers without routing the transactions through its branch office in the United States. The income or loss from sources within the United States for 1968 from sales of electronic equipment by the branch office, together with the income or loss from sources within the United States for that year from sales of wine by the home office, is treated as effectively connected for that year with the conduct of a business in the United States by S.

(c) *Fixed or determinable income and capital gains*—(1) *Principal factors to be taken into account* —(i) *In general.* In determining for purposes of paragraph (a) of this section whether any income for the taxable year from sources within the United States which is described in section 871(a)(1) or 881(a), relating to fixed or determinable annual or periodical gains, profits, and income and certain other gains, or whether gain or loss from sources within the United States for the taxable year from the sale or exchange of capital assets, is effectively connected for the taxable year with the conduct of a trade or business in the United States, the principal tests to be applied are *(a)* the asset-use test, that is, whether the income, gain, or loss is derived from assets used in, or held for use in, the conduct of the trade or business in the United States, and *(b)* the business-activities test, that is, whether the activities of the trade or business conducted in the United States were a material factor in the realization of the income, gain, or loss.

(ii) *Special rule relating to interest on certain deposits.* For purposes of determining under section 861(a)(1)(A) (relating to interest on deposits with banks, savings and loan associations, and insurance companies paid or credited before Jan. 1, 1976) whether the interest described therein is effectively connected for the taxable year with the conduct of a trade or business in the United States, such interest shall be treated as income from sources within the United States for purposes of applying this paragraph and § 1.864-5. If by reason of the application of this paragraph such interest is determined to be income which is not effectively connected for the taxable year with the conduct of a trade or business in the United States, it shall then be treated as interest from sources without the United States which is not subject to the application of § 1.864-5.

(2) *Application of the asset-use test* —(i) *In general.* For purposes of subparagraph (1) of this paragraph, the asset-use test ordinarily shall apply in making a determination with respect to income, gain, or loss of a passive type where the trade or business activities as such do not give rise directly to the realization of the income, gain, or loss. However, even in the case of such income, gain, or loss, any activities of the trade or business which materially contribute to the realization of such income, gain, or loss shall also be taken into account as a factor in determining whether the income, gain, or loss is effectively connected with the conduct of a trade or business in the United States. The asset-use test is of primary significance where, for example, interest income is derived from sources within the United States by a nonresident alien individual or foreign corporation that is engaged in the business of manufacturing or selling goods in the United States. See also subparagraph (5) of this paragraph for rules applicable to taxpayers conducting a banking, financing, or similar business in the United States.

(ii) *Cases where applicable.* Ordinarily, an asset shall be treated as used in, or held for use in,

Reg. § 1.864-4(c)(2)

the conduct of a trade or business in the United States if the asset is—

(*a*) Held for the principal purpose of promoting the present conduct of the trade or business in the United States; or

(*b*) Acquired and held in the ordinary course of the trade or business conducted in the United States, as, for example, in the case of an account or note receivable arising from that trade or business; or

(*c*) Otherwise held in a direct relationship to the trade or business conducted in the United States, as determined under paragraph (c)(2)(iv) of this section.

(iii) *Application of asset-use test to stock*—(*a*) *In general.* Except as provided in paragraph (c)(2)(iii)(*b*) of this section, stock of a corporation (whether domestic or foreign) shall not be treated as an asset used in, or held for use in, the conduct of a trade or business in the United States.

(*b*) *Stock held by foreign insurance companies.* [Reserved]

(iv) *Direct relationship between holding of asset and trade or business*—(*a*) *In general.* In determining whether an asset is held in a direct relationship to the trade or business conducted in the United States, principal consideration shall be given to whether the asset is needed in that trade or business. An asset shall be considered needed in a trade or business, for this purpose, only if the asset is held to meet the present needs of that trade or business and not its anticipated future needs. An asset shall be considered as needed in the trade or business conducted in the United States if, for example, the asset is held to meet the operating expenses of that trade or business. Conversely, an asset shall be considered as not needed in the trade or business conducted in the United States if, for example, the asset is held for the purpose of providing for (*1*) future diversification into a new trade or business, (*2*) expansion of trade or business activities conducted outside of the United States, (*3*) future plant replacement, or (*4*) future business contingencies.

(*b*) *Presumption of direct relationship.* Generally, an asset will be treated as held in a direct relationship to the trade or business if (*1*) the asset was acquired with funds generated by that trade or business, (*2*) the income from the asset is retained or reinvested in that trade or business, and (*3*) personnel who are present in the United States and actively involved in the conduct of that trade or business exercise significant management and control over the investment of such asset.

(*v*) *Illustration.* The application of paragraph (iv) may be illustrated by the following examples:

Example (1). M, a foreign corporation which uses the calendar year as the taxable year, is engaged in industrial manufacturing in a foreign country. M maintains a branch in the United States which acts as importer and distributor of the merchandise it manufactures abroad; by reason of these branch activities, M is engaged in business in the United States during 1968. The branch in the United States is required to hold a large current cash balance for business purposes, but the amount of the cash balance so required varies because of the fluctuating seasonal nature of the branch's business. During 1968 at a time when large cash balances are not required the branch invests the surplus amount in U.S. Treasury bills. Since these Treasury bills are held to meet the present needs of the business conducted in the United States they are held in a direct relationship to that business, and the interest for 1968 on these bills is effectively connected for that year with the conduct of the business in the United States by M.

Example (2). Foreign corporation M, which uses the calendar year as the taxable year, has a branch office in the United States where it sells to customers located in the United States various products which are manufactured by that corporation in a foreign country. By reason of this activity M is engaged in business in the United States during 1997. The U.S. branch establishes in 1997 a fund to which are periodically credited various amounts which are derived from the business carried on at such branch. The amounts in this fund are invested in various securities issued by domestic corporations by the managing officers of the U.S. branch, who have the responsibility for maintaining proper investment diversification and investment of the fund. During 1997, the branch office derives from sources within the United States interest on these securities, and gains and losses resulting from the sale or exchange of such securities. Since the securities were acquired with amounts generated by the business conducted in the United States, the interest is retained in that business, and the portfolio is managed by personnel actively involved in the conduct of that business, the securities are presumed under paragraph (c)(2)(iv)(*b*) of this section to be held in a direct relationship to that business. However, M is able to rebut this presumption by demonstrating that the fund was established to carry out a program of future expansion and not to meet the present needs of the business conducted in the United States. Consequently, the income, gains, and losses from the

Reg. § 1.864-4(c)(2)

securities for 1997 are not effectively connected for that year with the conduct of a trade or business in the United States by M.

(3) *Application of the business-activities test*—(i) *In general.* For purposes of subparagraph (1) of this paragraph, the business-activities test shall ordinarily apply in making a determination with respect to income, gain, or loss which, even though generally of the passive type, arises directly from the active conduct of the taxpayer's trade or business in the United States. The business-activities test is of primary significance, for example, where *(a)* dividends or interest are derived by a dealer in stocks or securities, *(b)* gain or loss is derived from the sale or exchange of capital assets in the active conduct of a trade or business by an investment company, *(c)* royalties are derived in the active conduct of a business consisting of the licensing of patents or similar intangible property, or *(d)* service fees are derived in the active conduct of a servicing business. In applying the business-activities test, activities relating to the management of investment portfolios shall not be treated as activities of the trade or business conducted in the United States unless the maintenance of the investments constitutes the principal activity of that trade or business. See also subparagraph (5) of this paragraph for rules applicable to taxpayers conducting a banking, financing, or similar business in the United States.

(ii) *Illustrations.* The application of this subparagraph may be illustrated by the following examples:

Example (1). Foreign corporation S is a foreign investment company organized for the purpose of investing in stocks and securities. S is not a personal holding company or a corporation which would be a personal holding company but for section 542(c)(7) or 543(b)(1)(C). Its investment portfolios consist of common stocks issued by both foreign and domestic corporations and a substantial amount of high grade bonds. The business activity of S consists of the management of its portfolios for the purpose of investing, reinvesting, or trading in stocks and securities. During the taxable year 1968, S has its principal office in the United States within the meaning of paragraph (c)(2)(iii) of § 1.864-2 and, by reason of its trading in the United States in stocks and securities, is engaged in business in the United States. The dividends and interest derived by S during 1968 from sources within the United States, and the gains and losses from sources within the United States for such year from the sale of stocks and securities from its investment portfolios, are effectively connected for 1968 with the conduct of the business in the United States by that corporation, since its activities in connection with the management of its investment portfolios are activities of that business and such activities are a material factor in the realization of such income, gains, and losses.

Example (2). N, a foreign corporation which uses the calendar year as the taxable year, has a branch in the United States which acts as an importer and distributor of merchandise; by reason of the activities of that branch, *N* is engaged in business in the United States during 1968. *N* also carries on a business in which it licenses patents to unrelated persons in the United States for use in the United States. The businesses of the licensees in which these patents are used have no direct relationship to the business carried on in N's branch in the United States, although the merchandise marketed by the branch is similar in type to that manufactured under the patents. The negotiations and other activities leading up to the consummation of these licenses are conducted by employees of N who are not connected with the U.S. branch of that corporation, and the U.S. branch does not otherwise participate in arranging for the licenses. Royalties received by N during 1968 from these licenses are not effectively connected for that year with the conduct of its business in the United States because the activities of that business are not a material factor in the realization of such income.

(4) *Method of accounting as a factor.* In applying the asset-use test or the business-activities test described in subparagraph (1) of this paragraph, due regard shall be given to whether or not the asset, or the income, gain, or loss, is accounted for through the trade or business conducted in the United States, that is, whether or not the asset, or the income, gain, or loss, is carried on books of account separately kept for that trade or business, but this accounting test shall not by itself be controlling. In applying this subparagraph, consideration shall be given to whether the accounting treatment of an item reflects the consistent application of generally accepted accounting principles in a particular trade or business in accordance with accepted conditions or practices in that trade or business and whether there is a consistent accounting treatment of that item from year to year by the taxpayer.

(5) *Special rules relating to banking, financing, or similar business activity*—(i) *Definition of banking, financing or similar business.* A nonresident alien individual or a foreign corporation shall be considered for purposes of this section and paragraph (b)(2) of § 1.864-5 to be engaged in the

Reg. § 1.864-4(c)(5)

active conduct of a banking, financing, or similar business in the United States if at some time during the taxable year the taxpayer is engaged in business in the United States and the activities of such business consist of any one or more of the following activities carried on, in whole or in part, in the United States in transactions with persons situated within or without the United States:

(a) Receiving deposits of funds from the public,

(b) Making personal, mortgage, industrial, or other loans to the public,

(c) Purchasing, selling, discounting, or negotiating for the public on a regular basis, notes, drafts, checks, bills of exchange, acceptances, or other evidences of indebtedness,

(d) Issuing letters of credit to the public and negotiating drafts drawn thereunder,

(e) Providing trust services for the public, or

(f) Financing foreign exchange transactions for the public.

Although the fact that the taxpayer is subjected to the banking and credit laws of a foreign country shall be taken into account in determining whether he is engaged in the active conduct of a banking, financing, or similar business, the character of the business actually carried on during the taxable year in the United States shall determine whether the taxpayer is actively conducting a banking, financing, or similar business in the United States. A foreign corporation which acts merely as a financing vehicle for borrowing funds for its parent corporation or any other person who would be a related person within the meaning of section 954(d)(3) if such foreign corporation were a controlled foreign corporation shall not be considered to be engaged in the active conduct of a banking, financing, or similar business in the United States.

(ii) *Effective connection of income from stocks or securities with active conduct of a banking, financing, or similar business.* Notwithstanding the rules in subparagraphs (2) and (3) of this paragraph with respect to the asset-use test and the business-activities test, any dividends or interest from stocks or securities, or any gain or loss from the sale or exchange of stocks or securities which are capital assets, which is from sources within the United States and derived by a nonresident alien individual or a foreign corporation in the active conduct during the taxable year of a banking, financing, or similar business in the United States shall be treated as effectively connected for such year with the conduct of that business only if the stocks or securities giving rise to such income, gain, or loss are attributable to the U.S. office through which such business is carried on and—

(a) Were acquired—

(1) As a result of, or in the course of making loans to the public,

(2) In the course of distributing such stocks or securities to the public, or

(3) For the purpose of being used to satisfy the reserve requirements, or other requirements similar to reserve requirements, established by a duly constituted banking authority in the United States, or

(b) Consist of securities (as defined in subdivision (v) of this subparagraph) which are—

(1) Payable on demand or at a fixed maturity date not exceeding 1 year from the date of acquisition,

(2) Issued by the United States, or any agency or instrumentality thereof, or

(3) Not described in (a) or in (1) or (2) of this (b).

However, the amount of interest from securities described in (b)(3) of this subdivision (ii) which shall be treated as effectively connected for the taxable year with the active conduct of a banking, financing, or similar business in the United States shall be an amount (but not in excess of the entire interest for the taxable year from sources within the United States from such securities) determined by multiplying the entire interest for the taxable year from sources within the United States from such securities by a fraction the numerator of which is 10 percent and the denominator of which is the same percentage, determined on the basis of a monthly average for the taxable year, as the book value of the total of such securities held by the U.S. office through which such business is carried on bears to the book value of the total assets of such office. The amount of gain or loss, if any, for the taxable year from the sale or exchange of such securities which shall be treated as effectively connected for the taxable year with the active conduct of a banking, financing, or similar business in the United States shall be an amount (but not in excess of the entire gain or loss for the taxable year from sources within the United States from the sale or exchange of such securities) determined by multiplying the entire gain or loss for the taxable year from sources within the United States from the sale or exchange of such securities by the fraction described in the immediately preceding sentence. The percentage of the denominator of the limiting fraction for such purposes shall be the percentage obtained by separately adding the book value of

Reg. § 1.864-4(c)(5)

such securities and such total assets held at the close of each month in the taxable year, dividing each such sum by 12, and then dividing the amount of securities so obtained by the amount of assets so obtained. This subdivision does not apply to dividends from stock owned by a foreign corporation in a domestic corporation of which more than 50 percent of the total combined voting power of all classes of stock entitled to vote is owned by such foreign corporation and which is engaged in the active conduct of a banking business in the United States. The application of this subdivision may be illustrated by the following example:

Example. Foreign corporation M, created under the laws of foreign country Y, has in the United States a branch, B, which during the taxable year is engaged in the active conduct of the banking business in the United States within the meaning of subdivision (i) of this subparagraph. During the taxable year M derives from sources within the United States through the activities carried on through B, $7,500,000 interest from securities described in subdivision *(b)(3)* of this subdivision (ii) and $7,500,000 gain from the sale or exchange of such securities. The monthly average, determined as of the last day of each month in the taxable year, of such securities held by B divided by the monthly average, as so determined, of the total assets held by B equals 15 percent. Under this subdivision, the amount of interest income from such securities that shall be treated as effectively connected for the taxable year with the active conduct by M of a banking business in the United States is $5 million ($7,500,000 interest × 10%/15%), and the amount of gain from the sale or exchange of such securities that shall be treated as effectively connected for such year with the active conduct of such business is $5 million ($7,500,000 gain × 10%/15%).

(iii) *Stocks or securities attributable to U.S. office—(a) In general.* For purposes of paragraph (c)(5)(ii) of this section, a stock or security shall be deemed to be attributable to a U.S. office only if such office actively and materially participated in soliciting, negotiating, or performing other activities required to arrange the acquisition of the stock or security. The U.S. office need not have been the only active participant in arranging the acquisition of the stock or security.

(b) *Exceptions.* A stock or security shall not be deemed to be attributable to a U.S. office merely because such office conducts one or more of the following activities:

(1) Collects or accounts for the dividends, interest, gain, or loss from such stock or security,

(2) Exercises general supervision over the activities of the persons directly responsible for carrying on the activities described in paragraph (c)(5)(iii)(a) of this section,

(3) Performs merely clerical functions incident to the acquisition of such stock or security,

(4) Exercises final approval over the execution of the acquisition of such stock or security, or

(5) Holds such stock or security in the United States or records such stock or security on its books or records as having been acquired by such office or for its account.

(c) *Effective date.* This paragraph (c)(5)(iii) shall be effective for income includible in taxable years beginning on or after June 18, 1984, except that 26 CFR § 1.864-4(c)(5)(iii) as it appeared in the Code of Federal Regulations revised as of April 1, 1983, shall apply to income received or accrued under a loan made by the taxpayer on or before May 18, 1984 or pursuant to a written binding commitment entered into on or before May 18, 1984.

(iv) *Acquisitions in course of making loans to the public.* For purposes of subdivision (ii) of this subparagraph—

(a) A stock or security shall be considered to have been acquired in the course of making a loan to the public where, for example, such stock or security was acquired as additional consideration for the making of the loan,

(b) A stock or security shall be considered to have been acquired as a result of making a loan to the public if, for example, such stock or security was acquired by foreclosure upon a bona fide default of the loan and is held as an ordinary and necessary incident to the active conduct of the banking, financing, or similar business in the United States, and

(c) A stock or security acquired on a stock exchange or organized over-the-counter market shall be considered not to have been acquired as a result of, or in the course of, making loans to the public.

(v) *Security defined.* For purposes of this subparagraph, a security is any bill, note, bond, debenture, or other evidence of indebtedness, or any evidence of an interest in, or right to subscribe to or purchase, any of the foregoing items.

(vi) *Limitations on application of subparagraph —(a) Other business activity.* This subparagraph provides rules for determining when

Reg. § 1.864-4(c)(5)

certain income from stocks or securities is effectively connected with the active conduct of a banking, financing, or similar business in the United States. Any dividends, interest, gain, or loss from sources within the United States which by reason of the application of subdivision (ii) of this subparagraph is not effectively connected with the active conduct by a nonresident alien individual or a foreign corporation of a banking, financing, or similar business in the United States may be effectively connected for the taxable year, under subparagraph (2) or (3) of this paragraph with the conduct by such taxpayer of another trade or business in the United States, such as, for example, the business of selling or manufacturing goods or merchandise or of trading in stocks or securities for the taxpayer's own account.

(b) *Other income.* For rules relating to income, gain, or loss from sources within the United States (other than dividends or interest from, or gain or loss from the sale or exchange of, stocks or securities referred to in subdivision (ii) of this subparagraph) derived in the active conduct of a banking, financing, or similar business in the United States, see subparagraphs (2) and (3) of this paragraph and paragraph (b) of this section.

(vii) *Illustrations.* The application of this subparagraph may be illustrated by the following examples:

Example (1). Foreign Corporation F, which is created under the laws of foreign country X and engaged in the active conduct of the banking business in country X and a number of other foreign countries, has in the United States a branch, B, which during the taxable year is engaged in the active conduct of the banking business in the United States within the meaning of subdivision (i) of this subparagraph. In the course of its banking business in foreign countries, F receives at its branches located in country X and other foreign countries substantial deposits in U.S. dollars which are transferred to the accounts of B in the United States. During the taxable year, B actively participates in negotiating loans to residents of the United States, such as call loans to U.S. brokers, which are financed from the U.S. dollar deposits transferred to B by F. In addition, B actively participates in purchasing on the New York Stock Exchange and over-the-counter markets long-term bonds and notes issued by the U.S. Government, U.S. Treasury bills, and long-term interest-bearing bonds issued by domestic corporations and having a maturity date of less than 1 year from the date of acquisition, all of which are purchased from the deposits transferred to B by F. All of the securities so acquired are held by B and recorded on its books in the United States. Pursuant to subdivision (ii) of this subparagraph, the interest received by F during the taxable year on these loans, bonds, notes, and bills is effectively connected for such year with the active conduct by F of a banking business in the United States.

Example (2). The facts are the same as in example (1) except that B also actively participates in using part of the U.S. dollar deposits, which are transferred to it by F, to purchase on the New York Stock Exchange shares of common stock issued by various domestic corporations. All of the shares so purchased are considered to be capital assets within the meaning of section 1221 and are recorded on B's books in the United States. None of the shares so purchased were acquired for the purpose of meeting reserve or other similar requirements. During the taxable year some of the shares are sold by B on the stock exchange. Pursuant to subdivision (ii) of this subparagraph, the dividends and gains received by F during the taxable year on these shares of stock are not effectively connected with the active conduct by F of a banking, financing, or similar business in the United States.

Example (3). The facts are the same as in example (1) except that B also uses part of the U.S. dollar deposits, which are transferred to it by F, to make a loan to domestic corporation M. As part of the consideration for the loan, M gives to B a number of shares of common stock issued by M. All of these shares of stock are considered to be capital assets within the meaning of section 1221 and are recorded on B's books in the United States. During the taxable year one-half of these shares of stock is sold by B on the New York Stock Exchange. Pursuant to subdivision (ii) of this subparagraph, the dividends and gains received by F during the taxable year on these shares of stock are effectively connected for such year with the active conduct by F of a banking business in the United States.

Example (4). The facts are the same as in example (1) except that during the taxable year the home office of F in country X actively participates in negotiating loans to residents of the United States, such as call loans to U.S. brokers, which are financed by the U.S. dollar deposits received at the home office and are recorded on the books of the home office. B does not participate in negotiating these loans. Pursuant to subdivision (ii) of this subparagraph the interest received by F during the taxable year on these loans made by the home office in country X is not effectively connected with the active conduct by

F of a banking, financing, or similar business in the United States.

Example (5). Foreign corporation Y, which is created under the laws of foreign country X and is engaged in the active conduct of a banking business in country X and other foreign countries, has a branch, C, in the United States that is engaged in the active conduct of a banking business in the United States, within the meaning of paragraph (c)(5)(i) of this section, during the taxable year. C handles the negotiation and acquisition of securities involved in loans made by Y to U.S. persons. C also presents interest coupons with respect to such securities for payment, presents all such securities for payment at maturity, and maintains complete photocopy files with respect to such securities. The activities of the office of Y in country X with respect to these securities consist of giving pro forma approval of the loans, storing the original securities, and recording the securities on the books of the country X office. Pursuant to paragraphs (c)(5)(ii) and (c)(5)(iii) of this section, the U.S. source interest income received by Y during the taxable year on these securities is effectively connected for such year with the active conduct by Y of a banking business in the United States.

(6) *Income related to personal services of an individual* —(i) *Income, gain, or loss from assets.* Income or gains from sources within the United States described in section 871(a)(1) and derived from an asset, and gain or loss from sources within the United States from the sale or exchange of capital assets realized by a nonresident alien individual engaged in a trade or business in the United States during the taxable year solely by reason of his performing personal services in the United States shall not be treated as income, gain, or loss which is effectively connected for the taxable year with the conduct of a trade or business in the United States, unless there is a direct economic relationship between his holding of the asset from which the income, gain, or loss results and his trade or business of performing the personal services.

(ii) *Wages, salaries, and pensions.* Wages, salaries, fees, compensations, emoluments, or other remunerations, including bonuses, received by a nonresident alien individual for performing personal services in the United States which, under paragraph (a) of § 1.864-2, constitute engaging in a trade or business in the United States, and pensions and retirement pay attributable to such personal services, constitute income which is effectively connected for the taxable year with the conduct of a trade or business in the United States by that individual if he is engaged in a trade or business in the United States at some time during the taxable year in which such income is received.

(7) *Effective date.* Paragraphs (c)(2) and (c)(6)(i) of this section are effective for taxable years beginning on or after June 6, 1996. [Reg. § 1.864-4.]

☐ [*T.D. 7216,* 11-2-72. *Amended by T.D. 7332,* 12-30-74; *T.D. 7958,* 5-17-84 *and T.D. 8657,* 3-5-96.]

[Reg. § 1.864-5]

§ 1.864-5. **Foreign source income effectively connected with U.S. business.**—(a) *In general.* This section applies only to a nonresident alien individual or a foreign corporation that is engaged in a trade or business in the United States at some time during a taxable year beginning after December 31, 1966, and to the income, gain, or loss of such person from sources without the United States. The income, gain, or loss of such person for the taxable year from sources without the United States which is specified in paragraph (b) of this section shall be treated as effectively connected for the taxable year with the conduct of a trade or business in the United States, only if he also has in the United States at some time during the taxable year, but not necessarily at the time the income, gain, or loss is realized, an office or other fixed place of business, as defined in § 1.864-7, to which such income, gain, or loss is attributable in accordance with § 1.864-6. The income of such person for the taxable year from sources without the United States which is specified in paragraph (c) of this section shall be treated as effectively connected for the taxable year with the conduct of a trade or business in the United States when derived by a foreign corporation carrying on a life insurance business in the United States. Except as provided in paragraphs (b) and (c) of this section, no income, gain, or loss of a nonresident alien individual or a foreign corporation for the taxable year from sources without the United States shall be treated as effectively connected for the taxable year with the conduct of a trade or business in the United States by that person. Any income, gain, or loss described in paragraph (b) or (c) of this section which, if it were derived by the taxpayer from sources within the United States for the taxable year, would not be treated under § 1.864-4 as effectively connected for the taxable year with the conduct of a trade or business in the United States shall not be treated under this section as effectively connected for the taxable year with the conduct of a trade or business in the United States.

(b) *Income other than income attributable to U.S. life insurance business.* Income, gain, or loss from sources without the United States other than

Reg. § 1.864-5(b)

income described in paragraph (c) of this section shall be taken into account pursuant to paragraph (a) of this section in applying §§ 1.864-6 and 1.864-7 only if it consists of—

(1) *Rents, royalties, or gains on sales of intangible property.* (i) Rents or royalties for the use of, or for the privilege of using, intangible personal property located outside the United States or from any interest in such property, including rents or royalties for the use, or for the privilege of using, outside the United States, patents, copyrights, secret processes and formulas, good will, trademarks, trade brands, franchises, and other like properties, if such rents or royalties are derived in the active conduct of the trade or business in the United States.

(ii) Gains or losses on the sale or exchange of intangible personal property located outside the United States or from any interest in such property, including gains or losses on the sale or exchange of the privilege of using, outside the United States, patents, copyrights, secret processes and formulas, good will, trademarks, trade brands, franchises, and other like properties, if such gains or losses are derived in the active conduct of the trade or business in the United States.

(iii) Whether or not such an item of income, gain, or loss is derived in the active conduct of a trade or business in the United States shall be determined from the facts and circumstances of each case. The frequency with which a nonresident alien individual or a foreign corporation enters into transactions of the type from which the income, gain, or loss is derived shall not of itself determine that the income, gain, or loss is derived in the active conduct of a trade or business.

(iv) This subparagraph shall not apply to rents or royalties for the use of, or for the privilege of using, real property or tangible personal property, or to gain or loss from the sale or exchange of such property.

(2) *Dividends or interest, or gains or loss from sales of stocks or securities*—(i) *In general.* Dividends or interest from any transaction, or gains or losses on the sale or exchange of stocks or securities, realized by *(a)* a nonresident alien individual or a foreign corporation in the active conduct of a banking, financing, or similar business in the United States or *(b)* a foreign corporation engaged in business in the United States whose principal business is trading in stocks or securities for its own account. Whether the taxpayer is engaged in the active conduct of a banking, financing, or similar business in the United States for purposes of this subparagraph shall be determined in accordance with the principles of paragraph (c)(5)(i) of § 1.864-4.

(ii) *Substitute payments.* For purposes of this paragraph (b)(2), a substitute interest payment (as defined in § 1.861-2(a)(7)) received by a foreign person subject to tax under this paragraph (b) pursuant to a securities lending transaction or a sale-repurchase transaction (as defined in § 1.861-2(a)(7)) with respect to a security (as defined in § 1.864-6(b)(2)(ii)(c)) shall have the same character as interest income paid or accrued with respect to the terms of the transferred security. Similarly, for purposes of this paragraph (b)(2), a substitute dividend payment (as defined in § 1.861-3(a)(6)) received by a foreign person pursuant to a securities lending transaction or a sale-repurchase transaction (as defined in § 1.861-3(a)(6)) with respect to a stock shall have the same character as a distribution received with respect to the transferred security. This paragraph (b)(2)(ii) is applicable to payments made after November 13, 1997.

(iii) *Incidental investment activity.* This subparagraph shall not apply to income, gain, or loss realized by a nonresident alien individual or foreign corporation on stocks or securities held, sold, or exchanged in connection with incidental investment activities carried on by that person. Thus, a foreign corporation which is primarily a holding company owning significant percentages of the stocks or securities issued by other corporations shall not be treated under this subparagraph as a corporation the principal business of which is trading in stocks or securities for its own account, solely because it engages in sporadic purchases or sales of stocks or securities to adjust its portfolio. The application of this subdivision may be illustrated by the following example:

Example. F, a foreign corporation, owns voting stock in foreign corporations M, N, and P, its holdings in such corporations constituting 15, 20, and 100 percent, respectively, of all classes of their outstanding voting stock. Each of such stock holdings by F represents approximately 20 percent of its total assets. The remaining 40 percent of F's assets consist of other investments, 20 percent being invested in securities issued by foreign governments and in stocks and bonds issued by other corporations in which F does not own a significant percentage of their outstanding voting stock, and 20 percent being invested in bonds issued by N. None of the assets of F are held primarily for sale; but, if the officers of that corporation were to decide that other investments would be preferable to its holding of such assets, F would sell the stocks and securities and reinvest the proceeds therefrom in other holdings. Any

Reg. § 1.864-5(b)(1)

income, gain, or loss which F may derive from this investment activity is not considered to be realized by a foreign corporation described in subdivision (i) of this subparagraph.

(3) *Sale of goods or merchandise through U.S. office.* (i) Income, gain, or loss from the sale of inventory items or of property held primarily for sale to customers in the ordinary course of business, as described in section 1221 (1), where the sale is outside the United States but through the office or other fixed place of business which the nonresident alien or foreign corporation has in the United States, irrespective of the destination to which such property is sent for use, consumption, or disposition.

(ii) This subparagraph shall not apply to income, gain, or loss resulting from a sales contract entered into on or before February 24, 1966. See section 102(e)(1) of the Foreign Investors Tax Act of 1966 (80 Stat. 1547). Thus, for example, the sales office in the United States of a foreign corporation enters into negotiations for the sale of 500,000 industrial bearings which the corporation produces in a foreign country for consumption in the Western Hemisphere. These negotiations culminate in a binding agreement entered into on January 1, 1966. By its terms delivery under the contract is to be made over a period of 3 years beginning in March of 1966. Payment is due upon delivery. The income from sources without the United States resulting from this sale negotiated by the U.S. sales office of the foreign corporation shall not be taken into account under this subparagraph for any taxable year.

(iii) This subparagraph shall not apply to gains or losses on the sale or exchange of intangible personal property to which subparagraph (1) of this paragraph applies or of stocks or securities to which subparagraph (2) of this paragraph applies.

(c) *Income attributable to U.S. life insurance business.* (1) All of the income for the taxable year of a foreign corporation described in subparagraph (2) of this paragraph from sources without the United States, which is attributable to its U.S. life insurance business, shall be treated as effectively connected for the taxable year with the conduct of a trade or business in the United States by that corporation. Thus, in determining its life insurance company taxable income from its U.S. business for purposes of section 802, the foreign corporation shall include all of its items of income from sources without the United States which would appropriately be taken into account in determining the life insurance company taxable income of a domestic corporation. The income to which this subparagraph applies shall be taken into account for purposes of paragraph (a) of this section without reference to §§ 1.864-6 and 1.864-7.

(2) A foreign corporation to which subparagraph (1) of this paragraph applies is a foreign corporation carrying on an insurance business in the United States during the taxable year which—

(i) Without taking into account its income not effectively connected for that year with the conduct of any trade or business in the United States, would qualify as a life insurance company under part I (section 801 and following) of subchapter L, chapter 1 of the Code, if it were a domestic corporation, and

(ii) By reason of section 842 is taxable under that part on its income which is effectively connected for that year with its conduct of any trade or business in the United States.

(d) *Excluded foreign source income.* Notwithstanding paragraphs (b) and (c) of this section, no income from sources without the United States shall be treated as effectively connected for any taxable year with the conduct of a trade or business in the United States by a nonresident alien individual or a foreign corporation if the income consists of—

(1) *Dividends, interest, or royalties paid by a related foreign corporation.* Dividends, interest, or royalties paid by a foreign corporation in which the nonresident alien individual or the foreign corporation described in paragraph (a) of this section owns, within the meaning of section 958(a), or is considered as owning, by applying the ownership rules of section 958(b), at the time such items are paid more than 50 percent of the total combined voting power of all classes of stock entitled to vote.

(2) *Subpart F income of a controlled foreign corporation.* Any income of the foreign corporation described in paragraph (a) of this section which is subpart F income for the taxable year, as determined under section 952(a), even though part of the income is attributable to amounts which, if distributed by the foreign corporation, would be distributed with respect to its stock which is owned by shareholders who are not U.S. shareholders within the meaning of section 951(b). This subparagraph shall not apply to any income of the foreign corporation which is excluded in determining its subpart F income for the taxable year for purposes of section 952(a). Thus, for example, this subparagraph shall not apply to—

(i) Foreign base company shipping income which is excluded under section 954(b)(2),

Reg. § 1.864-5(d)(2)

(ii) Foreign base company income amounting to less than 10 percent (30 percent in the case of taxable years of foreign corporations ending before January 1, 1976) of gross income which by reason of section 954(b)(3)(A) does not become subpart F income for the taxable year,

(iii) Any income excluded from foreign base company income under section 954(b)(4), relating to exception for foreign corporations not availed of to reduce taxes,

(iv) Any income derived in the active conduct of a trade or business which is excluded under section 954(c)(3), or

(v) Any income received from related persons which is excluded under section 954(c)(4).

This subparagraph shall apply to the foreign corporation's entire subpart F income for the taxable year determined under section 952(a), even though no amount is included in the gross income of a U.S. shareholder under section 951(a) with respect to that subpart F income because of the minimum distribution provisions of section 963(a) or because of the reduction under section 970(a) with respect to an export trade corporation. This subparagraph shall apply only to a foreign corporation which is a controlled foreign corporation within the meaning of section 957 and the regulations thereunder. The application of this subparagraph may be illustrated by the following examples:

Example (1). Controlled foreign corporation M, incorporated under the laws of foreign country X, is engaged in the business of purchasing and selling merchandise manufactured in foreign country Y by an unrelated person. M negotiates sales, through its sales office in the United States, of its merchandise for use outside of country X. These sales are made outside the United States, and the merchandise is sold for use outside the United States. No office maintained by M outside the United States participates materially in the sales made through its U.S. sales office. These activities constitute the only activities of M. During the taxable year M derives $100,000 income from these sales made through its U.S. sales office, and all of such income is foreign base company sales income by reason of section 954(d)(2) and paragraph (b) of § 1.954-3. The entire $100,000 is also subpart F income, determined under section 952(a). In addition, all of this income would, without reference to section 864(c)(4)(D)(ii) and this subparagraph, be treated as effectively connected for the taxable year with the conduct of a trade or business in the United States by M. Through its entire taxable year 60 percent of the one class of stock of M is owned within the meaning of section 958(a) by U.S. shareholders, as defined in section 951(b), and 40 percent of its one class of stock is owned within the meaning of section 958(a) by persons who are not U.S. shareholders, as defined in section 951(b). Although only $60,000 of the subpart F income of M for the taxable year is includible in the income of the U.S. shareholders under section 951(a), the entire subpart F income of $100,000 constitutes income which, by reason of section 864(c)(4)(D)(ii) and this subparagraph, is not effectively connected for the taxable year with the conduct of a trade or business in the United States by M.

Example (2). The facts are the same as in example (1) except that the foreign base company sales income amounts to $150,000 determined in accordance with paragraph (d)(3)(i) of § 1.954-1, and that M also has gross income from sources without the United States of $50,000 from sales, through its sales office in the United States, of merchandise for use in country X. These sales are made outside the United States. All of this income would, without reference to section 864(c)(4)(D)(ii) and this subparagraph, be treated as effectively connected for the taxable year with the conduct of a trade or business in the United States by M. Since the foreign base company income of $150,000 amounts to 75 percent of the entire gross income of $200,000, determined as provided in paragraph (d)(3)(ii) of § 1.954-1, the entire $200,000 constitutes foreign base company income under section 954(b)(3)(B). Assuming that M has no amounts to be taken into account under paragraphs (1), (2), (4), and (5) of section 954(b), the $200,000 is also subpart F income, determined under section 952(a). This subpart F income of $200,000 constitutes income which, by reason of section 864(c)(4)(D)(ii) and this subparagraph, is not effectively connected for the taxable year with the conduct of a trade or business in the United States by M.

(3) *Interest on certain deposits.* Interest which, by reason of section 861(a)(1)(A) (relating to interest on deposits with banks, savings and loan associations, and insurance companies paid or credited before January 1, 1976) and paragraph (c) of § 1.864-4, is determined to be income from sources without the United States because it is not effectively connected for the taxable year with the conduct of a trade or business in the United States by the nonresident alien individual or foreign corporation. [Reg. § 1.864-5.]

☐ [T.D. 7216, 11-2-72. Amended by T.D. 7893, 5-11-83 and T.D. 8735, 10-6-97.]

Reg. § 1.864-5(d)(3)

Determination of Sources of Income

See p. 20,601 for regulations not amended to reflect law changes

[Reg. § 1.864-6]

§ 1.864-6. Income, gain, or loss attributable to an office or other fixed place of business in the United States.—(a) *In general.* Income, gain, or loss from sources without the United States which is specified in paragraph (b) of § 1.864-5 and received by a nonresident alien individual or a foreign corporation engaged in a trade or business in the United States at some time during a taxable year beginning after December 31, 1966, shall be treated as effectively connected for the taxable year with the conduct of a trade or business in the United States only if the income, gain, or loss is attributable under paragraphs (b) and (c) of this section to an office or other fixed place of business, as defined in § 1.864-7, which the taxpayer has in the United States at some time during the taxable year.

(b) *Material factor test*—(1) *In general.* For purposes of paragraph (a) of this section, income, gain, or loss is attributable to an office or other fixed place of business which a nonresident alien individual or a foreign corporation has in the United States only if such office or other fixed place of business is a material factor in the realization of the income, gain, or loss, and if the income, gain, or loss is realized in the ordinary course of the trade or business carried on through that office or other fixed place of business. For this purpose, the activities of the office or other fixed place of business shall not be considered to be a material factor in the realization of the income, gain, or loss unless they provide a significant contribution to, by being an essential economic element in, the realization of the income, gain, or loss. Thus, for example, meetings in the United States of the board of directors of a foreign corporation do not of themselves constitute a material factor in the realization of income, gain, or loss. It is not necessary that the activities of the office or other fixed place of business in the United States be a major factor in the realization of income, gain, or loss. An office or other fixed place of business located in the United States at some time during a taxable year may be a material factor in the realization of an item of income, gain, or loss for that year even though the office or other fixed place of business is not present in the United States when the income, gain, or loss is realized.

(2) *Application of material factor test to specific classes of income.* For purposes of paragraph (a) of this section, an office or other fixed place of business which a nonresident alien individual or a foreign corporation, engaged in a trade or business in the United States at some time during the taxable year, had in the United States, shall be considered a material factor in the realization of income, gain, or loss consisting of—

(i) *Rents, royalties, or gains on sales of intangible property.* Rents, royalties, or gains or losses, from intangible personal property specified in paragraph (b)(1) of § 1.864-5, if the office or other fixed place of business either actively participates in soliciting, negotiating, or performing other activities required to arrange, the lease, license, sale, or exchange from which such income, gain, or loss is derived or performs significant services incident to such lease, license, sale, or exchange. An office or other fixed place of business in the United States shall not be considered to be a material factor in the realization of income, gain, or loss for purposes of this subdivision merely because the office or other fixed place of business conducts one or more of the following activities: (*a*) develops, creates, produces, or acquires and adds substantial value to, the property which is leased, licensed, or sold, or exchanged, (*b*) collects or accounts for the rents, royalties, gains, or losses, (*c*) exercises general supervision over the activities of the persons directly responsible for carrying on the activities or services described in the immediately preceding sentence, (*d*) performs merely clerical functions incident to the lease, license, sale or exchange or (*e*) exercises final approval over the execution of the lease, license, sale, or exchange. The application of this subdivision may be illustrated by the following examples:

Example (1). F, a foreign corporation, is engaged in the active conduct of the business of licensing patents which it has either purchased or developed in the United States. F has a business office in the United States. Licenses for the use of such patents outside the United States are negotiated by offices of F located outside the United States, subject to approval by an officer of such corporation located in the U.S. office. All services which are rendered to F's foreign licensees are performed by employees of F's offices located outside the United States. None of the income, gain, or loss resulting from the foreign licenses so negotiated by F is attributable to its business office in the United States.

Example (2). N, a foreign corporation, is engaged in the active conduct of the business of distributing motion picture films and television programs. N does not distribute such films or programs in the United States. The foreign distribution rights to these films and programs are acquired by N's U.S. business office from the U.S. owners of these films and programs. Employees of N's offices located in various foreign countries carry on in such countries all the solicitations and

Reg. § 1.864-6(b)(2)

negotiations for the licensing of these films and programs to licensees located in such countries and provide the necessary incidental services to the licensees. N's U.S. office collects the rentals from the foreign licensees and maintains the necessary records of income and expense. Officers of N located in the United States also maintain general supervision over the employees of the foreign offices, but the foreign employees conduct the day to day business of N outside the United States of soliciting, negotiating, or performing other activities required to arrange the foreign licenses. None of the income, gain, or loss resulting from the foreign licenses so negotiated by N is attributable to N's U.S. office.

(ii) *Dividends or interest, or gains or losses from sales of stock or securities*—(a) *In general.* Dividends or interest from any transaction, or gains or losses on the sale or exchange of stocks or securities, specified in paragraph (b)(2) of § 1.864-5, if the office or other fixed place of business either actively participates in soliciting, negotiating, or performing other activities required to arrange, the issue, acquisition, sale, or exchange, of the asset from which such income, gain, or loss is derived or performs significant services incident to such issue, acquisition, sale, or exchange. An office or other fixed place of business in the United States shall not be considered to be a material factor in the realization of income, gain, or loss for purposes of this subdivision merely because the office or other fixed place of business conducts one or more of the following activities: (*1*) collects or accounts for the dividends, interest, gains, or losses, (*2*) exercises general supervision over the activities of the persons directly responsible for carrying on the activities or services described in the immediately preceding sentence, (*3*) performs merely clerical functions incident to the issue, acquisition, sale, or exchange, or (*4*) exercises final approval over the execution of the issue, acquisition, sale, or exchange.

(*b*) *Effective connection of income from stocks or securities with active conduct of a banking, financing, or similar business.* Notwithstanding (*a*) of this subdivision (ii), the determination as to whether any dividends or interest from stocks or securities, or gain or loss from the sale or exchange of stocks or securities which are capital assets, which is from sources without the United States and derived by a nonresident alien individual or a foreign corporation in the active conduct during the taxable year of a banking, financing, or similar business in the United States, shall be treated as effectively connected for such year with the active conduct of that business shall be made by applying the principles of paragraph (c)(5)(ii) of § 1.864-4 for determining whether income, gain, or loss of such type from sources within the United States is effectively connected for such year with the active conduct of that business.

(*c*) *Security defined.* For purposes of this subdivision (ii), a security is any bill, note, bond, debenture, or other evidence of indebtedness, or any evidence of an interest in, or right to subscribe to or purchase, any of the foregoing items.

(*d*) *Limitations on application of rules on banking, financing, or similar business*—(*1*) *Trading for taxpayer's own account.* The provisions of (*b*) of this subdivision (ii) apply for purposes of determining when certain income, gain, or loss from stocks or securities is effectively connected with the active conduct of a banking, financing, or similar business in the United States. Any dividends, interest, gain, or loss from sources without the United States which by reason of the application of (*b*) of this subdivision (ii) is not effectively connected with the active conduct by a foreign corporation of a banking, financing, or similar business in the United States may be effectively connected for the taxable year, under (*a*) of this subdivision (ii), with the conduct by such taxpayer of a trade or business in the United States which consists of trading in stocks or securities for the taxpayer's own account.

(*2*) *Other income.* For rules relating to dividends or interest from sources without the United States (other than dividends or interest from, or gain or loss from the sale or exchange of, stocks or securities referred to in (*b*) of this subdivision (ii)) derived in the active conduct of a banking, financing, or similar business in the United States, see (*a*) of this subdivision (ii).

(iii) *Sale of goods or merchandise through U.S. office.* Income, gain, or loss from sales of goods or merchandise specified in paragraph (b)(3) of § 1.864-5, if the office or other fixed place of business actively participates in soliciting the order, negotiating the contract of sale, or performing other significant services necessary for the consummation of the sale which are not the subject of a separate agreement between the seller and the buyer. The office or other fixed place of business in the United States shall be considered a material factor in the realization of income, gain, or loss from a sale made as a result of a sales order received in such office or other fixed place of business except where the sales order is received unsolicited and that office or other fixed place of business is not held out to potential customers as the place to which such sales orders should be sent. The income, gain, or loss must be realized in the ordinary course of the trade or business car-

Reg. § 1.864-6(b)(2)

ried on through the office or other fixed place of business in the United States. Thus, if a foreign corporation is engaged solely in a manufacturing business in the United States, the income derived by its office in the United States as a result of an occasional sale outside the United States is not attributable to the U.S. office if the sales office of the manufacturing business is located outside the United States. On the other hand, if a foreign corporation establishes a sales office in the United States to sell for consumption in the Western Hemisphere merchandise which the corporation produces in Africa, the income derived by the sales office in the United States as a result of an occasional sale made by it in Europe shall be attributable to the U.S. sales office. An office or other fixed place of business in the United States shall not be considered to be a material factor in the realization of income, gain, or loss for purposes of this subdivision merely because of one or more of the following activities: (*a*) the sale is made subject to the final approval of such office or other fixed place of business, (*b*) the property sold is held in, and distributed from, such office or other fixed place of business, (*c*) samples of the property sold are displayed (but not otherwise promoted or sold) in such office or other fixed place of business, or (*d*) such office or other fixed place of business performs merely clerical functions incident to the sale. Activities carried on by employees of an office or other fixed place of business constitute activities of that office or other fixed place of business.

(3) *Limitation where foreign office is a material factor in realization of income*—(i) *Goods or merchandise destined for foreign use, consumption, or disposition.* Notwithstanding subparagraphs (1) and (2) of this paragraph, an office or other fixed place of business which a nonresident alien individual or a foreign corporation has in the United States shall not be considered, for purposes of paragraph (a) of this section, to be a material factor in the realization of income, gain or loss from sales of goods or merchandise specified in paragraph (b)(3) of § 1.864-5 if the property is sold for use, consumption, or disposition outside the United States and an office or other fixed place of business, as defined in § 1.864-7, which such nonresident alien individual or foreign corporation has outside the United States participates materially in the sale. For this purpose an office or other fixed place of business which the taxpayer has outside the United States shall be considered to have participated materially in a sale made through the office or other fixed place of business in the United States if the office or other fixed place of business outside the United States actively participates in soliciting the order resulting in the sale, negotiating the contract of sale, or performing other significant services necessary for the consummation of the sale which are not the subject of a separate agreement between the seller and buyer. An office or other fixed place of business which the taxpayer has outside the United States shall not be considered to have participated materially in a sale merely because of one or more of the following activities: (*a*) The sale is made subject to the final approval of such office or other fixed place of business, (*b*) the property sold is held in, and distributed from, such office or other fixed place of business, (*c*) samples of the property sold are displayed (but not otherwise promoted or sold) in such office or other fixed place of business, (*d*) such office or other fixed place of business is used for purposes of having title to the property pass outside the United States, or (*e*) such office or other fixed place of business performs merely clerical functions incident to the sale.

(ii) *Rules for determining country of use, consumption, or disposition*—(*a*) *In general.* As a general rule, personal property which is sold to an unrelated person shall be presumed for purposes of this subparagraph to have been sold for use, consumption, or disposition in the country of destination of the property sold; for such purpose, the occurrence in a country of a temporary interruption in shipment of property shall not cause that country to be considered the country of destination. However, if at the time of a sale of personal property to an unrelated person the taxpayer knew, or should have known from the facts and circumstances surrounding the transaction, that the property probably would not be used, consumed, or disposed of in the country of destination, the taxpayer must determine the country of ultimate use, consumption, or disposition of the property or the property shall be presumed to have been sold for use, consumption, or disposition in the United States. A taxpayer who sells personal property to a related person shall be presumed to have sold the property for use, consumption, or disposition in the United States unless the taxpayer establishes the use made of the property by the related person; once he has established that the related person has disposed of the property, the rules in the two immediately preceding sentences relating to sales to an unrelated person shall apply at the first stage in the chain of distribution at which a sale is made by a related person to an unrelated person. Notwithstanding the preceding provisions of this subdivision (*a*), a taxpayer who sells personal property to any person whose principal business consists of selling from inventory to retail customers at retail outlets outside the United States may assume at the time of the sale to that person that the prop-

Reg. § 1.864-6(b)(3)

erty will be used, consumed, or disposed of outside the United States. For purposes of this (a), a person is related to another person if either person owns or controls directly or indirectly the other, or if any third person or persons own or control directly or indirectly both. For this purpose, the term "control" includes any kind of control, whether or not legally enforceable, and however exercised or exercisable. For illustrations of the principles of this subdivision, see paragraph (a)(3)(iv) of § 1.954-3.

(b) *Fungible goods.* For purposes of this subparagraph, a taxpayer who sells to a purchaser personal property which because of its fungible nature cannot reasonably be specifically traced to other purchasers and to the countries of ultimate use, consumption, or disposition shall, unless the taxpayer establishes a different disposition as being proper, treat that property as being sold, for ultimate use, consumption, or disposition in those countries, and to those other purchasers, in the same proportions in which property from the fungible mass of the first purchaser is sold in the ordinary course of business by such first purchaser. No apportionment is required to be made, however, on the basis of sporadic sales by the first purchaser. This (b) shall apply only in a case where the taxpayer knew, or should have known from the facts and circumstances surrounding the transaction, the manner in which the first purchaser disposes of property from the fungible mass.

(iii) *Illustration.* The application of this subparagraph may be illustrated by the following example:

Example. Foreign corporation M has a sales office in the United States during the taxable year through which it sells outside the United States for use in foreign countries industrial electrical generators which such corporation manufactures in a foreign country. M is not a controlled foreign corporation within the meaning of section 957 and the regulations thereunder, and, by reason of its activities in the United States, is engaged in business in the United States during the taxable year. The generators require specialized installation and continuous adjustment and maintenance services. M has an office in foreign country X which is the only organization qualified to perform these installation, adjustment, and maintenance services. During the taxable year M sells several generators through its U.S. office for use in foreign country Y under sales contracts which also provide for installation, adjustment, and maintenance by its office in country X. The generators are installed in country Y by employees of M's office in country X, who also are responsible for the servicing of the equipment. Since the office of M in country X performs significant services incident to these sales which are necessary for their consummation and are not subject of a separate agreement between M and the purchaser, the U.S. office of M is not considered to be a material factor in the realization of the income from the sales and, for purposes of paragraph (a) of this section, such income is not attributable to the U.S. office of that corporation.

(c) *Amount of income, gain, or loss allocable to U.S. office*—(1) *In general.* If, in accordance with paragraph (b) of this section, an office or other fixed place of business which a nonresident alien individual or a foreign corporation has in the United States at some time during the taxable year is a material factor in the realization for that year of an item of income, gain, or loss specified in paragraph (b) of § 1.864-5, such item of income, gain, or loss shall be considered to be allocable in its entirety to that office or other fixed place of business. In no case may any income, gain, or loss for the taxable year from sources within the United States, or part thereof, be allocable under this paragraph to an office or other fixed place of business which a nonresident alien individual or a foreign corporation has in the United States if the taxpayer is at no time during the taxable year engaged in a trade or business in the United States.

(2) *Special limitation in case of sales of goods or merchandise through U.S. office.* Notwithstanding subparagraph (1) of this paragraph, in the case of a sale of goods or merchandise specified in paragraph (b)(3) of § 1.864-5, which is not a sale to which paragraph (b)(3)(i) of this section applies, the amount of income which shall be considered to be allocable to the office or other fixed place of business which the nonresident alien individual or foreign corporation has in the United States shall not exceed the amount which would be treated as income from sources within the United States if the taxpayer had sold the goods or merchandise in the United States. See, for example, section 863(b)(2) and paragraph (b) of § 1.863-3, which prescribes, as available method for determining the income from sources within the United States, the independent factory or production price method, the gross sales and property apportionment method, and any other method regularly employed by the taxpayer which more clearly reflects taxable income from such sources than those specifically authorized.

(3) *Illustrations.* The application of this paragraph may be illustrated by the following examples:

Reg. § 1.864-6(c)(1)

Determination of Sources of Income 46,135

See p. 20,601 for regulations not amended to reflect law changes

Example (1). Foreign corporation M, which is not a controlled foreign corporation within the meaning of section 957 and the regulations thereunder, manufactures machinery in a foreign country and sells the machinery outside the United States through its sales office in the United States for use in foreign countries. Title to the property which is sold is transferred to the foreign purchaser outside the United States, but no office or other fixed place of business of M in a foreign country participates materially in the sale made through its U.S. office. During the taxable year M derives a total taxable income (determined as though M were a domestic corporation) of $250,000 from these sales. If the sales made through the U.S. office for the taxable year had been made in the United States and the property had been sold for use in the United States, the taxable income from sources within the United States from such sales would have been $100,000, determined as provided in section 863 and 882(c) and the regulations thereunder. The taxable income which is allocable to M's U.S. sales office pursuant to this paragraph and which is effectively connected for the taxable year with the conduct of a trade or business within the United States by that corporation is $100,000.

Example (2). Foreign corporation N, which is not a controlled foreign corporation within the meaning of section 957 and the regulations thereunder, has an office in a foreign country which purchases merchandise and sells it through its sales office in the United States for use in various foreign countries, such sales being made outside the United States and title to the property passing outside the United States. No other office of N participates materially in these sales made through its U.S. office. By reason of its sales activities in the United States, N is engaged in business in the United States during the taxable year. During the taxable year N derives taxable income (determined as though N were a domestic corporation) of $300,000 from these sales made through its U.S. sales office. If the sales made through the U.S. office for the taxable year had been made in the United States and the property had been sold for use in the United States, the taxable income from sources within the United States from such sales would also have been $300,000, determined as provided in sections 861 and 882(c) and the regulations thereunder. The taxable income which is allocable to N's U.S. sales office pursuant to this paragraph and which is effectively connected for the taxable year with the conduct of a trade or business in the United States by that corporation is $300,000.

Example (3). The facts are the same as in example (2), except that N has an office in a foreign country which participates materially in the sales which are made through its U.S. office. The taxable income which is allocable to N's U.S. sales office is not effectively connected for the taxable year with the conduct of a trade or business in the United States by that corporation. [Reg. § 1.864-6.]

☐ [*T.D.* 7216, 11-2-72.]

[Reg. § 1.864-7]

§ 1.864-7. Definition of office or other fixed place of business.—(a) *In general.*—(1) This section applies for purposes of determining whether a nonresident alien individual or a foreign corporation that is engaged in a trade or business in the United States at some time during a taxable year beginning after December 31, 1966, has an office or other fixed place of business in the United States for purposes of applying section 864(c)(4)(B) and § 1.864-6 to income, gain, or loss specified in paragraph (b) of § 1.864-5 from sources without the United States or has an office or other fixed place of business outside the United States for purposes of applying section 864(c)(4)(B)(iii) and paragraph (b)(3)(i) of § 1.864-6 to sales of goods or merchandise for use, consumption, or disposition outside the United States.

(2) In making a determination under this section due regard shall be given to the facts and circumstances of each case, particularly to the nature of the taxpayer's trade or business and the physical facilities actually required by the taxpayer in the ordinary course of the conduct of his trade or business.

(3) The law of a foreign country shall not be controlling in determining whether a nonresident alien individual or a foreign corporation has an office or other fixed place of business.

(b) *Fixed facilities*—(1) *In general.* As a general rule, an office or other fixed place of business is a fixed facility, that is, a place, site, structure, or other similar facility, through which a nonresident alien individual or a foreign corporation engages in a trade or business. For this purpose an office or other fixed place of business shall include, but shall not be limited to, a factory; a store or other sales outlet; a workshop; or a mine, quarry, or other place of extraction of natural resources. A fixed facility may be considered an office or other fixed place of business whether or not the facility is continuously used by a nonresident alien individual or foreign corporation.

(2) *Use of another person's office or other fixed place of business.* A nonresident alien individual or a foreign corporation shall not be considered to have an office or other fixed place of

Reg. § 1.864-7(b)(2)

business merely because such alien individual or foreign corporation uses another person's office or other fixed place of business, whether or not the office or place of business of a related person, through which to transact a trade or business, if the trade or business activities of the alien individual or foreign corporation in that office or other fixed place of business are relatively sporadic or infrequent, taking into account the overall needs and conduct of that trade or business.

(c) *Management activity.* A foreign corporation shall not be considered to have an office or other fixed place of business merely because a person controlling that corporation has an office or other fixed place of business from which general supervision and control over the policies of the foreign corporation are exercised. The fact that top management decisions affecting the foreign corporation are made in a country shall not of itself mean that the foreign corporation has an office or other fixed place of business in that country. For example, a foreign sales corporation which is a wholly owned subsidiary of a domestic corporation shall not be considered to have an office or other fixed place of business in the United States merely because of the presence in the United States of officers of the domestic parent corporation who are generally responsible only for the policy decisions affecting the foreign sales corporation, provided that the foreign corporation has a chief executive officer, whether or not he is also an officer of the domestic parent corporation, who conducts the day-to-day trade or business of the foreign corporation from a foreign office. The result in this example would be the same even if the executive officer should (1) regularly confer with the officers of the domestic parent corporation, (2) occasionally visit the U.S. office of the domestic parent corporation, and (3) during such visits to the United States temporarily conduct the business of the foreign subsidiary corporation out of the domestic parent corporation's office in the United States.

(d) *Agent activity*—(1) *Dependent agents*—(i) *In general.* In determining whether a nonresident alien individual or a foreign corporation has an office or other fixed place of business, the office or other fixed place of business of an agent who is not an independent agent, as defined in subparagraph (3) of this paragraph, shall be disregarded unless such agent (*a*) has the authority to negotiate and conclude contracts in the name of the nonresident alien individual or foreign corporation, and regularly exercises that authority, or (*b*) has a stock of merchandise belonging to the nonresident alien individual or foreign corporation from which orders are regularly filed on behalf of such alien individual or foreign corporation. A person who purchases goods from a nonresident alien individual or a foreign corporation shall not be considered to be an agent for such alien individual or foreign corporation for purposes of this paragraph where such person is carrying on such purchasing activities in the ordinary course of its own business, even though such person is related in some manner to the nonresident alien individual or foreign corporation. For example, a wholly owned domestic subsidiary corporation of a foreign corporation shall not be treated as an agent of the foreign parent corporation merely because the subsidiary corporation purchases goods from the foreign parent corporation and resells them in its own name. However, if the domestic subsidiary corporation regularly negotiates and concludes contracts in the name of its foreign parent corporation or maintains a stock of merchandise from which it regularly fills orders on behalf of the foreign parent corporation, the office or other fixed place of business of the domestic subsidiary corporation shall be treated as the office or other fixed place of business of the foreign parent corporation unless the domestic subsidiary corporation is an independent agent within the meaning of subparagraph (3) of this paragraph.

(ii) *Authority to conclude contracts or fill orders.* For purposes of subdivision (i) of this subparagraph, an agent shall be considered regularly to exercise authority to negotiate and conclude contracts or regularly to fill orders on behalf of his foreign principal only if the authority is exercised, or the orders are filled, with some frequency over a continuous period of time. This determination shall be made on the basis of the facts and circumstances in each case, taking into account the nature of the business of the principal; but, in all cases, the frequency and continuity tests are to be applied conjunctively. Regularity shall not be evidenced by occasional or incidental activity. An agent shall not be considered regularly to negotiate and conclude contracts on behalf of his foreign principal if the agent's authority to negotiate and conclude contracts is limited only to unusual cases or such authority must be separately secured by the agent from his principal with respect to each transaction effected.

(2) *Independent agents.* The office or other fixed place of business of an independent agent, as defined in subparagraph (3) of this paragraph, shall not be treated as the office or other fixed place of business of his principal who is a nonresident alien individual or a foreign corporation, irrespective of whether such agent has authority to negotiate and conclude contracts in the name of his principal, and regularly exercises that authority, or maintains a stock of goods from which he regularly fills orders on behalf of his principal.

Reg. § 1.864-7(c)

(3) *Definition of independent agent* —(i) *In general.* For purposes of this paragraph, the term "independent agent" means a general commission agent, broker, or other agent of an independent status acting in the ordinary course of his business in that capacity. Thus, for example, an agent who, in pursuance of his usual trade or business, and for compensation, sell goods or merchandise consigned or entrusted to his possession, management, and control for that purpose by or for the owner of such goods or merchandise is an independent agent.

(ii) *Related persons.* The determination of whether an agent is an independent agent for purposes of this paragraph shall be made without regard to facts indicating that either the agent or the principal owns or controls directly or indirectly the other or that a third person or persons own or control directly or indirectly both. For example, a wholly owned domestic subsidiary corporation of a foreign corporation which acts as an agent for the foreign parent corporation may be treated as acting in the capacity of independent agent for the foreign parent corporation. The facts and circumstances of a specific case shall determine whether the agent, while acting for his principal, is acting in pursuance of his usual trade or business and in such manner as to constitute him an independent agent in his relations with the nonresident alien individual or foreign corporation.

(iii) *Exclusive agents.* Where an agent who is otherwise an independent agent within the meaning of subdivision (i) of this subparagraph acts in such capacity exclusively, or almost exclusively, for one principal who is a nonresident alien individual or a foreign corporation, the facts and circumstances of a particular case shall be taken into account in determining whether the agent, while acting in that capacity, may be classified as an independent agent.

(e) *Employee activity.* Ordinarily, an employee of a nonresident alien individual or a foreign corporation shall be treated as a dependent agent to whom the rules of paragraph (d)(1) of this section apply if such employer does not in and of itself have a fixed facility (as defined in paragraph (b) of this section) in the United States or outside the United States, as the case may be. However, where the employee, in the ordinary course of his duties, carries on the trade or business of his employer in or through a fixed facility of such employer which is regularly used by the employee in the course of carrying out such duties, such fixed facility shall be considered the office or other fixed place of business of the employer, irrespective of the rules of paragraph (d)(1) of this section. The application of this paragraph may be illustrated by the following example:

Example. M, a foreign corporation, opens a showroom office in the United States for the purpose of promoting its sales of merchandise which it purchases in foreign country X. The employees of the U.S. office, consisting of salesmen and general clerks, are empowered only to run the office, to arrange for the appointment of distributing agents for the merchandise offered by M, and to solicit orders generally. These employees do not have the authority to negotiate and conclude contracts in the name of M, nor do they have a stock of merchandise from which to fill orders on behalf of M. Any negotiations entered into by these employees are under M's instructions and subject to its approval as to any decision reached. The only independent authority which the employees have is in the appointment of distributors to whom M is to sell merchandise, but even this authority is subject to the right of M to approve or disapprove these buyers on receipt of information as to their business standing. Under the circumstances, this office used by a group of salesmen for sales promotion is a fixed place of business which M has in the United States.

(f) *Office or other fixed place of business of a related person.* The fact that a nonresident alien individual or a foreign corporation is related in some manner to another person who has an office or other fixed place of business shall not of itself mean that such office or other fixed place of business of the other person is the office or other fixed place of business of the nonresident alien individual or foreign corporation. Thus, for example, the U.S. office of foreign corporation M, a wholly owned subsidiary corporation of foreign corporation N, shall not be considered the office or other fixed place of business of N unless the facts and circumstances show that N is engaged in trade or business in the United States through that office or other fixed place of business. However, see paragraph (b)(2) of this section.

(g) *Illustrations.* The application of this section may be illustrated by the following examples:

Example (1). S, a foreign corporation, is engaged in the business of buying and selling tangible personal property. S is a wholly owned subsidiary of P, a domestic corporation engaged in the business of buying and selling similar property, which has an office in the United States. Officers of P are generally responsible for the policies followed by S and are directors of S, but S has an independent group of officers, none of whom are regularly employed in the United States. In addition to this group of officers, S has a chief executive officer, D, who is also an officer

Reg. § 1.864-7(g)

of P but who is permanently stationed outside the United States. The day-to-day conduct of S's business is handled by D and the other officers of such corporation, but they regularly confer with the officers of P and on occasion temporarily visit P's offices in the United States, at which time they continue to conduct the business of S. S does not have an office or other fixed place of business in the United States for purposes of this section.

Example (2). The facts are the same as in example (1) except that, on rare occasions, an employee of P receives an order which he, after consultation with officials of S and because P cannot fill the order, accepts on behalf of S rather than on behalf of P. P does not hold itself out as a person which those wishing to do business with S should contact. Assuming that orders for S are seldom handled in this manner and that they do not constitute a significant part of that corporation's business, S shall not be considered to have an office or other fixed place of business in the United States because of these activities of an employee of P.

Example (3). The facts are the same as in example (1) except that all orders received by S are subject to review by an officer of P before acceptance. S has a business office in the United States.

Example (4). S, a foreign corporation organized under the laws of Puerto Rico, is engaged in the business of manufacturing dresses in Puerto Rico and is entitled to an income tax exemption under the Puerto Rico Industrial Incentive Act of 1963. S is a wholly owned subsidiary of P, a domestic corporation engaged in the business of buying and selling dresses to customers in the United States. S sells most of the dresses it produces to P, the assumption being made that the income from these sales is derived from sources without the United States. P in turn sells these dresses in the United States in its name and through the efforts of its own employees and of distributors appointed by it. S does not have a fixed facility in the United States, and none of its employees are stationed in the United States. On occasion, employees of S visit the office of P in the United States, and executives of P visit the office of S in Puerto Rico, to discuss with one another matters of mutual business interest involving both corporations, including the strategy for marketing the dresses produced by S. These matters are also regularly discussed by such persons by telephone calls between the United States and Puerto Rico. S's employees do not otherwise participate in P's marketing activities. Officers of P are generally responsible for the policies followed by S and are directors of S, but S has a chief executive officer in Puerto Rico who, from its office therein, handles the day-to-day conduct of S's business. Based upon the facts presented, and assuming there are no other facts which would lead to a different determination, S shall not be considered to have an office or other fixed place of business in the United States for purposes of this section.

Example (5). The facts are the same as in example (4) except that the dresses are manufactured by S in styles and designs furnished by P and out of goods and raw materials purchased by P and sold to S. Based upon the facts presented, and assuming there are no other facts which would lead to a different determination, S shall not be considered to have an office or other fixed place of business in the United States for purposes of this section.

Example (6). The facts are the same as in example (5) except that pursuant to the instructions of P, the dresses sold by P are shipped by S directly to P's customers in the United States. Based upon the facts presented, and assuming there are no other facts which would lead to a different determination, S shall not be considered to have an office or other fixed place of business in the United States for purposes of this section. [Reg. § 1.864-7.]

☐ [T.D. 7216, 11-2-72.]

[Reg. § 1.864-8T]

§ 1.864-8T. Treatment of related person factoring income (temporary).—(a) *Applicability*—(1) *General rule.* This section applies for purposes of determining the treatment of income derived by a person from a trade or service receivable acquired from a related person. Except as provided in paragraph (d) of this section, if a person acquires (directly or indirectly) a trade or service receivable from a related person, any income (including any stated interest, discount or service fee) derived from the trade or service receivable shall be treated as if it were interest received on a loan to the obligor under the receivable. The characterization of income as interest pursuant to this section shall apply only for purposes of sections 551-558 (relating to foreign personal holding companies), sections 951-964 (relating to controlled foreign corporations), and section 904 (relating to the limitation on the foreign tax credit) of the Code and the regulations thereunder. The principles of sections 861 through 863 and the regulations thereunder shall be applied to determine the source of such interest income for purposes of section 904.

(2) *Override.* With respect to income characterized as interest under this section, the special rules of section 864(d) and this section override

Determination of Sources of Income

any conflicting provisions of the Code and regulations relating to foreign personal holding companies, controlled foreign corporations, and the foreign tax credit limitation. Thus, for example, pursuant to section 864(d)(5) and paragraph (e) of this section, stated interest derived from a factored trade or service receivable is not eligible for the subpart F de minimis rule of section 954(b)(3), the same country exception of section 954(c)(3)(A)(i), or the special rules for export financing interest of sections 904(d)(2) and 954(c)(2)(B), even if in the absence of this section the treatment of such stated interest would be governed by those sections.

(3) *Limitation.* Section 864(d) and this section apply only with respect to the tax treatment of income derived from a trade or service receivable acquired from a related person. Therefore, neither section 864(d) nor this section affects the characterization of an expense or loss of either the seller of a receivable or the obligor under a receivable. Accordingly, the obligor under a trade or service receivable shall not be allowed to treat any part of the purchase price of property or services as interest (other than amounts treated as interest under provisions other than section 864(d)).

(b) *Definitions.* The following definitions apply for purposes of this section and § 1.956-3T.

(1) *Trade or service receivable.* The term "trade or service receivable" means any account receivable or evidence of indebtedness, whether or not issued at a discount and whether or not bearing stated interest, arising out of the disposition by a related person of property described in section 1221(l) (hereinafter referred to as "inventory property") or the performance of services by a related person.

(2) *Related person.* A "related person" is:

(i) A person who is a related person within the meaning of section 267(b) and the regulations thereunder;

(ii) A United States shareholder (as defined in section 951(b)); or

(iii) A person who is related (within the meaning of section 267(b) and the regulations thereunder) to a United States shareholder.

(c) *Acquisition of a trade or service receivable*—(1) *General rule.* A trade or service receivable is considered to be acquired by a person at the time when that person is entitled to receive all or a portion of the income from the trade or service receivable. A person who acquires a trade or service receivable (hereinafter referred to as the "factor") is considered to have acquired a trade or service receivable regardless of whether:

(i) The acquisition is characterized for federal income tax purposes as a sale, a pledge of collateral for a loan, an assignment, a capital contribution, or otherwise;

(ii) The factor takes title to or obtains physical possession of the trade or service receivable;

(iii) The related person assigns the trade or service receivable with or without recourse;

(iv) The factor or some other person is obligated to collect the payments due under the trade or service receivable;

(v) The factor is liable for all property, excise, sales, or similar taxes due upon collection of the receivable;

(vi) The factor advances the entire face amount of the trade or service receivable transferred;

(vii) All trade or service receivables assigned by the related person are assigned to one factor; and

(viii) The obligor under the trade or service receivable is notified of the assignment.

(2) *Example.* The following example illustrates the application of paragraphs (a), (b), and (c)(1) of this section.

Example. P, a domestic corporation, owns all of the outstanding stock of FS, a controlled foreign corporation. P manufactures and sells paper products to customers, including X, an unrelated domestic corporation. As part of a sales transaction, P takes back a trade receivable from X and sells the receivable to FS. Because FS has acquired a trade or service receivable from a related person, the income derived by FS from P's receivable is interest income described in paragraph (a)(1) of this section.

(3) *Indirect acquisitions*—(i) *Acquisition through unrelated person.* A trade or service receivable will be considered to be acquired from a related person if it is acquired from an unrelated person who acquired (directly or indirectly) such receivable from a person who is a related person to the factor. The following example illustrates the application of this paragraph (c)(3)(i).

Example. A, a United States citizen, owns all of the outstanding stock of FPHC, a foreign personal holding company. A performs engineering services within and without the United States for customers, including X, an unrelated corporation. A performs engineering services for X and takes back a service receivable. A sells the receivable to Y, an unrelated corporation engaged in the factoring business. Y resells the receivable to FPHC. Because FPHC has indirectly acquired a service receivable from a related person, the income de-

Reg. § 1.864-8T(c)(3)

rived by FPHC from A's receivable is interest income described in paragraph (a)(1) of this section.

(ii) *Acquisition by nominee or pass-through entity.* A factor will be considered to have acquired a trade or service receivable held on its behalf by a nominee or by a partnership, simple trust, S corporation or other pass-through entity to the extent the factor owns (directly or indirectly) a beneficial interest in such partnership or other pass-through entity. The rule of this paragraph (c)(3)(ii) does not limit the application of paragraph (c)(3)(iii) of this section regarding the characterization of trade or service receivables of unrelated persons acquired pursuant to certain swap or pooling arrangements. The following example illustrates the application of this paragraph (c)(3)(ii).

Example. FS1, a controlled foreign corporation, acquires a 20 percent limited partnership interest in PS, a partnership. PS purchases trade or service receivables resulting from the sale of inventory property by FS1's domestic parent, P. PS does not purchase receivables of any person who is related to any other partner in PS. FS1 is considered to have acquired a 20 percent interest in the receivables acquired by PS. Thus, FS1's distributive share of the income derived by PS from the receivables of P. is considered to be interest income described in paragraph (a)(1) of this section.

(iii) *Swap or pooling arrangements.* A trade or service receivable of a person unrelated to the factor will be considered to be a trade or service receivable acquired from a related person and subject to the rules of this section if it is acquired in accordance with an arrangement that involves two or more groups of related persons that are unrelated to each other and the effect of the arrangement is that one or more related persons in each group acquire (directly or indirectly) trade or service receivables of one or more unrelated persons who are also parties to the arrangement, in exchange for reciprocal purchases of the first group's receivables. The following example illustrates the application of this paragraph (c)(3)(iii).

Example. Controlled foreign corporations A, B, C, and D are wholly-owned subsidiaries of domestic corporations M, N, O, and P, respectively. M, N, O, and P are not related persons. According to a prearranged plan, A, B, C, and D each acquire trade or service receivables of M, N, O, and/or P, except that neither A, B, C nor D acquires receivables of its own parent corporation. Because the effect of this arrangement is that the unrelated groups acquire each other's trade or service receivables pursuant to the arrangement, income derived by A, B, C, and D from the receivables acquired from M, N, O, and P is interest income described in paragraph (a)(1) of this section.

(iv) *Financing arrangements.* If a controlled foreign corporation (as defined in section 957(a)) participates (directly or indirectly) in a lending transaction that results in a loan to the purchaser of inventory property, services, or trade or service receivables of a related person (or a loan to a person who is related to the purchaser), and if the loan would not have been made or maintained on the same terms but for the corresponding purchase, then the controlled foreign corporation shall be considered to have indirectly acquired a trade or service receivable, and income derived by the controlled foreign corporation from such a loan shall be considered to be income described in paragraph (a)(1) of this section. For purposes of this paragraph (c)(3)(iv), it is immaterial that the sums lent are not, in fact, the sums used to finance the purchase of a related person's inventory property, services, or trade or service receivables. The amount of income derived by the controlled foreign corporation to be taken into account shall be the total amount of income derived from a lending transaction described in this paragraph (c)(3)(iv), if the amount lent is less than or equal to the purchase price of the inventory property, services, or trade or service receivables. If the amount lent is greater than the purchase price of the inventory property, services or receivables, the amount to be taken into account shall be the proportion of the interest charge (including original issue discount) that the purchase price bears to the total amount lent pursuant to the lending transaction. The following examples illustrate the application of this paragraph (c)(3)(iv).

Example (1). P, a domestic corporation, owns all of the outstanding stock of FS1, a controlled foreign corporation engaged in the financing business in Country X. P manufactures and sells toys, including sales to C, an unrelated corporation. Prior to P's sale of toys to C for $2,000, D, a wholly-owned Country X subsidiary of C, borrows $3,000 from FS1. The loan from FS1 to D would not have been made or maintained on the same terms but for C's purchase of toys from P. Two-thirds of the income derived by FS1 from the loan to D is interest income described in paragraph (a)(1) of this section.

Example (2). P, a domestic corporation, owns all of the outstanding stock of FS1, a controlled foreign corporation organized under the laws of Country X. FS1 has accumulated cash reserves. P has uncollected trade and service re-

Reg. § 1.864-8T(c)(3)

ceivables of foreign obligors. FS1 makes a $1,000 loan to U, a foreign corporation that is unrelated to P or FS1. U purchases P's trade and service receivables for $2,000. The loan would not have been made or maintained on the same terms but for U's purchase of P's receivables. The income derived by U from the receivables is not interest income within the meaning of paragraph (a) of this section. However, the interest paid by U to FS1 is interest income described in paragraph (a)(1) of this section.

Example (3). The facts are the same as in Example (2), except that U is a wholly-owned Country Y subsidiary of FS1. Because U is related to P within the meaning of paragraph (b)(2) of this section, under paragraph (c)(1) of this section, income derived by U from P's receivables is interest income described in paragraph (a)(1) of this section. In addition, the income derived by FS1 from the loan to U is interest income described in paragraph (a)(1) of this section.

(d) *Same country exception*—(1) *Income from trade or service receivables.* Income derived from a trade or service receivable acquired from a related person shall not be treated as interest income described in paragraph (a)(1) of this section if:

(i) The person acquiring the trade or service receivable and the related person are created or organized under the laws of the same foreign country;

(ii) The related person has a substantial part of its assets used in its trade or business located in such foreign country; and

(iii) The related person would not have derived foreign base company income, as defined in section 954(a) and the regulations thereunder, or income effectively connected with a United States trade or business from such receivable if the related person had collected the receivable.

For purposes of paragraph (d)(1)(ii) of this section, the standards contained in § 1.954-2(e) shall apply in determining the location of a substantial part of the assets of a related person. For purposes of paragraph (d)(1)(iii) of this section, a determination of whether the related person would have derived foreign base company income shall be made without regard to the de minimis test described in section 954(b)(3)(A). The following examples illustrate the application of this paragraph (d)(1).

Example (1). FS1, a controlled foreign corporation incorporated under the laws of Country X, owns all of the outstanding stock of FS2, which is also incorporated under the laws of Country X. FS1 has a substantial part of its assets used in its business in Country X. FS1 manufactures and sells toys for use in Country Y. The toys sold are considered to be manufactured in Country X under § 1.954-3(a)(2). FS1 is not considered to have a branch or similar establishment in Country Y that is treated as a separate corporation under section 954(d)(2) and § 1.954-3(b). Thus, gross income derived by FS1 from the toy sales is not foreign base company sales income. FS1 takes back receivables without stated interest from its customers. FS1 assigns those receivables to FS2. The income derived by FS2 from the receivables of FS1 is not interest income described in paragraph (a)(1) of this section, because it satisfies the same country exception under paragraph (d)(1) of this section.

Example (2). The facts are the same as in Example (1), except that the toys sold by FS1 are purchased from FS1's U.S. parent and are sold for use outside of Country X. Thus, any income derived by FS1 from the sale of the toys would be foreign base company sales income. Therefore, income derived by FS2 from the receivables of FS1 is interest income described in paragraph (a)(1) of this section. FS2 is considered to derive interest income from the receivable even if, solely by reason of the de minimis rule of section 954(b)(3)(A), FS1 would not have derived foreign base company income if FS1 had collected the receivable.

(2) *Income from financing arrangements.* Income derived by a controlled foreign corporation from a loan to a person that purchases inventory property or services of a person that is related to the controlled foreign corporation, or from other loans described in paragraph (c)(3)(iv) of this section, shall not be treated as interest income described in paragraph (a)(1) of this section if:

(i) The person providing the financing and the related person are created or organized under the laws of the same foreign country;

(ii) The related person has a substantial part of its assets used in its trade or business located in such foreign country; and

(iii) The related person would not have derived foreign base company income or income effectively connected with a United States trade or business:

(A) From the sale of inventory property or services to the borrower or from financing the borrower's purchase of inventory property or services, in the case of a loan to the purchaser of inventory property or services of a related person; or

(B) From collecting amounts due under the receivable or from financing the purchase of the receivable, in the case of a loan to the pur-

Reg. § 1.864-8T(d)(2)

46,142 Determination of Sources of Income

See p. 20,601 for regulations not amended to reflect law changes

chaser of a trade or service receivable of a related person.

For purposes of paragraph (d)(2)(ii) of this section, the standards contained in § 1.954-2(e) shall apply in determining the location of a substantial part of the assets of a related person. For purposes of paragraph (d)(2)(iii) of this section, a determination of whether the related person would have derived foreign base company income shall be made without regard to the de minimis test described in section 954(b)(3)(A). The following examples illustrate the application of this paragraph (d)(2).

Example (1). FS1, a controlled foreign corporation incorporated under the laws of Country X, owns all of the outstanding stock of FS2, which is also incorporated under the laws of Country X. FS1, which has a substantial part of its assets used in its business located in Country X, manufactures and sells toys for use in Country Y. The toys sold are considered to be manufactured in Country X under § 1.954-3(a)(2). FS1 is not considered to have a branch or similar establishment in Country Y that is treated as a separate corporation under section 954(d)(2) and § 1.954-3(b). Thus, the gross income derived by FS1 from the toy sales is not foreign base company sales income. FS2 makes a loan to FS3, a wholly-owned subsidiary of FS1 which is also incorporated under the laws of Country X, in connection with FS3's purchase of toys from FS1. FS3 does not earn any subpart F gross income. Thus, FS1 would not have derived foreign personal holding company interest income if FS1 had made the loan to FS3, because the interest would be covered by the same country exception of section 954(c)(3). Therefore, the income derived by FS2 from its loan to FS3 is not treated as interest income described in paragraph (a)(1) of this section, because it satisfies the same country exception under paragraph (d)(2) of this section. Such income is also not treated as foreign personal holding company income described in section 954(c)(1)(A) because the same country exception of section 954(c)(3) also applies to the interest actually derived by FS2 from its loan to FS3.

Example (2). FS1, a controlled foreign corporation incorporated under the laws of Country X, owns all of the outstanding stock of FS2, which is also incorporated under the laws of Country X. FS1 purchases toys from its U.S. parent and resells them for use outside of Country X. As part of a sales transaction, FS1 takes back trade receivables. FS2 makes a loan to U, an unrelated corporation, to finance U's purchase of FS1's trade receivables. Because FS1 would have derived foreign base company income if FS1 had collected the receivables or made the loan itself, the same country exception of paragraph (d)(2) of this section does not apply. Accordingly, under paragraph (c)(3)(iv) of this section, the income derived by FS2 from its loan to U is treated as interest income described in paragraph (a)(1) of this section.

(e) *Special rules*—(1) *Foreign personal holding companies and controlled foreign corporations.* For purposes of sections 551-558 (relating to foreign personal holding companies), the exclusion provided by section 552(c) for interest described in section 954(c)(3)(A) shall not apply to income described in paragraph (a)(1) of this section. For purposes of the sections 951-964 (relating to controlled foreign corporations), income described in paragraph (a)(1) of this section shall be included in a United States shareholder's pro rata share of a controlled foreign corporation's subpart F income without regard to the de minimis rule under section 954(b)(3)(A). However, income described in paragraph (a)(1) of this section shall be included in the computation of a controlled foreign corporation's foreign base company income for purposes of applying the de minimis rule under section 954(b)(3)(A) and the more than 70 percent of gross income test under section 954(b)(3)(B). In addition, income described in paragraph (a)(1) of this section shall be considered to be subpart F income without regard to the exclusions from foreign base company income provided by section 954(c)(2)(B) (relating to export financing interest derived in the conduct of a banking business) and section 954(c)(3)(A)(i) (relating to certain interest income received from related persons).

(2) *Foreign tax credit.* Income described in paragraph (a)(1) of this section shall be considered to be interest income for purposes of the section 904 foreign tax credit limitation and is not eligible for the exceptions for export financing interest provided in section 904(d)(2)(A)(iii)(II), (B)(ii), and (C)(iii). In addition, such income will be subject to the look-through rule for subpart F income set forth in section 904(d)(3) without regard to the de minimis exception provided in section 904(d)(3)(E).

(3) *Possessions corporations*—(i) *Limitation on credit.* Income described in paragraph (a)(1) of this section shall not be treated as income described in section 936(a)(1)(A) or (B) unless the income is considered under the principles of § 1.863-6 to be derived from sources within the possessions. Thus, the credit provided by section 936 is not available for income described in paragraph (a)(1) of this section unless the obligor under the receivable is a resident of a possession.

Reg. § 1.864-8T(e)(1)

Determination of Sources of Income

See p. 20,601 for regulations not amended to reflect law changes

In the case of a loan described in section 864(d)(6), the credit provided by section 936 is not available for income described in paragraph (a)(1) of this section unless the purchaser of the inventory property or services is a resident of a possession.

(ii) *Eligibility determination.* Notwithstanding the limitation on the availability of the section 936 credit for income described in paragraph (a)(1) of this section, if income treated as interest income under paragraph (a)(1) of this section is derived from sources within a possession (determined without regard to this section), such income shall be eligible for inclusion in a corporation's gross income for purposes of section 936(a)(2)(A). If such income is derived from the active conduct of a trade or business within a possession (determined without regard to this section), such income shall be eligible for inclusion in a corporation's gross income for purposes of section 936(a)(2)(B). (These rules apply for purposes of determining whether a corporation is eligible to elect the credit provided under section 936(a)).

(iii) *Example.* The following example illustrates the application of paragraph (e)(3) of this section.

Example. Corporation X is operating in a possession as a possessions corporation. In 1985, X earned $50,000 from the active conduct of a business in the possession, including $5,000 from trade or service receivables acquired from a related party. Obligors under the receivables acquired by X are not residents of the possession. Corporation X also earned $20,000 from activities other than its active conduct of business in the possession. The $5,000 derived by X from the receivables is not eligible for the section 936 credit. However, the $5,000 may be used by X to meet the percentage tests under section 936(a)(2) to the extent that such income is considered to be derived from sources within the possession (for purposes of section 936(a)(2)(A)) or is considered to be derived from the active conduct of a trade or business in the possession (for purposes of section 936(a)(2)(B)), in either case determined without regard to the characterization of such income under this section.

(f) *Effective date.* The provisions of this section shall apply with respect to accounts receivable and evidences of indebtedness transferred after March 1, 1984 and are effective June 14, 1988. [Temporary Reg. § 1.864-8T.]

☐ [T.D. 8209, 6-13-88.]

[Reg. § 1.865-1]

§ 1.865-1. **Loss with respect to personal property other than stock.**—(a) *General rules for allocation of loss*—(1) *Allocation against gain.* Except as otherwise provided in § 1.865-2 and paragraph (c) of this section, loss recognized with respect to personal property shall be allocated to the class of gross income and, if necessary, apportioned between the statutory grouping of gross income (or among the statutory groupings) and the residual grouping of gross income, with respect to which gain from a sale of such property would give rise in the hands of the seller. For purposes of this section, loss includes bad debt deductions under section 166 and loss on property that is marked-to-market (such as under section 475) and subject to the rules of this section. Thus, for example, loss recognized by a United States resident on the sale or worthlessness of a bond generally is allocated to reduce United States source income.

(2) *Loss attributable to foreign office.* Except as otherwise provided in § 1.865-2 and paragraph (c) of this section, and except with respect to loss subject to paragraph (b) of this section, in the case of loss recognized by a United States resident with respect to property that is attributable to an office or other fixed place of business in a foreign country within the meaning of section 865(e)(3), the loss shall be allocated to reduce foreign source income if a gain on the sale of the property would have been taxable by the foreign country and the highest marginal rate of tax imposed on such gains in the foreign country is at least 10 percent. However, paragraph (a)(1) of this section and not this paragraph (a)(2) will apply if gain on the sale of such property would be sourced under section 865(c), (d)(1)(B), or (d)(3).

(3) *Loss recognized by United States citizen or resident alien with foreign tax home.* Except as otherwise provided in § 1.865-2 and paragraph (c) of this section, and except with respect to loss subject to paragraph (b) of this section, in the case of loss with respect to property recognized by a United States citizen or resident alien that has a tax home (as defined in section 911(d)(3)) in a foreign country, the loss shall be allocated to reduce foreign source income if a gain on the sale of such property would have been taxable by a foreign country and the highest marginal rate of tax imposed on such gains in the foreign country is at least 10 percent.

(4) *Allocation for purposes of section 904.* For purposes of section 904, loss recognized with respect to property that is allocated to foreign source income under this paragraph (a) shall be allocated to the separate category under section

Reg. § 1.865-1(a)(4)

904(d) to which gain on the sale of the property would have been assigned (without regard to section 904(d)(2)(A)(iii)(III)). For purposes of § 1.904-4(c)(2)(ii)(A), any such loss allocated to passive income shall be allocated (prior to the application of § 1.904-4(c)(2)(ii)(B)) to the group of passive income to which gain on a sale of the property would have been assigned had a sale of the property resulted in the recognition of a gain under the law of the relevant foreign jurisdiction or jurisdictions.

(5) *Loss recognized by partnership.* A partner's distributive share of loss recognized by a partnership with respect to personal property shall be allocated and apportioned in accordance with this section as if the partner had recognized the loss. If loss is attributable to an office or other fixed place of business of the partnership within the meaning of section 865(e)(3), such office or fixed place of business shall be considered to be an office of the partner for purposes of this section.

(b) *Special rules of application*—(1) *Depreciable property.* In the case of a loss recognized with respect to depreciable personal property, the gain referred to in paragraph (a)(1) of this section is the gain that would be sourced under section 865(c)(1) (depreciation recapture).

(2) *Contingent payment debt instrument.* Loss described in the last sentence of § 1.1275-4(b)(9)(iv)(A) that is recognized with respect to a contingent payment debt instrument to which § 1.1275-4(b) applies (instruments issued for money or publicly traded property) shall be allocated to the class of gross income and, if necessary, apportioned between the statutory grouping of gross income (or among the statutory groupings) and the residual grouping of gross income, with respect to which interest income from the instrument (in the amount of the loss subject to this paragraph (b)(2)) would give rise.

(c) *Exceptions*—(1) *Foreign currency and certain financial instruments.* This section does not apply to loss governed by section 988 and loss recognized with respect to options contracts or derivative financial instruments, including futures contracts, forward contracts, notional principal contracts, or evidence of an interest in any of the foregoing.

(2) *Inventory.* This section does not apply to loss recognized with respect to property described in section 1221(a)(1).

(3) *Interest equivalents and trade receivables.* Loss subject to § 1.861-9T(b) (loss equivalent to interest expense and loss on trade receivables) shall be allocated and apportioned under the rules of § 1.861-9T and not under the rules of this section.

(4) *Unamortized bond premium.* If a taxpayer recognizing loss with respect to a bond (within the meaning of § 1.171-1(b)) did not amortize bond premium to the full extent permitted by section 171 and the regulations thereunder, then, to the extent of the amount of bond premium that could have been, but was not, amortized by the taxpayer, loss recognized with respect to the bond shall be allocated to the class of gross income and, if necessary, apportioned between the statutory grouping of gross income (or among the statutory groupings) and the residual grouping of gross income, with respect to which interest income from the bond was assigned.

(5) *Accrued interest.* Loss attributable to accrued but unpaid interest on a debt obligation shall be allocated to the class of gross income and, if necessary, apportioned between the statutory grouping of gross income (or among the statutory groupings) and the residual grouping of gross income, with respect to which interest income from the obligation was assigned. For purposes of this section, whether loss is attributable to accrued but unpaid interest (rather than to principal) shall be determined under the principles of §§ 1.61-7(d) and 1.446-2(e).

(6) *Anti-abuse rules*—(i) *Transactions involving built-in losses.* If one of the principal purposes of a transaction is to change the allocation of a built-in loss with respect to personal property by transferring the property to another person, qualified business unit, office or other fixed place of business, or branch that subsequently recognizes the loss, the loss shall be allocated by the transferee as if it were recognized by the transferor immediately prior to the transaction. If one of the principal purposes of a change of residence is to change the allocation of a built-in loss with respect to personal property, the loss shall be allocated as if the change of residence had not occurred. If one of the principal purposes of a transaction is to change the allocation of a built-in loss on the disposition of personal property by converting the original property into other property and subsequently recognizing loss with respect to such other property, the loss shall be allocated as if it were recognized with respect to the original property immediately prior to the transaction. Transactions subject to this paragraph shall include, without limitation, reorganizations within the meaning of section 368(a), liquidations under section 332, transfers to a corporation under section 351, transfers to a partnership under section 721, transfers to a trust, distributions by a partnership, distributions by a trust, transfers to or from a qualified business unit, office or other fixed place of business, or branch, or exchanges under section 1031. A person

Reg. § 1.865-1(a)(5)

Determination of Sources of Income 46,145

See p. 20,601 for regulations not amended to reflect law changes

may have a principal purpose of affecting loss allocation even though this purpose is outweighed by other purposes (taken together or separately).

(ii) *Offsetting positions.* If a taxpayer recognizes loss with respect to personal property and the taxpayer (or any person described in section 267(b) (after application of section 267(c)), 267(e), 318 or 482 with respect to the taxpayer) holds (or held) offsetting positions with respect to such property with a principal purpose of recognizing foreign source income and United States source loss, the loss shall be allocated and apportioned against such foreign source income. For purposes of this paragraph (c)(6)(ii), positions are offsetting if the risk of loss of holding one or more positions is substantially diminished by holding one or more other positions.

(iii) *Matching rule.* If a taxpayer (or a person described in section 1059(c)(3)(C) with respect to the taxpayer) engages in a transaction or series of transactions with a principal purpose of recognizing foreign source income that results in the creation of a corresponding loss with respect to personal property (as a consequence of the rules regarding the timing of recognition of income, for example), the loss shall be allocated and apportioned against such income to the extent of the recognized foreign source income. For an example illustrating a similar rule with respect to stock loss, see § 1.865-2(b)(4)(iv) *Example 3.*

(d) *Definitions*—(1) *Contingent payment debt instrument.* A contingent payment debt instrument is any debt instrument that is subject to § 1.1275-4.

(2) *Depreciable personal property.* Depreciable personal property is any property described in section 865(c)(4)(A).

(3) *Terms defined in § 1.861-8.* See § 1.861-8 for the meaning of *class of gross income, statutory grouping of gross income,* and *residual grouping of gross income.*

(e) *Examples.* The application of this section may be illustrated by the following examples:

Example 1. On January 1, 2000, *A*, a domestic corporation, purchases for $1,000 a machine that produces widgets, which *A* sells in the United States and throughout the world. Throughout *A*'s holding period, the machine is located and used in Country *X*. During *A*'s holding period, *A* incurs depreciation deductions of $400 with respect to the machine. Under § 1.861-8, *A* allocates and apportions depreciation deductions of $250 against foreign source general limitation income and $150 against U.S. source income. On December 12, 2002, *A* sells the machine for $100 and recognizes a loss of $500. Because the machine was used predominantly outside the United States, under sections 865(c)(1)(B) and 865(c)(3)(B)(ii) gain on the disposition of the machine would be foreign source general limitation income to the extent of the depreciation adjustments. Therefore, under paragraph (b)(1) of this section, the entire $500 loss is allocated against foreign source general limitation income.

Example 2. On January 1, 2002, *A*, a domestic corporation, loans $2,000 to *N*, its wholly-owned controlled foreign corporation, in exchange for a contingent payment debt instrument subject to § 1.1275-4(b). During 2002 through 2004, *A* accrues and receives interest income of $630, $150 of which is foreign source general limitation income and $480 of which is foreign source passive income under section 904(d)(3). Assume there are no positive or negative adjustments pursuant to § 1.1275-4(b)(6) in 2002 through 2004. On January 1, 2005, *A* disposes of the debt instrument and recognizes a $770 loss. Under § 1.1275-4(b)(8)(ii), $630 of the loss is treated as ordinary loss and $140 is treated as capital loss. Assume that $140 of interest income earned in 2005 with respect to the debt instrument would be foreign source passive income under section 904(d)(3). Under § 1.1275-4(b)(9)(iv), $150 of the ordinary loss is allocated against foreign source general limitation income and $480 of the ordinary loss is allocated against foreign source passive income. Under paragraph (b)(2) of this section, the $140 capital loss is allocated against foreign source passive income.

Example 3. (i) On January 1, 2003, *A*, a domestic corporation, purchases for $1,200 a taxable bond maturing on December 31, 2008, with a stated principal amount of $1,000, payable at maturity. The bond provides for unconditional payments of interest of $100, payable December 31 of each year. The issuer of the bond is a foreign corporation and interest on the bond is thus foreign source. Interest payments for 2003 and 2004 are timely made. *A* does not elect to amortize its bond premium under section 171 and the regulations thereunder, which would have permitted *A* to offset the $100 of interest income by $28.72 of bond premium in 2003, and by $30.42 in 2004. On January 1, 2005, *A* sells the bond and recognizes a $100 loss. Under paragraph (c)(4) of this section, $59.14 of the loss is allocated against foreign source income. Under paragraph (a)(1) of this section, the remaining $40.86 of the loss is allocated against U.S. source income.

(ii) The facts are the same as in paragraph (i) of this *Example 3*, except that *A* made the election to amortize its bond premium effective for taxable year 2004 (see § 1.171-4(c)). Under paragraph (c)(4) of this section, $28.72 of the loss is allocated against foreign source income. Under

Reg. § 1.865-1(e)

paragraph (a)(1) of this section, the remaining $71.28 of the loss is allocated against U.S. source income.

Example 4. On January 1, 2002, *A*, a domestic corporation, purchases for $1,000 a bond maturing December 31, 2014, with a stated principal amount of $1,000, payable at maturity. The bond provides for unconditional payments of interest of $100, payable December 31 of each year. The issuer of the bond is a foreign corporation and interest on the bond is thus foreign source. Between 2002 and 2006, *A* accrues and receives foreign source interest income of $500 with respect to the bond. On January 1, 2007, *A* sells the bond and recognizes a $500 loss. Under paragraph (a)(1) of this section, the $500 loss is allocated against U.S. source income.

Example 5. On January 1, 2002, *A*, a domestic corporation on the accrual method of accounting, purchases for $1,000 a bond maturing December 31, 2012, with a stated principal amount of $1,000, payable at maturity. The bond provides for unconditional payments of interest of $100, payable December 31 of each year. The issuer of the bond is a foreign corporation and interest on the bond is thus foreign source. On June 10, 2002, after *A* has accrued $44 of interest income, but before any interest has been paid, the issuer suddenly becomes insolvent and declares bankruptcy. *A* sells the bond (including the accrued interest) for $20. Assuming that *A* properly accrued $44 of interest income, *A* treats the $20 proceeds from the sale of the bond as payment of interest previously accrued and recognizes a $1,000 loss with respect to the bond principal and a $24 loss with respect to the accrued interest. See § 1.61-7(d). Under paragraph (a)(1) of this section, the $1,000 loss with respect to the principal is allocated against U.S. source income. Under paragraph (c)(5) of this section, the $24 loss with respect to accrued but unpaid interest is allocated against foreign source interest income.

(f) *Effective date*—(1) *In general.* Except as provided in paragraph (f)(2) of this section, this section is applicable to loss recognized on or after January 8, 2002. For purposes of this paragraph (f), loss that is recognized but deferred (for example, under section 267 or 1092) shall be treated as recognized at the time the loss is taken into account.

(2) *Application to prior periods.* A taxpayer may apply the rules of this section to losses recognized in any taxable year beginning on or after January 1, 1987, and all subsequent years, provided that—

(i) The taxpayer's tax liability as shown on an original or amended tax return is consistent with the rules of this section for each such year for which the statute of limitations does not preclude the filing of an amended return on June 30, 2002; and

(ii) The taxpayer makes appropriate adjustments to eliminate any double benefit arising from the application of this section to years that are not open for assessment.

(3) *Examples.* See § 1.865-2(e)(3) for examples illustrating an applicability date provision similar to the applicability date provided in this paragraph (f). [Reg. § 1.865-1.]

☐ [*T.D.* 8973, 12-27-2001.]

[Reg. § 1.865-2]

§ 1.865-2. **Loss with respect to stock.**—(a) *General rules for allocation of loss with respect to stock*—(1) *Allocation against gain.* Except as otherwise provided in paragraph (b) of this section, loss recognized with respect to stock shall be allocated to the class of gross income and, if necessary, apportioned between the statutory grouping of gross income (or among the statutory groupings) and the residual grouping of gross income, with respect to which gain (other than gain treated as a dividend under section 964(e)(1) or 1248) from a sale of such stock would give rise in the hands of the seller (without regard to section 865(f)). For purposes of this section, loss includes loss on property that is marked-to-market (such as under section 475) and subject to the rules of this section. Thus, for example, loss recognized by a United States resident on the sale of stock generally is allocated to reduce United States source income.

(2) *Stock attributable to foreign office.* Except as otherwise provided in paragraph (b) of this section, in the case of loss recognized by a United States resident with respect to stock that is attributable to an office or other fixed place of business in a foreign country within the meaning of section 865(e)(3), the loss shall be allocated to reduce foreign source income if a gain on the sale of the stock would have been taxable by the foreign country and the highest marginal rate of tax imposed on such gains in the foreign country is at least 10 percent.

(3) *Loss recognized by United States citizen or resident alien with foreign tax home*—(i) *In general.* Except as otherwise provided in paragraph (b) of this section, in the case of loss with respect to stock that is recognized by a United States citizen or resident alien that has a tax home (as defined in section 911(d)(3)) in a foreign country, the loss shall be allocated to reduce foreign source income if a gain on the sale of the stock would have been taxable by a foreign coun-

try and the highest marginal rate of tax imposed on such gains in the foreign country is at least 10 percent.

(ii) *Bona fide residents of Puerto Rico.* Except as otherwise provided in paragraph (b) of this section, in the case of loss with respect to stock in a corporation described in section 865(g)(3) recognized by a United States citizen or resident alien that is a bona fide resident of Puerto Rico during the entire taxable year, the loss shall be allocated to reduce foreign source income. If gain from a sale of such stock would give rise to income exempt from tax under section 933, the loss with respect to such stock shall be allocated to amounts that are excluded from gross income under section 933(1) and therefore shall not be allowed as a deduction from gross income. See section 933(1) and § 1.933-1(c).

(4) *Stock constituting a United States real property interest.* Loss recognized by a nonresident alien individual or a foreign corporation with respect to stock that constitutes a United States real property interest shall be allocated to reduce United States source income. For additional rules governing the treatment of such loss, see section 897 and the regulations thereunder.

(5) *Allocation for purposes of section 904.* For purposes of section 904, loss recognized with respect to stock that is allocated to foreign source income under this paragraph (a) shall be allocated to the separate category under section 904(d) to which gain on a sale of the stock would have been assigned (without regard to section 904(d)(2)(A)(iii)(III)). For purposes of § 1.904-4(c)(2)(ii)(A), any such loss allocated to passive income shall be allocated (prior to the application of § 1.904-4(c)(2)(ii)(B)) to the group of passive income to which gain on a sale of the stock would have been assigned had a sale of the stock resulted in the recognition of a gain under the law of the relevant foreign jurisdiction or jurisdictions.

(b) *Exceptions*—(1) *Dividend recapture exception*—(i) *In general.* If a taxpayer recognizes a loss with respect to shares of stock, and the taxpayer (or a person described in section 1059(c)(3)(C) with respect to such shares) included in income a dividend recapture amount (or amounts) with respect to such shares at any time during the recapture period, then, to the extent of the dividend recapture amount (or amounts), the loss shall be allocated and apportioned on a proportionate basis to the class or classes of gross income or the statutory or residual grouping or groupings of gross income to which the dividend recapture amount was assigned.

(ii) *Exception for de minimis amounts.* Paragraph (b)(1)(i) of this section shall not apply to a loss recognized by a taxpayer on the disposition of stock if the sum of all dividend recapture amounts (other than dividend recapture amounts eligible for the exception described in paragraph (b)(1)(iii) of this section (passive limitation dividends)) included in income by the taxpayer (or a person described in section 1059(c)(3)(C)) with respect to such stock during the recapture period is less than 10 percent of the recognized loss.

(iii) *Exception for passive limitation dividends.* Paragraph (b)(1)(i) of this section shall not apply to the extent of a dividend recapture amount that is treated as income in the separate category for passive income described in section 904(d)(2)(A) (without regard to section 904(d)(2)(A)(iii)(III)). The exception provided for in this paragraph (b)(1)(iii) shall not apply to any dividend recapture amount that is treated as income in the separate category for financial services income described in section 904(d)(2)(C).

(iv) *Examples.* The application of this paragraph (b)(1) may be illustrated by the following examples:

Example 1. (i) *P*, a domestic corporation, is a United States shareholder of *N*, a controlled foreign corporation. *N* has never had any subpart F income and all of its earnings and profits are described in section 959(c)(3). On May 5, 1998, *N* distributes a dividend to *P* in the amount of $100. The dividend gives rise to a $5 foreign withholding tax, and *P* is deemed to have paid an additional $45 of foreign income tax with respect to the dividend under section 902. Under the look-through rules of section 904(d)(3) the dividend is general limitation income described in section 904(d)(1)(I).

(ii) On February 6, 2000, *P* sells its shares of *N* and recognizes a $110 loss. In 2000, *P* has the following taxable income, excluding the loss on the sale of *N*:

(A) $1,000 of foreign source income that is general limitation income described in section 904(d)(1)(I);

(B) $1,000 of foreign source capital gain from the sale of stock in a foreign affiliate that is sourced under section 865(f) and is passive income described in section 904(d)(1)(A); and

(C) $1,000 of U.S. source income.

(iii) The $100 dividend paid in 1998 is a dividend recapture amount that was included in *P*'s income within the recapture period preceding the disposition of the *N* stock. The de minimis exception of paragraph (b)(1)(ii) of this section does not apply because the $100 dividend recap-

Reg. § 1.865-2(b)(1)

ture amount exceeds 10 percent of the $110 loss. Therefore, to the extent of the $100 dividend recapture amount, the loss must be allocated under paragraph (b)(1)(i) of this section to the separate limitation category to which the dividend was assigned (general limitation income).

(iv) *P*'s remaining $10 loss on the disposition of the *N* stock is allocated to U.S. source income under paragraph (a)(1) of this section.

(v) After allocation of the stock loss, *P*'s foreign source taxable income in 2000 consists of $900 of foreign source general limitation income and $1,000 of foreign source passive income.

Example 2. (i) *P*, a domestic corporation, owns all of the stock of *N1*, which owns all of the stock of *N2*, which owns all of the stock of *N3*. *N1*, *N2*, and *N3* are controlled foreign corporations. All of the corporations use the calendar year as their taxable year. On February 5, 1997, *N3* distributes a dividend to *N2*. The dividend is foreign personal holding company income of *N2* under section 954(c)(1)(A) that results in an inclusion of $100 in *P*'s income under section 951(a)(1)(A)(i) as of December 31, 1997. Under section 904(d)(3)(B) the inclusion is general limitation income described in section 904(d)(1)(I). The income inclusion to *P* results in a corresponding increase in *P*'s basis in the stock of *N1* under section 961(a).

(ii) On March 5, 1999, *P* sells its shares of *N1* and recognizes a $110 loss. The $100 1997 subpart F inclusion is a dividend recapture amount that was included in *P*'s income within the recapture period preceding the disposition of the *N1* stock. The de minimis exception of paragraph (b)(1)(ii) of this section does not apply because the $100 dividend recapture amount exceeds 10 percent of the $110 loss. Therefore, to the extent of the $100 dividend recapture amount, the loss must be allocated under paragraph (b)(1)(i) of this section to the separate limitation category to which the dividend recapture amount was assigned (general limitation income). The remaining $10 loss is allocated to U.S. source income under paragraph (a)(1) of this section.

Example 3. (i) *P*, a domestic corporation, owns all of the stock of *N1*, which owns all of the stock of *N2*. *N1* and *N2* are controlled foreign corporations. All the corporations use the calendar year as their taxable year and the U.S. dollar as their functional currency. On May 5, 1998, *N2* pays a dividend of $100 to *N1* out of general limitation earnings and profits.

(ii) On February 5, 2000, *N1* sells its *N2* stock to an unrelated purchaser. The sale results in a loss to *N1* of $110 for U.S. tax purposes. In 2000, *N1* has the following current earnings and profits, excluding the loss on the sale of *N2*:

(A) $1,000 of non-subpart F foreign source general limitation earnings and profits described in section 904(d)(1)(I);

(B) $1,000 of foreign source gain from the sale of stock that is taken into account in determining foreign personal holding company income under section 954(c)(1)(B)(i) and which is passive limitation earnings and profits described in section 904(d)(1)(A);

(C) $1,000 of foreign source interest income received from an unrelated person that is foreign personal holding company income under section 954(c)(1)(A) and which is passive limitation earnings and profits described in section 904(d)(1)(A).

(iii) The $100 dividend paid in 1998 is a dividend recapture amount that was included in *N1*'s income within the recapture period preceding the disposition of the *N2* stock. The de minimis exception of paragraph (b)(1)(ii) of this section does not apply because the $100 dividend recapture amount exceeds 10 percent of the $110 loss. Therefore, to the extent of the $100 dividend recapture amount, the loss must be allocated under paragraph (b)(1)(i) of this section to the separate limitation category to which the dividend was assigned (general limitation earnings and profits).

(iv) *N1*'s remaining $10 loss on the disposition of the *N2* stock is allocated to foreign source passive limitation earnings and profits under paragraph (a)(1) of this section.

(v) After allocation of the stock loss, *N1*'s current earnings and profits for 1998 consist of $900 of foreign source general limitation earnings and profits and $1,990 of foreign source passive limitation earnings and profits.

(vi) After allocation of the stock loss, *N1*'s subpart F income for 2000 consists of $1,000 of foreign source interest income that is foreign personal holding company income under section 954(c)(1)(A) and $890 of foreign source net gain that is foreign personal holding company income under section 954(c)(1)(B)(i). *P* includes $1,890 in income under section 951(a)(1)(A)(i) as passive income under sections 904(d)(1)(A) and 904(d)(3)(B).

Example 4. *P*, a foreign corporation, has two wholly-owned subsidiaries, *S*, a domestic corporation, and *B*, a foreign corporation. On January 1, 2000, *S* purchases a one-percent interest in *N*, a foreign corporation, for $100. On January 2, 2000, *N* distributes a $20 dividend to *S*. The $20 dividend is foreign source financial services in-

Reg. § 1.865-2(b)(1)

come. On January 3, 2000, S sells its N stock to B for $80 and recognizes a $20 loss that is deferred under section 267(f). On June 10, 2008, B sells its N stock to an unrelated person for $55. Under section 267(f) and § 1.267(f)-1(c)(1), S's $20 loss is deferred until 2008. Under this paragraph (b)(1), the $20 loss is allocated to reduce foreign source financial services income in 2008 because the loss was recognized (albeit deferred) within the 24-month recapture period following the receipt of the dividend. See §§ 1.267(f)-1(a)(2)(i)(B) and 1.267(f)-1(c)(2).

Example 5. The facts are the same as in Example 4, except P, S, and B are domestic corporations and members of the P consolidated group. Under the matching rule of § 1.1502-13(c)(1), the separate entity attributes of S's intercompany items and B's corresponding items are redetermined to the extent necessary to produce the same effect on consolidated taxable income as if S and B were divisions of a single corporation and the intercompany transaction was a transaction between divisions. If S and B were divisions of a single corporation, the transfer of N stock on January 3, 2000 would be ignored for tax purposes, and the corporation would be treated as selling that stock only in 2008. Thus, the corporation's entire $45 loss would have been allocated against U.S. source income under paragraph (a)(1) of this section because a dividend recapture amount was not received during the corporation's recapture period. Accordingly, S's $20 loss and B's $25 loss are allocated to reduce U.S. source income.

Example 6. (i) On January 1, 1998, P, a domestic corporation, purchases N, a foreign corporation, for $1,000. On March 1, 1998, P causes N to sell its operating assets, distribute a $400 general limitation dividend to P, and invest its remaining $600 in short-term government securities. P converted the N assets into low-risk investments with a principal purpose of holding the N stock without significant risk of loss until the recapture period expired. N earns interest income from the securities. The income constitutes subpart F income that is included in P's income under section 951, increasing P's basis in the N stock under section 961(a). On March 1, 2002, P sells N and recognizes a $400 loss.

(ii) Pursuant to paragraph (d)(3) of this section, the recapture period is increased by the period in which N's assets were held as low-risk investments because P caused N's assets to be converted into and held as low-risk investments with a principal purpose of enabling P to hold the N stock without significant risk of loss. Accordingly, under paragraph (b)(1)(i) of this section the $400 loss is allocated against foreign source general limitation income.

(2) *Exception for inventory.* This section does not apply to loss recognized with respect to stock described in section 1221(1).

(3) *Exception for stock in an S corporation.* This section does not apply to loss recognized with respect to stock in an S corporation (as defined in section 1361).

(4) *Anti-abuse rules*—(i) *Transactions involving built-in losses.* If one of the principal purposes of a transaction is to change the allocation of a built-in loss with respect to stock by transferring the stock to another person, qualified business unit (within the meaning of section 989(a)), office or other fixed place of business, or branch that subsequently recognizes the loss, the loss shall be allocated by the transferee as if it were recognized with respect to the stock by the transferor immediately prior to the transaction. If one of the principal purposes of a change of residence is to change the allocation of a built-in loss with respect to stock, the loss shall be allocated as if the change of residence had not occurred. If one of the principal purposes of a transaction is to change the allocation of a built-in loss with respect to stock (or other personal property) by converting the original property into other property and subsequently recognizing loss with respect to such other property, the loss shall be allocated as if it were recognized with respect to the original property immediately prior to the transaction. Transactions subject to this paragraph shall include, without limitation, reorganizations within the meaning of section 368(a), liquidations under section 332, transfers to a corporation under section 351, transfers to a partnership under section 721, transfers to a trust, distributions by a partnership, distributions by a trust, or transfers to or from a qualified business unit, office or other fixed place of business. A person may have a principal purpose of affecting loss allocation even though this purpose is outweighed by other purposes (taken together or separately).

(ii) *Offsetting positions.* If a taxpayer recognizes loss with respect to stock and the taxpayer (or any person described in section 267(b) (after application of section 267(c)), 267(e), 318 or 482 with respect to the taxpayer) holds (or held) offsetting positions with respect to such stock with a principal purpose of recognizing foreign source income and United States source loss, the loss will be allocated and apportioned against such foreign source income. For purposes of this paragraph (b)(4)(ii), positions are offsetting if the risk of loss

Reg. § 1.865-2(b)(4)

(iii) *Matching rule.* If a taxpayer (or a person described in section 1059(c)(3)(C) with respect to the taxpayer) engages in a transaction or series of transactions with a principal purpose of recognizing foreign source income that results in the creation of a corresponding loss with respect to stock (as a consequence of the rules regarding the timing of recognition of income, for example), the loss shall be allocated and apportioned against such income to the extent of the recognized foreign source income. This paragraph (b)(4)(iii) applies to any portion of a loss that is not allocated under paragraph (b)(1)(i) of this section (dividend recapture rule), including a loss in excess of the dividend recapture amount and a loss that is related to a dividend recapture amount described in paragraph (b)(1)(ii) (de minimis exception) or (b)(1)(iii) (passive dividend exception) of this section.

(iv) *Examples.* The application of this paragraph (b)(4) may be illustrated by the following examples. No inference is intended regarding the application of any other Internal Revenue Code section or judicial doctrine that may apply to disallow or defer the recognition of loss. The examples are as follows:

Example 1. (i) *Facts.* On January 1, 2000, P, a domestic corporation, owns all of the stock of N1, a controlled foreign corporation, which owns all of the stock of N2, a controlled foreign corporation. N1's basis in the stock of N2 exceeds its fair market value, and any loss recognized by N1 on the sale of N2 would be allocated under paragraph (a)(1) of this section to reduce foreign source passive limitation earnings and profits of N1. In contemplation of the sale of N2 to an unrelated purchaser, P causes N1 to liquidate with principal purposes of recognizing the loss on the N2 stock and allocating the loss against U.S. source income. P sells the N2 stock and P recognizes a loss.

(ii) *Loss allocation.* Because one of the principal purposes of the liquidation was to transfer the stock to P in order to change the allocation of the built-in loss on the N2 stock, under paragraph (b)(4)(i) of this section the loss is allocated against P's foreign source passive limitation income.

Example 2. (i) *Facts.* On January 1, 2000, P, a domestic corporation, forms N and F, foreign corporations, and contributes $1,000 to the capital of each. N and F enter into offsetting positions in financial instruments that produce financial services income. Holding the N stock substantially diminishes P's risk of loss with respect to the F stock (and vice versa). P holds N and F with a principal purpose of recognizing foreign source income and U.S. source loss. On March 31, 2000, when the financial instrument held by N is worth $1,200 and the financial instrument held by F is worth $800, P sells its F stock and recognizes a $200 loss.

(ii) *Loss allocation.* Because P held an offsetting position with respect to the F stock with a principal purpose of recognizing foreign source income and U.S. source loss, the $200 loss is allocated against foreign source financial services income under paragraph (b)(4)(ii) of this section.

Example 3. (i) *Facts.* On January 1, 2002, P and Q, domestic corporations, form R, a domestic partnership. The corporations and partnership use the calendar year as their taxable year. P contributes $900 to R in exchange for a 90-percent partnership interest and Q contributes $100 to R in exchange for a 10-percent partnership interest. R purchases a dance studio in Country X for $1,000. On January 2, 2002, R enters into contracts to provide dance lessons in Country x for a 5-year period beginning January 1, 2003. These contracts are prepaid by the dance studio customers on December 31, 2002, and R recognizes foreign source taxable income of $500 from the prepayments (R's only income in 2002). P takes into income its $450 distributive share of partnership taxable income. On January 1, 2003, P's basis in its partnership interest is $1,350 ($900 from its contribution under section 722, increased by its $450 distributive share of partnership income under section 705). On September 22, 2003, P contributes its R partnership interest to S, a newly-formed domestic corporation, in exchange for all the stock of S. Under section 358, P's basis in S is $1,350. On December 1, 2003, P sells S to an unrelated party for $1050 and recognizes a $300 loss.

(ii) *Loss allocation.* P recognized foreign source income for tax purposes before the income had economically accrued, and the accelerated recognition of income increased P's basis in R without increasing its value by a corresponding amount, which resulted in the creation of a built-in loss with respect to the S stock. Under paragraph (b)(4)(iii) of this section the $300 loss is allocated against foreign source income if P had a principal purpose of recognizing foreign source income and corresponding loss.

(c) *Loss recognized by partnership.* A partner's distributive share of loss recognized by a partnership shall be allocated and apportioned in accordance with this section as if the partner had recognized the loss. If loss is attributable to an office or other fixed place of business of the partnership within the meaning of section 865(e)(3), such office or fixed place of business shall be considered to be an office of the partner for purposes of this section.

(d) *Definitions*—(1) *Terms defined in § 1.861-8.* See § 1.861-8 for the meaning of *class of gross income, statutory grouping of gross income,* and *residual grouping of gross income.*

(2) *Dividend recapture amount.* A dividend recapture amount is a dividend (except for an amount treated as a dividend under section 78), an inclusion described in section 951(a)(1)(A)(i) (but only to the extent attributable to a dividend (including a dividend under section 964(e)(1)) included in the earnings of a controlled foreign corporation (held directly or indirectly by the person recognizing the loss) that is included in foreign personal holding company income under section 954(c)(1)(A)) and an inclusion described in section 951(a)(1)(B).

(3) *Recapture period.* A recapture period is the 24-month period ending on the date on which a taxpayer recognized a loss with respect to stock. For example, if a taxpayer recognizes a loss on March 15, 2002, the recapture period begins on and includes March 16, 2000, and ends on and includes March 15, 2002. A recapture period is increased by any period of time in which the taxpayer has diminished its risk of loss in a manner described in section 246(c)(4) and the regulations thereunder and by any period in which the assets of the corporation are hedged against risk of loss (or are converted into and held as low-risk investments) with a principal purpose of enabling the taxpayer to hold the stock without significant risk of loss until the recapture period has expired. In the case of a loss recognized after a dividend is declared but before such dividend is paid, the recapture period is extended through the date on which the dividend is paid.

(4) *United States resident.* See section 865(g) and the regulations thereunder for the definition of United States resident.

(e) *Effective date*—(1) *In general.* This section is applicable to loss recognized on or after January 11, 1999, except that paragraphs (a)(3)(ii), (b)(1)(iv) *Example 6*, (b)(4)(iii), (b)(4)(iv) *Example 3*, and (d)(3) of this section are applicable to loss recognized on or after January 8, 2002. For purposes of this paragraph (e), loss that is recognized but deferred (for example, under section 267 or 1092) shall be treated as recognized at the time the loss is taken into account.

(2) *Application to prior periods.* A taxpayer may apply the rules of this section to losses recognized in any taxable year beginning on or after January 1, 1987, and all subsequent years, provided that—

(i) The taxpayer's tax liability as shown on an original or amended tax return is consistent with the rules of this section for each such year for which the statute of limitations does not preclude the filing of an amended return on June 30, 2002; and

(ii) The taxpayer makes appropriate adjustments to eliminate any double benefit arising from the application of this section to years that are not open for assessment.

(3) *Examples.* The rules of this paragraph (e) may be illustrated by the following examples:

Example 1. (i) P, a domestic corporation, has a calendar taxable year. On March 10, 1985, P recognizes a $100 capital loss on the sale of N, a foreign corporation. Pursuant to sections 1211(a) and 1212(a), the loss is not allowed in 1985 and is carried over to the 1990 taxable year. The loss is allocated against foreign source income under § 1.861-8(e)(7). In 1999, P chooses to apply this section to all losses recognized in its 1987 taxable year and in all subsequent years.

(ii) Allocation of the loss on the sale of N is not affected by the rules of this section because the loss was recognized in a taxable year that did not begin after December 31, 1986.

Example 2. (i) P, a domestic corporation, has a calendar taxable year. On March 10, 1988, P recognizes a $100 capital loss on the sale of N, a foreign corporation. Pursuant to sections 1211(a) and 1212(a), the loss is not allowed in 1988 and is carried back to the 1985 taxable year. The loss is allocated against foreign source income under § 1.861-8(e)(7) on P's federal income tax return for 1985 and increases an overall foreign loss account under § 1.904(f)-1.

(ii) In 1999, P chooses to apply this section to all losses recognized in its 1987 taxable year and in all subsequent years. Consequently, the loss on the sale of N is allocated against U.S. source income under paragraph (a)(1) of this section. Allocation of the loss against U.S. source income reduces P's overall foreign loss account and increases P's tax liability in 2 years: 1990, a year that will not be open for assessment on June 30, 1999, and 1997, a year that will be open for assessment on June 30, 1999. Pursuant to paragraph (e)(2)(i) of this section, P must file an amended federal income tax return that reflects the rules of this section for 1997, but not for 1990.

Example 3. (i) P, a domestic corporation, has a calendar taxable year. On March 10, 1989, P recognizes a $100 capital loss on the sale of N, a foreign corporation. The loss is allocated against

Reg. § 1.865-2(e)(3)

Determination of Sources of Income

See p. 20,601 for regulations not amended to reflect law changes

foreign source income under § 1.861-8(e)(7) on P's federal income tax return for 1989 and results in excess foreign tax credits for that year. The excess credit is carried back to 1988, pursuant to section 904(c). In 1999, P chooses to apply this section to all losses recognized in its 1989 taxable year and in all subsequent years. On June 30, 1999, P's 1988 taxable year is closed for assessment, but P's 1989 taxable year is open with respect to claims for refund.

(ii) Because P chooses to apply this section to its 1989 taxable year, the loss on the sale of N is allocated against U.S. source income under paragraph (a)(1) of this section. Allocation of the loss against U.S. source income would have permitted the foreign tax credit to be used in 1989, reducing P's tax liability in 1989. Nevertheless, under paragraph (e)(2)(ii) of this section, because the credit was carried back to 1988, P may not claim the foreign tax credit in 1989.

[Reg. § 1.865-2.]

☐ [T.D. 8805, 1-8-99. Amended by T.D. 8973, 12-27-2001.]